**W9-AHF-351**

# SCOTT®

# 2007
# STANDARD POSTAGE
# STAMP CATALOGUE

ONE HUNDRED AND SIXTY-THIRD EDITION IN SIX VOLUMES

## VOLUME 5
### COUNTRIES OF THE WORLD
### P-SL

EDITOR — James E. Kloetzel

ASSOCIATE EDITOR — William A. Jones

ASSISTANT EDITOR/NEW ISSUES & VALUING — Martin J. Frankevicz

VALUING ANALYST — Steven R. Myers

ADMINISTRATIVE ASSISTANT/IMAGE COORDINATOR — Beth L. Brown

DESIGN MANAGER — Teresa M. Wenrick

ADVERTISING — Renee Davis

CIRCULATION/PRODUCT PROMOTION MANAGER — Tim Wagner

VICE PRESIDENT/EDITORIAL AND PRODUCTION — Steve Collins

VICE PRESIDENT/OPERATIONS — William Fay

Released August 2006

Includes New Stamp Listings through the August 2006 *Scott Stamp Monthly* Catalogue Update

Copyright© 2006 by

## *Scott Publishing Co.*

911 Vandemark Road, Sidney, OH 45365-0828

A division of AMOS PRESS, INC., publishers of *Scott Stamp Monthly, Linn's Stamp News, Coin World* and *Coin World's Coin Values.*

# Table of Contents



See Volume 1 for United States, United Nations and Countries of the World A-B
See Volumes 2, 3, 4, 6 for Countries of the World, C-O, So-Z.

Volume 2: C-F
Volume 3: G-I
Volume 4: J-O
Volume 6: So-Z

## Scott Publishing Mission Statement

The Scott Publishing Team exists to serve the recreational, educational and commercial hobby needs of stamp collectors and dealers.

We strive to set the industry standard for philatelic information and products by developing and providing goods that help collectors identify, value, organize and present their collections.

Quality customer service is, and will continue to be, our highest priority. We aspire toward achieving total customer satisfaction.

## Copyright Notice



## Trademark Notice



ISBN 0-89487-379-2

Library of Congress Card No. 2-3301

# Scott Publishing Co.

SCOTT®

911 VANDEMARK ROAD, SIDNEY, OHIO 45365   937-498-0802

Dear Scott Catalogue User:

## We're working on the last 1%.

We have now completed the conversion to full color of more than 99% of the stamp images in the *2007 Scott Standard Postage Stamp Catalogues*. There are fewer than 200 black and white images in this Volume 5 that need to be converted into color scans. The color image project is moving rapidly toward completion. It will be interesting to see what stamp becomes the final candidate for color scanning. Of course we continue to ask collectors and dealers to check their collections and stocks for any of the stamps that still appear in black and white in the catalogues. We still need your help to bring this project to a successful conclusion.

We took a computer and scanner to the very successful Washington 2006 international stamp show, and we were able to scan more than 75 stamps there that still appear in black and white in the catalogues. We thank those show dealers who graciously allowed us to borrow these stamps for the short time it took to scan them. We plan on repeating this scenario at the APS Stampshow in August in Chicago. We continue to be impressed with the cooperation we have received in response to our appeals for collector and dealer help. The response continues to be very encouraging, and we are glad to see so many individuals who share our vision for an all-color set of catalogues.

We have received more favorable feedback from customers concerning our printing of the catalogues in color than we have for any editorial enhancement this editor can remember. We will continue to upgrade the images, rescanning when necessary, until we are completely satisfied with the quality of all the color scans.

## What's new for Volume 5?

The many thousands of value changes that appear in Volume 5 are spread throughout the volume. The value changes in all the volumes this year, which overwhelmingly have been increases so far, have been driven almost totally by market prices and only indirectly, if at all, by currency exchange rates.

Countries with large numbers of value changes in Volume 5 include St. Vincent and St. Vincent Grenadines with 1,331 and 675 changes, respectively. Other countries with significant numbers of value changes include Pakistan, Papua New Guinea, Philippines, St. Kitts, St. Lucia, Samoa and Saudi Arabia.

In Pakistan, 350 value changes begin with the first set of 1947, Scott 1-19, in which many values for mint never hinged stamps rise somewhat and greater numbers of used values rise even more. Most changes are in the 1947 to 1900s period, and most are modest value increases. There are some value changes after the 1960s, such as the 2.25r Dr. Schweitzer issue of 1975, Scott 376, which jumps to $5 mint never hinged and $4 used, from $3.75 both ways in the 2006 Volume 5. One very modern item shows a large value increase. The 2004 Ninth SAF Games sheet of 16, Scott 1030, moves to $4.50 both mint never hinged and used from just $1.10 each way last year. There are very significant value increases in the 1947-48 Official sets, Scott O1-O26. Two stamps stand out for the size of their value increases. The 10r rose carmine and dark violet stamp of 1947, Scott O13, skyrockets in the used column to $90 in this 2007 volume, from only $35 last year. And the 1948 5r carmine, Scott O25, jumps in the mint never hinged column to $47.50, from just $30 in 2006.

But not every value change in the Pakistan listings is an increase (though in truth almost all of them are). The 10th Anniversary of the U.N. set of two from 1955, Scott 77-78, drops to just $4.25 mint never hinged and $8.50 used, from $18 mint never hinged and $25 used in 2006, as greater supplies have appeared on the market.

The 715 value changes in Papua New Guinea tend to be moderate value increases. The 1901 1/2p-2shop Lakatoi set, Scott 1-8, moves to $798.25 unused and $790.50 used, from $763.75 unused and $753 used last year. The 1906 large "Papua" overprinted set, Scott 11-18, jumps to $500 unused and $498.50 used, from

$444.50 unused and $487 used in 2006.

In Philippines, most of the 670 value changes are in the classic period and are generally increases in the 5-10 percent range. The changes occur in both the unused and used columns of the catalogue. Value changes in the 20th century listings are not nearly so numerous as in the 19th century listings.

Most value changes for the stamps of St. Vincent and St. Vincent Grenadines are for the issues of the 1980s and 1990s, and the changes tend to be moderate to large increases. An example of a large value increase is the 1986 10c-$3 Trees set, Scott 968-971, which jumps to $7.40 both mint never hinged and used, from $3.45 both ways in the 2006 Volume 5. There are many other value changes for the listings during these two decades that are quite significant. The 1989 10c-$5 World Cup Soccer Championships set, Scott 1236-1239, is a good example. From $5.10 both mint never hinged and used in the 2006 Volume 5, the set has risen in value to $8.50 mint never hinged and $6 used. The souvenir sheets for the set, Scott 1240 and 1241, move from $4.50 both mint never hinged and used to $7.50 both ways this year.

## What's new on the editorial side?

The most significant editorial changes in this year's Volume 5 occur in the listings of the Philippines. There are two major number additions to the classic "Habilitado Por La Nacion" overprints of 1868-74. The new Scott 24A is a 5c orange first design type A1, issued in 1874, with catalogue values of $7,000 unused and $6,000 used. Also added is Scott 27A, a 5c vermilion of the 1859 design type A5, with catalogue values of $3,000 unused and $1,500 used.

The complicated and at times frustrating Philippines National Symbols issues of 1993-98 have been extensively reworked in order to clarify and complete the listings. This has been accomplished with a minimum of renumberings (only three items). Several new major numbers have been added. See the Volume 5 Number Additions, Deletions & Changes list on page 1134 to see the changes, then turn to pages 256-7 and 263 for the complete listings. We are thankful for the help of Donald J. Peterson and the International Philippine Philatelic Society that made this revision possible.

Rounding out the changes to the Philippines, the listings for the stamps of the Filipino Revolutionary Government, 1898-99, have been brought over from the U.S. Specialized Catalogue and are now incorporated into the Standard Catalogue Volume 5 also. These five stamps and their varieties, Scott Y1-YP1, will be found at the end of the Philippine listings on page 282, and their listing here will help complete the philatelic history of the country.

Additional new lettered minor listings for errors and other varieties appear in Volume 5 for Ruanda-Urundi, Russia, St. Helena, Saudi Arabia and Singapore.

Six major Postal Fiscal numbers have been added to the listings of St. Christopher. Issued in 1883 and 1885, these are St. Kitts Nos. 22 and 28 overprinted "REVENUE" horizontally and "St. Christopher" diagonally, used postally in 1883, Scott AR1-2, and stamps of St. Christopher overprinted "SAINT KITTS/NEVIS/ REVENUE" in three lines, used postally in 1885, Scott AR3-AR6. A note after these listings states that other values exist with the overprints mentioned, but these others were not made available for postal purposes.

As always, collectors are urged to check the Catalogue Number Additions, Deletions & Changes listing for these and other catalogue changes.

Happy collecting,

*James E. Kloetzel*

James E. Kloetzel/Catalogue Editor

# Acknowledgments

Our appreciation and gratitude go to the following individuals who have assisted us in preparing information included in this year's Scott Catalogues. Some helpers prefer anonymity. These individuals have generously shared their stamp knowledge with others through the medium of the Scott Catalogue.

Those who follow provided information that is in addition to the hundreds of dealer price lists and advertisements and scores of auction catalogues and realizations that were used in producing the catalogue values. It is from those who noted here that we have been able to obtain information on items not normally seen in published lists and advertisements. Support from these people goes beyond data leading to catalogue values, for they also are key to editorial changes.

A. R. Allison
Roland Austin
Robert Ausubel (Great Britain Collectors Club)
Dr. H.U. Banz (S. W. Africa Stamp Study Group)
John Barone (Stamptracks)
Jack Hagop Barsoumian (International Stamp Co.)
Alan Bauer
Jules K. Beck (Latin American Philatelic Society)
Vladimir Berrio-Lemm (CEFIN_PANAMA)
George G. Birdsall (Northland Auctions)
John Birkinbine II
Roger S. Brody
Keith & Margie Brown
Mike Bush (Joseph V. Bush, Inc.)
Peter Bylen
Alan C. Campbell
John Cardoza
Tina & John Carlson (JET Stamps)
Joseph H. Chalhoub
Richard A. Champagne (Richard A. Champagne, Inc.)
Henry Chlanda
Bob Coale
Leroy P. Collins III
Laurie Conrad
Frank D. Correl
Andrew Cronin (Canadian Society of Russian Philately)
Stephen R. Datz
Tony Davis
Charles Deaton
John E. DeStefanis
Kenneth E. Diehl
Bob Dumaine
Esi Ebrani
Paul G. Eckman
Mehdi Esmaili (Iran Philatelic Study Circle)
David Esperson
Leon Finik (Loral Stamps)
Henry Fisher
Joseph E. Foley (Eire Philatelic Association)
Jeffrey M. Forster
Robert S. Freeman
Ernest E. Fricks (France & Colonies Philatelic Society)
Bob Genisol (Sultan Stamp Center)
Michael A. Goldman (Regency Superior, Ltd.)
Daniel E. Grau
Joe Hahn

John B. Head
Bruce Hecht (Bruce L. Hecht Co.)
Robert R. Hegland
Jack R. Hughes (Fellowship of Samoan Specialists)
Philip J. Hughes (Croatian Philatelic Society)
Wilson Hulme
Michael Jaffe (Michael Jaffe Stamps, Inc)
Peter C. Jeannopoulos
Stephen Joe (International Stamp Service)
Richard Juzwin (Richard Juzwin PTY LTD)
John Kardos
Allan Katz (Ventura Stamp Company)
Stanford M. Katz
Lewis Kaufman (The Philatelic Foundation)
Patricia A. Kaufmann
Dr. James W. Kerr
John R. Lewis (The William Henry Stamp Co.)
Roberto G. Liera (AMEXFIL)
Ulf Lindahl (Ethiopian Philatelic Society)
William A. Litle
Gary B. Little (Luxembourg Collectors Club)
Pedro Llach (Filatelia Llach S.L.)
William Thomas Lockard (Liberian Philatelic Society)
Dennis Lynch
Robert Manley
Robert L. Markovits (Quality Investors, Ltd.)
Marilyn R. Mattke
William K. McDaniel
Mark S. Miller (India Study Circle)
Allen Mintz (United Postal Stationery Society)
David Mordant
Gary M. Morris (Pacific Midwest Co.)
Peter Mosiondz, Jr.
Bruce M. Moyer (Moyer Stamps & Collectibles)
Richard H. Muller (Richard's Stamps)
James Natale
Albert Olejnik
Victor Ostolaza
John E. Pearson (Pittwater Philatelic Service)
Donald J. Peterson (International Philippine Philatelic Society)
Stanley M. Piller (Stanley M. Piller & Associates)
Virgil Pirvulescu
Todor Drumev Popov
Peter W. W. Powell
Ghassan D. Riachi
Peter A. Robertson
Omar Rodriguez
Michael Rogers (Michael Rogers, Inc.)

Wilford H. Ross
Michael Ruggiero
Frans H. A. Rummens (International Bulletin for Netherlands Philately)
Mehrdad Sadri (Persiphila)
Richard H. Salz
Jacques C. Schiff, Jr. (Jacques C. Schiff, Jr., Inc.)
Alex Schauss (Schauss Philatelics)
Bernard Seckler (Fine Arts Philatelists)
F. Burton Sellers
Guy Shaw
Sergio & Liane Sismondo (The Classic Collector)
Jay Smith
Robert M. Spaulding (International Society for Japanese Philately)
Frank Stanley, III
Richard Stark
Jerry Summers
Peter Thy (Philatelic Society for Greater Southern Africa)
Steve Unkrich
Philip T. Wall
William R Wallace
Daniel C. Warren
Richard A. Washburn
Giana Wayman (Asociacion Filatélica de Costa Rica)
William R. Weiss, Jr. (Weiss Auctions)
Ed Wener (Indigo)
Hans A. Westphal
Ken Whitby
Don White (Dunedin Stamp Centre)
Urmas Wompa
Robert F. Yacano (K-Line Philippines)
Ralph Yorio
Val Zabijaka
Dr. Michal Zika (Album)
John P. Zuckerman (Siegel Auction Galleries, Inc.)
Alfonso G. Zulueta, Jr.

A special acknowledgment to Liane and Sergio Sismondo of The Classic Collector for their extraordinary assistance and knowledge sharing that has aided in the preparation of this year's Standard and Classic Specialized Catalogues.

# Addresses, Telephone Numbers, Web Sites, E-Mail Addresses of General & Specialized Philatelic Societies

Collectors can contact the following groups for information about the philately of the areas within the scope of these societies, or inquire about membership in these groups. Aside from the general societies, we limit this list to groups that specialize in particular fields of philately, particular areas covered by the Scott Standard Postage Stamp Catalogue, and topical groups. Many more specialized philatelic society exist than those listed below. These addresses are updated yearly, and they are, to the best of our knowledge, correct and current. Groups should inform the editors of address changes whenever they occur. The editors also want to hear from other such specialized groups not listed.

Unless otherwise noted all website addresses begin with http://

**American Philatelic Society**
100 Match Factory Place
Bellefonte PA 16823-1367
Ph: (814) 933-3803
www.stamps.org
E-mail: apsinfo@stamps.org

**American Stamp Dealers Association**
Joseph Savarese
3 School St. Suite #205
Glen Cove NY 11542
Ph: (516) 759-7000
www.asdaonline.com
E-mail: asda@erols.com

**International Society of Worldwide Stamp Collectors**
Terry Myers, MD
PMB 200, 3308 Preston Rd. Suite 350
Plano TX 75093
www.iswsc.org
E-mail: iswsc@hotmail.com

**Royal Philatelic Society of Canada**
PO Box 929, Station Q
Toronto, ON, Canada M4T 2P1
Ph: (888) 285-4143
www.rpsc.org
E-mail:info@rpsc.org

**Young Stamp Collectors of America**
Janet Houser
100 Match Factory Place
Bellefonte PA 16823-1367
Ph: (814) 933-3820
www.stamps.org/ysca/intro.htm
E-mail: ysca@stamps.org

**Groups focusing on fields or aspects found in worldwide philately (some may cover U.S. area only)**

**American Air Mail Society**
Stephen Reinhard
PO Box 110
Mineola NY 11501
E-mail: sr1501@aol.com

**American First Day Cover Society**
Douglas Kelsey
PO Box 16277
Tucson AZ 85732-6277
Ph: (520) 321-0880
www.afdcs.org
E-mail: afdcs@aol.com

**American Revenue Association**
Eric Jackson
PO Box 728
Leesport PA 19533-0728
Ph: (610) 926-6200
www.revenuer.org
E-mail: eric@revenuer.com

**American Topical Association**
Ray E. Cartier
PO Box 57
Arlington TX 76004-0057
Ph: (817) 274-1181
americantopical.org
E-mail: americantopical@msn.com

**Errors, Freaks and Oddities Collectors Club**
Jim McDevitt
7643 Sequoia Dr., North
Mobile AL 36695-2809
Ph: (251) 607-9253
www.efoers.org
E-mail: cwousg@aol.com

**First Issues Collectors Club**
Kurt Streepy
P.O. Box 288
Clear Creek IN 47426-0288
www.firstissues.org
E-mail: orders@firstissues.org

**International Philatelic Society of Joint Stamp Issues Collectors**
Pascal Le Blond
60-600 Rue Cormier
Gatineau, QC, Canada J9H 6B4
http://rzimmerm.club.fr
E-mail: jointissues@yahoo.com

**National Duck Stamp Collectors Society**
Anthony J. Monico
PO Box 43
Harleysville PA 19438-0043
www.hwcn.org/link/ndscs
or www.ndscs.org
E-mail: ndscs@hwcn.org

**No Value Identified Club**
Albert Sauvanet
Le Clos Royal B, Boulevard des Pas Enchantes
St. Sebastien-sur Loire, France 44230
E-mail: alain.vailly@irin.univ nantes.fr

**The Perfins Club**
Kurt Ottenheimer
462 West Walnut St.
Long Beach NY 11561
Ph: (516) 431-3412
E-mail:oak462@optonline.net

**Postal History Society**
Kalman V. Illyefalvi
8207 Daren Court
Pikesville MD 21208-2211
Ph: (410) 653-0665

**Precancel Stamp Society**
Arthur Damm
176 Bent Pine Hill
North Wales PA 19454
Ph: (215) 368-6082
E-mail: sandadamm@enter.net

**United Postal Stationery Society**
Michael Davis
PO Box 3982
Chester VA 23831
www.upss.org
E-mail: upss@comcast.net

**United States Possessions Philatelic Society**
Eric A. Glohr
139 Richard Ave.
Lansing MI 48917
Ph: (517) 483-1797
E-mail: eglohr@lcc.edu

**Groups focusing on U.S. area philately as covered in the Standard Catalogue**

**Canal Zone Study Group**
Richard H. Salz
60 27th Ave.
San Francisco CA 94121-1026

**Carriers and Locals Society**
John D. Bowman
232 Leaf Lane
Alabaster AL 35007
Ph: (205) 621-8449
www.pennypost.org
E-mail: johndbowman@charter.net

**Confederate Stamp Alliance**
Kevin Baker
3015 Fieldview Dr.
Murfreesboro TN 37128
www.csalliance.org
E-mail: secretary@csalliance.org

**Hawaiian Philatelic Society**
Kay H. Hoke
PO Box 10115
Honolulu HI 96816-0115
Ph: (808) 521-5721

**Plate Number Coil Collectors Club**
Ronald E. Maifeld
PO Box 54622
Cincinnati OH 45254-0622
www.pnc3.org
E-mail: RON.MAIFELD@pnc3.org

**United Nations Philatelists**
Blanton Clement, Jr.
P.O. Box 146
Morrisvile PA 19067-0146
www.unpi.com
E-mail: bclemjr@yahoo.com

**United States Stamp Society**
Executive Secretary
PO Box 6634
Katy TX 77491-6631
www.usstamps.org
E-mail: webmaster@usstamps.org

**U.S. Cancellation Club**
Roger Rhoads
6160 Brownstone Ct.
Mentor OH 44060
www.geocities.com/athens/2088/usschome.htm
E-mail: rrrhoads@aol.com

**U.S. Philatelic Classics Society**
Mark D. Rogers
PO Box 80708
Austin TX 78708-0708
www.uspcs.org
E-mail: mrogers23@austin.rr.com

**Groups focusing on philately of foreign countries or regions**

**Aden & Somaliland Study Group**
Gary Brown
PO Box 106
Briar Hill, Victoria, Australia 3088
E-mail: garyjohn951@optushome.com.au

**American Society of Polar Philatelists (Antarctic areas)**
Alan Warren
PO Box 39
Exton PA 19341-0039
www.polarphilatelists.org
E-mail: alanwar@att.net

**Andorran Philatelic Study Circle**
D. Hope
17 Hawthorn Dr.
Stalybridge, Cheshire, United Kingdom
SK15 1UE
www.chy-an-piran.demon.co.uk/
E-mail: apsc@chy-an-piran.demon.co.uk

**Australian States Study Circle of The Royal Sydney Philatelic Club**
Ben Palmer
GPO 1751
Sydney, N.S.W., Australia 2001

**Austria Philatelic Society**
Ralph Schneider
PO Box 23049
Belleville IL 62223
Ph: (618) 277-6152
www.austriaphilatelicsociety.com
E-mail: rschneider39@charter.net

**American Belgian Philatelic Society**
Walter D. Handlin
1303 Bullens Lane.
Woodin, PA 19094
groups.hamptonroads.com/ABPS
E-mail: wdhandlin1@comcast.net

**Bechuanalands and Botswana Society**
Neville Midwood
69 Porlock Lane.
Furzton, Milton Keynes, United Kingdom MK4 1JY
www.nevsoft.com
E-mail: bbsoc@nevsoft.com

**Bermuda Collectors Society**
Thomas J. McMahon
PO Box 1949
Stuart FL 34995
www.bermudacollectorssociety.org

**Brazil Philatelic Association**
William V. Kriebel
1923 Manning St.
Philadelphia PA 19103-5728
Ph: (215) 735-3697
E-mail: kriebewv@drexel.edu

**British Caribbean Philatelic Study Group**
Dr. Reuben A. Ramkisson
3011 White Oak Lane
Oak Brook IL 60523-2513
Ph: (630) 963-1439
www.bcpsg.com
E-mail: rramkisson@juno.com

**British North America Philatelic Society (Canada & Provinces)**
H.P. Jacobi
6-2168 150A St.
Surrey, B.C., Canada V4A 9W4
http://bnaps.org
E-mail: pjacobi@shaw.ca

**British West Indies Study Circle**
W. Clary Holt
PO Drawer 59
Burlington NC 27216
Ph: (336) 227-7461

**Burma Philatelic Study Circle**
A. Meech
7208 91st Ave.
Edmonton, AB, Canada T6B 0R8
E-mail: ameech@telusplanet.net

**Ceylon Study Group**
R. W. P. Frost
42 Lonsdale Road, Cannington
Bridgewater, Somerset, United Kingdom TA5 2JS
E-mail: rodney.frost@tiscali

**Channel Islands Specialists Society**
Miss S. Marshall
3, La Marette, Alderney,
Channel Islands, United Kingdom,
GY9 3UQ
E-mail: am012e5300@blueyonder.co.uk

**China Stamp Society**
Paul H. Gault
PO Box 20711
Columbus OH 43220
www.chinastampsociety.org
E-mail: secretary@chinastampsociety.org

**Colombia/Panama Philatelic Study Group (COPAPHIL)**
PO Box 2245
El Cajon CA 92021
www.copaphil.org
E-mail: jimacross@cts.com

**Association Filatelic de Costa Rica**
Giana Wayman
c/o Interlink 102, PO Box 52-6770
Miami, FL 33152
E-mail: scotland@racsa.co.cr

**Society for Costa Rica Collectors**
Dr. Hector R. Mena
PO Box 14831
Baton Rouge LA 70808
www.socorico.org
E-mail: hrmena@aol.com

**Croatian Philatelic Society (Croatia & other Balkan areas)**
Ekrem Spanich
502 Romero, PO Box 696
Fritch TX 79036-0696
Ph: (806) 273-5609
www.croatianstamps.com
E-mail: eckSpanich@cableone.net

**Cuban Philatelic Society of America**
Ernesto Cuesta
PO Box 34434
Bethesda MD 20827
www.philat.com/cpsa

**Cyprus Study Circle**
Jim Wigmore
19 Riversmeet, Appledore
Bideford, N. Devon, United Kingdom EX39 1RE
www.cyprusstudycircle.org/index.htm
E-mail: jameswigmore@aol.com

**Society for Czechoslovak Philately**
Phil Rhoade
28168 Cedar Trail
Cleveland MN 56017
www.czechoslovakphilately.com
E-mail: philip.rhoade@mnsu.edu

**Danish West Indies Study Unit of the Scandinavian Collectors Club**
John L. Dubois
Thermalogic Corp.
22 Kane Industrial Drive
Hudson MA 01749
Ph: (800) 343-4492
dtwi.thlogic.com
E-mail: jld@thlogic.com

**East Africa Study Circle**
Jonathan Smalley
1 Lincoln Close
Tweeksbury, United Kingdom B91 1AE
easc.org.uk
E-mail: jpasmalley@tiscali.co.uk

**Egypt Study Circle**
Mike Murphy
109 Chadwick Road
London, United Kingdom SE15 4PY
egyptstudycircle.org.uk
E-mail: egyptstudycircle@hotmail.com

**Estonian Philatelic Society**
Juri Kirsimagi
29 Clifford Ave.
Pelham NY 10803
Ph: (914) 738-3713

**Ethiopian Philatelic Society**
Ulf Lindahl
21 Westview Place
Riverside CT 06878
Ph: (203) 866-3540
http://home.comcast.net/~fbheiser/ethiopia5.htm
E-mail: ulindahl@optonline.net

**Falkland Islands Philatelic Study Group**
Carl J. Faulkner
Williams Inn, On-the-Green
Williamstown MA 01267-2620
Ph: (413) 458-9371

**Faroe Islands Study Circle**
Norman Hudson
28 Enfield Road
Ellesmere Port, Cheshire, United Kingdom CH65 8BY
www.faroeislandssc.org.uk
E-mail: jntropics@hotmail.com

**Former French Colonies Specialist Society**
BP 628
75367 Paris Cedex 08, France
www.ifrance.com/colfra
E-mail: clubcolfra@aol.com

**France & Colonies Philatelic Society**
Edward Grabowski
741 Marcellus Drive
Westfield NJ 07090-2012
www.drunkenboat.net/frandcol/
E-mail: edjg@alum.mit.edu

**German Democratic Republic Study Group of the German Philatelic Society**
Ken Lawrence
PO Box 98
Bellefonte PA 16823-0098
Ph: (814) 422-0625
E-mail: apsken@aol.com

**Germany Philatelic Society**
PO Box 6547
chesterfield MO 63006
www.gps.nu

**Gibraltar Study Circle**
David R. Stirrups
34 Glamis Drive
Dundee, United Kingdom DD2 1QP
E-mail: drstirrups@dundee.ac.uk

**Great Britain Collectors Club**
Parker A. Bailey, Jr.
PO Box 773
Merrimack NH 03054-0773
www.gbstamps.com/gbcc
E-mail: pbaileyjr@worldnet.att.net

**Hellenic Philatelic Society of America (Greece and related areas)**
Dr. Nicholas Asimakopulos
541 Cedar Hill Ave.
Wyckoff NJ 07481
Ph: (201) 447-6262
E-mail: nick1821@aol.com

**Haiti Philatelic Society**
Ubaldo Del Toro
5709 Marble Archway
Alexandria VA 22315
www.haitiphilately.org
E-mail: u007ubl@aol.com

**Hong Kong Stamp Society**
Dr. An-Min Chung
3300 Darby Rd. Cottage 503
Haverford PA 19041-1064

**Society for Hungarian Philately**
Robert Morgan
2201 Roscomare Rd.
Los Angeles CA 90077-2222
www.hungarianphilately.org
E-mail: h.a.an.hoover@hungarianphilately.org

**India Study Circle**
John Warren
PO Box 7326
Washington DC 20044
Ph: (202) 564-6876
www.indiastudycircle.org
E-mail: warren_john@epa.gov

**Indian Ocean Study Circle**
K. B. Fitton
50 Firlands
Weybridge, Surrey, United Kingdom KT13 0HR
www.stampdomain.com/iosc
E-mail: keithfitton@intonet.co.uk

**Iran Philatelic Study Circle**
Mehdi Esmaili
PO Box 750090
Forest Hills NY 11375
www.iranphilatelic.org
E-mail: m.esmaili@earthlink.net

**Society of Indo-China Philatelists**
Ron Bentley
2000 North 24th Street.
Arlington VA 22207
www.sicp-online.org
E-mail: ron.bentley@verizon.net

**Eire Philatelic Association (Ireland)**
David J. Brennan
PO Box 704
Bernardsville NJ 07924
eirephilateliccassoc.org
E-mail: brennan704@aol.com

**Society of Israel Philatelists**
Paul S. Autrichtig
300 East 42nd St.
New York NY 10017

**Italy and Colonies Study Circle**
Andrew D'Anneo
1085 Dunweal Lane
Calistoga CA 94515
www.icsc.pwp.blueyonder.co.uk
E-mail: audanneo@napanet.net

**International Society for Japanese Philately**
Kenneth Kamholz
PO Box 1283
Haddonfield NJ 08033
www.isjp.org
E-mail: isjp@comcast.net

**Korea Stamp Society**
John E. Talmage
PO Box 6889
Oak Ridge TN 37831
www.pennfamily.org/KSS-USA
E-mail: jtalmage@usit.net

**Latin American Philatelic Society**
Jules K. Beck
30 1/2 Street #209
St. Louis Park MN 55426-3551

**Latvian Philatelic Society**
Aris Birze
569 Rougemount Dr.
Pickering, ON, Canada L1W 2C1

**Liberian Philatelic Society**
William Thomas Lockard
PO Box 106
Wellston OH 45692
Ph: (740) 384-2020
E-mail: tlockard@zoomnet.net

**Liechtenstudy USA (Liechtenstein)**
Ralph Schneider
PO Box 23049
Belleville IL 62223
Ph: (618) 277-6152
www.rschneiderstamps.com/Liechtenstudy.htm
E-mail: rsstamps@aol.com

**Lithuania Philatelic Society**
John Variakojis
3715 W. 68th St.
Chicago IL 60629
Ph: (773) 585-8649
www.filatelija.lt/lps/
E-mail: variakojis@earthlink.net

**Luxembourg Collectors Club**
Gary B. Little
7319 Beau Road
Sechelt, BC, Canada VON 3A8
www.luxcentral.com/stamps/LCC
E-mail: lcc@luxcentral.com

**Malaya Study Group**
David Tett
16 Broadway, Gustard Wood,
Wheathampstead, Herts, United Kingdom AL4 8LN
www.m s g/org/uk
E-mail: davidtett@aol.com

**Malta Study Circle**
Alec Webster
50 Worcester Road
Sutton, Surrey, United Kingdom SM2 6QB
E-mail: alecwebster50@hotmail.com

**Mexico-Elmhurst Philatelic Society International**
David Pietsch
PO Box 50997
Irvine CA 92619-0997
E-mail: mepsi@msn.com

**Society for Moroccan and Tunisian Philately**
206, bld. Pereire
75017 Paris, France
members.aol.com/Jhaik5814
E-mail: splm206@aol.com

**Nepal & Tibet Philatelic Study Group**
Roger D. Skinner
1020 Covington Road
Los Altos CA 94024-5003
Ph: (650) 968-4163
fuchs-online.com/ntpsc/
E-mail: colinhepper@hotmail.co.uk

**American Society of Netherlands Philately**
Jan Enthoven
221 Coachlite Ct. S.
Onalaska WI 54650
Ph: (608) 781-8612
www.cs.cornell.edu/Info/People/aswin/NL/neth
E-mail: jenthoven@centurytel.net

**New Zealand Society of Great Britain**
Keith C. Collins
13 Briton Crescent
Sanderstead, Surrey, United Kingdom CR2 0JN
www.cs.sttirac.uk/~rgc/nzsgb
E-mail: rgc@cs.sttirac.uk

**Nicaragua Study Group**
Erick Rodriguez
11817 S.W. 11th St.
Miami FL 33184-2501
clubs.yahoo.com/clubs/nicaraguastudygroup
E-mail: nsgsec@yahoo.com

**Society of Australasian Specialists/Oceania**
Henry Bateman
PO Box 4862
Monroe LA 71211-4862
Ph: (800) 571-0293 members.aol.com/stampsho/saso.html
E-mail: hbateman@jam.rr.com

**Orange Free State Study Circle**
J. R. Stroud
28 Oxford St.
Burnham-on-sea, Somerset, United Kingdom TA8 1LQ
www.ofssc.org
E-mail: jrstroud@classicfm.net

**Pacific Islands Study Circle**
John Ray
24 Woodvale Avenue
London, United Kingdom SE25 4AE
www.pisc.org.uk
E-mail: info@pisc.org.uk

**Pakistan Philatelic Study Circle**
Jeff Siddiqui
PO Box 7002
Lynnwood WA 98046
E-mail: jeffsiddiqui@msn.com

**Centro de Filatelistas Independientes de Panama**
Vladimir Berrio Lemm
Apartado 0823-02748
Plaza Concordia Panama, Panama
E-mail: panahistoria@yahoo.es

**Papuan Philatelic Society**
Steven Zirinsky
PO Box 49, Ansonia Station
New York NY 10023
Ph: (718) 706-0616
E-mail: szirinsky@cs.com

**International Philippine Philatelic Society**
Robert F. Yacano
PO Box 100
Toast NC 27049
Ph: (336) 783-0768
E-mail: ryacano@tria.d.rr.com

**Pitcairn Islands Study Group**
Dr. Everett L. Parker
719 Moosehead Lake Rd.
Greenville ME 04441-9727
Ph: (207) 695-3163
ourworld.compuserve.com/homepages/ ST_HELENA_ASCEN_TDC
E-mail: eparker@midmaine.net

**Plebiscite-Memel-Saar Study Group of the German Philatelic Society**
Clay Wallace
100 Lark Court
Alamo CA 94507
E-mail: clayw1@sbcglobal.net

**Polonus Philatelic Society (Poland)**
Chris Kulpinski
9350 E. Palm Tree Dr.
Scottsdale AZ 85255
Ph: (480) 585-7114
www.polonus.org
E-mail: ctk85255@yahoo.com

**International Society for Portuguese Philately**
Clyde Homen
1491 Bonnie View Rd.
Hollister CA 95023-5117
www.portugalstamps.com
E-mail: cjh1491@sbcglobal.net

**Rhodesian Study Circle**
William R. Wallace
PO Box 16381
San Francisco CA 94116
www.rhodesianstudycircle.org.uk
E-mail: bwall8rscr@earthlink.net

**Canadian Society of Russian Philately**
Andrew Cronin
PO Box 5722, Station A
Toronto, ON, Canada M5W 1P2
Ph: (905) 764-8968
www3.sympatico.ca/postrider/postrider
E-mail: postrider@sympatico.ca

**Rossica Society of Russian Philately**
Edward J. Laveroni
P.O. Box 320997
Los Gatos CA 95032-0116
www.rossica.org
E-mail: ed.laveroni@rossica.org

**Ryukyu Philatelic Specialist Society**
Carmine J. DiVincenzo
PO Box 381
Clayton CA 94517-0381

**St. Helena, Ascension & Tristan Da Cunha Philatelic Society**
Dr. Everett L. Parker
719 Moosehead Lake Rd.
Greenville ME 04441-9727
Ph: (207) 695 3163
ourworld.compuserve.com/homepages/ ST_HELENA_ASCEN_TDC
E-mail: eparker@midmaine.net

**St. Pierre & Miquelon Philatelic Society**
Jim Taylor
7704 Birch Bay Dr.
Blaine WA 98230
E-mail: jamestaylor@wavehome.com

**Associated Collectors of El Salvador**
Joseph D. Hahn
1015 Old Boalsburg Rd. Apt G-5
State College PA 16801-6149
www.elsalvadorphilately.org
E-mail: joehahn2@yahoo.com

**Fellowship of Samoa Specialists**
Jack R. Hughes
PO Box 1260
Boston MA 02117-1260
members.aol.com/tongajan/foss.html

**Sarawak Specialists' Society**
Stu Leven
PO Box 24764
San Jose CA 95154-4764
Ph: (408) 978-0193
www.britborneostamps.org.uk
E-mail: stulev@ix.netcom.com

**Scandinavian Collectors Club**
Donald B. Brent
PO Box 13196
El Cajon CA 92020
www.scc-online.org
E-mail: dbrent47@sprynet.com

**Slovakia Stamp Society**
Jack Benchik
PO Box 555
Notre Dame IN 46556

**Philatelic Society for Greater Southern Africa**
Alan J. Brooks
34 Seaton Drive
Aurora, ON, Canada L4G 2KI

**Spanish Philatelic Society**
Robert H. Penn
1108 Walnut Drive
Danielsville PA 18038
Ph: (610) 767-6793

**Sudan Study Group**
Charles Hass
PO Box 3435
Nashua NH 03061-3435
Ph: (603) 888-4160
E-mail: hassstamps@aol.com

**American Helvetia Philatelic Society (Switzerland, Liechtenstein)**
Richard T. Hall
PO Box 15053
Asheville NC 28813-0053
www.swiss-stamps.org
E-mail: secretary@swiss-stamps.org

**Tannu Tuva Collectors Society**
Ken Simon
513 Sixth Ave. So.
Lake Worth FL 33460-4507
Ph: (561) 588-5954
www.seflin.org/tuva
E-mail: p00311 5b@pb.seflin.org

**Society for Thai Philately**
H. R. Blakeney
PO Box 25644
Oklahoma City OK 73125
E mail: IIRBlakeney@aol.com

**Transvaal Study Circle**
J. Woolgar
132 Dale Street
Chatham, Kent ME4 6QH, United Kingdom
www.transvaalsc.org

**Ottoman and Near East Philatelic Society (Turkey and related areas)**
Bob Stuchell
193 Valley Stream Lane
Wayne PA 19087
www.oneps.org
E-mail: rstuchell@msn.com

**Ukrainian Philatelic & Numismatic Society**
George Slusarczuk
PO Box 303
Southfields NY 10975-0303
www.upns.org
E-mail: Yurko@warwick.net

**Vatican Philatelic Society**
Sal Quinonez
1 Aldersgate, Apt. 1002
Riverhead NY 11901-1830
Ph: (516) 727-6426
www.vaticanphilately.org
E-mail: pirozzi@vaticanphilately.org

**British Virgin Islands Philatelic Society**
Roger Downing
PO Box 11156
St. Thomas VI 00801-1156
www.islandsun.com/FEATURES/bviphil9198.html
E-mail: issun@candwbvi.net

**Chemistry & Physics on Stamps Study Unit**
Dr. Roland Hirsch
20458 Water Point Lane
Germantown MD 20874
www.cposu.org
E-mail: rhirsch@cposu.org

**Cats on Stamps Study Unit**
Mary Ann Brown
3006 Wade Rd.
Durham NC 27705
E-mail: ma.brown@duke.edu

**Captain Cook Study Unit**
Brian P. Sandford
173 Minuteman Dr.
Concord MA 01742-1923
www.captaincooksociety.com
E-mail: US@captaincooksociety.com/

**Canadiana Study Unit**
John Peebles
PO Box 3262, Station "A"
London, ON, Canada N6A 4K3
Ph: (619) 459-1194
Ph: (519) ... 
E-mail: john.peebles@sympatico.ca

**Biology Unit**
Alan Hanks
34 Seaton Dr.
Aurora, ON, Canada L4G 2K1
Ph: (905) 727-6993

**Bicycle Stamp Club**
Norman Batho
358 Iverson Place
East Windsor NJ 08520
Ph: (609) 448-9547
members.tripod.com/~bicyclestamps
E-mail: normbatho@worldnet.att.net

**Bird Stamp Society**
Mrs. Rosie Bradley
Crossway Green, 31 Park View,
Chepsow, Gwent, United Kingdom
NP16 5NA
E-mail: bradley666@lycos.co.uk

**Astronomy Study Unit**
George Young
PO Box 632
Tewksbury MA 01876-0632
Ph: (978) 851-8283
www.fandm.edu/departments/
astronomy/miscell/astunit.html
E-mail: george-young@msn.com

**Americana Unit**
Dennis Dengel
17 Peckham Rd.
Poughkeepsie NY 12603-2018
www.americanaunit.org
E-mail: info@americanaunit.org

## Topical Groups

**Yugoslavia Study Group of the Croatian Philatelic Society**
Michael Lenard
1514 North 3rd Ave.
Wausau WI 54401
Ph: (715) 675-2833
E-mail: mjlenard@aol.com

**Western Australia Study Group**
Brian Pope
PO Box 423
Claremont, Western Australia,
Australia 6910
www.wasc.org.uk/

**West Africa Study Circle**
Dr. Peter Newroth
5332 Sayward Hill Crescent
Victoria, BC, Canada V8Y 3H8

**Chess on Stamps Study Unit**
Anne Kasonic
7625 County Road #153
Interlaken NY 14847
E-mail: akasonic@capital.net

**Christmas Philatelic Club**
Linda Lawrence
312 Northwood Drive
Lexington KY 40505
Ph: (859) 293-0151
www.hwcn.org/link/cpc
E-mail: stamplinda@aol.com

**Christopher Columbus Philatelic Society**
Donald R. Ager
PO Box 71
Hillsboro NH 03244-0071
Ph: (603) 464-5379
E-mail: meganddon@tds.net

**Collectors of Religion on Stamps**
Verna Shackleton
425 North Linwood Avenue #110
Appleton WI 54914
www://myvbe.com/~cmfour/
coros1.htm
E-mail: corosec@sbcglobal.net

**Dogs on Stamps Study Unit**
Morris Raskin
202A Newport Rd.
Monroe Township NJ 08831
Ph: (609) 655-7411
www.dossu.org
E-mail: mraskin@cellurian.com

**Earth's Physical Features Study Group**
Fred Klein
515 Magdalena Ave.
Los Altos CA 94024
www.philately.com/society_news/
earths_physical.htm

**Ebony Society of Philatelic Events and Reflections (African-American topicals)**
Manuel Gilyard
800 Riverside Drive, Ste 4H
New York NY 10032-7412
www.esperstamps.org
E-mail: gilyardmani@aol.com

**Embroidery, Stitchery, Textile Unit**
Helen N. Cushman
1001 Genter St., Apt. 9H
La Jolla CA 92037
Ph: (619) 459-1194

**Europa Study Unit**
Donald W. Smith
PO Box 576
Johnstown PA 15907-0576
E-mail: eunity@aol.com or
donsmith65@msn.com

**Fine & Performing Arts**
Deborah L. Washington
6922 So. Jeffery Boulevard
#7 - North
Chicago IL 60649
E-mail: brasslady@comcast.net

**Fire Service in Philately**
Brian R. Engler, Sr.
726 1/2 W. Tilghman St.
Allentown PA 18102-2324
Ph: (610) 433-2782
www.firestamps.com
E-mail: brenglersr@enter.net

**Gay & Lesbian History on Stamps Club**
Joe Petronie
PO Box 190842
Dallas TX 75219-0842
www.glhsc.org
E-mail: glhsc@aol.com

**Gems, Minerals & Jewelry Study Unit**
George Young
PO Box 632
Tewksbury MA 01876-0632
Ph: (978) 851-8283
E-mail: george-young@msn.com

**Graphics Philately Association**
Mark H Winnegrad
PO Box 380
Bronx NY 10462-0380
www.graphics-stamps.org
E-mail: indybruce1@yahoo.com

**Journalists, Authors & Poets on Stamps**
Ms. Lee Strayer
P.O. Box 6808
Champaign IL 61826
E-mail: lstrayer@dcbnet.com

**Lighthouse Stamp Society**
Dalene Thomas
8612 West Warren Lane
Lakewood CO 80227-2352
Ph: (303) 986-6620
www.lighthousestampsociety.org
E-mail: dalene1@champmail.com

**Lions International Stamp Club**
John Bargus
304-2777 Barry Rd. RR 2
Mill Bay, BC, Canada V0R 2P0
Ph: (250) 743-5782

**Mahatma Gandhi On Stamps Study Circle**
Pramod Shivagunde
Pratik Clinic, Akluj
Solapur, Maharashtra, India 413101
E-mail: drnanda@bom6.vsnl.net.in

**Mask Study Unit**
Carolyn Weber
1220 Johnson Drive, Villa 104
Ventura CA 93003-0540
E-mail: cweber@venturalink.net

**Masonic Study Unit**
Stanley R. Longenecker
930 Wood St.
Mount Joy PA 17552-1926
E-mail: natsco@usa.net

**Mathematical Study Unit**
Estelle Buccino
5615 Glenwood Rd.
Bethesda MD 20817-6727
Ph: (301) 718-8898
www.math.ttu.edu/msu/
E-mail: m.strauss@ttu.edu

**Medical Subjects Unit**
Dr. Frederick C. Skvara
PO Box 6228
Bridgewater NJ 08807
E-mail: fcskvara@bellatlantic.net

**Napoleonic Age Philatelists**
Ken Berry
7513 Clayton Dr.
Oklahoma City OK 73132-5636
Ph: (405) 721-0044
E-mail: krb2@earthlink.net

**Old World Archeological Study Unit**
Caroline Scannel
11 Dawn Drive
Smithtown NY 11787-1761
www.owasu.org
E-mail: editor@owasu.org

**Petroleum Philatelic Society International**
Linda W. Corwin
5427 Pine Springs Court
Conroe TX 77304
Ph: (936) 441-0216
E-mail: corwin@pdq.net

**Philatelic Computing Study Group**
Robert de Violini
PO Box 5025
Oxnard CA 93031-5025
www.pcsg.org
E-mail: dviolini@adelphia.net

**Philatelic Lepidopterists' Association**
Alan Hanks
34 Seaton Dr.
Aurora, ON, Canada L4G 2K1
Ph: (905) 727-6933

**Rotary on Stamps Study Unit**
Richard J. Dickson
5540 N. Ocean Blvd. #207
Ocean Ridge FL 33435
rotaryonstamps.org
E-mail: roshq@kaballero.com

**Scouts on Stamps Society International**
Lawrence Clay
PO Box 6228
Kenewick WA 99336
Ph: (509) 735-3731
www.sossi.org
E-mail: tfrank@sossi.org

**Ships on Stamps Unit**
Les Smith
Site 12, Comp 11,
Kaleden, BC, Canada, V0H 1K0
www.shipsonstamps.org
E-mail: dilawren@vip.net

**Space Unit**
Carmine Torrisi
PO Box 780241
Maspeth NY 11378
Ph: (718) 386-7882
stargate1.usa.com/stamps/
E-mail: ctorrisi1@nyc.rr.com

**Sports Philatelists International**
Margaret Jones
5310 Lindenwood Ave.
St. Louis MO 63109-1758
www.sportsstamps.org

**Stamps on Stamps Collectors Club**
Alf Jordan
156 West Elm Street
Yarmouth ME 04096
Ph: (650) 234-1136
www.stampsonstamps.org
E-mail: ajordan1@maine.rr.com

**Windmill Study Unit**
Walter J. Hollien
PO Box 346
Long Valley NJ 07853-0346
Ph: (862) 812-0030
E-mail: whollien@earthlink.net

**Women on Stamps Study Unit**
Hugh Gottfried
2232 26th St.
Santa Monica CA 90405-1902
E-mail: hgottfried@adelphia.net

**Zeppelin Collectors Club**
Cheryl Ganz
PO Box 77196
Washington DC 20013

# Expertizing Services

The following organizations will, for a fee, provide expert opinions about stamps submitted to them. Collectors should contact these organizations to find out about their fees and requirements before submitting philatelic material to them. The listing of these groups here is not intended as an endorsement by Scott Publishing Co.

## General Expertizing Services

**American Philatelic Expertizing Service** (a service of the American Philatelic Society)
100 Match Factory Place
Bellefonte PA 16823-1367
Ph: (814) 237-3803
Fax: (814) 237-6128
www.stamps.org
E-mail: ambristo@stamps.org
Areas of Expertise: Worldwide

**B. P. A. Expertising, Ltd.**
PO Box 137
Leatherhead, Surrey, United Kingdom KT22 0RG
E-mail: sec.bpa@ccom.co.uk
Areas of Expertise: British Commonwealth, Great Britain, Classics of Europe, South America and the Far East

**Philatelic Foundation**
70 West 40th St., 15th Floor
New York NY 10018
Ph: (212) 221-6555
Fax: (212) 221-6208
www.philatelicfoundation.org
E-mail: philatelicfoundation@verizon.net
Areas of Expertise: U.S. & Worldwide

**Professional Stamp Experts**
PO Box 6170
Newport Beach CA 92658
Ph: (877) STAMP-88
Fax: (949) 833-7955
www.collectors.com/pse
E-mail: pseinfo@collectors.com
Areas of Expertise: Stamps and covers of U.S., U.S. Possessions, British Commonwealth

**Royal Philatelic Society Expert Committee**
41 Devonshire Place
London, United Kingdom W1N 1PE
www.rpsl.org.uk/experts.html
E-mail: experts@rpsl.org.uk
Areas of Expertise: All

## Expertizing Services Covering Specific Fields Or Countries

**Canadian Society of Russian Philately Expertizing Service**
PO Box 5722, Station A
Toronto, ON, Canada M5W 1P2
Fax: (416)932-0853
Areas of Expertise: Russian areas

**China Stamp Society Expertizing Service**
1050 West Blue Ridge Blvd
Kansas City MO 64145
Ph: (816) 942-6300
E-mail: hjmesq@aol.com
Areas of Expertise: China

**Confederate Stamp Alliance Authentication Service**
c/o Patricia A. Kaufmann
10194 N. Old State Road
Lincoln DE 19960-9797
Ph: (302) 422-2656
Fax: (302) 424-1990
www.webuystamps.com/csaauth.htm
E-mail: trishkauf@comcast.net
Areas of Expertise: Confederate stamps and postal history

**Croatian Philatelic Society Expertizing Service**
PO Box 696
Fritch TX 79036-0696
Ph: (806) 857-0129
E-mail: ou812@arn.net
Areas of Expertise: Croatia and other Balkan areas

**Errors, Freaks and Oddities Collectors Club Expertizing Service**
138 East Lakemont Dr.
Kingsland GA 31548
Ph: (912) 729-1573
Areas of Expertise: U.S. errors, freaks and oddities

**Estonian Philatelic Society Expertizing Service**
39 Clafford Lane
Melville NY 11747
Ph: (516) 421-2078
E-mail: esto4@aol.com
Areas of Expertise: Estonia

**Hawaiian Philatelic Society Expertizing Service**
PO Box 10115
Honolulu HI 96816-0115
Areas of Expertise: Hawaii

**Hong Kong Stamp Society Expertizing Service**
PO Box 206
Glenside PA 19038
Fax: (215) 576-6850
Areas of Expertise: Hong Kong

**International Association of Philatelics Experts**
United States Associate members:

**Paul Buchsbayew**
119 W. 57th St.
New York NY 10019
Ph: (212) 977-7734
Fax: (212) 977-8653
Areas of Expertise: Russia, Soviet Union

**William T. Crowe**
(see Professional Stamp Experts)
Areas of Expertise: United States

**John Lievsay**
(see American Philatelic Expertizing Service and Philatelic Foundation)
Areas of Expertise: France

**Robert W. Lyman**
P.O. Box 348
Irvington on Hudson NY 10533
Ph and Fax: (914) 591-6937
Areas of Expertise: British North America, New Zealand

**Robert Odenweller**
P.O. Box 401
Bernardsville, NJ 07924-0401
Ph and Fax: (908) 766-5460
Areas of Expertise: New Zealand, Samoa to 1900

**Alex Rendon**
P.O. Box 323
Massapequa NY 11762
Ph and Fax: (516) 795-0464
Areas of Expertise: Bolivia, Colombia, Colombian States

**Sergio Sismondo**
10035 Carousel Center Dr.
Syracuse NY 13290-0001
Ph: (315) 422-2331
Fax: (315) 422-2956
Areas of Expertise: British East Africa, Camerouns, Cape of Good Hope, Canada, British North America

**International Society for Japanese Philately Expertizing Committee**
32 King James Court
Staten Island NY 10308-2910
Ph: (718) 227-5229
Areas of Expertise: Japan and related areas, except WWII Japanese Occupation issues

**International Society for Portuguese Philately Expertizing Service**
PO Box 43146
Philadelphia PA 19129-3146
Ph: (215) 843-2106
Fax: (215) 843-2106
E-mail: s.s.washburne@worldnet.att.net
Areas of Expertise: Portugal and colonies

**Mexico-Elmhurst Philatelic Society International Expert Committee**
PO Box 1133
West Covina CA 91793
Areas of Expertise: Mexico

**Philatelic Society for Greater Southern Africa Expert Panel**
13955 W. 30th Ave.
Golden CO 80401
Areas of expertise: Entire South and South West Africa area, Bechuanalands, Basutoland, Swaziland

**Ukrainian Philatelic & Numismatic Society Expertizing Service**
30552 Dell Lane
Warren MI 48092-1862
Ph: (810) 751-5754
Areas of Expertise: Ukraine, Western Ukraine

**V. G. Greene Philatelic Research Foundation**
P.O. Box 204, Station Q
Toronto, ON, Canada M4T 2M1
Ph: (416) 921-2073
Fax: (416) 921-1282
E-mail: vggfoundation@on.aibn.com
www.greenefoundation.ca
Areas of Expertise: British North America

# Information on Catalogue Values, Grade and Condition

## Catalogue Value

The Scott Catalogue value is a retail value; that is, an amount you could expect to pay for a stamp in the grade of Very Fine with no faults. Any exceptions to the grade valued will be noted in the text. The general introduction on the following pages and the individual section introductions further explain the type of material that is valued. The value listed for any given stamp is a reference that reflects recent actual dealer selling prices for that item.

Dealer retail price lists, public auction results, published prices in advertising and individual solicitation of retail prices from dealers, collectors and specialty organizations have been used in establishing the values found in this catalogue. Scott Publishing Co. values stamps, but Scott is not a company engaged in the business of buying and selling stamps as a dealer.

Use this catalogue as a guide for buying and selling. The actual price you pay for a stamp may be higher or lower than the catalogue value because of many different factors, including the amount of personal service a dealer offers, or increased or decreased interest in the country or topic represented by a stamp or set. An item may occasionally be offered at a lower price as a "loss leader," or as part of a special sale. You also may obtain an item inexpensively at public auction because of little interest at that time or as part of a large lot.

Stamps that are of a lesser grade than Very Fine, or those with condition problems, generally trade at lower prices than those given in this catalogue. Stamps of exceptional quality in both grade and condition often command higher prices than those listed.

Values for pre-1900 unused issues are for stamps with approximately half or more of their original gum. Stamps with most or all of their original gum may be expected to sell for more, and stamps with less than half of their original gum may be expected to sell for somewhat less than the values listed. On rarer stamps, it may be expected that the original gum will be somewhat more disturbed than it will be on more common issues. Post-1900 unused issues are assumed to have full original gum. From breakpoints in most countries' listings, stamps are valued as never hinged, due to the wide availability of stamps in that condition. These notations are prominently placed in the listings and in the country information preceding the listings. Some countries also feature listings with dual values for hinged and never-hinged stamps.

## Grade

A stamp's grade and condition are crucial to its value. The accompanying illustrations show examples of Very Fine stamps from different time periods, along with examples of stamps in Fine to Very Fine and Extremely Fine grades as points of reference. When a stamp seller offers a stamp in any grade from fine to superb without further qualifying statements, that stamp should not only have the centering grade as defined, but it also should be free of faults or other condition problems.

**FINE** stamps (illustrations not shown) have designs that are quite off-center, with the perforations on one or two sides very close to the design but not quite touching it. There is white space between the perforations and the design that is minimal but evident to the unaided eye. Imperforate stamps may have small margins, and earlier issues may show the design just touching one edge of the stamp design. Very early perforated issues normally will have the perforations slightly cutting into the design. Used stamps may have heavier than usual cancellations.

**FINE-VERY FINE** stamps will be somewhat off center on one side, or slightly off center on two sides. Imperforate stamps will have two margins of at least normal size, and the design will not touch any edge. For perforated stamps, the perfs are well clear of the design, but are still noticeably off center. However, early issues of a country may be printed in such a way that the perforations may touch the design. In these cases, the perforations may cut

into the design very slightly. Used stamps will not have a cancellation that detracts from the design.

**VERY FINE** stamps will be just slightly off center on one or two sides, but the design will be well clear of the edge. The stamp will present a nice, balanced appearance. Imperforate stamps will be well centered within normal-sized margins. However, early issues of many countries may be printed in such a way that the perforations may touch the design on one or more sides. Where this is the case, a boxed note will be found defining the centering and margins of the stamps being valued. Used stamps will have light or otherwise neat cancellations. This is the grade used to establish Scott Catalogue values.

**EXTREMELY FINE** stamps are close to being perfectly centered. Imperforate stamps will have even margins that are slightly larger than normal. Even the earliest perforated issues will have perforations clear of the design on all sides.

**Scott Publishing Co. recognizes that there is no formally enforced grading scheme for postage stamps, and that the final price you pay or obtain for a stamp will be determined by individual agreement at the time of transaction.**

## Condition

Grade addresses only centering and (for used stamps) cancellation. Condition refers to factors other than grade that affect a stamp's desirability.

Factors that can increase the value of a stamp include exceptionally wide margins, particularly fresh color, the presence of selvage, and plate or die varieties. Unusual cancels on used stamps (particularly those of the 19th century) can greatly enhance their value as well.

Factors other than faults that decrease the value of a stamp include loss of original gum, regumming, a hinge remnant or foreign object adhering to the gum, natural inclusions, straight edges, and markings or notations applied by collectors or dealers.

Faults include missing pieces, tears, pin or other holes, surface scuffs, thin spots, creases, toning, short or pulled perforations, clipped perforations, oxidation or other forms of color changelings, soiling, stains, and such man-made changes as reperforations or the chemical removal or lightening of a cancellation.

## Stamp Illustrations Used in the Catalogue

It is important to note that the stamp images used for identification purposes in this catalogue may not be indicative of the grade of stamp being valued. Refer to the written discussion of grades on this page and to the grading illustrations on the following two pages for grading information.

## Grading Illustrations

On the following two pages are illustrations of various stamps from countries appearing in this volume. These stamps are arranged by country, and they represent early or important issues that are often found in widely different grades in the marketplace. The editors believe the illustrations will prove useful in showing the margin size and centering that will be seen on the various issues.

In addition to the matters of margin size and centering, collectors are reminded that the very fine stamps valued in the Scott catalogues also will possess fresh color and intact perforations, and they will be free from defects.

Examples shown are computer-manipulated images made from single digitized master illustrations.

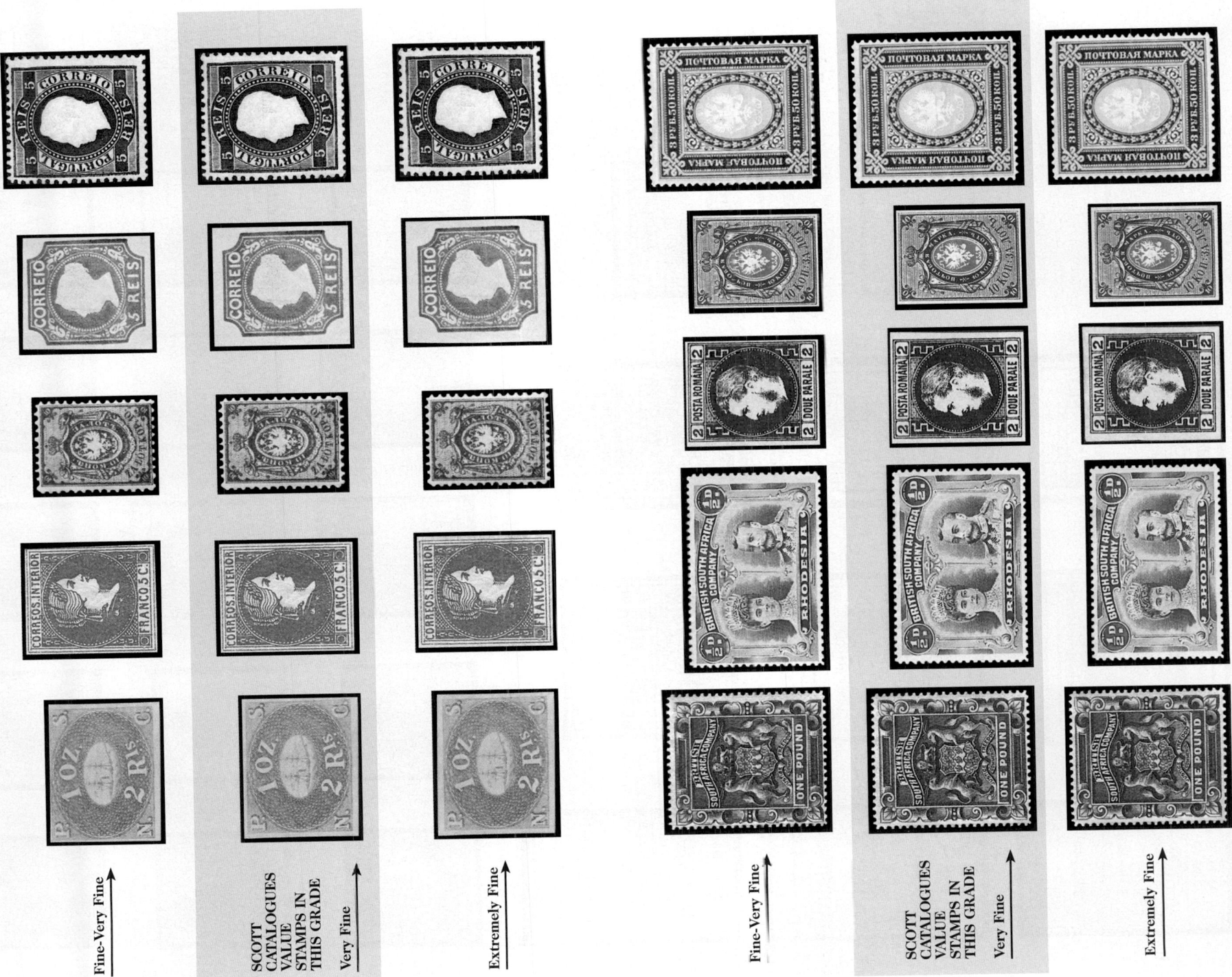

Fine-Very Fine

SCOTT CATALOGUES VALUE STAMPS IN THIS GRADE
Very Fine

Extremely Fine

Fine-Very Fine

SCOTT CATALOGUES VALUE STAMPS IN THIS GRADE
Very Fine

Extremely Fine

Very Fine

SCOTT
CATALOGUES
VALUE
STAMPS IN
THIS GRADE

Very Fine

SCOTT
CATALOGUES
VALUE
STAMPS IN
THIS GRADE

For purposes of helping to determine the gum condition and value of an unused stamp, Scott Publishing Co. presents the following chart which details different gum conditions and indicates how the conditions correlate with the Scott values for unused stamps. Used together, the Illustrated Grading Chart on the previous pages and this Illustrated Gum Chart should allow catalogue users to better understand the grade and gum condition of stamps valued in the Scott catalogues.

| Gum Categories: | MINT N.H. | | ORIGINAL GUM (O.G.) | | | | NO GUM |
|---|---|---|---|---|---|---|---|
| | **Mint Never Hinged** *Free from any disturbance* | **Lightly Hinged** *Faint impression of a removed hinge over a small area* | **Hinge Mark or Remnant** *Prominent hinged spot with part or all of the hinge remaining* | **Large part o.g.** *Approximately half or more of the gum intact* | **Small part o.g.** *Approximately less than half of the gum intact* | | **No gum** *Only if issued with gum* |
| Commonly Used Symbol: | ★★ | ★ | ★ | ★ | ★ | | (★) |
| Pre-1900 Issues (Pre-1890 for U.S.) | *Very fine pre-1900 stamps in these categories trade at a premium over Scott value* | | | Scott Value for "Unused" | | | Scott "No Gum" listings for selected unused classic stamps |
| From 1900 to breakpoints for listings of never-hinged stamps | Scott "Never Hinged" listings for selected unused stamps | Scott Value for "Unused" (Actual value will be affected by the degree of hinging of the full original gum.) | | | | | |
| From breakpoints noted for many countries | Scott Value for "Unused" | | | | | | |

**Never Hinged (NH; ★★):** A never-hinged stamp will have full original gum that will have no hinge mark or disturbance. The presence of an expertizer's mark does not disqualify a stamp from this designation.

**Original Gum (OG; ★):** Pre-1900 stamps should have approximately half or more of their original gum. On rarer stamps, it may be expected that the original gum will be somewhat more disturbed that it will be on more common issues. Post-1900 stamps should have full original gum. Original gum will show some disturbance caused by a previous hinge(s) which may be present or entirely removed. The actual value of a post-1900 stamp will be affected by the degree of hinging of the full original gum.

**Disturbed Original Gum:** Gum showing noticeable effects of humidity, climate or hinging over more than half of the gum. The significance of gum disturbance in valuing a stamp in any of the Original Gum categories depends on the degree of disturbance, the rarity and normal gum condition of the issue and other variables affecting quality.

**Regummed (RG; (★)):** A regummed stamp is a stamp without gum that has had some type of gum privately applied at a time after it was issued. This normally is done to deceive collectors and/or dealers into thinking that the stamp has original gum and therefore has a higher value. A regummed stamp is considered the same as a stamp with none of its original gum for purposes of grading.

# Understanding the Listings

On the opposite page is an enlarged "typical" listing from this catalogue. Below are detailed explanations of each of the highlighted parts of the listing.

**1 Scott number** — Scott catalogue numbers are used to identify specific items when buying, selling or trading stamps. Each listed postage stamp from every country has a unique Scott catalogue number. Therefore, Germany Scott 99, for example, can only refer to a single stamp. Although the Scott catalogue usually lists stamps in chronological order by date of issue, there are exceptions. When a country has issued a set of stamps over a period of time, those stamps within the set are kept together without regard to date of issue. This follows the normal collecting approach of keeping stamps in their natural sets.

When a country issues a set of stamps over a period of time, a group of consecutive catalogue numbers is reserved for the stamps in that set, as issued. If that group of numbers proves to be too few, capital-letter suffixes, such as "A" or "B," may be added to existing numbers to create enough catalogue numbers to cover all items in the set. A capital-letter suffix indicates a major Scott catalogue number listing. Scott uses a suffix letter only once. Therefore, a catalogue number listing with a capital-letter suffix will not also be found with the same number (lower case) used as a minor-letter listing. If there is a Scott 16A in a set, for example, there will not also be a Scott 16a. However, a minor-letter "a" listing may be added to a major number containing an "A" suffix (Scott 16Aa, for example).

Suffix letters are cumulative. A minor "b" variety of Scott 16A would be Scott 16Ab, not Scott 16b.

There are times when a reserved block of Scott catalogue numbers is too large for a set, leaving some numbers unused. Such gaps in the numbering sequence also occur when the catalogue editors move an item's listing elsewhere or have removed it entirely from the catalogue. Scott does not attempt to account for every possible number, but rather attempts to assure that each stamp is assigned its own number.

Scott numbers designating regular postage normally are only numerals. Scott numbers for other types of stamps, such as air post, semi-postal, postal tax, postage due, occupation and others have a prefix consisting of one or more capital letters or a combination of numerals and capital letters.

**2 Illustration number** — Illustration or design-type numbers are used to identify each catalogue illustration. For most sets, the lowest face-value stamp is shown. It then serves as an example of the basic design approach for other stamps not illustrated. Where more than one stamp use the same illustration number, but have differences in design, the design paragraph or the description line clearly indicates the design on each stamp not illustrated. Where there are both vertical and horizontal designs in a set, a single illustration may be used, with the exceptions noted in the design paragraph or description line.

When an illustration is followed by a lowercase letter in parentheses, such as "A2(b)," the trailing letter indicates which overprint or surcharge illustration applies.

Illustrations normally are 70 percent of the original size of the stamp. An effort has been made to note all illustrations not illustrated at that percentage. Virtually all souvenir sheet illustrations are reduced even more. Overprints and surcharges are shown at 100 percent of their original size if shown alone, but are 70 percent of original size if shown on stamps. In some cases, the illustration will be placed above the set, between listings or omitted completely. Overprint and surcharge illustrations are not placed in this catalogue for purposes of expertizing stamps.

**3** There are two principal types of catalogue listings: major and minor.

Major listings are in a larger type style than minor listings. The catalogue number is a numeral that can be found with or without a capital-letter suffix, and with or without a prefix.

Minor listings are in a smaller type style and have a small-letter suffix or (if the listing immediately follows that of the major number) may show only the letter. These listings identify a variety of each major item.

**4 Listing styles** — There are two principal types of catalogue listings: major and minor.

**5 Paper color** — The color of a stamp's paper is noted in italic type when the paper used is not white.

**6 Illustration number** — 
*(continued)*

**5 Basic information about a stamp or set** — Introducing each stamp issue is a small section (usually a line listing) of basic information about a stamp or set. This section normally includes the date of issue, method of printing, perforation, watermark and, sometimes, some additional information of note. *Printing method, perforation and watermark apply to the following listings until a change is noted.* Stamps created by overprinting or surcharging previous issues are assumed to have the same perforation, watermark and printing method as the original. Dates of issue are as precise as Scott is able to confirm and often reflect the dates on first-day covers, rather than the actual date of release.

Examples of major number listings include 16, 28A, B97, C13A, 10N5, and 10N6A. Examples of minor numbers are 16a and C13Ab.

Examples include perforation, color, watermark or printing method differences, multiples (some souvenir sheets, booklet panes and se-tenant combinations), and singles of multiples.

**6 Denomination** — This normally refers to the face value of the stamp; that is, the cost of the unused stamp at the post office at the time of issue. When a denomination is shown in parentheses, it does not appear on the stamp. This includes the non-denominated stamps of the United States, Brazil and Great Britain, for example.

**7 Color or other description** — This area provides information to solidify identification of a stamp. In many recent cases, a description of the stamp design appears in this space, rather than a listing of colors.

**8 Year of issue** — In stamp sets that have been released in a period that spans more than a year, the number shown in parentheses is the year that the stamp first appeared. Stamps without a date appeared during the first year of the issue. Dates are not always given for minor varieties.

**9 Value unused and Value used** — The Scott catalogue values are based on stamps that are in a grade of Very Fine unless stated otherwise. Unused values refer to items that have not been postal, revenue or any other duty for which they were intended. Pre-1900 unused stamps that were issued with gum must have at least most of their original gum. Later issues are assumed to have full original gum. From breakpoints specified in most countries' listings, stamps are valued as never hinged. Stamps issued without gum are noted. Modern issues with PVA or other synthetic adhesives may appear ungummed. Unused self-adhesive stamps are valued as appearing undisturbed on their original backing paper. Values for used self-adhesive stamps are for examples either on piece or off piece. For a more detailed explanation of these values, please see the "Catalogue Value," "Condition" and "Understanding Valuing Notations" sections elsewhere in this introduction.

In some cases, where used stamps are more valuable than unused stamps, the value is for an example with a contemporaneous cancel, rather than a modern cancel or a smudge or other unclear marking. For those stamps that were released for postal and fiscal purposes, the used value represents a postally used stamp. Stamps with revenue cancels generally sell for less.

Stamps separated from a complete se-tenant multiple usually will be worth less than a pro-rated portion of the se-tenant multiple, and stamps lacking the attached labels that are noted in the listings will be worth less than the values shown.

**10 Changes in basic set information** — Bold type is used to show any changes in the basic data given for a set of stamps. This includes perforation differences from one stamp to the next or a different paper, printing method or watermark.

**11 Total value of a set** — The total value of sets of three or more stamps issued after 1900 are shown. The set line also notes the range of Scott numbers and total number of stamps included in the grouping. The actual value of a set consisting predominantly of stamps having the minimum value of twenty cents may be less than the total value shown. Similarly, the actual value or catalogue value of se-tenant pairs or of blocks consisting of stamps having the minimum value of twenty cents may be less than the catalogue values of the component parts.

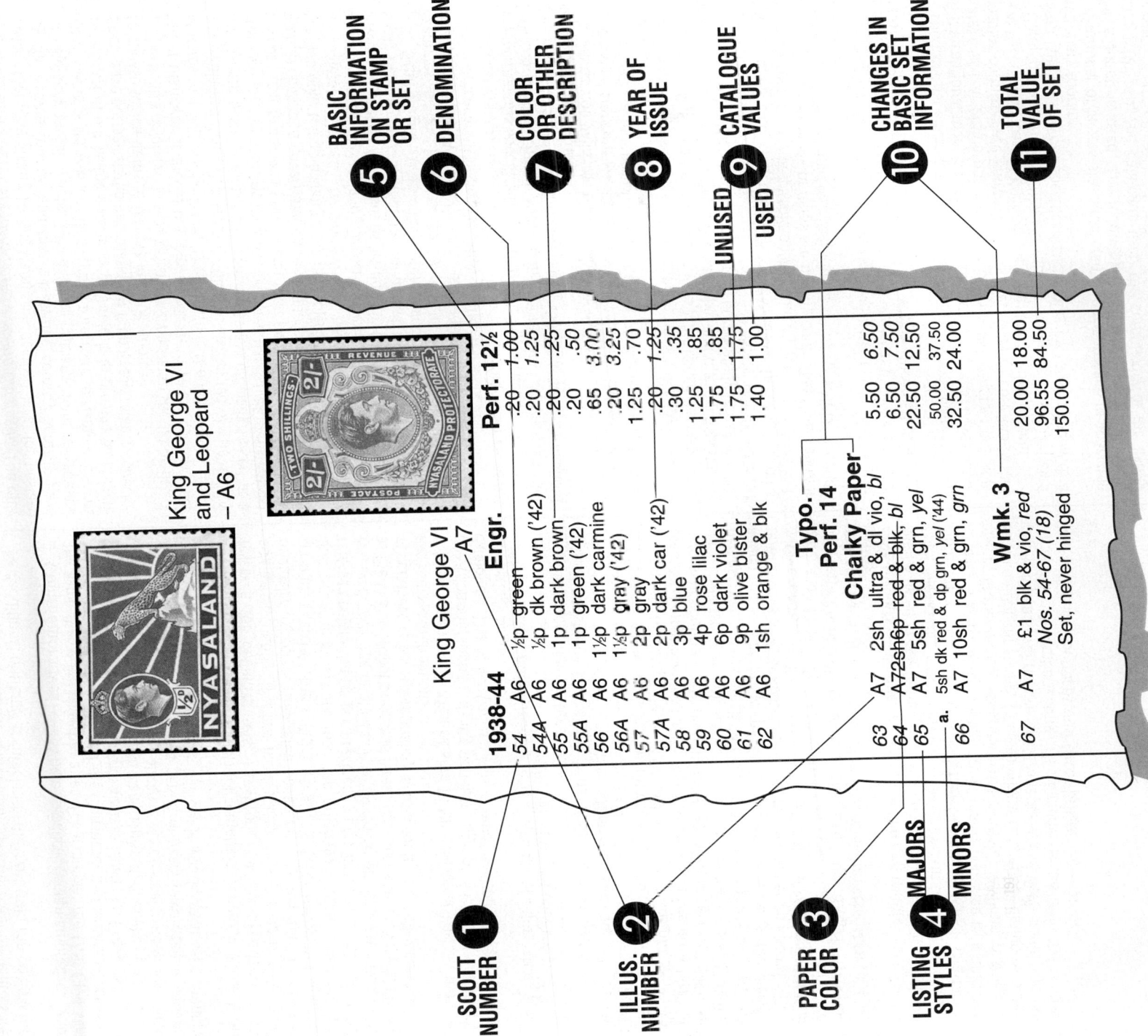

**5** BASIC INFORMATION ON STAMP OR SET

**6** DENOMINATION

**7** COLOR OR OTHER DESCRIPTION

**8** YEAR OF ISSUE

**9** CATALOGUE VALUES — UNUSED / USED

**10** CHANGES IN BASIC SET INFORMATION

**11** TOTAL VALUE OF SET

**1** SCOTT NUMBER

**2** ILLUS. NUMBER

**3** PAPER COLOR

**4** LISTING STYLES — MAJORS / MINORS

King George VI and Leopard — A6

King George VI A7

**1938-44   Engr.   Perf. 12½**

| Scott | Illus | Denom | Color/Description | Unused | Used |
|---|---|---|---|---|---|
| 54 | A6 | ½p | green | .20 | 1.00 |
| 54A | A6 | ½p | dk brown ('42) | .20 | 1.25 |
| 55 | A6 | 1p | dark brown | .20 | .25 |
| 55A | A6 | 1p | green ('42) | .20 | .50 |
| 56 | A6 | 1½p | dark carmine | .65 | 3.00 |
| 56A | A6 | 1½p | gray ('42) | .20 | 3.25 |
| 57 | A6 | 2p | gray | 1.25 | .70 |
| 57A | A6 | 2p | dark car ('42) | .20 | 1.25 |
| 58 | A6 | 3p | blue | .30 | .35 |
| 59 | A6 | 4p | rose lilac | 1.25 | .85 |
| 60 | A6 | 6p | dark violet | 1.75 | .85 |
| 61 | A6 | 9p | olive blster | 1.75 | 1.75 |
| 62 | A6 | 1sh | orange & blk | 1.40 | 1.00 |

**Typo.   Perf. 14   Chalky Paper**

| Scott | Illus | Denom | Color/Description | Unused | Used |
|---|---|---|---|---|---|
| 63 | A7 | 2sh | ultra & dl vio, bl | 5.50 | 6.50 |
| 64 | A7 | 2sh6p | red & blk, bl | 6.50 | 7.50 |
| 65 | A7 | 5sh | red & grn, yel | 22.50 | 12.50 |
| a. | | 5sh | dk red & dp grn, yel ('44) | 50.00 | 37.50 |
| 66 | A7 | 10sh | red & grn, grn | 32.50 | 24.00 |

**Wmk. 3**

| Scott | Illus | Denom | Color/Description | Unused | Used |
|---|---|---|---|---|---|
| 67 | A7 | £1 | blk & vio, red | 20.00 | 18.00 |
| | | | Nos. 54-67 (18) | 96.55 | 84.50 |
| | | | Set, never hinged | 150.00 | |

# Catalogue Listing Policy

It is the intent of Scott Publishing Co. to list all postage stamps of the world in the *Scott Standard Postage Stamp Catalogue*. The only strict criteria for listing is that stamps be decreed legal for postage by the issuing country and that the issuing country actually have an operating postal system. Whether the primary intent of issuing a given stamp or set was for sale to postal patrons or to stamp collectors is not part of our listing criteria. Scott's role is to provide basic comprehensive postage stamp information. It is up to each stamp collector to choose which items to include in a collection.

It is Scott's objective to seek reasons why a stamp should be listed, rather than why it should not. Nevertheless, there are certain types of items that will not be listed. These include the following:

1. Unissued items that are not officially distributed or released by the issuing postal authority. If such items are officially issued at a later date by the country, they will be listed. Unissued items consist of those that have been printed and then held from sale for reasons such as change in government, errors found on stamps or something deemed objectionable about a stamp subject or design.

2. Stamps "issued" by non-existent postal entities or fantasy countries, such as Nagaland, Occusi-Ambeno, Staffa, Sedang, Torres Straits and others. Also, stamps "issued" in the names of legitimate, stamp-issuing countries that are not authorized by those countries.

3. Semi-official or unofficial items not required for postage. Examples include items issued by private agencies for their own express services. When such items are required for delivery, or are valid as prepayment of postage, they are listed.

4. Local stamps issued for local use only. Postage stamps issued by governments specifically for "domestic" use, such as Haiti Scott 219-228, or the United States non-denominated stamps, are not considered to be locals, since they are valid for postage throughout the country of origin.

5. Items not valid for postal use. For example, a few countries have issued souvenir sheets that are not valid for postage. This area also includes a number of worldwide charity labels (some denominated) that do not pay postage.

6. Intentional varieties, such as imperforate stamps that look like their perforated counterparts and are usually issued in very small quantities. Also, other egregiously exploitative issues such as stamps sold for far more than face value, stamps purposefully issued in artificially small quantities or only against advance orders, stamps awarded only to a selected audience such as a philatelic bureau's standing order customers, or stamps sold only in conjunction with other products. All of these kinds of items are usually controlled issues and/or are intended for speculation. These items normally will be included in a footnote.

7. Items distributed by the issuing government only to a limited group, club, philatelic exhibition or a single stamp dealer or other private company. These items normally will be included in a footnote.

The fact that a stamp has been used successfully as postage, even on international mail, is not in itself sufficient proof that it was legitimately issued. Numerous examples of so-called stamps from non-existent countries are known to have been used to post letters that have successfully passed through the international mail system.

There are certain items that are subject to interpretation. When a stamp falls outside our specifications, it may be listed along with a cautionary footnote.

A number of factors are considered in our approach to analyzing how a stamp is listed. The following list of factors is presented to share with you, the catalogue user, the complexity of the listing process.

**Additional printings** — "Additional printings" of a previously issued stamp may range from an item that is totally different to cases where it is impossible to differentiate from the original. At least a minor number (a small-letter suffix) is assigned if there is a distinct change in stamp shade, noticeably redrawn design, or a significantly different perforation measurement. A major number (numeral or

numeral and capital-letter combination) is assigned if the editors feel the "additional printing" is sufficiently different from the original that it constitutes a different issue.

**Commemoratives** — Where practical, commemoratives with the same theme are placed in a set. For example, the U.S. Civil War Centennial set of 1961-65 and the Constitution Bicentennial series of 1989-90 appear as sets. Countries such as Japan and Korea issue such material on a regular basis, with an announced, or at least predictable, number of stamps known in advance. Occasionally, however, stamp sets that were released over a period of years have been separated. Appropriately placed footnotes will guide you to each set's continuation.

**Definitive sets** — Blocks of numbers generally have been reserved for definitive sets, based on previous experience with any given country. If a few more stamps were issued in a set than originally expected, they often have been inserted into the original set with a capital-letter suffix, such as U.S. Scott 1059A. If it appears that many more stamps than the originally allotted block will be released before the set is completed, a new block of numbers will be reserved, with the original one being closed off. In some cases, such as the U.S. Transportation and Great Americans series, several blocks of numbers exist. Appropriately placed footnotes will guide you to each set's continuation.

**New country** — Membership in the Universal Postal Union is not a consideration for listing status or order of placement within the catalogue. The index will tell you in what volume or page number the listings begin.

**"No release date" items** — The amount of information available for any given stamp issue varies greatly from country to country and even from time to time. Extremely comprehensive information about new stamps is available from some countries well before the stamps are released. By contrast some countries do not provide information about stamps or release dates. Most countries, however, fall between these extremes. A country may provide denominations or subjects of stamps from upcoming issues that are not issued as planned. Sometimes, philatelic agencies, those private firms hired to represent countries, add these later-issued items to sets well after the formal release date. This time period can range from weeks to years. If these items were officially released by the country, they will be added to the appropriate spot in the set. In many cases, the specific release date of a stamp or set of stamps may never be known.

**Overprints** — The color of an overprint is always noted if it is other than black. Where more than one color of ink has been used on overprints of a single set, the color used is noted. Early overprint and surcharge illustrations were altered to prevent their use by forgers.

**Se-tenants** — Connected stamps of differing features (se-tenants) will be listed in the format most commonly collected. This includes pairs, blocks or larger multiples. Se-tenant units are not always symmetrical. An example is Australia Scott 508, which is a block of seven stamps. If the stamps are primarily collected as a unit, the major number may be assigned to the multiple, with minors going to each component stamp. In cases where continuous-design or other unit se-tenants will receive significant postal use, each stamp is given a major Scott number listing. This includes issues from the United States, Canada, Germany and Great Britain, for example.

# Special Notices

## Classification of stamps

The *Scott Standard Postage Stamp Catalogue* lists stamps by country of issue. The next level of organization is a listing by section on the basis of the function of the stamps. The principal sections cover regular postage, semi-postal, air post, special delivery, registration, postage due and other categories. Except for regular postage, catalogue numbers for all sections include a prefix letter (or number-letter combination) denoting the class to which a given stamp belongs. When some countries issue sets containing stamps from more than one category, the catalogue will at times list all of the stamps in one category (such as air post stamps listed as part of a postage set).

The following is a listing of the most commonly used catalogue prefixes.

### Prefix... Category

C .....Air Post
M.....Military
P.......Newspaper
N......Occupation - Regular Issues
O......Official
Q......Parcel Post
J.......Postage Due
RA....Postal Tax
B......Semi-Postal
E......Special Delivery
MR ....War Tax

Other prefixes used by more than one country include the following:

H......Acknowledgment of Receipt
I.......Late Fee
CO.....Air Post Official
CQ....Air Post Parcel Post
RAC..Air Post Postal Tax
CF.....Air Post Registration
CB.....Air Post Semi-Postal
CBO..Air Post Semi-Postal Official
CE.....Air Post Special Delivery
EY.....Authorized Delivery
S.......Franchise
G.......Insured Letter
GY....Marine Insurance
MC....Military Air Post
MQ....Military Parcel Post
NC.....Occupation - Air Post
NO.....Occupation - Official
NJ......Occupation - Postage Due
NRA..Occupation - Postal Tax
NB.....Occupation - Semi-Postal
NE.....Occupation - Special Delivery
QY ....Parcel Post Authorized Delivery
AR ....Postal-fiscal
RAJ ....Postal Tax Due
RAB ....Postal Tax Semi-Postal
F.......Registration
EB.....Semi-Postal Special Delivery
EO .....Special Delivery Official
QE .....Special Handling

## New issue listings

Updates to this catalogue appear each month in the *Scott Stamp Monthly* magazine. Included in this update are additions to the listings of countries found in the *Scott Standard Postage Stamp Catalogue* and the *Specialized Catalogue of United States Stamps*, as well as corrections and updates to current editions of this catalogue.

From time to time there will be changes in the final listings of stamps from the *Scott Stamp Monthly* to the next edition of the catalogue. This occurs as more information about certain stamps or sets becomes available.

The catalogue update section of the *Scott Stamp Monthly* is the most timely presentation of this material available. Annual subscriptions to the *Scott Stamp Monthly* are available from Scott Publishing Co., Box 828, Sidney, OH 45365-0828.

## Number additions, deletions & changes

A listing of catalogue number additions, deletions and changes from the previous edition of the catalogue appears in each volume. See the Catalogue Number Additions, Deletions & Changes in the table of contents for the location of this list.

## Understanding valuing notations

The *minimum catalogue value* of an individual stamp or set is 20 cents. This represents a portion of the cost incurred by a dealer when he prepares an individual stamp for resale. As a point of philatelic-economic fact, the lower the value shown for an item in this catalogue, the greater the percentage of that value is attributed to dealer mark up and profit margin. In many cases, such as the 20-cent minimum value, that price does not cover the labor or other costs involved with stocking it as an individual stamp. The sum of minimum values in a set does not properly represent the value of a complete set primarily composed of a number of minimum-value stamps, nor does the sum represent the actual value of a packet made up of minimum-value stamps. Thus a packet of 1,000 different common stamps — each of which has a catalogue value of 20 cents — normally sells for considerably less than 200 dollars!

The *absence of a retail value* for a stamp does not necessarily suggest that a stamp is scarce or rare. A dash in the value column means that the stamp is known in a stated form or variety, but information is either lacking or insufficient for purposes of establishing a usable catalogue value.

Stamp values in *italics* generally refer to items that are difficult to value accurately. For expensive items, such as those priced at $1,000 or higher, a value in italics indicates that the affected item trades very seldom. For inexpensive items, a value in italics represents a warning. One example is a "blocked" issue where the issuing postal administration may have controlled one stamp in a set in an attempt to make the whole set more valuable. Another example is an item that sold at an extreme multiple of face value in the marketplace at the time of its issue.

One type of warning to collectors that appears in the catalogue is illustrated by a stamp that is valued considerably higher in used condition than it is as unused. In this case, collectors are cautioned to be certain the used version has a genuine and contemporaneous cancellation. The type of cancellation on a stamp can be an important factor in determining its sale price. Catalogue values do not apply to fiscal, telegraph or non-contemporaneous postal cancels, unless otherwise noted.

Some countries have released back issues of stamps in canceled-to-order form, sometimes covering as much as a 10-year period. The Scott Catalogue values for used stamps reflect canceled-to-order material when such stamps are found to predominate in the marketplace for the issue involved. Notes frequently appear in the stamp listings to specify which items are valued as canceled-to-order, or if there is a premium for postally used examples.

Many countries sell canceled-to-order stamps at a marked reduction of face value. Countries that sell or have sold canceled-to-order stamps at *full* face value include United Nations, Australia, Netherlands, France and Switzerland. It may be almost impossible to identify such stamps if the gum has been removed, because official government canceling devices are used. Postally used copies of these items on cover, however, are usually worth more than the canceled-to-order stamps with original gum.

## Abbreviations

Scott Publishing Co. uses a consistent set of abbreviations throughout this catalogue to conserve space, while still providing necessary information.

# COLOR ABBREVIATIONS

| | | |
|---|---|---|
| amb.amber | crim.crimson | ol....olive |
| anil.aniline | cr....cream | olvn.olivine |
| ap ...apple | dk ...dark | org...orange |
| aqua.aquamarine | dl...dull | pck..peacock |
| az...azure | dp...deep | pnksh pinkish |
| bis...bister | db...drab | Prus.Prussian |
| bl...blue | emer emerald | pur...purple |
| bld.blood | gldn.golden | redshreddish |
| blk...black | grysh grayish | res...reseda |
| bril.brilliant | gm...green | ros...rosine |
| brn..brown | grnshgreenish | ryl...royal |
| brnshbrownish | hel..heliotrope | sal....salmon |
| brnz.bronze | hn...henna | saph.sapphire |
| brt...bright | ind..indigo | scar..scarlet |
| brnt.burnt | int..intense | sep...sepia |
| car...carmine | lav..lavender | sien.sienna |
| cer ...cerise | lem..lemon | sil...silver |
| chlkychalky | lt.....light | sl....slate |
| chamchamois | lil...lilac | stl...steel |
| chnt.chestnut | mag.magenta | turq.turquoise |
| choc.chocolate | man.manila | ultra.ultramarine |
| chr...chrome | mar..maroon | Ven..Venetian |
| cit...citron | mv...mauve | ver...vermilion |
| cl...claret | multi multicolored | vio...violet |
| cob..cobalt | mlky milky | yel...yellow |
| cop...copper | myr..myrtle | yelsh yellowish |

When no color is given for an overprint or surcharge, black is the color used. Abbreviations for colors used for overprints and surcharges include: "(B)" or "(Blk)," black; "(Bl)," blue; "(R)," red; and "(G)," green.

Additional abbreviations in this catalogue are shown below:

| | | |
|---|---|---|
| Adm....Administration | | Intl....International |
| AFL....American Federation of Labor | | Invtd....Inverted |
| Anniv....Anniversary | | L....Left |
| APS....American Philatelic Society | | Lieut., lt....Lieutenant |
| Assoc....Association | | Litho....Lithographed |
| ASSR....Autonomous Soviet Socialist Republic | | LL....Lower left |
| b....Born | | LR....Lower right |
| BEP....Bureau of Engraving and Printing | | mm....Millimeter |
| Bicent....Bicentennial | | Ms....Manuscript |
| Bklt....Booklet | | Natl....National |
| Brit....British | | No....Number |
| btwn...Between | | NY....New York |
| Bur....Bureau | | NYC....New York City |
| c. or ca....Circa | | Ovpt....Overprint |
| Cat....Catalogue | | Ovptd....Overprinted |
| Cent....Centennial, century, centenary | | P....Plate number |
| CIO....Congress of Industrial Organizations | | Perf....Perforated, perforation |
| Conf....Conference | | Phil....Philatelic |
| Cong....Congress | | Photo....Photogravure |
| Cpl....Corporal | | PO....Post office |
| CTO....Canceled to order | | Pr....Pair |
| d....Died | | P.R....Puerto Rico |
| Dbl....Double | | Prec....Precancel, precanceled |
| EKU....Earliest known use | | Pres....President |
| Engr....Engraved | | PTT....Post, Telephone and Telegraph |
| Exhib....Exhibition | | Rio....Rio de Janeiro |
| Expo....Exposition | | Sgt....Sergeant |
| Fed....Federation | | Soc....Society |
| GB....Great Britain | | Souv....Souvenir |
| Gen....General | | SSR....Soviet Socialist Republic, see ASSR |
| GPO....General post office | | St....Saint, street |
| Horiz....Horizontal | | Surch....Surcharge |
| Imperf....Imperforate | | Typo....Typographed |
| Impt....Imprint | | UL....Upper left |
| | | Unwmkd....Unwatermarked |
| | | UPU....Universal Postal Union |
| | | UR....Upper Right |
| | | US....United States |
| | | USPOD....United States Post Office Department |
| | | USSR....Union of Soviet Socialist Republics |
| | | Vert....Vertical |
| | | VP....Vice president |
| | | Wmk....Watermark |
| | | Wmkd....Watermarked |
| | | WWI....World War I |
| | | WWII....World War II |

## Examination

Scott Publishing Co. will not comment upon the genuineness, grade or condition of stamps, because of the time and responsibility involved. Rather, there are several expertizing groups that undertake this work for both collectors and dealers. Neither will Scott Publishing Co. appraise or identify philatelic material. The company cannot take responsibility for unsolicited stamps or covers sent by individuals.

## How to order from your dealer

When ordering stamps from a dealer, it is not necessary to write the full description of a stamp as listed in this catalogue. All you need is the name of the country, the Scott catalogue number and whether the desired item is unused or used. For example, "Japan Scott 422 unused" is sufficient to identify the unused stamp of Japan listed as "422 A206 5y brown."

# Basic Stamp Information

A stamp collector's knowledge of the combined elements that make a given stamp issue unique determines his or her ability to identify stamps. These elements include paper, watermark, method of separation, printing, design and gum. On the following pages each of these important areas is briefly described.

## Paper

Paper is an organic material composed of a compacted weave of cellulose fibers and generally formed into sheets. Paper used to print stamps may be manufactured in sheets, or it may have been part of a large roll (called a web) before being cut to size. The fibers most often used to create paper on which stamps are printed include bark, wood, straw and certain grasses. In many cases, linen or cotton rags have been added for greater strength and durability. Grinding, bleaching, cooking and rinsing these raw fibers reduces them to a slushy pulp, referred to by paper makers as "stuff." Sizing and, sometimes, coloring matter is added to the pulp to make different types of finished paper.

After the stuff is prepared, it is poured onto sieve-like frames that allow the water to run off, while retaining the matted pulp. As fibers fall onto the screen and are held by gravity, they form a natural weave that will later hold the paper together. If the screen has metal bits that are formed into letters or images attached, it leaves slightly thinned areas on the paper. These are called watermarks.

When the stuff is almost dry, it is passed under pressure through smooth or engraved rollers - dandy rollers - or placed between cloth in a press to be flattened and dried.

Stamp paper falls broadly into two types: wove and laid. The nature of the surface of the frame onto which the pulp is first deposited causes the differences in appearance between the two. If deposited on a screen of fairly uniform thickness of the pulp will settle between the wires. The paper, when held to a light, will show alternate light and dark lines. The spacing and the thickness of the lines may vary, but on any one sheet of paper they are all alike. See Russia Scott 31-38 for examples of laid paper.

*Batonne*, from the French word meaning "a staff," is a term used if the lines in the paper are spaced quite far apart, like the printed ruling on a writing tablet. Batonne paper may be either wove or laid. If laid, fine laid lines can be seen between the batons.

*Quadrille* is the term used when the lines in the paper form little squares. *Oblong quadrille* is the term used when rectangles, rather than squares, are formed. See Mexico-Guadalajara Scott 35-37 for examples of oblong quadrille paper.

Paper also is classified as thick or thin, hard or soft, and by color if dye is added during manufacture. Such colors may include yellowish, greenish, bluish and reddish.

Brief explanations of other types of paper used for printing stamps, as well as examples, follow.

**Pelure** — Pelure paper is a very thin, hard and often brittle paper that is sometimes bluish or grayish in appearance. See Serbia Scott 169-170.

**Native** — This is a term applied to handmade papers used to produce some of the early stamps of the Indian states. Stamps printed on native paper may be expected to display various natural inclusions that are normal and do not negatively affect value. Japanese

paper, originally made of mulberry fibers and rice flour, is part of this group. See Japan Scott 1-18.

**Manila** — This type of paper is often used to make stamped envelopes and wrappers. It is a coarse-textured stock, usually smooth on one side and rough on the other. A variety of colors of manila paper exist, but the most common range is yellowish-brown.

**Silk** — Introduced by the British in 1847 as a safeguard against counterfeiting, silk paper contains bits of colored silk thread scattered throughout. The density of these fibers varies greatly and can include as few as one fiber per stamp or hundreds. U.S. revenue Scott R152 is a good example of an easy-to-identify silk paper stamp.

Silk-thread paper has uninterrupted threads of colored silk arranged so that one or more threads run through the stamp or postal stationery. See Great Britain Scott 5-6 and Switzerland Scott 14-19.

**Granite** — Filled with minute cloth or colored paper fibers of various colors and lengths, granite paper should not be confused with either type of silk paper. Austria Scott 172-175 and a number of Swiss stamps are examples of granite paper.

**Chalky** — A chalk-like substance coats the surface of chalky paper to discourage the cleaning and reuse of canceled stamps, as well as to provide a smoother, more acceptable printing surface. Because the designs of stamps printed on chalky paper are imprinted on what is often a water-soluble coating, any attempt to remove a cancellation will destroy the stamp. *Do not soak these stamps in any fluid.* To remove a stamp printed on chalky paper from an envelope, wet the paper from underneath the stamp until the gum dissolves enough to release the stamp from the paper. See St. Kitts-Nevis Scott 89-90 for examples of stamps printed on this type of chalky paper.

**India** — Another name for this paper, originally introduced from China about 1750, is "China Paper." It is a thin, opaque paper often used for plate and die proofs by many countries.

**Double** — In philately, the term double paper has two distinct meanings. The first is a two-ply paper, usually a combination of a thick and a thin sheet, joined during manufacture. This type was used experimentally as a means to discourage the reuse of stamps.

The design is printed on the thin paper. Any attempt to remove a cancellation would destroy the design. U.S. Scott 158 and other Banknote-era stamps exist on this form of double paper.

The second type of double paper occurs on a rotary press, when the end of one paper roll, or web, is affixed to the next roll to save time feeding the paper through the press. Stamp designs are printed over the joined paper and, if overlooked by inspectors, may get into post office stocks.

**Goldbeater's Skin** — This type of paper was used for the 1866 issue of Prussia, and was a tough, translucent paper. The design was printed in reverse on the back of the stamp, and the gum applied over the printing. It is impossible to remove stamps printed on this type of paper from the paper to which they are affixed without destroying the design.

**Ribbed** — Ribbed paper has an uneven, corrugated surface made by passing the paper through ridged rollers. This type exists on some copies of U.S. Scott 156-165.

Various other substances, or substrates, have been used for stamp manufacture, including wood, aluminum, copper, silver and gold foil, plastic, and silk and cotton fabrics.

## Watermarks

Watermarks are an integral part of some papers. They are formed in the process of paper manufacture. Watermarks consist of small designs, formed of wire or cut from metal and soldered to the surface of the mold or, sometimes, on the dandy roll. The designs may be in the form of crowns, stars, anchors, letters or other characters or symbols. These pieces of metal - known in the paper-making industry as "bits" - impress a design into the paper. The design sometimes may be seen by holding the stamp to the light. Some are more easily seen with a watermark detector. This important tool is a small black tray into which a stamp is placed face down and dampened with a fast-evaporating watermark detection fluid that brings up the watermark image in the form of dark lines against a lighter background. These dark lines are the thinner areas of the paper known as the watermark. Some watermarks are extremely difficult to locate, due to either a faint impression, watermark location or the color of the stamp. There also are electric watermark detectors that come with plastic filter disks of various colors. The disks neutralize the color of the stamp, permitting the watermark to be seen more easily.

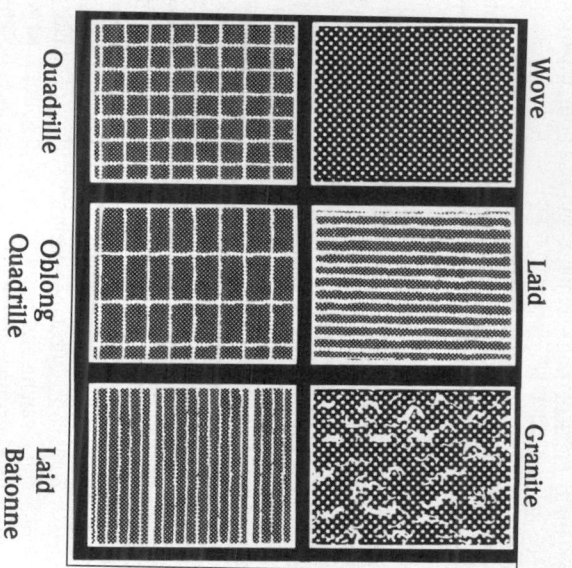

Wove

Laid

Granite

Quadrille

Oblong Quadrille

Laid Batonne

Multiple watermarks of Crown Agents and Burma

Watermarks of Uruguay, Vatican City and Jamaica

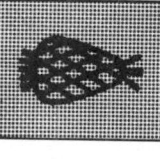

**WARNING: Some inks used in the photogravure process dissolve in watermark fluids (Please see the section on Soluble Printing Inks).** Also, see "chalky paper." Watermarks may be found normal, reversed, inverted, reversed and inverted, sideways or diagonal, as seen from the back of the stamp. The relationship of watermark to stamp design depends on the position of the printing plates or how paper is fed through the press. On machine-made paper, watermarks normally are read from right to left. The design is repeated closely throughout the sheet in a "multiple-watermark design." In a "sheet watermark," the design appears only once on the sheet, but extends over many stamps. Individual stamps may carry only a small fraction of the design.

"Marginal watermarks" occur in the margins of sheets or panes of stamps. They occur on the outside border of paper (ostensibly outside the area where stamps are to be printed). A large row of letters may spell the name of the country or the manufacturer of the paper, or a border of lines may appear. Careless press feeding may cause parts of these letters and/or lines to show on stamps of the outer row of a pane.

## Soluble Printing Inks

**WARNING:** Most stamp colors are permanent; that is, they are not seriously affected by short-term exposure to light or water. Many colors, especially of modern inks, fade from excessive exposure to light. There are stamps printed with inks that dissolve easily in water or in fluids used to detect watermarks. Use of these inks was intentional to prevent the removal of cancellations. Water affects all aniline inks, those on so-called safety paper and some photogravure printings - all such inks are known as *fugitive colors. Removal from paper of such stamps requires care and alternatives to traditional soaking.*

## Separation

"Separation" is the general term used to describe methods used to separate stamps. The three standard forms currently in use are perforating, rouletting and die-cutting. These methods are done during the stamp production process, after printing. Sometimes these methods are done on-press or sometimes as a separate step. The earliest issues, such as the 1840 Penny Black of Great Britain (Scott 1), did not have any means provided for separation. It was expected the stamps would be cut apart with scissors or folded and torn. These are examples of imperforate stamps. Many stamps were first issued in imperforate formats and were later issued with perforations. Therefore, care must be observed in buying single imperforate stamps to be certain they were issued imperforate and are not perforated copies that have been altered by having the perforations trimmed away. Stamps issued imperforate usually are valued as singles. However, imperforate varieties of normally perforated stamps should be collected in pairs or larger pieces as indisputable evidence of their imperforate character.

### PERFORATION

The chief style of separation of stamps, and the one that is in almost universal use today, is perforating. By this process, paper between the stamps is cut away in a line of holes, usually round, leaving little bridges of paper between the stamps to hold them together. Some types of perforation, such as hyphen-hole perfs, can be confused with roulettes, but a close visual inspection reveals that paper has been removed. The little perforation bridges, which project from the stamp when it is torn from the pane, are called the teeth of the perforation.

As the size of the perforation is sometimes the only way to differentiate between two otherwise identical stamps, it is necessary to be able to accurately measure and describe them. This is done with a perforation gauge, usually a ruler-like device that has dots or graduated lines to show how many perforations may be counted in the space of two centimeters. Two centimeters is the space universally adopted in which to measure perforations.

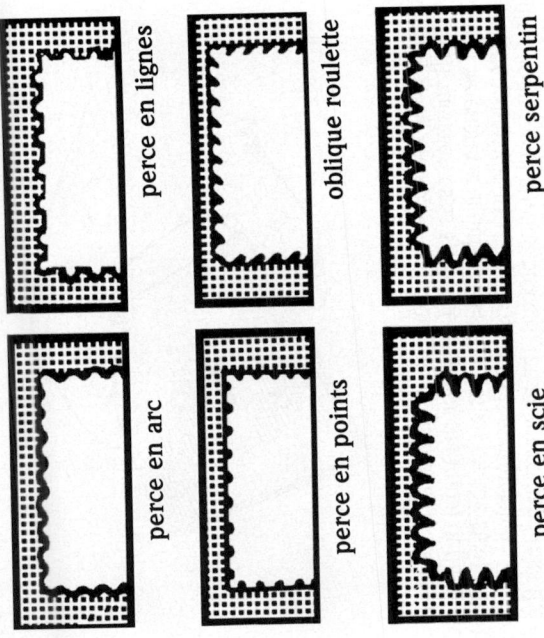

perce en arc — perce en lignes

perce en points — oblique roulette

perce en scie — perce serpentin

### Perforation gauge

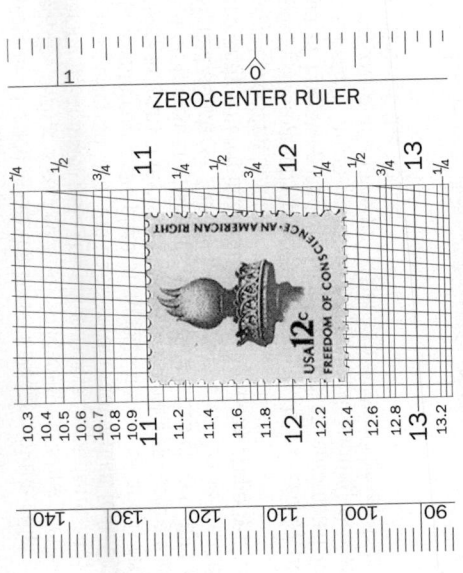

ZERO-CENTER RULER

To measure a stamp, run it along the gauge until the dots on it fit exactly into the perforations of the stamp. If you are using a graduated-line perforation gauge, simply slide the stamp along the surface until the lines on the gauge perfectly project from the center of the bridges or holes. The number to the side of the line of dots or lines that fit the stamp's perforation is the measurement. For example, an "11" means that 11 perforations fit between two centimeters. The description of the stamp therefore is "perf. 11." If the gauge of the perforations on the top and bottom of a stamp differs from that on the sides, the result is what is known as *compound perforations*. In measuring compound perforations, the gauge at top and bottom is always given first, then the sides. Thus, a stamp that measures 11 at top and bottom and 10 1/2 at the sides is "perf. 11 x 10 1/2." See U.S. Scott 632-642 for examples of compound perforations.

Stamps also are known with perforations different on three or all four sides. Descriptions of such items are clockwise, beginning with the top of the stamp.

A perforation with small holes and teeth close together is a "fine perforation." One with large holes and teeth far apart is a "coarse perforation." Holes that are jagged, rather than clean-cut, are "rough perforations." *Blind perforations* are the slight impressions left by the perforating pins if they fail to puncture the paper. Multiples of stamps showing blind perforations may command a slight premium over normally perforated stamps.

## ROULETTING

In rouletting, the stamp paper is cut partly or wholly through, with no paper removed. In perforating, some paper is removed. Rouletting derives its name from the French roulette, a spur-like wheel. As the wheel is rolled over the paper, each point makes a small cut. The number of cuts made in a two-centimeter space determines the gauge of the roulette, just as the number of perforations in two centimeters determines the gauge of the perforation.

The shape and arrangement of the teeth on the wheels varies. Various roulette types generally carry French names:

*Perce en lignes* - rouletted in lines. The paper receives short, straight cuts in lines. This is the most common type of rouletting. See Mexico Scott 500.

*Perce en points* - pin-rouletted or pin-perfed. This differs from a small perforation because no paper is removed, although round, equidistant holes are pricked through the paper. See Mexico Scott 242-256.

*Perce en arc* and *perce en scie* - pierced in an arc or saw-toothed designs, forming half circles or small triangles. See Hanover (German States) Scott 25-29.

*Perce en serpentin* - serpentine roulettes. The cuts form a serpentine or wavy line. See Brunswick (German States) Scott 13-18. Once again, no paper is removed by these processes, leaving the stamps easily separated, but closely attached.

## DIE-CUTTING

The third major form of stamp separation is die-cutting. This is a method where a die in the pattern of separation is created that later cuts the stamp paper in a stroke motion. Although some standard stamps bear die-cut perforations, this process is primarily used for self-adhesive postage stamps. Die-cutting can appear in straight lines, such as U.S. Scott 1551, or shapes, such as U.S. Scott 2522, imitating the appearance of perforations, such as New Zealand Scott 935A and 935B.

# Printing Processes

## ENGRAVING (Intaglio, Line-engraving, Etching)

**Master die** — The initial operation in the process of line engraving is making the master die. The die is a small, flat block of softened steel upon which the stamp design is recess engraved in reverse.

The term *syncopated perfs* describes intentional irregularities in the perforations. The earliest form was used by the Netherlands from 1925-33, where holes were omitted to create distinctive patterns. Beginning in 1992, Great Britain has used an oval perforation to help prevent counterfeiting. Several other countries have started using the oval perfs or other syncopated perf patterns.

A new type of perforation, still primarily used for postal stationery, is known as microperfs. Microperfs are tiny perforations (in some cases hundreds of holes per two centimeters) that allows items to be intentionally separated very easily, while not accidentally breaking apart as easily as standard perforations. These are not currently measured or differentiated by size, as are standard perforations.

Photographic reduction of the original art is made to the appropriate size. It then serves as a tracing guide for the initial outline of the design. The engraver lightly traces the design on the steel with his graver, then slowly works the design until it is completed. At various points during the engraving process, the engraver hand-inks the die and makes an impression to check his progress. These are known as progressive die proofs. After completion of the engraving, the die is hardened to withstand the stress and pressures of later transfer operations.

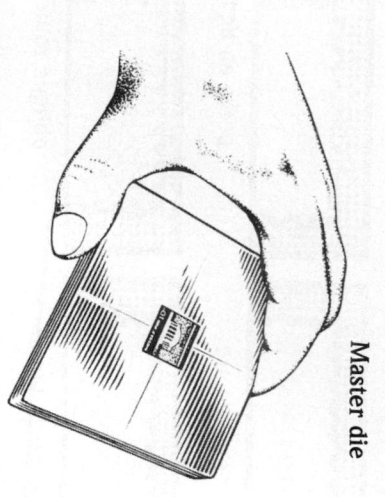

**Master die**

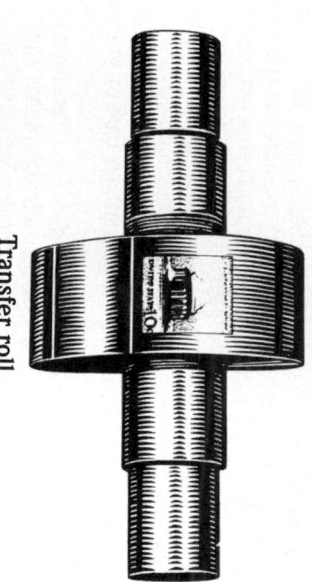

**Transfer roll**

**Transfer roll** — Next is production of the transfer roll that, as the name implies, is the medium used to transfer the subject from the master die to the printing plate. A blank roll of soft steel, mounted on a mandrel, is placed under the bearers of the transfer press to allow it to roll freely on its axis. The hardened die is placed on the bed of the press and the face of the transfer roll is applied to the die, under pressure. The bed or the roll is then rocked back and forth under increasing pressure, until the soft steel of the roll is forced into every engraved line of the die. The resulting impression on the roll is known as a "relief" or a "relief transfer." The engraved image is now positive in appearance and stands out from the steel. After the required number of reliefs are "rocked in," the soft steel transfer roll is hardened.

Different flaws may occur during the relief process. A defective relief may occur during the rocking in process because of a minute piece of foreign material lodging on the die, or some other cause. Imperfections in the steel of the transfer roll may result in a breaking away of parts of the design. This is known as a relief break, which will show up on finished stamps as small, unprinted areas. If a damaged relief remains in use, it will transfer a repeating defect to

**Plate** — The final step in pre-printing production is the making of the printing plate. A flat piece of soft steel replaces the die on the bed of the printing press. One of the reliefs on the transfer roll is positioned over this soft steel. Position, or layout, dots determine the correct position on the plate. The dots have been lightly marked on the plate. Deliberate alterations of reliefs sometimes occur. "Altered reliefs" designate these changed conditions.

the plate in advance. After the correct position of the relief is determined, the design is rocked in, by following the same method used in making the transfer roll. The difference is that at this time the image is being transferred from the transfer roll, rather than to it. Once the design is entered on the plate, it appears in reverse and is recessed. There are as many transfers entered on the plate as there are subjects printed on the sheet of stamps. It is during this process that double and shifted transfers occur, as well as re-entries. These are the result of improperly entered images that have not been properly burnished out prior to rocking in a new image.

Modern siderography processes, such as those used by the U.S. Bureau of Engraving and Printing, involve an automated form of rocking designs in on preformed cylindrical printing sleeves. The same process also allows for easier removal and re-entry of worn images right on the sleeve.

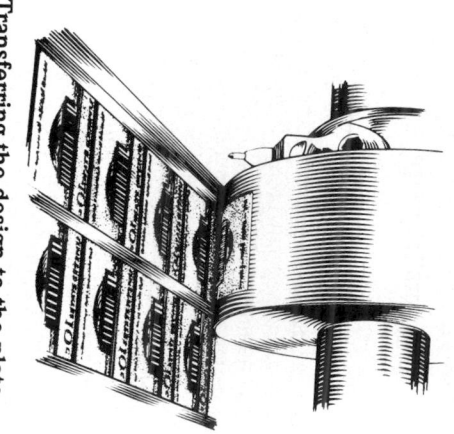

**Transferring the design to the plate**

Following the entering of the required transfers on the plate, the position dots, layout dots and lines, scratches and other markings generally are burnished out. Added at this time by the siderographer are any required *guide lines*, *plate numbers* or other *marginal markings*. The plate is then hand-inked and a proof impression is taken. This is known as a *plate proof*. If the impression is approved, the plate is machined for fitting onto the press, is hardened and sent to the plate vault ready for use.

On press, the plate is inked and the surface is automatically wiped clean, leaving ink only in the recessed lines. Paper is then forced under pressure into the engraved recessed lines, thereby receiving the ink. Thus, the ink lines on engraved stamps are slightly raised, and slight depressions (debossing) occur on the back of the stamp. Prior to the advent of modern high-speed presses and more advanced ink formulations, paper had to be dampened before receiving the ink. This sometimes led to uneven shrinkage by the time the stamps were perforated, resulting in improperly perforated stamps, or misperfs. Newer presses use drier paper, thus both *wet and dry printings* exist on some stamps.

**Rotary Press** — Until 1914, only flat plates were used to print engraved stamps. Rotary press printing was introduced in 1914, and slowly spread. Some countries still use flat-plate printing.

After approval of the plate proof, older *rotary press plates* require additional machining. They are curved to fit the press cylinder. "Gripper slots" are cut into the back of each plate to receive the "grippers," which hold the plate securely on the press. The plate is then hardened. Stamps printed from these bent rotary press plates are longer or wider than the same stamps printed from flat-plate presses. The stretching of the plate during the curving process is what causes this distortion.

**Re-entry** — To execute a re-entry on a flat plate, the transfer roll is re-applied to the plate, often at some time after its first use on the press. Worn-out designs can be resharpened by carefully burnishing out the original image and re-entering it from the transfer roll. If the original impression has not been sufficiently removed and the transfer roll is not precisely in line with the remaining impression, the resulting double transfer will make the re-entry obvious. If the registration is true, a re-entry may be difficult or impossible to distinguish. Sometimes a stamp printed from a successful re-entry is identified by having a much sharper and clearer impression than its neighbors. With the advent of rotary presses, post-press re-entries were not possible. After a plate was curved for the rotary press, it was impossible to make a re-entry. This is because the plate had already been bent once (with the design distorted).

However, with the introduction of the previously mentioned modern-style siderography machines, entries are made to the pre-formed cylindrical printing sleeve. Such sleeves are dechromed and softened. This allows individual images to be burnished out and re-entered on the curved sleeve. The sleeve is then rechromed, resulting in longer press life.

**Double Transfer** — This is a description of the condition of a transfer on a plate that shows evidence of a duplication of all, or a portion of the design. It usually is the result of the changing of the rocking in of the original entry. Double transfers also occur when only a portion of the design has been rocked in and improper position-ing is noted. If the worker elected not to burnish out the partial or completed design, a strong double transfer will occur for part or all of the design.

It sometimes is necessary to remove the original transfer from a plate and repeat the process a second time. If the finished re-worked image shows traces of the original impression, attributable to incom-plete burnishing, the result is a partial double transfer.

With the modern automatic machines mentioned previously, double transfers are all but impossible to create. Those partially doubled images on stamps printed from such sleeves are more than likely re-entries, rather than true double transfers.

**Re-engraved** — Alterations to a stamp design are sometimes neces-sary after some stamps have been printed. In some cases, either the original die or the actual printing plate may have its "temper" drawn (softened), and the design will be re-cut. The resulting impressions from such a re-engraved die or plate may differ slightly from the original issue, and are known as "re-engraved." If the alteration was made to the master die, all future printings will be consistently differ-ent from the original. If alterations were made to the printing plate, each altered stamp on the plate will be slightly different from each other, allowing specialists to reconstruct a complete printing plate.

**Dropped Transfers** — If an impression from the transfer roll has not been properly placed, a dropped transfer may occur. The final stamp image will appear obviously out of line with its neighbors.

**Short Transfer** — Sometimes a transfer roll is not rocked its entire length when entering a transfer onto a plate. As a result, the finished transfer on the plate fails to show the complete design, and the fin-ished stamp will have an incomplete design printed. This is known as a "short transfer." U.S. Scott No. 8 is a good example of a short transfer.

## TYPOGRAPHY (Letterpress, Surface Printing, Flexography, Dry Offset, High Etch)

Although the word "Typography" is obsolete as a term describing a printing method, it was the accepted term throughout the first century of postage stamps. Therefore, appropriate Scott listings in this catalogue refer to typographed stamps. The current term for this form of printing, however, is "letterpress."

As it relates to the production of postage stamps, letterpress print-ing is the reverse of engraving. Rather than having recessed areas trap the ink and deposit it on paper, only the raised areas of the design are inked. This is comparable to the type of printing seen by inking and using an ordinary rubber stamp. Letterpress includes all printing where the design is above the surface area, whether it is wood, metal or, in some instances, hardened rubber or polymer plastic.

For most letterpress-printed stamps, the engraved master is made in much the same manner as for engraved stamps. In this instance, however, an additional step is needed. The design is transferred to another surface before being transferred to the transfer roll. In this way, the transfer roll has a recessed stamp design, rather than one done in relief. This makes the printing areas on the final plate raised, or relief areas.

For less-detailed stamps of the 19th century, the area on the die not used as a printing surface was cut away, leaving the surface area raised. The original die was then reproduced by stereotyping or elec-trotyping. The resulting electrotypes were assembled in the required number and format of the desired sheet of stamps. The plate used in printing the stamps was an electroplate of these assembled elec-trotypes.

Once the final letterpress plates are created, ink is applied to the raised surface and the pressure of the press transfers the ink impres-sion to the paper. In contrast to engraving, the fine lines of letter-press are impressed on the surface of the stamp, leaving a debossed surface. When viewed from the back (as on a typewritten page), the corresponding line work on the stamp will be raised slightly (embossed) above the surface.

## PHOTOGRAVURE (Gravure, Rotogravure, Heliogravure)

In this process, the basic principles of photography are applied to a chemically sensitized metal plate, rather than photographic paper. The design is transferred photographically to the plate through a halftone, or dot-matrix screen, breaking the reproduction into tiny dots. The plate is treated chemically and the dots form depressions, called cells, of varying depths and diameters, depending on the degrees of shade in the design. Then, like engraving, ink is applied to the plate and the surface is wiped clean. This leaves ink in the tiny cells that is lifted out and deposited on the paper when it is pressed against the plate.

Gravure is most often used for multicolored stamps, generally using the three primary colors (red, yellow and blue) and black. By varying the dot matrix pattern and density of these colors, virtually any color can be reproduced. A typical full-color gravure stamp will be created from four printing cylinders (one for each color). The original multicolored image will have been photographically sepa-rated into its component colors.

Modern gravure printing may use computer-generated dot-matrix screens, and modern plates may be of various types including metal-coated plastic. The catalogue designation of Photogravure (or "Photo") covers any of these older and more modern gravure methods of printing.

For examples of the first photogravure stamps printed (1914), see Bavaria Scott 94-114.

## LITHOGRAPHY (Offset Lithography, Stone Lithography, Dilitho, Planography, Collotype)

The principle that oil and water do not mix is the basis for lithography. The stamp design is drawn by hand or transferred from engraving to the surface of a lithographic stone or metal plate in a greasy (oily) substance. This oily substance holds the ink, which will later be transferred to the paper. The stone (or plate) is wet with an acid fluid, causing it to repel the printing ink in all areas not covered by the greasy substance.

Transfer paper is used to transfer the design from the original stone or plate. A series of duplicate transfers are grouped and, in turn, transferred to the final printing plate.

**Photolithography** — The application of photographic processes to lithography. This process allows greater flexibility of design, related to use of halftone screens combined with line work. Unlike photogravure or engraving, this process can allow large, solid areas to be printed.

**Offset** — A refinement of the lithographic process. A rubber-covered blanket cylinder takes the impression from the inked lithographic plate. From the "blanket" the impression is *offset* or transferred to the paper. Greater flexibility and speed are the principal reasons offset printing has largely displaced lithography. The term "lithography" covers both processes, and results are almost identical.

## EMBOSSED (Relief) Printing

Embossing, not considered one of the four main printing types, is a method in which the design first is sunk into the metal of the die. Printing is done against a yielding platen, such as leather or linoleum. The platen is forced into the depression of the die, thus forming the design on the paper in relief. This process is often used for metallic inks.

Embossing may be done without color (see Sardinia Scott 4-6); with color printed around the embossed area (see Great Britain Scott 5 and most U.S. envelopes); and with color in exact registration with the embossed subject (see Canada Scott 656-657).

## HOLOGRAMS

For objects to appear as holograms on stamps, a model exactly the same size as it is to appear on the hologram must be created. Rather than using photographic film to capture the image, holography records an image on a photoresist material. In processing, chemicals eat away at certain exposed areas, leaving a pattern of constructive and destructive interference. When the photoresist is developed, the result is a pattern of uneven ridges that acts as a mold. This mold is then coated with metal, and the resulting form is used to press copies in much the same way phonograph records are produced.

A typical reflective hologram used for stamps consists of a reproduction of the uneven patterns on a plastic film that is applied to a reflective background, usually a silver or gold foil. Light is reflected off the background through the film, making the pattern present on the film visible. Because of the uneven pattern of the film, the viewer will perceive the objects in their proper three-dimensional relationships with appropriate brightness.

The first hologram on a stamp was produced by Austria in 1988 (Scott 1441).

## FOIL APPLICATION

A modern tecinique of applying color to stamps involves the application of metallic foil to the stamp paper. A pattern of foil is applied to the stamp paper by use of a stamping die. The foil usually is flat, but it may be textured. Canada Scott 1735 has three different foil applications in pearl, bronze and gold. The gold foil was textured using a chemical-etch copper embossing die. The printing of this stamp also involved two-color offset lithography plus embossing.

## COMBINATION PRINTINGS

Sometimes two or even three printing methods are combined in producing stamps. In these cases, such as Austria Scott 933 or Canada 1735 (described in the preceding paragraph), the multiple-printing technique can be determined by studying the individual characteristics of each printing type. A few stamps, such as Singapore Scott 684-684A, combine as many as three of the four major printing types (lithography, engraving and typography). When this is done it often indicates the incorporation of security devices against counterfeiting.

## INK COLORS

Inks or colored papers used in stamp printing often are of mineral origin, although there are numerous examples of organic-based pigments. As a general rule, organic-based pigments are far more subject to varieties and change than those of mineral-based origin.

The appearance of any given color on a stamp may be affected by many aspects, including printing variations, light, color of paper, aging and chemical alterations.

Numerous printing variations may be observed. Heavier pressure or inking will cause a more intense color, while slight interruptions in the ink feed or lighter impressions will cause a lighter appearance. Stamps printed in the same color by water-based and solvent-based inks can differ significantly in appearance. This affects several stamps in the U.S. Prominent Americans series. Hand-mixed ink formulas (primarily from the 19th century) produced under different conditions (humidity and temperature) account for notable color variations in early printings of the same stamp (see U.S. Scott 248-250, 279B, for example). Different sources of pigment can also result in significant differences in color.

Light exposure and aging are closely related in the way they affect stamp color. Both eventually break down the ink and fade colors, so that a carefully kept stamp may differ significantly in color from an identical copy that has been exposed to light. If stamps are exposed to light either intentionally or accidentally, their colors can be faded or completely changed in some cases.

Papers of different quality and consistency used for the same stamp printing may affect color appearance. Most pelure papers, for example, show a richer color when compared with wove or laid papers. See Russia Scott 181a, for an example of this effect.

The very nature of the printing processes can cause a variety of differences in shades or hues of the same stamp. Some of these shades are scarcer than others, and are of particular interest to the advanced collector.

## Luminescence

All forms of tagged stamps fall under the general category of luminescence. Within this broad category is fluorescence, dealing with forms of tagging visible under longwave ultraviolet light, and phosphorescence, which deals with tagging visible only under shortwave light. Phosphorescence leaves an afterglow and fluorescence does not. These treated stamps show up in a range of different colors when exposed to UV light. The differing wavelengths of the light activates the tagging material, making it glow in various colors that usually serve different mail processing purposes.

Intentional tagging is a post-World War II phenomenon, brought about by the increased literacy rate and rapidly growing mail volume. It was one of several answers to the problem of the need for more automated mail processes. Early tagged stamps served the purpose of triggering machines to separate different types of mail. A natural outgrowth was to also use the signal to trigger machines that faced all envelopes the same way and canceled them.

Tagged stamps come in many different forms. Some tagged stamps have luminescent shapes or images imprinted on them as a form of security device. Others have blocks (United States), stripes, frames (South Africa and Canada), overall coatings (United States), bars (Great Britain and Canada) and many other types. Some types of tagging are even mixed in with the pigmented printing ink (Australia Scott 306, Netherlands Scott 478 and U.S. Scott 1359 and 2443).

The means of applying taggant to stamps differs as much as the intended purposes for the stamps. The most common form of tagging is a coating applied to the surface of the printed stamp. Since the taggant ink is frequently invisible except under UV light, it does not interfere with the appearance of the stamp. Another common application is the use of phosphored papers. In this case the paper itself either has a coating of taggant applied before the stamp is printed, has taggant applied during the papermaking process (incorporating it into

the fibers), or has the taggant mixed into the coating of the paper. The latter method, among others, is currently in use in the United States.

Many countries now use tagging in various forms to either expedite mail handling or to serve as a printing security device against counterfeiting. Following the introduction of tagged stamps for public use in 1959 by Great Britain, other countries have steadily joined the parade. Among those are Germany (1961); Canada and Denmark (1962); United States, Australia, France and Switzerland (1963); Belgium and Japan (1966); Sweden and Norway (1967); Italy (1968); and Russia (1969). Since then, many other countries have begun using forms of tagging, including Brazil, China, Czechoslovakia, Hong Kong, Guatemala, Indonesia, Israel, Lithuania, Luxembourg, Netherlands, Penrhyn Islands, Portugal, St. Vincent, Singapore, South Africa, Spain and Sweden to name a few.

In some cases, including United States, Canada, Great Britain and Switzerland, stamps were released both with and without tagging. Many of these were released during each country's experimental period. Tagged and untagged versions are listed for the aforementioned countries and are noted in some other countries' listings. For at least a few stamps, the experimentally tagged version is worth far more than its untagged counterpart, such as the 1963 experimental tagged version of France Scott 1024.

In some cases, luminescent varieties of stamps were inadvertently created. Several Russian stamps, for example, sport highly fluorescent ink that was not intended as a form of tagging. Older stamps, such as early U.S. postage dues, can be positively identified by the use of UV light, since the organic ink used has become slightly fluorescent over time. Other stamps, such as Austria Scott 70a-82a (varnish bars) and Obock Scott 46-64 (printed quadrille lines), have become fluorescent over time.

Various fluorescent substances have been added to paper to make it appear brighter. These optical brighteners, as they are known, greatly affect the appearance of the stamp under UV light. The brightest of these is known as Hi-Brite paper. These paper varieties are beyond the scope of the Scott Catalogue.

Shortwave UV light also is used extensively in expertizing, since each form of paper has its own fluorescent characteristics that are impossible to perfectly match. It is therefore a simple matter to detect filled thins, added perforation teeth and other alterations that involve the addition of paper. UV light also is used to examine stamps that have had cancels chemically removed and for other purposes as well.

## Gum

The Illustrated Gum Chart in the first part of this introduction shows and defines various types of gum condition. Because gum condition has an important impact on the value of unused stamps, we recommend studying this chart and the accompanying text carefully.

The gum on the back of a stamp may be shiny, dull, smooth, rough, dark, white, colored or tinted. Most stamp gumming adhesives use gum arabic or dextrine as a base. Certain polymers such as polyvinyl alcohol (PVA) have been used extensively since World War II.

The *Scott Standard Postage Stamp Catalogue* does not list items by types of gum. The *Scott Specialized Catalogue of United States Stamps* does differentiate among some types of gum for certain issues.

Reprints of stamps may have gum differing from the original issues. In addition, some countries have used different gum formulas for different seasons. These adhesives have different properties that may become more apparent over time.

Many stamps have been issued without gum, and the catalogue will note this fact. See, for example, United States Scott 40-47. Sometimes, gum may have been removed to preserve the stamp. Germany Scott B68, for example, has a highly acidic gum that eventually destroys the stamps. This item is valued in the catalogue with gum removed.

## Reprints and Reissues

These are impressions of stamps (usually obsolete) made from the original plates or stones. If they are valid for postage and reproduce obsolete issues (such as U.S. Scott 102-111), the stamps are *reissues*. If they are from current issues, they are designated as *second, third, etc., printing.* If designated for a particular purpose, they are called *special printings.*

When special printings are not valid for postage, but are made from original dies and plates by authorized persons, they are *official reprints. Private reprints* are made from the original plates and dies by private hands. An example of a private reprint is that of the 1845 New Haven, Conn., postmaster's provisional. *Official reproductions* or imitations are made from new dies and plates by government authorization. Scott will list those reissues that are valid for postage if they differ significantly from the original printing.

The U.S. government made special printings of its first postage stamps in 1875. Produced were official imitations of the first two stamps (listed as Scott 3-4), reprints of the demonetized pre-1861 issues (Scott 40-47) and reissues of the 1861 stamps, the 1869 issues and the then-current 1875 denominations. Even though the official imitations and the reprints were not valid for postage, Scott lists all of these U.S. special printings.

Most reprints or reissues differ slightly from the original stamp in some characteristic, such as gum, paper, perforation, color or watermark. Sometimes the details are followed so meticulously that only a student of that specific stamp is able to distinguish the reprint or reissue from the original.

## Remainders and Canceled to Order

Some countries sell their stock of old stamps when a new issue replaces them. To avoid postal use, the *remainders* usually are canceled with a punch hole, a heavy line or bar, or a more-or-less regular-looking cancellation. The most famous merchant of remainders was Nicholas F. Seebeck. In the 1880s and 1890s, he arranged printing contracts between the Hamilton Bank Note Co., of which he was a director, and several Central and South American countries. The contracts provided that the plates and all remainders of the yearly issues became the property of Hamilton. Seebeck saw to it that ample stock remained. The "Seebecks," both remainders and reprints, were standard packet fillers for decades.

Some countries also issue stamps *canceled-to-order (CTO)*, either in sheets with original gum or stuck onto pieces of paper or envelopes and canceled. Such CTO items generally are worth less than postally used stamps. In cases where the CTO material is far more prevalent in the marketplace than postally used examples, the catalogue value relates to the CTO examples, with postally used examples noted as premium items. Most CTOs can be detected by the presence of gum. However, as the CTO practice goes back at least to 1885, the gum inevitably has been soaked off some stamps so they could pass as postally used. The normally applied postmarks usually differ slightly from standard postmarks, and specialists are able to tell the difference. When applied individually to envelopes by philatelically minded persons, CTO material is known as *favor canceled* and generally sells at large discounts.

## Cinderellas and Facsimiles

*Cinderella* is a catch-all term used by stamp collectors to describe phantoms, fantasies, bogus items, municipal issues, exhibition seals, local revenues, transportation stamps, labels, poster stamps and many other types of items. Some cinderella collectors include in their collections local postage issues, telegraph stamps, essays and proofs, forgeries and counterfeits.

A *fantasy* is an adhesive created for a nonexistent stamp-issuing

authority. Fantasy items range from imaginary countries (Occusi-Ambeno, Kingdom of Sedang, Principality of Trinidad or Torres Straits), to non-existent locals (Winans City Post), or nonexistent transportation lines (McKobish & Co.'s Acapulco-San Francisco Line).

On the other hand, if the entity exists and could have issued stamps (but did not) or was known to have issued other stamps, the items are considered *bogus* stamps. These would include the Mormon postage stamps of Utah, S. Allan Taylor's Guatemala and Paraguay inventions, the propaganda issues for the South Moluccas and the adhesives of the Page & Keyes local post of Boston.

*Phantoms* is another term for both fantasy and bogus issues.

*Facsimiles* are copies or imitations made to represent original stamps, but which do not pretend to be originals. A catalogue illustration is such a facsimile. Illustrations from the Moens catalogue of the last century were occasionally colored and passed off as stamps. Since the beginning of stamp collecting, facsimiles have been made for collectors as space fillers or for reference. They often carry the word "facsimile," "falsch" (German), "sanko" or "mozo" (Japanese), or "faux" (French) overprinted on the face or stamped on the back. Unfortunately, over the years a number of these items have had fake cancels applied over the facsimile notation and have been passed off as genuine.

## Forgeries and Counterfeits

Forgeries and counterfeits have been with philately virtually from the beginning of stamp production. Over time, the terminology for the two has been used interchangeably. Although both forgeries and counterfeits are reproductions of stamps, the purposes behind their creation differ considerably.

Among specialists there is an increasing movement to more specifically define such items. Although there is no universally accepted terminology, we feel the following definitions most closely mirror the items and their purposes as they are currently defined.

*Forgeries* (also often referred to as *Counterfeits*) are reproductions of genuine stamps that have been created to defraud collectors. Such spurious items first appeared on the market around 1860, and most old-time collections contain one or more. Many are crude and easily spotted, but some can deceive experts.

An important supplier of these early philatelic forgeries was the Hamburg printer Gebruder Spiro. Many others with reputations in this craft included S. Allan Taylor, George Hussey, James Chute, George Fortune, Benjamin & Sarpy, Julius Goldner, E. Oneglia and L.H. Mercier. Among the noted 20th-century forgers were Francois Fournier, Jean Sperati and the prolific Raoul DeThuin.

Forgeries may be complete replications, or they may be genuine stamps altered to resemble a scarcer (and more valuable) type. Most forgeries, particularly those of rare stamps, are worth only a small fraction of the value of a genuine example, but a few types, created by some of the most notable forgers, such as Sperati, can be worth as much or more than the genuine. Fraudulently produced copies are known of most classic rarities and many medium-priced stamps.

In addition to rare stamps, large numbers of common 19th- and early 20th-century stamps were forged to supply stamps to the early packet trade. Many can still be easily found. Few new philatelic forgeries have appeared in recent decades. Successful imitation of well-engraved work is virtually impossible. It has proven far easier to produce a fake by altering a genuine stamp than to duplicate a stamp completely.

*Counterfeit* (also often referred to as *Postal Counterfeit* or *Postal Forgery*) is the term generally applied to reproductions of stamps that have been created to defraud the government of revenue. Such items usually are created at the time a stamp is current and, in some cases, are hard to detect. Because most counterfeits are seized when the perpetrator is captured, postal counterfeits, particularly used on cover, are usually worth much more than a genuine example to spe-

cialists. The first postal counterfeit was of Spain's 4-cuarto carmine of 1854 (the real one is Scott 25). Apparently, the counterfeiters were not satisfied with their first version, which is now very scarce, and they soon created an engraved counterfeit, which is common. Postal counterfeits quickly followed in Austria, Naples, Sardinia and the Roman States. They have since been created in many other countries as well, including the United States.

An infamous counterfeit to defraud the government is the 1-shilling Great Britain "Stock Exchange" forgery of 1872, used on telegraph forms at the exchange that year. The stamp escaped detection until a stamp dealer noticed it in 1898.

## Fakes

*Fakes* are genuine stamps altered in some way to make them more desirable. One student of this part of stamp collecting has estimated that by the 1950s more than 30,000 varieties of fakes were known. That number has grown greatly since then. The widespread existence of fakes makes it important for stamp collectors to study their philatelic holdings and use relevant literature. Likewise, collectors should buy from reputable dealers who guarantee their stamps and make full and prompt refunds should a purchased item be declared faked or altered by some mutually agreed-upon authority. Because fakes always have some genuine characteristics, it is not always possible to obtain unanimous agreement among experts regarding specific items. These students may change their opinions as philatelic knowledge increases. More than 80 percent of all fakes on the philatelic market today are regummed, reperforated (or perforated for the first time), or bear forged overprints, surcharges or cancellations.

Stamps can be chemically treated to alter or eliminate colors. For example, a pale rose stamp can be re-colored to resemble a blue shade of high market value. In other cases, treated stamps can be made to resemble missing color varieties. Designs may be changed by painting, or a stroke or a dot added or bleached out to turn an ordinary variety into a seemingly scarcer stamp. Part of a stamp can be bleached and reprinted in a different version, achieving an inverted center or frame. Margins can be added or repairs done so deceptively that the stamps move from the "repaired" into the "fake" category.

Fakers have not left the backs of the stamps untouched either. They may create false watermarks, add fake grills or press out genuine grills. A thin India paper proof may be glued onto a thicker backing to create the appearance an issued stamp, or a proof printed on cardboard may be shaved down and perforated to resemble a stamp. Silk threads are impressed into paper and stamps have been split so that a rare paper variety is added to an otherwise inexpensive stamp. The most common treatment to the back of a stamp, however, is regumming.

Some in the business of faking stamps have openly advertised foolproof application of "original gum" to stamps that lack it, although most publications now ban such ads from their pages. It is believed that very few early stamps have survived without being hinged. The large number of never-hinged examples of such earlier material offered for sale thus suggests the widespread extent of regumming activity. Regumming also may be used to hide repairs or thin spots. Dipping the stamp into watermark fluid, or examining it under longwave ultraviolet light often will reveal these flaws.

Fakers also tamper with separations. Ingenious ways to add margins are known. Perforated wide-margin stamps may be falsely represented as imperforate when trimmed. Reperforating is commonly done to create scarce coil or perforation varieties, and to eliminate the naturally occurring straight-edge stamps found in sheet margin positions of many earlier issues. Custom has made straight-edged stamps less desirable. Fakers have obliged by perforating straight-edged stamps so that many are now uncommon, if not rare. Another fertile field for the faker is that of overprints, surcharges and cancellations. The forging of rare surcharges or overprints

began in the 1880s or 1890s. These forgeries are sometimes difficult to detect, but experts have identified almost all. Occasionally, overprints or cancellations are removed to create non-overprinted stamps or seemingly unused items. This is most commonly done by removing a manuscript cancel to make a stamp resemble an unused example. "SPECIMEN" overprints may be removed by scraping and repainting to create non-overprinted varieties. Fakers use inexpensive revenues or pen-canceled stamps to generate unused stamps for further faking by adding other markings. The quartz lamp or UV lamp and a high-powered magnifying glass help to easily detect removed cancellations.

The bigger problem, however, is the addition of overprints, surcharges or cancellations - many with such precision that they are very difficult to ascertain. Plating of the stamps or the overprint can be an important method of detection.

Fake postmarks may range from many spurious fancy cancellations to a host of markings applied to transatlantic covers, to addressing normally appearing postmarks to definitives of some countries with stamps that are valued far higher used than unused. With the increased popularity of cover collecting, and the widespread interest in postal history, a fertile new field for fakers has come about. Some have tried to create entire covers. Others specialize in adding stamps, tied by fake cancellations, to genuine stampless covers, or replacing less expensive or damaged stamps with more valuable ones. Detailed study of postal rates in effect at the time a cover in question was mailed, including the analysis of each handstamp used during the period, ink analysis and similar techniques, usually will unmask the fraud.

## Restoration and Repairs

Scott Publishing Co. bases its catalogue values on stamps that are free of defects and otherwise meet the standards set forth earlier in this introduction. Most stamp collectors desire to have the finest copy of an item possible. Even within given grading categories there are variances. This leads to a controversial practice that is not defined in any universal manner: stamp restoration.

There are broad differences of opinion about what is permissible when it comes to restoration. Carefully applying a soft eraser to a stamp or cover to remove light soiling is one form of restoration, as is washing a stamp in mild soap and water to clean it. These are fairly accepted forms of restoration. More severe forms of restoration include pressing out creases or removing stains caused by tape. To what degree each of these is acceptable is dependent upon the individual situation. Further along the spectrum is the freshening of a stamp's color by removing oxide build-up or the effects of wax paper left next to stamps shipped to the tropics.

At some point in this spectrum the concept of repair replaces that of restoration. Repairs include filling thin spots, mending tears by reweaving or adding a missing perforation tooth. Regumming stamps may have been acceptable as a restoration or repair technique many decades ago, but today it is considered a form of fakery.

Restored stamps may or may not sell at a discount, and it is possible that the value of individual restored items may be enhanced over that of their pre-restoration state. Specific situations dictate the resultant value of such an item. Repaired stamps sell at substantial discounts from the value of sound stamps.

# Terminology

**Booklets** — Many countries have issued stamps in small booklets for the convenience of users. This idea continues to become increasingly popular in many countries. Booklets have been issued in many sizes and forms, often with advertising on the covers, the panes of stamps or on the interleaving.

The panes used in booklets may be printed from special plates or made from regular sheets. All panes from booklets issued by the United States and many from those of other countries contain stamps that are straight edged on the sides, but perforated between. Others are distinguished by orientation of watermark or other identifying features. Any stamp-like unit in the pane, either printed or blank, that is not a postage stamp, is considered to be a label in the catalogue listings.

Scott lists and values booklet panes. Modern complete booklets also are listed and valued. Individual booklet panes are listed only when they are not fashioned from existing sheet stamps and, therefore, are identifiable from their sheet stamp counterparts.

Panes usually do not have a used value assigned to them because there is little market activity for used booklet panes, even though many exist used and there is some demand for them.

**Cancellations** — The marks or obliterations put on stamps by postal authorities to show that they have performed service and to prevent their reuse are known as cancellations. If the marking is made with a pen, it is considered a "pen cancel." When the location of the post office appears in the marking, it is a "town cancellation." A "postmark" is technically any postal marking, but in practice the term generally is applied to a town cancellation with a date. When calling attention to a cause or celebration, the marking is known as a "slogan cancellation." Many other types and styles of cancellations exist, such as duplex, numerals, targets, fancy and others. See also "precancels," below.

**Coil Stamps** — These are stamps that are issued in rolls for use in dispensers, affixing and vending machines. Those coils of the United States, Canada, Sweden and some other countries are perforated horizontally or vertically only, with the outer edges imperforate. Coil stamps of some countries, such as Great Britain and Germany, are perforated on all four sides and may in some cases be distinguished from their sheet stamp counterparts by watermarks, counting numbers on the reverse or other means.

**Covers** — Entire envelopes, with or without adhesive postage stamps, that have passed through the mail and bear postal or other markings of philatelic interest are known as covers. Before the introduction of envelopes in about 1840, people folded letters and wrote the address on the outside. Some people covered their letters with an extra sheet of paper on the outside for the address, producing the term "cover." Used airletter sheets, stamped envelopes and other items of postal stationery also are considered covers.

**Errors** — Stamps that have some major, consistent, unintentional deviation from the normal are considered errors. Errors include, but are not limited to, missing or wrong colors, wrong paper, wrong watermarks, inverted centers or frames on multicolor printing, inverted or missing surcharges or overprints, double impressions,

missing perforations, unintentionally omitted tagging and others. Factually wrong or misspelled information, if it appears on all examples of a stamp, are not considered errors in the true sense of the word. They are errors of design. Inconsistent or randomly appearing items, such as misperfs or color shifts, are classified as freaks.

**Color-Omitted Errors** — This term refers to stamps where a missing color is caused by the complete failure of the printing plate to deliver ink to the stamp paper or any other paper. Generally, this is caused by the printing plate not being engaged on the press or the ink station running dry of ink during printing.

**Color-Missing Errors** — This term refers to stamps where a color or colors were printed somewhere but do not appear on the finished stamp. There are four different classes of color-missing errors, and the catalog indicates with a two-letter code appended to each such listing what caused the color to be missing. These codes are used only for the United States' color-missing error listings.

EP = A piece of *extraneous paper* falling across the plate or stamp paper will receive the printed ink. When the extraneous paper is removed, an unprinted portion of stamp paper remains and shows partially or totally missing colors.

CM = A misregistration of the printing plates during printing will result in a *color misregistration*, and such a misregistration may result in a color not appearing on the finished stamp.

PS = A *perforation shift* after printing may remove a color from the finished stamp. Normally, this will occur on a row of stamps at the edge of the stamp pane.

FO = A *foldover* of the stamp sheet during printing may block ink from appearing on a stamp. Instead, the color will appear on the back of the foldover (where it might fall on the back of the stamp or perhaps on the back of the stamp or another stamp.) FO also will be used in the case of foldunders, where the paper may fold underneath the other stamp paper and the color will print on the platen.

**Overprints and Surcharges** — Overprinting involves applying wording or design elements over an already existing stamp. Overprints can be used to alter the place of use (such as "Canal Zone" on U.S. stamps), to adapt them for a special purpose ("Porto" on Denmark's 1913-20 regular issues for use as postage due stamps, Scott J1-J7) or to commemorate a special occasion (United States Scott 647-648).

A *surcharge* is a form of overprint that changes or restates the face value of a stamp or piece of postal stationery.
Surcharges and overprints may be handstamped, typeset or, occasionally, lithographed or engraved. A few hand-written overprints and surcharges are known.

**Personalized Stamps** — In 1999, Australia issued stamps with se-tenant labels that could be personalized with pictures of the customer's choice. Other countries quickly followed suit, with some offering to print the selected picture on the stamp itself within a frame that was used exclusively for personalized issues. As the picture used on these stamps or labels vary, listings for such stamps are for any picture within the common frame (or any picture on a se-tenant label), be it a "generic" image or one produced especially for a customer, almost invariably at a premium price.

**Precancels** — Stamps that are canceled before they are placed in the mail are known as precancels. Precanceling usually is done to expedite the handling of large mailings and generally allow the affected mail pieces to skip certain phases of mail handling. In the United States, precancellations generally identified the point of origin; that is, the city and state. This information appeared across the face of the stamp, usually centered between parallel lines. More recently, bureau precancels retained the parallel lines, but the city and state designations were dropped. Recent coils have a service inscription that is present on the original printing plate. These show the mail service paid for by the stamp. Since these stamps are not intended to receive further cancellations when used as intended, they are considered precancels. Such items often do not have parallel lines as part of the precancellation.

In France, the abbreviation *Affranchts* in a semicircle together with the word *Postes* is the general form of precancel in use. Belgian precancellations usually appear in a box in which the name of the city appears. Netherlands precancels have the name of the city enclosed between concentric circles, sometimes called a "lifesaver." Precancellations of other countries usually follow these patterns, but may be any arrangement of bars, boxes and city names.

Precancels are listed in the Scott catalogues only if the precancel changes the denomination (Belgium Scott 477-478); if the precancel is different from the non-precanceled version (such as untagged U.S. precancels); or if the stamp exists only precanceled (France Scott 1096-1099, U.S. Scott 2265).

**Proofs and Essays** — Proofs are impressions taken from an approved die, plate or stone in which the design and color are the same as the stamp issued to the public. Trial color proofs are impressions taken from approved dies, plates or stones in colors that vary from the final version. An essay is the impression of a design that differs in some way from the issued stamp. "Progressive die proofs" generally are considered to be essays.

**Provisionals** — These are stamps that are issued on short notice and intended for temporary use pending the arrival of regular issues. They usually are issued to meet such contingencies as changes in government or currency, shortage of necessary postage values or military occupation.

During the 1840s, postmasters in certain American cities issued stamps that were valid only at specific post offices. In 1861, postmasters of the Confederate States also issued stamps with limited validity. Both of these examples are known as "postmaster's provisionals."

**Se-tenant** — This term refers to an unsevered pair, strip or block of stamps that differ in design, denomination or overprint.
Unless the se-tenant item has a continuous design (see U.S. Scott 1451a, 1694a) the stamps do not have to be in the same order as shown in the catalogue (see U.S. Scott 2158a).

**Specimens** — The Universal Postal Union required member nations to send samples of all stamps they released into service to the International Bureau in Switzerland. Member nations of the UPU received these specimens as samples of what stamps were valid for postage. Many are overprinted, handstamped or initial-perforated "Specimen," "Cancelled" or "Muestra." Some are marked with bars across the denominations (China-Taiwan), punched holes (Czechoslovakia) or back inscriptions (Mongolia).
Stamps distributed to government officials or for publicity purposes, and stamps submitted by private security printers for official approval, also may receive such defacements.
The previously described defacement markings prevent postal use, and all such items generally are known as "specimens."

**Tete Beche** — This term describes a pair of stamps in which one is upside down in relation to the other. Some of these are the result of intentional sheet arrangements, such as Morocco Scott B10-B11. Others occurred when one or more electrotypes accidentally were placed upside down on the plate, such as Colombia Scott 57a. Separation of the tete-beche stamps, of course, destroys the tete beche variety.

# value priced **stockbooks**

Stockbooks are a classic and convenient storage alternative for many collectors. These German-made stockbooks feature heavyweight archival quality paper with 9 pockets on each page. The 8½" x 11⅝" pages are bound inside a handsome leatherette grain cover and include glassine interleaving between the pages for added protection. The Value Priced Stockbooks are available in two page styles, the white page stockbooks feature glassine pockets while the black page variety includes clear acetate pockets

## BLACK PAGE STOCKBOOKS ACETATE POCKETS

| ITEM | COLOR | PAGES | RETAIL |
|------|-------|-------|--------|
| ST16RD | Red | 16 pages | $10.95 |
| ST16GR | Green | 16 pages | $10.95 |
| ST16BL | Blue | 16 pages | $10.95 |
| ST16BK | Black | 16 pages | $10.95 |
| ST32RD | Red | 32 pages | $16.95 |
| ST32GR | Green | 32 pages | $16.95 |
| ST32BL | Blue | 32 pages | $16.95 |
| ST32BK | Black | 32 pages | $16.95 |
| ST64RD | Red | 64 pages | $29.95 |
| ST64GR | Green | 64 pages | $29.95 |
| ST64BL | Blue | 64 pages | $29.95 |
| ST64BK | Black | 64 pages | $29.95 |

## WHITE PAGE STOCKBOOKS GLASSINE POCKETS

| ITEM | DESCRIPTION | | RETAIL |
|------|-------------|--|--------|
| SW16BL | Blue | 16 pages | $6.95 |
| SW16GR | Green | 16 pages | $6.95 |
| SW16RD | Red | 16 pages | $6.95 |

Scott Value Priced Stockbooks are available from your favorite dealer or direct from:

**SCOTT**®

P.O. Box 828
Sidney OH 45365-0828
www.amosadvantage.com
1-800-572-6885

**AMOS** HOBBY PUBLISHING

# Currency Conversion

| Country | Dollar | Pound | S Franc | Yen | HK $ | Euro | Cdn $ | Aus $ |
|---|---|---|---|---|---|---|---|---|
| Australia | 1.3768 | 2.4007 | 1.0579 | 0.0116 | 0.1775 | 1.6662 | 1.1985 | |
| Canada | 1.1488 | 2.0032 | 0.8827 | 0.0097 | 0.1481 | 1.3903 | | 0.8344 |
| European Union | 0.8263 | 1.4408 | 0.6349 | 0.0070 | 0.1065 | | 0.7193 | 0.6002 |
| Hong Kong | 7.7556 | 13.523 | 5.9594 | 0.0656 | | 9.3859 | 6.7510 | 5.6331 |
| Japan | 118.27 | 206.23 | 90.881 | | 15.250 | 143.14 | 102.95 | 85.904 |
| Switzerland | 1.3014 | 2.2693 | | 0.0110 | 0.1678 | 1.5750 | 1.1328 | 0.9452 |
| United Kingdom | 0.5735 | | 0.4407 | 0.0048 | 0.0739 | 0.6940 | 0.4992 | 0.4165 |
| United States | — | 1.7437 | 0.7684 | 0.0085 | 0.1289 | 1.2102 | 0.8705 | 0.7263 |

| Country | Currency | U.S. $ Equiv. |
|---|---|---|
| Pakistan | rupee | .0167 |
| Palau | U.S. dollar | 1.00 |
| Palestinain Authority | Jordanian dinar | 1.411 |
| Panama | balboa | 1.00 |
| Papua New Guinea | kina | .3302 |
| Paraguay | guarani | .0002 |
| Penrhyn Island | New Zealand dollar | .6083 |
| Peru | new sol | .2978 |
| Philippines | peso | .0196 |
| Pitcairn Islands | New Zealand dollar | .6083 |
| Poland | zloty | .3045 |
| Portugal | euro | 1.2102 |
| Azores | euro | 1.2102 |
| Maderia | euro | 1.2102 |
| Qatar | riyal | .2747 |
| Romania | leu | .3449 |
| Russia | ruble | .0361 |
| Rwanda | franc | .0018 |
| St. Helena | British pound | 1.7437 |
| St. Kitts | East Caribbean dollar | .3745 |
| St. Lucia | East Caribbean dollar | .3745 |
| St. Pierre & Miquelon | euro | 1.2102 |
| St. Thomas & Prince | dobra | .0001 |
| St. Vincent | East Caribbean dollar | .3745 |
| St. Vincent Grenadines | East Caribbean dollar | .3745 |
| El Salvador | colon | .1143 |
| Samoa | tala (dollar) | .3515 |
| San Marino | euro | 1.2102 |
| Saudi Arabia | riyal | .2666 |
| Senegal | Community of French Africa (CFA) franc | .0018 |
| Serbia | dinar | .0139 |
| Montenegro | euro | 1.2102 |
| Seychelles | rupee | .1846 |
| Zil Elwannyen Sesel | rupee | .1846 |
| Sierra Leone | leone | .0004 |
| Singapore | dollar | .6223 |
| Slovakia | koruna | .0323 |
| Slovenia | tolar | .0051 |

## COMMON DESIGN TYPES

Pictured in this section are issues where one illustration has been used for a number of countries in the Catalogue. Not included in this section are over-printed stamps or those issues which are illustrated in each country.

### EUROPA
### Europa, 1956

The design symbolizing the cooperation among the six countries comprising the Coal and Steel Community is illustrated in each country.

Belgium........496-497
France........805-806
Germany........748-749
Italy........715-716
Luxembourg........318-320
Netherlands........368-369

### Europa, 1958

"E" and Dove — CD1

European Postal Union at the service of European integration.

1958, Sept. 13
Belgium........527-528
France........889-890
Germany........790-791
Italy........750-751
Luxembourg........341-343
Netherlands........375-376
Saar........317-318

### Europa, 1959

6-Link Enless Chain — CD2

1959, Sept. 19
Belgium........536-537
France........929-930
Germany........805-806
Italy........791-792
Luxembourg........354-355
Netherlands........379-380

### Europa, 1960

19-Spoke Wheel CD3

First anniversary of the establishment of C.E.P.T. (Conference Europeenne des Administrations des Postes et des Telecommunications.) The spokes symbolize the 19 founding members of the Conference.

1960, Sept.
Belgium........553-554
Denmark........379
Finland........376-377
France........970-971
Germany........818-820
Great Britain........377-378
Greece........688
Iceland........327-328
Ireland........175-176
Italy........809-810
Luxembourg........374-375
Netherlands........385-386
Norway........387
Portugal........866-867
Spain........941-942
Sweden........562-563
Switzerland........400-401
Turkey........1493-1494

### Europa, 1961

19 Doves Flying as One — CD4

The 19 doves represent the 19 members of the Conference of European Postal and Tele-communications Administrations C.E.P.T.

1961-62
Belgium........572-573
Cyprus........201-203
France........1005-1006
Germany........844-845
Great Britain........383-384
Greece........718-719
Iceland........340-341
Italy........845-846
Luxembourg........382-383
Netherlands........387-388
Spain........1010-1011
Switzerland........410-411
Turkey........1518-1520

### Europa, 1962

Young Tree with 19 Leaves CD5

The 19 leaves represent the 19 original members of C.E.P.T.

1962-63
Belgium........582-583
Cyprus........219-221
France........1045-1046
Germany........852-853
Greece........739-740
Iceland........348-349
Ireland........184-185
Italy........860-861
Luxembourg........386-387
Netherlands........394-395
Switzerland........416-417
Turkey........1553-1555

### Europa, 1963

Stylized Links, Symbolizing Unity — CD6

1963, Sept.
Belgium........598-599
Cyprus........229-231
Finland........419
France........1074-1075
Germany........867-868
Greece........768-769
Iceland........357-358
Ireland........188-189
Italy........880-881
Luxembourg........403-404
Norway........416-417
Sweden........441-442
Switzerland........429
Turkey........1602-1603

### Europa, 1964

Symbolic Daisy — CD7

5th anniversary of the establishment of C.E.P.T. The 22 petals of the flower symbolize the 22 members of the Conference.

1964, Sept.
Austria........738
Belgium........614-615
Cyprus........244-246
France........1109-1110
Germany........897-898
Greece........801-802
Iceland........367-368
Ireland........196-197
Italy........894-895
Luxembourg........411-412
Monaco........590-591
Netherlands........428-429
Norway........450
Portugal........931-933
Spain........1262-1263
Switzerland........438-439
Turkey........1628-1629

### Europa, 1965

Leaves and "Fruit" CD8

1965
Belgium........636-637
Cyprus........262-264
Finland........437
France........1131-1132
Germany........934-935
Iceland........375-376
Ireland........204-205
Italy........915-916
Luxembourg........432-433
Monaco........616-617
Netherlands........438-439
Norway........475-476
Portugal........958-960
Switzerland........469
Turkey........1665-1666

### Europa, 1966

Symbolic Sailboat — CD9

1966, Sept.
Andorra, French........172
Belgium........675-676
Cyprus........275-277
France........1163-1164
Greece........963-964
Iceland........862-863
Ireland........384-385
Italy........216-217
Liechtenstein........415
Luxembourg........440-441
Monaco........639-640
Netherlands........441-442
Norway........496-497
Portugal........980-982
Switzerland........477-478
Turkey........1718-1719

### Europa, 1967

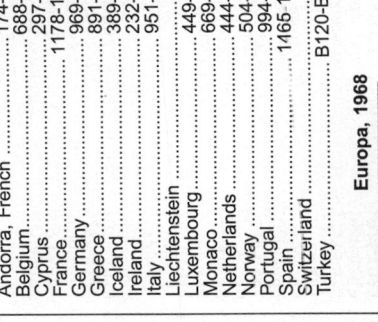

Cogwheels CD10

1967
Andorra, French........174-175
Belgium........688-689
Cyprus........297-299
France........1178-1179
Germany........969-970
Greece........891-892
Iceland........389-390
Ireland........232-233
Italy........951-952
Liechtenstein........420
Luxembourg........449-450
Monaco........669-670
Netherlands........444-447
Norway........504-505
Portugal........994-996
Spain........1465-1466
Switzerland........482
Turkey........B120-B121

### Europa, 1968

Golden Key with C.E.P.T. Emblem CD11

1968
Andorra, French........182-183
Belgium........705-706
Cyprus........314-316
France........1209-1210
Germany........983-984
Greece........916-917
Iceland........395-396
Ireland........242-243
Italy........979-980
Liechtenstein........442
Luxembourg........466-467
Monaco........689-691
Netherlands........452-453
Portugal........1019-1021
San Marino........687
Spain........1526
Turkey........1775-1776

### Europa, 1969

"EUROPA" and "CEPT" CD12

Tenth anniversary of C.E.P.T.

1969
Andorra, French........188-189
Austria........837
Belgium........718-719
Denmark........326-328
Finland........458
France........483
Germany........1245-1246
Great Britain........996-997
Greece........585
Iceland........947-948
Ireland........406-407
Italy........270-271
Liechtenstein........1000-1001
Luxembourg........453
Monaco........474-475
Norway........722-724
Portugal........475-476
San Marino........533-534
Spain........1038-1040
Sweden........701-702
Switzerland........1567
Turkey........814-816

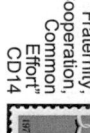

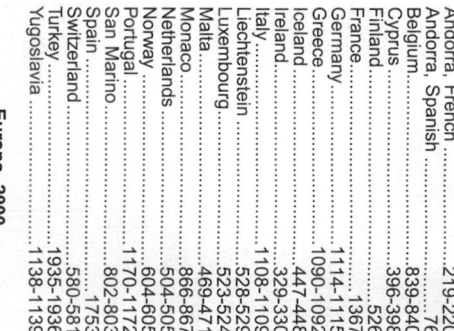

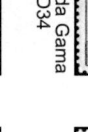

# 34A

Interwoven Threads
CD13

## Europa, 1970

### 1970

| | |
|---|---|
| Andorra, French | 196-197 |
| Belgium | 741-742 |
| Cyprus | 340-342 |
| France | 1271-1272 |
| Germany | 1018-1019 |
| Finland | 504 |
| Greece | 985, 987 |
| Iceland | 420-421 |
| Ireland | 279-281 |
| Italy | 1013-1014 |
| Liechtenstein | 470 |
| Luxembourg | 489-490 |
| Monaco | 769-770 |
| Netherlands | 483-484 |
| Portugal | 1060-1062 |
| San Marino | 729-730 |
| Spain | 1607 |
| Switzerland | 515-516 |
| Turkey | 1848-1849 |
| Yugoslavia | 1024-1025 |
| Switzerland | 500-501 |
| Turkey | 1799-1800 |
| Vatican | 470-472 |
| Yugoslavia | 1003-1004 |
| Monaco | |

"Fraternity, Cooperation, Common Effort"
CD14

## Europa, 1971

### 1971

| | |
|---|---|
| Andorra, French | 205-206 |
| Belgium | 803-804 |
| Cyprus | 365-367 |
| France | 1304 |
| Finland | 504 |
| Germany | 1064-1065 |
| Greece | 1029-1030 |
| Iceland | 429-430 |
| Ireland | 305-306 |
| Italy | 1038-1039 |
| Liechtenstein | 485 |
| Luxembourg | 500-501 |
| Malta | 425-427 |
| Monaco | 797-799 |
| Netherlands | 488-489 |
| Portugal | 1094-1096 |
| San Marino | 749-750 |
| Spain | 1675-1676 |
| Switzerland | 531-532 |
| Turkey | 1876-1877 |
| Yugoslavia | 1052-1053 |

Sparkles, Symbolic of Communications
CD15

## Europa, 1972

### 1972

| | |
|---|---|
| Andorra, French | 210-211 |
| Andorra, Spanish | 62 |
| Belgium | 825-826 |
| Cyprus | 380-382 |
| Finland | 512-513 |
| France | 1341 |
| Germany | 1089-1090 |
| Greece | 1049-1050 |
| Iceland | 439-440 |
| Ireland | 316-317 |
| Italy | 1065-1066 |
| Liechtenstein | 504 |
| Luxembourg | 512-513 |
| Malta | 450-453 |
| Monaco | 831-832 |

Post Horn and Arrows
CD16

## Europa, 1973

### 1973

| | |
|---|---|
| Andorra, French | 219-220 |
| Andorra, Spanish | 76 |
| Belgium | 839-840 |
| Cyprus | 396-398 |
| Finland | 526 |
| France | 1367 |
| Germany | 1114-1115 |
| Greece | 1090-1092 |
| Iceland | 447-448 |
| Ireland | 329-330 |
| Italy | 1108-1109 |
| Liechtenstein | 523-524 |
| Luxembourg | 523-529 |
| Malta | 469-471 |
| Monaco | 866-867 |
| Netherlands | 504-505 |
| Norway | 604-605 |
| Portugal | 1170-1172 |
| San Marino | 802-803 |
| Spain | 1753 |
| Switzerland | 580-581 |
| Turkey | 1935-1936 |
| Yugoslavia | 1138-1139 |
| Netherlands | 494-495 |
| Portugal | 1141-1143 |
| San Marino | 771-772 |
| Switzerland | 1718 |
| Turkey | 544-545 |
| Yugoslavia | 1100-1101 |

CD17

## Europa, 2000

### 2000

| | |
|---|---|
| Albania | 2621-2622 |
| Andorra, French | 522 |
| Andorra, Spanish | 262 |
| Armenia | 610-611 |
| Austria | 1814 |
| Azerbaijan | 698-699 |
| Belarus | 350 |
| Belgium | 1818 |
| Bosnia & Herzegovina (Moslem) | 358 |
| Bosnia & Herzegovina (Serb) | 111- |
| 112 | |
| Croatia | 428-429 |
| Cyprus | 959 |
| Czech Republic | 3120 |
| Denmark | 1189 |
| Estonia | 394 |
| Faroe Islands | 376 |
| Finland | 1129 |
| France | 2771 |
| Georgia | 228-229 |
| Germany | 2086-2087 |
| Gibraltar | 837-840 |
| Great Britain (Guernsey) | 805-809 |
| Great Britain (Jersey) | 935-936 |
| Great Britain (Isle of Man) | 883 |
| Greece | 1959 |
| Greenland | 363 |
| Hungary | 3699-3700 |
| Iceland | 910 |
| Ireland | 1230-1231 |
| Italy | 2349 |
| Latvia | 504 |
| Liechtenstein | 1178 |
| Lithuania | 668 |
| Luxembourg | 1035 |
| Macedonia | 187 |
| Malta | 1011-1012 |
| Moldova | 355 |
| Monaco | 2161-2162 |
| Poland | 3519 |
| Portugal | 2358 |
| Portugal (Azores) | 455 |
| Portugal (Madeira) | 208 |
| Romania | 4370 |
| Russia | 6589 |
| San Marino | 1480 |
| Slovakia | 355 |
| Slovenia | 424 |
| Spain | 3036 |
| Sweden | 2394 |
| Switzerland | 1074 |
| Turkey | 2762 |
| Turkish Rep. of Northern Cyprus | 500 |
| Ukraine | 379 |
| Vatican City | 1152 |

# COMMON DESIGN TYPES

## PORTUGAL & COLONIES
### Vasco da Gama

The Gibraltar stamps are similar to the stamp illustrated, but none have the design shown above. All other sets listed above include at least one stamp with the design shown, but some include stamps with entirely different designs. Bulgaria Nos. 2485-2486 are Europa and Yugoslavia Nos. 4131-4132 are Europa stamps with completely different designs.

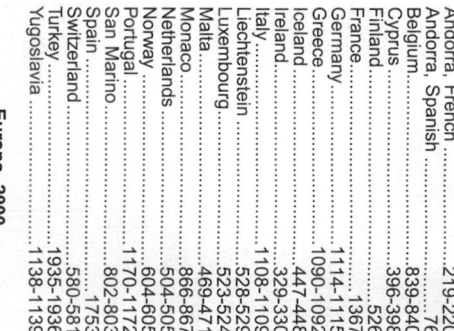

Fleet Departing
CD20

Fleet Arriving at Calicut — CD21

Embarking at Rastello
CD22

Muse of History
CD23

San Gabriel, da Gama and Camoens
CD24

Archangel Gabriel, the Patron Saint
CD25

Flagship San Gabriel — CD26

Vasco da Gama — CD27

### 1898

| | |
|---|---|
| Azores | 93-100 |
| Macao | 67-74 |
| Madeira | 37-44 |
| Portugal | 147-154 |
| Port. Africa | 1-8 |
| Port. Congo | 75-98 |
| Port. India | 189-196 |
| St. Thomas & Prince Islands | 170-193 |
| Timor | 45-52 |

Fourth centenary of Vasco da Gama's discovery of the route to India.

### Pombal
### POSTAL TAX
### POSTAL TAX DUES

Marquis de Pombal — CD28

Pombal Monument, Lisbon — CD30

Sebastiao Jose de Carvalho e Mello, Marquis de Pombal (1699-1782), statesman, rebuilt Lisbon after earthquake of 1755. Tax was for the erection of Pombal monument. Obligatory on all mail on certain days throughout the year. Postal Tax Dues are inscribed "Multa."

Planning Reconstruction of Lisbon, 1755 — CD29

### 1925

| | |
|---|---|
| Angola | RA1-RA3, RA1-RA3 |
| Azores | RA9-RA11, RA2-RA4 |
| Cape Verde | RA1-RA3, RA1-RA3 |
| Macao | RA1-RA3, RA1-RA3 |
| Madeira | RA1-RA3, RA1-RA3 |
| Mozambique | RA1-RA3, RA1-RA3 |
| Nyassa | RA11-RA13, RA1-RA3 |
| Port. Guinea | RA1-RA3, RA12-RA14 |
| Portugal | RA1-RA3, RA1-RA3 |
| Port. India | RA1-RA3, RA1-RA3 |
| St. Thomas & Prince Islands | RA1-RA3, RA1-RA3 |
| Timor | RA1-RA3, RA1-RA3 |

### 1938-39

Vasco da Gama
CD34

Mousinho de Albuquerque
CD35

Dam
CD36

Prince Henry the Navigator
CD37

Affonso de Albuquerque
CD38

Plane over Globe
CD39

| | |
|---|---|
| Angola | 274-291, C1-C9 |
| Cape Verde | 234-251, C1-C9 |
| Macao | 289-305, C7-C15 |
| Mozambique | 270-287, C1-C9 |
| Port. Guinea | 233-250, C1-C9 |
| Port. India | 439-453, C1-C8 |
| St. Thomas & Prince Islands | 302-319, 323-340, C1-C18 |
| Timor | 223-239, C1-C9 |

## ITU

ITU Emblem and the Archangel Gabriel — CD52

International Communications Union, Cent.

**1965, May 17**

| | |
|---|---|
| Angola | 511 |
| Cape Verde | 329 |
| Macao | 402 |
| Mozambique | 464 |
| Port. Guinea | 320 |
| St. Thomas & Prince Islands | 383 |
| Timor | 321 |

## National Revolution

40th anniv. of the National Revolution. Different buildings on each stamp.

CD53

**1966, May 28**

| | |
|---|---|
| Angola | 525 |
| Cape Verde | 338 |
| Macao | 403 |
| Mozambique | 465 |
| Port. Guinea | 329 |
| St. Thomas & Prince Islands | 392 |
| Timor | 322 |

## Navy Club

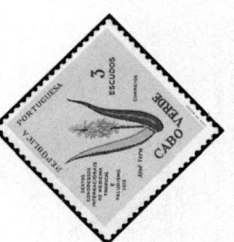

CD54

Centenary of Portugal's Navy Club. Each stamp has a different design.

**1967, Jan. 31**

| | |
|---|---|
| Angola | 527-528 |
| Cape Verde | 339-340 |
| Macao | 412-413 |
| Mozambique | 478-479 |
| Port. Guinea | 330-331 |
| St. Thomas & Prince Islands | 393-394 |
| Timor | 323-324 |

## Admiral Coutinho

CD55

Centenary of the birth of Admiral Carlos Viegas Gago Coutinho (1869-1959), explorer and aviation pioneer. Each stamp has a different design.

**1969, Feb. 17**

| | |
|---|---|
| Angola | 547 |
| Cape Verde | 355 |
| Macao | 417 |
| Mozambique | 484 |
| Port. Guinea | 335 |
| St. Thomas & Prince Islands | 397 |
| Timor | 335 |

## Sports

CD48

Each stamp shows a different sport.

**1962**

| | |
|---|---|
| Angola | 433-438 |
| Cape Verde | 320-325 |
| Macao | 394-399 |
| Mozambique | 424-429 |
| Port. Guinea | |
| St. Thomas & Prince Islands | 374-379 |
| Timor | 313-318 |

## Anti-Malaria

Anopheles Funestus and Malaria Eradication Symbol — CD49

World Health Organization drive to eradicate malaria.

**1962**

| | |
|---|---|
| Angola | 439 |
| Cape Verde | 326 |
| Macao | 400 |
| Mozambique | 430 |
| Port. Guinea | 305 |
| St. Thomas & Prince Islands | 380 |
| Timor | 319 |

## Airline Anniversary

Map of Africa, Super Constellation and Jet Liner — CD50

Tenth anniversary of Transportes Aereos Portugueses (TAP).

**1963**

| | |
|---|---|
| Angola | 490 |
| Cape Verde | 327 |
| Mozambique | 434 |
| Port. Guinea | 318 |
| St. Thomas & Prince Islands | 381 |

## National Overseas Bank

Antonio Teixeira de Sousa — CD51

Centenary of the National Overseas Bank of Portugal.

**1964, May 16**

| | |
|---|---|
| Angola | 509 |
| Cape Verde | 328 |
| Port. Guinea | 319 |
| St. Thomas & Prince Islands | 382 |
| Timor | 320 |

## Medical Congress

CD44

First National Congress of Tropical Medicine, Lisbon, 1952. Each stamp has a different design.

**1952**

| | |
|---|---|
| Angola | 358 |
| Cape Verde | 287 |
| Macao | 364 |
| Mozambique | 359 |
| Port. Guinea | 276 |
| Port. India | 516 |
| St. Thomas & Prince Islands | 356 |
| Timor | 271 |

## Postage Due Stamps

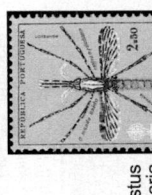

CD45

**1952**

| | |
|---|---|
| Angola | J37-J42 |
| Cape Verde | J31-J36 |
| Macao | J53-J58 |
| Mozambique | J40-J45 |
| Port. India | J47-J52 |
| St. Thomas & Prince Islands | J52-J57 |
| Timor | J31-J36 |

## Sao Paulo

Father Manuel de Nobrega and View of Sao Paulo — CD46

Founding of Sao Paulo, Brazil, 400th anniv.

**1954**

| | |
|---|---|
| Angola | 385 |
| Cape Verde | 297 |
| Macao | 382 |
| Mozambique | 395 |
| Port. Guinea | 291 |
| Port. India | 530 |
| St. Thomas & Prince Islands | 369 |
| Timor | 279 |

## Tropical Medicine Congress

CD47

Sixth International Congress for Tropical Medicine and Malaria, Lisbon, Sept. 1958. Each stamp shows a different plant.

**1958**

| | |
|---|---|
| Angola | 409 |
| Cape Verde | 303 |
| Macao | 392 |
| Mozambique | 404 |
| Port. Guinea | 295 |
| Port. India | 569 |
| St. Thomas & Prince Islands | 371 |
| Timor | 289 |

## Lady of Fatima

Our Lady of the Rosary, Fatima, Portugal — CD40

**1948-49**

| | |
|---|---|
| Angola | 315-318 |
| Cape Verde | 266 |
| Macao | 336 |
| Mozambique | 325-328 |
| Port. Guinea | 271 |
| Port. India | 480 |
| St. Thomas & Prince Islands | 351 |
| Timor | 254 |

A souvenir sheet of 9 stamps was issued in 1951 to mark the extension of the 1950 Holy Year. The sheet contains: Angola No. 316, Cape Verde No. 266, Macao No. 336, Mozambique No. 325, Portuguese Guinea No. 271, Portuguese India Nos. 480, 485, St. Thomas & Prince Islands No. 351, Timor No. 254. The sheet also contains a portrait of Pope Pius XII and is inscribed "Encerramento do Ano Santo, Fatima 1951." It was sold for 11 escudos.

## Holy Year

Angel Holding Candelabra CD42

Church Bells and Dove CD41

Holy Year, 1950.

**1950-51**

| | |
|---|---|
| Angola | 331-332 |
| Cape Verde | 268-269 |
| Macao | 339-340 |
| Mozambique | 330-331 |
| Port. Guinea | 273-274 |
| Port. India | 490-491, 496-503 |
| St. Thomas & Prince Islands | 353-354 |
| Timor | 258-259 |

A souvenir sheet of 8 stamps was issued in 1951 to mark the extension of the Holy Year. The sheet contains: Angola No. 331, Cape Verde No. 269, Macao No. 340, Mozambique No. 331, Portuguese Guinea No. 275, Portuguese India No. 490, St. Thomas & Prince Islands No. 354, Timor No. 258, some with colors changed. The sheet contains doves and is inscribed "Encerramento do Ano Santo, Fatima 1951." It was sold for 1/ escudos.

## Holy Year Conclusion

Our Lady of Fatima — CD43

**1951**

Conclusion of Holy Year. Sheets contain alternate vertical rows of stamps and labels bearing quotation from Pope Pius XII, different for each colony.

| | |
|---|---|
| Angola | 357 |
| Cape Verde | 270 |
| Macao | 352 |
| Mozambique | 356 |
| Port. Guinea | 275 |
| Port. India | 506 |
| St. Thomas & Prince Islands | 355 |
| Timor | 270 |

## Administration Reform

Centenary of the administration reforms of the overseas territories.

**1969, Sept. 25**

Angola ... 549
Cape Verde ... 357
Macao ... 419
Mozambique ... 491
Port. Guinea ... 337
St. Thomas & Prince Islands ... 399
Timor ... 338

Luiz Augusto Rebello da Silva — CD56

## Marshal Carmona

Birth centenary of Marshal Antonio Oscar Carmona de Fragoso (1869-1951), President of Portugal. Each stamp has a different design.

**1970, Nov. 15**

Angola ... 563
Cape Verde ... 359
Macao ... 422
Mozambique ... 493
Port. Guinea ... 340
St. Thomas & Prince Islands ... 403
Timor ... 341

CD57

## Olympic Games

20th Olympic Games, Munich, Aug. 26-Sept. 11. Each stamp shows a different sport.

**1972, June 20**

Angola ... 569
Cape Verde ... 361
Macao ... 426
Mozambique ... 504
Port. Guinea ... 342
St. Thomas & Prince Islands ... 408
Timor ... 343

CD59

## Lisbon-Rio de Janeiro Flight

50th anniversary of the Lisbon to Rio de Janeiro flight by Arturo de Sacadura and Coutinho, March 30-June 5, 1922. Each stamp shows a different stage of the flight.

**1972, Sept. 20**

Angola ... 570
Cape Verde ... 362
Macao ... 427
Mozambique ... 505
Port. Guinea ... 343
St. Thomas & Prince Islands ... 409
Timor ... 344

CD60

**1973, Dec. 15**

Angola ... 571
Cape Verde ... 363
Macao ... 429
Mozambique ... 509
Port. Guinea ... 344
St. Thomas & Prince Islands ... 410
Timor ... 345

## WMO Centenary

Centenary of international meteorological cooperation.

WMO Emblem — CD61

## FRENCH COMMUNITY

Upper Volta can be found under Burkina Faso in Vol. 1

Madagascar can be found under Malagasy in Vol. 3

## Colonial Exposition

People of French Empire CD70

Women's Heads CD71

France Showing Way to Civilization CD72

"Colonial Commerce" CD73

**1931**

International Colonial Exposition, Paris.

Cameroun ... 213-216
Chad ... 60-63
Dahomey ... 97-100
Fr. Guiana ... 152-155
Fr. Guinea ... 116-119
Fr. India ... 100-103
Fr. Polynesia ... 76-79
Fr. Sudan ... 102-105
Gabon ... 120-123
Guadeloupe ... 138-141
Indo-China ... 140-142
Ivory Coast ... 92-95
Madagascar ... 169-172
Martinique ... 129-132
Mauritania ... 65-68
Middle Congo ... 65-68
New Caledonia ... 176-179
Niger ... 73-76
Reunion ... 132-135
St. Pierre & Miquelon ... 138-141
Senegal ... 135-138
Somali Coast ... 254-257
Togo ... 82-85
Ubangi-Shari ... 66-69
Upper Volta ... 85-88
Wallis & Futuna Isls. ... 89

## Paris International Exposition
### Colonial Arts Exposition

"Colonial Resources" CD74

"Colonial Resources" CD77

Overseas Commerce CD75

Exposition Building and Women CD76

**1937**

Cameroun ... 223-224
Dahomey ... 111-112
Fr. Equatorial Africa ... 78-79
Fr. Guiana ... 169-170
Fr. Guinea ... 164-165
Fr. India ... 111-112
Fr. Polynesia ... 124-125
Fr. Sudan ... 116-117
Guadeloupe ... 155-156
Indo-China ... 203-204
Inini ... 42-43
Ivory Coast ... 163-164
Kwangchowan ... 121-122
Madagascar ... 209-210
Martinique ... 186-187
Mauritania ... 112-113
New Caledonia ... 215-216
Niger ... 87-88
Reunion ... 174-175
St. Pierre & Miquelon ... 205-206
Senegal ... 191-192
Somali Coast ... 179-180
Togo ... 268-269
Wallis & Futuna Isls. ... 90-91

## Paris International Exposition

"France and the Empire" CD78

Cultural Treasures of the Colonies CD79

Souvenir sheets contain one imperf. stamp.

**1937**

Cameroun ... 217-222A
Dahomey ... 101-107
Fr. Equatorial Africa ... 27-32, 73
Fr. Guiana ... 162-168
Fr. Guinea ... 120-126
Fr. India ... 104-110
Fr. Polynesia ... 117-123
Fr. Sudan ... 106-112
Guadeloupe ... 148-154
Indo-China ... 193-199
Inini ... 41
Ivory Coast ... 152-158
Kwangchowan ... 132
Madagascar ... 191-197
Martinique ... 179-185
Mauritania ... 69-75
New Caledonia ... 208-214
Niger ... 78-83
Reunion ... 167-173
St. Pierre & Miquelon ... 165-171
Senegal ... 172-178
Somali Coast ... 139-145
Togo ... 258-264
Wallis & Futuna Isls. ... 89

## Caille

Death centenary of Rene Caille (1799-1838), French explorer. All three denominations exist with colony name omitted.

Rene Caille and Map of Northwestern Africa — CD81

**1939**

Dahomey ... 108-110
Fr. Guiana ... 161-163
Fr. Guinea ... 113-115
Ivory Coast ... 160-162
Mauritania ... 109-111
Niger ... 84-86
St. Pierre & Miquelon ... 188-190
Somali Coast ... 265-267

## Curie

Pierre and Marie Curie CD80

40th anniversary of the discovery of radium. The surtax was for the benefit of the Intl. Union for the Control of Cancer.

**1938**

Cameroun ... B1
Dahomey ... B1-B2
Fr. Equatorial Africa ... B4-B8, CB1
France ... B76
Fr. Guiana ... B7-B11
Fr. Guinea ... B3-B7
Fr. India ... B1
Fr. Polynesia ... B2
Fr. Sudan ... B5
Guadeloupe ... B3
Indo-China ... B14
Ivory Coast ... B2
Madagascar ... B2
Martinique ... B2
New Caledonia ... B4
Niger ... B1
St. Pierre & Miquelon ... B3
Somali Coast ... B3
Togo ... B2
Inini ... B1

## New York World's Fair

Natives and New York Skyline CD82

**1939**

## French Revolution

Storming of the Bastille CD83

French Revolution, 150th anniv. The surtax was for the defense of the colonies.

**1939**

Cameroun ... B2-B6
Dahomey ... B3-B7
Fr. Equatorial Africa ... B4-B8, CB1
Fr. Guiana ... B7-B11
Fr. Guinea ... B3-B7
Fr. India ... B1
Fr. Polynesia ... B2
Fr. Sudan ... B5
Guadeloupe ... B2-B6
Indo-China ... B15-B19, CB1
Inini ... B1-B5
Ivory Coast ... B3-B7

# COMMON DESIGN TYPES

**1940**

Plane over Coastal Area — CD85

| | |
|---|---|
| Kwangchowan | B1-B5 |
| Madagascar | B3-B7, CB1 |
| Martinique | B3-B7 |
| Mauritania | B4-B8 |
| New Caledonia | B5-B9, CB1 |
| Niger | B2-B6 |
| Reunion | B5-B9, CB1 |
| St. Pierre & Miquelon | B4-B8, CB1 |
| Senegal | B3-B7 |
| Somali Coast | B2-B6 |
| Togo | B1-B5 |
| Wallis & Futuna Isls. | |

All five denominations exist with colony name omitted.

**1940**

Cross of Lorraine & Four-motor Plane CD87

| | |
|---|---|
| Dahomey | C1-C5 |
| Fr. Guinea | C1-C5 |
| Fr. Sudan | C1-C5 |
| Ivory Coast | C1-C5 |
| Mauritania | C1-C5 |
| Niger | C1-C5 |
| Senegal | C12-C16 |
| Togo | C1-C5 |

**Defense of the Empire**

Colonial Infantryman — CD86

**1941**

| | |
|---|---|
| Cameroun | B13B |
| Dahomey | B13 |
| Fr. Equatorial Africa | B8B |
| Fr. Guinea | D10 |
| Fr. Guinea | B13 |
| Fr. India | B13 |
| Fr. Sudan | B12 |
| Guadeloupe | B12 |
| Indo-China | B10 |
| Inini | B19B |
| Ivory Coast | B7 |
| Kwangchowan | B13 |
| Madagascar | B7 |
| Martinique | B9 |
| Mauritania | B9 |
| New Caledonia | B14 |
| Niger | B11 |
| Reunion | B12 |
| St. Pierre & Miquelon | B11 |
| Senegal | B8B |
| Somali Coast | B14 |
| Togn | B9 |
| Wallis & Futuna Isls. | B10B |
| | B7 |

**Colonial Education Fund**

CD86a

**1942**

| | |
|---|---|
| Cameroun | CB3 |
| Dahomey | CB4 |
| Fr. Equatorial Africa | CB5 |
| Fr. Guiana | CB4 |
| Fr. Guinea | CB4 |

---

Eboue

Wallis & Futuna Isls. ...... B9

CD91

Felix Eboue, first French colonial administrator to proclaim resistance to Germany after French surrender in World War II.

**1945**

| | |
|---|---|
| Cameroun | 296-297 |
| Fr. Equatorial Africa | 156-157 |
| Fr. Guiana | 171-172 |
| Fr. India | 210-211 |
| Fr. Polynesia | 150-151 |
| Fr. West Africa | 15-16 |
| Guadeloupe | 187-188 |
| Madagascar | 259-260 |
| Martinique | 196-197 |
| New Caledonia | 274-275 |
| Reunion | 238-239 |
| St. Pierre & Miquelon | 322-323 |
| Somali Coast | 238-239 |

**Victory**

Victory — CD92

European victory of the Allied Nations in World War II.

**1946, May 8**

| | |
|---|---|
| Cameroun | C8 |
| Fr. Equatorial Africa | C24 |
| Fr. Guiana | C11 |
| Fr. India | C7 |
| Fr. Polynesia | C10 |
| Fr. West Africa | C4 |
| Guadeloupe | C3 |
| Indo-China | C19 |
| Madagascar | C44 |
| Martinique | C3 |
| New Caledonia | C14 |
| Reunion | C25 |
| St. Pierre & Miquelon | C8 |
| Somali Coast | C8 |
| Wallis & Futuna Isls. | C1 |

**Chad to Rhine**

Leclerc's Departure from Chad — CD93

Battle at Cufra Oasis — CD94

---

**Tanks in Action, Mareth — CD95**

**Normandy Invasion — CD96**

**Entering Paris — CD97**

**Liboration of Strasbourg — CD98**

"Chad to the Rhine" march, 1942-44, by Gen. Jacques Leclerc's column, later French 2nd Armored Division.

**1946, June 6**

| | |
|---|---|
| Cameroun | C9-C14 |
| Fr. Equatorial Africa | C25-C30 |
| Fr. Guiana | C12-C17 |
| Fr. India | C8-C13 |
| Fr. Polynesia | C11-C16 |
| Fr. West Africa | C5-C10 |
| Guadeloupe | C4-C9 |
| Indo-China | C20-C25 |
| Madagascar | C45-C50 |
| Martinique | C4-C0 |
| New Caledonia | C15-C20 |
| Reunion | C26-C31 |
| St. Pierre & Miquelon | C9-C14 |
| Somali Coast | C9-C14 |
| Wallis & Futuna Isls. | C2-C7 |

**UPU**

French Colonials, Globe and Plane — CD99

Universal Postal Union, 75th anniv.

**1949, July 4**

| | |
|---|---|
| Cameroun | C29 |
| Fr. Equatorial Africa | C34 |
| Fr. India | C17 |
| Fr. Polynesia | C20 |
| Fr. West Africa | C15 |
| Indo-China | C26 |
| Madagascar | C55 |
| New Caledonia | C24 |
| St. Pierre & Miquelon | C18 |
| Somali Coast | C18 |
| Togo | C18 |
| Wallis & Futuna Isls. | C10 |

---

**Transport Plane CD88**

| | |
|---|---|
| Dahomey | C6-C13 |
| Fr. Guinea | C6-C13 |
| Fr. Sudan | C6-C13 |
| Ivory Coast | C6-C13 |
| Mauritania | C6-C13 |
| Niger | C17-C25 |
| Senegal | C6-C13 |
| Togo | |

**1942**

| | |
|---|---|
| Cameroun | C1-C7 |
| Fr. Equatorial Africa | C17-C23 |
| Fr. Guiana | C9-C10 |
| Fr. India | C3-C9 |
| Fr. Polynesia | C1-C3 |
| Fr. West Africa | C1-C2 |
| Guadeloupe | C37-C43 |
| Madagascar | C1-C2 |
| Martinique | C7-C13 |
| New Caledonia | C18-C24 |
| St. Pierre & Miquelon | C1-C7 |
| Somali Coast | C1-C7 |

**1941-5**

**Caravan and Plane CD89**

**Red Cross**

Marianne CD90

The surtax was for the French Red Cross and national relief.

**1944**

| | |
|---|---|
| Cameroun | B28 |
| Fr. Equatorial Africa | B38 |
| Fr. Guiana | B12 |
| Fr. India | B14 |
| Fr. Polynesia | B1 |
| Guadeloupe | B12 |
| Madagascar | B15 |
| Martinique | B11 |
| New Caledonia | B12 |
| Reunion | B15 |
| St. Pierre & Miquelon | B13 |
| Somali Coast | B13 |

## COMMON DESIGN TYPES

### 1950

CÔTE FRANÇAISE DES SOMALIS
ŒUVRES SOCIALES F.O.A.

Doctor
Treating
Infant
CD100

**Tropical Medicine**

The surtax was for charitable work.

| | |
|---|---|
| Cameroun | B29 |
| Fr. Equatorial Africa | B39 |
| Fr. India | B15 |
| Fr. Polynesia | B14 |
| Fr. West Africa | B14 |
| Madagascar | B3 |
| New Caledonia | B17 |
| St. Pierre & Miquelon | B14 |
| Somali Coast | B14 |
| Togo | B11 |

### 1952

CAMEROUN

Medal, Early Marine
and Colonial
Soldier — CD101

**Military Medal**

Centenary of the creation of the French Military Medal.

| | |
|---|---|
| Cameroun | 332 |
| Comoro Isls. | 39 |
| Fr. Equatorial Africa | 186 |
| Fr. India | 233 |
| Fr. Polynesia | 179 |
| Fr. West Africa | 57 |
| Madagascar | 286 |
| New Caledonia | 295 |
| St. Pierre & Miquelon | 345 |
| Somali Coast | 267 |
| Togo | 327 |
| Wallis & Futuna Isls. | 149 |

### 1952

CAMEROUN
LIBERATION

Allied Landing, Victory Sign and Cross
of Lorraine — CD102

**Liberation**

Liberation of France, 10th anniv.

| | |
|---|---|
| Cameroun | C32 |
| Comoro Isls. | C4 |
| Fr. Equatorial Africa | C38 |
| Fr. India | C18 |
| Fr. Polynesia | C22 |
| Fr. West Africa | C57 |
| Madagascar | C25 |
| New Caledonia | C19 |
| St. Pierre & Miquelon | C19 |
| Togo | C11 |

### 1954, June 6

Allied Landing, Victory Sign and Cross of Lorraine — CD102

### FIDES

CAMEROUN

Plowmen
CD103

Efforts of FIDES, the Economic and Social
Development Fund for Overseas Possessions.

| | |
|---|---|

---

### 1956

POSTES CÔTE FRANÇAISE DES SOMALIS
10e ANNIVERSAIRE
DÉCLARATION UNIVERSELLE DES DROITS DE L'HOMME

Sun, Dove
and U.N.
Emblem
CD105

**Human Rights**

10th anniversary of the signing of the Universal Declaration of Human Rights.

| | |
|---|---|
| Comoro Isls. | 44 |
| Fr. Equatorial Africa | 202 |
| Fr. Polynesia | 191 |
| Fr. West Africa | 85 |
| Madagascar | 300 |
| New Caledonia | 306 |
| St. Pierre & Miquelon | 356 |
| Somali Coast | 274 |
| Wallis & Futuna Isls. | 153 |

### 1958

| | |
|---|---|

(Fonds d'Investissement pour le Développement Economique et Social). Each stamp has a different design.

### 1956

RÉPUBLIQUE DU 1050

**Flower**

CD104

Each stamp shows a different flower.

| | |
|---|---|
| Cameroun | 326-329 |
| Comoro Isls. | 43 |
| Fr. Polynesia | 181 |
| Fr. West Africa | 65-72 |
| Madagascar | 292-295 |
| New Caledonia | 303 |
| Somali Coast | 268 |
| Togo | 331 |

### 1958-9

| | |
|---|---|
| Cameroun | 333 |
| Comoro Isls. | 45 |
| Fr. Equatorial Africa | 200-201 |
| Fr. Polynesia | 192 |
| Fr. So. & Antarctic Terr. | 11 |
| Fr. West Africa | 79-83 |
| Madagascar | 301-302 |
| New Caledonia | 304-305 |
| St. Pierre & Miquelon | 357 |
| Somali Coast | 270 |
| Togo | 348-349 |
| Wallis & Futuna Isls. | 152 |

### 1960

ÉTAT DU CAMEROUN
COMMISSION DE COOPÉRATION TECHNIQUE EN AFRIQUE AU SUD DU SAHARA
50F

CD106

**C.C.T.A.**

Commission for Technical Cooperation in
Africa south of the Sahara, 10th anniv.

| | |
|---|---|
| Cameroun | 335 |
| Cent. Africa | 3 |
| Congo, P.R. | 66 |
| Dahomey | 90 |
| Gabon | 138 |
| Ivory Coast | 150 |
| Madagascar | 317 |
| Mali | 9 |
| Mauritania | 104 |
| Niger | 117 |
| Upper Volta | 89 |

### 1962

RÉPUBLIQUE CENTRAFRICAINE
20F JEUX SPORTIFS

**Abidjan Games**

CD109

Abidjan Games, Ivory Coast, Dec. 24-31,
1961. Each stamp shows a different sport.

| | |
|---|---|
| Chad | 83-84 |
| Cent. Africa | 19-20 |
| Congo, P.R. | 103-104 |
| Gabon | 103-105 |
| Niger | 109-111 |
| Upper Volta | 163-164, C6 |

### 1962

PREMIER ANNIVERSAIRE DE L'UNION AFRICAINE ET MALGACHE
RÉPUBLIQUE CENTRAFRICAINE
30F POSTES

Flag of
Union
CD110

**African and Malagasy Union**

First anniversary of the Union.

| | |
|---|---|
| Cameroun | 373 |
| Cent. Africa | 21 |

---

## COMMON DESIGN TYPES

### 1958-9

Modern and Ancient Africa, Map and
Planes — CD107

**Air Afrique, 1961**

Founding of Air Afrique (African Airlines).

| | |
|---|---|
| Cameroun | C37 |
| Chad | C5 |
| Cent. Africa | C5 |
| Congo, P.R. | C7 |
| Dahomey | C18 |
| Gabon | C5 |
| Ivory Coast | C17 |
| Mauritania | C22 |
| Niger | C17 |
| Senegal | C31 |
| Upper Volta | C4 |

### 1961-62

RÉPUBLIQUE CENTRAFRICAINE
D'AIR-AFRIQUE
RF 25F POSTE AÉRIENNE
50f

**Anti-Malaria**

CD108

World Health Organization drive to eradicate malaria.

### 1962, Apr. 7

| | |
|---|---|
| Cameroun | B36 |
| Cent. Africa | B1 |
| Chad | B19 |
| Congo, P.R. | B1 |
| Dahomey | B16 |
| Gabon | B1 |
| Ivory Coast | B14 |
| Madagascar | B15 |
| Mauritania | B4 |
| Niger | B15 |
| Senegal | B19 |
| Somali Coast | B15 |
| Upper Volta | B1 |

### 1962-63

RF 25f
ARCHIPEL DES COMORES
11 JUILLET 1962 PLANSON TV PAR SATELLITE EUROPE-AMÉRIQUE

**Telstar**

Telstar and Globe Showing Andover
and Pleumeur-Bodou — CD111

First television connection of the United
States and Europe through the Telstar satellite, July 11-12, 1962.

| | |
|---|---|
| Andorra, French | 154 |
| Comoro Isls. | C7 |
| Fr. Polynesia | C29 |
| Fr. So. & Antarctic Terr. | C5 |
| New Caledonia | C33 |
| St. Pierre & Miquelon | C26 |
| Wallis & Futuna Isls. | C17 |

### 1963, Mar. 21

RÉPUBLIQUE CENTRAFRICAINE
CAMPAGNE MONDIALE CONTRE LA FAIM
25F5 POSTES

World Map
and Wheat
Emblem
CD112

**Freedom From Hunger**

U.N. Food and Agriculture Organization's
"Freedom from Hunger" campaign.

| | |
|---|---|
| Cameroun | B37-B38 |
| Cent. Africa | B2 |
| Chad | B2 |
| Congo, P.R. | B4 |
| Dahomey | B16 |
| Gabon | B5 |
| Ivory Coast | B21 |
| Madagascar | B17 |
| Mauritania | B15 |
| Niger | B17 |
| Senegal | B2 |
| Upper Volta | B2 |

### 1963, Sept. 2

50F
ARCHIPEL DES COMORES

**Red Cross Centenary**

CD113

Centenary of the International Red Cross.

| | |
|---|---|
| Comoro Isls. | 55 |
| Fr. Polynesia | 205 |
| New Caledonia | 328 |
| St. Pierre & Miquelon | 367 |
| Somali Coast | 297 |
| Wallis & Futuna Isls. | 165 |

### 1962, Sept. 8

| | |
|---|---|
| Chad | 85 |
| Congo, P.R. | 105 |
| Dahomey | 155 |
| Gabon | 165 |
| Ivory Coast | 198 |
| Madagascar | 332 |
| Mauritania | 170 |
| Niger | 112 |
| Senegal | 211 |
| Upper Volta | 106 |

# COMMON DESIGN TYPES

## African Postal Union, 1963

UAMPT Emblem, Radio Masts, Plane and Mail CD114

Establishment of the African and Malagasy Posts and Telecommunications Union.

**1963, Sept. 8**

| | |
|---|---|
| Cameroun | C47 |
| Cent. Africa | C10 |
| Chad | C9 |
| Congo, P.R. | C13 |
| Dahomey | C19 |
| Gabon | C13 |
| Ivory Coast | C25 |
| Madagascar | C75 |
| Mauritania | C22 |
| Niger | C27 |
| Rwanda | 36 |
| Senegal | C32 |
| Upper Volta | C9 |

## Air Afrique, 1963

Symbols of Flight — CD115

First anniversary of Air Afrique and inauguration of DC-8 service.

**1963, Nov. 19**

| | |
|---|---|
| Cameroun | C48 |
| Chad | C10 |
| Congo, P.R. | C14 |
| Gabon | C18 |
| Ivory Coast | C26 |
| Mauritania | C26 |
| Niger | C35 |
| Senegal | C33 |

## Europafrica

Europe and Africa Linked — CD116

Signing of an economic agreement between the European Economic Community and the African and Malagasy Union, Yaounde, Cameroun, July 20, 1963.

**1963-64**

| | |
|---|---|
| Cameroun | 402 |
| Chad | C11 |
| Cent. Africa | C12 |
| Congo, P.R. | C16 |
| Gabon | C19 |
| Ivory Coast | 217 |
| Niger | C43 |
| Upper Volta | C11 |

## Human Rights

Scales of Justice and Globe CD117

15th anniversary of the Universal Declaration of Human Rights.

**1963, Dec. 10**

| | |
|---|---|
| Comoro Isls. | 58 |
| Fr. Polynesia | 206 |
| New Caledonia | 329 |
| St. Pierre & Miquelon | 368 |
| Somali Coast | 300 |
| Wallis & Futuna Isls. | 166 |

## PHILATEC

Stamp Album, Champs Elysees Palace and Horses of Marly CD118

Intl. Philatelic and Postal Techniques Exhibition, Paris, June 5-21, 1964.

**1963-64**

| | |
|---|---|
| Comoro Isls. | 60 |
| France | 1078 |
| Fr. Polynesia | 207 |
| New Caledonia | 341 |
| St. Pierre & Miquelon | 369 |
| Somali Coast | 301 |
| Wallis & Futuna Isls. | 167 |

## Cooperation

CD119

Cooperation between France and the French-speaking countries of Africa and Madagascar.

**1964**

| | |
|---|---|
| Cameroun | 409-410 |
| Cent. Africa | 39 |
| Chad | 103 |
| Congo, P.R. | 121 |
| Dahomey | 193 |
| France | 1111 |
| Gabon | 175 |
| Ivory Coast | 221 |
| Madagascar | 360 |
| Mauritania | 181 |
| Niger | 143 |
| Senegal | 236 |
| Togo | 495 |

## ITU

Telegraph, Syncom Satellite and ITU Emblem CD120

Intl. Telecommunication Union, Cent.

## French Satellite A-1

**1965, May 17**

| | |
|---|---|
| Comoro Isls. | C14 |
| Fr. Polynesia | C33 |
| Fr. So. & Antarctic Terr. | C8 |
| New Caledonia | C40 |
| New Hebrides | 124-125 |
| St. Pierre & Miquelon | C29 |
| Somali Coast | C36 |
| Wallis & Futuna Isls. | C20 |

Diamant Rocket and Launching Installation — CD121

Launching of France's first satellite, Nov. 26, 1965.

**1965-66**

| | |
|---|---|
| Comoro Isls. | C15-C16 |
| France | 1137-1138 |
| Fr. Polynesia | C40-C41 |
| Fr. So. & Antarctic Terr. | C9-C10 |
| New Caledonia | C44-C45 |
| St. Pierre & Miquelon | C30-C31 |
| Somali Coast | C39-C40 |
| Wallis & Futuna Isls. | C22-C23 |

## French Satellite D-1

D-1 Satellite in Orbit — CD122

Launching of the D-1 satellite at Hammaguir Algeria, Feb. 17, 1966.

**1966**

| | |
|---|---|
| Comoro Isls. | C17 |
| France | 1148 |
| Fr. Polynesia | C42 |
| Fr. So. & Antarctic Terr. | C11 |
| New Caledonia | C46 |
| St. Pierre & Miquelon | C32 |
| Somali Coast | C40 |
| Wallis & Futuna Isls. | C24 |

## Air Afrique, 1966

Planes and Air Afrique Emblem — CD123

Introduction of DC-8F planes by Air Afrique.

**1966**

| | |
|---|---|
| Cameroun | C79 |
| Cent. Africa | C35 |
| Chad | C26 |
| Congo, P.R. | C42 |
| Dahomey | C47 |
| Gabon | C32 |
| Ivory Coast | C57 |
| Mauritania | C63 |
| Niger | C47 |
| Senegal | C54 |
| Togo | C31 |

## African Postal Union, 1967

Telecommunications Symbols and Map of Africa — CD124

Fifth anniversary of the establishment of the African and Malagasy Union of Posts and Telecommunications, UAMPT.

**1967**

| | |
|---|---|
| Cameroun | C90 |
| Cent. Africa | C46 |
| Chad | C37 |
| Congo, P.R. | C57 |
| Dahomey | C61 |
| Gabon | C58 |
| Ivory Coast | C34 |
| Madagascar | C85 |
| Mauritania | C65 |
| Niger | C75 |
| Rwanda | C1-C3 |
| Senegal | C60 |
| Togo | C81 |
| Upper Volta | C50 |

## Monetary Union

Gold Token of the Ashantis, 17-18th Centuries — CD125

West African Monetary Union, 5th anniv.

**1967, Nov. 4**

| | |
|---|---|
| Dahomey | 244 |
| Ivory Coast | 259 |
| Mauritania | 238 |
| Niger | 201 |
| Senegal | 294 |
| Togo | C23 |
| Upper Volta | 181 |

## WHO Anniversary

Sun, Flowers and WHO Emblem CD126

World Health Organization, 20th anniv.

**1968, May 4**

| | |
|---|---|
| Afars & Issas | 317 |
| Comoro Isls. | 73 |
| Fr. Polynesia | 241-242 |
| Fr. So. & Antarctic Terr. | 31 |
| New Caledonia | 367 |
| St. Pierre & Miquelon | 377 |
| Wallis & Futuna Isls. | 169 |

## Human Rights Year

Human Rights Flame — CD127

**1968, Aug. 10**

| | |
|---|---|
| Afars & Issas | 322-323 |

# COMMON DESIGN TYPES

Comoro Isls. ........ 76
Fr. Polynesia ........ 243-244
Fr. So. & Antarctic Terr. ........ 32
New Caledonia. ........ 382
St. Pierre & Miquelon. ........ 369
Wallis & Futuna Isls. ........ 170

Opening of PHILEXAFRIQUE, Abidjan, Feb. 14. Each stamp shows a local scene and stamp.

**1969, Feb. 14**
Cameroun. ........ C118
Cent. Africa ........ C65
Chad. ........ C48
Congo, P.R. ........ C77
Dahomey ........ C94
Gabon. ........ C82
Ivory Coast. ........ C38-C40
Madagascar. ........ C92
Mali. ........ C65
Mauritania. ........ C80
Niger. ........ C104
Senegal. ........ C68
Togo. ........ C104
Upper Volta ........ C62

## 2nd PHILEXAFRIQUE

CD128

**1969-70**
Afars & Issas ........ 337
Comoro Isls. ........ 83
Fr. Polynesia. ........ 251-252
Fr. So. & Antarctic Terr. ........ 35
New Caledonia. ........ 379
St. Pierre & Miquelon. ........ 396
Wallis & Futuna Isls. ........ 172

## Concorde

First flight of the prototype Concorde supersonic plane at Toulouse, Mar. 1, 1969.

Concorde in Flight CD129

**1969**
Afars & Issas ........ C56
Comoro Isls ........ C29
France ........ C42
Fr. Polynesia. ........ C50
New Caledonia ........ C18
Fr. So. & Antarctic Terr. ........ C63
St. Pierre & Miquelon. ........ C40
Wallis & Futuna Isls. ........ C30

## Development Bank

Bank Emblem — CD130

**1969**
African Development Bank, fifth anniv.
Cameroun ........ 499
Chad ........ 217
Congo, P.R. ........ 181-182
Ivory Coast ........ 281
Mali ........ 127-128
Mauritania ........ 267
Niger ........ 220
Senegal ........ 317-318
Upper Volta ........ 201

## ILO

Intl. Labor Organization, 50th anniv.

ILO Headquarters, Geneva, and Emblem — CD131

## ASECNA

10th anniversary of the Agency for the Security of Aerial Navigation in Africa and Madagascar (ASECNA, Agence pour la Sécurité de la Navigation Aérienne en Afrique et à Madagascar).

Map of Africa, Plane and Airport CD132

**1969-70**
Cameroun. ........ 500
Cent. Africa ........ 119
Chad ........ 222
Congo, P.R. ........ 197
Dahomey ........ 269
Gabon. ........ 260
Ivory Coast. ........ 287
Mali. ........ 130
Niger. ........ 321
Senegal. ........ 204
Upper Volta ........ 204

## U.P.U. Headquarters

New Universal Postal Union headquarters, Bern, Switzerland.

U.P.U. Headquarters CD133

**1970**
Afars & Issas ........ 342
Algeria ........ 443
Cameroun ........ 503-504
Cent. Africa ........ 125
Chad ........ 225
Comoro Isls ........ 84
Congo, P.R. ........ 216
Dahomey ........ 261-262
Fr. Polynesia. ........ 36
Gabon. ........ 258
Ivory Coast. ........ 295
Mali ........ 134-135
Madagascar. ........ 444
Mauritania ........ 283
New Caledonia ........ 282
Niger ........ 231-232
St. Pierre & Miquelon. ........ 397-398
Senegal ........ 328-329
Tunisia ........ 535
Wallis & Futuna Isls. ........ 173

## De Gaulle

First anniversary of the death of Charles de Gaulle, (1890-1970), President of France.

De Gaulle CD134

**1971-72**
Afars & Issas ........ 356-357
Comoro Isls. ........ 104-105
France ........ 1322-1325
Fr. Polynesia. ........ 270-271
Fr. So. & Antarctic Terr. ........ 52-53
New Caledonia. ........ 393-394
Reunion ........ 377, 380
St. Pierre & Miquelon. ........ 417-418
Wallis & Futuna Isls. ........ 177-178

## African Postal Union, 1971

10th anniversary of the establishment of the African and Malagasy Posts and Telecommunications Union, UAMPT. Each stamp has a different native design.

UAMPT Building, Brazzaville, Congo — CD135

**1971, Nov. 13**
Cameroun. ........ C177
Cent. Africa ........ C89
Chad ........ C94
Congo, P.R. ........ C136
Dahomey ........ C146
Gabon. ........ C120
Ivory Coast. ........ C47
Mauritania ........ C113
Niger. ........ C164
Rwanda ........ C8
Senegal ........ C105
Togo. ........ C166
Upper Volta ........ C97

## West African Monetary Union

West African Monetary Union, 10th anniv.

African Couple, City, Village and Commemorative Coin — CD136

**1972, Nov. 2**
Dahomey. ........ 300
Ivory Coast. ........ 331
Niger. ........ 299
Senegal. ........ 374
Togo. ........ 258
Upper Volta. ........ 280

## African Postal Union, 1973

11th anniversary of the African and Malagasy Posts and Telecommunications Union (UAMPT).

Telecommunications Symbols and Map of Africa — CD137

**1973, Sept. 12**
Cameroun. ........ 574
Cent. Africa ........ 194
Chad ........ 294
Congo, P.R. ........ 289
Dahomey ........ 311
Ivory Coast. ........ 320
Madagascar. ........ 361
Mauritania. ........ 500
Niger. ........ 287

## Philexafrique II — Essen

Philexafrique II — Essen CD138

Philexafrique II CD139

Designs: Indigenous fauna, local and German stamps. Types CD138-CD139, printed horizontally and vertically se-tenant in sheets of 10 (2x5). Label between horizontal pairs alternately commemorates Philexafrique II, Libreville, Gabon, June 1978, and 2nd International Stamp Fair, Essen, Germany, Nov. 1-5.

**1978-1979**
Benin ........ C285-C286
Central Africa ........ C200-C201
Chad ........ C238-C239
Congo Republic ........ C245-C246
Djibouti ........ C121-C122
Gabon. ........ C215-C216
Ivory Coast. ........ C64-C65
Mali. ........ C356-C357
Mauritania ........ C185-C186
Niger. ........ C291-C292
Rwanda ........ C12-C13
Senegal ........ C146-C147
Rwanda ........ 540
Senegal ........ 393
Togo ........ 849
Upper Volta ........ 297

# BRITISH COMMONWEALTH OF NATIONS

The listings follow established trade practices when these issues are offered as units by dealers. The Peace issue, for example, includes only one stamp from the Indian state of Hyderabad. The U.P.U. issue includes the Egypt set. Pairs are included for those varieties issues with bilingual designs se-tenant.

## Silver Jubilee

Reign of King George V, 25th anniv.

Windsor Castle and King George V — CD301

**1935**
Antigua ........ 77-80
Ascension ........ 33-36
Bahamas ........ 92-95
Barbados ........ 186-189
Basutoland ........ 11-14
Bechuanaland Protectorate ........ 117-120
Bermuda ........ 100-103
British Guiana ........ 223-226
British Honduras ........ 108-111
Cayman Islands ........ 81-84
Ceylon ........ 260-263
Cyprus ........ 136-139
Dominica ........ 90-93
Falkland Islands ........ 77-80
Fiji ........ 110-113
Gambia ........ 125-128
Gibraltar ........ 100-103
Gilbert & Ellice Islands ........ 33-36

# COMMON DESIGN TYPES

## Silver Jubilee (1935, continued)

Gold Coast......108-111
Grenada......124-127
Hong Kong......147-150
Jamaica......109-112
Kenya, Uganda, Tanganyika......42-45
Leeward Islands......96-99
Malta......184-187
Mauritius......204-207
Montserrat......85-88
Newfoundland......226-229
Nigeria......34-37
Northern Rhodesia......18-21
Nyasaland Protectorate......47-50
St. Helena......111-114
St. Kitts-Nevis......72-75
St. Lucia......91-94
St. Vincent......134-137
Seychelles......118-121
Sierra Leone......166-169
Solomon Islands......60-63
Somaliland Protectorate......77-80
Straits Settlements......213-216
Swaziland......20-23
Trinidad & Tobago......43-46
Turks & Caicos Islands......71-74
Virgin Islands......69-72

The following have different designs but are included in the omnibus set:

Great Britain......226-229
Offices in Morocco......67-70, 226-229, 422-425, 508-510
Australia......152-154
Canada......211-216
Cook Islands......98-100
India......142-148
Nauru......31-34
New Guinea......46-47
New Zealand......199-201
Niue......67-69
Papua......114-117
Samoa......163-165
South Africa......68-71
Southern Rhodesia......33-36
South-West Africa......121-124

249 stamps

## Coronation

Queen Elizabeth and King George VI — CD302

### 1937

Aden......13-15
Antigua......81-83
Ascension......37-39
Bahamas......97-99
Barbados......190-192
Basutoland......15-17
Bechuanaland Protectorate......121-123
Bermuda......115-117
British Guiana......227-229
British Honduras......112-114
Cayman Islands......97-99
Ceylon......275-277
Cyprus......140-142
Dominica......94-96
Falkland Islands......81-83
Fiji......114-116
Gambia......129-131
Gibraltar......104-106
Gilbert & Ellice Islands......37-39
Gold Coast......112-114
Grenada......128-130
Hong Kong......151-153
Jamaica......113-115
Kenya, Uganda, Tanganyika......60-62
Leeward Islands......100-102
Malta......188-190
Mauritius......208-210
Montserrat......89-91
Newfoundland......230-232
Nigeria......50-52
Northern Rhodesia......22-24
Nyasaland Protectorate......51-53
St. Helena......115-117
St. Kitts-Nevis......76-78
St. Lucia......107-109
St. Vincent......138-140
Seychelles......122-124
Sierra Leone......170-172
Solomon Islands......64-66
Somaliland Protectorate......81-83
Straits Settlements......235-237
Swaziland......24-26
Trinidad & Tobago......47-49
Turks & Caicos Islands......75-77
Virgin Islands......73-75

The following have different designs but are included in the omnibus set:

Great Britain......234
Offices in Morocco......82, 439, 514
Canada......237
Cook Islands......109-111
Nauru......35-38
Newfoundland......233-243
New Guinea......48-51
New Zealand......223-225
Niue......70-72
Papua......118-121
South Africa......74-78
Southern Rhodesia......38-41
South-West Africa......125-132

202 stamps

## Peace

King George VI and Parliament Buildings, London — CD303

Return to peace at the close of World War II.

### 1945-46

Aden......28-29
Antigua......96-97
Ascension......50-51
Bahamas......130-131
Barbados......207-208
Bermuda......131-132
British Guiana......242-243
British Honduras......127-128
Cayman Islands......112-113
Ceylon......293-294
Cyprus......156-157
Dominica......112-113
Falkland Islands......97-98
Falkland Islands Dep.......1L9-1L10
Fiji......137-138
Gambia......144-145
Gibraltar......119-120
Gilbert & Ellice Islands......52-53
Gold Coast......128-129
Grenada......143-144
Jamaica......136-137
Kenya, Uganda, Tanganyika......90-91
Leeward Islands......116-117
Malta......206-207
Mauritius......223-224
Montserrat......104-105
Nigeria......71-72
Northern Rhodesia......46-47
Nyasaland Protectorate......82-83
Pitcairn Island......9-10
St. Helena......128-129
St. Kitts-Nevis......91-92
St. Lucia......127-128
St. Vincent......152-153
Seychelles......149-150
Sierra Leone......186-187
Solomon Islands......80-81
Trinidad & Tobago......62-63
Turks & Caicos Islands......90-91
Virgin Islands......88-89

The following have different designs but are included in the omnibus set:

Great Britain......264-265
Offices in Morocco......523-524

## Silver Wedding

King George VI and Queen Elizabeth — CD304  CD305

### 1948-49

Aden......30-31
  Kathiri State of Seiyun......14-15
  Qu'aiti State of Shihr and Mukalla......14-15
Antigua......98-99
Ascension......52-53
Bahamas......148-149
Barbados......210-211
Basutoland......39-40
Bechuanaland Protectorate......147-148
Bermuda......133-134
British Guiana......244-245
British Honduras......129-130
Cayman Islands......116-117
Cyprus......158-159
Dominica......114-115
Falkland Islands......99-100
Falkland Islands Dep.......1L11-1L12
Fiji......139-140
Gambia......146-147
Gibraltar......121-122
Gilbert & Ellice Islands......124-125
Gold Coast......142-143
Grenada......145-146
Hong Kong......178-179
Jamaica......138-139
Kenya, Uganda, Tanganyika......92-93
Leeward Islands......118-119
Malaya
  Johore......128-129
  Kedah......55-56
  Kelantan......41-44
  Malacca......1-2
  Negri Sembilan......1-2
  Penang......1-2
  Perak......1-2
  Perlis......1-2
  Selangor......74-75
  Trengganu......47-48
Malta......223-224
Mauritius......229-230
Montserrat......106-107
Nigeria......73-74
North Borneo......238-239
Northern Rhodesia......48-49
Nyasaland Protectorate......85-86
Pitcairn Islands......11-12
St. Helena......130-131
St. Kitts-Nevis......93-94
St. Lucia......129-130
St. Vincent......154-155
Sarawak......174-175
Seychelles......151-152
Sierra Leone......188-189
Singapore......21-22
Solomon Islands......82-83
Somaliland Protectorate......110-111
Swaziland......48-49
Trinidad & Tobago......64-65
Turks & Caicos Islands......92-93
Virgin Islands......90-91
Zanzibar......224-225

The following have different designs but are included in the omnibus set:

Great Britain......264-265
Offices in Morocco......523-524
Aden
  Kathiri State of Seiyun......12-13
  Qu'aiti State of Shihr and Mukalla......12-13
Australia......200-202
Basutoland......29-31
Bechuanaland Protectorate......137-139
Burma......66-69
Cook Islands......127-130
Hong Kong......174-175
India......247-257
  Hyderabad......51
New Zealand......195-198
Niue......96
Pakistan-Bahawalpur......O16
Samoa......191-194
South Africa......100-102
Southern Rhodesia......67-70
South-West Africa......153-155
Swaziland......38-40
Zanzibar......222-223

164 stamps

## U.P.U.

Mercury and Symbols of Communications — CD306

Plane, Ship and Hemispheres — CD307

Mercury Scattering Letters over Globe CD308

U.P.U. Monument, Bern CD309

Universal Postal Union, 75th anniversary.

### 1949

Aden......32-35
  Kathiri State of Seiyun......16-19
  Qu'aiti State of Shihr und Mukalla......16-19
Antigua......100-103
Ascension......57-60
Bahamas......150-153
Barbados......212-215
Basutoland......41-44
Bechuanaland Protectorate......149-152
Bermuda......138, 141
British Guiana......246-249
British Honduras......137, 140
Brunei......79-82
Cayman Islands......118-121
Cyprus......160-163
Dominica......116-119
Falkland Islands......103-106
Falkland Islands Dep.......1L14-1L17
Fiji......141-144
Gambia......148-151
Gibraltar......123-126
Gilbert & Ellice Islands......56-59
Gold Coast......144-147
Grenada......147-150
Hong Kong......180-183
Jamaica......142-145
Kenya, Uganda, Tanganyika......94-97
Leeward Islands......126-129
Malaya
  Johore......151-154
  Kedah......57-60
  Kelantan......18-21
  Malacca......46-49
  Negri Sembilan......59-62
  Pahang......46-49
  Penang......23-26
  Perak......3-6
  Perlis......76-79
  Selangor......49-52
  Trengganu......94-97
Malta......225-228
Mauritius......231-234
Montserrat......108-111
New Hebrides, British......62-65
New Hebrides, French......79-82
Nigeria......75-78
North Borneo......240-243
Northern Rhodesia......50-53
Nyasaland Protectorate......87-90
Pitcairn Islands......13-16
St. Helena......132-135
St. Kitts-Nevis......95-98
St. Lucia......131-134
St. Vincent......170-173

The following have different designs but are included in the omnibus set:

Great Britain......267-268
Offices in Morocco......93-94, 525-526
Bahrain......62-63
Kuwait......82-83
Oman......25-26
St. Vincent......159

138 stamps

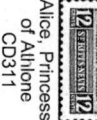

## Intl. Cooperation Year

ICY
Emblem
CD318

### 1965

| | |
|---|---|
| Antigua | 155-156 |
| Ascension | 94-95 |
| Bahamas | 222-223 |
| Basutoland | 103-104 |
| Bechuanaland Protectorate | 204-205 |
| Bermuda | 199-200 |
| British Guiana | 295-296 |
| British Honduras | 189-190 |
| Brunei | 118-119 |
| Cayman Islands | 174-175 |
| Dominica | 187-188 |
| Falkland Islands | 156-157 |
| Fiji | 213-214 |
| Gibraltar | 169-170 |
| Gilbert & Ellice Islands | 104-105 |
| Grenada | 207-208 |
| Hong Kong | 223-224 |
| Mauritius | 293-294 |
| Montserrat | 176-177 |
| New Hebrides, British | 110-111 |
| New Hebrides, French | 126-127 |
| Pitcairn Islands | 54-55 |
| St. Helena | 182-183 |
| St. Kitts-Nevis | 165-166 |
| St. Lucia | 199-200 |
| St. Vincent | 200-201 |
| Seychelles | 143-144 |
| Solomon Islands | 143-144 |
| South Arabia | 17-18 |
| Swaziland | 117-118 |
| Tristan da Cunha | 87-88 |
| Turks & Caicos Islands | 144-145 |
| Virgin Islands | 161-162 |

*64 stamps*

## Churchill Memorial

Winston
Churchill
and St.
Paul's,
London,
During Air
Attack
CD319

### 1066

| | |
|---|---|
| Antigua | 157-160 |
| Ascension | 96-99 |
| Bahamas | 224-227 |
| Barbados | 281-284 |
| Basutoland | 105-108 |
| Bechuanaland Protectorate | 206-209 |
| Bermuda | 201-204 |
| British Antarctic Territory | 16-19 |
| British Honduras | 191-194 |
| Brunei | 120-123 |
| Cayman Islands | 176-179 |
| Dominica | 189-192 |
| Falkland Islands | 158-161 |
| Fiji | 215-218 |
| Gibraltar | 171-174 |
| Gilbert & Ellice Islands | 106-109 |
| Grenada | 209-212 |
| Hong Kong | 225-228 |
| Mauritius | 295-298 |
| Montserrat | 178-181 |
| New Hebrides, British | 112-115 |
| New Hebrides, French | 128-131 |
| Pitcairn Islands | 56-59 |
| St. Helena | 184-187 |
| St. Kitts-Nevis | 167-170 |
| St. Lucia | 201-204 |
| St. Vincent | 241-244 |
| Seychelles | 222-225 |
| Solomon Islands | 145-148 |
| South Arabia | 19-22 |
| Swaziland | 119-122 |
| Tristan da Cunha | 89-92 |
| Turks & Caicos Islands | 146-149 |
| Virgin Islands | 163-166 |

*136 stamps*

## Royal Visit, 1966

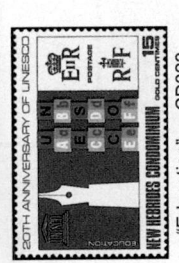

Royal Visit
to the
Caribbean
1966
ANTIGUA
6c

Queen
Elizabeth
II and
Prince
Philip
CD320

Caribbean visit, Feb. 4 - Mar. 6, 1966.

### 1966

| | |
|---|---|
| Antigua | 161-162 |
| Bahamas | 228-229 |
| Barbados | 285-286 |
| British Guiana | 299-300 |
| Cayman Islands | 180-181 |
| Dominica | 193-194 |
| Grenada | 213-214 |
| Montserrat | 182-183 |
| St. Kitts-Nevis | 171-172 |
| St. Lucia | 205-206 |
| St. Vincent | 245-246 |
| Turks & Caicos Islands | 150-151 |
| Virgin Islands | 167-168 |

*26 stamps*

## World Cup Soccer

NEW HEBRIDES
CONDOMINIUM
20

Soccer
Player
and Jules
Rimet
Cup
CD321

World Cup Soccer Championship, Wembley, England, July 11-30.

### 1966

| | |
|---|---|
| Antigua | 163-164 |
| Ascension | 100-101 |
| Bahamas | 245-246 |
| Bermuda | 205-206 |
| Brunei | 124-125 |
| Cayman Islands | 182-183 |
| Dominica | 195-196 |
| Fiji | 219-220 |
| Gibraltar | 175-176 |
| Gilbert & Ellice Islands | 125-126 |
| Grenada | 230-231 |
| New Hebrides, British | 116-117 |
| New Hebrides, French | 132-133 |
| Pitcairn Islands | 60-61 |
| St. Helena | 188-189 |
| St. Kitts-Nevis | 173 174 |
| St. Lucia | 207-208 |
| Seychelles | 226-227 |
| Solomon Islands | 167-168 |
| South Arabia | 23-24 |
| Tristan da Cunha | 93-94 |

*42 stamps*

## WHO Headquarters

New Hebrides
CONDOMINIUM
New Headquarters Building
25
WHO

World Health Organization
Headquarters, Geneva — CD322

### 1966

| | |
|---|---|
| Antigua | 165-166 |
| Ascension | 102-103 |
| Bahamas | 247-248 |
| Brunei | 126-127 |
| Dominica | 184-185 |
| Fiji | 197-198 |
| Gibraltar | 180-181 |
| Gilbert & Ellice Islands | 224-225 |
| Grenada | 232-233 |
| Hong Kong | 127-128 |
| Montserrat | 229-233 |
| New Hebrides, British | 118-119 |
| New Hebrides, French | 134-135 |
| Pitcairn Islands | 62-63 |
| St. Helena | 190-191 |
| St. Kitts-Nevis | 177-178 |
| St. Lucia | 209-210 |

## UNESCO Anniversary

EnR
POSTAGE
RF
15
UN
ESCO
"Education" — CD323

"Science" (Wheat ears & flask enclosing globe), "Culture" (lyre & columns). 20th anniversary of the UNESCO.

### 1966-67

| | |
|---|---|
| Antigua | 183-185 |
| Ascension | 108-110 |
| Bahamas | 249-251 |
| Barbados | 287-289 |
| Bermuda | 207-209 |
| Brunei | 128-130 |
| Cayman Islands | 186-188 |
| Dominica | 199-201 |
| Gibraltar | 183-185 |
| Gilbert & Ellice Islands | 129-131 |
| Grenada | 234-236 |
| Hong Kong | 231-233 |
| Mauritius | 299-301 |
| Montserrat | 186-188 |
| New Hebrides, British | 120-122 |
| New Hebrides, French | 136-138 |
| Pitcairn Islands | 64-66 |
| St. Helena | 192-194 |
| St. Kitts-Nevis | 179-181 |
| St. Lucia | 211-213 |
| St. Vincent | 249-251 |
| Seychelles | 230-232 |
| Solomon Islands | 171-173 |
| South Arabia | 27-29 |
| Swaziland | 123-125 |
| Tristan da Cunha | 101-103 |
| Turks & Caicos Islands | 155-157 |
| Virgin Islands | 176-178 |

*84 stamps*

## Silver Wedding, 1972

EnR
35
CENTIMES
RF
NEW HEBRIDES CONDOMINIUM

Queen Elizabeth II and Prince
Philip — CD324

Designs: borders differ for each country.

### 1972

| | |
|---|---|
| Anguilla | 161-162 |
| Antigua | 295-296 |
| Ascension | 164-165 |
| Bahamas | 344-345 |
| Bermuda | 296-297 |
| British Antarctic Territory | 43-44 |
| British Honduras | 306-307 |
| British Indian Ocean Territory | 48-49 |
| Brunei | 186-187 |
| Cayman Islands | 304-305 |
| Dominica | 352-353 |
| Falkland Islands | 223-224 |
| Fiji | 328-329 |
| Gibraltar | 292-293 |
| Gilbert & Ellice Islands | 206-207 |
| Grenada | 466-467 |
| Hong Kong | 271-272 |
| Montserrat | 286-287 |
| New Hebrides, British | 169-170 |
| Pitcairn Islands | 127-128 |
| St. Helena | 271-272 |
| St. Kitts-Nevis | 257-258 |
| St. Lucia | 328-329 |
| St. Vincent | 344-345 |
| Seychelles | 309-310 |
| Solomon Islands | 248-249 |
| South Georgia | 35-36 |

## Princess Anne's Wedding

EnR
95¢
THE WEDDING OF H.R.H.
THE PRINCESS ANNE
SEYCHELLES

Princess Anne
and Mark
Phillips — CD325

Wedding of Princess Anne and Mark Phillips, Nov. 14, 1973.

### 1973

| | |
|---|---|
| Anguilla | 179-180 |
| Ascension | 177-178 |
| Belize | 325-326 |
| Bermuda | 302-303 |
| British Antarctic Territory | 60-61 |
| Cayman Islands | 320-321 |
| Falkland Islands | 225-226 |
| Gibraltar | 305-306 |
| Gilbert & Ellice Islands | 216-217 |
| Hong Kong | 289-290 |
| Montserrat | 300-301 |
| Pitcairn Island | 135-136 |
| St. Helena | 277-278 |
| St. Kitts-Nevis | 274-275 |
| St. Lucia | 349-350 |
| St. Vincent Grenadines | 1-2 |
| Seychelles | 311-312 |
| Solomon Islands | 259-260 |
| South Georgia | 37-38 |
| Tristan da Cunha | 189-190 |
| Turks & Caicos Islands | 286-287 |
| Virgin Islands | 260-261 |

*44 stamps*

## Elizabeth II Coronation Anniv.

BARBADOS
50
Griffin of Edward III
CD326

BARBADOS
50
Coronation 1953
CD327

BARBADOS
50
Pelican
CD328

Designs: Royal and local beasts in heraldic form and simulated stonework. Portrait of Elizabeth II by Peter Grugeon. 25th anniversary of coronation of Queen Elizabeth II.

### 1978

| | |
|---|---|
| Ascension | 229 |
| Barbados | 474 |
| Belize | 397 |
| British Antarctic Territory | 71 |
| Cayman Islands | 404 |
| Christmas Island | 87 |
| Falkland Islands | 275 |
| Fiji | 384 |
| Gambia | 380 |
| Gibraltar | 312 |
| Mauritius | 464 |
| New Hebrides, British | 258 |
| St. Helena | 317 |
| St. Kitts-Nevis | 354 |
| Samoa | 472 |

Top-right corner listing:

| | |
|---|---|
| Tristan da Cunha | 178-179 |
| Turks & Caicos Islands | 257-258 |
| Virgin Islands | 241-242 |

*60 stamps*

St. Vincent listing (upper mid area):

| | |
|---|---|
| St. Vincent | 247-248 |
| Seychelles | 228-229 |
| Solomon Islands | 169-170 |
| South Arabia | 25-26 |
| Tristan da Cunha | 99-100 |

*46 stamps*

# COMMON DESIGN TYPES

## 1980

CD330

### Queen Mother Elizabeth's 80th Birthday

Designs: Photographs of Queen Mother Elizabeth. Falkland Islands issued in sheets of 50; others in sheets of 9.

20 sheets

| | |
|---|---|
| Solomon Islands | 368 |
| South Georgia | 51 |
| Swaziland | 302 |
| Tristan da Cunha | 238 |
| Virgin Islands | 337 |

12 stamps

| | |
|---|---|
| Ascension | 261 |
| Bermuda | 401 |
| Cayman Islands | 443 |
| Falkland Islands | 305 |
| Gambia | 412 |
| Gibraltar | 393 |
| Hong Kong | 364 |
| Pitcairn Islands | 193 |
| St. Helena | 341 |
| Samoa | 532 |
| Solomon Islands | 426 |
| Tristan da Cunha | 277 |

## Royal Wedding, 1981

CD331

### Prince Charles and Lady Diana — CD331

Wedding of Charles, Prince of Wales, and Lady Diana Spencer, St. Paul's Cathedral, London, July 29, 1981.

## 1981

| | |
|---|---|
| Antigua | 623-625 |
| Ascension | 294-296 |
| Barbados | 547-549 |
| Barbuda | 497-499 |
| Bermuda | 412-414 |
| Brunei | 268-270 |
| Cayman Islands | 471-473 |
| Dominica | 701-703 |
| Falkland Islands | 324-326 |
| Falkland Islands Dep. | 1L59-1L61 |
| Fiji | 442-444 |
| Gambia | 426-428 |
| Ghana | 759-761 |
| Grenada | 1051-1053 |
| Grenada Grenadines | 440-443 |
| Hong Kong | 373-375 |
| Jamaica | 500-503 |
| Lesotho | 335-337 |
| Maldive Islands | 906-908 |
| Mauritius | 520-522 |
| Norfolk Island | 280-282 |
| Pitcairn Islands | 206-208 |
| St. Helena | 353-355 |
| St. Lucia | 558-560 |
| Samoa | 509-517 |
| Sierra Leone | 450-452 |
| Solomon Islands | 382-384 |
| Swaziland | 294-296 |
| Turks & Caicos Islands | 486-488 |
| Uganda | 8-10 |
| Caicos Island | 314-316 |
| Vanuatu | 308-310 |
| Virgin Islands | 406-408 |

## Princess Diana

CD332

CD333

Designs: Photographs and portrait of Princess Diana, wedding or honeymoon photographs, royal residences, arms of issuing country. Portrait photograph by Clive Friend. Souvenir sheet margins show family tree, various people related to the princess, 21st birthday of Princess Diana of Wales, July 1.

## 1982

| | |
|---|---|
| Antigua | 663-666 |
| Ascension | 313-316 |
| Bahamas | 510-513 |
| Barbados | 585-588 |
| Barbuda | 544-546 |
| British Antarctic Territory | 92-95 |
| Cayman Islands | 486-489 |
| Dominica | 773-776 |
| Falkland Islands | 348-351 |
| Falkland Islands Dep. | 1L72-1L75 |
| Fiji | 470-473 |
| Gambia | 447-450 |
| Grenada | 1101A-1105 |
| Grenada Grenadines | 485-491 |
| Lesotho | 372-375 |
| Maldive Islands | 952-955 |
| Mauritius | 548-551 |
| Pitcairn Islands | 213-216 |
| St. Helena | 372-375 |
| St. Lucia | 591-594 |
| Sierra Leone | 531-534 |
| Solomon Islands | 471-474 |
| Swaziland | 406-409 |
| Tristan da Cunha | 310-313 |
| Turks and Caicos Islands | 530A-534 |
| Virgin Islands | 430-433 |

## 250th anniv. of first edition of Lloyd's List (shipping news publication) & of Lloyd's marine insurance.

CD335

Designs: First page of early edition of the list; historical ships, modern transportation or harbor scenes.

## 1984

| | |
|---|---|
| Ascension | 351-354 |
| Bahamas | 555-558 |
| Barbados | 627-630 |
| Cayes of Belize | 10-13 |
| Cayman Islands | 522-525 |
| Falkland Islands | 404-407 |
| Fiji | 509-512 |
| Gambia | 519-522 |
| Mauritius | 587-590 |
| Nauru | 280-283 |
| St. Helena | 412-415 |
| Samoa | 624-627 |
| Seychelles | 538-541 |
| Solomon Islands | 521-524 |
| Vanuatu | 368-371 |
| Virgin Islands | 466-469 |

## Queen Mother 85th Birthday

CD336

Designs: Photographs of Queen Mother Elizabeth. The high value in each set shows the same photograph taken of the Queen Mother holding the infant Prince Henry.

## 1985

| | |
|---|---|
| Ascension | 372-376 |
| Bahamas | 580-584 |
| Barbados | 660-664 |
| Bermuda | 469-473 |
| Falkland Islands | 420-424 |
| Falkland Islands Dep. | 1L92-1L96 |
| Fiji | 531-535 |
| Hong Kong | 447-450 |
| Jamaica | 599-603 |
| Dominica | 950-953 |
| Gambia | 604-608 |
| Grenada | 611-614 |
| Grenada Grenadines | 749-752 |
| Mauritius | 611-614 |
| Norfolk Island | 364-368 |
| St. Helena | 428-432 |
| Pitcairn Islands | 253-257 |
| Samoa | 649-653 |
| Seychelles | 567-571 |
| Solomon Islands | 543-547 |
| Swaziland | 476-480 |
| Tristan da Cunha | 372-376 |
| Uganda | 495-498 |

## 1986, April 21

## Queen Elizabeth II, 60th Birthday

CD337

## 1986

| | |
|---|---|
| Ascension | 389-393 |
| Bahamas | 592-596 |
| Barbados | 675-679 |
| Bermuda | 499-503 |
| Cayman Islands | 555-559 |
| Fiji | 544-548 |
| Hong Kong | 465-469 |
| Jamaica | 620-624 |
| Kiribati | 470-474 |
| Mauritius | 629-633 |
| Papua New Guinea | 640-644 |
| Pitcairn Islands | 270-274 |
| St. Helena | 451-455 |
| Samoa | 670-674 |
| Seychelles | 592-596 |
| Solomon Islands | 562-566 |
| South Georgia | 101-105 |
| Swaziland | 490-494 |
| Tristan da Cunha | 388-392 |
| Vanuatu | 414-418 |
| Zambia | 343-347 |
| Zil Elwannyen Sesel | 114-118 |

## Royal Wedding

CD338

### 1986, July 23

Marriage of Prince Andrew and Sarah Ferguson — CD338

| | |
|---|---|
| Ascension | 399-400 |
| Bahamas | 602-603 |
| Barbados | 687-688 |
| Cayman Islands | 560-561 |
| Jamaica | 501-504 |
| Pitcairn Islands | 275-276 |
| St. Helena | 460-461 |
| St. Kitts | 181-182 |

## Royal Wedding, 1986

CD340

Designs: Photographs of Prince Andrew and Sarah Ferguson during courtship, engagement and marriage.

## 1986

| | |
|---|---|
| Antigua | 939-942 |
| Barbuda | 809-812 |
| Dominica | 970-973 |
| Gambia | 635-638 |
| Grenada | 1385-1388 |
| Grenada Grenadines | 758-761 |
| Lesotho | 545-548 |
| Maldive Islands | 1181-1184 |
| Sierra Leone | 769-772 |
| Uganda | 510-513 |

## Queen Elizabeth II & Prince Philip, 1947 Wedding Portrait — CD339

Designs: Photographs tracing the life of Queen Elizabeth II.

## Queen Elizabeth II, 60th Birthday

CD339

| | |
|---|---|
| Seychelles | 602-603 |
| Solomon Islands | 567-568 |
| Tristan da Cunha | 397-398 |
| Zambia | 348-349 |
| Zil Elwannyen Sesel | 119-120 |

## Lloyds of London, 300th Anniv.

CD341

Designs: 17th century aspects of Lloyds, representations of each country's individual connections with Lloyds and publicized disasters insured by the organization.

## 1986

| | |
|---|---|
| Ascension | 454-457 |
| Bahamas | 655-658 |
| Barbados | 731-734 |
| Bermuda | 541-544 |
| Falkland Islands | 481-484 |
| Liberia | 1101-1104 |
| Malawi | 534-537 |
| Nevis | 571-574 |
| St. Helena | 501-504 |
| St. Lucia | 923-926 |
| Seychelles | 649-652 |
| Solomon Islands | 627-630 |

# COMMON DESIGN TYPES

## Moon Landing, 20th Anniv.

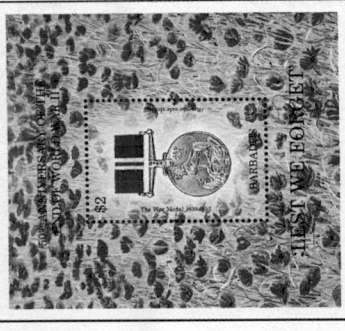

CD342

Designs: Equipment, crew photographs, spacecraft, official emblems and report profiles created for the Apollo Missions. Two stamps in each set are square in format rather than like the stamp shown; see individual country listings for more information.

**1989**
| | |
|---|---|
| Ascension Is. | 468-472 |
| Bahamas | 674-678 |
| Belize | 916-920 |
| Kiribati | 517-521 |
| Liberia | 1125-1129 |
| Nevis | 586-590 |
| St. Kitts | 248-252 |
| Samoa | 760-764 |
| Seychelles | 676-680 |
| Solomon Islands | 643-647 |
| Vanuatu | 507-511 |
| Zil Elwannyen Sesel | 154-158 |

## Queen Mother, 90th Birthday

CD343, CD344

Designs: Portraits of Queen Elizabeth, the Queen Mother. See individual country listings for more information.

**1990**
| | |
|---|---|
| Ascension Is. | 491-492 |
| Bahamas | 698-699 |
| Barbados | 782-783 |
| British Antarctic Territory | 170-171 |
| British Indian Ocean Territory | 106-107 |
| Cayman Islands | 622-623 |
| Falkland Islands | 527-528 |
| Kenya | 555-556 |
| Kiribati | 1145-1146 |
| Liberia | 336-337 |
| Pitcairn Islands | 532-533 |
| St. Helena | 969-970 |
| St. Lucia | 710-711 |
| Seychelles | 671-672 |
| Solomon Islands | 143-144 |
| South Georgia | 565-566 |
| Swaziland | 480-481 |
| Tristan da Cunha | 171-172 |

## Queen Elizabeth II, 65th Birthday, and Prince Philip, 70th Birthday

CD345

---

15c BAHAMAS — CD346

Designs: Portraits of Queen Elizabeth II and Prince Philip differ for each country. Printed in sheets of 10 + 5 labels (3 different) between. Stamps alternate, producing 5 different triptychs.

**1991**
| | |
|---|---|
| Ascension Is. | 505-506 |
| Bahamas | 730-731 |
| Belize | 969-970 |
| Bermuda | 617-618 |
| Kiribati | 571-572 |
| Mauritius | 733-734 |
| Pitcairn Islands | 348-349 |
| St. Helena | 554-555 |
| St. Kitts | 318-319 |
| Samoa | 790-791 |
| Seychelles | 723-724 |
| Solomon Islands | 688-689 |
| South Georgia | 149-150 |
| Swaziland | 586-587 |
| Vanuatu | 540-541 |
| Zil Elwannyen Sesel | 177-178 |

## Royal Family Birthday, Anniversary

Commonwealth of DOMINICA 10c — CD347

Queen Elizabeth II, 65th birthday, Charles and Diana, 10th wedding anniversary. Various photographs of Queen Elizabeth II, Prince Philip, Prince Charles, Princess Diana and their sons William and Henry.

**1991**
| | |
|---|---|
| Antigua | 1446-1455 |
| Barbuda | 1229-1238 |
| Dominica | 1326-1337 |
| Gambia | 1080-1089 |
| Grenada | 2006-2015 |
| Grenada Grenadines | 1331-1340 |
| Guyana | 2440-2451 |
| Lesotho | 871-875 |
| Maldive Islands | 1533-1542 |
| Nevis | 666-675 |
| St. Vincent | 1485-1494 |
| St. Vincent Grenadines | 769-778 |
| Sierra Leone | 1387-1396 |
| Turks & Caicos Islands | 913-922 |
| Uganda | 918-927 |

## Queen Elizabeth II's Accession to the Throne, 40th Anniv.

ANTIGUA & BARBUDA 10c — CD348

FALKLAND 7p — CD349

Various photographs of Queen Elizabeth II with local scenes.

**1992 - CD348**
| | |
|---|---|
| Antigua | 1513-1518 |
| Barbuda | 1306-1309 |
| Dominica | 1414-1419 |
| Gambia | 1172-1177 |
| Grenada | 2047-2052 |
| Grenada Grenadines | 1368-1373 |
| Lesotho | 881-885 |
| Maldive Islands | 1637-1642 |
| Nevis | 702-707 |
| St. Vincent | 1582-1587 |
| St. Vincent Grenadines | 829-834 |
| Sierra Leone | 1482-1487 |
| Turks and Caicos Islands | 978-987 |
| Uganda | 990-995 |
| Virgin Islands | 742-746 |

**1992 - CD349**
| | |
|---|---|
| Ascension Islands | 531-535 |
| Bahamas | 744-748 |
| Bermuda | 623-627 |
| British Indian Ocean Territory | 119-123 |
| Cayman Islands | 648-652 |
| Falkland Islands | 549-553 |
| Gibraltar | 605-609 |
| Hong Kong | 619-623 |
| Kenya | 563-567 |
| Kiribati | 582-586 |
| Pitcairn Islands | 362-366 |
| St. Helena | 570-574 |
| St. Kitts | 332-336 |
| Samoa | 805-809 |
| Seychelles | 734-738 |
| Solomon Islands | 708-712 |
| South Georgia | 157-161 |
| Tristan da Cunha | 508-512 |
| Vanuatu | 555-559 |
| Zambia | 561-565 |
| Zil Elwannyen Sesel | 183-187 |

## Royal Air Force, 75th Anniversary

15p FALKLAND ISLANDS — CD350

**1993**
| | |
|---|---|
| Ascension | 557-561 |
| Bahamas | 771-775 |
| Barbados | 842-846 |
| Belize | 1003-1008 |
| Bermuda | 648-651 |
| British Indian Ocean Territory | 136-140 |
| Falkland Is. | 573-577 |
| Fiji | 687-691 |
| Montserrat | 830-834 |
| St. Kitts | 351-355 |

## Royal Air Force, 80th Anniv.

35p ASCENSION ISLAND

Design CD350 Re-inscribed

**1998**
| | |
|---|---|
| Ascension | 697-701 |
| Bahamas | 907-911 |
| British Indian Ocean Terr. | 198-202 |
| Cayman Islands | 754-758 |
| Fiji | 814-818 |
| Gibraltar | 755-759 |
| Samoa | 957-961 |
| Turks & Caicos Islands | 1258-1265 |
| Tuvalu | 763-767 |
| Virgin Islands | 879-883 |

## End of World War II, 50th Anniv.

55c BARBADOS — CD351

---

$2 BARBADOS — LEST WE FORGET — CD352

**1995**
| | |
|---|---|
| Ascension | 613-617 |
| Bahamas | 824-828 |
| Barbados | 891-895 |
| Belize | 1047-1050 |
| British Indian Ocean Territory | 163-167 |
| Cayman Islands | 704-708 |
| Falkland Islands | 634-638 |
| Fiji | 720-724 |
| Kiribati | 662-668 |
| Liberia | 1175-1179 |
| Mauritius | 803-805 |
| St. Helena | 646-654 |
| St. Kitts | 389-393 |
| St. Lucia | 1018-1022 |
| Samoa | 890-894 |
| Solomon Islands | 799-803 |
| South Georgia & S. Sandwich Is. | 198-200 |
| Tristan da Cunha | 562-566 |

## UN, 50th Anniv.

15c BRITISH VIRGIN ISLANDS — CD353

**1995**
| | |
|---|---|
| Bahamas | 839-842 |
| Barbados | 901-904 |
| Belize | 1055-1058 |
| Jamaica | 847-851 |
| Liberia | 1187-1190 |
| Mauritius | 813-816 |
| Pitcairn Islands | 436-439 |
| St. Kitts | 390-401 |
| St. Lucia | 1023-1026 |
| Samoa | 900-903 |
| Tristan da Cunha | 568-571 |
| Virgin Islands | 807-810 |

## Queen Elizabeth, 70th Birthday

10c British Virgin Islands — CD354

**1996**
| | |
|---|---|
| Ascension | 632-635 |
| British Antarctic Territory | 240-243 |
| British Indian Ocean Territory | 176-180 |
| Falkland Islands | 653-657 |
| Pitcairn Islands | 446-449 |
| St. Helena | 672-676 |
| Samoa | 912-916 |
| Tokelau | 223-227 |
| Tristan da Cunha | 576-579 |
| Virgin Islands | 824-828 |

---

**South Georgia** ...131-134
**Trinidad & Tobago** ...484-487
**Tristan da Cunha** ...439-442
**Vanuatu** ...485-488
**Zil Elwannyen Sesel** ...146-149

## Diana, Princess of Wales (1961-97)

BAHAMAS 15c  CD355

| | |
|---|---|
| Ascension | 696 |
| Bahamas | 901A-902 |
| Barbados | 950 |
| Belize | 1091 |
| Bermuda | 753 |
| Botswana | 659-663 |
| British Antarctic Territory | 258 |
| British Indian Ocean Terr. | 197 |
| Cayman Islands | 752A-753 |
| Falkland Islands | 694 |
| Fiji | 819-820 |
| Gibraltar | 754 |
| Kiribati | 719A-720 |
| Namibia | 909 |
| Niue | 706 |
| Norfolk Island | 644-645 |
| Papua New Guinea | 937 |
| Pitcairn Islands | 487 |
| St. Kitts | 711 |
| St. Helena | 437A-438 |
| Samoa | 955A-956 |
| Seychelles | 802 |
| Solomon Islands | 866-867 |
| South Georgia & S. Sandwich Islands | |
| Tokelau | 220 |
| Tonga | 252B-253 |
| Niuafo'ou | 980 |
| Tristan da Cunha | 201 |
| Tuvalu | 618 |
| Vanuatu | 762 |
| Virgin Islands | 719 |
| | 878 |

## Wedding of Prince Edward and Sophie Rhys-Jones

ASCENSION ISLAND 50p
The Wedding of HRH Prince Edward
& Miss Sophie Rhys-Jones
Saturday 19 June 1997
CD356

### 1999

1st Manned Moon Landing, 30th Anniv.

ASCENSION ISLAND 15p
COMMAND AND SERVICE MODULES
CD357

| | |
|---|---|
| Ascension | 729-730 |
| Cayman Islands | 775-776 |
| Falkland Islands | 729-730 |
| Pitcairn Islands | 505-506 |
| St. Helena | 733-734 |
| Samoa | 971-972 |
| Tristan da Cunha | 636-637 |
| Virgin Islands | 908-909 |

### 1999

| | |
|---|---|
| Ascension | 731-735 |
| Bahamas | 942-946 |
| Barbados | 961-971 |
| Bermuda | 778 |
| Cayman Islands | 777-781 |

---

| | |
|---|---|
| Fiji | 853-857 |
| Jamaica | 889-893 |
| Kiribati | 746-750 |
| Nauru | 465-469 |
| St. Kitts | 460-464 |
| Samoa | 973-977 |
| Solomon Islands | 875-879 |
| Tuvalu | 800-804 |
| Virgin Islands | 910-914 |

## Queen Mother's Century

ASCENSION ISLAND 5p
1894 King George VI, 1854 Queen Elizabeth
and Sir Winston Churchill, September 1940
THE QUEEN MOTHER'S CENTURY
CD358

### 1999

| | |
|---|---|
| Ascension | 736-740 |
| Bahamas | 951-955 |
| Cayman Islands | 782-786 |
| Falkland Islands | 734-738 |
| Fiji | 858-862 |
| Norfolk Island | 688-692 |
| St. Helena | 740-744 |
| Samoa | 978-982 |
| Solomon Islands | 880-884 |
| South Georgia & South Sandwich Islands | 231-235 |
| Tristan da Cunha | 638-642 |
| Tuvalu | 805-809 |

## Prince William, 18th Birthday

Ascension Island 15p
CD359

### 2000

| | |
|---|---|
| Ascension | 755-759 |
| Cayman Islands | 797-801 |
| Falkland Islands | 762-766 |
| Fiji | 889-893 |
| South Georgia and South Sandwich Islands | 257-261 |
| Tristan da Cunha | 664-668 |
| Virgin Islands | 925-929 |

## Reign of Queen Elizabeth II, 50th Anniv.

CD360

### 2002

| | |
|---|---|
| Ascension | 790-794 |
| Bahamas | 1033-1037 |
| Barbados | 1019-1023 |
| Belize | 1152-1156 |
| Bermuda | 822-826 |
| British Antarctic Territory | 307-311 |
| British Indian Ocean Territory | 239- |
| | 243 |
| Cayman Islands | 844-848 |
| Falkland Islands | 804-808 |
| Gibraltar | 896-900 |
| Jamaica | 952-956 |
| Nauru | 491-495 |
| Norfolk Island | 758-762 |
| Papua New Guinea | 1019-1023 |
| Pitcairn Islands | 552 |
| St. Helena | 788-792 |
| St. Lucia | 1146-1150 |
| Solomon Islands | 931-935 |
| South Georgia & So. Sandwich Is. | |
| Swaziland | 274-278 |
| Tokelau | 706-710 |
| Tonga | 302-306 |
| | 1059 |

---

### 2003

| | |
|---|---|
| Ascension | 822 |
| Bermuda | 865 |
| British Antarctic Territory | 322 |
| British Indian Ocean Territory | 261 |
| Cayman Islands | 878 |
| Falkland Islands | 828 |
| St. Helena | 820 |
| South Georgia & South Sandwich Islands | 294 |
| Tristan da Cunha | 731 |
| Virgin Islands | 1003 |

## Coronation of Queen Elizabeth II, 50th Anniv.

ASCENSION ISLAND 40p
CD363

### 2003

| | |
|---|---|
| Ascension | 823-825 |
| Bahamas | 1073-1075 |
| Bermuda | 866-868 |
| British Indian Ocean Territory | 262- |
| | 264 |
| Cayman Islands | 879-881 |
| Jamaica | 970-972 |
| Kiribati | 825-827 |
| Pitcairn Islands | 577-581 |
| St. Helena | 821-823 |
| St. Lucia | 1171-1173 |
| Tokelau | 320-322 |
| Tristan da Cunha | 732-734 |
| Virgin Islands | 1004-1006 |

## Head of Queen Elizabeth II

Ascension Island £3
CD362

## Queen Mother Elizabeth (1900-2002)

Ascension Island 35p
CD361

| | |
|---|---|
| Niuafo'ou | 239 |
| Tristan da Cunha | 706-710 |
| Virgin Islands | 967-971 |

### 2002

| | |
|---|---|
| Ascension | 799-801 |
| Bahamas | 1044-1046 |
| Cayman Islands | 857-861 |
| Falkland Islands | 812-816 |
| Nauru | 499-501 |
| Pitcairn Islands | 561-565 |
| British Indian Ocean Territory | 245- |
| | 247 |
| Fiji | 808-812 |
| St. Helena | 808-812 |
| St. Lucia | 1155-1159 |
| Seychelles | 830 |
| Solomon Islands | 945-947 |
| South Georgia & So. Sandwich Isls. | 979-983 |
| Tokelau | 281-285 |
| Tristan da Cunha | 712-314 |
| Virgin Islands | 715-717 |

## Prince William, 21st Birthday

Ascension Island 75p
CD364

### 2003

| | |
|---|---|
| Ascension | 826 |
| British Indian Ocean Territory | 265 |
| Cayman Islands | 882-884 |
| Falkland Islands | 829 |
| South Georgia & South Sandwich Islands | 295 |
| Tokelau | 323 |
| Tristan da Cunha | 735 |
| Virgin Islands | 1007-1009 |

# British Commonwealth of Nations

## Dominions, Colonies, Territories, Offices and Independent Members

Comprising stamps of the British Commonwealth and associated nations.

A strict observance of technicalities would bar some or all of the stamps listed under Burma, Ireland, Kuwait, Nepal, New Republic, Orange Free State, Samoa, South Africa, South-West Africa, Stellaland, Sudan, Swaziland, the two Transvaal Republics and others but these are included for the convenience of collectors.

## 1. Great Britain

Great Britain: Including England, Scotland, Wales and Northern Ireland.

## 2. The Dominions, Present and Past

### AUSTRALIA

The Commonwealth of Australia was proclaimed on January 1, 1901. It consists of six former colonies as follows:

| | |
|---|---|
| New South Wales | Victoria |
| Queensland | Tasmania |
| South Australia | Western Australia |

The following islands and territories are, or have been, administered by Australia: Australian Antarctic Territory, Christmas Island, Cocos (Keeling) Islands, Nauru, New Guinea, Norfolk Island, Papua.

### CANADA

The Dominion of Canada was created by the British North America Act in 1867. The following provinces were former separate colonies and issued postage stamps:

| | |
|---|---|
| British Columbia and | Newfoundland |
| Vancouver Island | Nova Scotia |
| New Brunswick | Prince Edward Island |

### FIJI

The colony of Fiji became an independent nation with dominion status on Oct. 10, 1970.

### GHANA

This state came into existence Mar. 6, 1957, with dominion status. It consists of the former colony of the Gold Coast and the Trusteeship Territory of Togoland. Ghana became a republic July 1, 1960.

### INDIA

The Republic of India was inaugurated on January 26, 1950. It succeeded the Dominion of India which was proclaimed August 15, 1947, when the former Empire of India was divided into Pakistan and the Union of India. The Republic is composed of about 40 predominantly Hindu states of three classes: governor's provinces, chief commissioner's provinces and princely states. India also has various territories, such as the Andaman and Nicobar Islands.

The old Empire of India was a federation of British India and the native states. The more important princely states were autonomous. Of the more than 700 Indian states, these 43 are familiar names to philatelists because of their postage stamps.

#### CONVENTION STATES

| | |
|---|---|
| Chamba | Jhind |
| Faridkot | Nabha |
| Gwalior | Patiala |

#### NATIVE FEUDATORY STATES

| | |
|---|---|
| Alwar | Jammu |
| Bahawalpur | Jammu and Kashmir |
| Bamra | Jasdan |
| Barwani | Jhalawar |
| Bhopal | Jhind (1875-76) |
| Bhor | Kashmir |
| Bijawar | Kishangarh |
| Bundi | Las Bela |
| Bussahir | Morvi |
| Charkhari | Nandgaon |
| Cochin | Nowanuggur |
| Dhar | Orchha |
| Duttia | Poonch |
| Faridkot (1879-85) | Rajpeepla |
| Hyderabad | Sirmur |
| Idar | Soruth |
| Indore | Travancore |
| Jaipur | Wadhwan |

### NEW ZEALAND

Became a dominion on September 26, 1907. The following islands and territories are, or have been, administered by New Zealand:

| | |
|---|---|
| Aitutaki | Ross Dependency |
| Cook Islands (Rarotonga) | Samoa (Western Samoa) |
| Niue | Tokelau Islands |
| Penrhyn | |

### PAKISTAN

The Republic of Pakistan was proclaimed March 23, 1956. It succeeded the Dominion which was proclaimed August 15, 1947. It is made up of all or part of several Moslem provinces and various districts of the former Empire of India, including Bahawalpur and Las Bela. Pakistan withdrew from the Commonwealth in 1972.

### SOUTH AFRICA

Under the terms of the South African Act (1909) the self governing colonies of Cape of Good Hope, Natal, Orange River Colony and Transvaal united on May 31, 1910, to form the Union of South Africa. It became an independent republic May 3, 1961.

Under the terms of the Treaty of Versailles, South-West Africa, formerly German South-West Africa, was mandated to the Union of South Africa.

### SRI LANKA (CEYLON)

The Dominion of Ceylon was proclaimed February 4, 1948. The island had been a Crown Colony from 1802 until then. On May 22, 1972, Ceylon became the Republic of Sri Lanka.

## 3. Colonies, Past and Present; Controlled Territory and Independent Members of the Commonwealth

| | |
|---|---|
| Aden | Bechuanaland |
| Aitutaki | Bechuanaland Prot. |
| Antigua | Belize |
| Ascension | Bermuda |
| Bahamas | Botswana |
| Bahrain | British Antarctic Territory |
| Bangladesh | British Central Africa |
| Barbados | British Columbia and |
| Barbuda | Vancouver Island |
| Basutoland | British East Africa |
| Batum | British Guiana |

# COLLECT THE SCOTT WAY WITH

## Specialty Series Pages

### SCOTT ALBUMS FEATURE:

- High quality chemically neutral paper printed on one side. •
- All spaces identified by Scott numbers with either illustrations or descriptions. •
- All pages have matching borders. •
- Pages contain general postage issues, as well as complete back-of-the book materials. •
- Albums supplemented annually. •

For a complete list of Scott Specialty Series Pages available contact your local dealer, or call Scott Publishing at 1-800-5SCOTT5 or write to P.O. Box 828, Sidney, OH 45365.

| | | | |
|---|---|---|---|
| British Honduras | Kenya | New Hebrides | Southern Nigeria |
| British Indian Ocean Territory | Kenya, Uganda & Tanzania | New Republic | Southern Rhodesia |
| British New Guinea | Kuwait | New South Wales | South-West Africa |
| British Solomon Islands | Labuan | Niger Coast Protectorate | Stellaland |
| British Somaliland | Lagos | Nigeria | Straits Settlements |
| Brunei | Leeward Islands | Niue | Sudan |
| Burma | Lesotho | Norfolk Island | Swaziland |
| Bushire | Madagascar | North Borneo | Tanganyika |
| Cameroons | Malawi | Northern Nigeria | Tanzania |
| Cape of Good Hope | Malaya | Northern Rhodesia | Tasmania |
| Cayman Islands | Federated Malay States | North West Pacific Islands | Tobago |
| Christmas Island | Johore | Nova Scotia | Togo |
| Cocos (Keeling) Islands | Kedah | Nyasaland Protectorate | Tokelau Islands |
| Cook Islands | Kelantan | Oman | Tonga |
| Crete, | Malacca | Orange River Colony | Transvaal |
| British Administration | Negri Sembilan | Palestine | Trinidad |
| Cyprus | Pahang | Papua New Guinea | Trinidad and Tobago |
| Dominica | Penang | Penrhyn Island | Tristan da Cunha |
| East Africa & Uganda | Perak | Pitcairn Islands | Trucial States |
| Protectorates | Perlis | Prince Edward Island | Turks and Caicos |
| Egypt | Selangor | Queensland | Turks Islands |
| Falkland Islands | Singapore | Rhodesia | Tuvalu |
| Fiji | Sungei Ujong | Rhodesia & Nyasaland | Uganda |
| Gambia | Trengganu | Ross Dependency | United Arab Emirates |
| German East Africa | Malaysia | Sabah | Victoria |
| Gibraltar | Maldive Islands | St. Christopher | Virgin Islands |
| Gilbert Islands | Malta | St. Helena | Western Australia |
| Gilbert & Ellice Islands | Man, Isle of | St. Kitts | Zambia |
| Gold Coast | Mauritius | St. Kitts-Nevis-Anguilla | Zanzibar |
| Grenada | Mesopotamia | St. Lucia | Zululand |
| Griqualand West | Montserrat | St. Vincent | |
| Guernsey | Muscat | Samoa | |
| Guyana | Namibia | Sarawak | |
| Heligoland | Natal | Seychelles | |
| Hong Kong | Nauru | Sierra Leone | **POST OFFICES IN** |
| Indian Native States | Nevis | Solomon Islands | **FOREIGN COUNTRIES** |
| (see India) | New Britain | Somaliland Protectorate | Africa |
| Ionian Islands | New Brunswick | South Arabia | East Africa Forces |
| Jamaica | Newfoundland | South Australia | Middle East Forces |
| Jersey | New Guinea | South Georgia | Bangkok |
| | | | China |
| | | | Morocco |
| | | | Turkish Empire |

# Colonies, Former Colonies, Offices, Territories Controlled by Parent States

## Belgium
- Belgian Congo
- Ruanda-Urundi

## Denmark
- Danish West Indies
- Faroe Islands
- Greenland
- Iceland

## Finland
- Aland Islands

## France

**COLONIES PAST AND PRESENT, CONTROLLED TERRITORIES**
- Afars & Issas, Territory of
- Alaouites
- Alexandretta
- Algeria
- Alsace & Lorraine
- Anjouan
- Annam & Tonkin
- Benin
- Cambodia (Khmer)
- Cameroun
- Castellorizo
- Chad
- Cilicia
- Cochin China
- Comoro Islands
- Dahomey
- Diego Suarez
- Djibouti (Somali Coast)
- Fezzan
- French Congo
- French Equatorial Africa
- French Guiana
- French Guinea
- French India
- French Morocco
- French Polynesia (Oceania)
- French Southern & Antarctic Territories
- French Sudan
- French West Africa
- Gabon
- Germany
- Ghadames
- Grand Comoro
- Guadeloupe
- Indo-China
- Inini
- Ivory Coast
- Laos
- Latakia
- Lebanon
- Madagascar
- Martinique
- Mauritania
- Mayotte
- Memel
- Middle Congo
- Moheli
- New Caledonia
- New Hebrides
- Niger Territory
- Nossi-Be
- Obock
- Reunion
- Rouad, Ile
- Ste.-Marie de Madagascar
- St. Pierre & Miquelon
- Senegal
- Senegambia & Niger
- Somali Coast
- Syria
- Tahiti
- Togo
- Tunisia
- Ubangi-Shari
- Upper Senegal & Niger
- Upper Volta
- Viet Nam
- Wallis & Futuna Islands

**POST OFFICES IN FOREIGN COUNTRIES**
- China
- Crete
- Egypt
- Turkish Empire
- Zanzibar

## Germany

**EARLY STATES**
- Baden
- Bavaria
- Bergedorf
- Bremen
- Brunswick
- Hamburg
- Hanover
- Lubeck
- Mecklenburg-Schwerin
- Mecklenburg-Strelitz
- Oldenburg
- Prussia
- Saxony
- Schleswig-Holstein
- Wurttemberg

**FORMER COLONIES**
- Cameroun (Kamerun)
- Caroline Islands
- German East Africa
- German New Guinea
- German South-West Africa
- Kiauchau
- Mariana Islands
- Marshall Islands
- Samoa
- Togo

## Italy

**EARLY STATES**
- Modena
- Parma
- Romagna
- Roman States
- Sardinia
- Tuscany
- Two Sicilies
- Naples
- Neapolitan Provinces
- Sicily

**FORMER COLONIES, CONTROLLED TERRITORIES, OCCUPATION AREAS**
- Aegean Islands
- Calimno (Calino)
- Caso
- Cos (Coo)
- Karki (Carchi)
- Leros (Lero)
- Lipso
- Nisiros (Nisiro)
- Patmos (Patmo)
- Piscopi
- Rodi (Rhodes)
- Scarpanto
- Simi
- Stampalia
- Castellorizo
- Corfu
- Cyrenaica
- Eritrea
- Ethiopia (Abyssinia)
- Fiume
- Ionian Islands
- Cephalonia
- Ithaca
- Paxos
- Italian East Africa
- Libya
- Oltre Giuba
- Saseno
- Somalia (Italian Somaliland)
- Tripolitania

**POST OFFICES IN FOREIGN COUNTRIES**
"ESTERO"*
- Austria
- China
- Peking
- Tientsin
- Crete
- Tripoli
- Turkish Empire
- Constantinople
- Durazzo
- Janina
- Jerusalem
- Salonika
- Scutari
- Smyrna
- Valona

*Stamps overprinted "ESTERO" were used in various parts of the world.

## Netherlands
- Aruba
- Netherlands Antilles (Curacao)
- Netherlands Indies
- Netherlands New Guinea
- Surinam (Dutch Guiana)

## Portugal

**COLONIES PAST AND PRESENT, CONTROLLED TERRITORIES**
- Angola
- Angra
- Azores
- Cape Verde
- Funchal
- Horta
- Inhambane
- Kionga
- Lourenco Marques
- Macao
- Madeira
- Mozambique
- Mozambique Co.
- Nyassa
- Ponta Delgada
- Portuguese Africa
- Portuguese Congo
- Portuguese Guinea
- Portuguese India
- Quelimane
- St. Thomas & Prince Islands
- Tete
- Timor
- Zambezia

## Russia

**ALLIED TERRITORIES AND REPUBLICS, OCCUPATION AREAS**
- Armenia
- Aunus (Olonets)
- Azerbaijan
- Batum
- Estonia
- Far Eastern Republic
- Georgia
- Karelia
- Latvia
- Lithuania
- North Ingermanland
- Ostland
- Russian Turkestan
- Siberia
- South Russia
- Tannu Tuva
- Transcaucasian Fed. Republics
- Ukraine
- Wenden (Livonia)
- Western Ukraine

## Spain

**COLONIES PAST AND PRESENT, CONTROLLED TERRITORIES**
- Aguera, La
- Cape Juby
- Cuba
- Elobey, Annobon & Corisco
- Fernando Po
- Ifni
- Mariana Islands
- Philippines
- Puerto Rico
- Rio de Oro
- Rio Muni
- Spanish Guinea
- Spanish Morocco
- Spanish Sahara
- Spanish West Africa

**POST OFFICES IN FOREIGN COUNTRIES**
- Morocco
- Tangier
- Tetuan

# Dies of British Colonial Stamps

DIE A

DIE B

**DIE A:**
1. The lines in the groundwork vary in thickness and are not uniformly straight.
2. The seventh and eighth lines from the top, in the groundwork, converge where they meet the head.
3. There is a small dash in the upper part of the second line of the band of the crown.
4. The vertical color line in front of the throat stops at the sixth line of shading on the neck.

**DIE B:**
1. The lines in the groundwork are all thin and straight.
2. All the lines of the background are parallel.
3. There is no dash in the upper part of the crown.
4. The vertical color line in front of the throat stops at the eighth line of shading on the neck.

DIE I

DIE II

**DIE I:**
1. The base of the crown is well below the level of the inner white line around the vignette.
2. The labels inscribed "POSTAGE" and "REVENUE" are cut square at the top.
3. There is a white "bud" on the outer side of the main stem of the curved ornaments in each lower corner.
4. The second (thick) line below the country name is next to the crown cut diagonally.

DIE Ia.
1 as die II.
2 and 3 as die I.

DIE Ib.
1 and 3 as die II.
2 as die I.

**DIE II:**
1. The base of the crown is aligned with the underside of the white line around the vignette.
2. The labels curve inward at the top inner corners.
3. The "bud" has been removed from the outer curve of the ornaments in each corner.
4. The second line below the country name has the ends next to the crown cut vertically.

---

Wmk. 1
Crown and C C

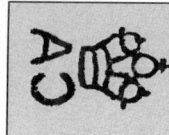

Wmk. 2
Crown and C A

Wmk. 3
Multiple Crown
and C A

Wmk. 4
Multiple Crown
and Script C A

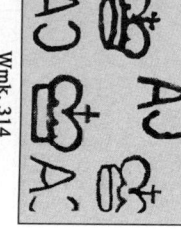

Wmk. 4a
St. Edward's Crown
and C A Multiple

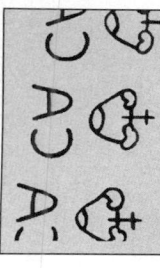

Wmk. 314

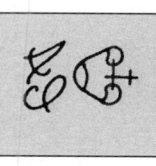

Wmk. 373

Wmk. 384

# British Colonial and Crown Agents Watermarks

Watermarks 1 to 4, 314, 373, and 384, common to many British territories, are illustrated here to avoid duplication.

The letters "CC" of Wmk. 1 identify the paper as having been made for the use of the Crown Colonies, while the letters "CA" of the others stand for "Crown Agents." Both Wmks. 1 and 2 were used on stamps printed by De La Rue & Co.

Wmk. 3 was adopted in 1904; Wmk. 4 in 1921; Wmk. 314 in 1957; Wmk. 373 in 1974; and Wmk. 384 in 1985.

In Wmk. 4a, a non-matching crown of the general St. Edwards type (bulging on both sides at top) was substituted for one of the Wmk. 4 crowns which fell off the dandy roll. The non-matching crown occurs in 1950-52 printings in a horizontal row of crowns on certain regular stamps of Barbados, Basutoland, British Guiana, Gold Coast, Grenada, Northern Rhodesia, St. Lucia, Swaziland and Trinidad and Tobago. A variation of Wmk. 4a, with the non-matching crown in a horizontal row of crown-CA-crown, occurs on regular stamps of Bahamas, St. Kitts-Nevis and Singapore.

Wmk. 314 was intentionally used sideways, starting in 1966. When a stamp was issued with Wmk. 314 both upright and sideways, the sideways varieties usually are listed also – with minor numbers. In many of the later issues, Wmk. 314 is slightly visible. Wmk. 373 is usually only faintly visible.

# PAKISTAN

'pa-ki-,stan

LOCATION — In southern, central Asia
GOVT. — Republic
AREA — 307,293 sq. mi.
POP. — 130,579,571 (1998)
CAPITAL — Islamabad

Pakistan was formed August 15, 1947, when India was divided into the Dominions of the Union of India and Pakistan, with some princely states remaining independent. Pakistan became a republic on March 23, 1956.

Pakistan had two areas made up of all or part of several predominantly Moslem provinces in the northwest and northeast corners of pre-1947 India. West Pakistan consists of the entire provinces of Baluchistan, Sind (Scinde) and "Northwest Frontier," and 15 districts of the Punjab. East Pakistan consisting of the Sylhet district in Assam and 14 districts in Bengal Province, became independent as Bangladesh in December 1971.

The state of Las Bela was incorporated into Pakistan.

12 Pies = 1 Anna
16 Annas = 1 Rupee
100 Paisa = 1 Rupee (1961)

**Catalogue values for all unused stamps in this country are for Never Hinged items.**

## Watermarks

Wmk. 274

Wmk. 351 — Crescent and Star Multiple

Stamps of India, 1937-43, Overprinted in Black:

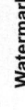

Wmk. 196

Nos. 1-12

Nos. 13-19

**1947, Oct. 1    Perf. 13½x14**

| | | | | |
|---|---|---|---|---|
| 1 | A83 | 3p slate | .20 | .20 |
| 2 | A83 | ½a rose violet | .20 | .20 |
| 3 | A83 | 9p lt green | .20 | .20 |
| 3A | A83 | 1a carmine rose | 1.60 | .20 |
| 4 | A84 | 1a3p bister (49) | 2.25 | |
| 4A | A84 | 1½a dk purple | .20 | .20 |
| 5 | A84 | 2a scarlet | .35 | .20 |
| 6 | A84 | 3a violet | .35 | .20 |
| 7 | A84 | 3½a ultra | 1.10 | .25 |
| 9 | A85 | 4a chocolate | .45 | .25 |
| 10 | A85 | 6a peacock blue | 1.00 | 1.00 |
| 11 | A85 | 8a blue violet | 1.75 | .70 |
| 12 | A85 | 12a carmine lake | 1.75 | 3.00 |
| 13 | A81 | 14a rose violet | 4.75 | .35 |
| 14 | A82 | 1r brn & slate | 3.00 | 1.25 |
| a. | | Inverted overprint | 175.00 | |
| b. | | Pair, one without ovpt. | 750.00 | |
| 15 | A82 | 2r dk brn & dk vio | 5.50 | 2.25 |
| 16 | A82 | 5r dp ultra & dk grn | 6.75 | 4.25 |
| 17 | A82 | 10r rose car & dk vio | 7.00 | 3.25 |
| 18 | A82 | 15r dk grn & dk brn | 62.50 | 82.50 |
| 19 | A82 | 25r dk vio & bl vio | 72.50 | 50.00 |
| | | Nos. 1-19 (20) | 170.60 | 155.25 |
| | | Set, hinged | 100.00 | |

Provisional use of stamps of India with handstamped or printed "PAKISTAN" was authorized in 1947-49. Nos. 4A, 14a 14b exist only as provisional issues.

Used values are for postal cancels. Telegraph cancels sell for much less.

Constituent Assembly Building, Karachi A1

Crescent and Urdu Inscription — A2

Designs: 2½a, Karachi Airport entrance. 3a, Lahore Fort gateway.

**1948, July 9    Unwmk.    Engr.**

| | | | | |
|---|---|---|---|---|
| 20 | A1 | 1½a bright ultra | .45 | .20 |
| 21 | A1 | 2½a green | .70 | .20 |
| 22 | A1 | 3a chocolate | .70 | .20 |

**Perf. 12**

| | | | | |
|---|---|---|---|---|
| 23 | A2 | 1r red | .60 | .60 |
| a. | | Perf. 14 | 4.75 | 5.00 |
| | | Nos. 20-23 (4) | 3.60 | 1.20 |

Pakistan's independence, Aug. 15, 1947. Value for No. 23a is for ctn. Postally used copies sell for much higher prices. For Nos. 23-43 and later issues, many "errors" exist from printer's waste.

Scales, Star and Crescent A3

Star and Crescent A4

Karachi Airport Building A5

Karachi Port Authority Building — A6

Khyber Pass — A7

2½a, 3½a, 4a, Ghulan Muhammed Dam, Indus River, Sind. 1r, 2r, 5r, Salimullah Hostel.

**1948-57    Perf. 12½, 14 (3a, 10a), 14x13½**
**(2½a, 3½a, 6a, 12a)    Unwmk.**

| | | | | |
|---|---|---|---|---|
| 24 | A3 | 3p org red, perf. 12½ | .20 | .20 |
| a. | | Perf. 13½ (54) | .40 | .40 |
| 25 | A3 | 6p pur, perf. 12½ | .85 | .20 |
| a. | | Perf. 13½ (54) | 1.60 | .75 |
| 26 | A3 | 9p grn, perf. 12½ | .50 | .20 |
| a. | | Perf. 13½ (54) | .65 | .50 |
| 27 | A4 | 1a dark blue | .20 | .30 |
| 28 | A4 | 1½a gray green | .20 | .20 |
| 29 | A4 | 2a orange red | .20 | .65 |
| 30 | A4 | 2½a green | 2.75 | 5.75 |
| 31 | A5 | 3a olive green | 7.25 | .80 |
| 32 | A5 | 3½a violet blue | 3.50 | 4.50 |
| 33 | A6 | 4a chocolate | .60 | .20 |
| 34 | A6 | 6a deep blue | .70 | .70 |
| 35 | A6 | 8a black | .50 | .90 |
| 36 | A5 | 10a red | 4.00 | 6.00 |
| 37 | A6 | 12a red | 6.50 | 1.10 |

**Perf. 14**

| | | | | |
|---|---|---|---|---|
| 38 | A5 | 1r ultra | 5.25 | .50 |
| a. | | Perf. 13½ (54) | 20.00 | 4.00 |
| 39 | A5 | 2r dark brown | 18.00 | .75 |
| a. | | Perf. 13½ (54) | 50.00 | 2.00 |

**Perf. 13½**

| | | | | |
|---|---|---|---|---|
| 40 | A5 | 5r car (54) | 12.00 | .75 |
| a. | | Perf. 13½x14 | 17.00 | .75 |

**Perf. 13**

| | | | | |
|---|---|---|---|---|
| 41 | A7 | 10r rose lilac (51) | 16.50 | 15.00 |
| a. | | Perf. 14 | 11.00 | 10.00 |
| b. | | Perf. 12 | 100.00 | 7.50 |
| 42 | A7 | 15r blue green (57) | 17.00 | 10.00 |
| b. | | Perf. 12 | 32.50 | 11.00 |

**Perf. 14**

| | | | | |
|---|---|---|---|---|
| 43 | A7 | 25r purple | 45.00 | 55.00 |
| a. | | Perf. 13 (54) | 62.50 | 29.00 |
| b. | | Perf. 13½ (54) | 142.50 | 103.50 |
| | | Nos. 24-43 (20) | | |
| | | Set, hinged | | |

See Nos. 259, types A9-A11. For surcharges and overprints see Nos. 124, O14-O26, O35-O37, O41-O43A, O52, O63, O68.

Imperfs of Nos. 24-43 are from proof sheets improperly removed from the printer's archives.

"Quaid-i-Azam" (Great Leader), "Mohammed Ali Jinnah" — A8

**1949, Sept. 11    Engr.    Perf. 13½x14**

| | | | | |
|---|---|---|---|---|
| 44 | A8 | 1½a brown | 1.75 | 1.00 |
| 45 | A8 | 3a dark green | 1.76 | 1.00 |
| 46 | A8 | 10a blk (English inscriptions) | 6.00 | 7.00 |
| | | Nos. 44-46 (3) | 9.50 | 9.00 |

1st anniv. of the death of Mohammed Ali Jinnah (1876-1948), Moslem lawyer, president of All-India Moslem League and first Governor General of Pakistan.

Re-engraved (Crescents Reversed)

A9

A10

A11

**1949-53    Perf. 12½, 13½x14 (3a, 10a), 14x13½ (6a, 12a)**

| | | | | |
|---|---|---|---|---|
| 47 | A10 | 1a dk blue (50) | 4.00 | .50 |
| 48 | A10 | 1½a gray green | 4.00 | .20 |
| a. | | Perf. 13 (55) | 4.00 | .20 |
| 49 | A10 | 2a orange red | 4.50 | .20 |
| a. | | Perf. 13 (52) | 11.50 | .80 |
| 50 | A9 | 3a olive | | .75 |
| 51 | A11 | 6a deep blue (50) | 8.50 | 1.75 |
| 52 | A11 | 8a black (50) | 9.00 | .90 |
| 53 | A9 | 10a red | 16.50 | 2.00 |
| 54 | A11 | 12a red (50) | 20.00 | 7.25 |
| | | Nos. 47-54 (8) | 78.00 | 7.25 |

For overprints see #O27-O31, O38-O40.

Vase and Plate — A12

Star and Crescent, Plane and Hour Glass — A13

Moslem Leaf Pattern — A14

Arch and Lamp of Learning A15

**1951, Aug. 14    Engr.    Perf. 13**

| | | | | |
|---|---|---|---|---|
| 55 | A12 | 2½a dark red | 1.50 | 1.00 |
| 56 | A13 | 3a dk rose lake | .75 | .20 |
| 57 | A12 | 3½a dp ultra (Urdu "½3") | 1.00 | 3.50 |
| 57A | A12 | 3½a dp ultra (Urdu "3½") (56) | 3.75 | 3.75 |
| 58 | A14 | 4a deep green | .75 | .20 |
| 59 | A14 | 6a red orange | 1.00 | .20 |
| 60 | A15 | 8a brown | 5.00 | .25 |
| 61 | A15 | 10a purple | 1.76 | 1.25 |
| 62 | A13 | 12a dk slate blue | 2.00 | .20 |
| | | Nos. 55-62 (9) | 17.50 | 10.55 |

Fourth anniversary of independence. On No. 57, the characters of the Urdu denomination at right appears as "½3." On the reengraved No. 57A, they read "3½."
Issue date: Dec. 1956.
See Nos. 88, O32-O34.
For surcharges see Nos. 255, 257.

Scinde District Stamp and Camel Train A16

**1952, Aug. 14    Perf. 13**

| | | | | |
|---|---|---|---|---|
| 63 | A16 | 3a olive green, *citron* | 1.25 | .50 |
| 64 | A16 | 12a dark brown, *salmon* | 2.00 | .50 |

5th anniv. of Pakistan's Independence and the cent. of the 1st postage stamps in the Indo-Pakistan sub-continent.

Peak K-2, Karakoram Mountains A17

**1954, Dec. 25**

| | | | | |
|---|---|---|---|---|
| 65 | A17 | 2a violet | .50 | .25 |

Conquest of K-2, world's 2nd highest mountain peak, in July 1954.

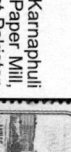

Gilgit Mountains — A19

Kaghan Valley — A18

Tea Garden, East Pakistan A20

Designs: 1a, Badshahi Mosque, Lahore. 1½a, Emperor Jahangir's Mausoleum, Lahore. 1r, Cotton field, 2r, River craft and jute field.

**1954, Aug. 14** **Engr.**

| | | | | |
|---|---|---|---|---|
| 66 | A18 | 6p rose violet | .20 | .20 |
| 67 | A19 | 9p blue | 3.75 | 1.25 |
| 68 | A19 | 1a dark green | .30 | .30 |
| 69 | A18 | 1½a carmine rose | .20 | .25 |
| 70 | A20 | 14a dark green | 1.50 | .60 |
| 71 | A20 | 1r yellow green | 3.00 | 1.25 |
| 72 | A20 | 2r orange | 12.00 | 1.00 |
| | | Nos. 66-72 (7) | 20.95 | 4.45 |

Seventh anniversary of independence.

Nos. 66, 69 exist in booklet panes of 4 torn from sheets. Value of booklet, $8.

For overprints & surcharges see #77, 101, 123, 126, O44-O50, O53-O56, O60-O62, O67, O69-O71.

Karnaphuli Paper Mill, East Pakistan (Urdu "½2") — A21

6a, Textile mill 8a, Jute mill 12a, Sui gas plant.

**1955, Aug. 14** **Unwmk.** **Perf. 13**

| | | | | |
|---|---|---|---|---|
| 73 | A21 | 2½a dk car (Urdu "½2") | .50 | 1.00 |
| 73A | A21 | 2½a dk car (Urdu "2½") ('56) | | |
| 74 | A21 | 6a dark blue | 1.00 | 1.00 |
| 75 | A21 | 8a violet | 3.75 | .20 |
| 76 | A21 | 12a car lake & org | 4.00 | .20 |
| | | Nos. 73-76 (5) | 9.60 | 2.60 |

**1955, Oct. 24**

| | | | | |
|---|---|---|---|---|
| 77 | A18 | 1½a red | 2.50 | 1.75 |
| 78 | A21 | 12a car lake & org | 5.00 | 3.50 |

Nos. 69 and 76 Overprinted in Ultramarine

Beware of forgeries.

Tenth Anniversary United Nations — A22

**1955, Dec. 7** **Unwmk.** **Perf. 13½x13**

| | | | | |
|---|---|---|---|---|
| 79 | A22 | 1½a dark green | .30 | .40 |
| 80 | A22 | 2a dark brown | .25 | .20 |
| 81 | A22 | 12a deep carmine | .90 | .30 |
| | | Nos. 79-81 (3) | 1.45 | .90 |

West Pakistan unification, Nov. 14, 1955.

Map of West Pakistan — A22

Cent. of the struggle for Independence (Indian Mutiny).

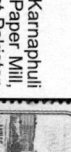

National Assembly A23

**1956, Mar. 23** **Litho.** **Perf. 13x12½**

| | | | | |
|---|---|---|---|---|
| 82 | A23 | 2a green | 1.25 | .20 |

Proclamation of the Republic of Pakistan, Mar. 23, 1956.

Crescent and Star — A24

**1956, Aug. 14** **Engr.** **Perf. 13**

| | | | | |
|---|---|---|---|---|
| 83 | A24 | 2a red | .75 | .20 |

Ninth anniversary of independence. For surcharges and overprints see Nos. 127, O57, O72-O73.

Map of East Pakistan — A25

**1956, Oct. 15** **Perf. 13½x13**

| | | | | |
|---|---|---|---|---|
| 84 | A25 | 1½a dark green | .50 | .75 |
| 85 | A25 | 2a dark brown | .50 | .20 |
| 86 | A25 | 12a deep red | .75 | .75 |
| | | Nos. 84-86 (3) | 1.50 | 1.70 |

1st Session at Dacca (East Pakistan) of the National Assembly of Pakistan.

Redrawn Types of 1951, 1955 and

Orange Tree — A26

**Perf. 13x13½, 13½x13** **Engr.**

| | | | | |
|---|---|---|---|---|
| 87 | A21 | 2½a dark carmine | .20 | .20 |
| 88 | A12 | 3½a bright blue | .30 | .20 |
| 89 | A26 | 10r dk green & orange | 1.25 | .80 |
| | | Nos. 87-89 (3) | | |

Nos. 87-89 inscribed "Pakistan" in English, Urdu and Bengali. Denomination in English only.

Islamic Republic of Pakistan, 1st anniv. See Nos. 95, 258, 475A. For surcharge and overprint see Nos. 159, O64.

Flag and Broken Chain — A27

**1957, May 10** **Litho.** **Perf. 13**

| | | | | |
|---|---|---|---|---|
| 90 | A27 | 1½a green | .75 | .20 |
| 91 | A27 | 12a blue | 1.75 | 1.00 |

Industrial Plants and Roses as Symbols of Progress A28

**1957, Aug. 14** **Unwmk.** **Perf. 13½**

| | | | | |
|---|---|---|---|---|
| 92 | A28 | 1½a light ultra | .20 | .25 |
| 93 | A28 | 4a orange vermilion | .50 | 1.00 |
| 94 | A28 | 12a red lilac | .50 | .45 |
| | | Nos. 92-94 (3) | 1.20 | 1.70 |

Type of 1957.

Design: 15r, Coconut Tree.

Tenth anniversary of independence.

Verse of Iqbal Poem A29

**1958, Mar. 23** **Engr.** **Perf. 13½x13**

| | | | | |
|---|---|---|---|---|
| 95 | A26 | 15r rose lilac & red | 5.25 | 3.50 |

Issued to commemorate the second anniversary of the Islamic Republic of Pakistan.

**1958, Apr. 21** **Photo.** **Perf. 14½x14** Black Inscriptions

| | | | | |
|---|---|---|---|---|
| 96 | A29 | 1½a citron | .60 | .20 |
| 97 | A29 | 2a orange brown | .20 | .20 |
| 98 | A29 | 14a aqua | 1.00 | 1.00 |
| | | Nos. 96-98 (3) | 2.20 | 1.40 |

20th anniv. of the death of Mohammad Iqbal (1877-1938), Moslem poet and philosopher.

Globe and Book — A30

**1958, Dec. 10** **Litho.** **Perf. 13**

| | | | | |
|---|---|---|---|---|
| 99 | A30 | 1½a Prus blue | .20 | .20 |
| 100 | A30 | 14a dark brown | .75 | 1.00 |

10th anniv. of the signing of the Universal Declaration of Human Rights.

Nos. 66 and 75 Overprinted:

"Pakistan Boy Scout 2nd National Jamboree Chittagong Dec. 58-Jan. 59"

**1958, Dec. 28** **Engr.** **Perf. 13**

| | | | | |
|---|---|---|---|---|
| 101 | A18 | 6p rose violet | .30 | .25 |
| 102 | A21 | 8a violet | .85 | .30 |

2nd National Boy Scout Jamboree held at Chittagong, Dec. 28-Jan. 4.

No. 74 Overprinted in Red: "Revolution Day, Oct. 27, 1959."

**1959, Oct. 27**

| | | | | |
|---|---|---|---|---|
| 103 | A21 | 6a dark blue | 1.00 | .20 |

First anniversary of the 1958 Revolution.

Red Cross — A31

**1959, Nov. 19** **Engr.; Cross Typo.** **Unwmk.** **Perf. 13**

| | | | | |
|---|---|---|---|---|
| 104 | A31 | 2a green & red | .40 | .20 |
| 105 | A31 | 10a dk blue & red | 1.10 | .60 |

Armed Forces Emblem — A32

**1960, Jan. 10** **Litho.** **Perf. 13**

| | | | | |
|---|---|---|---|---|
| 106 | A32 | 2a blue grn, red & ultra | .50 | .20 |
| 107 | A32 | 14a ultra & red | 1.25 | .60 |

Issued for Armed Forces Day.

Map Showing Disputed Areas A33

**1960, Mar. 23** **Engr.** **Unwmk.**

| | | | | |
|---|---|---|---|---|
| 108 | A33 | 6p purple | .45 | .20 |
| 109 | A33 | 2a copper red | .65 | .20 |
| 110 | A33 | 8a green | 1.40 | .20 |
| 111 | A33 | 1r blue | 2.00 | .20 |
| | | Nos. 108-111 (4) | 4.50 | .80 |

Publicizing the border dispute with India over Jammu and Kashmir, Junagarh and Manavadar.

For overprints and surcharges see Nos. 122, 125, 128, 178, O65-O66, O74-O75.

Uprooted Oak Emblem — A34

**1960, Apr. 7**

| | | | | |
|---|---|---|---|---|
| 112 | A34 | 2a carmine rose | .25 | .20 |
| 113 | A34 | 10a green | .35 | .60 |

Issued to publicize World Refugee Year, July 1, 1959-June 30, 1960.

House, Field and Column (Allegory of Democratic Development) A35

**1960, Oct. 27** **Photo.** **Perf. 13**

| | | | | |
|---|---|---|---|---|
| 114 | A35 | 2a brown, pink & grn | .20 | .20 |
| | a. | Green & pink omitted | 13.50 | |
| 115 | A35 | 14a multicolored | .35 | .60 |

Revolution Day, Oct. 27, 1960. No. 114a is easily counterfeited.

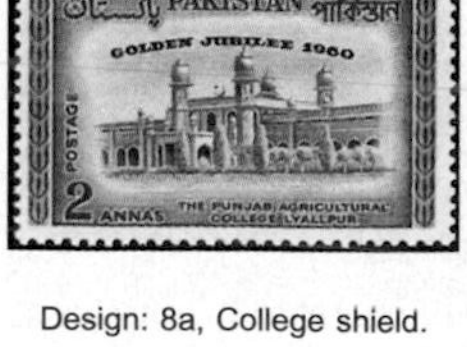

Punjab Agricultural College, Lyallpur A36

Design: 8a, College shield.

PAKISTAN

Map of Pakistan and Jasmine — A48

**1962, June 8**     **Unwmk.**     *Perf. 12*
162 A48 40p grn, yel grn & gray   1.10   .20

Introduction of new Pakistan Constitution.

Soccer
A49

13p, Hockey & Olympic gold medal. 25p, Squash rackets & British squash rackets championship cup. 40p, Cricket & Ayub challenge cup.

**1962, Aug. 14**    **Engr.**    *Perf. 12*½x13½
163 A49 7p blue & black     .20   .20
164 A49 13p green & black    .60   1.00
165 A49 25p lilac & black    .30   .20
166 A49 40p brown org & blk   2.00   2.00
    Nos. 163-166 (4)    3.10   3.40

Marble Fruit Dish and Clay Flask — A50

13p, Sporting goods. 25p, Camel skin lamp, brass jug. 40p, Wooden powder bowl, cane basket. 50p, Inlaid box, brassware.

**1962, Nov. 10**
167 A50 7p dark red     .20   .20
168 A50 13p dark green    3.50   2.25
169 A50 25p bright purple   .20   .20
170 A50 40p yellow green   .20   .20
171 A50 50p dull red     .20   .20
    Nos. 167-171 (5)    4.30   3.05

Children's Needs
A51

**1962, Dec. 11**   **Photo.**   *Perf. 13*½x14
172 A51 13p blue, plum & blk   .40   .20
173 A51 40p multicolored    .40   .20

16th anniv. of UNICEF.

No. 135a Overprinted in Red: "U.N. FORCE W. IRIAN"

**1963, Feb. 15**   **Engr.**   **Unwmk.**
174 A40 13p blue violet     .20   .30

Issued to commemorate the dispatch of Pakistani troops to West New Guinea.

Camel, Bull, Dancing Horse and Drummer A52

**1963, Mar. 13**   **Photo.**   *Perf. 12*
175 A52 13p multicolored    .20   .20

National Horse and Cattle Show, 1963.

---

Symbolic Flower — A43

**1961, Oct. 2**    **Unwmk.**    *Perf. 14*
151 A43 13p greenish blue    .50   .20
152 A43 90p red lilac     1.25   .25

Issued for Children's Day.

Roses — A44

**1961, Nov. 4**    *Perf. 13*½x13
153 A44 13p deep green & ver   .60   .20
154 A44 90p blue & vermilion   1.25   .40

Cooperative Day.

Police Crest and Traffic Policeman's Hand — A45

**1961, Nov. 30**   **Photo.**   *Perf. 13x12*½
155 A45 13p dk green, sil & blk   .50   .20
156 A45 40p red, silver & blk   1.10   .25

Centenary of the police force.

Eagle Locomotive, 1861 — A46

Design: 50pa, Diesel Engine, 1061.

**1961, Dec. 31**   **Engr.**   *Perf. 13*½x14
157 A46 13p yellow, green & blk   .90   .75
158 A46 50p green, blk & yellow   1.25   1.25

Centenary of Pakistan railroads.

No. 87 Surcharged in Red with New Value, Boeing 720-B Jetliner and: "FIRST JET FLIGHT KARACHI-DACCA"

**1962, Feb. 6**     **Engr.**     *Perf. 13*
159 A21 13p on 2 1/2a dk carmine   1.60   .75

1st jet flight from Karachi to Dacca, Feb. 6, 1962.

Mosquito and Malaria Eradication Emblem — A47

13p, Dagger pointing at mosquito, and emblem.

**1962, Apr. 7**   **Photo.**   *Perf. 13*½x14
160 A47 10p multicolored    .55   .20
161 A47 13p multicolored    .55   .20

WHO drive to eradicate malaria.

---

Chota Sona Masjid Gate — A41

Design: 10p, 13p, 25p, 40p, 50p, 75p, 90p, Shalimar Gardens, Lahore.

Type I

Type II

Two types of 1p, 2p and 5p:
I — First Bengali character beside "N" lacks appendage at left side of loop.
II — This character has a downward-pointing appendage at left side of loop, correcting "sh" to read "p".

On Nos. 129, 130, 132 the corrections were made individually on the plates, and each stamp may differ slightly. On No. 131a, the corrected letter is more clearly corrected and is uniform throughout the plate.

**1961-63**     **Engr.**     *Perf. 13*½x14
129 A40 1p violet (II)     .85   .20
   a. Type I               .80   .20
130 A40 2p rose red (II)    .85   .20
   a. Type I                .80   .20
131 A40 3p magenta     .35   .20
   a. Re-engraved die    6.00   6.00
132 A40 5p ultra (II)     3.75   .20
   a. Type I                .80   .20
133 A40 7p emerald     1.50   .20
134 A40 10p brown     .20   .20
135 A40 13p blue vio     .20   .20
136 A40 25p dark blue (62)   5.75   .20
137 A40 40p dull purple (62)   1.90   .20
138 A40 50p dull green (62)   .40   .20
139 A40 75p dk carmine (62)   .45   .20
140 A40 90p lt olive grn (62)   .55   .20
    *Perf. 13*½x13
141 A41 1r vermilion ('63)   2.40   .20
142 A41 1.25r purple     .95   .40
143 A41 2r orange ('63)   6.75   .20
144 A41 5r green ('63)   7.25   1.50
    Nos. 129-144 (16)   34.10   4.70

See #200-203. For surcharge and overprints see Nos. 184, O76-O82, O93-O93A.

Redrawn Bengali Inscription

**Designs Redrawn**

Bengali inscription redrawn with straight connecting line across top of characters. Shading of scenery differs, especially in Shalimar Gardens design at right are composed of horizontal lines instead of vertical lines and dots.

Designs as before; 15p, 20p, Shalimar Gardens.

**1963-70**        *Perf. 13*½x14
129b A40 1p violet     .20   .20
130b A40 2p rose red ('64)   .95   .40
131b A40 3p magenta ('70)   5.00   2.25
132b A40 5p ultra     5.75   2.25
133a A40 7p emerald ('64)   .20   .20
134a A40 10p brown     .20   .20
135a A40 13p blue violet    .20   .20
135B A40 20p rose lilac ('64)   .30   .20
135C A40 25p dark green ('70)   8.00   .20
136a A40 25p dark blue    .20   .20
137a A40 40p dull green ('64)   .20   .20
138a A40 50p dull green ('64)   .30   .20
139a A40 75p dark carmine ('64)   .30   .45
140a A40 90p lt olive green ('64)   .60   .60
    Nos. 129b-140a (14)   22.00   7.55

For overprints see #174, O76b, O77b, O78a, O79b, O80a, O81a, O82a, O83-O84A, O85a, O86a.

---

**1960, Oct.**    **Engr.**    *Perf. 12*½x14
116 A36 2a rose red & gray blue   .20   .20
117 A36 8a lilac & green    .20   .30

50th anniv. of the Punjab Agricultural College, Lyallpur.

Caduceus, College Emblem — A37

**1960, Nov. 16**   **Photo.**   *Perf. 13*½x13
118 A37 2a blue, yel & blk   .75   .20
119 A37 14a car rose, blk & emerald   2.50   1.00

King Edward Medical College, Lahore, cent.

Map of South-East Asia and Commission Emblem — A38

**1960, Dec. 5**     *Perf. 13*
120 A38 14a red orange   .40   .60

Conf. of the Commission on Asian and Far Eastern Affairs of the Intl. Chamber of Commerce, Karachi, Dec. 5-9.

"Kim's Gun" and Scout Badge A39

**1960, Dec. 24**   **Unwmk.**   *Perf. 12*½
121 A39 2a dk green, car & yel   .75   .20

3rd Natl. Boy Scout Jamboree, Lahore, Dec. 24-31.

No. 110 Overprinted in Red

**1961, Feb. 12**
122 A33 8a green     1.25   1.00

10th Lahore Stamp Exhibition, Feb. 12.

**New Currency**
Nos. 24, 68-69, 83, 108-109
Surcharged with New Value in Paisa

**1961**          *Perf. 13*
123 A18 1p on 1½a red    .20   .20
124 A33 2p on 3p orange red   .20   .20
125 A33 3p on 6p purple    .20   .20
126 A19 7p on 1a car rose   .20   .20
127 A24 13p on 2a red    .20   .20
128 A33 13p on 2a copper red   1.20   1.20
    Nos. 123-128 (6)   2.20   2.20

Various violet handstamped surcharges were applied to a variety of regular-issue stamps. Most of these repeat the denomination and some repeat the denomination of the basic stamp and add the new value. Example: "8 Annas (50 Paisa)" on No. 75. Many errors exist from printer's waste.
For overprints see Nos. O74-O75.

Warsak Dam, Kabul River A42

**1961, July 1**   **Engr.**   *Perf. 12*½x13½
150 A42 40p black & lt ultra   .75   .20

Dedication of hydroelectric Warsak Project.

Khyber Pass — A40

## Wheat and Tractor A53

Design: 50p, Hands and heap of rice.

**1963, Mar. 21  Engr.  Perf. 12½x13½**
176 A53 13p brown orange   2.75  .20
177 A53 50p brown   4.50  .40

FAO "Freedom from Hunger" campaign.

**1963, Mar. 23   Perf. 13**
178 A33 13p on 2a copper red   .65  .20

International Stamp Exhibition at Dacca.

No. 109 Surcharged with New Value and: "INTERNATIONAL/DACCA STAMP/EXHIBITION/1963"

## Centenary Emblem — A54

**1963, June 25  Engr. and Typo.  Perf. 13½x13½, 13½x12½**
179 A54 40p dark gray & red   2.50  .20

International Red Cross, cent.

## Paharpur Stupa A55

Designs: 13p, Cistern, Mohenjo-Daro, vert. 40p, Stupas, Taxila, 50pa, Stupas, Mainamati.

**1963, Sept. 16  Engr.  Unwmk.  Perf. 12½x13½, 13½x12½**
180 A55 7p ultra   .60  .20
181 A55 13p brown   .60  .20
182 A55 40p carmine rose   1.10  .20
183 A55 50p dark violet   1.25  .50
Nos. 180-183 (4)   3.55  1.10

**1963, Oct. 7   Perf. 13½x14**
184 A40 13p on 3pa magenta   .20  .20

No. 131 Surcharged and Overprinted: "100 YEARS OF P.W.D." "OCTOBER, 1963"

Centenary of Public Works Department.

## Atatürk Mausoleum, Ankara A56

**1963, Nov. 10  Engr.  Perf. 13x13½**
185 A56 50p red   .90  .20

25th anniv. of the death of Kemal Atatürk, pres. of Turkey.

## Globe and UNESCO Emblem A57

**1963, Dec. 10  Photo.  Perf. 13½x14**
186 A57 50p dk brn, vio blue & red   .60  .40

15th anniv. of the Universal Declaration of Human Rights.

## Multan Thermal Power Station A58

**1963, Dec. 25  Engr.  Perf. 12½x13½**
187 A58 13p ultra   .25  .20

Issued to mark the opening of the Multan Thermal Power Station.

### Type of 1961-63
**1963-65  Engr.  Perf. 13½x13  Wmk. 351**
200 A41 1r vermilion   .25  .20
201 A41 1.25r purple ('64)   1.60  .30
202 A41 2r orange   .85  .20
203 A41 5r green ('65)   5.20  1.20
Nos. 200-203 (4)

For overprints see Nos. O92-O93A.

## A59

**1964, Mar. 30  Engr.  Perf. 13x13½  Unwmk.**
204 A59 13p brick red & turq blue   .80  .20
205 A59 50p black & rose lilac   1.50  .30

UNESCO world campaign to save historic monuments in Nubia.

13p, Temple of Thot, Dakka, and Queen Nefertari with Goddesses Hathor and Isis. 50p, Ramses II, Abu Simbel, and View of Nile.

## Pakistan Pavilion and Unisphere A60

**1964, Apr. 22  Engr.  Perf. 12½x14, 14x12½  Unwmk.**
206 A60 13p ultramarine   .20  .20
207 A60 1.25r dp orange & ultra   .30  .25

New York World's Fair, 1964-65.

1.25r, Pakistan pavilion, Unisphere, vert.

## Mausoleum of Shah Abdul Latif — A61

**1964, June 25   Perf. 13½x13**
208 A61 50p magenta & ultra   2.25  .30

Bicentenary (?) of the death of Shah Abdul Latif of Bhit (1689-1752).

## Mausoleum of Jinnah — A62

**1964, Sept. 11  Unwmk.  Perf. 13**

Design: 15p, Mausoleum, horiz.
209 A62 15p green   .90  .20
210 A62 50p greenish gray   1.75  .30

16th anniv. of the death of Mohammed Ali Jinnah (1876-1948), the Quaid-i-Azam (Great Leader), founder and president of Pakistan.

## Bengali Alphabet on Slate and Slab with Urdu Alphabet A63

**1964, Oct. 5  Engr.**
211 A63 15p brown   .20  .20

Issued for Universal Children's Day.

## West Pakistan University of Engineering and Technology — A64

**1964, Dec. 21   Perf. 12½x14**
212 A64 15p henna brown   .20  .20

1st convocation of the West Pakistan University of Engineering & Technology, Lahore. Dec. 1964.

## Eyeglasses and Book — A65

**1965, Feb. 28  Litho.  Perf. 13x13½  Unwmk.**
213 A65 15p yellow & ultra   .20  .20

Issued to publicize aid for the blind.

## ITU Emblem, Telegraph Pole and Transmission Tower — A66

**1965, May 17  Engr.  Perf. 12½x14**
214 A66 15p deep claret   2.25  .25

Cent. of the ITU.

## ICY Emblem A67

**1965, June 26  Litho.  Perf. 13½**
215 A67 15p blue & black   .75  .20
216 A67 50p yellow & green   1.50  .30

International Cooperation Year, 1965.

## Hands Holding Book — A68

**1965, July 21  Litho.  Perf. 13½x13, 13x12½  Unwmk.**
217 A68 15p org brn, dk brn & buff   .55  .20
Size: 46x35mm
218 A68 50p multicolored   1.00  .30
Size: 54x30½mm

1st anniv. of the signing of the Regional Cooperation for Development Pact by Turkey, Iran and Pakistan.

50p, Map & flags of Turkey, Iran & Pakistan.

## Navy Emblem and Tanks, Army Emblem and Soldier — A69

**1965, Dec. 25  Litho.  Perf. 13½x13**
219 A69 7p multicolored   1.25  .20
220 A69 15p multicolored   2.00  .25
221 A69 50p multicolored   3.35  .35
Nos. 219-221 (3)   6.60  .75

Designs: 15p, Navy emblem, corvette No. O204 and officer. 50p, Air Force emblem, two F-104 Starfighters and pilot.

Issued to honor the Pakistani armed forces.

## Emblems of Pakistan Armed Forces — A70

**1966, Feb. 13  Litho.  Perf. 13½x13**
222 A70 15p buff, grn & dk bl   .70  .20

Issued for Armed Forces Day.

## Atomic Reactor, Islamabad — A71

**1966, Apr. 30  Engr.  Unwmk.  Perf. 13**
223 A71 15p black   .20  .20

Pakistan's first atomic reactor.

## Habib Bank Emblem A72

**1966, Aug. 25  Litho.  Unwmk.  Perf. 12½x13½**
224 A72 15p brown, org & dk grn   .20  .20

25th anniversary of the Habib Bank.

**Lithographed and Engraved** *Perf. 13*
1967, Oct. 26
244 A88 50p yellow, blue & lilac 1.75 .25
Coronation of Shah Mohammed Riza Pahlavi and Empress Farah of Iran.

Co-Operative Day — A89
"Each for all..." A89

1967, Nov. 4 *Perf. 13* Litho.
245 A89 15p multicolored .20 .20
Cooperative Day, 1967.

Mangla Dam — A90

1967, Nov. 23 *Perf. 13* Litho.
246 A90 15p multicolored .20 .20
Indus Basin Project, harnessing the Indus River for flood control and irrigation.

"Fight Against Cancer" — A91

Human Rights Flame — A92

1967, Dec. 26
247 A91 15p red & dk brown .70 .20
Issued to publicize the fight against cancer.

1968, Jan. 31 *Perf. 14x12½* Photo.
248 A92 15p Prus green & red .20 .20
249 A92 50p yellow, silver & red .25 .20
International Human Rights Year 1968.

Agricultural University and Produce A93

1968, Mar. 28 *Perf. 13½* Litho.
250 A93 15p multicolored .20 .20
Issued to publicize the first convocation of the East Pakistan Agricultural University.

WHO Emblem — A94

---

Flag of Valor — A83

1967, May 15 *Perf. 13* Litho.
238 A83 15p multicolored .20 .20
Flag of Valor awarded to the cities of Lahore, Sialkot and Sargodha.

Star and "20" — A84

1967, Aug. 14 *Unwmk.* Photo.
239 A84 15p red & slate green .20 .20
20th anniversary of independence.

Rice Plant and Globe A85

Cotton Plant, Bale and Cloth — A86

Design: 50p, Raw jute, bale and cloth.

1967, Sept. 26 *Perf. 13x13½* Photo.
240 A85 10p dk blue & yellow .20 .20
*Perf. 13*
241 A86 15p orange, bl grn & yel .25 .20
242 A86 50p blue grn, brn & tan .75 .65
Nos. 240-242 (3) .30 .25
Issued to publicize major export products.

Toys — A87

1967, Oct. 2 *Perf. 13* Litho.
243 A87 15p multicolored .20 .20
Issued for International Children's Day.

Shah and Empress Farah of Iran — A88

---

ITY Emblem — A78

1967, Jan. 1 *Perf. 13* Litho.
232 A78 15p bis brn, blue & blk .20 .20
International Tourist Year, 1967.

Red Crescent Emblem — A79

1967, Jan. 10 *Perf. 13½* Litho.
233 A79 15p brn, brn org & red .20 .20
Tuberculosis eradication campaign.

Scout Sign and Emblem A80

1967, Jan. 29 *Perf. 12½x13½* Photo.
234 A80 15p dp plum & brn org .25 .20
4th National Pakistan Jamboree. "Faisa" is a plate flaw, not an error.

Justice Holding Scales — A81

1967, Feb. 17 *Unwmk.* Litho.
235 A81 15p multicolored .20 .20
Centenary of High Court of West Pakistan.

Mohammad Iqbal — A82

1967, Apr. 21 *Perf. 13* Litho.
236 A82 15p red & brown .25 .20
237 A82 1r dk green & brn .75 .20
90th anniv. of the birth of Mohammad Iqbal (1877-1938), poet and philosopher.

---

Boy and Girl — A73

1966, Oct. 3 *Perf. 13x13½* Litho.
225 A73 15p multicolored .20 .20
Issued for Children's Day.

UNESCO Emblem A74

1966, Nov. 24 *Perf. 14* Unwmk.
226 A74 15p multicolored 3.50 .35
20th anniv. of UNESCO.

Secretariat Buildings, Islamabad, Flag and Pres. Mohammed Ayub Khan — A75

1966, Nov. 29 *Perf. 13* Litho.
227 A75 1bp multicolored .25 .20
228 A75 50p multicolored .50 .25
Publicizing the new capital, Islamabad.

Avicenna — A76

Mohammed Ali Jinnah — A77

1966, Dec. 3 *Perf. 13½*
229 A76 15p sal pink & slate grn .50 .20
Issued to publicize the Health Institute.

**Lithographed and Engraved** *Perf. 13*
1966, Dec. 25 *Unwmk.*
Design: 50p, Different frame.
230 A77 15p orange, blk & bl .30 .20
231 A77 50p lilac, blk & vio bl .50 .25
90th anniv. of the birth of Mohammed Ali Jinnah (1876-1948), 1st Governor General of Pakistan.

**1968, Apr. 7 Photo. Perf. 13½x12½**
251 A94 15p emerald & orange .20 .20
252 A94 50p orange & dk blue .25 .20
20th anniv. of WHO. "Pais" is a plate flaw, not an error.

Kazi Nazrul Islam A95

**Lithographed and Engraved**
**1968, June 25 Unwmk. Perf. 13**
253 A95 15p dull yellow & brown .35 .20
254 A95 50p rose & brown .75 .30
Kazi Nazrul Islam, poet and composer.

**1968, Sept. Engr. Perf. 13**
255 A13 4p on 3a dk rose lake .25 .75
256 A21 4p on 6a dk blue (R) .25 .75
257 A15 60p on 10a purple (R) .60 .35
  a. Black surcharge 1.50 .40
  Nos. 255-257 (3) 1.10 1.85

Nos. 56, 61 and 74 Surcharged with New Value and Bars in Black or Red

**1968 Types of 1948-57 Engr. Perf. 13**
258 A26 10r dk green & orange 3.00 3.00
259 A7 25r purple 5.00 7.00

Children with Hoops A96
GOOD HEALTH — A BASIC RIGHT OF EVERY CHILD

**1968, Oct. 7 Unwmk. Litho. Perf. 13**
260 A96 15p buff & multi .20 .20
Issued for International Children's Day.

Symbolic of Political Reforms — A97
LEADERSHIP THROUGH BASIC DEMOCRACIES

**Wmk. 351**
**1968, Oct. 27 Litho. Perf. 13**
261 A97 10p multicolored .20 .20
262 A97 15p multicolored .40 .20
263 A97 50p multicolored 2.10 .30
264 A97 60p multicolored .75 .30
  Nos. 261-264 (4) 3.45 1.00

Development Decade, 1958-1968.

Designs: 15p, Agricultural and industrial development. 50p, Defense. 60p, Scientific and cultural advancement.

Chittagong Steel Mill — A98
PAKISTAN'S FIRST STEEL MILL AT CHITTAGONG

**1969, Jan. 7 Unwmk. Perf. 13**
265 A98 15p gray grn, lt blue & blk .20 .20
Opening of Pakistan's first steel mill.

Family of Four A99
FAMILY PLANNING FOR PROSPERITY

**1969, Jan. 14 Litho. Perf. 13½**
266 A99 15p lt blue & plum .20 .20
Issued to publicize family planning.

Hockey Player and Medal — A100

**1969, Jan. 30 Photo. Perf. 13½**
267 A100 15p green, lt bl, blk & gold .20 .20
268 A100 1r grn, sal pink, blk & gold 3.25 .75
Pakistan's hockey victory at the 19th Olympic Games in Mexico.

Mirza Ghalib — A101

**1969, Feb. 15 Litho. Perf. 13**
269 A101 15p blue & multi .30 .20
270 A101 50p multicolored .60 .25
Mirza Ghalib (Asad Ullah Beg Khan, 1797-1869), poet who modernized the Urdu language.

Dacca Railroad Station A102

**1969, Apr. 27 Litho. Perf. 13**
271 A102 15p yel, grn, blk & dull bl .60 .20
Opening of the new railroad station in Kamalpur area of Dacca.

ILO Emblem and Ornamental Border — A103
1919-1969 INTERNATIONAL LABOUR ORGANISATION

**1969, May 15 Litho. Perf. 13½**
272 A103 15p brt grn & ocher .20 .20
273 A103 50p car rose & ocher .35 .20
50th anniv. of the ILO.

Lady on Balcony, Mogul Miniature, Pakistan A104

**1969, July 21 Litho. Perf. 13**
274 A104 20p multicolored .25 .20
275 A104 50p multicolored .30 .20
276 A104 1r multicolored .60 .20
  Nos. 274-276 (3) 1.15 .65

Designs: 20p, Lady Serving Wine, Safavi miniature, Iran. 1r, Sultan Suleiman Receiving Sheik Abdul Latif, 16th cent. miniature, Turkey.

5th anniv. of the signing of the Regional Cooperation for Development Pact by Turkey, Iran and Pakistan.

Eastern Refinery, Chittagong A105

**1969, Sept. 14 Photo. Perf. 13½**
277 A105 20p yel, blk & vio bl .20 .20
Opening of the 1st oil refinery in East Pakistan.

Children Playing — A106

**1969, Oct. 6 Litho. Perf. 13**
278 A106 20p blue & multi .20 .20
Issued for Universal Children's Day.

Japanese Doll, Map of Dacca-Tokyo Pearl Route — A107

**1969, Nov. 1 Litho. Perf. 13½x13**
279 A107 20p multicolored .75 .20
280 A107 50p ultra & multi 1.50 .30
Inauguration of the Pakistan International Airways Dacca-Tokyo "Pearl Route."

Reflection of Light Diagram — A108
FATHER OF OPTICS IBN-AL-HAITHAM (965-1039)

**1969, Nov. 4 Perf. 13**
281 A108 20p multicolored .20 .20
Alhazen (abu-Ali al Hasan ibn-al-Haytham, 965-1039), astronomer and optician.

Vickers Vimy and London-Darwin Route over Karachi — A109

**1969, Dec. 2 Photo. Perf. 13½x13**
282 A109 50p multicolored 1.10 .30
50th anniv. of the 1st England to Australia flight.

View of EXPO '70, Sun Tower, Flags of Pakistan, Iran and Turkey A110

**1970, Feb. 15 Litho. Perf. 13**
283 A110 50p multicolored .25 .25
Issued to publicize EXPO '70 International Exhibition, Osaka, Japan, Mar. 15-Sept. 13.

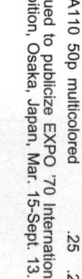
UPU Headquarters, Bern — A111
NEW U.P.U. HEADQUARTERS 1970

**1970, May 20 Litho. Perf. 13½x13**
284 A111 20p multicolored .30 .20
285 A111 50p multicolored .40 .30
Opening of new UPU headquarters in Bern. "A souvenir sheet of 2 exists, inscribed "U.P.U. Day 9th Oct. 1971". It contains stamps similar to Nos. 284-285, imperf. Value, $65.

UN Headquarters, New York — A112
25th ANNIVERSARY OF THE U.N.O.

**1970, June 26**
286 A112 20p green & multi .40 .20
287 A112 50p violet & multi .30 .20
Design: 50p, UN emblem.
25th anniversary of the United Nations.

Hockey Player and Cup — A127

**1971, Oct. 24**
312 A127 20p red & multi ... 3.00 .50
First World Hockey Cup, Barcelona, Spain, Oct. 15-24.

Great Bath at Mohenjo-Daro — A128

**1971, Nov. 4**
313 A128 20p dp org, dk brn & blk ... .25 .25
25th anniv. of UNESCO.

UNICEF Emblem A129

*Perf. 13*
**1971, Dec. 11** Litho.
314 A129 50p dull bl, org & grn ... .40 .40
25th anniv. of UNICEF.

King Hussein and Jordan Flag A130

**1971, Dec. 25**
316 A130 20p blue & multi ... .25 .20
50th anniversary of the Hashemite Kingdom of Jordan.

Pakistan Hockey Federation Emblem, and Cup — A131

**1971, Dec. 31**
316 A131 20p yellow & multi ... 4.75 .75
Pakistan, world hockey champions, Barcelona, Oct. 1971.

---

Cement Factory, Daudkhel — A123

*Perf. 13*
**1971, July 1** Litho.
304 A123 20p purple, blk & brn ... .20 .20
20th anniversary of Colombo Plan.

Badshahi Mosque, Lahore — A124

Designs: 10pa, Mosque of Selim, Edirne, Turkey. 50pa, Religious School, of Chaharbayli, Isfahan, Iran, vert.

*Perf. 13*
**1971, July 21** Litho.
305 A124 10p red & multi ... .20 .20
306 A124 20p green & multi ... .30 .25
307 A124 50p blue & multi ... .80 .30
Nos. 305-307 (3) ... 1.30 .75
7th anniversary of Regional Cooperation among Pakistan, Iran and Turkey.

Electric Train and Boy with Toy Locomotive — A125

*Perf. 13*
**1971, Oct. 4** Litho.
308 A125 20p slate & multi ... 2.75 .60
Children's Day.

Messenger and Statue of Cyrus the Great — A126

**1971, Oct. 15**
309 A126 10p green & multi ... .40 .25
310 A126 20p blue & multi ... .60 .30
311 A126 50p red & multi ... 1.00 1.05
Nos. 309-311 (3) ... 2.00 1.05
2500th anniversary of the founding of the Persian Empire by Cyrus the Great.
A souvenir sheet of 3 contains stamps similar to Nos. 309-311, imperf. Value, $60.

---

Flag and Inscription A119

*Perf. 13*
**1970, Oct. 5** Photo.
297 A118 20p multicolored ... .20 .20
Issued for Children's Day.

*Perf. 13½x13*
**1970, Dec. 7** Litho.
298 A119 20p violet & green ... .20 .20
299 A119 20p brt pink & green ... .20 .20
No. 298 inscribed "Elections for National Assembly 7th Dec. 1970." No. 299 inscribed "Elections for Provincial Assemblies 17th Dec. 1970."

Emblem and Burning of Al Aqsa Mosque — A120

*Perf. 13½x12½*
**1970, Dec. 26**
300 A120 20p multicolored ... .20 .20
Islamic Conference of Foreign Ministers, Karachi, Dec. 26-28.

Coastal Embankment — A121

*Perf. 13*
**1971, Feb. 25** Litho.
301 A121 20p multicolored ... .20 .20
Development of coastal embankments in East Pakistan.

Men of Different Races — A122

*Perf. 13*
**1971, Mar. 21** Litho.
302 A122 20p multicolored ... .20 .20
303 A122 50p lilac & multi ... .25 .25
Intl. Year against Racial Discrimination.

---

Education Year Emblem and Open Book — A113

*Perf. 13*
**1970, July 6** Litho.
288 A113 20p blue & multi ... .20 .20
289 A113 50p orange & multi ... .30 .20
International Education Year, 1970.

Saiful Malook Lake, Pakistan A114

Designs: 50p, Seeyo-Se-Pol Bridge, Esfahan, Iran. 1r, View, Fethiye, Turkey.

**1970, July 21**
290 A114 20p yellow & multi ... .20 .20
291 A114 50p yellow & multi ... .35 .30
292 A114 1r yellow & multi ... .55 .70
Nos. 290-292 (3) ... 1.10 .70
6th anniv. of the signing of the Regional Cooperation for Development Pact by Pakistan, Iran and Turkey.

Asian Productivity Year Emblem — A115

*Perf. 12½x14*
**1970, Aug. 18** Photo.
293 A115 50p black, yel & grn ... .35 .20
Asian Productivity Year, 1970.

Dr. Maria Montessori A116

*Perf. 13*
**1970, Aug. 31** Litho.
294 A116 20p red & multi ... .20 .20
295 A116 50p multicolored ... .25 .25
Maria Montessori (1870-1952) Italian educator and physician.

Tractor and Fertilizer Factory — A117

**1970, Sept. 12**
296 A117 20p yel grn & brn org ... .20 .20
10th Regional Food and Agricultural Organization Conf. for the Near East in Islamabad.

**1972, Jan. 15**
317 A132 20p brown, blk & blue .20 .25
International Book Year 1972.

Arab Scholars
A132

**1972, July 21** **Litho.** **Perf. 13**
322 A137 10p multicolored .35 .20
323 A137 20p multicolored .60 .25
324 A137 50p multicolored 1.50 .55
  Nos. 322-324 (3) 2.45 1.00

Regional Cooperation for Development Pact among Pakistan, Turkey and Iran, 8th anniversary.

Paintings: 10p, Fisherman, by Cevat Dereli (Turkey). 20p, Persian Woman, by Behzad.

---

Angels and Grand Canal, Venice — A133

**1972, Feb. 5** **Perf. 13**
318 A133 20p blue & multi .40 .25
UNESCO campaign to save Venice.

ECAFE Emblem A134

**1972, Mar. 28** **Litho.** **Perf. 13**
319 A134 20p blue & multi .20 .25
Economic Commission for Asia and the Far East (ECAFE), 25th anniversary.

"Your Heart is your Health" — A135

**1972, Apr. 7** **Perf. 13x13½**
320 A135 20p vio blue & multi .20 .25
World Health Day 1972.

"Only One Earth" A136

**1972, June 5** **Litho.** **Perf. 12½x14**
321 A136 20p ultra & multi .20 .25
UN Conference on Human Environment, Stockholm, June 5-16.

Young Man, by Abdur Rehman Chughtai A137

---

Jinnah and Independence Memorial A138

"Land Reforms" — A139

**1972, Aug. 14** **Perf. 13 (A138), 13½x12½ (A139)**
325 A138 10p shown .20 .20
326 A139 20p shown .20 .20
327 A139 20p Labor reforms .25 .20
328 A139 20p Education .25 .20
329 A139 20p Health care .25 .20
  a. Vert. strip of 4, #326-329 plus 4 labels 1.00 1.00
330 A138 60p rose lilac & car 1.75 1.30
  Nos. 325-330 (6) .55 .30

Designs: Nos. 326-329. Principal reforms. 60pa, State Bank, Islamabad, meeting-place of National Assembly, horiz.

25th anniversary of independence. No. 329a contains designs of Nos. 326-329, each with a decorative label, separated by simulated perfs.

---

Blood Donor, Society Emblem — A140

**1972, Sept. 6** **Litho.** **Perf. 14x12½**
331 A140 20p multicolored .30 .25
Pakistan National Blood Transfusion Service.

Census Chart A141

**1972, Sept. 16** **Litho.** **Perf. 13½**
332 A141 20p multicolored .20 .20
Centenary of population census.

---

Children Leaving Slum for Modern City — A142

**1972, Oct. 2** **Litho.** **Perf. 13**
333 A142 20p multicolored .20 .20
Children's Day.

Giant Book and Children A143

**1972, Oct. 23** **Perf. 13**
334 A143 20p purple & multi .20 .20
Education Week.

Nuclear Power Plant, Karachi A144

**1972, Nov. 28** **Litho.** **Perf. 13**
335 A144 20p multicolored .25 .25
Pakistan's first nuclear power plant.

---

Copernicus in Observatory, by Jan Matejko — A145

**1973, Feb. 19** **Litho.** **Perf. 13**
336 A145 20p multicolored .75 .25
500th birth anniversary of Copernicus.

Dancing Girl, Public Baths, Mohenjo-Daro — A146

**1973, Feb. 23** **Perf. 13½x13**
337 A146 20p multicolored .50 .25
Mohenjo-Daro excavations, 50th anniv.

---

Radar, Lightning, WMO Emblem — A147

**1973, Mar. 23** **Litho.** **Perf. 13**
338 A147 20p multicolored .25 .25
Cent. of intl. meteorological cooperation.

Prisoners of War — A148

**1973, Apr. 18** **Perf. 13**
339 A148 1.25 black & multi 2.00 2.00
A plea for Pakistani prisoners of war in India.

National Assembly, Islamabad A149

**1973, Apr. 21** **Perf. 12½x13½**
340 A149 20p green & multi .45 .30
Constitution Week.

---

State Bank and Emblem — A150

**1973, July 1** **Litho.** **Perf. 13**
341 A150 20p multicolored .20 .25
342 A150 1r multicolored .40 .35
State Bank of Pakistan, 25th anniversary.

---

Street, Mohenjo-Daro, Pakistan A151

**1973, July 21** **Perf. 13x13½**
343 A151 20p blue & multi .25 .20
344 A151 60p emerald & multi 1.00 .35
345 A151 1.25 red & multi 1.00 .75
  Nos. 343-345 (3) 2.25 1.30

Regional Cooperation for Development Pact among Pakistan, Turkey and Iran, 9th anniversary.

Designs: 20p, Statue of man, Shahdad, Kerman, Persia, 4000 B.C. 1.25r, Head from mausoleum of King Antiochus I (69-34 B.C.), Turkey.

## Pakistani Flag and Constitution — A152

**1973, Aug. 14   Litho.   Perf. 13**
346 A152 20p blue & multi   .25   .20
Independence Day.

## Mohammed Ali Jinnah — A153

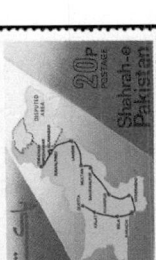

**1973, Sept. 11   Litho.   Perf. 13**
347 A153 20p emerald, yel & blk   .25   .20
Mohammed Ali Jinnah (1876-1948), president of All-India Moslem League.

## Wallago Attu — A154

Fish: 20p, Labeo rohita. 60p, Tilapia mossambica. 1r, Catla catla.

**1973, Sept. 24   Litho.   Perf. 13½**
348 A154 10p multicolored   1.25   1.10
349 A154 20p multicolored   1.25   1.10
350 A154 60p multicolored   2.50   1.75
351 A154 1r ultra & multi   2.50   1.75
a. Strip of 4, #348-351   7.50   7.50

## Book, Torch, Child and School — A155

**1973, Oct. 1   Litho.**
352 A155 20p multicolored   .35   .20
Universal Children's Day.

## Sindhi Farmer and FAO Emblem A156

**1973, Oct. 15   Litho.   Perf. 13**
353 A156 20p multicolored   .95   .35
World Food Organization, 10th anniv.

## Kemal Ataturk and Ankara — A157

**1973, Oct. 29**
354 A157 50p multicolored   .75   .40
50th anniversary of Turkish Republic.

## Scout Pointing to Planet and Stars — A158

**1973, Nov. 11   Litho.   Perf. 13½x12½**
355 A158 20p dull blue & multi   2.00   .50
25th anniversary of Pakistani Boy Scouts and Silver Jubilee Jamboree.

## Human Rights Flame, Sheltered Home — A159

**1973, Nov. 16**
356 A159 20p multicolored   .35   .25
25th anniversary of the Universal Declaration of Human Rights.

## al-Biruni and Jhelum Observatory — A160

**1973, Nov. 26   Litho.   Perf 13**
357 A160 20p multicolured   .50   .20
358 A160 1.25r multicolored   1.50   .50
International Congress on Millenary of abu-al-Rayhan al-Biruni, Nov. 26-Dec. 12.

## Dr. A. G. Hansen A161

**1973, Dec. 29**
359 A161 20p ultra & multi   1.50   .50
Centenary of the discovery by Dr. Armauer Gerhard Hansen of the Hansen bacillus, the cause of leprosy.

## Family and WPY Emblem A162

**1974, Jan. 1   Litho.   Perf. 13**
360 A162 20p yellow & multi   .25   .20
361 A162 1.25r salmon & multi   .30   .30
World Population Year 1974.

## Summit Emblem and Ornament — A163
## Emblem, Crescent and Rays A164

**1974, Feb. 22   Perf. 14x12½, 13**
362 A163 20p multicolored   .20   .20
363 A164 65p multicolored   .30   .40
a. Souvenir sheet of 2   3.25   3.25
Islamic Summit Meeting. No. 363a contains two stamps similar to Nos. 362-363 with simulated perforations.

## Metric Measures A165

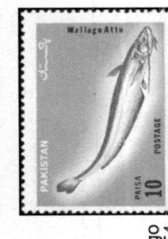

**1974, July 1   Litho.   Perf. 13**
364 A165 20p multicolored   .20   .20
Introduction of metric system.

## Kashan Rug, Lahore A166

Designs: 60p, Persian rug, late 16th century. 1.25r, Anatolian rug, 15th century.

**1974, July 21**
365 A166 20p multicolored   .20   .20
366 A166 60p multicolored   .50   .50
367 A166 1.25r multicolored   1.00   1.00
Nos. 365-367 (3)   1.70   1.70
10th anniversary of the Regional Cooperation for Development Pact among Pakistan, Iran and Turkey.

## Hands Protecting Sapling — A167

**1974, Aug. 9   Litho.   Perf. 13**
368 A167 20p multicolored   .50   .40
Arbor Day.

## Torch over Map of Africa with Namibia — A168

**1974, Aug. 26**
369 A168 60p green & multi   .45   .40
Namibia (South-West Africa) Day. See note after United Nations No. 241.

## Map of Pakistan with Highways and Disputed Area — A169

**1974, Sept. 23**
370 A169 20p multicolored   1.00   .75
Highway system under construction.

## Child and Students A170

**1974, Oct. 7   Litho.   Perf. 13**
371 A170 20p multicolored   .25   .25
Universal Children's Day.

## UPU Emblem — A171
## Liaqat Ali Khan — A172

2.25r, Jet, UPU emblem, mail coach.

**1974, Oct. 9**
**Size: 24x36mm**
372 A171 20p multicolored   .25   .20
**Size: 29x41mm**
373 A171 2.25r multicolored   .70   .70
a. Souv. sheet of 2, #372-373, imperf.   4.50   4.50
Centenary of Universal Postal Union.

**1974, Oct. 16   Litho.   Perf. 13x13½**
374 A172 20p black & red   .40   .25
Liaqat Ali Khan, Prime Minister 1947-1951.

**1974, Nov. 9 Litho. Perf. 13**
375 A173 20p multicolored .40 .25

Mohammad Allama Iqbal (1877-1938), poet and philosopher.

Mohammad Allama Iqbal — A173

Dr. Schweitzer on Ogowe River, 1915 — A174

**1975, Jan. 14 Litho. Perf. 13**
376 A174 2.25r multicolored 5.00 4.00

Dr. Albert Schweitzer (1875-1965), medical missionary, birth centenary.

Tourism Year 75 Emblem A175

**1975, Jan. 15**
377 A175 2.25r multicolored .50 .50

South Asia Tourism Year, 1975.

Flags of Participants, Memorial and Prime Minister Bhutto — A176

**1975, Feb. 22 Litho. Perf. 13**
378 A176 20p it blue & multi .55 .30
379 A176 1r brt pink & multi 1.25 1.00

2nd Lahore Islamic Summit, Feb. 22, 1st anniv.

IWY Emblem and Woman Scientist — A177

**1975, June 15 Litho. Perf. 13**
380 A177 20p multicolored .25 .20
381 A177 2.25r multicolored 1.75 1.75

International Women's Year 1975.

Design: 2.25r, Old woman and girl learning to read and write.

---

International Congress of Mathematical Sciences Dates, Arabic "X" — A178

**1975, July 14 Litho. Perf. 13**
382 A178 20p multicolored .95 .75

International Congress of Mathematical Sciences, Karachi, July 14-20.

Globe with Dates, Arabic "X" — A178

Camel Leather Vase, Pakistan A179

**1975, July 21**
383 A179 20p lilac & multi .40 .25
384 A179 60p violet blk & multi .80 .75
385 A179 1.25r blue & multi 1.25 1.10
Nos. 383-385 (3) 2.45 2.10

60p, Ceramic plate and RCD emblem, Iran, horiz. 1.25r, Porcelain vase, Turkey.

Regional Cooperation for Development Pact among Turkey, Iran and Pakistan.

Black Partridge A181

**1975, Aug. 9 Litho. Perf. 13x13½**
386 A180 20p multicolored .40 .30

Tree Planting Day.

Sapling, Trees and Ant — A180

**1975, Sept. 30 Litho. Perf. 13**
387 A181 20p blue & multi 1.75 .25
388 A181 2.25r yellow & multi 5.75 3.50

Wildlife Protection.

Girls — A182

**1975, Oct. 6**
389 A182 20p multicolored .30 .25

Universal Children's Day.

---

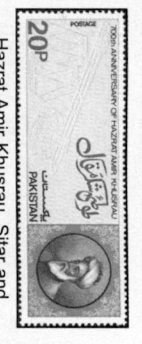

Hazrat Amir Khusrau, Sitar and Tabla — A183

**1975, Oct. 24 Litho. Perf. 14x12½**
390 A183 lt blue & multi .25 .30
391 A183 2.25r pink & multi .75 1.00

700th anniversary of Hazrat Amir Khusrau (1253-1325), musician who invented the sitar and tabla instruments.

Mohammad Iqbal — A184

**1975, Nov. 9**
392 A184 20p multicolored 2.00 .50

Mohammad Allama Iqbal (1877-1938), poet and philosopher, birth centenary.

Wild Sheep of the Punjab — A185

**1975, Dec. 31 Litho. Perf. 13**
393 A185 20p multicolored .75 .25
394 A185 3r multicolored 3.50 2.00

Wildlife Protection. See Nos. 410-411.

Mohenjo-Daro and UNESCO Emblem A186

**1976, Feb. 29 Litho. Perf. 13**
395 A186 10p multicolored 1.00 1.00
396 A186 20p multicolored 1.25 1.25
397 A186 65p multicolored 1.25 1.25
398 A186 3r multicolored 1.25 1.25
399 A186 4r multicolored 7.00 7.00
a. Strip of 5, #395-399 7.00 7.00

View of Mohenjo-Daro excavations.

UNESCO campaign to save Mohenjo-Daro excavations.

Dome and Minaret of Rauza-e-Mubarak Mausoleum — A187

---

**1976, Mar. 3 Photo. Perf. 13½x14**
400 A187 20p blue & multi .20 .20
401 A187 3r gray & multi .80 .60

International Congress on Seerat, the teachings of Mohammed, Mar. 3-15.

Alexander Graham Bell, 1876 Telephone and Dial — A188

**1976, Mar. 10 Litho. Perf. 13**
402 A188 3r blue & multi 2.50 2.50

Centenary of first telephone call by Alexander Graham Bell, Mar. 10, 1876.

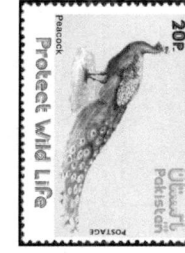

College Emblem — A189

**1976, Mar. 15 Litho. Perf. 13**
403 A189 20p multicolored .30 .30

Cent. of Natl. College of Arts, Lahore.

Peacock A190

**1976, Mar. 31 Litho. Perf. 13**
404 A190 20p lt blue & multi 1.75 .40
405 A190 3r pink & multi 5.50 4.75

Wildlife protection.

Eye and WHO Emblem — A191

**1976, Apr. 7**
406 A191 20p multicolored 1.40 .75

World Health Day: "Foresight prevents blindness."

Mohenjo-Daro, UNESCO Emblem, Bull (from Seal) — A192

**1976, May 31 Litho. Perf. 13**
407 A192 20p multicolored .30 .25

UNESCO campaign to save Mohenjo-Daro excavations.

PAKISTAN

**Trees — A207**

*Perf. 13*
.25 .25

**1977, Aug. 9   Litho.**
434 A207 20p multicolored
Tree planting program.

**Desert A208**

*Perf. 13*
.50 .25

**1977, Sept. 5   Litho.**
435 A208 65p multicolored
UN Conference on Desertification, Nairobi, Kenya. Aug. 29-Sept. 9.

**"Water for the Children" — A209**

*Perf. 14x12½*
.40 .25

**1977, Oct. 3   Litho.**
436 A209 50p multicolored
Universal Children's Day.

**Aga Khan III — A210**

*Perf. 13*
.95 .75

**1977, Nov. 2   Litho.   Rs.2**
437 A210 2r multicolored
Aga Khan III (1877-1957), spiritual ruler of Ismaili sect, statesman, birth centenary.

**Mohammad Iqbal — A211**

*Perf. 13*

**1977, Nov. 9**
438 A211 20p multicolored .60 .60
439 A211 65p multicolored .60 .60
440 A211 1.25r multicolored .70 .70
441 A211 2.25r multicolored .75 .75
442 A211 3r multicolored .85 .85
a. Strip of 5, #438-442 3.50 3.50

20p, Spirit appearing to Iqbal, painting by Behzad. 65p, Iqbal looking at Jamaluddin Afghani & Saeed Halim offering prayers, by Behzad. 1.25r, Verse in Urdu. 2.25r, Verse in Persian.
Mohammad Allama Iqbal (1877-1938), poet and philosopher, birth centenary.

---

**Children Reading A203**

1.25 .30

*Perf. 13*
.75 .30

**1976, Nov. 20**
427 A202 20p multicolored
Quaid-I-Azam Centenary Jamboree, Nov. 1976.

**1976, Dec. 15   Litho.**
428 A203 20p multicolored
Books for children.

**Mohammed Ali Jinnah — A204**

*Lithographed and Embossed*
*Perf. 12½*
3.75 3.75

**1976, Dec. 25**
429 A204 10r gold & green
Mohammed Ali Jinnah (1876-1948), 1st Governor General of Pakistan. An Imperf presentation sheet of 1 exists.

**Farm Family and Village, Tractor, Ambulance A205**

*Perf. 13*
.20 .20

**1977, Apr. 14   Litho.**
430 A205 20p multicolored
Social Welfare and Rural Development Year, 1976-77.

**Terracotta Bullock Cart, Pakistan — A206**

*Perf. 13*
.55 .20
.90 .30
1.25 1.25
2.70 1.75

**1977, July 21   Litho.**
431 A206 20p ultra & multi
432 A206 65p blue green & multi
433 A206 90p lilac & multi
Nos. 431-433 (3)

Designs: 20p, Terra-cotta jug, Turkey. 90p, Decorated jug, Iran.
Regional Cooperation for Development Pact among Pakistan, Turkey and Iran, 13th anniversary.

---

421 A196 1r multicolored .50 .40
422 A197 3r multicolored .75 .50
2.75 2.75
a. Block of 8, #415-422
Mohammed Ali Jinnah (1876-1948), first Governor General of Pakistan, birth centenary. Horizontal rows of types A196 and A197 alternate in sheet.

**Mohenjo-Daro and UNESCO Emblem — A198**

*Perf. 14*
.75 .50

**1976, Aug. 31**
423 A198 65p multicolored
UNESCO campaign to save Mohenjo-Daro excavations.

**Racial Discrimination Emblem — A199**

*Perf. 12½x13½*
.50 .40

**1976, Sept. 15   Litho.**
424 A199 65p multicolored
Fight against racial discrimination.

**Child's Head, Symbols of Health, Education and Food — A200**

*Perf. 13*
.50 .25

**1976, Oct. 4**
425 A200 20p blue & multi
Universal Children's Day.

**Verse by Allama Iqbal A201**

*Perf. 13*
.20 .20

**1976, Nov. 9   Litho.**
426 A201 20p multicolored
Mohammed Allama Iqbal (1877-1938), poet and philosopher, birth centenary.

**Scout Emblem, Jinnah Giving Salute — A202**

---

**Jefferson Memorial, US Bicentennial Emblem — A193**

**Declaration of Independence, by John Trumbull — A194**

*Perf. 13*
1.00 .50

**1976, July 4**
408 A193 90p multicolored

*Perf. 13½x13*
4.50 4.00

409 A194 4r multicolored
American Bicentennial.

**Wildlife Type of 1975**
Wildlife protection: 20p, 3r, Ibex.

**1976, July 12**
410 A185 20p multicolored .50 .35
411 A185 3r multicolored 3.50 2.50

**Mohammed Ali Jinnah — A195**

65p, Riza Shah Pahlavi. 90p, Kemal Ataturk.

**1976, July 21   Litho.   Perf. 14**
412 A195 20p multicolored 1.00 .50
413 A195 65p multicolored 1.00 .50
414 A195 90p multicolored 1.00 .50
a. Strip of 3, #412-414 3.25 3.25
Regional Cooperation for Development Pact among Pakistan, Turkey and Iran, 12th anniversary.

**Ornament A196**

**Jinnah and Wazir Mansion A197**

Designs (Jinnah and): 40p, Sind Madressah (building). 50p, Minar Qarardad (minaret). 3r, Mausoleum.

**1976, Aug. 14   Litho.   Perf. 13½**
415 A196 5p multicolored .25 .20
416 A196 10p multicolored .25 .20
417 A196 15p multicolored .25 .20
418 A197 20p multicolored .25 .20
419 A197 40p multicolored .25 .20
420 A197 50p multicolored .25 .20

## Holy Kaaba, Mecca A212

**1977, Nov. 21**    **Perf. 14**
443 A212 65p green & multi ... .50 .25
1977 pilgrimage to Mecca.

Healthy and Sick Bodies — A213

**1977, Dec. 19**    **Litho.**    **Perf. 13**
444 A213 65p blue green & multi ... .50 .25
World Rheumatism Year.

**1978, Feb. 5**    **Litho.**    **Perf. 12½x13½**
445 A214 75p multicolored ... .50 .20
Indonesia-Pakistan Economic and Cultural Cooperation Organization.

Woman from Rawalpindi-Islamabad — A214

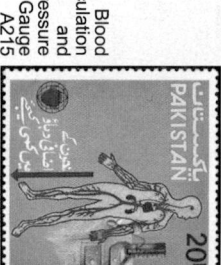

**1978, Apr. 20**    **Litho.**    **Perf. 13**
446 A215 20p blue & multi ... .30 .20
447 A215 2r yellow & multi ... 1.00 .75
Campaign against hypertension.

Blood Circulation and Pressure Gauge A215

Re.1

HENRY DUNANT 1828-1910

Henri Dunant, Red Cross, Red Crescent A216

**1978, May 8**    **Perf. 14**
448 A216 1r multicolored ... 2.00 .25
Henri Dunant (1828-1910), founder of Red Cross, 150th birth anniversary.

---

## Red Roses, Pakistan — A217

**1978, July 21**    **Litho.**    **Perf. 13½**
449 A217 20p multicolored ... .60 .20
450 A217 85p multicolored ... .85 .20
451 A217 90p multicolored ... 1.25 .35
a.   Strip of 3, #449-451 ... 2.75 2.75
Regional Cooperation for Development Pact among Turkey, Iran and Pakistan.

90p, Pink roses, Iran, 2r, Yellow rose, Turkey.

**1978, Nov. 20**    **Litho.**    **Perf. 13**
457 A222 1r multicolored ... .50 .20
Anti-Apartheid Year.

"Four Races" — A222

Hockey Stick and Ball, Championship Cup — A218

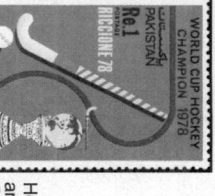

**1978, Aug. 26**    **Litho.**    **Perf. 13**
452 A218 1r multicolored ... 2.25 .25
453 A219 2r multicolored ... .75 .30
Riccione 78, 30th International Stamp Fair, Riccione, Italy, Aug. 26-28. No. 452 also commemorates Pakistan as World Hockey Cup Champion.

Fair Building, Fountain, Piazza Tourismo A219

**1978, Sept. 3**
454 A220 75p multicolored ... .50 .20
UN Conference on Technical Cooperation among Developing Countries, Buenos Aires, Argentina, Sept. 1978.

Globe and Cogwheels A220

St. Patrick's Cathedral, Karachi A221

**1978, Sept. 29**    **Litho.**    **Perf. 13**
455 A221 1r multicolored ... .20 .20
456 A221 2r multicolored ... .65 .25
St. Patrick's Cathedral, Karachi, centenary.

Design: 2r, Stained-glass window.

---

## Maulana Jauhar — A223

**1978, Dec. 10**    **Litho.**    **Perf. 13**
458 A223 50p multicolored ... .65 .25
Maulana Muhammad Ali Jauhar, writer, journalist and patriot, birth centenary.

Qararlad Monument A224

Type of 1957 and

Tomb of Ibrahim Khan Makli — A225a

Tractor A225

**1978-81**    **Engr.**
459 A224 2p dark green ... .20 .20
460 A224 3p black ... .20 .20
461 A224 5p violet blue ... .20 .20

**Engr.; Litho. (10p, 25p, 40p, 50p, 90p)**
462 A225 5p lt blue & blk ('79) ... .20 .20
463 A225 10p yel green ('79) ... .40 .20
464 A225 25p rose car & grn ('79) ... .20 .20
465 A225 40p carmine & blue ('79) ... .20 .20
466 A225 50p bl grn & vio ('79) ... .25 .20
467 A225 60p black ... .20 .20
468 A225 75p dull red ... .50 .20
469 A225 90p blue & carmine ... .20 .20

**Perf. 13½x13**
**Engr.**
470 A225a 1r olive ('80) ... .75 .20
471 A225a 1.50r dp orange ... .20 .20

**Wmk. 351**
472 A225a 2r car rose ('79) ... .20 .20
473 A225a 3r indigo ('80) ... .20 .20
474 A225a 4r black ('81) ... .20 .20
475 A225a 5r dk brn ('81) ... .20 .20
475A A26 15r rose lil & red ... .20 .20

**Perf. 14**
Nos. 459-475A (18) ... 1.50 1.50
... 6.00 4.90

Lithographed stamps, type A225, have bottom panel in solid color with colorless lettering and numerals 2mm high instead of 3mm. For overprints see Nos. O94-O110.

---

## Tornado Jet Fighter, de Havilland Rapide and Flyer A — A226

**1978, Dec. 24**    **Litho.**    **Unwmk.**    **Perf. 13**
476 A226 65p multicolored ... 1.60 1.60
477 A226 1r multicolored ... 1.90 1.90
478 A226 2r multicolored ... 2.00 2.00
479 A226 2.25r multicolored ... 2.00 2.00
a.   Block of 4, #476-479 ... 7.50 7.50
75th anniv. of 1st powered flight.

Wright Flyer A and; 1r, Phantom, F4F jet fighter & Tristar airliner; 2r, Bell X15 fighter & TU-104 airliner; 2.25r, MiG fighter & Concorde.

Koran Lighting the World and Mohammed's Tomb — A227

**1979, Feb. 10**    **Litho.**    **Perf. 13**
480 A227 20p multicolored ... .50 .20
Mohammed's birth anniversary.

Mother and Children A228

**1979, Feb. 25**
481 A228 50p multicolored ... .95 .25
APWA Services, 30th anniversary.

Lophophorus Impejanus — A229

**1979, June 17**    **Litho.**    **Perf. 13**
482 A229 20p multicolored ... 1.60 .40
483 A229 25p multicolored ... 1.60 .75
484 A229 40p multicolored ... 2.10 1.50
485 A229 1r multicolored ... 4.00 1.60
Nos. 482-485 (4) ... 9.30 4.25
Pheasants: 25p, Lophura leucomelana. 40p, Puccrasia macrolopha. 1r, Catreus wallichii.

For overprint see No. 525.

No. 485 Overprinted: "World Tourism Conference/Manila 80"

**1980, Sept. 27**
525 A229 1r multicolored ... 1.40 .50

World Tourism Conf., Manila, Sept. 27.

Birth Centenary of Mohammed Shairani — A245

**1980, Oct. 5**  *Litho.*  *Perf. 13*
526 A245 40p multicolored ... .50 .45

Aga Khan Architecture Award — A246

**1980, Oct. 23**  *Litho.*  *Perf. 13½*
527 A246 2r multicolored ... .75 .45

Rising Sun A247

**1981, Mar. 7**  *Litho.*  *Perf. 13*
Size: 30x41mm
528 A247 40p Hegira emblem ... .20 .40

**1980, Nov. 6**  *Litho.*  *Perf. 13*
529 A247 40p shown ... .20 .25

*Perf. 14*
Size: 33x33mm
530 A247 2r Moslem symbols ... .20 .35

Size: 31x54mm  *Perf. 13x13½*
531 A247 3r Globe, hands holding Koran ... .25 .50

**Souvenir Sheet**  *Imperf*
Nos. 528-531(4) ... .85 1.50

532 A247 4r Candles ... 1.00 .75

Hegira (Pilgrimage Year).

Airmail Service, 50th Anniversary — A248

Postal History: No. 533, Postal card cent.
No. 534, Money order service cent.

---

Pakistan International Airline, 25th Anniversary — A240

**1980, Jan. 10**  *Litho.*  *Perf. 13*
516 A240 1r multicolored ... 2.75 1.00

Infant, Rose — A241

**1980, Feb. 16**  *Perf. 13*
517 A241 50p multicolored ... 1.25 1.25

5th Asian Congress of Pediatric Surgery, Karachi, Feb. 16-19.

Conference Emblem A242

**1980, May 17**  *Litho.*  *Perf. 13*
518 A242 1r multicolored ... 1.10 .50

11th Islamic Conference of Foreign Ministers, Islamabad, May 17-21.

Lighthouse, Oil Terminal, Map Showing Karachi Harbor — A243

**1980, July 15**  *Perf. 13½*
519 A243 1r multicolored ... 2.50 1.10

Karachi Port, cent. of independent management.

Nos. 494-497 Overprinted in Red:
RICCIONE 80

**1980, Aug. 30**  *Litho.*  *Perf. 14x12½*
520 A233 40p multicolored ... .40 .60
521 A233 75p multicolored ... .50 .60
522 A233 1r multicolored ... .55 .65
523 A233 1r multicolored ... .75 .75
a. Block of 4, #520-523 ... 2.50 3.00

RICCIONE 80 International Stamp Exhibition, Riccione, Italy, Aug. 30-Sept. 2.

Quetta Command and Staff College, 75th Anniversary A244

**1980, Sept. 18**  *Litho.*  *Perf. 13*
524 A244 1r multicolored ... .20 .20

---

Fight Against Cancer A234

**1979, Nov. 12**  *Unwmk.*  *Litho.*  *Perf. 14*
499 A234 40p multicolored ... 1.10 .70

Pakistan Customs Service Centenary — A235

**1979, Dec. 10**  *Perf. 13x13½*
500 A235 1r multicolored ... .65 .25

"1378" is a plate flaw, not an error.

Tippu Sultan Shaheed — A236

**19/9, Mar. 23**  *Wmk. 351*  *Perf. 14*
501 A236 10r shown ... .75 .90
502 A236 15r Syed Ahmad Khan ... 1.00 1.10
503 A236 25r Altaf Hussain Hali ... 1.25 1.25
a. Strip of 3, #601 603 ... 3.25 6.00

Soo No. 600.

Ornament — A239

A237
A238
A239

**1980**  *Perf. 12x11½, 11½x12*  *Unwmk.*
506 A237 10p dk grn & yel org ... .20 .20
507 A237 15p dk grn & apple grn ... .20 .20
508 A237 25p multicolored ... .20 .25
509 A237 35p multicolored ... .20 .25
510 A238 40p red & lt brown ... .20 .25
511 A239 50p olive & vio bl ... .20 .30
512 A239 80p black & yel grn ... 1.40 1.65
Nos. 506-512 (7)

Issued: 25, 35, 50, 80p, 3/10; others, 1/15.
See Nos. 506-512.

---

At the Well, by Allah Baksh — A230

Paintings: 75p, Potters, by Kamalel Molk, Iran. 1.60r, Plowing, by Namik Ismail, Turkey.

**1979, July 21**  *Litho.*  *Perf. 14x13*
486 A230 40p multicolored ... .35 .20
487 A230 75p multicolored ... .35 .20
488 A230 1.60r multicolored ... .40 .20
a. Strip of 3, #486-488 ... 1.10 1.10

Regional Cooperation for Development Pact among Pakistan, Iran and Turkey, 15th anniversary.

Guj Embroidery — A231

Handicrafts: 1r, Enamel inlay brass plate. 1.50r, Baskets. 2r, Peacock, embroidered rug.

**1979, Aug. 23**  *Litho.*  *Perf. 14x13*
489 A231 40p multicolored ... .25 .20
490 A231 1r multicolored ... .30 .20
491 A231 1.50r multicolored ... .40 .20
492 A231 2r multicolored ... .45 .20
a. Block of 4, #489-492 ... 1.40 1.40

Children, IYC and SOS Emblems — A232

**1979, Sept. 10**  *Litho.*  *Perf. 13*
493 A232 50p multicolored ... .65 .30

SOS Children's Village, Lahore, opening.

Playground, IYC Emblem — A233

IYC Emblem and: Children's drawings.

**1979, Oct. 22**  *Perf. 14x12½*
494 A233 40p multicolored ... .25 .20
495 A233 75p multicolored ... .30 .20
496 A233 1r multicolored ... .40 .20
497 A233 1.50r multicolored ... .45 .20
a. Block of 4, #494-497 ... 1.40 1.40

**Souvenir Sheet**  *Imperf*
498 A233 2r multi, vert. ... 2.10 2.10

IYC. For overprints see #520-523.

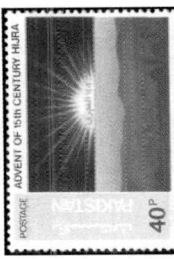

**1980-81**

| | | | |
|---|---|---|---|
| 533 | A248 | 40p multi, vert. | .50 .35 |
| 534 | A248 | 40p multi, vert. | .50 .35 |
| 535 | A248 | 1r multi | .90 .20 |

*Nos. 533-535 (3)*

Issued: #533, 12/27; #534, 12/20; #535, 2/15/81.

Heinrich von Stephan, UPU Emblem A249

**1981, Jan. 7**    **Perf. 13½**

536 A249 1r multicolored .50 .20

Von Stephan (1831-97), founder of UPU.

Conference Emblem, Afghan Refugee A250

Conference Emblem, UPU Emblem A249

Conference Emblem, Participants, Men — A251

Rs.2 AFGHAN REFUGEES

Conference Emblem, Map of Afghanistan — A252

85p 3rd Islamic Summit Conference

Conference Emblem in Ornament A253

Conference Emblem, Flags of Participants A254

**1981, Mar. 29**    **Litho.**    **Perf. 13**

| | | | |
|---|---|---|---|
| 537 | A250 | 40p multicolored | .45 .20 |
| 538 | A251 | 40p multicolored | .50 .20 |
| 539 | A250 | 1r multicolored | .80 .20 |

3rd Islamic Summit Conference, Makkah al-Mukarramah, Jan. 25-28.

**1981, Mar. 29**    **Perf. 13½**

| | | | |
|---|---|---|---|
| 540 | A251 | 1r multicolored | .80 .20 |
| 541 | A252 | 2r multicolored | .95 .35 |

*Nos. 537-541 (5)*    3.50 1.15

**1981, Mar. 29**    **Perf. 13½**

| | | | |
|---|---|---|---|
| 542 | A253 | 40p multicolored | .20 .20 |
| 543 | A254 | 40p multicolored | .20 .20 |
| 544 | A253 | 85p multicolored | .30 .25 |
| 545 | A254 | 85p multicolored | .40 .25 |

*Nos. 542-545 (4)*    1.10 .90

Kemal Ataturk (1881-1938), First President of Turkey — A255

**1981, May 19**    **Litho.**    **Perf. 13x13½**

546 A255 1r multicolored .35 .20

Green Turtle A256

**1981, June 20**    **Litho.**    **Perf. 12x11½**

547 A256 40p multicolored 1.75 .40

Palestinian Cooperation A257

FOR THE WELFARE OF THE FAMILIES OF MARTYRS AND FREEDOM FIGHTERS OF PALESTINE

**1981, July 25**    **Litho.**    **Perf. 13**

548 A257 2r multicolored .65 .25

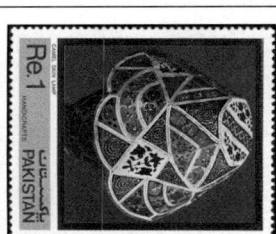

Mountain Ranges and Peaks — A258

**1981, Aug. 20**    **Perf. 14x13½**

| | | | |
|---|---|---|---|
| 549 | A258 | 40p Malubiting West. range | .65 .30 |
| 550 | | 40p Peak | .65 .30 |
| a. | | Pair, #549-550 | 1.40 1.40 |
| 551 | A258 | 1r Mt. Maramosh, range | 1.00 .40 |
| 552 | | 1r Mt. Maramosh, Peak | 1.00 .50 |
| a. | | Pair, #551-552 | 1.25 .60 |
| 553 | | 1.50 K6, range | 2.00 2.00 |
| 554 | | 1.50 Peak | 2.00 2.00 |
| a. | | Pair, #553-554 | 1.60 1.00 |
| 555 | | 2r K2, range | 2.50 2.50 |
| 556 | | 2r Peak | 3.25 3.25 |
| a. | | Pair, #555-556 | |

*Nos. 549-556 (8)*    9.00 4.80

Inauguration of Pakistan Steel Furnace No. 1, Karachi A260

**1981, Aug. 31**    **Perf. 13**    **Litho.**

| | | | |
|---|---|---|---|
| 557 | A260 | 40p multicolored | .25 .20 |
| 558 | A260 | 2r multicolored | .70 .75 |

Western Tragopan in Summer A261

**1981, Sept. 15**    **Litho.**    **Perf. 14**

| | | | |
|---|---|---|---|
| 559 | A261 | 40p shown | 2.50 .50 |
| 560 | A261 | 2r Winter | 6.00 3.25 |

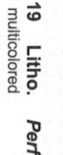

Intl. Year of the Disabled A262

**1981, Dec. 12**    **Litho.**    **Perf. 13**

| | | | |
|---|---|---|---|
| 561 | A262 | 40p multicolored | .30 .30 |
| 562 | A262 | 2r multicolored | 1.25 1.00 |

World Cup Championship A263

**1982, Jan. 31**    **Litho.**    **Perf. 13½x13**

| | | | |
|---|---|---|---|
| 563 | A263 | 1r Cup, flags in arc | 2.75 1.00 |
| 564 | A263 | 1r shown | 2.75 1.00 |
| a. | | Pair, #563-564 | 5.50 5.50 |

Camel Skin Lampshade A264

**1982, Feb. 20**    **Litho.**    **Perf. 14**

| | | | |
|---|---|---|---|
| 565 | A264 | 1r shown | .75 .50 |
| 566 | A264 | 1r Hala pottery | .75 .50 |

See Nos. 582-583.

Independence Day — A269

**1982, Aug. 14**    **Litho.**    **Perf. 13**

| | | | |
|---|---|---|---|
| 572 | A269 | 40p Flag | .20 .20 |
| 573 | A269 | 85p Map | .30 .30 |

**1982, Aug. 28**

574 A268 1r multicolored .30 .20

No. 571 Overprinted: "RICCIONE-82/1932-1982"

RICCIONE '82 Intl. Stamp Exhibition, Riccione, Italy, Aug. 28-30.

50th Anniv. of Sukkur Barrage — A268

**1982, July 17**    **Litho.**    **Perf. 13**

571 A268 1r multicolored .45 .25

For overprint see No. 574.

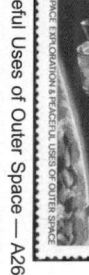

Peaceful Uses of Outer Space — A267

**1982, June 7**    **Litho.**    **Perf. 13**

570 A267 1r multicolored 3.00 1.00

No. 570 was printed with a vertical strip of labels, picturing different space satellites, in the middle of each sheet, allowing for pairs with label between.

Blind Indus Dolphin A266

**1982, Apr. 24**    **Litho.**    **Perf. 12x11½**

| | | | |
|---|---|---|---|
| 568 | A266 | 40p Dolphin | 3.00 .75 |
| 569 | A266 | 1r Dolphin, diff. | 5.00 1.50 |

TB Bacillus Centenary A265

**1982, Mar. 24**

567 A265 1r multicolored 1.75 .75

Jehangir Khan (b. 1963), World Squash Champion A286

**1984, Mar. 17** Litho. *Perf. 13*
605 A286 3r multicolored 3.50 1.25

Pakistan Intl. Airway China Service, 20th Anniv. A287

**1984, Apr. 29** Litho. *Perf. 13*
606 A287 3r Jet 8.00 5.00

Glass Work, Lahore Fort — A288

Various glass panels.

**1984, May 31** Litho. *Perf. 13*
607 A288 1r green & multi .35 .20
608 A288 1r purple & multi .35 .20
609 A288 1r vermilion & multi .35 .20
610 A288 1r brt blue & multi .36 .20
a. Nos. 607-610 (4) 1.40 .80

Forts — A289

**1984-88** Litho. *Perf. 11*
613 A289 5p Kot Diji .20 .20
614 A289 10p Rohtas .20 .20
615 A289 15p Bala Hissar ('86) .20 .20
616 A289 20p Attock .20 .20
617 A289 50p Hydorabad ('86) .20 .20
818 A289 60p Lahore .30 .20
619 A289 70p Sibi ('88) .30 .20
620 A289 80p Rankot ('86) .30 1.60
Nos. 613-620 (8) 1.70 1.60
Issued: 5p, 11/1; 10p, 9/25; 80p, 7/1.
For overprints see Nos. O118-O124.

Shah Rukn-i-Alam Tomb, Multan — A290

THE AGA KHAN AWARD FOR ARCHITECTURE

**1984, June 26** Litho. *Perf. 13*
624 A290 60p multicolored 2.75 1.25
Aga Khan Award for Architecture.

---

WORLD FOOD DAY

World Food Day A281

**1983, Oct. 9** Litho. *Perf. 13*
593 A280 2r multicolored .85 .25
Size: 33x33mm
594 A280 3r Symbol, diff. .30 .25

**1983, Oct. 24** Litho. *Perf. 13*
595 A281 3r Livestock 2.00 1.25
596 A281 3r Fruit 2.00 1.25
597 A281 3r Grain 2.00 1.25
598 A281 3r Seafood 2.00 1.25
a. Strip of 4, #595-598 8.25 7.50

A282

NATIONAL STAMP EXHIBITION 15, 18 NOV. 1983

**1983, Oct. 24** Litho. *Perf. 13½*
599 A282 60p multicolored .20 .20
National Fertilizer Corp.

A283

**1983, Nov. 13** Litho. *Perf. 13*
600 Strip of 6, View of Lahore City, 1852 4.00 4.00
a.-f. A283 60p any single .65 .40
PAKPHILEX '83 Natl. Stamp Exhibition.

Yachting Victory in 9th Asian Games, 1982 — A284

IX ASIAN GAMES DELHI 1982

**1983, Dec. 31** Litho. *Perf. 13*
601 A284 60p OK Dinghy 2.75 1.50
602 A284 60p Enterprise 2.75 1.50

Snow Leopard — A285

SNOW LEOPARD Panthera uncia

**1984, Jan. 21** *Perf. 14*
603 A285 40p lt green & multi 3.00 1.00
604 A285 1.60r blue & multi 8.75 5.00

---

TREKKING IN PAKISTAN

Yak Caravan, Zindiharam-Darkot Pass, Hindu Kush Mountains — A275

**1983, Apr. 28** Litho. *Perf. 13*
585 A275 1r multicolored 2.50 .50

MARSH CROCODILE Crocodilus palustre

Marsh Crocodile A276

**1983, May 19** *Perf. 13½x14*
586 A276 3r multicolored 5.75 1.50

**1983, June 20** Litho. *Perf. 14*
Size: 50x40mm
587 A276 1r Gazelle 4.00 1.50

36th Anniv. of Independence A277

**1983, Aug. 14**
588 A277 60p Star .20 .20
589 A277 4r Torch .35 .30

25th Anniv. of Indonesia-Pakistan Economic and Cultural Cooperation Org. — A278

Weavings.

**1983, Aug. 19** Litho. *Perf. 13*
590 A278 2r Pakistani (geometric) .30 .20
591 A278 2r Indonesian (figures) .30 .20

Siberian Cranes — A279

Grus leucogeranus

**1983, Sept. 8** *Perf. 13½*
592 A279 3r multicolored 6.00 3.00

WORLD COMMUNICATIONS YEAR 1983

World Communications Year — A280

---

100 YEARS OF THE UNIVERSITY OF THE PUNJAB 1882 1982

University of the Punjab Centenary — A270

**1982, Oct. 14** Litho. *Perf. 13½*
575 A270 40p multicolored 1.00 .30
No. 575 was printed with a vertical strip of labels, picturing different university buildings, in the middle of each sheet, allowing for pairs with label between.

Scouting Year — A271

75th ANNIVERSARY OF THE SCOUT MOVEMENT 1982

**1982, Dec. 23** Litho. *Perf. 13*
576 A271 2r Emblem .75 .35

Inauguration Quetta Natural Gas Line Project

Quetta Natural Gas Pipeline Project A272

**1983, Jan. 6** Litho. *Perf. 13*
577 A272 1r multicolored .30 .20

Common Peacock A273

Papilio polytes

**1983, Feb. 15** Litho. *Perf. 14*
578 A273 40p shown 1.75 .20
579 A273 50p Common rose 2.25 .20
580 A273 60p Plain tiger 2.50 .50
581 A273 1.50r Lemon butterfly 3.50 2.00
Nos. 578-581 (4) 10.00 2.90

Handicraft Type of 1982

**1983, Mar. 9**
582 A264 1r Straw mats .20 .20
583 A264 1r Five-flower cloth design .20 .20

THE AGA KHAN UNIVERSITY

Opening of Aga Khan University — A274

**1983, Mar. 16** *Perf. 13½*
584 A274 2r multicolored .30 .25
No. 584 was printed with a vertical strip of labels, picturing different university views, in the middle of each sheet, allowing for pairs with label between.

**1984, July 1**   Litho.   Perf. 13
625 A290a 3r multicolored   1.10 .50
Asia-Pacific Broadcasting Union, 20th Anniv. — A290a

**1984 Los Angeles Olympics**
1984 Summer Olympics, Los Angeles — A291
626 A291 3r Athletics   1.75 1.00
627 A291 3r Boxing   1.75 1.00
628 A291 3r Hockey   1.75 1.00
629 A291 3r Yachting   1.75 1.00
630 A291 3r Wrestling   8.75 5.00
Nos. 626-630 (5)
Issued in sheets of 10.

**1984, July 31**

**1984, Aug. 14**
631 A292 60p Jasmine   .20 .20
632 A292 4r Lighted torch   .45 .35
Independence, 37th Anniv. — A292

**1984, Sept. 1**
633 A293 60p multicolored   .65 .25
Intl. Trade Fair, Sept. 1-21, Karachi A293

1984 Natl Tourism Convention, Karachi, Nov. 5-8 — A293a

PAKISTAN TOURISM CONVENTION 1984

**1984, Nov. 5**   Litho.   Perf. 13½
634 Strip of 5   3.50 3.00
a.-e. A293a 1r any single   .70 .40
Shah Jahan Mosque: a, Main dome interior. b, Tile work. c, Entrance. d, Archways. e, Dome interior, diff.

---

**1984, Nov. 7**
635 A294 60p multicolored   .80 .50
United Bank Limited, 25th Anniv. A294

**1984, Dec. 24**   Perf. 14½x14
636 A294a 60p multicolored   1.00 .35
UNCTAD, UN Conference on Trade and Development, 20th Anniv. — A294a

**1984, Dec. 29**   Perf. 13½x14
637 A295 60p multicolored   .70 .20
638 A295 1r multicolored   .90 .20
Postal Life Insurance, Cent. — A295

**1984, Dec. 31**
639 A296 2r Unicorn, rock painting   2.00 .60
640 A296 2r Unicorn seal, round   4.25 4.25
a. Pair, #639-640   4.25
Restoration of Mohenjo-Daro.
UNESCO World Heritage Campaign A296

IYY, Girl Guides '75th Anniv. A297
**1985, Jan. 5**   Perf. 13½
641 A297 60p Emblems   4.00 1.25

---

Smelting A298

Pouring Steel — A299
**1985, Jan. 15**   Perf. 13
642 A298 60p multicolored   1.00 .30
643 A299 1r multicolored   1.60 .40

**1985, Mar. 20**   Litho.   Perf. 13
644 A300 60p Map, sunburst   1.25 .40
Referendum Reinstating Pres. Zia — A300

Minar-e-Qararadad-e-Pakistan Tower — A301
**1985, Mar. 23**
645 A301 1r multicolored   .90 .25
646 A302 1r multicolored   .90 .25
1985 Elections.
Ballot Box A302

Mountaineering — A303
KARAKORAM

---

**1985, May 27**   Litho.   Perf. 14
647 A303 40p Mt. Rakaposhi, Karakoram   3.00 .75
648 A303 2r Mt. Nangaparbat, Western Himalayas   6.75 5.00

Championship Pakistani Men's Field Hockey Team — A304
Design: 1984 Olympic gold medal, 1985 Dhaka Asia Cup, 1982 Bombay World Cup.
**1985, June 5**   Litho.   Perf. 13
649 A304 1r multicolored   4.00 1.25

King Edward Medical College, Lahore, 125th Anniv. — A305
**1985, July 28**   Litho.   Perf. 13
650 A305 3r multicolored   2.75 .75

Nat. Independence Day — A306
Designs: No. 651a, 37th Independence Day written in English. No. 651b, In Urdu.
**1985, Aug. 14**
651 Pair + 2 labels   .65 .65
a.-b. A306 60p any single   .30 .25
Printed in sheets of 4 stamps + 4 labels.

Sind Madressah-Tul-Islam, Karachi, Education Cent. — A307
**1985, Sept. 1**
652 A307 2r multicolored   2.50 .75

Mosque, Jinnah Avenue, Karachi — A308
**1985, Sept. 14**
653 A308 1r Mosque by day   1.25 .30
654 A308 1r At night   1.25 .30
35th anniv. of the Jamia Masjid Pakistan Security Printing Corporation's miniature replica of the Badshahi Mosque, Lahore.

Lawrence College, Murree, 125th Anniv. — A309

**1985, Sept. 21**
655 A309 3r multicolored   3.00 .75

UN, 40th Anniv. — A310

*Perf. 14x14½*   **Litho.**
**1985, Oct. 24**
656 A310 1r UN building, sun   .50 .20
657 A310 2r Building emblem   .80 .30

10th Natl. Scouting Jamboree, Lahore, Nov. 8-15 — A311

*Perf. 13*
**1985, Nov. 8**
658 A311 60p multicolored   3.76 1.50

Islamabad and Capital Development Authority Emblem — A312

*Perf. 14½*
**1985, Nov. 30**
659 A312 3r multicolored   2.75 .50
Islamabad, capital of Pakistan, 25th anniv.

Flags and Map of SAARC Nations A313

Flags as Flower Petals A314

*Perf. 13½, 13*
**1985, Dec. 8**
660 A313 1r multicolored   3.00 3.00
661 A314 2r multicolored   1.50 1.50
SAARC, South Asian Assoc. for Regional Cooperation.

---

Dove and World Map A315

*Perf. 13*
**1985, Dec. 14**
662 A315 60p multicolored   1.25 .40
UN Declaration on the Granting of Independence to Colonial Countries and Peoples, 25th Anniv.

Shaheen Falcon — A316

*Perf. 13½x14*
**1986, Jan. 20**
663 A316 1.50r multicolored   7.25 4.00

Agricultural Development Bank, Anniv. — A317

*Perf. 13*   **Litho.**
**1986, Feb. 18**
664 A317 60p multicolored   1.25 .35

Sadiq Egerton College, Bahawalpur, Cent. — A318

**1986, Apr. 25**
665 A318 1r multicolored   3.25 .75

A319

A320

*Perf. 13½*
**1986, May 11**
666 A319 1r multicolored   3.75 .75
Asian Productivity Organization, 25th anniv.

---

Independence Day, 39th anniv.

*Perf. 14½x14*   **Litho.**
**1986, Aug. 14**
667 A320 80p "1947-1986"   1.00 .30
668 A320 1r Urdu text, fireworks   1.00 .30

A321
A322

Intl. Literacy Day.

*Perf. 13*
**1986, Sept. 8**
669 A321 1r Teacher, students   1.60 .40

UN Child Survival Campaign.

*Perf. 13½x13*   **Litho.**
**1986, Oct. 28**
670 A322 80p multicolored   2.75 .35

Aitchison College, Lahore, Cent. — A323

*Perf. 13½*
**1986, Nov. 3**
671 A323 2.50r multicolored   .95 .25

Intl. Peace Year — A324

*Perf. 13*
**1986, Nov. 20**
672 A324 4r multicolored   .50 .30

4th Asian Cup Table Tennis Tournament, Karachi A325

*Perf. 14½*
**1986, Nov. 25**
673 A325 2r multicolored   3.25 .50

---

Marcopolo Sheep — A326

*Perf. 14*   **Litho.**
**1986, Dec. 4**
674 A326 2r multicolored   4.75 2.50
See No. 698.

Eco Philex '86 — A327

Mosques: No. 675a, Selimiye, Turkey. No. 675b, Gawhar Shad, Iran. No. 675c, Grand Mosque, Pakistan.

*Perf. 13*
**1986, Dec. 20**   Strip of 3
675 A327   6.25 5.00
a.-c. 3r, any single   2.00 1.00

St. Patrick's School, Karachi, 125th Anniv. — A328

*Perf. 13*   **Litho.**
**1987, Jan. 29**
676 A328 5r multicolored   2.75 .75

Savings Bank Week — A329

Birds, berries and: a. National defense. b. Education. c. Agriculture. d. Industry.

*Perf. 13*   **Litho.**
**1987, Feb. 21**
677 A329 Block of 4 + 2 labels   6.25 5.00
a.-d. 5r any single   1.50 .50

Parliament House Opening, Islamabad — A330

*Perf. 13*
**1987, Mar. 23**
678 A330 3r multicolored   .30 .20

**ERADICATE NARCOTICS** — A331

Fight Against
Drug Abuse
A331

**1987, June 30     Litho.**
679  A331  1r multicolored     .75  .20

Natl. flag and: 80p, Natl. anthem, written in Urdu. 3r, Jinnah's first natl. address, the Minar-e-Qararadad-e-Pakistan and natl. coat of arms.

Natl. Independence, 40th
Anniv. — A332

**1987, Aug. 14     Litho.     Perf. 13**
680  A332  80p multicolored     .30  .20
681  A332  3r  multicolored     1.00  .25

Miniature Sheet

Air Force, 40th Anniv. — A333

**1987, Sept. 7     Litho.     Perf. 13½**
682      Sheet of 10     20.00  17.50
a.-j.  A333  3r any single     1.50  1.00

Aircraft: a. Tempest II. b. Hawker Fury. c. Super Marine Attacker. d. F86 Sabre. e. F104 Star Fighter. f. C130 Hercules. g. F6. h. Mirage III. i. A5. j. F16 Fighting Falcon.

Tourism Convention 1987 — A334

**1987, Oct. 1     Perf. 13**
683      Block of 4     4.50  3.00
a.-d.  A334  1.50r any single     1.00  .30

Views along Karakoram Highway: a. Pasu Glacier. b. Apricot trees. c. Highway winding through hills. d. Khunjerab peak.

---

Shah Abdul Latif Bhitai
Mausoleum — A335

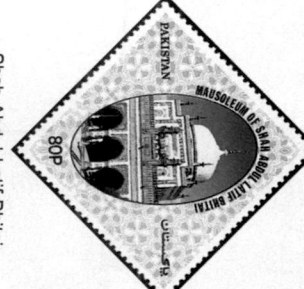

**1987, Oct. 8     Perf. 13**
684  A335  80p multicolored     .35  .20

D.J. Sind Government Science
College, Karachi, Cent. — A336

**1987, Nov. 7**
685  A336  80p multicolored     .35  .20

College of Physicians and Surgeons,
25th Anniv. — A337

**1987, Dec. 9     Litho.     Perf. 13**
686  A337  1r multicolored     1.00  .25

Intl. Year of
Shelter for the
Homeless
A338

**1987, Dec. 15**
687  A338  3r multicolored     .50  .25

Cathedral Church of the Resurrection,
Lahore, Cent. — A339

**1987, Dec. 20**
688  A339  3r multicolored     .65  .25

---

Radio
Pakistan
A341

**1987, Dec. 31**
690  A341  80p multicolored     .35  .20

Jamshed Nusserwanjee Mehta (1886-1952), Mayor of Karachi, Member of the Sind Legislative Assembly — A342

**1988, Jan. 7**
691  A342  3r multicolored     .45  .25

World Leprosy
Day — A343

**1988, Jan. 31**
692  A343  3r multicolored     .95  .25

World Health Organization, 40th
Anniv. — A344

**1988, Apr. 7     Litho.     Perf. 13**
693  A344  4r multicolored     .95  .30

Intl. Red Cross
and Red
Crescent
Organizations,
125th
Anniv. — A345

**1988, May 8**
694  A345  3r multicolored     .50  .25

---

Natl. Postal
Service,
40th Anniv.
A340

**1987, Dec. 28**
689  A340  3r multicolored     .65  .25

1988 Summer Olympics,
Seoul — A347

Miniature Sheet

**1988, Sept. 17     Litho.     Perf. 13½x13**
697      Sheet of 10-32 labels     17.00  14.00
a.-j.  A347  1r any single     1.50  .75

Labels contained in No. 697. Seoul Games character trademark or emblem. Size of No. 697: 261x214mm.

Events: a. Discus, shot put, hammer throw, javelin. b. Relay, hurdles, running, walking. c. High jump, long jump, triple jump, pole vault. d. Gymnastics floor exercises, rings, parallel bars. e. Table tennis, tennis, field hockey, baseball. f. Volleyball, soccer, basketball, team handball. g. Wrestling, judo, boxing, weight lifting. h. Sport pistol, fencing, rifle shooting, archery. i. Swimming, diving, yachting, quadruple-sculling, kayaking. j. Equestrian jumping, cycling, steeplechase.

Fauna Type of 1986

**1988, Oct. 29     Litho.     Perf. 14**
698  A326  2r Suleman markhor, vert.     1.00  .40

Pioneers of Freedom Type of 1979

**1989, Jan. 23     Litho.     Wmk. 351**
699  A236  3r Maulana Hasrat Mohani     .20  .20

---

Independence Day, 41st
Anniv. — A346

**1988, Aug. 14     Litho.     Perf. 13½**
695  A346  80p multicolored     .30  .25
696  A346  4r multicolored     .30  .25

Islamia College, Peshawar, 75th
Anniv. — A348

**1988, Dec. 22     Unwmk.     Perf. 13½**
700  A348  3r multicolored     .50  .20

SAARC Summit Conference,
Islamabad — A349

**1988, Dec. 29     Perf. 14**
701  A349  25r shown     1.75  1.00

**Size: 33x33mm**
702  A349  50r multicolored     4.00  2.00

Designs: 25r, Flags, symbols of commerce. 50r, Globe, communication and transportation. 75r, Bangladesh #69, Maldive Islands #1030, Bhutan #132, Pakistan #403, Ceylon #451, India #580, Nepal #437.

**Murray College, Sialkot, Cent. — A365**

*Perf. 14*

**1989, Dec. 18**
725 A365 6r multicolored   .75 .40

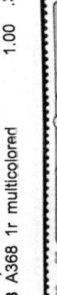

**Government College, Lahore, 125th Anniv. — A366**

*Perf. 13*

**1989, Dec. 21**
726 A366 6r multicolored   .75 .50

**Center on Integrated Rural Development for Asia and the Pacific (CIRDAP), 10th Anniv. — A367**

**1989, Dec. 31**
727 A367 3r multicolored   .75 .40

**Organization of the Islamic Conference (OIC), 20th Anniv. — A368**

*Perf. 13*   Litho.

**1990, Feb. 9**
728 A368 1r multicolored   1.00 .30

**7th World Field Hockey Cup, Lahore, Feb. 12-23 — A369**

Illustration reduced.

*Perf. 14x13½*

**1990, Feb. 12**
729 A369 2r multicolored   6.00 3.50

Pakistan Resolution Golden Jubilee 23rd March 1940-1990 — A370

---

Himalayan black bears and WWF emblem: a, Bear on slope, emblem UR. b, Bear on slope, emblem UL. c, Bear on top of rock, emblem UR. d, Seated bear, emblem UL.

*Perf. 14x13½*
Litho.   Unwmk.

**1989, Oct. 7**
719 A359 Block of 4   7.50 6.50
  a.-d. 4r, any single   1.50 1.00

**World Food Day — A360**

*Perf. 14x12½*

**1989, Oct. 16**
720 A360 1r multicolored   .50 .25

**Quilt and Bahishiti Darwaza (Heavenly Gate) — A361**

*Perf. 13*

**1989, Oct. 20**
721 A361 3r multicolored   .50 .20

800th Birth anniv. of Baba Farid.

**4th SAF Games, Islamabad — A362**

**1989, Oct. 20**
722 A362 1r multicolored   .35 .25

**Pakistan Television, 25th Anniv. — A363**

*Perf. 13½*   Litho.

**1989, Nov. 26**
723 A363 3r multicolored   .30 .20

**SAARC Year Against Drug Abuse and Drug Trafficking — A364**

*Perf. 13*

**1989, Dec. 8**
724 A364 7r multicolored   2.75 .75

---

**Asia-Pacific Telecommunity, 10th Anniv. — A355**

*Perf. 14½x14*

**1989, June 28**
709 Block of 4   .75 .60
  a.-d. A354 1r any single   .20 .20

**Laying the Foundation Stone for the 1st Integrated Container Terminal, Port Qasim — A356**

*Perf. 13½x14*

**1989, July 1**
710 A355 3r multicolored   .50 .20

**Mohammad Ali Jinnah — A357**

**1989, Aug. 5**
711 A356 6r Ship in berth   4.00 3.00

*Perf. 14*

**Litho. & Engr.   Wmk. 351**

*Perf. 13*

**1989, Aug. 14**
712 A357 1r multicolored   .65 .20
713 A357 1.50r multicolored   .80 .20
714 A357 2r multicolored   1.10 .30
715 A357 3r multicolored   1.40 .35
716 A357 4r multicolored   1.75 .40
717 A357 5r multicolored   1.90 .40
  Nos. 712-717 (6)   7.00 1.70

Independence Day. Nos. 712-717 exist overprinted "NATIONAL SEMINAR ON PHILATELY MULTAN 1992." These were available only at the seminar and were not sold in post offices. Value $125. Beware of forgeries.

**Abdul Latif Bhitai Memorial — A358**

**1989, Sept. 16**
718 A358 2r multicolored   .35 .20

Unwmk.   Litho.

245th death and 300th birth anniv. of Shah Abdul Latif Bhitai.

World Wildlife Fund — A359

---

**Size: 52x28mm**

*Perf. 13½x13*

703 A349 75r multicolored   4.75 3.00
     10.50 6.00
  Nos. 701-703 (3)

16th Asian Advertising Congress

**Adasia '89, 16th Asian Advertising Congress, Lahore, Feb. 18-22 — A350**

Litho.   *Perf. 13*

**1989, Feb. 18**
704 Strip of 3   3.75 2.75
  a. A350 1r deep rose lilac & multi   1.00 .75
  b. A350 1r green & multi   1.00 .75
  c. A350 1r bright vermilion & multi   1.00 .75

Printed in sheets of 9.

**Pres. Zulfikar Ali Bhutto (1928-1979), Ousted by Military Coup and Executed A351**

Portraits.

*Perf. 13*

**1989, Apr. 4**

Litho.

705 A351 1r shown   .20 .20
706 A351 2r multi, diff.   .25 .20

**Submarine Operations, 25th Anniv. — A352**

Submarines: a, *Agosta.* b, *Daphne.* c, *Fleet Snorkel.* Illustration reduced.

*Perf. 13½*

**1989, June 1**

Litho.

707 Strip of 3   5.25 5.25
  a.-c. A352 1r any single   1.50 1.00

**Oath of the Tennis Court, by David — A353**

*Perf. 13½*

**1989, June 24**
708 A353 7r multicolored   2.75 .75

Litho. French revolution, bicent.

**Archaeological Heritage — A354**

Terra cotta vessels excavated in Baluchistan: a, Pirak, c. 2200 B.C. b, Nindo Damb, c. 2300 B.C. c, Mehrgarh, c. 3600 B.C. d, Nausharo, c. 2600 B.C.

Pakistan Resolution, 50th Anniv. — A371

Designs: a. Allama Mohammad Iqbal addressing the Allahabad Session of the All-India Muslim League. b. Sir Syed Ahmad Khan as league secretary-general. c. Muslim fighter Maulana Mohammad Ali Jinnah at microphone. c. Muslim woman holding flag and swearing-in of Mohammad Ali Jinnah as governor-general of Pakistan, Aug. 14, 1947. 7r, English and Urdu translations of the resolution, natl. flag and Minar-e-Qaradade Pakistan.

**1990, Mar. 23    Litho.    Perf. 13**

| 730 | A370 | 1r any multicolored | 3.50 | 3.50 |
| a.-c. | Strip of 3 | | 1.10 | .75 |

| 731 | A371 | 7r multicolored | 2.75 | 1.75 |

Safe Motherhood South Asia Conference, Lahore — A372

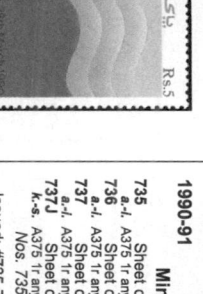

**1990, Mar. 24**    Size: 90x45mm    **Perf. 13½**

| 732 | A372 | 5r multicolored | .95 | .50 |

Painters of Pakistan

Calligraphic Painting of a Ghalib Verse, by Shakir Ali (1916-1975) — A373

**1990, Apr. 19    Litho.    Perf. 13½x13**

| 733 | A373 | 1r multicolored | 2.00 | .60 |

See Nos. 757-758.

Badr-1 First Satellite of Pakistan

Badr-1 Satellite — A374

**Litho.    Perf. 13**

| 734 | A374 | 3r multicolored | 3.75 | 2.50 |

Pioneers of Freedom

(1877-1938)
ALLAMA MOHAMMAD IQBAL

Pioneers of Freedom A375

**1990, July 26    Litho.    Perf. 13**

No. 735: a. Allama Mohammad Iqbal (1877-1938), b. Mohammad Ali Jinnah (1876-1948), c. Sir Syed Ahmad Khan (1817-98), d. Nawab Salimullah (1884-1915), e. Mohtarma Fatima Jinnah (1893-1967), f. Aga Khan III (1877-1957), g. Nawab Mohammad Ismail Khan (1884-1958), h. Hussain Shaheed Suhrawardy (1893-1963), i. Syed Ameer Ali (1849-1928).
No. 736: a. Nawab Bahadur Yar Jung (1905-44), b. Khawaja Nazimuddin (1894-1964), c. Maulana Obaidullah Sindhi (1872-1944), d. Sardar Abdul Qaiyum Khan (c. 1863-1937), e. Begum Jahanara Shah Nawaz (1896-1979), f. Sir Shujaat Hussain Hidayatullah (1879-1948), g. Qazi Mohammad Isa (1913-76), h. Sir Mir Shannawaz Khan Mamdot (1883-1942), i. Pir Shaib of Manki Sharif (1923-60).
No. 737: a. Liaquat Ali Khan (1895-1951), b. Maulvi A.K. Fazl-Ul-Haq (1873-1962), c. Allama Shabbir Ahmad Usmani (1885-1949), d. Sardar Abdur Rab Nishtar (1899-1958), e. Bi Amma (c. 1850-1924), f. Sir Abdullah Haroon (1872-1942), g. Chaudhry Rahmat Ali (1897-1951), h. Raja Sahib of Mahmudabad (1914-73), i. Hassanally Effendi (1830-1895).
No. 737J: k. Maulana Zafar Ali Khan (1873-1956), l. Maulana Mohamed Ali Jauhar (1878-1931), m. Chaudhry Khaliquzzaman (1889-1973), n. Hameed Nizami (1915-62), o. Begum Ra'ana Liaquat Ali Khan (1905-90), p. Mirza Abol Hassan Ispahani (1902-81), q. Raja Ghazanfar Ali Khan (1895-1963), r. Malik Barkat Ali (1886-1946), s. Mir Jaffer Khan Jamali (c. 1911-67).

**1990-91    Litho.    Perf. 13**
**Miniature Sheets**

| 735 | Sheet of 9 | | 3.75 | 3.00 |
| a.-i. | A375 1r any single | | .40 | .20 |
| 736 | Sheet of 9 | | 3.75 | 3.00 |
| a.-i. | A375 1r any single | | .40 | .20 |
| 737 | Sheet of 9 | | 3.75 | 3.00 |
| a.-i. | A375 1r any single | | .40 | .20 |
| 737J | Sheet of 9 ('91) | | 15.00 | 12.00 |
| k.-s. | A375 1r any single | | .40 | .20 |

Issued: #735-737, Aug. 19; #737J, 1991.
See Nos. 773, 792, 804, 859-860, 865, 875-876, 922-924.

Indonesia Pakistan Economic and Cultural Cooperation Organization, 1968-1990 — A376

**1990, Aug. 19**

| 738 | A376 | 7r multicolored | 2.00 | .90 |

Intl. Literacy Year — A377

**1990, Sept. 8**

| 739 | A377 | 3r multicolored | 1.50 | .75 |

Joint meeting of Royal College of Physicians, Edinburgh and College of Physicians and Surgeons, Pakistan.

A378

**1990, Sept. 22**

| 740 | A378 | 2r multicolored | 1.25 | .40 |

World Summit for Children A379

**1990, Sept. 19**

| 741 | A379 | 7r multicolored | .85 | .40 |

Year of the Girl Child A380

**1990, Nov. 21    Litho.    Perf. 13½**

| 742 | A380 | 2r multicolored | .95 | .50 |

Security Papers Ltd., 25th Anniv. — A381

**1990, Dec. 8**

| 743 | A381 | 3r multicolored | .90 | .75 |

Intl. Civil Defense Day — A382

**1991, Mar. 1    Litho.    Perf. 13**

| 744 | A382 | 7r multicolored | 1.75 | 1.00 |

South & West Asia Postal Union — A383

**1991, Mar. 21**

| 745 | A383 | 5r multicolored | 2.25 | 1.25 |

World Population Day — A384

**1991, July 11**

| 746 | A384 | 10r multicolored | 3.00 | 1.50 |

Intl. Special Olympics A385

**1991, July 19**

| 747 | A385 | 7r multicolored | 2.75 | 1.50 |

Habib Bank Limited, 50th Anniv. — A386

GOLDEN JUBILEE (1941-1991)

**1991, Aug. 25    Litho.    Perf. 13**

| 748 | A386 | 1r brt red & multi | 1.00 | .25 |
| 749 | A386 | 5r brt green & multi | 3.00 | 1.75 |

St. Joseph's Convent School, Karachi — A387

ST. JOSEPH'S CONVENT SCHOOL KARACHI – ESTABLISHED-1862

**1991, Sept. 8**

| 750 | A387 | 5r multicolored | 4.50 | 2.50 |

Emperor Sher Shah Suri (c. 1472-1545) A388

**1991, Oct. 5**

| 751 | A388 | 5r multicolored | 2.25 | 2.25 |

**Souvenir Sheet    Size: 90x81mm    Imperf**

| 752 | A388 | 7r multicolored | 2.50 | 2.50 |

Pakistani Scientific Expedition to Antarctica — A389

**1991, Oct. 28**

| 753 | A389 | 7r multicolored | 4.50 | 2.50 |

Houbara
Bustard — A390

**1991, Nov. 4**
754 A390 7r multicolored    3.50 2.00

Asian
Development
Bank, 25th
Anniv. — A391

**1991, Dec. 19**    **Litho.**    *Perf. 13*
755 A391 7r multicolored    3.00 1.50

Hazrat
Sultan
Bahoo,
300th
Death
Anniv.
A392

**1991, Dec. 22**
756 A392 7r multicoloured    1.75 .75

Painting Type of 1990

Paintings and artists: No. 757, Village Life,
by Allah Ustad Bux (1802-1978), No. 758,
Miniature of Royal Procession, by Muhammad
Haji Sharif (1889-1978).

**1991, Dec. 24**
757 A373 1r multicolored    2.50 1.00
758 A373 1r multicolored    2.50 1.00

American Express Travelers Cheques,
100th Anniv. — A393

Illustration reduced.

**1991, Dec. 26**    *Perf. 13½*
759 A393 7r multicolored    3.00 1.50

*First year of Privatisation*

Muslim Commercial Bank, First Year of
Private Operation — A394

7r, City skyline, worker, cogwheels, computer operators.

**1992, Apr. 8**    **Litho.**    *Perf. 13*
760 A394 1r multicolored    .30 .20
761 A394 7r multicolored    .65 .40

---

Pakistan, 1992 World Cricket
Champions — A395

World Cricket Cup and: 2r, Pakistani player,
vert. 7r, Pakistan flag, fireworks, vert.

**1992, Apr. 27**
762 A395 2r multicolored    1.00 .50
763 A395 5r multicolored    2.25 1.00
764 A395 7r multicolored    2.75 1.25
   Nos. 762-764 (3)    6.00 2.75

Intl. Space Year — A396

Design: 2r, Globo, satellite.

**1992, June 7**    **Litho.**    *Perf. 13*
771 A396 1r multicolored    .25 .20
772 A396 2r multicolored    .40 .25
   30th anniv. of first Pakistani rocket (#771).

Pioneers of Freedom Type of 1990

Designs: a, Syed Suleman Nadvi (1884-
1953). b, Nawab Iftikhar Hussain Khan
Mamdot (1906-1969). c, Maulana Muhammad
Shibli Naumani (1857-1914).

**1992, Aug. 14**    **Litho.**    *Perf. 13*
773 A375 1r Strip of 3, #a.-c.    4.00 3.50

World Population Day — A397

**1992, July 25**
774 A397 6r multicolored    1.10 1.00

Medicinal Plants — A398

**1992, Nov. 22**    **Litho.**    *Perf. 13*
775 A398 6r multicolored    2.50 2.25
   See No. 791.

Extraordinary Session of Economic
Cooperation Organization Council of
Ministers, Islamabad — A399

**1992, Nov. 28**
776 A399 7r multicolored    1.75 1.00

---

Intl.
Conference
on Nutrition,
Rome
A400

**1992, Dec. 5**    *Perf. 14*
777 A400 7r multicolored    1.00 1.00

A401

**1992, Dec. 14**    *Perf. 13*
778 A401 7r Alhambra, Spain    .75 .75

A402

Islamic cultural heritage.

**1992, Aug. 23**    *Perf. 14x12½*
779 A402 6th Jamboree    .85 .60
780 A402 6r 4th Conference    .85 .60
   Islamic Scouts, Islamabad

Government Islamia College, Lahore,
Cent. — A403

**1992, Nov. 1**    *Perf. 13*
781 A403 3r multicolored    .35 .35

Industries
A404

Designs: a, 10r, Surgical instruments. b,
15r, Leather goods. c, 25r, Sports equipment.

**1992, July 5**    **Litho.**    *Perf. 13½x13*
782 A404 Strip of 3, #a.-c.    5.00 5.00

World Telecommunications
Day — A405

**1993, May 17**    **Litho.**    *Perf. 13*
783 A405 1r multicolored    1.10 .30

---

21st Islamic
Foreign
Ministers
Conference
A406

**1993, Apr. 25**
784 A406 1r buff & multi    .50 .25
785 A406 6r green & multi    2.00 1.00

A407

DRESSES OF

A408

Traditional costumes of provinces.

**1993, Mar. 10**    *Perf. 14x13*
786 A407 6r Sindh    1.75 1.75
787 A407 6r North West Frontier    1.75 1.75
788 A407 6r Balluchistan    1.75 1.75
789 A407 6r Punjab    1.75 1.75
   Nos. 786-789 (4)    7.00 7.00

**1992, Dec. 31**
Birds: a, Gadwall. b, Common shelduck. c,
Mallard. d, Greylag goose. The order of the
birds is different on each row. Therefore the
arc of the rainbow is different on each of the 4
Gadwalls, etc.

790 A408 5r Sheet of 16    15.00 8.50
   a.   Horiz. strip of 4, #b-e    6.00
   b.-e.   Any single    .30 .30

**Medicinal Plants Type**

**1993, June 20**    **Litho.**    *Perf. 13*
791 A398 6r Fennel, chemistry
   equipment    3.25 1.00

Pioneers of Freedom Type of 1990

Designs: a, Rais Ghulam Mohammad Bhur-
gri (1878-1924). b, Mir Ahmed Yar Khan, Khan
of Kalat (1902-1977). c, Mohammad Abdul
Latif Pir Sahib Zakori Sharif (1914-1978).

**1993, Aug. 14**    **Litho.**    *Perf. 13*
792 A375 1r Strip of 3, #a.-c.    3.50 2.00

Gordon College, Rawalpindi,
Cent. — A410

**1993, Sept. 1**
793 A410 2r multicolored    1.75 1.75

**1993, Sept. 30**

Juniper Forests, Ziarat — A411

794 A411 7r multicolored    4.50 2.00

See No. 827.

**1993, Oct. 16**

795 A412 6r multicolored    1.25 1.25

World Food Day — A412

Perf. 14

A413

A414

**1993, Dec. 25**

796 A413 1r multicolored

Wazir Mansion, birthplace of Muhammad Ali Jinnah.

**1993, Oct. 28**

797 A414 7r multicolored

Burn Hall Institutions, 50th anniv.

Perf. 13x13½

Wmk. 351   Litho.   Perf. 14    1.10 .30

Unwmk.    2.40 2.40

**1993, Nov. 18**

798 A415 7r multicolored    2.40 2.40

South & West Asia Postal Union — A415

Perf. 13

**1993, Dec. 10**

799 A416 1r multicolored    1.25 .35

Pakistani College of Physicians & Surgeons, Intl. Medical Congress A416

**1994, Apr. 11**

800 A417 7r multicolored    1.40 1.40

ILO, 75th Anniv. A417

Perf. 13

**1994, Apr. 20**

801 A418 6r multicolored    2.75 2.75

a. Ratan jot, medicinal plant. b. Wetlands. c. Mahseer fish. d. Himalayan brown bear.

Strip or block of 4, #a.-d.

Litho.   Perf. 13½

Bio-diversity A418

**1994, May 15**

802 A419 7r multicolored    .95 .95

Intl. Year of the Family — A419

Perf. 13

**1994, July 11**

803 A420 7r multicolored    .95 .95

World Population Day — A420

Litho.   Perf. 13

**1994, Aug. 14**

804 A375 1r #a.-h. + label    2.00 2.00

Pioneers of Freedom Type of 1990

Miniature Sheet of 8

Litho.   Perf. 13

Designs: a. Nawab Mohsin-Ul-Mulk (1837-1907). b. Sir Shahnawaz Bhutto (1888-1957). c. Nawab Viqar-Ul-Mulk (1841-1917). d. Pir Ilahi Bux (1890-1975). e. Sheikh Sir Abdul Qadir (1874-1950). f. Dr. Sir Ziauddin Ahmed (1878-1947). g. Jam Mir Ghulam Qadir Khan (1920-88). h. Sardar Aurangzeb Khan (1899-1953).

**1994, Oct. 2**

805 A421 2r multicolored    1.00 .30

First Intl. Festival of Islamic Artisans.

Perf. 13x13½

A421

**1994, Sept. 8**

806 A422 7r multicolored    .65 .65

Intl. Literacy Day.

A422

**1994**

807 A423 6r multicolored    .95 .60

Hyoscyamus Niger — A423

Perf. 13

| | | | |
|---|---|---|---|
| **1994, Sept. 11** | **Litho. & Engr.** | **Wmk. 351** | **Perf. 13** |

Mohammed Ali Jinnah — A424

| 808 | A424 | 1r slate & multi | .20 | .20 |
|---|---|---|---|---|
| 809 | A424 | 2r claret & multi | .20 | .20 |
| 810 | A424 | 3r bright bl & multi | .20 | .20 |
| 811 | A424 | 4r emerald & multi | .20 | .20 |
| 812 | A424 | 5r lake & multi | .30 | .30 |
| 813 | A424 | 7r blue & multi | .30 | .30 |
| 814 | A424 | 10r green & multi | .50 | .50 |
| 815 | A424 | 12r orange & multi | .65 | .65 |
| 816 | A424 | 15r violet & multi | .80 | .80 |
| 817 | A424 | 20r rose & multi | 1.00 | 1.00 |
| 818 | A424 | 25r brown & multi | 1.25 | 1.25 |
| 819 | A424 | 30r olive brn & multi | 1.50 | 1.50 |
| | A424 | | 7.00 | 7.00 |

Nos. 808-819 (12)

**1994, Sept. 22**

820 A425 7r multicolored    .60 .40

2nd SAARC & 12th Natl. Scout Jamboree, Quetta — A425

Litho.   Perf. 13

**1994, Oct. 27**

821 A426 1r multicolored    .25 .25

Publication of Ferdowsi's Book of Kings, 1000th Anniv. — A426

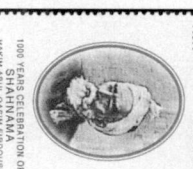

**1994, Aug. 19**

822 A427 10r Hala pottery    1.25 .60

823 A427 10r Lombok pottery    1.25 .60

a. Pair, #822-823    2.50 2.50

Indonesia-Pakistan Economic & Cultural Cooperation Organization — A427

See Indonesia Nos. 1585-1586.

**1994, Dec. 27**

824 A428 4r multicolored    .75 .75

Lahore Museum, Cent. — A428

Wmk. 351   Litho.   Perf. 13

**1994, Dec. 31**

825 A429 5r multicolored    .80 .40

Pakistan, 1994 World Cup Field Hockey Champions A429

**1995, Jan. 2**

826 A430 4r multicolored    .75 .30

World Tourism Organization, 20th Anniv. — A430

**1995, Feb. 14**

827 A431 1r like #794    .40 .20

Juniper Forests Type of 1993

Litho.   Perf. 13

Third Economic Cooperation Organization Summit, Islamabad — A431

THIRD ECO SUMMIT Rs.6
MARCH 14-15, 1995 ISLAMABAD ECONOMIC COOPERATION ORGANIZATION

**Perf. 14   Litho.**
**1995, Mar. 14**
828 A431 6r multicolored   1.10  1.10

Khushall Khan Khattak (1613-89) A432

Rs.7   KHUSHAL KHAN KHATTAK   1613-1689

**Perf. 13**
**1996, Feb. 28**
829 A432 7r multicolored   1.10  1.10

Earth Day A433

EARTH DAY   Rs.6

**Wmk. 351   Litho.   Perf. 13**
**1995, Apr. 20**
830 A433 6r multicolored   .95  .95

Snakes A434

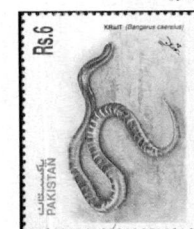

Rs.6   Krait (Bungarus caeruleus)

a, Krait. b, Cobra. c, Python. d, Viper.
**Perf. 13½   Unwmk.**
**1995, Apr. 15**
831 A434 6r Block of 4, #a.-d.   4.25  4.25

Traditional Means of Transportation — A435

Rs.5   KARACHI VICTORIA

**Wmk. 351   Litho.   Perf. 13**
**1995, May 22**
832 A435 5r Horse-drawn carriage   .85  .85

Louis Pasteur (1822-95) A436

Rs.5   100TH DEATH ANNIVERSARY OF LOUIS PASTEUR 1895-1995

**Wmk. 351   Litho.   Perf. 13**
**1995, Sept. 28**
833 A436 5r multicolored   .75  .55

UN, FAO, 50th Anniv. A437

FOOD FOR ALL   YEAR SERVICE TO HUMANITY UNITED NATIONS   Rs.1.25

**1995, Oct. 16**
834 A437 1.25r multicolored   .40  .20

Kinnaird College for Women, Lahore — A438

Over 80 Years of Women's Education   Rs.1.25

**Perf. 14x13**
**1995, Nov. 3**
835 A438 1.25r multicolored   .50  .20

4th World Conference on Women, Beijing — A439

**Perf. 13**

Women in various activities: a, Playing golf, Graduates, student, chemist, computer operator, reading gauge. b, repairing technical device. c, At sewing machine, working with textiles. d, Making rugs, police woman, laborers.

**1995, Sept. 15**
836 A439 1.25r Strip of 4, #a.-d.   1.25  1.25

Presentation Convent School, Rawalpindi, Cent. A440

Rs.1.25

**Wmk. 351   Litho.   Perf. 13½**
**1995, Sept. 8**
837 A440 1.25r multicolored   .50  .30

A440a

5 PAISA

Panel colors: 5p, Orange. 15p, Violet. 25p, Red. 75p, Red brown.
**Perf. 13½   Litho.   Unwmk.**
**1995-96**
837A-837D A440a Set of 4   .35  .25
Issued: 5p, 15p, 10/10/95; 25p, 9/28/95; 75p, 5/15/96.

Liaquat Ali Khan (1895-1951) — A441

PAKISTAN   Rs.1.25   1995-BIRTH CENTENARY OF LIAQUAT ALI KHAN

**Perf. 13**
**1995, Oct. 1**
838 A441 1.25r multicolored   .35  .25

1st Conference of Women Parliamentarians from Muslim Countries — A442

ISLAMABAD   Rs.5

Designs: No. 839, Dr. Tansu Ciller, Prime Minister of Turkey. No. 840, Mohtarma Benazir Bhutto, Prime Minister of Pakistan.

**Unwmk.**
**1995, Aug. 1**
839 A442 5r multicolored   1.10  1.10
840 A442 5r multicolored   1.10  1.10
a.   Pair, #839-840   2.25  2.25

Intl. Conference of Writers and Intellectuals A443

INTELLECTUALS   INTERNATIONAL CONFERENCE OF WRITERS &

**Perf. 14**
**Wmk. 351   Litho.**
**1995, Nov. 30**
841 A443 1.25r multicolored   .35  .25

Allama Iqbal Open University, 20th Anniv. — A444

AIOU   20 YEARS OF ALLAMA IQBAL OPEN UNIVERSITY

**Perf. 13**
**1995, Dec. 16**
842 A444 1.25r multicolored   .40  .30

Butterflies A445

Rs.6   ERASMIE

Designs: a, Érasmie. b, Catogramme. c, Ixias. d, Héliconie.
**Wmk. 351   Litho.   Perf. 13½**
**1995, Sept. 1**
843 A445 6r Strip of 4, #a.-d.   3.00  3.00

Fish — A446

Rs.6   SARDINE

Designs: a, Sardinella long. b, Tilapia mossambica. c, Salmo fario. d, Labeo rohita.
**Wmk. 351   Litho.   Perf. 13½**
**1995, Sept. 1**
844 A446 6r Strip of 4, #a.-d.   3.00  3.00

SAARC, 10th Anniv. — A447

First Decade of SAARC 1985-1995   Rs.1.25   PAKISTAN

**Perf. 13**
**1995, Dec. 8**
845 A447 1.25r multicolored   .35  .25

UN, 50th Anniv. — A448

ANNIVERSARY OF UNITED NATIONS   Rs.7

**Wmk. 351   Litho.   Perf. 13½**
**1995, Oct. 24**
846 A448 7r multicolored   .75  .75

Karachi '95, Natl. Water Sports Gala — A449

Rs.1.25   NATIONAL WATER SPORTS GALA KARACHI '95

Designs: a, Man on jet ski. b, Gondola race. c, Sailboard race. d, Man water skiing.
**Perf. 14x13**
**1995, Dec. 14**
847 A449 1.25r Block of 4, #a.-d.   1.40  1.40

University of Baluchistan, Quetta, 25th Anniv. — A452

Silver Jubilee UNIVERSITY OF BALUCHISTAN QUETTA 1970-1995   Rs.1.25

**Wmk. 351   Litho.   Perf. 13**
**1995, Dec. 31**
850 A452 1.25r multicolored   .35  .25

Zulfikar Ali Bhutto (1928-79), Politician, President — A455

Rs.4   17TH MARTYRDOM ANNIVERSARY OF (LATE) ZULFIKAR ALI BHUTTO   APRIL 4, 1996

Designs: 1.25r, Bhutto, flag, crowd of people, vert. 8r, like No. 855
**Wmk. 351   Litho.   Perf. 13**
**1996, Apr. 4**
855 A455 1.25r multicolored   .65  .25
856 A455 4r shown   2.00  .75
**Size: 114x69mm**
**Imperf**
857 A455 8r multicolored   3.00  3.00

PAKISTAN

Raja Aziz Bhatti Shaheed (1928-65) — A456

**1995, Sept. 5        Wmk. 351        Perf. 13**
858   A456   1.25r multicolored              1.00   .40

**Pioneers of Freedom Type of 1990**
#859, Maulana Shaukat Ali (1873-1938).
#860, Chaudhry Ghulam Abbas (1904-67).

**1995, Aug. 14        Unwmk.        Perf. 13**
859   A375   1r   green & brown              .50   .50
860   A375   1r   green & brown              .50   .50
a.   Pair, #859-860                          1.10   1.10

1996 Summer Olympic Games, Atlanta — A457

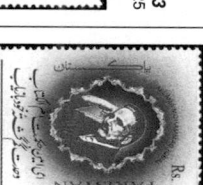

Design: 25r, #861-864 without denomina-tions, simulated perfs, Olympic rings. "100," Atlanta '96 emblem. Illustration reduced.

**1996, Aug. 3        Litho.        Perf. 13**
861   A457   5r   Wrestling                  .70   .70
862   A457   5r   Boxing                     .70   .70
863   A457   5r   Pierre de                  .70   .70
             Coubertin
864   A457   5r   Field hockey              2.80  2.80
Nos. 861-864 (4)

**Imperf**
864A   A457   25r multicolored              3.50  3.50

**Size: 111x101mm**

**Pioneers of Freedom Type of 1990**
Allama Abdullah Yousuf Ali (1872-1953).

**1996, Aug. 14        Unwmk.        Litho.        Perf. 13**
865   A375   1r green & brown               .35   .25

Restoration of General Post Office, Lahore — A458

**1996, Aug. 21        Wmk. 351        Perf. 14**
866   A458   5r multicolored                .45   .35

Intl. Literacy Day — A459

**1996, Sept. 8        Wmk. 351        Perf. 13**
867   A459   2r multicolored                .35   .25

---

Yarrow — A459a

MEDICINAL PLANTS OF PAKISTAN

**1996, Nov. 25        Wmk. 351        Perf. 13**
867A   A459a   3r multicolored              .75   .40

Faiz Ahmed Faiz, Poet, 86th Birthday — A460

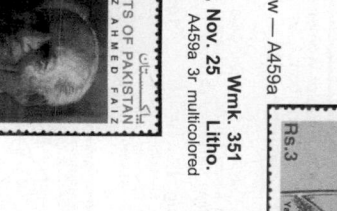
POETS OF PAKISTAN — FAIZ AHMED FAIZ

**1997, Feb. 13        Litho.        Perf. 13**
868   A460   3r multicolored                .35   .25

Tamerlane (1336-1405) — A461

**1997, Apr. 8        Unwmk.        Litho.        Perf. 13**
869   A461   3r multicolored                .35   .25

Designs: No. 870, Allama Mohammad Iqbal. No. 871, Jalal-Al-Din Moulana Rumi.

**1997, Apr. 21**
870   A462   3r multicolored                .20   .20
871   A462   3r multicolored                .20   .20

Famous Men — A462

Pakistani Independence, 50th Anniv. — A463

OIC — Golden Jubilee Celebrations of Organisation of Islamic Countries, 23rd March, 1997 Islamabad — PAKISTAN

**1997, Mar. 23        Perf. 13**
872   A463   2r multicolored                .20   .20

Special Summit of Organization of Islamic Countries, Islamabad.

---

WORLD POPULATION DAY — PAKISTAN

World Population Day — A464

**1997, July 11        Unwmk.        Litho.        Perf. 13**
873   A464   2r multicolored                .35   .25

Intl. Atomic Energy Agency-Pakistan Atomic Energy Commission Cooperation, 40th Anniv. — A465

40 YEARS OF IAEA-PAEC COOPERATION — PAKISTAN

**1997, July 29        Perf. 14**
874   A465   2r multicolored                .35   .25

**Pioneers of Freedom Type of 1990**
#875, Begum Salma Tassaduq Hussain (1908-95). #876, Mohammad Ayub Khuhro (1901-80).

**1997, Aug. 14        Litho.        Perf. 13**
875   A375   1r   green & brown             .20   .20
876   A375   1r   green & brown             .20   .20

Fruits of Pakistan — A466

FRUITS OF PAKISTAN — APPLE

**1997, May 8**
877   A466   2r   Apples                    .25   .25

Designs: a. Allama Mohammad Iqbal. b. Mohammad Ali Jinnah. c. Liaquat Ali Khan. d. Mohatrma Fatima Jinnah.

**1997, Aug. 14        Block of 4 + 2 Labels**
878   A467   3r #a.-d.                      2.25   .75

Independence, 50th Anniv. — A467

---

Lophophorus Impejanus — A468

PAKISTAN — PROJECT WILDLIFE — MONAL

**1997, Oct. 29        Wmk. 351        Perf. 13**
879   A468   2r multicolored                .60   .25

Lahore College for Women, 75th Anniv. — A469

75TH ANNIVERSARY OF LAHORE COLLEGE FOR WOMEN — PAKISTAN

**1997, Sept. 23**
880   A469   3r multicolored                .45   .35

Intl. Day of the Disabled — A470

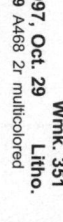
INTERNATIONAL DAY OF THE DISABLED — PAKISTAN

**1997, Dec. 3        Unwmk.        Litho.        Perf. 13**
881   A470   4r multicolored                .50   .40

Protection of the Ozone Layer — A471

SAVE THE OZONE LAYER — PAKISTAN

**1997, Nov. 15**
882   A471   3r multicolored                .45   .35

Pakistan Motorway, 50th Anniv. — A472

PAKISTAN MOTORWAY — GATEWAY TO PROSPERITY

**1997, Nov. 26        Perf. 13½**
883   A472   10r multicolored               .75   .75
a.   Souvenir sheet of 1                    3.00  3.00
No. 883a sold for 15r.

Karachi Grammar School, 150th Anniv. — A473

KARACHI GRAMMAR SCHOOL 1847-1997 — PAKISTAN

**1997, Dec. 30        Litho.        Perf. 13½**
884   A473   2r multicolored                .25   .25

## Medicinal Plants of Pakistan

**Garlic**
A474

**1997, Oct. 22**  **Perf. 13**  .40  .20
885  A474  2r multicolored

---

**Mirza Asad Ullah Khan Ghalib (1797-1869), Poet — A475**

.30  .30
**1998, Feb. 15**
886  A475  2r multicolored

---

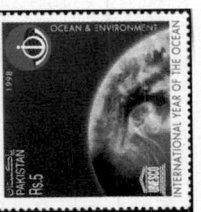

**Pakistan Armed Forces, 50th Anniv.**
A476

**1997, Mar. 23**  **Wmk. 351  Litho.**  **Perf. 13½**  .60  .60
887  A476  7r multicolored

---

**Sir Syed Ahmad Khan (1817-98), Educator, Jurist, Author — A477**

**1998, Mar. 27**  **Perf. 14**  .50  .50
888  A477  7r multicolored

---

**27th Natl. Games, Peshawar**
A478

**1998, Apr. 22**  **Wmk. 351  Litho.**  **Perf. 13**  .50  .50
889  A478  7r multicolored

---

## Medicinal Plants of Pakistan

Stramonium, Thornapple, Jimson Weed

**Jimsonweed**
A479

**1998, Apr. 27**  .20  .20
890  A479  2r multicolored

---

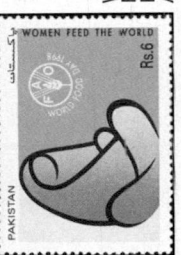

**Faisalabad Government College, Cent. (in 1997) — A480**

**1998, Aug. 14**  **Litho.**  **Perf. 13**  .35  .25
891  A480  5r multicolored

---

**Pakistan Senate, 25th Anniv.**
A481

**1998, Aug. 6**  **Perf. 13½**  .20  .20 / .25  .25
892  A481  2r green & multi
893  A481  5r blue & multi

---

**Mohammed Ali Jinnah — A482**

**1998-2001**  **Litho. & Engr.  Wmk. 351**  **Perf. 14**

| | | .20 | .20 |
|---|---|---|---|
| 893A | A482 1r red & black | .20 | .20 |
| 894 | A482 2r dk bl & rod | .20 | .20 |
| 895 | A482 2r slate grn & brn | .25 | .25 |
| 896 | A482 4r dp vio blk & org | .25 | .25 |
| 897 | A482 5r dp brn & grn | .35 | .25 |
| 898 | A482 6r dp grn & multi | .45 | .30 |
| 899 | A482 7r dp brn red & dp vio | .55 | .35 |
| | | 2.05 | 1.50 |

Nos. 894-899 (6)
Nos. 894 issued 8/14/98. No. 893A, 2001(?).

---

**21st Intl. Congress of Ophthalmology, Islamabad — A483**

**1998, Sept. 11**  **Wmk. 351  Litho.**  **Perf. 13**  .30  .30
900  A483  7r multicolored

---

**Syed Ahmed Shah Patrus Bukhari, Birth Cent.**
A484

**1998, Oct. 1**  .35  .25
901  A484  5r multicolored

---

**Philately in Pakistan, 50th Anniv. — A485**
Various portions of stamps inside "50," #20-23.

.40  .30
**1998, Oct. 4**
902  A485  6r multicolored

---

**World Food Day**
A486

**1998, Oct. 16**  **Wmk. 351  Photo.**  **Perf. 13**  .40  .30
903  A486  6r multicolored

---

**Mohammad Ali Jinnah (1876-1948)**
A487

**1998, Sept. 11**  **Wmk. 351  Photo.**  **Perf. 13½**  .90  .90 / 2.00  2.00
904  A487  13r multicolored
a. Souvenir sheet of 1, unwmk.
No. 904a sold for 20r.

---

**Universal Declaration of Human Rights, 50th Anniv.**
A488

**1998, Dec. 10**  **Wmk. 351**  **Perf. 13x14**  .35  .35
905  A488  6r multicolored

---

**Better Pakistan, 2010**
A489

#906, Harvesting grain. #907, Health care. #908, Satellite dishes. #909, Airplane.

**1998, Nov. 27**  **Unwmk.**
906  A489  2r multicolored  .20  .20
907  A489  2r multicolored  .20  .20
908  A489  2r multicolored  .20  .20
909  A489  2r multicolored  .80  .80
Nos. 906-909 (4)

---

**Dr. Abdus Salam, Scientist**
A490

---

**National Flag March**
A491

**1998, Nov. 21**  **Unwmk.  Litho.**  **Perf. 13**  .20  .20
910  A490  2r multicolored
See No. 916.

**Wmk. 351**  .20  .20

---

**Intl. Year of the Ocean**
A492

**1998, Dec. 16**
911  A491  2r multicolored

---

**Perf. 14**  .35  .35
**1998, Dec. 15**
912  A492  5r multicolored

---

**UNICEF in Pakistan, 50th Anniv.**
A493

a. Distributing water. b. Child holding book. c. Girl. d. Child receiving oral vaccine.

**1998, Dec. 15**  .40  .40
913  A493  2r Block of 4, #a.-d.

---

**Kingdom of Saudi Arabia, Cent. — A494**

**1999, Jan. 27**  **Perf. 13½  Litho.  Unwmk.**
914  A494  2r Emblem on sand  .50  .50
915  A494  15r Emblem on carpet  1.50  1.50
a. Souvenir sheet of 1  2.50  2.50
No. 915a sold for 20r.

---

**Scientists of Pakistan Type**
Dr. Salimuz Zaman Siddiqui (1897-1994).

**1999, Apr. 14**  **Perf. 13**  .35  .35
916  A490  5r multicolored

---

**Pakistani Nuclear Test, 1st Anniv. — A495**

**1999, May 28**  **Litho.**  **Perf. 13**  .35  .35
917  A495  5r multicolored

Completion of Data Darbar Mosque Complex — A496

**1999, May 31**   **Litho.**   **Perf. 13**
918   A496   7r multicolored   .40   .40

Fasting Buddha, c. 3-4 A.D. — A497

**1999, July 21**   **Litho.**   **Perf. 13½x13¾**
919   A497   7r shown   1.00   1.00
920   A497   7r Facing forward   1.00   1.00
a.   Souv. sheet of 2, #919-920   2.25   2.25

No. 920a sold for 25r. China 1999 World Philatelic Exhibition (No. 920a).

Geneva Conventions, 50th Anniv. — A498

**1999, Aug. 12**   **Perf. 12¾x13¾**
921   A498   5r pink, black & red   .35   .35

### Pioneers of Freedom Type of 1990

Designs: No. 922, Chaudhry Muhammad Ali (1905-80), 1st Secretary General. No. 923, Sir Adamjee Haji Dawood (1880-1948), banker. No. 924, Maulana Abdul Hamid Badayuni (1898-1970), religious scholar.

**1999, Aug. 14**   **Litho.**
922   A375   2r green & brown   .20   .20
923   A375   2r green & brown   .20   .20
924   A375   2r green & brown   .20   .20
Nos. 922-924 (3)   .60   .60

Ustad Nusrat Fateh Ali Khan (1948-97), Singer — A499

**1999, Aug. 16**
925   A499   2r multicolored   .20   .20

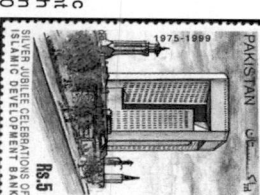      

Islamic Development Bank, 25th Anniv. (in 2000) — A500

**1999, Sept. 18**
926   A500   5r multicolored   .50   .50

---

People's Republic of China, 50th Anniv. — A501

**1999, Sept. 21**
927   A501   2r Gate of Heavenly Peace   .50   .50
928   A501   15r Arms, Mao Zedong, horiz.   1.25   1.25

A502

Universal Postal Union, 125th Anniv. — A502

A503

No. 929: a, Enterprise class. b, 470 class. c, Optimist class. d, Laser class. e, Mistral class.

**1999, Sept. 28**   **Perf. 13½x13¾**
929   A502   2r Strip of 5, #a.-e.   1.75   1.75

10th Asian Optimist Sailing Championships — A502a

Ninth Asian Sailing Championship.

**1999, Oct. 7**   **Litho.**   **Perf. 13½x13½**
929F   A502a   2r multi + label   .60   .60

**1999, Oct. 9**   **Perf. 14½**
930   A503   10r multicolored   .85   .85

UPU, 125th anniv.

Hakim Mohammed Said (1920-98), Physician — A504

**1999, Oct. 17**   **Litho.**   **Perf. 13**
931   A504   5r multicolored   .25   .25

National Bank of Pakistan, 50th Anniv. — A505

**1999, Nov. 8**   **Litho.**   **Wmk. 351**
932   A505   5r multi   **Perf. 13¼x13¾**   .20   .20

---

Shell Oil in Pakistan, Cent. — A506

**1999, Nov. 15**   **Perf. 13¼x13**
933   A506   4r multi   **Wmk. 351**   .20   .20

Rights of the Child, 10th Anniv. — A507

**1999, Nov. 20**   **Perf. 13x13¾**
934   A507   2r multi   **Unwmk.**   .20   .20

Allama Iqbal Open University, Islamabad — A508

Designs: 2r, University crest, flasks, microphone, mortarboard, book, computer. 3r, Similar to 2r, crest in center. 5r, Crest, map, mortarboard, book.

**1999, Nov. 20**   **Litho.**   **Unwmk.**
935   A508   2r bi grn & multi   .20   .20
936   A508   3r multi   .20   .20
937   A508   5r multi   .60   .60
Nos. 935-937 (3)   **Perf. 13**   .60   .60

Shabbir Hassan Khan Josh Malihabadi (1898-1982), Poet — A509

**1999, Dec. 5**
938   A509   5r multi   .20   .20

Dr. Afzal Qadri (1912-74), Entomologist — A510

**1999, Dec. 6**
939   A510   3r multi   .20   .20

---

Ghulam Bari Aleeg (1907-49), Journalist — A511

**1999, Dec. 10**   **Litho.**   **Perf. 13**
940   A511   5r multi   .20   .20

Plantain — A512

**1999, Dec. 20**
941   A512   5r multi   .20   .20

Eid-Ul-Fitr — A513

Illustration reduced.

**1999, Dec. 24**   **Litho.**   **Perf. 13¼x13½**
942   A513   2r green & multi   .50   .50
943   A513   15r blue & multi   1.50   1.50

SOS Children's Villages of Pakistan, 25th Anniv. — A514

**2000, Mar. 12**   **Perf. 13**
944   A514   2r multi   .20   .20

International Cycling Union, Cent. — A515

Illustration reduced.

**2000, Apr. 14**   **Litho.**   **Perf. 13¼**
945   A515   2r multi   .20   .20

Convention on Human Rights and Dignity — A516

Illustration reduced.

**2000, Apr. 21**   **Litho.**   **Unwmk.**
946   A516   2r multi   **Perf. 13¼**   .20   .20

Pakistan-People's Rep. of China Diplomatic Relations, 50th Anniv. — A534

Designs: No. 967, Yugur and Hunza women, flags. No. 968 — Paintings by Yao Youdou: a, Ma Gu's Birthday Offering. b, Two Pakistani Women Drawing Water.

**Perf. 13**

**2001, May 12**
| | | |
|---|---|---|
| 967 | A534 4r multi | .20 .20 |
| 968 | A534 4r Horiz. pair, #a-b | .30 .30 |

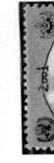

Mohammed Ali Jinnah (1876-1948)
A535

**2001, Aug. 14**
969 A535 4r multi .20 .20

Sindh Festival A536

**Unwmk.** **Litho.** **Perf. 13**

**2001, Sept. 22**
970 A536 4r multi .20 .20

Year of Dialogue Among Civilizations A537

**2001, Oct. 9**
971 A537 4r multi .20 .20

Turkmenistan, 10th Anniv. of Independence A538

**Perf. 13**

**2001, Oct. 27**
972 A538 5r multi .20 .20

---

Rotary Intl. Campaign Against Polio — A528

**2000, Dec. 13**
959 A528 2r multi .20 .20

UN High Commissioner for Refugees, 50th Anniv. — A529

**2000, Dec. 14**
960 A529 2r multi .20 .20

Poets — A530

Design: 2r, Hafeez Jalandhri (1900-82). 5r, Khawaja Ghulam Farid.

**Perf. 13** **Litho.**

**2001**
| | | |
|---|---|---|
| 961 | A530 2r multi | .20 .20 |
| 962 | A530 5r multi | .20 .20 |

Issued: 2r, 1/14. 5r, 9/25.

Habib Bank AG Zurich — A531

**Perf. 13** **Litho.**

**2001, Mar. 20**
963 A531 5r multi .20 .20

Chashma Nuclear Power Plant A532

**2001, Mar. 29**
964 A532 4r multi .20 .20

9th SAF Games, Islamabad A533

**Perf. 13½x13¼**

Background colors: No. 965, 4r, Light blue. No. 966, 4r, Lilac.

**2001, Apr. 9** **Set of 2**
965-966 A533 .30 .30

---

2000 Summer Olympics, Sydney — A523

No. 954: a, Runners. b, Field hockey. c, Weight lifting. d, Cycling. Illustration reduced.

**Perf. 14¼**

**2000, Sept. 20**
954 A523 4r Block of 4, #a-d 1.25 1.25

Natl. College of Arts, 125th Anniv. A524

**2000, Oct. 28**
955 A524 5r multi .20 .20

Creating the Future — A525

**Perf. 13½x13¼**

**2000, Nov. 4**
956 A525 5r multi .20 .20

Intl. Defense Exhibition and Seminar — A526

**Litho.** **Perf. 13**

**2000, Nov. 14**
957 A526 7r multi .30 .30

Licorice — A527

**Litho.** **Perf. 13**

**2000, Nov. 28**
958 A527 2r multi .20 .20

---

Edwardes College, Peshawar, Cent. — A517

**Perf. 13½**

**2000, Apr. 24**
947 A517 2r multi .20 .20

Mahomed Ali Habib (1904-59), Banker, Philantropist — A518

**Perf. 13** **Litho.**

**2000, May 15**
948 A518 2r multi .20 .20

Institute of Cost and Management Accountants, 50th Anniv. — A519

Design: 2r, Arrow. 15r, Globe.

**Perf. 13** **Litho.**

**2000, June 23**
| | | |
|---|---|---|
| 949 | A519 2r multi | .75 .75 |
| 950 | A519 15r multi | |

Ahmed E. H. Jaffer (1909-90), Politician A520

**Perf. 13** **Litho.**

**2000, Aug. 9**
951 A520 10r multi .60 .60

Creation of Pakistan, 53rd Anniv. — A521

a, No tree. b, Tree in foreground. c, Tree behind people, cart. d, Tree in distance.

**Perf. 13** **Litho.**

**2000, Aug. 14**
952 A521 5r Strip of 4, #a-d 1.50 1.50

**Nishan-e-Haider Medal Type of 1995**

Nishan-e-haider gallantry award winners: a, Capt. Muhammad Sarwar Shaheed (1910-48). b, Maj. Tufail Muhammad (1914-58). *Illustration reduced.*

**Perf. 13** **Litho.**

**2000, Sept. 6**
953 A456 5r Pair, #a-b .70 .70

## Convent of Jesus and Mary, Lahore, 125th Anniv. — A539

1876-2001

**2001, Nov. 15**    **Wmk. 351**
973 A539 4r multi ... .20 .20

## Men of Letters Type of 1999

Design: 4r, Dr. Ishtiaq Husain Qureshi (1903-81), historian.

**2001, Nov. 20**    **Unwmk.**
974 A511 4r multi ... .20 .20

## Birds — A540

**2001, Nov. 26**
975 A540 4r Block of 4, #a-d ... 1.50 1.50
    **Perf. 13½x13**

No. 975: a, Blue throat. b, Hoopoe. c, Pin-tailed sandgrouse. d, Magpie robin.

## Pakistan — United Arab Emirates Friendship, 30th Anniv. — A541

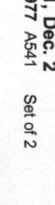

Rs.30 — 30 YEARS OF PAK-UAE FRIENDSHIP

Designs: 5r, Flags, handshake, vert. 30r, Sheik Zaid bin Sultan al Nahayan, Mohammed Ali Jinnah.

**2001, Dec. 2**    **Perf. 13**
976-977 A541 Set of 2 ... 3.00 3.00
     3.00 3.00

## Nishtar Medical College, Multan, 50th Anniv. — A542

Rs.5 — GOLDEN JUBILEE NISHTAR MEDICAL COLLEGE MULTAN — 1951-2001

**2001, Dec. 20**
978 A542 5r multi ... .20 .20

## Quaid Year — A543

Rs.4 — Quaid Year 2001

No. 979: a, Mohammed Ali Jinnah reviewing troops, 1948. b, Jinnah, soldiers, artillery gun, 1948.

No. 980, vert.: a, Jinnah taking oath as Governor General, 1947. b, Jinnah at opening ceremony of State Bank of Pakistan, 1948. c, Jinnah saluting at presentation of colors, 1948.

**2001, Dec. 25**    **Perf. 13**
979 A543 4r Horiz. pair ... .30 .30
  a.-b. A543 4r Any single ... .20 .20
980 A543 4r Horiz. strip of 3 ... .45 .45
  a.-c. A543 4r Any single ... .20 .20
    **Size: 33x56mm**
    **Perf. 13x13¼**

## Pakistan Ordnance Factories, 50th Anniv. — A544

Rs.4 — 50 YEARS OF PAKISTAN ORDNANCE FACTORIES — 1951-2001

**2001, Dec. 28**    **Perf. 13**
981 A544 4r multi ... .20 .20

## Men of Letters Type of 1999

Design: 5r, Syed Imtiaz Ali Taj (1900-70), playwright.

**2001, Oct. 13**    **Perf. 13½x13½**
982 A511 5r multi ... .20 .20

## Nishan-e-Haider Type of 1995

No. 983: a, Maj. Mohammad Akram Shaheed (1938-71). b, Maj. Shabbir Shaheeb (1943-71).

**2001, Sept. 6**    **Perf. 13**
983 A456 4r Any single ... .30 .30
  a.-b.   Horiz. pair ... .20 .20

## Peppermint — A545

Rs.4 — MEDICINAL PLANTS OF PAKISTAN — PEPPERMINT (Mentha x piperita)

Design: 5r, Hyssop.

**2001-02**   **Litho.**   **Wmk. 351**   **Perf. 13**
984 A545 4r multi ... .20 .20
985 A545 5r multi ... .20 .20

Issued: 4r, 11/12/01. 5r, 2/15/02.

## Poets Type of 2001

Design: Samandar Khan Samandar (1901-90).

**2002, Jan. 17**    **Litho.**
986 A530 5r multi ... .20 .20
    **Perf. 13**

## Pakistan — Japan Diplomatic Relations, 50th Anniv. — A546

Rs.5 — Amida BUDHA Japan / 50TH ANNIVERSARY OF PAKISTAN-JAPAN RELATIONS / Fasting BUDHA Pakistan / 2002

**2002, Apr. 28**    **Litho.**
987 A546 5r multi ... .20 .20
    **Perf. 14**

## Pakistan - Kyrgyzstan Diplomatic Relations, 10th Anniv. — A547

Rs.5 — 10TH ANNIVERSARY OF THE ESTABLISHMENT OF PAKISTAN DIPLOMATIC RELATIONS — 2002

**2002, May 27**    **Perf. 13½x12½**
988 A547 5r multi ... .20 .20

## Mangoes — A548

FRUITS OF PAKISTAN — CHAUNSA, ANWAR RATOL, SINDHRI, DUSHERI (Rs.4 each)

No. 989: a, Anwar Ratol. b, Dusheri. c, Chaunsa. d, Sindhri.

**2002, June 18**
989 A548 4r Block of 4, #a-d ... 1.25 1.25

## Independence, 55th Anniv. — A549

Famous people: No. 990, 4r, Noor-us-Sabah Begum (1908-78), Muslim leader and writer. No. 991, 4r, Prime Minister Ismail I. Chundrigar (1897-1960). No. 992, 4r, Habib Ibrahim Rahimtoola (1912-91), governmental minister. No. 993, 4r, Qazi Mureed Ahmed (1913-89), politician.

**2002, Aug. 14**    **Litho.**   **Perf. 13½x13**
990-993 A549 Set of 4 ... 1.50 1.50

## World Summit on Sustainable Development, Johannesburg. — A550

Rs.4 — PAKISTAN

Designs: No. 994, 4r, Children, Pakistani flag, dolphin, goat. No. 995, 4r, Water droplet, mountain (33x33mm).

**2002, Aug. 26**    **Perf. 13½, 14¼ (#995)**
994-995 A550 Set of 2 ... .30 .30

## Mohammad Aly Rangoonwala (1924-98), Philanthropist — A551

Rs.4 — MOHAMMAD ALY RANGOONWALA — THE PHILANTHROPIST

**2002, Aug. 31**    **Perf. 13**
996 A551 4r multi ... .20 .20

## Nishan-e-Haider type of 1995

No. 997: a, Lance Naik Muhammad Mahfuz Shaheed (1944-71). b, Sawar Muhammad Hussain Shaheed (1949-71).

**2002, Sept. 6**    **Perf. 13**
997 A456 4r Either single ... .30 .30
  a.-b.   Horiz. pair ... .20 .20

## Muhammad Iqbal Year — A552

Rs.4 — PAKISTAN — 2002 THE YEAR OF ALLAMA MUHAMMAD IQBAL

No. 998: a, Iqbal wearing hat, b, Iqbal without hat.

**2002, Nov. 9**    **Unwmk.**   **Litho.**   **Perf. 13**
998 A552 4r Horiz. pair, #a-b ... .30 .30

## Eid ul-Fitr — A553

Rs.4 — PAKISTAN — Eid Mubarak

**2002, Nov. 14**    **Wmk. 351**   **Perf. 13½x14**
999 A553 4r multi ... .30 .30

## Shifa-ul-Mulk Hakim Muhammad Hassan Qarshi (1896-1974), Physician — A554

Rs.4 — SHIFA-UL-MULK HAKIM MUHAMMAD HASSAN QARSHI

**2002, Dec. 20**    **Unwmk.**   **Perf. 13½**
1000 A554 4r multi ... .20 .20

## Pakistan 2003 Nat. Philatelic Exhibition, Karachi — A555

Rs.4 — PAKISTAN 2003 STAMP EXHIBITION

Illustration reduced.

**2003, Jan. 31**    **Wmk. 351**   **Litho.**   **Perf. 13**
1001 A555 4r multi + label ... .20 .20

## Pakistan Academy of Sciences, 50th Anniv. — A556

Rs.4 — GOLDEN JUBILEE 1953-2002 — PAKISTAN ACADEMY OF SCIENCES

**2003, Feb. 15**    **Unwmk.**   **Perf. 14½**
1002 A556 4r multi ... .20 .20

## North West Frontier Province, Cent. — A557

Rs.4 — PAKISTAN — 1901 — N. W. F. P. — CENTENARY CELEBRATIONS — 2001

**2003, Mar. 23**    **Wmk. 351**   **Litho.**   **Perf. 13½x13¼**
1003 A557 4r multi ... .20 .20

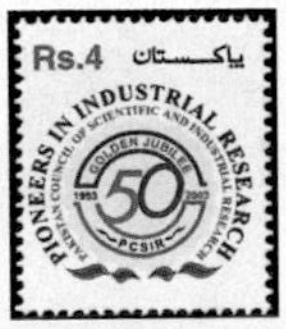

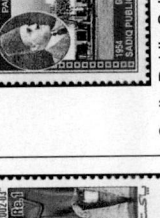

Pakistan Council of Scientific and Industrial Research, 50th Anniv. — A558

**2003, Mar. 31** ***Perf. 14x13¾***
**1004** A558 4r multi .20 .20

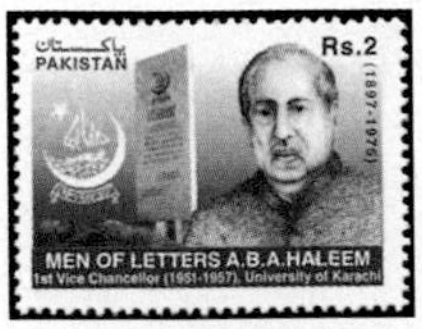

A. B. A. Haleem (1897-1975), Educator A559

**2003, Apr. 20** ***Perf. 13½x13¼***
**1005** A559 2r multi .20 .20

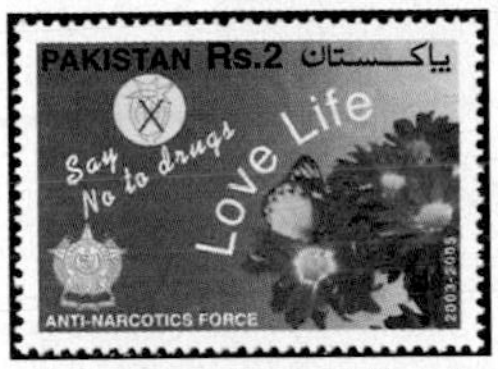

Campaign Against Illegal Drugs — A560

**2003, Apr. 21** ***Perf. 13***
**1006** A560 2r multi .20 .20

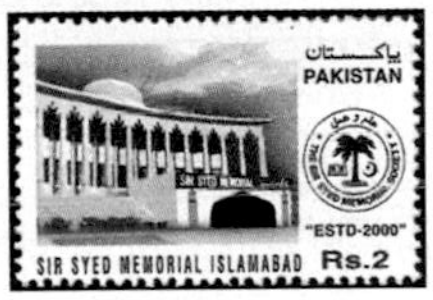

Sir Syed Memorial, Islamabad A561

**2003, Apr. 30** ***Perf. 13¼x13½***
**1007** A561 2r multi .20 .20

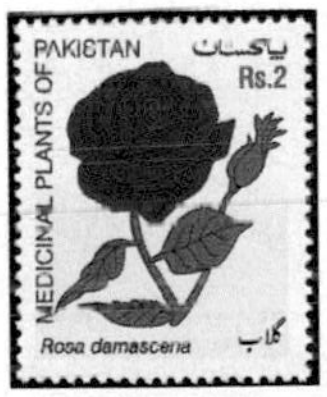

Rosa Damascena A562

***Perf. 13¼x12¾***
**2003, July 14** **Unwmk.**
**1008** A562 2r multi .20 .20

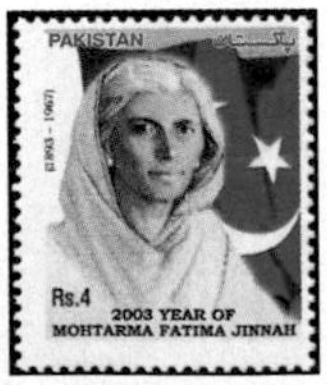

Mohtarma Fatima Jinnah (1893-1967), Presidential Candidate in 1964 — A563

**2003, July 31** **Litho.**
**1009** A563 4r multi .20 .20

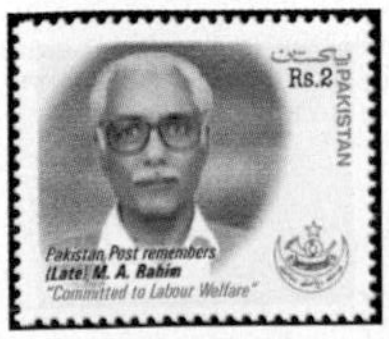

Famous Men — A564

Designs: No. 1010, 2r, M. A. Rahim (1919-2003), labor leader. No. 1011, 2r, Abdul Rahman (1959-2002), slain postal worker.

**2003, Aug. 3** ***Perf. 12¾x13¼***
**1010-1011** A564 Set of 2 .20 .20

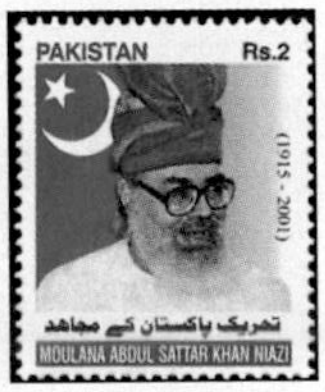

Famous Men — A565

Designs: No. 1012, 2r, Moulana Abdul Sattar Khan Niazi (1915-2001), politician. No. 1013, 2r, Muhammad Yousaf Khattak (1917-91), politician. No. 1014, 2r, Moulana Muhammad Ismail Zabeeh (1913-2001), political leader and journalist.

**2003, Apr. 14** ***Perf. 13¼x12¾***
**1012-1014** A565 Set of 3 .25 .25

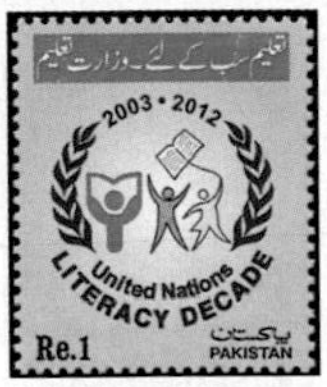

UN Literacy Decade, 2003-12 — A566

**2003, Sept. 6**
**1015** A566 1r multi .20 .20

**Nishan-e-Haider Type of 1995**

**2003, Sept. 7** ***Perf. 14***
**1016** A456 2r Pilot Officer Rashid Minhas Shaheed .20 .20

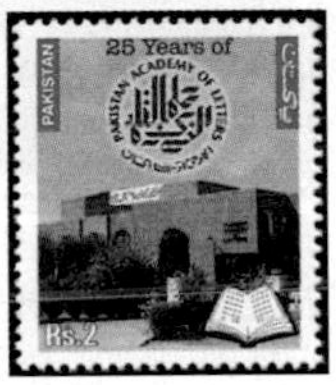

Pakistan Academy of Letters, 25th Anniv. — A567

**2003, Sept. 24** ***Perf. 13¼x12¾***
**1017** A567 2r multi .20 .20

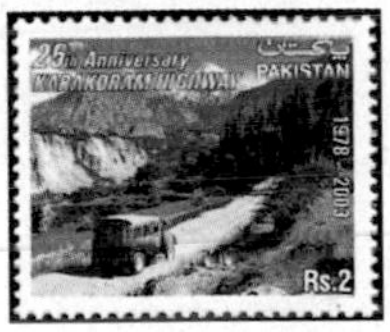

Karakoram Highway, 25th Anniv. — A568

***Perf. 12¾x13***
**2003, Oct. 1** **Litho.** **Unwmk.**
**1018** A568 2r multi .20 .20

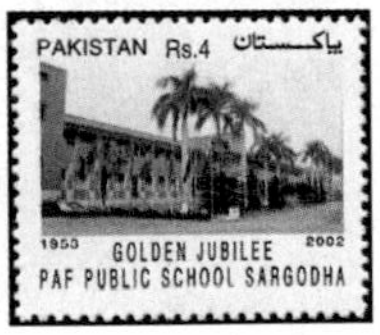

Pakistan Air Force Public School, Sargodha, 50th Anniv. — A569

***Perf. 13x13¼***
**2003, Oct. 10** **Litho.** **Wmk. 351**
**1019** A569 4r multi .20 .20

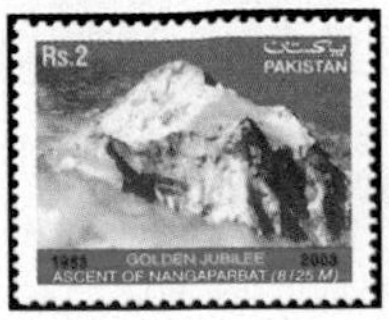

First Ascent of Nanga Parbat, 50th Anniv. — A570

***Perf. 12¾x13***
**2003, Oct. 6** **Litho.** **Unwmk.**
**1020** A570 2r multi .20 .20

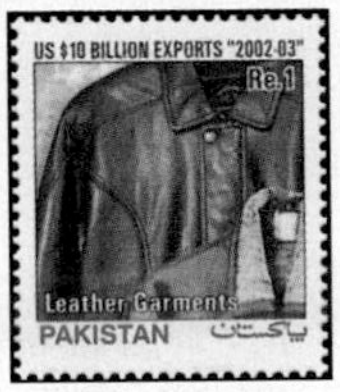

Exports — A571

No. 1021: a, Leather garments. b, Towels. c, Ready-made garments. d, Karachi Port Trust and Port Qasim. e, Fisheries. f, Yarn. g, Sporting goods. h, Fabrics. i, Furniture. j, Surgical instruments. k, Gems and jewelry. l, Leather goods. m, Information technology. n, Rice. o, Auto parts. p, Carpets. q, Marble and granite. r, Fruits. s, Cutlery. t, Engineering goods.

**2003, Oct. 20** ***Perf. 13x12¾***
**1021** Sheet of 20 3.00 3.00
*a.-t.* A571 1r Any single .20 .20

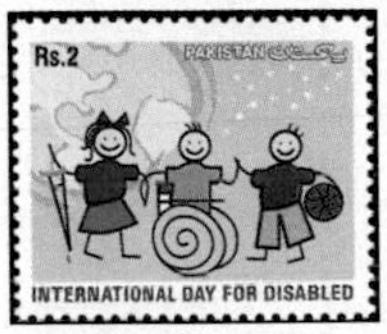

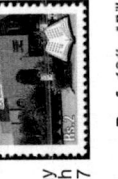

Intl. Day of the Disabled A572

**2003, Dec. 3** ***Perf. 12¾x13***
**1022** A572 2r multi .20 .20

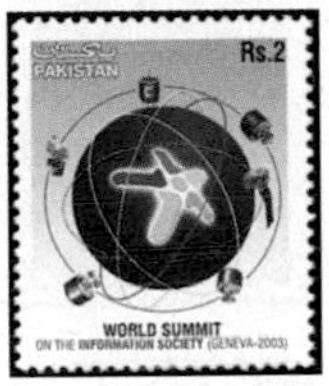

World Summit on the Information Society, Geneva, Switzerland A573

**2003, Dec. 10** ***Perf. 13x12¾***
**1023** A573 2r multi .20 .20

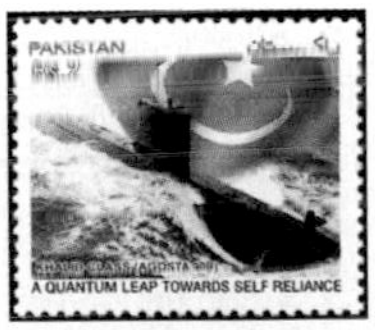

Submarines A574

Khalid Class (Agosta 90B) submarine and flag of: 1r, Pakistan Navy, vert. 2r, Pakistan.

**2003, Dec. 12** ***Perf. 13x12¾, 12¾x13***
**1024-1025** A574 Set of 2 .20 .20

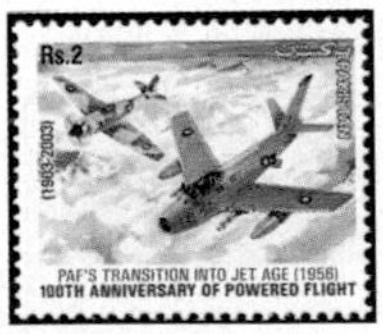

Powered Flight, Cent. — A575

Designs: No. 1026, 2r, Pakistan Air Force's transition into jet age, 1956. No. 1027, 2r, Air Force in action at Siachen, 1988-90.

**2003, Dec. 17** ***Perf. 12¾x13***
**1026-1027** A575 Set of 2 .20 .20

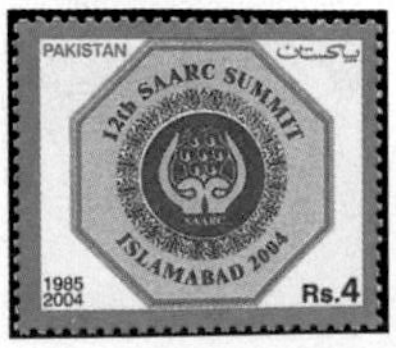

12th South Asian Association for Regional Cooperation Summit, Islamabad A576

**2004, Jan. 4**
**1028** A576 4r multi .20 .20

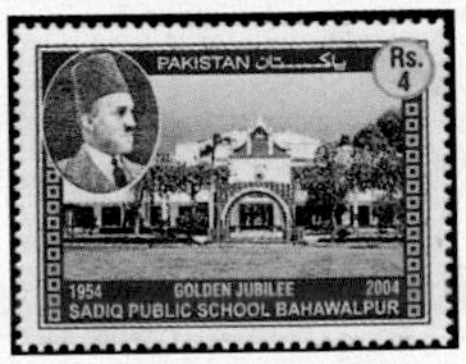

Sadiq Public School, Bahawalpur, 50th Anniv. — A577

**2004, Jan. 28** **Litho.** ***Perf. 14***
**1029** A577 4r multi .20 .20

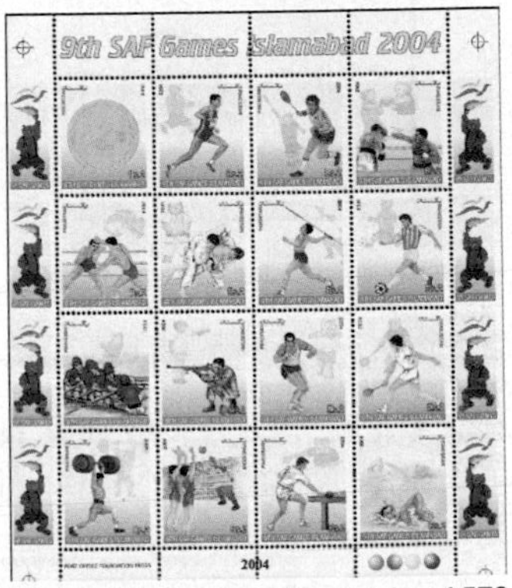

Ninth SAF Games, Islamabad — A578

No. 1030: a, Gold medal. b, Running. c, Squash (yellow and blue uniform). d, Boxing. e, Wrestling. f, Judo. g, Javelin. h, Soccer. i, Rowing. j, Shooting. k, Shot put. l, Badminton (white uniform). m, Weight lifting. n, Volleyball. o, Table tennis. p, Swimming.

**2004, Mar. 29** **Litho.** ***Perf. 13x12¾***
**1030** A578 2r Sheet of 16, #a-p 4.50 4.50

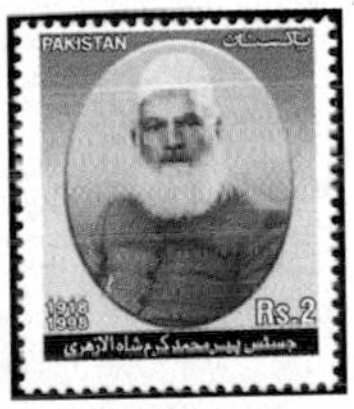

Pir Muhammad Karam Shah Al-Azhari (1918-98), Jurist — A579

**2004, Apr. 7**
**1031** A579 2r multi .20 .20

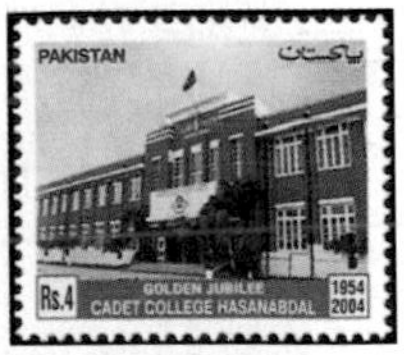

Cadet College, Hasan Abdal — A580

**2004, Apr. 8** ***Perf. 12¾x13***
**1032** A580 4r multi .20 .20

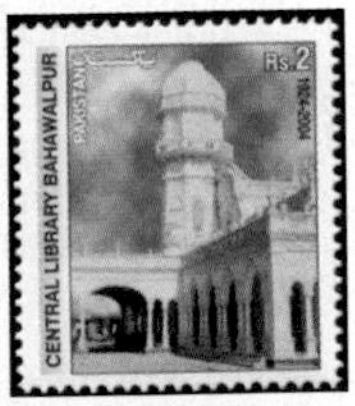

Central Library, Bahawalpur A581

**2004, Apr. 26** **Litho.** ***Perf. 13x12¾***
**1033** A581 2r multi .20 .20

**2004, May 12**

1034 A582 4r multi .20 .20

Mosque, Bhong — A582

**Perf. 12¾x13**

---

FIFA (Fédération Internationale de Football Association), Cent. — A583

No. 1035 — FIFA centenary emblem and: a. Player. b. Blue panel at bottom. c. Player, green panel at bottom.

**2004, May 21**

1035 A583 5r Any single 1.00 1.00
a.-c. .30 .30

Horiz. strip of 3

**Perf. 14**

---

**2004, June 7    Perf. 12¾x13, 13x12¾**

1036-1037 A584    Set of 2 .30 .30

Designs: No. 1036, 4r, Indus River near Chilas. No. 1037, 4r, Haramosh Peak near Gilgit, vert.

Silk Road — A584

---

Sui Southern Gas Company, 50th Anniv. — A585

**2004, July 24    Litho.    Perf. 12¾x13**

1038 A585 4r multi .20 .20

Protecting the National Heritage

National Heritage

---

**2004, July 31    Imperf**

1039 A586 5r shown .20 .20
1040 A586 30r Tent, K2 1.50 1.50

First Ascent of K2, 50th Anniv. — A586

**Size: 95x64mm**

---

**2004, Aug. 13    Perf. 13x12¾**

1041 A587 5r Any single .50 .50
a.-d. 2.00 2.00

Horiz. strip of 4

No. 1041: a. Track. b. Boxing. c. Field hockey. d. Wrestling.

2004 Summer Olympics, Athens — A587

XXVIII ATHENS OLYMPIC 2004    PAKISTAN    Rs.5

---

7 Lines of Text — A588

6 Lines of Text — A590

6½ Lines of Text — A589

6¾ Lines of Text — A591

Independence, 57th anniv.

**2004, Aug. 14**

1042    Horiz. strip of 4
a. A588 5r multi 1.25 1.25
b. A589 5r multi .30 .30
c. A590 5r multi .30 .30
d. A591 5r multi .30 .30

---

Maulvi Abdul Haq (1870-1961), Lexicographer — A592

"MEN OF LETTERS" MAULVI ABDUL HAQ
(1870 - 1961)
BABA-E-URDU

**2004, Aug. 16**

1043 A592 4r multi .20 .20

---

Fourth Intl. Calligraphy and Calligraphic Art Exhibition and Competition, Lahore — A593

PCG 4th International Calligraphy

**2004, Oct. 1**

1044 A593 5r multi .20 .20

---

Tropical Fish — A594

Paracheirodon innesi
Neon Tetra    Rs.2

**2004, Oct. 9**

1045 A594 2r Any single .35 .35
a.-e. .20 .20

Horiz. strip of 5

No. 1045: a. Neon tetra. b. Striped gourami. c. Black widow. d. Yellow dwarf cichlid. e. Tiger barb.

**Perf. 12½**

---

Japanese Economic Assistance, 50th Anniv. — A595

**2004, Nov. 8    Litho.    Perf. 12¾x13**

1046-1049 A595    Set of 4 .70 .70
1050    A595 multi .70 .70

**Imperf**

Designs: No. 1046, 5r, Training for handicapped. No. 1047, 5r, Polio eradication. No. 1048, 5r, Ghazi Barotha hydroelectric power project. No. 1049, 5r, Kohat Friendship Tunnel. Vignettes of Nos. 1046-1049, Friendship Tunnel.

---

Year of Child Welfare and Rights — A596

2004 Child Welfare and Rights    Rs.4

**2004, Nov. 20**

1051 A596 4r multi .20 .20

---

Allama Iqbal Open University, Islamabad, 30th Anniv. — A597

1974-2004
30 YEARS OF AIOU
Rs.20

**2004, Dec. 6    Perf. 12¾x13**

1052 A597 20r multi .70 .70

---

Khyber Medical College, Peshawar, 50th Anniv. — A598

50 Years
KHYBER MEDICAL COLLEGE    Rs.5

**2004, Dec. 30**

1053 A598 5r multi .20 .20

---

Prof. Ahmed Ali (1910-94), Writer — A599

PROFESSOR AHMED ALI
MEN OF LETTERS    Rs.5

**2005, Jan. 14    Litho.    Perf. 13x12¾**

1054 A599 5r multi .20 .20

---

Pakistan — Romania Friendship — A600

PAKISTAN
Dialogue Between Civilizations

**2005, Jan. 14**

1055-1056 A600    Set of 2 .35 .35

Poets Mihai Eminescu and Allama Iqbal and: No. 1055, 5r, Flags of Romania and Pakistan. No. 1056, 5r, Flags, monument to Eminescu and Iqbal by Emil Ghitulescu, Islamabad.

---

Saadat Hasan Manto (1912-55), Writer — A601

**2005, Jan. 18**

1057 A601 5r multi .20 .20

**Perf. 13x12¾**

---

Pakistan Air Force, 50th Anniv. — A605

A602
A603
A604

**2005, Mar. 23    Litho.    Perf. 13x12¾**

1058 A602 5r multi .20 .20
1059 A603 5r multi .20 .20
1060 A604 5r multi .20 .20
1061 A605 5r multi .20 .20
Nos. 1058-1061 (4) .80 .80

---

Command and Staff College, Quetta, Cent. — A606

**2005, Apr. 2    Perf. 12¾x13**

1062 A606 5r multi .20 .20

---

Turkish Grand National Assembly, 85th Anniv. — A607

**2005, Apr. 23    Perf. 14**

1063 A607 10r Horiz. pair, #a-b .70 .70

No. 1063 - Assembly building and: a. Kemal Ataturk, Turkish flag. b. Ataturk, Mohammed Ali Jinnah, Turkish and Pakistani flags. Illustration reduced.

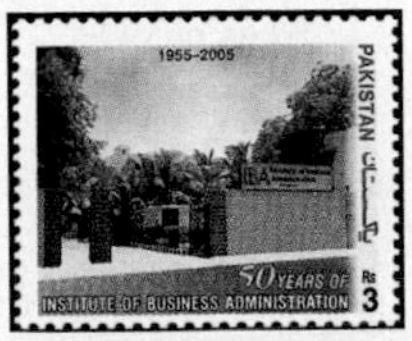


Institute of Business Administration, Karachi, 50th Anniv. — A608

Various views of campus with country name at: No. 1064, 3r, Right. No. 1065, 3r, Bottom.

**2005, Apr. 30** *Perf. 12¾x13*

| | | | |
|---|---|---|---|
| **1064-1065** A608 Set of 2 | .20 | .20 |

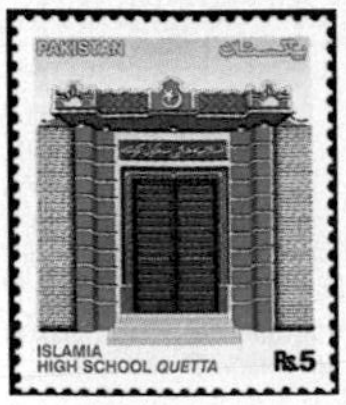


Islamia High School, Quetta, 95th Anniv. — A609

**2005, May 25** *Perf. 13x12¾*

| | | |
|---|---|---|
| **1066** A609 5r multi | .20 | .20 |

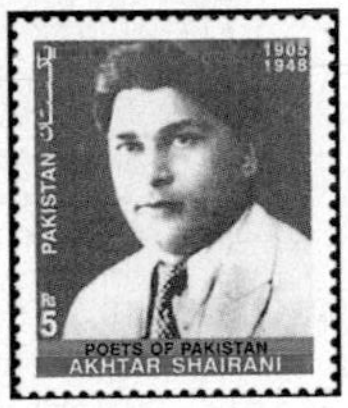


Akhtar Shairani (1905-48), Poet — A610

**2005, June 30**

| | | |
|---|---|---|
| **1067** A610 5r multi | .20 | .20 |

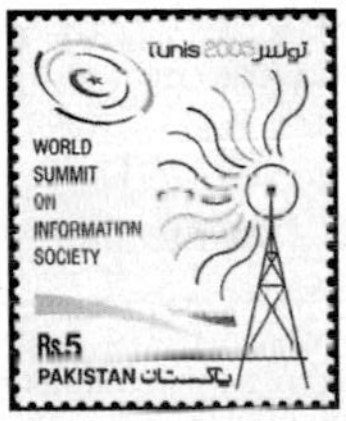


World Summit on Information Technology, Tunis, Tunisia — A611

**2005, July 15**

| | | |
|---|---|---|
| **1068** A611 5r multi | .20 | .20 |

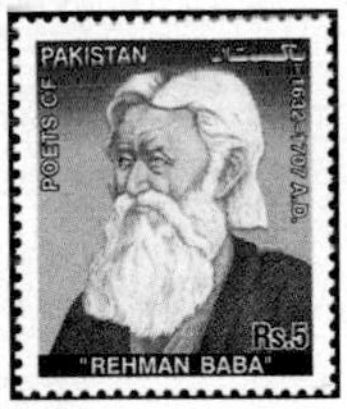


Abdul Rehman Baba (1632-1707), Poet — A612

**2005, Aug. 4**

| | | |
|---|---|---|
| **1069** A612 5r multi | .20 | .20 |

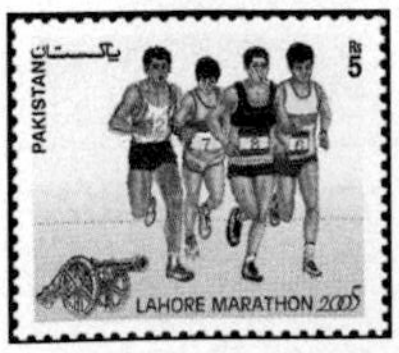


Lahore Marathon A613

**2005, Sept. 10** *Perf. 12¾x13*

| | | |
|---|---|---|
| **1070** A613 5r multi | .20 | .20 |

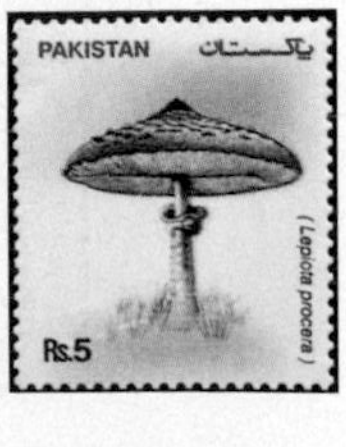


Mushrooms A614

No. 1071: a, Lepiota procera. b, Tricholoma gambosum. c, Amanita caesarea. d, Cantharellus cibarius. e, Boletus luridus. f, Morchella vulgaris. g, Amanita vaginata. h, Agaricus arvensis. i, Coprinus comatus. j, Clitocybe geotropa.

**2005, Oct. 1 Litho.** *Perf. 13¼x12¾*

| | | |
|---|---|---|
| **1071** Block of 10 | 1.75 | 1.75 |
| *a.-j.* A614 5r Any single | .20 | .20 |

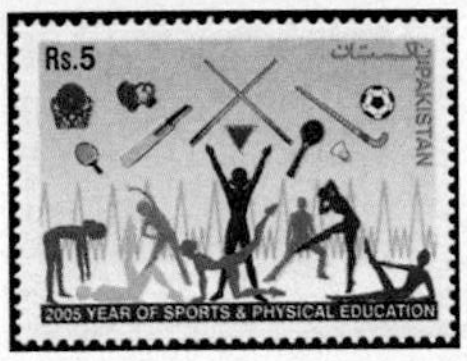


Intl. Year of Sports and Physical Education A615

**2005, Nov. 5** *Perf. 14*

| | | |
|---|---|---|
| **1072** A615 5r multi | .20 | .20 |

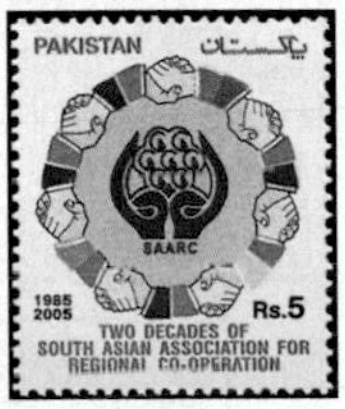


South Asian Association for Regional Cooperation, 20th Anniv. — A616

**2005, Nov. 12** *Perf. 13¼x12¾*

| | | |
|---|---|---|
| **1073** A616 5r multi | .20 | .20 |

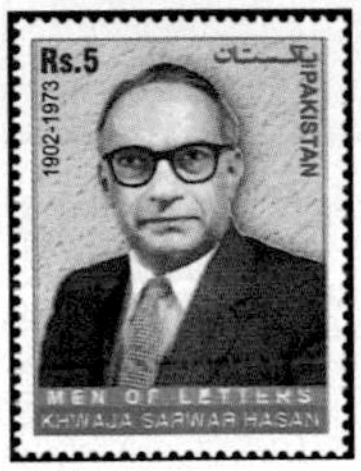


Khwaja Sarwar Hasan (1902-73), Diplomat — A617

**2005, Nov. 18** *Perf. 14*

| | | |
|---|---|---|
| **1074** A617 5r multi | .20 | .20 |

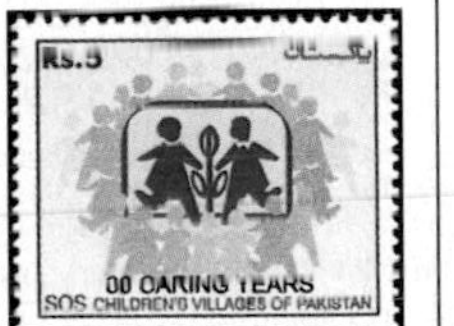


SOS Children's Villages in Pakistan, 30th Anniv. A618

**2005, Nov. 20** *Perf. 12¾x13¼*

| | | |
|---|---|---|
| **1075** A618 5r multi | .20 | .20 |

---

## OFFICIAL STAMPS

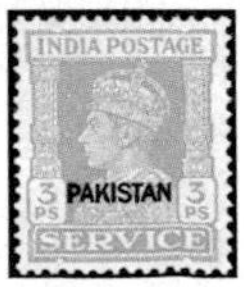


Official Stamps of India, 1939-43, Overprinted in Black

**1947-49 Wmk. 196** *Perf. 13½x14*

| | | | | |
|---|---|---|---|---|
| **O1** | O8 | 3p slate | 1.75 | .90 |
| **O2** | O8 | ½a dk rose vio | .35 | .20 |
| **O3** | O8 | 9p green | 5.50 | 2.00 |
| **O4** | O8 | 1a carmine rose | .35 | .20 |
| **O4A** | O8 | 1a3p bister ('49) | *7.50* | *10.00* |
| **O5** | O8 | 1½a dull purple | .35 | .20 |
| **O6** | O8 | 2a scarlet | .35 | .20 |
| **O7** | O8 | 2½a purple | 8.25 | 8.00 |
| **O8** | O8 | 4a dk brown | 1.60 | .65 |
| **O9** | O8 | 8a blue violet | 2.50 | 2.00 |

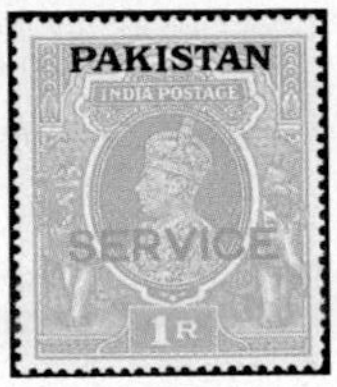


India Nos. O100-O103 Overprinted in Black

| | | | | |
|---|---|---|---|---|
| **O10** | A82 | 1r brown & slate | 1.00 | 2.00 |
| **O11** | A82 | 2r dk brn & dk vio | 5.00 | 5.00 |
| **O12** | A82 | 5r dp ultra & dk grn | 20.00 | *30.00* |
| | | Telegraph cancel | | *7.50* |
| **O13** | A82 | 10r rose car & dk vio | 50.00 | *90.00* |
| | | Telegraph cancel | | *5.00* |
| | | *Nos. O1-O13 (14)* | 104.50 | 151.35 |
| | | Set, hinged | 75.00 | |

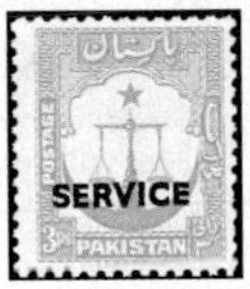


Regular Issue of 1948 Overprinted in Black or Carmine

*Perf. 12½, 13, 13½x14, 14x13½*

**1948, Aug. 14 Unwmk.**

| | | | | |
|---|---|---|---|---|
| **O14** | A3 | 3p orange red | .20 | .20 |
| **O15** | A3 | 6p purple (C) | .20 | .20 |
| **O16** | A3 | 9p dk green (C) | .20 | .20 |
| **O17** | A4 | 1a dk blue (C) | 4.25 | .20 |
| **O18** | A4 | 1½a gray grn (C) | 4.00 | .20 |
| **O19** | A4 | 2a orange red | 1.75 | .20 |
| **O20** | A5 | 3a olive green | 29.00 | 9.00 |
| **O21** | A6 | 4a chocolate | 1.25 | .20 |
| **O22** | A6 | 8a black (C) | 2.50 | *9.00* |
| **O23** | A5 | 1r ultra | 1.25 | .30 |
| **O24** | A5 | 2r dark brown | 17.50 | 10.00 |
| **O25** | A5 | 5r carmine | 47.50 | 11.00 |
| **O26** | A7 | 10r rose lil, perf. 14x13½ | 22.50 | *55.00* |
| *a.* | | Perf. 12 | 25.00 | *60.00* |
| *b.* | | Perf. 13 | 22.50 | *65.00* |
| | | *Nos. O14-O26 (13)* | 132.10 | 95.70 |
| | | Set, hinged | 72.50 | |

Issued: #O26a, 10/10/51; #O26b, 1954(?).

Nos. 47-50 and 52 Overprinted Type "a" in Black or Carmine

**1949-50** *Perf. 12½, 13½x14*

| | | | | |
|---|---|---|---|---|
| **O27** | A10 | 1a dark blue (C) | 1.10 | .20 |
| **O28** | A10 | 1½a gray green (C) | .35 | .20 |
| *a.* | | Inverted ovpt. | 150.00 | 40.00 |
| **O29** | A10 | 2a orange red | 1.10 | .20 |
| **O30** | A9 | 3a olive grn ('49) | 20.00 | 3.25 |
| **O31** | A11 | 8a black (C) | 30.00 | 11.00 |
| | | *Nos. O27-O31 (5)* | 52.55 | 14.85 |

Types of Regular Issue of 1951, "Pakistan" or "Pakistan Postage" Replaced by "SERVICE"

**Unwmk.**

**1951, Aug. 14 Engr.** *Perf. 13*

| | | | | |
|---|---|---|---|---|
| **O32** | A13 | 3a dark rose lake | 5.50 | *4.00* |
| **O33** | A14 | 4a deep green | 1.40 | .25 |
| **O34** | A15 | 8a brown | *7.00* | 1.75 |
| | | *Nos. O32-O34 (3)* | 13.90 | *6.00* |

Nos. 24-26, 47-49, 38-41 Overprinted in Black or Carmine

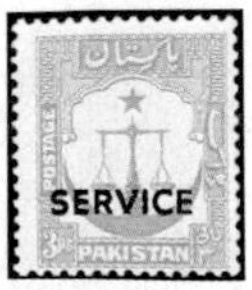


b

**1954**

| | | | | |
|---|---|---|---|---|
| **O35** | A3 | 3p orange red | .20 | .20 |
| **O36** | A3 | 6p purple (C) | .20 | .20 |
| **O37** | A3 | 9p dk green (C) | .20 | .20 |
| **O38** | A10 | 1a dk blue (C) | .20 | .20 |
| **O39** | A10 | 1½a gray green (C) | .20 | .20 |
| **O40** | A10 | 2a orange red | .20 | .20 |
| **O41** | A5 | 1r ultra | 8.50 | 2.00 |
| **O42** | A5 | 2r dark brown | 3.75 | .20 |
| **O43** | A5 | 5r carmine | 25.00 | 10.00 |
| **O43A** | A7 | 10r rose lilac | 22.50 | *40.00* |
| | | *Nos. O35-O43A (10)* | 60.95 | *53.40* |

Nos. 66-72 Overprinted Type "b" in Carmine or Black

**1954, Aug. 14**

| | | | | |
|---|---|---|---|---|
| **O44** | A18 | 6p rose violet (C) | .20 | *1.10* |
| **O45** | A19 | 9p blue (C) | 1.60 | *3.75* |
| **O46** | A19 | 1a carmine rose | .25 | .95 |
| **O47** | A18 | 1½a red | .25 | .95 |
| **O48** | A20 | 14a dk green (C) | 1.10 | *3.25* |
| **O49** | A20 | 1r yellow grn (C) | 1.40 | .20 |
| **O50** | A20 | 2r orange | 2.75 | .20 |
| | | *Nos. O44-O50 (7)* | 7.55 | *10.40* |

No. 75 Overprinted in Carmine Type "b" Overprint: 13x2½mm

**1955, Aug. 14 Unwmk.** *Perf. 13*

| | | | |
|---|---|---|---|
| **O51** A21 8a violet | .35 | .20 |

Nos. 24, 40, 66-72, 74-75, 83, 89 Overprinted in Black or Carmine

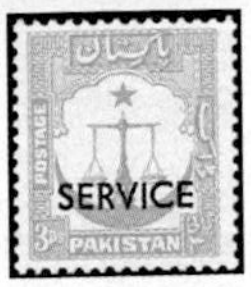


c

**1957-61**

| | | | | |
|---|---|---|---|---|
| **O52** | A3 | 3p org red ('58) | .20 | .20 |
| **O53** | A18 | 6p rose vio (C) | .20 | .20 |
| **O54** | A19 | 9p blue (C) ('58) | .20 | *.25* |
| **O55** | A19 | 1a carmine rose | .20 | .20 |
| **O56** | A18 | 1½a red | .20 | .20 |
| **O57** | A24 | 2a red ('58) | .20 | .20 |
| **O58** | A21 | 6a dk bl (C) ('60) | .20 | .20 |
| **O59** | A21 | 8a vio (C) ('58) | .20 | .20 |
| **O60** | A20 | 14a dk grn (C) ('58) | .40 | *2.00* |
| **O61** | A20 | 1r yel grn (C) ('58) | .40 | .20 |
| **O62** | A20 | 2r orange ('58) | 5.00 | .20 |
| **O63** | A5 | 5r carmine ('58) | 5.00 | .20 |
| **O64** | A26 | 10r dk grn & org (C) ('61) | 6.00 | 6.00 |
| | | *Nos. O52-O64 (13)* | 18.40 | 10.25 |

For surcharges see Nos. O67-O73.

Nos. 110-111 Overprinted Type "c"

**1961, Apr.**

| | | | | |
|---|---|---|---|---|
| **O65** | A33 | 8a green | .20 | .20 |
| **O66** | A33 | 1r blue | .20 | .20 |
| *a.* | | Inverted overprint | 7.50 | |

**New Currency**

Nos. O52, O55-O57 Surcharged with New Value in Paisa

**1961**

| | | | | |
|---|---|---|---|---|
| **O67** | A18 | 1p on 1½a red | .20 | .20 |
| *a.* | | Overprinted type "b" | 3.00 | 1.25 |
| **O68** | A3 | 2p on 3p orange red | .20 | .20 |
| *a.* | | Overprinted type "b" | 4.50 | 3.00 |
| **O69** | A19 | 6p on 1a car rose | .20 | .20 |
| **O70** | A19 | 7p on 1a car rose | .20 | .20 |
| *a.* | | Overprinted type "b" | 5.00 | 5.00 |
| **O71** | A18 | 9p on 1½a red | | |
| **O72** | A24 | 13p on 2a red ("PAISA") | .20 | .20 |
| **O73** | A24 | 13p on 2a red ("Paisa") | | |

Nos. O69, O71, O73 were locally overprinted at Mastung. On these stamps "paisa" is in lower case.

Forgeries of No. O69, O71 and O73 abound.

Nos. 125, 128 Overprinted Type "c"

**1961**

| | | | | |
|---|---|---|---|---|
| **O74** | A33 | 3p on 6p purple | .20 | .20 |
| **O75** | A33 | 13p on 2a copper red | .20 | .20 |

Various violet handstamped surcharges were applied to several official stamps. Most of these repeat the denomination of the basic stamp and add the new value. Example: "4 ANNAS (25 Paisa)" on No. O33.

Nos. 129-135, 135B, 135C, 136a, 137-140a Overprinted in Carmine

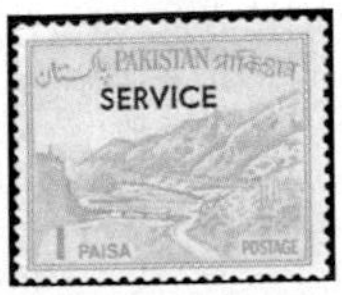


d

**1961-78** *Perf. 13½x14*

| | | | | |
|---|---|---|---|---|
| **O76** | A40 | 1p violet (II) | .20 | .20 |
| *a.* | | Type I | .40 | .40 |
| **O77** | A40 | 2p rose red (II) | .20 | .20 |
| *a.* | | Type I | .40 | .40 |
| **O78** | A40 | 3p magenta | .20 | .20 |
| **O79** | A40 | 5p ultra (II) | .20 | .20 |
| *a.* | | Type I | .40 | .40 |
| **O80** | A40 | 7p emerald | .20 | .20 |
| **O81** | A40 | 10p brown | .20 | .20 |
| **O82** | A40 | 13p blue violet | .20 | .20 |
| **O85** | A40 | 40p dull pur ('62) | .20 | .20 |
| **O86** | A40 | 50p dull grn ('62) | .20 | .20 |
| **O87** | A40 | 75p dk car ('62) | .20 | .20 |
| | | *Nos. O76-O87 (10)* | 2.00 | 2.00 |

Designs Redrawn

**1961-66**

| | | | | |
|---|---|---|---|---|
| *O76b* | A40 | 1p violet (#129b) ('63) | .20 | .20 |
| *O77b* | A40 | 2p rose red (#130b) ('64) | .20 | .20 |
| *O78a* | A40 | 3p mag (#131a) ('66) | 3.00 | 3.00 |
| *O79b* | A40 | 5p ultra (#132b) ('63) | .20 | .20 |
| *O80a* | A40 | 7p emerald (#133a) | 2.00 | .20 |
| *O81a* | A40 | 10p brown (#134a) ('64) | .20 | .20 |
| *O82a* | A40 | 13p blue vio (#135a) ('63) | .20 | .20 |

| | | | | |
|---|---|---|---|---|
| O82a | A40 | 13p blue & vio (#135a) | .20 | .20 |
| O83 | A40 | 15p rose lil (#135B; '63) | .30 | .30 |
| | | ('64) | | |
| O84 | A40 | 20p dl grn (#135C) | .20 | .20 |
| O84A | A40 | 25p dark blue | | |
| | | (#136a; '70) | .20 | .20 |
| O85a | A40 | 40p dull purple (#137a) | .35 | .20 |
| O86a | A40 | 50p dull grn (#138a) | .20 | .20 |
| O87a | A40 | 75p dark carmine | | |
| | | (#139a) | .20 | .20 |
| O88 | A40 | 90p lt ol grn (#140a; | | |
| | | '78) | 8.00 | 4.00 |

See Nos. O76b-O88 (14).

Nos. O84A and O88 for other stamps with designs redrawn.

**1963, Jan. 7 Unwmk. Perf. 13½x13**

Nos. 141, 143-144 Overprinted Type "c" in Black or Carmine

| O89 | A41 | 1r vermilion | .35 | .20 |
| O90 | A41 | 2r orange | 4.25 | 5.00 |
| O91 | A41 | 5r green (C) | 6.10 | 5.45 |

Nos. 200, 202-203 Overprinted Type "c"

**1968-? Wmk. 351 Perf. 13½x13**

| O92 | A41 | 1r vermilion | 1.00 | |
| O93 | A41 | 2r orange | 5.00 | .50 |
| O93A | A41 | 5r green (C) | 12.00 | 5.00 |

Nos. O92-O93A (3)    18.00   5.70

Nos. 459-468, 470-475 Overprinted Type "d" in Carmine or Black

**1979-84**

| O94 | A224 | 2p dark green | .20 | .20 |
| O95 | A225 | 3p black | .20 | .20 |
| O96 | A224 | 5p violet blue | .20 | .20 |
| O97 | A225 | 10p grnsh blue | .20 | .20 |
| O98 | A225 | 20p grnsh blue | .20 | .20 |
| O99 | A225 | 25p rose car | | |
| | | grn ('81) | .20 | .20 |
| O100 | A225 | 40p car & blk | .25 | .20 |
| O101 | A225 | 50p dp brn & vio | .30 | .20 |
| O102 | A225 | 60p black | 1.00 | .20 |
| O103 | A225 | 75p orange | 1.00 | .20 |
| O105 | A225 | 1r olive ('81) | 2.25 | .20 |
| O106 | A225a | 1.50r dp orange | 2.50 | .20 |
| O107 | A225a | 2r car rose | .90 | .20 |
| O108 | A225a | 3r indigo ('81) | 1.20 | .20 |
| O109 | A225a | 4r black ('84) | 1.25 | .20 |
| O110 | A225a | 5r dk brn ('84) | 1.25 | .35 |

Nos. O94-O110 (16)    9.00   3.35

Types A237-A239 Inscribed "SERVICE POSTAGE"

**1980 Litho. Perf. 12x11½, 11½x12**

| O111 | A237 | 10p dk grn & yel org | .20 | .20 |
| O112 | A237 | 15p dk grn & ap grn | .90 | .20 |
| O113 | A225 | 25p dp vio & rose car | .90 | .20 |
| O114 | A237 | 35p rose pink & brt | .20 | .20 |
| | | yel grn | .20 | .20 |
| O115 | A238 | 40p red & lt brn | .90 | .20 |
| O116 | A239 | 50p olive & vio bl | .25 | .20 |
| O117 | A239 | 80p blk & yel grn | 3.55 | 1.40 |

Nos. O111-O117 (7)

Issued: 10p, 15p, 40p, 1/15; others, 3/10.

Nos. 613-614, 616-620 Ovptd. "SERVICE" in Red

**1984-87 Litho. Perf. 11**

| O118 | A289 | 5p Kot Diji | .20 | .20 |
| O119 | A289 | 10p Rohtas | .20 | .20 |
| O120 | A289 | 40p Attock Fort | .20 | .20 |
| O121 | A289 | 50p Hyderabad | .20 | .20 |
| O122 | A289 | 60p Lahore ('86) | .20 | .20 |
| O123 | A289 | 70p Sibi | .20 | .20 |
| O124 | A289 | 80p Rankiot | 1.40 | 1.40 |

Nos. O118-O124 (7)

**1989, Dec. 24 Litho. & Engr.**

| O124A | A357 | 1r multicolored | 4.00 | 5.00 |

No. 712 Ovptd. "SERVICE" Litho. & Engr.

Issued: 10p, 9/25, 80p, 8/3/87.

National Assembly, Islamabad — O1

**1991-99 Litho. Wmk. 351 Perf. 13½**

| O125 | O1 | 1r green & red | .20 | .20 |
| O126 | O1 | 2r rose car & red | .20 | .20 |
| O127 | O1 | 3r ultra & red | .20 | .20 |
| O128 | O1 | 4r red brown & red | .20 | .20 |

| O129 | O1 | 5r rose lilac & red | .20 | .20 |
| O130 | O1 | 10r brown & red | .30 | .30 |

Issued: 10r, 2/6/99; others, 4/12/91.

**1999 Unwmk.**

| O131 | O1 | 2r rose car & red | .20 | .20 |

This is an expanding set. Numbers may change.

---

# BAHAWALPUR

LOCATION — A State of Pakistan.
AREA — 17,494 sq. mi.
POP. — 1,341,209 (1941)
CAPITAL — Bahawalpur

Bahawalpur was a State of India until 1947. These stamps had franking power solely within Bahawalpur.

Seventeen King George VI stamps of India exist overprinted with star, crescent and a line of Arabic. Their legitimacy is in dispute.

Used values are for c-t-o or favor cancels.

Amir Muhammad Bahawal Khan I Abbasi — A1

**1947, Dec. 1 Wmk. 274 Perf. 12½x12 Engr.**

1   A1   ½a brt car rose & blk   2.50   3.50

Bicentenary of the ruling family.

Nawab Sadiq Muhammad Khan V Abbasi Bahadur — A2

Tombs of the Amirs — A3

Mosque, Sadiq Garh — A4

Fort Dirawar A5

A9

**1948, Apr. 1 Wmk. 274**
**Perf. 12½ (A2), 12x12½ (A3, A5, A6, A7), 12½x12 (A4, A8), 13x13½ (A9) Engr.**

| 2 | A2 | 3p blue & blk | 1.50 | 2.50 |
| 3 | A2 | ½a lake & blk | 1.50 | 2.50 |
| 4 | A2 | 9p dk green & blk | 1.50 | 2.50 |
| 5 | A2 | 1a car & blk | 1.50 | 2.50 |
| 6 | A2 | 1½a violet & blk | 1.50 | 2.50 |
| 7 | A3 | 2a car & dp grn | 1.75 | 2.50 |
| 8 | A4 | 4a brn & org red | 2.00 | 2.50 |
| 9 | A5 | 6a blk & vio brn | 2.00 | 2.50 |
| 10 | A6 | 8a brt pur & car | 2.00 | 2.50 |
| 11 | A7 | 12a car & blk | 2.25 | 2.50 |
| 12 | A8 | 1r chocolate & vio | 2.50 | |
| 13 | A8 | 2r dp mag & dk | 22.50 | 20.00 |
| 14 | A8 | 5r purple & black | 37.50 | 42.50 |
| 15 | A9 | 10r black & car | 168.00 | 172.50 |

Nos. 2-15 (14)

See #18-21. For overprints see #O17-O24.

Palace, Sadiq Garh — A7

Nawab Sadiq Muhammad Khan V Abbasi Bahadur — A8

Nur-Mahal Palace — A6

Panjnad Weir — A12

**1948 Perf. 12x11½ Types of 1948**

| 18 | A8 | 1r orange & dp grn | 1.25 | 2.50 |
| 19 | A8 | 2r carmine & blk | 1.50 | 2.50 |
| 20 | A8 | 5r ultra & red brn | 1.75 | 2.50 |
| 21 | A9 | 10r green & red brn | 6.60 | 10.00 |

Nos. 18-21 (4)

**1949, Mar. 3 Perf. 14**

| 22 | A12 | 3p shown | .20 | 1.50 |
| 23 | A12 | ½a Wheat | .20 | 1.50 |
| 24 | A12 | 9p Cotton | .20 | 2.50 |
| 25 | A12 | 1a Sanwal Bull | .20 | 2.50 |

Nos. 22-25 (4)

25th anniv. of the acquisition of full ruling powers by Amir Khan V.

Panjnad Weir — A12

UPU Monument, Bern — A13

**1949, Oct. 10 Perf. 13**
**Center in Black**

| 26 | A13 | 9p green | .20 | 1.50 |
| 27 | A13 | 1a red violet | .20 | 1.50 |
| 28 | A13 | 1½a brown orange | .20 | 1.50 |
| 29 | A13 | 2½a blue | .80 | 6.00 |

Nos. 26-29 (4)

UPU, 75th anniv. Exist imperf. For overprints see Nos. O25-O28.

Panjnad Weir — O1

Tombs of the Amirs — A3

**1948, Oct. 15 Engr. Perf. 11½**
16   A10   1½a dp car & blk   1.40   2.50

Centenary of the Multan Campaign.

Camel and Colt — O2

Soldiers of 1848 and 1948 — A10

Antelopes O3

Amir Khan V and Mohammed Ali Jinnah — A11

**1948, Oct. 3 Engr. Perf. 13x12½**
17   A11   1½a grn & car rose   1.40   2.50

1st anniv. of the union of Bahawalpur with Pakistan.

---

**OFFICIAL STAMPS**

Two printings of Nos. O1-O10 exist. The first printing has brownish, streaky gum, and the second printing has clear, even gum.

Pelicans O4

## Pakistan — Bahawalpur

Juma Masjid Palace, Fort Derawar — O5

Temple at Pattan Munara — O6

**Red Overprint**
**Wmk. 274 Engr. Perf. 14**

**1945, Jan. 1**
| | | | |
|---|---|---|---|
| O1 | O5 | ½a brt grn & blk | 4.00 | 2.50 |
| O2 | O5 | 1a carmine & blk | 5.25 | 3.00 |
| O3 | O5 | 2a violet & blk | 4.50 | 3.00 |
| O4 | O4 | 4a olive & blk | 11.50 | 6.75 |
| O5 | O6 | 8a brown & blk | 26.00 | 8.75 |
| O6 | O6 | 1r orange & blk | 77.25 | 32.75 |
| | | Nos. O1–O6 (6) |

For types overprinted see Nos. O7–O9, O11–O13.

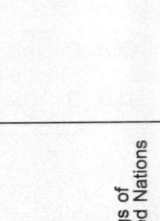

Types of 1945, Without Red Overprint, Surcharged in Black

**1945**
| | | | | Unwmk. |
|---|---|---|---|---|
| O7 | O5 | ½a on 8a lake & blk | 4.75 | 3.75 |
| O8 | O6 | 1½a on 1r org & blk | 40.00 | 12.50 |
| O9 | O6 | 1½a on 2r ultra & blk | 140.00 | 16.00 |
| | | Nos. O7–O9 (3) | 184.75 | 32.25 |

Camels — O7

**1945, Mar. 10**
| | | | | Red Overprint |
|---|---|---|---|---|
| O10 | O7 | 1a brown & black | | 42.50 | 50.00 |

Types of 1945, Without Red Overprint, Overprinted in Black

**1945**
| | | | | |
|---|---|---|---|---|
| O11 | O1 | ½a carmine & black | 1.75 | 3.00 |
| O12 | O1 | 1a carmine & black | 3.00 | 3.00 |
| O13 | O3 | 2a orange & black | 5.25 | 4.00 |
| | | Nos. O11–O13 (3) | 10.00 | 10.00 |

Nawab Sadiq Muhammad Khan V Abbasi Bahadur — O8

**1945**
| | | | | |
|---|---|---|---|---|
| O14 | O8 | 3p dp blue & blk | 3.50 | 5.00 |
| O15 | O8 | 1½a dp violet & blk | 20.00 | 10.50 |

**1946, May 1**
| | | | |
|---|---|---|---|
| O16 | O9 | 1½a emerald & gray | 2.25 | 2.50 |

Flags of Allied Nations O9

Victory of Allied Nations in World War II.

Stamps of 1948 Overprinted in Carmine or Black

**Perf. 12½, 12½x12, 12x11½, 13½**
**1948 Wmk. 274**
| | | | | |
|---|---|---|---|---|
| O17 | A2 | 3p dp bl & blk (C) | | 2.50 |
| O18 | A2 | 1a dp carmine & blk | 1.10 | 2.50 |
| O19 | A3 | 2a car & dp grn | 1.10 | 2.50 |
| O20 | A4 | 4a brown & org red | 1.10 | 2.50 |
| O21 | A8 | 1r org & dp grn (C) | 1.10 | 2.50 |
| O22 | A8 | 2r car & blk (C) | 1.10 | 2.50 |
| O23 | A8 | 5r ultra & red brn | | 2.50 |

| | | | (C) | |
|---|---|---|---|---|
| O24 | A9 | 10r grn & red brn (C) | 1.10 | 2.50 |
| | | Nos. O17–O24 (8) | 8.80 | 20.00 |

**Same Ovpt. in Carmine on #26-29**
**Perf. 13, 18**
**1949 Center in Black**
| | | | | |
|---|---|---|---|---|
| O25 | A13 | 9p green | .20 | 2.50 |
| O26 | A13 | 1a red violet | .20 | 2.50 |
| O27 | A13 | 1½a brown orange | .20 | 2.50 |
| O28 | A13 | 2 ½a blue | .80 | 10.00 |
| | | Nos. O25–O28 (4) | | |

75th anniv. of the UPU. Exist perf 17½x17 and Imperf.

---

## PALAU

pə-'lau

LOCATION — Group of 100 islands in the West Pacific Ocean about 1,000 miles southeast of Manila
AREA — 179 sq. mi.
POP. — 18,467 (1999 est.)
CAPITAL — Koror

Palau, the western section of the Caroline Islands (Micronesia), was part of the US Trust Territory of the Pacific, established in 1947. By agreement with the USPS, the republic began issuing its own stamps in 1984, with the USPS continuing to carry the mail to and from the islands.
On Jan. 10, 1986 Palau became a Federation as a Sovereign State in Compact of Free Association with the US.

100 Cents = 1 Dollar

**Catalogue values for all unused stamps in this country are for Never Hinged items.**

---

Palau Fruit Dove — A2

**1983, May 16** **Perf. 15**
| | | | | |
|---|---|---|---|---|
| 5 | A2 | 20c shown | .40 | .40 |
| 6 | A2 | 20c Palau morningbird | .40 | .40 |
| 7 | A2 | 20c Giant white-eye | .40 | .40 |
| 8 | A2 | 20c Palau fantail | .40 | .40 |
| | | Block of 4, #5-8 | 1.60 | 1.60 |

Sea Fan — A3

**Litho.** **Perf. 13½x14**
**1983-84**
| | | | | |
|---|---|---|---|---|
| 9 | A3 | 1c shown | .20 | .20 |
| 10 | A3 | 3c Map cowrie | .20 | .20 |
| 11 | A3 | 5c Jellyfish | .20 | .20 |
| 12 | A3 | 10c Hawksbill turtle | .20 | .20 |
| 13 | A3 | 13c Giant Clam | .20 | .20 |
| a. | | Booklet pane of 10 | 10.00 | |
| b. | | Bklt. pane of 10 (5 #13, 5 #14) | 11.00 | |
| 14 | A3 | 20c Parrotfish | .35 | .35 |
| a. | | Booklet pane of 10 | 10.50 | |
| 15 | A3 | 28c Chambered Nautilus | .45 | .45 |
| 16 | A3 | 30c Dappled sea cucumber | .50 | .50 |
| 17 | A3 | 37c Sea Urchin | .55 | .55 |
| 18 | A3 | 50c Starfish | .80 | .80 |
| 19 | A3 | $1 Squid | 1.60 | 1.60 |

**Perf. 15x14**
| | | | | |
|---|---|---|---|---|
| 20 | A3 | $2 Dugong | 4.25 | 4.25 |
| 21 | A3 | $5 Pink sponge | 10.50 | 10.50 |
| | | Nos. 9-21 (13) | 20.00 | 20.00 |

See Nos. 75-85.

Humpback Whale, World Wildlife Emblem — A4

**1983, Sept. 21** **Perf. 14**
| | | | | |
|---|---|---|---|---|
| 24 | A4 | 20c shown | .50 | .50 |
| 25 | A4 | 20c Blue whale | .50 | .50 |
| 26 | A4 | 20c Fin whale | .50 | .50 |
| 27 | A4 | 20c Great sperm whale | .50 | .50 |
| a. | | Block of 4, #24-27 | 2.00 | 2.00 |

Christmas 1983 — A5

Paintings by Charlie Gibbons, 1971.

**1983, Oct.** **Litho.** **Perf. 14½**
| | | | | |
|---|---|---|---|---|
| 28 | A5 | 20c First Child ceremony | .50 | .50 |
| 29 | A5 | 20c Spearfishing from Red Canoe | .50 | .50 |
| 30 | A5 | 20c Traditional feast at the Bai | .50 | .50 |
| 31 | A5 | 20c Taro gardening | .50 | .50 |
| 32 | A5 | 20c Spearfishing at New Moon | .50 | .50 |
| a. | | Strip of 5, #28-32 | 2.50 | 2.50 |

A6

Inauguration of Postal Service — A1

**1983, Mar. 10** **Litho.** **Perf. 14**
| | | | | |
|---|---|---|---|---|
| 1 | A1 | 20c Constitution preamble | .50 | .50 |
| 2 | A1 | 20c Hunters | .50 | .50 |
| 3 | A1 | 20c Fish | .50 | .50 |
| 4 | A1 | 20c Preamble, diff. | .50 | .50 |
| a. | | Block of 4, #1-4 | 2.00 | 2.00 |

---

Capt. Wilson's Voyage, Bicentennial — A7

**1983, Dec. 14** **Perf. 14x15**
| | | | | |
|---|---|---|---|---|
| 33 | A6 | 20c Capt. Henry Wilson | .45 | .45 |
| 34 | A7 | 20c Approaching Pelew | .45 | .45 |
| 35 | A7 | 20c Englishman's Camp on Ulong | .45 | .45 |
| 36 | A6 | 20c Prince Lee Boo | .45 | .45 |
| 37 | A7 | 20c King Abba Thulle | .45 | .45 |
| 38 | A7 | 20c Mooring in Koror | .45 | .45 |
| 39 | A7 | 20c Village scene of Pelew Islands | .45 | .45 |
| 40 | A6 | 20c Ludee | .45 | .45 |
| a. | | Block or strip of 8, #33-40 | 4.00 | 4.00 |

Local Seashells — A8

Shell paintings (dorsal and ventral) by Deborah Dudley Max.

**1984, Mar. 15** **Litho.** **Perf. 14**
| | | | | |
|---|---|---|---|---|
| 41 | A8 | 20c Triton trumpet, d. | .45 | .45 |
| 42 | A8 | 20c Horned helmet, d. | .45 | .45 |
| 43 | A8 | 20c Giant clam, d. | .45 | .45 |
| 44 | A8 | 20c Laciniate conch, d. | .45 | .45 |
| 45 | A8 | 20c Royal cloak scallop, d. | .45 | .45 |
| 46 | A8 | 20c Triton trumpet, v. | .45 | .45 |
| 47 | A8 | 20c Horned helmet, v. | .45 | .45 |
| 48 | A8 | 20c Giant clam, v. | .45 | .46 |
| 49 | A8 | 20c Laciniate conch, v. | .45 | .46 |
| 50 | A8 | 20c Royal cloak scallop, v. | .45 | .45 |
| a. | | Block of 10, #41-50 | 4.50 | 4.50 |

## 1984, June 19 — Litho. Perf. 14

Explorer Ships — A9

| | | | | | |
|---|---|---|---|---|---|
| 51 | A9 | 40c | Oroolong, 1783 | .85 | .85 |
| 52 | A9 | 40c | Duff, 1797 | .85 | .85 |
| 53 | A9 | 40c | Peiho, 1908 | .85 | .85 |
| 54 | A9 | 40c | Albatross, 1885 | .85 | .85 |
| a. | | | Block of 4, #51-54 | 3.50 | 3.50 |

UPU Congress.

AUSIPEX '84 — A10

| | | | | | |
|---|---|---|---|---|---|
| 55 | A10 | 20c | Throw spear fishing | .40 | .40 |
| 56 | A10 | 20c | Kite fishing | .40 | .40 |
| 57 | A10 | 20c | Underwater spear fishing | .40 | .40 |
| 58 | A10 | 20c | Net fishing | .40 | .40 |
| a. | | | Block of 4, #55-58 | 1.75 | 1.75 |

Fishing Methods.

## 1984, Sept. 6 — Litho. Perf. 14

Christmas Flowers — A11

| | | | | | |
|---|---|---|---|---|---|
| 59 | A11 | 20c | Mountain Apple | .40 | .40 |
| 60 | A11 | 20c | Beach Morning Glo- | .40 | .40 |
| 61 | A11 | 20c | Turmeric | .40 | .40 |
| 62 | A11 | 20c | Plumeria | .40 | .40 |
| a. | | | Block of 4, #59-62 | 1.75 | 1.75 |

## 1984, Nov. 28 — Litho. Perf. 14

Audubon Bicentenary — A12

| | | | | | |
|---|---|---|---|---|---|
| 63 | A12 | 22c | Shearwater chick | .85 | .85 |
| 64 | A12 | 22c | Shearwater's head | .85 | .85 |
| 65 | A12 | 22c | Shearwater in flight | .85 | .85 |
| 66 | A12 | 22c | Swimming | .85 | .85 |
| a. | | | Block of 4, #63-66, C5 (5) | 4.50 | 4.50 |

## 1985, Feb. 6 — Litho. Perf. 14½x14

Canoes and Rafts — A13

| | | | | | |
|---|---|---|---|---|---|
| 67 | A13 | 22c | Cargo canoe | .55 | .55 |
| 68 | A13 | 22c | War canoe | .55 | .55 |
| 69 | A13 | 22c | Bamboo raft | .55 | .55 |
| 70 | A13 | 22c | Racing/sailing canoe | .55 | .55 |
| a. | | | Block of 4, #67-70 | 2.25 | 2.25 |

## 1985, Mar. 27 — Litho. Perf. 14½x14

Marine Life Type of 1983

| | | | | | |
|---|---|---|---|---|---|
| 75 | A3 | 14c | Trumpet triton | .30 | .30 |
| a. | | | Booklet pane of 10 | 8.00 | — |

## 1985, June 11 — Litho.

| | | | | | |
|---|---|---|---|---|---|
| 76 | A3 | 22c | Bumphead par- rotfish | .55 | .55 |
| a. | | | Booklet pane of 10 | 10.00 | — |
| 77 | A3 | 25c | Soft coral, damsel fish | 11.00 | — |
| a. | | | Booklet pane 5 14c, 5 22c | | |
| 79 | A3 | 33c | Sea anemone, clownfish | .60 | .60 |
| 80 | A3 | 39c | Green sea turtle | .80 | .80 |
| 81 | A3 | 44c | Pacific sailfish | .95 | .95 |
| 85 | A3 | $10 | Spinner dolphins | 1.10 | 1.10 |
| | | | Nos. 75-85 (7) | 19.00 | 19.00 |
| | | | | 23.30 | 23.30 |

This is an expanding set. Numbers will change if necessary.

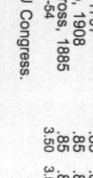

International Youth Year — A14

Christmas 1985 — A15

IYY emblem and children of all nationalities joined in a circle.

## 1985, July 15 — Litho. Perf. 14

| | | | | | |
|---|---|---|---|---|---|
| 86 | A14 | 44c | multicolored | .80 | .80 |
| 87 | A14 | 44c | multicolored | .80 | .80 |
| 88 | A14 | 44c | multicolored | .80 | .80 |
| 89 | A14 | 44c | multicolored | .80 | .80 |
| a. | | | Block of 4, #86-89 | 3.25 | 3.25 |

No. 89a has a continuous design.

## 1985, Oct. 21 — Litho. Perf. 14

Christmas: Island mothers and children.

| | | | | | |
|---|---|---|---|---|---|
| 90 | A15 | 14c | multicolored | .35 | .35 |
| 91 | A15 | 22c | multicolored | .50 | .50 |
| 92 | A15 | 33c | multicolored | .80 | .80 |
| 93 | A15 | 44c | multicolored | 1.10 | 1.10 |
| | | | Nos. 90-93 (4) | 2.75 | 2.75 |

Souvenir Sheet

Pan American Airways Martin M-130 China Clipper — A16

## 1985, Nov. 21 — Litho. Perf. 14

| | | | | | |
|---|---|---|---|---|---|
| 94 | A16 | $1 | multicolored | 2.50 | 2.50 |

1st Trans-Pacific Mail Flight, Nov. 22, 1935. See Nos. C10-C13.

Return of Halley's Comet A17

Fictitious local sightings.

## 1985, Dec. 21 — Litho. Perf. 14

| | | | | | |
|---|---|---|---|---|---|
| 95 | A17 | 44c | Kaeb canoe, 1758 | .75 | .75 |
| 96 | A17 | 44c | U.S.S. Vincennes, 1835 | .75 | .75 |
| 97 | A17 | 44c | S.M.S. Scharnhorst, 1910 | .75 | .75 |
| 98 | A17 | 44c | Yacht, 1986 | .75 | .75 |
| a. | | | Block of 4, #95-98 | 3.00 | 3.00 |

World of Sea and Reef — A19

Songbirds — A18

## 1986, Feb. 24 — Litho. Perf. 14

| | | | | | |
|---|---|---|---|---|---|
| 99 | A18 | 44c | Mangrove flycatcher | .85 | .85 |
| 100 | A18 | 44c | Cardinal honeyeater | .85 | .85 |
| 101 | A18 | 44c | Blue-faced par- rotfinch | .85 | .85 |
| 102 | A18 | 44c | Dusky and bridled white-eyes | .85 | .85 |
| a. | | | Block of 4, #99-102 | 3.50 | 3.50 |

Designs: a. Spear fisherman. b. Native raft. c. Sailing canoes. d. Rock islands, sailfish. e. Inter-island boat, flying fish. f. Bonefish. g. Common jack. h. Mackerel. i. Sailfish. j. Barracuda. k. Triggerfish. l. Dolphinfish. m. Spearfisherman, grouper. n. Manta ray. o. Marlin. p. Parrotfish. q. Wrasse. r. Red snapper. s. Herring. t. Dugong. u. Surgeonfish. v. Leopard ray. w. Hawksbill turtle. x. Needlefish. y. Tuna. z. Octopus. aa. Clownfish. ab. Squid. ac. Grouper. ad. Moorish idol. ae. Queen conch. af. Starfish. ag. Starfish, sting ray. ah. Lion fish. ai. Angel fish. aj. Butterfly fish. ak. Spiny lobster. al. Mangrove crab. am. Tridacna. an. Moray eel.

## 1986, May 22 — Litho. Perf. 15x14

| | | | | | |
|---|---|---|---|---|---|
| 103 | | Sheet of 40 | | 37.50 | |
| a.-an. | | A19 14c any single | | .25 | .25 |

AMERIPEX '86, Chicago, May 22-June 1

Seashells — A20

Commercial Trochus — Trochus niloticus

## 1986, Aug. 1 — Litho. Perf. 14

| | | | | | |
|---|---|---|---|---|---|
| 104 | A20 | 22c | Commercial trochus | .55 | .55 |
| 105 | A20 | 22c | Marble cone | .55 | .55 |
| 106 | A20 | 22c | Fluted giant clam | .55 | .55 |
| 107 | A20 | 22c | Bullmouth helmet | .55 | .55 |
| 108 | A20 | 22c | Golden cowrie | .55 | .55 |
| a. | | | Strip of 5, #104-108 | 2.75 | 2.75 |

See Nos. 150-154, 191-195, 212-216.

Int. Peace Year — A21

## 1986, Sept. 19 — Litho. Perf. 14

| | | | | | |
|---|---|---|---|---|---|
| 109 | A21 | 22c | Soldier's helmet | .65 | .65 |
| 110 | A21 | 22c | Plane wreckage | .65 | .65 |
| 111 | A21 | 22c | Woman playing guitar | .65 | .65 |
| 112 | A21 | 22c | Airai vista | .65 | .65 |
| a. | | | Block of 4, #109-112 | 2.75 | 2.75 |

Nos. 109-112,C17 (5) | 3.60 | 3.60 |

Indigenous Flowers — A25

Reptiles A22

## 1986, Oct. 28 — Litho. Perf. 14

| | | | | | |
|---|---|---|---|---|---|
| 113 | A22 | 22c | Gecko | .60 | .60 |
| 114 | A22 | 22c | Emerald tree skink | .60 | .60 |
| 115 | A22 | 22c | Estuarine crocodile | .60 | .60 |
| 116 | A22 | 22c | Leatherback turtle | .60 | .60 |
| a. | | | Block of 4, #113-116 | 2.40 | 2.40 |

Christmas — A23    Butterflies — A23a

Joy to the World, carol by Isaac Watts and Handel: No. 117, Girl playing guitar, boys, goat; No. 118, Girl carrying bouquet, boys, singing; No. 119, Palauan mother and child, singing; No. 120, Children, baskets of fruit. No. 121, Girl, fairy tern. Nos. 117-121 printed in a continuous design.

## 1986, Nov. 26 — Litho. Perf. 14

| | | | | | |
|---|---|---|---|---|---|
| 117 | A23 | 22c | multicolored | .40 | .40 |
| 118 | A23 | 22c | multicolored | .40 | .40 |
| 119 | A23 | 22c | multicolored | .40 | .40 |
| 120 | A23 | 22c | multicolored | .40 | .40 |
| 121 | A23 | 22c | multicolored | .40 | .40 |
| a. | | | Strip of 5, #117-121 | 2.00 | 2.00 |

## 1987, Jan. 5 — Litho. Perf. 14

| | | | | | |
|---|---|---|---|---|---|
| 121B | A23a | 44c | Tangadik, sour- sop | .90 | .90 |
| 121C | A23a | 44c | Dira amartai, sweet orange | .90 | .90 |
| 121D | A23a | 44c | Iihuochel, swamp cabbage | .90 | .90 |
| 121E | A23a | 44c | Bauosech, fig | .90 | .90 |
| f. | | | Block of 4, #121B-121E | 3.75 | 3.75 |

See Nos. 183-186.

Fruit Bats — A24

## 1987, Feb. 23 — Litho. Perf. 14

| | | | | | |
|---|---|---|---|---|---|
| 122 | A24 | 44c | In flight | .85 | .85 |
| 123 | A24 | 44c | Hanging | .85 | .85 |
| 124 | A24 | 44c | Eating | .85 | .85 |
| 125 | A24 | 44c | Head | .85 | .85 |
| a. | | | Block of 4, #122-125 | 3.50 | 3.50 |

## 1987-88 — Litho. Perf. 14

| | | | | | |
|---|---|---|---|---|---|
| 126 | A25 | 1c | Ixora casei | .20 | .20 |
| 127 | A25 | 3c | Lumnitzera littorea | .20 | .20 |
| 128 | A25 | 5c | Sonneratia alba | .20 | .20 |
| 129 | A25 | 10c | Tristellateia australasiae | .20 | .20 |
| 130 | A25 | 14c | Bikkia palauensis | .25 | .25 |
| 131 | A25 | 15c | Limnophila aromatica ('88) | 3.00 | — |
| 132 | A25 | 22c | Bruguiera gymnorhiza | .40 | .40 |
| a. | | | Booklet pane of 10 | 6.50 | — |
| b. | | | Booklet pane, 5 each 14c, 22c | 6.50 | — |

phosphate mine at Angaur. 33c, No. B1 and Japan Airways DC-2 over stone monuments at Badrulchau. 44c, No. 201 and Japanese post office, Koror. $1, Aviator's Grave, Japanese Cemetary, Peleliu, vert.

**1987, Oct. 16**    **Litho.**    **Perf. 14x13½**

| 164 | A28 | 14c | multicolored | .30 | .30 |
| 165 | A28 | 22c | multicolored | .45 | .45 |
| 166 | A28 | 33c | multicolored | .65 | .65 |
| 167 | A28 | 44c | multicolored | .85 | .85 |
| | | | Nos. 164-167 (4) | 2.25 | 2.25 |

**Souvenir Sheet**

**Perf. 13½x14**

| 168 | A28 | $1 | multicolored | 2.25 | 2.25 |

**Christmas — A30**

Verses from carol "I Saw Three Ships," Biblical characters, landscape and Palauans in outrigger canoes.

**1987, Nov. 24**    **Litho.**    **Perf. 14**

| 173 | A30 | 22c | I saw... | .45 | .45 |
| 174 | A30 | 22c | And what was... | .45 | .45 |
| 175 | A30 | 22c | Twas Joseph... | .45 | .45 |
| 176 | A30 | 22c | Saint Michael... | .45 | .45 |
| 177 | A30 | 22c | And the bells... | .45 | .45 |
| a. | | | Strip of 5, #173-177 | 2.25 | 2.25 |

**1987, Dec. 15**

#178, Snapping shrimp, goby. #179, Mauve vase sponge, sponge crab. #181, Pope's dam selfish, cleaner wrasse. #182, Clown anemone fish, sea anemone. #182, Four-color nudibranch, banded coral shrimp.

| 178 | A31 | 22c | multicolored | .50 | .50 |
| 179 | A31 | 22c | multicolored | .50 | .50 |
| 180 | A31 | 22c | multicolored | .50 | .50 |
| 181 | A31 | 22c | multicolored | .50 | .50 |
| 182 | A31 | 22c | multicolored | .50 | .50 |
| a. | | | Strip of 5, #178-182 | 2.75 | 2.75 |

**Symbiotic Marine Species—A31**


**Souvenir Sheet**

Palau Postal Independence Fifth Anniversary 1983-1988

**Postal Independence, 5th Anniv. — A33**

FINLANDIA '88: a, Kaep (pre-European outrigger sailboat). b, Spanish colonial cruiser. c, German colonial cruiser SMS Cormoran. c, 1885. d, Japanese mailbox, WWII machine gun, Koror Museum. e, US Trust Territory ship, Malakal Harbor. f, Koror post office.

**1988, June 8**    **Litho.**    **Perf. 14**

| 196 | A33 | $1 | Sheet of 6 | 2.50 | 2.50 |
| a.-f. | | | 25c multicolored | .40 | .40 |

**Souvenir Sheet**

U.S. Possessions Philatelic Society 1978 Hosting Palau at the Stamp Show

**US Possessions Phil. Soc., 10th Anniv. — A34**

PRAGA '88: a, "Collect Palau Stamps," original artwork for No. 196f and head of a man. b, Soc. emblem. c, Nos. 1-4. d, China Clipper original artwork and covers. e, Man and boy studying covers. f, Girl at show cancel booth.

**1988, Aug. 26**    **Litho.**    **Perf. 14**

| 197 | A34 | | Sheet of 6 | 4.25 | 4.25 |
| a.-f. | | | 45c any single | .70 | .70 |

**Christmas — A35**

Hark! The Herald Angels Sing: No. 198, Angels playing the violin, singing and sitting. No. 199, 3 angels and 3 children. No. 200, Nativity. No. 201, 2 angels, birds. No. 202, 3 children and 2 angels playing horns. Se-tenant in a continuous design.

**1988, Nov. 7**    **Litho.**    **Perf. 14**

| 198 | A35 | 25c | multicolored | .50 | .50 |
| 199 | A35 | 25c | multicolored | .50 | .50 |
| 200 | A35 | 25c | multicolored | .50 | .50 |
| 201 | A35 | 25c | multicolored | .50 | .50 |
| 202 | A35 | 25c | multicolored | .50 | .50 |
| a. | | | Strip of 5, #199-202 | 2.50 | 2.50 |

**Miniature Sheet**

**Chambered Nautilus — A36**

Designs: a, Fossil and cross section. b, Palauan bai symbols for the nautilus. c, Specimens trapped for scientific study. d, *Nautilus belauensis, pompillus, macromphalus.*


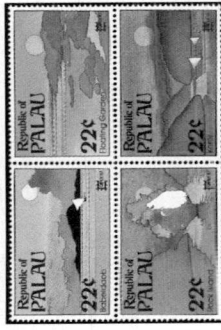

**45¢**

**1988, Dec. 23**    **Litho.**    **Perf. 14**

| 203 | A36 | | Sheet of 5 | 3.00 | 3.00 |
| a.-e. | | | 25c multicolored | .60 | .60 |

**PALAU 45**

**Endangered Birds of Palau — A37**

**1989, Feb. 9**    **Litho.**    **Perf. 14**

| 204 | A37 | 45c | Nicobar pigeon | .75 | .75 |
| 205 | A37 | 45c | Ground dove | .75 | .75 |
| 206 | A37 | 45c | Micronesian megapode | .75 | .75 |
| 207 | A37 | 45c | Owl | .75 | .75 |
| a. | | | Block of 4, #204-207 | 3.00 | 3.00 |

**Exotic Mushrooms — A38**

**1989, Mar. 16**    **Litho.**    **Perf. 14x14½**

| 208 | A38 | 45c | Gilled auricularia | .80 | .80 |
| 209 | A38 | 45c | Rock mushroom | .80 | .80 |
| 210 | A38 | 45c | Polyporous | .80 | .80 |
| 211 | A38 | 45c | Veiled stinkhorn | .80 | .80 |
| a. | | | Block of 4, #208-211 | 3.25 | 3.25 |

**Seashell Type of 1986**

**1989, Apr. 12**    **Litho.**    **Perf. 14**

| 212 | A20 | 25c | Robin redbreast triton | .50 | .50 |
| 213 | A20 | 25c | Hebrew cone | .50 | .50 |
| 214 | A20 | 25c | Tadpole triton | .50 | .50 |
| 215 | A20 | 25c | Lettered cone | .50 | .50 |
| 216 | A20 | 25c | Rugose miter | .50 | .50 |
| a. | | | Strip of 5, #212-216 | 2.50 | 2.50 |

**Souvenir Sheet**

IN MEMORIAM
Shōwa Emperor
Hirohito
1901-1989

平成

Thoughts on an Exotic Bird

He is a great lord,
with a mind that
flies as high
as that of the rukh,
so he will have
none of me,
who dares not climb
high.

*tyuka verse and Print by Ando Hiroshige, 1797-1858*

In Honor of Emperor Akihito

Heisei Era

PALAU $1

*A Little Bird, Amidst Chrysanthemums, 1830s, by Hiroshige (1797-1858)* — A39

**1989, May 17**    **Litho.**    **Perf. 14**

| 217 | A39 | $1 | multicolored | 2.10 | 2.10 |

Hirohito (1901-1989) and enthronement of Akihito as emperor of Japan.

## Lower left column

| 133 | A25 | 25c | Fagraea ksidl ('88) | .50 | .50 |
| a. | | | Booklet pane of 10 ('88) | 5.00 | — |
| b. | | | Booklet pane, 5 each 15c, 25c ('88) | 5.00 | — |
| 134 | A25 | 36c | Ophiorrhiza palauensis ('88) | .65 | .65 |
| 135 | A25 | 39c | Cerbera manghas | .70 | .70 |
| 136 | A25 | 44c | Sandera indica | .85 | .85 |
| 137 | A25 | 45c | Maesa canfieldiae ('88) | .85 | .85 |
| 138 | A25 | 50c | Dolichandrone spathacea | 1.00 | 1.00 |
| 139 | A25 | $1 | Barringtonia racemosa | 1.90 | 1.90 |
| 140 | A25 | $2 | Nepenthes mirabilis | 4.00 | 4.00 |
| 141 | A25 | $5 | Dendrobium palawense | 9.50 | 9.50 |

**Size: 49x28mm**

| 142 | A25 | $10 | Bouquet ('88) | 16.00 | 16.00 |
| | | | Nos. 126-142 (17) | 37.60 | 37.60 |

Issued: 3/12; $10, 3/17; 15c, 25c, 36c, 45c, 7/1; #131a, 133a-133b, 7/5.

Republic of PALAU 22¢

**CAPEX '87 — A26**

**1987, June 15**    **Litho.**    **Perf. 14**

| 146 | A26 | 22c | Babeldaob Is. | .50 | .50 |
| 147 | A26 | 22c | Floating Garden Isls. | .50 | .50 |
| 148 | A26 | 22c | Koror Is. | .50 | .50 |
| 149 | A26 | 22c | Koror | .50 | .50 |
| a. | | | A26 Block of 4, #146-149 | 2.00 | 2.00 |

**Seashells Type of 1986**

**1987, Aug. 25**    **Litho.**    **Perf. 14**

| 150 | A20 | 22c | Black-striped triton | .55 | .55 |
| 151 | A20 | 22c | Tapestry turban | .55 | .55 |
| 152 | A20 | 22c | Adusta murex | .55 | .55 |
| 153 | A20 | 22c | Little fox miter | .55 | .55 |
| 154 | A20 | 22c | Cardinal miter | .55 | .55 |
| a. | | | Strip of 5, #150-154 | 2.75 | 2.75 |

PALAU 14¢
Art. VIII, Sec. 1

**US Constitution Bicentennial A27**

Excerpts from Articles of the Palau and US Constitutions and Seals.

**1987, Sept. 17**    **Litho.**    **Perf. 14**

| 155 | A27 | 14c | Art. VIII, Sec. 1, Palau | .20 | .20 |
| 156 | A27 | 14c | Presidential seals | .20 | .20 |
| 157 | A27 | 14c | Art. II, Sec. 1, US | .20 | .20 |
| a. | | | Triptych + label, #155-157 | .70 | .70 |
| 158 | A27 | 22c | Art. IX, Sec. 1, Palau | .40 | .40 |
| 159 | A27 | 22c | Legislative seals | .40 | .40 |
| 160 | A27 | 22c | Art. I, Sec. 1, US | .40 | .40 |
| a. | | | Triptych + label, #158-160 | 1.40 | 1.40 |
| 161 | A27 | 44c | Art. X, Sec. 1, Palau | .75 | .75 |
| 162 | A27 | 44c | Supreme Court seals | .75 | .75 |
| 163 | A27 | 44c | Art. III, Sec. 1, US | .75 | .75 |
| a. | | | Triptych + label, #161-163 | 2.75 | 2.75 |
| | | | Nos. 155-163 (9) | 4.05 | 4.05 |

Nos. 156, 159 and 162 are each 28x42mm. Labels picture national flags.

## Lower middle column

PALAU 22¢

**1988, Jan. 25**

| 183 | A23a | 44c | multicolored | .75 | .75 |
| 184 | A23a | 44c | multicolored | .75 | .75 |
| 185 | A23a | 44c | multicolored | .75 | .75 |
| 186 | A23a | 44c | multicolored | .75 | .75 |
| a. | | | Block of 4, #183-186 | 3.00 | 3.00 |

**Butterflies and Flowers Type of 1987**

Designs: No. 183, Dannaus plexippus, Tournefotia argentia. No. 184, Papilio machaon, Citrus reticulata. No. 185, Captonsilia, Crataeva speciosa. No. 186, Collias philodice, Crataeva speciosa.

PALAU 44¢
WHIMBREL
Numenius phaeopus
GROUND DWELLERS

**Ground-dwelling Birds — A32**

**1988, Feb. 29**    **Litho.**    **Perf. 14**

| 187 | A32 | 44c | Whimbrel | .75 | .75 |
| 188 | A32 | 44c | Yellow bittern | .75 | .75 |
| 189 | A32 | 44c | Rufous night-heron | .75 | .75 |
| 190 | A32 | 44c | Banded rail | .75 | .75 |
| a. | | | Block of 4, #187-190 | 3.00 | 3.00 |

**Seashells Type of 1986**

**1988, May 11**    **Litho.**    **Perf. 14**

| 191 | A20 | 25c | Striped engina | .50 | .50 |
| 192 | A20 | 25c | Ivory cone | .50 | .50 |
| 193 | A20 | 25c | Plaited miter | .50 | .50 |
| 194 | A20 | 25c | Episcopal miter | .50 | .50 |
| 195 | A20 | 25c | Isabelle cowrie | .50 | .50 |
| a. | | | Strip of 5, #191-195 | 2.50 | 2.50 |

## Lower right column

PALAU 14¢

**Japanese Links to Palau — A28**

Japanese stamps, period cancellations and sedan used as mobile post office, near Ngerchelechuus Mountain. 22c, No. 347 and installations: 14c, No. 257 and 1937 Datsun sedan used as mobile post office, near Ngerchelechuus Mountain. 22c, No. 347 and

PALAU

## Miniature Sheet

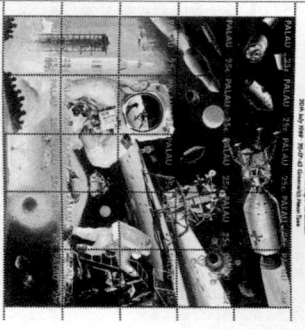

THE SEA OF TRANQUILITY

50th Anniversary APOLLO 11 — First Moon Landing

**First Moon Landing, 20th Anniv. — A40**

Apollo 11 mission: a, Third stage jettison. b, Lunar spacecraft. c, Module transposition (Eagle). d, Columbia module transposition (command module). e, Columbia module transposition (service module). f, Third stage burn. g, Vehicle entering orbit, Columbia and Eagle. h, Eagle on the Moon. i, Eagle in space. k, Three birds, Saturn V third stage, lunar spacecraft and escape tower. l, Astronaut's protective visor, pure oxygen system. m, American flag. n, Footsteps on lunar plain Sea of Tranquility. o, Armstrong descending from Eagle. p, Mobile launch tower, Saturn V thrust. v, Spectators, clouds of backwash. w, Parachute splashdown, U.S. Navy recovery ship and helicopter. x, Command module reentry. y, Jettison of service module prior to reentry.

**1989, July 20    Litho.    Perf. 14**
218    A40    25c any single    10.50    10.50
a.-y.    Sheet of 25    .40    .40

Palau $2.40

**1989, July 20    Perf. 13½x14**
219    A41    $2.40 multicolored    4.75    4.75
First Moon landing 20th anniv.

**Buzz Aldrin Photographed on the Moon by Neil Armstrong — A41**

PALAU 25

Literacy — A42

**1989, Oct. 13    Litho.    Perf. 14**
220    A42    25c any single    4.00    4.00
a.-y.    Block of 10    .40    .40

No. 220 printed in sheets containing two blocks of ten with strip of 5 labels between.

Imaginary characters and children reading: a, Youth astronaut. b, Boy riding dolphin. c, Cheshire cat in palm tree. d, Mother Goose. e, New York Yankee at bat. f, Girl reading. g, Boy reading. h, Mother reading to child. i, Girl holding flower and listening to story. j, Boy dressed in baseball uniform. Printed se-tenant in a continuous design.

---

## Miniature Sheet

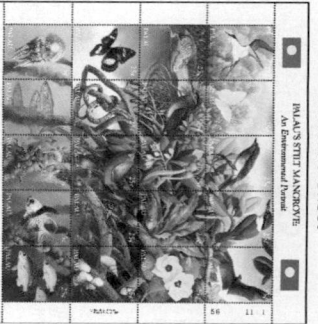

PALAU'S STILT MANGROVE
An Environmental Portrait

Inscribed labels contain book, butterflies and "Give Them / Books / Give Them / Wings."

**Stilt Mangrove Fauna — A43**

World Stamp Expo '89. a, Bridled tern. b, Sulphur butterfly. c, Mangrove flycatcher. b, Collared kingfisher. e, Fruit bat. f, Estuarine crocodile. p, Rufous night-heron. h, Stilt mangrove. i, Bird's nest fern. j, Beach hibiscus tree. k, Common egafly. l, Dog-faced watersnake. m, Jingle shell. n, Palau bark cricket. o, Periwinkle, mangrove oyster. p, Jellyfish. q, Striped mullet. r, Mussels, sea anemones, algae. s, Cardinalfish. t, Snapper.

**1989, Nov. 20    Litho.    Perf. 14½**
221    A43    25c any single    10.00    10.00
a.-t.    Block of 20    .50    .50

PALAU 25    soft corals

Christmas — A44    Soft Coral — A45

**1989, Dec. 18    Litho.    Perf. 14**
222    A44    25c multicolored    .50    .50
223    A44    25c multicolored    .50    .50
224    A44    25c multicolored    .50    .50
225    A44    25c multicolored    .50    .50
226    A44    25c multicolored    .50    .50
a.    Strip of 5, #222-226    2.75    2.75

*Whence Comes this Rush of Wings?* a carol: No. 222, Dusky tern, Audubon's shearwater, angels, island. No. 223, Fruit pigeon, angel. No. 224, Madonna and Child, ground pigeons, fairy terns, rails, sandpipers. No. 225, Angel, blue-headed green finch, red flycatcher, honeyeater. No. 226, Angel, blackheaded gulls. Printed se-tenant in a continuous design.

**1990, Jan. 3    Litho.    Perf. 14**
227    A45    25c Pink coral    .50    .50
228    A45    25c Pink & violet coral    .50    .50
229    A45    25c Yellow coral    .50    .50
230    A45    25c Red coral    .50    .50
a.    Block of 4, #227-230    2.00    2.00

---

## Miniature Sheet

PALAU 25

State Visit of Prince Lee Boo of Palau to England, 1784
A47

Prince Lee Boo, Capt. Henry Wilson and: a, HMS Victory docked at Portsmouth. b, St. James's Palace, London. c, Rotherhithe Docks, London. d, Capt. Wilson's residence, Devon. e, Lunardi's Grand English Air Balloon. f, St. Paul's and the Thames. g, Lee Boo's tomb, St. Mary's Churchyard, Rotherhithe. h, St. Mary's Church. i, Memorial tablet, St. Mary's Church.

**1990, May 6    Litho.    Perf. 14**
235    A47    25c any single    4.00    4.00
a.-i.    Sheet of 9    .45    .45

## Souvenir Sheet

PALAU
1890-1990    $1

Penny Black, 150th Anniv. — A48

**1990, May 6**
236    A48    $1 Great Britain #1    1.75    1.75
Stamp World London '90.

Orchids of PALAU 45

Orchids — A49

**1990, June 7    Perf. 14**
237    A49    45c Corymborkis veratrifolia    .75    .75
238    A49    45c Malaxis setipes    .75    .75
239    A49    45c Dipodium freycine-tianum    .75    .75
240    A49    45c Bulbophyllum micronesiacum    .75    .75
241    A49    45c Vanda teres and hookeriana    .75    .75
a.    Strip of 5, #237-241    3.75    3.75

---

## Birds of the Forest A46

PALAU 45c

**1990, Mar. 16    Perf. 14**
231    A46    45c Siberian rubythroat    .75    .75
232    A46    45c Palau bush-warbler    .75    .75
233    A46    45c Micronesian starling    .75    .75
234    A46    45c Cicadabird    .75    .75
a.    Block of 4, #231-234    3.00    3.00

PALAU 25c

Fairy Tern, Lesser Golden Plover, Sanderling A51

Lagoon life: b, Bidekill fisherman. c, Sailing yacht, insular halfbeaks. d, Palauan kaeps. e, White-tailed tropicbird. f, Spotted eagle ray. g, Great barracuda. h, Reef needlefish. i, Reef blacktip shark. j, Hawksbill turtle. k, Octopus. l,

## Miniature Sheet

Butterflies and Flowers A50

PALAU 45c

**1990, July 6    Litho.    Perf. 14**
242    A50    45c Wedelia striguosa    .70    .70
243    A50    45c Erthrina variegata    .70    .70
244    A50    45c Clerodendrum inerme    .70    .70
245    A50    45c Vigna marina    .70    .70
a.    Block of 4, #242-245    2.80    2.80

---

Batfish. m, Lionfish. n, Snowflake moray. o, Porcupine fish, sixkeeler threadfins. p, Blue sea star, regal angelfish, cleaner wrasse. q, Clown triggerfish. r, Spotted garden eel and orange chromis, sapphire damselfish, t, green chromis, Blue-lined sea bream, blue orangespine unicornfish, white-tipped soldierfish. u, Slatepencil sea urchin, leopard sea cucumber. v, Partridge tun shell. w, Mandarinfish. x, Tiger cowrie. y, Feather star-fish, orange-fin anemonefish.

**1990, Aug. 10    Litho.    Perf. 14½**
246    A51    25c Sheet of 25, #a.-    12.00    12.00
y.    Nos. 246a-246y inscribed on reverse.

PALAU 45c    PALAU 45c

Pacifica — A52

**1990, Aug. 24    Litho.    Perf. 14**
247    A52    45c Mailship, 1890    1.00    1.00
248    A52    45c US #803 on cover, fork-lift plane    2.25    2.25
a.    Pair, #247-248

Christmas — A53

PALAU 25

Here We Come A-Caroling: No. 250, Girl with music, poinsettias, doves, playing guitar, flute. No. 251, Boys and girls singing. No. 252, Family. No. 253, Three girls singing.

**1990, Nov. 28**
249    A53    25c multicolored    .40    .40
250    A53    25c multicolored    .40    .40
251    A53    25c multicolored    .40    .40
252    A53    25c multicolored    .40    .40
253    A53    25c multicolored    .40    .40
a.    Strip of 5, #249-253    2.00    2.00

## US Forces in Palau, 1944 A54

B-24S OVER PELELIU, 1944
PALAU 45c

Designs: No. 254, B-24s over Peleliu. No. 255, LCI launching rockets. No. 256, Marine Division launching offensive. No. 257, Soldier, children. No. 258, USS Peleliu.

**1990, Dec. 7    Perf. 14x13½**
254    A54    45c multicolored    .85    .85
255    A54    45c multicolored    .85    .85
256    A54    45c multicolored    .85    .85
257    A54    45c multicolored    .85    .85
a.    Block of 4, #254-257    3.50    3.50

## Souvenir Sheet

**Perf. 14x13½**
258    A54    $1 multicolored    2.25    2.25
See No. 339 for No. 258 with added inscription.

No. 258 contains one 51x38mm stamp.

PALAU

## Coral — A55    Litho.    Perf. 14

| | | | |
|---|---|---|---|
| 259 | A57 | 30c Staghorn | .55 .55 |
| 260 | A57 | 30c Velvet Leather | .55 .55 |
| 261 | A57 | 30c Van Gogh's Cypress | .55 .55 |
| 262 | A57 | 30c Violet Lace | .55 .55 |
| a. | A55 | Block of 4, #259-262 | 2.25 2.25 |

**1991, Mar. 4**

### Miniature Sheet

**Angaur, The Phosphate Island — A56**

**1991, Mar. 14**

263 A56 30c Sheet of 16, #a.-p.   9.00 9.00

Designs: a, Virgin Mary Statue, Nkulangelul Point. b, Angaur kaep, German colonial postmark. c, Eworofloch, Caroline Islands No. 13. d, Phosphate mine locomotive. e, Open slip off Lighthouse Hill. f, Dolphins. g, Estuarine crocodile. h, Workers cycling to phosphate plant. i, Ship loading phosphate. j, Hammerhead shark, German overseer. k, Marshall Islands No. 15. l, SMS Scharnhorst. m, SMS Emden. n, Crab-eating macaque monkey. o, Great sperm whale. p, HMAS Sydney.

Nos. 263b-263c, 263f-263g, 263j-263k, 263n-263o printed in continuous design showing map of island.

## Birds — A57

Perf. 14½x15, 13x13½    Litho.

**1991-92**

| | | | |
|---|---|---|---|
| 266 | A57 | 1c Palau bushwarbler | .20 .20 |
| 267 | A57 | 4c Common moorhen | .20 .20 |
| 268 | A57 | 6c Banded rail | .20 .20 |
| 269 | A57 | 19c Palau fantail | .30 .30 |
| a. | | Booklet pane, 10 #269b | 3.00 |
| 270 | A57 | 20c Mangrove flycatcher | .30 .30 |
| 271 | A57 | 23c Purple swamphen | .35 .35 |
| 272 | A57 | 29c Palau fruit dove | .45 .45 |
| a. | | Booklet pane, 5 each #270, #272 | 4.50 |
| b. | | Complete booklet, 10 #272a | 4.50 |
| | | Complete booklet, 10 #272b | 4.50 |
| 273 | A57 | 35c Great crested tern | .55 .55 |
| 274 | A57 | 40c Pacific reef heron | .60 .60 |
| 275 | A57 | 45c Micronesian pigeon | .70 .70 |
| 276 | A57 | 50c Great frigatebird | .75 .75 |
| 277 | A57 | 52c Little pied cormorant | .80 .80 |
| 278 | A57 | 75c Jungle night jar | 1.10 1.10 |
| 279 | A57 | 95c Cattle egret | 1.40 1.40 |
| 280 | A57 | $1.34 Great sulphur-crested cockatoo | 2.00 2.00 |
| 281 | A57 | $2 Blue-faced parrotfinch | 3.00 3.00 |
| 282 | A57 | $5 Eclectus parrot | 7.75 7.75 |

**Size: 52x30mm**

| | | | |
|---|---|---|---|
| 283 | A57 | $10 Palau bush warbler | 15.00 15.00 |
| | | Nos. 266-283 (18) | 35.65 35.65 |

The 1, 6, 20, 52, 75c, $10 are perf. 14½x15. Issued: 1, 6, 20, 52, 75c, $5, 4/6/92; $10, 9/10/92; #269b, 272a, 272b, 8/23/91; others, 4/18/91.

### Miniature Sheet

**Christianity in Palau, Cent. — A58**

Designs: a, Pope Leo XIII, 1891. b, Ibedul Ilengelekei, High Chief of Koror, 1871-1911. c, Fr. Marino de la Hoz, Br. Emilio Villar. f, Fr. Elias Fernandez. d, Fr. Edwin G. McManus (1908-1969), compiler of Palauan-English dictionary. e, Sacred Heart Church, Koror. f, Pope John Paul II.

**1991, Apr. 28    Perf. 14½**

288 A58 29c Sheet of 6, #a.-f.   2.75 2.75

### Miniature Sheet

**Marine Life A59**

Designs: a, Pacific white-sided dolphin. b, Common dolphin. c, Rough-toothed dolphin. d, Bottlenose dolphin. e, Harbor porpoise. f, Killer whale. g, Spinner dolphin. h, Dall's porpoise. i, Finless porpoise. j, Map of Palau, dolphins. k, Dusky dolphin. l, Southern right-whale dolphin. m, Striped dolphin. n, Fraser's dolphin. o, Peale's dolphin. p, Spectacled porpoise. q, Spotted dolphin. r, Hourglass dolphin. s, Risso's dolphin. t, Hector's dolphin.

**1991, May 24    Litho.    Perf. 14**

289 A59 29c Sheet of 20, #a.-t.   10.00 10.00

### Miniature Sheet

**Operations Desert Shield / Desert Storm — A60**

Designs: a, F-4G Wild Weasel fighter. b, F-117A Stealth fighter. c, AH-64A Apache helicopter. d, TOW missile launcher on M998 HMMWV. e, Pres. Bush. f, M2 Bradley fighting vehicle. g, Aircraft carrier USS Ranger. h, Corvette fast patrol boat. i, Battleship Wisconsin.

**1991, July 2    Litho.    Perf. 14**

290 A60 29c Sheet of 9, #a.-i.   3.25 3.25

**Size: 38x51mm**

291 A60 $2.90 Fairy tern, yellow ribbon   4.25 4.25

### Souvenir Sheet

292 A60 $2.90 like #291   4.50 4.50

No. 291 has a white border around design. No. 292 printed in continuous design.

## Republic of Palau, 10th Anniv. — A61

Designs: a, Palauan bai. b, Palauan bai interior, denomination UL. c, Same, denomination UR. d, Demi-god Chedechuul. e, Spider, denomination at UL. f, Money bird facing right. g, Money bird facing left. h, Spider, denomination at UR.

**1991, July 9    Perf. 14½**

293 A61 29c Sheet of 8, #a.-h.   4.00 4.00

See No. C21.

### Miniature Sheet

**Giant Clams A62**

Designs: a, Tridacna squamosa, Hippopus hippopus, Hippopus porcellanus, and Tridacna derasa. b, Tridacna gigas. c, Hatchery and tank culture. d, Diver, bottom-based clam nursery. e, Micronesian Mariculture Demonstration Center.

**1991, Sept. 17    Litho.    Perf. 14**

294 A62 50c Sheet of 5, #a.-e.   4.00 4.00

No. 294e is 109x17mm and imperf on 3 sides, perf 14 at top.

### Miniature Sheet

**Japanese Heritage in Palau A63**

Designs: No. 295: a, Marine research. b, Agricultural training. c, Agricultural research. e, Training in architecture and building. f, Air transportation. $1, Map, cancel from Japanese post office at Parao.

**1991, Nov. 19**

295 A63 29c Sheet of 6, #a.-f.   2.75 2.75

### Souvenir Sheet

296 A63 $1 multicolored   1.50 1.50

Phila Nippon '91.

### Miniature Sheet

**Peace Corps in Palau, 25th Anniv. A64**

Children's drawings: No. 297a, Flag, doves, children, and islands. b, Airplane, people being greeted. c, Red Cross instruction. d, Fishing industry. e, Agricultural training. f, Classroom instruction.

**1991, Dec. 6    Litho.    Perf. 13½**

297 A64 29c Sheet of 6, #a.-f.   3.00 3.00

## Christmas — A65

Silent Night: No. 298: a, Silent night, holy night. b, All is calm, all is bright. c, Round yon virgin, mother and Child. d, Holy Infant, so tender and mild. e, Sleep in heavenly peace.

**1991, Nov. 14    Perf. 14**

298 A65 29c Strip of 5, #a.-e.   2.25 2.25

### Miniature Sheet

**World War II in the Pacific A66**

Designs: No. 299a, Pearl Harbor attack begins. b, Battleship Nevada gets under way. c, USS Shaw explodes. d, Japanese aircraft carrier Akagi sunk. e, USS Wasp sunk off Guadalcanal. f, Battle of the Philippine Sea. g, US landing craft approach Saipan. h, US 1st Cavalry on Leyte. i, Battle of Bloody Nose Ridge, Peleliu. j, US troops land on Iwo Jima.

**1991, Dec. 6    Perf. 14½x15**

299 A66 29c Sheet of 10, #a.-j.   5.00 5.00

See No. C22.

**A67**

**A68**

Butterflies: a, Troides criton. b, Aethes zodiaca. c, Papillio poboroi. d, Vindula arsinoe.

Shells: a, Common hairy triton. b, Eglantine cowrie. c, Sulcate swamp cerith. d, Black-spined murex. e, Black-mouth moon.

**1992, Jan. 20    Litho.    Perf. 14**

300 A67 50c Block of 4, #a.-d.   3.00 3.00

**1992, Mar. 11**

301 A68 29c Strip of 5, #a.-e.   2.50 2.50

## Miniature Sheet

Age of Discovery
A69

**1992, May 25**      **Perf. 14**
302  A69  29c Sheet of 20, #a-t.                  10.50  10.50

### Miniature Sheet

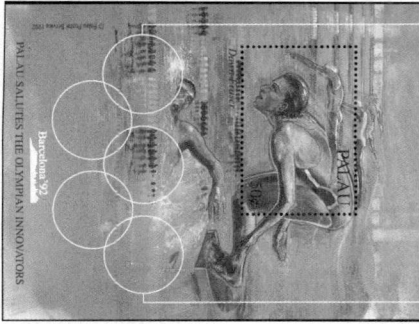

PALAU SALUTES THE OLYMPIAN INNOVATORS

Biblical Creation of the World — A70

Designs: a, "And darkness was..." b, Sun's rays. c, "Water, sun's rays. d, ...and it was good." e, "Let there be a..." f, Land forming. g, Water and land. h, ...and it was so." i, "Let the waters..." j, Tree branches. k, Shoreline. l, lights..." n, Comet, tree. m, "Let there be Sun, hillside. o, "Let the waters..." r, Birds. p, Fish, killer whale. t, Fish. u, "Let the earth..." v, Woman, man. w, Animals. x, ...and it was very good."

Nos. 303a-303d, 303e-303h, 303i-303l, 303m-303p, 303q-303t, 303u-303x, are blocks of 4.

**1992, June 5**      **Perf. 14½**
303  A70  29c Sheet of 24, #a-x.                  13.00  13.00

### Souvenir Sheets

PALAU  29¢

Let there be light, and there was light.

And darkness was upon the face of the deep. And the Spirit of God moved upon the face of the waters. And God said,

## 1992 Summer Olympics, Barcelona — A71

**1992, July 10**      **Perf. 14**
304  A71  50c  Dawn Fraser              .90  .90
305  A71  50c  Olga Korbut              .90  .90
306  A71  50c  Bob Beamon               .90  .90
307  A71  50c  Carl Lewis               .90  .90
308  A71  50c  Dick Fosbury             .90  .90
309  A71  50c  Greg Louganis            .90  .90
Nos. 304-309 (6)                       5.40  5.40

## Miniature Sheet

ELVIS PRESLEY

PALAU  29c

Elvis Presley
A72

**1992, Aug. 17**      **Perf. 13½x14**
310  A72  29c Sheet of 9, #a-i.                   6.00  6.00
Various portraits.
See No. 350.

## Christmas — A73

The Friendly Beasts carol depicting animals in Nativity Scene: No. 312a, "Thus Every Beast." b, "By Some Good Spell." c, "In The Stable Dark Was Glad to Tell." d, "Of The Gift He Gave Emanuel." e, "The Gift He Gave Emanuel."

PALAU  29c

**1992, Oct. 1**      **Perf. 14**
312  A73  29c Strip of 5, #a-e.                   2.50  2.50

## Fauna A74

PALAU  50c

Designs: a, Dugong. b, Masked booby. c, Macaque. d, New Guinean crocodile.

**1993, July 9**      **Litho.     Perf. 14**
313  A74  50c Block of 4, #a-d.                   3.25  3.25

## Seafood A75

GIANT DEEPWATER CRAB

PALAU  29

Designs: a, Giant crab. b, Scarlet shrimp. c, Smooth nylon shrimp. d, Armed nylon shrimp.

**1993, July 22**      **Litho.     Perf. 14½**
314  A75  29c Block of 4, #a-d.                   2.00  2.00

## Sharks A76

PALAU  50c

Designs: a, Oceanic whitetip. b, Great hammerhead. c, Leopard. d, Reef black-tip.

**1993, Aug. 11**      **Litho.     Perf. 14½**
315  A76  50c Block of 4, #a-d.                   3.25  3.25

## Miniature Sheet

PALAU  29c

World War II in the Pacific
A77

Actions in 1943: a, US takes Guadalcanal, Feb. b, Hospital ship Tranquility supports action. c, New Guineans join Allies in battle. d, US landings in New Georgia, June. e, USS California participates in every naval landing. f, Dauntless dive bombers over Wake Island, Oct. 6. g, US flamethrowers on Tarawa, Nov. h, US landings on Makin, Nov. i, B-25s bomb Simpson Harbor, Rabaul, Oct. 23. j, B-24s over Kwajalein, Dec. 8.

**1993, Sept. 23  Litho.     Perf. 14½x15**
316  A77  29c Sheet of 10, #a-j. + label                   6.00  6.00
See Nos. 325-326.

## Christmas — A78

PALAU  29c

Christmas carol, "We Wish You a Merry Christmas," with Palauan customs: a, Girl, goat. b, Goats, children holding leis, prow of canoe. c, Santa Claus. d, Children singing. e, Family with fruit, fish.

**1993, Oct. 22**      **Litho.     Perf. 14**
317  A78  29c Strip of 5, #a-e.                   2.50  2.50

## Prehistoric and Legendary Sea Creatures — A79

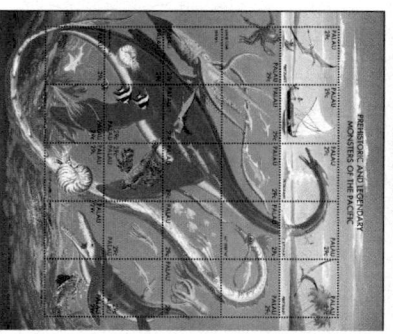

PREHISTORIC AND LEGENDARY MONSTERS OF THE PACIFIC

Illustration reduced.

**1993, Nov. 26**      **Litho.     Perf. 14**
318  A79  29c Sheet of 25, #a-y.                  12.50  12.50

## Miniature Sheet

Palau  29c

INTERNATIONAL YEAR 1993 INDIGENOUS PEOPLE

Paintings, by Charlie Gibbons: No. 319: a, After Child-birth Ceremony. b, Village in Early Palau.

Intl. Year of Indigenous People — A80

**1993, Dec. 8**      **Perf. 14x13½**
319  A80  29c Sheet, 2 ea #a-b.                   2.00  2.00
Storyboard carving, by Ngiraibuoch: $2.90, Quarrying of Stone Money, vert.

## Miniature Sheet

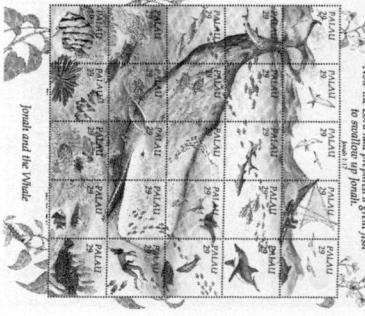

Now the Lord had prepared a great fish to swallow up Jonah.

Jonah 1:17

Jonah and the Whale

Jonah and the Whale — A81

**1993, Dec. 28**      **Litho.     Perf. 14**
320  A81  29c Sheet of 25, #a-y.                  13.00  13.00
Illustration reduced.

## Souvenir Sheet

**1993, Dec. 28**      **Perf. 13½x14**
321  A81  $2.90 multicolored                      5.00  5.00

## Hong Kong '94 A82

Hong Kong '94

PALAU  40¢

Rays: a, Manta (b). b, Spotted eagle (a). c, Coachwhip (d). d, Black spotted.

**1994, Feb. 18**      **Litho.     Perf. 14**
322  A82  40c Block of 4, #a-d.                   2.75  2.75

## Estuarine Crocodile A83

PALAU  20¢

Designs: a, With mouth open. b, Hatchling. c, Crawling on river bottom. d, Swimming.

**1994, Mar. 14**      **Litho.     Perf. 14**
323  A83  20c Block of 4, #a-d.                   2.00  2.00
World Wildlife Fund.

## Large Seabirds — A84

Red-footed Booby,   KUEL   Sula sula

Palau  50c

a, Red-footed booby. b, Great frigatebird. c, Brown booby. d, Little pied cormorant.

**1994, Apr. 22**      **Litho.     Perf. 14**
324  A84  50c Block of 4, #a-d.                   3.00  3.00

## World War II Type of 1993
### Miniature Sheets

Action in the Pacific, 1944: No. 325: a, US Marines capture Kwajalein, Feb. 1-7. b, Japanese enemy base at Truk destroyed, Feb. 17-18. c, SS-284 Tullibee participates in Operation Desecrate, March. d, US troops take Saipan, June 15-July 9. e, US troops take Peleliu, Sept. 15-Oct. Shoot, June 19-20. f, Guam liberated, July-Aug. g, US Marianas Turkey 14. h, Angaur secured in fighting, Sept. 17-22. i, Gen. Douglas MacArthur returns to Philippines, Oct. 20. j, US Army Memorial, Palau, Nov. 27.

Various scenes from Apollo moon missions.

**1994, July 20**
**Perf. 14½**

337 A87 29c #a.-t.     11.00 11.00

---

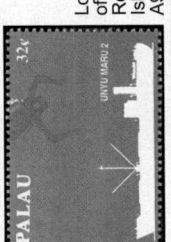

**1994, May**    **Sheets of 10**    **Perf. 14½**

325 A77 29c #a.-j. + label    5.00 5.00
326 A77 50c #a.-j. + label    8.50 8.50

**Pierre de Coubertin (1863-1937) — A85**

Winter Olympic medalists: No. 328, Anne-Marie Moser, witt. No. 329, James Craig. No. 330, Katarina Witt. No. 331, Eric Heiden, vert No. 332, Nancy Kerrigan. $2, Dan Jansen.

**1994, July 20**    **Litho.**    **Perf. 14**

327 A85 29c multicolored    .60 .60

**Souvenir Sheets**

328 A85 50c multicolored    .85 .85
329 A85 50c multicolored    .85 .85
330 A85 $1 multicolored    1.60 1.60
331 A85 $1 multicolored    1.60 1.60
332 A85 $1 multicolored    1.60 1.60
333 A85 $2 multicolored    3.25 3.25

Intl. Olympic Committee, cent.

**Miniature Sheets of 8**

---

**PHILAKOREA '94 — A86**

Wildlife carrying letters: No. 334: a, Sailfin goby. b, Sharpnose puffer. c, Lightning butterflyfish. d, Clown anemonefish. e, Parrotfish. f, Batfish. g, Clown triggerfish. h, twinspot wrasse.

No. 335a, Palau fruit bat. b, Crocodile. c, Dugong. d, Banded sea snake. e, Bottlenosed dophin. f, Hawksbill turtle. g, Octopus. h, Manta ray.

No. 336: a, Palau fantail. b, Banded crake. c, Island swiftlet. d, Micronesian kingfisher. e, Red-footed booby. f, Great frigatebird. g, Palau owl. h, Palau fruit dove.

**1994, Aug. 16**    **Litho.**    **Perf. 14**

334 A86 29c #a.-h.    4.75 4.75
335 A86 40c #a.-h.    6.50 6.50
336 A86 50c #a.-h.    8.00 8.00

No. 336 is airmail.

**Miniature Sheet of 20**

---

D-Day, Allied Invasion of Normandy, June 6, 1944: No. 326: a, C-47 transport aircraft dropping Allied paratroopers. b, Allied warships attack beach fortifications. c, Commandos attack from landing craft. d, Tanks land. e, Sherman flail tank beats path through minefields. f, Allied aircraft attack enemy reinforcements. g, Gliders deliver troops behind enemy lines. h, Pegasus Bridge, first French house liberated. i, Allied forces move inland to form bridgehead. j, View of beach at end of D-Day.

---

**Christmas — A91**

O Little Town of Bethlehem: a, Magi, cherubs. b, Angel, shepherds, sheep. c, Angels, nativity. d, Angels hovering over town, shepherd, sheep. e, Cherubs, doves.

**1994, Nov. 23**    **Litho.**    **Perf. 14**

345 A91 29c Strip of 5, #a-e    2.50 2.50

No. 345 is a continuous design and is printed in sheets containing three strips. The bottom strip is printed with se-tenant labels.

**Miniature Sheets of 12**

---

No. 258 with added text "50th ANNIVERSARY / INVASION OF PELELIU / SEPTEMBER 15, 1944"

**1994**    **Litho.**    **Perf. 14X13½**

339 A54 $1 multicolored    2.00 2.00

**Miniature Sheet of 9**

#338: b, Natl. seal. c, Pres. Kuniwo Nakamura, Palau, US Pres. Clinton. d, Palau, US flags. e, Musical notes of natl. anthem.

**1994, Oct. 1**    **Perf. 14**

338 A88 29c Strip of 5, #a.-e.    2.50 2.50

No. 338c is 57x42mm.

**Independence Day — A88**

---

**Disney Characters Visit Palau — A89**

No. 310: a, Mickey, Minnie arriving. b, Goofy finding way to hotel. c, Donald enjoying beach. d, Minnie, Daisy learning the Ngloik. e, Minnie, Mickey sailing to Natural Bridge. f, Scrooge finding money in Babeldaob jungle. g, Goofy, Napoleon Wrasse. h, Minnie, Clam Garden. i, Grandma Duck weaving basket.

No. 341, Mickey exploring underwater shipwreck. No. 342, Donald visiting Airai Bai on boat, vert.

**1994, Oct 14**    **Perf. 11¾x11**

340 A89   29c #a.-i.    5.00 5.00

**Souvenir Sheets**    **Perf. 14x13½**

341-342 A89   $1 each    2.25 2.25

343 A89 $2.90 multicolored    6.25 6.25

**Miniature Sheet of 12**

---

1994 World Cup Soccer Championships, US — A92

US coach, players: No. 346: a, Bora Milutinovic. b, Cle Kooiman. c, Ernie Stewart. d, Claudio Reyna. e, Thomas Dooley. f, Alexi Lalas. g, Dominic Kinnear. h, Frank Klopas. i, Paul Caliguiri. j, Mareolo Balboa. k, Oubi Jones. l, US flag, World Cup trohpy.

US players: No. 347a, Tony Meola. b, John Doyle. c, Eric Wynalda. d, Roy Wegerle. e, Fernando Clavijo. f, Hugo Perez. g, John Harkes. h, Mike Lapper. i, Mike Sorber. j, Brad Friedel. k, Tab Ramos. l, Joe-Max Moore.

No. 348: a, Bulvelu, Brazil. b, Romario, Rmzil. c, Franco Baresi, Italy. d, Roberto Baggio, Italy. e, Andoni Zubizarreta, Spain. f, Oleg Salenko, Russia. g, Gheorghe Hagi, Romania. h, Dennis Bergkamp, Netherlands. i, Iinsto Stoichkov, Bulgaria. j, Tomas Brolin, Sweden. k, Lothar Matthaus, Germany. l, Arrigo Sacchi, Italy & Brazil, World Cup trophy.

**1994, Dec. 23**

346 A92 29c #a.-l.    6.25 6.25
347 A92 29c #a.-l.    6.25 6.25
348 A92 50c #a.-l.    10.50 10.50

Elvis Presley Type of 1992
**Miniature Sheet**

Various portraits.

**1995, Feb. 28**    **Litho.**    **Perf. 14**

350 A72 32c Sheet of 9, #a.-i.    5.50 5.50

---

Intl. Year of the Family — A90

Story of Tebruchei: a, With mother as infant. b, Father. c, As young man. d, Wife-to-be. e, Bringing home fish. f, Pregnant wife. g, Elderly mother. h, Elderly father. i, With first born. j, Wife seated. k, Caring for mother. l, Father, wife and baby.

**1994, Nov. 1**    **Litho.**    **Perf. 14**

344 A90 20c #a.-l.    4.00 4.00

---

Fish — A93

1c, Cube trunkfish. 2c, Lionfish. 3c, Longjawed squirrelfish. 4c, Longnose filefish. 5c, Ornate butterflyfish. 10c, Yellow seahorse. 20c, Magenta dottyback. 32c, Reef lizardfish. 50c, Multibarred goatfish. 55c, Barred blenny. $1, Fingerprint sharpnose puffer. $2, Longnose hawkfish. $5, Mandarinfish. $10, Coral grouper.

**1995, Apr. 3**    **Litho.**    **Perf. 14½**

351 A93 1c multicolored    .20 .20
352 A93 2c multicolored    .20 .20
353 A93 3c multicolored    .20 .20
354 A93 4c multicolored    .20 .20
355 A93 5c multicolored    .20 .20
356 A93 10c multicolored    .20 .20
357 A93 20c multicolored    .30 .30
358 A93 32c multicolored    .45 .45
359 A93 50c multicolored    .70 .70
360 A93 55c multicolored    .75 .75
361 A93 $1 multicolored    1.50 1.50
362 A93 $2 multicolored    3.00 3.00
363 A93 $3 multicolored    4.50 4.50
364 A93 $5 multicolored    7.75 7.75

---

**Size: 48x30mm**

365 A93 $10 multicolored    16.00 16.00
   Nos. 351-365 (15)    36.15 36.15

**Booklet Stamps**
**Size: 18x21mm**
**Perf. 14x14½ Syncopated**

366 A93 20c multicolored    .40 .40
  a.   Booklet pane of 10    3.50
   Complete booklet, #366a   3.50
367 A93 32c multicolored    .60 .60
  a.   Booklet pane of 10    5.50
   Complete booklet, #367a   5.50
  b.   Booklet pane, 5 ea #366, 367   4.50
   Complete booklet, #367b   4.50

---

Lost Fleet of the Rock Islands A94

Underwater scenes, silhouettes of Japanese ships sunk during Operation Desecrate, 1944: a, Unyu Maru 2. b, Wakatake. c, Teshio Maru. d, Raizan Maru. e, Chuyo Maru. f, Shinsei Maru. g, Urakami Maru. h, Ose Maru. i, Iro. j, Shosei Maru. k, Patrol boat 31. l, Kibi Maru. m, Amatsu Maru. n, Gozan Maru. o, Matuoi Maru. p, Nagisan Maru. q, Akashi. r, Kamikazi Maru.

**1995, Mar. 30**    **Litho.**    **Perf. 14**

368 A94 32c #a.-r.    10.00 10.00

**Miniature Sheet of 18**

---

Flying Dinosaurs A95

Designs: a, Pteranodon sternbergi. b, Pteranodon ingens (e, c), c, Herodoctyls (b), d, Dorygnathus (e). e, Dimorphodon (f). f, Nyctosaurus (e). g, Pterodactylus kochi. h, Ornithodesmus (g, i). i, Diatryma (f). j, Archaeopteryx. k, Caenylugurilulides (j). l, Galiodactylus. m, Batrachognathus (j). n, Scaphognathus (j, k, m, o). o, Peteinosaurus (l). p, Ichthyornis. q, Ctenochiasma (m, p, r). r, Rhamphorhynchus (n, o, q).

**1995**    **Litho.**    **Perf. 14**

369 A95 32c #a.-r.    10.00 10.00

Earth Day, 25th anniv.

**Miniature Sheet**

---

Research & Experimental Jet Aircraft — A96

Designs: a, Fairey Delta 2. b, B-70 "Valkyrie." c, Douglas X-3 "Stilletto." d, Northrop/NASA HL-10. e, Bell XS-1. f, Tupolev Tu-144. g, Bell X-1. h, Boulton Paul P.111. i, EWR VJ 101C. j, Handley Page HP-115. k, Rolls Royce TMR "Flying Bedstead." l, North American X-15.

**1995**    **Litho.**    **Perf. 14**

370 A96 50c Sheet of 12, #a.-l.    10.00 10.00

**Souvenir Sheet**

371 A96 $2 multicolored    3.50 3.50

No. 370 is airmail. No. 371 contains one 85x29mm stamp.

PALAU 32c
Preparing Tin-Fish
by Wm.F.Draper
(U.S. Navy Combat Art Collection)

A101

**Miniature Sheets**

**1995, Sept. 15**    **Perf. 14½**
377   A100   20c   Block of 4, #a.-d.    1.40   1.40
378   A100   32c   multicolored    .55   .55

No. 377 was issued in sheets of 16 stamps.
No. 378 was issued in sheets of 16 stamps. See US No. 2999.

Designs: a, Fruit doves. b, Rock Islands. c, Map of islands. d, Orchid, hibiscus. 32c, Marine life.

**1995, Sept. 15**   **Litho.**   **Perf. 14**
**Souvenir Sheets**
375   A99   $2   multicolored    4.00   4.00
376   A99   $2   multicolored    4.00   4.00

374   A99   60c   Block of 4, #a.-d.    4.00   4.00

Designs: No. 374a, Outline of soldier's helmet, dove, peace. b, Turtle, diver, seabirds above. c, Fish, coral, crab. d, Coral fish, diff.

MARINE LIFE

PALAU 32

**UN, FAO, 50th Anniv. — A99**

**1995, Aug. 15**   **Litho.**   **Perf. 13½**
373   A98   32c   Block of 4, #a.-d.    2.25   2.25

No. 373 is a continuous design and was issued in sheets of 24 stamps.

Designs: a, Scuba gear. b, Cousteau diving saucer. c, Jim suit. d, Beaver IV. e, Ben Franklin. f, USS Nautilus. g, Deep Rover. h, Beebe Bathysphere. i, Deep Star IV. j, DSRV. k, Aluminaut. l, Nautile. m, Cyana. n, FNRS r, Trieste.

PALAU 32¢
SCUBA GEAR
500 feet

**1995, July 21**   **Litho.**   **Perf. 14**
372   A97   32c   #a.-r.    10.00   10.00

**Submersibles — A97**

**Miniature Sheet of 18**

Marine Life — A108

PALAU 32c
VERA-HATCHETFISH

**1996, Mar. 12**   **Litho.**   **Perf. 14**
387   A107   32c   Block of 4, #a.-d.    2.50   2.50

No. 387 was issued in sheets of 4.

Three different children from Palau in traditional costumes, child in middle wearing: a, Red flowerd costumes. b, Pink dress. c, Blue shorts. d, Red headpiece and shorts.

32¢
PALAU
unicef

**UNICEF, 50th Anniv. — A107**

**1996, Feb. 2**   **Litho.**   **Perf. 14**
385   A106   10c   Strip of 5, #a.-e.    1.25   1.25
**Miniature Sheet**
386   A106   60c   Sheet of 2, #a.-b.    2.50   2.50

No. 385 was issued in sheets of 2 + 4 labels like No. 386. Nos. 386a-386b are airmail and are each 56x43mm.

Stylized rats in parade: No. 385: a, One carrying flag, one playing horn. b, Three playing musical instruments. c, Two playing instruments. d, Family in front of house. Mirror images, diff. colors: No. 386: a, Like #385c-385d. b, Like #385a-385b.

PALAU 32¢

**New Year 1996 (Year of the Rat) — A106**

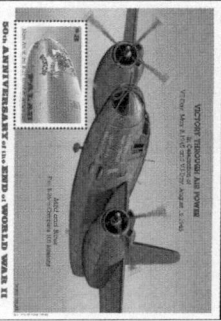

PALAU 32c
AKST RASSLER

**Miniature Sheet of 12**

**1995, Nov. 15**   **Litho.**   **Perf. 14**
383   A104   32c   2 each, #a.-f.    8.50   8.50

Small turtles, arrows representing routes during life cycle and: a, Large turtle. b, Upper half of turtle shell platter, Palau map. c, Rooster in tree, island scene. d, Native woman. e, Lower half of turtle shell platter, Palau map, Island couple. f, Fossil, palm trees, native house

**Life Cycle of the Sea Turtle — A104**

PALAU 32c

**Independence, 1st Anniv. — A100**

**1995, Oct. 18**    **Perf. 13½x14**
379   A101   32c   Sheet of 12, #a.-l    7.50   7.50
**Souvenir Sheet**
380   A101   60c   Sheet of 5, #a.-e.    6.00   6.00

**Perf. 14**
381   A102   $3   multicolored    5.00   5.00

Paintings by Wm. F. Draper. No. 379a, Preparing Tin-Fish. b, Hellcats Take-off into Palau's Rising Sun. c, Dauntless Dive Bombers over Malakal Harbor. d, Planes Return from The Landing. e, Communion Before Battle. f, The Landing. g, First Task Ashore. h, Fire Fighters Save Flak-torn Pilot. i, Marine Headed for Peleliu. j, Peleliu. k, Last Rites. l, The Thousand-Yard Stare.

Portraits by Albert Murray, vert.: No. 380a, Adm. Chester W. Nimitz. b, Adm. William F. Halsey. c, Adm. Raymond A. Spruance. d, Vice Adm. Marc A. Mitscher. e, Gen. Holland M. Smith, USMC.

$3, Nose art of B-29 Bock's Car.

**End of World War II, 50th Anniv. — A102**

CAPEX '96
PALAU 32
A109

**Sheets of 9**

Circumnavigators of the earth: No. 389: a, Ferdinand Magellan, ship Victoria. b, Charles Wilkes, ship Vincennes. c, Joshua Slocum, oyster boat Spray. d, Ben Carlin, amphibious vehicle Half-Safe. e, Edward L. Beach, submarine USS Triton. f, Naomi James, yacht Express Crusader. g, Sir Ranulf Fiennes, polar vehicle. h, Rick Hansen, wheel chair. i, Robin Knox-Johnson, catamaran Enza New Zealand.

No. 390: a, Lowell Smith, Douglas World Cruisers. b, Ernst Lehmann, Graf Zeppelin. c, Wiley Post, Lockheed Vega Winnie Mae. d, Yuri Gagarin, spacecraft Vostok I. e, Jerrie Mock, Cessna 180 Spirit of Columbus. f, Ross Perot, Jr., Bell Longranger III, Spirit of Texas. g, Brooke Knapp, Gulfstream III, The American Dream. h, Jeana Yeager, Dick Rutan, airplane Voyager. i, Fred Lasby, piper Commanche.

No. 391, Bob Martin, Mark Sullivan, Troy Bradley, Odyssey Gondola, No. 392, Sir Francis Chichester, yacht Gipsy Moth IV.

**1996, May 3**   **Litho.**   **Perf. 14**
389   A109   32c   Sheet of 9, #a.-i.    5.25   5.25
390   A109   60c   Sheet of 9, #a.-i.    10.00   10.00
**Souvenir Sheets**
391-392   A109   Sheet of 9, #a.-i.    5.50   5.50

No. 390 is airmail.

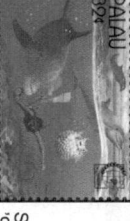

VICTORY THROUGH AIR POWER
50th ANNIVERSARY of the END of WORLD WAR II

**1995, Dec. 8**   **Litho.**   **Perf. 14**
384   A105   32c   multicolored    1.00   1.00

No. 384 was issued in sheets of 16.

**John Lennon (1940-80) — A105**

32¢
PALAU
JOHN

**Miniature Sheet**

## Bottom middle

PALAU
JENGE IMAGE CREATION
20c

**Biblical illustrations of the Old Testament appearing in "In Our Image," by Guy Rowe (1894-1969): a, Creation. b, Adam and Eve. c, Noah and his Wife. d, Abraham. e, Jacob's Blessing. f, Jacob Becomes Israel. g, Joseph and his Brethren. h, Moses and the Burning Bush. i, Moses and the Tablets. j, Balaam. k, Joshua. l, Gideon. m, Jephthah. n, Samson. o, Ruth and Naomi. p, Saul Anointed. q, Saul Denounced. r, David and Jonathan. s, David and Nathan. t, David Mourns. u, Solomon Praying. v, Solomon Judging. w, Elijah. x, Elisha. y, Job. z, Isaiah. aa, Jeremiah. ab, Ezekiel. ac, Nebuchadnezzar's Dream. ad, Amos.**

**Jerusalem, 3000th Anniv. — A111**

**1996, May 30**   **Litho.**   **Perf. 14x13½**
388   A108   32c   Strip of 5, #a.-e.    3.00   3.00

No. 388 was issued in miniature sheets of 3. China '96, Intl. Stamp Exhibition, Beijing.

Letter spelling "Palau" and: a, "P," fairy basslet, vermiculate parrotfish. b, "A," yellow cardinalfish. c, "L," Marten's butterflyfish. d, "A," starry moray, slate pencil sea urchin. e, "U," cleaner wrasse, coral grouper.

## Bottom right-middle

PALAU 1c
LOVE

**Disney Sweethearts — A110**

1c, like #393a. 2c, like #393c. 3c, #393d. 4c, like #393e. 5c, #393f. 6c, #393h.

No. #393: a, Simba, Nala, Timon. b, Bernard, Bianca, Mr. Chairman. c, Georgette, Tito, Oliver. d, Duchess, O'Malley, Marie. e, Bianca, Jake, Polly. f, Tod, Vixey, Copper. g, Robin Hood, Maiden Marian, Alan-a-Dale. h, Perdita, puppies. i, Pongo, Perdita, Lady, vert. #395, Bambi, Faline.

**1996, May 30**   **Litho.**   **Perf. 14x13½**
393   A110   60c   #a.-i.    11.00   11.00
**Sheet of 9**
393A-392F   A110   Set of 6    .75   .75
**Souvenir Sheets**
394-395   A110   $2   each    4.25   4.25

**Christmas — A103**

**1995, Oct. 31**   **Litho.**   **Perf. 14**
382   A103   32c   Strip of 5, #a.-e.    2.75   2.75

No. 382 is a continuous design and was issued in sheets of 15 stamps + 5 labels se-tenant with bottom row of sheet.

Native version of "We Three Kings of Orient Are": a, Angel, animals. b, Two wise men. c, Joseph, Mary, Jesus in manger. d, Wise man, shepherd, animals. e, Girl with fruit, goat, shepherd.

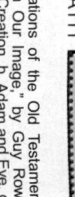

**1996, June 15   Perf. 14   Litho.**
396  A111  20c  Sheet of 30, a-ad   12.00 12.00

For overprint see No. 461.

**1996 Summer Olympics, Atlanta A112**

No. 397, Fanny Blankers Koen, gold medalist, 1948, vert. No. 398, Bob Mathias, gold medalist, 1948, 1952, vert. No. 399, Torchbearer entering Wembley Stadium, 1948. No. 400, Olympic flag, flags of Palau and U.K. before entrance to Stadium, Olympia, Greece. Athletes: No. 401: a, Hakeem Olajuwan, US. b, Pat McCormick, US. c, Jim Thorpe, US. d, Jesse Owens, US. e, Tatyana Gutsu, Unified Team. f, Michael Jordan, US. g, Fu Mingxia, China. h, Robert Zmelik, Czechoslovakia. i, Ivan Pedroso, Cuba. j, Nadia Comaneci, Romania. k, Jackie Joyner-Kersee, US. l, Michael Johnson, US. m, Kristin Otto, E. Germany. n, Vitali Scherbo, Unified Team. o, Johnny Weissmuller, US. p, Babe Didrikson, Hungary. s, Sawao Kato, Japan. t, Alexander Popov, Unified Team.

**1996, June 17   Litho.   Perf. 14**
397  A112  40c  multicolored   .80  .80
398  A112  40c  multicolored   .80  .80
a.  Pair, #397-398   1.60  1.60
399  A112  60c  multicolored   1.25  1.25
400  A112  60c  multicolored   1.25  1.25
a.  Pair, #399-400   2.50  2.50
401  A112  32c  Sheet of 20, #a.-t.   12.00 12.00

Nos. 398a, 400a were each issued in sheets of 20 stamps. No. 401 is a continuous design.

**Birds Over Palau Lagoon A113**

Designs: a, Lakkotsiang, female. b, Maledaob. c, Belochel (g). d, Lakkotsiang, male. e, Sechosech. f, Mechadelbedaoch (j). g, Laib. h, Cheloteachel. i, Deroech. j, Kerkirs. k, Dudek. l, Lakkulsiang. m, Bedauoll. n, Bedebedchaki. o, Kekerreirterrriil. q, Sechou (white Pacific reef-heron). r, Oohaieu. s, Oitirakladiai. t, Omechederiibabad.

**1996, July 10**
402  A113  50c  Sheet of 20, #a.-t.   19.00 19.00

**Aircraft A114**

Stealth, surveillance, and electronic warfare: No. 403: a, Lockheed U-2. b, General Dynamics EF-111A. c, Lockheed YF-12A. d, Lockheed SR-71. e, Teledyne-Ryan-Tiere II Plus. f, Lockheed XST. g, Lockhod ER-2. h, Lockheed F-117A Nighthawk. i, Lockheed EC-130E. j, Ryan Firebee. k, Lockheed Martin/Boeing "Darkstar". l, Boeing E-3A Sentry. No. 404: a, Northrop XB-35. b, Leduc O.21. c, Convair Model 118. d, Blohm und Voss BV 141. e, Vought V-173. f, McDonnell XF-85 Goblin. g, North American F-82B Twin Mustang. h, Lockheed XFV-1. i, Northrop XP-79B. j, Saunders Roe SR/A1. k, Caspian Sea Monster. l, Grumman X-29.
No. 405, Northrop B-2A Stealth Bomber. No. 406, Martin Marietta X-24B.

**1996, Sept. 9   Litho.   Perf. 14**
403  A114  40c  Sheet of 12, #a.-l.   9.50  9.50
404  A114  60c  Sheet of 12, #a.-l.   14.40 14.40

**Souvenir Sheets**
405  A114  $3  multicolored   6.00  6.00
406  A114  $3  multicolored   6.00  6.00

No. 404 is airmail. No. 406 contains one 85x28mm stamp.

**Independence, 2nd Anniv. — A115**

Paintings, by Koh Sekiguchi: No. 407, "In the Blue Shade of Trees-Palau (Kirie). No. 408 "The Birth of a New Nation (Kirie).

**1996, Oct. 1   Litho.   Perf. 14½**
407  20c  multicolored   .40  .40
408  20c  multicolored   .40  .40
a.  A115  Pair, #407-408   .80  .80

#408a issued in sheets of 16 stamps.

**Christmas — A116**

Christmas trees: a, Pandanus. b, Mangrove. c, Norfolk Island pine. d, Papaya. e, Casuarina.

**1996, Oct. 8   Perf. 14**
409  A116  32c  Strip of 5, #a.-e.   3.25  3.25

No. 409 was issued in sheets of 3.

**Voyage to Mars — A117**

No. 410: a, Viking 1 (US) in Mars orbit. b, Mars Lander fires de-orbit engines (top). c, Viking 1 symbol (top). d, Viking 1 symbol (bottom). e, Martian moon phobos. f, Mariner 9 in Mars orbit. g, Viking lander enters Martian atmosphere. h, Parachute deploys for Mars landing, heat shield jettisons. i, Proposed manned mission to Mars, 21st cent. j, US-Russian spacecraft (top). k, Lander descent engines fire for Mars landing. l, Viking 1 lands on Mars, July 20, 1976. m, NASA Mars rover. No. 412, NASA water probe on Mars. Illustration reduced.

**1996, Nov. 8   Litho.   Perf. 14x14½**
410  A117  32c  Sheet of 12, #a.-l.   7.75  7.75

**Souvenir Sheets**
411-412  A117  $3  each   6.00  6.00

No. 411 contains one 38x30mm stamp.

**Souvenir Sheet**

**New Year 1997 (Year of the Ox) — A117a**

Illustration reduced.

**1997, Jan. 2   Litho.   Perf. 14**
412A  A117a  $2  multicolored   4.00  4.00

**Souvenir Sheet**

Beautiful Palau Salutes South Pacific Commission 1947

**South Pacific Commission, 50th Anniv. — A118**

Illustration reduced.

**1997, Feb. 6   Litho.   Perf. 14**
413  A118  $1  multicolored   2.00  2.00

**Hong Kong '97 — A119**

Flowers: 1c, Pemphis acidula. 2c, Sea lettuce. 3c, Tropical almond. 4c, Guettarda. 5c, Pacific coral bean. $3, Sea hibiscus.
No. 420: a, Black mangrove. b, Cordia. c, Lantern tree. d, Palau rock-island flower.
No. 421: a, Fish-poison tree. b, Indian mulberry. c, Pacific poison-apple. d, Ailanthus.

**1997, Feb. 12   Perf. 14½, 13½ (#419)**
414-419  A119  Set of 6   6.25  6.25
420  A119  32c  Block of 4, #a.-d.   2.50  2.50
421  A119  50c  Block of 4, #a.-d.   4.00  4.00

Size of No. 419 is 73x48mm.
Nos. 420-421 were each issued in sheets of 16 stamps.

**Bicent. of the Parachute A120**

Uses of parachute: No. 422: a, Apollo 15 Command Module landing safely. b, "Caterpillar Club" flyer ejecting safely over land. c, Skydiving team formation. d, Parasailing. e, Military parachute demonstration teams. f, Parachute behind dragster. g, Dropping cargo from C-130 aircraft. h, "Goldfish Club" flyer ejecting safely at sea.
No. 423: a, Demonstrating parachute control. b, A.J. Garnerin, first successful parachute descent, 1797. c, Slowing down world land-speed record breaking cars. d, Dropping spies behind enemy lines. e, C-130E demonstrating "LAPES". f, Parachutes used to slow down high performance aircraft. g, ARD parachutes. g, US Army parachutist flying Parafoil.
No. 424 Training tower at Ft. Benning, Georgia. No. 425, "Funny Car" safety chute.

**1997, Mar. 13   Perf. 14½x14, 14x14½   Litho.**
422  A120  32c  Sheet of 8, #a.-h.   5.25  5.25
423  A120  60c  Sheet of 8, #a.-h.   9.75  9.75

**Souvenir Sheets   Perf. 14**
424-425  A120  $2  each   4.00  4.00

Nos. 422a-423a, 422b-423b, 422g-423g, 422h-423h are 20x48mm. No. 424 contains one 28x85mm, No. 425 one 57x42mm stamps.
No. 423 is airmail.
Postage Stamp Mega-Event, NYC, Mar. 1997 (#422-423).

**Native Birds A121**

a, Gray duck, banana tree. b, Red junglefowl, calamondin. c, Nicobar pigeon, fruited parinari tree. d, Cardinal honeyeater, wax apple tree. e, Yellow bittern, purple swamphen, giant taro, taro. f, Eclectus parrot, pangi football fruit tree. g, Micronesian pigeon, Rambutan. h, Micronesian starling, mango tree. i, Fruit bat, breadfruit tree. j, Collared kingfisher, coconut palm. k, Palau fruit dove, sweet orange tree. l, Chestnut mannikin, soursop tree.

**1997, Mar. 27   Litho.   Perf. 13½x14**
426  A121  20c  Sheet of 12, #a.-l.   4.75  4.75

50th Anniversary of UNESCO

**UNESCO, 50th Anniv. — A122**

Sites in Japan, vert: Nos. 427: a, c-h, Himeiji-jo. b, Kyoto.
Sites in Germany, Nos. 428: a-b, Augustusburg Castle. c, Falkenlust Castle. d, Roman ruins, Trier. e, Historic house, Trier.
No. 429, Forest, Shirakami-Sanchi, Japan. No. 430, Yakushima, Japan.

**1997, Apr. 7   Perf. 13½x14, 14x13½   Litho.**
**Sheets of 8 or 5 + Label**
427  A122  32c  #a.-h.   5.25  5.25
428  A122  60c  #a.-e.   6.00  6.00

**Souvenir Sheets**
429-430  A122  $2  each   4.00  4.00

A123

Palau 32¢

Hiroshige 1797-1858
Swallows and Peach Blossoms under a Full Moon

Palau 32¢

A124

Paintings by Hiroshige (1797-1858): No. 431: a, Swallows and Peach Blossoms under a Full Moon. b, A Parrot on a Flowering Branch. c, Crane and Rising Sun. d, Cock, Umbrella, and Morning Glories. e, A Titmouse Hanging Head Downward on a Camellia Branch.

No. 432, Falcon on a Pine Tree with the Rising Sun. No. 433, Kingfisher and Iris.

**1997, June 2          Litho.          Perf. 14**
431 A123 32c Sheet of 5, #a.-e.          3.75 3.75
432-433          **Souvenir Sheets**
432-433 A123 $2 each          4.00 4.00

**1997          Litho.          Perf. 14**
Volcano Goddesses of the Pacific: a, Darago, Philippines. b, Fuji, Japan. c, Pele, Hawaii. d, Pare, Maori. e, Dzalarhons, Haida. f, Chuginadak, Aleuts.
434 A124 32c Sheet of 6, #a.-f.          3.75 3.75
          PACIFIC 97.

**1997, Oct. 1**
Independence, 3rd Anniv. — A125
**1997, Oct. 1          Litho.          Perf. 14**
435 A125 32c multicolored          .65 .65
No. 435 was issued in sheets of 12.

3rd Anniversary of Independence
PALAU 32¢

Ships: No. 436: a, Albatross. b, Mabahiss. c, Atlantis II. d, Xarifa. e, Meteor. f, Egabrass III. g, Discoverer. h, Kaiyo. i, Ocean Defender.
No. 437, Jacques-Yves Cousteau (1910-97). No. 438, Cousteau, diff., vert. No. 439, Pete Seeger, vert.
Oceanographic Research — A126

PALAU 32¢
ALBATROSS

---

**1997, Oct. 1          Perf. 14x14½, 14½x14**
436 A126 32c Sheet of 9, #a.-i.          5.75 5.75
437-439          **Souvenir Sheets**
437-439 A126 $2 each          4.00 4.00

**1997, Nov. 26          Litho.          Perf. 14**
440 A127 60c multicolored          1.25 1.25
No. 440 was issued in sheets of 6.

Diana, Princess of Wales (1961-97) — A127

PALAU 32¢
EXERCISE YOUR RIGHT TO READ

Various Disney characters: 1c, like #447d. 3c, like #447l. 5c, like #447l. 10c, like #447h.
No. 447: a, "Exercise your right to read." b, "Reading is the ultimate luxury." c, "Share your knowledge." d, "Start them Young." e, "Reading is fundamental." f, "The insatiable reader." g, "Reading time is anytime." h, "Real men read." i, "I can read by myself." j, "The library is for everyone." k, vert. No. 449, Mickey, "Books are magical."

Disney's "Let's Read" — A128

**1997, Oct. 21          Perf. 14x13½, 13½x14**
441-446 A128          **Set of 6**
441-446 A128          5.75 5.75
447 A128 32c #a.-i.          .50 .50
          **Souvenir Sheets**
          **Sheet of 9**
448 A128 $2 multicolored          4.00 4.00
449 A128 $3 multicolored          6.00 6.00

**1997, Oct. 28          Perf. 14**
Children singing Christmas carol, "Some Children See Him": No. 450: a, Girl, boy in striped shirt. b, Boy, girl in pigtails. c, Girl, boy. Madonna and Child. d, Girl, two children. e, Boy, girl with long black hair.
450 A129 32c Strip of 5, #a.-e.          3.25 3.25
No. 450 was issued in sheets of 3 strips, bottom strip printed se-tenant with 5 labels containing lyrics.

Christmas — A129

PALAU 32¢

---

**1998, Jan. 2          Litho.          Perf. 14**
451 A130 50c multicolored          1.00 1.00
452 A130 50c multicolored          1.00 1.00

Chinese toys in shape of tiger: No. 451, White background. No. 452, Green background.
New Year 1998 (Year of the Tiger) — A130
Illustration reduced.

No. 453: a, Photograph of nucleus of galaxy M100. b, Top of Hubble telescope with solar arrays folded. c, Astronaut riding robot arm. d, Astronaut anchored to robot arm. e, Astronaut in cargo space with Hubble mounted to shuttle Endeavour. f, Hubble released after repair.
No. 454, Hubble cutaway, based on NASA schematic drawing. No. 455, Edwin Hubble (1889-1963), astronomer who proved existence of star systems beyond Milky Way. No. 456, Hubble Mission STS-82/Discovery.

Repair of Hubble Space Telescope A131

PALAU 32¢

**1998, Mar. 9          Litho.          Perf. 14**
453 A131 32c Sheet of 6, #a.-f.          3.75 3.75
454-456          **Souvenir Sheets**
454-456 A131 $2 each          4.00 4.00

Deep Sea Robots A133

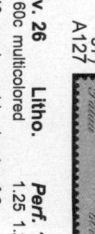 Mother Teresa
PALAU 60¢

Various portraits.
Mother Teresa (1910-97) — A132
**1998, Mar. 12          Litho.          Perf. 14**
457 A132 60c Sheet of 4, #a.-d.          4.75 4.75

No. 458: a, Ladybird ROV. b, Slocum Glider. c, Hornet. d, Scorpio. e, Odyssey AUV. f, Jamstec Survey System Launcher. g, Jamstec Survey System Finder/Salvager. i, Jamstec Survey System Vehicle. j, Jamstec Sub, h, Sea ROV. l, ABE. m, OBSS. n, RCV 225G

---

**Souvenir Sheets**
No. 396 Ovptd. in Silver

Palau 50
新年快乐
HAPPY NEW YEAR

**1998, Apr. 21          Souvenir Sheets**
458 A133 32c Sheet of 18, #a.-r.          11.50 11.50
459-460 A133 $2 each          4.00 4.00
UNESCO Intl. Year of the Ocean.

Swimming Eyeball. o, Japanese UROV. p, Benthos RPV. q, CURV. r, Smartie. No. 459, Jason Jr. inspecting Titanic. No. 460, Dolphin 3K.

**1998, May 13          Litho.          Perf. 14**
461 A111 20c Sheet of 30, a.-r.          12.00 12.00
          ad.
No. 461 is overprinted in sheet margin, "ISRAEL 98 — WORLD STAMP EXHIBITION / TEL AVIV 13-21 MAY 1998." Location of overprint varies.

PALAU 20¢

**1998, May 29          Litho.          Perf. 14**
462 A134 32c Sheet of 12, #a.-l.          9.50 9.50
#462: a, Bai (hut), people. b, Bai, lake. c, Bai, lake, person in canoe. d, Bird on branch over lake. e, Men rowing in canoe. f, Canoe, head of snake. g, Alligator under water. h, Fish, shark. i, Turtle, body of snake. j, Underwater bai, "gods". k, Snails, fish, Orachel swimming. l, Orachel's feet, coral, fish.
Legend of Orachel — A134

PALAU 32¢

**1998, June 5          Litho.          Perf. 14**
463 A135 50c Sheet of 8, #a.-h.          8.00 8.00
464          **Souvenir Sheet**
464 A135 $3 multicolored          6.00 6.00
Players, color of shirt — #463: a, Yellow, black & red. b, Blue, white & red. c, Green & white. d, White, red & blue. e, Green & white (black shorts). f, White, red & black. g, Blue & yellow. h, Red & white.
#463: a, Yellow, white, red & blue. g, Green & white. h, Pele.
1998 World Cup Soccer Championships, France — A135

PALAU 50¢
CELEBRATING WORLD CUP '98

Designs: a, Spear fishing. b, Spear throwing. c, Swimming. d, Pouring milk from coconut. e, Logo of games. f, Climbing coconut
4th Micronesian Games, Palau — A136

PALAU 32¢

trees. g, Canoeing. h, Husking coconut. i, Deep sea diving.

**1998, July 31    Perf. 14**
**Litho.**
465  A136  32c Sheet of 9, #a.-i.    5.75  5.75

## Rudolph The Red-Nosed Reindeer — A137

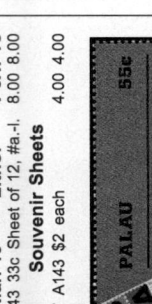

Christmas: a, Rudolph, two reindeer, girl. b, Two reindeer, girl holding flowers. c, Girl, two reindeer, boy. d, Two reindeer, girl smiling. e, Santa, children, Christmas gifts.

**1998, Sept. 15    Litho.    Perf. 14**
466  A137  32c Strip of 5, #a.-e.    3.25  3.25

No. 466 is a continuous design and was issued in sheets of 15 stamps.

## Disney/Pixar's "A Bug's Life" — A138

No. 467: a, Dot. b, Heimlich, Francis, Slim. c, Hopper. d, Princess Atta.
No. 468: Various scenes with Flik, Princess Atta.
No. 469, horiz.: a, Circous bugs. b, Slim, Francis, Heimlich. c, Manny. d, Francis.
No. 470: a, Slim, Flik. b, Heimlich, Slim, Francis performing. c, Manny, Flik. d, Gypsy, Manny, Rosie.
No. 471, Gypsy. No. 472, Princess Atta, Flik, horiz. No. 473, Slim, Francis, Heimlich, horiz. No. 474, Francis, Slim, Flik, Heimlich, horiz.

**1998, Dec. 1    Perf. 13½x14, 14x13½    Litho.**
**Sheets of 4**
467  A138  20c #a.-d.    1.60  1.60
468  A138  32c #a.-d.    2.50  2.50
469  A138  50c #a.-d.    4.00  4.00
470  A138  60c #a.-d.    4.75  4.75
**Souvenir Sheets**
471-474  A138  $2 each    4.00  4.00

Nos. 473-474 each contain one 76x51mm stamp.

## John Glenn's Return to Space — A139

No. 475, Various photos of Project Mercury, Friendship 7 mission, 1962.
No. 476, Various photos of Discovery Space Shuttle mission, 1998.

**1999, Jan. 7    Litho.    Perf. 14**
**Sheets of 8**
475-476  A139  60c #a.-h. each    9.50  9.50
**Souvenir Sheets**
477-478  A139  $2 each    4.00  4.00

Nos. 477-478 each contain one 28x42mm stamp.

## Environmentalists — A140

a, Rachel Carson. b, J.N. "Ding" Darling, US Duck stamp #RW1. c, David Brower. d, Jacques Cousteau. e, Roger Tory Peterson. f, Prince Philip. g, Joseph Wood Krutch. h, Aldo Leopold. i, Dian Fossey. j, US Vice-President Al Gore. k, David Attenborough. l, Paul McCready. m, Sting (Gordon Sumner). n, Paul Winter. o, Ian MacHarg. p, Denis Hayes.

**1999, Feb. 1    Litho.    Perf. 14½**
479  A140  33c Sheet of 16, #a.-p.    10.50 10.50

No. 479i shows Dian Fossey's name misspelled "Diane."

## MIR Space Station — A141

No. 480: a, Soyuz Spacecraft, Science Module. b, Spektr Science Module. c, Space Shuttle, Spacelab Module. d, Kvant 2, Scientific and Air Lock Module. e, Kristall Technological Module. f, Space Shuttle, Docking Module.
No. 481, Astronaut Charles Precourt, Cosmonaut Talgat Musabayev. No. 482, Cosmonaut Valeri Poliakov. No. 483, US Mission Specialist Shannon W. Lucid, Cosmonaut Yuri Y. Usachov. No. 484, Cosmonaut Anatoly Solovyov.

**1999, Feb. 18    Litho.    Perf. 14**
480  A141  33c Sheet of 6, #a.-f.    3.75  3.75
**Souvenir Sheets**
481-484  A141  $2 each    4.00  4.00

## Personalities — A142

1c, Haruo Remilik. 2c, Lazarus Salii. 20c, Charlie W. Gibbons. 22c, Adm. Raymond A. Spruance. 33c, Kuniwo Nakamura. 50c, Adm. William F. Halsey. 55c, Col. Lewis "Chesty" Puller. 60c, Franklin D. Roosevelt. 77c, Harry S Truman. $3.20, Jimmy Carter.

**1999, Mar. 4    Perf. 14x15**
485  A142  1c green    .20  .20
486  A142  2c purple    .20  .20
487  A142  20c violet    .40  .40
488  A142  22c bister    .45  .45
489  A142  33c brown    .65  .65
490  A142  50c brown    1.00  1.00
491  A142  55c blue green    1.10  1.10
492  A142  60c orange    1.25  1.25
493  A142  77c yellow brown    1.50  1.50
494  A142  $3.20 red violet    6.50  6.50
Nos. 485-494 (10)    13.25 13.25

Nos. 485, 492 exist dated 2001.

## Australia '99 World Stamp Expo — A143

Endangered species — #495: a, Leatherback turtle. b, Kemp's ridley turtle. c, Green turtle. d, Marine iguana. e, Green ghost frog. f, Spiny turtle. g, Hewitt's ghost frog. h, Geometric tortoise. i, Limestone salmander. j, Desert rain frog. k, Cape plantanna. l, Long-toed tree frog.
No. 496, Marine crocodile. No. 497, Hawksbill turtle.

**1999, Mar. 19    Litho.    Perf. 13**
495  A143  33c Sheet of 12, #a.-l.    8.00  8.00
**Souvenir Sheets**
496-497  A143  $2 each    4.00  4.00

## IBRA '99, Nuremburg — A144

498, Leipzig-Dresden Railway, Caroline Islands Type A4. No. 499, Gölsdorf 4-8-0, Caroline Islands Type A8, 10.

**1999, Apr. 27    Litho.    Perf. 14**
498-499  A144  55c Set of 2    2.25  2.25
**Souvenir Sheet**
500  A144  $2 multicolored    4.00  4.00

## Exploration of Mars — A145

No. 501: a, Mars Global Surveyor. b, Mars Climate Orbiter. c, Mars Polar Lander. d, Deep Space 2. e, Mars Surveyor 2001 Orbiter. f, Mars Surveyor 2001 Lander.
No. 502, Mars Global Surveyor. No. 503, Mars Climate Orbiter. No. 504, Mars Polar Lander. No. 505, Mars Surveyor 2001 Lander.

**1999, May 10    Litho.    Perf. 14**
501  A145  33c Sheet of 6, #a.-f.    4.00  4.00
**Souvenir Sheets**
502-505  A145  $2 each    4.00  4.00

Nos. 502-505 each contain one 38x50mm stamp. See Nos. 507-511.

### Space Type

International Space Station — #507: a, Launch 1R. b, Launch 14A. c, Launch 8A. d, Launch 1J. e, Launch 1E. f, Launch 16A. No. 508, Intl. Space Station. No. 509, Cmdr. Bob Cabana, Cosmonaut Sergei Krikalev. No. 510, Crew of Flight 2R, horiz. No. 511, X-38 Crew Return Vehicle, horiz.

**1999, June 12    Litho.    Perf. 14**
507  A145  33c Sheet of 6, #a.-f.    4.00  4.00
**Souvenir Sheets**
508-511  A145  $2 each    4.00  4.00

## Earth Day — A146

Pacific insects: a, Banza Natida. b, Drosophila heteroneura. c, Nesomicromus vagus. d, Megalagrian leptodemus. e, Pseudopsectra cookearum. f, Ampheida neacaledonia. g, Pseudopsectra swezeyi. h, Deinacrida heteracantha. i, Beech forest butterfly. j, Hercules moth. k, Striped sphinx moth. l, Tussock butterfly. m, Elytrochellus. n, Bush cricket. o, Longhorn beetle. p, Abathrus bicolor. q, Stylagymnusa subantartica. r, Moth butterfly. s, Paraconosoma naviculare. t, Ornithoptera priamus.

**1999, May 24    Litho.    Perf. 14**
506  A146  33c Sheet of 20, #a.-t.    13.50 13.50

## 20th Century Visionaries — A147

Designs: a, William Gibson, "Cyberspace." b, Danny Hillis, Massively Parallel Processing. c, Steve Wozniak, Apple Computer. d, Steve Jobs, Apple Computer. e, Nolan Bushnell, Atari, Inc. f, John Warnock, Adobe, Inc. g, Ken Thompson, Unix. h, Al Shugart, Seagate Technologies. i, Rand & Robyn Miller, "MYST". j, Nicolas Negroponte, MIT Media Lab. k, Bill Gates, Microsoft, Inc. l, Arthur C. Clarke, Orbiting Communications Satellite. m, Marshall McLuhan, "The Medium is the Message." n, Thomas Watson, Jr., IBM. o, Gordon Moore, Intel Corporation, "Moore's Law." p, James Gosling, Java. q, Sabeer Bhatia & Jack Smith, Hotmail.com. r, Esther Dyson, "Release 2.0." s, Jerry Yang, David Filo, Yahoo! t, Jeff Bezos, Amazon.com. u, Bob Kahn, TCP-IP. v, Jaron Lanter, "Virtual Reality." w, Andy Grove, Intel Corporation. x, Jim Clark, Silicon Graphics, Inc. y, Bob Metcalfe, Ethernet, 3com.

**1999, June 30    Litho.    Perf. 14**
512  A147  33c Sheet of 25, a.-y.    17.00 17.00

## Paintings by Hokusai (1760-1849) — A148

#513: a, Women Divers. b, Bull and Parasol. c, Drawings of Women (partially nude). d, Drawings of Women (seated, facing forward). o, Japanese spaniel. f, Portora in Landcapo.
#514: a, Bacchanalian Revelry. b, Bacchanalian Revelry (two seated back to back). c, Drawings of Women (crawling). d, Drawings of Women (facing backward). e, Ox-Herd. f, Ox-Herd (man on bridge).
No. 515, Mount Fuji in a Thunderstorm, vert. No. 516, At Swan Lake in Shinano.

**1999, July 20    Perf. 14x13¾**
**Sheets of 6**
513-514  A148  33c #a.-f., each    4.00  4.00
**Souvenir Sheets**
515-516  A148  $2 each    4.00  4.00

## Apollo 11, 30th Anniv. — A149

No. 517: a, Lift-off, jettison of stages. b, Earth, moon, capsule. c, Astronaut on lunar module ladder. d, Lift-off. e, Planting flag on moon. f, Astronauts Collins, Armstrong and Aldrin.
No. 518, Rocket on launch pad. No. 519, Astronaut on ladder, earth. No. 520, Lunar module above moon. No. 521, Capsule in ocean.

**1999, July 20    Litho.    Perf. 13½x14**
517  A149  33c Sheet of 6, #a.-f.    4.00  4.00
**Souvenir Sheets**
518-521  A149  $2 each    4.00  4.00

**Queen Mother (b. 1900) — A150**

No. 522: a, In Australia, 1958. b, In 1960. c, In 1970. d, In 1987. e, $2, Holding book, 1947.

**522** A150 60c Sheet of 4, #a-d. 4.75 4.75
+ label

**Gold Frames**
**Souvenir Sheet**
**Perf. 13¾**
**523** A150 $2 black 4.00 4.00

No. 523 contains one 38x51mm stamp.
See Nos. 636-637.

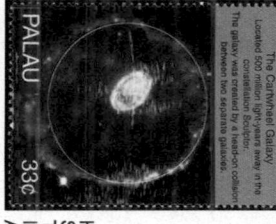

**Hubble Space Telescope Images A151**

PALAU 33c

The Cartwheel Galaxy... Located 500 million light-years away in the constellation Sculptor. The galaxy was created by a head-on collision between two separate galaxies.

No. 524: a, Cartwheel Galaxy. b, Stingray Nebula. c, NGC 3918. d, Cat's Eye Nebula (NGC 6543). e, NGC 7742. f, Eight-burst Nebula (NGC 3132).
No. 525, Eta Carinae. No. 526, Planetary nebula M2-9. No. 527, Supernova 1987-A. No. 528, Infrared aurora of Saturn.

**1999, Oct. 15 Litho. Perf. 13¾**
**524** A151 33c Sheet of 6, #a-f. 4.00 4.00
**Souvenir Sheets**
**525-528** A151 $2 each 4.00 4.00

**Christmas — A152**

**1999, Nov. 15 Perf. 14**
**529** A152 20c Strip of 5, #a-e. 2.00 2.00

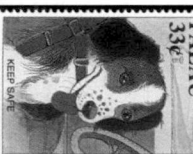

**Love for Dogs — A153**

No. 530: a, Keep safe. b, Show affection. c, A place of one's own. d, Communicate. e, Good food. f, Annual checkup. g, Teach rules. h, Exercise & play. i, Let him help. j, Unconditional love.
No. 531, Pleasure of your company. No. 532, Love is a gentle thing.

**1999, Nov. 23 Litho. Perf. 14**
**530** A153 33c Sheet of 10, #a-j. 6.75 6.75
**531-532** A153 $2 Sheet of 2,
**Souvenir Sheets**
**531-532** A153 $2 each 4.00 4.00

**Futuristic Space Probes A154**

PALAU 55¢

Text starting with — No. 533: a, Deep space probes like... b, This piggy-back... c, Deep space telescope... d, Mission planning... e, In accordance... f, Utilizing onboard...
No. 534, This secondary... No. 535, Deep space probes are an integral... No. 536, Deep space probes are our... No. 537, With the...

**2000, Jan. 18 Litho. Perf. 13¾**
**533** A154 55c Sheet of 6, #a-f. 3.50 3.50
**Souvenir Sheets**
**534-537** A154 $2 each 4.00 4.00

**Millennium A155**

Palau 20¢
Brazilian Indians, 1900

Highlights of 1800-50 — No. 538: a, Brazilian Indians. b, Haiti slave revolt. c, Napoleon becomes Emperor of France. d, Shaka Zulu. e, "Frankenstein" written. f, Simon Bolivar. g, Photography invented. h, First water purification works built. i, First all-steam railway. j, Michael Faraday discovers electromagnetism. k, First use of anesthesia. l, Samuel Morse completes first telegraph line. m, Women's rights convention in Seneca Falls, NY. n, Birth of Karl Marx. o, Revolution in German Confederation. p, Charles Darwin's voyages on the "Beagle" (60x40mm). q, Beijing, China.
Highlights of 1980-89 — No. 539: a, Lech Walesa organizes Polish shipyard workers. b, Voyager I photographs Saturn. c, Ronald Reagan elected US president. d, Identification of AIDS virus. e, Wedding of Prince Charles and Lady Diana Spencer. f, Compact discs go into production. g, Bhopal, India gas disaster. h, M. Pei's Pyramid entrance to the Louvre opens. i, Mikhail Gorbachev becomes leader of Soviet Union. j, Chernobyl nuclear disaster. k, Explosion of Space Shuttle "Challenger". l, Klaus Barbie convicted of crimes against humanity. m, Life of author Salman Rushdie threatened by Moslems. n, Benazir Bhutto becomes first woman prime minister of a Moslem state. o, Tiananmen Square revolt. p, Berlin Wall falls (60x40mm). q, World Wide Web.

**2000, Feb. 2 Litho. Perf. 12¾x12½**
**Sheets of 17, #a-q.**
**538-539** A155 20c each 7.00 7.00

Misspellings and historical inaccuracies abound on Nos. 538-539.
See No. 584.

**New Year 2000 (Year of the Dragon) — A156**

HAPPY LUNAR NEW YEAR $2
435.2
PALAU

Illustration reduced.

**2000, Feb. 5 Perf. 13¾**
**540** A156 $2 multi 4.00 4.00

**US Presidents — A157**

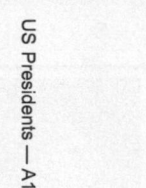

PALAU $1 Bill Clinton

**2000, Mar. 1 Litho. Perf. 13½x13¾**
**541** A157 $1 Bill Clinton 2.00 2.00
**542** A157 $2 Ronald Reagan 4.00 4.00
**543** A157 $3 Gerald Ford 6.00 6.00
**544** A157 $5 George Bush 10.00 10.00
**Size: 40x24mm**
**545** A157 $11.75 Kennedy 22.50 22.50
Nos. 541-545 (5) 44.50 44.50

**20th Century Discoveries About Prehistoric Life — A158**

Designs: a, Australopithecines. b, Australopithecine skull. c, Homo habilis. d, Hand axe. e, Homo habilis skull. f, Lucy. g, Australopithecine skeleton. h, Archaic Homo sapiens skull. i, Diapithicine skull. j, Homo erectus. k, Woodhut. k, Australopithecine ethiopsis skull. l, Dawn of mankind. m, Homo sapiens skull. n, Taung baby's skull. o, Homo erectus skull. p, Louis Leakey (1903-72). paleontologist. q, Neanderthal skull. r, Neanderthal. s, Evolution of the foot. t, Raymond Dart (1893-1988), paleontologist.

**2000, Mar. 15 Perf. 14¼**
**546** A158 20c Sheet of 20, #a-t. 8.00 8.00

Misspellings and historical inaccuracies are found on Nos. 549g, 546g, 546m, 546t and perhaps others.

**2000 Summer Olympics, Sydney A159**

Palau 33c

Designs: a, Charlotte Cooper, tennis player at 1924 Olympics. b, Women's shot put. c, Helsinki Stadium, site of 1952 Olympics. d, Ancient Greek athletes.

**2000, Mar. 31 Perf. 14**
**547** A159 33c Sheet of 4, #a-d. 2.75 2.75

**Future of Space Exploration A160**

PALAU 33¢

Text starting with — No. 548: a, This vehicle will be... b, This single stage... c, This robotic rocket... d, Dynamic... e, This fully... f, This launch vehicle...
No. 549, Increasingly, space travel... No. 550, Designed with projects... No. 551, Design is currently... No. 552, Inevitably, the future...

**2000, Apr. 10 Perf. 13¾**
**548** A160 33c Sheet of 6, #a-f. 4.00 4.00
**Souvenir Sheets**
**549-552** A160 $2 each 4.00 4.00

**Birds — A161**

PALAU 20c Slatey-legged Crake
Rallina eurizonoides

No. 553: a, Slatey-legged crake. b, Micronesian kingfisher. c, Little pied cormorant. d, Pacific reed egret. e, Nicobar pigeon. f, Rufous night heron.
No. 554: a, Mangrove flycatcher. d, Palau bush warbler. e, Palau fantail. f, Morningbird. scops owl. e, Palau ground dove. d, Palau No. 555, Palau fruit dove, horiz. No. 556, Palau white-eye, horiz.

**2000, Apr. 14 Litho. Perf. 14¼**
**553** A161 20c Sheet of 6, #a-f. 2.40 2.40
**554** A161 33c Sheet of 6, #a-f. 4.00 4.00
**Souvenir Sheets**
**555-556** A161 $2 each 4.00 4.00

**Visionaries of the 20th Century — A162**

VISIONAIRIES OF THE TWENTIETH CENTURY

a, Booker T. Washington. b, Buckminster Fuller. c, Marie Curie. d, Walt Disney. e, F. D. Roosevelt. f, Henry Ford. g, Betty Friedan. h, Sigmund Freud. i, Mohandas Gandhi. j, Mikhail Gorbachev. k, Stephen Hawking. l, Martin Luther King, Jr. m, Toni Morrison. Georgia O'Keeffe. o, Rosa Parks. p, Carl Sagan. q, Jonas Salk. r, Sally Ride. s, Nikola Tesla. t, Wilbur and Orville Wright.
Illustration reduced.

**2000, Apr. 28 Litho. Perf. 14¼x14½**
**557** A162 33c Sheet of 20, #a-t. 13.50 13.50

## 20th Century Science and Medicine Advances — A163

No. 558: a, James D. Watson, 1962 Nobel laureate. b, Har Gobind Khorana and Robert Holley, 1968 Nobel laureates. c, Hamilton O. Smith and Werner Arber, 1978 Nobel laureates. d, Extraction fo DNA from cells. e, Richard J. Roberts, 1993 Nobel laureate.

No. 559: a, Francis Crick, 1962 Nobel laureate. b, Marshall W. Nirenberg, 1968 Nobel laureate. c, Daniel Nathans, 1978 Nobel laureate. d, Harold E. Varmus and J. Michael Bishop, 1989 Nobel laureates. e, Phillip A. Sharp, 1993 Nobel laureate.

No. 560: a, Maurice H. F. Wilkins, 1962 Nobel laureate. b, DNA strand. c, Frederick Sanger and Walter Gilbert, 1980 Nobel laureates. d, Kary B. Mullis, 1993 Nobel laureate. e, Two DNA strands.

No. 561: a, Four winner, test tube. b, Two DNA strands, diagram of DNA fragments. c, Paul Berg, 1980 Nobel laureate. d, Michael Smith, 1993 Nobel laureate. e, Deer, DNA strands.

#562, Deer. #563, Dolly, 1st cloned sheep. Illustration reduced.

**2000, May 10** **Perf. 13¾**
**Sheets of 5, #a.-e.**
558-561 A163 33c each 3.50 3.50
**Souvenir Sheets**
562-563 A163 $2 each 4.00 4.00
Nos. 562-563 each contain one 38x50mm stamp.

## Marine Life — A164

DEEP-SEA FISH

No. 564: a, Prawn. b, Deep sea angler. c, Rooster fish. d, Grenadier. e, Platyberix opalescens. f, Lantern fish.
No. 565: a, Emperor angelfish. b, Nautilus. c, Moorish idol. d, Sea horse. e, Clown triggerfish. f, Clown fish.
No. 566, Giant squid. No. 567, Manta ray.
Illustration reduced.

## Millennium — A165

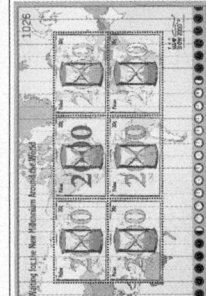

No. 568, horiz. — "2000," hourglass, and map of: a, North Pacific area. b, U.S. and Canada. c, Europe. d, South Pacific. e, South America. f, Southern Africa.
No. 569 — Clock face and: a, Sky. b, Building. c, Cove and lighthouse. d, Barn. e, Forest. f, Desert.
Illustration reduced.

**2000, May 25** **Perf. 13¾**
568 A165 20c Sheet of 6, #a-f 2.40 2.40
569 A165 55c Sheet of 6, #a-f 6.75 6.75
The Stamp Show 2000, London.

## New and Recovering Species — A166

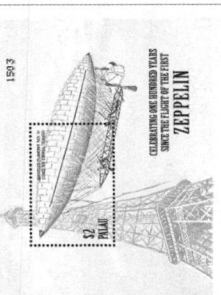
NEW AND RECOVERING SPECIES OF...

No. 570: a, Aleutian Canada goose. b, Western gray kangaroo. c, Palau scops owl. d, Jocotoco antpitta. e, Orchid. f, Red lechwe.
No. 571: a, Bald eagle. b, Small-whorled pogonia. c, Arctic peregrine falcon. d, Golden lion tamarin. e, American alligator. f, Brown pelican.
No. 572, Leopard. No. 573, Lahontan cutthroat trout, horiz.
Illustration reduced.

**2000, June 20** **Perf. 14**
**Sheets of 6, #a-f**
570-571 A166 33c each 4.00 4.00
**Souvenir Sheets**
572-573 A166 $2 each 4.00 4.00

## Dinosaurs — A167

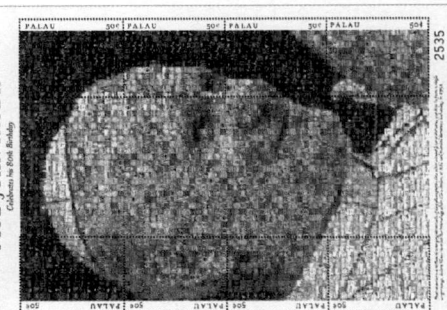
200 Million Years Ago — Dinosaurs of the Jurassic age

No. 574: a, Rhamphorhynchus. b, Ceratosaurus. c, Apatosaurus. d, Stegosaurus. e, Archaeopteryx. f, Allosaurus.
No. 575: a, Parasaurolophus. b, Pteranodon. c, Tyrannosaurus. d, Triceratops. e, Ankylosaurus. f, Velociraptor.
No. 576, Jurassic era view. No. 577, Cretaceous era view.
Illustration reduced.

**2000, June 20**
574 A167 20c Sheet of 6, #a-f 2.40 2.40
575 A167 33c Sheet of 6, #a-f 4.00 4.00
**Souvenir Sheets**
576-577 A167 $2 each 4.00 4.00

## Queen Mother, 100th Birthday — A168

Queen Mother

No. 578, 55c: a, With King George VI. b, Wearing brown hat.
No. 579, 55c: a, Wearing green hat. b, Wearing white hat.
Illustration reduced.

**2000, Sept. 1** **Litho.** **Perf. 14**
**Sheets of 4, 2 each #a-b**
578-579 A168 Set of 2 9.00 9.00
**Souvenir Sheet**
580 A168 $2 Wearing yellow hat 4.00 4.00

## First Zeppelin Flight, Cont. — A169

ZEPPELIN

No. 581: a, Le Jaune. b, Forlanini's Leonardo da Vinci. c, Baldwin's airship. d, Astra-Torres I. e, Parseval PL VII. f, Lebaudy's Liberte.
No. 582, $2, Santos-Dumont Daladouee No. 9. No. 583, $2, Santos-Dumont Daladouee No. 6.
Illustration reduced.

**2000, Sept. 1**
581 A169 55c Sheet of 6, #a-f 6.75 6.75
**Souvenir Sheets**
582-583 A169 Set of 2 8.00 8.00

## Millennium Type of 2000
### Sheet of 17

Undersea History and Exploration: a, Viking diver. b, Arab diver Issa. c, Salvage diver. d, Diver. e, Diving bell. f, Turtle. g, Siebe helmet. h, C.S.S. Hunley. i, Argonaut. j, Photosphere. k, Helmet diver. l, Bathysphere. m, Coelacanth. n, WWII charioteers. o, Trieste. p, Alvin visits geothermal vents (60x40mm). q, Jim suit.

**2000, Oct. 16** **Perf. 12½x12½**
584 A155 33c Sheet of 6, #a-q + label 11.50 11.50

## Photomosaic of Pope John Paul II — A170

POPE JOHN PAUL II
Celebration his 80th Birthday

## Various photos with religious themes. Illustration reduced.

**2000, Dec. 1** **Perf. 13¾**
585 A170 50c Sheet of 8, #a-h 8.00 8.00

## Souvenir Sheets

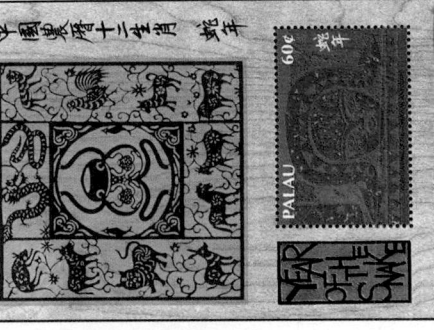
PALAU 60c
YEAR OF THE SNAKE

## New Year 2001 (Year of the Snake) — A171

Snake color: #586, Black. #587, Red.
Illustration reduced.

**2000, Dec. 1** **Perf. 14¼**
586-587 A171 60c Set of 2 2.40 2.40

## Pacific Ocean Marine Life — A172

Marine Life of the Pacific Ocean

No. 588: a, Scalloped hammerhead shark. b, Whitetip reef shark. c, Moon jellyfish. d, Lionfish. e, Seahorse. f, Spotted eagle ray.
Illustration reduced.

**2000** **Perf. 14½x14¼**
500 A172 55c Sheet of 6, #a-f 6.75 6.75

## Atlantic Ocean Fish — A173

Tropical Marine Fishes of the Atlantic Ocean

No. 589, horiz.: a, Reef bass. b, White shark. c, Sharptail eel. d, Sailfish. e, Southern stingray. f, Ocean triggerfish.
#590, Short bigeye. #591, Gafftopsail catfish.
Illustration reduced.

**2000** **Perf. 13¾**
589 A173 20c Sheet of 6, #a-f 2.40 2.40
**Souvenir Sheets**
590-591 A173 $2 Set of 2 8.00 8.00

## Pacific Arts Festival — A174

No. 592: a. Dancers, by S. Adelbai. b. Story Board Art, by D. Inabo. c. Traditional Money, by M. Takeshi. d. Clay Lamp and Bowl, by W. Watanabe. e. Meeting House, by Pasqual Tiaki. f. Outrigger Canoe, by S. Adelbai. g. Weaver, by M. Vitarelli. h. Rock Island Scene, by W. Marcil. i. Contemporary Music, by J. Imetuker.

**2000, Nov. 1**    **Litho.**    **Perf. 14¼**
592 A174 33c Sheet of 9, #a-i    6.00 6.00

## National Museum, 45th Anniv. — A175

No. 593: a. Kilt, turtle shell bracelet. b. Sculpture by H. Hijikata. c. Turtle shell, women's money by B. Sylvester. f. Prince Lebu. g. Money jar, by B. Sylvester. f. Prince Lebu by Ichikawa. g. Beach at Lild, by H. Hijikata. h. Traditional mask. i. Taro platter, by T. Rebluud. j. Meresebang, by Ichikawa. k. Wood sculpture, by B. Sylvester. l. Birth Ceremony, by I. Kishigawa.

**2000, Nov. 1**
593 A175 33c Sheet of 12, #a-l    8.00 8.00

Butterflies
A176

Designs: No. 594, 33c, Indian red admiral. No. 595, 33c, Fiery jewel. No. 596, 33c, Checkered swallowtail. No. 597, 33c, Yanifly. No. 598, 33c: a. Large green-banded blue. b. Union Jack. c. Broad-bordered grass yellow. d. Striped blue crow. e. Red lacewing. f. Palmfly.

No. 599, 33c: a. Cairn's birdwing. b. Meadow argus. c. Orange albatross. d. Glasswing. e. Beak. f. Great eggfly.
No. 600, $2, Clipper. No. 601, $2, Blue triangle.

**2000, Dec. 15**    **Perf. 14**
594-597 A176   Set of 4    2.75 2.75
   **Sheets of 6, #a-f**
598-599 A176   Set of 2    8.00 8.00
   **Souvenir Sheets**
600-601 A176   Set of 2    8.00 8.00

## Flora and Fauna — A177

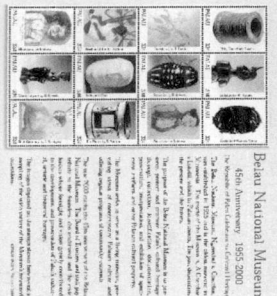

No. 602, 33c: a. Giant spiral ginger. b. Good luck plant. c. Ti tree, coconuts. d. Butterfly. e. Saltwater crocodile. f. Orchid.

No. 603, 33c: a. Little kingfisher. b. Mangrove snake. c. Bats, breadfruit. d. Giant tree frog. e. Giant centipede. f. Crab-eating macaque.
No. 604, $2, Soft coral, surgeonfish. No. 605, $2, Land crab, vert.

**2000, Dec. 29**   **Perf. 14x14¼, 14¼x14**
   **Sheets of 6, #a-f**
602-603 A177   Set of 2    8.00 8.00
   **Souvenir Sheets**
604-605 A177   Set of 2    8.00 8.00

Design: 11c, Lazarus Salii.

**2001**
606 A142 11c purple    .25 .25

## Personalities Type of 1999

Designs: 70c, Gen. Douglas MacArthur. 80c, Adm. Chester W. Nimitz. $12.25, John F. Kennedy.

**2001, June 10**    **Litho.**    **Perf. 14x14¾**
607 A142 70c lilac    1.40 1.40
608 A142 80c green    1.60 1.60
609 A142 $12.25 red    25.00 25.00
   Nos. 607-609 (3)    28.00 28.00

## Moths — A179

Designs: 20c, Veined tiger moth. 21c, Basker moth. 80c, White-lined sphinx moth. $1, Isabella tiger moth.

No. 620, 34c: a. Cinnabar moth. b. Beautiful tiger moth. c. Great tiger moth. d. Provence burnet moth. e. Jersey tiger moth. f. Ornate moth.

No. 621, 70c: a. Hoop pine moth. b. King's bee hawk moth. c. Banded bagnest moth. d. Io moth. e. Tau emperor moth. f. Lime hawkmoth. No. 622, $2, Spanish moon moth. No. 623, $2, Owl moth.

**2001, Oct. 15**    **Litho.**    **Perf. 14**
616-619 A179   Set of 4    4.50 4.50
   **Sheets of 6, #a-f**
620-621 A179   Set of 2    12.50 12.50
   **Souvenir Sheets**
622-623 A179   Set of 2    8.00 8.00

## Phila Nippon '01, Japan — A178

No. 610, 60c: a. Ono no Komachi Washing the Copybook, by Kiyomitsu Torii. b. Woman Playing Samisen and Woman Reading at Letter, by School of Matabei Iwasa. c. The Actor Danjura Ichikawa V as a Samurai in a Wrestling Arena Striking a Pose on a Go Board, by Shunsho Katsukawa. d. Gentleman Entertained by Courtesans, by Kiyonaga Torii. e. Geisha at a Teahouse in Shinagawa, by Kiyonaga Torii.

No. 611, 60c: a. Preparing Sashimi, by Utamaro. b. Ichimatsu Sanogawa I as Sogo no Goro and Kikugoro Onoe as Kyo no Jiro in Umewakana Futaba Soga, by Toyonobu Ishikawa. c. Courtesan Adjusting Her Comb, by Dohan Kaigetsudo. d. The Actor Tomijuro Nakamura I in a Female Role Dancing, by Shunsho Katsukawa. e. Woman with Poem Card and Writing Brush, by Gakutei Yashima.

No. 612, Six panels of screen, Kitano Shrine in Kyoto, by unknown artist.
No. 613, $2, Raiko Attacks a Demon Kite, by Hokkei Totoya. No. 614, $2, Beauty Writing a Letter, by Doshin Kaigetsudo. No. 615, $2, Fireworks at Ikenohata, by Kiyochika Kobayashi.

**2001, Oct. 30**
   **Sheets of 6, #a-f**
624-626 A180   Set of 3    22.50 22.50
   **Souvenir Sheets**
627-629 A180   Set of 3    12.00 12.00

## Nobel Prizes, Cent. — A180

Literature laureates — No. 624, 34c: a. Ivo Andric, 1961. b. Eyvind Johnson, 1974. c. Salvatore Quasimodo, 1959. d. Mikhail Sholokhov, 1965. e. Pablo Neruda, 1971. f. Saul Bellow, 1976.

No. 625, 70c: a. Boris Pasternak, 1958. b. Francois Mauriac, 1952. c. Frans Eemil Sillanpää, 1939. d. Roger Martin du Gard, 1937. e. Pearl Buck, 1938. f. André Gide, 1947.

No. 626, 80c: a. Karl Gjellerup, 1917. b. Anatole France, 1921. c. Sinclair Lewis, 1930. d. Jacinto Benavente, 1922. e. John Galsworthy, 1932. f. Erik A. Karlfeldt, 1931.
No. 627, $2, Luigi Pirandello, 1934. No. 628, $2, Bertrand Russell, 1950. No. 629, Harry Martinson, 1974.

## 2002 World Cup Soccer Championships, Japan and Korea — A181

The History of the World Cup

No. 630, 34c — World Cup posters from: a. 1950. b. 1954. c. 1958. d. 1962. e. 1966. f. 1970.
No. 631, 80c — World Cup posters from: a. 1978. b. 1982. c. 1986. d. 1990. e. 1994. f. 1998.
No. 632, $2, World Cup poster, 1930. No. 633, $2, Head and globe from World Cup trophy.

**2001, Nov. 29**    **Perf. 13¾x14¼**
   **Sheets of 6, #a-f**
630-631 A181   Set of 2    14.00 14.00
   **Souvenir Sheets**
632-633 A181   Set of 2    8.00 8.00

**2001, Aug. 13**    **Litho.**    **Perf. 14**
   **Sheets of 5, #a-e**
610-611 A178   Set of 2    12.00 12.00
612 A178 60c Sheet of 6, #a-f    7.25 7.25
   **Souvenir Sheets**
613-615 A178   Set of 3    12.00 12.00

Christmas — A182

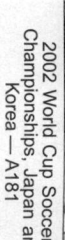

Denominations: 20c, 34c.

**2001, Nov. 29**    **Perf. 14**
634-635 A182   Set of 2    1.10 1.10

## Queen Mother Type of 1999 Redrawn

No. 636: a. In Australia, 1958. b. In 1960. c. In 1970. d. In 1987.
$2, Holding book, 1947.

**2001, Dec. 13**    **Perf. 14**
   **Souvenir Sheet**
636 A150 60c Sheet of 4, #a-d + label    4.75 4.75

## Yellow Orange Frames

**Perf. 13¾**
   **Souvenir Sheet**
637 A150 $2 black    4.00 4.00

Queen Mother's 101st birthday. No. 637 contains one 38x51mm stamp that is slightly darker than that found on No. 523. Sheet margins and frames found on Nos. 636-637 lack white embossing and gold arms and frames found on Nos. 522, 523.

## Pasturing Horses, by Han Kan — A183

**2001, Dec. 17**    **Perf. 14x14¾**
638 A183 60c multi    1.25 1.25

New Year 2002 (Year of the Horse). Printed in sheets of 4.

## Birds — A184

No. 639, 55c: a, Yellow-faced myna. b, Red-bellied pitta. c, Red-bearded bee-eater. d, Superb fruit dove. e, Coppersmith barbet. f, Diard's trogon.
No. 640, 60c: a, Spectacled monarch. b, Banded pitta. c, Rufous-backed kingfisher. d, Scarlet robin. e, Golden whistler. f, Jewel babbler.
No. 641, $2, Paradise flycatcher. No. 642, $2, Common kingfisher.

**2001, Dec. 26**    *Perf. 14*
639-640 A184   Sheets of 6, #a-f   14.00 14.00
    Set of 2     8.00 8.00
   **Souvenir Sheets**
      *Perf. 14¾*
641-642 A184   Set of 2     8.00 8.00

## Opening of Palau-Japan Friendship Bridge — A185

No. 040, 20c, No. 044, 34c: a, Diui un orange rock. b, Island, one palm tree. c, Island, three palm trees. d, Rocks, boat prow. e, Boat, bat. f, Cove, foliage. g, Red boat with two people. h, Buoy, birds. i, Birds, dolphin's tail. j, Dolphins. k, Person on raft. l, Two people standing in water. m, Person with fishing pole in water. n, Bridge tower. o, Bicyclist, taxi. p, Front of taxi. q, People walking on bridge. r, Truck, boat. s, School bus. t, Base of bridge tower. u, Birds under bridge. v, Birds under bridge. w, Base of bridge tower, tip of sail. x, Motorcyclist. y, Birds on black rock. z, Kayakers, aa, Kayak, boat. ab, Boat, sailboat. ac, Sailboat, jetty. ad, Jetski.

**2002, Jan. 11**    *Perf. 13*
643-644 A185   Sheets of 30, #a-ad   32.50 32.50
      Set of 2     32.50 32.50

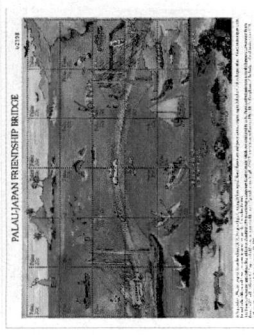

United We Stand — A186

**2002, Jan. 24**    *Perf. 14*
645 A186 $1 multi     2.00 2.00

---

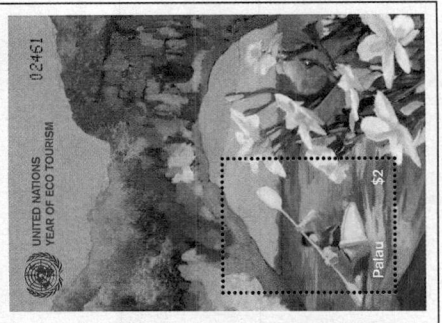

## Reign of Queen Elizabeth II, 50th Anniv. — A187

No. 646: a, In uniform. b, Wearing flowered hat. c, Prince Philip. d, Wearing tiara. $2, Wearing white dress.

**2002, Feb. 6**    *Perf. 14¾*
646 A187 80c Sheet of 4, #a-d   6.50 4.00
   **Souvenir Sheet**
647 A187   $2 multi     4.00 4.00

Birds — A188

Designs: 1c, Gray-backed white-eye. 2c, Great frigatebird. 3c, Eclectus parrot. 4c, Red-footed booby. 5c, Cattle egret. 10c, Cardinal honeyeater. 11b, Blue-faced parrot finch. 15c, Rufous fantail. 20c, White-faced storm petrel. 21c, Willie wagtail. 23c, Black-headed gull. 50c, Sanderling. 57c, White-tailed tropicbird. 70c, Rainbow lorikeet. 80c, Moorhen. $1, Buff-banded rail. $2, Beach thick-knee. $3, Common tern. $3.50, Ruddy turnstone. $3.95, White-collared kingfisher. $5, Sulphur-crested cockatoo. $10, Barn swallow.

**2002, Feb. 20**    *Perf. 14¾*
648 A188   1c multi    .20 .20
649 A188   2c multi    .20 .20
650 A188   3c multi    .20 .20
651 A188   4c multi    .20 .20
652 A188   5c multi    .20 .20
653 A188   10c multi    .20 .20
654 A188   11c multi    .20 .20
655 A188   15c multi    .30 .30
656 A188   20c multi    .40 .40
657 A188   21c multi    .40 .40
658 A188   23c multi    .45 .45
659 A188   50c multi    1.00 1.00
660 A188   57c multi    1.10 1.10
661 A188   70c multi    1.40 1.40
662 A188   80c multi    1.60 1.60
663 A188   $1 multi    2.00 2.00
664 A188   $2 multi    4.00 4.00
665 A188   $3 multi    6.00 6.00
666 A188   $3.50 multi   7.00 7.00
667 A188   $3.95 multi   8.00 8.00
668 A188   $5 multi    10.00 10.00
669 A188   $10 multi    20.00 20.00
     Nos. 648-669 (22)   65.05 65.05

Flowers — A189

Designs: 20c, Euanthe sanderiana. 34c, Ophiorrhiza palauensis. No. 672, 60c, Cerbera manghas. 80c, Mendinilla pterocaulia. No. 674, 60c: a, Bruguiera gymnorhiza. b, Samadera indicad. c, Maesa canfieldiae. d, Lumnitzera litorea. e, Dolichandrone palawense. f, Limnophila aromatica (red and white orchids).

---

No. 675, 60c: a, Sonneratia alba. b, Barringtonia racemosa. c, Ixora casei. d, Tristellateia australasiae. e, Nepenthes mirabilis. f, Limnophila aromatica (pink flowers). No. 676, $2, Fagraea ksid. No. 677, $2, Cerbera manghas, horiz.

**2002, Mar. 4**    *Perf. 14*
670-673 A189   Sheets of 4    4.00 4.00
674-675 A189   Set of 2    14.50 14.50
   **Souvenir Sheets**
676-677 A189   Set of 2    8.00 8.00

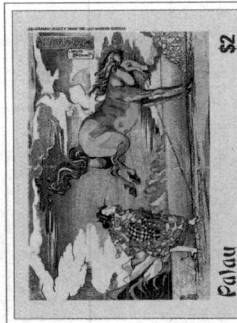

2002 Winter Olympics, Salt Lake City — A190

Skier with: No. 678, $1, Blue pants. No. 679, $1, Yellow pants.

**2002, Mar. 18**    *Perf. 14¾*
678-679 A190   Set of 2    4.00 4.00
679a   Souvenir sheet, #678-679   4.00 4.00

---

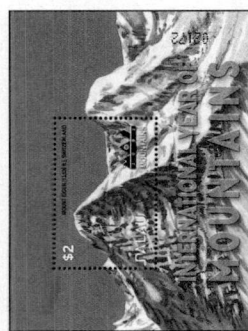

## Cats and Dogs — A191

No. 680, 50c, horiz.: a, Himalayan. b, Norwegian forest cat. c, Havana. d, Exotic shorthair. e, Persian. f, Maine coon cat.
No. 681, 50c, horiz.: a, Great Dane. b, Whippet. c, Bedlington terrier. d, Golden retriever. e, Papillon. f, Doberman pinscher.
No. 682, $2, British shorthair. No. 683, $2, Shetland sheepdog.

**2002, Mar. 18**   **Litho.**   *Perf. 14*
680-681 A191   Set of 2    12.00 12.00
   **Souvenir Sheets**
682-683 A191   Set of 2    8.00 8.00

## Intl. Year of Mountains — A192

No. 684: a, Mt. Fuji, Japan. b, Mt. Everest, Nepal and China. c, Mt. Owen, U.S. d, Mt. Huascarán, Peru. e, Mt. Eiger, Switzerland.

**2002, June 17**   **Litho.**   *Perf. 14*
684 A192 80c Sheet of 4, #a-d   6.50 6.50
   **Souvenir Sheet**
685 A192   $2 multi    4.00 4.00

Flags of Palau and its States — A193

No. 686: a, Palau (no inscription). b, Kayangel. c, Ngarchelong. d, Ngaraard. e, Ngardmau. f, Ngaremlengui. g, Ngiwal. h,

---

Ngatpang. i, Melekeor. j, Ngchesar. k, Aimeliik. l, Airai. m, Koror. n, Peleliu. o, Angaur. p, Sonsorol. q, Hatohobei.

**2002, July 9**
686 A193 37c Sheet of 17,   13.00 13.00
     #a-q
   All stamps on No. 686 lack country name.

## Winter Olympics Type of 2002 Redrawn with White Olympic Rings

Skier with: No. 687, $1, Blue pants. No. 688, $1, Yellow pants.

**2002, July 29**    *Perf. 13½*
687-688 A190   Set of 2    4.00 4.00
688a   Souvenir sheet, #687-688   4.00 4.00

## Intl. Year of Ecotourism — A194

No. 689: a, Divers, angelfish facing right. b, Ray. c, Sea cucumber. d, Emperor angelfish facing left. e, Sea turtle. f, Nautilus. $2, Person in canoe.

**2002, Apr. 26**    *Perf. 14¼x14¼*
689 A194 37c Sheet of 6, #a-f   7.25 7.25
   **Souvenir Sheet**
690 A194   $2 multi    4.00 4.00

## Japanese Art — A195

No. 691, vert. (38x50mm): a, The Actor Shuka Bando as Courtesan Shiraito, by Kunisada Utagawa. b, The Actor Danjuro Ichikawa VII as Sugawara no Michizane, by Kunisada Utagawa. c, The Actor Sojuro Sawamura III as Yuranosuke Oboshi, by Toyokuni Utagawa. d, The Actor Nizaemon Kataoka VII as Shihei Fujiwara, by Toyokuni Utagawa. e, Bust Portrait of the Actor Noshio Nakamura II, by Kunimasa Utagawa. f, The Actor Gon-Nosuke Kawarazaki as Daroku, by Kunichika Toyohara.
No. 692, 80c, vert. (27x88mm): a, Bush Clover Branch and Sweetfish, by Kuniyoshi Utagawa. b, Catfish, by Kuniyoshi Utagawa. c, Scene at Takanawa, by Eisen Keisai. d, Ochanomizu, by Keisai.
No. 693, 80c (50x88mm): a, Gaslight Hall, by Kiyochika Kobayashi. b, Cherry Blossoms at Night at Shin Yoshiwara, by Yasuji Inoue. c, Night Rain at Oyama, by Toyokuni Utagawa II. d, Kintai Bridge, by Keisai.
No. 694, $2, Okane, a Strong Woman of Omi, by Kuniyoshi Utagawa. No. 695, $2, Scene on the Banks of the Oumaya River, by Kuniyoshi Utagawa.

**2002, Sept. 23**
691 A195 60c Sheet of 6, #a-f   7.25 7.25
     *Perf. 14¼, 13½ (#692)*
692-693 A195   Sheets of 4, #a-d
     *Size: 105x85mm*
        *Imperf*
692-693 A195   Set of 2    13.00 13.00
694-695 A195   Set of 2    8.00 8.00

### Popeye — A196

**2002, Oct. 7**
696 A196 60c Sheet of 6, #a-f    7.25 7.25
  a. **Souvenir Sheet**
697 A196 $2 multi    4.00 4.00

No. 696, vert.: a, Wimpy. b, Swee'Pea. c, Popeye. d, Fish. e, Jeep. f, Brutus.
$2 Popeye golfing.

No. 705: a, Accountant bear. b, Computer programmer bear. c, Businesswoman bear. d, Lawyer bear.

**2002, Nov. 19**
705 A199 60c Sheet of 4, #a-d    5.00 5.00

### Teddy Bears, Cent. — A199

100th BIRTHDAY

### Christmas
**A198**

### Elvis Presley (1935-77) — A197

CHRISTMAS 2002 — SACRED CONVERSATION — PALAU 80c

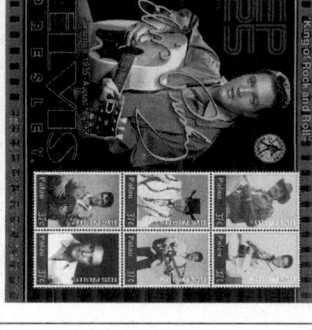

**2002, Oct. 23**
698 A197 37c Sheet of 6, #a-f    4.50 4.50

No. 698: a, On horse. b, Holding guitar, wearing white jacket, no hat. c, Wearing black hat. d, With guitar with two necks. e, Holding guitar, wearing colored jacket, no hat. f, Wearing shirt.

**2002, Nov. 5**
699-703 A198 Set of 5    6.00 6.00
  **Souvenir Sheet**
704 A198 $2 multi    4.00 4.00

Designs: 23c, Presentation of Jesus in the Temple, by Perugino, vert. 37c, Madonna and Child Enthroned Between Angels and Saints, by Domenico Ghirlandaio, vert. 60c, Maesta, by Simone Martini, vert. 80c, Sacred Conversation, by Giovanni Bellini. $1, Nativity, by Ghirlandaio. $2, Sacred Conversation (detail), by Bellini.
The painting shown on No. 704 does not appear to be a detail of the painting shown on No. 702.

### Queen Mother Elizabeth (1900-2002) — A200

H.M. The Queen Mother — IN MEMORIAM 1900-2002

**2002, Dec. 30**
706 A200 80c Sheet of 4, #a-d    6.50 6.50
  **Souvenir Sheet**
707 A200 $2 multi    4.00 4.00

No. 706: a, Holding bouquet. b, Wearing blue blouse and pearls. c, Wearing purple hat. d, Wearing tiara.
$2, Wearing flowered hat.

### 20th World Scout Jamboree, Thailand (in 2002) — A201

20. World Scout Jamboree, Thailand

Lord Robert Baden-Powell — $2

**2003, Jan. 13**    **Perf. 14**
708 A201 60c Sheet of 6, #a-f    7.25 7.25
  **Souvenir Sheet**
709 A201 $2 multi    4.00 4.00

No. 708, horiz.: a, Scout climbing rocks. b, Scout emblem, knife. c, Branches lashed together with rope. d, Cub scout (without cap). e, Knot. f, Boy scout (wearing cap).
$2 Lord Robert Baden-Powell.

### Shells — A202

Shells

Cymatium femorale — Palau — $2 — Angular Triton

**2003, Jan. 13**    **Perf. 14**
710 A202 60c Sheet of 6, #a-f    7.25 7.25
  **Souvenir Sheet**
711 A202 $2 multi    4.00 4.00

No. 710: a, Leafy murex. b, Trumpet triton. c, Giant tun. d, Queen conch. e, Spotted tun. f, Emperor helmet.
$2, Angular triton.

### New Year 2003 (Year of the Ram) — A203

Palau 37c

**2003, Jan. 27**    **Perf. 14¼x13¾**
712 A203 37c Vert. strip of 3, #a-c    2.25 2.25
  a.-c.    4.50
Sheet of 2 strips of 3.

No. 712: a, Ram facing right. b, Ram facing forward. c, Ram facing left.
No. 712 printed in sheets of 2 strips with slightly different backgrounds.

### Pres. John F. Kennedy (1917-63) — A204

**2003, Feb. 10**    **Perf. 14½x13¾**
713 A204 80c Sheet of 4, #a-d    6.50 6.50

No. 713: a, Wearing cap. b, Facing left. c, Facing right. d, Holding ship's wheel.

### Bird Type of 2002 With Unserified Numerals

**2003, Mar. 1**    **Perf. 14¼x13¾**
714 A188 26c multi    .55 .55
715 A188 37c multi    .75 .75

Designs: 26c, Golden whistler. 37c, Pale white-eye.

### Astronauts Killed in Space Shuttle Columbia Accident — A205

In Memoriam — The Crew of the Space Shuttle Columbia

**2003, Apr. 7**    **Perf. 13¾**
716 A205 37c Sheet of 7, #a-g    5.25 5.25

No. 716: a, Mission Specialist 1 David M. Brown. b, Commander Rick D. Husband. c, Mission Specialist 4 Laurel Blair Salton Clark. d, Mission Specialist 4 Kalpana Chawla. e, Payload Commander Michael P. Anderson. f, Pilot William C. McCool. g, Payload Specialist 4 Ilan Ramon.

### Orchids — A206

The Orchid — Palau — $2

**2003, Jan. 13    Litho.    Perf. 14**
717 A206 60c Sheet of 6, #a-f    7.25 7.25
  **Souvenir Sheet**
718 A206 $2 multi    4.00 4.00

No. 717: a, Phalaenopsis grex. b, Cattleya loddigesii. c, Phalaenopsis joline. d, Dendrobium. e, Laelia anceps. f, Cymbidium Stanley Fouracre.
$2, Vanda rothschildiana.

### Insects — A207

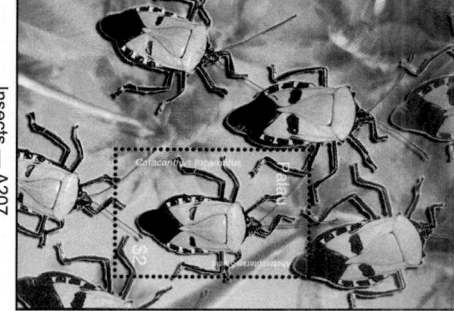

**2003, Jan. 13**
719 A207 60c Sheet of 6, #a-f    7.25 7.25
  **Souvenir Sheet**
720 A207 $2 multi    4.00 4.00

No. 719: a, Giant water bug. b, Weevil. c, Blister beetle. d, Bess beetle. e, Metallic stag beetle. f, Violin beetle.
$2, Anteropleran shield.

### First Non-stop Solo Transatlantic Flight, 75th Anniv. — A208

75th Anniversary of the First Solo Trans-Atlantic Flight

**2003, Feb. 10**
721 A208 60c Sheet of 6, #a-f    7.25 7.25

No. 721: a, Charles Lindbergh, Donald Hall and Spirit of St. Louis. b, Spirit of St. Louis, Apr. 28, 1927. c, Spirit of St. Louis, Curtiss Field, May 20, 1927. d, Spirit of St. Louis towed from Paris, May 20, 1927. e, Arrival in Paris, May 21, 1927. f, New York ticker tape parade.

## Sea Turtles — A219

LIFE CYCLE OF TURTLES

No. 746: a, Mating. b, Laying eggs at night. c, Hatching. d, Turtles going to sea. e, Growing up at sea. f, Returning to lay eggs.

2003, Feb. 6    **Perf. 14**
746 A219 60c Sheet of 6, #a-f   7.25 7.25
**Souvenir Sheet**
747 A219 $2 multi   4.00 4.00

## Paintings by Norman Rockwell — A220

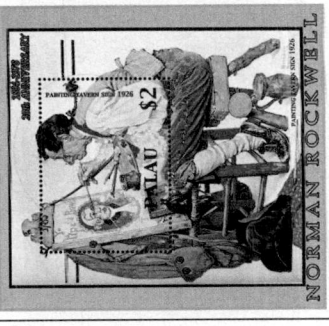

NORMAN ROCKWELL

No. 748, vert.: a, The Connoisseur. b, Artist Facing a Blank Canvas (Deadline). c, Art Critic. d, Stained Glass Artistry.
$2, Painting Tavern Sign.

2004, Feb. 6   **Litho.**   **Perf. 14¼**
748 A220 80c Sheet of 4, #a-d   6.50 6.50
**Souvenir Sheet**
749 A220 $2 multi   4.00 4.00

## Paintings by Pablo Picasso — A221

WOMAN DRESSING HER HAIR (DORA), 1940 — PALAU $2 — Pablo Picasso 1881–1973

No. 750: a, Dora Maar. b, The Yellow Sweater (Dora). c, Woman in Green (Dora). d, Woman in an Armchair (Dora). e, Woman Dressing Her Hair (Dora).

2004, Feb. 16   **Litho.**   **Perf. 14¼**
750 A221 80c Sheet of 4, #a-d   6.50 6.50
**Imperf**
751 A221 $2 multi   4.00 4.00
No. 750 contains four 37x50mm stamps.

## Paintings by James McNeill Whistler — A216

James McNeill Whistler 1834–1903 — Palau 37c

Designs: 37c, Blue and Silver: Trouville. 55c, The Last of Old Westminster. 60c, Wapping. $1 Cremorne Gardens, No. 2.
No. 737, vert.: a, Arrangement in Flesh Color and Black, Portrait of Theodore Duret. b, Arrangement in White and Black. c, Harmony in Pink and Gray, Portrait of Lady Meux. d, Arrangement in Black and Gold, Comte Robert de Montesquiou-Fezensac.
$2, Arrangement in Gray and Black No. 1, Portrait of Painter's Mother, vert.

2003, Sept. 22   **Perf. 14¼, 13¼ (#737)**
733-736 A216   Set of 4   5.25 5.25
737 A216 80c Sheet of 4, #a-d   6.50 6.50
**Souvenir Sheet**
738 A216 $2 multi   4.00 4.00
No. 737 contains four 35x71mm stamps.

## Circus Performers — A217

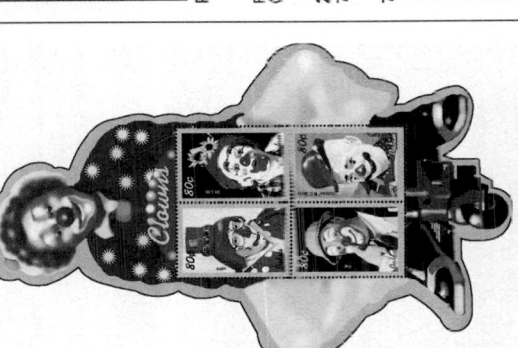

No. 739, 80c — Clowns: a, Apes. b, Mo Life. c, Gigi. d, "Buttons" McBride.
No. 740, 80c: a, Dngs. b, Olona Yakuenko. c, Mountain High. d, Chinese Circus.

2003, Sept. 29   **Perf. 14**
**Sheets of 4, #a-d**
739-740 A217   Set of 2   13.00 13.00

## Christmas A218

Designs: 37c, Madonna della Melagrana, by Botticelli. 60c, Madonna del Magnificat, by Botticelli. 80c, Madonna and Child with the Saints and the Angels, by Andrea del Sarto. $1, La Madonna del Roseto, by Botticelli. $2, Madonna and Child with the Angels and Saints, by Domenico Ghirlandaio.

2003, Dec. 1   **Perf. 14¼**
741-744 A218   Set of 4   5.75 5.75
**Souvenir Sheet**
745 A218 $2 multi   4.00 4.00

## Prince William, 21st Birthday — A213

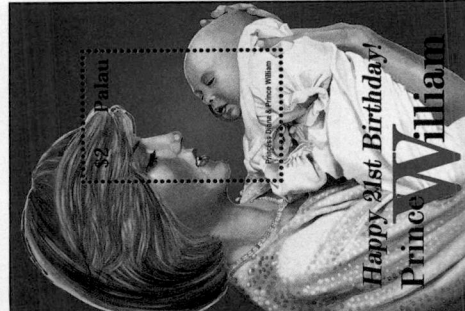

Happy 21st Birthday! Prince William

No. 727 — William: a, In yellow green shirt. b, As infant. c, In black sweater.
$2, As infant with Princess Diana.

2003, June 21
727 A213 $1 Sheet of 3, #a-c   6.00 6.00
**Souvenir Sheet**
728 A213 $2 multi   4.00 4.00

## Tour de France Bicycle Race, Cent. — A214

No. 729: a, Henri Pelissier, 1923. b, Ottavio Bottecchia, 1924. c, Bottoochia, 1925. d, Lucien Buysco, 1920.
$2, Philippe Thys, 1920.

2003, Aug. 23   **Perf. 13¼**
729 A214 60c Sheet of 4, #a-d   5.00 5.00
**Souvenir Sheet**
730 A214 $2 multi   4.00 4.00

## Powered Flight, Cent. — A215

No. 731: a, Fokker 70. b, Boeing 747-217B. c, Curtiss T-32 Condor. d, Vickers Viscount Type 761. e, Wright Flyer III. f, Avro Ten Achilles.
$2, Wright Flyer III, diff.

2003, Aug. 25   **Perf. 14**
731 A215 55c Sheet of 6, #a-f   6.75 6.75
**Souvenir Sheet**
732 A215 $2 multi   4.00 4.00

## Pres. Ronald Reagan — A209

RONALD REAGAN — 40TH U.S. PRESIDENT — RANCHER & COWBOY

Reagan with: a, Orange bandana. b, Red shirt. c, Blue shirt, head at left. d, Blue shirt, head at right.

2003, Feb. 10
722 A209 80c Sheet of 4, #a-d   6.50 6.50

## Princess Diana (1961-97) — A210

Princess Diana

Diana and clothing worn in: a, India. b, Canada. c, Egypt. d, Italy.

2003, Feb. 10
723 A210 80c Sheet of 4, #a-d   6.50 6.50

## Coronation of Queen Elizabeth II, 50th Anniv. — A211

50th Anniversary of the Coronation Ceremony of H.M. QUEEN ELIZABETH II

No. 724 — Queen with: a, Tiara. b, Pink dress. c, Hat.
$2, Tiara, diff.

2003, May 13
724 A211 $1 Sheet of 3, #a-c   6.00 6.00
**Souvenir Sheet**
725 A211 $2 multi   4.00 4.00

## Operation Iraqi Freedom — A212

OPERATION IRAQI FREEDOM — A salute to Our Heroes…

No. 726: a, Stealth bomber. b, F-18 fighter. c, MT Abrams tank. d, 203mm M-110s. e, USS Donald Cook. f, Tomahawk missile.

2003, May 14
726 A212 37c Sheet of 6, #a-f   4.50 4.50

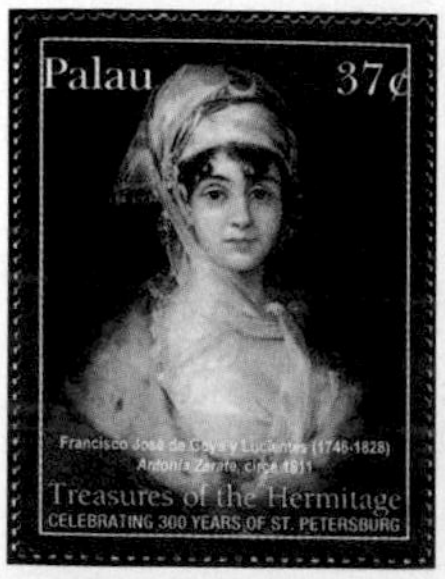


Paintings in the Hermitage, St. Petersburg, Russia
A222

Designs: 37c, Antonia Zarate, by Francisco de Goya. 55c, Portrait of a Lady, by Antonio Correggio. 80c, Portrait of Count Olivarez, by Diego Velázquez. $1, Portrait of a Young Man With a Lace Collar, by Rembrandt.
$2, Family Portrait, by Anthony Van Dyck.

**2004, Feb. 16 Litho. *Perf. 14¼***
**752-755** A222 Set of 4 5.50 5.50

**Size: 62x81mm**
***Imperf***

**756** A222 $2 multi 4.00 4.00

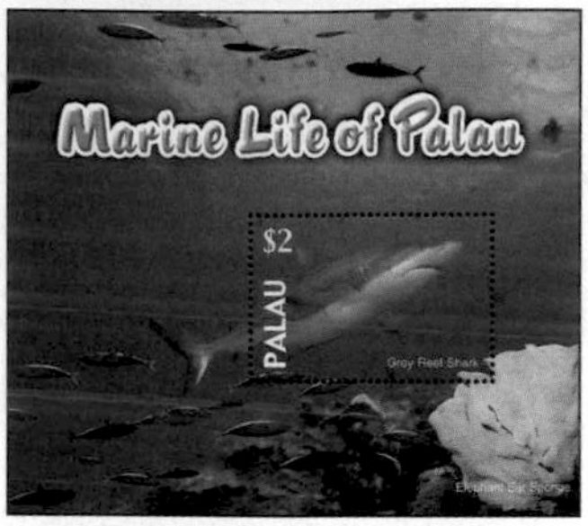


Marine Life — A223

No. 757: a, Coral hind. b, Sea octopus. c, Manta ray. d, Dugong. e, Marine crab. f, Grouper.
$2, Gray reef shark.

**2004, Feb. 16 *Perf. 14¼***
**757** A223 55c Sheet of 6, #a-f 6.75 6.75

**Souvenir Sheet**

**758** A223 $2 multi 4.00 4.00

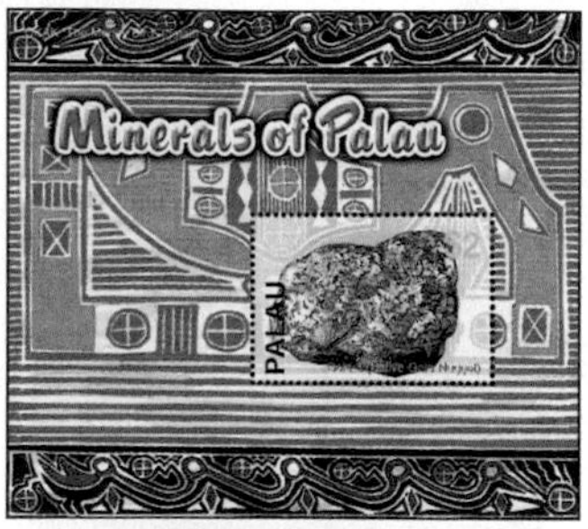


Minerals — A224

No. 759: a, Phosphate. b, Antimony. c, Limonite. d, Calcopyrite. e, Bauxite. f, Manganite.
$2, Gold.

**2004, Feb. 16**
**759** A224 55c Sheet of 6, #a-f 6.75 6.75

**Souvenir Sheet**

**760** A224 $2 multi 4.00 4.00

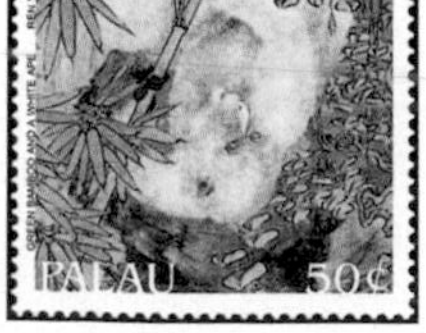


New Year 2004 (Year of the Monkey) A225

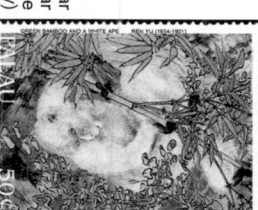

Green Bamboo and a White Ape, by Ren Yu: 50c, Detail. $1, Entire painting.

**2004, Mar. 9 *Perf. 13¼***
**761** A225 50c multi 1.00 1.00

**Souvenir Sheet**
***Perf. 13½x13¼***

**762** A225 $1 multi 2.00 2.00

No. 761 printed in sheets of 4. No. 762 contains one 27x83mm stamp.

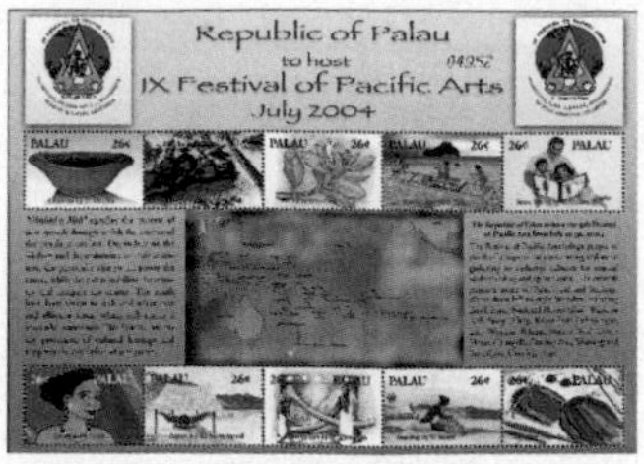


Ninth Festival of Pacific Arts — A226

No. 763, 26c: a, Oraschel, by M. Takeshi. b, Flute, by Sim Adelbai. c, Rur, by W. Watanabe. d, Bamboo Raft, by P. Tiakl. e, Story Telling, by K. Murret. f, Yek, by A. Imetuker. g, Canoe House, by W. Marsil. h, Carving Axe, by Watanabe. i, Weaving, by Marsil. j, Dancing Props, by Adelbai.
No. 764, 37c: a, Ongall, by Tiakl. b, Bai, by S. Weers. c, Taro Plant, by S. Smaserui. d, Toluk, by Watanabe. e, Medicinal Plants, by Smaserui. f, War Canoe, by Takeshi. g, Painting, by Adelbai. h, Pounding Taro, by Imetuker. h, Llengel, by Takeshi. i, Spear Technique, by Imetuker.

**2004, Apr. 13 *Perf. 13***
**Sheets of 10, #a-j**
**763-764** A226 Set of 2 13.00 13.00

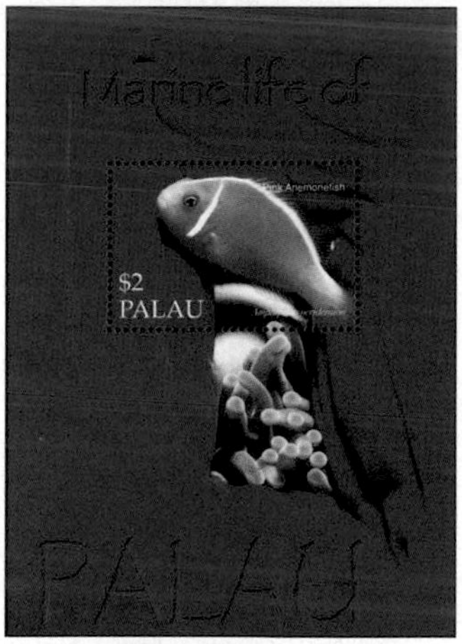


Marine Life — A227

No. 765, 26c: a, Cuttlefish. b, Long fin bannerfish. c, Red sponge, Medusa worm. d, Risbecia tryoni. e, Emperor angelfish. f, Chromodoris coi.
No. 766, 37c: a, Spotted eagle ray. b, Jellyfish. c, Nautilus. d, Gray reef shark. e, Tunicates. f, Manta ray.
No. 767, $2, Pink anemonefish. No. 768, $2, Dusky anemonefish.

**2004, May 20 *Perf. 14***
**Sheets of 6, #a-f**
**765-766** A227 Set of 2 7.75 7.75

**Souvenir Sheets**

**767-768** A227 Set of 2 8.00 8.00

No. 765 contains six labels.

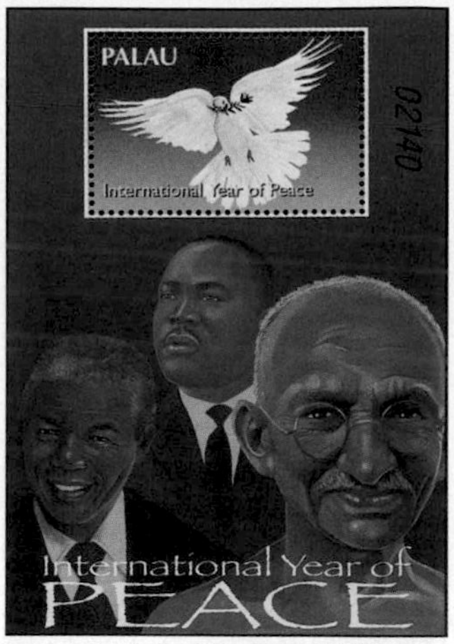


Intl. Year of Peace — A228

No. 769, vert.: a, Mahatma Gandhi. b, Nelson Mandela. c, Dr. Martin Luther King, Jr.
$2, Dove.

**2004, May 24 *Perf. 13½x13¼***
**769** A228 $3 Sheet of 3, #a-c 18.00 18.00

**Souvenir Sheet**
***Perf. 13¼x13½***

**770** A228 $2 multi 4.00 4.00

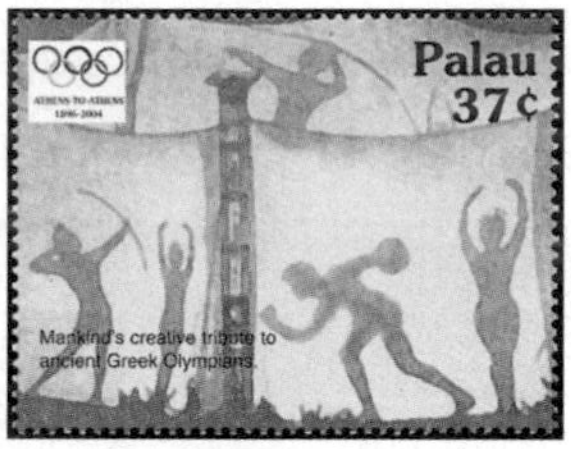


2004 Summer Olympics, Athens — A229

Designs: 37c, Athletes. 55c, Gold medals, Atlanta, 1996. 80c, Johannes Edström, Intl. Olympic Committee President, 1942-52, vert. $1, Women's soccer, Atlanta, 1996.

**2004, June 18 *Perf. 14¼***
**771-774** A229 Set of 4 5.50 5.50

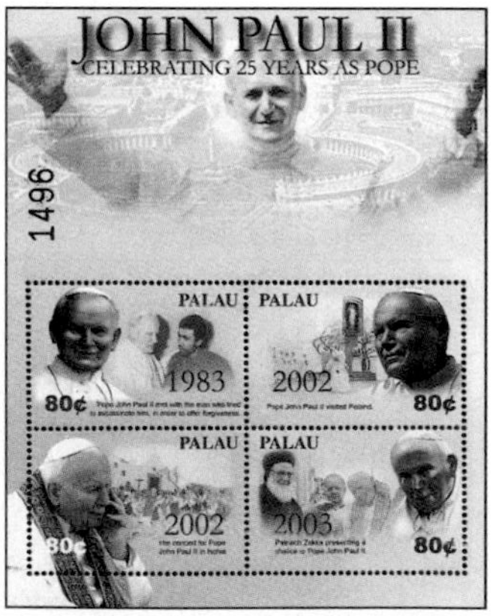


Election of Pope John Paul, 25th Anniv. (in 2003) — A230

Pope John Paul II: a, With Mehmet Agca, 1983. b, Visiting Poland, 2002. c, At concert in Ischia, Italy, 2002. d, With Patriarch Zakka, 2003.

**2004, June 18**
**775** A230 80c Sheet of 4, #a-d 6.50 6.50

Souvenir Sheet

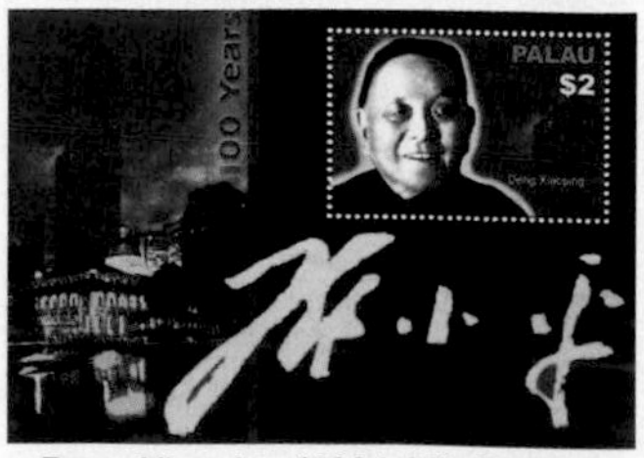


Deng Xiaoping (1904-97) Chinese Leader — A231

**2004, June 18**
**776** A231 $2 multi 4.00 4.00

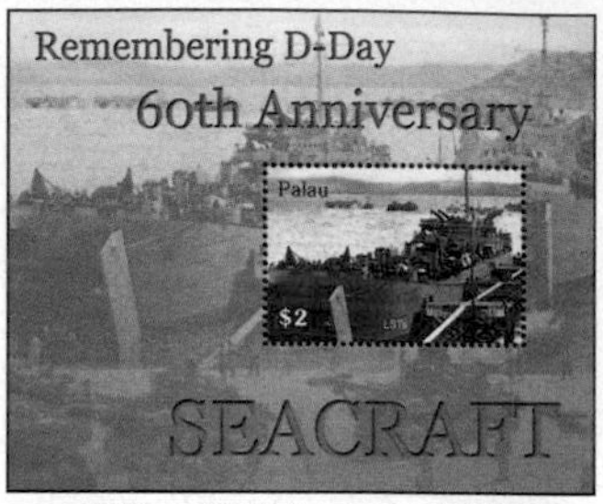


D-Day, 60th Anniv. — A232

No. 777: a, LCA 1377. b, Landing Craft, Infantry. c, LCVP. d, U-309. e, HMS Begonia. f, HMS Roberts.
$2, LSTs.

**2004, June 18**
**777** A232 50c Sheet of 6, #a-f 6.00 6.00

**Souvenir Sheet**

**778** A232 $2 multi 4.00 4.00

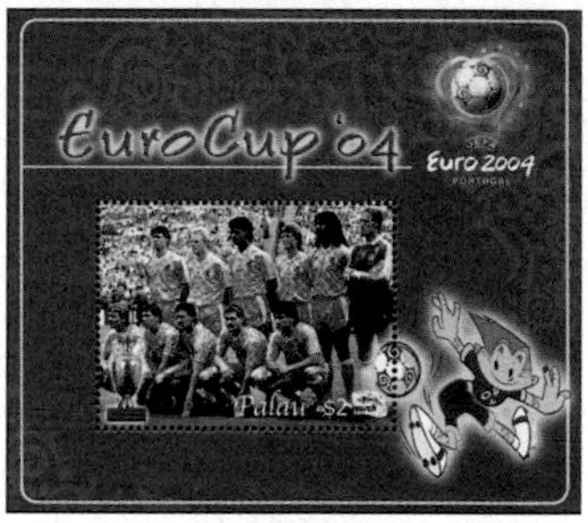


European Soccer Championships, Portugal — A233

No. 779, vert.: a, Rinus Michels. b, Rinat Dasaev. c, Marco Van Basten. d, Olympiastadion.
$2, 1988 Netherlands team.

**2004, June 18**
**779** A233 80c Sheet of 4, #a-d 6.50 6.50

**Souvenir Sheet**

**780** A233 $2 multi 4.00 4.00

No. 779 contains four 28x42mm stamps.

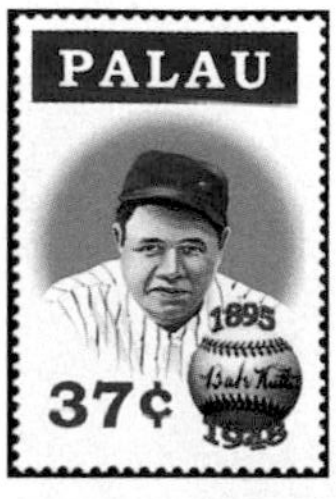


Babe Ruth (1895-1948), Baseball Player — A234

Ruth and: No. 781, 37c, Signed baseball. No. 782, 37c, World Series 100th anniversary emblem.

**2004, Sept. 3 *Perf. 13½x13¼***
**781-782** A234 Set of 2 1.50 1.50

Nos. 781-782 each printed in sheets of 8.

# HANS CHRISTIAN ANDERSEN
### 1805-1875

Hans Christian Andersen (1805-75), Author — A245

No. 814, vert. — Book covers: a. Hans Christian Andersen Fairy Tales. b. Hans Christian Andersen's The Ugly Duckling. c. Tales of Hans Christian Andersen.
$2, The Little Match Girl.

**2005, Apr. 4**
| | | | | |
|---|---|---|---|---|
| 814 | A245 | $1 Sheet of 3, #a-c | 6.00 | 6.00 |

**Souvenir Sheet**
| | | | | |
|---|---|---|---|---|
| 815 | A245 | $2 multi | 4.00 | 4.00 |

Battle of Trafalgar, Bicent. — A240

Various ships in battle: 37c, 55c, 80c, $1. $2, Admiral Horatio Nelson Wounded During Battle of Trafalgar.

**2005, Apr. 4**    *Perf. 14¼*
| | | | | |
|---|---|---|---|---|
| 816-819 | A246 | Set of 4 | 5.50 | 5.50 |

**Souvenir Sheet**
| | | | | |
|---|---|---|---|---|
| 820 | A246 | $2 multi | 4.00 | 4.00 |

# The Route to Victory

End of World War II, 60th Anniv. — A247

No. 821, 80c — Dambuster Raid: a. Pilots review routes prior to mission. b. Dambuster crew. c. Ground crews prepare Lancaster bomber. d. Bomber over Möhne Dam.
No. 822, 80c — Battle of Kursk: a. Russian tanks move forward. b. Tank commanders review maps. c. Russian and German armor clash. d. Destroyed German tank.
No. 823, $2, Squadron 617 leader Guy Gibson and "Highball Bouncing Bomb." No. 824, $2, Russian troops converge on destroyed German tank.

**2005, May 9**    *Perf. 13½*
| | | | | |
|---|---|---|---|---|
| 821-822 | A247 | Set of 2 | 13.00 | 13.00 |

**Souvenir Sheets**
| | | | | |
|---|---|---|---|---|
| 823-824 | A247 | Set of 2 | 8.00 | 8.00 |

---

**Souvenir Sheet**

## HAPPY LUNAR NEW YEAR

New Year 2005 (Year of the Rooster) — A242

No. 810: a. Rooster facing right, tail feathers at LL. b. Rooster facing left, tail feathers at LR. c. Rooster facing right, no tail feathers at LL. d. Rooster facing left, no tail feathers at LR.

**2005, Jan. 26**   *Litho.*   *Perf. 12½*
| | | | | |
|---|---|---|---|---|
| 810 | A242 | 50c Sheet of 4, #a-d | 4.00 | 4.00 |

**Souvenir Sheet**

Rotary International, Cent. — A243

No. 811: a. Rotary International emblem. b. Rotary Centennial bell. c. Flags of Rotary International, US, Great Britain, Canada, Germany, China and Italy. d. James Wheeler Davidson.

**2005, Apr. 4**    *Perf. 14*
| | | | | |
|---|---|---|---|---|
| 811 | A243 | 80c Sheet of 4, #a-d | 6.50 | 6.50 |

## POET · DRAMATIST · HISTORIAN

Friedrich von Schiller (1759-1805), Writer — A244

No. 812 — Schiller facing: a. Right (sepia tone). b. Right (color). c. Left (sepia tone).
$2, Facing left, diff.

**2005, Apr. 4**
| | | | | |
|---|---|---|---|---|
| 812 | A244 | $1 Sheet of 3, #a-c | 6.00 | 6.00 |

**Souvenir Sheet**
| | | | | |
|---|---|---|---|---|
| 813 | A244 | $2 multi | 4.00 | 4.00 |

---

FIFA (Fédération Internationale de Football Association), Cent. — A238

No. 799: a. Diego Maradona. b. David Seaman. c. Andreas Brehme. d. Paul Ince.
$2, Fernando Redondo.

**2004, Oct. 27**    *Perf. 12¾x12½*
| | | | | |
|---|---|---|---|---|
| 799 | A238 | 80c Sheet of 4, #a-d | 6.50 | 6.50 |

**Souvenir Sheet**
| | | | | |
|---|---|---|---|---|
| 800 | A238 | $2 multi | 4.00 | 4.00 |

National Basketball Association Players — A239

Designs: No. 801, 26c, Chris Bosh, Toronto Raptors. No. 802, 26c, Tim Duncan, San Antonio Spurs. No. 803, 26c, Kevin Garnett, Minnesota Timberwolves.

**2004, Nov. 3**    *Perf. 14*
| | | | | |
|---|---|---|---|---|
| 801-803 | A239 | Set of 3 | 1.60 | 1.60 |

Each stamp printed in sheets of 12.

Christmas — A240

Paintings of Madonna and Child by: 37c, Quentin Metsys. 60c, Adolphe William Bouguereau. 80c, William Dyce. $1, Carlo Crivelli. $2, Peter Paul Rubens, vert.

**2004, Dec. 23**    *Perf. 14¼*
| | | | | |
|---|---|---|---|---|
| 804-807 | A240 | Set of 4 | 5.75 | 5.75 |

**Souvenir Sheet**
| | | | | |
|---|---|---|---|---|
| 808 | A240 | $2 multi | 4.00 | 4.00 |

**Miniature Sheet**

Palau — Republic of China Diplomatic Relations, 5th Anniv. — A241

No. 809: a. Agricultural products. b. Republic of China Navy ship. c. Ngarachamayong Cultural Center. d. Palau National Museum.

**2004, Dec. 29**    *Perf. 14*
| | | | | |
|---|---|---|---|---|
| 809 | A241 | 80c Sheet of 4, #a-d | 6.50 | 6.50 |

---

Trains, Bicent. — A235

No. 783: a. ATSF 315. b. Amtrak 464. c. Railway N52. d. SD 70 MAC Diesel-electric locomotive. No. 784, 50c: a. CS SO2002. b. P 36 N0032. c. SW-600. d. Gambier LNV 9703 4-4-0 NG.
No. 785, $2, CN5700 locomotive. No. 786, $2, Eurostar.

**2004, Sept. 27**    *Perf. 13¼x13½*
| | | | | |
|---|---|---|---|---|
| 783 | A235 | 26c Sheet of 4, #a-d | 2.10 | 2.10 |
| 784 | A235 | 50c Sheet of 4, #a-d | 4.00 | 4.00 |

**Souvenir Sheet**
| | | | | |
|---|---|---|---|---|
| 785 | A235 | $2 multi | 4.00 | 4.00 |
| 786 | A235 | $2 multi | 4.00 | 4.00 |

Butterflies, Reptiles, Amphibians and Birds — A236

No. 787, 80c — Butterflies: a. Cethosia hypsea. b. Cethosia myrina. c. Charaxes durnfordi. d. Charaxos nitobia. No. 788, 80c — Reptiles: a. Bull snake. b. Garter snake. c. Yellow-lipped sea snake. d. Yellow-bellied sea snake.
No. 789, 80c, vert. — Birds: a. Blue faced parrot finch. b. Mangrove flycatcher. c. Palau swiftlet. d. Bridled white-eye.
No. 790, $2, Charaxes nitebis, diff. No. 791, $2, Glass frog. No. 792, $2, Dusky white-eye, vert.

**2004, Oct. 13**   *Litho.*   *Perf. 14*
**Sheets of 4, #a-d**
| | | | | |
|---|---|---|---|---|
| 787-789 | A236 | Set of 3 | 19.50 | 19.50 |

**Souvenir Sheets**
| | | | | |
|---|---|---|---|---|
| 790-792 | A236 | Set of 3 | 12.00 | 12.00 |

Dinosaurs — A237

No. 793, 26c, vert.: a. Kritosaurus. b. Triceratops. c. Hypselosaurus. d. Yingshanosaurus. No. 794, 80c: a. Hadrosaurus. b. Pterodaustro. c. Agilisaurus. d. Amargasaurus. No. 795, 80c, vert.: a. Corythosaurus. b. Dryosaurus. c. Euoplocephalus. d. Compsognathus. No. 796, $2, Ornithomimus. No. 797, $2, Archaeopteryx. No. 798, $2, Deinonychus, vert.

**2004, Oct. 13**
**Sheets of 4, #a-d**
| | | | | |
|---|---|---|---|---|
| 793-795 | A237 | Set of 3 | 15.00 | 15.00 |

**Souvenir Sheets**
| | | | | |
|---|---|---|---|---|
| 796-798 | A237 | Set of 3 | 12.00 | 12.00 |

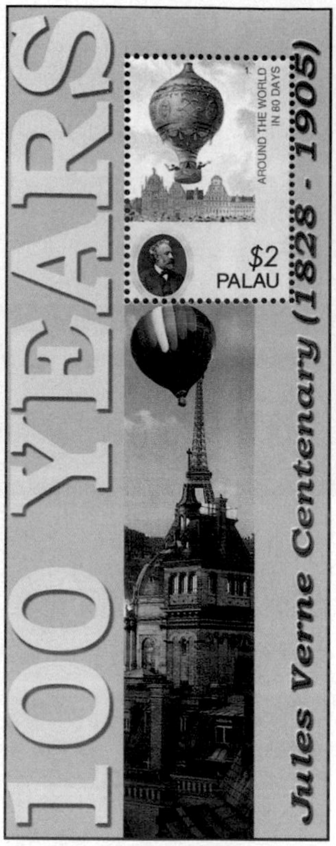
100 YEARS
AROUND THE WORLD IN 80 DAYS
$2
PALAU
Jules Verne Centenary (1828 - 1905)

Jules Verne (1828-1905), Writer — A248

No. 825, horiz.: a, 20,000 Leagues Under the Sea. b, Mysterious Island. c, Journey to the Center of the Earth.
$2, Around the World in 80 Days.

**2005, June 7** *Perf. 12¾*
**825** A248 $1 Sheet of 3, #a-c 6.00 6.00

**Souvenir Sheet**

**826** A248 $2 multi 4.00 4.00

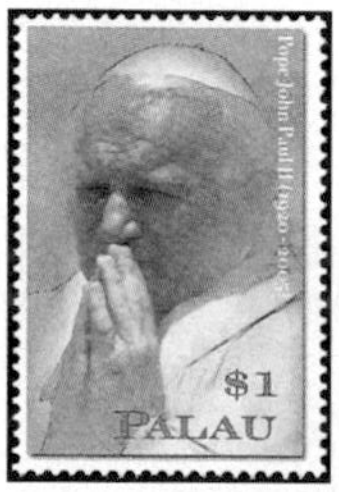
$1
PALAU

Pope John Paul II (1920-2005) A249

**2005, June 27** *Perf. 13½x13¼*
**827** A249 $1 multi 2.00 2.00

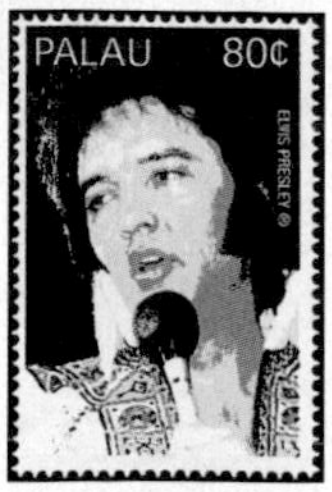
PALAU
80¢

A250

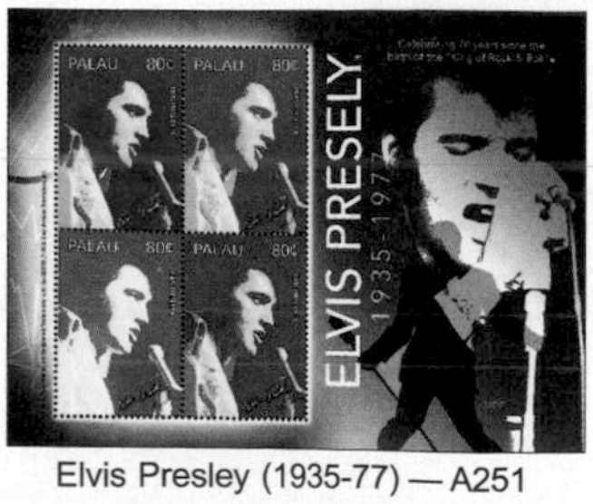
ELVIS PRESELY
1935-1977

Elvis Presley (1935-77) — A251

No. 829 — Color of Presley: a, Blue. b, Green. c, Yellow. d, Orange.

**2005, July 2** *Perf. 14*
**828** A250 80c multi 1.60 1.60
**829** A251 80c Sheet of 4, #a-d 6.50 6.50

No. 828 printed in sheets of 4.

**Trains Type of 2004**

No. 830: a, Birney N62 Interurban. b, C62-2-103103. c, WR MO 2007. d, Atchison, Topeka & Santa Fe locomotive 314.
$2, Royal Hudson #2860, vert.

**2005** *Perf. 13¼x13½*
**830** A235 80c Sheet of 4, #a-d 6.50 6.50

**Souvenir Sheet**
***Perf. 13½x13¼***

**831** A235 $2 multi 4.00 4.00

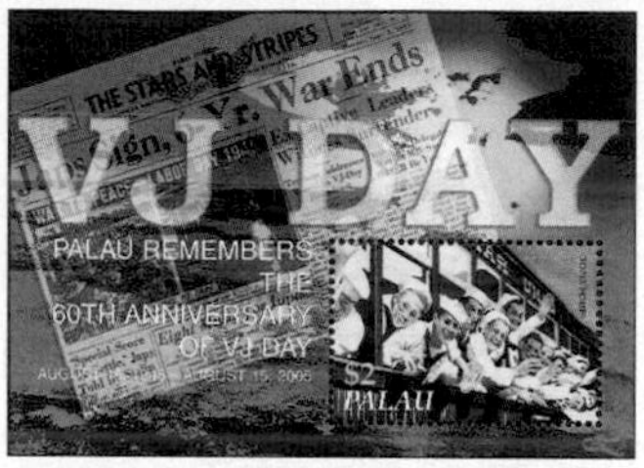
VJ DAY
PALAU REMEMBERS THE 60TH ANNIVERSARY OF VJ DAY
$2
PALAU

V-J Day, 60th Anniv. — A252

No. 832, vert.: a, Audie Murphy. b, John F. Kennedy. c, Fleet Admiral Chester W. Nimitz. d, Marines recapture Guam from the Japanese.
$2, Sailors going home.

**2005, June 7** **Litho.** *Perf. 12¾*
**832** A252 80c Sheet of 4, #a-d 6.50 6.50

**Souvenir Sheet**

**833** A252 $2 multi 4.00 4.00

Miniature Sheet

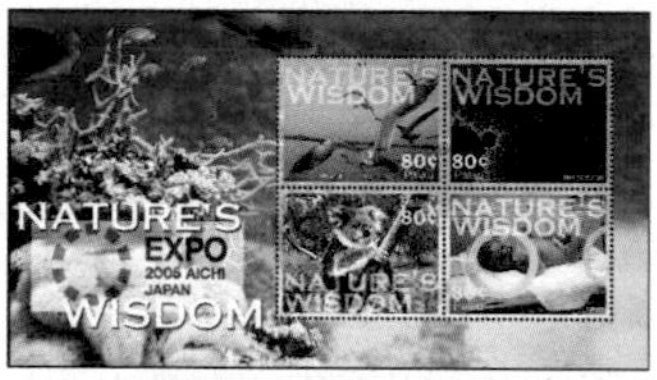
NATURE'S EXPO
WISDOM

Expo 2005, Aichi, Japan — A253

No. 834: a, Seagulls. b, The cosmos. c, Koala. d, Childbirth.

**2005, June 27** *Perf. 12*
**834** A253 80c Sheet of 4, #a-d 6.50 6.50

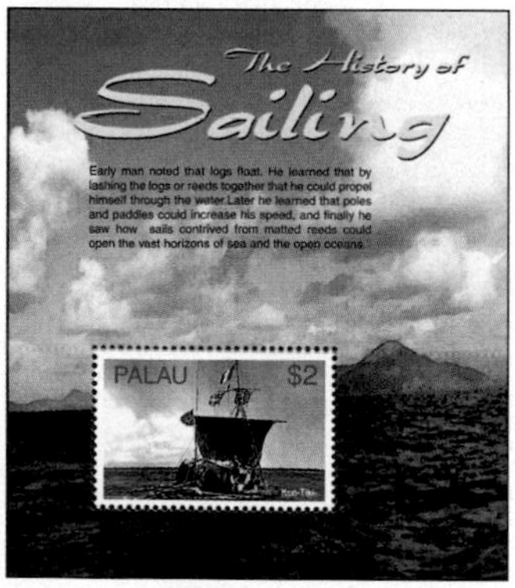
The History of Sailing
PALAU
$2

Sailing — A254

No. 835: a, Tepukei. b, Tainui. c, Palauan canoe. d, Yap outrigger.
$2, Kon-Tiki.

**2005, June 27** *Perf. 12¾*
**835** A254 80c Sheet of 4, #a-d 6.50 6.50

**Souvenir Sheet**

**836** A254 $2 multi 4.00 4.00

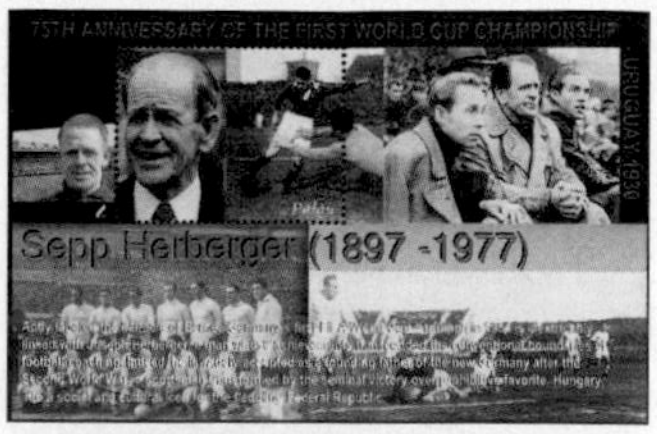
Sepp Herberger (1897 -1977)

World Cup Soccer Championships, 75th Anniv. — A255

No. 837, $1 — Scene from final match of: a, 1954. b, 1966. c, 1974.
No. 838, $1: a, Scene from 2002 final match. b, Lothar Matthias. c, Gerd Muller.
No. 839, $2, Sepp Herberger. No. 840, $2, Franz Beckenbauer.

**2005, July 19** *Perf. 12*

**Sheets of 3, #a-c**

**837-838** A255 Set of 2 12.00 12.00

**Souvenir Sheets**

**839** A255 $2 multi 4.00 4.00

***Perf. 12¾***

**840** A255 $2 multi 4.00 4.00

No. 840 contains one 42x28mm stamp.

PALAU
POSTE VATICANE
37¢
SEDE VACANTE

Vatican City No. 61 — A256

**2005, Aug. 9** *Perf. 13x13¼*
**841** A256 37c multi .75 .75

Printed in sheets of 12.

Miniature Sheet

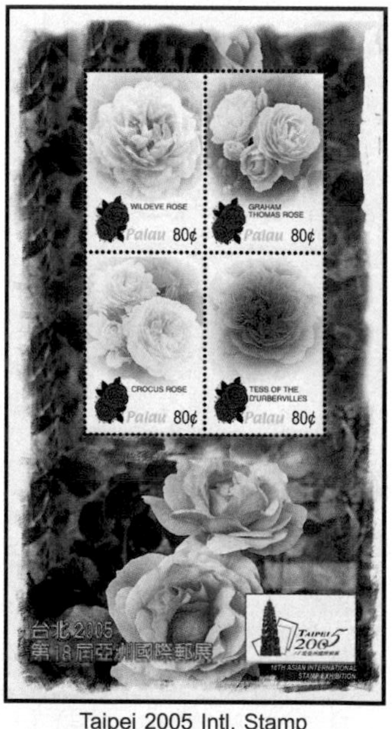
WILDEVE ROSE
GRAHAM THOMAS ROSE
CROCUS ROSE
TESS OF THE D'URBERVILLES
Palau 80¢

Taipei 2005 Intl. Stamp Exhibition — A257

No. 842: a, Wildeve rose. b, Graham Thomas rose. c, Crocus rose. d, Tes of the d'Urbervilles rose.

**2005, Aug. 19** *Perf. 14*
**842** A257 80c Sheet of 4, #a-d 6.50 6.50

Miniature Sheet

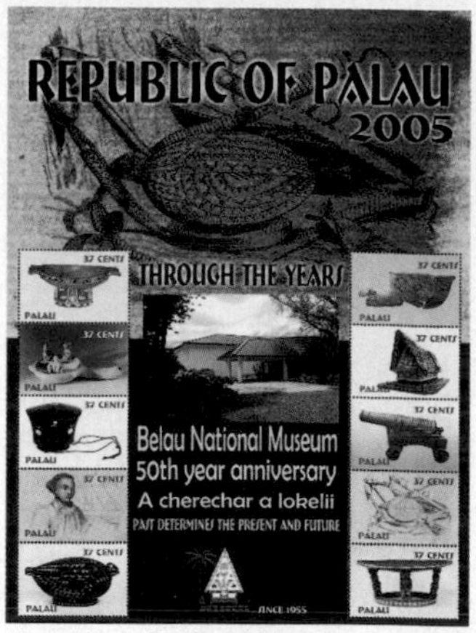
REPUBLIC OF PALAU
2005
THROUGH THE YEARS
Belau National Museum
50th year anniversary
A cherechar a lokelii
PAST DETERMINES THE PRESENT AND FUTURE

Items from National Museum — A258

No. 843: a, Decorated bowl, light yellow background. b, Potsherds, dull rose background. c, Sculpture with three people, blue background. d, Model of native house, light yellow background. e, Lidded container with strings. f, Cannon. g, Drawing of man on ship. h, Drawing of native craftwork. i, Bird-shaped figurine. j, Decorated bowl, pink background.

**2005, Sept. 30**
**843** A258 37c Sheet of 10, #a-j 7.50 7.50

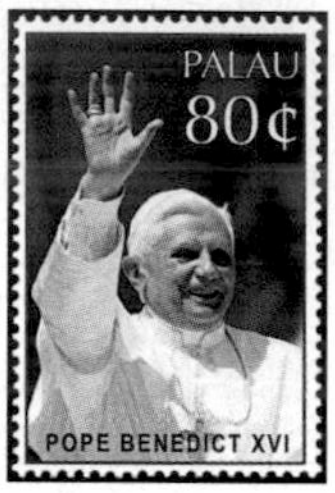
PALAU
80¢
POPE BENEDICT XVI

Pope Benedict XVI — A259

**2005, Nov. 21** *Perf. 13¾x13½*
**844** A259 80c multi 1.60 1.60

Printed in sheets of 4.

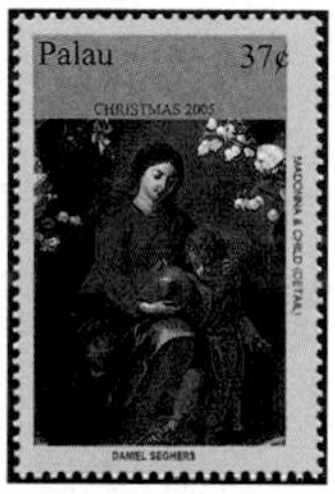
Palau
37¢

Christmas — A260

Paintings: 37c, Madonna and Child, by Daniel Seghers. 60c, Madonna and Child, by Raphael. 80c, The Rest on the Flight to Egypt, by Gerard David. $1, Granducci Madonna, by Raphael.
$2, Madonna and Child, by Bartolome Esteban Murillo.

**2005, Dec. 21** *Perf. 14*
**845-848** A260 Set of 4 5.75 5.75

**Souvenir Sheet**

**849** A260 $2 multi 4.00 4.00

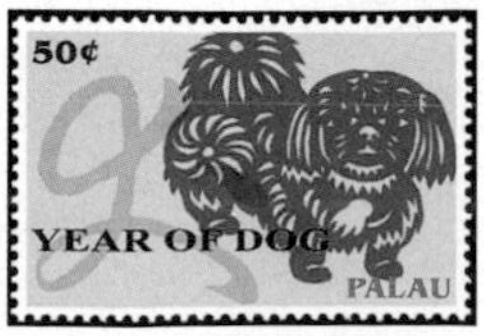
50¢
YEAR OF DOG
PALAU

New Year 2006 (Year of the Dog) A261

**2006, Jan. 3** *Perf. 13¼*
**850** A261 50c multi 1.00 1.00

Printed in sheets of 4.

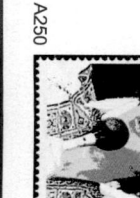

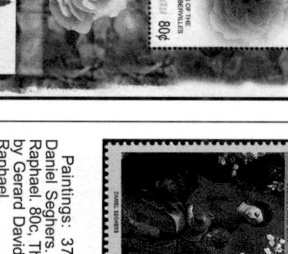

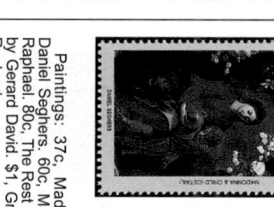

## PALAU

### Birds A262

Designs: 24c, Black oystercatcher. 39c, Great blue heron, vert.

**2006, Feb. 21    Litho.    Perf. 12**

| | | | |
|---|---|---|---|
| 851 | A262 | 24c multi | .50  .50 |
| 852 | A262 | 39c multi | .80  .80 |

### Worldwide Fund for Nature (WWF) — A263

No. 853 — Chambered nautilus: a, Two facing right. b, Two facing left. c, One, near coral. d, One, no coral.

**2006, Feb. 21    Perf. 12¾**

| | | | |
|---|---|---|---|
| 853 | A263 | 63c. Block of 4, #a-d | 5.25  5.25 |
| e. | | Sheet, ? each #853a 863d | 10.50  10.50 |

### SEMI-POSTAL STAMPS

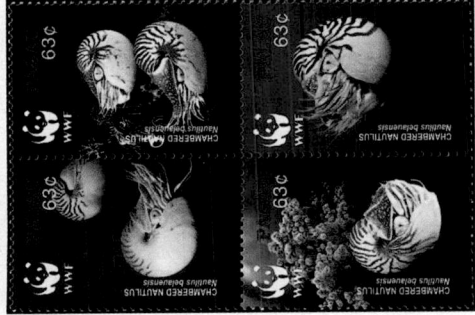

Olympic Sports SP1

**1988, Aug. 8    Litho.    Perf. 14**

| | | | |
|---|---|---|---|
| B1 | SP1 | 25c +5c Baseball glove, player | .50  .50 |
| B2 | SP1 | 25c +5c Running shoe, athlete | .50  .50 |
| a. | | Pair, #B1-B2 | 1.00  1.00 |
| B3 | SP1 | 45c +5c Goggles, swimmer | 1.25  1.25 |
| B4 | SP1 | 45c +5c Gold medal, diver | 1.25  1.25 |
| a. | | Pair, #B3-B4 | 2.50  2.50 |

### AIR POST STAMPS

White-tailed Tropicbird — AP1

**1984, June 12    Litho.    Perf. 14**

| | | | |
|---|---|---|---|
| C1 | AP1 | 40c shown | .75  .75 |
| C2 | AP1 | 40c Fairy tern | .75  .75 |
| C3 | AP1 | 40c Black noddy | .75  .75 |
| C4 | AP1 | 40c Black-naped tern | .75  .75 |
| a. | | Block of 4, #C1-C4 | 3.00  3.00 |

### Audubon Type of 1985

**1985, Feb. 6    Litho.    Perf. 14**

| | | | |
|---|---|---|---|
| C5 | A12 | 44c Audubon's Shearwater | 1.10  1.10 |

### Palau-Germany Political, Economic & Cultural Exchange Cent. — AP2

Germany Nos. 40, 65, Caroline Islands Nos. 19, 13 and: No. C6, German flag-raising at Palau, 1885. No. C7, Early German trading post in Angaur. No. C8, Abai architecture recorded by Prof. & Frau Kramer, 1908-1910. No. C9, S.M.S. Cormoran.

**1985, Sept. 19    Litho.    Perf. 14x13½**

| | | | |
|---|---|---|---|
| C6 | AP2 | 44c multicolored | .90  .90 |
| C7 | AP2 | 44c multicolored | .90  .90 |
| C8 | AP2 | 44c multicolored | .90  .90 |
| C9 | AP2 | 44c multicolored | .90  .90 |
| a. | | Block of 4, #C6-C9 | 3.75  3.75 |

### Trans-Pacific Airmail Anniv. Type of 1985

Aircraft: No. C10, 1951 Trans-Ocean Airways PBY-5A Catalina Amphibian. No. C11, 1968 Air Micronesia DC-6B Super Cloudmaster. No. C12, 1960 Trust Territory Airline SA-16 Albatross. No. C13, 1967 Pan American Douglas DC-4.

**1985, Nov. 21    Litho.    Perf. 14**

| | | | |
|---|---|---|---|
| C10 | A16 | 44c multicolored | .85  .85 |
| C11 | A16 | 44c multicolored | .85  .85 |
| C12 | A16 | 44c multicolored | .85  .85 |
| C13 | A16 | 44c multicolored | .85  .85 |
| a. | | Block of 4, #C10-C13 | 3.50  3.50 |

Haruo I. Remeliik (1933-1985), 1st President — AP3

Designs: No. C14, Presidential seal, excerpt from 1st inaugural address. No. C15, War canoe, address excerpt, diff. No. C16, Remeliik, US Pres. Reagan, excerpt from Reagan's speech, Pacific Basin Conference, Guam, 1984.

**1986, June 30    Litho.    Perf. 14**

| | | | |
|---|---|---|---|
| C14 | AP3 | 44c multicolored | 1.10  1.10 |
| C15 | AP3 | 44c multicolored | 1.10  1.10 |
| C16 | AP3 | 44c multicolored | 1.10  1.10 |
| a. | | Strip of 3, #C14-C16 | 3.50  3.50 |

Intl. Peace Year, Statue of Liberty Cent. — AP4

**1986, Sept. 19    Litho.**

| | | | |
|---|---|---|---|
| C17 | AP4 | 44c multicolored | 1.00  1.00 |

Aircraft — AP5

### Birds — AP6

**1989, May 17    Litho.    Perf. 14x14½**

| | | | |
|---|---|---|---|
| C18 | AP5 | 36c Cessna 207 Skywagon | .65  .65 |
| | | Booklet pane of 10 | 6.50 |
| C19 | AP5 | 39c Embraer EMB-110 Bandeirante | .85  .85 |
| a. | | Booklet pane of 10 | 7.25 |
| C20 | AP5 | 45c Boeing 727 | 1.00  1.00 |
| | | Booklet pane of 10 | 8.00 |
| b. | | Booklet pane, 5 each 36c, 45c | 7.50 |
| | | Nos. C18-C20 (3) | 2.50  2.50 |

### Palauan Bai Type

**1991, July 9    Litho.    Self-Adhesive    Die Cut**

| | | | |
|---|---|---|---|
| C21 | A61 | 50c like #293a | 1.50  1.50 |

### World War II in the Pacific Type
**Miniature Sheet**

Aircraft: No. C23: a, Grumman TBF Avenger, US Navy. b, Curtiss P-40C, Chinese Air Force "Flying Tigers." c, Mitsubishi A6M Zero-Sen, Japan. d, Hawker Hurricane, Royal Air Force. e, Consolidated PBY Catalina, Royal Netherlands Indies Air Force. f, Curtiss Hawk 75, Netherlands Indies. g, Boeing B-17E, US Army Air Force. h, Brewster Buffalo, Royal Australian Air Force. i, Supermarine Walrus, Royal Navy. j, Curtiss P-40E, Royal New Zealand Air Force.

**1992, Sept. 10    Litho.    Perf. 14½x15**

| | | | |
|---|---|---|---|
| C22 | A66 | 50c Sheet of 10, #a.. | 10.00  10.00 |
| | | j.. | 10.00  10.00 |

**1994, Mar. 24    Litho.    Perf. 14**

a, Palau swiftlet. b, Barn swallow. c, Jungle nightjar. d, White-breasted woodswallow.

| | | | |
|---|---|---|---|
| C23 | AP6 | 50c Block of 4, #a-d. | 3.75  3.75 |

No. C23 is printed in sheets of 16 stamps.

## PALESTINE

/ˈpa-lə-stin/

LOCATION—Western Asia bordering on the Mediterranean Sea
GOVT.— Former British Mandate
AREA — 10,429 sq. mi.
POP.— 1,605,816 (estimated)
CAPITAL— Jerusalem

Formerly a part of Turkey, Palestine was occupied by the Egyptian Expeditionary Forces of the British Army in World War I and was mandated to Great Britain in 1923. Mandate ended May 14, 1948.

## Watermark

Wmk. 33

10 Milliemes = 1 Piaster
1000 Milliemes = 1 Egyptian Pound
1000 Mils = 1 Palestine Pound (1928)

Jordan stamps overprinted with "Palestine" in English and Arabic are listed under Jordan.

## Issued under British Military Occupation

For use in Palestine, Transjordan, Lebanon, Syria and in parts of Cilicia and northeastern Egypt

A1

**Wmk. Crown and "GvR" (33). Litho. Rouletted 20**
**1918, Feb. 10**

| | | | | |
|---|---|---|---|---|
| 1 | A1 | 1pi deep blue | 175.00 | 105.00 |
| 2 | A1 | 1pi ultra | 2.40 | 2.40 |

### Nos. 2 & 1 Surcharged in Black

**1918, Feb. 16 — Typo. Perf. 15x14**

| | | | | |
|---|---|---|---|---|
| 3 | A1 | 5m on 1pi ultra | 4.25 | 3.25 |
| a. | | 5m on 1pi gray blue | 105.00 | 560.00 |

Nos. 1 and 3a were issued without gum. No. 3a is on paper with a surface sheen.

## Issued under British Administration
### Overprinted at Jerusalem

**1918 — Typo. Perf. 15x14**

| | | | | |
|---|---|---|---|---|
| 4 | A1 | 1m dark brown | .35 | .45 |
| 5 | A1 | 2m blue green | .35 | .35 |
| 6 | A1 | 3m light brown | .40 | .40 |
| 7 | A1 | 4m scarlet | .40 | .45 |
| 8 | A1 | 5m orange | .75 | .35 |
| 9 | A1 | 1pi indigo | .40 | .30 |
| 10 | A1 | 2pi olive green | 1.10 | .65 |
| 11 | A1 | 5pi plum | .40 | 2.00 |
| 12 | A1 | 9pi bister | 2.00 | 2.40 |
| 13 | A1 | 10pi ultramarine | 4.00 | 4.75 |
| 14 | A1 | 20pi gray | 3.25 | 3.25 |
| | | Nos. 4-14 (11) | 12.50 | 17.50 |
| | | | 25.50 | 31.00 |

Many shades exist.

Issued: 1m, 2m, 4m, 2pi, 5pi, 9pi; 5m, 9/25; 1pi, 11/9; 3m, 10pi, 12/17; 20pi, 12/27.

Nos. 4-11 exist with rough perforation.

Nos. 4-11 with overprint "O.P.D.A." (Ottoman Public Debt Administration) or "H.J.Z." (Hejaz-Jemen Railway) are revenue stamps; they exist postally used.

For overprints on stamps and types see #15-62 & Jordan #1-63, 73-90, 92-102, 130-144, J12-J23.

**1920, Sept. 1 — Wmk. 33 — Perf. 15x14**
**Arabic Overprint 8mm long**

| | | | | |
|---|---|---|---|---|
| 15 | A1 | 1m dark brown | 4.25 | 2.00 |
| 16 | A1 | 2m lt grn, perf. 14 | 1.60 | 1.50 |
| 17 | A1 | 3m lt brown | 8.00 | 4.75 |
| d. | | Perf 15x14 | 9.25 | 9.25 |
| e. | | "PALESTINE" omitted | 60.00 | — |
| 17a | A1 | 4m scarlet | 525.00 | 700.00 |
| 18 | A1 | 4m scarlet | 2.25 | 1.40 |
| e. | | Inverted overprint | 2.75 | 2.00 |
| 19 | A1 | 5m org, perf 14 | 1.40 | 4.50 |
| d. | | Perf 15x14 | 18.50 | |
| 20 | A1 | 1pi indigo (S) | 3.25 | .90 |
| 21 | A1 | 2pi olive green | 3.75 | 4.50 |
| 22 | A1 | 5pi plum | 19.50 | 22.50 |
| 23 | A1 | 9pi bister | 11.00 | 2.00 |
| 24 | A1 | 10pi ultra | 11.50 | 19.50 |
| 25 | A1 | 20pi gray | 30.00 | 19.50 |
| | | Nos. 15-25 (11) | 99.10 | 123.30 |

Forgeries exist of No. 17e.

### Stamps and Type of 1918 Overprinted in Black or Silver

Similar Overprint, with Arabic Line 10mm Long, Arabic "S" and "T" Joined, ".." at Left Extends Above Other Letters

**1921 — Perf. 15x14**

| | | | | |
|---|---|---|---|---|
| 37 | A1 | 1m dark brown | 1.40 | .35 |
| 38 | A1 | 2m blue green | 1.75 | .35 |
| 39 | A1 | 3m light brown | 1.75 | .20 |
| 40 | A1 | 4m scarlet | 2.25 | .40 |
| 41 | A1 | 5m orange | 1.75 | .35 |
| 42 | A1 | 1pi bright blue | 1.75 | .40 |
| 43 | A1 | 2pi olive green | 2.50 | .35 |
| 44 | A1 | 5pi plum | 7.00 | 5.75 |
| 45 | A1 | 9pi bister | 16.00 | 16.00 |
| 46 | A1 | 10pi ultra | 22.50 | 16.00 |
| 47 | A1 | 20pi gray | 57.50 | 575.00 |
| | | Nos. 37-47 (11) | 116.15 | 1,400. |
| | | | | 24.70 |

The 2nd character from left on bottom line that looks like quotation marks consists of long thin lines.

Deformed or damaged letters exist in all three lines of the overprint.

### Similar Overprint, with Arabic Line 10mm Long, Arabic "S" and "T" Separated and 6mm Between English and Hebrew Lines

**1920, Dec. 6**

| | | | | |
|---|---|---|---|---|
| 15b | A1 | 1m dk brn, perf 14 | 55.00 | 37.50 |
| 17b | A1 | 3m lt brn, perf 14 | 55.00 | 37.50 |
| 19b | A1 | 5m orange, perf 14 | 510.00 | 13,750. |
| d. | | Perf. 15x14 | 16,000. | |
| | | Nos. 15b-19b (3) | 112.50 | |

### Overprinted as Before, 7½mm Between English and Hebrew Lines, ".." at Left Even With Other Letters

**1921 — Perf. 15x14**

| | | | | |
|---|---|---|---|---|
| 15c | A1 | 1m dull brown | 12.50 | 2,300. |
| 16c | A1 | 2m blue green | 23.00 | 23.00 |
| 17c | A1 | 3m light brown | 29.00 | 6.25 |
| 18c | A1 | 4m scarlet | 30.00 | 4.00 |
| 19c | A1 | 5m orange | 32.50 | 1.10 |
| 20c | A1 | 1pi indigo (S) | 21.00 | .90 |
| 21c | A1 | 2pi olive green | 29.00 | 7.00 |
| 22c | A1 | 5pi plum | 57.50 | 9.00 |
| 23c | A1 | 9pi bister | 62.50 | 16.00 |
| 24c | A1 | 10pi ultra | 97.50 | 13,750. |
| 25c | A1 | 20pi pale gray | 449.50 | 212.00 |
| d. | | Perf. 14 | 2,900. | |
| | | Nos. 15c-25c (11) | | |

### Overprinted at London

**1920-21 — Perf. 15x14**

| | | | | |
|---|---|---|---|---|
| 15a | A1 | 1m dark brown | 1.40 | 1.10 |
| e. | | Perf. 14 | 625.00 | 800.00 |
| 16a | | As "a", invrtd. ovpt. | 450.00 | |
| d. | | Perf 15x14 | 7.50 | |
| 17a | A1 | 2m blue green | 7.50 | |
| e. | | "PALESTINE" omitted | 2,500. | 1,500. |
| f. | | Perf. 14 | 60.00 | |
| 18a | A1 | 3m light brown | 3.00 | 3.00 |
| 19a | A1 | 4m scarlet | 4.00 | 1.40 |
| 20a | A1 | 5m orange | 2.50 | 87.50 |
| 21a | A1 | 1pi indigo, perf. 14 (S) | | .90 |
| 22a | A1 | 2pi olive green ('21) | 57.50 | 1.25 |
| | | Nos. 15a-22a (8) | 190.90 | 51.40 |

This overprint often looks like grayish black. In the English line it looks grayish to grayish black, and the letters are frequently uneven and damaged.

### Similar Overprint on Type of 1921

**1922 — Wmk. 4 — Perf. 14**

| | | | | |
|---|---|---|---|---|
| 48 | A1 | 1m dark brown | 1.25 | .35 |
| a. | | Double overprint | 250.00 | 500.00 |
| b. | | Inverted overprint | 13,750. | |
| 49 | A1 | 2m yellow | 1.10 | .35 |
| 50 | A1 | 3m Prus blue | 1.75 | .20 |
| 51 | A1 | 4m rose | .75 | .20 |
| 52 | A1 | 5m orange | 2.25 | .35 |
| 53 | A1 | 6m blue green | 2.25 | .35 |
| 54 | A1 | 7m yellow brown | 1.75 | .35 |
| 55 | A1 | 8m red | 1.75 | .35 |
| 56 | A1 | 9m yellow bister | 2.25 | .35 |
| 57 | A1 | 13m ultra | 2.25 | .40 |
| 58 | A1 | 2pi olive green | 3.00 | .40 |
| a. | | Inverted overprint | 350.00 | 575.00 |
| 59 | A1 | 5pi yellow bister | 140.00 | 7.50 |
| a. | | Perf. 15x14 | 5.50 | 1.40 |
| 60 | A1 | 9pi bister | 10.00 | 10.00 |
| 61 | A1 | 10pi light blue | 8.50 | 8.50 |
| a. | | Perf. 14 | 1.00 | 3.00 |
| 62 | A1 | 20pi violet | 10.50 | 6.25 |
| a. | | Perf. 14 | 140.00 | 24.10 |
| | | Nos. 48-62 (15) | 55.35 | 24.10 |

The "E. F." for "E. E. F." on No. 61 is caused by damaged type.

The 2nd character from left on bottom line that looks like quotation marks consists of short thick lines.

### Rachel's Tomb — A3

### Citadel at Jerusalem — A5
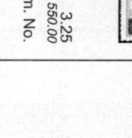

**1927-42 — Typo. Perf. 13½x14½**

| | | | | |
|---|---|---|---|---|
| 63 | A3 | 2m Prus blue | 1.10 | .20 |
| 64 | A3 | 3m yellow green | .85 | .20 |
| 65 | A4 | 4m rose red | 5.50 | 1.25 |
| 66 | A4 | 4m violet brn ('32) | 1.10 | .20 |
| 67 | A4 | 5m yellow org | 2.25 | .20 |
| a. | | Perf. 14 1½x14 (coil stamp) | | |
| 68 | A4 | 6m deep green | 16.00 | 20.00 |
| 69 | A5 | 7m deep red | .85 | .20 |
| 70 | A5 | 7m dk violet ('32) | .70 | |
| 71 | A5 | 8m dk violet ('32) | 13.50 | 6.75 |
| 72 | A4 | 8m yellow brown | 1.40 | .20 |
| 73 | A3 | 10m deep gray | 1.40 | .20 |
| a. | | Perf. 14 1½x14 (coil stamp) | | |
| 74 | A4 | 13m ultra | 23.50 | 26.00 |
| 75 | A4 | 13m olive bister | 8.00 | .40 |
| a. | | Perf. 14 ('38) | | |
| 76 | A5 | 15m ultra | 1.25 | .20 |
| 77 | A5 | 20m olive green | 1.40 | .20 |

### Tiberias and Sea of Galilee — A6 — Mosque of Omar (Dome of the Rock) — A4

| | | | | |
|---|---|---|---|---|
| 78 | A6 | 50m violet brown | 1.75 | .40 |
| 79 | A6 | 90m bister | 62.50 | 67.50 |
| 80 | A6 | 100m bister | 2.50 | .80 |
| 81 | A6 | 200m bright blue | 9.00 | 4.00 |
| 82 | A6 | 250m dp brown ('42) | 4.75 | 5.00 |
| 83 | A6 | 500m dk brown ('42) | 5.00 | 3.25 |
| 84 | A6 | £1 gray black | 141.35 | 93.55 |
| | | Nos. 63-84 (22) | 6.75 | 4.00 |

Issued: 3m, #74, 6/1; 2m, 5m, 6m, 10m, #65, 69, 71, 77-81, 8/14; #70, 72, 6/11/32; #5, 15m, 8/1/32; #66, 11/1/32; #82-84, 1/15/42.

## POSTAGE DUE STAMPS

D1

**1923 — Unwmk. — Typo. Perf. 11**

| | | | | |
|---|---|---|---|---|
| J1 | D1 | 1m bister brown | 17.50 | 27.50 |
| a. | | Horiz. pair, imperf. btwn. | 1,300. | |
| J2 | D1 | 2m green | 11.50 | 11.50 |
| a. | | Horiz. pair, imperf. btwn. | 8.00 | 11.50 |
| J3 | D1 | 4m red | 11.50 | 11.50 |
| J4 | D1 | 8m violet | 8.00 | 8.00 |
| a. | | Horiz. pair, imperf. btwn. | 2,100. | |
| J5 | D1 | 13m dark blue | 7.00 | 7.00 |
| a. | | Horiz. pair, imperf. btwn. | 975.00 | |
| | | Nos. J1-J5 (5) | 55.50 | 65.50 |

Imperfs. of 1m, 2m, 8m, are from proof sheets. Values for Nos. J1-J5 are for fine centered copies.

D2

D3

**1924, Dec. 1 — Wmk. 4**

| | | | | |
|---|---|---|---|---|
| J6 | D2 | 1m brown | 1.00 | 2.25 |
| J7 | D2 | 2m yellow | 2.50 | 2.00 |
| J8 | D2 | 4m green | 1.40 | 2.00 |
| J9 | D2 | 8m red | 3.50 | 1.00 |
| J10 | D2 | 13m ultramarine | 2.75 | 2.75 |
| J11 | D3 | 5pi violet | 9.75 | 2.25 |
| | | Nos. J6-J11 (6) | 22.25 | 11.40 |

## PALESTINIAN AUTHORITY

LOCATION — Areas of the West Bank and the Gaza Strip.
AREA — 2,410 sq. mi.
POP. — 2,825,000 (2000 est.)

1000 Fils (Mils) = 5 Israeli Shekels
1000 Fils = 1 Jordanian Dinar (Jan. 1, 1998)

**Catalogue values for all unused stamps in this country are for Never Hinged items.**

Hisham Palace, Jericho — A1

**1994**     **Litho.**     **Perf. 14**
| | | | |
|---|---|---|---|
| 1 | A1 | 5m multicolored | .20 .20 |
| 2 | A1 | 10m multicolored | .20 .20 |
| 3 | A1 | 20m multicolored | .20 .20 |
| 4 | A1 | 30m multicolored | .20 .20 |
| 5 | A1 | 40m multicolored | .20 .25 |
| 6 | A1 | 50m multicolored | .25 .25 |
| 7 | A1 | 75m multicolored | .25 .30 |
| 8 | A1 | 125m multicolored | .35 .35 |
| 9 | A1 | 150m multicolored | .40 .40 |
| 10 | A1 | 200m multicolored | .70 .70 |
| 11 | A1 | 300m multicolored | 1.00 1.00 |

**Size: 51x29mm**
| | | | |
|---|---|---|---|
| 12 | A1 | 500m multicolored | 1.75 1.75 |
| 13 | A1 | 1000m multicolored | 3.25 3.25 |
| | | *Nos. 1-13 (13)* | 9.00 9.00 |

Issued: 125m-500m, 8/15; others, 9/1.

Nos. 1-13 Surcharged "FILS" in English and Arabic in Black or Silver and with Black Bars Obliterating "Mils"

**1995, Apr. 10**     **Litho.**     **Perf. 14**
| | | | |
|---|---|---|---|
| 14 | A1 | 5f multicolored | .20 .20 |
| 15 | A1 | 10f multicolored | .20 .20 |
| 16 | A1 | 20f multicolored | .20 .20 |
| 17 | A1 | 30f multicolored (S) | .20 .25 |
| 18 | A1 | 40f multicolored (S) | .25 .25 |
| 19 | A1 | 50f multicolored (S) | .25 .25 |
| 20 | A1 | 75f multicolored (S) | .35 .35 |
| 21 | A1 | 125f multicolored | .45 .45 |
| 22 | A1 | 150f multicolored | .55 .55 |
| 23 | A1 | 200f multicolored | .90 .90 |
| 24 | A1 | 300f multicolored | 1.00 1.00 |

**Size: 51x29mm**
| | | | |
|---|---|---|---|
| 25 | A1 | 500f multicolored | 1.75 1.75 |
| 26 | A1 | 1000f multicolored | 3.25 3.25 |
| | | *Nos. 14-26 (13)* | 9.50 9.50 |

Pres. Yasser Arafat — A5

**1996, Mar. 20**
| | | | |
|---|---|---|---|
| 39 | A5 | 10f red violet & bluish black | .20 .20 |
| 40 | A5 | 20f yellow & bluish black | .20 .20 |
| 41 | A5 | 50f blue & bluish black | .20 .20 |
| 42 | A5 | 100f apple grn & bluish blk | .50 .50 |
| 43 | A5 | 1000f orange & bluish black | 3.50 3.50 |
| | | *Nos. 39-43 (5)* | 4.60 4.60 |

---

**1928-45**      **Perf. 14**
| | | | |
|---|---|---|---|
| J12 | D3 | 1m lt brown | .70 1.00 |
| | | *a.* Perf. 15x14 (45) | 37.50 75.00 |
| J13 | D3 | 2m yellow | 1.10 .70 |
| J14 | D3 | 4m green | 1.40 1.90 |
| | | *a.* 4m bluish grn, perf. 15x14 (45) | 62.50 90.00 |
| J15 | D3 | 6m brown org (33) | 17.50 5.75 |
| J16 | D3 | 8m red | 2.00 1.00 |
| J17 | D3 | 10m light gray | 1.50 .70 |
| J18 | D3 | 13m ultra | 2.25 2.00 |
| J19 | D3 | 20m olive green | 2.25 1.40 |
| J20 | D3 | 50m violet | 3.70 1.40 |
| | | *Nos. J12-J20 (9)* | 31.70 15.85 |

The Hebrew word for "mil" appears below the numeral on all values but the 1m. Issued: 6m, Oct. 1933; others, Feb. 1, 1928.

---

Illustration reduced.

**1995, May 17**     **Litho.**     **Perf. 14**
| | | | |
|---|---|---|---|
| 27 | A2 | 150f multicolored | .50 .50 |
| 28 | A2 | 350f multicolored | 1.10 1.10 |
| 29 | A2 | 500f multicolored | 1.60 1.60 |
| | | *Nos. 27-29 (3)* | 3.20 3.20 |

Christmas — A4

Traditional Costumes — A3

Women wearing various costumes.

**1995, May 31**
| | | | |
|---|---|---|---|
| 30 | A3 | 250f multicolored | .80 .80 |
| 31 | A3 | 300f multicolored | .95 .95 |
| 32 | A3 | 550f multicolored | 1.75 1.75 |
| 33 | A3 | 900f multicolored | 2.50 2.50 |
| | | *Nos. 30-33 (4)* | 6.00 6.00 |

**1995, Dec. 18**

Designs: 10f, Ancient view of Bethlehem. 20f, Modern view of Bethlehem. 50f, Entrance to grotto, Church of the Nativity. 100f, Yasser Arafat, Pope John Paul II. 1000f, Star of the Nativity, Church of the Nativity, Bethlehem. 10f, 20f, 100f, 1000f are horiz.
| | | | |
|---|---|---|---|
| 34 | A4 | 10f multicolored | .20 .20 |
| 35 | A4 | 20f multicolored | .20 .20 |
| 36 | A4 | 50f multicolored | .20 .60 |
| 37 | A4 | 100f multicolored | .60 .60 |
| 38 | A4 | 1000f multicolored | 4.70 4.70 |
| | | *Nos. 34-38 (5)* | | 

---

Illustration reduced.

**1996, May 20**
| | | | |
|---|---|---|---|
| 48 | A7 | 1250f multicolored | 4.50 4.50 |

1996 Summer Olympic Games, Atlanta — A8

Designs: 30f, Boxing. 40f, Medal. 1896. 50f, Runners. 150f, Olympic flame. 1000f, Palestinian Olympic Committee emblem.

**1996, July 19**     **Perf. 13½**
| | | | |
|---|---|---|---|
| 49 | A8 | 30f multicolored | .20 .20 |
| 50 | A8 | 40f multicolored | .20 .30 |
| 51 | A8 | 50f multicolored | .30 .30 |
| 52 | A8 | 150f multicolored | .65 .65 |
| | | *a.* Sheet of 3, #49, 51-52 | 8.75 |
| 53 | A8 | 1000f multicolored | 4.25 4.25 |
| | | *Nos. 49-53 (5)* | 5.60 5.60 |

Flowers — A9

**1996, Nov. 22**
| | | | |
|---|---|---|---|
| 54 | A9 | 10f Poppy | .20 .20 |
| 55 | A9 | 25f Hibiscus | .20 .20 |
| 56 | A9 | 100f Thyme | .50 .50 |
| 57 | A9 | 150f Lemon | .60 .60 |
| 58 | A9 | 750f Orange | 3.00 3.00 |
| | | *Nos. 54-58 (5)* | 4.50 4.50 |

**Souvenir Sheet**
| | | | |
|---|---|---|---|
| 59 | A9 | 1000f Olive | 4.25 4.25 |

---

**1996 Intl. Philatelic Exhibitions — A6**

Exhibition, site: 20f, CHINA '96, Summer Palace, Beijing. 50f, ISTANBUL '96, Hagia Sofia. 100f, ESSEN '96, Villa Hugel. 1000f, CAPEX '96, Toronto skyline.

**1996, May 18**
| | | | |
|---|---|---|---|
| 44 | A6 | 20f multicolored | .20 .20 |
| 45 | A6 | 50f multicolored | .35 .35 |
| 46 | A6 | 100f multicolored | .45 .45 |
| 47 | A6 | 1000f multicolored | 4.25 4.25 |
| | | *a.* Sheet, 2 each #44-47 + 2 labels | 10.00 |
| | | *Nos. 44-47 (4)* | 5.00 5.00 |

**Souvenir Sheet**

First Palestinian Legislative and Presidential Elections

1st Palestinian Parliamentary & Presidential Elections — A7

350f, Palestine #67. 500f, Palestine #72.

Palestine No. 63 — A2

---

**1997, May 29**

Birds — A11
| | | | |
|---|---|---|---|
| 61 | A11 | 25f Great tit | .20 .20 |
| 62 | A11 | 75f Blue rock thrush | .60 .60 |
| 63 | A11 | 150f Golden oriole | 1.40 1.40 |
| 64 | A11 | 400f Hoopoe | 2.25 2.25 |
| 65 | A11 | 600f Peregrine falcon | 4.65 4.65 |
| | | *Nos. 61-65 (5)* | |

Christmas — A10

**1996, Dec. 14**
| | | | |
|---|---|---|---|
| 60 | A10 | Sheet of 4, #a.-d. | 7.50 7.50 |

a, 150f, Magi. b, 350f, View of Bethlehem. c, 500f, Shepherds, sheep. d, 750f, Nativity scene.

**Souvenir Sheet**     **Perf. 14**

---

**1997, June 19**

Historic Views — A12
| | | | |
|---|---|---|---|
| 66 | A12 | 350f Gaza, 1839 | 1.50 1.50 |
| 67 | A12 | 600f Hebron, 1839 | 2.50 2.50 |

**Souvenir Sheet**

Return of Hong Kong to China — A13

**1997, July 1**
| | | | |
|---|---|---|---|
| 68 | A13 | 225f multicolored | 1.50 1.50 |

Friends of Palestine — A14

#69, Portraits of Yasser Arafat, Hans-Jürgen Wischnewski. #70, Wischnewski shaking hands with Arafat. #71, Mother Teresa with Arafat. #72, Mother Teresa.

**1997**     **Litho.**     **Perf. 14**
| | | | |
|---|---|---|---|
| 69 | A14 | 600f multicolored | 1.75 1.75 |
| 70 | A14 | 600f multicolored | 1.75 1.75 |
| | | *a.* Pair, #69-70 | 3.50 3.50 |
| 71 | A14 | 600f multicolored | 2.00 2.00 |
| 72 | A14 | 600f multicolored | 2.00 2.00 |
| | | *a.* Pair, #71-72 | 4.00 4.00 |
| | | *Nos. 69-72 (4)* | 7.50 7.50 |

#70a, 72a were issued in sheets of 4 stamps.
Issued: #69-70, 7/24; #71-72, 12/17.

Christmas — A15

**1997, Nov. 28**
| | | | |
|---|---|---|---|
| 73 | A15 | 350f multicolored | 1.25 1.25 |
| 74 | A15 | 700f multicolored | 2.25 2.25 |
| | | *a.* A15 Pair, #73-74 | 3.50 3.50 |

Mosaics from Floor of Byzantine Church, Jabalia-Gaza — A16

50f, Rabbit, palm tree. 125f, Goat, rabbit, dog. 200f, Basket, fruit tree, jar. 400f, Lion.

**1998, June 22    Litho.    Perf. 13½**
| | | | |
|---|---|---|---|
| 75 | A16 | 50f multicolored | .25 | .25 |
| 76 | A16 | 125f multicolored | .40 | .40 |
| 77 | A16 | 200f multicolored | .75 | .75 |
| 78 | A16 | 400f multicolored | 1.10 | 1.10 |
| | | Nos. 75-78 (4) | 2.50 | 2.50 |

**Souvenir Sheet**

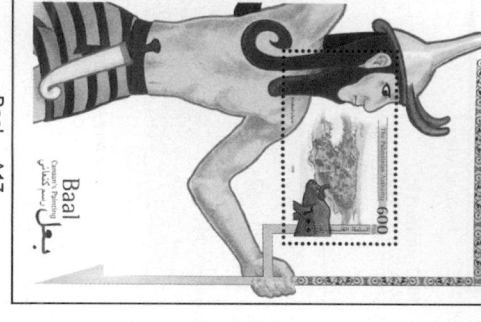

Baal — A17

Baal

**1998, June 15    Perf. 14**
79   A17   600f multicolored   2.50   2.50

A18

Raptors
A19

**1998, Sept. 30    Litho.    Perf. 14**
| | | | |
|---|---|---|---|
| 80 | A18 | 40f Urginea maritima | .20 | .20 |
| 81 | A18 | 80f Silybum marianum | .30 | .30 |
| 82 | A18 | 500f Foeniculum vulgare | 1.90 | 1.90 |
| 83 | A18 | 80f Inula viscosa | 3.25 | 3.25 |
| | | Nos. 80-83 (4) | 5.65 | 5.65 |

Medicinal plants.

**1998, Nov. 12    Litho.    Perf. 14**
| | | | |
|---|---|---|---|
| 84 | A19 | 20f Bonelli's eagle | .20 | .20 |
| 85 | A19 | 60f Hobby | .30 | .30 |
| 86 | A19 | 340f Verreaux's eagle | 1.25 | 1.25 |
| 87 | A19 | 600f Bateleur | 2.25 | 2.25 |
| 88 | A19 | 900f Buzzard | 3.25 | 3.25 |
| | | Nos. 84-88 (5) | 7.25 | 7.25 |

Granting of Additional Rights to
Palestinian Authority's Observer to
UN — A20

**1998, Dec. 3**
90   A21   Sheet of 4, #a.-d.   4.50   4.50

**Souvenir Sheet**

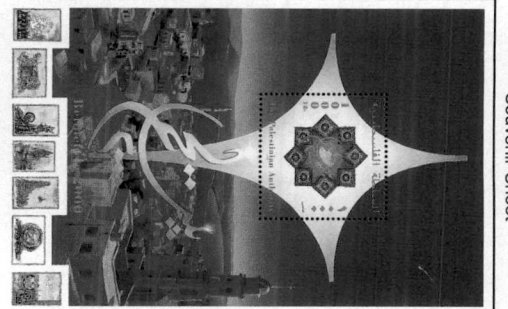

Christmas, Bethlehem 2000 — A22

**1998, Dec. 3**
91   A22   1000f multicolored   4.00   4.00

Illustration reduced.

**Souvenir Sheet**

Signing of Middle East Peace
Agreement, Wye River Conference,
Oct. 23, 1998 — A23

Palestinian Pres. Yasser Arafat and US
Pres. Bil Clinton. Illustration reduced.

**1999**
92   A23   900f multicolored   3.50   3.50

**Litho.    Perf. 14**

New
Airport,
Gaza
A24

**1999**
| | | | |
|---|---|---|---|
| 93 | A24 | 80f multicolored | .20 | .20 |
| 94 | A24 | 300f multicolored | .90 | .90 |
| 95 | A24 | 700f multicolored | 2.10 | 2.10 |
| | | Nos. 93-95 (3) | 3.20 | 3.20 |

Designs: 80f, Control tower, vert. 300f, Airplane. 700f, Terminal building.

**1998, Nov. 12**
89   A20   700f multicolored   2.50   2.50

Illustration reduced.

Butterflies
A21

Designs: a, 100f, Papilio alexanor. b, 200f,
Danaus chrysippus. c, 300f, Gonepleryx cleopatra. d, 400f, Melanargia titea.

**1999**
96   A25   Block of 6, #a.-f.   7.00   7.00

A26

Hebron: a, 400f. Lettering in white.
b, 500f, Lettering in gold.

**1999, Aug. 20    Litho.    Perf. 14**
97   A26   Pair, #a.-b.   2.75   2.75

**1999, Apr. 27**
98   A27   Strip of 5, #a.-e.   4.25   4.25

Arabian Horses (Various): a, 25f. b, 75f. c,
150f. d, 350f. e, 800f.

**Souvenir Sheet**

A27

**Souvenir Sheet**

**1999**
99   A28   750f multi   2.25   2.25

Illustration reduced.

Palestinian Sunbird — A28

**Perf. 13¾**
2.25   2.25

A29

Intl. Philatelic Exhibitions & UPU,
125th Anniv. — A25

a, 20f Buildings, China 1999. b, 260f, Buildings, Germany, IBRA '99. c, 80f, High-rise
buildings, Australia '99. d, 340f, Eiffel Tower,
Philex France '99. e, 400f, Aerial view of countryside, denomination LR, UPU, 125th anniv. f,
400f, like #96e, denomination LL.

**1999, Dec. 8    Litho.    Perf. 13¼x13**

**Background Color**
| | | | | |
|---|---|---|---|---|
| 100 | A29 | 60f black | .20 | .20 |
| 101 | A29 | 80f light blue | .25 | .25 |
| 102 | A29 | 100f dark gray | .30 | .30 |
| 103 | A29 | 280f lilac rose | .85 | .85 |
| 104 | A29 | 300f green | .90 | .90 |
| 105 | A29 | 400f red violet | 1.25 | 1.25 |
| 106 | A29 | 500f dark red | 1.50 | 1.50 |
| 107 | A29 | 560f light gray | 1.75 | 1.75 |

**Perf. 13¼**
| | | | | |
|---|---|---|---|---|
| 108 | A30 | 60f | Pair, #a.-b | 1.50 | 1.50 |
| 109 | A30 | 80f | Pair, #a.-b | 2.00 | 2.00 |
| 110 | A30 | 280f | Pair, #a.-b. | 3.25 | 3.25 |
| 111 | A30 | 460f | Pair, #a.-b. | 4.00 | 4.00 |
| 112 | A30 | 560f | Pair, #a.-b. | 4.00 | 4.00 |

**Litho. & Embossed Foil Application**
| | | | |
|---|---|---|---|
| 113 | A30 | 2000f multi | 7.00 | 7.00 |
| a. | | Booklet pane of 1 | 27.00 | 27.00 |

Nos. 100-113 (14)    27.00   27.00

Nos. 108-112 each printed in sheets of 10
containing 9 "a" +1 "b." No. 113 printed in
sheets of 4. Nos. 108a-112a also exist in
sheets of 10. Issued: No. 113a, 2000.

Giotto Paintings (Type A30): 200f, 280f,
2000f, The Nativity. 380f, 460f, The Adoration
of the Magi. 560f, The Flight into Egypt.
Inscription colors: Nos. 108a, 110a, Black.
Nos. 109a, 111a, White. No. 112a, Yellow.
Nos. 108b-112b have silver inscriptions and
frames.

Easter — A31

**2000    Litho.    Perf. 13¼**
114-118   A31   Set of 5   5.25   5.25

**Souvenir Sheet**

**Litho. & Embossed Foil Application**
| | | |
|---|---|---|
| 119 | A31 | 2000f multi | 6.00 | 6.00 |
| a. | | Booklet pane of 1 | 6.00 | |

Designs: 150f, Last Supper, by Giotto, white
inscriptions. 200f, Last Supper, yellow inscriptions. 300f, Lamentation, by Giotto, white
inscriptions. 350f, Lamentation, yellow inscriptions. 650f, Crucifix, by Giotto, orange frame.
2000f, Crucifix, gold frame.

Christmas
A32

Madonna of the Star by Fra Angelico.

**2000    Litho. & Embossed Foil Application    Perf. 13¾**
| | | |
|---|---|---|
| 120 | A32 | 2000f Bkt. pane of 1 | 6.00 | 6.00 |
| a. | | Miniature sheet of 1 | 20.00 | 20.00 |

Booklet, #113a, 119a, 120

**1999, Dec. 8**

Christmas, Bethlehem 2000 — A30

## Women's Traditional Clothing — A44a

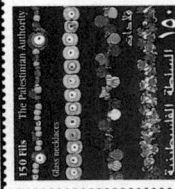

Various costumes: 50f, 100f, 500f.

**2002, June    Litho.    Perf. 14**
160A-160C  A44a  Set of 3
Souvenir Sheet
5.00  5.00

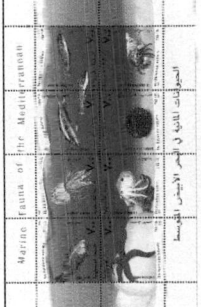

### Christmas — A45

**2002, Dec. 20    Perf. 14¼x14**
161  A45  1000f multi
3.75  3.75

Succulent
Plants — A46

Trees — A47

**Designs:** 550f, Prickly pear. 600f, Big-horned euphorbia. 750f, Century plant.

**2003, May 10    Litho.    Perf. 13¼x14**
162-164  A46    7.50  7.50
164a    Souvenir sheet, #162-164    7.50  7.50

**2003, July 12**

**Designs:** 300f, Olive tree. 700f, Blessing tree.
165-166  A47  Set of 2    4.00  4.00

### Universities — A48

**Designs:** 250f, Al-Azhar University, Gaza. 650f, Hebron University, Hebron. 800f, Arab American University, Jenin.

**2003, July 19    Set of 3**
167-169  A48    6.75  6.75

Handicrafts
A49

**Designs:** 150f, Glass necklaces. 200f, Headdress. 450f, Embroidery. 500f, Costume embroidery. 950f, Head veil.

**2003, Oct. 11    Litho.    Perf. 13¾**
170-174  A49  Set of 5    9.75  9.75

---

**No. 149:** a, 350f, Jerusalem After Rain. b, 550f, Mysticism. c, 850f, Ramallah. d, 900f, Remembrance.

**2001    Perf. 14x13¾**
149  A39    Sheet of 4, #a-d    8.00  8.00

### Worldwide Fund for Nature (WWF) — A40

**No. 150** — Houbara bustard, WWF emblem at: a, 350f, UR. b, 350f, LR. c, 750f, UL. d, 750f, LL.
Illustration reduced.

**2001    Litho.    Perf. 13¾x14**
150  A40    Block of 4, #a-d    10.50  10.50

Graf Zeppelin
Over Holy
Land — A41

**No. 150** — Zeppelin and: a, 200f, Map of voyage. 600f, Hills.

**2001    Perf. 13¾**
151-152  A41    Set of 2    2.75  2.75

Legends —
A42

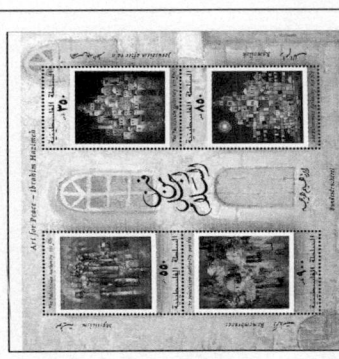

**Designs:** 300f, Man with magic lamp, buildings. 450f, Eagle, snake, gemstones, man. 650f, Man and woman on flying horse. 800f, Man hiding behind tree.

**2001    Perf. 13¾x14**
153  150  A42    Set of 4    6.75  6.75
Souvenir Sheet

### Peace for Bethlehem — A43

**2001    Perf. 14x13¾**
157  A42  950f multi    3.25  3.25

City
Views — A44

**Designs:** 450f, Jerusalem. 650f, El-Eizariya. 850f, Nablus.

**2002    Litho.    Perf. 13¾**
158-160  A44    Set of 3    7.25  7.25

---

## Souvenir Sheet

The Blue Madonna

### Blue Madonna — A37

**2000    Perf. 14x13¾**
133  A37    950f multi    3.00  3.00

### Christmas Type of 2000

**Designs:** No. 134, 100f. No. 138, 500f, Nativity, by Gentile da Fabriano, horiz. No. 135, 150f, Adoration of the Magi, by Fabriano, horiz. No. 136, 250f, Immaculate Conception, by Fabriano, horiz. No. 137, 350f, No. 139, 1000f, Like #120.

**2000    Litho.    Perf. 13¼**
134-139  A32    Set of 6    7.25  7.25

### Easter Type of 2000

**Designs:** 150f, Christ Carrying Cross, by Fra Angelico, blue inscriptions. 200f, Christ Carrying Cross, white inscriptions. 300f, Removal of Christ from Cross, by Fra Angelico, yellow inscriptions. 350f, Removal of Christ from the Cross, white inscriptions. 2000f, Crucifix, by Giotto, vert.

**2001    Litho.    Perf. 13¼**
140-143  A31    Set of 4    2.75  2.75
Souvenir Sheet
Litho. & Embossed
144  A31    2000f gold & multi    5.75  5.75

A38

Palestinian Authority flag and flag of various organizations: 50f, 100f, 200f, 500f.

**2001    Litho.    Perf. 13¾**
145-148  A38    Set of 4    2.50  2.50
Souvenir Sheet

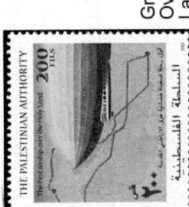

Art by Ibrahim Hazimeh

---

## Souvenir Sheet

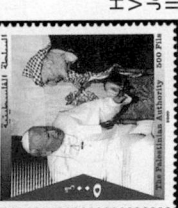

Holy Land
Visit of Pope
John Paul
II — A33

**Designs:** 500f, Pope, Yasser Arafat holding hands. 600f, Pope with miter. 750f, Pope touching Arafat's shoulder. 800f, Pope, creche. 1000f, Pope, back of Arafat's head.

**2000    Litho.    Perf. 13¾**
121-125  A33    Set of 5    11.00  11.00

Intl. Children's
Year — A34

**Designs:** 50f, Landscape. 100f, Children. 350f, Domed buildings. 400f, Family.

**2000**
126-129  A34    Set of 4    3.00  3.00

Pres.
Arafat's
Visit to
Germany
A35

Arafat and: 2001, German Chancellor Gerhard Schröder. 300f, German President Johannes Rau.

**2000    Perf. 14x14¼**
130-131  A35    Set of 2    2.00  2.00

### Marine Life — A36

**No. 132:** a, Parrotfish. b, Mauve stinger. c, Ornate wrasse. d, Rainbow wrasse. e, Red starfish. f, Common octopus. g, Purple sea urchin. h, Striated hermit crab.

**2000    Perf. 13¾**
132  A36  700f    Sheet of 8, #a-h    16.00  16.00

No. 175 — Chirac and: a, 200f, Yasser Arafat, French flag. b, 450f, Palestinian flag.

**2004**

175 A50     **Litho.**     **Perf. 14**
    Pair, #a-b     3.25   3.25

Printed in sheets containing two each of Nos. 175a-175b.

French President Jacques Chirac A50

Painting: View of Palestine, by Ibrahim Hazimen.

Illustration reduced.

**Souvenir Sheet**

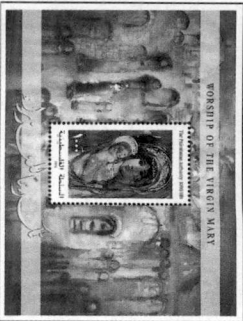

Worship of the Virgin Mary — A51

**2004**

176 A51 1000f multi     5.00   5.00

**Souvenir Sheet**

60 YEARS ARAB LEAGUE

Arab League, 60th Anniv. — A52

**2005**

177 A52 750f multi     **Perf. 13¾**
    3.50   3.50

**Litho.**

---

**SEMI-POSTAL STAMPS**

**Souvenir Sheet**

THE GAZA-JERICHO PEACE AGREEMENT

Gaza-Jericho Peace Agreement — SP1

Illustration reduced.

**1994, Oct. 7**     **Litho.**     **Perf. 14**
B1 SP1 750m +250m multi     6.50   6.50

For surcharge see No. B3.

Arab League, 50th Anniv. — SP2

**Souvenir Sheet**

50 YEARS ARAB LEAGUE

**1995, Mar. 22**     **Perf. 13½**
B2 SP2 750f +250f multi     3.75   3.75

No. B1 Surcharged "FILS" in English & Arabic and with Added Text at Left and Right

**1995, Apr. 10**     **Litho.**
B3 SP1 750f +250f multi     7.00   7.00

Honoring 1994 Nobel Peace Prize winners Arafat, Rabin and Peres.

---

**OFFICIAL STAMPS**

Natl. Arms — O1

**1994, Aug. 15**     **Litho.**     **Perf. 14**
O1 O1   50m yellow     .20   .20
O2 O1   100m green blue     .30   .30
O3 O1   125m blue     .10   .40
O4 O1   200m orange     .60   .60
O5 O1   250m olive     .80   .80
O6 O1   400m maroon     1.25   1.25
    Nos. O1-O6 (6)     3.55   3.55

Nos. O1-O6 could also be used by the general public, and non-official-use covers are known.

# PANAMA

'pa-na-,mä

LOCATION — Central America between Costa Rica and Colombia
GOVT. — Republic
AREA — 30,134 sq. mi.
POP. — 2,778,526 (1999 est.)
CAPITAL — Panama

Formerly a department of the Republic of Colombia, Panama gained its independence in 1903. Dividing the country at its center is the Panama Canal.

100 Centavos = 1 Peso
100 Centesimos = 1 Balboa (1904)

Catalogue values for unused stamps in this country are for Never Hinged items, beginning with Scott 350 in the regular postage section, Scott C82 in the airpost section, Scott CB1 in the airpost semi-postal section, and Scott RA21 in the postal tax section.

## Watermarks

Wmk. 229 — Wavy Lines

Wmk. 233 — "Harrison & Sons, London." in Script

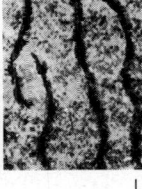

Wmk. 311 — Star and RP Multiple

Wmk. 334 — Rectangles

---

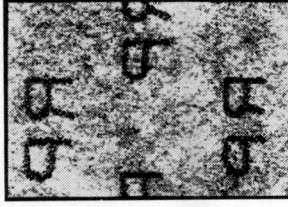

Wmk. 343 — RP Multiple

Wmk. 365 — Argentine Arms, Casa de Moneda de la Nacion & RA Multiple

Wmk. 377 — Interlocking Circles

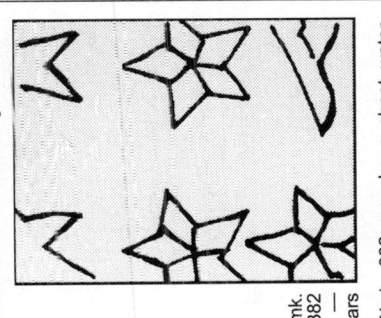

Wmk. 382 — Stars

Wmk. 382 may be a sheet watermark. It includes stars, wings with sun in middle and "Panama R de P".

### Issues of Panama Under Colombian Dominion

Valid only for domestic mail.

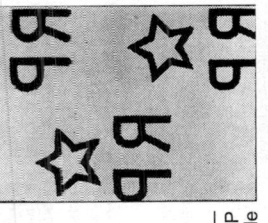

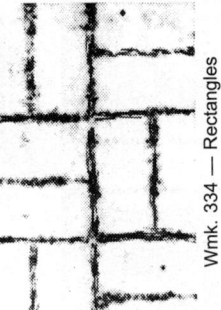

Coat of Arms

|      |    |        |       |       |
|------|----|--------|-------|-------|
| A1   | A2 | Imperf.|       |       |

1878  Unwmk.  Litho.  Thin Wove Paper
1  A1  5c gray green  25.00  30.00
a.  5c yellow green  25.00  30.00

---

### Issues of Colombia for use in the Department of Panama

Issued because of the use of different currency.

Map of Panama

|       |     |                    | A4 *Perf. 13½* |       |
|-------|-----|--------------------|----------------|-------|
| A3    |     |                    |                |       |

1887-88
8   A3  1c black, green          .90   .80
9   A3  2c black, pink ('88)    1.60  1.25
a.      2c black, salmon        1.60   .90
10  A3  5c black, blue           .90   .35
11  A3  10c black, yellow        .90   .40
a.      Imperf., pair
12  A3  20c black, lilac        1.00   .50
13  A3  50c brown (HH)          1.00
a.      imperf.                 7.30  4.30

Nos. 8-13 (6)

1892
14  A3  50c brown               2.50  1.10

### Pelure Paper
14  A3  50c brown               2.50  1.10

The stamps of this issue have been reprinted on papers of slightly different colors from those of the originals.

These are: 1c yellow green, 2c deep rose, 5c bright blue, 10c straw, 20c violet.

The 50c is printed from a very worn stone, in a lighter brown than the originals. The series includes a 10c on lilac paper.

All these stamps are to be found perforated, imperforate horizontally or imperforate vertically. At the same time that they were made, impressions were struck upon a variety of glazed and surface-colored papers.

See No. 14. For surcharges and overprints see Nos. 24-30, 107-108, 115-116, 137-139.

---

### Wove Paper

|          |     |                | Engr. | *Perf. 12* |      |
|----------|-----|----------------|-------|-----------|------|
| 1892-96  |     |                |       |           |      |
| 15       | A4  | 1c green       |       | .25       | .25  |
| 16       | A4  | 2c rose        |       | .40       | .25  |
| 17       | A4  | 5c blue        |       | 1.50      | .50  |
| 18       | A4  | 10c orange     |       | .35       | .25  |
| 19       | A4  | 20c violet ('95)|      | .50       | .35  |
| 20       | A4  | 50c bister brn ('96)|  | 6.50      | 4.00 |
| 21       | A4  | 1p lake ('96)  |       | 10.00     | 6.00 |

Nos. 15-21 (7)

In 1903 Nos. 15-21 were used in Cauca and three other southern Colombia towns. Stamps canceled in these towns are worth much more.

For surcharges and overprints see Nos. 22-23, 51-106, 109-114, 129-136, 139, 151-162, 181-184, F12-F15, H4-H5.

---

### Issues of the Republic Issued in the City of Panama

Stamps of 1892-96 Overprinted

1903, Nov. 16
#### Rose Handstamp
| 51 | A4 | 1c green       | 2.00  | 1.50  |
| 52 | A4 | 2c rose        | 2.00  | 3.00  |
| 53 | A4 | 5c blue        | 2.00  | 1.25  |
| 54 | A4 | 10c yellow     | 4.00  | 3.50  |
| 55 | A4 | 20c violet     | 4.00  | 7.00  |
| 56 | A4 | 50c bister brn | 10.00 | 40.00 |
| 57 | A4 | 1p lake        | 75.00 | 58.25 |

Nos. 51-57 (7)

#### Blue Black Handstamp
| 58 | A4 | 1c green       | 2.00  | 1.25  |
| 59 | A4 | 2c rose        | 1.00  | 1.00  |
| 60 | A4 | 5c blue        | 7.00  | 6.00  |
| 61 | A4 | 10c yellow     | 5.00  | 3.50  |
| 62 | A4 | 20c violet     | 10.00 | 7.50  |
| 63 | A4 | 50c bister brn | 10.00 | 7.50  |
| 64 | A4 | 1p lake        | 50.00 | 42.50 |

Nos. 58-64 (7)  85.00  69.25

The stamps of this issue are to be found with the handstamp placed horizontally, vertically or diagonally; inverted; double; double, one inverted; double, both inverted; in pairs, one without handstamp; etc.

---

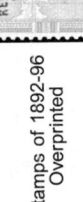

HABILITADO. 1894 1 CENTAVO.  (a)
HABILITADO. 1894 1 CENTAVOS.  (b)

Nos. 16, 12-14 Surcharged:

---

## Panama — top stamps

(d) HABILITADO. 1894 5 CENTAVOS.
(f) HABILITADO 1894 10 CENTAVOS.
(g) HABILITADO 1894 10 CENTAVOS.
(c) HABILITADO. 1894 5 CENTAVOS.
(e) HABILITADO 1894 5 CENTAVOS.

### Very Thin Wove Paper
2  A1  10c blue              60.00  60.00
3  A1  20c rose red          40.00  32.50
                            125.00

Nos. 1-3 (3)
4  A2  50c buff              1,500.

All values of this issue are known rouletted unofficially.

### Medium Thick Paper
5  A1  5c blue green         25.00  30.00
6  A1  10c blue              65.00  70.00
7  A2  50c orange            13.00
                            103.00

Nos. 5-7 (3)

Nos. 5-7 were printed before Nos. 1-4, according to Panamanian archives.

Values for used Nos. 1-5 are for handstamped postal cancellations.

These stamps have been reprinted in a number of shades, on thin to moderately thick, white or yellowish paper. They are without gum or with white, crackly gum. All values have been reprinted from new stones made from retouched dies. The marks of retouching are plainly to be seen in the sea and clouds. On the original 10c the shield in the upper left corner has two blank sections; on the reprints the design of this shield is completed. The impression of these reprints is frequently blurred.

Reprints of the 50c are rare. Beware of remainders of the 50c offered as reprints.

### Black Surcharge
1894
22  (a)  1c on 2c rose       .50   .40
a.       Inverted surcharge  2.50  2.50
b.       Double surcharge
23  (b)  1c on 2c rose       .40   .50
a.       "CCNTAVOS"          2.50  2.50
b.       Inverted surcharge
c.       Double surcharge    2.50  2.50

### Red Surcharge
24  5c on 20c black, III     2.50  1.50
a.   Inverted surcharge     12.50 12.50
c.   Without "HABILITADO"
25  5c on 20c black, III     3.50  3.00
a.   "CCNTAVOS"              7.50  7.50
b.   Inverted surcharge     12.50 12.50
c.   Without "HABILITADO"
26  (e)  5c on 20c black, III 6.00  5.00
a.       Inverted surcharge 12.50 12.50
b.       Double surcharge
27  (f)  10c on 50c brown    3.00  3.00
a.       Inverted surcharge
c.       "CCNTAVOS"         15.00
28  (g)  10c on 50c brown   12.50 12.50
a.       Inverted surcharge 32.50

### Pelure Paper
29  (f)  10c on 50c brown    4.00  3.00
a.       "CCNTAVOS"          7.50
b.       Inverted surcharge 12.50 12.50
30  (g)  10c on 50c brown   10.00 10.00
a.       "CCNTAVOS"
b.       Without "HABILITADO"
c.       Inverted surcharge 25.00 25.00
d.       Double surcharge   42.40 38.90

Nos. 22-30 (9)

There are several settings of those surcharges. Usually the surcharge is about 15½mm high, but in one setting, it is only 13mm. All the types are to be found with a comma after "CENTAVOS." Nos. 24, 25, 26, 29 and 30 exist with the surcharge printed sideways. Nos. 23, 24 and 29 may be found with an inverted "A" instead of "V" in "CENTAVOS." There are also varieties caused by dropped or broken letters.

This handstamp is known in brown rose on the 1, 5, 20 and 50c, in purple on the 1, 2, 50c, and 1p, and in magenta on the 5, 10, 20 and 50c.

Reprints were made in rose, black and other colors when the handstamp was nearly worn out, so that the "R" of "REPUBLICA" appears to be shorter than usual, and the bottom part of "LI" has been broken off. The "P" of "PANAMA" leans to the left and the tops of "NA" are broken. Many of these varieties are found inverted, double, etc.

**Overprinted**

## 1903, Dec. 3
### Bar in Similar Color to Stamp

**Black Overprint**

| | | |
|---|---|---|
| 65 | A4 2c rose | 2.50 2.50 |
| a. | "PANAMA" 15mm long | 3.50 |
| b. | Violet bar | 5.00 |
| 66 | A4 5c blue | 100.00 100.00 |
| a. | "PANAMA" 15mm long | 2.50 |
| b. | Double overprint, one in black | 2.50 |
| 67 | A4 10c yellow | 6.00 |
| a. | "PANAMA" 15mm long | 17.50 |
| b. | Horizontal overprint | |

*Nos. 65, 67-70 (5)*

**Gray Black Overprint**

| | | |
|---|---|---|
| 68 | A4 2c rose | 2.00 2.00 |
| a. | "PANAMA" 15mm long | 2.50 |

**Carmine Overprint**

| | | |
|---|---|---|
| 69 | A4 5c blue | 2.50 2.50 |
| a. | "PANAMA" 15mm long | 3.50 |
| 70 | A4 20c violet | 7.50 6.50 |
| a. | "PANAMA" 15mm long | 10.00 |
| b. | Double overprint, one in black | 17.00 16.00 |

This overprint was set up to cover fifty stamps. "PANAMA" is normally 13mm long and 1¾mm high but, in two rows in each sheet, it measures 15 to 16mm.

This word may be found with one or more of three inverted "V's" instead of "A's"; with an inverted "V" instead of "A," an inverted "N," an "A" with accent; and a fancy "P."

Owing to misplaced impressions, stamps exist with "PANAMA" once only, twice on one side, or three times.

**Overprinted in Red**

## 1903. Dec.

| | | |
|---|---|---|
| 71 | A4 1c green | .75 .60 |
| a. | "PANAMA" 15mm long | 1.25 |
| b. | "PANAMA" reading down | 3.00 |
| d. | Double overprint | 3.00 |
| 72 | A4 2c rose | .50 .40 |
| a. | "PANAMA" 15mm long | 1.00 |
| b. | "PANAMA" reading down | .75 |
| d. | Double overprint | |
| 73 | A4 20c violet | 4.00 |
| a. | "PANAMA" 15mm long | 1.50 1.00 |
| b. | "PANAMA" reading up and down | 2.25 |
| c. | Double overprint | |
| d. | Inverted overprint | |
| 74 | A4 50c bister brn | 8.00 8.00 |
| a. | "PANAMA" reading up and down | 18.00 18.00 |
| b. | Double overprint | 3.00 2.50 |
| d. | "PANAMA" 15mm long | 5.00 |
| 75 | A4 1p lake | 12.00 12.00 |
| a. | "PANAMA" reading up and down | 6.00 6.00 |
| b. | "PANAMA" 15mm long | 6.25 4.50 |
| c. | Double overprint | |
| d. | Inverted overprint | |

*Nos. 71-75 (5)*

This setting appears to be a re-arrangement (or two very similar re-arrangements) of the previous overprint. The overprint covers fifty stamps. "PANAMA" usually reads upward but sheets of the 1, 2 and 20c exist with the word reading upward on one half the sheet and downward on the other half.

In one re-arrangement one stamp has the word reading in both directions. Nearly all the varieties of the previous overprint are repeated in this setting excepting the inverted "Y" and fancy "P." There are also additional "PANAMA" 15mm long:

| | | |
|---|---|---|
| | | 15.00 15.00 |
| | | 11.75 9.00 |
| | | 25.00 |

**Handstamped in Magenta, Violet or Red**

| | | |
|---|---|---|
| 107 | A3 50c brown | 20.00 20.00 |
| | | 119.00 102.00 |

**On Stamps of 1887-92**

**Ordinary Wove Paper**

| | | |
|---|---|---|
| 108 | A3 50c brown | 70.00 |

*Nos. 101-107 (7)*

**Peluro Paper**

## 1903-04

**On Stamps of 1892-96**

| | | |
|---|---|---|
| 101 | A4 1c green | .75 .75 |
| 102 | A4 2c rose | .75 .75 |
| 103 | A4 5c blue | 1.00 1.00 |
| 104 | A4 10c yellow | 3.50 3.00 |
| 105 | A4 20c violet | 8.00 6.50 |
| 106 | A4 1p lake | 80.00 70.00 |

**Issued in Colon**

This overprint is set up to cover fifty stamps. In each fifty there are four stamps without accent on the "a" of "Republica" and one with a thick, upright "i."

Experts consider the black overprint on the 50c to be speculative.

The 20c violet and 50c bister brown exist with bar 2½mm instead of 2mm wide, including the error "PANAMA," but are not known to have been issued. Some copies have been canceled "to oblige."

**On Stamps of 1892-96**

| | | |
|---|---|---|
| 137 | A3 50c brown | 3.00 3.00 |
| 138 | A3 50c brown | 3.00 3.00 |
| a. | Double overprint | 14.00 |

**Blue Overprint**

**Ordinary Wove Paper**

**Peluro Paper**

## 1903-04

**Issued in Bocas del Toro**

Stamps of 1892-96 Overprinted

**Handstamped in Violet**

**R DE PANAMA**

| | | |
|---|---|---|
| 151 | A4 1c green | 20.00 20.00 |
| 152 | A4 2c rose | 20.00 20.00 |
| 153 | A4 5c blue | 20.00 14.00 |
| 154 | A4 10c yellow | 25.00 14.00 |
| 155 | A4 20c violet | 15.00 8.25 |
| 156 | A4 50c bister brn | 30.00 30.00 |
| 157 | A4 1p lake | 100.00 100.00 |
| | | 140.00 110.00 |
| | | 370.00 247.25 |

*Nos. 151-157 (7)*

The handstamp is known double and inverted. Counterfeits exist.

**Overprinted in Carmine**

**REPUBLICA DE PANAMA.**

## 1903-04

**On Stamp of 1892-96**

| | | |
|---|---|---|
| 139 | A4 20c violet | 200.00 |
| a. | Double overprint | |

Unknown with genuine cancels.

---

**Overprinted**

varieties of large letters and "PANAMA" occasionally has an "A" missing or inverted. There are misplaced impressions, as the previous setting.

## 1904-05

| | | |
|---|---|---|
| 76 | A4 1c green | .20 .20 |
| a. | Both words reading up | 1.50 |
| b. | Both words reading down | 2.75 |
| 77 | A4 2c rose | .20 |
| a. | Both words reading up | 15.00 |
| b. | Both words reading down | 20.00 |
| c. | Double overprint, one inverted | |
| d. | "PANAMA" | |
| e. | Inverted "M" in "PANAMA" | |
| 78 | A4 5c blue | .20 |
| a. | Both words reading up | 5.00 |
| b. | Both words reading down | 15.00 |
| c. | Pair, one without overprint | 20.00 |
| d. | Double overprint | |
| e. | Inverted "M" in "PANAMA" | |
| 79 | A4 10c yellow | .30 .20 |
| a. | Both words reading up | 2.50 |
| b. | Both words reading down | 5.00 |
| c. | Double overprint | 4.25 |
| d. | "PANAMA" | 12.50 |
| e. | Double overprint, one inverted | 25.00 |
| f. | "PANAMA" | 5.00 |
| g. | Inverted "M" in "PANAMA" | 5.00 |
| 80 | A4 20c violet | 20.00 20.00 |
| a. | Both words reading up | 5.00 |
| b. | Both words reading down | 5.00 |
| c. | Red brown overprint | 1.00 |
| d. | "PANAMA" | 3.50 |
| e. | Double overprint | |
| 81 | A4 50c bister brn | 2.00 1.00 |
| a. | Both words reading up | 2.00 |
| b. | Both words reading down | 10.50 |
| c. | Double overprint | 10.00 |
| d. | "PANAMA" | 1.60 |
| 82 | A4 1p lake | 5.00 5.00 |
| a. | Both words reading up | 5.00 |
| b. | Both words reading down | 12.50 |
| c. | Double overprint | 12.50 |
| d. | "PANAMA" | 10.00 |
| e. | Inverted "M" in "PANAMA" | |

*Nos. 76-82 (7)*

This overprint is also set up to cover fifty stamps. One stamp in each fifty has "PANAMA" reading upward at both sides. Another has the word reading downward at both sides. A third has an inverted "V" in place of the last "A" and a fourth has a small thick "N." In resetting all these varieties are corrected except the inverted "V." There are additional overprints as before.

Later printings show other varieties and have the bar 2½mm instead of 2mm wide. The colors of the various printings of Nos. 76-82 range from carmine to almost pink.

**Overprinted in Red**

Stamps with this overprint were a private speculation. They exist on cover. The overprint was to be used on postal cards.

**REPUBLICA DE PANAMA**

**On Stamps of 1892-96**

**Carmine Overprint**

| | | |
|---|---|---|
| 129 | A4 1c green | .40 .40 |
| a. | Inverted overprint | 6.00 |
| 130 | A4 2c rose | 2.25 |
| a. | Inverted overprint | 6.00 |
| b. | Double overprint, one inverted | .50 |
| c. | Double overprint | .50 .50 |

**Brown Overprint**

| | | |
|---|---|---|
| 131 | A4 1c green | 12.00 |
| a. | Double overprint, one inverted | |

**Black Overprint**

| | | |
|---|---|---|
| 132 | A4 1c green | 60.00 30.00 |
| a. | Vertical overprint | 42.50 |
| b. | Inverted overprint | 42.50 |
| c. | Double overprint, one inverted | 42.50 |
| 133 | A4 2c rose | .50 |
| a. | Inverted overprint | .50 |
| 134 | A4 10c yellow | .50 |
| a. | Inverted overprint | .50 |
| 135 | A4 20c violet | .50 |
| a. | Double overprint, one inverted | 4.00 |
| b. | Inverted overprint | 4.00 |
| 136 | A4 1p lake | 16.00 14.00 |
| a. | Double overprint, one inverted | .50 |

---

**REPUBLICA DE PANAMA**

Surcharged in Vermilion on Stamps of 1892-96 Issue:

**On Stamps of 1892-96**

**Ordinary Wove Paper**

| | | |
|---|---|---|
| 115 | A3 50c brown | 35.00 25.00 |
| | | 141.75 116.00 |

**Peluro Paper**

| | | |
|---|---|---|
| 116 | A3 50c brown | 50.00 37.50 |

The first note after No. 64 applies also to Nos. 109-116.

The handstamps on Nos. 109-116 have been counterfeited.

| | | |
|---|---|---|
| 109 | A4 1c green | 5.00 5.00 |
| 110 | A4 2c rose | 5.50 5.00 |
| 111 | A4 5c blue | 5.50 5.00 |
| 112 | A4 10c yellow | 8.25 7.00 |
| 113 | A4 20c violet | 10.00 9.00 |
| 114 | A4 1p lake | 70.00 60.00 |

*Nos. 109-115 (7)*

**General Issues**

## 1905, Feb. 4    Engr.    Perf. 12

| | | |
|---|---|---|
| 179 | A5 1c green | .60 .40 |
| 180 | A5 2c rose | .80 .50 |

A5

## 1906

| | | |
|---|---|---|
| 181 | A4 1c on 20c violet | .25 .25 |
| a. | "Pnnama" | 2.25 2.25 |
| b. | "Panrma" | 2.25 2.25 |
| c. | Inverted surcharge | 4.00 4.00 |
| d. | Double surcharge | 4.00 4.00 |
| e. | Double surcharge, one inverted | 3.50 3.50 |

| | | |
|---|---|---|
| 182 | A4 2c on 50c bister brn | .25 .25 |
| a. | 3rd "A" of "PANAMA" inverted | 2.25 2.25 |
| b. | "5" omitted | 4.00 4.00 |
| c. | Inverted surcharge | 4.00 4.00 |
| d. | Double surcharge | 2.50 |
| e. | Double surcharge, one inverted | |

The 2c on 20c violet was never issued to the public. All copies are inverted. Value, 75c.

**Carmine Surcharge**

| | | |
|---|---|---|
| 183 | A4 5c on 1p lake | .60 .40 |
| a. | Double surcharge | 6.00 6.00 |
| b. | "PANAMA" reading down | |

**On Stamp of 1903-04, No. 75**

| | | |
|---|---|---|
| 184 | A4 5c on 1p lake | .60 .40 |
| a. | "PANAMA" reading up and down | 5.50 5.50 |
| b. | "PANAMA" reading down | |
| c. | Inverted surcharge | |
| d. | Double surcharge | |
| e. | Double "PANAMA" reading down | |
| f. | 3rd "A" of "PANAMA" inverted | 1.70 1.30 |

*Nos. 181-184 (4)*

**National Flag — A6**

**Vasco Núñez de Balboa — A7**

PANAMA

José Vallarino — A41

Arms of Panama City — A40

Simón Bolívar — A43

"Land Gate" — A42

Statue of Cervantes — A44

Bolívar's Tribute — A45

Carlos de Ycaza — A46

Municipal Building in 1821 and 1921 — A47

Statue of Balboa — A48

Villa de Los Santos Church — A49

Fábrega — A51

Herrera — A50

**1921, Nov.**

| | | | | |
|---|---|---|---|---|
| 220 | A40 | ½c | orange | .80 | .25 |
| 221 | A41 | 1c | green | 1.00 | .20 |
| 222 | A42 | 2c | carmine | 1.25 | .25 |
| 223 | A43 | 2½c | red | 2.75 | 1.10 |
| 224 | A44 | 3c | dull violet | 2.75 | 1.10 |
| 225 | A45 | 5c | blue | 2.75 | .35 |
| 226 | A46 | 8c | olive green | 10.00 | 3.50 |
| 227 | A47 | 10c | violet | 6.75 | 1.50 |
| 228 | A48 | 15c | lt blue | 8.00 | 2.00 |
| 229 | A49 | 20c | olive brown | 14.50 | 3.50 |
| 230 | A50 | 24c | black brown | 14.50 | 4.25 |
| 231 | A51 | 50c | black | 25.00 | 8.00 |
| | | | | 90.05 | 26.00 |

Nos. 220-231 (12)

Centenary of independence. For overprints and surcharges see Nos. 264, 275-276, 299, 304, 308-310, C35.

---

| | | | | |
|---|---|---|---|---|
| 198 | A19 | 2c | red & blk | 1.00 | .30 |
| 199 | A20 | 2½c | red orange | 1.50 | .30 |
| a. | | | Booklet pane of 6 | 160.00 | |
| 200 | A21 | 5c | blue & blk | 2.00 | .30 |
| a. | | | Booklet pane of 6 | 160.00 | |
| 201 | A23 | 10c | violet & blk | 3.75 | 1.10 |
| a. | | | Booklet pane of 6 | | |

Nos. 195-201 (7) 10.95 3.40

For overprints and surcharges see #H23, I4-I7.

**1913, Sept.**

Balboa Sighting Pacific Ocean, His Dog "Leoncico" at His Feet — A24

202 A24 2½c dk grn & yel grn 1.75 .65

400th anniv. of Balboa's discovery of the Pacific Ocean.

**Panama-Pacific Exposition Issue**

Chorrera Falls — A25

Map of Panama Canal A26

Balboa Taking Possession of the Pacific A27

Ruins of Cathedral of Old Panama A28

Palace of Arts — A29

Gatun Locks — A30

Culebra Cut — A31

Santo Domingo Monastery's Flat Arch — A32

**1915-16** **Perf. 12**

| | | | | |
|---|---|---|---|---|
| 204 | A25 | ½c | ol grn & blk | .40 | .30 |
| 205 | A26 | 1c | dk green & blk | | |
| 206 | A27 | 2c | carmine & blk | .95 | .30 |
| a. | | 2c | ver & blk ('16) | .75 | .30 |

---

| | | | | |
|---|---|---|---|---|
| 208 | A28 | 2½c | scarlet & blk | .95 | .35 |
| 209 | A29 | 3c | violet & blk | 2.10 | .55 |
| 210 | A30 | 5c | blue & blk | 2.10 | .35 |
| a. | | | Center inverted | 800.00 | 650.00 |
| 211 | A31 | 10c | orange & blk | 10.50 | .70 |
| 212 | A32 | 20c | brown & blk | 300.00 | 3.25 |
| a. | | | Center inverted | 19.35 | 6.10 |

Nos. 204-212 (8)

For surcharges and overprints see Nos. 217, 233, E1-E2.

**1916**

Manuel J. Hurtado — A33

213 A33 8c violet & blk 9.00 4.25

For surcharge see No. 30.

S. S. Panama in Culebra Cut Aug. 11, 1914 A34

S. S. Panama in Culebra Cut Aug. 11, 1914 A35

S. S. Cristobal in Gatun Lock — A36

| | | | | |
|---|---|---|---|---|
| 214 | A34 | 12c | purple & blk | 15.00 | 5.75 |
| 215 | A35 | 15c | brt blue & blk | 10.00 | 3.50 |
| 216 | A36 | 24c | yellow brn & blk | 15.00 | 3.50 |
| | | | | 40.00 | 12.75 |

Nos. 211-216 (3)

**1918**

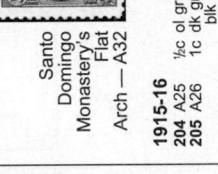

No. 208 Surcharged in Dark Blue

**1919, Aug. 15**

217 A28 2c on 2½c scar & blk .35 .35
a. Inverted surcharge 11.00 5.00
b. Double surcharge 15.00 6.00

City of Panama, 400th anniversary.

**1920**

Dry Dock at Balboa A38

Ship in Pedro Miguel Lock — A39

**Engr.**

218 A38 50c orange & blk 30.00 22.50
219 A39 1b dk violet & blk 40.00 27.50

For overprint and surcharge see Nos. C6, C37.

---

Fernández de Córdoba — A8

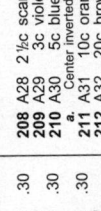

Coat of Arms — A9

Justo Arosemena A10

Manuel J. Hurtado A11

José de Obaldía A12

Tomás Herrera — A13

José de Fábrega — A14

**1906-07** **Engr.** **Perf. 11½**

| | | | | |
|---|---|---|---|---|
| 185 | A6 | ½c | orange & multi | .70 | .35 |
| 186 | A7 | 1c | dk green & blk | 1.00 | .35 |
| 187 | A8 | 2c | scarlet & blk | 1.00 | .35 |
| 188 | A9 | 2½c | red orange | 1.00 | .35 |
| 189 | A10 | 5c | blue & black | 1.75 | .65 |
| a. | | 5c | ultramarine & black | 2.00 | |
| 190 | A11 | 8c | purple & blk | 1.50 | .50 |
| 191 | A12 | 10c | violet & blk | 1.00 | .50 |
| 192 | A13 | 20c | brown & blk | 3.50 | 1.10 |
| 193 | A14 | 50c | black | 9.00 | 3.50 |
| | | | | 20.65 | 7.50 |

Nos. 185-193 (9)

Inverted centers exist of Nos. 185-187, 189, 189a, 190-193. Value, each $25. Nos. 185-193 exist imperf.

For surcharge see No. F29.

Map — A17

Balboa — A18

Córdoba — A19

Arms — A20

Obaldía A23

**1909-15**

| | | | | |
|---|---|---|---|---|
| 195 | A17 | ½c | orange ('11) | 1.00 | .30 |
| a. | | | Booklet pane of 6 | | |
| 196 | A17 | ½c | rose (15) | .70 | .60 |
| 197 | A18 | 1c | dk grn & blk | 1.00 | .50 |
| a. | | | Inverted center | 7,500. | |
| b. | | | Booklet pane of 6 | 160.00 | |

Arosemena A21

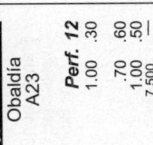

Hurtado — A52

Arms — A53

**1921, Nov. 28**

232 A52 2c dark green .65 .65

Manuel José Hurtado (1821-1887), president and folklore writer.
For overprints see Nos. 258, 301.

**No. 208 Surcharged in Black**

2 CENTESIMOS 2
1923

**1923**

233 A28 2c on 2½c scar & blk .45 .45

Surcharge varieties include wrong or omitted date, double surcharge and pair, one without surcharge. Value $2.50 each.
"Two stamps in each sheet have a bar above "CENTESIMOS.""

Bolivar — A54

Statue of Bolivar — A55

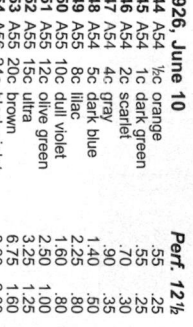

Bolivar Hall — A56

**1924, May**

**Engr.**

234 A53 ½c orange .20 .20
235 A53 1c dark green .25 .25
236 A53 2c carmine .25 .20
237 A53 2c dark blue .45 .20
238 A53 5c dark blue .60 .20
239 A53 10c dark violet .75 .40
240 A53 15c olive green .95 .40
241 A53 24c yellow brown 1.90 .60
242 A53 50c orange 4.50 1.10
243 A53 1b black 6.75 2.50
Nos. 234-243 (10) 16.55 6.00

For overprints see #277, 321A, 331-338, 352, C19-C20, C68, RA5, RA10-RA22.

**1926, June 10**

**Perf. 12½**

244 A54 ½c orange .55 .55
245 A54 1c dark green .55 .25
246 A54 2c scarlet .70 .30
247 A54 4c gray .90 .35
248 A54 5c dark blue 1.40 .50
249 A55 8c lilac 2.25 .80
250 A55 10c dull violet 1.60 .80
251 A55 12c olive green .95 .80
252 A55 15c ultra 3.25 1.25
253 A55 20c brown 6.75 1.60
254 A56 24c black 8.00 2.00
255 A56 50c black 13.50 5.00
Nos. 244-255 (12) 41.95 14.10

Bolivar Congress centennial.
For surcharges and overprints see Nos. 259-263, 266-267, 274, 298, 300, 302-303, 305-307, C33-C34, C36, C38-C39.

Lindbergh's "The Spirit of St. Louis" — A57

**1928, Jan. 9**  **Typo.**  **Rouletted 7**

256 A57 2c dk red & blk, salmon .40 .25
257 A58 5c dk blue, grn .60 .40

Visit of Colonel Charles A. Lindbergh to Central America by airplane.
No. 256 has black overprint.

Lindbergh's Airplane and Map of Panama — A58

**No. 232 Overprinted in Red**

**1928, Nov. 1**  **Perf. 12**

258 A52 2c dark green .25 .25

25th anniversary of the Republic.

**No. 247 Surcharged in Black**

**1930, Dec. 17**  **Perf. 12½, 13**

259 A54 1c on 4c gray .25 .20

Centenary of the death of Simón Bolívar, the Liberator.

**Nos. 244-246 Overprinted in Red or Blue**

**1932**  **Perf. 12½**

260 A54 ½c orange (R) .20 .20
261 A54 1c dark green (R) .35 .20
262 A54 2c scarlet (Bl) .35 .25
  a. Double overprint

**No. 252 Surcharged in Red**

HABILITADA 10 c.

263 A55 10c on 15c ultra 1.00 .50
  a. Double surcharge 55.00
Nos. 260-263 (4) 1.90 1.15

**1933**

264 A40 ½c orange .35 .20
  a. Overprint 17mm long

**No. 220 Overprinted as in 1932 in Black**
**Overprint 19mm Long**  **Perf. 12**

**1933, July 3**  **Engr.**  **Perf. 12½**

265 A60 2c dark red .50 .20

Dr. Manuel Amador Guerrero — A60

Centenary of the birth of Dr. Manuel Amador Guerrero, founder of the Republic of Panama and its first President.

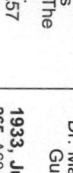

**No. 251 Surcharged in Red**

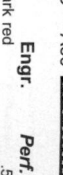

HABILITADA 10. c.

**1933**

266 A55 10c on 12c olive grn 1.25 .65

**No. 253 Overprinted in Red**

HABILITADA 20

267 A55 20c brown 2.25 1.75

José Domingo de Obaldía — A61

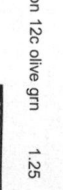

Quotation from Emerson — A63

National Institute — A64

Designs: 2c, Eusebio A. Morales, 12c, Justo A. Facio. 15c, Pablo Arosemena.

**1934, July**  **Engr.**  **Perf. 14**

268 A61 1c dark green 1.00 .50
269 A61 2c scarlet 1.00 .45
270 A63 5c dark blue .80 .80
271 A61 10c brown 3.25 1.50
272 A64 12c yellow green 6.50 2.00
273 A61 15c Prus blue 8.50 2.50
Nos. 268-273 (6) 21.50 7.75

25th anniv. of the Natl. Institute.

**Nos. 248, 227 Overprinted in Black or Red**

HABILITADA

**1935-36**

274 A54 5c dark blue .90 .30
275 A47 10c violet (R) ('36) 1.25 .60

Stamps of 1936 Overprinted in Red or Blue

4th Postal Congress of the Americas and Spain.

**1936**

**No. 225 Surcharged in Red**

276 A45 1c on 5c blue .40 .40
  a. Lines of surcharge 1½mm btwn. 6.50

**1936, Sept. 24**  **Perf. 11½**

277 A53 2c on 24c yellow brn .60 .50
  a. Double surcharge 20.00

Centenary of the birth of Pablo Arosemena, president of Panama in 1910-12. See Nos. C19-C20.

**No. 241 Surcharged in Blue**

HABILITADA B 0.01

**1936, Dec.**  **Engr.**  **Perf. 11½**

278 A67 ½c yellow org .55 .25
279 A67 1c yellow org .25 .20
280 A67 1c blue green .55 .20
281 A67 2c carmine rose .55 .20
282 A67 5c blue .80 .50
283 A67 10c dk violet 1.75 .75
284 A67 15c dk violet 1.75 .75
285 A67 20c red .75 .75
286 A67 20c black brn 3.50 2.00
287 A67 25c orange 7.75 5.00
  1b black 18.00 12.00
Nos. 278-287, C21-C26 (16) 62.70 39.90

Designs: 1c, Panama Tree. 2c, "La Pollera." 5c, Simon Bolivar. 10c, Cathedral Tower Ruins. Old Panama. 15c, Francisco Garcia y Santos. 20c, Madden Dam. Panama Canal. 25c, Columbus. 50c, Gaillard Cut. 1b, Panama Cathedral.

Ruins of Custom House, Portobelo — A67

**1937**

288 A67 ½c yellow org R .30
  a. Inverted overprint 18.00
289 A67 1c blue green (R) .45 .20
290 A67 2c carmine rose (Bl) .50 .20
291 A67 5c blue (R) .70 .25
292 A67 5c dk violet 1.75 .75
293 A67 10c dk vio (R) 5.25 3.25
294 A67 15c turq bl (R) .70 .35
295 A67 20c red (Bl) 2.00 1.25
295 A67 25c black brn (R) 2.75 1.25
296 A67 50c orange (Bl) 9.00 6.00
297 A67 1b black brn (R) 14.50 10.00
Nos. 288-297, C27-C32 (16) 84.60 54.05

Stamps of 1936 Overprinted in Red or Blue

1937-38

**1937, July**
**Stamps of 1921-26 Overprinted in Red or Blue**
**Perf. 12, 12½**

298 A54 ½c orange (R) 1.10 .80
  a. Inverted overprint 30.00

Flag of Panama — A103

Arms of Panama — A104

**Engraved; Flag on 2c Lithographed**
1947, Apr.    Perf. 12½    Unwmk.
350 A103 2c car, bl & red    .20  .20
351 A104 5c deep blue    .20  .20
Nat. Constitutional Assembly of 1945, 2nd anniv.

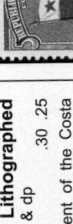

No. 241 Surcharged in Black

**1947**
352 A53 50c on 24c yel brn    2.00  1.50
a. "Habilitada"    2.00  2.00

**Perf. 12½**

Nos. C6C, C74, C75, and C87 Surcharged in Black or Carmine

353 AP5 ½c on 8c gray blk    .20  .20
a. "B/.0.0½ CORREOS" (transposed)    2.50  2.50
354 AP34 ½c on 8c dk brn & blk (C)    .20  .20
355 AP34 1c on 7c rose car    .20  .20
356 AP42 2c on 8c vio    2.80  2.30
Nos. 3b2-356 (5)

**Flag Type of 1942**

**Engr. and Litho.**

**1948**    ½c car, org, bl & dp car    .20  .20
357 A95 ½c car, org, bl & dp car    .20  .20

Monument to Firemen of Colon — A105

American-La France Fire Engine — A106

20c, Firemen & hose cart. 25c, New Central Fire Station, Colon. 50c, Maximino Walker. 1b, J. A. Ducruet.

**1948    Center in Black    Engr.**
358 A105 5c dp car    .65  .20
359 A106 10c orange    .90  .25
360 A106 20c gray bl    1.75  .40
361 A106 25c chocolate    1.75  .70
362 A105 50c purple    3.50  .70
363 A105 1b dp grm    5.00  1.50
Nos. 358-363 (6)    13.55  3.75

50th anniversary of the founding of the Colon Fire Department. For overprint see No. C125.

---

**1942    Engraved and Lithographed**
341 A94 2c rose red, dk bl & dp rose    .30  .25

1st anniv. of the settlement of the Costa Rica-Panama border dispute. See No. C73.

National Emblems — A95

Farm Girl in Work Dress — A96

Cart Laden with Sugar Cane (Inscribed "ACARRERO DE CAÑA") — A97

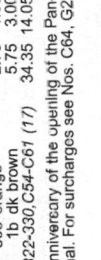

Balboa Taking Possession of the Pacific A98

San Blas Indian Woman and Child — A101

Santo Tomas Hospital A100

Golden Altar of San José — A99

Modern Highway A102

**1942    Engr.; Flag on ½c Litho.**
342 A95 ½c dl vio, bl & car    .20  .20
343 A96 1c dk green    .25  .20
344 A97 2c vermilion    .25  .20
345 A98 5c dp bl & blk    .25  .20
346 A99 10c car rose & org    .65  .50
347 A100 15c lt bl & blk    1.00  .50
348 A101 50c org red & ol blk    2.50  1.00
349 A102 1b black    3.50  1.00
Nos. 342-349 (8)    8.65  3.50

See Nos. 357, 365, 376-377, 380, 395, 409. For surcharges and overprints see Nos. 366-370, 373-375, 378-379, 381, 387-388, 396, C129-C130, RA23.

> **Catalogue values for unused stamps in this section, from this point to the end of the section, are for Never Hinged items.**

---

**1938, Dec. 7    Unwmk.**
**Engr. & Litho.    Perf. 12½**
**Center in Black; Flags in Red and Ultramarine**
317 A83 1c deep green    .35  .25
318 A83 2c carmine    .55  .30
319 A83 5c olive    .80  .30
320 A83 10c olive    1.40  .75
321 A83 15c brt ultra    1.75  1.25
Nos. 317-321,C49-C53 (10)    22.45  15.30

150th anniv. of the US Constitution.

NORMAL DE SANTIAGO JUNIO 5 1938

No. 236 Overprinted in Black

Gatun Lake A84

**1938, June 5    Perf. 12**
321A A53 2c carmine    .45  .25
b. Inverted overprint    22.50
Nos. 321A,C53A-C53B (3)    1.25  1.05

Opening of the Normal School at Santiago, Veraguas Province, June 5, 1938.

TELEGRAFOS — Liberty A93

Designs: 1c, Pedro Miguel Locks. 2c, Allegory. 5c, Culebra Cut. 10c, Ferryboat. 12c, Aerial View of Canal. 15c, Gen. William C. Gorgas. 50c, Dr. Manuel A. Guerrero. 1b, Woodrow Wilson.

**1939, Aug. 15    Engr.    Perf. 12½**
322 A84 ½c yellow    .20  .20
323 A84 1c dp blue grn    .55  .20
324 A84 2c dull rose    .65  .20
325 A84 5c dull blue    1.00  .20
326 A84 10c dk violet    1.10  .35
327 A84 12c olive green    1.10  .50
328 A84 15c ultra    1.10  .60
329 A84 50c orange    2.75  1.60
330 A84 1b dk brown    5.75  3.00
Nos. 322-330,C54-C61 (17)    34.35  14.05

25th anniversary of the opening of the Panama Canal. For surcharges see Nos. C64, G2.

CONSTITUCION 1941

Stamps of 1924 Overprinted in Black or Red

**1941, Jan. 2    Perf. 12**
331 A53 ½c orange    .35  .25
332 A53 1c dk grn (R)    .35  .30
333 A53 2c carmine    .35  .20
334 A53 5c dk bl (R)    .55  .30
335 A53 10c dk vio (R)    .80  .50
336 A53 15c ultra (R)    1.75  .65
337 A53 50c dp org    6.25  3.50
338 A53 1b blk    14.50  10.00
Nos. 331-338,C67-C71 (13)    49.90  31.20

New Panama constitution, effective 1/241.

**1942, Feb. 19    Black Overprint    Engr.**
339 A93 10c purple    1.40  1.00
**Surcharged with New Value**
340 A93 2c on 5c dk bl    1.75  .50
Nos. 339-340,C72 (3)    7.15  4.00

Flags of Panama and Costa Rica A94

---

299 A41 1c green (R)    .35  .25
a. Inverted overprint    30.00
300 A54 1c dk green (R)    .35  .35
301 A52 2c dk green (Bl)    .45  .35
302 A54 2c scarlet (Bl)    .55  .35

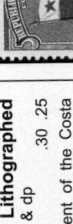

1937-38 2c

Stamps of 1921-26 Surcharged in Red

303 A54 2c on 4c gray    .70  .45
304 A46 2c on 8c ol grn    .70  .45
305 A55 2c on 8c lilac    .70  .45
306 A55 2c on 10c dl vio    .70  .50
307 A54 2c on 12c ol grn    .70  .60
308 A48 2c on 15c lt blue    .70  .60
309 A50 2c on 24c blk brn    .70  .35
310 A51 2c on 50c black    8.40  6.15
Nos. 298-310 (13)

Ricardo Arango A77

Juan A. Guizado A78

La Concordia Fire — A79

Modern Fire Fighting Equipment A80

Firemen's Monument A81

David H. Brandon A82

**1937, Nov. 25    Photo.    Wmk. 233**
**Perf. 14x14½, 14½x14**
311 A77 ½c orange red    2.10  .35
312 A78 1c green    2.10  .35
313 A79 2c red    2.10  .25
314 A80 5c brt blue    4.00  .50
315 A81 10c purple    7.25  1.25
316 A82 12c yellow grn    11.50  2.00
Nos. 311-316,C40-C42 (9)    44.80  7.05

50th anniversary of the Fire Department.

Old Panama Cathedral Tower and Statue of Liberty Enlightening the World, Flags of Panama and US — A83

## Cervantes — A107

**1948 Unwmk. Perf. 12½**

| | | | | |
|---|---|---|---|---|
| 364 | A107 | 2c car & blk | .80 | .20 |
| | | Nos. 364,C105-C106 (3) | 2.25 | .65 |

Miguel de Cervantes Saavedra, novelist, playwright and poet, 400th birth anniv.

Oxcart Type of 1942 Redrawn
Inscribed: "ACARREO DE CANA"

**1948 Perf. 12**

| | | | | |
|---|---|---|---|---|
| 365 | A97 | 2c vermilion | .60 | .20 |

No. 365 Surcharged or Overprinted in Black

**1949, May 23**

| | | | | |
|---|---|---|---|---|
| 366 | A96 | 1c on 2c ver | .25 | .20 |
| 367 | A97 | 2c vermilion | | .65 |
| a. | | Inverted overprint | | |
| | | Nos. 366-367,C108-C111 (6) | 3.00 | 3.00 |
| | | | 3.85 | 3.75 |

Incorporation of Chiriqui Province, cent.

**1949, Sept.**

| | | | | |
|---|---|---|---|---|
| 368 | A96 | 1c dk green | .25 | .20 |
| 369 | A97 | 2c ver (#365) | .45 | .20 |
| 370 | A98 | 5c blue (R) | .70 | .20 |
| | | Nos. 368-370,C114-C118 (8) | 3.85 | 4.35 |
| | | | 8.70 | |

75th anniv. of the UPU. Overprint on No. 368 is slightly different and smaller, 15½x12mm.

Francisco Javier de Luna — A108

**1949, Dec. 7 Perf. 12½**

| | | | | |
|---|---|---|---|---|
| 371 | A108 | 2c car & blk | .25 | .20 |

200th anniversary of the founding of the University of San Javier. See No. C119.

Dr. Carlos J. Finlay — A109

**1950, Jan. 12 Unwmk. Perf. 12**

| | | | | |
|---|---|---|---|---|
| 372 | A109 | 2c car & gray blk | .45 | .20 |

Issued to honor Dr. Carlos J. Finlay (1833-1915), Cuban physician and biologist who found that a mosquito transmitted yellow fever. See No. C120.

Stamps and Types of 1942-48 Issues Overprinted in Black or Red

**1950, Aug. 17**

| | | | | |
|---|---|---|---|---|
| 373 | A96 | 1c dk green | .20 | .20 |
| 374 | A95 | 2c on ½c car, org, bl & dp car (Bk) | .20 | .20 |
| 375 | A96 | 5c dp bl & blk | .30 | .20 |
| | | Nos. 373-375,C121-C125 (8) | 5.55 | 3.60 |

Gen. José de San Martin, death cent. The overprint is in four lines on No. 375.

**1950 Types of 1942**

| | | | | |
|---|---|---|---|---|
| 376 | A96 | 2c ver & blk | .20 | .20 |
| 377 | A98 | 5c blue | .25 | .20 |

No. 376 and 377 Overprinted in Green or Carmine

Nos. 376 and 377 is inscribed "ACARREO DE CANA."

**1951, Sept. 26 Engr.**

| | | | | |
|---|---|---|---|---|
| 378 | A97 | 2c ver & blk (G) | .25 | .20 |
| 379 | A98 | 5c blue (C) | .45 | .20 |

St. Jean-Baptiste de la Salle, 500th birth anniv.

The overprint exists (a) inverted on both stamps, (b) with top line omitted and second line repeated in its place. Value, each $12.50.

Altar Type of 1942

**1952 Engr. Perf. 12**

| | | | | |
|---|---|---|---|---|
| 380 | A99 | 10c pur & org | .75 | .25 |

No. 357 Surcharged "1952" and New Value in Black

**1952**

| | | | | |
|---|---|---|---|---|
| 381 | A95 | 1c on ½c multi | .20 | .20 |

Queen Isabella I and Arms — A110

**1952, Oct. 20 Center in Black Engr. Perf. 12½**

| | | | | |
|---|---|---|---|---|
| 382 | A110 | 1c green | .45 | .20 |
| 383 | A110 | 2c carmine | .45 | .20 |
| 384 | A110 | 5c dk bl | .45 | .20 |
| 385 | A110 | 10c purple | .70 | .25 |
| | | Nos. 382-385,C131-C136 (10) | 15.35 | 5.45 |

Queen Isabella I of Spain, 500th birth anniv.

No. 380 and Type of 1942 Surcharged "B/. 0.01 1953" in Black or Carmine

**1953 Perf. 12**

| | | | | |
|---|---|---|---|---|
| 387 | A99 | 1c on 10c pur & org | .20 | .20 |
| 388 | A100 | 1c on 15c black (C) | .20 | .20 |

A similar surcharge on No. 346 was privately applied.

General Remon Cantera, 1908-1955 — A115

**1955, June 1**

| | | | | |
|---|---|---|---|---|
| 399 | A115 | 3c lilac rose & blk | .20 | .20 |

See No. C153.

Tocumen International Airport A114

**1955**

| | | | | |
|---|---|---|---|---|
| 398 | A114 | ½c org brn | .45 | .20 |

For surcharges see Nos. 411-412.

---

Nos. 343, 357 and 345, Overprinted or Surcharged in Carmine or Black

**1953, Nov. 3 Engr. Perf. 12**

| | | | | |
|---|---|---|---|---|
| 389 | A111 | 2c purple | .45 | .20 |
| 390 | A112 | 5c red orange | .55 | .20 |
| 391 | A112 | 12c dp red vio | 1.25 | .95 |
| 392 | A112 | 20c slate gray | 2.25 | .25 |
| 393 | A96 | 50c org yel | 3.50 | .60 |
| 394 | A112 | 1b blue | 13.75 | 2.70 |
| | | Nos. 389-394 (6) | 5.75 | 1.25 |

Founding of the Republic of Panama, 50th anniv. See #C140-C145. For surcharge see #413.

A111

A112

**1954 Unwmk. Perf. 12**

| | | | | |
|---|---|---|---|---|
| 395 | A96 | 1c dp car rose | .20 | .20 |

Farm Girl Type of 1942 Surcharged with New Value

| | | | | |
|---|---|---|---|---|
| 396 | A96 | 3c on 1c dp car rose | .20 | .20 |

Monument to Gen. Tomas Herrera — A113

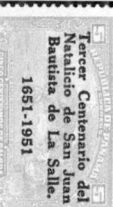

**1954 Litho. Perf. 12½**

| | | | | |
|---|---|---|---|---|
| 397 | A113 | 3c purple | .20 | .20 |
| | | Nos. 397,C148-C149 (3) | 4.45 | 2.65 |

Gen. Tomas Herrera, death cent.

2c, Baptism of the Flag, 5c; Manuel Amador Guerrero & Senora de Amador, 12c; Santos Jorge A. & Jeronimo de la Ossa, 20c, Revolutionary Junta, 50c, Old city hall, 1b, Natl. coinage.

Ferdinand de Lesseps — A117

First Excavation of Panama Canal A118

**1955, Nov. 16**

| | | | | |
|---|---|---|---|---|
| 401 | A117 | 3c rose brn, rose | .55 | .20 |
| 402 | A118 | 25c vio bl, lt bl | 2.25 | 1.40 |
| 403 | A117 | 50c vio bl, lt vio | 3.00 | 1.50 |
| | | Nos. 401-403,C155-C156 (5) | 11.15 | 5.80 |

Ferdinand de Lesseps, 150th birth anniv, French promoter, connected with building of Panama Canal. 75th anniv. of the 1st French excavations.

Imperfs exist, but were not sold at any post office.

Design: 50c, Theodore Roosevelt.

---

### Popes

A set of twelve stamps picturing various Popes exists. Value, approximately $100.

Arms of Panama City A119

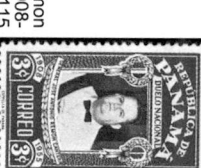

**1956, Aug. 17 Perf. 12½**

| | | | | |
|---|---|---|---|---|
| 404 | A119 | 3c green | .20 | .20 |

Sixth Inter-American Congress of Municipalities, Panama City, Aug. 14-19, 1956. For souvenir sheet see C182a.

Carlos A. Mendoza A120

**1956, Sept. 13 Litho. Unwmk.**

| | | | | |
|---|---|---|---|---|
| 405 | A120 | 10c rose red & dp grn | .35 | .20 |

Pres. Carlos A. Mendoza, birth cent.

National Archives A121

**1956, Nov. 27 Wmk. 311**

| | | | | |
|---|---|---|---|---|
| 406 | A121 | 15c shown | .70 | .20 |
| 407 | A121 | 25c Pres. Belisario Porras | | |
| | | Nos. 406-407,C183-C184 (4) | 1.00 | .50 |
| | | | 2.40 | 1.10 |

Centenary of the birth of Pres. Belisario Porras. For surcharge see No. 446.

Victor de la Guardia y Ayala and Miguel Chiari A116

**1955, Sept. 13**

| | | | | |
|---|---|---|---|---|
| 400 | A116 | 5c violet | .35 | .20 |

Centenary of province of Cocle.

PANAMA

Ruins of Old
Panama Cathedral
(1519-1671)
A139

Designs: 3c, David Cathedral. 5c, Natá
Church. 10c, Don Bosco Church. 15c,
Church of the Virgin of Carmen. 20c, Colon
Cathedral. 25c, Greek Orthodox Temple. 50c,
Cathedral of Panama. 1b, Protestant Church
of Colon.

**1962-64          Litho.          Wmk. 343**
**Buildings in Black**

| | | | | |
|---|---|---|---|---|
| 441 | A138 | 1c red & bl | .25 | .20 |
| 441A | A139 | 2c red & yel | .25 | .20 |
| 441B | A139 | 3c vio & yel | .25 | .20 |
| 441C | A139 | 5c rose & lt grn | .25 | .20 |
| 441D | A139 | 10c grn & yel | .25 | .20 |
| 441E | A139 | 10c red & bl ('64) | .35 | .25 |
| 441F | A139 | 15c ultra & lt grn | .35 | .25 |
| 441G | A139 | 20c red & pink | .55 | .35 |
| 441H | A138 | 25c grn & pink | .65 | .45 |
| 441I | A139 | 50c ultra & pink | 1.10 | .60 |
| 441J | A138 | 1b lilac & yel | 2.75 | 1.60 |
| | | Nos. 441-441J (11) | 6.90 | 4.30 |

Freedom of religion in Panama.
Issued #441E, 6/4/64; others, 7/20/62.
See #C256-C265; souvenir sheet #C264a.
For surcharges and overprints see Nos.
445A, 451, 467, C288, C296-C297, C299.

**1962, Oct. 12          Perf. 12½**
442  A140  3c carmine & gray          .20  .20

Bridge of the Americas during
Construction — A140

Opening of the Bridge of the Americas
(Thatcher Ferry Bridge), Oct. 12, 1962. See
No. C273. For surcharge see No. 445B.

Fire Brigade Exercises, Inauguration of
Aqueduct, 1906 — A141

Portraits of Fire Brigade Officials:  3c, Lt.
Col. Luis Carlos Endara P., Col. Raul Arango
N. and Major Ernesto Arosemena A. 5c, Guil-
lermo Patterson Jr., David F. de Castro, Pres.
T. Gabriel Duque, Telmo Rugliancich and
Tomas Leblanc.

**1963          Wmk. 311          Perf. 12½**

| | | | | |
|---|---|---|---|---|
| 443 | A141 | 1c emer & blk | .20 | .20 |
| 443A | A141 | 3c vio bl & blk | .30 | .20 |
| 444 | A141 | 5c mag & blk | .50 | .20 |
| | | Nos. 443-444,C279-C281 (6) | 2.70 | 1.50 |

75th anniversary (in 1962) of the Panamanian Fire Brigade.
For surcharge see No. 445C.

Nos. 440, 441A, 442, 443A and 407
Surcharged "VALE" and New Value in
Black or Red

**1963          Wmk. 343          Perf. 12½**

| | | | | |
|---|---|---|---|---|
| 445 | A137 | 4c on 3c ver & gray | .20 | .20 |
| 445A | A138 | 4c on 3c vio & yel | .20 | .20 |
| 445B | A140 | 4c on 3c car & gray | .20 | .20 |

**Wmk. 311**

| | | | | |
|---|---|---|---|---|
| 445C | A141 | 4c on 3c vio bl & blk | .20 | .20 |
| 446 | A121 | 10c on 25c dk car | | |
| | | rose & bluish | | |
| | | blk (R) | .35 | .20 |
| | | Nos. 445-446 (5) | 1.15 | 1.00 |

---

Agricultural
Products and
Cattle
A132

**1959, Jan.          Litho.          Perf. 12½          Wmk. 311**
422  A126  3c orange brown          .20  .20
          Nos. 422,C210-C212 (4)          2.00  1.45

Pope Pius XII, 1876-1958. See #C212a.

**1959, Apr. 14          Wmk. 311**

Design: 15c, Humanity looking into sun.

| | | | | |
|---|---|---|---|---|
| 423 | A127 | 3c maroon & olive | .20 | .20 |
| 424 | A127 | 15c orange & emer | .35 | .25 |
| | | Nos. 423-424,C213-C217 (7) | 3.85 | 3.10 |

10th anniv. (in 1958) of the signing of the
Universal Declaration of Human Rights.
For overprints see Nos. 425-426, C219-
C221.

Nos. 423-424
Overprinted in Dark
Blue

**1959, May 16**

| | | | | |
|---|---|---|---|---|
| 425 | A127 | 3c maroon & olive | .20 | .20 |
| 426 | A127 | 15c orange & emer | .35 | .20 |
| | | Nos. 425-426,C218-C221 (6) | 3.75 | 2.95 |

Issued to commemorate the 8th Reunion of
the Economic Commission for Latin America.

National
Institute
A129

Eusebio A.
Morales — A128

**1959, July 27          Litho.          Wmk. 311          Perf. 12½**

| | | | | |
|---|---|---|---|---|
| 427 | A128 | 3c shown | .20 | .20 |
| 428 | A128 | 13c Abel Bravo | .45 | .25 |
| 429 | A129 | 21c shown | .70 | .25 |
| | | Nos. 427-429,C222-C223 (5) | 1.75 | 1.10 |

50th anniversary, National Institute.

Soccer — A130

Fencing — A131

**1959, Oct. 26**

| | | | | |
|---|---|---|---|---|
| 430 | A130 | 1c shown | .20 | .20 |
| 431 | A130 | 3c Swimming | .35 | .20 |
| 432 | A130 | 3c Hurdling | .80 | .80 |
| | | 30c shown | 1.75 | 2.85 |
| | | Nos. 430-432,C224-C226 (6) | 6.10 | 2.85 |

3rd Pan American Games, Chicago, 8/27-
9/7/59.
For overprint and surcharge see #C289,
C349.

**1960, Sept. 22          Wmk. 343          Litho.          Perf. 12½**

| | | | | |
|---|---|---|---|---|
| 433 | A131 | 3c shown | .25 | .20 |
| 434 | A131 | 5c Soccer | .45 | .35 |
| | | Nos. 433-434,C234-C237 (6) | 4.85 | 2.35 |

17th Olympic Games, Rome, 8/25-9/11.
For surcharges & overprints see #C249-
C250, C254, C266-C270, C290, C298, C350,
RA40.

---

Pan-American Highway,
Panama — A122

**1957, Aug. 1**
408  A122  3c gray green          .20  .20
          Nos. 408,C185-C187 (4)          3.85  3.20

7th Pan-American Highway Congress.

**1957          Unwmk.          Engr.          Perf. 12**
409  A100  15c black          .50  .30

Hospital Type of 1942

Flags of 21
American
Nations — A124

Manuel Espinosa
Batista — A123

**1957, Sept. 20          Litho.          Wmk. 311**
410  A123  5c grn & ultra          .20  .20

Centenary of the birth of Manuel Espinosa
B., independence leader.

No. 398 Surcharged "1957" and New
Value in Violet or Black

**1957          Unwmk.**

| | | | | |
|---|---|---|---|---|
| 411 | A114 | 1c on ½c org brn (V) | .20 | .20 |
| 412 | A114 | 3c on ½c org brn | .20 | .20 |

No. 391 Surcharged "1958," New
Value and Dots

**1958          Engr.          Perf. 12**
413  A112  3c on 12c dp red vio          .20  .20

Organization of American States, 10th anniv.

**1958, July 10          Litho.          Perf. 12½          Unwmk.**
Center yellow & black; flags in
national colors

| | | | | |
|---|---|---|---|---|
| 414 | A124 | 1c lt gray | .20 | .20 |
| 415 | A124 | 1c org yel & emer | .20 | .20 |
| 416 | A124 | 3c red org | .20 | .20 |
| 417 | A124 | 5c ultra vio bl | .25 | .20 |
| | | Nos. 414-417,C203-C206 (8) | 4.30 | 3.40 |

Organization of American States, 10th anniv.

Brazilian
Pavilion,
Brussels
Fair — A125

3c, Argentina.  5c, Venezuela.  10c, Great
Britain.

**1958, Sept. 8          Wmk. 311**

| | | | | |
|---|---|---|---|---|
| 418 | A125 | 1c org yel & emer | .20 | .20 |
| 419 | A125 | 3c lt bl & olive | .20 | .20 |
| 420 | A125 | 5c lt brn & slate | .20 | .20 |
| 421 | A125 | 10c aqua & redsh brn | .20 | .20 |
| | | Nos. 418-421,C207-C209 (7) | 3.35 | 3.05 |

World's Fair, Brussels, Apr. 17-Oct. 19.

---

Agricultural
Products and
Cattle
A132

Children's
Hospital
A133

**1961, Mar. 3          Wmk. 311          Perf. 12½**
435  A132  3c blue green          .20  .20

Issued to publicize the second agricultural
and livestock census, Apr. 16, 1961.

**1961, May 2**
436  A133  3c greenish blue          .20  .20
          Nos. 436,C284-C286 (4)          2.30  .80

25th anniv. of the Lions Club of Panama.
See #C245-C247.

Flags of
Panama
and
Costa
Rica
A134

**1961, Oct. 2          Wmk. 343          Perf. 12½**
437  A134  3c car & bl          .20  .20

Meeting of Presidents Mario Echandi of
Costa Rica and Roberto F. Chiari of Panama
at Paso Canoa, Apr. 21, 1961. See No. C251.

Mercury and
Cogwheel — A136

Arms of
Colon — A135

**1962, Feb. 28          Litho.          Wmk. 311**
438  A135  3c car, yel & vio bl          .20  .20

3rd Central American Municipal Assembly,
Colon, May 13-17. See No. C255.

**1962, Mar. 16          Wmk. 343**
439  A136  3c red orange          .20  .20

First industrial and commercial census.

Social
Security
Hospital
A137

**1962, June 1          Perf. 12½**
440  A137  3c vermilion & gray          .20  .20

Opening of the Social Security Hospital.
For surcharge see No. 445.

San
Francisco
de la
Montana
Church,
Veraguas
A138

---

Pope Pius XII as Young
Man — A126

Manuel Espinosa
Batista — A123

UN
Headquarters
Building — A127

1964 Winter Olympics, Innsbruck — 141a

*Perf. 14x13½, 13½x14 (#447A, 447C)*

**1963, Dec. 20** **Litho.**

**447** A141a ½c Mountains .25 .20
**447A** A141a 1c Speed skating .25 .20
**447B** A141a 3c like No. 447 .55 .20
**447C** A141a 4c like No. 447A .65 .20
**447D** A141a 5c Slalom skiing .80 .25
**447E** A141a 15c like No. 447D 1.50 .60
**447F** A141a 21c like No. 447D 2.75 1.00
**447G** A141a 31c like No. 447D 4.00 1.50
*h.* Souv. sheet of 2, #447F-447G, perf. 13½x14 18.00 10.00
*Nos. 447-447G (8)* 10.75 4.15

#447D-447G are airmail. #447Gh exists imperf., with background colors switched. Value, $17.50.

Pres. Francisco J. Orlich, Costa Rica — A142

Vasco Nuñez de Balboa — A143

Flags and Presidents: 2c, Luis A. Somoza, Nicaragua. 3c, Dr. Ramon Villeda M., Honduras. 4c, Roberto F. Chiari, Panama.

*Perf. 12½x12*

**1963, Dec. 18** **Litho.** **Unwmk.**

**Portrait in Slate Green**

**448** A142 1c lt grn, red & ultra .20 .20
**448A** A142 2c lt bl, red & ultra .20 .20
**448B** A142 3c pale pink, red & ultra .20 .20
**448C** A142 4c rose, red & ultra .25 .20
*Nos. 448-448C,C292-C294 (7)* 3.15 2.50

Meeting of Central American Presidents with Pres. John F. Kennedy, San José, Mar. 18-20, 1963.

**1964, Jan. 22** **Photo.** ***Perf. 13***

**449** A143 4c green, *pale rose* .25 .20

450th anniv. of Balboa's discovery of the Pacific Ocean. See No. C295.

No. C231 Surcharged in Red: "Correos B/.0.10"

**1964** **Wmk. 311** **Litho.** ***Perf. 12½***

**450** AP74 10c on 21c lt bl .30 .20

Type of 1962 Overprinted in Red: "HABILITADA"

**1964** **Wmk. 343**

**451** A138 1b red, bl & blk 2.50 2.50

1964 Summer Olympics, Tokyo — A144

**1964, Apr.** ***Perf. 13½x14***

**452** A144 ½c shown .20 .20
**452A** A144 1c Torch bearer .20 .20

***Perf. 14x13½***

**452B** A144 5c Olympic stadium .30 .25
**452C** A144 10c like No. 452B .55 .30
**452D** A144 21c like No. 452B 1.10 .60
**452E** A144 50c like No. 452B 2.25 1.25
*f.* Souv. sheet of 1, perf. 13½x14 17.50 16.00
*Nos. 452-452E (6)* 4.60 2.80

Nos. 452B-452E are airmail. No. 452Ef exists imperf. with different colors. Value, $17.50.

Space Conquest — A145

½c, Projected Apollo spacecraft. 1c, Gemini, Agena spacecraft. 5c, Astronaut Walter M. Schirra. 10c, Astronaut L. Gordon Cooper. 21c, Schirra's Mercury capsule. 50c, Cooper's Mercury capsule.

**1964, Apr. 21** ***Perf. 14x14x13½***

**453** A145 ½c bl grn & multi .20 .20
**453A** A145 1c dk blue & multi .20 .20
**453B** A145 5c yel bis & multi .35 .35
**453C** A145 10c lil rose & multi .55 .45
**453D** A145 21c blue & multi 1.25 1.00
**453E** A145 50c violet & multi 5.75 5.00
*f.* Souvenir sheet of 1 22.50 22.50
*Nos. 453-453E (6)* 8.30 7.20

Nos. 453B-453E are airmail. No. 453Ef exists imperf. with different colors. Value, $22.50.

Aquatic Sports A146

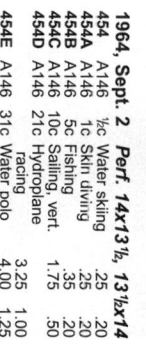

**1964, Sept. 2** ***Perf. 14x13½, 13½x14***

**454** A146 ½c Water skiing .25 .20
**454A** A146 1c Skin diving .25 .20
**454B** A146 5c Fishing .35 .20
**454C** A146 10c Sailing, vert. 1.75 .50
**454D** A146 21c Hydroplane racing 3.25 1.00
**454E** A146 31c Water polo 4.00 1.25
*f.* Souvenir sheet of 1 20.00 20.00
*Nos. 454-454E (6)* 9.85 3.35

Nos. 454B-454E are airmail.

Nos. 454-454Ef exist imperf in different colors. Value imperf, Nos. 454-454E $20. Value imperf, No. 454Ef $20.

Eleanor Roosevelt — A147

*Perf. 12x12½*

**1964, Oct. 9** **Litho.** **Unwmk.**

**455** A147 4c car & blk, *grnsh* .30 .20

Issued to honor Eleanor Roosevelt (1884-1962). See Nos. C330-C330a.

Canceled to Order

Canceled sets of new issues have been sold by the government. Postally used copies are worth more.

1964 Winter Olympics, Innsbruck — A147a

Olympic medals and winners: ½c, Women's slalom. 1c, Men's 500-meter speed skating. 2c, Four-man bobsled. 3c, Women's figure skating. 4c, Ski jumping. 5c, 15km cross country skiing. 6c, 50km cross country skiing. 7c, Women's 3000-meter speed skating. 10c, Men's figure skating. 21c, Two-man bobsled. 31c, Men's downhill skiing.

**Litho. & Embossed**

***Perf. 13½x14***

**1964, Oct. 14** **Unwmk.**

**456** A147a ½c bl grn & multi .25 .20
**456A** A147a 1c dk bl & multi .25 .20
**456B** A147a 2c brn vio & multi .25 .20
**456C** A147a 3c lil rose & multi .45 .20
**456D** A147a 4c brn lake & multi .70 .25
**456E** A147a 5c brt vio & multi .55 .30
**456F** A147a 6c grn bl & multi .70 .40
**456G** A147a 7c dp vio & multi 1.10 .65
**456H** A147a 10c emer grn & multi 1.75 1.00
**456I** A147a 21c ver & multi 2.00 1.10
**456J** A147a 31c ultra & multi 3.50 2.00
*k.* Souv. sheet of 3, #456H-456J 17.50 16.00
*Nos. 456-456J (11)* 11.50 6.50

Nos. 456E-456J are airmail.
No. 456Jk exists imperf. Value $17.50.
See Nos. 458-458J.

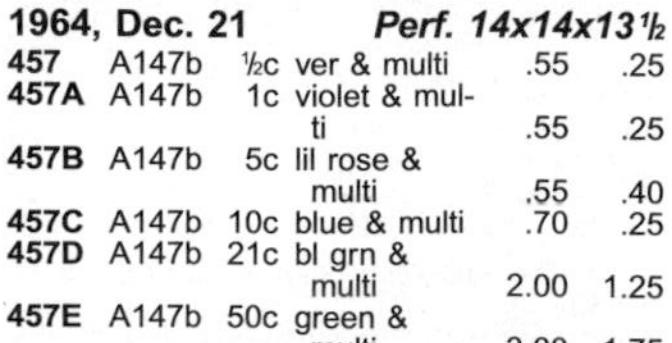

Satellites — A147b

Designs: ½c, Telstar 1. 1c, Transit 2A. 5c, OSO 1 Solar Observatory. 10c, Tiros 2 weather satellite. 21c, Weather station. 50c, Syncom 3.

**1964, Dec. 21** ***Perf. 14x14x13½***

**457** A147b ½c ver & multi .55 .25
**457A** A147b 1c violet & multi .55 .25
**457B** A147b 5c lil rose & multi .55 .40
**457C** A147b 10c blue & multi .70 .25
**457D** A147b 21c bl grn & multi 2.00 1.25
**457E** A147b 50c green & multi 3.00 1.75
*f.* Souvenir sheet of 1 17.50 16.00
*Nos. 457-457E (6)* 7.35 4.15

Nos. 457B-457E are airmail. No. 457Ef exists imperf in different colors. Value, $20.
For overprints see Nos. 489-489b.

1964 Olympic Medals Type

Summer Olympic Medals and Winners: ½c, Parallel bars. 1c, Dragon-class sailing. 2c, Individual show jumping. 3c, Two-man kayak. 4c, Team road race cycling. 5c, Individual dressage. 6c, Women's 800-meter run. 7c, 3000-meter steeplechase. 10c, Men's floor exercises. 21c, Decathlon. 31c, Men's 100-meter freestyle swimming.

**Litho. & Embossed**

**1964, Dec. 28** ***Perf. 13½x14***

**458** A147a ½c orange & multi .25 .20
**458A** A147a 1c plum & multi .25 .20
**458B** A147a 2c bl grn & multi .25 .20
**458C** A147a 3c red brn & multi .25 .20
**458D** A147a 4c lilac rose & multi .30 .20
**458E** A147a 5c dull grn & multi .60 .20
**458F** A147a 6c blue & multi .70 .25
**458G** A147a 7c dk vio & multi .85 .30
**458H** A147a 10c ver & multi 1.25 .40
**458I** A147a 21c dl vio & multi 1.90 .65
**458J** A147a 31c dk bl grn & multi 3.25 1.00
*k.* Souv. sheet of 3, #458H-458J 22.50 17.50
*Nos. 458-458J (11)* 9.85 3.80

#458E-458J are airmail. #458Jk exists imperf. Value, $25.

John F. Kennedy & Cape Kennedy — A147c

Designs: 1c, Launching of Titan II rocket, Gemini capsule. 2c, Apollo lunar module. 3c, Proposed Apollo command and service modules. 5c, Gemini capsule atop Titan II rocket. 6c, Soviet cosmonauts Komarov, Yegorov, Feoktistov. 11c, Ranger VII. 31c, Lunar surface.

Illustration reduced.

**1965, Feb. 25** **Litho.** ***Perf. 14***

**459** A147c ½c vio bl & multi .55 .20
**459A** A147c 1c blue & multi .55 .20
**459B** A147c 2c plum & multi .55 .20
**459C** A147c 3c ol grn & multi .70 .30
**459D** A147c 5c lilac rose & multi .70 .40
**459E** A147c 10c dull grn & multi 1.25 .70
**459F** A147c 11c brt vio & multi 2.00 1.10
**459G** A147c 31c green & multi 3.50 2.00
*h.* Souvenir sheet of 1 20.00 20.00
*Nos. 459-459G (8)* 9.80 5.10

Nos. 459D-459G are airmail. No. 459Gh exists imperf. in different colors. Value, $20.
For overprints see Nos. 491-491b.

Atomic Power for Peace — A147d

Designs: ½c, Nuclear powered submarine *Nautilus*. 1c, Nuclear powered ship *Savannah*. 4c, First nuclear reactor, Calderhall, England. 6c, Nuclear powered icebreaker *Lenin*. 10c, Nuclear powered observatory. 21c, Nuclear powered space vehicle.

Illustration reduced.

**1965, May 12**

**460** A147d ½c blue & multi
**460A** A147d 1c green & multi
**460B** A147d 4c red & multi
**460C** A147d 6c dl bl grn & multi
**460D** A147d 10c blue grn & multi
**460E** A147d 21c dk violet & multi
*f.* Souv. sheet of 2, #460D-460E 12.50 12.50
Set, #460-460E 6.75 3.50

Nos. 460C-460E are airmail.
Nos. 460-460Ef exists imperf in different colors. Value imperf, Nos. 460-460E $12.50. Value imperf, No. 460Ef $12.50.

## John F. Kennedy Memorial A147e

Kennedy and: ½c, UN emblem. 21c, Winston Churchill. 31c, Rocket launch at Cape Kennedy.

**1965, Aug. 23    Perf. 13½x13**

| | | | | |
|---|---|---|---|---|
| 461 | A147e | ½c multicolored | | |
| 461A | A147e | 1c multicolored | | |
| 461B | A147e | 10c + 5c, multi | | |
| 461C | A147e | 21c + 10c, multi | | |
| 461D | A147e | 31c + 15c, multi | | |
| e. | | Souv. sheet of 2, #461A, 461D, perf. 12½x12 | 12.50 | 6.00 |
| | | Set, #461-461D | 12.50 | 1.50 |

Nos. 461B-461D are airmail semipostal.
Nos. 461-461De exist imperf in different colors. Value $15.
For overprints see Nos. C367A-C367B.

## Keel-billed Toucan A148

**1965, Oct. 27    Unwmk.    Perf. 14**

Song Birds: 2c, Scarlet macaw. 3c, Red-crowned woodpecker. 4c, Blue-gray tanager.

| | | | | |
|---|---|---|---|---|
| 462 | A148 | 1c brt pink & multi | .65 | .20 |
| 462A | A148 | 2c multicolored | .65 | .20 |
| 462B | A148 | 3c brt vio & multi | 1.00 | .20 |
| 462C | A148 | 4c org yel & multi | 1.00 | .20 |
| | | Nos. 462-462C,C337-C338 (6) | 7.20 | 1.20 |

## Snapper — A149

**1965, Dec. 7    Litho.**

| | | | | |
|---|---|---|---|---|
| 463 | A149 | 1c shown | .35 | .20 |
| 463A | A149 | 2c Dorado | .35 | .20 |
| | | Nos. 463-463A,C339-C342 (6) | 3.95 | 1.40 |

## Pope Paul VI, Visit to UN — A149a

Designs: ½c, Pope on Balcony of St. Peters, Vatican City. 1c, Pope Addressing UN General Assembly. 5c, Arms of Vatican City, Panama, UN emblem. 10c, Lyndon Johnson, Pope Paul VI, Francis Cardinal Spellman. 31c, Ecumenical Council, Vatican II. 31c, Earlybird satellite.

**1966 Apr. 4    Perf. 12x12½**

| | | | | |
|---|---|---|---|---|
| 464 | A149a | ½c multicolored | .20 | .20 |
| 464A | A149a | 1c multicolored | | |
| 464B | A149a | 5c multicolored | | |
| 464C | A149a | 10c multicolored | | |
| 464D | A149a | 21c multicolored | | |
| 464E | A149a | 31c multicolored | 20.00 | 20.00 |
| f. | | Souv. sheet of 2, #464E, 464E, perf.13x13½ | 8.00 | 3.00 |
| | | Set, #464-464E | | |

Nos. 464B-464E are airmail. No. 464Ef exists imperf. with different margin color. Value $20.
For overprints see Nos. 490-490B.

## Famous Men — A149b

Designs: ½c, William Shakespeare. 10c, Dante Alighieri. 31c, Richard Wagner.

**1966, May 26    Perf. 14**

| | | | | |
|---|---|---|---|---|
| 465 | A149b | ½c multicolored | | |
| 465A | A149b | 10c multicolored | 15.00 | 15.00 |
| 465B | A149b | 31c multicolored | 6.75 | 3.25 |
| e. | | Souv. sheet of 2, #465A-465B, perf. 13½x14 | 15.00 | 3.25 |
| | | Set, #465-465B | | |

Nos. 465A-465B are airmail. No. 465Bc exists imperf. with different margin color. Value $20.

## Works by Famous Artists A149c

Paintings: ½c, Elizabeth Tucher by Durer. 10c, Madonna of the Rocky Grotto by Da Vinci. 31c, La Belle Jardiniere by Raphael.

**1966, May 26    Perf. 14**

| | | | | |
|---|---|---|---|---|
| 466 | A149c | ½c multicolored | | |
| 466A | A149c | 10c multicolored | 16.00 | 16.00 |
| 466B | A149c | 31c multicolored | 7.00 | 2.25 |
| | | Set, #466-466B | | |

Nos. 466A, 466B are airmail. No. 466Bc exists imperf. with different margin color. Value $30.

## No. 441H Surcharged

**1966, June 27    Wmk. 343    Perf. 12½**

| | | | | |
|---|---|---|---|---|
| 467 | A138 | 13c on 25c grn & pink | .40 | .25 |

The "25c" has not been obliterated.

---

**1966, July 11    Perf. 14**

| | | | | |
|---|---|---|---|---|
| 468 | A149d | ½c shown | | |
| 468A | A149d | .005b Uruguay, 1930 | | |
| | | Italy, 1934, 1930 | | |
| | | 1938 | | |
| 468B | A149d | 10c Brazil, 1958 | | |
| 468C | A149d | 10c 1962 | | |
| 468D | A149d | 21c Germany, 1954 | | |
| 468E | A149d | 21c Great Britain | 15.00 | 15.00 |
| f. | | Souv. sheet of 2, #468B, 468D | 12.50 | 11.00 |
| g. | | Souv. sheet of 2, #468, 468E, imperf. | 6.00 | 2.25 |
| | | Set, #468-465E | | |

World Cup Soccer Championships, Great Britain. Nos. 468B-468E are airmail. Nos. 468-468E exist imperf in different colors. Value, $22.50.
For overprints see Nos. 470-470g.

**1966, Aug. 12    Perf. 12x12½, 12½x12**

Italian Contributions to Space Research: ½c, Launch of Scout rocket. San Marco satellite. 1c, San Marco in orbit, horiz. 5c, Italian scientists, rocket. 10c, San Marco, at Panama, horiz. 21c, San Marco boosted into orbit, horiz.

| | | | | |
|---|---|---|---|---|
| 469 | A149e | ½c multicolored | | |
| 469A | A149e | 1c multicolored | | |
| 469B | A149e | 5c multicolored | | |
| 469C | A149e | 10c multicolored | 15.00 | 15.00 |
| 469D | A149e | 21c multicolored | 7.25 | 4.00 |
| | | Set, #469-469D | | |

Nos. 469B-469D are airmail. 
Nos. 469B-469D are airmail.

---

## Religious Paintings A149g

Paintings: ½c, Coronation of Mary. 1c, Holy Family with Angel. 2c, Adoration of the Magi. 3c, Madonna and Child. No. 471D, The Annunciation. No. 471E, The Nativity. No. 471Fh, Madonna and Child.

**1966, Oct. 24    Perf. 11**

Size of No. 471D: 32x34mm

| | | | |
|---|---|---|---|
| 471 | A149f | ½c Velazquez | |
| 471A | A149f | 1c Saraceni | |
| 471B | A149g | 2c Durer | |
| 471C | A149f | 3c Orazio | |
| 471D | A149g | 21c Rubens | |
| 471E | A149f | 21c Boticelli | |

**Souvenir Sheet    Perf. 14**

| | | | | |
|---|---|---|---|---|
| 471F | | Sheet of 2 | | |
| g. | | A149f 21c like No. 471E, black inscriptions | 12.50 | 11.00 |
| h. | | A149f 31c Mignard | 18.00 | 18.00 |
| | | Set, #471-471E | 9.00 | 1.25 |

Nos. 471D-471F exist imperf in different colors. Value imperf. Nos. 471-471E $10. Value imperf, No. 471F $17.50.

## Sir Winston Churchill, British Satellites — A149h

Churchill and: 10c, Blue Streak, NATO emblem. 31c, Europa 1, rocket engine.

**1966, Nov. 25    Perf. 12x12½**

| | | | | |
|---|---|---|---|---|
| 472 | A149h | ½c shown | | |
| 472A | A149h | 10c org & multi | | |
| 472B | A149h | 31c dk bl & multi | | |
| | | Souv. sheet of 2, #472A-472B, imperf. 13½x14 | 11.50 | 11.50 |
| | | | 6.25 | 2.00 |
| | | Set, #472-472B | | |

Nos. 472A-472B are airmail. No. 472Dc exists imperf in different colors. Value $12.50.
For overprints see Nos. 492-492B.

---

**1966, Sept. 28    Perf. 14**

| | | | | |
|---|---|---|---|---|
| 470 | A149d | ½c on #468 | | |
| 470A | A149d | .005b on #468A | | |
| 470B | A149d | 10c on #468B | | |
| 470C | A149d | 10c on #468C | | |
| 470D | A149d | 21c on #468D | | |
| 470E | A149d | 21c on #468E | | |
| f. | | on #468Ef | 30.00 | 30.00 |
| | | on #468Eg, imperf. | 13.50 | 3.75 |
| | | Set, #470-470E | | |

Nos. 470B-470E are airmail.

Nos. 468-468g Ovptd.

## John F. Kennedy, 3rd Death Anniv. — A149i

**1966, Nov. 25    Perf. 14**

| | | | | |
|---|---|---|---|---|
| 473 | A149i | ½c shown | | |
| 473A | A149i | 10c Kennedy, UN bldg. | | |
| 473B | A149i | 31c Kennedy, satellites & map | | |
| c. | | Souv. sheet of 2, #473A-473B | 18.00 | 18.00 |
| | | | 5.75 | 2.00 |
| | | Set, #473-473B | | |

No. 473A-473B are airmail. No. 473Bc exists imperf in different colors. Value $17.50.

A149f

Jules Verne (1828-1905), French Space Explorations — A149j

Designs: ½c, Earth, A-1 satellite. 1c, Verne, submarine. 5c, Earth, FR-1 satellite. 10c, Verne, telescope. 21c, Verne, capsule heading toward Moon. 31c, D-1 satellite over Earth.

**1966, Dec. 28** *Perf. 13½x14*

**474** A149j ½c bl & multi
**474A** A149j 1c bl grn & multi
**474B** A149j 5c ultra & multi
**474C** A149j 10c lil, blk & red
**474D** A149j 21c vio & multi
*f.* Souv. sheet of 2, #474C, 474D, imperf. 12.50 12.50
**474E** A149j 31c dl bl & multi
*g.* Souvenir sheet of 1 15.00 15.00
Set, #474-474E 8.50 2.00

Nos. 474B-474E are airmail.

Nos. 474-474Eg exist imperf in different colors. Value imperf. Nos. 474-474E $10. Value imperf, No. 474Eg $17.50.

Hen and Chicks A150

Domestic Animals: 3c, Rooster. 5c, Pig, horiz. 8c, Cow, horiz.

**1967, Feb. 3** **Unwmk.** *Perf. 14*

**475** A150 1c multi .20 .20
**475A** A150 3c multi .20 .20
**475B** A150 5c multi .20 .20
**475C** A150 8c multi .25 .20
*Nos. 475-475C,C353-C356 (8)* 4.10 2.30

Easter A150a

Paintings: ½c, Christ at Calvary. 1c, The Crucifixion. 5c, Pieta, horiz. 10c, Body of Christ. 21c, The Arisen Christ. No. 476E, ChristAscending into Heaven. No. 476F, Christ on the Cross. No. 476G, Madonna and Child.

**1967, Mar. 13** *Perf. 14x13½, 13½x14*

**476** A150a ½c Giambattista Tiepolo
**476A** A150a 1c Rubens
**476B** A150a 5c Sarto
**476C** A150a 10c Raphael Santi
**476D** A150a 21c Multscher
**476E** A150a 31c Grunewald
Set, #476-476E 7.50 3.00

**Souvenir Sheets**

*Perf. 12½x12x12½x13½*

**476F** A150a 31c Van der Weyden 20.00 20.00

*Imperf*

**476G** A150a 31c Rubens 20.00 20.00

Nos. 476B-476G are airmail.

1968 Summer Olympics, Mexico City — A150b

Indian Ruins at: ½c, Teotihuacan. 1c, Tajin. 5c, Xochicalco. 10c, Monte Alban. 21c, Palenque. 31c, Chichen Itza.

**1967, Apr.** *Perf. 12x12½*

**477** A150b ½c plum & multi
**477A** A150b 1c red lilac & multi
**477B** A150b 5c blue & multi
**477C** A150b 10c ver & multi
**477D** A150b 21c green bl & multi
**477E** A150b 31c green & multi
Set, #477-477E 8.00 3.00

**Souvenir Sheet**

*Perf. 12x12½x14x12½*

**477F** A150a 31c multi 18.00 18.00

Nos. 477B-477E are airmail.

New World Anhinga A151

Birds: 1c, Quetzals. 3c, Turquoise-browed motmot. 4c, Double-collared aracari, horiz. 5c, Macaw. 13c, Belted kingfisher. 50c, Hummingbird.

**1967, July 20** *Perf. 14*

**478** A151 ½c lt bl & multi 1.00 .20
**478A** A151 1c lt gray & multi 1.00 .20
**478B** A151 3c pink & multi 1.10 .20
**478C** A151 4c lt grn & multi 1.40 .20
**478D** A151 5c buff & multi 1.75 .20
**478E** A151 13c yel & multi 6.75 .75
*Nos. 478-478E (6)* 13.00 1.75

**Souvenir Sheet**

*Perf. 14½*

**478F** A151 50c Sheet of 1 15.00 15.00

No. 478A exists imperf. with blue background. Value $17.50.

Works of Famous Artists A151a

Paintings: No. 479, Maiden in the Doorway. No. 479A, Blueboy. No. 479B, The Promise of Louis XIII. No. 479C, St. George and the Dragon. No. 479D, The Blacksmith's Shop, horiz. No. 479E, St. Hieronymus. Nos. 479F-479K, Self-portraits.

*Perf. 14x13½, 13½x14*

**1967, Aug. 23**

**479** A151a 5c Rembrandt
**479A** A151a 5c Gainsborough
**479B** A151a 5c Ingres
**479C** A151a 21c Raphael
**479D** A151a 21c Velazquez
**479E** A151a 21c Durer
Set, #479-479E 7.25 2.00

**Souvenir Sheets**

***Various Compound Perfs.***

**479F** A151a 21c Gainsborough 8.50 5.00
**479G** A151a 21c Rembrandt 8.50 5.00
**479H** A151a 21c Ingres 8.50 5.00
**479I** A151a 21c Raphael 8.50 5.00
**479J** A151a 21c Velazquez 8.50 5.00
**479K** A151a 21c Durer 8.50 5.00

Nos. 479C-479K are airmail.

Red Deer, by Franz Marc — A152

Animal Paintings by Franz Marc: 3c, Tiger, vert. 5c, Monkeys. 8c, Blue Fox.

**1967, Sept. 1** *Perf. 14*

**480** A152 1c multi .20 .20
**480A** A152 3c multi .20 .20
**480B** A152 5c multi .20 .20
**480C** A152 8c multi .25 .20
*Nos. 480-480C,C357-C360 (8)* 3.65 1.90

Paintings by Goya A152a

Designs: 2c, The Water Carrier. 3c, Count Floridablanca. 4c, Senora Francisca Sebasa y Garcia. 5c, St. Bernard and St. Robert. 8c, Self-portrait. 10c, Dona Isabel Cobos de Porcel. 13c, Clothed Maja, horiz. 21c, Don Manuel Osoria de Zuniga as a child. 50c, Cardinal Luis of Bourbon and Villabriga.

**1967, Oct. 17** *Perf. 14x13½, 13½x14*

**481** A152a 2c multicolored
**481A** A152a 3c multicolored
**481B** A152a 4c multicolored
**481C** A152a 5c multicolored
**481D** A152a 8c multicolored
**481E** A152a 10c multicolored
**481F** A152a 13c multi, horiz.
**481G** A152a 21c multicolored
Set, #481-481G 9.00 2.25

**Souvenir Sheet**

**481H** A152a 50c multicolored 20.00 20.00

Nos. 481C-481H are airmail.

Life of Christ A152b

Paintings: No. 482, The Holy Family. No. 482A, Christ Washing Feet. 3c, Christ's Charge to Peter. 4c, Christ and the Money Changers in the Temple, horiz. No. 482D, Christ's Entry into Jerusalem, horiz. No. 482E, The Last Supper. No. 482Fl, Pastoral Adoration. No. 482Fm, The Holy Family. No. 482Gn, Christ with Mary and Martha. No. 482Go, Flight from Egypt. No. 482Hp, St. Thomas. No. 482Hq, The Tempest. No. 482Ir, The Transfiguration. No. 482Is, The Crucifixation. No. 482J, The Baptism of Christ, by Guido Reni. No. 482K, Christ at the Sea of Galilee, by Tintoretto, horiz.

**1968, Jan. 10** *Perf. 14x13½x13½x14*

**482** A152b 1c Michaelangelo
**482A** A152b 1c Brown
**482B** A152b 3c Rubens
**482C** A152b 4c El Greco
**482D** A152b 21c Van Dyck
**482E** A152b 21c de Juanes
Set, #482-482E 7.00 3.00

**Souvenir Sheets**

***Various Perfs.***

**482F** Sheet of 2 13.50 13.50
*l.* A152b 1c Schongauer
*m.* A152b 21c Raphael
**482G** Sheet of 2 13.50 13.50
*n.* A152b 3c Tintoretto
*o.* A152b 21c Caravaggio
**482H** Sheet of 2 13.50 13.50
*p.* A152b 21c Anonymous, 12th cent.
*q.* A152b 31c multicolored
**482I** Sheet of 2 13.50 13.50
*r.* A152b 21c Raphael
*s.* A152b 31c Montanez

*Imperf*

**482J** A152b 22c Sheet of 1 13.50 13.50
**482K** A152b 24c Sheet of 1 13.50 13.50

Nos. 482C-482K are airmail.

Butterflies — A152c

**1968, Feb. 23** *Perf. 14*

**483** A152c ½c Apodemia albinus
**483A** A152c 1c Caligo ilioneus, vert.
**483B** A152c 3c Meso semia tenera
**483C** A152c 4c Pamphila epictetus
**483D** A152c 5c Entheus peleus
**483E** A152c 13c Tmetoglene drymo
Set, #483-483E 22.00 4.00

**Souvenir Sheet**

*Perf. 14½*

**483F** A152c 50c Thymele chalco, vert. 15.00 15.00

Nos. 483D-483F are airmail.

No. 483F exists imperf with pink margin. Value $15.

10th Winter Olympics, Grenoble — A152d

**1968, May 7** *Perf. 14x13½, 13½x14*

**484** A152d ½c Emblem, vert.
**484A** A152d 1c Ski jumper
**484B** A152d 5c Skier
**484C** A152d 10c Mountain climber
**484D** A152d 21c Speed skater
**484E** A152d 31c Two-man bobsled
Set, #484-484E 7.00 1.50

**Souvenir Sheets**

*Perf. 14*

**484F** Sheet of 2 16.00 16.00
*h.* A152d 10c Emblem, snowflake
*i.* A152d 31c Figure skater
**484G** Sheet of 2 16.00 16.00
*j.* A152d 31c Biathlon
*k.* A152d 10c Skier on ski lift

Nos. 484B-484G are airmail.

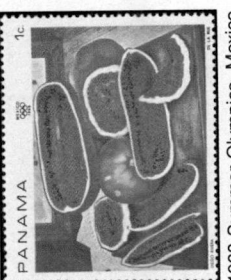

## Sailing Ships — A152e

Paintings by: ½c, Gamiero, vert. 1c, Lebreton. 3c, Van de Velde. 13c, Duncan. 50c, Anonymous Portuguese, vert.

**1968, May 7**    *Perf. 14*

| | | | |
|---|---|---|---|
| 485 | A152e | ½c multicolored | |
| 485A | A152e | 1c multicolored | |
| 485B | A152e | 3c multicolored | |
| 485C | A152e | 4c multicolored | |
| 485D | A152e | 5c multicolored | |
| 485E | A152e | 13c multicolored | |

Set, #485-485E   7.50   2.00

**Souvenir Sheet**

*Perf. 14½*

485F   A152e   50c multicolored   9.00   9.00

Nos. 485D-485E are airmail. No. 485F exists imperf. with light blue margin. Value $9.

## Tropical Fish — A152f

**1968, June 26**

| | | | |
|---|---|---|---|
| 486 | A152f | ½c | Ballistipus undulatus |
| 486A | A152f | 1c | Holacanthus ciliaris |
| 486B | A152f | 3c | Chaetodon ephippium |
| 486C | A152f | 4c | Epinephelus elongatus |
| 486D | A152f | 5c | Anisotremus virginicus |
| 486E | A152f | 13c | Ballistoides conspicillum |

Set, #486-486E   0.75   2.00

**Souvenir Sheet**

*Perf. 14½*

486F   A152f   50c   Raja texana, vert.   15.00   15.00

Nos. 486D-486F are airmail. No. 486F exists imperf. with pink margin. Value $15.

## Olympic Medals and Winners, Grenoble — A152g

Olympic Medals and Winners: 1c, Men's giant slalom. 2c, Women's downhill. 3c, Women's slalom. 4c, 5000-meter speed skating. 5c, 10,000-meter speed skating. 6c, Women's slalom. 8c, Women's 1000-meter speed skating. 13c, Women's 1500-meter speed skating. 30c, Two-man bobsled. 70c, Nordic combined.

**1968, July 30**   Litho. & Embossed   *Perf. 13½x14*

| | | | |
|---|---|---|---|
| 487 | A152g | 1c | pink & multi |
| 487A | A152g | 2c | vio & multi |
| 487B | A152g | 3c | grn & multi |
| 487C | A152g | 4c | plum & multi |
| 487D | A152g | 5c | red brn & multi |
| 487E | A152g | 6c | brt vio & multi |
| 487F | A152g | 8c | Prus bl & multi |
| 487G | A152g | 13c | bl & multi |
| 487H | A152g | 30c | rose lil & multi |

Set, #487-487H   6.75   2.00

**Souvenir Sheet**

487I   A152g   70c red & multi   18.00   18.00

Nos. 487G-487H are airmail.

**Miniature Sheet**

## Music — A152h

Paintings of Musicians, Instruments: 5c, Mandolin, by de la Hyre. 10c, Lute, by Caravaggio. 15c, Flute, by ter Brugghen. 20c, Violin, Chamber ensemble, by Tourmer. 25c, Violin, by Caravaggio. 30c, Piano, by Vermeer. 40c, Harp, by Memling.

**1968, Sept. 11**   Litho.   *Perf. 13½x14*

488   A152h   40c multicolored   10.00   2.00

| | | |
|---|---|---|
| a. | A152h | 5c multicolored |
| b. | A152h | 10c multicolored |
| c. | A152h | 15c multicolored |
| d. | A152h | 20c multicolored |
| e. | A152h | 25c multicolored |
| f. | A152h | 30c multicolored |

**Souvenir Sheet**

*Perf. 14*

488A   A152h   40c multicolored   18.00   18.00

**Nos. 457, 457E Ovptd. in Black**

**1968, Oct. 17**

| | | | | |
|---|---|---|---|---|
| 489 | A147b | ½c on No. 457 | 2.50 | .75 |
| 489A | A147f | 50c on No. 457E | 2.50 | .75 |
| b. | | Souv. sheet of 1, on No. 457EF | 22.50 | 22.50 |

Nos. 489-489A exist with gold overprint. Overprint differs on No. 489Ab.

**Nos. 464, 464D & 464Ef Ovptd. in Black or Gold**

**1968, Oct. 18**   *Perf. 12x12½*

| | | | | |
|---|---|---|---|---|
| 490 | A149a | ½c on No. 464 | 6.75 | |
| 490A | A149a | 21c on No. 464D | 6.75 | |

**Souvenir Sheet**

*Perf. 13x13½*

490B   on No. 464Ef (G)   27.50   27.50

Nos. 490A-490B are airmail. No. 490B exists imperf. with different colored border. Value same as No. 490B. Overprint differs on No. 490B.

**Nos. 459, 459G-459Gh Ovptd. in Black**

**1968, Oct. 21**   *Perf. 14*

| | | | | |
|---|---|---|---|---|
| 491 | A147c | ½c on No. 459 | 6.75 | |
| 491A | A147c | 31c on No. 459G | 6.75 | |
| b. | | on souv. sheet. No. 459Gh | 9.00 | 9.00 |

Nos. 491-491Ab are airmail.

Nos. 491-491A exist overprinted in gold. No. 491Ab exists imperf. overprinted in gold. Nos. 491-491A exist overprinted in different colors and black or gold overprints. Values, black $9, gold $90.

**Nos. 472-472A, 472Bc Overprinted in Black or Gold**

**1968, Oct. 22**   *Perf. 12x12½*

| | | | |
|---|---|---|---|
| 492 | A149h | ½c on No. 472 | 2.00 |
| 492A | A149h | 10c on No. 472A | 2.00 |

**Souvenir Sheet**

*Perf. 13½x14*

492B   on No. 472c   13.50   13.50

Nos. 492A-492B are airmail.

No. 492B exists imperf in different colors.

## Hunting on Horseback — A152i

Paintings and Tapestries: 1c, Koller. 3c, Courbet. 5c, Ischbein, the Elder. 10c, Gobelin, vert. 13c, Oudry. 30c, Rubens.

**1968, Oct. 29**   *Perf. 14*

| | | |
|---|---|---|
| 493 | A152i | 1c multicolored |
| 493A | A152i | 3c multicolored |
| 493B | A152i | 5c multicolored |
| 493C | A152i | 10c multicolored |
| 493D | A152i | 13c multicolored |
| 493E | A152i | 30c multicolored |

Set, #493-493E   5.75   2.00

Nos. 493D-493E are airmail.

**Miniature Sheet**

## Famous Race Horses — A152j

Horse Paintings: a, 5c, Lexington, by Edward Troye. b, 10c, American Eclipse, by Alvan Fisher. c, 15c, Plenipotentiary, by Abraham Cooper. d, 20c, Gimcrack, by George Stubbs. e, 25c, Flying Childers, by James Seymour. f, 30c, Eclipse, by Stubbs.

**1968, Oct. 29**   *Perf. 13½x14*

494   A152j   Sheet of 6, #a.-f.   15.00   12.50

## 1968 Summer Olympics, Mexico City — A152k

Mexican art: 1c, Watermelons, by Diego Rivera. 2c, Women, by Jose Clemente Orozco. 3c, Flower Seller, by Miguel Covarrubias, vert. 4c, Nuttall Codex, vert. 5c, Mayan statue, vert. 6c, Face sculpture, vert. 8c, Seated figure, vert. 13c, Ceramic angel, vert. 30c, Christ, by David Alfaro Siqueiros. 70c, Symbols of Summer Olympic events.

**1968, Dec. 23**   *Perf. 13½x14, 14x13½*

| | | |
|---|---|---|
| 495 | A152k | 1c multicolored |
| 495A | A152k | 2c multicolored |
| 495B | A152k | 3c multicolored |
| 495C | A152k | 4c multicolored |
| 495D | A152k | 5c multicolored |
| 495E | A152k | 6c multicolored |
| 495F | A152k | 8c multicolored |
| 495G | A152k | 13c multicolored |
| 495H | A152k | 30c multicolored |

Set, #495-495H   10.50   2.25

**Souvenir Sheet**

*Perf. 14*

495I   A152k   70c multicolored   16.00   16.00

Nos. 495G-495H are airmail.

## First Visit of Pope Paul VI to Latin America A152l

Paintings: 1c-3c, 5c-6c, Madonna and Child. 4c, The Annunciation. 7c-8c, Adoration of the Magi. 10c, Holy Family. 50c, Madonna and Child, angel.

**1969**

| | | | |
|---|---|---|---|
| 496 | A152l | 1c: | Raphael |
| 496A | A152l | 2c | Ferruzzi |
| 496B | A152l | 3c | Bellini |
| 496C | A152l | 4c | Portuguese School, 17th cent. |
| 496D | A152l | 5c | Van Dyck |
| 496E | A152l | 6c | Albani |
| 496F | A152l | 7c | Viennese master |
| 496G | A152l | 8c | Van Dyck |
| 496H | A152l | 10c | Portuguese School, 16th cent. |

Set, #496-496H   10.00   2.75

**Souvenir Sheet**

*Perf. 14½*

496I   A152l   50c Del Sarto   15.00   7.50

Nos. 496E-496I are airmail.

## Map of Americas and People — A153

**1969, Aug.**   Photo.   Wmk. 350

| | | | | |
|---|---|---|---|---|
| 500 | A153 | 5c violet blue | .20 | .20 |
| 501 | A153 | 10c bright rose lilac | .30 | .20 |

5c, Map of Panama, People and Houses, horiz.

Issued to publicize the 1970 census.

Cogwheel A154

**1969, Aug.**
502 A154 13c yel & dk bl gray .35 .20
50th anniv. of Rotary Intl. of Panama.

Cornucopia and Map of Panama A155

**1969, Oct. 10** Perf. 14½x15
Litho. Unwmk.
503 A155 10c lt bl & multi .35 .20
1st anniv. of the October 11 Revolution.

Map of Panama and Ruins — A156

Natá Church — A157

**1969-70** Perf. 14½x15, 15x14½
Litho. Unwmk.
504 A156 3c org & blk .20 .20
505 A156 5c lt bl grn ('70) .20 .20
506 A156 8c dl brn ('70) .25 .20
507 A156 13c emer & blk .35 .20
508 A156 13c vio brn ('70) .50 .25
509 A156 25c yellow ('70) .50 .50
510 A156 30c lt grn ('70) .65 .65
511 A156 30c black ('70) .80 .40
512 A156 34c org brn ('70) 1.00 .40
513 A156 38c brt bl ('70) 1.00 .40
514 A156 40c org yel ('70) 1.25 .60
515 A156 50c rose lil & blk 1.40 .70
516 A156 59c brt rose lil ('70) 2.00 .90
Nos. 504-516 (13) 10.10 5.20

Designs: 5c, Farmer, wife and mule. 13c, Hotel Continental. 20c, Church of the Virgin of Carmen. 21c, Gold altar, San José Church. 25c, Del Rey bridge. 30c, Dr. Justo Arosemena monument. 34c, Municipal Palace, Panama. 38c, Municipal Palace. 40c, French Plaza. 50c, Thatcher Ferry Bridge (Bridge of the Americas). 59c, National Theater.

For surcharges see Nos. 541, 543, 545-547, RA78-RA80.

Stadium and Discus Thrower A158

Flor del Espíritu Santo — A159

**1970, Jan. 6** Wmk. 365
Litho. Perf. 13½
517 A158 1c ultra & multi .20 .20
518 A158 2c ultra & multi .20 .20
519 A158 3c ultra & multi .20 .20
520 A158 5c ultra & multi .20 .20
521 A158 10c ultra & multi .30 .20
522 A158 13c ultra & multi .35 .20
523 A158 23c ultra & multi .40 .20
524 A159 23c pink & multi .85 .50
525 A158 30c ultra & multi .95 .75
Nos. 517-525,C368-C369 (11) 5.95 3.70
11th Central American and Caribbean Games, Feb. 28-Mar. 14.

Office of Comptroller General, 1970 — A160

**1971, Feb. 25** Litho. Wmk. 365
526 A160 3c yel & multi .20 .20
527 A160 5c brn, buff & gold .20 .20
528 A160 8c buff & gold .25 .20
529 A160 13c blk & multi .85 .80
Nos. 526-529 (4)

Designs: 5c, Alejandro Tapia and Martin Sosa, first Comptrollers, 1931-34, horiz. 8c, Comptroller's emblem. 13c, Office of Comptroller General, 1955-70, horiz.
Comptroller General's Office, 40th anniv.

Indian Alligator Design A161

**1971, Aug. 18** Wmk. 343 Perf. 13½
530 A161 8c multicolored .80 .20
SENAPI (Servicio Nacional de Artesanía y Pequeñas Industrias), 5th anniv.

Education Year Emblem, Map of Panama A162

**1971, Aug. 19** Litho.
531 A162 1b multicolored 3.50 2.50
International Education Year, 1970.
For surcharge see No. 542.

Congress Emblem — A163

**1972, Aug. 25**
532 A163 25c multicolored 1.00 .60
9th Inter-American Conference of Saving and Loan Associations, Panama City, Jan. 23-29, 1971.

UPU Headquarters, Bern — A164

Design: 30c, UPU Monument, Bern, vert.

**1971, Dec. 14** Wmk. 343 Perf. 13½
533 A164 8c multicolored .25 .20
534 A164 30c multicolored 1.00 .60
Inauguration of Universal Postal Union Headquarters, Bern, Switzerland.
For surcharge see No. RA77.

Cow, Pig and Produce A165

**1971, Dec. 15**
535 A165 3c yel, brn & blk .20 .20
3rd agricultural census.

Map of Panama and "4-S" Emblem A166

**1971, Dec. 16**
536 A166 2c multicolored .20 .20
Rural youth 4-S program.

UNICEF Emblem, Children A167

**1972, Sept. 12** Wmk. 365 Litho. Perf. 13½
537 A167 1c yel & multi .20 .20
25th anniv. (in 1971) of UNICEF. See No. C392a.
Nos. 537,C390-C392 (4) 1.90 1.20

Tropical Fruits A168

**1972, Sept. 13**
538 A168 1c shown .20 .20
539 A168 2c Isla de Noche .20 .20
540 A168 3c Carnival float, vert. .20 .20
Nos. 538-540,C393-C395 (6) 1.85 1.45
Tourist publicity.
For surcharges see Nos. RA75-RA76.

**1973, Mar. 16** Perf. 14½x15, 15x14½, 13½, Wmk. 343, Unwmkd.
541 A156 8c on 59c brt rose lil .20 .20
542 A162 10c on 1b multicolored .25 .25
543 A157 13c on 30c blk .25 .20
Nos. 541-543,C402 (4) 1.00 .95
UN Security Council Meeting, Panama City, Mar. 15-21. Surcharges differ in size and are adjusted to fit shape of stamp.

Nos. 516, 531 and 511 Surcharged in Red

José Daniel Crespo, Educator A169

**1973, June 20** Wmk. 365 Litho. Perf. 13½
544 A169 3c lt bl & multi .20 .20
Nos. 544,C403-C413 (12) 7.85 4.05
For overprints and surcharges see Nos. C414-C416, C418-C421, RA81-RA82, RA84.

Bolívar, Bridge of the Americas, Men with Flag — A170

**1974, Nov. 11** Perf. 15x14½, 14½x15
Litho. Unwmk.
545 A157 5c on 30c blk .20 .20
546 A156 10c on 59c brt rose lil .20 .20
547 A157 13c on 21c yel .20 .20
Nos. 545-547,C417-C421 (8) 1.65 1.60
Surcharge vertical on No. 546.

Nos. 511-512 and 509 Surcharged in Red

**1976, Mar. 30** Perf. 12½
Litho. Unwmk.
548 A170 6c multicolored .20 .20
Nos. 548,C426-C428 (4) 2.85 1.30
150th anniversary of Congress of Panama.

Evibacus Princeps A171

Marine life: 3c, Plitosarcus sinuosus, vert. 4c, Acanthaster planci. 7c, Starfish. 1b, Mitrax spinosissimus.

## Souvenir Sheet / National Lottery

Nicanor Villalaz, Designer of Coat of Arms — A174

PANAMA 5¢

National Lottery Building, Panama City — A175

**Perf. 12½**

**1976, Nov. 12   Litho.**
| | | | |
|---|---|---|---|
| 585 | A174 | 5c dk blue | .20 .20 |
| 586 | A175 | 6c multicolored | .20 .20 |

---

**Perf. 12½x13, 13x12½   Wmk. 377**

**1976, May 6   Litho.**
| | | | |
|---|---|---|---|
| 549 | A171 | 2c multi | .20 |
| 550 | A171 | 3c multi | .20 |
| 551 | A171 | 4c multi | .20 |
| 552 | A171 | 7c multi | .20 |

Nos. 549-552,C429-C430 (6)   3.75   1.50

**Souvenir Sheet**

*Imperf*

| | | | |
|---|---|---|---|
| 553 | A171 | 1b multi | 5.00 |

Bolivar from Bolivar Monument A172

PANAMA 20c

Bolivar and Argentine Flag A173

**Perf. 13½   Unwmk.**

**1976, June 22   Litho.**
| | | | |
|---|---|---|---|
| 554 | A172 | 20c shown | .50 |
| 555 | A173 | 20c shown | .50 |
| 556 | A173 | 20c Bolivia | .50 |
| 557 | A173 | 20c Brazil | .50 |
| 558 | A173 | 20c Chile | .50 |
| 559 | A172 | 20c Battle scene | .50 |
| 560 | A173 | 20c Colombia | .50 |
| 561 | A173 | 20c Costa Rica | .50 |
| 562 | A173 | 20c Cuba | .50 |
| 563 | A173 | 20c Ecuador | .50 |
| 564 | A173 | 20c El Salvador | .50 |
| 565 | A173 | 20c Guatemala | .50 |
| 566 | A173 | 20c Guyana | .50 |
| 567 | A173 | 20c Haiti | .50 |
| 568 | A172 | 20c Assembly | .50 |
| 569 | A173 | 20c Liberated people | .50 |
| 570 | A173 | 20c Honduras | .50 |
| 571 | A173 | 20c Jamaica | .50 |
| 572 | A173 | 20c Mexico | .50 |
| 573 | A173 | 20c Nicaragua | .50 |
| 574 | A173 | 20c Paraguay | .50 |
| 575 | A173 | 20c Peru | .50 |
| 576 | A172 | 20c Bolivar and flag | .50 |
| 577 | A173 | 20c Dominican Rep. | .50 |
| 578 | A172 | 20c Bolivar and flag bearer | .50 |
| 579 | A173 | 20c Surinam | .50 |
| 580 | A173 | 20c Trinidad-Tobago | .50 |
| 581 | A173 | 20c Uruguay | .50 |
| 582 | A173 | 20c Venezuela | .50 |
| 583 | A172 | 20c Indian delegation | .50 |
| a. | | Sheet of 30, #554-583 | 25.00 25.00 |

**Souvenir Sheet**
| | | | |
|---|---|---|---|
| 584 | | Sheet of 3 | 3.50 3.50 |
| a. | A172 | 30c Bolivar and flag bearer | .65 .65 |
| b. | A172 | 30c Monument, top | .65 |
| c. | A172 | 40c inscription tablet | .80 .80 |

Stamps of design A172 show details of Bolivar Monument, Panama City; design A173 shows head of Bolivar and flags of Latin American countries.

Amphictyonic Congress of Panama, sesquicentennial. No. 584 comes perf. and imperf. Values the same.

---

## Contadora Island

Contadora Island — A176

**Perf. 12½**

**1976, Dec. 29**
| | | | |
|---|---|---|---|
| 587 | A176 | 3c multicolored | .20 .20 |

Pres. Carter and Gen. Omar Torrijos Signing Panama Canal Treaties — A177

Design: 23c, like No. 588. Design includes Alejandro Orfila, Secretary General of OAS.

**1978, Jan.   Litho.   Perf. 12**

**Size: 90x40mm**
| | | | |
|---|---|---|---|
| 588 | A177 | 50c Strip of 3 | 8.00 8.00 |
| a. | | 3c multicolored | .20 .20 |
| b. | | 40c multicolored | 1.00 1.00 |
| c. | | 50c multicolored | 1.25 1.25 |

**Perf. 14**

**Size: 36x26mm**
| | | | |
|---|---|---|---|
| 589 | A177 | 23c multicolored | .45 .20 |

Signing of Panama Canal treaties, Washington, DC, Sept. 7, 1977.

Pres. Carter and Gen. Torrijos Signing Treaties — A178

**1978, Nov. 13   Litho.   Perf. 12**

**Size: 36x26mm**
| | | | |
|---|---|---|---|
| 590 | A178 | 5c Strip of 3 | 7.00 7.00 |
| a. | | 5c multi (30x40mm) | .25 .20 |
| b. | | 35c multi (30x40mm) | 1.00 1.00 |
| c. | | 41c multi (45x40mm) | 1.00 .40 |
| 591 | A178 | 3c Treaty signing | .20 .20 |

Signing of Panama Canal Treaties ratification documents, Panama City, Panama, June 6, 1978.

World Commerce Zone, Colon A179

REP DE PANAMA 6¢

**Perf. 12**

**1978**
| | | | |
|---|---|---|---|
| 592 | A179 | 6c multicolored | .20 .20 |

Free Zone of Colon, 30th anniversary.

---

## Melvin Jones, Lions Emblem

Melvin Jones, Lions Emblem A180

PANAMA 50c

**1978, Dec. 5**
| | | | |
|---|---|---|---|
| 593 | A180 | 50c multicolored | 1.25 .75 |

Birth centenary of Melvin Jones, founder of Lions International.

Torrijos with Children, Ship, Flag A181

PANAMA 3¢

"75," Coat of Arms A182

REPUBLICA DE PANAMA 6¢ — ANIVERSARIO 1904-1979 BANCO NACIONAL DE PANAMA

Rotary Emblem, "75" A183

PANAMA 17c — 75 A.R.O. SERVICIO

Gen. Torrijos and Pres. Carter, Flags, Ship A184

PANAMA 23¢

UPU Emblem, Globe — A185

PANAMA 35c

Boy and Girl Inside Heart — A186

ANO INTERNACIONAL DEL NIÑO — REP DE PANAMA 1979 50c

**1979, Oct. 1   Litho.   Perf. 14**
| | | | |
|---|---|---|---|
| 594 | A181 | 3c multicolored | .20 .20 |
| 595 | A182 | 6c multicolored | .20 .20 |
| 596 | A183 | 17c multicolored | .35 .30 |
| 597 | A184 | 23c multicolored | .45 .20 |
| 598 | A185 | 35c multicolored | .70 .60 |
| 599 | A186 | 50c multicolored | 1.00 .50 |

Nos. 594-599 (6)   2.90   2.00

Return of Canal Zone to Panama, Oct. 1 (3c, 23c); Natl. Bank, 75th anniv.; Rotary Intl., 75th anniv.; 18th UPU Cong., Rio, Sept.-Oct., 1979; Intl. Year of the Child.

Colon Station, St. Charles Hotel, Engraving A187

primer ferrocarril Panama 0.01

---

## Postal Headquarters / Census / Canal Centenary

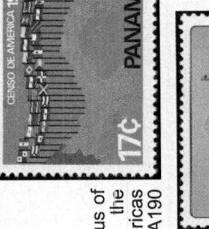

estafeta de correos, Balboa

PANAMA 0.03

Postal Headquarters, Balboa, Inauguration — A188

territorio nacional l'oct.1979 cerro ancón

PANAMA 6¢

Return of Canal Zone to Panama, Oct. 1, 1979 — A189

CENSO DE AMERICA 1980 — PANAMA 17¢

Census of the Americas A190

PANAMA 0.23

Panamanian Tourist and Convention Center Opening — A191

Banco Interamericano de Desarrollo — PANAMA 0.35

Inter-American Development Bank, 25th Anniversary — A192

EDG. LESSEPS — PANAMA 41c — CENTENARIO DEL CANAL

Canal Centenary A193

MOSCU 1980 — PANAMA 0.50

Olympic Stadium, Moscow '80 Emblem A194

**1980, June 17   Litho.   Perf. 12**
| | | | |
|---|---|---|---|
| 600 | A187 | 1c rose violet | .20 .20 |
| 601 | A188 | 3c multicolored | .20 .20 |
| 602 | A189 | 6c multicolored | .20 .20 |
| 603 | A190 | 17c multicolored | .35 .25 |
| 604 | A191 | 23c multicolored | .45 .20 |
| 605 | A192 | 35c multicolored | .70 .30 |
| 606 | A193 | 41c pale rose & blk | .90 .45 |
| 607 | A194 | 50c multicolored | 4.00 2.30 |

Nos. 600-607 (8)

Transpanamanian Railroad, 130th anniv. (1c); 22nd Summer Olympic Games, Moscow, July 19-Aug. 3 (50c).

La Salle Congregation, 75th Anniv. (1979) — A195

**1981, May 15**   Litho.   **Perf. 12**
608 A195 17c multicolored   .50 .20
Intl. Year of the Disabled.

Louis Braille — A196

**1981, May 15**   Litho.   **Perf. 12**
609 A196 23c multicolored   .45 .20

Bull's Blood — A197

Ramphocelus dimidiatus "sangre de toro"

**1981, June 26**   Litho.   **Perf. 12**
610 A197 3c shown            1.00 .20
611 A197 6c Lory, vert.      1.00 .20
612 A197 41c Hummingbird, vert.   4.25 .50
613 A197 50c Toucan          5.25 .40
Nos. 610-613 (4)            11.50 1.30

Apparition of the Virgin to St. Catherine Laboure, 150th Anniv. — A198

**1981, June 26**   Litho.   **Perf. 12**
614 A198 35c multicolored   .90 .35

Gen. Torrijos and Bayano Dam A199

**1982, Mar.**   Wmk. 311   Litho.   **Perf. 10½**
615 A199 17c multicolored   .35 .20

78th Anniv. of Independence Soldiers Institute — A200

**1981, Nov. 30**   Litho.   **Perf. 10½**
616 A200 3c multicolored   .20 .20

Gen. Omar Torrijos Herrera A201

First Death Anniv. of Gen. Omar Torrijos Herrera A201

**1982, May 14**   Litho.   **Perf. 10½**
617 A201 5c Aerial view      .20 .20
618 A201 6c Army camp        .20 .20
619 A201 50c Felipillo Engineering Works   1.00 .40
Nos. 617-619,C433-C434 (5)   3.50 1.60

Ricardo J. Alfaro (1882-1977), Statesman A202

**1982, Aug. 18**   Wmk. 382
620 A202 3c multicolored   .20 .20
See Nos. C436-C437.

1982 World Cup A203

**1982, Dec. 27**   Litho.   **Perf. 10½**
621 A203 50c Italian team   1.40 .50
See Nos. C438-C440.

Expo Comer '83, Intl. Panama Commerce Exposition, Jan. 12-16 A204

**1983**   Wmk. 382   **Perf. 10½**
622 A204 17c multicolored   .40 .30

Visit of Pope John Paul II — A205

Bank Emblem — A206

Various portraits of the Pope. 35c airmail.

**1983, Mar. 1**   **Perf. 12x11**   Litho.   Wmk. 382
623 A205 6c multicolored    .45 .20
624 A205 17c multicolored   .80 .25
625 A205 35c multicolored   1.75 .70
Nos. 623-625 (3)            3.00 1.15

**1983, Mar. 18**
626 A206 50c multicolored   1.25 .40
24th Council Meeting of Inter-American Development Bank, Mar. 21-23.

Simon Bolivar (1783-1830) A207

**1983, July 25**   Litho.   **Perf. 12**
627 A207 50c multicolored   1.25 .50

**Souvenir Sheet**
**Imperf**
628 A207 1b like 50c   2.50 .80

World Communications Year — A208

**1983, Oct. 9**   Litho.   **Perf. 14**
629 A208 30c UPAE emblem    .80 .25
630 A208 40c WCY emblem     1.00 .35
631 A208 50c UPU emblem     1.25 .45
632 A208 60c Dove in flight  1.60 .60
Nos. 629-632 (4)            4.65 1.60

633 A208 1b multicolored   2.75 2.75
No. 633 contains designs of Nos. 629-632 without denominations.

Freedom of Worship A209

**1983, Oct. 21**   Litho.   **Perf. 11½**
634 A209 3c Panama Mosque           .70 .25
635 A209 5c Bahai Temple            .20 .20
636 A209 5c St. Francis Church      .25 .20
637 A209 17c Kol Shearit Israel Synagogue   1.35 .85
Nos. 634-637 (4)

No. 637 incorrectly inscribed.

Famous Men: 3c, Richard Newman (1883-1946), educator. 5c, Cristobal Rodriguez Arosemena (1883-1943), politician. 6c, Alcibiades Arosemena (1883-1958), industrialist and financier. 35c, Cirilo Martinez (1883-1924), linguist.

Ricardo Miro (1883-1940), Poet — A210

**1983, Nov. 8**   Litho.   **Perf. 14**
638 A210 3c multicolored    .20 .20
639 A210 5c multicolored    .20 .20
640 A210 6c multicolored    .20 .20
641 A210 35c multicolored   .20 .20
642 A210 35c multicolored   1.00 .35
Nos. 638-642 (5)            1.80 1.15

The Prophet, by Alfredo Sinclair — A211

#643, Village House, by Juan Manuel Cedeno. #644, Large Nude, by Manuel Chong Neto. 3c, On Another Occasion, by Spiros Vamvas. 6c, Punta Chame Landscape, by Guillermo Trujillo. 28c, Neon Light, by Alfredo Sinclair. 41c, Highland Girls, by Al Sprague. 1b, Bright Morning, by Ignacio Mallol Pibernal.

**1983, Dec. 12**   **Perf. 12**
643 A211 1c multicolored    .20 .20
644 A211 1c multicolored    .20 .20
645 A211 3c multicolored    .20 .20
646 A211 3c multicolored    .20 .20
647 A211 28c multicolored   .70 .25
648 A211 35c multicolored   .90 .35
649 A211 41c multicolored   1.00 .40
650 A211 1b multicolored    2.75 1.00
Nos. 643-647, 650 horiz.
Nos. 643-650 (8)            6.15 2.80

Double Cup, Indian Period A212

Pottery: 40c, Raised dish, Tonosi period. 50c, Jug with face, Canazas period, vert. 60c, Bowl, Conte, vert.

**1984, Jan. 16**   Litho.   **Perf. 12**
651 A212 30c multicolored   1.10 .20
652 A212 40c multicolored   1.25 .30
653 A212 50c multicolored   1.60 .40
654 A212 60c multicolored   2.00 .95
Nos. 651-654 (4)            5.95 1.45

**Souvenir Sheet**
**Imperf**
655 A212 1b like 30c   2.75 2.75

Pre-Olympics — A213

**1984, June**   Litho.   **Perf. 14**
656 A213 19c Baseball            .90 .35
657 A213 19c Basketball, vert.   .90 .35
658 A213 19c Boxing              .90 .35
659 A213 19c Swimming, vert.     .90 .35
Nos. 656-659 (4)                3.60 1.40

Roberto Duran — A214

Paintings — A215

1984 Olympic Games — A214a

**Perf. 14**
**1984, June 14 Litho.**
660 A214 26c multicolored .60 .25

1st Panamanian to hold 3 boxing championships.

**1984 Litho. Perf. 14**
660A A214a 6c Shooting .20 .20
660B A214a 30c Weight lifting .90 .30
660C A214a 37c Wrestling 1.00 .40
660D A214a 1b Long jump 3.00 1.50
Nos. 660A-660D (4) 5.10 2.40

**Souvenir Sheet**
660E A214a 1b Running 3.00 3.00

Nos. 660B-660D are airmail. No. 660E contains one 45x45x64mm stamp.

**1984, Sept. 17 Litho. Perf. 14**

Paintings by Panamanian artists: 1c, Woman Thinking, by Manuel Chong Neto. 3c, The Child, by Alfredo Sinclair. 6c, A Day in the Life of Rumalda, by Brooke Alfaro. 30c, Highlands People, by Al Sprague. 37c, Intermission during the Dance, by Roberto Sprague. 44c, Punta Chame Forest, by Guillermo Trujillo. 50c, The Blue Plaza, by Juan Manuel Cedeno. 1b, Ira, by Spiros Vamvas.

661 A215 1c multi .20 .20
662 A215 3c multi, horiz. .20 .20
663 A215 6c multi, horiz. .20 .20
664 A215 30c multi .90 .30
665 A215 37c multi, horiz. 1.00 .40
666 A215 44c multi, horiz. 1.50 .55
667 A215 50c multi, horiz. 1.50 .55
668 A215 1b multi, horiz. 3.00 1.50
Nos. 661-668 (8) 8.85 3.85

Postal Sovereignty — A216
**Perf. 12**
**1984, Oct. 1 Litho.**
669 A216 19c Gen. Torrijos, canal .80 .30

Fauna A217
**Perf. 14**
**1984, Dec. 5 Engr.**
670 A217 3c Manatee .20 .20
671 A217 30c Gato negro 1.40 .50
672 A217 44c Tigrillo congo 2.00 .75
673 A217 50c Puerco de monte 2.25 .90
Nos. 670-673 (4) 5.85 2.35

**Souvenir Sheet**
674 A217 1b Perezoso de tres dedos, vert. 5.00 5.00

Nos. 671-673 are airmail.

Coins A218
**Perf. 11x12 Wmk. 353**
**1985, Jan. 17 Litho.**
675 A218 3c 1935 1c .20 .20
676 A218 3c 1904 10c .20 .20
677 A218 5c 1916 5c .25 .25
678 A218 30c 1904 50c 1.25 .50


679 A218 37c 1962 half-balboa 1.60 .60
680 A218 44c 1953 balboa 2.00 .70
Nos. 675-680 (6) 5.50 2.40
Nos. 678-680 are airmail.

**Contadora Type of 1985**
**Souvenir Sheet**
**Perf. 13½x13**
**1985, Oct. 1 Litho. Unwmk.**
680A AP108 1b Dove, flags, map 4.50 4.50

Cargo Ship in Lock A219
**Perf. 14**
**1985, Oct. 16**
681 A219 19c multicolored 1.10 .30
Panama Canal, 70th anniv. (1984).

UN 40th Anniv. A220
**Perf. 14**
**1986, Jan. 17 Litho.**
682 A220 23c multicolored .80 .35

Intl. Youth Year A221
**1986, Jan. 17**
683 A221 30c multicolored .90 .35

Waiting Her Turn, by Al Sprague — A222

Oil paintings: 5c, Aerobics, by Guillermo Trujillo (b. 1927). 19c, Cardboard House, by Eduardo Augustine (b. 1954). 30c, Door to the Homeland, by Juan Manuel Cedeno (b. 1914). 36c, Supper for Three, by Brooke Alfaro (b. 1949). 42c, Tenderness, by Alfredo Sinclair (b. 1915). 50c, Woman and Character, by Manuel Chong Neto (b. 1927). 60c, Calla lillies, by Maigualida de Diaz (b. 1950).

**1986, Jan. 21**
684 A222 3c multicolored .20 .20
685 A222 5c multicolored .20 .20
686 A222 19c multicolored .80 .30
687 A222 30c multicolored 1.25 .55
688 A222 36c multicolored 1.50 .65
689 A222 42c multicolored 1.75 .65
690 A222 50c multicolored 2.25 .80
691 A222 60c multicolored 2.75 1.00
Nos. 684-691 (8) 10.70 4.20

Miss Universe Pageant A223
**Perf. 12**
**1986, July 7 Litho.**
692 A223 23c Atlapa Center .80 .50
693 A223 60c Emblem, vert. 2.10 .80

Halley's Comet A224
30c, Old Panama Cathedral tower, vert.
**Perf. 13½**
**1986, Oct. 30 Litho.**
694 A224 23c multicolored .80 .35
695 A224 30c multicolored 1.00 .35
Size: 75x86mm
**Imperf**
695A A224 1b multicolored 4.00

A225 A226

1986 World Cup Soccer Championships, Mexico: Illustrations from Soccer History, by Sandoval and Meron.

**1986, Oct. 30**
696 A225 23c Argentina, winner .90 .35
697 A225 30c Fed. Rep. of Germany, 2nd 1.00 .35
698 A225 37c Argentina, Germany .25 1.00
Nos. 696-698 (3) 3.15 1.30

**Souvenir Sheet**
698A A225 1b Argentina, diff. 3.25

**1986, Nov. 21**
699 A226 20c shown .65 .25
700 A226 23c Montage of events .70 .35

15th Central American and Caribbean Games, Dominican Republic.

Christmas A227
**1986, Dec. 18**
701 A227 23c shown .70 .30
702 A227 36c Green tree 1.10 .55
703 A227 42c Silver tree 1.25 .55
Nos. 701-703 (3) 3.05 1.35

Intl. Peace Year — A228


Tropical Carnival, Feb.-Mar. A229

**Perf. 13½**
**1986, Dec. 30 Litho.**
704 A228 8c multicolored .25 .20
705 A228 19c multicolored .65 .25

**Perf. 13½**
**1987, Jan. 27 Litho.**
706 A229 20c Diablito Sucio mask .65 .30
707 A229 35c Sun 1.25 .50
Size: 74x84mm
**Imperf**
708 A229 1b like 35c 3.25 1.50
Nos. 706-708 (3) 5.15 2.30

1st Panamanian Eye Bank — A230
**Perf. 14**
**1987, Feb. 17 Litho.**
709 A230 37c multicolored 1.25 .75

Panama Lions Club, 50th Anniv. (in 1985). Dated 1986.

Flowering Plants — A231
Birds A232

**1987, Mar. 5**
710 A231 3c Brownea macrophylla .20 .20
711 A232 5c Thraupis episcopus .20 .20
712 A231 8c Solandra grandiflora .25 .20
713 A232 15c Tyrannus melancholicus .55 .25
714 A231 19c Barleria micans .70 .35
715 A232 23c Pelecanus occidentalis .80 .35
716 A231 30c Cordia dentata 1.10 .45
717 A232 36c Columba cayennensis 1.50 .55
Nos. 710-717 (8) 5.30 2.55

Dated 1986.

Monument and Octavio Mendez Pereira, Founder A233
**Perf. 14**
**1987, Mar. 26 Litho.**
718 A233 19c multicolored .65 .30

University of Panama, 50th anniv. (in 1985). Stamp dated "1986."

**1987, Apr. 9**    **Perf. 13½**
UNFAO, 40th Anniv. (in 1985)
A234

719 A234 10c blk, pale ol & yel grn .25 .20
720 A234 45c blk, dk grn & yel grn 1.50 .70

Nat'l Theater, 75th Anniv. A235

**1987, Apr. 28**    **Perf. 14**
721 A235 19c multicolored .55 .50
722 A235 30c shown .90 .50
723 A235 37c multicolored 1.00 .60
724 A235 60c multicolored 1.75 1.00
   Nos. 721-724 (4) 4.20 2.40
Baroque composers: 19c, Schutz (1585-1672), 37c, Bach. 60c, Handel. Nos. 721, 723-724 vert.

A236

**1987, May 13**    **Litho.**    **Perf. 14**
725 A236 23c multicolored .70 .45
Inter-American Development Bank, 25th anniv.

A237

**1987, Nov. 28**    **Litho.**    **Perf. 14**
726 A237 25c Fire wagon, 1887, and modern ladder truck 1.25 .40
727 A237 35c Fireman carrying victim 1.75 .60
Panama Fire Brigade, cent.

A238

A239

---

**1987, Dec. 11**
728 A238 15c Wrestling, horiz. .70 .20
729 A238 23c Tennis 1.00 .40
730 A238 30c Swimming, horiz. 1.25 .70
731 A238 41c Basketball 1.75 .70
732 A238 60c Cycling 2.50 1.00
   Nos. 728-732 (5) 7.20 2.85

**Souvenir Sheet**
733 A238 1b Weight lifting 3.75 3.75
10th Pan American Games, Indianapolis. For surcharges see Nos. 813, 817.

Int'l Year of Shelter for the Homeless A240

**1987, Dec. 17**
734 A239 22c multicolored .70 .35
735 A239 35c multicolored 1.10 .60
736 A239 37c multicolored 1.10 .60
   Nos. 734-736 (3) 2.90 1.55
Christmas (Religious paintings): 22c, Adoration of the Magi, by Albrecht Nentz (d. 1479). 35c, Virgin Adored by Angels, by Matthias Grunewald (d. 1528). 37c, The Virgin and Child, by Konrad Witz (c. 1400-1445).

**1987, Dec. 29**    **Perf. 14**
737 A240 45c multicolored 1.25 .75
738 A240 50c multicolored 1.40 .80
45c, by A. Sinclair. 50c, Woman, boy, girl, shack, housing in perspective by A. Pulido.
For surcharge see No. 814.

Reforestation Campaign A241

**1988, Jan. 14**
739 A241 35c dull grn & yel grn 1.10 .55
740 A241 40c red & pink 1.25 .70
741 A241 45c brn & lemon 1.50 .75
   Nos. 739-741 (3) 3.85 2.00
Dated 1987. For surcharge see No. 816.

Say No to Drugs A242

**1988, Jan. 14**    **Litho.**    **Perf. 14½x14**
742 A242 10c org lil rose .25 .20
743 A242 17c yel grn & lil rose .65 .30
744 A242 25c pink & sky blue 1.00 .40
   Nos. 742-744 (3) 1.90 .90

Child Survival Campaign A243

**1988, Feb. 29**    **Litho.**    **Perf. 14**
745 A243 20c Breast-feeding .65 .35
746 A243 31c Universal immunization 1.10 .60
747 A243 45c Growth and development, vert. 1.75 .90
   Nos. 745-747 (3) 3.50 1.85
For surcharge see No. 816A.

Fish A244

---

**1988, Mar. 14**
748 A244 7c Myripristis jacobus .25 .20
749 A244 35c Pomacanthus paru 1.10 .60
750 A244 60c Holocanthus tricolor 1.00 .60
751 A244 1b Equetus punctatus 2.00 1.00
   Nos. 748-751 (4) 6.85 3.40
   or 3.50 1.60
The 7c actually shows the Holocanthus tricolor, the 60c the Myripristis jacobus. For surcharge see No. 819.

Girl Guides, 75th Anniv. — A245

**1988, Apr. 14**
752 A245 35c multicolored 1.00 .60

Christmas A246

**1988, Dec. 29**    **Litho.**    **Perf. 12**
753 A246 17c multicolored .65 .30
754 A246 45c multicolored 1.50 .75
See No. C446.

St. John Bosco (1815-1888) A247

**1989, Jan. 31**
755 A247 10c Portrait .25 .20
756 A247 20c Minor Basilica .65 .35
Paintings: 17c, Virgin and Gift-givers. 45c, Virgin of the Rosary and St. Dominic.

1988 Summer Olympics, Seoul A248

**1989, Mar. 17**    **Litho.**    **Perf. 12**
757 A248 17c Running .55 .30
758 A248 25c Wrestling .80 .40
759 A248 60c Weight lifting 2.00 1.00
   Nos. 757-759 (3) 3.35 1.70

**Souvenir Sheet**
760 A248 1b Swimming, vert. 3.75 3.75
See No. C447.
Athletes and medals.

A249

---

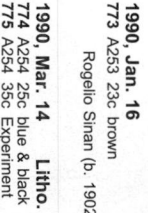
A250 AMERICA

**1989, Apr. 12**    **Litho.**    **Perf. 12**
761 A249 40c red, blk & blue 1.25 .75
762 A249 1b Emergency and rescue services 3.25 1.75
Int'l Red Cross and Red Crescent organizations, 125th anniv.

**1989, Oct. 12**    **Litho.**    **Perf. 12**
767 A250 20c Monolith of Barriles 1.25 .50
768 A250 35c Vessel 2.75 1.25
America Issue: Pre-Columbian artifacts.

French Revolution, Bicent. A251

**1989, Nov. 14**    **Perf. 13½**
769 A251 25c multicolored 1.10 .50
   Nos. 769,C450-C451 (3) 4.95 2.00

Christmas — A252

**1989, Dec. 1**    **Litho.**    **Perf. 12**
770 A252 17c multicolored .70 .30
771 A252 35c multicolored 1.50 .85
772 A252 45c multicolored 2.00 .85
   Nos. 770-772 (3) 4.20 1.80
17c, Holy family in Panamanian costume. 35c, Creche. 45c, Holy family, gift givers.

A253

**1990, Jan. 16**    **Litho.**
773 A253 23c brown .70 .45
Rogelio Sinan (b. 1902), writer.

A254

**1990, Mar. 14**    **Litho.**    **Perf. 13½**
774 A254 25c blue & black 1.00 .45
775 A254 35c Experiment 1.25 .60
776 A254 45c Beakers, test tubes, books 1.60 .75
   Nos. 774-776 (3) 3.85 1.80
Dr. Guillermo Patterson, Jr., chemist.

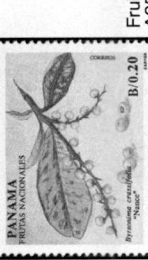

Fruits
A255

**1990, May 15**   *Perf. 13½*
777 A255 20c Byrsonima crassifolia   .55 .35
778 A255 35c Bactris gasipaes   1.10 .60
779 A255 40c Anacardium occidentale   1.50 .70
Nos. 777-779 (3)   3.15 1.65

B/0.35

Tortoises
A256

**1990, July 17**
780 A256 35c Pseudemys scripta   1.40 .60
781 A256 45c Lepidochelys olivacea   1.75 .75
782 A256 60c Geochelone carbonaria   2.50 1.00
Nos. 780-782 (3)   5.65 2.35

For surcharges see Nos. 815, 818.

AMERICA — PANAMA B/0.20

Native American
A257

**1990, Oct. 12**
783 A257 20c shown   1.40 .40
784 A257 35c Native, vert   2.25 .85

AMERICA — PANAMA B/0.35

Discovery of Isthmus of Panama, 490th Anniv. — A258

**1991, Nov. 19**   *Litho.*   *Perf. 12*
785 A258 35c multicolored   1.40 .65

450c

St. Ignatius of Loyola, 500th Birth Anniv. — A259

**1991, Nov. 29**
786 A259 20c multicolored   .65 .30
*a.* Tete beche pair   1.25 1.25

Society of Jesus, 450th anniv.

"Navidad 1991" — PANAMA B/0.35

Christmas
A260

**1991, Dec. 2**
787 A260 35c Luke 2:14   1.10 .65
788 A260 35c Nativity scene   1.10 .65
*a.* Pair, #787-788   2.25 2.25

---

10c

Social Security Administration, 50th Anniv. — A261

Design: No. 790, Dr. Arnulfo Arias Madrid (1901-1988), Constitution of Panama, 1941.

**1991**   *Litho.*   *Perf. 12*
789 A261 10c multicolored   .35 .20
790 A261 10c multicolored   .35 .20

Women's citizenship rights, 50th anniv. (No. 790).

EFIGENIA DE NUESTRO SEÑOR JESUCRISTO — PANAMA 10c

Epiphany — A262

**1992, Feb. 5**   *Litho.*   *Perf. 12*
791 A262 10c multicolored   .25 .20
*a.* Tete beche pair   .50 .30

PROYECTO — PANAMA CORREOS B/0.05

New Life Housing Project — A263

**1992, Feb. 17**
792 A263 5c multicolored   .25 .20
*a.* Tete beche pair   .50 .50

RICA Y PANAMA-1941-1991 — 50 ANIVERSARIO DE LA SOLUCION LIMITROFE ENTRE COSTA — B/0.20

Border Treaty Between Panama and Costa Rica, 50th Anniv. — A264

a, 20c, Hands clasped. b, 40c, Map. c, 50c, Pres. Rafael A. Calderon, Costa Rica, Pres. Arnulfo Arias Madrid, Panama.

**1992, Feb. 20**
793 A264 Strip of 3, #a.-c.   3.25 3.25

PANAMA 40c CORREOS — SALVEMOS LA CAPA DE OZONO

Causes of Hole in Ozone Layer — A265

**1992, Feb. 24**
794 A265 40c multicolored   1.75 .70
*a.* Tete beche pair   3.50 3.50

---

10c PANAMA CORREOS — X^A Versión

Expocomer '92, Intl. Commercial Exposition — A266

**1992, Mar. 11**
795 A266 10c multicolored   .25 .20

Dona Margot Fonteyn — 35c

Margot Fonteyn (1919-91), ballerina: a, 35c. Wearing dress. b, 45c, In costume.

**1992, Mar. 12**
796 A267   Pair, #a.-b.   4.50 4.50

PANAMA B/0.10 — 100 A NATALICIO DE MARIA OLIMPIA DE OBALDIA POETISA, 1891-1991

Maria Olimpia de Obaldia (1891-1985), poet.

**1992, June 22**   *Litho.*   *Perf. 12*
797 A268 10c multicolored   .25 .20
*a.* Tete beche pair   .50 .30

PANAMA 10c

1992 Summer Olympics, Barcelona — A269

**1992, June 24**   *Litho.*   *Perf. 12*
798 A269 10c multicolored   .25 .20
*a.* Tete beche pair   .50 .35

PANAMA B/0.20

Zion Baptist Church, Bocas del Toro, 1892 — A270

Baptist Church in Panama, Cent.

**1992, Oct. 1**   *Litho.*   *Perf. 12*
799 A270 20c multicolored   .65 .35
*a.* Tete beche pair   1.25 1.25

---

AMERICA — PANAMA B/0.20

Discovery of America, 500th Anniv. — A271

a, 20c, Columbus' fleet. b, 35c, Coming ashore.

**1992, Oct. 12**   *Perf. 12*
800 A271 Pair, #a.-b.   3.00 3.00

FAUNA PANAMEÑA EN VIAS DE EXTINCION — PANAMA B/0.05

801 A272 Strip of 4, #a.-d.   6.25 6.25
Endangered Wildlife: a, 5c, Agouti paca. b, 10c, Harpia harpyja. c, 15c, Folio onca. d, 20c, Iguana iguana.

**1992, Sept. 23**

EXPO-SEVILLA '92 — PANAMA CORREOS B/0.10

Expo '92, Seville.

**1992, Dec. 21**   *Litho.*
802 A273 10c multicolored   .25 .20
*a.* Tete beche pair   .50 .30

1992: AÑO DE LA SALUD DE LOS TRABAJADORES — PANAMA B/0.15

Worker's Health Year.

**1992, Dec. 21**
803 A274 15c multicolored   .45 .30
*a.* Tete beche pair   1.00 1.00

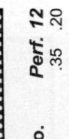
UNIFICACION EUROPEA — PANAMA B/0.10

Unification of Europe.

**1992, Dec. 21**   *Litho.*   *Perf. 12*
804 A275 10c multi + label   .35 .20

**Christmas — A276**

a, 20c, Angel announcing birth of Christ. b, 35c, Mary and Joseph approaching city gate.

**1992, Dec. 21**
805 A276 Pair, #a.-b.   1.75   1.75

Evangelism in America, 500th Anniv. (in 1992) — A277

**1993, Apr. 13**   **Litho.**   **Perf. 12**
806 A277 10c multicolored   .25   .20
  a. Tete beche pair   .50   .30

**1993, May 10**
807 A278 5c multicolored   .20   .20
  a. Tete beche pair   .50   .50

Natl. Day for the Disabled A278

Dr. Jose de la Cruz Herrera (1876-1961), Humanitarian A279

**1993, May 26**   **Litho.**   **Perf. 12**
808 A279 5c multicolored   .25   .20
  a. Tete beche pair   .50   .50

1992 Intl. Conference on Nutrition, Rome — A280

**1993, June 26**   **Litho.**   **Perf. 12**
809 A280 10c multicolored   .20   .20
  a. Tete beche pair   .50   .50

Columbus' Exploration of the Isthmus of Panama, 490th Anniv. — A281

**1994, June 2**   **Litho.**   **Perf. 12**
810 A281 50c multicolored   1.50   3.00
  a. Tete beche pair + 2 labels   3.00
Dated 1993.

Greek Community in Panama, 50th Anniv. A282

**1995, Feb. 16**   **Litho.**   **Perf. 12**
811 A282 20c multicolored   .45   .30

Designs: 20c, Greek influences in Panama, Panamanian flag, vert. No. 812a, Parthenon. No. 812b, Greek Orthodox Church.

**Souvenir Sheet**
812 A282 75c Sheet of 2, #a.-b.   4.00   2.50

Nos. 729, 731, 737, 741, 747, 750, 781-782 Surcharged

**1995**
813 A238 20c on 23c #729   .75   .35
814 A240 25c on 45c #737   .90   .45
815 A256 30c on 45c #781   1.00   .50
816 A241 35c on 45c #741   1.00   .50
816A A243 35c on 45c No. 747   .60
817 A238 40c on 41c #731   .65   .65
818 A256 50c on 60c #782   1.50   .70
819 A244 1b on 60c No. 750   2.25   1.00

Issued: #813-815, 816A-818, 819, 4/3; #816, 5/6.

Nos. 813-819 (8)   3.75   2.00
    12.50   6.20

**Perfs., Etc. as Before**

First Settlement of Panama, 475th Anniv. (in 1994) — A283

Designs: 15c, Horse and wagon crossing bridge. 20c, Arms of first Panama City, vert. 25c, Model of an original cathedral. 35c, Ruins of cathedral, vert.

**1996, Oct. 11**   **Litho.**   **Perf. 14**
820 A283 15c beige, black & brown   .45   .30
821 A283 20c multicolored   .65   .40
822 A283 25c beige, black & brown   .80   .45
823 A283 35c beige, black & brown   1.25   .70

Nos. 820-823 (4)   3.15   1.85

Endangered Species — A284

**1996, Oct. 18**   **Litho.**   **Perf. 14**
824 A284 20c Tinamus major   1.00   .40

Mammals A285

a, Nasua narica. b, Tamandua mexicana. c, Cyclopes didactylus. d, Felis concolor.

**1996, Oct. 18**
825 A285 25c Block of 4, #a.-d.   3.50   3.50

**1996, Oct. 22**   **Litho.**   **Perf. 14**
826 A286 40c multicolored   1.25   .75
Kiwanis Clubs of Panama, 25th anniv. (in 1993).
A286

**1996, Oct. 17**
827 A287 5b multicolored   15.00   9.50
Rotary Clubs of Panama, 75th anniv. (in 1994).
A287

**1996, Oct. 21**
828 A288 45c multicolored   1.40   .85
UN, 50th anniv. (in 1995).
A288

**1996, Oct. 21**
829 A289 35c multicolored   1.10   .70
Design: Ferdinand de Lesseps (1805-94), builder of Suez Canal.
A289

Andrés Bello Covenant, 25th Anniv. (in 1995) — A290

**1996, Oct. 23**
830 A290 35c multicolored   1.25   .70

Radiology, Cent. (in 1995) — A292

**1996, Oct. 23**   **Litho.**   **Perf. 14**
833 A292 1b multicolored   3.00   1.90

832 A291 1.50b multicolored   5.00   5.00
Patterns depicting four seasons: 1.50b, Invierno, Primavera, Verano, Otono.

Chinese Presence in Panama A291

**1996, June 10**   **Imperf.**
Size: 80x68mm

831 A291 60c multicolored   2.25   1.10
**1996, June 10**   **Litho.**   **Perf. 14½**

University of Panama, 60th Anniv. A293

**1996, Oct. 14**   **Litho.**   **Perf. 14**
834 A293 40c multicolored   1.25   .75

Christmas — A295

**1996, Oct. 24**   **Litho.**   **Perf. 14**
836 A295 35c multicolored   1.10   .70

Mail Train A296

**1996, Dec. 10**   **Litho.**   **Perf. 14**
837 A296 30c multicolored   1.60   .50
America issue.

Universal Congress of the Panama Canal A297

**1997, Sept. 9**   **Litho.**   **Perf. 14½x14**
838 A297 45c Pair, #a.-b.   2.75   2.75
No. 838: a, Pedro Miguel Locks. b, Miraflores Double Locks. 1.50b, Gatún Locks.
839 A297 1.50b multicolored   5.00   5.00
**Imperf**
Perforated portion of No. 839 is 76x31mm.

Torrijos-Carter Panama Canal Treaties, 20th Anniv. — A298

Designs: 20c, Painting, "Panama, More Than a Canal," by C. Gonzalez P. 30c, "Curtain of Our Flag," by A. Siever M. vert. 45c, "Huellas Perpetuas," by R. Marinez R. 50c, 1.50b, #588.

**1997, Sept. 9**    *Perf. 14*
840 A298 20c multicolored .65 .50
841 A298 30c multicolored 1.00 .75
842 A298 45c multicolored 1.40 1.10
843 A298 50c multicolored 1.60 1.25
      4.65 3.60
*Nos. 840-843 (4)* 5.00 5.00

     *Imperf*
844 A298 1.50b multicolored 5.00 5.00
Perforated portion of No. 844 is 114x50mm.

India's Independence, 50th Anniv. — A299

**1997, Oct. 2**    *Perf. 14x14½*
845 A299 50c Mahatma Gandhi 1.60 1.25

World Wildlife Fund: a, Heading right. b, Looking left. c, One in distance, one up close. d, With mouth wide open.

**1997, Nov. 18**    *Perf. 14½x14*
846 A300 25c Block of 4, #a.-d. 4.75 4.75

Crocodylus Acutus A300

**1997, Nov. 18**    *Perf. 14x14½*
847 A301 35c multicolored 1.75 .70

Christmas A301

**1997, Nov. 21**    *Litho.*
848 A302 20c multicolored .65 .50

Colon Fire Brigade, Cent. A302

---

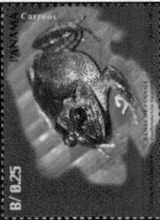

Frogs A303

Designs: a, Eleutherodactylus biporcatus. b, Hyla colymba. c, Hyla rufitela. d, Nelsonphryne aterrima.

**1997, Nov. 21**
849 A303 25c Block of 4, #a.-d. 3.25 3.25

National Costumes A304

**1997, Nov. 25**
850 A304 20c multicolored .65 .50
America issue.

Colon Chamber of Commerce, Agriculture and Industry, 85th Anniv. — A305

**1997, Nov. 27**    *Perf. 14x14½*
851 A305 1b multicolored 3.25 2.50

Justo Arosemena, Lawyer, Politician, Death Cent. (in 1996) — A306

**1997, Nov. 27**
852 A306 40c multicolored 1.25 1.00

Panamanian Aviation Co., 50th Anniv. — A307

Designs: a, Douglas DC-3. b, Martin-404. c, Avro HS-748. d, Electra L-168. e, Boeing B727-100. f, Boeing B737-200 Advanced.

**1997, Dec. 3**    *Perf. 14½x14*
853 A307 35c Block of 6, #a.-f. 6.75 6.75

Jerusalem, 3000th Anniv. — A308

20c, Jewish people at the Wailing Wall. 25c, Christians being led in worship at Church of the Holy Sepulchre. 60c, Muslims at the Dome of the Rock.

---

**1997, Dec. 29**    *Perf. 14x14½*
854 A308 20c multicolored .65 .50
855 A308 25c multicolored .80 .65
856 A308 60c multicolored 1.75 1.50
      3.20 2.65
*Nos. 854-856 (3)* 5.00 5.00

     *Imperf*
857 A308 1.50b like #854-856 5.00 5.00
Perforated portion of No. 857 is 90x40mm.

Tourism A309

10c, Old center of town, Panama City. 20c, Soberania Park. 25c, Panama Canal. 35c, Panama Bay. 40c, Fort St. Jerónimo. 45c, Rafting on Chagres River. 60c, Beach, Kuna Yana Region.

**1998, July 7**    *Perf. 14x14½, 14½x14*    *Litho.*
858 A309 10c multi, vert .25 .20
859 A309 20c multi, vert .65 .40
860 A309 25c multi .80 .50
861 A309 35c multi 1.10 .70
862 A309 40c multi 1.25 .80
863 A309 45c multi 1.50 .90
864 A309 60c multi 2.00 1.25
      7.55 4.75
*Nos. 858-864 (7)*

Organization of American States (OAS), 50th Anniv. — A310

**1998, Apr. 30**    *Perf. 14½x14*
865 A310 40c multicolored 1.25 1.00

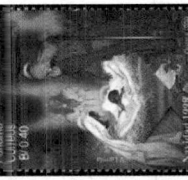

Colon Free Trade Zone, 50th Anniv. — A311

**1998, Feb. 2**    *Perf. 14½x14½*    *Litho.*    *Unwmk.*
866 A311 15c multi .70 .40

Protection of the Harpy Eagle — A312

Contest-winning art by students: a, Luis Melillo. b, Jorvisis Jiménez. c, Samuel Castro. d, Jorge Ramos.

**1998, Jan. 20**
867 A312 20c Block of 4, #a.-d. 4.50 4.50

---

Universal Declaration of Human Rights, 50th Anniv. — A313

**1998, Feb. 10**
868 A313 15c multi .70 .30

Panamanian Assoc. of Business Executives, 40th Anniv. — A314

**1998, Jan. 28**    *Perf. 14½x14*
869 A314 50c multi 2.25 1.00

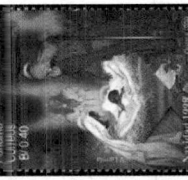

Beetles A315

Designs: a, Platyphora haroldi. b, Stilodes leoparda. c, Stilodes fuscollineata. d, Platyphora boucardi.

**1998**
870 A315 30c Block of 4, #a.-d. 6.75 6.75

Christmas A316

**1998, Jan. 14**    *Litho.*    *Perf. 14x14½*
871 A316 40c multi 1.40 .80

Panama Pavilion, Expo '98, Lisbon A317

**1998**    *Litho.*    *Perf. 14½x14*
872 A317 45c multi 1.60 .90

Panama Canal, 85th Anniv. (in 1999) — A318

No. 873: a, Canal builders and crane on train trestle. b, Partially built structures, construction equipment.

**2000, Sept. 7**    *Litho.*    *Perf. 14½x14*
873 A318 40c Pair, #a-b 4.00 4.00

     **Souvenir Sheet**
874 A318 1.50b Valley 7.50 7.50
No. 874 contains one label.

**2000, Sept. 7**    *Perf. 14½x14*
875-878 A319   Set of 4    6.25   3.50

Reversión of Papers of Panama Canal to Panama (in 1999)
A319

Various ships. Denominations: 20c, 35c, 40c, 45c.

Pres. Arnulfo Arias Madrid (1901-88) — A320

No. 879: a, 20c, Arias as medical doctor, with people. b, 20c, Arias giving speech, holding glasses. No. 880, a, 30c, Arias in 1941, 1951 and 1969, Panamanian flag. b, 30c, Arias giving speech, crowd. Illustration reduced.

**2001, Aug. 14**   *Litho.*   *Perf. 13x13½*
879-880   A320    *Horiz. pairs, #a-b*
     4.50   4.50

Christmas — A321

**2001, Dec. 4**    *Litho.*    *Perf. 14½x14½*
881 A321   35c multi      .80   .70
Dated 2000.

**2001, Dec. 4**
882 A322   20c multi      .90   .50
Dated 2000.

Holy Year (in 2000)
A322

18th UPAEP Congress (in 2000)
A323

**2001, Dec. 4**
883 A323   5b multi      22.50   12.50

Dreaming of the Future — A324

Children's art by: No. 884, 20c, I. Guerra. No. 885, 20c, D. Ortega. No. 886, 20c, horiz: a, J. Aguilar P. b, S. Sittón.

**2001, Dec. 4**   A324   Set of 2
884-885    *Perf. 14½x14½*
886 A324   75c Souvenir Sheet
   Sheet of 2, #a-b    1.75   1.00
Dated 2000.

Architecture of the 1990s — A325

Designs: No. 887, 35c, Los Defines Condominium, by Edwin Brown. No. 888, 35c, Banco General Tower, by Carlos Medina. No. 889, horiz: a, Building with round sides, by Ricardo Moreno. b, Building with three peaked roofs, by Moreno.

**2001, Dec. 4**   A325   Set of 2
887-888    *Perf. 14½x14½*
889 A325   75c Souvenir Sheet
   Sheet of 2, #a-b    6.75   6.75
Dated 2000.

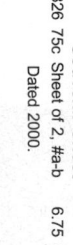

Orchids
A326

Designs: No. 890, 35c, Cattleya dowiana. No. 891, 35c, Psychopsis krameriana. No. 892: a, Peristeria clata. b, Miltoniopsis roezlii.

**2001, Dec. 4**    *Perf. 14½x14*
890-891   A326   Set of 2
892 A326   75c Sheet of 2, #a-b
     3.25   1.75
     6.75   6.75

Souvenir Sheet

San Fernando Hospital, 50th Anniv. (in 1999)
A327

**2001, Dec. 4**   *Litho.*   *Perf. 14½x14*
893 A327   20c multi      .90   .50
Dated 2000.

Pres. Mireya Moscoso
A328

**2002, Mar. 25**
894 A328   35c multi      1.60   .90
Dated 2000.

Independence From Spain, 180th Anniv. — A329

**2002, Apr. 30**    *Perf. 13½x13*
895-896 A329   Set of 2    1.25   .70
Dated 2001.

Discovery of the Isthmus, 500th Anniv. A330

Designs: 50c, Natives, ship, 5b, Native, European, crucifix, ships.

**2002, Apr. 30**    *Perf. 13½x13½*
897-898 A330   Set of 2    21.00   12.00
Dated 2001. No. 898 is airmail.

America Issue — UNESCO World Heritage — A331

No. 899, 15c: a, Castle of San Lorenzo. b, Salón Bolivar, Panama City. No. 900, 15c: a, Cathedral, Panama City. b, Portobelo Fortifications.

**2002, May 30**   *Perf. 13½x13, 13x13½*
899-900 A331    *Horiz. Pairs, #a-b*
     14.50   8.00
Dated 2001. No. 900 is airmail.

Murals by Roberto Lewis in Palacio de las Garzas
A332

No. 901: a, Heron, flagbearer and natives. b, Battle with natives. c, Woman, horse, men, fruit. d, Heron, woman in dress, woman picking fruit.

**2002, June 19**    *Perf. 13½x13½*
901    *Horiz. strip of 4, a.-d.*
   A332: 5c Any single    1.00   1.00
     .25   .20
Dated 2001.

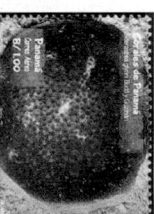

Corals
A333

No. 902: a, Montastraea annularis. b, Pavona chiriquiensis. c, Siderastrea glymi. 2b, Pocillopora.

**2002, June 28**
902 A333   10c Horiz. pair. #a-b
903 A333   1b multi
904 A333   2b multi
   Nos. 902-904 (3)
     .70   .40
     4.00   2.00
     8.00   4.00
     12.70   6.40
Dated 2001. Nos. 903-904 are airmail.

Butterflies and Caterpillars
A334

Details from mural by Roberto Lewis: No. 895, 15c, "180" at L. No. 896, 15c, "180" at R. Morpho peleides. 2b, Tarchon felderi.

**2002 ?**    *Litho.*    *Perf. 13x13½*
905-908 A334   Set of 4    14.50   8.00
Dated 2001. Nos. 907-908 are airmail.

Designs: No. 905, 10c, Ophioderes materna. No. 906, 10c, Rhuda focula. 1b, Ophioderes Amfitheatrismo Amfitre UPAYAP2002.

Christmas 2002
A335

**2003, June 16**    *Litho.*    *Perf. 14*
909 A335   15c multi      .30   .30
Dated 2002.

America Issue — Youth, Education and Literacy
A336

**2003, June 23**
910 A336   45c multi      1.40   .90
Dated 2002.

Clara González de Behringer, First Female Lawyer in Panama — A337

**2003, July 10**    *Perf. 13½x13*
911 A337   30c multi      1.00   .60
Dated 2002.

Colón, 150th Anniv. (in 2002) — A338

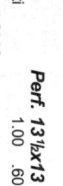

**2003, July 17**
912 A338   15c multi      .55   .30
Dated 2002.

Luis C. Russell (b. 1902), Jazz Musician
A339

**2003, Aug. 6**    *Perf. 14*
913 A339   10c multi      .35   .20
Dated 2002.

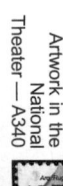

Artwork in the National Theater — A340

Designs: No. 914, 5c, Statue of Erato (holding lyre). No. 915, 5c, Statue of Melpomene (holding mask). 50c, Decoration on front of theater box, horiz. 60c, Theater facade and painting, horiz.

*Perf. 13½x13, 14 (50c), 13x13½ (60c)*

**2003, Aug. 12**
914-917 A340    Set of 4    4.00  2.40
Dated 2002. Nos. 916-917 are airmail.

St. Josemaría Escrivá de Balaguer (1902-75) — A341

*Perf. 14*
**2003, Aug. 13**    .35    .20
918 A341 10c multi
Dated 2002.

Republic of Panama, Cent. A342

Designs: 5c, National arms. 10c, First national flag. No. 921a, Manuel Amador Guerrero, first president. No. 921b, Pres. Mireya Moscoso. 25c, Declaration of Independence. 30c, Sterculia apetala. No. 923b, Peristeria elata. 35c, Revolutionary junta. 45c, Flag, Constitution of 1904, Constituent Delegates.

*Perf. 12*
**2003, Nov. 26**                    Litho.
919 A342  5c multi                .20    .20
920 A342  10c multi               .20    .20
921 A342  15c Horiz. pair, #a-b   .60    .60
922 A342  25c multi               .50    .50
923 A342  30c Horiz. pair, #a-b   .70    .70
924 A342  35c multi               .70    .70
925 A342  45c multi               .90    .90
                                 4.35  4.35
*Nos. 919-925 (7)*
Nos. 924-925 are airmail.

Republic of Panama, Cent. Type of 2003 Redrawn

*Perf. 12*
**2003, Nov. 26**                Litho.
925A    Souvenir booklet          3.50
 b.    Booklet pane, #f-g
 c.    Booklet pane, #h-i         .60
 d.    Booklet pane, #j, m        1.25
 e.    Booklet pane, #l           1.25
 f.    A342 5c Similar to #919    .20    .20
 g.    A342 10c Similar to #920   .20    .20
 h.    A342 15c Similar to #921a  .30    .30
 i.    A342 15c Similar to #921b  .30    .30
 j.    A342 25c Similar to #922   .50    .50
 k.    A342 30c Similar to #923a  .60    .60
 l.    A342 30c Similar to #923b  .60    .60
 m.    A342 35c Similar to #924   .70    .70

The text "1903 — Centenario de lar República de Panamá - 2003" is inscribed across the se-tenant pair stamps in each booklet pane. Other differences in text are also on each of Nos. 925Af-925Am.

Christmas A343

*Perf. 12*
**2003, Nov. 28**                  .20    .20
926 A343 10c multi

Panamá Correos
B/ 0.05

*Perf. 14½x14*    .70    .70
Panama, 2003 Iberoamerican Cultural Capital — A344

**2003, Dec. 4**
927 A344 5c multi

Pres. Mireya Moscoso A345

**2004, Aug. 10**  Litho.
928 A345 35c multi
Compare with Type A328. Dated 2000.

---

**AIR POST STAMPS**

CORREO AEREO 25
VEINTICINCO CENTESIMOS

Special Delivery Stamp No. E3 Surcharged in Dark Blue

*Perf. 12½*
**1929, Feb. 8**          Unwmk.
C1 SD1 25c on 10c org    1.00   .80
 a. Inverted surcharge  22.50  22.50

CORREO AEREO

Nos. C3-E4 Overprinted in Blue

**1929**
C2 SD1 10c orange         .50    .50
 a. Inverted overprint  16.00  14.00
 b. Double overprint    16.00  14.00

Some specialists claim the red overprint is a proof impression.

**With Additional Surcharge of New Value**
C3 SD1 15c on 10c org     .50    .50
C4 SD1 25c on 20c dk brn  1.10   1.00
 a. Double surcharge    14.00  14.00
  *Nos. C2-C4 (3)*        2.10   2.00

No. E3 Surcharged in Blue

CORREO AEREO 5 CENTESIMOS

*Perf. 12½*
**1930, Jan. 25**          .50    .50
C5 SD1 5c on 10c org

No. 219 Overprinted in Red

*Perf. 12*
**1930, Feb. 28**
C6 A39 1b dk vio & blk   16.00  12.50

---

AP5

Airplane over Map of Panama — AP6

*Perf. 12*                     Engr.
**1930-41**
C6A AP5  5c blue (41)     .20    .20
C6B AP5  7c rose car (41) .25    .20
C6C AP5  8c gray blk (41) .25    .20
C7  AP5  15c dp grn       .30    .20
C8  AP5  20c red          .35    .20
C9  AP5  25c deep blue    .65    .65
                         2.00   1.65
*Nos. C6A-C9 (6)*
See No. C112.

For surcharges and overprints see Nos. 353, C16-C16A, C53B, C69, C82-C83, C109, C122, C124.

*Perf. 12½*
**1930, Aug. 4**
C10 AP6  5c ultra         .20    .20
C11 AP6  10c orange       .30    .20
C12 AP6  30c rp vio       5.50   .50
C13 AP6  50c dp red       1.50   .50
C14 AP6  1b black        5.50   4.00
                        13.00   8.90
*Nos. C10-C14 (5)*

For surcharge and overprints see Nos. C53A, C70-C71, C115.

Amphibian AP7

*Typo.*
**1931, Nov. 24**   Without Gum
C15 AP7 5c deep blue     .80    1.00
 a. gray blue           .50    1.00
 b. Horiz. pair, imperf. btwn. 50.00

For the start of regular airmail service between Panama City and the western provinces, but valid only on Nov. 28-29 on mail carried by hydroplane "3 Noviembre." Many sheets have a papermaker's watermark "DOLPHIN BOND" in double-lined capitals.

HABILITADA
20 c.

No. C9 Surcharged in Red 19mm long

*Perf. 12*
**1932, Dec. 14**    Surcharge 17mm long
C16 AP5 20c on 25c dp bl   6.25   .70
C16A AP5 20c on 25c dp bl 200.00 2.50

CORREO AEREO 20

Special Delivery Stamp No. E4 Overprinted in Red or Black

**1934**
C17  SD1 20c dk brn       1.00    .50
C17A SD1 20c dk brn (Bk) 100.00 55.00

CORREO AEREO 10 CENTESIMOS

Surcharged In Black

**1935, June**
C18 SD1 10c on 20c dk brn  .80    .50

---

AEREO
1936-1936
5 CORREO CENTESIMOS

**Same Surcharge with Small "10"**
C18A SD1 10c on 20c dk brn  40.00  5.00
 b. Horiz. pair, imperf. vert. 100.00

Nos. 234 and 242 Surcharged in Blue

AEREO
5

**1936, Sept. 24**
C19 A53  5c on ½c org   400.00 250.00
C20 A53  5c on 50c org    1.00    .80
 a. Double surcharge    60.00  60.00

Centenary of the birth of President Pablo Arosemena.
It is claimed that No. C19 was not regularly issued. Counterfeits of No. C19 exist.

Urracá Monument AP8

REPUBLICA DE PANAMA
AEREO
100

Human Genius Uniting the Oceans AP9

20c, Panama City. 30c, Balboa Monument. 50c, Pedro Miguel Locks. 1b, Palace of Justice.

*Perf. 12*                Engr.
**1930, Mar. 1**
C21 AP8  5c blue          .65    .40
C22 AP9  10c yel org      .85    .60
C23 AP9  20c red          3.00   1.50
C24 AP8  30c dk vio       3.50   2.50
C25 AP9  50c car rose     8.00   5.75
C26 AP9  1b black         9.50   6.00
                        25.50  16.75
*Nos. C21-C26 (6)*

4th Postal Congress of the Americas and Spain.

Nos. C21-C26 Overprinted in Red or Blue

REPUBLICA DE PANAMA
AEREO
10

P.R.D

*Perf. 12*               Engr.
**1937, Mar. 29**
C27 AP8  5c blue (R)              .55    .30
 a. Inverted overprint          35.00
C28 AP9  10c yel org (Bl)        .75    .45
C29 AP9  20c red (Bl)            1.75   1.00
 a. Double overprint            35.00
C30 AP8  30c dk vio (R)          4.50   3.25
C31 AP8  50c car rose (Bl)      18.00  13.00
 a. Double overprint           120.00
C32 AP9  1b black (R)           22.50  13.00
                               48.55  31.00
*Nos. C27-C32 (6)*

CORREO AEREO 5c
15

Regular Stamps of 1921-26 Surcharged in Red

*Perf. 12, 12½*
**1937, June 30**
C33 A55  5c on 15c ultra   .75    .75
C34 A55  5c on 20c brn     .75    .75
C35 A47  5c on 10c vio     1.75   1.50

## Regular Stamps of 1920-26 Surcharged in Red

| | | | | |
|---|---|---|---|---|
| C36 | A56 | 5c on 24c blk vio | .75 | .75 |
| C37 | A39 | 5c on 1b dk vio & blk | .75 | .50 |
| C38 | A56 | 10c on 50c blk | 2.25 | 2.00 |
| a. | | Inverted surcharge | 20.00 | |

### No. 248 Overprinted in Red

| | | | | |
|---|---|---|---|---|
| C39 | A54 | 5c dark blue | .75 | .75 |
| a. | | Double overprint | 18.00 | |
| | | Nos. C33-C39 (7) | 7.75 | 7.00 |

**1937, Nov. 25  Perf. 14x14½  Photo.  Wmk. 233**

| | | | | |
|---|---|---|---|---|
| C40 | AP14 | 5c blue | 3.50 | .60 |
| C41 | AP15 | 10c orange | 1.00 | 1.00 |
| C42 | AP16 | 20c crimson | 7.25 | .75 |
| | | Nos. C40-C42 (3) | 15.75 | 2.35 |

50th anniversary of the Fire Department.

Fire Dept. Badge AP14

Florencio Arosemena AP15

José Gabriel Duque — AP16

---

**US Constitution Type**

**1938, Dec. 7  Unwmk.  Perf. 12½**

**Engr. & Litho. Center in Black, Flags in Red and Ultramarine**

| | | | | |
|---|---|---|---|---|
| C49 | A83 | 7c gray | .35 | .25 |
| C50 | A83 | 8c brt ultra | .35 | .35 |
| C51 | A83 | 15c red brn | .70 | .45 |
| C52 | A83 | 50c orange | 8.00 | 5.75 |
| C53 | A83 | 1b black | 17.60 | 12.55 |
| | | Nos. C49-C53 (5) | | |

### Nos. C12 and C7 Surcharged in Red

**1938, June 5  Perf. 12½, 12**

| | | | | |
|---|---|---|---|---|
| C53A | A6 | 7c on 30c dp vio | .40 | .40 |
| a. | | Double surcharge | 18.00 | |
| d. | | Inverted surcharge | 27.50 | |
| C53B | AP5 | 8c on 15c dp grn | .40 | .40 |
| d. | | Inverted surcharge | 22.50 | |

Opening of the Normal School at Santiago, Veraguas Province, June 5, 1938. The 8c surcharge has no bars.

Belisario Porras AP23

**1939, Aug. 15  Engr.**

| | | | | |
|---|---|---|---|---|
| C54 | AP23 | 1c dl rose | .40 | .20 |
| C55 | AP23 | 2c dp bl grn | .40 | .20 |
| C56 | AP23 | 5c indigo | .65 | .20 |
| C57 | AP23 | 10c dk vio | .70 | .20 |
| C58 | AP23 | 15c ultra | 1.60 | .35 |
| C59 | AP23 | 20c rose pink | 1.40 | 1.40 |
| C60 | AP23 | 50c dk brn | 5.00 | .70 |
| C61 | AP23 | 1b dp brn | 7.25 | 3.75 |
| | | Nos. C54-C61 (8) | 20.00 | 7.00 |

Opening of Panama Canal, 25th anniv. For surcharges see Nos. C63, C65, G1, G3.

Designs: 2c, William Howard Taft. 5c, Pedro J. Sosa. 10c, Lucien Bonaparte Wise. 15c, Armando Reclus. 20c, Gen. George W. Goethals. 50c, Ferdinand de Lesseps. 1b, Theodore Roosevelt.

**1941, Jan. 2  Perf. 12½, 12**

| | | | | |
|---|---|---|---|---|
| C67 | SD1 (e) | 7c on 10c org | 1.00 | 1.00 |
| C68 | A53 (f) | 15c on 24c yel brn (R) | | |
| C69 | AP5 (g) | 20c rose | 2.50 | 2.50 |
| C70 | AP6 (g) | 50c deep red | 4.00 | 4.00 |
| C71 | AP6 (g) | 1b black (R) | 13.50 | 10.00 |
| | | Nos. C67-C71 (5) | 25.00 | 19.50 |

New constitution of Panama which became effective Jan. 2, 1941.

**1940, Aug. 12**

| | | | | |
|---|---|---|---|---|
| C63 | AP23 a | 5c on 15c lt ultra | .25 | .25 |
| C64 | A84 | 7c on 15c ultra | 40.00 | 40.00 |
| C65 | AP23 c | 7c on 20c rose pink | .40 | .25 |
| C66 | AP31 | 8c on 15c blue | 1.45 | 1.00 |
| | | Nos. C63-C66 (4) | | |

Stamps of 1924-30 Overprinted in Black or Red:

d

e

f

g

c

b

a

---

**1938, Feb. 2  Perf. 14x14½, 14½x14**

| | | | | |
|---|---|---|---|---|
| C43 | AP17 | 1c shown | 2.25 | .20 |
| C44 | AP18 | 2c shown | 2.25 | .20 |
| C45 | AP18 | 7c Swimming | 3.00 | .20 |
| C46 | AP18 | 8c Boxing | 3.00 | .25 |
| C47 | AP17 | 15c Soccer | 5.00 | 1.25 |
| a. | | Souv. sheet of 5, #C43-C47 | 18.00 | 18.00 |
| b. | | As "a," No. C43 omitted | 2,500. | |
| | | Nos. C43-C47 (5) | 15.50 | 2.15 |

4th Central American Caribbean Games.

Basketball — AP17

Baseball AP18

**1940, Apr. 15  Unwmk.**

| | | | | |
|---|---|---|---|---|
| C62 | AP31 | 15c blue | .40 | .35 |

Pan American Union, 50th anniversary. For surcharge see No. C66.

Stamps of 1939-40 Surcharged in Black:

Flags of the 21 American Republics AP31

a

b

**1942, Feb. 19  Engr.**

| | | | | |
|---|---|---|---|---|
| C72 | AP32 | 20c chestnut brn | 4.00 | 2.50 |

**Black Overprint  Perf. 12**

Liberty — AP32

**Costa Rica - Panama Type**

**1942, Apr. 25  Engr. & Litho.  Unwmk.**

| | | | | |
|---|---|---|---|---|
| C73 | A94 | 15c dp grn, dk bl & dp rose | .70 | .20 |

Swordfish AP34

J. D. Arosemena Normal School — AP35

Alejandro Meléndez G. — AP40

---

### Nos. C6C and C7 Surcharged in Carmine

**1947, Mar. 8  Perf. 12**

| | | | | |
|---|---|---|---|---|
| C82 | AP5 | 5c on 8c gray blk | .25 | .20 |
| a. | | Double overprint | 25.00 | |
| C83 | AP5 | 10c on 15c dp grn | .55 | .40 |

### Nos. C74 to C76 Surcharged in Black or Carmine

| | | | | |
|---|---|---|---|---|
| C84 | AP34 | 5c on 7c rose car | | .25 |
| a. | | Double surcharge (Bk) | | |
| C85 | AP34 | 5c on 8c dk ol brn & blk | | 375.00 |
| C86 | AP34 | 10c on 15c dk vio | 30.00 | .20 |
| a. | | Double surcharge | 30.00 | .25 |
| | | Nos. C82-C86 (5) | 1.55 | 1.25 |

**1942, June 4  Engr.  Perf. 12**

| | | | | |
|---|---|---|---|---|
| C74 | AP34 | 7c rose carmine | .90 | .20 |
| C75 | AP34 | 8c dk ol brn & blk | .25 | .20 |
| C76 | AP34 | 15c dark violet | .45 | .20 |
| C77 | AP35 | 20c red brown | .65 | .20 |
| C78 | AP34 | 50c olive green | 1.10 | .40 |
| C79 | AP34 | 1b blk & org yel | 2.75 | .80 |
| | | Nos. C74-C79 (6) | 6.10 | 2.00 |

Designs: 8c, Gate of Glory, Portobelo. 15c, Taboga Island, Balboa Harbor. 50c, Firehouse. 1b, Gold animal figure.

**1943, Dec. 16**

| | | | | |
|---|---|---|---|---|
| C80 | AP40 | 3b dk olive gray | 5.25 | 4.50 |
| C81 | AP40 | 5b dark blue | 8.00 | 7.00 |

Design: 5b, Ernesto T. Lefevre.

See Nos. C96-C99, C113, C126. For surcharges and overprints see Nos. 354-355, C84-C86, C108, C110-C111, C114, C116, C118, C121, C123, C127-C128, C137.

For overprint & surcharge see #C117, C128A.

**Catalogue values for unused stamps in this section, from this point to the end of the section, are for Never Hinged items.**

**1947, Apr. 7  Engr.  Unwmk.**

| | | | | |
|---|---|---|---|---|
| C87 | AP42 | 8c violet | .40 | .25 |

Natl. Constitutional Assembly of 1945, 2nd anniv. For surcharge see No. 356.

National Theater — AP42

Manuel Amador Guerrero AP43

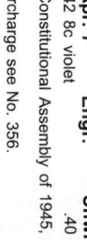

**No. C113 Surcharged "5 1953" in Carmine**

1953, Apr. 22      **Perf. 12**
C137 AP34 5c on 10c dk bl & blk   .35 .20

**Masthead of La Estrella — AP54**

1953, July
C138 AP54 5c rose carmine   .25 .20
C139 AP54 10c blue   .45 .20

Panama's 1st newspaper, La Estrella de Panama, cent.
For surcharges see Nos. C146-C147.

**Act of Independence AP55**

**Senora de Remon and Pres. José A. Remon Cantera AP56**

Designs: 7c, Pollera. 25c, National flower. 50c, Marcos A. Salazar, Esteban Huertas and Domingo Diaz A. 1b, Dancers

1953, Nov.
C140 AP55 2c deep ultra   .45 .20
C141 AP56 5c deep green   .45 .20
C142 AP56 7c gray   .55 .20
C143 AP56 25c black   3.50 .65
C144 AP56 50c dark brown   3.25 .75
C145 AP56 1b red orange   .75 1.90
C146 AP56   12.95 3.50
    Nos. C140-C145 (6)

Founding of republic, 50th anniversary.
For overprints see Nos. U227-C229.

**Nos. C138-C139 Surcharged with New Value in Black or Red**

1953-54
C146 AP51 1c on 5c rose car ('54)   .20 .20
C147 AP54 1c on 10c blue (R)   .20 .20

**Gen. Herrera at Conference Table AP57**

Design: 1b, Gen. Herrera leading troops.

1954, Dec. 4   Litho.   **Perf. 12½**
C148 AP57 6c deep green   4.00 2.25
C149 AP57 1b scarlet & blk

Death of Gen. Tomas Herrera, cent.
For surcharge see No. C198.

**Rotary Emblem and Map — AP58**

1955, Feb. 23
C150 AP58 6c rose violet   .25 .20
C151 AP58 21c red   .70 .35
C152 AP58 1b black   5.50 3.75
   a. 1b violet black   6.75 3.05
    Nos. C150-C152 (3)   6.45 3.05

Rotary International, 50th anniv.
For surcharge see No. C154.

**Cantera Type**

1955, June 1
C153 A115 6c rose vio & blk   .20 .20

Issued in tribute to Pres. José Antonio Remon Cantera, 1908-1955.

---

No. C115 has small overprint, 15½x12mm, like No. 368. Overprint on Nos. C114, C116 and C118 as illustrated. Surcharge on No. C117 is arranged vertically, 29x18mm.

**University of San Javier AP51**

1949, Dec. 7   Engr.   **Perf. 12½**
C119 AP51 5c dk blue & blk   .35 .20

See note after No. 371.

**Mosquito — AP52**

1950, Jan. 12      **Perf. 12**
C120 AP52 5c dp ultra & gray blk   1.60 .65

See note after No. 372.

**Nos. C96, C112, C113 and C9 Overprinted in Black or Carmine (5 or 4 lines)**

1950, Aug. 17     **Unwmk.**
C121 AP21 2c carmine   .55 .25
C122 AP5 5c orange   .65 .35
C123 AP34 10c dk bl & blk (C)   .65 .40
C124 AP5 25c deep blue (C)   1.00 .75

**Same on No. 362, Overprinted "AEREO"**
C125 A105 50c pur & blk (C)   2.00 1.25
   Nos. C121-C125 (5)   4.85 3.00

Gen. José de San Martin, death cent.

**Firehouse Type of 1942**   Engr.

1950, Oct. 30
C126 AP34 50c deep blue   3.50 1.00

**Nos. C113 and C81 Surcharged In Carmine or Orange**

1952, Feb. 20
C127 AP34 2c on 10c   .20 .20
   a. Inverted surcharge
C128 AP34 5c on 10c (O)   250.00
   a. Pair, one without surch.
C128A AP34 5c on 10c (O)   250.00
   b. Pair, one without surch.
C128A AP40 10c on 5b   29.00 20.00

The surcharge on No. C128A is arranged to fit stamp, with four bars covering value panel at bottom, instead of crosses.

1952, Aug. 1
C129 A97 5c on 2c ver & blk   .20 .20
   a. Inverted surcharge   22.50
C130 A99 25c on 10c pur & org   1.00 1.00

**Isabella Type of Regular Issue**   Engr.

1952, Oct. 20   Unwmk.   **Perf. 12½**
     Center in Black
C131 A110 4c red orange   .45 .20
C132 A110 5c olive green   .45 .20
C133 A110 10c gray blue   .65 .20
C134 A110 25c gray blue   1.75 .30
C135 A110 50c chocolate   2.50 .65
C136 A110 1b deep blue   13.30 4.60
   Nos. C131-C136 (6)

Queen Isabella I of Spain, 500th birth anniv.

---

**Monument to Cervantes AP50**

10c, Don Quixote attacking windmill.

1948, Nov. 15
C105 AP50 5c dk blue & blk   .55 .20
C106 AP50 10c purple & blk   .90 .25

400th anniv. of the birth of Miguel de Cervantes Saavedra, novelist, playwright and poet.

**No. C106 Overprinted in Carmine**

1949, Jan.
C107 AP50 10c purple & blk   .60 .40
   a. Inverted overprint   50.00

José Gabriel Duque (1849-1918), newspaper publisher and philanthropist.

**Nos. C96, C6A, C97 and C99 Overprinted in Black or Red**   **Perf. 12**

C108 AP34 2c carmine   .20 .20
C100 AP5(l) 5c blue (R)   5.00
C110 AP34(h) 15c olive gray   .65 .65
C111 AP34(h) 50c rose carmine   2.25 2.25
   Nos. C108-C111 (4)   3.35 3.35

Centenary of the incorporation of Chiriqui Province.
No. C74 exists with this overprint.

**Types of 1930-42**

Design: 10c, Gate of Glory, Portobelo.

1949, Aug. 4      **Perf. 12**
C112 AP5 5c orange   .20 .20
C113 AP34 10c dk blue & blk   .25 .20

For surcharge see No. C137.

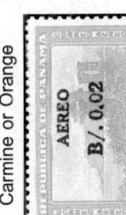

**Stamps of 1943-49 Overprinted or Surcharged in Black, Green or Red**

1949, Sept. 9
C114 AP34 2c carmine   .25 .20
   a. Inverted overprint   24.00
C115 AP5 5c orange (G)   .90 .35
   a. Inverted overprint   32.50
C116 AP34 10c dk bl & blk (R)   .90
   a. Double ovpt., one inverted   20.00
C117 AP40 25c on 3b dk bl or gray (R)   1.25 .70
C118 AP34 50c rose carmine   4.00 2.10
   Nos. C114-C118 (5)   7.30 3.75

75th anniv. of the UPU.

---

**Manuel Espinosa B. — AP44**

5c, José Agustin Arango. 10c, Federico Boyd. 15c, Ricardo Arias. 50c, Carlos Constantino Arosemena. 1b, Nicanor de Obarrio. 2b, Tomas Arias.

1948, Feb. 11     **Perf. 12½**
     Center in Black
C88 AP43 3c blue   .45 .20
C89 AP43 5c brown   .45 .20
C90 AP43 10c orange   .45 .20
C91 AP43 15c deep claret   .45 .20
C92 AP44 20c deep carmine   .80 .55
C93 AP44 50c dark gray   1.40 .80
C94 AP44 1b green   4.50 2.50
C95 AP44 2b yellow   18.50 10.65
   Nos. C88-C95 (8)

Members of the Revolutionary Junta of 1903.

**Types of 1942**     **Perf. 12**

1948, June 14
C96 AP34 2c carmine   .90 .20
C97 AP34 15c olive gray   .45 .20
C98 AP35 20c green   .45 .20
C99 AP34 50c rose carmine   7.25 3.00
   Nos. C96-C99 (4)   9.05 3.60

**Franklin D. Roosevelt and Juan D. Arosemena AP45**

**Four Freedoms AP46**

**Monument to F. D. Roosevelt — AP47**

**Map showing Boyd-Roosevelt Trans-Isthmian Highway — AP48**

**Franklin D. Roosevelt — AP49**

1948, Sept. 15     **Perf. 12½**
C100 AP45 5c dp car & blk   .25 .20
C101 AP46 10c yellow org   .35 .30
C102 AP47 20c dull green   .45 .35
C103 AP48 50c dp ultra & blk   .70 .60
C104 AP49 1b gray black   1.75 1.25
   Nos. C100-C104 (5)   3.50 2.70

Franklin Delano Roosevelt (1882-1945).
For surcharges see Nos. RA28-RA29.

For surcharge see No. C188.

**No. C151 Surcharged**

**1955, Dec. 7**

| | | | |
|---|---|---|---|
| C154 | AP58 | 15c on 21c red | .40 .35 |

Pedro J. Sosa — AP60

**1955, Nov. 22    Unwmk.    Litho.    Perf. 12½**

| | | | |
|---|---|---|---|
| C155 | AP60 | 5c grn, *lt grn* | .35 .20 |
| C156 | AP61 | 1b red lilac & blk | 5.00 2.50 |

150th anniversary of the birth of Ferdinand de Lesseps. Imperforates exist.

First Barge Going through Canal and de Lesseps AP61

Statue of Bolívar — AP63

Pres. Dwight D. Eisenhower — AP62

Bolívar Hall AP64

Portraits-Presidents: C158, Pedro Aramburu, Argentina; C159, Dr. Victor Paz Estenssoro, Bolivia; C160, Dr. Juscelino Kubitschek O., Brazil; C161, Gen. Carlos Ibáñez del Campo, Chile; C162, Gen. Gustavo Rojas Pinilla, Colombia; C163, Jose Figueres, Costa Rica; C164, Gen. Fulgencio Batista y Zaldivar, Cuba; C165, Gen. Hector B. Trujillo Molina, Dominican Rep.; C166, José Maria Velasco Ibarra, Ecuador; C167, Col. Carlos Castillo Armas, Guatemala; C168, Gen. Paul E. Magloire, Haiti; C169, Julio Lozano Diaz, Honduras; C170, Adolfo Ruiz Cortines, Mexico; C171, Gen. Anastasio Somoza, Nicaragua; C172, Ricardo Arias Espinosa, Panama; C173, Gen. Alfredo Stroessner, Paraguay; C174, Gen. Manuel Odria, Peru; C175, Col. Oscar Osorio, El Salvador; C176, Dr. Alberto F. Zubiria, Uruguay; C177, Gen. Marcos Perez Jimenez, Venezuela; 1b, Simon Bolivar.

**1956, July 18**

| | | | |
|---|---|---|---|
| C157 | AP62 | 6c rose car & vio | .45 .35 |
| C158 | AP62 | 6c brt grnsh bl & blk | .45 .20 |
| C159 | AP62 | 6c bl | .45 .20 |
| C160 | AP62 | 6c bister & blk | .45 .20 |
| C161 | AP62 | 6c emerald & blk | .45 .20 |
| C162 | AP62 | 6c lt grn & brn | .45 .20 |
| C163 | AP62 | 6c yellow & grn | .45 .20 |
| C164 | AP62 | 6c brt vio & grn | .45 .20 |
| C165 | AP62 | 6c dl pur & vio bl | .45 .20 |
| C166 | AP62 | 6c brt vio & grn | .45 .20 |
| C167 | AP62 | 6c citron & vio bl | .45 .20 |
| C168 | AP62 | 6c brn & vio bl | .45 .20 |
| C169 | AP62 | 6c brt car & grn | .45 .20 |
| C170 | AP62 | 6c red & brn | .45 .20 |
| C171 | AP62 | 6c lt bl & grn | .45 .20 |
| C172 | AP62 | 6c vio bl & grn | .45 .20 |
| C173 | AP62 | 6c orange & blk | .45 .20 |
| C174 | AP62 | 6c bluish gray & brn | .45 .20 |
| C175 | AP62 | 6c dk grn & | .45 .20 |
| C176 | AP62 | 6c sal rose & blk | .45 .20 |
| C177 | AP62 | 6c dk org brn & | .45 .20 |
| C178 | AP63 | 20c dk bluish gray | 1.10 .55 |
| C179 | AP64 | 50c green | 2.00 1.00 |
| C180 | AP63 | 1b brown | 5.00 1.75 |
| Nos. C157-C180 (24) | | | 17.55 7.70 |

Pan-American Conf., Panama City, July 21-22, 1956, and 130th anniv. of the 1st Pan-American Conf. Imperforates exist.

Ruins of First Town Council Building — AP65

**1956, Aug. 17**

Design: 50c, City Hall, Panama City.

| | | | |
|---|---|---|---|
| C181 | AP65 | 25c red | .65 .35 |
| C182 | AP65 | 50c black | 1.25 .90 |
| a. | | Souv. sheet of 3, #404, C181-C182, imperf. | 2.40 2.40 |

6th Inter-American Congress of Municipalities, Panama City, Aug. 14-19, 1956. No. C182a sold for 85c. For overprint see No. C187a.

Monument — AP66

St. Thomas Hospital AP67

Highway Construction AP68

**1956, Nov. 27    Wmk. 311**

| | | | |
|---|---|---|---|
| C183 | AP66 | 5c dk green | .25 .20 |
| C184 | AP67 | 15c dk carmine | .45 .20 |

Centenary of the birth of Pres. Belisario Porras.

**1957, Aug. 1    Wmk. 311    Perf. 12½**

| | | | |
|---|---|---|---|
| C185 | AP68 | 10c black | .25 .20 |
| C186 | AP68 | 20c dk gray & blk | .65 .55 |
| C187 | AP68 | 1b green | 2.75 2.25 |
| Nos. C185-C187 (3) | | | 3.65 3.00 |
| a. | | Souv. sheet of 3, unwmkd. | 16.00 16.00 |

7th Pan-American Highway Congress, black: No. C187a is No. C182a overprinted in black: "VII degree CONGRESSO INTER-AMERICANO DE CARRETERAS 1957."

**No. C153 Surcharged "1957" and New Value**

**1957, Aug. 13    Unwmk.**

| | | | |
|---|---|---|---|
| C188 | AP59 | 10c on 6c rose vio & blk | .20 .20 |

Customs House, Portobelo AP70

Remon Polyclinic — AP69

**1957    Wmk. 311**

Buildings: #C191, Portobelo Castle. #C192, San Jeronimo Castle. #C193, Remon Hippodrome. #C194, Legislature. #C195, Interior & Treasury Department. #C196, El Panama Hotel. #C197, San Lorenzo Castle.

**1957, Oct.    Design in Black**

| | | | |
|---|---|---|---|
| C189 | AP69 | 10c lt blue | .25 .20 |
| C190 | AP70 | 10c lilac | .25 .20 |
| C191 | AP70 | 10c gray | .25 .20 |
| C192 | AP70 | 10c lilac rose | .25 .20 |
| C193 | AP70 | 10c ultra | .25 .20 |
| C194 | AP70 | 10c brown ol | .25 .20 |
| C195 | AP70 | 10c orange yel | .25 .20 |
| C196 | AP70 | 10c yellow grn | .25 .20 |
| C197 | AP70 | 1b red | 4.25 3.20 |
| Nos. C189-C197 (9) | | | 4.25 3.20 |

**1957, Feb. 11    Unwmk.**

| | | | |
|---|---|---|---|
| C198 | AP57 | 5c on 6c dp grn | .20 .20 |

**No. C148 Surcharged with New Value and "1958" in Red**

Flags of Panama and UN AP72

United Nations Emblem — AP71

**1958, Mar. 5    Litho.    Wmk. 311**

| | | | |
|---|---|---|---|
| C199 | AP71 | 10c brt green | .25 .20 |
| C200 | AP71 | 21c lt ultra | .45 .25 |
| C201 | AP71 | 50c orange | 1.10 .85 |
| C202 | AP72 | 1b gray, ultra & car | 2.25 1.60 |
| a. | | Souv. sheet of 4, #C199-C202, imperf. | 5.25 5.25 |
| Nos. C199-C202 (4) | | | 4.05 2.90 |

**OAS Type of Regular Issue, 1958**

Designs: 10c, 1b, Flags of 21 American Nations. 50c, Headquarters in Washington.

Portraits: 5c, Justo A. Facio, Rector. 10c, Ernesto de la Guardia, Jr., Pres. of Panama.

**1959, July 27    Wmk. 311    Litho.    Perf. 12½**

| | | | |
|---|---|---|---|
| C222 | A128 | 5c emer & bl (R) | .25 .20 |
| C223 | A128 | 10c black | .20 .20 |

**Type of Regular Issue, 1959**

**1959, Oct. 26    Wmk. 311    Perf. 12½**

| | | | |
|---|---|---|---|
| C224 | A130 | 5c Boxing | .35 .20 |
| C225 | A130 | 10c Baseball | .70 .20 |
| C226 | A130 | 50c Basketball | 2.75 1.25 |
| Nos. C224-C226 (3) | | | 3.80 1.65 |

For surcharge see No. C349.

1b, Map of Americas showing Pan-American Highway.

20c, Road through jungle, Darien project.

10th anniv. of the UN (in 1955). The sheet also exists with the 10c and 50c omitted.

**1958, July 10    Unwmk.    Perf. 12½**

**Center yellow and black; flags in national colors**

| | | | |
|---|---|---|---|
| C203 | A124 | 5c lt blue | .25 .20 |
| C204 | A124 | 10c carmine rose | .25 .20 |
| C205 | A124 | 50c gray | .70 .60 |
| C206 | A124 | 1b black | 2.25 1.60 |
| Nos. C203-C206 (4) | | | 3.45 2.60 |

**Type of Regular Issue**

Pavilions: 15c, Vatican City. 50c, United States. 1b, Belgium.

**1958, Sept. 8    Wmk. 311    Perf. 12½**

| | | | |
|---|---|---|---|
| C207 | A125 | 15c gray & lt vio | .25 .20 |
| C208 | A125 | 50c dk gray & org brn | .70 .65 |
| C209 | A125 | 1b brt vio & bluish | 1.60 1.40 |
| a. | | Souv. sheet of 7, #418-421, C207-C209 | 5.25 5.25 |
| Nos. C207-C209 (3) | | | 2.55 2.25 |

No. C209a sold for 2b.

**Pope Type of Regular Issue**

Portraits of Pius XII: 5c, as cardinal. 30c, wearing papal tiara. 50c, Enthroned.

**1959, Jan. 21    Litho.    Wmk. 311**

| | | | |
|---|---|---|---|
| C210 | A126 | 5c violet | .25 .20 |
| C211 | A127 | 30c dk lilac rose | .65 .40 |
| C212 | A126 | 50c blue gray | .90 .65 |
| a. | | Souv. sheet of 4, #422, C210-C212, imperf. | 2.25 2.25 |
| Nos. C210-C212 (3) | | | 1.80 1.25 |

#C212a is watermarked sideways and sold for 1b. The sheet also exists with 30c omitted. #C212a with C.E.P.A.L. overprint is listed as #C221a.

**Human Rights Issue Type**

Designs: 5c, Humanity looking into sun. 10c, 20c, Torch and UN emblem. 50c, UN Flag; 1b, UN Headquarters building.

**1959, Apr. 14    Litho.    Perf. 12½**

| | | | |
|---|---|---|---|
| C213 | A127 | 5c emerald & bl | .25 .20 |
| C214 | A127 | 10c gray & org brn | .25 .20 |
| C215 | A127 | 20c brown & gray | .25 .20 |
| C216 | A127 | 50c green & ultra | .80 .65 |
| C217 | A127 | 1b red & blue | 1.75 1.40 |
| Nos. C213-C217 (5) | | | 3.30 2.65 |

**Nos. C213-C215, C212a Overprinted and C216 Surcharged in Red or Dark Blue**

**1959, May 16    Unwmk.**

| | | | |
|---|---|---|---|
| C218 | A127 | 5c emer & bl (R) | .25 .20 |
| C219 | A127 | 10c gray & org brn (Bl) | .45 .25 |
| C220 | A127 | 20c brown & gray & org brn (R) | .25 .20 |
| C221 | A127 | 50c on 50c grn & ultra (R) | 3.20 2.55 |
| a. | | Souv. sheet of 4, #C218-C221 (4) | 6.25 6.25 |

8th Reunion of the Economic Commission for Latin America. This overprint also exists on Nos. C216-C217. These were disavowed by Panama's postmaster general. No. C221a is No. C212a with two-line black overprint at top of sheet: "8a. REUNION DE LA C.E.P.A.L. MAYO 1959."

Nos. C143-C145 Overprinted in Vermilion, Red or Black

**Unwmk.**

**1960, Feb. 6** **Engr.** ***Perf. 12***
**C227** AP56 25c black (V) .90 .20
**C228** AP56 50c dk brown (R) 1.25 .40
**C229** AP56 1b red orange 2.00 1.25
*Nos. C227-C229 (3)* 4.15 1.85

World Refugee Year, July 1, 1959-June 30, 1960.

The revenues from the sale of Nos. C227-C229 went to the United Nations Refugee Fund.

Administration Building, National University — AP74

Designs: 21c, Humanities building. 25c, Medical school. 30c, Dr. Octavio Mendez Pereira first rector of University.

**Wmk. 311**

**1960, Mar. 23** **Litho.** ***Perf. 12½***
**C230** AP74 10c brt green .25 .20
**C231** AP74 21c lt blue .55 .20
**C232** AP74 25c ultra .80 .35
**C233** AP74 30c black 1.00 .40
*Nos. C230-C233 (4)* 2.60 1.15

National University, 25th anniv.

For surcharges see Nos. 450, C248, C253, C287, C291.

### Olympic Games Type

5c, Basketball. 10c, Bicycling, horiz. 25c, Javelin thrower. 50c, Athlete with Olympic torch.

**1960, Sept. 22** **Wmk. 343** ***Perf. 12½***
**C234** A131 5c orange & red .25 .20
**C235** A131 10c ocher & blk .55 .20
**C236** A131 25c lt bl & dk bl 1.10 .55
**C237** A131 50c brown & blk 2.25 1.00
*a.* Souv. sheet of 2, #C236-C237 4.50 4.50
*Nos. C234-C237 (4)* 4.15 1.95

For surcharges see Nos. C249-C250, C254, C266-C270, C290, O050, RA40.

Citizens' Silhouettes AP75

10c, Heads and map of Central America.

**1960** **Litho.** **Wmk. 229**
**C238** AP75 5c black .25 .20
**C239** AP75 10c brown .25 .20

6th census of population and the 2nd census of dwellings (No. C238), Dec. 11, 1960, and the All America Census, 1960 (No. C239).

Boeing 707 Jet Liner AP76

**1960, Dec. 1** **Wmk. 343** ***Perf. 12½***
**C240** AP76 5c lt grnsh blue .25 .20
**C241** AP76 10c emerald .25 .20
**C242** AP76 20c red brown .45 .25
*Nos. C240-C242 (3)* .95 .65

1st jet service to Panama. For surcharge see No. RA41.

Souvenir Sheet

UN Emblem — AP77

**Wmk. 311**

**1961, Mar. 7** **Litho.** ***Imperf.***
**C243** AP77 80c blk & car rose 2.25 2.25

15th anniv. (in 1960) of the UN.
Counterfeits without control number exist.

### No. C243 Overprinted in Blue with Large Uprooted Oak Emblem and "Ano de los Refugiados"

**1961, June 2**
**C244** AP77 80c blk & car rose 2.50 2.50

World Refugee Year, July 1, 1959-June 30, 1960.

### Lions International Type

Designs: 5c, Helen Keller School for the Blind. 10c, Children's summer camp. 21c, Arms of Panama and Lions emblem.

**1961, May 2** **Wmk. 311** ***Perf. 12½***
**C245** A133 5c black .20 .20
**C246** A133 10c emerald .20 .20
**C247** A133 21c ultra, yel & red .40 .25
*Nos. C245-C247 (3)* .80 .65

For overprints see Nos. C284-C286.

Nos. C230 and C236 Surcharged in Black or Red

**1961** **Wmk. 311 (1c); Wmk. 343**
**C248** AP74 1c on 10c .20 .20
**C249** A131 1b on 25c (Bk) 2.10 2.00
**C250** A131 1b on 25c (R) 2.10 2.00
*Nos. C248-C250 (3)* 4.40 4.20

Pres. Roberto F. Chiari and Pres. Mario Echandi AP78

**Wmk. 343**

**1961, Oct. 2** **Litho.** ***Perf. 12½***
**C251** AP78 1b black & gold 2.75 1.60

Meeting of the Presidents of Panama and Costa Rica at Paso Canoa, Apr. 21, 1961.

Dag Hammarskjold AP79

**1961, Dec. 27** ***Perf. 12½***
**C252** AP79 10c black .20 .20

Dag Hammarskjold, UN Secretary General, 1953-61.

No. C230 Surcharged

**1962, Feb. 21** **Wmk. 311**
**C253** AP74 15c on 10c brt grn .30 .20

No. C236 Surcharged

**Wmk. 343**
**C254** A131 1b on 25c 2.75 1.25

City Hall, Colon AP80

**1962, Feb. 28** **Litho.** **Wmk. 311**
**C255** AP80 5c vio bl & blk .20 .20

Issued to publicize the third Central American Municipal Assembly, Colon, May 13-17.

### Church Type of Regular Issue, 1962

Designs: 5c, Church of Christ the King. 7c, Church of San Miguel. 8c, Church of the Sanctuary. 10c, Saints Church. 15c, Church of St. Ann. 21c, Canal Zone Synagogue (Now used as USO Center). 25c, Panama Synagogue. 30c, Church of St. Francis. 50c, Protestant Church, Canal Zone. 1b, Catholic Church, Canal Zone.

**Wmk. 343**

**1962-64** **Litho.** ***Perf. 12½***

**Buildings in Black**

**C256** A138 5c purple & buff .25 .20
**C257** A138 7c lil rose & brt pink .25 .20
**C258** A139 8c purple & bl .25 .20
**C259** A130 10c lilac & sal .25 .20
**C259A** A139 10c grn & dl red brn ('64) .25 .20
**C260** A139 15c red & buff .35 .20
**C261** A138 21c brown & blue .55 .40
**C262** A138 25c blue & pink .65 .35
**C263** A139 30c lil rose & bl .70 .40
**C264** A138 50c lilac & lt grn 1.10 .65
*a.* Souv. sheet of 4, #441H-441J, C262, C264, imperf. 5.75 5.75
**C265** A139 1b bl & sal 2.25 1.40
*Nos. C256-C265 (11)* 6.85 4.40

Freedom of religion in Panama. Issue dates: #C259A, June 4, 1964; others, July 20, 1962.

For overprints and surcharges see Nos. C288, C296-C297, C299.

### Nos. C234 and C236 Overprinted and Surcharged "IX JUEGOS C.A. Y DEL CARIBE KINGSTON-1962" and Games Emblem in Black, Green, Orange or Red

**1962** **Wmk. 343** ***Perf. 12½***
**C266** A131 5c org & red .20 .20
**C267** A131 10c on 25c (G) .65 .35
**C268** A131 15c on 25c (O) .80 .45
**C269** A131 20c on 25c (R) .90 .50
**C270** A131 25c lt bl & dk bl 1.00 .55
*Nos. C266-C270 (5)* 3.55 2.05

Ninth Central American and Caribbean Games, Kingston, Jamaica, Aug. 11-25.

Nos. CB1-CB2 Surcharged

**1962, May 3** **Wmk. 311**
**C271** SPAP1 10c on 5c + 5c 1.40 .75
**C272** SPAP1 20c on 10c + 10c 2.10 1.50

### Type of Regular Issue, 1962

Design: 10c, Canal bridge completed.

**1962, Oct. 12** **Wmk. 343**
**C273** A140 10c blue & blk .20 .20

John H. Glenn, "Friendship 7" Capsule — AP81

UPAE Emblem — AP82

Designs: 10c, "Friendship 7" capsule and globe, horiz. 31c, Capsule in space, horiz. 50c, Glenn with space helmet.

**1962, Oct. 19** **Wmk. 311** ***Perf. 12½***
**C274** AP81 5c rose red .20 .20
**C275** AP81 10c yellow .35 .20
**C276** AP81 31c blue 1.50 .80
**C277** AP81 50c emerald 1.75 1.00
*a.* Souv. sheet of 4, #C274-C277, imperf. 4.00 4.00
*Nos. C274-C277 (4)* 3.80 2.20

1st orbital flight of US astronaut Lt. Col. John H. Glenn, Jr., Feb. 20, 1962. No. C277a sold for 1b.

For surcharges see Nos. C290A-C290D, C367, CB4-CB7.

**1963, Jan. 8** **Litho.** **Wmk. 343**
**C278** AP82 10c multi .35 .20

50th anniversary of the founding of the Postal Union of the Americas and Spain, UPAE.

### Type of Regular Issue

10c, Fire Engine "China", Plaza de Santa Ana. 15c, 14th Street team. 21c, Fire Brigade emblem.

**1963, Jan. 22** **Wmk. 311** ***Perf. 12½***
**C279** A141 10c orange & blk .35 .20
**C280** A141 15c lilac & blk .45 .20
**C281** A141 21c gold, red & ultra .90 .50
*Nos. C279-C281 (3)* 1.70 .00

"FAO" and Wheat Emblem — AP83

**1963, Mar. 21** **Litho.**
**C282** AP83 10c green & red .35 .20
**C283** AP83 15c ultra & red .45 .20

FAO "Freedom from Hunger" campaign.

### No. C245 Overprinted in Yellow, Orange or Green: "XXII Convención / Leonística / Centroamericana / Panama, 18-21 / Abril 1963"

**1963, Apr. 18** **Wmk. 311** ***Perf. 12½***
**C284** A133 5c black (Y) .70 .20
**C285** A133 5c black (O) .70 .20
**C286** A133 5c black (G) .70 .20
*Nos. C284-C286 (3)* 2.10 .60

22nd Central American Lions Congress, Panama, Apr. 18-21.

No. C230 Surcharged:

HABILITADO
Vale B/.0.04

**1963, June 11**
C287 AP74 4c on 10c brt grn .25 .20

Nos. 445 and 432 Overprinted "AEREO" Vertically

**1963** Wmk. 343 Perf. 12½
C288 A139 10c green, yel & blk .25 .20

Wmk. 311
C289 A130 20c emerald & red brn .65 .25

No. C234 Overprinted: "LIBERTAD DE PRENSA 20-VIII-63"
**1963, Aug. 20** Wmk. 343
C290 A131 5c orange & red .25 .20
Freedom of Press Day, Aug. 20, 1963.

HABILITADO
10¢

"Visita Astronautas Glenn-Schirra Sheppard Cooper a Panamá"

No. C274, C277 and C277a Overprinted or Surcharged — a

No. C274 Surcharged in Black — b

**1963, Aug. 21** Wmk. 311 Litho. Perf. 12½
C290B AP81(a) 5c on #C274 3.25
C290A AP81(a) 10c on 5c
C290B AP81(b) 10c on 25c ultra

**1963, Oct. 9** Wmk. 311 Perf. 12½
C291 AP74 10c on 25c ultra .20 .20

No. C232 Surcharged in Red: "VALE 10¢"
**1963, Aug. 21** Litho. Perf. 12½
C290A AP81(a) 5c on #C274 .50
C290C AP81(b) 10c on 5c #C274 9.00

Souvenir Sheet
Imperf.
C290D AP81(a) Sheet of 4, #C277a 50.00

Overprint on No. C290D has names in capital letters and covers all four stamps.

**1964, Feb. 17** Unwmk. Engr. Perf. 12
Center in Black

(C300-C321 table)
C300 AP84 21c olive 1.40 .90
C301 AP84 21c chocolate 1.40 .90
C302 AP84 21c aqua 1.40 .90
C303 AP84 21c red brown 1.40 .90
C304 AP84 21c magenta 1.40 .90
C305 AP84 21c orange red 1.40 .90
C306 AP84 21c blue 1.40 .90
C307 AP84 21c green 1.40 .90
C308 AP84 21c emerald 1.40 .90
C309 AP84 21c dp violet 1.40 .90
C310 AP84 21c violet bl 1.40 .90
C311 AP84 21c dk slate grn 1.40 .90
C312 AP84 21c violet 1.40 .90
C313 AP84 21c black 1.40 .90
C314 AP84 21c emerald .90 .90
C315 AP84 21c blue .90 .90
C316 AP84 21c dp violet .90 .90
C317 AP84 21c carmine rose .90 .90
C318 AP84 21c Prus green .90 .90
C319 AP84 21c dark brown 1.40 .90
C320 AP84 21c dark blue 7.50 5.00
C321 AP84 2b yellow green 14.50 9.00
Nos. C300-C321 (22) 15.00 15.00
a. Souv. sheet of 6 32.00 15.00

Cathedrals: #C301, St. Stephen's, Vienna, Paris. #C302, St. Sofia, Sofia. #C303, Notre Dame, London. #C306, Cologne. #C305, St. Paul's, St. Elizabeth's, Kosice, Czechoslovakia (inscr. Kassa, Hungary). #C308, New Delhi. #C309, Milan. #C310, Guadalupe Basilica. #C311, New Church, Delft, Netherlands. #C312, Lima. #C313, St. John's. #C314, Toledo. #C315, St. Basil's, Moscow. #C316, Lisbon. #C317, Stockholm. #C318, Basel. #C319, St. George's, Patriarchal Church, Istanbul. St. Panama City, 2b, St. Peter's Basilica, Rome.

Nos. 434 and 444 Surcharged: "Aéreo B/.0.10"
**1964** Wmk. 343 Perf. 12½
C298 A131 10c on 5c bl grn & emer .20 .20
C299 A139 10c on 5c rose, lt grn & blk .20 .20

St. Patrick's Cathedral, New York — AP84

Vatican II, the 21st Ecumenical Council of the Roman Catholic Church.
No. C321a contains 6 imperf. stamps similar to Nos. C300, C303, C305, C315, C320 and C321. Size: 198x138mm. Sold for 3.85b.
Six stamps of this set (Nos. C300, C305, C309, C319, C321a) were overprinted "1964." The overprint in olive bister on the stamps, yellow on the souvenir sheet. The overprint is reported to exist also in yellow gold on the same six stamps and in olive bister on the souvenir sheet.

**1964, Feb. 17** Unwmk. Engr. Perf. 12
Center in Black

**1964** Perf. 13½x14
Unwmk.
C327 AP84b 21c black & blue 1.00 .60
C328 AP84b 21c black & blue 1.00 .60

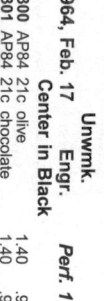

AP84b

AP84c

Hammarskjold Memorial, UN Day. No. C327, C329a, Dag Hammarskjold. No. C328, C329b, UN emblem.

**1964, Sept. 24** Perf. 13½x14 Unwmk.
Souvenir Sheet
Imperf
C329 Sheet of 2 6.75 6.75
a.-b. AP84b 21c blk & grn, any single 1.25 1.25

Nos. C327-C328 exist imperf in black and green. Value $4.50.

Roosevelt Type of Regular Issue
**1964, Oct. 9** Litho. Perf. 12½x12½
C330 A147 20c grn & blk, buff .40 .30
a. Souv. sheet of 2, #C332 imperf.

**1964**
C331 AP84c 21c shown .75 .50
C332 AP84c 21c Papal coat of arms .75 .50
a. Souv. sheet of 2, #C331-C332 6.00 5.00

Pope John XXIII (1881-1963). Nos. C331-C332 exist imperf in different colors. Value $20.

**1965**
C333 AP84d 10c blue & multi 2.00 .75
C334 AP84d 21c green & multi 2.00 .75
a. Souv. sheet of 2, #C333-C334

21c, Galileo, studies of gravity. Illustration reduced.

Galileo, 400th Birth Anniv. — AP84d

Nos. C333-C334a exist imperf in different colors. Value, $11.

World's Fair, New York AP84a

**1963, Dec. 18** Litho. Unwmk.
Portrait in Slate Green
C292 A142 5c yel, red & ultra .30 .25
C293 A142 10c bl, red & ultra .50 .35
C294 A142 21c org yel, red & ul-tra
Nos. C292-C294 (3) 1.50 1.10
2.30 1.70

Balboa Type of Regular Issue, 1964
**1964, Jan. 22** Photo. Perf. 13
C295 A143 10c dk vio, pale pink .20 .20

No. C261 Surcharged in Red: "VALE B/.0.50"
**1964** Wmk. 343 Litho. Perf. 12½
C296 A138 50c on 21c brn, bl & blk 1.00 .70

Type of 1962 Overprinted: "HABILITADA"
C297 A139 1b emer, yel & blk 2.00 2.00

Type of Regular Issue, 1963
Flags and Presidents: 5c, Julio A. Rivera, El Salvador. 10c, Miguel Ydigoras F., Guatemala. 21c, John F. Kennedy, US.

Souvenir Sheet
Perf. 12
C326 AP84a 21c ultra & blk 6.00 6.00

5c, 10c, 15c, Various pavilions. 21c, Unisphere.

No. C326 contains one 49x35mm stamp. Exists imperf. Value, same as No. C326.

**1965**
C335 AP84e 10c Peace Medal, obv. 15.00 15.00
C336 AP84e 10c Peace Medal, rev. 2.25 .75
a. Souv. sheet of 2, #C335-C336 2.25 .75

Alfred Nobel (1833-1896), Founder of Nobel Prize — AP84e

Litho. & Embossed
Perf. 14
2.00 .75
2.00 .75

Nos. C335-C336a exist imperf in different colors. Value, $4.50.

ITU Cent. AP85a

**1966, Aug. 12** Perf. 13½x14
Souvenir Sheet
C351 AP86a 31c multicolored —
C352 AP86a 31c multicolored 4.50

No. C352 exists imperf, with blue green background. Value $15.

Animal Type of Regular Issue, 1967
**1967, Feb. 3** Unwmk. Perf. 14
C353 A160 10c multi .45 .20
C354 A160 13c multi .55 .20
C355 A150 30c multi 1.00 .50
C356 A150 30c multi 1.25 .60
Nos. C353-C356 (4) 3.25 1.50

Domestic Animals: 10c, Pekingese dog. 13c, Zebu, horiz. 30c, Cat. 40c, Horse, horiz.

50th anniv. of the Junior Chamber of Commerce.

Nos. C224 and C236 Surcharged
**1966, June 27** Wmk. 311 Perf. 12½
C349 A130 3c on 5c blk & red .20 .20
C350 A131 13c on 25c lt & dk bl .35 .25
The old denominations are not obliterated on Nos. C349-C350.

Junior Chamber of Commerce Emblem and: #C343, Hibiscus. #C344, Water lily. #C347, Orchid. #C345, Crimson-backed tanager. #C346, Gladiolus. #C348, Flor del Espíritu Santo.

**1966, Mar. 16**
C339 A149 8c brt pink & multi .90 .35
C340 A149 12c multi .90 .35
C341 A149 13c multi .70 .25
C342 A149 25c multi 1.40 .35
Nos. C339-C342 (4) 3.25 1.00

AP84c

English Daisy and Emblem — AP85

**1965, Mar. 16**
C343 AP85 30c brt pink & multi .90 .35
C344 AP85 30c salmon & multi .90 .35
C345 AP85 30c pale yel & multi 1.25 .35
C346 AP85 40c lt grn & multi 1.25 .35
C347 AP85 40c multi 1.25 .35
C348 AP85 40c pink & multi 1.25 .35
Nos. C343-C348 (6) 6.45 2.10

Bird Type of Regular Issue, 1965
Song Birds: 5c, Common troupial, horiz. 10c, Crimson-backed tanager, horiz.

**1965, Oct. 27** Unwmk. Perf. 14
Litho.
C337 A148 5c dp orange & multi 1.40 .20
C338 A148 10c brt blue & mul-ti 1.70 .25
a. Souv. sheet of 6, #462- 462C, C337-C338 22.50 22.50

No. C338a exists imperf. Value, $22.50.

Fish Type of Regular Issue
Designs: 8c, Shrimp. 12c, Hammerhead. 13c, Atlantic sailfish. 25c, Seahorse, vert.

**1965, Dec. 7** Litho.
C339 A149 45 .20

## Young Hare, by Dürer — AP86

10c, St. Jerome and the Lion, by Albrecht Dürer. 20c, Lady with the Ermine, by Leonardo Da Vinci. 30c, The Hunt, by Delacroix, horiz.

**1967, Sept. 1**

| | | | | |
|---|---|---|---|---|
| C357 | AP86 | 10c black, buff & car | .35 | .20 |
| C358 | AP86 | 13c lt yellow & multi | .55 | .25 |
| C359 | AP86 | 20c multicolored | .80 | .25 |
| C360 | AP86 | 30c multicolored | 1.10 | .45 |
| | | Nos. C357-C360 (4) | 2.80 | 1.10 |

## Panama-Mexico Friendship — AP86a

Designs: 1b, Pres. Gustavo Díaz Ordaz of Mexico and Pres. Marco A. Robles of Panama, horiz.

**1968, Jan. 20**    *Perf. 14*

| | | | | |
|---|---|---|---|---|
| C361 | AP86a | 50c shown | 2.00 | .60 |
| C361A | AP86a | 1b multi | 4.00 | 1.10 |
| | | Souv. sheet of 2, #C361-C361A, imperf. | 8.00 | 8.00 |

For overprints see Nos. C364-C364B.

## Souvenir Sheet

**Olympic Equestrian Events — AP86b**

**1968, Oct. 29**    *Imperf.*

| | | | | |
|---|---|---|---|---|
| C362 | AP86b | Sheet of 2 | 45.00 | 45.00 |
| a. | | 0c Dressage | 1.50 | 3.50 |
| b. | | 30c Show jumping | 5.00 | 3.50 |

## Intl. Human Rights Year — AP86c

**1968, Dec. 18**    *Perf. 14*

| | | | | |
|---|---|---|---|---|
| C363 | AP86c | 40c multicolored | 11.50 | 7.50 |
| a. | | Miniature sheet of 1 | 30.00 | 30.00 |

## Nos. C361-C361b Ovptd. in Red or Black

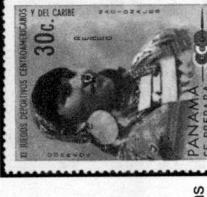

**1969, Jan. 31**

| | | | | |
|---|---|---|---|---|
| C364 | AP86a | 50c on #C361 (R) | 6.25 | 1.50 |
| C364A | AP86a | 1b on #C361A (B) | 6.25 | 1.50 |
| | | **Souvenir Sheet** | | |
| C364B | | on #C361b (R) | 11.50 | 11.50 |

Intl. Philatelic and Numismatic Expo. Overprint larger on No. C364A, larger and in different arrangement on No. C364B.

## Intl. Space Exploration — AP86d

**1969, Mar. 14**

| | | | | |
|---|---|---|---|---|
| C365 | | Sheet of 6 | 18.00 | 18.00 |
| a. | AP86d | 5c France, Diadem I | .50 | .25 |
| b. | AP86d | 10c Italy, San Marco | 1.00 | .40 |
| c. | AP86d | 15c Great Britain, UK | 1.50 | .50 |
| d. | AP86d | 20c US, Saturn | 2.00 | .75 |
| e. | AP86d | 25c US, Surveyor 7 | 3.00 | 1.00 |
| f. | AP86d | 30c Europe/US, Esro 2 | 4.00 | 1.25 |

## Satellite Transmission of Summer Olympics, Mexico, 1968 — AP86e

**1969, Mar. 14**    *Perf. 14½*

| | | | | |
|---|---|---|---|---|
| C300 | AP86e | 1b multi | 3.00 | 1.00 |
| a. | | Miniature sheet of 1 | 10.00 | 2.00 |

Nos. CB4, 461B & 461C Surcharged

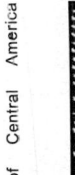

Decreto No 112 (de 6 de marzo de 1969)
B/. 0.05

**1969, Mar. 26**    *Perf. 13½x13*

| | | | | |
|---|---|---|---|---|
| C367 | AP81 | 5c on 5c+5c | 3.50 | .50 |
| C367A | A147e | 5c on 10c+5c | 3.50 | .50 |
| C367B | A147e | 10c on 21c+10c | 3.50 | .50 |

## Games Type of Regular Issue and San Blas Indian Girl — AP87

Design: 13c, Bridge of the Americas.

**1970, Jan. 6**    *Litho.*    *Perf. 13½*

| | | | | |
|---|---|---|---|---|
| C368 | A158 | 13c multi | 1.00 | .30 |
| C369 | AP87 | 13c multi | 1.25 | .75 |
| a. | | "AEREO" omitted | 50.00 | 50.00 |

See notes after No. 525.

## Juan D. Arosemena and Arosemena Stadium — AP88

Designs: 2c, 3c, 5c, like 1c. No. C374, Basketball. No. C375, New Panama Gymnasium. No. C376, Revolution Stadium. No. C377, Panamanian man and woman in Stadium. 30c, Stadium, eternal flame, arms of Mexico, Puerto Rico and Cuba.

**1970, Oct. 7**    *Wmk. 365*    *Perf. 13½*

| | | | | |
|---|---|---|---|---|
| C370 | AP00 | 1c multi | .20 | .20 |
| C371 | AP88 | 2c pink & multi | .20 | .20 |
| C372 | AP88 | 3c pink & multi | .20 | .20 |
| C373 | AP88 | 5c pink & multi | .20 | .20 |
| C374 | AP88 | 13c lt blue & multi | .45 | .20 |
| C375 | AP88 | 13c lilac & multi | .45 | .20 |
| C376 | AP88 | 13c yellow & multi | .45 | .20 |
| C377 | AP88 | 13c pink & multi | .45 | .20 |
| C378 | AP00 | 30c yellow & multi | 1.25 | .50 |
| a. | | Souv. sheet of 1, imperf. | 2.00 | 2.10 |
| | | Nos. C370-C378 (9) | 3.85 | 2.10 |

11th Central American and Caribbean Games, Feb. 28-Mar. 14.

## US astronauts Charles Conrad, Jr., Richard F. Gordon, Jr. and Alan L. Bean. — AP89

**1971**    *Wmk. 343*    *Perf. 13½*

| | | | | |
|---|---|---|---|---|
| C379 | AP89 | 13c gold & multi | .50 | .35 |
| C380 | AP89 | 13c lt green & multi | .50 | .35 |

Man's first landing on the moon, Apollo 11, July 20, 1969 (No. C379) and Apollo 12 moon mission, Nov. 14-24, 1969. Issued: No. C379, Aug. 20; No. C380, Aug. 23.

#C379, Astronaut on Moon.

## EXPO '70 Emblem and Pavilion — AP90

**1971, Aug. 24**    *Litho.*

| | | | | |
|---|---|---|---|---|
| C381 | AP90 | 10c pink & multi | .25 | .25 |

EXPO '70 International Exposition, Osaka, Japan, Mar. 15-Sept. 13.

## Flag of Panama — AP91

Design: 13c, Map of Panama superimposed on Western Hemisphere, and tourist year emblem.

**1971, Dec. 11**    *Wmk. 343*

| | | | | |
|---|---|---|---|---|
| C382 | AP91 | 5c multi | .20 | .20 |
| C383 | AP91 | 13c multi | .25 | .25 |

Proclamation of 1972 as Tourist Year of the Americas.

## Mahatma Gandhi — AP92

**1971, Dec. 17**

| | | | | |
|---|---|---|---|---|
| C384 | AP92 | 10c black & multi | .60 | .35 |

Centenary of the birth of Mohandas K. Gandhi (1869-1948), leader in India's fight for independence.

## Central American Independence Issue

Flags of Central American States — AP92a

**1971, Dec. 20**

| | | | | |
|---|---|---|---|---|
| C385 | AP92a | 13c multi | .35 | .25 |

160th anniv. of Central America independence.

AP93

**1971, Dec. 21**

| | | | | |
|---|---|---|---|---|
| C386 | AP93 | 8c Panama #4 | .25 | .25 |

2nd National Philatelic and Numismatic Exposition, 1970.

AP94

**1972, Sept. 7**    *Wmk. 365*

| | | | | |
|---|---|---|---|---|
| C387 | AP94 | 40c Natá Church | .80 | .60 |

450th anniversary of the founding of Natá.

For surcharges see Nos. C402, RA85.

**Telecommunications Emblem — AP95**

**1972, Sept. 8**
C388 AP95 13c lt bl, dp bl & blk ... .40 .40
3rd World Telecommunications Day (in 1971).

No. C387 Surcharged in Red Similar to No. 542

C402 13c on 40c multi ... .35 .30
UN Security Council Meeting, Panama City, Mar. 15-21.

**1973, Mar. 16    Wmk. 365    Perf. 13½**
C400 AP99 50c green & multi ... 1.50 .60
C401 AP99 1b multicolored ... 3.00 1.00
Nos. C396-401 (6) ... 6.05 2.45

7th Bolivar Games, Panama City, 2/17-3/3.

Portrait Type of Regular Issue 1973

Designs: 5c, Isabel Herrera Obaldia, educator, 8c, Nicolas Victoria Jaén, educator, 10c, Forest Scene, by Roberto Lewis. 10c, Portrait of a Lady, by Manuel E. Amador, poet. 13c, Ricardo Miró, poet, 20c, Manuel Amador Guerrero, statesman, 25c, Belisario Porras, statesman, 30c, Juan Demostenes Arosemena, statesman, 34c, Octavio Mendez Pereira, writer, 38c, Ricardo J. Alfaro, writer.

**1973, June 20    Litho.    Perf. 13½**
C403 A169 5c pink & multi ... .20 .20
C404 A169 8c pink & multi ... .25 .20
C405 A169 10c gray & multi ... .35 .20
C406 A169 13c pink & multi ... .55 .20
C407 A169 13c pink & multi ... .55 .20
C408 A169 20c blue & multi ... .70 .40
C409 A169 21c yellow & multi ... .80 .40
C410 A169 25c pink & multi ... .80 .40
C411 A169 30c gray & multi ... 1.00 .45
C412 A169 34c lt blue & multi ... 1.10 .60
C413 A169 38c lt blue & multi ... 1.25 .60
Nos. C403-C413 (11) ... 7.65 3.85

Famous Panamanians.

**Apollo 14 — AP96**

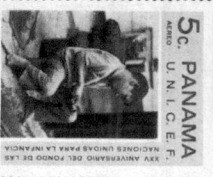

**1972, Sept. 11**
C389 AP96 13c tan & multi ... .90 .50
Apollo 14 US moon mission, 1/1-2/9/71.

**Shoeshine Boy Counting Coins — AP97**

**1972, Sept. 12**
C390 AP97 5c shown ... .20 .20
C391 AP97 8c Mother & Child ... .25 .25
C392 AP97 50c UNICEF emblem ... 1.25 .55
a. Souv. sheet of 1, imperf. ... 1.75 1.75
Nos. C390-C392 (3) ... 1.70 1.00
25th anniv. (in 1971) of the UNICEF.

**San Blas Cloth, Cuna Indians AP98**

**1972, Sept. 13**
C393 AP98 5c shown ... .20 .20
C394 AP98 8c Beaded necklace, Guaymi Indians ... .25 .20
C395 AP98 25c View of Portobelo ... .80 .45
a. Souv. sheet of 2, #C393, C395, imperf. ... 3.50 3.50
Nos. C393-C395 (3) ... 1.25 .85
For surcharges see Nos. C417, RA83.
Tourist publicity.

**Baseball Games' Emblem AP99**

**1973, Feb. 9    Litho.    Perf. 12½    Unwmk.**
C396 AP99 8c rose red & yel ... .25 .20
C397 AP99 10c black & ultra ... .25 .20
C398 AP99 13c blue & multi ... .35 .20
C399 AP99 25c blk, yel grn & red ... .70 .25

Games' Emblem and: 10c, Basketball, vert. 13c, Torch, vert. 25c, Boxing, 50c, Map and flag of Panama, Bolivar, 1b, Medals.

50th anniversary of the Isabel Herrera Obaldia Professional School.

**1973, Sept. 14    Litho.    Perf. 13½**
C414 A169 5c pink & multi ... .20 .20
C415 A169 25c pink & multi ... .90 .40
C416 A169 34c bl & multi (R) ... 1.10 .75
Nos. C414-C416 (3) ... 2.20 1.40

For overprints and surcharges see Nos. C414-C416, C418-C421.

Nos. C403, C410, and C412 Overprinted in Black or Red

Nos. C395, C408, C413, C412 and C409 Surcharged in Red

**1974, Nov. 11    Litho.    Perf. 13½**
C417 AP98 1c on 25c multi ... .20 .20
C418 A169 3c on 20c multi ... .20 .20
C419 A169 3c on 38c multi ... .20 .20
C420 A169 10c on 34c multi ... .20 .20
C421 A169 13c on 21c multi ... .20 .20
Nos. C417-C421 (5) ... 1.00 1.00

**Women's Hands, Panama Map, UN and IWY Emblems AP100**

**1975, May 6    Litho.    Unwmk.**
C422 AP100 17c blue & multi ... .70 .20
a. Souv. sheet, imperf., no gum ... 1.50 1.50
International Women's Year 1975.

**Victoria Sugar Plant, Sugar Cane, Map of Veraguas Province AP101**

**1975, Oct. 9    Litho.    Perf. 12½**
C423 AP101 17c bl, buff & blk ... .70 .30
C424 AP101 27c ultra & yel grn ... 1.00 .35
C425 AP101 33c bl & multi ... 1.10 .40
Nos. C423-C425 (3) ... 2.80 1.10

Designs: 17c, Bayano electrification project and map of Panama, horiz. 33c, Tocumen International Airport and map, horiz.

Oct. 11, 1968, Revolution, 7th anniv.

**Bolivar Statue and Flags — AP102**

**Bolivar Hall, Panama City AP103**

**1976, Mar.    Perf. 13x12½, 12½x13**
C426 AP102 23c multi ... .65 .20
C427 AP103 35c multi ... 1.00 .30
C428 AP102 41c multi ... 1.60 .60
Nos. C426-C428 (3) ... 2.65 1.10

Design: 41c, Bolivar with flag of Panama, ruins of Old Panama City.

150th anniversary of Congress of Panama. Issue dates: 23c, Mar. 15; others Mar. 30.

Marine Life Type of 1976

**1976, May 6    Litho.    Wmk. 377**
C429 A171 17c multi ... .90 .30
C430 A171 27c multi ... 1.25 .40
Perf. 13½

Marine life: 17c, Diodon hystrix, vert. 27c, Pocillopora damicornis.

**Cerro Colorado — AP104**

**1976, Nov. 12    Litho.    Perf. 12½**
C431 AP104 23c multi ... .55 .20
Cerro Colorado copper mines, Chiriqui Province.

**Gen. Omar Torrijos Herrera (1929-1981) AP105**

**1982, Feb.    Litho.    Perf. 10½**
C432 AP105 23c multi ... .65 .20

Torrijos Type of 1982

**1982, May 14    Litho.    Wmk. 311**
C433 A201 41c Torrijos Airport ... 1.10 .50
C434 A201 35c Security Council reunion, 1973 ... 1.00 .30
Perf. 10½

**Souvenir Sheet    Imperf**
C435 A201 23c like #C432 ... 3.00 3.00
No. C435 sold for 1b.

Alfaro Type of 1982

**1982, Aug. 18    Wmk. 382**
C436 A202 17c multi ... .45 .20
C437 A202 23c multi ... .65 .20
Photos by Luiz Gutierrez Cruz.

World Cup Type of 1982

**1982, Dec. 27    Litho.    Perf. 10½**
C438 A203 23c Map ... .70 .20
C439 A203 35c Pele, vert. ... 1.00 .30
C440 A203 41c Cup, vert. ... 1.25 .40
Nos. C438-C440 (3) ... 2.95 .90

1b imperf. souvenir sheet exists in design of 23c; black control number. Value $13.50.

**Nicolas A. Solano (1882-1943), Tuberculosis Researcher AP106**

**1983, Feb. 8    Litho.    Wmk. 382 (Stars)    Perf. 10½**
C441 AP106 23c brown ... .50 .50

**World Food Day — AP107**

**1984, Oct. 16    Litho.    Perf. 12**
C442 AP107 30c Hand grasping fork ... 1.25 .50

**Contadora Group for Peace — AP108**

**1985, Oct. 1    Litho.    Perf. 14**
C443 AP108 10c multi ... .45 .20
C444 AP108 20c multi ... .90 .30
C445 AP108 30c multi ... 1.25 .50
Nos. C443-C445 (3) ... 2.60 1.00
See No. 680A.

## SPECIAL DELIVERY STAMPS

Nos. 211-212 Overprinted in Red

**1926 Unwmk. Perf. 12**
E1 A31 10c org & blk 7.50 3.25
E2 A32 20c brn & blk 40.00 3.25
  a. "EXPRESO" 10.00 3.25
  b. Double overprint 40.00
     35.00 35.00

Bicycle Messenger SD1

**1929 Engr. Perf. 12½**
E3 SD1 10c orange 1.25 1.00
E4 SD1 20c dk brn 4.75 2.50

For surcharges and overprints see Nos. C1-C5, C17-C18A, C67

## REGISTRATION STAMPS

Issued under Colombian Dominion

R1

**1888 Unwmk. Engr. Perf. 13½**
F1 R1 10c black, gray 8.00 5.25

*Imperforate and part-perforate copies without gum and those on surface-colored paper are reprints.*

R2

Magenta, Violet or Blue Black Handstamped Overprint

**1898 Perf. 12**
F2 R2 10c yellow 7.00 6.50

The handstamp on No. F2 was also used as a postmark.

R3

**1900 Litho. Perf. 11**
F3 R3 10c blk, lt bl 4.00 3.50

**1901**
F4 R3 10c brown red 30.00 20.00

R4

**1902 Blue Black Surcharge**
F5 R4 20c on 10c brn red 20.00 16.00

## AIR POST SEMI-POSTAL STAMPS

**Catalogue values for unused stamps in this section are for Never Hinged items.**

"The World Against Malaria" — SPAP1

**1961, Dec. 20 Litho. Perf. 12½**
CB1 SPAP1 5c + 5c car rose .50 .50
CB2 SPAP1 10c + 10c vio bl .50 .50
CB3 SPAP1 15c + 15c dk grn 1.50 1.50
Nos. CB1-CB3 (3)

WHO drive to eradicate malaria.
For surcharges see Nos. C271-C272.

Nos. C274-C276 Surcharged in Red

**Wmk. 311**
**1963, Mar. 4 Litho. Perf. 12½**
CB4 AP81 5c +5c on #C274 1.00 .75
CB5 AP81 10c +10c on #C275 2.00 1.50
CB6 AP81 15c +15c on #C276 2.00 1.50

Surcharge on No. CB4 differs to fit stamp. See No. CB7.

"Centenario Cruz Roja Internacional"

No. CB4 Surcharged in Black

CB7 AP81 10c on 5c+5c 6.00 5.00
Intl. Red. Cross cent.

---

## AIR POST (Commemorative)

Christmas Type of 1988
**1988, Dec. 29 Litho. Perf. 12**
C446 A246 35c St. Joseph and the Infant 1.10 .40

Olympics Type of 1989
**1989, Mar. 17 Litho. Perf. 12**
C447 A248 35c Boxing 1.10 .40

Opening of the Panama Canal, 75th Anniv. AP109
**1989, Sept. 29 Litho. Perf. 13½**
C448 AP109 35c Ancon in lock, 1914 1.25 .65
C449 AP109 60c Ship in lock, 1989 2.00 1.10

Revolution Type of 1989
**1989, Nov. 14 Litho.**
C450 A251 35c Storming of the Bastille 1.75 .65
C451 A251 45c multi, emblem, bicent. 2.10 .85
French revolution, bicent.

Christmas 2001 AP110
**2002, Apr. 30 Litho. Perf. 13x13½**
C452-C454 AP110 Set of 3 14.50 14.50
Dated 2001.

La Salle Schools in Panama, Cent. (in 2002) AP111
**2003, May 15 Litho. Perf. 13x13½**
C455 AP111 5b multi 16.00 10.00
Dated 2002.

Natá, 480th Anniv. (in 2002) AP112
**2003, May 20 Litho. Perf. 13x13½**
C456 AP112 1b multi 3.25 2.00
Dated 2002.

Trains AP113
Designs: 40c, Colón locomotive. 50c, Panama Railroad, vert.
**Perf. 13x13½, 14 (50c)**
**2003, July 16 Set of 2**
C457-C458 AP113 3.00 1.90
Dated 2002.

Santa María de Belén, 500th Anniv. AP114
**2003, July 31 Perf. 14 Litho.**
C459 AP114 1.50b multi 5.00 3.00
Dated 2002.

Fourth Voyage of Christopher Columbus, 500th Anniv. (in 2002) AP115
**2003, Jan. 31 Perf. 13x13½**
C460 AP115 2b multi 6.75 4.00
Dated 2002.

Kuna Indians AP116

Designs: No. C461, 50c, Village, people in canoe, woman. No. C462, 50c, Man and woman, vert. No. C463, 60c, Woman sewing. No. C464, 60c, Dancers. No. 1.50b, Fish.

**Perf. 14 (#C461), 13½x13 (#C462), 13x13½**
**2003, Aug. 12 Souvenir Sheet Perf. 13½x14**
C461-C464 AP116 Set of 4 7.00 4.50
C465 AP116 1.50b multi 5.75 5.75
Dated 2002. No. C465 contains one 50x45mm stamp.

Medicine in Panama AP117
**Perf. 12**
Designs: No. C466, 50c, Santo Tomás de Villanueva Hospital, 300th anniv. No. C467, 50c, Gorgas Memorial Institute of Tropical and Preventative Medicine, 75th anniv.
**2003**
C466-C467 AP117 Set of 2 2.00 2.00
Issued: No. C466, 11/11; No. C467, 11/17.

Jewelry AP118
Designs: 45c, Necklaces. 60c, Brooches.
**2003, Nov. 24 Set of 2**
C468-C469 AP118 2.10 2.10

America Issue - Endangered Species — AP119
**2003, Nov. 26**
C470 AP119 2b multi 4.00 4.00

La Estrella de Panama Newspaper, 150th Anniv. — AP120
**2003, Dec. 3**
C471 AP120 40c multi .80 .80

## Issues of the Republic

### Issued in the City of Panama

Registration Stamps of Colombia Handstamped

**Handstamped in Blue**
Black or Rose

R9

**1903-04**

| | | Imperf. | |
|---|---|---|---|
| F6 | R9 20c red brn, bl | 45.00 | 42.50 |
| F7 | R9 20c blue, blue (R) | 45.00 | 42.50 |

For surcharges and overprints see Nos. F8-F11, F16-F26.

Reprints exist of Nos. F6 and F7; see note after No. 64.

**1903-04**

| F8 | R9 10c on 20c red brn, bl | 60.00 | 55.00 |
|---|---|---|---|
| b. | "10" in blue black | 60.00 | 55.00 |
| F9 | R9 10c on 20c bl, bl | 60.00 | 45.00 |

**Handstamped in Rose**

With Additional Surcharge in Rose

| F10 | R9 10c on 20c red brn, bl | 60.00 | 55.00 |
|---|---|---|---|
| F11 | R9 10c on 20c blue, blue | 45.00 | 42.50 |

### Issued in Colon

Regular Issues Handstamped "R/COLON" in Circle (as on F2) Together with Other Overprints and Surcharges

**Handstamped**

**1903-04**

| F12 | A4 10c yellow | 3.00 | 2.50 |
|---|---|---|---|

**F13** A4 10c yellow

**Handstamped**

**Overprinted in Red**

PANAMA

Handstamped

PANAMA PANAMA

**F14** A4 10c yellow 3.00 2.50

**Overprinted in Black**

República de Panamá

**Colombia No. F13 Handstamped Like No. F12 in Violet**

| | | Imperf | |
|---|---|---|---|
| F15 | A4 10c yellow | 7.50 | 5.00 |

The handstamps on Nos. F12 to F15 are in magenta, violet or red; various combinations of these colors are to be found. They are struck in various positions, including double, inverted, one handstamp omitted, etc.

| F16 | R9 20c red brn, bl | 60.00 | 55.00 |
|---|---|---|---|

---

**Overprinted Like No. F15 in Black**

| F17 | R9 20c red brn, bl | 6.00 | 5.75 |
|---|---|---|---|

**No. F17 Surcharged in Manuscript**

| F18 | R9 20c red brn, bl | 60.00 | 55.00 |
|---|---|---|---|

**No. F17 Surcharged in Purple**

| F19 | R9 10c on 20c | 82.50 | 80.00 |
|---|---|---|---|

**No. F17 Surcharged in Violet**

10

| F20 | R9 10c on 20c | 82.50 | 80.00 |
|---|---|---|---|

The varieties of the overprint which are described after No. 138 are also to be found on the Registration and Acknowledgment of Receipt stamps. It is probable that Nos. F17 to F20 inclusive owe their existence more to speculation than to postal necessity.

**1903-04**

| F21 | R9 20c blue, blue | 125.00 | 125.00 |
|---|---|---|---|
| F22 | R9 20c red brn, blue | 125.00 | 125.00 |

**No. F21 Surcharged in Violet or Red**

| F23 | R9 10c on 20c bl, bl | 150.00 | 140.00 |
|---|---|---|---|

### Issued in Bocas del Toro

Colombia Nos. F17 and F13 Handstamped in Violet

**R DE PANAMA**

Surcharged in Manuscript (a) "10cs" in Red "10cs" in Red (b)

| F25 | R9 10 on 20c red | 70.00 | 65.00 |
|---|---|---|---|
| F26 | R9 10cs on 20c bl, bl | 55.00 | 50.00 |
| | brn, bl | 525.00 | 505.00 |

No. F25 without surcharge is bogus, according to leading experts.

Reprints exist of Nos. F21-F26 (5).

### Colombia Nos. F13, F17 Handstamped in Violet

**General Issue**

R5

**1904**

| F27 | R5 10c green | Engr. | |
|---|---|---|---|
| | | Perf. 12 | |
| | | 1.00 | .50 |

Nos. 190 and 213 Surcharged in Red

**1916-17**

| F29 | A11 5c on 8c pur & blk | 3.00 | 2.25 |
|---|---|---|---|
| a. | "5" inverted | 3.00 | |
| b. | Large, round "5" | 55.00 | |
| c. | Inverted surcharge | 12.50 | 11.00 |
| d. | Tête bêche surcharge | | |
| F30 | A33 5c on 8c vio & blk | | |
| | ("17") | 3.50 | .80 |
| a. | Inverted surcharge | 10.00 | 8.25 |
| b. | Tête bêche surcharge | | |
| c. | Double surcharge | 40.00 | |

#F29-F30

#F29b

Experts consider this handstamp—"A.R. / COLON / COLOMBIA"—to be a cancellation or a marking intended for a letter to receive special handling. It was applied at Colon to various stamps in 1897-1904 in different colored inks for philatelic sale. It exists on cover, usually with the bottom line removed by masking the handstamp.

**1902**

| H4 | A4 5c blue | 5.00 | 5.00 |
|---|---|---|---|
| H5 | A4 10c yellow | 10.00 | 10.00 |

This handstamp was also used as a postmark.

**1903-04**

| H9 | A4 10c blue, blue | Imperf. | |
|---|---|---|---|
| | | 10.00 | 8.00 |

Reprints exist of No. H9, see note after No. 64.

**No. H9 Surcharged with New Value**

| H10 | AR2 5c on 10c bl, bl | 5.00 | 5.00 |
|---|---|---|---|

### Issues of the Republic
Issued in the City of Panama
Colombia No. H3 Handstamped

**Handstamped in Rose**

AR2

| H11 | AR2 10c blue, blue | 17.50 | 14.00 |
|---|---|---|---|

---

## INSURED LETTER STAMPS

Stamps of 1939 Surcharged in Black

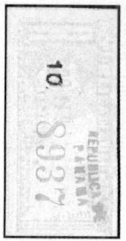

**1942**

| | | Unwmk. | Perf. 12½ | |
|---|---|---|---|---|
| G1 | AP23 5c on 1b blk | .50 | .50 | |
| G2 | A84 10c on 1b dk brn | .80 | .80 | |
| G3 | AP23 25c on 50c dk brn | 2.00 | 2.00 | |
| | Nos. G1-G3 (3) | 3.30 | 3.30 | |

### ACKNOWLEDGMENT OF RECEIPT STAMPS

Issued under Colombian Dominion

**1904**

| H21 | AR2 5c on 10c blue, blue | 11.00 | 8.00 |
|---|---|---|---|

No. H21, unused, without surcharge is bogus.

### Issued in Bocas del Toro
Colombia No. H3 Handstamped in Violet and Surcharged in Red Like Nos. F25-F26

**No. H19 Surcharged in Manuscript**

| H20 | AR2 10c on 10c | 100.00 | 82.50 |
|---|---|---|---|

**1904**

| H22 | AR3 5c blue | Engr. | |
|---|---|---|---|
| | | Perf. 12 | |
| | | 1.00 | .80 |

AR3

**General Issue**

No. 199 Overprinted in Violet

**1916**

| H23 | A20 2½c red orange | 1.00 | .80 |
|---|---|---|---|
| a. | "R.A." for "A.R." | 50.00 | |
| b. | Double overprint | 8.00 | |
| c. | Inverted overprint | 8.00 | |

A.R.

---

### INSURED LETTER STAMPS

Stamps of 1939 Surcharged in Black

Handstamped in Magenta or Violet

**H17** AR2 10c blue, blue 15.00 15.00

**Handstamped**

| | | Imperf | |
|---|---|---|---|
| H18 | AR2 10c blue, blue | 82.50 | 70.00 |

**Overprinted in Black**

PANAMA

**H19** AR2 10c blue, blue 11.00 8.00

República de Panamá.

### Issued in Colon
Colombia No. H3 Handstamped in Violet or Blue Black

**Colombia No. 14 Handstamped in Rose or Blue Black**

Panamá

### Issues of the Republic
Issued in the City of Panama

### LATE FEE STAMPS

**1903-04**

| I1 | LF3 5c pur, rose | Unwmk. | Imperf. | |
|---|---|---|---|---|
| | | 12.50 | 9.00 | |
| I2 | LF3 5c pur, rose (Bl Blk) | 17.50 | 12.50 | |

Reprints exist of #I1-I2; see note after #64.

LF3

REPÚBLICA DE PANAMA

REPÚBLICA DE PANAMA

## General Issue

**LF4**

**Engr.    Perf. 12**

**1904**

| | | | | |
|---|---|---|---|---|
| I3 | LF4 | 2½c lake | 1.00 | .65 |

**No. 199 Overprinted with Typewriter**

*Retardo*

**1910, Aug. 12**

| | | | | |
|---|---|---|---|---|
| I4 | A20 | 2½c red orange | 125.00 | 100.00 |

Counterfeits abound. Used only on Aug. 12-13.

**Handstamped**

*RETARDO*

**1910**

| | | | | |
|---|---|---|---|---|
| I5 | A20 | 2½c red orange | 60.00 | 50.00 |

Counterfeits abound.

**No. 195 Surcharged in Green**

**1917**

| | | | | |
|---|---|---|---|---|
| I6 | A17 | 1c on ½c orange | .80 | .80 |
| a. | | "UN CENTESIMO" inverted | 50.00 | 50.00 |
| b. | | Double surcharge | 10.00 | 10.00 |
| c. | | Inverted surcharge | 6.50 | 6.50 |

**Same Surcharge on No. 196**

**1921**

| | | | | |
|---|---|---|---|---|
| I7 | A17 | 1c on ½c rose | 25.00 | 20.00 |

## POSTAGE DUE STAMPS

Statue of Columbus — D2

San Geronimo Castle Gate, Portobelo — D1

Pedro J. Sosa — D4

Design: 4c, Capitol, Panama City.

**1915    Unwmk.    Engr.    Perf. 12**

| | | | | |
|---|---|---|---|---|
| J1 | D1 | 1c olive brown | 3.00 | .75 |
| J2 | D2 | 2c olive brown | 4.50 | .65 |
| J3 | D4 | 4c olive brown | 4.50 | 1.25 |
| J4 | D4 | 10c olive brown | 18.00 | 4.40 |
| | | Nos. J1-J4 (4) | | |

Type D1 was intended to show a gate of San Lorenzo Castle, Chagres, and is so labeled. It actually shows the main gate of San Geronimo Castle, Portobelo.

**1930    Perf. 12½**

| | | | | |
|---|---|---|---|---|
| J5 | D5 | 1c emerald | 1.00 | .60 |
| J6 | D5 | 2c dark red | 1.00 | .60 |
| J7 | D5 | 4c dark blue | 1.60 | .80 |
| J8 | D5 | 10c violet | 5.20 | 2.80 |
| | | Nos. J5-J8 (4) | | |

## POSTAL TAX STAMPS

Pierre and Marie Curie — PT1

**1939    Unwmk.    Engr.**

| | | | | |
|---|---|---|---|---|
| RA1 | PT1 | 1c rose carmine | .65 | .20 |
| RA2 | PT1 | 1c green | .65 | .20 |
| RA3 | PT1 | 1c orange | .65 | .20 |
| RA4 | PT1 | 1c blue | 2.60 | .80 |
| | | Nos. RA1-RA4 (4) | | |

See Nos. RA6-RA18, RA24-RA27, RA30.

**Stamp of 1924 Overprinted in Black**

Inscribed 1940

**1940**

| | | | | |
|---|---|---|---|---|
| RA5 | A53 | 1c dark green | 1.40 | .75 |

**1941**

| | | | | |
|---|---|---|---|---|
| RA6 | PT1 | 1c rose carmine | .65 | .20 |
| RA7 | PT1 | 1c green | .65 | .20 |
| RA8 | PT1 | 1c orange | .65 | .20 |
| RA9 | PT1 | 1c blue | 2.60 | .80 |
| | | Nos. RA6-RA9 (4) | | |

Inscribed 1942

**1942**

| | | | | |
|---|---|---|---|---|
| RA10 | PT1 | 1c violet | .40 | .20 |

Inscribed 1943

**1943**

| | | | | |
|---|---|---|---|---|
| RA11 | PT1 | 1c rose carmine | .40 | .20 |
| RA12 | PT1 | 1c green | .40 | .20 |
| RA13 | PT1 | 1c orange | .40 | .20 |
| RA14 | PT1 | 1c blue | 1.60 | .80 |
| | | Nos. RA11-RA14 (4) | | |

Inscribed 1945

**1945**

| | | | | |
|---|---|---|---|---|
| RA15 | PT1 | 1c rose carmine | .90 | .20 |
| RA16 | PT1 | 1c green | .90 | .20 |
| RA17 | PT1 | 1c orange | .90 | .20 |
| RA18 | PT1 | 1c blue | 3.60 | .80 |
| | | Nos. RA15-RA18 (4) | | |

**Nos. 234 and 235 Surcharged in Black or Red**

**1946    Unwmk.    Perf. 12**

| | | | | |
|---|---|---|---|---|
| RA19 | A53 | 1c on ½c orange | .60 | .20 |
| RA20 | A53 | 1c on 1c dk grn (R) | .60 | .20 |

> Catalogue values for unused stamps in this section, from this point to the end of the section, are for Never Hinged items.

**Same Surcharged in Black on Nos. 239 and 241**

**1947**

| | | | | |
|---|---|---|---|---|
| RA21 | A53 | 1c on 12c ol grn | 1.00 | .30 |
| RA22 | A53 | 1c on 24c yel brn | 1.00 | .30 |

**Surcharged in Red on No. 342**

| | | | | |
|---|---|---|---|---|
| RA23 | A95 | 1c on ½c dl vio, bl & car | 1.00 | .20 |

**Type of 1939 Inscribed 1947**

**1947**

| | | | | |
|---|---|---|---|---|
| RA24 | PT1 | 1c rose carmine | 1.25 | .20 |
| RA25 | PT1 | 1c green | 1.25 | .20 |
| RA26 | PT1 | 1c orange | 1.25 | .20 |
| RA27 | PT1 | 1c blue | 5.00 | .80 |
| | | Nos. RA24-RA27 (4) | | |

**Nos. C100 and C101 Surcharged in Black**

**1949, Feb. 16    Unwmk.    Perf. 12½**

| | | | | |
|---|---|---|---|---|
| RA28 | AP45 (a) | 1c on 5c | .65 | .20 |
| a. | | Inverted surcharge | 10.00 | |
| RA29 | AP46 (b) | 1c on 10c yel org | .65 | .20 |

**Type of 1939 Inscribed 1949**

**1949**

| | | | | |
|---|---|---|---|---|
| RA30 | PT1 | 1c brown | 2.00 | .20 |

The tax from the sale of Nos. RA1-RA30 was used for the control of cancer.

Juan D. Arosemena Stadium — PT2

Torch Emblem — PT3

Discobolus — PT4

#RA33, Adan Gordon Olympic Swimming Pool.

**1951    Unwmk.    Engr.    Perf. 12½**

| | | | | |
|---|---|---|---|---|
| RA31 | PT2 | 1c carmine & blk | 1.60 | .25 |
| RA32 | PT3 | 1c dk bl & blk | 1.60 | .25 |
| RA33 | PT2 | 1c grn & blk | 4.80 | .75 |
| | | Nos. RA31-RA33 (3) | | |

**1952**

Design: No. RA34, Turners' emblem.

| | | | | |
|---|---|---|---|---|
| RA34 | PT3 | 1c org & blk | 1.60 | .25 |
| RA35 | PT4 | 1c pur & blk | 1.60 | .25 |

The tax from the sale of Nos. RA31-RA35 was used to promote physical education.

Boys Doing Farm Work — PT5

**Type of 1958 Inscribed 1959**

**1958    Wmk. 311    Litho.    Perf. 12½    Size: 35x24mm**

| | | | | |
|---|---|---|---|---|
| RA36 | PT5 | 1c rose red & gray | .20 | .20 |

**1959    Size: 35x24mm**

| | | | | |
|---|---|---|---|---|
| RA37 | PT5 | 1c gray & emerald | .20 | .20 |
| RA38 | PT5 | 1c vio bl & gray | .20 | .20 |

**Type of 1958 Inscribed 1960**

**1960    Litho.    Wmk. 334    Size: 32x23mm    Perf. 13½**

| | | | | |
|---|---|---|---|---|
| RA39 | PT5 | 1c carmine & gray | .20 | .20 |

**Nos. C235 and C241 Surcharged in Black or Red**

**1961    Wmk. 343    Perf. 12½**

| | | | | |
|---|---|---|---|---|
| RA40 | A131 | 1c on 10c ocher & blk | .20 | .20 |
| RA41 | AP76 | 1c on 10c emer (R) | .20 | .20 |

Girl at Sewing Machine — PT6

**1961, Nov. 24    Wmk. 343    Litho.    Perf. 12½**

| | | | | |
|---|---|---|---|---|
| RA42 | PT6 | 1c brt vio | .25 | .20 |
| RA43 | PT6 | 1c rose lilac | .25 | .20 |
| RA44 | PT6 | 1c yellow | .25 | .20 |
| RA45 | PT6 | 1c blue | .25 | .20 |
| RA46 | PT6 | 1c emerald | .25 | .20 |
| | | Nos. RA42-RA46 (5) | 1.25 | 1.00 |

**1961, Dec. 1**

Design: Boy with hand saw.

| | | | | |
|---|---|---|---|---|
| RA47 | PT6 | 1c red lilac | .25 | .20 |
| RA48 | PT6 | 1c rose | .25 | .20 |
| RA49 | PT6 | 1c orange | .25 | .20 |
| RA50 | PT6 | 1c blue | .25 | .20 |
| RA51 | PT6 | 1c gray | .25 | .20 |
| | | Nos. RA47-RA51 (5) | 1.25 | 1.00 |

Map of Panama, Flags — PT8

Boy Scout — PT7

Designs: Nos. RA57-RA61, Girl Scout.

**1964, Feb. 7    Wmk. 343**

| | | | | |
|---|---|---|---|---|
| RA52 | PT7 | 1c olive | .25 | .20 |
| RA53 | PT7 | 1c gray | .25 | .20 |
| RA54 | PT7 | 1c lilac | .25 | .20 |
| RA55 | PT7 | 1c carmine rose | .25 | .20 |
| RA56 | PT7 | 1c blue | .25 | .20 |
| RA57 | PT7 | 1c bluish green | .25 | .20 |
| RA58 | PT7 | 1c violet | .25 | .20 |
| RA59 | PT7 | 1c orange | .25 | .20 |
| RA60 | PT7 | 1c yellow | .25 | .20 |
| RA61 | PT7 | 1c brn org | .25 | .20 |
| | | Nos. RA52-RA61 (10) | 2.50 | 2.00 |

The tax from Nos. RA36-RA61 was for youth rehabilitation.

**1973, Jan. 22    Unwmk.**

| | | | | |
|---|---|---|---|---|
| RA62 | PT8 | 1c black | .20 | .20 |

7th Bolivar Sports Games, Feb. 17-Mar. 3, 1973. The tax was for a new post office in Panama City.

Post Office — PT9

Designs: No. RA63, Farm Cooperative. No. RA64, 5b silver coin. No. RA65, Victoriano Lorenzo. No. RA66, RA69, Cacique Urraca. No. RA67, RA70, Post Office.

## PANAMA (continued)

**1973-75**

| | | | | |
|---|---|---|---|---|
| RA63 | PT9 | 1c brt yel grn & ver | .45 | .20 |
| RA64 | PT9 | 1c gray & red | .45 | .20 |
| RA65 | PT9 | 1c ocher & red | .45 | .20 |
| RA66 | PT9 | 1c org & red | .45 | .20 |
| RA67 | PT9 | 1c bl & red | .45 | .20 |
| RA68 | PT9 | 1c blue ('74) | .45 | .20 |
| RA69 | PT9 | 1c orange ('74) | .45 | .20 |
| RA70 | PT9 | 1c vermilion ('75) | .45 | .20 |

Nos. RA63-RA70 (8)  3.60  1.60

The tax was for a new post office in Panama City.

Stamps of 1969-1973 Surcharged in Violet Blue, Yellow, Black or Carmine

**1975**

| | | | | |
|---|---|---|---|---|
| RA75 | A168 | 1c on 1c (#538; VB) | | .20 |
| RA76 | A168 | 1c on 2c (#539; Y) | | .20 |
| RA77 | A164 | 1c on 30c (#534; B) | | .20 |
| RA78 | A157 | 1c on 30c (#511; B) | | .20 |
| RA79 | A156 | 1c on 40c (#514; B) | | .20 |
| RA80 | A156 | 1c on 50c (#515; B) | | .20 |
| RA81 | A169 | 1c on 20c (#C408, C) | | .20 |
| RA82 | A169 | 1c on 25c (#C410; C) | | .20 |
| RA83 | AP98 | 1c on 25c (#C395; B) | | .20 |
| RA84 | A169 | 1c on 30c (#C411; B) | | .20 |
| RA85 | AP94 | 1c on 40c (#C387; C) | | .20 |

Nos. RA75-RA85 (11)  2.20  2.20

The tax was for a new post office in Panama City. Surcharge vertical, reading down on No. RA75 and up on Nos. RA76, RA78 and RA83. Nos. RA75-RA85 were obligatory on all mail.

PT10

**1980, Dec. 3    Litho.    Perf. 12**

| | | | |
|---|---|---|---|
| RA86 | PT10 | 2c Boys | .20 |
| RA87 | PT10 | 2c Boy and chicks | .20 |
| RA88 | PT10 | 2c Working in fields | .20 |
| RA89 | PT10 | 2c Boys feeding piglet | .20 |
| a. | | Souv. sheet of 4, #RA86-RA89 | .60 |

Tax was for Children's Village (Christmas 1980). #RA89a sold for 1b.

PT11

**1981, Nov. 1    Litho.    Perf. 12**

| | | | |
|---|---|---|---|
| RA90 | PT11 | 2c Boy, pony | .20 |
| RA91 | PT11 | 2c Nativity | .20 |
| RA92 | PT11 | 2c Tree | .20 |
| RA93 | PT11 | 2c Church | .20 |
| a. | | Block of 4, #RA90-RA93 | .60 |

**Souvenir Sheet**

RA94  Sheet of 4  12.50
a.-d.  PT11 2c, Children's drawings

Tax was for Children's Village. No. RA94 sold for 5b.

PT12

**1982, Nov. 1    Litho.    Perf. 13½x12½**

| | | | | |
|---|---|---|---|---|
| RA95 | PT12 | 2c Carpentry | .20 | .20 |
| RA96 | PT12 | 2c Beekeeping | .20 | .20 |
| a. | | Pair, #RA95-RA96 | | |
| RA97 | PT12 | 2c Pig farming, vert. | .20 | .20 |
| RA98 | PT12 | 2c Gardening, vert. | .20 | .20 |
| a. | | Pair, #RA97-RA98 | | |

Tax was for Children's Village (Christmas 1982).

PANAMA — PAPUA NEW GUINEA

Children's Drawings — PT13

**1983, Nov. 1    Litho.    Perf. 14½**

| | | | | |
|---|---|---|---|---|
| RA99 | PT13 | 2c Annunciation | .20 | .20 |
| RA100 | PT13 | 2c Bethlehem and Star | .20 | .20 |
| RA101 | PT13 | 2c Church and Houses | .20 | .20 |
| RA102 | PT13 | 2c Flight into Egypt | .80 | .80 |

Nos. RA99-RA102 (4)

Souvenir sheets exist showing unnominated designs of Nos. RA99, RA101 and RA102 respectively. They sold for 2b each. Value $5.50 each.

Children's Village, Boy — PT14

**1984, Nov. 1    Litho.    Perf. 12x12½**

| | | | | |
|---|---|---|---|---|
| RA103 | PT14 | 2c White-collared shirt | .20 | .20 |
| RA104 | PT14 | 2c T-shirt | .20 | .20 |
| RA105 | PT14 | 2c Checked shirt | .20 | .20 |
| RA106 | PT14 | 2c Scout uniform | .60 | .60 |
| a. | | Block of 4, #RA103-RA106 | | |

Tax was for Children's Village. An imperf. souvenir sheet sold for 2b, with designs similar to Nos. RA103-RA106, exists. Value $7.50.

Christmas 1985 — PT15

**1985, Dec. 10    Litho.    Perf. 13½x13**

| | | | | |
|---|---|---|---|---|
| RA107 | PT15 | 2c multi | .20 | .20 |
| RA108 | PT15 | 2c multi | .20 | .20 |
| RA109 | PT15 | 2c multi | .20 | .20 |
| RA110 | PT15 | 2c multi | .60 | .60 |
| a. | | Block of 4, #RA107-RA110 | | |

Inscriptions: No. RA107, "Ciudad del Nino es... mi vida." No. RA108, "Feliz Navidad." No. RA109, "Feliz Ano Nuevo." No. RA110, "Gracias."

Tax was for Children's Village. A souvenir sheet, perf. and imperf., sold for 2b, with designs of Nos. RA107-RA110.

Children's Village, 20th Anniv. — PT16

**1986, Nov. 1    Litho.    Perf. 13½**

| | | | | |
|---|---|---|---|---|
| RA111 | PT16 | 2c multi | .20 | .20 |
| RA112 | PT16 | 2c multi | .20 | .20 |
| RA113 | PT16 | 2c multi | .20 | .20 |
| RA114 | PT16 | 2c multi | .80 | .80 |
| a. | | Block of 4, #RA111-RA114 (4) | | |

Inscriptions and Embera, Cuna, Embera and Guaymies tribal folk figures: No. RA111, "1966-1986." No. RA112, "Ciudad del Nino es... mi vida." No. RA113, "20 anos de fundacion." No. RA114, "Gracias."

Nos. RA111-RA114 obligatory on all mail through Nov., Dec. and Jan.; tax for Children's Village. Printed Nov., Dec. and Jan. Sold for 2b. Sheet exists perf. and imperf., with one 58x68mm 2b stamp showing similar characters. Value $6.75 each.

---

# PAPUA NEW GUINEA

'pa-pya-wa 'nü 'gi-nē

LOCATION — Eastern half of island of New Guinea, north of Australia
GOVT. — Independent state in British Commonwealth.
AREA — 185,136 sq. mi.
POP. — 4,705,126 (1999 est.)
CAPITAL — Port Moresby

In 1884 a British Protectorate was proclaimed over this part of the island, called "British New Guinea." In 1905 the administration was transferred to Australia and in 1906 the name was changed to Territory of Papua.

In 1949 the administration of Papua and New Guinea was unified, as the 1952 issue indicates. In 1972 the name was changed to Papua New Guinea. In 1973 came self-government, followed by independence on September 16, 1975.

Issues of 1925-39 for the mandated Territory of New Guinea are listed under New Guinea.

Catalogue values for unused stamps in this country are for Never Hinged items, beginning with Scott #22 in the regular postage section and Scott J1 in the postage due section.

12 Pence = 1 Shilling
20 Shillings = 1 Pound
100 Cents = 1 Dollar (1966)
100 Toea = 1 Kina (1975)

## Watermarks

Wmk. 13 — Crown and Double-Lined A

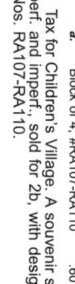

Wmk. 74 — Crown and Single-Lined A Sideways

Wmk. 228 — Small Crown and C of A Multiple

Wmk. 387

Wmk. 47 — Multiple Rosette

The paper varies in thickness and the watermark is found in two positions, with the greater width of the rosette either horizontal or vertical. For overprints see Nos. 11-26.

**British New Guinea**

Lakatoi — A1

**1901, July 1    Wmk. 47    Perf. 14
Engr.
Center in Black**

| | | | | |
|---|---|---|---|---|
| 1 | A1 | ½p yellow green | 8.75 | 4.50 |
| 2 | A1 | 1p carmine | 5.00 | 4.00 |
| 3 | A1 | 2p violet | 12.00 | 7.00 |
| 4 | A1 | 2½p ultra | 17.50 | 20.00 |
| 5 | A1 | 4p black brown | 40.00 | 40.00 |
| 6 | A1 | 6p dark green | 62.50 | 75.00 |
| 7 | A1 | 1sh orange | 600.00 | 600.00 |
| 8 | A1 | 2sh6p brown ('05) | 798.25 | 790.50 |

Nos. 1-8 (8)

**1906, Nov. 8    Wmk. 47    Perf. 14**

Stamps of British New Guinea, Overprinted

**Papua**

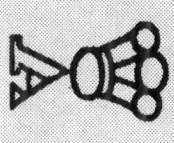

Large Overprint
Center in Black

| | | | | |
|---|---|---|---|---|
| 11 | A1 | ½p yellow green | 6.00 | 22.50 |
| 12 | A1 | 1p carmine | 16.00 | 20.00 |
| 13 | A1 | 2p violet | 3.50 | 7.00 |
| 14 | A1 | 2½p ultra | 4.50 | 3.50 |
| 15 | A1 | 4p black brown | 200.00 | 150.00 |
| 16 | A1 | 6p dark green | 23.00 | 45.00 |
| 17 | A1 | 1sh orange | 175.00 | 45.00 |
| 18 | A1 | 2sh6p brown | 200.00 | 175.00 |

Nos. 11-18 (8)  500.25  498.50

Small Overprint
Center in Black

| | | | | |
|---|---|---|---|---|
| 19 | A1 | ½p yellow green | 9.25 | 11.50 |

**1907**

**Small "PAPUA"**

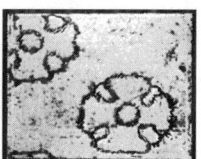

| | | | | |
|---|---|---|---|---|
| 20 | A1 | 1p carmine | 2,000. | |
| a. | | Vertical overprint, up | 5.50 | |
| 21 | A1 | 2p violet | 2,500. | |
| 22 | A1 | 2½p ultra | 5.25 | 3.50 |
| 23 | A1 | 4p violet | 11.00 | 22.50 |
| a. | | Double overprint | | |

**Large Overprint
Center in Black**

| | | | | |
|---|---|---|---|---|
| 24 | A1 | 6p dark green | 35.00 | 60.00 |
| a. | | Double overprint | 3,000. | 47.50 |
| 25 | A1 | 1sh orange | 35.00 | 5,000. |
| a. | | Double overprint | 32.50 | 50.00 |
| 26 | A1 | 2sh6p brown | 8,000. | 50.00 |
| a. | | Double overprint | 5,000. | 50.00 |
| b. | | Vert. ovpt. ('08) | 4,600. | 65.00 |
| c. | | 2sh6p brown ('08) | 12.50 | 18.00 |
| d. | | Double horiz. ovpt. | 3,500. | |

Nos. 19-26 (8)  183.50  267.00

**1907-08    Litho.**

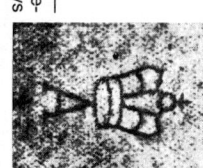

A2

**Perf. 11, 12½    Wmk. 13**

| | | | | |
|---|---|---|---|---|
| 28 | A2 | 1p carmine ('08) | 5.50 | 5.75 |
| 29 | A2 | 2p violet ('08) | 10.50 | 6.00 |
| 30 | A2 | 2½p ultra ('08) | 7.00 | 7.00 |
| 31 | A2 | 4p black brown | 6.75 | 11.50 |
| 32 | A2 | 6p dk green ('08) | 12.50 | 18.00 |
| 33 | A2 | 1sh orange ('08) | 27.50 | 24.00 |

Nos. 28-33 (6)  69.75  72.75

**1909-10    Wmk. Sideways**

**Perf. 12½    Center in Black**

| | | | | |
|---|---|---|---|---|
| 30a | A2 | 2½p | 150.00 | 140.00 |
| 31a | A2 | 4p | 12.00 | 9.25 |
| 33a | A2 | 1sh | 97.50 | 70.00 |

Nos. 30a-33a (3)  259.50  219.25

**1909-10    Wmk. Sideways**

| | | | | |
|---|---|---|---|---|
| 34 | A2 | ½p yellow green | 3.50 | 6.00 |
| a. | | Perf. 11x12½ | 2,600. | 2,600. |
| b. | | Perf. 11 | 2.75 | 4.25 |

**35** A2 1p carmine 8.00 *14.00*
*a.* Perf. 11 11.00 *9.25*
**36** A2 2p violet ('10) 6.00 *12.00*
*a.* Perf. 11x12½ 975.00
*b.* Perf. 11 13.50 *10.50*
**37** A2 2½p ultra ('10) 6.00 *22.50*
*a.* Perf. 12½ 10.50 *45.00*
**38** A2 4p black brn ('10) 5.50 *11.00*
*a.* Perf. 11x12½ 8,500.
**39** A2 6p dark green 13.00 21.00
*a.* Perf. 12½ 3,250. *4,250.*
**40** A2 1sh orange ('10) 17.50 *42.50*
*a.* Perf. 11 55.00 *70.00*
*Nos. 34-40 (7)* 59.50 *129.00*

One stamp in each sheet has a white line across the upper part of the picture which is termed the "rift in the clouds."

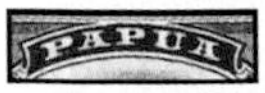

Large "PAPUA"

2sh6p:
Type I — The numerals are thin and irregular. The body of the "6" encloses a large spot of color. The dividing stroke is thick and uneven.
Type II — The numerals are thick and well formed. The "6" encloses a narrow oval of color. The dividing stroke is thin and sharp.

**1910** **Wmk. 13**
**Center in Black**

**41** A2 ½p yellow green 4.00 *12.50*
**42** A2 1p carmine 10.50 *9.75*
**43** A2 2p violet 5.75 *5.75*
**44** A2 2½p blue violet 6.50 *20.00*
**45** A2 4p black brown 6.50 *11.50*
**46** A2 6p dark green 10.00 *8.50*
**47** A2 1sh orange 7.50 *22.50*
**48** A2 2sh6p brown, type II 45.00 *52.50*
*a.* Type I 50.00 *62.50*
*Nos. 41-48 (8)* 95.75 *143.00*

**Wmk. Sideways**

**49** A2 2sh6p choc, type I 80.00 *100.00*

**1911** **Typo.** **Wmk. 74** ***Perf. 12½***
**50** A2 ½p yellow green .60 *2.75*
**51** A2 1p lt red .90 1.00
**52** A2 2p lt violet .90 1.00
**53** A2 2½p ultra 6.00 *10.00*
**54** A2 4p olive green 2.75 *12.50*
**55** A2 6p orange brown 4.25 *5.75*
**56** A2 1sh yellow 12.00 *45.00*
**57** A2 2sh6p rose 37.50 *42.50*
*Nos. 50-57 (8)* 64.90 *120.50*

For surcharges see Nos. 74-79.

**1915, June** ***Perf. 14***
**59** A2 1p light red 7.50 2.25

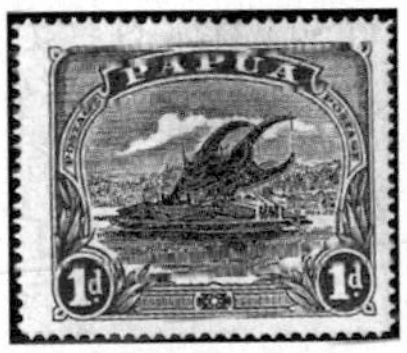

A3

**1916-31**
**60** A3 ½p pale yel grn & myr grn ('19) .95 1.10
**61** A3 1p rose red & blk 1.75 .75
**62** A3 1½p yel brn & gray bl ('25) 1.75 .95
**63** A3 2p red vio & vio brn ('19) 2.25 .85
**64** A3 2p red brn & vio brn ('31) 2.50 .85
*a.* 2p cop red & vio brn ('31) 29.00 2.25
**65** A3 2½p ultra & dk grn ('19) 6.00 *16.00*
**66** A3 3p emerald & blk 2.25 2.25
*a.* 3p dp bl grn & blk 5.25 9.25
**67** A3 4p org & lt brn ('19) 3.25 5.75
**68** A3 5p ol brn & sl ('31) 4.75 *19.00*
**69** A3 6p vio & dl vio ('23) 3.75 *11.00*
**70** A3 1sh ol grn & dk brn ('19) 4.25 *8.00*
**71** A3 2sh6p rose & red brn ('19) 25.00 *47.50*
**72** A3 5sh dp grn & blk 55.00 *60.00*
**73** A3 10sh gray bl & grn ('25) 160.00 *200.00*
*Nos. 60-73 (14)* 273.45 *374.00*

Type A3 is a redrawing of type A2.
The lines of the picture have been strengthened, making it much darker, especially the sky and water.
For surcharges & overprints see #88-91, O1-O10.

Stamps of 1911 Surcharged

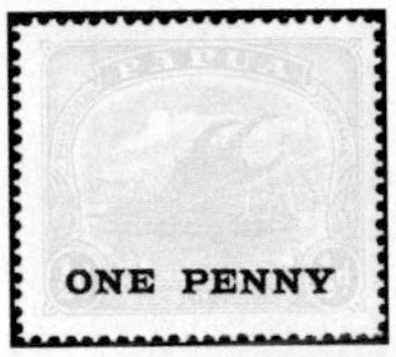

**1917** ***Perf. 12½***
**74** A2 1p on ½p yellow grn 1.10 1.40
**75** A2 1p on 2p lt violet 14.00 *17.50*
**76** A2 1p on 2½p ultra 1.40 *4.50*
**77** A2 1p on 4p olive green 2.00 *5.25*
**78** A2 1p on 6p org brn 9.25 *20.00*
**79** A2 1p on 2sh6p rose 2.00 *7.00*
*Nos. 74-79 (6)* 29.75 *55.65*

No. 62 Surcharged

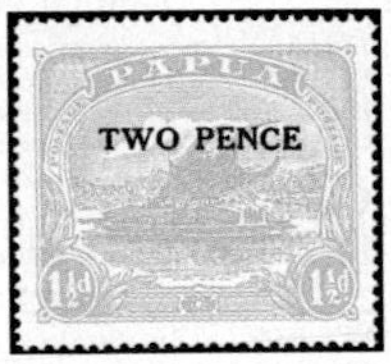

**1931, Jan. 1** ***Perf. 14***
**88** A3 2p on 1½p yellow brn & gray blue 1.50 *2.50*

Nos. 70, 71 and 72 Surcharged in Black

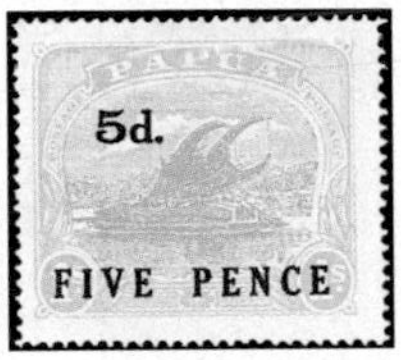

**1931**
**89** A3 5p on 1sh #70 2.00 4.00
**90** A3 9p on 2sh6p #71 7.00 *10.00*
**91** A3 1sh3p on 5sh #72 5.00 *10.50*
*Nos. 89-91 (3)* 14.00 *24.50*

Type of 1916 Issue

**1932** **Wmk. 228** ***Perf. 11***
**92** A3 9p dp violet & gray 7.50 *37.50*
**93** A3 1sh3p pale bluish green & grayish violet 12.00 *37.50*

For overprints see Nos. O11-O12.

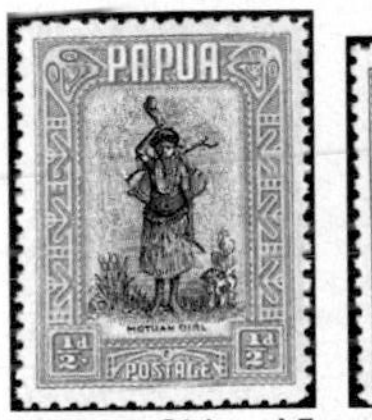

Motuan Girl — A5

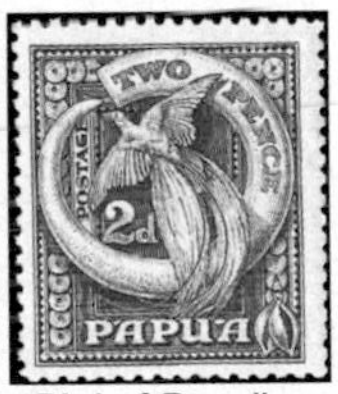

Bird of Paradise and Boar's Tusk — A6

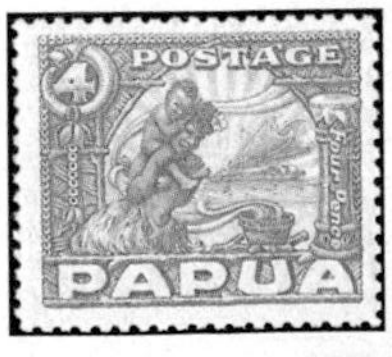

Mother and Child — A7

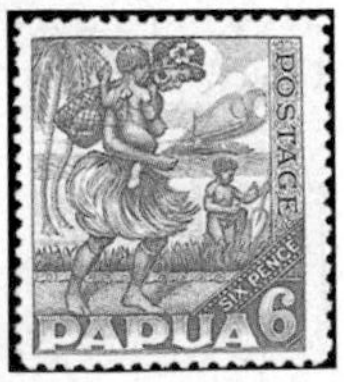

Papuan Motherhood — A8

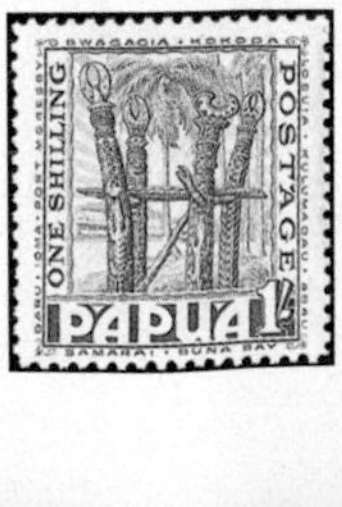

Dubu (Ceremonial Platform) — A9

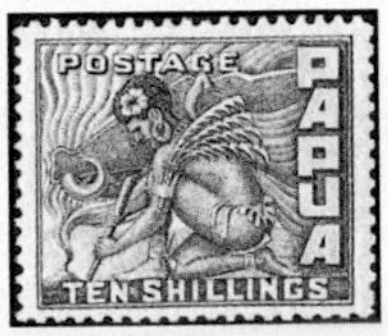

Fire Maker — A10

Designs: 1p, Steve, son of Oala. 1½p, Tree houses. 3p, Papuan dandy. 5p, Masked dancer. 9p, Shooting fish. 1sh3p, Lakatoi. 2sh, Delta art. 2sh6p, Pottery making. 5sh, Sgt.-Major Simoi. £1, Delta house.

**Unwmk.**

**1932, Nov. 14** **Engr.** ***Perf. 11***
**94** A5 ½p orange & blk 1.75 *3.75*
**95** A5 1p yel grn & blk 2.00 *.70*
**96** A5 1½p red brn & blk 1.75 *9.25*
**97** A6 2p light red 12.50 *.35*
**98** A5 3p blue & blk 3.75 *7.50*
**99** A7 4p olive green 6.25 *11.00*
**100** A5 5p grnsh sl & blk 3.50 3.50
**101** A8 6p bister brown 8.50 6.25
**102** A5 9p lilac & blk 11.50 *24.00*
**103** A9 1sh bluish gray 4.50 *9.75*
**104** A5 1sh3p brown & blk 17.50 *29.00*
**105** A5 2sh bluish slate & blk 17.50 *26.00*
**106** A5 2sh6p rose lilac & blk 29.00 *42.50*
**107** A5 5sh olive & blk 62.50 62.50
**108** A10 10sh gray lilac 97.50 97.50
**109** A5 £1 lt gray & black 210.00 175.00
*Nos. 94-109 (16)* 490.00 508.55

For overprints see Nos. 114-117.

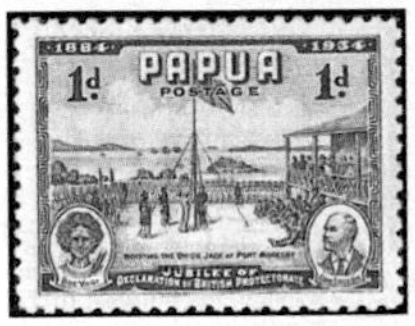

Hoisting Union Jack at Port Moresby A21

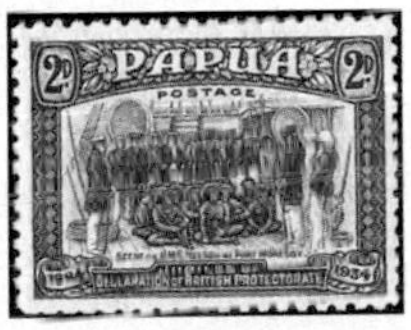

H. M. S. "Nelson" at Port Moresby A22

**1934, Nov. 6**
**110** A21 1p dull green 1.10 *3.50*
**111** A22 2p red brown 1.50 *3.00*
**112** A21 3p blue 1.50 *3.00*
**113** A22 5p violet brown 10.00 *13.00*
*Nos. 110-113 (4)* 14.10 *22.50*
Set, never hinged 25.00

Declaration of British Protection, 50th anniv.

**Silver Jubilee Issue**

Stamps of 1932 Issue Overprinted in Black:

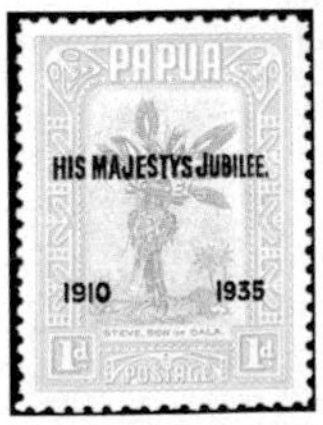

a

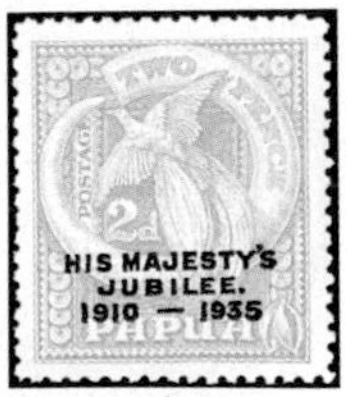

b

**1935, July 9**
**Glazed Paper**
**114** A5(a) 1p yellow grn & blk .85 *2.75*
**115** A6(b) 2p light red 2.25 *2.75*
**116** A5(a) 3p lt blue & blk 2.00 *2.75*
**117** A5(a) 5p grnsh slate & blk 2.75 *2.75*
*Nos. 114-117 (4)* 7.85 *11.00*
Set, never hinged 13.00

25th anniv. of the reign of George V.

**Coronation Issue**

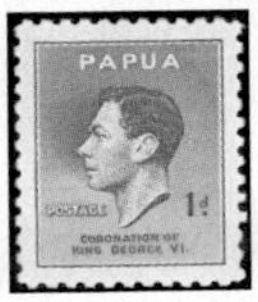

King George VI — A22a

**Unwmk.**

**1937, May 14** **Engr.** ***Perf. 11***
**118** A22a 1p green .45 .20
**119** A22a 2p salmon rose .45 .40
**120** A22a 3p blue .45 .55
**121** A22a 5p brown violet .45 .85
*Nos. 118-121 (4)* 1.80 2.00
Set, never hinged 2.50

**Catalogue values for unused stamps in this section, from this point to the end of the section, are for Never Hinged items.**

**Papua and New Guinea**

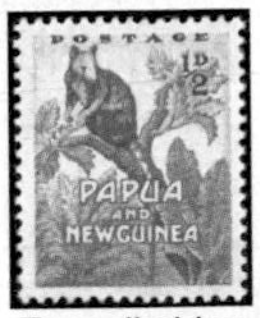

Tree-climbing Kangaroo A23

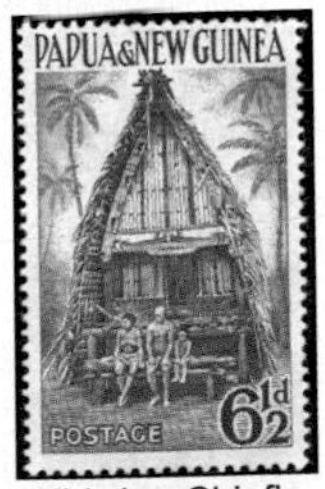

Kiriwina Chief's House A24

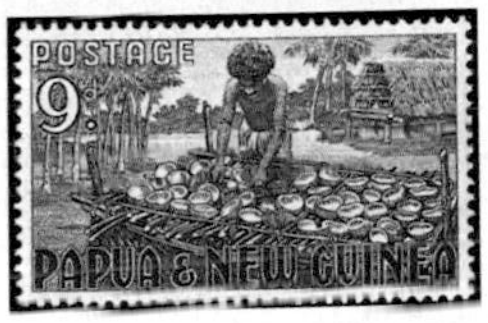

Copra Making A25

Designs: 1p, Buka head-dress. 2p, Youth. 2½p, Bird of paradise. 3p, Policeman. 3½p, Chimbu headdress. 7½p, Kiriwina yam house. 1sh, Trading canoe. 1sh6p, Rubber tapping. 2sh, Shields and spears. 2sh6p, Plumed shepherd. 10sh, Map. £1, Spearing fish.

**Unwmk.**

**1952, Oct. 30** **Engr.** ***Perf. 14***
**122** A23 ½p blue green .30 .20
**123** A23 1p chocolate .25 .20
**124** A23 2p deep ultra .50 .20
**125** A23 2½p orange 3.50 .60
**126** A23 3p dark green .85 .20
**127** A23 3½p dk carmine .85 .20
**128** A24 6½p vio brown 2.25 .20
**129** A24 7½p dp ultra 4.00 1.50
**130** A25 9p chocolate 4.75 .75
**131** A25 1sh yellow green 2.75 .20
**132** A24 1sh6p dark green 8.50 1.00
**133** A24 2sh deep blue 7.50 .20
**134** A25 2sh6p dk red brown 7.00 .75
**135** A25 10sh gray black 55.00 14.00
**136** A24 £1 chocolate 60.00 14.00
*Nos. 122-136 (15)* 158.00 34.20
Set, hinged 100.00

See #139-141. For surcharges & overprints see #137-138, 147, J1-J3, J5-J6.

Nos. 125 and 131 Surcharged with New Values and Bars

**1957, Jan. 29** ***Perf. 14***
**137** A23 4p on 2½p orange .85 .20
**138** A25 7p on 1sh yellow green .60 .25

Type of 1952 and

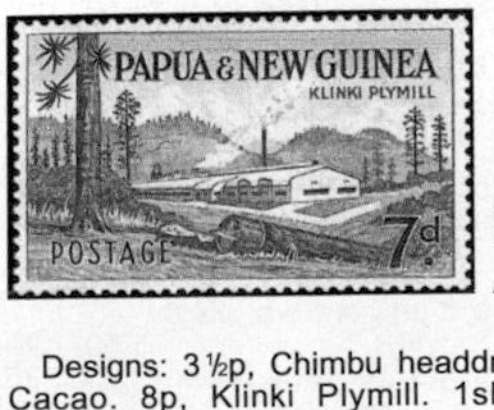

Klinki Plymill A26

Designs: 3½p, Chimbu headdress. 4p, 5p, Cacao. 8p, Klinki Plymill. 1sh7p, Cattle. 2sh5p, Cattle. 5sh, Coffee, vert.

**1958-60** **Engr.** ***Perf. 14***
**139** A23 3½p black 6.50 1.00
**140** A23 4p vermilion .75 .20
**141** A23 5p green ('60) .75 .20

| | | | |
|---|---|---|---|
| 142 | A26 | 7p gray green | 7.50 .20 |
| 143 | A26 | 8p dk ultra | 1.00 1.00 |
| 144 | A26 | 1sh7p red brown | 19.00 14.50 |
| 145 | A26 | 2sh6p vermilion | 4.50 2.50 |
| 146 | A26 | 5sh gray olive & brn red | 11.00 2.10 |
| | | Nos. 139-146 (8) | 51.00 21.70 |

Issued: June 2, 1958, Nov. 10, 1960. For surcharge see No. J4.

**1959, Dec. 1**
| 147 | A23 | 5p on ½p blue green | .75 .20 |
|---|---|---|---|

No. 122 Surcharged with New Value

**1961, Apr. 10 Photo. Perf. 14½x14**
| 148 | A27 | 5p green & yellow | 1.00 .20 |
|---|---|---|---|
| 149 | A27 | 2sh3p grn & salmon | 8.00 5.00 |

Reconstitution of the Legislative Council.

Council Chamber and Frangipani Flowers A27

Woman's Head — A28

Red-plumed Bird of Paradise — A29

Port Moresby Harbor A30

View of Rabaul, by Samuel Terarup Cham — A33

Constable Ragas Annis Matia, Port Moresby A32

Woman Dancer A31

Elizabeth II A34

Designs: 3p, Man's head. 6p, Golden opossum. 2sh, Male dancer with drum. 2sh3p, Piaggio transport plane landing at Tapini.

**Perf. 14 (A28, A31, A32), 14x13½ (A29, A33), 14x13½ (A30), 14½ (A34)**
**1961-63 Engr. Unwmk.**
| 153 | A28 | 1p dk carmine | 1.25 .30 |
|---|---|---|---|
| 154 | A28 | 3p bluish black | .20 .20 |

**Photo.**
| 155 | A29 | 5p lt brn, red brn & yel | 1.50 .20 |
|---|---|---|---|
| 156 | A29 | 6p gray, ocher & slate | .75 1.25 |

**Engr.**
| 157 | A30 | 8p green | .30 .20 |
|---|---|---|---|
| 158 | A31 | 1sh gray green | 4.00 .20 |
| 159 | A31 | 2sh rose lake | .45 .20 |
| 160 | A30 | 2sh3p dark blue | .50 .40 |
| 161 | A32 | 3sh green | 2.25 1.40 |

| 162 | A33 | 10sh multicolored | 16.50 10.00 |
|---|---|---|---|
| 163 | A34 | £1 brt grn, blk & gold | 31.80 17.75 |

**Photo.**
The 5p and 6p are on granite paper.
Issued: 3sh, 9/5/62; 10sh, 2/13/63; 5p, 6p, 3/27/63; 8p, 2sh3p, 5/8/63; £1, 7/3/63; others, 7/26/61.

Malaria Eradication Emblem — A35

**1962, Apr. 7 Litho. Perf. 14**
| 164 | A35 | 5p lt blue & maroon | .75 .40 |
|---|---|---|---|
| 165 | A35 | 1sh lt brown & red | 1.40 .60 |
| 166 | A35 | 2sh yellow green & blk | 1.60 1.75 |
| | | Nos. 164-166 (3) | 3.75 2.75 |

WHO drive to eradicate malaria.

Map of Australia and South Pacific A36

**1962, July 9 Engr. Unwmk.**
| 167 | A36 | 5p dk red & lt grn | .85 .20 |
|---|---|---|---|
| 168 | A36 | 1sh6p dk violet & red | 2.25 .90 |
| 169 | A36 | 2sh6p dk blue & lt blue | 5.35 3.00 |
| | | Nos. 167-169 (3) | |

5th So. Pacific Conf., Pago Pago, July 1962.

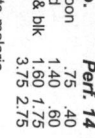

High Jump — A37

Games Emblem — A38

**1962, Oct. 24 Photo. Perf. 11½**
| 171 | A37 | 5p shown | .35 .25 |
|---|---|---|---|
| 172 | A37 | 5p Javelin | .35 .25 |

**Size: 26x21mm**
**Granite Paper**

| 173 | A37 | 2sh3p runners | 1.75 1.75 |
|---|---|---|---|
| | | Nos. 171-173 (3) | 2.45 2.25 |

British Empire and Commonwealth Games, Perth, Australia, Nov. 22-Dec. 1. Nos. 171 and 172 printed in alternating horizontal rows in sheet.

Red Cross Centenary Emblem — A38a

**1963, May 1 Perf. 13½**
| 174 | A38a | 5p blue grn, gray & red | .55 .20 |
|---|---|---|---|

**1963, Aug. 14 Engr. Perf. 13½x14**
| 176 | A38 | 5p olive bister | .20 .20 |
|---|---|---|---|
| 177 | A38 | 1sh green | .60 .25 |

So. Pacific Games, Suva, Aug. 29-Sept. 7.

Top of Wooden Shield — A39

Casting Ballot — A40

Various Carved Heads.

**1964, Feb. 5 Unwmk. Perf. 11½**
| 178 | A39 | 1p multicolored | .55 .20 |
|---|---|---|---|
| 179 | A39 | 2sh5p multicolored | .60 1.00 |
| 180 | A39 | 2sh6p multicolored | .60 .20 |
| 181 | A39 | 5sh multicolored | .75 .20 |
| | | Nos. 178-181 (4) | 2.50 1.60 |

First Common Roll elections.

**1964, Mar. 4 Unwmk. Perf. 11½**
**Granite Paper Photo.**
| 182 | A40 | 5p dk brn & pale brn | .20 .20 |
|---|---|---|---|
| 183 | A40 | 2sh3p dk brn & lt bl | .70 .40 |

A41

A42

**1964, Aug. 5 Engr. Perf. 14**
| 184 | A41 | 5p violet | .20 .20 |
|---|---|---|---|
| 185 | A41 | 8p green | .20 .20 |
| 186 | A41 | 1sh deep ultra | .40 .30 |
| 187 | A41 | 1sh2p rose brown | 1.00 .90 |
| | | Nos. 184-187 (4) | |

Designs: 5p, Patients at health center clinic. 8p, Dentist and school child patient. 1sh, Nurse holding infant. 1sh2p, Medical student using microscope.
Territorial health services.

**1964-65 Unwmk. Photo. Perf. 11½**
| 188 | A42 | 1p brt cit & dk brn | .35 .20 |
|---|---|---|---|
| 189 | A42 | 3p gray & dk brn | .45 .20 |
| 190 | A42 | 6p sal pink & blk | .50 .20 |
| 191 | A42 | 6p pale grn & blk | .50 .20 |
| 192 | A42 | 8p pale lil & dk | .20 |

**Size: 25x36mm**
| 193 | A42 | 1sh salmon & blk | 1.25 .20 |
|---|---|---|---|
| 194 | A42 | 2sh blue & dk brn | .25 .25 |
| 195 | A42 | 2sh3p lt grn & dk brn | .70 .70 |
| 196 | A42 | 3sh yel & dk brn | .60 .70 |
| 197 | A42 | 5sh lt ultra & dk brn | 1.00 |
| 198 | A42 | 10sh dk blue | 2.10 |

**Size: 21x26mm**
**Birds in Natural Colors**

Designs: 1p, Striped gardener bower birds. 3p, New Guinea regent bower birds. 5p, Blue birds of paradise. 6p, Lawes six-wired birds of paradise. 1sh, Emperor birds of paradise. 2sh, Brown sickle-billed bird of paradise. 3sh, Magnificent bird of paradise. 2sh3p, Lesser bird of paradise. 5sh, Twelve-wired bird of paradise. 10sh, Magnificent rifle birds.

| | | Nos. 188-198 (11) | 22.60 13.50 |
|---|---|---|---|

Issued: 6p, 8p, 1sh, 10sh, 10/28/64; others, 1/20/65.

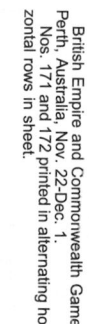

Carved Crocodile's Head — A43

**1965, Mar. 24 Photo. Perf. 11½**
| 199 | A43 | 4p multicolored | .40 .20 |
|---|---|---|---|
| 200 | A43 | 1sh6p gray brown & dk brown | 1.90 1.75 |
| 201 | A43 | 1sh6p lil, dk brown & buff | .80 .35 |
| 202 | A43 | 4sh bl, dk vio & mar | 3.50 2.50 |
| | | Nos. 199-202 (4) | |

Designs: Wood carvings from Sepik River Region used as ship's prows and as objects of religious veneration.

**1965, Apr. 14 Perf. 13½x13**
| 203 | A43a | 2sh3p brt grn, sep & blk | .50 .50 |
|---|---|---|---|

"Simpson and His Donkey" by Wallace Anderson — A43a
ANZAC issue. See note after Australia No. 387.

**1965, July 7 Photo. Perf. 11½**
| 204 | A44 | 6p multicolored | .20 .20 |
|---|---|---|---|
| 205 | A44 | 1sh multicolored | .20 .20 |

Urbanized Community and Stilt House — A44
6th South Pacific Conf., Lae, July, 1965.
Design: 1sh, Stilt house at left.

UN Emblem, Mother and Child A45

**1965, Oct. 13 Unwmk. Perf. 11½**
| 206 | A45 | 5p dull pur, grnsh bl & | .20 .20 |
|---|---|---|---|
| 207 | A45 | 1sh dull pur, blue & org | .20 .20 |
| 208 | A45 | 2sh dp blue, pale grn & grn | .60 .60 |
| | | Nos. 206-208 (3) | |

UN Emblem and: 1sh, Globe and orbit, vert. 2sh, Four globes in orbit, vert.
20th anniversary of the United Nations.

New Guinea Birdwing A46

**1966 Photo. Granite Paper Perf. 11½**
| 209 | A46 | 1c salmon, blk & aqua | .40 .80 |
|---|---|---|---|
| 210 | A46 | 3c gray grn, brn & org | .40 .80 |
| 211 | A46 | 4c multicolored | .40 .80 |
| 212 | A46 | 5c multicolored | .40 .80 |
| 213 | A46 | 10c multicolored | .45 .25 |
| 214 | A46 | 12c salmon & multi | .55 .25 |
| 215 | A46 | 15c pale vio, dk brn & buff | 2.50 2.00 |
| 216 | A46 | 20c yel bister, dk brn & yel orange | 1.75 .70 |
| 217 | A46 | 25c gray, blk & yel orange | .65 .25 |
| 218 | A46 | 50c multicolored | 1.40 1.40 |

Butterflies: 1c, Blue emperor, vert. 3c, White-banded map butterfly, vert. 4c, Mountain swallowtail, vert. 5c, Port Moresby terinos, vert. 12c, Blue crow. 15c, Euchenor butterfly. 20c, White-spotted parthenos. 25c, Orange Jezebel. 50c, New Guinea emperor. $1, Blue-spotted leaf-wing. $2, Paradise birdwing.

Hydroelectric Power — A52

**Perf. 11½**

Beetles: 10c, Eupholus schoenherri. 20c, Sphingnotus albertisi. 25c, Cyphogastra albertisi.

**1967, Apr. 12  Unwmk.**

| | | | | |
|---|---|---|---|---|
| 237 | A51 | 5c | blue & multi | .20 .20 |
| 238 | A51 | 10c | lt green & multi | .30 .25 |
| 239 | A51 | 20c | rose & multi | .50 .50 |
| 240 | A51 | 25c | yellow & multi | .55 .40 |
| | | | Nos. 237-240 (4) | 1.55 1.15 |

**1967, June 28  Photo.  Perf. 12x12½**

Designs: 10c, Pyrethrum (Chrysanthemum cinerariaefolium). 20c, Tea. 25c, like 5c.

| | | | | |
|---|---|---|---|---|
| 241 | A52 | 5c | multicolored | .20 .20 |
| 242 | A52 | 10c | multicolored | .20 .20 |
| 243 | A52 | 20c | multicolored | .30 .30 |
| 244 | A52 | 25c | multicolored | 1.00 .80 |
| | | | Nos. 241-244 (4) | |

Completion of part of the Laloki River Hydroelectric Works near Port Moresby, and the Hydrological Decade (UNESCO), 1965-74.

Leaf Beetle — A51

**PAPUA AND NEW GUINEA 5c**

---

Molala Harai and Paiva Streamer — A47

Myths of Elema People: 7c, Marai, the fisherman. 30c, Meavea Kivovia and the Black Cockatoo. 60c, Toivita Tapavita (symbolic face decorations).

**1966, June 8  Photo.  Perf. 11½**
**Granite Paper**

| | | | | |
|---|---|---|---|---|
| 221 | A47 | 2c | black & carmine | .25 .20 |
| 222 | A47 | 7c | blue, blk & yel | .25 .20 |
| 223 | A47 | 30c | blk, yel grn & car | .30 .20 |
| 224 | A47 | 60c | blk, org & car | .75 .30 |
| | | | Nos. 221-224 (4) | 1.55 .90 |

Discus — A48

**1966, Aug. 31  Perf. 11½**
**Granite Paper**

| | | | | |
|---|---|---|---|---|
| 225 | A48 | 5c | shown | .20 .20 |
| 226 | A48 | 10c | Soccer | .25 .20 |
| 227 | A48 | 20c | Tennis | .35 .35 |
| | | | Nos. 225-227 (3) | .80 .75 |

Second South Pacific Games, Noumea, New Caledonia, Dec. 8-18.

**SOUTH PACIFIC GAMES NOUMEA 1966**
**PAPUA & NEW GUINEA 5c**

---

| | | | | |
|---|---|---|---|---|
| 219 | A46 | $1 | pale blue, dk brn & dp org | 1.75 3.50 |
| 220 | A46 | $2 | multicolored | 6.25 8.50 |
| | | | Nos. 209-220 (12) | 29.25 18.70 |

In 1967 Courvoisier made new plates for the $1 and $2. Stamps from these plates show many minor differences and slight variations in shade.

Issued: 12c, 10/10; others, 2/14.

**PAPUA AND NEW GUINEA 2c**

Book and Pen ("Fine Arts") — A50

Flowers: 10c, Tecomanthe dendrophila. 20c, Rhododendron macgregoriae. 60c, Rhododendron konori.

**1966, Dec. 7  Photo.**

| | | | | |
|---|---|---|---|---|
| 228 | A49 | 2c | multicolored | .20 .20 |
| 229 | A49 | 10c | blue & multi | .20 .20 |
| 230 | A49 | 20c | brown & multi | .50 .20 |
| 231 | A49 | 60c | multicolored | 1.25 1.50 |
| | | | Nos. 228-231 (4) | 2.15 2.10 |

d'Albertis' Creeper — A49

**1967, Feb. 8  Photo.  Perf. 12½x12**

3c, "Surveying," transit, view finder, pencil. 4c, "Civil Engineering," buildings, compass. 5c, "Science," test tubes, chemical formula. 20c, "Justice," Justitia, scales.

| | | | | |
|---|---|---|---|---|
| 232 | A50 | 1c | orange & multi | .20 .20 |
| 233 | A50 | 3c | blue & multi | .20 .20 |
| 234 | A50 | 4c | brown & multi | .20 .20 |
| 235 | A50 | 5c | green & multi | .20 .20 |
| 236 | A50 | 20c | pink & multi | 1.00 1.00 |
| | | | Nos. 232-236 (5) | |

Issued to publicize the development of the University of Papua and New Guinea and the Institute of Higher Technical Education.

**HIGHER EDUCATION 1c**
**PAPUA & NEW GUINEA**

---

Frogs — A56

**1968, Apr. 24  Photo.  Perf. 11½**

| | | | | |
|---|---|---|---|---|
| 257 | A56 | 5c | Tree | .35 .35 |
| 258 | A56 | 10c | Tree, diff. | .35 .35 |
| 259 | A56 | 15c | Swamp | .35 .20 |
| 260 | A56 | 20c | Tree, diff. | .45 .35 |
| | | | Nos. 257-260 (4) | 1.50 1.10 |

**PAPUA & NEW GUINEA 10c**

Human Rights Flame and Headdress A57

Symbolic Designs: 10c, Human Rights Flame surrounded by the world. 20c, 25c, "Universal Suffrage" in 2 abstract designs.

**1968, June 26  Litho.  Perf. 14x13**

| | | | | |
|---|---|---|---|---|
| 261 | A57 | 5c | black & multi | .20 .20 |
| 262 | A57 | 10c | black & multi | .20 .20 |
| 263 | A57 | 20c | black & multi | .30 .30 |
| 264 | A57 | 25c | black & multi | 1.00 1.00 |
| | | | Nos. 261-264 (4) | |

Issued for Human Rights Year, 1968, and to publicize free elections.

**HUMAN RIGHTS YEAR**
**PAPUA & NEW GUINEA 5c**

---

Frilled Clam — A58

Sea Shells. 1c, Egg cowry. 3c, Crested stromb. 4c, Lithograph cone. 5c, Marble cone. 7c, Orange-spotted miter. 10c, Red volute. 12c, Checkerboard helmet shell. 15c, Scorpion shell. 25c, Chocolate-flamed Venus shell. 30c, Giant murex. 40c, Chambered nautilus. 60c, Triton's trumpet. $1, Emerald snails. $2, Glory of the sea, vert.

**1968-69  Perf. 12x12½, 12x12½**
**Granite Paper**

| | | | | |
|---|---|---|---|---|
| 265 | A58 | 1c | multicolored | .20 .20 |
| 266 | A58 | 3c | multicolored | .35 .35 |
| 267 | A58 | 4c | multicolored | .20 1.25 |
| 268 | A58 | 5c | multicolored | .30 .20 |
| 269 | A58 | 7c | multicolored | .40 .20 |
| 270 | A58 | 10c | multicolored | .50 .20 |
| 271 | A58 | 12c | multicolored | 1.40 2.00 |
| 272 | A58 | 15c | multicolored | .65 1.00 |
| 273 | A58 | 25c | multicolored | .75 1.00 |
| 274 | A58 | 30c | multicolored | .75 .40 |
| 275 | A58 | 40c | multicolored | .75 1.00 |
| 276 | A58 | 50c | multicolored | .80 1.00 |
| 277 | A58 | 60c | multicolored | .75 .60 |
| 278 | A58 | $1 | multicolored | 1.25 5.50 |
| 279 | A58 | $2 | multicolored | 13.00 16.00 |
| | | | Nos. 265-279 (15) | 22.05 |

Issued: 5c, 20c, 25c, 30c, 60c, 8/28/68; 3c, 10c, 15c, 40c, $1, 10/30/68; others, 1/29/69.

**20c PAPUA & NEW GUINEA**

---

Myths of Elema People: No. 281, 5c inscribed "Iko." No. 282, 10c inscribed "Luvuapo." No. 283, 10c inscribed "Miro."

**Perf. 12½x13½xRoul. 9xPerf. 13½**
**#280 & 282:**
**Roul. 9 x Perf. 13½x12½x13½**
**#281 & 283:**

**1969, Apr. 9  Litho.  Unwmk.**

| | | | | |
|---|---|---|---|---|
| 280 | A59 | 5c | black, yellow & red | .20 .20 |
| 281 | A59 | 5c | black, yellow & red | .20 .20 |
| a. | | Vert. pair, #280-281 | | .40 .40 |
| 282 | A59 | 10c | black, gray & red | .25 .25 |
| 283 | A59 | 10c | black, gray & red | .25 .25 |
| a. | | Vert. pair, #282-283 | | .50 .60 |
| | | | Nos. 280-283 (4) | .90 .90 |

Nos. 281a, 283a have continuous designs, rouletted between.

**Perf. 14x14½, 14½x14  Engr.**

**1969, June 25**

Designs: 10c, Games' swimming pool, Boroko, horiz. 20c, Main Games area, Konedobu, horiz.

| | | | | |
|---|---|---|---|---|
| 284 | A60 | 5c | black | .20 .20 |
| 285 | A60 | 10c | bright violet | .30 .30 |
| 286 | A60 | 20c | green | .70 .70 |
| | | | Nos. 284-286 (3) | |

3d S. Pacific Games, Port Moresby, Aug. 13-23.

Potter A62

Dendrobium Ostringianum A61

Orchids: 10c, Dendrobium lawesii. 20c, Dendrobium pseudofrigidum. 30c, Dendrobium conanthum.

**1969, Aug. 27  Photo.  Perf. 11½**
**Granite Paper**

| | | | | |
|---|---|---|---|---|
| 287 | A61 | 5c | multicolored | .25 .25 |
| 288 | A61 | 10c | multicolored | .55 .50 |
| 289 | A61 | 20c | multicolored | .70 .75 |
| 290 | A61 | 30c | multicolored | .80 .50 |
| | | | Nos. 287-290 (4) | 2.50 2.00 |

Issued to publicize the 6th World Orchid Conference, Sydney, Australia, Sept. 1909.

**5c PAPUA & NEW GUINEA**

---

**1969, Sept. 24  Photo.  Perf. 11½**
**Granite Paper**

| | | | | |
|---|---|---|---|---|
| 291 | A62 | 5c | multicolored | .25 .20 |

50th anniv. of the ILO.

Seed Pod Rattle (Tareko) A64

**TAREKO**
**PAPUA AND NEW GUINEA 5c**

Bird of Paradise A63

**Coil Stamps**
**Perf. 14½ Horiz.**

**1969-71**

| | | | | |
|---|---|---|---|---|
| 291A | A63 | 2c | red, dp blue & blk | .20 .20 |
| 292 | A63 | 5c | orange & emerald | .20 .20 |

Issue dates: 5c, Sept. 24, 2c, Apr. 1, 1971.

**1969, Oct. 29  Photo.  Perf. 12½**

Musical Instruments: 10c, Hand drum (garamut). 25c, Pan pipes (iviliko). 30c, Hourglass drum (kundu).

| | | | | |
|---|---|---|---|---|
| 293 | A64 | 10c | multicolored | .20 .20 |
| 294 | A64 | 10c | multicolored | .20 .25 |
| 295 | A64 | 25c | multicolored | .70 .35 |
| 296 | A64 | 30c | multicolored | 1.40 1.00 |
| | | | Nos. 293-296 (4) | |

**5c Papua and New Guinea**

---

Legend of Tito-Iko — A59

Fireball Class Sailboat, Port Moresby Harbor — A60

**PORT MORESBY 1969**
**PAPUA & NEW GUINEA 5c**
**THIRD SOUTH PACIFIC GAMES**

Battle of Milne Bay — A53

Designs: 5c, Soldiers on Kokoda Trail, vert. 20c, The coast watchers. 50c, Battle of the Coral Sea.

**1967, Aug. 30  Unwmk.  Perf. 11½**

| | | | | |
|---|---|---|---|---|
| 245 | A53 | 2c | multicolored | .25 .35 |
| 246 | A53 | 5c | multicolored | .25 .20 |
| 247 | A53 | 20c | multicolored | .30 .20 |
| 248 | A53 | 50c | multicolored | .55 .50 |
| | | | Nos. 245-248 (4) | 1.35 1.25 |

25th anniv. of the battles in the Pacific, which stopped the Japanese from occupying Papua and New Guinea.

**MILNE BAY 2c PAPUA & NEW GUINEA**

Chimbu District Headdress A55

**1967, Nov. 29  Photo.  Perf. 12**

Parrots: 5c, Fairy lory. 20c, Dusk-orange lory. 25c, Edward's fig parrot.

| | | | | |
|---|---|---|---|---|
| 249 | A54 | 5c | multicolored | .40 .20 |
| 250 | A54 | 7c | multicolored | .50 .75 |
| 251 | A54 | 20c | multicolored | .75 .20 |
| 252 | A54 | 25c | multicolored | 2.40 1.35 |
| | | | Nos. 249-252 (4) | |

Pesquet's Parrot A54

**1968, Feb. 21  Photo.  Unwmk.**
**Perf. 12x12½, 12½x12**

Headdress from: 10c, Southern Highlands District, horiz. 20c, Western Highlands District. 60c, Chimbu District (different from 5c).

| | | | | |
|---|---|---|---|---|
| 253 | A55 | 5c | multi | .20 .20 |
| 254 | A55 | 10c | multi | .20 .20 |
| 255 | A55 | 20c | multi, horiz. | .50 .50 |
| 256 | A55 | 30c | multi | 1.40 1.10 |
| | | | Nos. 253-256 (4) | |

**5c PAPUA & NEW GUINEA**

Prehistoric
Ambum Stone
and Skull — A65

**1970, Feb. 11** **Photo.** **Perf. 12½**
297 A65 5c violet brown & multi .25 .20
298 A65 10c ocher & multi .35 .20
299 A65 25c org brn & multi .50 .35
300 A65 30c olive green & multi 1.00 .60
Nos. 297-300 (4) 2.00 1.15

Designs: 10c, Masawa canoe of the Kula Circuit. 25c, Map of Papua and New Guinea made by Luis Valez de Torres, 1606. 30c, H.M.S. Basilisk, 1873.

King of Saxony
Bird of
Paradise — A66

Birds of Paradise: 10c, King. 15c, Augusta Victoria. 25c, Multi-crested.

**1970, May 13** **Photo.** **Perf. 11½**
301 A66 5c tan & multi 1.00 .20
302 A66 10c multicolored 1.25 .60
303 A66 15c lt blue & multi 1.75 1.00
304 A66 25c multicolored 2.00 1.15
Nos. 301-304 (4) 6.50 2.55

Canceled to Order

Starting in 1970 or earlier, the Philatelic Bureau at Port Moresby began to sell new issues canceled to order at face value.

Douglas DC-3
Volcano — A67

Aircraft: No. 305, DC-6B and Mt. Wilhelm. No. 306, Lockheed Mark II Electra and Mt. Yule. No. 307, Boeing 727 and Mt. Giluwe. No. 308, Fokker F27 Friendship and Manam Island Volcano. 30c, Boeing 707 and Hornbm's Bluff.

**1970, July 8** **Photo.** **Perf. 14½x14**
305 A67 5c "TAA" on tail .35 .25
306 A67 5c Striped tail .35 .25
307 A67 5c "T" on tail .35 .25
308 A67 5c Red tail .35 .25
a. Block of 4, #305-308 1.50 1.50
309 A67 25c multicolored 1.50 .80
310 A67 30c multicolored .80 .55
Nos. 305-310 (6) 3.00 1.95

Development of air service during the last 25 years between Australia and New Guinea.

National Handicraft: 10c, Lime pot. 30c, Album sago storage pot. 30c, bowl, horiz.

**1970, Oct. 28** **Photo.** **Perf. 11½**
315 A69 5c multicolored .20 .20
317 A69 10c multicolored .30 .20
318 A69 30c multicolored .40 .40
Nos. 315-318 (4) 1.20 1.00

Wogeo Island
Food
Bowl — A69

Eastern
Highlands
House — A70

**1971, Jan. 27** **Photo.** **Perf. 12½**
319 A70 7c dark olive & multi .25 .20
320 A70 7c Prus blue & multi .30 .20
321 A70 10c deep org & multi .30 .60
322 A70 40c brown & multi 1.60 1.75
Nos. 319-322 (4)

Local Architecture: 7c, Milne Bay house. 10c, Purari Delta house. 40c, Sepik or Men's Spirit House.

Basketball
A72

4th South Pacific Games

**1971, Mar. 31** **Photo.** **Perf. 11½**
323 A71 5c blue green & multi .35 .20
324 A71 10c multicolored .50 .20
325 A71 15c multicolored .90 .70
326 A71 25c dull yellow & multi 1.25 .70
327 A71 30c olive & multi 4.25 2.25
Nos. 323-327 (5)

Animals: 10c, Brown and white striped possum. 15c, Feather-tailed possum, anteater, horiz. 30c, Good-fellow's tree-climbing kangaroo, horiz.

Spotted
Cuscus — A71

Bartering Fish
for Coconuts
and Taro — A73

Siaa
Dancer — A74

Primary industries: 9c, Man stacking yams and taro. 14c, Market scene. 30c, Farm couple tending yams.

**1971, June 9** **Litho.** **Perf. 14**
328 A72 7c shown .20 .20
329 A72 14c Yachting .35 .25
330 A72 21c Boxing .35 .35
331 A72 28c Field events 1.25 1.10
Nos. 328-331 (4)

Fourth South Pacific Games, Papeete, French Polynesia, Sept. 8-19.

Nicolaus N. de Miklouho-Maclay,
Explorer, and Mask — A68

Designs: 10c, Bronislaw Kaspar Malinowski, anthropologist, and hut. 15c, Count Tommaso Salvadori, ornithologist, and cassowary. 20c, Friedrich R. Schlechter, botanist, and orchid.

**1970, Aug. 19** **Photo.** **Perf. 11½**
311 A68 5c brown, blk & lilac .20 .20
313 A68 15c dull lilac & multi .45 .30
314 A68 20c slate & multi .80 .30
Nos. 311-314 (4) 1.70 1.00

42nd Cong. of the Australian and New Zealand Assoc. for the Advancement of Science, Port Moresby, Aug. 17-21.

Pitted-shelled
Turtle — A77

**1972, Mar. 15** **Photo.** **Perf. 11½**
344 A77 7c multicolored .50 .20
345 A77 14c car rose & multi 1.25 1.00
346 A77 21c yellow & multi 1.25 1.25
347 A77 30c yel green & multi 1.60 1.00
Nos. 344-347 (4) 4.60 3.45

Designs: 14c, Angle-headed agamid. 21c, Green python. 30c, Water monitor.

South Pacific Commission, 25th anniv.

**1972, Jan. 26**
342 A76 15c brt green & multi .50 .40
343 A76 15c brt green & multi .50 .40
a. Pair, #342-343 1.50 1.50

Papua New
Guinea Map,
South Pacific
Commission
Emblem — A76

#343, Man's head, So. Pacific Commission flag.

Papua New
Guinea and
Australia
Arms — A75

**1972, Jan. 26** **Perf. 12½x12**
340 A75 7c gray blue, org & blk .35 .30
341 A75 7c gray blue, blk, red & .35 .30
a. Pair, #340-341

#341, Papua New Guinea & Australia flags.

Constitutional development for the 1972 House of Assembly elections.

**1971, Aug. 18** **Photo.** **Perf. 11½**
332 A73 7c multicolored .20 .20
333 A73 9c multicolored .25 .25
334 A73 14c multicolored .40 .20
335 A73 30c multicolored .60 .50
Nos. 332-335 (4) 1.45 1.15

**1971, Oct. 27** **Photo.** **Perf. 11½**
336 A74 7c orange & multi .25 .20
337 A74 9c yel green & multi .30 .20
338 A74 20c bister & multi .70 .55
339 A74 28c multicolored 1.25 .90
Nos. 336-339 (4) 2.50 1.90

Designs: 9c, Urasena masked dancer. 20c, Two Siassi masked dancers, horiz. 28c, Three Siaa dancers, horiz.

Curtiss Seagull MF 6 and Ship — A78

**1972, June 7** **Granite Paper**
348 A78 7c dp yellow & multi .30 .20
349 A78 14c dp orange & multi .85 1.00
350 A78 20c olive & multi 1.40 1.00
351 A78 25c multicolored 4.15 3.20
Nos. 348-351 (4)

Designs: 14c, De Havilland 37 & porters from gold fields. 20c, Junkers G 31 & heavy machinery. 25c, Junkers F 13 & Lutheran mission church.

50th anniv. of aviation in Papua New Guinea.

National Day Unity
Emblem — A79

**1972, Aug. 16** **Perf. 12½x12½**
352 A79 7c violet blue & multi .20 .20
353 A79 10c orange & multi .30 .20
354 A79 30c vermilion & multi .50 .50
Nos. 352-354 (3) 1.00 .90

Designs: 10c, Unity emblem and kundu (drum). 30c, Unity emblem and conch.

National Day, Sept. 15, 1972.

Rev. Copland
King — A80

**1972, Oct. 25** **Photo.** **Perf. 11½**
355 A80 7c dark blue & multi .30 .35
356 A80 7c dark red & multi .30 .35
357 A80 7c dark green & multi .30 .35
358 A80 7c dark olive bister & multi 1.20 1.40
Nos. 355-358 (4)

Pioneering Missionaries: No. 356, Pastor Ruatoka. No. 357, Bishop Stanislaus Henry Verjus. No. 358, Rev. Dr. Johannes Flierl.

Christmas 1972.

Relay Station on Mt. Tomavatur — A81

**1973, Jan. 24** **Photo.** **Perf. 12½**
359 A81 7c shown .30 .20
360 A81 7c Mt. Kerigomna .30 .20
361 A81 7c Satelburg .30 .20
362 A81 7c Wideru .30 .20
363 A81 9c Teleprinter 1.25 .85
364 A81 30c Map of network .85
a. Block of 4, #359-362 2.85 1.85
Nos. 359-364 (6)

Telecommunications development 1968-1972. No. 363a has a unifying frame.

Queen Carol's Bird
of Paradise — A82

**1973, Mar. 30** **Photo.** **Perf. 11½**
365 A82 7c citron & multi 1.00 .35
366 A82 14c dull green & multi 2.50 1.00
367 A82 21c lemon & multi 2.75 1.50
368 A82 28c lt blue & multi 3.75 1.75
Nos. 365-368 (4) 10.00 4.60

Birds of Paradise: 14c, Goldie's. 21c, Ribbon-tailed astrapia. 28c, Princess Stephanie's.

**Size: 17x48mm**

**Size: 22½x38mm**

## Wood Carver, Milne Bay — A83

Designs: 3c, Wig makers, Southern Highlands. 5c, Bagana Volcano, Bougainville. 6c, Pig Exchange, Western Highlands. 7c, Coastal village, Central District. 8c, Arawe mother, West New Britain. 9c, Fire dancers, East New Britain. 10c, Tifalmin hunter, West Sepik District. 14c, Crocodile hunters, Western District. 15c, Mt. Elimbari, Chimbu. 20c, Canoe racing, Manus District. 21c, Making sago, Gulf District. 25c, Council House, East Sepik. 28c, Menyamya bowmen, Morobe. 30c, Shark snaring, Madang. 40c, Fishing canoes, Madang. 60c, Women making tapa cloth, Northern District. $1, Asaro mudmen, Eastern Highlands. $2, Sing festival, Enga District.

**1973-74    Photo.    Perf. 11½**
**Granite Paper**

| | | | | |
|---|---|---|---|---|
| 369 | A83 | 1c multicolored | .20 | .20 |
| 370 | A83 | 3c multi ('74) | .35 | .20 |
| 371 | A83 | 5c multicolored | .55 | .35 |
| 372 | A83 | 6c multi ('74) | .75 | 1.00 |
| 373 | A83 | 7c multicolored | .30 | .20 |
| 374 | A83 | 8c multi ('74) | .35 | .20 |
| 375 | A83 | 9c multicolored | .40 | .20 |
| 376 | A83 | 10c multicolored | .60 | .20 |
| 377 | A83 | 14c multicolored | .45 | .60 |
| 378 | A83 | 15c multicolored | .50 | .30 |
| 379 | A03 | 20c multi ('74) | 1.00 | .30 |
| 380 | A83 | 21c multicolored | .50 | .90 |
| 381 | A83 | 25c multicolored | .50 | .90 |
| 382 | A83 | 28c multicolored | .50 | .90 |
| 383 | A83 | 30c multicolored | .50 | .40 |
| 386 | A83 | 60c multi ('74) | .60 | .75 |
| 387 | A83 | $1 multi ('74) | .85 | 1.50 |
| 388 | A83 | $2 multicolored | 3.50 | 6.00 |
| Nos. 369-383,385-388 (19) | | | 12.85 | 14.95 |

Issued: 1c, 7c, 15c, 25c, 40c, 6/13; 5c, 14c, 21c, 28c, 30c; Aug.; 3c, 8c, 10c, 20c, 60c; $1, 1/23/74.

## Papua New Guinea No. 7 — A84

1c, Ger. New Guinea #1,2. 6c, Ger. New Guinea #17. 7c, New Britain #43. 25c, New Guinea #1. 30c, Papua New Guinea #108.

**Litho. (1c, 7c); Litho. & Engr. (others)**
**1973, Oct. 24    Perf. 13½x14**
**Size: 54x31mm**

| | | | | |
|---|---|---|---|---|
| 389 | A84 | 1c gold, brn, grn & blk | .20 | .20 |
| 390 | A84 | 6c silver, blue & indigo | .25 | .20 |
| 391 | A84 | 7c gold, red, blk & buff | .25 | .25 |

**Perf. 14x14½**
**Size: 45x38mm**

| | | | | |
|---|---|---|---|---|
| 392 | A84 | 9c gold, org, blk & brn | .30 | .30 |
| 393 | A84 | 25c gold & orange | .70 | .90 |
| 394 | A84 | 30c silver & dp lilac | .75 | 1.00 |
| Nos. 389-394 (6) | | | 2.45 | 2.85 |

75th anniv. of stamps in Papua New Guinea.

## Masks — A85

**1973, Dec. 5    Photo.    Perf. 12½**
**Granite Paper**

| | | | | |
|---|---|---|---|---|
| 395 | A85 | 7c multicolored | .30 | .20 |
| 396 | A85 | 10c violet blue & multi | .60 | .60 |

Self-government.

## Queen Elizabeth II A86

**1974, Feb. 22    Photo.    Perf. 14x14½**

| | | | | |
|---|---|---|---|---|
| 397 | A86 | 7c dp carmine & multi | .40 | .20 |
| 398 | A86 | 30c vio blue & multi | 1.00 | 1.00 |

Visit of Queen Elizabeth II and the Royal Family, Feb. 22-27.

## Wreathed Hornbill — A87

Size of No. 400, 32½x48mm.

**1974, June 12    Perf. 12, 11½ (10c)    Photo.**
**Granite Paper**

| | | | | |
|---|---|---|---|---|
| 399 | A87 | 7c shown | 1.50 | .75 |
| 400 | A87 | 10c Great cassowary | 2.50 | 3.25 |
| 401 | A87 | 30c Kapul eagle | 5.50 | 7.50 |
| Nos. 399-401 (3) | | | 9.50 | 11.50 |

## Dendrobium Bracteosum — A88

Orchids: 10c, Dendrobium anosmum. 20c, Dendrobium smillieae. 30c, Dendrobium insigne.

**1974, Nov. 20    Photo.    Perf. 11½**
**Granite Paper**

| | | | | |
|---|---|---|---|---|
| 402 | A88 | 7c dark green & multi | .65 | .20 |
| 403 | A88 | 10c dark blue & multi | .50 | .40 |
| 404 | A88 | 20c bister & multi | .75 | 1.00 |
| 405 | A88 | 30c green & multi | 1.10 | 1.40 |
| Nos. 402-405 (4) | | | 3.00 | 3.00 |

## Motu Lakatoi A89

Traditional Canoes: 10c, Tami two-master morobe. 25c, Aramia racing canoe. 30c, Buka Island canoe.

**1975, Feb. 26    Photo.    Perf. 11½**
**Granite Paper**

| | | | | |
|---|---|---|---|---|
| 406 | A89 | 7c multicolored | .25 | .20 |
| 407 | A89 | 10c orange & multi | .45 | .45 |
| 408 | A89 | 25c apple green & multi | .90 | 1.75 |
| 409 | A89 | 30c citron & multi | 2.50 | 3.40 |
| Nos. 406-409 (4) | | | 1.00 | 1.00 |

## Paradise Birdwing Butterfly, 1t Coin — A90

## Ornate Butterfly Cod on 2t and Plateless Turtle on 5t — A91

New coinage: 10t, Cuscus on 10t. 20t, Cassowary on 20t. 1k, River crocodiles on 1k coin with center hole; obverse and reverse of 1k.

**1975, Apr. 21    Perf. 11, 11½ (A91)    Photo.**
**Granite Paper**

| | | | | |
|---|---|---|---|---|
| 410 | A90 | 1t green & multi | .20 | .20 |
| 411 | A91 | 7t brown & multi | .45 | .45 |
| 412 | A90 | 10t violet blue & multi | .45 | .45 |
| 413 | A90 | 20t multicolored | .90 | .90 |
| 414 | A91 | 1k dull blue & multi | 2.50 | 2.50 |
| Nos. 410-414 (5) | | | 4.50 | 4.50 |

## Ornithoptera Alexandrae A92

Birdwing Butterflies: 10t, O. victoriae regis. 30t, O. allottei. 40t, O. chimaera.

**1975, June 11    Photo.    Granite Paper**

| | | | | |
|---|---|---|---|---|
| 415 | A92 | 7t multicolored | .40 | .20 |
| 416 | A92 | 10t multicolored | .50 | .50 |
| 417 | A92 | 30t multicolored | 1.50 | 1.50 |
| 418 | A92 | 40t multicolored | 2.00 | 3.25 |
| Nos. 415-418 (4) | | | 4.40 | 5.45 |

## Boxing and Games' Emblem — A93

**1975, Aug. 2    Photo.    Perf. 11½**
**Granite Paper**

| | | | | |
|---|---|---|---|---|
| 419 | A93 | 7t shown | .25 | .20 |
| 420 | A93 | 20t Track and field | .45 | .16 |
| 421 | A93 | 25t Basketball | .50 | .60 |
| 422 | A93 | 30t Swimming | 1.70 | 2.00 |
| Nos. 419-422 (4) | | | | |

5th South Pacific Games, Guam, Aug. 1-10.

## Map of South East Asia and Flag of PNG A94

Design: 30t, Map of South East Asia and Papua New Guinea coat of arms.

**1975, Sept. 10    Photo.    Perf. 11½**
**Granite Paper**

| | | | | |
|---|---|---|---|---|
| 423 | A94 | 7t red & multi | .20 | .20 |
| 424 | A94 | 30t blue & multi | .60 | .60 |
| a. | | Souvenir sheet of 2, #423-424 | 1.50 | 1.50 |

Papua New Guinea independence, Sept. 16, 1975.

## M. V. Bulolo A95

Ships of the 1930's: 15t, M.V. Macdhui. 25t, M.V. Malaita. 60t, S.S. Montoro.

**1976, Jan. 21    Photo.    Perf. 11½**
**Granite Paper**

| | | | | |
|---|---|---|---|---|
| 425 | A95 | 7t multicolored | .25 | .20 |
| 426 | A95 | 15t multicolored | .40 | .30 |
| 427 | A95 | 25t multicolored | .70 | .45 |
| 428 | A95 | 60t multicolored | 1.65 | 1.75 |
| | | | 3.00 | 2.70 |
| Nos. 425-428 (4) | | | | |

## Rorovana Carvings A96

Bougainville Art: 20t, Upe hats. 25t, Kapkaps (tortoise shell ornaments). 30t, Carved canoe paddles.

**1976, Mar. 17    Photo.    Perf. 11½**
**Granite Paper**

| | | | | |
|---|---|---|---|---|
| 429 | A96 | 7t multicolored | .25 | .20 |
| 430 | A96 | 20t blue & multi | .45 | .45 |
| 431 | A96 | 25t dp orange & multi | .50 | .50 |
| 432 | A96 | 30t multicolored | .55 | .70 |
| | | | 1.75 | 1.85 |
| Nos. 429-432 (4) | | | | |

## Houses A97

**1976, June 9    Photo.    Perf. 11½**
**Granite Paper**

| | | | | |
|---|---|---|---|---|
| 433 | A97 | 7t Rabaul | .20 | .20 |
| 434 | A97 | 15t Aramia | .30 | .25 |
| 435 | A97 | 30t Telefomin | .60 | .50 |
| 436 | A97 | 40t Tapini | .65 | .90 |
| | | | 1.75 | 1.85 |
| Nos. 433-436 (4) | | | | |

## Boy Scouts and Scout Emblem A98

Designs: 15t, Sea Scouts on outrigger canoe, Scout emblem. 60t, Plane on water.

**1976, Aug. 18    Photo.    Perf. 11½**
**Granite Paper**

| | | | | |
|---|---|---|---|---|
| 437 | A98 | 7t multicolored | .35 | .20 |
| 438 | A98 | 15t lilac & multi | .35 | .45 |
| 439 | A98 | 15t multicolored | .45 | .45 |
| 440 | A99 | 60t multicolored | 1.10 | 1.75 |
| | | | 2.25 | 2.65 |
| Nos. 437-440 (4) | | | | |

50th anniversaries: Papua New Guinea Boy Scouts; 1st flight from Australia.

## Father Ross and Mt. Hagen A100

**1976, Oct. 28    Photo.    Perf. 11½**
**Granite Paper**

| | | | | |
|---|---|---|---|---|
| 441 | A100 | 7t multicolored | .40 | .25 |

Rev. Father William Ross (1896-1973), American missionary in New Guinea.

## 1976, Oct. 28 — Granite Paper

Clouded Rainbow Fish — A101

| | | | | |
|---|---|---|---|---|
| 442 | A101 | 5t multicolored | .25 | .20 |
| 443 | A101 | 15t multicolored | .75 | .40 |
| 444 | A101 | 30t multicolored | 1.40 | .75 |
| 445 | A101 | 40t multicolored | 1.75 | .95 |
| | | Nos. 442-445 (4) | 4.15 | 2.30 |

Tropical Fish: 15t, Imperial angelfish. 30t, Freckled rock cod. 40t, Threadfin butterflyfish.

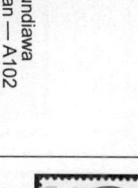
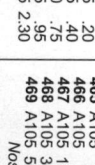

Mekeo Headdress A103
Kundiawa Man — A102

## 1977-78

**Perf. 14½x14**
Sizes: 25x30mm (1, 5, 20t), 26x26mm (10, 15, 25, 30, 50t), 23x38mm (35, 40t)

| | | | | |
|---|---|---|---|---|
| 446 | A102 | 1t multicolored | .20 | .20 |
| 447 | A102 | 5t multicolored | .20 | .20 |
| 448 | A102 | 10t multicolored | .25 | .20 |
| 449 | A102 | 15t multicolored | .25 | .25 |
| 450 | A102 | 20t multicolored | .40 | .25 |
| 451 | A102 | 25t multicolored | .30 | .30 |
| 452 | A102 | 30t multicolored | .35 | .30 |
| 453 | A102 | 35t multicolored | .40 | .30 |
| 454 | A102 | 50t multicolored | .55 | .30 |
| 455 | A102 | 60t multicolored | .80 | .30 |

**Perf. 14½x14**
Size: 28x35½mm
| 456 | A102 | 1k multicolored | .80 | 1.40 |
|---|---|---|---|---|

Size: 33x23mm
| 457 | A103 | 2k multicolored | 1.40 | 2.75 |
|---|---|---|---|---|
| | | | 6.00 | 6.85 |

Issued: #456-457, 1/12/77; #448, 450, 453, 455, 6/7/78; others, 3/29/78.

Headdresses: 5t, Masked dancer, East Sepik Province. 10t, Dancer, Koiari area. 15t, Hanuabada woman. 20t, Young woman, Orokaiva. 25t, Haus Tambaran dancer, East Sepik Province. 30t, Asaro Valley man. 35t, Garaina man, Morobe. 40t, Waghi Valley man. 50t, Trobriand dancer, Milne Bay. 1k, Wasara.

**Perf. 12 (15, 25, 30t), 11½ (others)**

Silver Jubilee 1977

## 1977, Mar. 16 — Photo. Perf. 15x14

Elizabeth II and P.N.G. Arms A104

| | | | | |
|---|---|---|---|---|
| 462 | A104 | 7t multicolored | .30 | .20 |
| 463 | A104 | 15t multicolored | .60 | .70 |
| 464 | A104 | 35t multicolored | .70 | 1.25 |
| | | Nos. 462-464 (3) | 1.30 | 1.25 |

Designs: 7t, Queen and P.N.G. flag. 35t, Queen and map of P.N.G.
25th anniv. of the reign of Elizabeth II.

---

Whitebreasted Ground Dove — A105

## 1977, June 8 — Granite Paper — Photo. Perf. 11½

| | | | | |
|---|---|---|---|---|
| 465 | A105 | 5t multicolored | .40 | .20 |
| 466 | A105 | 7t multicolored | .40 | .20 |
| 467 | A105 | 15t multicolored | .75 | .65 |
| 468 | A105 | 30t multicolored | 1.00 | .90 |
| 469 | A105 | 50t multicolored | 1.75 | 3.00 |
| | | Nos. 465-469 (5) | 4.30 | 4.95 |

Protected Birds: 7t, Victoria crowned pigeon. 15t, Pheasant pigeon. 30t, Orange-fronted fruit dove. 50t, Banded imperial pigeon.

Girl Guides and Gold Badge A106

## 1977, Aug. 10 — Litho. Perf. 14½

| | | | | |
|---|---|---|---|---|
| 470 | A106 | 7t multicolored | .20 | .20 |
| 471 | A106 | 15t multicolored | .30 | .20 |
| 472 | A106 | 30t multicolored | .55 | .40 |
| 473 | A106 | 35t multicolored | .65 | 1.30 |
| | | Nos. 470-473 (4) | 1.65 | 1.30 |

Designs (Girl Guides): 15t, Mapping and blue badge. 30t, Doing laundry in brook and red badge. 35t, Wearing grass skirts, cooking and green badge.
Papua New Guinea Girl Guides, 50th anniv.

Legend of Kari Marupi — A107

## 1977, Oct. 19 — Litho. Perf. 13½

| | | | | |
|---|---|---|---|---|
| 474 | A107 | 7t black & multi | .20 | .20 |
| 475 | A107 | 20t black & multi | .45 | .35 |
| 476 | A107 | 30t black & multi | .50 | .60 |
| 477 | A107 | 35t black & multi | .60 | .60 |
| | | Nos. 474-477 (4) | 1.65 | 1.75 |

Myths of Elema People: 20t, Oa-Laea. 30t, Oa-Iarapo. 35t, Savoripi Clan.

Blue-tailed Skink A108

## 1978, Jan. 25 — Granite Paper — Photo. Perf. 11½

| | | | | |
|---|---|---|---|---|
| 478 | A108 | 10t blue & multi | .30 | .20 |
| 479 | A108 | 15t lilac & multi | .40 | .25 |
| 480 | A108 | 35t olive & multi | .60 | .75 |
| 481 | A108 | 40t orange & multi | .80 | .80 |
| | | Nos. 478-481 (4) | 2.10 | 2.00 |

Lizards: 15t, Green tree skink. 35t, Crocodile skink. 40t, New Guinea blue-tongued skink.

Roboastra Arika — A109

Sea Slugs: 15t, Chromodoris fidelis. 35t, Flabellina macassarana. 40t, Chromodoris trimarginata.

## 1978, Aug. 29 — Photo. Perf. 11½

| | | | | |
|---|---|---|---|---|
| 482 | A109 | 10t multicolored | .30 | .30 |
| 483 | A109 | 15t multicolored | .40 | .30 |
| 484 | A109 | 35t multicolored | .65 | .65 |
| 485 | A109 | 40t multicolored | .75 | .75 |
| | | Nos. 482-485 (4) | 2.10 | 1.90 |

Mandated New Guinea Constabulary A110

## 1978, Oct. 26 — Photo. Perf. 14½x14

| | | | | |
|---|---|---|---|---|
| 486 | A110 | 10t multicolored | .20 | .20 |
| 487 | A110 | 15t multicolored | .30 | .30 |
| 488 | A110 | 20t multicolored | .35 | .35 |
| 489 | A110 | 25t multicolored | .40 | .40 |
| 490 | A110 | 30t multicolored | .50 | .50 |
| | | Nos. 486-490 (5) | 1.75 | 1.75 |

Constabulary and Badge: 10t, Royal Papua New Guinea. 15t, Armed British New Guinea. 20t, German New Guinea police. 30t, Royal Papua and New Guinea.

---

## PAPUA NEW GUINEA

Oenetus A114

Ocarina, Chimbu Province — A111

## 1979, Jan. 24 — Litho. Perf. 14½x14, 14x14½

| | | | | |
|---|---|---|---|---|
| 491 | A111 | 7t multicolored | .30 | .30 |
| 492 | A111 | 20t multicolored | .30 | .30 |
| 493 | A111 | 28t multicolored | .35 | .40 |
| 494 | A111 | 35t multicolored | .50 | .50 |
| | | Nos. 491-494 (4) | 1.40 | 1.40 |

Musical Instruments: 20t, Musical bow, New Britain, horiz. 28t, Launut, New Ireland. 35t, New Hanover, horiz. Nose flute, horiz.

Prow and Paddle, East New Britain — A112

## 1979, Mar. 28 — Litho. Perf. 14½

| | | | | |
|---|---|---|---|---|
| 495 | A112 | 14t multicolored | .20 | .20 |
| 496 | A112 | 21t multicolored | .30 | .25 |
| 497 | A112 | 25t multicolored | .35 | .30 |
| 498 | A112 | 40t multicolored | .45 | .60 |
| | | Nos. 495-498 (4) | 1.30 | 1.35 |

Canoe Prows and Paddles: 21t, Trobriand Islands. 25t, Sepik war canoe. 40t, Milne Bay.

Belt of Shell Disks — A113

## 1979, June 6 — Litho. Perf. 12½x12

| | | | | |
|---|---|---|---|---|
| 499 | A113 | 7t multicolored | .20 | .20 |
| 500 | A113 | 15t multicolored | .25 | .25 |
| 501 | A113 | 25t multicolored | .45 | .45 |
| 502 | A113 | 35t multicolored | .55 | .65 |
| | | Nos. 499-502 (4) | 1.45 | 1.55 |

Traditional Currency: 15t, Tusk chest ornament. 25t, Shell armband. 35t, Shell necklace.

## 1979, Aug. 29 — Photo. Perf. 11½

| | | | | |
|---|---|---|---|---|
| 503 | A114 | 7t multicolored | .20 | .20 |
| 504 | A114 | 15t multicolored | .35 | .35 |
| 505 | A114 | 20t multicolored | .40 | .50 |
| 506 | A114 | 30t multicolored | .60 | .70 |
| 507 | A114 | 35t multicolored | 2.00 | 2.40 |
| | | Nos. 503-507 (5) | | |

Moths: 15t, Celerina vulgaris. 20t, Alcidis aurora. 25t, Phyllodes conspicillator. 30t, Nyctalemon patroclus, vert.

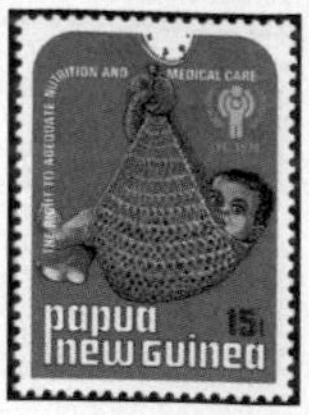

Baby in String Bag Scale — A115

## 1979, Oct. 24 — Litho. Perf. 14x13½

| | | | | |
|---|---|---|---|---|
| 508 | A115 | 7t multicolored | .20 | .20 |
| 509 | A115 | 15t multicolored | .25 | .25 |
| 510 | A115 | 30t multicolored | .35 | .35 |
| 511 | A115 | 60t multicolored | 1.40 | 1.40 |
| | | Nos. 508-511 (4) | | |

IYC (Emblem and): 7t, Mother nursing baby. 30t, Boy playing with dog and ball. 60t, Girl in classroom.

Mail Sorting, Mail Truck A116

## 1980, Jan. 23 — Litho. Perf. 13½x14

| | | | | |
|---|---|---|---|---|
| 512 | A116 | 7t multicolored | .20 | .20 |
| 513 | A116 | 25t multicolored | .30 | .30 |
| 514 | A116 | 35t multicolored | .40 | .40 |
| 515 | A116 | 40t multicolored | .50 | .50 |
| | | Nos. 512-515 (4) | 1.40 | 1.40 |

UPU Membership: 25t, Wartime mail delivery. 35t, UPU monument, airport and city. 40t, Hand canceling, letter carrier.

Male Dancer, Betrothal Ceremony — A117

## 1980, Mar. 26 — Granite Paper — Photo. Perf. 11½

| | | | | |
|---|---|---|---|---|
| 516 | A117 | 20t single stamp | 1.25 | 1.25 |
| 516a. | | Strip of 5 | .25 | .25 |

Third South Pacific Arts Festival, Port Moresby (Mini Betrothal Ceremony Mural): No. 516 has continuous design.

National Census — A118

## 1980, June 4 — Litho. Perf. 14

| | | | | |
|---|---|---|---|---|
| 517 | A118 | 7t shown | .20 | .20 |
| 518 | A118 | 15t Population symbol | .25 | .25 |
| 519 | A118 | 40t P.N.G. map | .55 | .55 |
| 520 | A118 | 50t Faces | .75 | .75 |
| | | Nos. 517-520 (4) | 1.70 | 1.70 |

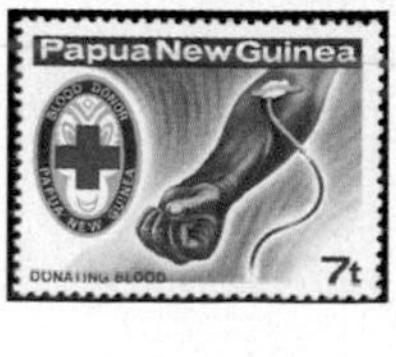

Blood Transfusion, Donor's Badge — A119

## Coral Type of 1982

**1983, Nov. 9**    **Photo.**    **Perf. 11½**

588 A130 20t Isis sp. .80 .75
589 A130 25t Acropora sp. 1.00 1.00
590 A130 35t Stylaster elegans 1.50 1.50
591 A130 45t Turbinarea sp. 2.00 1.90
Nos. 588-591 (4) 5.30 5.15
Nos. 588-591 vert.

## Turtles A135

**1984, Feb. 8**    **Granite Paper**    **Photo.**

592 A135 5t Chelonia depressa .20 .20
593 A135 10t Chelonia mydas .30 .30
594 A135 15t Eretkmochelys imbricata .50 .50
595 A135 20t Lepidochelys olivacea .60 .60
596 A135 25t Caretta caretta .80 .80
597 A135 40t Dermochelys coriacea 1.40 1.40
Nos. 592-597 (6) 3.80 3.80

## Papua-Australia Airmail Service, 50th Anniv. — A136

Mail planes.

**1984, May 8**    **Litho.**    **Perf. 14½x14**

598 A136 20t Avro X VH-UXX .45 .45
599 A136 25t DH86B VH-UYU .55 .55
600 A136 40t Westland Widgeon Carmania 1.00 1.00
601 A136 60t Consolidated Catalina NC777 1.40 1.40
Nos. 598-601 (4) 3.40 3.40

## Parliament House Opening — A137

**1984, Aug. 7**    **Litho.**    **Perf. 13½x14**

602 A137 10t multicoloured .45 .45

## Bird of Paradise A138

**1984, Aug. 7**    **Granite Paper**    **Photo.**    **Perf. 11½**

603 A138 5k multicolored 9.50 9.50

## Ceremonial Shield — A139

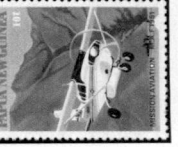

---

## Coral A130

**1982, July 21**    **Photo.**    **Granite Paper**    **Perf. 11½**

566 A130 1t Stylophora sp. .20 .20
567 A130 5t Acropora numilis .20 .20
568 A130 15t Distichopora sp. .40 .30
569 A130 1k Xenia sp. 2.25 2.00
Nos. 566-569 (4) 3.05 3.70
See Nos. 575-579, 588-591, 614.

## Centenary of Catholic Church in Papua New Guinea — A131

**1982, Sept. 15**    **Photo.**    **Perf. 11½**

570 Strip of 3 .80 .80
a. A131 10t any single .25 .25

## 12th Commonwealth Games, Brisbane, Australia, Sept. 30-Oct. 9 — A132

**1982, Oct. 6**    **Litho.**    **Perf. 14½**

571 A132 10t Running .20 .20
572 A132 15t Boxing .30 .30
573 A132 45t Shooting .90 .90
574 A132 50t Lawn bowling 1.00 1.00
Nos. 571-574 (4) 2.40 2.40

## Coral Type of 1982

**1903, Jan. 12**    **Photo.**    **Granite Paper**    **Perf. 11½**

575 A130 3t Dendrophylla .70 1.00
576 A130 3t Dendronephthya .85 .80
577 A130 30t Dendrone-phthya, diff. 1.40 .90
578 A130 40t Antipathes 1.50 1.50
579 A130 3k Distichopoura 7.00 7.00
Nos. 575-579 (5) 11.45 11.20
Nos. 575-579 vert.

## Commonwealth Day — A133

**1983, Mar. 9**    **Litho.**    **Perf. 14**

580 A133 10t Flag, arms .20 .20
581 A133 15t Youth, recreation .25 .25
582 A133 20t Technical assistance .30 .30
583 A133 50t Export assistance .85 .85
Nos. 580-583 (4) 1.60 1.60

## World Communications Year — A134

**1983, Sept. 7**    **Litho.**    **Perf. 14**

584 A134 10t Mail transport .20 .20
585 A134 25t Writing & receiving letter .50 .50
586 A134 30t Telephone calls .60 .60
587 A134 60t Family reunion 1.20 1.20
Nos. 584-587 (4) 2.50 2.50

---

## PAPUA NEW GUINEA

543 A124 30t multicolored .50 .50
544 A124 35t multicolored .55 .55
Nos. 540-544 (5) 1.80 1.80

## Scoop Net Fishing A125

**1981, Aug. 26**

545 A125 10t shown .20 .20
546 A125 15t Kite fishing .25 .25
547 A125 30t Rod fishing .45 .45
548 A125 60t Scissor net fishing .95 .95
Nos. 545-548 (4) 1.85 1.85

## Forcartia Buhleri A126

**1981, Oct. 28**    **Photo.**    **Granite Paper**    **Perf. 12**

549 A126 5t shown .20 .20
550 A126 15t Naninia citrina .30 .30
551 A126 20t Papulina adonis .35 .35
552 A126 30t Papustyla hindei, Papustyla hermione, Papustyla novae-pommeraniae .55 .55
553 A126 40t Rhynchotrochus strabo .70 .70
Nos. 549-553 (5) 2.10 2.10

## 75th Anniv. of Boy Scouts A127

**1082, Jan. 20**    **Photo.**    **Granite Paper**    **Perf. 11½**

554 A127 15t Lord Baden-Powell, flag raising .30 .30
555 A127 25t Leader, campfire .50 .50
556 A127 35t Scout, hut building .65 .65
557 A127 50t Percy Chatterton, first aid 1.00 1.00
Nos. 554-557 (4) 2.45 2.45

## Wanigela Pottery A128

**1982, Mar. 24**    **Litho.**    **Size: 29x29mm**    **Perf. 14**

558 A128 10t Boiken, East Sepik .20 .20
559 A128 20t Gumalu, Madang .30 .30

**Size: 36x23mm**    **Perf. 14½**

560 A128 40t shown .60 .60
561 A128 50t Ramu Valley, Madang .75 .75
Nos. 558-561 (4) 1.85 1.85

## Nutrition A129

**1982, May 5**    **Litho.**    **Perf. 14½x14**

562 A129 10t Mother, child .20 .20
563 A129 15t Protein .25 .25
564 A129 25t Fruits, vegetables .55 .55
565 A129 40t Carbohydrates .75 .75
Nos. 562-565 (4) 1.80 1.80

---

**1980, Aug. 27**    **Litho.**    **Perf. 14½**

521 A119 7t shown .20 .20
522 A119 15t Donating blood .20 .20
523 A119 30t Map of donation centers .45 .45
524 A119 60t Blood components and types .80 .80
Nos. 521-524 (4) 1.65 1.65

## Dugong A120

**1980, Oct. 29**    **Photo.**    **Perf. 11½**

525 A120 7t shown .20 .20
526 A120 30t Native spotted cat, vert. .40 .40
527 A120 35t Tube-nosed bat, vert. .50 .50
528 A120 45t Raffray's bandicoot .75 .75
Nos. 525-528 (4) 1.85 1.85

## Beach Kingfisher A121

**1981, Jan. 21**    **Photo.**    **Granite Paper**    **Perf. 12**

529 A121 3t shown .20 .20
530 A121 7t Forest kingfisher .20 .20
531 A121 20t Sacrud kingfisher .50 .50

**Size: 26x45½mm**

532 A121 25t White-tailed paradise kingfisher .55 .55

**Size: 26x36mm**

533 A121 60t Blue-winged kookaburra 1.00 1.00
Nos. 529-533 (5) 2.95 2.05

## Mask A122

**Coil Stamps**    **Perf. 14½ Horiz.**

**1981, Jan. 21**    **Photo.**

534 A122 2t shown .20 .20
535 A122 5t Hibiscus .20 .20
For surcharge see No. 615.

## Defense Force Soldiers Firing Mortar — A123

## Missionary Aviation Fellowship Plane — A124

**1981, Mar. 25**    **Photo.**    **Perf. 13½x14**

536 A123 7t shown .20 .20
537 A123 35t DC-3 military plane .25 .25
538 A123 40t Patrol boat Elatpe .65 .65
539 A123 50t Medics treating civilians .80 .80
Nos. 536-539 (4) 1.90 1.90

**1981, June 17**    **Litho.**    **Perf. 14**

540 A124 10t multicolored .20 .20
541 A124 15t multicolored .25 .25
542 A124 20t multicolored .30 .30

Planes of Missionary Organizations: 15t, Holy Ghost Society, 20t, Summer Institute of Linguistics, 30t, Lutheran Mission, 35t, Seventh Day Adventist.

## PAPUA NEW GUINEA

**1984, Sept. 21**
| | | | |
|---|---|---|---|
| 604 | A139 | 10t Central Province | .25 | .25 |
| 605 | A139 | 20t West New Britain | .60 | .60 |
| 606 | A139 | 30t Madang | .90 | .90 |
| 607 | A139 | 50t East Sepik | 1.65 | 1.65 |
| | | *Nos. 604-607 (4)* | 3.40 | 3.40 |

See Nos. 677-680.

British New Guinea Proclamation
Centenary — A140

**1984, Nov. 6    Litho.    Perf. 14½x14**
| | | | |
|---|---|---|---|
| 608 | A140 | 10t Nelson, Port Moresby, 1884 | .55 | .55 |
| a. | | 10t Pair, #608-609 | .25 | .25 |
| 609 | A140 | 10t Port Moresby, 1884 | .25 | .25 |
| b. | | 10t Pair | .25 | .25 |
| | | Pair | 2.50 | 2.50 |
| 612 | A142 | 40t shown | 1.25 | 1.25 |
| 613 | A142 | 60t Dali Beach, Vanimo | 2.00 | 2.00 |
| b. | | 45t Elizabeth, Rabaul, 1884 | 1.25 | 1.25 |
| | | *Nos. 610-613 (4)* | 4.35 | 4.35 |

Chimbu
Gorge
A142

**1985, Feb. 6    Photo.    Perf. 11½**
| | | | |
|---|---|---|---|
| 610 | A142 | 10t Fergusson Island, vert. | .30 | .30 |
| 611 | A142 | 25t Sepik River, vert. | .80 | .80 |

Coral Type of 1982

**1985, May 29    Photo.    Perf. 11½**
| | | | |
|---|---|---|---|
| 614 | A130 | 12t Dendronephthya sp. | .75 | .75 |

For surcharge see No. 686.

No. 536 Surcharged

**1985, Apr. 1    Litho.    Perf. 13½x14**
| | | | |
|---|---|---|---|
| 615 | A123 | 12t on 7t multi | 2.75 | 2.75 |
| a. | | Inverted surcharge | — | |

Ritual Structures
A143

Designs: 15t, Dubu platform, Central Province. 20t, Tamunial house, West New Britain. 30t, Yam tower, Trobriand Island. 60t, Huli grave, Tari.

**1985, May 1    Perf. 13x13½**
| | | | |
|---|---|---|---|
| 616 | A143 | 15t multicolored | .50 | .50 |
| 617 | A143 | 20t multicolored | .70 | .70 |
| 618 | A143 | 30t multicolored | 1.00 | 1.00 |
| 619 | A143 | 60t multicolored | 1.75 | 1.75 |
| | | *Nos. 616-619 (4)* | 3.95 | 3.95 |

Indigenous Birds of Prey — A144

**1985, Aug. 26    Perf. 14x14½**
| | | | |
|---|---|---|---|
| 620 | A144 | 12t Accipiter brachyurus | .50 | .50 |
| 621 | A144 | 12t In flight | .50 | .50 |
| a. | | A144 Pair, #620-621 | 1.00 | 1.00 |
| 622 | A144 | 30t Megatriorchis doriae | 1.25 | 1.25 |
| 623 | A144 | 30t In Flight | 1.25 | 1.25 |
| a. | | A144 Pair, #622-623 | 2.50 | 2.50 |
| 624 | A144 | 60t Henicopernis longicauda | 2.50 | 2.50 |
| 625 | A144 | 60t In flight | 2.50 | 2.50 |
| a. | | A144 Pair, #624-625 | 5.00 | 5.00 |
| | | *Nos. 620-625 (6)* | 8.50 | 8.50 |

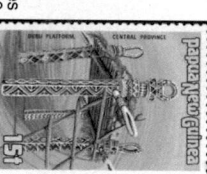

Post Office
Centenary
A146

Designs: 12t, No. 631a, 1901 Postal card, aerogramme, spectacles and inkwell. 30t, No. 631b, Queensland Type A15, No. 628. 40t, No. 631c, Plane and news clipping, 1885. 60t, No. 631d, 1892 German canceler, 1985 first day cancel.

**1985, Oct. 9    Perf. 14½x14**
| | | | |
|---|---|---|---|
| 627 | A146 | 12t multicolored | .35 | .35 |
| 628 | A146 | 30t multicolored | 1.00 | 1.00 |
| 629 | A146 | 40t multicolored | 1.50 | 1.50 |
| 630 | A146 | 60t multicolored | 2.00 | 2.00 |
| | | *Nos. 627-630 (4)* | 4.85 | 4.85 |

Souvenir Sheet

| | | | |
|---|---|---|---|
| 631 | | Sheet of 4 | 6.75 | 6.75 |
| a. | A146 | 12t multicolored | .50 | .50 |
| b. | A146 | 30t multicolored | 1.25 | 1.25 |
| c. | A146 | 40t multicolored | 1.50 | 1.50 |
| d. | A146 | 60t multicolored | 2.25 | 2.25 |

Nombowai Cave
Carved Funerary
Totems — A147

**1985, Nov. 13    Perf. 11½**
| | | | |
|---|---|---|---|
| 632 | A147 | 12t Bird Rulowlaw, headman | .50 | .30 |
| 633 | A147 | 30t Barn owl Raus, headman | 1.25 | .75 |
| 634 | A147 | 60t Melerawuk | 2.00 | 2.00 |
| 635 | A147 | 80t Cockerel, woman | 2.50 | 3.75 |
| | | *Nos. 632-635 (4)* | 6.25 | 6.80 |

Conch
Shells — A148

**1986, Feb. 12    Litho.    Perf. 11½**
| | | | |
|---|---|---|---|
| 636 | A148 | 15t Cypraea valenta | .75 | .45 |
| 637 | A148 | 35t Oliva buelowi | 1.50 | 1.50 |
| 638 | A148 | 35t Oliva parkinsoni | 2.00 | 2.00 |
| 639 | A148 | 70t Cypraea aurantium | 2.00 | 3.75 |
| | | *Nos. 636-639 (4)* | 6.75 | 7.70 |

Common Design Types pictured following the introduction.

Queen Elizabeth II 60th Birthday
Common Design Type

Designs: 15t, In ATS officer's uniform, 1945. 35t, Silver wedding anniv., portrait by Patrick Litchfield, Balmoral, 1972. 50t, Inspecting troops, Port Moresby, 1982. 60t, Banquet aboard Britannia, state tour, 1982. 70t, Visiting Crown Agents' offices, 1983.

**1986, Apr. 21    Perf. 14½**
| | | | |
|---|---|---|---|
| 640 | CD337 | 15t scar, blk & sil | .30 | .30 |
| 641 | CD337 | 35t ultra & multi | .70 | .70 |
| 642 | CD337 | 50t green & multi | 1.00 | 1.00 |

AMERIPEX '86
A149

| | | | |
|---|---|---|---|
| 643 | CD337 | 60t violet & multi | 1.10 | 1.10 |
| 644 | CD337 | 70t rose vio & multi | 1.40 | 1.40 |
| | | *Nos. 640-644 (5)* | 4.50 | 4.50 |

Small birds.

**1986, May 22    Photo.    Perf. 12½
Granite Paper**
| | | | |
|---|---|---|---|
| 645 | A149 | 15t Pitta erythrogaster | .65 | .65 |
| 646 | A149 | 35t Melanocharis stria-tiventris | 1.50 | 1.50 |
| 647 | A149 | 45t Rhipidura rufifrons | 1.90 | 1.90 |
| 648 | A149 | 70t Poecilodryas placens, vert. | 3.00 | 3.00 |
| | | *Nos. 645-648 (4)* | 7.05 | 7.05 |

Lutheran
Church,
Cent. — A150

**1986, July 7    Litho.    Perf. 14x15**
| | | | |
|---|---|---|---|
| 649 | A150 | 15t Monk, minister | .55 | .55 |
| 650 | A150 | 70t Churches from 1886, 1986 | 2.50 | 2.50 |

Indigenous
Orchids — A151

**1986, Aug. 4    Litho.    Perf. 14½x14**
| | | | |
|---|---|---|---|
| 651 | A151 | 15t Dendrobium vexil-larius | .65 | .65 |
| 652 | A151 | 35t Dendrobium lineale | 1.75 | 1.50 |
| 653 | A151 | 45t Dendrobium john-soniae | 2.00 | 1.90 |
| 654 | A151 | 70t Dendrobium cuthbertsonii | 3.00 | 3.00 |
| | | *Nos. 651-654 (4)* | 7.60 | 7.05 |

Folk
Dancers — A152

**1986, Nov. 12    Litho.    Perf. 14**
| | | | |
|---|---|---|---|
| 655 | A152 | 15t Maprik | .65 | .65 |
| 656 | A152 | 35t Kiriwina | 1.50 | 1.50 |
| 657 | A152 | 35t Kundiawa | 1.90 | 1.90 |
| 658 | A152 | 70t Fasu | 3.00 | 3.00 |
| | | *Nos. 655-658 (4)* | 7.05 | 7.05 |

Fish
A153

**1987, Apr. 15    Unwmk.    Litho.    Perf. 15**
| | | | |
|---|---|---|---|
| 659 | A153 | 17t White-cap anemonefish | .65 | .50 |
| 660 | A153 | 30t Black anemonefish | 1.25 | 1.00 |
| 661 | A153 | 35t Tomato clownfish | 1.40 | 1.25 |
| 662 | A153 | 70t Spine-cheek anemonefish | 2.25 | 4.00 |
| | | *Nos. 659-662 (4)* | 5.55 | 6.75 |

For surcharges see Nos. 720, 823, 868.

Ships — A154

**1987-88    Photo.    Unwmk.    Perf. 11½
Granite Paper**
| | | | |
|---|---|---|---|
| 663 | A154 | 1t La Boudeuse, 1768 | .40 | .50 |
| 664 | A154 | 5t Roebuck, 1700 | .75 | .90 |
| 665 | A154 | 10t Swallow, 1767 | 1.00 | .90 |
| 666 | A154 | 15t Fly, 1845 | 1.25 | .60 |
| 667 | A154 | 17t Ilke 15t | 1.25 | .50 |
| 668 | A154 | 20t Rattlesnake, 1849 | 1.25 | .45 |
| 669 | A154 | 30t Viitaz, 1871 | 1.25 | 1.50 |
| 670 | A154 | 35t San Pedrico, Zabre, 1606 | .75 | .90 |
| 671 | A154 | 40t L'Astrolabe, 1827 | 1.50 | 1.50 |
| 672 | A154 | 45t Neva, 1876 | .90 | .80 |
| 673 | A154 | 60t Caravel of Jor-ge De Meneses, 1526 | 2.00 | 2.00 |
| 674 | A154 | 70t Eendracht, 1616 | 1.50 | 1.50 |
| 675 | A154 | 1k Blanche, 1872 | 2.75 | 2.75 |
| 676 | A154 | 2k Merrie En-gland, 1889 | 4.25 | 4.25 |
| 676A | A154 | 3k Samoa, 1884 | 28.30 | 26.55 |
| | | *Nos. 663-676A (15)* | | |
| | | Issued: 5, 35, 45, 70t, 2k, 6/15/87; 15, 20, 40, 60t, 2/17/88; 17t, 1k, 3/1/88; 1, 10, 30t, 3k, 11/16/88. | | |
| | | See Nos. 960-963. For surcharge see No. 824. | | |

War shields.

**1987, Aug. 19    Perf. 11½x12    Photo.    Unwmk.**
| | | | |
|---|---|---|---|
| 677 | A139 | 15t Elema shield, Gulf Province, c. 1880 | .30 | .30 |
| 678 | A139 | 35t East Sepik Prov-ince | .75 | .75 |
| 679 | A139 | 45t Simbai region, Madang Province | .95 | .95 |
| 680 | A139 | 70t Telefomin region, West Sepik | 1.45 | 1.45 |
| | | *Nos. 677-680 (4)* | 3.45 | 3.45 |

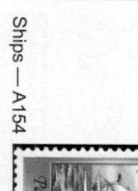

Starfish
A156

**1987, Sept. 30    Litho.    Perf. 14**
| | | | |
|---|---|---|---|
| 682 | A156 | 17t Protoreaster nodosus | .60 | .40 |
| 683 | A156 | 35t Gomophia egeriae | 1.25 | .90 |
| 684 | A156 | 45t Choriaster granu-latus | 1.90 | 1.10 |
| 685 | A156 | 70t Neoferdina ocellata | 5.25 | 5.15 |
| | | *Nos. 682-685 (4)* | 2.75 | |

Aircraft
A157

No. 614
Surcharged

**1987, Sept. 23    Photo.    Perf. 11½
Granite Paper**
| | | | |
|---|---|---|---|
| 686 | A130 | 15t on 12t multi | .90 | .90 |

Designs: 15t, Cessna Stationair 6, Rabaraba Airstrip. 35t, Britten-Norman Islander over Hombrum Bluff. 45t, DHC Twin Otter over the Highlands. 70t, Fokker F28 over Madang.

**1987, Nov. 11 Unwmk. Litho. Perf. 14**

| | | | | |
|---|---|---|---|---|
| 687 | A157 | 15t multicolored | .75 | .45 |
| 688 | A157 | 35t multicolored | 1.25 | 1.00 |
| 689 | A157 | 45t multicolored | 1.50 | 1.25 |
| 690 | A157 | 70t multicolored | 2.25 | 4.00 |
| | | Nos. 687-690 (4) | 5.75 | 6.70 |

**Royal Papua New Guinea Police Force, Cent. — A158**

Historic and modern aspects of the force: 17t, Motorcycle constable and pre-independence native officer wearing a lap-lap. 35t, Sir William McGregor, Armed Native Constabulary founder, 1890, and recruit. 45t, Badges. 70t, Albert Hahl, German official credited with founding the island's police movement in 1888, and badge, early officer.

**1988, June 15 Unwmk. Perf. 14x15 Litho.**

| | | | | |
|---|---|---|---|---|
| 691 | A158 | 17t multicolored | .45 | .45 |
| 692 | A158 | 35t multicolored | .85 | .85 |
| 693 | A158 | 45t multicolored | 1.10 | 1.10 |
| 694 | A158 | 70t multicolored | 1.65 | 1.65 |
| | | Nos. 691-694 (4) | 4.05 | 4.05 |

**Sydney Opera House and a Lakatoi (ship) — A159**

**Fireworks and Globes — A160**

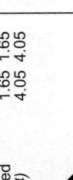

**1988, July 30 Litho. Perf. 13½**

| | | | | |
|---|---|---|---|---|
| 695 | A159 | 35t multicolored | .80 | .80 |
| 696 | A160 | Pair | 1.80 | 1.80 |
| a.-b. | | 35t any single | .90 | .90 |
| c. | | Souvenir sheet of 2, #a.-b. | 2.00 | 2.00 |

SYDPEX '88, Australia (No. 695); Australia bicentennial (No. 696).

**World Wildlife Fund A161**

Metamorphosis of a Queen Alexandra's birdwing butterfly.

**1988, Sept. 19 Perf. 14½**

| | | | | |
|---|---|---|---|---|
| 697 | A161 | 5t Courtship | 1.25 | 1.50 |
| 698 | A161 | 17t Ovipositioning and larvae, vert. | 2.25 | 1.25 |
| 699 | A161 | 25t Emergence from pupa, vert. | 3.00 | 2.75 |
| 700 | A161 | 35t Adult male on leaf | 3.50 | 3.50 |
| | | Nos. 697-700 (4) | 10.00 | 9.00 |

**1988 Summer Olympics, Seoul A162**

**1988, Sept. 19 Litho. Perf. 13½**

| | | | | |
|---|---|---|---|---|
| 701 | A162 | 17t Running | .40 | .40 |
| 702 | A162 | 45t Weight lifting | 1.10 | 1.10 |

**Rhododendrons A163**

**Wmk. 387**

**1989, Jan. 25 Litho. Perf. 14**

| | | | | |
|---|---|---|---|---|
| 703 | A163 | 3t R. zoelleri | .20 | .20 |
| 704 | A163 | 20t R. cruthwelli | .50 | .50 |
| 705 | A163 | 60t R. superbum | 1.50 | 1.50 |
| 706 | A163 | 70t R. christianae | 1.75 | 1.75 |
| | | Nos. 703-706 (4) | 3.95 | 3.95 |

**Intl. Letter Writing Week — A164**

**Perf. 14½**

**1989, Mar. 22**

| | | | | |
|---|---|---|---|---|
| 707 | A164 | 20t Writing letter | .40 | .40 |
| 708 | A164 | 35t Mailing letter | .65 | .65 |
| 709 | A164 | 60t Stamping letter | 1.10 | 1.10 |
| 710 | A164 | 70t Reading letter | 1.40 | 1.40 |
| | | Nos. 707-710 (4) | 3.55 | 3.55 |

**Thatched Dwellings — A165**

**Wmk. 387**

**1989, May 17 Perf. 15**

| | | | | |
|---|---|---|---|---|
| 711 | A165 | 20t Buka Is., 1880s | .50 | .50 |
| 712 | A165 | 35t Koiari tree houses | .90 | .90 |
| 713 | A165 | 60t Lauan, New Ireland, 1890s | 1.50 | 1.50 |
| 714 | A165 | 70t Basilaki, Milne Bay Province, 1930s | 1.75 | 1.75 |
| | | Nos. 711-714 (4) | 4.65 | 4.65 |

**Small Birds — A166**

**1989, July 12 Unwmk. Perf. 14½**

| | | | | |
|---|---|---|---|---|
| 715 | A166 | 20t Oreocharis arfaki female, shown | 1.00 | .90 |
| 716 | A166 | 20t Male | 1.00 | .90 |
| a. | | Pair, #715-716 | 2.25 | 2.25 |
| 717 | A166 | 35t Ifrita kowaldi | 1.50 | 1.50 |
| 718 | A166 | 45t Poecilodryas albonotata | 1.60 | 1.60 |
| 719 | A166 | 70t Sericornis nouhuysi | 2.50 | 2.50 |
| | | Nos. 715-719 (5) | 7.60 | 7.40 |

**No. 659 Surcharged**

**1989, July 12 Unwmk. Perf. 15**

| | | | | |
|---|---|---|---|---|
| 720 | A153 | 20t on 17t multi | .75 | .75 |
| a. | | Double surcharge | | 150.00 |

**Traditional Dance — A167**

Designs: 20t, Motumotu, Gulf Province. 35t, Baining, East New Britain Province. 60t, Vailala River, Gulf Province. 70t, Timbunke, East Sepik Province.

**1989, Sept. 6 Litho. Perf. 14x14½ Wmk. 387**

| | | | | |
|---|---|---|---|---|
| 721 | A167 | 20t multicolored | .65 | .60 |
| 722 | A167 | 35t multicolored | 1.10 | 1.00 |
| 723 | A167 | 60t multicolored | 2.00 | 2.00 |
| 724 | A167 | 70t multicolored | 2.25 | 2.25 |
| | | Nos. 721-724 (4) | 6.00 | 5.85 |

For surcharge see No. 860.

**Christmas A168**

Christmas 1989

Designs: 20t, Hibiscus, church and symbol from a gulf gope board, Kavaumai. 35t, Rhododendron, madonna and child, and mask, Murik Lakes region. 60t, D'Albertis creeper, candle, and shield from Oksapmin, West Sepik highlands. 70t, Pacific frangipani, peace dove and flute mask from Chungrehu, a Ran village in Ramu.

**1989, Nov. 8 Perf. 14x14½ Litho.**

| | | | | |
|---|---|---|---|---|
| 725 | A168 | 20t multicolored | .55 | .55 |
| 726 | A168 | 35t multicolored | .90 | .90 |
| 727 | A168 | 60t multicolored | 1.75 | 1.75 |
| 728 | A168 | 70t multicolored | 2.00 | 2.00 |
| | | Nos. 725-728 (4) | 5.20 | 5.20 |

**Waterfalls — A169**

**1990, Feb. 1 Unwmk. Litho. Perf. 14**

| | | | | |
|---|---|---|---|---|
| 729 | A169 | 20t Guni Falls | .60 | .50 |
| 730 | A169 | 35t Rouna Falls | .90 | .85 |
| 731 | A169 | 60t Ambua Falls | 1.60 | 1.50 |
| 732 | A169 | 70t Wawoi Falls | 1.75 | 1.75 |
| | | Nos. 729-732 (4) | 4.85 | 4.60 |

For surcharges see Nos. 866, 870.

**Natl. Census A170**

**1990, May 2 Perf. 14½x15**

| | | | | |
|---|---|---|---|---|
| 733 | A170 | 20t Three youths, form | .50 | .50 |
| 734 | A170 | 70t Man, woman, child, form | 1.90 | 1.65 |

For surcharge see No. 869.

**Gogodala Dance Masks — A171**

**1990, July 11 Litho. Perf. 13½**

| | | | | |
|---|---|---|---|---|
| 735 | A171 | 20t shown | .85 | .40 |
| 736 | A171 | 35t multi. diff. | 1.25 | .75 |
| 737 | A171 | 60t multi. diff. | 2.00 | 3.00 |
| 738 | A171 | 70t multi. diff. | 2.25 | 3.00 |
| | | Nos. 735-738 (4) | 6.35 | 7.15 |

For surcharges see Nos. 867, 871.

**Waitangi Treaty, 150th Anniv. — A172**

Designs: 20t, Dwarf Cassowary, Great Spotted Kiwi. No. 740, Double Wattled Cassowary, Brown Kiwi. No. 741, Sepik mask and Maori carving.

**1990, Aug. 24 Litho. Perf. 14½**

| | | | | |
|---|---|---|---|---|
| 739 | A172 | 20t multicolored | 1.00 | .50 |
| 740 | A172 | 35t multicolored | 1.25 | .80 |
| 741 | A172 | 70t multicolored | 3.50 | 2.10 |
| | | Nos. 739-741 (3) | | |

No. 741 for World Stamp Exhibition, New Zealand 1990.

For surcharges see Nos. 862-863.

**Birds A173**

**1990, Sept. 26 Litho. Perf. 14**

| | | | | |
|---|---|---|---|---|
| 742 | A173 | 20t Whimbrel | .95 | .60 |
| 743 | A173 | 35t Sharp-tailed sandpiper | 1.25 | .95 |
| 744 | A173 | 60t Ruddy turnstone | 2.25 | 3.00 |
| 745 | A173 | 70t Terek sandpiper | 7.20 | 7.55 |
| | | Nos. 742-745 (4) | | |

**Musical Instruments A174**

**1990, Oct. 31 Litho. Perf. 13**

| | | | | |
|---|---|---|---|---|
| 746 | A174 | 20t Jew's harp | .65 | .50 |
| 747 | A174 | 35t Musical bow | 1.00 | .80 |
| 748 | A174 | 60t Wantoat drum | 1.75 | 2.00 |
| 749 | A174 | 70t Gogodala rattle | 2.00 | 2.00 |
| | | Nos. 746-749 (4) | 5.40 | 5.30 |

For surcharge see No. 861.

**Snail Shells A174a**

Designs: 21t, Rhynchotrochus weigmani. 40t, Forcartia globula, Canefriula azonata. 50t, Planispira deaniana. 80t, Papuina chancel, Papuina xanthochelia.

A175

A176

**1991, Mar. 6**    **Litho.**    **Perf. 14x14½**

| 750 | A174a | 21t multicolored | .65 | .55 |
|---|---|---|---|---|
| 751 | A174a | 40t multicolored | 1.25 | 1.00 |
| 752 | A174a | 50t multicolored | 1.75 | 1.75 |
| 753 | A174a | 80t multicolored | 2.25 | 2.75 |
| | | Nos. 750-753 (4) | 5.90 | 6.05 |

For surcharge see No. 864.

**1991-94**

**Litho.**    **Perf. 14½**

| 755 | A175 | 1t Ptiloris magnificus | .20 | .20 |
|---|---|---|---|---|
| 756 | A175 | 5t Loria loriae | .20 | .20 |
| 757 | A175 | 10t Cnemophilus macgregorii | .20 | .40 |
| 758 | A175 | 20t Parotia wahnesi | .40 | .40 |
| 759 | A175 | 21t Manucodia chalybata | .45 | .45 |
| 760 | A175 | 30t Paradisaea decora | .60 | .60 |
| 761 | A175 | 40t Loboparadisea sericea | .80 | .80 |
| 762 | A175 | 45t Cicinnurus regius | 2.00 | .95 |
| 763 | A175 | 50t Paradigalla brevicauda | 1.00 | 1.00 |
| 764 | A175 | 60t Parotia carolae | 3.50 | 1.30 |
| 765 | A175 | 90t Paradisaea guilielmi | 3.50 | 1.95 |
| 766 | A175 | 1k Diphyllodes magnificus | 2.00 | 2.00 |
| 767 | A175 | 2k Lophorina superba | 4.00 | 4.00 |
| a. | | Strip of 4, #761, 763, 766-767 + label | 4.00 | 4.00 |
| 768 | A175 | 5k Phonygammus keraudrenii | 8.00 | 8.00 |

**Perf. 13**

| 769 | A176 | 10k Paradisaea minor | 10.00 | 10.00 |
|---|---|---|---|---|
| | | Nos. 755-769 (15) | 49.85 | 45.05 |

No. 767a for Hong Kong '94 and sold for 4k. Stamps in No. 767a do not have "1992."
BIRD OF PARADISE" at bottom of design.
Issued: 21t, 45t, 60t, 90t, 3/25/92; 5k, 40t, 50t, 1k, 2k, 9/2/92; 1t, 10t, 20t, 30t, 1993; 10k, 5/1/91; No. 767a, 2/18/94.
For surcharges see #878A, 878C.

Large T — A176a

**1993**    **Litho.**    **Perf. 14½**

| 770 | A176a | 21t like #759 | 1.00 | .50 |
|---|---|---|---|---|
| 770A | A176a | 45t like #762 | 2.00 | 1.10 |
| 770B | A176a | 60t like #765 | 2.25 | 2.00 |
| 770C | A176a | 90t like #765 | 2.75 | 3.25 |
| 770D | | Nos. 770A-770D (4) | 8.00 | 6.85 |

Originally scheduled for release on Feb. 19, 1992, #770A-770D were withdrawn when the denomination was found to have an upper case "T." Corrected versions with a lower case "T" are #759, 762, 764-765. A quantity of the original stamps appeared in these items, which prevent speculation in the market and to Administration of Papua New Guinea released the stamps with the upper case "T."
For surcharges see #878B, 878D.

A181

---

A178

**1991, June 26**    **Litho.**    **Perf. 13**

| 771 | A177 | 21t Cricket | 1.50 | .50 |
|---|---|---|---|---|
| 772 | A177 | 40t Running | 1.50 | 1.00 |
| 773 | A177 | 50t Baseball | 1.50 | 1.50 |
| 774 | A177 | 80t Rugby | 2.75 | 3.50 |
| | | Nos. 771-774 (4) | 7.00 | 6.50 |

1991 South Pacific Games A177

Anglican Church in Papua New Guinea, Cent. A178

**1991, Aug. 7**    **Litho.**    **Perf. 14½**

| 775 | A178 | 21t multicolored | 1.25 | .50 |
|---|---|---|---|---|
| 776 | A178 | 40t multicolored | 2.50 | 1.25 |
| 777 | A178 | 80t multicolored | 4.25 | 4.25 |
| | | Nos. 775-777 (3) | | |

Churches: 21t, Cathedral of St. Peter & St. Paul, Dogura. 40t, Kaleta Shrine, Anglican landing site. 80t, First thatched chapel, modawa tree.

**1991, Oct. 16**    **Litho.**    **Perf. 13**

| 778 | A179 | 21t multicolored | .65 | .50 |
|---|---|---|---|---|
| 779 | A179 | 40t multicolored | 1.25 | .95 |
| 780 | A179 | 50t multicolored | 2.00 | 1.25 |
| 781 | A179 | 80t multicolored | 5.40 | 5.70 |
| | | Nos. 778-781 (4) | | |

Traditional Headdresses A179

Designs: 21t, Rambutso, Manus Province. 40t, Marawaka, Eastern Highlands. 50t, Tufi, Oro Province. 80t, Sina Sina, Simbu Province.

Discovery of America, 500th Anniv. A180

**1992, Apr. 15**    **Litho.**    **Perf. 14**

| 782 | A180 | 21t Nina | .60 | .45 |
|---|---|---|---|---|
| 783 | A180 | 40t Pinta | 1.50 | 1.00 |
| 784 | A180 | 60t Santa Maria | 1.75 | 1.75 |
| 785 | A180 | 90t Columbus, ships | 2.50 | 3.00 |
| a. | | Souvenir sheet of 2, #784-785 | 6.00 | 6.00 |
| | | Nos. 782-785 (4) | 6.35 | 6.20 |

World Columbian Stamp Expo '92, Chicago. Issue date: No. 785a, June 3.

---

A182

**1992, June 3**    **Litho.**    **Perf. 14**

| 786 | A181 | 21t multicolored | .65 | .50 |
|---|---|---|---|---|
| 787 | A181 | 45t multicolored | 1.25 | 1.00 |
| 788 | A181 | 60t multicolored | 1.50 | 1.40 |
| 789 | A181 | 90t multicolored | 2.25 | 2.25 |
| | | Nos. 786-789 (4) | 5.65 | 5.15 |

Papuan Gulf Artifacts: 21t, Canoe prow shield, Bamu. 45t, Skull rack, Kerewa. 60t, Ancestral figure, Era River. 90t, Gope (spirit) board, Urama.

**1992, July 22**    **Litho.**    **Perf. 14**

| 790 | A182 | 21t multicolored | .75 | .50 |
|---|---|---|---|---|
| 791 | A182 | 45t multicolored | 1.40 | 1.00 |
| 792 | A182 | 60t multicolored | 2.00 | 1.75 |
| 793 | A182 | 90t multicolored | 2.50 | 2.25 |
| | | Nos. 790-793 (4) | 6.65 | 5.50 |

Soldiers from: 21t, Papuan Infantry Battalion. 45t, Australian Militia. 60t, Japanese Nankai Force. 90t, US Army.
World War II, 50th anniv.

A183

**1992, Oct. 28**    **Litho.**    **Perf. 14**

| 794 | A183 | 21t Hibiscus tiliaceus | .75 | .50 |
|---|---|---|---|---|
| 795 | A183 | 45t Castanospermum australe | 1.50 | 1.00 |
| 796 | A183 | 60t Cordia subcordata | 2.50 | 2.00 |
| 797 | A183 | 90t Acacia auriculiformis | 7.75 | 7.25 |
| | | Nos. 794-797 (4) | | |

Flowering Trees — A183

Mammals A184

**1993, Apr. 7**    **Litho.**    **Perf. 14**

| 798 | A184 | 21t Myoictis melas | .50 | .50 |
|---|---|---|---|---|
| 799 | A184 | 45t Microperoryctes longicauda | 1.10 | 1.10 |
| 800 | A184 | 60t Mallomys rothschildi | 1.50 | 1.50 |
| 801 | A184 | 90t Pseudocheirus forbesi | 2.25 | 2.25 |
| | | Nos. 798-801 (4) | 5.35 | 5.35 |

Small Birds — A185

**1993, June 9**    **Litho.**    **Perf. 14**

| 802 | A185 | 21t Clytomyias insignis | .50 | .45 |
|---|---|---|---|---|
| 803 | A185 | 45t Pitta superba | 1.00 | .95 |
| 804 | A185 | 60t Rhagologus leucostigma | 1.50 | 1.25 |
| 805 | A185 | 90t Toxorhamphus poliopterus | 2.25 | 2.50 |
| | | Nos. 802-805 (4) | 5.25 | 5.15 |

---

Nos. 802-805 Redrawn with Taipei '93 emblem in Blue and Yellow

**1993, Aug. 13**    **Litho.**    **Perf. 14**

| 806 | A185 | 21t multicolored | .75 | .50 |
|---|---|---|---|---|
| 807 | A185 | 45t multicolored | 1.50 | 1.00 |
| 808 | A185 | 60t multicolored | 1.75 | 1.40 |
| 809 | A185 | 90t multicolored | 2.25 | 3.50 |
| | | Nos. 806-809 (4) | 6.25 | 6.50 |

Freshwater Fish A186

**1993, Sept. 29**    **Litho.**    **Perf. 14x14½**

| 810 | A186 | 21t multicolored | .60 | .50 |
|---|---|---|---|---|
| 811 | A186 | 45t multicolored | 1.25 | 1.00 |
| 812 | A186 | 60t multicolored | 2.25 | 2.25 |
| 813 | A186 | 90t multicolored | 5.60 | 5.25 |
| | | Nos. 810-813 (4) | | |

For surcharges see Nos. 876-878.

Designs: Iriatherina werneri. 45t, Tateurndina ocellicauda. 60t, Melanotaenia affinis. 90t, Pseudomugil connieae.

**1993, Oct. 27**    **Litho.**    **Perf. 14**

| 814 | A187 | 21t DC3 | .75 | .50 |
|---|---|---|---|---|
| 815 | A187 | 45t F27 | 1.50 | 1.00 |
| 816 | A187 | 60t Dash 7 | 2.00 | 1.75 |
| 817 | A187 | 90t Airbus A310-300 | 2.50 | 2.50 |
| a. | | Souvenir sheet of 4, #814-817 Airbus A310-300 | 6.75 | 6.75 |
| | | Nos. 814-817 (4) | | |

Air Niugini, 20th Anniv. A187

Souvenir Sheet

Paradisaea Rudolphi — A188

**1993, Sept. 29**    **Litho.**    **Perf. 14**

| 818 | A188 | 2k Bangkok '93 | 7.50 | 7.50 |
|---|---|---|---|---|

Bangkok '93.

Huon Tree Kangaroo — A189

**1994, Jan. 19**    **Litho.**    **Perf. 14½**

| 819 | A189 | 21t Domesticated joey | .50 | .45 |
|---|---|---|---|---|
| 820 | A189 | 45t Adult male | 1.00 | 1.00 |
| 821 | A189 | 60t Female, joey in pouch | 1.50 | 1.40 |
| 822 | A189 | 90t Adolescent | 2.00 | 2.75 |
| | | Nos. 819-822 (4) | 5.00 | 5.60 |

No. 661 Surcharged

## No. 671 Surcharged

**1994, Mar. 23**
### Perfs. and Printing Methods as Before
| | | | | |
|---|---|---|---|---|
| 823 | A153 | 21t on 35t multi | 10.00 | .80 |
| 824 | A154 | 1.20k on 40t multi | 4.00 | 1.60 |

No. 824 exists with double surcharge. Other varieties may exist.

## Artifacts — A190

Designs: 1t, Hagen ceremonial axe, Western Highlands. 2t, Telefomin war shield, West Sepik. 20t, Head mask, Gulf of Papua. 21t, Kanganaman stool, East Sepik. 45t, Trobriand lime gourd, Milne Bay. 60t, Yuat River flute stopper, East Sepik. 90t, Tami island dish, Morobe. 1k, Kundu drum, Ramu River estuary. 5k, Gogodala dance mask, Western Province. 10k, Malanggan mask, New Ireland.

**1994-95  Litho.  Perf. 14½**
| | | | | |
|---|---|---|---|---|
| 825 | A190 | 1t multicolored | .20 | .20 |
| 826 | A190 | 2t multicolored | .20 | .20 |
| 828 | A190 | 20t multicolored | .35 | .35 |
| 829 | A190 | 21t multicolored | .35 | .35 |
| 833 | A190 | 45t multicolored | .80 | .80 |
| 835 | A190 | 60t multicolored | 1.10 | 1.10 |
| 836 | A190 | 90t multicolored | 1.65 | 1.65 |
| 837 | A190 | 1k multicolored | 1.85 | 1.85 |
| 839 | A190 | 3k multicolored | 9.00 | 9.00 |
| 840 | A190 | 10k multicolored | 15.00 | 15.00 |
| | | | 30.30 | 30.30 |

Nos. 825-840 (10)

Issued: 21, 45, 60, 90t, 1/23; 1, 2, 20t, 5k, 6/29/94; 1k, 10k, 4/12/95. This is an expanding set. Numbers may change.

## Classic Cars A191

**1994, May 11  Litho.  Perf. 14**
| | | | | |
|---|---|---|---|---|
| 841 | A191 | 21t Model T Ford | .60 | .50 |
| 842 | A191 | 45t Chevrolet 490 | 1.25 | 1.00 |
| 843 | A191 | 60t Baby Austin | 1.75 | 1.40 |
| 844 | A191 | 90t Willys Jeep | 2.50 | 2.75 |
| | | | 6.10 | 5.65 |

Nos. 841-844 (4)

## PHILAKOREA '94 — A192

**1994, Aug. 10  Litho.  Perf. 14**
| | | | | |
|---|---|---|---|---|
| 845 | A192 | Sheet of 2, #a.-b. | 5.50 | 5.50 |

Tree kangaroos: 90t, Dendrolagus inustus. 1.20k, Dendrolagus dorianus.

## Moths A193

Designs: 21t, Daphnis hypothous pallescens. 45t, Tanaorhinus unipuncta. 60t, Neodiphthera sciron. 90t, Parotis maginata.

**1994, Oct. 26  Litho.  Perf. 14**
| | | | | |
|---|---|---|---|---|
| 846 | A193 | 21t multicolored | .50 | .45 |
| 847 | A193 | 45t multicolored | 1.25 | 1.00 |
| 848 | A193 | 60t multicolored | 1.50 | 1.25 |
| 849 | A193 | 90t multicolored | 2.50 | 2.50 |
| | | | 5.75 | 5.20 |

Nos. 846-849 (4)

## Beatification of Peter To Rot — A194

**1995, Jan. 11  Litho.  Perf. 14**
| | | | | |
|---|---|---|---|---|
| 850 | A194 | 21t Peter To Rot | .45 | .45 |
| 851 | A194 | 1k on 90t Pope John Paul II | 2.25 | 2.25 |
| | | | 3.50 | 3.50 |
| a. | | Pair, #850-851 + label | | |

No. 851 was not issued without surcharge.

## Tourism A195

#852, Cruising. #853, Handicrafts. #854, Resorts. #855, Trekking adventure. #856, #857, White-water rafting. #858, Boat, diver. #859, Divers, sunken plane.

**1995, Jan. 11  Litho.**
| | | | | |
|---|---|---|---|---|
| 852 | A195 | 21t multicolored | .45 | .45 |
| 853 | A195 | 21t multicolored | .45 | .45 |
| 854 | A195 | 50t on 45t multi | .90 | .90 |
| 855 | A195 | 50t on 45t multi | 1.10 | 1.10 |
| a. | | Pair, #852-853 | 2.25 | 2.25 |
| 856 | A195 | 65t on 60t multi | 1.40 | 1.40 |
| | | #861 866 | 32.50 | |
| 857 | A195 | 65t on 60t multi | 1.40 | 1.40 |
| a. | | Pair, #856-857 | 2.75 | 2.75 |
| 858 | A195 | 1k on 90t multi | 2.25 | 2.25 |
| 859 | A195 | 1k on 90t multi | 2.25 | 2.25 |
| a. | | Pair, #858-859 | 4.50 | 4.50 |
| | | | 10.40 | 10.40 |

Nos. 852-859 (8)

Nos. 854-859 were not issued without surcharge.

## Thick "t" in Surcharge

Nos. 662, 722, 730, 732, 734, 736, 738, 740-741, 747, 753, 762, 765, 770B, 770D Surcharged

**1994  Perfs., Etc. as Before**
| | | | | |
|---|---|---|---|---|
| 860 | A167 | 5t on 35t #722 | 5.75 | 1.00 |
| 861 | A174 | 5t on 35t #747 | 24.00 | 17.50 |
| 862 | A172 | 10t on 35t #740 | 22.50 | 7.50 |
| 863 | A172 | 10t on 35t #741 | 17.50 | 6.50 |
| 864 | A174a | 21t on 80t #753 | 32.50 | 17.50 |
| 866 | A169 | 50t on 35t #730 | 32.50 | 32.50 |
| 867 | A169 | 50t on 35t #736 | 72.50 | 32.50 |
| | | | 650.00 | |
| a. | | Inverted surcharge | | |
| 868 | A153 | 65t on 70t #662 | 4.00 | 1.75 |
| 869 | A170 | 65t on 70t #734 | 4.00 | 4.00 |
| 870 | A171 | 1k on 70t #732 | 20.00 | 6.50 |
| 871 | A171 | 50t on 70t #738 | 27.50 | 20.50 |
| | | | 262.75 | 98.50 |

Nos. 860-871 (11)

Size, style and location of surcharge varies.

No. 861 exists in pair, one without surcharge. Other varieties exist.
Issued: #862, 8/23/94; #864, 8/28/94; #861, 863, 864, 10/3/94; #860, 871, 10/6/94; #866-868, 869-870, 11/28/94.

## Mushrooms A196

25t, Lentinus umbrinus. 50t, Amanita hemibapha. 65t, Boletellus emodensis. 1k, Ramaria zippellii.

**1995, June 21  Litho.  Perf. 14**
| | | | | |
|---|---|---|---|---|
| 872 | A196 | 25t multicolored | .40 | .40 |
| a. | | Complete booklet, 10 #872 | 4.00 | |
| 873 | A196 | 50t multicolored | .85 | .85 |
| a. | | Complete booklet, 10 #873 | 8.50 | |
| 874 | A196 | 65t multicolored | 1.10 | 1.10 |
| 875 | A196 | 1k multicolored | 1.75 | 1.75 |
| | | | 4.10 | 4.10 |
| | | Nos. 872-875 (4) | | |

**1996  Litho.  Perf. 12**
| | | | | |
|---|---|---|---|---|
| 875A | A196 | 25t like #872 | 2.50 | 2.50 |

No. 875A has a taller vignette, a smaller typeface for the description, denomination, and country name and does not have a date inscription like #872.

## Thin "t" in Surcharge

Nos. 811-813 Surcharged Thick "t"
Nos. 762, 765, 770B, 770D Surcharged Thin "t"

See illustration above #860.

**1995  Litho.  Perf. 14x14½**
| | | | | |
|---|---|---|---|---|
| 876 | A186 | 21t on 45t #811 | 1.00 | .35 |
| 877 | A186 | 21t on 45t #812 | 1.00 | 1.75 |
| 878 | A186 | 21t on 90t #813 | 1.00 | .70 |
| 878A | A175 | 21t on 45T #762 | 8.00 | .70 |
| 878B | A176a | 21t on 45T | 1.76 | |
| | | #770B | | .70 |
| 878C | A175 | 21t on 90t #765 | 12.00 | 12.00 |
| 878D | A176a | 21t on 90t | 50.00 | 1.75 |
| | | #770D | 125.00 | 7.70 |

Nos. 876-870D (7)

Nos. 878A-878D exist with thick surcharge. This printing of 3200 each does not seem to have seen much, if any, public sale.
Issued: #876-878, 6/20; #878A-878B, 5/16; #878C, 3/27; #878D, 4/25.

## Independence, 20th Anniv. — A197

Designs: 50t, 1k, "20" emblem.

**1995, Aug. 30**
| | | | | |
|---|---|---|---|---|
| 879 | A197 | 21t shown | .40 | .40 |
| 880 | A197 | 50t blue & multi | .90 | .90 |
| 881 | A197 | 1k green & multi | 1.75 | 1.75 |
| | | | 3.05 | 3.05 |

Nos. 879-881 (3)

## Souvenir Sheet

Singapore '95 — A198

Orchids: a, 21t, Dendrobium rigidifolium. b, 45t, Dendrobium convolutum. c, 60t, Dendrobium spectabile. d, 90t, Dendrobium tapiniense.

**1995, Aug. 30  Litho.  Perf. 14**
| | | | | |
|---|---|---|---|---|
| 882 | A198 | Sheet of 4, #a.-d. | 5.50 | 5.50 |

No. 882 sold for 3k.

## Souvenir Sheet

New Year 1995 (Year of the Boar) — A199

Illustration reduced.

**1995, Sept. 14**
| | | | | |
|---|---|---|---|---|
| 883 | A199 | 3k multicolored | 5.50 | 5.50 |

Beijing '06.

## Eruption of Rabaul Volcano, 1st Anniv. A200

**1995, Sept. 19**
| | | | | |
|---|---|---|---|---|
| 884 | A200 | 2k multicolored | 3.50 | 3.50 |

## Crabs A201

**1995, Oct. 25  Litho.  Perf. 14**
| | | | | |
|---|---|---|---|---|
| 885 | A201 | 21t Zosimus aeneus | .40 | .40 |
| 886 | A201 | 50t Cardisoma carnifex | 1.00 | 1.00 |
| 887 | A201 | 65t Uca tetragonon | 1.30 | 1.30 |
| 888 | A201 | 1k Eriphia sebana | 4.70 | 4.70 |

Nos. 885-888 (4)

For surcharge see #939B.

## Parrots — A202

Taipei '96, 10th Asian Intl. Philatelic Exhibition — A207

a. Dr. Sun Yat-sen (1866-1925). b, Dr. John Guise (1914-91). Illustration reduced.

**1996, Oct. 16** ... **Litho.** ... **Perf. 14**
906 A207 65t Sheet of 2, #a.-b. 3.75 3.75

---

Beetles — A203

Designs: 25t, Psittrichas haematodus. 50t, Trichoglossus haematodus. 65t, Alisterus chloropterus. 1k, Aprosmictus erythropterus.

**1996, Jan. 17** ... **Litho.** ... **Perf. 12**
889 A202 25t multicolored .75 .40
890 A202 50t multicolored .75 .40
891 A202 65t multicolored 1.50 1.60
892 A202 1k multicolored 2.00 2.00
Nos. 889-892 (4) 6.00 4.75

Designs: 25t, Lagriomorpha indigacea. 50t, Eupholus geoffroy. 65t, Promechus pulcher. 1k, Callistola pulchra.

**1996, Mar. 20** ... **Litho.** ... **Perf. 12**
893 A203 25t multicolored .65 .65
894 A203 50t multicolored 1.30 1.30
895 A203 65t multicolored 1.70 1.70
896 A203 1k multicolored 2.60 2.60
Nos. 893-896 (4) 6.25 6.25

Souvenir Sheet

Zhongshan Memorial Hall, Guangzhou, China — A204

Illustration reduced.

CHINA '96, 9th Asian Int. Philatelic Exhibition.

**1996, Apr. 22** ... **Litho.** ... **Perf. 14**
897 A204 70t multicolored 2.00 2.00

---

1996 Summer Olympics, Atlanta A205

**1996, July 24** ... **Litho.** ... **Perf. 12**
898 A205 25t Shooting .40 .40
899 A205 50t Track .75 .75
900 A205 65t Weight lifting 1.25 1.00
901 A205 1k Boxing 1.75 1.50
Nos. 898-901 (4) 4.15 3.65

Olymphilex '96.

---

Radio, Cent. A206

25t, Air traffic control. 50t, Commercial broadcasting. 65t, Gerehu earth station. 1k, 1st transmission in Papua New Guinea.

**1996, Sept. 11** ... **Litho.** ... **Perf. 12**
902 A206 25t multicolored .40 .40
903 A206 50t multicolored .75 .75
904 A206 65t multicolored 1.00 1.00
905 A206 1k multicolored 1.50 1.50
Nos. 902-905 (4) 3.65 3.65

---

Flowers A208

Designs: 1t, Hibiscus rosa-sinensis. 5t, Bougainvillea spectabilis. 65t, Plumeria rubra. 1k, Mucuna novo-guineensis.

**1996, Nov. 27** ... **Litho.** ... **Perf. 14**
907 A208 1t multicolored .30 .20
908 A208 5t multicolored .30 .20
909 A208 50t multicolored 1.10 1.00
910 A208 1k multicolored 1.50 1.50
Nos. 907-910 (4) 3.20 2.90

---

Souvenir Sheet

Oxen and Natl. Flag — A209

**1997, Feb. 3** ... **Litho.** ... **Perf. 14**
911 A209 1.50k multicolored 3.00 3.00

Hong Kong '97.

---

Boat Prows A210

**1997, Mar. 19** ... **Litho.** ... **Perf. 14½x14**
912 A210 25t Gogodala .40 .40
913 A210 50t East New Britain .75 .75
914 A210 65t Trobriand Island 1.00 1.00
915 A210 1k Walomo 1.50 1.50
Nos. 912-915 (4) 3.65 3.65

---

Queen Elizabeth II and Prince Philip, 50th Wedding Anniv. — A211

**1997, June 25** ... **Litho.** ... **Perf. 13½**
916 A211 25t multicolored .40 .40
917 A211 25t multicolored .40 .40
a. Pair, #916-917 .80 .80

Designs: 25t, Princess Anne, polo players. #917, Queen up close. #918, Queen, another person riding attire. #919, Queen, another person riding horses. #920, Grandsons riding horses, Prince waving. #921, Queen waving, riding pony. 2k, Queen, Prince riding in open carriage.

Souvenir Sheet

918 A211 50t multicolored .75 .75
919 A211 1k multicolored .75 .75
a. Pair, #918-919 1.50 1.50
920 A211 1k multicolored 1.50 1.50
921 A211 1k multicolored 1.50 1.50
a. Pair, #920-921 3.00 3.00
922 A211 2k multicolored 2.50 2.50
Nos. 916-921 (6) 5.30 5.30

---

Air Niugini, First Flight, Port Moresby-Osaka — A212

Souvenir Sheet

Illustration reduced.

**1997, July 19** ... **Litho.** ... **Perf. 12**
923 A212 3k multicolored 5.75 5.75

---

1997 Pacific Year of Coral Reef A213

Designs: 25t, Pocillopora woodjonesi. 50t, Subergorgia mollis. 65t, Oxypora glabra. 1k, Turbinaria reniformis.

**1997, Aug. 27** ... **Litho.** ... **Perf. 12**
924 A213 25t multicolored .40 .40
925 A213 50t multicolored .75 .75
926 A213 65t multicolored 1.00 1.00
927 A213 1k multicolored 1.50 1.50
Nos. 924-927 (4) 3.65 3.65

---

Flowers — A214

Designs: 10t, Thunbergia fragrans. 20t, Caesalpinia pulcherrima. 25t, Hoya. 30t, Heliconia. 50t, Amomum goliathensis.

**1997, Nov. 26** ... **Litho.** ... **Perf. 12**
928 A214 10t multicolored .25 .20
929 A214 20t multicolored .35 .30
930 A214 25t multicolored .40 .40
931 A214 30t multicolored .55 .55
932 A214 50t multicolored .85 .85
Nos. 928-932 (5) 2.45 2.30

---

Birds A215

Designs: 25t, Tyto tenebricosa. 50t, Aepypodius arfakianus. 65t, Accipiter poliocephalus. 1k, Zonerodius heliosylus.

**1998, Jan. 28** ... **Litho.** ... **Perf. 12**
933 A215 25t multicolored .60 .60
934 A215 50t multicolored .85 .85
935 A215 65t multicolored 1.25 1.25
936 A215 1k multicolored 1.75 2.00
Nos. 933-936 (4) 4.45 4.40

---

Diana, Princess of Wales (1961-97)
Common Design Type

**1998, Apr. 29** ... **Litho.** ... **Perf. 14½x14**
937 CD355 1k Sheet of 4, #a.-d. 7.00 7.00

Designs: a, In beige colored dress. b, In violet dress with lace collar. c, Wearing plaid jacket. d, Holding flowers.

---

Mother Teresa (1910-97) A216

**1998, Apr. 29** ... **Litho.** ... **Perf. 14½**
938 A216 65t With child 1.00 1.00
939 A216 1k shown 1.50 1.50
a. Pair, #938-939 3.25 3.25

No. 937 sold for 4k + 50t with surtax from international sales being donated to the Princess Diana Memorial fund and surtax from national sales being donated to designated local charity.

---

No. 887 Surcharged

**1998, May 28** ... **Litho.** ... **Perf. 14**
939B A201 25t on 65t multi .60 .60

---

Moths A217

Designs: 25t, Daphnis hypothous pallescens. 50t, Theretra polistratus. 65t, Psilogramma casuarina. 1k, Meganoton hyloicoides.

**1998, June 17** ... **Litho.** ... **Perf. 14**
940 A217 25t multicolored .40 .40
941 A217 50t multicolored .75 .75
942 A217 65t multicolored 1.00 1.00
943 A217 1k multicolored 1.50 1.50
Nos. 940-943 (4) 3.65 3.65

---

First Orchid Spectacular A219

A218

Designs: 25t, Coelogyne fragrans. 50t, Den. cuthbertsonii. 65t, Den. vexillarius. 1k, Den. finisterrae.

**1998, Sept. 15** ... **Litho.** ... **Perf. 14**
944 A218 25t multicolored .40 .40
945 A218 50t multicolored .75 .75
946 A218 65t multicolored 1.00 1.00
947 A218 1k multicolored 1.50 1.50
Nos. 944-947 (4) 3.65 3.65

## Mission Aviation Fellowship, 50th Anniv. in Papua New Guinea—A234

Designs: 35t, Cessna 170, pig, bird, Bibles. 70t, Harry Hartwig (1916-51), Auster Autocar. 90t, Pilot and Cessna 260. 1.40k, Twin Otter and plane mechanics.

**2001, Oct. 17    Set of 4    Perf. 13¼x13¾**
1001-1004  A234    2.75  2.75

## Papua New Guinea — People's Republic of China Diplomatic Relations, 25th Anniv. A235

Designs: 10t, Flags, world map. 50t, Dragon, bird of paradise. 2k, Tien An Men Square, Papua New Guinea Parliament Building.

**2001, Oct. 12    Litho.    Perf. 12**
1005-1007  A235  Set of 3    2.50  2.50

### Methods and Perfs As Before

Nos. 850, 968, 972, 976 and 992 Surcharged

**2001, Dec. 1**
1008  A194  50t  on 21t #850    .90  .70
  a.  Horiz. pair, 1008, 851 + central label    2.25  2.25
1009  A231  50t  on 25t #992    .50  .30
1010  A224  50t  on 65t #968    .50  .30
1011  A225  2.65k  on 65t #972    1.75  1.75
1012  A226  2.65k  on 65t #976    1.75  1.75
Nos. 1008-1012 (5)    5.40  4.80

## Provincial Flags A236

**2001, Dec. 12    Litho.    Perf. 14**
1013  A236  10t  Enga    .30  .20
1014  A236  15t  Simbu    .30  .20
1015  A236  20t  Manus    .30  .20
1016  A236  50t  Central    .60  .25
1017  A236  2k  New Ireland    2.25  2.00
1018  A236  5k  Sandaun    3.50  3.50
Nos. 1013-1018 (6)    7.25  6.35

### Reign Of Queen Elizabeth II, 50th Anniv. Issue
#### Common Design Type

Designs: Nos. 1019, 1023a, 1.25k, Princess Elizabeth with Queen Mother and Princess Margaret, 1941. Nos. 1020, 1023b, 1.45k, Wearing tiara, 1975. Nos. 1021, 1023c, 2k, With Princes Philip and Charles, 1951. Nos. 1022, 1023d, 2.65k, Wearing red hat. Nos. 1023e, 5k, 1955 portrait by Annigoni (38x50mm).

**2002, Feb. 6    Litho.    Wmk. 373**
**Perf. 14¼x14½, 13½ (#1023e)**

**With Gold Frames**
1019-1022  CD360  Set of 4    6.00  6.00

**Souvenir Sheet**
**Without Gold Frames**
1023  CD360  Sheet of 5, #a-e    6.75  6.75

---

## Shells A229

Designs: 25t, Turbo petholatus. 50t, Charonia tritonis. 65t, Cassis cornuta. 1k, Ovula ovum.

**2000, Feb. 23    Litho.    Perf. 14**
984-987  A229  Set of 4    2.50  2.50

## Independence, 25th Anniv. — A230

Designs: 25t, Shell. 50t, Bird of Paradise. 65t, Ring. 1k, Coat of arms.
Illustration reduced.

**2000, June 21    Perf. 14**
988-991  A230  Set of 4    3.00  3.00
991a  Souvenir sheet, #988-991, no labels    3.00  3.00

### Stamps with se-tenant label
Strips with two stamps alternating with two different labels exist for Nos. 989 and 990.

## 2000 Summer Olympics, Sydney A231

Designs: 25t, Running. 50t, Swimming. 65t, Boxing. 1k, Weight lifting.

**2000, July 12    Perf. 14¼**
992-995  A231  Set of 4    3.00  3.00

## Olymphilex 2000, Sydney — A232

**2000, July 12    Perf. 14¼**
996  A232  3k  multi    4.25  4.25

**Souvenir Sheet**
Sold for 3.50k.

## Birds A233

Designs: 35t, Comb-crested Jacana. 70t, Masked lapwing. 90t, White ibis. 1.40k, Black-tailed godwit.

**2001, Mar. 21    Litho.    Perf. 14**
997-1000  A233  Set of 4    3.00  3.00

---

## Millennium A224

Map and: 25t, Stopwatch, computer keyboard. 50t, Concentric circles. 65t, Internet page, computer user. 1k, Computers, satellite dish.

**1999    Litho.    Perf. 12¾**
966  A224  25t  multicolored    .35  .20
967  A224  50t  multicolored    .50  .35
968  A224  65t  multicolored    .80  .80
969  A224  1k  multicolored    1.25  1.25
Nos. 966-969 (4)    2.90  2.60

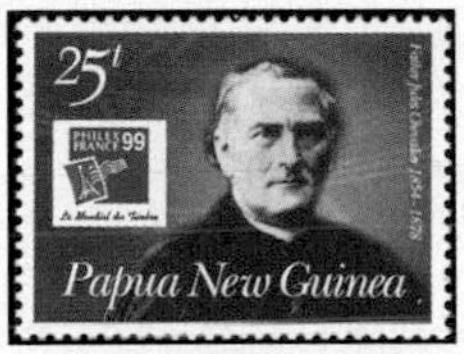

## PhilexFrance '99 A225

Frenchmen with historical ties to Papua New Guinea: 25t, Father Jules Chevalier. 50t, Bishop Alain-Marie. 65t, Chevalier D'Entrecasteaux. 1k, Count de Bougainville.

**1999, Mar. 2    Litho.    Perf. 12¾**
970  A225  25t  multi    .25  .15
971  A225  50t  multi    .45  .35
972  A225  65t  multi    .55  .55
973  A225  1k  multi    .90  .90
Nos. 970-973 (4)    2.15  2.00

## Hiri Moale Festival A226

Designs: 25t, Clay pots, native. 50t, Hanenamo, native. 65t, Lakatoi, native. #977, 1k, Sorcerer, native.
No. 978: a, Sorcerer. b, Clay pots. c, Lakatoi.

**1999, Sept. 8    Litho.    Perf. 12¾**
974  A226  25t  multi    .25  .20
975  A226  50t  multi    .50  .35
976  A226  65t  multi    .65  .65
977  A226  1k  multi    .90  .90
Nos. 974-977 (4)    2.30  2.10

**Souvenir Sheet**
978  A226  1k  Sheet of 3, #a-c.    3.00  3.00

## Year of the Rabbit (in 1999) — A227

Color of rabbit: a, Gray. b, Tan. c, White. d, Pink.
Illustration reduced.

**2000, Apr. 21    Litho.    Perf. 12¾**
979  A227  65t  Sheet of 4, #a-d.    3.50  3.50

## Queen Mother, 100th Birthday A228

Various photos. Color of frame: 25t, Yellow. 50t, Lilac. 65t, Green. 1k, Dull orange.

**2000, Aug. 4    Perf. 14**
980-983  A228  Set of 4    3.00  3.00

---

## 1998, Oct. 5    Litho.    Perf. 14

Sea Kayaking World Cup. Manus Island: 25t, Couple in kayak. 50t, Competitor running through Loniu Caves. 65t, Man standing in boat with sail, man seated in kayak. 1k, Competitor in kayak, bird of paradise silhouette.
948  A219  25t  multicolored    .40  .40
949  A219  50t  multicolored    .75  .75
950  A219  65t  multicolored    1.00  1.00
951  A219  1k  multicolored    1.50  1.50
Nos. 948-951 (4)    3.65  3.65

## 1998 Commonwealth Games, Kuala Lumpur — A220

**1998, Sept. 30    Litho.    Perf. 14**
952  A220  25t  Weight lifting    .25  .25
953  A220  50t  Lawn bowls    .45  .45
954  A220  65t  Rugby    .60  .60
955  A220  1k  Squash    .95  .95
Nos. 952-955 (4)    2.25  2.25

## Christmas A221

Designs: 25t, Infant in manger. 50t, Mother breastfeeding infant. 65t, "Wise men" in traditional masks, headdresses looking at infant. 1k, Map of Papua New Guinea.

**1998, Nov. 18    Litho.    Perf. 14**
956  A221  25t  multicolored    .25  .20
957  A221  50t  multicolored    .55  .40
958  A221  65t  multicolored    .75  .75
959  A221  1k  multicolored    1.25  1.25
Nos. 956-959 (4)    2.80  2.60

## Australia '99, World Stamp Expo — A222

Ships: 25t, "Boudeuse," 1768. 50t, "Neva," 1876. 65t, "Merrir England," 1889. 1k, "Samoa," 1884.
#964: a, 5t, Rattlesnake, 1849. b, 10t, Swallow, 1767. c, 15t, Roebeck, 1700. d, 20t, Blanche, 1872. e, 30t, Vitiaz, 1871. f, 40t, San Pedrico and Eabre, 1606. g, 60t, Jorge de Menesis, 1526. h, 1.20k, L'Astrolabe, 1827.

**1999, Mar. 17**
960  A222  25t  multicolored    .35  .25
961  A222  50t  multicolored    .65  .50
962  A222  65t  multicolored    1.00  1.00
963  A222  1k  multicolored    3.25  3.00

**Sheet of 8**
964  A222  #a-h.    4.25  4.25
No. 964a is incorrectly inscribed "Simpson Blanche 1872."

## IBRA '99, World Philatelic Exhibition, Nuremberg — A223

Exhibition emblem and: a, German New Guinea #17. b, German New Guinea #1, #2.

**1999    Litho.    Perf. 14**
965  A223  1k  Pair, #a-b.    2.00  2.00

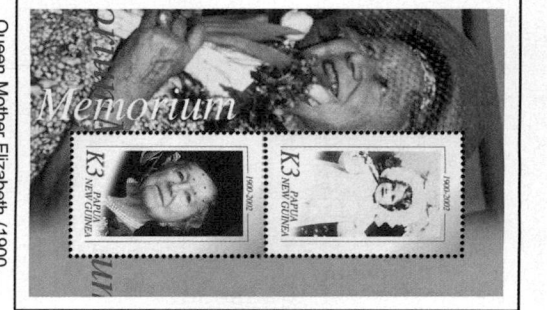

*Memorium*

## Lakatoi Type of 1901 Inscribed "Papua New Guinea"

British New Guinea stamps, cent. (in 2001).

**2002, June 5    Litho.    Unwmk.**

**Perf. 14½x14**

Center in Brown Black

1024-1029  A1    Set of 6    9.00  9.00
a.    Souvenir sheet, #1024-    9.00  9.00
1029

Frame colors: 5t, Red. 15t, Brown violet. 20t, Light blue. 1.25k, Brown. 1.45k, Green. 10k, Orange.

Orchids — A237

1037  A237  7k multi    6.50  6.50

**2002, Aug. 28    Perf. 14**

1036  A237  2k    5.75  5.75
1030-1035  A237    Set of 6    10.00  10.00

**Souvenir Sheet**

1038-1043  A238    Set of 6    11.00
            11.00  11.00

Designs: 5t, Cadetia tayloiri. 30t, Dendrobium. anosmum. 45t, Dendrobium bigibbum. 1.25k, Dendrobium cuthbertsonii. 1.45k, Spriantnes sinensis. 2.65k, Thelymitra carnea. No. 1036, horiz.: a, Dendrobium bracteosum. b, Calochilus campestris. c, Anastomus oscitans. d, Thelymitra carnea, diff. e, Dendrobium macrophyllum. f, Dendrobium johnsoniae. 7k, Bulbophyllum graveolens, horiz.

Thelymitra carnea

**2002**

1045-1046  A239    Set of 2    8.00  8.00

**2002, Nov. 20    Litho.    Perf. 14**

1047  A240  50t multi    .50  .50
1048  A241  50t multi    .50  .50

No. 1048 was printed in sheets of 4.

**2002, Nov. 20    Perf. 14¾**

1044  A239  2k Sheet of 7, #a-g  11.00  11.00

**Souvenir Sheets**

**Perf. 13½x14¼ (#1044d), Compound × 14¼ (#1044c, 1044e) 13¼x10¾**

No. 1046, blue shading in UL of stamps: a, 3k, Wearing white hat. b, 3k, Wearing hat and brooch.

No. 1046, blue shading in UL of stamps: a, 3k, Wearing white hat. b, 3k, Wearing hat and brooch.

Int'l Year of Mountains A242

**2002, Nov. 20**

1049-1052  A242    Set of 4    5.00  5.00

Designs: 50t, Mt. Wilhelm, Papua New Guinea. 1.25k, Matterhorn, Switzerland. 1.45k, Mt. Fuji, Japan. 2.65k, Massif des Aravis, France.

**2003, June 18**

1062-1067  A245    Set of 6    8.00  8.00
1068  A245  2k Sheet of 6, #a-f  8.25  8.25

**2003, Apr. 30    Litho.    Perf. 14**

1069  A245  8k multi    5.50  5.50

**Souvenir Sheet**

Prince William: No. 1070, 65t, Wearing colored sports shirt. No. 1071, 65t, Wearing white shirt. 1.50k, As child. No. 1073, 2k, Wearing suit and tie, gray green background. 2.50k, Wearing plaid shirt. 4k, On polo pony. No. 1076, 2k — Lilac background: a, As toddler. b, Wearing sunglasses. c, Wearing suit (full face). d, Wearing suit and tie (profile). e, Wearing deep blue shirt. f, Wearing yellow shirt with black collar. 8k, Wearing suit and tie, gray green background, diff.

1070-1075  A246    Set of 6    7.50  7.50
1076  A246  2k Sheet of 6, #a-f  8.00  8.00

**Souvenir Sheet**

1077  A246  8k multi    5.00  5.00

Prince William, 21st birthday.

Various portraits of Queen Elizabeth II with background colors of: No. 1062, 65t, Purple. No. 1063, 65t, Olive green. 1.50k, Dark blue. No. 1065, 2k, Red. 2.50k, Dull green. 4k, Orange. No. 1068, 2k — Yellow orange background with Queen: a, Wearing hat. b, Wearing crown and sash. c, Wearing red dress. d, Wearing tiara. e, Wearing red dress. f, Wearing black hat. 8k, Wearing black robe, gray green background. Coronation of Queen Elizabeth, 50th anniv.

United We Stand A241

**United We Stand**

A245

A246    Prince William

**2003, Oct. 15    Perf. 14½x14¾**

**1090**    Horiz. strip of 4    6.50  6.50
a.    A249  66t multi    .50  .50
b.    A249  1.50k multi    1.00  1.00
c.    A249  2.50k multi    1.75  1.75
d.    A249  4k multi    2.50  2.50

**With White Frames**

**1091**    Sheet, 2 each #a-d    12.00  12.00
a.    A249  66t multi    .50  .50
b.    A249  1.50k multi    1.00  1.00
c.    A249  2.50k multi    1.75  1.75
d.    A249  4k multi    2.50  2.50

**Without White Frames**

Tree kangaroos: Nos. 1090a, 1091a, Dendrolagus inustus. Nos. 1090b, 1091b, Dendrolagus matschiei. Nos. 1090c, 1091c, Dendrolagus dorianus. Nos. 1090d, 1091d, Dendrolagus goodfellowi.

Worldwide Fund for Nature (WWF)

Endangered Dolphins — A250

**2003, Nov. 19    Perf. 13½**

1092-1097  A250    Set of 6    8.75  8.75
1098  A250  1.50k Sheet of 6, #a-f  6.75  6.75

Designs: No. 1092, 65t, Humpback dolphin. No. 1093, 65t, Bottlenose dolphins. No. 1094, 1.50k, Bottlenose dolphin, with frame line. 2k, Irrawaddy dolphin. 2.50k, Humpback dolphin and fishermen. 4k, Irrawaddy dolphin and diver. No. 1098, 1.50k: a, Humpback dolphin and sailboat. b, Bottlenose dolphin, without frame line. c, Bottlenose dolphins, diff. d, Irrawaddy dolphin and diver, diff. e, Irrawaddy dolphin, diff. f, Humpback dolphin underwater.

Clay Pots — A243

**2003, Jan. 22**

1053-1057  A243    Set of 5    7.00  7.00

Designs: 65t, Sago storage pot. 1k, Smoking pot. 1.50k, Water jar. 2.50k, Water jar, diff. 4k, Ridge pot.

Coastal Villages A247

**2003, July 24**

1078-1083  A247    Set of 6    8.00  8.00

Designs: No. 1078, 65t, Gabagaba. No. 1079, 65t, Wanigela (Koki). 1.50k, Tubuserea. 2k, Hanuabada. 2.50k, Barakau. 4k, Porebada.

Freshwater Fish — A251

**2004, Jan. 30    Perf. 14¼**

1099-1104  A251    Set of 6    22.50  22.50
a.    Complete booklet, 10    5.00
#1099
b.    Complete booklet, 10    5.00
#1100

Designs: No. 1099, 70t, Lake Wanam rainbowfish. No. 1100, 70t, Kokoda mogurnda. 1k, Sepik grunter. 2.70k, Papuan black bass. 4.60k, Lake Tebera rainbowfish. 20k, Wichmann's mouth almighty.

20th World Scout Jamboree, Thailand — A244

**2003, Feb. 12**

1058-1061  A244    Set of 4    4.75  4.75

Designs: 50t, Group of scouts. 1.25k, Two scouts seated. 1.45k, Scouts on tower. 2.65k, Two scouts standing.

Powered Flight, Cent. A248

**2003, Aug. 27**

1084-1087  A248    Set of 4    6.50  6.50
1088  A248  2.50k Sheet of 4, #a-  8.00  8.00
d

Designs: 65t, Orville Wright circles plane over Fort Myer, Va., 1908. 1.50k, Orville Wright pilots "Baby Grand" Belmont, 1910. No. 1086, 2.50k, Wilbur Wright holding anemometer, Pau, France, 1909. 4k, Wilbur Wright pilots Model A, Pau, France, 1909. No. 1088, 2.50k — 1903 photos from Kitty Hawk: a, Untried airplane outside hangar. b, Rollout of plane from hangar. c, Preparing airplane for takeoff. d, Airplane takes off. 10k, Airplane takes off, diff.

**Souvenir Sheet**

1089  A248  10k multi    8.00  8.00

Dinosaurs A252

**2004, Feb. 25    Perf. 14**

1105-1110  A252    Set of 6    10.00  10.00
1111  A252  1.50k Sheet of 6, #a-f  7.00  7.00

Designs: 70t, Ankylosaurus. 1k, Oviraptor. 2k, Tyrannosaurus. 2.70k, Gigantosaurus. 2.70k, Centrosaurus. 4.60k, Carcharodontosaurus. No. 1111: a, Edmontonia. b, Struthiomimus. c, Psittacosaurus. d, Gastonia. e, Shunosaurus. f, Iguanodon. 7k, Afrovenator.

**Souvenir Sheet**

1112  A252  7k multi    5.25  5.25

Queen Mother Elizabeth (1900-2002) — A239

No. 1044, horiz.: a With Queen Elizabeth II women (28x23mm). b With Elizabeth and two other women (28x23mm). c, With pearl necklace visible at left (26x23mm). d. Color photograph (40x29mm). e, With pearl necklace visible at right (26x29mm). f, With man in top hat at right (28x23mm). 9, With King George VI (28x23mm). No. 1045, blue shading in UR of stamps : a, 3k, As child. b, 3k, Wearing black hat.

## Beetles A264

Designs: No. 1182, 75t, Promechus pulcher. No. 1183, 75t, Callistola pulchra. 1k, Lagriomorpha indigacea. 3k, Hellerhinus papuanus. 3.10k, Aphorina australis. 5.20k, Bothricara pulchella.

| | | | | |
|---|---|---|---|---|
| **2005, June 29** | | **Perf. 14** | | |
| 1182-1187 A264 | | Set of 6 | 9.00 | 9.00 |

### Souvenir Sheet

Pope John Paul II (1920-2005) — A265

No. 1188 — Denomination and country name in: a, Blue. b, Green. c, Orange. d, Red violet.

| | | | | |
|---|---|---|---|---|
| **2005, Aug. 10** | **Litho.** | | **Perf. 12¾** | |
| 1188 A265 2k Sheet of 4, #a-d | | | 5.25 | 5.25 |

## Provincial Flags A266

Province: No. 1189, 76t, Gulf. No. 1100, 76t, Southern Highlands. 1k, North Solomons. 3k, Oro. 3.10k, Western Highlands. 5.20k, Western.

| | | | | |
|---|---|---|---|---|
| **2005, Sept. 21** | | **Perf. 14** | | |
| 1189-1194 A266 | | Set of 6 | 9.25 | 9.25 |

## Cats and Dogs — A267

Designs: No. 1195, 75t, Somali Rudy cat. No. 1196, 75t, Balinese Seal Lynx Point cat. 3k, Sphynx Brown Mackerel Tabby and White cat. 3.10k, Korat Blue cat. 5.20k, Bengal Brown Spotted Tabby cat.

No. 1200: a, Yorkshire terrier. b, Basenji. c, Neapolitan mastiff. d, Poodle. 10k, Boston terrier, horiz.

| | | | | |
|---|---|---|---|---|
| **2005, Nov. 2** | | **Perf. 12¾** | | |
| 1195-1199 A267 | | Set of 5 | 8.50 | 8.50 |
| 1200 A267 2.50k Sheet of 4, #a- | | | 6.75 | 6.75 |

### Souvenir Sheet

| | | | |
|---|---|---|---|
| 1201 A267 10k multi | | 6.75 | 6.75 |

Summer Institute of Languages in Papua New Guinea, 50th Anniv. — A268

---

## Methods and Perfs as Before

| | | | |
|---|---|---|---|
| **2005, Jan. 3** | | | |
| 1154 A251 75t on 70t #1099 | | .50 | .50 |
| 1155 A251 75t on 70t #1100 | | .50 | .50 |
| 1156 A254 75t on 70t #1126 | | .50 | .50 |
| 1157 A254 75t on 70t #1127 | | .50 | .50 |
| Nos. 1154-1157 (4) | | 2.00 | 2.00 |

## Birds A260

Designs: 5t. Little egret. No. 1159, 75t, Nankeen night heron. 3k, Crested tern. 3.10k, Bar-tailed godwit. 5.20k, Little pied heron.
White-faced heron.

| | | | | |
|---|---|---|---|---|
| **2005, Jan. 26** | **Litho.** | | **Perf. 14** | |
| 1158-1163 A260 | | Set of 6 | 8.50 | 8.50 |

## Rotary International, Cent. — A261

Designs: 75t, Mobilizing communities in the fight against HIV and AIDS. 3k, Barefoot child, PolioPlus and Rotary centennial emblems. 3.10k, Co-founders of first Rotary Club. 5.20k, Chicago skyline.

No. 1168, vert.: a, Silvester Schiele (1870-1945), first Rotary President. b, Paul Harris, founder. c, Children. 10k, Emblem and globe, vert.

| | | | | |
|---|---|---|---|---|
| **2005, Feb. 23** | **Litho.** | | **Perf. 14** | |
| 1164-1167 A261 | | Set of 4 | 8.00 | 8.00 |
| 1168 A261 4k Sheet of 3, #a-c | | | 8.00 | 8.00 |

### Souvenir Sheet

| | | | |
|---|---|---|---|
| 1169 A261 10k multi | | 6.50 | 6.50 |

## Frangipani Varieties — A262

Designs: No. 1170, 75t, Evergreen. No. 1171, 75t, Lady in Pink. 1k, Carmine Flush. 3k, Cultivar acutifolia. 3.10k, American Beauty. 5.20k, Golden Kiss.

| | | | |
|---|---|---|---|
| **2005, Apr. 6** | **Perf. 12¾** | | |
| 1170-1175 A262 | Set of 6 | 9.00 | 9.00 |

## Mushrooms A263

Designs: No. 1176, 75t, Gymnopilus spectabilis. No. 1177, 75t, Melanogaster ambiguus. 3.10k, Microporus xanthopus. 5.20k, Psilocybe subcubensis. No. 1180: a, Amanita muscaria. b, Amanita rubescens. c, Suillus luteus. d, Stropharia cubensis. e, Aseroes rubra. f, Psilocybe aucklandii. 10k, Mycena pura.

| | | | |
|---|---|---|---|
| **2005, May 18** | | | |
| 1176-1179 A263 | Set of 4 | 6.50 | 6.50 |
| 1180 A263 2k Sheet of 6, #a-f | | 8.00 | 8.00 |

### Souvenir Sheet

| | | | |
|---|---|---|---|
| 1181 A263 10k multi | | 6.50 | 6.50 |

---

## National Soccer Team — A256

Various players in action: 70t, 2.65k, 2.70k, 4.60k.

| | | | | |
|---|---|---|---|---|
| **2004, Sept. 8** | | **Perf. 14¼** | | |
| 1136-1139 A256 | | Set of 4 | 9.00 | 9.00 |

## FIFA (Fédération Internationale de Football Association), Cent. — A257

No. 1140: a, Bruno Conti. b, Oliver Kahn. c, Mario Kempes. d, Bobby Moore. 10k, Bobby Robson.

| | | | | |
|---|---|---|---|---|
| **2004, Sept. 8** | | **Perf. 13¼x13½** | | |
| 1140 A257 2.50k Sheet of 4, #a-d | | | 8.75 | 8.75 |

### Souvenir Sheet

| | | | |
|---|---|---|---|
| 1141 A257 10k multi | | 8.75 | 8.75 |

## Provincial Flags A258

Province: No. 1142, 70t, East New Britain. No. 1143, 70t, Madang. 2.65k, Eastern Highlands. 2.70k, Morobe. 4.60k, Milno Bay. 10k, East Sepik.

| | | | | |
|---|---|---|---|---|
| **2004, Oct. 20** | | **Perf. 14** | | |
| 1142-1147 A258 | | Set of 6 | 15.00 | 15.00 |

## Shells A259

Designs: No. 1148, 70t, Phalium areola. No. 1149, 70t, Conus auratus. 2.65k, Oliva miniacea. 2.70k, Lambis chiragra. 4.60k, Conus suratensis. 10k, Architectonica perspectiva.

| | | | |
|---|---|---|---|
| **2004, Nov. 17** | | | |
| 1148-1153 A259 | Set of 6 | 15.00 | 15.00 |

Nos. 1099, 1100, 1126, 1127 Surcharged

---

Nos. 1015, 1078, 1079, 1092 and 1093 Surcharged

a

b

## Methods and Perfs As Before

| | | | |
|---|---|---|---|
| **2004** | | | |
| 1113 A236(a) 5t on 20t #1015 | | .25 | .25 |
| 1114 A247(b) 70t on 65t #1078 | | .25 | .60 |
| 1115 A247(b) 70t on 65t #1079 | | .60 | .60 |
| 1116 A250(a) 70t on 65t #1092 | | .60 | .60 |
| 1117 A250(a) 70t on 65t #1093 | | .60 | .60 |
| Nos. 1113-1117 (5) | | 2.65 | 2.65 |

Issued: Nos. 1114-1115, 1/20; others, 6/2.

## Orchids A253

Designs: 70t, Phalaenopsis amabilis. 1k, Phaius tankervilloae. No. 1120, 2lt, Dulbophyllum macranthum. 2.65k, Dendrobium rhodostictum. 2.70k, Diplocaulobium ridleyanum. 4.60k, Spathoglottis papuana.

No. 1124, 2k: a, Dendrobium cruttwellii. b, Dendrobium coeloglossum. c, Dendrobium alaticaulinum. d, Dendrobium obtusisepalum. e, Dendrobium johnsoniae. f, Dendrobium magno.

7k, Dendrobium biggibum.

| | | | | |
|---|---|---|---|---|
| **2004, May 19** | **Litho.** | | **Perf. 14** | |
| 1118-1123 A253 | | Set of 6 | 10.00 | 10.00 |
| 1124 A253 2k Sheet of 6, #a-f | | | 9.00 | 9.00 |

### Souvenir Sheet

| | | | |
|---|---|---|---|
| 1125 A253 7k multi | | 5.25 | 5.25 |

## Headdresses — A254

Province of headdress: No. 1126, 70t, Simbu. No. 1127, 70t, East Sepik. 2.65k, Southern Highlands. 2.70k, Western Highlands. 4.60k, Eastern Highlands. 5k, Central.

| | | | |
|---|---|---|---|
| **2004, June 2** | | | |
| 1126-1131 A254 | Set of 6 | 12.00 | 12.00 |
| Complete booklet, 10 #1126 | | | 5.00 |
| Complete booklet, 10 #1127 | | | 5.00 |

## 2004 Summer Olympics, Athens — A255

Designs: 70t, Swimming. 2.65k, Weight lifting, vert. 2.70k, Torch race, vert. 4.60k, Poster for 1952 Helsinki Olympics, vert.

| | | | | |
|---|---|---|---|---|
| **2004, Aug. 11** | | **Perf. 13¼** | | |
| 1132-1135 A255 | | Set of 4 | 9.00 | 9.00 |

## AIR POST STAMPS

Regular Issue of 1916 Overprinted

No. C1 exists on white and on yellowish paper. No. C1d on yellowish paper only.

### 1929 — Wmk. 74, Perf. 14

| | | | | |
|---|---|---|---|---|
| C1 | A3 | 3p blue grn & dk gray | 2.00 | 12.50 |
| b. | | Vert. pair, one without ovpt. | | |
| c. | | Horiz. pair, one without | | |
| d. | | 3p blue grn & sepia blk | 4,250. | 3,750. |
| e. | | Overprint on back, vert. | | |

### 1930, Sept. 15 — Wmk. 74, Perf. 14

| | | | | |
|---|---|---|---|---|
| C2 | A3 | 3p blue grn & blk | 2.00 | 7.00 |
| a. | | Yellowish paper | 1,850. | 1,400. |
| b. | | Double overprint | | |
| C3 | A3 | 3p ultra | 8.00 | 11.50 |
| a. | | Yellowish paper | | |
| b. | | Inverted overprint | 4,000. | |
| C4 | A3 | 6p violet & dull vio | 6.00 | 17.50 |
| | | | 10.00 | 26.00 |
| | | Nos. C2-C4 (3) | 16.00 | 36.00 |

Port Moresby AP1

### 1938, Sept. 6 — Unwmk. Engr., Perf. 11

| | | | | |
|---|---|---|---|---|
| C5 | AP1 | 2p carmine | 2.75 | 3.50 |
| C6 | AP1 | 3p ultra | 2.75 | 2.50 |
| C7 | AP1 | 5p dark green | 2.75 | 3.50 |
| C8 | AP1 | 8p red brown | 6.50 | 16.50 |
| C9 | AP1 | 1sh violet | 17.50 | 17.50 |
| | | Set, never hinged | 32.25 | 42.50 |
| | | Nos. C5-C9 (5) | 40.00 | |

Papua as a British possession, 50th anniv.

Papuans Poling Rafts — AP2

### 1939-41

| | | | | |
|---|---|---|---|---|
| C10 | AP2 | 2p carmine | 2.25 | 3.50 |
| C11 | AP2 | 3p ultra | 2.25 | 7.50 |
| C12 | AP2 | 5p dark green | 2.25 | 1.50 |
| C13 | AP2 | 8p red brown | 6.00 | 2.50 |
| C14 | AP2 | 1sh violet | 7.50 | 7.00 |
| C15 | AP2 | 2sh6p lt olive (41) | 22.50 | 32.50 |
| | | Set, never hinged | 42.75 | 54.50 |
| | | Nos. C10-C15 (6) | 60.00 | |

## POSTAGE DUE STAMPS

Designs: No. 1202, 80t, Postal services. No. 1203, 80t, Literacy; 1k, Jim Dean, first director. 3.20k, Tokpies preschools; 3.25k, Aviation. 5.35k, Community development.

### 2006, Jan. 4 — Litho., Perf. 13½

| | | | | |
|---|---|---|---|---|
| 1202-1207 | A268 | Set of 6 | 9.50 | 9.50 |

Nos. 128, 122, 129, 139 and 125 Surcharged in Black, Blue, Red or Orange

### 1960 — Unwmk. Engr., Perf. 14

| | | | | |
|---|---|---|---|---|
| J1 | A24 | 1p on 6½p | 7.00 | 7.00 |
| J2 | A23 | 3p on ½p (Bl) | 8.25 | 5.00 |
| a. | | Double surcharge | | |
| J3 | A24 | 6p on 7½p (R) | 25.00 | 12.00 |
| a. | | Double surcharge | 600.00 | |
| J4 | A23 | 1sh3p on 3½p (O) | 9.50 | 7.50 |
| J5 | A23 | 3sh on 2½p | 25.00 | 15.00 |
| | | Nos. J1-J5 (5) | 74.75 | 46.50 |

## POSTAL CHARGES

Regular Issues of 1916-23 Overprinted in Red

No. 129 Surcharged with New Value in Red

| | | | | |
|---|---|---|---|---|
| J6 | A24 | 6p on 7½p | 675. | 375. |
| a. | | Double surcharge | 3,000. | 1,750. |

Surcharge forgeries exist.

D1

### 1960, June 2 — Litho., Perf. 13½x14, Wmk. 228

| | | | | |
|---|---|---|---|---|
| J7 | D1 | 1p orange | .70 | .55 |
| J8 | D1 | 3p ocher | .75 | .55 |
| J9 | D1 | 6p light ultra | .80 | .30 |
| J10 | D1 | 9p vermilion | .80 | 1.25 |
| J11 | D1 | 1sh emerald | 1.10 | .40 |
| J12 | D1 | 1sh3p bright violet | 4.50 | 1.50 |
| J13 | D1 | 1sh6p light blue | 5.00 | 1.00 |
| J14 | D1 | 3sh yellow | 14.95 | 10.05 |
| | | Nos. J7-J14 (8) | | |

## OFFICIAL STAMPS

### 1931 — Wmk. 74, Perf. 14½

| | | | | |
|---|---|---|---|---|
| O1 | A3 | ½p #60 | 2.40 | 5.50 |
| O2 | A3 | 1p #61 | 4.75 | 8.75 |
| O3 | A3 | 1½p #62 | 1.90 | 14.00 |
| O4 | A3 | 2p #63 | 4.50 | 10.50 |
| O5 | A3 | 3p #66 | 3.00 | 25.00 |
| O6 | A3 | 4p #67 | 3.00 | 21.00 |
| O7 | A3 | 5p #68 | 7.00 | 42.50 |
| O8 | A3 | 6p #69 | 4.75 | 9.75 |
| O9 | A3 | 1sh #70 | 10.50 | 45.00 |
| O10 | A3 | 2sh6p #71 | 45.00 | 97.50 |

### 1932 — Wmk. 228, Perf. 11½

| | | | | |
|---|---|---|---|---|
| O11 | A3 | 9p #92 | 35.00 | 55.00 |
| O12 | A3 | 1sh3p #93 | 35.00 | 55.00 |
| | | Nos. O1-O12 (12) | 156.80 | 379.50 |

# PARAGUAY

'par-ə-ˌgwī

LOCATION — South America, bounded by Bolivia, Brazil and Argentina
GOVT. — Republic
AREA — 157,042 sq. mi.
POP. — 5,434,095 (1999 est.)
CAPITAL — Asuncion

10 Reales = 100 Centavos = 1 Peso
100 Centimos = 1 Guarani (1944)

Catalogue values for unused stamps in this country are for Never Hinged items, beginning with Scott 430 in the regular postage section, Scott B11 in the semi-postal section, and Scott C154 in the airpost section.

## Watermarks

Wmk. 319 — Stars and R P Multiple

Wmk. 320 — Interlacing Lines

Wmk. 347 — RP Multiple

Vigilant Lion Supporting Liberty Cap
A1   A2   A3

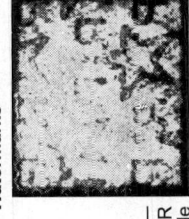

**1870, Aug. 1   Unwmk.   Litho.   Imperf.**

| | | | |
|---|---|---|---|
| 1 | A1 1r rose | 5.00 | 9.00 |
| 2 | A2 2r blue | 90.00 | 100.00 |
| 3 | A3 3r black | 275.00 | 319.00 |

Unofficial reprints of 2r in blue and other colors are on thicker paper than originals. They show a colored dot in upper part of "S" of "DOS" in upper right corner.
For surcharges see Nos. 4-9, 19.

## Handstamp Surcharged

**1878**

**Black Surcharge**

| | | | |
|---|---|---|---|
| 4 | A1 5c on 1r rose | 80.00 | 110.00 |
| 5 | A2 5c on 2r blue | 325.00 | 300.00 |
| 5E | A3 5c on 3r black | 450.00 | 450.00 |
| | Nos. 4-5E (3) | 855.00 | 860.00 |

**Blue Surcharge**

| | | | |
|---|---|---|---|
| 5F | A1 5c on 1r rose | 80.00 | 110.00 |
| 5H | A2 5c on 2r blue | 425.00 | 1,000. |
| 6 | A3 5c on 3r black | 425.00 | 425.00 |
| | Nos. 5F-6 (3) | 1,505. | 1,535. |

The surcharge may be found inverted, double, sideways and omitted.
The originals are surcharged in dull black or dull blue. The reprints are in intense black and bright blue. The reprint surcharges are over-inked and show numerous breaks in the handstamp.

## Handstamp Surcharged

**Black Surcharge**

| | | | |
|---|---|---|---|
| 7 | A2 5c on 2r blue | 500.00 | 425.00 |
| 8 | A3 5c on 3r black | 425.00 | 425.00 |

**Blue Surcharge**

| | | | |
|---|---|---|---|
| 9 | A3 5c on 3r black | 250.00 | 250.00 |
| a. | Dbl. surch., large & small "5" | 1,175. | 1,100. |
| | Nos. 7-9 (3) | | |

The surcharge on Nos. 7, 8 and 9 is usually placed sideways. It may be found double or inverted on Nos. 8 and 9.
Nos. 4 to 9 have been extensively counterfeited.
Two examples recorded of No. 9a, one without gum, the other with full but disturbed original gum

---

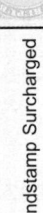

| | | | |
|---|---|---|---|
| 16 | A7 4c brown | .80 | .70 |
| a. | Imperf., pair | 25.00 | 25.00 |
| b. | Horiz. pair, imperf. vert. | 25.00 | 25.00 |
| c. | Vert. pair, imperf. horiz. | | |

### No. 11 Surcharged

**Handstamped in Black or Gray**

**1881, July   Perf. 12½**

| | | | |
|---|---|---|---|
| 17 | A4 1c on 10c blue grn | 10.00 | 9.00 |
| 18 | A4 2c on 10c blue grn | 10.00 | 9.00 |

Gray handstamps sell for much more than black.

### No. 1 Surcharged

**1884, May 8   Handstamped   Imperf.**

| | | | |
|---|---|---|---|
| 19 | A1 1c on 1r rose | 5.00 | 4.50 |

The surcharges on Nos. 17-19 exist double, inverted and in pairs with one omitted. Counterfeits exist.

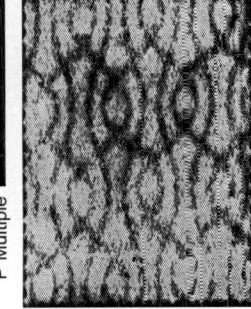

A4a

**1879   Litho.   Perf. 12½**

**Thin Paper**

| | | | |
|---|---|---|---|
| 10 | A4 5r orange | 1.25 | |
| 11 | A4 10r red brown | 1.50 | |
| a. | Imperf. | 40.00 | |
| b. | Horiz. pair, imperf. vert. | | |

Nos. 10 and 11 were never placed in use.
For surcharges see Nos. 17-18.

**1879-81**

**Thin Paper**

| | | | |
|---|---|---|---|
| 12 | A4a 5c orange brown | 2.50 | 3.00 |
| 13 | A4a 10c blue grn (81) | 3.50 | 12.00 |
| a. | Imperf., pair | 12.00 | |

Reprints of Nos. 10-13 are imperf., perf. 11½, 12, 12½ or 14. They have yellowish gum and the 10c is deep green.

### Seal of the Treasury
A11   A12

**1004, Aug. 3   Litho.   Perf. 11½, 12½**

| | | | |
|---|---|---|---|
| 20 | A11 1c green | .70 | .65 |
| 21 | A11 2c rose pink | .70 | .65 |
| 22 | A11 5c pale blue, yellowish | 2.10 | 1.95 |
| | Nos. 20-22 (3) | | |

Shades exist.
For overprints see Nos. O1, O8, O15.

**Imperf., Pairs**

| | | | |
|---|---|---|---|
| 20a | A11 1c green | 12.50 | |
| 21a | A11 2c rose red | 16.00 | |
| 22a | A11 5c blue | 44.50 | |
| | Nos. 20a 22a (3) | | |

A5   A6   A7

**1881, Aug.   Litho.   Perf. 11½-13½**

| | | | |
|---|---|---|---|
| 14 | A5 1c blue | .80 | .70 |
| a. | Imperf., pair | | |
| b. | Horiz. pair, imperf. btwn. | | |
| 15 | A6 2c rose red | .80 | .70 |
| a. | Imperf., pair | 1.00 | .90 |
| b. | 2c dull orange red | | |
| c. | Horiz. pair, imperf. vert. | 25.00 | 25.00 |
| d. | Vert. pair, imperf. horiz. | 25.00 | 25.00 |

**1887   Perf. 11½, 11½x12, 12½x11½   Typo.**

| | | | |
|---|---|---|---|
| 23 | A12 1c green | .25 | .20 |
| 25 | A12 5c blue | .40 | .30 |
| 26 | A12 7c brown | .70 | .40 |
| 27 | A12 10c lilac | .50 | .30 |
| 28 | A12 15c orange | .50 | .30 |
| 29 | A12 20c pink | 3.10 | 2.00 |
| | Nos. 23-29 (7) | | |

See #42-45. For surcharges & overprints see #46, 49-50, 71-72, 167-170A, O20-O41, O49.

---

## Overprint Handstamped in Violet

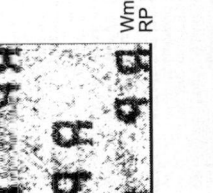

**1892, Oct. 12   Perf. 12x12½**

| | | | |
|---|---|---|---|
| 31 | A15 10c violet blue | 7.00 | 3.50 |

Discovery of America by Columbus, 400th anniversary. Overprint reads: "1492 / 12 DE OCTUBRE / 1892." Sold only on day of issue.

### Juan G. González — A15

1c, Cirilo A. Rivarola. 2c, Salvador Jovella-nos. 4c, Juan B. Gil. 5c, Higinio Uriarte. 10c, Candido Bareiro. 14c, Gen. Bernardino Caballero. 20c, Gen. Patricio Escobar.

**1892-96   Litho.   Perf. 12x12½**

| | | | |
|---|---|---|---|
| 32 | A15 1c gray (centavos) | .20 | .20 |
| 33 | A15 1c gray (centavn) (96) | .70 | .70 |
| 34 | A15 2c green | .20 | .20 |
| 35 | Chalky paper ('96) | | |
| 35 | A15 4c carmine | .20 | .20 |
| | Chalky paper ('96) | | |
| 36 | A15 5c violet ('93) | .20 | .20 |
| a. | Chalky paper ('96) | | |
| 37 | A15 10c vio bl (punched) ('93) | | .20 |
| | Unpunched ('96) | 4.00 | |
| 38 | A15 10c dull blue ('96) | .20 | .40 |
| 39 | A15 14c yellow brown | .60 | .40 |
| 40 | A15 20c red ('93) | 1.00 | .40 |
| 41 | A15 30c light green | 1.50 | .65 |
| | Nos. 32-41 (10) | 4.50 | 2.85 |

The 10c violet blue (No. 37) was, until 1090, issued punched with a circular hole in order to prevent it being fraudulently overprinted as No. 31.
Nos. 33 and 38 are on chalky paper.
For surcharge see No. 70.

### Seal Typo of 1887

**1892   Typo.**

| | | | |
|---|---|---|---|
| 42 | A12 40c slate blue | 2.00 | .90 |
| 43 | A12 60c yellow | 1.00 | .40 |
| 44 | A12 80c light blue | .90 | .40 |
| 45 | A12 1p olive green | 4.80 | 2.10 |
| | Nos. 42-45 (4) | | |

Nos. 47-48

No. 46

**1895, Aug. 1   Perf. 11½x12**

| | | | |
|---|---|---|---|
| 46 | A12 5c on 7c brown, #26 | .50 | .50 |

### Telegraph Stamps Surcharged

**1896, Apr.   Engr.   Perf. 11½**

**Denomination In Black**

| | | | |
|---|---|---|---|
| 47 | 5c on 2c brown & gray | .60 | .40 |
| a. | Inverted surcharge | 10.00 | 10.00 |
| 48 | 5c on 4c yellow & gray | .60 | .40 |
| a. | Inverted surcharge | 7.50 | 7.50 |

### Symbols of Liberty from Coat of Arms — A13

**1889, Feb.   Litho.   Perf. 11½**

| | | | |
|---|---|---|---|
| 30 | A13 15c red violet | 2.50 | 2.00 |
| a. | Imperf., pair | 10.00 | 8.00 |

For overprints see Nos. O16-O19.

### Nos. 28, 42 Surcharged

**1898-99   Typo.**

| | | | |
|---|---|---|---|
| 49 | A12 10c on 15c org ('99) | .60 | .35 |
| a. | Double surcharge | 14.00 | 14.00 |
| b. | | 9.00 | |
| 50 | A12 10c on 40c slate bl | .30 | .20 |

Surcharge on No. 49 has small "c."

## Telegraph Stamps Surcharged

The basic telegraph stamps are like those used for Nos. 47-48, but the surcharges on Nos. 50A-50B consist of "5" and "10 10" above a blackout rectangle covering the engraved denominations.

A 40c red, bluish gray and black telegraph stamp (basic type of A24) was used as provisional in August, 1900, for postage. Value, postally used, $5.

**1900, May 14**  **Engr.**  **Perf. 11½**
| 50A | A25 | 5c grn, gray & blk | 4.00 | 2.50 |
| 50B | A25 | 10c on 50c blk | 1.75 | 1.00 |

Seal of the Treasury
A25

J. B.
Egusquiza
A26

**1900, Sept.**  **Engr.**  **Perf. 11½, 12**
| 51 | A25 | 1c gray | .20 | .20 |
| 52 | A25 | 2c gray | .20 | .20 |
| 53 | A25 | 3c orange brown | .20 | .20 |
| 54 | A25 | 5c dark green | .50 | .20 |
| 54A | A25 | 8c dark brown | | |
| 55 | A25 | 10c carmine rose | .50 | .20 |
| 56 | A25 | 24c deep blue | 1.90 | 1.20 |

See Nos. 57-67. For surcharges see Nos. 69, 74, 76, 156-157.

**1901, Apr.**  **Litho.**  **Perf. 11½**  **Small Figures**
| 57 | A25 | 2c rose | .20 | .20 |
| 58 | A25 | 5c violet brown | .70 | .25 |
| 59 | A25 | 40c blue | 1.10 | .65 |

Nos. 57-59 (3)

**1901-02**  **Larger Figures**
| 60 | A25 | 1c gray green ('02) | .20 | .20 |
| 61 | A25 | 2c gray | .20 | .20 |
| a. | Half used as 1c on cover | | 10.00 |
| 62 | A25 | 4c pale blue | .20 | .20 |
| 63 | A25 | 5c violet | .20 | .20 |
| 64 | A25 | 8c gray brown ('02) | .50 | .20 |
| 65 | A25 | 10c rose red ('02) | .50 | .20 |
| 66 | A25 | 20c orange ('02) | 1.00 | .20 |
| 67 | A25 | 40c blue | 3.00 | 1.60 |

Nos. 60-67 (8)

**1901, Sept. 24**  **Typo.**  **Perf. 12x12½**  **Chalky Paper**
| 68 | A26 | 1p slate | .30 | .20 |

For surcharge see No. 73.

**1902, Aug.**  **Red Surcharge**
| 69 | A25 | 20c on 24c dp blue | .25 | .20 |
| a. | Inverted surcharge | 6.25 | |

Counterfeit surcharges exist.

No. 56 Surcharged

Habilitado
en un
1 cent. 1

Habilitado
en cinco
5 cent. 5

**1902, Sept.**
| 70 | | No. 70 | | |

**1902, Dec. 22**  **Perf. 12x12½**
| 70 | A15 | 1c on 14c yellow | .20 | .20 |
| a. | No period after "cent" | .75 | |
| b. | Comma after "cent" | .65 | |
| c. | Accent over "Un" | .50 | |

Nos. 39, 43-44 Surcharged  **Perf. 11½**
| 71 | A12 | 5c on 60c yellow | .20 | .25 |
| 72 | A12 | 5c on 80c lt blue | .20 | .20 |

Nos. 71-72

---

**1902-03**  **Perf. 11½**
| 73 | A26 | 1c on 1p slate ('03) | .20 | .20 |
| a. | No period after "cent" | 1.60 | 1.50 |

#73

Habilitado
en un
1 cent.

Habilitado
en cinco
5 cent. 5

#76

Habilitado
en
5 cent.

#74

**1902-03**  **Perf. 12**
| 74 | A25 | 5c on 8c gray brown | .25 | .20 |
| a. | No period after "cent" | .90 | .75 |
| 76 | A25 | 5c on 20c orange | 3.50 | 3.00 |
| b. | Comma after "cent" | .25 | .20 |

The surcharge on Nos. 73 and 74 is found reading both upward and downward.

Nos. 73-76 (3)
| 76 | | | .70 | .60 |

Sentinel Lion with Right Paw
Ready to Strike for "Peace and
Justice"

A32  A33

**1903, Feb. 28**  **Litho.**  **Perf. 11½**  **Unwmk.**
| 77 | A32 | 1c gray | .20 | .20 |
| 78 | A32 | 2c blue green | .30 | .20 |
| 79 | A32 | 3c red orange | .40 | .20 |
| 80 | A32 | 5c orange brown | .50 | .20 |
| 81 | A32 | 20c carmine | .60 | .20 |
| 82 | A32 | 30c deep blue | 1.40 | .65 |
| 83 | A32 | 60c purple | 3.90 | 1.85 |

Nos. 77-83 (7)

For surcharges and overprints see Nos. 139-140, 166, O50-O56.

**1903, Sept.**  **Engr.**
| 84 | A33 | 1c yellow green | .20 | .20 |
| 85 | A33 | 2c blue green | .20 | .20 |
| 86 | A33 | 5c purple | .20 | .20 |
| 87 | A33 | 10c purple | .30 | .20 |
| 88 | A33 | 20c dark green | .70 | .30 |
| 89 | A33 | 30c ultramarine | 1.00 | .70 |
| 90 | A33 | 60c ocher | 3.90 | 1.80 |

Nos. 84-90 (7)

Nos. 84-90 exist imperf. Value for pairs, $3 each for 1c-20c, $4 for 30c, $5 for 60c.

The three-line overprint "Gobierno provisorio Ago. 1904" is fraudulent.

Sentinel Lion at Rest
A35  A36

**1905-10**  **Perf. 11½, 12, 11½x12**  **Engr.**
Dated "1904"
| 91 | A35 | 1c orange | .30 | .20 |
| 92 | A35 | 1c vermilion ('07) | .20 | .20 |
| 93 | A35 | 1c grnish bl ('07) | .20 | .20 |
| 94 | A35 | 2c vermilion ('07) | .20 | .20 |
| 95 | A35 | 2c olive grn ('07) | 40.00 | |
| 96 | A35 | 2c dark green ('08) | .20 | .20 |
| 97 | A35 | 5c car rose ('08) | .30 | .20 |
| 98 | A35 | 5c dark blue | .20 | .20 |
| 99 | A35 | 5c yellow ('06) | .20 | .20 |
| 100 | A35 | 5c bister ('06) | .20 | .20 |
| 101 | A35 | 10c emerald ('07) | .20 | .20 |
| 102 | A35 | 10c violet ('08) | .30 | .20 |
| 103 | A35 | 20c dp ultra ('06) | .30 | .20 |
| 104 | A35 | 20c bister ('07) | .30 | .20 |

---

**1904, Aug.**  **Litho.**  **Perf. 11½**
| 112 | A36 | 10c light blue | .25 | .20 |
| a. | Imperf., pair | 3.00 | |

All but Nos. 92 and 104 exist imperf. Value for pair, $10 each, except No. 95 at $35 and Nos. 109-111 at $15 each pair.

For surcharges and overprints see Nos. 129-130, 146-155, 174-190, 266.

| 105 | A35 | 20c apple grn ('07) | .30 | .20 |
| 106 | A35 | 30c turq bl ('06) | .45 | .20 |
| 107 | A35 | 30c blue gray ('06) | .45 | .20 |
| 108 | A35 | 60c dull lilac ('08) | .60 | .20 |
| 109 | A35 | 60c choc ('08) | .40 | .20 |
| 110 | A35 | 60c red brown | .60 | .20 |
| 111 | A35 | 60c salmon pink ('10) | .40 | .20 |

Nos. 91-94,96-111 (20)  6.10
Nos. 91-111 (21)

**1904, Dec.**
| 113 | A36 | 30c on 10c light blue | .40 | .25 |

Peace and peace between a successful revolutionary party and the government previously in power.

No. 112 Surcharged
in Black

Governmental
Palace,
Asunción — A37

Dated "1904"
**1906-10**  **Engr.**  **Perf. 11½, 12**  **Center in Black**
| 114 | A37 | 1p bright rose | 1.25 | .75 |
| 115 | A37 | 1p brown org ('07) | .50 | .25 |
| 116 | A37 | 2p brown org ('07) | .50 | .25 |
| 117 | A37 | 2p ol gray ('07) | .50 | .25 |
| 118 | A37 | 2p turquoise ('07) | .25 | .20 |
| 119 | A37 | 5p ol grn ('10) | .30 | .20 |
| 120 | A37 | 5p brn org ('10) | .75 | .25 |
| 121 | A37 | 5p lake ('09) | .25 | .20 |
| 122 | A37 | 5p dull bl ('10) | .75 | .50 |
| 123 | A37 | 10p brown org ('10) | .75 | .50 |
| 124 | A37 | 10p dp blue ('10) | .70 | .50 |
| 125 | A37 | 10p dp blue ('10) | .75 | .50 |
| 126 | A37 | 20p olive grn ('07) | 1.75 | 1.60 |
| 127 | A37 | 20p olive grn ('07) | 1.75 | 1.60 |
| 128 | A37 | 20p yellow ('10) | 1.75 | 1.60 |

Nos. 114-128 (15)  12.70  9.65

---

**Official Stamps of
1906-08 Overprinted**

Habilitado

**Same Surcharge on Official Stamps
of 1903**
| 139 | A32 | 5c on 30c dp blue | 1.25 | 1.10 |
| 140 | A32 | 5c on 60c purple | .50 | .30 |
| a. | Double surcharge | 2.50 | |

Nos. 139-138 (8)

Official Stamps of
1906-08 Surcharged

Habilitado
en
5
CENTAVOS

**1907**
| 129 | A35 | 5c on 2c vermilion | .30 | .20 |
| a. | "5" omitted | 1.00 | 1.00 |
| b. | Double surcharge | .30 | .20 |
| 130 | A35 | 5c on 2c olive grn | .40 | .20 |
| b. | Double surcharge, one invtd. | 1.00 | |
| c. | Inverted surcharge | 6.00 | |
| d. | Double surcharge, both invtd. | 1.00 | |

Nos. 94 and 95
Surcharged

Habilitado
en
5
CENTAVOS

**1908**
| 131 | O17 | 5c on 1c bister | 2.00 | 2.00 |
| a. | Inverted surcharge | 2.00 | 2.00 |
| 132 | O17 | 5c on 10c violet | 2.00 | 2.00 |
| 133 | O17 | 5c on 20c emerald | .30 | .20 |
| 134 | O17 | 5c on 20c violet | .30 | .20 |
| a. | Inverted surcharge | 2.25 | 2.25 |

**Same Surcharge on Official Stamps
of 1901-02**
| 135 | O17 | 5c on 30c slate bl | .65 | .65 |
| 136 | O17 | 5c on 30c turq bl | 1.00 | .65 |
| a. | Inverted surcharge | | |
| 137 | O17 | 5c on 60c choc | .30 | .20 |
| a. | Double surcharge | 6.00 | |
| b. | Bar omitted | .60 | |
| 138 | O17 | 5c on 60c red brown | .40 | .20 |
| a. | Inverted surcharge | 4.10 | 2.50 |

Nos. 131-138 (8)

**Regular Issues of
1906-08 Surcharged**

**1908**
| 141 | O17 | 5c deep blue | .20 | .20 |
| a. | Bar omitted | 1.50 | |
| b. | Inverted overprint | 1.50 | |
| 142 | O17 | 5c slate blue | 2.00 | 1.50 |
| 143 | O17 | 5c greenish blue | 1.75 | 1.25 |
| a. | Inverted overprint | 4.50 | |
| 144 | O18 | 1p brown org & blk | .25 | .25 |
| a. | Bar omitted | 3.75 | |
| 145 | O18 | 1p brt rose & blk | .45 | .35 |
| a. | Triple overprint, two inverted | 2.25 | |
| b. | Double overprint, one inverted | 1.25 | |
| c. | Triple overprint | 1.25 | |

Nos. 141-145 (5)  1.35  1.20

**Same Surcharge on Regular Issue
of 1901-02**
| 146 | A35 | 5c on 1c grnish bl | .20 | .20 |
| a. | Double surcharge | 1.00 | |
| b. | Inverted surcharge | 7.00 | |
| 147 | A35 | 5c on 2c car rose | 1.00 | 1.00 |
| a. | Double surcharge | 1.75 | |
| 148 | A35 | 5c on 60c brn, invd. | 2.50 | 2.50 |
| b. | Double surcharge, one inverted | 2.00 | |
| c. | Double surcharge, one invd. | 2.00 | |
| d. | Inverted surcharge | 2.00 | |
| 149 | A35 | 5c on 60c org brn | 2.00 | 2.00 |
| a. | Double surcharge, one invtd. | .50 | |
| 150 | A35 | 5c on 60c choc | 3.50 | 3.50 |
| a. | Double surcharge | .50 | |
| 151 | A35 | 5c on 1c grnish bl | .20 | .20 |
| a. | Inverted surcharge | 5.00 | |
| 152 | A35 | 5c on 2c ver | 5.00 | 5.00 |
| 153 | A35 | 5c on 2c car rose | 12.50 | 3.50 |
| 154 | A35 | 5c on 30c dl lil | 3.50 | 3.00 |
| a. | Inverted surcharge | 1.50 | |
| 155 | A35 | 5c on 30c turq bl | 1.50 | 1.50 |

Nos. 146-155 (10)  12.40  10.90

**Same Surcharge on No. O52**
| 166 | A32 | 20c on 5c blue | 1.25 | 1.00 |
| a. | Inverted surcharge | 3.75 | 1.80 |

**Same Surcharge on Official Issue
of 1908**
| 156 | A25 | 5c on 28c org | 1.25 | 1.10 |
| 157 | A25 | 5c on 40c dk bl | .40 | .30 |
| a. | Inverted surcharge | 4.00 | 4.00 |

**Same Surcharge on Regular Issue
of 1901-02**
| 158 | A35 | 5c on 10c emer | .20 | .20 |
| 159 | O17 | 5c on 10c red lil | 7.00 | |
| a. | "5" omitted | 1.00 | |
| 160 | A35 | 5c on 20c bis | 1.00 | |
| a. | Double surcharge | .40 | |
| 161 | O17 | 5c on 20c sal pink | 1.50 | |
| a. | Inverted surcharge | 1.75 | |
| 162 | O17 | 5c on 30c bl gray | .20 | |
| a. | "5" omitted | 1.50 | |
| 163 | O17 | 5c on 30c yel | .20 | |
| a. | Double surcharge | 1.50 | |
| 164 | O17 | 5c on 60c org brn | 6.00 | |
| a. | "5" omitted | 6.00 | |
| 165 | O17 | 5c on 60c dp ultra | 2.50 | |
| b. | Inverted surcharge | 2.50 | |

Nos. 158-165 (8)

A42

**1922, Feb. 8  Litho.  Perf. 11½**
243 A42 50c car & dk blue ... .20 .20
  a. Imperf. pair ... 10.00 10.00
  b. Center inverted ... .50 .50
244 A42 1p dk blue & brn ... 12.50 12.50
  a. Imperf. pair
  b. Center inverted
For overprints see Nos. L1-L2.

**Rendezvous of Conspirators A43**

**1922-23**
245 A43 1p deep blue ... .20 .20
246 A43 1p scar & dk bl ('23) ... .20 .20
247 A43 1p red vio & gray ('23) ... .20 .20
248 A43 1p org & gray ('23) ... .20 .20
249 A43 5p dark violet ... .60 .60
250 A43 5p dk bl & org brn ('23) ... .60 .60
251 A43 5p dl red & lt bl ('23) ... .60 .60
252 A43 5p emer & blk ('23) ... 3.20 1.60
Nos. 245-252 (8)

National Independence.

**No. 218 Surcharged "Habilitado en $1:-1924" in Red**

**1924**
253 A40 1p on 1.25p pale blue ... .20 .20

This stamp was for use in Asunción. Nos. L3 to L5 were for use in the interior, as is indicated by the "C" in the surcharge.

**Map of Paraguay — A44**

**1924  Litho.  Perf. 11½**
254 A44 1p dark blue ... .20 .20
255 A44 2p carmine rose ... .20 .20
256 A44 4p light blue ... .40 .60
  a. Perf. 12 ... .60 .60
Nos. 254-256 (3)
#254-256 exist imperf. Value $3 each pair.
For surcharges and overprint see Nos. 267, C5, C15-C16, C54-C55, L7.

**Columbus — A46**

**Gen. José E. Díaz — A45**

**1925-26  Perf. 11½, 12**
257 A45 50c red ... .20 .20
258 A45 1p dark blue ... .20 .20
259 A45 1p emerald ('26) ... .60 .60
Nos. 257-259 (3)
#257-258 exist imperf. Value $1 each pair.
For overprints see Nos. L6, L8, L10.

**1925  Perf. 11½**
260 A46 1p blue ... .20 .20
  a. Imperf. pair ... 2.00
For overprint see No. L9.

---

**Nos. J10 and 214 Surcharged**
224 D2 5c on 40c yellow brn ... .20 .20
225 A40 30c on 40c rose ... 1.20 1.20
Nos. 220-225 (6)

Nos. 220-225 exist with surcharge inverted, double and double with one inverted. The surcharge "Habilitado-1918-5 cents 5" on the 1c gray official stamps of 1914, is bogus.

**No. J11 Overprinted**

**1920**
229 D2 1p yellow brown ... .20 .20
  a. Inverted overprint ... .65 .65
  e. as "9.", "HABILITADO" ... .75 .75
  f. as "9.", "1929" for "1920" ... .75 .75
  g. Overprint lines 8mm apart ... .20 .20

**Nos. 216 and 219 Surcharged**

**1920**
230 A40 50c on 80c yellow ... .20 .20
231 A40 1.75p on 3p grnsh bl ... .75 .65
**Same Surcharge on No. J12**
232 D2 1p on 1.50p yel brn ... 1.40 1.25
Nos. 229-232 (4)

Nos. 229-232 exist with various surcharge errors, including inverted, double, double inverted and double with one inverted. Those that were issued are listed.

**Parliament Building A41**

**1920  Litho.  Perf. 11½**
233 A41 50c red & black ... .25 .20
234 A41 1p lt blue & blk ... 1.50 1.50
235 A41 1.75p dk blue & blk ... .20 .20
236 A41 3p orange & blk ... 2.10 .90
Nos. 233-236 (4)

50th anniv. of the Constitution.
All values exist imperforate on Nos. 233, 235 and 236 with center inverted. It is doubtful that any of these varieties were regularly issued.

**No. 215 Surcharged**

**1920**
237 A40 50c on 75c deep blue ... .30 .20

**Nos. 200, 215 Surcharged**

**1921**
241 A38 50c on 75c deep blue ... .20 .20
242 A40 50c on 75c deep blue ... .20 .20

---

**"The Republic" A39**

**Coat of Arms above Numeral of Value A38**

**1910-21  Litho.  Perf. 11½**
191 A38 1c gray black ... .20 .20
192 A38 5c bright violet ... 1.00 1.00
  a. Pair, imperf. between
193 A38 5c blue grn ('19) ... .20 .20
194 A38 5c lt blue ('21) ... .20 .20
195 A38 10c yellow green ('19) ... .20 .20
196 A38 10c dp vio ('19) ... .20 .20
197 A38 10c red ('21) ... .20 .20
198 A38 20c red ... .20 .20
199 A38 50c car rose ... .30 .20
200 A38 75c deep blue ... .30 .20
  a. Diag. half perforated ('11) ... 2.10 2.00
Nos. 191-200 (10)

Nos. 191-200 exist imperforate.
No. 200a was authorized for use as 20c.
For surcharges see #208, 241, 261, 265.

**1911  Engr.**
201 A39 1c olive grn & blk ... .30 .20
202 A39 2c dk blue & blk ... .30 .20
203 A39 5c carmine & indigo ... .30 .20
204 A39 10c dp blue & brn ... .30 .20
205 A39 20c olive grn & ind ... .40 .20
206 A39 50c lilac & indigo ... .50 .20
207 A39 75c ol grn & red lil ... 2.50 1.40
Nos. 201-207 (7)

Centenary of National Independence.
The 1c, 2c, 10c and 50c exist imperf. Value for pairs, $1.50 each.

**No. 199 Surcharged**

**1912**
208 A38 20c on 50c car rose ... .20 1.25
  a. Inverted surcharge ... 1.25 1.25
  b. Double surcharge ... 1.75 1.75
  c. Bar omitted

**National Coat of Arms — A40**

**1913  Engr.  Perf. 11½**
209 A40 1c gray ... .20 .20
210 A40 5c orange ... .20 .20
211 A40 5c lilac ... .20 .20
212 A40 10c green ... .20 .20
213 A40 20c dull red ... .20 .20
214 A40 40c rose ... .20 .20
215 A40 75c deep blue ... .20 .20
216 A40 80c yellow ... .20 .20
217 A40 1p light blue ... .20 .20
218 A40 1.25p pale blue ... .30 .30
219 A40 3p greenish blue ... 2.50 2.20
Nos. 209-219 (11)

For surcharges see Nos. 225, 230-231, 237, 242, 253, 262-263, L3-L4.

**Nos. J7-J10 Overprinted**

**1918**
220 D2 5c yellow brown ... .20 .20
221 D2 10c yellow brown ... .20 .20
222 D2 20c yellow brown ... .20 .20
223 D2 40c yellow brown ... .20 .20

---

**Surcharged**

**On Stamp of 1887**
**1908**
167 A12 20c on 2c car ... 2.50 2.00
  a. Inverted surcharge ... 7.50

**On Official Stamps of 1892**
168 A12 5c on 15c org ... 2.50 1.75
169 A12 5c on 20c pink ... 40.00 32.50
170 A12 5c on 50c gray ... 17.50 12.50
170A A12 20c on 5c blue ... 1.50 1.25
  b. Inverted surcharge ... 8.75 8.75
Nos. 167-170A (5) ... 64.00 50.00

Nos. 151, 152, 153, 155, 167, 170A, while duly authorized, all appear to have been sold to a single individual, and although they paid postage, it is doubtful whether they can be considered as ever having been placed on sale to the public.

**Nos. O82-O84 Surcharged (Date in Red)**

**1908-09**
171 O18 1c on 1p brt rose & blk ... .20 .20
172 O18 1c on 1p lake & blk ... .20 .20
173 O18 1c on 1p brn org & blk ... .90 .60
  (09) ... 1.30 1.00
Nos. 171-173 (3)

Varieties of surcharge on Nos. 171-173 include: "CETTAVO"; date omitted, double or inverted; third line double or unitted.

**Types of 1905-1910 Overprinted**

**1908, Mar. 5  Perf. 11½**
174 A35 1c emerald ... .20 .20
175 A35 5c yellow ... .20 .20
176 A35 10c lilac brown ... .20 .20
177 A35 20c yellow orange ... .25 .20
178 A35 30c red ... .20 .20
179 A35 60c magenta
180 A37 1p light blue ... 1.45 1.40
Nos. 174-180 (7)

**Overprinted**

**1909, Sept.**
181 A35 1c blue gray ... .20 .20
182 A35 5c scarlet ... .20 .20
183 A35 5c dark green ... .20 .20
184 A35 5c deep orange ... .20 .20
185 A35 10c rose ... .20 .20
186 A35 10c bister brown ... .20 .20
187 A35 20c violet ... .20 .20
188 A35 20c orange brown ... .30 .30
189 A35 30c dull blue ... .30 .30
190 A35 30c dull brown ... 2.20 2.00
Nos. 181-190 (10)

Counterfeits exist.

## 1926

| 261 | A38 | 1c on 5c lt blue | .20 | .20 |
|---|---|---|---|---|
| 262 | A40 | 7c on 40c rose | .20 | .20 |
| 263 | A40 | 15c on 75c dp bl (R) | .20 | .20 |
| 264 | D2 | 1.50p on 1.50p yel brn | .80 | .80 |

Nos. 261-264 (4)

## 1927

Nos. 194, 179 and 256 Surcharged "Habilitado" and New Values

| 265 | A38 | 2c on 5c lt blue | .20 | .20 |
|---|---|---|---|---|
| 266 | A35 | 50c on 60c magenta | .20 | .20 |
| a. | Inverted surcharge | 2.00 | |
| 267 | A44 | 4p lt blue | .20 | .20 |

## Official Stamp of 1914 Surcharged "Habilitado" and New Value

Habilitado en 7 centavos

| 268 | O19 | 50c on 75c dp bl | .80 | .80 |

Nos. 265-268 (4)

National Emblem — A47

Map of Paraguay — A49

Pedro Juan Caballero — A48

Ignacio Iturbe — A51

Oratory of the Virgin, Asunción — A52

Fulgencio Yegros — A50

## 1927-38
Perf. 12, 11, 11½, 11x12
Typo.

| 269 | A47 | 1c lt red ('31) | .20 | .20 |
|---|---|---|---|---|
| 270 | A47 | 2c org red ('30) | .20 | .20 |
| 271 | A47 | 7c lilac | .20 | .20 |
| 272 | A47 | 7c emerald ('29) | .20 | .20 |
| 273 | A47 | 10c gray grn ('28) | .20 | .20 |
| a. | 10c light green ('31) | .20 | |
| 274 | A47 | 10c lil rose ('30) | .20 | .20 |
| 275 | A47 | 10c light bl ('35) | .20 | .20 |
| 276 | A47 | 20c dull brn ('30) | .20 | .20 |
| 277 | A47 | 20c dull bl ('28) | .20 | .20 |
| 278 | A47 | 20c lt vio ('31) | .20 | .20 |
| 279 | A47 | 50c rose ('35) | .20 | .20 |
| 280 | A47 | 50c ultramarine | .20 | .20 |
| 281 | A47 | 50c dl red ('28) | .20 | .20 |
| 282 | A47 | 50c orange ('30) | .20 | .20 |
| 283 | A47 | 50c gray ('31) | .20 | .20 |
| 284 | A47 | 50c brn vio ('34) | .20 | .20 |
| 285 | A47 | 70c ultra ('28) | .20 | .20 |
| 286 | A48 | 1p emerald | .20 | .20 |
| 287 | A48 | 1p org red ('30) | .20 | .20 |
| 288 | A48 | 1p brown ('34) | .20 | .20 |
| 289 | A47 | 1.50p brown | .20 | .20 |
| 290 | A47 | 1.50p ultramarine | .20 | .20 |
| 291 | A49 | 1.50p lilac ('28) | .20 | .20 |
| 292 | A49 | 1.50p rose red ('32) | .20 | .20 |
| 293 | A50 | 2.50p bister | .20 | .20 |
| 294 | A51 | 3p gray | .20 | .20 |
| 295 | A51 | 3p rose red ('36) | .20 | .20 |
| 296 | A51 | 3p violet ('36) | .20 | .20 |
| 297 | A52 | 5p chocolate | .20 | .20 |
| 298 | A52 | 5p rose org ('36) | .20 | .20 |
| 299 | A52 | 5p pale org | .20 | .20 |
| 300 | A49 | 5p red ('29) | .20 | .20 |
| 301 | A49 | 20p emerald ('38) | .20 | .20 |
| 302 | A49 | 20p vio brn ('29) | .40 | .40 |

Nos. 269-302 ('34)
9.50

No. 281 is also known perf. 10½x11½.
Papermaker's watermarks are sometimes found on No. 271 ("GLORIA BOND") in double-lined circle) and No. 280 ("Extra Vencedor Bond" or "ADBANCEIM M. C"). For surcharges and overprints see Nos. 312, 403, C4, C6, C13-C14, C17-C18, C32, C34-C35, L11-L30, O94-O96, O98.

## 1928, Aug. 15
Arms of Juan de Salazar de Espinosa A53

Columbus A54

| 303 | A53 | 10p violet brown | 1.75 | 1.25 |

Perf. 12

Juan de Salazar de Espinosa, founder of Asunción. A papermaker's watermark ("INDIAN BOND EXTRA STRONG S.&C") is sometimes found on Nos. 303, 305-307.

## 1928
Litho.

| 304 | A54 | 10p ultra | .80 | .50 |
|---|---|---|---|---|
| 305 | A54 | 10p vermilion | .80 | .50 |
| 306 | A54 | 10p deep red | .80 | .50 |

Nos. 304-306 (3)
2.40 1.50

For surcharge & overprint see #C33, L37.

## 1928, Nov. 20
President Rutherford B. Hayes of US and Villa Occidental — A55

| 307 | A55 | 10p gray brown | 5.00 | 2.25 |
|---|---|---|---|---|
| 308 | A55 | 10p red brown | 5.00 | 2.25 |

Perf. 12

50th anniv. of the Hayes' Chaco decision.

Portraits of Archbishop Bogarin — A56

## 1930, Aug. 15

| 309 | A56 | 1.50p lake | 1.00 | .75 |
|---|---|---|---|---|
| 310 | A56 | 1.50p turq blue | 1.00 | .75 |
| 311 | A56 | 1.50p dull vio | 3.00 | 2.25 |

Nos. 309-311 (3)

Archbishop Juan Sinforiano Bogarin, first archbishop of Paraguay. For overprints see Nos. 321-322.

### No. 272 Surcharged

No. 272 Surcharged

## 1930

| 312 | A47 | 5c on 7c emer | .20 | .20 |

A57

Habilitado en CINCO

## 1930-39
Typo. Perf. 11½, 12

| 313 | A57 | 10p brown | .50 | .20 |
|---|---|---|---|---|
| 314 | A57 | 10c brn red, bl ('31) | .50 | .20 |
| 315 | A57 | 10p dk bl, pink ('32) | .50 | .20 |
| 316 | A57 | 10p gray brn ('36) | .40 | .20 |
| 317 | A57 | 10p gray ('37) | .40 | .20 |
| 318 | A57 | 10p blue ('39) | .40 | .20 |

Nos. 313-318 (6)
2.50 1.20

1st Paraguayan postage stamp, 60th anniv. For overprint see No. L31.

Gunboat "Humaitá" — A58

## 1931

| 319 | A58 | 1.50p purple | .40 | .25 |

Perf. 12

Nos. 319, C39-C53 (16)
6.40 6.10

Constitution, 60th anniv. For overprint see No. L33.

View of San Bernardino — A59

## 1931, Aug.

| 320 | A59 | 1p light green | .25 | .20 |

Founding of San Bernardino, 50th anniv. For overprint see No. L32.

Nos. 309-310 Overprinted in Blue or Red

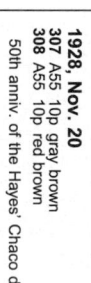

## 1931, Dec. 31

| 321 | A56 | 1.50p lake (Bl) | 1.00 | 1.00 |
|---|---|---|---|---|
| 322 | A56 | 1.50p turq blue (R) | 1.00 | 1.00 |

Map of the Gran Chaco — A60

## 1932-35
Typo. Perf. 12

| 323 | A60 | 1.50p deep violet | .20 | .20 |
|---|---|---|---|---|
| 324 | A60 | 1.50p rose ('35) | .20 | .20 |

For overprints see Nos. L34-L36, O97.

### Nos. C74-C78 Surcharged

CORREOS 1 PESO FELIZ AÑO NUEVO 1933

## 1933
Litho.

| 325 | AP18 | 50c on 4p ultra | .25 | .20 |
|---|---|---|---|---|
| 326 | AP18 | 1p on 8p red | .50 | .40 |
| 327 | AP18 | 1.50p on 12p bl grm | .50 | .40 |

Carlos Antonio López — A65

José Eduvigis Díaz — A66

Oratory of the Virgin, Asunción — A64

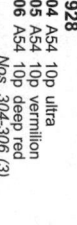

Monstrance A62

Arms of Asunción A63

## 1937, Aug.
Unwmk. Perf. 11½

| 338 | A62 | 1p brn, yel & red | .20 | .20 |
|---|---|---|---|---|
| 339 | A62 | 3p dk blue, yel & red | .20 | .20 |
| 340 | A62 | 10p blue & red | .60 | .60 |

Nos. 338-340 (3)

1st Nat. Eucharistic Congress, Asuncion.

## 1937, Aug.

| 341 | A63 | 50c violet & buff | .20 | .20 |
|---|---|---|---|---|
| 342 | A63 | 1p bis & lt grn | .20 | .20 |
| 343 | A63 | 3p red & lt bl | .20 | .20 |
| 344 | A63 | 10p car rose & red | .30 | .30 |
| 345 | A63 | 20p blue & drab | .30 | .30 |

Nos. 341-345 (5)
1.50 1.00

Founding of Asuncion, 400th anniv.

## 1938-39
Typo. Perf. 11, 12

| 346 | A64 | 5p olive green | .30 | .20 |
|---|---|---|---|---|
| 347 | A64 | 5p pale rose ('39) | .40 | .20 |
| 348 | A61 | 11p violet brwn | 1.00 | .25 |

Nos. 346-348 (3)
.55

Founding of Asuncion, 400th anniv.

### Flag of the Race Issue
Flag with Three Crosses; Caravels of Columbus — A61

## 1933, Oct. 10
Litho. Perf. 11

| 328 | AP18 | 2p on 16p dk vio | .50 | .40 |
|---|---|---|---|---|
| 329 | AP18 | 5p on 20p org brn | 1.10 | .30 |

Nos. 325-329 (5)
2.85 2.30

| 330 | A61 | 10c multicolored | .30 | .20 |
|---|---|---|---|---|
| 331 | A61 | 20c multicolored | .30 | .20 |
| 332 | A61 | 50c multicolored | .30 | .20 |
| 333 | A61 | 1p multicolored | .30 | .20 |
| 334 | A61 | 1.50p multicolored | .30 | .20 |
| 335 | A61 | 5p multicolored | .60 | .25 |
| 336 | A61 | 10p multicolored | .60 | .50 |
| 337 | A61 | 10p multicolored | .60 | .50 |

Nos. 330-337 (8)
3.30 2.25

441st anniv. of the sailing of Christopher Columbus from the port of Palos, Aug. 3, 1492, on his first voyage to the New World. Nos. 332, 334 and 335 exist with Maltese crosses omitted.

Arms of Irala — A95

Domingo Martinez de Irala and His Vision — A94

**1942, Aug. 15**    **Engr.**    **Perf. 12**
| | | | |
|---|---|---|---|
| 395 | A93 | 2p green | 65 | .30 |
| 396 | A94 | 5p rose | 65 | .30 |
| 397 | A95 | 7p sapphire | 9.45 | 5.90 |

*Nos. 395-397, C131-C133 (6)*

400th anniversary of Asuncion.

Pres. Higinio Morinigo, Scenes of Industry & Agriculture A96

**1943, Aug. 15**    **Unwmk.**
| | | | |
|---|---|---|---|
| 398 | A96 | 7p blue | .20 | .20 |

For surcharges see Nos. 404, 428.

**1943, Aug. 15**
| | | | |
|---|---|---|---|
| 399 | A97 | 50c violet | .20 | .20 |
| 400 | A97 | 1p gray brn | .20 | .20 |
| 401 | A97 | 5p dark grn | .50 | .20 |
| 402 | A97 | 7p brt ultra | .25 | .20 |

*Nos. 399-402 (4)*    1.15 | .80

Discovery of America, 450th anniv.

For surcharges see Nos. 405, 429.

Christopher Columbus A97

No. 296 Surcharged in Black

**1944**    **Perf. 12, 11, 11½, 11x12**
| | | | |
|---|---|---|---|
| 403 | A51 | 1c on 3p brt vio | .20 | .20 |

Nos. 398 and 402 Surcharged "1944 / 5 Centimos 5" in Red

**1944**    **Perf. 12**
| | | | |
|---|---|---|---|
| 404 | A96 | 5c on 7p blue | .20 | .20 |
| 405 | A97 | 5c on 7p brt ultra | .20 | .20 |

Imperforates Starting with No. 406, many Paraguayan stamps exist imperf.

Primitive Postal Service among Indians — A98

---

**1940, Aug. 15**    **Photo.**    **Perf. 13½**
| | | | |
|---|---|---|---|
| 378 | A86 | 1p aqua & brt red vio | .50 | .25 |
| 379 | A87 | 5p dp yel grn & red brn | .65 | .65 |
| 380 | A86 | 6p org brn & ultra | 1.50 | 1.00 |
| 381 | A86 | 10p ver & black | 4.15 | 2.20 |

*Nos. 378-381 (4)*

Postage stamp centenary.

Dr. José Francia A90    A91

**1940, Sept. 20**    **Engr.**    **Perf. 12**
| | | | |
|---|---|---|---|
| 382 | A90 | 50c carmine rose | .20 | .20 |
| 383 | A91 | 50c plum | .20 | .20 |
| 384 | A90 | 1p bright green | .20 | .20 |
| 385 | A91 | 5p deep blue | .80 | .80 |

*Nos. 382-385 (4)*

Centenary of the death of Dr. Jose Francia (1766-1840), dictator of Paraguay, 1814-1840.

No. 366 Surcharged In Black

**1940, Sept. 7**    **Perf. 12½**
| | | | |
|---|---|---|---|
| 386 | A77 | 5p on 50c dp org | .20 | .20 |

In honor of Pres. Jose F. Estigarribia who died in a plane crash Sept. 7, 1940.

**Visita al Paraguay Agosto de 1941**

No. 360 Overprinted in Black

**1941, Aug.**    **Perf. 12**
| | | | |
|---|---|---|---|
| 387 | A70 | 6p multi | .20 | .20 |

Visit to Paraguay of Pres. Vargas of Brazil.

Nos. C113-C115 Overprinted "HABILITADO" and Bars in Blue or Red

**1942, Jan. 17**    **Perf. 12½**
| | | | |
|---|---|---|---|
| 388 | A69 | 1p multi (Bl) | .20 | .20 |
| 389 | A69 | 3p multi (R) | .20 | .20 |
| 390 | A70 | 5p multi (R) | .60 | .60 |

*Nos. 388-390 (3)*

Coat of Arms — A92

**1942-43**    **Litho.**    **Perf. 11, 12, 11x12**
| | | | |
|---|---|---|---|
| 391 | A92 | 1p light green | .20 | .20 |
| 392 | A92 | 4p orange ('43) | .30 | .30 |
| 393 | A92 | 7p light blue | .20 | .20 |
| 394 | A92 | 7p yel brn ('43) | .80 | .80 |

*Nos. 391-394 (4)*

Nos. 391-394 exist imperf.

The Indian Francisco — A93

---

Cowboys — A79

Plowing — A80

Design: 5p, Pres. Carlos Antonio Lopez (1790-1862) and Gen. José Eduvigis Diaz in the National Pantheon, Asuncion.

Oxcart A82

View of Paraguay River — A81

Pasture A83

Pirareta Falls — A84

**Perf. 12½**
| | | | |
|---|---|---|---|
| 366 | A77 | 50c deep orange | .20 | .20 |
| 367 | A78 | 1p brt red violet | .20 | .20 |
| 368 | A79 | 3p bright green | .20 | .20 |
| 369 | A80 | 5p chestnut | .20 | .20 |
| 370 | A81 | 10p magenta | .20 | .30 |
| 371 | A82 | 20p violet | .40 | .30 |
| 372 | A83 | 50p cobalt blue | .90 | .45 |
| 373 | A84 | 100p black | 1.90 | 1.40 |

*Nos. 366-373 (8)*    4.20 | 3.15

**1940, Jan. 1**    **Photo.**

Second Buenos Aires Peace Conference. For surcharge see No. 386.

Map of the Americas — A85

**1940, May**    **Engr.**    **Perf. 12**
| | | | |
|---|---|---|---|
| 374 | A85 | 50c red orange | .20 | .20 |
| 375 | A85 | 1p green | .30 | .30 |
| 376 | A85 | 5p dark blue | .75 | .50 |
| 377 | A85 | 10p brown | 4.85 | 3.75 |

*Nos. 374-377, C127-C130 (8)*

Pan American Union, 50th anniversary.

Sir Rowland Hill — A87

Reproduction of Type A1 — A86

Designs: 6p, Type A2. 10p, Type A3.

---

**1939**    **Perf. 12**
| | | | |
|---|---|---|---|
| 349 | A65 | 2p lt ultra & pale brn | .30 | .20 |
| 350 | A66 | 2p lt ultra & brn | .30 | .20 |

Reburial of ashes of Pres. Carlos Antonio Lopez (1790-1862) and Gen. José Eduvigis Diaz in the National Pantheon, Asuncion.

Pres. Patricio Escobar and Ramon Zubizarreta A67

**1939-40**    **Litho.**    **Perf. 11½**

**Heads in Black**
| | | | |
|---|---|---|---|
| 351 | A67 | 50c dull org ('40) | .20 | .20 |
| 352 | A67 | 1p violet ('40) | .20 | .20 |
| 353 | A67 | 2p red brown ('40) | .25 | .25 |
| 354 | A67 | 5p ultra | .25 | .20 |

*Nos. 351-354, C122-C123, O99-O104 (12)*    9.40 | 9.30

Founding of the University of Asuncion, 50th anniv.

Varieties of this issue include inverted heads (50c, 1p, 2p); doubled heads; Caballero and Decoud heads in 50c frame: imperforates and part-perforates. Copies with inverted heads were not officially issued.

Coats of Arms — A69

Pres. Baldomir of Uruguay, Flags of Paraguay, Uruguay A70

**1939**    **Engr.; Flags Litho.**    **Perf. 12**

**Flags in National Colors**
| | | | |
|---|---|---|---|
| 355 | A69 | 50c violet blue | .20 | .20 |
| 356 | A70 | 1p olive | .20 | .20 |
| 357 | A70 | 2p blue green | .20 | .25 |
| 358 | A70 | 3p sepia | .20 | .25 |
| 359 | A70 | 5p orange | .25 | .40 |
| 360 | A70 | 6p dull violet | .50 | .40 |
| 361 | A70 | 10p bister brn | .40 | .25 |

*Nos. 355-361, C113-C121 (16)*    14.95 | 10.45

Designs: 2p, Pres. Benavides, Peru. 3p, US Eagle and Shield. 5p, Pres. Alessandri, Chile. 6p, Pres. Vargas, Brazil. 10p, Pres. Ortiz, Argentina.

First Buenos Aires Peace Conference. For overprint & surcharge see #387, B10.

Coats of Arms of New York and Asuncion A76

**1939, Nov. 30**
| | | | |
|---|---|---|---|
| 362 | A76 | 5p scarlet | .20 | .20 |
| 363 | A76 | 10p deep blue | .30 | .30 |
| 364 | A76 | 11p dk blue grn | .40 | .30 |
| 365 | A76 | 22p olive blk | .50 | .40 |

*Nos. 362-365, C124-C126 (7)*    9.55 | 8.85

New York World's Fair.

Paraguayan Soldier — A77

Paraguayan Woman — A78

Ruins of Humaitá Church — A99

Locomotive of early Paraguayan Railroad — A100

Early Merchant Ship — A102

Marshal Francisco S. Lopez — A101

Port of Asunción — A103

Birthplace of Paraguay's Liberation — A104

Monument to Heroes of Itororó — A105

**1945**
414 A101 5c on 7c light blue .20 .20

No. 409 Surcharged in Red

**1944-45** **Unwmk.** **Engr.** **Perf. 12½**
| | | | |
|---|---|---|---|
| 406 | A98 | 1c black | .20 .20 |
| 407 | A99 | 2c copper brn ('45) | .20 .20 |
| 408 | A100 | 5c light olive | 1.00 .20 |
| 409 | A101 | 7c light blue ('45) | .40 .25 |
| 410 | A102 | 10c green ('45) | .50 .25 |
| 411 | A103 | 15c dark blue ('45) | .50 .30 |
| 412 | A104 | 50c black brown | .65 .30 |
| 413 | A105 | 1g dk rose car ('45) | 1.90 .40 |

Nos. 406-413 (8) 5.35 1.00
Nos. 406-413/8) 16.85 13.95

See Nos. 406-413,C134-C146, C158-C162.
For surcharges see #414, 427.

Designs: 3c, Venezuela Flag, 5c, Colombia Flag. 2g, Peru Flag.

Handshake, Map and Flags of Paraguay and Panama A106

Engr.; Flags Litho. in Natl. Colors
**1945, Aug. 15** **Unwmk.** **Perf. 12½**
| | | | |
|---|---|---|---|
| 415 | A106 | 1c dark green | .20 .20 |
| 416 | A106 | 3c lake | .20 .20 |
| 417 | A106 | 5c blue blk | .20 .20 |
| 418 | A106 | 2g brown | 1.10 .75 |

Nos. 415-418,C147-C153 (11) 8.30 7.95
Goodwill visits of Pres. Higinio Morinigo during 1943.

Nos. B6 to B9 Surcharged "1945" and New Value in Black

**1945** **Engr.** **Perf. 12**
| | | | |
|---|---|---|---|
| 419 | A96 | 2c on + 3p red brn | .20 .20 |
| 420 | A97 | 2c on + 3p purple | .20 .20 |
| 421 | SP4 | 2c on + 3p car rose | .20 .20 |
| 422 | SP4 | 2c on + 3p saph | .20 .20 |
| 423 | SP4 | 5c on + 3p red brn | .20 .20 |
| 424 | SP4 | 5c on + 3p purple | .20 .20 |
| 425 | SP4 | 5c on + 3p car rose | .20 .20 |
| 426 | SP4 | 5c on + 3p saph | .20 .20 |

Nos. 419-426 (8) 1.60 1.60

Similar Surcharge in Red on Nos. 409, 398 and 402
| | | | |
|---|---|---|---|
| 427 | A101 | 7c lt blue | .20 .20 |
| 428 | A96 | 5c on 7p purple | .20 .20 |
| 429 | A97 | 5c on 7p brt ultra | .60 .60 |

Nos. 427-429 (3)
Nos. 427-429 exist with black surcharge.

Catalogue values for unused stamps in this section, from this point to the end of the section, are for Never Hinged items.

Monument to Antequera A112

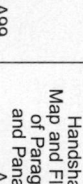

**1946, Sept. 21** **Engr.** **Perf. 12½**
| | | | |
|---|---|---|---|
| 435 | A102 | 1c rose car | .20 .20 |
| 436 | A111 | 2c purple | .20 .20 |
| 437 | A98 | 5c ultra | .20 .20 |
| 438 | A112 | 10c org yel | .20 .20 |
| 439 | A105 | 15c org olive | .25 .20 |
| 440 | A113 | 50c deep grn | .35 .20 |
| 441 | A104 | 1g brt ultra | 2.00 1.60 |

Nos. 435-441 (7) .65 .40

See Nos. C135-C138, C143.

Coat of Arms ("U.P.U." at bottom) — A110

**1946** **Litho.** **Perf. 11, 12, 11x12**
430 A110 5c gray .20 .20

See Nos. 459-463, 478-480, 498-506, 525-536, 646-658.
For overprints see Nos. 464-466.

Nos. B6 to B9 Surcharged "1946" and New Value in Black

**1946** **Perf. 12**
| | | | |
|---|---|---|---|
| 431 | SP4 | 5c on 7p red brn | .40 .30 |
| 432 | SP4 | 5c on 7p purple | .40 .30 |
| 433 | SP4 | 5c on 7p car rose | .40 .30 |
| 434 | SP4 | 5c on 7p saph | 1.60 1.20 |

Nos. 431-434 (4)

First Telegraph in South America A111

Types of 1944-45 and

Colonial Jesuit Altar — A113

Marshal Francisco Solano Lopez — A114

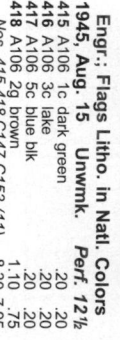

**1947, May 15** **Perf. 12**
| | | | |
|---|---|---|---|
| 442 | A114 | 1c purple | .20 .20 |
| 443 | A114 | 2c org red | .20 .20 |
| 444 | A114 | 5c green | .20 .20 |
| 445 | A114 | 15c ultra | .65 .65 |
| 446 | A114 | 50c dark grn | .65 .65 |

Nos. 442-446,C163-C167 (10) 7.40 7.40

Juan Sinforiano Bogarin, Archbishop of Asunción — A115

Projected Monument of the Sacred Heart of Jesus — A117

Archbishopric Coat of Arms — A116

Monument to Antequera A112

"Political Enlightenment" A119

C. A. Lopez, J. N. Gonzalez and Freighter Paraguari A120

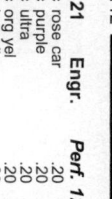

**1948, Sept. 11** **Engr. & Litho.**
| | | | |
|---|---|---|---|
| 451 | A119 | 5c car red & bl | .20 .20 |
| 452 | A119 | 15c red org, red & bl | .20 .20 |

Nos. 451-452,C176-C177 (4) 6.30 4.30

Issued to honor the Barefeet, a political group.

**1949** **Litho.**
Centers in Carmine, Black, Ultramarine and Blue
| | | | |
|---|---|---|---|
| 453 | A120 | 2c orange | .20 .20 |
| 454 | A120 | 5c car | .20 .20 |
| 455 | A120 | 10c violet | .20 .20 |
| 456 | A120 | 15c violet | .25 .20 |
| 457 | A120 | 50c blue grn | .25 .20 |
| 458 | A120 | 1g dull vio brn | 1.35 1.25 |

Nos. 453-458 (6)

Paraguay's merchant fleet centenary.

**1950** **Unwmk.** **Perf. 10½**
| | | | |
|---|---|---|---|
| 459 | A110 | 5c red | .20 .20 |
| 460 | A110 | 10c blue vio | .20 .20 |
| 461 | A110 | 15c black | .20 .20 |
| 462 | A110 | 50c blue lilac | .20 .20 |
| 457 | A110 | 1g pale violet | .20 .20 |

Type of 1946

**1951** **Coarse Impression**
463 A110 30c green .20 .20

Nos. 459-463 (5) 1.00 1.00

Colonial Jesuit Altar — A113

**1946** **Unwmk.** **Engr.** **Perf. 12½**
GUARANI 1

**1946** Types of 1944-45 and New Value in Black

Vision of Projected Monument A118

**1948, Jan. 6** **Engr.** **Perf. 12½**
| | | | |
|---|---|---|---|
| 447 | A115 | 2c dark blue | .20 .20 |
| 448 | A116 | 5c deep car | .20 .20 |
| 449 | A117 | 10c gray blk | .35 .25 |
| 450 | A118 | 15c green | 9.85 9.75 |

Nos. 447-450,C168-C175 (12)

Archbishopric of Asunción, 50th anniv.

Illustration reduced one-half.

**1951, Apr. 18**
| | | | |
|---|---|---|---|
| 464 | A110 | 5c red (Bk) block | .75 .75 |
| 465 | A110 | 10c blue (R) block | 1.25 1.25 |
| 466 | A110 | 30c green (V) block | 2.00 2.00 |

Nos. 464-466 (3) 4.00 4.00

Blocks of Four of Nos. 459, 460 and 463 Overprinted in Various Colors

PRIMER CONGRESO
DE ENTIDADES ECONOMICAS DEL PARAGUAY
18 — 17 — 1951

1st Economic Cong. of Paraguay, 4/18/51.

Columbus Lighthouse — A121

**1952, Feb. 11** **Perf. 10**
| | | | |
|---|---|---|---|
| 467 | A121 | 2c org brn | .20 .20 |
| 468 | A121 | 5c light ultra | .20 .20 |
| 469 | A121 | 10c rose | .20 .20 |
| 470 | A121 | 15c light blue | .20 .20 |
| 471 | A121 | 20c lilac | .20 .20 |

**1960, Mar. 18 Photo. Perf. 12½**
| | | | | |
|---|---|---|---|---|
| 556 | A131 | 30c brt red & bl grn | .20 | .20 |
| 557 | A131 | 50c plum & bl | .20 | .20 |
| 558 | A131 | 75c ol grn & org | .20 | .20 |
| 559 | A131 | 1.50g dk vio & bl grn | 1.60 | 1.60 |

Nos. 556-559,C262-C264 (7)

Olympic Games of 1960.

**1960, Apr. 7 Litho. Perf. 11**
| | | | | |
|---|---|---|---|---|
| 560 | A132 | 25c sal & yel grn | .60 | .20 |
| 561 | A132 | 50c lt yel grn & red org | .60 | .20 |
| 562 | A132 | 70c lt brn & lil rose | .75 | .20 |
| 563 | A131 | 1.50g lt bl & ultra | .75 | .20 |
| 564 | A132 | 3g gray & bis brn | 1.40 | .45 |

Nos. 560-564,C265-C268 (9) 9.90 4.55

World Refugee Year, July 1, 1959-June 30, 1960 (1st issue).

UN Emblem and Dove — A133

Flags of UN and Paraguay and UN Emblem A134

UN Declaration of Human Rights: 3g, Hand holding scales. 6g, Hands breaking chains. 20g, Flame.

**1960, Apr. 21 Perf. 12½x13**
| | | | | |
|---|---|---|---|---|
| 565 | A133 | 1g dk car & bl | .30 | .20 |
| 566 | A133 | 3g blue & org | .30 | .20 |
| 567 | A133 | 6g gray grn & sal | .40 | .20 |
| 568 | A133 | 20g ver & yel | .55 | .25 |

Nos. 565-568,C269-C271 (†) 2.05

Miniature sheets exist, perf. and imperf., containing one each of Nos. 565-568, all printed in purple and orange.

15th anniversary of the United Nations.

**1960, Oct. 24 Perf. 13x13½ Photo. Unwmk.**
| | | | | |
|---|---|---|---|---|
| 569 | A134 | 30c lt bl, red & bl | .20 | .20 |
| 570 | A134 | 75c yel, rod & bl | .20 | .20 |
| 571 | A134 | 00c pale lil, red & bl | 1.00 | 1.00 |

Nos. 569-571,C272-C273 (5)

Truck Carrying Logs — A136

International Bridge, Arms of Brazil, Paraguay — A135

**1961, Jan. 26 Litho. Perf. 14**
| | | | | |
|---|---|---|---|---|
| 572 | A135 | 15c green | .20 | .20 |
| 573 | A135 | 30c dull blue | .20 | .20 |
| 574 | A135 | 50c orange | .20 | .20 |
| 575 | A135 | 75c vio blue | .20 | .20 |
| 576 | A135 | 1g violet | 2.90 | 2.70 |

Nos. 572-576,C274-C277 (9)

Inauguration of the International Bridge between Paraguay and Brazil.

**1961, Apr. 10 Unwmk. Photo. Perf. 13**
| | | | | |
|---|---|---|---|---|
| 577 | A136 | 25c yel grn & rose car | .20 | .20 |
| 578 | A136 | 90c blue & yel | .20 | .20 |
| 579 | A136 | 1g car rose & grn | .20 | .20 |
| 580 | A136 | 5g lilac & emer | .20 | .20 |
| 581 | A136 | 6g violet | 3.30 | 2.95 |

Nos. 577-581,C278-C281 (9)

Paraguay's progress, "Paraguay en Marcha."

---

1.50g, St. Ignatius and San Ignacio Monastery.

**1958, Mar. 15 Wmk. 319 Litho. Perf. 11**
| | | | | |
|---|---|---|---|---|
| 520 | A128 | 5c dk red brn | .20 | .20 |
| 521 | A129 | 50c lt bl grn | .20 | .20 |
| 522 | AP91 | 1.50g brt vio | .20 | .20 |
| 523 | A128 | 3g light brn | .20 | .20 |
| 524 | A129 | 6.25g rose car | 1.00 | 1.00 |

Nos. 520-524 (5)

St. Ignatius of Loyola (1491-1556). See Nos. 935-935.

**Arms Type of 1946**
**1958-64 Litho. Perf. 10, 11**
| | | | | |
|---|---|---|---|---|
| 525 | A110 | 45c gray olive | .20 | .20 |
| 526 | A110 | 50c rose vio | .20 | .20 |
| 527 | A110 | 70c lt brn ('59) | .20 | .20 |
| 527A | A110 | 90c vio blue | .20 | .20 |
| 528 | A110 | 1g violet | .20 | .20 |
| 529 | A110 | 1.50g lilac ('59) | .20 | .20 |
| 529A | A110 | 2g bister ('64) | .20 | .20 |
| 530 | A110 | 3g lt bis ('59) | .20 | .20 |
| 531 | A110 | 3g olive | .20 | .20 |
| 531A | A110 | 4.50g lt ultra ('59) | .20 | .20 |
| 531B | A110 | 5g rose red ('59) | .20 | .25 |
| 532 | A110 | 10g bl grn ('59) | .20 | .20 |
| 533 | A110 | 12.45g yel green | .20 | .20 |
| 534 | A110 | 15g orange | .30 | .20 |
| 535 | A110 | 30g citron | .30 | .30 |
| 536 | A110 | 50g brown red | .40 | .65 |
| | A110 | 100g gray vio | .85 | |

Nos. 525-536 (16) 4.15 3.75

Pres. Alfredo Stroessner A130

**1958, Aug. 15 Wmk. 320 Litho. Perf. 13½**
**Center in Slate**
| | | | | |
|---|---|---|---|---|
| 537 | A130 | 5c sal pink | .20 | .20 |
| 538 | A130 | 10c sal grn | .20 | .20 |
| 539 | A130 | 25c yel grn | .20 | .20 |
| 540 | A130 | 30c light fawn | .20 | .20 |
| 541 | A130 | 50c rose car | .20 | .20 |
| 542 | A130 | 75c light ultra | .20 | .20 |
| 543 | A130 | 1g lt grn | .35 | .25 |
| 544 | A130 | 10g brown | 7.80 | 6.70 |

Nos. 537-544,C246-C251 (14)

Re-election of President General Alfredo Stroessner

Nos. 491-497 Surcharged in Red

---

Santa Maria Cornice — A126

Jesuit Ruins: 20c, Corridor at Trinidad. 2.50g, Tower of Santa Rosa. 5g, San Cosme gate. 15g, Church of Jesus. 25g, Niche at Trinidad.

**1955, June 19 Perf. 12½x12, 12x12½ Engr. Unwmk.**
| | | | | |
|---|---|---|---|---|
| 491 | A125 | 5c org yel | .20 | .20 |
| 492 | A125 | 20c olive bister | .20 | .20 |
| 493 | A126 | 50c lt red brn | .20 | .20 |
| 494 | A126 | 2.50g olive | .20 | .20 |
| 495 | A125 | 2g ocher | .20 | .20 |
| 496 | A125 | 15g blue grn | .45 | .25 |
| 497 | A126 | 25g deep grn | 3.50 | 3.20 |

Nos. 491-497,C225-C232 (15) 3.50 3.20

25th anniv. of the priesthood of Monsignor Rodriguez.
For surcharges see Nos. 545-551.

**Arms Type of 1946**
**1956-58 Perf. 10, 11 (No. 500) Unwmk.**
| | | | | |
|---|---|---|---|---|
| 498 | A110 | 5c brown ('57) | .20 | .20 |
| 499 | A110 | 30c red brn ('57) | .20 | .20 |
| 500 | A110 | 45c gray olive | .20 | .20 |
| 500A | A110 | 90c lt vio bl | .20 | .20 |
| 501 | A110 | 2g ocher | .20 | .20 |
| 502 | A110 | 2.20g lil rose | .20 | .20 |
| 503 | A110 | 3g ol bis ('58) | .20 | .20 |
| 503A | A110 | 4.20g emer ('57) | .20 | .20 |
| 504 | A110 | 5g ver ('57) | .20 | .20 |
| 505 | A110 | 10g lt grn ('57) | .20 | .20 |
| 506 | A110 | 20g blue ('57) | 2.30 | 2.20 |

Nos. 498-506 (11)

No. 500A exists with four-line, carmine overprint: "DIA N. UNIDAS 24 Octubre 1945-1956". It was not regularly issued and no decree authorizing it is known.

Soldiers, Angel and Asuncion Cathedral — A127

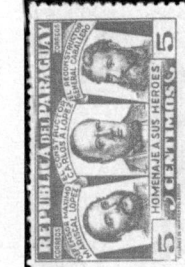

**1957, June 12 Perf. 13½ Photo. Unwmk.**
**Granite Paper**
**Flags in Red and Blue**
| | | | | |
|---|---|---|---|---|
| 508 | A127 | 5c bl grn | .20 | .20 |
| 509 | A127 | 10c carmine | .20 | .20 |
| 510 | A127 | 15c ultra | .20 | .20 |
| 511 | A127 | 20c dp claret | .20 | .20 |
| 512 | A127 | 25c gray blk | .20 | .20 |
| 513 | A127 | 30c lt bluo | .20 | .20 |
| 514 | A127 | 40c gray blk | .20 | .20 |
| 515 | A127 | 50c dark car | .20 | .20 |
| 516 | A127 | 1g bluish grn | .20 | .20 |
| 517 | A127 | 1.30g ultra | .20 | .40 |
| 518 | A127 | 1.50g dp claret | .40 | .40 |
| 519 | A127 | 2g claret | 2.40 | 2.40 |

Nos. 508-519 (12)

#513-519, Soldier & nurse in medallion & flags.

Heroes of the Chaco war. See #C233-C245.

Goalkeeper Catching Soccer Ball — A131

WRY Emblem — A132

Blessed Roque Gonzales and St. Ignatius A129

Statue of St. Ignatius (Guarani Carving) — A128

---

| | | | | |
|---|---|---|---|---|
| 472 | A121 | 50c orange | .20 | .20 |
| 473 | A121 | 1g bluish grn | 1.40 | 1.40 |

Nos. 467-473 (7)

Silvio Pettirossi, Aviator — A122

**1954, Mar. Litho. Perf. 10**
| | | | | |
|---|---|---|---|---|
| 474 | A122 | 5c blue | .30 | .20 |
| 475 | A122 | 20c rose pink | .30 | .20 |
| 476 | A122 | 50c vio brn | .30 | .20 |
| 477 | A122 | 60c lt vio | 2.45 | 1.65 |

Nos. 474-477,C201-C204 (8)

**Arms Type of 1946**
**1954 Perf. 11**
| | | | | |
|---|---|---|---|---|
| 478 | A110 | 10c vermilion | .20 | .20 |

**Perf. 10**
| | | | | |
|---|---|---|---|---|
| 478A | A110 | 10c ver, redrawn | .20 | .20 |
| 479 | A110 | 10g orange | .25 | .20 |
| 480 | A110 | 50g vio brn | 1.75 | 1.40 |

Nos. 478-480 (4) 2.40 2.00

No. 478A measures 20½x24mm, has 5 frame lines at left and 6 at right. No. 478 measures 20x24½mm, has 6 frame lines at left and 5 at right.

Three National Heroes — A123

**1954, Aug. 15 Litho.**
| | | | | |
|---|---|---|---|---|
| 481 | A123 | 5c light vio | .25 | .20 |
| 482 | A123 | 10c light blue | .25 | .20 |
| 483 | A123 | 50c rose pink | .25 | .20 |
| 484 | A123 | 1g org brn | .25 | .20 |
| 485 | A123 | 2g blue grn | .25 | .20 |

Nos. 481-485,C216-C220 (10) 10.25 9.80

Marshal Francisco S. Lopez, Pres. Carlos A Lopez and Gen. Bernardino Caballero.

Pres. Alfredo Stroessner and Pres. Juan D. Peron — A124

**1955, Apr. Wmk. 90 Perf. 13x13½**
**Photo. & Litho.**
| | | | | |
|---|---|---|---|---|
| 486 | A124 | 5c multicolored | .25 | .20 |
| 487 | A124 | 10c multicolored | .25 | .20 |
| 488 | A124 | 50c multicolored | .25 | .20 |
| 489 | A124 | 1.30g multicolored | .35 | .25 |
| 490 | A124 | 2.20g multicolored | 2.20 | 1.85 |

Nos. 486-490,C221-C224 (9)

Visit of Pres. Juan D. Peron of Argentina.

Jesuit Ruins, Trinidad Belfry A125

**P. J. Caballero, José G. R. Francia, F. Yegros, Revolutionary Leaders — A137**

**1961, May 16    Litho.    Perf. 14½**
| | | | |
|---|---|---|---|
| 582 | A137 | 30c green | .20 .20 |
| 583 | A137 | 30c lil rose | .20 .20 |
| 584 | A137 | 90c violet | .20 .20 |
| 585 | A137 | 1.50g Prus bl | .20 .20 |
| 586 | A137 | 3g olive bis | .20 .20 |
| 587 | A137 | 4g ultra | .20 .20 |
| 588 | A137 | 5g brown | .20 .20 |

Nos. 582-588,C282-C287 (13)   5.00  4.50
150th anniv. of Independence (1st issue).

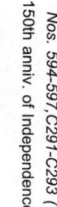

**"Chaco Peace" — A138**

**Puma — A139**

**1961, June 12    Perf. 14x14½**
| | | | |
|---|---|---|---|
| 589 | A138 | 25c vermilion | .20 .20 |
| 590 | A138 | 30c green | .20 .20 |
| 591 | A138 | 50c red brn | .20 .20 |
| 592 | A138 | 1g bright vio | .20 .20 |
| 593 | A138 | 2g dk bl gray | .20 .20 |

Nos. 589-593,C288-C290 (8)   3.90  3.55
Chaco Peace; 150th anniv. of Independence (2nd issue).

**1961, Aug. 16    Unwmk.    Perf. 14**
| | | | |
|---|---|---|---|
| 594 | A139 | 75c dull vio | .50 .20 |
| 595 | A139 | 1.50g brown | .50 .20 |
| 596 | A139 | 4.50g green | .50 .25 |
| 597 | A139 | 10g Prus blue | .50 .25 |

Nos. 594-597,C291-C293 (7)   7.75  5.35
150th anniv. of Independence (3rd issue).

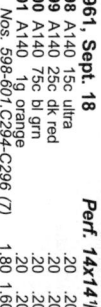

**University Seal — A140**

**1961, Sept. 18    Perf. 15**
| | | | |
|---|---|---|---|
| 598 | A140 | 15c ultra | .20 .20 |
| 599 | A140 | 25c dk red | .20 .20 |
| 600 | A140 | 75c bl grn | .20 .20 |
| 601 | A140 | 1g orange | .20 .20 |

Nos. 598-601,C294-C296 (7)   1.80  1.60
Founding of the Catholic University in Asuncion; 150th anniv. of Independence (4th issue).

**Hotel Guarani A141**

**1961, Oct. 14    Litho.    Perf. 15**
| | | | |
|---|---|---|---|
| 602 | A141 | 50c slate bl | .20 .20 |
| 603 | A141 | 1g green | .20 .20 |
| 604 | A141 | 4.50g lilac | 1.60 1.60 |

Nos. 602-604,C297-C300 (7)   1.60  1.60
Opening of the Hotel Guarani; 150th anniv. of Independence (5th issue).

**Tennis Racket and Balls in Flag Colors — A142**

**1961, Oct. 16    Litho.    Perf. 11**
| | | | |
|---|---|---|---|
| 605 | A142 | 35c multi | .20 .20 |
| 606 | A142 | 75c multi | .20 .20 |
| 607 | A142 | 1.50g multi | .20 .20 |
| 608 | A142 | 2.25g multi | .20 .20 |
| 609 | A142 | 4g multi | 1.00 1.00 |

Nos. 605-609 (5)
28th South American Tennis Championships, Asuncion, Oct. 15-23 (1st issue). Imperforates exist in changed colors as well as two imperf. souvenir sheets with stamps in changed colors. Values: stamps, set $6; souvenir sheets, pair $30.

**Alan B. Shepard, First US Astronaut A143**

**1961, Dec. 22    Litho.    Perf. 11**
| | | | |
|---|---|---|---|
| 610 | A143 | 10c blue & brown | .25 .20 |
| 611 | A143 | 25c blue & car rose | .25 .20 |
| 612 | A143 | 50c blue & yel | .25 .20 |
| 613 | A143 | 75c blue & green | .25 .20 |
| 614 | A143 | 18.15g green & blue | 8.00 5.00 |
| 615 | A143 | 36g orange & blue | 8.00 5.00 |
| 616 | A143 | 50g car rose & blue | 11.00 7.50 |
| a. | | Souvenir sheet of 1 | 30.00 |

Nos. 610-616 (7)   28.00  18.30
18.15g, 36g, 50g, Shepard, Saturn, horiz.
Also exist imperf in different colors. Value, set $30; souvenir sheet $160.
Nos. 614-616a are airmail.

**Uprooted Oak Emblem — A145**

**1961, Dec. 30    Unwmk.    Perf. 11**
| | | | |
|---|---|---|---|
| 619 | A145 | 10c ultra & lt bl | .20 .20 |
| 620 | A145 | 15c maroon & org | .20 .20 |
| 621 | A145 | 25c car rose & pink | .20 .20 |
| 622 | A145 | 75c dk bl & yel grn | .80 .80 |

Nos. 619-622 (4)
World Refugee Year, 1959-60 (2nd issue). Imperforates in changed colors and souvenir sheets exist. Some specialists question the status of this issue. See Nos. C307-C309.

**Europa A146**

**1961, Dec. 31**
| | | | |
|---|---|---|---|
| 623 | A146 | 50c multicolored | .20 .20 |
| 624 | A146 | 75c multicolored | .30 .20 |
| 625 | A146 | 1g multicolored | .30 .20 |

Design: 20g, 50g, Dove.

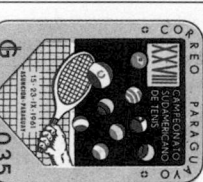

| | | | |
|---|---|---|---|
| 626 | A146 | 1.50g multicolored | .30 .20 |
| 627 | A146 | 4.50g multicolored | .75 .70 |
| a. | | Souvenir sheet of 5, #623-627 | |
| 628 | A146 | 20g multicolored | 17.50 |
| 629 | A146 | 50g multicolored | 15.00 |
| a. | | Souvenir sheet of 1 | 70.00 |

Nos. 623-629 (7)   31.95  1.50
Nos. 628-629 are airmail.

**Tennis Player — A147**

**1962, Jan. 5    Perf. 15x14½**
| | | | |
|---|---|---|---|
| 630 | A147 | 35c Prussian bl | .55 .20 |
| 631 | A147 | 75c dark vio | .55 .20 |
| 632 | A147 | 1.50g red brn | .55 .20 |
| 633 | A147 | 2.25g emerald | .55 .20 |
| 634 | A147 | 4g carmine | .55 .20 |
| 635 | A147 | 12.45g red lil | 1.10 .40 |
| 636 | A147 | 20g org brn | 1.60 .65 |
| 637 | A147 | 50g org brn | 6.00 2.25 |

Nos. 630-637 (8)
28th South American Tennis Championships, 1961 (2nd issue) and the 150th anniv. of Independence (6th issue). Nos. 634-637 are airmail.

**Scout Bugler — A148**

**Lord Baden-Powell A148a**

**1962, Feb. 6    Perf. 11**
*Olive Green Center*
| | | | |
|---|---|---|---|
| 638 | A148 | 10c dp magenta | .20 .20 |
| 639 | A148 | 20c red orange | .20 .20 |
| 640 | A148 | 25c dk brown | .20 .20 |
| 641 | A148 | 30c emerald | .20 .20 |
| 642 | A148 | 50c indigo | .20 .20 |
| 643 | A148a | 12.45g car rose & bl | 2.75 2.75 |
| 644 | A148a | 36g car rose & emer | 6.45 6.45 |
| 645 | A148a | 50g car rose & org yel | 2.00 2.00 |

Nos. 638-645 (8)
Issued to honor the Boy Scouts. Imperfs in changed colors exist and imperf souvenir sheets exist. Value, set $22, souvenir sheet $70. Some specialists question the status of this issue.
Nos. 643-645 are airmail.

**UN Emblem A150**

**1962, Apr. 23    Perf. 15**
Design: #670-673, UN Headquarters, NYC.
| | | | |
|---|---|---|---|
| 666 | A150 | 50c bister brn | .20 .20 |
| 667 | A150 | 75c dp claret | .20 .20 |
| 668 | A150 | 1g Prussian bl | .20 .20 |
| 669 | A150 | 2g orange brn | .20 .20 |
| 670 | A150 | 12.45g ol dvo | .35 .35 |
| 671 | A150 | 18.15g ol grn | .65 .65 |
| 672 | A150 | 23.40g brn red | 1.10 1.10 |
| 673 | A150 | 30g carmine | 3.85 3.85 |

Nos. 666-673 (8)
UN; Independence, 150th anniv. (8th issue). Nos. 670-673 are airmail.

**Map and Laurel Branch — A149**

**1962, Apr. 14    Perf. 14x14½    Unwmk.**
| | | | |
|---|---|---|---|
| 659 | A149 | 50c ocher | .20 .20 |
| 660 | A149 | 75c vio blue | .20 .20 |
| 661 | A149 | 1g purple | .20 .20 |
| 662 | A149 | 1.50g brt grn | .20 .20 |
| 663 | A149 | 4.50g vermilion | .20 .20 |
| 664 | A149 | 20g lil rose | .60 .60 |
| 665 | A149 | 20g orange | 1.80 1.80 |

Nos. 659-665 (7)
Day of the Americas; 150th anniv. of Independence (7th issue). Nos. 664-665 are airmail.
Design: 20g, 50g, Hands holding globe.

**Arms Type of 1946**

**1962-68    Litho.    Wmk. 347**
| | | | |
|---|---|---|---|
| 646 | A110 | 50c steel bl ('63) | .20 .20 |
| 647 | A110 | 70c dull lil ('63) | .20 .20 |
| 648 | A110 | 15g violet ('63) | .20 .20 |
| 649 | A110 | 3g dp bl ('68) | .20 .20 |
| 650 | A110 | 4.50g redsh brn ('67) | .20 .20 |
| 651 | A110 | 5g lilac ('64) | .20 .20 |
| 652 | A110 | 10g car rose ('63) | .20 .20 |
| 653 | A110 | 12.45g ultra | .20 .20 |
| 654 | A110 | 15.45g org ver | .20 .20 |
| 655 | A110 | 18.15g lilac | .20 .20 |
| 656 | A110 | 20g lt brn ('63) | .20 .20 |
| 657 | A110 | 100g dl red brn ('67) | .70 .40 |
| 658 | A110 | 100g bl gray ('63) | 3.25 2.80 |

Nos. 646-658 (13)

**Malaria Eradication Emblem and Mosquito A151**

**1962, May 23    Perf. 14x13½    Wmk. 346**
| | | | |
|---|---|---|---|
| 674 | A151 | 30c pink, ultra & blk | .20 .20 |
| 675 | A151 | 50c bis, grn & blk | .20 .20 |
| 676 | A151 | 75c rose red, blk & bis | .20 .20 |
| 677 | A151 | 1g brt grn, blk & bis | .20 .20 |
| 678 | A151 | 1.50g dl red brn, blk & bis | .20 .20 |
| 679 | A151 | 3g bl, red & blk | .20 .20 |
| 680 | A151 | 4.50g dl vio | .20 .20 |
| 681 | A151 | 12.45g ol bis, grn & blk | .20 .25 |
| 682 | A151 | 18.15g rose lil, red & blk | .40 .30 |
| 683 | A151 | 36g rose red, vio bl & blk | 1.00 .75 |

Nos. 674-683 (10)   3.00  2.70
WHO drive to eradicate malaria. Imperforates exist in changed colors. Value, $8. Also, two souvenir sheets exist, one containing one copy of No. 683, the other an imperf 36g in blue, red & black. Value, each $20.
Some specialists question the status of this issue.
Nos. 679-683 are airmail.

Stadium — A152

Soccer Players and Globe A152a

**Perf. 13½x14   Litho.   Wmk. 346**
**1962, July 28**
| 684 | A152 | 15c | yel & dk brn | .20 | .20 |
| 685 | A152 | 25c | brt grn & dk brn | .20 | .20 |
| 686 | A152 | 30c | lt vio & dk brn | .20 | .20 |
| 687 | A152 | 40c | dl org & dk brn | .20 | .20 |
| 688 | A152 | 50c | brt yel grn & brn | .20 | .20 |
| 689 | A152a | 12.45g | brt rose, blk & brn | .70 | .35 |
| 690 | A152a | 18.15g | lt red brn, blk & vio | 1.00 | .45 |
| 691 | A152a | 36g | gray grn, blk & brn | 2.25 | .80 |
| | | | Nos. 684-691 (8) | 4.95 | 2.60 |

World Soccer Championships, Chile, May 30–June 17.
Imperfs exist. Value $8. A souvenir sheet containing one No. 691 exists, both perforated and imperf. Value, $20 and $50, respectively. Some specialists question the status of this issue.
Nos. 689-691 are airmail.

Freighter A153

Ship's Wheel — A153a

Designs: Various merchantmen. 44g, Like 12.45g with diagonal colorless band in background.

**Perf. 14½x15   Unwmk.**
**1962, July 31**
| 692 | A153 | 30c | bister brn | .25 | .25 |
| 693 | A153 | 90c | slate bl | .25 | .25 |
| 694 | A153 | 1.50g | brown red | .25 | .25 |
| 695 | A153 | 2g | green | .25 | .25 |
| 696 | A153 | 4.20g | vio blue | .30 | .25 |

**Perf. 15x14½**
| 697 | A153a | 12.45g | dk red | .30 | .25 |
| 698 | A153a | 44g | blue | .60 | .35 |
| | | | Nos. 692-698 (7) | 2.20 | 1.85 |

Issued to honor the merchant marine.
Nos. 697-698 are airmail.

Friendship 7 over South America — A154

Lt. Col. John H. Glenn, Jr., Lt. Cmdr. Scott Carpenter A154a

**Perf. 13½x14   Litho.   Wmk. 346**
**1962, Sept. 4**
| 699 | A154 | 15c | dk bl & bis | .25 | .25 |
| 700 | A154 | 25c | vio brn & bis | .30 | .25 |
| 701 | A154 | 30c | dk sl grn & bis | .30 | .25 |
| 702 | A154 | 40c | dk gray & bis | .30 | .25 |
| 703 | A154 | 50c | dk vio & bis | .30 | .25 |
| 704 | A154 | 12.45g | car lake & gray | .30 | .25 |
| 705 | A154a | 18.15g | red lil & gray | .30 | .45 |
| 706 | A154a | 36g | dl cl & gray | .55 | |
| | | | Nos. 699-706 (8) | 2.65 | 2.20 |

US manned space flights. Imperfs. in changed colors and two souvenir sheets exist. Some specialists question the status of this issue.
Nos. 704-706 are airmail.

Discus Thrower — A155

Olympic flame &: 12.45g, Melbourne, 1956. 18.15g, Rome, 1960. 36g, Tokyo, 1964.

**Litho.**
**1962, Oct. 1**
| 707 | A155 | 15c | blk & yel | .75 | .25 |
| 708 | A155 | 25c | blk & lt grn | .75 | .25 |
| 709 | A155 | 30c | blk & pink | .75 | .25 |
| 710 | A155 | 40c | blk & pale vio | .75 | .25 |
| 711 | A155 | 50c | blk & lt bl | .75 | .25 |
| 712 | A155 | 12.45g | blk grn, lt grn & choc | .85 | .75 |
| 713 | A155 | 18.15g | nl brn, yel & choc | .85 | .75 |
| 714 | A155 | 36g | rose red, pink & choc | 1.50 | 1.00 |
| | | | Nos. 707-714 (8) | 6.95 | 3.75 |

Olympic Games from Amsterdam 1928 to Tokyo 1964. Each stamp is inscribed with date and place of various Olympic Games. Imperfs. in changed colors and two souvenir sheets exist. Some specialists question the status of this issue.
Nos. 712-714 are airmail.

Peace Dove and Cross A156

Dove Symbolizing Holy Ghost — A156a

**Perf. 14½   Litho.**
**1962, Oct. 11   Unwmk.**
| 715 | A156 | 50c | olive | .20 | .20 |
| 716 | A156 | 70c | dark blue | .20 | .20 |
| 717 | A156 | 1.50g | bister | .20 | .20 |
| 718 | A156 | 2g | violet | .20 | .20 |
| 719 | A156 | 3g | brick red | .20 | .20 |
| 720 | A156a | 5g | vio bl | .20 | .20 |
| 721 | A156a | 12.45g | lake | .35 | .30 |
| 722 | A156a | 12.45g | brt grn | .40 | |
| 723 | A156a | 18.15g | orange | .80 | .30 |

| 724 | A156a | 23.40g | violet | 1.00 | .40 |
| 725 | A156a | 36g | rose red | 1.25 | .50 |
| | | | Nos. 715-725 (11) | 5.00 | 2.80 |

Vatican II, the 21st Ecumenical Council of the Roman Catholic Church, which opened Oct. 11, 1962.
Nos. 720-725 are airmail.

Europa A157

**Perf. 11**
**1962, Dec. 17**
| 726 | A157 | 4g | yel, red & brn | 30.00 | |
| 727 | A157 | 36g | multi; diff. | 13.00 | |
| a. | | | Souvenir sheet of 2, #726-727 | | |
| | | | Set, #726-727 | | |

No. 727 is airmail.

Solar System A158

12.45g, 36g, 50g, Inner planets, Jupiter & rocket.

**Perf. 14x13½**
**Wmk. 346**
**1962, Dec. 17**
| 728 | A158 | 10c | org & purple |
| 729 | A158 | 20c | org & brn vio |
| 730 | A158 | 25c | org & dark vio |
| 731 | A158 | 30c | org & ultra |
| 732 | A158 | 50c | org & dull green |
| 733 | A158 | 12.45g | org & brown |
| 734 | A158 | 36g | org & blue |
| 735 | A158 | 50g | org & green |
| a. | | | Souvenir sheet of 1 | 12.00 |
| | | | Sot, #728-735 | 22.50 |

Nos. 733-735 are airmail.

The following stamps exist imperf. in different colors: Nos. 736-743a, 744-751a, 752-759a, 760-766a, 775-782a, 783-790a, 791-798a, 799-805a, 806-813a, 814-821a, 828-835a, 836-843, 841a, 850-857a, 858-865a, 871-878, 870a, 88/-894a, 895-902, 900a, 903-910a, 911-918a, 919-926a, 927-934a, 943-950a, 951-958a, 959-966a, 978-985a, 986-993a, 994-1001a, 1002-1003, 1003d, 1004-1007a, 1051-1059, B12-B19.

Pierre de Coubertin (1836-1937), Founder of Modern Olympic Games — A159

**Perf. 14x13½**
**Wmk. 346**
Summer Olympic Games sites and: Nos. 12.45g, 18.15g, 36g, Torch bearer in stadium.
**1963, Feb. 16**
| 736 | A159 | 15c | Athens, 1896 |
| 737 | A159 | 25c | Paris, 1900 |
| 738 | A159 | 30c | St. Louis, 1904 |
| 739 | A159 | 40c | London, 1908 |
| 740 | A159 | 50c | Stockholm, 1912 |
| 741 | A159 | 12.45g | No games, 1916 |
| 742 | A159 | 18.15g | Antwerp, 1920 |
| 743 | A159 | 36g | Paris, 1924 | 55.00 | 15.00 |
| a. | | | Souvenir sheet of 1 | | |
| | | | Set, #736-743 | | |

Nos. 741-743a are airmail.

Walter M. Schirra, US Astronaut — A160

Design: 12.45g, 36g, 50g, Schirra.
**Perf. 13½x14**
**1963, Mar. 16**
| 744 | A160 | 10c | brn org & blk |
| 745 | A160 | 20c | car & blk |
| 746 | A160 | 25c | lake & blk |
| 747 | A160 | 30c | ver & blk |
| 748 | A160 | 50c | mag & blk |
| 749 | A160 | 12.45g | bl blk & lake |
| 750 | A160 | 36g | dl gray vio & lake |
| 751 | A160 | 50g | dk grn bl & lake | 19.00 | 12.00 |
| a. | | | Souvenir sheet of 1 | 21.00 | |
| | | | Nos. 744-751 | | |

Nos. 749-751a are airmail.

Winter Olympics A161

Games sites and: 12.45g, 36g, 50g, Snowflake.
**Perf. 14x13½**
**1963, May 16**
| 752 | A161 | 10g | Chamonix, 1924 |
| 753 | A161 | 20c | St. Moritz, 1928 |
| 754 | A161 | 25c | Lake Placid, 1932 |
| 755 | A161 | 30c | Garmisch-Partenkirchen, 1936 |
| 756 | A161 | 50c | Ol. Muniz, 1948 |
| 757 | A161 | 12.45g | Oslo, 1952 |
| 758 | A161 | 36g | Cortina d'Ampezzo, 1956 |
| 759 | A161 | 50g | Squaw Valley, 1960 | 17.00 | 15.00 |
| a. | | | Souvenir sheet of 1 | | |
| | | | Nos. 752-759 | | |

Nos. 757-759a are airmail.

Freedom from Hunger A162

**Perf. 13½x14, 14x13½**
**1963, May 31**
| 760 | A162 | 10c | yel grn & brn |
| 761 | A162 | 25c | lt bl & brn |
| 762 | A162 | 50c | lt grn bl & brn |
| 763 | A162 | 75c | lt lil & brn |
| 764 | A162 | 18.15g | yel org & brn | 22.50 |
| 765 | A162 | 36g | lt bl grn & brn | 9.00 |
| 766 | A162 | 50g | bis & brn | 7.00 |
| a. | | | Souvenir sheet of 1 | |
| | | | Nos. 760-766 | |

#760-763 are vert. #764-766a are airmail.

Pres. Alfredo Stroessner A163

**Perf. 11**
**Wmk. 347**
**1963, Aug. 6**
| 767 | A163 | 50c | ol gray & sep | .25 | .20 |
| 768 | A163 | 75c | buff & sepia | .25 | .20 |
| 769 | A163 | 1.50g | lt sep & sep | .25 | .20 |
| 770 | A163 | 3g | emer & sepia | .25 | .20 |
| 771 | A163 | 12.45g | pink & claret | .25 | .20 |

772 A163 18.15g pink & grn   .30   .20
773 A163 36g pink & vio   1.00   .70
Nos. 767-773 (7)   2.55   1.90
Nos. 771-773 are airmail.

Third presidential term of Alfredo Stroessner. A 36g imperf souvenir sheet exists.

## MUESTRA

"Illustrations may show the word "MUESTRA." This means specimen and is not on the actual stamps. The editors would like to borrow stamps so that replacement illustrations can be made.

### Souvenir Sheet

Dag Hammarskjold, UN Secretary General — A164

**1963, Aug. 21**   **Unwmk.**   **Imperf.**
774 A164 2g Sheet of 2   27.50

Project Mercury Flight of L. Gordon Cooper A165

**1963, Aug. 23**   **Litho.**   **Wmk. 346**
**Perf. 14x13½, 13½x14**
775 A165 15c choc & red
776 A165 25c gray grn & red
777 A165 30c brn & blue
778 A165 40c brn & violet
779 A165 50c brn & green
780 A165 dp bl & red
781 A165 18.15g brn & bl grn
782 A165 50g brn & pink
  a. Souvenir sheet of 1   30.00
Nos. 780-782 are airmail.
12.45g, 18.15g, 50g, L. Gordon Cooper, vert.

15.00   8.00

1964 Winter Olympics, Innsbruck A166

**1963, Oct. 28**   **Perf. 14x13½, 13½x14**   **Unwmk.**
783 A166 15c choc & red
784 A166 25c gray grn & red
785 A166 30c plum & red
786 A166 40c sl grn & red
787 A166 50c dp bl & red
788 A166 12.45g grn bl & red
789 A166 18.15g grn bl & red
790 A166 50g grn bl & red
  a. Souvenir sheet of 1
Nos. 788-790 are airmail.
Design: 12.45g, 18.15g, 50g, Innsbruck Games emblem, vert.

22.50   16.00   9.00

---

1964 Summer Olympics, Tokyo — A167

**1964, Jan. 8**   **Perf. 13½x14**
791 A167 15c blue & red
792 A167 25c org & red
793 A167 30c tan & red
794 A167 40c vio brn & red
795 A167 50c grn & red
796 A167 12.45g vio & red
797 A167 18.15g brn & red
798 A167 50g grn bl & red
  a. Souvenir sheet of 1   37.50
Nos. 796-798 are airmail.
12.45g, 18.15g, 50g, Tokyo games emblem.

8.00   6.00

Int'l Red Cross, Cent. A168

**1964, Feb. 4**   **Perf. 14x13½, 13½x14**
799 A168 10c vio brn & red
800 A168 25c bl grn & red
801 A168 30c dk bl & red
802 A168 50c ol blk & red
803 A168 18.15g choc, red, & pink
804 A168 36g brn & red
805 A168 50g vio & red
  a. Souvenir sheet of 1
Nos. 803-805 are airmail.

20.00   7.00   7.00

Designs: 10c, Helicopter. 25c, Space ambulance. 30c, Red Cross symbol, vert. 50c, Clara Barton, founder of American Red Cross. 18.15g, Jean Henri Dunant, founder of Int'l Red Cross, vert. 36g, Red Cross space hospital, space ambulance. 50g, Plane, ship, ambulance, vert.

Space Research A169

**1964, Mar. 11**
806 A169 15c vio & tan
807 A169 25c grn & tan
808 A169 30c gm & tan
809 A169 40c brt bl & tan
810 A169 50c si grn & tan
811 A169 12.45g dk bl & tan
812 A169 18.15g dk grn bl & tan
813 A169 50g dp vio & tan
  a. Souvenir sheet of 1 (#811-813a)
Nos. 811-813a are airmail.

17.00   14.00   9.00

Designs: 15c, 25c, 30c, Gemini spacecraft rendezvous with Agena rocket. 40c, 50c, Future Apollo and LunarModules. 50g, Telstar communications satellite. Olympic rings, vert.

Rockets and Satellites A170

1964 Summer Olympic Games, Tokyo (#811-813a). Nos. 811-813a are airmail.

15c, 25c, Apollo command module mockup. 30c, Tiros 7 weather satellite, vert. 40c, 50c, Ranger 6. 12.45g, 18.15g, 50g, Saturn I lift-off, vert.

---

**1964, Apr. 25**   **Perf. 13½x14**
814 A170 15c brn & tan
815 A170 25c vio & tan
816 A170 30c Prus bl & lake
817 A170 40c ver & tan
818 A170 50c ultra & tan
819 A170 12.45g bl grn & choc
820 A170 18.15g bl grn & choc
821 A170 50g lil rose & choc
  a. Souvenir sheet of 1
Nos. 819-821a are airmail.
17.00   8.00   8.00

Popes Paul VI, John XXIII and St. Peter's, Rome A171

**1964, May 23**   **Wmk. 347**
822 A171 1.50g claret & org   .25   .25
823 A171 3g claret & dk grn   .20   .20
824 A171 4g claret & bister   .25   .25
825 A171 si grn & lem   .25   .25
826 A171 18.15g pur & lem   .45   .30
827 A171 36g vio bl & lem   1.60   1.10
  a. Souvenir sheet of 6   3.10   2.25
Nos. 822-827 are airmail.
National holiday of St. Maria Auxiliadora (Our Lady of Perpetual Help).

Design: 12.45g, 18.15g, 36g, Asuncion Cathedral, Popes Paul VI and John XXIII.

United Nations A172

**1964, July 30**
**Size: 35x35mm (#830, 834), 40x29mm (#831-832, 835)**
**Perf. 14x13½, 14 (15c, 25c, 12.45g)**   **Unwmk.**
828 A172 15c blk & brn
829 A172 25c blk & brn
830 A172 30c blk & red
831 A172 30c blk & ver
832 A172 40c blk & sep
833 A172 12.45g blk & car
834 A172 50c vio & car
835 A172 18.15g blk & grn

Designs: 15c, John F. Kennedy. 25c, Pope Paul VI and Patriarch Atenagoras. 30c, Eleanor Roosevelt, Chairman of UN Commission on Human Rights. 40c, Relay, Syncom and Telstar satellites. 50c, Echo 2 satellite. 18.15g, U Thant, UN Sec. Gen. 50g, Rocket, flags of Europe, vert.

**Perf. 13½x14**
835 A172 50g multicolored
  a. Souvenir sheet of 1
Nos. 833-835a are airmail.
Set, #828-835   32.50
4.00   3.00

Space Achievements — A173

**1964, Sept. 12**   **Perf. 12½x12**
836 A173 10c bl & blk
837 A173 15c yel grn & brt pink
838 A173 20c yel org & bl
839 A173 30c mag & bl
840 A173 40c yel org, bl & blk

Designs: 10c, 30c, Ranger 7, Moon, vert. 15c, 12.45+6g, Wernher von Braun looking through telescope, vert. 20c, 20+10g, John F. Kennedy, rockets, vert. 40c, 18.15+9g, Rockets, von Braun.

---

**1964, Oct. 6**   **Wmk. 347**
841 A173 12.45g red & bl
842 A173 20g +6g red & bl
843 A173 20g +10g red & bl
  a. Souvenir sheet of 2, #840-841   30.00
Set, #836-843   11.00   8.00
Nos. 841-843 are airmail.

Coats of Arms of Paraguay and France A174

**1964, Oct. 6**   **Wmk. 347**
844 A174 1.50g brown   .20   .20
845 A174 3g ultramarine   .20   .20
846 A174 4g gray   .20   .20
847 A174 12.45g lilac   .25   .25
848 A174 18.15g bl grn   .35   .35
849 A174 36g magenta   1.60   1.00
  a. Souvenir sheet of 6   2.80   2.20
Nos. 844-849 (6)
Visit of Pres. Charles de Gaulle of France.
Designs: 3g, 12.45g, 36g, Presidents Stroessner and de Gaulle. 18.15g, Coats of Arms of Paraguay and France.

Boy Scout Jamborees — A175

**1965, Jan. 15**   **Unwmk.**   **Perf. 14**
850 A175 10c Argentina, 1961
851 A175 15c Peru, cancelled
852 A175 20c Chile, 1959
853 A175 30c Brazil, 1954
854 A175 40c Uruguay, 1957
855 A175 12.45g Brazil, 1960
856 A175 18.15g Venezuela, 1964
857 A175 36g Brazil, 1963
  a. Souvenir sheet of 1, perf. 12x12½
Nos. 855-857a are airmail.

Designs: 15c, 18.15g, Lord Robert Baden-Powell (1867-1941), Boy Scouts founder. 20c, 30c, 12.45g, Boy Scout emblem, map, marl.

A176    A177

**1965, Mar. 30**   **Litho. & Embossed**   **Perf. 13½x13**
858 A176 15c multicolored
859 A176 25c multicolored
860 A176 30c multicolored

Olympic and Paraguayan Medals; 25c, John F. Kennedy. 30c, Medal of Peace and Justice, reverse. 40c, Gens. Stroessner and DeGaulle, profiles. 50c, 18.15g, DeGaulle and Stroessner in uniform. 12.45g, Medal of Peace and Justice, obverse.

**1965, Apr. 26**    Wmk. 347    *Perf. 11*
| | | | | |
|---|---|---|---|---|
| 866 | A177 | 1.50g dull grn | .20 | .20 |
| 867 | A177 | 3g car red | .20 | .20 |
| 868 | A177 | 4g dark blue | .20 | .20 |
| 869 | A177 | 12.45g blue & blk | .50 | .35 |
| 870 | A177 | 36g brt lil & blk | 1.30 | 1.15 |

*Nos. 869-870 are airmail.*

Overprint: "Centenario de la Epopeya Nacional 1.864-1.870."

Design: Map of Americas.

Scientists — A178

**1965, June 5**    Unwmk.    Litho.    *Perf. 14*
| | | | | |
|---|---|---|---|---|
| 871 | A178 | 1.50g Newton | .20 | .20 |
| 872 | A178 | 15c Copernicus | .20 | .20 |
| 873 | A178 | 20c Galileo | .20 | .20 |
| 874 | A178 | 30c like #871 | .20 | .20 |
| 875 | A178 | 40c Einstein | .20 | .20 |
| 876 | A178 | 12.45g +6g like #873 | | 12.50 |
| a. | Souvenir sheet of 2, perf. 13½x14 | | | |
| 877 | A178 | 18.15g +9g like #875 | | |
| 878 | A178 | 20g +10g like #872 | | 5.00 |

*Nos. 876-878 are airmail.*

*Set, #871-878 (8)*

Cattleya Warscewiczii A179

Ceibo Tree — A179a

**1965, June 28**    Unwmk.    *Perf. 14½*
| | | | | |
|---|---|---|---|---|
| 879 | A179 | 20c purple | .20 | .20 |
| 880 | A179 | 30c blue | .20 | .20 |
| 881 | A179 | 90c bright mag | .20 | .20 |
| 882 | A179 | 1.50g green | .80 | .80 |
| 883 | A179a | 3g brn red | .80 | .80 |
| 884 | A179a | 4g green | .80 | .80 |
| 885 | A179a | 4.50g orange | .20 | .20 |
| 886 | A179a | 66g brn org | 3.40 | 3.40 |

*Nos. 883-884, 886 are airmail.*

150th anniv. of Independence (1811-1961).

John F. Kennedy and Winston Churchill — A180

*Perf. 12½x12*
| | | | | |
|---|---|---|---|---|
| 861 | A176 | 40c multicolored | | |
| 862 | A176 | 50c multicolored | | |
| 863 | A176 | 12.45g multicolored | | |
| 864 | A176 | 18.15g multicolored | | |
| 865 | A176 | 50g multicolored | 30.00 | |
| a. | Souv. sheet of 1, perf. 13½x13 | | 10.00 | 8.00 |

*Nos. 863-865a are airmail. Medal on No. 865a is gold foil.*

Designs: 15c, Kennedy, PT 109. 25c, Kennedy family. 30c, 12.45g, Churchill, Parliament building. 40c, Kennedy, Alliance for Progress emblem. 50c, 18.15g, Kennedy, rocket launch at Cape Canaveral. 50g, John Glenn, Kennedy, Lyndon Johnson examining Friendship 7.

*Perf. 12x12½*
| | | | | |
|---|---|---|---|---|
| 887 | A180 | 15c bl & brn | | |
| 888 | A180 | 25c red & brn | | |
| 889 | A180 | 30c vio & blk | | |
| 890 | A180 | 40c org & sep | | |
| 891 | A180 | 50c bl grn & sep | | |
| 892 | A180 | 12.45g yel & blk | 20.00 | |
| 893 | A180 | 18.15g car & blk | | |
| 894 | A180 | 50g grn & blk | 10.00 | 6.00 |
| a. | Souvenir sheet of 1 | | | |

*Nos. 892-894a are airmail.*

*Set, #887-894*

ITU, Cent. — A181

Satellites: 10c, 40c, Ranger 7 transmitting to Earth. 15c, 20g+10g, Syncom, Olympic rings. 20c, 18.15g+9g, Early Bird. 30c, 12.45g+6g, Relay, Syncom, Telstar, Echo 2.

**1965, Sept. 30**
| | | | | |
|---|---|---|---|---|
| 895 | A181 | 10c dull bl & sep | | |
| 896 | A181 | 15c lilac & blk | | |
| 897 | A181 | 20c ol grn & sep | | |
| 898 | A181 | 30c blue & sepia | | |
| 899 | A181 | 40c grn & sep | | |
| 900 | A181 | 12.45g +6g ver & sep | 22.50 | |
| a. | Souvenir sheet of 2, #899-900 | | | |
| 901 | A181 | 18.15g +9g org & sep | | |
| 902 | A181 | 20g +10g vio & sep | | |

*Nos. 900-902 are airmail.*

*Set, #895-902*

Pope Paul VI, Visit to UN A182

Designs: 10c, 50c, Pope Paul VI, U Thant. A. Fanfani. 15c, 12.45g, Pope Paul VI, Lyndon B. Johnson. 20c, 36g, Early Bird satellite, globe, papal arms. 30c, 18.15g, Pope Paul VI, Unisphere.

**1965, Nov. 19**
| | | | | |
|---|---|---|---|---|
| 903 | A182 | 10c multicolored | | |
| 904 | A182 | 15c multicolored | | |
| 905 | A182 | 20c multicolored | | |
| 906 | A182 | 30c multicolored | | |
| 907 | A182 | 50c multicolored | | |
| 908 | A182 | 12.45g multicolored | | |
| 909 | A182 | 18.15g multicolored | 22.50 | |
| 910 | A182 | 36g multicolored | 5.00 | 5.00 |
| a. | Souvenir sheet of 1 | | | |

*Nos. 908-910a are airmail.*

*Set, #903-910*

Astronauts and Space Exploration — A183

15c, 50g, Edward White walking in space, 6/3/65. 25c, 18.15g, Gemini 7 & 8 docking, 12/16-18/65. 30c, 40c, 50c, Edward White, Young, 3/23/65. 40c, 50c, Edward White, James McDivitt, 6/3/65. 12.45g, Photographs of lunar surface.

*Perf. 12x12½*
| | | | | |
|---|---|---|---|---|
| 911 | A183 | 15c multicolored | | |
| 912 | A183 | 25c multicolored | | |
| 913 | A183 | 30c multicolored | | |
| 914 | A183 | 40c multicolored | | |
| 915 | A183 | 50c multicolored | | |
| 916 | A183 | 12.45g multicolored | 37.50 | |
| 917 | A183 | 18.15g multicolored | 3.00 | 2.50 |
| 918 | A183 | 50g multicolored | | |
| a. | Souvenir sheet of 1 | | | |

*Nos. 916-918a are airmail.*

*Set, #911-918*

Events of 1965 — A184

10c, Meeting of Pope Paul VI & Cardinal Spellman, 10/4/65. 15c, Intl. Phil. Exposition, Vienna. 20c, OAS. 75th anniv. 30c, 36g, Intl. Quiet Sun Year, 1964-65. 50c, 18.15g, Saturn rockets at NY World's Fair. 12.45g, UN Intl. Cooperation Year.

**1966, Mar. 9**
| | | | | |
|---|---|---|---|---|
| 919 | A184 | 10c multicolored | | |
| 920 | A184 | 15c multicolored | | |
| 921 | A184 | 20c multicolored | | |
| 922 | A184 | 30c multicolored | | |
| 923 | A184 | 50c multicolored | | |
| 924 | A184 | 12.45g multicolored | 35.00 | |
| 925 | A184 | 18.15g multicolored | 2.75 | 2.75 |
| 926 | A184 | 36g multicolored | | |
| a. | Souvenir sheet of 1 | | | |

*Nos. 924-926a are airmail.*

*Set, #919-926*

1968 Summer Olympics, Mexico City — A185

*Perf. 12½x12 (Nos. 927, 929, 931, 933), 13½x13*
| | | | | |
|---|---|---|---|---|
| 927 | A185 | 10c shown | | |
| 928 | A185 | 15c God of Death | | |
| 929 | A185 | 20c Aztec calendar stone | | |
| 930 | A185 | 30c like No. 928 | | |
| 931 | A185 | 50c Zapotec deity | 18.00 | |
| 932 | A185 | 12.45g like No. 931 | 10.00 | 6.00 |
| 933 | A185 | 18.15g like No. 927 | | |
| 934 | A185 | 36g like No. 929 | | |
| a. | Souvenir sheet of 1 | | | |

*Nos. 932-934a are airmail.*

*Set, #927-934*

St. Ignatius Type of 1958 and St. Ignatius and San Ignacio Monastery A185a

**1966, Apr. 20**    Wmk. 347    *Perf. 11*
| | | | | |
|---|---|---|---|---|
| 935 | A129 | 15c ultramarine | .20 | .20 |
| 936 | A129 | 25c ultramarine | .20 | .20 |
| 937 | A129 | 75c ultramarine | .20 | .20 |
| 938 | A129 | 90c ultramarine | .20 | .20 |
| 939 | A185a | 3g brown | .20 | .20 |
| 940 | A185a | 12.45g sepia | | |

German Contributors in Space Research — A186

Designs: 10c, 36g, Paraguay #835, C97, Germany #C40. 15c, 50c, 18.15g, 3rd stage of Europa I rocket, vert. 20c, 12.45g, Hermann Oberth, jet propulsion engineer, vert. 30c, Reinhold K. Tiling, builder of 1st German rocket, 1931, vert.

*Perf. 12x12½ (Nos. 943, 950), 12½x12 (Nos. 945, 947, 949), 13½x13*
| | | | | |
|---|---|---|---|---|
| 941 | A185a | 18.15g sepia | .20 | .20 |
| 942 | A185a | 23.40g sepia | .25 | .20 |
| | | | 1.65 | 1.60 |

*Nos. 935-942 (8)*

350th anniv. of the founding of San Ignacio Guazu Monastery. *Nos. 939-942 are airmail.*

Unwmk.
| | | | | |
|---|---|---|---|---|
| 943 | A186 | 10c multicolored | | |
| 944 | A186 | 15c multicolored | | |
| 945 | A186 | 20c multicolored | | |
| 946 | A186 | 30c multicolored | | |
| 947 | A186 | 50c multicolored | | |
| 948 | A186 | 12.45g multicolored | 19.00 | |
| 949 | A186 | 18.15g multicolored | 4.00 | 4.50 |
| 950 | A186 | 36g multicolored | | |
| a. | Souvenir sheet of 1, perf. 12x13½x13x13½ | | | |

*Nos. 948-950a are airmail.*

*Set, #943-950*

Writers — A187

**1966, May 16**    *Perf. 12x12½*
| | | | | |
|---|---|---|---|---|
| 951 | A187 | 10c Dante | | |
| 952 | A187 | 15c Moliere | | |
| 953 | A187 | 20c Goethe | | |
| 954 | A187 | 30c Shakespeare | | |
| 955 | A187 | 50c like #952 | | |
| 956 | A187 | 12.45g like #953 | 17.00 | |
| 957 | A187 | 18.15g like #954 | 5.00 | 5.00 |
| 958 | A187 | 36g like #951 | | |
| a. | Souvenir sheet of 1, perf. 13½x14 | | | |

*Nos. 956-958a are airmail.*

*Set, #951-958*

Italian Contributors in Space Research — A188

10c, 36g, Italian satellite, San Marco 1. 15c, 18.15g, Drafting machine, Leonardo Da Vinci. 20c, 12.45g, Map, Italo Balbo (1896-1940), aviator. 30c, 50c, Floating launch & control facility, satellite.

**1966, July 11**
| | | | | |
|---|---|---|---|---|
| 959 | A188 | 10c multicolored | | |
| 960 | A188 | 15c multicolored | | |
| 961 | A188 | 20c multicolored | | |
| 962 | A188 | 30c multicolored | | |
| 963 | A188 | 50c multicolored | | |
| 964 | A188 | 12.45g multicolored | 15.00 | |
| 965 | A188 | 18.15g multicolored | 7.00 | 5.00 |
| 966 | A188 | 36g multicolored | | |
| a. | Souvenir sheet of 1, perf. 13x13½ | | | |

*Nos. 964-966a are airmail.*

*Set, #959-966*

## Rubén Darío — A189
"Paraguay de Fuego" by Darío — A189a

**1966, July 16 — Wmk. 347**

| | | | | |
|---|---|---|---|---|
| 967 | A189 | 50c ultramarine | .20 | .20 |
| 968 | A189 | 70c bister brn | .20 | .20 |
| 969 | A189 | 1.50g rose car | .20 | .20 |
| 970 | A189 | 3g violet | .20 | .20 |
| 971 | A189 | 4g greenish bl | .20 | .20 |
| 972 | A189 | 5g black | .20 | .20 |
| 973 | A189 | 12.45g blue | .20 | .20 |
| 974 | A189 | 18.15g red lil | .25 | .20 |
| 975 | A189a | 23.40g org brn | .25 | .20 |
| 976 | A189a | 36g brt grn | .55 | .45 |
| 977 | A189a | 50g rose car | .85 | .60 |
| a. | | Souvenir sheet of 1, perf. 13x13½ | 3.25 | 2.85 |

Nos. 967-977 (11)

50th death anniv. of Rubén Darío (pen name of Félix Rubén García Sarmiento, 1867-1916), Nicaraguan poet, newspaper correspondent and diplomat.
Nos. 973-977 are airmail.

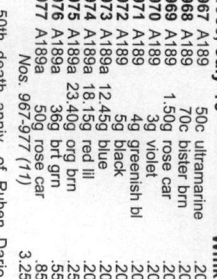

## Space Missions — A190

**1966, Aug. 25 — Unwmk.**

| | | | | |
|---|---|---|---|---|
| 978 | A190 | 10c Gemini 8 | .20 | .20 |
| 979 | A190 | 15c Gemini 9 | .20 | .20 |
| 980 | A190 | 20c Surveyor 1 | .20 | .20 |
| 981 | A190 | 30c Gemini 10 on moon | .20 | .20 |
| 982 | A190 | 50c Gemini 11 | .20 | .20 |
| 983 | A190 | 12.45g | .20 | .20 |
| 984 | A190 | 18.15g | .20 | .20 |
| 985 | A190 | 36g | | |
| a. | | Souvenir sheet of 1, perf. 13x13½ | 24.00 | |

Nos. 983-985a are airmail.

## 1968 Winter Olympics, Grenoble — A191

**1966, Sept. 30 — Perf. 14**

| | | | | |
|---|---|---|---|---|
| 986 | A191 | 10c Figure skating | 27.50 | 5.50 |
| 987 | A191 | 15c Downhill skiing | | |
| 988 | A191 | 20c Speed skating | | |
| 989 | A191 | 30c 2-man luge | | |
| 990 | A191 | 50c like #986 | | |
| 991 | A191 | 12.45g like #988 | | |
| 992 | A191 | 18.15g like #987 | | |
| 993 | A191 | 36g like #986 | | |
| a. | | Souvenir sheet of 1 #986-993 | 25.00 | 12.00 |

Nos. 987, 992, 993, World Skiing Championships, Portillo, Chile, 1966. Nos. 991-993a are airmail.

## Pres. John F. Kennedy, 3rd Death Anniv. — A192

**1966, Nov. 7 — Perf. 12x12½, 13½x14 (#997-998, 1001)**

| | | | | |
|---|---|---|---|---|
| 994 | A192 | 10c Echo 1 & 2 | | |
| 995 | A192 | 15c Telstar 1 & 2 | | |
| 996 | A192 | 20c Relay 1 & 2 | | |
| 997 | A192 | 30c Syncom 1, 2 & 3, Early Bird | | |
| 998 | A192 | 50c like #997 | | |
| 999 | A192 | 12.45g like #995 | | |
| 1000 | A192 | 18.15g like #996 | | |
| 1001 | A192 | 36g like #994 | | |
| a. | | Souvenir sheet of 1, perf. 13x14/13½x14 | 24.00 | |
| Set, #994-1001 | | | 8.00 | 5.00 |

Nos. 999-1001a are airmail.

## Paintings A193

Portraits of women by: No. 1002a, 10c, De Largillière. b, 15c, Rubens. c, 20c, Titian. d, 30c, Hans Holbein. e, 50c, Sánchez Coello. Paintings: No. 1003a, 12.45g, Venus with United by Love by Veronese. b, 18.15g, Allegory of Prudence, Peace and Abundance by Vouet. c, 36g, Madonna and Child by Andres Montegna.

**1966, Dec. 10 — Perf. 14x13½**

| | | | | |
|---|---|---|---|---|
| 1002 | A193 | Strip of 5, #a.-e. | | |
| 1003 | A193 | Strip of 1, #1003c | | |
| d. | | Souvenir sheet of 1, #1003c | 22.50 | |

Nos. 1002-1003
Set, #1002-1003

Nos. 1003a-1003d are airmail. No. 1003d has green pattern in border and is perf. 12½x12.

## Holy Week Paintings A194

Life of Christ by: No. 1004a, 10c, Raphael. b, 15c, Rubens. c, 20c, Da Ponte. d, 30c, El Greco. e, 50c, Murillo, horiz. 12.45g, G. Reni. 18.15g, Tintoretto. 36g, Da Vinci, horiz.

**1967, Feb. 28 — Perf. 14x13½, 13½x14**

| | | | | |
|---|---|---|---|---|
| 1004 | A194 | Strip of 5, #a.-e. | | |
| 1005 | A194 | 12.45g multicolored | 15.00 | |
| 1006 | A194 | 18.15g multicolored | 8.00 | 5.00 |
| 1007 | A194 | 36g multicolored | | |
| a. | | Souvenir sheet of 1 | | |

Nos. 1005-1007a are airmail. No. 1007a has salmon pattern in border and contains one 60x40mm, perf. 14 stamp.

## Birth of Christ by Barocci — A195

16th Cent. Paintings: 12.45g, Madonna and Child by Caravaggio. 18.15g, Mary of the Holy Family (detail) by El Greco. 36g, Assumption of the Virgin by Vasco Fernandes.

**1967, Mar. 10 — Perf. 14½**

| | | | | |
|---|---|---|---|---|
| 1008 | A195 | 10c lt bl & multi | | |
| 1009 | A195 | 15c lt grn & multi | | |
| 1010 | A195 | 20c lt brn & multi | | |
| 1011 | A195 | 30c lil & multi | | |
| 1012 | A195 | 50c pink & multi | | |
| 1013 | A195 | 12.45g lt grn & multi | | |
| 1014 | A195 | 18.15g brt pink & multi | | |
| 1015 | A195 | 36g lt vio & multi | | |
| a. | | Souv. sheet of 1, sep & multi | 22.50 | |
| Set, #1008-1015 | | | 8.00 | 5.00 |

Nos. 1013-1015a are airmail. Exist imperf. with changed borders.

## Globe and Lions Emblem — A196

## Medical Laboratory "Health" A196a

Designs: 1.50g, 3g, Melvin Jones, Lions' Headquarters, Chicago. 4g, 5g, 18.15g, Library "Education."

**1967, May 9 — Litho. — Wmk. 347**

| | | | | |
|---|---|---|---|---|
| 1016 | A196 | 50c light vio | .20 | .20 |
| 1017 | A196 | 70c blue | .20 | .20 |
| 1018 | A196 | 1.50g ultra | .20 | .20 |
| 1019 | A196 | 3g brown | .20 | .20 |
| 1020 | A196 | 4g Prussian grn | .20 | .20 |
| 1021 | A196 | 5g gray | .20 | .20 |
| 1022 | A196 | 12.45g dk brn | .20 | .20 |
| 1023 | A196 | 18.15g violet | .20 | .20 |
| 1024 | A196 | 23.40g rose cl | .20 | .20 |
| 1025 | A196 | 36g Prus blue | .30 | .20 |
| 1026 | A196a | 50g rose car | .35 | .20 |
| Set, #1016-1026 (11) | | | 2.45 | 2.20 |

50th anniversary of Lions International. Nos. 1022-1026 are airmail.

## Vase of Flowers by Chardin A197

Still Life Paintings by: No. 1027b, 15c, Fontanesi, horiz. c, 20c, Gogh. e, 50c, Renoir. Paintings: 12.45g, Cha-U-Kao at the Moulin Rouge by Toulouse-Lautrec. 18.15g, Gabrielle Escalier, Shepherd of Provence by Renoir. 36g, Patience Escalier, horiz. c, 20c, Cezanne. d, 30c, Van Gogh. e, 50c, Renoir. 12.45g, Cha-U-Kao at the Moulin Rouge by Jean Renoir by Renoir. 36g, Patience by Van Gogh.

**1967, May 16 — Perf. 12½x12**

| | | | | |
|---|---|---|---|---|
| 1027 | A197 | #a.-e. Strip of 5 | | |
| 1028 | A197 | 12.45g multicolored #a.-e. Strip of 5 | | |

**Perf. 14x13½**

| | | | | |
|---|---|---|---|---|
| 1029 | A197 | 18.15g multicolored | 22.50 | 5.75 |
| 1030 | A197 | 36g multicolored | 5.75 | |
| a. | | Souvenir sheet of 1, perf. 14x12x14x13½ | | |
| Set, #1027-1030 | | | | |

Nos. 1028-1030a are airmail. No. 1030a has a green pattern in border. No. 1030a has a green pattern in border. Exist imperf. with changed borders.

## Famous Paintings — A198

**1967, July 16 — Perf. 12x12½**

| | | | | |
|---|---|---|---|---|
| 1031 | A198 | 10c Jan Steen | | |
| 1032 | A198 | 15c Frans Hals, vert. | | |
| 1033 | A198 | 20c Jordaens | | |
| 1034 | A198 | 25c Rembrandt | | |
| 1035 | A198 | 30c de Marees | | |
| 1036 | A198 | 50c Quentin, vert. | | |
| 1037 | A198 | 12.45g Nicolaes Maes, vert. | | |
| 1038 | A198 | 18.15g Vigee-Lebrun, vert. | | |
| 1039 | A198 | 36g Rubens, vert. | | |
| Set, #1031-1039 | | | 8.00 | 5.00 |

**Souvenir Sheet — Perf. 12x12½**

| | | | | |
|---|---|---|---|---|
| 1040 | A198 | 50g G. B. Tiepolo | 12.00 | |

Nos. 1037-1039 are airmail. An imperf. souvenir sheet of 3, #1037-1039 exists with dark green pattern in border.

## John F. Kennedy, 50th Birth Anniv. A199

Kennedy and: 10c, Recovery of Alan Shepard's capsule, Lyndon Johnson, Mrs. Kennedy. 15c, John Glenn. 20c, Mr. and Mrs. M. Scott Carpenter. 25c, Rocket 2nd stage, Wernher Von Braun. 30c, Mr. and Mrs. Walter Schirra. 50c, Syncom 2 satellite, horiz. 12.45g, Launch of Atlas rocket. 18.15g, Theorized lunar landing, horiz. 36g, Portrait of Kennedy by Torres. 50g, Apollo lift-off.

**1967, Aug. 19 — Perf. 14x13½, 13½x14**

| | | | | |
|---|---|---|---|---|
| 1041 | A199 | 10c multicolored | | |
| 1042 | A199 | 15c multicolored | | |
| 1043 | A199 | 20c multicolored | | |
| 1044 | A199 | 25c multicolored | | |
| 1045 | A199 | 30c multicolored | | |
| 1046 | A199 | 50c multicolored | | |
| 1047 | A199 | 12.45g multicolored | | |
| 1048 | A199 | 18.15g multicolored | | |
| 1049 | A199 | 36g multicolored | | |
| Set, #1041-1049 | | | 13.00 | 6.00 |

**Souvenir Sheet**

| | | | | |
|---|---|---|---|---|
| 1050 | A199 | 50g multicolored | 22.50 | |

Nos. 1047-1050 are airmail. An imperf. souvenir sheet of 3 containing #1047-1049 exists with violet border.

## Sculptures A200

**1967, Oct. 16** — *Perf. 14x13½*
| | | | |
|---|---|---|---|
| 1051 | A200 | 10c | Head of athlete |
| 1052 | A200 | 15c | Myron's Discobolus |
| 1053 | A200 | 20c | Apollo of Belvedere |
| 1054 | A200 | 25c | Artemis |
| 1055 | A200 | 30c | Venus De Milo |
| 1056 | A200 | 50c | Winged Victory, Samothrace |
| 1057 | A200 | 12.45g | Laocoon Group |
| 1058 | A200 | 18.15g | Moses |
| 1059 | A200 | 50g | Pieta | 5.75 4.75 |

Set, #1051-1059

Nos. 1057-1059 are airmail.

## Mexican Art — A201

Designs: 10c, Bowl, Veracruz. 15c, Knobbed vessel, Colima. 20c, Mixtec jaguar pitcher. 25c, Head, Veracruz. 30c, Vessel depicting a woman, Teotihuacan. 50c, Vessel seated woman, Aztec. 12.45g, Mixtec bowl, horiz. 18.15g, Three-legged vessel, Teotihuacan, horiz. 36g, Golden mask, Teotihuacan, horiz. 50g, The Culture of the Totonac by Diego Rivera, 1950, horiz.

**1967, Nov. 29** — *Perf. 14x13½*
| | | | |
|---|---|---|---|
| 1060 | A201 | 10c | multicolored |
| 1061 | A201 | 15c | multicolored |
| 1062 | A201 | 20c | multicolored |
| 1063 | A201 | 25c | multicolored |
| 1064 | A201 | 30c | multicolored |
| 1065 | A201 | 50c | multicolored |

*Perf. 13½x14*
| | | | |
|---|---|---|---|
| 1066 | A201 | 12.45g | multicolored |
| 1067 | A201 | 18.15g | multicolored |
| 1068 | A201 | 36g | multicolored | 16.00 9.00 |

Set, #1060-1068

**Souvenir Sheet**
*Perf. 14*
| | | | |
|---|---|---|---|
| 1069 | A201 | 50g | multicolored 19.00 |

1968 Summer Olympics, Mexico City (#1065-1069). Nos. 1066-1069 are airmail. An imperf. souvenir sheet of 3 containing #1066-1068 exists with green pattern in border. Value $30.

## Paintings of the Madonna and Child A202

**1968, Jan. 27** — *Perf. 14x13½, 13½x14*
| | | | |
|---|---|---|---|
| 1070 | A202 | 10c | Bellini |
| 1071 | A202 | 15c | Raphael |
| 1072 | A202 | 20c | Correggio |
| 1073 | A202 | 25c | Luini |
| 1074 | A202 | 50c | Bronzino |
| 1075 | A202 | 50c | Van Dyck |
| 1076 | A202 | 12.45g | Vignon, horiz. |
| 1077 | A202 | 18.15g | de Ribera, horiz. | 6.50 3.75 |
| 1078 | A202 | 36g | Botticelli | 3.75 |

Set, #1070-1078

Nos. 1076-1078 are airmail and also exist as imperf. souvenir sheet of 3 with olive brown pattern in border. Value $37.50.

## Paintings of Winter Scenes — A203
## 1968 Winter Olympics Emblem A204

**1968, Apr. 23** — *Perf. 13½x14, 14x13½*
| | | | |
|---|---|---|---|
| 1079 | A203 | 10c | Pissarro |
| 1080 | A203 | 15c | Utrillo, vert. |
| 1081 | A203 | 20c | Monet |
| 1082 | A203 | 25c | Breitner, vert. |
| 1083 | A203 | 30c | Sisley |
| 1084 | A203 | 50c | Brueghel, vert. |
| 1085 | A203 | 12.45g | Avercampe, vert. |
| 1086 | A203 | 18.15g | Brueghel, diff. |
| 1087 | A203 | 36g | P. Limbourg & brothers, vert. | 5.75 3.75 |

Set, #1070-1087

**Souvenir Sheet**
| | | | |
|---|---|---|---|
| 1088 | | | Shoot of 2 | 30.00 |
| a. | A204 | 50g | multicolored | |

Nos. 1087-1088, 1088a are airmail. No. 1088 contains #1088a and #1087 with red pattern.

## Paintings A206

#1099-1106, paintings of children. #1107-1108, paintings of sailboats at sea.

**1968, July 9** — *Perf. 14x13½, 13½x14*
| | | | |
|---|---|---|---|
| 1099 | A206 | 10c | Russell |
| 1100 | A206 | 15c | Velazquez |
| 1101 | A206 | 20c | Romney |
| 1102 | A206 | 25c | Lawrence |
| 1103 | A206 | 30c | Caravaggio |
| 1104 | A206 | 50c | Gentileschi |
| 1105 | A206 | 12.45g | Renoir |
| 1106 | A206 | 18.15g | Copley |
| 1107 | A206 | 36g | Sessions, horiz. | 10.00 4.75 |

Set, #1099-1107

**Souvenir Sheet**
*Perf. 14*
| | | | |
|---|---|---|---|
| 1108 | | | Sheet of 2 | 17.60 |
| a. | A206 | 50g | Currier & Ives, horiz. | |

1968 Summer Olympics, Mexico City (Nos. 1107-1108). No. 1106-1108a are airmail. No. 1108 contains No. 1108a and No. 1107 with a red pattern in border.

Paraguayan Stamps, Cent. (in 1970) — A205

**1968, June 3** — *Perf. 13½x14, 14x13½* — **Litho.**
| | | | |
|---|---|---|---|
| 1089 | A205 | 10c | #1, 4 |
| 1090 | A205 | 15c | #21, 310, vert. |
| 1091 | A205 | 20c | #203, C140 |
| 1092 | A205 | 25c | #C72, C61, vert. |
| 1093 | A205 | 30c | #638, 711 |
| 1094 | A205 | 50c | #406, C38, vert. |
| 1095 | A205 | 12.45g | #B2, B7 |
| 1096 | A205 | 18.15g | #C10, C11, vert. |
| 1097 | A205 | 36g | #828, C76, vert. | 14.00 8.00 |

Set, #1089-1097

**Souvenir Sheet**
*Perf. 14*
| | | | |
|---|---|---|---|
| 1098 | | | Sheet of 2 | 35.00 27.50 |
| a. | A205 | 50g | #929 & #379 | |

Nos. 1095-1098a are airmail. No. 1098 contains No. 1098a and No. 1097 with light brown pattern in border.

A207

Emblem — A207a

**1968, Aug. 12** — **Wmk. 347** — *Perf. 11*
| | | | | |
|---|---|---|---|---|
| 1109 | A207 | 3g | bluish grn | .20 .20 |
| 1110 | A207 | 4g | brt pink | .20 .20 |
| 1111 | A207 | 5g | bister brn | .20 .20 |
| 1112 | A207 | 10g | violet | .20 .20 |
| 1113 | A207a | 36g | blk brn | .30 .25 |
| 1114 | A207a | 50g | rose claret | .35 .25 |
| 1115 | A207a | 100g | brt bl | .80 .60 |
| | | | Nos. 1109-1115 (7) | 2.25 1.85 |

WHO, 20th anniv.; cent. of the natl. epic.

## 39th Intl. Eucharistic Congress A208

Paintings of life of Christ by various artists (except No. 1125a).

**1968, Sept. 25** — *Perf. 14x13½* — **Litho.** — **Unwmk.**
| | | | |
|---|---|---|---|
| 1116 | A208 | 10c | Caravaggio |
| 1117 | A208 | 15c | El Greco |
| 1118 | A208 | 20c | Del Sarto |
| 1119 | A208 | 25c | Van der Weyden |
| 1120 | A208 | 30c | De Patinier |
| 1121 | A208 | 50c | Plockhorst |
| 1122 | A208 | 12.45g | Correggio |
| 1123 | A208 | 18.15g | Raphael |
| 1124 | A208 | 36g | Correggio | 11.00 5.00 |

Set, #1116-1124

**Souvenir Sheet**
*Perf. 14*
| | | | |
|---|---|---|---|
| 1125 | | | Sheet of 2 | 15.00 |
| a. | A208 | 36g | Pope Paul VI | |
| b. | A208 | 50g | Tiepolo | |

Pope Paul VI's visit to South America (No. 1125). Nos. 1122-1125b are airmail.

## Events of 1968 — A209

Designs: 10c, Mexican 25p Olympic coin. 15c, Rentry of Echo 1 satellite. 20c, Visit of Pope Paul VI to Fatima, Portugal. 25c, Dr. Christian Barnard, 1st heart transplant. 30c, Martin Luther King, assassination. 50c, Pres. Alfredo Stroessner laying wreath at grave of Pres. Kennedy. 12.45g, Pres. Stroessner, Pres. Lyndon B. Johnson. 18.15g, John F. Kennedy, Abraham Lincoln, Robert Kennedy. 50g, Summer Olympics, Mexico City, satellite transmissions, vert.

**1968, Dec. 21** — *Perf. 13½x14, 14x13½*
| | | | |
|---|---|---|---|
| 1126 | A209 | 10c | multicolored |
| 1127 | A209 | 15c | multicolored |
| 1128 | A209 | 20c | multicolored |
| 1129 | A209 | 25c | multicolored |
| 1130 | A209 | 30c | multicolored |
| 1131 | A209 | 50c | multicolored |
| 1132 | A209 | 12.45g | multicolored |
| 1133 | A209 | 18.15g | multicolored |
| 1134 | A209 | 50g | multicolored | 11.00 5.00 |

Set, #1126-1134

Nos. 1132-1134 are airmail. Set exists imperf. in sheets of 3 in changed colors.

## 1968 Summer Olympics, Mexico City A210

## Olympic Stadium A210a

Gold Medal Winners: 10c, Felipe Munoz, Mexico, 200-meter breast stroke. 15c, Daniel Rebillard, France, 4000-meter cycling. 20c, David Hemery, England, 400-meter hurdles. 25c, Bob Seagren, US, pole vault. 30c, Francisco Rodriguez, Venezuela, light flyweight boxing. 50c, Bjorn Ferm, Sweden, modern pentathlon. 12.45g, Klaus Dibiasi, Italy, platform diving. 50g, Ingrid Becker, West Germany, fencing, women's pentathlon.

**1969, Feb. 13** — *Perf. 14x13½*
| | | | |
|---|---|---|---|
| 1135 | A210 | 10c | multicolored |
| 1136 | A210 | 15c | multicolored |
| 1137 | A210 | 20c | multicolored |
| 1138 | A210 | 25c | multicolored |
| 1139 | A210 | 30c | multicolored |
| 1140 | A210 | 50c | multicolored |
| 1141 | A210 | 12.45g | multicolored |

1142 A210a 18.15g multicolored
1143 A210 50g multicolored  8.50  5.00
Nos. 1141-1143 are airmail. Set exists imperf. in sheets of 3 in changed colors.

## Space Missions — A211

**1969, Mar. 10    Perf. 13½x14**

Designs: 10c, Apollo 7, John F. Kennedy. 15c, Apollo 8, Kennedy. 20c, Apollo 8, Kennedy, diff. 25c, Study of solar flares. ITU emblem. 30c, Canary Bird satellite. 50c, ESRO satellite. 12.45g, Werner von Braun, rocket launch. 18.15g, Global satellite. Coverage. ITU emblem. 50g, Otto Lilienthal, Graf Zeppelin, Hermann Oberth, evolution of flight.

1144 A211 10c multicolored
1145 A211 15c multicolored
1146 A211 20c multicolored
1147 A211 25c multicolored
1148 A211 30c multicolored
1149 A211 50c multicolored
1150 A211 12.45g multicolored
1151 A211 18.15g multicolored
1152 A211 50g multicolored
Set, #1144-1152  6.00  3.25
Nos. 1150-1152 are airmail. Set exists imperf. in sheets of 3 in changed colors.

"World United in Peace" — A212

Peace Week.

**1969, June 28    Wmk. 347    Perf. 11**

1153 A212 50c rose  .20  .20
1154 A212 70c ultra  .20  .20
1155 A212 1.50g light brn  .20  .20
1156 A212 3g lil rose  .20  .20
1157 A212 4g emerald  .20  .20
1158 A212 5g violet  .20  .20
1159 A212 10g brt lilac  .20  .20
Set, #1153-1159 (7)  1.40  1.40

## Birds
A213

**1969, July 9    Perf. 13½x14, 14x13½    Unwmk.**

1160 A213 10c multicolored
1161 A213 15c multicolored
1162 A213 20c multicolored
1163 A213 25c multicolored
1164 A213 30c multicolored
1165 A213 50c multicolored
1166 A213 75c multicolored
1167 A213 12.45g multicolored
1168 A213 18.15g multicolored
Set, #1160-1168  21.00  3.50

Designs: 10c, Pteroglossus viridis. 15c, Phytotoma rutila. 20c, Porphyrula martinica. 25c, Oxyruncus cristatus. 30c, Spizaetus ornatus. 50c, Phoenicopterus ruber. 75c, Amazona ochrocephala. 12.45g, Ara ararauna. Ara macao. 18.15g, Colibri coruscans.
Nos. 1167-1168 are airmail. Nos. 1161, 1164-1168 are vert.

## Olympic Soccer Champions, 1900-1968 A215

**1969, Nov. 26    Perf. 14**

1178 A215 10c multicolored
1179 A215 15c multicolored
1180 A215 20c multicolored
1181 A215 25c multicolored
1182 A215 30c multicolored
1183 A215 50c multicolored
1184 A215 75c multicolored
1185 A215 12.45g multicolored
1186 A215 18.15g multicolored
Set, #1178-1186  10.00  4.00

Souvenir Sheet

1187 A215 23.40g multi  10.00  —
1188 A215 23.40g multi  15.00  —

Nos. 1185-1188 are airmail. No. 1187 contains one 49x60mm stamp. No. 1188 contains one 50x61mm stamp.

Designs: 10c, Great Britain, Paris, 1900. 15c, Canada, St. Louis, 1904. 20c, Great Britain, London, 1908 and Stockholm, 1912. 25c, Belgium, Antwerp, 1920. 30c, Uruguay, Paris, 1924 and Amsterdam, 1928. 50c, Italy, Berlin, 1936. 75c, Sweden, London, 1948; USSR, Melbourne, 1956. 12.45g, Yugoslavia, Rome, 1960. 18.15g, Hungary, Helsinki, 1952, Tokyo, 1964 and Mexico, 1968.

A216

World Cup or South American Soccer Champions: 10c, Paraguay, 1953. 15c, Uruguay, 1930. 20c, Italy, 1934. 25c, Italy, 1938. 30c, Uruguay, 1950. 50c, Germany, 1954. horiz. 75c, Brazil, 1958. 12.45g, Brazil, 1962. 18.15g, England, 1966. No. 1198, Trophy. No. 1199, Soccer player, satellite.

**1969, Nov. 26    Perf. 14**

1189 A216 10c multicolored
1190 A216 15c multicolored
1191 A216 20c multicolored
1192 A216 25c multicolored
1193 A216 30c multicolored
1194 A216 50c multicolored
1195 A216 75c multicolored
1196 A216 12.45g multicolored
1197 A216 18.15g multicolored
Set, #1189-1197  4.50  2.50

Souvenir Sheets
**Perf. 13½, Imperf(#199)**
1198 A216 23.40g multicolored  35.00
1199 A216 23.40g multicolored  20.00
Nos. 1196-1199 are airmail. No. 1198 contains one 50x60mm stamp. No. 1199 contains one 45x57mm stamp.

## Fauna — A214

**1969, July 9**

1169 A214 10c Porcupine
1170 A214 15c Lemur, vert.
1171 A214 20c 3-toed sloth, vert.
1172 A214 25c Puma
1173 A214 30c Alligator
1174 A214 50c Jaguar
1175 A214 75c Anteater
1176 A214 12.45g Tapir
1177 A214 18.15g Capybara
Set, #1169-1177  2.75  1.75
Nos. 1176-1177 are airmail.

## Paintings by Francisco de Goya (1746-1828) — A217

**1969, Nov. 29    Litho.    Perf. 14x13½**

1200 A217 10c multicolored
1201 A217 15c multicolored
1202 A217 20c multicolored
1203 A217 25c multicolored
1204 A217 30c multicolored
1205 A217 50c multicolored
1206 A217 75c multicolored
1207 A217 12.45g multicolored
1208 A217 18.15g multicolored
Set, #1200-1208  5.00  3.00

Souvenir Sheet
**Perf. 14**
1209 A217 23.40g multicolored  27.50
Nos. 1207-1209 are airmail.

Designs: 10c, Miguel de Lardibazal. 15c, Francisca Sabasa y Gracia. 20c, Don Manuel Osorio. 25c, Young Women with a Letter. 30c, The Water Carrier. 50c, Truth, Time and History. 75c, The Forge. 12.45g, The Spell. 18.15g, "Duke of Wellington on Horseback. 23.40g, "La Maja Desnuda."

## Christmas A218

Various paintings of The Nativity or Madonna and Child.

**1969, Nov. 29    Perf. 13½**

1210 A218 10c Master Bertram
1211 A218 15c Procaccini
1212 A218 20c Di Credi
1213 A218 25c De Flemalle
1214 A218 30c Correggio
1215 A218 50c Borgianni
1216 A218 75c Botticelli
1217 A218 12.45g El Greco
1218 A218 18.15g De Morales
Set, #1210-1218  9.00  4.00

Souvenir Sheet
**Perf. 13½**
1219 A218 23.40g Isenheimer Altar  22.50
Nos. 1217-1219 are airmail.

## Souvenir Sheet
European Space Program — A219

**1969, Nov. 29    Litho.    Perf. 14**
1220 A219 23.40g ESRO 1B  20.00
**Imperf**
1221 A219 23.40g Ernst Stuhlinger  24.00

## Francisco Solano — A220

**1970, Mar. 1    Wmk. 347    Perf. 11**

1222 A220 1g bis brn  .20  .20
1223 A220 2g violet  .20  .20
1224 A220 4g brt pink  .20  .20
1225 A220 5g blue  .20  .20
1226 A220 6g rose claret  .20  .20
1227 A220 10g bright grn  .20  .20
1228 A220 15g lt Prus bl  .20  .20
1229 A220 20g org brn  .20  .20
1230 A220 30g gray grn  .20  .20
1231 A220 40g gray grn  .25  .20
Set, #1222-1231 (10)  2.15  2.00

Marshal Francisco Solano Lopez (1827-1870), President of Paraguay. Nos. 1228-1231 are airmail.

## 1st Moon Landing, Apollo 11 — A221

**1970, Mar. 11    Unwmk.    Perf. 14**

1232 A221 10c multicolored
1233 A221 15c multicolored
1234 A221 20c multicolored
1235 A221 25c multicolored
1236 A221 30c multicolored
1237 A221 50c multicolored
1238 A221 75c multicolored
1239 A221 12.45g multicolored
1240 A221 18.15g multicolored
Set, #1232-1240  5.50  2.75

Souvenir Sheets
**Imperf**
1241 A221 23.40g multicolored  15.00
1242 A221 23.40g multicolored  20.00
1243 A221 23.40g multicolored  15.00
Nos. 1239-1243 are airmail. Nos. 1241-1242 contain one 50x60mm stamp. No. 1242 contain one 60x50mm stamp.

Designs: 10c, Wernher von Braun, lift-off. 15c, Eagle and Columbia in lunar orbit. 20c, Deployment of lunar module. 25c, Landing on Moon. 30c, First steps on lunar surface. 50c, Gathering lunar soil. 75c, Lift-off from Moon. 12.45g, Rendezvous of Eagle and Columbia. 18.15g, Pres. Kennedy, von Braun, splashdown. No. 1241, Gold medal of Armstrong, Aldrin and Collins. No. 1242, Moon landing medal, Kennedy, von Braun. No. 1243, Apollo 12 astronauts Charles Conrad and Alan Bean on moon, and Dr. Kurl Debus.

## Easter — A222

Designs: 10c, 15c, 20c, 25c, 30c, 50c, 75c, Stations of the Cross. 12.45g, 18.15g, Christ appears to soldiers, vert. 18.15g, The sad Madonna, vert.

1970, Mar. 11
1244 A222 10c multicolored
1245 A222 15c multicolored
1246 A222 20c multicolored
1247 A222 25c multicolored
1248 A222 30c multicolored
1249 A222 50c multicolored
1250 A222 75c multicolored
1251 A222 12.45g multicolored
1252 A222 18.15g multicolored
Set, #1244-1252   4.50   3.00

Souvenir Sheet
Perf. 13½
1253 A222 23.40g multicolored   10.00
Nos. 1251-1253 are airmail. No. 1253 contains one 50x60mm stamp.

## Paraguay No. 2 — A223

Designs (First Issue of Paraguay): 2g, 10g, #1. 3g, #3. 5g, #2. 15g, #3. 30g, #2. 36g, #1.

1970, Aug. 15   Litho.   Wmk. 347
1254 A223 1g car rose   .20 .20
1255 A223 2g ultra   .20 .20
1256 A223 3g org brn   .20 .20
1257 A223 5g violet   .20 .20
1258 A223 10g lilac   .20 .20
1259 A223 15g vio brn   .25 .20
1260 A223 30g dp grn   .45 .40
1261 A223 36g brt pink   .50 .40
Set, #1254-1261 (8)   2.20 2.00
Centenary of stamps of Paraguay. #1259-1261 are airmail.

## 1972 Summer Olympics, Munich A224

No. 1262: a, 10c, Discus. b, 15c, Cycling. c, 20c, Men's hurdles. d, 25c, Fencing. e, 30c, Swimming.
50c, Shotput. 75c, Sailing. 12.45g, Equestrian, horiz. No. 1267, Flags, Olympic coins. No. 1268, 1269, Frauenkirche Church, Munich, horiz. Olympic Village, Munich, horiz.

1970, Sept. 28   Unwmk.   Perf. 14
1262 A224   Strip of 5, #a-e.
1263 A224 50c multicolored
1264 A224 75c multicolored
1265 A224 12.45g multicolored
1266 A224 18.15g multicolored
Set, #1262-1266   6.00 3.00

Souvenir Sheet
Perf. 13½
1267 A224 23.40g multicolored   12.50

Imperf
1268 A224 23.40g multicolored   60.00
1269 A224 23.40g multicolored   22.50
Nos. 1265-1269 are airmail. Nos. 1267-1269 each contain one 50x60mm stamp.

## Paintings, Pinakothek, Munich, 1972 A225

Nudes by: No. 1270a, 10c, Cranach. b, 15c, Baldung. c, 20c, Tintoretto. d, 25c, Rubens. e, 30c, Boucher, horiz. 50c, Baldung, diff. 75c, Cranach, diff.
12.45g, Self-portrait, Durer. 18.15g, Alterpiece, Altdorfer. 23.40g, Madonna and Child.

1970, Sept. 28   Perf. 14
1270 A225   Strip of 5, #a-e.
1271 A225 50c multicolored
1272 A225 75c multicolored
1273 A225 12.45g multicolored
1274 A225 18.15g multicolored
Set, #1270-1274   8.00 4.00

Souvenir Sheet
Perf. 13½
1275 A225 23.40g multicolored   22.50
Nos. 1273-1275 are airmail. No. 1275 contains one 50x60mm stamp.

## Apollo Space Program — A226

No. 1276: a, 10c, Ignition, Saturn 5. b, 15c, Apollo 1 mission emblem, vert. c, 20c, Apollo 7, Oct. 1968. d, 25c, Apollo 8, Dec. 1968. e, 30c, Apollo 9, Mar. 1969.
50c, Apollo 10, May 1969. 75c, Apollo 11, July 1969. 12.45g, Apollo 12, Nov. 1969. 18.15g, Apollo 13, Apr. 1970. No. 1281, Lunar landing sites. No. 1282, Wernher von Braun, rockets. No. 1283, James A. Lovell, John L. Swigert, Fred W. Haise.

1970, Oct. 10   Perf. 14
1276 A226   Strip of 5, #a-e.
1277 A226 50c multicolored
1278 A226 75c multicolored
1279 A226 12.45g multicolored
1280 A226 18.15g multicolored
Set, #1276-1280   5.00 3.00

Souvenir Sheets
Perf. 13½
1281 A226 23.40g multicolored   10.00

Imperf
1282 A226 23.40g multicolored   50.00
1283 A226 23.40g multicolored   20.00
Nos. 1279-1283 are airmail. Nos. 1281-1283 each contain one 60x50mm stamp.

Future Space Projects: No. 1284a, 10c, Space station, 2000. b, 15c, Lunar station. c, 20c, Space transport. d, 25c, Lunar rover. e, 30c, Skylab.
50c, Space station, 1971. 75c, Lunar vehicle. 12.45g, Lunar vehicle, diff. vert. 18.15g, Vehicle rising above lunar surface. 23.40g, Moon stations, transport.

1970, Oct. 19   Perf. 14
1284 A226   Strip of 5, #a-e.
1285 A226 50c multicolored
1286 A226 75c multicolored
1287 A226 12.45g multicolored
1288 A226 18.15g multicolored
Set, #1284-1288   5.00 2.50

## EXPO '70, Osaka, Japan A228

Souvenir Sheet
Perf. 13½
1289 A226 23.40g multicolored   15.00
Nos. 1287-1289 are airmail. No. 1289 contains one 50x60mm stamp. For overprints see Nos. 2288-2290, C653.

Paintings from National Museum, Tokyo: No. 1290a, 10c, Buddha. b, 15c, Fire, people. c, 20c, Demon, Ogata Korin. d, 25c, Japanese play, Hishikawa Moronobu. e, 30c, Birds.
50c, Woman, Utamaro. 75c, Samurai, Wantabe Kazan. 12.45g, Women Beneath Tree, Kano Hideroi. 18.15g, Courtesans, Torri Kiyonaga. 50g, View of Mt. Fuji, Hokusai, horiz. No. 1296, Courtesan, Kaigetsudo Ando. No. 1297, Emblem of Expo '70. No. 1298, Emblem of 1972 Winter Olympics, Sapporo.

1970, Nov. 26   Litho.   Perf. 14
1290 A228   Strip of 5, #a-e.
1291 A228 50c multicolored
1292 A228 75c multicolored
1293 A228 12.45g multicolored
1294 A228 18.15g multicolored
1295 A228 50g multicolored
Set, #1290-1295   6.00 4.00

Souvenir Sheets
Perf. 13½
1296 A228 20g multicolored   10.00
1297 A228 20g multicolored   17.50
1298 A228 20g multicolored   30.00
Nos. 1293-1298 are airmail. Nos. 1296-1298 each contain one 50x60mm stamp.

## Flower Paintings A229

Artists: No. 1299a, 10c, Von Jawlensky. b, 15c, Purrmann. c, 20c, De Vlaminck. d, 25c, Monet. e, 30c, Renoir.
50c, Van Gogh. 75c, Cezanne. 12.45g, Van Huysum. 18.15g, Ruysch. 50g, Walscappelle. 20g, Bosschaert.

1970, Nov. 26   Perf. 14
1299 A229   Strip of 5, #a-e.
1300 A229 50c multicolored
1301 A229 75c multicolored
1302 A229 12.45g multicolored
1303 A229 18.15g multicolored
1304 A229 50g multicolored
Set, #1299-1304   5.00 3.00

Souvenir Sheet
Perf. 13½
1305 A229 20g multicolored   10.00
Nos. 1302-1305 are airmail. No. 1305 contains one 50x60mm stamp.

## Paintings from The Prado, Madrid — A230

Nudes by: No. 1306a, 10c, Titian. b, 15c, Velazquez. c, 20c, Van Dyck. d, 25c, Tintoretto. e, 30c, Rubens.
50c, Venus and Sleeping Adonis, Veronese. 75c, Adam and Eve, Titian. 12.45g, The Holy Family, Goya. 18.15g, Shepherd Boy, Murillo. 50g, The Holy Family, El Greco.

1970, Dec. 16   Perf. 14
1306 A230   Strip of 5, #a-e.
1307 A230 50c multicolored
1308 A230 75c multicolored
1309 A230 12.45g multicolored
1310 A230 18.15g multicolored
1311 A230 50g multicolored
Set, #1306-1311   6.00 4.00
#1309-1311 are airmail. #1307-1311 are vert.

1970, Dec. 16
Paintings by Albrecht Durer (1471-1528): No. 1312a, 10c, Adam and Eve. b, 15c, St. Jerome in the Wilderness. c, 20c, St. Eustachius and George. d, 25c, Lucretia's Suicide. e, 30c, Piper and drummer.
50c, Oswald Krel. 75c, Stag Beetle. 12.45g, Paul and Mark. 18.15g, Lot's Flight. 50g, Nativity.

1312 A230   Strip of 5, #a-e.
1313 A230 50c multicolored
1314 A230 75c multicolored
1315 A230 12.45g multicolored
1316 A230 18.15g multicolored
1317 A230 50g multicolored
Set, #1312-1317   6.00 4.00
Nos. 1315-1317 are airmail. See No. 1273.

## Christmas A232

Paintings: No. 1318a, 10c, The Annunciation, Van der Weyden. b, 15c, The Madonna, Zeitblom. c, 20c, The Nativity, Von Soest. d, 25c, Adoration of the Magi, Mayno. e, 30c, Adoration of the Magi, Fabriano.
50c, Flight From Egypt, Masters of Martyrdom. 75c, Presentation of Christ, Memling. 12.45g, The Holy Family, Poussin, horiz. 18.15g, The Holy Family, Rubens. 20g, Adoration of the Magi, Giorgione, horiz. 50g, Madonna and Child, Batoni.

1971, Mar. 23   Perf. 14
1318 A232   Strip of 5, #a-e.
1319 A232 50c multicolored
1320 A232 75c multicolored
1321 A232 12.45g multicolored
1322 A232 18.15g multicolored
1323 A232 50g multicolored
Set, #1318-1323   6.00 4.00

Souvenir Sheet
Perf. 13½
1324 A232 20g multicolored   17.50
Nos. 1321-1324 are airmail. No. 1324 contains one 60x50mm stamp.

Olympic decathlon. gold medalists: No. 1325a, 10c. Hugo Wieslander, Stockholm 1912. b, 15c. Helge Loviand, Antwerp 1920. c, 20c. Harold M. Osborn, Paris 1924. d, 25c. Paavo Yrjola, Amsterdam 1928. e, 30c, James Bausch, Los Angeles 1932.
50c, Glenn Morris, Berlin 1936. 75c, Bob Mathias, London 1948, Helsinki 1952. 12.45g, Milton Campbell, Melbourne 1956. 18.15g, Rafer Johnson, Rome 1960. 50g, Willi Holdorf, Tokyo 1964. No. 1331, Bill Toomey, Mexico City 1968.
No. 1332, Pole vaulter, Munich, 1972.

**1971, Mar. 23**    **Perf. 14**
1325 A233   Strip of 5,
1326 A233     #a–e.
1327 A233   50c multicolored
1328 A233   75c multicolored
1329 A233   12.45g multicolored
1330 A233   18.15g multicolored
     50g multicolored
Set, #1325-1330    6.00   3.00

**Souvenir Sheets**
**Perf. 13½**
1331 A233   20g multicolored   14.00   14.00
1332 A233   20g multicolored   14.00   14.00
Nos. 1328-1332 are airmail. Nos. 1331-1332 each contain one 50x60mm stamp.

Paintings by: No. 1333a, 10c, Van Dyck. b, 15c. Titian. c, 20c, Van Dyck, diff. d, 25c, Walter. e, 30c, Orsi.
50c, 17th cent. Japanese artist, horiz. 75c, David. 12.45g, Huguet. 18.15g, Perugino. 20g, Van Eyck. 50g, Witz.

Art — A234

**1971, Mar. 26**    **Perf. 14**
1333 A234   Strip of 5,
1334 A234     #a–e.
1335 A234   50c multicolored
1336 A234   75c multicolored
1337 A234   12.45g multicolored
1338 A234   18.15g multicolored
     50g multicolored
Set, #1333-1338    6.00   4.00

**Souvenir Sheet**
**Perf. 13½**
1339 A234   20g multicolored   19.00
Nos. 1336-1339 are airmail. No. 1339 contains one 50x60mm stamp.

Paintings from the Louvre, Paris
Portraits of women by: No. 1340a, 10c, De la Tour. b, 15c, Boucher. c, 20c, Delacroix. d, 25c, 16th cent. French artist. e, 30c, Ingres.
50c, Ingres, horiz. 75c, Watteau, horiz. 12.45g, 2nd cent. artist. 18.15g, Renoir. 20g, Mona Lisa, Da Vinci. 50g, Liberty Guiding the People, Delacroix.

**1971, Mar. 26**    **Perf. 14**
1340 A234
1341 A234   Strip of 5,
1342 A234     #a–e.
1343 A234   50c multicolored
1344 A234   75c multicolored
1345 A234   12.45g multicolored
     18.15g multicolored
     50g multicolored
Set, #1340-1345    6.00   4.00

---

**1346 A234**   20g multicolored   14.00
Nos. 1343-1346 are airmail. No. 1346 contains one 50x60mm stamp.

**Souvenir Sheet**
**Perf. 13½**

Paintings
A236

Artist: No. 1347a, 10c, Botticelli. b, 15c, Titian. c, 20c, Raphael. d, 25c, Pellegrini. e, 30c, Caracci.
50c, Titian. horiz. 75c, Ricci, horiz. 12.45g, Courtines. 18.15g, Rodas. 50g, Murillo.

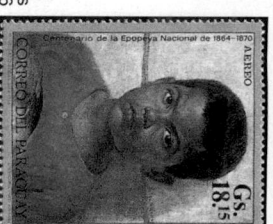

**1971, Mar. 29**    **Perf. 14**
1347 A236   Strip of 5, #a–e.
1348 A236   50c multicolored
1349 A236   75c multicolored
1350 A236   12.45g multicolored
1351 A236   18.15g multicolored
1352 A236   50g multicolored
Set, #1347-1352    6.00   4.00
Nos. 1350-1352 are airmail.

Different Paintings by: No. 1353a, 10c, Gozzoli, vert. b, 15c, Velazquez, vert. c, 20c, Brun. d, 25c, Fontainebleau School, 1550, vert. e, 30c, Uccello, vert.
50c, P. De Vos, 75c, Vernet. 12.45g, 18.15g, 50g, Alken & Sutherland. No. 1360, Paul & Derveaux. No. 1360, Degas.

Hunting Scenes — A237

**1971, Mar. 29**    **Perf. 14**
1353 A237   Strip of 5,
1354 A237     #a–e.
1355 A237   50c multicolored
1356 A237   75c multicolored
1357 A237   12.45g multicolored
1358 A237   18.15g multicolored
     50g multicolored
Set, #1353-1358    6.00   4.00

**Souvenir Sheets**
**Perf. 13½**
1359 A237   20g multicolored   12.00
1360 A237   20g multicolored   12.00
Nos. 1356-1360 are airmail. Nos. 1359-1360 each contain one 60x50mm stamp.

Designs: Nos. 1361a-1361e, 10c, 15c, 20c, 25c, 30c. Different flowers. Gukel. 50c, Birds. Lu Chi. 75c. Flowers. Sakai Hoitsu. 12.45g, Man and Woman. Utamaro. 18.15g, Tea Ceremony, from Tea museum. 50c, Bathers. Utamaro. No. 1367, Woman. Kamakura Period. No. 1368, Japan #1, #821, #904,

Philatokyo
'71 — A238

**1367 A238**   20g multicolored   15.00
**1368 A238**   20g multicolored   15.00
Set, #1361-1366    6.00   4.00
Nos. 1364-1368 are airmail. Nos. 1367-1368 each contain one 50x60mm stamp. See Nos. 1375-1376.

**Souvenir Sheets**
**Perf. 13½**

**1971, Apr. 7**    **Perf. 14**
1361 A238
1362 A238   Strip of 5,
1363 A238     #a–e.
1364 A238   50c multicolored
1365 A238   75c multicolored
1366 A238   12.45g multicolored
     18.15g multicolored
     50g multicolored

Paintings of women by: No. 1369a, 10c, Harunobu. b, 15c, Hosoda. c, 20c, Harunobu, diff. d, 25c, Uemura Shoen. e, 30c, Ketao.
50c, Three Women, Torii. 75c, Old Man, Kakizaki. 12.45g, 2-man bobsled. 18.15g, Ice sculptures, horiz. 50g, Mt. Fuji, Hokusai, horiz. No. 1375, Skier, horiz. No. 1376, Sapporo Olympic emblems.

**1971, Apr.**    **Perf. 14**
1369 A239   Strip of 5,
1370 A239     #a–e.
1371 A239   50c multicolored
1372 A239   75c multicolored
1373 A239   12.45g multicolored
1374 A239   18.15g multicolored
     50g multicolored
Set, #1369-1374    6.00   4.00

**Souvenir Sheets**
**Perf. 14½**
1375 A239   20g multicolored   17.00
1376 A239   20g multicolored   17.00
Nos. 1372-1376 are airmail. No. 1375 contains one 35x25mm stamp with PhilaTokyo 71 emblem. No. 1376 contains one 50x60mm stamp.
For Japanese painting stamps with white border and Winter Olympics emblem see #1409-1410.

**Wmk. 347**
**Litho.**    **Perf. 11**
**1971, May 18**
1377 A240   3g ultra   .20   .20
1378 A240   5g lilac   .20   .20
1379 A240   10g emerald   .20   .20
1380 A240   20g claret   .20   .20
1381 A240   25g brt pink   .20   .20
1382 A240   30g brown   .20   .20
1383 A240   50g gray olive   .35   .25
Set, #1377-1383 (7)    1.55   1.45
International Education Year.
Nos. 1380-1383 are airmail.

UNESCO and Paraguay
Emblems, Globe, Teacher and Pupil
A240

Artists: 10c, Caravaggio. No. 1385: a, 15c, Venezian. 50g, Holbein. 25c, Cranach. 30c, 12.45g, Cranach, diff. 18.15g, Durer. 50g, Schongauer.

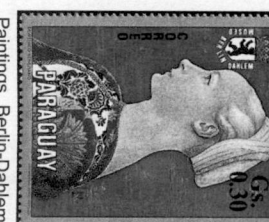

Paintings, Berlin-Dahlem Museum — A241

**1971, Dec. 24**    **Unwmk.**
     b, 20c, Di Cosimo. 25c, Cranach. 30c, 12.45g, Cranach, diff. 18.15g, Durer. 50g, continuous design.
1384 A241   10c multicolored
1385 A241   Pair. #a–b.
1386 A241   25c multicolored
1387 A241   30c multicolored
1388 A241   50c multicolored
1389 A241   75c multicolored
1390 A241   12.45g multicolored
1391 A241   18.15g multicolored
1392 A241   50g multicolored
Set, #1384-1392    6.00   4.00
Nos. 1390-1392 are airmail. No. 1385 has continuous design.

**Perf. 14**

Paintings: No. 1393a, 10c, Desiree Clary. Gerin. b, 15c, Josephine de Beauharnais, Gros. c, 20c, Maria Luisa, Gerard. d, 25c, Juliette Recamier, Gerard. e, 30c, Maria Walewska, Gerard.
50c, Victoria Kraus, unknown artist, horiz. 75c, Napoleon on Horseback, Chabord. 12.45g, Trafalgar. A. Mayer, horiz. 18.15g, Napoleon Leading Army, Gautherot, horiz. 50g, Napoleon's tomb.

**1971, Dec. 24**    **Perf. 14**
1393 A242   Strip of 5, #a–e.
1394 A242   50c multicolored
1395 A242   75c multicolored
1396 A242   12.45g multicolored
1397 A242   18.15g multicolored
1398 A242   50g multicolored
Set, #1393-1398    6.00   4.00
Nos. 1396-1398 are airmail.

Designs: No. 1399a, 10c, Trevithick, Great Britain, 1804. b, 15c, Blenkinsops, 1812. c, 20c, G. Stephenson #1, 1825. d, 25c, Marc Seguin, France, 1829. e, 30c, "Adler," Germany, 1835.
50c, Sampierdarena #1, Italy, 1854. 75c, Paraguay #1, 1861. 12.45g, "Munich," Germany. 1841. 18.15g, US, 1875. 20g, Japanese locomotives, 1872-1972. 50g, Mikado D-50, Japan, 1923.

Locomotives — A243

**1972, Jan. 6**
1399 A243
1400 A243   Strip of 5,
1401 A243     #a–e.
1402 A243   50c multicolored
1403 A243   75c multicolored
     12.45g multicolored
     18.15g multicolored

1404 A243 50g multicolored 6.00 4.00
Set, #1399-1404
**Souvenir Sheet** *Perf. 13½*
1405 A243 20g multicolored 12.00 5.00
Nos. 1402-1405 are airmail. No. 1405 contains one 60x50mm stamp. See Nos. 1476-1480.

## 1972 Winter Olympics, Sapporo — A244

Designs: Nos. 1406a, 10c, Hockey player. b, 15c, Jean-Claude Killy. c, 20c, Gaby Seyfert. d, 25c, 4-Man bobsled. e, 30c, Luge. 50c, Ski jumping, horiz. 75c, Slalom skiing, horiz. 12.45g, Painting, Kuniyoshi. 10.15g, Winter Scene, Hiroshige, horiz. 18.15g, man in traditional dress.

*Perf. 14*
**1972, Jan. 6** Strip of 5, #a.-e.
1406 A244
1407 A244 50c multicolored
1408 A244 75c multicolored
1409 A244 12.45g multicolored
1410 A244 18.15g multicolored
1411 A244 50g multicolored 9.00 4.00
Set, #1406-1411
**Souvenir Sheet** *Perf. 13½*
1412 A244 20g Skier 17.00
1413 A244 20g Flags 22.50
Nos. 1409-1413 are airmail. Nos. 1412-1413 each contain one 50x60mm stamp. For Winter Olympic overprint see Nos. 2295-2297. For overprint stamps with gold border, see Nos. 1372-1373.

## UNICEF, 25th Anniv. (in 1971) — A245

**1972, Jan. 24** Granite Paper
1414 A245 1g red brn .20 .20
1415 A245 2g ultra .20 .20
1416 A245 3g lil rose .20 .20
1417 A245 4g violet .20 .20
1418 A245 5g emerald .20 .20
1419 A245 10g claret .20 .20
1420 A245 20g brt bl .20 .20
1421 A245 25g lt ol .20 .20
1422 A245 30g dk brn .20 .20
Nos. 1414-1422 (9) 1.80 1.80
Nos. 1420-1422 are airmail.

## Race Cars A246

No. 1423: a, 10c, Ferrari. b, 15c, B.R.M. c, 20c, Brabham. d, 25c, March. e, 30c, Honda. 50c, Matra-Simca MS 650. 75c, Porsche. 12.45g, Maserati-8 CTF, 1938. 18.15g, Bugatti 35B, 1929. 20g, Lotus 72 Ford. 50g, Mercedes, 1924.

**1972, Mar. 20** Unwmk. Strip of 5, #a.-e.
1423 A246
1424 A246 50c multicolored
1425 A246 75c multicolored
1426 A246 12.45g multicolored

1427 A246 18.15g multicolored
1428 A246 50g multicolored 12.00 5.00
Set, #1423-1428
**Souvenir Sheet** *Perf. 13½*
1429 A246 20g multicolored 22.50
Nos. 1426-1429 are airmail. No. 1429 contains one 60x50mm stamp.

## Sailing Ships — A247

Paintings: No. 1430a, 10c, Intrepid. b, 15c, Holbein. c, 20c, Nagasaki print. d, 25c, Portuguese ship, unknown artist. e, 30c, Roux. 50c, Santa Maria, Mount Vernon, US, 1798, Corne. 75c, Van Eertvelt, vert. 12.45g, Royal Prince, 1679, Van Beecq. 18.15g, Van Bree. 50g, Book of Arms, 1497, vert.

*Perf. 14*
**1972, Mar. 29** Strip of 5, #a.-e.
1430 A247
1431 A247 50c multicolored
1432 A247 75c multicolored
1433 A247 12.45g multicolored
1434 A247 18.15g multicolored
1435 A247 50g multicolored 4.50 3.00
Set, #1430-1435
Nos. 1433-1435 are airmail.

## Paintings in Vienna Museum A248

Nudes by: No. 1436a, 10c, Rubens. b, 15c, Bellini. c, 20c, Carracci. d, 25c, Cagnacci. e, 30c, Mandolin Player, Strozzi. 75c, Woman in Red Hat, Cranach the elder. 12.45g, Adam and Eve, Coxcie. 18.15g, Legionary on Horseback, Poussin. 50g, Madonna and Child, Bronzino.

**1972, May 22** Strip of 5, #a.-e.
1436 A248
1437 A248 50c multicolored
1438 A248 75c multicolored
1439 A248 12.45g multicolored
1440 A248 18.15g multicolored
1441 A248 50g multicolored 5.50 4.00
Set, #1436-1441
Nos. 1439-1441 are airmail.

## Paintings in Asuncion Museum A249

No. 1442: a, 10c, Man in Straw Hat, Holden Jara. b, 15c, Portrait, Tintoretto. c, 20c, Indians, Holden Jara. d, 25c, Nude, Bouchard. e, 30c, Nude, Italian School. 50c, Reclining Nude, Berisso, horiz. 75c, Carracci, horiz. 12.45g, Reclining Nude, Schiaffino, horiz. 18.15g, Reclining Nude, Lostow, horiz. 50g, Madonna and Child, 17th cent. Italian School.

**1972, May 22**
1442 A249
1443 A249 50c multicolored
1444 A249 75c multicolored
1445 A249 12.45g multicolored
1446 A249 18.15g multicolored
1447 A249 50g multicolored 4.00 3.00
Set, #1442-1447
Nos. 1445-1447 are airmail.

## Presidential Summit — A250

No. 1448: a, 10c, Map of South America. b, 15c, Brazil natl. arms. c, 20c, Argentina natl. arms. d, 25c, Bolivia natl. arms. e, 30c, Paraguay natl. arms. 50c, Pres. Emilio Garrastazu, Brazil. 75c, Pres. Alejandro Lanusse, Argentina. 12.45g, Pres. Hugo Banzer Suarez, Bolivia. 18.15, Pres. Stroessner, Paraguay, horiz. 23.40g, Flags.

**1972, Nov. 18** Strip of 5, #a.-e.
1448 A250
1449 A250 50c multicolored
1450 A250 75c multicolored
1451 A250 12.45g multicolored
1452 A250 18.15g multicolored
Set, #1448-1452
**Souvenir Sheet** *Perf. 13½*
1453 A250 23.40g multicolored 1.75
Nos. 1451-1453 are airmail. No. 1453 contains one 50x60mm stamp. For overprint see No. 2144.

## Pres. Stroessner's Visit to Japan — A251

No. 1454: a, 10c, Departure of first Japanese mission to US & Europe, 1871. b, 15c, First railroad, Tokyo-Yokahama, 1872. c, 20c, Samurai. d, 25c, Geishas. e, 30c, Cranes, Hiroshige. 50c, Honda race car. 75c, Pres. Stroessner, Emperor Hirohito, Mt. Fuji, bullet train, horiz. 12.45g, Rocket. 18.15g, Stroessner, Hirohito, horiz. No. 1459, Mounted samurai, Masanobu, 1740. No. 1460, Hirohito's speech, state dinner, horiz. No. 1461, Delegations at Tokyo airport, horiz.

**1972, Nov. 18** Strip of 5, #a.-e.
1454 A251
1455 A251 50c multicolored
1456 A251 75c multicolored
1457 A251 12.45g multicolored
1458 A251 18.15g multicolored 6.75
Nos. 1454-1458 (5)
**Souvenir Sheets** *Perf. 13½*
1459 A251 23.40g multicolored 17.50
1460 A251 23.40g multicolored 17.50
*Imperf*
1461 A251 23.40g multicolored
Nos. 1457-1461 are airmail. Nos. 1459-1460 each contain one 50x60mm stamp. No. 1461 contains one 85x42mm stamp with simulated perforations. For overprints see Nos. 2192-2194, 2267.

## Wildlife A252

*Perf. 14*
Paintings — #1462: a, 10c, Cranes, Boke. b, 15c, Tiger, Utamaro. c, 20c, Horses, Arenys. d, 25c, Pheasant, Dietzsch. e, 30c, Monkey, Brueghel, the Elder. All vert. 50c, Deer, Marc. 75c, Crab, Durer. 12.45g, Rooster, Jakuchu, vert. 18.15g, Swan, Asselyn.

**1972, Nov. 18** Strip of 5, #a.-e.
1462 A252 50c multicolored
1463 A252 75c multicolored
1464 A252 12.45g multicolored
1465 A252 18.15g multicolored
1466 A252 50g multicolored
Set, #1462-1466 4.50 2.50
Nos. 1465-1466 are airmail.

## Acaray Dam A253

Designs: "70, Francisco Solano Lopez monument. 3g, Friendship Bridge. 5g, Tebicuary River Bridge. 10g, Hotel Guarani. 20g, Bus and car on highway. 25g, Hospital of Institute for Social Service. 50g, "Presidente Stroessner" of state merchant marine. 100g, "Electra" C of Paraguayan airlines.

*Perf. 13½x10* Wmk. 347
**1972, Nov. 16** Granite Paper
1467 A253 1g sepia .20 .20
1468 A253 2g brown .20 .20
1469 A253 3g brt ultra .20 .20
1470 A253 5g brt pink .20 .20
1471 A253 10g dl grn .20 .20
1472 A253 20g rose car .20 .20
1473 A253 25g gray .20 .20
1474 A253 50g violet .35 .25
1475 A253 100g brt lil .70 .50
Nos. 1467-1475 (9) 2.45 2.15
Tourism Year of the Americas.
Nos. 1472-1475 are airmail.

## Locomotives Type

No. 1176: a, 10c, Stephenson's Rocket, 1829. b, 15c, First Swiss railroad, 1847. c, 20c, 1st Spanish locomotive, 1848. d, 2c, Norris, US, 1850. e, 30c, Ansaldo, Italy, 1859. 50c, Badenia, Germany, 1863. 75c, 1st Japanese locomotive, 1895. 12.45g, P.L.M., France, 1924. 18.15g, Stephenson's Northumbrian.

*Perf. 14*
**1972, Nov. 25** Unwmk. Strip of 5, #a.-e.
1476 A243 50c multicolored
1477 A243 75c multicolored
1478 A243 12.45g multicolored
1479 A243 18.15g multicolored
1480 A243 50g multicolored
Set, #1476-1480 9.00 4.00
Nos. 1479-1480 are airmail.

## South American Wildlife — A254

No. 1481: a, 10c, Tetradactyla. b, 15c, Nasua socialis. c, 20c, Priodontes giganteus. d, 25c, Blastocerus dichotomus. e, 30c, Felis pardalis.

**1972, Nov. 25**

1481 A254 50c multicolored
1482 A254 50c multicolored
1483 A254 75c multicolored
1484 A254 12.45g multicolored
1485 A254 18.15g multicolored
Set, #1481-1485 multicolored
Nos. 1484-1485 are airmail.

11.00 4.00

50c, Aotes, vert. 75c, Rhea americana. 12.45g, Desmodus rotundus. 18.15g, Urocyon cinereo-argenteus.

OAS Emblem — A255

**1973**

Nos. 1492-1495 are airmail

**Perf. 13x13½**

**Litho.** **Wmk. 347**
**Granite Paper**

1486 A255 1g multi .20 .20
1487 A255 2g multi .20 .20
1488 A255 3g multi .20 .20
1489 A255 4g multi .20 .20
1490 A255 5g multi .20 .20
1491 A255 10g multi .20 .20
1492 A255 20g multi .20 .20
1493 A255 25g multi .20 .20
1494 A255 50g multi .35 .25
1495 A255 100g multi .70 .25
Set, #1486-1495 (10) 2.65 2.35

Org. of American States, 25th anniv.
Nos. 1486-1495 on airmail

Paintings in Florence Museum A256

**1973**

**Litho.** **Wmk. 347**

1496 A256 Strip of 7, #a.-g.
1497 A256 Strip of 3, #a.-c.
Set, #1496-1497 5.50 3.50

No. 1497 is airmail.

**Perf. 14 Unwmk.**

Artists: No. 1496: a, 10c, Cranach, the Elder. b, 15c, Caravaggio. c, 20c, Florentino. d, 25c, Di Credi. e, 30c, Liss. f, 50c, Botticelli. g, 75c, Titian, horiz. No. 1497: a, 5g, Titian, horiz. b, 10g, Del Piombo, horiz. c, 20g, Di Michelino, horiz.

**MUESTRA**

Butterflies — A257

#1498: a, 10c, Catagramma patazza. b, 15c, Agrias narcissus. c, 20c, Papilio zagreus. d, 25c, Heliconius chestertoni. e, 30c, Metamorphaphido. f, 50c, Catagramma astarte. g, 75c, Papilio brasiliensis.
No. 1499a, 5g, Agrias sardanapalus. b, 10g, Callithea saphhira. c, 20g, Jemadia hospita.

**1973, Mar. 13**

1498 A257 Strip of 7, #a.-g.
1499 A257 Strip of 3, #a.-c.
Set, #1498-1499 8.00 4.50

No. 1499 is airmail.

---

Cats A258

**1973, June 29**

1500 A258 Strip of 7, #a.-g.
1501 A258 Strip of 3, #a.-c.
Set, #1500-1501 9.00 4.50

No. 1500 is airmail. For other cat designs, see type A287.

Faces of Cats: No. 1500: a, 10c. b, 15c. c, 20c. d, 25c. e, 30c. f, 50c. g, 75c. No. 1501a, 5g, Cat under rose bush, by Desportes. b, 10g, Two cats, by Marc, horiz. c, 20g, Man with cat, by Rousseau.

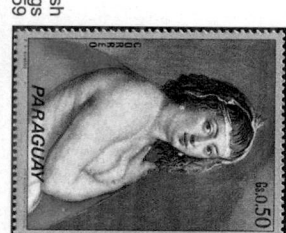

Flemish Paintings A259

**1973, June 29**

**Litho.** **Perf. 14**

1502 A259 Strip of 7, #a.-g.
1503 A259 Strip of 3, #a.-c.
Set, #1502-1503 6.00 4.00

No. 1503 is airmail.

Nudes by: No. 1502: a, 10c, Spranger. b, 15c, Jordaens. c, 20c, de Clerck. d, 25c, Spranger, diff. e, 30c, Goltzius. f, 50c, Rubens. g, 75c, Vase of flowers, J. Brueghel. No. 1503a, 5g, Nude, de Clerck, horiz. b, 10g, Woman with mandolin, de Vos. c, 20g, Men, horses, Rubens, horiz.

Hand Holding Letter — A260

**1973, July 10**

**Litho.** **Perf. 11**

1504 A260 2g lil rose & blk .20 .20

No. 1504 was issued originally as a nonobligatory stamp to benefit mailmen, but its status was changed to regular postage.

EXPOPAR 73, Paraguayan Industrial Exhib. — A261

**1973, Aug. 11**

**Granite Paper**

**Wmk. 347** **Perf. 13x13½**

1505 A261 1g org brn .20 .20
1506 A261 2g vermilion .20 .20
1507 A261 3g blue .20 .20
1508 A261 4g emerald .20 .20
1509 A261 5g lilac .20 .20
1510 A261 20g lilac rose .20 .20
1511 A261 25g rose claret .20 .20
Nos. 1505-1511 (7) 1.40 1.40

Nos. 1510-1511 are airmail.

---

1974 World Cup Soccer Championships, Munich — A262

**1973**

**Litho.** **Unwmk.** **Perf. 14**

1512 A262 Strip of 7, #a.-g.
1513 A262 5g multicolored
1514 A262 Pair, #a.-b.
Set, #1512-1514 9.00 5.00

**Souvenir Sheets**

**Perf. 13½**

1515 A262 25g multicolored 17.50
1516 A262 25g multicolored 17.50

Nos. 1513-1514, 1516, Oct. 8 & No. 1515, June 29. For overprint see No. 2131.

No. 1512: a, 10c, Uruguay vs. Paraguay. b, 15c, Crerand, England and Eusebio, Portugal. c, 20c, Bobby Charlton, England. d, 25c, Franz Beckenbauer, Germany. e, 30c, Erler, Germany and McNab, England. f, 50c, Pele, Brazil and Willi Schulz, Germany. g, 75c, Arsenio Erico, Paraguay.
5g, Brian Labone, Gerd Mueller, Bobby Moore. No. 1514a, 10g, Luigi Riva, Italy. No. 1514b, 20g, World Cup medals. No. 1515, World Cup trophy. 25g, Player scoring goal.

**MUESTRA**

Paintings A263

Details from paintings, artist: No. 1517a, Venus and Mars, Pittoni. c, 20c, Rape of Europa, Veronese. d, 25c, Susannah and the Elders, Tintoretto. e, 30c, Euphrosyne, Amigoni. f, 50c, Allegory of Moderation, Veronese. g, 75c, Ariadne, Tintoretto.
10g, Portrait of Woman in Fur Hat, G.D. Tiepolo. b, 20g, Dialectic of Industry, Veronese.

**1973, Oct. 8**

**Perf. 14**

1517 A263 Strip of 7, #a.-g.
1518 A263 5g multicolored
1519 A263 Pair, #a.-b.
Set, #1517-1519 5.50 3.00

Nos. 1518-1519 are airmail.

Birds A264

No. 1520: a, 10c, Tersina viridis. b, 15c, Pipile cumanensis. c, 20c, Rupicola rubinus. d, 25c, Andigena laminirostris. e, 30c, Pyrocephalus

---

Space Exploration — A265

1523 A264 25g multicolored 12.50
tains one 50x60mm stamp.

**Souvenir Sheet**

**Perf. 13½**

1520 A264 Strip of 7, #a.-g.
1521 A264 5g multicolored
1522 A264 Pair, #a.-b.
Set, #1520-1522 6.00 5.00

Nos. 1521-1523 are airmail. No. 1523 con-

**1973, Nov. 14**

No. 1524a, 10c, Apollo 11. b, 15c, Apollo 12. c, 20c, Apollo 13. d, 25c, Apollo 14. e, 30c, Apollo 15. f, 50c, Apollo 16. g, 75c, Apollo 17.
5g, Skylab. 10g, Apollo-Soyuz mission. b, 20g, Apollo 17. Space shuttle. neer 11, Jupiter. No. 1528, Pioneer 10, Jupiter, vert.

1524 A265 Strip of 7, #a.-g.
1525 A265 5g multicolored
1526 A265 Pair, #a.-b.
Set, #1524-1526 6.00 5.00

**Souvenir Sheet**

**Perf. 14½**

1527 A265 25g multicolored 17.00

**Perf. 13½**

1528 A265 25g multicolored 15.00

#1525-1528 are airmail. #1527 contains on 35x25mm stamp. #1528 one 50x60mm stamp.

REPUBLICA DEL PARAGUAY

Women of Avignon, Pablo Picasso — A266

Souvenir Sheet

**1973, Nov. 14**

**Perf. 13½**

1529 A266 25g multicolored 11.00

Illustration reduced.

Traditional Costumes A267

**1973, Nov. 14**

**Perf. 14**

No. 1530: a, 25c, Indian girl. b, 50c, Bottle dance costume. c, 75c, Dancer balancing vase on head. d, 1g, Dancer with flowers. e, 1.50g, Weavers. f, 1.75g, Man, woman in

Origin of the Milky Way, Tintoretto. 15g, Rider and Hounds, Pisanello.

**1975, Apr. 25    Unwmk.    Perf. 14**
1556  A276  5c  multicolored
1557  A276  10c  multicolored
1558  A276  15c  multicolored
1559  A276  20c  multicolored
1560  A276  35c  multicolored
1561  A276  40c  multicolored
1562  A276  40c  multicolored
1563  A276  50c  multicolored
Set, #1556-1563                 8.00  3.00

**Souvenir Sheet**
**Perf. 13½**
1564  A276  15g multicolored         15.00

No. 1564 is airmail, contains one 50x60mm stamp and price includes a 5g surtax for a monument to Francisco Solano Lopez.

Dogs
A277

**1975, June 7**
1565  A277  5c  Boxer
1566  A277  10c  Poodle
1567  A277  15c  Basset hound
1568  A277  20c  Collie
1569  A277  25c  Chihuahua
1570  A277  35c  German shepherd
1571  A277  40c  Pekinese
1572  A277  50c  Chow
Set, #1565-1572               4.50  1.50

**Souvenir Sheet**
**Perf. 13½**
1573  A277  15g  Fox hound, horse      20.00

No. 1573 is airmail, contains one 50x50mm stamp and price includes a 5g surtax for a monument to Francisco Solano Lopez.

South American Fauna — A278

Designs: No. 1574a, 5c, Piranha (Pirana). b, 10c, Anaconda. c, 15c, Turtle (Tortuga). d, 20c, Iguana. e, 25c, Mono, vert. f, 35c, Mara. g, 40c, Marmota, vert. h, 50c, Peccary.

**1975, Aug. 20    Litho.    Perf. 14**
1574  A278  Strip of 8, #a.-h.       3.00  1.50

**Souvenir Sheet**
**Perf. 13½**
1575  A278  15g  Aguara guazu        10.00

No. 1575 is airmail, contains and one 60x50mm stamp, and price includes a 5g surtax for a monument to Francisco Solano Lopez.
For overprints see Nos. 2197.

Michelangelo (1475-1564), Italian Sculptor and Painter — A279

---

Details from works and artists: No. 1545a, 5c, Portrait, Romano. b, 10c, Boy Carrying Fruit, Caravaggio. c, 15c, A Sybil, Domenichino. d, 20c, Nude, Titian. e, 25c, The Danae, Correggio. f, 35c, Nude, Savoldo. g, 40c, Nude, da Vinci. h, 50c, Nude, Rubens. 15g, Christ Child, Piero di Cosimo.

**1975, Jan. 15    Perf. 14**
1545  A273  Strip of 8, #a.-h.       2.00  1.50

**Souvenir Sheet**
**Perf. 14½**
1546  A273  15g multicolored          6.00

No. 1546 is airmail and price includes a 5g surtax used for a monument to Franciso Solano Lopez.

Christmas
A274

Paintings, artists: No. 1547a, 5c, The Annunciation, della Robbia. b, 10c, The Nativity, G. David. c, 15c, Madonna and Child, Memling. d, 20c, Adoration of the Shepherds, Giorgione. e, 25c, Adoration of the Magi, French school, 1400. f, Madonna and Child with Saints, Pulzone. 35c, 40c, Madonna and Child, van Orley. h, 50c, Flight From Egypt, Pacher. 15g, Adoration of the Magi, Raphael.

**1975, Jan. 17    Perf. 14**
1547  A274  Strip of 8, #a.-h.       2.00  1.50

**Souvenir Sheet**
**Perf. 14½**
1548  A274  15g multicolored         10.00

No. 1548 is airmail and price includes a 5g surtax for a monument to Francisco Solano Lopez.

"U.P.U.," Pantheon, Carrier Pigeon, Globe — A275

**1975, Feb.    Wmk. 347    Perf. 13½x13**
1549  A275  1g  blk & lilac              .20  .20
1550  A275  2g  blk & rose red           .25  .20
1551  A275  3g  blk & ultra              .25  .20
1552  A275  5g  blk & blue               .25  .20
1553  A275  10g  blk & lil rose          .25  .20
1554  A275  20g  blk & brn               .25  .20
1555  A275  25g  blk & emer             1.75  1.40
Nos. 1549-1555 (7)                      1.40

Centenary of Universal Postal Union.
Nos. 1554-1555 are airmail.

Paintings in National Gallery, London A276

Details from paintings, artist: 5c, The Rokeby Venus, Velazquez, horiz. 10c, (The Range of Love), Watteau. 15c, Venus (The School of Love), Gainsborough. 20c, Mrs. Sarah Siddons, Gainsborough. 25c, Cupid Complaining to Venus, L. Cranach the Elder. 35c, Portrait, Lotto. 40c, Nude, Rembrandt. 50c, Venus.

---

25c, Bavaria. e, 30c, Painting by C.C. Henderson. f, 50c, Austria, vert. g, 75c, Zurich, vert. 5g, Hot air balloon, Apollo spacecraft, airplane, Graf Zeppelin. No. 1538a, 10g, Steam locomotive. b, 20g, Ocean liner, sailing ship. No. 1539, Airship, balloon. No. 1540, Mail coach crossing river.

**1974, Mar. 20    Perf. 14**
1536  A271  Strip of 7, #a.-g.
1537  A271  5g  multicolored
1538  A271  Pair, #a.-b.
Set, #1536-1538                 8.00  6.00

**Souvenir Sheets**
**Perf. 14½**
1539  A271  15g multicolored          35.00
**Perf. 13½**
1540  A271  15g multicolored          40.00

Nos. 1537-1540 are airmail. No. 1539 contains one 50x35mm stamp. No. 1540 one 60x50mm stamp. Nos. 1539-1540 each include a 5g surtax for a monument to Francisco Solano Lopez. For overprint see No. 2127.

Paintings
— A272

Details from works, artist: No. 1541a, 10c, Adam and Eve, Mabuse. b, 15c, Portrait, Piero di Cosimo. c, 20c, Bathsheba in her Bath, Cornelisz. d, 25c, Toilet of Venus, Boucher. e, 30c, The Bathers, Renoir. f, 50c, Lot and his Daughters, Dix. g, 75c, Bouquet of Flowers, van Kessel. 5g, King's Pet Horse, Seele. No. 1543a, 10g, Woman with Paintbrushes, Batoni. b, 20g, Three Musicians, Flemish master.

**1974, Mar. 20**
1541  A272  Strip of 7, #a.-g.
1542  A272  5g  multicolored
1543  A272  Pair, #a.-b.
Set, #1541-1543                12.00  6.00

Nos. 1542-1543 are airmail.

Sailing Ships — A272a

Designs: No. 1544a, 5c, Ship, map. b, 10c, English ships. 15c, Dutch ship. d, 20c, Whaling ships. e, 25c, Spanish ship. f, 35c, USS Constitution. g, 40c, English frigate. h, 50c, "Fanny", 1832.

**1974, Sept. 13    Perf. 14½**
1544  A272a  Strip of 8, #a.-h.      2.00  1.00

Strip price includes a 50c surtax.

Paintings in Borghese Gallery, Rome A273

---

dance costumes. g, 2.25g, Musicians in folk dress, horiz.

**1973, Dec. 30    Perf. 14**
1530  A267  Strip of 7, #a.-g.       2.00  1.00

Flowers
A268

Designs: No. 1531a, 10c, Passion flower. b, 20c, Dahlia. c, 25c, Bird of paradise. d, 30c, Freesia. e, 40c, Anthurium. f, 50c, Water lily. g, 75c, Orchid.

**1973, Dec. 31**
1531  A268  Strip of 7, #a.-g.       8.00  3.00

Roses A269

Designs: No. 1532a, 10c, Hybrid perpetual. b, 15c, Tea scented. c, 20c, Japanese rose. d, 25c, Bouquet of roses and flowers. e, 30c, Rose of Provence. f, 50c, Hundred petals rose. g, 75c, Bouquet of roses, dragonfly.

**1974, Feb. 2**
1532  A269  Strip of 7, #a.-g.       7.00  5.00

Paintings in Gulbenkian Museum A270

Designs and artists: No. 1533a, 10c, Cupid and Three Graces, Boucher. b, 15c, Bath of Venus, Burne-Jones. c, 20c, Mirror of Venus, Burne-Jones. d, 25c, Two Women, Natoire. e, 30c, Fighting Cockerels, de Vos. f, 50c, Portrait of a Young Girl, Bugiardini. g, 75c, Madonna and Child, J. Gossaert. No. 1534a, 10g, Woman with Harp, Lawrence. b, 20g, Centaurs Embracing, Rubens.

**1974, Feb. 4**
1533  A270  Strip of 7, #a.-g.
1534  A270  5g  multicolored
1535  A270  Pair, #a.-b.
Set, #1533-1535                 7.00  5.00

Nos. 1534-1535 are airmail.

UPU Cent. A271

Horse-drawn mail coaches: No. 1536a, 10c, London. b, 15c, France. c, 20c, England. d,

No. 1583: Statues. a, 5c, David. b, 10c, Aurora.
Paintings. c, 15c, Original Sin. d, 20c, The Banishment. e, 25c, The Deluge. f, 35c, Eve. g, 40c, Mary with Jesus and John. h, 50c, Judgement Day.
No. 1585a, 5g, Adam Receiving Life from God, horiz. 4g, Adam...
No. 1586, 5g, Libyan Sybil. b, 10g, Delphic Sybil. No. 1586, God Creating the Heaven and the Earth, horiz. No. 1587, The Holy Family.

**1975, Aug. 23**   **Litho.**   **Perf. 12**

| 1583 | A279 | 15g multicolored | | |
| 1584 | A279 | 4g multicolored | 1.00 | .75 |
| | | Strip of 8, #a.-h. | 1.50 | 1.50 |
| | | Pair, #a.-b. | | |
| 1585 | A279 | | 6.00 | 4.25 |

**Souvenir Sheets   Perf. 14**

| 1586 | A279 | 15g multicolored | 17.50 |
| 1587 | A279 | 15g multicolored | 17.50 |

Nos. 1586-1587 sold for 20g with surtax for a monument to Francisco Solano Lopez. Nos. 1584-1587 are airmail.

Winter Olympics, Innsbruck, 1976 — A280

**1975, Aug. 27**   **Litho.**   **Perf. 14**

| 1596 | A280 | 1g Luge | | |
| | | Strip of 4, #a.-d. | | |
| 1597 | A280 | | | |
| 1598 | A280 | | | |
| 1599 | A280 | 20g 4-Man bobsled | | |
| | | Set, #1596-1599 | | |
| 1600 | A280 | 25g Ski jumper | 8.00 | 8.00 |
| 1601 | A280 | 25g Woman figure skater | 17.50 | |

**Souvenir Sheet   Perf. 13½**

| 1600 | A280 | 25g Ski jumper | 27.50 |
| 1601 | A280 | 25g Woman figure skater | 17.50 |

#1597a, 2g, Slalom skier. b, 3g, Cross country skier. c, 4g, Speed skater. d, 5g, Downhill skier.
Nos. 1596, 1598-1601 are horiz. Nos. 1598-1601 are airmail. Nos. 1600-1601 each contain one 60x50mm stamp.

Summer Olympics, Montreal, 1976 — A281

No. 1606: a, 1g, Weightlifting. b, 2g, Kayak. c, 3g, Hildegard Flack, 800 meter run. d, Lasse Viren, 5,000 meter run.
No. 1607: a, 5g, Dieter Kottysch, boxing. b, 10g, Lynne Evans, archery. c, 15g, Akinori Nakayama, balance rings. 20g, Heide Rosendahl, broad jump. No. 1609, Decathlon. No. 1610, Liselott Linsenhoff, dressage, horiz.

**1975, Aug. 28**   **Perf. 14**

| 1606 | A281 | Strip of 4, #a.-d. | | |
| 1607 | A281 | Strip of 3, #a.-c. | | |
| 1608 | A281 | 20g multicolored | | |
| | | Set, #1606-1608 | 8.00 | 5.00 |

**Souvenir Sheets   Perf. 14½**

| 1609 | A281 | 25g multicolored | 20.00 |
| 1610 | A281 | 25g multicolored | 20.00 |

Nos. 1607b-1610 are airmail.

---

Ships.
US, Bicent. — A282

**1975, Oct. 20**   **Litho.**   **Unwmk.**   **Perf. 14**

| 1616 | A282 | 5c Sachem, vert. | | |
| 1617 | A282 | 10c Reprisal, Lexington | | |
| 1618 | A282 | 15c Mosquito, Spy | | |
| 1619 | A282 | 20c Wasp | | |
| 1620 | A282 | 25c Providence, vert. | | |
| 1621 | A282 | 35c Yankee Hero, Milford | | |
| 1622 | A282 | 40c Cabot, vert. | | |
| 1623 | A282 | 50c Hornet, vert. | | |
| | | Set, #1616-1623 | | |

**Souvenir Sheet**

| 1624 | A282 | 15g Montgomery | 22.50 |

No. 1624 is airmail and contains one 50x70mm stamp.

5.00 2.00

Details from paintings, artists: No. 1625a, 5c, The Collector, Kahill. b, 10c, Morning Interlude, Brackman. vert. c, 15c, White Cloud, Catlin. vert. d, 20c, Man From Kentucky, Benton. vert. e, 25c, The Emigrants, Remington. f, 35c, Spirit of '76, Willard. vert. g, John Paul Jones capturing Serapis, unknown artist. h, 50c, Declaration of Independence, Trumbull. 15g, George Washington, Stuart and Jefferson, Peale.

US, Bicent. — A283

**1975, Nov. 20**   **Perf. 14**

| 1625 | A283 | Strip of 8, #a.-h. | 6.00 | 3.00 |

**Souvenir Sheet   Perf. 13½**

| 1625A | A283 | 15g multicolored | 30.00 |

No. 1625A is airmail, contains one 60x50mm stamp and price includes a 5g surtax for a monument to Francisco Solano Lopez.

No. 1628 is airmail.

**1976, Mar. 16**   **Litho.**   **Perf. 13½x13**   **Wmk. 347**

| 1626 | A284 | 5g vio, blk & red | .20 | .20 |
| 1627 | A284 | 10g ultra, blk & red | .20 | .20 |
| 1628 | A284 | 30g brn, blk & red | .25 | .60 |
| | | Nos. 1626-1628 (3) | .25 | .60 |

Inauguration of Institute of Higher Education, Sept. 23, 1974.

Institute of Higher Education — A284

---

No. 1631 is airmail.

**1976, Mar. 16**   **Perf. 13½x13½**

| 1629 | A285 | 3g blk, bl & citron | .20 | .20 |
| 1630 | A285 | 4g car, bl & citron | .20 | .20 |
| 1631 | A285 | 25g emer, bl & lemon | .60 | .60 |
| | | Nos. 1629-1631 (3) | | |

Rotary Intl., 70th Anniv. — A285

Int'l Women's Year (1975).
No. 1634 is airmail.

**1976, Mar. 16**

| 1632 | A286 | 1g ultra & brn | .20 | .20 |
| 1633 | A286 | 1g car & brn | .20 | .20 |
| 1634 | A286 | 20g grn & brn | .60 | .60 |
| | | Set, #1632-1634 (3) | | |

IWY Emblem, Woman's Head — A286

Various cats: No. 1635a, 5c. b, 10c. c, 15c. d, 20c. e, 25c. f, 35c. g, 40c. h, 50c. 15g.

Cats A287

**1976, Apr. 2**   **Unwmk.**   **Perf. 14**

| 1635 | A287 | Strip of 8, #a.-h. | 3.00 | 1.50 |

**Souvenir Sheet   Perf. 13½**

| 1636 | A287 | 15g multicolored | 21.00 |

No. 1636 is airmail, contains one 50x60mm stamp and price includes a 5g surtax for a monument to Francisco Solano Lopez. See Nos. 2132-2133, 2201-2202, 2274-2275. For overprint see No. 2212.

Locomotives: 1g, Planet, England, 1830. 2g, Koloss, Austria, 1844. 3g, Tarasque, France, 1846. 4g, Lawrence, Canada, 1853. 5g, Carlsruhe, Germany, 1854. 10g, Great Sagua, US, 1856. 15g, Berga, Spain, 1929. 25g, Encarnacion, Paraguay. 25g, English locomotive, 1825.

Railroads, 150th Anniv. (in 1975) — A288

**1976, Mar. 16**   **Litho.**   **Perf. 13x13½**

| 1637 | A288 | 1g multicolored | | |
| 1638 | A288 | 2g multicolored | | |
| 1639 | A288 | 2g multicolored | | |
| 1640 | A288 | 4g multicolored | | |
| 1641 | A288 | 5g multicolored | | |
| 1642 | A288 | 10g multicolored | | |

---

Painting by Spanish Artists — A289

Paintings: 1g, The Naked Maja by Goya. 2g, Nude by J. de Torres. 3g, Nude holding oranges by de Torres, vert. 4g, Woman playing piano by Z. Velazquez. vert. 5g, Knight on white horse by Esquivel. 10g, The Shepherd by Murillo. 15g, The Immaculate Conception by Antolinez. vert. 20g, Nude by Zuloaga. 25g, Prince Baltasar Carlos on Horseback by D. Velazquez.

**1976, Apr. 2**   **Perf. 13x13½, 13½x13**

| 1646 | A289 | 1g multicolored | | |
| 1647 | A289 | 2g multicolored | | |
| 1648 | A289 | 3g multicolored | | |
| 1649 | A289 | 4g multicolored | | |
| 1650 | A289 | 5g multicolored | | |
| 1651 | A289 | 10g multicolored | | |
| 1652 | A289 | 15g multicolored | | |
| 1653 | A289 | 20g multicolored | | |
| | | Set, #1646-1653 | 6.00 | 3.00 |

**Souvenir Sheet**

| 1654 | A289 | 25g multicolored | 7.50 |

Nos. 1651-1654 are airmail. No. 1654 contains one 58x82mm stamp.

| 1643 | A288 | 25g multicolored | | |
| 1644 | A288 | 25g multicolored | | |
| | | Set, #1637-1644 | 14.00 | 5.00 |

**Souvenir Sheet**

| 1645 | A288 | 25g multicolored | 40.00 |

Nos. 1642-1645 are airmail. No. 1645 contains one 40x27mm stamp.

No. 1655: a, 5c. Prepona praeneste. b, 10c. Prepona proschion. c, 15c. Pereute leucodrosime. d, 20c. Agrias amydon. e, 25c. Morpho aega gynandromorphe. f, 35c. Pseudatteria leopardina. g, 40c. Morpho helena. h, 50c. Morpho hecuba.

Butterflies — A290

**1976, May 12**   **Unwmk.**   **Perf. 14**

| 1655 | A290 | Strip of 8, #a.-h. | 7.00 | 3.00 |

Farm Animals — A291

**1976, June 15**

| 1656 | A291 | 1g Rooster, vert. | | |
| 1657 | A291 | 2g Hen, vert. | | |
| 1658 | A291 | 3g Turkey, vert. | | |
| 1659 | A291 | 4g Sow | | |
| 1660 | A291 | 5g Donkeys | | |
| 1661 | A291 | 10g Brahma cattle | | |
| 1662 | A291 | 15g Holstein cow | | |
| 1663 | A291 | 15g Horse | | |
| | | Set, #1656-1663 | 4.00 | 3.00 |

Nos. 1661-1663 are airmail.

3g, Luann Ryan, US, archery, vert. d, 4g, Jennifer Chandler, US, diving. e, 5g, Shirley Babashoff, US, swimming. f, 10g, Christine Stuckelberger, Switzerland, equestrian. g, 15g, Japan, volleyball, vert.
20g, Annegret Richter, W. Germany, running, vert. f, 10g, Bruce Jenner, US, decathlon. No. 1705, Bruce Jenner, US, decathlon. No. 1706, Alwin Schockemohle, equestrian. No. 1707, Medals list, vert.

**1976, Dec. 18**    Unwmk.    **Perf. 14**
1703 A297   20g multicolored    8.00 3.00
    Set, #1703-1704

**Souvenir Sheets**
**Perf. 14½**
1705 A297   25g multicolored    30.00
1706 A297   25g multicolored    30.00
1707 A297   25g multicolored    30.00
Nos. 1705-1707 are airmail. Nos. 1705-1706 each contain one 50x40mm stamp. No. 1707 contains one 50x70mm stamp.

Titian, 500th Birth Anniv. A298

Details from paintings: No. 1708a, 1g, Venus and Adonis. b, 2g, Diana and Callisto. c, 3g, Perseus and Andromeda. d, 4g, Venus of the Mirror. e, 5g, Venus Sleeping, horiz. f, 10g, Bacchanal, horiz. g, 15g, Venus, Cupid and the Lute Player. 20g, Venus and the Organist, horiz.

**1976, Dec. 18**    Strip of 7, #a.-g.    **Perf. 14**
1708 A298     10.00 3.00
1709 A298   20g multicolored    10.00 3.00
    Set, #1708-1709
Nos. 1700l-1709g are airmail.

Peter Paul Rubens, 400th Birth Anniv. A299

Paintings: No. 1710a, 1g, Adam and Eve. b, 2g, Tiger and Lion Hunt. c, 3g, Bathsheba Receiving David's Letter. d, 4g, Susanna in the Bath. e, 5g, Perseus and Andromeda. f, 10g, Andromeda Chained to the Rock. g, 15g, Shivering Venus. 20g, St. George Slaying the Dragon. 25g, Birth of the Milky Way, horiz.

**1977, Feb. 18**    Strip of 7, #a.-g.
1710 A299    
1711 A299   20g multicolored    8.00 4.00
    Set, #1710-1711

**Souvenir Sheet**
**Perf. 14½**
1712 A299   25g multicolored    37.50
Nos. 1710f-1710g, 1711-1712 are airmail.

US, Bicent.— A300

Gold Medal Winners: No. 1703a, 1g, Nadia Comaneci, Romania, gymnastics, vert. b, 2g, Kornelia Ender, East Germany, swimming. c,

---

Space exploration: No. 1713a, 1g, John Glenn, Mercury 7. b, 2g, Pres. Kennedy. Apollo 11. c, 3g, Wernher von Braun. Apollo 17. d, 4g, Mercury, Venus, Mariner 10. e, 5g, Jupiter, Saturn, Jupiter 10/11. f, 10g, Viking Mars. g, 15g, Viking A on Mars. 20g, Viking B on Mars. No. 1715, Future space projects on Mars, vert. No. 1716, Future land rover on Mars.

**1977, Mar. 3**    Strip of 7, #a.-g.    **Perf. 14**
1713 A300
1714 A300   20g multicolored    8.00 4.00
    Set, #1713-1714

**Souvenir Sheets**
**Perf. 13½**
1715 A300   25g multicolored    37.50
1716 A300   25g multicolored    27.50
Nos. 1713f-1713g, 1714-1716 are airmail. No. 1715 contains one 50x60mm stamp. No. 1716 one 60x50mm stamp.

Olympic History A301

Designs: 1g, Spiridon Louis, marathon 1896, Athens, Pierre de Coubertin. 2g, Giuseppe Delfino, fencing 1960, Rome, Pope John XXIII. 3g, Jean Claude Killy, skiing 1968, Grenoble, Charles de Gaulle. 4g, Ricardo Delgado, boxing 1968, Mexico City, G. Diaz Ordaz. 5g, Hayata, gymnastics 1964, Tokyo, Emperor Hirohito. 10g, Klaus Wolfermann, javelin 1972, Munich, Avery Brundage. 15g, Michel Vaillancourt, equestrian 1976, Montreal, Queen Elizabeth II. 20g, Franz Klammer, skiing 1976, Innsbruck, Austrian national arms. 25g, Emblems of 1896 Athens games and 1976 Montreal games.

**1977, June 7**
1717 A301   1g multicolored
1718 A301   2g multicolored
1719 A301   3g multicolored
1720 A301   4g multicolored
1721 A301   5g multicolored
1722 A301   10g multicolored
1723 A301   15g multicolored
1724 A301   20g multicolored
    Set, #1717-1724    6.00 3.00

**Souvenir Sheet**
**Perf. 13½**
1725 A301   25g multicolored    22.50
Nos. 1722-1725 are airmail. No. 1725 contains one 49x60mm stamp.

LUPOSTA '77, Intl. Stamp Exibition, Berlin A302

Graf Zeppelin 1st South America flight and: 1g, German girls in traditional costumes. 2g, Bull fighter, Seville. 3g, Dancer, Rio de Janeiro. 4g, Gaucho breaking bronco, Uruguay. 5g, Like #1530b. 10g, Argentinian gaucho. 15g, Ceremonial indian costume, Bolivia. 20g, Indian on horse, US. No. 1734, Zeppelin over sailing ship. No. 1735, Ferdinand Von Zeppelin, zeppelin over Berlin, horiz.

**1977, June 9**    **Perf. 14**
1726 A302   1g multicolored
1727 A302   2g multicolored
1728 A302   3g multicolored
1729 A302   4g multicolored
1730 A302   5g multicolored
1731 A302   10g multicolored
1732 A302   15g multicolored
1733 A302   20g multicolored    11.00 4.00
    Set, #1726-1733

---

PARAGUAY

US and US Post Office, Bicent.— A292

Designs: 1g, Pony Express rider. 2g, Stagecoach. 3g, Steam locomotive, vert. 4g, American steamship. 5g, Curtiss Jenny biplane. 10g, Mail bus. 15g, Mail car, rocket mail, vert. 20g, First official missile mail. No. 1672, First flight cover, official missile mail. No. 1673, US #C76 tied to cover by moon landing cancel.

**1976, June 18**
1664 A292   1g multicolored
1665 A292   2g multicolored
1666 A292   3g multicolored
1667 A292   4g multicolored
1668 A292   5g multicolored
1669 A292   10g multicolored
1670 A292   15g multicolored
1671 A292   20g multicolored
    Set, #1664-1671

**Souvenir Sheets**
**Perf. 14½**
1672 A292   25g multicolored    20.00
1673 A292   25g multicolored    20.00
Nos. 1669-1673 are airmail and each contain one 50x40mm stamp.

PARAGUAY

Mythological Characters — A293

Details from paintings, artists: No. 1674a, 1g, Jupiter, Ingres. b, 2g, Saturn, Rubens. c, 3g, Neptune, Tiepolo. d, 4g, Uranus and Aphrodite, Merlina, horiz. e, 5g, Pluto and Proserpine, Giordano, horiz. f, 10g, Venus, Ingres. g, 15g, Mercury, de la Hyre. 20g, Mars and Venus, Veronese.

**1976, July 18**    Strip of 7, #a.-g.    **Perf. 14**
1674 A293
1675 A293   20g multicolored    8.00 5.00
    Set, #1674-1675

**Souvenir Sheet**
**Perf. 14½**
1676 A293   25g multicolored    50.00
Nos. 1674-1674g, 1675-1676 are airmail.

PARAGUAY

Sailing Ships — A294

Paintings: No. 1677a, 1g, Venice frigate of the Spanish Armada, vert. b, 2g, Swedish war ship, Vasa, 1628, vert. c, 3g, Spanish galleon being attacked by pirates by Puget. d, 4g, Combat by Dawson. e, 5g, European boat in Japan, vert. f, 10g, Elizabeth Grange in Liverpool by Walters. g, 15g, Pussen, 1903, by Holst. 20g, Grand Duchess Elizabeth, 1902, by Bohrdt.

---

PARAGUAY

German Sailing Ships — A295

Ship, artist: 1g, Bunte Kuh, 1402, Zeeden. 2g, Arms of Hamburg, 1667, Wichman, vert. 3g, Kaiser Leopold, 1667, Wichman, vert. 4g, Deutschland, 1848, Pollack, vert. 5g, Humboldt, 1851, Fedeler. 10g, Borussia, 1855, Seitz. 15g, Gorch Fock, 1958, Stroh, vert. 20g, Grand Duchess Elizabeth, 1902, Bohrdt. 25g, SS Pamir, Zeytline, vert.

**1976, Aug. 20**    Litho.
1685 A295   1g multicolored
1686 A295   2g multicolored
1687 A295   3g multicolored
1688 A295   4g multicolored
1689 A295   5g multicolored
1690 A295   10g multicolored
1691 A295   15g multicolored
1692 A295   20g multicolored
    Set, #1685-1692    8.00 4.00

**Souvenir Sheet**
**Perf. 14½**
1693 A295   25g multicolored    20.00
Intl. German Naval Exposition, Hamburg; NORDPOSTA '76 (No. 1693). Nos. 1690-1693 are airmail.

PARAGUAY

US Bicentennial — A296

Western Paintings by: No. 1694a, 1g, E. C. Ward. b, 2g, William Robinson Leigh. c, 3g, A. J. Miller. d, 4g, Charles Russell. e, 5g, Frederic Remington. f, 10g, Remington, horiz. g, 15g, Carl Bodmer. No. 1695, A. J. Miller. No. 1696, US #1, 2, 245, C76.

**1976, Sept. 9**    Unwmk.    Litho.    **Perf. 14**
1694 A296    Strip of 7, #a.-g.
1695 A296   20g multicolored    15.00 5.00
    Set, #1694-1695

**Souvenir Sheet**
**Perf. 13x13½**
1696 A296   25g multicolored    47.50
Nos. 1694-1694g, 1695-1696 are airmail. No. 1696 contains one 65x55mm stamp.

---

**1976, July 15**    Strip of 7, #a.-g.    **Perf. 14**
1677 A294
1678 A294   20g multicolored    6.00 3.00
    Set, #1677-1678
Nos. 16771-1678 are airmail.

**1976 Summer Olympics, Montreal — A297**

PARAGUAY

**Souvenir Sheets**
**Perf. 13½**
1734 A302 25g multicolored 60.00
1735 A302 25g multicolored 25.00
#1731-1735 are airmail. #1734 contains one 49x60mm stamp. #1735 one 60x49mm stamp.

Mburucuya
Flowers
A303

**1977**
**Perf. 13x13½**   **Litho.**   **Wmk. 347**
1736 A304 1g multicolored .20
1737 A304 2g multicolored .20
1738 A304 3g multicolored .20
1739 A304 5g multicolored .20
1740 A304 20g multicolored .25
1741 A304 25g multicolored .30
Issued: 2g, 3g, 20g, 4/25; 1g, 5g, 25g, 6/27.
Nos. 1740-1741 are airmail.

Designs: No. 1742a, 1g, Orville and Wilbur Wright, Wright Flyer, 1903; b, 2g, Alberto Santos-Dumont, Canard, 1906; c, 3g, Louis Bleriot, Bleriot 11, 1909; d, 4g, Otto Lilienthal, Glider, 1891; f, 5g, Igor Sikorsky, Avion le Grande, 1913; f, 10g, Juan de la Cierva, Autogiro, g, 15g, Silvio Pettirossi, Deperdussin acrobatic plane. No. 1743, Concorde jet. No. 1744, Lindbergh, Spirit of St. Louis, Statue of Liberty, Eiffel Tower. No. 1745, Design of flying machine by da Vinci.

**1977, July 18**   **Unwmk.**   **Perf. 14**
1742 A305 25g multicolored
Strip of 7, #a-g.
1743 A305 20g multicolored

**Souvenir Sheet**
**Perf. 14½**
1744 A305 25g multicolored 35.00
1745 A305 25g multicolored 35.00
Set, #1742-1743 8.00 4.00
Nos. 1742-1745 are airmail. No. 1745 contains one label.

Francisco Solano
Lopez — A306

Weaver with
Spider Web
Lace — A304

Designs: 1g, Ostrich feather panel, 2g, Black palms, 20g, Rose tabebuia, 25g, Woman holding ceramic pot.

Aviation History — A305

---

Paintings by: No. 1755a, 1g, Gabrielle Rainer Istvanffy, b, 2g, L.C. Hoffmeister, c, 3g, Frans Floris, d, 4g, Gerard de Lairesse, e, 5g, David Teniers I, f, 10g, Jacopo Zucchi, g, 15g, Pierre Paul Prudhon. 20g, Francois Boucher, 25g, Ingres, 5g-25g vert.

**1977, July 25**   **Perf. 14**
1755 A307 1g multicolored
Strip of 7, #a-g.
1756 A307 20g multicolored 5.00 3.00
Set, #1755-1756

**Souvenir Sheet**
**Perf. 14½**
1757 A307 25g multicolored 20.00
Nos. 1755f-1757 are airmail.

Marshal Francisco Solano Lopez (1827-1870), President of Paraguay, Nos. 1753-1754 are airmail.

**Perf. 13x13½**   **Litho.**   **Wmk. 347**
1752 A306 10g brown .20 .20
1753 A306 50g dk vio .50 .40
1754 A306 100g green 1.00 .75
Set, 1752-1754 (3) 1.70 1.35
Nos. 1752-1754 are airmail.

Paintings — A307

---

Designs: No. 1764a, 1g, De Beurs van Amsterdam; b, 2g, Katharina von Blankenese, c, 3g, Cuxhaven, d, 4g, Rhein, e, 5g, Churprinz and Marian, f, 10g, Bark of Bremen, vert. g, 15g, Elbe II, vert. 20g, Karacke, 25g, Admiral Karpeanger.

**1977, Aug. 27**   **Unwmk.**   **Perf. 14**
1764 A308 1g multicolored
Strip of 7, #a-g.
1765 A308 20g multicolored
Set, #1764-1765 8.00 4.00

**Souvenir Sheet**
**Perf. 13½**
1766 A308 25g multicolored 12.00
Nos. 1764f-1766 are airmail. No. 1766 contains one 40x30mm stamp.

German Sailing Ships — A308

---

Posters and World Cup Champions: No. 1782a, 1g, Uruguay, 1930, b, 2g, Italy, 1934, c, 3g, Italy, 1938, d, 4g, Uruguay, 1950, e, 5g, Germany, 1954, f, 10g, Soccer player by Fritz Genkinger, g, 15g, Soccer player, orange shirt by Genkinger.
No. 1783a, 1g, Brazil, 1958, b, 2g, Brazil, 1962, c, 3g, England, 1966, d, 4g, Brazil, 1970, e, 5g, Germany, 1974, f, 10g, Player #4 by Genkinger, g, 15g, Player #1 by Genkinger, horiz.
No. 1784, World Cup Trophy. No. 1785, German players, Argentina '78. No. 1786, The Loser, g, 15g, Player #11 by Genkinger. (player #11) by Genkinger.

**1977, Oct. 28**   **Unwmk.**   **Perf. 14**
1782 A310 1g multicolored
Strip of 7, #a-g.
1783 A310 1g multicolored
Strip of 7, #a-g.
1784 A310 20g multicolored
1785 A310 20g multicolored
Set, #1782-1785 16.00 8.00

**Souvenir Sheets**
**Perf. 14½**
1786 A310 25g red & multi 40.00
1787 A310 25g black & multi 40.00
Nos. 1782f-1782g, 1783f-1783g, 1784-1787 are airmail.

1978 World Cup Soccer
Championships, Argentina — A310

---

Details from paintings: No. 1788a, 1g, Rubens and Isabella Brant under Honeysuckle Bower; b, 2g, Judgment of Paris, c, 3g, Union of Earth and Water, d, 4g, Daughters of Kekrops Discovering Erichthonius, e, 5g, Holy Family with the Lamb, f, 10c, Adoration of Magi, g, 15c, Philip II on Horseback. 20g, Education of Marie de Medici, horiz. 25g, Triumph of Eucharist Over False Gods.

**1978, Jan. 19**   **Unwmk.**   **Perf. 14**
1788 A312 1g multicolored
Strip of 7, #a-g.
1789 A312 20g multicolored
Set, #1788-1789

**Souvenir Sheet**
**Perf. 14½**
1790 A312 25g multicolored, gold 16.00
1790A A312 25g multicolored, silver 22.50
Nos. 1788f-1788g, 1789-1790 are airmail. No. 1790 contains one 50x70mm stamp and exists inscribed in gold or silver.

Peter Paul Rubens, 400th Birth Anniv. A312

---

**Souvenir Sheet**
**Perf. 14½**
1775 A309 25g multicolored 47.50
Nos. 1773f-1775 are airmail.

1978 World Cup Soccer
Championships, Argentina — A310

Authors and scenes from books: No. 1773a, 1g, John Steinbeck, Grapes of Wrath, vert. b, 2g, Ernest Hemingway, Death in the Afternoon, c, 3g, Pearl S. Buck, The Good Earth, vert. d, 4g, George Bernard Shaw, Pygmalion, vert. e, 5g, Maurice Maeterlinck, Joan of Arc, vert. f, 10g, Rudyard Kipling, The Jungle Book, g, Henryk Sienkiewicz, Quo Vadis, 20g, C. Theodor Mommsen, History of Rome. 25g, Nobel prize medal.

**1977, Sept. 5**   **Perf. 14**
1773 A309 1g multicolored
Strip of 7, #a-g.
1774 A309 20g multicolored
Set, #1773-1774 8.00 4.00

Nobel Laureates for Literature — A309

---

Paintings of chess players: No. 1791a, 1g, De Cremone, b, 2g, L. van Leyden, c, 3g, H. Muehlich, d, 4g, Arabian artist, e, 5g, Benjamin Franklin playing chess, f, May. f, 10g, G. Cruikshank, g, 15g, 17th cent. tapestry, 20g, Napoleon playing chess on St. Helena, 25g, Illustration from chess book, Shah Name.

**1978, Jan. 23**   **Perf. 14**
1791 A313 1g multicolored
Strip of 7, #a-.
1792 A313 20g multicolored 40.00 14.00
Set, #1791-1792

**Souvenir Sheet**
**Perf. 14½**
1793 A313 25g multicolored 45.00
Nos. 1791f-1791g, 1792-1793 are airmail. No. 1793 contains one 50x40mm stamp.

1978 World Chess Championships,
Argentina — A313

---

Paintings: No. 1794a, 3g, Satyr and the Nymphs, b, 4g, Satyr with Peasant, c, 5g, Allegory of Fertility, d, 6g, Upbringing of Jupiter, e, 7g, Holy Family, f, 8g, Adoration of the Shepherds, g, 20g, Jordaens with his family, 10g, Meleagro with Atalanta, horiz. No. 1796, Feast for a King, horiz. No. 1797, Holy Family with Shepherds.

**1978, Jan. 25**   **Perf. 14**
1794 A314 3g multicolored
Strip of 7, #a-g.
1795 A314 10g multicolored
1796 A314 25g multicolored
Set, #1794-1796 18.00 6.00

**Souvenir Sheet**
**Perf. 14½**
1797 A314 25g multicolored 14.00
Nos. 1795-1797 are airmail. No. 1797 contains one 50x70mm stamp.

Jacob Jordaens, 300th Death Anniv. A314

---

Monograms and details from paintings: No. 1804a, 3g, Temptation of the Idler 7g, Adam and Eve, c, 5g, Satyr Family, d, 6g, Eve, e, 7g, Adam, f, 8g, Portrait of a Young Man, g, 20g, Squirrels and Acorn. 10g, Madonna and Child. No. 1806, Brotherhood of the Rosary (Lute-playing Angel). No. 1607, Soldier on Horseback with a Lance.

**1978, Mar. 10**   **Perf. 14**
1804 A315 3g multicolored
Strip of 7, #a-g.
1805 A315 10g multicolored
1806 A315 25g multicolored
Set, #1804-1806 12.00 5.00

Albrecht Durer, 450th Death Anniv. A315

**Souvenir Sheet**
**Perf. 13½**
1807 A315 25g blk, buff & sil  37.50
Nos. 1805-1807 are airmail. No. 1807 contains one 30x40mm stamp.

## Francisco de Goya, 150th Death Anniv. A316

Paintings: No. 1814a, 3g, Allegory of the Town of Madrid. b, 4g, The Clothed Maja. c, 5g, The Parasol. d, 6g, Dona Isabel Cobos de Porcel. e, 7g, The Drinker. f, 8g, The 2nd of May 1908. g, 20g, General Jose Palafox on Horseback. 10g, Savages Murdering a Woman. 25g, The Naked Maja, horiz.

1978, May 11  Perf. 14
1814 A316  Strip of 7, #a-g.
1815 A316 10g multicolored
1816 A316 25g multicolored
Set, #1814-1816  10.00 4.00
Nos. 1815-1816 are airmail.

## Future Space Projects — A317

Various futuristic space vehicles and imaginary creatures: No. 1816a, 3g, b, 4g, c, 5g, d, 6g, e, 7g, f, 8g, g, 20g.

1978, May 16  Strip of 7, #a-g.
1817 A317  10g multicolored
1818 A317
1819 A317 25g multi, diff.
Set, #1817-1819  10.00 5.00
Nos. 1818-1819 are airmail.

## Racing Cars — A318

No. 1820: a, 3g, Tyrell Formula I. b, 4g, Lotus Formula 1. c, 5g, McLaren Formula 1. d, 6g, Brabham Alfa Romeo Formula 1. e, 7g, Renault Turbo Formula 1. f, 8g, Wolf Formula 1. g, 20g, Porsche 935. 10g, Mercedes Benz W196, Stirling Moss, driver. No. 1823, Ferrari 312T.

1978, June 28  Perf. 14
1820 A318  Strip of 7, #a-g.
1821 A318 10g multicolored
1822 A318 25g multicolored
Set, #1820-1822  8.00 4.00
Souvenir Sheet
Perf. 14½
1823 A318 25g multicolored  20.00
Nos. 1821-1823 are airmail. No. 1823 contains one 50x35mm stamp.

## Paintings by Peter Paul Rubens A319

3g, Holy Family with a Basket. 4g, Amor Cutting a Bow. 5g, Adam & Eve in Paradise. 6g, Crown of Fruit, horiz. 7g, Kidnapping of Ganymede. 8g, The Hunting of Crocodile & Hippopotamus. 10g, The Reception of Marie de Medici at Marseilles. 20g, Two Satyrs. 25g, Felicity of the Regency.

1978, June 30  Perf. 14
1824 A319  3g multicolored
1825 A319  4g multicolored
1826 A319  5g multicolored
1827 A319  6g multicolored
1828 A319  7g multicolored
1829 A319  8g multicolored
1830 A319 10g multicolored
1831 A319 20g multicolored
1832 A319 25g multicolored
Set, #1824-1832  10.00 6.00
Nos. 1830, 1832 are airmail.

## National College A320

Perf. 13½x13
Litho.  Wmk. 347

| 1978 | | | |
|---|---|---|---|
| 1833 A320 | 3g claret | .20 | .20 |
| 1834 A320 | 4g violet blue | .20 | .20 |
| 1835 A320 | 5g lilac | .20 | .20 |
| 1836 A320 | 6g brown | .20 | .20 |
| 1837 A320 | 25g violet black | .20 | .20 |
| 1838 A320 | 30g bright green | .25 | 1.20 |
| Set, #1833-1838 (6) | | 1.25 | 1.20 |

Centenary of National College in Asuncion. Nos. 1836-1838 are airmail.

## José Estigarribia, Bugler, Flag of Paraguay A321

Perf. 13x13½
Litho.

| 1978 | | | |
|---|---|---|---|
| 1839 A321 | 3g multi | .20 | .20 |
| 1840 A321 | 5g multi | .20 | .20 |
| 1841 A321 | 10g multi | .20 | .20 |
| 1842 A321 | 20g multi | .20 | .20 |
| 1843 A321 | 25g multi | .20 | .20 |
| 1844 A321 | 30g multi | .25 | 1.20 |
| Set, #1839-1844 (6) | | 1.25 | 1.20 |

Induction of Jose Felix Estigarribia (1888-1940), general and president of Paraguay, into Salon de Bronce (National Heroes' Hall of Fame).
Nos. 1842-1844 are airmail.

## Queen Elizabeth II Coronation, 25th Anniv. A322

Flowers and: 3g, Barbados #234. 4g, Tristan da Cunha #13. 5g, Bahamas #157. 6g, Seychelles #172. 7g, Solomon Islands #88. 8g, Cayman Islands #150. 10g, New Hebrides #77. 20g, St. Lucia #156. 25g, St. Helena #139.
No. 1854, Solomon Islands #368a-368c, Gilbert Islands #312a-312c. No. 1855, Great Britain #313-316.

1978, July 25  Unwmk.  Perf. 14
1845 A322  3g multicolored
1846 A322  4g multicolored
1847 A322  5g multicolored
1848 A322  6g multicolored
1849 A322  7g multicolored
1850 A322  8g multicolored
1851 A322 10g multicolored
1852 A322 20g multicolored
1853 A322 25g multicolored
Set, #1845-1853  18.00 6.00
Souvenir Sheets
Perf. 13½
1854 A322 25g multicolored  60.00
1855 A322 25g multicolored  60.00
Nos. 1851, 1853-1855 are airmail. Nos. 1854-1855 each contain one 60x40mm stamp.

## Intl. Philatelic Exhibitions A323

Various paintings, ship, nudes, etc. for: No. 1866a, 3g, Nordposta 78. b, 4g, Riccione 70. c, 5g, Uruguay '79. d, 6g, ESSEN '78. e, 7g, PRAGA '78. f, 8g, London '80. 8, 20g, ESPAMER '79. f, 8g, London '80. 8, 20g, EUROPA 78. No. 1858, Eurphila 78.
No. 1859, Francisco de Pinedo, map of his flight.

1978, July 10  Strip of 7, #a-g.
1856 A323  10g multicolored
1857 A323  20g multicolored
1858 A323  25g multicolored
Set, #1856-1858  12.00 4.00
Souvenir Sheet
Perf. 13½x13
1859 A323  25g multicolored  30.00
No. 1859 fur Riccione '78 and Eurphila '78 and contains one 54x34mm stamp. Nos. 1857-1859 are airmail. Nos. 1856b-1858 are vert.

## Intl. Year of the Child A324

Grimm's Snow White and the Seven Dwarfs: No. 1866a, 3g, Snow White pricking her finger. b, 4g, Queen and mirror. c, 5g, Man with dagger. d, 6g, Snow White in forest. e, 7g, Snow White asleep, seven dwarfs. f, 8g, Snow White dancing with dwarfs. g, 20g, Snow White being offered apple. 10g, Snow Charming in repose. 25g, Snow White, Prince Charming on horseback.

1978, Oct. 26  Strip of 7, #a-g.
1866 A324  10g multicolored
1867 A324  20g multicolored
1868 A324  25g multicolored
Set, #1866-1868  11.00 5.00
Nos. 1867-1868 are airmail. See Nos. 1893-1896, 1916-1919.

## Mounted South American Soldiers A325

No. 1869a, 3g, Gen. Jose Felix Bogado (1771-1829). b, 4g, Colonel, First Volunteer Regiment, 1806. c, 5g, Colonel wearing dress uniform, 1860. d, 6g, Soldier, 1864-1870. e, 7g, Dragoon, 1865. f, 8g, Lancer. g, 20g, Soldier, 1865. 10g, Gen. Bernardo O'Higgins, 200th birth anniv. 25g, Jose de San Martin, 200th birth anniv.

1978, Oct. 31  Strip of 7, #a-g.
1869 A325  10g multicolored
1870 A325  multicolored
1871 A325  25g multicolored
Set, #1869-1871  7.00 3.00
Nos. 1870-1871 are airmail.

## 1978 World Cup Soccer Championships, Argentina — A326

Soccer Players: No. 1872a, 3g, Paraguay, vert. b, 4g, Austria, Sweden. c, 5g, Argentina, Poland. d, 6g, Italy, Brazil. e, 7g, Netherlands, Austria. f, 8g, Scotland, Peru. g, 20g, Germany, Italy. 10g, Argentina, Holland. 25g, Germany, Tunisia.

1979, Jan. 9  Strip of 7, #a-g.
1872 A326  10g multicolored
1873 A326  10g multicolored
1874 A326  25g multicolored
Set, #1872-1874  8.50 3.00
Souvenir Sheet
Perf. 13½
1875 A326 25g multicolored  50.00
Nos. 1873-1875 are airmail. No. 1875 contains one 60x40mm stamp. For overprint see No. C610.

## Christmas A327

Paintings of the Nativity and Madonna and Child by: No. 1876a, 3g, Giorgione, horiz. b, 4g, Titian. c, 5g, Titian, diff. d, 6g, Raphael. e, 7g, Schongauer. f, 8g, Muratti. e, Oost. 10g, Memling. No. 1878, Rubens. No. 1879, Madonna and Child Surrounded by a Garland and Boy Angels, Rubens.

1979, Jan. 10  Litho.  Perf. 14
1876 A327  Strip of 7, #a-g.
1877 A327 10g multicolored
1878 A327 25g multicolored
Set, #1876-1878  7.00 3.50
Souvenir Sheet
Photo. & Engr.
Perf. 12
1879 A327 25g multicolored  75.00
Nos. 1877-1879 are airmail.

## First Powered Flight, 75th Anniv. (in 1978) — A328

Airplanes: No. 1880a, 3g, Eole. c, 5g, Ader, 1890. b, 4g, Flyer III, Wright Brothers. c, 5g, Voisin. d, 6g, Henri Farman, 1908. d, 6g, Curtiss. Eugene Ely. e, 7g, Etrich-Taube A11. f, 8g, Fokker EIII. g, 20g, Albatros C.1915. 10g, Boeing 747 carrying space shuttle. No. 1882, Boeing 707 carrying Zeppelin flight commemorative cancels.

**1979, Apr. 24**  **Litho.**  **Perf. 14**
1880  A328  b.10 multicolored
1881  A328  10g multicolored
1882  A328  25g multicolored
Set, #1880-1882

**Souvenir Sheet**
**Perf. 14½**
1883  A328  25g blue & black  8.00  3.00

1883  A328  25g blue & black  70.00

Nos. 1881-1883 are airmail. Nos. 1880-1883 incorrectly commemorate 75th anniv. of ICAO. No. 1883 contains one 50x40mm stamp.

## Albrecht Dürer, 450th Death Anniv. (in 1978) A329

Paintings: No. 1884a, 3g, Virgin with the Dove. b, 4g, Virgin Praying. c, 5g, Mater Dolorosa. d, 6g, Virgin with a Carnation. e, 7g, Madonna and Sleeping Child. f, 8g, Virgin Before the Archway. g, 20g, Flight Into Egypt.
No. 1885, Madonna of the Haller family. No. 1886, Virgin with a Pear.
No. 1887, Lamentation Over the Dead Christ for Albrecht Glimm. No. 1888, Space station, horiz., with Northern Hemisphere of Celestial Globe in margin.

**1979, Apr. 28**  **Perf. 14**
1884  A329  25g multicolored
1885  A329  10g multicolored
1886  A329  25g multicolored
Set, #1884-1886

**Souvenir Sheets**
**Perf. 13½**
1887  A329  25g multicolored  17.00  17.00
1888  A329  25g multicolored  10.00  5.00

Intl. Year of the Child (#1885-1886). Nos. 1885-1886, 1888 are airmail. No. 1888 contains one 30x40mm stamp, No. 1887 contains one 40x30mm stamp.

## Sir Rowland Hill, Death Cent. — A330

Hill and: No. 1889a, 3g; Newfoundland #C1, vert. b, 4g; France #C14, c, 5g; Spain #B106, d, 6g; Similar to Ecuador to #C2, vert. e, 7g, US #C3a, f, 8g, Gelber Hund inverted overprint, vert. g, 20g, Switzerland #C20a.
1891, Privately issued Zeppelin stamp, No. 1891, Paraguay #C82, #C96, vert. No. 1892, Italy No. 1892A, France #C3-C4.

**1979, June 11**  **Perf. 14**
1889  A330  g.  13.00  5.00
Strip of 7, #a.-g.
1890  A330  25g multicolored  30.00
1891  A330  10g multicolored
Set, #1889-1891

**Perf. 14½**
1892  A330  25g multicolored  20.00
1892A A330  25g multicolored

Issue dates: No. 1892A, Aug. 28. Others, June 11. Nos. 1890-1892A are airmail.

## Grimm's Fairy Tales Type of 1978

Cinderella: No. 1893a, 3g, Two stepsisters watch Cinderella cleaning. b, 4g, Cinderella, father, stepsisters. c, 5g, Cinderella with birds while working. d, 6g, Finding dress. e, 7g, Going to ball. f, 8g, Dancing with prince. g, 20g, Losing slipper leaving ball. 10g, Prince Charming trying slipper on Cinderella's foot. No. 1895, Couple riding to castle. No. 1896, Couple entering ballroom.

**1979, June 24**  **Perf. 14½**
1893  A324  25g multicolored
1894  A324  10g multicolored
1895  A324  25g multicolored
Set, #1893-1895

**Souvenir Sheet**
**Perf. 13½**
1896  A324  25g multicolored  15.00

Intl. Year of the Child.

## 1980 Winter Olympics, Lake Placid — A332

#1899: a, 3g, Monica Schefischik, luge. b, 4g, E. Deufl, Austria, downhill skiing. c, 5g, G. Thoeni, Italy, slalom skiing. d, 6g, Canada Two-man bobsled. e, 7g, Germany vs. Finland, ice hockey. f, 8g, Hoenl, Russia, ski jump. g, 20g, Dianne De Leeuw, Netherlands, figure skating, vert.
10g, Hanni Wenzel, Liechtenstein, slalom skiing. No. 1901, Frommelt, Liechtenstein, slalom skiing. No. 1902, Kulakova, Russia, cross country skier. No. 1903, Dorothy Hamill, US, figure skating, vert. No. 1904, Brigitte Totschnig, skier.

**1979**  **Unwmk.**  **Perf. 14**
1899  A332  g.
Strip of 7, #a.-g.
1900  A332  25g multicolored
1901  A332  10g multicolored
Set, #1899-1907

**Souvenir Sheets**
**Perf. 13½**
1902  A332  25g multicolored  20.00
1903  A332  10g multicolored  22.50
1904  A332  25g multicolored  10.00  5.00

Nos. 1900-1904 are airmail. Nos. 1902-1903 each contain one 40x30mm stamp, #1902-1903, #1904, one 25x36mm stamp. Issued: #1899-1902, 8/22; #1903, 6/11; #1904, 4/24.

## Congress Emblem A331

**1979, Aug.**  **Litho.**  **Perf. 13x13½**
1897  A331  10g red, blue & black  .20  .20
1898  A331  50g red, blue & black  .40  .30

22nd Latin-American Tourism Congress, Asuncion. No. 1898 is airmail.

## Sailing Ships — A333

No. 1905: a, 3g, Caravel, vert. b, 4g, Warship. c, 5g, Warship, by Jan van Beeck. d, 6g, H.M.S. Britannia, vert. e, 7g, Salamis, vert. f, 8g, Ariel, vert. g, 20g, Warship, by Robert Salmon.

**1979, Aug. 28**  **Perf. 14**
1905  A333  g.  8.00  3.00
Strip of 7, #a.-g.
1906  A333  10g Lisette
1907  A333  25g Holstein, vert.
Set, #1905-1907

Nos. 1906-1907 are airmail.

## Intl. Year of the Child A334

Various kittens: No. 1908a, 3g. b, 4g. c, 5g. d, 6g. e, 7g. f, 8g. g, 20g.

**1979, Nov. 29**  **Perf. 14**
1908  A334  g.  8.00  3.00
Strip of 7, #a.-g.
1909  A334  10g multicolored
1910  A334  25g multicolored
Set, #1909-1910

Nos. 1909-1910 are airmail.

## Grimm's Fairy Tales Type of 1978

Little Red Riding Hood: No. 1916a, 3g, Leaving with basket. b, 4g, Meets wolf. c, 5g, Picks flowers. d, 6g, Wolf puts on Granny's gown. e, 7g, Wolf in bed. f, 8g, Hunter arrives. g, 20g, Saved by the hunter.
10g, Hunter enters house. No. 1918, Hunter leaves. No. 1919, Overall scene.

**1979, Dec. 4**  **Perf. 14**
1916  A324  g.
Strip of 7, #a.-g.
1917  A324  10g multicolored
1918  A324  25g multicolored
Set, #1916-1918

**Souvenir Sheet**
**Perf. 14½**
1919  A324  25g multicolored  24.00

Intl. Year of the Child. No. 1919 contains one 50x70mm stamp.

## Greek Athletes A335

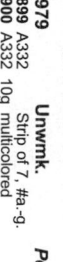

Paintings on Greek vases: No. 1926a, 3g, 3 runners. b, 4g, 2 runners. c, 5g, Throwing contest. d, 6g, Discus. e, 7g, Wrestlers. f, 8g, Wrestlers, diff. 9, 10g, Horse and rider, 20g, 2 runners, 25g, 4 warriors with shields, horiz.

**1979, Dec. 20**  **Perf. 14**
1926  A335  g.
Strip of 7, #a.-g.
1927  A335  10g multicolored
1928  A335  25g multicolored
Set, #1926-1928  9.00  3.00

Nos. 1927-1928 are airmail.

## Electric Trains — A336

No. 1929: a, 3g, First electric locomotive, Siemens, 1879, vert. b, 4g, Switzerland, 1897. c, 5g, Model E71 28, Switzerland. d, 6g, Mountain train, Switzerland. e, 7g, Electric locomotive used in Benelux countries. f, 8g, Locomotive "Rheinpfeil", Germany. g, 20g, Model BB-9004, France.
10g, 200-Km/hour train, Germany. 25g, Japanese bullet train.

**1979, Dec. 24**  **Litho.**  **Perf. 14**
1929  A336  g.  11.00  5.00
Strip of 7, #a.-g.
1930  A336  10g multicolored
1931  A336  25g multicolored
Set, #1929-1931

Nos. 1930-1931 are airmail.

## Sir Rowland Hill, Death Cent. — A337

Hill and: No. 1938a, 3g, Spad S XIII, 1917-18. b, 4g, P-51 D Mustang. c, 5g, Mitsubishi A6M6c Zero-Sen, 1944. d, 6g, Deperdussin float plane, 1913. e, 7g, Savoia-Marchetti SM 7911, 1936. f, 8g, Messerschmitt Me 262B, 1942-45. g, 20g, Nieuport 24bis, 1917-18.
10g, Zeppelin LZ 104-/l59, 1917. No. 1940, Fokker Dr-1 Caza, 1917. No. 1941, Vickers Supermarine "Spitfire" Mk.IX, 1942-45.

**1980, Apr. 8**  **Perf. 14**
1938  A337  g.
Strip of 7, #a.-g.
1939  A337  10g multicolored
1940  A337  25g multicolored
Set, #1938-1940  11.00  5.00

**Souvenir Sheet**
**Perf. 13½**
1941  A337  25g multicolored  25.00

Incorrectly commemorates 75th anniv. of ICAO. Nos. 1939-1941 are airmail. No. 1941 contains one 37x27mm stamp.

## Sir Rowland Hill, Paraguayan Stamps — A338

Hill and: No. 1948a, 3g, #1. b, 4g, #5. c, 5g, #6. d, 6g, #379. e, 7g, #381. f, 8g, #384. 9, 10g, #C83, horiz. No. 1950, #C54, horiz. No. 1951, #C54, horiz. No. 1952, #C1, horiz.

**1980, Apr. 14**  **Litho.**  **Perf. 14**
1948  A338  g.
Strip of 7, #a.-g.
1949  A338  10g multicolored
1950  A338  25g multicolored
Set, #1948-1950  11.00  5.00

**Souvenir Sheets**
**Perf. 14½**
1951  A338  25g multicolored  30.00
1952  A338  25g multicolored  30.00

#1949-1952 are airmail. #1951 contains one 50x40mm stamp. #1952 one 50x35mm stamp.

**1980 Winter Olympics, Lake Placid A339**

No. 1953: a, 3g, Thomas Wassberg, Sweden, cross country skiing. b, 4g, Scharer & Benz, Switzerland, 2-man bobsled. c, 5g, Annemarie Moser-Proll, Austria, women's downhill skiing. d, 6g, Hockey team, US. e, 7g, Leonhard Stock, Austria, men's downhill skiing. g, 20g, Christa Kinshofer, Germany, slalom skiing.
10g, Ingemar Stenmark, slalom, Sweden. No. 1955, Robin Cousins, figure skating, Great Britain. No. 1956, Eric Heiden, speed skating, US, horiz.

1980, June 4    *Perf. 14*
1953 A339    Strip of 7, #a-g.
1954 A339 10g multi, horiz.
1955 A339 25g multi, horiz.
*Set, #1953-1955*    12.00 6.00
**Souvenir Sheet**
*Perf. 13½*
1956 A339 25g multicolored    25.00
Nos. 1954-1956 are airmail. No. 1956 contains one 60x49mm stamp.

**Composers and Paintings of Young Ballerinas A340**

Paintings of ballerinas by Cydney or Degas and: No. 1957a, 3g, Gioacchino Rossini. b, 4g, Johann Strauss, the younger. c, 5g, Debussy. d, 6g, Beethoven. e, 7g, Chopin. f, 8g, Richard Wagner. g, 20g, Johann Sebastian Bach, horiz. 10g, Robert Stoltz. 25g, Verdi.

1980, July 1    *Perf. 14*
1957 A340    Strip of 7, #a-g.
1958 A340 10g multicolored
1959 A340 25g multicolored    10.00 5.00
*Set, #1957-1959*
Birth and death dates are incorrectly inscribed on 4g, 8g, 10g. No. 1957f is incorrectly inscribed "Adolph" Wagner. Nos. 1958-1959 are airmail. For overprints see Nos. 1998-1999.

**Christmas, Intl. Year of the Child A342**

No. 1968: a, 3g, Christmas tree. b, 4g, Santa filling stockings. c, 5g, Nativity scene. d, 6g, Adoration of the Magi. e, 7g, Three children, presents. f, 8g, Children, dove, fruit. g, 20g, Children playing with toys. 10g, Madonna and Child, horiz. No. 1970, Children blowing bubbles, horiz. No. 1971, Five children, horiz.

1980, Aug. 4    **Unwmk.**    *Perf. 14*
1968 A342    Strip of 7, #a-g.
1969 A342 10g multicolored
1970 A342 25g multicolored
*Set, #1960-1970*
**Souvenir Sheet**
1971 A342 25g multicolored    25.00
Nos. 1969-1970 are airmail.

**Pilar City Bicentennial — A341**

1980, July 17    **Wmk. 347**
*Perf. 13½x13*    **Litho.**
1966 A341 5g multi    .20 .20
1967 A341 25g multi    .20 .20
No. 1967 is airmail.

---

**Paraguay Airlines Boeing 707 Service Inauguration — A345**

1980, Sept. 17    *Perf. 13½x13*    **Litho.**    **Wmk. 347**
1976 A345 100g multi    .20 .20
1977 A345 100g multi    .80 .65
No. 1977 is airmail.

**World Cup Soccer Championships, Spain — A346a**

Various soccer players, winning country: No. 1978a, 3g, Uruguay 1930, 1950. b, 4g, Italy 1934, 1938. c, 5g, Germany 1954, 1974. d, 6g, Brazil 1958, 1962, 1970. e, 7g, England, 1966. f, 8g, Argentina, 1978. g, 20g, Espana '82 emblem.
10g, World Cup trophy, flags. 25g, Soccer player from Uruguay.

1980, Dec. 10    **Unwmk.**    *Perf. 14*
1978 A346    Strip of 7, #a-g.
1979 A346 10g multicolored
1980 A346 25g multicolored
*Set, #1978-1980*    14.00 5.00
**Souvenir Sheet**
*Perf. 14½*
1981 A346a 25g Sheet of 1 + 2 labels    22.50
Nos. 1979-1981 are airmail.

**Ships A313**

Emblems and ships: No. 1972a, 3g, ESPAMER '80, Spanish Armada. b, 4g, NORWEX '80, Viking longboat. c, 5g, RICCIONE '80, Battle of Lepanto. d, 6g, ESSEN '80, Great Harry of Cruickshank. e, 7g, US Dicentennial, Mount Vernon. f, 8g, LONDON '80, H.M.S. Victory. g, 20g, ESSEN '80, Gorch Fock. 25g, PHILATOKYO '81, Nippon Maru. horiz.

1980, Sept. 15    *Perf. 14*
1972 A343    Strip of 7, #a-g.
1973 A343 10g multicolored
1974 A343 25g multicolored    10.00 5.00
*Set, #1972 1974*
Nos. 1973-1974 are airmail. For overprint see No. 2278.

---

**1980 World Chess Championships, Mexico — A347**

Illustrations from The Book of Chess: No. 1982a, 3g, Two men, chess board. b, 4g, Circular chess board, players. c, 5g, Four-person chess match. d, 6g, King Alfonso X of Castile and Leon. e, 7g, Two players, chess board, horiz. f, 8g, Two veiled women, chess board, horiz. g, 20g, Two women in robes, chess board, horiz.
10g, Crusader knights, chess board, horiz. 25g, Three players, chess board, horiz.

1980, Dec. 15    **Litho.**    *Perf. 14*
1982 A347    Strip of 7, #a-g.
1983 A347 10g multicolored
1984 A347 25g multicolored
*Set, #1982-1984*    13.00 4.00
See Nos. C506-C510. Compare with illustration AP199.

**King Juan Carlos — A344**

**Souvenir Sheet**
1980, Sept. 19    *Perf. 14½*
1975 A344 25g multicolored    15.00

---

PARAGUAY Gs.4

**1980 Winter Olympics, Lake Placid A348**

Olympic scenes, gold medalists: No. 1985a, 25c, Lighting Olympic flame. b, 50c, Hockey team, US. c, 1g, Eric Heiden, US, speed skating. d, 2g, Robin Cousins, Great Britain, figure skating. e, 3g, Thomas Wassberg, Sweden, cross country skiing. f, 4g, Annie Borckinck, Netherlands, speed skating. g, 5g, Gold, silver, and bronze medals.
No. 1986, Irene Epple, silver medal, slalom, Germany. 10g, Ingemar Stenmark, slalom, giant slalom, Sweden. 30g, Annemarie Moser-Proll, downhill, Austria. 25g, Baron Pierre de Coubertin.

1981, Feb. 4    **Litho.**    *Perf. 14*
1985 A348    Strip of 7, #a-g.
1986 A348 5g multicolored
1987 A348 10g multicolored
1988 A348 30g multicolored
*Set, #1985-1988*    7.00 3.50
**Souvenir Sheet**
*Perf. 13½*
1988A A348 25g multicolored    20.00
No. 1985 exists in strips of 4 and 3. Nos. 1986-1988A are airmail. No. 1988A contains one 30x40mm stamp.

**Locomotives — A349**

No. 1989, 25c, Electric model 242, Germany. b, 50c, Electric, London-Midlands-Lancashire, England. c, 1g, Electric, Switzerland. d, 2g, Diesel-electric, Montreal-Vancouver, Canada. e, 3g, Electric, Austria. f, 4g, Electric inter-urban, Lyons-St. Etienne, France, vert. g, 5g, First steam locomotive in Paraguay.
No. 1991, Steam locomotive, Japan. 10g, Stephenson's steam engine, 1830 England. 30g, Crocodile locomotive, Switzerland. 25g, Stephenson's Rocket, 1829, England, vert.

1981, Feb. 9    **Litho.**    *Perf. 14*
1989 A349    Strip of 7, #a-g.
1990 A349 5g multicolored
1991 A349 10g multicolored
1992 A349 30g multicolored
*Set, #1989-1992*    14.00 5.00
**Souvenir Sheet**
*Perf. 13½x13*
1993 A349 25g multicolored    32.50
Electric railroads, cent. (#1989a-1989f), steam-powered railway service, 150th anniv. (#1989g, 1990-1991), Liverpool-Manchester Railway, 150th anniv. (#1992). Swiss Railways, 75th anniv. (#1993).
Nos. 1990-1993 are airmail. No. 1993 contains one 54x34mm stamp.

**Intl. Year of the Child A350**

PARAGUAY

Portraits of children with assorted flowers:
No. 1994a, 10g. b, 25g. c, 50g. d, 100g. e,
200g. f, 300g. g, 400g.

**1981, Apr. 13          Litho.          Perf. 14**
**1994** A350          Strip of 7, #a–g.
**1995** A350     75g multicolored
**1996** A350     500g multicolored
**1997** A350     1000g multicolored
Set, #1994–1997          42.50   21.00

Nos. 1995–1997 are airmail.

**1981, May 22**
**1998** A340     4g on #1957b          1.00   .60
**1999** A340     10g on #1958          2.00   1.00

No. 1999 is airmail.

Nos. 1957b and 1958 Overprinted in
Red

The following stamps were issued in
sheets of 8 with 1 label: Nos. 2001,
2013, 2037, 2044, 2047, 2055, 2140.

The following stamp was issued in
sheets of 10 with 2 labels: No. 1994a.

The following stamps were issued in
sheets of 6 with 3 labels: Nos. 2017,
2029, 2035, 2104, 2145.

The following stamps were issued in
sheets of 3 with 6 labels: Nos. 2079, 2143.

The following stamps were issued in
sheets of 5 with 4 labels: Nos. 2050-
2051, 2057, 2059, 2061, 2067, 2069,
2077, 2082, 2089, 2092, 2107, 2117,
2120, 2121, 2123, 2125, 2129, 2135,
2138, 2142, 2146, 2148, 2151, 2160,
2163, 2165, 2169, 2172, 2176, 2179,
2182, 2190, 2196, 2202, 2204, 2214,
2222, 2224, 2232, 2244, 2246, 2248,
2261, 2263, 2265, 2271, 2273, 2275,
2277.

The following stamps were issued in
sheets of 4 with 5 labels: Nos. 2307,
2310, 2313, 2316, 2324, 2329.

Peter Paul
Rubens,
Paintings
A354

Details from paintings: No. 2012: a, 25c,
Madonna Surrounded by Saints, b, 50c, Judg-
ment of Paris, c, 1g, Duke of Buckingham.
Conducted to the Temple of Virtus, d, 2g,
Minerva Protecting Peace from Mars, e, 3g,
Henry IV Receiving the Portrait of Marie de
Medici, f, 4g, Triumph of Juliers, 5g, Madonna
and Child Reigning Among Saints (Cherubs).

**1981, July 9          Litho.          Perf. 14**
**2012** A354          Strip of 6, #a–f.
**2013** A354     5g multicolored
Set, #2012–2013          2.00   1.00

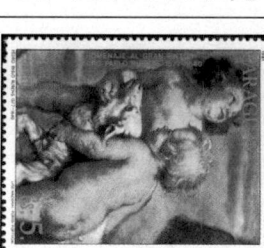

Jean Auguste-Dominique Ingres
(1780–1867), Painter — A355

Details from paintings: No. 2014: a, 25c, c,
1g, d, 2g, f, 4g, The Turkish Bath. b, 50c, The
Water Pitcher. e, 3g, Oedipus and the
Sphinx. g, 5g, The Bathing Beauty.

**1981, Oct. 13          Litho.          Perf. 14**
**2014** A355          Strip of 7, #a–g.          2.50   1.50

A horiz. strip of 5 containing Nos. 2014a–
2014e exists.

For overprints see No. 2045.

No. 2014f and 2014g exist in sheet of 8 (four
each) plus label.

Royal Wedding of Prince Charles and
Lady Diana Spencer — A351

Prince Charles, sailing ships: No. 2000a,
25c, Royal George. b, 50c, Great Britain. c,
1g, Taeping. d, 2g, Star of India. e, 3g, Tor-
rens. f, 4g, Loch Etive. No. 2001, Medway.

**1981, June 27**
**2000** A351          Strip of 6, #a–f.
**2001** A351     5g multicolored          25.00
Set, #2000–2004          13.00   6.00

**Souvenir Sheet**
          **Perf. 13½**
**2005** A351     25g multicolored

Nos. 2002–2005 are airmail. No. 2005 contains one 50x60mm stamp. For overprint see
No. 2253.

No. 2005 has an orange margin. It also
exists in gray margin. Same value.

Christmas
A358

**1981, Dec. 17          Perf. 14**
**2028** A358          Strip of 6, #a–f.

**Size: 28x45mm**

**Perf. 13½**
**2029** A358     5g multicolored

Intl. Year of the Child (Nos. 2028-2029). For
overprints see No. 2042.

Intl. Year of
the Child
A359

Story of Puss 'n Boots: No. 2030a, 25c,
Boy, Puss. b, 50c, Puss, rabbits. c, 1g,
Puss, king. 2g, Prince, princess, king.
3g, Giant ogre, Puss. 4g, Christmas
mouse. 5g, Princess, prince, Puss.

**1982, Apr. 16          Litho.          Perf. 14**
**2030** A359          Pair, #a–b.
**2031** A359     1g multicolored
**2032** A359     2g multicolored
**2033** A359     3g multicolored
**2034** A359     4g multicolored
**2035** A359     5g multicolored
Set, #2030–2035          9.00   2.50

Souvenir Sheets
          **Perf. 14½**
**2026** A357     25g like #2022d          37.50
**2027** A357     25g Wedding portrait          37.50

No. 2022g exists in sheets of 8 plus label.
Nos. 2023–2027 are airmail. Nos. 2026-2027
contain one each 50x70mm stamp.

Royal
Wedding of
Prince
Charles
and Lady
Diana
A357

Designs: No. 2022a–2022c, 25c, 50c, 1g,
Diana, Charles, flowers. d, 2g, Couple. e, 3g,
Couple leaving church. f, 4g, Couple, Queen
Elizabeth II waving from balcony. 2022g, 5g,
Diana. No. 2023, Wedding party, horiz. 10g,
Riding in royal coach, horiz. 30g, Yeomen of
the guard, horiz.

**1981, Dec. 4          Litho.          Perf. 14**
**2022** A357          Strip of 6, #a–f.
**2022G** A357     5g multicolored
**2023** A357     5g multicolored
**2024** A357     10g multicolored
**2025** A357     30g multicolored
Set, #2022–2025          21.00   8.00

Scouting, 75th Anniv. and Lord Baden-
Powell, 125th Birth Anniv. — A360

No. 2036: a, 25c, Tetradactyla, Scout hand
salute. b, 50c, Nandu (rhea), Cub Scout and
trefoil. c, 1g, Peccary, Wolf's head totem. d,
2g, Coatimundi, emblem on buckle. e, 3g,
Mara, Scouting's Intl. Communications
emblem. f, 4g, Deer, boy scout.

**1982, Apr. 21**
**2036** A360          Strip of 6, #a–f.
**2037** A360     5g multicolored
**2038** A360     5g multicolored
**2039** A360     10g multicolored
**2040** A360     30g multicolored

No. 2038, Ocelot, scouts cooking. 10g, Collie,
boy scout. 30g, Armadillo, two scouts planting
tree. 25g, Lord Baden-Powell, founder
of Boy Scouts.

Women in various traditional costumes: a,
10g. b, 25g. c, 50g. d, 100g. e, 200g. f, 300g.
g, 400g, President Stroessner, Itaipu Dam.

**1981, June 30          Perf. 14**
**2006** A352          Strip of 7, #a–g.

For overprints see No. 2281.

Traditional
Costumes
and Itaipu
Dam
A352

UPU Membership Centenary — A353

**1981, Aug. 18          Litho.          Perf. 13½x13**
**2007** A353     5g rose lake & blk          .20   .20
**2008** A353     10g lil & blk          .20   .20
**2009** A353     25g grn & blk          .20   .20
**2010** A353     25g lt red brn & blk          .40   .30
**2011** A353     30g brn & blk          1.20   1.10
Nos. 2007-2011 (5)

Nos. 2015-2016 Oyptd. in Gold

**1981, Oct. 25**
**2020** A356          on #2015a-2015b
**2021** A356          on #2016a-2016d
Set, #2020–2021          3.00   .75

Espamer '81 Philatelic Exhibition.

Nos. 2015-2016 Oyptd. in Silver

**1981, Oct. 22**
**2018** A356          on #2015a-2015b
**2019** A356          on #2016a-2016d
Set, #2018–2019          2.50   1.25

Philatelia '81, Frankfurt.

Designs: No. 2015: a, 25c, Women Running
on the Beach. b, 50c, Family on the Beach.
No. 2016: a, 1g, Still-life. b, 2g, Bullfighter. c,
3g, Children Drawing. d, 4g, Seated Woman.
5g, Paul as Clown.

**1981, Oct. 19**
**2015** A356          Pair, #a–b.
**2016** A356          Strip of 4, #a–d.
**2017** A356     5g multicolored
Set, #2015–2017          6.00   3.00

Pablo Picasso, Birth Cent. — A356

Designs: No. 2028a, 25c, Jack-in-the-box.
b, 50c, Jesus and angel. c, 1g, Santa, angels.
d, 2g, Angels lighting candle. e, 3g, Christmas
plant. f, 4g, Nativity scene. 5g, Children singing by Christmas tree.

Set, #2036-2040

**Souvenir Sheet**    *Perf. 14½*
2041   A360   25g multicolored    16.00
Nos. 2038-2041 are airmail. For overprint see No. 2140.

**No. 2028 Overprinted with ESSEN 82 Emblem**
**1982, Apr. 28**    *Perf. 14*
2042   A358   on #2028a-2028f    2.50   1.75
Essen '82 Intl. Philatelic Exhibition.

### Cats and Kittens — A361

Various cats or kittens: No. 2043a, 25c. b, 50c. c, 1g. d, 2g. e, 3g, f, 4g.
**1982, June 7**    *Perf. 14*
2043   A361   Strip of 6, #a.-f.
2044   A361   5g multi, vert.    2.50   1.00
Set, #2043-2044
For overprints see Nos. 2054-2055.

**Nos. 2014a-2014e Ovptd. PHILEXFRANCE 82 Emblem ans "PARIS 11-21.6.82" in Blue**
**1982, June 11**
2045   A355   Strip of 5, #a.-e.    2.00   1.00
Philexfrance '82 Intl. Philatelic Exhibition. Size of overprint varies.

### World Cup Soccer Championships, Spain — A362

Designs: 2046a, 25c, Brazilian team. b, 50c, Chilean team. c, 1g, Honduran team. d, 2g, Peruvian team. e, 3g, Salvadoran team. f, 4g, Globe as soccer ball, flags of Latin American finalists. No. 2047, Ball of flags. No. 2048, Austrian team. No. 2049, Players from Brazil, Austria. No. 2050, Spanish team. No. 2051, Two players from Argentina, Brazil, vert. No. 2052, W. German team. No. 2053, Players from Argentina, Brazil. No. 2053A, World Cup trophy, world map on soccer balls. No. 2053B, Players from W. Germany, Mexico, vert.
**1982**    *Litho.*    *Perf. 14*
2046   A362   Strip of 6, #a.-f.
2047   A362   5g multicolored
2048   A362   5g multicolored
2049   A362   5g multicolored
2050   A362   10g multicolored
2051   A362   10g multicolored
2052   A362   30g multicolored
2053   A362   30g multicolored    13.00   6.00
Set, #2046-2053
**Souvenir Sheets**    *Perf. 14½*
2053A   A362   25g multicolored    17.00
2053B   A362   25g multicolored    17.00
Issued: #2049, 2051, 2053, 2053A, 4/19; others, 6/13.
Nos. 2047 exists in sheets of 8 plus label. Nos. 2048-2053B are airmail. For overprints see Nos. 2086, 2286, C593.

---

**Nos. 2043-2044 Overprinted in Silver With PHILATECIA 82 and Intl. Year of the Child Emblems**
**1982, Sept. 12**    *Perf. 14*
2054   A361   Strip of 5, #a.-e.
2055   A361   5g on #2044    3.00   2.00
Set, #2054-2055
Philatelia '82, Hanover, Germany and Intl. Year of the Child.

### Raphael, 500th Birth Anniv. A363

Details from paintings: No. 2056a, 25c, Adam and Eve (The Fall). b, 50c, Creation of Eve. c, 1g, Portrait of a Young Woman (La Fornarina). d, 2g The Three Graces. e, 3g, f, 4g, Cupid and the Three Graces. 5g, Leda and the Swan.
**1982, Sept. 27**    *Perf. 14*
2056   A363   Strip of 6, #a.-f.
2057   A363   5g multicolored    7.00   2.50
Set, #2056-2057
Nos. 2056e-2056f have continuous design.

### Christmas A364

Entire works or details from paintings by Raphael: No. 2058a, 25c, The Belvedere Madonna. b, 50c, The Ansidei Madonna. c, 1g, La Belle Jardiniere. d, 2g, The Aldobrandini (Garvagh) Madonna. e, 3g, Madonna of the Goldfinch. f, 4g, The Alba Madonna. No. 2059, Madonna of the Grand duke. 10g, The Alba Madonna, diff. 25g, The Holy Family with St. Elizabeth and the Infant St. John and Two Angels. 30g, The Canigiani Holy Family.
**1982**    *Perf. 14, 13x13½ (#2061)*
2058   A364   Strip of 6, #a.-f.
2059   A364   5g multicolored
2060   A364   5g multicolored
2061   A364   10g multicolored
2062   A364   30g multicolored    15.00   5.00
Set, #2058-2062
**Souvenir Sheet**    *Perf. 14½*
2063   A364   25g multicolored    17.50
Issued: #2058-2059, 9/30; others, 12/17. Nos. 2058a-2058f and 2059 exist perf. 13. Nos. 2060-2063 are airmail and have silver lettering. For overprint see No. 2087.

### Life of Christ, by Albrecht Durer A365

Details from paintings: No. 2064a, 25c, The Flight into Egypt. b, 50c, Christ Among the Doctors. c, 1g, Christ Carrying the Cross. d, 2g, Nailing of Christ to the Cross. e, 3g, Christ

---

on the Cross. f, 4g, Lamentation Over the Dead Christ. 5g, The Circumcision of Christ.
**1982, Dec. 14**    *Perf. 14*
2064   A365   Strip of 6, #a.-f.
   *Perf. 13x13½*
2065   A365   5g multicolored    9.50   3.50
Set, #2064-2065
For overprint see No. 2094.

### South American Locomotives — A366

Locomotives from: No. 2066a, 25c, Argentina. b, 50c, Uruguay. c, 1g, Ecuador. d, 2g, Bolivia. e, 3g, Peru. f, 4g, Brazil. 5g, Paraguay.
**1983, Jan. 17**    *Litho.*    *Perf. 14*
2066   A366   Strip of 6, #a.-f.
2067   A366   5g multicolored    3.50   1.75
Set, #2066-2067
For overprint see No. 2093.

### Race Cars A367

No. 2068: a, 25c, ATS-Ford D 06. b, 50c, Ferrari 126 C 2. c, 1g, Brabham BMW BT 50. d, 2g, Renault RE 30 B. e, 3g, Porsche 956. f, 4g, Talbot-Ligier-Matra JS 19. 5g, Mercedes Benz C-111.
**1983, Jan. 19**    *Perf. 14*
2068   A367   Strip of 6, #a.-f.
   *Perf. 13½x13*
2069   A367   5g multicolorod    6.00   1.75
Set, #2068-2069
For overprint see No. 2118.

### Itaipua Dam, Pres. Stroessner — A368

**1983, Jan. 22**    *Litho.*    *Wmk. 347*
2070   A368   5g multi    .20   .20
2071   A368   5g multi    .20   .20
2072   A368   10g multi    .20   .20
2073   A368   20g multi    .20   .20
2074   A368   25g multi    .40   .30
2075   A368   50g multi    1.40   1.30
25th anniv. of Stroessner City.
Nos. 2070-2075 (6)

### 1984 Winter Olympics, Sarajevo — A369

---

ice skaters: No. 2076a, 25c, Marika Kilius, Hans-Jurgens Baumler, Germany, 1964. b, 50c, Tai Babilonia, Randy Gardner, US, 1976. c, 1g, Anett Poetzsch, E. Germany, 1980, vert. d, 2g, Tina Riegel, Andreas Nischwitz, Germany, 1980, vert. e, Dagmar Lurz, Germany, 1980, vert. f, 4g, Trixi Schuba, Austria, 1972, vert. 5g, Peggy Fleming, US, 1968, vert.
   *Perf. 13½x13, 13x13½*    **Unwmk.**
**1983, Feb. 23**    Strip of 6, #a.-f.
2076   A369   5g multicolored
2077   A369   5g multicolored    3.50   1.75
Set, #2076-2077
For overprints see Nos. 2177, 2266.

### Pope John Paul II A370

#2078: a, 25c, Virgin of Caacupe. b, 50c, Cathedral of Caacupe. c, 1g, Cathedral of Asuncion. d, 2g, Pope holding crucifix. e, 3g, Our Lady of the Assumption. f, 4g, Pope giving blessing. 5g, Pope with hands clasped. 25g, Madonna & child.
**1983, June 11**    *Litho.*    *Perf. 14*
2078   A370   Strip of 6, #a.-f.
2079   A370   5g multicolored    8.25   3.00
Set, #2078-2079
**Souvenir Sheet**    *Perf. 14½*
2080   A370   25g multicolored    16.00
No. 2080 is airmail. For overprint see No. 2143.

### Antique Automobiles — A371

No. 2081: a, 25c, Bordino Steamcoach, 1854. b, 50c, Panhard & Levassor, 1892. c, 1g, Benz Velo, 1894. d, 2g, Peugeot-Daimler, 1894. e, 3g, 1st car with patented Lutzmann system, 1898. f, 4g, Benz Victory, 1891-92. No. 2082, Ceirano 5CV. No. 2083, Mercedes Simplex PS 32 Turismo, 1902. 10g, Stae Electric, 1909. 25g, Benz Velocipede, 1885. 30g, Rolls Royce Silver Ghost, 1913.
**1983, July 18**    *Perf. 14*
2081   A371   Strip of 6, #a.-f.
2082   A371   5g multicolored
2083   A371   5g multicolored
2084   A371   10g multicolored
2085   A371   30g multicolored    9.00   3.00
Set, #2081-2085
**Souvenir Sheet**    *Perf. 14½*
2085A   A371   25g   Sheet of 1 + label    20.00
Nos. 2083-2085A are airmail.

**No. 2046 Ovptd. in Red, No. 2058 Ovptd. in Black with "52o CONGRESO F.I.P." and Brasiliana 83 Emblem**
**1983, July 27**    *Perf. 14*
2086   A362   Strip of 6, #a.-f.
2087   A364   Strip of 6, #a.-f.
Brasiliana '83, Rio de Janiero and 52nd FIP Congress. No. 2087 exists perf. 13.

## Aircraft Carriers — A372

PARAGUAY Gs.1

Carriers and airplanes: No. 2088a, 25c, 25 de Mayo, A-4Q Sky Hawk, Argentina. b, 50c, Minas Gerais, Brazil. c, 1g, Akagi, A6M3 Zero, Japan. d, 2g, Giuseppe Miraglia, Italy. e, 3g, Enterprise, S-3A Viking, US. f, 4g, Dedalo, AV-8A Matador, Spain. 5g, Schwabenland, Dornier DO-18, Germany. No aircraft on Nos. 2088b, 2088d.

25g, US astronauts Donn Eisele, Walter Schirra & Walt Cunningham, Earth & Apollo 7.

**1983, Aug. 29** — **Perf. 14**
2088 A372 Strip of 6, #a.-f.    6.25 2.25
2089 A372 5g multicolored
Set, #2088-2089

**Souvenir Sheet** — **Perf. 13½**
2090 A372 25g multicolored    21.00
No. 2090 is airmail and contains one 55x45mm stamp.

### Birds A373

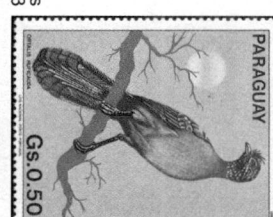

PARAGUAY Gs.0.50

#2091: a, 25c, Pulsatrix perspicillata. b, 50c, Ortalis ruficauda. c, 1g, Chloroceryle amazona. d, 2g, Trogon violaceus. e, 3g, Pezites militaris. f, 4g, Bucco capensis. 5g, Cyanerpes cyaneus.

**1983, Oct. 22** — **Perf. 14**
2091 A373 Strip of 6, #a.-f.

No. 2066 Ovptd. for PHILATELICA 83 in Silver
2092 A373 5g multicolored
Set, #2091-2092    6.00 1.25

**1983, Oct. 28**
2093 A366 Strip of 6, #a.-f.    3.00 2.00
Philatelia '83, Dusseldorf, Germany.

**1983, Nov. 5**
2094 A365 Strip of 6, #a.-f.    4.50 2.00
Exfivia '83 Philatelic Exhibition, La Paz, Bolivia.

### Re-election of President Stroessner — A374

PARAGUAY Gs.75.

**1983, Nov. 24**
2095 A374 10g multicolored
2096 A374 25g multicolored
2097 A374 50g multicolored
   **Perf. 14**

10g, Passion flower, vert. 25g, Miltonia phalaenopsis, vert. 50g, Natl. arms, Chaco soldier. 75g, Acaray hydroelectric dam. 100g, Itaipu hydroelectric dam. 200g, Pres. Alfredo Stroessner, vert.

---

2098 A374 75g multicolored    5.00 2.50
   **Perf. 13**
2099 A374 100g multicolored
2100 A374 200g multicolored
Set, #2095-2100
#2099-2100 are airmail. #2096 exists perf. 13. For overprint see #C577.

### Montgolfier Brothers' 1st Flight, Bicent. — A375

PARAGUAY Gs.1

No. 2101: a, 25c, Santos-Dumont's Biplane, 1906. b, 50c, Airship. c, 1g, Paulhan's biplane over Juvisy. d, 2g, Zeppelin LZ-3, 1907. e, 3g, Biplane of Henri Farman. f, 4g, Graf Zeppelin over Friedrichshafen. 5g, Lebaudy's dirigible. 25g, Detail of painting, Great Week of Aviation at Betheny, 1910.

**1984, Jan. 7** — **Perf. 13**
2101 A375 Strip of 6, #a.-f.    5.00 2.00
   **Perf. 14**
2104 A375 5g multicolored
Set, #2101-2104

**Souvenir Sheet** — **Perf. 13½**
2105 A375 25g multicolored    21.00
No. 2105 is airmail and contains one 75x55mm stamp. For overprint see No. 2145.

### Dogs A376

PARAGUAY Gs.2

#2106: a, 25c, German Shepherd. b, 50c, Great Dane, vert. c, 1g, Poodle, vert. d, 2g, Saint Bernard. e, 3g, Greyhound. f, 4g, Dachshund. 5g, Boxer.

**1984, Jan. 11** — **Litho.**
2106 A376 Strip of 6, #a.-f.    3.50 1.75
2107 A376 5g multicolored
Set, #2106-2107
   **Perf. 14**

### Animals, Anniversaries — A377

PARAGUAY Gs.10

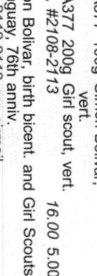

**1984, Jan. 24** — **Perf. 13**
2108 A377 10g Puma
2109 A377 25g Alligator
2110 A377 50g Jaguar
2111 A377 75g Peccary
2112 A377 100g Simon Bolivar, vert.
2113 A377 200g Girl scout, vert.
Set, #2108-2113    16.00 5.00
Simon Bolivar, birth bicent. and Girl Scouts of Paraguay, 76th anniv. Nos. 2112-2113 are airmail.

### Christmas A378

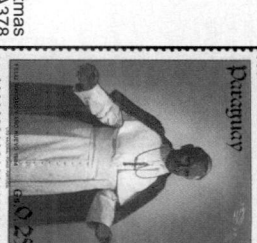

Paraguay 0.25

Designs: No. 2114a, 25c, Pope John Paul II. b, 50c, Christmas tree. c, 1g, Children. d, 2g, Nativity Scene. e, 3g, Three Kings. f, 4g, Madonna and Child. 5g, Madonna and Child by Raphael.

**1984, Mar. 23** — **Perf. 13x13½**
2114 A378 Strip of 6, #a.-f.
2115 A378 5g multicolored
Set, #2114-2115    8.25 2.00

### Troubadour Knights A379

Paraguay Gs.0.25 — MUESTRA

Illustrations of medieval miniatures: No. 2116a, 25c, Ulrich von Liechtenstein. b, 50c, Ulrich von Gutenberg. c, 1g, Der Putter. d, 2g, Walther von Metz. e, 3g, Hartman von Aue. f, 4g, Lutok von Seuen. 5g, Werner von Teufen.

**1984, Mar. 27** — **Perf. 14**
2116 A379 Strip of 6, #a.-f.
2117 A379 5g multicolored
Set, #2116-2117    5.50 2.00
   **Perf. 13**
For overprint see No. 2121.

No. 2068 Ovptd. in Silver with ESSEN 84 Emblem
2118 A367 Strip of 6, #a.-f.    2.50 1.25
**1984, May 10**
Essen '84 Int. Philatelic Exhibition.

### UPU Congress, Hamburg '84 — A381

PARAGUAY Gs.5

Sailing ships: No. 2122a, 25c, Admiral of Hamburg. b, 50c, Neptune. c, 1g, Archimedes. d, 2g, Passat. e, 3g, Finkenwerder cutter off Heligoland. f, 4g, Four-masted ship. 5g, Deutschland.

**1984, June 19** — **Perf. 13**
2122 A381 Strip of 6, #a.-f.
2123 A381 5g multicolored
Set, #2122-2123    4.00 2.00
For overprints see Nos. 2146, 2279-2280.

### British Locomotives — A382

PARAGUAY Gs.0.50 — LIDERES DEL MUNDO

No. 2124: a, 25c, Pegasus 097, 1868. b, 50c, Pegasus 097, diff. c, 1g, Cornwall, 1847. d, 2g, Cornwall, 1847, diff. e, 3g, Patrick Stirling #1, 1870. f, 4g, Patrick Stirling #1, 1870, diff. 5g, Stepney Brighton Terrier, 1872.

**1984, June 20** — **Perf. 13**
2124 A382 Strip of 6, #a.-f.
2125 A382 5g multicolored
Set, #2124-2125    9.00 3.00
   **Perf. 14**

No. C486 Overprinted in Silver with UN emblem and "40o Aniversario de la / Fundacion de las / Naciones Unidas 26.6.1944"
2126 AP161 25g on No. C486    20.00
**1984, Aug. 1** — **Litho.**

No. 1536 Ovptd. in Orange (#a.-d.) or Silver (#e.-g.) with AUSIPEX 84 Emblem and:

### Endangered Animals — A380

PARAGUAY Gs.0.50

#2119: a, 25c, Priodontes giganteus. b, 50c, Catagonus wagneri. c, 1g, Felis pardalis. d, 2g, Chrysocyon brachyurus. e, 3g, Burmeisteria retusa. f, 4g, Myrmecophaga tridactyla. 5g, Caiman crocodilus.

**1984, June 16** — **Perf. 13**
2119 A380 Strip of 6, #a.-f.
2120 A380 5g multicolored
Set, #2119-2120    6.25 2.50
For overprint see No. 2129.

No. 2117 Ovptd. in Silver with Emblems, etc., for U.P.U. 19th World Congress, Hamburg
2121 A379 5g on #2117    2.50 1.25
**1984, June 19** — **Perf. 13**

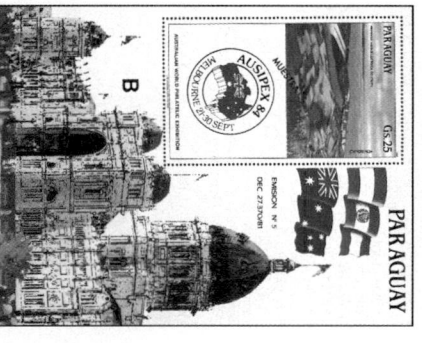

2127 A271
2128 A383 25g multicolored    12.00
   **Perf. 14**
**1984, Aug. 21**
**Souvenir Sheet** — **Perf. 14½**
   3.50 1.75
Ausipex '84 Int. Philatelic Exhibition, Melbourne, Australia. No. 2128 is airmail.

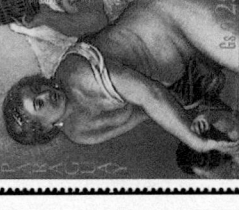

**1984**

2129 A380    5g on #2120    2.00 2.00

Nos. 2120 and C551 Ovptd. in Black and Red

**Perf. 13**

2130 AP178 30g on #C551    4.00 4.00

**Perf. 14**

Issued: #2129, Sept. 20; #2130, Aug. 30. No. 2130 is airmail.

No. 1512 Ovptd. "VER STUTTGART CAMPEON NACIONAL DE FUTBOL DE ALEMANIA 1984" and Emblem

**1984, Sept. 5**

2131 A263 Strip of 7, #a.-g.    2.50 1.25

VFB Stuttgart, 1984 German Soccer Champions.

Cat Type of 1976

Various cats: No. 2132: a, 25c. b, 50c. c, 1g. d, 2g. e, 3g. f, 4g.

**1984, Sept. 10    Perf. 13x13½**

2132 A287    Strip of 6, #a.-f.

2133 A287 5g multicolored    6.00 2.00

**Souvenir Sheet**

**Perf. 13½**

2134 A384    Strip of 6, #a.-f.

2135 A384 5g multicolored    6.00 2.00

**Litho.**

2136 A384 30g multicolored    17.00

No. 2136 is airmail and contains one 50x60mm stamp. For overprints see Nos. 2174, 2199, 2200. Compare with type A399.

World Wildlife Fund — A386

Endangered or extinct species: No. 2139a, 25c, Capybara. b, 50c, Mono titi, vert. c, 1g, Rana cornuda adornada. d, 2g, Priodontes giganteus, digging. e, 3g, Priodontes giganteus, by water. f, 4g, Myrmecophaga tridactyla. g, 5g, Myrmecophaga tridactyla, with young.

**1985, Jan. 19    Perf. 14**

2137 A385    Strip of 6, #a.-f.

2138 A385 5g multicolored    17.00 6.00

Set, #2137-2138

**Perf. 14**

2139 A386    Strip of 7, #a.-g.    47.50 10.00

See Nos. 2166-2167.

**1985, Mar. 13    Perf. 14**

2140 A360 5g on No. 2037    2.00 1.00

No. 2037 Ovptd. in Red with ISRAPHIL Emblem

**1985, Apr. 10**

Israel '85 Intl. Philatelic Exhibition.

John James Audubon, Birth Bicent. A387

Birds: No. 2141a, 25c, Piranga flava. b, 50c, Polyborus plancus. c, 1g, Chrysmitris caudata. d, 2g, Xolmis irupero. e, 3g, Phloeoccastes leucopogon. f, 4g, Thraupis bonariensis. 5g, Parula pitiayumi, horiz.

**1985, Apr. 18    Perf. 13**

2141 A387    Strip of 6, #a.-f.

2142 A387 5g multicolored    5.00 1.50

Set, #2141-2142

**Perf. 14**

2143 A370 5g on #2079    4.00 1.50

No. 2079 Ovptd. in Silver with Italia '85 Emblem

**1985, May 20**

Italia '85 Intl. Philatelic Exhibition.

No. 1448e Red on Silver

No. 1448e Ovptd. in Red on Silver

**1985, June 12**

2144 A250 30c on #1448e    1.50 .75

No. 2104 Ovptd. in Silver and Blue with LUPO 85 Congress Emblem

**1985, July 5**

2145 A375 5g on No. 2104    1.00 .50

LUPO '85, Lucerne, Switzerland.

**1985, July 5    Perf. 13**

2146 A381 5g on #2123    1.00 .50

No. 2123 Ovptd. in Silver and Blue with MOPHILA 85 Emblem and "HAMBURGO 11-12. 9. 85"

Mophila '85 Intl. Philatelic Exhibition, Hamburg.

Intl. Youth Year A388

Scenes from Tom Sawyer and Huckleberry Finn: No. 2147a, 25c, Mississippi riverboat. b, 50c, Finn. c, 1g, Finn and friends by campfire. d, 2g, Finn and Joe, sinking riverboat. e, 3g, Finn, friends, riverboat. f, 4g, Cemetery. 5g, Finn, Sawyer, 25g, Raft, riverboat.

**1985, Aug. 5    Perf. 13½x13**

2147 A000    Strip of 6, #a.-f.

2148 A388 5g multicolored    6.50 2.00

Set, #2147-2148

**Souvenir Sheet**

**Perf. 14½**

2149 A388 25g multicolored    17.50

No. 2149 is airmail. For overprint see No. C612.

German Railroads, 150th Anniv. — A389

Locomotives: No. 2150a, 25c, T3, 1883. b, 50c, T18, 1912. c, 1g, T16, 1014. d, 2g, #01 118, Historic Trains Society, Frankfurt. e, 3g, #06 001 Express, Nuremberg. Transit Museum. f, 4g, #10 002 Express, 1957. 5g, Der Adler, 1835. 25g, Painting of 1st German Train, Dec. 7, 1835.

**1985, Aug. 8    Perf. 14**

2150 A389    Strip of 6, #a.-f.

2151 A389 5g multicolored    6.00 2.00

Set, #2150-2151

**Souvenir Sheet**

**Perf. 13**

2152 A389 25g multicolored    17.50

No. 2152 is airmail and contains one 75x53mm stamp. For overprint see No. 2165.

Development Projects — A390

Pres. Stroessner and: 10g, Soldier, map, vert. 25g, Model of Yaci Reta Hydroelectric Project. 50g, Itaipu Dam. 75g, Merchantman Lago Ipoa. 100g, 1975 Coin, vert. 200g, Asuncion Intl. Airport.

**1985, Sept. 17    Litho.    Perf. 13**

2153 A390 10g multicolored    1.00 .50

2154 A390 25g multicolored

2155 A390 50g multicolored

2156 A390 75g multicolored

Nudes by Peter Paul Rubens A391

2157 A390 100g multicolored    5.00 2.50

2158 A390 200g multicolored

Chaco Peace Agreement, 50th Anniv. (#2153, 2157). Nos. 2157-2158 are airmail. For overprints see Nos. 2254-2259.

Details from paintings: No. 2159a, 25c, b, 50c, Venus in the Forge of Vulcan. c, 1g, Cimon and Iphigenia, horiz. d, 2g, The Horrors of War. e, 3g, Apotheosis of Henry IV and The Proclamation of the Regency. f, 4g, The Reception of Marie de Medici at Marseilles. 5g, Union of Earth and Water. 25g, Nature Attended by the Three Graces.

**1985, Oct. 18    Perf. 14**

2159 A391    Strip of 6, #a.-f.

**Perf. 13x13½**

2160 A391 5g multicolored    10.00 4.00

Set, #2159-2160

**Souvenir Sheet**

**Perf. 14**

2161 A391 25g multicolored    20.00 17.00

No. 2161 is airmail.

**1986, Jan. 16    Perf. 14**

Nudes by Titian: details from paintings. No. 2162a, 25c, Venus, an Organist, Cupid and a Little Dog. b, 50c, c, 1g, Diana and Actaeon. d, 2g, Danae. e, 3g, Nymph and a Shepherd. f, 4g, Venus of Urbino. 5g, Cupid Blindfolded by Vonus, vert. 25g, Diana and Callisto, vert

2162 A391    Strip of 6, #a.-f.

**Perf. 13**

2163 A391 5g multicolored    10.00 3.00

Set, #2162-2163

**Souvenir Sheet**

**Perf. 13½**

2164 A391 25g multicolored    20.00 20.00

No. 2164 is airmail and contains one 50x60mm stamp.

Nos. 2150 Ovptd. in Red

**1986, Feb. 25    Perf. 14**

2165 A389    Strip of 6, #a.-f.    2.00 1.00

Essen '86 Intl. Philatelic Exhibition.

Mushrooms Type of 1985

Designs: No. 2166a, 25g, Lepiota procera. b, 50c, Tricholoma albo-brunneum. c, 1g, Clavaria. d, 2g, Volvaria. e, 3g, Lcoperdon perlatum. f, 4g, Dictyophora duplicata. 5g, Polyporus rubrum.

**1986, Mar. 17    Perf. 13**

2166 A385    Strip of 6, #a.-f.

2167 A385 5g multicolored    3.50 1.75

Set, #2166-2167

1984 Summer Olympics, Los Angeles — A384

Gold medalists: No. 2134a, 25c Michael Gross, W. Germany, swimming. b, 50c, Peter Vidmar, US, gymnastics. c, 1g, Fredy Schmirtke W. Germany, cycling. d, 2g, Philippe Boisgo, France, fencing. e, 3g, Ulrike Meyfarth, W. Germany, women's high jump. f, 4g, Games emblem. 5g, Mary Lou Retton, US, women's all-around gymnastics, vert. 300, Rolf Milser, W. Germany, weight lifting, vert.

Mushrooms A385

#2137: a, 25c, Boletus luteus. b, 50c, Agaricus campester. c, 1g, Pholiota spectabilis. d, 2g, Tricholoma terreum. e, 3g, Laccaria laccata. f, 4g, Amanita phalloides. 5g, Scleroderma verrucosum.

# PARAGUAY

Automobile, Cent. — A393

**PARAGUAY**
Gs.4.

No. 2168: a, 25c, Wolseley, 1904. b, 50c, Peugeot, 1892. c, 1g, Panhard, 1895. d, 2g, Cadillac, 1903. e, 3g, Fiat, 1902. f, 4g, Stanley Steamer, 1898. 5g, Carl Benz Velociopede, 1885. 25g, Carl Benz (1844-1929), automotive engineer.

**1986, Apr. 28    Litho.    Perf. 13½x13**
2168  A393  f.
2169  A393  5g multicolored            6.00  3.00
  Set, #2168-2169

No. 2170 is airmail and contains one 30x40mm stamp.

2170  A393  25g multicolored        17.00  17.00

---

World Cup Soccer Championships, Mexico City — A394

**PARAGUAY**
Gs.0.50

Various match scenes, Paraguay vs.: No. 2171a, 25c. b, 50c, US, 1930. c, 1g, Belgium, 1930. d, 2g, US, 1930. e, 3g, Brazil, 1985. 5g, Natl. Team, 1986. 25g, Player, vert.

**1986, Mar. 12    Perf. 13½x13**
2171  A394  Strip of 6, #a.-f.
2172  A394  5g multicolored          7.00  3.50
  Set, #2171-2172

**Souvenir Sheet**
**Perf. 14½**
2173  A394  25g multicolored      17.00  17.00

---

No. 2135 Ovptd. in Silver "JUEGOS / PANAMERICANOS / INDIANAPOLIS / 1987"

**1986, June 9    Perf. 13**
2174  A384  5g on No. 2135          2.50  1.25

1987 Pan American Games, Indianapolis.

---

Maybach Automobiles — A395

**PARAGUAY**
MAYBACH, TIPO W-6 (1900-36)
Gs.0.25

No. 2175: a, 25c, W-6, 1930-36. b, 50c, SW-38 convertible. c, 1g, SW-38 hardtop, 1938. d, 2g, W-6/DSG, 1933. e, 3g, Zeppelin DS-8, 1931. f, 4g, Zeppelin DS-8, 1936. 5g, Zeppelin DS-8, aerodynamic cabriolet, 1936.

**1986, June 19    Perf. 13½x13**
2175  A395  Strip of 6, #a.-f.
2176  A395  5g multicolored          5.00  2.50
  Set, #2175-2176

---

**1986, July 9    Perf. 13**
2177  A369  5g on #2077             2.50  1.25

No. 2077 Overprinted in Bright Blue with Olympic Rings and "CALGARY 1988"

1988 Winter Olympics, Calgary.

---

Statue of Liberty, Cent. — A396

**PARAGUAY**
Gs.4.

Passenger liners: No. 2178a, 25c, City of Paris, England, 1867. b, 50c, Mauretania, England. c, 1g, Normandie, France, 1932. d, 2g, Queen Mary, England, 1938. e, 3g, Kaiser Wilhelm the Great III, Germany, 1897. f, 4g, United States, US, 1952. 5g, Bremen, Germany, 1928. 25g, Sailing ship Gorch Fock, Germany, 1976, vert.

**1986, July 25    Perf. 13**
2178  A396  f.
2179  A396  5g multicolored        12.50  2.00
  Set, #2178-2179

**Souvenir Sheet**
**Perf. 14½**
2180  A396  25g multicolored       13.00 13.00

No. 2180 is airmail and contains one 50x70mm stamp.

---

Dog Type of 1984

#2181: a, 25c, German shepherd. b, 50c, Icelandic sheepdog. c, 1g, Collie. d, 2g, Boxer. e, 3g, Scottish terrier. f, 4g, Welsh springer spaniel. 5g, Painting of Labrador retriever by Ellen Krebs, vert.

**1986, Aug. 28    Perf. 14½**
2181  A376  Strip of 6, #a.-f.
2182  A376  5g multicolored         5.00  1.50
  Set, #2181-2182

---

Paraguay Official Stamps, Cent. — A397

**OFFICIAL**
5 G PARAGUAY
CENTENARIO DEL PRIMER SELLO OFICIAL

Designs: No. 2183-2185, #O1. #2186-2188, #O4.

**1986, Aug. 28    Litho.    Perf. 13x13½**
2183  A397  5g  multi             .20  .20
2184  A397  15g  multi            .20  .20
2185  A397  40g  multi            .20  .20
2186  A397  65g  multi            .25  .20
2187  A397  100g  multi           .40  .30
2188  A397  150g  multi           1.45  1.30
  Set, #2183-2188 (6)

Nos. 2186-2188 are airmail.

---

Tennis Players
A398

**PARAGUAY**
Gs.2

Designs: No. 2189a, Victor Pecci, Paraguay. b, 50c, Jimmy Connors, US. c, 1g, Gabriela Sabatini, Argentina. d, 2g, Boris Becker, W. Germany. e, 3g, Claudia Kohde, E. Germany. f, 4g, Sweden, 1985 Davis Cup team champions. horiz. 5g, Steffi Graf, W. Germany. 25g,

---

1988 Summer Olympics, Seoul
A399

MARY LOU RETTON (ESTADOS UNIDOS) MEGALLA DE ORO
GIMNASIA (DISCIPLINAS VARIAS — INDIVIDUAL)
**PARAGUAY**
Gs.2

Athletes, 1984 Olympic medalists: No. 2195a, 25c, Runner. b, 50c, Boxer. c, 1g, Joaquim Cruz, Brazil, 800-meter run. d, 2g, Mary Lou Retton, US, individual all-around gymnastics. e, 3g, Carlos Lopes, Portugal, marathon. f, 4g, Fredy Schmidtke, W. Germany, 1000-meter cycling. horiz. 5g, Joe Fargis, US, equestrian, horiz.

**1986, Oct. 29    Perf. 13x13½, 13½x13**
2195  A399  Strip of 6, #a.-f.
2196  A399  5g multicolored         5.00  3.00
  Set, #2195-2196

For overprints see Nos. 2227-2228, 2230.

---

Olympics Type of 1985 Overprinted in Silver with Olympic Rings and 500th Anniv. of the Discovery of America Emblems and "BARCELONA 92 / Sede de las Olimpiadas en el ano del 500o Aniversario del Descubrimiento de America

Designs like Nos. 2134a-2134f.

**1987, Apr. 24    Perf. 14**
2199  A384  Strip of 6, #a.-f.     8.00  8.00

1992 Summer Olympics, Barcelona and discovery of America, 500th anniv. in 1992.

---

No. 2135 Overprinted in Silver "ROMA / OLYMPHILEX" / Olympic Rings / "SEOUL / CALGARY / 1988"

**1987, Apr. 30    Perf. 13**
2200  A384  5g on No. 2135         2.50  2.50

Olymphilex '87 Intl. Philatelic Exhibition, Rome.

---

Various cats and kittens: No. 2201: a, 1g, b, 2g, c, 3g, d, 5g, 60g, Black cat.

Cat Type of 1976

**1987, May 22    Perf. 13x13½**
2201  A287  Strip of 4, #a.-d.
2202  A287  60g multicolored        2.50  1.25
  Set, #2201-2202

No. 2202 also exists perf. 14. For overprint see No. 2212.

---

**1986, Sept. 17    Unwmk.**
2189  A398  Strip of 6, #a.-f.
2190  A398  5g multicolored         3.50  1.50
  Set, #2189-2190

**Souvenir Sheet**
**Perf. 13½**
2191  A398  25g multicolored      14.00 14.00

No. 2191 is airmail and contains one 75x55mm stamp. For overprints see No. 2229.

---

Nos. 1454-1456 Ovptd. in Red or Silver (#2192c, 2192d): "Homenage a la visita de Sus Altezas Imperiales los Principees Hitachi --28.9-3.10.86"

**1986, Sept. 28    Perf. 14**
2192  A251  Strip of 5, #a.-e.
2193  A251  50c on #1455
2194  A251  75c on #1456            3.00  3.00
  Set, #2192-2194

---

Paintings by Rubens
A400

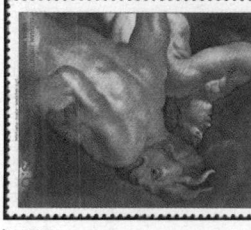

**PARAGUAY**
Gs.10
MUESTRA

No. 2203: a, 1g, The Four Corners of the World. horiz. b, 2g, Jupiter and Calisto. c, 3g, Susana and the Elders. d, 5g, Marriage of Henry IV and Marie de Medici in Lyon. 60g, The Last Judgment. 100g, The Holy Family with St. Elizabeth and John the Baptist. No. 2205A, War and Peace.

**1987    Litho.    Perf. 13x13½, 13½x13**
2203  A400  Strip of 4,
2204  A400  60g multicolored        8.50  2.00
  Set, #2203-2204

**Souvenir Sheets**
2205  A400  100g multicolored    14.00 14.00
2205A  A400  100g multicolored   14.00 14.00
  Issued: #2204, May 25; #2205, May 26. Nos. 2205-2205A are airmail and contain one 54x68mm stamp.

Christmas 1986 (#2205).

---

Places and Events — A401

**PARAGUAY**
Gs.10

10g, ACEPAR Industrial Plant. 25g, Franciscan monk, native, vert. 50g, Yaguaron Church altar, vert. 75g, Founding of Asuncion, 450th anniv. 100g, Paraguay Airlines passenger jet. 200g, Pres. Stoessner, vert.

**1987, June 2    Litho.    Perf. 13**
2206  A401  10g multicolored
2207  A401  25g multicolored
2208  A401  50g multicolored
2209  A401  75g multicolored
2210  A401  100g multicolored
2211  A401  200g multicolored
  Set, #2206-2211                  21.00  7.50

Nos. 2210-2211 are airmail. For overprints see Nos. 2225-2226, C685, C722.

---

**1987, Mar. 20    Litho.    Perf. 14**
2197  A278  Strip of 5, #a.-e.
2198  AP176  10g multicolored       5.00  5.00
  Set, #2197-2198

500th Anniv. of the discovery of America and the 12th Spanish-American Stamp & Coin Show, Madrid.

---

No. 2201 Ovptd. in Blue

**PARAGUAY**
CAPEX 87
Gs.1.

**1987, June 12    Perf. 13½x13**
2212  A287  Strip of 4, #a.-d.     1.50  1.50

Berlin, 750th Anniv. A409

Paintings: No. 2245a, 1g, Virgin and Child, by Jan Gossaert. b, 2g, Virgin and Child, by Rubens. c, 3g, Virgin and Child, by Hans Memling. d, 5g, Madonna, by Albrecht Durer. 60g, Adoration of the Shepherds, by Martin Schongauer.

**1988, Apr. 8    Perf. 13**
2245 A409    Strip of 4, #a.-d.
2246 A409 60g multicolored    10.00 5.00
Set, #2245-2246
Christmas 1987. See Nos. C727-C731.

Visit of Pope John Paul II A410

Religious art: No. 2247a, 1g, Pope John Paul II, hands clasped. b, 2g, Statue of the Virgin. c, 3g, Czestochowa Madonna r 5g, Our Lady of Caacupe. Nos. 2247a-2247d are vert.

**1988, Apr. 11    Perf. 13**
2247 A410    Strip of 4, #a.-d.
2248 A410 60g multicolored    4.00 2.00
Set, #2247-2248

Visit of Pope John Paul II — A411

Rosette window and crucifix.

**1988, May 5    Litho.    Perf. 13x13½**
2249 A411 10g blue & blk    .20 .20
2250 A411 20g blue & blk    .20 .20
2251 A411 50g blue & blk    .25 .20
Nos. 2249-2251 (3)    .65 .60

**World Wildlife Fund Type of 1985**

Endangered Animals: No. 2252a, 1g, like #2139g. b, 2g, like #2139f. c, 3g, like #2139d. d, 5g, like #2139e.

**1988, June 14    Unwmk.    Perf. 14**
2252 A386    Strip of 4, #a.-d.    8.00 3.50
Nos. 2252a-2252d have denomination and border in blue.

Nos. 2000a-2000d Ovptd. in Gold with Emblem and "Bicentenario de / AUSTRALIA / 1788-1988"

**1988, June 17    Perf. 14**
2253 A351    Strip of 4, #a.-d.    3.50 3.50
Australia, bicent.

Types of 1985 Overprinted in 2 or 4 Lines in Gold "NUEVO PERIODO PRESIDENCIAL CONSTITUCIONAL 1988-1993"

**1988, Aug. 12    Perf. 14**
2254 A390    like #2153
2255 A390 25g    like #2154
2256 A390 50g    like #2155
2257 A390 75g    like #2156

---

No. 2233 is airmail and contains one 54x75mm stamp.

1988 Winter Olympics, Calgary — A407

#2237: a, 5g, Joel Gaspoz. b, 60g, Peter Mueller.

**1987, Dec. 31    Perf. 14**
2234 A407    1g Maria Walliser
2235 A407    2g Erika Hess
2236 A407    3g Pirmin Zurbriggen    10.00 4.00
Set, #2234-2236

**Miniature Sheet    Perf. 13½x13**
2237 A407    Sheet of 4
each #2237a, 2237b+label

**Souvenir Sheet    Perf. 14½**
2238 A407 100g Walliser, Zurbriggen    13.00 13.00
No. 2238 is airmail. For overprints see Nos. 2240-2242.

No. 2221 Ovptd. in Silver "AEROPEX 88 / ADELAIDE"

**1988, Jan. 29    Perf. 13**
2239 A404    Strip of 4, #a.-d.    8.00 4.00
Aeropex '88, Adelaide, Australia.

Nos. 2234-2236 Ovptd. in Gold with Olympic Rings and "OLYMPEX / CALGARY 1900"

**1988, Feb. 13    Perf. 14**
2240 A407 1g on #2234
2241 A407 2g on #2235
2242 A407 3g on #2236    4.50 4.50
Olympex '88, Calgary. Size and configuration of overprint varies.

1988 Summer Olympics, Seoul — A408

Equestrians: No. 2243a, 1g, Josef Neckermann, W. Germany, on Venetia. b, 2g, Henri Chammartin, Switzerland. c, 3g, Christine Stueckelberger, Switzerland, on Granat. d, 5g, Liselott Linsenhoff, W. Germany, on Piaff. 60g, Hans-Guenter Winkler, W. Germany.

**1988, Mar. 7    Perf. 13**
2243 A408    Strip of 4, #a.-d.
2244 A408 60g multicolored    8.00 4.00
Set, #2243-2244
For overprint see No. 2291.

---

Discovery of America, 500th Anniv. (in 1992) — A402

Discovery of America anniv. emblem and ships: No. 2213a, 1g, Spanish galleon. 17th cent. b, 2g, Victoria, 1st to circumnavigate the globe, 1519-22. c, 3g, San Hermenegildo. 5g, San Martin, c.1582. 60g, Santa Maria, c.1492, vert.

**1987, Sept. 9    Perf. 14**
2213 A402    Strip of 4, #a.-d.
2214 A402 60g multicolored    7.50 3.00
Set, #2213-2214

Colorado Party, Cent. — A403

Bernardino Caballero (founder), President Stroessner and: 5g, 10g, 25g, three-lane highway. 150g, 170g, 200g, Power lines.

**1987, Sept. 11    Wmk. 347**
2215 A403    5g multi    .20 .20
2216 A403    10g multi    .20 .20
2217 A403    25g multi    .20 .20
2218 A403    150g multi    .40 .25
2219 A403    170g multi    .45 .35
2220 A403    200g multi    .50 .40
Nos. 2215-2220 (6)    2.00 1.60
Nos. 2218-2220 are airmail.

Berlin, 750th Anniv. — A404

Berlin Stamps and Coins: No. 2221: a, 1g, #9NB145. b, 2g, #9NB154. c, 3g, #9N57, vert. d, 5g, #9N170, vert. 60g, 1987 Commemorative coin, vert.

**1987, Sept. 12    Perf. 13½x13, 13½x13    Unwmk.**
2221 A404    Strip of 4, #a.-d.
2222 A404 60g multicolored    10.00 5.00
Set, #2221-2222
For overprints see Nos. 2239, 2294.

**Perf. 14**
2224 A405 60g multicolored    3.00 2.00
Set, #2223-2224

Nos. 2209-2210 Ovptd. in Bright Blue

EXFIVIA 87 BOLIVIA 4 al 13.12.87

**1987, Sept. 30    Perf. 13**
2225 A401    75g on #2209
2226 A401 100g on #2210    1.50 1.50
Set, #2225-2226
EXFIVIA '87 Intl. Philatelic Exhibition, LaPaz, Bolivia. No. 2226 is airmail.

Nos. 2195d-2195f, 2196 Overprinted in Black or Silver

OLYMPHILEX'88 SEUL 1988

**1987, Oct. 1    Perf. 13½x13**
2227 A399    Strip of 3, #a.-c.
2228 A399 5g on No. 2190 (6)    5.00 5.00
Olymphilex '87 Intl. Phil. Exhib., Seoul.

No. 2189 Ovptd. with Emblem and "PHILATELIA '87," etc.

**1987, Oct. 15    Perf. 13½x13½, 13½x13**
2229 A398    Strip of 6, #a.-f.    3.00 3.00
PHILATELIA '87 Intl. Phil. Exhib., Cologne. Size and configuration of overprint varies.

Nos. 2195a-2195b Ovptd. in Bright Blue for EXFILNA '87 and BARCELONA 92

**1987, Oct. 24    Perf. 13x13½**
2230 A399    Pall, #a.-b.    1.00 4.00
Exfilna '87 Intl. Philatelic Exhibition.

Ship Paintings A406

No. 2231: a, 1g, San Juan Nepomuceno. b, 2g, San Eugenio. c, 3g, San Telmo. d, 5g, San Carlos. 60g, Spanish galleon, 16th cent. 100g, One of Columbus ships.

**1987    Litho.    Perf. 14**
2231 A406    Strip of 4, #a.-d.

**Perf. 13½x13½**
2232 A406    60g multicolored    10.00 4.00
Set, #2231-2232

**Souvenir Sheet    Perf. 13½**
2233 A406 100g multicolored    13.00 13.00
Discovery of America, 500th anniv. in 1992 (#2233). Issue dates: Nos. 2231-2232, Dec. 10. No. 2233, Dec. 12.

Race Cars A405

No. 2223: a, 1g, Audi Sport Quattro. b, 2g, Lancia Delta S 4. c, 3g, Fiat 131. d, 5g, Porsche 911 4x4. 60g, Lancia Rally.

**1987, Sept. 27    Perf. 13**
2223 A405    Strip of 4, #a.-d.

**2258** A390 100g like #2157
**2259** A390 200g like #2158 3.50 3.50
Set, #2254-2259

Pres. Stroessner's new term in office. Nos. 2258-2259 are airmail.

Olympic Tennis, Seoul — A412

**1988, Aug. 16** **Perf. 13**
**2260** A412 60g multicolored 15.00 7.00
**2261** A412 60g multicolored
Strip of 4, #a.-d.
Set, #2260-2267

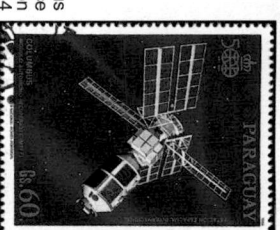

PARAGUAY — MUESTRA

1992 Summer Olympics, Barcelona — A413

Olympic medalists from Spain: No. 2262a, 1g, Ricardo Zamora, soccer, Antwerp, 1920, vert. b, 2g, Equestrian team, Amsterdam, 1928. c, 3g, Angel Leon, shooting, Helsinki, 1952. d, 5g, Kayak team, Montreal, 1976. 60g, Francisco Fernandez Ochoa, slalom, Sapporo, 1972, vert. 100g, Olympic Stadium, Barcelona, vert.

**1989, Jan. 5** **Perf. 14**
**2262** A413 Strip of 4, #a.-d.

**2263** A413 60g multicolored 9.00 4.50
Set, #2262-2263

Souvenir Sheet
**Perf. 13½**
**2264** A413 100g multicolored 12.00 12.00

Discovery of America 500th anniv. (in 1992). No. 2264 is airmail and contains one 50x60mm stamp. For overprint see No. 2293.

Columbus Space Station A414

**1989, Jan. 7** **Litho.** **Perf. 13x13½**
**2265** A414 60g multicolored 4.00 2.00

Discovery of America 500th anniv. (in 1992).

No. 2076 Overprinted in Silver, Red and Blue with Olympic Rings, "1992" and Emblem

**1989, Jan. 10** **Perf. 13½x13, 13x13½**
**2266** A369 Strip of 6, #a.-f. 5.00 5.00

1992 Winter Olympics, Albertville. Location and configuration of overprint varies.

---

PARAGUAY — Gs.1.

Olympic Tennis, Seoul A412

**1989, Feb. 8** **Perf. 14**
**2267** A251 Strip of 5, #a.-e. 3.00 3.00

Death of Emperor Hirohito of Japan.

No. 1454 Ovptd. in Silver "HOMENAJE AL EMPERADOR HIROITO DE JAPON 29.IV.1901-6.1.1989"

Paintings by Titian — A416

No. 2270: a, 1g, Bacchus and Ariadne (Bacchus); b, 2g, Bacchus and Ariadne (tutelary spirit); c, 3g, Death of Actaeon. d, 5g, Portrait of a Young Woman with a Fur Cape. 60g, Concert in a Field. 100g, Holy Family with Donor.

**1989, Apr. 17** **Perf. 13x13½**
**2270** A416 Strip of 4, #a.-d.

**2271** A416 60g multicolored 10.00 4.00
Set, #2270-2271

Souvenir Sheet
**Perf. 13½**
**2271A** A416 100g multicolored 12.00

No. 2271A is airmail and contains one 60x49mm stamp. Issue date: May 27.

PARAGUAY — Gs.1.

Formula 1 Drivers, Race Cars — A415

No. 2268: a, 1g, Stirling Moss, Mercedes W196. b, 2g, Emerson Fittipaldi, Lotus. c, 3g, Nelson Piquet, Lotus. d, 5g, Juan Manuel Fangio, Maserati 250F.

**1989, Mar. 6** **Perf. 13**
**2268** A415 Strip of 4, #a.-d.
**2269** A415 60g multicolored 9.00 4.50
Set, #2268-2269

**1989, May 29** **Perf. 14½**

Miniature Sheet
**2278** A343 Sheet of 7+label, like #1972 18.00

Discovery of America 500th anniv. (in 1992).

---

Athletes: No. 2272a, 1g, Torbjorn Lokken, 1987 Nordic combined world champion. b, 2g, Atle Skardal, skier, Norway. c, 3g, Geir Karlstad, Norway, world 10,000-meter speed skating champion, 1987. d, 5g, Franck Piccard, France, 1988 Olympic medalist, skiing. 60g, Roger Ruud, ski jumper, Norway.

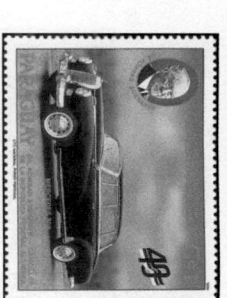

PARAGUAY — PARAFIL '89

MENSAJERO DEL AMOR 500

**1989, May 23** **Perf. 13½x13**
**2272** A417 Strip of 4, #a.-d.
**2273** A417 60g multicolored 17.00 8.00
Set, #2272-2273

1994 Winter Olympics, Lillehammer — A417

**1989, May 25** **Perf. 13**
**2274** A287 Strip of 4, #a.-d.
**2275** A287 60g Siamese 12.50 4.00
Set, #2274-2275

Cat Type of 1976
Various cats: #2274a, 1g. b, 2g. c, 3g. d, 5g.

---

Nos. 2046, 2172 Overprinted in Metallic Red and Silver "PARAGUAY CLASIFICADO EN 1930, 1950, 1958 Y 1986" and Emblems or "ITALIA '90"

**1989, Sept. 15** **Litho.** **Perf. 13½x13**
**2286** A362 Strip of 6, #a.-f.

**1989, Sept. 15** **Litho.** **Perf. 14**
**2287** A394 5g multicolored 20.00 8.00
Set, #2286-2287

1990 World Cup Soccer Championships, Italy. Location and size of overprint varies.

Parafil '89, Paraguay-Argentina philatelic exhibition.

---

Nos. 2171 Overprinted in Metallic Red and Silver with FIFA and Italia 90 Emblems and "PARAGUAY PARTICIPO EN 13 CAMPEONATOS MUNDIALES"

**1989, Sept. 14** **Litho.** **Perf. 13½x13**
**2283** A394 Strip of 6, #a.-f. 15.00 15.00

Size and configuration of overprint varies.

**1989, July 5** **Perf. 14**
**2281** A352 Pair, #a.-b. 2.00 1.00

Nos. 2006a-2006b Ovptd. "BRASILIANA / 89"

**1989, May 30** **Litho.** **Perf. 13½x13**
**2279** A381 Strip of 4, #a.-d.
**2280** A381 5g on #2123 15.00 15.00
Set, #2279-2280

No. 2122a Overprinted with Hamburg Emblem and Nos. 2122b-2122f, 2123 Ovptd. with Diff. Emblem in Red or Silver

No. 2122a Overprinted with Discovery of America, 500th Anniv. Emblem in Red on Silver

City of Hamburg, 800th anniv.

---

Nos. C738, C753 Overprinted in metallic red with Italia '90 emblem and "SUDAMERICA-GRUPO 2 / PARAGUAY-COLOMBIA / PARAGUAY-ECUADOR / COLOMBIA-PARAGUAY / ECUADOR-PARAGUAY" and in metallic red on silver with FIFA emblem

**1989, Sept. 14** **Litho.** **Perf. 13**
**2284** AP228 25g on #C738
**2285** AP232 25g on #C753 15.00 7.00
Nos. 2283-2285 (8)

Nos. 2251, C724 Overprinted

---

Famous men and automobiles: No. 2276a, 1g, Konrad Adenauer, chancellor, 1949-1963, Mercedes. b, 2g, Ludwig Erhard, chancellor, 1963-1966, Volkswagen Beetle. c, 3g, Felix Wankel, engine designer, 1963 NSU Spider. d, 5g, Franz Josef Strauss, President of Bavarian Cabinet, BMW 502. 60g, Pres. Richard von Weizsacker and Dr. Josef Neckermann.

**1989, May 27** **Perf. 13½x13**
**2276** A418 Strip of 4, #a.-d.
**2277** A418 60g multicolored 12.00 6.00
Set, #2276-2277

For overprints see No. 2369.

Ship Type of 1980 Overprinted with Discovery of America, 500th Anniv. Emblem in Red on Silver

**1989, Sept. 18** **Perf. 13**
**2291** A226 Strip of 4, #a.-e.
**2292** AP233 25g on #C764 (G) 10.00 10.00
Set, #2291-2292

1992 Summer Olympics, Barcelona, Spain. Size and location of overprint varies.

Nos. 2243, C764 Overprinted in Silver or Gold with Emblem and "ATENAS 100 ANOS DE LOS JUEGOS OLIMPICOS 1896-1996"

---

Federal Republic of Germany, 40th Anniv. — A418

Wernher von Braun's Signature and UN and Space Emblems

**1989, Sept. 16** **Perf. 14**
**2288** A226 50c multicolored
**2289** A226 50c multicolored
**2290** A226 75c multicolored 12.00 12.00
Set, #2288-2290

Location, size and configuration of overprint varies.

Nos. 1284-1286 Ovptd. in Gold "...BIEN ESTUVIMOS EN LA LUNA AHORA NECESITAMOS LOS MEDIOS PARA LLEGAR A LOS PLANETAS"

Nos. 2262a-2262d Ovptd. in Silver with Heads of Steffi Graf or Boris Becker and:
"WIMBLEDON 1988 / SEUL 1988 / WIMBLEDON 1989 / EL TENIS NUEVAMENTE EN / LAS OLIMPIADAS 1988-1992"
or Similar

**1989, Sept. 19** **Perf. 14**
**2293** A413 Strip of 4, #a.-d. 8.00 8.00

Addition of tennis as an Olympic sport in 1992. Size and configuration of overprint varies.

No. 2221 Ovptd. in Gold and Blue "PRIMER AEROPUERTO PARA / COHETES, BERLIN 1930 OBERTH. / NEBEL, RITTER, VON BRAUN" space emblem and "PROF. DR. HERMANN / OBERTH 95o ANIV. / NACIMIENTO 25.6.1989"

**1989, Sept. 20** **Perf. 13½x13, 13x13½**
**2294** A404 Strip of 4, #a.-d. 18.00 6.00

Dr. Hermann Oberth, rocket scientist, 95th birth anniv. Overprint size, etc. varies.

Nos. 1406-1408 Ovptd. with Emblems and Silver "OLIMPIADAS / DE INVIERNO / ALBERTVILLE 1992" in 2 or 3 Lines

**1989, Sept. 21** **Perf. 14**
**2295** A244 Strip of 5, #a.-e.
**2296** A244 50c multicolored
**2297** A244 75c multicolored 20.00 10.00
Set, #2295-2297

1992 Winter Olympics, Albertville. Size and configuration of overprint varies.

**1989, Oct. 9** **Litho.** **Wmk. 347**
**2298** A411 50g on #2251 3.00 3.00
**2299** AP226 120g on #C724 8.00 8.00

## Birds Facing Extinction — A419

**Perf. 13½x13  Litho.  Wmk. 347**
**1989, Dec. 19**
| 2300 | A419 | 50g Ara chloroptera | .20 | .20 |
| 2301 | A419 | 100g Mergus octosetaceus | .20 | .20 |
| 2302 | A419 | 300g Rhea americana | .50 | .40 |
| 2303 | A419 | 500g Ramphastos toco | .80 | .65 |
| 2304 | A419 | 1000g Crax fasciolata | 1.60 | 1.40 |
| 2305 | A419 | 2000g Ara araruna | 3.25 | 2.50 |
|  |  |  | 6.55 | 5.35 |

Nos. 2300-2305 (6)

Nos. 2302-2305 airmail. Nos. 2300 & 2305 vert. Frames and typestyles vary greatly. Watermark on 50g, 100g, 300g is 8mm high.

## 1992 Summer Olympics, Barcelona — A420

Athletes: No. 2306a, 1g, A. Fichtel and S. Bau, W. Germany, foils, 1988. b, 2g, Spanish basketball team, 1984. c, 3g, Jackie Joyner-Kersee, heptathlon and long jump, 1988. d, 5g, L. Bootbaum, W. Germany, show jumping, team, 1988. 60g, W. Brinkmann, W. Germany, show jumping, team, 1988. 100g, Emilio Sánchez, tennis.

**1989, Dec. 26  Unwmk.  Litho.  Perf. 14**
| 2306 | A420 | Strip of 4, #a.-d.  Perf. 13 |  |  |
| 2307 | A420 | 60g multicolored | 13.00 | 6.00 |

Set, #2306-2307

**Souvenir Sheet  Perf. 13½**
| 2308 | A420 | 100g multicolored | 15.00 |

No. 2308 is airmail and contains one 47x57mm stamp.

## World Cup Soccer Championships, Italy — A421

1986 World Cup soccer players in various positions: No. 2309a, 1g, England vs. Paraguay. b, 2g, Spain vs. Denmark. c, 3g, France vs. Italy. d, 5g, Germany vs. Morocco. 60g, Mexico vs. Italy. 100g, Paraguay. Germany vs. Argentina.

**1989, Dec. 29  Perf. 14**
| 2309 | A421 | Strip of 4, #a.-d.  Perf. 13½ |  |  |
| 2310 | A421 | 60g multicolored | 11.00 | 5.00 |

Set, #2309-2310

**Souvenir Sheet  Perf. 14½**
| 2311 | A421 | 100g multicolored | 15.00 |

No. 2311 is airmail and contains one 40x50mm stamp.

For overprints see Nos. 2355-2356.

## Organization of American States, Cent. — A425

**Perf. 13½x13**
**1990, Feb. 9  Litho.  Wmk. 347**
| 2320 | A425 | 50g multicolored | .20 | .20 |
| 2321 | A425 | 100g multicolored | .30 | .25 |
| 2322 | A425 | 200g Map of Paraguay | .60 | .45 |
|  |  |  | 1.10 | .90 |

Nos. 2320-2322 (3)

## 1992 Summer Olympics, Barcelona — A422

Barcelona '92, proposed Athens '96 emblems and: No. 2312a, 1g, Greece #128. b, 2g, Greece #126, vert. c, 3g, Greece #127, vert. d, 5g, Greece #123, vert. 60g, Paraguay #736. 100g, Horse and rider, vert.

**1990, Jan. 4  Perf. 13½x13, 13x13½**
| 2312 | A422 | Strip of 4, #a.-d. | 17.00 | 6.00 |

**Souvenir Sheet  Perf. 13½**
| 2313 | A422 | 60g multicolored |  |  |

Set, #2312-2313

**Souvenir Sheet  Perf. 13½**
| 2314 | A422 | 100g multicolored | 15.00 |

No. 2314 is airmail and contains one 50x60mm stamp and exists with either white or yellow border. Stamps inscribed 1989. For overprints see No. 2357.

## 1992 Winter Olympics, Albertville — A426

Calgary 1988 skiers: No. 2323a, 1g, Alberto Tomba, Italy, slalom and giant slalom. b, 2g, Vreni Schneider, Switzerland, women's slalom and giant slalom, vert. c, 3g, Luc Alphand, France, skier, vert. d, 5g, Matti Nykaenen, Finland, ski-jumping.
60g, Marina Kiehl, W. Germany, women's downhill. 100g, Frank Piccard, France, super giant slalom.

**1990, Mar. 7  Unwmk.  Perf. 14**
| 2323 | A426 | Strip of 4, #a.-d.  Perf. 13 |  |  |
| 2324 | A426 | 60g multicolored | 8.00 | 5.00 |

Set, #2323-2324

**Souvenir Sheet  Perf. 14½**
| 2325 | A426 | 100g multicolored | 15.00 |

No. 2325 is airmail, contains one 40x50mm stamp and exists with either white or yellow border.

## Swiss Confederation, 700th Anniv. — A423

#2315: a, 3g, Monument to William Tell. b, 5g, Manship Globe, UN Headquarters, Geneva. 60g, 15th cent. messenger, Bern. #2317, 1st Swiss steam locomotive, horiz. #2318, Jean Henri Dunant, founder of the Red Cross, horiz.

**1990, Jan. 25  Perf. 14**
| 2315 | A423 | Pair, #a.-b.  Perf. 13 |  |  |
| 2316 | A423 | 60g multicolored | 12.50 | 5.00 |

Set, #2315-2316

**Souvenir Sheets  Perf. 14½**
| 2317 | A423 | 100g multicolored | 25.00 |
| 2318 | A423 | 100g multicolored | 25.00 |

Nos. 2317-2318 are airmail. For overprints see Nos. 2352-2354.

## Pre-Columbian Art, Customs A427

UPAE Emblem and: 150g, Pre-Columbian basket. 500g, Aboriginal ceremony.

**Perf. 13**
**1990, Mar. 8  Wmk. 347**
| 2326 | A427 | 150g multicolored | 1.00 | .75 |
| 2327 | A427 | 500g multicolored | 2.50 | 1.50 |

No. 2327 is airmail.
For overprints see Nos. 2345-2346.

## Wood Carving A424

**Perf. 14**
**1990, Jan. 26**
| 2319 | A424 | Pair, #a.-b. + label | 3.00 | 1.00 |

Discovery of America, 500th anniv. emblem &: #2319: a, 1g, 1st cathechism in Guarani. b, 2g, shown. #2319 has continuous design.

---

c, 3g, Baden #4b on cover. d, 5g, Roman States #4 on cover. 60g, Paraguay #C38 and four #C54 on cover.

**1990, Mar. 12  Unwmk.  Perf. 14**
| 2328 | A428 | Strip of 4, #a.-d.  Perf. 13½x13 |  |  |
| 2329 | A428 | 60g multicolored |  |  |

## Postal Union of the Americas and Spain (UPAE) A429

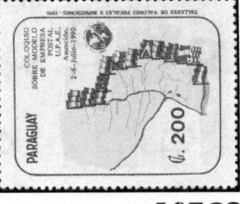

**1990, July 2  Perf. 13½x13½**
| 2330 | A429 | 200g Map, flags | .60 | .30 |
| 2331 | A429 | 250g Paraguay #1 | .70 | .35 |
| 2332 | A429 | 350g FDC of #2326-2327, horiz. | 1.60 | .45 |
|  |  |  | 2.90 | 1.10 |

Nos. 2330-2332 (3)

## National University, Cent. (in 1989) — A430

**1990, Sept. 8**
| 2333 | A430 | 300g Future site | .90 | .70 |
| 2334 | A430 | 400g Present site | 1.25 | .95 |
| 2335 | A430 | 600g Old site | 1.75 | 1.50 |
|  |  |  | 3.90 | 3.15 |

Nos. 2333-2335 (3)

## Franciscan Churches — A431

**1990, Sept. 25  Litho.  Perf. 13½x13  Wmk. 347**
| 2336 | A431 | 50g Guarambare | .20 | .20 |
| 2337 | A431 | 100g Yaguaron | .30 | .25 |
| 2338 | A431 | 200g Ita | .60 | .45 |
|  |  |  | 1.10 | .90 |

Nos. 2336-2338 (3)
For overprints see Nos. 2366-2368.

## Democracy in Paraguay — A432

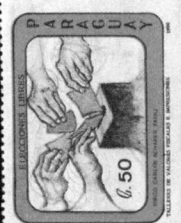

Designs: 100g, State and Catholic Church, vert. 200g, Human rights, vert. 300g, Freedom of the Press, vert. 500g, Return of the exiles. 3000g, People and democracy.

**Perf. 13½x13, 13x13½  Litho.  Wmk. 347**
**1990, Oct. 5**
| 2339 | A432 | 50g multicolored | .20 | .20 |
| 2340 | A432 | 100g multicolored | .20 | .20 |
| 2341 | A432 | 200g multicolored | .40 | .35 |
| 2342 | A432 | 300g multicolored | .60 | .55 |
| 2343 | A432 | 500g multicolored | 1.00 | .90 |
| 2344 | A432 | 3000g multicolored | 6.00 | 5.50 |
|  |  |  | 8.40 | 7.70 |

Nos. 2339-2344 (6)
Nos. 2343-2344 are airmail.

## First Postage Stamp, 150th Anniv. — A428

Penny Black, Mail Transportation 500th anniv. emblem and: No. 2328a, 1g, Penny Black on cover. b, 2g, Mauritius #1-2 on cover.

## Nos. 2326-2327 Overprinted in Magenta

**1990 Litho. Wmk. 347 Perf. 13**

| | | | |
|---|---|---|---|
| 2345 | A427 | 150g multicolored | .45 .40 |
| 2346 | A427 | 500g multicolored | 1.50 1.25 |

No. 2346 is airmail.

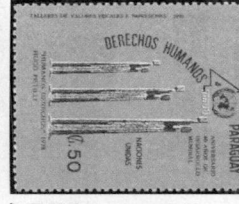

Visita de sus Majestades Los Reyes de España 22-24 Octubre 1990

**UN Development Program, 40th Anniv. — A433**

Designs: 50m, Human Rights, sculpture by Hugo Pistilli. 100m, United Nations, sculpture by Hermann Guggiani. 150m, Miguel de Cervantes Literature Award, won by Augusto Roa Bastos.

**1990, Oct. 26**

| | | | |
|---|---|---|---|
| 2347 | A433 | 50g lilac & multi | .30 .20 |
| 2348 | A433 | 100g gray & multi | .45 .25 |
| 2349 | A433 | 150g green & multi | .70 .40 |
| | | Nos. 2347-2349 (3) | 1.45 .85 |

America A434

**1990, Oct. 31 Perf. 13½x13 Wmk. 347**

| | | | |
|---|---|---|---|
| 2350 | A434 | 50g multicolored | .60 .30 |
| 2351 | A434 | 250g multicolored | 1.25 1.00 |

No. 2351 is airmail.

50g, Paraguay River banks. 250g, Chaco land.

## Nos. 2315-2316, 2318 Ovptd. in Metallic Red and Silver

700 Aniv. Confederacion Helvetica 1291-1991 · 125 años

**1991, Apr. 2 Unwmk. Litho. Perf. 14**

| | | | |
|---|---|---|---|
| 2352 | A423 | Pair, #a-b. | .60 .30 |

**Perf. 13**

| | | | |
|---|---|---|---|
| 2353 | A423 | 60g on #2316 | 8.00 8.00 |

Set, #2352-2353

**Souvenir Sheet Perf. 14½**

| | | | |
|---|---|---|---|
| 2354 | A423 | 100g on #2318 | 17.00 17.00 |

Swiss Confederation, 700th anniv. and Red Cross, 125th anniv. No. 2354 is airmail. No. 2352 exists perf. 13. Location of overprint varies.

## Nos. 2309-2310 Ovptd. in Silver

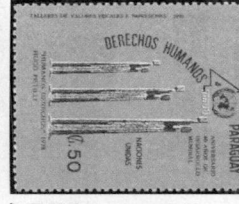

USA 94 — Adjudicacion Campeonato Mundial de Fútbol

1994 World Cup Soccer Championships. Location of overprint varies.

**1991, Apr. 4 Perf. 14**

| | | |
|---|---|---|
| 2355 | A421 | Strip of 4, #a-d. |
| 2356 | A421 | 60g on #2310 |

10.00 10.00

Set, #2355-2356

## Nos. 2312, C822, C766 Ovptd. in Silver

**1991, Apr. 4 Perf. 13**

| | | |
|---|---|---|
| 2357 | A422 | |
| 2358 | AP246 | 25g on #C822 |
| 2359 | AP233 | 30g on #C766 |

Participation of reunified Germany in 1992 Summer Olympics. Nos. 2356-2359 are airmail. Location of overprint varies.

Participación de Alemania Unificada en las Olimpiadas Barcelona 92 · 200 Aniv. 1791-1991 · Gs.l.

**Professors A435**

Designs: 50g, Julio Manuel Morales, gynecologist. 100g, Carlos Gatti, clinician. 200g, Gustavo Gonzalez, geologist. 300g, Juan Max Boettner, physician, geologist, musician. 350g, Juan Boggino, pathologist. 500g, Andres Barbero, physician, founder of Paraguayan Red Cross.

PROF. DR. JULIO MANUEL MORALES — Maestro de la Ginecología

**1991, Apr. 5 Litho. Wmk. 347**

| | | | |
|---|---|---|---|
| 2360 | A435 | 50g multicolored | .20 .20 |
| 2361 | A435 | 100g multicolored | .25 .25 |
| 2362 | A435 | 200g multicolored | .40 .35 |
| 2363 | A435 | 300g multicolored | .50 .55 |
| 2364 | A435 | 350g multicolored | .60 .55 |
| 2365 | A435 | 500g multicolored | .90 .60 |
| | | Nos. 2360-2365 (6) | 3.10 2.80 |

Nos. 2364-2365 are airmail.

**1991 Wmk. 347 Perf. 13½x13**

| | | | |
|---|---|---|---|
| 2366 | A431 | 50g on #2336 | .25 .20 |
| 2367 | A431 | 100g on #2337 | .25 .20 |
| 2368 | A431 | 200g on #2338 | .35 .35 |
| | | Nos. 2366-2368 (3) | 1.00 .75 |

Espamer '91 Philatelic Exhibition.

## Nos. 2276c-2276d Ovptd. in Silver

Unificación de Alemania para la Paz del Mundo

**1991**

| | | |
|---|---|---|
| 2369 | A418 | Strip of 4, #a-d. **Perf. 13** |

5.25 5.00

## Nos. 2276a-2276b Ovptd. in Silver

200 Aniv. Lilienthal — Unificación de Alemania para la Paz del Mundo

**Writers and Musicians — A436**

Designs: 50g, Ruy Diaz de Guzman, historian. 100g, Maria Talavera, war correspondent, vert. 150g, Augusto Roa Bastos, writer, vert. 200g, Jose Asuncion Flores, composer, vert. 250g, Felix Perez Cardozo, harpist. 300g, Juan Carlos Moreno Gonzalez, composer.

PARAGUAY — RUY DIAZ DE GUZMAN — PRIMER HISTORIADOR PARAGUAYO — G. 50

**1991, Aug. 27 Litho. Wmk. 347 Perf. 13½x13, 13½x13**

| | | | |
|---|---|---|---|
| 2373 | A436 | 50g multicolored | .20 .20 |
| 2374 | A436 | 100g multicolored | .25 .25 |
| 2375 | A436 | 150g multicolored | .40 .35 |
| 2376 | A436 | 200g multicolored | .50 .45 |
| 2377 | A436 | 250g multicolored | .60 .55 |
| 2378 | A436 | 300g multicolored | .75 .65 |
| | | Nos. 2373-2378 (6) | 2.70 2.45 |

Nos. 2376-2378 are airmail.

America A437 — AMERICA — La Guerra de Tavare — PARAGUAY — G. 100

100g, War of Tavare. 300g, Arrival of Spanish explorer Domingo Martinez de Irala in Paraguay.

**1991, Oct. 9 Litho. Wmk. 347 Perf. 13½x13**

| | | | |
|---|---|---|---|
| 2379 | A437 | 100g multicolored | .25 .25 |
| 2380 | A437 | 300g multicolored | .75 .65 |

No. 2380 is airmail.

## Nos. 2336-2338 Ovptd. in Black and Red

ESPAMER Buenos Aires — PARAGUAY — G. 50

Nos. 2364-2365 are airmail.

**Paintings A438**

Designs: 50g, Compass of Life, by Alfredo Morales. 100g, The Lighted Alley, by Michael Burt. 150g, Earring, by Lucy Yegros. 200g, Migrant Workers, by Hugo Bogado Barrios. 250g, Passengers Without a Ship, by Bernardo Ismachoviez. 300g, Native Guarani, by Lotte Schulz.

Compás de la vida · ALFREDO MORALES · PARAGUAY · G.50

**1991, Nov. 12 Litho. Wmk. 347 Perf. 13½x13**

| | | | |
|---|---|---|---|
| 2381 | A438 | 50g multicolored | .20 .20 |
| 2382 | A438 | 100g multicolored | .25 .25 |
| 2383 | A438 | 150g multicolored | .40 .45 |
| 2384 | A438 | 200g multicolored | .50 .45 |
| 2385 | A438 | 250g multicolored | .60 .55 |
| 2386 | A438 | 300g multicolored | .75 .65 |
| | | Nos. 2381-2386 (6) | 2.70 2.45 |

Nos. 2384-2386 are airmail.

**Endangered Species — A439**

PARAGUAY — Felis pardalis — G. 100

Designs: 50g, Catagonus wagneris, vert. 100g, Felis pardalis. 150g, Tapirus terrestri. 200g, Chrysocyon brachyurus.

**1992, Jan. 28 Litho. Wmk. 347 Perf. 13½x13, 13½x13**

| | | | |
|---|---|---|---|
| 2387 | A439 | 50g multicolored | .20 .20 |
| 2388 | A439 | 100g multicolored | .25 .25 |
| 2389 | A439 | 150g multicolored | .40 .35 |
| 2390 | A439 | 200g multicolored | .50 .45 |
| | | Nos. 2387-2390 (4) | 1.35 1.25 |

**Tile Designs of Christianized Indians A440**

PARAGUAY — MOTIVO GEOMETRICO

**1992, Mar. 2 Litho. Wmk. 347 Perf. 13½x13**

| | | | |
|---|---|---|---|
| 2391 | A440 | 50g Geometric | .25 .20 |
| 2392 | A440 | 100g Church | .25 .20 |
| 2393 | A440 | 150g Missionary ship | .35 .35 |
| 2394 | A440 | 200g Plant | .35 .35 |

Discovery of America, 500th anniv.

**Leprosy Society of Paraguay, 60th Anniv. — A441**

PATRONATO DE LEPROSOS — PARAGUAY — G. 50

Designs: 50g, Society emblem, Malcolm L. Norment, founder. 250g, Gerhard Henrik Armauer Hansen (1841-1912), discoverer of leprosy bacillus.

**1992, Apr. 28 Litho. Wmk. 347 Perf. 13½x13**

| | | | |
|---|---|---|---|
| 2395 | A441 | 50g multicolored | .20 .20 |
| 2396 | A441 | 250g multicolored | .60 .55 |

**Earth Summit, Rio de Janeiro — A442**

Earth Summit emblem, St. Francis of Assisi, and: 50g, Hands holding symbols of clean environment. 100g, Butterfly, industrial pollution. 250g, Globe, calls for environmental protection.

**1992, June 9**

| | | | | |
|---|---|---|---|---|
| 2397 | A442 | 50g | multicolored | .20 .20 |
| 2398 | A442 | 100g | multicolored | .25 .25 |
| 2399 | A442 | 250g | multicolored | .55 .55 |
| | | | | 1.00 1.00 |

*Nos. 2397-2399 (3)*

For overprints see Nos. 2422-2424.

**Natl. Census A443**

**1992, July 30    Perf. 13½x13, 13x13½**

| | | | | |
|---|---|---|---|---|
| 2400 | A443 | 50g | Economic activity | .20 .20 |
| 2401 | A443 | 200g | Houses, vert. | .45 .45 |
| 2402 | A443 | 250g | Population, vert. | .60 .55 |
| 2403 | A443 | 300g | Education | .75 .65 |
| | | | | 2.00 1.85 |

*Nos. 2400-2403 (4)*

**1992 Summer Olympics, Barcelona — A444**

**1992, Sept. 1    Perf. 13½x13, 13½x13**

| | | | | |
|---|---|---|---|---|
| 2404 | A444 | 50g | Soccer, vert. | .20 .20 |
| 2405 | A444 | 100g | Tennis, vert. | .25 .25 |
| 2406 | A444 | 150g | Running, vert. | .40 .35 |
| 2407 | A444 | 200g | Swimming | .50 .40 |
| 2408 | A444 | 250g | Judo, vert. | .60 .55 |
| 2409 | A444 | 350g | Fencing | .85 .75 |
| | | | | 2.80 2.50 |

*Nos. 2404-2409 (6)*

**Evangelism in Paraguay, 500th Anniv. — A445**

Designs: 50g, Fríar Luis Bolanos. 100g, Fríar Juan de San Bernardo. 150g, San Roque Gonzalez de Santa Cruz. 200g, Father Amancio Gonzalez. 250g, Monsignor Juan Sinforiano Bogarin, vert.

**1992, Oct. 9    Rough Perf. 13½x13, 13x13½    Unwmk.**

| | | | | |
|---|---|---|---|---|
| 2410 | A445 | 50g | multicolored | .20 .20 |
| 2411 | A445 | 100g | multicolored | .25 .25 |
| 2412 | A445 | 150g | multicolored | .40 .35 |
| 2413 | A445 | 200g | multicolored | .50 .45 |
| 2414 | A445 | 250g | multicolored | .60 .55 |
| | | | | 1.95 1.80 |

*Nos. 2410-2414 (5)*

For overprints see Nos. 2419-2421.

---

**America A446**

Designs: 150g, Columbus, fleet arriving in New World. 350g, Columbus, vert.

**1992, Oct. 12    Rough Perf. 13½x13, 13x13½**

| | | | | |
|---|---|---|---|---|
| 2415 | A446 | 150g | multicolored | .40 .35 |
| 2416 | A446 | 350g | multicolored | .85 .75 |

No. 2416 is airmail.

**Ovptd. "PARAFIL 92" in Blue**

**1992, Nov. 9**

| | | | | |
|---|---|---|---|---|
| 2417 | A446 | 150g | multicolored | .40 .35 |
| 2418 | A446 | 350g | multicolored | .85 .75 |

No. 2418 is airmail.

**Nos. 2410-2412 Ovptd. in Green**

**1992, Nov. 6    Rough Perf. 13½x13**

| | | | | |
|---|---|---|---|---|
| 2419 | A445 | 50g | multicolored | .20 .20 |
| 2420 | A445 | 100g | multicolored | .25 .25 |
| 2421 | A445 | 150g | multicolored | .40 .35 |
| | | | | .85 .80 |

*Nos. 2419-2421 (3)*

**Nos. 2397-2399 Ovptd. in Blue**

**1992, Oct. 24    Wmk. 347**

| | | | | |
|---|---|---|---|---|
| 2422 | A442 | 50g | multicolored | .20 .20 |
| 2423 | A442 | 100g | multicolored | .25 .25 |
| 2424 | A442 | 250g | multicolored | .55 .55 |
| | | | | 1.00 1.00 |

*Nos. 2422 2424 (3)*

**Inter-American Institute for Cooperation in Agriculture, 50th Anniv. — A447**

Designs: 50g, Field workers. 100g, Test tubes, cattle in pasture. 200g, Hands holding flower. 250g, Cows, corn, city.

**1992, Nov. 27    Perf. 13x13½    Unwmk.**

| | | | | |
|---|---|---|---|---|
| 2425 | A447 | 50g | multicolored | .20 .20 |
| 2426 | A447 | 100g | multicolored | .25 .25 |
| 2427 | A447 | 200g | multicolored | .50 .45 |
| 2428 | A447 | 250g | multicolored | .60 .55 |
| | | | | 1.55 1.45 |

*Nos. 2425-2428 (4)*

For overprints see Nos. 2461-2462.

---

**Notary College of Paraguay, Cent. — A448**

Designs: 50g, Yolanda Bado de Artecona. 100g, Jose Ramon Silva. 150g, Abelardo Brugada Valpy. 200g, Tomas Varela. 250g, Jose Livio Lezcano. 300g, Francisco I. Fernandez.

**1992, Nov. 29    Rough Perf. 13x13½**

| | | | | |
|---|---|---|---|---|
| 2429 | A448 | 50g | multicolored | .20 .20 |
| 2430 | A448 | 100g | multicolored | .25 .25 |
| 2431 | A448 | 150g | multicolored | .40 .35 |
| 2432 | A448 | 200g | multicolored | .50 .45 |
| 2433 | A448 | 250g | multicolored | .60 .55 |
| 2434 | A448 | 300g | multicolored | .70 .65 |
| | | | | 2.65 2.45 |

*Nos. 2429-2434 (6)*

**Opening of Lopez Palace, Cent. A449**

Paintings of palace by: 50g, Michael Burt. 100g, Esperanza Gill. 200g, Emili Aparici. 250g, Hugo Bogado Barrios, vert.

**1993, Mar. 9    Perf. 13½x13½, 13x13½**

| | | | | |
|---|---|---|---|---|
| 2435 | A449 | 50g | multicolored | .20 .20 |
| 2436 | A449 | 100g | multicolored | .25 .25 |
| 2437 | A449 | 200g | multicolored | .50 .45 |
| 2438 | A449 | 250g | multicolored | .60 .55 |
| | | | | 1.55 1.45 |

*Nos. 2435-2438 (4)*

For overprints see Nos. 2453-2456.

**Treaty of Asuncion, 1st Anniv. — A450**

**1993, Mar. 10    Wmk. 347**

| | | | | |
|---|---|---|---|---|
| 2439 | A450 | 50g | Flags, map | .20 .20 |
| 2440 | A450 | 350g | Flags, globe | .85 .75 |

**Rough Perf. 13x13½**

**Santa Isabel Leprosy Assoc., 50th Anniv. — A451**

Various flowers.

**1993, May 24    Perf. 13x13½    Unwmk.**

| | | | | |
|---|---|---|---|---|
| 2441 | A451 | 50g | multicolored | .20 .20 |
| 2442 | A451 | 100g | multicolored | .50 .45 |
| 2443 | A451 | 250g | multicolored | .60 .80 |
| 2444 | A451 | 350g | multicolored | .85 .80 |
| | | | | 2.15 2.00 |

*Nos. 2441-2444 (4)*

---

**Goethe College, Cent. — A452**

Designs: 50g, Goethe, by Johann Heinrich Lips, inscription. 100g, Goethe (close-up), by Johann Heinrich Wilhelm Tischbein.

**1993, June 18**

| | | | | |
|---|---|---|---|---|
| 2445 | A452 | 50g | multicolored | .20 .20 |
| 2446 | A452 | 100g | multicolored | .50 .45 |

For overprints see Nos. 2451-2452.

**World Friendship Crusade, 35th Anniv. — A453**

Designs: 50g, Stylized globe. 100g, Map, Dr. Ramon Artemio Bracho. 200g, Children. 250g, Two people embracing.

**1993, July 1**

| | | | | |
|---|---|---|---|---|
| 2447 | A453 | 50g | multicolored | .20 .20 |
| 2448 | A453 | 100g | multicolored | .25 .25 |
| 2449 | A453 | 200g | multicolored | .50 .45 |
| 2450 | A453 | 250g | multicolored | .60 .55 |
| | | | | 1.55 1.45 |

*Nos. 2447-2450 (4)*

For overprint see No. 2486.

**Nos. 2445-2446 Ovptd. "BRASILIANA 93"**

**1993, July 12**

| | | | | |
|---|---|---|---|---|
| 2451 | A452 | 50g | multicolored | .20 .20 |
| 2452 | A452 | 200g | multicolored | .50 .46 |

**Nos. 2435-2430 Ovptd.**

**Perf. 13½x13, 13x13½**

**1993, Aug. 13**

| | | | | |
|---|---|---|---|---|
| 2453 | A449 | 50g | multicolored | .20 .20 |
| 2454 | A449 | 100g | multicolored | .25 .25 |
| 2455 | A449 | 200g | multicolored | .50 .45 |
| 2456 | A449 | 250g | multicolored | .60 .55 |
| | | | | 1.55 1.45 |

*Nos. 2453-2456 (4)*

Size of overprint varies.

**Church of the Incarnation, Cent. — A454**

Design: 50g, Side view of church, vert.

**1993, Oct. 8    Litho.    Unwmk.    Perf. 13**

| | | | | |
|---|---|---|---|---|
| 2457 | A454 | 50g | multicolored | .20 .20 |
| 2458 | A454 | 350g | multicolored | .40 .35 |

**Endangered Animals—A455**

America: 50g, Myrmecophaga tridactyla. 250g, Speothos venaticus.

**1993, Oct. 27**

| | | | | |
|---|---|---|---|---|
| 2459 | A455 | 50g multicolored | .60 | .25 |
| 2460 | A455 | 250g multicolored | 1.00 | .25 |

No. 2459 is airmail.

**Nos. 2426-2427 Ovptd.**

**1993, Nov. 16**

| | | | Perf. 13x13½ | |
|---|---|---|---|---|
| 2461 | A447 | 100g multicolored | .20 | .20 |
| 2462 | A447 | 200g multicolored | .25 | .20 |

**Christmas A456**

**1993, Nov. 24**

| | | | | |
|---|---|---|---|---|
| 2463 | A456 | 50g shown | .20 | .30 |
| 2464 | A456 | 250g Stars, wise men | .30 | .25 |

**Scouting in Paraguay, 80th Anniv.—A457**

50g, Girl scouts watching scout instructor. 100g, Boy scouts learning crafts. 200g, Lord Robert Baden-Powell. 250g, Girl scout with flag.

**1993, Dec. 30**

| | | | | |
|---|---|---|---|---|
| 2465 | A457 | 50g multicolored | .20 | .20 |
| 2466 | A457 | 100g multicolored | .20 | .20 |
| 2467 | A457 | 200g multicolored | .20 | .25 |
| 2468 | A457 | 250g multicolored | .30 | .90 |
| | | Nos. 2465-2468 (4) | .85 | |

**First Lawyers to Graduate from Natl. University of Asuncion, Cent.—A458**

**1994, Apr. 8**

| | | | Perf. 13 | |
|---|---|---|---|---|
| 2469 | A458 | 50g Cecilio Baez | .20 | .20 |
| 2470 | A458 | 100g Benigno Ri-queleme, vert. | .20 | .20 |

**Phoenix Sports Corporation, 50th Anniv.—A459**

Designs: 50g, Basketball player, vert. 200g, Soccer players, vert. 250g, Pedro Garcia Arias, founder, tennis player.

**1994, May 20 — Litho. Perf. 13**

| | | | | |
|---|---|---|---|---|
| 2473 | A459 | 50g multicolored | .20 | .20 |
| 2474 | A459 | 200g multicolored | .90 | .25 |
| 2475 | A459 | 250g multicolored | .30 | .25 |
| | | Nos. 2473-2475 (3) | .75 | .65 |

| | | | | |
|---|---|---|---|---|
| 2471 | A458 | 250g Emeterio Gon-zalez | .30 | .25 |
| 2472 | A458 | 500g J. Gaspar Vil-lamayor | .50 | .50 |
| | | Nos. 2469-2472 (4) | 1.20 | 1.15 |

**1994 World Cup Soccer Championships, U.S.—A460**

Various soccer plays.

**1994, June 2**

| | | | | |
|---|---|---|---|---|
| 2476 | A460 | 250g multicolored | .30 | .25 |
| 2477 | A460 | 500g multicolored | .50 | .50 |
| 2478 | A460 | 1000g multicolored | 1.00 | .85 |
| | | Nos. 2476-2478 (3) | 1.80 | 1.60 |

For overprints see Nos. 2483-2485.

**Intl. Olympic Committee, Cent.—A461**

**1994, June 23 — Unwmk. Litho. Perf. 13**

| | | | | |
|---|---|---|---|---|
| 2479 | A461 | 350g Runner | .40 | .35 |
| 2480 | A461 | 400g Lighting Olympic flame | .45 | .40 |

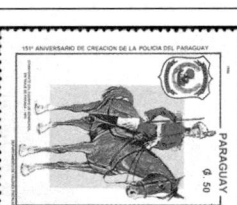

**World Congress on Physical Education, Asuncion—A462**

Designs: 1000g, Stylized family running to break finish line, vert.

**1994, July 19 — Perf. 13½x13, 13x13½ Litho.**

| | | | | |
|---|---|---|---|---|
| 2481 | A462 | 200g multicolored | .40 | .30 |
| 2482 | A462 | 1000g multicolored | 1.75 | 1.50 |

**Nos. 2476-2478 Ovptd.**

**1994, Aug. 2 — Perf. 13**

| | | | | |
|---|---|---|---|---|
| 2483 | A460 | 250g multicolored | .45 | .40 |
| 2484 | A460 | 500g multicolored | .90 | .75 |
| 2485 | A460 | 1000g multicolored | 1.75 | 1.50 |
| | | Nos. 2483-2485 (3) | 3.10 | 2.65 |

**No. 2448 Ovptd.**

**1994, Aug. 3**

| | | | Perf. 13x13½ | |
|---|---|---|---|---|
| 2486 | A453 | 100g multicolored | .20 | .20 |

**Agustin Pio Barrios Mangore (1885-1944), Musician A463**

**1994, Aug. 5 — Perf. 13x13½**

| | | | | |
|---|---|---|---|---|
| 2487 | A463 | 250g In tuxedo | .45 | .40 |
| 2488 | A463 | 500g In traditional costume | .90 | .75 |

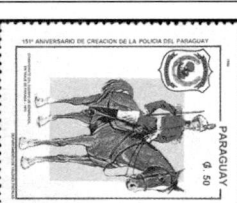

**Paraguayan Police, 151st Anniv.—A464**

50g, 1913 Guardsman on horseback. 250g, Pedro Nolasco Fernandez, 1st capital police chief; Carlos Bernadino Cacabelos, 1st commissioner.

**1994, Aug. 26 — Perf. 13x13½**

| | | | | |
|---|---|---|---|---|
| 2489 | A464 | 50g multicolored | .20 | .20 |
| 2490 | A464 | 250g multicolored | .45 | .40 |

For overprint see Nos. 2569-2570.

**Parafil '94 A465**

Birds: 100g, Ciconia maguari. 400g, Paroaria capitata. 500g, Jabiru mycteria, vert. 150g, Chloroceryle ameri-cana, vert.

**1994, Sept. 9 — Perf. 13**

| | | | | |
|---|---|---|---|---|
| 2491 | A465 | 100g multicolored | .35 | .25 |
| 2492 | A465 | 150g multicolored | .50 | .25 |
| 2493 | A465 | 400g multicolored | 1.25 | .60 |
| 2494 | A465 | 500g multicolored | 1.75 | .75 |
| | | Nos. 2491-2494 (4) | 3.85 | 1.80 |

**Solar Eclipse A466**

Designs: 50g, Eclipse, Copernicus. 200g, Sundial, Johannes Kepler.

**1994, Sept. 23 — Unwmk. Litho. Perf. 13**

| | | | | |
|---|---|---|---|---|
| 2495 | A466 | 50g multicolored | .20 | .20 |
| 2496 | A466 | 200g multicolored | .40 | .30 |

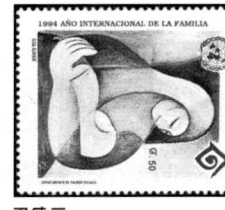

**America Issue A467**

**1994, Oct. 11 — Perf. 13½**

| | | | | |
|---|---|---|---|---|
| 2497 | A467 | 100g Derelict loco-motive | .20 | .20 |
| 2498 | A467 | 1000g Motorcycle | 2.00 | 1.60 |

**Intl. Year of the Family—A468**

**1994, Oct. 25 — Perf. 13x13½**

| | | | | |
|---|---|---|---|---|
| 2499 | A468 | 50g Mother, child | .20 | .20 |
| 2500 | A468 | 250g Family faces | .50 | .40 |

**Christmas—A469**

Ceramic figures: 150g, Nativity, 700g, Joseph, infant Jesus, Mary, vert.

**1994, Nov. 4 — Perf. 13½**

| | | | | |
|---|---|---|---|---|
| 2501 | A469 | 150g multicolored | .30 | .25 |
| 2502 | A469 | 700g multicolored | 1.40 | 1.10 |

**Paraguayan Red Cross, 75th Anniv.—A470**

Designs: 150g, Boy Scouts, Jean-Henri Dunant. 700g, Soldiers, paramedics, Dr. Andres Barbero.

## Top row

**Founding of Society of Salesian Fathers in Paraguay, Cent. — A485**

Pope John Paul II, St. John Bosco (1815-88), and: 200g, Men, boys from Salesian Order, vert. flag. 300g, Madonna and Child, vert. 1000g, Map of Paraguay, man following light.

**1996, July 22**   *Perf. 13½x13, 13x13½*
| | | | | |
|---|---|---|---|---|
| 2537 | A485 | 200g multicolored | .20 | .20 |
| 2538 | A485 | 300g multicolored | .30 | .20 |
| 2539 | A485 | 1000g multicolored | 1.50 | 1.00 |
| | | Nos. 2537-2539 (3) | | |

**UNICEF, 50th Anniv. — A486**

Children's paintings: 1000g, Outdoor scene, by S. Báez. 1300g, Four groups of children, by C. Pérez.

**1996, Sept. 27**   *Perf. 13½x13*
| | | | | |
|---|---|---|---|---|
| 2540 | A486 | 1000g multicolored | 1.00 | .60 |
| 2541 | A486 | 1300g multicolored | 1.25 | .85 |

**Visit of Pope John Paul II to Caacupe, Site of Apparition of the Virgin — A487**

Design: 200g, Pope John Paul II, church, Virgin of Caacupe, vert.

**1996, Oct. 4**   *Perf. 13x13½, 13x13*
| | | | | |
|---|---|---|---|---|
| 2542 | A487 | 200g multicolored | .20 | .20 |
| 2543 | A487 | 1300g multicolored | 1.25 | .85 |

**Traditional Costumes A488**

America issue: 500g, Woman in costume. 1000g, Woman, man, in costumes.

**1996, Oct. 11**   *Perf. 13x13*
| | | | | |
|---|---|---|---|---|
| 2544 | A488 | 500g multicolored | .50 | .30 |
| 2545 | A488 | 1000g multicolored | 1.00 | .60 |

**UN Year for Eradication of Poverty — A489**

## Second row

**Christmas A480**

**1995, Nov. 7**
| | | | | |
|---|---|---|---|---|
| 2525 | A480 | 200g shown | .20 | .20 |
| 2526 | A480 | 1000g Nativity | 1.00 | .70 |

**Jose Marti (1853-95) — A481**

Designs: 200g, Hedychium coronarium, Marti, vert. 1000g, Hedychium coronarium, map & flag of Cuba, Marti.

**1995, Dec. 19**   *Litho.*   *Perf. 13½*
| | | | | |
|---|---|---|---|---|
| 2527 | A481 | 200g multicolored | .25 | .20 |
| 2528 | A481 | 1000g multicolored | 1.10 | .75 |

**Lion's Clubs of South America & the Caribbean, 25th Anniv. — A482**

**1996, Jan. 11**
| | | | | |
|---|---|---|---|---|
| 2529 | A482 | 200g Railway station | .25 | .20 |
| 2530 | A482 | 1000g Viola House | 1.10 | .75 |

**Orchids A483**

Designs: 100g, Cattleya nobilior. 200g, Oncidium varicosum. 1000g, Oncidium jonesianum, vert. 1150g, Sophronitis cernua.

**1996, Apr. 22**   *Perf. 13½x13, 13x13½*   *Litho.*
| | | | | |
|---|---|---|---|---|
| 2531 | A483 | 100g multicolored | .20 | .20 |
| 2532 | A483 | 200g multicolored | .20 | .20 |
| 2533 | A483 | 1000g multicolored | 1.00 | .60 |
| 2534 | A483 | 1150g multicolored | 1.10 | .65 |
| | | Nos. 2531-2534 (4) | 2.50 | 1.65 |

**1996 Summer Olympic Games, Atlanta A484**

**1996, June 6**   *Perf. 13½x13*
| | | | | |
|---|---|---|---|---|
| 2535 | A484 | 500g Diving | .50 | .30 |
| 2536 | A484 | 1000g Running | 1.00 | .60 |

## Third row

**1995, July 6**
| | | | | |
|---|---|---|---|---|
| 2512 | A475 | 100g Parula pitiayumi | .20 | .20 |
| 2513 | A475 | 200g Chirroxiphia caudata | .30 | .20 |
| 2514 | A475 | 600g Icterus icterus | 1.25 | .60 |
| 2515 | A475 | 1000g Carduelis magellanica | 2.00 | 1.00 |
| | | Nos. 2512-2515 (4) | 3.75 | 2.00 |

**Fifth Intl. Symposium on Municipalities, Ecology & Tourism A476**

Designs: 1150g, Rio Monday rapids. 1300g, Areguá Railroad Station.

**1995, Aug. 4**   *Litho.*   *Perf. 13½*
| | | | | |
|---|---|---|---|---|
| 2516 | A476 | 1150g multicolored | 1.25 | .85 |
| 2517 | A476 | 1300g multicolored | 1.40 | .90 |

**Volleyball, Cent. — A477**

**1995, Sept. 28**
| | | | | |
|---|---|---|---|---|
| 2518 | A477 | 300g shown | .30 | .20 |
| 2519 | A477 | 600g Ball, net | .60 | .40 |
| 2520 | A477 | 1000g Hands, ball, net | 1.00 | .70 |
| | | Nos. 2518-2520 (3) | 1.90 | 1.30 |

**America Issue A478**

Preserve the environment: 950g, Macizo Monument, Achay Reserve, Chaco, vert. 2000g, Tinfunique.

**1995, Oct. 12**
| | | | | |
|---|---|---|---|---|
| 2521 | A478 | 950g multicolored | 1.50 | .65 |
| 2522 | A478 | 2000g multicolored | 2.75 | 1.40 |

**UN, 50th Anniv. — A479**

Designs: 200g, Flags above olive branch. 3000g, UN emblem, stick figures.

**1995, Oct. 20**
| | | | | |
|---|---|---|---|---|
| 2523 | A479 | 200g multicolored | .20 | .20 |
| 2524 | A479 | 3000g multicolored | 3.00 | 2.00 |

## Fourth row

**1994, Nov. 25**   *Perf. 13½x13*
| | | | | |
|---|---|---|---|---|
| 2503 | A470 | 150g multicolored | .30 | .25 |
| 2504 | A470 | 700g multicolored | 1.40 | 1.10 |

A 500g showing "75" inside a red cross, with ambulance and emblem with black cross in center was part of this set. When it was discovered that the emblem contained a black instead of a red cross it was withdrawn. The editors are gathering information on this stamp.

**San Jose College, 90th Anniv. — A471**

Pope John Paul II and: 200g, Eternal flame. 250g, College entrance.

**1994, Dec. 4**
| | | | | |
|---|---|---|---|---|
| 2505 | A471 | 200g multicolored | .40 | .30 |
| 2506 | A471 | 250g multicolored | .50 | .40 |

**Louis Pasteur (1822-95) A472**

**1995, Mar. 24**   *Litho.*   *Perf. 13½*
| | | | | |
|---|---|---|---|---|
| 2507 | A472 | 1000g multicolored | 1.50 | 1.00 |

**Fight Against AIDS — A473**

**1995, May 4**
| | | | | |
|---|---|---|---|---|
| 2508 | A473 | 500g Faces | .75 | .50 |
| 2509 | A473 | 1000g shown | 1.50 | 1.00 |

**FAO, 50th Anniv. A474**

**1995, June 23**
| | | | | |
|---|---|---|---|---|
| 2510 | A474 | 950g Bread, pitcher | 1.40 | 1.00 |
| 2511 | A474 | 2000g Watermelon | 3.00 | 2.00 |

**Fifth Neotropical Ornithological Congress — A475**

**1996, Oct. 17**    *Perf. 13½x13, 13x13½*
2546 A489 1000g Food products   1.00   .60
2547 A489 1150g Boy, fruit, vert.   1.10   .75

Christmas
A490

**1996, Nov. 7**    *Perf. 13x13½*
2548 A490 200g multicolored   .20   .20
2549 A490 1000g multicolored   1.00   .60
Madonna and Child, by: 200g, Koki Ruiz. 1000g, Hernán Miranda.

Butterflies
A491

**1997, Mar. 5**   **Litho.**   *Perf. 13½x13½*
2550 A491 200g multicolored   .20   .20
2551 A491 500g multicolored   .85   .30
2552 A491 1000g multicolored   1.75   .55
2553 A491 1150g multicolored   2.00   .65
  Nos. 2550-2553 (4)   4.80   1.70
Designs: 200g, Eryphanis automedon. 500g, Dryadula phaetusa. 1000g, Vanessa myrinna. 1150g, Heliconius ethilla.

Official Buildings — A492

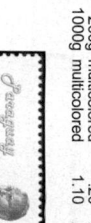

**1997, May 5**    *Perf. 13x13½*
2554 A492 200g multicolored   .20   .20
2555 A492 1000g multicolored   1.10   .65
200g, 1st Legislature. 1000g, Postal Headquarters.

**1997, Year of Christ — A493**
1997, June 10    *Perf. 13x13½*
2556 A493 1000g multicolored   .95   .60
1997, Year of Jesus Christ — A493
Crucifix, Pope John Paul II

Environmental and Climate Change — A495

**1997, Aug. 25**    *Perf. 13½x13, 13x13½*
2558 A495 300g multi   .30   .20
2559 A495 500g multi, vert.   .50   .30
2560 A495 1000g multi   1.00   .60
  Nos. 2558-2560 (3)   1.80   1.10
Flowers: 300g, Opuntia elata. 500g, Bromelia balansae. 1000g, Monvillea kroenlaini.

1st Philatelic Exposition of MERCOSUR Countries, Chile and Bolivia — A496

**1997, Aug. 29**    *Perf. 13½x13, 13x13½*
2561 A496 200g multicolored   .20   .20
2562 A496 1000g multicolored   .95   .60
2563 A496 1150g multicolored   1.10   .65
  Nos. 2561-2563 (3)   2.25   1.45
Fauna: 200g, Felis tigrina. 1000g, Alouatta caraya, vert. 1150g, Agouti paca.

MERCOSUR (Common Market of Latin America) A497

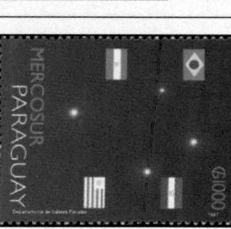

**1997, Sept. 26**    *Perf. 13x13½*
2564 A497 1000g multicolored   .95   .60
See Argentina #1975, Bolivia #1019, Brazil #2646, Uruguay #1681.

America Issue — A498

Life of a postman: 1000g, Postman, letters going around the world, vert. 1150g, Window

11th Summit of the Rio Group Chiefs of State, Asunción — A494

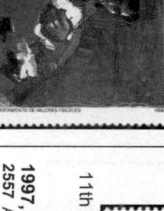

**1997, Aug. 23**    *Perf. 13½x13*
2557 A494 1000g multicolored   .95   .60

**1997, Oct. 10**   *Perf. 13½x13½, 13½x13*
2565 A498 1000g multicolored   1.00   .60
2566 A498 1150g multicolored   1.10   .65
with six panes showing weather conditions, different roads, postman.

Nat. Council on Sports, 50th Anniv. — A499

**1997, Oct. 16**    *Perf. 13½x13½*
2567 A499 200g multicolored   .25   .20
2568 A499 1000g multicolored   1.25   .75
200g, Neri Kennedy throwing javelin. 1000g, Ramón Miliciades Gimenez Gaona throwing discus.

Nos. 2489-2490 Ovptd. in Red

**1997, Nov. 14**
2569 A464 50g multicolored   .50   .30
2570 A464 250g multicolored   2.50   1.50

Christmas A500

**1997, Nov. 17**
2571 A500 200g multicolored   .20   .20
2572 A500 1000g multicolored   1.10   .65
Paintings of Madonna and Child: 200g, By Olga Blinder. 1000g, By Hernán Miranda.

UN Fund for Children of the World with AIDS — A501

**1997, Dec. 5**
2573 A501 500g multicolored   .50   .30
2574 A501 1000g multicolored   1.00   .60
Children's paintings: 500g, Boy. 1000g, Girl.

Rotary Club of Asunción, 70th Anniv. — A502

**1997, Dec. 11**
2575 A502 1150g multicolored   1.10   .65

1998 World Cup Soccer Championships, France — A503

**1998, Jan. 22**   **Litho.**   *Perf. 13½*
2576 A503 200g multicolored   .20   .20
2577 A503 500g multicolored   .55   .30
2578 A503 1000g multicolored   1.00   .60
  Nos. 2576-2578 (3)   1.70   1.10
200g, Julio César Romero, vert. 500g, Carlos Gamarra, vert. 1000g, 1998 Paraguayan team.

Fish A504

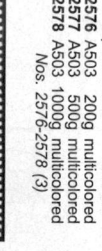

**1998, Apr. 17**   **Litho.**   *Perf. 13*
2579 A504 200g multicolored   .25   .20
2580 A504 300g multicolored   .30   .20
2581 A504 500g multicolored   .55   .30
2582 A504 1000g multicolored   1.25   .60
  Nos. 2579-2582 (4)   2.35   1.30
Designs: 200g, Tetragonopterus argenteus. 300g, Pseudoplatystoma coruscans. 500g, Salminus brasiliensis. 1000g, Acestrorhynchus altus.

Contemporary Paintings — A505

**1998, June 5**    *Perf. 13½*
2583 A505 200g multi, vert.   .20   .20
2584 A505 300g multi, vert.   .25   .20
2585 A505 400g multi, vert.   .35   .20
2586 A505 1000g multi, vert.   .80   .50
  Nos. 2583-2586 (4)   1.60   1.10
Designs: 200g, Hands, geometric shape, by Carlos Colombino. 300g, Mother nursing infant, by Félix Toranzos. 400g, Flowers, by Edith Gimenez. 1000g, Woman lifting tray of food, by Ricardo Migliorisi.

Mushrooms A506

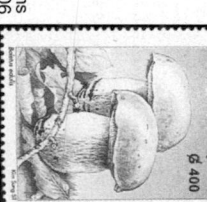

## Organization of American States (OAS), 50th Anniv. — A507

400g, Boletus edulis. 600g, Macrolepiota procera. 1000g, Geastrum triplex.

**1998, June 26**
2587 A506 400g multicolored .40 .20
2588 A506 600g multicolored .60 .35
2589 A506 1000g multicolored 1.00 .60
Nos. 2587-2589 (3) 2.00 1.15

Designs: 500g, Home of Carlos A. López, Asunción. 1000g, Palmerola Villa, Areguá.

**1998, July 16**
2590 A507 500g multicolored .40 .20
2591 A507 1000g multicolored .80 .50

Episcopacy of Hernando de Trejo y Sanabria, 400th Anniv. — A508

Pope John Paul II and: 400g, Sacrarium doors, Caazapá Church, vert. 1700g, Statue of St. Francis of Assisi, Atyrá Church.

**1998, Sept. 5** *Perf. 13x13½, 13½x13*
2592 A508 400g multi .35 .25
2593 A508 1700g multi 1.75 1.25

Ruins of Jesuit Mission Church A509

**1998, Sept. 16 Litho.** *Perf. 13½x13*
2594 A509 5000g multicolored 5.75 3.75

Flowers A510

Designs: 100g, Acacia caven. 600g, Cordia trichotoma. 1900g, Glandularia sp.

**1998, Sept. 16 Litho.** *Perf. 13x13½*
2595 A510 100g multi .20 .20
2596 A510 600g multi .60 .40
2597 A510 1900g multi 2.00 1.50
Nos. 2595-2597 (3) 2.80 2.10

America Issue A511

---

Universal Declaration of Human Rights, 50th Anniv. — A512

Artwork by: 500g, Carlos Colombino. 1000g, José Filartiga.

**1998, Oct. 23** *Perf. 13½x13*
2600 A512 500g multi .35 .25
2601 A512 1000g multi .70 .45

Christmas Creche Figures — A513

**1998, Sept. 16** *Perf. 13½x13, 13x13½*
2602 A513 300g shown .20 .20
2603 A513 1600g 3Jubilé, vert. 1.10 .65

Designs: 100g, Micrurus frontalis. 300g, Ameiva ameiva. 1600g, Geochelone carbonaria. 1700g, Caiman yacare.

Reptiles A514

**1999, May 13 Litho.** *Perf. 13½x13*
2604-2607 A514 Set of 4 4.25 2.75

Paintings — A515

Paintings by: 500g, Ignacio Nuñez Soler. 1600g, Modesto Delgado Rodas. 1700g, Jaime Bestard.

**1999, June 23 Litho.** *Perf. 13½x13*
2608 A515 500g multi .50 .30
2609 A515 1600g multi 1.75 1.10
2610 A515 1700g multi 3.75 2.40
Nos. 2608-2610 (3)

America Soccer Cup A516

---

Famous women and buildings: 1600g, Serafina Davalos (1883-1957), first woman lawyer, National College building. 1700g, Adela Speratti (1865-1902), director of Normal School.

Designs: 300g, Carlos Humberto Paredes, vert. 500g, South American Soccer Confederation Building, Luque. 1900g, Feliciano Cáceres Stadium, Luque.

*Perf. 13½x13½, 13x13*
**1999, June 24**
2611 A516 300g multi .20 .20
2612 A516 500g multi .50 .30
2613 A516 1900g multi 1.75 1.25
Nos. 2611-2613 (3) 2.45 1.75

SOS Children's Villages, 50th Anniv. — A517

**1999, July 16** *Perf. 13½x13, 13x13½*
2614 A517 1700g Toucan 1.25 1.00
2615 A517 1900g Toucan, vert. 1.75 1.25

Protests of Assassination of Vice-President Luis Maria Argaña — A518

Designs: 100g, Protest at Governmental Palace. 500g, Argaña, vert. 1500g, Protest at National Congress.

**1999, Aug. 26**
2616 A518 100g multi .20 .20
2617 A518 500g multi .50 .40
2618 A518 1500g multi 1.75 1.25
Nos. 2616-2618 (3) 2.45 1.85

Medicinal Plants — A519

Designs: 600g, Cochlospermum regium. 700g, Borago officinalis. 1700g, Passiflora cincinnata.

**1999, Sept. 8** *Perf. 13½x13½*
2619 A519 600g multi .35 .35
2620 A519 700g multi .45 .45
2621 A519 1700g multi 1.00 1.00
Nos. 2619-2621 (3) 1.80 1.80

America Issue, A New Millennium Without Arms — A520

Various artworks by Ricardo Migliorisi.

*Perf. 13½x13, 13½x13½*
**1999, Oct. 12 Litho.**
2622 A520 1500g multi, vert. .90 .55
2623 A520 3000g multi, vert. 1.90 1.25

---

Intl. Year of the Elderly A521

Designs by: 1000g, Olga Blinder. 1900g, Maria de los Reyes Ornella Herrero, vert.

*Perf. 13½x13, 13x13½* **Litho.**
2624-2625 A521 Set of 2 1.75 1.75

Christmas A522

Artwork by: 300g, Manuel Viedma. 1600g, Federico Ordiñana.

**1999, Nov. 11 Litho.** *Perf. 13x13½*
2626 A522 300g multi .20 .20
2627 A522 1600g multi .95 .60

City of Pedro Juan Caballero, Cent. — A523

Flowers: 1000g, Tabebuia impetiginosa. 1600g, Tabobuia pulcherrima, vert.

**1999, Dec. 1** *Perf. 13½x13, 13x13½* **Litho.**
2628 A523 1000g multi .60 .60
2629 A523 1600g multi 1.00 1.00

Inter-American Development Bank, 40th Anniv. — A524

Designs: 600g, Oratory of Our Lady of Asuncion and Pantheon of Heroes, Asuncion. 700g, Governmental Palace.

**1999, Dec. 6** *Perf. 13½x13*
2630 A524 600g multi .35 .35
2631 A524 700g multi .45 .45

Intl. Women's Day — A525

Carmen Casco de Lara Castro and sculpture: 400g, Conjunction, by Domingo Rivarola. 2000g, Violation, by Gustavo Beckelmann.

**2000, Apr. 7** **Litho.** ***Perf. 13x13½***
**2632-2633** A525 Set of 2 1.40 1.40

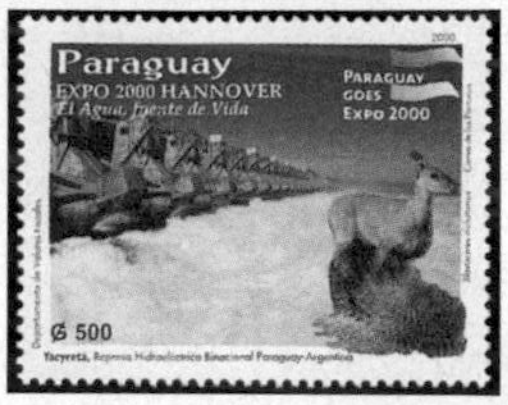


Expo 2000, Hanover
A526

Designs: 500g, Yacyreta Dam and deer. 2500g, Itaipú Dam, tapir.

**2000, May 5** ***Perf. 13½x13***
**2634-2635** A526 Set of 2 1.75 1.75

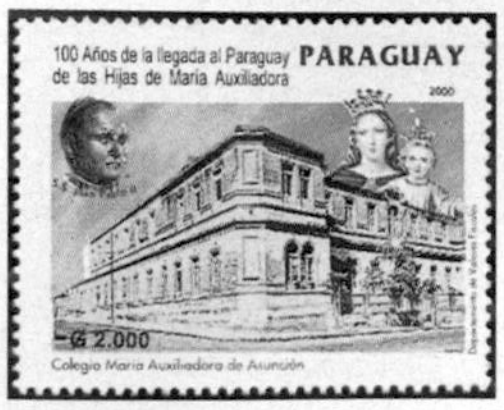


Salesians in Paraguay, Cent. — A527

Madonna and Child, Pope John Paul II and: 600g, Salesians, vert. 2000g, College building.

***Perf. 13x13½, 13½x13***
**2000, May 19** **Litho.**
**2636-2637** A527 Set of 2 1.50 1.50

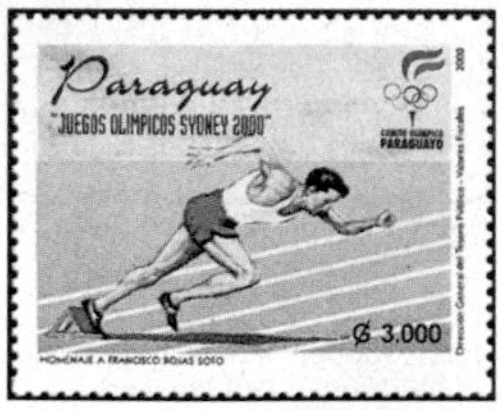


2000 Summer Olympics, Sydney — A528

Designs: 2500g, Soccer, vert. 3000g, Runner Francisco Rojas Soto.

**2000, July 28** ***Perf. 13x13½, 13½x13***
**2638-2639** A528 Set of 2 3.25 3.25

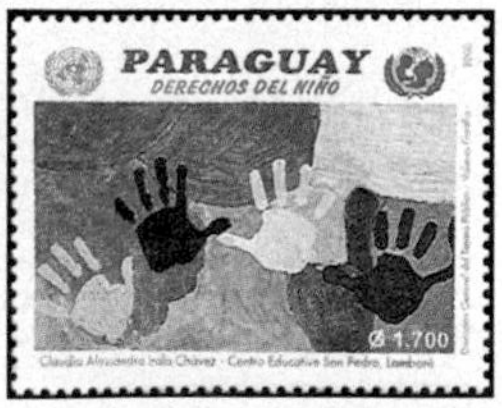


Rights of the Child
A529

Designs: 1500g, Child between hands, vert. 1700g, Handprints.

***Perf. 13x13½, 13½x13***
**2000, Aug. 16**
**2640-2641** A529 Set of 2 1.90 1.90

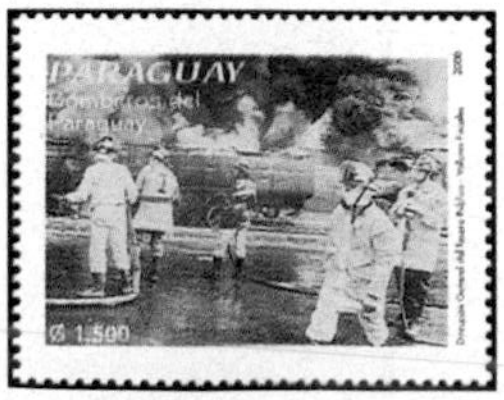


Fire Fighters
A530

Designs: 100g, Fire fighters, white truck, vert. 200g, Fire fighter in old uniform, emblem, vert. 1500g, Fire fighters at fire. 1600g, Fire fighters, yellow truck.

***Perf. 13x13½, 13½x13***
**2000, Sept. 28**
**2642-2645** A530 Set of 4 2.00 2.00

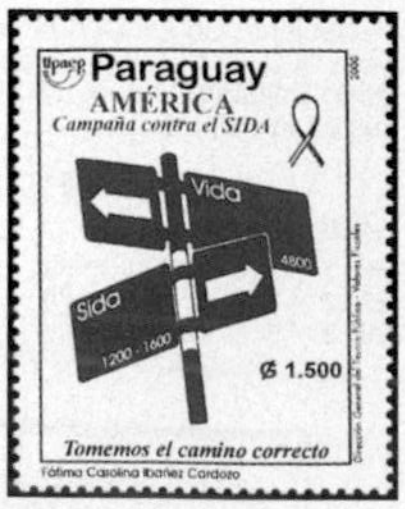


America Issue, Fight Against AIDS — A532

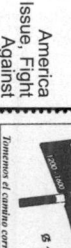

Designs: 1500g, Signs with arrows. 2500g, Tic-tac-toe game.

**2000, Oct. 19** ***Perf. 13x13½***
**2648-2649** A532 Set of 2 2.40 2.40

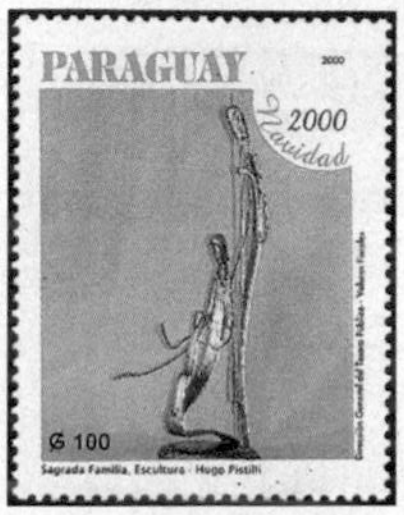


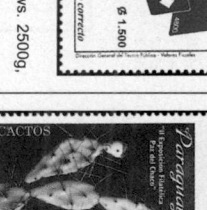

Christmas
A534

Designs: 100g, Holy Family, sculpture by Hugo Pistilli. 500g, Poem by José Luis Appleyard. 2000g, Creche figures, horiz.

***Perf. 13x13½, 13½x13***
**2000, Nov. 17** **Litho.**
**2652-2654** A534 Set of 3 2.75 2.75

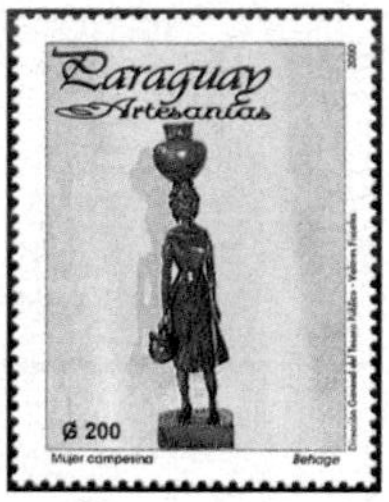


Artisan's Crafts — A535

Designs: 200g, Campesina Woman, by Behage. 1500g, Cattle horns, by Quintin Velazquez, horiz. 2000g, Silver filigree orchid, by Quirino Torres.

***Perf. 13¼x13½, 13½x13¼***
**2000, Nov. 28** **Litho.**
**2655-2657** A535 Set of 3 4.00 4.00

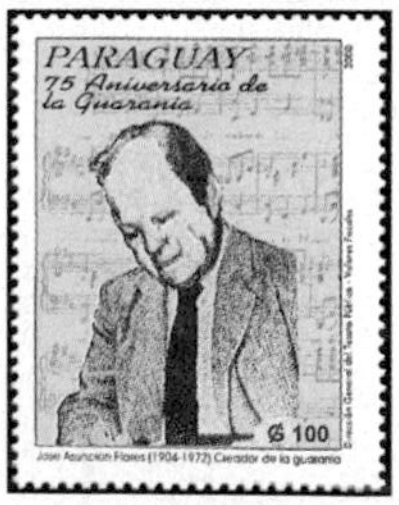


Guarania Music, 75th Anniv. — A536

Designs: 100g, José Asunción Flores (1904-72), composer. 1500g, Violin. 2500g, Trombone.

**2000, Dec. 20** ***Perf. 13¼x13½***
**2658-2660** A536 Set of 3 4.25 4.25

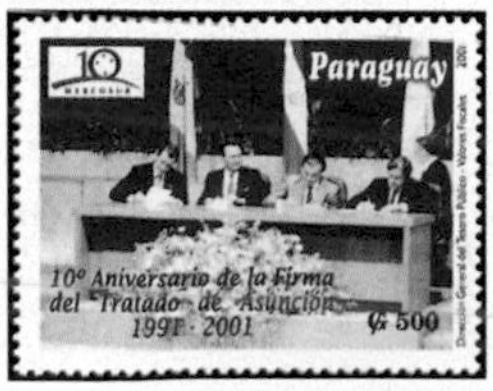


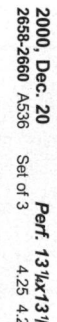

Signing of Asunción Treaty, 10th Anniv.
A537

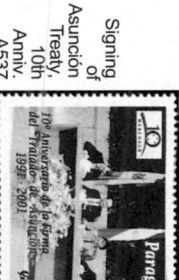

Designs: 500g, Delegates signing treaty. 2500g, Map of South America with signatory nations colored, vert.

***Perf. 13½x13¼, 13¼x13½***
**2001, June 20**
**2661-2662** A537 Set of 2 1.60 1.60

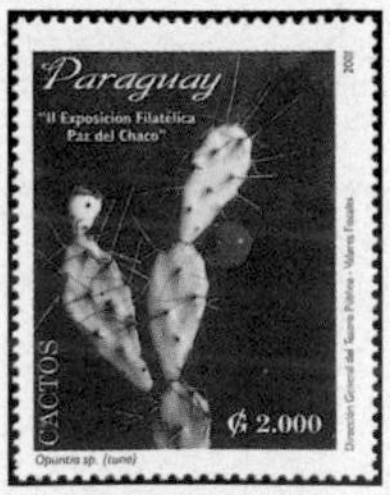


Cacti — A538

Designs: 2000g, Opuntia sp. 2500g, Cereus stenogonus.

**2001, June 29** ***Perf. 13¼x13½***
**2663-2664** A538 Set of 2 2.40 2.40

Second Paz del Chaco Philatelic Exhibition.

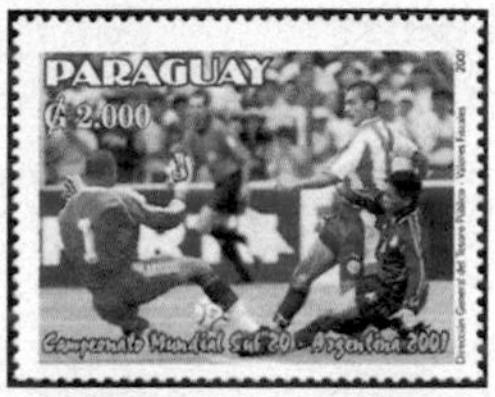


Under 20 Soccer Championships, Argentina — A539

Designs: 2000g, Players. 2500g, Players, diff., vert.

***Perf. 13½x13¼, 13¼x13½***
**2001, June 29**
**2665-2666** A539 Set of 2 2.40 2.40

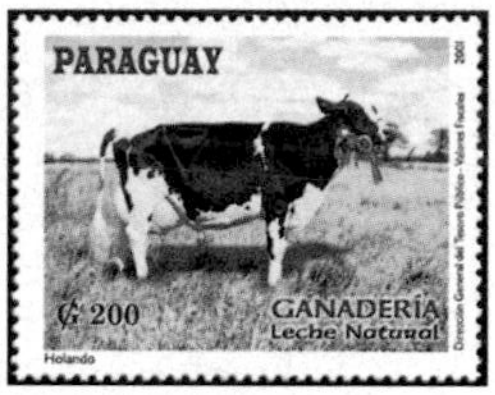


Cattle
A540

Designs: 200g, Holando-Argentino. 500g, Nelore. 1500g, Pampa Chaqueño.

**2001, July 20** ***Perf. 13½x13¼***
**2667-2669** A540 Set of 3 1.25 1.25

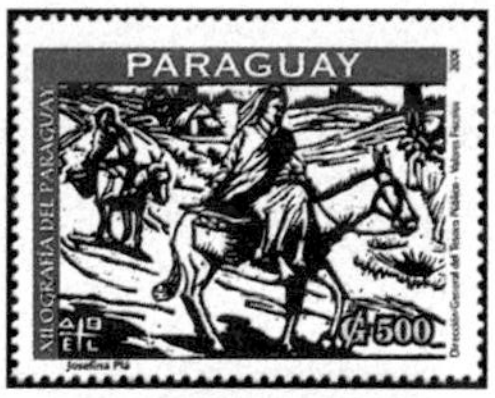


Engravings — A541

Woodcuts by: No. 2670, 500g, Josefina Plá. No. 2671, 500g, Leonor Cecotto, vert. 1500g, Jacinto Rivero. 2000g, Livio Abramo.

***Perf. 13½x13¼, 13¼x13½***
**2001, Aug. 28**
**2670-2673** A541 Set of 4 2.40 2.40

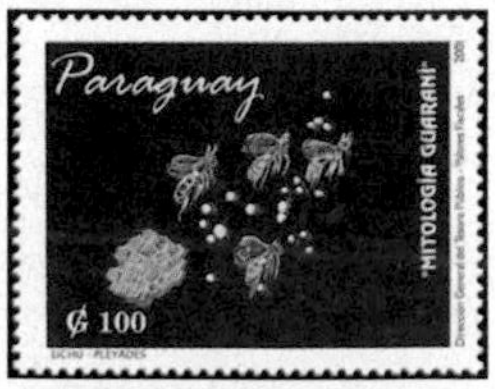


Mythological Heavens of the Guarani — A542

Designs: 100g, Elchu (Pleiades). 600g, Mborevi Rape (Milky Way). 1600g, Jagua Ho'u Jasy (lunar eclipse).

**2001, Sept. 24** ***Perf. 13½x13¼***
**2674-2676** A542 Set of 3 1.25 1.25

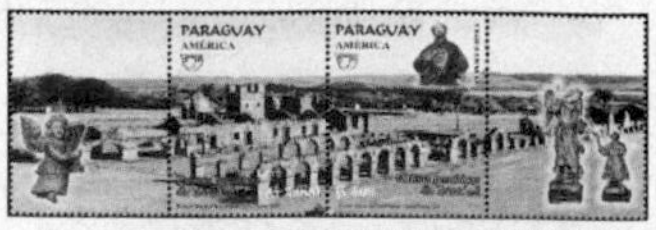

America Issue — UNESCO World Heritage Sites — A543

No. 2677: a, 500g, St. Ignatius of Loyola, Jesuit Mission Ruins, Trinidad. b, 2000g, Jesuit Mission Ruins.
Illustration reduced.

**2001, Oct. 9** ***Perf. 13¼x13½***
**2677** A543 Horiz. pair, #a-b, + 2 flanking labels 1.40 1.40

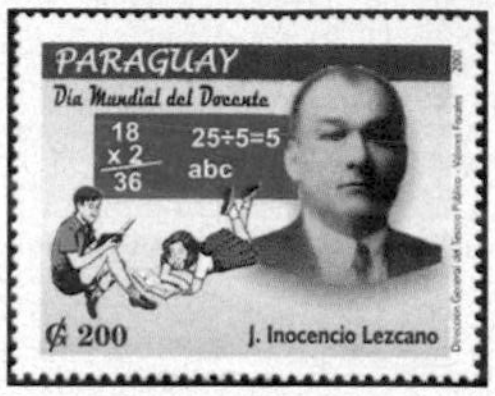


World Teachers' Day — A544

Designs: 200g, Children studying, school blackboard, J. Inocencio Lezcano (1889-1935), educator. 1600g, Symbols of education, Ramón I. Cardozo (1876-1943), educator.

**2001, Oct. 9** ***Perf. 13½x13¼***
**2678-2679** A544 Set of 2 1.10 1.10

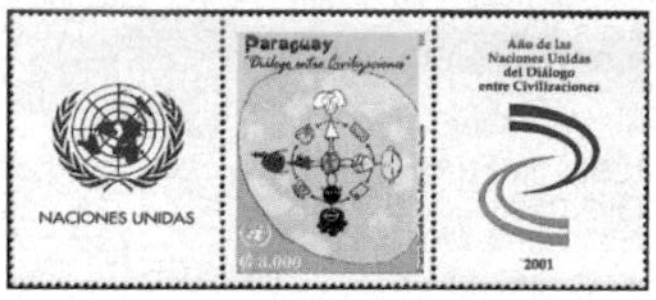


Year of Dialogue Among Civilizations — A545

Illustration reduced.

**2001, Oct. 23** ***Perf. 13¼x13½***
**2680** A545 3000g multi + 2 flanking labels 1.40 1.40

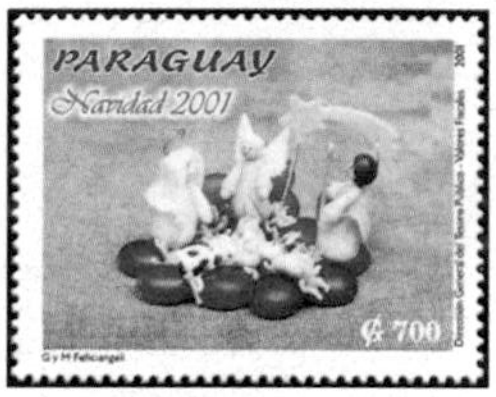


Christmas — A546

Nativity scenes by: 700g, Gladys and Maria de Feliciangeli. 4000g, Mercedes Servin.

**2001, Nov. 29** ***Perf. 13½x13¼***
**2681-2682** A546 Set of 2 2.50 2.50

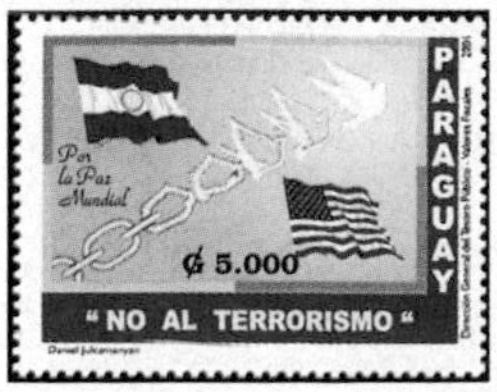


No to Terrorism
A547

Designs: 700g, Statue of Liberty, World Trade Center, vert. 5000g, Flags of Paraguay and U.S., chain becoming doves.

***Perf. 13¼x13½, 13½x13¼***
**2001, Dec. 19** **Litho.**
**2683-2684** A547 Set of 2 3.00 3.00

Passiflora
Caerulea
A548

**2001, Dec. 21**          *Perf. 13½x13½*
2685  A548  4000g multi          2.10  2.10

Paraguayan,
Bolivian, and
Argentinian
Scout
Jamboree,
Boquerón
Province
A549

**2002, Jan. 24**          *Perf. 13½x13½*
2686  A549  6000g multi          .40  .40

El Mbiguá Social Club, Asunción,
25th Anniv. — A550

**2002, May 3**          *Perf. 13½x13½*
2687  A550  700g multi          .40  .40

Juan de
Salazar Spanish
Cultural Center,
25th
Anniv. — A551

Jesuit wood carvings, 18th cent.: 2500g,
Pieta. 5000g, St. Michael Archangel.
**2002, May 7**          *Perf. 13½x13½*
2688-2689  A551          Set of 2          3.25  3.25

2002 World Cup Soccer
Championships, Japan and
Korea — A552

Designs: 3000g, Paraguay team. 5000g,
Players in action, vert.
**2002, May 18**  *Perf. 13½x13½, 13½x13½*
2690-2691  A552          Set of 2          3.25  3.25
For overprint see No. 2705.

---

Arrival of Mennonites in Paraguay,
75th Anniv. — A553

Cross, plow, Menno Simons (1496-1561),
Religious Leader, and: 2000g, Mennonite
Church, Filadelfia. 4000g, Mennonite Church,
Loma Plata.
**2002, June 25**          *Perf. 13½x13½*
2692-2693  A553          Set of 2          2.50  2.50

Horses
A554

Designs: 700g, Criollo. 1000g, Cuarto de
Milla (quarterhorse), 6000g, Arabian.
**2002, July 12**
2694-2696  A554          Set of 3          3.25  3.25

Olimpia Soccer Team, Cent. — A555

Illustration reduced.
**2002, July 24**          *Perf. 13½x13½*
2697  A555  700g multi + 2 flanking labels

Pan-American
Health
Organization,
Cent. — A556

Medicinal plants: 4000g, Stevia rebaudiana
bertoni. 5000g, Ilex paraguayensis.
**2002, Sept. 16**          *Perf. 13½x13½*
2698-2699  A556          Set of 2          3.75  3.75

International Forum on Postal Service
Modernization and Reform — A557

Forum emblem and statues by Serafín Mar-
sal: 1000g, Campesina. 4000g, Quyuga-vera.
**2002, Sept. 30**          *Perf. 13½x13½*
2700-2701  A557          Set of 2          2.10  2.10

Paraguay — Republic of China
Diplomatic Relations, 45th
Anniv. — A558

---

Illustration reduced.
**2002, Oct. 10**          *Perf. 13½x13½*
2702  A558  4000g multi + 2 flanking labels          1.90  1.90

America Issue — Youth, Education
and Literacy — A559

Designs: 3000g, Classroom. 6000g, Children playing.
**2002, Oct. 12**          *Perf. 13½x13½*
2703-2704  A559          Set of 2          3.75  3.75

No. 2690 Overprinted

**2002**
2705  A552  3000g on #2690          1.40  1.40

Christmas — A560

Various creche figures: a, 1000g. b, 4000g.
c, 700g.
Illustration reduced.
**2002, Dec. 2     Litho.          *Perf. 13¼*
2706  A560     Horiz. strip of 3, #a-
c          2.60  2.60

Church,
Areguá — A561

**2002, Dec. 18**
2707  A561  4000g multi          1.90  1.90

District of San Antonio, Cent. — A562

**2003, Apr. 21     Litho.          *Perf. 13¼*
2708  A562  700g multi          .35  .35

---

Josefina Plá (1903-99), Artist — A563

Designs: 700g, Plate. 6000g, Carving.
**2003, May 30     Litho.          *Perf. 13¼*
2709-2710  A563          Set of 2          3.00  3.00

Parrots — A564

Designs: 1000g, Amazona aestiva. 2000g,
Myiopsitta monachus. 4000g, Aratinga
leucophtalmus.
**2003, June 9**
2711-2713  A564          Set of 3          3.25  3.25

Paraguay Philatelic Center, 90th anniv.
(#2711). Paz del Chaco Bi-national Philatelic
Exhibition (#2712). PARAFIL Bi-national Philatelic Exhibition (#2713).

Legislative Palace — A565

Illustration reduced.
**2003, June 24          *Perf. 13½x13¼*
2714  A565  4000g multi + label          1.90  1.90
Printed in sheets of 12 stamps and 18
labels.

Pontificate of Pope John Paul II, 25th
Anniv. — A566

Illustration reduced.
**2003, June 27          *Perf. 13¼*
2715  A566  6000g multi + label          2.75  2.75

Farm
Animals
A567

Designs: 1000g, Pig. 3000g, Sheep. 8000g,
Goat.
**2003, July 18**
2716-2718  A567          Set of 3          5.50  5.50

## Foods A568

**2003, July 25**
2719-2721 A568 Set of 3 2.60 2.60
Designs: 700g, Peanuts, honey and nougat. 2000g, Sopa Paraguaya. 3000g, Chipá.

## Folk Artists A569

**2003, Sept. 12**
2722-2724 A569 Set of 3 1.75 1.75
Designs: 700g, Julio Correa (1890-1953), playwright. 1000g, Emiliano Rivarola Fernández (1894-1949), singer. 2000g, Manuel Ortiz Guerrero (1894-1933), poet.

## Dances A570

**2003, Sept. 23**
2725-2727 A570 Set of 3 3.50 3.50
Designs: 700g, Golondriana. 3000g, Polka. 4000g, Galopera.

## Guaraní Soccer Team, Cent. — A571

**2003, Oct. 9**
2728 A571 700g multi + label .40 .40
Illustration reduced.

## Native Clothing A572

**2003, Oct. 22**
2729-2730 A572 Set of 2 4.00 4.00
Designs: 4000g, Sixty-strip poncho, Paraí. 5000g, Shirt, Ao Poí.

## Christmas A573

**2003, Nov. 12**
2731-2733 A573 Set of 3 2.60 2.60
Designs: 700g, Journey to Egypt. 1000g, Adoration of the Shepherds. 4000g, Nativity.

## Indoor Soccer World Cup Championships, Paraguay — A574

**2003, Nov. 14**
2734 A574 Horiz. pair, #a-b 4.00 4.00
No. 2734 — Various players: a, 4000g. b, 5000g.
Printed in sheets with two pairs of five pairs separated by a column of labels.

## America Issue - Flowers A575

**2003, Nov. 26**
2735-2737 A575 Set of 3 5.00 5.00
Designs: 1000g, Cordia bordasii. No. 2736, 5000g, Bulnesia sarmientoi. No. 2737, 5000g, Chorisia insignis.

## Comics by Robin Wood — A576

**2004, May 24**
2738-2740 A576 Set of 3 4.00 4.00
Designs: 1000g, Anahí. 3000g, Nippur de Lagash. 5000g, Dago.

## National Soccer Team, Cent. — A577

**2004, June 25**
2741 A577 700g multi + label .35 .35
Illustration reduced.

## San José College, Cent. — A578

**2004, July 2** Litho. Perf. 13¼
2742 A578 700g multi .35 .35

## Pablo Neruda (1904-73), Poet — A579

**2004, July 6** Litho. Perf. 13¼
2743 A579 5000g multi 2.25 2.25

## World of the Guaranís — A580

**2004, July 7**
2744-2745 A580 Set of 2 3.00 3.00
Designs: 700g, Monday Waterfalls. 6000g, Entrance to Ciudad de Tobatí.
Nos. 2744 and 2745 were issued in sheets of 15 stamps and 10 labels.

## Independence House — A581

**2004, Aug. 13** Litho. Perf. 13¼
2746-2747 A581 Set of 2 2.60 2.60
Designs: Dr. Carlos Pussineri and: José Laterza Parodi. 700g, Mural by House. 5000g, Independence House.

## José Asunción Flores (1904-72), Composer A582

**2004, Aug. 24** Litho. Perf. 13¼
2748 A582 5000g multi 2.25 2.25

## Museo del Barro, 25th Anniv. A583

**2004, Aug. 26** Litho. Perf. 13¼
2749-2751 A583 Set of 3 4.00 4.00
Designs: 2000g, Painting by Enrique Careaga. 3000g, Anthropomorphic jug, vert. 4000g, Christ of the Column, vert.

## Paraguayan Railroads, 150th Anniv. — A584

**2004, Sept. 22** Perf. 13¼
2752-2753 A584 Set of 2 2.25 2.25
2754 A584 6000g multi 2.75 2.75
Roulette 5¼
**Souvenir Sheet**
No. 2754 contains one 50x40mm stamp.
Designs: 2000g, Locomotive No. 151, Camello. 3000g, Locomotive No. 104, El Coquelo, horiz. 6000g, Locomotive No. 10, Sapucai, horiz.

## America Issue — Environmental Protection — A585

**2004, Oct. 11** Litho. Perf. 13¼
2755 A585 6000g multi 2.75 2.75
2756 A585 6000g multi 2.75 2.75
Rouletted 5¼
**Souvenir Sheet**
Designs: No. 2755, Procnias nudicollis. No. 2756, Ceratophrys cranwelli.

## Water Conservation — A586

**2004, Oct. 22**
2757-2758 A586 Set of 2 3.25 3.25
Designs: 3000g, Felis pardalis, storks, telephone poles. 4000g, Hydrochoerus hydrochaeris, Myrmecophaga tridactyla, Chauna torquata.

PARAGUAY

## Airplanes — AP3

**Typo.**    **Perf. 12**

**1929-31**

| | | | | |
|---|---|---|---|---|
| C7 | AP1 | 2.85p gray green | .50 | .45 |
| | a. | imperf., pair | 37.50 | |
| C8 | AP1 | 2.85p turq grn ('31) | .25 | .20 |
| C9 | AP2 | 5.65p brown | .75 | .35 |
| C10 | AP2 | 5.65p scar ('31) | .40 | .25 |
| C11 | AP3 | 11.30p chocolate | .50 | .35 |
| | a. | imperf., pair | 37.50 | |
| C12 | AP3 | 11.30p dp blue ('31) | .25 | .25 |
| | | Nos. C7-C12 (6) | 2.65 | 1.85 |

Sheets of these stamps sometimes show portions of a papermaker's watermark "Indian Bond C. Extra Strong." Excellent counterfeits are plentiful.

## Regular Issues of 1924-28 Surcharged in Black or Red

**Perf. 11½, 12**

**1929**

| | | | | |
|---|---|---|---|---|
| C13 | A47 | 95c on 7c lilac | .20 | .20 |
| C14 | A47 | 1.90p on 20c dull bl | .20 | .20 |
| C15 | A44 | 3.40p on 4p lt bl (R) | .25 | .20 |
| | a. | Double surcharge | .40 | |
| C16 | A44 | 4.75p on 4p lt bl (R) | .45 | .40 |
| | a. | Double surcharge | 2.00 | |
| C17 | A51 | 6.80p on 3p gray | .50 | .50 |
| | a. | Double surcharge | 3.00 | |
| C18 | A52 | 17p on 5p choc | 1.50 | 1.50 |
| | a. | Horiz. pair, imperf. between | 75.00 | |
| | | Nos. C13-C18 (6) | 3.10 | 3.00 |

Six stamps in the sheet of No. C17 have the "$" and numerals thinner and narrower than the normal type.

Airplane and Arms — AP4

Cathedral of Asunción AP5

Airplane and Globe — AP6

**Perf. 12**

**1930**

| | | | | |
|---|---|---|---|---|
| C19 | AP4 | 95c dp red, pink | .25 | .25 |
| C20 | AP4 | 95c dk bl, blue | .25 | .25 |
| C21 | AP5 | 1.90p lt red, pink | .25 | .25 |
| C22 | AP5 | 1.90p violet, blue | .25 | .25 |
| C23 | AP6 | 6.80p blk, lt bl | .25 | .25 |
| C24 | AP6 | 6.80p green, pink | .30 | .30 |
| | | Nos. C19-C24 (6) | 1.50 | 1.55 |

Sheets of Nos. C19-C24 have a papermaker's watermark: "Extra Vencedor Bond." Counterfeits exist.

---

Various coins and coat of arms.

**Litho. & Engr.**    **Perf. 12x12½**

**1964, Dec. 11**

| | | | |
|---|---|---|---|
| B12 | SP5 | 20g +10g multicolored | |
| B13 | SP5 | 30g +15g multicolored | |
| B14 | SP5 | 50g +25g multicolored | |
| B15 | SP5 | 100g +50g multicolored | |
| | a. | Souvenir sheet of 4, #B12-B15 | 22.50 |
| | | Nos. B12-B15 (4) | |

Buildings and Coats of Arms of Popes John XXIII & Paul VI — SP6

#B16, Dome of St. Peters. #B17, Site of Saint Peter's tomb. #B18, Saint Peter's Plaza. #B19, Taj Mahal.

**1964, Dec. 12**

| | | | |
|---|---|---|---|
| B16 | SP6 | 20g +10g multicolored | |
| B17 | SP6 | 30g +15g multicolored | |
| B18 | SP6 | 50g +25g multicolored | |
| B19 | SP6 | 100g +50g multicolored | |
| | a. | Souvenir sheet of 4, #B16-B19 | 110.00 |
| | | R19 | 20.00 |
| | | Nos. B16-B19 (4) | |

## AIR POST STAMPS

## Official Stamps of 1913 Surcharged

**Perf. 11½**    **Unwmk.**

| | | | | |
|---|---|---|---|---|
| C1 | O19 | 2.85p on 5c lilac | .75 | .65 |
| C2 | O19 | 5.65p on 10c grn | .50 | .40 |
| C3 | O19 | 11.30p on 50c rose | .75 | .50 |
| | | Nos. C1-C3 (3) | 2.00 | 1.55 |

Counterfeits of surcharge exist.

## Regular Issues of 1924-27 Surcharged as in 1929

**Perf. 12**

**1929, Feb. 26**

| | | | | |
|---|---|---|---|---|
| C4 | A51 | 3.40p on 3p gray | 1.75 | 1.10 |
| | a. | Surch. "Correo / en $3.40 / Habilitado / Aereo" | 8.75 | |
| | b. | Double surcharge | 8.75 | |
| C5 | A44 | 6.80p on 4p lt bl | 1.75 | 1.10 |
| | a. | "Aéreo" instead of "Aéreo" Surch. "Correo / Aereo / en $6.80 / Habilitado" | 8.75 | |
| C6 | A52 | 17p on 5p choc | 1.75 | 1.10 |
| | a. | Surch. "Correo / Habilitado / Aereo / en 17p" | 4.50 | |
| | b. | Double surcharge 17p | 5.25 | 3.30 |
| | | Nos. C4-C6 (3) | | |

Wings AP1

Pigeon with Letter AP2

---

College of Agriculture — SP2

**1930**

| | | | | |
|---|---|---|---|---|
| B4 | SP2 | 1.50p + 50c blue, pink | .30 | .30 |

Surtax for the Agricultural Institute. The sheet of No. B4 has a papermaker's watermark: "Vencedor Bond." A 1.50p+50c red on yellow was prepared but not regularly issued. Value, 20 cents.

Red Cross Headquarters SP3

**1932**

| | | | | |
|---|---|---|---|---|
| R5 | SP3 | 50c + 50c rose | .30 | .25 |

Our Lady of Asunción — SP4

**Engr.**

**1941**

| | | | | |
|---|---|---|---|---|
| B6 | SP4 | 7p + 3p red brown | .30 | .25 |
| B7 | SP4 | 7p + 3p purple | .30 | .25 |
| B8 | SP4 | 7p + 3p carmine rose | .30 | .25 |
| B9 | SP4 | 7p + 3p sapphire | .30 | .25 |
| | | Nos. B6-B9 (4) | 1.20 | 1.00 |

### No. 361 Surcharged in Black

**1944**

| | | | | |
|---|---|---|---|---|
| B10 | A70 | 10c on 10µ multicolored | .35 | .25 |

The surtax was for the victims of the San Juan earthquake in Argentina.

**Catalogue values for unused stamps in this section, from this point to the end of the section, are for Never Hinged items.**

### No. C169 Surcharged in Carmine "AYUDA AL ECUADOR 5 + 5"

**1949**    **Unwmk.**    **Perf. 12½**

| | | | | |
|---|---|---|---|---|
| B11 | A117 | 5c + 5c on 30c dk blue | .20 | .20 |

Surtax for the victims of the Ecuador earthquake.

38th Intl. Eucharistic Congress, Bombay — SP5

---

Crops — A587

Designs: 2000g, Corn. 4000g, Cotton. 6000g, Soybeans.

**2004, Oct. 22**    **Litho.**    **Perf. 13¼**

| | | | | |
|---|---|---|---|---|
| 2759-2761 | A587 | Set of 3 | 5.50 | 5.50 |

Christmas — A588

Paintings by Ricardo Migliorisi: 3000g, Madonna and Child. 5000g, Angel, vert.

**2004, Nov. 12**

| | | | | |
|---|---|---|---|---|
| 2762-2763 | A588 | Set of 2 | 3.75 | 3.75 |

Latin American Parliament, 40th Anniv. — A589

**2004, Nov. 16**

| | | | | |
|---|---|---|---|---|
| 2764 | A589 | 4000g multi + label | 1.90 | 1.90 |

Itaipú Dam, 30th Anniv. — A590

Designs: 4000g, Dam and spillway. 5000g, Aerial view of dam, vert.

**2004, Dec. 10**    **Litho.**    **Perf. 13¼**

| | | | | |
|---|---|---|---|---|
| 2765-2766 | A590 | Set of 2 | 4.00 | 4.00 |

## SEMI-POSTAL STAMPS

Red Cross Nurse SP1

**1930, July 22**    **Typo.**    **Perf. 12**

**Unwmk.**

| | | | | |
|---|---|---|---|---|
| B1 | SP1 | 1.50p + 50c gray violet | 1.25 | .75 |
| B2 | SP1 | 1.50p + 50c deep rose | 1.25 | .75 |
| B3 | SP1 | 1.50p + 50c dark blue | 1.25 | .75 |
| | | Nos. B1-B3 (3) | 3.75 | 2.25 |

The surtax was for the benefit of the Red Cross Society of Paraguay.

## Stamps and Types of 1927-28 Overprinted in Red

### 1930
| | | | | |
|---|---|---|---|---|
| C25 | A47 | 10c olive green | .20 | .20 |
| C26 | A47 | 20c dull blue | 3.00 | .20 |
| a. | A47 | 20c dull blue | .20 | .20 |

b. "CORREO CORREO" instead of "CORREO AEREO"

| | | | | |
|---|---|---|---|---|
| C27 | A48 | 1p emerald | 2.50 | |
| C28 | A51 | 3p gray | .50 | .50 |
| | | | .40 | .40 |

Counterfeits of Nos. C26a and C26b exist.

Nos. 273, 282, 286, 288, 300, 302, 305 Surcharged in Red or Black

 CORREO AEREO CINCO #C31

 CORREO AEREO VEINTE CENTAVOS

 CORREO AEREO SEIS #C33

  CORREO AEREO DIEZ #C34-C35

 CORREO AEREO 10 #C29-C30, C32

Nos. C25-C26 (2)

### 1930

### Red or Black Surcharge
| | | | | |
|---|---|---|---|---|
| C29 | A47 | 5c on 10c gray grn (R) | .20 | .20 |
| a. | | "AEREO" omitted | 15.00 | |
| b. | | Vert. pair, imperf. between | 20.00 | |
| C30 | A47 | 5c on 70c ultra (R) | .20 | .20 |
| C31 | A48 | 20c on 1p org red | .20 | .20 |
| b. | | "CORREO CORREO" double | 3.00 | 3.00 |
| C32 | A47 | 40c on 50c org (R) | 3.00 | 3.00 |
| a. | | "AEREO" double | 3.00 | |
| b. | | "CORREO CORREO" double | 4.50 | 4.50 |
| c. | | "AEREO" omitted | 4.50 | 4.50 |
| C33 | A54 | 6p on 10p red | 3.00 | 3.00 |
| a. | | "CORREO CORREO" double | 4.50 | |
| C34 | A49 | 10p on 20p red | .75 | .70 |
| C35 | A49 | 10p on 20p vio brn | 3.00 | 2.75 |
| | | Nos. C29-C35 (7) | 7.55 | 7.00 |

Declaration of Independence AP11

### 1930, May 14
| | | | | |
|---|---|---|---|---|
| C36 | AP11 | 2.85p dark blue | .20 | .20 |
| C37 | AP11 | 3.40p dark green | .25 | .20 |
| C38 | AP11 | 4.75p deep lake | .75 | .65 |
| | | Nos. C36-C38 (3) | | |

Typo. Perf. 11½, 12

Nat. Independence Day, May 14, 1811.

### 1931-39
Gunboat "Paraguay."

Gunboat Type
| | | | | |
|---|---|---|---|---|
| C39 | A58 | 1p claret | .20 | .20 |
| C40 | A58 | 1p dk blue ('36) | .20 | .20 |
| C41 | A58 | 2p orange | .20 | .20 |
| C42 | A58 | 2p dk brn ('36) | .25 | .25 |
| C43 | A58 | 3p turq green ('36) | .25 | .25 |
| C44 | A58 | 3p lt ultra ('36) | .25 | .25 |
| C45 | A58 | 3p brt rose ('39) | .30 | .30 |
| C46 | A58 | 3p violet ('36) | .30 | .30 |
| C47 | A58 | 6p dk green | .25 | .25 |
| C48 | A58 | 6p dull bl ('39) | .25 | .25 |
| C49 | A58 | 6p vermilion | .70 | .60 |
| C50 | A58 | 10p bluish grn ('35) | 1.00 | 1.00 |
| C51 | A58 | 10p yel brn ('36) | .75 | .75 |

---

Regular Issue of 1924 Surcharged

1st constitution of Paraguay as a Republic and the "Humaita." Counterfeits of #C39-C53 are plentiful.

| | | | | |
|---|---|---|---|---|
| C52 | A58 | 10p dk blue ('36) | .50 | .50 |
| C53 | A58 | 10p lt pink ('39) | .65 | .65 |
| | | Nos. C39-C53 (15) | 6.00 | 5.85 |

### 1931, Aug. 22

 "Graf Zeppelin"

| | | | | |
|---|---|---|---|---|
| C54 | A44 | 3p on 4p lt bl | 8.00 | 6.00 |

Overprinted

 "Graf Zeppelin"

| | | | | |
|---|---|---|---|---|
| C55 | A44 | 4p lt blue | 7.00 | 5.00 |

On Nos. C54-C55 the Zeppelin is hand-stamped. The rest of the surcharge or overprint is typographed.

---

War Memorial AP13

Orange Tree and Yerba Mate — AP14

Yerba Mate — AP15

Palms — AP16

Eagle — AP17

### 1931-36
| | | | | |
|---|---|---|---|---|
| C56 | AP17 | 5c lt blue | 6.25 | .20 |

Litho.
| | | | | |
|---|---|---|---|---|
| C57 | AP13 | 5c dp grn ('33) | .20 | .20 |
| C58 | AP13 | 5c red ('33) | .20 | .20 |
| C59 | AP13 | 5c violet ('33) | .20 | .20 |
| C60 | AP14 | 10c brn violet | .20 | .20 |
| C61 | AP14 | 10c dp violet | .20 | .20 |
| C62 | AP14 | 10c brn lake ('33) | .20 | .20 |
| C63 | AP14 | 10c ultra ('35) | .20 | .20 |
| C64 | AP15 | 20c red | .20 | .20 |
| C65 | AP15 | 20c dl blue ('33) | .20 | .20 |

### 1932, Apr.
Airship "Graf Zeppelin" — AP18

| | | | | |
|---|---|---|---|---|
| C66 | AP15 | 20c emer ('33) | .20 | .20 |
| C67 | AP15 | 20c yel brn ('33) | .20 | .20 |
| a. | | Imperf. pair | 3.75 | |
| C68 | AP16 | 40c dp green | .20 | .20 |
| C69 | AP16 | 40c red ('36) | .20 | .20 |
| C70 | AP16 | 40c slate bl ('35) | .20 | .20 |
| C71 | AP17 | 80c dull blue | .20 | .20 |
| C72 | AP17 | 80c dl grn ('33) | .20 | .20 |
| C73 | AP17 | 80c scar ('33) | 3.60 | 3.60 |
| | | Nos. C56-C73 (18) | | |

| | | | | |
|---|---|---|---|---|
| C74 | AP18 | 4p ultra | .85 | .85 |
| a. | | Imperf. pair | 5.00 | |
| C75 | AP18 | 8p red | 1.40 | 1.00 |
| C76 | AP18 | 12p blue grn | 1.10 | .85 |
| C77 | AP18 | 16p dk violet | 2.25 | 1.50 |
| C78 | AP18 | 20p orange brn | 2.25 | 1.50 |
| | | Nos. C74-C78 (5) | 7.85 | 6.20 |

For surcharges see Nos. 325-329.

Litho.

"Graf Zeppelin" over Brazilian Terrain AP19

### 1933, May 5
"Graf Zeppelin" over Atlantic — AP20

| | | | | |
|---|---|---|---|---|
| C79 | AP19 | 4.50p dp blue | 2.00 | 1.25 |
| C80 | AP19 | 9p dp rose | 3.00 | 2.25 |
| a. | | Horiz. pair, imperf. between | 150.00 | |
| C81 | AP19 | 13.50p blue grn | 4.00 | 3.00 |
| C82 | AP20 | 22.50p bis brn | 8.00 | 6.00 |
| C83 | AP20 | 45p dull vio | 10.00 | 10.00 |
| | | Nos. C79-C83 (5) | 27.00 | 22.50 |

For overprints see Nos. C88-C97.

Posts and Telegraph Building, Asunción — AP21

### 1934-37
| | | | | |
|---|---|---|---|---|
| C84 | AP21 | 33.75p ultra | 2.00 | 1.50 |
| C85 | AP21 | 33.75p car ('35) | 1.50 | 1.25 |
| C86 | AP21 | 33.75p rose ('37) | 1.25 | 1.25 |
| a. | | Horiz. pair, imperf. between | | |
| C87 | AP21 | 33.75p bis brn ('36) | 2.00 | 1.50 |
| | | Nos. C84-C87 (4) | 5.50 | 4.50 |

Perf. 11½

Excellent counterfeits exist. For surcharge see No. C107.

### 1934, May 26
Nos. C79-C83 Overprinted in Black

| | | | | |
|---|---|---|---|---|
| C88 | AP19 | 4.50p deep bl | 2.00 | 1.50 |
| C89 | AP19 | 9p dp rose | 2.50 | 2.00 |
| C90 | AP19 | 13.50p blue grn | 7.00 | 4.00 |
| C91 | AP20 | 22.50p bis brn | 9.00 | 7.00 |
| C92 | AP20 | 45p dull vio | 26.50 | 19.50 |
| | | Nos. C88-C92 (5) | | |

---

### 1935
Types of 1933 Overprinted in Black

| | | | | |
|---|---|---|---|---|
| C93 | AP19 | 4.50p rose red | 3.00 | 2.00 |
| C94 | AP19 | 9p lt green | 4.00 | 2.00 |
| C95 | AP19 | 13.50p brown | 6.50 | 6.00 |
| C96 | AP20 | 22.50p violet | 7.00 | 6.00 |
| C97 | AP20 | 45p scar | 20.00 | 12.00 |
| | | Nos. C93-C97 (5) | 43.00 | 28.00 |

### 1935-39
Tobacco Plant — AP22

Typo.
| | | | | |
|---|---|---|---|---|
| C98 | AP22 | 17p lt brown | 2.00 | 1.50 |
| C99 | AP22 | 17p carmine | 3.75 | 3.75 |
| C100 | AP22 | 17p dark blue | 2.50 | 2.50 |
| C101 | AP22 | 17p pale yel grn | 9.75 | 9.75 |
| | | Nos. C98-C101 (4) | | |

Excellent counterfeits are plentiful.

### 1935-38
Church of Incarnation AP23

| | | | | |
|---|---|---|---|---|
| C102 | AP23 | 102p carmine | 3.75 | 2.50 |
| C103 | AP23 | 102p blue | 3.75 | 2.50 |
| C103A | AP23 | 102p indigo ('36) | 2.75 | 2.40 |
| C104 | AP23 | 102p yellow brn | | |
| a. | | Imperf. pair | 15.00 | |
| C105 | AP23 | 102p violet ('37) | 1.25 | 1.25 |
| C106 | AP23 | 102p blue grn | | |
| | | Nos. C102-C106 (6) ('38) | 1.10 | 1.10 |
| | | | 14.85 | 12.00 |

Excellent counterfeits are plentiful. For surcharges see Nos. C108-C109.

### 1937, Aug. 1
Types of 1934-35 Surcharged in Red

| | | | | |
|---|---|---|---|---|
| C107 | AP21 | 24p on 33.75p sl bl | .50 | .35 |
| C108 | AP23 | 65p on 102p dl bls | 1.25 | .90 |
| C109 | AP23 | 84p on 102p bl grn | 1.25 | .75 |
| | | Nos. C107-C109 (3) | 3.00 | 2.00 |

### 1939, Aug. 3
Plane over Asunción AP24

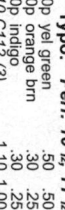

| | | | | |
|---|---|---|---|---|
| C110 | AP24 | 3.40p yel green | .50 | .30 |
| C111 | AP24 | 3.40p orange brn | .30 | .25 |
| C112 | AP24 | 3.40p indigo | 1.10 | 1.00 |
| | | Nos. C110-C112 (3) | | |

Typo. Perf. 10½, 11½

# PARAGUAY

## Buenos Aires Peace Conference Type and

Map of Paraguay with New Chaco Boundary — AP28

Designs: 1p, Flags of Paraguay and Bolivia. 5p, Pres. Ortiz of Argentina, flags of Paraguay, Argentina. 10p, Pres. Vargas, Brazil. 30p, Pres. Alessandri, Chile. 50p, US Eagle and Shield. 100p, Pres. Benavides, Peru. 200p, Pres. Baldomir, Uruguay.

**Engr.; Flags Litho.** **Perf. 12½**

**1939, Nov. Flags in National Colors**

| | | | | |
|---|---|---|---|---|
| C113 | A69 | 1p red brown | .20 | .20 |
| C114 | A69 | 3p dark blue | .20 | .20 |
| C115 | A70 | 5p olive blk | .20 | .20 |
| C116 | A70 | 10p violet | .20 | .20 |
| C117 | A70 | 30p orange | .20 | .20 |
| C118 | A70 | 50p black brn | .30 | .30 |
| C119 | A70 | 100p brt green | .45 | .30 |
| C120 | A70 | 200p green | 1.25 | 1.25 |
| C121 | A70 | 500p blue | 9.00 | 6.00 |
| | | Nos. C113-C121 (9) | 13.00 | 10.75 |

For overprints see Nos. 388-390.

## University of Asuncion Type

Pres. Bernardino Caballero and Senator José S. Decoud.

**Perf. 12** **Litho.**

**1939, Sept.**

| | | | | |
|---|---|---|---|---|
| C122 | A67 | 28p rose & blk | 3.25 | 3.25 |
| C123 | A67 | 90p yel grn & blk | 4.00 | 4.00 |

Map with Asunción to New York Air Route — AP35

New York World's Fair.

**1939, Nov. 30** **Engr.**

| | | | | |
|---|---|---|---|---|
| C124 | AP35 | 3p brown | 1.90 | 1.50 |
| C125 | AP35 | 80p orange | 2.25 | 2.25 |
| C126 | AP35 | 90p purple | 4.00 | 4.00 |
| | | Nos. C124-C126 (3) | 8.15 | 7.75 |

**1940, May** **Perf. 12**

| | | | | |
|---|---|---|---|---|
| C127 | A85 | 20p rose car | .20 | .20 |
| C128 | A85 | 70p violet bl | .45 | .50 |
| C129 | A85 | 100p Prus grn | .50 | .50 |
| C130 | A85 | 500p purple | 2.25 | 1.75 |
| | | Nos. C127-C130 (4) | 3.40 | 2.65 |

Pan American Union Type

**1942, Aug. 15 Asuncion 400th Anniv. Type**

| | | | | |
|---|---|---|---|---|
| C131 | A93 | 20p deep plum | .75 | .40 |
| C132 | A94 | 70p fawn | 1.75 | 1.10 |
| C133 | A95 | 90p olive gray | 5.00 | 3.50 |
| | | Nos. C131-C133 (3) | 7.50 | 5.00 |

### Imperforates

Starting with No. C134, many Paraguayan air mail stamps exist imperforate.

Port of Asunción — AP40

---

First Telegraph in South America — AP41

Early Merchant Ship — AP42

Birthplace of Paraguay's Liberation — AP43

Monument to Antequera — AP44

Locomotive of First Paraguayan Railroad — AP45

Monument to Heroes of Itororó — AP46

Government House — AP47

Primitive Postal Service among Indians — AP48

Colonial Jesuit Altar — AP49

Ruins of Humaitá Church — AP50

Oratory of the Virgin — AP51

Marshal Francisco S. Lopez — AP52

**1944-45** **Unwmk.**

| | | | | |
|---|---|---|---|---|
| C134 | AP40 | 1c blue | .20 | .20 |
| C135 | AP41 | 2c green | .20 | .20 |
| C136 | AP42 | 3c brown vio | .20 | .20 |
| C137 | AP43 | 5c brt bl grn | .20 | .20 |
| C138 | AP44 | 10c dk violet | .20 | .20 |
| C139 | AP45 | 20c orange | .20 | .20 |
| C140 | AP46 | 30c dk brown | .20 | .20 |
| C141 | AP47 | 40c olive | .35 | .10 |
| C142 | AP48 | 70c brown red | .60 | .60 |
| C143 | AP49 | 1g orange yel | .80 | .90 |
| C144 | AP50 | 2g copper brn | 1.00 | .90 |
| C145 | AP51 | 5g black brn | 2.75 | 2.75 |
| C146 | AP52 | 10g indigo | 5.00 | 5.00 |
| | | Nos. C134-C146 (13) | 11.50 | 11.15 |

See Nos. C158-C162. For surcharges see Nos. C154-C157.

### Flags Type

20c, Ecuador. 40c, Bolivia. 70c, Mexico. 1g, Chile. 2g, Brazil. 5g, Argentina. 10g, US.

**Engr.; Flags Litho. in Natl. Colors**

**1945, Aug. 15**

| | | | | |
|---|---|---|---|---|
| C147 | A106 | 20c orange | .20 | .20 |
| C148 | A106 | 40c olive | .20 | .20 |
| C149 | A106 | 70c lake | .35 | .35 |
| C150 | A106 | 1g slate bl | .50 | .50 |
| C151 | A106 | 2g blue vio | 1.40 | 1.40 |
| C152 | A106 | 5g green | 3.75 | 3.75 |
| C153 | A106 | 10g brown | 6.60 | 6.60 |
| | | Nos. C147-C153 (7) | 13.00 | 13.00 |

Sizes: Nos. C147-C151, 30x26mm; 5g, 32x28mm; 10g, 33x30mm.

> **Catalogue values for unused stamps in this section, from this point to the end of the section, are for Never Hinged items.**

**Nos. C139-C142 Surcharged "1946" and New Value in Black**

**Perf. 12½**

**1946**

| | | | | |
|---|---|---|---|---|
| C154 | AP45 | 5c on 20c dk brn | .40 | .40 |
| C155 | AP46 | 5c on 30c lt blue | .40 | .40 |
| C156 | AP47 | 5c on 40c olive | .40 | .40 |
| C157 | AP48 | 5c on 70c brn red | .40 | .40 |
| | | Nos. C154-C157 (4) | 1.60 | 1.60 |

**Types of 1944-45**

**1946, Sept. 21** **Engr.**

| | | | | |
|---|---|---|---|---|
| C158 | AP50 | 10c dp car | .20 | .20 |
| C159 | AP40 | 20c emerald | .30 | .30 |
| C160 | AP47 | 20c brown org | .35 | .35 |
| C161 | AP52 | 5g purple | 1.00 | 1.00 |
| C162 | AP51 | 10g rose car | 2.75 | 2.75 |
| | | Nos. C158-C162 (5) | 4.50 | 4.50 |

### Marshal Francisco Solano Lopez Type

**1947, May. 15** **Perf. 12**

| | | | | |
|---|---|---|---|---|
| C163 | A114 | 32c car lake | .20 | .20 |
| C164 | A114 | 64c orange brn | .30 | .30 |
| C165 | A114 | 1g brown org | .60 | .60 |
| C166 | A114 | 5g Prus grn & brn vio | 1.60 | 1.60 |
| C167 | A114 | 10g dk car rose & dk yel grn | 3.25 | 3.25 |
| | | Nos. C163-C167 (5) | 5.95 | 5.95 |

---

## Archbishopric of Asunción Types

**1948, Jan. 6** **Unwmk.** **Perf. 12½**

Size: 25½x31mm

| | | | | |
|---|---|---|---|---|
| C168 | A116 | 20c gray blk | .20 | .20 |
| C169 | A117 | 30c dark blue | .20 | .20 |
| C170 | A118 | 40c lilac | .35 | .35 |
| C171 | A115 | 70c orange red | .45 | .45 |
| C172 | A112 | 1g brown red | .45 | .45 |
| C173 | A118 | 2g red | 1.25 | 1.25 |

Size: 25½x34mm

| | | | | |
|---|---|---|---|---|
| C174 | A115 | 5g brt car & dk bl | 2.25 | 2.25 |
| C175 | A116 | 10g dk grn & brn | 3.75 | 3.75 |
| | | Nos. C168-C175 (8) | 8.90 | 8.90 |

For surcharges see Nos. B11, C178.

## Type of Regular Issue of 1948 Inscribed "AEREO"

**1948, Sept. 11** **Engr. & Litho.**

| | | | | |
|---|---|---|---|---|
| C176 | A119 | 69c dk grn, red & bl | .90 | .90 |
| C177 | A119 | 5g dk bl, red & bl | 5.00 | 3.00 |

The Barefeet, a political group.

No. C171 Surcharged in Black

**1949, June 29**

| | | | | |
|---|---|---|---|---|
| C178 | A115 | 5c on 70c org red | .20 | .20 |

Archbishop Juan Sinforiano Bogarin (1863-1949).

Franklin D. Roosevelt AP66

Symbols of UPU — AP65

**1950, Sept. 4** **Engr.**

| | | | | |
|---|---|---|---|---|
| C179 | AP65 | 20c green & violet | .20 | .20 |
| C180 | AP65 | 30c rose vio & brn | .20 | .20 |
| C181 | AP65 | 50c gray & green | .25 | .25 |
| C182 | AP65 | 1g blue & brown | .35 | .35 |
| C183 | AP65 | 5g rose & black | 1.00 | .55 |
| | | Nos. C179-C183 (5) | 2.00 | 1.35 |

UPU, 75th anniv. (in 1949).

**Engr.; Flags Litho.** **Perf. 12½**

**1950, Oct. 2 Flags in Carmine & Violet Blue.**

| | | | | |
|---|---|---|---|---|
| C184 | AP66 | 20c red | .20 | .20 |
| C185 | AP66 | 30c black | .20 | .20 |
| C186 | AP66 | 50c claret | .20 | .20 |
| C187 | AP66 | 1g dk gray grn | .40 | .40 |
| C188 | AP66 | 5g deep blue | 1.20 | 1.20 |
| | | Nos. C184-C188 (5) | | |

Franklin D. Roosevelt (1882-1945).

Urn Containing Remains of Columbus AP67

**1952, Feb. 11** **Litho.** **Perf. 10**

| | | | | |
|---|---|---|---|---|
| C189 | AP67 | 10c ultra | .20 | .20 |
| C190 | AP67 | 30c green | .20 | .20 |
| C191 | AP67 | 30c lilac | .20 | .20 |
| C192 | AP67 | 40c rose | .20 | .20 |
| C193 | AP67 | 50c bister brn | .20 | .20 |
| C194 | AP67 | 1g blue | .25 | .25 |
| C195 | AP67 | 2g orange | .40 | .40 |
| C196 | AP67 | 5g red brown | .30 | .30 |
| | | Nos. C189-C196 (8) | 1.70 | 1.70 |

PARAGUAY

Queen Isabella I — AP68

**1952, Oct. 12**
| | | | |
|---|---|---|---|
| C197 | AP68 | 1g vio blue | .20 .20 |
| C198 | AP68 | 2g chocolate | .25 .25 |
| C199 | AP68 | 5g dull green | .55 .55 |
| C200 | AP68 | 10g lilac rose | 1.20 1.20 |

Nos. C197-C200 (4)

500th birth anniv. of Queen Isabella I of Spain (in 1951).

**1954, Mar.**
Pettirossi Type
| | | | |
|---|---|---|---|
| C201 | A122 | 40c brown | .30 .20 |
| C202 | A122 | 55c green | .30 .20 |
| C203 | A122 | 80c dull green | .35 .20 |
| C204 | A122 | 1.30g gray blue | 1.25 .85 |

Nos. C201-C204 (4)

Church of San Roque AP70

**1954, June 20** Engr. Perf. 12x13
| | | | |
|---|---|---|---|
| C205 | AP70 | 20c carmine | .20 .20 |
| C206 | AP70 | 30c brown vio | .20 .20 |
| C207 | AP70 | 50c ultra | .20 .20 |
| C208 | AP70 | 1g red brn & bl grn | .20 .20 |
| C209 | AP70 | 1g red brn & lil rose | .20 .20 |
| C210 | AP70 | 1g red brn & blk | .20 .20 |
| C211 | AP70 | 1g red brn & vio | .20 .20 |

a. Min. sheet of 4, #C208-C211, perf. 12x12½ 2.00 .30

**1954, Aug. 15**
Heroes Type
Unwmk. Perf. 12x13
| | | | |
|---|---|---|---|
| C212 | AP70 | 5g dk red brn & vio | 2.00 |
| C213 | AP70 | 5g dk red brn & ol | .20 .20 |

a. Min. sheet of 4 #C212-C215, perf. 12x12½ 2.20 2.20

| | | | |
|---|---|---|---|
| C214 | AP70 | 5g dk red brn & grn | .20 .20 |
| C215 | AP70 | 5g dk red brn & org yel | .20 .20 |

Nos. C205-C215 (11)

Centenary (in 1953) of the establishment of the Church of San Roque, Asuncion. Nos. C211a and C215a issued without gum.

**1955, Apr.** Photo. & Litho.
Peron Visit Type
Perf. 13x13½
Frames & Flags in Blue & Carmine
| | | | |
|---|---|---|---|
| C216 | AP70 | 5g dk red brn & ol | .20 .20 |

**1955, Apr.** Litho. Perf. 10
Heroes Type
Unwmk.
| | | | |
|---|---|---|---|
| C217 | A123 | 5g violet | .25 .20 |
| C218 | A123 | 10g olive green | .50 .40 |
| C219 | A123 | 20g gray green | .75 .70 |
| C220 | A123 | 50g vermilion | 1.75 1.75 |
| C221 | A123 | 100g blue | 9.00 8.80 |

Nos. C216-C220 (5)

**1955, Apr. 15** Engr. Perf. 12x13
Frames & Flags in Blue & Carmine
| | | | |
|---|---|---|---|
| C221 | A124 | 60c grn & cream | .25 .20 |
| C222 | A124 | 2g bl grn & cream | .25 .20 |
| C223 | A124 | 4g lt blue grn | .25 .20 |
| C224 | A124 | 4.10g brt rose pink & | |

Nos. C221-C224 (4)

Monsignor Rodriguez Type
Jesuit Ruins: 3g, Corridor at Trinidad. 6g, Tower of Santa Rosa. 10g, San Cosme gate. 20g, Church of Jesus. 30g, Niche at Trinidad. 50g, Sacristy at Trinidad.

**1955, June 19** Engr. Perf. 12½x12, 12x12½ Unwmk.
| | | | |
|---|---|---|---|
| C225 | A126 | 2g aqua | .20 .20 |
| C226 | A125 | 3g olive grn | .20 .20 |
| C227 | A126 | 4g lt blue grn | .20 .20 |
| C228 | A126 | 6g brown | .20 .20 |
| C229 | A126 | 10g rose | .20 .20 |
| C230 | A125 | 20g brown ol | .20 .20 |
| C231 | A126 | 30g dp green | .30 .25 |
| C232 | A126 | 50g dk green | 1.85 1.75 |

For surcharges see Nos. C225-C232.

Map and UN Emblem AP78

Uprooted Oak Emblem AP79

**1959, Aug. 27** Typo. Perf. 11
| | | |
|---|---|---|
| C260 | AP77 5g ocher & ultra | .50 .40 |

Visit of Dag Hammarskjold, Secretary General of the UN, Aug. 27-29.

**1959, Oct. 24** Unwmk.
| | | | |
|---|---|---|---|
| C261 | AP78 | 12.45g blue & salmon | .20 .20 |

United Nations Day, Oct. 24, 1959.

UN Emblem AP77

Nos. C225-C232 Surcharged like #545-551 in Red

**1959, May 26** Perf. 12½x12, 12x12½ Engr. Unwmk.
| | | | |
|---|---|---|---|
| C252 | A125 | 4g on 2g aqua | .25 .20 |
| C253 | A125 | 12.45g on 3g ol grn | .25 .20 |
| C254 | A126 | 18.15g on 6g brown | .35 .25 |
| C255 | A125 | 23.40g on 10g rose | .50 .40 |
| C256 | A125 | 34.80g on 20g brn ol | .70 .55 |
| C257 | A125 | 36g on 4g lt bl grn | .90 .60 |
| C258 | A126 | 43.95g on 30g dk grn | .90 .55 |
| C259 | A126 | 100g on 50g dk grn | 5.95 4.15 |

Nos. C252-C259 (8)

The surcharge is made to fit the stamps. Counterfeits of surcharge exist.

"Republic" and Soldier — AP76

**1957, June 12** Photo. Perf. 13½
Granite Paper
Flags in Red and Blue
| | | | |
|---|---|---|---|
| C233 | AP75 | 10c ultra | .20 .20 |
| C234 | AP75 | 15c dp claret | .20 .20 |
| C235 | AP75 | 20c red | .20 .20 |
| C236 | AP75 | 25c light blue | .20 .20 |
| C237 | AP75 | 50c bluish grn | .20 .20 |
| C238 | AP75 | 1g rose car | .20 .20 |
| C239 | AP75 | 1.30g grn ol | .20 .20 |
| C240 | AP75 | 2g emerald | .20 .20 |
| C241 | AP75 | 1.50g light blue | .20 .20 |
| C242 | AP76 | 5g red | .20 .20 |
| C243 | AP76 | 4.10g gray black | .20 .20 |
| C244 | AP76 | 10g bluish grn | .25 .20 |
| C245 | AP76 | 25g ultra | 2.65 2.60 |

Nos. C233-C245 (13)

Heroes of the Chaco war.

Stroessner Type of Regular Issue
**1958, Aug. 16** Litho. Wmk. 320
Center in Slate
| | | | |
|---|---|---|---|
| C246 | A130 | 12g rose lilac | .45 .35 |
| C247 | A130 | 18g orange | .50 .45 |
| C248 | A130 | 23g orange brn | .60 .60 |
| C249 | A130 | 40g emerald | 1.00 .90 |
| C250 | A130 | 50g citron | 1.25 1.25 |
| C251 | A130 | 66g gray | 6.05 5.05 |

Nos. C246-C251 (6)

Re-election of Pres. General Alfredo Stroessner.

"Paraguay en Marcha" Type of 1961
12.45g, Truck carrying logs. 18.15g, Logs on river barge. 22g, Radio tower. 36g, Jet plane.

**1961, Apr. 10** Photo. Perf. 13
| | | | |
|---|---|---|---|
| C278 | A136 | 12.45g yel & vio bl | .35 .30 |
| C279 | A136 | 18.15g pur & ocher | .50 .40 |
| C280 | A136 | 22g ultra & ocher | .55 .45 |
| C281 | A136 | 36g brn grn & yel | 2.30 1.95 |

Nos. C278-C281 (4)

Inauguration of the International Bridge between Paraguay and Brazil.

"Republic" and Soldier — AP76

**1960, Apr. 21** Perf. 12½x13
Human Rights Type of Regular Issue, 1960
| | | | |
|---|---|---|---|
| C269 | A133 | 40g dk ultra & red | .30 .30 |
| C270 | A133 | 60g grnish bl & red | .65 .65 |
| C271 | A133 | 100g dk ultra & red | 1.20 1.20 |

Nos. C269-C271 (3)

An imperf. miniature sheet exists, containing one each of Nos. C269-C271, all printed in green and vermilion.

UN Type of Regular Issue
**1960, Oct. 24** Photo. Perf. 13x13½
| | | | |
|---|---|---|---|
| C272 | A134 | 3g orange, red & bl | .25 .25 |
| C273 | A134 | 4g pale grn, red & bl | .20 .20 |

International Bridge, Paraguay-Brazil AP80

**1961, Jan. 26** Litho. Unwmk.
| | | | |
|---|---|---|---|
| C274 | AP80 | 3g carmine | .20 .20 |
| C275 | AP80 | 12.45g brown lake | .35 .30 |
| C276 | AP80 | 18.15g rose | .45 .40 |
| C277 | AP80 | 36g dk blue | .90 .80 |

a. Souv. sheet of 4, #C274-C277, imperf.

Nos. C274-C277 (4)

"Paraguay" and Clasped Hands — AP82

**1960, Mar. 18** Photo. Perf. 12½
| | | | |
|---|---|---|---|
| C262 | A131 | 12.45g red & dk bl | .20 .20 |
| C263 | A131 | 18.15g lilac & gray ol | .20 .20 |
| C264 | A131 | 36g bl grn & rose | .40 .40 |

Nos. C262-C264 (3)

The Paraguayan Philatelic Agency reported as spurious the imperf. souvenir sheet reproducing one of No. C264.

**1960, Apr. 7** Litho. Perf. 11
| | | | |
|---|---|---|---|
| C265 | AP79 | 4g green & pink | .70 .60 |
| C266 | AP79 | 12.45g bl & yel grn | 1.25 .65 |
| C267 | AP79 | 18.15g car & ocher | 1.75 .75 |
| C268 | AP79 | 23.40g red org & bl | 5.80 3.30 |

Nos. C265-C268 (4)

World Refugee Year, July 1, 1959-June 30, 1960 (1st issue).

**1961, June 12** Perf. 14x14½
South American Tapir — AP83
| | | | |
|---|---|---|---|
| C288 | AP82 | 3g vio blue | .30 .25 |
| C289 | AP82 | 4g rose claret | .35 .30 |
| C290 | AP82 | 100g gray green | 2.90 2.55 |

Nos. C288-C290 (3)

Catholic University Type of 1961
**1961, Sept. 18** Perf. 14x14½
| | | | |
|---|---|---|---|
| C291 | A140 | 3g bister brn | 1.50 1.00 |
| C292 | AP83 | 12.45g claret | 1.50 1.00 |
| C293 | AP83 | 18.15g ultra | .50 .40 |
| C294 | A140 | 12.45g lilac rose | 1.00 .80 |

Nos. C291-C293 (3)

**1961, Oct. 16** Litho. Unwmk. Perf. 11
Tennis Type
| | | | |
|---|---|---|---|
| C295 | A140 | 3g bister brn | 1.50 1.00 |
| C296 | A140 | 12.45g lilac rose | 1.00 .80 |

**1961, Oct. 14** Litho. Perf. 15
| | | | |
|---|---|---|---|
| C297 | A141 | 3g dull red brn | .20 .20 |
| C298 | A141 | 4g grn | .25 .25 |
| C299 | A141 | 18.15g orange | .25 .25 |
| C300 | A141 | 36g rose car | .35 .35 |

Nos. C297-C300 (4)

Hotel Guarani Type of 1961
Design: Hotel Guarani, different view.

**1961, Oct. 16** Litho. Unwmk. Perf. 11
| | | | |
|---|---|---|---|
| C301 | A142 | 12.45g multi | .50 |
| C302 | A142 | 20g multi | 3.00 |
| C303 | A142 | 50g multi | 4.75 |

Nos. C301-C303 (3)

Some specialists question the status of this issue.

Declaration of Independence — AP81

**1961, May 16** Litho. Perf. 14½
| | | | |
|---|---|---|---|
| C282 | AP81 | 12.45g dl red brn | .30 .20 |
| C283 | AP81 | 18.15g dk blue | .35 .35 |
| C284 | AP81 | 23.40g green | .50 .45 |
| C285 | AP81 | 30g lilac | .65 .50 |
| C286 | AP81 | 36g rose | .80 .75 |
| C287 | AP81 | 44g olive | 3.60 3.10 |

Nos. C282-C287 (6)

150th anniv. of Independence (1st issue).

Olympic Games Type of Regular Issue
Design: Basketball.

**1959, Oct. 24** Litho. Perf. 10
| | | | |
|---|---|---|---|
| C261 | AP78 | 12.45g blue & salmon | .20 .20 |

Design: Oak emblem rooted in ground, wavy-lined frame.

WRY Type
Design: Oak emblem rooted in ground, wavy-lined frame.

**1961, Dec. 30**
| | | | |
|---|---|---|---|
| C307 | A145 | 18.15g brn & red | .35 |
| C308 | A145 | 36g car & emer | .90 |
| C309 | A145 | 50g mint | 1.25 |

Nos. C307-C309 (3)

Some imperf. souvenir sheets exist of this issue.

Two imperf. souvenir sheets exist containing four 12.45g stamps each in a different color with simulated perforations and black marginal inscription.

Imperforates in changed colors and souvenir sheets exist. Some specialists question the status of this issue.

Pres. Alfredo Stroessner and Prince Philip AP84

Portraits in Ultramarine

**1962, Mar. 9** Litho.
| | | | |
|---|---|---|---|
| C310 | AP84 | 12.45g grn & buff | .20 .20 |
| C311 | AP84 | 18.15g red & pink | .20 .20 |
| C312 | AP84 | 36g brn & yel | .70 .70 |

Nos. C310-C312 (3)

Visit of Prince Philip, Duke of Edinburgh. Imperf. and imperf. souvenir sheets exist.

## Souvenir Sheets

**Emblems of Apollo Space Missions — AP94**

Designs: No. C332, Apollo 7, 8, 9, & 10. No. C333, Apollo 11, 12, 13, & 14.

| | | | |
|---|---|---|---|
| **1971, Mar. 26** | | **Perf. 14** | |
| C332 | AP94 | 20g multicolored | 15.00 |
| C333 | AP94 | 20g multicolored | 15.00 |

### Souvenir Sheet

**Charles de Gaulle — AP95**

| | | | |
|---|---|---|---|
| **1971, Dec. 24** | | **Perf. 13½** | |
| C334 | AP95 | 20g multicolored | 22.50 |

### Souvenir Sheet

**Taras Shevchenko (1814-1861), Ukrainian Poet — AP96**

| | | | |
|---|---|---|---|
| **1971, Dec. 24** | | **Perf. 13½** | |
| C335 | AP96 | 20g multicolored | 11.00 |

### Souvenir Sheets

**Johannes Kepler (1571-1630), German Astronomer — AP97**

Kepler and: No. C336, Apollo lunar module over moon. No. C337, Astronaut walking in space.

---

| | | | | |
|---|---|---|---|---|
| **1969, June 28** | **Wmk. 347** | | **Perf. 11** | |
| C318 | AP90 | 36g blue | .75 | .40 |
| C319 | AP90 | 50g bister brn | 1.00 | .75 |
| C320 | AP90 | 100g rose car | 2.00 | 1.25 |
| Nos. C318-C320 (3) | | | 3.75 | |

National drive for teachers' homes.

### Souvenir Sheets

**U.S. Space Program — AP91**

John F. Kennedy, Wernher von Braun, moon and: No. C321, Apollo 11 en route to moon. No. C322, Saturn V lift-off. No. C323, Apollo 9. No. C324, Apollo 10.

| | | | |
|---|---|---|---|
| **1969, July 9** | | **Perf. 14** | |
| C321 | AP91 | 23.40g multicolored | 15.00 |
| C322 | AP91 | 23.40g multicolored | 22.50 |
| | | ***Imperf*** | |
| C323 | AP91 | 23.40g multicolored | 27.50 |
| C324 | AP91 | 23.40g multicolored | 27.50 |

Nos. C323-C324 each contain one 56x46mm stamp.

### Souvenir Sheets

**Events and Anniversaries — AP92**

#C325, Apollo 14. #C326, Dwight D. Eisenhower, 1st death anniv. #C327, Napoleon Bonaparte, birth bicent. #C328, Brazil, winners of Julca Rimet World Cup Soccer Trophy.

| | | | |
|---|---|---|---|
| **1970, Dec. 16** | | **Perf. 13½** | |
| C325 | AP92 | 20g multicolored | 30.00 |
| C326 | AP92 | 20g multicolored | 15.00 |
| C327 | AP92 | 20g multicolored | 17.00 |
| C328 | AP92 | 20g multicolored | 20.00 |

### Souvenir Sheets

**Paraguayan Postage Stamps, Cent. — AP93**

No. C329, Marshal Francisco Solano Lopez, Pres. Alfredo Stroessner, Paraguay #1. No. C330, #3, 1014, 1242. No. C331, #1243, C8. C74.

| | | | |
|---|---|---|---|
| **1971, Mar. 23** | | | |
| C329 | AP93 | 20g multicolored | 10.00 |
| C330 | AP93 | 20g multicolored | 17.00 |
| C331 | AP93 | 20g multicolored | 17.00 |

Issued: #C329, 3/23; #C330-C331, 3/29.

---

### Souvenir Sheet

**Cattleya Cigas — AP87**

| | | | | |
|---|---|---|---|---|
| **1963, Aug. 21** | | **Litho.** | | |
| C315 | AP87 | 66g multicolored | 62.50 | 15.00 |

### Souvenir Sheet

**Pres. Alfredo Stroessner — AP88**

| | | | |
|---|---|---|---|
| **1964, Nov. 3** | | | |
| C316 | AP88 | 36g multicolored | 9.00 |

### Souvenir Sheet

**Saturn V Rocket, Pres. John F. Kennedy — AP89**

| | | | |
|---|---|---|---|
| **1968, Jan. 27** | | **Perf. 14** | |
| C317 | AP89 | 50g multicolored | 17.00 |

Pres. Kennedy, 4th death anniv. (in 1967).

**Torch, Book, Houses — AP90**

---

Illustrations AP85-AP89, AP92-AP94, AP96-AP97, AP99-AP105, AP107-AP110, AP113-AP115, AP117, AP123, AP127a, AP132-AP133, AP136, AP138, AP140, AP142, AP144-AP145, AP149-AP150, AP152-AP153, AP156, AP158-AP159, AP165, AP167, AP171, AP180, AP183-AP184, AP187, AP196, AP202, AP205, AP208, AP211, AP221-AP222, AP224-AP225, AP229, AP234-AP235, AP237 and AP240 are reduced.

### Souvenir Sheet

**Abraham Lincoln (1809-1865), 16th President of U.S. — AP85**

| | | | |
|---|---|---|---|
| **1963, Aug. 21** | **Litho.** | ***Imperf.*** | |
| C313 | AP85 | 36g gray & vio brn | 10.00 |

**Limited Distribution Issues**

Beginning with No. C313, stamps with limited distribution are not valued.

### Souvenir Sheet

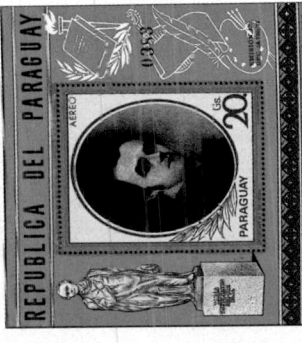

**1960 Summer Olympics, Rome — AP86**

| | | | |
|---|---|---|---|
| **1963, Aug. 21** | | **Litho. & Engr.** | |
| C314 | AP86 | 50g lt bl, vio brn & sep | 90.00 |

**MUESTRA**

Illustrations may show the word "MUESTRA." This means specimen and is not on the actual stamps.

**1971, Dec. 24**
C336 AP97 20g multicolored    17.00
C337 AP97 20g multicolored    17.00

Souvenir Sheet

Republica del Paraguay

10 years of U.S. Space Program — AP98

**1972, Jan. 6**    *Perf. 13½*
C338 AP98 20g multicolored    17.00

Souvenir Sheet

Republica del Paraguay

Apollo 16 Moon Mission — AP99

**1972, Mar. 29**    *Litho.*    *Perf. 13½*
C339 AP99 20g multicolored    20.00

Souvenir Sheets

History of the Olympics — AP100

Designs: No. C340, Pierre de Coubertin (1863-1937), founder of modern Olympics. No. C341, Skier, Garmisch-Partenkirchen, 1936. No. C342, Olympic flame, Sapporo, 1972. No. C343, French, Olympic flags, No. C344, Javelin thrower, Paris, 1924. No. C345, Equestrian event.

**1972, Mar. 29**    *Perf. 14½*
C340 AP100 20g multicolored    15.00
C341 AP100 20g multicolored    15.00
C342 AP100 20g multicolored    20.00
C343 AP100 20g multicolored    20.00
C344 AP100 20g multicolored    20.00
C345 AP100 20g multicolored    22.50

Souvenir Sheet

Republica del Paraguay

Medal Totals, 1972 Winter Olympics, Sapporo — AP101

**1972, Nov. 18**    *Perf. 13½*
C346 AP101 23.40g multicolored    20.00

Souvenir Sheets

French Contributions to Aviation and Space Exploration — AP102

Georges Pompidou, Charles de Gaulle and: No. C347, Concorde. No. C348, Satellite D2A; Mirage G 8 jets.

**1972, Nov. 25**
C347 AP102 23.40g multicolored    60.00
C348 AP102 23.40g multicolored    55.00

Souvenir Sheets

Summer Olympic Gold Medals, 1896-1972 — AP103

**1972, Nov. 25**
C349 AP103 23.40g 9 medals, 1896-1932.    17.00
C350 AP103 23.40g 8 medals, 1936-1972    17.00

Souvenir Sheet

Republica del Paraguay

Adoration of the Shepherds by Murillo — AP104

**1972, Nov. 25**
C351 AP104 23.40g multicolored    17.00

Christmas.

Souvenir Sheet

CORREO DE LA REPUBLICA DEL PARAGUAY

Apollo 17 Moon Mission — AP105

**1973, Mar. 13**
C352 AP105 25g multicolored    27.50

Souvenir Sheet

Medal Totals, 1972 Summer Olympics, Munich — AP106

**1973, Mar. 15**    *Perf. 13½*
C353 AP106 25g multicolored    30.00

Souvenir Sheets

The Holy Family by Peter Paul Rubens — AP107

Design: No. C355, In the Forest at Pierrefonds by Alfred de Dreux.

**1973, Mar. 15**
C354 AP107 25g multicolored    25.00
C355 AP107 25g multicolored    15.00

Souvenir Sheet

IBRA

German Championship Soccer Team F.C. Bayern, Bavaria — AP108

IBRA '73 Intl. Philatelic Exhibition, Munich.

**1973, June 29**    *Imperf.*
C356 AP108 25g multicolored    7.50

Souvenir Sheet

REPUBLICA DEL PARAGUAY

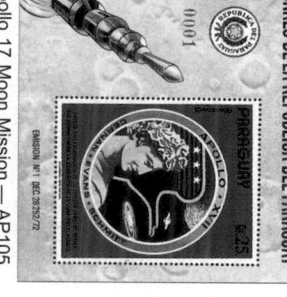

Copernicus, 500th Birth Anniv. and Space Exploration — AP109

#C357, Lunar surface, Apollo 11. #C358, Copernicus, position of Earth at solstices and equinoxes. #C359, Skylab space laboratory.

**1973, June 29**    *Perf. 13½*
C357 AP109 25g multicolored    15.00
C358 AP109 25g multicolored    15.00
C359 AP109 25g multicolored    25.00

Souvenir Sheets

Exploration of Mars — AP110

**1973, Oct. 8**
C360 AP110 25g Mariner 9    25.00
C361 AP110 25g Viking probe, horiz.    37.50

Pres. Stroessner's Visit to Europe and Morocco — AP111

Designs: No. C362a, 5g Arms of Paraguay, Spain, Canary Islands, b. 10g, Gen. Franco, Stroessner, vert. c. 25g, Arms of Paraguay, Germany. d. 50g, Stroessner, Giovanni Leone, Italy, vert. No. C363, Itaipu Dam between Paraguay and Brazil.

## German World Cup Soccer Champions — AP120

Design: No. C399, Hemispheres, emblems of 1974 and 1978 World Cup championships.

1974, Dec. 20 — **Perf. 14**
C395 AP120  4g Holding World Cup trophy, vert.    7.00  5.00

**Souvenir Sheets    Perf. 13½**
C396 AP120  5g Team on field    25.00
C397 AP120 10g Argentina 78 emblem, vert.    25.00
Set, #C395-C397
C398 AP120 15g Players holding trophy, vert.
C399 AP120 15g multicolored    '24.00

No. C398 contains one 50x60mm stamp, and No. C399 contains one 60x50mm stamp. Face value of each sheet was 15g plus 5g extra for a monument to Francisco Solano Lopez.

### Souvenir Sheet

## Apollo-Soyuz — AP121

1974, Dec. 20 — **Perf. 13½**
C400 AP121 15g multicoloured    '24.00

## Expo 75 — AP122

1975, Feb. 24 — **Perf. 14**
C401 AP122  4g Ryuky-umurasaki, vert.
C402 AP122  5g Hibiscus
C403 AP122 10g Ancient sailing ship    4.00  2.00
Set, #C401-C403

**Souvenir Sheet    Perf. 14½**
C404 AP122 15g Expo emblem, vert.    14.00

No. C404 face value was 15g plus 5g extra for a monument to Francisco Solano Lopez.

---

### Souvenir Sheet

## First Balloon Flight over English Channel — AP117

1974, Sept. 13 — **Imperf.**
C383 AP117 15g multicolored    32.50

No. C383 face value was 15g plus 5g extra for a monument for Francisco Solano Lopez.

## Anniversaries and Events — AP118

Designs: 4g, US #C76 on covers that went to Moon; Nn C366a, 0g, Pres. Pinochet of Chile. No. C385b, 10g, Pres. Stroessner's visit to South Africa. No. C386, Mariner 10 over Mercury, horiz.

1974, Dec. 2 — **Perf. 14**
C384 AP118  4g multicolored    8.00  8.00
C385 AP118  4g multicolored
Set, #C384-C385  Pair #a.-b.

**Souvenir Sheet    Perf. 13½**
C386 AP118 15g multicolored    20.00

Nos. C386 contains one 60x50mm stamp. Face value was 15g plus 5g extra for a monument to Francisco Solano Lopez. Compare No. C386 with No. C392.

## Anniversaries and Events — AP119

Designs: 4g, UPU, cent. 5g, 17th Congress, UPU, Lausanne. 10g, Intl. Philatelic Exposition, Montevideo, Uruguay. No. C392, Mariner 10 orbiting Mercury, horiz. No. C393, Figure skater, horiz. No. C394, Innsbruck Olympic emblem.

1974, Dec. 7 — **Perf. 14**
C389 AP119  4g multicolored    20.00
C390 AP119  5g multicolored    20.00
C391 AP119 10g multicolored    7.00  5.00
Set, #C389-C391

**Souvenir Sheets    Perf. 13½**
C392 AP119 15g bl & multi    20.00
C393 AP119 15g multicolored    17.00
C394 AP119 15g multicolored    17.00

UPU centennial (#C389), Nos. C392-C394 each contain one 60x50mm stamp and face value was 15g plus 5g extra for a monument to Francisco Solano Lopez.

---

C373 AP114 25g Skylab 2 astronauts, horiz.    15.00
C374 AP114 25g Olympic Flame    15.00

UPU centennial (#C371-C372). 1976 Olympic Games (#C374).

### President Stroessner Type of 1973

100g, Stroessner, Georges Pompidou. 200g, Stroessner and Pope Paul VI.

1974, Apr. 25 — **Perf. 14**
C375 AP111 100g multicolored    2.00  1.00

**Souvenir Sheet    Perf. 13½**
C376 AP111 200g multicolored    5.00

No. C376 contains one 60x50mm stamp.

## Lufthansa Airlines Intercontinental Routes, 40th Anniv. — AP115

1974, July 13 — **Perf. 13½**
C377 AP115 15g multicolored    17.00

No. C377 face value was 15g plus 5g extra for a monument to Francisco Solano Lopez.

### Souvenir Sheet

## Hermann Oberth, 80th Anniv. of Birth — AP115a

1974, July 13 — **Litho.    Perf. 13½**
C378 AP115a 15g multi    40.00

No. C378 face value was 15g plus 5g extra for a monument to Francisco Solano Lopez.

## 1974 World Cup Soccer Championships, West Germany — AP116

1974, July 13 — **Perf. 14**
C379 AP116  4g Goalie
C380 AP116  5g Soccer ball
C381 AP116 10g shown    21.00  10.00
Set, #C379-C381

**Souvenir Sheet    Perf. 13½**
C382 AP116 15g Soccer ball, diff.    27.50

No. C382 contains one 53x46mm stamp. No. C382 face value was 15g plus 5g extra for a monument for Francisco Solano Lopez.

---

1973, Dec. 30 — **Perf. 14**
C362 AP111    Strip of 4, #a.-d.
C363 AP111 150g multicolored    5.00  2.50
Set, #C362-C363

**Souvenir Sheet    Imperf**
C364 AP111 100g multicolored    3.00

No. C364 contains one 60x50mm stamp.

## 1974 World Cup Soccer Championships, Munich — AP112

Abstract paintings of soccer players: No. C366a, 10g, Player seated on globe. b, 20g, Player as viewed from under foot. No. C367, Player kicking ball. No. C368, Goalie catching ball, horiz.

1974, Jan. 31 — **Perf. 14**
C365 AP112  5g shown
C366 AP112  5g Pair, #a.-b.    15.00  6.00
Set, #C365-C366

**Souvenir Sheets    Perf. 13½**
C367 AP112 25g multicolored    20.00
C368 AP112 25g multicolored    20.00

Nos. C367-C368 each contain one 50x60mm stamp.

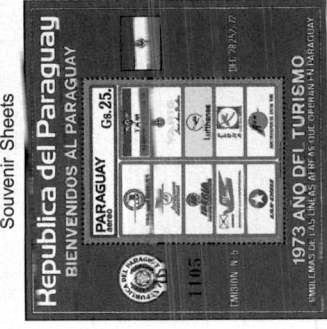

## Tourism Year — AP113

Design: No. C370, Painting, Birth of Christ by Louis le Nain (1593-1648), horiz.

1974, Feb. 4 — **Perf. 13½**
C369 AP113 25g multicolored    12.00
C370 AP113 25g multicolored    7.00

**Souvenir Sheets**

Christmas (No. C370).

## Events and Anniversaries — AP114

1974, Mar. 20
C371 AP114 25g Rocket lift-off    22.50
C372 AP114 25g Solar system, horiz.    25.00

# REPUBLICA DEL PARAGUAY

**Anniversaries and Events — AP123**

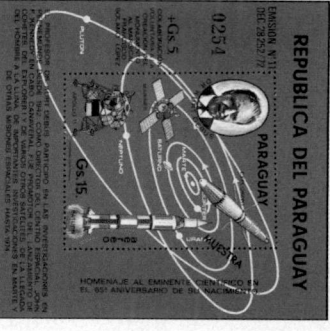

Designs: No. C405, Dr. Kurt Debus, space scientist, 65th birth anniv. No. C406, 1976 Summer Olympics, Montreal, horiz.

**1975, Feb. 24    Perf. 13½**

| | | |
|---|---|---|
| C405 | AP123 15g multicolored | 17.00 |
| C406 | AP123 15g multicolored | 17.00 |

Nos. C405-C406 face value was 15g plus 5g extra for a monument to Francisco Solano Lopez.

## Souvenir Sheets

**REPUBLICA DEL PARAGUAY**

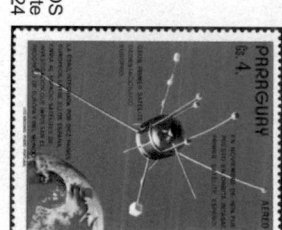

Designs: No. C408a, 5g, ESPANA 75, b, 10g, Mother and Child, Murillo.

**1975, Aug. 21    Perf. 14**

| | | |
|---|---|---|
| C407 | AP124 4g shown | |
| C408 | AP124 Pair, #1.-b. | |
| | Set, #C407-C408. | 5.00 3.00 |

### Souvenir Sheet

GEOS Satellite AP124

**Perf. 13½**

| | | |
|---|---|---|
| C409 | AP124 15g Spain #1139, 1838, C167, charity | 40.00 |
| C410 | AP124 15g Zeppelin, plane, satellites | 50.00 |

**Perf. 14½**

| | | |
|---|---|---|
| C411 | AP124 15g Jupiter | 22.50 |

Nos. C409-C411 face value was 15g plus 5g extra for a monument to Francisco Solano Lopez.

Size of stamps: No. C409, 45x55mm; C410, 55x45mm; C411, 32x22mm.

## Souvenir Sheets

Republica del Paraguay

**Anniversaries and Events — AP125**

#C413, UN emblem, Intl. Women's Year, vert. #C414, Helios space satellite.

**1975, Aug. 26    Perf. 13½**

| | | |
|---|---|---|
| C413 | AP125 15g multicolored | 15.00 |
| C414 | AP125 15g multicolored | 15.00 |

Nos. C413-C414 face value was 15g plus 5g extra for a monument to Francisco Solano Lopez.

**Anniversaries and Events — AP125a**

Designs: 4g, First Zeppelin flight, 75th anniv. 5g, Emblem of 1978 World Cup Soccer Championships, Argentina, vert. 10g, Emblem of Nordposta 75, statue.

**1975, Oct. 13    Litho.    Perf. 14**

| | | |
|---|---|---|
| C415-C417 | AP125a Set of 3 | 6.00 4.00 |

## Souvenir Sheets

**REPUBLICA DEL PARAGUAY**

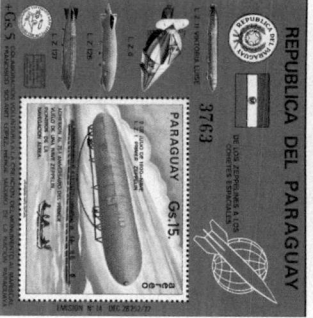

No. C418, Zeppelin, boats. No. C419, Soccer, Intelsat IV, vert. No. C420, Viking Mars landing.

**1975, Oct. 13    Perf. 13½**

| | | |
|---|---|---|
| C418 | AP126 15g multicolored | 20.00 |
| C419 | AP126 15g multicolored | 20.00 |
| C420 | AP126 15g multicolored | 20.00 |

Nos. C418-C420 face value was 15g plus 5g extra for a monument to Francisco Solano Lopez.

**Anniversaries and Events — AP126**

#C421: a, 4g, Lunar tower; b, 5g, Ford Elite, 1975; c, 10g, Ford, 1896. Nos. C422, Airplanes and spacecraft. No. C423, Arms of Paraguay & US.

### United States, Bicent. — AP127

**1975, Nov. 28    Litho.    Perf. 14**

| | | |
|---|---|---|
| C421 | AP127 Strip of 3, #a.-c. | 6.00 4.00 |

### Souvenir Sheets

**Perf. 13½**

| | | |
|---|---|---|
| C422 | AP127 15g multicolored | 27.50 |
| C423 | AP127 15g multicolored | 26.00 |

Nos. C422-C423 each contain one 60x50mm stamp and face value was 15g plus 20g with 5g surtax for a monument to Francisco Solano Lopez.

### Souvenir Sheet

La Musique by Francois Boucher — AP127a

Republica del Paraguay

**1975, Nov. 28    Perf. 13½**

| | | |
|---|---|---|
| C424 | AP127a 15g multicolored | 10.00 |

No. C424 face value was 15g plus 5g extra for a monument to Francisco Solano Lopez.

**Anniversaries and Events — AP128**

Designs: 4g, Flight of Concorde jet, 5g, JU 52/3M, Lufthansa Airlines, 50th anniv, 10g, EXFILMO '75 and ESPAMER '75. No. C428, Concorde, diff. No. C429, Dr. Albert Schweitzer, missionary and Konrad Adenauer, German statesman. No. C430, Porsche, auto designer, birth cent., vert.

**1975, Dec. 20    Perf. 14**

| | | |
|---|---|---|
| C425 | AP128 4g multicolored | |
| C426 | AP128 5g multicolored | |
| C427 | AP128 10g multicolored | |
| | Set, #C425-C427. | 6.00 4.00 |

### Souvenir Sheets

**Perf. 13½**

| | | |
|---|---|---|
| C428 | AP128 15g multicolored | 27.50 |
| C429 | AP128 15g multicolored | 15.00 |
| C430 | AP128 15g multicolored | 80.00 |

Nos. C428-C430 face value was 15g plus 5g extra for a monument to Francisco Solano Lopez. No. C428 contains one 54x34mm stamp, No. C429 one 60x50mm stamp, No. C430 one 30x40mm stamp.

**Anniversaries and Events — AP129**

Details: 4g, The Transfiguration by Raphael, vert. 5g, Nativity by Del Mayno. Detail from Adoration of the Shepherds by Ghirlandaio. No. C434, Detail from Adoration of... by Vignon. No. C435, Austria, 1000th anniv., Leopold I, natl. arms, vert. No. C436, Sepp Herberger and Helmut Schon, coaches for German soccer team.

**1976, Feb. 2    Litho.    Perf. 14**

| | | |
|---|---|---|
| C431 | AP129 4g multicolored | |
| C432 | AP129 5g multicolored | |
| C433 | AP129 10g multicolored | |
| | Set, #C431-C433. | 6.00 3.00 |

### Souvenir Sheets

**Perf. 13½**

| | | |
|---|---|---|
| C434 | AP129 15g multicolored | 5.00 |
| C435 | AP129 15g multicolored | 50.00 |

**Perf. 13½x13**

| | | |
|---|---|---|
| C436 | AP129 15g multicolored | 100.00 |

Nos. C434-C436 face value was 15g plus 5g extra for a monument to Francisco Solano Lopez. No. C434 contains one 40x30mm stamp, No. C435 one 30x40mm stamp, No. C436 one 54x34mm stamp.

### Souvenir Sheet

Apollo-Soyuz — AP130

**1976, Apr. 2    Perf. 13½x13**

| | | |
|---|---|---|
| C437 | AP130 25g multicolored | 22.50 |

### Souvenir Sheet

Lufthansa, 50th Anniv. — AP131

**1976, Apr. 7    Perf. 13½x13**

| | | |
|---|---|---|
| C438 | AP131 25g multicolored | 17.50 |

### Souvenir Sheet

Interphil 76 — AP132

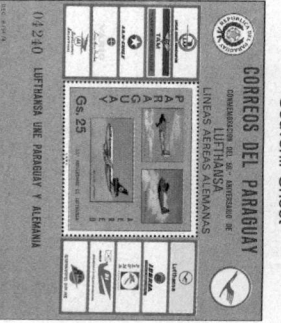

**1976, May 12    Perf. 13½**

| | | |
|---|---|---|
| C439 | AP132 15g multicolored | 12.00 |

No. C439 face value was 15g plus 5g extra for a monument to Francisco Solano Lopez.

## Souvenir Sheets

**REPUBLICA DEL PARAGUAY**

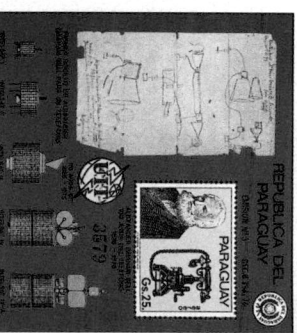

Designs: No. C440, Alexander Graham Bell, telephone cent. No. C441, Gold, silver and bronze medals, 1976 Winter Olympics, Innsbruck. No. C442, Gold medalist Rosi Mittermaier, downhill and slalom, vert. No. C443, Viking probe on Mars. No. C444, UN Postal Administration, 25th anniv. and UPU cent., vert. No. C445, Prof. Hermann Oberth, Wernher von Braun. No. C446, Madonna and Child by Durer, vert.

**Anniversaries and Events — AP133**

**1976    Perf. 13½**

| | | |
|---|---|---|
| C440 | AP133 25g multicolored | 40.00 |
| C441 | AP133 25g multicolored | 22.50 |
| C442 | AP133 25g multicolored | 175.00 |

**Perf. 14½**

| | | | |
|---|---|---|---|
| C443 | AP133 | 25g multicolored | 32.50 |
| C444 | AP133 | 25g multicolored | 35.00 |
| C445 | AP133 | 25g multicolored | 90.00 |
| C446 | AP133 | 25g multicolored | 70.00 |

No. C442 contains one 35x54mm stamp, No. C443 one 46x36mm stamp, No. C444 one 25x35mm stamp.
Issued: #C440-C441, 6/15; #C443, 7/8; #C442, C444, 7/15; #C445, 8/20; #C446, 9/9.

Souvenir Sheet

UN Offices in Geneva #22, UN #42 — AP136

**Perf. 13½**

1976, Dec. 18
C447 AP136 25g multicolored 17.50
UN Postal Administration, 26th anniv. and telephone, cent.

Souvenir Sheet

Ludwig van Beethoven (1770-1827) — AP137

**Perf. 14¼**

1977, Feb. 28 Litho.
C448 AP137 25g multi 6.00

Souvenir Sheet

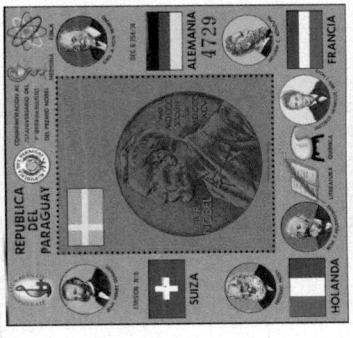

Alfred Nobel, 80th Death Anniv. and First Nobel Prize, 75th Anniv. — AP138

**Perf. 13½**

1977, June 7
C449 AP138 25g multicolored 27.50

Souvenir Sheet

Coronation of Queen Elizabeth II, 25th Anniv. — AP139

**Perf. 14½**

1977, July 25
C450 AP139 25g multicolored 30.00

Souvenir Sheet

URUGUAY '77 Intl. Philatelic Exhibition — AP140

**Perf. 13½**

1977, Aug. 27 Litho.
C451 AP140 25g multicolored 18.00

Souvenir Sheets

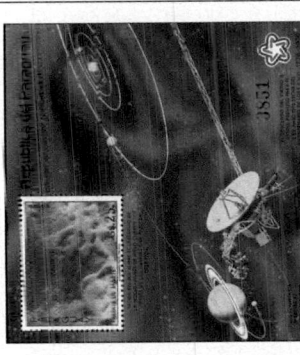

Exploration of Mars — AP141

**Perf. 13½**

1977, Sept. 5
C452 AP141 25g Martian craters 45.00

**Perf. 14¼x14½**

1977, Nov. 28
C453 AP141 25g Wernher von Braun 65.00

**Perf. 13½**

1977, Oct. 28 Litho.
C454 AP141 25g Projected Martian lander 80.00

Souvenir Sheet

Sepp Herberger, German Soccer Team Coach — AP142

**Perf. 13½**

1978, Jan. 23 Litho.
C455 AP142 25g multicolored 42.50

Souvenir Sheet

REPUBLICA DEL PARAGUAY
JUEGOS OLIMPICOS 1976-1980

Austria #B331, Canada #681, US #716, Russia #B66 — AP143

**Perf. 14½**

1978, Mar. 10 Litho.
C456 AP143 25g multicolored 30.00
Inner perforations are simulated.

Souvenir Sheet

Alfred Nobel — AP144

**Perf. 13½**

1978, Mar. 15 Litho.
C457 AP144 25g multicolored 42.50

Souvenir Sheets

Anniversaries and Events — AP145

Designs: No. C458, Queen Elizabeth II wearing St. Edward's Crown, holding orb and scepter. No. C459, Queen Elizabeth II presenting World Cup Trophy to English team captain. No. C460, Flags of nations participating in 1978 World Cup Soccer Championships. No. C461, Soccer action. No. C462, Argentina, 1978 World Cup Champions.

**1978**
**Perf. 14½, 13½ (#C461)**

| | | | |
|---|---|---|---|
| C458 | AP145 | 25g multicolored | 15.00 |
| C459 | AP145 | 25g multicolored | 30.00 |
| C460 | AP145 | 25g multicolored | 37.50 |
| C461 | AP145 | 25g multicolored | 30.00 |
| C462 | AP145 | 25g multicolored | 30.00 |

Coronation of Queen Elizabeth II, 25th Anniv. (#C458-C459). 1978 World Cup Soccer Championships, Argentina (#C460-C462).
No. C460 contains one 70x50mm stamp. No. C461 one 39x57mm stamp.
Issued: #C458, 5/11; #C459-C460, 5/16; #C461, 6/30; #C462, 10/26.

Souvenir Sheet

Jean-Henri Dunant, 150th Birth Anniv. — AP146

**Perf. 14½**

1978, June 28
C463 AP146 25g multicolored 27.50

Souvenir Sheet

Capt. James Cook, 250th Birth Anniv. — AP147

**Perf. 13½**

1978, July 19
C464 AP147 25g multicolored 20.00
Discovery of Hawaii. Death of Capt. Cook. bicentennial; Hawaii Statehood, 20th anniv.

Aregua Satellite Communication Station>AP148' — C465

Coat of Arms>

**Perf. 14** Litho.

1978, Aug. 15
C465 AP148 75g multi —
C466 AP148a 500g multi —
An additional stamp was issued in this set. The editors would like to examine any examples.

**1978, Oct. 31** Souvenir Sheet

Adoration of the Magi by Albrecht Durer — AP149

C468 AP149 25g multicolored **Perf. 13½**
10.00

**1978, Oct. 31** Souvenir Sheet

Prof. Hermann Oberth, 85th Birth Anniv. — AP150

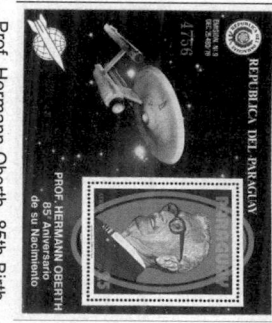

**1979, Aug. 28**
C469 AP150 25g multicolored **Perf. 13½**
25.00

World Cup Soccer Championships — AP151

Souvenir Sheet

**1979, Nov. 29**
C470 AP151 25g multicolored
32.50

Helicopters — AP152

Souvenir Sheet

**1979, Nov. 29** **Litho.** **Perf. 13½**
C471 AP152 25g multicolored
27.50

1980 Summer Olympics, Moscow — AP153

Souvenir Sheet

**1979, Dec. 20** **Perf. 14½**
C472 AP153 25g Two-man canoe
35.00

Republica del Paraguay

1982 World Cup Soccer Championships, Spain — AP154

Souvenir Sheet

**1979, Dec. 24** **Litho.** **Perf. 13x13½**
C473 AP154 25g Sheet of 1 + label
30.00

Maybach DS-8 "Zeppelin" — AP155

Wilhelm Maybach, 50th death anniv. Karl Maybach, 100th birth anniv.

Souvenir Sheet

**1980, Apr. 8**
C474 AP155 25g multicolored **Perf. 14½**
50.00

Rotary Intl., 75th Anniv. — AP156

Souvenir Sheet

**1980, July 1** **Litho.** **Perf. 14½**
C475 AP156 25g multicolored
22.50

Apollo 11 Type of 1970

Design: 1st steps on lunar surface.

Souvenir Sheet
**Size: 36x26mm**

**1980, July 30** **Perf. 13½**
C476 A221 25g multicolored
22.50

Virgin Surrounded by Animals by Albrecht Durer — AP158

Souvenir Sheet

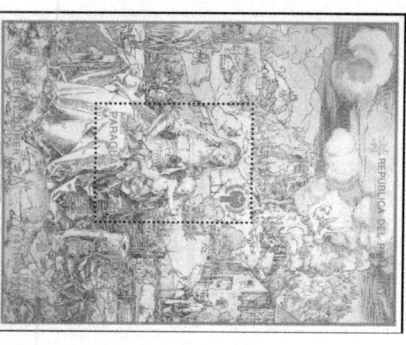

1980 Olympic Games — AP159

Souvenir Sheet

**1980, Dec. 15** **Litho.** **Perf. 14**
C478 AP159 25g multi
30.00

**1980, Sept. 24** **Photo. & Engr.** **Perf. 12**
C477 AP158 25g multicolored
175.00

Metropolitan Seminary Centenary — AP160

**1981, Mar. 26** **Litho.** **Wmk. 347**
C479 AP160 5g ultra .20 .20
C480 AP160 10g red brn .20 .20
C481 AP160 25g green .20 .20
C482 AP160 50g gray .40 .30
Nos. C479-C482 (4) 1.00 .90

Anniversaries and Events — AP161

Paintings: 5g, Queen with the Child by Stefan Lochner. 10g, Our Lady of Caacupe. 25g, Altar of the Virgin by Albrecht Durer. 30g, Virgin and Child by Matthias Grunewald.

5g, George Washington, 250th birth anniv. (in 1982). 10g, Queen Mother Elizabeth, 80th birthday (in 1980). 30g, Phila Tokyo '81, No. C486, Emperor Hirohito, 80th birthday, No. C487, Washington Crossing the Delaware.

**1981, July 10** **Unwmk.** **Perf. 14**
C483 AP161 5g multicolored
C484 AP161 10g multicolored
C485 AP161 25g multicolored
Set, #C483-C485 12.50 3.00

Souvenir Sheets **Perf. 14½**
C486 AP161 25g multicolored 10.00
C487 AP161 25g multicolored 27.50

For overprints see Nos. 2126, C590-C591, C611.

No. C484 issued in sheets of 8 plus a label.

Pres. Ronald Reagan and; 5g, Columbia in Earth orbit. 10g, Astronauts John Young and Robert Crippen. 30g, Columbia landing. George Washington and: No. C491, Columbia re-entering atmosphere. No. C492, Columbia inverted above Earth.

**1981, Oct. 9** **Perf. 13½**
C488 AP162 5g multicolored
C489 AP162 10g multicolored
C490 AP162 30g multicolored
Set, #C488-C490 18.00 5.00

Souvenir Sheets **Perf. 14**
C491 AP162 25g multicolored 22.50
C492 AP162 25g multicolored 22.50

Nos. C491-C492 each contain one 60x50mm stamp. Inauguration of Pres. Reagan, George Washington, 250th birth anniv. (in 1982) (#C491-C492).

World Cup Soccer, Spain, 1982 — AP163

**1981, Oct. 15 Color of Shirts** **Perf. 14**
C493 AP163 5g yellow, green
C494 AP163 10g blue, white
C495 AP163 30g white & black, orange
Set, #C493-C495 6.00 3.00

Souvenir Sheet **Perf. 14½**
C496 AP163 25g Goalie 21.00

No. C494 exists in sheets of 5 plus 4 labels.

Christmas AP164

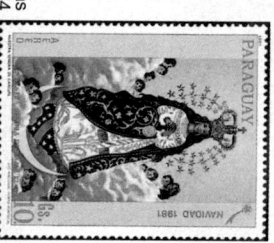

**1981, Dec. 21** **Perf. 14**
C497 AP164 5g multicolored
C498 AP164 10g multicolored
C499 AP164 30g multicolored
Set, #C497-C499 13.00 4.00

Souvenir Sheet **Perf. 13½**
C500 AP164 25g multicolored 20.00

No. C500 contains one 54x75mm stamp.

First Space Shuttle Mission — AP162

Graf Zeppelin's First Flight to South America, 50th Anniv. — AP165

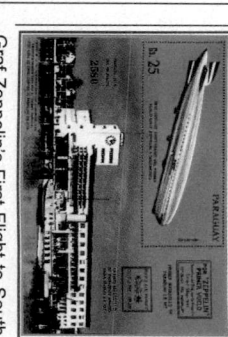

**1981, Dec. 28** **Perf. 14½**
C501 AP165 25g multicolored
30.00

PARAGUAY Gs.5

1984 Summer Olympics, Los Angeles AP174

**Perf. 14**

1932 Gold medalists: 5g, Wilson Charles, US, 100-meter dash. 10g, Ellen Preis, Austria, fencing. 25g, Rudolf Ismayr, Germany, weight lifting. 30g, John Anderson, US, discus.

**1983, June 13**

| | | | |
|---|---|---|---|
| C535 | AP174 | 5g multicolored | |
| C536 | AP174 | 10g multicolored | |
| C537 | AP174 | 30g multicolored | 4.00 2.00 |

Set, #C535-C537

**Souvenir Sheet**

**Perf. 14½**

C538 AP174 25g Sheet of 1 + label ... 25.00

No. C535 incorrectly credits Charles with gold medal.

PARAGUAY Gs.5

**Perf. 14**

Flowers AP175

**1983, Aug. 31**

| | | | |
|---|---|---|---|
| C539 | AP175 | 5g Epidend. | |
| C540 | AP175 | 10g Lilium | |
| C541 | AP175 | 30g Heliconia | 2.50 1.00 |

Set, #C539-C541

PARAGUAY Gs.5

Intl. Maritime Organization, 25th Anniv. — AP176

5g, Brigantine Undine. 10g, Training ship Sofia, 1881, horiz. 30g, Training ship Stein, 1879. No. C545, Santa Maria. No. C546, Santa Maria and Telstar communications satellite.

**Perf. 14, 13½x13 (10g)     Litho.**

**1983, Oct. 24**

| | | | |
|---|---|---|---|
| C542 | AP176 | 5g multicolored | |
| C543 | AP176 | 10g multicolored | |
| C544 | AP176 | 30g multicolored | 4.00 2.00 |

Set, #C542-C544

**Souvenir Sheets**

**Perf. 14½**

C545 AP176 25g multicolored ... 18.00

**Perf. 13½**

C546 AP176 25g multicolored ... 18.00

No. C546 contains one 90x57mm stamp. Discovery of America, 490th Anniv. (in 1982) (#C545-C546). For overprint see No. 2198.

---

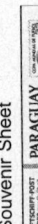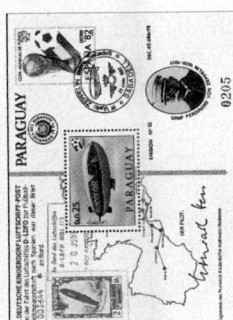

**Souvenir Sheet**

PARAGUAY

1982 World Cup Soccer Championships, Spain — AP171

**Perf. 13½**

**1983, Jan. 21**

C522 AP171 25g Fuji blimp ... 20.00

AEREO PARAGUAY Gs.5

German Rocket Scientists — AP172

**Perf. 14**

Designs: 5g, Dr. Walter R. Dornberger. V2 rocket ascending. 10g, Nebel, Ritter, Oberth, Riedel, and Von Braun examining rocket mock-up. 30g, Dr. A. F. Staats, Cyrus B research rocket.

No. C526, Dr. Eugen Sanger, rocket design. No. C527, Fritz Von Opel, Opel-Sander rocket plane. No. C528, Friedrich Schmiedl, first rocket used for mail delivery.

**1983**

| | | | |
|---|---|---|---|
| C523 | AP172 | 6g multicolored | |
| C524 | AP172 | 10g multicolored | |
| C525 | AP172 | 30g multicolored | 8.00 3.00 |

Set, #C523-C525

**Souvenir Sheets**

**Perf. 14½**

| | | | |
|---|---|---|---|
| C526 | AP172 | 25g multicolored | |
| C527 | AP172 | 25g multicolored | 40.00 |
| C528 | AP172 | 25g multicolored | 65.00 |

Issued: No. C528, Apr. 13; others, Jan. 24.

PARAGUAY Gs.5

First Manned Flight, 200th Anniv. AP173

Balloons: 5g, Montgolfier brothers, 1783. 10g, Baron von Lutgendorf's, 1786. 30g, Adorne's, 1784. No. C532, Montgolfier brothers, diff. No. C533, Profiles of Montgolfier Brothers. No. C534, Bicentennial emblem, nova.

**Perf. 14, 13 (10g)**

**1983**

| | | | |
|---|---|---|---|
| C529 | AP173 | 5g multicolored | |
| C530 | AP173 | 10g multicolored | |
| C531 | AP173 | 30g multicolored | 8.00 2.00 |

Set, #C529-C531

**Souvenir Sheets**

**Perf. 13½**

| | | | |
|---|---|---|---|
| C532 | AP173 | 25g multicolored | 10.50 |
| C533 | AP173 | 25g multicolored | 10.50 |
| C534 | AP173 | 25g multicolored | 26.00 |

Nos. C532-C533 each contain one 50x60mm stamp, No. C534 one 30x40mm stamp.

---

PARAGUAY Gs.5

Italy, Winners of 1982 World Cup Soccer Championships — AP168

**Perf. 14**

Players: 5g, Klaus Fischer, Germany. 10g, Altobelli holding World Cup Trophy. 25g, Forster, Altobelli, horiz. 30g, Fischer, Gordillo.

**1982, Oct. 20**

| | | | |
|---|---|---|---|
| C511 | AP168 | 5g multicolored | |
| C512 | AP168 | 10g multicolored | |
| C513 | AP168 | 30g multicolored | 8.00 4.00 |

Set, #C511-C513

**Souvenir Sheet**

**Perf. 14½**

C513A AP168 25g multicolored ... 17.00

Christmas — AP169

Paintings by Peter Paul Rubens: 5g, The Nativity. 10g, The Massacre of the Innocents. 25g, The Madonna Adored by Four Penitents and Saints. 20g, The Flight to Egypt.

**Perf. 14**

**1982, Oct. 23**

| | | | |
|---|---|---|---|
| C514 | AP169 | 5g multicolored | |
| C515 | AP169 | 10g multicolored | |
| C516 | AP169 | 30g multicolored | 7.00 2.00 |

Set, #C514-C516

**Souvenir Sheet**

**Perf. 14½**

C517 AP169 25g multicolored ... 1.50

No. C517 contains one 50x70mm stamp.

The Sampling Officials of the Draper's Guild by Rembrandt — AP170

Details from Rembrandt Paintings: 10g, Self portrait, vert. 25g, Night Watch, vert. 30g, Self portrait, diff., vert.

**Perf. 14, 13 (10g)**

**1983, Jan. 21**

| | | | |
|---|---|---|---|
| C518 | AP170 | 5g multicolored | |
| C519 | AP170 | 10g multicolored | |
| C520 | AP170 | 30g multicolored | 7.00 2.00 |

Set, #C518-C520

**Souvenir Sheet**

**Perf. 13½**

C521 AP170 25g multicolored ... 15.00

No. C521 contains one 50x60mm stamp.

---

Mother Maria Mazzarello (1837-1881), Co-Founder of Daughters of Mary AP166

**Perf. 13x13½     Wmk. 347**

**1981, Dec. 30     Litho.**

| | | | |
|---|---|---|---|
| C502 | AP166 | 20g blk & grn | .20 .20 |
| C503 | AP166 | 25g blk & red brn | .20 .20 |
| C504 | AP166 | 50g blk & gray vio | .80 .70 |

Nos. C502-C504 (3)

**Souvenir Sheet**

The Magus (Dr. Faust) by Rembrandt — AP167

**Litho. & Typo.**

**Perf. 14½     Unwmk.**

**1982, Apr. 23**

C505 AP167 25g blk, buff & gold ... 25.00

Johann Wolfgang von Goethe, 160th death anniv.

The following stamps were issued 4 each in sheets of 8 with 1 label: Nos. C590-C591, C669-C670, C677-C678, C682-C683, C690-C691, C699-C700, C718-C719, C747-C748.

The following stamps were issued in sheets of 4 with 5 labels: Nos. C765-C766, C774, C779-C780, C785, C803, C813, C818, C823.

The following stamps were issued in sheets of 3 with 6 labels: Nos. C739, C754.

The following stamps were issued in sheets of 5 with 4 labels: Nos. C507, C512, C515, C519, C524, C529, C535, C539, C542, C548, C550, C559, C569, C572, C579, C582, C585, C588, C596, C598, C615, C622, C626, C634, C642, C647, C650, C656, C705, C711, C731, C791, C798, C808.

The following stamp was issued in sheets of 7 with 2 labels: No. C660.

**World Chess Championships Type of 1980**

Illustrations from "The Book of Chess": 5g, The Game of the Virgins. 10g, Two gothic ladies. 30g, Chess game at apothecary shop. No. C509, Christians and Jews preparing to play in garden. No. C510, Indian prince introducing chess to Persia.

**Perf. 13½     Litho.**

**1982, June 10**

| | | | |
|---|---|---|---|
| C506 | A347 | 5g multicolored | |
| C507 | A347 | 10g multicolored | |
| C508 | A347 | 30g multicolored | 8.00 4.00 |

Set, #C506-C508

**Souvenir Sheets**

**Perf. 13½**

C509 A347 25g multicolored ... 15.00

**Perf. 14½**

C510 A347 25g multicolored ... 15.00

No. C509 contains one 50x60mm stamp, No. C510 50x70mm stamp. For overprint see No. C665.

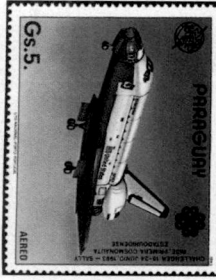

## Space Achievements — AP177

Designs: 5g, Space shuttle Challenger. 10g, Pioneer 10, vert. 30g, Herschel's telescope, Cerro Tololo Observatory, Chile, vert.

**1984, Jan. 9** — **Perf. 14**
C547 AP177 5g multicolored
C548 AP177 10g multicolored
C549 AP177 30g multicolored
Set, #C547-C549          7.00 2.00

### Summer Olympics, Los Angeles AP178

**1984, Jan.** — **Perf. 14**
5g, 400-meter hurdles. 10g, Small bore rifle, horiz. 25g, Equestrian, Christine Stuckleberger. 30g, 100-meter dash.
C550 AP178 5g multicolored
C551 AP178 10g multicolored
C552 AP178 30g multicolored
Set, #C550-C552          6.00 2.00

**Souvenir Sheet** — **Perf. 14½**
C553 AP178 25g multicolored          35.00
For overprint see No. 2130.

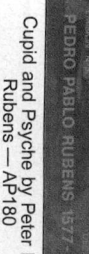

### 1984 Winter Olympics, Sarajevo AP179

**1984, Mar. 24** — **Perf. 14, 13x13½ (10g)**
C554 AP179 5g Steve Podborski, downhill
C555 AP179 10g Olympic Flag
C556 AP179 30g Gaetan Boucher, speed skating
Set, #C554-C556          5.00 2.00
No. C555 printed se-tenant with label.

## Cupid and Psyche by Peter Paul Rubens — AP180

Design: No. C558, Satyr and Maenad (copy of Rubens' Bacchanal) by Jean-Antoine Watteau (1684-1721).

**1984, Mar. 26** — **Perf. 13½**
C557 AP180 25g multicolored          17.00 17.00
C558 AP180 25g multicolored          17.00 17.00
No. C558 contains one 78x57mm stamp.

### 1982, 1986 World Cup Soccer Championships, Spain, Mexico City — AP181

Soccer players: 5g, Tardelli, Breitner. 10g, Zamora, Stielike. 30g, Walter Schachner, player on ground.
No. C562, Player from Paraguay. No. C563, World Cup Trophy. Player from Paraguay, Spanish, Mexican characters, horiz.

**1984, Mar. 29** — **Perf. 14, 13 (10g)**
C559 AP181 5g multicolored
C560 AP181 10g multicolored
C561 AP181 30g multicolored
Set, #C559-C561          5.00 2.00

**Souvenir Sheets** — **Perf. 14½**
C562 AP181 25g multicolored          20.00
C563 AP181 25g multicolored          20.00

### ESPANA '84 — AP182

**1984, Mar. 31**
C564 AP182 25g multicolored          14.00 14.00
No. C564 has one stamp and a label.

## Souvenir Sheets

### ESPANA '84 — AP183

No. C565, Holy Family of the Lamb by Raphael. No. C566, Adoration of the Magi by Rubens.

**1984, Apr. 16** — **Perf. 13½**
C565 AP183 25g multicolored          21.00 21.00
C566 AP183 25g multicolored          21.00 21.00

### 19th UPU Congress — AP184

**1984, June 9**
C567 AP184 25g multicolored          7.50 7.50

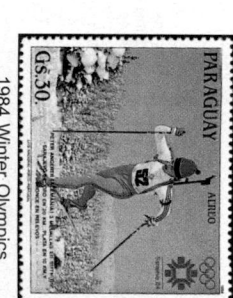

### Int'l. Chess Federation, 60th Anniv. — AP185

**1984, June 18** — **Perf. 14, 13x13½ (10g)**
C568 AP185 5g shown
C569 AP185 10g Woman holding chess piece
C570 AP185 30g Bishop, knight
Set, #C568-C570          9.00 4.00

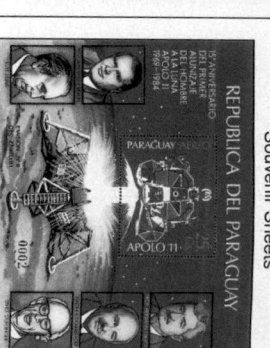

### First Europe to South America Airmail Flight by Lufthansa, 50th Anniv. — AP186

## Souvenir Sheets

### First Moon Landing, 15th Anniv. — AP187

**1984, June 23** — **Perf. 14½**
C574 AP187 25g Apollo 11 lunar module          45.00 45.00
C575 AP187 25g Prof. Hermann Oberth          45.00 45.00
Hermann Oberth, 90th Birthday (#C575).

**1984, June 22** — **Perf. 14, 13½x13 (10g)**
Designs: 5g, Lockheed Superconstellation. 10g, Dornier Wal. 30g, Boeing 707.
C571 AP186 5g multicolored
C572 AP186 10g multicolored
C573 AP186 30g multicolored
Set, #C571-C573          5.00 2.00
For overprint see No. C592.

## The Holy Family with John the Baptist — AP188

No. 2099 Overprinted in Red: ANIVERSARIO GOBIERNO CONSTRUCTIVO Y DE LA PAZ DEL PRESIDENTE CONSTITUCIONAL GRAL. DE EJERCITO ALFREDO STROESSNER 15 / 8 / 1964

**1984, Aug. 3** — **Photo. & Engr.** — **Perf. 14**
C576 AP188 20g multicolored          65.00 65.00
Raphael, 500th birth anniv. (in 1983).

**1984, Aug. 15** — **Perf. 13**
C577 A374 100g on No. 2099          1.50 1.50

### 1984 Winter Olympics, Sarajevo — AP189

Gold medalists: 10g, Max Julen, giant slalom, Switzerland. 10g, Hans Stanggassinger, Franz Wembacher, luge, West Germany. 30g, Peter Angerer, biathlon, Germany.

PARAGUAY

**Jean-Henri Dunant, Founder of Red Cross, 75th Death Anniv. — AP198**

Dunant and: 5g, Enclosed ambulance. 10g, Nobel Peace Prize. Red Cross emblem. 30g, Open ambulance with passengers.

1985, Aug. 6    *Perf. 13*
C614 AP198 5g multicolored
C615 AP198 10g multicolored
C616 AP198 30g multicolored
Set, #C614-C616    20.00 5.00

**World Chess Congress, Austria — AP199**

5g, The Turk, copper engraving, Book of Chess by Racknitz, 1789. 10g, King seated, playing chess. Book of Chess, 14th cent. 25g, Margrave Otto von Brandenburg playing chess with his wife, Great Manuscript of Heidelberg Songs, 13th cent. 30g, Three men playing chess, Book of Chess, 14th cent.

1985, Aug. 9    *Litho.*    *Perf. 13*
C617 AP199 5g multicolored
C618 AP199 10g multicolored
C619 AP199 30g multicolored
Sol, II/C617 C610    11.00 4.00

**Souvenir Sheet**    *Perf. 13½*
C620 AP199 25g multicolored    30.00 30.00
No. C620 contains one 60x50mm stamp.

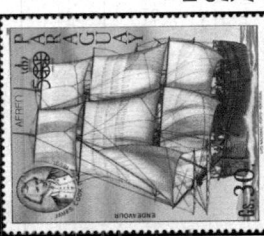

**Discovery of America 500th Anniv. AP200**

Explorers, ships: 5g, Marco Polo and ship. 10g, Vicente Yanez Pinzon, Nina, horiz. 25g, Christopher Columbus, Santa Maria. 30g, James Cook, Endeavor.

1985, Oct. 19    *Perf. 14, 13½x13 (10g)*    *Litho.*
C621 AP200 5g multicolored
C622 AP200 10g multicolored
C623 AP200 30g multicolored
Set, #C621-C623    5.00 3.00

**Souvenir Sheet**    *Perf. 14½*
C624 AP200 25g multicolored    17.00 17.00
Year of Cook's death is incorrect on No. C623. For overprint see No. C756.

---

**Souvenir Sheet**

**Visit of Pope John Paul II to South America — AP196**

1985, Apr. 22    *Litho.*    *Perf. 13½*
C603 AP196 25g silver & multi    17.00 17.00
No. C603 also exists with gold inscriptions.

**Inter-American Development Bank, 25th Anniv. — AP197**

1985, Apr. 25    *Litho.*    *Wmk. 347*
C604 AP197 3g dl red brn, org & yel    20   20
C605 AP197 5g vio, org & yel    20   20
C606 AP197 10g rose vio, org & yel    20   20
C607 AP197 50g sep, org & yel    20   20
C608 AP197 65g bl, org & yel    20   20
C609 AP197 95g pale bl grn, org & yel    1.20 1.20
Nos. C604-C609 (6)

No. 1875 Ovptd. in Black in Margin "V EXPOSICION MUNDIAL / ARGENTINA 85" and

1985, May 24    *Unwmk.*    *Perf. 13½*
C610 A326 25g on No. 1875    12.00 12.00

No. C485 Ovptd. in Dark Blue with Emblem and:
"Expo '85/TSUKUBA"

1985, July 5    *Perf. 14*
C611 AP161 30g on No. C485    3.00 1.50

No. 2149 Ovptd. in Dark Blue in Margin with UN emblem and "26.6.1985 — 40-ANIVERSARIO DE LA / FUNDACION DE LAS NACIONES UNIDAS"

1985, Aug. 5    *Perf. 14½*
C612 A388 25g on No. 2149    17.50 17.00

---

No. C572 Ovptd. in Vermilion

1985, Feb. 16    *Perf. 13½x13*
C592 AP186 10g on No. C572    4.00 2.00

No. 2053A Ovptd. "FINAL / ALEMANIA 1 : 3 ITALIA"

1985, Mar. 7    *Perf. 14½*
C593 A362 25g multicolored    17.00 17.00

**Souvenir Sheets**

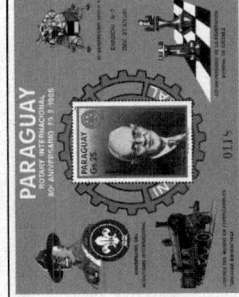

**Rotary Intl., 80th Anniv. — AP193**

Designs: No. C594, Paul Harris, founder of Rotary Intl. No. C595, Rotary Intl. Headquarters, Evanston, IL, horiz.

1985, Mar. 11
C594 AP193 25g multicolored    40.00
C595 AP193 25g multicolored    70.00

No. C579 Ovptd. "OLYMPHILEX 85" in Black and Olympic Rings in Silver

1985, Mar. 18    *Perf. 13½x13*
C596 AP189 10g on No. C579    3.00 1.50

**Music Year — AP194**

Designs: 5g, Agustin Barrios (1885-1944), musician, vert. 10g, Johann Sebastian Bach, composer, score. 30g, Folk musicians.

1985, Apr. 16    *Perf. 14, 13½x13 (10g)*
C597 AP194 5g multicolored
C598 AP194 10g multicolored
C599 AP194 30g multicolored
Set, #C597-C599    4.00 2.00

**1st Paraguayan Locomotive, 1861 — AP195**

1985, Apr. 20    *Perf. 14*
C600 AP195 5g shown
C601 AP195 10g Transrapid 06, Germany
C602 AP195 30g TGV, France
Set, #C600-C602    15.00 5.00

---

**Motorcycles, Cent. — AP190**

1984, Nov. 9    *Perf. 14, 13½x13 (10g)*
C581 AP190 5g Reitwagen, Daimler-Maybach, 1885
C582 AP190 10g BMW, 1980
C583 AP190 30g Opel, 1930
Set, #C581-C583    5.00 2.00

**Christmas AP191**

1985, Jan. 18    *Perf. 13*
C584 AP191 5g shown
C585 AP191 10g Girl playing guitar
C586 AP191 30g Girl, candle, basket
Set, #C584-C586    4.00 2.00

No. C484 Ovptd. in Silver

1985, Feb. 6    *Perf. 14*
C590 AP161 10g INTERPEX / 1985    1.50 .75
C591 AP161 10g STAMPEX / 1985    1.50 .75

**1986 World Cup Soccer Championships, Mexico — AP192**

Various soccer players.

1985, Jan. 21    *Perf. 13x13½, 13½x13*

**Color of Shirt**
C587 AP192 5g red & white
C588 AP192 10g white & black, horiz.
C589 AP192 30g blue
Set, #C587-C589    4.00 2.00

## ITALIA '85 — AP201

Nudes (details): 5g, La Fortuna, by Guido Reni, vert. 10g, The Triumph of Galatea, by Raphael. 25g, The Birth of Venus, by Botticelli, vert. 30g, Sleeping Venus, by Il Giorgione.

**1985, Dec. 3**    **Perf. 14**
C625 AP201 5g multicolored
C626 AP201 10g multicolored
C627 AP201 30g multicolored
Set, #C625-C627

**Souvenir Sheet**    **Perf. 13½**
C628 AP201 25g multicolored    45.00 42.50
No. C628 contains one 49x60mm stamp.    10.00 3.00

## Maimonides, Philosopher, 850th Birth Anniv. — AP202

**1985, Dec. 31**    **Perf. 13½**
C629 AP202 25g multicolored    25.00 25.00

## UN, 40th Anniv. AP203

**1986, Feb. 27**    **Wmk. 392**
C630 AP203 5g bl & sepia    .20  .20
C631 AP203 10g bl & gray    .20  .20
C632 AP203 50g bl & grysh brn    .60  .60
Set, #C630-C632 (3)
For overprint see No. C726.

## AMERIPEX '86 AP204

Discovery of America 500th anniv. emblem and: 5g, Spain #424, 10g, US #233, 25g, Spain #426, horiz. 30g, Spain #421.

**1986, Mar. 19**    **Perf. 14, 13½x13 (10g)**    **Unwmk.**
C633 AP204 5g multicolored
C634 AP204 10g multicolored
C635 AP204 30g multicolored

---

**Souvenir Sheet**    **Perf. 13½**
C636 AP204 25g multicolored
No. C636 contains one 60x40mm stamp.
For overprint see No. C755.

## 1984 Olympic Gold Medalist, Dr. Reiner Klimke on Ahlerich — AP205

**1986, Mar. 20**    **Perf. 14½**
C637 AP205 25g multicolored    22.50 22.50

## Tennis Players AP206

Designs: 5g, Martina Navratilova, US. 10g, Boris Becker, W. Germany. 30g, Victor Pecci, Paraguay.

**1986, Mar. 26**    **Perf. 14, 13 (10g)**
C638 AP206 5g multicolored
C639 AP206 10g multicolored
C640 AP206 30g multicolored
Set, #C638-C640    9.00 5.00
Nos. C638-C640 exist with red inscriptions, perf. 13. For overprints see Nos. C672-C673.

## Halley's Comet — AP207

Designs: 5g, Bayeux Tapestry, c. 1066, showing comet. 10g, Edmond Halley, comet. 25g, Giotto probe. 30g, Rocket lifting off. Giotto probe, vert.

**1986, Apr. 30**    **Perf. 14, 13½x13 (10g)**
C641 AP207 5g multicolored
C642 AP207 10g multicolored
C643 AP207 30g multicolored
Set, #C641-C643    12.00 4.00

**Souvenir Sheet**    **Perf. 14½**
C644 AP207 25g multicolored    25.00 25.00

---

## Madonna by Albrecht Durer — AP208

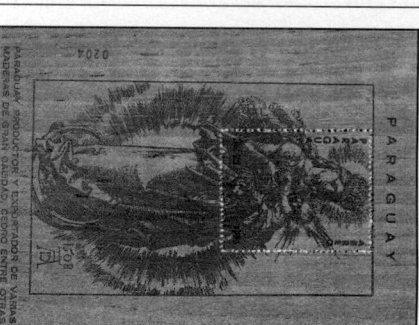

**1986, June 4**    **Typo.**    **Rough Perf. 11**    **Self-Adhesive**
C645 AP208 25g black & red    25.00 25.00
No. C645 was printed on cedar.

## Locomotives — AP209

**1986, June 23**    **Litho.**    **Perf. 13**
C646 AP209 5g #3038
C647 AP209 10g Canadian Pacific A1E, 1887
C648 AP209 30g 1D1 #483, 1925
Set, #C646-C648    6.00 3.00

## 1986 World Cup Soccer Championships — AP210

Paraguay vs.: 5g, Colombia. 10g, Chile. 30g, Chile, diff. Paraguay Natl. team.

**1986, June 24**    **Perf. 13, 13½x13 (10g)**
C649 AP210 5g multicolored
C650 AP210 10g multicolored
C651 AP210 30g multicolored
Set, #C649-C657    6.00 3.00

**Souvenir Sheet**    **Perf. 14½**
C652 AP210 25g multicolored    13.00 13.00
No. C652 contains one 81x75mm stamp.
For overprints see Nos. C693-C695.

**1986, July 11**    **Perf. 13½**
C653 A226 23.40g on No. 1289    13.00 13.00
No. 1289 Ovptd. in Silver on Dark Blue with Mercury Capsule and "MERCURY / 5-V-1961 / 25 Anos Primer / Astronauta / Americano / Alan B. Shepard / 1986"

---

## Trajectory Diagram of Halley's Comet, Giotto Probe — AP211

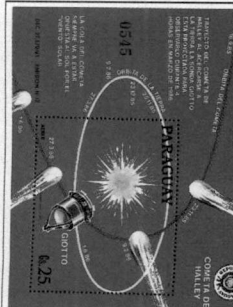

**1986, July 28**    **Souvenir Sheet**
C654 AP211 25g multicolored    20.00

## German Railroads, 150th Anniv. — AP212

25g, Christening of the 1st German Train, 1835, by E. Shilling & B. Goldschmidt.

**1986, Sept. 1**    **Perf. 13½x13**
C655 AP212 5g VT 10 501DB, 1954
C656 AP212 10g 1st Electric, 1879
C657 AP212 30g Hydraulic diesel, class 218
Set, #C655-C657    10.00 3.00

**Souvenir Sheet**    **Perf. 13½**
C658 AP212 25g multicolored    18.00 18.00
No. C658 contains one 54x75mm stamp.

## Intl. Peace Year AP213

Details from The Consequences of War, by Rubens: 5g, Two women. 10g, Woman nursing child. 30g, Two men.

**1986, Oct. 27**    **Perf. 13**
C659 AP213 5g multicolored
C660 AP213 10g multicolored
C661 AP213 30g multicolored
Set, #C659-C667    10.00 5.00

## Japanese Emigrants in Paraguay, 50th Anniv. — AP214

**1986, Nov. 6**    **Perf. 13½x13, 13x13½**
C662 AP214 5g La Colemna Vineyard    .20 .20
C663 AP214 10g Cherry, lapacho flowers    .20 .20

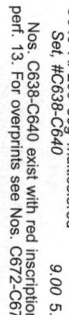

## Souvenir Sheet

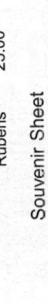

Christmas — AP221

**1988, Jan. 4**    **Perf. 13½**
C713 AP221 100g Madonna, by Rubens   25.00

## Souvenir Sheet

1988 Summer Olympics, Seoul — AP222

**1988, Jan. 18**    **Perf. 14½**
C714 AP222 100g gold & multi   14.00

Exists with silver lettering and frame.

5g, NASA-ESA space station. 10g, Eurospace module Columbus docked at space station. 20g, NASA space sation. 25g, Ring section of space station, vert. 30g, Space station living quarters in central core, vert.

Colonization of Space — AP223

**1988, Mar. 9**   **Litho.**   **Perf. 13½x13**
C715 AP223 5g multicolored
C716 AP223 10g multicolored
C717 AP223 20g multicolored
  **Perf. 13x13½**
C718 AP223 25g multicolored
C719 AP223 30g multicolored
*Set, #C715-C719*   17.00 7.00

---

20g, Judith with the Head of Holofernes, 1617. 25g, Assembly of the Gods of Olympus. 30g, Venus, Cupid, Bacchus and Ceres.

**1987, Dec. 14**    **Perf. 13**
C696 AP218 5g multicolored
C697 AP218 10g multicolored
C698 AP218 20g multicolored
  **Perf. 13x13½**
C699 AP218 25g multicolored
C700 AP218 30g multicolored
*Set, #C696-C700*   12.00 6.00

Christmas AP219

Details from paintings: 5g, Virgin and Child with St. Joseph and St. John the Baptist, anonymous. 10g, Madonna and Child under the Veil with St. Joseph and St. John, by Marco da Siena. 20g, Sacred Conversation with the Donors, by Titian. 25g, The Brotherhood of the Rosary, by Durer. 30g, Madonna with Standing Child, by Rubens. 100g, Madonna and Child, engraving by Albrecht Durer.

**1987**   **Litho.**   **Perf. 14**
C701 AP219 5g multicolored
C702 AP219 10g multicolored
C703 AP219 20g multicolored
C704 AP219 25g multicolored
  **Perf. 13x13½**
C705 AP219 30g multicolored   7.00 3.50
*Set, #C701-C705.*
**Souvenir Sheet**
  **Perf. 14½**
C706 AP219 100g multi   30.00 25.00
Issued: #C701-C705, 12/16; #C706, 12/17.

Locomotives: 5g, Steam #3669, 1899. 10g, Steam #GZ 44074. 20g, Steam, diff. 25g, Diesel-electric. 30g, Austria No. 1067.

Austrian Railways, Sesquicentennial — AP220

**1988, Jan. 2**    **Perf. 14**
C707 AP220 5g multicolored
C708 AP220 10g multicolored
C709 AP220 20g multicolored
C710 AP220 25g multicolored
  **Perf. 13½x13**
C711 AP220 30g multicolored   10.00 5.00
*Set, #C707-C711*
**Souvenir Sheet**
  **Perf. 13½**
C712 AP220 100g multicolored   30.00
No. C712 contains one 50x60mm stamp.

---

Gold medalists or Olympic competitors: 5g, Michela Figini, Switzerland, downhill, 1984, vert. 10g, Hanni Wenzel, Liechtenstein, slalom and giant slalom, 1980. 20g, 4-Man bobsled, Switzerland, 1956, 1972. 25g, Markus Wasmeier, downhill. 30g, Ingemar Stenmark, Sweden, slalom and giant slalom, 1980. 100g, Pirmin Zurbriggen, Switzerland, vert. (downhill, 1988).

**1987, Sept. 10**    **Perf. 14**
C679 AP216 5g multicolored
C680 AP216 10g multicolored
C681 AP216 20g multicolored
  **Perf. 13½x13**
C682 AP216 25g multicolored
C683 AP216 30g multicolored   11.00 5.00
**Souvenir Sheet**
  **Perf. 13½**
C684 AP216 100g multicolored   14.00 14.00
No. C684 contains one 45x57mm stamp.

Nos. 2211 and C467 Ovptd. in Red on Silver "11.IX.1887 - 1987 / Centenario de la fundación de / la A.N.R. (Partido Colorado) / Bernardino Caballero Fundador / General de Ejercito / D. Alfredo Stroessner Continuador"

**1987, Sept. 11**    **Perf. 13, 14**
C685 A401 200g on No. 2211   4.00 4.00
C686 AP148 1000g on No. C467
*Set, #C685-C686*

1988 Summer Olympics, Seoul — AP217

Medalists and competitors: 5g, Sabine Everts, West Germany, javelin. 10g, Carl Lewis, US, 100 and 200-meter run. 20g, Darrell Pace, US, archery, 1976, 1984. 25g, Juergen Hingsen, West Germany, decathalon, 1984. 30g, Claudia Losch, West Germany, shot put, 1984. 100g, Fredy Schmidtke, West Germany, cycling, 1984.

**1987, Sept. 22**    **Perf. 14**
C687 AP217 5g multi
C688 AP217 10g multi
C689 AP217 20g multi
  **Perf. 13½x13**
C690 AP217 25g multi, vert.
C691 AP217 30g multi, vert.   8.00 4.00
*Set, #C687-C691*
**Souvenir Sheet**
  **Perf. 14½**
C692 AP217 100g multi, vert.   13.00 13.00

Nos. C650-C652 Ovptd. in Violet or Blue (#C694) with Soccer Ball and "ZURICH 10.VI.87 / Lanzamiento ITALIA '90 / Italia 3 - Argentina 1"

**1987, Oct. 19**   **Litho.**
C693 AP210 10g on No. C650
C694 AP210 30g on No. C651   5.00 5.00
*Set, #C693-C694*
**Souvenir Sheet**
  **Perf. 14½**
C695 AP210 25g on No. C652   15.00 15.00

Paintings by Rubens AP218

Details from: 5g, The Virtuous Hero Crowned. 10g, The Brazen Serpent, 1635.

---

C664 AP214 20g Integration monument, vert.   .20 .20
   .60 .60

No. C507 Ovptd. in Silver "XXVII-DUBAI / Olimpiada de / Ajedrez - 1986"

**1986, Dec. 30**   **Unwmk.**   **Perf. 14**
C665 A347 10g on No. C507   6.00 2.00

1986 World Cup Soccer Championships, Mexico — AP214a

Match scenes.

**1987, Feb. 19**    **Perf. 14**
C666 AP214a 5g England vs. Paraguay
C667 AP214a 10g Larios catching ball
C668 AP214a 20g Trejo, Ferreira
  **Perf. 13½x13**
C669 AP214a 25g Torales, Flores, Romero
C670 AP214a 30g Mendonza   11.00 6.00
**Souvenir Sheet**
  **Perf. 14½**
C671 AP214a 100g Romero   13.00 13.00
Nos. C669-C670 are horiz. No. C671 contains one 40x50mm stamp.

Nos. C639-C640 Ovptd. in Silver including Olympic Rings and "NUEVAMENTE EL / TENIS EN LAS / OLYMPIADAS 1988 / SEOUL COREA"

**1987, Apr. 15**    **Perf. 13**
C672 AP206 10g on No. C639
C673 AP206 30g on No. C640

Automobiles — AP215   **Litho.**   **Perf. 13½**

**1987, May 29**
C674 AP215 5g Mercedes 300 SEL 6.3
C675 AP215 10g Jaguar Mk II 3.8
C676 AP215 20g BMW 635 CSI
C677 AP215 25g Alfa Romeo GTA
C678 AP215 30g BMW 1800 Tisa
*Set, #C674-C678*   11.00 5.00

1988 Winter Olympics, Calgary—AP216

**Souvenir Sheet**

**1988, Mar. 10    Litho.    Perf. 14½**
C720 AP224 100g multicolored    25.00

Berlin, 750th Anniv. — AP224

LUPOSTA '87.

**1988, June 15    Wmk. 392**
C726 AP203 10g blue & gray    .20 .20

Paraguay Philatelic Center, 75th Anniv.

**Berlin, 750th Anniv. Paintings Type of 1988**

5g, Venus and Cupid, 1742, by Francois Boucher. 10g, Perseus Liberates Andromeda, 1662, by Rubens. 20g, Venus and the Organist by Titian. 25g, Leda and the Swan by Correggio. 30g, St. Cecilia by Rubens.

**1988, June 15    Unwmk.    Perf. 13**
C727 A409 5g multi, horiz.
C728 A409 10g multi, horiz.
C729 A409 20g multi, horiz.
C730 A409 25g multi, horiz.
C731 A409 30g multicolored
Set, #C727-C731    7.00 4.00

Founding of "New Germany" and 1st Cultivation of Herbal Tea, Cent. — AP227

**1988, June 18    Wmk. 347**
**Litho.    Perf. 13x13½, 13½x13**
C732 AP227 90g Cauldron, vert.    .40 .30
C733 AP227 105g Farm workers carrying crop    .50 .35
C734 AP227 120g like 105g    .55 .45
Nos. C732-C734 (3)    1.45 1.10

**Perf. 13½**
**1988, Aug. 5    Wmk. 347**
**Litho.    Perf. 13½**
C741 AP230 200g multi    .40 .30
C742 AP230 500g multi    1.00 1.00
C743 AP230 1000g multi    2.00 2.00
Nos. C741-C743 (3)    3.40 3.30

Pres. Stroessner's new term in office. 1988-1993. Size of letters in watermark on 200g, 5mm. On 500g, 10mm.

Government Palace and Pres. Stroessner — AP230

**1988, Apr. 12**
C721 AP225 100g multicolored    25.00

Apollo 15 Launch, 1971 — AP225

No. 2210 Ovptd. in Metallic Red with

**1988, Apr. 28    Perf. 13**
C722 A401 100g on No. 2210    2.00 2.00

Caacupe Basilica and Pope John Paul II — AP226

**1988, May 5    Perf. 13½x13**
**Litho.    Wmk. 347**
C723 AP226 100g multi    .45 .35
C724 AP226 120g multi    .55 .40
C725 AP226 150g multi    .70 .50
Nos. C723-C725 (3)    1.70 1.25

Visit of Pope John Paul II.

No. C631 Overprinted

75° ANIVERSARIO DE FUNDACION CENTRO FILATELICO DEL PARAGUAY 15 JUNIO-1913-1988

---

**1988, Aug. 3    Perf. 14½**
C740 AP229 100g multicolored    25.00

Count Ferdinand von Zeppelin, Airship Designer, Birth Sesquicentennial — AP229

**Souvenir Sheet**

C739 AP228 30g multicolored
Set, #C735-C739    15.00 5.00
For overprint see No. 2284.

**1988, Aug. 1    Unwmk.    Perf. 13**
C735 AP228 5g multicolored
C736 AP228 10g multicolored
C737 AP228 20g multicolored
C738 AP228 25g multicolored

**Perf. 13½x13**

1990 World Cup Soccer Championships, Italy — AP228

5g, Machine slogan cancel from Montevideo, May 21, 1930. 10g, Italy #324, vert. 20g, France #349. 25g, Brazil #696, vert. 30g, Paraguayan commemorative cancel for ITALIA 1990.

**1988, Sept. 2    Unwmk.**
**Perf. 13½x13**
C744 AP231 5g multicolored
C745 AP231 10g multicolored
C746 AP231 20g multicolored
C747 AP231 25g multicolored
C748 AP231 30g multicolored
Set, #C744-C748    10.00 5.00

**Souvenir Sheet**
C749 AP231 100g multicolored    15.00

1988 Winter Olympics, Calgary — AP231

Gold medalists: 5g, Hubert Strolz, Austria, Alpine combined. 10g, Alberto Tomba, Italy, giant slalom and slalom. 20g, Franck Piccard, France, super giant slalom. 25g, Thomas Muller, Hans-Peter Pohl and Hubert Schwarz, Federal Republic of Germany, Nordic combined team, vert. 30g, Vreni Schneider, Switzerland, giant slalom and slalom. 100g, Marina Kiehl, Federal Republic of Germany, downhill, vert.

---

**1988, Nov. 25    Perf. 14**
C756 AP200 30g on No. C623    2.00 2.00

No. C623 Ovptd. in Gold

**1988, Nov. 25    Perf. 14**
C755 AP204 30g Ovptd. on No. C635    2.00 2.00

No. C635 Ovptd. in Metallic Red:

1990 World Cup Soccer Championships, Italy — AP232

**1988, Oct. 4    Perf. 13**
C750 AP232 5g multicolored
C751 AP232 10g multicolored
C752 AP232 20g multicolored
C753 AP232 25g multicolored
**Perf. 14**
C754 AP232 30g multicolored
Set, #C750-C754    9.00 4.50
For overprint see No. 2285.

Designs: 5g, Mexico #C350. 10g, Germany #1146. 20g, Argentina #1147, vert. 25g, Spain #2211. 30g, Italy #1742.

1988 Summer Olympics, Seoul — AP233

Gold medalists: No. C757, Nicole Uphoff, individual dressage. No. C758, Anja Fichtel, Sabine Bau, Zita Funkenhauser, Anette Kluge and Christine Weber, team foil. No. C759, Silvia Sperber, smallbore standard rifle. No. C760, Mathias Baumann, Claus Erhorn, Thies Kaspareit and Ralph Ehrenbrink, equestrian team 3-day event. No. C761, Anja Fichtel, individual foil, vert. No. C762, Franke Sloothaak, Dirk Hafemeister, Wolfgang Brinkmann and Ludger Beerbaum, equestrian team jumping. No. C763, Arnd Schmitt individual epee, vert. No. C764, Jose Luis Doreste, Finn class yachting. No. C765, Steffi Graf, tennis. No. C766, Michael Gross, 200-meter butterfly, vert. No. C768, Nicole Uphoff, Monica Theodorescu, Ann Kathrin Linsenhoff and Reiner Klimke, team dressage.

**1989**
C757 AP233 5g multicolored
C758 AP233 5g multicolored
C759 AP233 10g multicolored
C760 AP233 10g multicolored
C761 AP233 20g multicolored
C762 AP233 20g multicolored
C763 AP233 25g multicolored
C764 AP233 25g multicolored
**Perf. 13½x13**
C765 AP233 30g multicolored
C766 AP233 30g multicolored
Set, #C757-C766    10.00 5.00

**Souvenir Sheets    Perf. 14½**
C767 AP233 100g multicolored    12.00
C768 AP233 100g multicolored    12.00

Nos. C767-C768 each contain one 80x50mm stamp. Issue dates: Nos. C757, C759, C761, C763, C765, and C767, Mar. 3. Others, Mar. 20. For overprints see Nos. 2292, 2359.

No. C631 Ovptd. in Metallic Red:

**Souvenir Sheet**

Intl. Red Cross, 125th Anniv. (in 1988). — AP234

**1989, Apr. 17**    **Litho.**    **Perf. 13½**
C769 AP234 100g in changed colors    12.00

No. C769 has perforated label picturing Nobel medal.

**Olympics Type of 1989**

1988 Winter Olympic medalists or competitors: 5g, Pirmin Zurbriggen, Peter Mueller, Switzerland, and Franck Piccard, France, Alpine skiing. 10g, Sigrid Wolf, Austria, super giant slalom, vert. 20g, Czechoslovakia vs. West Germany, hockey, vert. 25g, Piccard, skiing, vert. 30g, Piccard, wearing medal, vert.

**1989, Apr. 17**    **Perf. 13½x13**
C770 AP233 5g multicolored
   **Perf. 13x13½**
C771 AP233 10g multicolored
C772 AP233 20g multicolored
C773 AP233 25g multicolored
C774 AP233 30g multicolored    8.00 4.00
Set, #C770-C774

**Souvenir Sheet**

Luis Alberto del Parana and the Paraguayans — AP237

**1989, May 25**    **Perf. 14½**
C780A AP237 100g multicolored    30.00

A clear plastic phonograph record is affixed to the souvenir sheet.

Hamburg, 800th Anniv. — AP238

Hamburg anniv. emblem, SAIL '89 emblem, and: 5g, Galleon and Icarus, woodcut by Pieter Brueghel. 10g, Windjammer, vert. 20g, Old Hamburg by A.E. Schliecker, vert. 25g, Commemorative coin issued by Federal Republic of Germany. 100g, Hamburg, 13th cent. illuminated manuscript, vert.

**1989, May 26**    **Perf. 13½x13, 13x13½**
C781 AP238 5g multicolored
C782 AP238 10g multicolored
C783 AP238 20g multicolored
C784 AP238 25g multicolored
C785 AP238 30g multicolored    12.00 6.00
   **Souvenir Sheet**    **Perf. 14½**
C786 AP238 100g multicolored    20.00

No. C786 contains one 40x50mm stamp.

**Souvenir Sheet**

1990 World Cup Soccer Championships, Italy — AP235

**1989, Apr. 21**    **Perf. 14½**
C775 AP235 100g Sheet of 1 + label    13.00

1st Moon Landing, 20th Anniv. — AP236

Designs: 5g, Wernher von Braun, Apollo 11 launch, vert. 10g, Michael Collins, lunar module on moon. 20g, Neil Armstrong, astronaut on lunar module ladder, vert. 25g, Buzz Aldrin, solar wind experiment, vert. 30g, Kurt Debus, splashdown of Columbia command module, vert.

**1989, May 24**    **Perf. 13**
C776 AP236 5g multicolored
C777 AP236 10g multicolored
C778 AP236 20g multicolored
C779 AP236 25g multicolored
C780 AP236 30g multicolored    12.00 6.00
Set, #C776-C780

French Revolution, Bicent. — AP239

Details from paintings: 5g, Esther Adorns Herself for her Presentation to King Ahasuerus, by Theodore Chasseriau, vert. 10g, Olympia, by Manet, vert. 20g, The Drunker Erigone with a Panther, by Louis A. Reisener. 25g, Anniv. emblem and natl. coats of arms. 30g, Liberty Leading the People, by Delacroix, vert. 100g, The Education of Maria de Medici, by Rubens, vert.

**1989, May 27**    **Perf. 13x13½, 13½x13**
C787 AP239 5g multicolored
C788 AP239 10g multicolored
C789 AP239 20g multicolored
C790 AP239 25g multicolored
C791 AP239 30g multicolored    12.00 6.00
Set, #C787-C791
   **Souvenir Sheet**    **Perf. 14½**
C792 AP239 100g multicolored    17.00

**Souvenir Sheet**

Railway Zeppelin, 1931 — AP240

**1989, May 27**    **Litho.**    **Perf. 13½**
C793 AP240 100g multicolored    18.00

Jupiter and Calisto by Rubens AP241

Details from paintings by Rubens: 10g, Boreas Abducting Oreithyia (1619-20). 20g, Fortuna (1625). 25g, Mars with Venus and Cupid (1625). 30g, Virgin with Child (1620).

**1989, Dec. 27**    **Litho.**    **Perf. 14**
C794 AP241 5g multicolored
C795 AP241 10g multicolored
C796 AP241 20g multicolored
C797 AP241 25g multicolored
   **Perf. 13**
C798 AP241 30g multicolored    10.00 5.00
Set, #C794-C798

Death of Rubens, 350th anniversary.

Penny Black, 150th Anniv. AP242

Penny Black, 500 years of postal services emblem, and: 5g, World '90 emblem and: 5g, Brazil #1. 10g, British Guiana #2. 20g, Chile #1. 25g, Uruguay #1. 30g, Paraguay #1.

**1989, Dec. 30**    **Perf. 14**
C799 AP242 5g multicolored
C800 AP242 10g multicolored
C801 AP242 20g multicolored
C802 AP242 25g multicolored
   **Perf. 13**
C803 AP242 30g multicolored    10.00 5.00
Set, #C799-C803

Animals AP243

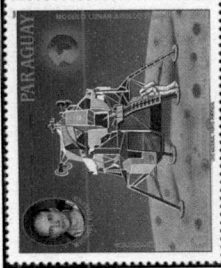

Designs: 5g, Martucha. 5g, Mara. 20g, Lobo de crin. 25g, Rana cornuda tintorera, horiz. 30g, Jaguar, horiz. Inscribed 1989.

**1990, Jan. 8**    **Perf. 13x13½, 13½x13**
C804 AP243 5g multicolored
C805 AP243 10g multicolored
C806 AP243 20g multicolored
C807 AP243 25g multicolored    12.00 6.00
C808 AP243 30g multicolored
Set, #C804-C808

Columbus' Fleet AP244

Discovery of America 500th anniversary emblem and: 10g, Olympic rings, stylized basketball player, horiz. 20g, Medieval nave, Expo '92 emblem. 25g, Four-masted barkentine, Expo '92 emblem, horiz. 30g, Similar to Spain Scott 2571, Expo '92 emblem.

**1990, Jan. 27**    **Perf. 14**
C809 AP244 5g multicolored
C810 AP244 10g multicolored
C811 AP244 20g multicolored
C812 AP244 25g multicolored
   **Perf. 13½x13**
C813 AP244 30g multicolored    8.00 4.00
Set, #C809-C813

Postal Transportation, 500th Anniv. — AP245

500th Anniv. Emblem and: 5g, 10g, 20g, 25g, Penny Black and various post coaches, 10g, vert. 30g, Post coach.

**1990, Mar. 9**    **Perf. 13½x13, 13x13½**
C814 AP245 5g multicolored
C815 AP245 10g multicolored
C816 AP245 20g multicolored
C817 AP245 25g multicolored
C818 AP245 30g multicolored    12.00 7.00
Set, #C814-C818

Fort and City of Arco by Durer — AP246

Paintings by Albrecht Durer, postal transportation 500th anniversary emblem and: 10g, Trent Castle. 20g, North Innsbruck. 25g, Fort yard of the Animals. No. C824, Madonna and Child, vert. No. C825, Postrider, vert.

**1990, Mar. 14**    **Perf. 14**
C819 AP246 5g multicolored
C820 AP246 10g multicolored
C821 AP246 20g multicolored
C822 AP246 25g multicolored
   **Perf. 13**
C823 AP246 30g multicolored    13.00 6.00
Set, #C819-C823
   **Souvenir Sheets**    **Perf. 14½**
C824 AP246 100g multicolored    20.00
C825 AP246 100g multicolored    20.00

Nos. C824-C825 each contain one 40x50mm stamp. For overprint see No. 2358.

## POSTAGE DUE STAMPS

| 1986-887 | | Photo. |
|---|---|---|
| C826 | AP247 | 40g red lilac |
| C827 | AP247 | 60g bright green |
| | | ('88) |

**Wmk. 347**

AP247

| 1924-26 | | | Perf. 11 | |
|---|---|---|---|---|
| L6 | A45 | 50c red ('25) | 1.00 | .85 |
| L7 | A44 | 4c green | | |
| L8 | A45 | 1p dk bl (R) ('25) | | |
| L9 | A45 | 1p blue (R) ('25) | | |
| L10 | A45 | 1p emerald ('26) | 1.50 | 1.25 |

Nos. L6, L8-L9 exist imperf. Value $2.50
each pair.

D1   D2

**1927-39**

Same Overprint on Stamps and Type
of 1927-36 in Red or Black

| L11 | A47 | 50c ultra ('26) | | | .20 | .20 |
|---|---|---|---|---|---|---|
| L12 | A47 | 50c df red ('28) | | | .20 | .20 |
| L13 | A47 | 5c red | | | .20 | .20 |
| L14 | A47 | 10c orange ('29) | | | .20 | .20 |
| L15 | A47 | 50c gray (R) ('31) | | | .20 | .20 |
| L16 | A47 | 50c bluish grn ('36) | | | .20 | .20 |
| L17 | A47 | 50c vio (R) ('34) | | | .20 | .20 |
| L18 | A48 | 1p emerald | | | .20 | .20 |
| L19 | A48 | 1p org red ('29) | | | .20 | .20 |
| L20 | A48 | 1p lil brn ('31) | | | .20 | .20 |
| L21 | A48 | 1p dk bl (R) ('33) | | | .20 | .20 |
| L22 | A48 | 1p vio (R) ('36) | | | .20 | .20 |
| L23 | A49 | 1.50p brown | | | .20 | .20 |
| L24 | A49 | 1.50p lilac ('28) | | | 1.50 | |
| L25 | A49 | 1.50p dull bl ('34) | | | .20 | .20 |
| L26 | A50 | 2.50p bister ('28) | | | .20 | .20 |
| L27 | A50 | 2.50p vio (R) ('36) | | | .20 | .20 |
| L28 | A51 | 3p gray ('31) | | | .20 | .20 |
| L29 | A51 | 3p rose red ('36) | | | .20 | .20 |
| L30 | A52 | 5p vio (R) ('36) | | | .20 | .20 |
| L31 | A57 | 10p gray brn ('39) | | | .20 | .20 |

Nos. L11-L31 (21)   4.30   4.25

**1931-36**

Types of 1931-35 and No. 305
Overprinted in Black or Red

| L32 | A59 | 1p light red | .20 | .20 |
|---|---|---|---|---|
| L33 | A58 | 1.50p dp red ('32) | .20 | .20 |
| L34 | A60 | 1.50p org brn ('32) | .20 | .20 |
| L35 | A60 | 1.50p bis brn ('34) | .20 | .20 |
| L36 | A60 | 1.50p grn ('34) | .20 | .20 |
| L37 | A54 | 10p vermilion | 2.25 | 2.25 |

Nos. L32-L37 (6)   1.25   1.25

## INTERIOR OFFICE ISSUES

The "C" signifies "Campana" (rural).
These stamps were sold by Postal
Agents in country districts, who
received a commission on their sales.
These stamps were available for postage in the interior but not in Asuncion or
abroad.

Nos. 243-
244
Overprinted
in Red

**1904**

Nos. 215, 218, J12 Surcharged

| 1913 | | Unwmk. | Litho. | Perf. 11½ |
|---|---|---|---|---|
| J1 | D1 | 1c yellow brown | | .20 .20 |
| J2 | D1 | 2c yellow brown | | .20 .20 |
| J3 | D1 | 5c yellow brown | | .20 .20 |
| J4 | D1 | 20c green | | .80 .80 |

Nos. J1-J4 (4)

**1904**   **Engr.**

| J5 | D2 | 1c yellow brown | .20 .20 |
|---|---|---|---|
| J6 | D2 | 2c yellow brown | .20 .20 |
| J7 | D2 | 5c yellow brown | .20 .20 |
| J8 | D2 | 10c yellow brown | .20 .20 |
| J9 | D2 | 20c yellow brown | .20 .20 |
| J10 | D2 | 40c yellow brown | .20 .20 |
| J11 | D2 | 1p yellow brown | .20 .20 |
| J12 | D2 | 1.50p yellow brown | 1.60 1.60 |

Nos. J5-J12 (8)

For overprints and surcharges see Nos.
220-224, 229, 232, 264, L5.

**1922**

| L1 | A42 | 50c car & dk bl | .20 .20 |
|---|---|---|---|
| L2 | A42 | 1p dk bl & blk | .20 .20 |

The overprint on No. L2 exists double or
inverted. Counterfeits exist. Double or inverted
overprints on No. L1 and all overprints in black
are counterfeit.

**1924**

| L3 | A40 | 50c on 75c deep bl | .20 .20 |
|---|---|---|---|
| L4 | A40 | 1p on 1.25p pale bl | .20 .20 |
| L5 | D2 | 1p on 1.50p yel brn | .60 .60 |

Nos. L3-L5 (3)

The stamps L3-L4 exist imperf.

## OFFICIAL STAMPS

Nos. 254, 257-260 Overprinted in
Black or Red

O7

| 1886, Aug. 20 | | Unwmk. | Litho. | Imperf. |
|---|---|---|---|---|
| O1 | O1 | 1c orange | 3.00 3.00 |
| O2 | O1 | 2c violet | 3.00 3.00 |
| O3 | O1 | 5c green | 3.00 3.00 |
| O4 | O1 | 7c green | 3.00 3.00 |
| O5 | O1 | 10c slate blue | 3.00 3.00 |
| O6 | O1 | 15c emerald | 1.25 |
| O7 | O1 | 20c claret | 21.00 21.00 |

a.   Wavy lines on face of stamp
b.   "OFICIAL" omitted   21.00 21.00

Nos. O1-O7 (7)

Nos. O1 to O7 have the date and various
control marks and letters printed on the back
of each stamp in blue and black.
The overprints exist inverted on all values.
Nos. O1 to O7 have been reprinted from
new stones made from slightly retouched dies.

Types of 1886 With
Overprint

| 1886 | | | Perf. 11½ |
|---|---|---|---|
| O8 | O1 | 1c dark green | .50 .50 |
| O9 | O1 | 2c scarlet | .50 .50 |
| O10 | O1 | 5c dull blue | .50 .50 |
| O11 | O1 | 7c orange | .50 .50 |
| O12 | O1 | 10c lake | .50 .50 |
| O13 | O1 | 15c brown | .50 .50 |
| O14 | O1 | 20c blue | 3.50 3.50 |

Nos. O8-O14 (7)

The overprint exists inverted on all values.
Value, each $1.50.

**1886, Sept. 1**

No. 20 Overprinted

O15   A11   1c dark green   1.50   1.50

**1889**

Types of 1889
Regular Issue
Surcharged

| | | | Perf. 11½ |
|---|---|---|---|
| O16 | A13 | 3c on 15c violet | 1.50 1.00 |
| O17 | A13 | 5c on 15c brn | 1.50 1.00 |

**Imperf.**

| O18 | A13 | 1c on 15c maroon | 1.50 1.00 |
|---|---|---|---|
| O19 | A13 | 2c on 15c maroon | 6.00 4.00 |

Nos. O16-O19 (4)

Counterfeits of Nos. O16-O19 abound.

**1889**

Handstamped Surcharge in Black

Regular Issue of 1887
Handstamp
Overprinted in Violet

Regular Issue of 1903
Overprinted

No. 45 Overprinted

**1901, Feb.**   **Engr.**   **Perf. 11½, 12½**

| O20 | O16 | 1c dull blue | .20 .20 |
|---|---|---|---|
| O21 | O16 | 2c rose red | .20 .20 |
| O22 | O16 | 4c dark brown | .20 .20 |
| O43 | O16 | 5c dark green | .20 .20 |
| O44 | O16 | 8c orange brn | .20 .20 |
| O45 | O16 | 10c deep blue | .20 .20 |
| O46 | O16 | 20c deep green | 1.40 1.40 |

O48   A12c deep green, type O16,
but not issued.

A 12c deep green, type O16,
was prepared but not issued.

Nos. O42-O48 (7)

O16

**1893**

No. 26 Overprinted

O41   A12   7c brown   10.00   5.00

Counterfeits of No. O41 exist.

**1892**

Stamps and Type of
1887 Regular Issue
Overprinted in Black

| O33 | A12 | 1c green | .20 .20 |
|---|---|---|---|
| O34 | A12 | 2c rose red | .20 .20 |
| O35 | A12 | 7c brown | 1.00 |
| O36 | A12 | 10c lilac | 1.75 1.00 |
| O37 | A12 | 15c orange | .65 .25 |
| O38 | A12 | 20c orange | .25 .25 |
| O39 | A12 | 50c pink | .20 .20 |
| O40 | A12 | 50c gray | 3.65 2.45 |

Nos. O33-O40 (8)

**1890**   **Perf. 11½-12½ & Compounds**   **Typo.**

| O20 | A12 | 1c green | .20 .20 |
|---|---|---|---|
| O21 | A12 | 2c rose red | .20 .20 |
| O22 | A12 | 5c blue | 3.75 2.50 |
| O23 | A12 | 7c brown | .20 .20 |
| O24 | A12 | 10c lilac | .65 .25 |
| O25 | A12 | 15c orange | .45 .30 |
| O26 | A12 | 20c pink | 5.40 3.85 |

Nos. O20-O26 (7)

Nos. O20-O26 exist with double overprint
and all but the 20c with inverted overprint.
Nos. O20-O22, O24-O26 exist with blue
overprint. The status is questioned.

**1902**

No. 45 Overprinted

O49   A12   1p olive grn   .20 .20
a.   Inverted overprint   10.00

Counterfeits of No. O49a exist.

**1903**   **Perf. 11½**

| O50 | A32 | 1c gray | .20 .20 |
|---|---|---|---|
| O51 | A32 | 2c blue green | .20 .20 |
| O52 | A32 | 5c blue | .20 .20 |
| O53 | A32 | 10c orange brn | .20 .20 |
| O54 | A32 | 20c carmine | .20 .20 |

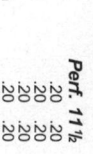

O3   O1

O4   O2

O5   O6

Rarotongan Chief (Te Po) — A16

**1927**    **Engr.**    **Wmk. 61**
31 A16 2½p blue & red brn   4.00 30.00

Types of 1920 Issue

**1928-29**
33 A10 ½p yellow grn & blk   6.25 24.00
34 A11 1p carmine rose & blk   6.25 21.00

## PENRHYN
### Northern Cook Islands

POP. — 606 (1996).

The Northern Cook Islands include six besides Penrhyn that are inhabited: Nassau, Palmerston (Avarua), Manihiki (Humphrey), Rakahanga (Reirson), Pukapuka (Danger) and Suwarrow (Anchorage).

100 Cents = 1 Dollar

**Catalogue values for unused stamps in this section are for Never Hinged items.**

PENRHYN / NORTHERN COOK ISLANDS

Cook Islands Nos. 200-201, 203, 205-208, 211-212, 215-217 Overprinted

**1973**   **Photo.**   **Unwmk.**   **Perf. 14x13½**
35 A34 1c gold & multi   .20
36 A34 2c gold & multi   .20
37 A34 3c gold & multi   .20
38 A34 4c gold & multi   .20 35.00
  a. Overprinted on #204   35.00
39 A34 5c gold & multi   .20
40 A34 6c gold & multi   .25
41 A34 15c gold & multi   .35
42 A34 20c gold & multi   .45
43 A34 50c gold & multi   .60
44 A34 50c gold & multi   1.50 1.90
45 A35 $1 gold & multi   1.25 2.00
46 A35 $2 gold & multi   1.25 4.50
Nos. 35-46 (12)   7.00 10.85

Nos. 45-46 are overprinted "Penrhyn" only. Overprint exists with broken "E" or "O". Issued with and without fluorescent security underprinting.
Issued: #35-45, Oct. 24; #46, Nov. 14.

Cook Islands Nos. 369-371 Overprinted in Silver: "PENRHYN / NORTHERN"

**1973, Nov. 14**   **Photo.**   **Perf. 14**
47 A60 25c Princess Anne   .35 .25
48 A60 30c Mark Phillips   .35 .25
49 A60 50c Princess and Mark Phillips   .35 .75
Nos. 47-49 (3)   1.05 1.25

Wedding of Princess Anne and Capt. Mark Phillips.

**Fluorescence**

Starting with No. 50, stamps carry a "fluorescent security underprinting" in a multiple pattern combining a sailing ship, "Penrhyn Northern Cook Islands" and stars.

Ostracion A17

---

Tahi Siling.   f

**1903**     **Wmk. 61**
10 A23(d) 3p yel brn (C)   11.50 24.00
11 A26(e) 6p rose (Bl)   17.50 40.00
12 A29(f) 1sh org red (Bl)   62.50 62.50
  a. 1sh brown red (Bl)   62.50 62.50
  b. 1sh bright red (Bl)   91.50 126.50
Nos. 10-12 (3)

**1914-15**   **Perf. 14, 14x14½**
13 A41(a) ½p yel grn (C)   .90 9.25
  a. No period after "PENI"   29.00 85.00
14 A41(a) ½p yel grn (V)   .90 9.25
  a. No period after "ISLAND"   11.50 52.50
    ('15)
15 A41(e) 6p car rose   45.00 10.00
16 A41(f) 1sh ver (Bl)   26.00 80.00
  a. No period after "ISLAND"   47.50 110.00
Nos. 13-16 (4)   75.30 208.50

New Zealand Stamps of 1915-19 Overprinted in Red or Dark Blue

PENRHYN ISLAND

**Typo.**
**Perf. 14x13½, 14x14½**
17 A43 ½p yel grn (R) ('20)   1.10 2.25
18 A47 1½p gray black (R)   7.50 20.00
19 A47 1½p brn org (R) ('19)   .70 20.00
20 A43 3p choc (Bl)   4.00 22.50

**Engr.**
**1917-20**
21 A44 2½p dull bl (R) ('20)   2.25 7.50
22 A45 3p vio brn (Bl) ('18)   11.00 80.00
23 A45 6p car rose (Bl) ('18)
24 A45 1sh vermilion (Bl)   5.75 21.00
Nos. 17-24 (8)   14.00 37.50
   16.30 210.75

Avarua Waterfront A11 — Landing of Capt. Cook A10 — Coconut Palm — A13 — Capt. James Cook — A12 — Avarua Harbor — A15 — Arorangi Village, Rarotonga — A14

**1920**   **Unwmk.**   **Perf. 14**
25 A10 ½p emerald & blk   1.10 19.00
  a. Center inverted   625.00
26 A11 1p red & black   1.75 17.50
  a. Center inverted   850.00
27 A12 1½p violet & blk   7.50 22.50
28 A13 3p red org & blk   3.00 9.75
29 A14 6p dk brn & red brn
30 A15 1sh dull bl & blk   3.75 22.50
   11.50 30.00
Nos. 25-30 (6)   28.60 121.25

---

## PENRHYN ISLAND

pen-'rin 'i-land

(Tongareva)

AREA — 3 sq. mi.
POP. — 395 (1926)

Stamps of Cook Islands were used in Penrhyn from 1932 until 1973.

12 Pence = 1 Shilling

**Catalogue values for unused stamps in this country are for Never Hinged items, beginning with Scott 35 in the regular postage section, Scott B1 in the semi-postal section and Scott O1 in the officials section.**

**Watermarks**

Wmk. 63 — Double-lined N Z and Star

Wmk. 61 — N Z Double-lined and Star Close Together

On watermark 61 the margins of the sheets are watermarked "NEW ZEALAND POSTAGE" and parts of the double-lined letters of these words are frequently found on the stamps. It occasionally happens that a stamp shows no watermark whatever.

Stamps of New Zealand Surcharged in Carmine, Vermilion, Brown or Blue:

½ pence   1 pence   2½ pence

**1902**   **Wmk. 63**
1 A18 ½p green (C)   .90 6.50
  a. No period after "ISLAND"   175.00 225.00
2 A35 1p carmine (Br)   3.75 17.50
  a. Perf. 11   1,000. 1,000.
  b. Perf. 11x14   1,000. 1,000.

**Wmk. 61**
5 A18 ½p green (V)   2.25 6.50
6 A35 1p carmine (Bl)   1.40 4.50
  a. No period after "ISLAND"   55.00 200.00
  b. Perf. 11x14   9,000. 8,500.

**Unwmk.**
8 A22 2½p blue (C)   3.50 9.00
  a. "½" and "PENI" 2mm apart   17.50 35.00
9 A22 2½p blue (V)   3.50 9.00
  a. "½" and "PENI" 2mm apart   17.50 35.00
Nos. 1-9 (9)   15.30 53.00

Stamps with compound perfs. also exist perf. 11 or 14 on one or more sides.

e

d

---

O55 A32 30c deep blue   .20 .20
O56 A32 60c purple   1.40 1.40
Nos. O50-O56 (7)

O17   O18

**1905-08**   **Engr.**   **Perf. 11½, 12**
O57 O17 1c gray grn   .20 .20
O58 O17 1c ol grn ('05)   .20 .20
O59 O17 1c brn org ('06)   .45 .45
O60 O17 1c ver ('08)   .20 .20
O61 O17 2c brown org   .25 .25
O62 O17 2c gray grn ('05)   .75 .25
O63 O17 2c red ('06)   .40 .20
O64 O17 2c gray ('08)   .20 .20
O65 O17 5c deep bl ('06)   1.50 1.00
O66 O17 5c gray bl ('08)   .75 .65
O67 O17 5c grnsh bl ('08)   .20 .20
O68 O17 10c violet ('06)   .70 .40
O69 O17 20c violet ('08)   6.00 4.10
Nos. O57-O69 (13)

**1908**
O70 O17 10c bister   3.50
O71 O17 10c emerald   3.50
O72 O17 10c red lilac   4.50
O73 O17 20c green   3.00
O74 O17 20c salmon pink   3.50
O75 O17 20c green   3.50
O76 O17 20c dull red   3.50
O77 O17 30c blue gray   3.50
O78 O17 30c yellow   1.50
O79 O17 60c chocolate   4.00
O80 O17 60c orange brn   5.00
O81 O17 60c deep ultra   24.00
O82 O18 1p brt rose & blk   24.00
O83 O18 1p lake & blk   25.00
O84 O18 1p brn org & blk   110.00
Nos. O70-O84 (15)

Nos. O70-O84 were not issued, but were surcharged or overprinted for use as regular postage stamps. See Nos. 131-138, 141-145, 158-165, 171-173.

O19   **Perf. 11½**

**1913**
O85 O19 1c gray   .20 .20
O86 O19 2c orange   .20 .20
O87 O19 5c lilac   .20 .20
O88 O19 10c green   .20 .20
O89 O19 20c dull red   .20 .20
O90 O19 30c rose   .20 .20
O91 O19 75c deep blue   .20 .25
O92 O19 1p dull blue   .20 .20
O93 O19 2p yellow   1.80 1.80
Nos. O85-O93 (9)

For surcharges see Nos. 268, C1-C3.

Type of Regular Issue of 1927-38 Overprinted in Red

OFICIAL 50

**1935**   **Unwmk.**
O94 A47 10c light ultra   .20 .20
O95 A47 50c violet   .20 .20
O96 A48 1p orange   .20 .20
O97 A60 1.50p green   .20 .20
O98 A50 2.50p orange   1.00 1.00
Nos. O94-O98 (5)

Overprint is diagonal on 1.50p.

University of Asunción Type

**Litho.**   **Perf. 12**
**1940**
O99 A67 50c red brn & blk   .20 .20
O100 A67 1p carmine & blk   .20 .20
O101 A67 2p lt bl grn & blk   .20 .20
O102 A67 5p ultra & blk   .20 .20
O103 A67 10p lt vio & blk   .30 .25
O104 A67 50p dp org & blk   1.30 1.25
Nos. O99-O104 (6)

PENRHYN
NORTHERN COOK ISLANDS
$2
Aerial View of Penrhyn Atoll — A18

Designs: ½c-$1, Various fish of Penrhyn. $5, Map showing Penrhyn's location.

**1974-75 Photo. *Perf. 13½x14***

| | | | | |
|---|---|---|---|---|
| **50** | A17 | ½c multicolored | .20 | .20 |
| **51** | A17 | 1c multicolored | .20 | .20 |
| **52** | A17 | 2c multicolored | .20 | .20 |
| **53** | A17 | 3c multicolored | .20 | .20 |
| **54** | A17 | 4c multicolored | .20 | .20 |
| **55** | A17 | 5c multicolored | .20 | .20 |
| **56** | A17 | 8c multicolored | .20 | .20 |
| **57** | A17 | 10c multicolored | .20 | .20 |
| **58** | A17 | 20c multicolored | .85 | .45 |
| **59** | A17 | 25c multicolored | .90 | .50 |
| **60** | A17 | 60c multicolored | 2.25 | 1.25 |
| **61** | A17 | $1 multicolored | 3.75 | 2.00 |
| **62** | A18 | $2 multicolored | 9.25 | *9.00* |
| **63** | A18 | $5 multicolored | 9.25 | 5.00 |
| | | *Nos. 50-63 (14)* | 27.85 | 19.80 |

Issued: $2, 2/12/75; $5, 3/12/75; others 8/15/74.

For surcharges and overprints see Nos. 72, 352-353, O1-O12.

PENRHYN
NORTHERN COOK ISLANDS
CENTENARY OF THE UNIVERSAL POSTAL UNION 1874 · 1974
25c
Map of Penrhyn and Nos. 1-2 — A19

UPU, cent.: 50c, UPU emblem, map of Penrhyn and Nos. 27-28.

**1974, Sept. 27 *Perf. 13***

| | | | | |
|---|---|---|---|---|
| **64** | A19 | 25c violet & multi | .35 | .35 |
| **65** | A19 | 50c slate grn & multi | .75 | .75 |

Penrhyn
5c
NORTHERN COOK ISLANDS
CHRISTMAS 1974
Adoration of the Kings, by Memling — A20

Christmas: 10c, Adoration of the Shepherds, by Hugo van der Goes. 25c, Adoration of the Kings, by Rubens. 30c, Holy Family, by Orazio Borgianni.

**1974, Oct. 30**

| | | | | |
|---|---|---|---|---|
| **66** | A20 | 5c multicolored | .20 | .20 |
| **67** | A20 | 10c multicolored | .25 | .25 |
| **68** | A20 | 25c multicolored | .50 | .50 |
| **69** | A20 | 30c multicolored | .60 | .60 |
| | | *Nos. 66-69 (4)* | 1.55 | 1.55 |

PENRHYN NORTHERN COOK ISLANDS
30c
SIR WINSTON CHURCHILL CENTENARY · 1874-1974
Churchill Giving "V" Sign — A21

**1974, Nov. 30 Photo.**

| | | | | |
|---|---|---|---|---|
| **70** | A21 | 30c shown | .40 | .60 |
| **71** | A21 | 50c Portrait | .60 | .90 |

Winston Churchill (1874-1965).

PENRHYN
NORTHERN COOK ISLANDS
KIA ORANA ASTRONAUTS
$5
No. 63 Overprinted

**1975, July 24 *Perf. 13½x13***

| | | | | |
|---|---|---|---|---|
| **72** | A18 | $5 multicolored | 2.50 | 2.50 |

Safe splashdown of Apollo space capsule.

CHRISTMAS 1975
7c
Penrhyn
NORTHERN COOK ISLANDS
Madonna, by Dirk Bouts — A22

EASTER 1975
15c
PENRHYN
NORTHERN COOK ISLANDS
Pietà, by Michelangelo — A23

Madonna Paintings: 15c, by Leonardo da Vinci. 35c, by Raphael.

**1975, Nov. 21 Photo. *Perf. 14½x13***

| | | | | |
|---|---|---|---|---|
| **73** | A22 | 7c gold & multi | .60 | .20 |
| **74** | A22 | 15c gold & multi | 1.00 | .40 |
| **75** | A22 | 35c gold & multi | 1.40 | .60 |
| | | *Nos. 73-75 (3)* | 3.00 | 1.20 |

Christmas 1975.

**1976, Mar. 19 Photo. *Perf. 14x13***

| | | | | |
|---|---|---|---|---|
| **76** | A23 | 15c gold & dark brown | .30 | .25 |
| **77** | A23 | 20c gold & deep purple | .45 | .40 |
| **78** | A23 | 35c gold & dark green | .65 | .60 |
| | *a.* | Souvenir sheet of 3, #76-78 | 1.75 | 1.75 |
| | | *Nos. 76-78 (3)* | 1.40 | 1.25 |

Easter and for the 500th birth anniv. of Michelangelo Buonarroti (1475-1564), Italian sculptor, painter and architect.

AMERICAN REVOLUTION BICENTENNIAL
Penrhyn Penrhyn Penrhyn
The Spirit of '76, by Archibald M. Willard — A24

No. 79, Washington Crossing the Delaware, by Emmanuel Leutze.

**1976, May 20 Photo. *Perf. 13½***

| | | | | |
|---|---|---|---|---|
| **79** | A24 | Strip of 3 | 1.10 | 1.10 |
| | *a.* | 30c Boatsman | .35 | .35 |
| | *b.* | 30c Washington | .35 | .35 |
| | *c.* | 30c Men in boat | .35 | .35 |
| **80** | A24 | Strip of 3 | 2.00 | 2.00 |
| | *a.* | 50c Drummer boy | .55 | .55 |
| | *b.* | 50c Old drummer | .55 | .55 |
| | *c.* | 50c Fifer | .55 | .55 |
| | *d.* | Souvenir sheet, #79-80 | 3.75 | 3.75 |

American Bicentennial. Nos. 79-80 printed in sheets of 15, 5 strips of 3 and 3-part corner labels.

For overprint see No. O13.

XXI OLYMPIC GAMES · MONTREAL 1976
PENRHYN
NORTHERN COOK ISLANDS
25c
Running — A25

Montreal Olympic Games Emblem and: 30c, Long jump. 75c, Javelin.

**1976, July 9 Photo. *Perf. 13½***

| | | | | |
|---|---|---|---|---|
| **81** | A25 | 25c multicolored | .30 | .25 |
| **82** | A25 | 30c multicolored | .35 | .30 |
| **83** | A25 | 75c multicolored | .85 | .75 |
| | *a.* | Souvenir sheet of 3, #81-83, perf. 14½x13½ | 2.00 | 2.00 |
| | | *Nos. 81-83 (3)* | 1.50 | 1.30 |

21st Olympic Games, Montreal, Canada, July 17-Aug. 1. Nos. 81-83 printed in sheets of 6 (2x3).

7c
PENRHYN
NORTHERN COOK ISLANDS
Flight into Egypt, by Dürer — A26

Etchings by Albrecht Dürer: 15c, Adoration of the Shepherds. 35c, Adoration of the Kings.

**1976, Oct. 20 Photo. *Perf. 13x13½***

| | | | | |
|---|---|---|---|---|
| **84** | A26 | 7c silver & dk brown | .20 | .20 |
| **85** | A26 | 15c silver & slate grn | .25 | .25 |
| **86** | A26 | 35c silver & purple | .55 | .45 |
| | | *Nos. 84-86 (3)* | 1.00 | .90 |

Christmas. Nos. 84-86 printed in sheets of 8 (2x4) with decorative border.

SILVER JUBILEE
EIIR
50c
PENRHYN
NORTHERN COOK ISLANDS
Elizabeth II and Westminster Abbey — A27

$1, Elizabeth II & Prince Philip. $2, Elizabeth II.

**1977, Mar. 24 Photo. *Perf. 13½x13***

| | | | | |
|---|---|---|---|---|
| **87** | A27 | 50c silver & multi | .20 | .20 |
| **88** | A27 | $1 silver & multi | .40 | .40 |
| **89** | A27 | $2 silver & multi | .80 | .80 |
| | *a.* | Souvenir sheet of 3, #87-89 | 1.60 | 1.60 |
| | | *Nos. 87-89 (3)* | 1.40 | 1.40 |

25th anniversary of reign of Queen Elizabeth II. Nos. 87-89 issued in sheets of 4.

For overprints see Nos. O14-O15.

CHRISTMAS 1977
PENRHYN
NORTHERN · COOK ISLANDS
7c
Annunciation — A28

Designs: 15c, Announcement to Shepherds. 35c, Nativity. Designs from "The Bible in Images," by Julius Schnorr von Carolsfeld (1794-1872).

**1977, Sept. 23 Photo. *Perf. 13½***

| | | | | |
|---|---|---|---|---|
| **90** | A28 | 7c multicolored | .30 | .30 |
| **91** | A28 | 15c multicolored | .75 | .75 |
| **92** | A28 | 35c multicolored | 1.50 | 1.50 |
| | | *Nos. 90-92 (3)* | 2.55 | 2.55 |

Christmas. Issued in sheets of 6.

20c
Penrhyn
NORTHERN COOK ISLANDS
20c
Penrhyn
NORTHERN COOK ISLANDS
A29

#93a, Red Sickle-bill (I'wii). #93b, Chief's Feather Cloak. #94a, Crimson creeper (apapane). #94b, Feathered head of Hawaiian god. #95a, Hawaiian gallinule (alae). #95b, Chief's regalia: feather cape, staff (kahili) and helmet. #96a, Yellow-tufted bee-eater (o'o). #96b, Scarlet feathered image (head).

Birds are extinct; their feathers were used for artifacts shown.

**1978, Jan. 19 Photo. *Perf. 12½x13***

| | | | | |
|---|---|---|---|---|
| **93** | A29 | 20c Pair, #a.-b. | 1.90 | .90 |
| **94** | A29 | 30c Pair, #a.-b. | 2.00 | 1.00 |
| **95** | A29 | 35c Pair, #a.-b. | 2.25 | 1.25 |
| **96** | A29 | 75c Pair, #a.-b. | 3.50 | 1.75 |
| | *c.* | Souv. sheet, #93a, 94a, 95a, 96a | 5.50 | 5.50 |
| | *d.* | Souv. sheet, #93b, 94b, 95b, 96b | 5.50 | 5.50 |
| | | *Nos. 93-96 (4)* | 9.65 | 4.90 |

Bicentenary of Capt. Cook's arrival in Hawaii. Printed in sheets of 8 (4x2).

EASTER 1978
10c
PENRHYN
NORTHERN COOK ISLANDS
A31

PENRHYN
PENRHYN
PENRHYN
PENRHYN
PENRHYN
PENRHYN
A32

Rubens' Paintings: 10c, St. Veronica by Rubens. 15c, Crucifixion. 35c, Descent from the Cross.

**1978, Mar. 10 Photo. *Perf. 13½x13***

**Size: 25x36mm**

| | | | | |
|---|---|---|---|---|
| **101** | A31 | 10c multicolored | .20 | .20 |
| **102** | A31 | 15c multicolored | .30 | .30 |
| **103** | A31 | 35c multicolored | .70 | .70 |
| | *a.* | Souvenir sheet of 3 | 1.50 | 1.50 |
| | | *Nos. 101-103 (3)* | 1.20 | 1.20 |

Easter and 400th birth anniv. of Peter Paul Rubens (1577-1640). Nos. 101-103 issued in sheets of 6. No. 103a contains one each of Nos. 101-103 (27x36mm).

Miniature Sheet

**1978, May 24 Photo. *Perf. 13***

| | | | | |
|---|---|---|---|---|
| **104** | | Sheet of 6 | 2.00 | 2.00 |
| | *a.* | A32 90c Arms of United Kingdom | .40 | .30 |
| | *b.* | A32 90c shown | .40 | .30 |
| | *c.* | A32 90c Arms of New Zealand | .40 | .30 |
| | *d.* | Souvenir sheet of 3, #104a-104c | 2.00 | 2.00 |

25th anniv. of coronation of Elizabeth II.

No. 104 contains 2 horizontal se-tenant strips of Nos. 104a-104c, separated by horizontal gutter showing coronation.

CHRISTMAS 1978
30c
PENRHYN
NORTHERN · COOK ISLANDS
A33

Paintings by Dürer: 30c, Virgin and Child. 35c, Virgin and Child with St. Anne.

**1978, Nov. 29 Photo. *Perf. 14x13½***

| | | | | |
|---|---|---|---|---|
| **105** | A33 | 30c multicolored | .75 | .75 |
| **106** | A33 | 35c multicolored | .85 | .85 |
| | *a.* | Souvenir sheet of 2, #105-106 | 1.40 | 1.40 |

Christmas and 450th death anniv. of Albrecht Dürer (1471-1528), German painter. Nos. 105-106 issued in sheets of 6.

PENRHYN
75c
PENRHYN
75c
POSTAGE
ONE PENNY
CENTENARY OF THE DEATH OF ROWLAND HILL
A34

**PENRHYN ISLAND**

#107a, Penrhyn #64-65. #107b, Rowland Hill, Penny Black. #108a, Penrhyn #104b. #108b, Hill portrait.

**1979, Sept. 26    Photo.    Perf. 14**
107  A34  75c  Pair, #a.-b.     1.25  1.25
108  A34  90c  Pair, #a.-b.     1.50  1.50
 c. Souvenir sheet of 4, #107-108    3.25  3.25

Sir Rowland Hill (1795-1879), originator of penny postage. Issued in sheets of 8.

Max and Moritz, IYC Emblem — A35

IYC: Scenes from Max and Moritz, by Wilhelm Busch (1832-1908).

**1979, Nov. 20    Photo.    Perf. 13x12½**
111  Sheet of 4     1.00
 a. A35 12c shown     .25
 b. A35 12c Looking down chimney     .25
 c. A35 12c With stolen chickens     .25
 d. A35 12c Woman and dog, empty pan     .25
112  Sheet of 4     1.25
 a. A35 15c Sawing bridge     .30
 b. A35 15c Man falling into water     .30
 c. A35 15c Broken bridge     .30
 d. A35 15c Running away     .30
113  Sheet of 4     1.60
 a. A35 20c Baker     .40
 b. A35 20c Sneaking into bakery     .40
 c. A35 20c Falling into dough     .40
 d. A35 20c Baked into breads     .40
 Nos. 111-113 (3)     3.85

Sheets come with full labels at top and bottom showing text from stories or trimmed with text removed. Values of 3 sheets with full labels $11.

Easter (15th Century Prayerbook Illustrations): 12c, Jesus Carrying the Cross. 20c, Crucifixion, by William Vreland. 35c, Descent from the Cross.

**1980, Mar. 28    Photo.    Perf. 13x13½**
114  A36  12c  multicolored     .20  .20
115  A36  20c  multicolored     .35  .35
116  A36  35c  multicolored     .60  .60
 a. Souvenir sheet of 3, #114-116     1.10  1.10
 Nos. 114-116 (3)     1.15  1.15

See Nos. B4-B6.

**1980, Sept. 17    Photo.**
117  A37  $1 multicolored     1.75  1.75
 **Souvenir Sheet    Perf. 13**
118  A37  $2.50 multicolored     3.25  3.25

Queen Mother Elizabeth, 80th birthday.

Platform diving: #119a, Martina Jäschke, DDR. #119b, Falk Hoffman, DDR. Archery: #120a, Tomi Polkolainen. #120b, Kete Losaberidze. Soccer: #121a, Czechoslovakia, gold. #121b, DDR, silver. Running: #122a, Barbel Wockel. #122b, Pietro Mennea.

**1980, Nov. 14    Photo.    Perf. 13½**
119  A38  10c  Pair, #a.-b.     .25  .25
120  A38  20c  Pair, #a.-b.     .50  .50
121  A38  30c  Pair, #a.-b.     .75  .75
122  A38  50c  Pair, #a.-b.     1.25  1.25
 **Souvenir Sheet**
123  A38  Sheet of 8     2.75  2.75

22nd Summer Olympic Games, Moscow, July 19-Aug. 3.
No. 123 contains #119-122 with gold borders and white lettering at top and bottom.

Christmas (15th Century Virgin and Child Paintings by): 20c, Virgin and Child, by Luis Dalmau. 35c, Serra brothers. 50c, Master of the Porciuncula.

**1980, Dec. 5    Photo.    Perf. 13**
127  A39  20c  multicolored     .25  .25
128  A39  35c  multicolored     .40  .40
129  A39  50c  multicolored     .50  .50
 a. Souvenir sheet of 3, #127-129     2.50  2.50
 Nos. 127-129 (3)     1.15  1.15

See Nos. B7-B9.

#160a, 165a, Amatasi. #160b, 165a, Ndrua. #160c, 165a, Waka. #160d, 165a, Tongiaki. #161a, 166a, Va'a teu'ua. #161b, 166b, Victoria, 1500. #161c, 166c, Golden Hinde, 1560. #161d, 166d, Boudeuse, 1760. #162a, 167a, Bounty, 1787. #162b, 167b, Astrolabe, 1811. #162c, 167c, Star of India, 1861. #162d, 167d, Great Rep., 1853. #163a, 168a, Balcutha, 1886. #163b, 168b, Coonatto, 1863. #163c, 168c, Antiope, 1866. #163d, 168d, Teaping, 1863. #164a, 169a, Preussen, 1902. #164b, 169b, Pamir, 1921. #164c, 169c, Cap Hornier, 1910. #164d, 169d, Patriarch, 1869.

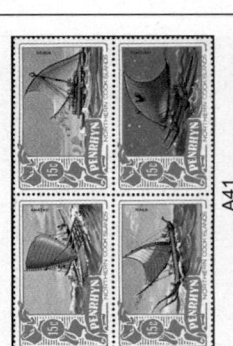

**1981    Photo.    Perf. 14**
160  A40  1c  Block of 4, #a.-d.     .20  .20
161  A40  3c  Block of 4, #a.-d.     .20  .20
162  A40  4c  Block of 4, #a.-d.     .40  .40
163  A40  6c  Block of 4, #a.-d.     .55  .55
164  A40  10c  Block of 4, #a.-d.     1.00  1.00
 **Perf. 13½x14½**
165  A41  15c  Block of 4, #a.-d.     1.60  1.60
166  A41  20c  Block of 4, #a.-d.     2.00  2.00
167  A41  30c  Block of 4, #a.-d.     3.25  3.25
168  A41  50c  Block of 4, #a.-d.     5.00  5.00
169  A41  $1  Block of 4, #a.-d.     10.00  10.00
 **Perf. 13½**
170  A42  $2  shown     5.00  5.00
171  A42  $4  Mermerus, 1872     10.00  10.00
172  A42  $6  Resolution, Discovery, 1776     17.00  17.00
 Nos. 160-172 (13)     56.20  56.20

Cutty Sark, 1869
A42

Christ with Crown of Thorns, by Titan — A44

Issued: 30c, Jesus at the Grove, by Paolo Veronese. 50c, Pieta, by Van Dyck.

**1981, Apr. 5**
173  A44  30c  multicolored     .50  .35
174  A44  40c  multicolored     .65  .65
175  A44  50c  multicolored     .85  .75
 a. Souv. sheet of #173-175, perf 13½     3.75  3.75
 Nos. 173-175 (3)     2.00  1.60

See Nos. B10-B12.

Designs: Portraits of Prince Charles.

**1981, July 10    Photo.    Perf. 14**
176  A45  40c  multicolored     .20  .20
177  A45  50c  multicolored     .25  .25
178  A45  60c  multicolored     .30  .30
179  A45  70c  multicolored     .40  .40
180  A45  80c  multicolored     .45  .45
 a. Souv. sheet of 5, #176-180+label     2.50  2.50
 Nos. 176-180 (5)     1.60  1.60

Royal wedding. Nos. 176-180 each issued in sheets of 5 plus label showing couple.
For overprints and surcharges see Nos. 195-199, 244-245, 248, 299-300, B13-B18.

Shirts: #181: a, Red. b, Striped. c, Blue. #182: a, Blue. b, Red. c, Striped. #183: a, Orange. b, Purple. c, Black.

**1981, Dec. 7    Photo.    Perf. 13**
181  A46  15c  Strip of 3, #a.-c.     1.00  .60
182  A46  35c  Strip of 3, #a.-c.     2.25  1.75
183  A46  50c  Strip of 3, #a.-c.     6.50  3.60
 Nos. 181-183 (3)

1982 World Cup Soccer. See No. B19.

Christmas — A47
21st Birthday of Princess Diana — A48

Dürer Engravings: 30c, Virgin on a Crescent, 1508. 40c, Virgin at the Fence, 1503. 50c, Holy Virgin and Child, 1505.

**1981, Dec. 15    Photo.    Perf. 13x13½**
184  A47  30c  multicolored     1.10  1.10
185  A47  40c  multicolored     1.50  1.50
186  A47  50c  multicolored     1.90  1.90
 a. Souvenir sheet of 3     4.00  4.00
 Nos. 184-186 (3)     4.50  4.50
 **Souvenir Sheets    Perf. 14x13½**
187  A47  70c + 5c like #184     1.50  1.50
188  A47  70c + 5c like #185     1.50  1.50
189  A47  70c + 5c like #186     1.50  1.50

No. 186a contains Nos. 184-186 each with 2c surcharge. Nos. 187-189 each contain one 25x40mm stamp. Surtaxes were for childrens' charities.

Designs: Portraits of Diana.

**1982, July 1    Photo.    Perf. 13½**
190  A48  30c  multicolored     1.00  1.00
191  A48  50c  multicolored     1.25  1.25
192  A48  70c  multicolored     1.50  1.50
193  A48  90c  multicolored     1.75  1.75
194  A48  $1.40  multicolored     3.50  3.50
 a. Souv. sheet, #190-194 + label     9.00  9.00
 Nos. 190-194 (5)     9.00  9.00

For new inscriptions, overprints and surcharges, see Nos. 200-204, 246-247, 249-250, 301-302.

Nos. 176-100a Overprinted: "BIRTH OF PRINCE WILLIAM OF WALES 21 JUNE 1982"

**1982, July 30**
195  A45  40c  multicolored     .50  .50
196  A45  50c  multicolored     .65  .65
197  A45  60c  multicolored     .75  .75
198  A45  70c  multicolored     1.00  1.00
199  A45  80c  multicolored     1.10  1.10
 a. Souv. sheet, #195-199 + label     6.00  6.00
 Nos. 195-199 (5)

Nos. 190-194a Inscribed in Silver: 21 JUNE 1982 BIRTH OF/PRINCE WILLIAM OF WALES (a) or COMMEMORATING THE BIRTH OF/PRINCE WILLIAM OF WALES (b)

**1982**
200  A48  30c  Pair, #a.-b.     .60  .60
201  A48  50c  Pair, #a.-b.     .90  .90
202  A48  70c  Pair, #a.-b.     1.50  1.50
203  A48  80c  Pair, #a.-b.     1.75  1.75
204  A48  $1.40  Pair, #a.-b.     3.25  3.25
 c. Souv. sheet of 5, #200a, 201a, 202a, 203a, 204a + label     8.00  8.00
 Nos. 200-204 (5)

Miniature sheets of each denomination were issued containing 2 "21 JUNE 1982..." 3 "COMMEMORATING..." and label. Value, set of 5 sheets, $21.
Se-tenant pairs come with or without label. For surcharges see Nos. 247, 250, 253.

Christmas: Virgin and Child Paintings.

## PENRHYN ISLAND

Various whale hunting scenes.

Save the Whales Campaign — A52

**1982, Dec. 10  Photo.  Perf. 14**
205  A49  35c Joos Van Cleve (1485-1540)  .70  .70
206  A49  48c Filippino Lippi (1457-1504)  .90  .90
207  A49  60c Cima Da Conegliano (1459-1517)  1.10  1.10
a.  Souvenir sheet of 3
  Nos. 205-207 (3)  2.70  2.70

208  A49  70c + 5c like 35c  1.75  1.75
209  A49  70c + 5c like 48c  1.75  1.75
210  A49  70c + 5c like 60c  1.75  1.75

Nos. 205-207 were printed in sheets of five plus label. No. 207a contains no (1459-1517) on each stamp, perf. 13½. Surtaxes were for childrens' charities.

Nos. 205-207 each contain one stamp, perf. 13½. Nos. 208-210 each contain one stamp, with 2c surcharge. Surtaxes were for childrens' charities.

Scouting Year A51

Emblem and various tropical flowers.

**1983, Mar. 14  Perf. 13½x13**
211  A50  60c Block of 4, #a.-d., Map.  2.75  2.75

#a, Red coral. #b, Aerial view. #c, Roosevelt, grass skirt. #d, Map.

Commonwealth day. For surcharges see No. O27-O30.

**1983, Apr. 5  Perf. 13½x14½**
215  A51  36c multicolored  1.90  .60
216  A51  48c multicolored  2.25  .80
217  A51  60c multicolored  3.00  1.00
  Nos. 215-217 (3)  7.15  2.40

**Souvenir Sheet**
218  A51  $2 multicolored  4.25  4.25

15th World Boy Scout Jamboree.

**1983, July 8  Photo.  Perf. 13½x14½**
219  A51  36c multicolored  1.90  1.60
220  A51  48c multicolored  2.50  1.00
221  A51  60c multicolored  2.90  2.60
  Nos. 219-221 (3)  6.90  2.60

**Souvenir Sheet**
222  A51  $2 multicolored  4.25  4.25

WORLD JAMBOREE / CANADA / 1983"

Nos. 215-218 Overprinted: "XV /

---

A50

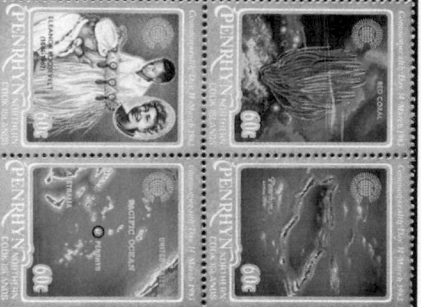

**1983, July 29  Photo.  Perf. 13**
223  A52  8c multicolored  .90  .30
224  A52  15c multicolored  1.40  .40
225  A52  35c multicolored  2.75  .75
226  A52  60c multicolored  4.50  1.50
227  A52  $1 multicolored  7.25  2.50
  Nos. 223-227 (5)  16.80  5.45

World Communications Year — A53

Designs: Cable laying Vessels.

**1983, Sept.  Photo.  Perf. 13**
228  A53  36c multicolored  1.10  .60
229  A53  48c multicolored  1.40  .80
230  A53  60c multicolored  1.75  1.00
  Nos. 228-230 (3)  4.25  2.40

**Souvenir Sheet**
231  Sheet of 3  3.00  3.00
a.  A53  36c + 3c like No. 228  1.10  .75
b.  A53  48c + 3c like No. 229  1.00  1.00
c.  A53  60c + 3c like No. 230  1.10  1.10

Surtax was for local charities.

Nos. 164, 166-167, 170, 172, 178-180, 192-194, 202-204 Surcharged

**1983  Perf. 14, 13½x14½, 13½**
**Blocks of 4, #a.-d. (#241-243)**
**Pairs, #a.-b. (#247, 250, 253)  Photo.**
241  A40  18c on 10c #164  1.75  1.75
242  A41  18c on 10c #166  3.00  3.00
243  A41  36c on 30c #167  3.00  3.00
244  A45  36c on 30c #170  1.25  1.00
245  A45  72c on 70c #172  1.75  1.75
247  A48  36c on 70c #178  3.75  3.75
248  A48  96c on 80c #179  2.25  2.25
249  A48  96c on 80c #180  2.25  2.25
250  A42  36c on 80c #192  3.75  3.75
251  A42  96c on 80c #193  4.00  4.00
252  A42  $1.20 on #194  4.00  4.00
253  A48  $1.20 on #202  3.75  3.75
254  A42  $5.60 on $6 multi  15.00  15.00
  Nos. 241-254 (14)  50.75  50.75

Issued: #241-243, 245, 251, Sept. 26; #244, 246, 249, 252, 254, Oct. 28; others Dec. 1.

First Manned Balloon Flight, 200th Anniv. — A54

Designs: 36c, Airship, Sir George Cayley (1773-1857). 48c, Man-powered airship, Dupuy de Lome (1818-1885). 60c, Brazilian Aviation Pioneer, Alberto Santos Dumont (1873-1932). 96c, Practical Airship, Paul Lebaudy (1858-1937). $1.32, Graf Zeppelin.

**1983, Oct. 31  Litho.  Perf. 13**
255  A54  36c multicolored  1.25  1.25
256  A54  48c multicolored  1.75  1.75
257  A54  60c multicolored  2.00  2.00
258  A54  96c multicolored  3.00  3.00
259  A54  $1.32 multicolored  4.50  4.50
a.  Souvenir sheet of 5, #255-259  12.00  12.00
  Nos. 255-259 (5)  12.50  12.50

Nos. 255-259 se-tenant with labels. Sheets of 5 for each value exist. Nos. 255-259 are misspelled "ISLANS." For correcting overprints see Nos. 287-291.

---

**PENRHYN ISLAND**

Christmas A55

**1983, Nov. 30  Photo.  Perf. 13x13½**
260  A55  36c multicolored  .90  .55
261  A55  42c multicolored  1.10  .65
262  A55  48c multicolored  1.40  .75
263  A55  60c multicolored  1.50  .95
  Nos. 260-263 (4)  4.90  2.90

**Souvenir Sheets**
264  A55  75c + 5c like #260  1.25  1.25
265  A55  75c + 5c like #261  1.25  1.25
266  A55  75c + 5c like #262  1.25  1.25
267  A55  75c + 5c like #263  1.25  1.25

Raphael Paintings: 36c, Madonna in the Meadow. 42c, Tempi Madonna. 48c, Cowper Madonna. 60c, Madonna Della Tenda.

No. 263a contains Nos. 260-263 each with 3c surcharge. Nos. 264-267 each contain one 29x41mm stamp. Issued Dec. 28. Surtaxes were for children's charities.

Waka Canoe — A56

**1984  Photo.  Perf. 14½**
268  A56  2c shown  .20  .20
269  A56  4c Amatasi fishing boat  .20  .20
270  A56  5c Ndrua canoe  .20  .20
271  A56  8c Tongiaki canoe  .20  .20
272  A56  10c Victoria, 1500  .40  .40
273  A56  18c Golden Hind, 1560  .55  .55
274  A56  20c Boudeuse, 1760  .65  .65
275  A56  30c Bounty, 1787  .90  .90
276  A56  36c Astrolabe, 1811  1.10  1.10
277  A56  48c Great Republic, 1853  1.50  1.50
278  A56  50c Star of India, 1861  1.60  1.60
279  A56  60c Coonatto, 1863  1.60  1.60
280  A56  72c Antiope, 1866  1.75  1.75
281  A56  80c Balcutha, 1886  2.25  2.25
282  A56  96c Cap Hornier, 1910  2.50  2.50
283  A56  $1.20 Pamir, 1921  3.25  3.25
  Pamir, 1921  1.60  1.60

**Size: 42x34mm**
284  A56  $3 Mermerus, 1872  3.25  3.25
285  A56  $5 Cutty Sark, 1869  6.75  6.75
286  A56  $9.60 Resolution, Discovery  11.00  11.00
  Resolution, Discovery  20.00  20.00
  Nos. 268-286 (19)  56.60  56.60

Issue dates: Nos. 268-277, Feb. 8, Nos. 278-283, Mar. 23, Nos. 284-286 June 15.

Nos. 255-259a Ovptd. with Silver Bar and "NORTHERN COOK ISLANDS" in Black

**1984**
287  A54  36c multicolored  .85  .85
288  A54  48c multicolored  1.10  1.10
289  A54  60c multicolored  1.40  1.40
290  A54  96c multicolored  2.25  2.25
291  A54  $1.32 multicolored  3.00  3.00
a.  Souvenir sheet of 5, #287-291  8.60  8.60
  Nos. 287-291 (5)  8.75  8.75

For overprints and surcharges see Nos. O16-O26, O31-O34, O36, O38, O40.

---

1984 Los Angeles Summer Olympic Games A57

**1984, July 20  Photo.  Perf. 13½x13**
292  A57  35c Olympic flag  .90  .90
293  A57  60c Torch, flags  .60  .60
294  A57  $1.80 Classic runners, Memorial Coliseum
  Sheet of 3 + label  2.40  2.40
  Nos. 292-294 (3)  3.90  3.90

**Souvenir Sheet**
295  Sheet of 3 + label  3.50  3.50
a.  A57  35c + 5c like #292  .40  .40
b.  A57  60c + 5c like #293  .65  .65
c.  A57  $1.80 + 5c like #294  2.25  2.25

Surtax for amateur sports.

---

Audubon Bicentenary — A59

**1985, Apr. 9  Photo.  Perf. 13½x13**
311  A59  20c Harlequin duck  1.60  1.60
312  A59  55c Sage grouse  4.25  4.25
313  A59  65c Solitary sandpiper  5.00  5.00
314  A59  75c Red-backed sandpiper  5.75  5.75
  Nos. 311-314 (4)  16.60  16.60

**Souvenir Sheets**
315  A59  95c Like #311  3.00  3.00
316  A59  95c Like #312  3.00  3.00
317  A59  95c Like #313  3.00  3.00
318  A59  95c Like #314  3.00  3.00

For surcharges see Nos. 391-394.

Paintings: 36c, Virgin and Child, by Giovanni Bellini. 48c, Virgin and Child, by Lorenzo di Credi. 60c, Virgin and Child, by Palma, the Older. 96c, Virgin and Child, by Raphael.

**1984, Oct. 18**
299  A45  $2 on 40c  2.00  2.00
300  A45  $2 on 50c  2.00  2.00
301  A48  $2 on 30c  2.00  2.00
302  A48  $2 on 50c  2.00  2.00
  Nos. 299-302 (4)  8.00  8.00

**Souvenir Sheet**
298  Sheet of 2  3.50  3.50
a.  A57a  96c like #296  1.75  1.75
b.  A57a  96c like #297  1.75  1.75

For surcharge see No. 345.

Nos. 176-177, 190-191 Ovptd. "Birth of/Prince Henry/15 Sept. 1984" and Surcharged in Black or Gold

Nos. 299-302 printed in sheets of 5 plus one label each picturing a couple or an heraldic griffin.

AUSIPEX '84 — A57a

**1984, Sept. 20**
296  A57a  60c Nos. 136, 108, 180, 104b  1.10  1.10
297  A57a  $1.20 Nos. 63 of South Pacific  2.25  2.25

Christmas 1984 — A58

**1984, Nov. 15  Photo.  Perf. 13x13½**
303  A58  36c multicolored  .65  .65
304  A58  48c multicolored  1.10  1.10
305  A58  60c multicolored  1.25  1.25
306  A58  96c multicolored  1.75  1.75
a.  Souvenir sheet of 4  4.50  4.50
  Nos. 303-306 (4)  5.00  5.00

**Souvenir Sheets**
307  A58  96c + 10c like #303  1.75  1.75
308  A58  96c + 10c like #304  1.75  1.75
309  A58  96c + 10c like #305  1.75  1.75
310  A58  96c + 10c like #306  1.75  1.75

No. 306a contains Nos. 303-306, each with 5c surcharge. Nos. 307-310 issued Dec. 10. Surtax for children's charities.

**1985, June 24 Photo.** *Perf. 13x13½*
319 A60 75c Photograph, 1921 .60 .65
320 A60 95c New mother, 1926 .80 .80
321 A60 $1.20 Coronation day, 1937 1.10 1.00
322 A60 $2.80 70th birthday 2.50 2.50
  a. Souvenir sheet of 4, #319-322 19.00 19.00
    *Nos. 319-322 (4)* 5.00 4.95

**Souvenir Sheet**
323 A60 $5 Portrait, c. 1980 4.25 4.25
No. 322a issued on 8/4/86, for 86th birthday.

Intl. Youth Year — A61

Grimm Brothers' fairy tales.

**1985, Sept. 10** *Perf. 13x13½*
324 A61 75c House in the Wood 2.25 2.25
325 A61 95c Snow White and Rose Red 3.50 3.50
326 A61 $1.15 Goose Girl 5.00 5.00
    *Nos. 324-326 (3)* 10.75 10.75

Christmas 1985 A62

**1985, Nov. 25 Photo.**
327 A62 75c multicolored 1.75 1.75
328 A62 $1.15 multicolored 2.50 2.50
329 A62 $1.80 multicolored 4.25 4.25
    *Nos. 327-329 (3)* 8.50 8.50

**Souvenir Sheets** *Perf. 13½*
330 Sheet of 3 4.75 4.75
  a.-c. A62 95c any single 1.50 1.50
331 A62 $1.20 like #327 1.75 1.75
332 A62 $1.45 like #328 2.25 2.25
333 A62 $2.75 like #329 4.00 4.00

Halley's Comet — A63

**1986, Feb. 4** *Perf. 13½x13*
334 A63 $1.50 Comet head 4.25 4.25
335 A63 $1.50 Comet tail 4.25 4.25
  a. Pair, #334-335 8.50 8.50

**Size: 109x43mm** *Imperf*
336 A63 $3 multicolored 6.50 6.50
    *Nos. 334-336 (3)* 15.00 15.00

---

For surcharges see Nos. B20-B23.

**Souvenir Sheets**

Statue of Liberty, Cent. — A68

Photographs: No. 350a, Workmen, crown. No. 350b, Ellis Is., aerial view. No. 350c, Immigration building, Ellis Is. No. 350d, Buildings, opposite side of Ellis Is. No. 350e, Workmen inside torch structure. No. 351a, Liberty's head and torch. No. 351b, Torch. No. 351c, Workmen on scaffold. No. 351d, Statue, full figure. No. 351e, Workmen beside statue. Nos. 351a-351e vert.

**1987, Apr. 15 Litho.** *Perf. 14*
350 Sheet of 5 + label 6.50 6.50
  a.-e. A68 65c any single 1.25 1.25
351 Sheet of 5 + label 6.50 6.50
  a.-e. A68 65c any single 1.25 1.25

Nos. 62-63 Ovptd. "Fortieth Royal Wedding / Anniversary 1947-87" in Lilac Rose

**1987, Nov. 20 Photo.** *Perf. 13½x14*
352 A18 $2 multicolored 2.25 2.25
353 A18 $5 multicolored 6.00 6.00

Christmas A69

Paintings (details) by Raphael: 95c, No. 357a, The Garvagh Madonna; 95c, No. 357b, The Alba Madonna, the National Gallery of Art, Washington. $2.25, No. 357c, $4.80, The Madonna of the Fish, Prado Museum, Madrid.

**1987, Dec. 11 Photo.** *Perf. 13½*
354 A69 95c multicolored 2.50 2.50
355 A69 $1.60 multicolored 3.25 3.25
356 A69 $2.25 multicolored 5.00 5.00
    *Nos. 354-356 (3)* 10.75 10.75

**Souvenir Sheets**
357 Sheet of 3 + label 18.00 18.00
  a.-c. A69 $1.15 any single 5.50 5.50
358 A69 $4.80 multicolored 17.50 17.50
No. 358 contains one 31x39mm stamp.

1988 Summer Olympics, Seoul — A70

Events and: 55c, $1.25, Seoul Games emblem. 95c, Obverse of a $50 silver coin issued in 1987 to commemorate the participation of Cook Islands athletes in the Olympics for the 1st time. $1.50, Coin reverse.

**1988, July 29** *Perf. 13½x13, 13x13½* **Photo.**
359 A70 55c Running 1.40 1.40
360 A70 95c High jump, vert. 2.75 2.75
361 A70 $1.25 Shot put 3.00 3.00
362 A70 $1.50 Swim, vert. 5.25 5.25
    *Nos. 359-362 (4)* 12.40 12.40

**Souvenir Sheet**
363 Sheet of 2 11.50 11.50
  a. A70 $2.50 like 95c 5.50 5.50
  b. A70 $2.50 like $1.50 5.50 5.50

---

Nos. 359-363 Ovptd. for Olympic Gold Medalists
  a. "CARL LEWIS / UNITED STATES / 100 METERS"
  b. "LOUISE RITTER / UNITED STATES / HIGH JUMP"
  c. "ULF TIMMERMANN / EAST GERMANY / SHOT-PUT"
  d. "STEFFI GRAF / WEST GERMANY / WOMEN'S TENNIS"
  e. "JACKIE / JOYNER-KERSEE / United States / Heptathlon"
  f. "STEFFI GRAF / West Germany / Women's Tennis / MILOSLAV MECIR / Czechoslovakia / Men's Tennis"

**1988, Oct. 14** *Perf. 13½x13, 13x13½* **Photo.**
364 A70(a) 55c on No. 359 1.25 1.25
365 A70(b) 95c on No. 360 2.25 2.25
366 A70(c) 95c on No. 361 2.50 2.50
367 A70(d) $1.50 on No. 362 5.25 5.25
    *Nos. 364-367 (4)* 11.25 11.25

**Souvenir Sheet**
368 Sheet of 2 11.50 11.50
  a. A70(e) $2.50 on No. 363a 5.50 5.50
  b. A70(f) $2.50 on No. 363b 5.50 5.50

Christmas A71

*Virgin and Child paintings by Titian.*

**1988, Nov. 9** *Perf. 13x13½*
369 A71 70c multicolored 1.75 1.75
370 A71 85c multi. diff. 2.00 2.00
371 A71 95c multi. diff. 2.50 2.50
372 A71 $1.25 multi. diff. 3.00 3.00
    *Nos. 369-372 (4)* 9.25 9.25

**Souvenir Sheet** *Perf. 13*
373 A71 $6.40 multi. diff. 11.00 11.00
No. 373 contains one diamond-shaped stamp, size: 55x55mm.

1st Moon Landing, 20th Anniv. A72

Apollo 11 mission emblem, US flag and: 55c, First step on the Moon. 75c, Astronaut carrying experiment. 95c, Conducting experiment. $1.25, Crew members Armstrong, Collins and Aldrin. $1.75, Armstrong and Aldrin aboard lunar module.

**1989, July 24 Photo.** *Perf. 14*
374-378 A72 Set of 5 13.00 13.00

Christmas A73

Details from *The Nativity*, by Albrecht Durer, 1498, center panel of the Paumgartner altarpiece: 55c, center panel. 70c, Christ child, cherubs. 85c, Joseph. $1.25, Attendants. $6.40, Entire painting.

**1989, Nov. 17 Photo.** *Perf. 13x13½*
379-382 A73 Set of 4 7.25 7.25

**Souvenir Sheet**
383 A73 $6.40 multicolored 11.00 11.00
No. 383 contains one 31x50mm stamp.

**Queen Mother, 90th Birthday — A74**

**1990, July 24**   **Photo.**   **Perf. 13½**
| 384 | A74 | $2.25 multicolored | 4.00 | 4.00 |

**Souvenir Sheet**
| 385 | A74 | $7.50 multicolored | 18.00 | 18.00 |

**Christmas — A75**
| 390 | A75 | $6.40 multicolored | 13.50 | 13.50 |

**1990, Nov. 26**   **Litho.**   **Perf. 14**

**Souvenir Sheet**
| 386-389 | A75 | Set of 4 | 11.50 | 11.50 |

Paintings: 55c, Adoration of the Magi by Veronese. 70c, Virgin and Child by Quentin Metsys. 85c, Virgin and Child Jesus by Van Der Goes. $1.50, Adoration of the Kings by Jan Gossaert. $6.40, Virgin and Child with Saints Francis, John the Baptist, Zenobius and Lucy by Domenico Veneziano.

**1990, Dec. 5**   **Photo.**   **Perf. 13**
| 391 | A59 | $1.50 on 20c (R) | 3.25 | 3.25 |
| 392 | A59 | $1.50 on 55c | 3.25 | 3.25 |
| 393 | A59 | $1.50 on 65c | 3.25 | 3.25 |
| 394 | A59 | $1.50 on 75c (R) | 3.25 | 3.25 |
| | | Nos. 391-394 (4) | 13.00 | 13.00 |

Birdpex '90, 20th Intl. Ornithological Cong., New Zealand. Surcharge appears in various locations.

Nos. 311-314. Surcharged in Red or Black

No. 172 Overprinted
"COMMEMORATING 65th BIRTHDAY OF H.M. QUEEN ELIZABETH II"

**1991, Apr. 22**   **Photo.**   **Perf. 13½**
| 395 | A42 | $6 multicolored | 14.00 | 14.00 |

**Christmas — A76**

**1991, Nov. 11**   **Litho.**   **Perf. 14**
| 396-399 | A76 | Set of 4 | 10.00 | 10.00 |

**Souvenir Sheet**
| 400 | A76 | $6.40 multicolored | 17.50 | 17.50 |

Paintings: 55c, Virgin and Child with Saints, by Gerard David. 85c, The Nativity, by Tintoretto. $1.15, Mystic Nativity, by Botticelli. $1.85, Adoration of the Shepherds, by Murillo. $6.40, Madonna and the Chair, by Raphael.

**1992 Summer Olympics, Barcelona — A77**

**1992, July 27**   **Litho.**   **Perf. 14**
| 401 | A77 | 75c Runners | 2.50 | 2.50 |
| 402 | A77 | 95c Boxing | 3.00 | 3.00 |
| 403 | A77 | $1.15 Swimming | 3.50 | 3.50 |
| 404 | A77 | $1.50 Wrestling | 4.00 | 4.00 |
| | | Nos. 401-404 (4) | 13.00 | 13.00 |

**6th Festival of Pacific Arts, Rarotonga — A78**

**1992, Oct. 16**   **Litho.**   **Perf. 14x15**
| 405 | A78 | $1.15 multicolored | 3.25 | 3.25 |
| 406 | A78 | $1.75 multicolored | 3.50 | 3.50 |
| 407 | A78 | $1.95 multicolored | 4.00 | 4.00 |
| | | Nos. 405-407 (3) | 10.75 | 10.75 |

Festival poster and: $1.15, Marquesan canoe. $1.75, Statue of Tangaroa. $1.95, Manihiki canoe.

For overprints see Nos. 455-457.

Overprinted 'ROYAL VISIT'

**1992, Oct. 16**
| 408 | A78 | $1.15 on #405 | 2.75 | 2.75 |
| 409 | A78 | $1.75 on #406 | 3.75 | 3.75 |
| 410 | A78 | $1.95 on #407 | 4.50 | 4.50 |
| | | Nos. 408-410 (3) | 11.00 | 11.00 |

**Christmas A79**

**1992, Nov. 18**   **Litho.**   **Perf. 13½**
| 411-414 | A79 | Set of 4 | 9.50 | 9.50 |

**Souvenir Sheet**
| 415 | A79 | $6.40 multicolored | 12.50 | 12.50 |

No. 415 contains one 38x48mm stamp.

Paintings by Ambrogio Borgognone: 55c, Virgin with Child and Saints. 85c, Virgin on Throne. $1.05, Virgin on Carpet. $1.85, Virgin of the Milk.

**Discovery of America, 500th Anniv. — A80**

**1992, Dec. 4**   **Litho.**   **Perf. 15x14**
| 416 | A80 | $1.15 multicolored | 3.25 | 3.25 |
| 417 | A80 | $1.35 multicolored | 3.25 | 3.25 |
| 418 | A80 | $1.75 multicolored | 4.75 | 4.75 |
| | | Nos. 416-418 (3) | 11.25 | 11.25 |

Designs: $1.15, Vicente Yanez Pinzon, Nina. $1.35, Martin Alonso Pinzon, Pinta. $1.75, Columbus, Santa Maria.

**Coronation of Queen Elizabeth II, 40th Anniv. — A81**

**1993, June 4**   **Litho.**   **Perf. 14x14½**
| 419 | A81 | $6 multicolored | 11.50 | 11.50 |

**Marine Life — A82**    **Marine Life — A82a**

**1993-98**   **Litho.**   **Perf. 14**
| 420 | A82 | 5c Helmet shell | .20 | .20 |
| 421 | A82 | 10c Daisy coral | .20 | .20 |
| 422 | A82 | 15c Hydroid coral | .20 | .20 |
| 423 | A82 | 20c Feather star | .25 | .25 |
| 424 | A82 | 25c Sea star | .30 | .30 |
| 425 | A82 | 50c Nudibranch | .40 | .40 |
| 426 | A82 | 50c Smooth sea star | .55 | .55 |
| 427 | A82 | 70c Black pearl oyster | .65 | .55 |
| 428 | A82 | 80c Pyjama nudi-branch | 1.00 | .80 |
| 429 | A82 | 85c Prickly sea cucumber | 1.10 | .90 |
| 430 | A82 | 90c Organ pipe coral | 1.25 | .95 |
| 431 | A82 | $1 Aeolid nudi-branch | 1.40 | 1.00 |
| 432 | A82 | $2 Textile cone shell | 2.75 | 1.10 |
| 433 | A82a | $3 pink & multi | 2.75 | 2.25 |
| 434 | A82a | $5 lilac & multi | 4.00 | 3.25 |
| 435 | A82a | $8 blue & multi | 7.00 | 5.50 |
| 435A | A82a | $10 grn & multi | 14.00 | 11.00 |
| | | Nos. 420-435A (17) | 50.00 | 39.80 |

For overprints see #O41-O53.

Issued: 80c, 85c, 90c, $1, $2, 12/3/93; $3, $5, 11/21/94; $8, 11/17/97; $10, 10/1/98; others, 10/18/93. This is an expanding set. Numbers will change if necessary.

**Christmas — A83**

Details from Virgin on Throne with Child, by Cosimo Tura: 55c, Madonna and Child. 85c, Musicians. $1.05, Musicians, diff. $1.95, Woman. $4.50, Entire painting.

**1993, Nov. 2**   **Litho.**   **Perf. 14**
| 436 | A83 | 55c multicolored | 1.40 | 1.40 |
| 437 | A83 | 85c multicolored | 2.25 | 2.25 |
| 438 | A83 | $1.05 multicolored | 2.50 | 2.50 |
| 439 | A83 | $1.95 multicolored | 3.75 | 3.75 |

**Size: 32x47mm**
| 440 | A83 | $4.50 multicolored | 8.25 | 8.25 |
| | | Nos. 436-440 (5) | 18.15 | 18.15 |

**First Manned Moon Landing, 25th Anniv. A84**

**1994, July 20**   **Litho.**   **Perf. 14**
| 441 | A84 | $3.25 multicolored | 11.50 | 11.50 |

**End of World War II, 50th Anniv. — A86**

**1995, Sept. 4**   **Litho.**   **Perf. 13**
| 444 | A86 | $3.75 Pair, #a-b. | 24.00 | 24.00 |

Designs: a, Battleships on fire, Pearl Harbor, Dec. 7, 1941. b, B-29 bomber Enola Gay, A-bomb cloud, Aug. 1945.

**Christmas — A85**

**1994, Nov. 30**   **Litho.**   **Perf. 14**
| 442 | A85 | 90c Block of 4, #a-d. | 6.75 | 6.75 |
| 443 | A85 | $1 Block of 4, #a-d. | 7.25 | 7.25 |

Details or entire paintings: No. 442a, Virgin and Child with Saints Paul & Jerome, by Vivarini. b, The Virgin and Child with Saints by B. Luini. c, The Virgin and Child with Saints Jerome & Dominic, by F. Lippi. d, Virgin and Child, by Murillo. No. 443a, Adoration of the Kings, by Reni. b, Madonna & Child with the Infant Baptist, by Raphael. c, Adoration of the Kings, by Reni, diff. d, Virgin and Child, by Bergognone.

**Queen Mother, 95th Birthday A87**

**1995, Sept. 14**   **Litho.**   **Perf. 13½**
| 445 | A87 | $4.50 multicolored | 12.00 | 12.00 |

No. 445 was issued in sheets of 4.

**UN, 50th Anniv. — A88**

**1995, Oct. 20**   **Litho.**   **Perf. 13½**
| 446 | A88 | $4 multicolored | 6.50 | 6.50 |

No. 446 was issued in sheets of 4.

**1995, Year of the Sea Turtle — A89**

No. 447: a, Loggerhead. b, Hawksbill.
No. 448: a, Olive ridley. b, Green.

**1995, Dec. 7    Litho.    Perf. 13½**
447  A89  $1.15  Pair, #a-b.    5.50  4.00
448  A89  $1.65  Pair, #a-b.    8.25  5.00

Queen Elizabeth II, 70th Birthday — A90

**1996, June 20    Litho.    Perf. 14**
449  A90  $4.25  multicolored    8.00  8.00

No. 449 was issued in sheets of 4.

1996 Summer Olympic Games, Atlanta — A91

**1996, July 12    Litho.    Perf. 14**
450  A91  $5  multicolored    11.00  11.00

**Souvenir Sheet**
451  A92  $3  multicolored    4.25  4.25

No. 452 is a continuous design.

**1997, Nov. 20    Litho.    Perf. 14**
452  A92  $4  multicolored    6.00  6.00

Queen Elizabeth II and Prince Philip, 50th Wedding Anniv. — A92

**Souvenir Sheet**
453  A93  $3.75  like #453    4.50  4.50

No. 453 was issued in sheets of 5 + label.
For surcharge see #B24.

Diana, Princess of Wales (1961-97) — A93

**1998, May 7    Litho.    Perf. 14**
453  A93  $1.50  multicolored    1.75  1.75

**Souvenir Sheet**
454  A93  $3.75  like #453

Nos. 405-407 Ovptd. "KIA ORANA / THIRD MILLENNIUM"
Methods and Perfs as before

**1999, Dec. 31**
455  A77  $1.15  multi    1.25  1.25
456  A77  $1.75  multi    2.10  2.10
457  A77  $1.95  multi    2.40  2.40
      Nos. 455-457 (3)    5.75  5.75

The Queen Mother's 100th Birthday

Queen Mother, 100th Birthday — A94

No. 458: a, With King George VI. b, With Princess Elizabeth. c, With King George VI, Princesses Elizabeth and Margaret. d, With Princesses.

**2000, Oct. 20    Litho.    Perf. 14**
458  A94  $2.50  Sheet of 4, #a-    10.50  10.50
      d

**Souvenir Sheet**
459  A94  $10  Portrait    10.50  10.50

2000 Summer Olympics, Sydney — A95

No. 460, horiz.: a, Ancient javelin. b, Javelin. c, Ancient discus. d, Discus.

**2000, Dec. 14**
460  A95  $2.75  Sheet of 4, #a-    12.50  12.50
      d

**Souvenir Sheet**
461  A95  $3.50  Torch relay    4.00  4.00

Worldwide Fund for Nature (WWF) A96

Various photos of ocean sunfish: 80c, 90c, $1.15, $1.95.

**2003, Feb. 24    Litho.    Perf. 14**
462-465  A96  Set of 4    6.75  6.75

Each printed in sheets of 4.

United We Stand — A97

**2003, Sept. 30    Litho.    Perf. 14**
466  A97  $1.50  multi    5.00  5.00

Printed in sheets of 4.

Pope John Paul II (1920-2005) A98

**2005, Nov. 11    Litho.    Perf. 14**
467  A98  $1.45  multi    2.10  2.10

Printed in sheets of 5 + label.

---

# SEMI-POSTAL STAMPS

Easter Type of 1978
Souvenir Sheets

Rubens Paintings: No. B1, like #101. No. B2, like #102. No. B3, like #103.

**1978, Apr. 17    Photo.    Perf. 13½x13**
B1  A31  60c + 5c multi    .60  .60
B2  A31  60c + 5c multi    .60  .60
B3  A31  60c + 5c multi    .60  .60
      Nos. B1-B3 (3)    1.80  1.80

Surtax was for school children.

Easter Type of 1980
Souvenir Sheets

**1980, Mar. 28    Photo.    Perf. 13x13½**
B4  A36  70c + 5c like #114    .60  .60
B5  A36  70c + 5c like #115    .60  .60
B6  A36  70c + 5c like #116    .60  .60
      Nos. B4-B6 (3)    1.80  1.80

Surtax was for local charities.

Christmas Type of 1980
Souvenir Sheets

**1980, Dec. 5    Photo.    Porf. 13**
B7  A39  70c + 5c like #127    1.25  1.25
B8  A39  70c + 5c like #128    1.25  1.25
B9  A39  70c + 5c like #129    1.25  1.25
      Nos. B7-B9 (3)    3.75  3.75

Surtax was for local charities.

Easter Type of 1981
Souvenir Sheets

**1981, Apr. 5    Photo.    Perf. 13½**
B10  A44  70c + 5c like #173    1.25  1.25
B11  A44  70c + 5c like #174    1.25  1.25
B12  A44  70c + 5c like #175    3.75  3.75
      Nos. B10-B12 (3)

Surtax was for local charities.

Nos. 176-180a Surcharged

**1981, Nov. 30    Photo.    Perf. 14**
B13  A45  40c + 5c like #176    .85  .45
B14  A45  50c + 5c like #177    .85  .50
B15  A45  60c + 5c like #178    1.25  .75
B16  A45  70c + 5c like #179    1.25  1.25
B17  A45  80c + 5c like #180    5.45  4.20
      Nos. B13-B17 (5)

**Souvenir Sheet**
Sheet of 5    7.00  7.00
a.  A45  40c + 10c like #176    1.25  1.25
b.  A45  50c + 10c like #177    1.25  1.25
c.  A45  60c + 10c like #178    1.25  1.25
d.  A45  70c + 10c like #179    1.25  1.25
e.  A45  80c + 10c like #180    1.25  1.25

B18

Intl. Year of the Disabled. Surtax was for the disabled.

Soccer Type of 1981

**1981, Dec. 7    Perf. 13**
B19  A46  Sheet of 9    6.50  3.00

No. B19 contains Nos. 181-183. Surtax was for local sports.

Nos. 346-349 Surcharged "..SOUTH PACIFIC PAPAL VISIT ..21 TO 24 NOVEMBER 1986" in Metallic Blue

**1986, Nov. 24    Litho.    Perf. 13x13½**
B20  A67  65c + 10c multi    4.25  4.25
B21  A67  $1.75 + 10c multi    7.00  7.00
B22  A67  $2.50 + 10c multi    8.50  8.50
      Nos. B20-B22 (3)    19.75  19.75

**Souvenir Sheet**
**Perf. 13½x13**
B23  Sheet of 3    24.00  24.00
a.-c.  A67  $1.50 + 10c like #349a-    7.50  7.50
      349c.

No. B23 inscribed "COMMEMORATING FIRST PAPAL VISIT TO SOUTH PACIFIC / VISIT OF POPE JOHN PAUL II. NOVEMBER 1986."

No. 454 Surcharged "CHILDREN'S CHARITIES" in Silver

**Souvenir Sheet**
**1998, Nov. 19    Litho.    Perf. 14**
B24  A93  $3.75  +$1 multi    6.00  6.00

---

# OFFICIAL STAMPS

O.H.M.S.

Nos. 51-60, 80, 88-89 Overprinted or Surcharged in Black, Silver or Gold

**1978, Nov. 14    Perf. 13½x14, 13½, 13½x13    Photo.**
O1  A17  1c multi    .20  .20
O2  A17  2c multi    .20  .20
O3  A17  3c multi    .25  .25
O4  A17  4c multi    .25  .25
O5  A17  5c multi    .25  .20
O6  A17  8c multi    .40  .20
O7  A17  10c multi    .50  .50
O8  A17  15c on 60c multi    .55  .35
O9  A17  18c on 60c multi    .60  .35
O10  A17  20c multi    .60  .35
O11  A17  25c multi (S)    .65  .40
O12  A17  25c multi (G)    .70  .45
O13  A24  Strip of 3, multi    3.25  2.25
      a.    50c, 80c multi
      b.    50c, 80c (S)    1.00  .75
      c.    50c, 80c (G)    1.00  .75
O14  A27  $1 multi (S)    2.75  .65
O15  A27  $2 multi (G)    4.75  .70
      Nos. O1-O15 (15)    16.00  6.90

Overprint on No. O14 diagonal.

Nos. 268-276, 278, 277, 211-214, 280, 282, 281, 283, 170, 284, 171, 285, 172, 286 Surcharged with Bar and New Value or Ovptd. "O.H.M.S." in Silver or Metallic Red

**1985-87    Photo.    Perfs. as before**
O16  A56  2c multi    .20  .20
O17  A56  4c multi    .20  .20
O18  A56  5c multi    .20  .20
O19  A56  10c multi    .20  .20
O20  A56  16c multi    .20  .20
O21  A56  18c multi    .20  .20
O22  A56  20c multi    .30  .30
O23  A56  30c multi    .40  .40
O24  A56  40c on 36c    .40  .40
O25  A56  50c multi    .50  .50
O26  A56  55c multi    .55  .55
O27  A50  55c on 48c    .55  .65
O28  A50  65c on 60c #211a    .65  .65
O29  A50  65c on 60c #211b    .65  .65
O30  A50  65c on 60c #211c    .65  .65
O31  A56  65c on 60c #211d    .65  .65
O32  A56  75c on 72c    .75  .75
O33  A56  75c on 96c    .75  .75
O34  A56  $1.20 multi    1.00  .80
O35  A42  $2 multi (R)    1.75  1.50
O36  A56  $3 multi (R)    2.75  2.10
O37  A42  $4 multi (R)    3.50  2.50
O38  A56  $5 multi (R)    4.50  3.50
O39  A42  $6 multi (R)    5.50  4.00
O40  A56  $9.60 multi    9.00  6.50
      Nos. O16-O40 (25)    36.15  29.15

Issued: #O16-O30, 8/15; #O31-O37, 4/29/86; #O38-O40, 11/2/87.

Nos. 420-432 Ovptd. "O.H.M.S." in Silver

**1998    Litho.    Perf. 14**
O41  A82  5c multicolored    .20  .20
O42  A82  10c multicolored    .20  .20
O43  A82  15c multicolored    .20  .20
O44  A82  20c multicolored    .20  .20
O45  A82  25c multicolored    .20  .20
O46  A82  30c multicolored    .35  .35
O47  A82  50c multicolored    .45  .45
O48  A82  70c multicolored    .60  .60
O49  A82  80c multicolored    .80  .80

| | | | | |
|---|---|---|---|---|
| O50 | A82 | 85c multicolored | .80 | .80 |
| O51 | A82 | 90c multicolored | .85 | .85 |
| O52 | A82 | $1 multicolored | .95 | .95 |
| O53 | A82 | $2 multicolored | 2.00 | 2.00 |
| | | Nos. O41-O53 (13) | 7.80 | 7.80 |

Nos. O41-O52 were not sold unused to local customers. Issued: $2, 9/30; others, 7/20.

# PERU

pə-ˈrü

LOCATION — West coast of South America
GOVT. — Republic
AREA — 496,093 sq. mi.
POP. — 24,800,768 (1998 est.)
CAPITAL — Lima

8 Reales = 1 Peso (1857)
100 Centimos = 8 Dineros =
4 Pesetas = 1 Peso (1858)
100 Centavos = 1 Sol (1874)
100 Centimos = 1 Inti (1985)
100 Centimos = 1 Sol (1991)

**Catalogue values for unused stamps in this country are for Never Hinged items, beginning with Scott 426 in the regular postage section, Scott B1 in the semi-postal section, Scott C78 in the airpost section, Scott CB1 in the airpost semi-postal section, and Scott RA31 in the postal tax section.**

**Watermark**

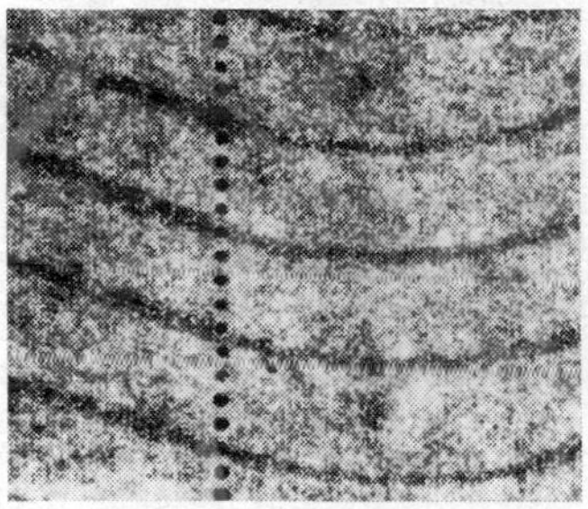

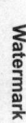

Wmk. 346 — Parallel Curved Lines

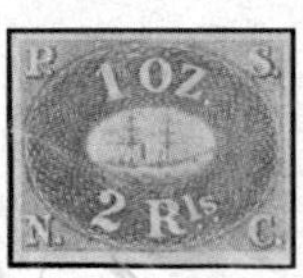

Sail and Steamship — A1

Design: 2r, Ship sails eastward.

**Unwmk.**

**1857, Dec. 1** **Engr.** ***Imperf.***
**1** A1 1r blue, *blue* 1,250. 1,450.
**2** A1 2r brn red, *blue* 1,350. 1,600.

The Pacific Steam Navigation Co. gave a quantity of these stamps to the Peruvian government so that a trial of prepayment of postage by stamps might be made.

Stamps of 1 and 2 reales, printed in various colors on white paper, laid and wove, were prepared for the Pacific Steam Navigation Co. but never put in use. Value $50 each on wove paper, $400 each on laid paper.

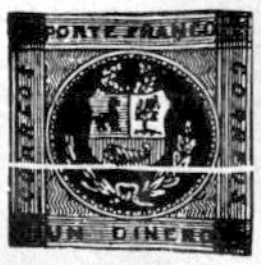
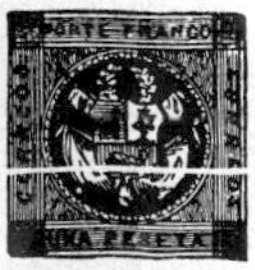

Coat of Arms
A2 A3

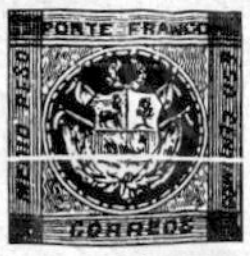

A4

Wavy Lines in Spandrels

**1858, Mar. 1** **Litho.**
**3** A2 1d deep blue 200. 27.50
**4** A3 1p rose red 850. 125.
**5** A4 ½peso rose red *3,750.* *3,000.*
**6** A4 ½peso buff *1,600.* 300.
*a.* ½peso orange yellow *1,600.* 300.

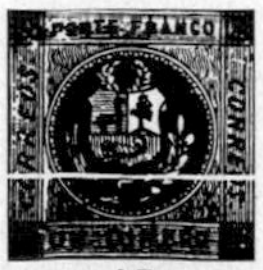
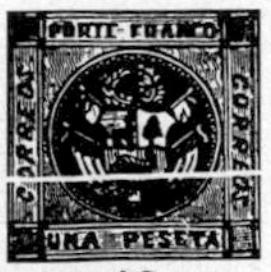

A5 A6

Large Letters

**1858, Dec.**
**Double-lined Frame**
**7** A5 1d slate blue 250.00 27.50
**8** A6 1p red 250.00 37.50

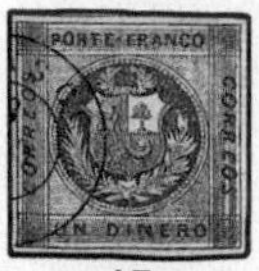
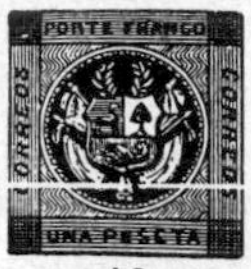

A7 A8

**1860-61**
**Zigzag Lines in Spandrels**
**9** A7 1d blue 100.00 6.50
*a.* 1d Prussian blue 100.00 12.00
*b.* Cornucopia on white ground 225.00 47.50
*c.* Zigzag lines broken at angles 125.00 14.00
**10** A8 1p rose 250.00 25.00
*a.* 1p brick red 250.00 25.00
*b.* Cornucopia on white ground 250.00 30.00

**Retouched, 10 lines instead of 9 in left label**
**11** A8 1p rose 125.00 25.00
*a.* Pelure paper 200.00 25.00
*Nos. 9-11 (3)* 475.00 56.50

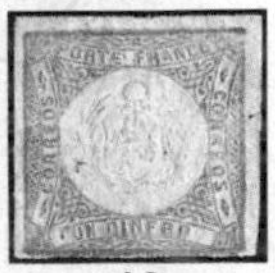
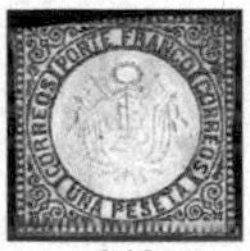

A9 A10

**1862-63** **Embossed**
**12** A9 1d red 13.00 3.50
*a.* Arms embossed sideways 425.00 90.00
*b.* Thick paper 27.50 8.00
*c.* Diag. half used on cover 140.00
**13** A10 1p brown ('63) 72.50 24.00
*a.* Diag. half used on cover 1,000.

Counterfeits of Nos. 13 and 15 exist.

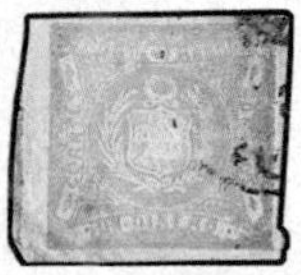

A11

**1868-72**
**14** A11 1d green 11.00 2.25
*a.* Arms embossed inverted *1,250.* *750.00*
*b.* Diag. half used on cover 350.00
**15** A10 1p orange ('72) 90.00 32.50
*a.* Diag. half used on cover —

Nos. 12-15, 19 and 20 were printed in horizontal strips. Stamps may be found printed on two strips of paper where the strips were joined by overlapping.

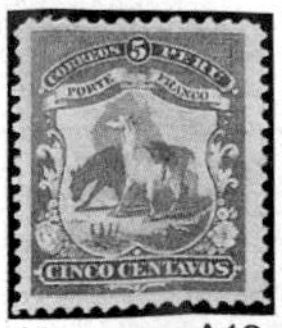

Llamas — A12

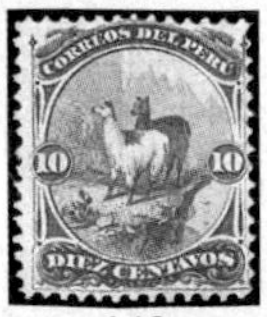

A13

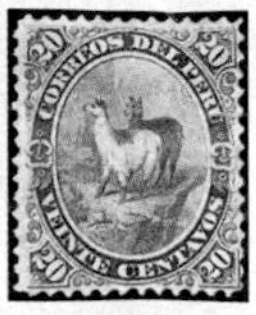

A14

**1866-67** **Engr.** ***Perf. 12***
**16** A12 5c green 6.00 .60
**17** A13 10c vermilion 6.00 1.40
**18** A14 20c brown 20.00 4.00
*a.* Diagonal half used on cover 375.00
*Nos. 16-18 (3)* 32.00 6.00

See Nos. 109, 111, 113.

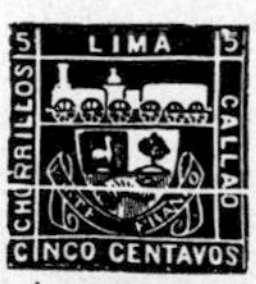

Locomotive and Arms — A15

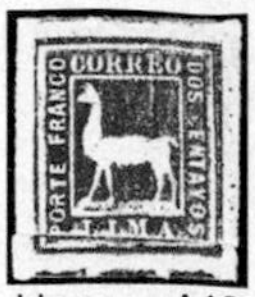

Llama — A16

**1871, Apr.** **Embossed** ***Imperf.***
**19** A15 5c scarlet 75.00 25.00
*a.* 5c pale red 75.00 25.00

20th anniv. of the first railway in South America, linking Lima and Callao.

The so-called varieties "ALLAO" and "CALLA" are due to over-inking.

**1873, Mar.** ***Rouletted Horiz.***
**20** A16 2c dk ultra 30.00 *250.00*

Counterfeits are plentiful.

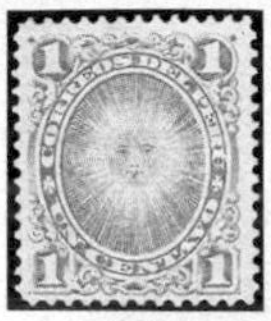

Sun God of the Incas — A17

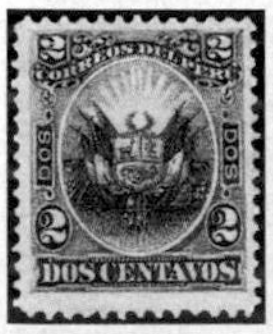
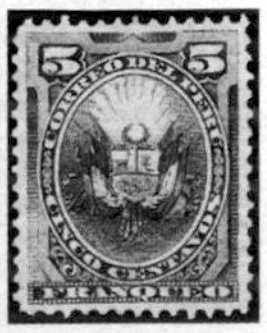

Coat of Arms
A18 A19

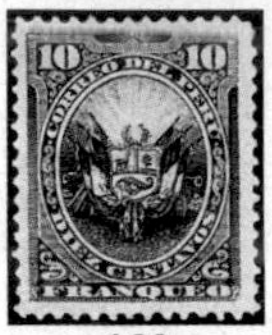
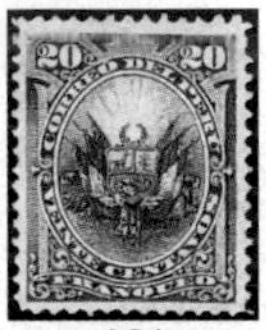

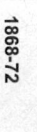

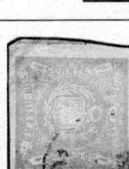

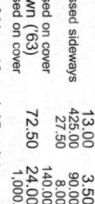

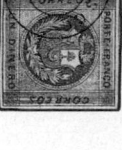

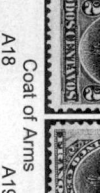

A20 A21

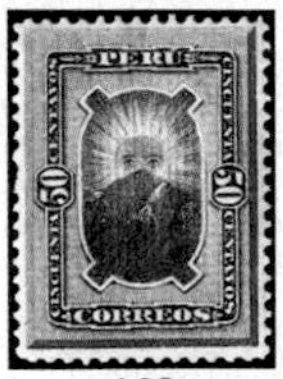
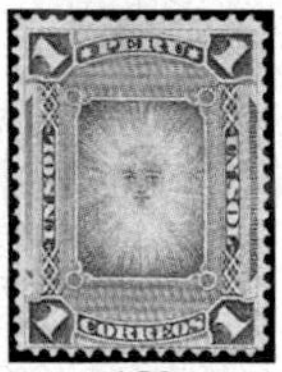

A22 A23

Embossed with Grill

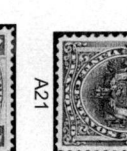

**1874-84** **Engr.** ***Perf. 12***
**21** A17 1c orange ('79) .50 .40
**22** A18 2c dk violet .65 .50
**23** A19 5c blue ('77) .85 .25
**24** A19 5c ultra ('79) 8.50 2.00
**25** A20 10c green ('76) .25 .20
*a.* Imperf., pair 25.00
**26** A20 10c slate ('84) 2.00 .25
*a.* Diag. half used as 5c on cover —
**27** A21 20c brown red 2.00 .65
**28** A22 50c green 9.00 2.50
**29** A23 1s rose 1.50 1.50
*Nos. 21-29 (9)* 25.25 8.25

No. 25a lacks the grill.

No. 26 with overprint "DE OFICIO" is said to have been used to frank mail of Gen. A. A. Caceres during the civil war against Gen. Miguel Iglesias, provisional president. Experts question its status.

**1880**
**30** A17 1c green 2.00
**31** A18 2c rose 2.00

Nos. 30 and 31 were prepared for use but not issued without overprint.

See Nos. 104-108, 110, 112, 114-115.

For overprints see Nos. 32-103, 116-128, J32-J33, O2-O22, N11-N23, 1N1-1N9, 3N11-3N20, 5N1, 6N1-6N2, 7N1-7N2, 8N7, 8N10-8N11, 9N1-9N3, 10N3-10N8, 10N10-10N11, 11N1-11N5, 12N1-12N3, 13N1, 14N1-14N16, 15N5-15N8, 15N13-15N18, 16N1-16N22.

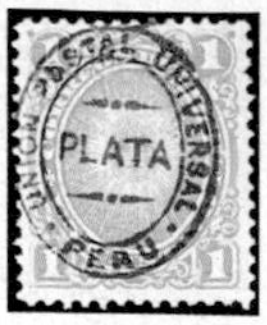

Stamps of 1874-80 Overprinted in Red, Blue or Black

Reduced illustration

**1880, Jan. 5**
**32** A17 1c green (R) .50 .40
*a.* Inverted overprint 10.00 10.00
*b.* Double overprint 13.50 13.50
**33** A18 2c rose (Bl) 1.00 .65
*a.* Inverted overprint 10.00 10.00
*b.* Double overprint 14.00 12.00
**34** A18 2c rose (Bk) 45.00 35.00
*a.* Inverted overprint
*b.* Double overprint
**35** A19 5c ultra (R) 2.00 1.00
*a.* Inverted overprint 10.00 10.00
*b.* Double overprint 14.00 14.00
**36** A22 50c green (R) 27.50 17.50
*a.* Inverted overprint 45.00 45.00
*b.* Double overprint 55.00 55.00
**37** A23 1s rose (Bl) 70.00 45.00
*a.* Inverted overprint 110.00 110.00
*b.* Double overprint 110.00 110.00
*Nos. 32-37 (6)* 146.00 99.55

Stamps of 1874-80 Overprinted in Red or Blue

Reduced illustration

**1881, Jan. 28**
**38** A17 1c green (R) .75 .60
*a.* Inverted overprint 8.25 8.25
*b.* Double overprint 14.00 14.00
**39** A18 2c rose (Bl) 14.00 9.00
*a.* Inverted overprint 17.50 15.00
*b.* Double overprint 25.00 20.00
**40** A19 5c ultra (R) 1.50 .75
*a.* Inverted overprint 14.00 14.00
*b.* Double overprint 20.00 20.00
**41** A22 50c green (R) 450.00 250.00
*a.* Inverted overprint 600.00
**42** A23 1s rose (Bl) 82.50 55.00
*a.* Inverted overprint 150.00

*Reprints of Nos. 38 to 42 were made in 1884. In the overprint the word "PLATA" is 3mm high instead of 2½mm. The cross bars of the letters "A" of that word are set higher than on the original stamps. The 5c is printed in blue instead of ultramarine.*

For stamps of 1874-80 overprinted with Chilean arms or small UPU "horseshoe," see Nos. N11-N23.

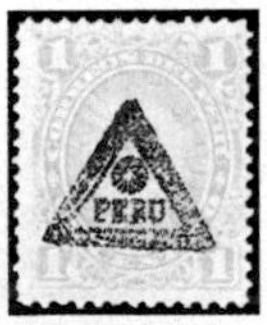

Stamps of 1874-79 Handstamped in Black or Blue

**1883**
**65** A17 1c orange (Bk) .85 .65
**66** A17 1c orange (Bl) 45.00
**68** A19 5c ultra (Bk) 7.50 5.00
**69** A20 10c green (Bk) .75 .65
**70** A20 10c green (Bl) 5.00 4.00
**71** A22 50c green (Bk) 7.00 3.50
**73** A23 1s rose (Bk) 10.00 6.00
*Nos. 65-73 (7)* 76.10
*Nos. 65,68-73 (6)* 31.10 19.80

This overprint is found in 11 types.

The 1c green, 2c dark violet and 20c brown red, overprinted with triangle, are fancy varieties made for sale to collectors and never placed in regular use.

Overprinted Triangle and "Union Postal Universal Peru" in Oval

**1883**
**77** A22 50c grn (R & Bk) 125.00 60.00
**78** A23 1s rose (Bl & Bk) 140.00 90.00

The 1c green, 2c rose and 5c ultramarine, over printed with triangle and "U. P. U. Peru" oval, were never placed in regular use.

Overprinted Triangle and "Union Postal Universal Lima" in Oval

**1883**
**79** A17 1c grn (R & Bl) 50.00 37.50
**80** A17 1c grn (R & Bk) 4.00 4.00
*a.* Oval overprint inverted
*b.* Double overprint of oval
**81** A18 2c rose (Bl & Bk) 4.00 4.00
**82** A19 5c ultra (R & Bk) 6.50 6.00

**PERU**

| | | | | |
|---|---|---|---|---|
| 83 | A19 | 5c ultra (R & Bl) | 6.50 | 6.00 |
| 84 | A22 | 50c grn (R & Bk) | 140.00 | 90.00 |
| 85 | A23 | 1s rose (Bl & Bk) | 150.00 | 125.00 |
| | | Nos. 79-85 (7) | 361.00 | 272.50 |

Some authorities question the status of No. 79.

*Nos. 80, 81, 84, and 85 were reprinted in 1884. They have the second type of oval overprint with "PLATA" 3mm high.*

Pres. Remigio Morales Bermúdez

**Overprinted Triangle and**

**1894, Oct. 23**

| | | | | |
|---|---|---|---|---|
| 118 | A17 | 1c orange | .60 | .40 |
| a. | | Inverted overprint | 7.00 | 7.00 |
| b. | | Double overprint | 7.00 | |
| 119 | A17 | 1c green | .40 | .35 |
| a. | | Inverted overprint | 3.50 | 3.50 |
| b. | | Dbl. inverted ovpt. | .40 | .35 |
| 120 | A18 | 2c violet | 7.00 | 7.00 |
| a. | | Diagonal half used as 1c | | |
| b. | | Inverted overprint | 7.00 | |
| c. | | Double overprint | .40 | .35 |
| 121 | A18 | 2c rose | 7.00 | 7.00 |
| a. | | Double overprint | 1.75 | |
| b. | | Inverted overprint | 2.50 | |
| 122 | A19 | 5c blue | 4.25 | 2.00 |
| 122A | A19 | 5c ultra | 10.00 | |
| 123 | A20 | 10c green | .40 | .35 |
| a. | | Inverted overprint | 7.00 | |
| 124 | A22 | 50c green | 1.40 | 1.25 |
| | | Nos. 118-124 (8) | 10.35 | 6.80 |

**Same, with Additional Overprint of Horseshoe**

| | | | | |
|---|---|---|---|---|
| 125 | A18 | 2c vermilion | .35 | .25 |
| a. | | Head inverted | 2.50 | 2.50 |
| 126 | A19 | 5c blue | .70 | .70 |
| a. | | Head inverted | 1.00 | 1.00 |
| b. | | Head double | | |
| 127 | A22 | 50c rose | 42.50 | 30.00 |
| a. | | Head inverted | 55.00 | 45.00 |
| b. | | Head double | | |
| 128 | A23 | 1s ultra | 100.00 | 90.00 |
| a. | | Both overprints inverted | 125.00 | 110.00 |
| b. | | Head double | 125.00 | 110.00 |
| | | Nos. 125-128 (4) | 143.85 | 120.75 |

**Overprinted Horseshoe Alone**

**1883, Oct. 23**

| | | | | |
|---|---|---|---|---|
| 95 | A17 | 1c green | 1.25 | 1.25 |
| 96 | A18 | 2c vermilion | 1.25 | 4.00 |
| a. | | Double overprint | | |
| 97 | A19 | 5c blue | 2.00 | 2.00 |
| 98 | A19 | 5c ultra | 20.00 | 15.00 |
| 99 | A22 | 50c rose | 57.50 | 57.50 |
| 100 | A23 | 1s | 30.00 | 30.00 |
| | | Nos. 95-100 (6) | 112.00 | 102.25 |

Stamps of 1874-80 Overprinted in Black

No. 23 Overprinted in Black

The 2c violet overprinted with the above design in red and triangle in black also the 1c green overprinted with the same combination plus the horseshoe in black, are fancy varieties made for sale to collectors.

**1884, Apr. 28**

| | | | | |
|---|---|---|---|---|
| 103 | A19 | 5c blue | .65 | .40 |
| a. | | Double overprint | 5.00 | 6.00 |

Stamps of 1c and 2c with the above overprint, also with the "U. P. U. LIMA" oval in blue or "CORREOS LIMA" in a double-lined circle in red, were made to sell to collectors and were never placed in use.

**Without Overprint or Grill**

**1886-95**

| | | | | |
|---|---|---|---|---|
| 104 | A17 | 1c dull violet | .50 | .20 |
| 105 | A17 | 1c vermilion ('95) | .40 | .20 |
| 106 | A17 | 1c green | .75 | .20 |
| 107 | A18 | 2c dp ultra ('95) | .35 | .20 |
| 108 | A18 | 2c orange | .60 | .30 |
| 109 | A12 | 5c claret ('95) | 1.25 | .50 |
| 110 | A20 | 10c slate | .40 | .20 |
| 111 | A13 | 10c orange ('95) | .60 | .35 |
| 112 | A21 | 20c blue | 5.00 | .65 |
| 113 | A14 | 20c orange ('95) | 6.00 | 1.40 |
| 114 | A22 | 50c red | 1.50 | .50 |
| 115 | A23 | 1s brown | 18.60 | 5.35 |
| | | Nos. 104-115 (12) | | |

**Overprinted Horseshoe in Black and Triangle in Rose Red**

**1889**

| | | | | |
|---|---|---|---|---|
| 116 | A17 | 1c green | .75 | .50 |
| a. | | Horseshoe inverted | 7.50 | |

Nos. 30 and 25 Overprinted "Union Postal Universal Lima" in Oval in Red

**1889, Sept. 1**

| | | | | |
|---|---|---|---|---|
| 117 | A17 | 1c green | 1.50 | 1.25 |
| 117A | A20 | 10c green | 1.50 | 1.50 |

The overprint on Nos. 117 and 117A is of the second type with "PLATA" 3mm high.

---

Manco Capac, Founder of Inca Dynasty — A24

Francisco Pizarro Conqueror of the Inca Empire — A25

General José de La Mar — A26

**1896-1900**

| | | | | |
|---|---|---|---|---|
| 141 | A24 | 1c ultra | .50 | .20 |
| a. | | 1c blue (error) | 40.00 | 35.00 |
| 142 | A24 | 1c yel grn ('98) | .50 | .20 |
| 143 | A24 | 2c blue | .50 | .20 |
| 144 | A24 | 2c scar ('99) | .75 | .20 |
| 145 | A25 | 5c indigo | .75 | .20 |
| 146 | A25 | 5c green ('97) | 1.00 | .20 |
| 147 | A25 | 5c grnsh bl ('99) | .50 | .20 |
| 148 | A25 | 10c yellow | 1.00 | .25 |
| 149 | A25 | 10c gray blk ('00) | 1.00 | .25 |
| 150 | A26 | 20c orange | 2.00 | .80 |
| 151 | A26 | 50c car rose | 5.00 | .80 |
| 152 | A26 | 1s orange red | 7.50 | 1.00 |
| 153 | A26 | 2s claret | 2.25 | 4.70 |
| | | Nos. 141-153 (13) | 22.75 | |

The 5c in black is a chemical changeling. For surcharges and overprints see Nos. 187-188, E1, O23-O26.

Paucartambo Bridge A27

Post and Telegraph Building, Lima — A28

Pres. Nicolás de Piérola — A29

**1897, Dec. 31**

| | | | | |
|---|---|---|---|---|
| 154 | A27 | 1c dp ultra | .65 | .35 |
| 155 | A28 | 2c brown | .65 | .25 |
| 156 | A29 | 5c bright rose | 1.00 | .25 |
| | | Nos. 154-156 (3) | 2.30 | .85 |

Opening of new P.O. in Lima.

A30, A31

**1897, Nov. 8**

| | | | | |
|---|---|---|---|---|
| 157 | A30 | 1c bister | .50 | .45 |
| a. | | Inverted overprint | 2.50 | 2.50 |
| b. | | Double overprint | 10.00 | 10.00 |

**Perf. 11½**

**Vermilion Surcharge**

**1895**

| | | | | |
|---|---|---|---|---|
| 129 | A23a | 5c on 5c grn | 10.00 | 7.50 |
| 130 | A23a | 10c on 10c ver | 10.00 | 6.00 |
| 131 | A23a | 20c on 20c brn | 8.50 | 6.50 |
| 132 | A23a | 50c on 50c ultra | 10.00 | 7.50 |
| 133 | A23a | 1s on 1s red brn | 46.50 | 35.50 |
| | | Nos. 129-133 (5) | | |

Nos. 129-133 were used only in Tumbes. The basic stamps were prepared by revolutionaries in northern Peru.

A23a

"Liberty" A23b, A23c

**1895, Sept. 8**

Engr.

| | | | | |
|---|---|---|---|---|
| 134 | A23b | 1c gray violet | 1.40 | .80 |
| 135 | A23b | 2c green | 1.40 | .80 |
| 136 | A23b | 5c yellow | 1.40 | .80 |
| 137 | A23c | 10c ultra | 1.40 | .80 |
| 138 | A23c | 20c orange | 7.25 | 5.50 |
| 139 | A23c | 50c dark blue | 40.00 | 27.50 |
| 140 | A23c | 1s car lake | 54.25 | 37.20 |
| | | Nos. 134-140 (7) | | |

Success of the revolution against the government of General Cáceres and of the election of President Piérola.

---

Admiral Miguel L. Grau — A33

Pres. Eduardo de Romaña — A32

**1899**

| | | | | |
|---|---|---|---|---|
| 158 | A31 | 5s orange red | 1.60 | 1.60 |
| 159 | A31 | 10s blue green | 500.00 | 350.00 |

For surcharge see No. J36.

**1900   Frame Litho., Center Engr.**

| | | | | |
|---|---|---|---|---|
| 160 | A32 | 22c yel grn & blk | 8.00 | .85 |

**1901, Jan.**

2c, Col. Francisco Bolognesi. 5c, Pres. Romaña.

| | | | | |
|---|---|---|---|---|
| 161 | A33 | 1c green & blk | 1.00 | .25 |
| 162 | A33 | 2c red & black | 1.00 | .25 |
| 163 | A33 | 5c dull vio & blk | 3.00 | .75 |
| | | Nos. 161-163 (3) | | |

Advent of 20th century.

A34

Municipal Hygiene Institute Lima — A35

**1902**

Engr.

| | | | | |
|---|---|---|---|---|
| 164 | A34 | 22c green | .35 | .20 |

**1905**

| | | | | |
|---|---|---|---|---|
| 165 | A35 | 12c dp blue & blk | 1.00 | .25 |

For surcharges see Nos. 166-167, 186, 189.

**Same Surcharged in Red or Violet**

**1907**

| | | | | |
|---|---|---|---|---|
| 166 | A35 | 1c on 12c (R) | .25 | |
| a. | | Inverted surcharge | 8.00 | |
| 167 | A35 | 2c on 12c (V) | .50 | .35 |
| a. | | Inverted surcharge | 8.00 | |
| b. | | Double surcharge | 8.00 | |

Admiral Grau — A37

Monument of Bolognesi — A36

Llama — A38

Statue of Bolívar — A39

City Hall, Lima, formerly an Exhibition Building — A40

School of Medicine, Lima — A41

Post and Telegraph Building, Lima — A42

Grandstand at Santa Beatrix Race Track — A43

Columbus Monument — A44

**1907**

| | | | | |
|---|---|---|---|---|
| **168** | A36 | 1c yel grn & blk | .35 | .20 |
| **169** | A37 | 2c red & violet | .35 | .20 |
| **170** | A38 | 4c olive green | 5.50 | .75 |
| **171** | A39 | 5c blue & blk | .60 | .20 |
| **172** | A40 | 10c red brn & blk | 1.00 | .25 |
| **173** | A41 | 20c dk grn & blk | 22.50 | .50 |
| **174** | A42 | 50c black | 22.50 | 1.00 |
| **175** | A43 | 1s purple & grn | 125.00 | 2.50 |
| **176** | A44 | 2s dp bl & blk | 125.00 | 100.00 |
| | | *Nos. 168-176 (9)* | 302.80 | 105.60 |

For surcharges and overprint see #190-195, E2.

Manco Capac A45

Columbus A46

Pizarro A47

San Martin A48

Bolívar A49

La Mar A50

Ramón Castilla A51

Grau A52

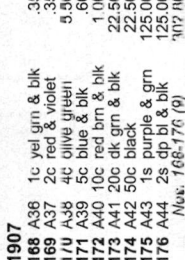

Bolognesi — A53

**1909**

| | | | | |
|---|---|---|---|---|
| **177** | A45 | 1c gray | .20 | .20 |
| **178** | A46 | 2c green | .20 | .20 |
| **179** | A47 | 4c vermilion | .30 | .20 |
| **180** | A48 | 5c violet | .20 | .20 |
| **181** | A49 | 10c deep blue | .50 | .20 |
| **182** | A50 | 12c pale blue | 1.00 | .20 |
| **183** | A51 | 20c brown red | 1.10 | .25 |
| **184** | A52 | 50c yellow | 5.00 | .35 |
| **185** | A53 | 1s brn red & blk | 10.00 | .35 |
| | | *Nos. 177-185 (9)* | 18.50 | 2.15 |

See types A54, A78-A80, A81-A89.
For surcharges and overprint see Nos. 196-200, 208, E3.

No. 165 Surcharged In Red

**1913, Jan.**

| | | | | |
|---|---|---|---|---|
| **186** | A35 | 8c on 12c dp bl & blk | .65 | .25 |

Stamps of 1899-1908 Surcharged in Magenta

a

b

c

**1915**

**On Nos. 142, 149**

| | | | | |
|---|---|---|---|---|
| **187** | A24(a) | 1c on 1c | 16.50 | 12.00 |
| *a.* | | Inverted surcharge | 22.50 | 18.00 |
| **188** | A25(a) | 1c on 10c | .80 | .75 |

**On No. 165**

| | | | | |
|---|---|---|---|---|
| **189** | A35(c) | 2c on 12c | .25 | .20 |
| *a.* | | Inverted surcharge | | |

**On Nos. 168-170, 172-174**

| | | | | |
|---|---|---|---|---|
| **190** | A36(a) | 1c on 1c | .65 | .65 |
| **191** | A37(a) | 1c on 2c | 1.00 | 1.00 |
| **192** | A38(b) | 1c on 4c | 1.60 | 1.60 |
| *a.* | | Inverted surcharge | 6.00 | 6.00 |
| **193** | A40(b) | 1c on 10c | .35 | .30 |
| *a.* | | Inverted surcharge | 2.50 | 2.50 |
| **193C** | A40(c) | 2c on 10c | 100.00 | 80.00 |
| **194** | A41(c) | 2c on 20c | 14.00 | 12.00 |
| **195** | A42(c) | 2c on 50c | 2.00 | 2.00 |
| | | *Nos. 187-195 (10)* | 137.15 | 110.50 |

Nos. 182-184, 179, 185 Surcharged in Red, Green or Violet

d

e

f

**1916**

| | | | | |
|---|---|---|---|---|
| **196** | A50(d) | 1c on 12c (R) | .20 | .20 |
| *a.* | | Double surcharge | 2.00 | 2.00 |
| *b.* | | Green surcharge | 4.50 | 4.50 |
| **197** | A51(d) | 1c on 20c (G) | .20 | .20 |
| **198** | A52(d) | 1c on 50c (G) | .20 | .20 |
| *a.* | | Inverted surcharge | 2.00 | 2.00 |
| **199** | A47(e) | 2c on 4c (V) | .20 | .20 |
| **200** | A53(f) | 10c on 1s (G) | .50 | .20 |
| *a.* | | "VALF" | 3.50 | 3.50 |
| | | *Nos. 196-200 (5)* | 1.30 | 1.00 |

Official Stamps of 1909-14 Overprinted or Surcharged in Green or Red:

g

h

**1916**

| | | | | |
|---|---|---|---|---|
| **201** | O1(g) | 1c red (G) | .20 | .20 |
| **202** | O1(h) | 2c on 50c ol grn (R) | .20 | .20 |
| **203** | O1(g) | 10c bis brn (G) | .20 | .20 |

**Postage Due Stamps of 1909 Surcharged in Violet-Black**

| | | | | |
|---|---|---|---|---|
| **204** | D7 | 2c on 1c brown | .40 | .40 |
| **205** | D7 | 2c on 5c brown | .20 | .20 |
| **206** | D7 | 2c on 10c brown | .20 | .20 |
| **207** | D7 | 2c on 50c brown | .20 | .20 |
| | | *Nos. 201-207 (7)* | 1.60 | 1.60 |

Many copies of Nos. 187 to 207 have a number of pin holes. It is stated that these holes were made at the time the surcharges were printed.

The varieties which we list of the 1915 and 1916 issues were sold to the public at post offices. Many other varieties which were previously listed are now known to have been delivered to one speculator or to have been privately printed by him from the surcharging plates which he had acquired.

No. 179 Surcharged in Black

**1917**

| | | | | |
|---|---|---|---|---|
| **208** | A47 | 1c on 4c ver | .25 | .20 |
| *a.* | | Double surcharge | 4.00 | 4.00 |
| *b.* | | Inverted surcharge | 4.00 | 4.00 |

San Martín — A54

Columbus at Salamanca — A62

Funeral of Atahualpa A63

Battle of Arica, "Arica, the Last Cartridge" A64

Designs: 2c, Bolivar. 4c, José Gálvez. 5c, Manuel Pardo. 8c, Grau. 10c, Bolognesi. 12c, Castilla. 20c, General Cáceres.

**1918** **Engr.**

**Centers in Black**

| | | | | |
|---|---|---|---|---|
| **209** | A54 | 1c orange | .20 | .20 |
| **210** | A54 | 2c green | .20 | .20 |
| **211** | A54 | 4c lake | .30 | .20 |
| **212** | A54 | 5c dp ultra | .25 | .20 |
| **213** | A54 | 8c red brn | .75 | .25 |
| **214** | A54 | 10c grnsh bl | .35 | .20 |
| **215** | A54 | 12c dl vio | 1.00 | .20 |
| **216** | A54 | 20c ol grn | 1.25 | .20 |
| **217** | A62 | 50c vio brn | 5.00 | .35 |
| **218** | A63 | 1s greenish bl | 12.00 | .50 |
| **219** | A64 | 2s deep ultra | 21.00 | .65 |
| | | *Nos. 209-219 (11)* | 42.30 | 3.15 |

For surcharges see Nos. 232-233, 255-256.

Augusto B. Leguía — A65

**1919, Dec.** **Litho.**

| | | | | |
|---|---|---|---|---|
| **220** | A65 | 5c bl & blk | .20 | .20 |
| *a.* | | Imperf. | .35 | .35 |
| *b.* | | Center inverted | 11.00 | 11.00 |
| **221** | A65 | 5c brn & blk | .20 | .20 |
| *a.* | | Imperf. | .35 | .35 |
| *b.* | | Center inverted | 11.00 | 11.00 |

Constitution of 1919.

San Martín — A66

Thomas Cochrane — A70

Oath of Independence — A69

Designs: 2c, Field Marshal Arenales. 4c, Field Marshal Las Heras. 10c, Martin Jean Guisse. 12c, Vidal. 20c, Leguia. 50c, San Martin monument. 1s, San Martin and Leguia.

**1921, July 28** **Engr.; 7c Litho.**

| | | | | |
|---|---|---|---|---|
| **222** | A66 | 1c ol brn & red brn | .30 | .20 |
| *a.* | | Center inverted | 375.00 | 350.00 |
| **223** | A66 | 2c green | .30 | .20 |
| **224** | A66 | 4c car rose | .80 | .60 |
| **225** | A69 | 5c ol brn | .40 | .20 |
| **226** | A70 | 7c violet | .65 | .25 |
| **227** | A66 | 10c ultra | .80 | .40 |
| **228** | A66 | 12c blk & slate | 2.50 | .60 |
| **229** | A66 | 20c car & gray blk | 2.50 | .80 |
| **230** | A66 | 50c vio brn & dl vio | 7.25 | 2.50 |
| **231** | A69 | 1s car rose & yel grn | 12.00 | 3.75 |
| | | *Nos. 222-231 (10)* | 27.50 | 9.50 |

Centenary of Independence.

Nos. 213, 212 Surcharged in Black or Red Brown

**1923-24**

| | | | | |
|---|---|---|---|---|
| **232** | A54 | 5c on 8c No. 213 | .50 | .25 |
| **233** | A54 | 4c on 5c (RB) ('24) | .35 | .20 |
| *a.* | | Inverted surcharge | 5.00 | 5.00 |
| *b.* | | Double surcharge, one inverted | 6.00 | 6.00 |

A78

A79

Simón Bolívar — A80

## 1924

**Perf. 14, 14x14½, 14½, 13½**
**Engr.; Photo. (4c, 5c)**

José Tejada Rivadeneyra A81 — Iturregui A83 — Mariano Melgar A82

| No. | Type | Denom | | |
|---|---|---|---|---|
| 234 | A78 | 2c olive grn | .30 | .20 |
| 235 | A79 | 4c yellow grn | .50 | .20 |
| 236 | A79 | 5c black | 1.00 | .20 |
| 237 | A80 | 10c carmine | 1.60 | .20 |
| 238 | A78 | 20c ultra | 1.25 | .80 |
| 239 | A78 | 50c dull violet | 3.75 | .80 |
| 240 | A78 | 1s yellow brn | 2.50 | |
| 241 | A78 | 2s dull blue | 21.00 | 11.00 |
| | | Nos. 234-241 (8) | 38.40 | 15.30 |

Centenary of the Battle of Ayacucho which ended Spanish power in South America.
No. 237 exists imperf.

Statue of Maria Bellido — A87 — De Saco — A88 — Monument of José Olaya — A86 — Leguia A84 — José de La Mar — A85

## 1924-29

José Leguia — A89
**Engr. Size: 18½x23mm Perf. 12**

| No. | Type | Denom | | |
|---|---|---|---|---|
| 242 | A81 | 2c olive gray | .20 | .20 |
| 243 | A82 | 4c dk grn | .20 | .20 |
| 244 | A83 | 8c black | .20 | .20 |
| 245 | A84 | 10c org red | 2.00 | 2.00 |
| 245A | A84 | 15c dp bl ('28) | .60 | .20 |
| 246 | A85 | 20c blue | .80 | .20 |
| 247 | A86 | 20c yel ('29) | 1.50 | .20 |
| 248 | A87 | 50c violet | 5.00 | .30 |
| 249 | A88 | 1s bis brn | 9.00 | .80 |
| 250 | A89 | 2s ultra | 42.00 | 9.30 |

See Nos. 258, 260, 276-282.
For surcharges and overprint see Nos. 251-253, 257-260, 262, 268-271, C1.

No. 246 Surcharged in Red:

## 1925

a — DOS Centavos 1925 — b

---

## 1925

No. 245 Overprinted

"Plebiscito"

| 251 | A86(a) | 2c on 20c blue | 350.00 | |
| a. | A86(b) | 2c on 20c blue | .80 | .50 |
| 252 | A86(b) | 2c on 20c blue | 35.00 | 35.00 |
| a. | | Inverted surcharge | 50.00 | 50.00 |
| b. | | Double surch., one inverted | | |

No. 247 Surcharged

"Habilitada 15 cts."

**1929**

| 257 | A86 | 15c on 20c yellow | .75 | .75 |
| a. | | Inverted surcharge | 2.25 | 2.25 |
| | | Nos. 255-257 (3) | 7.50 | 7.50 |

**1929**

| 258 | A81 | 2c olive gray | .75 | .75 |
| 260 | A84 | 10c orange red | 2.25 | 2.25 |

**Coil Stamps**
Stamps of 1924 Issue
**Perf. 14 Horizontally**

| 261 | PT6 | 2c dark violet | 40.00 | 20.00 |
| a. | | Inverted overprint | 45.00 | 17.50 |

**1930**

"Habilitada Franqueo 2 Cts. 1930"

| 262 | A86 | 2c on 20c yellow | .25 | .25 |

No. 247 Surcharged

"Habilitada 2 Cts. 1930"
**Perf. 12**

| | | | .35 | .35 |
| | | | 2.50 | 2.50 |

Postal Tax Stamp of 1928 Overprinted

Air Post Stamp of 1928 Surcharged

| 263 | AP1 | 2c on 50c dk grn | .20 | .20 |
| a. | | "Habilitada" | 1.00 | 1.00 |

---

## 1925

| 253 | A84 | 10c org red | 1.00 | 1.00 |
| a. | | Inverted overprint | 17.50 | 17.50 |

This stamp was for exclusive use on letters from the plebiscite provinces of Tacna and Arica, and posted on the Peruvian transport "Ucayali" anchored in the port of Africa.

No. 213 Surcharged

"Habilitada 2 centavos 1929"

**Habilitada 2 Cts. 1929**
a — b

| 255 | A54(a) | 2c on 8c | .75 | .75 |
| 256 | A54(b) | 2c on 8c | .75 | .75 |

Coat of Arms — A91

Lima Cathedral A92

**1929, July 5**
**Perf. 12x11½, 11½x12 Litho.**

| 264 | A91 | 2c green | 1.10 | .75 |
| 265 | A92 | 5c scarlet | 1.90 | 1.25 |
| 266 | A92 | 10c dark blue | 1.40 | 1.00 |
| 267 | A91 | 50c bister brown | 22.50 | 12.00 |
| | | Nos. 264-267 (4) | 26.90 | 15.00 |

6th Pan American Congress for Child Welfare. By error the stamps are inscribed "Seventh Congress."

**1930, July 5**
10c, Children's Hospital. 50c, Madonna & Child.

---

**1930, Dec. 22 Photo. Perf. 15x14**

Type of 1924 Overprinted in Black, Green or Blue
**Size: 18½x22mm**

| 268 | A84 | 10c orange red (Bk) | 1.00 | .80 |
| a. | | Inverted overprint | 10.00 | 10.00 |
| b. | | Without overprint | 6.60 | 6.60 |
| 269 | A84 | 2c on 10c org red (G) | .20 | .20 |
| 270 | A84 | 4c on 10c org red (G) | .20 | .20 |
| a. | | Inverted surcharge | 12.00 | |
| 271 | A84 | 15c on 10c org red | 8.25 | 8.25 |
| a. | | Inverted surcharge | | |
| b. | | Double surcharge | | |
| | | Nos. 268-271 (4) | | |

**Same with Additional Surcharge of Numerals in Each Corner**

| | | | .30 | .20 |
| | | | 10.00 | 10.00 |
| | | | 10.00 | 10.00 |
| | | | 1.70 | 1.40 |

**Engr. Perf. 12**
**Size: 19x23½mm**

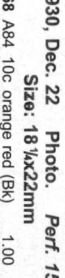 

Bolivar — A95

**1930, Dec. 16 Litho. Perf. 15x14**

| 272 | A95 | 2c olive green | .35 | .35 |
| 273 | A95 | 4c red | .65 | .35 |
| 274 | A95 | 15c deep blue | .35 | .35 |
| 275 | A95 | 15c deep green | .65 | .65 |
| a. | A95 | 15c slate gray | 2.00 | 1.75 |
| | | Nos. 272-275 (4) | | |

Death cent. of General Simón Bolivar.
For surcharges see Nos. RA14-RA16.

## 1931

Types of 1924-29 Issues
Size: 18x22mm
**Photo. Perf. 15x14**

| 276 | A81 | 2c olive green | .25 | .20 |
| 277 | A82 | 4c dark green | .25 | .20 |
| 279 | A85 | 15c yellow | .75 | .20 |
| 280 | A86 | 20c yellow | 1.25 | .25 |
| 281 | A87 | 50c violet | 1.25 | .25 |
| 282 | A88 | 1s olive brown | 5.75 | 1.40 |
| | | Nos. 276-282 (6) | | |

---

Old Stone Bridge, Lima — A97

Pizarro — A96

1st Peruvian Phil. Exhib., Lima, July, 1931.

**1931, July 28 Litho. Perf. 11**

| 283 | A96 | 2c slate blue | 1.60 | 1.40 |
| 284 | A96 | 4c deep brown | 1.60 | 1.40 |
| 285 | A96 | 10c dark green | 1.60 | 1.40 |
| 286 | A97 | 10c rose red | 1.60 | 1.40 |
| 287 | A97 | 10c mag & lt grn | 1.60 | 1.40 |
| 288 | A97 | 15c yel & lt grn | 1.60 | 1.40 |
| 289 | A97 | 15c dk slate & red | 11.20 | 9.80 |
| | | Nos. 283-289 (7) | | |

Llamas A106

Manco Capac A99

Oil Refinery A100

Picking Cotton A103

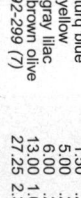 

Arms of Piura A107 — Mining A105 — Sugar Cane Field A102 — Guano Deposits A104

**1931-32**
**Perf. 11, 11x11½**

| 292 | A99 | 2c olive black | .25 | .20 |
| 293 | A100 | 4c dark green | .50 | .20 |
| 295 | A102 | 10c red orange | .20 | .20 |
| a. | | Vertical pair, imperf. between | 30.00 | |
| 296 | A103 | 15c turq blue | 1.50 | .20 |
| 297 | A104 | 20c yellow | .60 | .25 |
| 298 | A105 | 50c gray lilac | 5.00 | .25 |
| 299 | A106 | 1s brown olive | 13.00 | 1.00 |
| | | Nos. 292-299 (7) | 27.25 | 2.30 |

**1932, July 28 Perf. 11½x12**

| 300 | A107 | 10c dark blue | 6.25 | 6.00 |
| 301 | A107 | 15c deep violet | 32.50 | 31.00 |
| | | Nos. 300-301,C3 (3) | | |

400th anniv. of the founding of the city of Piura. On sale one day. Counterfeits exist.

## Aerial View of Callao A135

## Plan of Walls of Callao in 1746 A137

Packetboat "Sacramento" — A139

Viceroy José Antonio Manso de Velasco — A140

Fort Maipú — A141

Plan of Fort Real Felipe A142

Design: 15c, Docks and Custom House.

**1936, Aug. 27    Photo.    Perf. 12½**

| 341 | A132 | 2c black | .55 | .25 |
|---|---|---|---|---|
| 342 | A133 | 4c bl grn | .55 | .25 |
| 343 | A134 | 5c yel brn | .55 | .25 |
| 344 | A135 | 10c bl gray | .55 | .25 |
| 345 | A135 | 15c green | .55 | .25 |
| 346 | A137 | 20c brn | .70 | .25 |
| 347 | A138 | 50c purple | 1.40 | .40 |
| 348 | A139 | 1s olive grn | 8.75 | 1.40 |

**Engr.**

| 349 | A140 | 2s violet | 15.00 | 15.00 |
|---|---|---|---|---|
| 350 | A141 | 5s carmine | 20.00 | 15.00 |
| 351 | A142 | 10s red org & brn | 50.00 | 40.00 |
| Nos. 341-351,C13 (12) | | | 101.60 | 66.45 |

Province of Callao founding, cent.

Nos. 340, 321 and 323 Surcharged in Black

**1936    Perf. 13½, 13**

| 353 | A131 | 2c on 4c bl grn | .20 | .20 |
|---|---|---|---|---|
| 354 | A118 | 10c on 20c dp bl | .25 | .20 |
| a. | | "0.20" for "0.02" | 3.50 | 3.50 |
| b. | | Double surcharge | 3.50 | |
| | | Inverted surcharge | 3.50 | |
| 355 | A119 | 10c on 1s dk vio | .35 | .35 |
| | | | .80 | .75 |

Many varieties of the surcharge are found on these stamps; no period after "S," no

---

Zuniga y Velazco and Philip IV — A129

Supreme God of the Nazcas — A130

**1935, Jan. 17    Engr.; Photo. (10c)    Perf. 12½**

| 332 | A125 | 4c gray blue | .80 | .80 |
|---|---|---|---|---|
| 333 | A126 | 5c dark car | .30 | .30 |
| 334 | A127 | 10c magenta | 3.25 | 1.60 |
| 335 | A126 | 20c green | 1.25 | 1.25 |
| 336 | A128 | 35c dark car | 6.50 | 4.00 |
| 337 | A129 | 50c org & brn | 4.50 | 4.00 |
| 338 | A130 | 1s pur & red | 13.00 | 10.00 |
| Nos. 332-338 (7) | | | 29.60 | 22.45 |

Founding of the City of Ica, 300th anniv.

Pizarro and the Thirteen — A131

**1935-36    Photo.    Perf. 13½**

| 339 | A131 | 2c dp claret | .25 | .20 |
|---|---|---|---|---|
| 340 | A131 | 4c bl grn (36) | .25 | .20 |

For surcharge and overprints see Nos. 353, J53, RA25-RA26.

 "San Cristobal," First Peruvian Warship — A132

 Grand Marshal José de La Mar — A138

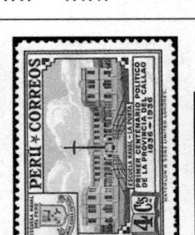 Naval College at Punta — A133

 Independence Square, Callao — A134

---

Pizarro and the Thirteen A120

Belle of Lima — A122

Francisco Pizarro — A123

**1935, Jan. 18    Perf. 13½**

| 324 | A120 | 2c brown | .35 | .20 |
|---|---|---|---|---|
| 325 | A120 | 4c violet | .50 | .40 |
| 326 | A122 | 10c rose red | .50 | .60 |
| 327 | A123 | 15c ultra | .80 | .75 |
| 328 | A120 | 25c slate gray | 1.40 | 1.50 |
| 329 | A122 | 50c olive grn | 2.00 | 2.00 |
| 330 | A122 | 1s Prus bl | 4.50 | 3.00 |
| 331 | A123 | 2s org brn | 10.50 | 8.00 |
| Nos. 324-331,C6-C12 (15) | | | 66.10 | 46.15 |

Founding of Lima, 4th cent.

4c, Lima Cathedral. 1s, Veiled woman of Lima.

 View of Ica — A125

Lake Huacachina, Health Resort — A126

Grapes — A127

Cotton Boll — A128

---

Parakas A108

Inca — A110

Chimu A109

**1932, Oct. 15    Perf. 11½, 12, 11½x12**

| 302 | A108 | 10c dk vio | .20 | .20 |
|---|---|---|---|---|
| 303 | A109 | 15c brn red | .40 | .20 |
| 304 | A110 | 50c dk brn | 1.50 | .60 |
| Nos. 302-304 (3) | | | | |

4th cent. of the Spanish conquest of Peru.

Arequipa and El Misti — A111

President Luis M. Sánchez Cerro — A112

Statue of Liberty — A116

Monument to Simón Bolívar at Lima — A115

**1932 '34    Photo.**

| 305 | A111 | 2c black | .20 | .20 |
|---|---|---|---|---|
| 306 | A111 | 2c blue blk | .20 | .20 |
| 307 | A111 | 2c grn ('34) | .20 | .20 |
| 308 | A111 | 4c dk brn | .20 | .20 |
| 309 | A111 | 4c org ('34) | .20 | .20 |
| 310 | A112 | 10c vermilion | .20 | .70 |
| 311 | A115 | 15c ultra | .40 | .20 |
| 312 | A115 | 15c mag ('34) | 14.50 | 10.00 |
| 313 | A115 | 20c red brn | .40 | .20 |
| 314 | A115 | 20c vio ('31) | .85 | .20 |
| 315 | A115 | 50c dk grn ('33) | .05 | .20 |
| 316 | A115 | 1s dp org | .85 | .35 |
| 317 | A115 | 1s org brn | 6.75 | .20 |
| Nos. 305-317 (13) | | | 33.85 | 12.55 |

For overprint see No. RA24.

The Inca — A119

Pizarro — A117

Coronation of Huascar — A118

**1934**

| 318 | A116 | 10c rose | .50 | .20 |
|---|---|---|---|---|

**1934-35    Perf. 13**

| 319 | A117 | 10c crimson | .25 | .20 |
|---|---|---|---|---|
| 320 | A117 | 15c ultra | .75 | .20 |
| 321 | A118 | 20c deep bl ('35) | 1.25 | .20 |
| 322 | A118 | 50c red brm | 1.00 | .35 |
| 323 | A119 | 1s dark vio | 3.00 | .35 |
| Nos. 319-323 (5) | | | 6.25 | 1.15 |

For surcharges and overprint see Nos. 354-355, J54, O32.

period after "Cts.," period after "2," "S" omitted, various broken letters, etc.
The surcharge on No. 355 is horizontal.

Peruvian
Cormorants
(Guano
Deposits) — A143

Oil Well at
Talara — A144

Avenue of
the
Republic,
Lima
A146

Post Office,
Lima — A149

San Marcos
University
at Lima
A148

Viceroy Manuel
de Amat y
Junyent — A150

Designs: 10c, "El Chasqui" (Inca Courier).
20c, Municipal Palace and Museum of Natural
History. 5s, Joseph A. de Pando y Riva. 10s,
Dr. José Dávila Condemarín.

**1936-37**

| | | | | Photo. Perf. 12½ | |
|---|---|---|---|---|---|
| 356 | A143 | 2c | lt brn | .60 | .20 |
| 357 | A143 | 2c | grn ('37) | .75 | .20 |
| 358 | A143 | 4c | blk brn | .60 | .20 |
| 359 | A144 | 4c | int blk ('37) | .35 | .20 |
| 360 | A143 | 10c | crimson | .35 | .20 |
| 361 | A143 | 10c | ver ('37) | .65 | .20 |
| 362 | A143 | 15c | ultra | .35 | .20 |
| 363 | A146 | 15c | brt bl ('37) | .65 | .20 |
| 364 | A146 | 15c | brt bl ('37) | .35 | .20 |
| 365 | A146 | 20c | black | .25 | .20 |
| 366 | A148 | 50c | blk brn ('37) | .20 | .20 |
| 367 | A148 | 50c | dk gray yel | 2.50 | .60 |
| | | | (37) | | |
| 368 | A149 | 1s | brn vio | .75 | .20 |
| 369 | A149 | 1s | ultra ('37) | 1.40 | .20 |

| | | | Engr. | | |
|---|---|---|---|---|---|
| 370 | A150 | 2s | ultra | 10.00 | 2.25 |
| 371 | A150 | 2s | dk vio ('37) | 3.25 | .60 |
| 372 | A150 | 5s | slate bl | 10.00 | 2.25 |
| 373 | A150 | 10s | dk vio & brn | 55.00 | 24.00 |

Nos. 356-373 (18) 92.65 32.80

**1937**
374 A150 1s on 2s ultra 2.75 2.50

No. 370
Surcharged in
Black

Habilit.
Un Sol

Highway Map
of Peru — A155

Government Palace — A165

Children's Holiday
Center,
Ancon — A153

Chavin
Pottery — A154

Lima Coat
of Arms
A164

Palace
Square
A163

Toribio de
Luzuriaga
A159

Industrial Bank
of Peru — A157

Archaeological
Museum,
Lima — A156

Historic Fig Tree
A160

Worker's Houses,
Lima — A158

Idol from
Temple of
Chavin — A161

Mt.
Huascarán — A162

Imprint: "Waterlow & Sons Limited,
Londres"

**1938, July 1 Photo. Perf. 12½, 13**

| 375 | A153 | 2c | emerald | .20 | .20 |
|---|---|---|---|---|---|
| 376 | A154 | 4c | org brn | .20 | .20 |
| 377 | A155 | 10c | scarlet | .20 | .20 |
| 378 | A156 | 15c | ultra | .20 | .20 |
| 379 | A157 | 20c | magenta | .20 | .20 |
| 380 | A158 | 50c | greenish blue | .40 | .20 |

| | | | Engr. | | |
|---|---|---|---|---|---|
| 381 | A159 | 1s | dp claret | 1.00 | .20 |
| 382 | A160 | 2s | green | 3.00 | .20 |
| 383 | A161 | 5s | dl vio & brn | 7.00 | .40 |
| 384 | A162 | 10s | blk & ultra | 12.00 | .50 |

Nos. 375-384 (10) 24.45 2.50

See Nos. 410-418, 426-433, 438-441.
For surcharges see Nos. 388, 406, 419,
445-446A, 456, 758.

Gonzalo
Pizarro and
Orellana
A167

Francisco de
Orellana — A168

Francisco
Pizarro — A169

Overprint: "FRANQUEO
POSTAL"

**1941 Litho. Perf. 12**

| 389 | A166 | 50c | dull yel | 2.00 | .20 |
|---|---|---|---|---|---|
| 390 | A166 | 1s | violet | 2.00 | .20 |
| 391 | A166 | 2s | dl gray grn | 4.00 | .60 |
| 392 | A166 | 5s | fawn | 22.50 | 6.75 |
| 393 | A166 | 10s | rose vio | 35.00 | 5.25 |

Nos. 389-393 (5) 65.50 13.00

"FRANQUEO
POSTAL"

National Radio
Station
A166

**1940**
388 A155 5c on 10c scarlet
a. Inverted surcharge

No. 377 Surcharged
in Black

**1938, Dec. 9 Photo. Perf. 12½**
385 A163 10c slate green .50 .35

**Engraved and Lithographed**
386 A164 15c blk, gold, red & bl .80 .45

**Photo.**
387 A165 1s olive 2.00 1.25
Nos. 385-387,C62-C64 (6) 6.80 4.55
8th Pan-American Conf., Lima, Dec. 1938.

No. 377
Surcharged
in Black

Perf. 13
.20 .20

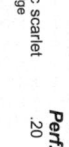

Gonzalo
Pizarro
A171

Discovery of the
Amazon River
A172

Map of South
America with
Amazon as
Spaniards
Knew It in
1542 — A170

**1943, Feb. Perf. 12½**

| 394 | A167 | 2c | crimson | .20 | .20 |
|---|---|---|---|---|---|
| 395 | A168 | 4c | slate | .20 | .20 |
| 396 | A169 | 10c | yel brn | .20 | .20 |
| 397 | A170 | 15c | vio blue | .50 | .20 |
| 398 | A171 | 20c | yel olive | .50 | .20 |
| 399 | A172 | 25c | dull org | 1.60 | .40 |
| 400 | A167 | 30c | dp magenta | .40 | .20 |
| 401 | A170 | 50c | blue grn | .40 | .30 |
| 402 | A167 | 70c | violet | 2.25 | .80 |
| 403 | A171 | 80c | lt bl | 2.25 | .80 |
| 404 | A172 | 1s | cocoa brn | 4.00 | .60 |
| 405 | A169 | 5s | intense blk | 8.00 | 4.00 |

Nos. 394-405 (12) 20.20 8.10
400th anniv. of the discovery of the Amazon
River by Francisco de Orellana in 1542.

No. 415 Surcharged
in Black

Habilitada
S o. 0.20

**1946**
419 A159 20c on 1s vio brn .30 .20
a. Surcharge reading down 8.25 8.25

Samuel Finley
Breese
Morse — A173

**1944**
407 A173 15c light blue .20 .20
408 A173 30c olive gray .50 .20
Centenary of invention of the telegraph.

Types of 1938
Imprint: "Columbian Bank Note Co."

**1945-47 Litho. Perf. 12½**

| 410 | A153 | 2c | green | .20 | .20 |
|---|---|---|---|---|---|
| 411 | A154 | 4c | org brn ('46) | .20 | .20 |
| 412 | A155 | 10c | ultra | .20 | .20 |
| 413 | A156 | 15c | magenta | 1.60 | .20 |
| 414 | A158 | 20c | grnish bl | .25 | .20 |
| 415 | A159 | 1s | vio brn | .65 | .20 |
| 416 | A160 | 2s | dl grn | .50 | .20 |
| 417 | A161 | 5s | dl vio & brn | 4.00 | .50 |
| 418 | A162 | 10s | blk & ultra ('47) | 12.30 | .75 |

Nos. 410-418 (9) 12.30 2.65

**1943**
406 A155 10c on 10c scar

Perf. 13
.20 .20

A174

Engineering School A182

Vicuña — A183

Contour Farming, Cuzco A184

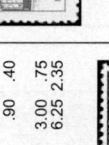

Monument to Admiral Miguel L. Grau — A179

Water Promenade A180

Post Boy — A181

Gen. Marcos Perez Jimenez — A185

Wheat Emblem and Symbol of Agriculture, Industry A189

Pacific Fair Emblem — A191

Alliance for Progress Emblem — A190

Symbols of the Eucharist A186

Trumpeting Angels A187

---

**1960, Aug. 10     Photo.     Perf. 11½**
479 A186 50c Cross and "JHS"    .20  .20
480 A186  1s shown              .25  .25

Nos. 479-480 were intended for voluntary use to help finance the 6th National Eucharistic Congress at Piura, Aug. 25-28, 1960. Authorized for payment of postage on day of issue only, Aug. 10, but through misunderstanding within the Peruvian postal service they were accepted for payment of postage by some post offices until late in December. Reauthorized for postal use, they were again sold and used, starting in July, 1962. See Nos. RA37-RA38.

**1961, Dec. 20     Litho.     Perf. 10½**
481 A187 20c bright blue        .30  .20

Christmas. Valid for postage for one day, Dec. 20. Used thereafter as a voluntary seal to benefit a fund for postal employees.

Centenary Cedar, Main Square, Pomabamba — A188

**1962, Sept. 7     Engr.     Perf. 13     Unwmk.**
482 A188  1s red & green        .40  .20

Cent. (in 1961) of Pomabamba province.

Types of 1952-53

Designs: 20c, Vicuña. 30c, Port of Matarani. 40c, Guimbal. 50c, Contour farming. 60c, Tourist hotel, Taona. 1s, Paramonga Inca fortress.

Imprint: "Thomas De La Rue & Co. Ltd."

**Perf. 13x13½, 13½x13, 12 (A184)**
**1962, Nov. 19     Litho.     Wmk. 346**
483 A183 20c rose claret        .20  .20
484 A182 30c dark blue          .20  .20
485 AP49 40c orange             .20  .20
486 A184 50c lt bluish grn      .20  .20
487 A182 60c grnsh brn          .20  .20
488 A184  1s rose               .25  .20
Nos. 483-488 (6)                1.25 1.20

**1963, July 23     Unwmk.     Perf. 12½**
489 A189  1s red org & ocher    .20  .20

FAO "Freedom from Hunger" campaign. See No. C190.

---

Designs: 2c, Tourist Hotel, Tacna. 5c, Fishing boat and principal fish. 10c, Matarani. 15c, Locomotive No. 80 and coaches. 30c, Ministry of Public Health and Social Assistance. 1s, Paramonga fortress. 2s, Monument to Native Farmer.

Imprint: "Thomas De La Rue & Co. Ltd."

**Perf. 13, 12 (A184)**
**1952-53     Litho.     Unwmk.**
457 A182  2c red lil ('53)      .20  .20
458 A182  5c green              .20  .20
459 A182 10c yel grn ('53)      .20  .20
460 A182 15c gray ('53)         .20  .20
461 A183 20c red brn ('53)      .40  .20
462 A182 25c rose red           .20  .20
463 A182 30c Indigo ('53)       .20  .20
464 A184  1s green ('53)        .20  .20
465 A184  1s brown              .30  .20
466 A184  2s Prus grn ('53)     2.70 2.00

See Nos. 468-478, 483-490, 107 501 C184-C185, C209.
For surcharges see Nos. C434, C437, C440-C441, C454, C494.

**1956, July 25     Engr.     Perf. 13½x13**
467 A185 25c brown              .20  .20

Visit of Gen. Marcos Perez Jimenez, Pres. of Venezuela, June 195b.

Types of 1952-53
Imprint: "Thomas De La Rue & Co. Ltd."
Designs as before.

**1957-59     Litho.     Perf. 13, 12**
468 A182 15c brown ('59)        .40  .20
469 A182 25c green ('59)        .40  .20
470 A182 30c dull pur           .30  .20
471 A184 50c dull pur           .30  .20
472 A184  1s lt vio bl          .50  .20
473 A184  2s gray ('58)         2.20 1.20
Nos. 468-473 (6)

Types of 1952-53
Imprint: "Joh. Enschedé en Zonen-Holland"
Designs as before.

**Perf. 12½x13½, 13½x12½, 13x14**
**1960     Litho.     Unwmk.**
474 A183 20c lt red brn         .20  .20
475 A182 30c lilac rose         .20  .20
476 A184 50c rose vio           .20  .20
477 A184  1s rose vio           .20  .20
478 A184  2s gray               .40  .20
Nos. 474-478 (5)                1.20 1.00

#475 measures 33x22mm, #470 32x22½mm.

---

**Engr.     Perf. 12½**
432 A161  5s ultra & red brn ('50)   .90  .40
433 A162 10s dk bl grn & blk ('51)   3.00 .75
Nos. 426-433 (8)                     6.25 2.35

**1949, June 6     Perf. 12½**
434 A179 10c ultra & bl grn     .20  .20

Imprint: "Inst. de Grav. Paris."

**1951     Perf. 12½x12, 12x12½**
438 A156 15c peacock grn        .20  .20
439 A157 20c violet             .20  .20
440 A158 50c org brn            .20  .20
441 A159  1s dark brn           .30  .20
Nos. 438-441 (4)                .90  .80

Nos. 375 and 438 Surcharged in Black

**1951-52     Perf. 12½x12**
445 A153  1c on 2c              .20  .20
446 A156 10c on 15c             .20  .20
446A A156 10c on 15c ('52)      .60  .60
Nos. 445-446A (3)

On No. 446A "S/. 0.10" is in smaller type measuring 11½mm. See No. 456.
Nos. 445-446A exist with surcharge double.

Overprint: "V Congreso Panamericano de Carreteras 1951"

**1951, Oct. 13     Unwmk.     Perf. 12**
**Black Overprint**
447 A180  2c dk grn             .20  .20
448 A180  4c brt red            .20  .20
449 A181 15c gray              .20  .20
450 A180 20c ol brn             .20  .20
451 A180 50c dp plum            .25  .20
452 A180  1s blue               .30  .20
453 A180  2s deep blue          .45  .20
454 A180  5s brn lake           1.25 1.25
455 A180 10s chocolate          5.30 3.90
Nos. 447-455 (9)

Designs: 4c, 50c, 1s, 2s, Various buildings, Lima. 20c, Post Office Street, Lima. 5s, Lake Llangamuco, Ancachs. 10s, Ruins of Machu-Picchu.

5th Pan-American Congress of Highways, 1951.

No. 438 Surcharged in Black

**1952     Unwmk.     Perf. 12½x12**
456 A156  5c on 15c pck grn     .20  .20

---

A175

A176

A177

A178

Imprint: "Waterlow & Sons Limited, Londres."

**1947, Apr. 15     Litho.     Perf. 12½     Unwmk.**
420 A174 15c blk & car          .25  .20
421 A175  1s olive grn          .45  .30
422 A176 1.35s yel grn          .45  .35
423 A177  3s Prus blue          .85  .60
424 A178  5s dull grn           1.75 1.25
Nos. 420-424 (5)                3.75 2.70

1st National Tourism Congress, Lima. The basic stamps were prepared, but not issued, for the 5th Pan American Highway Congress of 1944.

Overprinted in Black
**Perf. 12½**

Types of 1938
**Perf. 13x13½, 13½x13     Photo.**
**1949-51**
426 A154  4c chocolate          .20  .20
428 A156 15c aquamarine         .20  .20
427 A157 20c blue vio           .20  .20
429 A158 50c red brn            .20  .20
430 A159  5s blk brn            .50  .20
431 A160  2s ultra              1.00 .20

Catalogue values for unused stamps in this section, from this point to the end of the section, are for Never Hinged items.

**1964, June 22**    **Litho.**    **Perf. 12x12½**
490   A190   40c multi    .65   .65
Nos. 490,C192-C193 (3)
Alliance for Progress. See note after US No. 1234.

**1965, Oct. 30**    **Litho.**    **Perf. 12x12½**
491   A191   1.50s multi    .20   .20
492   A191   2.50s multi    .20   .20
493   A191   3.50s multi    .70   .20
Nos. 491-493 (3)
4th Intl. Pacific Fair, Lima, Oct. 30-Nov. 14.

Santa Claus and Letter — A192

**1965, Nov. 2**    **Perf. 11**
494   A192   20c red & blk    .20   .20
495   A192   50c grn & blk    .20   .20
496   A192   1s blk & blk    .35   .20
Nos. 494-496 (3)    .75   .60
Christmas. Valid for postage for one day, Nov. 2. Used Nov. 3, 1965-Jan. 31, 1966, as voluntary seals for the benefit of a fund for postal employees. See #641-643.

Types of 1952-62
20c, Vicuña. 30c, Port of Matarani. 40c, Gunboat. 50c, Contour farming. 1s, Paramonga, Inca fortress.

Imprint: "I.N.A."

**1966, Aug. 8**    **Litho.**    **Unwmk.**
497   A183   20c brn red    .20   .20
498   A182   30c dk bl    .20   .20
499   AP49   40c orange    .20   .20
500   A184   50c gray grn    .20   .20
501   A184   1s rose    .20   .20
Nos. 497-501 (5)    1.00   1.00

**Perf. 12, 13½x14 (A184)**

Postal Tax Stamps Nos. RA40, RA43 Surcharged

a       b

**Perf. 14x14½, 12½x12**

**1966, May 9**
501A   PT11 (a)   10c on 2c lt brn    .20   .20
501B   PT14 (b)   10c on 3c lt car    .20   .20

**1966, Nov. 24**    **Photo.**    **Perf. 13½x14**
502   A193   70c blk, bl & vio bl    .20   .20
Opening of the Huinco Hydroelectric Center. See No. C205.

6-year building program. See No. C212.

Inca Wind Vane and Sun — A194

**1967, Apr. 18**    **Photo.**    **Unwmk.**
503   A194   90c dp lil rose, blk & gold    .20   .20

**Perf. 13½x14**

---

**1967, Oct. 9**    **Photo.**    **Perf. 12**
504   A195   1s gold, dk grn & blk    .20   .20
5th Intl. Pacific Fair, Lima, Oct. 27-Nov. 12. See No. C216.

Gold Alligator, Mochica Culture A196

**1968, Aug. 16**    **Photo.**    **Perf. 12**
505   A196   1.90s dp magenta    1.25   .20
506   A196   2.60s black    1.75   .20
507   A196   3.60s dp magenta    2.00   .30
508   A196   4.60s black    2.50   .35
509   A196   5.60s dp magenta    5.00   .40
Nos. 505-509 (5)
Designs (gold sculptures of the pre-Inca Yunca tribes): 2.60s, Bird, vert. 3.60s, Lizard. 4.60s, Bird, horiz. 5.60s, Jaguar.
See Nos. B1-B5.

**Sculptures in Gold Yellow and Brown**

**1969, Mar. 3**    **Litho.**    **Perf. 11**
510   A197   2.50s on 90c brn & yel    .20   .20
511   A197   3s on 90c lil & brn    .20   .20
512   A197   4s on 90c rose &    .35   .20
     grn
Nos. 510-512,C232-C233 (5)    1.35   1.00

**Black Surcharge**
Designs: 3s, 4s, Farmer digging in field.

#510-512 were not issued without surcharge. For surcharge see No. 685.

Indian and Wheat — A197

---

**1969, Apr. 9**    **Litho.**    **Perf. 12**
513   A198   2.50s multi    .20   .20
514   A198   3s gray & multi    .20   .20
515   A198   4s lil & multi    .25   .20
516   A198   5.50s lt bl & multi    .85   .80
Nos. 513-516 (4)
Nationalization of the Brea Parinas oilfields, Oct. 9, 1968.

Flag, Worker Holding Oil Rig and Map A198

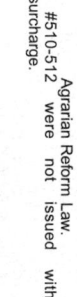

**1969, June 17**    **Litho.**    **Perf. 11**
517   A199   2.50s dp bl & multi    .20   .20
Nos. 517,C238-C241 (5)    1.00   1.00
1st Peruvian Airlines (APSA) flight to Europe.

Kon Tiki Raft, Globe and Jet — A199

---

Pacific Fair Emblem — A195

Freed Andean Farmer A201

**1969, Aug. 28**    **Litho.**    **Perf. 11**
519   A201   2.50s dk bl, lt bl & red    .20   .20
Nos. 519,C246-C247 (3)    .60   .60
Enactment of the Agrarian Reform Law of June 24, 1969.

Adm. Miguel Grau A202?

**1969, Oct. 8**    **Litho.**    **Perf. 11**
520   A202   50s dk bl & multi    3.00   2.25
Issued for Navy Day.

Capt. José A. Quiñones Gonzales (1914-41), Military Aviator — A200

**1969, July 23**    **Litho.**    **Perf. 11**
518   A200   20s red & multi    1.25   .60
See No. C243.

---

**1969, Nov. 14**    **Litho.**    **Perf. 12**
521   A203   2.50s gray & multi    .20   .20
Nos. 521,C251-C252 (3)    .65   .60
6th Intl. Pacific Trade Fair, Lima, Nov. 14-30.

Flags and "6" — A203

**1969, Dec. 1**    **Litho.**    **Perf. 11**
522   A192   20c red & blk    .25   .20
523   A192   50c org & blk    .25   .20
524   A192   20c brn & blk    .75   .60
Nos. 522-524 (3)
Design: Santa Claus and letter inscribed "FELIZ NAVIDAD Y PROSPERO ANO NUEVO."
Christmas. Valid for postage for one day, Dec. 1, 1969. Used after that date as postal tax stamps.
Santa Claus Type of 1965

Gen. Francisco Bolognesi and Soldier — A204

---

Ministry of Transport and Communications A206

**1970, Apr. 1**    **Litho.**    **Perf. 11**
527   A206   40c org & gray    .30   .20
528   A206   40c multi    .30   .20
529   A206   40c gray & lt gray    .30   .20
530   A206   40c brick red & lt gray    .30   .20
531   A206   40c org brn & gray    .30   .20
Nos. 527-531 (5)    1.50   1.00
Ministry of Transport and Communications, 1st anniv.

**1970, Feb. 23**    **Litho.**    **Perf. 11**
526   A205   2.50s buff, blk & brn    .40   .20
Nos. 526,C281-C284 (5)    1.50   1.30

**1969, Dec. 9**
525   A204   1.20s lt ultra, blk & gold    .35   .20
Army Day, Dec. 9. See No. C253.

Puma-shaped Jug, Vicus Culture — A205

---

Anchovy A207

**1970, Apr. 30**    **Litho.**    **Perf. 11**
532   A207   2.50s org & multi    .80   .20
533   A207   2.50s vio bl & multi    .80   .20
a.   Strip of 5, #532-533, C285-C287    7.50   7.50
Fish: No. 533, Pacific hake.

Composite Head; Soldier and Farmer A208

**1970, June 24**    **Litho.**    **Perf. 11**
534   A208   2.50s gold & multi    .20   .20
Nos. 534,C290-C291 (3)    .75   .60
"United people and army building a new Peru."

Cadets, Chorrilos College, and Arms — A209

Coat of Arms and: No. 536, Cadets of La Punta Naval College. No. 537, Cadets of Las Palmas Air Force College.

**1970, July 27  Litho.  Perf. 11**

| | | | | |
|---|---|---|---|---|
| 535 | A209 | 2.50s blk & multi | .40 | .20 |
| 536 | A209 | 2.50s blk & multi | .40 | .20 |
| 537 | A209 | 2.50s blk & multi | .40 | .20 |
| a. | | Strip of 3, #535-537 | 1.25 | .75 |

Peru's military colleges.

Courtyard, Puruchuco Fortress, Lima — A210

**1970, Aug. 6**

| | | | | |
|---|---|---|---|---|
| 538 | A210 | 2.50s multi | .20 | .20 |
| | | Nos. 538,C294-C297 (5) | 1.40 | 1.40 |

Issued for tourist publicity.

Nativity, Cuzco School A211

Christmas paintings: 1.50s, Adoration of the Kings, Cuzco School. 1.80s, Adoration of the Shepherds, Peruvian School.

**1970, Dec. 23  Litho.  Perf. 11**

| | | | | |
|---|---|---|---|---|
| 539 | A211 | 1.20s multi | .35 | .20 |
| 540 | A211 | 1.50s multi | .35 | .20 |
| 541 | A211 | 1.80s multi | .40 | .60 |
| | | Nos. 539-541 (3) | 1.10 | 1.40 |

St. Rosa of Lima — A212

**1971, Apr. 12  Litho.  Perf. 11**

| | | | | |
|---|---|---|---|---|
| 542 | A212 | 2.50s multi | .20 | .20 |

300th anniv. of the canonization of St. Rosa of Lima (1586-1617), first saint born in the Americas.

Tiahuanacoide Cloth — A213

Design: 2.50s, Chancay cloth.

**1971, Apr. 19**

| | | | | |
|---|---|---|---|---|
| 543 | A213 | 1.20s bl & multi | .30 | .20 |
| 544 | A213 | 1.20s yel & multi | .30 | 1.00 |
| | | Nos. 543-544,C306-C308 (5) | 1.60 | 1.00 |

---

Nazca Sculpture, 5th Century, and Seriolella A214

**1971, June 7  Litho.  Perf. 11**

| | | | | |
|---|---|---|---|---|
| 545 | A214 | 1.50s multi | .50 | .20 |
| | | Nos. 545,C309-C312 (5) | 3.95 | 1.40 |

Publicity for 200-mile zone of sovereignty of the high seas.

Mateo Garcia Pumacahua A215

#547, Mariano Melgar. #548, Micaela Bastidas. #549, Jose Faustino Sanchez Carrion. #550, Francisco Antonia de Zela. #551, Jose Baquijano y Carrillo. #552, Martin Jorge Guise.

**1971**

| | | | | |
|---|---|---|---|---|
| 546 | A215 | 1.20s ver & blk | .20 | .20 |
| 547 | A215 | 1.20s dk & multi | .20 | .20 |
| 548 | A215 | 1.50s dk & multi | .20 | .20 |
| 549 | A215 | 2s dk bl & multi | .20 | .70 |
| 550 | A215 | 2.50s ultra & multi | .20 | .20 |
| 551 | A215 | 3s gray & multi | .20 | .20 |
| 552 | A215 | 2.50s dk bl & multi | .20 | .20 |
| | | Nos. 546-552,C313 C325 (20) | 4.65 | 4.00 |

150th anniv. of independence, and to honor the heroes of the struggle for independence.

Issue dates: Nos. 546, 550, May 10; Nos. 547, 551, July 9; Nos. 548, 549, 552, July 27

Gongora Portentiosa A216

Designs: Various Peruvian orchids.

**1971, Sept. 27  Perf. 13½x13**

| | | | | |
|---|---|---|---|---|
| 553 | A216 | 1.50s pink & multi | .25 | .20 |
| 554 | A216 | 2s pink & multi | .30 | .20 |
| 555 | A216 | 2.50s pink & multi | .40 | .20 |
| 556 | A216 | 3s pink & multi | .45 | .20 |
| 557 | A216 | 3.50s pink & multi | .55 | 1.00 |
| | | Nos. 553-557 (5) | 1.95 | 1.00 |

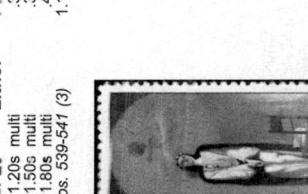

"Progress of Liberation," by Teodoro Nuñez Ureta A217

**1971, Nov. 4  Perf. 13x13½**

| | | | | |
|---|---|---|---|---|
| 558 | A217 | 1.20s multi | .25 | .20 |
| 559 | A217 | 3.50s multi | .75 | 1.40 |
| | | Nos. 558-559,C331 (3) | 3.75 | 1.40 |

2nd Ministerial meeting of the "Group of 77."

---

EXFILIMA71

Plaza de Armas, Lima, 1843 A218

3.50s, Plaza de Armas, Lima, 1971.

**1971, Nov. 6**

| | | | | |
|---|---|---|---|---|
| 560 | A218 | 3s pale grn & blk | .35 | .20 |
| 561 | A218 | 3.50s lt brick red & blk | .45 | .20 |

3rd Annual Intl. Stamp Exhibition, EXFILIMA '71, Lima, Nov. 6-14.

Army Coat of Arms — A219

**1971, Dec. 9  Litho.  Perf. 13½x13**

| | | | | |
|---|---|---|---|---|
| 562 | A219 | 8.50s multi | .75 | .20 |

Sesquicentennial of Peruvian Army.

Flight into Egypt A220

Old Stone Sculptures of Huamanga: 2.50s, Three Kings. 3s, Nativity.

**1971, Dec. 18  Perf. 13x13½**

| | | | | |
|---|---|---|---|---|
| 563 | A220 | 1.80s multi | .25 | .20 |
| 564 | A220 | 2.50s multi | .35 | .20 |
| 565 | A220 | 3s gray & multi | .80 | .60 |
| | | Nos. 563-565 (3) | | |

Christmas  See Nos. 597-599

Fisherman, by J. M. Ugarte Elespuru — A221

Gold Staluette, Chimu, c. 1500 — A222

Paintings by Peruvian Workers: 4s, Threshing Grain in Cajamarca, by Camilo Blas. 6s, Huanca Highlanders, by José Sabogal.

**1971, Dec. 30  Perf. 13½x13**

| | | | | |
|---|---|---|---|---|
| 566 | A221 | 3.50s blk & multi | .40 | .20 |
| 567 | A221 | 4s blk & multi | .50 | .20 |
| 568 | A221 | 6s blk & multi | .75 | .60 |
| | | Nos. 566-568 (3) | 1.65 | 1.00 |

To publicize the revolution and change of order.

**1972, Jan. 31  Litho.  Perf. 13½x13**

Ancient Jewelry: 4s, Gold drummer, Chimu. 4.50s, Quartz figurine, Lambayeque culture.

---

5th century. 5.40s, Gold necklace and pendant, Mochiqua. 4th century. 6s, Gold insect, Lambayeque culture, 14th century.

| | | | | |
|---|---|---|---|---|
| 569 | A222 | 3.90s red, blk & ocher | .65 | .20 |
| 570 | A222 | 4s red, blk & ocher | .65 | .20 |
| 571 | A222 | 4.50s brt blk & ocher | .80 | .20 |
| 572 | A222 | 5.40s red, blk & ocher | .95 | .20 |
| 573 | A222 | 6s red, blk & ocher | .95 | .20 |
| | | Nos. 569-573 (5) | 4.00 | 1.00 |

Popeye Catalufa A223

Fish: 1.50s, Guadara. 2.50s, Jack mackerel.

**1972, Mar. 20  Perf. 13x13½**

| | | | | |
|---|---|---|---|---|
| 574 | A223 | 1.20s lt bl & multi | .55 | .20 |
| 575 | A223 | 1.50s lt bl & multi | .55 | .20 |
| 576 | A223 | 2.50s lt bl & multi | .55 | 1.00 |
| | | Nos. 574-576,C333-C334 (5) | 2.45 | 1.40 |

Seated Warrior, Mochica — A224

"Bringing in the Harvest" (July) — A225

Painted pottery jugs of Mochica culture, 5th cent'. 1.20s, Helmeted head. 2c, Kneeling deer. 2.50s, Helmeted head. 3s, Kneeling warrior.

**1972, May 8  Perf. 13½x13**

| | | | | |
|---|---|---|---|---|
| 577 | A224 | 1.20s multi | .40 | .20 |
| 578 | A224 | 2s multi | .60 | .20 |
| 579 | A224 | 2s multi | .60 | .20 |
| 580 | A224 | 2.60s multi | .65 | .20 |
| 581 | A224 | 3s multi | .80 | .20 |
| | | Nos. 577-581 (5) | 2.95 | 1.00 |

Emerald Background

**Black Vignette & Inscriptions**

**1972-73  Litho.  Perf. 13½x13**

Monthly woodcuts from Calendario Incaico.

| | | | | |
|---|---|---|---|---|
| 582 | A225 | 2.50s red brn (July) | .40 | .20 |
| 583 | A225 | 3s grn (Aug.) | .40 | .20 |
| 584 | A225 | 2.50s rose (Sept.) | .40 | .20 |
| 585 | A225 | 3s lt bl (Oct.) | .55 | .20 |
| 586 | A225 | 2.50s org (Nov.) | .55 | .20 |
| 587 | A225 | 3s lil (Dec.) | .55 | .20 |
| 588 | A225 | 2.50s brn (Jan.) ('73) | .75 | .20 |
| 589 | A225 | 3s pale grn (Feb.) ('73) | .55 | .20 |
| 590 | A225 | 2.50s bl (Mar.) ('73) | .55 | .20 |
| 591 | A225 | 3s org (Apr.) ('73) | .40 | .20 |
| 592 | A225 | 2.50s lil rose (May) ('73) | .40 | .20 |
| 593 | A225 | 3s yel & blk (June) ('73) | .55 | 2.40 |
| | | Nos. 582-593 (12) | 6.30 | 2.40 |

Family Tilling Field — A226

400th anniv. of publication of the Calendario Incaico by Felipe Guaman Poma de Ayala.

Oil Derricks — A228

**1972, Oct. 31**  Perf. 13½x13, 13x13½  **Litho.**
594 A226 2s multi .40 .20
595 A226 2.50s multi .40 .20
596 A228 3s gray & multi 1.20 .60
Nos. 594-596 (3)

Sovereignty of the Sea (Inca Frieze) — A227

4th anniversaries of land reforms and the nationalization of the oil industry and the 15th anniv. of the claim to a 200-mile zone of sovereignty of the sea.

**Christmas Type of 1971**

Sculptures from Huamanga, 17-18th cent.: 1.50s, Holy Family, wood, vert. 2s, Holy Family with lambs, stone. 2.50s, Holy Family in stable, stone, vert.

**1972, Nov. 30**  **Litho.**  **Perf. 13**
597 A220 1.50s buff & multi .25 .20
598 A220 2s buff & multi .25 .20
599 A220 2.50s buff & multi .75 .60
Nos. 597-599 (3)

Morning Glory — A228a

Mayor on Horseback, by Fierro — A229

**1972, Dec. 29**  **Litho.**  **Perf. 13**
600 A228a 1.50s shown .20 .20
601 A228a 2.50s Amaryllis .35 .20
602 A228a 3s Liabum excel-sum .50 .20
603 A228a 3.50s Bletia (orchid) .70 .20
604 A228a 5s Cantua buxifolia .55 .20
Nos. 600-604 (5) 2.30 1.00

**1973, Aug. 13**  **Litho.**  **Perf. 13**
605 A229 1.50s salmon & multi .20 .20
606 A229 2s salmon & multi .20 .20
607 A229 2.50s salmon & multi .25 .20
608 A229 3.50s salmon & multi .35 .20
609 A229 4.50s salmon & multi .55 .20
Nos. 605-609 (5) 1.55 1.00

Paintings by Francisco Pancho Fierro (1803-1879): 2s, Man and Woman, 1830. 2.50s, Padre Abregu Riding Mule, 3.50s, Dancing Couple. 4.50s, Bullfighter Estevan Arredondo on Horseback.

Presentation in the Temple — A230

**1973, Nov. 30**  **Litho.**  **Perf. 13½x13½**
610 A230 1.50s multi .20 .20
611 A230 2s multi .20 .20
612 A230 2.50s multi .60 .60
Nos. 610-612 (3)

Christmas Paintings of the Cuzqueña School: 2s, Holy Family, vert. 2.50s, Adoration of the Kings.

Peru No. 20 — A231

**1974, Mar. 1**  **Litho.**  **Perf. 13**
613 A231 6s gray & dk bl .45 .25
Peruvian Philatelic Assoc., 25th anniv.

Non-ferrous Smelting Plant, La Oroya A232

**1974**  **Litho.**  **Perf. 13x13½**
614 A232 1.50s blue .20 .20
615 A233 2s multi .20 .20
616 A232 3s rose claret .20 .20
617 A232 4.50s green .25 .20
618 A233 8s multi .35 .20
619 A233 10s multi .45 .20
Nos. 614-619 (6) 1.65 1.20

"Peru Determines its Destiny."
Issued: 2s, 8s, 10s, 7/1; 1.50s, 3s, 4.50s, 12/6.

Colombia Bridge, San Martin A233

Designs: 8s, 10s, Different views, Santiago Antunez Dam, Tayacaja.

**1974**  **Litho.**  **Perf. 13x13½**
620 A234 1.50s multi .20 .20
621 A234 2s multi .20 .20
622 A234 2.50s multi .20 .20
623 A234 3s multi .35 .20
Nos. 620-623 (4) 1.00 .80

Battle of Junin, by Felix Yañez A234

2s, 3s, Battle of Ayacucho, by Felix Yañez.

**1974**  **Perf. 13x13½**
Sesquicentennial of the Battles of Junin and Ayacucho.
Issued: 1.50s, 2.50s, Aug. 6; 2s, 3s, Oct. 9.
See Nos. C400-C404.

Indian Madonna — A235

**1974, Dec. 20**  **Litho.**  **Perf. 13½x13**
624 A235 1.50s multi .20 .20
Christmas. See No. C417.

Maria Parado de Bellido A236

International Women's Year Emblem — A237

IWY Emblem, Peruvian Colors and: 2s, Micaela Bastidas. 2.50s, Juana Alarco de Dammert.

**1975, Sept. 8**  **Perf. 13x13½, 13½x13**  **Litho.**
625 A236 1.50s bl grn, red & blk .20 .20
626 A237 2s blk & red .20 .20
627 A236 2.50s pink, blk & red .20 .20
628 A237 3s red, blk & ultra .25 .20
Nos. 625-628 (4) .85 .80

International Women's Year.

St. Juan Macias — A238

**1975, Nov. 14**  **Perf. 13½x13**
629 A238 5s blk & multi .25 .20
Canonization of Juan Macias in 1975.

Louis Braille A239

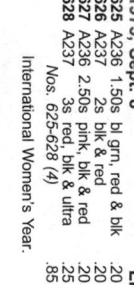

**1976, Mar. 2**  **Litho.**  **Perf. 13½x13½**
630 A239 4.50s gray, red & blk .20 .20
Sesquicentennial of the invention of Braille system of writing for the blind by Louis Braille (1809-1852).

Peruvian Flag A240

**1976, Aug. 29**  **Litho.**  **Perf. 13½x13½**
631 A240 5s gray, blk & red .20 .20
Revolutionary Government, phase II, 1st anniv.

St. Francis, by El Greco — A241

**1976, Dec. 9**  **Litho.**  **Perf. 13½x13**
632 A241 5s gold, buff & brn .25 .20
St. Francis of Assisi, 750th death anniv.

Indian Mother — A242

**1976, Dec. 23**
633 A242 4s multi .25 .20
Christmas.

Chasqui Messenger A243

**1977**  **Litho.**  **Perf. 13½x13**
634 A243 6s grnsh bl & blk .20 .20
635 A243 8s red & blk .20 .20
636 A243 10s ultra & blk .25 .20
637 A243 12s lt grn & blk .40 .35
Nos. 634-637,C465-C467 (7) 4.05 2.40
For surcharge see No. C502.

"X" over Flags — A244

**1977, Nov. 25**  **Litho.**  **Perf. 13½x13**
638 A244 10s multi .20 .20
10th Int'l Pacific Fair, Lima, Nov. 16-27.

Billiard Balls — A258

**1979, June 4**    *Perf. 13½x13*
700   A258   34s multicolored    .25   .25
For surcharge see No. 714.

**1979, June 24**
701   A259   50s multicolored    .35   .20
Inca Sun Festival, Cuzco.

Arms of Cuzco — A259

Peru Colors, Tacna Monument A260

**1979, Aug. 28**   Litho.   *Perf. 13½x13*
702   A260   16s multicolored    .20   .20
Return of Tacna Province to Peru, 50th anniv.
For surcharge see No. 712.

Telecom 79 — A261

**1979, Sept. 20**
703   A261   15s multicolored    .20   .20
3rd World Telecommunications Exhibition, Geneva, Sept. 20-26.

Caduceus A262

Gold Jewelry — A264

---

**1978, July-Aug.**

| No. | Type | Description | | |
|---|---|---|---|---|
| 674 | PT11(a) | 2s on 2c (O) | .20 | .20 |
| 675 | PT11(b) | 3s on 2c (Bk) | .20 | .20 |
| 676 | PT11(a) | 4s on 2c (V) | .20 | .20 |
| 677 | PT11(a) | 5s on 2c (V) | .20 | .20 |
| 678 | PT11(b) | 6s on 2c (DBl) | .20 | .20 |
| 679 | SP1 | 20s on 1.90s + 90c (G) | .75 | .75 |
| 680 | SP1 | 30s on 2c + 1.30s (Bl) | .75 | .75 |
| 681 | PT11(c) | 35s on 2c (C) | .25 | .25 |
| 682 | SP1 | 50s on 2c (LiBl) | 2.00 | 2.00 |
| 683 | SP1 | 55s on 3.60s + | 1.00 | 1.00 |
| 684 | SP1 | 65s on 4.60s + 2.30s (Go) | 1.00 | 1.00 |
| 685 | A196 | 80s on 5.60s (VBl) | .75 | .75 |
| 686 | SP1 | 85s on 20s + 10s (Bk) | 1.50 | 1.50 |
| | | Nos. 674-686 (13) | 9.00 | 9.00 |

Surcharge on Nos. 679-680, 683-684. 686 includes heavy bar over old denomination.

Battle of Iquique A254

Heroes' Crypt — A255

Col. Francisco Bolognesi A256

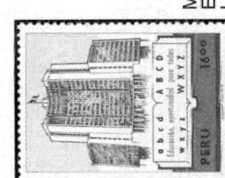

War of the Pacific: No. 688, Col. Jose J. Inclan. No. 689, Corvette Union running Arica blockade. No. 690, Battle of Angamos, Aguirre, Miguel Grau (1888-18/9), Peru. No. 690A, Lt. Col. Pedro Ruiz Gallo. 85s, Marshal Andres A. Caceres. No. 693, Naval Battle of Angamos. No. 693, Battle of Tarapaca. 115s, Adm. Miguel Crau. No. 697, Col. Bolognesi's Reply, by Angeles de la Cruz. No. 698, Col. Alfonso Ugarte on horseback.

*Perf. 13½x13, 13x13½*

**1979-80**    Litho.

| No. | Type | Description | | |
|---|---|---|---|---|
| 687 | A254 | 14s multicolored | .20 | .20 |
| 688 | A256 | 25s multicolored | .35 | .20 |
| 689 | A254 | 25s multicolored | .25 | .20 |
| 690 | A254 | 25s multicolored | .25 | .20 |
| 690A | A254 | 25s multicolored ('80) | .25 | .20 |
| 691 | A256 | 85s multicolored | .50 | .50 |
| 692 | A254 | 100s multicolored | .65 | .30 |
| 693 | A254 | 100s multicolored | .65 | .30 |
| 694 | A256 | 115s multicolored | 1.25 | .75 |
| 695 | A255 | 200s multicolored | 4.00 | 3.00 |
| 696 | A256 | 200s multicolored | 1.25 | 1.00 |
| 697 | A254 | 200s multicolored | 1.25 | 1.00 |
| 698 | A254 | 200s multicolored | 1.25 | 1.00 |
| | | Nos. 687-698 (13) | 12.00 | 8.85 |

For surcharges see Nos. 713, 732.

Peruvian Red Cross, Cent. A257

*Perf. 13x13½*
**1979, May 4**
699   A257   16s multicolored    .20   .20

---

Thomas Faucett, Planes of 1928, 1978 A249

**1978, Oct. 19**   Litho.   *Perf. 13*    .40   .25
655   A249   40s multicolored    .40   .25
Faucett Aviation, 50th anniversary.

Nazca Bowl, Huaco A250

**1978-79**    Litho.    *Perf. 13x13½*

| No. | Type | Description | | |
|---|---|---|---|---|
| 656 | A250 | 16s violet bl ('79) | .20 | .20 |
| 657 | A250 | 20s green ('79) | .20 | .20 |
| 658 | A250 | 25s lt green ('79) | .25 | .25 |
| 659 | A250 | 35s rose red ('79) | .40 | .25 |
| 660 | A250 | 45s dk brown | .45 | .25 |
| 661 | A250 | 50s black | .55 | .30 |
| 662 | A250 | 55s car rose ('79) | .55 | .30 |
| 663 | A250 | 70s lilac rose ('79) | .65 | .55 |
| 664 | A250 | 75s blue | .75 | .45 |
| 665 | A250 | 80s salmon ('79) | .75 | .45 |
| 666 | A250 | 200s brt vio ('79) | 1.90 | 1.40 |
| 667 | A250 | 4.60s | 6.65 | 4.55 |
| | | Nos. 656-667 (11) | | |

For surcharges see Nos. 715, 731.

Peruvian Nativity — A252

**1978, Dec. 28**   Litho.   *Perf. 13½x13*
672   A252   16s multicolored    .20   .20

Ministry of Education, Lima — A253

**1979, Jan. 4**
673   A253   16s multicolored    .20   .20
National Education Program.

Nos. RA40, B1-B5 and 509 Surcharged in Various Colors. No. RA40 Surcharged also:

a    b    c

---

Republican Guard Badge — A245

**1977, Dec. 1**
639   A245   12s multi    .25   .20
58th anniversary of Republican Guard.

Indian Nativity — A246

**1977, Dec. 23**
640   A246   8s multi    .20   .20
Christmas. See No. C484.

Nos. 495, 494, 496 Surcharged with New Value and Bar in Red, Dark Blue or Black: "FRANQUEO / 10.00 / RD-0161-77"

**1977, Dec.**    *Perf. 11*

| No. | Type | Description | | |
|---|---|---|---|---|
| 641 | A192 | 10s on 50c (R) | .25 | .25 |
| 642 | A192 | 20s on 20c (DB) | .50 | .40 |
| 643 | A192 | 30s on 1s (B) | 1.40 | .90 |
| | | Nos. 641-643 (3) | | |

Inca Head — A247

**1978**    Litho.    *Perf. 13½x13*

| No. | Type | Description | | |
|---|---|---|---|---|
| 644 | A247 | 6s bright green | .20 | .20 |
| 645 | A247 | 10s red | .20 | .20 |
| 646 | A247 | 16s red brown | .20 | .20 |
| | | Nos. 644-646,C486-C489 (7) | 3.80 | 2.85 |

For surcharges see Nos. C498-C499, C501.

Flags of Germany, Argentina, Austria, Brazil A248

Argentina '78 Emblem and Flags of Participants: No. 648, 652, Hungary, Iran, Italy, Mexico. No. 649, 653, Scotland, Spain, France, Netherlands. No. 650, 654, Peru, Poland, Sweden and Tunisia. No. 651, like No. 647.

**1978**    Litho.    *Perf. 13x13½*

| No. | Type | Description | | |
|---|---|---|---|---|
| 647 | A248 | 10s blue & multi | .30 | .20 |
| 648 | A248 | 10s blue & multi | .30 | .20 |
| 649 | A248 | 10s blue & multi | .30 | .20 |
| 650 | A248 | 10s blue & multi | .35 | .20 |
| a. | | Block of 4, #647-650 | 1.50 | 1.50 |
| 651 | A248 | 16s blue & multi | .35 | .20 |
| 652 | A248 | 16s blue & multi | .35 | .20 |
| 653 | A248 | 16s blue & multi | .35 | .20 |
| 654 | A248 | 16s blue & multi | .35 | .20 |
| a. | | Block of 4, #651-654 | 1.50 | 1.60 |
| | | Nos. 647-654 (8) | 2.65 | 1.60 |

11th World Soccer Cup Championship, Argentina, June 1-25.
Issued: #647-650, 6/28; #651-654, 12/4.

World Map, "11," Fair Emblem — A263

**1979, Nov. 13**
704 A262 25s multicolored .20 .20

World Map, 4th Intl. "11," Fair Feria Internacional del Pacifico–Lima.

**1979, Nov. 24**
705 A263 55s multicolored .40 .25

Stomatology Academy of Peru, 50th anniv.; 11th Pacific Intl. Trade Fair, Lima, 11/14-25.

**1979, Dec. 19** Perf. 13½x13
706 A264 85s multicolored .55 .40

Larco Herrera Archaeological Museum.

Queen Sofia and King Juan Carlos I, Visit to Peru A266

**1979, Dec. 27** Litho. Perf. 13½x13
707 A265 25s multicolored .20 .20

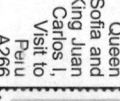

Christmas A265

**1979** Litho. Perf. 13x13½
708 A266 75s multicolored .55 .25

No. RA40 Surcharged in Black, Green or Blue

**1979, Oct. 8**
709 PT11 7s on 2c brown .20 .20
710 PT11 9s on 2c brown (G) .20 .20
711 PT11 15s on 2c brown (B) .60 .60

Nos. 702, 687, 700, 663 Surcharged

**1980, Apr. 14** Perf. 13½x13, 13x13½
Litho.
712 A260 20s on 16s multi .25 .20
713 A254 25s on 14s multi .30 .25
714 A258 65s on 34s multi .50 .40
715 A250 80s on 70s lilac rose .50 .30
Nos. 712-715,C501-C502 (6) 2.50 1.70

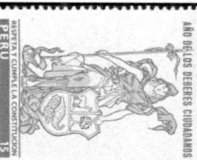

Liberty Holding Arms of Peru — A267

Chimu Cult Cup — A268

Civic duties: 15s, Respect the Constitution. 20s, Honor country. 25s, Vote. 30s, Military service. 35s, Pay taxes. 45s, Contribute to national progress. 50s, Respect rights.

---

**1980**
716 A267 15s greenish blue .20 .20
717 A267 20s salmon pink .20 .20
718 A267 25s ultra .20 .20
719 A267 30s black .20 .20
720 A267 35s black .20 .20
721 A267 45s light blue green .20 .20
722 A267 50s brown .50 .25
Nos. 716-722 (7) 1.85 1.50

Map of Peru and Liberty—A269

**1980, July 9**
723 A268 35s multicolored .25 .20

Return to Civilian Government — A270

**1980, Sept. 9** Litho.
724 A269 25s multicolored .20 .20
725 A270 35s multicolored .25 .25

For surcharge see No. 730.

Machu Picchu A271

**1980, Nov. 10** Litho. Perf. 13x13½
726 A271 25s multicolored .20 .20

World Tourism Conf., Manila, Sept. 27.

Tupac Amaru Rebellion Bicent.— A272

**1981** Perf. 13½x13, Rouletted 11 (#737A)
737B, 11½ (#737A)

Cross, Unleavened Bread, Wheat A276a

Chalice, Host A276b

**1981** Litho., Photo. (#737A-737B)
735 PT17 40s on 10c multi .20 .20
736 A275 40s on 25s on #733 .50 .25
737 A275 130s on #733 .50 .25
737A A276a 140s on 50c brn, yel & red .30 .25
(DB)
737B A276b 140s on 1s multi .30 .25
737C A275 140s on 25s #733 .50 .25
Nos. 735-737C (6) 2.30 1.45

Issued: #735, Apr. 12; #736, Apr. 15; #737A, Apr. 6; #737B, Apr. 15; #737C, Apr. 28.

---

Christmas A273

**1980, Dec. 22** Litho. Perf. 13½x13
727 A272 25s multicolored .20 .20

**1980, Dec. 31** Litho. Perf. 13
728 A273 15s multicolored .20 .20

Nos. 725, 667, 694 Surcharged

**1981** Litho. Perf. 13½x13½
729 A274 40s multicolored .30 .25

**1981, Jan. 28** Litho. Perf. 13½x13½
730 A270 25s on 35s multi .30 .25
731 A250 85s on 200s brt violet .65 .50
732 A256 100s on 115s multi .75 .50
Nos. 730-732 (3) 1.60 1.30

Return to Constitutional Government, July 28, 1980 — A275

**1981, Mar. 26** Litho. Perf. 13½x13
733 A275 25s multicolored .25 .20

For surcharges see Nos. 736-737, 737C.

Tupac Amaru and Micaela Bastidas, Bronze Sculptures, by Miguel Baca-Rossi A276

**1981, May 18** Litho. Perf. 13x13½
734 A276 60s multicolored .45 .35

Rebellion of Tupac Amaru and Micaela Bastidas, bicentenary.

Nos. 733, RA41 and Voluntary Postal Tax Stamps of 1965 Surcharged in Black, Dull Brown or Lake

---

Inca Messenger, by Guaman Poma (1526-1613) A280

**1981**
752 A280 30s lilac & blk .25 .20
753 A280 40s vermilion & blk .20 .20
754 A280 130s brt yel grn & blk .50 .40

Int'l Year of the Disabled A280a

**1981** Litho. Perf. 12

Carved Stone Head, Pallasca Tribe A277

**1981-82** Litho. Perf. 13½x13, 13x13½
738 A277 30s dp rose lilac .25 .25
739 A277 40s orange ('82) .30 .30
740 A277 40s ultra .30 .30
742 A277 80s brown ('82) .75 .40
743 A277 80s red ('82) .75 .40
745 A277 100s lilac rose 1.00 .70
748 A277 140s lt blue grn 1.00 .70
749 A277 180s green ('82) 1.25 1.25
749A A277 180s green ('82) 1.05 1.00
749B A277 280s violet ('82) 1.40 1.00
Nos. 738-749B (10) 8.25 5.70

#739, 742, 749 Pottery vase, Inca, vert. #740, Head, diff. vert. #743, Huaco idol (fish), Nazca. 100s, Pallasca, vert. 140s, Puma.

For surcharges see #789, 798-799, 1026.

**1981, May 31** Perf. 13½x13
750 A278 130s multicolored .60 .60

Postal and Philatelic Museum, 50th anniv.

150th Death Anniv. of Simon Bolivar (in 1980) — A274

**1981, Oct. 7** Litho. Perf. 13½x13
751 A279 30s purple & gray .25 .25

1979 Constitution Assembly President Victor Raul Haya de la Torre.

## 10th Anniv. of State Security Service A296

**1983, Mar. 8**
784 A296 100s blue & orange .20 .20

## Horseman's Ornamental Silver Shoe, 19th Cent. A297

**1983, Mar. 18**
785 A297 250s multicolored .45 .30

## 30th Anniv. of Santiago Declaration A298

## 75th Anniv. of Lima and Callao State Lotteries — A300

## 25th Anniv. of Lima-Bogota Airmail Service — A299

**1983, Mar. 25**
786 A298 280s Map .50 .50
For surcharge see No. 796.

**1983, Apr. 8**
787 A299 150s Jet .30 .20

**1983, Apr. 26**
788 A300 100s multicolored .20 .20

Nos. 739, 773, 771, 778, 780, 782, 781, 786, 777, 749, 774 Surcharged in Black or Green

**1983** **Litho.**
| | | | | |
|---|---|---|---|---|
| 789 | A277 | 100s on 40s orange | .25 | .20 |
| 790 | A285 | 100s on 70s multi | .25 | .20 |
| 791 | A283 | 100s on 80s blk & red | .25 | .20 |
| 792 | A290 | 100s on 240s multi | .25 | .20 |
| 793 | A292 | 100s on 240s multi | .25 | .25 |
| 794 | A294 | 100s on 240s ol grn | .25 | .25 |
| 795 | A293 | 150s on 240s multi | .30 | .30 |
| 796 | A298 | 150s on 280s multi | .30 | .30 |
| 797 | A289 | 150s on 280s multi | .35 | .35 |
| 798 | A277 | 300s on 180s green | .45 | .45 |
| 799 | A277 | 400s on 180s green | .70 | .70 |
| 800 | A286 | 500s on 80s multi | .90 | .90 |
| | | | 1.10 | 1.10 |
| | | | 5.25 | 4.70 |

Nos. 789-800 (12)

## Military Ships A301

---

## Pedro Vilcapaza A290

**Perf. 13½x13**
**1982**
777 A289 280s Holy Family .50 .50
For surcharge see No. 797.

**Perf. 13½x13**
**1982, Dec. 2**
778 A290 240s black & lt brn .45 .30

Death centenary of Indian leader against Spanish during Andes Rebellion.
For surcharges see Nos. 792.

## Jose Davila Condemarin (1799-1882), Minister of Posts (1849-76) — A291

**Perf. 13x13½**
**1982, Dec. 10**
779 A291 150s blue & blk .25 .25
For surcharge see No. 793.

## 10th Anniv. of Intl. Potato Study Center, Lima A292

**Perf. 13x13½**
**1982, Dec. 27**
780 A292 240s multicolored .45 .30
For surcharge see No. 793.

## 150th Anniv. of City of San Miguel de Piura A293

**Perf. 13x13½**
**1982, Dec. 31**
781 A293 280s Arms .50 .50
For surcharge see No. 795.

## TB Bacillus Centenary A294

**Perf. 12**
**1983, Jan. 18**
782 A294 240s Microscope, slide .45 .45
For surcharge see No. 794.

## St. Teresa of Jesus of Avila (1515-1582), by Jose Espinoza de los Monteros, 1682 — A295

**1983, Mar. 1**
783 A295 100s multicolored .20 .20

---

## Rights of the Disabled — A284

**Perf. 12**
**1982, Oct. 18**
771 A283 80s black & red .20 .20
For surcharge see No. 791.

## Brena Campaign Centenary A285

**1982, Oct. 22**
772 A284 200s blue & red .35 .25

**Perf. 13½x13**
**1982, Oct. 26**
773 A285 70s Andres Caceres medallion .20 .20
For surcharge see No. 790.

## 1982 World Cup — A286

## 16th Intl. Congress of Latin Notaries, Lima, June — A287

**Perf. 12**
**1982, Nov. 2**
774 A286 80s multicolored .20 .20
For surcharge see No. 800.

**1982, Nov. 6**
775 A287 500s Emblem .90 .60

## Handicrafts Year A288

**Perf. 13x13½**
**1982, Nov. 24**
776 A288 200s Clay bull figurine .35 .25

## Christmas A289

---

| | | | |
|---|---|---|---|
| 755 | A280 | 140s brt blue & blk | .50 .50 |
| 756 | A280 | 200s yellow brn & blk | .75 .75 |
| | | | 2.20 2.25 |

Nos. 752-756 (5)

Christmas. Issue dates: 30s, 40s, 200s, Dec. 21; others, Dec. 31.

**1981** **Litho.** **Perf. 13½x13**
756A A280a 100s multicolored .60 .40

Nos. 377, C130, C143, J56, O33, RA36, RA39, RA40, RA42, RA43 Surcharged in Brown, Black, Orange, Red, Green or Blue

**1982**
| | | | | |
|---|---|---|---|---|
| 757 | PT11 | 10s on 2c (#RA40, Br) | .25 | .25 |
| 758 | A155 | 10s on 10c (#377) | .20 | .20 |
| 758A | AP60 | 40s on 1.25s (#C143) | .20 | .20 |
| 758B | PT15 | 70s on 5c (#RA36, R) | .20 | .20 |
| 759 | D7 | 80s on 10c (#J56) | .20 | .20 |
| 760 | O1 | 80s on 10c (#O33) | .20 | .20 |
| 761 | PT14 | 80s on 3c (#RA43, R) | .20 | .20 |
| 762 | PT17 | 100s on 10c (#RA42, R) | .25 | .20 |
| 763 | AP57 | 100s on 2.20s (#C130, R) | .25 | .25 |
| 764 | PT14 | 150s on 3c (#RA39, G) | .35 | .35 |
| 765 | PT14 | 180s on 3c (#RA43, R) | .40 | .40 |
| 766 | PT14 | 200s on 3c (#RA43, Bl) | .50 | .50 |
| 767 | AP60 | 240s on 1.25s (#C143, R) | .60 | .60 |
| 768 | PT15 | 280s on 5c (#RA36) | .70 | .70 |
| | | | 4.50 | 4.50 |

Nos. 757-768 (14)

Nos. 758A, 763, 767 airmail. Nos. 759 and 760 surcharged "Habilitado / Franq. Postal / 80 Soles".

## Jorge Basadre (1903-1908), Historian — A281

## Julio C. Tello (1882-1947), Archaeologist — A282

**Perf. 13½x13, 13x13½** **Litho.**
**1982, Oct. 13**
769 A281 100s pale green & blk .25 .20
770 A282 200s lt green & dk bl .50 .30

## 9th Women's World Volleyball Championship, Sept. 12-26 — A283

**1983, May 2** Perf. 12
801 A301 150s Cruiser Almirante Grau, 1907 .25 .20
802 A301 350s Submarine Ferre, 1913 .65 .40

Simon Bolivar Birth Bicentenary A302

Christmas A303

**1983, Dec. 13** Perf. 14
803 A302 100s black & lt bl .20 .20

**1983, Dec. 16**
804 A303 100s Virgin and Child .20 .20

25th Anniv. of Intl. Pacific Fair—A304

Col. Leoncio Prado (1853-83) A306

World Communications Year (in 1983)—A305

**1983**
805 A304 350s multicolored .65 .40

**1984, Jan. 27** Litho.
806 A305 700s multicolored 1.40 .90

**1984, Feb. 3** Litho. Perf. 14
807 A306 150s ol & ol brn .20 .20

Postal Building A307

Pottery—A308

Shipbuilding and Repair—A309

Arms of City of Callao—A310

Peruvian Flora—A311

Peruvian Fauna—A312

A313

**1984**
808 A307 50s Ministry of Posts, Lima

**Litho. Perf. 14**
809 A308 100s Water jar .20 .20
810 A308 150s Llama .20 .20
811 A308 200s Painted vase .20 .20
812 A309 250s shown .20 .20
813 A309 300s Mixed cargo ship .20 .20
814 A310 350s shown .25 .20
815 A310 400s Arms of Caja- marca .30 .20
816 A310 500s Arms of Ayacu- cho .40 .20
817 A311 700s Canna edulis ker .50 .30
818 A312 1000s Lagothrix flavi- cauda .75 .40

Issued: 50s, 8/29; 100s-200s, 300s, 2/22; 350s, 4/23; 400s, 6/21; 500s, 6/22; 700s, 9/12; 1000s, 7/3.
See Nos. 844-853, 880-885.

Nos. 808-818 (11) 3.50 2.50

Admiral Grau—A317

Independence Declaration Act—A316

Naval Battle—A318

Designs: 50s, Hipolito Unanue (1758-1833). 200s, Ricardo Palma (1833-1919), Writer.

**1984, Mar. 30** Litho. Perf. 14
819 A313 50s dull green .20 .20
820 A313 200s purple .20 .20

Issue dates: 50s, Nov. 14; 200s, Mar. 20. See No. 828.

**1984**
821 A315 500s Shooting .50 .25
822 A315 750s Hurdles 1.00 .35

1984 Summer Olympics.

A315

**1984, July 18** Litho. Perf. 14
823 A316 350s Signing document .20 .20

**1984, Oct. 8** Litho. Perf. 12½
824 Block of 4 2.25 .75
a. A317 600s Knight of the Seas, by Pablo Muniz .55 .20
b. A318 600s Battle of Angamos .55 .20
c. A317 600s Congressional seat .55 .20
d. A318 600s Battle of Iquique .55 .20

Admiral Miguel Grau, 150th birth anniv.

Peruvian Naval Vessels A319

**1984, Dec.** Litho. Perf. 14
825 A319 250s Destroyer Almi- rante Guise, 1934 .20 .20
826 A319 400s Gunboat America, 1905 .20 .20

Christmas A320

Famous Peruvians Type of 1984

**1984, Dec. 11** Litho. Perf. 13x13½
827 A320 1000s multi .45 .30

**1984, Dec. 14** Litho. Perf. 14
828 A313 100s brown lake .20 .20

Victor Andres Belaunde (1883-1967), Pres. of UN General Assembly, 1959-60.

15th Pacific Intl. Fair, Lima A323

**1984, Dec. 20** Litho. Perf. 13½x13
829 A322 1000s Street scene .40 .30

450th Anniv., Founding of Cuzco—A322

**1984, Dec. 28** Litho.
830 A323 1000s Llama .40 .30

Visit of Pope John Paul II—A325

**1985, Jan. 17** Litho. Perf. 13½x13
831 A324 1500s The Foundation of Lima, by Francisco Gamarra .50 .35

**1985, Jan. 31** Litho. Perf. 13½x13
832 A325 2000s Portrait .50 .35

450th Anniv., Lima—A324

Microwave Tower—A326

## Jose Carlos Mariategui (1894-1924), Author — A327

**1985, Feb. 28  Litho.  Perf. 13½x13**
833 A326 1100s multi   .75  .20
ENTEL Peru, Natl. Telecommunications Org., 15th anniv.

**1985-86  Photo.  Perf. 13½x13**
Designs: 500s, Francisco Garcia Calderon (1832-1905), president. No. 838, Oscar Miro Quesada (1884-1981), jurist. No. 839, Cesar Vallejo (1892-1938), author. No. 840, Jose Santos Chocano (1875-1934), poet.

| 836 | A327 | 500s lt olive grn | .20 | .20 |
| 837 | A327 | 800s dull red | .20 | .20 |
| 838 | A327 | 800s dk olive grn | .20 | .20 |
| 839 | A327 | 800s Prus blue ('86) | .20 | .20 |
| 840 | A327 | 800s dk red brn ('86) | .20 | .20 |
| | | Nos. 836-840 (5) | 1.00 | 1.00 |

See Nos. 901-905.

## American Air Forces Cooperation System, 25th Anniv. — A328

**1985, Apr. 16**
842 A328 400s Member flags, emblem   .20  .20

## Jose A. Quinones Gonzales (1914-1941), Air Force Captain — A329

**1985, Apr. 22  Perf. 13½x13**
843 A329 1000s Portrait, bomber   .45  .20

### Types of 1984

Design: 200s, Entrance arch and arcade, Central PO admin. building, vert. No. 845, Spotted Robles Moqo bisque vase, Pacheco, Ica. No. 846, Huaura bisque cat. No. 847, Robles Moqo bisque llama head. No. 848, Huancavelica city arms. No. 849, Huanuco city arms. No. 850, Puno city arms. No. 851, Llama wool industry. No. 852, Hymenocallis amancaes. No. 853, Penguins, Antarctic landscape.

**1985-86  Litho.  Perf. 13½x13**

| 844 | A307 | 200s slate blue | .20 | .20 |
| 845 | A308 | 500s bister brn | .25 | .20 |
| 846 | A308 | 500s dull yellow brn | .25 | .20 |
| 847 | A308 | 500s black brn | .25 | .20 |
| 848 | A310 | 700s brt org yel | .30 | .20 |
| 849 | A310 | 700s brt brn ('86) | .30 | .20 |
| 850 | A310 | 900s brown ('86) | .40 | .20 |
| 851 | A309 | 1100s multicolored | .50 | .20 |
| 852 | A311 | 1500s multicolored | .50 | .20 |
| 853 | A312 | 1500s multicolored | .70 | .20 |
| | | Nos. 844-853 (10) | 3.65 | 2.00 |

## Natl. Aerospace Institute Emblem, Globe A330

**1985, May 24  Perf. 13½x13**
858 A330 900s ultra   .20  .20
14th Inter-American Air Defense Day.

## Founding of Constitution City — A333

**1985, July  Litho.  Perf. 13½x13**
859 A333 300s Map, flag, crucifix   .20  .20

## Natl. Radio Society, 55th Anniv. A334

**1985, July 24**
860 A334 1300s bl & brt org   .20  .20

## San Francisco Convent Church — A335

**1985, Oct. 12  Perf. 13½x13**
061 A335 1300s multicolored   .20  .20

## Doctrina Christiana Frontispiece, 1585, Lima — A336

**1985, Oct. 23**
862 A336 300s pale buff & blk   .20  .20
1st printed book in South America, 400th anniv.

## Intl. Civil Aviation Org., 40th Anniv. A337

**1985, Oct. 31  Perf. 13½x13**
863 A337 1100s 1920 Curtis Jenny   .20  .20

## Christmas A338

### Postman, Child — A338a

**1985, Dec. 30  Litho.  Perf. 13½x13**
864 A338 2.50i Virgin and child, 17th cent.   .50  .20

**1985, Dec. 30  Litho.  Perf. 13½x13**
864A A338a 2.50i multi   1.00  .25
Christmas charity for children's and postal workers' funds.

## Founding of Trujillo, 450th Anniv. — A339

**1986, Mar. 5  Litho.  Perf. 13½x13**
865 A339 3i City arms   .40  .25

## Restoration of Chan Chan Ruins, Trujillo Province A340

**1986, Apr. 5  Litho.  Perf. 13½x13**
866 A340 50c Bas-relief   .20  .20

## Saint Rose of Lima, Birth Quadricent. A341

**1986, Apr. 30  Litho.  Perf. 13½x13**
867 A341 7i multicolored   1.10  .60

### 16th Intl. Pacific Fair — A342

**1986, May 20**
868 A342 1i Natl. products symbols   .40  .20

## Intl. Youth Year A343

**1986, May 23  Perf. 13½x13**
869 A343 3.50i multicolored   .40  .30

**1986, June 27  Litho.  Perf. 13x13½**
870 A344 50c brown   .20  .20
Pedro Vilcapazza (1740-81), independence hero.

**1986, Aug. 8  Litho.  Perf. 13x13½**
871 A345 3.50i multi   .65  .30
UN, 40th anniv.

**1986, Aug. 11  Litho.  Perf. 13x13½**
872 A346 50c grysh brown   .25  .20
Fernando and Justo Albujar Fayaque, Manuel Guarniz Lopez, natl. heroes.

A344

A345

A346

## Peruvian Navy A347

**1986, Aug. 19  Perf. 13x13½**
873 A347 1.50i R-1, 1926   .20  .20
874 A347 2.50i Abtao, 1954   .30  .25

### Flora Type of 1984

**1986  Litho.  Perf. 13x13**

| 880 | A311 | 80c Tropaeolum majus | .20 | .20 |
| 881 | A311 | 80c Datura candida | .20 | .20 |
| 884 | A312 | 2i Canis nudus | .25 | .20 |
| 885 | A312 | 2i Penelopo albipennis | .35 | .30 |
| | | Nos. 880-885 (4) | 1.00 | .90 |

## Canchis Province Folk Costumes A348

**1986, Aug. 26  Litho.  Perf. 13½x13**
890 A348 3i multicolored   .35  .25

Tourism Day A349

**1986, Aug. 29** **Perf. 13x13½**
891 A349 4i Sacsayhuaman .50 .35
**1986, Oct. 12 Litho.** **Perf. 13x13½**
891A A349 4i Intihuatana, Cuzco .55 .40

**1986, Sept. 4**
892 A350 1i multicolored .60 .20
Interamerican Development Bank, 25th Anniv. — A350

Beatification of Sr. Ana de Los Angeles — A351
**1986, Sept. 15**
893 A351 6i St. Ana, Pope John Paul II .70 .55

Jorge Chavez (1887-1910), Aviator, and Bleriot XI
1M — A352
**1986, Sept. 23** **Perf. 13½x13**
894 A352 5i multicolored .85 .45
Chavez's flight over the Alps, 75th anniv.

VAN '86 — A353
**1986, Sept. 26**
895 A353 50c light blue .20 .20
Ministry of Health vaccination campaign, Sept. 27-28, Oct. 25-26, Nov. 22-23.

**1986, Oct. 1**
Natl. Journalism Day — A354
896 A354 1.50i multi .20 .20

Peruvian Navy A355
**1986, Oct. 7 Litho.** **Perf. 13x13½**
897 A355 1i Brigantine Gamarra, 1848 .30 .20
898 A355 1i Monitor Manco Ca-pac, 1880 .30 .20

Institute of Higher Military Studies, 35th Anniv. A356
**1986, Oct. 31 Litho.** **Perf. 13x13½**
899 A356 1i multicolored .20 .20

Boy, Girl — A357
**1986, Nov. 3** **Perf. 13½x13**
900 A357 2.50i red, brn & blk .40 .30
Christmas charity for children and postal workers' funds.

Famous Peruvians Type of 1985
**1986-87**
901 A327 50c Carrion .20 .20
902 A327 50c Barrenechea .20 .20
904 A327 80c Jose de la Riva Aguero .80 .80
905 A327 80c Barrenechea .80 .80
Nos. 901-905 (4)
Issued: #904, 10/22/87; #905, 11/9/87. This is an expanding set. Numbers will change if necessary.

Christmas A358
**1986, Dec. 3** **Perf. 13½x13**
908 A358 5i St. Joseph and Child .75 .60

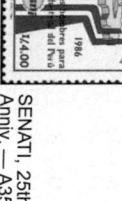

SENATI, 25th Anniv. — A359
**1986, Dec. 19** **Perf. 13½x13**
909 A359 4i multicolored .70 .45

Shipibo Tribal Costumes A360

World Food Day — A361
**1987, Apr. 24 Litho.** **Perf. 13½x13**
910 A360 3i multicolored .45 .35

**1987, May 26**
911 A361 50c multicolored .40 .20

Preservation of the Nasca Lines — A362
**1987, June 13 Litho.** **Perf. 13½x13**
912 A362 8i multicolored 1.25 .90
Design: Nasca Lines and Dr. Maria Reiche (b. 1903), archaeologist.

A363

A364

A365

**1987, July 15 Litho.** **Perf. 13½x13**
913 A363 50c violet .20 .20
Mariano Santos (1850-1900), "The Hero of Tarapaca," 1879, Chilean war. Dated 1986.

**1987, July 19** **Perf. 13½x13**
914 A364 3i multicolored .45 .35
Natl. Horse Club, 50th anniv. Dated 1986.

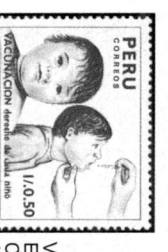

**1987, Aug 13** **Perf. 13½x13**
915 A365 2i multicolored .30 .25
Gen. Felipe Santiago Salaverry (1806-1836), revolution leader. Dated 1986.

AMIFIL '87 — A367
Colca's Canyon — A366
**1987, Sept. 8 Litho.** **Perf. 13½x13**
916 A366 6i multicolored 1.00 .40
10th Natl. Philatelic Exposition, Arequipa. Dated 1986.

**1987, Sept. 10**
917 A367 1i Nos. 1-2 .20 .20
Dated 1986.

Jose Maria Arguedas (b. 1911), Anthropologist, Author — A368
**1987, Sept. 19**
918 A368 50c brown .20 .20

Arequipa Chamber of Commerce & Industry A369
**1987, Sept. 23** **Perf. 13½x13**
919 A369 2i multicolored .25 .20

Vaccinate Every Child Campaign A370
**1987, Sept. 30 Litho.** **Perf. 13½x13**
920 A370 50c orange brown .20 .20

Argentina, Winner of the 1986 World Cup Soccer Championships — A371
**1987, Nov. 18**
921 A371 4i multicolored .60 .25

Restoration of Chan Chan Ruins, Trujillo Province — A372

Chimu culture (11th-15th cent.) bas-relief.

**1987, Nov. 27**
922 A372 50c multicolored ... .20 .20
See No. 936.

**1987, Dec. 7**
923 A373 4i Comet, Giotto satellite ... .30 .25

Halley's Comet A373

Jorge Chavez Dartnell (1887-1910), Aviator — A374

Founding of Lima, 450th Anniv. (in 1985) — A375

**1987, Dec. 15** *Perf. 13½x13*
924 A374 2i yel bis, claret brn & gold ... .40 .20

**1987, Dec. 18** **Litho.** *Perf. 13½x13*
925 A375 2.50i Osambela Palace ... .30 .20
Dated 1985.

Discovery of the Ruins at Machu Picchu, 75th Anniv. (in 1986) A376

**1987, Dec.** *Perf. 13½x13*
926 A376 9i multicolored ... .65 .50
Dated 1986.

St. Francis's Church, Cajamarca A377

**1988, Jan. 23** **Litho.** *Perf. 13½x13*
927 A377 2i multicolored ... .30 .20
Cultural Heritage. Dated 1986.

---

Participation of Peruvian Athletes in the Olympics, 50th Anniv. — A378

Design: Athletes on parade, poster publicizing the 1936 Berlin Games.

**1988, Mar. 1** **Litho.** *Perf. 13½x13*
928 A378 1.50i multicolored ... .40 .20
Dated 1986.

Ministry of Education, 150th Anniv. A379

**1988, Mar. 10** *Perf. 13x13½*
929 A379 1i multicolored ... .30 .20

Coronation of the Virgin of the Evangelization by Pope John Paul II — A380

**1988, Mar. 14** **Litho.** *Perf. 13½x13*
930 A380 10i multicolored ... .50 .25
Dated 1986.

Rotary Intl. Involvement in Anti-Polio Campaign A381

**1988, Mar. 16**
931 A381 2i org, gold & dark blue ... .20 .20

Postman, Cathedral A382

St. John Bosco (1815-1888), Educator — A384

---

Meeting of 8 Latin-American Presidents, Acapulco, 1st Anniv. — A383

**1988, Apr. 29** **Litho.** *Perf. 13½x13*
932 A382 9i brt blue ... .30 .20

Christmas charity for children and postal workers funds.

**1988, May 4** *Perf. 13x13½*
933 A383 9i multicolored ... .30 .20

**1988, June 1** *Perf. 13x13½*
934 A384 5i multicolored ... .20 .20

1st Peruvian Scientific Expedition to the Antarctic A385

**1988, June 2** *Perf. 13½x13½*
935 A385 7i Ship Humboldt, globe ... .20 .20

Restoration of Chan Chan Ruins, Trujillo Province A386

**1988, June 7**
936 A386 4i Bas-relief ... .35 .20

Cesar Vallejo (1892-1938), Poet — A387

Journalists' Fund — A388

**1988, June 15** *Perf. 13½x13*
937 A387 25i buff, blk & brn ... 1.00 .30

**1988, July 12** **Litho.** *Perf. 13½x13*
938 A388 4i buff & deep ultra ... .20 .20

Type A44 — A389

**1988, Sept. 1** **Litho.** *Perf. 13½x13*
939 A389 20i blk, lt pink & ultra ... .20 .20
EXFILIMA '88, discovery of America 500th anniv.

---

17th Intl. Pacific Fair A390

**1988, Sept. 6** *Perf. 13x13½*
940 A390 4i multicolored ... .20 .20

Painting by Jose Sabogal (1888-1956) — A391

**1988, Sept. 7**
941 A391 12i multicolored ... .20 .20

Peru Kennel Club Emblem, Dogs — A392

**1988, Sept. 9** *Perf. 13½x13*
942 A392 20i multicolored ... .35 .20
CANINE '88 Intl. Dog Show, Lima.

Alfonso de Silva (1902-1934), Composer, and Score to Esplandido de Flores — A393

**1988, Sept. 27** **Litho.** *Perf. 13½x13*
943 A393 20i multicolored ... .20 .20

2nd State Visit of Pope John Paul II — A394

1988 Summer Olympics, Seoul — A395

**1988, Oct. 10** *Perf. 13½x13*
944 A394 50i multicolored ... .40 .20

**1988, Nov. 10** **Litho.** *Perf. 13½x13*
945 A395 25i Women's volleyball ... .40 .20

Women's Volleyball Championships (1982) — A396

Chavin Culture Ceramic Vase — A397

**1988, Nov. 16**    *Perf. 12*
946 A396 95i on 300s multi   .80 .40
No. 946 not issued without overprint. Christmas charity for children's and postal workers' funds.

**1988**    *Litho.*    *Perf. 12*
**Surcharged in Red**
947 A397 40i on 100s red brn   .20 .20
948 A397 80i on 10s blk   .30 .20
Nos. 947-948 not issued without surcharge. Issue dates: 40i, Dec. 15; 80i, Dec. 22.

Rain Forest Border Highway — A398

Codex of the Indian Kings, 1681 — A399

**1989, Jan. 27**    *Litho.*    *Perf. 12*
**Surcharged in Black**
949 A398 70i on 80s multi   .20 .20
Not issued without surcharge.

**1989, Feb. 10**
**Surcharged in Olive Brown**
950 A399 230i on 300s multi   .50 .25
Not issued without surcharge.

Credit Bank of Peru, Cent. A400

**1989, Apr. 9**    *Litho.*    *Perf. 13x13½*
951 A400 500i Huari Culture weaving   .90 .45

---

Postal Services A401

**1989, Apr. 20**    *Perf. 13*
952 A401 50i SESPO, vert.   .20 .20
953 A401 100i CAN   .20 .20

El Comercio, 150th Anniv. — A402

**1989, May 15**
954 A402 600i multi   .60 .30

Garcilaso de la Vega (1539-1616), Historian Called "The Inca" — A403

**1989, July 11**    *Litho.*    *Perf. 12½*
955 A403 300i multi   .40 .20

Express Mail Service A404

**1989, July 12**
956 A404 100i dark red, org & dark blue   .20 .20

Federation Emblem and Roca — A405

**1989, Aug. 29**    *Litho.*    *Perf. 13*
957 A405 100i multi   .20 .20
Luis Loli Roca (1925-1988), founder of the Federation of Peruvian Newspaper Publishers.

Restoration of Chan Chan Ruins, Trujillo Province A406

**1989, Sept. 17**    *Perf. 12½*
958 A406 400i multi   .45 .25
Chimu culture (11th-15th cent.) bas-relief.

---

Geographical Society of Lima, Cent. — A407

**1989, Sept. 18**    *Perf. 13*
959 A407 600i Early map of So. America   .65 .30

Founders of Independence Soc. — A408

**1989, Sept. 28**    *Litho.*    *Perf. 12½*
960 A408 300i multicolored   .30 .20

3rd Meeting of the Presidential Consultative and Planning Board — A409

**1989, Oct. 12**    *Perf. 13*
961 A409 1300i Huacachina Lake   1.60 .80
For surcharge see No. 1017.

Children Mailing Letters — A410

**1989, Nov. 29**    *Litho.*    *Perf. 12½*
962 A410 1200i multicolored   .30 .20
Christmas charity for children's and postal workers' funds.

Cacti A411

**1989, Dec. 21**    *Litho.*    *Perf. 13*
963 A411 500i Loxanthocereus acanthurus   .20 .20
964 A411 500i Corycactus huincoensis   .20 .20
965 A411 500i Haageocereus clavispinus   .20 .20
966 A411 500i Trichocereus pervianus   .20 .20
967 A411 500i Matucana cereoides   .20 .20
Nos. 963-967 (5)   1.00 1.00
Nos. 965-967 vert. For surcharges see Nos. 1028-1031.

---

America Issue — A412

**1989, Dec. 28**    *Perf. 12½*
968 A412 5000i shown   4.00 2.00
969 A412 5000i multi, diff.   4.00 2.00
UPAE emblem and pre-Columbian medicine jars.

 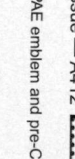

Belen Church, Cajamarca A413

**1990, Feb. 1**    *Litho.*    *Perf. 12½*
970 A413 600i multicolored   .20 .20
Historic patrimony of Cajamarca and culture of the Americas.

Huascaran Natl. Park — A414

 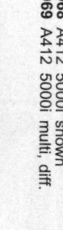

**1990, Feb. 4**    *Perf. 13*
971 A414 900i Llanganuco Lagoons   .20 .20
972 A414 900i Mountain climber, Andes, vert.   .20 .20
973 A414 1000i Alpamayo mountain   .20 .20
974 A414 1000i Puya raimondii, vert.   .20 .20
975 A414 1100i Condor and Quenual   .20 .20
976 A414 1100i El Huascaran   1.20 1.20
Nos. 971-976 (6)

Pope and Icon of the Virgin — A415

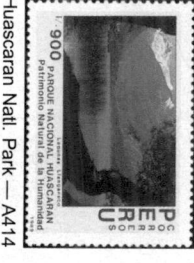

**1990, Feb. 6**    *Perf. 12½*
977 A415 1250i multicolored   .50 .25
Visit of Pope John Paul II. For surcharge see No. 1039.

Butterflies — A416

**1990, Feb. 11**    *Perf. 13*
978 A416 1000i Amydon   .20 .20
979 A416 1000i Agrias beata, female   .20 .20
980 A416 1000i Sardanapalus, male   .20 .20
981 A416 1000i Sardanapalus, female   .20 .20

Sir Rowland Hill and Penny Black — A431

**1992, Jan. 15**   **Litho.**   **Perf. 13**
1015 A431 .40im gray, blk & bl .85 .45
Penny Black, 150th anniv. (in 1990).

**1992, Jan. 28**
1016 A432 .30im multicolored .65 .35
Our Lady of Guadalupe College, 150th anniv. (in 1990)

**1992, Jan. 30**   **Perf. 13½x13**
1017 A433 10c multicolored .20
Entre Nous Society, 80th anniv.

Peru-Bolivia Port Access Agreement — A434

**1992, Feb. 25**   **Litho.**   **Perf. 12½**
1018 A434 20c multicolored .30 .20

Restoration of Chan-Chan Ruins — A435

**1992, Mar. 17**
1019 A435 .15im multicolored .35 .20
Dated 1990.

---

Maria Jesus Castaneda de Pardo, First Woman President of Peruvian Red Cross — A426

**1991, May 15**   **Litho.**   **Perf. 12½**
1004 A426 .15im on 2500i red & blk .60 .30
Dated 1990. Not issued without surcharge.

2nd Peruvian Scientific Expedition to Antarctica — A427

**1991, June 20**
40im, Penguins, man. .45im, Peruvian research station, skua. .50im, Whale, map, research station.
1005 A427 .40im on 50,000i 1.60 .80
1006 A427 .45im on 80,000i 1.75 .90
1007 A427 .50im on 100,000i 2.00 1.00
Nos. 1005-1007 (3) 5.35 2.70
Not issued without surcharge.

St. Anthony Natl. Univ., Cuzco, 300th Anniv.: 10c, Siphonandra elliptica. 20c, Don Manuel de Mollinedo y Angulo, founder. 1s, University coat of arms.

**1991, Sept. 26**   **Perf. 13½x13**
1008 A428 10c multicolored .25 .20
1009 A428 20c multicolored .50 .25
1010 A428 1s multicolored 2.40 1.25
Nos. 1008-1010 (3) 3.15 1.70

**1991, Dec. 3**   **Litho.**   **Perf. 13½x13**
Paintings: No. 1011, Madonna and child. No. 1012, Madonna with lambs and angels.
1011 A429 70c multicolored 1.50 .75
1012 A429 70c multicolored 1.50 .75
Postal Workers' Christmas fund.

America Issue — A430

**1991, Dec. 23**   **Perf. 13**
1013 A430 .50im Mangrove swamp 1.10 .55
1014 A430 .50im Gera waterfall, vert. 1.10 .55
Dated 1990.

---

Arequipa, 450th Anniv. — A421

**1990, Aug. 15**   **Litho.**   **Perf. 13**
990 A421 50,000i multi .50 .25

Lighthouse A422

Design: 230,000i; Hospital ship Morona.

**1990, Sept. 19**   **Surcharged in Black**   **Perf. 12½**
991 A422 110,000i on 200i blue .85 .45
992 A422 230,000i on 400i blue 1.75 .90
Not issued without surcharge.

**1990-91**   **Litho.**   **Perf. 13**
993 A423 110,000i Torch bearer .55 .30
994 A423 280,000i Shooting 1.40 .70
995 A423 290,000i Running, horiz.
996 A423 300,000i Soccer 1.40 .70
997 A423 560,000i Swimming, horiz. 1.50 .75
998 A423 580,000i Equestrian 2.25 1.10
999 A423 600,000i Sailing 2.40 1.25
1000 A423 620,000i Tennis 2.50 1.25
Nos. 993-1000 (8) 14.50 7.30
4th South American Games, Lima. Issue dates: #993-996, Oct. 19. #997-1000, Feb. 5, 1991.

**1990, Nov. 22**   **Litho.**   **Self-Adhesive**   **Die Cut**
1001 A424 250,000i No. 1 1.50 .75
1002 A424 350,000i No. 2 2.25 1.10
Pacific Steam Navigation Co., 150th anniv.

Postal Workers' Christmas Fund — A425

**1990, Dec. 7**   **Litho.**   **Perf. 12½**
1003 A425 310,000i multi 1.75 .90

---

982 A416 10001 Agrias beata, male .20 .20
Nos. 978-982 (5) 1.00 1.00
For surcharges see Nos. 1033-1037.

Victor Raul Haya de La Torre and Seat of Government.
**1990, Feb. 24**   **Perf. 12½**
983 A417 2100i multicolored .55 .25
Return to constitutional government, 10th anniv.

**1990, May 24**   **Litho.**   **Perf. 12½**
984 A418 300i multicolored .30 .20
Peruvian Philatelic Assoc., 50th anniv. Dated 1989. For surcharge see No. 1038.

World Exposition of Stamp & Literature Printers, Buenos Aires. Dated 1989. For surcharge see No. 1032.
**1990, May 29**
985 A419 300i multicolored .20 .20

French Revolution, Bicentennial — A420

#986, Liberty. #987, Storming the Bastille. #988, Lafayette celebrating the Republic. #989, Rousseau & symbols of the Revolution.
**1990, June 5**
986 A420 2000i multicolored .85 .45
987 A420 2000i multicolored .85 .45
988 A420 2000i multicolored .85 .45
989 A420 2000i shown .85 .45
a. Strip of 4, #986-989 + label 3.50 3.50
Dated 1989.

Antonio Raimondi, Naturalist and Publisher, Death Cent. — A436

PERU CORREOS 1/m 0.30

**1992, Mar. 31**
1020 A436 .30im multicolored .75 .40

---

Newspaper "Diario de Lima", Bicent. (in 1990) — A437

PERU CORREOS 1/m 0.35

**1992, May 22    Litho.    Perf. 13**
1021 A437 .35im pale yel & black .65 .35
Dated 1990.

---

Mariano Melgar (1790-1815), Poet — A438

1790 1990    PERU S/ 0.60

**1992, Aug. 5    Litho.    Perf. 12½x13**
1022 A438 60c multicolored 1.40 .70

---

8 Reales, 1568. First Peruvian Coinage A439

PERU S/. 0.70

**1992, Aug. 7    Perf. 13x12½**
1023 A439 70c multicolored 1.00 .50

---

Catholic University of Peru, 75th Anniv. — A440

PERU años 1917-1992 S/0.90

**1992, Aug. 18    Perf. 12½**
1024 A440 90c black & tan 1.25 .65

---

Pan-American Health Organization, 90th Anniv. — A441

PERU CORREOS PRO SALUTE MUNDI    S/. 3.00

---

Nos. 749, 961 Surcharged

PERU CORREOS S/. 0.40

**1992, Nov. 18    Litho.    Perf. 13½x13, 13**
1026 A277 50c on 180s #749 .65 .35
1027 A409 1s on 1300i #961 1.25 .65

---

Nos. 963, 965-967, 977-982, & 984-985 Surcharged

**1992, Dec. 24    Perfs. as Before    Litho.**
1028 A411 40c on 500i #963 3.50 1.50
1029 A411 40c on 500i #965 3.50 1.50
1030 A411 40c on 500i #966 3.50 1.50
1031 A411 40c on 500i #967 3.50 1.50
1032 A419 50c on 300i #985 3.50 1.50
1033 A416 50c on 1000i #977 3.50 1.50
1034 A416 50c on 1000i #978 3.50 1.50
1035 A416 50c on 1000i #980 3.50 1.50
1036 A416 50c on 1000i #981 3.50 1.50
1037 A416 50c on 1000i #982 3.50 1.50
1038 A418 50c on 1250i #984 3.50 1.50
1039 A415 1s on 1250i #977 7.50 1.50
Nos. 1028-1039 (12) 50.00 18.00

---

**1992, Dec. 2    Litho.    Die Cut    Self-Adhesive**
1025 A441 3s multicolored 4.50 2.25

PERU S/. 0.50    MUSEO CULTURA INCA

---

Virgin with a Spindle, by Urbina — A442

PERU S/0.80    VIRGEN NIÑA HILANDERA

**1993, Feb. 10    Litho.    Die Cut    Self-Adhesive**
1040 A442 80c multicolored 1.40 .70

---

Various artifacts.
Sican Culture A443

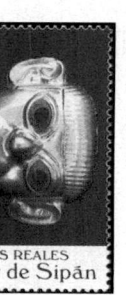

PERU S/.2.00    SICAN

**1993, Feb. 10    Self-Adhesive**
1041 A443 2s multicolored 2.75 1.40
1042 A443 5s multi, vert. 6.75 3.50

---

Evangelization in Peru, 500th Anniv. — A444

PERU S/1.00

**1993, Feb. 12    Self-Adhesive**
1043 A444 1s multicolored 1.75 .90

---

Dancers, by Monica Rojas — A446

PERU S/.1.50

Fruit Sellers, by Angel Chavez — A445

PERU S/.1.50    EXPRESIONES FOLKLORICAS DEL PERU

**1993, Feb. 12    Self-Adhesive**
1044 A445 1.50s multicolored 2.00 1.00
1045 A446 1.50s multicolored 2.00 1.00

---

Statue of Madonna and Child — A447

CENTENARIO SALESIANO 1891 1991    PERU S/.0.70

Salesian Brothers in Peru, cent. (in 1991).

**1993, Feb. 24    Litho.    Die Cut    Self-Adhesive**
1046 A447 70c multicolored 1.10 .55

---

America Issue — A448

AMERICA AMERICA    liPerú PERU S/.0.90    PERU S/.1.00

UPAEP: No. 1047a, 90c, Francisco Pizarro, sailing ship. b. 1s, Sailing ship, map of north-west coast of South America.

**1993, Mar. 19    Perf. 12½**
1047 A448 Pair, #a.-b. 2.40 1.25

---

Sipan Gold Head — A449

liPerú    JOYAS REALES    Señor de Sipán    S/.0.50

**1993, Apr. 1**
1048 A449 50c multicolored 6.00 6.00

---

Beatification of Josemaría Escrivá, 1st Anniv. — A450

Primer Aniversario 1993    PERU S/0.30    Beatificación de Josemaría Escrivá    Roma 17 de Mayo de 1992

**1993, July 7    Litho.    Die Cut    Self-Adhesive**
1049 A450 30c multicolored .70 .35

---

Peru-Japan Treaty of Peace and Trade, 120th Anniv. — A451

PERU S/.0.90

Designs: 1.50s, Flowers, 1.70s, Peruvian, Japanese children, mountains.

**1993, Aug. 21    Litho.    Perf. 11**
1050 A451 1.50s multicolored 2.00 1.00
1051 A451 1.70s multicolored 2.25 1.10

---

Sea Lions — A452

PERU S/.0.90    AMERICA

**1993, Sept. 20    Litho.    Perf. 11**
1052 A452 90c shown 1.10 .55
1053 A452 1s Parrot, vert. 1.40 .70
Amfil '93 (#1052), Brasiliana '93 (#1053).

---

A453    PERU S/0.50    A454    PERU S/0.50

**1993, Nov. 9    Litho.    Die Cut    Self-Adhesive**
1054 A453 50c olive brown
Honorio Delgado, Physician and Author, Birth Cent. (in 1992).

**1993, Nov. 12    Self-Adhesive**
1055 A454 80c orange brown 1.60 .80
Rosalia De LaValle De Morales Macedo, Social Reformer, Birth Cent.

---

A455    PERU S/.2.00

Sculptures depicting Peruvian ethnic groups.

**1993, Nov. 22    Self-Adhesive**
1056 A455 2s Quechua 3.25 1.60
1057 A455 3.50s Orejon 5.75 3.00

---

Int'l Pacific Fair, Lima — A456

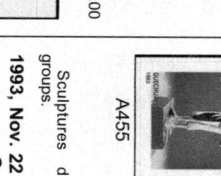

PERU S/.1.50    FERIA

**1993, Nov. 25    Litho.    Perf. 11**
1058 A456 1.50s multicolored 2.75 1.50

---

Based on available exchange rates, the face value of Nos. 1056-1057 is about $2.53. It appears that Peruvian stamps are appearing in the market at significantly higher prices. We have left some of Peru's new issues unvalued until we have more information on the relationship between face value and current retail prices.

Christmas — A457

Cultural Artifacts — A458

Design: 1s, Madonna of Loreto.

**1993, Nov. 30**
1059 A457 1s multicolored

**1993, Nov. 30** **Die Cut**
2.50s, Sican artifacts 4s, Sican mask. 10s, Chancay ceramic statue, vert. 20s, Chancay textile.

**Self-Adhesive**
| | | | | |
|---|---|---|---|---|
| 1060 | A458 | 2.50s multicolored | 4.00 | 2.40 |
| 1061 | A458 | 4s multicolored | 5.50 | 3.50 |
| 1062 | A458 | 10s multicolored | 14.50 | 8.75 |
| 1063 | A458 | 20s multicolored | 29.00 | 17.50 |

Nos. 1060-1063 (4) 53.00 32.15

See Nos. 1079-1082.

Cultural Artifacts A469

Mochican art: 40c, Pitcher with figures beneath blanket, 80c, Jeweled medallion. 90c, Figure holding severed head.

**1995, Mar. 27** **Perf. 14**
| | | | | |
|---|---|---|---|---|
| 1091 | A469 | 40c multicolored | .35 | .35 |
| 1092 | A469 | 80c multicolored | .70 | .35 |
| 1093 | A469 | 90c multicolored | .80 | .40 |

Nos. 1091-1093 (3) 1.85 .95

Dated 1994.

Union Club, Fountain, Plaza of Arms A474

Design: 1s, Santo Domingo Convent, Lima.

**1995, Apr. 19** **Litho.** **Perf. 14**
| | | | | |
|---|---|---|---|---|
| 1101 | A474 | 90c multicolored | 1.50 | .75 |
| 1102 | A474 | 1s multicolored | 1.75 | .90 |

Cultural history of Lima.

Prevention of AIDS — A459

**1993, Dec. 1** **Litho.** **Perf. 11**
1064 A459 1.50s multicolored 2.00 .75

A460

**1994, Mar. 4** **Litho.** **Die Cut**
**Self-Adhesive**
1065 A460 1s multicolored 1.60 .80

Natl. Council on Science and Technology (Concytec), 25th Anniv. Dated 1993.

**1994**
20c, 40c, 50c, Bridge of Huaman Poma de Ayala.

**Self-Adhesive**
| | | | | |
|---|---|---|---|---|
| 1066 | A461 | 20c blue | .35 | .20 |
| 1067 | A461 | 40c orange | .65 | .35 |
| 1068 | A461 | 50c purple | .85 | .45 |

Nos. 1066-1068 (3) 1.85 1.00

**Litho.** **Perf. 12x11**
| | | | | |
|---|---|---|---|---|
| 1073 | A461 | 30c brown | .45 | .25 |
| 1074 | A461 | 40c black | .70 | .35 |
| 1075 | A461 | 50c vermilion | .85 | .45 |

Nos. 1073-1075 (3) 2.00 1.05

Issued: Nos. 1066-1068, 3/11/94; Nos. 1073-1075, 5/13/94.
This is an expanding set. Numbers may change.

Cultural Artifacts Type of 1993

No. 1079, Engraved silver container, vert. No. 1080, Engraved medallion. No. 1081, Carved bull, Pucara. No. 1082, Plate with fish designs.

A461

Juan Parra del Riego, Birth Cent. — A470

No. 1095, Jose Carlos Mariategui, birth cent.

**1995, Mar. 28** **Perf. 14**
1094 A470 90c multicolored 1.40 .70

**Perf. 13½x13**
1095 A470 90c multicolored 1.40 .70

Dated 1994.

Ethnic Groups — A475

**Perf. 13½x13**
| | | | | |
|---|---|---|---|---|
| 1103 | A475 | 1s Bora girl | 1.75 | .90 |
| 1104 | A475 | 1.80s Aguaruna man | 3.00 | 1.50 |

**Self-Adhesive**
| | | | | |
|---|---|---|---|---|
| 1079 | A458 | 1.50s multicolored | 2.50 | 1.25 |
| 1080 | A458 | 1.50s multicolored | 2.50 | 1.25 |
| 1081 | A458 | 3s multicolored | 4.75 | 2.40 |
| 1082 | A458 | 3s multicolored | 4.75 | 2.40 |

Nos. 1079-1082 (4) 14.50 7.30

Dated 1993.

Sipan Artifacts A464

**1994, May 19** **Litho.** **Perf. 11**
1083 A464 3s Peanut-shaped beads 4.75 2.40
1084 A464 5s Mask, vert. 8.00 4.00

El Brujo Archaeological Site, Trujillo — A465

**1994, Nov. 3** **Litho.** **Perf. 14**
1085 A465 70c multicolored .65 .35

Christmas A466

Ceramic figures: 1.80s, Christ child. 2s, Nativity scene. Dated 1994.

**1995, Mar. 17** **Litho.** **Perf. 13½x13**
1086 A466 1.80s multicolored 1.60 .80
1087 A466 2s multicolored 1.75 .90

1994 World Cup Soccer Championships, U.S. — A467

**1995, Mar. 20** **Perf. 13½x13**
1088 A467 60c shown .75 .40
1089 A467 4.80s Mascot, flags 7.25 3.75

Dated 1994.

Las Carmelitas Monastery, 350th Anniv. A471

**1995, Mar. 31** **Litho.** **Perf. 13**
1096 A471 70c multicolored 1.10 .55

Dated 1994.

Peru's Volunteer Fireman's Assoc. A472

Fire trucks: 50c, Early steam ladder. 90c, Modern aerial ladder.

**1995, Apr. 12** **Perf. 14**
1097 A472 50c multicolored .85 .40
1098 A472 90c multicolored 1.50 .75

Dated 1994.

Ministry of Transportation, 25th Anniv. — A468

**1995, Mar. 22** **Perf. 13x13½**
1090 A468 20c multicolored .20 .20

Dated 1994.

World Food Program, 30th Anniv. A476

**1995, May 3** **Perf. 13x13½**
1105 A476 1.80s multicolored 3.00 1.50

Solanum Ambosinum A477

Reed Boat, Lake Titicaca — A478

Design: 2s, Mochica ceramic representation of papa flower.

**1995, May 8** **Perf. 13½x13**
1106 A477 1.80s multicolored 3.00 1.50
1107 A477 2s multicolored 3.50 1.75

**1995, May 12**
1108 A478 2s multicolored 3.50

Musical Instruments A473

**1995, Apr. 10** **Litho.** **Perf. 13½x13**
1099 A473 20c Cello .35 .20
1100 A473 40c Drum .70 .35

Fauna A479

**1995, May 18** **Perf. 13½x13, 13½x13½**
1109 A479 1s American owl, vert. 1.75 .90
1110 A479 1.80s Jaguar 3.00 1.50

**Andes Development Corporation, 25th Anniv. — A480**

1995, Aug. 29    Litho.    Perf. 14
1111 A480 5s multicolored    8.00 4.00

**World Tourism Day A481**

1995, Sept. 27
1112 A481 5.40s multicolored    8.50 4.25
Dated 1994.

**World Post Day A482**

1995, Oct. 9
1113 A482 1.80s Antique mail box    2.75 1.40

**America Issue A483**

1995, Oct. 12    Perf. 13½x14, 14x13½ (#1115)
1114 A483 1.50s Landing of Columbus    2.50 1.25
1115 A483 1.70s Guanaco, vert.    2.75 1.40
1116 A483 1.80s Early mail cart    2.75 1.40
1117 A483 2s Postal trucks    3.25 1.60
Nos. 1114-1117 (4)    11.25 5.65
No. 1116-1117 are dated 1994.

**UN, 50th Anniv. A484**

1995, Oct. 28    Perf. 14
1118 A484 90c multicolored    1.50 .75
Design: 90c, Peruvian delegates, 1945.

**Entrys, Lima Cathedrals A485**

Designs: 30c, St. Apolonia. 70c, St. Louis, side entry to St. Francis.

**Artifacts from Art Museums A486**

1995, Oct. 20
1119 A485 30c multicolored    .55 .30
1120 A485 70c multicolored    1.25 .65
Dated 1994.

1995, Oct. 31    Perf. 14½x14
Carvings and sculptures: No. 1121, St. James on horseback, 19th cent. No. 1122, Church, 40c, 1123, Woman on pedestal, 50c.
1121 A486 20c multicolored    .35 .20
1122 A486 20c multicolored    .35 .20
1123 A486 40c multicolored    .65 .35
1124 A486 50c multicolored    .80 .40
Nos. 1121-1124 (4)    2.15 1.15
Dated 1994.

**Scouting — A487**

1995, Nov. 9    Litho.    Perf. 13½x13
Designs: a, 80c, Lady Olave Baden-Powell. b, 1s, Lord Robert Baden-Powell.
1125 A487 Pair, #a-b.    2.75 1.40
Dated 1994.

A488    A489

1995, Nov. 16
1126 A488 1.80s multicolored    2.75 1.40
1127 A488 2s multicolored    3.00 1.50
Folk Dances: 1.80s, Festejo. 2s, Marinera limena, horiz.
Dated 1994.

Perf. 14
1995, Nov. 23
1128 A489 50c multicolored    .85 .45
1129 A489 90c multicolored    1.50 .75
Biodiversity: 50c, Manu Natl. Park. 90c, Anolis punctatus, horiz.

**Electricity for Development A490**

1995, Nov. 27
1130 A490 20c multicolored    .30 .20
1131 A490 40c multicolored    .60 .30
Electricity for Development: 20c, Toma de Huinco. 40c, Antacoto Lake.
Dated 1994.

A490

**Peruvian Saints A491**

1995, Dec. 4
Peruvian Saints: 90c, St. Toribio de Mogrovejo. 1s, St. Franciso Solano.
1132 A491 90c multicolored    1.40 .70
1133 A491 1s multicolored    1.50 .75
Dated 1994.

A491

**FAO, 50th Anniv. A492**

1996, Apr. 24    Litho.    Perf. 14
1134 A492 60c multicolored    .90 .55

**Christmas 1995 A493**

1996, May 2
1135 A493 30c multicolored    .45 .25
1136 A493 70c multicolored    1.00 .60
Local crafts: 30c, Nativity scene with folding panels, vert. 70c, Carved statues of three Magi.

**America Issue A494**

1996, May 9
1137 A494 30c multicolored    .45 .25
1138 A494 70c multicolored    1.00 .60
Designs: 30c, Rock formations of Lachay. 70c, Coastal black crocodile.

**Int'l Pacific Fair — A495**

1996, May 16
1139 A495 60c multicolored    .90 .55

**1992 Summer Olympic Games, Barcelona A496**

1996, June 10    Litho.    Perf. 12½
1140 A496 60c Block of 4, #a.-d.    3.00 1.75
a, Shooting. b, Tennis. c, Swimming. d, Weight lifting.
Dated 1992. For surcharges see #1220-1223.

**Expo '92, Seville A497**

1996, June 17
1141 A497 1.50s multicolored    2.25 1.40
Dated 1992.

**Cesar Vallejo (1892-1938), Writer — A498**

1996, June 25
1142 A498 50c black & gray    .75 .45
Dated 1992.

**Lima, City of Culture — A499**

1996, July 1
1143 A499 30c brown & tan    .45 .25
Dated 1992. For surcharge see No. 1219.

Heinrich von Stephan (1831-97) — A510

**1997, Oct. 9**
1162 A510 10s multicolored   13.00 9.75

America Issue — A511

1163 A511 2.70s Early post carrier   3.50 2.75
1164 A511 2.70s Modern letter carrier   3.50 2.75

**1997, Oct. 12**

13th Bolivar Games — A512

a, Tennis. b, Soccer. c, Basketball. d, Shot put.

*Perf. 14x13½*
**1997, Oct. 17** Litho. Block of 4, #a.-d.   14.00 10.50
1165 A512 2.70s multicolored

Marshal Ramon Castilla (1797-1867) — A513

**1997, Oct. 17**
1166 A513 1.80s multicolored   2.50 1.90

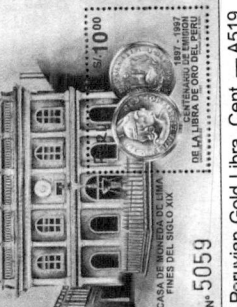

Treaty of Tlatelolco Banning Nuclear Weapons in Latin America, 30th Anniv. — A514

**1997, Nov. 3**
1167 A514 20s multicolored   26.00 20.00

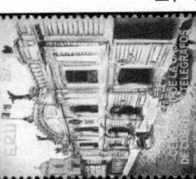

Manu Natl. Park — A515

---

Birds: a, Kingfisher. b, Woodpecker. c, Crossbill. d, Eagle. e, Jabiru. f, Owl.

**1997, Oct. 24** **Sheet of 6**
1168 A515 3.30s #a.-f. + label   25.00 19.00

8th Peruvian Antarctic Scientific Expedition A516

**1997, Nov. 10**
1169 A516 6s multicolored   7.75 5.75

Christmas A517

**1997, Nov. 26**
1170 A517 2.70s multicolored   3.50 2.75

Hipolito Unanue Agreement, 25th Anniv. — A518

*Perf. 14x13½*
**1997, Dec. 18** Litho.
1171 A518 1s multicolored   1.25 .95

Souvenir Sheet

Peruvian Gold Libra, Cent. — A519

**1997, Dec. 18**
1172 A519 10s multicolored   13.00 9.75

Dept. of Post and Telegraph, Cent. — A520

**1997, Dec. 31**
1173 A520 1s multicolored   1.25 .95

---

Kon-Tiki Expedition, 50th Anniv. A500

**1997, Apr. 28** *Perf. 12½* Litho.
1144 A500 3.30s multicolored   2.50 1.90

Beginning with No. 1145, most stamps have colored lines printed on the back creating a granite paper effect.

UNICEF, 50th Anniv. (in 1996) A501

**1997, Aug. 7** Litho. *Perf. 13½x14*
1145 A501 1.80s multicolored   2.40 1.75

Mochica Pottery — A502

**1997, Aug. 18** Litho. *Perf. 14½*

Designs: 20c, Owl. 30c, Ornamental container. 50c, Goose jar. 1s, Two monkeys on jar. 1.30s, Duck pitcher. 1.50s, Cat pitcher.

| | | |
|---|---|---|
| 1146 | A502 20c green | .25 .20 |
| 1147 | A502 30c lilac | .40 .30 |
| 1148 | A502 50c black | .65 .50 |
| 1149 | A502 1s red brown | 1.25 .95 |
| 1150 | A502 1.30s red | 1.75 1.25 |
| 1151 | A502 1.50s brown | 2.00 1.50 |
| | | 6.30 4.70 |

*Nos. 1146-1151 (6)*

See Nos. 1179-1183, 1211-1214.

1996 Summer Olympics, Atlanta — A503

a, Shooting. b, Gymnastics. c, Boxing. d, Soccer.

**1997, Aug. 25** *Perf. 14x13½*
1152 A503 2.70s Strip of 4, #a.-d.   13.50 10.25

College of Biology, 25th Anniv. — A504

**1997, Aug. 26**
1153 A504 5s multicolored   6.25 4.75

---

Scouting, 90th Anniv. — A505

**1997, Aug. 29**
1154 A505 6.80s multicolored   8.50 6.50

8th Intl. Conference Against Corruption, Lima A506

**1997, Sept. 7** *Perf. 13½x14*
1155 A506 2.70s multicolored   2.00 1.50

Montreal Protocol on Substances that Deplete Ozone Layer, 10th Anniv. — A507

**1997, Sept. 16** *Perf. 14x13½*
1156 A507 6.80s multicolored   8.25

Lord of Sipan Artifacts A508

Designs: 2.70s, Animal figure with large hands, feet. 3.30s, Medallion with warrior figure, vert. 10s, Tomb of Lord of Sipan, vert.

**1997, Sept. 22** Litho. *Perf. 13½x14*
1157 A508 2.70s multicolored   3.50 2.75
1158 A508 3.30s multicolored   4.30 3.25

**Souvenir Sheet**
1159 A508 10s multicolored   13.00 9.75

Peruvian Indians — A509

**1997, Oct. 12** Litho. *Perf. 14x13½*
1160 A509 2.70s Man   3.50 2.75
1161 A509 2.70s Woman   3.50 2.75

America Issue. Nos. 1160-1161 are dated 1996.

### Organization of American States (OAS), 50th Anniv. — A521

**1998, Apr. 30**   Litho.   **Perf. 14x13½**
1174  A521  2.70s multicolored   3.50  3.50

### Chorrillos Military School, Cent. — A522

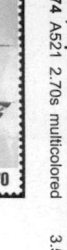

**1998, May 22**   **Perf. 13½x14**
1175  A522  2.70s multicolored   3.50  3.50

### Tourism — A523

**1998, June 22**   Litho.   **Perf. 14x13½**
1176  A523  5s multicolored   5.75  5.75

### Peruvian Horse — A524
CABALLO PERUANO DE PASO

**1998, June 5**
1177  A524  2.70s pale violet & violet   3.25  3.25

### 1998 World Cup Soccer Championships, France — A525
COPA MUNDIAL DE FUTBOL FRANCIA 98

**1998, June 26**
1178  A525  Pair, #a.-b.   7.00  7.00
a, 2.70s, Goalie. b, 3.30s, Two players.

**Souvenir Sheet**
**Perf. 13½x14**
1178C A525  10s multicolored   12.00  12.00

### Mochica Pottery Type of 1997

**1998, June 19**   Litho.   **Perf. 14½**
1179  A502  1s slate        1.25  1.25
1180  A502  1s violet       1.60  1.60
1181  A502  1.30s pale blue 1.60  1.60
1182  A502  1.50s bister    3.50  3.50
1183  A502  2.70s black brown  4.00  4.00
1183  A502  3.30s black brown  4.00  4.00
Nos. 1179-1183 (5)   12.25  12.25
1s, like #1149. 1.30s, like #1146. 1.50s, like #1151. 2.70s, like #1148. 3.30s, like #1150.

---

### Aero Peru, 25th Anniv. — A526

**1998, May 22**   **Perf. 13½x14**
1184  A526  1.50s multicolored   1.90  1.90
1185  A526  2.70s multicolored   3.50  3.50

### Restoration of the Cathedral of Lima, Cent. — A527
BANCO WIESE

**1998, June 15**   **Perf. 14x13½**
1186  A527  2.70s multicolored   3.25  3.25

### Inca Rulers — A528
AÑO INTERNACIONAL DE LOS OCEANOS

**1998, July 17**   Litho.   **Perf. 14x13½**
1187  A528  2.70s Lloque Yupanqui   3.25  3.25
1188  A528  2.70s Sinchi Roca       3.25  3.25
1189  A528  9.70s Manco Ca-pac      18.00 18.00
Nos. 1187-1189 (3)   24.50  24.50
See Nos. 1225-1228.

### Intl. Year of the Ocean — A529

**1998, Aug. 8**
1190  A529  6.80s multicolored   8.00  8.00

### Natl. Symphony Orchestra, 60th Anniv. — A530
60 ANIVERSARIO DE LA ORQUESTA SINFONICA NACIONAL  1938-1998

**1998, Aug. 11**
1191  A530  2.70s multicolored   3.25  3.25
**Perf. 14x13½**

### Mother Teresa (1910-97) — A531
MADRE TERESA DE CALCUTA

**1998, Sept. 5**
1192  A531  2.70s multicolored   3.25  3.25

---

### Peruvian Children's Foundation — A532
FUNDACION POR LOS NIÑOS DEL PERU

**1998, Sept. 17**   Litho.   **Perf. 14x13½**
1193  A532  8.80s multicolored   10.50  10.50

### Heroes of the Cenepa River — A533
HEROES DEL CENEPA

**Souvenir Sheet**
**1998, June 5**
1194  A533  10s multicolored   12.00  12.00
Illustration reduced.

### Princesa De Ampato — A534
PRINCESA DE AMPATO
El cuerpo prehispánico mejor conservado de América Latina

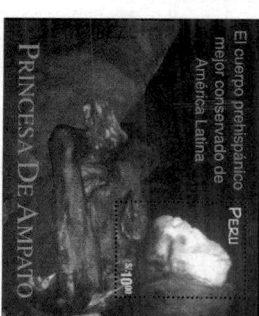

**1998, Sept. 8**
1195  A534  10s multicolored   12.00  12.00
Illustration reduced.

### Fauna of Manu Natl. Park — A535
FAUNA DEL MANU

**1998, Sept. 27**   Litho.   **Perf. 14x13½**
1196  A535  1.50s multicolored   1.75  1.75

### America Issue — A536
AMERICA

**1998, Oct. 12**
1197  A536  2.70s Chabuca   3.00  3.00

---

### Stamp Day — A537
DIA MUNDIAL DEL SELLO

**1998, Oct. 9**
1198  A537  6.80s No. 3   7.75  7.75

### Frogs — A538

Agalychnis craspedopus

**1998, Oct. 23**   Litho.   **Perf. 14x13½**
1199  A538  3.30s Block of 6, #a.-f. + label   13.50  13.50
No. 1199: a, Agalychnis craspedopus. b, Ceratophrys cornuta. c, Eppedobates macero. d, Phyllomedusa vaillanti. e, Dendrobates biolat. f, Hemiphractus proboscideus.

### Christmas — A539
NAVIDAD 98  NACIMIENTO DE CHULUCANAS

**1998, Nov. 16**
1200  A539  3.30s multicolored   2.25  2.25
**Perf. 13½x14**

### Universal Declaration of Human Rights, 50th Anniv. — A540

**1998, Dec. 10**   Litho.   **Perf. 13½x14**
1201  A540  5s multicolored   3.50  3.50

### Peru-Ecuador Peace Treaty — A541
Acuerdo de Paz  PERU-ECUADOR  Brasilia-1998

**1998, Nov. 26**   Litho.   **Perf. 13½x14**
1202  A541  2.70s multicolored   2.25  2.25
Brasilia '98.

### 19th World Scout Jamboree, Chile — A542
XIX JAMBOREE MUNDIAL SCOUT  CHILE 1999  SIEMPRE LISTO

**1999, Jan. 5**   Litho.   **Perf. 14x13½**
1203  A542  5s Pair, #a.-b.   6.50  6.50
Designs: a, Scouting emblem, stylized tents. b, Emblem, tents, "SIEMPRE LISTO."

**Peruvian Philatelic Assoc., 50th Anniv. — A543**

**1999, Jan. 10**
1204  A543  2.70s No. 19  1.75  1.75

**Paintings by Pancho Fierro (1809-79) — A544**

Designs: 2.70s, Once Upon a Time in a Shaded Grove. 3.30s, Sound of the Devil.

**1999, Jan. 16**
1205  A544  2.70s multicolored  1.75  1.75
1206  A544  3.30s multicolored  2.25  2.25

**Regional Dance — A545**

*Perf. 14x13½*  **Litho.**
**1999, Feb. 10**
1207  A545  3.30s multicolored  2.00  2.00

**CENDAF, 25th Anniv. A546**

*Perf. 13½x14*
**1999, Mar. 1**
1208  A546  1.80s multicolored  1.10  1.10

**Ernest Malinowski (1818-99), Central Railroad A547**

**1999, Mar. 3**
1209  A547  5s multicolored  3.00  3.00

**Peruvian Foundation for Children's Heart Disease A548**

**1999, Mar. 6**
1210  A548  2.70s multicolored  1.60  1.60

**Mochica Pottery Type of 1997**

Designs: 1s, like #1151. 1.50s, like #1148. 1.80s, like #1146. 2s, like #1150.

**1999, Feb. 16  Litho.**  *Perf. 14½*
1211  A502  1s lake  .65  .65
1212  A502  1.50s dark blue blk  1.00  1.00
1213  A502  1.80s brown  1.10  1.10
1214  A502  2s orange  1.25  1.25
Nos. 1211-1214 (4)  4.00  4.00

**Fauna of the Peruvian Rain Forest — A549**

*Perf. 14x13½*
**1999, Apr. 23**
1215  A549  5s multicolored  3.25  3.25

**Souvenir Sheet**
**Fauna of Manu Natl. Park — A550**

Illustration reduced.

*Perf. 13½x14*
**1999, Apr. 23**
1216  A550  10s multicolored  6.50  6.50

**Milpo Mining Co., 50th Anniv. A551**

*Perf. 13½x14*
**1999, Apr. 6**
1217  A551  1.50s multicolored  1.00  1.00
See note after No. 1145.

**Japanese Immigration to Peru, Cent. — A552**

*Perf. 14x13½*
**1999, Apr. 3**
1218  A552  6.80s multicolored  4.50  4.50

**Nos. 1140, 1143 Surcharged in Black, Brown, Dark Blue, Red or Green**

**1999**  **Litho.**  *Perf. 12½*
1219  A499  2.40s on 30c (Br) multi  1.40  1.40
**Blocks of 4**
1220  A496  1s on 60c #a-d.  2.40  2.40
1221  A496  1.50s on 60c (DB) #a.-d.  3.50  3.50

1222  A496  2.70s on 60c (R) #a.-  6.50  6.50
  d.
1223  A496  3.30s on 60c (G) #a.-  8.00  8.00
  d.
Size and location of surcharge varies.

**Antarctic Treaty, 40th Anniv. A553**

*Perf. 13½x14*
**1999, May 24**
1224  A553  6.80s multicolored  4.00  4.00

**Inca Rulers Type of 1998**  *Perf. 14x13½*
**1999, June 24  Litho.**
1225  A528  3.30s Capac Yupanqui  2.00  2.00
1226  A528  3.30s Yahuar Huaca  2.00  2.00
1227  A528  3.30s Inca Roca  2.00  2.00
1228  A528  3.30s Maita Capac  8.00  8.00
Nos. 1225-1228 (4)

**Souvenir Sheet**
**Nazca Lines — A554**

Illustration reduced.

**1999, June 8**
1229  A554  10s multicolored  6.00  6.00
Margin shows Maria Reiche (1903-98), expert in Nazca Lines.

**Minerals A555**

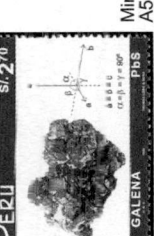

*Perf. 13½x14*
**1999, July 3**
1230  A555  2.70s multicolored  1.60  1.60
1231  A555  3.30s multicolored  2.00  2.00
1232  A555  5s multicolored  3.00  3.00
  6.60  6.60
Nos. 1230-1232 (3)
Designs: 2.70s, Galena. 3.30s, Scheelite. 5s, Virgotrigonia peterseni.

**Virgin of Carmen — A556**

*Perf. 14x13½*
**1999, July 16**
1233  A556  3.30s multicolored  2.00  2.00

**Santa Catalina Monastery — Arequipa — A557**

*Perf. 14x13½*  **Litho.**
**1999, Aug. 15**
1234  A557  2.70s multicolored  1.75  1.75

**Chinese Immigration to Peru, 150th Anniv. A558**

*Perf. 13½x14*
**1999**
1235  A558  1.50s red & black  .85  .85

**Peruvian Medical Society, 25th Anniv. — A559**

*Perf. 14x13½*
**1999  Litho.**
1236  A559  1.50s multicolored  .85  .85

**UPU, 125th Anniv. A560**

*Perf. 13½x14*  **Litho.**
**1999, Oct. 9**
1237  A560  3.30s multicolored  1.90  1.90

**America Issue, A New Millennium Without Arms A561**

*Perf. 14x13½, 13½x14*
**1999, Oct. 12**  Earth, sunflower, vert.
1238  A561  2.70s Earth, sunflower  1.60  1.60
1239  A561  3.30s shown  1.90  1.90

**Señor de los Milagros Religious Procession A562**

*Perf. 14x13½*
**1999, Oct. 18**
1240  A562  1s Incense burner  .65  .65
1241  A562  1.50s Procession  .95  .95

**1999, Oct. 22**
Inter-American Development Bank, 40th Anniv. — A563
*Perf. 13½x14*
1242 A563 1.50s multicolored .95 .95

Butterflies A564

Designs: a. Pterourus zagreus chrysome-lus. b. Asterope buckleyi. c. Parides chabrias. d. Mimoides pausanias. e. Nessaea obrina. f. Pterourus zagreus zagreus.

**1999, Oct. 23** *Perf. 14½x13½*
Block of 6 + Label
1243 A564 3.30s #a.-f. 11.50 11.50

**1999, Oct. 26** *Perf. 13½x14, 14x13½*
1244 A565 1s multicolored .65 .65
1245 A565 1s multicolored .65 .65
1246 A565 1s multicolored .65 .65
Nos. 1244-1246 (3) 1.95 1.95

Border Disputes Settled by Brasilia Peace Accords A565

Maps of regions from: No. 1244, Cusumasa Bumburiza to Yaupi, Santiago. No. 1245, Lagatococha to Güeppi, vert. No. 1246, Cunhuime Sur to 20 de Noviembre, vert.

**1999, Nov. 22** *Perf. 14x13½*
1247 A566 2.70s multicolored 1.60 1.60
Peruvian Postal Services, 5th Anniv. — A566

**1999, Dec. 1** *Litho.* *Perf. 14x13½*
1248 A567 2.70s multicolored 1.60 1.60
Christmas A567

**1999, Dec. 29** *Litho.* *Perf. 13½x14*
1249 A568 2.70s multi 1.60 1.60
Ricardo Bentín Mujica (1899-1979), Businessman — A568

**2000, Jan. 1**
1250 A569 10s multi 5.75 5.75
Millennium — A569
Souvenir Sheet

**2000, Jan. 17** *Perf. 14x13½*
1251 A570 1.50s multi .90 .90
Printed se-tenant with label.
Ricardo Cillóniz Oberti, Businessman A570

**2000, Jan. 27** *Litho.* *Perf. 14x13½*
a. Alpacas at right. b. Alpacas at left.
1252 A571 1.50s Pair, #a.-b. 1.75 1.75
Alpaca Wool Industry — A571

**2000, Feb. 4**
1253 A572 4s multi 2.40 2.40
Nuclear Energy Institute — A572

**2000, Feb. 7**
1254 A573 1s Pair, #a.-b. 1.25 1.25
Retamas S.A. Gold Mine — A573
Miner, mine and buildings: a. Text in blue violet. b. Text in white.

**2000, Feb. 28** *Perf. 13½x14*
1255 A574 3.30s multi 2.00 2.00
Comptroller General, 70th Anniv. A574

**2000, Mar. 19** *Litho.* *Perf. 13½x14*
1256 A575 1.60s multi 1.00 1.00
Emilio Guimoye, Field of Flowers A575

**2000, May 3** Granite Paper *Perf. 14x13½*
1257 A576 1.80s multi + label 1.10 1.10
1999 Natl. Scholastic Games — A576

**2000, July 20** Granite Paper *Perf. 13½x14*
1258 A577 1.30s multi .85 .85
Machu Picchu A577

**2000, Aug. 22** *Litho.* *Perf. 13½x14* Granite Paper
1259 A578 3.80s multi 2.25 2.25
Campaign Against Domestic Violence A578

**2000, Aug. 23** Granite Paper
1260 A579 3.20s multi 1.90 1.90
Holy Year 2000 A579

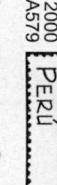

Designs: No. 1261, 3.20s, Lake Yarinacocha, by Mari Trini Ramos Vargas. No. 1262, 3.20s, Ahuashiyacu Falls, by Susan Hidalgo Bacalla. No. 1263, 3.80s, Arequipa Countryside, by Anibal Lajo Yañez.

**2000, Aug. 25** Granite Paper
*Perf. 13½x14, 14x13½*
1261-1263 A580 Set of 3 6.00 6.00
Children's Drawing Contest Winners A580

**2000, Aug. 28** Granite Paper *Perf. 13½x14*
1264 A581 3.20s multi 1.90 1.90
"Millennium Assembly" of UN General Assembly A581

**2000, Sept. 1** Granite Paper
1265 A582 3.80s multi 2.25 2.25
Gen. José de San Martin (1777-1850) — A582

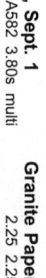

**2000, Sept. 3** Granite Paper *Perf. 14x13½*
1266 A583 Pair, #a-b 2.25 2.25
Ormeño Bus Co., 30th Anniv. — A583
No. 1266: a. 1s, Bus and map of South America. b. 2.70s, Bus and map of North America. Illustration reduced.

**2000, Sept. 11** Granite Paper *Perf. 13½x14*
1267 A584 3.20s multi 1.90 1.90
Intl. Cycling Union, Cent. A584

World Meteorological Organization, 50th Anniv. — A585

**2000, Sept. 13**    Granite Paper
1268 A585 1.50s multi    .90 .90

Lizards of Manu Natl. Park — A586

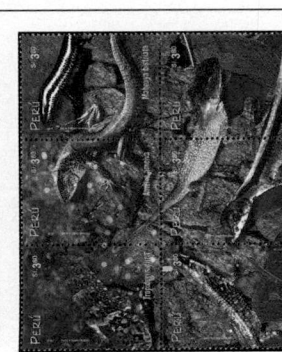

No. 1269: a, Tropidurus plica. b, Ameiva ameiva. c, Mabouya bistriata. d, Neusticurus ecpleopus. e, Anolis fuscoauratus. f, Enyalioides palpebralis. Illustration reduced.

*Perf. 14x13½*

**2000, Sept. 15**    Granite Paper
1269 A586 3.80s Block of 6, #a-f    13.50 13.50

Matucana Madisonitorum — A587

*Perf. 13½x14*

**2000, Sept. 18**    Granite Paper
1270 A587 3.80s multi    2.25 2.25

Carlos Noriega, First Peruvian Astronaut A588

**2000, Sept. 20**    Granite Paper
1271 A588 3.80s multi    2.25 2.25

Toribio Rodriguez de Mendoza (1750-1825), Theologian A589

*Perf. 14x13½*

**2000, Sept. 21**    Granite Paper
1272 A589 3.20s multi    1.90 1.90

Ucayali Province, Cent. A590

---

Pisco Wine A591

*Perf. 13½x14*

**2000, Sept. 25**    Granite Paper
1273 A590 3.20s multi    1.90 1.90

**2000, Sept. 27**    Granite Paper
1274 A591 3.80s multi    2.25 2.25

Latin American Integration Association, 20th Anniv. — A592

*Perf. 14x13½*

**2000, Sept. 29**    Granite Paper
1275 A592 10.20s multi    4.75 4.75

Peruvian Journalists Federation, 50th Anniv. — A593

**2000, Sept. 30**    Granite Paper
1276 A593 1.50s multi    .90 .90

Sexi Petrified Forest A594

*Perf. 13½x14*

**2000, Oct. 3**    Granite Paper
1277 A594 1.50s multi    .90 .90

America Issue, Campaign Against Aids A595

**2000, Oct. 12**    Granite Paper
1278 A595 3.80s multi    2.25 2.25

Supreme Court A596

**2000, Oct. 16**    Granite Paper
1279 A596 1.50s multi    .90 .90

---

Salvation Army in Peru, 90th Anniv. — A597

*Perf. 14x13½*

**2000, Nov. 3**    Granite Paper
1280 A597 1.50s multi    .90 .90

Peruvian Cancer League's Fight Against Cancer, 50th Anniv. A598

*Perf. 13½x14*

**2000, Nov. 9**    Granite Paper
1281 A598 1.50s multi    .90 .90

Border Map Type of 1999

Flags and maps of border separating Peru and: 1.10s, Chile, vert. 1.50s, Brazil, vert. 2.10s, Colombia. 3.20s, Ecuador. 3.80s, Bolivia, vert.

*Perf. 14x13½, 13½x14*

**2000, Nov. 27**    Granite Paper
1282-1286 A565    Set of 5    7.00 7.00

Railroads in Peru, 150th Anniv. A599

*Perf. 13½x14*

**2000, Nov. 27**    Granite Paper
1287 A599 1.50s multi    .90 .90

Luis Alberto Sanchez (1900-94), Politician — A600

*Perf. 14x13½*

**2000, Nov. 27**    Granite Paper
1288 A600 3.20s multi    1.90 1.90

National Congress A601

*Perf. 13½x14*

**2000, Dec. 7**    Granite Paper
1289 A601 3.80s multi    2.25 2.25

---

Caretas Magazine, 50th Anniv. A602

**2000, Dec. 15**    Granite Paper
1290 A602 3.20s multi    1.90 1.90

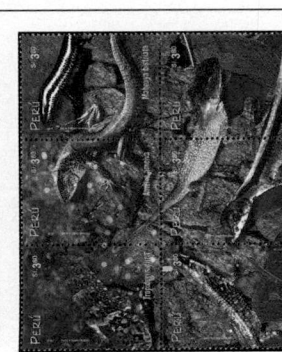

Cacti A603

Designs: 1.10s, Haageocereus acranthus, vert. 1.50s, Cleistocactus xylorhizus, vert. No. 1293, 2.10s, Mila caespitosa, vert. No. 1294, 2.10s, Haageocereus setosus, vert. 3.20s, Opuntia pachypus. 3.80s, Haageocereus tenuis.

*Perf. 13½x13¾, 13¾x13½*    Litho.

**2001, Aug. 24**    A603
1291-1296 A603    Set of 6    8.00 8.00

San Marcos University, 450th Anniv. — A604

*Perf. 13½x13¾*

**2001, Sept. 4**
1297 A604 1.50s multi    .85 .85

Alianza Lima Soccer Team, Cent. — A605

No. 1298: a. Players. b, Players, ball.

**2001, Sept. 6**
1298 A605 3.20s Horiz. pair, #a-b    3.75 3.75

Anti-Drug Campaign — A606

*Perf. 13½x13½*

**2001, Sept. 7**
1299 A606 1.10s multi    .65 .65

**Gen. Roque Sáenz Peña (1851-1914), Pres. of Argentina — A607**

**2001, Sept. 7**
1300 A607 3.80s multi    2.25 2.25

---

**Lurin River Valley A608**

**2001, Sept. 10**
1301 A608 1.10s multi    .65 .65

**Amphipoda Hyalella — A609**

**2001, Sept. 10**
1302 A609 1.80s multi    1.00 1.00

---

**Postal and Philatelic Museum, 70th Anniv. — A610**

**2001, Oct. 9**    **Perf. 13½x13¾**
1303 A610 3.20s multi    1.90 1.90

---

9th Iberoamerican Summit of Heads of State — A611

**2002, Mar. 6**    **Litho.**    **Perf. 14x13½**
1304 A611   Horiz. pair, #a-b    2.25 2.25
Dated 2001.

Country names and: a, 1.10s, Rectangle. b, 2.70s, Angled line.

---

**Peru — Costa Rica Diplomatic Relations, 150th Anniv. — A612**

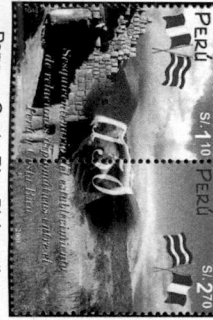

Flags, handshake and: a, 1.10s, Ruins. b, 2.70s, Grassland.

**2002, Mar. 12**
1305 A612   Horiz. pair, #a-b    2.25 2.25
Dated 2001.

---

**World Conference Against Racism, Durban, South Africa A613**

**2002, Mar. 13**    **Perf. 14x13½**
1306 A613 3.80s multi    2.25 2.25
Dated 2001.

**Intl. Day of Indigenous People — A614**

**2002, Mar. 13**    **Perf. 14x13½**
1307 A614 5.80s multi    3.50 3.50
Dated 2001.

---

**Intl. Organization for Migration, 50th Anniv. — A615**

**2002, Apr. 2**    **Perf. 13½x14**
1308 A615 3.80s multi    2.25 2.25
Dated 2001.

---

**Pan-American Health Organization, Cent. — A616**

**2002, Apr. 8**
1309 A616 3.20s multi    1.90 1.90
Dated 2001.

---

**La Molina Agricultural University, Cent. — A617**

Arms and: a, 1.10s, Sepia photograph of building. b, 2.70s, Color photograph of building.

**2002, Apr. 16**    **Perf. 14x13½**
1310 A617   Horiz. pair, #a-b    2.25 2.25
Dated 2001.

---

**Pisco Distilling A618**

Designs: 3.20s, Alembics, 3.80s, Jugs. 10s, La Fiesta de la Chicha y el Pisco, by José Sabogal.

**2002, Apr. 18**    **Perf. 13½x14**
1311-1312 A618   Set of 2    4.25 4.25
**Souvenir Sheet**
1313 A618 10s multi    5.75 5.75
Dated 2001.

---

**Orchids — A619**

Designs: 1.50s, Stanhopea sp. 3.20s, Chloraea pavoni. 3.80s, Psychopsis sp.

**2002, Apr. 30**    **Perf. 14x13½**
1314-1316 A619   Set of 3    5.00 5.00
Dated 2001.

---

**Flowers of Tuber Plants A620**

Designs: 1.10s, Solanum stenotomum. 1.50s, Ipomoea batatas. 2.10s, Ipomoea purpurea.

**2002, May 7**    **Perf. 13½x14**
1317-1319 A620   Set of 3    2.75 2.75

---

**America Issue — UNESCO World Heritage Sites — A621**

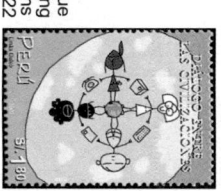

Balconies of Lima buildings: 2.70s, Palacio de Osambela. 5.80s, Palacio de Torre Tagle.

**2002, May 14**    **Litho.**    **Perf. 14x13½**
1320-1321 A621   Set of 2    5.00 5.00
Dated 2001.

---

**Year of Dialogue Among Civilizations A622**

Designs: 1.50s, Flower. 1.80s, shown.

**2002, May 16**
1322-1323 A622   Set of 2    1.90 1.90
Dated 2001.

---

**Paracas National Reserve A623**

Designs: 1.10s, Sula dactilatra, vert. 1.50s, Sula variegata. 3.20s, Haematopus palliatus. 3.80s, Grapsus grapsus.

**2002, May 21**    **Perf. 14x13½, 13½x14**
1324-1327 A623   Set of 4    5.50 5.50
Dated 2001.

---

**Endangered Animals — A624**

Souvenir Sheet

**2002, May 22**    **Perf. 13½x14**
1328 A624 8s multi    4.75 4.75
Dated 2001.

---

**Scouting in Peru, 90th Anniv. — A625**

No. 1329: a, Lord Robert Baden-Powell. b, 10.20s, First Peruvian Scouts.

**2002, June 4**    **Perf. 14x13½**
1329 A625   3.20s Horiz. pair, #a-b    3.75 3.75
**Souvenir Sheet**
1330 A625 10.20s multi    6.00 6.00
Dated 2001.

---

**Folk Dances — A626**

Designs: 2.10s, Zamacueca. 2.70s, Alcatraz.

**2002, June 4**
1331-1332 A626   Set of 2    2.75 2.75
Dated 2001.

## Treaty of Friendship, Commerce and Navigation Between Peru and Italy, 150th Anniv. — A643

No. 1358: a, Maps of Peru and Western Hemisphere. b, Map of Italy and Eastern Hemisphere.

Perf. 14x13½
2003, Nov. 13
1358 A643 2s Horiz. pair, #a-b  2.40 2.40

## Water Snake Bilingual Education Project — A644

No. 1359: a, Head of snake, project emblem. b, Tail of snake, children's drawing.

2003, Nov. 28
1359 A644 2s Horiz. pair, #a-b  2.40 2.40

## UNESCO Associated Schools Project Network, 50th Anniv. A645

Perf. 13½x14  .70 .70
2003, Nov.
1360 A645 1.20s multi

## America Issue - Fauna — A646

No. 1361: a, Four Rupicola peruviana and butterfly. b, One Rupicola peruviana.

Perf. 14x13½
2003, Dec. 1
1361 A646 2s Horiz. pair, #a-b  2.40 2.40

## Peru — Panama Diplomatic Relations, Cent. — A647

2003, Dec. 12
1362 A647 4r multi  2.40 2.40

## Powered Flight, Cent. — A648

---

## Hydrography and Navigation Dept., Cent. — A637

Perf. 14x13½  Litho.  .65 .65
2003, June 13
1352 A637 1.10s multi

## Manuela Ramos Movement, 25th Anniv. — A638

2.25 2.25
2003, July 1
1353 A638 3.80s multi

## Radioprogramas del Peru Network, 40th Anniv. — A639

Perf. 13½x14  2.40 2.40
2003, Oct. 1  Litho.
1354 A639 4s multi

## Pres. Fernando Belaunde Terry (1912-2002) A640

Perf. 14x13½  .90 .90
2003, Oct. 7
1355 A640 1.60s multi

## Canonization of St. Josemaria Escrivá de Balaguer — A641

Perf. 13½x14  .70 .70
2003, Oct. 11
1356 A641 1.20s multi

## Sister Teresa de la Cruz Candamo (1875-1953), Founder of Canonesas de la Cruz — A642

2.40 2.40
2003, Nov. 3
1357 A642 4s multi

---

## Admiral Miguel Grau A631

Perf. 13½x14  2.25 2.25
2002, July 23
1346 A631 3.80s multi
Dated 2001.

## Peruvian — Spanish Business Meeting A632

2.25 2.25
2002, Aug. 7
1347 A632 3.80s multi
Dated 2001.

## National Fisheries Society, 50th Anniv. A633

Perf. 13½x13¾
1.90 1.90
3.80 3.80
2002, Nov. 12
1348 A633 3.20s multi
a. Tête beche pair

## Alexander von Humboldt's Visit to Peru, Bicent. — A634

Illustration reduced.

Perf. 13½x13½
1.00 1.90
3.80
2002, Nov. 20
1349 A634 3.20s multi + label
a. Tête beche strip 2 #1349 +2 central labels

## Peru - Bolivia Integration for Development — A635

Perf. 13½x14
1.90 1.90
2002, Nov. 29
1350 A635 3.20s multi

## Natl. Commission on Andean and Amazonian Peoples A636

.85 .85
2002, Dec. 12
1351 A636 1.50s multi

---

## International Express Service A627

Perf. 13½x14
11.50 11.50
2002, June 10
1333 A627 20s multi
Dated 2001.

## Rulers — A628

Inca

Designs: 1.50s, Viracocha. 2.70s, Pachacutec. 3.20s, Inca Yupanqui. 3.80s, Tupac Inca Yupanqui.

Perf. 14x13½  Litho.  Set of 4
6.50 6.50
2002, June 24
1334-1337 A628
Dated 2001.

## Primates — A629

No. 1338: a, Aotus miconax. b, Pithecia irrorata. c, Pithecia aequatorialis. d, Cebus albifrons. e, Saimiri boliviensis. f, Aotus vociferans.

Illustration reduced.

13.00 13.00
2002, June 25
1338 A629 3.80s Block of 6, #a-f
Dated 2001.

### Minerals Type of 1999

Designs: 1.80s, Chalcopyrite. No. 1340, 3.20s, Sphalerite. No. 1341, 3.20s, Pyrargyrite.

Perf. 13½x14  Set of 3
4.75 4.75
2002, July 3
1339-1341 A555
Dated 2001.

## Pre-Columbian Artifacts — A630

Designs: 1.50s, Crab-like man, Sipán. 3.20s, Warrior, Sicán. 3.80s, Gold breastplate, Kuntur Wasi, horiz. 10.20s, Pinchudo, Gran Pajatén, horiz.

Perf. 14x13½, 13½x14  Set of 3
5.00 5.00
2002, July 3
1342-1344 A630

Souvenir Sheet
6.00 6.00
1345 A630 10.20s multi
Dated 2001.

Illustration reduced.

**2003, Dec. 17**
1363 A648 4.80s multi + label ... **Perf. 13½x14** ... 2.75 2.75

Cajón A649

**2003, Dec. 18**
1364 A649 4.80s multi ... 2.75 2.75

Chess A650

**2004, Jan. 5**
1365 A650 1.20s multi ... Dated 2003. ... .70 .70

National Rehabilitation Institute — A651

**2004, Jan. 5**
1366 A651 1.20s multi ... Dated 2003. ... .70 .70

Swimming A652

**2004, Jan. 5**
1367 A652 1.20s multi ... Dated 2003. ... **Perf. 14x13½** ... .70 .70

National Civil Defense System, 30th Anniv. (in 2002) — A653

**2004, Jan. 14**
1368 A653 4.80s multi ... Dated 2002. ... 2.75 2.75

**2004, Jan. 14**
1369 A654 4.80s multi ... Dated 2002.

Christmas 2003 A664

**Perf. 13½x14** ... 2.75 2.75

PERU

Cebiche A655

**2004, Jan. 14**
1370 A655 4.80s multi ... Dated 2003. ... 2.75 2.75

Viceroys — A656

No. 1371: a, 1.20s, Antonio de Mendoza (1495-1552), b, 1.20s, Andrés Hurtado de Mendoza (1500-61), c, 1.20s, Diego Lopez de Zúñiga y Velasco (d. 1564), d, 4.80s, Blasco Nuñez de Vela (d. 1546).

**2004, Jan. 14**
1371 A656 Block of 4, #a-d ... Dated 2003. ... **Perf. 14x13½** ... 5.00 5.00

Minerals A657

Designs: 1.20s, Rhodochrosite. 1.20s, Orpiment. 4.80s,

**2004, Jan. 21**
1372-1373 A657 Set of 2 ... Dated 2002. ... **Perf. 13½x14** ... 3.50 3.50

Peruvian Saints A658

Designs: No. 1374, 4.80s, St. Rose of Lima (1586-1617). No. 1375, 4.80s, St. Martin de Porres (1579-1639), vert.

**2004, Jan. 21**
1374-1375 A658 Set of 2 ... Dated 2002. ... **Perf. 13½x14, 14x13½,** vert. ... 5.50 5.50

Orchids A659

Jorge Basadre (1903-80), Historian — A660

**2004, Jan. 30**
1379 A660 4.80s blue ... Dated 2003. ... **Engr.** ... 2.75 2.75

Trains A661

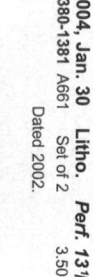

Designs: 1.20s, Locomotive and train station. 4.80s, Train on Galeras Bridge.

**2004, Jan. 30**
1380-1381 A661 Set of 2 ... Dated 2002. ... **Litho.** ... 3.50 3.50

Endangered Species — A662

Designs: 1.80s, Londra felina. No. 1383, 1.80s, Ara couloni, vert.

**2004, Jan. 30**
1382-1383 A662 Set of 2 ... Dated 2002. ... **Perf. 13½x14, 14x13½,** vert. ... 2.10 2.10

Fire Fighting A663

Designs: No. 1384, 2.20s, Firefighters with hose. No. 1385, 2.20s, Fire truck.

**2004, Jan. 30**
1384-1385 A663 Set of 2 ... Dated 2002. ... **Perf. 13½x14** ... 2.50 2.50

Incan Emperors A664

Huáscar

Designs: No. 1386, 1.20s, Huáscar (d. 1533). No. 1387, 1.20s, Atahualpa (d. 1533). 4.80s, Huayna Cápac (d. 1525).

**2004, Jan. 30**
1386-1388 A664 Set of 3 ... Dated 2002. ... **Perf. 14x13½** ... 4.25 4.25

Designs: 1.20s, Chaubardia heteroclita, vert. 2.20s, Cochleanthera amazonica, vert. 4.80s, Sobralia sp.

**2004, Jan. 21**
1376-1378 A659 Set of 3 ... Dated 2002. ... **Perf. 14x13½, 13½x14** ... 4.75 4.75

Rubén Vargas Ugarte, Historian A665

**2004, Feb. 4**
1389 A665 4.80s multi ... Dated 2002. ... **Perf. 13½x14** ... 2.75 2.75

2002 World Cup Soccer Championships, Japan and Korea — A666

National Stadium, 50th Anniv. (in 2002) A667

**2004, Feb. 4**
1390 A666 4.80s multi ... Dated 2002. ... 2.75 2.75

**2004, Feb. 4**
1391 A667 4.80s multi ... Dated 2002. ... 2.75 2.75

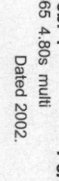  

National Day of Biological Diversity, May 22, 2002 A668

**2004, Feb. 4**
1392 A668 4.80s multi ... Dated 2002. ... 2.75 2.75

World Population Day A669

**2004, Feb. 4**
1393 A669 4.80s multi ... Dated 2002. ... 2.75 2.75

José Jiménez Borja (1901-82), Writer — A670

**2004, Feb. 4**
1394 A670 4.80s multi ... Dated 2002. ... **Perf. 14x13½** ... 2.75 2.75

 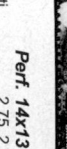

## Cacti — A671

Designs: No. 1395, 1.20s, Eriosyce islayensis. No. 1395, 1.20s, Matucana haynei. 4.80s, Pigmaeocereus bylesianus.

**2004, Feb. 4**
1395-1397 A671 Set of 3   4.25 4.25
Dated 2002.

## Antarctic Fauna A672

Designs: No. 1398, 1.80s, Leucocarbo atriceps, vert. No. 1399, 1.80s, Pygoscelis papua, vert. No. 1400, 1.80s, Asteroidea sp., vert.

**Perf. 13½x14, 14x13½**
**2004, Feb. 4**
1398-1400 A672 Set of 3   3.25 3.25
Dated 2002.

## Pisco Sour A673

**Perf. 13½x14**
**2004, Feb. 10**
1401 A673 4.80s multi   2.76 2.75

## Daniel Alcides Carrión (1857-1885), Medical Martyr — A674

**Perf. 14x13½  Litho.**
**2004, Feb. 19**
1402 A674 4.80s multi   2.75 2.75
Dated 2002.

## Souvenir Sheet

**Foundation of Jauja, by Wenceslao Hinostroza — A675**
**Perf. 13½x14**
**2004, Feb. 20**
1403 A675 7s multi   4.00 4.00
Dated 2002.

## Animals — A676

**Perf. 14x14½**
**2004, Feb. 23**
1404 A676 20c Alpaca   .20 .20
1405 A676 30c Vicuna   .20 .20
1406 A676 40c Guanaco   .25 .25
1407 A676 50c Llama   .30 .30
Nos. 1404-1407 (4)   .95 .95
Dated 2002.

## Vipers — A677

*Víboras del Perú*

No. 1408: a, Bothrops roedingeri. b, Micrurus lemniscatus. c, Bothrops atrox. d, Bothrops microphthalmus. e, Micrurus surinamensis. f, Bothrops barnetti.

**Perf. 14x13½**
**2004, Feb. 23**
1408 A677 1.80s Block of 6, #a-f, + label   6.25 6.25
Dated 2003.

## Souvenir Sheet

**Intl. Year of Mountains (in 2002) — A678**
**Perf. 13½x14**
**2004, Feb. 23**
1409 A678 7s multi   4.00 4.00
Dated 2002.

## Royal Tombs of Sipán Museum A679

**2004, Feb. 24**
1410 A679 4.80s multi   2.75 2.75
Dated 2003.

## Lighthouses — A680

*Faros del Perú*

No. 1411: a, Punta Capones Lighthouse. b, Chincha Islands Lighthouse.

**Perf. 14x13½**
**2004, Feb. 26**
1411 A680 2s Horiz. pair, #a-b   2.40 2.40
Dated 2003.

## Volunteer Firefighters of Peru, 130th Anniv. — A681

**2004, Mar. 2**
1412 A681 4.80s multi   2.75 2.75

## Miniature Sheet

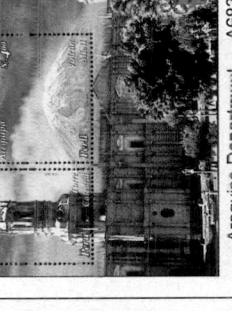

*Peces del Mar del Perú*

## Fish — A682

No. 1413: a, Trachurus murphyi. b, Mugil cephalus. c, Engraulis ringens. d, Odontesthes regia regia. e, Merluccius gayi peruanus.

**Perf. 13½x14**
**2004, Mar. 3**
1413 A682 1.60s Sheet of 5, #a-e   4.75 4.75
Dated 2002.

## Souvenir Sheet

**Arequipa Department — A683**

No. 1414: a, Cathedral tower. b, Misti Volcano, horiz.

**Perf. 14x13½, 13½x14 (#1414b)**
**2004, Mar. 18**
1414 A683 4s Sheet of 2, #a-b   4.75 4.75
Dated 2002.

## Machu Picchu — A684

*Machu Picchu — Patrimonio Cultural de la Humanidad*

No. 1415: a, 1.20s, Sundial. b, 1.20s, Temple of the Three Windows. c, 1.20s, Waterfall, Huayna Picchu. d, 4.80s, Aerial view of Machu Picchu.

**Perf. 14x13½**
**2004, Mar. 20**
1415 A684 Block of 4, #a-d   5.00 5.00
Dated 2003.

## Medicinal Plants A685

*Vista de gato — Uncaria tomentosa — S/.4.80*

Designs: No. 1416, 4.80s, Uncaria tomentosa. No. 1417, 4.80s, Myrciaria dubia. No. 1418, 4.80s, Lepidium meyenii.

**Perf. 13½x14**
**2004, Mar. 26**
1416-1418 A685 Set of 3   8.50 8.50

## Annual Assembly of Governors of the Inter-American Development Bank — A686

Reunión Anual de la Asamblea de Gobernadores en cit Lima 2004  PERU

**2004, Mar. 26**
1419 A686 4.80s multi   2.75 2.75

## Dogs — A687

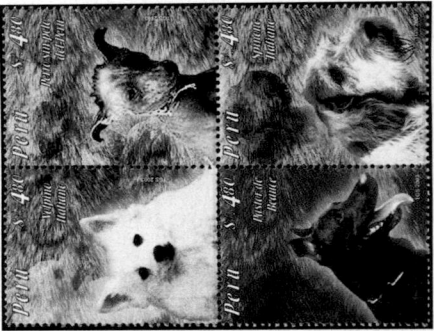

No. 1420: a, Italian Volpino. b, Peruvian hairless dog. c, Beauceron. d, Italian Spinone.

**2004, Mar. 29**

Dances — A688

**2004, Apr. 2**    **Perf. 14x13½**
1420 A687 4.80s Block of 4, #a-d    11.00 11.00
Dated 2003.

**2004**
1421-1422 A688   Set of 2   1.40 1.40
Issued: No. 1421, 4/16; No. 1422, 5/28.
Dated 2003.

Designs: No. 1421, 1.20s, Huayno. No. 1422, 1.20s, Huaylash.

Preparation for "El Niño" — A689

**2004, Apr. 21**    **Perf. 13½x14**
1423 A689 4.80s multi   2.75 2.75
Dated 2002.

Tourism
A690

**2004**    **Perf. 13½x14, 14x13½**
1424-1427 A690   Set of 4   11.00 11.00
Issued: No. 1424, 4/22; No. 1425, 4/29; No. 1426, 5/6; No. 1427, 6/10. Dated 2002 (#1425-1427) or 2003 (#1424).

Designs: No. 1424, 4.80s, Lake Paca, Jauja. No. 1425, 4.80s, Ballestas Islands, Ica, vert. No. 1426, 4.80s, Inca Baths, Cajamarca, vert. No. 1427, 4.80s, Huanchaco, Trujillo, vert.

Santiago Apostol Temple, Puno
A691

**2004, July 2**    **Perf. 13½x14**
1428 A691 1.80s multi   1.10 1.10
Dated 2003.

America Issue —
Youth, Education and Literacy — A692

**2004, July 5**    **Perf. 14x13½, 13½x14**
1429-1430 A692   Set of 2   3.50 3.50
Dated 2002 (#1429) or 2003 (#1430).

Designs: 1.20s, Children, stylized flower. 4.80s, Computer operator, horiz.

---

**PERU**

2004 Copa America Soccer Tournament, Peru — A693

**2004, July 9**    **Perf. 14x14½**
1431 A693 5s multi   3.00 3.00

Souvenir Sheet

Horses — A694

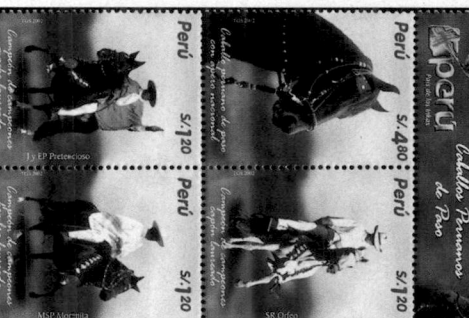

**2004, Aug. 6**    **Perf. 14x13½**
1432 A694   Block of 4, #a-d + label   5.00 5.00
Dated 2002.

No. 1432: a, 1.20s, White horse. b, 1.20s, Black horse, rider with raised hand. c, 1.20s, Black horse, rider with white poncho. d, 4.80s, Horse's head.

Miniature Sheet

Fauna en vías de extinción

Worldwide Fund for Nature (WWF) — A695

**2004, Oct. 15**    **Litho.**
1433 A695   Sheet of 4, #a-d   2.40 2.40

No. 1433 — Pteronura brasiliensis: a, 30c. Looking. b, 50c. With mouth open. c, 1.50s, Eating. d, 1.50s, Sleeping.

---

America Issue — Environmental Protection — A696

**2004, Oct. 25**    **Perf. 13½x14**
1434 A696 4.50s multi   2.75 2.75

Railroads
A697

**2004, Oct. 29**    **Perf. 13½x14**
1435 A697 5s multi   3.00 3.00
1436 A697 10s multi   6.00 6.00

Souvenir Sheet
**Perf. 13½x14**
1437 A698 10s multi   6.00 6.00

Peruvian Song Day, 60th Anniv. A698

**2004, Oct. 31**    **Perf. 13½x14**
1438 A699 5s multi   3.00 3.00

FIFA (Fédération Internationale de Football Association), Cent. — A699

**2004, Nov. 2**    **Perf. 13½x14**
1439 A700 5s multi   3.00 3.00

Election of Pope John Paul II, 25th Anniv. (in 2003) A700

**2004, Nov. 2**    **Perf. 14x13½**
1440 A701 5s multi   3.00 3.00

Canonization of Mother Teresa — A701

---

Musicians — A702

Miniature Sheet

**2004, Nov. 12**    **Perf. 14x13½, 14x14x13½x14**
1441 A702 2s Sheet of 5, #a-e   6.00 6.00

No. 1441: a, Juan Diego Flórez. b, Susana Baca. c, Gianmarco. d, Eva Ayllón, horiz. e, Líbido, horiz. (#1441a, 1441e)

Flora Tristan Women's Center, 25th Anniv. — A703

**2004, Nov. 9**    **Litho.**
1442 A703 5s multi   3.00 3.00    **Perf. 14**

Exporter's Day — A704

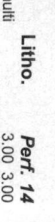

**2004, Nov. 9**    **Perf. 14**
1443 A704 5s multi   3.00 3.00

Latin American Parliament, 40th Anniv. — A705

**2004, Nov. 16**    **Perf. 13½x14**
1444 A705 2.50s Horiz. pair, #a-b   3.00 3.00

No. 1444: a, Parliament emblem. b Andrés Townsend Escurra, first President of Latin American Parliament, and flags. Illustration reduced.

Lima Bar Association, 200th Anniv. — A706

**2004, Nov. 17**
1445 A706 5s multi   3.00 3.00

Houses of
Worship
A722

Designs: 4.50s, San Cristóbal Church,
Huamanga. 5s, Huancayo Cathedral.

**2005, Feb. 7**    **Litho.**    *Perf. 13½x14*
1467-1468  A722    Set of 2    6.00  6.00

Abolition of
Slavery,
150th
Anniv.
A723

**2005, Feb. 25**
1469  A723  5s claret

**Engr.**
3.25  3.25

Armed Forces — A724

No. 1470: a, 1.80s, Army tank. b, 1.80s,
Navy submarine. c, 1.80s, Air Force Mirage
jets. d, 3.20s, Air Force Sukhoi jet. e, 3.20s,
Army soldiers. f, 3.20s, Navy frigate.
Illustration reduced.

**2005, Feb. 28**    **Litho.**
1470  A724    Block of 6, #a-f, +    9.25  9.25
label

Frult
A725

Designs: No. 1471, 4.50s, Eugenia stipitata.
No. 1472, 4.50s, Maurilla flexuosa. 5s, Solanum sessiflorum dunal, vert.

**2005, Mar. 4**    *Perf. 13½x14, 14x13½*
1471-1473  A725    Set of 3    0.75  8.75

Parque de las Leyendes, 40th
Anniv. — A718

No. 1463: a, Cantua buxifolia. b, Puma
concolor.

**2005, Jan. 14**    *Perf. 14x13½*
1463  A718  5s Horiz. pair, #a-b    6.25  6.25
Dated 2004.

Championship
Trophies Won By
Cienciano Soccer
Team — A719

**2005, Jan. 22**    3.25  3.25
1464  A719  5s multi

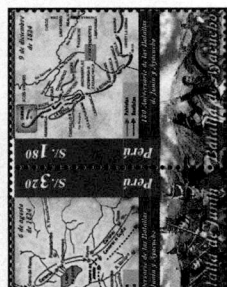

Stomatology
Academy of
Peru, 75th
Anniv. — A720

**2005, Jan. 24**    3.26  3.26
1465  A720  60 multi
Dated 2004.

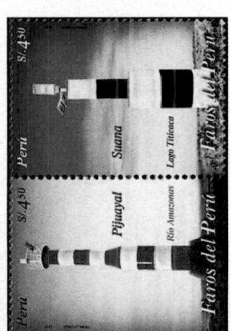

National Health Crusade — A721

Illustration reduced.

**2005, Feb. 2**    **Perf. 14**
1466  A721  2s multi + label    1.25  1.25
Dated 2004.

Various ceramic pieces with background
colors of: No. 1455, 4.50s, Dark blue. No.
1456, 4.50s, Red violet. 5s, Blue, horiz.

**2004, Dec. 6**    *Perf. 14x14½, 14½x14*
1455-1457  A712    Set of 3    8.50  8.50

Third Meeting of
South American
Presidents
A713

**2004, Dec. 8**    *Perf. 14x13½*
1458  A713  5s multi    3.00  3.00

Lima Museum of
Art, 50th
Anniv. — A714

**2004, Dec. 9**    **Litho.**
1459  A714  5s multi    3.00  3.00

Battles, 180th Anniv. — A715

No. 1460: a, 1.80s, Map and scene of Battle
of Ayacucho. b, 3.20s, Map and scene of Bat-
lle of Junin.

**2004, Dec. 9**
1460  A715    Horiz. pair, #a-b    3.00  3.00

Lighthouses — A716

No. 1461: a, Pijuayal Lighthouse, Amazon
River. b, Suana Lighthouse, Lake Titicaca.

**2004, Dec. 10**
1461  A716  4.50s Horiz. pair,    5.50  5.50
#a-b

Souvenir Sheet

Sacred City of Caral — A717

**2004, Dec. 15**    *Perf. 13½x14*
1462  A717  10s multi    6.25  6.25

Serpost,
10th Anniv.
A707

**2004, Nov. 22**    3.00  3.00
1446  A707  5s multi

Jungle
River
Fauna
A708

Designs: 2s, Serrasalmus. 4.50s, Ponto-
poria blainvillei. 5s, Arapaima gigas, vert.

**2004, Nov. 30**    *Perf. 13½x14, 14x13½*
1447-1449  A708    Set of 3    7.00  7.00

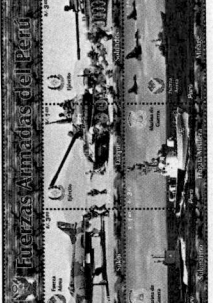

Christmas
A709

**2004, Dec. 2**    *Perf. 14x13½*
1450  A709  5s multi    3.00  3.00

Antarctica
A710

Designs: 1.50s, Machu Picchu Scientific
Base, King George Island. 2s, Megaptera
novaeangliae, horiz. 4.50s, Orcinus orca,
horiz.

**2004, Dec. 3**    *Perf. 14x13½, 13½x14*
1451-1453  A710    Set of 3    5.00  5.00

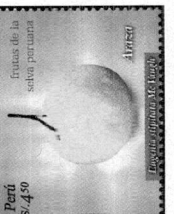

Prehistoric Animals — A711

No. 1454: a, 1.80s, Drawings of Smilodon
neogaeus and Toxodon platensis Owen.
3.20s, Fossils, depiction of body of Toxodon
platensis.

**2004, Dec. 6**    *Perf. 14x13½*
1454  A711    Horiz. pair, #a-b    3.00  3.00

Mochica
Ceramics — A712

## Opera Singer Luis Alva Talledo, Founder of Prolírica — A726

**2005, Mar. 10** | **Perf. 13½x14**
1474 A726 1.50s multi — .95 .95

## Reserva de Allpahuayo / Mishana -Iquitos-

**2005, Mar. 21** | **Perf. 14x13½**
1475 A727 4.50s Block of 4, #a-d + label — 11.00 11.00

No. 1475: a, Hormiguero norteño de cola castaña. b, Tiranuelo de Mishana. c, Rana arborícola. d, Sacha runa.

### Allpahuayo Reserve Wildlife — A727

### Souvenir Sheet

### Science of Antonio Raimondo — A729

**2005, Apr. 18**
1477 A729 Block of 4, #a-d + label — 9.00 9.00

No. 1477: a, 1.80s, Sculptures, Chavin de Huantar. b, 3.20s, Bird and bat. c, 4.50s, Stanopheea. d, 5s, Fossil of N. C. Roemoceras Subplanum Hyatt.

### Europa Stamps, 50th Anniv. (in 2006) — A734

**2005, Nov. 24** | **Litho.** | **Perf. 14**
1482 A734 2s Sheet of 4, #a-d — 4.75 4.75

No. 1482: a, Mochica headdress and Spain #1526. b, Chimú ceremonial jewelry and Spain #941. c, Mochica earrings and Spain #1567. d, Mochica headdress and Spain #1607.

### Souvenir Sheet

## Catalogue values for unused stamps in this section are for Never Hinged items.

## SEMI-POSTAL STAMPS

## Paintings — A728

*Pintura Peruana*

**2005, Apr. 4**
1476 A728 2s Block of 6, #a-f, + label — 7.50 7.50

No. 1476 — Unidentified paintings by: a, Pancho Fiero. b, Ignacio Moreno. c, Daniel Hernández. d, Camilo Blas. e, Ricardo Grau. f, Fernando de Szyszlo. Illustration reduced.

## Penelope Albipennis — A730

*Para Alblanca — Tras 100 años de extinción*

**2005, May 2**
1478 A730 10s multi — 6.25 6.25

## Architecture — A731

*Arquitectura Peruana*

**2005, May 18** | **Perf. 13½x14**
1479 A731 Block of 4, #a-d, + label — 12.00 12.00

Designs: a, 4.50s, Government Palace. b, 4.50s, Italian Art Museum. c, 5s, Mega Plaza. d, 5s, Larco Mar. Illustration reduced.

## Postal Money Orders — A732

*Giros Postales*

**2005, May 30**
1480 A732 5s multi — 3.25 3.25

## Gold Funerary Mask — SP1

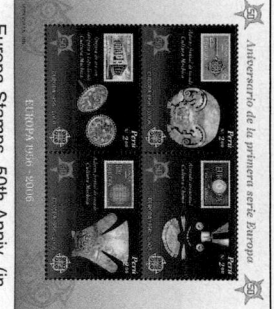

ORO DEL PERU 1.90 +0.90

**1966, Aug. 16** | **Photo.** | **Perf. 12x12½, 12½x12** | **Unwmk.**
B1 SP1 1.90s + 90c multi — .50 .40
B2 SP1 2.60s + 1.30s multi — .60 .50
B3 SP1 3.60s + 1.80s multi — .90 .75
B4 SP1 4.60s + 2.30s multi — 1.25 1.00
B5 SP1 20s + 10s multi — 4.75 4.00
Nos. B1-B5 (5) — 8.00 6.65

Designs: 2.60s+1.30s, Ceremonial knife. 4.60s+2.30s, Goblet with precious stones. 20s+10s, Earplug.

The designs show gold objects of the 12th-13th centuries Chimu culture. The surtax was for tourist publicity. For surcharges see Nos. 679-680, 683-684, 686.

## AIR POST STAMPS

### No. 248 Overprinted in Black

*Servicio Aéreo*

**1927, Dec. 10** | **Unwmk.** | **Perf. 12**
C1 A87 50c violet — 37.50 20.00

Two types of overprint. Counterfeits exist.

### President Augusto Bernardino Leguía — AP1

**1928, Jan. 12** | **Engr.**
C2 AP1 50c dark green — .65 .35

For surcharge see No. 263.

### Coat of Arms of Piura Type

**1932, July 28** | **Litho.**
C3 A107 50c scarlet — 20.00 19.00

Counterfeits exist.

### Airplane in Flight — AP3

**1934, Feb. 7** | **Engr.** | **Perf. 12½**
C4 AP3 2s blue — 4.00 .35
C5 AP3 5s brown — 8.00 .75

### Palace of Torre-Tagle — AP7

Funeral of Atahualpa AP4

**1935, Jan. 18** | **Photo.** | **Perf. 13½**
C6 AP4 5c emerald — .25 .20
C7 AP4 35c brown — .35 .30
C8 AP4 50c orange yel — .70 .60
C9 AP4 1s plum — 1.25 .90
C10 AP7 2s red orange — 2.00 1.75
C11 AP4 5s dp claret — 8.50 5.25
C12 AP4 10s dk blue — 32.50 5.25
Nos. C6-C12 (7) — 45.55 31.50

Designs: 35c, Mt. San Cristobal. 50c, Avenue of Barefoot Friars. 10s, Pizarro and the Thirteen.

4th centenary of founding of Lima. Nos. C6-C12 overprinted "Radio Nacional" are revenue stamps.

### "La Callao," First Locomotive in South America — AP9

**1936, Aug. 27** | **Perf. 12½**
C13 AP9 35c gray black — 3.00 1.40

Founding of the Province of Callao, cent.

### Nos. C4-C5 Surcharged "Habilitado" and New Value, like Nos. 353-355.

**1936, Nov. 4**
C14 AP3 5c on 2s blue — .35 .20
C15 AP3 25c on 5s brown — .65 .35
a. Double surcharge — 13.50 13.50
b. No period btwn. "o" & "25" — 16.50
c. Inverted surcharge — 1.40 1.40

There are many broken letters in this setting.

### Mines of Peru — AP10

CORREOS DEL PERU

Manuel Ferreyros, José Gregorio Paz Soldán and Antonio Arenas — AP42

**1938, Dec. 9**    **Photo.**    *Perf. 12½*

| | | | |
|---|---|---|---|
| C62 | AP40 | 25c brt ultra | .65 | .45 |
| C63 | AP41 | 1.50s brown vio | 1.75 | 1.50 |
| C64 | AP42 | 2s black | 1.10 | .55 |
| | | *Nos. C62-C64 (3)* | 3.50 | 2.50 |

8th Pan-American Conference at Lima.

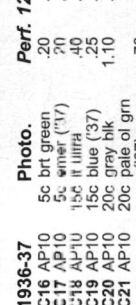

No. C52 Surcharged in Black

**1942**    *Perf. 13*
C65 AP30 15c on 25c dp grn   1.00   .20

Types of 1938
Imprint: "Columbian Bank Note Co."
**1945-46**   **Unwmk.**   **Litho.**   *Perf. 12½*

| | | | |
|---|---|---|---|
| C73 | AP27 | 5c violet brown | .20 | .20 |
| C74 | AP31 | 30c orange | .20 | .25 |
| C75 | AP36 | 1.50s purple (46) | .70 | .65 |
| | | *Nos. C73-C75 (3)* | | |

Nos. C73 and C54 Overprinted in Black

**1947, Sept. 25**    *Perf. 12½, 13*
C76 AP27 5c violet brown   .20   .20
C77 AP32 50c green   .20   .20

1st Peru Intl. Airways flight from Lima to New York City, Sept. 27-28, 1947.

Catalogue values for unused stamps in this section, from this point to the end of the section, are for Never Hinged items.

Peru-Great Britain Air Route — AP43

Basketball Players — AP44

Designs: 5s, Discus thrower. 10s, Rifleman.

**1948, July 29**    **Photo.**    *Perf. 12½*
C78 AP43 1s blue   2.25   1.50

**Carmine Overprint, "AEREO"**

| | | | |
|---|---|---|---|
| C79 | AP44 | 2s red brown | 3.00 | 2.00 |
| C80 | AP44 | 5s yellow green | 3.25 | 3.25 |
| C81 | AP44 | 10s yellow | 6.25 | 4.00 |
| a. | | Souv. sheet, #C78-C81, perf 13 | 27.50 | 27.50 |
| | | *Nos. C78-C81 (4)* | 16.50 | 10.75 |

Peru's participation in the 1948 Olympic Games held at Wembley, England, during July and August. Postally valid for four days, July 29-Aug. 1, 1948. Proceeds went to the Olympic Committee.

---

Mountain Road — AP34

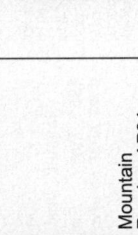

Plaza San Martin, Lima — AP35

Stele from Chavin Temple AP37

National Radio of Peru AP36

Ministry of Public Works, Lima — AP38

Crypt of the Heroes, Lima — AP39

Imprint: "Waterlow & Sons Limited, Londres."

**1938, July 1**    **Photo.**    *Perf. 12½, 13*

| | | | |
|---|---|---|---|
| C49 | AP27 | 5c violet brn | .20 | .20 |
| C50 | AP28 | 15c dk brown | .20 | .30 |
| C51 | AP29 | 20c dp magenta | .30 | .20 |
| C52 | AP30 | 25c dp green | .20 | .20 |
| C53 | AP31 | 30c orange | .20 | .20 |
| C54 | AP32 | 50c green | .25 | .20 |
| C55 | AP33 | 70c slate bl | .40 | .70 |
| C56 | AP34 | 80c olive | | .70 |
| C57 | AP35 | 1s slate grn | 5.50 | .70 |
| C58 | AP36 | 1.50s purple | 1.25 | 2.50 |

**Engr.**

| | | | |
|---|---|---|---|
| C59 | AP37 | 2s ind & org brn | 2.00 | .50 |
| C60 | AP38 | 5s brown | 10.00 | 1.00 |
| C61 | AP39 | 10s ol grn & ind | 40.00 | 24.00 |
| | | | 61.20 | 29.80 |

See Nos. C73-C75, C89-C93, C103. For surcharges see Nos. C65, C76-C77, C82-C88, C108.

Torre-Tagle Palace — AP40

National Congress Building — AP41

---

Jorge Chávez AP14

Aerial View of Peruvian Coast AP16

View of the "Sierra" — AP17

St. Rosa of Lima — AP22

Designs: 5c, La Mar Park, Lima. 15c, Native Steamer "Inca" on Lake Titicaca. 20c, Native Queña (flute) Player and Llama. 30c, Ram at Mudel Ferru, Puno. 1s, Train in Mountains. 1.50s, Jorge Chávez Aviation School. 2s, Transport Plane. 5s, Aerial View of Virgin Forests.

**1936-37**    **Photo.**    *Perf. 12½*

| | | | |
|---|---|---|---|
| C16 | AP10 | 5c brt green | .20 | .20 |
| C17 | AP10 | 5c winer ('37) | .20 | .20 |
| C18 | AP10 | 15c lt ultra | .40 | .25 |
| C19 | AP10 | 15c blue ('37) | .25 | .20 |
| C20 | AP10 | 20c gray blk | 1.10 | .20 |
| C21 | AP10 | 20c pale ol grn | | .25 |
| C22 | AP14 | 25c mag ('37) | .70 | .25 |
| C23 | AP10 | 25c henna brn | .35 | .35 |
| C24 | AP10 | 30c dk ol brn ('37) | 3.50 | 1.00 |
| C25 | AP14 | 30c brown | 1.00 | .95 |
| C26 | AP10 | 35c brown | 2.00 | .26 |
| C27 | AP10 | 50c yellow | .35 | .20 |
| C28 | AP16 | 50c brn vio ('37) | .50 | .20 |
| C29 | AP16 | 70c Prus grn | 4.25 | 4.50 |
| C30 | AP17 | 70c pdk grn ('37) | .70 | .65 |
| C31 | AP17 | 80c brn blk | 5.00 | 4.50 |
| C32 | AP10 | 80uc ol grn ('37) | 1.00 | 1.00 |
| C33 | AP10 | 1s ultra | .45 | .45 |
| C34 | AP14 | 1s red brn ('37) | 3.50 | .35 |
| C35 | AP14 | 1.50s red brn | 1.75 | .20 |
| | | 1.50s org yel ('37) | 5.50 | 5.00 |
| | | | 3.50 | .35 |

**Engr.**

| | | | |
|---|---|---|---|
| C36 | AP10 | 2s deep blue | 10.00 | 6.50 |
| C37 | AP10 | 2s yel grn | .70 | |
| | | ('37) | 6.75 | 3.25 |
| C38 | AP16 | 5s green | 12.50 | 3.25 |
| C39 | AP22 | 10s car & brn | 100.00 | 92.50 |
| | | grn | 165.00 | 124.00 |
| | | *Nos. C16-C39 (24)* | | |

Nos. C23, C25, C28, C30, C36 Surcharged in Black or Red

Habilit. Un Sol

**1936, June 26**

| | | | |
|---|---|---|---|
| C40 | AP10 | 15c on 30c hn brn | .30 | |
| C41 | AP14 | 15c on 35c brown | .50 | .50 |
| C42 | AP16 | 15c on 70c Prus | .20 | |
| C43 | AP17 | 25c on 80c brn blk grn (R) | 3.25 | 2.75 |
| C44 | AP10 | 1s on 2s dp bl | 3.25 | 2.75 |
| | | | 5.25 | 3.75 |
| | | *Nos. C40-C44 (5)* | 12.75 | 9.75 |

Surcharge on No. C43 is vertical, reading down.

---

Jorge Chávez — AP24

Map of Aviation Lines from Peru — AP26

Airport of Limatambo at Lima — AP25

Designs: 10c, Juan Bielovucic (1889-?) flying over Lima race course, Jan. 14, 1911. 15c, Jorge Chávez-Dartnell (1887-1910), French-born Peruvian aviator who flew from Brixen to Domodossola in the Alps and died of plane-crash injuries.

**1937, Sept. 15**    **Engr.**    *Perf. 12*

| | | | |
|---|---|---|---|
| C45 | AP23 | 10c violet | .35 | .20 |
| C46 | AP24 | 15c dk green | .50 | .20 |
| C47 | AP25 | 25c gray brn | .35 | .20 |
| C48 | AP26 | 1s black | 1.60 | 1.75 |
| | | *Nos. C45-C48 (4)* | 2.80 | 1.85 |

Inter-American Technical Conference of Aviation, Sept. 1937.

Monument on the Plains of Junin — AP28

Government Restaurant at Callao — AP27

View of Tarma — AP30

Rear Admiral Manuel Villar — AP29

Dam, Ica River — AP31

Highway and Railroad Passing AP33

View of Iquitos AP32

First Flight in Peru, 1911 — AP23

PERU

A surtax of 2 soles on No. C81a was for the Children's Hospital.

Remainders of Nos. C78-C81 and C81a were overprinted "Melbourne 1956" and placed on sale Nov. 19, 1956, at all post offices as "voluntary stamps" with no postal validity. Clerks were permitted to postmark them to please collectors, and proceeds were to help pay the cost of sending Peruvian athletes to Australia. On April 14, 1957, postal authorities declared these stamps valid for one day, April 15, 1957. The overprint was applied to 10,000 sets and 21,000 souvenir sheets.

Value, set, $20; sheet, $15.

No. C55 Surcharged in Red

**1948, Dec.** Perf. 13
| | | |
|---|---|---|
| C82 | AP33 10c on 70c slate blue | .20 .20 |
| C83 | AP33 20c on 70c slate blue | .20 .20 |
| C84 | AP33 55c on 70c slate blue | .60 .60 |
| | Nos. C82-C84 (3) | |

Nos. C52, C55 and C56 Surcharged in Black

S/. 0.10

**1949, Mar. 25**
| | | |
|---|---|---|
| C85 | AP30 5c on 25c dp grn | .20 .20 |
| C86 | AP30 10c on 25c dp grn | .20 .20 |
| C87 | AP33 15c on 70c slate bl | .20 .20 |
| C88 | AP33 30c on 80c olive | .65 .20 |
| | Nos. C85-C88 (4) | 1.25 .80 |

The surcharge reads up, on No. C87.

Imprint: "Waterlow & Sons Limited, Londres."

Types of 1938
**1949-50** Perf. 13x13½, 13½x13 Photo.
| | | |
|---|---|---|
| C89 | AP27 5c olive bister | .20 .20 |
| C90 | AP31 30c red | .20 .20 |
| C91 | AP33 70c blue | .25 .20 |
| C92 | AP34 80c cerise | .40 .20 |
| C93 | AP36 1.50s vio blu ('50) | .50 .20 |
| | Nos. C89-C93 (5) | 1.55 1.00 |

Air View, Reserva Park, Lima — AP45

Flags of the Americas and Spain AP46

**1951, Apr. 2** Engr.
| | | |
|---|---|---|
| C94 | AP45 5c blue grn | |
| C95 | AP45 30c black & car | |

Overprinted "U. P. U. 1874-1949" in Red or Black

**1951,** Perf. 12
| | | |
|---|---|---|
| C96 | AP45 5c blue grn | .20 .20 |
| C97 | AP45 30c black & car | .20 .20 |
| C98 | AP45 55c yel grn (Bk) | .20 .20 |
| C99 | AP45 95c dk green | .20 .20 |
| C100 | AP45 1.50s dp car (Bk) | .20 .20 |
| C101 | AP45 2s deep blue | .25 .20 |
| C102 | AP45 5s rose car (Bk) | .20 .20 |
| | AP45 10s purple | .25 .20 |
| | AP46 20s dk grn & ul- | 3.50 |
| | tra | 5.50 |

Nos. C94-C102 (9) 6.75 5.50

UPU, 75th anniv. (in 1949).

Nos. C94-C102 exist without overprint, but were not regularly issued. Value, set, $200.

---

Type of 1938 Surcharged in Black

**1951, May.** Engr. Perf. 12½x12
C103 AP27 5c olive bister .20 .20

Imprint: "Inst. de Grav. Paris."

Type of 1938 Surcharged in Black

HABILITADA S/. 0.25

**1951**
C108 AP31 25c on 30c rose red .20 .20

Designs: 50c, Church and convent of Santo Domingo. 1.20s, P. de Peralta Barnuevo, T. de San Martin y Contreras and J. Baquijano y Carrillo de Cordova. 2s, T. Rodriguez de Mendoza, J. Hipolito Unanue y Garcia. 5s, Arms of the University, 1571 and 1735.

San Marcos University — AP48

**1951, Dec. 10** Perf. 11½x12½
| | | |
|---|---|---|
| C109 | AP47 30c gray | .20 .20 |
| C110 | AP47 40c ultra | .20 .20 |
| C111 | AP48 50c car rose | .20 .20 |
| C112 | AP47 1.20s emerald | .40 .20 |
| C113 | AP47 2s slate | .25 .20 |
| C114 | AP47 5s multicolored | .50 .20 |
| | Nos. C109-C114 (6) | 1.55 1.00 |

400th anniv. of the founding of San Marcos University.

River Gunboat Marañón AP49

Peruvian Cormorants — AP50

**1951, Dec. 10** Perf. 11½x12½ Litho.
| | | |
|---|---|---|
| | AP49 30c gray | .20 .20 |
| | AP50 40c ultra | .20 .20 |
| | AP49 50c car rose | .20 .20 |
| | | 1.10 .20 |
| | Nos. C123-C126 (4) | 2.15 1.20 |

National Airport, Lima AP51

**1953, June 18** Engr. Perf. 12½x11½, 11½x12½
| | | |
|---|---|---|
| C123 | AP55 40c dp carmine | .20 .20 |
| C124 | AP56 1.25s emerald | .40 .30 |
| C125 | AP55 2.15s dp plum | .40 .30 |
| C126 | AP56 2.20s black | .65 .30 |
| | Nos. C123-C126 (4) | 1.45 1.00 |

Designs: 50c, Eiffel Tower and Cathedral of Lima. 1.25s, Admiral Dupetit-Thouars and frigate "La Victorieuse." 2.20s, Presidents Coty and Prado and exposition hall.

---

Thomas de San Martín y Contreras and Jerónimo de Aliaga y Ramírez — AP47

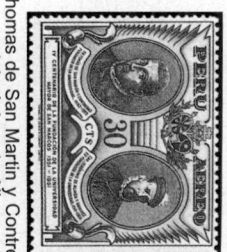

**1953-60** Unwmk. Perf. 13, 12
| | | |
|---|---|---|
| C115 | AP49 40c yellow grn | .20 .20 |
| a. | 40c blue green ('57) | .20 .20 |
| C116 | AP50 75c dk brown | .75 .20 |
| C116A | AP50 80c pale brn red | |
| | ('60) | |
| C117 | AP51 1.25s blue | .40 .20 |
| C118 | AP49 1.50s cerise | .20 .20 |
| C119 | AP51 2.20s dk blue | .20 .20 |
| C120 | AP52 3s brown | .95 .20 |
| C121 | AP53 5s bister | .75 .20 |
| C122 | AP54 10s dull vio brn | 1.75 .35 |
| | 10s dull bro brn | 6.00 2.00 |
| | Nos. C115-C122 (9) | |

For surcharges see #C158-C162, C182-C183, C186-C189. C210-C211.

Designs: 1.50s, Housing Unit No. 3, 2.20s, Inca Solar Observatory.

Imprint: "Thomas De La Rue & Co. Ltd."

Garcilaso de la Vega AP53

Tobacco Plant AP52

Manco Capac Monument AP54

Pre-Stamp Postal Markings — AP58

**1957, Sept. 16** Perf. 13
| | | |
|---|---|---|
| C127 | AP57 40c claret, grn & | .20 .20 |
| | ultra | |
| C128 | AP57 50c grn, blk & hn | .20 .20 |
| C129 | AP57 1.25s bl, ind & dk grn | .20 .20 |
| C130 | AP57 2.20s bluish blk, bl & | |
| | red brn | .40 .40 |
| | Nos. C127-C130 (4) | 1.00 1.00 |

French Exposition, Lima, Sept. 15-Oct. 1. For surcharges see Nos. 763, C503-C505.

**1957, Dec. 1** Engr. Unwmk. Perf. 12½x13
| | | |
|---|---|---|
| C131 | AP58 5c silver & blk | .20 .20 |
| C132 | AP58 10c lil rose & bl | .20 .20 |
| C133 | AP58 15c grn & red brn | .20 .20 |
| C134 | AP58 25c org yel & bl | .20 .20 |
| C135 | AP58 30c vio brn & bl | .20 .20 |
| | black & bis | .20 .20 |
| C136 | AP58 40c black & bis | .20 .20 |
| C137 | AP58 45c dk bl & dk brn | .30 .25 |
| C138 | AP58 2.20s red & sl bl | .30 .25 |
| C139 | AP58 5s lil rose & mar | 1.25 1.00 |
| C140 | AP58 10s sil grn & lil | 1.75 1.75 |
| | Nos. C131-C140 (10) | 5.25 4.70 |

Centenary of Peruvian postage stamps. No. C140 issued to publicize the Peruvian Centenary Phil. Exhib. (PEREX).

---

Design: 1s, Ramon Castilla.

Flags of France and Peru — AP61

Arms of Lima and Bordeaux AP57

EXPOSICION PERU

Designs: 50c, National flag. 55c, Huancayo Hotel. 96c, Blanca-Ancash Cordillera. 1.50s, Arequipa Hotel. 2s, Coal chute and dock, Chimbote. 5s, Town hall, Miraflores. 10s, Hall of National Congress, Lima.

---

Queen Isabella I — AP55

**1951, June 18**
500th birth anniv. (in 1951) of Queen Isabella I of Spain.
For surcharge see No. C475.

Port of Callao and Pres. Manuel Prado AP60

Carlos Paz Soldan — AP59

**1958, Apr. 7** Litho. Wmk. 116 Perf. 14x13½, 13½x14
| | | |
|---|---|---|
| C141 | AP59 40c brn & pale rose | .20 .20 |
| C142 | AP59 1s grn & lt grn | .20 .20 |
| C143 | AP60 1.25s dull pur & ind | .60 .60 |
| | Nos. C141-C143 (3) | |

Centenary of the telegraph connection between Lima and Callao and the centenary of the political province of Callao.
For surcharges see Nos. 758A, 767.

Fleet of Columbus — AP56

PERU

Agriculture, Industry and Archaeology AP76

**1962, Sept. 7  Litho.  Perf. 14x13½**
C181 AP76 1s black & gray  .20  .20
Cent. (in 1961) of Pallasca Ancash province.

### Types of 1953-60

1.30s, Guanayes. 1.50s, Housing Unit No. 3. 1.80s, Locomotive No. 80 (like #460). 2s, Monument to Native Farmer. 3s, Tobacco plant. 4.30s, Inca Solar Observatory. 5s, Garcilaso de la Vega. 10s, Inca Monument.
Imprint: "Thomas De La Rue & Co. Ltd."

**1962-63  Wmk. 346  Litho.  Perf. 13**
C182 AP50 1.30s pale yellow  .20  .20
C183 AP49 1.50s claret  .25  .25
C184 A182 1.80s dark blue  .25  .20

**Perf. 12**
C185 A184 2s emerald ('63)  .25  .20
C186 A52 3s lilac rose  .35  .20
C187 A51 4.30s orange  .65  .25
C188 A53 5s citron  .65  .35

**Perf. 13½x14**
C189 A54 10s vio bl ('63)  1.25  .50
Nos. C182-C189 (8)  3.85  2.10

### Freedom from Hunger Type

**1963, July 23  Unwmk.  Perf. 12½**
C190 A189 4.30s lt grn & ocher  .50  .50

Jorge Chávez and Wing — AP77

Fair Poster — AP78

**1964, Feb. 20  Engr.  Perf. 13**
C191 AP77 5s org brn, dk brn & bl  .65  .35
1st crossing of the Alps by air (Sept. 23, 1910) by the Peruvian aviator Jorge Chávez, 50th anniv.

### Alliance for Progress Type

Design: 1.30s, Same, horizontal.

**1964, June 22  Perf. 12½x12, 12x12½  Litho.**
C192 A190 1.30s multi  .20  .20
C193 A190 3s multi  .25  .25

**1965, Jan. 15  Unwmk.  Perf. 14½**
C194 AP78 1s multi  .20  .20
3rd International Pacific Fair, Lima 1963.

Basket, Globe, Pennant — AP79

St. Martin de Porres — AP80

---

### Machu Picchu Sheet

A souvenir sheet was issued Sept. 11, 1961, to commemorate the 50th anniversary of the discovery of the ruins of Machu Picchu, ancient Inca city in the Andes, by Hiram Bingham. It contains two bi-colored imperf. airmail stamps, 5s and 10s, lithographed in a single design picturing the mountaintop ruins. The sheet was valid for one day and was sold in a restricted manner. Value $20.

Fair Emblem and Llama — AP73

Olympic Torch, Laurel and Globe — AP72

**1961, Dec. 13  Unwmk.  Perf. 13**
C172 AP72 5s gray & ultra  .40  .35
C173 AP73 10s gray & car  .85  .60
a.  Souv. sheet of 2, #C172-C173, imperf.  2.50  2.25
17th Olympic Games, Rome, 8/25-9/11/60.

**1962, Jan.  Litho.  Perf. 10½x11**
C174 AP73 1s multi  .20  .20
2nd International Pacific Fair, Lima, 1961.

Map Showing Disputed Border, Peru-Ecuador — AP74

**1962, May 25  Perf. 10½**
**Gray Background**
C175 AP74 1.30s blk, red & car rose  .20  .20
C176 AP74 1.50s blk, red & emer  .20  .20
C177 AP74 2.50s blk, red & dk bl  .25  .65
Nos. C175-C177 (3)  .65  .65
Settlement of the border dispute with Ecuador by the Protocol of Rio de Janeiro, 20th anniv.

Cahuide and Cuauhtémoc — AP75

**1962, May 25  Engr.  Perf. 13**
C178 AP75 1s dk car rose, red & brt grn  .20  .20
C179 AP75 2s grn, red & brt grn  .20  .20
C180 AP75 3s grn, red & brt grn  .25  .60
Nos. C178-C180 (3)  .65  .60
Exhibition of Peruvian art treasures in Mexico.

---

**1958, Nov. 13**
**Star in Blue and Olive Bister**
C154 AP66 80c emerald  .20  .20
C155 AP66 1.10s red orange  .20  .20
C156 AP66 1.20s ultra  .20  .20
C157 AP66 1.50s lilac rose  .80  .80
Nos. C154-C157 (4)
Lima Bar Assoc., 150th anniv.

### Types of 1953-57

Designs: 80c, Peruvian cormorants. 3.80s, Map of Peru Solar Observatory.
Imprint: "Joh. Enschedé en Zonen-Holland"

**Perf. 12½x14, 14x13, 13x14**
**1959, Dec. 9  Unwmk.**
C158 AP50 80c brown red  .20  .20
C159 A52 3s lt green  .60  .25
C160 AP51 3.80s orange  1.00  .25
C161 AP53 5s brown  .60  .25
C162 AP54 10s orange ver  1.25  .40
Nos. C158-C162 (5)  3.65  1.35

WRY Emblem, Dove, Rainbow and Farmer — AP67

Peruvian Cormorant Over Ocean — AP68

**1960, Apr. 7  Litho.  Perf. 14x13**
C163 AP68 80c multi  .25  .25
C164 AP67 4.30s multi  .55  .55
a.  Souv. sheet of 2, #C163-C164, imperf.  6.00  7.00
World Refugee Year, 7/1/59-6/30/60.
No. C164a sold for 15s.

**1960, May 30  Perf. 14x13½**
C165 AP68 1s multi  .35  .20
Intl. Pacific Fair, Lima, 1959.

Lima Coin of 1659 AP69

**1961, Jan. 19  Unwmk.  Perf. 13x14**
C166 AP69 1s org brn & gray  .20  .20
C167 AP69 2s Prus bl & gray  .20  .20
1st National Numismatic Exposition, Lima, 1959; 300th anniv. of the first dated coin (1659) minted at Lima.

The Earth AP70

**1961, Mar. 8  Litho.  Perf. 13½x14**
C168 AP70 1s multicolored  .75  .20
International Geophysical Year.

Frigate Amazonas AP71

**1961, Mar. 8  Engr.  Perf. 13½**
C169 AP71 50c brown & grn  .20  .20
C170 AP71 80c dl vio & red org  .20  .20
C171 AP71 1s green & sepia  .60  .60
Nos. C169-C171 (3)
Centenary (in 1958) of the trip around the world by the Peruvian frigate Amazonas.

---

Cathedral of Lima and Lady AP62

1.50s, Horseback rider & mail in Lima. 2.50s, Map of Peru showing national products.

**1958, May 20  Engr.  Unwmk.**
C144 AP61 50c dl vio, bl & car  .20  .20
C145 AP62 65c multi  .20  .20
C146 AP61 1.10s red orange  .20  .20
C147 AP61 2.50s sl grn, grnsh bl & claret  .25  .85
Nos. C144-C147 (4)  .80  .80
Peruvian Exhib. in Paris, May 20-July 10.

Bro. Martin de Porres Velasquez AP63

First Royal School of Medicine (Now Ministry of Government and Police) — AP64

Designs: 1.20s, Daniel Alcides Carrion Garcia. 1.50s, José Hipolito Unanue Pavon.

**Perf. 13x13½, 13½x13**
**1958, July 24  Litho.**
C148 AP63 60c multi  .20  .20
C149 AP63 1.20s multi  .20  .20
C150 AP63 1.50s multi  .20  .20
C151 AP64 2.20s black  .80  .80
Nos. C148-C151 (4)
Daniel A. Carrion (1857-85), medical martyr.

Gen. Ignacio Álvarez Thomas AP65

**1958, Nov. 13  Perf. 13x12½**
C152 AP65 1.10s brn lake, bis & ver  .20  .20
C153 AP65 1.20s blk, bis & ver  .20  .20
General Thomas (1787-1857), fighter for South American independence.

"Justice" and Emblem — AP66

**1965, Apr. 19**    *Perf. 12x12½*
C195 AP79 1.30s violet & red    .25 .25
C196 AP79 4.30s bis brn & red    .55 .55
4th Women's Intl. Basketball Championship.
For surcharge see No. C493.

**1965, Oct. 29    Litho.    *Perf. 11***
C197 AP80 1.30s gray & multi    .20 .20
C198 AP80 1.80s gray & multi    .20 .20
C199 AP80 4.30s gray & multi    .50 .50
Nos. C197-C199 (3)    .90 .90
Canonization of St. Martin de Porres Velasquez (1579-1639), on May 6, 1962.
For surcharges see Nos. C439, C496.

Designs: 1.80s, St. Martin's miracle: dog, cat and mouse feeding from same dish. 4.30s, St. Martin with cherubim in Heaven.

Victory Monument, Lima, and Battle Scene — AP81

**1966, May 2    Photo.    *Perf. 14x13½***
C200 AP81 1.90s multicolored    .25 .25
C201 AP81 3.60s brn, yel, & bis    .40 .40
C202 AP81 4.60s multicolored    .60 .60
Nos. C200-C202 (3)    1.25 1.25
Centenary of Peru's naval victory over the Spanish Armada at Callao, May, 1866.

Designs: 3.60s, Monument and Callao Fortress. 4.60s, Monument and José Galvez.

Civil Guard Emblem AP82

**1966, Aug. 30    Photo.    *Perf. 13½x14***
C203 AP82    90c multicolored    .20 .20
C204 AP82 1.90s dp lil rose, gold & blk    .20 .20
Centenary of the Civil Guard.
1.90s, Various activities of Civil Guard.

Sun Symbol, Ancient Carving — AP83

**1966, Nov. 24    Photo.    *Perf. 13½x14***
C205 A193 1.90s lil, blk & vio bl    .20 .20

Hydroelectric Center Type

**1967, Feb. 16    Litho.    *Perf. 14x13½, 13½x14***
C206 AP83 2.60s red org & blk    .25 .20
C207 AP83 3.60s dp blue & blk    .35 .25
C208 AP83 4.60s tan & multi    .40 .30
Nos. C206-C208 (3)    1.00 .75
Photography exhibition "Peru Before the World" which opened simultaneously in Lima, Madrid, Santiago de Chile and Washington, Sept. 27, 1966.
For surcharges see #C444, C470, C492.

Types of 1953-60
Designs: 3.60s, Map of Peru and spiral, horiz. 4.60s, Globe with map of Peru.
2.60s, Monument to Native Farmer. 3.60s, Tobacco plant. 4.60s, Inca Solar Observatory.

---

St. Rosa of Lima by Angelino Medoro — AP84

**1967, Jan.    Imprint: "I.N.A."    *Perf. 13½x14, 14x13½***
C209 A184 2.60s brt green    .25 .20
C210 A184 3.60s brt green    .35 .20
C211 AP51 4.60s orange    .40 .25
Nos. C209-C211 (3)    1.00 .65

Wind Vane and Sun Type of Regular Issue
**1967, Apr. 18    Photo.    *Perf. 13½x14***
C212 A194 1.90s yel brn, blk & gold    .25 .20

**1967, Aug. 30    Photo.    Black, Gold & Multi    *Perf. 13½***
C213 AP84 1.90s    .25 .20
C214 AP84 2.60s    .40 .20
C215 AP84 3.60s    1.25 .65
Nos. C213-C215 (3)    1.25 .65
St. Rosa Painted by: 2.60s, Carlo Maratta. 3.60s, Cuzquena School, 17th century.

Fair Type of Regular Issue
**1967, Oct. 27    Photo.    *Perf. 12***
C216 A195 1.90s brt red lil & blk    .20 .20

Lions Emblem — AP85

**1967, Dec. 29    Litho.    *Perf. 14x13½***
C217 AP85 1.60s brt bl & vio bl, grysh    .25 .20
350th death anniv. of St. Rosa of Lima. For surcharge see No. C477.
50th anniversary of Lions International.

---

Decorated Jug, Nazca Culture — AP86

Antarqui, Inca Messenger AP87

**1968, June 4    Photo.    *Perf. 12***
C218 AP86 1.90s multi    .25 .20
C219 AP86 2.60s multi    .35 .20
C220 AP86 3.60s black & multi    .35 .20
C221 AP86 4.60s brown & multi    .45 .25
C222 AP86 5.60s gray & multi    .90 .25
Nos. C218-C222 (5)    2.30 1.35
For surcharges see #C445-C453, C497, C500.

Designs: Painted pottery juge of pre-Inca Nazca culture: 2.60s, Falcon. 3.60s, Round jug decorated with grain-eating bird. 4.60s, Two-headed snake. 5.60s, Marine bird.

**1968, Sept. 2    Litho.    *Perf. 12***
C223 AP87 3.60s multi    .30 .30
C224 AP87 5.60s red, blk & brn    .45 .45
Design: 5.60s, Alpaca and jet liner.
12th anniv. of Peruvian Airlines (APSA). For surcharges see Nos. C480-C482.

---

Human Rights Flame — AP88

**1968, Sept. 5    Photo.    *Perf. 14x13½***
C225 AP88 6.50s brn, red & grn    .25 .20
International Human Rights Year.

Discobolus and Mexico Olympics Emblem AP89

**1968, Oct. 19    Photo.    *Perf. 13½***
C226 AP89 2.30s yel, brn & dk bl    .20 .20
C227 AP89 3.50s yel grn, sil bl & red    .20 .20
C228 AP89 5s brt pink, blk & ultra    .25 .20
C229 AP89 6.50s blk & brn    .30 .20
C230 AP89 8s lil, ultra & car    .40 .25
C231 AP89 9s org, vio & grn    .40 .30
Nos. C226-C231 (6)    1.85 1.46
19th Olympic Games, Mexico City, 10/12-27.

Hand, Corn and Field AP90

**1969, Mar. 3    Litho.    *Perf. 11***
C232 AP90 5.50s on 1.90s grn & yel    .25 .20
C233 AP90 6.50s on 1.90s bl grn & yel    .35 .20
Agrarian Reform Law. Not issued without surcharge.

---

Peruvian Silver 8-reales Coin, 1568 AP91

**1969, Mar. 17    Litho.    *Perf. 12***
C234 AP91 5s yellow, gray & blk    .20 .20
C235 AP91 5s sil grn, gray & blk    .20 .20
400th anniv. of the first Peruvian coinage.

Ramon Castilla Monument AP92

**1969, May 30    Photo.    *Perf. 13½***
Size: 21x37mm
C236 AP92 5s emerald & indigo    .35 .20

**1969, June 17    Litho.    *Perf. 12***
Size: 27x40mm
C237 AP92 10s plum & brn    .65 .30
Ramon Castilla (1797-1867), president of Peru (1845-1851 and 1855-1862), on the occasion of the unveiling of the monument in Lima.

Design: 10s, Pres. Ramon Castilla.

Airline Type of Regular Issue
**1969, June 17    Litho.    *Perf. 11***
C238 A199 3s org & multi    .20 .20
C239 A199 4s multi    .20 .20
C240 A199 5.50s ver & multi    .20 .20
C241 A199 6.50s vio & multi    .80 .80
Nos. C238-C241 (4)    1.40 1.40
First Peruvian Airlines (APSA) flight to Europe.

---

Radar Antenna, Satellite and Earth — AP93

**1969, July 14    Litho.    *Perf. 11***
C242 AP93 20s multi    1.25 .55
Souv. sheet    1.50 1.50
Opening of the Lurin satellite earth station near Lima.
No. C242a contains one imperf. stamp with simulated perforations similar to No. C242.

Gonzales Type of Regular Issue inscribed "AEREO"
**1969, July 23    *Perf. 11***
C243 A200 20s red & multi    1.25 .55

---

WHO Emblem AP94

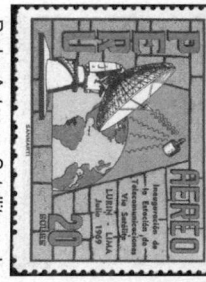

**1969, Aug. 14    Photo.    *Perf. 12***
C244 AP94 5s gray, red brn, gold & blk    .20 .20
C245 AP94 6.50s dp org, gray bl, gold & blk    .20 .20
WHO, 20th anniv.

Agrarian Reform Type of Regular Issue
**1969, Aug. 28    Litho.    *Perf. 11***
C246 A201 3s lil & blk    .20 .20
C247 A201 4s brn & buff    .20 .20

Garcilaso de la Vega — AP95

**1969, Sept. 18    Litho.    *Perf. 12x12½***
C248 AP95 2.40s emer, sil & blk    .20 .20
C249 AP95 3.50s ultra, red & blk    .20 .20
C250 AP95 5s sil, yel, blk & brn    .60 .60
a.    Souv. sheet of 3, #C248-C250, imperf.    1.10 1.10
Nos. C248-C250 (3)    ...
Garcilaso de la Vega, called "Inca" (1539-1616), historian of Peru.
Designs: 2.40s, De la Vega's coat of arms. 3.50s, Title page of "Commentarios Reales que tratan del origen de los Yncas," Lisbon, 1609.

## Fair Type of Regular Issue, 1969

**1969, Nov. 14**    **Litho.**    **Perf. 11**
C251 A203 3s bis & multi .20 .20
C252 A203 4s multi .25 .20

## Bolognesi Type of Regular Issue

**1969, Dec. 9**    **Litho.**    **Perf. 11**
C253 A204 50s lt brn, blk & gold 3.00 1.40

## Soldier-Farmer Type of Regular Issue

**1970, June 24**    **Litho.**    **Perf. 11**
C290 A208 3s gold & multi .20 .20
C291 A208 5.50s gold & multi .35 .20

UN Headquarters, NY—AP100

**1970 June 26**
C292 AP100 3s vio bl & lt bl .20 .20
25th anniversary of United Nations.

Rotary Club Emblem—AP101

**1970, July 18**
C293 AP101 10s blk, red & gold .70 .50
Rotary Club of Lima, 50th anniversary.

## Tourist Type of Regular Issue

3s, Ruins of Sun Fortress, Trujillo. 4s, Sacsayhuaman Arch, Cuzco. 5.50s, Arch & Lake Titicaca, Puno. 10s, Machu Picchu, Cuzco.

**1970, Aug. 6**    **Litho.**    **Perf. 11**
C294 A210 3s multi .20 .20
C295 A210 4s multi, vert. .20 .20
C296 A210 5.50s multi, vert. .30 .30
C297 A210 10s multi, vert. .50 .50
a. Souvenir sheet of 5 1.60 1.60
Nos. C294-C297 (4) 1.20 1.20

No. C297a contains 5 imperf. stamps similar to Nos. 538, C294-C297 with simulated perforations.

Procession, Lord of Miracles—AP102

4s, Cockfight, by T. Nuñez Ureta. 5.50s, Altar of Church of the Nazarene, vert. 6.50s, Procession, by J. Vinatea Reinoso. 8s, Procession, by José Sabogal, vert.

**1970, Nov. 30**    **Litho.**    **Perf. 11**
C298 AP102 3s blk & multi .20 .20
C299 AP102 4s blk & multi .20 .20
C300 AP102 5.50s blk & multi .25 .20
C301 AP102 6.50s blk & multi .35 .20
C302 AP102 8s blk & multi 1.40 1.00
Nos. C298-C302 (5)
October Festival in Lima.

"Tight Embrace" (from ancient monolith) AP103

**1971, Feb. 8**    **Litho.**    **Perf. 11**
C303 AP103 4s ol gray, yel & red .35 .20
C304 AP103 5.50s dk bl, pink & red .40 .20
C305 AP103 6.50s sl, buff & red .45 .20
Nos. C303-C305 (3) 1.20 .60

Issued to express Peru's gratitude to the world for aid after the Ancash earthquake, May 31, 1970.

Arms of Amazonas—AP96

**1970, Jan. 6**    **Litho.**    **Perf. 11**
C254 AP96 10s multi .50 .50

ILO Emblem AP97

**1970, Jan. 16**    **Photo.**    **Perf. 13½x14**
C278 AP97 3s dk vio bl & lt ultra .25 .25
ILO, 50th anniv.

Motherhood and UNICEF Emblem AP98

**1970, Jan. 16**    **Perf. 13½x14**
C279 AP98 5s yel, gray & blk .25 .20
C280 AP98 6.50s brt pink, gray & blk .35 .20

## Vicus Culture Type of Regular Issue

Ceramics of Vicus Culture, 6th-8th Centuries: 3s, Squatting warrior. 4s, Jug. 5.50s, Twin jugs. 6.50s, Woman and jug.

**1970, Feb. 23**    **Litho.**    **Perf. 11**
C281 A205 3s buff, blk & brn .20 .20
C282 A205 4s buff, blk & brn .20 .20
C283 A205 5.50s buff, blk & brn .30 .30
C284 A205 6.50s buff, blk & brn .40 .40
Nos. C281-C284 (4) 1.10 1.10

## Fish Type of Regular Issue

**1970, Apr. 30**    **Litho.**    **Perf. 11**
C285 A207 3s Swordfish .20 .20
C286 A207 3s Yellowfin tuna .20 .20
C287 A207 5.50s Wolf fish .30 .30
Nos. C285-C287 (3) .70 .70

Telephone—AP99

**1970, June 12**    **Litho.**    **Perf. 11**
C288 AP99 5s multi .25 .20
C289 AP99 10s multi .55 .25
Nationalization of the Peruvian telephone system, Mar. 25, 1970.

## Textile Type of Regular Issue

Designs: 3s, Chancay tapestry, vert. 4s, Chancay lace. 5.50s, Paracas cloth, vert.

**1971, Apr. 19**    **Litho.**    **Perf. 11**
C306 A213 3s multi .25 .20
C307 A213 4s grn & multi .35 .20
C308 A213 5.50s multi 1.00 .60

## Fish Type of Regular Issue

Fish Sculptures and Fish: 3.50s, Chimu Inca culture, 14th century and Chilean sardine. 4s, Mochica culture, 5th century, and engraulis ringens. 5.50s, Chimu culture, 13th century, and meriuccios peruanos. 8.50s, Nazca culture, 3rd century, and brevoortis maculatachilcae.

**1971, June 7**    **Litho.**    **Perf. 11**
C309 A214 3.50s multi .55 .20
C310 A214 4s multi .75 .20
C311 A214 4.50s multi .90 .20
C312 A214 8.50s multi 1.25 .80
Nos. C309-C312 (4) 3.45 .80

## Independence Type of 1971

Paintings: No. C313, Toribio Rodriguez de Mendoza. No. C314, José de la Riva Aguero. No. C315, Francisco Vidal. 3.50s, José de San Martin. No. C316, Juan P. Viscardo y Guzman. No. C318, Hipolito Unanue. 4.50s, José G. Condorcanqui-Tupac Amaru. No. C320, Liberation Monument, Paracas. No. C321, Francisco J. de Luna Pizarro. 6s, March of the Numancia Battalion, horiz. 7.50s, Peace Tower, monument for Alvarez de Arenales, horiz. 9s, Liberators' Monument, Lima, horiz. 10s, Independence Proclamation in Lima, horiz.

**1971**    **Litho.**    **Perf. 11**
C313 A215 3s brt mag & blk .20 .20
C314 A215 3s gray & multi .20 .20
C315 A215 3s dk bl & multi .20 .20
C316 A215 3.50s dk bl & multi .20 .20
C317 A215 4s emer & blk .20 .20
C318 A215 4s gray & multi .20 .20
C319 A215 4.50s brn & blk .20 .20
C320 A215 4.50s dk bl & multi .25 .20
C321 A215 5.50s brn & blk .20 .20
C322 A215 6s dk bl & multi .25 .20
C323 A215 7.50s dk bl & multi .30 .20
C324 A215 9s dk bl & multi .40 .20
C325 A215 10s dk bl & multi .40 .20
Nos. C313-C325 (13) 3.25 2.60

150th anniversary of independence, and to honor the heroes of the struggle for independence. Sizes: 6s, 10s, 45x35mm, 7.50s, 9s, 41x39mm. Others 31x49mm.

Issued: #C313, C317, C320, 5/10; #C314, C010, C021, 7/6; others ////.

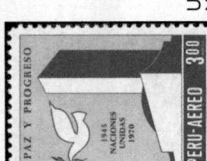

Ricardo Palma—AP104

**1971, Aug. 27**    **Perf. 13**
C326 AP104 7.50s ol bis & blk .60 .20
Sesquicentennial of National Library. Ricardo Palma (1884-1912) was a writer and director of the library.

Weight Lifter—AP105

**1971, Sept. 15**
C327 AP105 7.50s brt bl & blk .50 .20
25th World Weight Lifting Championships, Lima.

Flag, Family, Soldier's Head—AP106

**1971, Oct. 4**
C328 AP106 7.50s blk, lt bl & red .50 .20
a. Souv. sheet of 1, imperf. 1.25 1.00
3rd anniv. of the revolution of the armed forces.

"Sacramento"—AP107

**1971, Oct. 8**
C329 AP107 7.50s lt bl & dk bl .40 .20
Sesquicentennial of Peruvian Navy.

Peruvian Order of the Sun AP108

**1971, Oct. 8**
C330 AP108 7.50s multi .40 .40
Sesquicentennial of the Peruvian Order of the Sun.

## Liberation Type of Regular Issue

Design: 50s, Detail from painting "Progress of Liberation," by Teodoro Nuñez Ureta.

**1971, Nov. 1**    **Litho.**    **Perf. 13x13½**
C331 A217 50s multi 3.25 1.00
2nd Ministerial meeting of the "Group of 77."

Fair Emblem AP109

**1971, Nov. 12**    **Perf. 13**
C332 AP109 4.50s multi .30 .20
7th Pacific International Trade Fair.

## Fish Type of Regular Issue

3s, Pontinus furcirhinus dubius. 5.50s, Hogfish.

**1972, Mar. 20**    **Litho.**    **Perf. 13x13½**
C333 A223 3s lt bl & multi .30 .20
C334 A223 5.50s lt bl & multi .50 .20

Teacher and Children, by Teodoro Nuñez Ureta AP110

**1972, Apr. 10**    **Litho.**    **Perf. 13x13½**
C335 AP110 6.50s multi .30 .20
Enactment of Education Reform Law.

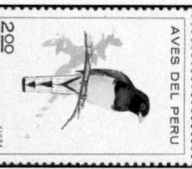

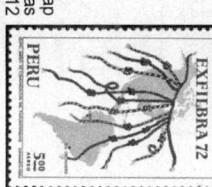

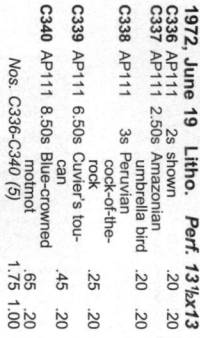

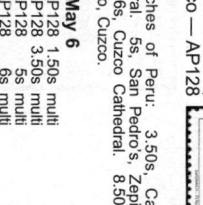

214

PERU

**AVES DEL PERU**

White-tailed Trogon — AP111

**1972, June 19    Litho.    Perf. 13½x13**

| | | | |
|---|---|---|---|
| C336 | AP111 | 2s shown | .20 .20 |
| C337 | AP111 | 2.50s Amazonian umbrella bird | .20 .20 |
| C338 | AP111 | 3s Peruvian cock-of-the-rock | .25 .20 |
| C339 | AP111 | 6.50s Cuvier's toucan | .45 .20 |
| C340 | AP111 | 8.50s Blue-crowned motmot | .65 .20 |

Nos. C336-C340 (5)    1.75 1.00

Quipu and Map of Americas AP112

**EXFILBRA 72**

**1972, Aug. 21**

C341 AP112 5s blk & multi    .30 .20

4th Interamerican Philatelic Exhibition, EXFILBRA, Rio de Janeiro, Aug. 26-Sept. 2.

Inca Runner, Olympic Rings — AP113

**1972, Aug. 28**

C342 AP113 8s buff & multi    .55 .35

20th Olympic Games, Munich, 8/26-9/11.

Woman of Catacaos, Piura — AP114

**TRAJES TIPICOS CATACAOS PIURA**

**1972-73**

| | | | |
|---|---|---|---|
| C343 | AP114 | 2s | .20 .20 |
| C344 | AP114 | 3.50s | .30 .30 |
| C345 | AP114 | 4s | .35 .35 |
| C346 | AP114 | 4.50s | .40 .40 |
| C347 | AP114 | 5s | .40 .40 |
| C347A | AP114 | 6.50s | .50 .50 |
| C347B | AP114 | 8s | .60 .60 |

Regional Costumes: 2s, Tupe (Yauyos) woman of Lima. 4s, Indian with bow and arrow, from Conibo, Loreto. 4.50s, Man with calabash, Cajamarca. 5s, Moche woman, Trujillo. 6.50s, Man and woman of Ocongate, Cuzco. 8s, Chucupana woman of Junin. 10s, Woman of Puno dancing "Pandilla."

Funerary Tower, Sillustani, Puno — AP115

**1972, Oct. 16    Litho.**

Archaeological Monuments: 1.50s, Stone of the 12 angles, Cuzco. 3.50s, Stone of Ancash. 5s, Wall and gate, Chavin. 8s, Ruins of Machu Picchu.

| | | | |
|---|---|---|---|
| C349 | AP115 | 1.50s multi, horiz. | .65 .65 |
| C350 | AP115 | 3.50s multi, horiz. | .25 .20 |
| C351 | AP115 | 5s multi, horiz. | .45 .25 |
| C352 | AP115 | 8s multi, horiz. | .85 .35 |
| C353 | AP115 | | 1.20 |

Nos. C349-C353 (5)    2.30 1.20

AP116

**Perf. 13½x13, 13x13½**

| | | | |
|---|---|---|---|
| C347B | AP114 | 8.50s blk & multi | |
| C348 | AP114 | 10s blk & multi | .75 .75 |

Nos. C343-C348 (9)    4.15 4.15

Issued: 3.50s, 4s, 6.50s, 9/29/72; 2s, 4.50s, 10s, 4/30/73; 5s, 8s, 8.50s, 10/15/73.

**TEJIDOS DEL PERU**

AP117

Inca ponchos, various textile designs.

**1973, Jan. 29    Litho.    Perf. 13½x13**

| | | | |
|---|---|---|---|
| C354 | AP116 | 2s multi | .20 .20 |
| C355 | AP116 | 2.50s multi | .20 .20 |
| C356 | AP116 | 3.50s multi | .20 .20 |
| C357 | AP116 | 4s multi | .25 .20 |
| C358 | AP116 | 8s multi | .50 .20 |

Nos. C354-C358 (5)    1.35 1.00

Antique Jewelry: 1.50s, Goblets and Ring, Mochica, 10th cent. 2.50s, Golden hands and arms, Lambayeque, 12th cent. 3.50s, Gold male statuette, Mochica, 8th cent. 4s, Gold male brooches, Nazca, 8th cent. 8s, Flayed puma, Mochica, 8th cent.

**1973, Mar. 19    Litho.    Perf. 13½x13**

| | | | |
|---|---|---|---|
| C359 | AP117 | 1.50s multi | .20 .20 |
| C360 | AP117 | 2.50s multi | .20 .20 |
| C361 | AP117 | 4s multi | .25 .25 |
| C362 | AP117 | 4s multi | .25 .25 |
| C363 | AP117 | 8s multi | .50 .20 |

Nos. C359-C363 (5)    1.35 1.05

Andean Condor — AP118

**PERU FAUNA PROTEGIDA**

**1973, Apr. 16    Litho.    Perf. 13½x13**

| | | | |
|---|---|---|---|
| C364 | AP118 | 4s blk & multi | .25 .20 |
| C365 | AP118 | 5s blk & multi | .40 .20 |
| C366 | AP118 | 8s blk & multi | .75 .25 |

Nos. C364-C366 (3)    1.40 .65

Protected Animals: 5s, Vicuña. 8s, Spectacled bear.

See Nos. C372-C376, C411-C412.

Indian Guide, by José Sabogal — AP119

**1973, May 7    Litho.    Perf. 13½x13**

Peruvian Paintings: 8.50s, Portrait of a Lady, by Daniel Hernandez. 20s, Man Holding Figurine, by Francisco Laso.

| | | | |
|---|---|---|---|
| C367 | AP119 | 1.50s multi | .20 .20 |
| C368 | AP119 | 8.50s multi | .40 .20 |
| C369 | AP119 | 20s multi | .90 .50 |

Nos. C367-C369 (3)    1.50 1.00

Basket and World Map AP120

**1973, May 26    Perf. 13x13½**

| | | | |
|---|---|---|---|
| C370 | AP120 | 5s green | .25 .20 |
| C371 | AP120 | 20s lil rose | 1.10 .50 |

1st International Basketball Festival.

**PERU    BASKETBALL 1973**

Orchid — AP122

**ORQUIDEAS DEL PERU**

Darwin's Rhea — AP121

**PERU FAUNA PROTEGIDA**

**1973, Sept. 3    Litho.    Perf. 13½x13**

| | | | |
|---|---|---|---|
| C372 | AP121 | 2.50s shown | .30 .20 |
| C373 | AP121 | 3.50s Giant otter | .45 .25 |
| C374 | AP121 | 6s Greater flamingo | .60 .25 |
| C375 | AP121 | 8.50s Bush dog, horiz. | .75 .50 |
| C376 | AP121 | 10s Chinchilla, horiz. | 2.70 1.55 |

Nos. C372-C376 (5)

Protected animals.

**1973, Sept. 27**

Designs: Various orchids.

| | | | |
|---|---|---|---|
| C377 | AP122 | 1.50s blk & multi | .20 .20 |
| C378 | AP122 | 2.50s blk & multi | .25 .20 |
| C379 | AP122 | 3s blk & multi | .30 .20 |
| C380 | AP122 | 3.50s blk & multi | .35 .20 |
| C381 | AP122 | 8s blk & multi | .75 .20 |

Nos. C377-C381 (5)    1.85 1.00

Pacific Fair Emblem — AP123

**PERU-LIMA 1973    FERIA INTERNACIONAL DEL PACIFICO**

**1973, Nov. 14    Litho.    Perf. 13½x13**

C382 AP123 8s blk, red & gray    .60 .30

8th International Pacific Fair, Lima.

Cargo Ship ILO AP124

**EL PERU DETERMINA SU DESTINO    PERU**

Designs: 2.50s, Boats of Pescaperu fishing organization. 8s, Jet and seagull.

Moral House, Arequipa AP127

**PERU**

Bridge at Yananacu, by Enrique Camino Brant AP126

**2.50s, El Misti Mountain, Arequipa. 5s, Puya Raymondi (cacti), vert. 6s, Huascaran Mountain. 8s, Lake Querococha. Views on 5s, 6s, 8s are views in White Cordilleras Range, Ancash Province.**

**1974, Feb. 11    Perf. 13x13½, 13½x13**

| | | | |
|---|---|---|---|
| C387 | AP126 | 8s multi | .40 .20 |
| C388 | AP126 | 10s multi | .50 .25 |
| C389 | AP126 | 50s multi | 2.25 1.25 |

Nos. C387-C389 (3)    3.15 1.70

**1974, Feb. 11**

| | | | |
|---|---|---|---|
| C390 | AP127 | 1.50s multi | .20 .20 |
| C391 | AP127 | 2.50s multi | .20 .20 |
| C392 | AP127 | 5s multi | .30 .20 |
| C393 | AP127 | 6s multi | .30 .20 |
| C394 | AP127 | 8s multi | .65 .20 |

Nos. C390-C394 (5)    1.75 1.00

Lima Monument AP125

**PERU**

**1973, Nov. 27    Perf. 13**

C386 AP125 8.50s red & multi

50th anniversary of Air Force Academy. Monument honors Jorge Chavez, Peruvian aviator.

**1973, Dec. 14    Litho.    Perf. 13**

| | | | |
|---|---|---|---|
| C383 | AP124 | 1.50s multi | .25 .20 |
| C384 | AP124 | 2.50s multi | .40 .30 |
| C385 | AP124 | 8s multi | 1.45 .70 |

Nos. C383-C385 (3)

Issued to promote government enterprises.

San Jeronimo's, Cuzco — AP128

**PERU**

Churches of Peru: 3.50s, Cajamarca Cathedral. 5s, San Pedro's, Lima. 6s, Cuzco Cathedral. 8.50s, Santo Domingo, Cuzco.

**1974, May 6**

| | | | |
|---|---|---|---|
| C395 | AP128 | 1.50s multi | .45 .20 |
| C396 | AP128 | 3.50s multi | .50 .20 |
| C397 | AP128 | 5s multi | .75 .20 |
| C398 | AP128 | 6s multi | .90 .20 |
| C399 | AP128 | 8.50s multi | 1.40 .20 |

Nos. C395-C399 (5)    4.00 1.00

Surrender at Ayacucho, by Daniel Hernandez AP129

**PERU**

## C442–C455

| No. | Type | Surcharge | | |
|---|---|---|---|---|
| C442 | AP52 | 4s on 3.60s (77) | | .25 .20 |
| C443 | AP51 | 5s on 4.30s (R) #C187 | | .30 .20 |
| C444 | AP83 | 6s on 4.60s (Bk) ('77) #C208 | | .35 .20 |
| C445 | AP51 | 6s on 4.60s ('77) #C211 | | .35 .25 |
| C446 | AP51 | 7s on 4.30s (Bk) #C187 ('77) | | .25 .25 |
| C447 | AP52 | 7.50s on 3.60s (DBl) #C210 | | .45 .25 |
| C448 | AP52 | 8s on 3.60s (O) #C210 | | .50 .30 |
| C449 | AP51 | 10s on 4.30s (Bk) #C187 ('77) | | .30 .20 |
| C450 | AP51 | 10s on 4.60s (DBl) #C211 | | .60 .20 |
| C451 | AP86 | 24s on 3.60s (Bk) #C220 ('77) | | 1.75 .60 |
| C452 | AP86 | 28s on 4.60s (Bk) #C221 ('77) | | 1.00 .60 |
| C453 | AP86 | 32s on 5.60s (Bk) #C222 ('77) | | 1.00 .60 |
| C454 | A184 | 50s on 2.60s (O) #C209 ('77) | | 2.50 1.00 |
| C455 | AP52 | 50s on 3.60s (G) #C210 | | 12.85 7.10 |

Nos. C436-C455 (20)

Map of Tacna and Tarata Provinces. — AP144

Investigative Police badge. — AP145

1076, Aug. 28 Litho. Perf. 13½x13
C456 AP144 10s multi .45 .25
Re-incorporation of Tacna Province into Peru, 47th anniversary.

1976, Sept. 15 Litho. Perf. 13½x13
C457 AP145 20s multi .05 .35
Investigative Police of Peru, 54th anniv.

"Declaration of Bogota." — AP147

AP146

1976, Sept. 22
C458 AP146 10s multi .40 .20
Declaration of Bogota for cooperation and world peace, 10th anniversary.

---

Fair Poster — AP140

Col. Francisco Bolognesi AP141

1975, Nov. 21 Litho. Perf. 13½x13
C425 AP140 6s blk, bis & red .45 .25
9th International Pacific Fair, Lima, 1975.

1975, Dec. 23 Litho. Perf. 13½x13
C426 AP141 20s multi 1.00 .50
160th birth anniv. of Col. Bolognesi.

Indian Mother and Child — AP142

Inca Messenger, UPAE Emblem — AP143

1976, Feb. 23 Litho. Perf. 13½x13
C427 AP142 6s gray & multi .40 .25
Christmas 1975.

1976, Mar. 19 Litho. Perf. 13½x13
C428 AP143 5s red, blk & tan .40 .25
11th Congress of the Postal Union of the Americas and Spain, UPAE.

Nos. C187, C211, C160, C209, C210
Surcharged in Dark Blue or Violet Blue (No Bar)

1976
C429 AP51 2s on 4.30s org .20 .20
C430 AP51 3.50s on 4.60s org .20 .20
C431 AP51 4.50s on 3.80s org .20 .20
C432 AP51 4.50s on 4.30s org .30 .20
C433 AP51 6s on 4.60s org .40 .25
C434 A184 10s on 2.60s brt grn .55 .20
C435 AP52 50s on 3.60s lil rose (VB) 2.10 1.75
3.95 3.00
Nos. C429-C435 (7)

Stamps of 1962-67 Surcharged with New Value and Heavy Bar in Black, Red, Green, Dark Blue or Orange
1976-77 As Before
C436 AP52 1.50s on 3.60s (Bk) #C210 .20 .20
C437 A184 2s on 2.60s (R) #C209 ('77) .20 .20
C438 AP52 2s on 3.60s (G) #C210 .20 .20
C439 AP80 2s on 4.30s org #C199 .20 .20
C440 A184 3s on 2.60s (Bk) #C209 ('77) .20 .20
C441 A184 4s on 2.60s (DBl) #C209 .25 .20

---

Designs: 6s, Battle of Junin, by Felix Yañez. 7.50s, Battle of Ayacucho, by Felix Yañez.
1974 Litho. Perf. 13x13½
C400 AP129 3.50s multi .25 .20
C401 AP129 6s multi .25 .20
C402 AP129 7.50s multi .45 .20
C403 AP129 8.50s multi .50 .20
C404 AP129 10s multi .65 1.00
2.10 1.00
Nos. C400-C404 (5)

Sesquicentennial of the Battles of Junin and Ayacucho and of the surrender at Ayacucho. Issued: 7.50s, 8/6; 6s, 10/9; others, 12/9.

Pedro Paulet and Aerial Torpedo AP135

1974, Nov. 28 Litho. Perf. 13x13½
C416 AP135 8s bl & vio .50 .30
UPU, cent. Pedro Paulet, inventor of the mail-carrying aerial torpedo.

Christmas Type of 1974
Design: 6.50s, Indian Nativity scene.
1974, Dec. 20 Perf. 13½x13
C417 A235 6.50s multi .25 .20

Andean Village, Map of South American West Coast AP136

1974, Dec. 30
C418 AP136 6.50s multi .35 .25
Meeting of Communications Ministers of Andean Pact countries.

Map of Peru, Modern Buildings, UN Emblem — AP137

1975, Mar. 12 Litho. Perf. 13x13
C419 AP137 6s blk, gray & red .20 .20
2nd United Nations Industrial Development Organization Conference, Lima.

Nos. C187, C211 and C160 Surcharged with New Value and Heavy Bar in Dark Blue
1975, April Litho. Wmk. 346
C420 AP51 2s on 4.30s org .20 .20
Perf. 13½x14, 13x14 Unwmk.
C421 AP51 2.50s on 4.60s org .25 .20
C422 AP51 5s on 3.80s org .70 .60
Nos. C420-C422 (3)

World Map and Peruvian Colors AP138

1975, Aug. 25 Litho. Perf. 13x13½
C423 AP138 6.50s lt bl, vio bl & red .25 .20
Conference of Foreign Ministers of Nonaligned Countries.

Map of Peru and Flight Route AP139

1975, Oct. 23 Litho. Perf. 13x13½
C424 AP139 8s red, pink & blk .35 .20
AeroPeru's first flights: Lima-Rio de Janeiro, Lima-Los Angeles.

---

Chavin Stone, Ancash AP130

Machu Picchu, Cuzco AP131

#C407, C409, Different bas-reliefs from Chavin Stone. #C408, Baths of Tampumacchay, Cuzco. #C410, Ruins of Kencco, Cuzco.

1974, Mar. 25 Perf. 13½x13, 13x13½
C405 AP130 3s multi .20 .20
C406 AP131 3s multi .20 .20
C407 AP130 5s multi .20 .30
C408 AP131 5s multi .30 .20
C409 AP130 10s multi .60 .20
C410 AP131 20s multi .60 1.20
2.20 1.20
Nos. C405-C410 (6)

Cacajao Rubicundus AP132

1974, Oct. 21 Perf. 13½x13
C411 AP132 8s multi .50 .25
C412 AP132 20s multi 1.25 .40
Protected animals.

Inca Gold Mask AP133

1974, Nov. 8
C413 AP133 8s yel & multi .50 .20
8th World Mining Congress, Lima.

Chalan, Horseman's Cloak — AP134

1974, Nov. 11 Litho. Perf. 13½x13
C414 AP134 5s multi .50 .20
C415 AP134 8.50s multi .50 .25

**1976, Nov. 2 — Litho. — Perf. 13½x13**
C459 AP147 7s ultra & blk .40 .20
Pal Losonczi and map of Hungary.
Visit of Pres. Pal Losonczi of Hungary, Oct. 1976.

**1976, Dec. 16 — Litho. — Perf. 13**
C460 AP148 10s bl & multi .35 .20
Map of Amazon Basin, Colors of Peru and Brazil — AP148
Visit of Gen. Ernesto Geisel, president of Brazil, Nov. 5, 1976.

**1977, Mar. 9 — Litho. — Perf. 13x13½**
C461 AP149 20s red buff & blk .75 .40
Liberation Monument, Lima — AP149
Army Day.

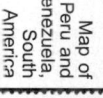

**1977, Mar. 14 — Litho. — Perf. 13½x13**
C462 AP150 12s buff & multi .80 .30
Map of Peru and Venezuela, South America — AP150
Meeting of Pres. Francisco Morales Bermúdez Cerrutti of Peru and Pres. Carlos Andres Perez of Venezuela, Dec. 1976.

**1977, May 30 — Litho. — Perf. 13½x13**
C463 AP151 20s gray, red & blk 1.20 .30
Electronic Tree — AP151
World Telecommunications Day.

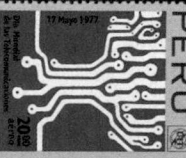

**1977, July 13 — Litho. — Perf. 13½x13**
C464 AP152 14s multi .45 .30
Map of Peru, Refinery, Tanker — AP152
Development of Bayovar oil complex.

**1977**
Messenger Type of 1977 — Perf. 13½x13
C465 A243 24s mag & blk .75 .40
C466 A243 28s bl & blk 1.25 .40
C467 A243 32s rose brn & blk 2.75 1.30
Nos. C465-C467 (3) 2.75 1.30

---

**1977, Oct. 8 — Litho. — Perf. 13½x13**
C468 AP153 10s multi .20 .20
Arms of Arequipa — AP153
Gold of Peru Exhibition, Arequipa 1977.

**1977, Sept. 3 — Litho. — Perf. 13½x13**
C469 AP154 36s multi .55 .25
Gen. Jorge Rafael Videla — AP154
Visit of Jorge Rafael Videla, president of Argentina.

**1977 — As Before**
Stamps of 1953-67 Surcharged with New Value and Heavy Bar in Black, Dark Blue or Green
C470 AP83 2s on 3.60s multi .20 .20
C471 AP51 2s on 4.60s .20 .20

**1977**
C472 AP51 4s on 4.60s #C211 .20 .20
C473 AP51 5s on 4.30s #C187 .35 .20
C474 AP51 5s on 4.60s #C210 .20 .20
C475 AP52 10s on 2.15s #C125 .40 .20
C476 AP52 10s on 3.60s #C210 .20 .20
C477 AP84 10s on 3.60s (DB) #C215 .65 .20
C478 AP52 20s on 3.60s (DB) .50 .20
C479 AP51 100s on 3.80s (G) #C160 1.75 .25
Nos. C470-C479 (10) 5.20 3.60

Stamps of 1965-67 Surcharged with "Habilitado / R.D. No. O118" and New Value in Red, Green, Violet Blue or Black

Nos. C223-C224 Surcharged with New Value, Heavy Bars and: "FRANQUEO"
**1977 — Litho. — Perf. 12**
C480 A87 6s on 3.60s multi .45 .25
C481 A87 8s on 3.60s multi .55 .35
C482 A87 8s on 5.60s multi 1.55 1.00
Nos. C480-C482 (3) 1.55 1.00

---

**1977, Dec. 15 — Litho. — Perf. 13½x13**
C483 AP155 28s multi .40 .25
Adm. Miguel Grau — AP155
Navy Day. Miguel Grau (1838-1879), Peruvian naval commander.

**1977, Dec. 23**
Christmas Type of 1977
C484 A246 20s Indian Nativity .50 .20

**1978, Jan. 12 — Litho. — Perf. 13**
C485 AP156 30s multi .40 .30
Andres Bello, Flag and Map of Participants — AP156

8th Meeting of Education Ministers honoring Andrés Bello, Lima.

---

**1978**
Inca Type of 1978 — Perf. 13½x13
C486 A247 24s dp rose lil .35 .30
C487 A247 30s salmon .45 .30
C488 A247 65s brt bl 1.00 .65
C489 A247 95s dk bl 1.40 1.00
Nos. C486-C489 (4) 3.20 2.25

Antenna, ITU Emblem — AP157

**1978, July 3 — Litho. — Perf. 13½x13**
C490 AP157 50s gray & multi .70 .65
10th World Telecommunications Day.

**1978, Sept. 4 — Litho. — Perf. 13½x13**
C491 AP158 30s multi .45 .40
San Martin, Flag Colors of Peru and Argentina — AP158
Gen. José de San Martin (1778-1850), soldier and statesman, protector of Peru.

**1978 — Litho.**
Stamps of 1965-67 Surcharged "Habilitado / R.D. No. O118" and New Value in Red, Green, Violet Blue or Black
C492 AP83 34s on 4.60s multi (R) #C208 .30 .25
C493 AP79 40s on 4.30s multi (G) #C196 .35 .30
C494 A184 70s on 2.60s brt grn (VB) #C209 .60 .50
C495 AP52 110s on 3.60s lil rose (Bk) #C210 .90 .75
C496 AP80 265s on 4.30s gray & multi (Bk) #C199 4.40 3.80
Nos. C492-C496 (5) 2.25 2.00

Stamps and Type of 1968-78 Surcharged in Violet Blue, Black or Red
**1978 — Litho.**
C497 AP86 25s on 4.60s (VB) #C220 .25 .25
C498 A247 45s on 28s dk grn (R) #C221 .40 .25
C499 A247 75s on 28s dk grn (Bk) #C222 .65 .40
C500 AP86 105s on 5.60s (R) #C222 1.25 1.00
Nos. C497-C500 (4) 2.55 1.90

Nos. C498-C499 not issued without surcharge.

**1980, Apr. 14 — Litho. — Perf. 13½x13**
C501 A247 35s on 24s dp rose lil .30 .25
C502 A243 45s on 32s rose brn & blk .40 .30

No. C130 Surcharged in Black
**1981, Nov. — Engr. — Perf. 13**
C503 A49 35s on 2.20s multi .30 .30

No. C130 Surcharged and Overprinted in Green: "12 Feria / Internacional / del / Pacifico 1981"
**1981, Nov. 30**
C504 A57 40s on 2.20s multi .30 .25
C505 AP57 140s on 2.20s multi 1.10 .75
12th Int. Pacific Fair.

---

**AIR POST SEMI-POSTAL STAMPS**

Chavin Griffin — SPAP1

**1963, Apr. 18 — Litho. — Wmk. 346**
Perf. 12½x12, 12x12½
Design in Gray and Brown
CB1 SPAP1 1s + 50c sal pink .20 .20
CB2 SPAP1 1.50s + 1s multi .20 .20
CB3 SPAP1 2s + 2.50s lit grn .50 .50
CB4 SPAP1 4.30s + 3s green .80 .80
CB5 SPAP1 6s + 4s citron 1.00 1.00
Nos. CB1-CB5 (5) 2.70 2.70

The designs are from ceramics found by archaeological excavations of the 14th century Chavin culture. The surtax was for the excavations fund.

Design: 1.50s+1s, Bird. 3s+2.50s, Mythological figure, vert. 6s+4s, Chavin god, vert.

**1964, Jan. 29 — Litho. — Unwmk.**
Perf. 12½x12
CB6 SPAP2 1.30s + 70c multi .30 .20
CB7 SPAP2 4.30s + 1.70s multi .70 .40
Henri Dunant and Centenary Emblem — SPAP2
Centenary of International Red Cross.

---

**SPECIAL DELIVERY STAMPS**

No. 149 Overprinted in Black
**1908 — Unwmk. — Perf. 12**
E1 A25 10c gray black 20.00 15.00

No. 172 Overprinted in Violet
**1909 — Perf. 12**
E2 A40 10c red brn & blk 25.00 14.00

**1910**
E3 A49 10c deep blue 14.00 12.00

Two handstamps were used to make No. E2. Impressions from them measure 22½x6½mm and 24x6½mm. Counterfeits exist of Nos. E1-3.

No. 1819 Handstamped in Violet

---

**POSTAGE DUE STAMPS**

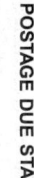

Coat of Arms — D1

## Steamship and Llama

D2   D3   D4   D5

### 1874-79 Unwmk. Engr. Perf. 12

| No. | Type | Description | | |
|---|---|---|---|---|
| J1 | D1 | 1c bister ('79) | .25 | .20 |
| J2 | D2 | 5c vermilion | .30 | .25 |
| J3 | D3 | 10c orange | .35 | .25 |
| J4 | D4 | 20c blue | .60 | .35 |
| J5 | D5 | 50c brown | 9.00 | 3.50 |
| | | | 10.50 | 4.50 |

Nos. J1-J5 (5)

A 2c green exists, but was not regularly issued.

For overprints and surcharges see Nos. 157, J6-J31, J37-J38, 8N14-8N15, 14N18.

### 1902-07 Without Grill

| No. | Type | Description | |
|---|---|---|---|
| J1a | D1 | 1c bister | .20 |
| J2a | D2 | 5c vermilion | .20 |
| J3a | D3 | 10c orange | .35 |
| J4a | D4 | 20c blue | .95 |

Nos. J1a-J4a (4)

### 1881 "PLATA" 2½mm High

| No. | Type | Description | | |
|---|---|---|---|---|
| J6 | D1 | 1c bis (Bl) | 3.60 | 6.50 |
| J7 | D2 | 5c ver (Bl) | | 6.00 |
| a. | | Double overprint | | 17.00 |
| J8 | D3 | 10c org (Bl) | 6.50 | 17.00 |
| a. | | Inverted overprint | 7.00 | 17.00 |
| J9 | D4 | 20c bl (R) | 25.00 | 20.00 |
| J10 | D5 | 50c brn (Bl) | 55.00 | 50.00 |
| a. | | Double overprint | 96.50 | 85.00 |

Nos. J6-J10 (5)

Nos. J1-J5 Overprinted in Blue or Red

In the reprints of this overprint "PLATA" is 3mm high instead of 2½mm. Besides being struck in the regular colors it was also applied to the 1, 5, 10 and 50c in red and the 20c in blue.

### 1881 Overprinted in Red

| No. | Type | Description | | |
|---|---|---|---|---|
| J11 | D1 | 1c bister | 5.00 | 5.00 |
| J12 | D2 | 5c vermilion | 6.50 | 6.50 |
| J13 | D3 | 10c orange | 8.00 | 8.00 |
| J14 | D4 | 20c blue | 25.00 | 20.00 |
| J15 | D5 | 50c brown | 124.50 | 102.50 |

Nos. J11-J15 (5)

Originals of Nos. J11 to J15 are overprinted in brick-red, oily ink; reprints in thicker, bright red ink. The 5c exists with reprinted overprint in blue.

---

### Overprinted "Union Postal Universal Lima Plata", in Oval in first named color and Triangle in second named color

### 1883

| No. | Type | Description | | |
|---|---|---|---|---|
| J16 | D1 | 1c bis (Bl & Bk) | 5.00 | 3.50 |
| J17 | D1 | 1c ver (Bk & Bl) | 7.50 | 7.00 |
| J18 | D2 | 5c ver (Bl & Bk) | 7.50 | 7.00 |
| J19 | D3 | 10c org (Bl & Bk) | 7.50 | 6.00 |
| J20 | D4 | 20c bl (R & Bk) | 450.00 | 450.00 |
| J21 | D5 | 50c brn (Bl & Bk) | 55.00 | 42.50 |

Reprints of Nos. J16 to J21 have the oval overprint with "PLATA" 3mm. high. The 1c also exists with the oval overprint in red.

### Overprinted in Black

### 1884

| No. | Type | Description | | |
|---|---|---|---|---|
| J22 | D1 | 1c bister | .50 | .50 |
| J23 | D2 | 5c vermilion | .50 | .50 |
| J24 | D3 | 10c orange | .50 | .50 |
| J25 | D4 | 20c blue | 1.00 | .90 |
| J26 | D5 | 50c brown | 3.00 | .90 |
| | | | 5.50 | 2.90 |

Nos. J22-J26 (5)

The triangular overprint is found in 11 types.

### Overprinted "Lima Correos" in Circle In Red and Triangle in Black

### 1884

| No. | Type | Description | | |
|---|---|---|---|---|
| J27 | D1 | 1c bister | 12.50 | 11.00 |

Reprints of No. J27 have the overprint in bright red. At the time they were made the overprint was also printed on the 5, 10, 20 and 50c Postage Due stamps.

Postage Due stamps overprinted with Sun and "CORREOS LIMA" (as shown above No. 103), alone or in combination with the "U.P.U. LIMA" oval and "LIMA CORREOS" in double-lined circle, are fancy varieties made to sell to collectors and never placed in use.

### Overprinted

### 1896-97

| No. | Type | Description | | |
|---|---|---|---|---|
| J28 | D1 | 1c bister | .35 | .30 |
| J29 | D2 | 5c vermilion | .45 | .25 |
| a. | | Double overprint | | |
| J30 | D3 | 10c orange | .55 | .35 |
| a. | | Inverted overprint | | |
| J31 | D4 | 20c blue | .65 | .50 |
| a. | | Double overprint | | |
| J32 | A22 | 10c red ('97) | .75 | .50 |
| J33 | A23 | 1s brown ('97) | 1.00 | .65 |
| a. | | Double overprint | | |
| b. | | Inverted overprint | 3.75 | 2.55 |

Nos. J28-J33 (6)

### Liberty — D6

### 1899

| No. | Type | Description | | |
|---|---|---|---|---|
| J34 | D6 | 5s yel grn | 5.00 | 5.00 |
| J35 | D6 | 10s dl vio | 900.00 | 900.00 |

For surcharge see No. J39.

---

### 1902 On No. 159

| No. | Type | Description | | |
|---|---|---|---|---|
| J36 | A31 | 5c on 10s bl grn | 1.00 | .80 |
| a. | | Double surcharge | 12.00 | 12.00 |

### On No. J4

| No. | Type | Description | | |
|---|---|---|---|---|
| J37 | D4 | 1c on 20c blue | .50 | .40 |
| a. | | "DEFICIT" omitted | 6.50 | 2.00 |
| b. | | "DEFICIT" double | 6.00 | 2.00 |
| c. | | "UN CENTAVO" double | 8.25 | 6.00 |
| d. | | "UN CENTAVO" omitted | | |

### Surcharged Vertically

| No. | Type | Description | | |
|---|---|---|---|---|
| J38 | D4 | 5c on 20c blue | 1.50 | 1.00 |

### On No. J35

| No. | Type | Description | | |
|---|---|---|---|---|
| J39 | D6 | 1c on 10s dull vio | .60 | .50 |
| | | | 3.60 | 2.70 |

Nos. J36-J39 (4)

D7

### 1909 Engr. Perf. 12

| No. | Type | Description | | |
|---|---|---|---|---|
| J40 | D7 | 1c red brown | .50 | .20 |
| J41 | D7 | 5c red brown | .50 | .20 |
| J42 | D7 | 10c red brown | .60 | .20 |
| J43 | D7 | 50c red brown | .90 | .20 |
| | | | 2.50 | .80 |

Nos. J40-J43 (4)

### 1921 Size: 18¼x22mm

| No. | Type | Description | | |
|---|---|---|---|---|
| J44 | D7 | 1c violet brown | .25 | .20 |
| J45 | D7 | 2c violet brown | .25 | .20 |
| J46 | D7 | 5c violet brown | .35 | .25 |
| J47 | D7 | 10c violet brown | .50 | .25 |
| J48 | D7 | 50c violet brown | 1.60 | .75 |
| J49 | D7 | 1s violet brown | 7.50 | 3.00 |
| J50 | D7 | 2s violet brown | 12.00 | 3.50 |
| | | | 22.45 | 8.10 |

Nos. J44-J50 (7)

Nos. J40 and J50 have the circle at the center replaced by a shield containing "S/.", in addition to the numeral.

In 1929 during a shortage of regular postage stamps, 2mm of the Postage Due stamps of 1921 were used instead.

See Nos. J50A-J52, J55-J56, 204-207, 757. For surcharges see Nos. J19-J22.

### Type of 1909-22 Size: 18¾x23mm

| No. | Type | Description | | |
|---|---|---|---|---|
| J50A | D7 | 2c violet brown | .75 | .20 |
| J50B | D7 | 10c violet brown | .75 | .20 |

### 1932 Photo. Perf. 14½x14

### Type of 1909-22 Issues

| No. | Type | Description | | |
|---|---|---|---|---|
| J51 | D7 | 2c violet brown | .75 | .25 |
| J52 | D7 | 10c violet brown | .75 | .25 |

### Regular Stamps of 1934-35 Overprinted in Black

### 1935 Perf. 13

| No. | Type | Description | | |
|---|---|---|---|---|
| J53 | A131 | 2c deep claret | .75 | .50 |
| J54 | A117 | 10c crimson | .75 | .50 |

Imprint: "Waterlow & Sons, Limited, Londres."

### Type of 1909-32 Size: 19x23mm

### 1936 Engr. Perf. 12½

| No. | Type | Description | | |
|---|---|---|---|---|
| J55 | D7 | 2c light brown | .20 | .20 |
| J56 | D7 | 10c gray green | .50 | .50 |

---

## OFFICIAL STAMPS

### Regular Issue of 1886 Overprinted in Red

### 1890, Feb. 2

| No. | Type | Description | | |
|---|---|---|---|---|
| O2 | A17 | 1c dl vio | 1.40 | 1.40 |
| O3 | A18 | 2c green | 8.25 | 8.25 |
| a. | | Double overprint | 1.40 | 1.40 |
| O4 | A19 | 5c orange | 8.25 | 8.25 |
| a. | | Inverted overprint | 2.00 | 1.60 |
| b. | | Double overprint | 8.25 | 8.25 |
| O5 | A20 | 10c slate | 1.00 | .65 |
| a. | | Double overprint | 8.25 | 8.25 |
| O6 | A21 | 20c blue | 3.00 | 2.00 |
| a. | | Inverted overprint | 8.25 | 8.25 |
| O7 | A22 | 50c red | 4.00 | 2.00 |
| a. | | Double overprint | | 12.00 |
| O8 | A23 | 1s brown | 5.00 | 4.50 |
| a. | | Inverted overprint | 17.00 | 17.00 |
| b. | | Double overprint | 17.80 | 13.55 |

Nos. O2-O8 (7)

### 1894, Oct.

Nos. 118-124 (Bermudez Ovpt.) Overprinted Type "a" in Red

| No. | Type | Description | | |
|---|---|---|---|---|
| O9 | A17 | 1c green | 6.50 | 5.50 |
| a. | | "Gobierno" and head invtd. | 22.50 | 20.00 |
| O10 | A17 | 1c orange | 1.40 | 1.40 |
| b. | | Dbl. ovpt. of "Gobierno" | 10.00 | 10.00 |
| O11 | A18 | 2c rose | 1.40 | 1.40 |
| O12 | A18 | 2c violet | 22.50 | 20.00 |
| a. | | Overprinted head inverted | | |
| O13 | A19 | 5c ultra | | |
| a. | | "Gobierno" double | | |
| O14 | A19 | 5c blue | 10.00 | 9.00 |
| b. | | Both overprints inverted | | |
| O15 | A20 | 10c green | 3.50 | 3.50 |
| O16 | A22 | 50c green | 5.00 | 5.00 |
| a. | | Both overprints inverted | 67.70 | 61.70 |

Nos. O9-O16 (8)

### Nos. 125-126 ("Horseshoe" Ovpt.) Overprinted Type "a" in Red

| No. | Type | Description | | |
|---|---|---|---|---|
| O17 | A18 | 2c vermilion | 2.00 | 2.00 |
| O18 | A19 | 5c blue | 2.00 | 2.00 |

### 1895, May

Nos. 105, 107, 109, 113 Overprinted Type "a" in Red

| No. | Type | Description | | |
|---|---|---|---|---|
| O19 | A17 | 1c vermilion | 8.25 | 8.25 |
| O20 | A18 | 2c dp ultra | 6.50 | 6.50 |
| O21 | A12 | 5c claret | 6.50 | 6.50 |
| O22 | A14 | 20c dp ultra | 29.50 | 29.50 |
| a. | | Double overprint | | |

Nos. O19-O22 (4)

Nos. O2-O22 have been extensively counterfeited.

### Nos. 141, 148, 149, 151 Overprinted in Black

### 1896-1901

| No. | Type | Description | | |
|---|---|---|---|---|
| O23 | A24 | 1c ultra | .20 | .20 |
| O24 | A25 | 1c yellow | 1.00 | .50 |
| a. | | Double overprint | | |
| O25 | A25 | 10c gray blk ('01) | .20 | .20 |
| O26 | A26 | 50c brt rose (4) | .40 | .25 |
| | | | 1.80 | 1.15 |

Nos. O23-O26 (4)

O1

### 1909-14 Engr. Perf. 12 Size: 18½x22mm

| No. | Type | Description | | |
|---|---|---|---|---|
| O27 | O1 | 1c red | .20 | .20 |
| a. | | 1c brown red | .20 | .20 |
| O28 | O1 | 1c orange ('14) | .50 | .35 |
| O29 | O1 | 10c bis brn ('14) | .20 | .20 |
| a. | | 10c violet brown | .20 | .20 |

**1933 Photo. Perf. 15x14**

No. 319 Overprinted in Black — "Servicio Oficial"

| O31 | O1 | 10c violet brown | .50 | .20 |
|---|---|---|---|---|

**1935 Unwmk. Perf. 13**

| O32 | A117 | 10c crimson | .20 | .20 |
|---|---|---|---|---|

Imprint: "Waterlow & Sons, Limited, Londres."

Type of 1909-33
Size: 19x23mm   Perf. 12½

**1936 Engr.**

| O33 | O1 | 10c light brown | .20 | .35 |
|---|---|---|---|---|
| O34 | O1 | 50c gray green | .20 | .35 |

| O30 | O1 | 50c c gm (14) | .60 | .35 |
|---|---|---|---|---|
| | | Size: 18¾x23½mm | | |
| a. | | 50c blue green | 1.00 | .35 |
| O30B | O1 | 10c vio brn | 2.00 | 1.30 |

See Nos. O31, O33-O34. For overprints and surcharge see Nos. 201-203, 760.

## PARCEL POST STAMPS

Porte de Conducción — 5 CENTAVOS (PP2)
Porte de Conducción — 2 CENTAVOS (PP1)
Porte de Conducción — 1 CENTAVO (PP3)

## POSTAL TAX STAMPS

### Plebiscite Issues

These stamps were not used in Tacna and Arica (which were under Chilean occupation) but were used in Peru to pay a supplementary tax on letters, etc.

It was intended that the money derived from the sale of these stamps should be used to help defray the expenses of the plebiscite.

Morro — Arica — PT1

Adm. Grau and Col. Bolognesi Reviewing Troops — PT2

Bolognesi Monument — PT3

**1925-26 Unwmk. Litho. Perf. 12**

| RA1 | PT1 | 5c dp bl | 1.50 | .35 |
|---|---|---|---|---|
| RA2 | PT1 | 5c rose red | .80 | .25 |
| RA3 | PT1 | 5c yel grn | .70 | .25 |
| RA4 | PT2 | 10c brown | .80 | .80 |
| RA5 | PT3 | 50c bl grn | 25.00 | 10.65 |
| | | Nos. RA1-RA5 (5) | 19.00 | 9.00 |

**1926**

| RA6 | PT4 | 2c orange | .30 | .20 |
|---|---|---|---|---|

**1927-28**

| RA7 | PT5 | 2c org | .60 | .20 |
|---|---|---|---|---|
| RA8 | PT5 | 2c red brn | .60 | .20 |
| RA9 | PT5 | 2c dk bl | .40 | .20 |
| RA10 | PT5 | 2c gray vio | .40 | .20 |
| RA11 | PT5 | 2c bl grn ('28) | .40 | .20 |
| RA12 | PT5 | 20c red | 2.50 | 1.00 |
| | | Nos. RA7-RA12 (6) | 5.10 | 2.00 |

**1928 Engr.**

| RA13 | PT6 | 2c dk vio | .20 | .20 |
|---|---|---|---|---|

The use of the Plebiscite stamps was discontinued July 26, 1929, after the settlement of the Tacna-Arica controversy with Chile.

For overprint see No. 261.

### Unemployment Fund Issues

These stamps were required in addition to the ordinary postage, on every letter or piece of postal matter. The money obtained by their sale was to assist the unemployed.

Nos. 273-275 Surcharged

"Labor" PT7
Blacksmith PT8

**1931**

| RA14 | A95 | 2c on 4c red | .65 | .50 |
|---|---|---|---|---|
| RA15 | A95 | 2c on 10c bl grn | 3.50 | 3.50 |
| a. | | Inverted surcharge | 3.50 | 3.50 |
| RA16 | A95 | 2c on 15c sl gray | 3.50 | 3.50 |
| a. | | Inverted surcharge | 3.50 | 3.50 |
| | | Nos. RA14-RA16 (3) | 1.65 | 1.50 |

Two types of Nos. RA17-RA18:
I — Imprint 15mm.
II — Imprint 13¾mm.

**1931-32 Litho. Perf. 12x11½, 11½x12**

| RA17 | PT7 | 2c emer (I) | .20 | .20 |
|---|---|---|---|---|
| a. | | Type II | | |
| RA18 | PT7 | 2c rose car (I) ('32) | .20 | .20 |
| a. | | Type II | | |

**1932-34**

| RA19 | PT8 | 2c dp gray | .20 | .20 |
|---|---|---|---|---|
| RA20 | PT8 | 2c pur ('34) | .20 | .20 |

Monument of 2nd of May — PT9

**1933-35 Perf. 13, 13½, 13x13½**

| RA21 | PT9 | 2c bl vio | .20 | .20 |
|---|---|---|---|---|
| RA22 | PT9 | 2c org ('34) | .20 | .20 |
| RA23 | PT9 | 2c brn vio ('35) | .20 | .20 |
| | | Nos. RA21-RA23 (3) | .60 | .60 |

For overprint see No. RA27.

No. 307 Overprinted in Black

**1934 Photo.**

| RA24 | A111 | 2c green | .20 | .20 |
|---|---|---|---|---|
| a. | | Inverted overprint | 2.00 | 2.00 |

Perf. 13½

No. 339 Overprinted Type "a" in Black

"Pro-Desocupados"

**1935**

| RA25 | A131 | 2c deep claret | .20 | .20 |
|---|---|---|---|---|

**1936 Unwmk. Perf. 13½**

No. 339 Overprinted in Black

| RA26 | A131 | 2c deep claret | .20 | .20 |
|---|---|---|---|---|

No. RA23 Overprinted in Black — "Ley 8310"

**1936 Perf. 13x13½**

| RA27 | PT9 | 2c brn vio | .20 | .20 |
|---|---|---|---|---|
| a. | | Double overprint | | 1.40 |
| b. | | Overprint reading down | | 1.40 |
| c. | | Overprint double, reading down | | 1.40 |

St. Rosa of Lima — PT10

Imprint: "American Bank Note Company"

**1937 Engr. Perf. 12**

| RA28 | PT10 | 2c car rose | .20 | .20 |
|---|---|---|---|---|

"Protection" by John Q. A. Ward — PT11

Imprint: "American Bank Note Company"

**1938 Litho.**

| RA29 | PT11 | 2c brown | .20 | .20 |
|---|---|---|---|---|

Nos. RA27 and RA28 represented a tax to help erect a church.

The tax was to help the unemployed. See Nos. RA30, RA34, RA40. For surcharges see Nos. 501A, 674-678, 681-682, 709-711, 757.

**1943 Perf. 12½**

| RA30 | PT11 | 2c dl claret brn | .20 | .20 |
|---|---|---|---|---|

Type of 1938 Redrawn
Imprint: "Columbian Bank Note Company."

See note above #RA14. See #RA34, RA40.

Catalogue values for unused stamps in this section, from this point to the end of the section, are for Never Hinged items.

**1949 Black Surcharge**

| RA31 | PT12 | 3c on 4c vio bl | .55 | .20 |
|---|---|---|---|---|
| RA32 | PT13 | 3c on 10c blue | .55 | .20 |

The tax was for an education fund.

Symbolical of Education PT14   Perf. 12½, 12

Emblem of Congress PT15   Perf. 14

**1950 Typo. Size: 16½x21mm**

| RA33 | PT14 | 3c dp car | .20 | .20 |
|---|---|---|---|---|

For surcharges see Nos. RA35, RA39, RA43, 766, RA45-RA48, RA58.

---

**1897 Typeset Unwmk. Perf. 12**

| Q1 | PP1 | 1c dull lilac | 2.25 | 1.90 |
|---|---|---|---|---|
| Q2 | PP2 | 2c bister | 2.50 | 2.25 |
| a. | | 2c olive | 2.50 | 2.25 |
| Q3 | PP3 | 2c yellow | 2.75 | |
| c. | | Laid paper | | |
| Q4 | PP3 | 5c dk bl | 6.50 | |
| a. | | Tête bêche pair | 375.00 | |
| Q5 | PP3 | 10c vio brn | 10.00 | |
| Q6 | PP3 | 20c rose red | 17.00 | 14.00 |
| Q7 | PP3 | 50c bl grn | 45.00 | 37.50 |
| | | Nos. Q1-Q6 (6) | 90.75 | 72.15 |

**1903-04 Surcharged in Black**

UN CENTAVO

| Q7 | PP3 | 1c on 20c rose red | 12.00 | 10.00 |
|---|---|---|---|---|
| Q8 | PP3 | 1c on 50c bl grn | 12.00 | 10.00 |
| Q9 | PP3 | 5c on 10c vio brn | 80.00 | 65.00 |
| a. | | Double surcharge | 125.00 | 110.00 |
| b. | | Inverted surcharge | 104.00 | 85.00 |
| | | Nos. Q7-Q9 (3) | | |

## OCCUPATION STAMPS

### Issued under Chilean Occupation

Stamps formerly listed as Nos. N1-N10 are regular issues of Chile canceled in Peru.

Stamps of Peru, 1874-80, Overprinted in Red, Blue or Black

**1881-82**
- N11 A17 1c org (Bl) .50 1.00
  - a. Inverted overprint
- N12 A18 2c dk vio (Bk) .50 4.00
  - a. Inverted overprint 16.50
  - b. Double overprint 22.50
- N13 A18 2c rose (Bk) 1.60 18.00
  - a. Inverted overprint
- N14 A19 5c bl (R) 55.00 62.50
  - a. Inverted overprint

- N15 A19 5c ultra (R) 90.00 100.00
- N16 A20 10c grn (R) .50 1.60
  - a. Double overprint 6.50 6.50
  - b. Inverted overprint 12.00 12.00
- N17 A21 20c brn red (Bl) 80.00 125.00
- Nos. N11-N17 (7) 228.10 312.10

Reprints of No. N17 have the overprint in bright blue; on the originals it is in dull ultramarine. Nos. N11 and N12 exist with reprinted overprint in red or yellow. There are numerous counterfeits with the overprint in both correct and fancy colors.

Same, with Additional Overprint in Black

**1882**
- N19 A17 1c grm (R) .50 .80
  - a. Arms inverted .80
  - b. Arms double 8.25 10.00
  - c. Horseshoe inverted 5.50 6.50
- N20 A19 5c bl (R) .80 13.50
  - a. Arms double .80
- N21 A22 50c rose (Bk) 13.50 15.00
  - a. Arms double 1.60 2.00
- N22 A22 50c rose (Bl) 1.60 2.75
- N23 A23 1s ultra (R) 3.25 4.50
  - a. Arms inverted 13.50
  - b. Horseshoe inverted 16.50
  - c. Arms and horseshoe inverted 20.00
  - d. Arms double 13.50
- Nos. N19-N23 (5) 7.75 10.85

## PROVISIONAL ISSUES

### Stamps Issued in Various Cities of Peru during the Chilean Occupation of Lima and Callao

During the Chilean-Peruvian War which took place in 1879 to 1882, the Chilean forces occupied the two largest cities in Peru, Lima & Callao. As these cities were the source of supply of postage stamps, Peruvians in other sections of the country were left without stamps and were forced to the expedient of making provisional issues from whatever material was at hand. Many of these were former canceling devices made over for this purpose. Counterfeits exist of many of the overprinted stamps.

### ANCACHS

(See Note under "Provisional Issues")

Regular Issue of Peru, Overprinted in Manuscript in Black

**1884 Unwmk. Perf. 12**
- 1N1 A19 5c blue 5/.50 55.00

Regular Issues of Peru, Overprinted in Black

**FRANCA**

Overprinted FRANCA
- 1N2 A19 5c blue 18.00 16.50

Overprinted
- 1N3 A19 5c blue 90.00 82.50
- 1N4 A20 10c green 55.00 40.00
- 1N5 A20 10c slate 55.00 35.00

Same, with Additional Overprint "FRANCA"
- 1N6 A20 10c green 82.50 42.50

Overprinted
- 1N7 A19 5c blue 30.00 25.00
- 1N8 A20 10c green 30.00 25.00

Same, with Additional Overprint "FRANCA"
- 1N9 A20 10c green

Revenue Stamp of Peru, 1878-79, Overprinted in Black "CORREO Y FISCAL" and "FRANCA"
- 1N10 A1 10c yellow 37.50 37.50

A1

### APURIMAC

(See Note under "Provisional Issues")

Provisional Issue of Arequipa Overprinted in Black

ADMON. PRAL. DE CORREOS DEL DEPTO DE APURIMAC ===ABANCAY===

**1885 Unwmk. Imperf.**
- 2N1 A6 10c gray 100.00 90.00

Some experts question the status of No. 2N1.

### AREQUIPA

(See Note under "Provisional Issues")

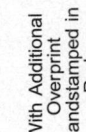

Coat of Arms
A1     A2

Overprint ("PROVISIONAL 1881-1882") in Black

**1881, Jan. Unwmk. Imperf.**
- 3N1 A1 10c blue 2.50 3.50
  - a. 10c ultramarine 2.50 4.00
  - b. Double overprint 12.00 13.50
    Overprinted on back of stamp
- 3N2 A2 25c rose 8.25 10.00
  - a. 25c rose invld. 2.50 6.00
    "2" in upper left corner
  - b. "Centavos" 8.25 10.00
  - c. Double overprint 12.00 13.50

The overprint also exists on 5s yellow. The overprints "1883" in large figures or "Habilitado 1883" are fraudulent. For overprints see Nos. 3N3, 4N1, 8N1, 10N1, 15N1-15N3.

With Additional Overprint Handstamped in Red

---

Type of 1938
Imprint: "Thomas De La Rue & Co. Ltd."

**1951 Litho.**
- RA34 PT11 2c lt redsh brn .20 .20

Type of 1950
Imprint: "Thomas De La Rue & Company, Limited."

**1952 Unwmk. Perf. 14, 13**
Size: 16½x21½mm
- RA35 PT14 3c brn car .20 .20

**1954 Rouletted 13**
- RA36 PT15 5c bl & red .25 .20

The tax was to help finance the National Marian Eucharistic Congress. For surcharges see Nos. 758B, 768.

Piura Arms and Congress Emblem — PT16

**1960 Litho. Perf. 10½**
- RA37 PT16 10c ultra, red, grn & yel .20 .20
- RA38 PT16 10c ultra & red .25 .20
  - a. Green ribbon inverted

Nos. RA37-RA38 were used to help finance the 6th National Eucharistic Congress, Piura, Aug. 25-28. Obligatory on all domestic mail until Dec. 31, 1960. Both stamps exist imperf.

Type of 1950
Imprint: "Bundesdruckerei Berlin"

**1961 Perf. 14**
Size: 17½x22½mm
- RA39 PT14 3c dp car .20 .20

Type of 1938
Imprint: "Harrison and Sons Ltd"

**1962, Apr. Litho. Perf. 14x14½**
- RA40 PT11 2c lt brn .20 .20

Symbol of Eucharist — PT17

**1962**
Imprint: "Iberia"
- RA41 PT17 10c bl & org .20 .20

Type of 1950

**1962, May 8 Rouletted 11**
- RA42 PT17 10c bl & org .20 .20

Type of 1950
Imprint: "Thomas de La Rue"

**1965, Apr. Litho. Perf. 12½x12**
Size: 18x22mm
- RA43 PT14 3c light carmine .20 .20

Type of 1962 Overprinted in Red with three "X," Bars and: "Periodista / Peruano / LEY / 16078"

**1966, July 2 Litho. Pin Perf.**
Imprint: "Iberia"
- RA44 PT17 10c vio & org .20 .20

No. RA43 Surcharged in Green or Black

HABILITADO "Fondo del Periodista Peruano" Ley 16078 S/o. 0.10

HABILITADO "Fondo del Periodista Peruano" Ley 16078 S/o. 0.10

**1966-67 Perf. 12x12½**
- RA45 PT14 (b) 10c on 3c (G) .80 .20
- RA46 PT14 (c) 10c on 3c (Bk) .80 .20
- RA47 PT14 (c) 10c on 3c (G) .20 .20
- RA48 PT14 (c) 10c on 3c (G) 2.00 .80
- Nos. RA45-RA48 (4)

The surtax of Nos. RA44-RA48 was for the Peruvian Journalists' Fund.

Pen Made of Newspaper PT18

**1967, Dec. Litho. Perf. 11**
- RA49 PT18 10c dk red & blk .20 .20

The surtax was for the Peruvian Journalists' fund. For surcharges see Nos. RA56-RA57.

Temple at Chan-Chan PT19

**1967, Dec. 27**
Designs: No. RA51, Side view of temple. Nos. RA52-RA55, Various stone bas-reliefs from Chan-Chan.
- RA50 PT19 20c bl & grn .20 .20
- RA51 PT19 20c multi .20 .20
- RA52 PT19 20c brt bl & blk .20 .20
- RA53 PT19 20c emer & blk .20 .20
- RA54 PT19 20c sep & blk .20 .20
- RA55 PT19 20c lil rose & blk 1.20 1.20
- Nos. RA50-RA55 (6)

The surtax was for the excavations at Chan-Chan, northern coast of Peru. (Mochica-Chimu pre-Inca period).

Type of 1967 Surcharged in Red: "VEINTE / CENTAVOS / R.S. 16-8-68"
- RA56 PT19 20c on 50c multi .50 .50
- RA57 PT19 20c on 1s multi .50 .50

Nos. RA56-RA57 without surcharge were not obligatory tax stamps. No. C199 surcharged "PRO NAVIDAD/ Veinte Centavos/R.S. 5-11-68" was not a compulsory postal tax stamp.

Designs: No. RA56, Handshake. No. RA57, Globe and pen.

#RA43 Surchd. Similar to Type "c"

**1968, Oct.**
- RA58 PT14 20c on 3c lt car .20 .20

Surcharge lacks quotation marks and 4th line reads: Ley 17050.

## 1881, Feb.
3N3 A1 10c blue ... 3.50 3.50
a. 10c ultramarine ... 13.50 8.25

A4

## 1883
3N7 A4 10c dull rose ... 3.50 5.00
a. 10c vermilion ... 3.50 5.00

**Overprinted in Blue like No. 3N3**

Litho.
3N9 A4 10c vermilion ... 5.00 4.00
a. 10c dull rose ... 5.00 4.00

See No. 3N10. For overprints see Nos. 8N2, 8N9, 10N2, 15N4.

Reprints of No. 3N9 are in different colors from the originals, orange, bright red, etc. They are printed in sheets of 20 instead of 25.

3N10 A4 10c brick red (Bl) ... 160.00

**Redrawn**

The redrawn stamp has small triangles without arabesques in the lame lower spandrels. The palm branch at left of the shield and other parts of the design have been redrawn.

Nos. 3N11-3N20 (7)

## 1884 Embossed with Grill Perf. 12
Magenta On Regular Issues of Peru

3N11 A17 1c org (Bk, V or M) ... 6.50 6.50
3N13 A19 5c bl (Bk, V or M) ... 6.50 6.50
3N15 5c ultramarine (Bk or M) ... 2.00 1.40
3N16 A20 10c sl (Bk) ... 3.50 6.50
3N16 A21 20c brn red (Bk) ... 3.50 2.50
3N18 A22 50c grn (Bk or V) ... 25.00 25.00
3N20 A23 1s rose (Bk or V) ... 26.00 25.00
... 35.00 35.00
... 103.50 101.00

**Same Overprint in Black, Violet or**

A5

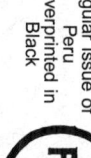

A6

Rear Admiral
M. L. Grau
A7

Col. Francisco
Bolognesi
A8

## 1885
Same Overprint as on Previous Issues

Imperf.
3N22 A5 5c olive (Bk) ... 5.25 5.25
3N23 A6 10c gray (Bk) ... 5.25 4.75
3N25 A7 5c blue (Bk) ... 5.25 4.75
3N26 A8 10c olive (Bk) ... 5.25 3.25
... 21.00 18.00

For overprints see Nos. 2N1, 8N5-8N6, 8N12-8N13, 10N9, 10N12, 15N10-15N12.

**Without Overprint**
3N22a A5 5c olive ... 4.00 3.25
3N23a A6 10c gray ... 4.00 3.25
3N25a A7 5c blue ... 4.00 3.25
3N26a A8 10c olive ... 17.25 15.00

These stamps have been reprinted without overprint; originals are on thicker paper with distinct mesh, reprints on paper without mesh.

Nos. 3N22a-3N26a (4)

## AYACUCHO
Provisional Issue of Arequipa Overprinted in Black

(See Note under "Provisional Issues")

 (CORREO DE AYACUCHO)

## 1883
8N9 A4 10c red ... 10.00 10.00

## 1881
4N1 A1 10c blue ... 82.50 70.00
a. 10c ultramarine ... 82.50 70.00

**Regular Issue of Arequipa Overprinted in Black**

Unwmk. Imperf.

**CHACHAPOYAS**

(See Note under "Provisional Issues")

## 1884
5N1 A19 5c ultra ... 100.00 90.00

**Regular Issue of Peru Overprinted in Black**

Unwmk. Perf. 12

**CHALA**

(See Note under "Provisional Issues")

 (CHALA)

## 1884
6N1 A19 5c blue ... 8.25 6.50
6N2 A20 10c slate ... 10.00 8.25

**Regular Issues of Peru Overprinted in Black**

Unwmk. Perf. 12

**CHICLAYO**

(See Note under "Provisional Issues")

## 1884
7N1 A19 5c blue ... 16.50 10.00

**Same, Overprinted**

7N2 A19 5c blue ... 35.00 22.50

**Regular Issue of Peru Overprinted in Black**

 FRANCA

## CUZCO
(See Note under "Provisional Issues")

**Overprinted "CUZCO" in an oval of dots**

 (18° DISTRITO)

Imperf.
70.00 60.00
70.00 60.00

**Regular Issue of Peru Overprinted in Black "CUZCO" in a Circle**

Perf. 12
50.00 50.00

## HUACHO
(See Note under "Provisional Issues")

 (T)

## 1881
8N14 D1 10c on 1c bis ... 110.00 100.00
8N15 D3 10c on 10c org ... 110.00 100.00

Postage Due Stamps of Peru Surcharged in Black

Perf. 12

**Same Overprint in Black on Provisional Issues of Arequipa**

## 1884
8N10 A19 5c blue ... 16.50 10.00
8N11 A20 10c slate ... 16.50 10.00

Imperf

**Same Overprint in Black on Regular Issues of Arequipa**

8N12 A5 5c olive ... 27.50 27.50
8N13 A6 10c gray ... 8.00 8.00

8N7 A19 5c blue ... 50.00 50.00

## MOQUEGUA
(See Note under "Provisional Issues")

 (MOQUE-GUA.)

## 1884
9N1 A19 5c blue ... 8.00 8.00
9N2 A20 10c green ... 6.00 6.00
9N3 A20 10c slate ... 30.00 30.00
Nos. 9N1-9N3 (3)

Unwmk. Perf. 12

**Regular Issues of Peru Overprinted in Black**

**PAITA**
(See Note under "Provisional Issues")

 (PAITA)

## 1884
10N10 A19 5c blue ... 65.00
10N11 A20 10c slate ... 25.00

Imperf

**Same Overprint in Violet on Provisional Issue of Arequipa**

10N12 A6 10c gray ... 70.00 65.00

## 1885
10N9 A6 10c gray ... 57.50 50.00

**Same Overprint in Violet on Provisional Issue of Arequipa**

Imperf.

**Regular Issues of Peru Overprinted in Violet**

**PASCO**
(See Note under "Provisional Issues")

 (PASCO)

## 1884
12N1 A19 5c blue (M) ... 16.00 12.50
12N2 A20 10c green (M) ... 35.00 30.00
12N3 A20 10c slate (Bk) ... 65.00 57.50
Nos. 12N1-12N3 (3) ... 116.00 100.00

Unwmk. Perf. 12

**Regular Issues of Peru Overprinted in Magenta or Black**

**PISCO**
(See Note under "Provisional Issues")

 (PISCO)

## 1884
13N1 A19 5c blue ... 190.00 160.00

Unwmk. Perf. 12

**Regular Issue of Peru Overprinted in Black**

**PIURA**
(See Note under "Provisional Issues")

 (PIURA)

## 1884
11N4 A19 5c blue ... 22.50 22.50

**Red Overprint**
11N5 A19 5c ultra ... 22.50 22.50
a. 5c blue ... 22.50 22.50

Violet Overprint. Letters 5½mm High

Overprint lacks ornaments on #11N4-11N5.

**Black Overprint**
11N1 A19 5c blue ... 16.00 15.00
11N2 A20 10c green ... 65.00 30.00
11N3 A20 10c slate ... 65.00 22.50

Unwmk. Perf. 12

## PERU

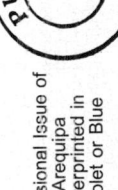

**1884 Unwmk.**    **Perf. 12**
14N1 A19 5c blue ... 20.00 10.00
  a. 5c ultramarine ... 13.50
14N2 A21 20c brn red ... 82.50 82.50
14N3 A22 50c green ... 200.00 200.00

**Same Overprint in Black on Provisional Issues of Peru of 1881**
14N4 A17 1c orange (Bl) ... 22.50 22.50
14N5 A18 2c rose (Bl) ... 40.00 40.00
14N6 A19 5c ultra (R) ... 50.00 50.00

**Regular Issues of Peru Overprinted in Violet, Black or Blue**
14N7 A19 5c bl (V) ... 16.00 10.00
  a. 5c ultramarine (Bk) ... 16.00 10.00
  b. 5c ultramarine (Bk) ... 16.00 10.00
14N8 A21 20c brn red (Bk) ... 82.50 82.50
14N9 A21 20c brn red (Bl) ... 82.50 82.50

**Same Overprint in Black on Provisional Issues of Peru of 1881**
14N10 A17 1c grn (R) ... 22.50 22.50
14N11 A19 5c bl (R) ... 22.50 22.50
  a. 5c ultramarine (R) ... 40.00 40.00

**(PIURA)**
**Regular Issues of Peru Overprinted in Black**
14N13 A19 5c blue ... 4.00 3.50
14N14 A21 20c brn red ... 82.50 82.50

**(PIURA / VAPOR)**
**Regular Issues of Peru Overprinted in Black**
14N15 A19 5c blue ... 70.00 65.00
14N16 A21 20c brn red ... 140.00 125.00

**Same Overprint on Postage Due Stamp of Peru**
14N18 D3 10c orange ... 80.00 67.50

**(PUNO 17)**
**Provisional Issue of Arequipa Overprinted in Violet or Blue**

**1882-83 Unwmk.**    **Imperf.**
15N1 A1 10c blue (V) ... 16.00 16.00
  a. 10c ultramarine (V) ... 20.00 20.00
15N3 A2 25c red (V) ... 25.00 25.00
15N4 A4 10c dl rose (Bl) ... 25.00 25.00
  a. 10c vermilion (Bl) ... 25.00 25.00

The overprint also exists on 5s yellow of Arequipa.

Diameter of outer circle 20½mm, PUNO 11½mm wide, M 3½mm wide. Other types of this overprint are fraudulent.

**1884**    **Perf. 12**
15N5 A17 1c orange ... 12.00 12.00
15N6 A18 2c violet ... 35.00 35.00
15N7 A19 5c blue ... 8.25 8.25

**Violet Overprint**
15N8 A19 5c blue ... 8.25 8.25
  a. 5c ultramarine ... 12.00 12.00

**Same Overprint in Black on Provisional Issues of Arequipa**
**1885**    **Imperf.**
15N10 A5 5c olive ... 16.50 13.50
15N11 A6 10c gray ... 5.50 5.50
15N12 A8 10c olive ... 10.00 10.00

---

**Regular Issues of Peru Overprinted in Magenta**

   **Perf. 12**
   10.00 8.25
   13.50 12.00
   5.50 5.50
   11.00 11.00
   82.50 82.50

**1884**
15N13 A17 1c orange
15N14 A18 2c violet
15N15 A19 5c ultramarine
  a. 5c ultramarine
15N16 A20 10c green
15N17 A21 20c brn red
15N18 A22 50c green

**(YCA)**
**YCA**
(See Note under "Provisional Issues")

**Regular Issues of Peru Overprinted in Violet**

**1884 Unwmk.**    **Perf. 12**
16N1 A17 1c orange ... 40.00 40.00
16N3 A19 5c blue ... 12.00 6.75

**Black Overprint**
16N5 A19 5c blue ... 10.00 5.25

**Magenta Overprint**
16N6 A19 5c blue ... 10.00 5.25
16N7 A20 10c slate ... 30.00 30.00

**(YCA / VAPOR)**
**Regular Issues of Peru Overprinted in Black**
16N12 A19 5c blue ... 150.00 140.00
16N13 A21 20c brown ... 190.00 160.00

**Regular Issues of Peru Overprinted in Carmine**
16N14 A19 5c blue ... 150.00 140.00
16N15 A20 10c slate ... 190.00 160.00

**(YCA / VAPOR)**
**Same, with Additional Overprint**
16N21 A19 5c blue ... 160.00 150.00
16N22 A21 20c brn red ... 250.00 225.00

Various other stamps exist with the overprints "YCA" and "YCA VAPOR" but they are not known to have been issued. Some of them were made to fill a dealer's order and others are reprints or merely cancellations.

# PHILIPPINES

ˌfi-lə-ˈpēnz

LOCATION — Group of about 7,100 islands and islets in the Malay Archipelago, north of Borneo, in the North Pacific Ocean
GOVT. — Republic
AREA — 115,830 sq. mi.
POP. — 68,614,536 (1995)
CAPITAL — Manila

The islands were ceded to the United States by Spain in 1898. On November 15, 1935, they were given their independence, subject to a transition period which ended July 4, 1946. On that date the Commonwealth became the Republic of the Philippines.

20 Cuartos = 1 Real
100 Centavos de Peso = 1 Peso (1864)
100 Centimos de Escudo = 1 Escudo (1871)
100 Centimos de Peseta = 1 Peseta (1872)
1000 Milesimas de Peso = 100 Centimos or Centavos = 1 Peso (1878)
100 Cents = 1 Dollar (1899)
100 Centavos = 1 Peso (1906)
100 Centavos (Sentimos) = 1 Peso (Piso) (1946)

**Catalogue values for unused stamps in this country are for Never Hinged items, beginning with Scott 500 in the regular postage section, Scott B1 in the semi-postal section, Scott C64 in the air post section, Scott E11 in the special delivery section, Scott J23 in the postage due section, and Scott O50 in the officials section.**

### Watermarks

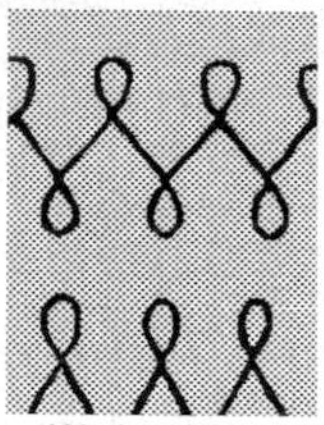
Wmk. 104 — Loops

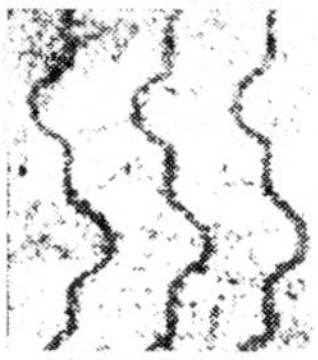
Wmk. 257 — Curved Wavy Lines

Watermark 104: loops from different watermark rows may or may not be directly opposite each other.

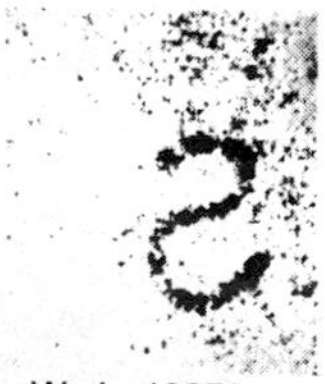
Wmk. 190PI — Single-lined PIPS

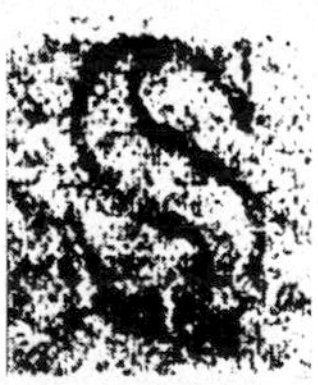
Wmk. 191PI — Double-lined PIPS

Watermark 191 has double-lined USPS.

Wmk. 233 — "Harrison & Sons, London." in Script

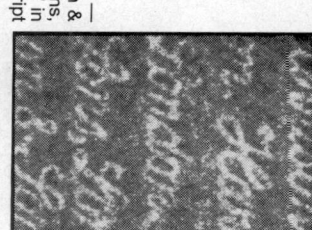

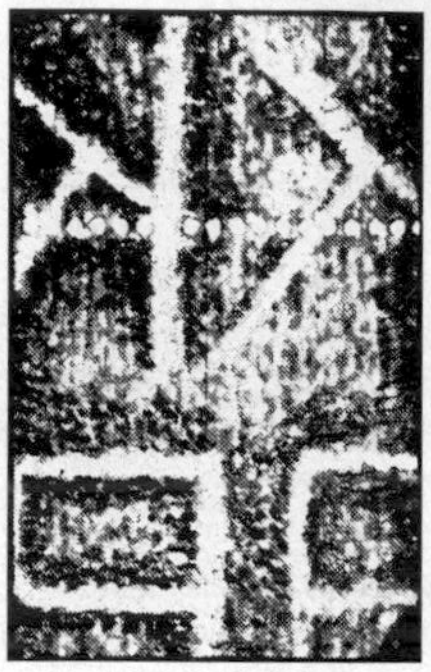
Wmk. 372 — "K" and "P" Multiple

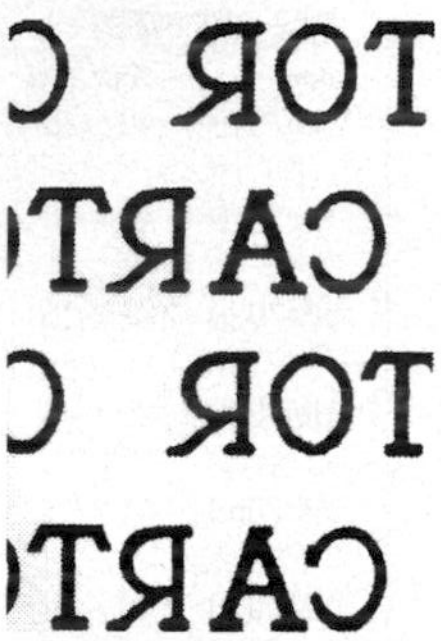
Wmk. 385

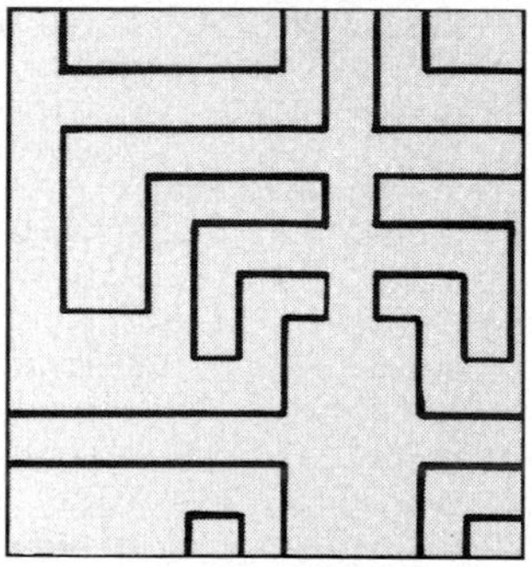
Wmk. 389

Wmk. 391 — Natl. Crest, Rising Sun and Eagle, with inscr. "REPUBLIKA / NG / PILIPINAS," "KAWANIHAN / NG / KOREO"

### Issued under Spanish Dominion

The stamps of Philippine Islands punched with a round hole were used on telegraph receipts or had been withdrawn from use and punched to indicate that they were no longer available for postage. In this condition they sell for less, as compared to postally used copies.

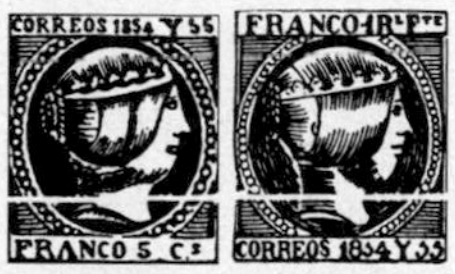
Queen Isabella II
A1 A2

| 1854 | Unwmk. | Engr. | *Imperf.* |
|---|---|---|---|
| 1 | A1 5c orange | 1,800. | 300. |
| *a.* | 5c brown orange | 2,000. | 375. |
| 2 | A1 10c carmine | 550. | 240. |
| *a.* | 10c pale rose | 875. | 375. |
| 4 | A2 1r blue | 600. | 275. |
| *a.* | 1r slate blue | 775. | 300. |
| *b.* | 1r ultramarine | 750. | 300. |
| *c.* | "CORROS," (pos. 26) | *3,400.* | *1,250.* |
| 5 | A2 2r green | 950. | 190. |
| *a.* | 2r yellow green | 825. | 425. |

Forty varieties of each value.
The 10c black was never issued. Value $5,000.
For overprints see Nos. 25-25A.

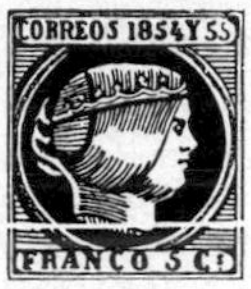
A3

| 1855 | | | Litho. |
|---|---|---|---|
| 6 | A3 5c red | 1,500. | 425. |

Four varieties.

**Redrawn**

| | | | |
|---|---|---|---|
| 7 | A3 5c vermilion | *7,500.* | *850.* |

In the redrawn stamp the inner circle is smaller and is not broken by the labels at top and bottom. Only one variety.

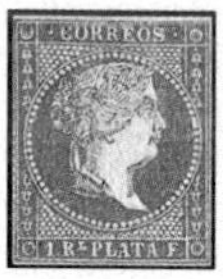
Queen Isabella II — A4

| 1856 | Typo. | Wmk. 104 | |
|---|---|---|---|
| 8 | A4 1r gray green | 55.00 | 80.00 |
| 9 | A4 2r carmine | 275.00 | 190.00 |

Nos. 8 and 9 used can be distinguished from Cuba Nos. 2 and 3 only by the cancellations.
For overprints, see Nos. 26-27.

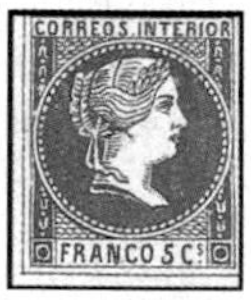
Queen Isabella II — A5

Dot after "CORREOS"

| 1859, Jan. 1 | Litho. | Unwmk. | |
|---|---|---|---|
| 10 | A5 5c vermilion | 12.50 | 6.25 |
| *a.* | 5c scarlet | 17.00 | 8.50 |
| *b.* | 5c orange | 25.00 | 12.00 |
| 11 | A5 10c rose | 12.50 | *20.00* |

Four varieties of each value, repeated in the sheet.
For overprint see No. 28.

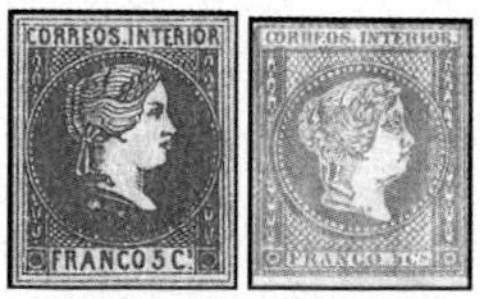
Dot after CORREOS
A6 A7

| 1861-62 | | | |
|---|---|---|---|
| 12 | A6 5c vermilion | 29.00 | 32.50 |
| 13 | A7 5c dull red ('62) | 150.00 | 50.00 |

No. 12, one variety only, repeated in sheet.
For overprint see No. 29.

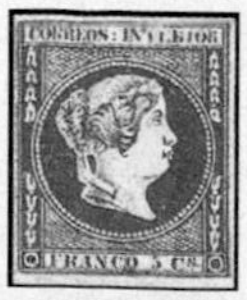
Colon after CORREOS — A8

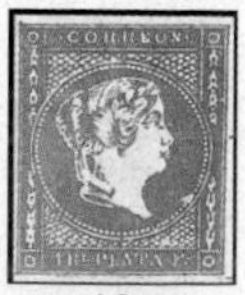
A8a

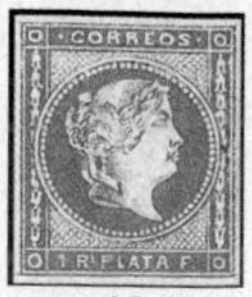
A9

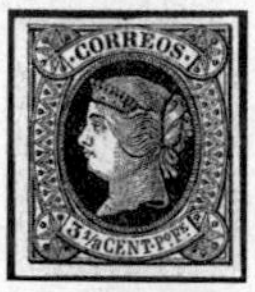
A10

| 1863 | | | | |
|---|---|---|---|---|
| 14 | A8 | 5c vermilion | 11.00 | 7.00 |
| 15 | A8 | 10c carmine | 30.00 | *55.00* |
| 16 | A8 | 1r violet | 625.00 | 350.00 |
| 17 | A8 | 2r blue | 525.00 | 300.00 |
| 18 | A8a | 1r gray grn | 250.00 | 125.00 |
| 20 | A9 | 1r emerald | 140.00 | 40.00 |
| *a.* | | 1r green | 150.00 | 42.50 |
| | | *Nos. 14-20 (6)* | 1,581. | 877.00 |

No. 18 has "CORREOS" 10½mm long, the point of the bust is rounded and is about 1mm from the circle which contains 94 pearls.
No. 20 has "CORREOS" 11mm long, and the bust ends in a sharp point which nearly touches the circle of 76 pearls.
For overprints see Nos. 30-34.

| 1864 | | | | Typo. |
|---|---|---|---|---|
| 21 | A10 | 3⅛c blk, *yel* | 3.25 | 1.60 |
| 22 | A10 | 6⅞c grn, *rose* | 5.75 | 1.60 |
| 23 | A10 | 12⅘c blue, *sal* | 6.00 | 1.40 |
| 24 | A10 | 25c red, *buff* | 8.50 | 3.00 |
| | | *Nos. 21-24 (4)* | 23.50 | 7.60 |

For overprints see Nos. 35-38.

Cuba Nos. 2-3 and Preceding Issues Handstamped

**HABILITADO**
**POR LA**
**NACION**

| 1868-74 | | | | |
|---|---|---|---|---|
| 24A | A1 | 5c orange ('74) | *7,000.* | *6,000.* |
| 25 | A2 | 1r sl bl ('74) | *1,850.* | *800.00* |
| *b.* | | "CORROS," (pos. 26) | | *3,000.* |
| 25A | A2 | 2r grn ('74) | *3,500.* | *775.00* |
| 26 | A4 | 1r grn, *bl* ('73) | 160.00 | 70.00 |
| 27 | A4 | 2r car, *bl* ('73) | 300.00 | 200.00 |
| 27A | A5 | 5c vermilion ('74) | *3,000.* | *1,500.* |
| 28 | A5 | 10c rose ('74) | 60.00 | 40.00 |
| 29 | A7 | 5c dull red ('73) | 225.00 | 110.00 |
| 30 | A8 | 5c ver ('72) | 100.00 | 30.00 |
| 31 | A8 | 1r vio ('72) | 650.00 | 375.00 |
| 32 | A8 | 2r bl ('72) | 475.00 | 275.00 |
| 33 | A8a | 1r gray grn ('71) | 150.00 | 40.00 |
| 34 | A9 | 1r emer ('71) | 45.00 | 19.00 |
| *a.* | | 1r green | 50.00 | 24.00 |
| 35 | A10 | 3⅛c blk, *yellow* | 9.00 | 4.50 |
| 36 | A10 | 6⅞c grn, *rose* | 9.00 | 4.50 |
| 37 | A10 | 12⅘c bl, *salmon* | 30.00 | 15.00 |
| 38 | A10 | 25c red, *buff* | 27.50 | 14.00 |

Imperforates

Imperforates of designs A11-A14 probably are from proof or trial sheets.

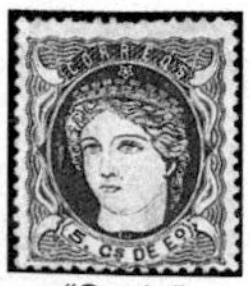
"Spain"
A11

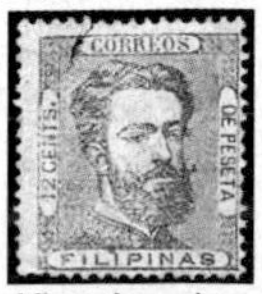
King Amadeo
A12

| 1871 | | Typo. | *Perf. 14* | |
|---|---|---|---|---|
| 39 | A11 | 5c blue | 55.00 | 5.50 |
| 40 | A11 | 10c deep green | 7.25 | 4.50 |
| 41 | A11 | 20c brown | 65.00 | 30.00 |
| 42 | A11 | 40c rose | 80.00 | 35.00 |
| | | *Nos. 39-42 (4)* | 207.25 | 75.00 |

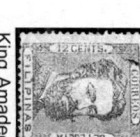

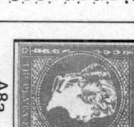

## 1872

| No. | Type | Description | Unused | Used |
|---|---|---|---|---|
| 43 | A12 | 12c rose | 12.50 | 4.00 |
| 44 | A12 | 16c blue | 120.00 | 27.50 |
| 45 | A12 | 25c gray lilac | 9.25 | 4.00 |
| 46 | A12 | 62c violet | 27.50 | 7.00 |
| 47 | A12 | 1p25c yellow brn | 55.00 | 22.50 |
| | | | 224.25 | 65.00 |

Nos. 43-47 (5)

A 12c in deep blue and a 62c in rose exist but were not issued. Value $30 each.

"Peace" A13

## 1874

| No. | Type | Description | Unused | Used |
|---|---|---|---|---|
| 48 | A13 | 12c gray lilac | 17.00 | 4.00 |
| 49 | A13 | 25c ultra | 6.00 | 2.00 |
| 50 | A13 | 62c rose | 50.00 | 4.00 |
| 51 | A13 | 1p25c brown | 250.00 | 62.50 |
| | | | 323.00 | 72.50 |

Nos. 48-51 (4)

King Alfonso XII A14

## 1875-77

| No. | Type | Description | Unused | Used |
|---|---|---|---|---|
| 52 | A14 | 2c rose | 3.00 | .75 |
| 53 | A14 | 2c dk blue ('77) | 200.00 | 80.00 |
| 54 | A14 | 6c ultra ('77) | 11.00 | 13.00 |
| 55 | A14 | 10c blue ('77) | 4.00 | .75 |
| 56 | A14 | 10c lilac ('76) | 4.00 | .75 |
| 57 | A14 | 20c vio brn ('76) | 13.00 | 9.25 |
| 58 | A14 | 25c dp green ('76) | 11.00 | 2.00 |
| | | | 246.00 | 106.50 |

Nos. 52-58 (7)

Nos. 52, 63 Handstamp Surcharged in Black or Blue

## 1877-79

| No. | Type | Description | Unused | Used |
|---|---|---|---|---|
| 59 | A14 | 12c on 2c rose (Bk) | 67.50 | 21.00 |
| 60 | A16 | 12c on 25m blk (Bk) ('79) | 80.00 | 35.00 |
| 61 | A16 | 12c on 25m blk (Bl) ('79) | 275.00 | 150.00 |
| | | | 422.50 | 206.00 |

Nos. 59-61 (3)

Surcharge exists inverted on Nos. 59 and 60, values unused, $525, $775, respectively. Surcharge exists double on No. 59, value unused $400.

Imperforates of type A16 probably are from proof or trial sheets.
For surcharges see Nos. 60-61, 72-75.

Stamps of 1878-79 Surcharged:

UNIVERSAL DE CONVENIO

A16

## 1878-79 Typo.

| No. | Type | Description | Unused | Used |
|---|---|---|---|---|
| 62 | A16 | 25m black | 3.25 | .40 |
| 63 | A16 | 25m green ('79) | 65.00 | 60.00 |
| 64 | A16 | 50m dull lilac | 32.50 | 9.75 |
| 65 | A16 | 0.0625 (62½m) gray | 62.50 | 14.50 |
| 66 | A16 | 100m car ('79) | 105.00 | 35.00 |
| 67 | A16 | 100m yel grn ('79) | 9.75 | 2.50 |
| 68 | A16 | 125m blue | 5.75 | .45 |
| 69 | A16 | 200m rose ('79) | 35.00 | 5.50 |
| 70 | A16 | 200m vio rose ('79) | 600.00 | |
| 71 | A16 | 250m bister ('79) | 12.50 | 2.50 |
| | | | 631.25 | 730.60 |

Nos. 62-71 (10)

## 1879

| No. | Type | Description | Unused | Used |
|---|---|---|---|---|
| 72 | A16 (a) | 2c on 25m grn | 40.00 | 8.00 |
| b. | | Inverted surcharge | 300.00 | 175.00 |
| 73 | A16 (a) | 8c on 100m car | 35.00 | 6.50 |
| a. | | "COREROS" | 110.00 | 57.50 |

UNIVERSAL DE CONVENIO
CORREOS
HABILITADO 2 cent de peso

a / b

| No. | Type | Description | Unused | Used |
|---|---|---|---|---|
| 74 | A16 (a) | 2c on 25m grn | 160.00 | 40.00 |
| 75 | A16 (b) | 8c on 100m car | 160.00 | 94.50 |
| | | | 395.00 | |

Nos. 72-75 (4)

A19

Original state: The medallion is surrounded by a heavy line of color of nearly even thickness, touching the line below "Filipinas"; the opening in the hair above the temple is narrow and pointed.

1st retouch: The line around the medallion is thin, except at the upper right, and does not touch the horizontal line above it; the opening in the hair is slightly wider and rounded; the lock of hair above the forehead is shaped like a broad "V" and ends in a point; there is a faint white line below it, which is not found on the original. The shape of the hair and the width of the white line vary.

2nd retouch: The lock of hair is less pointed; the white line is much broader.

## 1880-88 Typo.

| No. | Type | Description | Unused | Used |
|---|---|---|---|---|
| 76 | A19 | 2c carmine | .75 | .65 |
| 77 | A19 | 2c brown | 6.50 | 1.50 |
| 78 | A19 | 2½c ultra ('82) | 1.00 | 1.75 |
| 79 | A19 | 2½c ultra, 1st retouch ('83) | .75 | 1.50 |
| 80 | A19 | 2½c ultra, 2nd retouch ('86) | 8.50 | 3.50 |
| 81 | A19 | 5c gray ('82) | .75 | 1.50 |
| 82 | A19 | 5c gray blue | 1.25 | 9.00 |
| 83 | A19 | 8c dp green ('82) | 5.75 | 5.25 |
| 84 | A19 | 8c yellow brn | 30.00 | 3.50 |
| 85 | A19 | 10c green ('88) | 375.00 | 3.50 |
| 86 | A19 | 10c brown violet | 3.00 | 1.50 |
| 87 | A19 | 12½c brt rose ('82) | 1.50 | 3.75 |
| 88 | A19 | 25c dk brm ('82) | 65.25 | 32.65 |

Nos. 76-83,85-88 (12)

See #89, 110-111. For surcharges see #89-108, 110-111.

Surcharges exist double or inverted on many of Nos. 89-136.

Stamps and Type of 1880-86 Handstamp Surcharged in Black, Green, Yellow or Red:

Design A19 Black Surcharge

## 1881-88

| No. | Type | Description | Unused | Used |
|---|---|---|---|---|
| 89 | (c) | 2c on 2½c brn | 3.75 | 2.00 |
| 91 | (f) | 10c on 2½c ultra (#80) ('87) | 1.75 | 2.75 |
| 92 | (d) | 20c on 8c on 2r bl ('83) | 5.50 | 2.75 |
| 93 | (d) | 20c on 8c (#78) ('83) | 8.50 | |
| | | | 160.00 | 275.00 |
| 94 | (d) | 2r on 2½c ultra (#78; '83) | 1.75 | 85.00 |
| a. | | On No. 79 | 5.50 | 50.00 |
| b. | | On No. 80 | 50.00 | 85.00 |

Most used copies of No. 93 are hole-punched. Postally used copies (#98A) are rare.

## Green or Yellow (#98A) Surcharge

| No. | Type | Description | Unused | Used |
|---|---|---|---|---|
| 95 | (e) | 8c on 2c car | 6.00 | 1.90 |
| 95A | (d+e) | 8c on 1r on 2c car ('83) | 95.00 | 175.00 |
| 96 | (d) | 10c on 2c car | 4.75 | 1.90 |
| 97 | (d) | 1r on 2c car ('83) | 110.00 | 35.00 |
| 98 | (d) | 1r on 5c gray bl ('83) | 5.50 | 2.75 |
| 98A | (d) | 1r on 5c gray | 105.00 | 175.00 |
| 99 | (d) | 1r on 8c brn ('83) | 8.50 | 2.75 |

## Red Surcharge

| No. | Type | Description | Unused | Used |
|---|---|---|---|---|
| 100 | (f) | 1c on 2½c ultra (#79; '87) | 1.00 | .75 |
| 101 | (f) | 1c on 2½c ultra (#80; '87) | 3.00 | 1.50 |
| 102 | (d) | 16c on 2½c ultra (#78; '83) | 8.50 | 2.75 |
| 103 | (d) | 1r on 2c car ('83) | 5.50 | 2.75 |
| 104 | (d) | 1r on 5c bl gray ('83) | 16.00 | 4.50 |

Handstamp Surcharged in Magenta

## 1887

| No. | Type | Description | Unused | Used |
|---|---|---|---|---|
| 105 | A19 (g) | 8c on 2½c (#79) | 1.00 | .75 |
| 106 | A19 (g) | 8c on 2½c (#80) | 3.75 | 2.50 |

## 1888

| No. | Type | Description | Unused | Used |
|---|---|---|---|---|
| 107 | A19 (h) | 2½c on 1c gray grn | 1.50 | .85 |
| 108 | A19 (h) | 2½c on 5c bl gray | 1.70 | .75 |
| 110 | N1 (h) | 2½c on 50m bis | 1.60 | .70 |
| 111 | A19 (h) | 2½c on 10c grm | 1.60 | .55 |
| | | Nos. 107-111 (5) | 8.00 | 3.95 |

No. 109 is surcharged on a newspaper stamp of 1886-89 and has the inscriptions shown on cut N1.

On Revenue Stamps

R1  / R2  / R3

Handstamp Surcharged or Overprinted in Black, Yellow, Green, Red, Blue or Magenta:

HABILITADO PARA CORREOS

m

## 1881-88 Black Surcharge

| No. | Type | Description | Unused | Used |
|---|---|---|---|---|
| 112 | R1 (c) | 2c on 10c bis | 42.50 | 11.00 |
| 113 | R1 (i) | 2½c on 10c bis | 9.00 | 1.50 |
| 114 | R1 (i) | 2½c on 2r bl | 175.00 | 110.00 |
| 115 | R1 (i) | 8c on 10c bis | 360.00 | 260.00 |
| 116 | R1 (i) | 8c on 10c bis | 7.25 | 1.75 |
| 117 | R1 (d) | 1r on 10c bis gray bl ('83) | 6.75 | 3.25 |
| 118 | R1 (d) | 1r on 12½c gray bl ('82) | 10.00 | 3.50 |
| 119 | R1 (d) | 1r on 10c bis ('82) | 6.00 | 1.90 |

## Yellow Surcharge

| No. | Type | Description | Unused | Used |
|---|---|---|---|---|
| 120 | R2 (e) | 2c on 200m grn ('82) | 5.50 | 2.50 |
| 121 | R1 (d) | 16c on 2r bl ('83) | 4.50 | 2.25 |

## Green Surcharge

| No. | Type | Description | Unused | Used |
|---|---|---|---|---|
| 122 | R1 (d) | 1r on 10c bis ('83) | 5.50 | 3.25 |

## Red Surcharge

| No. | Type | Description | Unused | Used |
|---|---|---|---|---|
| 123 | R1 (d+e) | 2r on 8c on 2r blue | 40.00 | 25.00 |
| a. | | On 8c on 2r blue (d+d) | 60.00 | 55.00 |

j / k

| No. | Type | Description | Unused | Used |
|---|---|---|---|---|
| 124 | R1(d) | 1r on 12½c gray bl ('83) | 14.00 | 11.00 |
| 125 | R1(k) | 6½c on 12½c gray bl ('85) | 5.75 | 11.00 |
| 126 | R3(d) | 1r on 10p bis ('83) | 85.00 | 20.00 |
| 127 | R1(m) | 1r green | 290.00 | 360.00 |
| 127A | R1(m) | 2r blue | 525.00 | 625.00 |
| 127B | R1(d) | 1r on 1r green | 375.00 | 360.00 |
| 128 | R2(d) | 1r on 1p grn ('83) | 30.00 | 13.00 |
| 129 | R2(d) | 1r on 200m grn ('83) | 70.00 | 130.00 |
| 129A | R1(d) | 2r on 2r blue ('83) | 250.00 | 425.00 |

The surcharge on No. 129A is pale red.

## Blue Surcharge

| No. | Type | Description | Unused | Used |
|---|---|---|---|---|
| 129B | R1(m) | 1r on 2c car ('81) | 350.00 | 525.00 |

## Magenta Surcharge

| No. | Type | Description | Unused | Used |
|---|---|---|---|---|
| 130 | R2(h) | 2½c on 200m grn ('88) | 3.75 | 1.50 |
| 131 | R2(h) | 2½c on 20c bis ('88) | 11.00 | 5.00 |

On Telegraph Stamps

T1  / T2

Surcharged in Red, or Black

## 1883-88

| No. | Type | Description | Unused | Used |
|---|---|---|---|---|
| 132 | T1 (d) | 2r on 250m ultra (R) | 6.75 | 3.25 |
| 133 | T1 (d) | 20c on 250m ultra (R) | 575.00 | 325.00 |
| 134 | T1 (d) | 2r on 250m ultra | 8.75 | 4.00 |
| 135 | T1 (d) | 1r on 20c on 250m ultra (R & Bk) | 8.00 | 4.00 |

## Magenta Surcharge

| No. | Type | Description | Unused | Used |
|---|---|---|---|---|
| 136 | T2 (h) | 2½c on 1c bis ('88) | .80 | .55 |

Most, if not all, used copies of No. 133 are hole-punched. Used value is for examples with hole punches.

Type of 1880-86 Redrawn

## 1887-89

| No. | Type | Description | Unused | Used |
|---|---|---|---|---|
| 137 | A19 | 50m bister | .55 | 5.00 |
| 138 | A19 | 1c gray green ('88) | .55 | 4.00 |
| 139 | A19 | 8c yellow brn ('88) | .60 | .50 |
| | | | 8.50 | 40.00 |

Nos. 107,110,139 (3)

King Alfonso XIII — A36

## 1890-97 Typo.

| No. | Type | Description | Unused | Used |
|---|---|---|---|---|
| 140 | A36 | 1c violet ('92) | .60 | 1.90 |
| 141 | A36 | 1c rose ('95) | 15.00 | 11.00 |
| 142 | A36 | 1c blue grn | 2.00 | 3.25 |
| 143 | A36 | 2c claret ('97) | 12.00 | 25.00 |
| 144 | A36 | 2c violet ('92) | .20 | .20 |
| 145 | A36 | 2c claret | .20 | .20 |
| 146 | A36 | 2c dk brown | .20 | .20 |
| 147 | A36 | 2c gray brn ('94) | .20 | .30 |
| 148 | A36 | 2c ultra ('96) | .30 | 1.90 |
| 149 | A36 | 2½c dull blue ('92) | .70 | 1.90 |
| 150 | A36 | 2½c ol gray ('92) | .25 | 1.10 |
| 151 | A36 | 5c dark blue | .45 | 1.10 |
| 152 | A36 | 5c dk gray | .70 | 1.10 |
| 153 | A36 | 5c green ('92) | .60 | .50 |
| 155 | A36 | 5c violet brn | 8.00 | 11.00 |
| 156 | A36 | 5c blue grn ('96) | 5.25 | 6.25 |
| 157 | A36 | 6c brown vio ('92) | .25 | 1.10 |
| 158 | A36 | 6c red orange ('94) | 1.00 | 1.90 |
| 159 | A36 | 6c car rose ('96) | 5.25 | 6.25 |
| 160 | A36 | 8c yellow grn | .25 | .25 |
| 161 | A36 | 8c ultra ('92) | .60 | .25 |
| 162 | A36 | 8c red brown ('94) | .70 | .70 |
| 163 | A36 | 10c blue grn ('91) | 1.50 | 1.90 |
| 164 | A36 | 10c pale claret | 1.25 | .35 |
| 165 | A36 | 10c claret ('92) | .70 | .25 |
| 166 | A36 | 10c ol yel brn ('96) | .70 | .25 |
| 167 | A36 | 12½c yellow ('92) | .25 | 1.10 |
| 168 | A36 | 12½c red orange ('92) | .70 | 1.10 |
| 169 | A36 | 15c car ('92) | .70 | .25 |

170 A36 15c rose ('94) 1.75 .70
171 A36 15c bl grn ('96) 1.90 1.75
172 A36 20c rose 65.00 32.50
173 A36 20c sal ('91) 19.00 16.00
174 A36 20c gray brn ('92) 3.75 *9.00*
175 A36 20c dk vio ('94) 15.00 *16.00*
176 A36 20c org ('96) 4.00 2.00
177 A36 25c brown 8.00 4.00
178 A36 25c dull bl ('91) 2.00 *3.25*
179 A36 40c dk vio ('97) 14.00 *37.50*
180 A36 80c claret ('97) 30.00 *42.50*
*Nos. 140-180 (40)* 225.05 *246.45*

Many of Nos. 140-180 exist imperf and in different colors. These are considered to be proofs.

Stamps of Previous Issues Handstamp Surcharged in Blue, Red, Black or Violet

**1897**

**Blue Surcharge**

181 A36 5c on 5c green 3.75 2.50
182 A36 15c on 15c red brn 5.50 1.75
183 A36 20c on 20c gray brn 12.00 *12.00*

**Red Surcharge**

185 A36 5c on 5c green 4.50 4.75

**Black Surcharge**

187 A36 5c on 5c green 67.50 *175.00*
188 A36 15c on 15c rose 5.50 1.75
189 A36 20c on 20c dk vio 35.00 18.00
190 A36 20c on 25c brown 25.00 *25.00*

**Violet Surcharge**

191 A36 15c on 15c rose 9.75 6.50
*Nos. 181-191 (9)* 168.50 247.25

Inverted, double and other variations of this surcharge exist.

The 5c on 5c blue gray (#81a) was released during US Administration. The surcharge is a mixture of red and black inks.

*Impressions in violet black are believed to be reprints. The following varieties are known: 5c on 2⁴⁄₈c olive gray, 5c on 5c blue green, 5c on 25c brown, 15c on 15c rose, 15c on 15c red brown, 20c on 20c gray brown, 20c on 20c dark violet, 20c on 25c brown. These surcharges are to be found double, inverted, etc.*

King Alfonso XIII — A39

**1898** **Typo.**

192 A39 1m orange brown .20 1.00
193 A39 2m orange brown .20 *1.25*
194 A39 3m orange brown .20 *1.25*
195 A39 4m orange brown 7.00 *30.00*
196 A39 5m orange brown .20 2.00
197 A39 1c black violet .20 .45
198 A39 2c dk bl grn .20 .45
199 A39 3c dk brown .20 .45
200 A39 4c orange 17.50 *35.00*
201 A39 5c car rose .20 .45
202 A39 6c dk blue .95 *1.25*
203 A39 8c gray brown .40 .25
204 A39 10c vermilion 1.50 1.00
205 A39 15c dull ol grn 1.50 .85
206 A39 20c maroon 1.60 1.10
207 A39 40c violet .95 *1.25*
208 A39 60c black 3.50 3.00
209 A39 80c red brown 16.50 4.00
210 A39 1p yellow green 11.50 *13.00*
211 A39 2p slate blue 25.00 *16.00*
*Nos. 192-211 (20)* 89.50 *114.00*

Nos. 192-211 exist imperf. Value $800.

The Spanish surrendered in May 1898. Some Filipinos continued to fight until 1901. During this period provisional stamps were created in several areas. Some of these stamps may have been totally philatelic. See the Scott Specialized Catalogue of U. S. Stamps for stamps issued by Gen. Aguinaldo's Filipino Revolutionary Government.

## Issued under US Administration

Regular Issues of the United States Overprinted in Black

On US No. 260

**1899-1900** **Unwmk.** ***Perf. 12***

212 A96 50c orange 375.00 225.00

On US Nos. 279, 279d, 267, 268, 281, 282C, 283, 284, 275 and 275a

**Wmk. 191**

213 A87 1c yellow grn 3.00 .60
*a.* Inverted overprint *32,500.*
214 A88 2c red, IV 1.25 .60
*a.* 2c org red, type IV ('01) 1.25 .60
*b.* Booklet pane, 6 #214 ('00) 250.00 200.00
*c.* 2c reddish car, type IV 1.90 .90
*d.* 2c rose car, type IV 2.25 1.10
215 A89 3c purple 7.50 1.25
216 A91 5c blue 7.50 .90
*a.* Inverted overprint *3,750.*
217 A94 10c brown, I 25.00 4.00
217A A94 10c org brn, II 125.00 25.00
218 A95 15c olive grn 40.00 8.00
219 A96 50c orange 125.00 37.50
*a.* 50c red orange 250.00
*Nos. 213-219 (8)* 334.25 77.85

No. 216a is valued in the grade of fine.

On US Nos. 280b, 282 and 272

**1901**

220 A90 4c orange brn 27.50 5.00
221 A92 6c lake 35.00 7.00
222 A93 8c violet brn 35.00 7.50
*Nos. 220-222 (3)* 97.50 19.50

**On US Nos. 276, 276A, 277a and 278**

**Red Overprint**

223 A97 $1 blk, type I 475. 275.
223A A97 $1 blk, type II 2,400. 750.
224 A98 $2 dk blue 475. 350.
225 A99 $5 dk green 825. *900.*

On US Nos. 300-313 and shades

**1903-04**

226 A115 1c blue green 5.00 .30
227 A116 2c carmine 7.50 1.10
228 A117 3c brt violet 67.50 12.50
229 A118 4c brown ('04) 75.00 22.50
*a.* 4c orange brown 75.00 20.00
230 A119 5c blue 13.50 1.00
231 A120 6c brnsh lake ('04) 80.00 22.50
232 A121 8c vio blk ('04) 45.00 15.00
233 A122 10c pale red brn ('04) 25.00 2.25
*a.* 10c red brown 30.00 3.00
*b.* Pair, one without ovpt. *1,500.*
234 A123 13c purple blk 35.00 17.50
*a.* 13c brown violet 35.00 17.50
235 A124 15c olive grn 60.00 15.00
236 A125 50c orange 125.00 35.00
*Nos. 226-236 (11)* 538.50 144.65

**Red Overprint**

237 A126 $1 black 475. 275.
238 A127 $2 dk blue ('04) 800. 850.
239 A128 $5 dk green ('04) 975. *5,000.*

On US Nos. 319, 319c in Black

**1904**

240 A129 2c carmine 5.50 2.25
*a.* Booklet pane of 6 *1,100.*
*b.* 2c scarlet 6.25 2.75
*c.* As "b," booklet pane of 6

José Rizal — A40

Arms of Manila — A41

4c, McKinley. 6c, Magellan. 8c, Miguel Lopez de Legaspi. 10c, Gen. Henry W. Lawton. 12c, Lincoln. 16c, Adm. William T. Sampson. 20c, Washington. 26c, Francisco Carriedo. 30c, Franklin.

Each Inscribed "Philippine Islands / United States of America"

**1906, Sept. 8** **Engr.** **Wmk. 191PI**

241 A40 2c dp green .25 .20
*a.* 2c yellow green ('10) .40 .20
*b.* Booklet pane of 6 750.00
242 A40 4c carmine .50 .20
*a.* 4c carmine lake ('10) .80 .20
*b.* Booklet pane of 6 650.00
243 A40 6c violet 1.25 .20
244 A40 8c brown 2.50 .70
245 A40 10c blue 1.75 .20
*a.* 10c dark blue 1.75 .20
246 A40 12c brown lake 5.00 2.00
247 A40 16c violet blk 3.75 .20
248 A40 20c orange brn 4.00 .30
249 A40 26c violet brn 6.00 2.25
250 A40 30c olive grn 4.75 1.50
251 A41 1p orange 27.50 7.00
252 A41 2p black 35.00 1.25
253 A41 4p dk blue 100.00 15.00
254 A41 10p dk green 225.00 70.00
*Nos. 241-254 (14)* 417.25 101.00

See Nos. 255-304, 326-353. For surcharges see Nos. 368-369, 450. For overprints see Nos. C1-C28, C36-C46, C54-C57, O5-O14.

Change of Colors

**1909-13** ***Perf. 12***

255 A40 12c red orange 8.50 2.50
256 A40 16c olive green 3.50 .75
257 A40 20c yellow 7.50 1.25
258 A40 26c blue green 1.75 .75
259 A40 30c ultra 10.00 3.25
260 A41 1p pale violet 30.00 5.00
260A A41 2p vio brn ('13) 85.00 2.75
*Nos. 255-260A (7)* 146.25 16.25

**1911** **Wmk. 190PI** ***Perf. 12***

261 A40 2c green .65 .20
*a.* Booklet pane of 6 800.00
262 A40 4c car lake 2.50 .20
*a.* 4c carmine — —
*b.* Booklet pane of 6 600.00
263 A40 6c dp violet 2.00 .20
264 A40 8c brown 8.50 .45
265 A40 10c blue 3.25 .20
266 A40 12c orange 2.50 .45
267 A40 16c olive grn 2.50 .20
*a.* 16c pale olive green 2.50 .20
268 A40 20c yellow 2.50 .20
*a.* 20c orange 3.00 .20
269 A40 26c blue green 3.00 .20
270 A40 30c ultra 3.50 .40
271 A41 1p pale violet 22.50 .55
272 A41 2p violet brn 27.50 .75
273 A41 4p dp blue 625.00 80.00
274 A41 10p dp green 225.00 25.00
*Nos. 261-274 (14)* 930.90 109.00

**1914**

275 A40 30c gray 10.00 .40

**1914-23** ***Perf. 10***

276 A40 2c green 2.00 .20
*a.* Booklet pane of 6 *750.00*
277 A40 4c carmine 2.00 .20
*a.* Booklet pane of 6 *750.00*
278 A40 6c lt violet 37.50 9.00
*a.* 6c deep violet 42.50 6.00
279 A40 8c brown 40.00 10.00
280 A40 10c dk blue 25.00 .20
281 A40 16c olive grn 75.00 4.50
282 A40 20c orange 22.50 .85
283 A40 30c gray 55.00 2.75
284 A41 1p pale vio 110.00 3.00
*Nos. 276-284 (9)* 369.00 30.70

**1918-26** ***Perf. 11***

285 A40 2c green 20.00 4.25
*a.* Booklet pane of 6 *750.00*
286 A40 4c carmine 25.00 2.50
*a.* Booklet pane of 6 *1,350.*
287 A40 6c dp violet 35.00 1.75
287A A40 8c lt brown 200.00 25.00
288 A40 10c dk blue 52.50 1.50
289 A40 16c olive grn 90.00 6.75
289A A40 20c orange 60.00 7.50
289C A40 30c gray 55.00 12.50
289D A41 1p pale violet 70.00 14.00
*Nos. 285-289D (9)* 607.50 75.75

**1917-25** **Unwmk.** ***Perf. 11***

290 A40 2c yellow grn .20 .20
*a.* 2c dark green .20 .20
*b.* Vert. pair, imperf. horiz. *1,500.*
*c.* Horiz. pair, imperf. btwn. *1,500.* —
*d.* Vert. pair, imperf. btwn. *1,750.* *1,000.*
*e.* Booklet pane of 6 *27.50*
291 A40 4c carmine .20 .20
*a.* 4c light rose .20 .20
*b.* Booklet pane of 6 17.50 —
292 A40 6c deep violet .30 .20
*a.* 6c lilac .35 .20
*b.* 6c red violet .35 .20
*c.* Booklet pane of 6 *550.00* —
293 A40 8c yellow brown .20 .20
*a.* 8c orange brown .20 .20
294 A40 10c deep blue .20 .20
295 A40 12c red orange .30 .20
296 A40 16c lt ol grn 55.00 .25
*a.* 16c olive bister 55.00 .40
297 A40 20c orange yel .30 .20
298 A40 26c green .45 .45
*a.* 26c blue green .55 .25
299 A40 30c gray .55 .20
300 A41 1p pale violet 35.00 1.00
*a.* 1p red lilac 35.00 1.00
*b.* 1p pale rose lilac 35.00 1.10
301 A41 2p violet brn 26.00 1.00
302 A41 4p blue 24.00 .75
*a.* 4p dark blue 24.00 .75
*Nos. 290-302 (13)* 142.70 5.05

**1923-26**

Design: 16c, Adm. George Dewey.

303 A40 16c olive bister .90 .20
*a.* 16c olive green 1.25 .20
304 A41 10p deep green ('26) 45.00 5.00

Legislative Palace A42

**1926, Dec. 20** **Unwmk.** ***Perf. 12***

319 A42 2c green & blk .40 .25
*a.* Horiz. pair, imperf. btwn. *300.00*
*b.* Vert. pair, imperf. btwn. *575.00*
320 A42 4c carmine & blk .40 .35
*a.* Horiz. pair, imperf. btwn. *325.00*
*b.* Vert. pair, imperf. btwn. *600.00*
321 A42 16c ol grn & blk .75 .65
*a.* Horiz. pair, imperf. btwn. *350.00*
*b.* Vert. pair, imperf. btwn. *625.00*
*c.* Double impression of center *675.00*
322 A42 18c lt brown & blk .85 .50
*a.* Double impression of center *1,250.*
*b.* Vert. pair, imperf. btwn. *675.00*
323 A42 20c orange & blk 1.25 .80
*a.* 20c orange & brown *600.00* —
*b.* Imperf., pair *575.00* *575.00*
*c.* As "a," imperf., pair *1,750.*
*d.* Vert. pair, imperf. btwn. *700.00*
324 A42 24c gray & blk .85 .55
*a.* Vert. pair, imperf. btwn. *700.00*
325 A42 1p rose lil & blk 47.50 32.50
*a.* Vert. pair, imperf. btwn. *675.00*
*Nos. 319-325 (7)* 52.00 35.60

Opening of the Legislative Palace.
For overprints see Nos. O1-O4.

Coil Stamp
Rizal Type of 1906

**1928** ***Perf. 11 Vertically***

326 A40 2c green 8.00 *16.00*

Types of 1906-23

**1925-31** **Unwmk.** ***Imperf.***

340 A40 2c yel grn ('31) .20 .20
*a.* 2c green ('25) .30 .20
341 A40 4c car rose ('31) .20 .20
*a.* 4c carmine ('25) .50 .25
342 A40 6c violet ('31) 1.00 1.00
*a.* 6c deep violet('25) 9.00 4.50
343 A40 8c brown ('31) .90 .90
*a.* 8c yellow brown ('25) 6.75 3.50
344 A40 10c blue ('31) 1.75 1.40
*a.* deep blue ('25) 27.50 8.00
345 A40 12c dp org ('31) 2.50 2.10
*a.* red orange ('25) 27.50 8.00
346 A40 16c olive green (Dewey) ('31) 2.00 1.50
*a.* bister green ('25) 22.50 6.00
347 A40 20c dp yel org ('31) 2.00 1.50
*a.* yel org ('25) 22.50 6.00
348 A40 26c green ('31) 2.00 1.50
*a.* blue green ('25) 27.50 8.00
349 A40 30c light gray ('31) 2.25 1.75
*a.* gray ('25) 27.50 8.00
350 A41 1p lt violet ('31) 4.50 4.50
*a.* violet ('25) 100.00 40.00
351 A41 2p brn vio ('31) 11.00 11.00
*a.* violet brown ('25) 225.00 85.00
352 A41 4p blue ('31) 37.50 32.50
*a.* deep blue ('25) 1,100. 425.00
353 A41 10p green ('31) 110.00 110.00
*a.* deep green ('25) 2,250. 850.00
*Nos. 340-353 (14)* 177.80 170.05
*Nos. 340a-353a (14)* 3,846. 1,452.

Mount Mayon, Luzon A43

Post Office, Manila A44

Pier No. 7, Manila Bay — A45

## 1936, June 19 — Perf. 12

| | | |
|---|---|---|
| 402 A68 | 2c yellow brown | .20 .20 |
| 403 A68 | 6c slate blue | .20 .20 |
| a. | Horiz. pair, imperf. vert. | 1,350. |
| 404 A68 | 36c red orange | .45 .85 |
| | Nos. 402-404 (3) | .90 |

75th anniv. of the birth of José Rizal.

## 1936, Nov. 15 — Perf. 11

| | | |
|---|---|---|
| 408 A69 | 2c orange brown | .20 .20 |
| 409 A69 | 6c yellow green | .20 .20 |
| 410 A69 | 12c ultra | .60 .60 |
| | Nos. 408-410 (3) | |

1st anniversary of the Commonwealth.
For overprints see Nos. 467, 475.

**Stamps of 1935 with Large Overprint in Black**

a

b

## 1936-37 — Perf. 11

| | | |
|---|---|---|
| 411 A53 (a) | 2c rose | .20 .20 |
| a. | Booklet pane of 6 | 4.00 |
| 412 A54 | 4c yel grn ('37) | 3.00 4.00 |
| 413 A55 | 6c dark brown | .50 .50 |
| 414 A56 | 8c violet ('37) | .25 .25 |
| 415 A57 | 10c rose carmine | .20 .20 |
| a. | "Commonwealth" | — |
| 416 A58 | 12c black ('37) | .20 .20 |
| 417 A59 | 16c dk blue | .20 .20 |
| 418 A60 | 20c lt ol grn ('37) | .65 .40 |
| 419 A61 | 26c indigo ('37) | .65 .35 |
| 420 A62 | 30c orange red | .45 .45 |
| 421 A63 | 1p red org & blk | .65 .20 |
| 422 A64 | 2p bis brn & blk ('37) | 6.00 2.75 |
| 423 A65 (b) | 4p bl & blk ('37) | 25.00 5.00 |
| 424 A66 (b) | 5p grn & blk ('37) | 39.85 1.50 |
| | Nos. 411, 413-424 (13) | 11.60 |

Arms of Manila A71

Map of Philippines A70

## 1937, Feb. 3

| | | |
|---|---|---|
| 425 A70 | 2c yellow green | .20 .20 |
| 426 A70 | 6c lt brown | .20 .20 |
| 427 A70 | 12c sapphire | .25 .25 |
| 428 A70 | 20c dp orange | .50 .40 |
| 429 A70 | 36c dp violet | .65 .35 |
| 430 A70 | 50c carmine | 2.00 1.55 |
| | Nos. 425-430 (6) | |

33rd Eucharistic Congress.

## 1937, Aug. 27 — Perf. 11

| | | |
|---|---|---|
| 431 A71 | 10p gray | 5.00 1.40 |
| 432 A71 | 20p henna brown | 3.00 1.40 |

For surcharges see Nos. 495-496. For overprints see Nos. 451, C58.

---

Battle of Manila Bay, 1898, A64

Montalban Gorge A65

George Washington A66

## 1935, Feb. 15 — Engr. — Perf. 11

| | | |
|---|---|---|
| 383 A53 | 2c rose | .20 .20 |
| 384 A54 | 4c yellow grn | .20 .20 |
| 385 A55 | 6c dk brown | .20 .20 |
| 386 A56 | 8c violet | .20 .20 |
| 387 A57 | 10c rose car | .25 .25 |
| 388 A58 | 12c black | .25 .30 |
| 389 A59 | 16c dark blue | .25 .30 |
| 390 A60 | 20c light olive green | .30 .40 |
| 391 A61 | 26c indigo | .30 .25 |
| 392 A62 | 30c orange red & black | |
| 393 A63 | 1p red orange & black | 1.25 1.25 |
| 394 A64 | 2p red brn & black | 1.75 1.25 |
| 395 A65 | 4p blue & black | 5.00 3.00 |
| 396 A66 | 5p green & black | 14.00 3.50 |
| | Nos. 383-396 (14) | 28.10 11.35 |

For overprints see Nos. 411-424, 433-446, 463-466, 468, 472-474, 478-484, 485-494, C52-C53, O15-O36, O38, O40-O43, N2-N3, NO6. For surcharges see Nos. 449, N4-N9, N28, NO2 NO5.

## Commonwealth Issues

The Temples of Human Progress — A67

## 1935, Nov. 15

| | | |
|---|---|---|
| 397 A67 | 2c carmine rose | .20 .20 |
| 398 A67 | 6c dp violet | .20 .20 |
| 399 A67 | 16c blue | .30 .30 |
| 400 A67 | 20c yellow grn | .35 .55 |
| 401 A67 | 50c dp violet | .55 .55 |
| | Nos. 397-401 (5) | 1.50 1.45 |

Inauguration of the Philippine Commonwealth, Nov. 15, 1935.

President Manuel L. Quezon — A69

Jose Rizal — A68

---

José Rizal — A53

Woman and Carabao A54

La Filipina — A55

Pearl Fishing A56

Fort Santiago A57

Salt Spring — A58

Magellan's Landing, 1521 — A59

"Juan de la Cruz" — A60

Rice Terraces A61

"Blood Compact," 1565 — A62

Barasoain Church, Malolos A63

---

(See footnote) — A46

Rice Planting A47

Rice Terraces A48

Baguio Zigzag A49

## 1932, May 3 — Perf. 11

| | | |
|---|---|---|
| 354 A43 | 2c yellow green | .40 .20 |
| 355 A44 | 4c rose carmine | .35 .25 |
| 356 A45 | 12c orange | .50 .50 |
| 357 A46 | 18c red orange | 26.00 9.50 |
| 358 A47 | 20c yellow | .65 .65 |
| 359 A48 | 24c deep violet | 1.00 .65 |
| 360 A49 | 32c olive brown | 1.00 .70 |
| | Nos. 354-360 (7) | 29.90 12.35 |

The 18c vignette was intended to show Pagsanjan Falls in Laguna, central Luzon, and is so labeled. Through error the stamp pictures Vernal Falls in Yosemite National Park, California.
For overprints see #C29-C35, C47-C51, C63.

**Nos. 302, 302a Surcharged in Orange or Red**

## 1932

| | | |
|---|---|---|
| 368 A41 | 1p on 4p blue (O) | 2.50 .50 |
| a. | 1p on 4p dark blue (o) | 3.00 1.25 |
| 369 A41 | 2p on 4p dk bl (R) | 4.00 .80 |
| a. | 2p on 4p bl (R) | 4.00 .80 |

Baseball Players A50

Basketball Players — A52

Tennis Player — A51

Perf. 11½
1.75 .90
.25 .20

## 1934, Apr. 14 — Typo. — Perf. 11½

| | | |
|---|---|---|
| 380 A50 | 2c yellow brn | 1,250. |
| 381 A51 | 6c ultra | .25 .20 |
| a. | Vert. pair, imperf. bwn. | 1,250. |
| 382 A52 | 16c violet brown | .50 .50 |
| a. | Vert. pair, imperf. horiz. | 1,250. |
| | Nos. 380-382 (3) | 2.50 1.60 |

Tenth Far Eastern Championship Games.

### Stamps of 1935 with Small Overprint in Black

**1938-40**    *Perf. 11*

| | | | | |
|---|---|---|---|---|
| 433 | A53 (a) | 2c rose ('39) | 4.00 | — |
| a. | | Booklet pane of 6 | 3.50 | |
| b. | | As "a," lower left-hand stamp overprinted "WEALTH COMMON." | 2.50 | 2.50 |
| 434 | A54 (a) | 4c yel grn ('40) | 30.00 | |
| c. | | Hyphen omitted | | |
| 435 | A55 (a) | 6c dk brn ('39) | .20 | .20 |
| 436 | A56 (a) | 8c golden brown | .20 | .20 |
| a. | | 8c violet ('39) | 90.00 | |
| 437 | A57 (b) | 10c rose car | .20 | .20 |
| a. | | "Commonwealth" ('39) | 1.40 | .70 |
| 438 | A58 (b) | 12c black ('40) | .20 | .20 |
| 439 | A59 (b) | 16c dk blue | .20 | .20 |
| 440 | A60 (a) | 20c lt ol grn | .20 | .20 |
| a. | | "Commonwealth" | .40 | .20 |
| 441 | A61 (b) | 26c indigo ('40) | .20 | .20 |
| 442 | A62 (b) | 30c org red | .60 | .75 |
| 443 | A63 (b) | 1p red org & blk | 8.00 | |
| 444 | A64 (b) | 2p bis brn & blk | 3.25 | |
| 445 | A65 (b) | 4p bl & blk | 350.00 | 350.00 |
| 446 | A66 (b) | 5p grn & blk | 367.90 | 386.50 |

Overprint "b" measures 18½x1¾mm. No. 433b occurs in booklet pane, No. 433a, position 5; all copies are straight-edged, left and bottom.

Nos. 433-446 (14)

### Stamps of 1917-37 Surcharged in Red, Violet or Black

b — FIRST FOREIGN TRADE WEEK, MAY 21-27, 1939, 6 centavos 6
a — FIRST FOREIGN TRADE WEEK, MAY 21-27, 1939, 2
c — FIRST FOREIGN TRADE WEEK, MAY 21-27, 1939, 50 centavos 50

**Triumphal Arch — A72**

**1939, July 5**

| | | | | |
|---|---|---|---|---|
| 449 | A54 | 2c on 4c yel grn (R) | .20 | .20 |
| 450 | A40 | 6c on 26c grn | .20 | .30 |
| 451 | A71 | 50c on 20p hn brn (Bk) | 1.00 | 1.00 |
| a. | | 6c on 26c bl grn (V) | 1.00 | 1.00 |
| | | Nos. 449-451 (3) | 1.40 | 1.40 |

Foreign Trade Week.

**Malacañan Palace — A73**

**1939, Nov. 15**    *Perf. 11*

| | | | | |
|---|---|---|---|---|
| 452 | A72 | 2c yellow green | .20 | .20 |
| 453 | A72 | 12c carmine | .20 | .20 |
| 454 | A72 | 12c bright blue | .20 | .20 |
| | | Nos. 452-454 (3) | .60 | .60 |

For overprints see Nos. 469, 476.

**1939, Nov. 15**    *Perf. 11*

| | | | | |
|---|---|---|---|---|
| 455 | A73 | 2c green | .20 | .20 |
| 456 | A73 | 6c orange | .20 | .20 |
| 457 | A73 | 12c carmine | .60 | .60 |
| | | Nos. 455-457 (3) | | |

For overprint see No. 470.

Nos. 452-457 commemorate the 4th anniv. of the Commonwealth.

**Pres. Quezon Taking Oath of Office — A74**

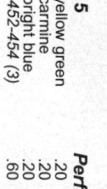

**1940, Feb. 8**

| | | | | |
|---|---|---|---|---|
| 458 | A74 | 2c orange | .20 | .20 |
| 459 | A74 | 6c dk green | .25 | .20 |
| 460 | A74 | 36c purple | .65 | .60 |
| | | Nos. 458-460 (3) | | |

4th anniversary of Commonwealth.
For overprints see Nos. 471, 477.

**José Rizal — A75**

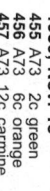

**1941, Apr. 14**    Rotary Press Printing
Size: 19x22½mm   *Perf. 11x10½*

| | | | | |
|---|---|---|---|---|
| 461 | A75 | 2c apple green | .20 | .50 |

**1941-43**    Flat Plate Printing
Size: 18¾x22mm   *Perf. 11*

| | | | | |
|---|---|---|---|---|
| 462 | A75 | 2c apple green ('43) | .20 | .50 |
| a. | | 2c pale apple green ('43) | .50 | |
| b. | | Bklt. pane of 6 #462 | 1.25 | 5.00 |
| c. | | Bklt. pane of 6 #462a | 2.50 | 2.75 |

No. 462 was issued only in booklet panes and all copies have straight edges.
Further printings were made in 1942 and 1943 in different shades from the first supply of stamps sent to the islands.
For type A75 overprinted see Nos. 464, O37, O39, N1, NO1.

### Philippine Stamps of 1935-41, Handstamped in Violet

 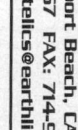 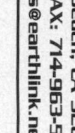   

(VICTORY)

**1944**    *Perf. 11, 11x10½*

| | | | | |
|---|---|---|---|---|
| 463 | A53 | 2c (#411) | 325.00 | 160.00 |
| a. | | Booklet pane of 6 | 12,500. | |
| 463B | A53 | 2c (#433) | 1,400. | 1,350. |
| 464 | A75 | 2c (#461) | 3.75 | |
| 465 | A54 | 4c (#384) | 42.50 | 42.50 |
| 466 | A55 | 6c (#385) | 3,250. | 2,000. |
| 467 | A69 | 6c (#409) | 150.00 | 110.00 |
| 468 | A55 | 6c (#413) | 3,500. | 825.00 |
| 469 | A72 | 10c (#453) | 350.00 | 725.00 |
| 470 | A73 | 16c (#456) | 1,750. | 725.00 |
| 471 | A74 | 2c (#459) | 225.00 | 200.00 |
| 472 | A73 | 16c (#459) | 17.50 | 24.00 |
| 473 | A56 | 8c (#436) | 200.00 | 90.00 |
| 474 | A57 | 10c (#415) | 175.00 | 140.00 |
| 475 | A69 | 10c (#437) | 1,100. | 400.00 |
| 476 | A57 | 10c (#439) | 5,500. | 190.00 |
| 477 | A74 | 12c (#454) | 275.00 | 2,250. |
| 478 | A59 | 16c (#417) | 350.00 | |
| 479 | A59 | 16c (#389) | 2,000. | 550.00 |
| 480 | A60 | 20c (#440) | 650.00 | 200.00 |
| 481 | A60 | 20c (#420) | 110.00 | 325.00 |
| 482 | A62 | 30c (#442) | 350.00 | 325.00 |
| 483 | A62 | 30c (#420) | 750.00 | 375.00 |
| 484 | A63 | 1p (#443) | 6,250. | 4,500. |

Nos. 463-484 are valued in the grade of fine to very fine.

### Types of 1935-37 Overprinted

a — VICTORY COMMON-WEALTH
b — VICTORY COMMONWEALTH

**1945**    *Perf. 11*

| | | | | |
|---|---|---|---|---|
| 485 | A53 (a) | 2c rose | .20 | .20 |
| 486 | A54 (a) | 4c yellow grn | .20 | .20 |
| 487 | A55 (a) | 6c golden brn | .20 | .20 |
| 488 | A56 (a) | 8c violet | .20 | .20 |
| 489 | A57 (b) | 10c rose car | .20 | .20 |
| 490 | A58 (b) | 12c black | .25 | .20 |
| 491 | A59 (b) | 16c dk blue | .20 | .20 |
| 492 | A60 (a) | 20c lt olive grn | .30 | .20 |
| 493 | A62 (b) | 30c orange red & blk | .40 | .35 |
| 494 | A63 (b) | 1p red org & blk | 1.10 | .25 |
| 495 | A71 | 10p gray | 40.00 | 13.50 |
| 496 | A71 | 20p henna brown | 35.00 | 15.00 |
| | | Nos. 485-496 (12) | 78.25 | 30.70 |

**José Rizal — A76**

**1946, May 28**    Rotary Press Printing
497 A76 2c sepia   *Perf. 11x10½*   .20   .20
For overprints see Nos. 503, O44.

**Philippine Girl Holding Flag of the Republic — A77**

Republic

**1946, July 4**    Unwmk.   Engr.

| | | | | |
|---|---|---|---|---|
| 500 | A77 | 2c carmine | .50 | .25 |
| 501 | A77 | 6c green | .50 | .35 |
| 502 | A77 | 12c blue | 1.00 | .35 |
| | | Nos. 500-502 (3) | 2.00 | .85 |

Philippine independence, July 4, 1946.

**1946, Dec. 30**    *Perf. 11x10½*
503 A76 2c sepia   .40   .20
50th anniv. of the execution of José Rizal.

No. 497 Overprinted in Brown
No. 431-432 Overprinted in Black

**Rizal Monument — A78**

**Bonifacio Monument — A79**

**Jones Bridge — A80**

**Santa Lucia Gate — A81**

**Mayon Volcano — A82**

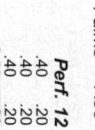

**Avenue of Palms — A83**

**1947**    Engr.   *Perf. 12*

| | | | | |
|---|---|---|---|---|
| 504 | A78 | 4c black brown | .40 | .20 |
| 505 | A79 | 6c red orange | .40 | .20 |
| 506 | A80 | 10c deep blue | 1.00 | .20 |
| 507 | A81 | 16c slate gray | 2.50 | .60 |
| 508 | A82 | 20c red brown | 2.50 | .20 |

**Headman of Barangay Inspecting Harvest — A102**

**1951, Mar. 31  Litho.  Perf. 12½**
| | | | |
|---|---|---|---|
| 554 | A102 | 5c dull green | .75 .20 |
| 555 | A102 | 6c red brown | .40 .25 |
| 556 | A102 | 18c violet blue | 1.55 .75 |
| | | Nos. 554-556 (3) | |

**Imperf., Pairs**
| | | | |
|---|---|---|---|
| 554a | A102 | 5c dull green | 3.25 2.00 |
| 555a | A102 | 6c red brown | 1.90 .90 |
| 556a | A102 | 18c violet blue | 1.40 .75 |
| | | Nos. 554a-556a (3) | 6.55 3.65 |

The government's Peace Fund campaign.

**Arms of Cebu A104**

**Arms of Iloilo A106**

**Arms of Manila A103**

**Arms of Zamboanga A105**

**1951  Engr.  Perf. 12**

*Various Frames*
| | | | |
|---|---|---|---|
| 557 | A103 | 5c purple | 1.25 .25 |
| 558 | A103 | 6c gray | .95 .25 |
| 559 | A103 | 18c bright ultra | .60 .40 |

*Various Frames*
| | | | |
|---|---|---|---|
| 560 | A104 | 5c crimson rose | 1.25 .25 |
| 561 | A104 | 6c bister brown | .60 .25 |
| 562 | A104 | 18c violet | .95 .40 |

*Various Frames*
| | | | |
|---|---|---|---|
| 563 | A105 | 5c blue green | 1.60 .25 |
| 564 | A105 | 6c red brown | .95 .25 |
| 565 | A105 | 18c light blue | .95 .40 |

*Various Frames*
| | | | |
|---|---|---|---|
| 566 | A106 | 5c bright green | 1.60 .25 |
| 567 | A106 | 6c violet | .95 .25 |
| 568 | A106 | 18c deep blue | .95 .40 |
| | | Nos. 557-568 (12) | 12.60 3.60 |

Issued: A103, 2/3; A104, 4/27; A105, 6/19; A106, 8/26.
For surcharges see Nos. 634-636.

**Liberty Holding Declaration of Human Rights — A108**

**1951, Dec. 10  Perf. 12**
| | | | |
|---|---|---|---|
| 572 | A108 | 5c green | .40 .25 |
| 573 | A108 | 6c red orange | .85 .35 |
| 574 | A108 | 18c ultra | 3.10 .85 |
| | | Nos. 572-574 (3) | |

Universal Declaration of Human Rights.

**UN Emblem and Girl Holding Flag — A107**

**1951, Oct. 24  Unwmk.  Perf. 11½**
| | | | |
|---|---|---|---|
| 569 | A107 | 5c red | 1.40 .25 |
| 570 | A107 | 6c blue green | .85 .35 |
| 571 | A107 | 18c violet blue | 3.10 .85 |
| | | Nos. 569-571 (3) | |

United Nations Day, Oct. 24, 1951.

---

**Red Lauan Tree — A97**

**1950, Mar. 1**
| | | | |
|---|---|---|---|
| 537 | A96 | 2c purple | .30 .20 |
| 538 | A96 | 6c dk green | .40 .20 |
| 539 | A96 | 18c dp blue | 5.15 1.75 |
| | | Nos. 537-539, C68-C69 (5) | |

5th World Cong. of the Junior Chamber of Commerce, Manila, Mar. 1-8, 1950.
For surcharge see No. 825.

**Globe — A96**

**Lions Club Emblem — A99**

**1950, Apr. 14**
| | | | |
|---|---|---|---|
| 540 | A97 | 2c green | .45 .20 |
| 541 | A97 | 4c purple | .55 .20 |

50th anniversary of the Bureau of Forestry.

**F. D. Roosevelt with his Stamps — A98**

**1950, May 22**
| | | | |
|---|---|---|---|
| 542 | A98 | 4c dark brown | .80 .20 |
| 543 | A98 | 6c carmine rose | .35 .25 |
| 544 | A98 | 18c blue | 1.50 .70 |
| | | Nos. 542-544 (3) | |

Honoring Franklin D. Roosevelt and for the 25th anniv. of the Philatelic Association of the Philippines. See No. C70.

**Engr.**

**1950, June 4**
| | | | |
|---|---|---|---|
| 545 | A99 | 2c orange | .95 .30 |
| 546 | A99 | 4c violet | 5.65 1.70 |
| | | Nos. 545-546, C71-C72 (4) | |

Convention of the Lions Club, Manila, June 1950.

**Pres. Elpidio Quirino Taking Oath — A100**

**1950, July 4  Unwmk.  Perf. 12**
| | | | |
|---|---|---|---|
| 547 | A100 | 2c car rose | .25 .20 |
| 548 | A100 | 4c magenta | .40 .25 |
| 549 | A100 | 6c blue green | .90 .65 |
| | | Nos. 547-549 (3) | |

Republic of the Philippines, 4th anniv.

**No. 527 Surcharged in Black**

**1950, Sept. 20**
| | | | |
|---|---|---|---|
| 550 | A91 | 1c on 2c bright green | .60 .20 |

**Dove over Globe — A101**

**1950, Oct. 23**
| | | | |
|---|---|---|---|
| 551 | A101 | 5c green | .60 .20 |
| 552 | A101 | 6c rose carmine | .45 .35 |
| 553 | A101 | 18c ultra | 1.50 .75 |
| | | Nos. 551-553 (3) | |

Baguio Conference of 1950.
For surcharge see No. 828.

---

**José — A91**

Rizal

**Manuel A. Roxas — A90**

**1948, July 15  Engr.  Perf. 12**
| | | | |
|---|---|---|---|
| 525 | A90 | 2c black | .25 .20 |
| 526 | A90 | 4c black | .35 .20 |

Issued in tribute to President Manuel A. Roxas who died April 15, 1948.

**1948, June 19  Unwmk.**
| | | | |
|---|---|---|---|
| 527 | A91 | 2c bright green | .40 .20 |
| a. | | Booklet pane of 6 | 3.00 2.10 |

For surcharges see Nos. 550, O56. For overprint see No. O53.

**Sampaguita, National Flower — A93**

**Scout Saluting — A92**

**1948, Oct. 31  Typo.  Imperf.**
| | | | |
|---|---|---|---|
| 528 | A92 | 2c chocolate & green | 1.00 .30 |
| a. | | Perf. 11½ | 1.00 .75 |
| 529 | A92 | 4c chocolate & pink | 1.75 .40 |
| a. | | Perf. 11½ | 1.50 1.10 |

Boy Scouts of the Philippines, 25th anniv. No. 528 exists part perforate.

**1948, Dec. 8  Perf. 12½**
| | | | |
|---|---|---|---|
| 530 | A93 | 3c blk, pale bl & grm | .60 .30 |

**UPU Monument, Bern — A94**

**1949, Oct. 9  Unwmk.  Engr.  Perf. 12**
| | | | |
|---|---|---|---|
| 531 | A94 | 4c green | .70 .20 |
| 532 | A94 | 6c dull violet | .40 .20 |
| 533 | A94 | 18c blue gray | 1.50 .60 |
| | | Nos. 531-533 (3) | |

**Souvenir Sheet  Imperf**
| | | | |
|---|---|---|---|
| 534 | | Sheet of 3 | 3.00 2.00 |
| a. | A94 | 4c green | .70 .35 |
| b. | A94 | 6c dull violet | .70 .35 |
| c. | A94 | 18c blue | .70 .35 |

75th anniv. of the UPU.
In 1960 an unofficial, 3-line overprint ("President D. D. Eisenhower /Visit to the Philippines/June 14-16, 1960") was privately applied to No. 534. For surcharge & overprint see #806, 901.

**Gen. Gregorio del Pilar at Tirad Pass — A95**

**1949, Dec. 2  Perf. 12**
| | | | |
|---|---|---|---|
| 535 | A95 | 2c red brown | .35 .20 |
| 536 | A95 | 4c green | .55 .20 |

50th anniversary of the death of Gen. Gregorio P. del Pilar and fifty-two of his men at Tirad Pass.

---

| | | | |
|---|---|---|---|
| 509 | A83 | 50c dull green | 2.00 .35 |
| 510 | A83 | 1p violet | 2.75 .35 |
| | | Nos. 504-510 (7) | 10.95 2.10 |

For surcharges see Nos. 613-614, 809. For overprints see Nos. 609, O50-O52, O54-O55.

**Manuel L. Quezon — A84**

**1947, May 1**
| | | | |
|---|---|---|---|
| 511 | A84 | 1c green | |

See No. 515.

**Typo.**
| | | | |
|---|---|---|---|
| 511 | A84 | 1c green | .40 .20 |

**Pres. Manuel A. Roxas Taking Oath of Office — A85**

**1947, July 4  Unwmk.  Perf. 12½**
| | | | |
|---|---|---|---|
| 512 | A85 | 4c carmine rose | .50 .20 |
| 513 | A85 | 6c dk green | .75 .45 |
| 514 | A85 | 16c purple | 1.25 .85 |
| | | Nos. 512-514 (3) | 2.50 1.50 |

First anniversary of republic.

**Quezon Type  Souvenir Sheet  Imperf.**

**1947, Nov. 28**
| | | | |
|---|---|---|---|
| 515 | | Sheet of 4 | 1.75 1.25 |
| a. | A84 | 1c bright green | .20 .20 |

**United Nations Emblem A87**

**1947, Nov. 24  Perf. 12½**
| | | | |
|---|---|---|---|
| 516 | A87 | 4c dk car & pink | 1.75 1.00 |
| a. | | Imperf. | 3.60 2.60 |
| 517 | A87 | 6c pur & pale vio | .75 .85 |
| a. | | Imperf. | 3.00 2.50 |
| 518 | A87 | 12c dp bl & pale bl | 3.50 2.50 |
| a. | | Imperf. | 6.00 3.50 |
| | | Nos. 516-518 "3" | 20.00 7.50 |

Nos. 516a-518a "3"†
Conference of the Economic Commission in Asia and the Far East, held at Baguio.

**Gen. Douglas MacArthur — A88**

**1948, Feb. 3  Engr.  Perf. 12**
| | | | |
|---|---|---|---|
| 519 | A88 | 4c purple | .75 .40 |
| 520 | A88 | 6c rose car | 1.00 .40 |
| 521 | A88 | 16c brt ultra | 3.00 1.40 |
| | | Nos. 519-521 (3) | |

**Threshing Rice — A89**

**1948, Feb. 23  Typo.  Perf. 12½**
| | | | |
|---|---|---|---|
| 522 | A89 | 2c grn & pale yel grn | 1.00 .40 |
| 523 | A89 | 6c brown & cream | 1.75 .40 |
| 524 | A89 | 18c dp bl & pale bl | 3.25 1.25 |
| | | Nos. 522-524 (3) | 6.00 2.05 |

Conf. of the FAO held at Baguio. No. 524 exists imperf. See No. C67.

**Students and Department Seal — A109**

**1952, Jan. 31**
575 A109 5c orange red .60 .30
50th anniversary (in 1951) of the Philippine Educational System.

**Presidents Quirino and Sukarno — A116**

**1953, Apr. 30**
585 A115 5c turq green .55 .25
586 A115 6c vermilion .45 .25
Philippines International Fair.

**1953, Oct. 5 Engr. & Litho.**
587 A116 5c multicolored .65 .35
588 A116 6c multicolored .35 .30
2nd anniversary of the visit of Indonesia's President Sukarno.

---

**Milkfish and Map A111**

**1952, Oct. 27 Perf. 12½**
578 A111 5c orange brown 1.00 .30
579 A111 6c deep blue .50 .30
4th Indo-Pacific Fisheries Council Meeting, Quezon City, Oct. 23-Nov. 7, 1952.

**Maria Clara — A112**

**1952, Nov. 16**
580 A112 5c deep blue 1.00 .30
581 A112 6c brown .75 .30
1st Pan-Asian Philatelic Exhibition, PANAPEX, Manila, Nov. 16-22.
Nos. 580-581,C73 (3) 3.75 1.35

**Wright Park, Baguio City — A113**

**1952, Dec. 15 Perf. 12**
582 A113 5c red orange .90 .30
583 A113 6c dp blue green .60 .30
3rd Lions District Convention, Baguio City.

**Francisco Baltazar, Poet — A114**

**1953, Mar. 27**
584 A114 5c citron .60 .30

**"Gateway to the East" — A115**

National Language Week.

---

**Marcelo H. del Pilar — A117**

**1952-60 Perf. 12, 12½, 13, 14x13½ Engr.**
589 A117 1c red brn ('53) .30 .20
590 A117 2c gray ('60) .25 .20
591 A117 3c brick red ('59) .30 .20
592 A117 5c crim rose .30 .20
595 A117 10c ultra ('55) .50 .20
597 A117 20c car lake ('55) .80 .20
598 A117 25c yel grn ('58) 1.00 .20
599 A117 50c org ver ('59) 1.25 .20
600 A117 60c org ver ('58) 1.50 .20
601 A117 2p violet 5.00 1.00
Nos. 589-601 (10) 11.20 3.10

1c, Manuel L. Quezon. 2c, José Abad Santos (diff. frame). 3c, Apolinario Mabini (diff. frame). 10c, Father José Burgos. 20c, Lapu-Lapu. 25c, Gen. Antonio Luna. 50c, Cayetano Arellano. 60c, Andres Bonifacio. 2p, Graciano L. Jaena.

For overprints & surcharges see #608, 626, 641-642, 647, 830, 871, 875-877, 057-061.

**Doctor Examining Boy A118**

**1953, Dec. 16**
603 A118 5c lilac rose .65 .25
604 A118 6c ultra .60 .25
50th anniversary of the founding of the Philippine Medical Association.

**First Philippine Stamps, Magellan's Landing and Manila Scene A119**

**1954, Apr. 25 Stamp of 1854 in Orange**

**Perf. 13**
605 A119 5c purple .65 .30
606 A119 18c deep blue 1.60 .85
607 A119 30c green 4.00 2.00
Nos. 605-607,C74-C76 (6) 21.25 9.00
Centenary of Philippine postage stamps. For surcharge see No. 829.

---

**Discus Thrower and Games Emblem A120**

**1954, May 31 Perf. 13**
610 A120 5c shown 2.75 .80
611 A120 18c Swimmer .90 .40
612 A120 30c Boxers 2.25 1.50
Nos. 610-612 (3) 5.90 2.70
2nd Asian Games, Manila, May 1-9.

Nos. 505 and 508 Surcharged in Blue

**1954, Sept. 6 Perf. 12**
613 A79 5c on 10c red org .75 .45
614 A82 18c on 20c red brn .75 .45
The surcharge is arranged to obliterate the original denomination. Manila Conference, 1954.

No. 592 Overprinted

**Allegory of Independence A121**

**1954, Nov. 30 Perf. 13**
615 A121 5c dark carmine 1.00 .30
616 A121 18c deep blue .65 .30
56th anniversary of the declaration of the first Philippine Independence. For surcharge see No. 826.

**"Immaculate Conception," by Murillo A122**

**1954, Dec. 30 Perf. 12**
617 A122 5c blue .65 .25
Issued to mark the end of the Marian Year.

---

**1954, Apr. 23 Perf. 12**
608 A117 5c crimson rose 1.50 .85
609 A83 18c on 50c dull grn 2.25 1.25
1st National Boy Scout Jamboree, Quezon City, April 23-30, 1954. The surcharge on No. 609 is reduced to fit the size of the stamp.

Nos. 592 and 509 Overprinted or Surcharged in Black

**Allegory of Labor — A124**

**Pres. Ramon Magsaysay A125**

**1955, May 26 Perf. 13x12½**
620 A124 5c brown .60 .25
Issued in connection with the Labor-Management Congress, Manila, May 26-28, 1955.

**1955, July 4**
621 A125 5c blue .50 .20
622 A125 20c red 1.25 .50
623 A125 30c green 3.00 1.20
Nos. 621-623 (3)
9th anniversary of the Republic.

**Village Well A126**

**1956, Mar. 16 Perf. 12½x13½**
624 A126 5c violet .60 .25
625 A126 20c dull green 1.00 .40
Issued to publicize the drive for improved health conditions in rural areas.

**1956, Aug. 1 Unwmk. Perf. 12**
626 A117 5c crimson rose .55 .35
5th Annual Conf. of the World Confederation of Organizations of the Teaching Profession, Manila, Aug. 1-8, 1956.

No. 592 Overprinted

**Nurse and Disaster Victims A127**

**1956, Aug. 30 Perf. 12**
627 A127 5c violet .40 .30
628 A127 20c gray brown 1.25 .60
Engraved; Cross Lithographed in Red
50 years of Red Cross Service in the Philippines.

Monument to US Landing, Leyte — A128

**1956, Oct. 20**   **Litho.**   **Perf. 12½**
629 A128 5c carmine rose   .65 .25
  a. Imperf, pair ('57)   5.75 3.00

Landing of US forces under Gen. Douglas MacArthur on Leyte, Oct. 20, 1944. Issue date: No. 629a, Feb. 16.

Santo Tomas University A129

**1956, Nov. 13**   **Photo.**   **Perf. 11½**
630 A129 5c brown car & choc   .50 .35
631 A129 60c lilac & red brn   3.25 1.60

Statue of Christ by Rizal — A130

**1956, Nov. 28**   **Unwmk.**   **Engr.**   **Perf. 12**
632 A130 5c gray olive   .40 .25
633 A130 20c rose carmine   1.10 .60

2nd Natl. Eucharistic Cong., Manila, Nov. 28-Dec. 2, and for the centenary of the Feast of the Sacred Heart.

Nos. 561, 564 and 567 Surcharged with New Value in Blue or Black

**1956**   **Perf. 12**
634 A104 5c on 6c big brn (Bl)   .50 .25
635 A106 6c on 6c red brn (Hl)   .50 .25
636 A108 5c on 6c vio (Bk)   1.50 .75
  Nos. 634-636 (3)

Girl Scout, Emblem and Tents A131

**1957, Jan. 19**   **Litho.**   **Perf. 12½**
637 A131 5c dark blue   .60 .30
  a. Imperf, pair   5.75 3.50

Centenary of the Scout movement and for the Girl Scout World Jamboree, Quezon City, Jan. 19-Feb. 2, 1957.
Copies of Nos. 637 and 637a (No. 48 in sheet) exist with heavy black rectangular handstamps obliterating erroneous date at left, denomination and cloverleaf emblem.

Pres. Ramon Magsaysay (1907-57) — A132

**1957, Aug. 31**   **Engr.**   **Perf. 12**
638 A132 5c black   .35 .20

---

"Spoliarium" by Juan Luna — A133

**1957, Oct. 23**   **Perf. 14x14½**
639 A133 5c rose carmine   .35 .20

Centenary of the birth of Juan Luna, painter.

Sergio Osmena and First National Assembly — A134

**1957, Oct. 16**   **Perf. 12½x13½**
640 A134 5c blue green   .35 .20

1st Philippine Assembly and honoring Sergio Osmeña, Speaker of the Assembly.

Nos. 595 and 597 Surcharged in Carmine or Black

**1957, Dec. 30**   **Perf. 14x13½**
641 A117 5c on 10c ultra (C)   .65 .25
642 A117 10c on 20c car lake   .65 .30

Inauguration of Carlos P. Garcia as president and Diosdado Macapagal as vice-president, Dec. 00.

University of the Philippines — A135

**1958**   **Engr.**   **Perf. 13½x13**
643 A135 5c dk carmine rose   .35 .20

50th anniversary of the founding of the University of the Philippines.

Pres. Carlos P. Garcia — A136

**1958**   **Photo.**   **Perf. 11½**   **Granite Paper**
644 A136 5c multicolored   .25 .20
645 A136 20c multicolored   .50 .30

12th anniversary of Philippine Republic.

---

Manila Cathedral — A137

**1958, Dec. 8**   **Perf. 13x13½, 12**   **Engr.**
646 A137 5c multicolored   .35 .20

Issued to commemorate the inauguration of the rebuilt Manila Cathedral, Dec. 8, 1958.

No. 592 Surcharged

OneCentavo

**1959**   **Perf. 12**
647 A117 1c on 5c crim rose   .35 .20

Nos. B4-B5 Surcharged with New Values and Bars

**1959, Feb. 3**   **Perf. 13**
648 SP4 1c on 2c + 2c red   .25 .20
649 SP5 6c on 4c + 4c vio   .25 .20

14th anniversary of the liberation of Manila from the Japanese forces.

Philippine Flag A138

**1959, Feb. 8**   **Unwmk.**   **Perf. 13**
650 A138 6c dp ultra, yel & dp car   .20 .20
651 A138 20c dp car, yel & dp ultra   .45 .20

---

Seal of Bulacan Province A139

Seal of Bacolod City A140

**1959**   **Engr.**   **Perf. 13**
652 A139 6c lt yellow grn   .20 .20
653 A139 20c rose red   .40 .20

60th anniversary of the Malolos constitution. For surcharge see No. 848.

**1959**
Design: 6c, 25c, Seal of Capiz Province and portrait of Pres. Roxas.
654 A139 6c lt brown   .25 .20
655 A139 25c purple   .35 .25

Pres. Manuel A. Roxas, 11th death anniv.

**1959**
656 A140 6c blue green   .20 .20
657 A140 10c rose lilac   .40 .20

Nos. 658-803 were reserved for the rest of a projected series showing seals and coats of arms of provinces and cities.

Camp John Hay Amphitheater, Baguio — A141

---

**Perf. 13½ (6c, 25c), 12 (6c)**
**1959, Sept. 1**
804 A141 6c bright green   .20 .20
805 A141 25c rose red   .35 .20

50th anniversary of the city of Baguio.

No. 533 Surcharged in Red

**1959, Oct. 24**   **Perf. 12**
806 A94 6c on 18c blue   .40 .20

Issued for United Nations Day, Oct. 24.

Maria Cristina Falls — A142

**1959, Nov. 18**   **Photo.**   **Perf. 13½, 12**
807 A142 6c vio & dp yel grn   .25 .20
808 A142 30c green & brown   .75 .30

No. 504 Surcharged with New Value and Bars

**1959**   **Engr.**   **Perf. 12**
809 A78 1c on 4c blk brn   .35 .20

Manila Athenaeum Emblem — A143

**1959, Dec. 10**   **Perf. 13½, 12**
810 A143 6c ultra   .20 .20
811 A143 30c rose red   .40 .25

Centenary of the Manila Atheneum (Ateneo de Manila), a school, and to mark a century of progress in education.

Manuel Quezon — A144

José Rizal — A145

**1959-60**   **Engr.**   **Perf. 13**
812 A144 1c olive gray ('60)   .30 .20
813 A145 6c gray blue   .40 .20
**Perf. 14x12**

For overprint see No. O62.

Constitution of the Philippines — A146

***Perf. 12½x13½***

**1960** **Unwmk.** **Photo.**
**814** A146 6c brown & gold .65 .20

25th anniversary of the Philippine Constitution. See No. C82.

Site of Manila Pact A147

**1960** **Engr.** ***Perf. 12½***
**815** A147 6c emerald .20 .20
**816** A147 25c orange .40 .20

5th anniversary (in 1959) of the Congress of the Philippines establishing the South-East Asia Treaty Organization (SEATO).
For overprints see Nos. 841-842.

Sunset at Manila Bay and Uprooted Oak Emblem — A148

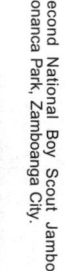

**1960, Apr. 7** **Photo.** ***Perf. 13½***
**817** A148 6c multicolored .30 .20
**818** A148 25c multicolored .70 .20

World Refugee Year, 7/1/59-6/30/60.

A149

**1960, July 29** ***Perf. 13½***
**819** A149 5c lt grn, red & gold .30 .20
**820** A149 6c bl, red & gold .30 .20

Philippine Tuberculosis Society, 50th anniv.

Basketball — A150

**1960, Nov. 30** ***Perf. 13x13½***
**821** A150 6c shown .35 .20
**822** A150 10c Runner .50 .20
*Nos. 821-822,C85-C86 (4)* 2.35 1.45

17th Olympic Games, Rome, 8/25-9/11.

Presidents Eisenhower and Garcia and Presidential Seals — A151

**1960, Dec. 30** ***Perf. 13½***
**823** A151 6c multi .20 .20
**824** A151 20c ultra, red & yel .30 .20

Visit of Pres. Dwight D. Eisenhower to the Philippines, June 14, 1960.

Nos. 539, 616, 619, 553, 606 and 598 Surcharged with New Values and Bars in Red or Black

**1960-61** **Engr.** ***Perf. 12, 13, 12½***
**825** A96 1c on 18c dp bl (R) .30 .20
**826** A121 5c on 18c dp bl (R) .55 .25
**827** A123 5c on 18c dp car rose .55 .20
**828** A101 10c on 18c ultra (R) .55 .25
**829** A119 10c on 18c dp bl & org (R) .55 .20
**830** A117 20c on 25c yel grn ('61) .55 .25
*Nos. 825-830 (6)* 3.05 1.35

On No. 830, no bars are overprinted, the surcharge "20 20" serving to cancel the old denomination.

Mercury and Globe — A152

**1961, Jan. 23** **Photo.** ***Perf. 13½***
**831** A152 6c red brn, bl, blk & gold .95 .20

Manila Postal Conf., Jan. 10-23. See #C87.

Nos. B10, B11 and B11a Surcharged "2nd National Boy Scout Jamboree Pasonanca Park" and New Value in Black or Red

**1961, May 2** **Engr.** ***Perf. 13***
**Yellow Paper**
**832** SP8 10c on 6c + 4c car .35 .20
**833** SP8 30c on 25c + 5c bl (R) .55 .35
*a.* Tete beche, *wht* (10c on 6c + 4c & 30c on 25c + 5c) (Bk) 1.25 1.00

Second National Boy Scout Jamboree, Pasonanca Park, Zamboanga City.

De la Salle College, Manila A153

**1961, June 16** **Photo.** ***Perf. 11½***
**834** A153 6c multi .25 .20
**835** A153 10c multi .25 .20

De la Salle College, Manila, 50th anniv.

José Rizal as Student A154

6c, Rizal & birthplace at Calamba, Laguna. 10c, Rizal & parents. 20c, Rizal with Juan Luna & F. R. Hidalgo in Madrid. 30c, Rizal's execution.

**1961** **Unwmk.** ***Perf. 13½***
**836** A154 5c multi .20 .20
**837** A154 6c multi .20 .20
**838** A154 10c grn & red brn .25 .20
**839** A154 20c brn red & grnsh bl .30 .25
**840** A154 30c vio, lil & org brn .50 .30
*Nos. 836-840 (5)* 1.45 1.15

Centenary of the birth of José Rizal.

Nos. 815-816 Overprinted

**1961, July 4** **Engr.** ***Perf. 12½***
**841** A147 6c emerald .20 .20
**842** A147 25c orange .30 .25

15th anniversary of the Republic.

Colombo Plan Emblem and Globe Showing Member Countries — A155

**1961, Oct. 8** **Photo.** ***Perf. 13x11½***
**843** A155 5c multi .25 .20
**844** A155 6c multi .25 .20

7th anniversary of the admission of the Philippines to the Colombo Plan.

Government Clerk — A156

**1961, Dec. 9** **Unwmk.** ***Perf. 12½***
**845** A156 6c vio, bl & red .25 .20
**846** A156 10c gray bl & red .50 .20

Honoring Philippine government employees.

No. C83 Surcharged

**1961, Nov. 30** **Engr.** ***Perf. 14x14½***
**847** AP11 6c on 10c car .35 .20

Philippine Amateur Athletic Fed., 50th anniv.

No. 655 Surcharged with New Value and: "MACAPAGAL-PELAEZ INAUGURATION DEC. 30, 1961"

**1961, Dec. 30** ***Perf. 12½***
**848** A139 6c on 25c pur .35 .20

Inauguration of Pres. Diosdado Macapagal and Vice-Pres. Emanuel Pelaez.

No. B8 Surcharged

**1962, Jan. 23** **Photo.** ***Perf. 13½x13***
**849** SP7 6c on 5c grn & red .50 .20

Vanda Orchids — A157

Apolinario Mabini — A158

Orchids: 6c, White mariposa. 10c, Sander's dendrobe. 20c, Sanggumay.

**1962, Mar. 9** **Photo.** ***Perf. 13½x14***
**Dark Blue Background**
**850** 5c rose, grn & yel .60 .20
**851** 6c grn & yel .60 .20
**852** 10c grn, car & brn .60 .20
**853** 20c lil, brn & grn .60 .20
*a.* A157 Block of 4, #850-853 2.50 2.25
*b.* As "a," imperf. 3.50 3.00

***Perf. 13½; 14 (1s); 13x12 (#857, 10s)***
**1962-69** **Engr.** **Unwmk.**

Portraits: 1s, Manuel L. Quezon. 5s, Marcelo H. del Pilar. No. 857, José Rizal. No. 857A, Rizal (wearing shirt). 10s, Father José Burgos. 20s, Lapu-Lapu. 30s, Rajah Soliman. 50s, Cayetano Arellano. 70s, Sergio Osmena. No. 863, Emilio Jacinto. No. 864, José M. Panganiban.

**854** A158 1s org brn ('63) .20 .20
**855** A158 3s rose red .20 .20
**856** A158 5s car rose ('63) .20 .20
**857** A158 6s dk red brn .25 .20
**857A** A158 6s pck bl ('64) .25 .20
**858** A158 10s brt pur ('63) .25 .20
**859** A158 20s Prus bl ('63) .30 .20
**860** A158 30s vermilion .75 .20
**861** A158 50s vio ('63) 1.00 .20
**862** A158 70s brt bl ('63) 1.25 .20
**863** A158 1p grn ('63) 2.40 .35
**864** A158 1p dp org ('69) .80 .30
*Nos. 854-864 (12)* 7.85 2.65

For surcharges & overprints see #873-874, 946, 969, 1054, 1119, 1209, O63-O69.

Pres. Macapagal Taking Oath of Office — A159

## 1962
### Photo. Perf. 13½
### Vignette Multicolored

| | | | |
|---|---|---|---|
| 865 | A159 | 6s blue | .20 .20 |
| 866 | A159 | 10s green | .20 .20 |
| 867 | A159 | 30s violet | .50 .60 |

Nos. 865-867 (3)

Swearing in of President Diosdado Macapagal, Dec. 30, 1961.

Volcano in Lake Taal and Malaria Eradication Emblem — A160

### 1962, Oct. 24 Unwmk.
### Granite Paper Perf. 11½

| | | | |
|---|---|---|---|
| 868 | A160 | 6s multi | .20 .20 |
| 869 | A160 | 10s multi | .50 .50 |
| 870 | A160 | 30s multi | .90 .90 |

Nos. 868-870 (3)

Issued on UN Day for the WHO drive to eradicate malaria.

No. 598 Surcharged in Red

### 1962, Nov. 15 Engr. Perf. 12

| | | | |
|---|---|---|---|
| 871 | A117 | 20s on 25c yel grn | .50 .20 |

Issued to commemorate the bicentennial of the Diego Silang revolt in Ilocos Province.

No. B6 Overprinted with Sideways Chevron Obliterating Surtax
### 1962, Dec. 23 Perf. 12

| | | | |
|---|---|---|---|
| 872 | SP6 | 5c on 5c + 1c dp bl | .50 .20 |

Nos. 855, 857 Surcharged with New Value and Old Value Obliterated
### 1963 Perf. 13½

| | | | |
|---|---|---|---|
| 873 | A158 | 1s on 3s rose red | .25 .20 |

### Perf. 13x12

| | | | |
|---|---|---|---|
| 874 | A158 | 5s on 6s red brn | .25 .20 |

No. 601 Surcharged

### 1963, June 12 Perf. 13½

| | | | |
|---|---|---|---|
| 875 | A117 | 6s on 2p vio | .30 .20 |
| 876 | A117 | 20s on 2p vio | .45 .20 |
| 877 | A117 | 70s on 2p vio | .75 .70 |
| | | Nos. 875-877 (3) | 1.50 .70 |

Diego Silang Bicentennial Art and Philatelic Exhibition, ARPHEX, Manila, May 28-June 30.

Pres. Manuel Roxas — A161

### 1963-73 Engr. Perf. 13½

| | | | |
|---|---|---|---|
| 878 | A161 | 6s brt bl & blk, bluish | .35 .20 |
| 879 | A161 | 30s brn & blk | .80 .20 |

**Pres. Ramon Magsaysay**

| | | | |
|---|---|---|---|
| 880 | A161 | 6s lil & blk (65) | .35 .20 |
| 881 | A161 | 30s yel grn & blk | .80 .20 |

**Pres. Elpidio Quirino**

| | | | |
|---|---|---|---|
| 882 | A161 | 6s grn & blk (65) | .35 .20 |
| 883 | A161 | 30s rose lil & blk (65) | .80 .20 |

**Gen. (Pres.) Emilio Aguinaldo**

| | | | |
|---|---|---|---|
| 883A | A161 | 6s dk cl & blk (66) | .35 .20 |
| 883B | A161 | 30s bl & blk (66) | .80 .20 |

**Pres. José P. Laurel**

| | | | |
|---|---|---|---|
| 883C | A161 | 6s lt red brn & blk (66) | .20 .20 |

**Pres. Manuel L. Quezon**

| | | | |
|---|---|---|---|
| 883D | A161 | 30s bl & blk (66) | .35 .20 |
| 883E | A161 | 10s lt gray & blk (67) | .35 .20 |
| 883F | A161 | 1s vio & blk ('67) | .55 .20 |

**Pres. Sergio Osmeña**

| | | | |
|---|---|---|---|
| 883G | A161 | 10s rose lil & blk (70) | .35 .20 |

**Pres. Carlos P. Garcia**

| | | | |
|---|---|---|---|
| 883H | A161 | 40s grn & blk (70) | .20 .20 |
| 883I | A161 | 10s multi (73) | .35 .20 |
| 883J | A161 | 70s multi (73) | 8.60 3.20 |

Nos. 878-883J honor former presidents. For surcharges see Nos. 984-985, 1120, 1146, 1160-1161.

Globe, Flags of Thailand, Korea, China, Philippines — A162

### 1963, Aug. 26 Photo. Perf. 13½x13

| | | | |
|---|---|---|---|
| 884 | A162 | 6s dk grn & multi | .50 .20 |
| 885 | A162 | 30s dk grn & multi | .35 .20 |

Asian-Oceanic Postal Union, 1st anniv. For surcharge see No. 1078.

Red Cross Centenary Emblem — A163

### 1963, Sept. 1 Perf. 11½

| | | | |
|---|---|---|---|
| 886 | A163 | 5s lt vio, gray & red | .30 .20 |
| 887 | A163 | 6s ultra, gray & red | .30 .20 |
| 888 | A163 | 20s grn, gray & red | .90 .60 |

Nos. 886-888 (3)

Centenary of the International Red Cross.

Bamboo Dance — A164

Folk Dances: 6s, Dance with oil lamps. 10s, Duck dance. 20s, Princess Gandingan's rock dance.

### 1963, Sept. 15 Unwmk. Perf. 14

| | | | |
|---|---|---|---|
| 889 | A164 | 5s multi | .40 .20 |
| 890 | A164 | 6s multi | .40 .20 |
| 891 | A164 | 10s multi | .40 .20 |
| 892 | A164 | 20s multi | 1.90 1.50 |
| a. | A164 | Block of 4, #889-892 | |

For surcharges and overprints see #1043-1046.

Pres. Macapagal and Filipino Family — A165

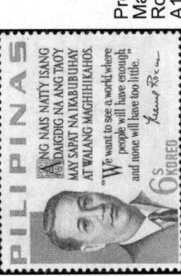

### 1963, Sept. 28 Perf. 14

| | | | |
|---|---|---|---|
| 893 | A165 | 5s bl & multi | .25 .20 |
| 894 | A165 | 6s yel & multi | .40 .20 |
| 895 | A165 | 20s multi | .90 .60 |

Nos. 893-895 (3)

Issued to publicize Pres. Macapagal's 5-year Socioeconomic Program. For surcharge see No. 1181.

Presidents Lopez Mateos and Macapagal — A166

### 1963, Sept. 28 Photo. Perf. 13½

| | | | |
|---|---|---|---|
| 896 | A166 | 6s multi | .20 .20 |
| 897 | A166 | 30s multi | .30 .30 |

Visit of Pres. Adolfo Lopez Mateos of Mexico to the Philippines. For surcharge see No. 1166.

Andres Bonifacio — A167

### 1963, Nov. 30 Unwmk. Perf. 12

| | | | |
|---|---|---|---|
| 898 | A167 | 5s gold, brn, gray & red | .20 .20 |
| 899 | A167 | 6s sil, brn, gray & red | .35 .20 |
| 900 | A167 | 25s brnz, brn, gray & red | .50 .60 |
| | | Nos. 898-900 (3) | 1.05 1.00 |

Centenary of the birth of Andres Bonifacio, national hero and poet. For surcharges see Nos. 1147, 1162.

No. 534 Overprinted: "UN ADOPTION/DECLARATION OF HUMAN RIGHTS/15TH ANNIVERSARY DEC. 10, 1963"
### 1963, Dec. 10 Engr. Imperf.
Souvenir Sheet

| | | | |
|---|---|---|---|
| 901 | A94 | Sheet of 3 | 3.25 2.50 |

15th anniv. of the Universal Declaration of Human Rights.

Woman holding Sheaf of Rice — A168

### 1963, Dec. 20 Photo. Perf. 13½x13

| | | | |
|---|---|---|---|
| 902 | A168 | 6s brn & multi | .50 .20 |
| | | Nos. 902, C88-C89 (3) | 1.25 .70 |

FAO "Freedom from Hunger" campaign.

Bamboo Organ — A169

### 1964, May 4 Perf. 13½

| | | | |
|---|---|---|---|
| 903 | A169 | 5s multi | .25 .20 |
| 904 | A169 | 6s multi | .50 .25 |
| 905 | A169 | 20s multi | 1.00 .65 |

Nos. 903-905 (3)

The bamboo organ in the Church of Las Pinas, Rizal, was built by Father Diego Cera, 1816-1822. For surcharge see No. 1055.

Apolinario Mabini — A170

### 1964, July 23 Wmk. 233 Photo. Perf. 14½

| | | | |
|---|---|---|---|
| 906 | A170 | 6s pur & gold | .20 .20 |
| 907 | A170 | 10s red brn & gold | .25 .20 |
| 908 | A170 | 30s brt grn & gold | .75 .60 |

Nos. 906-908 (3)

Apolinario Mabini (1864-1903), national hero and a leader of the 1898 revolution. For surcharge see No. 1056.

Pres. Macapagal Signing Code — A172

Flags Surrounding SEATO Emblem — A171

### 1964, Sept. 8 Unwmk. Photo.
### Flags and Emblem Multicolored Perf. 13

| | | | |
|---|---|---|---|
| 909 | A171 | 6s dk bl & yel | .20 .20 |
| 910 | A171 | 10s dp grn & yel | .30 .20 |
| 911 | A171 | 25s dk brn & yel | .40 .60 |
| | | Nos. 909-911 (3) | .90 .60 |

10th anniversary of the South-East Asia Treaty Organization (SEATO). For surcharge see No. 1121.

### 1964, Dec. 21 Wmk. 233 Perf. 14½

| | | | |
|---|---|---|---|
| 912 | A172 | 3s multi | .45 .20 |
| 913 | A172 | 6s multi | .45 .60 |
| | | Nos. 912-913,C90 (3) | 1.40 .60 |

Signing of the Agricultural Land Reform Code. For surcharges see Nos. 970, 1234.

Basketball — A173

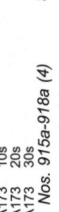

Sport: 10s, Women's relay race. 20s, Hurdling. 30s, Soccer.

### 1964, Dec. 28 Perf. 14½x14

| | | | |
|---|---|---|---|
| 915 | A173 | 6s lt bl, dk grn & gold | .20 .20 |
| 916 | A173 | 10s gold, pink & dk brn | .25 .20 |
| b. | | Gold omitted | |
| 917 | A173 | 20s gold, dk brn & yel | .45 .20 |
| 918 | A173 | 30s emer, dk brn & gold | .60 .20 |
| | | | 1.50 .80 |

Nos. 915-918 (4)

18th Olympic Games, Tokyo, Oct. 10-25. For overprints and surcharge see Nos. 962-965, 1079.

### Imperf., Pairs

| | | | |
|---|---|---|---|
| 915a | A173 | 6s | 1.25 .75 |
| 916a | A173 | 10s | 1.25 .75 |
| 917a | A173 | 20s | 2.75 1.75 |
| 918a | A173 | 30s | 8.00 5.00 |

Nos. 915a-918a (4)

Presidents Lubke and Macapagal and Coats of Arms — A174

### 1965, Apr. 19 Unwmk. Perf. 13½

| | | | |
|---|---|---|---|
| 919 | A174 | 6s ol grn & multi | .20 .20 |
| 920 | A174 | 10s dp bl & multi | .40 .20 |
| 921 | A174 | 25s dp bl & multi | .90 .60 |

Nos. 919-921 (3)

Visit of Pres. Heinrich Lubke of Germany, Nov. 18-23, 1964. For surcharge see No. 1167.

Emblems of Manila Observatory and Weather Bureau — A175

**1965, May 22 Photo. Perf. 13½**

| 922 | A175 | 6s lt ultra & multi | .20 | .20 |
|---|---|---|---|---|
| 923 | A175 | 20s lt vio & multi | .30 | .20 |
| 924 | A175 | 50s bl grn & multi | .40 | .25 |
| | | Nos. 922-924 (3) | .90 | .65 |

Issued to commemorate the centenary of the Meteorological Service in the Philippines. For surcharge see No. 1069.

Pres. John F. Kennedy (1917-63) — A176

**1965, May 29 Perf. 14½x14 Wmk. 233**

Center Multicolored

| 925 | A176 | 6s gray | .20 | .20 |
|---|---|---|---|---|
| 926 | A176 | 10s brt vio | .30 | .20 |
| 927 | A176 | 30s ultra | .40 | .20 |
| | | Nos. 925-927 (3) | .90 | .60 |

Nos. 925-927 exist with ultramarine of tie omitted. The 6s and 30s exist imperf. Value, each $30.

For surcharges see Nos. 1148, 1210.

King and Queen of Thailand, Pres. and Mrs. Macapagal — A177

**1965, June 12 Perf. 12½x13**

| 928 | A177 | 2s brt bl & multi | .20 | .20 |
|---|---|---|---|---|
| 929 | A177 | 6s blk & multi | .30 | .20 |
| 930 | A177 | 30s red & multi | .40 | .20 |
| | | Nos. 928-930 (3) | .90 | .60 |

Visit of King Bhumibol Adulyadej and Queen Sirikit of Thailand, July 1963.

For surcharge see No. 1122.

Princess Beatrix and Evangelina Macapagal A178

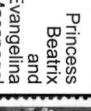

**1965, July 4 Photo. Perf. 13x12½**

| 931 | A178 | 2s brt & multi | .20 | .20 |
|---|---|---|---|---|
| 932 | A178 | 6s blk & multi | .20 | .20 |
| 933 | A178 | 10s multi | .75 | .60 |
| | | Nos. 931-933 (3) | | |

Visit of Princess Beatrix of the Netherlands, Nov. 21-23, 1962.

For surcharge see No. 1188.

Map of Philippines, Cross and Legaspi-Urdaneta Monument — A179

Design: 3s, Cross and Rosary held before map of Philippines.

**1965, Oct. 4 Unwmk. Perf. 13**

| 934 | A179 | 3s multi | .25 | .20 |
|---|---|---|---|---|
| 935 | A179 | 6s multi | 2.00 | .95 |
| | | Nos. 934-935,C91-C92 (4) | | |

400th anniv. of the Christianization of the Philippines. See souvenir sheet No. C92a. For overprint see No. C108.

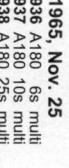

Presidents Sukarno and Macapagal and Prime Minister Tunku Abdul Rahman A180

**1965, Nov. 25 Perf. 13**

| 936 | A180 | 6s multi | .20 | .20 |
|---|---|---|---|---|
| 937 | A180 | 10s multi | .30 | .20 |
| 938 | A180 | 25s multi | .40 | .20 |
| | | Nos. 936-938 (3) | .90 | .60 |

Signing of the Manila Accord (Maphilindo) by Malaya, Philippines and Indonesia. For surcharge see No. 1182.

Bicyclists and Globe A181

**1965, Dec. 5 Perf. 13½**

| 939 | A181 | 6s multi | .20 | .20 |
|---|---|---|---|---|
| 940 | A181 | 10s multi | .30 | .20 |
| 941 | A181 | 25s multi | .40 | .20 |
| | | Nos. 939-941 (3) | .90 | .60 |

Second Asian Cycling Championship, Philippines, Nov. 28-Dec. 5.

Nos. B21-B22 Surcharged

MARCOS-LOPEZ INAUGURATION DEC. 30, 1965 PILIPINAS

**1965, Dec. 30 Engr.**

| 942 | SP12 | 10s on 6s + 4s | .30 | .20 |
|---|---|---|---|---|
| 943 | SP12 | 30s on 30s + 5s | .45 | .25 |

Inauguration of President Ferdinand Marcos and Vice-President Fernando Lopez.

Antonio Regidor — A182

**1966, Jan. 21 Engr. Perf. 12x11**

| 944 | A182 | 6s blue | .25 | .20 |
|---|---|---|---|---|
| 945 | A182 | 30s brown | .35 | .20 |

Dr. Antonio Regidor, Sec. of the High Court of Manila and Pres. of Public Instruction.

For surcharges see Nos. 1110-1111.

No. 857A Overprinted in Red: "HELP ME STOP / SMUGGLING / Pres. MARCOS"

**1966, May 1 Engr. Perf. 13½**

| 946 | A158 | 6s peacock blue | .35 | .20 |
|---|---|---|---|---|

Anti-smuggling drive.

Exists with overprint inverted, double, double inverted and double with one inverted.

For surcharge see No. 1209.

Girl Scout Giving Scout Sign A183

**1966, May 26 Litho. Perf. 13x12½**

| 947 | A183 | 3s ultra & multi | .20 | .20 |
|---|---|---|---|---|
| 948 | A183 | 6s emer & multi | .20 | .20 |
| 949 | A183 | 20s brn & multi | .75 | .60 |
| | | Nos. 947-949 (3) | | |

Philippine Girl Scouts, 25th anniversary. For surcharge see No. 1019.

Pres. Marcos Taking Oath of Office — A184

**1966, June 12 Perf. 12½**

| 950 | A184 | 6s bl & multi | .20 | .20 |
|---|---|---|---|---|
| 951 | A184 | 20s emer & multi | .30 | .20 |
| 952 | A184 | 30s yel & multi | .40 | .20 |
| | | Nos. 950-952 (3) | .90 | .60 |

Inauguration of Pres. Ferdinand E. Marcos, 12/30/65. For overprints & surcharge see #960-961, 1050.

Seal of Manila and Historical Scenes — A185

**1966, June 24 Perf. 13½**

| 953 | A185 | 6s multi | .25 | .20 |
|---|---|---|---|---|
| 954 | A185 | 30s multi | .35 | .20 |

Adoption of the new seal of Manila. For surcharges see Nos. 1070, 1118, 1235.

Old and New Philippine National Bank Buildings — A186

**1966, July 22 Photo. Perf. 14x13½**

| 955 | A186 | 6s gold, ultra, sil & blk | .25 | .20 |
|---|---|---|---|---|
| 956 | A186 | 10s multi | .35 | .20 |

Designs: 6s, Entrance to old bank building and 1p silver coin.

Post Office, Annex Three A187

**1966, Oct. 1 Wmk. 233 Perf. 14½**

| 957 | A187 | 6s lt vio, yel & grn | .20 | .20 |
|---|---|---|---|---|
| 958 | A187 | 10s rose cl, yel & grn | .25 | .20 |
| 959 | A187 | 20s ultra, red & grn | .75 | .60 |
| | | Nos. 957-959 (3) | | |

50th anniv. of the Philippine Natl. Bank. See #C93. For surcharges see #1071, 1100, 1236.

60th anniversary of Postal Savings Bank. For surcharges see Nos. 1104, 1112, 1189.

Nos. 950 and 952 Overprinted in Emerald or Black

**1966, Oct. 24 Litho. Perf. 12½**

| 960 | A184 | 6s multi (E) | .25 | .20 |
|---|---|---|---|---|
| 961 | A184 | 30s multi | .35 | .20 |

Manila Summit Conference, Oct. 23-27.

Nos. 915a-918a Overprinted

**Wmk. 233**

**1967, Jan. 14 Photo. Imperf.**

| 962 | A173 | 6s lt bl, dk brn & gold | .30 | .30 |
|---|---|---|---|---|
| 963 | A173 | 10s gold, dk brn & pink | .35 | .35 |
| 964 | A173 | 20s gold, dk brn & yel | .45 | .20 |
| 965 | A173 | 30s emer, dk brn & gold | .60 | .40 |
| | | Nos. 962-965 (4) | 1.75 | 1.00 |

Lions Intl. 50th anniv. The Lions emblem is in the lower left corner on the 10s and in the upper left corner on the 6s and in the upper right corner on the 30s.

"Succor" by Fernando Amorsolo — A188

PILIPINAS 5s 25TH ANNIVERSARY BATTLE OF BATAAN 1942-1967 KOREO

**1967, May 15 Litho. Unwmk. Perf. 14**

| 966 | A188 | 5s sepia & multi | .30 | .30 |
|---|---|---|---|---|
| 967 | A188 | 20s blue & multi | .70 | .20 |
| 968 | A188 | 2p green & multi | 1.50 | .90 |
| | | Nos. 966-968 (3) | 2.50 | |

25th anniversary of the Battle of Bataan.

Nos. 857A and 913 Surcharged

**1967, Aug. Engr. Perf. 13½**

| 969 | A158 | 4s on 6s pck bl | .25 | .20 |
|---|---|---|---|---|
| 970 | A172 | 5s on 6s multi | .35 | .20 |

25th anniversary of the Battle of Bataan.

Issue dates: 4s, Aug. 10; 5s, Aug. 7.

Gen. Douglas MacArthur and Paratroopers Landing on Corregidor — A189

**1967, Aug. 31 Unwmk. Litho. Perf. 14**

| 971 | A189 | 6s multi | .35 | .20 |
|---|---|---|---|---|
| 972 | A189 | 5p multi | 5.75 | 3.00 |

25th anniversary, Battle of Corregidor.

Bureau of Posts, Manila, Jones Bridge over Pasig River — A190

**1967, Sept. 15    Litho.    Perf. 14x13½**
973  A190  4s multi & blk          .20  .20
974  A190  20s multi & red        .30  .30
975  A190  50s multi & vio         .40  .25
                                   .90  .65
65th anniversary of the Bureau of Posts.
For overprint see No. 1015.

Philippine Nativity Scene — A191

**1967, Dec. 1    Photo.    Perf. 13½**
976  A191  10s multi              .25  .20
977  A191  40s multi              .35  .25
Christmas 1967.

Chinese Garden, Rizal Park, Presidents Marcos and Chiang Kai-shek — A192

Presidents' heads & scenes in Chinese Garden, Rizal Park, Manila: 10s, Gate. 20s, Landing pier.

**1967-68    Photo.    Perf. 13½**
978  A192   5s multi              .20  .20
979  A192  10s multi ('68)        .35  .20
980  A192  20s multi              1.25  .60
                Nos. 978-980 (3)
Sino-Philippine Friendship Year 1966-67.

Makati Center Post Office, Mrs. Marcos and Rotary Emblem — A193

**1968, Jan. 9    Litho.    Perf. 14**
981  A193  10s bl & multi         .20  .20
982  A193  20s grn & multi        .30  .20
983  A193  40s multi              .50  .35
                Nos. 981-983 (3)  1.00  .75
1st anniv. of the Makati Center Post Office.

Nos. 882, 883C and B27 Surcharged with New Value and Two Bars

---

**1968**
984  A161   5s on 6s grn & blk    .55  .20
985  A161   5s on 6s lt red brn &
                blk               .55  .20
986  SP14  10s on 6s + 5s ultra
                & red             .65  .20
                                  1.75  .60
                Nos. 984-986 (3)
For similar surcharge see No. 1586.

Felipe G. Calderon, Barasoain Church and Malolos Constitution — A194

**1968, Apr. 4    Litho.    Perf. 14**
987  A194  10s lt ultra & multi   .20  .20
988  A194  40s grn & multi        .30  .30
989  A194  75s multi              .60  .30
                Nos. 987-989 (3)  1.10  .70
Calderon (1868-1909), lawyer and author of the Malolos Constitution.

Earth and Transmission from Philippine Station to Satellite — A195

**1968, Oct. 21    Photo.    Perf. 13½**
990  A195  10s blk & multi        .30  .20
991  A195  40s multi              .55  .55
992  A195  75s multi              .90  .90
                Nos. 990-992 (3)  1.75  .75
Issued to commemorate the inauguration of the Philcomsat Station in Tany, Luzon, May 2, 1968.

Tobacco Industry and Tobacco Board's Emblem — A196

**1968, Nov. 15    Photo.    Perf. 13½**
993  A196  10s blk & multi        .20  .20
994  A196  40s bl & multi         .35  .30
995  A196  70s crim & multi       .60  .60
                Nos. 993-995 (3)  1.15  1.00
Philippine tobacco industry.

Kudyapi — A197

Philippine Musical Instruments: 20s, Ludag (drum). 30s, Kulintangan. 50s, Subing (bamboo flute).

**1968, Nov. 22    Photo.    Perf. 13½**
996  A197  10s multi              .20  .20
997  A197  20s multi              .30  .20
998  A197  30s multi              .50  .25
999  A197  50s multi              .75  .45
                Nos. 996-999 (4)  1.75  1.10

Concordia College A198

---

**1968, Dec. 8    Perf. 13x13½**
1000  A198  10s multi             .25  .20
1001  A198  20s multi             .35  .20
1002  A198  70s multi             .65  .70
                Nos. 1000-1002 (3)  1.25  1.10
Centenary of the Colegio de la Concordia, Manila, a Catholic women's school. Issued Dec. 8 (Sunday), but entered the mail Dec. 9.

Singing Children — A199

**1968, Dec. 16    Perf. 13½**
1003  A199  10s multi             .20  .20
1004  A199  40s multi             .45  .35
1005  A199  75s multi             .85  .60
                Nos. 1003-1005 (3)  1.50  1.15
Christmas 1968.

Animals A200

**1969, Jan. 8    Photo.    Perf. 13½**
1006  A200   2s Tarsier           .20  .20
1007  A200  10s Tamarau           .30  .20
1008  A200  40s Carabao           .60  .20
1009  A200  75s Mouse deer        1.90  .75
                Nos. 1006-1009 (4)  3.00  1.35
Opening of the hunting season.

Emilio Aguinaldo and Historical Building, Cavite — A201

**1969, Jan. 23    Litho.    Perf. 14**
1010  A201  10s yel & multi       .20  .20
1011  A201  40s bl & multi        .50  .25
1012  A201  70s multi             .80  .55
                Nos. 1010-1012 (3)  1.50  1.00
Emilio Aguinaldo (1869-1964), commander of Filipino forces in rebellion against Spain.

Guard Turret, San Andres Bastion, Manila, and Rotary Emblem — A202

**1969, Jan. 29    Photo.    Perf. 12½**
1013  A202  10s ultra & multi     .50  .20
                A202, C96-C97 (3)  1.75  .80
50th anniv. of the Manila Rotary Club.

Senator Claro M. Recto (1890-1960), Lawyer and Supreme Court Judge — A203

**1969, Feb. 10    Engr.    Perf. 13**
1014  A203  10s bright rose lilac  .35  .20

---

No. 973 Overprinted

**1969, Feb. 14    Litho.    Perf. 14x13½**
1015  A190  4s multi & blk         .35  .20
Philatelic Week, Nov. 24-30, 1968.

José Rizal College, Mandaluyong — A204

**1969, Feb. 19    Photo.    Perf. 13**
1016  A204  10s multicolored      .20  .20
1017  A204  40s multicolored      .35  .20
1018  A204  50s multicolored      .70  .25
                Nos. 1016-1018 (3)  1.25  .65
Founding of Rizal College, 50th anniv.

No. 948 Surcharged in Red with New Value, 2 Bars and: "4th NATIONAL BOY / SCOUT JAMBOREE / PALAYAN CITY-MAY, 1969"

**1969, May 12    Litho.    Perf. 13x12½**
1019  A183  5s on 6s multi        .35  .20

A205    A206

Map of Philippines, Red Crescent, Cross, Lion and Sun emblems.

**1969, May 26    Photo.    Perf. 12½**
1020  A205  10s gray, ultra & red  .20  .20
1021  A205  40s lt ultra, dk bl &
                red              .35  .25
1022  A205  75s bister, brn & red  .70  .30
                Nos. 1020-1022 (3)  1.25  .75
League of Red Cross Societies, 50th anniv.

**1969, June 13    Photo.    Perf. 14**
Pres. and Mrs. Marcos harvesting miracle rice.
1023  A206  10s multicolored      .20  .20
1024  A206  40s multicolored      .25  .25
1025  A206  75s multicolored      .70  .30
                Nos. 1023-1025 (3)  1.25  .75
Introduction of IR8 (miracle) rice, produced by the International Rice Research Institute.

Holy Child of Leyte and Map of Leyte — A207

**1969, June 30    Perf. 13½**
1026  A207  5s emerald & multi    .25  .20
1027  A207  10s crimson & multi   .35  .20
80th anniv. of the return of the image of the Holy Child of Leyte to Tacloban. See No. C98.

## 1969, Sept. 12 — Photo. — Perf. 13½
Philippine Development Bank — A208

| | | | |
|---|---|---|---|
| 1028 | A208 | 10s dk blk & grn | .20 .20 |
| 1029 | A208 | 40s rose car, blk & grn | .40 .25 |
| 1030 | A208 | 75s brown, blk & grn | .75 .30 |
| | | Nos. 1028-1030 (3) | 1.35 .75 |

Inauguration of the new building of the Philippine Development Bank in Makati, Rizal.

## 1969, Sept. 15 — Photo. — Perf. 13½
Butterflies: 20s, Tailed jay. 30s, Red Helen. 40s, Birdwing.

Common Birdwing A209

| | | | |
|---|---|---|---|
| 1031 | A209 | 10s multicolored | .45 .20 |
| 1032 | A209 | 20s multicolored | 1.10 .20 |
| 1033 | A209 | 30s multicolored | .90 .25 |
| 1034 | A209 | 40s multicolored | .90 .35 |
| | | Nos. 1031-1034 (4) | 3.35 1.00 |

## 1969, Oct. 6 — Photo. — Perf. 13½x14
World's Children and UNICEF Emblem A210

| | | | |
|---|---|---|---|
| 1035 | A210 | 10s blue & multi | .30 .20 |
| 1036 | A210 | 20s multicolored | .30 .20 |
| 1037 | A210 | 30s multicolored | .90 .60 |
| | | Nos. 1035-1037 (3) | |

15th anniversary of Universal Children's Day.

## 1969, Oct. 20 — Perf. 13½
Monument and Leyte Landing — A211

| | | | |
|---|---|---|---|
| 1038 | A211 | 5s lt grn & multi | .30 .20 |
| 1039 | A211 | 10s yellow & multi | .30 .20 |
| 1040 | A211 | 40s pink & multi | .90 .60 |
| | | Nos. 1038-1040 (3) | |

25th anniv. of the landing of the US forces under Gen. Douglas MacArthur on Leyte, Oct. 20, 1944.

## 1969, Nov. 4 — Photo. — Perf. 13½
Philippine Cultural Center, Manila — A212

| | | | |
|---|---|---|---|
| 1041 | A212 | 10s ultra | .30 .30 |
| 1042 | A212 | 30s brt rose lilac | .45 .20 |

Cultural Center of the Philippines, containing theaters, a museum and libraries.

---

Nos. 889-892 Surcharged or Overprinted: "1969 PHILATELIC WEEK"

## 1969, Nov. 24 — Photo. — Perf. 14

| | | | |
|---|---|---|---|
| 1043 | A164 | 5s multicolored | .40 .20 |
| 1044 | A164 | 5s on 6s multicolored | .40 .20 |
| 1045 | A164 | 10s multicolored | .40 .25 |
| 1046 | A164 | 10s on 20s multi | 1.75 1.25 |
| a. | | Block of 4, #1043-1046 | |

Philatelic Week, Nov. 23-29.

## 1969, Nov. 30 — Photo. — Perf. 12½
Melchora Aquino — A213

| | | | |
|---|---|---|---|
| 1047 | A213 | 10s multicolored | .20 .20 |
| 1048 | A213 | 20s multicolored | .30 .20 |
| 1049 | A213 | 30s dk bl & multi | .90 .60 |
| | | Nos. 1047-1049 (3) | |

Melchora Aquino (Tandang Sora; 1812-1919), the Grand Old Woman of the Revolution.

## 1969, Dec. 30 — Litho. — Perf. 12½
No. 950 Surcharged with New Value, 2 Bars and: "PASINAYA, IKA-2 / PANUNUNGKULAN / PANGULONG / FERDINAND E. MARCOS / DISYEMBRE 30, 1969"

| | | | |
|---|---|---|---|
| 1050 | A184 | 5s on 6s multi | .55 .20 |

Inauguration of Pres. Marcos and Vice Pres. Fernando Lopez for 2nd term, 12/30.

---

## 1970, Jan. 20 — Photo. — Perf. 13½

Pouring Ladle and Iligan Steel Mills — A214

| | | | |
|---|---|---|---|
| 1051 | A214 | 10s ver & multi | .20 .20 |
| 1052 | A214 | 20s multicolored | .30 .20 |
| 1053 | A214 | 30s ultra & multi | .40 .20 |
| | | Nos. 1051-1053 (3) | |

Iligan Integrated Steel Mills, Northern Mindanao, the first Philippine steel mills.

Nos. 857A, 904 and 906 Surcharged with New Value and Two Bars

## 1970, Apr. 30 — As Before

| | | | |
|---|---|---|---|
| 1054 | A158 | 4s on 6s peacock bl | .50 .20 |
| 1055 | A169 | 5s on 6s multi | .75 .20 |
| 1056 | A170 | 5s on 6s pur & gold | 2.00 .60 |
| | | Nos. 1054-1056 (3) | |

## 1970, May 20 — Unwmk. — Photo.
New UPU Headquarters and Monument, Bern — A215

| | | | |
|---|---|---|---|
| 1057 | A215 | 10s bl, dk bl & yel | .25 .20 |
| 1058 | A215 | 30s lt grn, dk bl & yel | .35 .20 |

Opening of the new UPU Headquarters in Bern.

---

## 1970, Sept. 6 — Photo. — Perf. 13½x14
Emblem, Mayon Volcano and Filipina — A216

| | | | |
|---|---|---|---|
| 1059 | A216 | 10s brt blue & multi | .30 .20 |
| 1060 | A216 | 20s multicolored | .30 .20 |
| 1061 | A216 | 30s multicolored | .90 .60 |
| | | Nos. 1059-1061 (3) | |

15th International Conference on Social Welfare, Manila, Sept. 6-12.

## 1970, Oct. 5 — Perf. 13x13½
Crab, by Alexander Calder, and Map of Philippines A217

| | | | |
|---|---|---|---|
| 1062 | A217 | 10s emerald & multi | .20 .20 |
| 1063 | A217 | 40s multicolored | .30 .30 |
| 1064 | A217 | 50s ultra & multi | .40 .30 |
| | | Nos. 1062-1064 (3) | |

Campaign against cancer.

## 1970, Oct. 19 — Photo. — Perf. 13½
Sea Shells: 10s, Royal spiny oyster. 20s, Venus comb. 40s, Glory of the sea.

Scaled Tridacna A218

| | | | |
|---|---|---|---|
| 1065 | A218 | 5s black & multi | .40 .20 |
| 1066 | A218 | 10s dk grn & multi | .70 .20 |
| 1067 | A218 | 20s multicolored | .75 .25 |
| 1068 | A218 | 40s dk blue & multi | 1.25 .30 |
| | | Nos. 1065-1068 (4) | 3.10 .95 |

## 1970, Oct. 26 — Photogravure; Lithographed — Perf. 13½, 12½
Nos. 922, 953 and 955 Surcharged

| | | | |
|---|---|---|---|
| 1069 | A175 | 4s on 6s multi | .70 .70 |
| 1070 | A185 | 4s on 6s multi | 1.10 .20 |
| 1071 | A186 | 4s on 6s multi | 1.10 .20 |
| | | Nos. 1069-1071 (3) | 2.90 .60 |

On No. 1070, old denomination is obliterated by two bars. One line surcharge on No. 1071.

## 1970, Nov. 16 — Photo. — Perf. 13½
Map of Philippines and FAPA Emblem — A219

| | | | |
|---|---|---|---|
| 1072 | A219 | 10s dp org & multi | .20 .20 |
| 1073 | A219 | 50s lt violet & multi | .35 .20 |

Opening of the 4th General Assembly of the Federation of Asian Pharmaceutical Assoc. (FAPA) & the 3rd Asian Cong. of Pharmaceutical Sciences.

---

## 1970, Nov. 12 — Perf. 12½x13½
Hundred Islands of Pangasinan, Peddler's Cart — A220

| | | | |
|---|---|---|---|
| 1074 | A220 | 10s multicolored | .20 .20 |
| 1075 | A220 | 20s multicolored | .30 .20 |
| 1076 | A220 | 30s multicolored | .75 .25 |
| 1077 | A220 | 2p multicolored | 2.50 1.00 |
| | | Nos. 1074-1077 (4) | 3.75 1.65 |

20s, Tree house in Pasonanca Park, Zamboanga City. 30s, Sugar industry, Negros Island, Mt. Kanlaon. Woman & Carabao statue, symbolizing agriculture. 2p, Miagao Church, Iloilo, & horse-drawn calesa.
Tourist publicity. See Nos. 1086-1097.

No. 884 Surcharged: "UPU-AOPU / Regional Seminar / Nov. 23-Dec. 5, 1970 / TEN 10s"

## 1970, Nov. 22 — Photo. — Perf. 13½x13

| | | | |
|---|---|---|---|
| 1078 | A162 | 10s on 6s multi | .50 .20 |

Universal Postal Union and Asian-Oceanic Postal Union Regional Seminar, 11/23-12/5.

No. 915 Surcharged Vertically: "1970 PHILATELIC WEEK"

## 1970, Nov. 22 — Perf. 14½x14
Wmk. 233

| | | | |
|---|---|---|---|
| 1079 | A173 | 10s on 6s multi | .35 .20 |

Philatelic Week, Nov. 22-28.

## 1970, Nov. 27 — Photo. — Perf. 13½x14
Pope Paul VI, Map of Far East and Australia — A221

| | | | |
|---|---|---|---|
| 1080 | A221 | 10s ultra & multi | .35 .25 |
| 1081 | A221 | 30s multicolored | 1.70 .75 |
| | | Nos. 1080-1081,C99 (3) | |

Visit of Pope Paul VI, Nov. 27-29, 1970.

## 1970, Dec. 30 — Engr. — Perf. 14½
Mariano Ponce — A222

| | | | |
|---|---|---|---|
| 1082 | A222 | 10s rose carmine | .35 .20 |

Mariano Ponce (1863-1918); editor and legislator. See #1136-1137. For surcharges & overprint see #1190, 1231, O70.

PATA Emblem A223

## No. 953 Surcharged

**1972, Apr. 20**
1118 A185 5s on 6s multi — .90 .20 — *Perf. 12½*

No. O69 with Two Bars over "G" and "O"

**1972, May 16 Engr. *Perf. 13½***
1119 A158 50s violet — .90 .20

Nos. 883A, 909 and 929 Surcharged with New Value and 2 Bars

**1972, May 29**
1120 A161 10s on 6s dp cl & blk — 1.10 .20
1121 A177 10s on 6s multi — .90 .20
1122 A177 10s on 6s multi — — .60
Nos. 1120-1122 (3) — 3.10

## No. 944 Surcharged

*Perf. 12x11 Engr. Unwmk.*

**1971, Nov. 24**
1110 A182 4s on 6s blue — .30 .20
1111 A182 5s on 6s blue — .30 .20

## No. 957 Surcharged

*Perf. 14½*

**1971, Nov. 24 Photo.**
1112 A187 5s on 6s multi — .50 .20

Philatelic Week, 1971.

**Wmk. 233**

## Independence Monument, Manila — A233

**1972, May 31 Photo. *Perf. 13x12½***
1123 A233 5s brt blue & multi — .20 .20
1124 A233 30s red & multi — .45 .20
1125 A233 60s emerald & multi — .65 .20
Nos. 1123-1125 (3) — 1.30 .60

Visit ASEAN countries (Association of South East Asian Nations).

## "K," Skull and Crossbones — A234

Development of Philippine Flag: No. 1126, 3 "K's" in a row ("K" stands for Katipunan). No. 1127, 3 "K's" as triangle. No. 1128, One "K." No. 1130, 3 "K's, sun over mountain on white triangle. No. 1131, Sun over 3 "K's. No. 1132, Tagalog "K" in sun. No. 1133, Sun with human face. No. 1134, Tricolor flag, forerunner of present flag. No. 1135, Present flag. Nos. 1126, 1128, 1130-1131, 1133, 1135 inscribed in Tagalog.

**1972, June 12 Photo. *Perf. 13***
1126 A234 30s ultra & red — 1.75 .30
1127 A234 30s ultra & red — 1.75 .30
1128 A234 30s ultra & red — 1.75 .30
1129 A234 30s ultra & blk — 1.75 .30
1130 A234 30s ultra & red — 1.75 .30
1131 A234 30s ultra & red — 1.75 .30
1132 A234 30s ultra & red — 1.75 .30
1133 A234 30s ultra & red — 1.75 .30
1134 A234 30s ultra, red & blk — 1.75 .30
1135 A234 30s ultra, yel & red — 1.75 .30
a. Block of 10 — 20.00 10.00

**Portrait Type of 1970**
40s, Gen. Miguel Malvar. 1p, Julian Felipe.

**1972 Engr. *Perf. 14***
1136 A222 40s rose red — .25 .20
1137 A222 1p deep blue — .55 .20

Honoring Gen. Miguel Malvar (1865-1911), revolutionary leader, and Julian Felipe (1861-1944), composer of Philippine national anthem. Issue dates: 40s, July 10; 1p, June 26.

---

## Radar with Map of Far East and Oceania — A230

**1972, Feb. 29 Photo. *Perf. 14x14½***
1113 A230 5s org yel & multi — .25 .20
1114 A230 40s red org & multi — .35 .20

Electronics Conferences, Manila, 12/1-7/71.

## Fathers Gomez, Burgos and Zamora — A231

**1972, Apr. 3 *Perf. 13x12½***
1115 A231 5s gold & multi — .35 .20
1116 A231 60s gold & multi — .55 .20

Centenary of the deaths of Fathers Mariano Gomez, José Burgos and Jacinto Zamora, martyrs for Philippine independence from Spain.

## Digestive Tract — A232

**1972, Apr. 11 Photo. *Perf. 12½x13***
1117 A232 20s ultra & multi — .60 .20

4th Asian Pacific Congress of Gastroenterology, Manila, Feb. 5-12. See No. C103.

---

**Tourist Type of 1970**

**Manila Anniversary Emblem — A226**

**1971, June 24**
1102 A226 10s multicolored — 1.25 .35

Founding of Manila, 400th anniv. See #C101.

## Santo Tomas University, Arms of Schools of Medicine and Pharmacology — A227

**1971, July 8 Photo. *Perf. 13½***
1103 A227 5s yellow & multi — 1.50 .35

Centenary of the founding of the Schools of Medicine and Surgery, and Pharmacology at the University of Santo Tomas, Manila. See No. C102.

## No. 957 Surcharged

**1071, July 11 Wmk. 233 *Perf. 14½***
1104 A187 5s on 6s multi — .50 .20

World Congress of University Presidents, Manila.

## Our Lady of Guia Appearing to Filipinos and Spanish Soldiers — A228

**1971, July 8 Photo. *Perf. 13½***
1105 A228 30s multi — .25 .20
1106 A228 75s multi — 1.00 .35

4th centenary of appearance of the statue of Our Lady of Guia, Ermita, Manila.

## Bank Building, Plane, Car and Workers — A229

**1971, Sept. 14 Photo. *Perf. 12½***
1107 A229 10s blue & multi — .30 .20
1108 A229 30s lt grn & multi — .30 .20
1109 A229 1p multicolored — 1.25 .70
Nos. 1107-1109 (3) —

1st Natl. City Bank in the Philippines, 70th anniv.

---

**1971, Jan. 21 Photo. *Perf. 14½***
1083 A223 5s brt green & multi — .30 .20
1084 A223 10s blue & multi — .45 .20
1085 A223 70s brown & multi — .75 .70
Nos. 1083-1085 (3) — 1.50

Pacific Travel Association (PATA), 20th annual conference, Manila, Jan. 21-29.

Designs: 10s, Filipina and Ang Nayong (7 village replicas around man-made lakes). 20s, Woman and fisherman, Estancia. 30s, Pagsanjan Falls. 5p, Watch Tower, Punta Cruz, Boho.

**Perf. 12½x13½**
**1971, Feb. 15 Photo.**
1086 A220 10s multicolored — .35 .20
1087 A220 20s multicolored — .35 .20
1088 A220 30s multicolored — .90 .30
1089 A220 5p multicolored — 3.50 1.75
Nos. 1086-1089 (4) — 5.10 2.45

**1971, Apr. 19**
Designs: 10s, Cultured pearl farm, Davao. 20s, Coral divers, Davao, Mindanao. 40s, Moslem Mosque, Zamboanga. 1p, Rice terraces, Banaue.
1090 A220 10s multicolored — .30 .20
1091 A220 20s multicolored — .45 .20
1092 A220 40s multicolored — 1.00 .25
1093 A220 1p multicolored — 1.75 .40
Nos. 1090-1093 (4) — 3.50 1.05

**1971, May 3**
10s, Spanish cannon, Zamboanga. 30s, Magellan's cross, Cebu City. 50s, Big Jar monument in Calamba, Laguna. 70s, Mayon Volcano, Legaspi.
1094 A220 10s multicolored — .30 .20
1095 A220 30s multicolored — .45 .20
1096 A220 50s multicolored — 1.00 .25
1097 A220 70s multicolored — 1.25 .35
Nos. 1094-1097 (4) — 3.00 1.00

## No. 955 Surcharged

**Family and Emblem A224**

**1971, Mar. 21 Photo. *Perf. 13½***
1098 A224 20s lt grn & multi — .25 .20
1099 A224 40c pink & multi — .35 .20

Regtional Conf. of the Intl. Planned Parenthood Federation for SE Asia & Oceania, Baguio City, Mar. 21-27.

## No. 955 Surcharged

**1971, June 10 Photo. *Perf. 14x13½***
1100 A186 5s on 6s multi — .60 .25

## Allegory of Law A225

**1971, June 15 Photo. *Perf. 13***
1101 A225 15s orange & multi — 1.50 .35

60th anniversary of the University of the Philippines Law College. See No. C100.

## Parrotfish A235

**1972, Aug. 14**    Photo.    **Perf. 13**
1138 A235 5s shown .35 .20
1139 A235 10s Sunburst butterf. .20
1140 A235 20s Moorish idol
    Iyfish 1.40 .25
Nos. 1138-1140, C104 (4) 4.60 1.10
Tropical fish.

## Development Bank of the Philippines A236

**1972, Sept. 12**
1141 A236 10s gray blue & multi .20
1142 A236 20s lilac & multi .30
1143 A236 60s tan & multi .90
Nos. 1141-1143 (3) .40
Development Bank of the Philippines, 25th anniv.

## Pope Paul VI A237

FIRST ANNIVERSARY OF THE VISIT OF HIS HOLINESS, POPE PAUL VI 1970-NOVEMBER 27-1971

**1972, Sept. 26**   Unwmk.   **Perf. 14**
1144 A237 10s green & multi .50 .20
1145 A237 50s lt violet & multi 1.00 .30
Nos. 1144-1145,C105 (3) 2.25 .85
First anniversary (in 1971) of the visit of Pope Paul VI to the Philippines, and for his 75th birthday.

## Charon's Bark, by Resurreccion Hidalgo — A238

LA BARCA DE AQUERONTE · R. Hidalgo · SANAY NG SELYO AT PILATELIA

Nos. 880, 899 and 925 Surcharged with New Value and 2 Bars

**1972, Sept. 29**    As Before
1146 A176 10s on 6s lil & blk 1.10 .20
1147 A167 10s on 6s multi 1.10 .20
1148 A176 10s on 6s multi 3.10 .60
Nos. 1146-1148 (3) .60

Paintings: 10s, Rice Workers' Meal, by F. Amorsolo. 30s, "Spain and the Philippines," by Juan Luna. vert. 70s, Song of Maria Clara, by F. Amorsolo.

**1972, Oct. 16**   Unwmk.   Photo.
Size: 38x40mm
1149 A238 5s silver & multi .35 .20
1150 A238 10s silver & multi .35 .20
Size: 24x56mm
1151 A238 30s silver & multi .75 .20

1152 A238 70s silver & multi .75 .30
Nos. 1149-1152 (4) 2.20 .90
25th anniversary of the organization of the Stamp and Philatelic Division.

Size: 38x40mm

## Lamp, Nurse, Emblem — A239

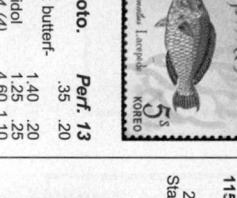

PHILIPPINE NURSES ASSOCIATION 1922 · 50th ANNIVERSARY · 1972

**1972, Oct. 22**    **Perf. 12½x13½**
1153 A239 5s violet & multi .20 .20
1154 A239 5s blue & multi .30 .20
1155 A239 70s orange & multi .40 .25
Nos. 1153-1155 (3) .65
Philippine Nursing Association, 50th anniv.

## Heart, Map of Philippines A240

PUSO MO'Y IYONG KALUSUGAN PANDAIGDIG NA BUWAN NG PUSO ABRIL 1972

**1972, Oct. 24**    **Perf. 13**
1156 A240 5s purple, emer & red .20 .20
1157 A240 10s blue, emer & red .30 .20
1158 A240 30s emerald, bl & red .40 .20
Nos. 1156-1158 (3) .60

"Your heart is your health," World Health Month.

## First Mass on Limasawa, by Carlos V. Francisco — A241

450th ANNIVERSARY OF THE FIRST MASS IN LIMASAWA 1521 1971

**1972, Oct. 31**    **Perf. 14**
1159 A241 10s brown & multi .90 .20
450th anniversary of the first mass in the Philippines, celebrated by Father Valderama on Limasawa, Mar. 31, 1521. See No. C106.

## Torch, Olympic Emblems — A242

Munich 1972

**1972, Nov. 13**    **As Before**
1160 A161 10s on 6s bl & blk .85 .30
1161 A161 10s on 6s grn & blk 1.25 .30
1162 A167 10s on 6s multi .90 .30
Nos. 1160-1162 (3) 3.00 .90
20th Olympic Games, Munich, 8/26-9/11. For surcharges see Nos. 1297, 1759-1760.

Nos. 896 and 919 Surcharged with New Value, Two Bars and: "1972 PHILATELIC WEEK"

**1972, Nov. 15**    **Perf. 12½x13½**
1163 A242 5s blue & multi .50 .20
1164 A242 5s multicolored .50 .20
1165 A242 70s orange & multi .90 .40
Nos. 1163-1165 (3) 1.60 .60
Philatelic Week 1972.

## Manunggul Burial Jar, 890-710 B.C. — A243

MANUNGGUL BURIAL JAR

**1972, Nov. 23**    Photo.    **Perf. 13½**
1166 A166 10s on 6s multi .50 .50
1167 A174 10s on 6s multi .50 .20

**1972, Nov. 29**
1168 A243 10s green & multi .40 .20
1169 A243 10s lilac & multi .40 .20
1170 A243 10s blue & multi .40 .20
1171 A243 10s yellow & multi .40 .20
Nos. 1168-1171 (4) 1.60 .80
#1169, Ngipet Duldug Cave ritual earthenware vessel, 155 B.C. #1170, Metal age chalice, 200-600 A.D. #1171, Earthenware vessel, 15th cent.

## College of Pharmacy and Univ. of the Philippines Emblems — A244

60TH YEAR OF NATIONAL SERVICE TRAINING MANPOWER FOR THE PHARMACEUTICAL SCIENCES · U.P. COLLEGE OF PHARMACY

**1972, Dec. 11**    **Perf. 12½x13½**
1172 A244 5s lt vio & multi .25 .20
1173 A244 10s yel grn & multi .25 .20
1174 A244 10s ultra & multi .90 .65
Nos. 1172-1174 (3) .65
60th anniversary of the College of Pharmacy and Univ. of the Philippines.

## Christmas Lantern Makers, by Jorge Pineda — A245

MALIGAYANG PASKO AT MANIGONG BAGONG TAON

**1972, Dec. 14**    Photo.    **Perf. 12½**
1175 A245 10s dk bl & multi .20 .20
1176 A245 30s brown & multi .50 .20
1177 A245 50s green & multi 1.45 .65
Nos. 1175-1177 (3) .75 .25
Christmas 1972.

## Red Cross Flags, Pres. Roxas and Mrs. Aurora Quezon A246

**1972, Dec. 21**    Photo.    **Perf. 14, 13**
1178 A246 5s ultra & multi .20 .20
1179 A246 10s multicolored .30 .20
1180 A246 30s brown & multi .90 .40
Nos. 1178-1180 (3) .60
25th anniv. of the Philippine Red Cross.

Nos. 894 and 936 Surcharged with New Value and 2 Bars

**1973, Jan. 22**    Photo.    **Perf. 14, 13**
1181 A165 10s on 6s multi .65 .20
1182 A180 10s on 6s multi .65 .20

## San Luis University, Luzon — A247

IKA-60 ANIBERSARYO NG PAMANTASAN NG SAN LUIS

**1973, Mar. 1**    Photo.    **Perf. 13½x14**
1183 A247 5s multicolored .25 .20
1184 A247 5s yellow & multi .35 .20
1185 A247 75s multicolored 1.00 .65
Nos. 1183-1185 (3) .65
60th anniversary of San Luis University, Baguio City, Luzon. For surcharge see No. 1305.

## Col. Jesus Villamor and Fighter Planes — A248

COL. JESUS VILLAMOR

**1973, Apr. 9**    Photo.    **Perf. 13½x14**
1186 A248 10s multicolored .25 .20
1187 A248 2p multicolored 1.25 .70
Col. Jesus Villamor (1914-1971), World War II aviator who fought for liberation of the Philippines. For surcharge see No. 1230.

Nos. 932, 957, O70 Surcharged with New Values and 2 Bars

**1973, Apr. 23**    As Before
1188 A178 5s on 6s multi 1.10 .20
1189 A187 15s on 10s multi .80 .20
1190 A222 15s on 10s rose car 3.00 .60
Nos. 1188-1190 (3) .60
Two additional bars through "G.O." on No. 1190.

## ITI Emblem, Performance and Actor Vic Silayan — A249

1st THIRD WORLD THEATRE FESTIVAL · UNESCO/PETA

**1973, May 15 Photo. *Perf. 13x12½***

**1191** A249 5s blue & multi .20 .20
**1192** A249 10s yel grn & multi .25 .20
**1193** A249 50s orange & multi .45 .20
**1194** A249 70s rose & multi .60 .25
*Nos. 1191-1194 (4)* 1.50 .85

1st Third World Theater Festival, sponsored by the UNESCO affiliated International Theater Institute, Manila, Nov. 19-30, 1971.
For surcharge see No. 1229.

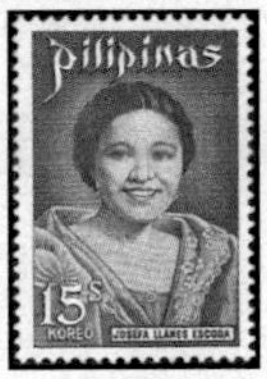

Josefa Llanes Escoda — A250

#1196, Gabriela Silang. No. 1197, Rafael Palma. 30s, Jose Rizal. 60s, Marcela Agoncillo. 90s, Teodoro R. Yangco. 1.10p, Dr. Pio Venezuela. 1.20p, Gregoria de Jesus. #1204, Pedro A. Paterno. #1205, Teodora Alonso. 1.80p, Edilberto Evangelista. 5p, Fernando M. Guerrero.

**1973-78 Engr. *Perf. 14½***

**1195** A250 15s sepia .20 .20

**Litho. *Perf. 12½***

**1196** A250 15s violet ('74) .20 .20
**1197** A273 15s emerald ('74) .20 .20
**1198** A250 30s vio bl ('78) .20 .20
**1199** A250 60s dl red brn .55 .25
**1200** A273 90s brt bl ('74) .75 .20
**1202** A273 1.10p brt bl ('74) .90 .20
**1203** A250 1.20p dl red ('78) .60 .20
**1204** A250 1.50p lil rose 1.25 .45
**1205** A273 1.50p brown ('74) 1.25 .20
**1206** A250 1.80p green 2.00 .55
**1208** A250 5p blue 4.50 1.75
*Nos. 1195-1208 (12)* 12.60 4.60

**1973-74 *Imperf.***

*1196a* A250 15s violet ('74) .25 .25
*1197a* A273 15s emerald ('74) .25 .25
*1199a* A250 60s dull red brown 1.40 .65
*1200a* A273 90s bright blue ('74) 1.60 1.25
*1202a* A273 1.10p bright blue ('74) 2.10 1.60
*1204a* A250 1.50p lilac rose 2.40 1.90
*1205a* A273 1.50p brown ('74) 2.75 2.25
*1206a* A250 1.80p green 3.25 2.50
*1208a* A250 5p blue 8.00 5.25
*Nos. 1196a-1208a (9)* 22.00 15.90

Honoring: Escoda (1898-194?), leader of Girl Scouts and Federation of Women's Clubs. Silang (1731-63), "the Ilocana Joan of Arc". Palma (1874-1939), journalist, statesman, educator. Rizal (1861-96), natl. hero. Agoncillo (1859-1946), designer of 1st Philippine flag, 1898. Yangco (1861-1939), patriot and philanthropist. Valenzuela (1869-1956), physician and newspaperman.

Gregoria de Jesus, independence leader. Paterno (1857-1911), lawyer, writer, patriot. Alonso (1827-1911), mother of Rizal. Evangelista (1862-97), army engineer, patriot. Guerrero (1873-1929), journalist, political leader.

For overprint & surcharges see #1277, 1311, 1470, 1518.

No. 946 surcharged with New Value

**1973, June 4 Engr. *Perf. 13½***

**1209** A158 5s on 6s peacock bl .60 .20

Anti-smuggling campaign.

No. 925 Surcharged

**1973, June 4 Wmk. 233**

**1210** A176 5s on 6s multi .60 .20

10th anniv. of death of John F. Kennedy.

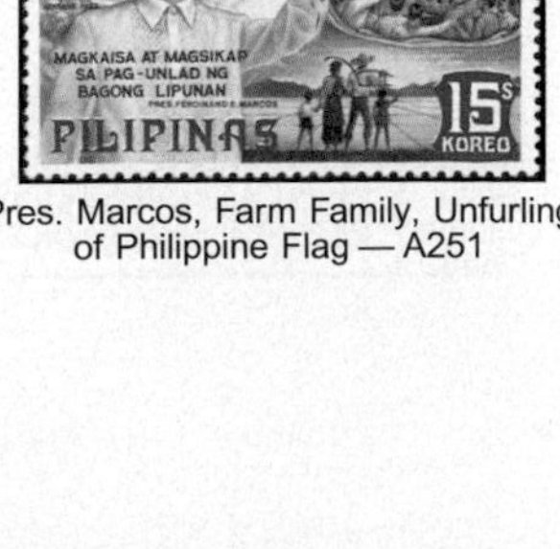

Pres. Marcos, Farm Family, Unfurling of Philippine Flag — A251

***Perf. 12½x13½***

**1973, Sept. 24 Photo. Unwmk.**

**1211** A251 15s ultra & multi .25 .20
**1212** A251 45s red & multi .50 .20
**1213** A251 90s multi .75 .25
*Nos. 1211-1213 (3)* 1.50 .65

75th anniversary of Philippine independence and 1st anniversary of proclamation of martial law.

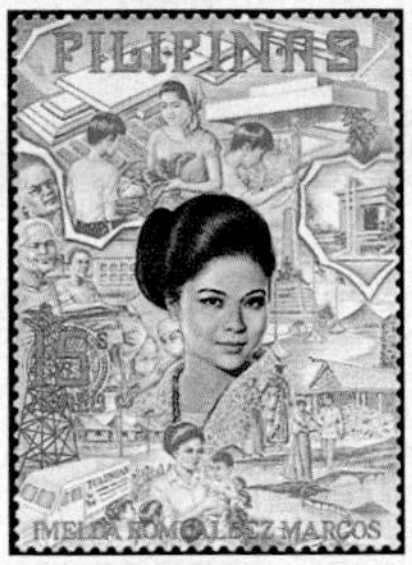

Imelda Romualdez Marcos, First Lady of the Philippines A252

**1973, Oct. 31 Photo. *Perf. 13***

**1214** A252 15s dl bl & multi .20 .20
**1215** A252 50s multicolored .40 .20
**1216** A252 60s lil & multi .60 .25
*Nos. 1214-1216 (3)* 1.20 .65

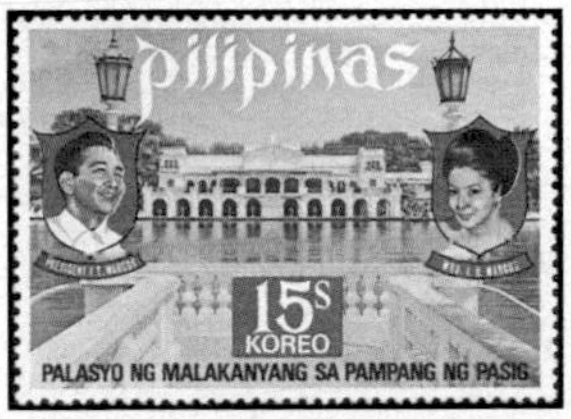

Presidential Palace, Manila, Pres. and Mrs. Marcos — A253

**1973, Nov. 15 Litho. *Perf. 14***

**1217** A253 15s rose & multi .20 .20
**1218** A253 50s ultra & multi .50 .20
*Nos. 1217-1218,C107 (3)* 1.45 .70

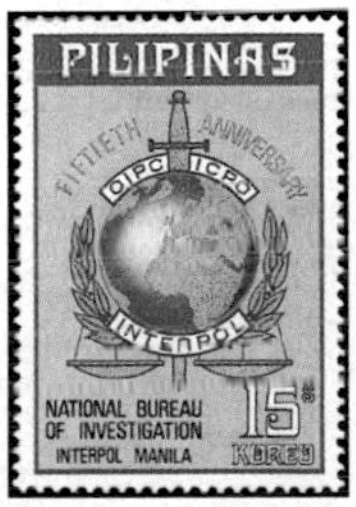

INTERPOL Emblem — A254

**1973, Dec. 18 Photo. *Perf. 13***

**1219** A254 15s ultra & multi .30 .20
**1220** A254 65s lt grn & multi .45 .20

Intl. Criminal Police Organization, 50th anniv.

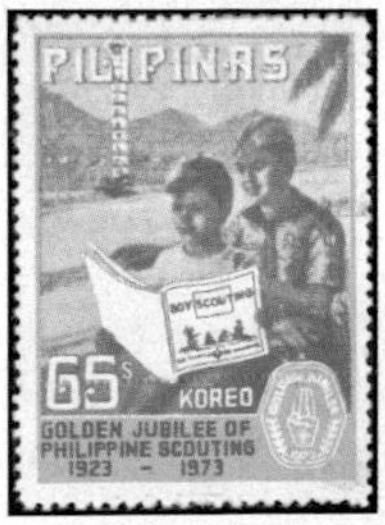

Cub and Boy Scouts — A255

15s, Various Scout activities; inscribed in Tagalog.

**1973, Dec. 28 Litho. *Perf. 12½***

**1221** A255 15s bister & emer .40 .20
*a.* Imperf, pair ('74) 2.50 1.50
**1222** A255 65s bister & brt bl .75 .30
*a.* Imperf, pair ('74) 3.50 2.00

50th anniv. of Philippine Boy Scouts.
Nos. 1221a-1222a issued Feb. 4, although first day covers are dated Dec. 28, 1973.

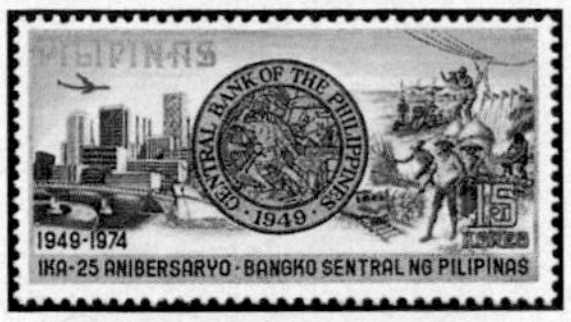

Manila, Bank Emblem and Farmers — A256

Designs: 60s, Old bank building. 1.50p, Modern bank building.

**1974, Jan. 3 Photo. *Perf. 12½x13½***

**1223** A256 15s silver & multi .20 .20
**1224** A256 60s silver & multi .35 .20
**1225** A256 1.50p silver & multi 1.10 .40
*Nos. 1223-1225 (3)* 1.65 .80

Central Bank of the Philippines, 25th anniv.

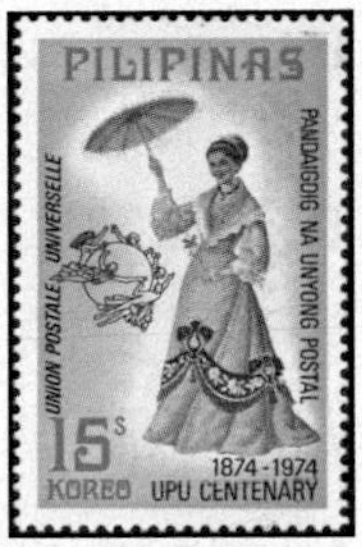

UPU Emblem, Maria Clara Costume — A257

Filipino Costumes: 60s, Balintawak and UPU emblem. 80s, Malong costume and UPU emblem.

**1974, Jan. 15 *Perf. 12½***

**1226** A257 15s multicolored .20 .20
**1227** A257 60s multicolored .45 .20
**1228** A257 80s multicolored .80 .35
*Nos. 1226-1228 (3)* 1.45 .75

Centenary of Universal Postal Union.

No. 1192 Surcharged in Red with New Value, 2 Bars and: "1973 / PHILATELIC WEEK"

**1974, Feb. 4 Photo. *Perf. 13x12½***

**1229** A249 15s on 10s multi .60 .20

Philatelic Week, 1973. First day covers exist dated Nov. 26, 1973.

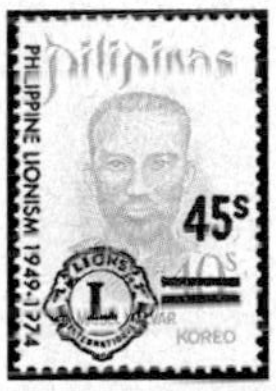

Nos. 1186 and 1136 Overprinted and Surcharged

**1974, Mar. 25 Photo. *Perf. 13½x14***

**1230** A248 15s on 10s multi .60 .20

**Engr. *Perf. 14***

**1231** A222 45s on 40s rose red .60 .20

Lions Intl. of the Philippines, 25th anniv. The overprint on #1230 arranged to fit shape of stamp.

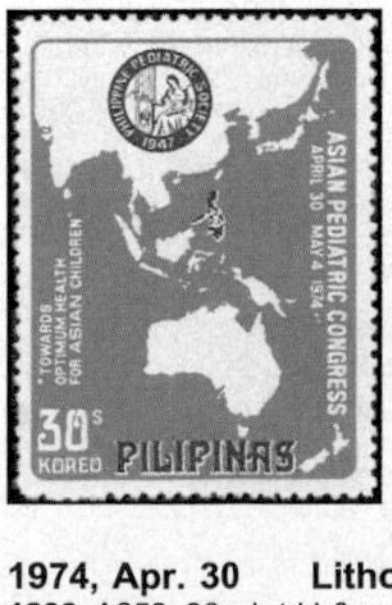

Pediatrics Congress Emblem and Map of Participating Countries A258

**1974, Apr. 30 Litho. *Perf. 12½***

**1232** A258 30s brt bl & red .50 .20
*a.* Imperf, pair 2.50 1.50
**1233** A258 1p dl grn & red 1.00 .30
*a.* Imperf, pair 5.00 3.50

Asian Congress of Pediatrics, Manila, Apr. 30-May 4.

Nos. 912, 954-955 Surcharged with New Value and Two Bars

**1974, Aug. 1 As Before**

**1234** A172 5s on 3s multi .75 .25
**1235** A185 5s on 6s multi 1.00 .25
**1236** A186 5s on 6s multi 1.25 .25
*Nos. 1234-1236 (3)* 3.00 .75

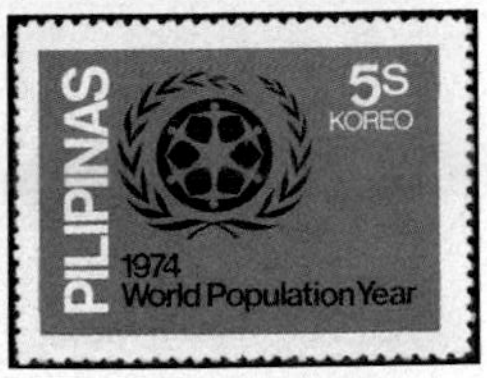

WPY Emblem A259

**1974, Aug. 15 Litho. *Perf. 12½***

**1237** A259 5s org & bl blk .40 .20
*a.* Imperf. 1.50 .75
**1238** A259 2p lt grn & dk bl 1.60 .60
*a.* Imperf. 9.50 7.00

World Population Year, 1974.

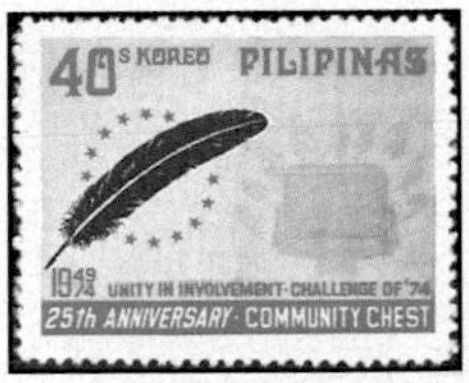

Red Feather Community Chest Emblem A260

**Wmk. 372**

**1974, Sept. 5 Litho. *Perf. 12½***

**1239** A260 15s brt bl & red .20 .20
**1240** A260 40s emer & red .65 .20
**1241** A260 45s red brn & red .65 .20
*Nos. 1239-1241 (3)* 1.50 .60

Philippine Community Chest, 25th anniv.

**Imperf. Pairs**

*1239a* A260 15s 3.75 3.50
*1240a* A260 40s 1.75 1.25
*1241a* A260 45s 1.75 1.25
*Nos. 1239a-1241a (3)* 7.25 6.00

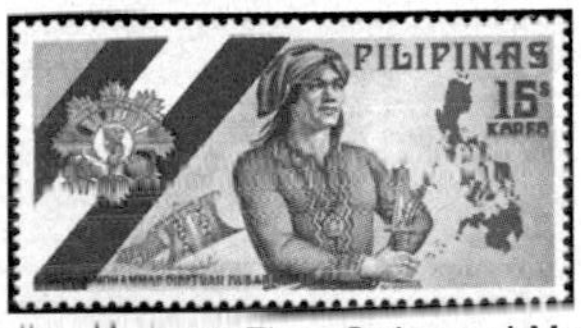

Sultan Kudarat, Flag, Order and Map of Philippines — A261

***Perf. 13½x14***

**1975, Jan. 13 Photo. Unwmk.**

**1242** A261 15s multicolored .36 .20

Sultan Mohammad Dipatuan Kudarat, 16th-17th century ruler.

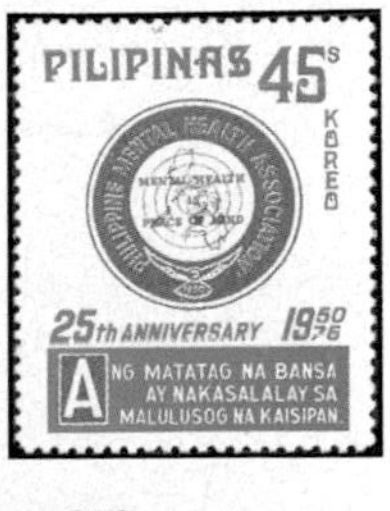

Mental Health Association Emblem A262

**Wmk. 372**

**1975, Jan. 20 Litho. *Perf. 12½***

**1243** A262 45s emer & org .35 .20
*a.* Imperf, pair 2.00 1.50
**1244** A262 1p emer & pur .80 .30
*a.* Imperf, pair 4.00 3.00

Philippine Mental Health Assoc., 25th anniv.

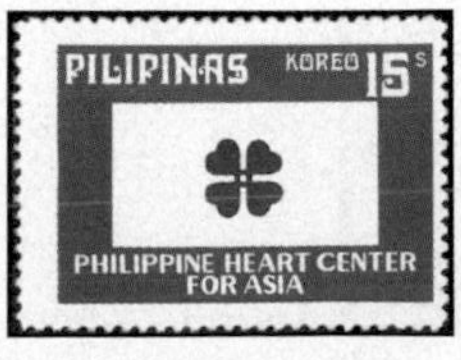

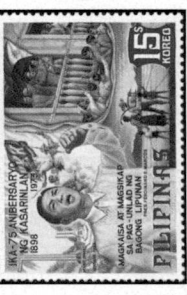

4-Leaf Clover A263

**1975, Feb. 14**
| | | | | |
|---|---|---|---|---|
| 1245 | A263 | 15s vio bl & red | .35 | .20 |
| | a. | Imperf, pair | 2.50 | 1.50 |
| 1246 | A263 | 50s emer & red | .80 | .35 |
| | a. | Imperf, pair | 4.50 | 3.00 |

Philippine Heart Center for Asia, inauguration.

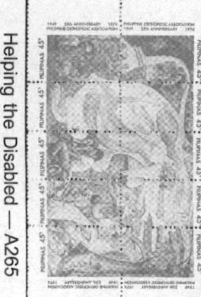

Military Academy, Cadet and Emblem — A264

**1975, Feb. 17**    **Perf. 13½x14**
| | | | | |
|---|---|---|---|---|
| 1247 | A264 | 15s grn & multi | .35 | .20 |
| 1248 | A264 | 45s plum & multi | .55 | .25 |

Philippine Military Academy, 70th anniv.

Helping the Disabled — A265

**1975, Mar. 17**    **Perf. 12½, Imperf.**
| | | | | |
|---|---|---|---|---|
| 1249 | A265 | 45s grn, any single | 7.50 | 6.00 |
| | a.-j. | Block of 10 | .55 | .35 |

25th anniversary (in 1974) of Philippine Orthopedic Association. For surcharge see No. 1635. No. 1249 exists imperf. Value unused, $12.

Nos. B43, B50-B51 Surcharged with New Value and Two Bars

**1975, Apr. 15**    **Unwmk.**
| | | | | |
|---|---|---|---|---|
| 1250 | SP18 | 5s on 15s + 5s | .60 | .20 |
| 1251 | SP18 | 60s on 70s + 5s | .90 | .20 |
| 1252 | SP18 | 1p on 1.10p + 5s | 2.75 | .75 |
| | | Nos. 1250-1252 (3) | | |

"Grow and Conserve Forests" — A266

**1975, Apr. 15**    **Wmk. 372**
| | | | | |
|---|---|---|---|---|
| 1253 | | 45s "Grow" | .45 | .20 |
| 1254 | | 45s "Conserve" | .45 | .20 |
| | a. | Pair, #1253-1254 | .90 | .75 |

Forest conservation.

Jade Vine — A268

**1975, May 19**    **Litho.**    **Perf. 14½**
| | | | | |
|---|---|---|---|---|
| 1255 | A268 | 15s multicolored | .35 | .20 |

Imelda R. Marcos, IWY Emblem — A269

**1975, June 9**    **Photo.**    **Perf. 14½**

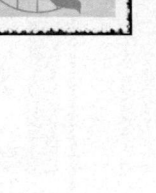

Civil Service Emblem — A270

**1975, July 2**    **Wmk. 372**    **Litho.**
| | | | | |
|---|---|---|---|---|
| 1256 | A269 | 15s bl & blk | .35 | .20 |
| 1257 | A269 | 80s pink, bl & blk | .55 | .25 |

International Women's Year 1975. For surcharges see Nos. 1500, 1505.

**1975, Sept. 19**    **Litho.**    **Perf. 12½**
| | | | | |
|---|---|---|---|---|
| 1258 | A270 | 15s multicolored | .35 | .20 |
| 1259 | A270 | 50s multicolored | .55 | .25 |
| | a. | Imperf, pair | 3.75 | 3.75 |

For surcharges see Nos. 1517, 1520.

Dam and Emblem A271

**1975, Sept. 30**    **Litho.**    **Perf. 12½**
| | | | | |
|---|---|---|---|---|
| 1260 | A271 | 40s org & vio bl | .25 | .20 |
| 1261 | A271 | 1.50p brt rose & vio bl | 2.00 | 2.00 |
| | a. | Imperf, pair | .90 | .35 |

For surcharges see Nos. 1517, 1520.

Manila Harbor, 1875 A272

**1975, Nov. 4**    **Unwmk.**    **Perf. 13x13½**
| | | | | |
|---|---|---|---|---|
| 1262 | A272 | 1.50p red & multi | 1.25 | .35 |

Hong Kong and Shanghai Banking Corporation, centenary of Philippines service.

Norberto Romualdez (1875-1941), Scholar and Legislator — A272

Jose Rizal Monument, Luneta Park — A273a

Noted Filipinos: No. 1264, Rafael Palma (1874-1939), journalist, statesman, educator. No. 1265, Rajah Kalantiaw, chief of Panay, author of ethical-penal code (1443). 65s, Emilio Jacinto (1875-1899), patriot. No. 1269, Gen. Gregorio del Pilar (1875-1899), military hero. No. 1270, Lope K. Santos (1879-1963), grammarian, writer. 1.60p, Felipe Agoncillo (1859-1941), lawyer, cabinet member.

**1975-81**    **Wmk. 372**    **Litho.**    **Perf. 12½**
| | | | | |
|---|---|---|---|---|
| 1264 | A273 | 30s brn ('77) | .30 | .20 |
| 1265 | A273 | 30s dp rose ('78) | .30 | .20 |
| 1266 | A273 | 40s yel & blk ('81) | .60 | .20 |
| 1267 | A273 | 60s violet | 1.00 | .20 |
| 1268 | A273 | 65s lilac rose | 2.50 | 2.50 |
| | a. | Imperf, pair | .75 | .20 |
| 1269 | A273 | 90s lilac rose | 2.00 | 2.00 |
| | a. | Imperf, pair | 1.25 | 2.50 |
| 1270 | A273 | 90s grn ('78) | 1.25 | .20 |
| | a. | Imperf, pair | 3.00 | 3.00 |
| 1272 | A273 | 1.60p blk ('76) | 2.25 | .20 |
| | | Nos. 1264-1272 (8) | 6.95 | 1.60 |

See #1195-1208. For overprint & surcharges see #1278, 1310, 1367, 1440, 1469, 1514, 1562, 1574, 1758-1760.

PAL Planes of 1946 A278

1st landing of the Pan American World Airways China Clipper in the Philippines, 40th anniv.

A274

**1975, Nov. 22**    **Litho.**    **Perf. 12½**
| | | | | |
|---|---|---|---|---|
| 1275 | A274 | 60s multicolored | .75 | .20 |
| 1276 | A274 | 1.50p multicolored | 1.75 | .50 |

Nos. 1199 and 1205 Overprinted

**1975, Nov. 22**    **Unwmk.**
| | | | | |
|---|---|---|---|---|
| 1277 | A250 | 60s dl red brn | .50 | .25 |
| 1278 | A273 | 1.50p brown | 1.25 | .30 |

Airmail Exhibition, Nov. 22-Dec. 9.

APO Emblem — A275

**1975, Nov. 24**    **Wmk. 372**
| | | | | |
|---|---|---|---|---|
| 1279 | A276 | 5s ultra & multi | .25 | .20 |
| 1280 | A276 | 1p bl & multi | 1.50 | 1.50 |
| | a. | Imperf, pair | 6.00 | 6.00 |

Amateur Philatelists' Org., 25th anniv. For surcharge see No. 1338.

Philippine Churches: 20s, San Agustin Church. 30s, Morong Church, Basilica of Taal. 45s, San Sebastian Church.

**1975, Dec. 23**    **Litho.**    **Perf. 12½**
| | | | | |
|---|---|---|---|---|
| 1281 | A276 | 20s bluish grn | .50 | .20 |
| 1282 | A276 | 30s yel org & blk | .50 | .20 |
| 1283 | A276 | 45s rose, brn & blk | .75 | .30 |
| 1284 | A276 | 60s org, bis & blk | 1.25 | .30 |
| | | Nos. 1281-1284 (4) | 3.00 | .95 |

Holy Year 1975.

A277

**1976, Jan. 27**    **Imperf. Pairs**
| | | | | |
|---|---|---|---|---|
| 1281a | A276 | 20s | 2.00 | 1.40 |
| 1282a | A276 | 30s | 2.00 | 1.40 |
| 1283a | A276 | 45s | 3.50 | .25 |
| 1284a | A276 | 60s | 3.50 | .60 |
| | | Nos. 1281a-1284a (4) | 12.50 | 8.30 |

Manila Symphony Orchestra, 50th anniversary.

Conductor's hands.

**1976, Feb. 14**
| | | | | |
|---|---|---|---|---|
| 1285 | A277 | 5s org & multi | .35 | .20 |
| 1286 | A277 | 50s multicolored | .55 | .20 |

**1976, Feb. 14**
| | | | | |
|---|---|---|---|---|
| 1287 | A278 | 60s bl & multi | .60 | .20 |
| 1288 | A278 | 1.50p red & multi | 1.90 | .60 |

Philippine Airlines, 30th anniversary.

National University A279

**1976, Mar. 30**
| | | | | |
|---|---|---|---|---|
| 1289 | A279 | 45s bl, vio bl & yel | .40 | .20 |
| 1290 | A279 | 60s lt bl, vio bl & pink | .75 | .20 |

National University, 75th anniversary.

Eye Exam — A280

**1976, Apr. 7**    **Litho.**    **Perf. 12½**
| | | | | |
|---|---|---|---|---|
| 1291 | A280 | 15s multicolored | .50 | .20 |

World Health Day: "Foresight prevents blindness."

Book and Emblem — A281

**1976, May 24**    **Litho.**    **Unwmk.**    **Perf. 12½**
| | | | | |
|---|---|---|---|---|
| 1292 | A281 | 1.50p grn & multi | 1.25 | .30 |

National Archives, 75th anniversary.

Santo Tomas University, Emblems A282

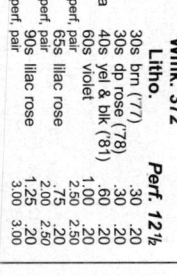

ASEAN
Emblem
A296

**1977, Aug. 8**
1329 A296 1.50p grn & multi        1.25   .25
Association of South East Asian Nations
(ASEAN), 10th anniversary.

Cable-laying Ship, Map Showing Cable
Route — A297

**1977, Aug. 26    Litho.    Perf. 12½**
1330 A297 1.30p multicolored        .85   .25
Inauguration of underwater telephone cable
linking Okinawa, Luzon and Hong Kong.

President Marcos — A298

**1977, Sept. 11    Wmk. 372**
1331 A298 30s multicolored        .30   .20
1332 A298 2.30p multicolored        1.20   .25
Ferdinand E. Marcos, president of the Philippines, 60th birthday.

People Raising
Flag — A299

**1977, Sept. 21    Litho.    Perf. 12½**
1333 A299 30s multicolored        .35   .20
1334 A299 2.30p multicolored        1.10   .35
5th anniversary of "New Society."

Bishop Gregorio
Aglipay — A300

**1977, Oct. 1    Litho.    Perf. 12½**
1335 A300 30s multicolored        .40   .20
1336 A300 90s multicolored        1.10   .25
Philippine Independent Aglipayan Church,
75th anniversary.

---

Emblem,
Flags,
Map of
AOPU
A291

**1977, Apr. 1    Wmk. 372**
1322 A291 50s multicolored        .40   .25
1323 A291 1.50p multicolored        1.10   .35
Asian-Oceanic Postal Union (AOPU), 15th
anniv.

Cogwheels and
Worker — A292

**1977, Apr. 21    Perf. 12½**
1324 A292 90s blk & multi        .50   .25
1325 A292 2.30p blk & multi        1.25   .45
Asian Development Bank, 10th anniversary.

Farmer at
Work and
Receiving
Money
A293

**1977, May 14    Wmk. 372**
1326 A293 30s org rod & multi        .05   .20
National Commission on Countryside Credit
and Collection, campaign to strengthen the
rural credit system.

Solicitor
General's
Emblem
A294

**1977, June 30    Litho.    Perf. 12½**
1327 A294 1.65p multicolored        1.25   .25
Office of the Solicitor General, 75th anniv.
For surcharges see Nos. 1483, 1519.

Conference
Emblem
A295

**1977, July 29    Litho.    Perf. 12½**
1328 A295 2.20p bl & multi        1.25   .25
8th World Conference of the World Peace
through Law Center, Manila, Aug. 21-26.
For surcharge see No. 1576.

---

Virgin of
Antipollo
A287

**1976, Oct. 4    Litho.    Perf. 12½**
1301 A286 60s multicolored        .40   .20
1302 A286 1.50p multicolored        1.10   .35
Joint Annual Meeting of the Board of Governors of the International Monetary Fund and
the World Bank, Manila, Oct. 4-8.
For surcharge see No. 1575.

**1976, Nov. 26    Perf. 12½**
1303 A287 30s multicolored        .40   .20
1304 A287 90s multicolored        1.10   .25
Virgin of Antipollo, Our Lady of Peace and
Good Voyage, 350th anniv. of arrival of statue
in the Philippines and 50th anniv. of the
canonical coronation.

No. 1184 Surcharged with New Value
and 2 Bars and Overprinted "1976
PHILATELIC WEEK"

**Perf. 13½x14**
**1976, Nov. 26    Photo.    Unwmk.**
1305 A247 30s on 10s multi        .60   .20
Philatelic Week 1976.

People
Going to
Church
A288

**1976, Dec. 1    Litho.    Perf. 12½**
1306 A288 15s bl & multi        .50   .20
1307 A288 30s bl & multi        1.00   .20
Christmas 1976.

Symbolic
Diamond and
Book — A289

Galicano
Apacible — A290

**1976, Dec. 13    Unwmk.**
1308 A289 30s grn & multi        .50   .20
1309 A289 75s grn & multi        .75   .70
Philippine Educational System, 75th anniv.

No. 1202 and 1208 Surcharged with
New Value and 2 Bars

**1977, Jan. 17**
1310 A273 1.20p on 1.10p bl        1.00   .20
1311 A250 3p on 5p bl        2.50   .70

**1977    Litho.    Wmk. 372    Perf. 12½**
1313 A290 30s multicolored        .25   .25
1318 A290 2.30p multicolored        1.25   .25
Design: 30s, José Rizal.
Dr. José Rizal (1861-1896) physician, poet
and national hero (30s). Dr. Galicano
Apacible (1864-1949), physician, statesman
(2.30p).
Issue dates: 30s, Feb. 16; 2.30p, Jan. 24.

---

**1976, June 7    Wmk. 372**
1293 A282 15s yel & multi        .30   .20
1294 A282 50s multicolored        .60   .20
Colleges of Education and Science, Santo
Tomas University, 50th anniversary.

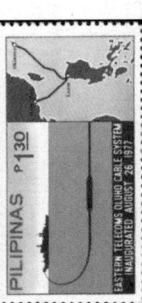

Maryknoll College — A283

**1976, July 26    Wmk. 372    Litho.**
1295 A283 15s lt bl & multi        .35   .20
1296 A283 1.50p bis & multi        .90   .25
Maryknoll College, Quezon City, 50th anniv.

No. 1164 Surcharged in Dark Violet

**1976, July 30    Photo.    Perf. 12½x13½**
1297 A242 15s on 10s multi        .75   .25
21st Olympic Games, Montreal, Canada,
July 17-Aug. 1.

Police College, Manila — A284

**1976, Aug. 8    Litho.    Perf. 12½**
1298 A284 15s multicolored        .25   .20
        a.    Imperf, pair        1.75   1.75
1299 A284 60s multicolored        .60   .25
        a.    Imperf, pair        5.75   5.75
Philippine Constabulary, 75th anniversary.

Surveyors — A285

**1976, Sept. 2    Wmk. 372**
1300 A285 80s multicolored        1.25   .30
Bureau of Lands, 75th anniversary.

Monetary Fund
and World Bank
Emblems — A286

Fokker F VIIa over World Map A301

**1977, Oct. 28**    **Wmk. 372**
1337 A301 2.30p multicolored   1.90 .50
First scheduled Pan American airmail service, Havana to Key West, 50th anniversary.

**1977, Nov. 22**    **Litho.**    **Perf. 12½**
1338 A275 90s on 1p multi   .90 .25
No. 1280 Surcharged with New Value, 2 Bars and Overprinted in Red: "1977 / PHILATELIC / WEEK"
Philatelic Week.

Children Celebrating and Star from Lantern — A302

**1977, Dec. 1**    **Unwmk.**
1339 A302 30s multicolored   .30 .20
1340 A302 45s multicolored   .60 .20
Christmas 1977.

Scouts and Map showing Jamboree Locations A303

**1977, Dec. 27**
1341 A303 30s multicolored   .50 .20
National Boy Scout Jamboree, Tumauini, Isabela; Capitol Hills, Cebu City; Mariano Marcos, Davao, Dec. 27, 1977-Jan. 5, 1978.

Far Eastern University Arms — A304

**1977, Dec. 27**    **Litho.**    **Wmk. 372**
1342 A304 30s gold & multi   .40 .20
Far Eastern University, 50th anniversary.

Sipa A305

**1978, Feb. 28**    **Perf. 12½**
1343 A305 5s bl & multi   .20 .20
1344 A305 10s bl & multi   .30 .20
1345 A305 40s bl & multi   .50 .25
1346 A305 75s bl & multi   .75 .25
a. Block, #1343-1346   1.90 1.40
Various positions of Sipa ball-game.
No. 1346a has continuous design.

Arms of Meycauayan A306

**1978, Apr. 21**    **Litho.**    **Perf. 12½**
1347 A306 1.05p multicolored   .90 .25
Meycauayan, founded 1578-1579. For surcharge see No. 1560.

Moro Vinta and UPU Emblem — A307

**1978, June 9**    **Litho.**    **Perf. 13½**
1348 A307 2.50p multicolored   1.50 .40
1349 A307 5p multicolored   2.25 .80

**Souvenir Sheet**
**Perf. 12½x13**
1350 Sheet of 4   15.00 12.50
a.-d. A307 7.50p, any single   3.25 3.25
e. Sheet, imperf   15.00 12.50
   A307 7.50p, any single, imperf   15.00 12.50
CAPEX International Philatelic Exhibition, Toronto, Ont., June 9-18. No. 1350 contains 36½x25mm stamps. No. 1350 exists imperf. in changed colors.

Andres Bonifacio Monument, by Guillermo Tolentino — A308

**1978, July 10**    **Litho.**    **Perf. 12½**
1351 A308 30s multicolored   .50 .20

Rook, Knight and Globe A309

**1978, July 17**
1352 A309 30s vio bl & red   .40 .20
1353 A309 2p vio bl & red   1.50 .30
World Chess Championship, Anatoly Karpov and Viktor Korchnoi, Baguio City, 1978.

Miners A310

**1978, Aug. 12**    **Litho.**    **Perf. 12½**
1354 A310 2.30p multicolored   1.90 .35
Benguet gold mining industry, 75th anniv.

Manuel Quezon and Quezon Memorial A311

**1978, Aug. 19**
1355 A311 30s multicolored   .25 .20
1356 A311 1p multicolored   1.00 .25
Manuel Quezon (1878-1944), first president of Commonwealth of the Philippines.

Law Association Emblem, Philippine Flag — A312

**1978, Aug. 27**    **Litho.**    **Perf. 12½**
1357 A312 2.30p multicolored   1.25 .35
58th Int'l. Law Conf., Manila, 8/27-9/2.

Pres. Sergio Osmeña (1878-1961) A313

**1978, Sept. 8**
1358 A313 30s multicolored   .30 .20
1359 A313 1p multicolored   .90 .25
For surcharge see No. 1501.

Map Showing Cable Route, Cablelaying Ship — A314

**1978, Sept. 30**
1360 A314 1.40p multicolored   1.25 .25
ASEAN Submarine Cable Network, Philippines-Singapore cable system, inauguration.

Basketball, Games Emblem A315

**1978, Oct. 1**
1361 A315 30s multicolored   .40 .20
1362 A315 2.30p multicolored   1.50 .40
8th Men's World Basketball Championship, Manila, Oct. 1-15.

San Lazaro Hospital and Dr. Catalino Gavino A316

**1978, Oct. 13**    **Litho.**    **Perf. 12½**
1363 A316 50s multicolored   .50 .20
1364 A316 90s multicolored   .75 .25
San Lazaro Hospital, 400th anniversary. For surcharge see No. 1512.

Nurse Vaccinating Child — A317

**1978, Oct. 24**
1365 A317 30s multicolored   .40 .20
1366 A317 1.50p multicolored   1.50 .40
Eradication of smallpox.

No. 1268 Surcharged

**1978, Nov. 23**
1367 A273 60s on 65s lil rose   .75 .20
Philatelic Week.

"The Telephone Across Country and World" — A318

**1978, Nov. 28**    **Wmk. 372**    **Litho.**    **Perf. 12½**
1368 A318 30s multicolored   .40 .20
1369 A318 2p multicolored   1.40 .40
a. A318 2p Pair, #1368-1369   1.90 1.90
Philippine Long Distance Telephone Company, 50th anniversary.

Decade of the Filipino Child Traveling Family — A320

**1978, Nov. 28**    **Litho.**    **Perf. 12½**
1370 A320 30s multicolored   .40 .20
1371 A320 1.35p multicolored   1.10 .25
Decade of Philippine children. For surcharges see Nos. 1504, 1561.

Church and Arms of Agoo A321

Agoo Quadricentennial Commemoration

## 1979, June 25 — Archdiocese of Manila

Patrol Boat, Naval Arms A337

Perf. 12½

| 1417 | A336 | 30s multi | .30 | .20 |
|---|---|---|---|---|
| 1418 | A336 | 75s multi | .60 | .20 |
| 1419 | A336 | 90s multi | .85 | .25 |
| | | | 1.75 | .65 |

Nos. 1417-1419 (3)

Archdiocese of Manila, 400th anniversary.

## 1979, June 26

| 1420 | A337 | 30s multi | .50 | .20 |
|---|---|---|---|---|
| 1421 | A337 | 45s multi | .75 | .20 |

Philippine Navy Day.

Man Breaking Chains, Broken Syringe — A338

## 1979, July 23 — Litho.

Perf. 12½

| 1422 | A338 | 30s multi | .25 | .20 |
|---|---|---|---|---|
| 1423 | A338 | 90s multi | .75 | .25 |
| 1424 | A338 | 1.05p multi | .85 | .25 |
| | | | 1.85 | .65 |

Nos. 1422-1424 (3)

Fight drug abuse. For surcharge see Nos. 1480, 1513.

Afghan Hound A339

## 1979, Aug. 6 — Litho.

Perf. 14

Designs: 90s, Striped tabbies. 1.20p, Dobermann pinscher. 2.20p, Siamese cats. 2.00p, German shepherd, 5p, Chinchilla cats.

| 1425 | A339 | 30s multi | .50 | .20 |
|---|---|---|---|---|
| 1426 | A339 | 90s multi | 1.00 | .30 |
| 1427 | A339 | 1.20p multi | 1.25 | .45 |
| 1428 | A339 | 2.20p multi | 2.00 | .45 |
| 1429 | A339 | 2.30p multi | 4.25 | .85 |
| 1430 | A339 | 5p multi | 11.00 | 2.65 |

Nos. 1425-1430 (6)

Children Playing IYC Emblem A340

## 1979, Aug. 31 — Litho.

Perf. 12½

| 1431 | A340 | 15s multi | .25 | .20 |
|---|---|---|---|---|
| 1432 | A340 | 20s multi | .40 | .20 |
| 1433 | A340 | 25s multi | .40 | .20 |
| 1434 | A340 | 1.20p multi | .75 | .20 |
| | | | 1.80 | .80 |

Nos. 1431-1434 (4)

Children playing and IYC emblem, diff.

Hands Holding Emblem — A341

International Year of the Child.

---

UNCTAD Emblem A332

## 1979, May 3 — Wmk. 372 — Litho.

Perf. 12½

| 1401 | A332 | 1.20p multi | .75 | .25 |
|---|---|---|---|---|
| 1402 | A332 | 2.30p multi | 1.50 | .40 |

5th Session of UN Conference on Trade and Development, Manila, May 3-June 1.

Civet Cat A333

## 1979, May 14 — Litho.

Perf. 14

Philippine Animals: 1.20p, Macaque. 2.20p, Wild boar. 2.30p, Dwarf leopard. No. 1407, Asiatic dwarf otter. No. 1408, Anteater.

| 1403 | A333 | 30s multi | .30 | .20 |
|---|---|---|---|---|
| 1404 | A333 | 1.20p multi | .90 | .30 |
| 1405 | A333 | 2.20p multi | 1.50 | .45 |
| 1406 | A333 | 2.30p multi | 1.50 | .80 |
| 1407 | A333 | 5p multi | 3.25 | .80 |
| 1408 | A333 | 5p multi | 3.50 | .80 |
| | | | 10.95 | 3.00 |

Nos. 1403-1408 (6)

Dish Antenna — A334

## 1979, May 17

Perf. 12½

| 1409 | A334 | 90s multi | 1.10 | .30 |
|---|---|---|---|---|
| 1410 | A334 | 1.30p World map | 1.10 | .30 |

11th World Telecommunications Day, 5/17.

Mussaenda Donna Evangelina — A335

## 1979, June 11 — Litho.

Perf. 14

Philippine Mussaendas: 1.20p, Dona Esperanza. 2.20p, Dona Hilaria. 2.30p, Dona Aurora. No. 1415, Gining Imelda. No. 1416, Dona Trining.

| 1411 | A335 | 30s multi | .30 | .20 |
|---|---|---|---|---|
| 1412 | A335 | 1.20p multi | .90 | .30 |
| 1413 | A335 | 2.20p multi | 1.50 | .45 |
| 1414 | A335 | 2.30p multi | 1.50 | .80 |
| 1415 | A335 | 5p multi | 3.25 | .80 |
| 1416 | A335 | 5p multi | 3.50 | .80 |
| | | | 10.95 | 3.00 |

Nos. 1411-1416 (6)

Manila Cathedral, Coat of Arms — A336

---

Rotary Emblem and "60" — A327

Rosa Sevilla de Alvero — A328

## 1979, Jan. 26 — Wmk. 372 — Litho.

Perf. 12½

| 1387 | A327 | 30s multi | .35 | .20 |
|---|---|---|---|---|
| 1388 | A327 | 2.30p multi | 1.25 | .40 |

Rotary Club of Manila, 60th anniversary.

## 1979, Mar. 4 — Litho.

Perf. 12½

| 1389 | A328 | 30 rose | .40 | .20 |
|---|---|---|---|---|

Rosa Sevilla de Alvero, educator and writer, birth centenary.

For surcharges see Nos. 1479-1482.

Oil Well and Map of Palawan A329

## 1979, Mar. 21 — Wmk. 372 — Litho.

Perf. 12½

| 1390 | A329 | 30s multi | .35 | .20 |
|---|---|---|---|---|
| 1391 | A329 | 45s multi | .55 | .20 |

First Philippine oil production, Nido Oil Reef Complex, Palawan.

Merrill's Fruit Doves — A330

Birds: 1.20p, Brown tit babbler. 2.20p, Mindoro imperial pigeons. 2.30p, Steere's pittas. No. 1396, Koch's and red-breasted pittas. No. 1397, Philippine eared nightjar.

## 1979, Apr. 16 — Litho.

Perf. 14x13½

Unwmk.

| 1392 | A330 | 30s multi | .30 | .25 |
|---|---|---|---|---|
| 1393 | A330 | 1.20p multi | 1.10 | .75 |
| 1394 | A330 | 2.20p multi | 2.75 | .75 |
| 1395 | A330 | 2.30p multi | 2.75 | .75 |
| 1396 | A330 | 5p multi | 11.00 | 1.75 |
| 1397 | A330 | 5p multi | 11.00 | 1.75 |
| | | | 28.90 | 5.50 |

Nos. 1392-1397 (6)

Association Emblem and Reader A331

## 1979, Apr. 3 — Wmk. 372 — Litho.

Perf. 12½

| 1398 | A331 | 30s multi | .25 | .20 |
|---|---|---|---|---|
| 1399 | A331 | 1p multi | .45 | .30 |
| 1400 | A331 | | 1.10 | .20 |
| | | | 1.80 | .70 |

Nos. 1398-1400 (3)

Association of Special Libraries of the Philippines, 25th anniversary.

---

Church and Arms of Balayan A322

## 1978, Dec. 7 — Litho.

Perf. 12½

| 1372 | A321 | 30s multicolored | .45 | .20 |
|---|---|---|---|---|
| 1373 | A321 | 45s multicolored | .45 | .20 |

400th anniversary of the founding of Agoo.

## 1978, Dec. 8

| 1374 | A322 | 30s multicolored | .30 | .20 |
|---|---|---|---|---|
| 1375 | A322 | 90s multicolored | .60 | .20 |

400th anniv. of the founding of Balayan.

Dr. Honoria Acosta Sison (1888-1970), 1st Philippine Woman Physician — A323

## 1978, Dec. 15

| 1376 | A323 | 30s multicolored | .40 | .20 |
|---|---|---|---|---|

Family, Houses, UN Emblem — A324

## 1978, Dec. — Litho.

Perf. 12½

| 1377 | A324 | 30s multicolored | .40 | .20 |
|---|---|---|---|---|
| 1378 | A324 | 3p multicolored | 1.75 | .50 |

30th anniversary of Universal Declaration of Human Rights.

Chaetodon Trifasciatus — A325

Fish: 1.20p, Ballistoides niger. 2.20p, Rhinecanthus aculeatus. 2.30p, Chelmon rostratus. No. 1383, Chaetodon mertensi. No. 1384, Euxiphipops xanthometapon.

## 1978, Dec. 29 — Litho.

Perf. 14

| 1379 | A325 | 30s multi | .30 | .20 |
|---|---|---|---|---|
| 1380 | A325 | 1.20p multi | .90 | .30 |
| 1381 | A325 | 2.20p multi | 1.40 | .40 |
| 1382 | A325 | 2.30p multi | 1.40 | .40 |
| 1383 | A325 | 5p multi | 3.50 | .90 |
| 1384 | A325 | 5p multi | 3.50 | .90 |
| | | | 11.00 | 3.10 |

Nos. 1379-1384 (6)

Carlos P. Romulo, UN Emblem A326

## 1979, Jan. 14 — Litho.

Perf. 12½

| 1385 | A326 | 30s multi | .40 | .20 |
|---|---|---|---|---|
| 1386 | A326 | 2p multi | 1.40 | .40 |

Carlos P. Romulo (1899-1985), pres. of UN General Assembly and Security Council.

**1979, Sept. 27**    Litho.    **Perf. 12½**
1435 A341 30s multi .25 .20
1436 A341 1.35p multi 1.00 .25
Methodism in the Philippines, 80th anniv.

Emblem and Coins A342

**1979, Nov. 15**   Wmk. 372   Litho.   **Perf. 12½**
1437 A342 30s multi .50 .20
Philippine Numismatic and Antiquarian Society, 50th anniversary.

Concorde over Manila and Paris A343

**1979, Nov. 22**
Design: 2.20p, Concorde over Manila.
1438 A343 1.05p multi 1.00 .40
1439 A343 2.20p multi 2.50 .75
Air France service to Manila, 25th anniversary.

**1979, Nov. 27**
No. 1272 Surcharged in Red
1440 A273 90s on 1.60 blk .90 .25
Philatelic Week. Surcharge similar to No. 1367.

Transport Association Emblem A344

**1979, Nov. 27**    Litho.
1441 A344 75s multi .60 .20
1442 A344 2.20p multi 1.75 .40
International Air Transport Association, 35th annual general meeting, Manila.

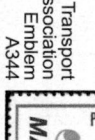

Local Government Year — A345

**1979, Dec. 14**    Litho.    **Perf. 12½**
1443 A345 30s multi .20 .20
1444 A345 45s multi .45 .20
For surcharge, see No. 1481.

Mother and Children, Ornament — A346

**1979, Dec. 17**
1445 A346 30s shown .30 .20
1446 A346 90s Stars .95 .20
Christmas. For surcharge see No. 1515.

---

Emblem and Congress Emblem A347

**1980, Jan. 20**   Wmk. 372   Litho.   **Perf. 12½**
1447 A347 30s multi .25 .20
1448 A347 90s multi 2.25 .30
Southeast Asia and Pacific Area League Against Rheumatism, 4th Congress, Manila, Jan. 19-24.

Gen. Douglas MacArthur A348

**1980, Jan. 26**   Wmk. 372   **Perf. 12½**
1449 A348 30s multi .30 .20
1450 A348 75s multi .50 .20
1451 A348 2.30p multi 1.75 .60
    Nos. 1449-1451 (3) 2.55 1.00

**Souvenir Sheet**
**Imperf**
1452 A348 5p multi 4.00 3.25
Gen. Douglas MacArthur (1880-1964). For overprint see No. 2198.

Design: 30s, MacArthur's birthplace (Little Rock, ARI) & burial place (Norfolk, VA). 2.30p, MacArthur's cap. Sunglasses & pipe. 5p, MacArthur & troops wading ashore at Leyte, Oct. 20, 1944.

Knights of Columbus of Philippines, 75th Anniversary A349

**1980, Feb. 14**
1453 A349 30s multi .25 .20
1454 A349 1.35p multi 1.00 .25
Knights of Columbus of Philippines, 75th anniversary.

Philippine Military Academy, 75th Anniversary — A350

**1980, Feb. 17**   Wmk. 372   Litho.
1455 A350 30s multi .50 .20
1456 A350 1.20p multi 1.00 .20

Philippines Women's University, 75th Anniversary — A351

**1980, Feb. 21**    **Perf. 12½**
1457 A351 30s multi .75 .20
1458 A351 1.05p multi 2.25 .40

---

Rheumatic Pain Spots and Congress Emblem A347

Rotary International, 75th Anniversary (Paintings by Carlos Botong Francisco): Nos. 1459 and 1460 each in continuous design.

**1980, Feb. 23**    **Perf. 12½**
1459    Strip of 5 5.00 5.00
  a. A362 30s single stamp .70 .70
1460    Strip of 5 12.00 12.00
  a. A362 2.30p single stamp 1.75 1.75

Disaster Relief A352

A353

**1980, Mar. 28**   Wmk. 372   Litho.   **Perf. 12½**
1461 A353 30s multi .75 .20
1462 A353 1.30p multi 2.00 .30
6th centenary of Islam in Philippines.

A354

**1980, Apr. 7**
1463 A354 30s multi .50 .30
1464 A354 75s multi 2.50 .75
World Health Day (Apr. 7); anti-smoking campaign.

Philippine Girl Scouts, 40th Anniversary A355

**1980, May 26**   Wmk. 372   Litho.   **Perf. 12½**
1465 A355 30s multi .40 .20
1466 A355 2p multi 1.40 .35

Jeepney (Public Jeep) A356

**1980, June 24**    Litho.    **Perf. 12½**
1467 A356 30s Jeepney, diff. .40 .20
1468 A356 1.20p multi 1.25 .35
For surcharge see No. 1503.

**1980, Aug. 1**
Nos. 1272, 1206 Surcharged in Red
1469 A273 1.35p on 1.60p blk 1.90 .35
1470 A250 1.50p on 1.80p grn .60 .60
Independence, 82nd Anniversary.

---

Association Emblem — A357

**1980, Aug. 1**   Wmk. 372   Litho.   **Perf. 12½**
1471 A357 30s multi .25 .20
1472 A357 2.30p multi 1.50 .40
International Association of Universities, 7th General Conference, Manila, Aug. 25-30.

Congress Emblem, Map of Philippines A358

**1980, Aug. 18**   Wmk. 372   Litho.   **Perf. 12½**
1473 A358 30s lt grn & blk .25 .20
1474 A358 75s lt bl & blk 1.10 .30
1475 A358 2.30p sal & blk 1.75 .70
    Nos. 1473-1475 (3)
Intl. Federation of Library Associations and Institutions, 46th Congress, Manila, 8/18-23.

Kabataang Barangay (New Society), 5th Anniversary — A359

**1980, Sept. 19**    Litho.    **Perf. 12½**
1476 A359 30s multi 1.00 1.00
1477 A359 40s multi .35 .20
1478 A359 1p multi .80 .35
    Nos. 1476-1478 (3) 1.40 .65

**1980, Sept. 26**   Wmk. 372   Litho.   **Perf. 12½**
1479 A328 40s on 30s rose (Bl) 1.00 .20
1480 A338 40s on 30s multi 1.00 .20
1481 A345 40s on 30s multi 1.00 .20
1482 A346 40s on 30s multi (R) 2.00 .20
1483 A294 2p on 1.65p multi (R) 4.00 .30
    Nos. 1479-1483 (5) 9.00 1.10
Nos. 1389, 1422, 1443, 1445, 1327 Surcharged in Blue, Black or Red
Nos. 1476-1478 (3)

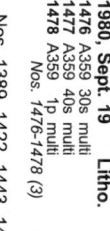

Catamaran, Conference Emblem — A360

**1980, Sept. 27**
1484 A360 30s multi .30 .20
1485 A360 2.30p multi 1.50 .50
World Tourism Conf., Manila, Sept. 27.

Stamp Day — A361

UN, 35th Anniv. — A362

**1980, Oct. 9**

| | | | |
|---|---|---|---|
| 1486 | A361 | 40s multi | .40 .20 |
| 1487 | A361 | 1p multi | .85 .25 |
| 1488 | A361 | 2p multi | 1.75 .55 |
| | | | 3.00 1.00 |

Nos. 1486-1488 (3)

**1980, Oct. 20**

Designs: 40s, UN Headquarters and Emblem. Flag of Philippines. 3.20p, UN and Philippine flags, UN headquarters.

| | | | |
|---|---|---|---|
| 1489 | A362 | 40s multi | .35 .20 |
| 1490 | A362 | 3.20p multi | 2.25 .65 |

Murex Alabaster A363

**1980, Nov. 2**

| | | | |
|---|---|---|---|
| 1491 | A363 | 40s shown | .85 .20 |
| 1492 | A363 | 60s multi | .60 .20 |
| 1493 | A363 | 1.20p Homalocantha zamboi | .85 .25 |
| 1494 | A363 | 2p Xenophora pallidula | 1.60 .35 |
| | | | 3.90 1.00 |

Nos. 1491-1494 (4)

INTERPOL Emblem on Globe — A364

**1980, Nov. 5   Wmk. 372**
**Litho.**

| | | | |
|---|---|---|---|
| 1495 | A364 | 40s multi | .30 .20 |
| 1496 | A364 | 1p multi | .60 .20 |
| 1497 | A364 | 3.20p multi | 1.60 .55 |
| | | | 2.50 .95 |

Nos. 1495-1497 (3)

49th General Assembly Session of INTERPOL (Intl. Police Organization), Manila, Nov. 13-21.

Central Philippine University, 75th Anniversary A365

**1980, Nov. 17   Unwmk.**

| | | | |
|---|---|---|---|
| 1498 | A365 | 40s multi | .75 .20 |
| 1499 | A365 | 3.20p multi | 2.25 .80 |

No. 1257 Surcharged
**Wmk. 372**
**1980, Nov. 21   Litho.   Perf. 12½**

| | | | |
|---|---|---|---|
| 1500 | A269 | 1.20p on 80s multi | 1.50 .35 |

Philatelic Week. Surcharge similar to No. 1367.

No. 1358 Surcharged
**1980, Nov. 30**

| | | | |
|---|---|---|---|
| 1501 | A313 | 40s on 30s multi | 1.25 .35 |

APO Philatelic Society, 30th anniversary.

Christmas Tree, Present and Candy Cane — A366

---

**Perf. 12½   Litho.   Unwmk.**
**1980, Dec. 15**

| | | | |
|---|---|---|---|
| 1502 | A366 | 40s multi | .55 .20 |

Christmas 1980.

No. 1467 Surcharged
**1981, Jan. 2**

| | | | |
|---|---|---|---|
| 1503 | A356 | 40c on 30s multi | 2.00 .30 |

Nos. 1370, 1257 Surcharged in Red or Black

**1981**

| | | | |
|---|---|---|---|
| 1504 | A320 | 10s on 30s (R) multi | 1.00 .25 |
| 1505 | A269 | 85s on 80s multi | 2.00 .30 |

Issue dates: 10s, Jan. 12; 85s, Jan. 2.

Heinrich Von Stephan, UPU Emblem A367

**1981, Jan. 30**

| | | | |
|---|---|---|---|
| 1506 | A367 | 3.20p multi | 2.50 .75 |

Heinrich von Stephan (1831-1897), founder of UPU, birth sesquicentennial.

Pope John Paul II Greeting Crowd — A368

Designs: 90s, Pope, signature, vert. 1.2/lyn, Pope, cardinals, vert. 3p, Pope giving blessing, Vatican arms, Manila Cathedral. 7.50p, Pope, light on map of Philippines, vert.

**1981, Feb. 17   Perf. 13½x14   Unwmk.**

| | | | |
|---|---|---|---|
| 1507 | A368 | 90s multi | .75 .25 |
| 1508 | A368 | 1.20p multi | .80 .25 |
| 1509 | A368 | 2.30p multi | 1.75 .50 |
| 1510 | A368 | 3p multi | 2.50 .65 |
| | | | 5.80 1.65 |

Nos. 1507-1510 (4)

**Souvenir Sheet**

| | | | |
|---|---|---|---|
| 1511 | A368 | 7.50p multi | 4.25 5.00 |

Visit of Pope John Paul, Feb. 17-22.

Nos. 1364, 1423, 1268, 1446, 1261, 1206, 1327 Surcharged

**1981   Litho.   Perf. 12½**

| | | | |
|---|---|---|---|
| 1512 | A316 | 40s on 90s multi | .90 .25 |
| 1513 | A338 | 40s on 1.20p multi | .90 .20 |
| 1514 | A272 | 40s on 65s lil rose | .90 .25 |
| 1515 | A346 | 40s on 90s multi | 1.50 .35 |
| 1517 | A271 | 1p on 1.50p brt rose & vio bl | 1.50 .25 |
| 1518 | A250 | 1.20p on 1.80p grn | 2.10 .40 |
| 1519 | A294 | 1.20p on 1.65p multi | 2.75 .40 |
| 1520 | A271 | 2p on 1.50p brt rose & vio bl | 3.50 .35 |
| | | | 14.05 2.45 |

Nos. 1512-1520 (8)

---

A370

**1981, Apr. 20   Wmk. 372**

| | | | |
|---|---|---|---|
| 1521 | A369 | 2p multi | 1.25 .40 |
| 1522 | A369 | 3.20p multi | 1.75 .65 |

68th Spring Meeting of the Inter-Parliamentary Union, Manila, Apr. 20-25.

Unless otherwise stated, Nos. 1523-1580 are on granite paper.

**1981, May 22   Wmk. 372   Litho.   Perf. 12½**

| | | | |
|---|---|---|---|
| 1523 | A370 | 40s Bubble coral | .90 .20 |
| 1524 | A370 | 40s Branching coral | .90 .20 |
| 1525 | A370 | 40s Brain coral | .90 .20 |
| 1526 | A370 | 40s Table coral | .90 .20 |
| | | | 4.00 |
| a. | A370 | Block of 4, #1523-1526 | 4.00 |

Philippine Motor Vehicles, A3000, 50th Anniv. — A371

Vintage cars.

**1981, May 25**

| | | | |
|---|---|---|---|
| 1527 | A371 | 40s President's car | .80 .20 |
| 1528 | A371 | 1930 | .80 .20 |
| 1529 | A371 | 1937 | .80 .20 |
| 1530 | A371 | 40s shown | .80 .20 |
| | | | 3.50 |
| a. | A371 | Block of 4, #1627-1530 | 3.50 |

Re-inauguration of Pres. Ferdinand E. Marcos — A372

**1981, June 30**

| | | | |
|---|---|---|---|
| 1531 | A372 | 40s multi | .50 .20 |

**Souvenir Sheet   Imperf**

| | | | |
|---|---|---|---|
| 1532 | A372 | 5p multi | 4.00 5.00 |

No. 1531 exists imperf. Value $1. For overprint see No. 1753.

St. Ignatius Loyola, Founder of Jesuit Order A373

400th Anniv. of Jesuits in Philippines: No. 1534, Jose Rizal, Ateneo University. No. 1535, Father Federico Faura, Manila Observatory. No. 1536, Father Saturnino Urios, map of Philippines.

A369

---

A374

A375

**1981, July 31**

| | | | |
|---|---|---|---|
| 1533 | A373 | 40s multi | .70 .20 |
| 1534 | A373 | 40s multi | .70 .20 |
| 1535 | A373 | 40s multi | .70 .20 |
| 1536 | A373 | 40s multi | .70 .20 |
| | | | 3.00 3.00 |

**Souvenir Sheet   Imperf**

| | | | |
|---|---|---|---|
| 1537 | A373 | 2p multi | 4.00 4.75 |

#1537 contains vignettes of #1533-1536. For surcharge see No. 1737.

Design: 40s, Isabelo de los Reyes (1867-1938), labor union founder. 1p, Gen. Gregorio del Pilar (1875-1899). No. 1540, Francisco Dagohoy. No. 1543, Ambrosia R. Bautista, signer of Declaration of Independence, 1898. No. 1544, Juan Sumulong (1875-1942), statesman. 2.30p, Nicanor Abelardo (1893-1934), composer. 3.20p, Gen. Vicente Lim (1888-1945), first Philippine graduate of West Point.

**Wmk. 372   Perf. 12½**
**1981-82   Litho.**

| | | | |
|---|---|---|---|
| 1538 | A374 | 40s grnsh bl ('82) | .35 .20 |
| 1539 | A374 | 1p blk & red brn | .60 .20 |
| 1540 | A374 | 1.20p blk & lt red brn | .95 .25 |
| 1541 | A374 | 1.20p brown ('82) | 1.50 .35 |
| 1543 | A374 | 2p blk & red brn | 1.10 .35 |
| 1544 | A374 | 2p rose lil ('82) | 1.50 .35 |
| 1545 | A374 | 2.30p lt red brn ('82) | 1.75 .40 |
| 1546 | A374 | 3.20p gray bl ('82) | 2.25 .65 |
| | | | 10.00 2.75 |

Nos. 1538-1546 (8)

See Nos. 1672-1660, 1002 1683, 1685. For surcharges see Nos. 1668-1669.

**1981, Sept. 2**

| | | | |
|---|---|---|---|
| 1551 | A375 | 40s multi | .50 .20 |

Chief Justice Fred Ruiz Castro, 67th birth anniv.

A376

A376a

**1981, Oct. 24   Wmk. 372   Litho.   Perf. 12½**

| | | | |
|---|---|---|---|
| 1552 | A376 | 40s multi | .40 .20 |
| 1553 | A376 | 3.20p multi | 2.10 .65 |

Intl. Year of the Disabled.

**1981, Nov. 7**

| | | | |
|---|---|---|---|
| 1554 | A376a | 40s multi | .30 .20 |
| 1555 | A376a | 2p multi | 1.40 .45 |
| 1556 | A376a | 3.20p multi | 3.70 .60 |
| | | | 3.70 1.25 |

Nos. 1554-1556 (3)

24th Intl. Red Cross Conf., Manila, 117-14.

**1981, Nov. 13**
Intramuros Gate, Manila — A377
1557 A377 40s black .50 .20

**Manila Park Zoo Concert Series, Nov 20-30 A378**
**1981, Nov. 20**
1558 A378 40s multi .50 .20

No. 1329 Overprinted "1981 Philatelic Week" and Surcharged
**1981, Nov. 20**
1559 A296 1.20p on 1.50p multi 1.90 .40

Nos. 1205, 1347, 1371 Surcharged
**1981, Nov. 25**   Wmk. 372   Litho.   *Perf. 12½*
1560 A306 40s on 1.05p multi 1.25 .25
1561 A320 40s on 1.35p multi 1.25 .25
1562 A273 1.20p on 1.50p brn 3.50 .85
Nos. 1560-1562 (3) 6.00 .85

**11th Southeast Asian Games, Manila, Dec. 6-15 A379**
**1981, Dec. 3**
1563 A379 40s Running .55 .20
1564 A379 1p Bicycling 1.10 .20
1565 A379 2p Pres. Marcos, Intl. Olympic Pres. Samaranch 2.25 .30
1566 A379 2.30p Soccer 2.75 .50
1567 A379 2.80p Shooting 3.50 .65
1568 A379 3.20p Bowling 3.75 .85
Nos. 1563-1568 (6) 13.90 2.70

**Manila Intl. Film Festival, Jan. 18-29 A380**
**1982, Jan. 18**   Wmk. 372   Litho.   *Perf. 12½*
1569 A380 40s Film Center .40 .20
1570 A380 2p Golden trophy, vert. 1.75 .45
1571 A380 3.20p Trophy, diff., vert. 4.65 1.40
Nos. 1569-1571 (3) 2.50 .75

**Manila Metropolitan Waterworks and Sewerage System Centenary — A381**
**1982, Jan. 22**
1572 A381 40s blue .40 .20
1573 A381 1.20p brown 1.25 .30

**1982, Jan. 28**
1574 A273 1p on 65s lil rose 1.25 .40
1575 A286 1p on 1.50p multi 1.25 .40
1576 A295 3.20p on 2.20p multi 8.50 1.80
Nos. 1268, 1302, 1328 Surcharged
Nos. 1574-1576 (3) 6.00 1.00

---

**Scouting Year — A382**
**1982, Feb. 22**
1577 A382 40s Portrait .45 .20
1578 A382 2p Scout giving salute 1.75 .55

**25th Anniv. of Children's Museum and Library Foundation A383**
**1982, Feb. 25**
1579 A383 40s Mural .30 .20
1580 A383 1.20p Children playing 1.25 .35

**77th Anniv. of Philippine Military Academy A384**
**1982, Mar. 25**   Wmk. 372   Litho.   *Perf. 12½*
1581 A384 40s multi .40 .20
1582 A384 1p multi .85 .25

**40th Bataan Day A385**
**Souvenir Sheet**
*Imperf*
**1982, Apr. 9**
1583 A385 40s multi .40 .20
1584 A385 2p Soldier "Reunion for Peace" 1.40 .30
1585 A385 3.20p Cannon, flag 3.50 4.00

No. 1585 contains one 38x28mm stamp. No. 1585 comes on two different papers, the second being thicker with cream gum. For surcharge see No. 2114.

**1982**
No. B27 Surcharged
Photo.   *Perf. 13½*
1586 SP14 10s on 6 + 5s multi .75 .25

---

Aurora Aragon Quezon (1888-1949), former First Lady. — A387
**1982, Apr. 28**   Litho.   *Perf. 12½*
1587 A386 1p rose pink 1.50 .20
There are three types of No. 1587. See Nos. 1684-1684A.

**1982, May 1**
1588 A387 40s Man holding award .50 .20
1589 A387 1.20p 7th Towers Awards. 1.50 .25

**UN Conf. on Human Environment, 10th Anniv. — A388**
**1982, June 5**
1590 A388 40s Turtle .65 .25
1591 A388 3.20p Philippine eagle 3.75 1.00

**75th Anniv. of Univ. of Philippines College of Medicine A389**
**1982, June 10**
1592 A389 40s multi .50 .20
1593 A389 3.20p multi 2.00 .75

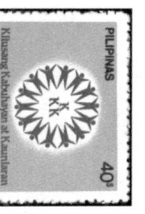

**Natl. Livelihood Movement A390**
**1982, June 12**
1594 A390 40s multi .50 .20
See #1681-1681A. For overprint see #1634.

**Adamson Univ., 50th Anniv. — A391**
**1982, June 21**
1595 A391 40s bl & multi .35 .20
1596 A391 1.20p lt vio & multi 1.10 .25

**Social Security, 25th Anniv. — A392**

---

**Pres. Marcos, 65th Birthday — A393**
**1982, Sept. 1**   *Perf. 13½x13*
1597 A393 40s multi .30 .20
1598 A392 1.20p multi .90 .25

**1982, Sept. 11**   *Perf. 13½x13*
1599 A393 40s sil & multi .50 .20
1600 A393 3.20p sil & multi 2.00 .75
a. Souv. sheet of 2, #1599-1600, imperf. 4.00 4.00
For surcharge see No. 1666.

**15th Anniv. of Assoc. of Southeast Asian Nations (ASEAN) A394**
**1982, Sept. 22**   Litho.   *Perf. 12½*
1601 A394 40s Flags .65 .20

**St. Teresa of Avila (1515-1582) — A395**
**1982, Oct. 15**   *Perf. 13x13½*
1602 A395 40s Text .35 .20
1603 A395 1.20p Map .75 .25
1604 A395 2p like #1603 1.50 .25
Nos. 1602-1604 (3) 2.60 .70

**10th Anniv. of Tenant Farmers' Emancipation Decree — A396**
**1982, Oct. 21**   Litho.   Wmk. 372
1605 A396 40s Pres. Marcos signing law 1.60 .25
See No. 1654.

**350th Anniv. of St. Isabel College A397**
**1982, Oct. 22**   *Perf. 13x13½*
1606 A397 40s multi .30 .20
1607 A397 1p multi 1.25 .40

**Reading Campaign A398**

**1982, Nov. 4**
1608 A398 40s yel & multi .30 .20
1609 A398 2.30p grn & multi 1.50 .60
For surcharge see No. 1713.

42nd Skal Club World Congress, Manila, Nov. 7-12 A399

**1982, Nov. 7**
1610 A399 40s Heads .35 .20
1611 A399 2p Chief 2.25 .75

25th Anniv. of Bayanihan Folk Arts Center A400

Designs: Various folk dances.
*Perf. 13x13½* **Litho.**
**1982, Nov. 10**
1612 A400 40s multi .35 .25
1613 A400 2.80p multi 2.75 .65

TB Bacillus Centenary A401

**Wmk. 372**
**1982, Dec. 7**
1614 A401 40s multi .35 .20
1615 A401 2.80p multi 2.25 .75

Christmas 1982 A402

**1982, Dec. 10**
1616 A402 40s multi 1.00 .20
1617 A402 1p multi 2.75 .75

Philatelic Week, Nov. 22-28 A403

*Perf. 13x13½* **Litho.** **Wmk. 372**
**1982, Nov. 28**
1618 A403 40s yel & multi .30 .20
1619 A403 1p sil & multi .90 .20
For surcharge see No. 1667.

Visit of Pres. Marcos to the US, Sept. A404

**1982, Dec. 18**
1620 A404 40s multi .35 .20
1621 A404 3.20p multi 2.75 .75
a. Souv. sheet of 2, #1620-1621 4.00 4.75

---

UN World Assembly on Aging, July 26-Aug. 6 — A405

Senate Pres. Eulogio Rodriguez, Sr. (1883-1964) A406

**1982, Dec. 24**
1622 A405 1.20p Woman 1.10 .20
1623 A405 2p Man 1.50 .30

**1983, Jan. 21**
1624 A406 40s grn & multi .30 .20
1625 A406 1.20p org & multi .90 .00

1983 Manila Intl. Film Festival, Jan. 24-Feb. 4 A407

**1983, Jan. 24**
1626 A407 40s blk & multi .35 .20
1627 A407 3.20p pink & multi 2.75 .75

Beatification of Lorenzo Ruiz (1981) — A408

*Perf. 13x13½* **Litho.** **Wmk. 372**
**1983, Feb. 18**
1628 A408 40s multi .35 .20
1629 A408 1.20p multi 1.10 .20

400th Anniv. of Local Printing Press A409
FIRST LOCAL PRINTING PRESS

**1983, Mar. 14**
1630 A409 40s blk & grn .50 .20

Safety at Sea — A410

*Perf. 13½x13*
**1983, Mar. 17**
1631 A410 40s multi .20
25th anniv. of Inter-Governmental Maritime Consultation Org. Convention.

---

Intl. Org. of Supreme Audit Institutions, 11th Congress, Manila, Apr. 19-27 A411

*Perf. 13x13½* **Wmk. 372** **Litho.**
**1983, Apr. 8**
1632 A411 40s Symbols .40 .20
1633 A411 2.80p Emblem 1.75 .60
a. Souv. sheet of 2, 1632-1633, imperf. 4.25 5.00

No. 1633a comes on two papers: cream gum, normal watermark; white gum, watermark made up of smaller letters.

Type of 1982 Overprinted in Red: "7th BSP NATIONAL JAMBOREE 1983"
*Perf. 12½*
**1983, Apr. 13**
1634 A400 40s multi .50 .20
Boy Scouts of Philippines jamboree.

No. 1249 Surcharged
**1983, Apr. 15**
1635 Block of 10 10.00 10.00
a.-j. A265 40s on 45s, any single .90 .90

HAPPINESS IS A SET OF GOOD TEETH A412

75th anniv. of Dental Assoc.
*Perf. 13½x13* **Litho.**
**1983, May 9**
1636 A412 40s multi .50 .20

UP DIAMOND JUBILEE YEAR A413

*Perf. 13½x13* **Litho.**
**1983, June 17**
1637 A413 40s Statue .30 .20
1638 A413 1.20p Statue, diamond 1.00 .25
75th anniv. of University of the Philippines.

Visit of Japanese Prime Minister Yasuhiro Nakasone, May 6-8 — A414

*Perf. 13½x13½* **Wmk. 372** **Litho.**
**1983, June 20**
1639 A414 40s multi .50 .20

25th Anniv. of Natl. Science and Technology Authority A415
National Science and Technology Authority 1958-1983

---

**1983, July 11**
1640 A415 40s Animals, produce .45 .20
1641 A415 40s Heart, food, pill .45 .20
1642 A415 40s Factories, windmill, car .45 .20
1643 A415 40s Chemicals, house, book .45 .20
1.90 1.60
a. Block of 4, #1640-1643
Science Week.

World Communications Year — A416

*Perf. 12½*
**Wmk. 372** **Litho.**
**1983, Oct. 24**
1644 A416 3.20p multi 2.25 .75

Philippine Postal System Bicentennial — A417

**1983, Oct. 31**
1645 A417 40s multi .50 .20

Christmas — A418
Star of the East and festival scene in continuous design.
**1983, Nov. 15** **Litho.**
1646 3up of 6 3.75 3.25
.75 .90
4.00 4.75
a.-e. A418 40s single stamp
f. Souvenir sheet

Xavier University, 50th Anniv. A419

*Perf. 12½*
**1983, Dec. 1** **Litho.**
1647 A419 40s multi .40 .20
1648 A419 60s multi .90 .20

*Perf. 14*
Ministry of Labor and Employment A420

A421

**1983, Dec. 8**    **Litho.**    **Perf. 12½**
| 1649 | A420 | 40s brt ultra & multi | .90 | .20 |
| 1650 | A420 | 60s gold & multi | .90 | .20 |

Ministry of Labor and Employment, golden jubilee.

**1983, Dec. 7**
| 1651 | A421 | 40s multi | .40 | .20 |
| 1652 | A421 | 60s multi | .90 | .20 |

50th anniv. of Women's Suffrage Movement.

Philatelic Week — A422

**1983, Dec. 20**
| 1653 | A422 | 50s multi | .40 | .20 |
a.-e.   A422 50s any single

Stamp Collecting: a, Cutting. b, Soaking. d, Affixing hinges. e, Mounting stamp.

Emancipation Type of 1982

**1983**    **Litho.**    **Perf. 13**
Size: 32x22mm
| 1654 | A396 | 40s multi | 2.50 | .45 |

PILIPINAS 40

RELIGIOUS OF THE VIRGIN MARY · 1684-1984

**1983, Dec. 20**
| 1653 | ... | Strip of 5 | 4.00 | 4.00 |
| a.-e. | | A422 50s any single | .75 | .75 |

PILIPINAS P3.00 Doña Concha Felix de Calderon

Princess Tarhata Kiram — A424

**1984, Jan. 16**    **Wmk. 372**    **Perf. 13**
| 1661 | A424 | 3p grn & red | 1.90 | .35 |

Philippine Cockatoo — A423

**1984, Jan. 9**    **Unwmk.**    **Perf. 14**
| 1655 | A423 | 40s shown | .45 | .25 |
| 1656 | A423 | 2.30p Guaiabero | 1.40 | .50 |
| 1657 | A423 | 2.80p Crimson-spotted racket-tailed parrots | 1.75 | .55 |
| 1658 | A423 | 3.20p Large-billed parrot | 2.10 | .60 |
| 1659 | A423 | 3.60p Tanygnathus sumatranus | 2.25 | .60 |
| 1660 | A423 | 5p Hanging parakeets | 3.00 | .75 |

There were 500,000 of each value created cto with Jan 9 1984 cancel in the center of each block of 4. These were sold at a small fraction of face value. Used values are for ctos.

Nos. 1655-1660 (6)   10.95   3.25

Order of Virgin Mary, 300th Anniv. A425

**1984, Jan. 23**    **Perf. 13½x13**
| 1662 | A425 | 40s blk & multi | .60 | .20 |
| 1663 | A425 | 60s red & multi | 1.25 | .20 |

**1984, Feb. 9**    **Perf. 13**
| 1664 | A426 | 60s blk & bl grn | .60 | .20 |
| 1665 | A426 | 3.60p red & bl grn | 1.75 | .25 |

Dona Concha Felix de Calderon A426

---

No. 1685 Portrait Type of 1981

Designs: No. 1672, Gen. Artemio Ricarte. No. 1673, Teodoro M. Kalaw. No. 1674, Pres. Carlos P. Garcia. No. 1675, Senator Quintin Paredes. No. 1676, Dr. Deogracias V. Villadolid (1896-1976), 1st director, Bureau of Fisheries. No. 1677, Santiago Fonacier (1885-1940), archbishop. No. 1678, Dr. Vicente Orestes Romualdez (1885-1970), lawyer. 3p. Francisco Dagohoy.

**1984-85**    **Litho.**
| 1672 | A374 | 60s blk & lt brn | 1.40 | .20 |
| 1673 | A374 | 60s blk & pur | 1.75 | .20 |
| 1674 | A374 | 60s black | 1.75 | .20 |
| 1675 | A374 | 60s dull blue | .70 | .20 |
| 1676 | A374 | 60s dk red ('85) | .70 | .20 |
| 1677 | A374 | 60s brn blk ('85) | .50 | .20 |
| 1678 | A374 | 60s cobalt blue | .50 | .20 |

Types of 3p:
Type I — Medium heavy denomination.
Type II — Large "PILIPINAS," large, heavy denomination.
Type III — Large "PILIPINAS," medium denomination.

| 1679 | A374 | 2p brt rose ('85) | .85 | .20 |
| 1680 | A374 | 3p pale brn, type I | 3.50 | .40 |
| 1680A | A374 | 3p pale brn, type III | 5.25 | .30 |

Nos. 1672-1680A (10)   22.65   2.45

Issued: #1672, 3/22; #1673, 3/31; #1674, 6/14; #1675, 9/12; #1676, 3/22; #1677, 5/21; #1678, 2p, 7/3; 3p, 9/7.

Type of 1982

Types of 3.60p:
Type I — Thick Frame line, large "P," "360" with line under "60."
Type II — Medium Frame line, small "p," "3.60."

**1984-86**
| 1681 | A390 | 60s green & multi | .25 | .20 |
| 1681A | A390 | 60s red & multi | .25 | .20 |
| 1682 | A374 | 1.80p multi | .70 | .20 |
| 1683 | A374 | 2.40p multi | 1.10 | .20 |
| 1684 | A386 | 3.60p Quezon, type I | .50 | .20 |
| 1684A | A386 | As #1684, type II | 1.60 | .40 |
| 1685 | A374 | 4.20p Quezon, type II | 2.10 | .40 |

Nos. 1681-1685 (7)   8.55   1.85

Issued: #1681A, 10/19; #1684A, 2/14/86; others 3/26.

Nos. 1546, 1599, 1618 Surcharged

**1984, Feb. 20**
| 1666 | A393 | 60s on 40s | .35 | .20 |
| 1667 | A403 | 60s on 40s | .40 | .20 |
| 1668 | A374 | 3.60p on 40s (R) | 3.25 | .40 |

Nos. 1666-1668 (3)   4.00   1.40

No. 1685 Surcharged

**1985, Oct. 21**    **Litho.**    **Perf. 12½**
| 1669 | A374 | 3.60p on 4.20p rose | 5.50 | .90 |

---

PILIPINAS P3.00 Princess Tarhata Kiram

Philippine Princess Tarhata Kiram — A424

**1984, Apr. 25**    **Litho.**    **Perf. 13x13½**
| 1686 | A427 | 70s multi | .50 | .25 |
| 1687 | A427 | 3.60p multi | 2.25 | .75 |

Night Views of Manila.

Ayala Corp. Sesquicentenary — A427

ESPAÑA '84 A428 PILIPINAS P2.50

Designs: 2.50p, No. 1690d, Our Lady of the Most Holy Rosary, with St. Dominic, by C. Francisco. 5p, No. 1690a, Spoliarium, by Juan Luna. No. 1690b, Blessed Virgin of Manila as Patroness of Voyages, Galleon showing map of Panama-Manila. No. 1690c, Illustrations from The Monkey and the Turtle, by Rizal (first children's book published in Philippines, 1885).

**1984, Apr. 27**    **Unwmk.**    **Perf. 14**
| 1688 | A428 | 2.50p multi | 1.00 | 1.00 |
| 1689 | A428 | 5p multi | 2.00 | 2.00 |
| a. | | Pair, #1688-1689 | 3.75 | |

**Souvenir Sheet Perf. 14½x15, Imperf.**
| 1690 | | Sheet of 4 | 19.00 | 19.00 |
| a.-d. | A428 7.50p, any single | | 4.00 | 4.00 |

Maria Pax Mendoza Guzon — A429

PILIPINAS 60s Dr. Maria Paz Mendoza Guazon 1884-1984

**1984, May 26**    **Wmk. 372**    **Perf. 13**
| 1691 | A429 | 60s brt blue & red | 1.00 | .25 |
| 1692 | A429 | 65s brt blue, red & blk | .85 | .25 |

Butterflies — A430

PILIPINAS 60s ADOLIAS AMKANA

**1984, Aug. 2**    **Unwmk.**    **Litho.**    **Perf. 14**
| 1693 | A430 | 60s Adolias amkana | .60 | .20 |
| 1694 | A430 | 2.40p Papilio daedalus | 1.25 | .35 |
| 1695 | A430 | 3p Prothoe frankii semperi | 1.50 | .50 |
| 1696 | A430 | 3.60p Troides magoi | 1.50 | .50 |
| 1697 | A430 | 4.20p Yoma sabina vasuki | 1.50 | .50 |
| 1698 | A430 | 5p Chilasa idaeoides | 2.10 | .60 |

Nos. 1693-1698 (6)   8.45   2.75

There were 500,000 of each value created cto with Jul 5 1984 cancel in the center of each block of 4. These were sold at a small fraction of face value. Used values are for ctos.

---

**1984, Feb. 7**   —   (various listings per column)

PILIPINAS 60 1984 OLYMPICS LOS ANGELES

Summer Olympics, Los Angeles, 1984 — A431

**1984, Aug. 9**    **Unwmk.**    **Litho.**    **Perf. 14**
| 1699 | A431 | 60s multi | .25 | .20 |
| 1700 | A431 | 2.40p multi | 1.00 | .30 |
| 1701 | A431 | 6p multi | 2.50 | .50 |
| 1702 | A431 | 7.20p multi | 3.00 | .70 |
| 1703 | A431 | 8.40p multi | 3.25 | .85 |
| 1704 | A431 | 20p multi | 8.00 | 1.00 |

Nos. 1699-1704 (6)   18.00   3.55

**Souvenir Sheet**
| 1705 | | Sheet of 4 | 15.00 | 15.00 |
| a.-d. | A431 6p, any single | | 2.50 | 2.50 |

Designs: 60s, Running (man). 2.40p, Swimming. 7.20p, Windsurfing. 8.40p, Boxing. 6p, Running (woman). 20p, Cycling.

There were 500,000 of each value created cto with Aug 8 1984 cancel in the center of each block of 4. These were sold at a fraction of face value. Used value, set of 6 ctu, $1.25.

Nos. 1699-1705 were also issued imperf, with blue, instead of red, stars at sides. Value, set of 6 stamps $100, souvenir sheet $50.

Baguio City, 75th Anniv. A432

PILIPINAS ¹20

---

PILIPINAS 50s CUTTING

No. 1, Australia No. 59 and Koalas A434

AUSIPEX '84.

**1984, Sept. 21**    **Perf. 14½x15**    **Unwmk.**
| 1708 | A434 | 3p multi | 3.00 | 1.00 |
| 1709 | A434 | 3.60p multi | 4.00 | 1.00 |

**Souvenir Sheet**
| 1710 | | Sheet of 3 | 24.00 | 24.00 |
| a. | A434 20p multi | | 6.00 | 6.00 |

AUSIPEX '84. No. 1710 exists imperf.

No. 1609 Surcharged with 2 Black Bars and Ovptd. "14-17 NOV. '84 / R.I. ASIA REGIONAL CONFERENCE"

**1984, Nov. 11**    **Wmk. 372**    **Litho.**
| 1713 | A398 | 1.20p on 2.30p multi | 1.60 | .40 |

Philatelic Week — A435

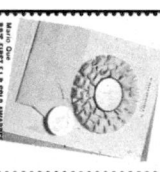

Maria Que AUSIPEX '84

**1984, Nov. 22**    **Perf. 13½x13**
| 1714 | | 1.20p Gold medal | .50 | .35 |
| 1715 | | 3p Winning stamp exhibit | 1.50 | .80 |
| a. | A435 Pair, #1714-1715 | | 2.75 | 2.75 |

AUSIPEX '84 and Maria Que, 1st Philippine exhibitor to win FIP Gold Award. For overprints see Nos.

Light Rail Transit A433

PILIPINAS ¹20 LIGHT RAIL TRANSIT The Mansion

**1984, Sept. 10**    **Wmk. 372**    **Litho.**    **Perf. 12½**
| 1706 | A432 | 1.20p The Mansion | 1.25 | .35 |

**1984, Aug. 24**    **Litho.**    **Perf. 13x13½**
| 1707 | A433 | 1.20p multi | 1.25 | .35 |

A similar unlisted issue shows a streetcar facing left on the 1.20p.

---

Ships A436

PILIPINAS 60s CARACOA

**1984, Nov.**    **Unwmk.**    **Perf. 13½x13**    **Litho.**
| 1718 | A436 | 60s Caracoa canoes | .40 | .25 |
| 1719 | A436 | 1.20p Chinese junk | .40 | .30 |
| 1720 | A436 | 6p Spanish galleon | 1.75 | .45 |
| 1721 | A436 | 7.20p Casco | 2.25 | .60 |
| 1722 | A436 | 8.40p Steamboat | 2.50 | .65 |
| 1723 | A436 | 20p Cruise liner | 12.55 | 3.25 |

Nos. 1718-1723 (6)

There were 500,000 of each value created cto with Oct 5 1984 cancel in the center of each block of 4. These were sold at a small fraction of face value. Value, set of 6 cto, $1.25.

Ateneo de Manila University, 125th Anniv. A438

**1984, Dec. 7** *Perf. 13½x13½* **Wmk. 372** **Litho.**
1730 A438 60s ultra & gold .55 .20
1731 A438 1.20p dk ultra & sil 1.10 .30

A438a

60s, Manila-Dagupan, 1892. 1.20p, Light rail transit, 1984. 6p, Bicol Express, 1955. 7.20p, Tranvis (1905, electric street car). 8.40, Commuter train, 1984. 20p, Early street car pulled by horses, 1898.

**1984, Dec. 18** *Perf. 14x13¾* **Unwmk.**
1731A A438A 60s multi .40 .25
1731B A438a 1.20p multi .85 .30
1731C A438a 6p multi 2.50 .45
1731D A438a 7.20p multi 3.25 .60
1731E A438a 8.40p multi 3.50 .65
1731F A438a 20p multi 7.50 1.00
     18.00 3.25
*Nos. 1731A-1731F (6)*

There were 500,000 of each value created cto with Dec. 5 1984 cancel in the center of each block of 4. These were sold at a small fraction of face value. Value, set of 6 cto, $1.50.

For surcharges see #1772-1773.

Christmas A439

**1984, Dec. 8** *Perf. 13½x13* **Wmk. 372**
1732 A439 60s Madonna and Child .75 .25
1733 A439 1.20p Holy family 2.50 .60
   a. Pair, #1732-1733 2.25 2.25

**1984, Dec. 19**
Philippines Jaycees Commitment to Youth Development.
Abstract painting by Raoul G. Isidro.
1734 Strip of 10 24.00 24.00
   a.-e. A440 60s any single .75 .75
   f.-j. A440 3p any single 3.00 3.00

Natl. Jaycees Awards, 25th anniv. — A440

**1985, Jan. 14** *Perf. 13x13½*
1735 A441 60s multicolored .35 .25
1736 A441 3p multicolored 1.90 .85

Philippine-Virginia Tobacco Admin., 25th anniv.

Dried Tobacco Leaf and Plant A441

---

No. 1537 Surcharged

**1985, Jan.** **Litho.** *Imperf.*
1737 A373 3p on 2p multi 4.75 3.50
     First printing had missing period ("p300").
Value $12.

Nos. 1714-1715 Overprinted "Philatelic Week 1984"

**1985, Jan.** *Perf. 13½x13*
1737A A435 1.20p Gold medal .50 .35
1737B A435 3p Winning stamp exhibit 1.50 .85
     2.75 2.75
   c. Pair, #1737A-1737B

Natl. Research Council Emblem A442

**1985, Feb. 3** **Litho.** *Perf. 13x13½*
1738 A442 60s bl, dk bl & blk .30 .20
1739 A442 1.20p org, dk bl & blk 1.00 .25

Pacific Science Assoc., 5th intl. congress, Manila, Feb. 3-7.

Medicinal Plants A443

**1985, Mar. 15** *Perf. 12½*
1740 A443 60s Carmona retusa 1.25 .25
1741 A443 1.20p Orthosiphon aristatus 2.40 .50
1742 A443 2.40p Vitex negundo 3.76 .65
1743 A443 3p Aloe barbadensis 3.75 .75
1744 A443 3.60p Quisqualis indica 4.75 .90
1745 A443 4.20p Blumea balsamifera 6.50 1.00
     22.40 4.00
*Nos. 1740-1745 (6)*

INTELSAT, 20th Anniv. A444

**1985, Apr. 6** *Perf. 13x13½*
1746 A444 60s multicolored .35 .20
1747 A444 3p multicolored 2.25 .75

A444a

Philippine Horses: 60s, Pintos. 1.20p, Palomino. 6p, Bay. 7.20p, Brown. 8.40p, Gray. 20p, Chestnut.
#1747G: h, as 1.20p. i, as 7.20p. j, as 6p. k, as 20p.

**1984, Dec. 18** **Unwmk.**
1747A A444a 60s multi .40 .25
1747B A444a 1.20p multi .85 .35
1747C A444a 6p multi 2.00 .75
1747D A444a 7.20p multi 2.75 .90
1747E A444a 8.40p multi 3.25 1.00
1747F A444a 20p multi 6.75 1.25
     16.00 4.50
*Nos. 1747A-1747F (6)*

*Perf. 14x13¾*
**Souvenir Sheet of 4**
1747G A444a 8.40p h.-k. 15.00 15.00

There were 500,000 each of #1747A-1747F created cto with Apr 12 1985 cancel in the center of each block of 4. These were sold at a small fraction of face value. Value, set of 6 cto, $1.50.

---

**1985, July 29**
1756 A450 60s Immunization, research .35 .20
1757 A450 1.20p Charity seal .65 .25
   a. Pair, #1756-1757 1.25 1.25

No. 1297 Surcharged with Bars, New Value and Scout Emblem in Gold, Ovptd. "GSP" and "45th Anniversary Girl Scout Charter" in Black

**1985, Aug. 19** **Unwmk.** **Photo.**
1758 A242 2.40p on 15s on 10s 1.50 .45
1759 A242 4.20p on 15s on 10s 2.50 .65
1760 A242 20p on 15s on 10s 3.50 .90
     7.50 2.00
*Nos. 1758-1760 (3)*

Virgin Mary Birth Bimillennium A451

Statues and paintings.

**1985, Sept. 8** **Wmk. 372** *Perf. 13½x13*
1761 A451 1.20p Fatima .70 .20
1762 A451 2.40p Beaterio 1.60 .40
1763 A451 3p Penafrancia 2.25 .60
1764 A451 3.60p Guadalupe 2.75 1.00
     7.30 2.20
*Nos. 1761-1764 (4)*

Intl. Youth Year A452

Prize-winning children's drawings.

**1985, Sept. 23** *Perf. 13x13½*
1765 A452 2.40p Agriculture 1.00 .35
1766 A452 3.60p Education 2.00 .75

Girl and Rice Terraces A453

**1985, Sept. 26**
1767 A453 2.40p multi 2.25 .65

World Tourism Organization, 6th general assembly, Sofia, Bulgaria, Sept. 17-26.

Export Year — A454

---

Institutionalization of Tax Research 1960-1985

Tax Research Institute, 25th Anniv. — A445

**1985, Apr. 22** **Wmk. 372** *Perf. 13½x13*
1748 A445 60s multicolored .60 .20

Intl. Rice Research Institute, 25th Anniv. — A446

**1985, May 27** *Perf. 13x13½*
1749 A446 60s Planting .40 .20
1750 A446 3p Paddies 2.25 .20

1st Spain-Philippines Peace Treaty, 420th Anniv. — A447

Designs: 1.20p, Blessed Infant of Cebu, statue, shrine and basilica. 3.60p, King Tupas of Cebu and Miguel Lopez de Logaspi signing treaty, 1565.

**1985, June 4** *Perf. 12½*
1751 A447 1.20p multi .50 .20
1752 A447 3.60p multi 1.00 .30
   a. Pair, #1751-1752 + label 4.50 4.50

No. 1532 Ovptd. "10th Anniversary Philippines and People's Republic of China Diplomatic Relations 1975-1985"

**1985, June 8** *Imperf.*
1753 A372 5p multi 6.00 7.00

Arbor Week, June 9-15 — A448

**1985, June 9** *Perf. 13½x13*
1754 A448 1.20p multi 1.25 .35

Battle of Bessang Pass, 40th Anniv. A449

**1985, June 14** *Perf. 13x13½*
1755 A449 1.20p multi 1.25 .35

Natl. Tuberculosis Soc., 75th Anniv. — A450

**University of the Philippines, College of Law, 75th anniv. See No. 1838.**

**1986, Jan. 12**
1778 A459 60s lilac rose & blk .40 .25
1779 A459 3p brt grn, lil rose & blk .40 .25

Scales of Justice
A459

University of the Philippines, College of Law, 75th anniv. See No. 1838.

**1985, Dec. 8** **Perf. 13x13½**
1776 A458 60s Panuluyan .50 .25
1777 A458 3p Pagdalaw 2.50 .75

Christmas 1985
A458

**1985, Nov. 24** **Perf. 12½**
1774 A457 60s multicolored .20
1775 A457 3p multicolored .75

Natl. Bible Week
A457

**1985, Nov. 22** **Perf. 13x13½**
1770 A456 3p China Clipper on water 2.25 .75
1771 A456 3.60p China Clipper, map 2.75 .75

1st Transpacific Airmail Service, 50th Anniv. — A456

Nos. 1731C-1731D Surcharged with Bars, New Value and "PHILATELIC WEEK 1985" in Black
**1985, Nov. 24** **Unwmk.**
1772 A438a 60s on 6p .75 .35
1773 A438a 3p on 7.20p 3.25 1.00
No. 1773 is airmail.

**Perf. 14x13¾**

**1985, Oct. 24**
1769 A455 3.60p multi 2.50 .65

**1985, Oct. 8** **Perf. 13½x13**
1768 A454 1.20p multi 1.25 .35

UN, 40th Anniv. — A455

Design: 60s, Noli Me Tangere.
**1986** **Wmk. 391** **Litho.** **Perf. 13**
1780 A460 60s violet .30 .20
1781 A460 1.20p bluish grn 1.25 .20
1782 A460 3.60p redsh brn 2.25 .75
Issued: 60s, 1.20p, Feb. 21; 3.60p, July 10.
For surcharges see Nos. 1834, 1913.

Flores de Heidelberg, by Jose Rizal — A460

**1986** **Wmk. 391**
1788 A463 60s multicolored .40 .20
1789 A463 3p multicolored 2.10 .55

EXPO '86, Vancouver
A463

**1986, May 2** **Perf. 13x13½**

Asian Productivity Organization, 25th Anniv. — A464

**1986**
1790 A464 60s multicolored .40 .20
1791 A464 3p multicolored 2.25 .75

**1986, Apr. 12** **Perf. 13½x13, 13x13½**
1786 A462 60s Refinery, vert. .40 .20
1787 A462 3p shown 2.00 .75

Bataan Oil Refining Corp., 25th Anniv. A462

**1986, Mar. 15** **Wmk. 372**
1783 A461 60s, any single .40 .20
a-d. Block of 4 7.50 7.50
1784 A461 60s, any single .50 .30
a-d. Block of 4 7.50 7.50
1785 A461 3.60p, any single 5.25 5.25
a-b. Pair 15.00 15.00
Nos. 1783-1785 (3).

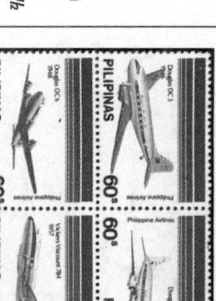

Philippine Airlines, 45th Anniv. — A461

**1986, May 22** **Perf. 13½x13**
1793 A465 60s No. 241 .40 .20
1794 A465 3p No. 390 2.00 .70
See No. 1835.

Election of Corazon Aquino, 7th Pres. — A466

**1986, May 25** **Wmk. 372**
1795 A466 60s multi .25 .20
1796 A466 1.20p multi .40 .30
1797 A466 2.40p multi 1.10 .30
1798 A466 3.60p multi 1.25 .50
Nos. 1795-1798 (4).

**Souvenir Sheet** **Imperf**
1799 A466 7.20p multi 4.00 4.75
For surcharge see No. 1939.

**1986, June 16** **Perf. 13x13½**
1800 A467 60s grn, blk & pink .50 .20
1801 A467 2.40p grn, blk & bl 1.25 .35
1802 A467 3p grn, blk & yel 2.00 .60
Nos. 1800-1802 (3).

**Souvenir Sheet** **Imperf**
1803 A467 7.20p grn & blk 5.00 6.00
For surcharge see No. 1940.

De La Salle University, 75th Anniv. A467

A468

**Size: 30x22mm**
1792 A464 3p pale brown 1.25 .30
Nos. 1790-1792 (3) 3.90 1.25
Issued: #1790-1791, 5/15; #1792, 7/10.

AMERIPEX '86 — A465

**1986, Aug. 21** **Perf. 13½x13, 13x13½**
1804 A468 60s dl bluish grn .40 .20
1805 A469 2p shown 1.00 .35
1806 A469 3.60p The Filipino is worth dying for, horiz.
Nos. 1804-1806 (3) 1.60 .45

**Souvenir Sheet** **Imperf**
1807 A469 10p Hindi ka nag-iisa, horiz. 4.75 5.50
See No. 1836. For surcharges see Nos. 1914 and 2706A.

Memorial to Benigno S. Aquino, Jr. (1932-83) A469

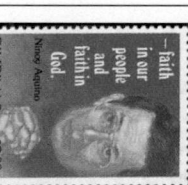

**1986, Aug. 28** **Perf. 13½x13**
1808 A470 60s Vanda sander-ana .50 .25
1809 A470 1.20p Epigeneium ly-onii 1.50 .40
1810 A470 2.40p Paphiopedilum philippinense 2.75 .60
1811 A470 3p Anesiella philippinensis 3.50 .90
Nos. 1808-1811 (4) 8.25 2.15
For surcharge see No. 1941.

Indigenous Orchids — A470

**1986, Aug. 29** **Wmk. 391**
1812 A471 60s pink, blk & lake .35 .25
1813 A471 3.60p pale grn, blk & dk ultra 2.50 .75
For surcharge see No. 1915.

Quiapo District, 400th Anniv. — A471

**1986, Sept. 1** **Perf. 13½x13**
1814 A472 60s bl & multi .30 .20
1815 A472 3p grn & multi 1.75 .40
See No. 1841. For surcharge see No. 1888.

General Hospital, 75th Anniv. — A472

Halley's Comet
A473

**1986, Sept. 25 — Perf. 13x13½ — Wmk. 389**
1816 A473 60s Comet, Earth .50 .20
1817 A473 2.40p Comet, Earth, Moon 2.00 .50

For surcharge see No. 1942.

74th FDI World Dental Congress, Manila A474

**1986, Nov. 10 — Litho. — Perf. 13x13½**
1818 A474 60s Handshake .75 .25
1819 A474 3p Jeepney bus 4.25 1.00

See Nos. 1837, 1840.

Insects A475

Intl. Peace Year — A476

**1986, Nov. 21 — Perf. 13x13½, 13½x13**
1820 A475 60s Butterfly, beetles 1.00 .30
1821 A476 1p blue & blk 2.00 .45
1822 A475 3p Dragonflies 3.00 .75
Nos 1820-1822 (3) 6.00 1.50

Philately Week.

Manila YMCA, 75th Anniv. — A477

**1986, Nov. 28 — Perf. 13x13½**
1823 A477 2p blue 1.25 .40
1824 A477 3.60p red 3.25 .60

See No. 1839. For surcharge see No. 1916.

Philippine Normal College, 85th Anniv. A478

Various arrangements of college crest and buildings, 1901-1986.

**1986, Dec. 12 — Wmk. 389**
1825 A478 60s multi 1.00 .25
1826 A478 3.60p buff, ultra & gldn brn 2.75 .60

For surcharge see No. 1917.

Christmas A479

**1986, Dec. 15 — Perf. 13½x13, 13x13½**
1827 A479 60s Holy family .50 .20
1828 A479 60s Mother and child, doves .50 .20
1829 A479 60s Child touching mother's face .50 .20

1830 A479 1p Adoration of the shepherds .75 .25
1831 A479 1p Mother, child signaling peace .75 .25
1832 A479 1p Holy family, lamb .75 .25
1833 A479 1p Mother, child blessing food .75 .25
Nos. 1827-1833 (7) 4.50 1.60

No. 1780 Surcharged

**1987, Jan. 6 — Wmk. 391 — Litho.**
1834 A460 1p on 60s vio 1.00 .20

Types of 1986

Designs: 75s. No. 390, AMERIPEX '86. 1p, Benigno S. Aquino, Jr. 3.25p, Handshake, 74th World Dental Congress. 3.50p, Scales of Justice. 4p, Manila YMCA emblem. 4.75p, Jeepney bus. 5p, General Hospital. 5.50p, Boeing 747, 1980.

Types of 4p
Type I — "4" is taller than "0's."
Type II — "4" is same height as "0's."

**1987 — Litho. — Perf. 13**
**Size: 22x31mm, 31x22mm**
1835 A465 75s brt yel grn .40 .20
1836 A468 1p blue .45 .20
1837 A474 3.25p dull grn 1.25 .35
1838 A459 3.50p dark car 1.75 .35
1839 A477 4p blue, type I 1.75 .30
1839A A477 4p blue, type II 3.50 .45
1840 A474 4.75p dl yel grn 2.10 .45
1841 A472 5p olivo bister 2.25 .50
1842 A461 5.50p dk bl gray 2.50 .50
Nos. 1835-1842 (9) 15.95 3.30

All No. 1839 dated "1-1-87."
Issued: #1839A, 12/16; others, 1/16.

Manila Hotel, 75th Anniv. A480

**1087, Jan. 30 — Wmk. 389 — Perf. 13x13½**
1843 A480 1p Hotel, c. 1912 .50 .25
1844 A480 4p Hotel, 1987 2.10 .45
1845 A480 4.75p Lobby 2.50 .50
1846 A480 5.50p Foyer 4.00 .90
Nos. 1843-1046 (4) 9.10 2.10

Intl. Eucharistic Congress, Manila, 50th Anniv. A481

**1987, Feb. 7 — Perf. 13½x13, 13x13½**
1847 A481 75s Emblem, vert. .50 .20
1848 A481 1p shown .70 .20

Pres. Aquino Taking Oath A482

Text — A483

**1987, Mar. 4 — Perf. 13½x13, 13x13½**
1849 A482 1p multi .40 .25
1850 A483 5.50p bl & deep bis 2.40 .65

Ratification of the new constitution.
See No. 1905. For surcharge see No. 2005.

Lyceum College and Founder, Jose P. Laurel A484

**1987, May 7 — Litho. — Perf. 13x13½**
1851 A484 1p multi .50 .25
1852 A484 2p multi 1.25 .60

Lyceum of the Philippines, 35th anniv.

Government Service Insurance System — A485

**1987, June 1 — Perf. 13½x13**
1853 A485 1p Salary and policy loans .45 .20
1854 A485 1.25p Disability, medicare .65 .20
1855 A485 2p Retirement benefits 1.10 .35
1856 A485 3.50p Life insurance 1.60 .55
Nos. 1853-1856 (4) 3.80 1.30

Davao City, 50th Anniv. A486

**1987, Mar. 16 — Litho. — Perf. 13x13½**
1857 A486 1p Falconer, woman planting, city seal .75 .20

Salvation Army in the Philippines, 50th Anniv. — A487

Natl. League of Women Voters, 50th Anniv. — A488

**1987, June 5 — Photo. — Perf. 13x13½**
1858 A487 1p multi .50 .20

**1987, July 15**
1859 A488 1p pink & blue .75 .20

A489

A490

#1851, Gen. Vicente Lukban (1860-1916). #1862, Wenceslao Q. Vinzons (1910-1942).

#1863, Brig.-gen. Mateo M. Capinpin (1887-1958). #1864, Jesus Balmori (1882-1948).

**1987 — Litho. — Wmk. 391**
**Perf. 13x13½, 12½ (#1862)**
1861 A489 1p olive grn .50 .20
1862 A489 1p dull greenish blue .60 .20
1863 A489 1p dull red brn .60 .20
1864 A489 1p rose red & rose claret .50 .80
Nos. 1861-1864 (4) 2.20 .80

Issued: #1861, 7/31; #1862, 9/9; #1863, 10/15; #1864, 12/17.

**1987, July 22 — Litho. — Perf. 13½x13 — Wmk. 389**
Nuns (1862-1987), children, Crucifix, Sacred Heart.
1881 A490 1p multi .90 .25

Daughters of Charity of St. Vincent de Paul in the Philippines, 125th anniv.

Map of Southeast Asia, Flags of ASEAN Members A491

**1987, Aug. 7 — Perf. 13x13½**
1882 A491 1p multi .90 .25

ASEAN, 20th anniv.

Exports Campaign A492

**1987, Aug. 11 — Wmk. 391 — Perf. 13**
1883 A492 1p shown .40 .20
1884 A492 2p Worker, gearwheel .06 .20

See No. 1904.

Canonization of Lorenzo Ruiz by Pope John Paul II, Oct. 18 — A493

First Filipino saint: 1p, Ruiz, stained glass window showing Crucifixion. 5.50p, Ruiz at prayer, execution in 1637.

**1987, Oct. 10 — Litho. — Wmk. 389 — Perf. 13x13½**
1885 A493 1p multi .75 .25
1886 A493 5.50p multi 3.00 .85
**Size: 57x57mm**
**Imperf**
1887 A493 8p like 5.50p 4.50 3.50
Nos. 1885-1887 (3) 8.25 4.60

No. 1887 has denomination at LL.

No. 1841 Surcharged

**1987, Oct. 12 — Wmk. 391 — Perf. 13**
1888 A472 4.75p on 5p olive bis 1.90 .55

Order of the Good Shepherd Sisters in Philippines, 65th Anniv. A494

**1987, Oct. 27** — Wmk. 389 — Perf. 13x13½
1889 A494 1p multi — 1.50 .35

Design: Worker, gearwheel.
Exports Type of 1987

1901 A499 8p Pig, holiday foods — 4.00 .75
1902 A499 9.50p Traditional foods — 4.50 .85
1903 A499 11p Serving meal — 5.25 1.00
Nos. 1896-1903 (8) — 22.15 4.40

**1987, Dec. 16** — Wmk. 391 — Litho. — Perf. 13
1904 A492 4.75p lt blue & blk — 1.40 .25

Constitution Ratification Type of 1987
**1987, Dec. 16**
1905 A483 5.50p brt yel grn & fawn — 1.60 .45
Size: 22x31½mm — Perf. 13

Founders: J. Vargas, M. Camus, J.E.H. Stevenot, A.N. Luz, V. Lim, C. Romulo and G.A. Daza.

Nat'l. Boy Scout Movement, 50th Anniv. A495

**1987, Oct. 28** — Litho. — Perf. 13½x13½
1890 A495 1p multi — 1.25 .25

Philippine Philatelic Club, 50th Anniv. A496

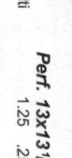

**1987, Nov. 7** — Perf. 13½x13½
1891 A496 1p multi — 1.25 .25

3rd ASEAN Summit Meeting, Dec. 14-15, 1987

**1987, Dec. 5** — Perf. 13½x13½
1895 A498 4p multicolored — 2.50 .70

Designs: 1p. First missionaries, shipwrecked church and image of the Virgin, vert. 4.75p. J.A. Jeronino Guerrero, Br. Diego de St. Maria and Letran Dominican College. 5.50p. Pope with Dominican representatives.

Order of the Dominicans in the Philippines, 400th Anniv. A497

**1987, Nov. 11** — Perf. 13½x13, 13x13½
1892 A497 1p multi — .30 .20
1893 A497 4.75p multi — 1.75 .40
1894 A497 5.50p multi — 4.55 1.20
Nos. 1892-1894 (3)

Philippine Postal Service Pasko 1987

**1987, Dec. 8** — Perf. 13½x13
1896 A499 1p Postal service — .45 .25
1897 A499 5-Pointed stars — .45 .25
1898 A499 4p Procession, church — .45 .25
1899 A499 4.75p Gift exchange — 2.25 .35
1900 A499 5.50p Bamboo cannons — 3.00 .60
Christmas 1987 — A499

Grand Masonic Lodge of the Philippines, 75th Anniv. A500

**1987, Dec. 19** — Wmk. 389
1906 A500 1p multi — 1.50 .35
Perf. 13½x13½

United Nations Projects A501

Designs: a. Int'l. Fund for Agricultural Development (IFAD). b. Transport and Communications Decade for Asia and the Pacific. c. Int'l. Year of Shelter for the Homeless (IYSH). d. World Health Day, 1987.

**1987, Dec. 22** — Litho. — Perf. 13½x13½
1907 A501 1p, any single — 9.00 9.00
a.-d. Strip of 4 + label — 2.00 2.00
Label, pictures UN emblem. Exists imperf. Value $30.

Designs: 1p. Official seals of the Senate and Quezon City House of Representatives, gavel, vert. 5.50p. Congress in session.

7th Opening of Congress A502

**1988, Jan. 25** — Perf. 13½x13, 13x13½
1908 A502 1p multi — .75 .25
1909 A502 5.50p multi — 3.00 .85

St. John Bosco (1815-1888), Educator — A503

**1988, Jan. 31** — Perf. 13½x13½
1910 A503 1p multi — .30 .25
1911 A503 5.50p multi — 2.40 .60

BUY PHILIPPINE MADE MOVEMENT MONTH

Buy Philippine Goods — A504

**1988, Feb. 1** — Litho. — Perf. 13½x13
1912 A504 1p buff, ultra, blk & scar — .60 .20

Nos. 1782, 1806, 1813, 1824, 1826 Surcharged

Wmk. 389 (#1914, 1917), 391 (#1913, 1915, 1916)
**1988, Feb. 14** — Perf. 13 (#1782), 13x13½
1913 A460 3p on 3.60p redsh brn — 2.50 .40
1914 A469 3p on 3.60p multi — 2.50 .40
1915 A471 3p on 3.60p pale grn, blk & dark ultra — 3.00 .40
1916 A477 3p on 3.60p red ultra & golden — 3.50 .50
1917 A478 3p on 3.60p buff, brn — 3.50 .50
Nos. 1913-1917 (5) — 15.00 2.20

Use Zip Codes — A505

**1988, Feb. 25** — Wmk. 391 — Perf. 13
1918 A505 60s multi — .35 .20
1919 A505 1p multi — .55 .20

Insects That Prey on Other Insects — A506

**1988, Mar. 11** — Perf. 13
1920 A506 1p Vesbius purpureus — .40 .20
1921 A506 5.50p Campsomeris aurulenta — 2.25 .65

Solar Eclipse 1988 A507

TOTAL SOLAR ECLIPSE '88 Philippines

**1988, Mar. 18** — Unwmk. — Perf. 13
1922 A507 1p multi — .50 .20
5.50p multi — 2.50 .50

Toribio M. Teodoro (1887-1965), Shoe Manufacturer A508

**1988, Apr. 27** — Wmk. 391 — Litho. — Perf. 13
1923 A508 1p multicolored — .60 .20
1924 A508 1.20p multicolored — .90 .20

75 YEARS OF SERVICE COLLEGE OF THE HOLY SPIRIT A510

College of the Holy Spirit, 75th anniv.; 1p. Emblem and motto "Truth in Love." 4p. Arnold Janssen, founder, and Sr. Edelwina, director 1920-1947.

INTERNATIONAL CONFERENCE OF NEWLY RESTORED DEMOCRACIES A509

Int'l. Conf. of Newly Restored Democracies.

**1988, May 22** — Perf. 13½x13
1926 A509 1p blk, mar & gold — .35 .20

**1988, June 4** — Litho. — Unwmk.
1927 A509 4p blk, ol grn & mar — 2.00 .55
1928 A510 4p dark ultra, brt blue & blk — 2.25 .65

Juan Luna and Felix Hidalgo.

First Nat'l. Juan Luna and Felix Resurreccion Hidalgo Commemorative Exhibition, June 15-Aug. 15. Artists Luna and Hidalgo won medals at the 1884 Madrid Fine Arts Exhibition.

A511

**1988, June 15** — Wmk. 391 — Perf. 13
1929 A511 1p multi — .40 .20
1930 A511 5.50p multi — 1.90 .55

A512

Nat'l. Irrigation Administration, 25th anniv.
**1988, June 22** — Litho. — Wmk. 372
1931 A512 1p multi — .40 .20
1932 A512 5.50p multi — 2.25 .65

Designs: 1p. Scuba diving, Siquijor Is. 1.20p. Big game fishing, Aparri, Cagayan Province. 4p. Yachting, Manila Central. 5.50p. Climbing Mt. Apo. 8p. Golf, Cebu, Cebu Is. 11p. Cycling through Marawi, Mindanao Is.

Nat'l. Olympic Committee Emblem and Sporting Events A513

**1988, July 11** — Perf. 13½x13½
1933 A513 1p multi — .40 .25
1934 A513 1.20p multi — .40 .25
1935 A513 4p multi — 1.60 .40
1936 A513 4p multi — 1.60 .40
1937 A513 8p multi — 2.75 .40
1938 A513 11p multi — 3.95 1.10
Nos. 1933-1938 (6) — 10.90 3.00

Exist imperf. 4p, 8p, 1p and 5.50p also exist in strips of 4 plus center label, perf and imperf, picturing torch and inscribed "Philippine Olympic Week, May 1-7, 1988."

**Philatelic Week, Nov. 24-30, 1988 — A530**

**1988, Nov. 28    Wmk. 391    Perf. 13**
1974 A529 1p Communications tower    .60    .20

**1988, Nov. 24    Wmk. 391**
Emblem and: a. Post Office. b. Stamp counter. c. Framed stamp exhibits, four people. d. Exhibits, 8 people. Has a continuous design.
1975 A530 Block of 4    2.50  2.00
a.-d.    1p any single    .55  .25
e.    As "a," dated "1938" (error)    10.00  10.00

**Christmas A531**
Designs: 75s, Handshake, peave dove, vert. 1p, Children making ornaments. 2p, Boy carrying decoration. 3.50p, Tree, vert. 4.75p, Candle, vert. 5.50p, Man, star, heart.

**1988, Dec. 2**
1976 A531 75s multi    .50  .20
1977 A531 1p multi    .50  .25
1978 A531 2p multi    1.00  .25
1979 A531 3.50p multi    1.50  .35
1980 A531 4.75p multi    2.00  .35
1981 A531 5.50p multi    2.50  .50
    8.00  1.85
Nos. 14/6 1981 (6)

**Gen. Santos City, 50th Anniv. A532**

**Perf. 13x13½    Litho.**
**1989, Feb. 27**
1982 A532 1p multi    .60  .20

**Guerrilla Fighters — A533**
Emblem and: No. 1983, Miguel Z. Ver (1918-42). No. 1984, Eleuterio L. Adevoso (1922-75). Printed in continuous design.

**1989, Feb. 18    Wmk. 372**
1983 1p multi    .40  .20
1984 1p multi    .40  .20
    .90  .90
a.    A533 Pair, #1983-1984

---

**Bacolod City Charter, 50th Anniv. A524**

**Perf. 13½x13½    Wmk. 372**
**1988, Oct. 19    Litho.**
1967 A524 1p multi    .60  .20

**Dona Aurora Aragon Quezon (b. 1888) — A526**

**Perf. 13½x13    Wmk. 391**
**1988, Nov. 7**
1969 A526 1p multi    .30  .20
1970 A526 5.50p multi    2.00  .55

**UST Graduate School, 50th Anniv. — A525**

**1988, Dec. 20    Litho.**
1968 A525 1p multi    .60  .20

**Malate Church, 400th Anniv. — A527**
a, Church, 1776. b, Statue & anniv. emblem. c, Church, 1880. d, Church, 1988. Continuous design.

**1988, Dec. 16    Wmk. 391**
1971 A527 Block of 4    1.50  1.50
a.-d.    1p any single    .35  .35

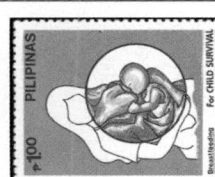

**UN Declaration of Human Rights, 40th Anniv. A528**

**1988, Dec. 9    Wmk. 372**
1972 A528 1p shown    .45  .20
1973 A528 1p Commission on human rights    .45  .20
a.    Pair. Nos. 1972-1973    1.00  1.00

**Long Distance Telephone Company A529**

**Perf. 13½x13**

---

**Perf. 13½x13    Wmk. 372**
**1988, Sept. 19**
1955 A519 1p Women's archery    .45  .20
1956 A519 1.20p Women's tennis    .50  .20
1957 A519 4p Boxing    1.40  .35
1958 A519 5.50p Women's running    1.90  .45
1959 A519 8p Swimming    2.00  .55
1960 A519 11p Cycling    2.75  .65
    9.00  2.40
Nos. 1955-1960 (6)

**Souvenir Sheet**
**Imperf**
1961    Sheet of 4    10.00  8.00
a.    A519 5.50p Weight lifting    2.25  2.25
b.    A519 5.50p Basketball, horiz.    2.25  2.25
c.    A519 5.50p Judo    2.25  2.25
d.    A519 5.50p Shooting, horiz.    2.25  2.25
Nos. 1955-1960 exist imperf. Value $19.

**Department of Justice, Cent. A520**

**Perf. 13½x13½    Wmk. 372**
**1988, Sept. 26**
1962 A520 1p multi    .60  .20

**Intl. Red Cross and Red Crescent Organizations, 125th Anniv. — A521**

**Perf. 13½x13**
**1988, Sept. 30**
1963 A521 1p multi    .50  .20
1964 A521 5.50p multi    2.50  .70

**Christian Children's Fund, 50th Anniv. — A522**

**1988, Oct. 6**
1965 A522 1p multi    .60  .20

**UN Campaigns A523**
Designs: a, Breast-feeding. b, Growth monitoring. c, Immunization. d, Oral rehydration. e, Oral rehydration therapy. f, Youth on crutches.

**1988, Oct. 24    Litho.    Perf. 13½x13**
1966    Strip of 5    3.00  2.50
a.-e.    A523 1p any single    .60  .25
Child Survival Campaign (Nos. 1966a-1966d); Decade for Disabled Persons (No. 1966e).

---

Nos. 1797, 1801, 1810 and 1817 Surcharged with 2 Bars and New Value in Black or Gold (#1942)

**As Before**
**1988, Aug. 1**
1939 A466 1.90p on 2.40p #1797    1.25  .35
1940 A467 1.90p on 2.40p #1801    1.25  .60
1941 A470 1.90p on 2.40p #1810    1.25  .35
1942 A473 1.90p on 2.40p #1817    1.25  .35
    5.00  1.65
Nos. 1939-1942 (4)

**Land Bank of the Philippines, 25th Anniv. A514**

**1988, Aug. 1**

**Philippine Intl. Commercial Bank, 50th Anniv. A515**

**Perf. 13½x13½    Wmk. 372**
**1988, Aug. 8    Litho.**
1943 A514 1p shown    .40  .20
1944 A515 1p shown    .40  .20
1945 A515 5.50p like No. 1943    2.75  .40
1946 A515 5.50p like No. 1944    6.30  1.20
Nos. 1943-1946 (4)
Nos. 1943-1944 and 1945-1946 exist in se-tenant pairs from center rows of the sheet.

**Profile of Francisco Balagtas Baltasar (b. 1788), Tagalog Language Poet, Author — Ab1b**

**Wmk. 391    Perf. 13**
**1988, Aug. 8    Litho.**
1947 A516 1p Facing right    .35  .20
1948 A516 1p Facing left    .35  .65
a.    Pair. #1947-1948    .90  .90

**Quezon Institute, 50th Anniv. A517**
Philippine Tuberculosis Soc.

**Perf. 13½x13½    Wmk. 372**
**1988, Aug. 18    Litho.**
1949 A517 1p multi    .50  .25
1950 A517 5.50p multi    3.25  .65

**1988 Summer Olympics, Seoul A519**

**Mushrooms A518**

**Wmk. 391    Perf. 13**
**1988, Sept. 13**
1951 A518 60s Brown    .25  .20
1952 A518 1p Rat's ear fungus    .40  .20
1953 A518 2p Abalone    1.10  .25
1954 A518 4p Straw    1.40  .30
    3.15  .95
Nos. 1951-1954 (4)

**Oblates of Mary Immaculate, 50th Anniv. — A534**

1989, Feb. 17    **Perf. 13½x13**
| | | | Wmk. 372 | |
|---|---|---|---|---|
| 1985 | A534 | 1p multicolored | .60 | .20 |

**Fiesta Islands '89 — A535**

1989-90   **Perf. 13 (Nos. 1991, 1994, 1997), 13½x14**
Litho.   Wmk. 391   Unwmk.

| | | | | | |
|---|---|---|---|---|---|
| 1986 | A535 | 60s | Turumba | .25 | .20 |
| 1987 | A535 | 75s | Pahiyas | .30 | .20 |
| 1988 | A535 | 1p | Pagoda Sa Wawa | .25 | .20 |
| 1988 | A535 | 1p | Masskara | .35 | .20 |
| 1989 | A535 | 1p | Independence Day | .25 | .20 |
| 1990 | A535 | 1p | like #1995 | .95 | .20 |
| 1990A | A535 | 4p | | 2.25 | .40 |
| 1991 | A535 | 3.50p | Sinulog | 2.25 | .25 |
| 1992 | A535 | 4.75p | Cagayan de Oro | 1.10 | .25 |
| 1993 | A535 | 4.75p | Grand Canao | 1.10 | .35 |
| 1994 | A535 | 4.75p | Iloilo Paraw regatta | 1.90 | .40 |
| 1995 | A535 | 5.50p | Penafrancia | 1.40 | .55 |
| 1996 | A535 | 5.50p | Firmonrkfe | 1.50 | .45 |
| 1997 | A535 | 6.25p | Lenten festival | 1.10 | .60 |
| | | Nos. 1986-1997 (13) | | 13.55 | 4.30 |

Issued: #1991, 1994, 6.25p, 60s, 75s, 3.50p, 6/28/89; #1988, 1992, 1995, 9/1/89; #1989, 1993, 1996, 12/1/89; 4p, 8/6/90.

**Great Filipinos — A536**

Don Tomas B. Mapua 1888-1989

1989, May 18   **Perf. 14x13½**
Litho.   Wmk. 391   Unwmk.

| | | | | |
|---|---|---|---|---|
| 1998 | A536 | 1p any single | 2.25 | 2.25 |
| a.-e. | | A536 Strip of 5 | .35 | .35 |

See Nos. 2022, 2089, 2151, 2240, 2360, 2414, 2486, 2536.

Men and women: a. Don Tomas B. Mapua (1888- ), educator. b. Camilo O. Osias (1889- ), educator. c. Dr. Olivia D. Salamanca (1889- ), physician. d. Dr. Francisco I. Santiago (1889- ), composer. e. Leandro H. Fernandez (1889- ), educator.

**26th World Congress of the Intl. Federation of Landscape Architects — A537**

1989, May 31
| | | | Wmk. 391 | |
|---|---|---|---|---|
| 1999 | A537 | Block of 4 | 1.50 | 1.50 |
| a.-d. | | 1p any single | .35 | .35 |

Designs: a. Adventure Pool. b. Paco Park. c. Beautification of Malacanang area streets. d. Erosion control at an upland farm.
Printed in continuous design.

---

**French Revolution, Bicent. — A538**

1989, July 1   **Perf. 14**
| | | | | |
|---|---|---|---|---|
| 2000 | A538 | 1p multi | .30 | .20 |
| 2001 | A538 | 5.50p multi | 1.90 | .60 |

**Supreme Court — A539**

1989, June 11   Wmk. 372
| | | | | |
|---|---|---|---|---|
| 2002 | A539 | 1p multi | .60 | .20 |

**Natl. Science and Technology Week — A540**

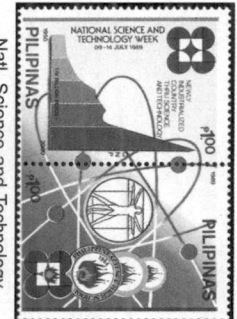

1989, July 14   Wmk. 391   **Perf. 13**
| | | | | |
|---|---|---|---|---|
| 2003 | A540 | 1p GNP chart, School emblem | .40 | .20 |
| 2004 | A540 | 1p Science High | .90 | .90 |
| a. | | A540 Pair. #2003-2004 | 1.25 | .35 |

**No. 1905 Surcharged**

1989, June 5   Litho.   Wmk. 391   **Perf. 13**
| | | | | |
|---|---|---|---|---|
| 2005 | A483 | 4.75p on 5.50p | 1.25 | .35 |

**Philippine Environment Month — A542**

1989, Aug. 21   Litho.   **Perf. 14**
| | | | | |
|---|---|---|---|---|
| 2006 | A542 | 1p Palawan peacock pheasant | .60 | .20 |
| 2007 | A542 | 1p Palawan bear cat | .60 | .20 |
| a. | | A542 Pair. #2006-2007 | 1.25 | 1.25 |

**Asia-Pacific Telecommunity, 10th Anniv. — A544**

1989, Oct. 30   Wmk. 372   Litho.   **Perf. 14**
| | | | | |
|---|---|---|---|---|
| 2008 | A544 | 1p multicolored | .60 | .20 |

---

**Dept. of Natl. Defense, 50th Anniv. — A545**

1989, Oct. 23
| | | | | |
|---|---|---|---|---|
| 2009 | A545 | 1p multicolored | .60 | .20 |

**Intl. Maritime Organization — A546**

1989, Nov. 13   Wmk. 372   **Perf. 14**
| | | | | |
|---|---|---|---|---|
| 2010 | A546 | 1p multicolored | .60 | .20 |

**World Stamp Expo '89 — A546a**

1989, Nov. 17   Litho.   **Perf. 14**
| | | | | |
|---|---|---|---|---|
| 2010A | A546a | 1p #1, Y1 | .60 | .60 |
| 2010B | A546a | 4p #219, 398 | 2.00 | 2.00 |
| 2010C | A546a | 5.50p #N1, 500 | 3.00 | 3.00 |
| a. | | A546a 5.50p #N1, 500 | 5.60 | 5.60 |
| | | Nos. 2010A-2010C (3) | 5.60 | 5.60 |

Nos. 2010A-2010C withdrawn from sale week of release.

**Teaching Philately in the Classroom, Close-up of Youth Collectors A547**

1989, Nov. 20   **Perf. 14x13½**
| | | | | |
|---|---|---|---|---|
| 2011 | A547 | 1p shown | .50 | .20 |
| 2012 | A547 | 1p Class, diff. | .50 | .20 |

**Christmas — A548**

Pasko '89

1989   **Perf. 13½x14**
| | | | | |
|---|---|---|---|---|
| 2013 | A548 | 60s Annunciation | .20 | .20 |
| 2014 | A548 | 75s Visitation | .30 | .20 |
| 2015 | A548 | 1p Journey to Bethlehem | .20 | .20 |
| 2016 | A548 | 2p Search for the inn | .35 | .20 |
| 2017 | A548 | 4p Appearance of the star | .65 | .25 |
| 2018 | A548 | 4.75p Birth of Jesus Christ | 1.00 | .35 |
| | | Nos. 2013-2018 (6) | 3.75 | 1.60 |

---

**Beer Production, Cent. — A550**

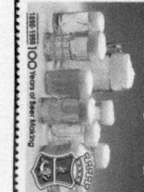

1990, Feb. 12   Wmk. 391   Photo.   **Perf. 14**
| | | | | |
|---|---|---|---|---|
| 2019 | A549 | 5.50p black, dark red & deep blue | 1.25 | .35 |

11th World Cardiology Congress A549

1990, Apr. 16
| | | | | |
|---|---|---|---|---|
| 2020 | A550 | 1p multicolored | .25 | .20 |
| 2021 | A550 | 5.50p multicolored | 1.25 | .35 |

**1990 Census — A551**

1990, Apr. 30   Wmk. 391   Photo.   **Perf. 14**
Color of Buildings
| | | | | |
|---|---|---|---|---|
| 2023 | A551 | 1p light blue | .45 | .20 |
| 2024 | A551 | 1p beige | .45 | .20 |
| a. | | A551 Pair. #2023-2024 | 1.00 | 1.00 |

**Great Filipinos Type of 1989**

1990, June 1   Litho.   Unwmk.   **Perf. 14x13½**
| | | | | |
|---|---|---|---|---|
| 2022 | A536 | Strip of 5, #a-e. | 2.00 | 2.00 |

Designs: a. Claro M. Recto (1890-1960), politician. b. Manuel H. Bernabe. c. Guillermo E. Tolentino. d. Epidio R. Quirino (1890-1956), politician. e. Bienvenido Ma. Gonzalez.

**Legion of Mary, 50th Anniv. — A552**

1990, July 21   Photo.   **Perf. 14**
| | | | | |
|---|---|---|---|---|
| 2025 | A552 | 1p multicolored | .60 | .20 |

**Girl Scouts of the Philippines, 50th Anniv. A553**

1990, May 21   Photo.   **Perf. 14**
| | | | | |
|---|---|---|---|---|
| 2026 | A553 | 1p yellow & multi | .30 | .20 |
| 2027 | A553 | 1.20p lt lilac & multi | .45 | .20 |

**Asian Pacific Postal Training Center, 20th Anniv. A554**

1990, Sept. 10   Wmk. 391   Photo.   **Perf. 14**
| | | | | |
|---|---|---|---|---|
| 2028 | A554 | 1p red & multi | .30 | .20 |
| 2029 | A554 | 4p blue & multi | 1.25 | .35 |

### Natl. Catechetical Year — A555

**1990, Sept. 28**
| | | | | |
|---|---|---|---|---|
| 2030 | A555 | 1p blk & multi | .25 | .20 |
| 2031 | A555 | 3.50p grm & multi | 1.00 | .30 |

### Intl. Literacy Year A556

**1990, Oct. 24** — **Photo.** — **Perf. 14**
| | | | | |
|---|---|---|---|---|
| 2032 | A556 | 1p blk, org & grn | .25 | .20 |
| 2033 | A556 | 5.50p blk, yel & grn | 1.60 | .40 |

### UN Development Program, 40th Anniv. — A557

**1990, Oct. 24**
| | | | | |
|---|---|---|---|---|
| 2034 | A557 | 1p yel & multi | .25 | .20 |
| 2035 | A557 | 5.50p orange & multi | 1.60 | .40 |

### Flowers — A558

**1990** — **Photo.** — **Wmk. 391** — **Perf. 14**
| | | | | |
|---|---|---|---|---|
| 2036 | A558 | 1p Waling waling | .50 | .20 |
| 2037 | A558 | 4p Sampaguita | 1.75 | .50 |

29th Orient and Southeast Asian Lions forum.
Issued: 1p, Oct. 3; 4p, Oct. 18.

### Christmas A560

Drawings of the Christmas star: a, Yellow star, pink beading. b, Yellow star, white beading. c, Green, blue, yellow and orange star. d, Red star, white outlines.

**1990, Dec. 3**
| | | | | |
|---|---|---|---|---|
| 2038 | A559 | 1p any single | 1.25 | 1.25 |
| a.-d. | | Strip of 4 | | .30 |
| 2039 | A560 | 5.50p multicolored | 1.75 | .50 |

### Blind Safety Day A561

**1990, Dec. 7** — **Photo.** — **Perf. 14**
| | | | | |
|---|---|---|---|---|
| 2040 | A561 | 1p bl, blk & yel | .50 | .20 |

### Publication of Rizal's "Philippines After 100 Years," Cent. A562

**1990, Dec.17**
| | | | | |
|---|---|---|---|---|
| 2041 | A562 | 1p multicolored | .50 | .20 |

### Philatelic Week A563

Paintings: 1p, Family by F. Amorsolo. 4.75p, The Builders by V. Edades. 5.50p, Laughter by A. Magsaysay-Ho.

**1990, Nov. 16**
| | | | | |
|---|---|---|---|---|
| 2042 | A563 | 1p multicolored | .25 | .20 |
| 2043 | A563 | 4.75p multi, vert. | 1.25 | .40 |
| 2044 | A563 | 5.50p multi, vert. | 1.50 | .50 |
| | | Nos. 2042-2044 (3) | 3.00 | 1.10 |

### 2nd Plenary Council of the Philippines. A564

**1991, Jan. 30**
| | | | | |
|---|---|---|---|---|
| 2045 | A564 | 1p multicolored | .50 | .20 |

### A565

Philippine Airlines, 50th anniv. No. 2047 is airmail.

**1991, Mar. 15** — **Litho.** — **Perf. 14**
| | | | | |
|---|---|---|---|---|
| 2046 | A565 | 1p multicolored | .20 | .20 |
| 2047 | A565 | 5.50p multicolored | 1.40 | .35 |

### Flowers — A566

Flowers: 1p, 2p, Plumeria. 4p, Ixora. 4.75p, 7p, Bougainvillea. 5.50p, 8p, Hibiscus.

**1991** — **Photo.** — **Perf. 14x13½**
| | | | | |
|---|---|---|---|---|
| 2048 | A566 | 60s Gardenia | .35 | .20 |
| 2049 | A566 | 75s Allamanda | .35 | .20 |
| 2050 | A566 | 1p yellow | .40 | .20 |
| 2051 | A566 | 1p red | .40 | .20 |
| 2052 | A566 | 1p salmon | .40 | .20 |
| 2053 | A566 | 1p white | .40 | .20 |
| a. | | Block of 4, #2050-2053 | 1.75 | 1.75 |
| 2053B | A566 | 1p like #2049 | .40 | .20 |
| 2054 | A566 | 1.20p Nerium | .50 | .20 |
| 2055 | A566 | 1.50p like #2048 | .50 | .20 |
| 2056 | A566 | 2p yellow | 1.00 | .30 |
| 2057 | A566 | 2p red | 1.00 | .30 |
| 2058 | A566 | 2p rose & yel | 1.00 | .30 |
| 2059 | A566 | 2p white & multi | 1.00 | .30 |
| a. | | Block of 4, #2056-2059 | 4.25 | |
| 2060 | A566 | 3p like #2054 | 1.40 | .70 |
| 2061 | A566 | 3.25p Cananga | 1.50 | .40 |
| 2062 | A566 | 4p dull rose | 1.75 | .50 |
| 2063 | A566 | 4p pale yellow | 1.75 | .50 |
| 2064 | A566 | 4p orange yel | 1.75 | .50 |
| 2065 | A566 | 4p scarlet | 1.75 | .50 |
| a. | | Block of 4, #2062-2065 | 8.25 | |
| 2066 | A566 | 4.75p vermilion | 2.10 | .70 |
| 2067 | A566 | 4.75p brt rose III | 2.10 | .70 |
| 2068 | A566 | 4.75p white | 2.10 | .70 |
| 2069 | A566 | 4.75p lilac rose | 2.10 | .70 |
| a. | | Block of 4, #2066-2069 | 9.00 | |
| 2070 | A566 | 5p Canna | 2.50 | .80 |
| 2071 | A566 | 5p red | 2.50 | .80 |
| 2072 | A566 | 5.50p yellow | 2.50 | .85 |
| 2073 | A566 | 5.50p white | 2.50 | .85 |
| 2074 | A566 | 5.50p pink | 2.50 | .85 |
| a. | | Block of 4, #2072-2075 | 11.00 | |
| 2076 | A566 | 6p dull rose | 3.00 | 1.00 |
| 2077 | A566 | 6p pale yellow | 3.00 | 1.00 |
| 2078 | A566 | 6p orange yel | 3.00 | 1.00 |
| 2079 | A566 | 6p scarlet | 3.00 | 1.00 |
| a. | | Block of 4, #2076-2079 | 13.00 | |
| 2080 | A566 | 7p vermilion | 3.50 | 1.10 |
| 2081 | A566 | 7p white | 3.50 | 1.10 |
| 2082 | A566 | 7p brt rose III | 3.50 | 1.10 |
| 2083 | A566 | 7p dp lil rose | 3.50 | 1.10 |
| a. | | Block of 4, #2080-2083 | 14.50 | |
| 2084 | A566 | 8p red | 3.75 | 1.25 |
| 2085 | A566 | 8p white | 3.75 | 1.25 |
| 2086 | A566 | 8p pink | 3.75 | 1.25 |
| 2087 | A566 | 8p deep pink | 3.75 | 1.25 |
| a. | | Block of 4, #2084-2087 | 16.00 | |
| 2088 | A566 | 10p like #2070 | 5.00 | 4.00 |
| | | Nos. 2048-2088 (42) | 87.2b | 30.95 |

Issued: 60s, 75s, #2053a, 5.50p, 3/30; 1.20p, 4p, 4.75p, 5/17 (FDC, on sale 5/7), #2053B, 1/23/93.
Inscribed "1991" except for No. 2053B, which is inscribed "1992."
Nos. 2048, 2053a, 2055, 2059a, 2060, 2070, 2079a, 2083a, 2087a, 2088 exist with "1992." Value for set, $175.

### Great Filipinos Type of 1989

Designs: a, Jorge B. Vargas (1890-1980). b, Ricardo M. Paras (1891-1984). c, Jose P. Laurel (1891-1959), politician. d, Vicente Fabella (1891-1959). e, Maximo M. Kalaw (1891-1954).

**1991, June 3** — **Litho.** — **Perf. 14x13½**
| | | | | |
|---|---|---|---|---|
| 2089 | A536 | 1p Strip of 5, #a.-e. | .50 | 1.50 |

### 12th Asia-Pacific Boy Scout Jamburee A567

**1991, Apr. 22** — **Perf. 14x13½**
| | | | | |
|---|---|---|---|---|
| 2090 | A567 | 1p Square knot | .30 | .20 |
| 2091 | A567 | 4p Sheepshank knot | .90 | .25 |
| 2092 | A567 | 4.75p Figure 8 knot | 1.10 | .30 |
| a. | | Souv. sheet of 3, #2090-2092, imperf. | 4.50 | 4.50 |
| | | Nos. 2090-2092 (3) | 2.30 | .75 |

No. 2092a sold for 16.50p and has simulated perfs.

### Antipolo by Carlos V. Francisco A568

**1991, June 23** — **Litho.** — **Granite Paper** — **Perf. 14**
| | | | | |
|---|---|---|---|---|
| 2093 | A568 | 1p multicolored | .60 | .20 |

### Pithecophaga Jefferyi — A569

**Photo.**
| | | | | |
|---|---|---|---|---|
| 2094 | A569 | 1p Head | .60 | .20 |
| 2095 | A569 | 4.75p Perched on limb | 1.75 | .25 |
| 2096 | A569 | 5.50p In flight | 3.00 | .40 |
| 2097 | A569 | 8p Feeding young | 3.50 | .60 |
| | | Nos. 2094-2097 (4) | 8.85 | 1.45 |

World Wildlife Fund.

**1991, July 31**

### Philippine Bar Association, Cent. — A570

**1991, Aug. 20** — **Perf. 14**
| | | | | |
|---|---|---|---|---|
| 2098 | A570 | 1p multicolored | .50 | .20 |

### A571

**Wmk. 391** — **Photo.**
**1991, Aug. 29**
| | | | | |
|---|---|---|---|---|
| 2099 | A571 | 1p multicolored | .70 | .20 |

**Size: 82x88mm** — **Imperf**
| | | | | |
|---|---|---|---|---|
| 2100 | A571 | 16p like #2099 | 6.00 | 6.00 |

Induction of Filipinos into USAFFE (US Armed Forces in the Far East), 50th Anniv. For overprint see No. 2193.

### A572

Independence Movement, cent.: a, Basil at graveside. b, Simon carrying lantern. c, Father Florentino, treasure chest. d, Sister Juli with rosary.

**1991, Sept. 18**
| | | | | |
|---|---|---|---|---|
| 2101 | A572 | 1p Block of 4, #a.-d. | 2.00 | 2.00 |

### A573

**Wmk. 391** — **Photo.**
**1991, Oct. 15**
| | | | | |
|---|---|---|---|---|
| 2102 | A573 | 1p multicolored | .50 | .20 |

**Size: 60x60mm** — **Imperf**
| | | | | |
|---|---|---|---|---|
| 2103 | A573 | 16p multicolored | 4.00 | 3.00 |

St. John of the Cross, 400th death anniv.

### United Nations Agencies A574

**1991, Oct. 24** — **Perf. 14**

| 2104 | A574 | 1p multicolored | .20 | .20 |
|---|---|---|---|---|
| 2105 | A574 | 4p multicolored | .90 | .25 |
| 2106 | A574 | 5.50p multicolored | 2.40 | .65 |
| | | Nos. 2104-2106 (3) | | |

Designs: 1p, UNICEF, children, 4p, High Commissioner for Refugees, hands support-ing boat people 5.50p, Postal Administration, 40th anniv. UN #29, #C3.

**Philatelic Week A575**

**1991, Nov. 20**

| 2107 | A575 | 7p multicolored | .35 | .20 |
|---|---|---|---|---|
| 2108 | A575 | 7p multicolored | 1.50 | .40 |
| 2109 | A575 | 8p multicolored | 1.90 | .50 |
| | | Nos. 2107-2109 (3) | 3.75 | 1.10 |

Paintings: 2p, Bayanihan by Carlos Fran-cisco. 7p, Sari-sari Vendor by Mauro Malang Santos. 8p, Give Us This Day by Vincente Manansala.

**16th Southeast Asian Games, Manila A576**

**1991, Nov. 22** — **Wmk. 391 Photo. Perf. 14**

| 2110 | A576 | 2p multicolored | .35 | .20 |
|---|---|---|---|---|
| 2111 | A576 | 2p multicolored | .35 | .20 |
| 2112 | A576 | 6p multicolored | .75 | .75 |
| 2113 | A576 | 6p multicolored | 1.00 | .35 |
| a. | A576 | Pair, #2112-2113 | 2.25 | 2.25 |
| b. | | Souv. sheet of 2, #2112-2113, imperf. | 2.25 | 2.25 |
| c. | | Souv. sheet of 4, #2112-2113 | 3.00 | 3.50 |
| | | | 4.00 | 4.75 |
| | | Nos. 2110-2113 (4) | 2.70 | 1.10 |

Designs: #2110, Gymnastics, games emblem at UR. #2111, Gymnastics, games emblem at LR. #2112, Martial arts, games emblem at LL. #2113, Martial arts, games emblem at LR, vert.

No. 2113b has simulated perforations.

No. 1585 Surcharged in Red

**1991, Nov. 27** — **Souvenir Sheet Wmk. 372 Imperf.**

| 2114 | A385 | 4p on 3.20p | 3.00 | 3.50 |
|---|---|---|---|---|

First Philippine Philatelic Convention.

**Children's Christmas Paintings — A577**

**1991, Dec. 4** — **Wmk. 391 Perf. 14**

| 2115 | A577 | 2p shown | .40 | .20 |
|---|---|---|---|---|
| 2116 | A577 | 6p Wrapped gift | 1.10 | .35 |
| 2117 | A577 | 7p Santa, tree | 1.40 | .40 |
| 2118 | A577 | 8p Tree, star | 1.50 | .45 |
| | | Nos. 2115-2118 (4) | 4.40 | 1.40 |

---

**Insignias of Military Groups Inducted into USAFFE — A578**

White background: No. 2119a, 1st Regular Div. b, 2nd Regular Div. c, 11th Div. d, 21st Div. e, 31st Div. f, 41st Div. g, 51st Div. h, 61st Div. i, 71st Div. j, 81st Div. k, 91st Div. l, 101st Div. m, Bataan Force. n, Philippine Div. o, Philippine Army Air Corps. p, Offshore Patrol. Nos. 2120a-2120p, like #2119a-2119p with yellow background.

**1991, Dec. 8** — **Perf. 14x13½ Photo. Wmk. 391**

| 2119 | A578 | 2p Block of 16, #a.-p. | 15.00 | 15.00 |
|---|---|---|---|---|
| 2120 | A578 | 2p Block of 16, #a.-p. | 15.00 | 15.00 |
| q. | | Block of 32, #2119-2120 | 45.00 | 45.00 |

Induction of Filipinos into USAFFE, 50th anniv. Nos. 2119-2120 were printed in sheets of 200 containing 5 #2120q plus five blocks of 8.

**Basketball, Cent. A579**

**1991, Dec. 19** — **Wmk. 391 Litho. Perf. 14**

| 2121 | A579 | 2p multicolored | .60 | .20 |
|---|---|---|---|---|
| 2122 | A579 | 6p multicolored | 1.50 | .50 |
| 2123 | A579 | 7p multicolored | 1.65 | .65 |
| 2124 | A579 | 8p multicolored | 2.50 | .75 |
| a. | | Souv. sheet of 4, #2121-2124. | 7.25 | 7.25 |
| | | Nos. 2121-2124 (4) | 6.85 | 2.10 |

Designs: 2p, PBA Games, vert. 6p, Map, player dribbling. 7p, Early players. 8p, Men shooting basketball, vert. 16p, Tip-off.

**Souvenir Sheet Imperf**

| 2125 | A579 | 16p multicolored | 5.25 | 5.25 |
|---|---|---|---|---|

No. 2125 has simulated perforations.

**New Year 1992, Year of the Monkey A580**

**1991, Dec. 27** — **Wmk. 391 Litho. Perf. 14**

| 2126 | A580 | 2p violet & multi | 1.25 | .30 |
|---|---|---|---|---|
| 2127 | A580 | 6p green & multi | 3.25 | .65 |

See Nos. 2459a, 2460a.

---

**Services and Products A581**

**1992, Jan. 15** — **Wmk. 391 Litho. Perf. 14**

| 2128 | A581 | 2p Mailing center | .40 | .20 |
|---|---|---|---|---|
| 2129 | A581 | 6p Housing project | 1.10 | .35 |
| 2130 | A581 | 7p Livestock | 1.40 | .45 |
| 2131 | A581 | 8p Handicraft | 1.60 | .55 |
| | | Nos. 2128-2131 (4) | 4.50 | 1.55 |

**Medicinal Plants — A582**

**1992, Feb. 7** — **Wmk. 391 Litho. Perf. 14**

| 2132 | A582 | 2p Curcuma longa | .75 | .20 |
|---|---|---|---|---|
| 2133 | A582 | 6p Centella asiatica | 1.60 | .40 |
| 2134 | A582 | 7p Cassia alata | 2.00 | .50 |
| 2135 | A582 | 8p Ervatamia panda-cagui | | |
| | | Nos. 2132-2135 (4) | 6.75 | 1.70 |

**Love A583**

**1992, Feb. 10** — **Wmk. 391 Photo. Perf. 14**

| 2137 | A583 | 2p Pair, #a.-b. | 1.00 | 1.00 |
|---|---|---|---|---|
| 2138 | A583 | 6p Pair, #a.-b. | 2.75 | 2.75 |
| 2139 | A583 | 7p Pair, #a.-b. | 3.50 | 3.50 |
| 2140 | A583 | 8p Pair, #a.-b. | 8.00 | 8.00 |
| | | Nos. 2137-2140 (4) | 15.25 | 15.25 |

"I Love You" in English on Nos. 2137a-2140a, in Filipino on Nos. 2137b-2140b with designs: No. 2137, Letters, map, heart. 2p, Heart, doves. No. 2139, Bouquet of flowers, No. 2140, Map, Cupid with bow and arrow.

---

**A584**

**1992, Apr. 12** — **Wmk. 391 Litho. Perf. 14**

| 2141 | A584 | 2p blue & multi | .40 | .20 |
|---|---|---|---|---|
| 2142 | A584 | 8p red vio & multi | 1.90 | .40 |

Our Lady of Sorrows of Porta Vaga, 400th anniv.

**A585**

**1992, Mar. 27**

| 2143 | A585 | 2p multicolored | .40 | .20 |
|---|---|---|---|---|
| 2144 | A585 | 8p multicolored | 1.90 | .40 |

Expo '92, Seville: 2p, Man and woman cele-brating. 8p, Philippine discovery scenes. 16p, Pavilion, horiz.

**Souvenir Sheet Imperf**

| 2145 | A585 | 16p multicolored | 7.50 | 7.50 |
|---|---|---|---|---|

---

**Department of Agriculture, 75th Anniv. — A586**

**1992, May 4**

| 2146 | A586 | 2p Strip of 3, #a.-c. | 1.90 | 1.90 |
|---|---|---|---|---|

a, Man planting seed. b, Fish trap. c, Pigs.

**Manila Jockey Club, 125th Anniv. A588**

**1992, May 14** — **Wmk. 391 Litho. Perf. 14**

| 2149 | A588 | 2p multicolored | .75 | .25 |
|---|---|---|---|---|

**Souvenir Sheet Imperf**

| 2150 | A588 | 8p multicolored | 4.00 | 4.75 |
|---|---|---|---|---|

No. 2150 has simulated perfs.

**Great Filipinos Type of 1989**

Designs: a, Pres. Manuel A. Roxas (1892-1948). b, Justice Natividad Almeda-Lopez (1892-1977). c, Justice Roman A. Ozaeta (b. 1892). d, Engracia Cruz-Reyes (1892-1975). e, Fernando Amorsolo (1892-1972).

**1992, June 1** — **Perf. 14x13½ Wmk. 391**

| 2151 | A536 | 2p Strip of 5, #a.-e. | 1.90 | 1.90 |
|---|---|---|---|---|

**30th Chess Olympiad, Manila A589**

**1992, June 7** — **Wmk. 391 Perf. 14**

| 2152 | A589 | 2p No. 1352 | .40 | .20 |
|---|---|---|---|---|
| 2153 | A589 | 6p No. B21 | 1.40 | .35 |

**Souvenir Sheet Imperf**

| 2154 | A589 | 8p Sheet of 2, #a.-b. | 4.50 | 5.25 |
|---|---|---|---|---|

#2154: a, like #2152. b, like #2153.

No. 2154 has simulated perfs.

2p, Bataan, cross. 6p, Insignia of defenders of Bataan & Corregidor. 8p, Corregidor. Monument. #2158, Cross, map of Bataan. #2159, Monument, map of Corregidor.

**Size: 63x76mm, 76x63mm**

**1992, June 12** **Wmk. 391** **Photo.** **Perf. 14**
| | | | | |
|---|---|---|---|---|
| 2155 | A590 | 2p multicolored | .40 | .20 |
| 2156 | A590 | 6p multicolored | 1.25 | .35 |
| 2157 | A590 | 8p multicolored | 1.60 | .45 |

**Imperf**
| | | | | |
|---|---|---|---|---|
| 2158 | A590 | 16p multicolored | 5.00 | 5.00 |
| 2159 | A590 | 16p multicolored | 5.00 | 5.00 |
| | | | 13.25 | 11.00 |
Nos. 2155-2159 (5)

Nos. 2158-2159 have simulated perforations.

President Corazon C. Aquino and President-Elect Fidel V. Ramos — A591

Anniversary of Democracy.

**1992, June 30** **Perf. 14**
2160 A591 2p multicolored .60 .20

Jose Rizal's Exile to Dapitan, Cent. A592

**1992, June 17**
| | | | | |
|---|---|---|---|---|
| 2161 | A592 | 2p Dapitan shrine | .95 | .25 |
| 2162 | A592 | 2p Portrait, vert. | .95 | .25 |

Contemporary paintings: Nos. 2163, 2165, Spirit of ASEAN. Nos. 2164, 2166, ASEAN Sea.

**1992, July 18** **Wmk. 391** **Litho.** **Perf. 14**
| | | | | |
|---|---|---|---|---|
| 2163 | A593 | 2p multicolored | .40 | .20 |
| 2164 | A593 | 2p multicolored | .40 | .20 |
| 2165 | A593 | 6p multicolored | 1.25 | .35 |
| 2166 | A593 | 6p multicolored | 1.25 | .35 |
| | | | 3.30 | 1.10 |
Nos. 2163-2166 (4)

ASEAN, 25th Anniv. A593

World War II, 50th Anniv. — A590

Founding of Katipunan, Cent. A594

Details or entire paintings of revolutionaries, by Carlos "Botong" Francisco: No. 2167a, Preparing for battle. No. 2167b, Attack leader (detail), vert. No. 2168a, Attack. No. 2168b, Signing papers.

**1992, July 27** **Wmk. 391** **Photo.** **Perf. 14**
| | | | | |
|---|---|---|---|---|
| 2167 | A594 | 2p Pair, #a.-b. | 1.50 | 1.50 |
| 2168 | A594 | 2p Pair, #a.-b. | 1.50 | 1.50 |

Philippine League, Cent. A595

**1992, July 31** **Wmk. 391** **Photo.** **Perf. 14**
2169 A595 2p multicolored .75 .25

1992 Summer Olympics, Barcelona A596

**1992, Aug. 4** **Wmk. 391** **Litho.**
| | | | | |
|---|---|---|---|---|
| 2170 | A596 | 2p Swimming | .30 | .20 |
| 2171 | A596 | 6p Boxing | 1.50 | .45 |
| 2172 | A596 | 8p Hurdling | 2.00 | .55 |
| | | | 3.80 | 1.20 |
Nos. 2170-2172 (3)

**Souvenir Sheet**

**Imperf**
2172A A596 Sheet of 3, 2171-2172, 2172Ab | 4.50 | 5.25 |
a. 1p like #2170 | .50 | .50 |

No. 2172A has simulated perforations.

Religious of the Assumption in Philippines, Cent. — A597

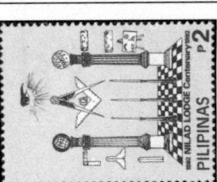

Cathedral of San Sebastian, Cent. — A597a

**1992, Aug. 15** **Wmk. 391** **Photo.** **Perf. 14**
| | | | | |
|---|---|---|---|---|
| 2173 | A597 | 2p multicolored | .60 | .20 |
| 2174 | A597a | 2p multicolored | .60 | .20 |

Various Masonic symbols and: 6p, A. Luna. 8p, M.H. Del Pilar.

**1992, Aug. 15** **Wmk. 391** **Photo.** **Perf. 14**
| | | | | |
|---|---|---|---|---|
| 2175 | A598 | 2p green & black | .35 | .20 |
| 2176 | A598 | 6p yellow, black & brown | 1.50 | .40 |
| 2177 | A598 | 8p blue, black & violet | 1.90 | .55 |
| | | | 3.75 | 1.15 |
Nos. 2175-2177 (3)

Founding of Nilad Masonic Lodge, Cent. — A598

Pres. Fidel V. Ramos Taking Oath of Office, June 30, 1992 A599

**1992, July 30**
| | | | | |
|---|---|---|---|---|
| 2178 | A599 | 2p Ceremony, people | .35 | .20 |
| 2179 | A599 | 8p Ceremony, flag | 1.50 | .60 |

Freshwater Aquarium Fish A600

Designs: No. 2180a, Red-tailed guppy. b, Tiger lacetail guppy. c, Flamingo guppy. d, Neon tuxedo guppy. e, King cobra guppy. No. 2181a, Black moor. b, Bubble eye. c, Pearl scale goldfish. d, Red cap. e, Lionhead goldfish.
No. 2182, Golden arowana.
No. 2183a, Delta topsail variatus. b, Orange spotted hi-fin platy. c, Red lyretail swordtail. d, Bleeding heart hi-fin platy.
No. 2184a, 6p, Green discus. b, 6p, Brown discus. c, 7p, Red discus. d, 7p, Blue discus.

**1992, Sept. 9** **Perf. 14**
2180 A600 1.50p Strip of 5, #a.- | 4.00 | 4.00 |
e.
**Imperf**
2181 A600 2p Strip of 5, #a.- | 4.00 | 4.00 |
e.

**Size: 65x45mm**
2182 A600 8p multicolored | 3.00 | 3.00 |

**Souvenir Sheets of 4**

**Perf. 14**
| | | | | |
|---|---|---|---|---|
| 2183 | A600 | 4p #a.-d. | 4.75 | 5.75 |
| 2184 | A600 | 6p, 7p #a.-d. | 8.25 | 9.25 |

Nos. 2182 and 2184 were overprinted "PHILIPPINE STAMP EXHIBITION 1992 — TAIPEI" in margins. Most of this overprinted issue was sold to the dealer to co-sponsored the exhibit.
See Nos. 2253-2257.

Birthday Greetings A601

**1992, Sept 28** **Perf. 14**
| | | | | |
|---|---|---|---|---|
| 2185 | A601 | 2p Couple dancing | .35 | .20 |
| 2186 | A601 | 6p like #2185 | 1.25 | .50 |
| 2187 | A601 | 7p Cake, balloons | 1.60 | .75 |
| 2188 | A601 | 8p like #2187 | 4.45 | 1.95 |
Nos. 2185-2188 (4)

Columbus' Discovery of America, 500th Anniv. A602

Various fruits and vegetables.

**1992, Oct. 14**
| | | | | |
|---|---|---|---|---|
| 2189 | A602 | 2p multicolored | .40 | .20 |
| 2190 | A602 | 6p multi. diff. | 1.40 | .35 |
| 2191 | A602 | 6p multi. diff. | 2.00 | .45 |
| | | | 3.80 | 1.00 |
Nos. 2189-2191 (3)

Intl. Conference on Nutrition, Rome A603

**1992, Oct. 27**
2192 A603 2p multicolored .60 .20

No. 2100 Ovptd. in Blue "Second / National Philatelic Convention / Cebu, Philippines, Oct. 22-24, 1992"

**1992, Oct. 15** **Wmk. 391** **Photo.**
2193 A571 16p multicolored 6.00 5.25

**Imperf.**

Various pictures of mother and child.

Christmas A604

**1992, Nov. 5** **Wmk. 391** **Litho.** **Perf. 14**
| | | | | |
|---|---|---|---|---|
| 2194 | A604 | 2p multicolored | .35 | .20 |
| 2195 | A604 | 6p multicolored | 1.25 | .35 |
| 2196 | A604 | 7p multicolored | 1.25 | .40 |
| 2197 | A604 | 8p multicolored | 1.75 | .45 |
| | | | 4.60 | 1.40 |
Nos. 2194-2197 (4)

No. 1452 Ovptd. "INAUGURATION OF THE PHILIPPINE POSTAL MUSEUM / AND PHILATELIC LIBRARY, / NOVEMBER 10, 1992" in Red

**1992, Nov. 10** **Wmk. 372** **Litho.**

**Souvenir Sheet**
2198 A348 5p multicolored 2.50 2.50

Fight Against Drug Abuse.

A605

A606

**1992, Nov. 15** **Wmk. 391** **Litho.** **Perf. 14**
| | | | | |
|---|---|---|---|---|
| 2199 | A605 | 2p People, boat | .35 | .20 |
| 2200 | A605 | 8p People, boat, diff. | 1.50 | .45 |

Paintings: 2p, Family, by Cesar Legaspi. 6p, Pounding Rice, by Nena Saguil. 7p, Fish Vendors, by Romeo V. Tabuena.

**1992, Nov. 24**
| | | | | |
|---|---|---|---|---|
| 2201 | A606 | 2p multicolored | .35 | .20 |
| 2202 | A606 | 6p multicolored | 1.25 | .30 |
| 2203 | A606 | 7p multicolored | 1.40 | .40 |
| | | | 3.00 | .90 |
Nos. 2201-2203 (3)

Philatelic Week.

PHILIPPINES

Birds
A607

Designs: No. 2204a, Black shama. b, Philippine cockatoo. c, Sulu hornbill. d, Mindoro imperial pigeon. e, Blue-headed fantail. No. 2205a, Philippine trogon, vert. b, Rufous hornbill, vert. c, White-bellied woodpecker, vert. d, Spotted wood kingfisher, vert. No. 2206a, Brahminy kite. b, Philippine falconet. c, Pacific reef egret. d, Philippine mallard.

**1992, Nov. 25    Litho.    Perf. 14**

**Wmk. 391**

| 2204 | A607 | 2p Strip of 5, #a.-e. | 3.00 | 3.00 |
| 2205 | A607 | 2p Sheet of 4, #a.-d. | 2.25 | 2.75 |
| 2206 | A607 | 2p Sheet of 4, #a.-d. | 2.25 | 2.75 |

**Souvenir Sheets**

No. 2204 printed in sheets of 10 with designs in each row shifted one space to the right from the preceding row. Two rows in each sheet are tete-beche.

The 1st printing of this set was rejected. The unissued stamps do not have the frame around the birds. The denominations on the sheet stamps and the 2nd souvenir sheet are larger. On the 1st souvenir sheet they are smaller. For overprint see No. 2405.

New Year 1993, Year of the Rooster
A608

**1992**

| 2207 | A608 | 2p Native fighting cock | .40 | .20 |

**2208 A608 6p Legendary**
Maranao bird          1.40    .40
a.    Souvenir sheet of 2,
      2208 + 2 labels     2.50    3.00
b.    As "a", ovptd. in sheet margin    2.50    3.00

Nos. 2208a and 2208b exist imperf. Overprint on No. 2208b reads: "PHILIPPINE STAMP EXHIBIT / TAIPEI, DECEMBER 1992" in English and Chinese.
Issued: #2207-2208, 11/27; #2208b, 12/1.
See Nos. 2459b, 2460b.

PILIPINAS ₱2   PHILIPPINE GUERRILLA UNITS OF WORLD WAR II
PILIPINAS ₱2   PHILIPPINE GUERRILLA UNITS OF WORLD WAR II

Guerrilla Units of World War II — A609

**1992, Dec. 7**

| 2209 | A609 | 2p Block of 4, #a.-d. | 3.50 | 3.50 |

Units: a. Bulacan Military Area, Anderson's Command, Luzon Guerrilla Army Forces. b, Marking's Fil-American Guerrillas, Hunters ROTC Guerrillas. c, 61st Division, 71st Division. President Quezon's Own Guerrillas. d, 48th Chinese Guerrilla Squadron, 101st Division. Vinzons Cebu Area Command. d, 48th Chinese Guerrillas. Cebu Guerrillas, 101st Division.

National Symbols:

A610   National Flag
A610a

National Symbols: A610

| 2210 | A610 | 60s (R) | .80 | .25 |
| 2211 | A610b | 1p (R) | .25 | .25 |
| 2211A | A610b | 1p (Br) | .25 | .25 |
| 2212 | A610a | 1p (R) | .25 | .25 |
| 2212A | A610a | 1p (Br) | .25 | .25 |
| 2213 | A610c | 1.50p (R) | .25 | .25 |
| 2214 | A610c | 1.50p (B) | .25 | .20 |
a.    Dated "1995"

Nos. 2212A and 2214 have blue security printing.
Issued: #2210, 6/12/93; #2211, 5/3/94; #2211A, 2/6/95; #2212, 4/29/93; #2212A, 2/12/96; #2213, 6/12/3; #2213a, 2/6/95; #2214, 2/12/6.

Nos. 2210-2236 inscribed with year of issue unless noted otherwise
**1993-98    Litho.    Perf. 14x13½**
Wmk. 391, except #2212A, 2214, 2215, 2216A, 2218A, 2220, 2222 (Unwmk.)

**Red (R) and Blue (B) "PILIPINAS" on bottom, except #2212 (Brown (Br) "PILIPINAS" on top)**

National Animal
A610d

National Flower
A610b

National Bird — A610t

National Sport — A610t

José Rizal
National Hero
A610r

National Dance
A610s

National House
A610p

National Fruit
A610n

National Leaf
A610j

National Costume
A610m

**Blue Security Printing**

| 2215 | A610 | 2p Block of 14, #a.- | 9.00 | 15.00 |
| | | n. | | |
| a. | A610d | 2p multi | .30 | .25 |
| b. | A610b | 2p multi | .30 | .25 |
| c. | A610e | 2p multi | .30 | .25 |
| d. | A610p | 2p multi | .30 | .25 |
| e. | A610n | 2p multi | .30 | .25 |
| f. | A610o | 2p multi | .30 | .25 |
| g. | A610s | 2p multi | .30 | .25 |
| h. | A610f | 2p multi | .30 | .25 |
| i. | A610r | 2p multi | .30 | .25 |
| j. | A610i | 2p multi | .30 | .25 |
| k. | A610k | 2p multi | .30 | .25 |
| l. | A610t | 2p multi | .30 | .25 |
| m. | A610g | 2p multi | .30 | .25 |
| n. | A610c | 2p multi | .30 | .25 |
Issued 11/2/95.

**Red "PILIPINAS" on bottom, except #2216, 2217, 2217a (Brown "PILIPINAS" on top)**

**No Security Printing**

| 2216 | A610d | 2p multi | .30 | .30 |
| 2216A | A610e | 2p multi | .30 | .25 |
| 2217 | | 2p Block of 14, #a.- | 9.00 | 15.00 |
| | | n. | | |
| a. | A610d | 2p multi | .30 | .25 |
| b. | A610b | 2p multi | .30 | .25 |
| c. | A610e | 2p multi | .30 | .25 |
| d. | A610p | 2p multi | .30 | .25 |
| e. | A610n | 2p multi | .30 | .25 |
| f. | A610o | 2p multi | .30 | .25 |
| g. | A610s | 2p multi | .30 | .25 |
| h. | A610f | 2p multi | .30 | .25 |
| i. | A610r | 2p multi | .30 | .25 |
| j. | A610i | 2p multi | .30 | .25 |
| k. | A610k | 2p multi | .30 | .25 |
| l. | A610t | 2p multi | .30 | .25 |
| m. | A610g | 2p multi | .30 | .25 |
| n. | A610c | 2p multi | .30 | .25 |
Issued: #2216, 4/29/93; #2216A, 2/10/94; #2217, 10/28/93.

No. 2217a is a later printing of #2216, in which the word "watawat" is much smaller. #2217h is a later printing of #2216A, in which the date is lowered near the middle of "PILIPINAS," rather than near the top of "PILIPINAS."

**Red "PILIPINAS" on bottom, except #2218a (Blue "PILIPINAS" on bottom)**

| 2218 | A610f | 3p multi | .50 | .35 |
| a. | Dated "1994" | | .50 | .35 |
| b. | Dated "1995" | | .50 | .35 |
| 2218C | A610g | 3p multi | .50 | .35 |
"PILIPINAS" red: #2218, 2218a, 2218C. Blue security printing: #2218, 6/12/93; #2218C, 3/1/96.
Issued: #2218, 6/12/93; #2218a, 4/19/94; #2218b, 2/1/95; #2218C, 3/1/96.

Illustrations reduced.

National House (bahay kubo)
A610p   A610q   House   Various

National Fruit (mangga)
A610n   A610o   Fruit

National Leaf (anahaw)
A610j   A610k   Leaf

National Costume (barong tagalog at baro't saya)
A610m   Costume

National Bird (agila)
A610h   A610i   Bird

National Animal (kalabaw)
A610f   A610g   Animal

National Flag (watawat)
A610d   A610e   Flag

National Flower (sampaguita)
A610a   A610b   Flower

National Fish (bangus)
A610c   Fish

National Hero (Dr. José P. Rizal)
A610r

National Dance (tinikling)
A610s

National Sports (sipa)
A610t

Tree
A610

**Blue "PILIPINAS" on bottom, except #2219n (Blue "PILIPINAS" on top)**

**Blue Security Printing**

| 2219 | | 4p Block of 14, #a.- | 15.00 | 25.00 |
| | | n. | | |
| a. | A610d | 4p multi | .75 | .40 |
| b. | A610b | 4p multi | .75 | .40 |
| c. | A610e | 4p multi | .75 | .40 |
| d. | A610p | 4p multi | .75 | .40 |
| e. | A610n | 4p multi | .75 | .40 |
| f. | A610o | 4p multi | .75 | .40 |
| g. | A610s | 4p multi | .75 | .40 |
| h. | A610f | 4p multi | .75 | .40 |
| i. | A610r | 4p multi | .75 | .40 |
| j. | A610i | 4p multi | .75 | .40 |
| k. | A610k | 4p multi | .75 | .40 |
| l. | A610t | 4p multi | .75 | .40 |
| m. | A610g | 4p multi | .75 | .40 |
| n. | A610c | 4p multi | .75 | .40 |
Issued 1/8/96. Stamps are dated "1995."

**Blue "PILIPINAS" on bottom, except #2220a (Blue "PILIPINAS" on top)**

**Blue Security Printing**

| 2220 | A610h | 4p multi | 1.50 | .60 |
| a. | Dated "1994" | | 15.00 | 25.00 |
| b. | Dated "1995" | | 1.50 | .60 |

Issued 2/12/96.

**Red "PILIPINAS" on bottom (R): #2221-2221b, 2223B, 2223c, 2224B, 2224c, 2226, 2226a, 2228-2228b. Blue "PILIPINAS" on bottom (B): #2222, 2223A, 2224A, 2227, 2229. Brown "PILIPINAS" on top (Br): #2223, 2224, 2225.**

| 2221 | A610h | 5p (R) | 1.50 | .60 |
| a. | Dated "1994" | | 7.00 | .60 |
| b. | Dated "1995" | | 1.50 | .60 |
| 2222 | A610h | 5p (B) | 1.50 | .60 |
| 2223 | A610j | 6p (Br) | 2.50 | 1.00 |
| 2223A | A610j | 6p (B) | 2.50 | 1.00 |
| 2223B | A610j | 6p (R) | 2.50 | 1.00 |
| 2224 | A610i | 7p (Br) | 3.00 | 1.25 |
| 2224A | A610i | 7p (B) | 3.00 | 1.25 |
| 2224B | A610m | 7p (R) | 3.00 | 1.25 |
| 2225 | A610m | 7p (Br) | 3.00 | 1.25 |
| 2226 | A610o | 8p (R) | 3.50 | 1.50 |
| 2227 | A610o | 8p (B) | 3.50 | 1.50 |
| 2228 | A610c | 8p (R) | 3.50 | 1.50 |
| a. | Dated "1994" | | 4.00 | 2.00 |
| b. | Dated "1995" | | 4.00 | 2.00 |
| 2229 | A610p | 10p (B) | 4.00 | 2.00 |
Nos. 2210-2229 (28)          89.90   103.10
Blue security printing: #2222, 2223A, 2224A, 2227, 2229.
Issued: #2221, 2228, 6/12/93; #2221a, 2224A, 4/19/94; #2221b, 2/1/95; #2222, 2/12/96; #2223, 2224, 2225, #2223A, 11/21/96; #2223B, #2223Bc, #2223c, 4/29/93; #2223A, 4/3/95; #2224A, 12/1/94; #2223Bc, 4/19/96; #2224B, #2224A, 2227, 2229, 10/4/93; 3/14/95; #2224B, 7/6/94.

**Souvenir Sheets**

CENTENARY OF PHILIPPINE INDEPENDENCE
1898-1998
Series I PHILIPPINE FLAG WITH NATIONAL SYMBOLS

NATIONAL ANTHEM (Lupang Hinirang)

Philippine Flag with National Symbols — A610u

PHILIPPINES

A615

A616

Natl. Coconut Week.

| | | | |
|---|---|---|---|
| 2252 | A615 | 2p multicolored | .60 .20 |

**1993, Aug. 24**

**Fish Type of 1992**

No. 2253: a, Paradise fish. b, Pearl gourami. c, Red-tailed black shark. d, Tiger barb. e, Cardinal tetra.
No. 2254: a, Albino ryukin goldfish. b, Black oranda goldfish. c, Lionhead goldfish. d, Colestial-eye goldfish. e, Pompon goldfish.
No. 2255: a, Pearl-scale angelfish. b, Zebra angelfish. c, Marble angelfish. d, Black angelfish.
No. 2256: a, Neon betta. b, Libby betta. c, Split-tailed betta. d, Butterfly betta. e, Albino oscar.

**1993** *Unwmk.* *Perf. 14*

| | | | | |
|---|---|---|---|---|
| 2253 | A600 | 2p Strip of 5, #a.-e. | 2.50 | 2.50 |
| 2254 | A600 | 2p Strip of 5, #a.-e. | 2.50 | 2.50 |

**Souvenir Sheets**

*Perf. 14*

| | | | | |
|---|---|---|---|---|
| 2255 | A600 | 2p Sheet of 4, #a.-d. | 2.00 | 2.50 |
| 2256 | A600 | 3p Sheet of 4, #a.-d. | 3.00 | 3.50 |
| e. | | Ovptd. in margin | 3.75 | 4.50 |

*Imperf* **Stamp Size: 70x45mm**

| | | | | |
|---|---|---|---|---|
| 2257 | A000 | 6p multicolored | 1.50 | 1.50 |
| a. | | Ovptd. in black | 2.25 | 2.25 |

Nos. "2256e, 2257a overprinted in black "QUEEN SIRIKIT NATIONAL CONVENTION CENTER / 1-10 OCTOBER 1993," "BANG-KOK WORLD PHILATELIC EXHIBITION 1993" with Bangkok '93 show emblem in purple in margin.
Nos. 2255a-2255d are vert.
Issued: #2256e, 2257a, 9/20; others, 9/9.

A617

16th World Law Conference, Manila — A617

6p, Globe on scales, gavel, flag, vert. 7p, Justice holding scales, courthouse. 8p, Fisherman, vert.

**1993, Sept. 20** *Photo.* *Perf. 14*

| | | | | |
|---|---|---|---|---|
| 2258 | A616 | 2p multicolored | .50 | .20 |

Basic Petroleum and Minerals, Inc., 25th anniv.

**1993, Sept. 30** *Litho.* *Unwmk.*

*Perf. 14*

| | | | | |
|---|---|---|---|---|
| 2259 | A617 | 6p multicolored | .30 | .20 |
| 2260 | A617 | 6p multicolored | 1.00 | .30 |
| 2261 | A617 | 7p multicolored | 1.10 | .35 |
| 2262 | A617 | 8p multicolored | 1.40 | .40 |
| | | Nos. 2259-2262 (4) | 3.80 | 1.25 |

---

Great Filipinos Type of 1989

Designs: a, Nicanor Abelardo, composer. b, Pilar Hidalgo-Lim, mathematician, educator. c, Manuel Viola Gallego, lawyer, educator. d, Maria Ylagan Orosa (1893-1943), pharmacist, health advocate. e, Eulogio B. Rodriguez, historian.

**1993, June 10** *Perf. 13½*

| | | | | |
|---|---|---|---|---|
| 2240 | A536 | 2p Strip of 5, #a.-e. | 2.25 | 2.25 |

17th South East Asia Games, Singapore A612

Judo

Boxing PILIPINAS ₱2

No. 2241: a, Weight lifting, archery, fencing, shooting. b, Boxing, judo. c, Track, cycling, gymnastics, golf.
No. 2242: a, Table tennis, soccer, volleyball, badminton. b, Billiards, bowling. c, Swimming, water polo, yachting, diving.
No. 2243, Basketball, vert.

**1993, June 18** *Perf. 13*

| | | | | |
|---|---|---|---|---|
| 2241 | A612 | 2p Strip of 3, #a.-c. | 1.25 | 1.25 |
| 2242 | A612 | 6p Strip of 3, #a.-c. | 3.75 | 3.75 |

**Souvenir Sheet**

| | | | | |
|---|---|---|---|---|
| 2243 | A612 | 10p multicolored | 5.00 | 6.00 |

#2241a, 2241c, 2241d, 2242a, 2242c are 80x30mm. No. 2243 contains one 30x4umm stamp. No. 2242a exists inscribed "June 13-20, 1993."

Orchids — A613

No. 2244: a, Spathoglottis chrysantha. b, Arachnis longicaulis. c, Phalaenopsis mannii. d, Coelogyne marmorata. e, Dendrobium sanderae.
No. 2245: a, Dendrobium serratilabium. b, Phalaenopsis equestris. c, Vanda merrillii. d, Vanda luzonica. e, Grammatophyllum martae.
No. 2246, Aerides quinquevulnera. No. 2247, Vanda lamellata.

**1993, Aug. 14** *Unwmk.* *Perf. 14*

| | | | | |
|---|---|---|---|---|
| 2244 | A613 | 2p Block of 5, #a.-e. | 2.25 | 2.25 |
| 2245 | A613 | 3p Block of 5, #a.-e. | 3.75 | 3.75 |

**Souvenir Sheets**

*Imperf*

| | | | | |
|---|---|---|---|---|
| 2246 | A613 | 8p multicolored | 2.50 | 3.00 |
| a. | | With additional inscription | 2.50 | 3.00 |
| 2247 | A613 | 8p multicolored | 2.50 | 3.00 |
| a. | | With additional inscription | 2.50 | 3.00 |

No. 2246 contains one 27x78mm stamp. No. 2246a, 2247a inscribed in sheet margin with Taipei '93 emblem in blue and yellow. Additional black inscription in English and Chinese reads: "ASIAN INTERNATIONAL INVITATION STAMP EXHIBITION / TAIPEI '93."

Greetings — A614

"Thinking of You" in English on Nos. 2248a-2251a, in Filipino on Nos. 2248b-2251b with designs: 2p, Flowers, dog at window. 8p, Dog looking at alarm clock. 7p, Dog looking at calendar. 8p, Dog with slippers.

**1993, Aug. 20** *Wmk. 391* *Litho.*

*Perf. 14*

| | | | | |
|---|---|---|---|---|
| 2248 | A614 | 2p Pair, #a.-b. | 1.00 | 1.00 |
| 2249 | A614 | 6p Pair, #a.-b. | 3.25 | 3.25 |
| 2250 | A614 | 7p Pair, #a.-b. | 3.25 | 3.25 |
| 2251 | A614 | 8p Pair, #a.-b. | 4.25 | 4.25 |
| | | Nos. 2248-2251 (4) | 11.75 | 11.75 |

---

**CENTENARY OF PHILIPPINE INDEPENDENCE**
1898-1998
SERIES 5: HISTORICAL EVENTS AND PERSONAGES (1897)

NATIONAL ANTHEM (Ang Lupang Hinirang) Part 5

Historical Events and Personages (1897) — A610y

Designs: a, Ediberto Evangelista; b, Vicente Alvarez; c, Francisco Del Castillo; d, Pantaleon Valllegas.
Nos. 2235a-2235d have blue security printing.

| | | | | |
|---|---|---|---|---|
| 2235 | A610q | 4p, Sheet of 4, #a.-d. | 8.00 | 12.00 |
| a. | | A610y 4p multi | 1.00 | 2.00 |
| b. | | A610q 4p multi | 1.00 | 2.00 |
| c. | | A610q 4p multi | 1.00 | 2.00 |
| d. | | A610q 4p multi | 1.00 | 2.00 |

Issued 6/12/97.

**CENTENARY OF PHILIPPINE INDEPENDENCE**
1898-1998
SERIES 6: HISTORICAL EVENTS OF 1898

NATIONAL ANTHEM (Ang Lupang Hinirang) Part 6

Historical Events of 1898 — A610z

Designs: a, Tres de Abril Uprising in Cebu; b, Negros Uprising, 1898; c, Iligan Uprising, 1898; d, Philippine Centennial Logo, Kalayaan.
Nos. 2236a-2236d have blue security printing.

| | | | | |
|---|---|---|---|---|
| 2236 | A610z | 4p, Sheet of 4, #a.-d. | 8.00 | 12.00 |
| a. | | A610q 4p multi | 1.00 | 2.00 |
| b. | | A610q 4p multi | 1.00 | 2.00 |
| c. | | A610q 4p multi | 1.00 | 2.00 |
| d. | | A610q 4p multi | 1.00 | 2.00 |

Issued 6/12/98.

Butterflies A611

PILIPINAS ₱2

Euploea mulciber

Designs: No. 2237a, Euploea mulciber. b, Cheritra orpheus. c, Delias henningia. d, Mycalesis ita. e, Delias diaphana.
No. 2238a, Papilio rumanzobia. b, Papilio palinurus. c, Trogonoptera trojana. d, Graphium agamemnon.
No. 2239, Papilio lowi, Valeria boebera, Delias themis.

**1993** *Litho.* *Wmk. 391* *Perf. 14*

| | | | | |
|---|---|---|---|---|
| 2237 | A611 | 2p Strip of 5, #a.- | 3.00 | 3.00 |

**Souvenir Sheets**

| | | | | |
|---|---|---|---|---|
| 2238 | A611 | 2p Sheet of 4, #a.-d. | 2.50 | 3.00 |
| e. | | Ovptd. in sheet margin | 2.50 | 4.25 |
| 2239 | A611 | 10p multicolored | 3.50 | 4.25 |
| a. | | Ovptd. in sheet margin | 14.00 | 15.00 |
| b. | | Ovptd. in blue in sheet margin | | |

Issue dates: Nos. 2237-2239, May 28. Nos. 2238e, 2239a, May 29. No. 2239b, July 1. Nos. 2238a-2238d are vert. No. 2239 contains one 116x28mm stamp.
Overprint on Nos. 2238e, 2239a reads "INDOPEX '93 / INDONESIA PHILATELIC EXHIBITION 1993" and "6th ASIAN INTERNATIONAL PHILATELIC EXHIBITION / 29th MAY-4th JUNE 1993 SURABAYA-INDONESIA."
Overprint on No. 2239b reads "Towards the Year 2000 / 46th PAF Anniversary 1 July 1993" and includes Philippine Air Force emblem and jet.

---

*Perf. 13½*
*Unwmk.*

| | | | | |
|---|---|---|---|---|
| 2231 | A610u | 1p, Sheet of 12, #a.-j,+2 labels | 15.00 | 25.00 |
| a. | | A610e 1p multi | 1.00 | 2.00 |
| b. | | A610q 1p multi | 1.00 | 2.00 |
| c. | | A610m 1p multi | 1.00 | 2.00 |
| d. | | A610 1p multi | 1.00 | 2.00 |
| e. | | A610K 1p multi | 1.00 | 2.00 |
| f. | | A610K 1p multi | 1.00 | 2.00 |
| g. | | A610K 1p multi | 1.00 | 2.00 |
| h. | | A610l 1p multi | 1.00 | 2.00 |
| i. | | A610f 1p multi | 1.00 | 2.00 |
| j. | | A610f 1p multi | 1.00 | 2.00 |

No. 2231e does not have the blue security printing, present on No. 2212A.
Issued: 6/12/93.

**CENTENARY OF PHILIPPINE INDEPENDENCE**
1898-1998
SERIES 2: PHILIPPINE FLAG WITH NATIONAL LANDMARKS

NATIONAL ANTHEM (Lupang Hinirang) Part 2

Philippine Flag with National Landmarks — A610v

Designs: a, Aquinaldo Shrine; b, Rizal Shrine; Barasoian Shrine, d, Mabini Shrine.

| | | | | |
|---|---|---|---|---|
| 2232 | A610v | 2p, 3p, #a.-d. | 8.00 | 12.00 |
| a. | | A610q 2p multi | 1.00 | 2.00 |
| b. | | A610q 2p multi | 1.00 | 2.00 |
| c. | | A610q 3p multi | 1.00 | 2.00 |
| d. | | A610q 3p multi | 1.00 | 2.00 |

Issued 6/12/94.

**CENTENARY OF PHILIPPINE INDEPENDENCE**
1898-1998
SERIES 3: 1872 CAVITE MUTINY

NATIONAL ANTHEM (Ang Lupang Hinirang) Part 3

1872 Cavite Mutiny — A610w

Designs: a, Cavite Arsenal; b, La Fuerza de San Felipe-Cavite; c, Commemorative marker; d, Cristanto de Los Reyes y Mendoza.

| | | | | |
|---|---|---|---|---|
| 2233 | A610w | 2p, 3p, Sheet of 4, #a.-r | 8.00 | 12.00 |
| a. | | A610q 2p multi | 1.00 | 2.00 |
| b. | | A610q 2p multi | 1.00 | 2.00 |
| c. | | A610q 3p multi | 1.00 | 2.00 |
| d. | | A610q 3p multi | 1.00 | 2.00 |

Issued 6/12/9b.

**CENTENARY OF PHILIPPINE INDEPENDENCE**
1898-1998
SERIES 4: 1896 PHILIPPINE REVOLUTION

NATIONAL ANTHEM (Ang Lupang Hinirang) Part 4

1896 Philippine Revolution — A610x

Designs: a, Cry of Pugdalawin; b, Battle of Pinaglabanan; c, Cry of Nueca Ecija; d, Battle of Binakayan.

| | | | | |
|---|---|---|---|---|
| 2234 | A610x | 4p, Sheet of 4, #a.-d. | 8.00 | 12.00 |
| a. | | A610q 4p multi | 1.00 | 2.00 |
| b. | | A610q 4p multi | 1.00 | 2.00 |
| c. | | A610q 4p multi | 1.00 | 2.00 |
| d. | | A610q 4p multi | 1.00 | 2.00 |

Issued 6/12/96.

**Our Lady of the Rosary of la Naval, 400th Anniv. A618**

1993, Oct. 18 — Wmk. 391
2263 A618 2p multicolored .50 .20

**Intl Year of Indigenous People — A619**

People wearing traditional costumes.

1993, Oct. 24 — Unwmk.
2264 A619 2p multicolored .45 .25
2265 A619 6p multicolored 1.40 .35
2266 A619 7p multicolored 1.40 .40
2267 A619 8p multicolored 1.75 .50
Nos. 2264-2267 (4) 5.00 1.50

Philately Week.

**Environmental Protection — A620**

Paintings: 2p, Trees. 6p, Marine life. 7p, Bird, trees. 8p, Man and nature.

1993, Nov. 22
2268 A620 2p multicolored .45 .25
2269 A620 6p multicolored 1.40 .35
2270 A620 7p multicolored 1.40 .40
2271 A620 8p multicolored 1.75 .50
Nos. 2268-2271 (4) 5.00 1.50

Filipino Inventors Society, Inc, 50th Anniv.

1993, Nov. 30 — Unwmk. Litho. Perf. 14
2272 A621 2p Pair, #a-b. .90 .90
a, Lunar buggy. b, Floating power tiller.

1993, Nov. 30
2273 A622 2p multicolored .50 .20
Printing of Doctrina Christiana in Spanish and Tagalog. 400th anniv.

**A623 — Christmas**

Christmas: 2p, Nativity scene. 6p, Church, people. 7p, Water buffalo carrying fruits, vegetables, sea food. 8p, Christmas lantern, carolers.

1993, Dec. 1
2274 A623 2p multicolored .35 .20
2275 A623 6p multicolored 1.00 .30
2276 A623 7p multicolored 1.25 .35
2277 A623 8p multicolored 1.40 .45
Nos. 2274-2277 (4) 4.00 1.30

1993, Dec. 10
Maps, Philippine guerrilla units of World War II: a, US Army Forces in the Philippines Northern Luzon. b, Bohol Area Command. c, Leyte Area Command. d, Palawan Special Battalion, Sulu Area Command.
2278 A624 2p Block or strip of 4, #a-d. 2.50 2.50

**Philippines 2000 A625 — Peace and Order**

Designs: 2p, Peace and Order. 6p, Transportation, communications. 7p, Infrastructure. No. 2282, People empowerment. No. 2283, Transportation, communications, buildings, people.

1993, Dec. 14 — Unwmk. Litho. Perf. 14
2279 A625 2p multicolored .25 .20
2280 A625 6p multicolored .90 .30
2281 A625 7p multicolored 1.10 .35
2282 A625 8p multicolored 1.25 .40
Nos. 2279-2282 (4) 3.50 1.25

Souvenir Sheet
Imperf
Size: 110x85mm
2283 A625 8p multicolored 3.00 3.00

**A626 — New Year 1994 (Year of the Dog)**

1993, Dec. 15 — Unwmk. Litho. Perf. 14
2284 A626 2p Manigong bagong taon .40 .20
2285 A626 6p Happy new year 1.40 .40
a. Souvenir sheet of 2, #2284-2285 + labels 3.00 3.00
No. 2285a exists imperf.
See Nos. 2459c, 2460c.

**First ASEAN Scout Jamboree, Mt. Makiling — A627**

2p, Flags of ASEAN countries, Boy Scout emblem. 6p, Flags, Boy Scout emblem.

1993, Dec. 28
2286 A627 2p multicolored .35 .25
2287 A627 6p multicolored 1.10 .35
a. Souv. sheet of 2, #2286-2287 3.50 3.50

**Rotary Club of Manila, 75th Anniv. A628**

1994, Jan. 19 — Unwmk. Litho. Perf. 14
2288 A628 2p multicolored .50 .20

**17th Asian Pacific Dental Congress, Manila A629**

2p, Healthy teeth. 6p, Globe, flags, teeth.

1994, Feb. 3
2289 A629 2p multicolored .50 .25
2290 A629 6p multicolored 1.50 .35

**Corals A630**

1994, Feb. 15 — Litho. Perf. 14
#2291: a, Acropora microphthalma. b, Seriatopora hystrix. c, Acropora latistella. d, Millepora tenella. e, Millepora tenella, up close. f, Pachyseris valenciennesi. g, Pavona decussata. h, Galaxea fascicularis. i, Acropora formosa. j, Acropora humilis.
#2292: a, Isis. b, Plexaura. c, Dendronephthya. d, Heteroxenia.
diff. c, Dendrophyllia gracilis. d, Plerogyra sinuosa.

2291 A630 2p Block of 10, #a-j. 5.00 5.00

Souvenir Sheets
2292 A630 2p Sheet of 4, #a-d. 2.00 2.50
2293 A630 3p Sheet of 4, #a-d. 3.00 3.50
a. With added inscription 6.75 7.75

No. 2293e is inscribed in sheet margin "NAPHILCON '94 / 1ST NATIONAL / PHILATELIC CONGRESS / 21 FEBRUARY - 5 MARCH 1994 / PHILATELY 2000." Issued: No. 2293e, 2/21.

**Hong Kong '94 — A631**

1994, Feb. 18
2294 A631 2p multicolored .35 .25
2295 A631 6p multicolored 1.10 .35
a. Souvenir sheet of 2, #2294-2295, blue 2.50 3.00
b. As 'a', green 2.50 3.00
Backgrounds differ on Nos. 2295a, 2295b.

**Philippine Military Academy Class of 1944, 50th Anniv. A632**

1994, Feb. 20
2296 A632 2p multicolored .50 .20

**A633**

1994, Mar. 1
2297 A633 2p multicolored .50 .20
Federation of Filipino-Chinese Chambers of Commerce and Industry, 40th Anniv.

**A634**

1994, Apr. 15
2298 A634 2p Pair, #a-b. 1.00 1.00
2299 A634 2p Pair, #a-b. 1.00 1.00
2300 A634 2p Pair, #a-b. 1.00 1.00
2301 A634 2p Pair, #a-b. 1.00 1.00
Nos. 2298-2301 (4) 4.00 4.00

"Congratulations" in English on Nos. 2298a-2301a, in Tagalog on Nos. 2298b-2301b with designs: No. 2298, Books, diploma, mortarboard No. 2299. 2300, Baby carried by stork. No. 2300, Valentine bouquet with portraits in heart. No. 2301, Bouquet.

**A635**

1994, May 5 — Litho. Perf. 14
2302 A635 2p Pair, #a-b. 1.00 1.00
2303 A635 3p Pair, #a-b. 1.50 1.50

Souvenir Sheet
2304 A635 8p Sheet of 2, #a-b. 3.50 4.25

1994 Miss Universe Pageant, Manila: Nos. 2302a (2p), 2304a, Gloria Diaz, 1969 winner. Nos. 2302b (6p), Crown, Philippine jeepney. winner. No. 2303a (2p), 2304b, Margie Moran, 1973 winner. Nos. 2303b (7p), Pageant participant. Kalesa horse-drawn cart.

**Great Filipinos Type of 1989**

Designs: a, Antonio J. Molina, musician. b, Jose Yulo, politician. c, Josefa Jara-Martinez, social worker. d, Nicanor Reyes, Sr., accountant. e, Sabino B. Padilla, lawyer.

1994, June 10
2307 A636 2p Strip of 5, #a-e. 2.25 2.25

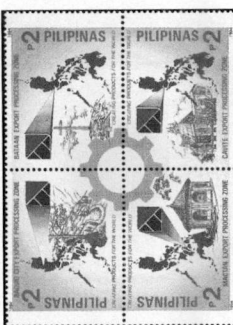

**Philippine Export Processing Zones — A637**

No. 2308: a, Baguio City. b, Bataan. c, Mactan. d, Cavite.

No. 2309a, 7p, Map of Philippines, export products. b, 8p, Export products flowing around world map.

**1994, July 4    Litho.    Perf. 14**

**Unwmk.**

| | | | | |
|---|---|---|---|---|
| 2308 | A637 | 2p Block of 4, #a.-d. | 1.75 | 1.75 |
| 2309 | A637 | Pair, #a.-b. | 2.75 | 2.75 |

**Fight Illegal Recruitment Year — A638**

**1994, July 15**

| | | | | |
|---|---|---|---|---|
| 2310 | A638 | 2p multicolored | .50 | .20 |

**Wildlife — A639**

a, Palawan bearcat. b, Philippine tarsier. c, Scaly anteater. d, Palawan porcupine.

**1994, Aug. 12    Litho.    Perf. 14**

| | | | | |
|---|---|---|---|---|
| 2311 | A639 | 6p Block of 4, #a.-d. | 4.50 | 4.50 |

**Souvenir Sheet**

| | | | | |
|---|---|---|---|---|
| 2312 | A639 | 12p multicolored | 3.25 | 4.00 |
| a. | | Ovptd. in margin | 3.25 | 4.00 |

No. 2312a overprinted in white, black and red in sheet margin with "SINGPEX '94 / 31 August-3 September 1994" and show emblem.

**PHILAKOREA '94 — A640**

Shells: a, Conus gloriamaris. b, Conus striatus. c, Conus geographus. d, Conus textile.

No. 2314a, Conus marmoreus. b, Conus geographus, diff. No. 2315a, Conus striatus, diff. No. 2315b, Conus marmoreus, diff.

**1994, Aug. 16**

| | | | | |
|---|---|---|---|---|
| 2313 | A640 | 2p Block of 4, #a.-d. | 2.50 | 2.50 |

**Souvenir Sheets**

| | | | | |
|---|---|---|---|---|
| 2314 | A640 | 6p Sheet of 2, #a.-b. | 3.00 | 3.75 |
| 2315 | A640 | 6p Sheet of 2, #a.-b. | 3.00 | 3.75 |

**Landings at Leyte Gulf, 50th Anniv. A641**

Designs: a, Pres. Sergio Osmena, Sr. b, Gen. MacArthur wading ashore. c, Dove of Peace. d, Carlos P. Romulo.

**1994, Sept. 15**

| | | | | |
|---|---|---|---|---|
| 2316 | A641 | 2p Block of 4, #a.-d. | 2.25 | 2.25 |

See Nos. 2391a-2391d.

**Intl. Anniversaries & Events — A642**

**Unwmk.**

**1994, Oct. 24    Litho.    Perf. 14**

| | | | | |
|---|---|---|---|---|
| 2317 | A642 | 2p Family | .30 | .25 |
| 2318 | A642 | 6p Labor workers | .90 | .35 |
| 2319 | A642 | 7p Bells | 1.10 | .50 |
| | | Feather, clouds | | |
| | | Nos. 2317-2319 (3) | 2.30 | 1.10 |

Intl. Year of the Family (#2317), ILO, 75th anniv. (#2318). ICAO, 50th anniv. (#2319).

**Visit of US Pres. Bill Clinton A643**

**1994, Nov. 12**

| | | | | |
|---|---|---|---|---|
| 2320 | A643 | 2p green & multi | .20 | .20 |
| 2321 | A643 | 8p blue & multi | 1.60 | .45 |

**East Asian Business Convention, Davao — A644**

**1994, Nov. 15**

| | | | | |
|---|---|---|---|---|
| 2322 | A644 | 2p violet & multi | .30 | .20 |
| 2323 | A644 | 6p brown & multi | .90 | .30 |

Nos. 2322-2323 not issued without overprint "Nov. 15-20, 1994" and obliterator covering original date at lower left.

**Philatelic Week — A645**

Portraits by Philippine artists: 2p, Soteranna Puson Y Quintos de Ventenilla, by Dionisio de Castro. 6p, Quintina Castor de Sadie, by Simon Flores y de la Rosa. 7p, Artist's mother, by Felix Eduardo Resurreccion Hidalgo y Padilla. 8p, Una Bulaquena, by Juan Luna y Novicio. 12p, Cirilo and Severina Quiason Family, by Simon Flores y de la Rosa.

**1994, Nov. 21**

| | | | | |
|---|---|---|---|---|
| 2324 | A645 | 2p multicolored | .25 | .20 |
| 2325 | A645 | 6p multicolored | .80 | .35 |
| 2326 | A645 | 7p multicolored | .95 | .45 |
| 2327 | A645 | 8p multicolored | 1.00 | .55 |
| | | Nos. 2324-2327 (4) | 3.00 | 1.55 |

**Souvenir Sheet**

| | | | | |
|---|---|---|---|---|
| 2328 | A645 | 12p multicolored | 3.00 | 3.75 |

No. 2328 contains one 29x80mm stamp.

**Christmas A646**

**1994, Nov. 25**

| | | | | |
|---|---|---|---|---|
| 2329 | A646 | 2p Wreath | .20 | .20 |
| 2330 | A646 | 6p Angels | .75 | .25 |
| 2331 | A646 | 7p Bells | .90 | .30 |
| 2332 | A646 | 8p Basket | 1.25 | .35 |
| | | Nos. 2329-2332 (4) | 3.10 | 1.10 |

**ASEANPEX '94 — A647**

#2333: a, Blue-naped parrot. b, Bleeding heart pigeon. c, Palawan peacock pheasant. d, Koch's pitta.

No. 2334, Philippine eagle, vert.

**1994**

| | | | | |
|---|---|---|---|---|
| 2333 | A647 | 2p Block of 4, #a.-d. | 2.25 | 2.25 |

**Souvenir Sheet**

| | | | | |
|---|---|---|---|---|
| 2334 | A647 | 12p multicolored | 4.00 | 4.75 |

**A648**

**Philippine Guerrilla Units in World War II — A649**

No. 2335: a, Troops entering prison. b, Prisoners escaping. Bombed building and — #2336: a, Emblem of East Central Luzon Guerrilla Area. b, Map, Mindoro Provincial Battalion, Marinduque Guerrilla Force. c, Map, Zambales Military District, Masbate Guerrilla Regiment. d, Map, Samar Area Command.

**1994    Litho.    Unwmk.    Perf. 14**

| | | | | |
|---|---|---|---|---|
| 2335 | A648 | 2p Pair, #a.-b. | 1.00 | 1.00 |
| 2336 | A649 | 2p Block of 4, #a.-d. | 2.25 | 2.25 |

No. 2335 is a continuous design. See Nos. 2392a-2392b.

**New Year 1995 (Year of the Boar) A650**

**1994**

| | | | | |
|---|---|---|---|---|
| 2337 | A650 | 2p shown | .40 | .20 |
| 2338 | A650 | 6p Boy, girl pigs | 1.50 | .35 |
| a. | | Souvenir sheet of 2, #2337-2338 + 2 labels | 3.00 | 3.75 |

No. 2338 exists imperf. Value, unused $3.

See Nos. 2459d, 2460d.

**Kalayaan, Cent. (in 1998) — A651**

a, Flag, 1898. b, Philippine flag. c, Cent. emblem.

**1994**

| | | | | |
|---|---|---|---|---|
| 2339 | A651 | 2p Strip of 3, #a.-c. | 1.50 | 1.50 |

**AIDS Awareness A652**

**1994**

| | | | | |
|---|---|---|---|---|
| 2340 | A652 | 2p multicolored | 1.00 | .30 |

**Visit of Pope John Paul II A653**

Pope John Paul II and: #2342, Papal arms, globe showing Philippines. 6p, Emblem, map of Asia. #2344, Children. a, Archdiocese of Manila. b, Diocese of Cebu. c, Diocese of Caceres. d, Diocese of Nueva Segovia. #2345, Pros. Fidel V. Ramos, Pope John Paul II.

**1995, Jan. 2**

| | | | | |
|---|---|---|---|---|
| 2341 | A653 | 2p Block of 4, #a.-d. | 1.40 | 1.40 |
| 2342 | A653 | 2p multicolored | .30 | .20 |
| 2343 | A653 | 6p multicolored | 1.00 | .25 |
| 2344 | A653 | 8p multicolored | 1.40 | .35 |
| | | Nos. 2341-2344 (4) | 4.10 | 2.20 |

**Souvenir Sheet**

| | | | | |
|---|---|---|---|---|
| 2345 | A653 | 8p multicolored | 3.25 | 3.25 |
| a. | | Overprinted in margin | 3.25 | 3.25 |

Federation of Asian Bishops' Conferences (#2343). 10th World Youth Day (#2344). Overprint in margin of No. 2345a reads "CHRISTYPEX '95 / JANUARY 4-16, 1995 / University of Santo Tomas, Manila / PHILIPPINE PHILATELIC FEDERATION."

**Lingayen Gulf Landings, 50th Anniv. — A654**

a, Map of Lingayen Gulf, ships, troops. b, Map, emblems of 6th, 37th, 40th, 43rd Divisions.

**1995, Jan. 9**

| | | | | |
|---|---|---|---|---|
| 2346 | A654 | 2p Pair, #a.-b. | 1.00 | 1.00 |

No. 2346 is a continuous design. See Nos. 2391e-2391f.

## Liberation of Manila, 50th Anniv. — A655

**1995, Feb. 3**
2347 A655 2p magenta & multi   .45 .20
2348 A655 8p blue & multi   1.75 .60
See Nos. 2392m, 2392r.

Statue honoring victims and: 2p, 8p, Various destroyed buildings. Illustration reduced.

## Jose W. Diokno, Politician — A656
(1922-87)

**1995, Feb. 26**
2349 A656 2p multicolored   .50 .20

## Intl. School, Manila, 75th Anniv. A657

**1995, Mar. 4**
    Unwmk.   Litho.   Perf. 14
2350 A657 2p shown   .35 .20
2351 A657 8p Globe, cut out figures   1.50 .40

## Wildlife — A658

**1995, Mar. 20**
2352 A658 2p Block of 4, #a-d.   2.00 2.00
    Souvenir Sheet
2353 A658 8p Sheet of 2, #a.-b.   3.25 3.25

No. 2352: a, Mousedeer. b, Tamaraw. c, Visayan warty pig. d, Palm civet. No. 2353, vert. a, Flying lemur. b, Philippine deer.

## Battles of World War II, 50th Anniv. A659

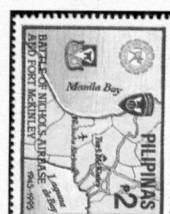
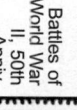

**1995, Apr. 9**
2354 A659 2p multicolored   .65 .20
2355 A659 2p Pair, #a-b.   1.25 1.25
See Nos. 2391g-2391h, 2392c.

Unit emblems and and maps showing: No. 2354, Battle of Nichols Airbase and Ft. Mckinley. No. 2355: a, Nasugbu landings. b, Tagaytay landings.

## Liberation of Baguio, 50th Anniv. A660

**1995, Apr. 27**
2356 A660 2p multicolored   .75 .25
See No. 2392d.

## Liberation of Internment Camps, 50th Anniv. A661

**1995, May 28**
2357 A661 2p UST   .75 .20
2358 A661 2p Cabanatuan   .75 .20
2359 A661 2p Los Banos   .75 .20
    Nos. 2357-2359 (3)   2.25 .60
See Nos. 2392e-2392g.

## Great Filipinos Type of 1989

**1995, June 1**
    Perf. 14x13½
    Litho.   Unwmk.
2360 A636 2p Strip of 5, #a.-e.   1.90 1.90

Persons born in 1895: a, Victorio C. Edades. b, Jovita Fuentes. c, Candido M. Africa. d, Asuncion Arriola-Perez. e, Eduardo A. Quisumbing.

## Catholic Bishops' Conference of the Philippines, 50th Anniv. A662

**1995, July 22**
    Perf. 14
2361 A662 2p multicolored   .50 .20

## A663    A664

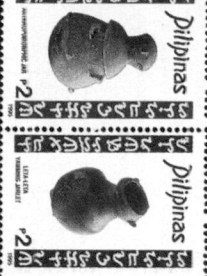

**1995, Aug. 2**
2362 A663 2p multicolored   .50 .20

Jaime N. Ferrer (1916-87).

**1995, Aug. 4**
2363 A664 12p multi, no show gin   .75 .25
   a.   Show emblem in margin   3.00 3.00
    Souvenir Sheet
2364 A664 12p Block of 4, #a.-d.   2.00 2.00
   a.   Show emblem in margin   3.00 3.00

Jars — #2363: a, Manunggul. b, Non-anthropomorphic. c, Anthropomorphic. d, Leta-leta yawning jarlet. 12p, Double spouted and legged vessel, presentation tray.

Archaeological finds. No. 2363 contains one 80x30mm stamp. No. 2364a has Jakarta '95 show emblem in margin. Issued 8/19/95.

## ASEAN Environment Year 1995 — A665

**1995, Aug. 10**
2365 A665 2p Pair, #a.-b.   1.25 1.25
    Souvenir Sheet
2366 A665 8p Sheet of 2, #a.-b.   5.50 5.50

Designs: Nos. 2365a, 2366a. Left hand holding turtle, wildlife scene. Nos. 2365b, 2366b. Right hand below fish, bird, wildlife scene.

Nos. 2365-2366 are each continuous designs.

## Philippine Eagle, New Natl. Bird — A666

**1995, Aug. 11**
2367 A666 16p multicolored   4.00 4.00

Illustration reduced.

## Mercury Drug Co., 50th Anniv. A667

**1995, Aug. 15**
2368 A667 2p multicolored   .60 .20

## Parish of St. Louis Bishop, 400th Anniv. A668

**1995, Aug. 18**
2369 A668 2p multicolored   .50 .20

## Asian-Pacific Postal Training Center, 25th Anniv. — A669

**1995, Sept. 1**
2370 A669 6p multicolored   1.00 .40
    Unwmk.   Litho.   Perf. 14

## UN, 50th Anniv. — A670

**1995, Sept. 25**
2371 A670 2p Block of 4, #a.-d.   2.40 2.40
2371E A670 2p Cesar C. Bengzon   20.00 20.00
   f.   Block of 4, #2371b-2371d, 2371E   150.00
    Souvenir Sheet
2372 A670 16p multicolored   3.00 3.00

Filipinos serving in UN: No. 2371a, #2371b, Carlos P. Romulo. b, Rafael M. Salas. c, Salvador P. Lopez. d, Jose D. Ingloo.

No. 2371E was issued with the wrong portrait and was withdrawn after two days.

## FAO, 50th Anniv. A671

**1995, Sept. 25**
2373 A671 8p multicolored   1.50 .65

## Manila Overseas Press Club, 50th anniv. A672

**1995, Oct. 5**
    Unwmk.   Litho.   Perf. 14
2373A A671a 2p multicolored   .50 .20

## Fish A687

PILIPINAS P4 — EMPEROR ANGELFISH (Pomacanthus imperator)

No. 2402: a. Emperor fish. b. Mandarinfish. c., Regal angelfish. d. Clown triggerfish. e, Raccoon butterflyfish. g., Powder brown tang. h, Two-banded anemonefish. i, Moorish idol. j, Blue tang. k, Majestic angelfish.
No. 2403: a, like #2402d. b, like #2402k. c, like #2402c. d, like #2402h.

**1996, Mar. 12**
2402 A687 4p Strip of 5, #a.-e. 5.50 5.50
2402F A687 4p Strip of 5, #g.-k. 5.50 5.50

**Miniature Sheet**
2403 A687 4p Sheet of 4, #a.-d. 3.00 3.00
 e. #2403 with new inscriptions 3.00 3.00

**Souvenir Sheet**
2404 A687 12p Lionfish 2.00 2.00
 a. #2404 with new inscriptions 2.00 2.00

Nos. 2402, 2402F have blue compressed security printing at left, black denomination, white background, margin. Nos. 2403-2404 have blue background, violet denomination, continuous design.
Nos. 2403e, 2404a inscribed in sheet margins with various INDONESIA '96 exhibition emblems. Issued: Nos. 2403e, 2404a, 3/21/96.
See Nos. 2410-2413.

BRAHMINY KITE (Haliastur indus)
PILIPINAS P2

No. 2206 Ovptd. in Green on all 4 Stamps
**1996 Litho. Wmk. 391 Perf. 14**
2405 A607 2p Sheet of 4, #a.-d. 2.50 2.50
Ovpt. in sheet margin reads: "THE YOUNG PHIL ATELISTS' SOCIETY 10TH ANNIVERSARY".

## Souvenir Sheet

PILIPINAS P10 — PALARONG PAMBANSA '96 SOCSARGEN

**Basketball — A688**

Illustration reduced.

**1996, Apr. 14**
2406 A688 10p multicolored 12.50 12.50
PALARONG/PAMBANSA '96.

PILIPINAS P4 — FRANCISCO B. ORTIGAS SR.

Francisco B. Ortigas, Sr. — A689
**1996, Apr. 30 Unwmk.**
2407 A689 4p multicolored .50 .20

---

#2355, red. Nos. 2391i-2391l, map of Philippines with blue background showing sites of Allied landings.
No. 2392: a-b, like #2335, white. c, like #2354, red. d, like #2356, white. e, like #2358, white. f, like #2357, white. g, like #2359, white. h.-l., like #2389a-2389e, purple. m, like #2347, red. n.-q., map of Philippines with green background showing location of prison camps. r, like #2348, red.

**1995, Dec. 27 Litho. Perf. 14**
2391 A681 2p Sheet of 12, #a.-l. 7.00 7.00
2392 A681 2p Sheet of 18, #a.-r. 11.00 11.00

PILIPINAS P2 — 23rd International Congress of Internal Medicine

## 23rd Intl. Congress of Internal Medicine — A682

**1996, Jan. 10 Litho. Perf. 14**
2393 A682 2p multicolored .50 .20

PILIPINAS P2 — Centennial 1895-1995 — Sun Life Assurance

## Sun Life Assurance Company of Canada in the Philippines, Cent. A683

**1996, Jan. 26**
2394 A683 2p shown .30 .20
2395 A683 8p Sun over horizon 1.40 .60

PILIPINAS P2 — Happy Valentine / I Love You

## Valentine's Day — A684

"I Love You" on Nos. 2396a-2399a, "Happy Valentine" on Nos. 2396b-2399b and: No. 2396, Pair of love birds. No. 2397, Cupid with bow and arrow. No. 2398, Box of chocolates. No. 2399, Bouquet of roses, butterfly.

**1996, Feb. 9**
2396 A684 2p Pair, #a.-b. .75 .75
2397 A684 6p Pair, #a.-b. 2.25 2.25
2398 A684 7p Pair, #a.-b. 2.50 2.50
2399 A684 8p Pair, #a.-b. 3.00 3.00
 Nos. 2396-2399 (4) 8.50 8.50

50 — PILIPINAS P2 — SANTO TOMAS University Hospital

## St. Thomas University Hospital, 50th Anniv. A685

**1996, Mar. 5**
2400 A685 2p multicolored .50 .20

Araneta University Foundation — Golden Jubilee — 1946 1996 — PILIPINAS P2

## Gregorio Araneta University Foundation, 50th Anniv. — A686

**1996, Mar. 5**
2401 A686 2p multicolored .50 .20

---

**1995, Dec. 1**
2386 A677 2p shown .30 .20
2387 A677 6p Outline of rat .95 .45
 a. Souv. sheet, #2386-2387+2 labels 3.00 3.00
No. 2387a exists imperf. Value, $5.
See Nos. 2459e, 2460e.

PILIPINAS P2 — BICOL BRIGADE — EAFT VETERANS LEGION, INC. — PHILIPPINE GUERRILLA UNITS OF WWII

## Philippine Guerrilla Units of World War II — A678

Designs: a. Emblem, FIL-American Irregular Troops (FAIT). b, Emblem, BICOL Brigade. c, Map, FIL-American Guerrilla Forces (Cavite). d, Map, South Tarlac, Northwest Pampanga Military Districts.

**1995, Dec. 8 Litho. Perf. 14**
2388 A678 2p Block of 4, #a.-d. 3.50 3.50

PILIPINAS P2 — LIBERATION OF PANAY AND ROMBLON

## Significant Events of World War II, 50th Anniv. A679

Designs: a, Map, liberation of Panay and Romblon. b, Map, Liberation of Cebu, American Division. c, Battle of Ipo Dam, 43rd Division, FIL-American Guerrillas. d, Map, Battle of Bacocang Pass, 37th Division. e, Sculpture, surrender of Gen. Yamashita.

**1995, Dec. 15**
2389 A679 2p Strip of 5, #a.-e. 6.00 6.00
See Nos. 2392h-2392l.

PILIPINAS P2 — Jose Rizal, Andres Bonifacio, Apolinario Mabini

## Revolutionary Heroes — A680

a, Jose P. Rizal (1861-96) b, Andres Bonifacio, (1863-97). c, Apolinario Mabini (1864-1903).

**1995, Dec. 27**
2390 A680 2p Set of 3, #a.-c. 1.75 1.75

## Miniature Sheets World War II Types of 1994-95 and Map of Philippines — A681

END OF WORLD WAR II, 50th ANNIVERSARY

Color of Pilipinas and denomination: Nos. 2391a-2391d, blue. #2316, red. Nos. 2391e-2391f, like #2346, red. Nos. 2391g-2391h, like

---

**1995, Oct. 24**
2374 A672 2p Total Eclipse of the Sun .85 .35

NATIONAL STAMP COLLECTING MONTH (NOVEMBER) — TWO IGOROT WOMEN, Victorio Edades — GREAT ACHIEVERS IN PHILIPPINE ART — PILIPINAS P2

## Natl. Stamp Collecting Month A673

Paintings: 2p, Two Igorot Women, by Victorio Edades. 6p, Serenade, by Carlos "Botong" Francisco. 7p, Tuba Drinkers, by Vincente Manansala. 8p, Genesis, by Fernando Ocampo. 12p, The Builders, by Edades.

**1995, Nov. 6**
2375 A673 2p multicolored .30 .20
2376 A673 6p multicolored .95 .40
2377 A673 7p multicolored 1.00 .50
2378 A673 8p multicolored 1.25 .60
 Nos. 2375-2378 (4) 3.50 1.70

**Souvenir Sheet**
2379 A673 12p multicolored 3.00 3.00
No. 2379 contains one 76x26mm stamp.

PILIPINAS P2

## Christmas A674

Musical instruments, Christmas carols.

**1995, Nov. 22**
2380 A674 2p Tambourine .30 .20
2381 A674 6p Maracas .95 .45
2382 A674 7p Guitar 1.00 .50
2383 A674 8p Drum 1.25 .65
 Nos. 2380 2383 (4) 3.50 1.80

PILIPINAS P2 — SGV & Co — 1946 1996

## Sycip Gorres Velayo & Co. Accounting Firm, 50th Anniv. A675

**1995, Nov. 27**
2384 A675 2p Abacus .50 .20

PRES. FIDEL V. RAMOS SIGNING PROCLAMATION 404

## Souvenir Sheet

Pres. Fidel V. Ramos Proclaiming November as Natl. Stamp Collecting Month — A676

**1995, Nov. 29**
2385 A676 8p multicolored 3.00 3.00

PILIPINAS P2 — ARNISONG BAGONG TAON — YEAR OF THE RAT

## New Year 1996 (Year of the Rat) A677

**PHILIPPINES**

**1996, Apr. 30**
2408 A690 4p multicolored .20

Discovery of Radioactivity, Cent. — A690

---

**1996, Apr. 30**
2409 A691 4p multicolored .20

Congregation of Dominican Sisters of St. Catherine of Siena, 300th Anniv. — A691

---

**Fish Type of 1996**

No. 2410: a, Long-horned cowfish. b, Queen angelfish. c, Long-nosed butterflyfish. d, Yellow tang. e, Blue-faced angelfish.

No. 2411: a, Saddleback butterflyfish. b, Sailfin tang. c, Harlequin tuskfish. d, Clown wrasse. e, Spotted boxfish.

No. 2412: a, like #2410e. b, like #2410c. c, like #2410b. d, like #2411c.

No. 2413, vert: a, Purple firefish. b, Pacific seahorse. c, Red-faced batfish. d, Long-nosed hawkfish.

**1996**
2410 A687 4p Strip of 5, #a-e. 5.50 5.50
2411 A687 4p Strip of 5, #a-e. 5.50 5.50
2412 A687 4p Sheet of 4, #a-d. 2.50 2.50
   e. With added inscription 2.50 2.50
2413 A687 4p Sheet of 4, #a-d. 2.50 2.50
   e. With added inscription 2.50 2.50

Nos. 2412-2413 have white background. Nos. 2410-2411 have blue background. ASEANPEX '96 (#2412-2413) inscription in sheet margin of #2412e. Added includes CHINA '96 emblem and "CHINA '96 9th Asian International Exhibition" in red. Issued: #2410-2413, 5/10; #2412e, 2413e, 5/16.

---

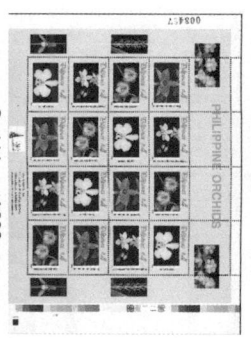

**Great Filipinos Type of 1989**

Designs: a, Carlos P. Garcia (1896-1971), politician. b, Casimiro del Rosario (1896-1962), physicist. c, Geronima T. Pecson (1896-1989), politician. d, Cesar C. Bengson (1896-1992), lawyer. e, Jose Corazon de Jesus (1896-1932), writer.

**1996, June 1    Litho.    Unwmk.**
2414 A536 4p Strip of 5, #a-e. 2.50 2.50

**1996, June 1    Perf. 13½**
2414 A536 4p Strip of 5, #a-e. 2.50 2.50

---

ABS CBN (Broadcasting Network), 50th Anniv. — A692

**1996, June 13    Perf. 14**
2415 A692 4p shown .50 .20
2416 A692 8p Rooster, world map 1.00 .40

---

**1996, June 24**
2417 A693 4p multicolored .50 .25

Manila, Convention City A693

---

**1996, July 3**
2418 A694 4p multicolored .50 .25

Jose Cojuangco, Sr. (1896-1976), Businessman, Public Official — A694

---

**Symbols of Philippines, U.S.: 4p, Hats. 8p, National birds. 16p, Flags, vert.**

**1996, July 4**
2419 A695 4p multicolored .50 .25
2420 A695 8p multicolored 1.40 .50

Philippine-American Friendship Day — A695

**Souvenir Sheet**
2421 A695 16p multicolored 3.50 3.50

Modern Olympic Games, Cent. A696

---

No. 2426a, Boxing. 6p. No. 2426b, Athletics. 7p. No. 2426c, Swimming. 8p. No. 2426d, Equestrian.

**1996, July 19    Unwmk.**
**Litho.    Perf. 14**
2422 A696 4p multicolored .50 .25
2423 A696 6p multicolored .70 .40
2424 A696 7p multicolored .85 .45
2425 A696 8p multicolored .50 .50

**Miniature Sheet**
2426 A696 4p Sheet of 4, #a-d. 3.50 3.50

Nos. 2422-2425 have colored background, blue security code at right, denominations at LR. Nos. 2426a-2426d have colored circles on white background, blue security code at top, and denominations at UR, UL, LR, LL, respectively.

---

**1996, Aug. 15**
2427 A697 4p multicolored .50 .25

University of the East, 50th Anniv. A697

---

**Orchids — A698**

No. 2428: a, Dendrobium anosmum. b, Phalaenopsis equestris-alba. c, Vanda javieri.

No. 2429: a, Renanthera philippinensis. b, Dendrobium schuetzei. c, Dendrobium taurinum. d, Vanda lamellata.

No. 2430: a, Coelogyne pandurata. b, Vanda merrillii. c, Cymbidium aliciae. d, Dendrobium topaziacum.

**1996, Sept. 26**
2428 A698 4p Block or strip of 4, #a-d. 2.25 2.25
2429 A698 4p Block or strip of 4, #a-d. 2.25 2.25

**Miniature Sheet**
2430 A698 4p Sheet of 4, #a-d. 3.50 3.50

Nos. 2428-2429 were printed in sheets of 16 stamps. ASEANPEX '96 (#2430). Complete sheets of Nos. 2428-2429 have ASEANPEX emblem in selvage.

---

**1996, Sept. 30**
2431 A699 4p multicolored .50 .25

6th Asia Pacific Intl. Trade Fair A699

---

12p, Pamela Hetherington, "Coronation." Living Gold "Erin Treasure," Eleanor Spicer "White Bouquet."

**1996, Oct. 9**
2432 A700 4p Block of 4, #a-d. 2.00 2.00

**Souvenir Sheet**
2433 A700 16p multicolored 3.00 3.00

Orchids: No. 2434: a, Fran's Fantasy "Alea." b, Malvarosa Green Goddess "Nani." c, Ports of Paradise "Emerald Isle." d, Mem. Conrada Perez "Nani."

No. 2435: a, Pokai tangerine "Lea." b, Mem. Roselyn Reisman "Diana." c, Mem. Benigno Aquino "Flying Aces."

**TAIPEX '96 — A701**

**1996, Oct. 21    Litho.    Perf. 14**
2434 A701 4p Block of 4, #a-d. 2.25 2.25
2435 A701 4p Block of 4, #a-d. 2.25 2.25

**Souvenir Sheet**
2436 A701 12p multicolored 3.50 3.50

Nos. 2434-2435 were issued in sheets of 16 stamps. No. 2436 contains one 80x30mm stamp.

1996 Asia-Pacific Economic Cooperation — A702

---

Winning entries of stamp design competition: 4p, Ship behind mountains, airplane, skyscrapers, tower, ship, satellite dish, vert. 7p, Skyscrapers. 8p, Flags of nations beside path, globe, skyscrapers, sun, vert.

**1996, Oct. 30**
2437 A702 4p multicolored .55 .25
2438 A702 6p shown .85 .40
2439 A702 7p multicolored 1.00 .45
2440 A702 8p multicolored 1.10 .50

Nos. 2437-2440 (4) 3.50 1.60

---

**UNICEF, 50th Anniv. — A700**

Children in montage of scenes studying, working, playing — #2432: a, Blue & multi. b, Purple & multi. c, Green & multi. d, Red & multi.

16p, Four children, horiz.

---

Designs: 4p, Philippine Nativity scene, vert. 6p, Midnight Mass. 7p, Carolers. 8p, Carolers with Carabao, vert.

**Christmas A703**

**1996, Nov. 5**
2441 A703 4p multicolored .55 .25
2442 A703 6p multicolored .85 .40
2443 A703 7p multicolored 1.00 .45
2444 A703 8p multicolored 1.00 .50

Nos. 2441-2444 (4) 3.50 1.60

---

**1996, Nov. 11**
2445 A704 4p multicolored .55 .25

Eugenio P. Perez (1896-1957), Politician — A704

---

New Year 1997 (Year of the Ox) A705

**1996, Dec. 1    Litho.    Perf. 14**
2446 A705 4p Carabao .60 .25
2447 A705 6p Tamaraw .90 .40
   a. Souv. sheet of 2, #2446-2447 2.75 2.75

No. 2447a exists imperf. Value, $2.50. See Nos. 2459f, 2460f.

## ASEANPEX '96, Intl. Philatelic Exhibition, Manila — A706

## Independence, Cent. (in 1998) — A707

Jose P. Rizal (1861-96): No. 2448: a, At 14 years. b, At 18. c, At 25. d, At 31.
No. 2449: a, "Noli Me Tangere." b, Gomburza to whom Rizal dedicated "El Filibusterismo." c, Oyang Dapitana, by Rizal. d, Ricardo Camicero, by Rizal.
No. 2450, horiz: a, Rizal's house, Calamba. b, University of St. Tomas, Manila, 1611. c, Orient Hotel, Manila. d, Dapitan during Rizal's time.
No. 2451, horiz: a, Central University, Madrid. b, British Museum, London. c, Botanical Garden, Madrid. d, Heidelberg, Germany. No. 2452, Rizal at 14, horiz. No. 2453, Rizal at 18, horiz. No. 2454, Rizal at 25, horiz. No. 2455, Rizal at 31, horiz.

**1996**

| | | | | |
|---|---|---|---|---|
| 2448 | A706 | 4p Block of 4, #a.-d. | 2.25 | 2.25 |
| 2449 | A706 | 4p Block of 4, #a.-d. | 2.25 | 2.25 |
| 2450 | A706 | 4p Block of 4, #a.-d. | 2.25 | 2.25 |
| 2451 | A706 | 4p Block of 4, #a.-d. | 2.25 | 2.25 |

**Souvenir Sheets**

| | | | | |
|---|---|---|---|---|
| 2452 | A706 | 12p multicolored | 2.50 | 2.50 |
| 2453 | A706 | 12p multicolored | 2.50 | 2.50 |
| 2454 | A706 | 12p multicolored | 2.50 | 2.50 |
| 2455 | A706 | 12p multicolored | 2.50 | 2.50 |

Issued: #2448, #2452, 12/14; #2449, 2453, 12/15; #2450, 2454, 12/16; #2451, 2455, 12/17. Nos. 2448-2451 were issued in sheets of 16 stamps.

**1996, Dec. 20**

Revolutionary heroes: a, Fr. Mariano C. Gomez (1799-1872). b, Fr. Jose A. Burgos (1837-72). c, Fr. Jacinto Zamora (1835-72).

| | | | | |
|---|---|---|---|---|
| 2456 | A707 | 4p Strip of 3, #a.-c. | 2.50 | 2.50 |

Jose Rizal — A709

**1996, Dec. 30      Litho.      Perf. 14**

| | | | | |
|---|---|---|---|---|
| 2458 | A709 | 4p multicolored | .65 | .25 |

**New Year Types of 1991-96**

**1997, Feb. 12      Litho.      Unwmk.**

| | | | | |
|---|---|---|---|---|
| 2459 | | Sheet of 6 | 3.75 | 3.75 |
| a. | A580 | 4p like #2126 | .60 | .60 |
| b. | A608 | 4p like #2208 | .60 | .60 |
| c. | A626 | 4p like #2284 | .60 | .60 |
| d. | A650 | 4p like #2337 | .60 | .60 |
| e. | A677 | 4p like #2386 | .60 | .60 |
| f. | A705 | 4p like #2446 | .60 | .60 |
| 2460 | | Sheet of 6 | 5.25 | 5.25 |
| a. | A580 | 6p like #2127 | .85 | .85 |
| b. | A608 | 6p like #2207 | .85 | .85 |
| c. | A626 | 6p like #2285 | .85 | .85 |
| d. | A650 | 6p like #2338 | .85 | .85 |
| e. | A677 | 6p like #2387 | .85 | .85 |
| f. | A705 | 6p like #2447 | .85 | .85 |

Hong Kong '97.
Nos. 2459a-2459b, 2460a-2460b have white margins, color differences. Nos. 2459c-2459d, 2459f, 2460c-2460d, 2460f do not have blue security printing, and have color differences. Nos. 2459e, 2460e, do not have blue security printing, and have color differences.
Nos. 2459a-2459f, 2460a-2460f are all dated "1997".

## Holy Rosary Seminary, Bicent. A710

**1997, Feb. 18      multicolored**

| | | | | |
|---|---|---|---|---|
| 2461 | A710 | 4p multicolored | .55 | .25 |

## Philippine Army, Cent. A711

**1997, Feb. 18      multicolored**

| | | | | |
|---|---|---|---|---|
| 2462 | A711 | 4p multicolored | .55 | .25 |

## Natl. Symbols Type of 1993-96 and:

Gem — A711a

*Blue "PILIPINAS" on bottom, except #2464 (Black)*

| 1997 | | Litho. Unwmk. | Perf. 14x13½ | |
|---|---|---|---|---|
| 2463 | A610h | 1p like #2212A | .25 | .25 |
| 2463A | A610u | 2p lilac #2217A | .30 | .25 |
| 2463B | A610o | 3p like #2212A | .50 | 1.75 |
| 2464 | A711a | 4p multicolored | .75 | .50 |
| 2465 | A610i | 5p like #2222 | .75 | 1.00 |
| 2465A | A610i | 5p like #2222 | .75 | 1.00 |
| 2466 | A610k | 6p like #2223A | 2.50 | 1.00 |
| 2466A | A610k | 6p like #2223A | 2.50 | 1.00 |
| 2467 | A610m | 7p like #2224A | 3.00 | 1.25 |
| 2467A | A610m | 7p like #2224A | 3.00 | 1.25 |
| 2468 | A610o | 8p like #2227 | 3.50 | 1.50 |
| 2468A | A610o | 8p like #2227 | 3.50 | 1.50 |
| 2469 | A610p | 10p like #2229 | 4.00 | 2.00 |
| 2469A | A610p | 10p like #2229 | 4.00 | 2.00 |
| | | Nos. 2463-2469A (14) | 29.30 | 16.25 |

Nns. 2463, 2465, 2466, 2467, 2468 and 2469 do not have blue compressed security printing at top and are dated "1997."
Nos. 2463A-2464, 2465A, 2466A, 2467A, 2468A, and 2469A have blue compressed security printing at top and are dated "1997." Issued: #2463, 2469, 2/27/97; 2463A, 4/15; 2463B, 2466A, 4/18; 2465A, 4/29; #2464, 6/10; #2465, 2/26; #2466, 3/10; #2467, 3/7; #2467A, 5/8; #2468, 3/6; #2468A, 5/8; #2469A, 4/22.

## Dept. of Finance, Cent. A712

**1997, Apr. 8      multicolored      Perf. 14**

| | | | | |
|---|---|---|---|---|
| 2471 | A712 | 4p multicolored | .55 | .25 |

## Philippine Red Cross, 50th Anniv. A713

**1997, Apr. 8      multicolored**

| | | | | |
|---|---|---|---|---|
| 2472 | A713 | 4p multicolored | .55 | .25 |

## Philamlife Insurance Co., 50th Anniv. A714

**1997, Apr. 8      multicolored**

| | | | | |
|---|---|---|---|---|
| 2473 | A714 | 4p multicolored | .55 | .25 |

## J. Walter Thompson Advertising, 50th Anniv. in Philippines A715

**1997, Apr. 18      multicolored**

| | | | | |
|---|---|---|---|---|
| 2474 | A715 | 4p multicolored | .55 | .25 |

**Souvenir Sheet**

World Philatelic Exhibition
May 29 – June 8, 1997
San Francisco, California U.S.A.
PILIPINAS P16
PACIFIC 97
PHILIPPINE-AMERICAN FRIENDSHIP DAY
REPUBLIC DAY
1946-1996 50TH ANNIVERSARY

Philippine-American Friendship Day, Republic Day, 50th Anniv. — A716

Illustration reduced.

**1997, May 29**

| | | | | |
|---|---|---|---|---|
| 2475 | A716 | 16p multicolored PACIFIC 97. | 4.25 | 4.25 |

## Wild Animals — A717

World Wildlife Fund: No. 2476, Visayan spotted deer. No. 2477, Visayan spotted deer (doe & fawn). No. 2478, Visayan warty pig. No. 2479, Visayan warty pig (adult, young).

**1997, July 24**

| | | | | |
|---|---|---|---|---|
| 2476 | | 4p multicolored | .65 | .30 |
| a. | | Sheet of 8 | 5.50 | 5.50 |
| 2477 | | 4p multicolored | .65 | .30 |
| a. | | Sheet of 8 | 5.50 | 5.50 |
| 2478 | | 4p multicolored | .65 | .30 |
| a. | | Sheet of 8 | 5.50 | 5.50 |
| 2479 | | 4p multicolored | .65 | .30 |
| a. | | Sheet of 8 | 5.50 | 5.50 |
| b. | A717 | 6p like #2447 | 2.75 | 2.75 |
| | | Set of 4 sheets, #2476a-2479a | 22.00 | 22.00 |

No. 2479b was issued in sheets of 16 stamps.

## ASEAN, 30th Anniv. — A718

Founding signatories: No. 2480, Adam Malik, Indonesia, Tun Abdul Razak, Malaysia, Narcisco Ramos, Philippines, S. Rajaratnam, Singapore, Thanat Khoman, Thailand. No. 2481, Natl. flags of founding signatories. No. 2482, Flags of current ASEAN countries. No. 2483, Flags of ASEAN countries surrounding globe.

**1997, Aug. 7      Perf. 14**

| | | | | |
|---|---|---|---|---|
| 2480 | | 4p multicolored | .40 | .25 |
| 2481 | | 4p multicolored | .40 | .25 |
| a. | A718 | Pair, #2480-2481 | 1.00 | 1.00 |
| 2482 | | 6p multicolored | .70 | .40 |
| 2483 | | 6p multicolored | .70 | .40 |
| a. | A718 | Pair, #2482-2483 | 1.50 | 1.50 |
| | | Nos. 2480-2483 (4) | 2.20 | 1.30 |

## World Scout Parliamentary Union, 2nd General Assembly A719

**1997, Aug. 17**

| | | | | |
|---|---|---|---|---|
| 2484 | A719 | 4p multicolored | .60 | .25 |

## Manuel L. Quezon University, 50th Anniv. A720

**1997, Aug. 19**

| | | | | |
|---|---|---|---|---|
| 2485 | A720 | 4p multicolored | .60 | .25 |

## Great Filipinos Type of 1989

Famous people: a, Justice Roberto Regala (1897-1979). b, Doroteo Espiritu, dental surgeon, inventor. c, Elisa R. Ochoa (1897-1978), nurse, tennis champion. d, Mariano and Marcos (1907-1945), lawyer, educator. e, Jose F. Romero (1897-1978), editor.

**1997, June 1      Perf. 14x13½      Litho.      Unwmk.**

| | | | | |
|---|---|---|---|---|
| 2486 | A536 | 4p Strip of 5, #a.-e. | 2.25 | 2.25 |

## Battle of Candon, 1898 A721

4p, Don Federico Isabelo Abaya, revolutionary leader against Spanish. 6p, Soldier on horseback.

**1997, Sept. 24      Perf. 14**

| | | | | |
|---|---|---|---|---|
| 2487 | A721 | 4p multi, vert. | .45 | .25 |
| 2488 | A721 | 6p multi | .75 | .40 |

St. Therese of Lisieux (1873-97) — A722

**1997, Oct. 16**
2489 A722 6p multicolored ... .75 .40

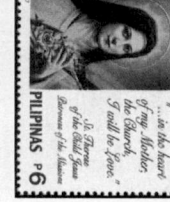

Stamp and Philatelic Division, 50th Anniv. — A723

**1997, Nov. 4** Litho. Perf. 14
2490 A723 4p multicolored ... .40 .25
2491 A723 6p multicolored ... .60 .40
2492 A723 7p multicolored ... .70 .40
2493 A723 8p multicolored ... .80 .55
Nos. 2490-2493 (4) ... 2.50 1.70

Heinrich von Stephan (1831-97) — A724

**1997, Oct. 24** Litho. Perf. 14
2494 A723 16p multicolored ... 3.50 3.50

Souvenir Sheet

No. 2494 contains one 80x30mm stamp.

Asian and Pacific Decade of Disabled Persons — A725

**1997, Oct. 24** Litho. Perf. 14
2495 A724 4p multicolored ... .60 .25

**1997, Oct. 24**
2496 6p multicolored ... .90 .45
2497 A726 8p multicolored ... 1.25 .50

Souvenir Sheet
2498 A726 16p multicolored ... 4.25 4.25

No. 2498 is a continuous design.

Intl. Year of the Reef — A726

Illustration reduced.

Natl. Stamp Collecting Month — A726a

Paintings: 4p, Dalagang Bukid, by Fernando Amorsolo, vert. 6p, Bagong Taon, by Arturo Luz, vert. 7p, encounter of the Nuestra Sra. de Cavadonga and the Centurion, by Alfredo Carmelo. 16p, Pista sa Nayon, by Carlos Francisco.

**1997, Nov. 7** Litho. Perf. 14
2499 A727 4p multicolored ... .40 .25
2500 A727 6p multicolored ... .75 .40
2501 A727 7p multicolored ... .85 .45
2502 A727 8p multicolored ... 1.00 .50
Nos. 2499-2502 (4) ... 3.00 1.60

Independence, Cent. — A728

Various stained glass windows.

**1997, Nov. 30**
2503 A728 4p Strip of 3, #a.-c. ... 1.75 1.75

Various monuments to Andres Bonifacio (1863-97), revolutionary. Katipunan: a, red & multi. b, yellow & multi. c, blue & multi.

New Year 1998 (Year of the Tiger) — A729

**1997, Dec. 1**
2504 A729 4p shown ... .60 .25
2505 A729 6p Tigers diff. ... .90 .40
a. Souvenir sheet, 2 labels ... 3.25 3.25

No. 2505a exists imperf. Value, $2.50.

Philippine Eagle — A730

National Bird PHILIPPINE EAGLE

**1997, Dec. 5**
2506 A730 20p Looking right ... 2.75 1.25
2507 A730 30p Looking forward ... 4.25 2.00
2508 A730 50p On cliff ... 7.00 3.50
Nos. 2506-2508 (3) ... 14.00 6.75

Game Cocks — A731

No. 2509: a, Hatch grey. b, Spangled roundhead. c, Racey mug. d, Silver grey. No. 2510, vert: a, Groy. b, Kelso. c, Bruner roundhead. d, Democrat.

Christmas — A727

2498E A726a 16p multicolored ... 3.50 3.50

Souvenir Sheet

No. 2498E contains one 80x30mm stamp.

Nos. 2498A-2498D (4)
2498A A726a 4p multicolored ... .40 .25
2498B A726a 6p multicolored ... .60 .40
2498C A726a 7p multicolored ... .70 .45
2498D A726a 8p multicolored ... .80 .50

Souvenir Sheet
2509 A731 12p multicolored ... 1.75 1.75
2510 A731 16p multicolored ... 2.00 2.00

Nos. 2509, 2510 ... 
No. 2511, Cock fight, vert. No. 2512, Cocks facing each other ready to fight.

2511 A731 12p multicolored ... 1.75 1.75
2512 A731 16p multicolored ... 2.75 2.75

Souvenir Sheets

No. 2512 contains one 80x30mm stamp.

**1997, Dec. 18**
2509 A731 4p Block of 4, #a.-d. ... 2.00 2.00
2510 A731 4p Block of 4, #a.-d. ... 2.00 2.00

Art Association of the Philippines, 50th Anniv. — A732

Stylized designs: No. 2513, Colors of flag, sunburst. No. 2514, Association's initials, clenched fist holding artist's implements.

**1998, Feb. 14** Unwmk. Litho. Perf. 14
2513 A732 4p multicolored ... .65 .25
2514 A732 4p multicolored ... .65 .25
a. Pair, #2513-2514 ... 1.50 1.50

Club Filipino Social Organization, Cent. — A733

SAGISAG NG KARANGALAN AT KALAYAAN

**1998, Feb. 14**
2515 A733 4p multicolored ... .60 .25

Blessed Marie Eugenie (1817-98) — A734

**1998, Feb. 25**
2516 A734 4p multicolored ... .60 .25

Fulbright Educational Exchange Program in the Philippines, 50th Anniv. — A735

**1998, Feb. 25**
2517 A735 4p multicolored ... .60 .25

Heroes of the Revolution — A736

National flag and: 4p, Melchora Aquino (1812-1919). 11p, Andres Bonifacio (1863-97). 13p, Apolinario Mabini (1864-1903). 15p, Emilio Aguinaldo (1869-1964).

**1998** Litho. Unwmk. Perf. 13½
2518 A736 4p multicolored ... .60 .30
2519 A736 11p multicolored ... 1.50 .65
2520 A736 13p multicolored ... 1.60 .80
2521 A736 15p multicolored ... 1.90 .90
Nos. 2518-2521 (4) ... 5.60 2.65

Issued: 4p, 3/3/98. 11p, 13p, 15p, 3/24/98. #2519-2521 exist dated "1999."

Apo View Hotel, 50th Anniv. — A737

**1998, Mar. 20** Perf. 14
2522 A737 4p multicolored ... .60 .30

Philippine Cultural High School, 75th Anniv. — A738

2523 A738 4p multicolored ... .60 .30

Victorino Mapa High School, 75th Anniv. — A739

**1998, May 5**
2524 A739 4p multicolored ... .60 .30

Philippine Navy, Cent. — A740

**1998, May 5**
2525 A740 4p multicolored ... .60 .30

University of Baguio, 50th Anniv. — A741

**1998, May 5**
2526 A741 4p multicolored ... .60 .30

Philippine Maritime Institute, 50th Anniv. — A742

**1998, May 5**
2527 A742 4p multicolored ... .60 .30

Heroes of the Revolution Type of 1998

Design: Gen. Antonio Luna (1866-99).

**1998, Apr. 30** Litho. Unwmk. Perf. 13½
2528 A736 5p multicolored ... .60 .30

See Nos. 2528, 2546-2550, 2578-2597, 2607.

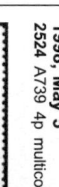
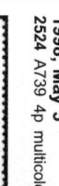
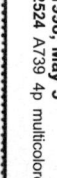

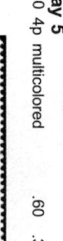

PHILIPPINE POSTAL SERVICE 1898 CENTENNIAL 1998 — PILIPINAS P6
PILIPINAS P6 — PHILIPPINE POSTAL SERVICE 1898 CENTENNIAL 1998

A754

Pasko '98 — PILIPINAS P6

A755

Philippine Postal Service, Cent.— #2555: a, Child placing envelope into mailbox, globe. b, Arms encircling globe, envelopes, Philippine flag as background. c, Airplane, globe, various stamps over building. d, Child holding up hands, natl. flag colors, envelopes. 15p, Child holding envelope as it crisscrosses globe.

**1998, Nov. 4**
2555 A754 6p Block of 4, #a.-d.   3.00 3.00
    **Souvenir Sheet**
2556 A754 15p multicolored   4.00 4.00
   No. 2556 contains one 76x30mm stamp.

**1998, Nov. 5**
   Pilipinas; Various star lanterns.
2557 A755 6p multicolored   .65 .35
2558 A755 11p multicolored   1.25 .70
2559 A755 13p multicolored   1.60 .85
2560 A755 15p multicolored   1.75 1.00
     Nos. 2557-2560 (4)   5.25 2.90
     Pasko '98.

**Souvenir Sheets**

PILIPINAS '98

Philippines '98, Philippine Cent. Invitational Intl. Philatelic Exhibition — A756

Revolutionary scenes, stamps of revolutionary govt.: No. 2561, Soldiers celebrating, #Y1-Y2. No. 2562, Signing treaty, telegraph stamps, #YF1, "Recibos" (Official receipt) stamps. No. 2564, Procession, #Y3, perf. examples of #YP1. No. 2565, New government convening, "Trans de Ganades" (cattle transfer) stamp, Libertad essay. Illustration reduced.

**1998**
2561 A756 15p multicolored   5.50 5.50
2562 A756 15p multicolored   5.50 5.50
2563 A756 15p multicolored   5.50 5.50
2564 A756 15p multicolored   5.50 5.50
2565 A756 15p multicolored   27.50 27.50
     Nos. 2561-2565 (5)

No. 2561 exists imperf. The first printing has varying amounts of black offset on the reverse. Value, $60. The second printing does not have the offset. Value, $12.50.
Nos. 2561-2565 were issued one each day from 11/5-11/9.

---

Issued: 4p, 10p, 18p, 5/18/98. 2p, 8p, 7/20/98.

Pilipinas P4

Philippine Centennial — A749a

No. 2550A: a, Spoliarium, by Juan Luna. c, 1st display of Philippine flag, 1898. d, Execution of Jose Rizal, 1896. e, Andres Bonifacio. f, Church, Malolos.

**1998, July**
2550A A749a   Souv. booklet   32.50
   b.   4p multicolored   .55
   c.   8p multicolored   1.10
   d.-e.   16p multicolored   2.25
   f.   20p multicolored   2.75
No. 2550A contains panes of 4 each of Nos. 2550Ab-2550Ac and one pane of 1 each of Nos. 2550Ad-2550Af.

PILIPINAS P4 — Philippine Coconut Industry, Cent. A750

*Perf. 14*
**1998, Oct. 9**
2551 A750 4p multicolored   1.00 .30

PILIPINAS P4 — Holy Spirit Adoration Distoro in Philippines, 75th Anniv. A751

*Perf. 14*
**1990, Oct. 9**
2652 A751 1p multicolored   1.25 .30

Universal Delciration of Human Rights, 50th Anniv. — A752

PILIPINAS P4

**1998, Oct. 24**
2553 A752 4p multicolored   .90 .30

Intl. Year of the Ocean — A753

PILIPINAS P15

**1998, Oct. 24**
2554 A753 15p multicolored   2.60 1.10
   a.   Souvenir sheet, #2554   4.50 4.50
Illustration reduced (#2554).
No. 2554a is a continuous design.

---

P4 — Melchora Aquino
P4 — Nazaria Lagos
P4 — Agueda Kahabagan

Philippine Independence, Cent.— A747

Patriots of the revolution: a, Melchora Aquino. b, Nazaria Lagos. c, Agueda Kahabagan.

**1998, June 9   Litho.   Unwmk.   *Perf. 14***
2540 A747 4p Strip of 3, #a.-c.   1.50 1.50

Sa pisong ibibigay, ilog Pasig ay mabubuhay — PILIPINAS P4

Pasig River Campaign for Waste Management — A748

**1998, June 19**
2541 A748 4p multicolored   .60 .20

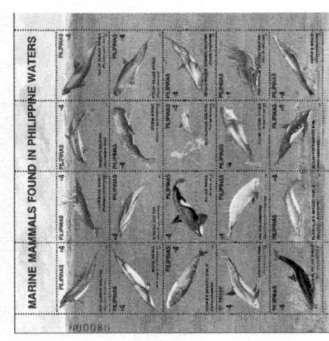

MARINE MAMMALS FOUND IN PHILIPPINE WATERS

Marine Mammals — A749

No. 2542: a, Bottlenose dolphin. b, Humpback whale. c, Fraser's dolphin. d, Melon-headed whale. e, Minke whale. f, Striped dolphin. g, Sperm whale. h, Pygmy killer whale. i, Cuvier's beaked whale. j, Killer whale. k, Bottlenose dolphin. l, Long-snouted spinner dolphin. m, Risso's dolphin. n, Finless porpoise. o, Pygmy sperm whale. p, Pantropical spotted dolphin. q, False killer whale. r, Blainville's beaked whale. s, Rough-toothed dolphin. t, Bryde's whale. 15p, Dugong.

**1998, June 19**
2542 A749 4p Sheet of 20, #a.-t.   10.00 10.00
     **Souvenir Sheet**
2543 A749 15p multicolored   4.00 4.00

Nos. 2218a, 2218b, 2220 Ovptd. in Gold with Philippine Centennial Centennial Emblem

**1998   Litho.   Unwmk.   *Perf. 14x13½***
2544 A610f   3p multi, dated "1995" (#2218b)   .25
2544A A610f   3p multi, dated 1994 (#2218a)   60.00 60.00
2545 A610g   4p Block of 14, #a.-n.   15.00 25.00
   a.-n.   Any single   .75 .75
Issued: No. 2544, 7/7/98; 2545, 6/12/9.
No. 2544A, dated "1994," was overprinted in error.

**Heroes of the Revolution Type of 1998**

2p, Emilio Jacinto. 4p, Jose P. Rizal. 8p, Marcelo H. del Pilar. 10p, Gregorio del Pilar. 18p, Juan Luna.

*Perf. 13½*
**1998**
2546 A736 2p multicolored   .60 .25
2547 A736 4p multicolored   .60 .30
2548 A736 8p multicolored   1.00 .50
2549 A736 10p multicolored   1.25 .70
2550 A736 18p multicolored   2.50 1.25
     Nos. 2546-2550 (5)   5.95 3.00
   #2548 and 2549 exist dated "1999."

---

FILIPINAS P15 — EXPO 98

Expo '98, Lisbon A743

4p, Boat on lake, vert. 15p, Vinta on water. 15p, Main lobby, Philippine Pavilion.

*Perf. 14*
**1998, May 22**
2529 A743 4p multicolored   .50 .25
2530 A743 15p multicolored   2.00 1.00
     **Souvenir Sheet**
2531 A743 15p multicolored   3.50 3.50
   No. 2531 contains one 80x30mm stamp.

Clark Special Economic Zone — A744

PILIPINAS P15

Illustration reduced.

**1998, May 28**
2532 A744 15p multicolored   1.90 1.00

Flowers — A745

P4 — Artabotrys hexapetalus GUMAMELA
P4 — Hibiscus rosa-sinensis SAMPAGUITA
P4 — Gardenia jasminoides ADELFA
P4 — Nerium oleander ILANG-ILANG

#2533: a, Artabotrys hexapetalus. b, Hibiscus rosa-sinensis. c, Norium oleander. d, Jasminum sambac.
#2534, vert: a, Gardenia jasminoides. b, Ixora coccinea. c, Erythrina indica. d, Abelmoschus moschatus.
#2535, Medinilla magnifica.

**1998, May 29**
2533 A745 4p Block of 4, #a.-d.   2.25 2.25
2534 A745 4p Block of 4, #a.-d.   2.25 2.25
     **Souvenir Sheet**
2535 A745 15p multicolored   4.00 4.00

**Great Filipinos Type of 1989**

Designs: a, Andres R. Soriano (1898-1964). b, Tomas Fonacier (1898-1991). c, Josefa L. Escoda (1898-1945). d, Lorenzo M. Tañada (1898-1992). e, Lazaro Francisco (1898-1980).

*Perf. 14x13½*
**1998, June 1**
2536 A536 4p Strip of 5, #a.-e.   2.25 2.25

PILIPINAS P15

Philippine Independence, Cent.— A746

No. 2537, Mexican flag, sailing ship. 2538, Woman holding Philippine flag, monument, sailing ship, map of Philippines. No. 2539, Spanish flag, Catholic Church, religious icon, Philippine flag.

*Perf. 14*
**1998, June 3**
2537 A746 15p multicolored   1.40 .40
2538 A746 15p multicolored   1.40 .40
2539 A746 15p multicolored   1.40 .40
   a.   Strip of 3, #2537-2539   4.50 4.50
   b.   Souvenir sheet, #2537-2539 + 3 labels   5.00 5.00
See Mexico #2079-2080, Spain #2949. For overprint see #2629.

## 1998, Nov. 10

| | | | |
|---|---|---|---|
| 2566 | A757 | 6p Taking oath | .75 .40 |
| 2567 | A757 | 15p Giving speech | 1.75 1.00 |

Pres. Joseph Ejercito Estrada A757

**Shells — A758**

## 1998, Nov. 6
**Unwmk.** **Litho.** **Perf. 14**

| | | | |
|---|---|---|---|
| 2568 | A758 | 4p Block of 4, #a.-d. | 2.25 2.25 |
| 2569 | A758 | 4p Block of 4, #a.-d. | 2.25 2.25 |

**Souvenir Sheet**

2570 A758 8p Sheet of 2, #a.-b. 5.00 5.00
a. Souvenir sheet, Type II 10.00 10.00

No. 2568: a, Mitra papalis. b, Vexillum citrinum. c, Vexilum rugosum. d, Volema carinfera.

No. 2569: a, Teramachia dalii. b, Nassarius vitiensis. c, Cymbiola imperialis. d, Cymbiola aulica.

No. 2570: a, Nassarius papillosus. b, Fasci-olaria trapezium.

c. Cloud in sheet margin touches "s's" of Shells. On #2570c, cloud does not touch "s's" of Shells. Colors are dark on #2570c, lighter on #2570.

PILIPINAS P6

Natl. Stamp Collecting Month — A759

## 1998, Nov. 25

| | | | |
|---|---|---|---|
| 2571 | A759 | 6p black & blue | .60 .40 |
| 2572 | A759 | 11p black & brown | 1.25 .70 |
| 2573 | A759 | 13p black & lilac | 1.40 .80 |
| 2574 | A759 | 15p black & green | 1.75 .95 |
| | | Nos. 2571-2574 (4) | 5.00 2.85 |

**Souvenir Sheet**

2575 A759 15p black 3.25 3.25
No. 2575 contains one 26x76mm stamp.

Motion picture, director, 6p, "Ang Sawa Sa Lumang Simboryo," Gerardo de Leon. 11p, "Dyesebel," Gerardo de Leon. 13p, "Prinsipe Amante," Lamberto V. Avellana. No. 2574, "Anak Dalita," Lamberto V. Avellana. No. 2575, "Siete Infantes de Lara," costume design by Carlos "Botong" Francisco.

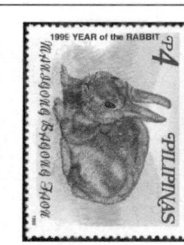

1996 YEAR of the RABBIT
PILIPINAS P4

## 1998, Dec. 1

| | | | |
|---|---|---|---|
| 2576 | A760 | 4p shown | .50 .25 |
| 2577 | A760 | 11p Two rabbits | 1.50 .70 |
| a. | | Souvenir sheet, #2576-2577 | 3.75 3.75 |

No. 2577a exists imperf. Value, $5.

New Year 1999 (Year of the Rabbit) A760

## 1998, Nov. 20
**Unwmk.** **Litho.** **Imperf.**

| | | | |
|---|---|---|---|
| 2575A | A759a | 15p multi | 2.50 2.50 |
| 2575B | A759a | 15p multi | 2.50 2.50 |
| 2575C | A759a | 15p multi | 2.50 2.50 |
| 2575D | A759a | 15p multi | 2.50 2.50 |
| 2575E | A759a | 15p multi | 2.50 2.50 |
| 2575F | A759a | 15p multi | 2.50 2.50 |
| | | Nos. 2575A-2575F (6) | 15.00 15.00 |

Pride, various women and. No. 2575A, Eagle (Resources). No. 2575B, Costume (Heritage). No. 2575C, Flag (Filipino People). No. 2575D, Artifacts with text (Literature). No. 2575E, Rice terraces (Engineering). No. 2575F, "Noli Me Tangere" (Citizenry).

Nos. 2575A-2575F have simulated perforations.

## Philippine Centennial — A759a

PILIPINAS P15

## Heroes of the Revolution Type of 1998
**Booklet Stamps**
**Yellow Background**

## 1998, Dec. 15
**Litho.** **Perf. 13½**

| | | | |
|---|---|---|---|
| 2578 | A736 | 15p like #2518 | .70 .40 |
| 2579 | A736 | 15p like #2519 | .70 .40 |
| 2580 | A736 | 15p like #2520 | .70 .40 |
| 2581 | A736 | 15p like #2521 | .70 .40 |
| 2582 | A736 | 15p like #2528 | .70 .40 |
| 2583 | A736 | 15p like #2547 | .70 .40 |
| 2584 | A736 | 15p like #2549 | .70 .40 |
| 2585 | A736 | 15p like #2550 | .70 .40 |
| 2586 | A736 | 15p like #2546 | .70 .40 |
| 2587 | A736 | 6p like #2548 | .70 .40 |
| a. | | Booklet pane, #2578-2587 | 8.00 8.00 |
| | | Complete booklet, #2578-2587 | 8.00 |

**Green Background**

| | | | |
|---|---|---|---|
| 2588 | A736 | 15p like #2546 | 2.00 1.00 |
| 2589 | A736 | 15p like #2518 | 2.00 1.00 |
| 2590 | A736 | 15p like #2547 | 2.00 1.00 |
| 2591 | A736 | 15p like #2521 | 2.00 1.00 |
| 2592 | A736 | 15p like #2548 | 2.00 1.00 |
| 2593 | A736 | 15p like #2549 | 2.00 1.00 |
| 2594 | A736 | 15p like #2519 | 2.00 1.00 |
| 2595 | A736 | 15p like #2520 | 2.00 1.00 |
| 2596 | A736 | 15p like #2521 | 2.00 1.00 |
| a. | | Booklet pane, 2c #2546, 8c #2548, 2 each 11c, 13c, #2596 | 13.00 13.00 |
| 2597 | A736 | 15p like #2550 | 13.00 13.00 |
| | | Complete booklet, #2588-2597 | 19.00 |
| | | Booklet pane, #2597a | 19.00 19.00 |
| | | Complete booklet, #2597a | 19.00 |

Nos. 2587a, 2596a, 2597a were made available to collectors unattached to the booklet cover.

PILIPINAS P5
THRIFT STAMP

## Philippine Centennial — A762

Pagsilang ng Sambayanang Pilipino

Designs: a, Centennial emblem. b, Proclamation of independence. c, Malolos Congress. d, Nov. 5th uprising. e, Cry of Santa Barbara Iloilo. f, Victory over colonial forces. g, Flag raising, Butuan City. h, Ratification of Malolos Constitution. i, Philippine Republic formed. j, Barasoain Church.

## 1999, Jan. 11

2599 A762 6p Sheet of 10, #a-j 10.00 10.00

**Scouting — A762a**

PILIPINAS P5

## 1999, Jan. 16
**Litho.** **Unwmk.**
**Perf. 13½**

| | | | |
|---|---|---|---|
| 2599K | A762a | 5p multicolored | 1.50 .30 |
| 2599L | A762a | 5p multicolored | 1.50 .30 |

Designs: No. 2599K, Girl Scout, boys planting tree. No. 2599L, Boy Scout, Girl Scout, flag, people representing various professions.

Nos. 2599K-2599L are dated 1995, inscribed "THRIFT STAMP," and were valid for postage due to stamp shortage.

## Philippine Central Bank, 50th Anniv. A761

PILIPINAS P6

## 1999, Jan. 3
**Litho.** **Perf. 14**

2598 A761 6p multicolored .90 .30

## Dept. of Transportation and Communications, Cent. — A763

PILIPINAS P6 PILIPINAS P6

Emblem and: a, Ship. b, Jet. c, Control tower. d, Satellite dish, bus. e, Control, 15p, Philpost Headquarters, truck, motorcycle on globe.

## 1999, Jan. 20

2600 A763 6p Block of 4, #a-d. 3.25 3.25

**Souvenir Sheet**

2601 A763 15p multicolored 3.00 3.00
No. 2601 contains one 80x30mm stamp.

## Filipino-American War, Cent. — A764

PILIPINAS P5

## 1999, Feb. 4

2602 A764 5p multicolored .60 .30

## Philippine Military Academy, Cent. A765

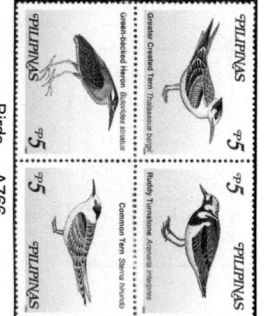
P5
PHILIPPINE MILITARY ACADEMY

## 1999-2001

2603 A765 5p multicolored .60 .30
a. Small "P" in denomination 1.25 .65

"P" in denomination is 1¾mm tall on No. 2603, 1½mm tall on No. 2603a.
Issue dates: No. 2603, 2/4/99. No. 2063a, 2001.

## Birds — A766

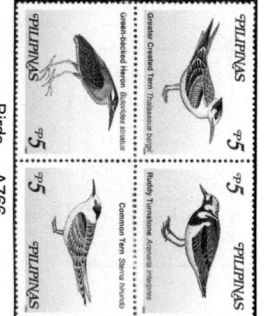
PILIPINAS P5 / P5 / P5

## 1999
**Litho.** **Perf. 14**

| | | | |
|---|---|---|---|
| 2604 | A766 | 5p Block of 4, #a-d. | 2.25 2.25 |
| 2605 | A766 | 5p Block of 4, #a-d. | 2.25 2.25 |

**Souvenir Sheets**

2606 A766 8p Sheet of 2, #a.-b. 3.50 3.50
a. As #2606, diff. sheet margin, inscription 4.50 4.50

No. 2604: a, Greater crested tern. b, Ruddy turnstone. c, Green-backed heron. d, Common tern. No. 2605: a, Black-winged stilt. b, Asiatic dowitcher. c, Whimbrel. d, Reef heron. No. 2606: a, Spotted greenshank. b, Tufted duck.

Issued: #2604-2606, 2/22; #2606a, 3/19.

PHILIPPINES

Senate — A781

CHIANG KAI SHEK COLLEGE
A782

1999, Oct. 15
2630 A781 5p multi .80 .20

1999, Oct. 20
2631 A782 5p multi .80 .20
New Building of Chiang Kai-shek College, Manila.

Issued in sheets of 10.

Tanza National Comprehensive High School, 50th Anniv. — A783

1999, Oct. 24
2632 A783 5p multi .80 .20

San Agustin Church, Paoay, World Heritage Site
A784

Intl. Year of Older Persons
A785

World Teachers' Day
A786

1999, Oct. 24
2633 A784 5p multi .80 .20
2634 A785 11p multi 1.75 .50
2635 A785 15p multi 2.50 .75
Nos. 2633-2635 (3) 5.05 1.45

United Nations Day.

Christmas
A787

Basko ng

PILIPINAS P5

---

## Diplomatic Relations Type of 1999

Philippines-Korea diplomatic relations. 50th anniv., flowers: 5p, 11p, Jasminum sambac, hibiscus syriacus.

**1999, Aug. 9        Litho.        Perf. 14**
2623 A774 5p multicolored .70 .35
2624 A774 11p multicolored 1.50 .75

Order of flowers from top is reversed on 11p value.

Issued in sheets of 20 (10 of each denomination in two rows of 5, separated by a central gutter). Most sheets of 20 were cut in half through the central gutter.

Community Chest, 50th Anniv.
A777

1999, Aug. 30
2625 A777 5p multicolored .80 .20

A778

A779

Philippine Bible Society, cent.

1999, Aug. 30
2626 A778 5p multicolored .80 .20

St. Francis of Assisi Parish, Cariaya, 400th anniv.

1999, Sept. 3
2627 A779 5p multicolored .80 .20

National Anthem, Cent.
A780

1999, Sept. 3
2628 A780 5p multicolored .80 .20

Souvenir Sheet

No. 2539b Overprinted in Silver "25th ANNIVERSARY IPPS"

**1999, Sept. 24        Litho.        Perf. 14**
2629 A746 15p Sheet of 3, #a.-c., + 3 labels 4.50 4.50

Ovpt. in sheet margin has same inscription twice, "25th ANNIVERSARY INTERNATIONAL PHILIPPINE PHILATELIC SOCIETY 1974-99" and two society emblems.

---

No. 2614: a. Sea squirt. b. Banded sea snake. c. Manta ray. d. Painted rock lobster. No. 2615: a. Sea grapes. b. Branching coral. c. Sea urchin.

**1999, May 11        Litho.        Perf. 14**
2614 A771 5p Block of 4, #a.-d. 2.50 2.50
**Sheet of 3**
2615 A771 5p #a.-c. + label 5.00 5.00

Juan F. Nakpil, Architect, Birth Cent.
A772

1999, May 25
2616 A772 5p multicolored .65 .30

UPU, 125th Anniv.
A773

**1999, May 26        Litho.        Perf. 14**
2617 A773 5p multicolored .65 .30
2618 A773 15p multicolored 1.90 .95

Designs: 5p, Globe, boy writing letter. 15p, Globe, girl looking at stamp collection.

Philippines-Thailand Diplomatic Relations, 50th Anniv. — A774

Orchids: 5p, 11p, Euanthe sanderiana, cattleya Queen Sirikit.

**1999, June 13        Litho.        Perf. 14**
2619 A774 5p multicolored .65 .30
2620 A774 11p multicolored 1.40 .70

Order of flowers from top is reversed on 11p value.

Issued in sheets of 20 (10 of each denomination in two rows of 5, separated by a central gutter). Most sheets of 20 were cut in half through the central gutter.
See #2623-2624, 2640-2641.

Masonic Charities for Crippled Children, Inc., 75th Anniv.
A775

1999, July 5
2621 A775 5p multicolored .65 .30

Production of Eberhard Faber "Mongol" Pencils, 150th Anniv. — A776

1999, July 5
2622 A776 5p multicolored .65 .30

---

No. 2606a contains inscription, emblem for Australia 99 World Stamp Expo.

## Heroes of the Revolution Type

**Pink Background**
**1999, Mar. 12    Litho.        Unwmk.**
2607 A736 5p like #2547 .55 .30

Manila Lions Club, 50th Anniv.
A767

**Perf. 14**
1999, Mar. 20
2608 A767 5p multicolored .60 .30

Design: Emblem, Francisco "Paquito" Ortigas, Jr., first president.

**Perf. 13½**

Philippine Orthopedic Assoc., 50th Anniv. — A768

1999, Mar. 20
2609 A768 5p multicolored .60 .30

La Union Botanical Garden, San Fernando
A769

Designs: No. 2610, Entrance sign, birdhouse. No. 2611, Ticket booth at entrance.

1999, Mar. 20
2610 A769 5p multicolored .60 .30
2611 A769 5p multicolored .60 .30
a. Pair, #2610-2611 1.25 1.25

Frogs — A770

#2612: a. Woodworth's frog. b. Giant Philippine frog. c. Gliding tree frog. d. Common forest frog. #2613: a. Spiny tree frog. b. Truncate-toed chorus frog. c. Variable-backed frog.

**1999, Apr. 5**
2612 A770 5p Block of 4, #a.-d. 2.50 2.50
**Sheet of 3**
2613 A770 5p #a.-c. + label 5.00 5.00

Marine Life — A771

**1999, Oct. 27**

**Color of Angel's Gown**

| | | | | |
|---|---|---|---|---|
| 2636 | A787 | 5p red violet | 1.00 | .20 |
| 2637 | A787 | 11p yellow | 2.00 | .45 |
| 2638 | A787 | 13p blue | 2.25 | .55 |
| 2639 | A787 | 15p green | 2.75 | .65 |
| a. | | Sheet of 4, #2636-2639 | 8.00 | 8.00 |
| | | Nos. 2636-2639 (4) | 8.00 | 1.85 |

Nos. 2636-2639 each issued in stamps with two central labels.

**1999, Nov. 15**  Perf. 14

| | | | | |
|---|---|---|---|---|
| 2640 | A774 | 5p multi | .75 | .25 |
| 2641 | A774 | 15p multi | 2.75 | .75 |

**Diplomatic Relations Type of 1999**

Philippines-Canada diplomatic relations, 50th anniv., mammals: 5p, 15p, Tamaraw, polar bear.

Order of mammals from top is reversed on 15p value. Issued in sheets of 20 (10 of each denomination in two rows of 5, separated by a central gutter). Most sheets of 20 were cut in half through central gutter.

**Renovation of Araneta Coliseum A788**

**1999, Nov. 19**  Litho.

| | | | | |
|---|---|---|---|---|
| 2642 | A788 | 5p multi | 1.00 | .25 |

**3rd ASEAN Informal Summit.**

**1999, Nov. 19**

| | | | | |
|---|---|---|---|---|
| 2643 | A789 | 5p dark blue | .75 | .20 |
| 2644 | A789 | 11p blue green | 2.25 | .50 |

National Stamp Collecting Month.

**1999, Nov. 29**

| | | | | |
|---|---|---|---|---|
| 2645 | A790 | 5p multi | 1.00 | .20 |
| 2646 | A790 | 11p multi | 2.00 | .45 |
| 2647 | A790 | 13p multi | 2.25 | .55 |
| 2648 | A790 | 15p multi | 2.75 | .65 |
| | | Nos. 2645-2648 (4) | 8.00 | 1.85 |

Sculptures: No. 2645, Kristo, by Arturo Luz. 11p, Homage to Dodgie Laurel, by J. Elizalde Navarro. 13p, Hilitan, by Napoleon Abueva. No. 2648, Mother and Child, by Abueva. Rizal, horiz. b, 15p, El Ermitano, by José Rizal, horiz.

**Souvenir Sheet**

| | | | | |
|---|---|---|---|---|
| 2649 | A790 | Sheet of 2, #a.-b. | 4.00 | 4.00 |

**New Year 2000 (Year of the Dragon) A791**

**1999, Dec. 1**  Perf. 14

| | | | | |
|---|---|---|---|---|
| 2650 | A791 | 5p Dragon in water | .75 | .20 |
| 2651 | A791 | 11p Dragon in sky | 2.75 | .75 |
| a. | | Sheet of 2, #2650-2651 | 2.25 | .25 |
| b. | | As "a," imperf. | 5.75 | 5.75 |

**Battle of Tirad Pass, Cent. A792**

**1999, Dec. 2**  Perf. 14

| | | | | |
|---|---|---|---|---|
| 2652 | A792 | 5p multi | .80 | .20 |

**Orchids — A793**

**1999, Dec. 3**  Litho.

| | | | | |
|---|---|---|---|---|
| 2653 | A793 | 5p Block of 4, #a.-d. | 4.00 | 4.00 |
| 2654 | A793 | 5p Sheet of 4, #a.-d. | 5.00 | 5.00 |

No. 2653: a, Paphiopedium urbanianum. b, Phalaenopsis schilleriana. c, Dendrobium amethystoglossum. d, Paphiopedium barbatum.

No. 2654, horiz.: a, Paphiopedium haynaldianum. b, Phalaenopsis stuartiana. c, Trichoglottis brachiata. d, Ceratostylis rubra.

**Battle of San Mateo, Cent. A794**

**1999, Dec. 19**  Litho.

| | | | | |
|---|---|---|---|---|
| 2655 | A794 | 5p multicolored | .80 | .20 |

**People Power — A795**

**1999, Dec. 31**

| | | | | |
|---|---|---|---|---|
| 2656 | A795 | 5p Strip of 3, #a.-c. | 3.50 | 3.50 |

People and: a, Tank. b, Tower. c, Crucifix.

**Natl. Commission on the Role of Filipino Women — A796**

**2000, Jan. 7**  Litho.  Perf. 14

| | | | | |
|---|---|---|---|---|
| 2657 | A796 | 5p multi | .80 | .20 |

"Women Empowerment for Gender Equality"

**Manila Bulletin, Cent. A797**

**2000, Feb. 2**  Litho.  Perf. 14

| | | | | |
|---|---|---|---|---|
| 2658 | A797 | 5p multi | .50 | .20 |
| a. | A797 | 5p multi | .50 | .20 |

Manila Bulletin celebrates 100th year

Issued: No. 2658a, 6/7.

**La Union Province, 150th Anniv. — A798**

**2000, Mar. 2**

| | | | | |
|---|---|---|---|---|
| 2659 | A798 | 5p Block of 4, #a.-d. | 2.50 | 2.50 |

Arms of province and: a, Sailboat, golfer. b, Tractor, worker, building. c, Building, flagpole. d, Airplane, ship, telephone tower, people on telephone, computer.

**Civil Service Commission, Cent. — A799**

**2000, Mar. 20**

| | | | | |
|---|---|---|---|---|
| 2660 | A799 | 5p multi | .50 | .20 |

**Millennium A800**

**2000, Mar. 31**

| | | | | |
|---|---|---|---|---|
| 2661 | A800 | 5p Strip of 3, #a.-c. | 1.50 | 1.50 |

Designs: a, Golden Garuda of Palawan. b, First sunrise of the millennium, Pusan Point. c, Golden Tara of Agusan.

**GMA Radio and Television Network, 50th Anniv. A802**

**2000, Mar. 1**  Litho.  Perf. 14

| | | | | |
|---|---|---|---|---|
| 2662 | A802 | 5p multi | .50 | .20 |

**Philippine Presidents — A803**

Joseph Ejercito Estrada

**2000**  Perf. 13½

| | | | | |
|---|---|---|---|---|
| 2662A | A803 | Pair | 1.25 | 1.25 |
| b.-c. | A803 | 5p Any single | .55 | .20 |
| 2663 | | Block of 10 | 7.50 | 7.50 |
| a.-j. | A803 | 5p Any single | .60 | .20 |

**Diplomatic Relations Type of 1999**

5p, Sarimanok, Great Wall of China, 11p, Phoenix, Banaue rice terraces. a, 5p, Great Wall, horiz. b, 11p, Rice terraces, horiz.

Nos. 2662b-2662c have presidential seal but lack blue lines at bottom. No. 2663a has denomination at left. Nos. 2663b-2663c have small Presidential seal at bottom.

Issued: No. 2662A, 2/6. No. 2663, 3/16.

See Type A828 for stamps showing Presidential seal with colored background.

See Nos. 2672-2676.

**2000, May 8**  Perf. 14

| | | | | |
|---|---|---|---|---|
| 2664-2665 | A774 | Set of 2 | 3.00 | 3.00 |

**Souvenir Sheet**

| | | | | |
|---|---|---|---|---|
| 2666 | A774 | Sheet of 2, #a.-b. | 1.50 | 1.50 |

**Diplomatic Relations Type of 1999**

Issued in sheets of 20 (10 of each denomination in two rows of 5, separated by a central gutter). Most sheets of 20 were cut in half through central gutter.

**St. Thomas Aquinas Parish, Mangaldan, 400th Anniv. A805**

**2000, June 1**

| | | | | |
|---|---|---|---|---|
| 2667 | A805 | 5p multi | .50 | .20 |

**Battle Centenaries — A806**

**2000, June 19**

| | | | | |
|---|---|---|---|---|
| 2668-2671 | A806 | 5p Set of 4 | 2.00 | 2.00 |

Battles in Philippine Insurrection: #2668, Mabitac. #2669, Paye, vert. #2670, Makahambus Hill, vert. #2671, Pulang Lupa.

**Presidents Type of 2000 Redrawn**

**2000**  Litho.  Perf. 13½

**Blue Lines at Bottom**

| | | | | |
|---|---|---|---|---|
| 2672 | A803 | 5p Block of 10 | 9.50 | 9.50 |
| a.-j. | | Any single | .75 | .75 |
| 2673 | A803 | 10p Any single | 3.75 | 3.75 |
| a.-b. | | Pair | 3.75 | 3.75 |
| 2674 | A803 | 11p Any single | 4.25 | 4.25 |
| a.-b. | | Pair | 4.25 | 4.25 |
| 2675 | A803 | 13p Any single | 1.50 | 1.50 |
| a.-b. | | Pair | 4.75 | 4.75 |
| 2676 | A803 | 15p Any single | 1.75 | 1.75 |
| a.-b. | | Pair | 5.50 | 5.50 |
| | | Pair | 2.00 | 2.00 |
| | | | 27.75 | 27.75 |

No. 2672: a, Presidential seal. b, Joseph Ejercito Estrada. c, Fidel V. Ramos. d, Corazon C. Aquino. e, Ferdinand E. Marcos. f, Diosdado Macapagal. g, Carlos P. Garcia. h, Ramon Magsaysay. i, Elpidio Quirino. j, Manuel Roxas.

No. 2673: a, Magsaysay. b, Garcia. No. 2674: a, Macapagal. b, Marcos. No. 2675: a, Aquino. b, Ramos. No. 2676: a, Estrada. b, Presidential seal.

Issued: No. 2672, 7/3; Nos. 2673-2674, 8/4. Nos. 2675-2676, 6/19.

No. 2672a has denomination at R, while No. 2672b has denomination at L. Nos. 2672b-2672j have no presidential seal, while Nos. 2662Ab-2662Ac, 2663b-2663j) have seal.

## No. 1806 Handstamp Surcharged in Red

**Perf. 13x13½    Litho.    Wmk.**

2000, Nov. 24

2706A A469 5p on 3.60p multi    5.00 5.00

---

### New Year 2001 (Year of the Snake) A822

**Perf. 14    Unwmk.**

2000, Dec. 20

2707-2708 A822    Set of 2    2.50 2.50

2708a    Souvenir sheet, #2707-2708 + 2 labels    7.00 7.00

Snakes with inscription in: 5p, Tagalog. 11p, English.

No. 2708a exists imperf.

---

### Millennium A823

No. 2709: a. Trade and progress. b. Education and knowledge. c. Communication and information.

2000, Dec. 28

2709 A823    4.00 4.00

a.    Horiz. strip of 3    .50 .20

---

### Bank of the Philippine Islands, 150th Anniv. A824

**Litho.**

2001, Jan. 30

2710 A824 5p multi    .50 .20

---

### Hong Kong 2001 Stamp Exhibition A825

Designs: No. 2711a, 5p. No. 2712, 11p, Tamaraw. No. 2711b, 5p. No. 2713, 11p, Agila. No. 2711c, 5p. No. 2714, 11p, Tarsier. No. 2711d, 5p. No. 2715, 11p, Tarsier orchid. No. 2711e, 5p. No. 2716, 11p, Pawikan.

2001, Feb. 1

2711 A825    Horiz. strip of 5    4.00 4.00

a.-e.    A825 5p Any single    .60 .20

**Souvenir Sheets**

2712-2716 A825    Set of 5    12.50 12.50

2713a    Ovptd. in margin in red    2.50 2.50

2715a    Ovptd. in margin in red    2.50 2.50

Nos. 2712-2716 have show emblem on sheet margin instead of on stamp.

Issued: Nos. 2713a, 2715a, 6/30/01. Overprint in margin on Nos. 2713a, 2715a has Chinese inscriptions and English text "PHILIPPINE-CHINESE PHILATELIC SOCIETY / 1951 GOLDEN JUBILEE 2001."

---

### Clothing Exhibit at Metropolitan Museum of Manila — A818

No. 2690, 5p: a, Kalinga / Gaddang cotton loincloth. b, Portrait of Leticia Jimenez, by unknown artist.

No. 2691, 5p, horiz.: a, B'laan female upper garment. b, T'boli T'nalak abaca cloth.

No. 2692: a, 5p, Portrait of Teodora Devera Ygnacio, by Justiniano Asunción. b, 15p, Detail of Tawsug silk sash.

Illustration reduced.

**Perf. 14**

2000, Nov. 15

2690-2691 A818    Pairs, #a-b    2.00 2.00

Set of 2    2.00 2.00

**Souvenir Sheet**

2692 A818    Sheet of 2, #a-b    3.00 3.00

---

### Natl. Stamp Collecting Month A819

Designs: 5p, Portrait of an Unkown Lady, by Juan Luna, vert. 11p, Nude, by José Joya. 13p, Lotus Odalisque, by Rodolfo Paras-Perez. No. 2696, 15p, Untitled Nude, by Fernando Amorsolo. No. 2697, The Memorial, by Cesar Legaspi.

**Perf. 14**

2000, Nov. 20

2693-2696 A819    Set of 4    6.50 6.50

**Souvenir Sheet**

2697 A819 11p multi    4.00 4.00

No. 2697 contains one 80x29 stamp and label.

---

### Christmas A820

Angels: No. 2698, 5p, In pink robe, with bouquet of flowers. No. 2699, 5p, As #2698, with Holy Year 2000 emblem and inscription. 11p, In green robe. 13p, In orange robe. 15p, In red robe, with garland of flowers.

**Litho.**

2000, Nov. 22

2698-2702 A820    Set of 5    6.00 6.00

---

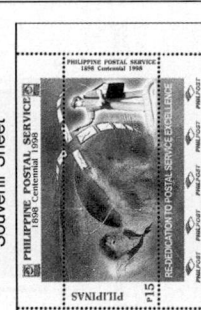

### APO Philatelic Society, 50th Anniv. — A821

Emblem and stamps: No. 2703, 5p, #620 (yellow background). No. 2704, 5p, #639 (light blue background), horiz. No. 2705, 5p, #850 (dull green background). No. 2706, 5p, #B21 (pink background), horiz.

2000, Nov. 23

2703-2706 A821    Set of 4    2.75 2.75

---

### 2000 Olympics, Sydney — A813

No. 2684: a, Running. b, Archery. c, Shooting. d, Diving.

No. 2685, horiz.: a, Boxing. b, Equestrian. c, Rowing. d, Taekwondo.

Illustration reduced.

2000, Sept. 30

2684 A813 5p Block of 4, #a-d    2.40 2.40

**Souvenir Sheet**

2685 A813 5p Sheet of 4, #a-d    5.00 5.00

---

### Teresian Association in the Philippines, 50th Anniv. A814

2000, Oct. 10

2686 A814 5p multi    .50 .20

---

### House of Representatives A815

**Perf. 14**

2000, Oct. 15

2687 A815 5p multi    .50 .20

---

### Marine Corps, 50th Anniv. A816

2000, Oct. 18

2688 A816 5p multi    .50 .20

---

**Souvenir Sheet**

### Postal Service, Cent. (in 1998) — A817

2000, Nov. 6

2689 A817 15p multi    3.00 3.00

---

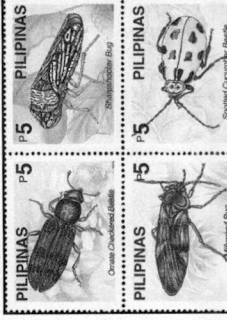

### Insects—A807

No. 2677: a, Ornate checkered beetle. b, Sharpshooter bug. c, Milkweed bug. d, Spotted cucumber beetle.

No. 2678: a, Green June beetle. b, Convergent ladybird. c, Eastern Hercules beetle. d, Harlequin cabbage bug.

Illustration reduced.

**Perf. 14**

2000, July 21

2677 A807 5p Block of 4, #a-d    2.00 2.00

e.    Souvenir sheet, #2677    2.50 2.50

2678 A807 5p Block of 4, #a-d    2.00 2.00

e.    Souvenir sheet, #2678    2.50 2.50

---

### Occupational Health Nurses Association, 50th Anniv. — A808

2000, Aug. 30

2679 A808 5p multi    .50 .20

---

### Diocese of Lucena, 50th Anniv. A809

2000, Aug. 30

2680 A809 5p multi    .50 .20

---

### Millennium A810

Boats: a, Balanghai. b, Vinta. c, Caracoa.

2000, Sept. 21

2681 A810    Horiz. strip of 3    4.00 4.00

a.-c.    A810 5p Any single    .75 .20

---

### Equitable PCI Bank, 50th Anniv. A811

2000, Sept. 26

2682 A811 5p multi    .50 .20

---

### Year of the Overseas Filipino Worker A812

**Litho.**

2000, Sept. 29

2683 A812 5p multi    .50 .40

Gen. Paciano Rizal (1851-1930) — A826

**2001, Mar. 7    Litho.    Perf. 14**
2717  A826  5p multi    .50  .20

San Beda College, Cent. — A827

**2001, Mar. 9**
2718  A827  5p multi    .50  .20

**Diplomatic Relations Type of 1999**
Philippines-Vatican City diplomatic relations, 50th anniv.; main altars at: 5p, St. Peter's Basilica, Vatican City. No. 2720, 15p, San Agustin Church, Manila.
No. 2721: a, Adam, from Creation of Adam, by Michelangelo. b, God, from Creation of Adam.

**2001, Mar. 14**
2719-2720  A774    Set of 2    2.50  2.50

**Souvenir Sheet**
2721  A774  15p  Sheet of 2, #a-b    4.50  4.50

Nos. 2719-2720 issued in two rows of 5, rated by a central gutter). Most sheets of 20 were cut in half through central gutter.

Presidential Seal With Colored Background — A828

Tourist Spots A829

**2001, Apr. 5    Background Colors    Perf. 13¾**
2722  A828  5p yellow    .50  .20
2723  A828  15p blue    1.50  .45

Stamps of the same denomination showing the Presidential Seal with white backgrounds are listed as Nos. 2663a, 2672a and 2676b.

El Nido
PILIPINAS P5
PALAWAN
P5 PILIPINAS

No. 2724: a, El Nido, Palawan Province. b, Vigan House, Ilocos Sur Province. c, Boracay, Aklan Province. d, Chocolate Hills, Bohol Province.
15p, Banaue Rice Terraces, Ifugao Province.

**2000, Apr. 14    Perf. 14**
2724  A829  Horiz. strip of 4    2.00  2.00
a-d  A829  5p Any single    .50  .20

**Souvenir Sheet**
2725  A829  15p multi    2.00  2.00

No. 2725 contains one 80x30mm stamp. No. 2725 exists with washed-out colors and a larger year date.

---

Pres. Macapagal-Arroyo PILIPINAS

Pres. Gloria Macapagal-Arroyo A831

**2001, Apr. 22**
2726  A830  5p multi    .50  .20

Canonical Coronation of Our Lady of Manaoag, 75th Anniv. — A830

Pres. Macapagal-Arroyo: No. 2727, 5p, Waving. No. 2728, 5p, Taking oath of office.

**2001, Apr. 29**
2727-2728  A831    Set of 2    1.00  1.00

**Diplomatic Relations Type of 1999**
Philippines-Australia diplomatic relations, landmarks: 5p, Nos. 2730-2731, 13p, Sydney Opera House, Cultural Center of the Philippines. No. 2731 is horiz.

**2001, May 21**
2729-2730  A774    Set of 2    2.00  .75

**Souvenir Sheet**
2731  A774  13p multi    3.50  3.50

No. 2731 contains one 80x30mm stamp.

Silliman University Centennial PILIPINAS P5

**2001, May 31**
2732  A832  5p multi    .50  .20

Silliman University, Dumaguete City, Cent. A833

**2001, June 1**
2733  A833  5p multi    .50  .20

Supreme Court, Cent. A832

PHILIPPINE NORMAL UNIVERSITY PILIPINAS P5

Philippine Normal University, Cent. A834

**2001, June 1**
2734  A834  5p multi    .50  .20

DON JOAQUIN ORTEGA PILIPINAS P5

Joaquin J. Ortega (1870-1943), First Civil Governor of La Union Province — A835

**2001, July 12**
2735  A835  5p multi    .35  .20

---

THE MOROS OF LUZON ca 1590 P5 PILIPINAS
VISAYAN COUPLE ca 1590 P5 PILIPINAS
THE MOROS OF LUZON ca 1590 P5 PILIPINAS
TAGALOG COUPLE ca 1590 P5 PILIPINAS

Illustrations from Boxer Codex, c. 1590 — A837

No. 2737: a, Visayan couple. b, Tagalog couple. c, Moros of Luzon (multicolored frame). d, Moros of Luzon (blue frame).
No. 2738: a, Pintados (denomination at left). b, Pintados (denomination at right). c, Cagayan female. d, Zambal.

**2001, Aug. 1**
2737  A837  5p Block of 4, #a-d    1.25  1.25

**Souvenir Sheet**
2738  A837  5p Sheet of 4, #a-d    2.50  2.50
e.    Sheet of 4, #a-d, with Philia Nippon '01 margin    2.50  2.50

CENTENARY OF THE FILIPINO-AMERICAN EDUCATORS P5 PILIPINAS

Arrival of American Educators (Thomasites), Cent. — A838

Designs: 5p, Thomasite teachers, US transport ship Thomas. 15p, Philippine students.

**2001, Aug. 23**
2739-2740  A838    Set of 2    1.50  1.50

TECHNOLOGICAL UNIVERSITY OF THE PHILIPPINES 2001 PILIPINAS P5

Technological University of the Philippines, Cent. — A839

**2001, Aug. 20    Litho.    Perf. 14**
2741  A839  5p multi    .35  .20

---

100 YEARS ANNIVERSARY 1901-2001 NATIONAL MUSEUM OF THE PHILIPPINES PILIPINAS P5

National Museum of the Philippines, Cent. — A840

**2001, Sept. 3**
2742  A840  5p multi    .35  .20

Lands Management Bureau, Cent. — A841

**2001, Sept. 17**
2743  A841  5p multi    .35  .20

Colegio de San Jose and San Jose Seminary, 400th Anniv. — A842

**2001, Oct. 1**
2744  A842  5p multi    .35  .20

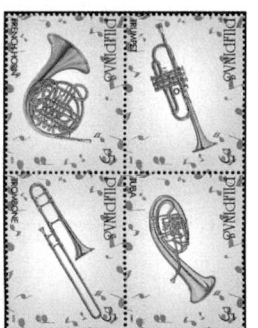

COLEGIO de SAN JOSE • SAN JOSE SEMINARY 400 YEARS 1601 • 2001 PILIPINAS P5

Makati City Financial District A843

**2001, Oct. 1**
2745  A843  5p multi    .35  .20

Presidential Seal With Colored Background Type of 2001

No. 2749: a, Trumpet. b, Tuba. c, French horn. d, Trombone.
No. 2750, vert.: a, Bass drum. b, Clarinet, oboe. c, Xylophone. d, Sousaphone. Illustration reduced.

**2001, Oct. 5    Background Colors    Perf. 13¾**
2746  A828  10p green    .60  .30
2747  A828  11p pink    .65  .30
2748  A828  13p gray    .75  .40
Nos. 2746-2748 (3)    2.00  1.00

Musical Instruments — A844

**2001, Oct. 8    Perf. 14**
2749  A844  5p Block of 4, #a-d    2.00  2.00

**Souvenir Sheet**
2750  A844  5p Sheet of 4, #a-d    2.50  2.50

Malampaya Deep Water Gas Power Project A845

Frame colors: 5p, Silver. 15p, Gold.

**2001, Oct. 16**
2751-2752 A845 Set of 2
1.25 1.25

Intl. Volunteers Year A846

**2001, Oct. 24**
2753 A846 5p multi
.35 .20

Year of Dialogue Among Civilizations A847

**2001, Oct. 24**
2754 A847 15p multi
.90 .45

Christmas A848

Designs: 5p, Herald Angels. 11p, Kumuku-tikitikitap. 13p, Pasko ni Bitoy. 15p, Pasko na naman.

**2001, Oct. 30**
2755-2758 A848 Set of 4
2.75 2.75

Philippines — Switzerland Relations, 150th Anniv. — A849

Monument statues by Richard Kissling: 5p, William Tell. No. 2760, 15p, Jose P. Rizal. No. 2761, 15p, Mayon Volcano, Philippines, and Matterhorn, Switzerland.

**2001, Nov. 26**
2759-2760 A849 Set of 2
1.25 1.25

**Souvenir Sheet**

2761 A849 15p multi
2.50 2.50

No. 2761 contains one 79x29mm stamp. Nos. 2759-2760 issued in sheets of 20 (10 of each denomination in two rows of 5, separated by a central gutter). Most sheets of 20 were cut in half through central gutter.

Drawings of Manila Inhabitants, c. 1840 — A850

Designs: 17p, Woman with hat, man with green pants. 21p, Woman with veil, man with brown pants. 22p, Man, woman at mortar and pestle.

---

**2001, Dec. 1** **Perf. 13¾**
2762 A850 17p multi 1.00 .60
2763 A850 21p multi 1.25 .70
2764 A850 22p multi 1.40 .70
3.65 1.80

Nos. 2762-2764 (3)
No. 2762 exist dated "2002."
No. 2762 exists dated "2003."

Solicitor General, Cent. — A851

**2001, Dec. 7** **Perf. 14**
2765 A851 5p multi .35 .20

Natl. Stamp Collecting Month A852

**2001, Dec. 7** **Litho.**
2766-2769 A852 Set of 4
4.00 4.00

**Souvenir Sheet**

2770 A852 22p multi 2.50 2.50

No. 2770 contains one 79x29mm stamp.

New Year 2002 (Year of the Horse) A853

Horse color: 5p, Red. 17p, White.

**2001, Dec. 14** **Perf. 14**
2771-2772 A853 Set of 2 1.50 .70
2772a Souvenir sheet, #2771-2772, + 2 labels 5.00 5.00

No. 2772a exists imperf.

Josemaria Escrivá (1902-75), Founder of Opus Dei — A854

**2002, Jan. 9**
2773 A854 5p multi .35 .20

World Heritage Sites A855

Vigan City sites: 5p, St. Paul's Metropolitan Cathedral. 22p, Calle Crisologo.

**2002, Jan. 22**
2774-2775 A855 Set of 2 1.60 1.60

---

Salvador Z. Araneta, Statesman, Birth Cent. — A856

**2002, Jan. 31**
2776 A856 5p multi .35 .20

Customs Service, Cent. A857

**2002, Feb. 1**
2777 A857 5p multi .35 .20

Valentine's Day — A858

No. 2778: a, Envelope. b, Man and woman. c, Cat and dog. d, Balloon.

**2002, Feb. 8**
2778 A858 5p Block of 4, #a-d 1.50 1.50

Drawings of Manila inhabitants Type of 2001

**2002, Mar. 1** **Litho.** **Perf. 13¾**
2779 A850 5p Man, woman on horses .30 .20

Exists dated "2003."

Baguio General Hospital and Medical Center, Cent. A859

**2002, Mar. 22** **Perf. 14**
2780 A859 5p multi .30 .20

Beatification of Blessed Pedro Calungsod A860

Designs: 5p, Calungsod with palm frond. 22p, Map of Guam, ship, Calungsod with cross.

**2002, Apr. 2** **Perf. 14**
2781 A860 5p multi .30 .20

---

Size: 102x72mm
*Imperf*
2782 A860 22p multi 2.00 2.00

Negros Occidental High School, Cent. — A861

**2002, Apr. 12** **Perf. 14**
2783 A861 5p multi .30 .20

La Consolacion College, Manila, Cent. A862

**2002, Apr. 12**
2784 A862 5p multi .30 .20

Vesak Day — A863

**2002, May 26**
2785 A863 5p multi .30 .20

Presidents Type of 2000 Redrawn
**Without Years of Service**

No. 2786: a, Gloria Macapagal-Arroyo. b, Joseph Ejercito Estrada. c, Fidel V. Ramos. d, Corazon C. Aquino. e, Ferdinand E. Marcos. f, Diosdado Macapagal. g, Carlos P. Garcia. h, Ramon Magsaysay. i, Elpidio Quirino. j, Manuel Roxas.

**2002, June 12** **Perf. 13½**
**Without Presidential Seal**
**Blue Lines at Bottom**
2786 Block of 10 3.00 3.00
a.-r. A803 5p Any single .30 .20

Cavite National High School, Cent. A864

**2002, June 19** **Perf. 14**
2787 A864 5p multi .30 .20

Mangroves A865

Fish A866

Fish
A867

Hands and Small Fish
A868

**2002, June 24**    **Unwmk.**

**Litho.**    **Perf. 14**

| | | | | |
|---|---|---|---|---|
| 2788 | A865 | 5p multi | .40 | .20 |
| 2789 | A866 | 5p multi | .40 | .20 |
| 2790 | A867 | 5p multi | .40 | .20 |
| 2791 | A868 | 5p multi | .40 | .20 |
| Nos. 2788-2791 (4) | | | 1.60 | .80 |

**Souvenir Sheet**

| | | | | |
|---|---|---|---|---|
| 2792 | A865 | Sheet of 4, #a-d | 1.60 | 1.60 |

No. 2792: a, Monitors in boats at marine sanctuary. b, Mangrove reforestation. c, Monitors checking reefs. d, Seaweed farming. Coastal resources conservation.

Iglesia Filipina Independiente, Cent. — A869

**2002, July 4**    **Souvenir Sheet**

| | | | | |
|---|---|---|---|---|
| 2793 | A869 | 5p multi | .40 | .20 |

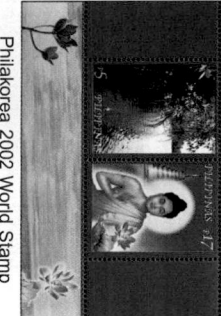
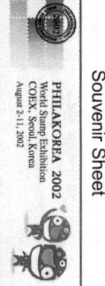

Philakorea 2002 World Stamp Exhibition, Seoul — A870

**2002, Aug. 2**    **Unwmk.**

| | | | | |
|---|---|---|---|---|
| 2794 | A870 | Sheet of 2, #a-b | 2.00 | 2.00 |

No. 2794: a, 5p, Mangrove. b, 17p, Buddhist, temple and flower.
No. 2794 exists imperf. with changed background color.

No. 2210 Surcharged

**Method & Perf. as Before**

**Wmk. 391**

**2002, Aug. 15**

| | | | | |
|---|---|---|---|---|
| 2795 | A610 | 3p on 60s multi | .25 | .20 |

---

Telecommunications Officials Meetings, Manila — A870a

**2002, Aug. 22**    **Litho.**    **Perf. 14**

| | | | | |
|---|---|---|---|---|
| 2795A | A870a | 5p multi | .40 | .20 |

Second Telecommunications Ministerial Meeting, Third ASEAN Telecommunications Senior Officials Meeting, Eighth ASEAN Telecommunications Regulators Council Meeting.

Marikina, Shoe Capital of the Philippines — A871

**2002, Oct. 15**    **Unwmk.**

**Litho.**    **Perf. 14**

| | | | | |
|---|---|---|---|---|
| 2796 | A871 | 5p multi | .40 | .20 |

**Souvenir Sheet**

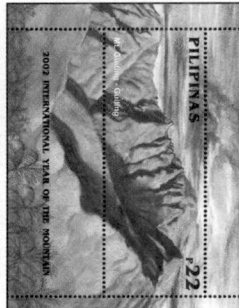

**2002, Oct. 28**

| | | | | |
|---|---|---|---|---|
| 2797 | A872 | 22p multi | 1.75 | .90 |

Int'l. Year of Mountains — A872

Stamp Collecting Month A874

**2002, Nov. 5**

| | | | | |
|---|---|---|---|---|
| 2798-2801 | A873 | Set of 4 | 5.25 | 2.60 |

Various holiday foods: 5p, 17p, 21p, 22p.

Christmas — A873

**2002, Nov. 2**

| | | | | |
|---|---|---|---|---|
| 2802-2805 | A874 | Set of 4 | 5.25 | 5.25 |

**Size: 99x74mm**

**Imperf**

| | | | | |
|---|---|---|---|---|
| 2806 | A874 | 22p multi | 2.00 | 2.00 |

Designs: 5p, Gerardo de Leon (1913-81), movie director. 17p, Francisca Reyes Aquino (1899-1983), founder of Philippine Folk Dance Society. 21p, Pablo S. Antonio (1901-75), architect. No. 2805, 22p, Jose Garcia Villa (1912-97), writer. No. 2806, 22p, Honorata de la Rama (1902-91), singer and actress.

---

First Circumnavigation of the World, 480th Anniv. — A875

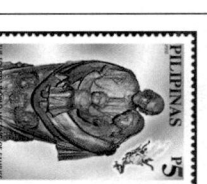

**2002, Nov. 11**

| | | | | |
|---|---|---|---|---|
| 2807 | A875 | 5p Vert. strip of 4, #a-d | 1.60 | 1.60 |

No. 2807 — Ship and: a, Antonio Pigafetta. b, Ferdinand Magellan. c, King Charles I of Spain. d, Sebastian Elcano. World Map and King Charles I of Spain.

**Size: 104x85mm**

**Imperf**    **Perf. 14**

| | | | | |
|---|---|---|---|---|
| 2808 | A875 | 22p multi | 2.00 | 2.00 |

Fourth World Meeting of Families — A876

**2002, Nov. 23**

| | | | | |
|---|---|---|---|---|
| 2809-2810 | A876 | Set of 2 | 1.40 | 1.40 |

Designs: 5p, Sculpture of Holy Family. 11p, Family, crucifix, Holy Spirit.

New Year 2003 (Year of the Ram) A877

**2002, Dec. 1**

**Perf. 14**

| | | | | |
|---|---|---|---|---|
| 2811-2812 | A877 | Set of 2 | 1.75 | 1.75 |
| a. Souvenir sheet, #2811-2812 + 2 labels | | | 1.75 | 1.75 |

Ram facing: 5p, Left. 17p, Right.
No. 2812a exists imperf.

Lyceum of the Philippines, 50th Anniv. — A878

**2002, Dec. 5**

**Perf. 14**

| | | | | |
|---|---|---|---|---|
| 2813 | A878 | 5p multi | .40 | .20 |

---

Orchids — A879

**2002, Dec. 19**

**Perf. 14**

| | | | | |
|---|---|---|---|---|
| 2814 | A879 | 5p Block of 4, #a-d | 1.60 | 1.60 |

**Souvenir Sheet**

**Imperf**

| | | | | |
|---|---|---|---|---|
| 2815 | A879 | 22p multi | 1.75 | 1.75 |

No. 2814: a, Luisia teretifolia. b, Dendrobium victoria-reginae, horiz. c, Gedorum densiflorum. d, Nervilia plicata, horiz. 22p, Grammatophyllum scriptum, horiz.
No. 2815 contains one 69x40mm stamp. No. 2814 was reprinted with a larger "2002" date.

La Union National High School, Cent. A880

**2003, Jan. 22**

**Perf. 14**

| | | | | |
|---|---|---|---|---|
| 2816 | A880 | 5p multi | .40 | .20 |

St. Luke's Medical Center, Cathedral Heights, Cent. A881

**2003, Jan. 23**

| | | | | |
|---|---|---|---|---|
| 2817 | A881 | 5p multi | .40 | .20 |

Far Eastern University, 75th Anniv. A882

**2003, Jan. 28**

| | | | | |
|---|---|---|---|---|
| 2818 | A882 | 5p multi | .40 | .20 |

Manila Electric Railroad and Light Company, Cent. A883

**2003, Jan. 31**

| | | | | |
|---|---|---|---|---|
| 2819 | A883 | 5p multi | .40 | .20 |

PHILIPPINES

philippinensis. 30p, Mariposa. 50p, Sanggumay. 75p, Lady's slipper. 100p, Waling-waling.

**2003-04**     *Perf. 14½*

| 2849 | A888 | 6p multi | .50 | .25 |
| 2849A | A888 | 9p multi | .70 | .35 |
| 2850 | A888 | 10p multi | .80 | .40 |
| | | With space between "P" and "10," dated 2004 (04) | | |
| 2851 | A888 | 17p multi | .80 | .80 |
| | a. | Base of "P" even with base of "17," dated 2004 (04) | 1.40 | .70 |
| 2852 | A888 | 21p multi | 1.40 | 1.40 |
| | a. | Base of "P" even with base of "21," dated 2004 (04) | 1.75 | .85 |
| 2853 | A888 | 100p multi | 1.75 | 1.75 |
| | a. | Base of "P" even with base of "22," dated 2004, plant name 14mm long (04) | 1.75 | .90 |
| | b. | As "a," plant name 12½mm long (04) | 1.75 | .90 |

**Perf. 14**

| 2854 | A897 | 30p multi | 2.40 | 1.25 |
| 2855 | A897 | 50p multi | 4.00 | 2.00 |
| 2856 | A897 | 75p multi | 6.00 | 3.00 |
| 2857 | A897 | 100p multi | 8.00 | 4.00 |
| | | Nos. 2849-2857 (10) | 27.30 | 13.70 |

Designs: 6p, 10p, 17p, 22p, 8/8; 30p, 100p. 8/21; 50p, 75p, 9/9, 9p, 11/4. No. 2850a, 6/2/04; No. 2851a, 8/2/04; No. 2852a, 7/21/04; No. 2853a, 6/10/04. No. 2853b, 2004.

See Nos. 2904-2912.

Philippine — Spanish Friendship Day — A894

Designs: 6p, Poster for Madoura Exhibit, by Pablo Picasso. 22p, Flashback, by José T. Joya.

**2003, June 30**    *Litho.*

| 2845-2846 | A894 | | .25 .25 |
| | | Set of 2 | .25 .25 |

Philippines Chamber of Commerce, Cent. A895

**2003, July 15**
2847   A895   6p multi    .50   .25

Benguet Corporation, Cent. A896

**2003, Aug. 12**
2848   A896   6p multi    .50   .25

**Orchid Type of 2003 With Plant Names and**

A897

Designs: 6p, Dendrobium uniflorum. 9p, Paphiopedilum urbanianum. 10p, Kingidium philippinense. 17p, Epigeneium lyonii. 21p, Thrixspermum subulatum. 22p, Trichoglottis

PHILIPPINES — MEXICO 50 YEARS OF DIPLOMATIC RELATIONS

Our Lady of Guadalupe

Philippines — Mexico Diplomatic Relations, 50th Anniv. — A898

Designs: 5p, Our Lady of Guadalupe. No. 2859, 22p, Miraculous Image of the Black Nazarene.

**2003, Apr. 23**

2858-2859   A898    2.25 2.25
   Set of 2

**Souvenir Sheet**

2860   A898   22p multi    1.75 1.75

No. 2860 contains one 40x30mm stamp.

Our Lady of Caysasay, 400th Anniv. — A899

**2003, Sept. 8**
2861   A899   6p multi    .50   .25

CORNELIO T. VILLAREAL 1903 BIRTH CENTENARY 2003

Cornelio T. Villareal, Sr., House Speaker, Birth Cent. — A900

**2003, Sept. 11**
2862   A900   6p multi    .50   .25

---

Waterfalls — A893

No. 2843: a, Maria Cristina Falls. b, Katibawasan Falls. c, Bagongbong Falls. d, Pagsanjan Falls.

No. 2844: a, Casiawan Falls. b, Pangi Falls. c, Tinago Falls. d, Kipot Twin Falls.

**2003, June 27**
2843   A893   6p Block of 4, #a-d    2.00 2.00

**Souvenir Sheet**

2844   A893   6p Sheet of 4, #a-d    4.00 4.00

---

**2003, May 16**    *Perf. 14½, 13¾ (9p)*

| 2830 | A888 | 6p multi | .50 | .25 |
| 2831 | A888 | 9p multi | .70 | .35 |
| 2832 | A888 | 9p multi | 1.40 | .70 |
| 2833 | A888 | 21p multi | 1.75 | .85 |
| | | Set of 4 | 4.35 | 2.15 |

See Nos. 2849-2853 for stamps with flower names.

No. 2722 Surcharged in Black or Red

**2003**    *Perf. 13¾*

| 2834 | A828 | 1p on 5p multi | .20 | .20 |
| 2835 | A828 | 1p on 5p multi (R) | .20 | .20 |
| 2836 | A828 | 5p on 5p multi | .50 | .25 |
| | | Nos. 2834-2836 (3) | .90 | .65 |

Issued: Nos. 2834-2835, 5/19; No. 2836, 6/4.

Philippine Medical Association, Cent. — A889

**2003, May 21**    *Perf. 14*
2837   A889   6p multi    .50   .25

Rural Banking, 50th Anniv. — A890

**2003, May 22**
2838   A890   6p multi    .50   .25

Mountains — A891

No. 2839: a, Mt. Makiling. b, Mt. Kanlaon. c, Mt. Kitanglad. d, Mt. Mating-oy.

No. 2840: a, Mt. Iraya. b, Mt. Hibok-Hibok. c, Mt. Apo. d, Mt. Santo Tomas.

Illustration reduced.

**2003, June 16**
2839   A891   6p Block of 4, #a-d    2.00 2.00

**Souvenir Sheet**

2840   A891   6p Sheet of 4, #a-d    2.00 2.00

Chinese Roots of José Rizal A892

Designs: 6p, Rizal Monument, Rizal Park, Jinjiang, People's Republic of China, vert. 17p, Rizal and Pagoda, Jinjiang.

**2003, June 19**
2841-2842   A892    1.90 1.90
   Set of 2

---

Mahal Kita

St. Valentine's Day — A884

Mailman and: 5p, Heart-shaped strawberry. 17p, Hearts and mountains. 21p, Hearts and clouds. 22p, Butterflies and heart-shaped flowers.

**2003, Feb. 11**
2820-2823   A884   Set of 4    5.25 5.25

**Souvenir Sheets**

50 Years in the Philippines

Partners in Language Development

Summer Institute of Linguistics, 50th Anniv. in Philippines — A885

Int'l. Decade of the World's Indigenous People.

No. 2824: a, 5p, Yakan weaving. b, 6p, Ifugao weaving. c, 5p, Kagayanen weaving. d, Bagobo Abaca weaving.

No. 2825, 11p: a, Ayta bow and arrows. b, Ibatan baskets. c, Palawano gong. d, Mindanao instruments.

No. 2826: a, 17p, Iboli cross-stitch. b, 5p, Aklanon Piña weaving. c, Kalinga weaving. d, Manobo beadwork.

**2003, Feb. 28**    *Litho.*

**Sheets of 4, #a-d**

2824-2826   A885   Set of 3    9.00 9.00

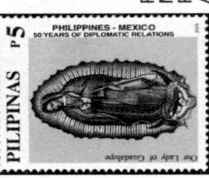

Arrival of Japanese Workers for Construction of Kennon Road, Cent A886

**2003, Feb. 20**    *Perf. 14*
2827   A886   5p multi    .40   .20

National Heroes A887

Designs: No. 2828, 6p, Apolinario Mabini (1864-1903), independence advocate. No. 2829, 6p, Luciano San Miguel (1875-1903), military leader.

**2003, May 13**    *Litho.*    *Perf. 14*
2828-2829   A887   Set of 2    1.00 1.00

Orchids — A888

Designs (no flower names shown): 6p, Dendrobium uniflorum. 9p, Paphiopedilum urbanianum. 17p, Epigeneium lyonii. 21p, Thrixspermum subulatum.

# PHILIPPINES

## National Teachers College, 75th Anniv. — A901

PILIPINAS P6

**2003, Sept. 15**
2863 A901 6p multi ... .50 .25

## Sanctuary of San Antonio Parish, 50th Anniv. — A902

**2003, Oct. 4** Litho.
2864 A902 6p multi ... .50 .25

## Int'l. Year of Fresh Water — A903

*Souvenir Sheet*

Int'l. Year of Freshwater 2003

**Nos. 2722-2723 Overprinted in Red**

**2003, Oct. 17** Perf. 13¾
2865 A828 5p multi ... .40 .20
2866 A828 15p multi ... 1.25 .60

**2003, Oct. 24** Perf. 14
2867 A903 22p multi + label ... 2.00 2.00

## Federation of Free Farmers, 50th Anniv. — A904

FFF — Federation of Free Farmers 1953-2003
PILIPINAS P6

**2003, Oct. 25**
2868 A904 6p multi ... .50 .25

## Christmas A905

PASKO 2003
PILIPINAS P6

**2003, Oct. 28**
2869-2872 A905 6p multi ... Set of 4 ... 5.25 5.25

Inscriptions: 6p, Mano po ninong ii: 17p, Himig at kulay ng Pasko, vert. 21p, Noche buena, vert. 22p, Karoling sa jeepney.

## National Stamp Collecting Month A906

PILIPINAS P21 SAKAY'N'MOY

**2003, Nov. 1**
2873-2876 A906 6p multi ... Set of 4 ... 5.25 2.60

*Souvenir Sheet*
2877 A906 22p multi ... 1.75 1.75

No. 2877 contains one 80x30mm stamp.

Cartoon art: 6p, Kenkoy, by Tony Velasquez, vert. 17p, Ikabod, by Nonoy Marcelo, vert. 21p, Sakay N'Moy, by Hugo C. Yonzon, Jr. No. 2876, 22p, Kalabong en Bosyo, by Larry Alcala. No. 2877, 22p, Hugo, the Sidewalk Vendor, by Rodolfo V. Ragodon.

## Winning Children's Art in National Anti-Drug Stamp Design Contest — A907

ANG BATANG PINOY LABAN SA DROGA P6 PILIPINAS

**2003, Nov. 3**
2878 A907 6p Block of 4, #a-d ... 2.00 2.00

No. 2878: a, Globe, child with broom, by Nicole Fernan L. Caminian. b, Children, "No Drugs" symbol, by Jairus Cabajar. c, Children painting over "Drug Addiction" picture, by Genevieve V. Lazarte. d, Child chopping tree with hatchet, by Martin F. Rivera.

## Nos. 2550Ab, 2550Ac, 2550Ad and 2550Ae Surcharged

**2003, Nov. 11** Perf. 14
2879 A749a 17p on 4p #2550Ab ... 1.40 .70
2880 A749a 17p on 8p #2550Ac ... 1.40 .70
2881 A749a 22p on 16p #2550Ad ... 1.75 .90
2882 A749a 22p on 16p #2550Ae ... 1.75 .90
Nos. 2879-2882 (4) ... 6.30 3.20

Nos. 2879-2882 were sold removed from the booklet. The basic stamps were in the booklet.

## First Philippine Stamps, 150th Anniv. — A908

PILIPINAS P.22 / P17

*Souvenir Sheet*

**2003, Nov. 14**
2883 A908 22p multi ... 2.00 2.00

## Camera Club of the Philippines, 75th Anniv. A909

THE CAMERA CLUB PHILIPPINES — PILIPINAS P6 1928·2003

**2003, Dec. 1** Litho.
2884 A909 6p multi ... .50 .25

Camera Club of the Philippines, 75th Anniv. of Manila.

Filipinas 2004 Stamp Exhibition, Mandaluyong City. See Nos. 2891-2897.

## New Year 2004 (Year of the Monkey) A910

PILIPINAS P6 — 2004 YEAR OF THE MONKEY — MAONGKONG BAGONG TAON

**2003, Dec. 1**
2885-2886 A910 ... Set of 2 ... 1.90 .95
2886a Souvenir sheet, #2885-2886 + 2 labels ... 1.90 1.90

Monkey: 6p, Perched on branch. 17p, Hanging from branch.

No. 2886a exists imperf.

## Architecture — A912

ARCHITECTURAL HERITAGE — PILIPINAS P6

**2003, Dec. 22**
2889 A912 6p Block of 4, #a-d ... 2.00 2.00

No. 2889: a, Luneta Hotel. b, Hong Kong Shanghai Bank. c, El Hogar. d, Regina Building. No. 2890, horiz.: a, Pangasinan Capitol. b, Metropolitan Theater. c, Philtrust. d, University of Manila.

*Souvenir Sheet*
2890 A912 6p Sheet of 4, #a-d ... 2.00 2.00

## Succulent Plants — A911

PILIPINAS P6

**2003, Dec. 5**
2887 A911 6p Block of 4, #a-d ... 2.00 2.00

*Souvenir Sheet*
2888 A911 6p Sheet of 4, #a-d ... 2.00 2.00

No. 2887: a, Mammilaria spinosissima (yellow frame). b, Epithelantha bokei. c, Rebutia spinosissima. d, Turbinicarpus alonsoi. No. 2888: a, Aloe humilis. b, Euphorbia golisana. c, Gymnocalycium spinosissima. d, Mammilaria spinosissima (green frame).

## Powered Flight, Cent. — A911a

100 Years of AVIATION 1903-2003 — PILIPINAS P6

**2003, Dec. 17** Litho. Perf. 14
2888E A911a 6p Horiz. pair, #f-g ... 1.00 1.00

No. 2888E — Do24TT: f, Green background. g, Yellow background. Illustration reduced.

## Background Colors / Souvenir Sheets

**2003-04** Perf. 14
2891 A908 6p Any single ... .50 .25
a.-d. Horiz. strip of 4 ... 2.00 2.00

2892 A908 22p dk to lt rose ... 1.75 1.75
2893 A908 22p dk to lt blue ... 1.75 1.75
2894 A908 22p blue to lt grn ... 1.75 1.75
2895 A908 22p dk to lt pink ... 1.75 1.75
2896 A908 22p dk to lt yellow ... 1.75 1.75
2897 A908 22p brn to yellow ... 1.75 1.75
a. A908 22p white

No. 2891 (36x26mm each): a, Blue to lilac background, #1. b, Orange to yellow background, #2. c, Light to dark green background, #4. d, Dark to light pink background, #5. Nos. 2892-2897: Like #2883. A sheet containing a block of four of perf. and imperf. examples of Nos. 2891a-2891d sold for 100p.

With Postpex 2004 inscription added in red and black in sheet margin. Filipinas 2004 Stamp Exhibition, Mandaluyong City. Issued: No. 2892, 12/15/03; No. 2893, 1/15/04; No. 2894, 1/30/04; No. 2895, 1/31/04; Nos. 2896, 2897, 2/1/04; No. 2897a, 4/19/04.

## First Philippine Stamps, 150th Anniv. — A908

Visit PILIPINAS — FIRST PHILIPPINE MAIL — MANDALUYONG CITY

*Souvenir Sheet*

## Arrival in Philippines of Sisters of St. Paul of Chartres, Cent. — A913

THE LOVE OF CHRIST IMPELS US — PILIPINAS P6 — 100

**2004, Jan. 22** Perf. 14
2898 A913 6p multi ... .50 .25

## Polytechnic University of the Philippines, Cent. — A914

PILIPINAS P6 — POLYTECHNIC UNIVERSITY OF THE PHILIPPINES — 100

**2004, Jan. 22**
2899 A914 6p multi ... .50 .25

Tanduay Distillers, Inc., 150th Anniv. — A915

**2004, Jan. 22**    Litho.
2900 A915 6p multi    .50   .25

Grepalife Life Insurance Co., 50th Anniv. — A916

**2004, Jan. 22**
2901 A916 6p multi    .50   .25

2003 State Visit of U.S. Pres. George W. Bush A917

Flags of U.S. and Philippines, George W. Bush and: 6p, Crowd, 22p, Philippines Pres. Gloria Macapagal-Arroyo, Malacañang Palace.

**2004, Feb. 23**   Litho.   **Perf. 13x13½**
2902-2903 A917   Set of 2    2.25   1.10

**Orchid Type of 2003 With Plant Names**

Designs: 1p, Liparis latifolia. 2p, Cymbidium finlaysonianum. 3p, Phalaenopsis philippinensis. 4p, Phalaenopsis fasciata. 5p, Spathoglottis plicata.

No. 2909: a, Phalaenopsis fuscata. b, Phalaenopsis stuartiana. c, Renanthera monachia. d, Aerides quinquevulnera. 8p, Phalaenopsis schilleriana. 9p, Phalaenopsis pulchra. 20p, Phaius tankervilleae.

Two types of 1p and 5p:

I — Denomination and year date not touching edges of background color, digits of year date touching.

II — Denomination and year date touch edges of background color, digits of year date spaced.

Three types of 2p:

I — Plant name 13½mm long and 1mm from year date, denomination and year date not touching edges of background color.

II — Plant name 13½ mm long and 2mm from year date, denomination and year date touching edges of background color.

III — Plant name 14mm long and 1½mm from year date, denomination and year date touching edges of background color.

| **2004** | | Litho. | **Perf. 14½** | |
|---|---|---|---|---|
| 2904 | A888 | 1p multi, type I | .20 | .20 |
| a. | | Type II | .20 | .20 |
| 2905 | A888 | 2p multi, type I | .20 | .20 |
| a. | | Type II | .20 | .20 |
| b. | | Type III | .20 | .20 |
| 2906 | A888 | 3p multi | .25 | .20 |
| 2907 | A888 | 4p multi | .30 | .20 |
| 2908 | A888 | 5p multi, type I | .40 | .20 |
| a. | | Type II | .50 | .25 |
| 2909 | A888 | Block of 4 | 2.00 | 2.00 |
| a.-d. | A888 | 6p Any single | .65 | .35 |
| 2910 | A888 | 8p multi | .70 | .35 |
| 2911 | A888 | 9p multi | .80 | .35 |
| 2912 | A888 | 20p multi | 1.60 | .80 |
| | | Nos. 2904-2912 (9) | 6.30 | 4.45 |

Issued: Nos. 2904, 2908, 3/9; Nos. 2904a, 2905, 2905b, 2910, 4/1: Nos. 2905a, 2908a, 4/28; Nos. 2906, 2907, 2911, 2912, 6/11; No. 2909, 12/20.

---

Pfizer Pharmaceuticals, 50th Anniv. in Philippines A918

**2004, Apr. 30**    **Perf. 14**
2913 A918 6p multi    .50   .25

Our Lady of Piat, 400th Anniv. — A919

**2004, June 21**
2914 A919 6p multi    .50   .25

Bonsai A920

No. 2915, vert. — Orange to yellow background: a, Bantigue. b, Kamuning Binangonan with thick trunk, dark brown pot. c, Balete. d, Mulawin aso. e, Kamuning Binangonan with root-like trunk, dark brown pot f, Logwood. g, Kamuning Binangonan, orange clay pot. h, Bantolinao.

No. 2916 — Purple to white background: a, Bantigue with thick trunk, brown pot. b, Chinese elm. c, Bantigue with two trunks, brown pot. d, Bantigue, white pot. e, Balete with many green leaves, black and brown pot. f, Balete with few green leaves, brown pot. g, Bantigue, light brown rectangular pot. h, Mansanita.

Nos. 2917a, 2918a, Lomonsito. Nos. 2917b, 2918b, Bougainvillea, pot on table. Nos. 2917c, 2918c, Bougainvillea, orange brown pot. Nos. 2917d, 2918d, Kalyos.

| **2004** | | | **Perf. 14** | |
|---|---|---|---|---|
| 2915 | | Block of 8 | 4.00 | 4.00 |
| a.-h. | A920 | 6p Any single | .50 | .25 |
| 2916 | | Block of 8 | 4.00 | 4.00 |
| a.-h. | A920 | 6p Any single | .50 | .25 |

**Souvenir Sheets**

**Solid Blue Background**

| 2917 | | Sheet of 4 | 2.00 | 2.00 |
|---|---|---|---|---|
| a.-d. | A920 | 6p Any single | .50 | .25 |

**Blue to White Background**

| 2918 | | Sheet of 4 | 2.00 | 2.00 |
|---|---|---|---|---|
| a.-d. | A920 | 6p Any single | .50 | .25 |

Issued: Nos. 2915-2917, 7/27; No. 2918, 8/28. 2004 World Stamp Championship, Singapore (No. 2918).

---

Miguel Lopez de Legazpi (c. 1510-72), Founder of Manila — A922

**2004, Aug. 20**    Litho.   .25
2924 A922 6p multi    .50   .25

Admiral Tomas A. Cloma, Sr. (1904-96) A923

**2004, Aug. 20**
2925 A923 6p multi    .50   .25

Animals of the Lunar New Year Cycle — A924

Designs: Nos. 2926a, 2927a, Rat. Nos. 2926b, 2927b, Ox. Nos. 2926c, 2927c, Tiger. Nos. 2926d, 2927d, Rabbit. Nos. 2926e, 2927e, Dragon. Nos. 2926f, 2927f, Snake. Nos. 2926g, 2928a, Horse. Nos. 2926h, 2928b, Goat. Nos. 2926i, 2928c, Monkey. Nos. 2926j, 2928d, Cock. Nos. 2926k, 2928e, Dog. Nos. 2926l, 2928f, Pig.

**2004, Sept. 9**    **Perf. 14**

**English Inscriptions at Left**
2926 A924 6p Sheet of 12, #a-l, + 3 labels   6.00   6.00

**Chinese Inscriptions at Left**
2927 A924 6p Sheet of 6, #a-f, + 6 labels   3.00   3.00
2928 A924 6p Sheet of 6, #a-f, + 6 labels   3.00   3.00

---

2004 Summer Olympics, Athens A921

Designs: 6p, Shooting. 17p, Taekwondo. 21p, Swimming. No. 2922, 22p, Archery. No. 2923, 22p, Boxing.

**2004, Aug. 13**   Set of 4    5.50   2.75
2919-2922 A921   **Souvenir Sheet**
2923 A921 22p multi    1.75   .90

---

Manila Central University, Cent. A925

**2004, Sept. 21**    .50   .25
2929 A925 6p multi
a. Miniature sheet of 8   4.00   4.00

Christmas A926

Various Christmas trees: 6p, 17p, 21p, 22p.

**2004, Oct. 1**   Set of 4    5.50   5.50
2930-2933 A926

Filipino-Chinese General Chamber of Commerce, Cent. — A927

No. 2934: a, Intramuros, Philippines. b, Great Wall of China. Illustration reduced.

**2004, Oct. 12**
2934 A927 6p Horiz. pair, #a-b   1.00   1.00

Winning Designs in Rice Is Life National Stamp Design Contest — A928

No. 2935, 6p: a, By Maria Enna T. Alegre. b, By Lady Fatima M. Velasco.
No. 2936, 6p: a, By Sean Y. Pajaron. b, By Lijan B. Delgado.
No. 2937, 6p: a, By Michael O. Villadolid. b, By Gary M. Manalo.

**2004, Oct. 15**    Litho.

**Horiz. Pairs, #a-b**
2935-2937 A928   Set of 3    3.00   3.00
2937c   Miniature sheet #2935a-2935b, 2936a-2936b, 2937a-2937b   3.00   3.00

Intl. Year of Rice.

Natl. Stamp Collecting Month A929

Comic strip and comic book illustrations: No. 2938, 6p, Darna. b, By Nestor P. Redondo. No. 2939, 6p, Kulafu, by Francisco Reyes. No. 2940, 6p, El Vibora, by Federico C. Javinal, vert. No. 2941, 6p, Lapu-Lapu, by Francisco V. Coching, vert.

**2004**
2938-2941 A929   Set of 4    2.00   2.00
**Souvenir Sheet**
2942 A929 22p multi    2.00   2.00

No. 2942 contains one 30x80mm stamp.

San Agustin Church, Manila, 400th Anniv. — A930

No. 2943: a, Denomination at left. b, Denomination at right.

**2004, Nov. 13**
2943 A930 6p Horiz. pair, #a-b   1.00   1.00

**New Year 2005 (Year of the Rooster)**
A931

Designs: 6p, Rooster's head. 17p, Rooster.

| | | |
|---|---|---|
| **2004, Dec. 1** | | |
| 2944-2945 A931 | Souvenir sheet, 2 each #2944-2945 | |
| 2944 | | 1.90 1.90 |
| 2945 | | 4.00 4.00 |

Owls: No. 2946, 6p, Giant Scops owl. No. 2947, 6p, Philippine eagle owl. No. 2948, 6p, Negros Scops owl. No. 2949, 6p, West Visayan hawk owl.

| | | |
|---|---|---|
| **2004, Dec. 22** | | |
| 2946-2949 A932 | Set of 4 | 2.00 2.00 |
| 2949a | Block of 4, #2946-2949 | 2.00 2.00 |

**Worldwide Fund for Nature (WWF) — A932**

**Liceo de Cagayan University**
A933

| | | |
|---|---|---|
| **2005, Feb. 5** | | Litho. |
| 2950 A933 | 6p multi | .50 .25 |

**Seventh-Day Adventist Church in the Philippines, Cent. — A934**

| | | |
|---|---|---|
| **2005, Feb. 18** | | Perf. 14 |
| 2951 A934 | 6p multi | .50 .25 |

**Baguio Country Club, Cent. — A935**

No. 2952: a. Club in 1905. b, Club in 2005. Illustration reduced.

| | | |
|---|---|---|
| **2005, Feb 18** | | |
| 2952 A935 | 6p Horiz. pair, #a-b | 1.00 1.00 |

**Butterflies — A936**

Designs: 1p, Arisbe decolor stratos. No. 2954: a. Parantica noeli. b, Chilasa osmana osmana. c, Graphium sandawanum joreli. d, Papilio xuthus benguetanus.

| | | |
|---|---|---|
| **2005** | | Litho. Perf. 14½ |
| 2953 A936 | 1p multi | .20 .20 |
| 2954 A936 | Block of 4 | 7.00 3.50 |
| a.-d. | A936 22p Any single | 1.75 .85 |

See Nos. 2978-2981.

Issued: 1p, 4/12; No. 2954, 3/3.

---

**Shells — A937**

No. 2955: a, Chicoreus saulii. b, Spondylus variants. c, Spondylus linquaefelis. d, Spondylus broderipii.
No. 2956: a, Chlamys senatoria. b, Sipho-nofusus vicdani. c, Epitonium scalare. d, Harpa harpa.
No. 2957: a, Siliquaria armata. b, Argonauta argo. c, Perotrochus vicdani. d, Corcuium cardissa.

| | | |
|---|---|---|
| **2005, Apr. 15** | | Perf. 14 |
| 2955 A937 | Block of 4 | 2.00 1.00 |
| a.-d. | 6p Any single | .50 .25 |
| 2956 A937 | Block of 4 | 2.00 1.00 |
| a.-d. | 6p Any single | .50 .25 |
| 2957 A937 | Souvenir Sheet | |
| | Sheet of 4 + 2 la-bels | 2.00 1.00 |
| a.-d. | 6p Any single | .50 .25 |

**State Visit of Hu Jintao, Pres. of People's Republic of China**
A938

Flags of Philippines and People's Republic of China, Philippines Pres. Gloria Macapagal-Arroyo and, 6p, Pres. Hu at right. 17p, Pres. Hu at left.

| | | |
|---|---|---|
| **2005, Apr. 27** | | |
| 2958-2959 A938 | Set of 2 | 1.90 .95 |
| 2959a | Souvenir sheet, #2958-2959 | 1.90 .95 |

**Architecture — A939**

No. 2960: a, Ernesto de la Cruz Ancestral House. b, Limjoco Residence. c, Pelaez Ancestral House. d, Vergara House.
No. 2961: a, Gliceria Marela Villavicencio.
b, Lasala-Guarin House. c, Claparols House. d, Ilagan Ancestral House. Illustration reduced.

| | | |
|---|---|---|
| **2005, May 7** | | |
| 2960 A939 | Block of 4 | 2.00 1.00 |
| a.-d. | 6p Any single | .50 .25 |
| 2961 A939 | Souvenir Sheet | |
| | Sheet of 4 | 2.00 1.00 |
| a.-d. | 6p Any single | .50 .25 |

**Central Philippine University, Cent.**
A940

| | | |
|---|---|---|
| **2005, May 13** | | |
| 2962 A940 | 6p multi | .50 .25 |

---

**Rotary International, Cent. — A941**

Denomination: 6p. At left, in red. At right, in red.

| | | |
|---|---|---|
| **2005, May 31** | | |
| 2963-2964 A941 | Set of 2 | 1.90 .95 |
| 2964a | Miniature sheet, 6 #2963, 2 #2964 | 6.00 3.00 |

**San Bartolome Parish, 400th Anniv.**
A942

| | | |
|---|---|---|
| **2005, July 25** | | Litho. Perf. 14 |
| 2965 A942 | 6p multi | .50 .25 |

**Senator Blas F. Ople (1927-2003)**
A943

| | | |
|---|---|---|
| **2005, July 28** | | |
| 2966 A943 | 6p multi | .50 .25 |

**Shells — A944**

No. 2967, 6p: a, Chrysallis fischeri. b, Helicostyla bicolorata. c, Helicostyla dobiosa. d, Helicostyla portei.
No. 2968, 6p: a, Cochlostyla imperator. b, Helicostyla turbinoides. c, Helicostyla lignaria.
d. Amphidromus dubius.
No. 2969, horiz.: a, Calocochlia depressa. b, Cochlostyla sarcinosa. c, Calocochlia schadenbergi. d, Helicostyla pulcherrina.

| | | |
|---|---|---|
| **2005** | | Perf. 14 |
| 2967-2968 A944 | Set of 2 | |
| | Souvenir Sheets | |
| | Set of 4, #a-d | 4.00 2.00 |
| 2969 A944 | 6p Souvenir Sheet | |
| | Sheet of 4, #a-d + 2 labels | 2.00 1.00 |
| 2970 | | |
| a. | A944 2p Like #2969a, 2969b | 1.40 .70 |
| b. | A944 3p Like #2969c | .20 .20 |

Issued: Nos. 2967-2969, 8/8; No. 2970, 8/19. Upper left label on No. 2970 has Taipei 2005 Exhibition emblem; lower right label has "Greetings from the Philippines" inscription.

---

**Intl. Year of the Eucharist**
A945

Winning pictures in stamp design contest by: No. 2971, 6p, Carlos Vincent H Ruiz. No. 2972, 6p, Carlos Vincent H Ruiz. No. 2973, 6p, Telly Farolan-Somera. No. 2974, 6p, Allen A. Moran. No. 2975, 6p, Elouiza Athena Tentativa. No. 2976, 6p, Jianina Marishka C. Montealto.

| | | |
|---|---|---|
| **2005, Sept. 8** | | |
| 2971-2976 A945 | Set of 6 | 3.00 1.50 |
| 2976a | Souvenir sheet, #2971-2976, + 6 labels | 3.00 1.50 |

**No. 1887 Surcharged in Red**

| | | |
|---|---|---|
| **2005, Sept. 14** | Wmk. 389 Litho. Imperf. |
| 2977 A493 | 15p on 8p multi | 1.25 .60 |

**Butterflies Type of 2005 and Souvenir Sheet**

Designs: 5p, Parantica danatti pinensis. No. 2979: a, Hebenoia glaucippe philippinensis. b, Moduza urdaneta aynii. c, Lexias satrapes hiwaga. d, Cheritra orpheus orpheus.
e, Achillides chikae chikae. f, Arisbe ideaoiedes ideaoiedes. g, Dellas schoenigi hermeli. h, Achillides palinurus daedalus. i, Dellas levicki justini. j, Troides magellanus magellanus.
No. 2980: a, Idea electra electra. b, Charaxes bajula adoracion. c, Tanaecia calliphorus calliphorus. d, Trogonoptera trojana.
e, Charaxes bajula adoracion. diff.
No. 2981: a, Cethosia biblis barangingi. b, Menalaides polytes ledebouria. c, Appias nero palawanica. d, Udara tyotaroi.

| | | |
|---|---|---|
| **2005** | | Unwmk. Perf. 14½ |
| 2978 A936 | 5p multi | .40 .20 |
| 2979 A936 | Block of 10 | 5.00 2.50 |
| a.-j. | A936 6p Any single | .50 .25 |
| 2980 | | Block of 4, #a-d | 5.50 2.75 |
| a. | A936 17p multi | 1.25 .60 |
| b. | A936 17p multi | 1.25 .60 |
| c. | A936 17p multi | 1.25 .60 |
| d. | A936 17p multi | 1.25 .60 |
| e. | A947 17p multi | .60 |
| 2981 | | Block of 4, #2980a, 2980c, 2980d, 2980e | 6.75 3.50 |
| a.-d. | A936 21p Any single | 1.60 .80 |

Issued: No. 2978, 11/22; No. 2979, 12/9; Nos. 2978-2981, 12/2.

A946

A947

PHILIPPINES

## SEMI-POSTAL STAMPS

Catalogue values for unused stamps in this section are for Never Hinged items.

### Republic

Epifanio de los Santos, Trinidad H. Pardo and Teodoro M. Kalaw — SP1

Doctrina Christiana, Cover Page — SP2

"Noli Me Tangere," Cover Page — SP3

**1949, Apr. 1  Unwmk.  Engr.  Perf. 12**

| | | | |
|---|---|---|---|
| B1 | SP1 4c + 2c sepia | 1.50 | 1.50 |
| B2 | SP2 6c + 4c violet | 5.00 | 5.00 |
| B3 | SP3 18c + 7c blue | 5.50 | 5.50 |
| | Nos. B1-B3 (3) | 12.00 | 12.00 |

War Widow and Children — SP4

Disabled Veteran — SP5

The surtax was for restoration of war-damaged public libraries.

---

**1950, Nov. 30**

| | | | |
|---|---|---|---|
| B4 | SP4 2c + 2c red | .30 | .20 |
| B5 | SP5 4c + 4c violet | .40 | .30 |

The surtax was for war widows and children and disabled veterans of World War II. For surcharges see Nos. 648-649.

Mrs. Manuel L. Quezon — SP6

**Perf. 12**

**1952, Aug. 19**

| | | | |
|---|---|---|---|
| B6 | SP6 5c + 1c dp bl | .30 | .20 |
| B7 | SP6 2c + 2c car rose | .45 | .30 |

The surtax was used to encourage planting and care of fruit trees among Philippine children. For surcharge see No. 872.

Quezon Institute — SP7

**1958, Aug. 19  Photo.  Perf. 13½, 12**

**Cross in Red**

| | | | |
|---|---|---|---|
| B8 | SP7 5c + 5c grn | .20 | .20 |
| B9 | SP7 10c + 5c dp vio | .30 | .30 |

These stamps were obligatory on all mail from Aug. 19-Sept. 30. For surcharges see Nos. 849, B12-B13, B16.

The surtax on all semi-postals from Nos. B8-B9 onward was for the Philippine Tuberculosis Society unless otherwise stated.

Scout — SP8

**1959  Engr.  Perf. 13**

**Yellow Paper**

| | | | |
|---|---|---|---|
| B10 | SP8 6c + 4c shown | .20 | .20 |
| B11 | SP8 25c + 5c Archery | .55 | .45 |
| a. | Nos. B10-B11 tete beche, white | 1.00 | .85 |
| | Nos. B10-B11,CB1-CB3 (5) | 2.75 | 2.50 |

10th Boy Scout World Jamboree, Makiling National Park, July 17-26. The surtax was to finance the Jamboree. For souvenir sheet see No. CB3a. For surcharges see Nos. 832-833, C111.

**Nos. B8-B9 Surcharged in Red**

**1959  Photo.  Perf. 13½, 12**

| | | | |
|---|---|---|---|
| B12 | SP7 3c + 5c on 5c + 5c | .25 | .20 |
| a. | "3 + 5" and bars omitted | | |
| B13 | SP7 6c + 5c on 10c + 5c | .35 | .25 |

---

Third Asian Para Games — A956

Designs: 6p, Runner with amputated arm. 17p, Wheelchair racer.

**2005, Dec. 6**

| | | | |
|---|---|---|---|
| 3004-3005 | A956  Set of 2 | 1.90 | .95 |

---

23rd Southeast Asia Games, Philippines — A953

No. 2992: a, Boxing. b, Cycling. c, Wushu. d, Bowling. e, Badminton. f, Billiards. Eagle has black beak on all stamps.

No. 2993, horiz.: a, Track. b, Soccer. c, Taekwondo. d, Judo. e, Chess. f, Karate. g, Gymnastics. h, Pencaksilat. i, Dragon boat racing. j, Swimming.

No. 2994: a, Baseball. b, Shooting. c, Archery. d, Bowling (eagle with brown beak). e, Volleyball. f, Boxing (eagle with brown beak). g, Cycling (eagle with brown beak). h, Badminton (eagle with brown beak).

No. 2995: a, Shooting. b, Archery. c, Equestrian.

No. 2996, horiz.: a, Arnis. b, Chess. c, Dragon boat racing.

**2005, Nov. 22**

**Red Frames**

| | | | |
|---|---|---|---|
| 2992 | Block of 6 | 3.00 | 1.50 |
| a.-f. | A953 6p Any single | .50 | .25 |
| 2993 | Sheet of 10 + 8 large labels | 8.00 | 8.00 |
| a.-j. | A953 6p Any single | .75 | .75 |
| 2994 | Sheet of 10, #2992c, 2992f, 2994a-2994h, + 20 labels | 8.00 | 8.00 |
| a.-h. | A953 6p Any single | .75 | .75 |

**Blue Frames**

| | | | |
|---|---|---|---|
| 2995 | Sheet of 3 | 1.40 | .70 |
| a. | A953 5p multi | .40 | .20 |
| b.-c. | A953 6p Either single | .50 | .25 |
| 2996 | Sheet of 3 | 1.40 | .70 |
| a. | A953 5p multi | .40 | .20 |
| b.-c. | A953 6p Either single | .50 | .25 |

No. 2992 was printed in sheets containing two blocks. Nos. 2993a-2993j lack perforations between the stamp and the adjacent labels that are the same size as the stamp. There are perforations between the stamps and labels on No. 2994. The labels to the right of the stamps could be personalized. Nos. 2993 and 2994 each sold for 99p with generic flag labels, and for 350p with personalized labels.

---

National Stamp Collecting Month — A954

Prints: No. 2997, 6p, Pinoy Worker Abr'd., by Ben Cab. No. 2998, 6p, Bulbs, by M. Parial. No. 2999, 6p, The Fourth Horseman, by Tequi. No. 3000, 6p, Breaking Ground, by R. Olazo. 22p, Form XV, by Brenda Fajardo, horiz.

**2005, Nov. 28**

| | | | |
|---|---|---|---|
| 2997-3000 | A954  Set of 4 | 2.00 | 1.00 |

**Souvenir Sheet**

| | | | |
|---|---|---|---|
| 3001 | A954 22p multi | 1.75 | .90 |

No. 3001 contains one 80x30mm stamp.

---

Intl. Year of Sports and Physical Education — A948

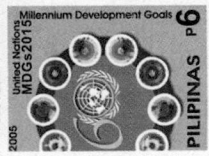

UN Millennium Development Goals — A949

**2005, Oct. 19  Perf. 14**

| | | | |
|---|---|---|---|
| 2982 | A948 6p Horiz. pair, #a-b | 1.00 | .50 |
| c. | 6p single | .50 | .25 |
| d. | Horiz. pair, #2982a, 2982c | 1.00 | .50 |
| 2983 | A949 6p single | .50 | .25 |

**Souvenir Sheet**

| | | | |
|---|---|---|---|
| 2984 | Sheet, #2982a, 2982b, 2984a | 1.75 | .90 |
| a. | A949 10p single | .75 | .50 |
| b. | Sheet, #2982a, 2982c, 2984a | 1.75 | .90 |

United Nations, 60th anniv.

No. 2982: a, Dove, open book, Philippines flag, basketball, emblem at LL. b, Torch, sports equipment, people with joined hands, dove flying to right, emblem at LR. c, Torch, sports equipment, people with joined hands, dove flying to left, emblem at LL.

---

Bureau of Corrections, Cent. — A950

**2005, Nov. 4**

| | | | |
|---|---|---|---|
| 2985 | A950 6p multi | .50 | .25 |

---

Inauguration of Pres. Gloria Macapagal-Arroyo — A951

Pres. Macapagal-Arroyo: 6p, Taking oath. 22p, Giving inaugural speech.

**2005, Nov. 9**

| | | | |
|---|---|---|---|
| 2986-2987 | A951  Set of 2 | 2.25 | 1.10 |

---

New Year 2006 (Year of the Dog) — A955

Dog and inscription: a, 6p, "Manigong Bagong Taon." b, 17p, "Happy New Year."

**2005, Dec. 1**

| | | | |
|---|---|---|---|
| 3002-3003 | A955  Set of 2 | 1.90 | .95 |
| 3002a | Souvenir sheet, 2 each #3002-3003 | 4.00 | 1.90 |

---

Christmas — A952

Various department store window Christmas displays: 6p, 17p, 21p, 22p.

**2005, Nov. 16**

| | | | |
|---|---|---|---|
| 2988-2991 | A952  Set of 4 | 5.50 | 2.75 |

## Bohol Sanatorium — SP9

**1959, Aug. 19**    **Engr.**    **Perf. 12**

**Cross in Red**

| | | | |
|---|---|---|---|
| B14 | SP9 | 6c + 5c yel grn | .20 .20 |
| B15 | SP9 | 25c + 5c vio bl | .40 .30 |

No. B8 Surcharged "Help Prevent TB" and New Value

**1960, Aug. 19**    **Photo.**    **Perf. 13½, 12**

| | | | |
|---|---|---|---|
| B16 | SP7 | 6c + 5c on 5c + 5c | .50 .20 |

## Roxas Memorial T.B. Pavilion SP10

**1961, Aug. 19**    **Unwmk.**    **Photo.**

**Perf. 11½**

**Cross in Red**

| | | | |
|---|---|---|---|
| B17 | SP10 | 6c + 5c brn & red | .50 .20 |

## José Rizal Playing Chess SP12

**1962, Aug. 19**

**Cross in Red**

| | | | |
|---|---|---|---|
| B18 | SP11 | 6s + 5s dk vio | .20 .20 |
| B19 | SP11 | 30s + 5s ultra | .35 .20 |
| B20 | SP11 | 70s + 5s brt bl | 1.25 .90 |

Nos. B18-B20 (3)

## Emiliano J. Valdes T.B. Pavilion SP11

**1962, Dec. 30**    **Engr.**    **Perf. 13**

| | | | |
|---|---|---|---|
| B21 | SP12 | 6s + 4s grn & rose lil | .35 .20 |
| B22 | SP12 | 30s + 5s brt bl & cl | .90 .45 |

Design: 30s+5s, Rizal fencing.

## Map of Philippines and Cross — SP13

## Negros Oriental T.B. Pavilion SP14

**1963, Aug. 19**    **Unwmk.**    **Perf. 13**

| | | | |
|---|---|---|---|
| B23 | SP13 | 6s + 5s vio & red | .20 .20 |
| B24 | SP13 | 10s + 5s grn & red | .30 .20 |
| B25 | SP13 | 50s + 5s brn & red | 1.25 .75 |

Nos. B23-B25 (3)

Surtax for Rizal Foundation. For surcharges see Nos. 942-943.

---

## Stork-billed Kingfisher — SP15

**1964, Aug. 19**    **Photo.**    **Perf. 13½**

**Cross in Red**

| | | | |
|---|---|---|---|
| B26 | SP14 | 5s + 5s brt pur | .20 .20 |
| B27 | SP14 | 6s + 5s ultra | .20 .20 |
| B28 | SP14 | 30s + 5s brown | .30 .25 |
| B29 | SP14 | 70s + 5s green | .55 .50 |

Nos. B26-B29 (4)

No. B27 Surcharged in Red with New Value and Two Bars

**1965, Aug. 19**    **Cross in Red**

| | | | |
|---|---|---|---|
| B30 | SP14 | 1s + 5s on 6s + 5s | .25 .20 |
| B31 | SP14 | 3s + 5s on 6s + 5s | .35 .20 |

For surcharges see Nos. 986, 1586.

**1967, Aug. 19**    **Photo.**    **Perf. 13½**

**Cross in Red**

| | | | |
|---|---|---|---|
| B32 | SP15 | 1s + 5s multi | .20 .20 |
| B33 | SP15 | 5s + 5s multi | .30 .20 |
| B34 | SP15 | 10s + 5s multi | .60 .25 |
| B35 | SP15 | 30s + 5s multi | 2.40 .70 |

Nos. B32-B35 (4)

Birds: 5s+5s, Rufous hornbill. 10s+5s, Monkey-eating eagle. 30s+5s, Great-billed parrot.

**1969, Aug. 15**    **Litho.**    **Perf. 13½**

**Cross in Red**

| | | | |
|---|---|---|---|
| B36 | SP15 | 1s + 5s multi | .20 .20 |
| B37 | SP15 | 5s + 5s multi | .50 .20 |
| B38 | SP15 | 10s + 5s multi | 1.00 .60 |
| B39 | SP15 | 40s + 5s multi | 3.70 1.30 |

Nos. B36-B39 (4)

Birds: 1s+5s, Three-toed woodpecker. 5s+5s, Philippine trogon. 10s+5s, Mt. Apo lorikeet. 40s+5s, Scarlet minivet.

## Julia V. de Ortigas and Tuberculosis Society Building — SP16

**1970, Aug. 3**    **Photo.**    **Perf. 13½**

| | | | |
|---|---|---|---|
| B40 | SP16 | 1s + 5s multi | .20 .20 |
| B41 | SP16 | 5s + 5s multi | .30 .20 |
| B42 | SP16 | 30s + 5s multi | 1.00 .45 |
| B43 | SP16 | 70s + 5s multi | 2.75 1.40 |

Nos. B40-B43 (4)

Mrs. Julia V. de Ortigas was president of the Philippine Tuberculosis Soc., 1932-69. For surcharge see No. 1251.

## Mabolo, Santol, Chico, Papaya SP17

**1972, Aug. 1**    **Litho.**    **Perf. 13**

| | | | |
|---|---|---|---|
| B44 | SP17 | 1s + 5s multi | .20 .20 |
| B45 | SP17 | 5s + 5s multi | .30 .20 |
| B46 | SP17 | 40s + 5s multi | .65 .25 |
| B47 | SP17 | 1p + 5s multi | 2.75 1.15 |

Nos. B44-B47 (4)

Philippine Fruits: 10s+5s, Balimbing, atis, mangosteen, macupa, bananas. 40s+5s, Susong-kalabao, avocado, duhat, watermelon, guava, mango. 1p+5s, Lanzones, oranges, sirhuelas, pineapple.

**1973, June 15**

Nos. B45-B46 Surcharged with New Value and 2 Bars

| | | | |
|---|---|---|---|
| B48 | SP17 | 15s + 5s on 10s + 5s | .35 .20 |
| B49 | SP17 | 60s + 5s on 40s + 5s | .90 .35 |

## Dr. Basilio J. Valdes and Veterans Memorial Hospital — SP18

**1974, July 8**    **Litho.**    **Perf. 12½**

**Cross in Red**

| | | | |
|---|---|---|---|
| B50 | SP18 | 15s + 5s blue grn | .35 .20 |
| a. | | Imperf. | — .75 |
| B51 | SP18 | 1.10p + 5s vio blue | .90 .30 |
| a. | | Imperf. | 3.00 3.00 |

Dr. Valdes (1892-1970) was president of Philippine Tuberculosis Society. For surcharges see Nos. 1250, 1252.

---

# AIR POST STAMPS

## Madrid-Manila Flight Issue

Regular Issue of 1917-26 Overprinted in Red or Violet

**1926, May 13**    **Unwmk.**    **Perf. 11**

| | | | |
|---|---|---|---|
| C1 | A40 | 2c green (R) | 12.50 12.50 |
| C2 | A40 | 4c carmine | 15.00 15.00 |
| a. | | Inverted overprint | 3,000. |
| C3 | A40 | 6c org brown | 55.00 |
| C4 | A40 | 8c deep blue | 57.50 |
| C5 | A40 | 10c deep blue | 57.50 57.50 |
| C6 | A40 | 12c red orange | 57.50 57.50 |
| C7 | A40 | 16c lt olive green (Sampson) | 57.50 57.50 |
| C8 | A40 | 16c ol bister (Sampson) (R) | 1,600. |
| C9 | A40 | 16c olive green (Dewey) | 3,000. |
| C10 | A40 | 20c orange yellow | 5,000. |
| C11 | A40 | 26c blue green | 70.00 30.00 |
| C12 | A40 | 30c gray | 70.00 70.00 |
| C13 | A40 | 2p vio brown (R) | 70.00 70.00 |
| C14 | A41 | 4p dark blue (R) | 550.00 300.00 |
| C15 | A41 | 10p deep green | 750.00 500.00 |
| | | | 1,350. 700.00 |

**Same Overprint on No. 269**

**Perf. 12**    **Wmk. 190PI**

| | | | |
|---|---|---|---|
| C16 | A40 | 26c blue green | 6,250. |

**Same Overprint on No. 284**

| | | | |
|---|---|---|---|
| C17 | A41 | 1p pale violet | 210.00 175.00 |

Flight of Spanish aviators Gallarza and Loriga from Madrid to Manila.

## London-Orient Flight Issue

**1928, Nov. 9**    **Unwmk.**    **Perf. 11**

| | | | |
|---|---|---|---|
| C18 | A40 | 4c carmine | .60 .50 |
| C19 | A40 | 4c green | .75 |
| C20 | A40 | 6c violet | 2.40 1.75 |
| C21 | A40 | 8c orange brown | |
| C22 | A40 | 10c deep blue | 2.50 1.90 |
| C23 | A40 | 12c red orange | 2.50 1.90 |
| C24 | A40 | 16c olive (Dewey) | 3.50 2.75 |
| C25 | A40 | 20c orange yellow | 3.00 |
| C26 | A40 | 26c blue green | 3.75 2.75 |
| C27 | A40 | 30c gray | 10.00 6.50 |
| | | | 10.00 6.50 |

## Regular Issue of 1917-25 Overprinted

Visit of Capt. Wolfgang von Gronau on his round-the-world flight.

**1932, Sept. 27**    **Unwmk.**    **Perf. 11**

| | | | |
|---|---|---|---|
| C29 | A43 | 2c yellow green | .40 .35 |
| C30 | A44 | 4c rose carmine | .50 .35 |
| C31 | A45 | 12c yellow | .70 .35 |
| C32 | A46 | 18c red orange | 4.00 3.25 |
| C33 | A47 | 20c yellow | 2.00 1.50 |
| C34 | A48 | 24c deep violet | 2.00 1.50 |
| C35 | A49 | 32c olive brown | 11.70 9.00 |

Nos. C29-C35 (7)

**Same Overprint on No. 271**

**Perf. 12**    **Wmk. 190PI**

| | | | |
|---|---|---|---|
| C28 | A41 | 1p pale violet | 50.00 25.00 |
| | | | 89.00 51.75 |

Nos. 354-360 Overprinted

Commemorating an airplane flight from London to Manila.

**1933, Apr. 11**

| | | | |
|---|---|---|---|
| C36 | A40 | 2c green | .40 .35 |
| C37 | A40 | 4c carmine | .45 .35 |
| C38 | A40 | 6c deep violet | .80 .75 |
| C39 | A40 | 8c orange brn | 1.50 1.00 |
| C40 | A40 | 10c dk blue | 2.25 1.00 |
| C41 | A40 | 12c orange | 2.00 1.00 |
| C42 | A40 | 16c ol grn (Dewey) | 1.50 1.00 |
| C43 | A40 | 20c yellow | 1.75 1.00 |
| C44 | A40 | 26c green | 3.00 1.75 |
| C45 | A40 | 30c gray | 17.65 10.20 |

Nos. C36-C45 (10)

Regular Issue of 1917-25 Overprinted

**1933, May 26**    **Unwmk.**    **Perf. 11**

| | | | |
|---|---|---|---|
| C46 | A40 | 2c green | .50 .40 |

Commemorating the flight from Madrid to Manila of aviator Fernando Rein y Loring.

**No. 290a Overprinted**

Regular Issue of 1917-25 Overprinted in Red

| | | | |
|---|---|---|---|
| C47 | A44 | 4c rose carmine | .20 .20 |
| C48 | A45 | 12c orange | .30 .20 |
| C49 | A47 | 20c yellow | .30 .20 |
| C50 | A48 | 24c deep violet | .40 .25 |
| C51 | A49 | 32c olive brown | 2.20 1.60 |

Nos. C46-C51 (6)

## Nos. 387, 392 Overprinted in Gold

**1935, Dec. 2**

| | | | |
|---|---|---|---|
| C52 | A57 | 10c rose carmine | .30 .30 |
| C53 | A62 | 30c orange red | .50 .50 |

China Clipper flight from Manila to San Francisco, December 2-5, 1935.

## Regular Issue of 1917-25 Surcharged in Various Colors

**1936, Sept. 6** — Perf. 11
C54 A40 2c on 4c car (Bl) .20 .20
C55 A40 6c on 12c red org (V) .20 .20
C56 A40 16c on 26c bl grn (Bk) .50 .70
 Nos. C54-C56 (3) .65 .60

Manila-Madrid flight by aviators Antonio Arnaiz and Juan Calvo.

## Regular Issue of 1917-37 Surcharged in Black or Red

**1939, Feb. 17** — Perf. 11
C57 A40 8c on 26c bl grn (Bk) .75 .40
 3.75 .80
C58 A71 1p on 10p gray (R) 3.00 2.25

1st Air Mail Exhibition, held Feb. 17-19, 1939.

## Moro Vinta and Clipper AP1

**1941, June 30**
C59 AP1 8c carmine 1.00 .60
C60 AP1 20c ultra 1.25 .45
C61 AP1 60c blue green 1.75 1.00
C62 AP1 1p sepia .70 .60
 Nos. C59-C62 (4) 4.70 2.55

For overprint see No. NO7. For surcharges see Nos. N10-N11, N35-N36.

**1944, Dec. 3** — Unwmk. — Perf. 11
C63 A44 4c rose carmine 2.750. 2.750.

No. C47 Handstamped in Violet

**Catalogue values for unused stamps in this section, from this point to the end of the section, are for Never Hinged items.**

## Republic

Manuel L. Quezon and Franklin D. Roosevelt AP2

**1947, Aug. 19** — Unwmk. — Engr. — Perf. 12
C64 AP2 6c dark orange .50 .50
C65 AP2 40c red orange 1.00 1.00
C66 AP2 80c deep blue 2.75 2.75
 Nos. C64-C66 (3) 4.25 4.25

## FAO Type

**1948, Feb. 23** — Typo. — Perf. 12½
C67 A89 40c dk car & pink 10.00 6.50

## Junior Chamber Type

**1950, Mar. 1** — Engr. — Perf. 12
C68 A96 30c deep orange 1.40 .40
C69 A96 50c carmine rose 2.50 .70

## F. D. Roosevelt Type — Souvenir Sheet

**1950, May 22** — Imperf.
C70 A98 80c deep green 3.00 2.50

---

## Lions Club Type

**1950, June 2** — Perf. 12
C71 A99 30c emerald 1.75 .45
C72 A99 50c ultra 2.00 .60
 a. Souvenir sheet of 2, #C71-C72 3.00 2.50

## Maria Clara Type

**1952, Nov. 16** — Perf. 12½
C73 A112 30c rose carmine 2.00 .75

## Postage Stamp Cent. Type

**1954, Apr. 25** — Perf. 13
C74 A119 10c dark brown 2.50 1.00
C75 A119 20c dark green 4.00 1.60
C76 A119 50c blue green 8.50 3.25
 Nos. C74-C76 (3) 15.00 5.85

## Rotary Intl. Type

**1955, Feb. 23**
C77 A123 50c blue green 2.50 1.00

## Lt. José Gozar AP10

20c, 50c, Lt. Gozar. 30c, 70c, Lt. Dasa.

**1955** — Engr. — Perf. 13
C78 AP10 20c deep violet .45 .20
C79 AP10 30c red .50 .20
C80 AP10 50c bluish green .70 .20
C81 AP10 70c blue 1.10 .90
 Nos. C78-C81 (4) 2.75 1.50

Lt. José Gozar and Lt. Cesar Fernando Basa, Filipino aviators in World War II.

## Constitution Type of Regular Issue

**1960, Feb. 8** — Photo. — Perf. 12½x13½
C82 A116 30c brt bl & silver .50 .25

Air Force Plane of 1935 and Jet AP11

## Olympic Type of Regular Issue

**1960, May 2** — Engr. — Perf. 14x14½
C83 AP11 10c carmine .30 .20
C84 AP11 20c ultra .45 .25

25th anniversary of Philippine Air Force. For surcharge see No. 847.

## Olympic Type of Regular Issue

**1960, Nov. 30** — Photo. — Perf. 13x13½
C85 A150 30c orange & brn .50 .35
C86 A150 70c grnsh bl & vio brn 1.00 .70

30c, Sharpshooter. 70c, Woman swimmer.

## Postal Conference Type

**1961, Feb. 23** — Photo. — Perf. 13½x13
C87 A152 30c multicolored .50 .25

## Freedom from Hunger Type

**1963, Dec. 20** — Photo.
C88 A168 30s lt grn & multi .30 .20
C89 A168 50s multicolored .45 .30

## Land Reform Type

**1964, Dec. 21** — Wmk. 233 — Perf. 14½
C90 A172 30s multicolored .50 .20

Mass Baptism by Father Andres de Urdaneta, Cebu — AP12

70s, World map showing route of the Cross from Spain to Mexico to Cebu, and two galleons.

---

**1965, Oct. 4** — Unwmk. — Photo. — Perf. 13
C91 AP12 30s multicolored .50 .20
C92 AP12 70s multicolored 1.00 .35
 a. Souvenir sheet of 4 3.00 2.50

400th anniv. of the Christianization of the Philippines. No. C92a contains four imperf. stamps similar to Nos. 934-935 and C91-C92 with simulated perforation.
For surcharge see No. C108.

## Souvenir Sheet

Family and Progress Symbols — AP13

**1966, July 22** — Photo. — Imperf.
C93 AP13 70s multicolored 4.25 1.40

50th anniv. of the Philippine Natl. Bank. No. C93 contains one stamp with simulated perforation superimposed on a facsimile of a 50p banknote of 1916.

Eruption of Taal Volcano and Refugees — AP14

**1967, Oct. 1** — Photo. — Perf. 13½x13½
C94 AP14 70s multicolored .60 .45

Eruption of Taal Volcano, Sept. 28, 1965.

Eruption of Taal Volcano — AP15

**1968, Oct. 1** — Litho. — Perf. 13½
C95 AP15 70s multicolored .60 .55

Eruption of Taal Volcano, Sept. 20, 1965.

## Rotary Type of 1969

**1969, Jan. 29** — Photo. — Perf. 12½
C96 A202 40s green & multi .40 .40
C97 A202 75s red & multi .85 .40

## Holy Child Type of Regular Issue

**1969, June 30** — Photo. — Perf. 13½
C98 A207 40s ultra & multi .75 .25

## Pope Type of Regular Issue

**1970, Nov. 27** — Photo. — Perf. 13½x14
C99 A221 40s violet & multi .80 .30

## Law College Type of Regular Issue

**1971, June 15** — Photo. — Perf. 13
C100 A225 1p green & multi .80 .45

## Manila Type of Regular Issue

**1971, June 24** — Photo.
C101 A226 1p multi & blue .80 .45

## Santo Tomas Type of Regular Issue

**1971, July 8** — Photo. — Perf. 13½
C102 A227 2p lt blue & multi 1.25 .80

## Congress Type of Regular Issue

**1972, Apr. 11** — Photo. — Perf. 13½x13
C103 A232 40s green & multi .50 .25

## Tropical Fish Type of Regular Issue

**1972, Aug. 14** — Photo. — Perf. 13
C104 A235 50s Dusky angelfish 1.60 .45

---

## Pope Paul VI Type of Regular Issue

**1972, Sept. 26** — Photo. — Perf. 14
C105 A237 60s lt blue & multi .75 .35

## First Mass Type of Regular Issue

**1972, Oct. 31** — Photo. — Perf. 14
C106 A241 60s multicolored .60 .25

## Presidential Palace Type of Regular Issue

**1973, Nov. 15** — Litho. — Perf. 14
C107 A253 60s multicolored .75 .30

## No. C92a Surcharged and Overprinted with US Bicentennial Emblems and: "U.S.A. BICENTENNIAL / 1776-1976" in Black or Red

**1976, Sept. 20** — Photo. — Unwmk. — Imperf.
C108 Sheet of 4 1.50 1.25
 a. A179 5s on 3s multi .20 .20
 b. A179 5s on 6s multi .20 .20
 c. A179 15s on 30s multi .30 .30
 d. A179 50s on 70s multi .75 .35

American Bicentennial. Nos. C108a-C108d are overprinted with Bicentennial emblem and 2 bars over old denomination. Inscription and 2 Bicentennial emblems overprinted in margin.

## Souvenir Sheet

Netherlands No. 1 and Philippines No. 1 and Windmill AP16

**1977, May 26** — Litho. — Perf. 14½
C109 Sheet of 3 10.00 10.00
 a. AP16 7.50p multicolored 2.75 2.10

AMPHILEX '77, International Stamp Exhibition, Amsterdam, May 26-June 5. Exists imperf. Value $20.

## Souvenir Sheet

Philippines and Spain Nos. 1, Bull and Matador AP17

**1977, Oct. 7** — Litho. — Perf. 12½x13
C110 Sheet of 3 10.00 10.00
 a. AP17 7.50p multicolored 2.75 2.00

ESPAMER '77 (Exposicion Filatelica de America y Europa), Barcelona, Spain, 10/7-13.
Exists imperf. Value $18.

Nos. B10 and CB3a Surcharged

**1979, July 5** — Engr. — Perf. 13
C111 SP8 90s on 6c + 4c car, yel 1.25 .45

## Souvenir Sheet — White Paper

C112 Sheet of 5 3.00 3.00
 a. SP8 50s on 6c + 4c carmine .50 .35
 b. SP8 50s on 25c + 5c blue .50 .35
 c. SP8 50s on 35c + 10c green .50 .35
 d. SP8 50s on 70c + 20c red brown .50 .35
 e. SP8 50s on 80c + 20c violet .50 .35

First Manila Philatelic Exhibition, Quezon City, July 4-14, commemorating 25th anniversary of First National Jamboree. No. C111 includes "AIR-MAIL." Surcharge on No. C112 overprinted with heavy bars; new commemorative inscriptions and Scout emblem added.

# AIR POST SEMI-POSTAL STAMPS

## Type of Semi-Postal Issue, 1959

Designs: 30c+10c, Bicycling. 70c+20c, Scout with plane model. 80c+20c, Pres. Carlos P. Garcia and scout shaking hands.

**1959, July 17**    **Unwmk.**    **Engr.**    **Perf. 13**
CB1 SP8 30c + 10c green .30 .30
CB2 SP8 70c + 20c red brown .70 .65
CB3 SP8 80c + 20c violet 1.00 .90
a. Souvenir sheet of 5 2.00 1.85

Nos. CB1-CB3 (3)

10th Boy Scout World Jamboree, Makiling Natl. Park, July 17-26. Surtax was for the Jamboree.
No. CB3a measures 17x89mm. and contains one each of Nos. CB1-CB3 and types of Nos. B10-B11 on white paper. Sold for 4p. For surcharge see No. C112.

---

# SPECIAL DELIVERY STAMPS

**1901, Oct. 15**    **Wmk. 191**    **Perf. 12**
E1 SD3 10c dark blue 125.00 100.00

United States No. E5

**1906**
Overprinted in Red
E2A SD4 10c ultra 2,750.

**1907**
E2A SD4 10c ultra

United States No. E6

**Special Printing**
Overprinted in Red as No. E1 on United States No. E6

See Nos. E3-E6. For overprints see Nos. E7-E10, EO1.

**1906**    **Wmk. 191PI**    **Perf. 11**
E2 SD2 20c ultra 30.00 7.50
b. 20c pale ultra 30.00 7.50

**1911**
E3 SD2 20c dp ultra

Type of 1906
**1916**
E4 SD2 20c dp ultra

**1919**    **Unwmk.**    **Perf. 10**
E5 SD2 20c ultra 175.00 75.00

**1925-31**    **Imperf.**
E6 SD2 20c pale blue .60 .20
b. 20c dull violet .60 .20
E6 SD2 20c dull vio ('31) 20.00 52.50
a. 20c violet blue ('28) 42.50 30.00

**1939**    **Perf. 11**
E7 SD2 20c blue violet .25 .20

Type of 1919 Overprinted in Black

Nos. E5b and E7 Handstamped in Violet

Post Office Clerk—D3

---

**1944**    **Perf. 11**
E8 SD2 20c dull vio (#E5b) 1,400. 550.00
E9 SD2 20c blue vio (#E7) 500.00 225.00

**1945**
E10 SD2 20c blue violet .70 .55
a. "IC" close together 3.25 2.75

Type SD2 Overprinted "VICTORY" As No. 486.

## Republic

**1947, Dec. 22**    **Unwmk.**    **Engr.**    **Perf. 12**
E11 SD3 20c blue lilac .50 .40

Manila Post Office and Messenger SD3

**1962, Jan. 23**    **Perf. 13½x13**
E12 SD4 20c lilac rose .60 .30

---

# SPECIAL DELIVERY OFFICIAL STAMP

O.B.

**1931**    **Unwmk.**    **Perf. 11**
EO1 SD2 20c dull violet .75 80.00
a. No period after "B" 40.00 —
b. Double overprint

Type of 1906 Issue Overprinted

It is strongly recommended that expert opinion be acquired for No. EO1 used.

---

# POSTAGE DUE STAMPS

PHILIPPINES

Postage Due Stamps of the United States Nos. J38 to J44 Overprinted in Black

**1899, Aug. 16**    **Wmk. 191**    **Perf. 12**
J1 D2 1c deep claret 8.50 1.50
J2 D2 2c deep claret 6.50 1.25
J3 D2 5c deep claret 15.00 1.25
J4 D2 10c deep claret 15.00 2.50
J5 D2 50c deep claret 200.00 5.50

**1901, Aug. 31**
J6 D2 3c deep claret .75 7.00
J7 D2 30c deep claret 200.00 100.00

Nos. J1-J7 (7)

No. J1 was used to pay regular postage September 5-19, 1902.

---

D4

## Republic

**1947, Oct. 20**    **Unwmk.**    **Engr.**    **Perf. 12**
J23 D4 3c rose carmine .25 .20
J24 D4 4c brt violet blue .45 .25
J25 D4 6c olive green .60 .40
J26 D4 10c orange .70 .50

Nos. J23-J26 (4) 2.00 1.35

---

# OFFICIAL STAMPS

## Official Handstamped Overprints

"Officers purchasing stamps for government business may, if they so desire, overprint them with the letters 'O.B.' either in writing with black ink or by rubber stamps but in such a manner as not to obliterate the stamp that postmasters will be unable to determine whether the stamps have been previously used." C. M. Cotterman, Director of Posts, Dec. 26, 1905. Beginning with Jan. 1, 1906, all branches of the Insular Government used postage stamps to prepay postage instead of franking them as before. Some officials used manuscript, some utilized typewriters, some made press-printed overprints, but by far the larger number used rubber stamps. The majority of these read "O.B." but other forms were: "OFFICIAL BUSINESS" or "OFFICIAL MAIL" in two lines, with variations on many of these.

These "O.B." overprints are known on US 1899-1901 stamps; on 1903-06 stamps in red and blue; on 1906 stamps in red, blue, black, yellow and green. Beginning in 1926 the Philippines, per order of May 25, 1907, overprinted and issued by the Post Office, but some government stamps were also made on 1906 stamps in red, blue, black, yellow and green in red and blue; on 1906 stamps in red, blue, black, yellow and green. Beginning in 1926 the government continued to handstamp "O.B."

Nos. 383-392 Overprinted in Black:

a

b

**1938-40**    **Perf. 11**
O27 A53(a) 2c rose .20 .20
a. Hyphen omitted .20 .20
O28 A54(b) 4c yellow grn .20 .20
a. No period after "B" .20 .20
O29 A55(a) 6c dk brown .20 .20
O30 A56(b) 8c violet .20 .20
O31 A57(b) 10c rose car .40 .20
a. No period after "B" 40.00
O32 A58(b) 12c black .20 .20
O33 A59(b) 16c dark blue .20 .20
O34 A60(a) 20c lt ol grm ('40) .25 .20
O35 A61(b) 26c indigo .20 .20
O36 A62(b) 30c orange red .20 .20

Nos. O27-O36 (10) 2.20 2.20

---

## PHILIPPINES

**1937**
J15 D3 3c on 4c brown red .20 .20

Nos. J8 to J14 Handstamped in Violet

VICTORY

**1944**    **Unwmk.**    **Engr.**    **Perf. 11**
J8 D3 4c brown red .20 .20
J9 D3 6c brown red .20 .20
J10 D3 8c brown red .20 .20
J11 D3 10c brown red .20 .20
J12 D3 12c brown red .20 .20
J13 D3 16c brown red .20 .20
J14 D3 20c brown red 1.40 1.40

Nos. J8-J14 (7)

For overprints see Nos. O16-O22, NJ1. For surcharge see No. J15.

**1928, Aug. 21**    **Unwmk.**    **Engr.**    **Perf. 11**
J16 D3 4c brown red 140.00
J17 D3 6c brown red 90.00
J18 D3 8c brown red 95.00
J19 D3 10c brown red 90.00
J20 D3 12c brown red 95.00
J21 D3 16c brown red 95.00
J22 D3 20c brown red 695.00

Nos. J16-J22 (7)

**1937**
J15 D3 3c on 4c brown red

No. J8 Surcharged in Blue

---

OFFICIAL

Regular Issue of 1917-26 Overprinted in Red

**1926, Dec. 20**    **Unwmk.**    **Perf. 12**
O1 A42 2c green & blk 2.25 1.00
O2 A42 4c carmine & blk 2.25 1.25
a. Vert. pair, imperf. btwn. 750.00
O3 A42 18c brn & blk 6.75 1.75
O4 A42 20c orange & blk 18.25 8.00

Nos. O1-O4 (4)

Opening of the Legislative Palace.

Regular Issue of 1917-26 Overprinted in Red

**1931**    **Perf. 11**
O5 A40 2c green .20 .20
a. No period after "b" 15.00 5.00
O6 A40 4c carmine 20.00 5.00
a. No period after "O"
O7 A40 6c dp violet .20 .20
O8 A40 8c yellow brn .20 .20
O9 A40 10c deep blue .20 .20
O10 A40 12c red orange .20 .20
O11 A40 16c lt ol grn (Dewey) .25 .20
a. 16c olive brn 1.25 .25
O12 A40 20c orange yel .40 .30
O13 A40 26c green 1.00 .65
O14 A40 30c gray .30 .25

Nos. O5-O14 (10) 2.55 2.15

Same Overprint on Nos. 383-392

**1935**
O15 A53 2c green .20 .20
a. No period after "b" 15.00 5.00
O16 A54 4c yellow green 20.00 8.50
a. No period after "b"
O17 A55 6c dk brown 35.00 17.50
a. No period after "b"
O18 A56 8c violet 15.00 5.00
O19 A57 10c rose carmine 20.00 5.00
a. No period after "b"
O20 A58 12c black .20 .20
O21 A59 16c dark blue .20 .20
O22 A60 lt olive grn .20 .20
O23 A61 26c indigo .30 .20
O24 A62 30c orange red 2.15 2.05

Nos. O15-O24 (10)

Same Overprint on Nos. 411, 418

**1937-38**    **Perf. 11**
O25 A53 2c rose .20 .20
a. No period after "B" 2.25 2.25
O26 A60 20c lt ol grm ('38) .65 .50

## Official Stamps

**No. 461 Overprinted in Black**

O. B.    Unwmk.

**1941, Apr. 14**    *Perf. 11x10½*

| O37 | A75 | 2c apple green | .20 | .20 |

### Official Stamps Handstamped in Violet

VICTORY / O. B.

**1944**    *Perf. 11, 11x10½*    Unwmk.

| O38 | A53 | 2c (#O27) | 375.00 | 150.00 |
| O39 | A75 | 2c (#O37) | 25.00 | |
| O40 | A54 | 4c (#O16) | 6.50 | 3.00 |
| O40A | A55 | 10c (#O31) | 42.50 | 30.00 |
| O41 | A57 | 10c (#O31) | 6,500. | |
| O42 | A60 | 20c (#O22) | 6,000. | |
| O43 | A60 | 20c (#O26) | 1,750. | |

**No. 497 Overprinted Type "c" in Black**

*Perf. 11x10½*    Unwmk.

| O44 | A76 | 2c sepia | .20 | .20 |

> Catalogue values for unused stamps in this section, from this point to the end of the section, are for Never Hinged items.

### Republic

O. B.

**Nos. 504, 505 and 507 Overprinted in Black — d**

**1948**    Unwmk.

| O50 | A78 | 4c black brown | .50 | .20 |
| a. | Inverted overprint | | 25.00 | |
| b. | Double overprint | | 25.00 | |
| O51 | A79 | 10c red orange | .50 | .20 |
| O52 | A81 | 16c slate gray | 3.00 | .55 |
| | | Nos. O50-O52 (3) | 4.00 | .95 |

The overprint on No. O51 comes in two sizes: 13mm, applied in Manila, and 12½mm, applied in New York.

O. B. "2"

**Nos. 527, 508 and 509 Overprinted in Black — e**

**1949**

| O53 | A91 | 2c bright green | .50 | .20 |

Overprint Measures 14mm

| O54 | A82 | 20c red brown | 1.00 | .20 |

Overprint Measures 12mm

| O55 | A83 | 50c dull green | 1.50 | .55 |

**No. 550 Overprinted Type "e" in Black**
Overprint Measures 14mm

**1950**

| O56 | A91 | 1c on 2c brt green | .50 | .20 |

O. B.

**Nos. 589, 592, 595 and 597 Overprinted in Black — f**

Overprint Measures 15mm

**1952-55**

| O57 | A117 | 1c red brown (53) | .50 | .20 |
| O58 | A117 | 5c crim rose | .50 | .20 |
| O59 | A117 | 10c ultra (55) | 1.50 | .20 |
| O60 | A117 | 20c car lake (55) | 3.00 | .80 |
| | | Nos. O57-O60 (4) | | |

O. B.    OneCentavo

**No. 647 Overprinted — g**

**1959**    Engr.    *Perf. 12*

| O61 | A117 | 1c on 5c crim rose | .50 | .20 |

**No. 813 Overprinted Type "f"**
Overprint measures 16½mm

**1959**

| O62 | A145 | 6c gray blue | .60 | .20 |

**Nos. 856-861 Overprinted**

PILIPINAS G.O. (h)    pilipinas G.O. MARIANO PONCE (i)

PILIPINAS G.O. (j)    PILIPINAS G.O. (k)

*Perf. 13¾*    .20

| O63 | A158(i) | 5s car rose ('03) | .50 | .20 |

**1962-64**    *Perf. 13x12*

| O64 | A158(h) | 6s dk red brn | .50 | .20 |

*Perf. 13½*

| O65 | A158(k) | 6s pck blue ('64) | .50 | .20 |
| O66 | A158(j) | 10s brt purple (63) | .50 | .20 |
| O67 | A158(j) | 20s Prus blue (63) | .50 | .20 |
| O68 | A150(l) | 30s vermilion | .75 | .20 |
| O69 | A158(k) | 5s violet ('63) | 1.00 | 1.20 |
| | | Nos. O63-O69 (7) | 4.25 | 1.40 |

"G.O." stands for "Gawaing Opisyal," Tagalog for "Official Business."
On 6s overprint "k" is 10mm wide.
For overprint see No. 1119.

**No. 1082 Overprinted Type "I"**

**1970, Dec. 30**    Engr.    *Perf. 14*

| O70 | A222 | 10s rose carmine | .50 | .20 |

## POSTAL TAX STAMPS

Mt. Pinatubo Fund — PT1

25c, Lahar flow. #RA2, Erupting volcano. #RA3, Animals after eruption. #RA4, Village after eruption. #RA5, People clearing ash.

**Wmk. 391**

**1992, Nov. 16**    Litho.    *Perf. 13¾*

| RA1 | PT1 | 25c multi | | .20 |
| RA2 | PT1 | 1p multi | .60 | .60 |
| RA3 | PT1 | 1p multi | .60 | .60 |
| RA4 | PT1 | 1p multi | .60 | .60 |
| RA5 | PT1 | 1p multi | .60 | .60 |
| a. | Block of 4, #RA2-RA5 | | 2.40 | 2.40 |
| | | Nos. RA1-RA5 (5) | 2.60 | 2.60 |

Use of Nos. RA1-RA5 as postal tax stamps was suspended on 2/1/93. These stamps subsequently became valid for postage.

## OCCUPATION STAMPS

### Issued under Japanese Occupation

**Nos. 461, 438 and 439 Overprinted with Bars in Black**

**1942-43**    Unwmk.    *Perf. 11x10½, 11*

| N1 | A75 | 2c apple green | .20 | .60 |
| a. | Pair, one without overprint | | | |
| N2 | A58 | 12c black ('13) | .20 | .60 |
| N3 | A60 | 16a dark lilac | 5.40 | 6.20 |
| | | Nos. N1-N3 (3) | | |

**Nos. 435, 442, 443 and 423 Surcharged in Black**

5 (a)    16 (b)    50 CENTAVOS (c)    ONE PESO (d)

*Perf. 11*

| N4 | A55 | 5c on 6c gldn brn | | .20 |
| a. | Top bar shorter, thinner | | | |
| b. | 5(c) on 6c dk brn | | .20 | .20 |
| c. | As "b," top bar shorter and thinner | | | .20 |
| N5 | A62 | 16c on 30c (43) | .25 | .25 |
| N6 | A63 | 50c on 1p (43) | .60 | .60 |
| N7 | A65 | 1p on 4p (43) | 100.00 | 200.00 |
| a. | Double surcharge | | | 300.00 |

On Nos. N4 and N4b, the top bar measures 1½x22½mm. On Nos. N4a and N4c, the top bar measures 1x21mm and the "5" is smaller and thinner.

**No. 384 Surcharged in Black**

**1942, May 18**

| N8 | A54 | 2c on 4c yel grn | 6.00 | 6.00 |

Japan's capture of Bataan and Corregidor. The American-Filipino forces finally surrendered May 7, 1942.

**No. 384 Surcharged in Black**

**1942, Dec. 8**

| N9 | A54 | 5c on 4c yel grn | .50 | .50 |

1st anniv. of the "Greater East Asia War."

**Nos. C59 and C62 Surcharged in Black**

**1943, Jan. 23**

| N10 | AP1 | 2c on 8c carmine | .25 | .25 |
| N11 | AP1 | 5c on 1p sepia | .50 | .50 |

Philippine Executive Commission, 1st anniv.

Rice Planting OS2    Moro Vinta — OS4

Nipa Hut OS1    Mt. Mayon and Mt. Fuji — OS3

**Engr., Typo. (2c, 6c, 25c)**    Wmk. 257    *Perf. 13*

**1943-44**

| N12 | OS1 | 1c deep orange | .20 | .20 |
| N13 | OS2 | 2c bright green | .20 | .20 |
| N14 | OS1 | 4c slate green | .20 | .20 |
| N15 | OS3 | 5c orange brown | .20 | .20 |
| N16 | OS3 | 6c red | .20 | .20 |
| N17 | OS3 | 10c blue green | .20 | 1.00 |
| N18 | OS4 | 12c steel blue | 1.00 | 1.00 |
| N19 | OS4 | 16c dark brown | 1.25 | 1.25 |
| N20 | OS4 | 20c rose violet | 1.25 | 1.25 |
| N21 | OS2 | 21c violet | .20 | .20 |
| N22 | OS2 | 25c pale brown | .20 | .20 |
| N23 | OS3 | 50c deep carmine | .75 | .75 |
| N24 | OS4 | 2p dull violet | 5.50 | 5.50 |
| N25 | OS4 | 5p dark olive | 14.00 | 14.00 |
| | | Nos. N12-N25 (14) | 24.30 | 24.30 |

For surcharges see Nos. NB5-NB7.

---

| P12 | N2 | 1m ultra ('96) | .35 | .20 |
| P13 | N2 | 2m dark violet | .25 | .45 |
| P14 | N2 | 2m green ('92) | 2.50 | 13.00 |
| P15 | N2 | 2m olive gray ('94) | .25 | .45 |
| P16 | N2 | 2m brown ('96) | .30 | 1.10 |
| P17 | N2 | 5m dark violet | .25 | |
| P18 | N2 | 5m green ('92) | 200.00 | 55.00 |
| P19 | N2 | 5m olive gray ('94) | .25 | .45 |
| P20 | N2 | 5m dp blue grn ('96) | 2.50 | 1.40 |
| | | Nos. P5-P20 (16) | 218.75 | 89.40 |

Imperfs. exist of Nos. P8, P9, P11, P12, P16, P17 and P20.

## NEWSPAPER STAMPS

FILIPINAS — N2    FILIPINAS — N1

**1886-89**    Unwmk.    Typo.    *Perf. 14*

| P1 | N1 | ⅛c yellow green | .30 | 3.25 |
| P2 | N1 | 1m rose (89) | .30 | 21.00 |
| P3 | N1 | 2m blue (89) | .30 | 21.00 |
| P4 | N1 | 5m dk brown (89) | 1.20 | 66.25 |
| | | Nos. P1-P4 (4) | | |

**1890-96**

| P5 | N2 | ⅛c dark violet | .25 | .20 |
| P6 | N2 | ⅛c green ('92) | 8.00 | 10.00 |
| P7 | N2 | ⅛c orange brn ('94) | | |
| P8 | N2 | ⅛c dull blue ('96) | .25 | .25 |
| P9 | N2 | 1m dark violet | .85 | .60 |
| P10 | N2 | 1m green ('92) | 2.25 | 5.50 |
| P11 | N2 | 1m olive gray ('94) | .25 | .45 |

## 1943, May 7 — Photo. Unwmk.

Map of Manila Bay Showing Bataan and Corregidor — OS5

| | | |
|---|---|---|
| N26 OS5 2c carmine red | .20 | .40 |
| N27 OS5 5c bright green | .25 | .50 |

Fall of Bataan & Corregidor, 1st anniv.

## 1943, June 20 — Engr. Perf. 11

| | | |
|---|---|---|
| N28 A60 12c on 20c lt ol grn | .20 | — |
| a. Double surcharge | | |

No. 440 Surcharged in Black

350th anniversary of the printing press in the Philippines. "Limbagan" is Tagalog for "printing press."

Rizal Monument, Filipina and Philippine Flag — OS6

## 1943, Oct. 14 — Photo. Perf. 12

| | | |
|---|---|---|
| N29 OS6 5c light blue | .20 | .20 |
| N30 OS6 12c orange | .20 | .20 |
| a. Imperf. | | |
| N31 OS6 17c rose pink | .20 | .20 |
| a. Imperf. | | |
| Nos. N29-N31 (3) | .60 | .60 |

"Independence of the Philippines." Japan granted "independence" Oct. 14, 1943, when the puppet republic was founded. The imperforate stamps were issued without gum. See No. NB4.

 José Rizal — OS7

 Rev. José Burgos — OS8

## 1944, Feb. 17 — Litho. Perf. 12

| | | |
|---|---|---|
| N32 OS7 5c blue | .20 | .20 |
| a. Imperf. | | |
| N33 OS8 12c carmine | .20 | .20 |
| a. Imperf. | | |
| N34 OS7 17c deep orange | .20 | .20 |
| a. Imperf. | | |
| Nos. N32-N34 (3) | .60 | .60 |

Design: 17c, Apolinario Mabini.

## 1944, May 7 — Perf. 11

| | | |
|---|---|---|
| N35 AP1 5c on 20c ultra | .50 | .50 |
| N36 AP1 12c on 60c blue grn | 1.25 | 1.25 |

Fall of Bataan & Corregidor, 2nd anniv.

Nos. C60 and C61 Surcharged in Black

See No. NB8.

---

 José P. Laurel — OS10

## 1945, Jan. 12 — Litho. Imperf.

Without Gum

| | | |
|---|---|---|
| N37 OS10 5c dull violet brn | .20 | .20 |
| N38 OS10 7c blue green | .20 | .20 |
| N39 OS10 20c chalky blue | .20 | .20 |
| Nos. N37-N39 (3) | .60 | .60 |

Issued belatedly to commemorate the 1st anniv. of the puppet Philippine Republic, 10/14/44. "S" stands for "sentimos."

# OCCUPATION SEMI-POSTAL STAMPS

Woman, Farming and Cannery — OSP1

## 1942, Nov. 12 — Unwmk. Litho. Perf. 12

| | | |
|---|---|---|
| NB1 OSP1 2c + 1c pale violet | .20 | .60 |
| NB2 OSP1 5c + 1c brt green | .20 | .60 |
| NB3 OSP1 16c + 2c orange | 32.50 | 32.50 |

Campaign to produce and conserve food. The surtax aided the Red Cross.

## "Independence of the Philippines" Type

### 1943, Oct. 14 — Souvenir Sheet Without Gum Imperf.

| | | |
|---|---|---|
| NB4 Sheet of 3 | 65.00 | 10.00 |

No. NB4 contains one each of Nos. N29a-N31a. Lower inscription from Rizal's "Last Farewell." Size: 127x177mm. Sold for 2.50p. The value for No. NB4 used is for a stamp from a first day cover. Commercially used examples are extremely scarce and worth much more.

## 1943, Dec. 8 — Wmk. 257 Perf. 13

| | | |
|---|---|---|
| NB5 OS4 12c + 21c steel blue | .20 | .40 |
| NB6 OS1 20c + 36c rose violet | .20 | .40 |
| NB7 OS3 21c + 40c violet | .60 | 1.20 |
| Nos. NB5-NB7 (3) | | |

The surtax was for the benefit of victims of a Luzon flood. "Baha" is Tagalog for "flood."

Nos. N18, N20 and N21 Surcharged in Black

## Type of 1944 Souvenir Sheet

### 1944, Feb. 9 — Litho. Without Gum Imperf.

| | | |
|---|---|---|
| NB8 Sheet of 3 | 5.00 | 4.00 |

#NB8 contains 1 each of #N32a-N34a. Sheet sold for 1p, surtax going to a fund for the care of heroes' monuments. The value for No. NB8 used is for a stamp from a first day cover.

# OCCUPATION POSTAGE DUE STAMP

No. J15 Overprinted with Bar in Blue

## 1942, Oct. 14 — Unwmk. Perf. 11

| | | |
|---|---|---|
| NJ1 D3 3c on 4c brown red | 35.00 | 20.00 |

On copies of No. J15, two lines were drawn in India ink with a ruling pen across "United States of America" by employees of the Short

---

Paid Section of the Manila Post Office to make a provisional 3c postage due stamp which was used from Sept. 1, 1942. (when the letter rate was raised from 2c to 5c) until Oct. 14 when No. NJ1 went on sale.

# OCCUPATION OFFICIAL STAMPS

Nos. 461, 413, 435, 435a and 442 Overprinted or Surcharged in Black and with Bars and

## 1943-44 — Unwmk. Perf. 11x10½, 11

| | | |
|---|---|---|
| NO1 A75 2c apple green | .20 | .20 |
| NO2 A55 5(c) on 6c gldn brn (#413) (#44) | 500.00 | |
| NO3 A55 5(c) on 6c dk brn (#435a) | 45.00 | 45.00 |
| a. Narrower spacing between bars | .20 | .20 |
| b. 5(c) on 6c dark brown (#435) | .20 | .20 |
| a. As "b," narrower spacing between bars | .20 | — |
| NO4 A62 16c on 30c org red | .30 | .30 |
| d. Double overprint | .30 | .30 |
| a. Wider spacing between bars | .30 | .30 |

On Nos. NO3 and NO3b, the bar deleting "United States of America" is 9¾mm to 10mm above the bar deleting "Common." On Nos. NO3a and NO3c, the spacing is 8mm to 8½mm.

On No. NO4 the center bar is 19mm long, 3½mm below the top bar and 6mm above the Japanese characters. On No. NO4a, the center bar is 20½mm long, 9mm below the top bar and 1mm above the Japanese characters. "K. P." stands for Kagamiitang Pampamahalaan, "Official Business" in Tagalog.

Nos. 435 and 435a Surcharged in Black

## 1944

| | | |
|---|---|---|
| NO5 A55 5c on 6c golden brown | .20 | .20 |
| a. 5c on 6c dark brown | .20 | .20 |

Nos. O34 and C62 Overprinted in Black

## 1944 — Perf. 11

| | | |
|---|---|---|
| NO6 A60(a) 20c light olive green | .25 | .25 |
| NO7 AP1(b) 1p sepia | .65 | .65 |
| Nos. NO5-NO7 (3) | 1.10 | 1.10 |

---

# PHILIPPINES

# POSTAGE ISSUES

of Katipunan origin. The letters "K K K" on these stamps are the initials of this society whose complete name is "Kataas-taasang, Kagalang-galang Katipunan nang Manga Anak nang Bayan," meaning "Sovereign Worshipful Association of the Sons of the Country."

The regular postage and telegraph stamps were in use on Luzon as early as Nov. 10, 1898. Owing to the fact that stamps for the different purposes were not always available, together with a lack of proper instructions, any of the adhesives were permitted to be used in the place of the other. Hence telegraph and revenue stamps were accepted for postage and postage stamps for revenue or telegraph charges. In addition to the regular postal emissions, there are a number of provisional stamps, issues of local governments of islands and towns.

 A1

Coat of Arms — A3

A2

## 1898-99 — Unwmk. Perf. 11½

| | | |
|---|---|---|
| Y1 A1 2c red | 175.00 | 125.00 |
| a. Double impression | | |
| Y2 A2 2c red | 225.00 | .20 |
| b. Double impression | | |
| Y3 A3 2c red | 150.00 | .25 |
| d. Horiz. pair, imperf. between | 200.00 | |
| e. Vert. pair, imperf. between | 200.00 | 200.00 |
| a. A3 2c red | 150.00 | 200.00 |

Imperf pairs and pairs, imperf horizontally, have been created from No. Y2e.

# REGISTRATION STAMP

 RS1

| | | |
|---|---|---|
| YF1 RS1 8c green | 2.50 | |
| a. Imperf, pair | 400.00 | |
| b. Imperf, vertically, pair | | |

# NEWSPAPER STAMP

 N1

| | | |
|---|---|---|
| YP1 N1 1m black | 1.00 | |
| a. Imperf, pair | 1.00 | |

# FILIPINO REVOLUTIONARY GOVERNMENT

The Filipino Republic was instituted by Gen. Emilio Aguinaldo on June 23, 1899. At the same time he assumed the office of President. Aguinaldo dominated the greater part of the island of Luzon and some of the smaller islands until late in 1899. He was taken prisoner by United States troops on March 23, 1901.

The devices composing the National Arms, adopted by the Filipino Revolutionary Government, are emblems of the Katipunan political secret society or

## PITCAIRN ISLANDS

ˈpit-ˌkarn ˈī-lənds

LOCATION — South Pacific Ocean, nearly equidistant from Australia and South America
GOVT. — British colony under the British High Commissioner in New Zealand
AREA — 18 sq. mi. (includes all islands)
POP. — 49 (1999 est.)

The district of Pitcairn also includes the uninhabited islands of Ducie, Henderson and Oeno.

Postal affairs are administered by New Zealand.

12 Pence = 1 Shilling
100 Cents = 1 Dollar (1967)

**Catalogue values for all unused stamps in this country are for Never Hinged items.**

Cluster of Oranges A1

Fletcher Christian with Crew and View of Pitcairn Island — A2

John Adams and His House A3

William Bligh and H. M. Armed Vessel "Bounty" A4

Map of Pitcairn and Pacific Ocean — A5

Bounty Bible — A6

H.M. Armed Vessel "Bounty" A7

Pitcairn School, 1949 — A8

Fletcher Christian and View of Pitcairn Island — A9

Fletcher Christian with Crew and Coast of Pitcairn A10

***Perf. 12½, 11½x11***

**1940-51 Engr. Wmk. 4**

| | | | | |
|---|---|---|---|---|
| 1 | A1 | ½p blue grn & org | .40 | *.65* |
| 2 | A2 | 1p red lil & rose vio | .55 | *.75* |
| 3 | A3 | 1½p rose car & blk | .55 | .55 |
| 4 | A4 | 2p dk brn & brt grn | 1.75 | 1.50 |
| 5 | A5 | 3p dk blue & yel grn | 1.25 | *1.50* |
| 5A | A6 | 4p dk blue grn & blk | 16.00 | 11.00 |
| 6 | A7 | 6p sl grn & dp brn | 5.00 | 1.75 |
| 6A | A8 | 8p lil rose & grn | 16.00 | 8.00 |
| 7 | A9 | 1sh slate & vio | 3.00 | 2.00 |
| 8 | A10 | 2sh6p dk brn & brt grn | 8.00 | 4.00 |
| | | *Nos. 1-8 (10)* | 52.50 | 31.70 |

Nos. 1-5, 6 and 7-8 exist in a booklet of eight panes of one. Value $2,000.
Issued: 4p, 8p, 9/1/51; others, 10/15/40.

Common Design Types pictured following the introduction.

### Peace Issue
Common Design Type

**1946, Dec. 2** ***Perf. 13½x14***

| | | | | |
|---|---|---|---|---|
| 9 | CD303 | 2p brown | .35 | .35 |
| 10 | CD303 | 3p deep blue | .65 | .65 |

### Silver Wedding Issue
Common Design Types

**1949, Aug. 1 Photo.** ***Perf. 14x14½***

| | | | | |
|---|---|---|---|---|
| 11 | CD304 | 1½p scarlet | 1.50 | .75 |

**Engraved; Name Typographed**
***Perf. 11½x11***

| | | | | |
|---|---|---|---|---|
| 12 | CD305 | 10sh purple | 65.00 | *70.00* |

### UPU Issue
Common Design Types

**Engr.; Name Typo. on 3p & 6p**

**1949, Oct. 10** ***Perf. 13½, 11x11½***

| | | | | |
|---|---|---|---|---|
| 13 | CD306 | 2½p red brown | 5.00 | 2.00 |
| 14 | CD307 | 3p indigo | 5.00 | 2.00 |
| 15 | CD308 | 6p green | 10.00 | 4.00 |
| 16 | CD309 | 1sh rose violet | 17.50 | 8.00 |
| | | *Nos. 13-16 (4)* | 37.50 | 16.00 |

### Coronation Issue
Common Design Type

**1953, June 2** ***Perf. 13½x13***

| | | | | |
|---|---|---|---|---|
| 19 | CD312 | 4p dk green & blk | 2.50 | 1.75 |

Ti Plant — A11

Map — A12

Designs: 2p, John Adams and Bounty Bible. 2½p, Handicraft (Carving). 3p, Bounty Bay. 4p, School (actually Schoolteacher's House). 6p, Fiji-Pitcairn connection (Map). 8p, Inland scene. 1sh, Handicraft (Ship model). 2sh, Wheelbarrow. 2sh6p, Whaleboat.

***Perf. 13x12½, 12½x13***

**1957, July 2 Engr. Wmk. 4**

| | | | | |
|---|---|---|---|---|
| 20 | A11 | ½p lilac & green | .85 | .50 |
| 21 | A12 | 1p olive grn & blk | 4.00 | 1.50 |
| 22 | A12 | 2p blue & brown | 1.50 | .50 |
| 23 | A11 | 2½p orange & brn | .60 | .55 |
| 24 | A11 | 3p ultra & emer | .95 | .75 |
| 25 | A11 | 4p ultra & rose red *(Pitcairn School)* | 1.10 | .95 |
| 26 | A11 | 6p indigo & buff | 1.60 | 1.25 |
| 27 | A11 | 8p magenta & grn | .75 | *1.50* |
| 28 | A11 | 1sh brown & blk | 2.75 | 1.40 |
| 29 | A12 | 2sh dp org & grn | 18.00 | 13.50 |
| 30 | A11 | 2sh6p mag & ultra | 27.50 | 12.00 |
| | | *Nos. 20-30 (11)* | 59.60 | 34.40 |

See Nos. 31, 38.

Type of 1957 Corrected

**1958, Nov. 5** ***Perf. 13x12½***

| | | | | |
|---|---|---|---|---|
| 31 | A11 | 4p ultra & rose red *(School-teacher's House)* | 5.50 | 1.50 |

Simon Young and Pitcairn A13

Designs: 6p, Maps of Norfolk and Pitcairn Islands. 1sh, Schooner Mary Ann.

***Perf. 14½x13½***

**1961, Nov. 15 Photo. Wmk. 314**

| | | | | |
|---|---|---|---|---|
| 32 | A13 | 3p yellow & black | .50 | .50 |
| 33 | A13 | 6p blue & red brown | 1.25 | 1.00 |
| 34 | A13 | 1sh brt green & dp org | 1.25 | 1.00 |
| | | *Nos. 32-34 (3)* | 3.00 | 2.50 |

Pitcairn Islanders return from Norfolk Island.

### Freedom from Hunger Issue
Common Design Type

**1963, June 4** ***Perf. 14x14½***

| | | | | |
|---|---|---|---|---|
| 35 | CD314 | 2sh6p ultra | 15.00 | 7.50 |

### Red Cross Centenary Issue
Common Design Type

**1963, Dec. 9 Litho.** ***Perf. 13***

| | | | | |
|---|---|---|---|---|
| 36 | CD315 | 2p black & red | .50 | .25 |
| 37 | CD315 | 2sh6p ultra & red | 9.50 | 5.75 |

Type of 1957
***Perf. 13x12½***

**1963, Dec. 4 Engr. Wmk. 314**

| | | | | |
|---|---|---|---|---|
| 38 | A11 | ½p lilac & green | 1.00 | 1.00 |

Pitcairn Longboat A14

Queen Elizabeth II — A15

1p, H.M. Armed Vessel Bounty. 2p, Oarsmen rowing longboat. 3p, Great frigate bird. 4p, Fairy tern 6p, Pitcairn reed warbler. 8p, Red-footed booby. 10p, Red-tailed tropic birds. 1sh, Henderson Island flightless rail. 1sh6p, Henderson Island lory. 2sh6p, Murphy's petrel. 4sh, Henderson Island fruit pigeon.

**1964-65 Photo.** ***Perf. 14x14½***

| | | | | |
|---|---|---|---|---|
| 39 | A14 | ½p multicolored | .20 | *.30* |
| 40 | A14 | 1p multicolored | .30 | .30 |
| 41 | A14 | 2p multicolored | .30 | .30 |
| 42 | A14 | 3p multicolored | .60 | .30 |
| 43 | A14 | 4p multicolored | .65 | .30 |
| 44 | A14 | 6p multicolored | .75 | .35 |
| 45 | A14 | 8p multicolored | .75 | .45 |
| a. | | Gray (beak) omitted | 300.00 | |
| 46 | A14 | 10p multicolored | .85 | .55 |
| 47 | A14 | 1sh multicolored | .85 | .75 |
| 48 | A14 | 1sh6p multicolored | 5.50 | 1.25 |
| 49 | A14 | 2sh6p multicolored | 5.00 | 1.75 |
| 50 | A14 | 4sh multicolored | 7.00 | 2.75 |
| 51 | A15 | 8sh multicolored | 3.50 | 2.75 |
| | | *Nos. 39-51 (13)* | 26.25 | 12.10 |

Issued: ½p-4sh, 8/5/64; 8sh, 4/5/65.
For surcharges see Nos. 72-84.

### ITU Issue
Common Design Type

**1965, May 17 Litho.** ***Perf. 11x11½***

| | | | | |
|---|---|---|---|---|
| 52 | CD317 | 1p red lilac & org brn | .40 | .20 |
| 53 | CD317 | 2sh6p grnsh blue & ultra | 11.50 | 5.75 |

### Intl. Cooperation Year Issue
Common Design Type

**1965, Oct. 25** ***Perf. 14½***

| | | | | |
|---|---|---|---|---|
| 54 | CD318 | 1p bl grn & cl | .35 | .20 |
| 55 | CD318 | 1sh6p lt vio & grn | 14.00 | 8.00 |

### Churchill Memorial Issue
Common Design Type

**1966, Jan. 24 Photo.** ***Perf. 14***
**Design in Black, Gold and Carmine Rose**

| | | | | |
|---|---|---|---|---|
| 56 | CD319 | 2p brt blue | 1.40 | .75 |
| 57 | CD319 | 3p green | 4.00 | 1.00 |
| 58 | CD319 | 6p brown | 4.25 | 2.00 |
| 59 | CD319 | 1sh violet | 6.25 | 4.25 |
| | | *Nos. 56-59 (4)* | 15.90 | 8.00 |

### World Cup Soccer Issue
Common Design Type

**1966, Aug. 1 Litho.** ***Perf. 14***

| | | | | |
|---|---|---|---|---|
| 60 | CD321 | 4p multi | 1.00 | .75 |
| 61 | CD321 | 2sh6p multi | 6.00 | 3.25 |

### WHO Headquarters Issue
Common Design Type

**1966, Sept. 20 Litho.** ***Perf. 14***

| | | | | |
|---|---|---|---|---|
| 62 | CD322 | 8p multi | 4.25 | 1.50 |
| 63 | CD322 | 1sh6p multi | 8.75 | 5.50 |

### UNESCO Anniversary Issue
Common Design Type

**1966, Dec. 1 Litho.** ***Perf. 14***

| | | | | |
|---|---|---|---|---|
| 64 | CD323 | ½p "Education" | .20 | .20 |
| 65 | CD323 | 10p "Science" | 4.25 | 2.00 |
| 66 | CD323 | 2sh "Culture" | 9.00 | 4.50 |
| | | *Nos. 64-66 (3)* | 13.45 | 6.70 |

Mangarevan Canoe, c. 1325, and Pitcairn Island — A16

Designs: 1p, Pedro Fernandez de Quiros and galleon, 1606. 8p, "San Pedro," 17th century Spanish brigantine, 1606. 1sh, Capt. Philip Carteret and H.M.S. Swallow. 1sh6p, "Hercules," 1819.

**Wmk. 314**

**1967, Mar. 1 Photo.** ***Perf. 14½***

| | | | | |
|---|---|---|---|---|
| 67 | A16 | ½p multicolored | .20 | .20 |
| 68 | A16 | 1p multicolored | .20 | .20 |
| 69 | A16 | 8p multicolored | .30 | .25 |
| 70 | A16 | 1sh multicolored | .50 | .40 |
| 71 | A16 | 1sh6p multicolored | .75 | .70 |
| | | *Nos. 67-71 (5)* | 1.95 | 1.75 |

Bicentenary of the discovery of Pitcairn Islands by Capt. Philip Carteret.

Nos. 39-51 Surcharged in Gold

**1967, July 10** ***Perf. 14x14½***

| | | | | |
|---|---|---|---|---|
| 72 | A14 | ½c on ½p | .20 | .20 |
| a. | | Brown omitted | 575.00 | |
| 73 | A14 | 1c on 1p | .20 | .20 |
| 74 | A14 | 2c on 2p | .20 | .20 |
| 75 | A14 | 2½c on 3p | .20 | .20 |
| 76 | A14 | 3c on 4p | .25 | .25 |
| 77 | A14 | 5c on 6p | .40 | .35 |
| 78 | A14 | 10c on 8p | .85 | .50 |
| a. | | "10c" omitted | *700.00* | |
| 79 | A14 | 15c on 10p | 1.10 | .75 |
| 80 | A14 | 20c on 1sh | 1.60 | 1.00 |
| 81 | A14 | 25c on 1sh6p | 1.75 | 1.25 |

| | | | |
|---|---|---|---|
| 82 | A14 | 30c on 2sh6p | 2.25 |
| 83 | A14 | 40c on 4sh | 2.50 |
| 84 | A15 | 45c on 8sh | 2.25 |

Nos. 72-84 (13) 18.00 12.65

Size of gold rectangle and anchor varies. The anchor symbol is designed after the anchor of H.M.S. Bounty.

ONE HUNDREDTH ANNIVERSARY OF THE DEATH OF BLIGH

Admiral Bligh and Bounty's Launch — A17

**1967, Dec. 7**    **Unwmk.**    **Litho.**    **Perf. 13**

| | | | | |
|---|---|---|---|---|
| 85 | A17 | 1c ultra, lt blue & blk | .20 | .20 |
| 86 | A17 | 8c brt rose, yel & blk | .25 | .25 |
| 87 | A17 | 20c brown, yel & blk | .60 | .55 |

Nos. 85-87 (3) 1.05 1.00

150th anniv. of the death of Admiral William Bligh (1754-1817), capt. of the Bounty.

Designs: 8c, Bligh and his followers adrift in a boat. 20c, Bligh's tomb, St. Mary's Cemetery, Lambeth, London.

Human Rights Flame — A18

**1968, Mar. 4**    **Litho.**    **Perf. 13½x13**

| | | | | |
|---|---|---|---|---|
| 88 | A18 | 1c rose & multi | .20 | .20 |
| 89 | A18 | 10c ocher & multi | .20 | .20 |
| 90 | A18 | 25c multicolored | .90 | .80 |

Nos. 88-90 (3)

International Human Rights Year.

WORLD HEALTH 1948-1968

Microscope, Cell, Germs and WHO Emblem — A20

**1968, Aug. 19**    **Photo.**    **Wmk. 314**
**Perf. 14½x14, 14x14½**

| | | | | |
|---|---|---|---|---|
| 91 | A19 | 5c chocolate & multi | .20 | .20 |
| 92 | A19 | 10c dp green & multi | .20 | .20 |
| 93 | A19 | 15c brt violet & multi | .30 | .25 |
| 94 | A19 | 20c black & multi | .40 | .35 |

Nos. 91-94 (4) 1.10 1.00

See Nos. 194-197.

Flower and Wood of Miro Tree — A19

Pitcairn Handicraft. 10c. Carved flying fish. 15c. Two "hand" vases, vert. 20c. Old and new woven baskets, vert.

**1968, Nov. 25**    **Litho.**    **Perf. 14**

| | | | | |
|---|---|---|---|---|
| 95 | A20 | 2c vio blue, grnsh bl & blk | .20 | .20 |
| 96 | A20 | 20c black, magenta & org | .60 | .50 |

20c, Hypodermic and jars containing pills.
20th anniv. of WHO.

---

PITCAIRN ISLANDS

Capt. Bligh and his Larcum-Kendall Chronometer — A21

**1969, Sept. 17**    **Litho.**    **Wmk. 314**
**Perf. 13x12½, 12½x13**

| | | | | |
|---|---|---|---|---|
| 97 | A21 | 1c brn, yel & gold | 1.25 | 1.00 |
| 98 | A21 | 1c brn, yel & gold | .20 | .20 |
| 99 | A21 | 3c red, blk & gold | .20 | .20 |
| 100 | A21 | 4c buff, brn & gold | .20 | .20 |
| 101 | A21 | 5c gold & multi | .30 | .30 |
| 102 | A21 | 6c gold & multi | .35 | .30 |
| 103 | A21 | 8c gold & multi | .40 | .30 |
| 104 | A21 | 10c gold & multi | .40 | .40 |
| 105 | A21 | 15c gold & multi | .85 | .85 |
| 106 | A21 | 20c gold & multi | 1.25 | 1.00 |
| 107 | A21 | 25c gold & multi | 1.40 | 1.40 |
| 108 | A21 | 30c gold & multi | 2.75 | 3.25 |
| 109 | A21 | 40c red lil, blk & gold | 3.50 | 3.25 |

Nos. 97-109 (13) 20.30 14.75

For overprint see No. 118.

1c, Pitcairn Island. 3c, Bounty's anchor, vert. 4c, Plan of the Bounty, drawn 1787. 5c, Breadfruit and method of transporting young plants. 6c, Bounty Bay. 8c, Pitcairn longboat. 10c, Ship, Landing Point and palms. 15c, Fletcher Christian's Cave. 25c, "Thursday October Christian's house. 25c, "Flying Fox," Thursday Fox," vert. 30c, Radio Station at Taro Ground. 40c, Bounty Bible.

---

Lantana — A22

**1970, Mar. 23**    **Litho.**    **Perf. 14**

| | | | | |
|---|---|---|---|---|
| 110 | A22 | 1c black & multi | .20 | .20 |
| 111 | A22 | 2c black & multi | .20 | .20 |
| 112 | A22 | 5c black & multi | .45 | .20 |
| 113 | A22 | 25c black & multi | 3.50 | 1.75 |

Nos. 110-113 (4) 4.35 2.35

Pitcairn Flowers: 2c, Indian shot (canna indica). 5c, Pulau (hibiscus tiliaceus). 25c, Wild gladioli.

Rudderfish (Dream Fish) — A23

**1970, Oct. 12**    **Photo.**    **Wmk. 314**
**Perf. 14½x14**

| | | | | |
|---|---|---|---|---|
| 114 | A23 | 5c black & multi | 1.25 | .60 |
| 115 | A23 | 10c grnsh bl & blk | 2.00 | 1.00 |
| 116 | A23 | 15c multicolored | 3.25 | 1.00 |
| 117 | A23 | 20c multicolored | 4.50 | 1.75 |

Nos. 114-117 (4) 11.00 4.85

Fish: 5c, Groupers (Auntie and Anni). 15c, Wrasse (Elwyn's trousers). 20c, Wrasse (Whistling daughter).

POLYNESIAN ARTIFACTS

Polynesian Artifacts — A24

No. 104 Overprinted in Silver: "ROYAL VISIT 1971"

**1971, Feb. 22**    **Litho.**    **Perf. 13½x12½**

| | | | | |
|---|---|---|---|---|
| 118 | A21 | 10c gold & multi | 5.00 | 3.75 |

---

Health Care — A25

Polynesian Art on Pitcairn: 5c, Rock carvings. 15c, Making of stone fishhook. 20c, Seated deity, vert.

**1971, May 3**    **Litho.**    **Perf. 13½**
**Queen's Head in Gold**

| | | | | |
|---|---|---|---|---|
| 119 | A24 | 5c dk brown & bis | .85 | .65 |
| 120 | A24 | 10c ol green & blk | 1.40 | 1.10 |
| 121 | A24 | 15c black & blk | 2.50 | 1.50 |
| 122 | A24 | 20c blk & rose red | 3.00 | 1.75 |

Nos. 119-122 (4) 7.75 5.00

4c, South Pacific Commission flag & Southern Cross, vert. 18c, Education (elementary school). 20c, Economy (country store).

**1972, Apr. 4**    **Litho.**    **Perf. 14x14½**

| | | | | |
|---|---|---|---|---|
| 123 | A25 | 4c vio bl, yel & ultra | .65 | .50 |
| 124 | A25 | 8c brown & multi | 1.10 | 1.10 |
| 125 | A25 | 18c yellow grn & multi | 1.75 | 1.50 |
| 126 | A25 | 20c orange & multi | 2.00 | 1.75 |

Nos. 123-126 (4) 5.50 4.75

So. Pacific Commission, 25th anniv.

Silver Wedding Issue, 1972
Common Design Type

Design: Queen Elizabeth II, Prince Philip, skuas and longboat.

**1972, Nov. 20**    **Photo.**    **Wmk. 314**

| | | | | |
|---|---|---|---|---|
| 127 | CD324 | 4c slate grn & multi | .25 | .20 |
| 128 | CD324 | 20c ultra & multi | .85 | .60 |

---

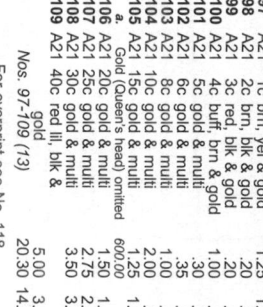

PITCAIRN ISLANDS

Pitcairn Coat of Arms — A26

**1973, Jan. 2**    **Litho.**    **Perf. 14½x14**

| | | | | |
|---|---|---|---|---|
| 129 | A26 | 50c multicolored | 3.50 | 8.00 |

Rose Apple — A27

**1973, June 25**    **Perf. 14**

| | | | | |
|---|---|---|---|---|
| 130 | A27 | 5c shown | .75 | .25 |
| 131 | A27 | 8c Mountain apple | 1.25 | .50 |
| 132 | A27 | 10c Lata (myrtle) | 2.25 | 1.00 |
| 133 | A27 | 20c Cassia | 4.00 | 2.00 |
| 134 | A27 | 35c Guava | 5.00 | 5.00 |

Nos. 130-134 (5)

Princess Anne's Wedding Issue
Common Design Type

**1973, Nov. 14**    **Litho.**    **Perf. 14**

| | | | | |
|---|---|---|---|---|
| 135 | CD325 | 10c lilac & multi | .20 | .20 |
| 136 | CD325 | 25c gray grn & multi | .40 | .35 |

Miter and Horn Shells A28

| | | | | |
|---|---|---|---|---|
| 137 | A28 | 4c shown | .50 | .40 |
| 138 | A28 | 10c Dove shells | 1.00 | .90 |
| 139 | A28 | 18c Limpets and false limpet | 1.75 | 1.50 |
| 140 | A28 | 50c Lucine shells | 4.50 | 4.00 |
| a. | | Souvenir sheet of 4, #137-140 | 11.00 | 11.00 |

Nos. 137-140 (4) 7.75 6.80

**1974, Apr. 15**

---

UPU Emblem A29

Pitcairn Post Office, UPU Emblem A29

UPU, cent.: 20c, Stampless cover, "Posted at Pitcairn Island No Stamps Available. 35c, Longboat leaving Bounty Bay for ship offshore.

**1974, July 22**    **Wmk. 314**    **Perf. 14½**

| | | | | |
|---|---|---|---|---|
| 141 | A29 | 4c multicolored | .20 | .20 |
| 142 | A29 | 20c multicolored | .60 | .50 |
| 143 | A29 | 35c multicolored | 2.05 | 1.70 |

Nos. 141-143 (3)

PITCAIRN ISLANDS

Churchill: "Lift up your hearts . . ." — A30

Design: 35c, Churchill and "Give us the tools and we will finish the job."

**1974, Nov. 30**    **Litho.**    **Wmk. 373**

| | | | | |
|---|---|---|---|---|
| 144 | A30 | 20c black & citron | .50 | .40 |
| 145 | A30 | 35c black & yellow | .75 | .60 |

Sir Winston Churchill (1874-1965).

---

Queen Elizabeth II — A31

**1975, Apr. 21**    **Wmk. 314**    **Perf. 14½**

| | | | | |
|---|---|---|---|---|
| 146 | A31 | $1 multicolored | 9.50 | 14.00 |

Mailboats — A32

**1975, July 22**    **Litho.**    **Perf. 14½**

| | | | | |
|---|---|---|---|---|
| 147 | A32 | 4c Seringapatam, 1830 | .20 | .20 |
| 148 | A32 | 18c Pitcairn, 1890 | .55 | .55 |
| 149 | A32 | 18c Athenic, 1901 | 1.00 | 1.00 |
| 150 | A32 | 50c Gothic, 1948 | 2.75 | 2.75 |
| a. | | Souvenir sheet of 4, #147-150, perf. 14 | | |

Nos. 147-150 (4) 13.50 13.50   4.50 4.50

PITCAIRN WASP

Pitcairn Wasp A33

**1975, Nov. 9**    **Wmk. 314**    **Litho.**    **Perf. 14½**

| | | | | |
|---|---|---|---|---|
| 151 | A33 | 4c blue grn & multi | .40 | .25 |
| 152 | A33 | 6c shown | .65 | .50 |
| 153 | A33 | 10c carmine & multi | 1.00 | .75 |
| 154 | A33 | 15c purple & multi | 1.00 | 1.00 |
| 155 | A33 | 20c multicolored | 1.75 | 1.50 |

Nos. 151-155 (5) 5.30 4.00

Insects: 6c, Grasshopper. 10c, Pitcairn moths. 15c, Dragonfly. 20c, Banana moth.

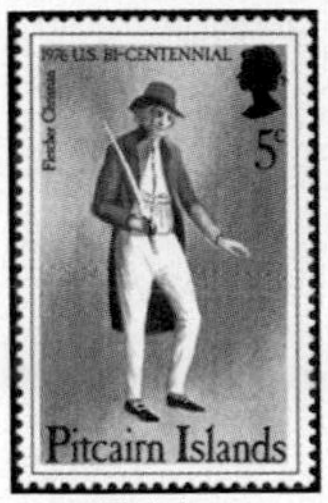

Fletcher Christian — A34

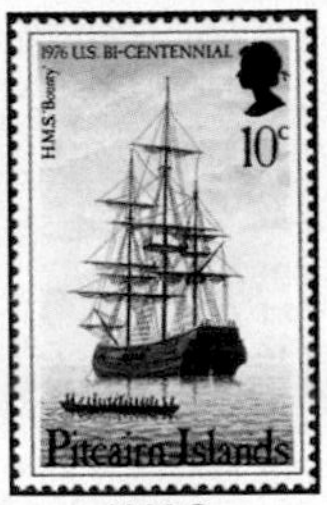

H.M.S. Bounty — A35

American Bicentennial: 30c, George Washington. 50c, Mayflower.

**1976, July 4 Wmk. 373 *Perf. 13½***
**156** A34 5c multicolored .20 .20
**157** A35 10c multicolored .40 .35
**158** A34 30c multicolored 1.00 .90
*a.* Pair, #156, 158 1.40 1.40
**159** A35 50c multicolored 1.25 1.00
*a.* Pair, #157, 159 1.65 1.65
*Nos. 156-159 (4)* 2.85 2.45

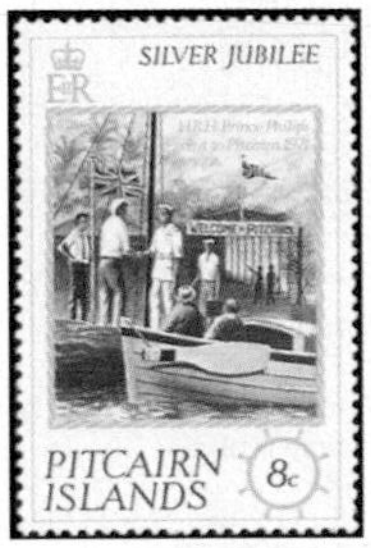

Prince Philip's Arrival, 1971 Visit — A36

20c, Chair of homage. 50c, The enthronement.

**1977, Feb. 6 *Perf. 13***
**160** A36 8c silver & multi .20 .20
**161** A36 20c silver & multi .30 .30
**162** A36 50c silver & multi .75 .75
*Nos. 160-162 (3)* 1.25 1.25

25th anniv. of the reign of Elizabeth II.

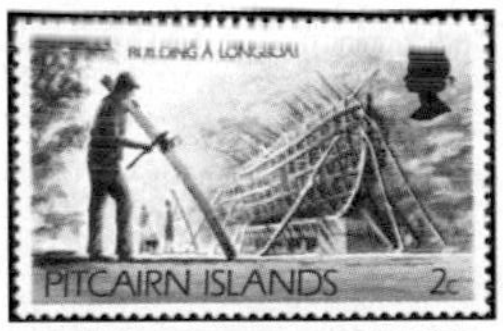

Building Longboat — A37

Designs: 1c, Man ringing Island Bell, vert. 5c, Landing cargo. 6c, Sorting supplies. 9c, Cleaning wahoo (fish), vert. 10c, Farming. 15c, Sugar mill. 20c, Women grating coconuts and bananas. 35c, Island church. 50c, Gathering miro logs, Henderson Island. 70c, Burning obsolete stamps, vert. $1, Prince Philip and "Britannia." $2, Elizabeth II, vert.

**1977-81 Litho. *Perf. 14½***
**163** A37 1c multicolored .30 .65
**164** A37 2c multicolored .30 .65
**165** A37 5c multicolored .35 .65
**166** A37 6c multicolored .35 .65
**167** A37 9c multicolored .35 .65
**168** A37 10c multicolored .35 .65
**168A** A37 15c multicolored 1.25 2.25
**169** A37 20c multicolored .35 .65
**170** A37 35c multicolored .45 .85
**171** A37 50c multicolored .45 .85
**171A** A37 70c multicolored 1.25 2.40
**172** A37 $1 multicolored .70 1.25
**173** A37 $2 multicolored .75 1.40
*Nos. 163-173 (13)* 7.20 13.55

Issued: #168A, 171A, 10/1/81; others, 9/12/77.

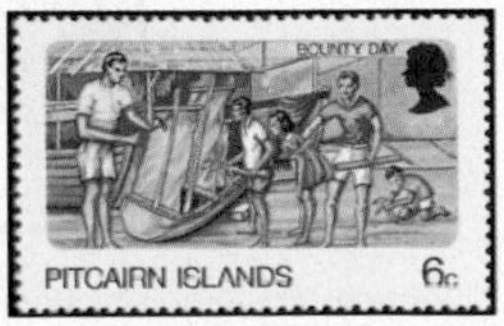

Building "Bounty" Model — A38

Bounty Day: 20c, Bounty model afloat. 35c, Burning Bounty.

**1978, Jan. 9 *Perf. 14½***
**174** A38 6c yellow & multi .20 .20
**175** A38 20c yellow & multi .85 .65
**176** A38 35c yellow & multi 1.25 1.00
*a.* Souvenir sheet of 3, #174-176 8.50 8.50
*Nos. 174-176 (3)* 2.30 1.85

Souvenir Sheet

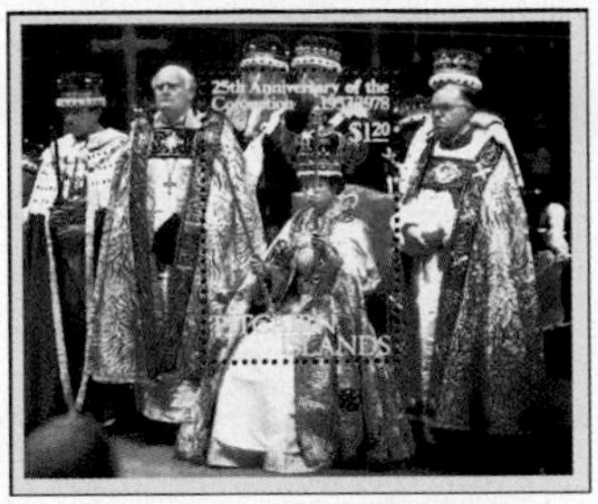

Elizabeth II in Coronation Regalia — A39

**Wmk. 373**
**1978, Sept. Litho. *Perf. 12***
**177** A39 $1.20 silver & multi 2.00 2.00

25th anniv. of coronation of Elizabeth II.

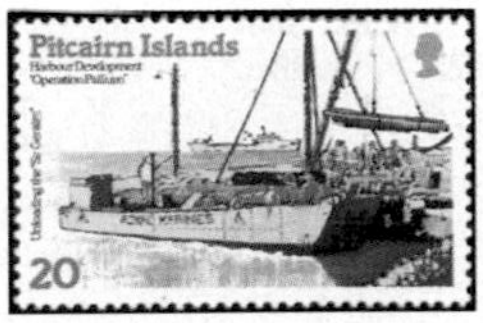

Unloading "Sir Geraint" — A40

Designs: 15c, Harbor before development. 30c, Work on the jetty. 35c, Harbor after development.

**Wmk. 373**
**1978, Dec. 18 Litho. *Perf. 13½***
**178** A40 15c multicolored .20 .20
**179** A40 20c multicolored .35 .35
**180** A40 30c multicolored .60 .60
**181** A40 35c multicolored .65 .65
*Nos. 178-181 (4)* 1.80 1.80

Development of new harbor on Pitcairn.

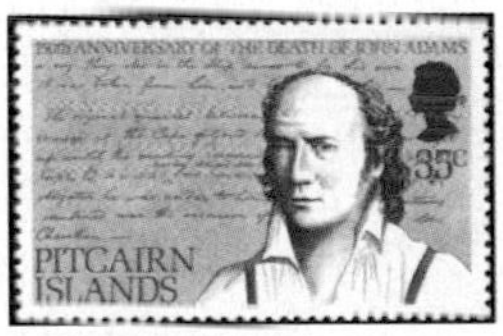

John Adams — A41

Design: 70c, John Adams' grave.

**1979, Mar. 5 Litho. *Perf. 14½***
**182** A41 35c multicolored .30 .50
**183** A41 70c multicolored .60 .75

John Adams (1760-1829), founder of Pitcairn Colony, 150th death anniversary.

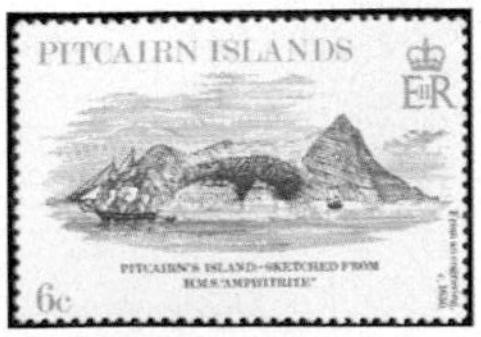

Pitcairn Island Seen from "Amphitrite" — A42

Engravings (c. 1850): 9c, Bounty Bay and Pitcairn Village, 20c, Lookout Ridge. 70c, Church and schoolhouse.

**1979, Sept. 12 Litho. *Perf. 14***
**184** A42 6c multicolored .20 .20
**185** A42 9c multicolored .20 .20
**186** A42 20c multicolored .20 .20
**187** A42 70c multicolored .50 .50
*Nos. 184-187 (4)* 1.10 1.10

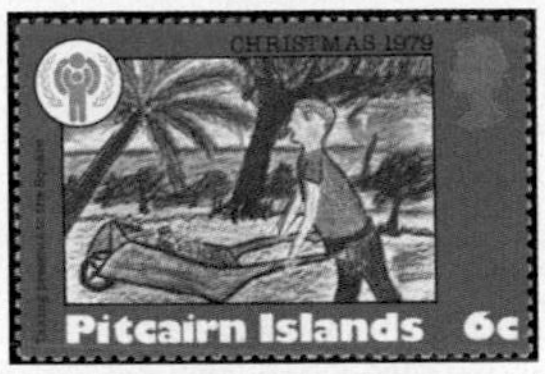

Taking Presents to the Square, IYC Emblem — A43

IYC Emblem and Children's Drawings: 9c, Decorating trees with presents. 20c, Distributing presents. 35c, Carrying the presents home.

**Wmk. 373**
**1979, Nov. 28 Litho. *Perf. 13½***
**188** A43 6c multicolored .20 .20
**189** A43 9c multicolored .20 .20
**190** A43 20c multicolored .30 .30
**191** A43 35c multicolored .50 .50
*a.* Souvenir sheet of 4, #188-191 1.50 2.00
*Nos. 188-191 (4)* 1.20 1.20

Christmas and IYC.

Souvenir Sheet

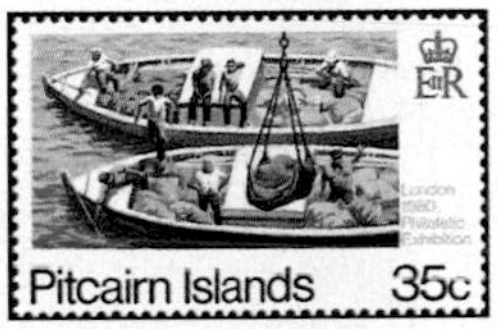

Mail Transport by Longboat — A44

**Wmk. 373**
**1980, May 6 Litho. *Perf. 14½***
**192** Sheet of 4 1.25 1.25
*a.* A44 35c shown .25 .25
*b.* A44 35c Mail crane lift .25 .25
*c.* A44 35c Tractor transport .25 .25
*d.* A44 35c Arrival at post office .25 .25

London 80 Intl. Phil. Exhib., May 6-14.

**Queen Mother Elizabeth Birthday Issue**
Common Design Type
**Wmk. 373**
**1980, Aug. 4 Litho. *Perf. 14***
**193** CD330 50c multicolored .50 .50

Handicraft Type of 1968
***Perf. 14½x14, 14x14½***
**1980, Sept. 29 Litho. Wmk. 373**
**194** A19 9c Turtles .20 .20
**195** A19 20c Wheelbarrow .20 .20
**196** A19 35c Gannet, vert. .25 .25
**197** A19 40c Bonnet and fan, vert. .35 .35
*Nos. 194-197 (4)* 1.00 1.00

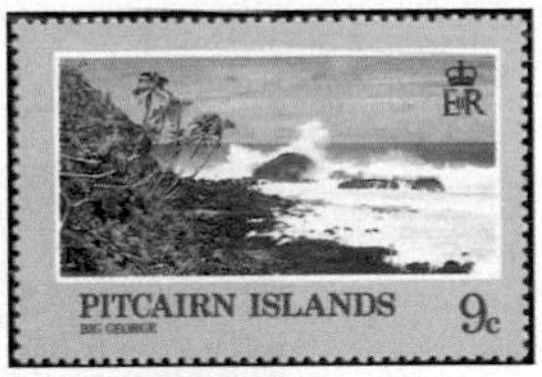

Big George — A45

**Wmk. 373**
**1981, Jan. 22 Litho. *Perf. 14***
**198** A45 6c View of Adamstown .20 .20
**199** A45 9c shown .20 .20
**200** A45 20c Christian's Cave, Gannet's Ridge .20 .20
**201** A45 35c Pawala Valley Ridge .25 .25
**202** A45 70c Tatrimoa .40 .40
*Nos. 198-202 (5)* 1.25 1.25

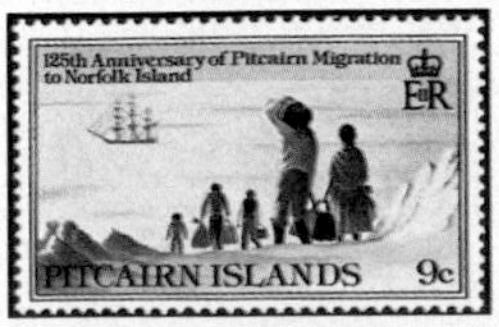

Citizens Departing for Norfolk Island — A46

**1981, May 3 Photo. *Perf. 13x14½***
**203** A46 9c shown .20 .20
**204** A46 35c Norfolk Isld. from Morayshire .35 .35
**205** A46 70c Morayshire .70 .70
*Nos. 203-205 (3)* 1.25 1.25

Migration to Norfolk Is., 125th anniv.

**Royal Wedding Issue**
Common Design Type
**Wmk. 373**
**1981, July 22 Litho. *Perf. 14***
**206** CD331 20c Bouquet .20 .20
**207** CD331 35c Charles .20 .20
**208** CD331 $1.20 Couple .75 .75
*Nos. 206-208 (3)* 1.15 1.15

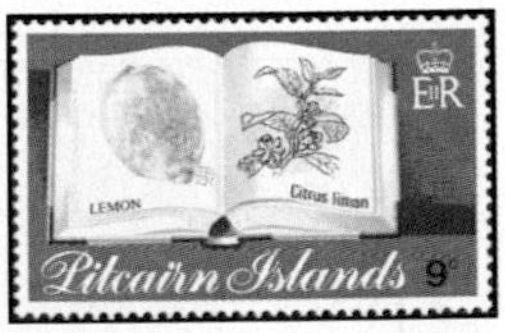

Lemon — A47

**1982, Feb. 23 Litho. *Perf. 14½***
**209** A47 9c shown .20 .20
**210** A47 20c Pomegranate .30 .30
**211** A47 35c Avocado .40 .40
**212** A47 70c Pawpaw .85 .85
*Nos. 209-212 (4)* 1.75 1.75

**Princess Diana Issue**
Common Design Type
**1982, July 1 Litho. *Perf. 14½x14***
**213** CD333 6c Arms .20 .20
**214** CD333 9c Diana .45 .45
**215** CD333 70c Wedding .75 .75
**216** CD333 $1.20 Portrait 1.40 1.40
*Nos. 213-216 (4)* 2.80 2.80

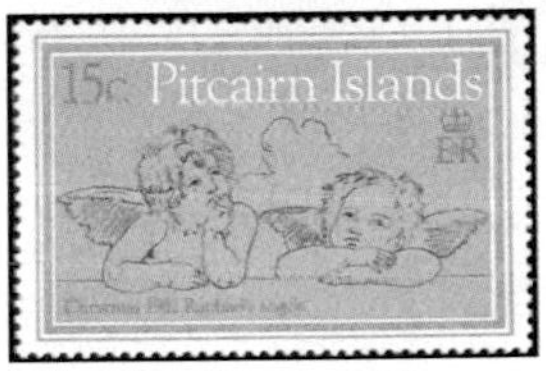

Christmas — A48

Designs: Various paintings of angels by Raphael. 50c, $1 vert.

**1982, Oct. 19 Litho. *Perf. 14***
**217** A48 15c multicolored .25 .25
**218** A48 20c multicolored .25 .25
**219** A48 50c multicolored .40 .40
**220** A48 $1 multicolored .60 .60
*Nos. 217-220 (4)* 1.50 1.50

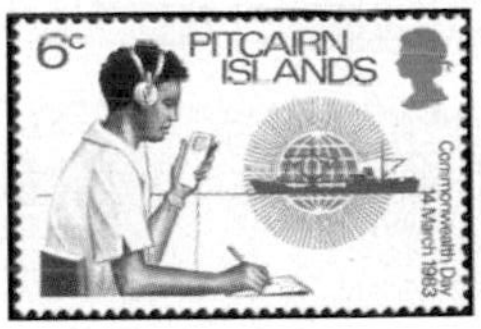

A48a

**1983, Mar. 14**
**221** A48a 6c Radio operator .20 .20
**222** A48a 9c Postal clerk .20 .20
**223** A48a 70c Fisherman .50 .50
**224** A48a $1.20 Artist .85 .85
*Nos. 221-224 (4)* 1.75 1.75

Commonwealth Day.

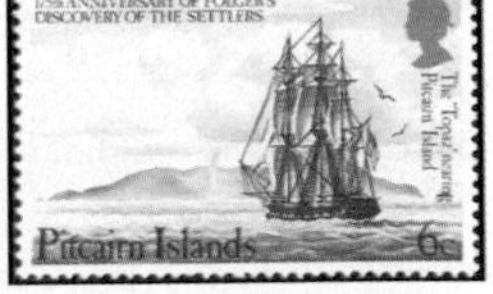

175th Anniv. of Capt. Folger's Discovery of the Settlers — A49

**Wmk. 373**
**1983, June 14 Litho. *Perf. 14***
**225** A49 6c Topaz off Pitcairn Isld. .35 .30
**226** A49 20c Topaz, islanders .50 .45
**227** A49 70c John Adams welcoming Folger .80 .80
**228** A49 $1.20 Presentation of Chronometer 1.25 1.25
*Nos. 225-228 (4)* 2.90 2.80

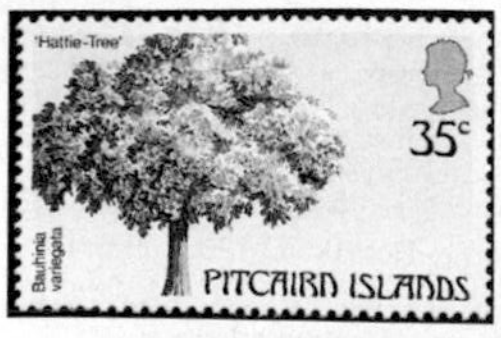


Local Trees
A50

**1983, Oct. 6** **Litho.** ***Perf. 13½***
**229** Pair .75 .75
*a.* A50 35c Hattie .40 .40
*b.* A50 35c Branch, wood painting .40 .40
**230** Pair 1.25 1.25
*a.* A50 70c Pandanus .65 .65
*b.* A50 70c Branch, basket weaving .65 .65

See Nos. 289-290.

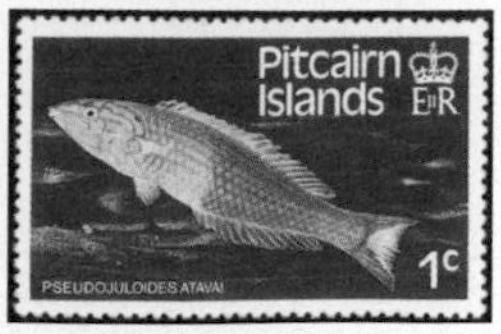


Pseudojuloides Atavai — A51

**Wmk. 373**

**1984, Jan. 11** **Litho.** ***Perf. 14½***
**231** A51 1c shown .25 .30
**232** A51 4c Halichoeres melas-mapomus .45 .30
**233** A51 6c Scarus longip-pinis .45 .35
**234** A51 9c Variola louti .45 .35
**235** A51 10c Centropyge hotumatua .45 .40
**236** A51 15c Stegastes emeryi .45 .40
**237** A51 20c Chaetodon smithi .55 .50
**238** A51 35c Xanthichthys mento .75 .70
**239** A51 50c Chrysiptera galba .75 *1.00*
**240** A51 70c Genicanthus spinus 1.00 *1.40*
**241** A51 $1 Myripristis tiki 1.00 *1.75*
**242** A51 $1.20 Anthias ventral-is 1.10 *1.75*
**243** A51 $2 Pseudocaranx dentex 1.75 *4.00*
*Nos. 231-243 (13)* 9.40 13.20

See Nos. 295-296.

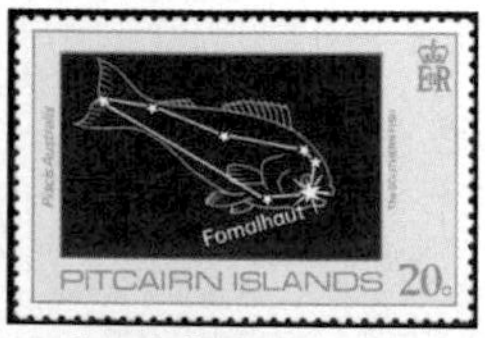


Constellations — A52

**1984, May 14** **Wmk. 373**
**244** A52 15c Crux Australis .25 .25
**245** A52 20c Piscis Australis .35 .35
**246** A52 70c Canis Minor .90 .90
**247** A52 $1 Virgo 1.25 1.25
*Nos. 244-247 (4)* 2.75 2.75

Souvenir Sheet

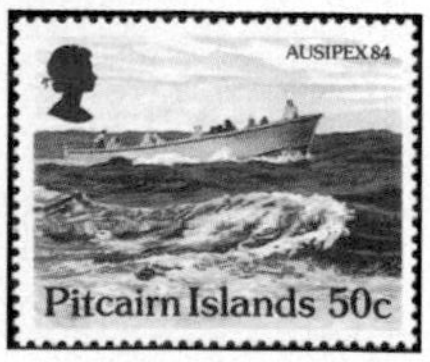


AUSIPEX '84 — A53

Longboats.

**1984, Sept. 21** **Litho.** **Wmk. 373**
**248** Sheet of 2 2.50 2.50
*a.* A53 50c multicolored .50 .50
*b.* A53 $2 multicolored 2.00 2.00

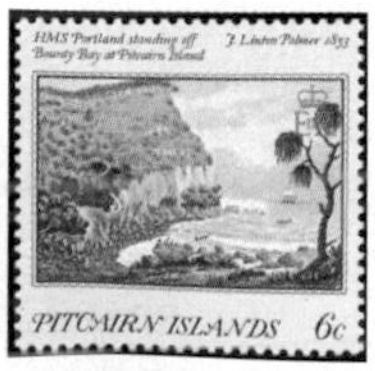


HMS Portland off Bounty Bay, by J. Linton Palmer, 1853 — A54

Paintings by J. Linton Palmer, 1853, and William Smyth, 1825: 9c, Christian's Look Out at Pitcairn Island. 35c, The Golden Age. $2, View of Village, by Smyth.

**Wmk. 373**

**1985, Jan. 16** **Litho.** ***Perf. 14***
**249** A54 6c multicolored .35 .35
**250** A54 9c multicolored .35 .35
**251** A54 35c multicolored .70 .70

**Size: 48x32mm**

**252** A54 $2 multicolored 2.50 2.50
*Nos. 249-252 (4)* 3.90 3.90

Copies of No. 252 with "1835" date were not issued. Value, $85.
See Nos. 291-294.

**Queen Mother 85th Birthday**
Common Design Type

***Perf. 14½x14***

**1985, June 7** **Litho.** **Wmk. 384**
**253** CD336 6c In Dundee, 1964 .20 *.30*
**254** CD336 35c At 80th birth-day celebra-tion .40 *.50*
**255** CD336 70c Queen Mother .70 .70
**256** CD336 $1.20 Holding Prince Henry 1.40 1.40
*Nos. 253-256 (4)* 2.70 2.90

**Souvenir Sheet**

**257** CD336 $2 In coach at the Races, Ascot 3.25 3.25

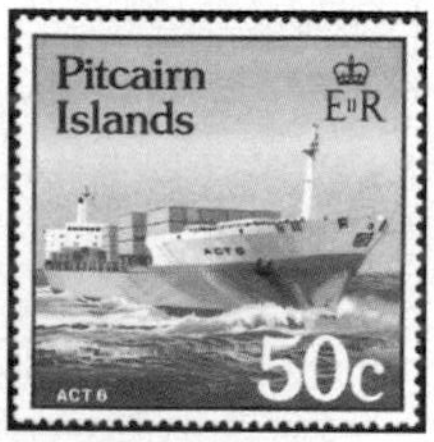


Act 6 — A55

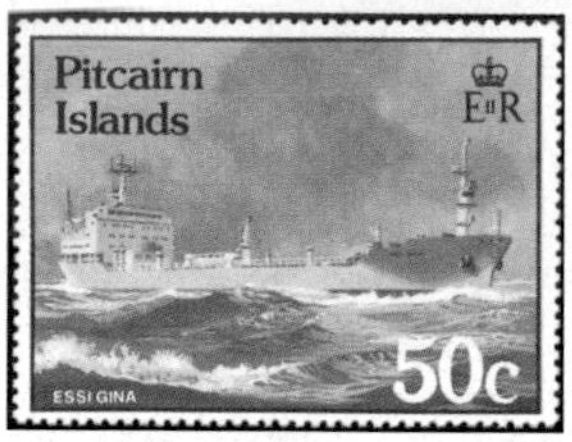


Essi Gina A56

**1985, Aug. 28** ***Perf. 14½x14***
**258** A55 50c shown 1.25 1.25
**259** A55 50c Columbus Louisiana 1.25 1.25

***Perf. 14***

**260** A56 50c shown 1.25 1.25
**261** A56 50c Stolt Spirit 1.25 1.25
*Nos. 258-261 (4)* 5.00 5.00

See Nos. 281-284.

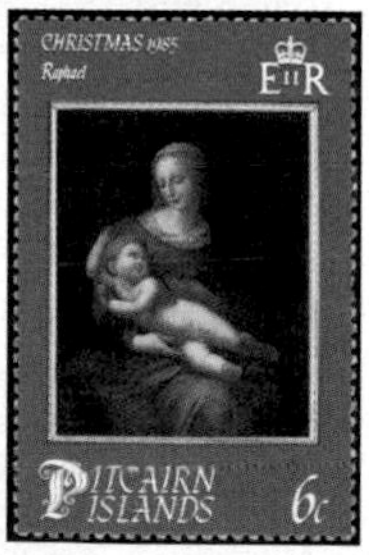


Christmas A57

Madonna & child paintings: 6c, by Raphael. 9c, by Krause. 35c, by Andreas Mayer. $2, by an unknown Austrian master.

**1985, Nov. 26** ***Perf. 14***
**262** A57 6c multicolored .40 .40
**263** A57 9c multicolored .40 .40
**264** A57 35c multicolored .95 .95
**265** A57 $2 multicolored 5.25 5.25
*Nos. 262-265 (4)* 7.00 7.00

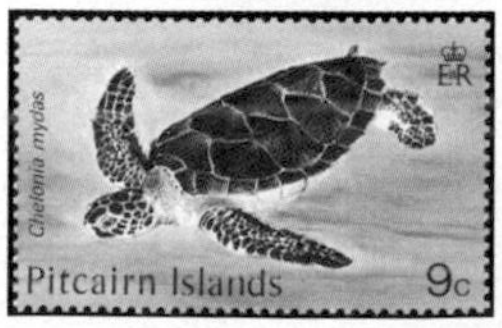


Turtles A58

Designs: 9c, 20c, Chelonia mydas. 70c, $1.20, Eretmochelys imbricata.

**Wmk. 384**

**1986, Feb. 12** **Litho.** ***Perf. 14½***
**266** A58 9c multicolored 1.25 1.25
**267** A58 20c multi, diff. 2.00 2.00
**268** A58 70c multicolored 3.75 3.75
**269** A58 $1.20 multi, diff. 4.00 4.00
*Nos. 266-269 (4)* 11.00 11.00

**Queen Elizabeth II 60th Birthday**
Common Design Type

Designs: 6c, In Royal Lodge garden, Windsor, 1946. 9c, Wedding of Princess Anne and Capt. Mark Philips, 1973. 20c, Wearing mantle and robes of Order of St. Paul's Cathedral, 1961. $1.20, Concert, Royal Festival Hall, London, 1971. $2, Visting Crown Agents' offices, 1983.

**1986, Apr. 21** **Litho.** ***Perf. 14½***
**270** CD337 6c multi .20 .20
**271** CD337 9c multi .20 .20
**272** CD337 20c multi .20 .20
**273** CD337 $1.20 multi 1.00 1.00
**274** CD337 $2 multi 1.75 1.75
*Nos. 270-274 (5)* 3.35 3.35

**Royal Wedding Issue, 1986**
Common Design Type

Designs: 20c, Informal portrait. $1.20, Andrew aboard royal navy vessel.

**Wmk. 384**

**1986, July 23** **Litho.** ***Perf. 14***
**275** CD338 20c multi .35 .35
**276** CD338 $1.20 multi 2.40 2.40

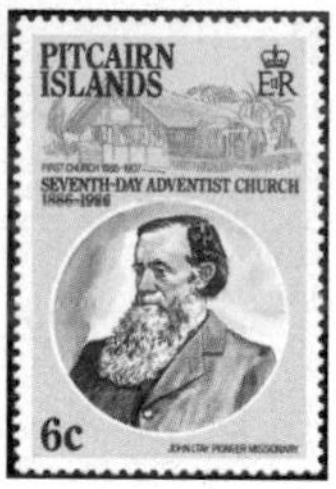


7th Day Adventist Church, Cent. — A59

Designs: 6c, First church, 1886, and John I. Tay, missionary. 20c, Second church, 1907, and mission ship Pitcairn, 1890. 35c, Third church, 1945, baptism and Down Isaac. $2, Church, 1954, and sailing ship.

**1986, Oct. 18**
**277** A59 6c multicolored .25 .25
**278** A59 20c multicolored .70 .70
**279** A59 35c multicolored 1.25 1.25
**280** A59 $2 multicolored 6.50 6.50
*Nos. 277-280 (4)* 8.70 8.70

Ship Type of 1985

**1987, Jan. 20** ***Perf. 14x14½***
**281** A55 50c Brussel 1.60 1.60
**282** A55 50c Samoan Reefer 1.60 1.60

***Perf. 14***

**283** A56 50c Australian Exporter 1.60 1.60
**284** A56 50c Taupo 1.60 1.60
*Nos. 281-284 (4)* 6.40 6.40

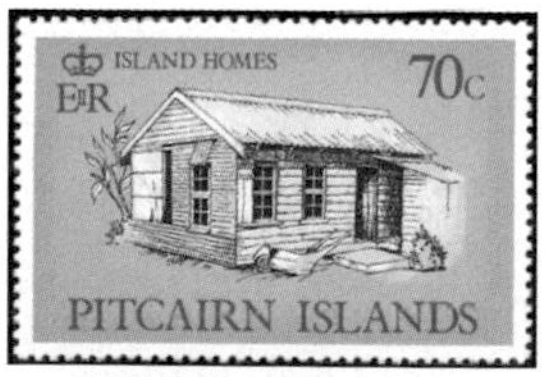


Island Houses — A60

**1987, May 21** **Wmk. 373** ***Perf. 14***
**285** A60 70c lt greenish blue, blu-ish grn & blk .70 .70
**286** A60 70c cream, yel bister & blk .70 .70
**287** A60 70c lt blue, brt blue & blk .70 .70
**288** A60 70c lt lil, brt vio & blk .70 .70
*Nos. 285-288 (4)* 2.80 2.80

Tree Type of 1983

**1987, Aug. 10** **Wmk. 384** ***Perf. 14½***
**289** Pair 1.50 1.50
*a.* A50 40c Leaves, blossoms .75 .75
*b.* A50 40c Monkey puzzle tree .75 .75
**290** Pair 5.50 5.50
*a.* A50 $1.80 Leaves, blossoms, nuts 2.75 2.75
*b.* A50 $1.80 Duduinut tree 2.75 2.75

Art Type of 1985

Paintings by Lt. Conway Shipley, 1848: 20c, House and Tomb of John Adams. 40c, Bounty Bay, with H.M.S. Calypso. 90c, School House and Chapel. $1.80, Pitcairn Island with H.M.S. Calypso.

**1987, Dec. 7** **Litho.** ***Perf. 14***
**291** A54 20c multi .60 .60
**292** A54 40c multi 1.00 1.00
**293** A54 90c multi 1.75 1.75

**Size: 48x32mm**

**294** A54 $1.80 multi 2.50 2.50
*Nos. 291-294 (4)* 5.85 5.85

Fish Type of 1984
**Wmk. 384**

**1988, Jan. 14** **Litho.** ***Perf. 14½***
**295** A51 90c Variola louti 3.75 2.75
**296** A51 $3 Gymnothorax eurostus 6.25 4.75

Souvenir Sheet

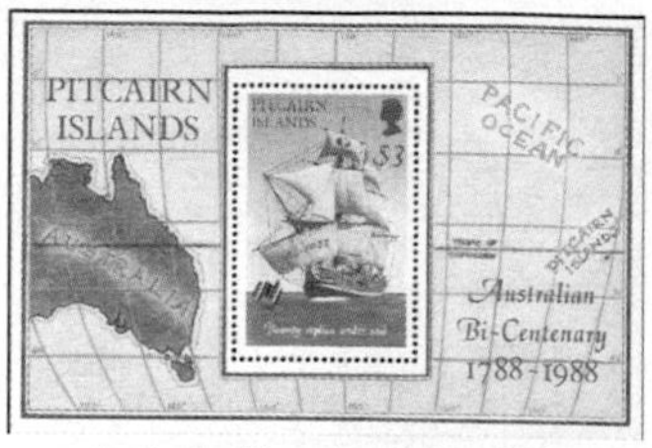


Australia Bicentennial — A61

**1988, May 9** **Wmk. 384** ***Perf. 14***
**297** A61 $3 HMS *Bounty* replica under sail 5.50 5.50

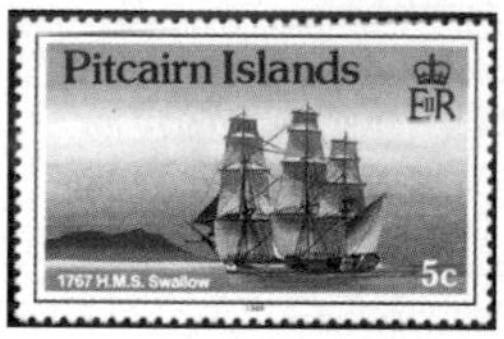


Visiting Ships A62

**Wmk. 373**

**1988, Aug. 14** **Litho.** ***Perf. 13½***
**298** A62 5c HMS *Swallow*, 1767 .20 .20
**299** A62 10c HMS *Pandora*, 1791 .20 .20
**300** A62 15c HMS *Briton* and HMS *Tagus*, 1814 .20 .20
**301** A62 20c HMS *Blossom*, 1825 .20 .20
*a.* Wmk. 384 1.60 *1.60*
*b.* Booklet pane of 4, #301a 5.75
**302** A62 30c S.V. *Lucy Anne*, 1831 .40 .40
**303** A62 35c S.V. *Charles Doggett*, 1831 .45 .45
**304** A62 40c HMS *Fly*, 1838 .50 .50
**305** A62 60c LMS *Camden*, 1840 .75 .75
**306** A62 90c HMS *Virago*, 1853 1.10 1.10
*a.* Wmk. 384 1.60 *1.60*
*b.* Booklet pane of 4, #306a 5.75
**307** A62 $1.20 S.S. *Rakaia*, 1867 1.50 1.50
**308** A62 $1.80 HMS *Sappho*, 1882 2.25 2.25
**309** A62 $5 HMS *Champion*, 1893 5.75 5.75
*Nos. 298-309 (12)* 13.50 13.50

20c, 90c exist dated "1990."
Issued: #301a-301b, 306a-306b, 5/3/90.

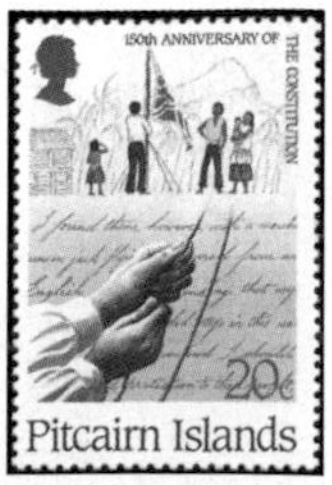


Constitution, 150th Anniv. — A63

Text and: 20c, Raising the Union Jack. 40c, Signing of the constitution aboard the H.M.S. "Fly," 1838. $1.05, Suffrage. $1.80, Equal education.

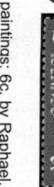

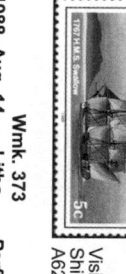

## Christmas A63

**1988, Nov. 30**   Wmk. 373   **Perf. 14**
| | | | | |
|---|---|---|---|---|
| 315 | A63 | 20c multicolored | .35 | .35 |
| 316 | A63 | 40c multicolored | .55 | .55 |
| 317 | A63 | $1.05 multicolored | 1.25 | 1.25 |
| 318 | A63 | $1.80 multicolored | 2.10 | 2.10 |
| | | Nos. 315-318 (4) | 4.25 | 4.25 |

## Christmas A64

a, Angel, animals in stable. b, Holy Family. c, Two Magi. d, Magus and shepherd boy.

**1988, Nov. 30**   Wmk. 384   **Perf. 14**
| | | | | |
|---|---|---|---|---|
| 319 | | Strip of 4 + label | 4.25 | 4.25 |
| a.-d. | A64 | 90c any single | 1.00 | 1.00 |

## Miniature Sheets — Pitcairn Isls., Bicent.

No. 320 (*Bounty* sets sail for the South Seas, Dec. 23, 1787): a, Fitting out the *Bounty* at Deptford. b, *Bounty* leaving Spithead. c, *Bounty* trying to round Cape Horn. d, Anchored in Adventure Bay, Tasmania. e, Ship's mates collecting breadfruit. f, Breadfruit in great cabin.

No. 321 (the mutiny, Apr. 28, 1789): a, *Bounty* leaving Matavai Bay. b, Mutineers waking Capt. Bligh. c, Confrontation between Fletcher Christian and Bligh. d, Bligh and crew set adrift in an open boat. e, Castaways. f, Throwing breadfruit overboard.

No. 322: a, like No. 321e. b, Isle of Man #393 A, Norfolk Is. #453.

**1989**   Litho.   Wmk. 373
| | | | | |
|---|---|---|---|---|
| 320 | | Sheet of 6 | 7.50 | 7.50 |
| a.-f. | A66 | 20c any single | .80 | .80 |
| 321 | | Sheet of 6 | 17.00 | 17.00 |
| a.-f. | A65 | 90c any single | 2.10 | 2.10 |

**Souvenir Sheet**   Wmk. 384
| | | | | |
|---|---|---|---|---|
| 322 | | Sheet of 3 + label | 6.25 | 6.25 |
| a.-c. | A65 | 90c any single | 2.00 | 2.00 |

See #331, Isle of Man #389-394 and Norfolk Is. #452-456. Issued: #320, Feb. 22; #321-322, Apr. 28. Difference between #. 321e and 327a is inscription at bottom of #322a: "C. Abbott 1989 BOT."

## Aircraft A66

**1989, July 25**   Wmk. 384   Litho.   **Perf. 14½**
| | | | | |
|---|---|---|---|---|
| 323 | A66 | 20c RNZAF Orion | .50 | .50 |
| 324 | A66 | 80c Beechcraft Queen Air | 2.25 | 2.25 |
| 325 | A66 | $1.05 Navy helicopter, USS Breton | 3.25 | 3.25 |
| 326 | A66 | $1.30 RNZAF Hercules | 4.00 | 4.00 |
| | | Nos. 323-326 (4) | 10.00 | 10.00 |

Second mail drop on Pitcairn, Mar. 21, 1985 (20c); photo mission from Tahiti, Jan. 14, 1983 (80c); diesel fuel delivery by the navy, Feb. 12, 1969 ($1.05); and parachute delivery of a bulldozer, May 31, 1983 ($1.30).

## The Islands A67

**1989, Oct. 23**   Wmk. 373   Litho.   **Perf. 14**
| | | | | |
|---|---|---|---|---|
| 327 | A67 | 15c Ducie Is. | .35 | .35 |
| 328 | A67 | 90c Henderson Is. | 1.50 | 1.50 |
| 329 | A67 | $1.05 Oeno Is. | 1.90 | 1.90 |
| 330 | A67 | $1.30 Pitcairn Is. | 2.50 | 2.50 |
| | | Nos. 327-330 (4) | 6.25 | 6.25 |

## Bicentennial Type of 1989 — Miniature Sheet

Designs: a, Mutineers aboard *Bounty* anticipating landing on Pitcairn. b, Landing. c, Exploration of the island. d, Carrying goods ashore. e, Burning the *Bounty*. f, Settlement.

**1990, Jan. 15**   Wmk. 384   **Perf. 14**
| | | | | |
|---|---|---|---|---|
| 331 | | Sheet of 6 + 3 labels | 10.00 | 10.00 |
| a.-f. | A65 | 40c any single | 1.25 | 1.25 |

## Stamp World London '90 — A68

Links with the UK: 80c, Peter Heywood and Ennerdale, Cumbria. 90c, John Adams and The Tower of St. Augustine, Hackney. $1.05, William Bligh and The Citadel Gateway, Plymouth. $1.30, Fletcher Christian and birthplace, Cockermouth.

**1990, May 3**   Wmk. 373   **Perf. 14**
| | | | | |
|---|---|---|---|---|
| 332 | A68 | 80c multicolored | 1.10 | 1.10 |
| 333 | A68 | 90c multicolored | 1.25 | 1.25 |
| 334 | A68 | $1.05 multicolored | 1.50 | 1.50 |
| 335 | A68 | $1.30 multicolored | 1.90 | 1.90 |
| | | Nos. 332-335 (4) | 5.75 | 5.75 |

## Queen Mother 90th Birthday — Common Design Types

**1990, Aug. 4**   Wmk. 384   **Perf. 14x15**
| | | | | |
|---|---|---|---|---|
| 336 | CD343 | 40c Portrait, 1037 | .75 | .50 |

**Perf. 14½**
| | | | | |
|---|---|---|---|---|
| 337 | CD344 | $3 King, Queen in carriage | 4.50 | 3.25 |

## First Pitcairn Island Postage Stamps, 50th Anniv. — A69

Historical items and Pitcairn Islands stamps.

**Perf. 13½x14**
**1990, Oct. 15**   Wmk. 373
| | | | | |
|---|---|---|---|---|
| 338 | A69 | 20c Chronometer, #2 | .40 | .40 |
| 339 | A69 | 90c Bounty's Bible, #31 | 1.60 | 1.60 |
| 340 | A69 | 90c Bounty's Bell, #108 | 2.00 | 2.00 |
| 341 | A69 | $1.05 Bounty, #172 | 2.40 | 2.40 |
| 342 | A69 | $1.30 Penny Black, #300 | 3.25 | 3.25 |
| | | Nos. 338-342 (5) | 9.65 | 9.65 |

## Birds — A70

**1990, Dec. 5**   Wmk. 373   **Perf. 14**
| | | | | |
|---|---|---|---|---|
| 343 | A70 | 20c Redbreast | .40 | .40 |
| 344 | A70 | 90c Wood pigeon | 2.00 | 2.00 |
| 345 | A70 | $1.30 Sparrow | 2.75 | 2.75 |
| 346 | A70 | $1.80 Flightless chicken | 4.00 | 4.00 |
| | | Nos. 343-346 (4) | 9.15 | 9.15 |

Birdpex '90, 20th Intl. Ornithological Congress, New Zealand.

## Miniature Sheet — Pitcairn Islands, Bicent. A71

Bicentennial celebrations: a, Re-enacting the landing. b, Commemorative plaque. c, Memorial church service. d, Cricket match. e, Bounty model burning. f, Fireworks.

**1991, Mar. 24**   Wmk. 384   Litho.   **Perf. 14½**
| | | | | |
|---|---|---|---|---|
| 347 | A71 | 80c Sheet of 6, #a.-f. | 17.00 | 17.00 |

## Elizabeth & Philip, Birthdays — Common Design Types

**1991, July 12**   Wmk. 384   Litho.   **Perf. 14½**
| | | | | |
|---|---|---|---|---|
| 348 | CD346 | 20c multicolored | .40 | .40 |
| 349 | CD345 | $1.30 multicolored | 3.00 | 3.00 |
| a. | | Pair, #348-349 + label | 3.50 | 3.50 |

## Cruise Ships A72

**1991, June 17**   **Perf. 14**
| | | | | |
|---|---|---|---|---|
| 350 | A72 | 15c Europa | .45 | .45 |
| 351 | A72 | 80c Royal Viking Star | 2.25 | 2.25 |
| 352 | A72 | $1.30 World Discoverer | 3.50 | 3.50 |
| 353 | A72 | $1.80 Sagafjord | 5.25 | 5.25 |
| | | Nos. 350-353 (4) | 11.45 | 11.45 |

## Island Vehicles A73

**1991, Sept. 25**   Wmk. 373   **Perf. 14**
| | | | | |
|---|---|---|---|---|
| 354 | A73 | 20c Bulldozer | .65 | .65 |
| 355 | A73 | $1 Motorcycle | 1.75 | 1.75 |
| 356 | A73 | $1.30 Tractor | 1.75 | 1.75 |
| 357 | A73 | $1.80 All-terrain vehicle | 3.25 | 3.25 |
| | | Nos. 354-357 (4) | 7.40 | 7.40 |

## Christmas — A74

**1991, Nov. 18**   **Perf. 14x14½**
| | | | | |
|---|---|---|---|---|
| 358 | A74 | 20c The Annunciation | .40 | .40 |
| 359 | A74 | 80c Shepherds | 1.40 | 1.40 |
| 360 | A74 | $1.30 Nativity scene | 2.25 | 2.25 |
| 361 | A74 | $1.80 Three wise men | 3.00 | 3.00 |
| | | Nos. 358-361 (4) | 7.05 | 7.05 |

## Queen Elizabeth II's Accession to the Throne, 40th Anniv. — Common Design Type

**1992, Feb. 6**   Wmk. 384   Litho.
| | | | | |
|---|---|---|---|---|
| 362 | CD349 | 20c multicolored | .40 | .40 |
| 363 | CD349 | 60c multicolored | 1.25 | 1.25 |
| 364 | CD349 | 90c multicolored | 1.50 | 1.50 |
| 365 | CD349 | $1 multicolored | 1.50 | 1.50 |

**Wmk. 373**
| | | | | |
|---|---|---|---|---|
| 366 | CD349 | $1.80 multicolored | 2.50 | 2.50 |
| | | Nos. 362-366 (5) | 7.15 | 7.15 |

## Sharks — A75

Designs: 20c, Carcharhinus galapagensis. $1, Eugomphodus taurus. $1.50, Carcharhinus melanopterus. $1.80, Carcharhinus amblyrhynchos.

**1992, June 30**   Wmk. 373   **Perf. 15x14½**   Litho.
| | | | | |
|---|---|---|---|---|
| 367 | A75 | 20c multicolored | .50 | .50 |
| 368 | A75 | $1 multicolored | 2.40 | 2.40 |
| 369 | A75 | $1.50 multicolored | 3.25 | 3.25 |
| 370 | A75 | $1.80 multicolored | 4.75 | 4.75 |
| | | Nos. 367-370 (4) | 10.90 | 10.90 |

## Sir Peter Scott Commemorative Expedition to Pitcairn Islands, 1991-92 — A76

Designs: 20c, Montastrea, acropora coral sticks. $1, Henderson sandalwood. $1.50, Murphy's petrel. $1.80, Henderson hawkmoth.

**1992, Sept. 11**   **Perf. 14x15**   Litho.   Wmk. 373
| | | | | |
|---|---|---|---|---|
| 371 | A76 | 20c multicolored | .50 | .50 |
| 372 | A76 | $1 multicolored | 2.50 | 2.50 |
| 373 | A76 | $1.50 multicolored | 3.75 | 3.75 |
| 374 | A76 | $1.80 multicolored | 5.25 | 5.25 |
| | | Nos. 371-374 (4) | 12.00 | 12.00 |

## Captain William Bligh, 175th Anniv. of Death A77

20c, Bligh's birthplace, St. Tudy, Cornwall, HMAV Resolution. $1, On deck of HMAV Bounty, breadfruit plant. $1.50, Voyage in open boat, Bligh's Bounty. $1.80, Portrait by Rachel H. Combe, Battle of Camperdown, 1797.

**1992, Dec. 7**   Wmk. 373   Litho.
| | | | | |
|---|---|---|---|---|
| 375 | A77 | 20c multicolored | .40 | .40 |
| 376 | A77 | $1 multicolored | 2.00 | 2.00 |
| 377 | A77 | $1.50 multicolored | 2.75 | 2.75 |
| 378 | A77 | $1.80 multicolored | 3.25 | 3.25 |
| | | Nos. 375-378 (4) | 8.40 | 8.40 |

## Royal Naval Vessels A78

**1993, Mar. 10**   Wmk. 384   Litho.   **Perf. 14**
| | | | | |
|---|---|---|---|---|
| 379 | A78 | 15c HMS Chichester | .40 | .40 |
| 380 | A78 | 20c HMS Jaguar | .60 | .60 |

## PITCAIRN ISLANDS

```
381  A78  $1.80 HMS Andrew      5.50   5.50
382  A78  $3 HMS Warrior        8.75   8.75
          Nos. 379-382 (4)     15.25  15.25
```

Coronation of Queen Elizabeth II, 40th Anniv. A79

**1993, June 17      Wmk. 373      Perf. 13**

```
383  A79  $5 multicolored      10.50  10.50
```

### Scenic Views A80

Designs: 20c, Pawala Valley Ridge. 90c, St. Pauls. $1.20, Matt's Rocks from Water Valley. $1.50, Ridge Rope to St. Paul's Pool. $1.80, Ship Landing Point.

**1993, Sept. 8      Wmk. 373      Perf. 14**

```
384  A80  10c multicolored      .35    .35
385  A80  90c multicolored     1.50   1.50
386  A80  $1.20 multicolored   2.00   2.00
387  A80  $1.50 multicolored   2.40   2.40
388  A80  $1.80 multicolored   3.00   3.00
          Nos. 384-388 (5)     9.25   9.25
```

### Lizards A81

Designs: 20c, Indopacific tree gecko. No. 390, Stump-toed gecko. No. 391, Mourning gecko. $1, Moth skink No. 393, Snake-eyed skink. No. 394, White-bellied skink.

**1993, Dec. 14      Litho.      Wmk. 373      Perf. 13x13½**

```
389  A81  20c multicolored      .75    .75
390  A81  45c multicolored     1.25   1.25
391  A81  $1 multicolored      2.75   2.75
392  A81  $1 multicolored      3.25   3.25
393  A81  $1.50 multicolored   4.50   4.50
394  A81  $1.80 multicolored   4.50   4.50
          Nos. 389-394 (6)    15.50  15.50
```

Nos. 390-391, 393-394 Ovptd. with Hong Kong '94 Emblem

**1994, Feb. 18      Litho.      Wmk. 373      Perf. 13x13½**

```
395  A81  45c on #390          1.10   1.10
396  A81  45c on #391          1.10   1.10
  a.      Pair, #395-396       2.25   2.25
397  A81  $1.50 on #393        4.00   4.00
398  A81  $1.50 on #394        4.00   4.00
  a.      Pair, #397-398       8.00   8.00
          Nos. 395-398 (4)    10.20  10.20
```

### Early Pitcairners — A82

Designs: 5c, Friday October Christian, 20c, Moses Young, $1.80, James Russell McCoy, $3, Rosalind Amelia Young.

**1994, Mar. 7      Perf. 14**

```
399  A82  5c multicolored       .35    .35
400  A82  20c multicolored      .40    .40
401  A82  $1.80 multicolored   3.50   3.50
402  A82  $3 multicolored      5.50   5.50
          Nos. 399-402 (4)     9.75   9.75
```

### Shipwrecks A83

Designs: 20c, Wildwave, Oeno Island 1858. 90c, Cornwallis, Pitcairn Island 1875. $1.80, Acadia, Ducie Island, 1881. $3, Oregon, Oeno Island, 1883.

**1994, June 22      Wmk. 373      Litho.      Perf. 14**

```
403  A83  20c multicolored      .55    .55
404  A83  90c multicolored     2.10   2.10
405  A83  $1.80 multicolored   4.25   4.25
406  A83  $3 multicolored      7.25   7.25
          Nos. 403-406 (4)    14.15  14.15
```

### Corals A84

Designs: 20c, Fire coral, vert. 90c, Cauliflower coral, arc-eye hawkfish. $1, Snubnose chub, lobe coral, butterflyfish, vert. $3, Coral garden, butterflyfish, vert.

**1994, Sept. 15      Wmk. 373      Litho.      Perf. 14**

```
407  A84  20c multicolored      .75    .75
408  A84  90c multicolored     3.00   3.00
409  A84  $1 multicolored      3.25   3.25
          Nos. 407-409 (3)     7.00   7.00
```

Souvenir Sheet

```
410  A84  $3 multicolored      6.75   6.75
```

### Christmas A85

Flowers: 20c, Morning glory. 90c, Hibiscus, vert. $1, Frangipani. $3, Ginsey, vert.

**1994, Nov. 24      Wmk. 373      Litho.      Perf. 14**

```
411  A85  20c multicolored      .35    .35
412  A85  90c multicolored     1.60   1.60
413  A85  $1 multicolored      1.75   1.75
414  A85  $3 multicolored      5.50   5.50
          Nos. 411-414 (4)     9.20   9.20
```

### Birds A86

Designs: 5c, Fairy tern. 10c, Red-tailed tropicbird chick, vert. 15c, Henderson rail. 20c, Red-footed booby, vert. 45c, Blue-gray noddy. 50c, Henderson reed warbler. 90c, Common noddy. $1, Masked booby, chick, vert. $1.80, Henderson fruit dove. $2, Murphy's petrel. $3, Christmas shearwater. $5, Red-tailed tropicbird juvenile.

**1995, Mar. 8      Wmk. 373      Litho.      Perf. 13½**

```
415  A86  5c multicolored       .35    .35
416  A86  10c multicolored      .35    .35
417  A86  15c multicolored      .45    .45
418  A86  20c multicolored      .45    .45
419  A86  45c multicolored      .65    .70
420  A86  50c multicolored      .75    .80
421  A86  90c multicolored     1.25   1.25
422  A86  $1 multicolored      1.40   1.40
423  A86  $1.80 multicolored   2.25   2.25
424  A86  $2 multicolored      2.50   2.50
425  A86  $3 multicolored      3.75   3.75
426  A86  $5 multicolored      6.25   6.25
          Nos. 415-426 (12)   20.40  21.10
```

### Oeno Island Vacation — A87

Designs: 20c, Boating. 90c, Volleyball on the beach. $1.80, Picnic. $3, Sing-a-long.

**1995, June 26      Wmk. 373      Perf. 14x15**

```
427  A87  30c multicolored      .30    .30
428  A87  90c multicolored     1.60   1.60
429  A87  $1.80 multicolored   3.25   3.25
430  A87  $3 multicolored      5.25   5.25
          Nos. 427-430 (4)    10.40  10.40
```

### Queen Mother, 95th Birthday — A88

**1995, Aug. 4      Perf. 14½**

Souvenir Sheet

```
431  A88  $5 multicolored     10.00  10.00
```

### Radio, Cent. — A89

Designs: 20c, Guglielmo Marconi, radio equipment, 1901. $1, Man, Pitcairn radio, 1938. $1.50, Woman, satellite earth station equipment, 1994. $3, Satellite in orbit, 1992.

**1995, Sept. 5      Wmk. 373      Perf. 13**

```
432  A89  20c multicolored      .30    .30
433  A89  $1 multicolored      1.60   1.60
434  A89  $1.50 multicolored   2.25   2.25
435  A89  $3 multicolored      5.25   5.25
          Nos. 432-435 (4)     9.90   9.90
```

### UN, 50th Anniv. Common Design Type

Designs: 20c, Lord Mayor's Show. $1, RFA Brambleleaf. $1.50, UN ambulance. $3, Royal Air Force Tristar.

**1995, Oct. 24      Wmk. 373      Litho.      Perf. 14**

```
436  CD353  20c multicolored     .35    .35
437  CD353  $1 multicolored     1.90   1.90
438  CD353  $1.50 multicolored  3.00   3.00
439  CD353  $3 multicolored     6.00   6.00
            Nos. 436-439 (4)   11.25  11.25
```

### Supply Ship Day — A90

### Queen Elizabeth II, 70th Birthday

Common Design Type

Various portraits of Queen, scenes from Pitcairn Islands: 20c, Bounty Bay. 90c, Jetty, Rocks. $3, St. Paul's. Landing Point, Bounty Bay. $1.80, Matt's.

**1996, Jan. 30      Perf. 14x14½**

```
440  A90  20c Early morning     .50    .50
441  A90  40c Meeting ship      .80    .80
442  A90  90c Unloading sup-
              plies            1.75   1.75
443  A90  $1 Landing work      2.00   2.00
444  A90  $1.50 Supply sorting 2.75   2.75
445  A90  $1.80 Last load      3.50   3.50
          Nos. 440-445 (6)    11.30  11.30
```

### CHINA '96, 9th Asian Intl. Philatelic Exhibition — A91

**1996, Apr. 21      Perf. 13½x14**

```
446  CD354  20c multicolored     .40    .40
447  CD354  90c multicolored    1.60   1.60
448  CD354  $1.80 multicolored  3.25   3.25
449  CD354  $3 multicolored     5.25   5.25
            Nos. 446-449 (4)   10.50  10.50
```

Souvenir Sheet

```
450  A91  20c multicolored     3.50   3.50
451  A91  $1.80 multicolored   3.50   3.50
452  A91  90c Sheet of 2, #a.-b.  3.75   3.75
```

#450, Chinese junk #451, HMAV Bounty. No. 452: a. Chinese rat. b. Polynesian rat.

### Amateur Radio — A92

Designs: 20c, Call signs of members in Amateur Radio Operator's Club, 1996. No. 454, VR6 1M calling for medical assistance. No. 455, Operator receiving transmission, physician standing by, $2.50, Andrew Young, Pitcairn's first operator, 1938.

**1996, Sept. 4      Wmk. 384      Perf. 14**

```
453  A92  20c multicolored      .55    .55
454  A92  $1 multicolored      3.25   3.25
455  A92  $1.50 multicolored   5.00   5.00
456  A92  $2.50 multicolored   7.00   7.00
          Nos. 453-456 (4)    12.55  12.55
```

### Birds A93

World Wildlife Fund. 5c, Henderson Island reed-warbler, vert. 10c, Stephen's lorikeet, vert. 20c, Henderson rail, vert. 90c, Henderson Island fruit-dove, vert. No. 461, Masked booby. No. 462, Common fairy-tern.

**1996, Nov. 20      Wmk. 373      Perf. 14**

```
457  A93  5c multicolored       .20    .20
458  A93  10c multicolored      .20    .20
459  A93  20c multicolored      .35    .35
460  A93  90c multicolored     1.60   1.60
461  A93  $1 multicolored      1.25   1.25
462  A93  $2 multicolored      3.50   3.50
          Nos. 457-462 (6)     9.35   7.50
```

## Souvenir Sheet A94

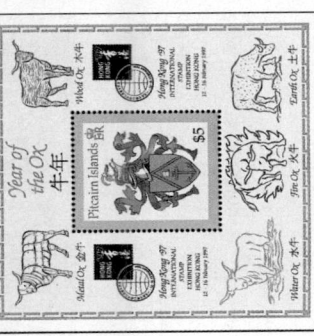

Year of the Ox 牛年

Illustration reduced.

**Coat of Arms — A95**

**Perf. 14½x14**
**1997, Feb. 12**
463  A94  $5 multicolored  9.00  9.00
Hong Kong '97.

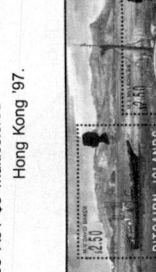

a, MV David Baker. b, MV McLachlan.

**Perf. 13½x14**
**1997, May 26  Litho.**
464  A95  $2.50  Sheet of 2, #a.-b.  10.00  10.00

## South Pacific Commission, 50th Anniv. — A96

## Health Care A96

Designs: 20c, New Health Center. $1, Resident nurse treating patient. $1.70, Dental officer treating patient. $3, Patient being taken aboard ship.

**Wmk. 373    Perf. 14**
**1997, Sept. 12    Litho.**
465  A96  20c multicolored  .40  .40
466  A96  $1 multicolored  1.75  1.75
467  A96  $1.70 multicolored  3.00  3.00
468  A96  $3 multicolored  5.00  5.00
Nos. 465-468 (4)  10.15  10.15

## Queen Elizabeth II and Prince Philip, 50th Wedding Anniv. — A97

Designs: No. 469, Prince driving team of horses. No. 470, Queen wearing wide-brimmed hat. No. 471, Prince in formal riding attire. No. 472, Queen, horse. No. 473, Queen and Prince standing behind flowers. No. 474, Prince Charles riding horse.

**Wmk. 373    Perf. 13**
**1997, Nov. 20    Litho.**
469  20c multicolored  .25  .25
470  20c multicolored  .25  .25
a.  A97  Pair, #469-470  .50  .50
471  $1 multicolored  1.75  1.75
472  $1 multicolored  1.75  1.75
a.  A97  Pair, #471-472  3.50  3.50
473  $1.70 multicolored  2.75  2.75
474  $1.70 multicolored  2.75  2.75
a.  A97  Pair, #473-474  5.50  5.50
Nos. 469-474 (6)  9.50  9.50

## Christmas A98

Flower, picture: 20c, Gardenia taitensis, view of Island at night. 80c, Bauhinia variegata, ringing public bell. $1.20, Metrosideros collina, children's baskets hanging on line. $3, Hibiscus tiliaceus, Pitcairn Church, Square at Adamstown.

**Wmk. 373    Perf. 13½**
**1997, Dec. 1    Litho.**
475  A98  20c multicolored  .25  .25
476  A98  80c multicolored  1.25  1.25
477  A98  $1.20 multicolored  1.75  1.75
478  A98  $3 multicolored  4.50  4.50
Nos. 475-478 (4)  7.75  7.75

## Views of Christian's Cave — A99

5c, Dorcas Apple, looking across Adamstown. 20c, Rocks near Betty's Edge looking past Tatinanny. 35c, Cave mouth. $5, Cave from near where Fletcher Christian built home.

**Wmk. 384    Perf. 13½**
**1998, Feb. 9    Litho.**
479  A99  5c multi  .25  .25
480  A99  20c multi  .45  .45
481  A99  35c multi, vert.  .75  .75
482  A99  $5 multi, vert.  6.50  6.50
Nos. 479-482 (4)  7.95  7.95

## Sailing Ships A100

Designs: 20c, HMS Bounty, 1790. 90c, HMS Swallow, 1767. $1.80, HMS Briton & HMS Tagus, 1814. $3, HMS Fly, 1838.

**Wmk. 373    Perf. 14½x14**
**1998, May 28    Litho.**
483  A100  20c multicolored  .50  .50
484  A100  90c multicolored  1.25  1.25
485  A100  $1.80 multicolored  2.50  2.50
486  A100  $3 multicolored  4.50  4.50
Nos. 483-486 (4)  8.75  8.75

## Diana, Princess of Wales (1961-97)
Common Design Type of 1998

**Wmk. 373    Perf. 14½x14**
**1998, Aug. 31    Litho.**
487  CD355  90c  Sheet of 4, #a.-d.  5.50  5.50
a, In evening dress. b, Wearing white hat, pearls. c, In houndstooth top. d, Wearing white hat, top.

No. 487 sold for $3.60 + 40c with surtax being donated to the Princess Diana Memorial Fund.

## Flowers A101

20c, Bidens mathewsii. 90c, Hibiscus. $1.80, Osteomeles anthyllidifolia. $3, Ipomoea littoralis.

**Wmk. 373    Perf. 14**
**1998, Oct. 20    Litho.**
488  A101  20c multicolored  .85  .85
489  A101  90c multicolored  2.00  2.00
490  A101  $1.80 multicolored  3.00  3.00
491  A101  $3 multicolored  5.00  5.00
Nos. 488-491 (4)  10.85  10.85
Flowers are below inscriptions on Nos. 489, 491.

## Int'l Year of the Ocean A102

Designs: 20c, Fishing. 90c, Divers, vert. $1.80, Reef fish. $3, Murphy's petrel, vert.

**Unwmk.    Perf. 14**
**1998, Dec. 16**
492  A102  20c multicolored  .80  .80
493  A102  90c multicolored  2.00  2.00
494  A102  $1.80 multicolored  3.00  3.00
495  A102  $3 multicolored  4.50  4.50
a.  Souv. sheet of 4, #492-495 + label  11.00  11.00
Nos. 492-495 (4)  10.30  10.30

## Government Education on Pitcairn, 50th Anniv. — A103

Scenes on pages of books: 20c, Schoolmaster George Hunn Nobbs, students, 1828. 90c, Schoolmaster Simon Young, daughter Rosalind, teacher Hattie Andre, 1893. $1.80, teacher Roy Clark, 1932. $3, Modern school at Palau, 1999.

**Unwmk.    Perf. 14**
**1999, Feb. 15    Litho.**
496  A103  20c multicolored  .20  .20
497  A103  90c multicolored  1.25  1.25
498  A103  $1.80 multicolored  2.50  2.50
499  A103  $3 multicolored  4.25  4.25
Nos. 496-499 (4)  8.20  8.20

## Archaeological Expedition to Survey Wreck of the Bounty — A104

Scenes of ship during last voyage and: a, 50c, Anchor. b, $1, Cannon. c, $1.50, Chronometer. d, $2, Copper caldron.

**1999, Mar. 19**
500  A104  Sheet of 4, #a.-d.  7.25  7.25

## 19th Cent. Pitcairn Island A105

Designs: 20c, John Adams (d. 1829), Bounty Bay. 90c, Topaz, 1808. $1.80, George Hunn Nobbs, Norfolk Island. $3, HMS Champion, 1893.

**Perf. 14½x14    Wmk. 373**
**1999, May 25    Litho.**
501  A105  20c multicolored  .60  .60
502  A105  90c multicolored  1.40  1.40
503  A105  $1.80 multicolored  2.75  2.75
504  A105  $3 multicolored  8.75  8.75
Nos. 501-504 (4)

## Wedding of Prince Edward and Sophie Rhys-Jones
Common Design Type

**Perf. 13¾x14    Wmk. 384**
**1999, June 18    Litho.**
505  CD356  $2.50  Separate portraits  3.00  3.00
506  CD356  $2.50  Couple  3.00  3.00

## Honey Bees A106

Designs: 20c, Beekeepers, hives. $1, Bee, white and purple flower. $1.80, Bees, honeycomb. $3, Bee on flower, honey jar.

**1999, Sept. 12    Litho.**
**Die Cut Perf. 9    Self-Adhesive**
507  A106  20c multicolored  .75  .75
508  A106  $1 multicolored  1.60  1.60
a.  Souvenir sheet of 1  2.75  2.75
509  A106  $1.80 multicolored  4.50  4.50
510  A106  $3 multicolored  9.60  9.60
Nos. 507-510 (4)
China 1999 World Philatelic Exhibition, No. 508a Issued 8/21.

## Protection of Galapagos Tortoise "Mr. Turpen" A107

Designs: a, 5c, Arrival of the ship Yankee, 1937. b, 20c, Off-loading Mr. Turpen to a longboat. c, 35c, Mr. Turpen. d, $5, Close-up of tortoise's head.

**Perf. 14¼    Litho.    Unwmk.**
**2000, Jan. 14**
511  A107  Strip of 4, #a.-d., + label  10.00  10.00

## Flowers A108

Designs: 10c, Guettarda speciosa. 15c, Hibiscus tiliaceus. 20c, Selenicereus grandiflorus. 30c, Metrosideros collina. 50c, Alpinia zerumbet. $1, Syzygium jambos. $1.50, Commelina diffusa. $1.80, Canna indica. $2, Allamanda cathartica. $3, Calophyllum inophyllum. $5, Ipomea indica. $10, Bauhinia monandra (40x40mm).

**Litho., Litho. with Foil Application ($10)**
**Perf. 13¾x13¼, 13½x13¾ ($10)    Unwmk.**
**2000, May 22**
512-523  A108  Set of 12  26.00  26.00
520a  Souvenir sheet, #518, 520  6.00  6.00
The Stamp Show 2000, London (No. 520a).

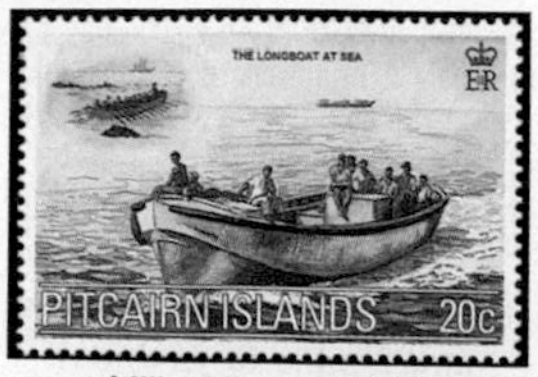


Millennium — A109

Old and modern pictures: 20c, Longboat at sea. 90c, Landing and longboat house. $1.80, Transportation of crops. $3, Communications.

**Wmk. 373**

**2000, June 28 Litho. *Perf. 13¾***
**524-527** A109 Set of 4 6.75 6.75

Souvenir Sheets

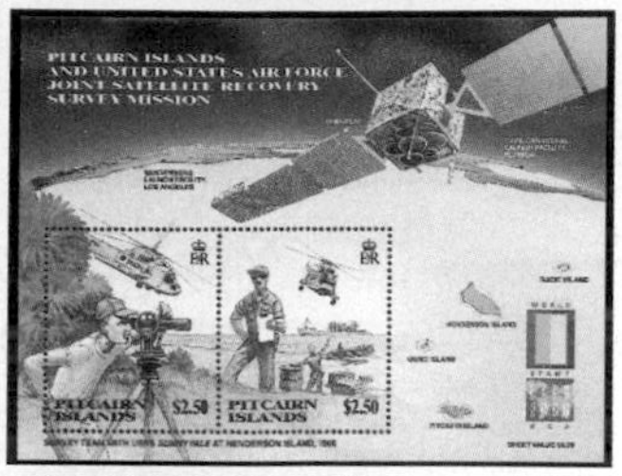

Satellite Recovery Mission — A110

No. 528: a, Surveryor, helicopter. b, Military personnel, boat, ship, helicopter.
Illustration reduced.

**2000, July 7 Unwmk. *Perf. 14¼***
**528** A110 $2.50 Sheet of 2, #a-b 9.00 9.00

World Stamp Expo 2000, Anaheim.
Illustration shows lower half of the entire sheet. The upper half, which has descriptive text, and is printed on the reverse, is the same size as the lower half. The entire sheet is folded where the halves meet.

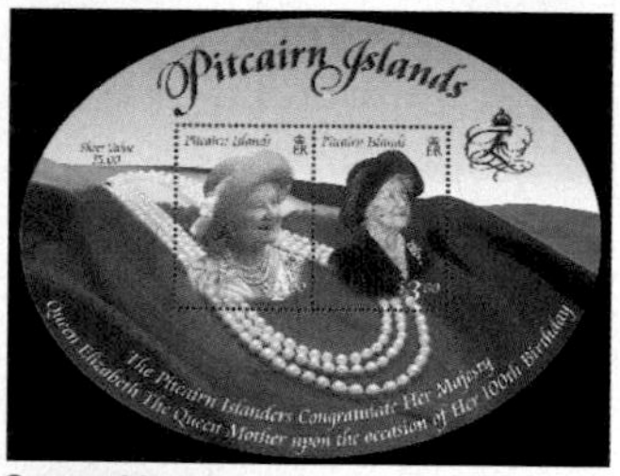


Queen Mother, 100th Birthday — A111

No. 529: a, $2, Blue hat. b, $3, Maroon hat.
Illustration reduced.

**2000, Aug. 4 *Perf. 14***
**529** A111 Sheet of 2, #a-b 9.00 9.00

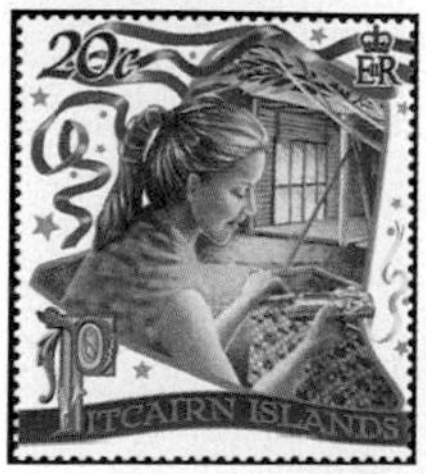


Christmas A112

***Perf. 14½***

**2000, Nov. 22 Litho. Unwmk.**
**530** Strip of 4 7.00 7.00
*a.* A112 20c Woman .50 .50
*b.* A112 80c Man, boy 1.50 1.50
*c.* A112 $1.50 Woman, child 2.00 2.00
*d.* A112 $3 Three children 3.00 3.00

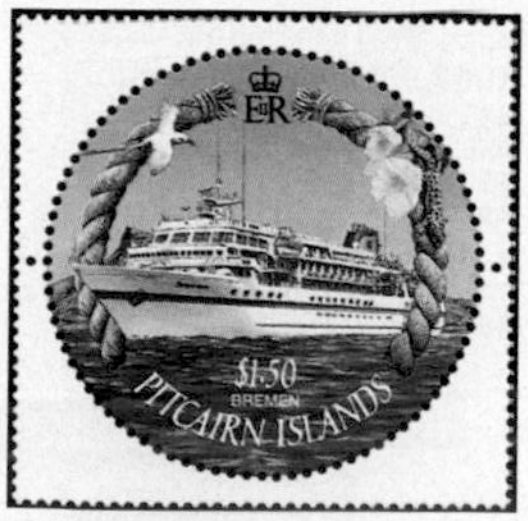


Cruise Ships A113

Designs: No. 531, $1.50, Bremen. No. 532, $1.50, MV Europa. No. 533, $1.50, MS Rotterdam. No. 534, $1.50, Saga Rose.

***Perf. 14¾***

**2001, Feb. 1 Litho. Unwmk.**
**531-534** A113 Set of 4 8.00 8.00

Values are for copies with surrounding selvage.

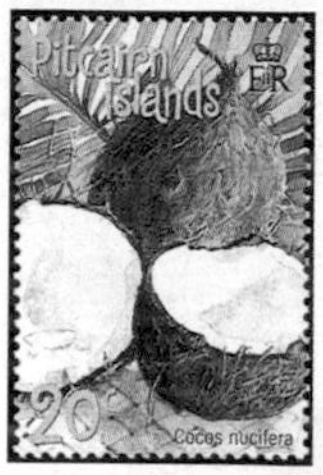


Tropical Fruit — A114

Designs: 20c, Cocos nucifera. 80c, Punica granatum. $1, Passiflora edulis. $3, Ananas comosus.

**2001, Apr. 6 Litho. *Perf. 13½x13¼***
**535-538** A114 Set of 4 6.50 6.50
*538a* Souvenir sheet, #536, 538 5.50 5.50

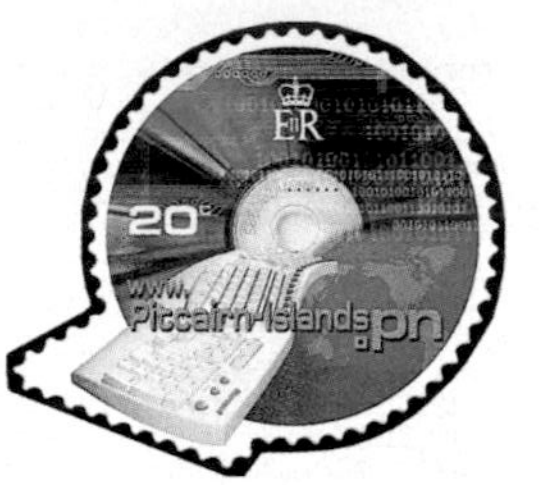


Allocation of ".pn" Internet Domain Suffix — A115

CD and: 20c, Computer keyboard. 50c, Circuit board. $1, Integrated circuit. $5, Mouse.

**2001, June 11 *Serpentine Die Cut***
**Self-Adhesive**
**539-542** A115 Set of 4 9.50 9.50

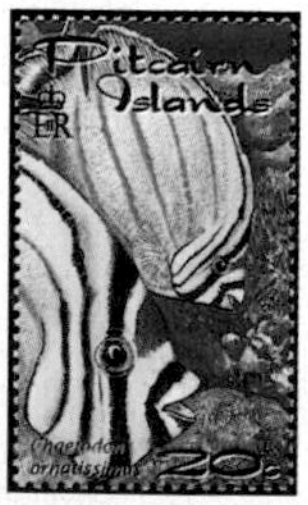


Tropical Fish — A116

Designs: 20c, Chaetodon ornatissimus. 80c, Chaetodon reticulatus. $1.50, Chaetodon lunula. $2, Henochus chrysostomus.

***Perf. 13x13¼***

**2001, Sept. 4 Litho. Unwmk.**
**543-546** A116 Set of 4 6.25 6.25
*546a* Souvenir sheet, #543, 546 3.50 3.50

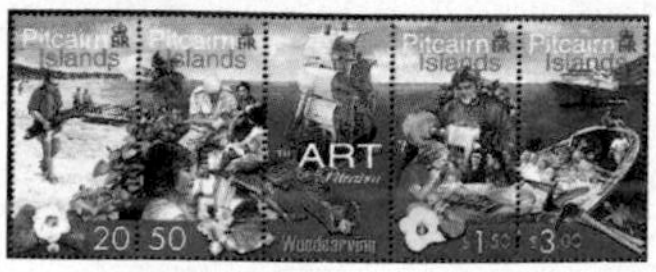


Wood Carving — A117

No. 547: a, 20c, Miro flower, man on beach carrying log. b, 50c, Toa flower, artisans carving fish. c, $1.50, Pulau flower, man using machine, woman looking at carved objects. d, $3, Ship, boat, carved objects.

**2001, Oct. 11**
**547** A117 Horiz. strip of 4, #a-d, + central label 6.50 6.50

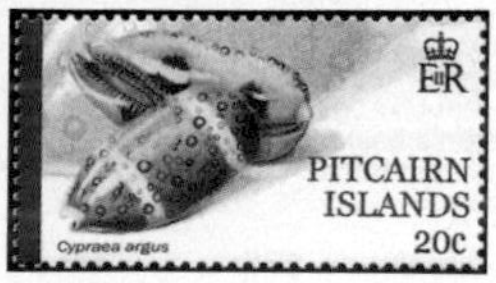


Cowrie Shells A118

Designs: 20c, Cypraea argus. 80c, Cypraea isabella. $1, Cypraea mappa. $3, Cypraea mauritana.

**2001, Dec. 6 *Perf. 13¼x13***
**548-551** A118 Set of 4 6.25 6.25

**Reign Of Queen Elizabeth II, 50th Anniv. Issue**

Common Design Type

Souvenir Sheet

No. 552: a, 50c, With Queen Mother and Princess Margaret. b, $1, Wearing tiara. c, $1.20, Without hat. d, $1.50, Wearing hat. e, $2, 1955 portrait by Annigoni (38x50mm).

***Perf. 14¼x14½, 13¾ (#552e)***

**2002, Feb. 6 Litho. Wmk. 373**
**552** CD360 Sheet of 5, #a-e 9.25 9.25

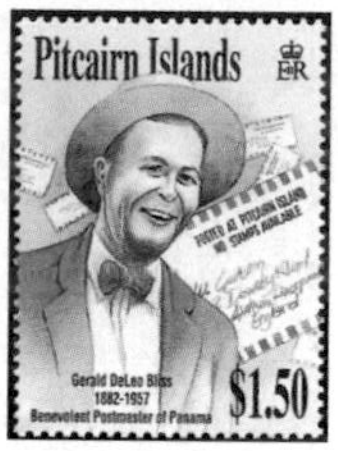


Famous Men — A119

Designs: No. 553, $1.50, Gerald DeLeo Bliss (1882-1957), Panamanian postmaster who expedited Pitcairn mail. No. 554, $1.50, Capt. Arthur C. Jones (1898-1987), shipper of trees to Pitcairn. No. 555, $1.50, James Russell McCoy (1845-1924), missionary. No. 556, $1.50, Adm. Sir Fairfax Moresby (1786-1877), philanthropist.

***Perf. 14¼x14¾***

**2002, Apr. 5 Litho. Unwmk.**
**553-556** A119 Set of 4 9.25 9.25

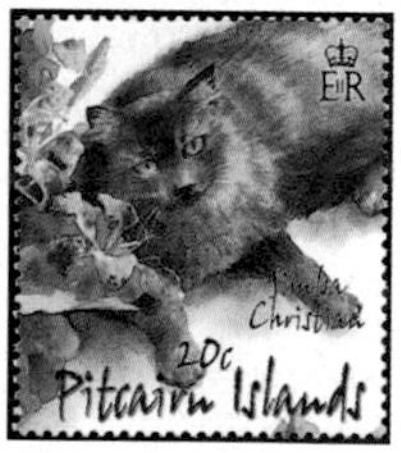


Cats — A120

Local cats: 20c, Simba Christian. $1, Miti Christian. $1.50, Nala Brown. $3, Alicat Pulau.

***Perf. 13¼x13***

**2002, June 28 Litho. Unwmk.**
**557-560** A120 Set of 4 6.50 6.50
*a.* Souvenir sheet of 2, #557, 560 6.50 6.50

**Queen Mother Elizabeth (1900-2002)**

Common Design Type

Designs: 40c, As child, c. 1910 (black and white photograph). Nos. 562, 565a, $1, As young woman, without hat. $1.50, Wearing flowered hat. Nos. 564, 565b, $2, Wearing blue hat.

**Wmk. 373**

**2002, Aug. 5 Litho. *Perf. 14¼***
**With Purple Frames**
**561-564** CD361 Set of 4 8.50 8.50

**Souvenir Sheet**
**Without Purple Frames**
***Perf. 14½x14¼***
**565** CD361 Sheet of 2, #a-b 4.75 4.75

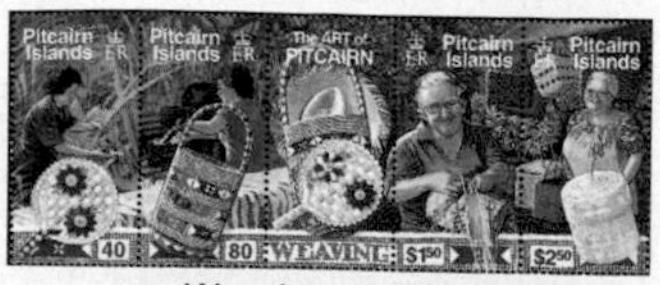


Weaving — A121

No. 566: a, 40c, Woman cutting thatch. b, 80c, Woman dyeing thatch. c, $1.50, Millie Christian weaving. d, $2.50, Thelma Brown with finished products.

***Perf. 13¼x12¾***

**2002, Oct. 18 Litho. Unwmk.**
**566** A121 Horiz. strip of 4, #a-d + central label 7.50 7.50

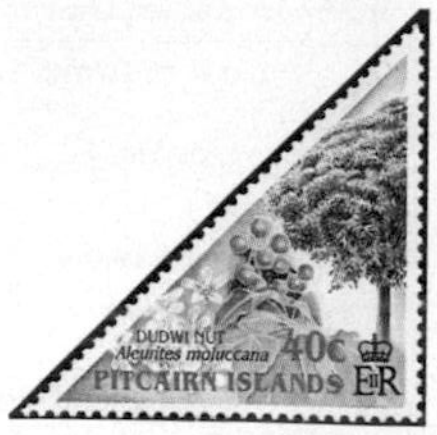


Trees A122

Designs: 40c, Dudwi nut. $1, Toa. $1.50, Miro. $3, Hulianda.

***Perf. 13¼***

**2002, Dec. 1 Litho. Unwmk.**
**567-570** A122 Set of 4 7.50 7.50

Souvenir Sheet

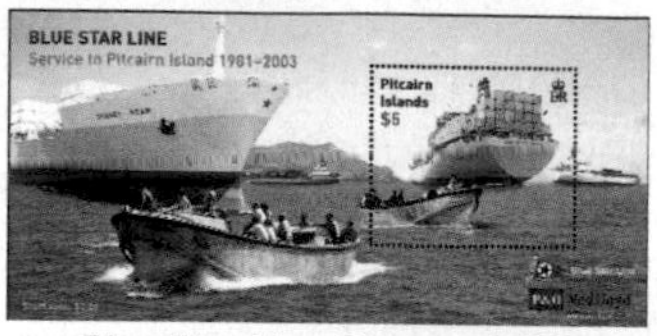


Blue Star Line Ships — A123

**2003, Jan. 8 Litho. *Perf. 14x13¼***
**571** A123 $5 multi 8.50 8.50

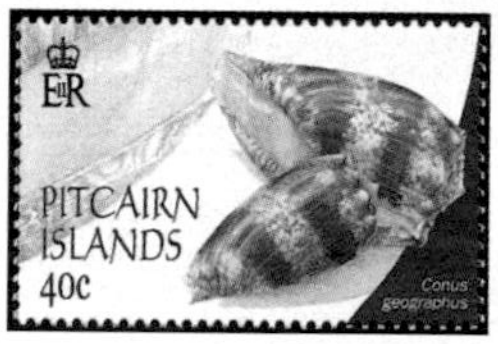


Cone Shells A124

Designs: 40c, Conus geographus. 80c, Conus textile. $1, Conus striatus. $1.20, Conus marmoreus. $3, Conus litoglyphus.

***Perf. 13½x13¾***

**2003, Mar. 14 Litho. Unwmk.**
**572-576** A124 Set of 5 7.00 7.00

**Coronation of Queen Elizabeth II, 50th Anniv.**

Common Design Type

Designs: Nos. 577, 581a, 40c, Queen wearing tiara. No. 578, 80c, Carriage in procession. No. 579, $1.50, Queen wearing tiara, diff. Nos. 580, 581b, $3, Queen in procession at coronation.

***Perf. 14¼x14½***

**2003, June 2 Litho. Wmk. 373**
**Vignettes Framed, Red Background**
**577-580** CD363 Set of 4 6.75 6.75

**Souvenir Sheet**
**Vignettes Without Frame, Purple Panel**
**581** CD363 Sheet of 2, #a-b 4.00 4.00

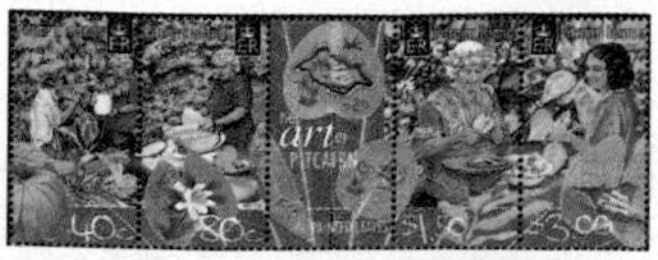

Painted Leaves — A125

No. 582: a, 40c, Women putting leaves in earthenware jar. b, 80c, Washing leaves. c, $1.50, Leaf painter. d, $3, Leaf painter, diff.

*Perf. 13¼*

**2003, Aug. 18 Litho. Unwmk.**
**582** A125 Horiz. strip of 4, #a-d, + central label 6.75 6.75

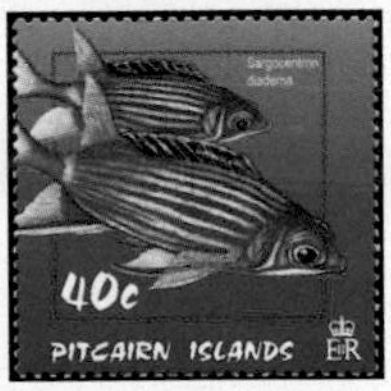


Squirrelfish
A126

Designs: 40c, Sargocentron diadema. 80c, Sargocentron spiniferum. $1.50, Sargocentron caudimaculatum. $3, Neoniphon sammara.

*Perf. 13¼*

**2003, Oct. 8 Litho. Unwmk.**
**583-586** A126 Set of 4 7.00 7.00
*586a* Souvenir sheet of 1 3.75 3.75

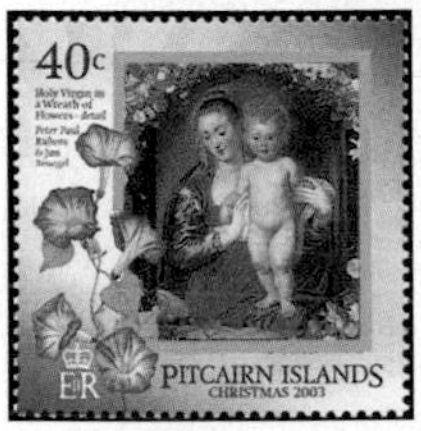


Christmas
A127

Morning glory and: 40c, Holy Virgin in a Wreath of Flowers, by Peter Paul Rubens and Jan Brueghel. $1, Madonna della Rosa, by Raphael. $1.50, Stuppacher Madonna, by Matthias Grünewald. $3, Madonna with Cherries, by Titian.

**Litho. with Foil Application**

**2003, Nov. 17** *Perf. 13¾*
**587-590** A127 Set of 4 7.25 7.25

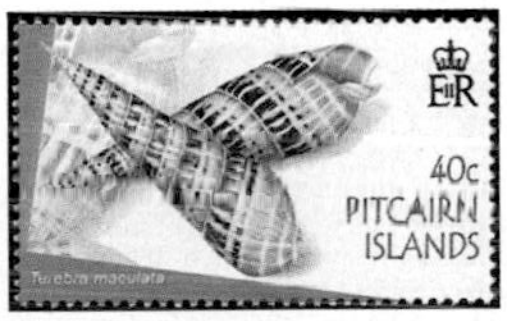


Shells
A128

Designs: 40c, Terebra maculata. 80c, Terebra subulata. $1.20, Terebra crenulata. $3, Terebra dimidata.

*Perf. 14x14½*

**2004, Jan. 21 Litho. Unwmk.**
**591-594** A128 Set of 4 7.25 7.25

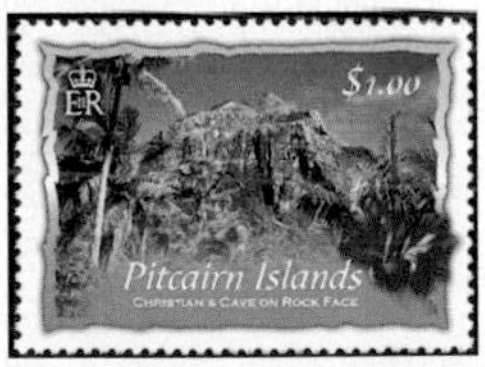


Scenery
A129

Designs: 50c, Anchor, Bounty Bay and Hill of Difficulty, vert. $1, Flower, Christian's Cave on Rock Face. $1.50, Shells, St. Paul's Pool, vert. $2.50, Bird, Ridge Rope towards St. Paul's Point.

*Perf. 13¼*

**2004, Apr. 28 Litho. Unwmk.**
**595-598** A129 Set of 4 9.25 9.25

Souvenir Sheet

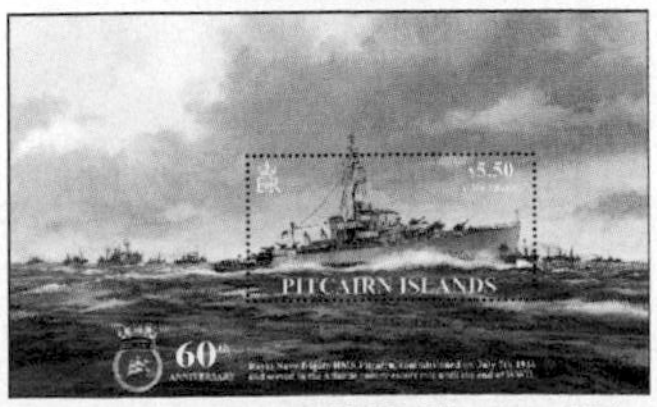


Commissioning of HMS Pitcairn, 60th Anniv. — A130

*Perf. 13¼*

**2004, July 7 Litho. Unwmk.**
**599** A130 $5.50 multi 11.50 11.50

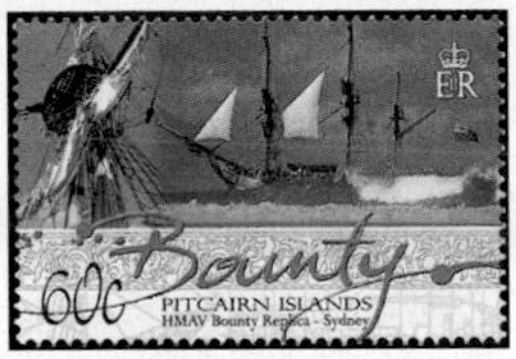


HMAV Bounty Replica, Sydney
A131

Replica and: 60c, Sail and mast. 80c, Stern. $1, Figurehead. $3.50, Rigging.

**2004, Sept. 8** *Perf. 14¼x14*
**600-603** A131 Set of 4 11.50 11.50
*603a* Souvenir sheet of 1 7.00 7.00

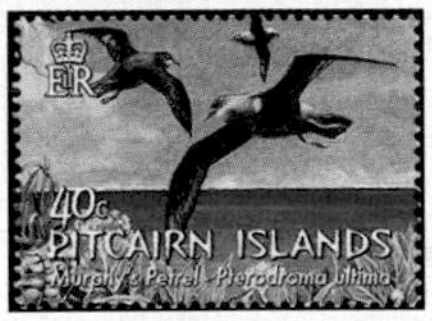


Murphy's Petrel
A132

Designs: 40c, Three in flight. 50c, Adult and chicks. $1, Adult nesting, flower, vert. $2, Head of adult, vert. $2.50, In flight.

**2004, Nov. 17 Litho.** *Perf. 14½*
**604-608** A132 Set of 5 9.25 9.25
*608a* Souvenir sheet, #604-608 9.25 9.25

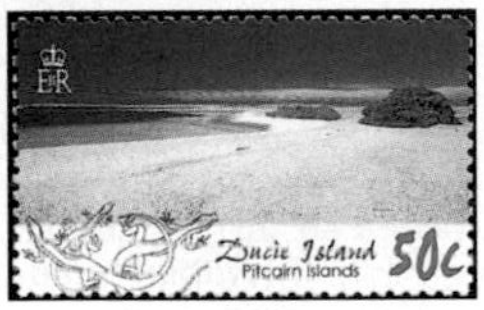


Views of Ducie and Oeno Islands
A133

Designs: 50c, Beach, Ducie Island, lizards. 60c, Rocks off Ducie Island, starfish. 80c, Sun on horizon, Ducie Island, birds. $1, Boat off Oeno Island, palm tree. $1.50, Beach and palm trees, Oeno Island, shells. $2.50, Boat with fishermen off Oeno Island, fish.

**2005, Feb. 10 Litho.** *Perf. 13¼*
**609-614** A133 Set of 6 10.00 10.00

Souvenir Sheet

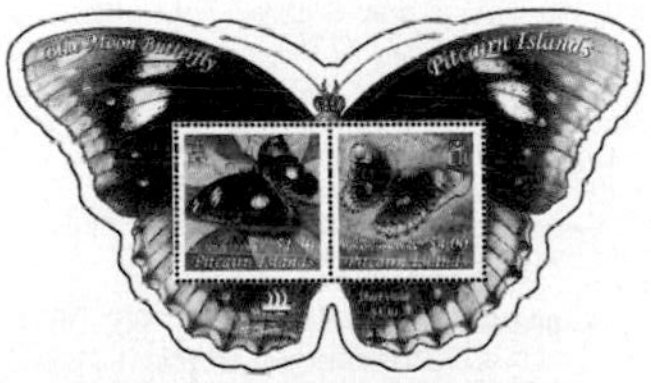


Blue Moon Butterfly — A134

No. 615: a, $1.50, Male. b, $4, Female.

**2005, Apr. 8 Litho.** *Perf. 14½*
**615** A134 Sheet of 2, #a-b 8.00 8.00

Souvenir Sheet

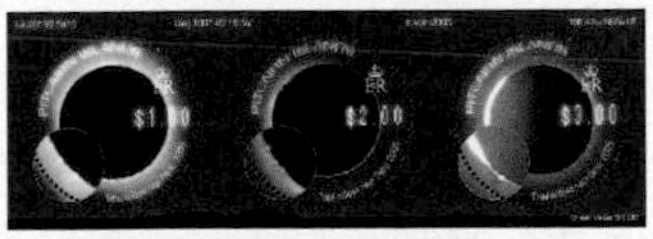

Apr. 8, 2005 Solar Eclipse — A135

No. 616 — Eclipse and various solar prominences: a, $1. b, $2. c, $3.

**2005, Apr. 8** *Perf.*
**616** A135 Sheet of 3, #a-c 8.75 8.75

No. 616 contains three 38mm diameter stamps.

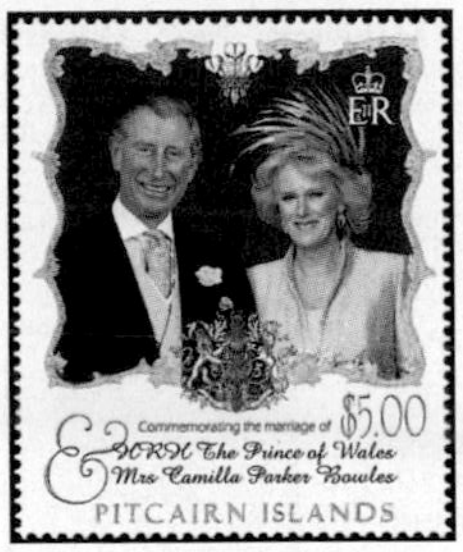


Wedding of Prince Charles and Camilla Parker Bowles
A136

**Litho. With Foil Application**

**2005, Apr. 9** *Perf. 14x14½*
**617** A136 $5 multi 7.25 7.25

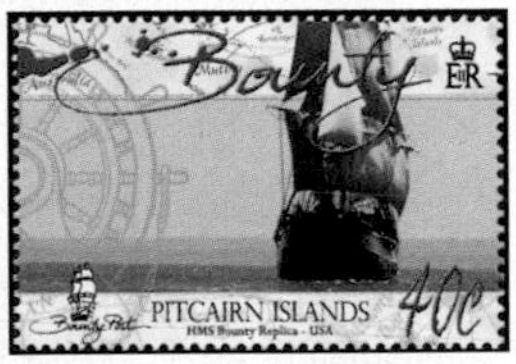


HMS Bounty Replica, US
A137

Replica, map, emblem for Bounty Post and: 40c, Ship's wheel. $1, Lantern. $1.20, Bell. $3, Rigging.

**2005, June 21 Litho.** *Perf. 14¼x14*
**618-621** A137 Set of 4 7.75 7.75
*621a* Souvenir sheet of 1 4.25 4.25

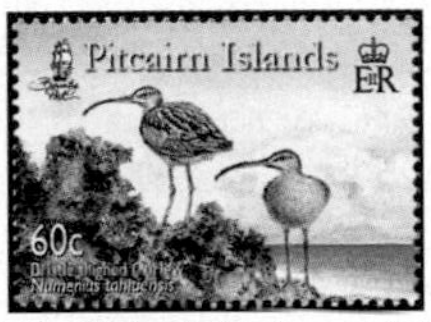


Bristle-thighed Curlew — A138

Designs: 60c, Curlews on rock. $1, Head of curlew. $1.50, Curlew with open beak, vert. $1.80, Head of curlew, two curlews in flight, vert. $2, Curlew on driftwood.

**2005, Sept. 14 Litho.** *Perf. 14½*
**622-626** A138 Set of 5 9.75 9.75
*626a* Souvenir sheet, #622-626 9.75 9.75

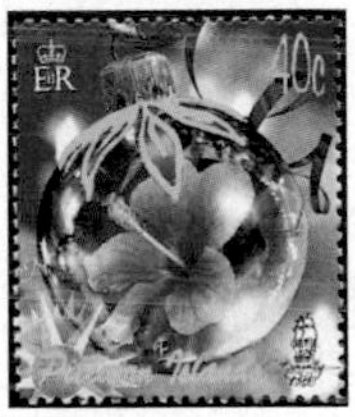


Christmas
A139

Christmas ornament with: 40c, Hibiscus flower. 80c, Seabird. $1.80, Coat of arms. $2.50, HMS Bounty.

**Litho. with Foil Application**

**2005, Nov. 23** *Perf. 13¼*
**627-630** A139 Set of 4 8.00 8.00

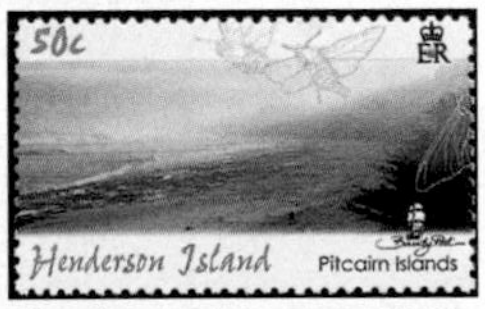


Henderson Island — A140

Various scenes of Henderson Island and: 50c, Insects. 60c, Parrots. $1, Sea birds. $1.20, Lobsters. $1.50, Octopi. $2, Turtles.

**2006, Feb. 15 Litho.** *Perf. 13¼*
**631-636** A140 Set of 6 9.25 9.25

# POLAND

'pō-lənd

LOCATION — Europe between Russia and Germany
GOVT. — Republic
AREA — 120,628 sq. mi.
POP. — 38,608,929 (1999 est.)
CAPITAL — Warsaw

100 Kopecks = 1 Ruble
100 Fenigi = 1 Marka (1918)
100 Halerzy = 1 Korona (1918)
100 Groszy = 1 Zloty (1924)

**Catalogue values for unused stamps in this country are for Never Hinged items, beginning with Scott 534 in the regular postage section, Scott B63 in the semi-postal section, Scott C28 in the airpost section, Scott CB1 in the airpost semi-postal section, and Scott J146 in the postage due section.**

**Watermarks**

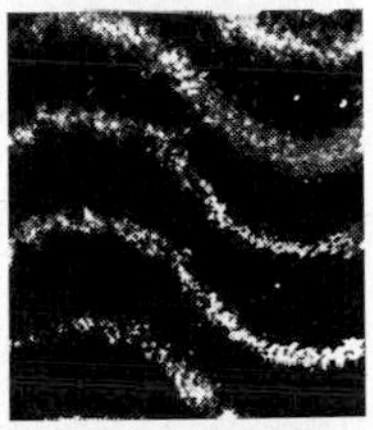

Wmk. 145 — Wavy Lines

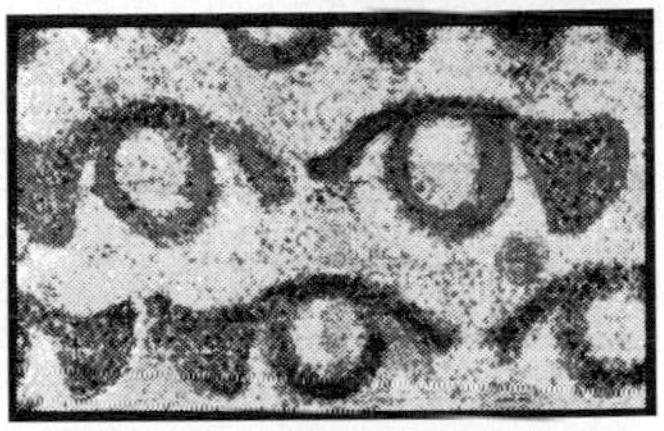

Wmk. 234 — Multiple Post Horns

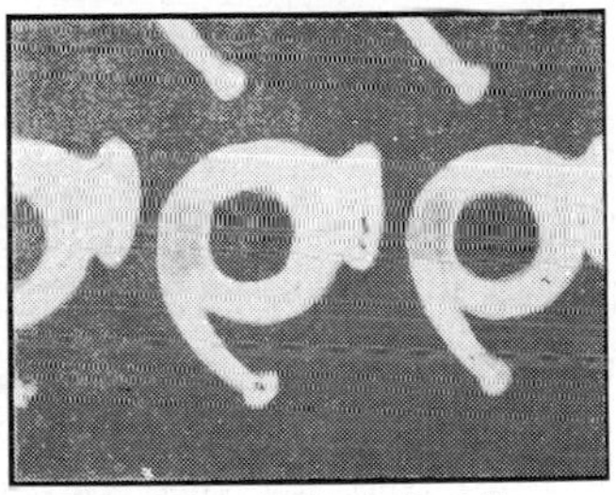

Wmk. 326 — Multiple Post Horns

**Issued under Russian Dominion**

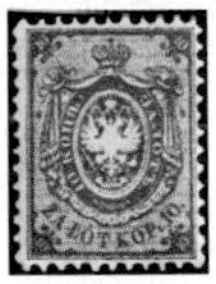

Coat of Arms — A1

*Perf. 11½ to 12½*

**1860 Typo. Unwmk.**

| | | | |
|---|---|---|---|
| 1 | A1 10k blue & rose | 800. | 200. |
| a. | 10k blue & carmine | 950. | 275. |
| b. | 10k dark blue & rose | 950. | 275. |
| c. | Added blue frame for inner oval | 1,400. | 475. |
| d. | Imperf. | | |

Used for letters within the Polish territory and to Russia. Postage on all foreign letters was paid in cash.

These stamps were superseded by those of Russia in 1865.

Counterfeits exist.

**Issues of the Republic**

Local issues were made in various Polish cities during the German occupation.

In the early months of the Republic many issues were made by overprinting the German occupation stamps with the words "Poczta Polska" and an eagle or bars often with the name of the city.

These issues were not authorized by the Government but were made by the

local authorities and restricted to local use. In 1914 two stamps were issued for the Polish Legion and in 1918 the Polish Expeditionary Force used surcharged Russian stamps. The regularity of these issues is questioned.

Numerous counterfeits of these issues abound.

### Warsaw Issues

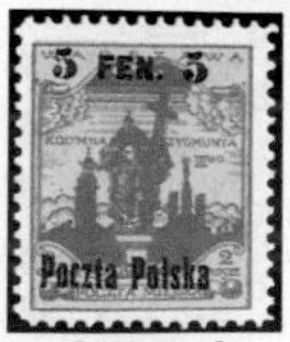

Statue of Sigismund III — A2

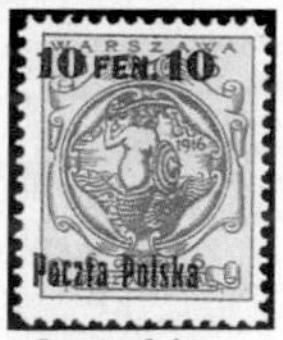

Coat of Arms of Warsaw — A3

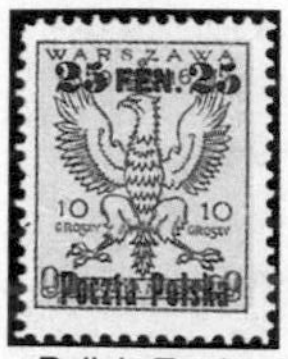

Polish Eagle A4

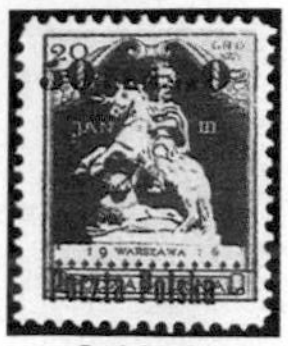

Sobieski Monument A5

Stamps of the Warsaw Local Post Surcharged

**1918, Nov. 17 Wmk. 145 *Perf. 11½***

| | | | | |
|---|---|---|---|---|
| **11** | A2 | 5f on 2gr brn & buff | .60 | .35 |
| a. | | Inverted surcharge | 37.50 | 32.50 |
| **12** | A3 | 10f on 6gr grn & buff | .40 | .35 |
| a. | | Inverted surcharge | 4.50 | 4.00 |
| **13** | A4 | 25f on 10gr rose & buff | 4.75 | 1.75 |
| a. | | Inverted surcharge | 9.00 | 8.00 |
| **14** | A5 | 50f on 20gr bl & buff | 4.25 | 4.25 |
| a. | | Inverted surcharge | 125.00 | 100.00 |
| | | *Nos. 11-14 (4)* | 10.00 | 6.70 |

Counterfeits exist.

Occupation Stamps Nos. N6-N16 Overprinted or Surcharged:

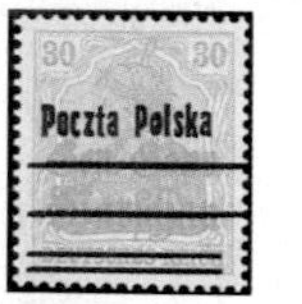

a

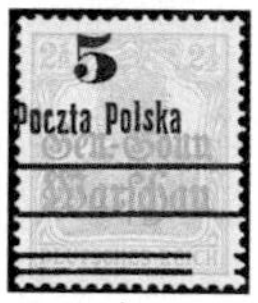

b

**1918-19 Wmk. 125 *Perf. 14, 14½***

| | | | | |
|---|---|---|---|---|
| **15** | A16 | 3pf brown ('19) | 19.00 | 12.00 |
| **16** | A22 | 5pf on 2½pf gray | .30 | .30 |
| **17** | A16 | 5pf on 3pf brown | 3.50 | 2.25 |
| **18** | A16 | 5pf green | .65 | .50 |
| **19** | A16 | 10pf carmine | .20 | .20 |
| **20** | A22 | 15pf dark violet | .20 | .20 |
| **21** | A16 | 20pf blue | .20 | .20 |
| a. | | 20pf ultramarine | 750.00 | 1,500. |
| **23** | A22 | 25pf on 7½pf org | .30 | .20 |
| **24** | A16 | 30pf org & blk, *buff* | .20 | .20 |
| **25** | A16 | 40pf lake & black | .45 | .45 |
| **26** | A16 | 60pf magenta | .65 | .65 |
| | | *Nos. 15-26 (11)* | 25.65 | 17.15 |

There are two settings of this overprint. The first printing, issued Dec. 5, 1918, has space of 3½mm between the middle two bars. The second printing, issued Jan. 15, 1919, has space of 4mm. No. 15 comes only in the second setting; all others in both. The German overprint on No. 21a is very glossy.

Varieties of this overprint and surcharge are numerous: double; inverted; misspellings (Pocata, Poczto, Pelska); letters omitted, inverted or wrong font; 3 bars instead of 4, etc.

No. 21a requires competent expertization. A number of shades of the blue No. 21 exist. Counterfeits exist.

### Lublin Issue

Austrian Military Semi-Postal Stamps of 1918 Overprinted

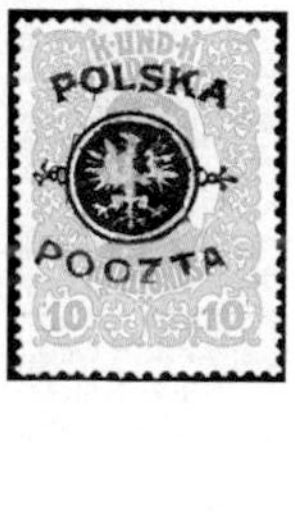

**1918, Dec. 5 Unwmk. *Perf. 12½x13***

| | | | | |
|---|---|---|---|---|
| **27** | MSP7 | 10h gray green | 7.50 | 5.50 |
| a. | | Inverted overprint | 19.00 | 19.00 |
| **28** | MSP8 | 20h magenta | 6.25 | 5.50 |
| a. | | Inverted overprint | 19.00 | 19.00 |
| **29** | MSP7 | 45h blue | 5.50 | 5.50 |
| a. | | Inverted overprint | 19.00 | 19.00 |
| | | *Nos. 27-29 (3)* | 19.25 | 16.50 |

Austrian Military Stamps of 1917 Surcharged

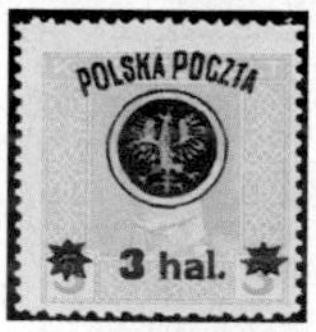

**1918-19 *Perf. 12½***

| | | | | |
|---|---|---|---|---|
| **30** | M3 | 3hal on 3h ol gray | 17.50 | 13.00 |
| a. | | Inverted surcharge | 225.00 | 225.00 |
| b. | | Perf. 11½ | 17.50 | 13.00 |
| c. | | Perf. 11½x12½ | 24.00 | 22.50 |
| **31** | M3 | 3hal on 15h brt rose | 3.00 | 2.50 |
| a. | | Inverted surcharge | 20.00 | 20.00 |

Surcharged in Black

| | | | | |
|---|---|---|---|---|
| **32** | M3 | 10hal on 30h sl grn | 3.00 | 2.50 |
| a. | | Inverted surcharge | 20.00 | 20.00 |
| b. | | Brown surcharge (error) | 60.00 | 50.00 |
| **34** | M3 | 25hal on 40h ol bis | 6.25 | 5.25 |
| a. | | Inverted surcharge | 30.00 | 30.00 |
| b. | | Perf. 11½ | 10.00 | 7.75 |
| **35** | M3 | 45hal on 60h rose | 3.00 | 2.50 |
| a. | | Inverted surcharge | 20.00 | 20.00 |
| **36** | M3 | 45hal on 80h dl blue | 4.25 | 3.25 |
| a. | | Inverted surcharge | 30.00 | 30.00 |
| **37** | M3 | 50hal on 60h rose | 6.25 | 6.25 |
| a. | | Inverted surcharge | 20.00 | 20.00 |

**Similar surcharge with bars instead of stars over original value**

| | | | | |
|---|---|---|---|---|
| **38** | M3 | 45hal on 80h dl blue | 5.00 | 3.50 |
| a. | | Inverted surcharge | 20.00 | 20.00 |

Overprinted

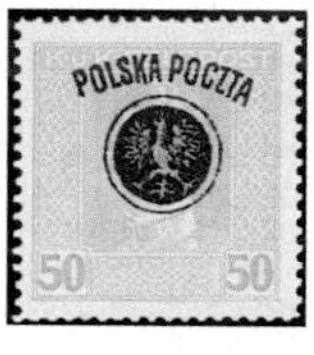

| | | | | |
|---|---|---|---|---|
| **39** | M3 | 50h deep green | 15.00 | 13.00 |
| a. | | Inverted overprint | 80.00 | 80.00 |
| **40** | M3 | 90h dark violet | 4.25 | 2.50 |
| a. | | Inverted overprint | 20.00 | 20.00 |
| | | *Nos. 30-40 (10)* | 67.50 | 54.25 |

### Counterfeits

**All Cracow issues, Nos. 41-60, J1-J12 and P1-P5, have been extensively counterfeited. Competent expertization is necessary. Prices apply only for authenticated stamps with identified plating position. Cost of certificate is not included in the catalogue value.**

### Cracow Issues

Austrian Stamps of 1916-18 Overprinted

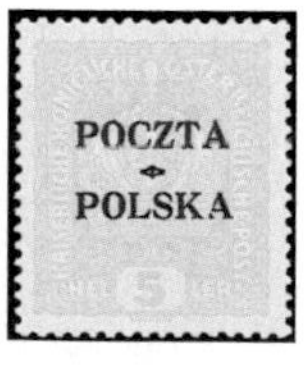

**1919, Jan. 17 Typo.**

| | | | | |
|---|---|---|---|---|
| **41** | A37 | 3h brt violet | 190.00 | 200.00 |
| **42** | A37 | 5h lt green | 190.00 | 210.00 |
| **43** | A37 | 6h deep orange | 25.00 | 19.50 |
| a. | | Inverted overprint | 6,000. | |
| **44** | A37 | 10h magenta | 190.00 | 190.00 |
| **45** | A37 | 12h lt blue | 35.00 | 35.00 |
| **46** | A39 | 40h olive green | 13.00 | 13.00 |
| a. | | Inverted overprint | 100.00 | 100.00 |
| b. | | Double overprint | 400.00 | |
| **47** | A39 | 50h blue green | 7.00 | 7.00 |
| a. | | Inverted overprint | | 8,000. |
| **48** | A39 | 60h deep blue | 4.00 | 4.00 |
| a. | | Inverted overprint | 100.00 | 75.00 |
| **49** | A39 | 80h orange brown | 4.00 | 4.50 |
| a. | | Inverted overprint. | 100.00 | 100.00 |
| b. | | Double overprint | 125.00 | 125.00 |
| **50** | A39 | 90h red violet | 625.00 | 725.00 |
| **51** | A39 | 1k carmine, *yel* | 7.00 | 6.00 |

**Engr.**

| | | | | |
|---|---|---|---|---|
| **52** | A40 | 2k blue | 4.00 | 4.50 |
| **53** | A40 | 3k carmine rose | 75.00 | 60.00 |
| **54** | A40 | 4k yellow green | 125.00 | 100.00 |
| **55** | A40 | 10k deep violet | 4,000. | 5,000. |

The 3k is on granite paper.

The overprint on Nos. 52-55 is litho. and slightly larger than illustration with different ornament between lines of type.

Same Overprint on Nos. 168-171

**1919 Typo.**

| | | | | |
|---|---|---|---|---|
| **56** | A42 | 15h dull red | 25.00 | 6.50 |
| **57** | A42 | 20h dark green | 125.00 | 125.00 |
| **58** | A42 | 25h blue | 1,250. | 850.00 |
| **59** | A42 | 30h dull violet | 225.00 | 190.00 |

Austria No. 157 Surcharged

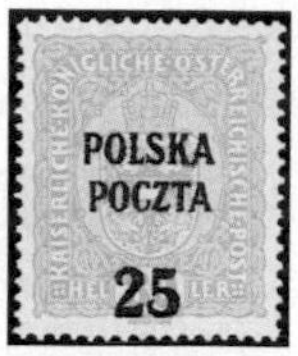

**1919, Jan. 24**

| | | | | |
|---|---|---|---|---|
| **60** | A39 | 25h on 80h org brn | 2.75 | 2.75 |
| a. | | Inverted surcharge | 100.00 | 60.00 |

Excellent counterfeits of Nos. 27 to 60 exist.

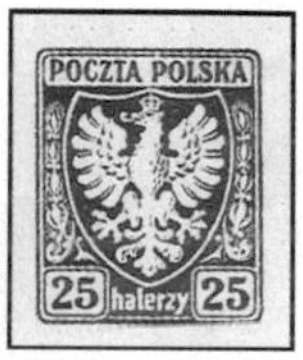

Polish Eagle — A9

**1919, Feb. 25 Litho. *Imperf.***

**Without gum**

**Yellowish Paper**

| | | | | |
|---|---|---|---|---|
| **61** | A9 | 2h gray | .30 | .35 |
| **62** | A9 | 3h dull violet | .30 | .35 |
| **63** | A9 | 5h green | .20 | .20 |
| **64** | A9 | 6h orange | 13.00 | 19.00 |
| **65** | A9 | 10h lake | .20 | .20 |
| **66** | A9 | 15h brown | .20 | .20 |
| **67** | A9 | 20h olive green | .30 | .35 |

**Bluish Paper**

| | | | | |
|---|---|---|---|---|
| **68** | A9 | 25h carmine | .20 | .20 |
| **69** | A9 | 50h indigo | .20 | .20 |
| **70** | A9 | 70h deep blue | .30 | .35 |
| **71** | A9 | 1k ol gray & car | .55 | .95 |
| | | *Nos. 61-71 (11)* | 15.75 | 22.35 |

Nos. 61-71 exist with privately applied perforations.

Counterfeits exist.

For surcharges see Nos. J35-J39.

### Posen (Poznan) Issue

Germany Nos. 84-85, 87, 96, 98 Overprinted in Black

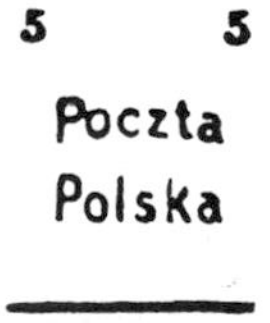


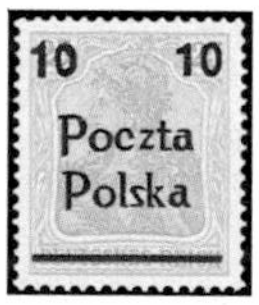

***Perf. 14, 14½***

**1919, Aug. 5 Wmk. 125**

| | | | | |
|---|---|---|---|---|
| **72** | A22 | 5pf on 2pf gray | 18.00 | 15.00 |
| **73** | A22 | 5pf on 7½pf org | 1.90 | 1.25 |
| a. | | Inverted surcharge | 100.00 | |
| **74** | A16 | 5pf on 20pf bl vio | 1.50 | 1.10 |
| **75** | A16 | 10pf on 25pf org & blk, *yel* | 3.75 | 3.00 |
| **76** | A16 | 10pf on 40pf lake & blk | 2.00 | 1.25 |
| | | *Nos. 72-76 (5)* | 27.15 | 21.60 |

Counterfeits exist.

Germany Nos. 96 and 98 Surcharged in Red or Green

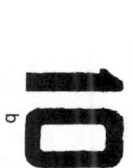

a b

**1919, Sept. 15**

| | | | | |
|---|---|---|---|---|
| **77** | A22 | 5pf on 2pf (R) | 250.00 | 150.00 |
| a. | | Inverted surcharge | 4,250. | |
| **78** | A22 | 10pf on 7½pf (G) | 150.00 | 110.00 |

Nos. 77-78 are a provisional issue for use in Gniezno. Counterfeit surcharges abound.

Eagle and Fasces, Symbolical of United Poland A10 A11

"Agriculture" A12

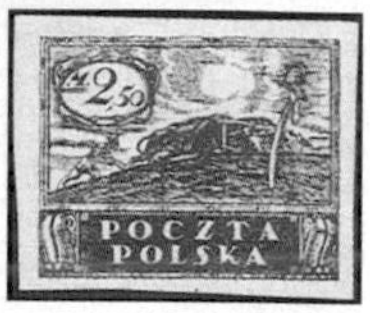

"Peace" — A13

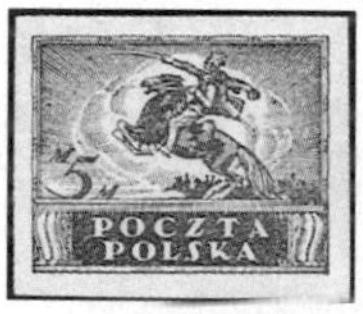

Polish Cavalryman A14

### For Northern Poland

Denominations as "F" or "M"

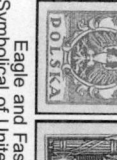

**1919, Jan. 27 *Imperf.***

**Wove or Ribbed Paper**

| | | | | |
|---|---|---|---|---|
| **81** | A10 | 3f bister brn | .20 | .20 |
| **82** | A10 | 5f green | .20 | .20 |
| **83** | A10 | 10f red violet | .20 | .20 |
| **84** | A10 | 15f deep rose | .20 | .20 |
| **85** | A11 | 20f deep blue | .20 | .20 |
| **86** | A11 | 25f olive green | .25 | .20 |
| **87** | A11 | 50f blue green | .25 | .20 |
| **88** | A12 | 1m violet | 2.50 | 2.00 |
| **89** | A12 | 1.50m deep green | 4.50 | 2.50 |
| **90** | A12 | 2m dark brown | 3.75 | 2.50 |
| **91** | A13 | 2.50m orange brn | 16.00 | 11.00 |
| **92** | A14 | 5m red violet | 20.00 | 11.00 |
| | | *Nos. 81-92 (12)* | 48.25 | 30.40 |

***Perf. 10, 11, 11½, 10x11½, 11½x10***

**1919-20**

| | | | | |
|---|---|---|---|---|
| **93** | A10 | 3f bister brn | .20 | .20 |
| **94** | A10 | 5f green | .20 | .20 |
| **95** | A10 | 10f red violet | .20 | .20 |
| **96** | A10 | 10f brown ('20) | .20 | .20 |
| **97** | A10 | 15f deep rose | .20 | .20 |
| **98** | A10 | 15f vermilion ('20) | .20 | .20 |
| **99** | A11 | 20f deep blue | .20 | .20 |
| **100** | A11 | 25f olive green | .20 | .20 |
| **101** | A11 | 40f brt violet ('20) | .20 | .20 |
| **102** | A11 | 50f blue green | .20 | .20 |
| **103** | A12 | 1m violet | .45 | .20 |
| **105** | A12 | 1.50m deep green | .75 | .40 |
| **106** | A12 | 2m dark brown | .75 | .40 |
| **107** | A13 | 2.50m orange brn | 1.25 | 1.00 |
| **108** | A14 | 5m red violet | 2.00 | 1.00 |
| | | *Nos. 93-108 (15)* | 7.20 | 5.00 |

Several denominations among Nos. 81-132 are found with double impression or in pairs imperf. between.

See #109-132, 140-152C, 170-175. For surcharges & overprints see #153, 199-200, B1-B14, 2K1-2K10, Eastern Silesia 41-50.

### For Southern Poland

Denominations as "H" or "K"

**1919, Jan. 27 *Imperf.***

| | | | | |
|---|---|---|---|---|
| **109** | A10 | 3h red brown | .30 | .20 |
| **110** | A10 | 5h emerald | .20 | .20 |
| **111** | A10 | 10h orange | .20 | .20 |
| **112** | A10 | 15h vermilion | .20 | .20 |
| **113** | A11 | 20h gray brown | .20 | .20 |
| **114** | A11 | 25h light blue | .20 | .20 |
| **115** | A11 | 50h orange brn | .30 | .20 |
| **116** | A12 | 1k dark green | .50 | .20 |
| **117** | A12 | 1.50k red brown | 2.50 | 4.00 |
| **118** | A12 | 2k dark blue | 2.50 | 2.25 |
| **119** | A13 | 2.50k dark violet | 8.50 | 6.50 |
| **120** | A14 | 5k slate blue | 24.00 | 8.25 |
| | | *Nos. 109-120 (12)* | 39.60 | 22.60 |

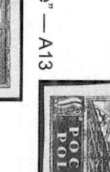

POLAND

## No. 191 Surcharged

| | | | | |
|---|---|---|---|---|
| 198 | A27 | 25000m on 20m car | .50 | .20 |
| | | | 5.00 | 5.00 |
| a. | Double surcharge | | | 7.50 |
| b. | Inverted surcharge | | | |

### No. 150 Surcharged with New Value

**1924**

| | | | | |
|---|---|---|---|---|
| 199 | A10 | 20000m on 2m gray | .70 | .20 |
| | | grn | 7.50 | 7.50 |
| | | | 5.00 | 5.00 |
| a. | Inverted surcharge | | | |
| b. | Double surcharge | | | |

### Type of 1919 Issue Surcharged with New Value

| | | | | |
|---|---|---|---|---|
| 200 | A10 | 100000m on 5m red brn | .30 | .20 |
| | | | 7.50 | 7.50 |
| a. | Double surcharge | | | |
| b. | Inverted surcharge | | 2.70 | 1.20 |

Nos. 195-200 (6)

---

Arms of Poland — A35

### Perf. 10 to 14½ and Compound    Litho.
**1924    Thin Paper**

| | | | | |
|---|---|---|---|---|
| 205 | A35 | 10,000m lilac brn | .30 | .25 |
| 206 | A35 | 20,000m olive grn | .30 | .25 |
| 207 | A35 | 30,000m scarlet | 1.10 | .35 |
| 208 | A35 | 50,000m apple grn | 2.25 | .35 |
| 209 | A35 | 100,000m brn org | .30 | .30 |
| 210 | A35 | 200,000m lt blue | .60 | .35 |
| 211 | A35 | 500,000m red vio | .60 | .65 |
| 212 | A35 | 1,000,000m brown | | |
| 213 | A35 | pale rose | .60 | 8.00 |
| 214 | A35 | 2,000,000m dk green | 1.10 | 100.00 |
| | | | 7.75 | 110.65 |

Set, never hinged    20.00

Nos. 205-214 (10)

---

President Stanislaus Wojciechowski A37

Arms of Poland A36

### Perf. 10 to 13½ and Compound
**1924**

| | | | | |
|---|---|---|---|---|
| 215 | A36 | 1g orange brown | .35 | .20 |
| 216 | A36 | 2g dark brown | .35 | .20 |
| 217 | A36 | 3g orange | .40 | .20 |
| 218 | A36 | 5g olive green | .90 | .20 |
| 219 | A36 | 10g blue green | 1.10 | .20 |
| 220 | A36 | 15g red | 1.10 | .20 |
| 221 | A36 | 20g blue | 2.25 | .35 |
| 222 | A36 | 25g red brown | 3.00 | .35 |
| a. | | 25g gray blue | 4,250. | |
| 223 | A36 | 30g deep violet | 3,000. | .25 |
| 224 | A36 | 40g indigo | 21.00 | |
| 225 | A36 | 50g magenta | 4.00 | .30 |
| | | | 3.75 | |

### Perf. 11½, 12

| | | | | |
|---|---|---|---|---|
| 226 | A37 | 1z scarlet | 22.50 | 1.25 |

Nos. 215-226 (12)    60.70    3.90

Set, never hinged    125.00

For overprints see Nos. 1K1-1K11.

Poznan Town Hall — A39

Holy Gate of Wilno (Vilnius) — A38

---

### Perf. 9 to 14½ and Compound
**1922-23**

| | | | | |
|---|---|---|---|---|
| 170 | A10 | 5f blue | .20 | .25 |
| 171 | A10 | 10f lt violet | .20 | .25 |
| 172 | A11 | 20f pale red | .20 | .50 |
| 173 | A11 | 40f violet brn | .20 | 1.00 |
| 174 | A11 | 75f orange | .20 | .25 |
| 175 | A11 | 50f orange brn | .20 | .25 |
| 176 | A32 | 1m black | .20 | .25 |
| 177 | A32 | 1.25m dark green | .20 | .25 |
| 178 | A32 | 1.50m deep rose | .20 | .25 |
| 179 | A32 | 3m emerald | .20 | .25 |
| 180 | A32 | 4m deep ultra | .20 | .50 |
| 181 | A32 | 5m yellow brn | .20 | .25 |
| 182 | A32 | 6m red orange | .20 | 1.00 |
| 183 | A32 | 10m lilac brn | .20 | 1.00 |
| 184 | A32 | 20m deep violet | .40 | 3.50 |
| 185 | A32 | 50m olive green | .40 | 4.50 |
| 187 | A32 | 80m vermilion ('23) | 1.50 | 4.50 |
| 188 | A32 | 100m violet ('23) | | 5.00 |
| 189 | A32 | 200m orange ('23) | 10.00 | 23.00 |
| 190 | A32 | 300m pale blue ('23) | | |

Nos. 170-190 (20)

Union of Upper Silesia with Poland. There were 2 printings of Nos. 176 to 190. The 1st being from flat plates, the 2nd from rotary press on thin paper, perf. 12½. Nos. 173 and 175 are printed from new plates showing larger value numerals and a single "1".

### Sower Type Redrawn
Size: 25x21mm

**1922    Thick or Thin Wove Paper**

| | | | | |
|---|---|---|---|---|
| 191 | A27 | 20m carmine | .30 | .20 |

In this stamp the design has been strengthened and made more distinct, especially the ground and the numerals in the upper corners.

---

Nicolaus Copernicus A33

### Perf. 10 to 12½
**1923**

| | | | | |
|---|---|---|---|---|
| 192 | A33 | 1000m indigo | .80 | .30 |
| 193 | A34 | 3000m brown | 45 | 15.00 |
| 194 | A33 | 5000m rose | 15.00 | .80 |
| | | | 2.05 | .90 |

Nos. 192-194 (3)

Nicolaus Copernicus (1473-1543), astronomer (Nos. 192, 194); Stanislaus Konarski (1700-1773), educator, and the creation by the Polish Parliament of the Commission of Public Instruction (No. 193).

Father Stanislaus Konarski — A34

---

### No. 163 Surcharged

**1923    Perf. 9 to 14½ and Compound on 25m**

| | | | | |
|---|---|---|---|---|
| 195 | A31 | 10000m on 25m | .30 | .20 |
| a. | Double surcharge | | 5.00 | |
| b. | Inverted surcharge | | 7.50 | |

---

### Stamps of 1921 Surcharged

**1923    Perf. 9 to 14½ and Compound**

| | | | | |
|---|---|---|---|---|
| 196 | A27 | 25000m on 20m red | .60 | .20 |
| a. | Double surcharge | | 5.00 | 5.00 |
| b. | Inverted surcharge | | 10.00 | |
| 197 | A27 | 50000m on 10m grnsh bl | .30 | .20 |
| | | | 5.00 | 5.00 |
| a. | Double surcharge | | | |
| b. | Inverted surcharge | | 7.50 | 7.50 |

---

### Perf. 10, 11½, 10x11½, 11½x10

| | | | | |
|---|---|---|---|---|
| 121 | A10 | 3h red brown | .20 | .20 |
| 122 | A10 | 5h emerald | .20 | .20 |
| 123 | A10 | 10h orange | .20 | .20 |
| 124 | A10 | 15h vermilion | .20 | .20 |
| 125 | A11 | 50h light blue | .20 | .20 |
| 126 | A11 | 25h gray brown | .20 | .35 |
| 127 | A11 | 50h orange brn | .50 | .50 |
| 128 | A12 | 1k dark green | .50 | .50 |
| 129 | A12 | 1.50k red brown | 1.10 | .50 |
| 130 | A12 | 2k dark blue | 1.25 | .65 |
| 131 | A13 | 2.50k dark violet | 2.00 | 1.10 |
| 132 | A14 | 5k slate blue | 7.35 | 4.50 |

Nos. 121-132 (12)

### National Assembly Issue

A20

25f, Gen. Josef Pilsudski 1m, Griffin.

**1919-20    Wove or Ribbed Paper**

| | | | | |
|---|---|---|---|---|
| 133 | A20 | 10f red violet | .20 | .20 |
| 134 | A21 | 15f brown red | .40 | .25 |
| a. | Imperf. pair | | 26.00 | |
| 135 | A21 | 20f dp brown (21x25mm) | 26.00 | |
| 136 | A22 | 20f dp green (17x20mm) ('20) | .30 | .25 |
| a. | Pair, imperf. vert. | | | |
| 137 | A21 | 25f olive green | .60 | .80 |
| 138 | A24 | 50f Prus blue | .20 | .20 |
| 139 | A24 | 1m purple | .30 | .25 |

Nos. 133-139 (7)    2.25    2.15

First National Assembly of Poland.

Ignacy Jan Paderewski — A21

Adalbert Trampczynski — A22

Eagle Watching Ship — A24

---

### General Issue
**1919    Perf. 9 to 14½ and Compound**
Thin Laid Paper

| | | | | |
|---|---|---|---|---|
| 140 | A11 | 25f olive green | .20 | .20 |
| 141 | A11 | 50f blue green | .20 | .20 |
| 142 | A12 | 1m dark gray | .35 | .20 |
| 143 | A12 | 2m bister brn | 1.10 | .20 |
| 144 | A13 | 3m red brown | 5.00 | 5.75 |
| a. | Pair, imperf. vert. | | 5.00 | |
| 145 | A14 | 5m red violet | .20 | .20 |
| 146 | A14 | 6m deep rose | .20 | .20 |
| a. | Pair, imperf. vert. | | | |
| 147 | A14 | 10m brown red | 6.50 | 6.50 |
| a. | Horizontal pair, imperf. | .35 | .25 |
| 148 | A14 | 20m gray green | .75 | .40 |

Nos. 140-148 (9)    3.85    2.05

### Type of 1919 Redrawn
**1920-22    Perf. 9 to 14½ and Compound**
Thin Laid or Wove Paper

| | | | | |
|---|---|---|---|---|
| 149 | A10 | 1m red | .20 | .20 |
| 150 | A10 | 2m gray green | .20 | .20 |
| 151 | A10 | 3m light blue | .20 | .20 |
| 152A | A10 | 4m rose red | .20 | .20 |
| 152A | A10 | 5m dark violet | 5.25 | 5.25 |
| a. | Horiz. pair, imperf. vert. | | | |
| 152C | A10 | 8m gray brown ('22) | 1.35 | 1.25 |

Nos. 149-152C (6)    2.70    1.80

The word "POCZTA" is in smaller letters and the numerals have been enlarged. The color of No. 152A varies from dark violet to red brown.

---

Sun (Peace) Breaking into Darkness (Despair) — A28

"Peace" and "Agriculture" — A29

"Peace" — A30

### Perf. 11, 11½, 12, 12½, 13 and Compound
**1921, May 2**

| | | | | |
|---|---|---|---|---|
| 156 | A28 | 2m green | 1.40 | .65 |
| 157 | A28 | 3m blue | 1.40 | .60 |
| 158 | A28 | 4m red | .90 | .60 |
| 159 | A29 | 4m carmine rose (error) | | 300.00 |
| 160 | A29 | 6m carmine rose | 1.00 | .80 |
| 161 | A30 | 25m dk violet | 2.50 | 1.90 |
| 162 | A30 | 50m slate bl & buff | 1.50 | 1.10 |

Nos. 156-162 (7)    10.10    6.25

---

Polish Eagle — A31

Issued to commemorate the Constitution.

### Perf. 9 to 14½ and Compound
**1921-23**

| | | | | |
|---|---|---|---|---|
| 163 | A31 | 25m violet & buff | .20 | .20 |
| 164 | A31 | 50m carmine & buff | .20 | .20 |
| a. | Vert. pair, imperf. horiz. | | | |
| 165 | A31 | 100m blk brn & org | .35 | .35 |
| 166 | A31 | 200m black & rose ('23) | .35 | .35 |
| 167 | A31 | 300m olive grn ('23) | .35 | .35 |
| 168 | A31 | 400m brown ('23) | .35 | .35 |
| 169A | A31 | 500m brn vio ('23) | .35 | .35 |
| 169 | A31 | 1000m orange ('23) | .35 | .25 |
| 169B | A31 | 2000m dull blue ('23) | 2.70 | 1.80 |

Nos. 163-169B (9)

For surcharge see No. 195.

---

### Perf. 10, 11½, 11½x10    Perf. 11½

Sower and Rainbow of Hope — A27

### Perf. 9 to 14½ and Compound    Litho.
**1921    Thin Laid or Wove Paper**
Size: 28x22mm

| | | | | |
|---|---|---|---|---|
| 154 | A27 | 10m slate blue | .20 | .20 |
| 155 | A27 | 15m light brown | .40 | .20 |
| 155A | A27 | 20m red | .80 | .60 |

Nos. 154-155A (3)

Signing of peace treaty with Russia. See No. 191. For surcharges see Nos. 196-198.

### Perf. 10, 11½, 10x11½, 11½x10    Thick Wove Paper
**1921, Jan. 25**

| | | | | |
|---|---|---|---|---|
| 153 | A11 | 3m on 40f brt vio | .20 | .20 |
| a. | Double surcharge | | 20.00 | 20.00 |
| b. | Inverted surcharge | | 20.00 | |

---

Miner — A32

Type of 1919 and

No. 101 Surcharged

Sigismund Monument, Warsaw — A40

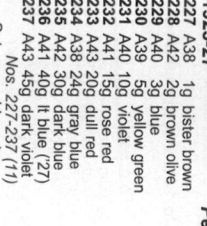

Wawel Castle at Cracow — A41

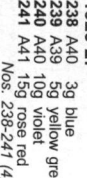

Sobieski Statue at Lwow — A42

Ship of State — A43

**1925-27**     **Perf. 10 to 13**

| No. | Type | Denomination | | |
|---|---|---|---|---|
| 227 | A38 | 1g bister brown | .40 | .40 |
| 228 | A42 | 2g brown olive | .25 | .25 |
| 229 | A40 | 2g blue | .45 | .25 |
| 230 | A39 | 3g yellow green | 1.75 | .20 |
| 231 | A39 | 5g blue | 1.75 | .20 |
| 232 | A41 | 15g rose red | 1.90 | .20 |
| 233 | A43 | 20g dull red | 1.65 | .20 |
| 234 | A38 | 24g gray green | 1.90 | .20 |
| 235 | A42 | 30g gray blue | 7.50 | 1.10 |
| 236 | A41 | 40g dark blue | 3.00 | .20 |
| 237 | A43 | 45g dark violet | 7.50 | .20 |

Set, never hinged   31.15   3.15
Nos. 227-237 (11)   42.50

For overprints see Nos. 1K11A-1K17.

**1926-27**   **Redrawn**

| No. | Type | Denomination | | |
|---|---|---|---|---|
| 238 | A40 | 3g blue | 2.75 | .45 |
| 239 | A39 | 5g yellow green | 3.25 | .50 |
| 240 | A40 | 10g deep ultra | 4.75 | .20 |
| 241 | A41 | 15g rose red | 4.75 | .20 |

Set, never hinged   15.50   1.05
Nos. 238-241 (4)   22.50

On Nos. 229-232 the lines representing clouds touch the numerals. On the redrawn stamps the numerals have white outlines, separating them from the cloud lines.

For overprint see No. 1K18.

Frederic Chopin — A45

**1927**   **Typo.**   **Perf. 12½, 11½**

| No. | Type | Denomination | | |
|---|---|---|---|---|
| 242 | A44 | 20g red brown | 3.25 | .20 |
| 243 | A45 | 40g deep ultra | 16.00 | 1.75 |

Set, never hinged   27.50

See No. 250. For overprint see No. 1K18.

Marshal Pilsudski — A44

President Ignacy Moscicki — A46

**1927, May 4**   **Perf. 11½**

| 245 | A46 | 20g red | 5.50 | .45 |
|---|---|---|---|---|

    7.00

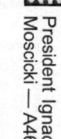

---

Dr. Karol Kaczkowski A47

Juliusz Slowacki A48

**1927, May 27**   **Perf. 11½, 12½**

| No. | Type | Denomination | | |
|---|---|---|---|---|
| 246 | A47 | 10g gray green | 2.75 | 2.25 |
| 247 | A47 | 25g carmine | 6.50 | 3.00 |
| 248 | A47 | 40g dark blue | 8.75 | 3.00 |

Nos. 246-248 (3)   18.00   8.25
Set, never hinged   8.25

4th Intl. Congress of Military Medicine and Pharmacy, Warsaw, May 30-June 4.

**1927, June 28**   **Perf. 12½**

| 249 | A48 | 20g rose | 6.00 | .50 |
|---|---|---|---|---|

Never hinged   8.00

Transfer from Paris to Cracow of the remains of Julius Slowacki, poet.

**1928**   **Perf. 11½, 12x11½, 12½x13**

| 250 | A44 | 25g yellow brown | 2.75 | .25 |
|---|---|---|---|---|

Never hinged   6.00

Pilsudski Type of 1927

**Design Redrawn**

**1928, May 3**   **Engr.**   **Perf. 12½**

| 251 | A49 | Sheet of 2 | 250.00 | 325.00 |
|---|---|---|---|---|

Never hinged   375.00
a. 50g black brown   110.00   140.00
b. 1z black brown   110.00   140.00

1st Natl. Phil. Exhib., Warsaw, May 3-13. Sold to each purchaser of a 1.50z ticket to the Warsaw Philatelic Exhibition. Counterfeits exist.

A49   Souvenir Sheet

Marshal Pilsudski A49a

Pres. Moscicki A50

**1928-31**   **Perf. 10½ to 14 and Compound**

**Wove Paper**

| 253 | A49a | 50g bluish slate | 4.00 | .20 |
|---|---|---|---|---|
| 254 | A49a | 50g blue grn ('31) | 12.50 | .20 |

Set, never hinged   22.50

See No. 315.

**1928**   **Perf. 12x12½, 11½ to 13½ and Compound**

| 255 | A50 | 1z black, cream | 11.00 | .20 |
|---|---|---|---|---|

Never hinged   17.00
a. Horizontally laid paper ('30)   90.00   2.50
Never hinged

**Laid Paper**

See Nos. 305, 316. For surcharges and overprints see Nos. J92-J94, 1K19, 1K24.

Kosciuszko, Washington, Pulaski — A57

**1932, May 3**   **Laid Paper**   **Perf. 11½**

| 267 | A57 | 30g brown | 2.75 | .30 |
|---|---|---|---|---|

  3.50

200th birth anniv. of George Washington.

---

General Josef Bem A51

Henryk Sienkiewicz A52

**1928, May**   **Typo.**   **Wove Paper**   **Perf. 12½**

| 256 | A51 | 25g rose red | 4.00 | .25 |
|---|---|---|---|---|

  5.25

Return from Syria to Poland of the ashes of General Josef Bem.

**1928, Oct.**

| 257 | A52 | 15g ultra | 2.00 | .20 |
|---|---|---|---|---|

Never hinged   3.25

For overprint see No. 1K23.

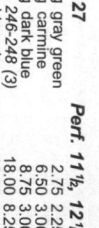

Eagle Arms — A53

"Swiatowid," Ancient Slav God — A54

**1928-29**   **Perf. 12½x12½**

| No. | Type | Denomination | | |
|---|---|---|---|---|
| 258 | A53 | 5g dark violet | .35 | .20 |
| 259 | A53 | 10g green | 1.00 | .20 |
| 260 | A53 | 25g red brown | 1.90 | .60 |

Nos. 258-260 (3)   3.75
Set, never hinged

**1928, Dec. 15**   **Perf. 12½x12**

| 261 | A54 | 25g brown | 2.50 | .20 |
|---|---|---|---|---|

Never hinged   3.25

Poznan Agricultural Exhibition.

See design A58. For overprints see Nos. 1K20-1K22.

King John III Sobieski A55

Stylized Soldiers A56

**1930, Nov. 1**   **Perf. 12½**

| No. | Type | Denomination | | |
|---|---|---|---|---|
| 263 | A56 | 5g violet brown | .35 | .20 |
| 264 | A56 | 15g dark blue | 2.25 | .35 |
| 265 | A56 | 25g red brown | 1.25 | .20 |
| 266 | A56 | 30g dull red | 3.75 | .20 |

Nos. 263-266 (4)
Set, never hinged

**1930, July**   **Perf. 12½x12½**

| 262 | A55 | 75g claret | 5.75 | .25 |
|---|---|---|---|---|

  7.50

---

A58

**1932-33**   **Typo.**   **Perf. 12x12½**

| No. | Type | Denomination | | |
|---|---|---|---|---|
| 268 | A58 | 5g dull vio ('33) | .35 | .20 |
| 269 | A58 | 5g green | .35 | .20 |
| 270 | A58 | 10g green | .35 | .20 |
| 271 | A58 | 15g red brown ('33) | .75 | .20 |
| 272 | A58 | 20g gray | .95 | .20 |
| 273 | A58 | 25g buff | 3.25 | .20 |
| 274 | A58 | 60g blue | 19.00 | .35 |

Nos. 268-274 (7)
Set, never hinged
a. 60g deep rose   25.00   1.35
  32.50

For overprints and surcharge see Nos. 280-281, 284, 292, 1K25-1K27.

Torun City Hall — A59

**1933, Jan. 2**   **Engr.**   **Perf. 11½**

| 275 | A59 | 60g blue | 37.50 | .75 |
|---|---|---|---|---|

  80.00

700th anniversary of the founding of the City of Torun by the Grand Master of the Knights of the Teutonic Order.

See No. B28.

Altar Panel of St. Mary's Church, Cracow — A60

**1933, July 10**   **Perf. 11½-12½ & Compound**   **Unwmk.**

| 277 | A60 | 80g red brown | 15.00 | 1.50 |
|---|---|---|---|---|

Never hinged   21.00

400th death anniv. of Veit Stoss, sculptor and woodcarver. For surcharge see No. 285.

John III Sobieski and Allies before Vienna, painted by Jan Matejko — A61

**1933, Sept. 12**   **Laid Paper**

| 278 | A61 | 1.20z indigo | 37.50 | 6.00 |
|---|---|---|---|---|

Never hinged   60.00

250th anniv. of the deliverance of Vienna by the Polish and allied forces under command of John III Sobieski, King of Poland, when besieged by the Turks in 1683.
For surcharge see No. 286.

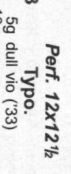

Cross of Independence A62

**1933, Nov. 11**   **Wmk. 234**   **Typo.**

| 279 | A62 | 30g scarlet | 7.50 | .40 |
|---|---|---|---|---|

Never hinged   8.75

15th anniversary of independence.

Josef Pilsudski A63

**1933**   **Perf. 12½**

Skier — A98

Poland Welcoming Teschen People — A97

**1938, Nov. 11**

| | | | |
|---|---|---|---|
| 334 | A97 | 25g dull violet | 1.50 .45 |
| | | Never hinged | 2.00 |

Restoration of the Teschen territory ceded by Czechoslovakia.

**1939, Feb. 6**

| | | | |
|---|---|---|---|
| 335 | A98 | 15g orange brown | 1.00 1.10 |
| 336 | A98 | 25g dull violet | 1.75 .50 |
| 337 | A98 | 30g rose red | 2.25 1.10 |
| 338 | A98 | 55g brt ultra | 4.00 4.00 |
| | | Set, never hinged | 15.00 6.70 |
| | | Nos. 335-338 (4) | 25.00 |

Intl. Ski Meet, Zakopane, Feb. 11-19.

**Type of 1938**

15g, King Ladislas II Jagello, Queen Hedwig.

**Re-engraved**  *Perf. 12½*

**1939, Mar. 2**  .25 .20

| | | | |
|---|---|---|---|
| 339 | A83 | 15g redsh brown | .55 |
| | | Never hinged | |

No. 322 with crossed swords and helmet at lower left. No. 339, swords and helmet have been removed.

Marshal Pilsudski Reviewing Troops — A99

*Engr.*

**1939, Aug. 1**  .60 .50

| | | | |
|---|---|---|---|
| 340 | A99 | 25g dull rose violet | .80 |

Polish Legion, 25th anniv. See No. B35a.

### Polish Peoples Republic

Tadeusz Kosciuszko A101

Polish Eagle — A103

Romuald Traugutt A100

Design: 1z, Jan Henryk Dabrowski.

**Perf. 11½**  **Litho.**  **Unwmk.**

**1944, Sept. 7**  **Without Gum**

| | | | |
|---|---|---|---|
| 341 | A100 | 25g crimson rose | 37.50 40.00 |
| 342 | A101 | 50g deep green | 45.00 52.50 |
| 343 | A101 | 1z deep ultra | 40.00 52.50 |
| | | Nos. 341-343 (3) | 122.50 145.00 |

Counterfeits exist.

For surcharges see Nos. 362-363.

Grunwald Monument, Cracow — A104

---

Kosciuszko, Paine and Washington and View of New York City — A82

*Perf. 12x12½*

**1938, Mar. 17**  1.25 1.75

| | | | |
|---|---|---|---|
| 319 | A82 | 1z gray blue | 2.00 |
| | | Never hinged | |

150th anniv. of the US Constitution.

Marshal Pilsudski — A95

Boleslaus I and Emperor Otto III at Gnesen — A83

Designs: 10g, King Casimir III. 15g, King Ladislas II Jagello and Queen Hedwig. 20g, King Casimir IV. 25g, Treaty of Lublin. 30g, King Stephen Bathory commending Wielock, the peasant. 45g, Stanislas Zolkiewski and Jan Chodkiewicz. 50g, John III Sobieski entering Vienna. 55g, Union of nobles, commoners and peasants. 75g, Dabrowski, Kosciuszko and Poniatowski. 1z, Polish soldiers. 2z, Romuald Traugutt.

*Perf. 12½*

**1938, Nov. 11**  *Engr.*

| | | | |
|---|---|---|---|
| 320 | A83 | 5g red orange | .20 .20 |
| 321 | A83 | 10g green | .20 .20 |
| 322 | A83 | 15g fawn | .30 .20 |
| 323 | A83 | 20g peacock blue | .40 .20 |
| 324 | A83 | 25g dull violet | .40 .20 |
| 325 | A83 | 30g rose red | .65 .20 |
| 326 | A83 | 45g black | .40 .20 |
| 327 | A83 | 50g brt red vio | 2.75 .20 |
| 328 | A83 | 55g ultra | .85 .20 |
| 329 | A83 | 75g dull green | 2.00 1.50 |
| 330 | A83 | 1z orange | 1.60 1.40 |
| 331 | A83 | 2z carmine rose | 11.00 8.00 |
| 332 | A95 | 3z gray black | 9.00 14.00 |
| | | Nos. 320-332 (13) | 29.55 26.70 |
| | | Set, never hinged | 37.50 |

20th anniv. of Poland's independence. See No. 339. For surcharges see Nos. N33-N47.

### Souvenir Sheet

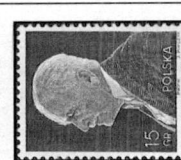

Souvenir Sheet

Marshal Pilsudski, Gabriel Narutowicz, President Moscicki, Marshal Smigly-Rydz — A96

*Perf. 12½*

**1938, Nov. 11**  Sheet of 4

| | | | |
|---|---|---|---|
| 333 | A96 | | 16.00 18.00 |
| | | Never hinged | 21.00 |
| a. | | 25g dull violet (Pilsudski) | 1.75 |
| b. | | 25g dull violet (Narutowicz) | 1.75 |
| c. | | 25g dull violet (Moscicki) | 1.75 |
| d. | | 25g dull violet (Smigly-Rydz) | 1.75 |

20th anniv. of Poland's independence.

---

Type of 1932 Overprinted in Red or Black

Wyst. Filat. 1934 Katowice

**1934, May 5**  *Perf. 12*

| | | | |
|---|---|---|---|
| 280 | A58 | 20g gray (R) | 30.00 24.00 |
| 281 | A58 | 30g deep rose | 30.00 24.00 |
| | | Set, never hinged | 100.00 |

Katowice Philatelic Exhibition. Counterfeits exist.

*Perf. 11½ to 12½ and Compound*

**1934, Aug. 6**  *Engr.*  **Unwmk.**

| | | | |
|---|---|---|---|
| 282 | A63 | 25g gray blue | 1.25 .25 |
| 283 | A63 | 30g black brown | 3.00 .40 |
| | | Set, never hinged | 5.25 |

Polish Legion, 20th anniversary.
For overprint see No. 293.

Nos. 274, 277-278 Surcharged in Black or Red

**1934**  **Wmk. 234**  *Perf. 12x12½*

| | | | |
|---|---|---|---|
| 284 | A58 | 55g on 60g blue | 6.00 .50 |

*Perf. 11½-12½ & Compound*  **Unwmk.**

| | | | |
|---|---|---|---|
| 285 | A60 | 25g on 80g red brn | 6.50 .65 |
| 286 | A61 | 1z on 1.20z ind (R) | 16.00 2.50 |
| a. | | Figure "1" in surcharge 5mm high instead of 4½mm | 18.00 21.00 2.50 |
| | | Never hinged | 28.50 3.65 |
| | | Nos. 284-286 (3) | 48.00 |

Surcharge of No. 286 includes bars.

Marshal Pilsudski — A64

*Perf. 11 to 13 and Compound*

**1935**  *Perf. 12x12½*

| | | | |
|---|---|---|---|
| 287 | A64 | 5g black | .40 .20 |
| 288 | A64 | 15g black | .40 .20 |
| 289 | A64 | 25g black | 1.65 1.00 |
| 290 | A64 | 45g black | 6.75 2.40 |
| 291 | A64 | 1z black | 10.75 5.00 |
| | | Never hinged | 19.95 8.00 |

*Perf. 11½, 11½x12½*  **Unwmk.**

24.00

Nos. 287-291 (5)

Pilsudski mourning issue.
Nos. 287-290 aro typo., Nos. 290-291 litho. No. 289 exists both typo. and litho.
See No. B35b.

Kopiec Marszałka Piłsudskiego

**1935**  **Wmk. 234**

| | | | |
|---|---|---|---|
| 292 | A58 | 15g red brown | 1.00 .45 |

*Perf. 11½, 11½x12½*  **Unwmk.**

| | | | |
|---|---|---|---|
| 293 | A63 | 25g gray blue (R) | 3.25 1.50 |
| | | Set, never hinged | 5.75 |

Issued in connection with the proposed memorial to Marshal Pilsudski, the stamps were sold at Cracow exclusively.

---

**1935-36**  **Typo.**  *Perf. 12½x13*

| | | | |
|---|---|---|---|
| 294 | A65 | 5g violet blue | .60 .20 |
| 295 | A65 | 10g yellow green | .60 .20 |
| 296 | A65 | 15g Prus green | 1.90 .20 |
| 297 | A65 | 20g violet black | .95 .20 |

*Engr.*

| | | | |
|---|---|---|---|
| 298 | A65 | 25g myrtle green | .80 .20 |
| 299 | A65 | 30g rose red | 2.00 .30 |
| 300 | A65 | 45g plum ('36) | 1.00 .30 |
| 301 | A65 | 50g blue ('36) | 1.00 .10 |
| 302 | A65 | 55g brown ('36) | .60 .60 |
| 303 | A65 | 1z brown ('36) | 9.50 .60 |
| 304 | A75 | 3z black brown | 24.35 6.65 |
| | | Set, never hinged | 32.50 |

See Nos. 308-311. For overprints see Nos. 306-307, 1K28-1K32.

Type of 1928 inscribed "1926. 3. VI. 1936" on Bottom Margin

**1936, June 3**  7.50 6.00

| | | | |
|---|---|---|---|
| 305 | A50 | 1z ultra | 9.50 |
| | | Never hinged | |

Presidency of Ignacy Moscicki, 10th anniv.

Nos. 299, 302 Overprinted in Blue or Red

POCZTA POLSKA GORDON-BENNETT 30.VIII.1936

| | | | |
|---|---|---|---|
| | | | 12.00 6.00 |
| 306 | A65 | 30g rose red | 12.00 6.00 |
| 307 | A65 | 55g blue (R) | 30.00 |
| | | Set, never hinged | |

Gordon-Bennett Intl. Balloon Race. Counterfeits exist.

**Scenic Type of 1935-36**

Designs: 5g, Church at Czestochowa. 10g, Maritime Terminal, Gdynia. 15g, University, Lwow. 20g, Municipal Building, Katowice.

**1937**  *Engr.*

| | | | |
|---|---|---|---|
| 308 | A65 | 5g violet blue | .20 .20 |
| 309 | A66 | 10g green | .55 .20 |
| 310 | A65 | 15g red brown | .40 .20 |
| 311 | A65 | 20g orange brown | .55 .20 |
| | | Nos. 308-311 (4) | 1.70 .80 |
| | | Set, never hinged | 3.00 |

For overprints see Nos. 1K31-1K32.

President Moscicki A81

*Perf. 12½x13*

**1937**  .25 .20

| | | | |
|---|---|---|---|
| 312 | A80 | 25g slate green | .60 .20 |
| 313 | A80 | 55g blue | 1.50 |
| | | Set, never hinged | |

For surcharges see Nos. N30, N32.

**Types of 1928-37 Souvenir Sheets**

**1937**

| | | | |
|---|---|---|---|
| 314 | | Sheet of 4 | 25.00 25.00 |
| a. | A80 | 25g, dark brown | 2.75 2.75 |
| 315 | | Sheet of 4 | 25.00 25.00 |
| a. | A49a | 50g, deep blue | 2.75 2.75 |
| 316 | | Sheet of 4 | 25.00 25.00 |
| a. | A50 | 1z, gray black | 2.75 2.75 |

Visit of King Carol of Romania to Poland, June 26-July 1.  110.00
See No. B35c.

Marshal Smigly-Rydz A80

**1938, Feb. 1**  *Perf. 12½*

| | | | |
|---|---|---|---|
| 317 | A81 | 15g slate green | .20 .20 |
| 318 | A81 | 30g rose violet | .60 .20 |
| | | Set, never hinged | 1.10 |

71st birthday of President Moscicki. For surcharge see No. N31.

"The Dog Cliff" — A65

President Ignacy Moscicki — A75

Designs: 10g, "Eye of the Sea." 15g, M. S. "Pilsudski." 20g, View of Pleniny. 25g, Belvedere Palace. 30g, Castle in Mira. 45g, Castle at Podhorce. 50g, Cloth Hall, Cracow. 55g, Raczynski Library, Poznan. 1z, Cathedral, Wilno.

## 1944, Sept. 13 — Photo. Perf. 12½

344 A103 25g deep red .60 .35
a. 25g dull red, typo. .85 1.10
345 A104 50g dk slate green .45 .20
Set, never hinged 1.65

No. 344a was not put on sale without surcharge. See Nos. 346, 349a. For surcharges see Nos. 345A-356, 364, B54, C19-C20.

## 1944-45

345A A103 1z on 25g ('45) 1.90 2.00
345B A103 2z on 25g ('45) 1.90 2.00
345C A103 3z on 25g ('45) 5.70 6.00
Nos. 345A-345C (3) 7.00

Issued to honor Polish government agencies, K. R. N. — Krajowa Rada Narodowa (Polish National Council); P. K. W. N. — Polski Komitet Wyzwolenia Narodu (Polish National Liberation Committee) and R. T. R. P. — Rząd Tymczasowy Rzeczypospolitej Polskiej (Temporary Administration of the Polish Republic). Counterfeits exist.

a — 31.XII.1943 K. R. N. 31.XII.1944
b — 3 zł 31.XII.1944 R. T. R. P.
c — 2 zł 31.XII.1944 P. K. W. N.

### No. 344 Surcharged in Black

## 1945, Sept. 1

346 A103 1.50z on 25g dull red .45 .70
Counterfeits of No. 346a exist.

### No. 344a Surcharged in Brown

1.50 ZŁ

### No. 344 Surcharged in Blue

3 zł — Kielce 15. I. 1945

## 1945, Feb. 12

347 A103 25g deep red 4.25 6.25
348 A103 3z on 25g (Radom, 16. I. 1945)
349 A103 3z on 25g (Warszawa, 17. I. 1945) 3.00 3.50
a. 3z on 25g dull red #344a 110.00 125.00
350 A103 3z on 25g (Czestochowa, 17. I. 1945) 6.25 7.00
351 A103 3z on 25g (Krakow, 19. I. 1945) 3.00 3.50
352 A103 3z on 25g (Lodz, 19. I. 1945) 3.00 3.50
353 A103 3z on 25g (Gniezno, 22. I. 1945) 3.00 3.50

354 A103 3z on 25g (Bydgoszcz, 23. I. 1945) 3.00 3.50
355 A103 3z on 25g (Kalisz, 24. I. 1945) 3.00
356 A103 3z on 25g (Zakopane, 29. I. 1945) 3.00 3.50
Nos. 347-356 (10) 34.50 42.50
Set, never hinged 41.25

Dates overprinted are those of liberation for each city. Counterfeits exist.

---

### Copernicus Memorial — A108

POCZTA POLSKA

### Wawel Castle — A109

## 1945, Apr. 10 — Photo. Perf. 10½, 11

357 A105 50g dk violet brn .20 .35
a. 50g dark brown .45 1.00
358 A106 1z henna brown .30 .25
359 A107 2z sapphire .45 .35
360 A108 3z dp red violet 1.25 .50
361 A109 3z blue green 2.75 3.25
Nos. 357-361 (5) 4.95 4.55
Set, never hinged 6.25

Liberation of Cracow Jan. 19, 1945. Nos. 357-361 exist imperforate. No. 357a is a coarser printing from a new plate showing designer's name (J. Wilczyk) in lower left margin. No. 357 does not show his name.

### Kosciuszko Statue, Cracow — A106

POCZTA POLSKA

### Cloth Hall, Cracow — A107

### Grunwald Monument, Cracow — A105

POCZTA POLSKA

---

### No. 345 Surcharged in Brown

## 1945, Sept. 10

364 A104 1z on 50g dk sl grn .40 .20
Never hinged .60

### No. 345 Surcharged in Black

1 ZŁ — Perf. 12½

---

### Lodz Skyline A110

POCZTA POLSKA

### Kosciuszko Monument, Lodz A111

POCZTA POLSKA

### Flag Bearer Carrying Wounded Comrade — A112

## 1945 — Litho. Perf. 11, 9 (3z)

365 A110 1z dp ultra .55 .20
366 A111 3z dull red violet .60 .45
367 A112 5z deep carmine 2.00 1.90
Nos. 365-367 (3) 3.15 2.55
Set, never hinged 4.00

Nos. 365 and 367 commemorate the liberation of Lodz and Warsaw.

### Grunwald Battle Scene — A113

POLSKA

## 1945, July 16

368 A113 5z deep blue 7.00 9.00
Never hinged 10.00
Battle of Grunwald (Tannenberg), July 15, 1410.

### Eagle Breaking Fetters and Manifesto of Freedom — A114

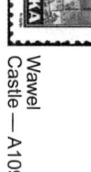
POLSKA

## 1945, July 22

369 A114 3z rose carmine 10.00 15.00
Never hinged 15.00
1st anniv. of the liberation of Poland.

---

### Crane Tower, Gdansk — A115

POCZTA POLSKA GDANSK

### Stock Tower, Gdansk — A116

POCZTA POLSKA GDANSK

### Ancient High Gate, Gdansk A117

## 1945, Sept. 15 — Photo. Unwmk.

370 A115 1z olive .20 .20
371 A116 2z sapphire .60 .25
372 A117 3c dark violet 1.00 .65
Nos. 370-372 (3) 1.50
Set, never hinged

Recovery of Poland's access to the sea at Gdansk (Danzig). Exist imperf. Value, set $25.

### Civilian and Soldiers in Rebellion — A118

10 zł POWSTANIE LISTOPADOWE 1830 29.XI 1945

## 1945, Nov. 29

373 A118 10z black 7.75 9.00
Never hinged
115th anniv. of the "November Uprising" against the Russians, Nov. 29, 1830.

### Holy Cross Church — A119

POLSKA

## 1945-46 — Unwmk. Imperf.

374 A119 1.50z crimson .20 .20
375 A119 1.50z dark blue .40 .40
376 A119 3z dark blue .40 .40
377 A119 3.50z lt blue grn .95 .40
378 A119 8z brown 1.90 .40
379 A119 10z dark violet ('46) .80 .30
Nos. 374-379 (6) 4.65 1.75

Views of Warsaw, 1939 and 1945: 1.50z, Warsaw Castle, 1939 and 1945; 3z, Cathedral of St. John; 3.50z, City Hall; 6z, Post Office; 8z, Army General Staff Headquarters.

Nos. 374-379 Overprinted in Black

POLSKA WARSZAWA WOLNA 17 Styczeń 1945—1946

## 1946, Jan. 17

383 A119 1.50z crimson 1.25 2.25
384 A119 3z dark blue 1.25 2.25
385 A119 3.50z lt blue grn .95 .40
386 A119 6z gray black .40 .40
387 A119 8z brown 1.25 2.25
388 A119 10z dark violet ('46) 1.25 2.25
Nos. 383-388 (6) 7.50 13.50
Set, never hinged 10.00

Liberation of Warsaw, 1/17/45, 1st anniv. Counterfeits exist.

---

Nos. 341-342 Surcharged in Black or Red:

POCZTA POLSKA 22.I.1863 5 zł

d

POCZTA POLSKA 24.III.1794 5 zł.

e

## 1945

362 A100(d) 5z on 25g 27.50 32.50
363 A101(e) 5z on 50g (R) 6.00 9.00
Never hinged
No. 362 was issued without gum.

Perf. 11½

---

### Polish Revolutionist A125

POLSKA

### Infantry Advancing A126

POLSKA

## 1946, Jan. 22 — Perf. 11

389 A125 6z slate blue 6.00 9.00
Never hinged 7.50
Revolt of Jan. 22, 1863.

## 1946, May 9

390 A126 3z brown .30 .20
Never hinged
Polish freedom, first anniversary.

Premier Edward Osubka-Morawski, Pres. Boleslaw Bierut and Marshal Michael Rola-Zymierski — A127

## 1946, July 22 Unwmk.
**Perf. 11x10½**

391 A127 3z purple 3.00 4.00
Never hinged

For surcharge see No. B53.

Bedzin Castle — A128

## 1946, Sept. 1 Photo. Imperf.

392 A128 5z olive gray .20 .20
393 A128 5z brown .20 .20

**Perf. 10½**

394 A129 6z gray black .30 .20

**Imperf**

395 A130 10z deep blue .65 .20
Set, never hinged 1.35 .80
2.00

Perforated copies of Nos. 392, 393 and 395 have been privately made.
For surcharge see No. 404.

Duke Henry IV of Silesia, from Tomb at Wroclaw — A129

Lanckrona Castle A130

Jan Matejko, Jacek Malczewski, Josef Chelmonski — A131

Adam Chmielowski (Brother Albert) — A132

---

Designs: 3z, Chopin. 5z, Wojciech Boguslawski, Helena Modjeska and Stefan Jaracz. 6z, Alexander Swietochowski, Stephen Zeromski and Boleslaw Prus. 10z, Marie Sklodowska Curie. 15z, Stanislaw Wyspianski, Juliusz Slowacki and Jan Kasprowicz. 20z, Adam Mickiewicz.

## 1947
**Perf. 11**

396 A131 1z blue .20 .20
397 A132 2z brown .35 .20
398 A132 2z Prus green .45 .20
399 A131 5z olive green .65 .20
400 A131 6z gray green 1.00 .20
401 A132 10z gray brown 1.10 .40
402 A131 15z sepia 1.25 .50
403 A132 20z gray black 1.50 .70
Nos. 396-403 (8) 6.50 2.60
Set, never hinged 9.00
Set exists imperf, value $12.

No. 394 Surcharged in Red

## 1947, Feb. 25 Perf. 10½

404 A129 5z on 6z gray blk .40 .20
Never hinged .70

### Types of 1947
## 1947 Photo. Perf. 11, Imperf.

405 A131 1z slate gray .20 .20
406 A132 2z orange .20 .20
407 A132 3z olive green 1.40 .35
408 A131 5z olive green .30 .20
409 A131 6z carmine rose .50 .20
410 A132 10z blue .90 .20
411 A131 15z chestnut brn .75 .30
412 A132 20z dark violet .50 .50
a. Souv. sheet of 8, #405-412 140.00 200.00
Never hinged 175.00
Nos. 405-412 (8) 4.75 2.15
Set, never hinged 7.00
No. 412a sold for 500z.

Farmer — A140

Miner A142

Fisherman A141

Laborer — A139

## 1947, Aug. 20 Engr. Perf. 13

413 A139 5z rose brown .70 .20
414 A140 10z brt blue green .20 .20
415 A141 15z dark blue .75 .20
416 A142 20z brown black 2.15 .80
Nos. 413-416 (4) 3.00
Set, never hinged

---

Allegory of the Revolution A143

Insurgents A144

## 1948, Mar. 15 Photo. Perf. 11

417 A143 15z brown .25 .20
Revolution of 1848. See Nos. 430-432.

## 1948, Apr. 19

418 A144 15z gray black 1.25 1.40
Never hinged 2.00
Ghetto uprising, Warsaw, 5th anniv.

Decorated Bicycle Wheel A145

## 1948, May 1

419 A145 15z brt rose & blue 2.00 1.10
Never hinged 3.00
1st Intl. Bicycle Peace Race, Warsaw-Prague-Warsaw.

Launching Ship — A146

Loading Freighter A147

35z, Radau yacht "Gen. Mariusz Zaruski."

## 1948, June 22

420 A146 6z violet 1.10 2.75
421 A147 15z brown car 2.25 3.50
422 A147 35z slate gray 4.60 3.75
Nos. 420-422 (3) 10.00
Set, never hinged
Polish Merchant Marine.

Cyclists A148

A149

## 1948, June 22

423 A148 3z gray 1.25 3.00
424 A148 6z brown 1.25 3.75
425 A148 15z green 4.50 4.50
Nos. 423-425 (3) 6.00 11.25
Set, never hinged
Poland Bicycle Race, 7th Circuit, 6/22-7/4.

---

## 1948, July 15

426 A149 6z blue .35 .30
427 A149 15z red .75 .30
428 A149 18z rose brown .65 .20
429 A149 35z dark brown 2.40 1.10
Nos. 426-429 (4) 3.75
Set, never hinged
Exhibition to commemorate the recovery of Polish territories, Wroclaw, 1948.

Gen. Henryk Dembinski and Gen. Josef Bem — A150

Symbolical of United Youth — A151

Designs: 35z, S. Worcell, P. Sciegienny and E. Dembowski. 60z, Friedrich Engels and Karl Marx.

## 1948, July 15

430 A150 30z dark brown .50 .40
431 A150 35z olive green 2.25 .55
432 A150 60z bright rose 3.45 1.35
Nos. 430-432 (3) 5.00
Set, never hinged
Revolution of 1848, cent. See No. 417.

## 1948, Aug. 8

433 A151 15z blue .45 .25
Never hinged .75
Intl. Congress of Democratic Youth, Warsaw, Aug.

Stagecoach Leaving Torun Gate — A152

## 1948, Sept. 4

434 A152 15z brown .45 .30
Never hinged .75
Philatelic Exhibition, Torun, Sept.

Clock Dial and Locomotive A153

## 1948, Oct. 6
**Perf. 11½**

435 A153 18z blue 4.00 10.00
European Railroad Schedule Conference, Cracow.

Pres. Boleslaw Bierut A154

## 1948-49 Unwmk. Perf. 11, 11½

436 A154 2z orange ('49) .20 .20
437 A154 3z blue grn ('49) .20 .20
438 A154 5z brown .20 .20
439 A154 5z slate .40 .20
440 A154 10z violet ('49) .40 .20
441 A154 15z dp carmine .45 .25
442 A154 18z gray green .20 .20
443 A154 30z gray green .75 .30
444 A154 35z violet brown 4.60 2.00
Nos. 436-444 (9) 8.00
Set, never hinged

## Workers Carrying Flag A155

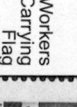

Designs: 15z, Marx, Engels, Lenin and Stalin. 25z, Ludwig Waryński.
Inscribed: "Kongres Jedności Klasy Robotniczej 8. XII. 1948."

**1948, Dec. 8**    **Perf. 11**
445 A155 5z crimson   .50 .25
446 A155 15z dull violet   .50 .65
447 A155 25z dark green   1.25 1.45
  Set, never hinged   3.50

Congress of the Union of the Working Class, Warsaw, Dec. 1948.

**Redrawn**
Dated: "XII. 1948"

**1948, Dec. 15**    **Perf. 11½**
448 A155 5z brown carmine   1.75 1.25
449 A155 15z bright blue   1.75 2.50
450 A155 25z dark green   2.25 2.50
  Set, never hinged   7.50

Designs as before.

"Socialism" A156

Designs: 5z, "Labor." 15z, "Peace."

**1949, May 31**   **Unwmk.**   **Perf. 11½**   **Photo.**
451 A156 3z carmine rose   .75 1.00
452 A156 5z deep blue   .90 1.00
453 A156 15z deep green   1.10 1.40
  Nos. 451-453 (3)   2.75 3.40
  Set, never hinged   3.75

8th Trade Union Congress, June 5, 1949.

Warsaw Scene — A157
Radio Station — A159
Pres. Bolesław Bierut — A158

**1949, July 22**   **Perf. 13x12½, 12½x13**   **Litho.**
454 A157 10z gray black   2.00 2.00
455 A158 15z lilac rose   1.25 1.25
456 A159 35z gray blue   4.50 4.50
  Set, never hinged   6.00

5th anniv. of "People's Poland."

A160

UPU, 75th Anniv.: 6z, Stagecoach and world map. 30z, Ship and map. 80z, Plane and map.

**1949, Oct. 10**   **Engr.**   **Perf. 13x12½**
457 A160 6z gray purple   .85 1.75
458 A160 30z blue   1.40 1.75
459 A160 80z dull green   3.75 4.25
  Nos. 457-459 (3)   6.00 7.50
  Set, never hinged   7.25

**1949**    **Perf. 13½x13**

Symbolical of United Poland.
460 A161 5z brown red   .70 .20
461 A161 10z rose red   .25 .20
462 A161 15z green   .25 .20
463 A161 35z dark brown   .70 .40
  Nos. 460-463 (4)   1.90 1.00
  Set, never hinged   2.75

Congress of the People's Movement for Unity.

Adam Mickiewicz A162
Frederic Chopin A163

Design: 35z, Juliusz Słowacki.

**1949, Dec. 5**   **Perf. 12½**
464 A162 10z brown violet   2.00 1.75
465 A163 15z brown rose   2.00 1.75
466 A162 35z deep blue   6.00 5.25
  Nos. 464-466 (3)     8.75
  Set, never hinged   8.75

Mail Delivery — A164
Adam Mickiewicz and Pushkin — A165

**1950, Jan. 21**   **Perf. 12½**
467 A164 15z red violet   2.00 2.50
  Never hinged   3.00

3rd Congress of PTT Trade Unions, Jan. 21-23, 1950.

**1949, Dec. 15**
468 A165 15z lilac   2.00 2.50
  Never hinged   3.50

Polish-Soviet friendship.

Pres. Bolesław Bierut A166
Julian Marchlewski A167

**1950, Feb. 25**   **Engr.**   **Perf. 12x12½**
469 A166 15z red   .30 .30
  Never hinged   .30

See Nos. 478-484, 490-496. For surcharge see No. 522.

A161

**1950**   25th death anniv. of Julian Marchlewski, author and political leader.

**1950, Mar. 23**   **Photo.**   **Perf. 11x10½**
470 A167 15z gray black   .55 .30
  Never hinged   .30

**1950, Apr. 15**
471 A168 5z dark brown   .20 .20
  Never hinged   .25

See No. 497.

Reconstruction, Warsaw — A168

**1950, Apr. 15**   **Perf. 11, 12 and Compounds of 13**

Worker Holding Hammer, Flag and Olive Branch — A169
Workers of Three Races with Flag — A170

**1950, Apr. 26**   **Perf. 11½**
472 A169 10z deep lilac rose   1.10 .20
473 A170 15z brown olive   1.10 .20
  Set, never hinged   3.50

60th anniversary of Labor Day.

Freedom Monument, Poznan — A171
Dove on Globe — A172

**1950, Apr. 27**
474 A171 15z chocolate   .25 .20
  Never hinged   .40

Poznan Fair, Apr. 29-May 14, 1950.

**1950, May 15**   **Unwmk.**
475 A172 10z deep green   .65 .20
476 A172 15z dark brown   1.50 .20
  Set, never hinged   .30

Day of Intl. Action for World Peace.

Polish Workers — A173
Hibner, Kniewski and Rutkowski A174

**1950, July 20**   **Perf. 12½x13**
477 A173 15z violet blue   .20 .20
  Never hinged   .30

Poland's 6 year plan. See Nos. 507A-510, 539.

**1950, Aug. 18**   **Photo.**   **Perf. 12½**
485 A174 15z gray black   1.75 .70
  Never hinged   2.50

25th anniv. of the execution of three Polish revolutionists, Władysław Hibner, Władysław Kniewski and Henryk Rutkowski.

Worker and Dove — A175
Dove by Picasso — A176

**1950, Aug. 31**   **Engr.**   **Perf. 12½**
486 A175 15z green   .30 .20
  Never hinged   .50

Polish Peace Congress, Warsaw, 1950.

Bierut Type of 1950, No Frame

**1950**   **Engr.**   **Perf. 11**
478 A166 5z dull green   .20 .20
479 A166 10z dull red   .20 .20
480 A166 15z deep blue   .65 .20
481 A166 20z violet brown   .20 .20
482 A166 25z yellow brown   .30 .20
482A A166 30z rose brown   .35 .20
483 A166 40z brown   .25 .20
484 A166 50z olive   1.10 .25
  Nos. 478-484 (8)   3.25 1.65
  Set, never hinged   6.00

"GROSZY"

To provide denominations needed as a result of the currency revaluation of Oct. 28, 1950, each post office was authorized to surcharge stamps of its current stock with the word "Groszy." Many types and sizes of this surcharge exist. The surcharge was applied to most of Poland's 1946-1950 issues. All stamps of that period could receive the surcharge upon request of anyone. Counterfeits exist.

Josef Bem and Battle Scene — A177

**1950, Nov. 13**
487 A176 40g blue   1.25 .30
488 A176 45g brown red   .40 .20
  Set, never hinged   2.50

2nd World Peace Congress.

**1950, Dec. 10**
489 A177 45g blue   2.00 1.50
  Never hinged   3.00

Death centenary of Gen. Josef Bem.

Type of 1950 with Frame Omitted

**1950, Dec. 16**   **Engr.**   **Perf. 12x12½**
490 A166 5g brown violet   .20 .20
491 A166 10g bluish green   .20 .20
492 A166 15g dp yellow grn   .20 .20
493 A166 25g dark red   .20 .20
493A A166 30g red   .25 .20
494 A166 40g vermilion   .95 .20
495 A166 45g deep blue   .20 .20
496 A166 75g brown   .60 .20
  Nos. 490-496 (8)   2.80 1.60
  Set, never hinged   4.00

Reconstruction Type of 1950

**1950**   **Perf. 11, 11x11½, 13x11**
497 A168 15g green   .20 .20
  Never hinged   .25

See No. B63.

**1952, Mar. 8** — **Perf. 12½x12**
536 A196 1.20z deep carmine .40 .20
Intl. Women's Day. See No. B64.

Gen. Karol Swierczewski-Walter — A197
Pres. Boleslaw Bierut — A198

**1952, Mar. 28** — **Perf. 12½**
537 A197 90g blue gray .40 .20
Gen. Karol Swierczewski-Walter (1896-1947). See No. B65.

**1952, Apr. 18**
538 A198 90g dull green .70 .45
  Nos. 530,B66-B67 (3) 1.70 .85
60th birth anniv. of Pres. Boleslaw Bierut.

### Souvenir Sheet

A199

**1951, Nov. 15** — Sheet of 4 — 20.00 12.50
539 A199 1.40
 a. 45g rod brown (A173) 1.40
 b. 75g red brown (A173) 1.40
 c. 1.15z red brown (A173) 1.40
 d. 1.20z red brown (A173) 1.40
Polish Philatelic Association Congress, Warsaw, 1951. Sold for 5 zloty.

J. I. Kraszewski — A201
Workers with Flag — A200

**1952, May 1** — **Unwmk.** — **Perf. 12½**
540 A200 75g deep green .45 .20
Labor Day, May 1, 1952. See No. B70.

**1952, May**
541 A201 25g brown violet .35 .20
542 A201 1z yellow green .40 .20
543 A201 1.15z red green .75 .35
  Nos. 541-543,B71-B72 (5) 2.25

### Various Frames

---

Type of 1950 with Frame Omitted
Surcharged with New Value in Black

**1951, Sept. 1** — **Engr.** — **Perf. 12½x11½**
522 A166 45g on 35z red .30 .20
  Never hinged

**1951, Aug. 5** — **Photo.** — **Perf. 12½x11**
523 A190 40g deep ultra .60 .20
  Never hinged .95
3rd World Youth Festival, Berlin, Aug. 5-19.

Frederic Chopin and Stanislaw Moniuszko — A192
Festival of Polish Music, 1951.

Joseph V. Stalin — A191

**1951, Oct. 30** — **Engr.** — **Perf. 12½**
524 A191 45g lake .20 .20
525 A191 90g gray black .40 .20
Month of Polish-Soviet friendship, Nov. 1951.

**1951, Nov. 15** — **Unwmk.**    **Perf. 12½x11½**
526 A192 45g gray .20 .20 / .20 .20
527 A192 90g brownish red .90 .25 / .40 .20
Set, never hinged 1.75 / 1.25

Coal Mining — A194
Apartment House Construction — A193

Design #429-530, Electrical installation

Inscribed: "Plan 6," etc.
**1951-52**
528 A193 30g dull green .20 .20
529 A193 30g gray black (52) .20 .20
530 A193 45g red (52) .25 .20
531 A193 90g chocolate .40 .20
532 A193 1.15z violet brn (52) .40 .20
533 A194 1.20z deep blue ('52) 3.10 1.95
  Nos. 528-533,B66-B69A (9) 4.00
Set, never hinged
Poland's 6-year plan.

**Catalogue values for unused stamps in this section, from this point to the end of the section, are for Never Hinged items.**

Flag, Workman, Mother and Child — A196
Pawel Finder — A195
Portrait: 1.15z, Malgorzata Fornalska.

**1952, Jan. 18**
534 A195 90g chocolate .25 .20
535 A195 1.15z red orange .30 .20
  Nos. 534-535,B63 (3) .75 .60
Polish Workers Party, 10th anniv.

---

Congress Emblem — A186
Stanislaw Staszyk — A184

Z. F. von Wroblewski and Karol S. Olszewski — A185

Portraits: 40g, Marie Sklodowska Curie. 60g, Marceli Nencki. 1.15z, Nicolaus Copernicus.

**Perf. 12½, 14x11**
**1951, Apr. 25** — **Photo.**
511 A184 25g carmine rose 1.90 1.50
512 A184 40g ultra .25 .20
513 A185 45g purple 7.00 1.50
514 A184 60g green .55 .20
515 A184 1.15z claret 1.90 .75
516 A186 1.20z gray 1.40 .60
  Nos. 511-516 (6) 13.00 4.75
  Set, never hinged 16.00
1st Congress of Polish Science.

Feliks E. Dzerzhinski — A187

**1951, July 5** — **Engr.** — **Perf. 12x12½**
517 A187 45g chestnut brown .20 .20
25th death anniv. of Feliks E. Dzerzhinski, Polish revolutionary, organizer of Russian secret police.

Pres. Boleslaw Bierut — A188

**1951, July 22** — **Perf. 12½**
518 A188 45g dark carmine .50 .25
519 A188 60g deep green 12.00 6.75
520 A188 90g deep blue 1.50 .50
  Nos. 518-520 (3) 13.50 7.50
Set, never hinged 19.00
7th anniv. of the formation of the Polish People's Republic.

Youths Encircling Globe — A190

Flag and Sports Emblem — A189

**1951, Sept. 8** — **Perf. 12½, 14x11**
521 A189 45g green 1.00 .50
1.65
National Sports Festival, 1951.

---

Woman and Doves — A178

**1951, Mar. 2** — **Engr.** — **Perf. 12½**
498 A178 45g dark red .30 .20
.50
Congress of Women, Mar. 3-4, 1951.

Gen. Jaroslaw Dabrowski — A179

**1951, Mar. 24** — **Perf. 12x12½**
499 A179 45g dark green .20 .20
.35
80th anniv. of the Insurrection of Paris and the death of Gen. Jaroslaw Dabrowski.

Dove Type of 1950 Surcharged
**1951, Apr. 20** — **Perf. 12½**
500 A176 45g on 15z brn red .60 .20
  Never hinged .60

Worker and Flag — A180

Steel Mill, Nowa Huta — A181

**1951, Apr. 25** — **Photo.** — **Perf. 14x11**
501 A180 45g scarlet .35 .20
  Never hinged .55
Labor Day, May 1.

**1951** — **Engr.**
502 A181 40g dark blue .20 .20
503 A181 45g black .20 .20
504 A181 60g brown .20 .20
505 A181 90g dark carmine .40 .20
  Nos. 502-505 (4) 1.00 .80
2.50

Pioneer Saluting — A182
Boy and Girl Pioneers — A183

**1951, Apr. 1** — **Photo.**
506 A182 30g olive brown .50 .50
507 A183 45g brt grnsh blue 6.00 .75
Set, never hinged 8.00
Issued to publicize Children's Day, June 1, 1951.

Workers Type of 1950
**1951** — **Unwmk.** — **Engr.** — **Perf. 12½x13**
507A A173 45g violet blue .20 .20
508 A173 75g black green .20 .20
509 A173 1.15z dark green .40 .20
510 A173 1.20z dark red .25 .20
  Nos. 507A-510 (4) 1.05 .80
Set, never hinged 2.50
Issued to publicize Poland's 6-year plan.

## Nikolai Gogol A202

**1952, June 5**
544 A202 25g deep green .75 .40
100th death anniv. of Nikolai V. Gogol, writer.

## Gymnast A203

**1952, June 21 Photo. Perf. 13**
545 A203 1.15z Runners 1.40 .90
546 A203 1.20z blue .90 .50
Nos. 545-546,B75-B76 (4) 7.50 3.15

## Racing Cyclists — A204

**1952, Apr. 25 Perf. 13½**
547 A204 40g blue 1.25 .40
5th Intl. Peace Bicycle Race, Warsaw-Berlin-Prague.

## Concrete Works, Wierzbica A206

## Shipyard Worker and Collier — A205

**1952, June 28 Engr. Perf. 12½**
548 A205 90g violet brown .95 .60
Shipbuilders' Day, 1952.

**1952, June 17**
549 A206 3z gray .95 .40
550 A206 10z brown red 1.50 .25

## Bugler A207

**1952, July 17 Perf. 12½x12**
551 A207 90g brown .45 .20
Youth Festival, 1952. See Nos. B79-B80.

## Celebrating New Constitution A208

## Power Plant, Jaworzno A209

**1952, July 22 Photo. Perf. 12½**
552 A208 3z vio & dk brn .40 .25
Proclamation of a new constitution. See No. B81.

**1952, Aug. 7 Engr.**
553 A209 1z black .65 .25
554 A209 1.50z deep green 1.95 .65
Nos. 553-554,B82 (3)

## Grywald — A210

**1952, Aug. 18**
555 A210 60g dark green 1.60 .50
556 A210 1z red ("Niedzica") 2.50 1.00
a. 1z red ("Niedzica") 6.00 .90
Nos. 555-556,B85 (3)

## Parachute Descent — A211

**1952, Aug. 23**
557 A211 90g deep blue .70 .45
Nos. 557,B86-B87 (3) 3.50 1.65
Aviation Day, Aug. 23.

## Avicenna A212

**1952, Sept. 1**
558 A212 75g red brown .35 .20
559 A212 90g sepia .25 .20
Anniversaries of the births of Avicenna (1000th) and Victor Hugo (150th).

## Shipbuilding A213

**1952, Sept. 10**
560 A213 5g deep green .20 .20
561 A213 15g red brown .20 .20
Portrait: 90g, Victor Hugo.

## Assault on the Winter Palace, 1917 A214

**1952, Nov. 7 Perf. 12x12½**
562 A214 60g dark brown .55 .30
Russian Revolution, 35th anniv. See #562, B92 exist imperf. Value $30.
Reconstruction of Gdansk shipyards.

## Auto Assembly Plant, Zeran — A215

**1952, Dec. 12**
563 A215 1.15z brown .48 .20
See No. B99.

## Dove — A216

**1952, Dec. 12 Photo. Perf. 12½**
564 A216 30g green .55 .20
565 A216 60g ultra 1.25 .50
Congress of Nations for Peace, Vienna, Dec. 12-19, 1952.

## Copernicus Watching Heavens, by Jan Matejko — A222

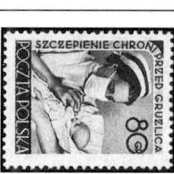

## Nicolaus Copernicus — A223

## Soldier with Flag — A217

**1953, Feb. 2 Unwmk. Perf. 11**
566 A217 60g olive gray 4.50 1.60
567 A217 80g blue gray 1.00 .40
10th anniv. of the Battle of Stalingrad.

## Karl Marx — A218

**1953, Mar. 14 Perf. 12½**
568 A218 60g dull blue 19.00 10.00
569 A218 80g dark brown 1.00 .30
70th death anniv. of Karl Marx.

## Cyclists and Arms of Warsaw — A219

**1953, Apr. 30**
570 A219 80g dark brown 1.25 .50
571 A219 80g dark green 1.25 .50
572 A219 80g red 15.00 9.00
Nos. 570-572 (3) 17.50 10.00
6th Intl. Peace Bicycle Race, Warsaw-Berlin-Prague.

## Flag and Globe — A220

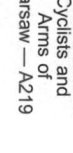

**1953, Apr. 28**
573 A220 60g vermilion 4.25 3.25
574 A220 80g carmine .70 .35
Labor Day, May 1, 1953.
Arms: No. 571, Berlin. No. 572, Prague.

## Boxer — A221

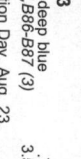

**1953, May 17**
575 A221 40g red brown 1.00 .50
576 A221 80g orange 10.00 6.25
577 A221 95g violet brown 1.00 1.00
Nos. 575-577 (3) 12.00 7.25
European Championship Boxing Matches, Warsaw, May 17-24, 1953.
Design: 95g, Boxing match.

## Nurse Feeding Baby — A228

**1953, Nov. 21**
587 A228 80g rose carmine 8.75 5.00
588 A228 1.75z deep green .25 .20
Poland's Social Health Service.
Design: 1.75z, Nurse instructing mother.

**1953, May 22 Perf. 12x12½, 12½x12 Engr.**
578 A222 20g green 1.50 .50
579 A223 80g deep blue 12.00 10.00
480th birth anniv. of Nicolaus Copernicus, astronomer.

## Old Part of Warsaw — A225

## Fishing Boat — A224

**1953, July 15 Perf. 12½**
580 A224 80g dark green 1.10 .45
581 A224 1.35z deep blue 2.00 1.50
Issued for Merchant Marine Day.
Design: 1.35z, Freighter "Czech."

**1953, July 15 Photo.**
582 A225 20g red brown .40 .35
583 A225 2.35z blue 3.50 3.00
36th anniv. of the proclamation of "People's Poland."

1.35z, Congress badge (similar to AP7).

## Students of Two Races — A226

**1953, Aug. 24**
584 A226 40g dark brown .50 .20
585 A227 1.35z green 1.00 .20
586 A227 1.50z blue 2.50 3.00
Nos. 584-586,C32-C33 (5) 6.50 4.65
3rd World Congress of Students, Warsaw, 1953.

## Schoolgirl and Dove — A227

## Mieczyslaw Kalinowski A229

## Battle Scene, Polish and Soviet Flags A230

**1953, Oct. 10**
589 A229 45g brown 3.50 2.25
590 A230 80g brown lake .55 .25
591 A229 1.75z olive gray 4.60 2.65
Nos. 589-591 (3)
10th anniv. of Poland's People's Army.
Portrait: 1.75z, Roman Pazinski.

## Chopin and Piano — A254

Cities: 45g, Gdansk. 60g, Torun. 1.40z, Malbork. 1.55z, Olsztyn.

**1954, Oct. 16** — Engr. — *Perf. 12x12½*

| | | | | |
|---|---|---|---|---|
| 639 | A253 | 20g dk car, bl | 2.75 | .70 |
| 640 | A253 | 45g brown, yel | .20 | .20 |
| 641 | A253 | 60g dk green, cit | .25 | .20 |
| 642 | A253 | 1.40z dk blue, pink | .50 | .20 |
| 643 | A253 | 1.55z dk vio brn, cr | 1.25 | .20 |
| | | Nos. 639-643 (5) | 5.00 | 1.50 |

Pomerania's return to Poland, 500th anniv. For overprint see No. 866.

**1954, Nov. 8** — Photo. — *Perf. 12½*

| | | | | |
|---|---|---|---|---|
| 644 | A254 | 45g dark brown | .50 | .20 |
| 645 | A254 | 60g dark green | .95 | .20 |
| 646 | A254 | 1z dark blue | 2.25 | .55 |
| | | Nos. 644-646 (3) | 3.70 | .95 |

5th Intl. Competition of Chopin's Music.

## Coal Mine — A255

Designs: 20g, Soldier, flag and map. 25g, Steel mill. 45g, Relaxing worker in deck chair. 60g, Tractor in field. 1.15z, Lublin Castle. 1.40z, Books and publications. 1.55z, Loading ship. 2.10z, Attacking tank.

Photo.; Center Engr. — *Perf. 12½x12*

**1954-55**

| | | | | |
|---|---|---|---|---|
| 647 | A255 | 10g red brn & choc | 1.25 | .20 |
| 648 | A255 | 20g rose & grnsh blk | .65 | .30 |
| 649 | A255 | 25g bister & blk | 1.50 | .20 |
| 650 | A255 | 40g yel org & ohoo | .90 | .20 |
| 651 | A255 | 45g claret & vio brn | .95 | .20 |
| 652 | A255 | 60g emerald & red brn | .95 | .25 |
| 653 | A255 | 1.15z brt bl grn & sep | .95 | .50 |
| 654 | A255 | 1.40z orange & choc | 9.25 | 2.25 |
| 655 | A255 | 1.55z blue & indigo | 1.75 | .65 |
| 656 | A255 | 2.10z ultra & indigo | 3.00 | 1.40 |
| | | Nos. 647-656 (10) | 20.75 | 6.15 |

10th anniversary of "People's Poland." Issued: 25g, 60g, 1955, others, 12/23/54.

## Insurgents Attacking Russians — A256

Photo.; Center Litho.

60g, Gen. Tadeusz Kosciuszko and insurgents. 1.40z, Kosciuszko leading attack in Cracow.

**1954, Nov. 30** — Engr. — *Perf. 12½*

| | | | | |
|---|---|---|---|---|
| 657 | A256 | 40g grnsh black | .40 | .20 |
| 658 | A256 | 60g violet brown | .60 | .20 |
| 659 | A256 | 1.40z dark gray | 1.65 | .70 |
| | | Nos. 657-659 (3) | 2.65 | 1.10 |

160th anniv. of the Insurrection of 1794.

---

## Handstand on Horizontal Bars — A248

**1954, May 31** — Photo. — *Perf. 12½*

60g, Glider, flags. 1.35z, Glider, large cloud.

| | | | | |
|---|---|---|---|---|
| 624 | A246 | 45g dark green | .20 | .20 |
| 625 | A246 | 60g purple | 4.00 | .80 |
| 626 | A246 | 60g brown | .90 | .30 |
| 627 | A246 | 1.35z blue | 6.00 | 1.50 |
| | | Nos. 624-627 (4) | | |

Intl. Glider Championships, Leszno.

## Fencing — A247

Design: 1z, Relay racers.

**1954, July 17**

| | | | | |
|---|---|---|---|---|
| 628 | A247 | 25g violet brown | 1.40 | .35 |
| 629 | A248 | 60g Prus blue | 1.40 | .25 |
| 630 | A247 | 1z violet blue | 2.75 | .65 |
| | | Nos. 628-630 (3) | 5.55 | 1.25 |

## Javelin Throwers A249

## Studzianki Battle Scene — A250

*Perf. 12*

**1954, July 17**

| | | | | |
|---|---|---|---|---|
| 631 | A249 | 60g rose brn & dk red brn | 1.25 | .25 |
| 632 | A249 | 1.55z gray & black | 1.10 | .35 |

Nos. 628-632 were issued to publicize the second Summer Spartacist Games, 1954.

**1954, Aug. 24** — *Perf. 12½*

| | | | | |
|---|---|---|---|---|
| 633 | A250 | 60g dark green | 1.40 | .25 |
| 634 | A250 | 1z dark green | 6.00 | 2.75 |

Design: 1z, Soldier and flag bearer.
10th anniversary, Battle of Studzianki.

## Farmer Picking Fruit — A252

## Railway Signal — A251

Design: 60g, Modern train.

**1954, Sept. 9**

| | | | | |
|---|---|---|---|---|
| 635 | A251 | 60g dull blue | 4.00 | 1.00 |
| 636 | A251 | 60g black | 2.00 | .50 |

Issued to publicize Railwaymen's Day.

**1954, Sept. 15**

| | | | | |
|---|---|---|---|---|
| 637 | A252 | 40g violet | 1.40 | .60 |
| 638 | A252 | 60g black | .60 | .20 |

Month of Polish-Soviet friendship.

## View of Elblag A253

---

## Krynica Spa A239

## Dunajec Canyon, Pieniny Mountains A240

Designs: 80g, Morskie Oko, Tatra Mts. 2z, Windmill and framework, Ciechocinek.

**1953, Dec. 16**

| | | | | |
|---|---|---|---|---|
| 608 | A239 | 20g blue & rose brn | .25 | .20 |
| 609 | A240 | 80g bl grn & dk vio | 1.90 | 1.25 |
| 610 | A240 | 1.75z ol bis & dk grn | .75 | .20 |
| 611 | A239 | 2z brick red & blk | 1.10 | .20 |
| | | Nos. 608-611 (4) | 4.00 | 1.85 |

## Spinning Mill Worker — A242

## Electric Passenger Train — A241

Design: 80g, Electric locomotive and cars.

**1954, Jan. 26** — Engr.

| | | | | |
|---|---|---|---|---|
| 612 | A241 | 60g deep blue | 6.25 | 4.25 |
| 613 | A241 | 80g red brown | .75 | .25 |

**1954, Mar. 24** — Photo.

Designs: 40g, Woman letter carrier. 80g, Woman tractor driver.

| | | | | |
|---|---|---|---|---|
| 614 | A242 | 20g deep green | 1.50 | .45 |
| 615 | A242 | 40g deep blue | .60 | .20 |
| 616 | A242 | 80g dark brown | .70 | .20 |
| | | Nos. 611-616 (3) | 2.50 | .05 |

## "Peace" Uniting Three Capitals — A244

## Flags and May Flowers — A243

**1954, Apr. 28** — *Perf. 12½x12*

| | | | | |
|---|---|---|---|---|
| 617 | A243 | 40g chocolate | .75 | .30 |
| 618 | A243 | 60g deep blue | .75 | .20 |
| 619 | A243 | 80g carmine rose | .75 | .25 |
| | | Nos. 617-619 (3) | 2.25 | .75 |

Labor Day, May 1, 1954.

**1954, Apr. 29** — *Perf. 12½x12*

| | | | | |
|---|---|---|---|---|
| 620 | A244 | 80g red brown | .50 | .20 |
| 621 | A244 | 80g deep blue | .50 | .20 |

No. 621, Dove, olive branch and wheel.
7th Intl. Bicycle Tour, May 2-17, 1954.

## Glider and Framed Clouds — A246

A245

**1954, Apr. 30** — Engr. — *Perf. 11½*

| | | | | |
|---|---|---|---|---|
| 622 | A245 | 25g gray | .95 | .20 |
| 623 | A245 | 80g brown carmine | .30 | .20 |

3rd Trade Union Congress, Warsaw 1954.

---

## Courtyard, Wawel Castle A232

## Jan Kochanowski A231

Portrait: 1.35z, Mikolaj Rej.

**1953, Nov. 10** — Engr.

| | | | | |
|---|---|---|---|---|
| 592 | A231 | 20g red brown | .20 | .20 |
| 593 | A232 | 80g deep plum | .40 | 1.00 |
| 594 | A231 | 1.35z gray black | 1.75 | 1.00 |
| | | Nos. 592-594 (3) | 2.35 | 1.40 |

Issued for the "Renaissance Year." For surcharges see Nos. 733-736.

## Palace of Culture, Warsaw A233

Designs: 1.75z, Constitution Square. 2z, Old Section, Warsaw.

**1953, Nov. 30** — *Perf. 12x12½*

| | | | | |
|---|---|---|---|---|
| 595 | A233 | 80g vermillion | 9.00 | 1.25 |
| 596 | A233 | 1.75z deep blue | .65 | .40 |
| 597 | A233 | 2z violet brown | 5.50 | 2.50 |
| | | Nos. 595-597 (3) | 15.15 | 4.15 |

Issued for the reconstruction of Warsaw.

## Skier — A237

## Ice Dancer — A236

Design: 2.05z, Ice hockey player.

**1953, Dec. 31** — Litho. — *Perf. 12½*

| | | | | |
|---|---|---|---|---|
| 602 | A236 | 80g blue | 1.25 | .30 |
| 603 | A237 | 05g blue green | 1.75 | .50 |
| 604 | A236 | 2.85z dark red | 4.75 | 2.00 |
| | | Nos. 602-604 (3) | 7.75 | 2.80 |

### Canceled to Order

The government stamp agency began late in 1951 to sell canceled sets of new issues. Until 1990, at least, values in the second ("used") column are for these canceled-to-order stamps. Postally used copies are worth more.

## Children at Play — A238

Designs: 80g, Girls on the way to school. 1.50z, Two students in class.

**1953, Dec. 31** — Photo.

| | | | | |
|---|---|---|---|---|
| 605 | A238 | 10g violet | .20 | .20 |
| 606 | A238 | 60g red brown | .80 | .30 |
| 607 | A238 | 1.50z dark green | 7.00 | 2.50 |
| | | Nos. 605-607 (3) | | |

**Bison — A257**

60g, European elk, 1.90z, Chamois, 3z, Beaver.

**1954, Dec. 22    Engr.; Background Photo.**
| | | | | |
|---|---|---|---|---|
| 660 | A257 | 45g yel grn & blk brn | .40 | .20 |
| 661 | A257 | 60g emerald & dk brn | .60 | .20 |
| 662 | A257 | 1.90z blue & blk brn | 1.75 | .50 |
| 663 | A257 | 3z bl grn & dk brn | 3.15 | 1.10 |

Exist imperf. Value, set $4.50.

**Liberators Entering Warsaw — A258**

**1955, Jan. 17    Engr.**
| | | | | |
|---|---|---|---|---|
| 664 | A258 | 40g red brown | .85 | .30 |
| 665 | A258 | 60g dull blue | 2.25 | .65 |

Liberation of Warsaw, 10th anniversary.

**Frederic Chopin A259**

**Sigismund III A261**

**1955, Feb. 22    Photo.**
| | | | | |
|---|---|---|---|---|
| 666 | A259 | 40g dark brown | .35 | .20 |
| 667 | A259 | 60g indigo | .65 | .20 |

5th Intl. Competition of Chopin's Music, Feb. 22-Mar. 21.

**Nicolaus Copernicus A260**

Allegory of freedom (Warsaw Mermaid).

Warsaw monuments: 5g, Mermaid, 10g, Feliks E. Dzerzhinski; 40g, Brothers in Arms Monument; 45g, Marie Sklodowska Curie; 60g, Adam Mickiewicz; 1.55z, Jan Kilinski.

**1955, May 3    Unwmk.    Perf. 12½**
| | | | | |
|---|---|---|---|---|
| 668 | A260 | 5g dk grn, grnsh | .20 | .20 |
| 669 | A260 | 10g vio brn, yel | .20 | .20 |
| 670 | A261 | 15g blk brn, blush | .20 | .20 |
| 671 | A260 | 20g dk bl, pink | .20 | .20 |
| 672 | A260 | 45g vio, vio | .80 | .20 |
| 673 | A261 | 45g vio brn, cr | .60 | .20 |
| 674 | A261 | 60g dk bl, gray | .80 | .25 |
| 675 | A261 | 1.55z sl bl, grysh | 1.65 | .30 |
| | | Nos. 668-675 (8) | 4.45 | 1.75 |

See Nos. 737-739.

Design: 60g, Monument.

**Palace of Culture and Flags of Poland and USSR — A262**

**1955, Apr. 21    Perf. 12½x12, 11    Photo.**
| | | | | |
|---|---|---|---|---|
| 676 | A262 | 40g rose red | .20 | .20 |
| 677 | A262 | 40g lt brown | .60 | .30 |
| 678 | A262 | 60g Prus blue | .25 | .20 |
| 679 | A262 | 60g dk olive brn | 1.30 | .90 |
| | | Nos. 676-679 (4) | | |

Polish-USSR treaty of friendship, 10th anniv.

**Arms and Bicycle Wheels — A263**

**1955, Apr. 25    Photo.**
| | | | | |
|---|---|---|---|---|
| 680 | A263 | 40g chocolate | .40 | .20 |
| 681 | A263 | 60g ultra | .25 | .20 |

**Poznan Town Hall and Fair Emblem — A264**

Design: 60g, Three doves above road.

**1955, June 10    Perf. 12½**
| | | | | |
|---|---|---|---|---|
| 682 | A264 | 40g brt ultra | .30 | .20 |
| 683 | A264 | 60g dull red | .20 | .20 |

24th Intl. Fair at Poznan, July 3-24, 1955.

**"Laikonik" Carnival Costume A265**

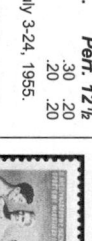

A265a

**1955, June 16    Typo.    Perf. 12**
Multicolored Centers
| | | | | |
|---|---|---|---|---|
| 684 | A265 | 20g emerald & henna | .30 | .25 |
| 685 | A265a | 40g brt org & lil | .45 | .30 |
| 686 | A265 | 60g blue & carmine | 1.25 | .75 |
| | | Nos. 684-686 (3) | 2.00 | |

Cracow Celebration Days.

**Pansies — A266**

40g, (#690), Dove & Tower of Palace of Science & Culture, 45g, Pansies, 60g, (#691), 1z, "Peace" (POKO), & Warsaw Mermaid.

**1955, July 13    Litho.    Perf. 12**
| | | | | |
|---|---|---|---|---|
| 687 | A266 | 25g vio brn, org & car | .20 | .20 |
| 688 | A266 | 40g gray bl & gray blk | .35 | .20 |
| 689 | A266 | 45g brn lake, yel & car | .35 | .20 |
| 690 | A266 | 60g sepia & orange | .30 | .20 |
| 691 | A266 | 60g ultra & lt blue | .30 | .20 |
| 692 | A266 | 1z purple & lt blue | .90 | .50 |
| | | Nos. 687-692 (6) | 2.25 | 1.50 |

5th World Festival of Youth, Warsaw, July 31-Aug. 14, 1955. Exist imperf. Value, set $3.

---

**Motorcyclists A267**

**1955, July 20    Photo.    Perf. 12½**
| | | | | |
|---|---|---|---|---|
| 693 | A267 | 40g chocolate | .30 | .20 |
| 694 | A267 | 60g dk green | .25 | .20 |

13th Intl. Motorcycle Race in the Tatra Mountains, Aug. 7-9, 1955.

**Stalin Palace of Culture and Science, Warsaw A268**

**1955, July 21**
| | | | | |
|---|---|---|---|---|
| 695 | A268 | 60g ultra | .20 | .20 |
| 696 | A268 | 60g gray | .45 | .20 |
| 697 | A268 | 75g blue green | .45 | .20 |
| 698 | A268 | 75g brown | 1.30 | .80 |
| | | Nos. 695-698 (4) | | |

Polish National Day, July 22, 1955. Sheets contain alternating copies of the 60g values or the 75g values respectively.

**Athletes — A269**

**Stadium — A270**

**1955, July 27    Unwmk.    Perf. 12½**
| | | | | |
|---|---|---|---|---|
| 699 | A269 | 20g chocolate | .20 | .20 |
| 700 | A269 | 40g plum | .20 | .20 |
| 701 | A270 | 40g dull blue | .20 | .20 |
| 702 | A269 | 1z orange ver | .55 | .20 |
| 703 | A269 | 1z dull violet | .70 | .20 |
| 704 | A269 | 1.35z peacock green | 1.25 | .50 |
| | | Nos. 699-704 (6) | 3.20 | 1.50 |

Designs: 40g, Hammer throwing, 1z, Basketball, 1.35z, Sculling, 1.55z, Swimming. 2nd International Youth Games, 1955. Exist imperf. Value, set $4.

**Town Hall, Szczecin (Stettin) — A271**

**Rebels with Flag — A272**

**1955, Sept. 22    Engr.    Perf. 11½**
| | | | | |
|---|---|---|---|---|
| 705 | A271 | 25g dull green | .20 | .20 |
| 706 | A271 | 40g red brown | .30 | .20 |
| 707 | A271 | 60g violet blue | .30 | .20 |
| 708 | A271 | 95g dark gray | 2.00 | .90 |
| | | Nos. 705-708 (4) | | |

Designs: 40g, Cathedral, Wroclaw (Breslau) 60g, Town Hall, Zielona Gora (Grunberg), 95g, Town Hall, Opole (Oppeln).
10th anniv. of the acquisition of Western Polish Territories.

**1955, Sept. 30    Photo.    Perf. 12½x12½**
| | | | | |
|---|---|---|---|---|
| 709 | A272 | 40g dark brown | .25 | .20 |
| 710 | A272 | 60g dk carmine rose | .20 | .20 |

Revolution of 1905, 50th anniversary.

**Adam Mickiewicz — A273**

---

**Mickiewicz Monument, Paris — A274**

**1955, Oct. 10    Perf. 12½x12½, 12½**
| | | | | |
|---|---|---|---|---|
| 711 | A273 | 20g dark brown | .20 | .20 |
| 712 | A274 | 40g brn org & dk brn | .25 | .20 |
| 713 | A274 | 40g green & brown | .25 | .20 |
| 714 | A274 | 95g brn red & blk | 2.15 | 1.10 |
| | | Nos. 711-714 (4) | | |

60g, Death mask; 95g, Statue, Warsaw.
Death cent. of Adam Mickiewicz, poet, and to publicize the celebration of Mickiewicz year.

**Teacher and Child — A275**

**1955, Oct. 21    Perf. 12½x13**
| | | | | |
|---|---|---|---|---|
| 715 | A275 | 40g brown | 1.50 | .50 |
| 716 | A275 | 60g ultra | 2.50 | .85 |

Polish Teachers' Trade Union, 50th anniv.
Design: 60g, Flame and open book.

**Rook and Hands — A276**

**1956, Feb. 9    Perf. 12½    Unwmk.**
| | | | | |
|---|---|---|---|---|
| 717 | A276 | 40g dark red | 1.00 | .85 |
| 718 | A276 | 60g blue | 1.50 | .20 |

First World Chess Championship of the Deaf and Dumb, Feb. 9-23.
Design: 60g, Chess knight and hands.

**Captain and S.S. Kilinski A277**

**1956, Mar. 16    Engr.    Perf. 12½x12½**
| | | | | |
|---|---|---|---|---|
| 719 | A277 | 5g green | .20 | .20 |
| 720 | A277 | 10g carmine lake | .20 | .20 |
| 721 | A277 | 20g deep ultra | .20 | .20 |
| 722 | A277 | 45g rose brown | .70 | .20 |
| 723 | A277 | 95g dull blue | 1.85 | 1.00 |
| | | Nos. 719-723 (5) | | |

10g, Sailor and barges, 20g, Dock worker and worker, 45g, Shipyard and worker, 60g, Fisherman, S.S. Chopin and trawlers.

**Ice Skates — A278**

**Snowflake and Cyclist — A279**

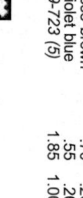

**1956, Mar. 7    Photo.    Perf. 12½**
| | | | | |
|---|---|---|---|---|
| 724 | A278 | 20g brt ultra & blk | 4.00 | 1.50 |
| 725 | A278 | 40g brn grn & vio bl | .55 | .20 |
| 726 | A278 | 60g lilac & lake | 5.10 | 1.90 |
| | | Nos. 724-726 (3) | | |

Designs: 40g, Snowflake and Ice Hockey sticks, 60g, Snowflake and Skis.
XI World Students Winter Sport Championship, Mar. 7-13.

**1956, Apr. 25    Unwmk.**
| | | | | |
|---|---|---|---|---|
| 727 | A279 | 40g dark blue | 1.25 | .40 |
| 728 | A279 | 60g dark green | .20 | .20 |

9th Intl. Peace Bicycle Race, Warsaw-Berlin-Prague, May 1-15.

Zakopane Mountains and Shelter — A280

40g, Map, compass & knapsack. 60g, Map of Poland & canoe. 1.15z, Skis & mountains.

**1956, May 25**
| | | | | |
|---|---|---|---|---|
| 729 | A280 | 30g dark green | .30 | .20 |
| 730 | A280 | 40g lt red brown | .30 | .20 |
| 731 | A280 | 60g blue | 1.10 | .50 |
| 732 | A280 | 1.15z dull purple | .55 | .20 |
| | | Nos. 729-732 (4) | 2.25 | 1.10 |

Polish Tourist industry.

No. 593 Surcharged with New Values

**1956, July 6    Engr.    Perf. 12½**
| | | | | |
|---|---|---|---|---|
| 733 | A232 | 10g on 80g dp plum | .35 | .20 |
| 734 | A232 | 40g on 80g dp plum | .30 | .20 |
| 735 | A232 | 60g on 80g dp plum | .55 | .20 |
| 736 | A232 | 1.35z on 80g dp plum | 1.25 | .70 |
| | | Nos. 733-736 (4) | 2.45 | 1.30 |

The size and type of surcharge and obliteration of old value differ for each denomination.

Type of 1955

Warsaw Monuments: 30g, Ghetto Monument. 40g, John III Sobieski. 1.55z, Prince Joseph Poniatowski.

**1956, July 10**
| | | | | |
|---|---|---|---|---|
| 737 | A260 | 30g black | .25 | .20 |
| 738 | A260 | 40g red brn, grnsh | .50 | .25 |
| 739 | A260 | 1.55z vio brn, pnksh | 1.45 | .70 |
| | | Nos. 737-739 (3) | | |

No. 737 measures 22½x28mm, instead of 21x27mm.

Polish and Russian Dancers A281

**1956, Sept. 14    Litho.    Perf. 12**
| | | | | |
|---|---|---|---|---|
| 740 | A281 | 40g brn red & brn | .35 | .20 |
| 741 | A281 | 60g bister & red | .20 | .20 |

Polish-Soviet Friendship month.

Ludwiga Warzynska and Children — A282

**1956, Sept. 17    Photo.    Perf. 12½**
| | | | | |
|---|---|---|---|---|
| 742 | A282 | 40g dull red brown | .70 | .20 |
| 743 | A282 | 60g blue | .30 | .20 |

Issued in honor of a heroic school teacher who saved three children from a burning house.

Bee on Clover and Beehive — A283

**1956, Oct. 30    Litho.    Unwmk.**
| | | | | |
|---|---|---|---|---|
| 744 | A283 | 40g org yel & brn | .95 | .35 |
| 745 | A283 | 60g yellow & brn | .30 | .20 |

50th death anniv. of Father Jan Dzierzon, the inventor of the modernized beehive.

Design: 60g, Father Jan Dzierzon.

"Lady with the Ermine" by Leonardo da Vinci A284

40g, Niobe. 60g, Madonna by Veit Stoss.

**1956    Engr.    Perf. 11½x11**
| | | | | |
|---|---|---|---|---|
| 746 | A284 | 40g dark green | 2.50 | 1.25 |
| 747 | A284 | 60g dark violet | .75 | .20 |
| 748 | A284 | 1.55z chocolate | 1.75 | .70 |
| | | | 5.00 | 1.65 |
| | | Nos. 746-748 (3) | | |

Intl. Museum Week (UNESCO), Oct. 8-14.

Fencer A285

Designs: 20g, Boxer. 25g, Sculling. 40g, Steeplechase racer. 60g, Javelin thrower. No. 755, Woman gymnast. No. 756, Woman broad jumper.

**1956    Engr.    Perf. 11½**
| | | | | |
|---|---|---|---|---|
| 750 | A285 | 10g slate & chnt | .20 | .20 |
| 751 | A285 | 20g lt brn & dl vio | .25 | .20 |
| a. | | Center inverted | | |
| 752 | A285 | 25g lt blue & blk | .40 | .20 |
| 753 | A285 | 40g brt brn & redsh brn | .30 | .20 |
| 754 | A285 | 60g rose car & ol brn | .40 | .20 |
| 755 | A285 | 1.55z lt vio & sepia | 1.50 | 1.00 |
| 756 | A285 | 1.55z orange & chnt | 1.00 | 2.25 |
| | | | 4.05 | 2.25 |
| | | Nos. 750-756 (7) | | |

16th Olympic Games, Melbourne, 11/22-12/8.

Design: 60g, Open book and cogwheels.

15th Century Mailman — A286

**Lithographed and Engraved**
**1956, Nov. 30    Unwmk.    Perf. 12½**
| | | | | |
|---|---|---|---|---|
| 757 | A286 | 60g lt blue & blk | 1.65 | .80 |

Reopening of the Postal Museum in Wroclaw.

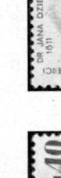

Ski Jumper and Snowflake — A288

Skier and Snowflake A287

Design: 1z, Skier in right corner.

**1957, Jan. 18    Photo.    Perf. 12½**
| | | | | |
|---|---|---|---|---|
| 758 | A287 | 40g blue | .25 | .20 |
| 759 | A288 | 60g dark green | .25 | .20 |
| 760 | A287 | 1z purple | 1.00 | .70 |
| | | Nos. 758-760 (3) | | |

50 years of skiing in Poland.

Globe and Tree A289

UN Emblem — A290

UN Building, NY — A291

**1957, Feb. 26    Photo.    Perf. 12**
| | | | | |
|---|---|---|---|---|
| 761 | A289 | 5g mag & brt grnsh bl | .35 | .20 |
| 762 | A290 | 15g blue & gray | .40 | .20 |
| 763 | A291 | 40g brt bl grn & gray | .75 | .45 |
| | | | 1.50 | .85 |

Issued in honor of the United Nations.
Exist imperf. Value, set $4.25.

An imperf. souvenir sheet exists, containing a 1.50z stamp in a redrawn design similar to A291. The stamp is blue and bright bluish green. Value, $25 unused, $14 canceled.

Skier — A292

Sword, Foil and Saber on World Map — A293

**1957, Mar. 22    Perf. 12½**
| | | | | |
|---|---|---|---|---|
| 764 | A292 | 60g blue | .60 | .25 |
| 765 | A292 | 60g brown | .00 | .30 |

12th anniv. of the death of the skiers Bronislaw Czech and Hanna Maruszarzowna.

**1957, Apr. 20    Unwmk.    Perf. 12½**
Designs: No. 767, Fencer facing right. No. 768, Fencer facing left.
| | | | | |
|---|---|---|---|---|
| 766 | A293 | 40g deep plum | .55 | .30 |
| 767 | A293 | 60g carmine | .40 | .20 |
| 768 | A293 | 60g ultra | 1.25 | .50 |
| a. | | Pair. #767-768 | | |

World Youth Fencing Championships, Warsaw.
No. 768a has continuous design.

Bicycle Wheel and Carnation A295

Dr. Sebastian Petrycy A294

Doctors' Portraits: 20g, Wojciech Oczko. 40g, Jedrzej Sniadecki. 60g, Tytus Chalubinski. 1z, Wladyslaw Bieganski. 1.35z, Jozef Dietl. 2.50z, Benedykt Dybowski. 3z, Henryk Jordan.

**Portraits Engr., Inscriptions Typo.**
**1957          Perf. 11½**
| | | | | |
|---|---|---|---|---|
| 769 | A294 | 10g sepia & ultra | .20 | .20 |
| 770 | A294 | 20g emerald & claret | .20 | .20 |
| 771 | A294 | 40g gray & org red | .20 | .20 |
| 772 | A294 | 60g blue & pale brn | .50 | .20 |
| 773 | A294 | 1z org & dk blue | .20 | .20 |
| 774 | A294 | 1.35z gray brn & grn | .20 | .20 |
| 775 | A294 | 2.50z dull vio & lil rose | .25 | .20 |
| 776 | A294 | 3z violet & brn | 2.00 | 1.60 |
| | | Nos. 769-776 (8) | | |

**1957, May 4    Photo.    Perf. 12½**
| | | | | |
|---|---|---|---|---|
| 777 | A295 | 60g shown | .55 | .20 |
| 778 | A295 | 1.50z Cyclist | .20 | .20 |

10th Intl. Peace Bicycle Race, Warsaw-Berlin-Prague.

Poznan Fair Emblem — A296

Turk's Cap — A297

**1957, June 8    Litho.    Unwmk.**
| | | | | |
|---|---|---|---|---|
| 779 | A296 | 60g ultramarine | .25 | .20 |
| 780 | A296 | 2.50z lt blue green | .30 | .20 |

Issued to publicize the 26th Fair at Poznan.

**1957, Aug. 12    Photo.    Perf. 12**
Flowers: 20g, Carline Thistle. No. 783, Sea Holly. No. 784, Edelweiss. No. 785, Lady's-slipper.
| | | | | |
|---|---|---|---|---|
| 781 | A297 | 60g bl grn & claret | .25 | .20 |
| 782 | A297 | 60g gray, grn & yol | .25 | .20 |
| 783 | A297 | 60g lt bluc & grn | .25 | .20 |
| 784 | A297 | 60g lt yel grn | .20 | .20 |
| 785 | A297 | 60g lt grn, mar & yel | 1.00 | .25 |
| | | Nos. 781-785 (5) | 2.00 | 1.05 |

Town Hall, Leipzig and Congress Emblem — A299

Fire Fighter — A298

60g, Child & flames. 2.50z, Grain & flames.

**1957, Sept. 11    Perf. 12**
| | | | | |
|---|---|---|---|---|
| 786 | A298 | 40g black & red | .20 | .20 |
| 787 | A298 | 60g dk grn & org red | .50 | .20 |
| 788 | A298 | 2.50z violet & blk | .90 | .60 |
| | | Nos. 786-788 (3) | | |

**1957, Sept. 25    Photo.    Perf. 12½**
| | | | | |
|---|---|---|---|---|
| 789 | A299 | 60g violet | .20 | .20 |

4th Intl. Trade Union Cong., Leipzig, Oct. 4-15.

"Girl Writing Letter" by Fragonard A300

## Karol Libelt — A301

**1957, Oct. 9** — **Perf. 12**
790 A300 2.50z dark blue green — .50 .20
Issued for Stamp Day, Oct. 9.

**1957, Nov. 15** — **Photo.** — **Perf. 12½**
791 A301 60g carmine lake — .20 .20
Centenary of the Poznan Scientific Society and to honor Karol Libelt, politician and philosopher.

## Jan A. Komensky (Comenius) A303

## Broken Chain and Flag — A302

**1957, Nov. 7**
792 A302 60g brt blue & red — .25 .20
793 A302 2.50z black & red brn — .25 .20
40th anniv. of the Russian Revolution.

**1957, Dec. 11** — **Unwmk.** — **Perf. 12**
794 A303 2.50z brt carmine — .25 .20
300th anniv. of the publication of "Didactica Opera Omnia."

Design: 2.50z, Lenin Statue, Poronin.

## Henri Wieniawski A304
## Andrzej Strug A305

**1957, Dec. 2** — **Perf. 12½**
795 A304 2.50z blue — .25 .20
3rd Wieniawski Violin Competition in Poznan.

**1957, Dec. 16** — **Unwmk.** — **Perf. 12½**
796 A305 2.50z brown — .20 .20
20th death anniv. of Andrzej Strug, novelist.

## Joseph Conrad and "Torrens" A306

**1957, Dec. 30** — **Engr.** — **Perf. 12x12½**
797 A306 60g brown, grnsh — .20 .20
798 A306 2.50z dk blue, pink — .45 .20
Birth cent. of Joseph Conrad, Polish-born English writer.

## Postillion and Stylized Plane — A307
## Town Hall at Biecz — A308

**1958**
Designs: 40g, plane and satellite. 60g, St. Mary's Church, Cracow, mail coach and plane. 95g, Mail coach and postal bus. 2.10z, Medieval postman and train. 3.40z, Medieval galleon and modern ships.

799 A307 40g lt blue & vio brn — .20 .20
800 A307 60g pale vio & blk — .20 .20
801 A307 95g lemon & violet — .45 .35
802 A307 2.10z gray & ultra — .45 .35
803 A307 2.50z brt blue & blk — .35 .35
804 A307 3.40z aqua & maroon — .35 .25
Nos. 799-804 (6) — 1.75 1.40
400th anniversary of the Polish posts. Imperfs. exist of all but No. 803.

**1958, Mar. 29** — **Engr.** — **Perf. 12½**
Town Halls: 40g, Wroclaw. 60g, Tarnow, horiz. 2.10z, Danzig. 2.50z, Zamosc.
805 A308 20g green — .20 .20
806 A308 40g brown — .20 .20
807 A308 60g dark blue — .30 .20
808 A308 2.10z rose lake — .30 .20
809 A308 2.50z violet — .45 .20
Nos. 805-809 (5) — 1.35 1.00

## Giant Pike Perch A309

**1958, Apr. 22** — **Photo.** — **Perf. 12**
Fishes: 60g, Salmon, vert. 2.10z, Pike, vert. 2.50z, Trout, vert. 6.40z, Grayling.
810 A309 40g bl, blk, grn & yel — .20 .20
811 A309 60g yel grn, dk grn & bl — .20 .20
812 A309 2.10z dk bl, grn & yel — .40 .20
813 A309 2.50z pur, blk & yel grn — 1.50 .30
814 A309 6.40z bl grn, brn & red — .90 .35
Nos. 810-814 (5) — 3.20 1.25

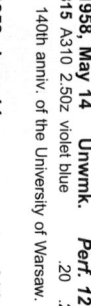

## Casimir Palace, Warsaw University A310
## Stylized Glider and Cloud A311

**1958, May 14** — **Unwmk.** — **Perf. 12½**
815 A310 2.50z violet blue — .20 .20
140th anniv. of the University of Warsaw.

**1958, June 14** — **Litho.**
816 A311 60g gray blue & blk — .20 .20
817 A311 2.50z gray & blk — .35 .20
7th Intl. Glider Competitions.
Design: 2.50z, Design reversed.

## Fair Emblem — A312
## Armed Postman and Mail Box — A313

**1958, June 9** — **Perf. 11**
818 A312 2.50z black & rose — .20 .20
27th Fair at Poznan.

**1958, Sept. 1** — **Engr.** — **Perf. 11**
819 A313 60g dark blue — .20 .20
19th anniv. of the defense of the Polish post office at Danzig (Gdansk). Inscribed: "You were the first."

## Letter, Quill and Postmark A314
## Polar Bear A315

**1958, Sept. 30** — **Photo.** — **Perf. 12½x12**
Design: 2.50z, Rocket and Sputnik.
821 A315 60g black — .20 .20
822 A315 2.50z dark blue — .55 .20
Intl. Geophysical Year.

**1958, Oct. 9** — **Litho.**
820 A314 60g blk, brn & ver — .50 .25
Issued for Stamp Day. Exists imperf.

## Partisan's Cross — A316

**1958, Oct. 10** — **Perf. 11**
823 A316 40g black, grn & ochre — .20 .20
824 A316 60g black, blue & yel — .20 .20
825 A316 2.50z multicolored — .60 .20
Nos. 823-825 (3) — 1.00 .60
Designs: 60g, Virtuti Militari Cross. 2.50z, Grunwald Cross. Polish People's Army, 15th anniv.

## 17th Century Ship — A317
## UNESCO Building, Paris — A318

Design: 2.50z, Polish immigrants.

## Stagecoach — A319

**1958, Oct. 26** — **Engr.** — **Perf. 12½**
829 A319 2.50z slate, buff — 1.00 .50
a. Souvenir sheet of 6 — 7.50 7.50
Philatelic exhibition in honor of the 400th anniv. of the Polish post, Warsaw, Oct. 25-Nov. 10.

**1958, Oct. 29** — **Perf. 11**
826 A317 60g slate grn — .20 .20
827 A317 2.50z carmine rose — .25 .20
350th anniversary of the arrival of the first Polish immigrants in America.

**1958, Nov. 3** — **Unwmk.**
828 A318 2.50z yellow grn & blk — .45 .20
UNESCO Headquarters in Paris, opening, Nov. 3.

**1958, Dec. 12** — **Unwmk.** — **Imperf.**
**Souvenir Sheet** — **Printed on Silk**
**Wmk. 326**
830 A319 50z dark blue — 12.00 10.00
400th anniversary of the Polish posts.

## Stanislaw Wyspianski A320
## Kneeling Figure A321

**1958, Nov. 25** — **Engr.** — **Perf. 12½**
Portrait: 2.50z, Stanislaw Moniuszko.
831 A320 60g dark violet — .35 .20
832 A320 2.50z dk slate grn — .35 .20
Stanislaw Wyspianski, painter and poet, and Stanislaw Moniuszko, composer.

## Red Flag — A322
## Sailing — A323

**1958, Dec. 10** — **Litho.**
833 A321 2.50z lt brn & red brn — .35 .20
Signing of the Universal Declaration of Human Rights, 10th anniv.

**1958, Dec. 16** — **Photo.**
834 A322 60g plum & red — .20 .20
Communist Party of Poland, 40th anniv.

**1959, Jan. 3**
835 A323 40g lt bl & vio bl — .20 .20
836 A323 60g salmon & brn vio — .30 .20
837 A323 95g green & brn vio — .30 .20
838 A323 2z dp bl & lt grn — 1.00 .80
Nos. 835-838 (4)
Sports: 60g, Girl archer. 95g, Soccer. 2z, Horsemanship.

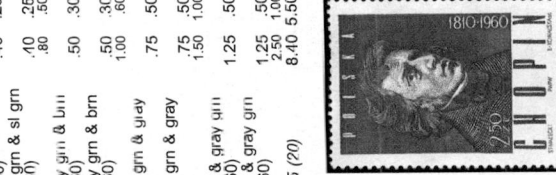

Man from Rzeszow — A341

Woman from Rzeszow — A342

Regional Costumes: 40g, Cracow. 60g, Kurpiow. 1z, Silesia. 2z, Lowicz. 2.50z, Mountain people. 3.10z, Kujawy. 3.40z, Lublin. 5.60z, Szamotuli. 6.50z, Lubuski.

### Engraved and Photogravure

**1959-60  Wmk. 326  Perf. 12, Imperf.**

| | | | |
|---|---|---|---|
| 886 | A341 | 20g slate grn & blk | .20 .20 |
| 887 | A341 | 20g slate grn & blk | .20 .20 |
| | | Pair, #886-887 | |
| 888 | A341 | 40g lt bl & rose car | .20 .20 |
| | | (60) | |
| 889 | A342 | 40g rose car & bl | .20 .20 |
| | | (60) | |
| | a. | Pair, #888-889 | |
| 890 | A341 | 60g black & pink | .20 .20 |
| 891 | A341 | 60g black & pink | .20 .20 |
| | a. | Pair, #890-891 | |
| 892 | A341 | 1z grnsh red & dk red | .20 |
| 893 | A342 | 1z grnsh bl & dk red | .20 |
| | a. | Pair, #892-893 | |
| 894 | A341 | 2z yel & ultra (60) | .20 .25 |
| 895 | A342 | 2z yel & ultra (60) | .20 .20 |
| | | Pair, #894-895 | .40 |
| 896 | A341 | 2.50z green & rose lll | .30 .30 |
| 897 | A342 | 2.50z green & rose lll bl | .30 .40 |
| | | Pair, #896-897 | .60 |
| 898 | A341 | 3.10z yel grn & sl grn (60) | .40 .25 |
| 899 | A342 | 3.10z yel grn & sl grn (60) | .40 |
| | a. | Pair, #898-899 | .80 .50 |
| 900 | A341 | 3.40z gray grn & brn (60) | .50 .30 |
| 901 | A342 | 3.40z gray grn & brn (60) | .50 |
| | a. | Pair, #900-901 | 1.00 .60 |
| 902 | A341 | 5.60z yel grn & gray bl (60) | .75 .50 |
| 903 | A342 | 5.60z yel grn & gray bl (60) | .75 |
| | a. | Pair, #902-903 | 1.50 1.00 |
| 904 | A311 | 6.50z vio & gray grn (60) | 1.25 .50 |
| 905 | A312 | 6.50z vio & gray grn (60) | 1.25 |
| | a. | Pair, #904-905 | 2.50 1.00 |
| | | Nos. 886-905 (20) | 8.40 5.50 |

Frederic Chopin — A344

Piano — A343

Design: 1.50z, Musical note and manuscript.

**1960, Feb. 22  Litho.  Perf. 12**

| | | | |
|---|---|---|---|
| 906 | A343 | 60g brt violet & blk | .40 .35 |
| 907 | A343 | 1.50z black, gray & red | .60 .25 |

**Engr.**

| | | | |
|---|---|---|---|
| 908 | A344 | 2.50z black | 2.50 .90 |
| | | Nos. 906-908 (3) | 3.50 1.50 |

150th anniversary of the birth of Frederic Chopin and to publicize the Chopin music competition.

---

**Perf. 11  Size: 23x23mm**

| | | | |
|---|---|---|---|
| 870 | A335 | 2.50z red, pink & blk | .65 .35 |
| | | Nos. 868-870 (3) | 1.05 .75 |

Polish Red Cross, 40th anniv.; Red Cross, cent.

Flower Made of Stamps — A337

Polish-Chinese Friendship Society Emblem — A336

**Wmk. 326**

**1959, Sept. 28  Litho.  Perf. 11**

| | | | |
|---|---|---|---|
| 871 | A336 | 60g multicolored | .45 .20 |
| 872 | A336 | 2.50z multicolored | .30 .20 |

Polish-Chinese friendship.

**1959, Oct. 9  Perf. 12½**

| | | | |
|---|---|---|---|
| 873 | A337 | 60g lt grnsh bl, grn & red | .20 .20 |
| 874 | A337 | 2.50z red, grn & vio | .35 .20 |

Issued for Stamp Day, 1959.

Sputnik 3 — A338

60g, Luna I, sun. 2.50z, Earth, moon, Sputnik 2.

**1959, Nov. 7  Photo.  Wmk. 326**

| | | | |
|---|---|---|---|
| 875 | A338 | 40g Prus blue & gray | .25 .20 |
| 876 | A338 | 60g maroon & black | .30 .20 |
| 877 | A338 | 2.50z green & dk blue | .90 .50 |
| | | Nos. 875-877 (3) | 1.45 .90 |

42nd anniv. of the Russian Revolution and the landing of the Soviet moon rocket. Exist imperf. Value, set $3.

Charles Darwin A340

Child Doing Homework A339

Design: 60g, Three children leaving school.

### Lithographed and Engraved

**1959, Nov. 14  Perf. 11½**

| | | | |
|---|---|---|---|
| 878 | A339 | 40g green & dk brn | .20 .20 |
| 879 | A339 | 60g blue & red | .20 .20 |

"1,000 Schools" campaign for the 1,000th anniversary of Poland.

Scientists: 40g, Dmitri I. Mendeleev. 60g, Albert Einstein. 1.50z, Louis Pasteur. 1.55z, Isaac Newton. 2.50z, Nicolaus Copernicus.

**1959, Dec. 10  Engr.  Perf. 11**

| | | | |
|---|---|---|---|
| 880 | A340 | 20g dark brn | .20 .20 |
| 881 | A340 | 40g olive gray | .20 .20 |
| 882 | A340 | 60g claret | .20 .20 |
| 883 | A340 | 1.55z dk violet brn | .20 .20 |
| 884 | A340 | 1.55z dark green | .45 .20 |
| 885 | A340 | 2.50z violet | 1.00 .50 |
| | | Nos. 880-885 (6) | 2.25 1.50 |

---

Map of Austria and Flower A331

Lazarus Ludwig Zamenhof A330

Design: 1.50z, Star, globe and flag.

**1959, July 24  Perf. 12½**

| | | | |
|---|---|---|---|
| 859 | A330 | 60g blk & grn, ol | .20 .20 |
| 860 | A330 | 1.50z ultra, grn & red, gray | .40 .20 |

Centenary of the birth of Lazarus Ludwig Zamenhof, author of Esperanto, and in conjunction with the Esperanto Congress in Warsaw.

**1959, July 27  Litho.**

| | | | |
|---|---|---|---|
| 861 | A331 | 60g sep, red & grn, yel | .20 .20 |
| 862 | A331 | 2.50z bl, red, & grn, gray | .45 .20 |

7th World Youth Festival, Vienna, July 26-Aug. 14.

Symbolic Plane — A332

**1959, Aug. 24  Wmk. 326  Perf. 12½**

| | | | |
|---|---|---|---|
| 863 | A332 | 60g vio bl, grnsh bl & blk | .20 .20 |

30th anniv. of LOT, the Polish airline.

Sejm (Parliament) Building — A333

**1959, Aug. 27  Photo.  Perf. 12x12½**

| | | | |
|---|---|---|---|
| 864 | A333 | 60g lt grn, blk & red | .20 .20 |
| 865 | A333 | 2.50z vio gray, blk & red | .40 .20 |

48th Interparliamentary Conf., Warsaw.

No. 640 Overprinted in Blue: "BALPEX — GDANSK 1959"

**1959, Aug. 30  Engr.  Unwmk.**

| | | | |
|---|---|---|---|
| 866 | A253 | 45g brown, red | .65 .50 |

Intl. Phil. Exhib. of Baltic States at Gdansk.

Red Cross Nurse — A335

Stylized Dove and Globe — A334

**1959, Sept. 1  Wmk. 326  Photo.  Perf. 12½**

| | | | |
|---|---|---|---|
| 867 | A334 | 60g blue & gray | .20 .20 |

World Peace Movement, 10th anniv.

**1959, Sept. 21  Litho.  Perf. 12½**

Designs: 60g, Nurse. 2.50z, Henri Dunant.

**Size: 21x26mm**

| | | | |
|---|---|---|---|
| 868 | A335 | 40g red, lt grn & blk | .20 .20 |
| 869 | A335 | 60g bis brn, brn & red | .20 .20 |

---

Hand at Wheel — A324

Wheat, Hammer and Flag — A325

**1959, Mar. 10  Wmk. 326  Perf. 12½**

| | | | |
|---|---|---|---|
| 839 | A324 | 40gr shown | .20 .20 |
| 840 | A325 | 60gr shown | .20 .20 |
| 841 | A324 | 1.55z Factory | .40 .60 |
| | | Nos. 839-841 (3) | |

3rd Workers Congress.

Amanita Phalloides — A326

Designs: Various mushrooms.

**1959, May 8  Photo.  Perf. 11½**

| | | | |
|---|---|---|---|
| 842 | A326 | 20g yel, grn & brn | 1.40 .75 |
| 843 | A326 | 30g multicolored | .20 .20 |
| 844 | A326 | 40g multicolored | .60 .20 |
| 845 | A326 | 60g yel grn, brn & ocher | .20 .20 |
| 846 | A326 | 1z multicolored | .60 .20 |
| 847 | A326 | 2.50z dull purple | .40 .40 |
| 848 | A326 | 3.40z multicolored | 1.10 .40 |
| 849 | A326 | 5.60z dl yel, brn & grn | 3.00 1.50 |
| | | Nos. 842-849 (8) | 8.10 3.65 |

"Storks," by Jozef Chelmonski A327

Paintings by Polish Artists: 60g, Mother and Child, Stanislaw Wyspianski, vert. 1z, Mme. de Romanet, Henryk Rodakowski, vert. 1.50z, Old Man and Death, Jacek Malczewski, vert. 6.40z, River Scene, Aleksander Gierymski.

**1959  Engr.  Perf. 12, 12½x12**

| | | | |
|---|---|---|---|
| 850 | A326 | 40g gray green | .20 .20 |
| 851 | A327 | 60g dull purple | .25 .20 |
| 852 | A327 | 1z intense black | .30 .30 |
| 853 | A327 | 1.50z brown | .50 .30 |
| 854 | A327 | 6.40z blue | 2.25 .70 |
| | | Nos. 850-854 (5) | 3.50 1.60 |

Nos. 850 and 854 measure 36x28mm; Nos. 851 and 853, 28x36mm; No. 852, 28x37mm.

Miner and Globe A328

**1959, July 1  Litho.**

| | | | |
|---|---|---|---|
| 855 | A328 | 2.50z multicolored | .45 .20 |

3rd Miners' Conf., Katowice, July 1959.

**1959, July 21  Wmk. 326  Perf. 12x12½**

Symbol of Industry A329

Map of Poland and: 40g, Map of Poland and Symbol of Industry. 1.50z, Symbol of art and science.

| | | | |
|---|---|---|---|
| 856 | A329 | 40g black, bl & grn | .20 .20 |
| 857 | A329 | 60g black & ver | .20 .20 |
| 858 | A329 | 1.50z black & blue | .60 .60 |
| | | Nos. 856-858 (3) | |

15 years of the Peoples' Republic of Poland.

Stamp of 1860
A345

100 LAT POLSKIEGO ZNACZKA POCZTOWEGO

Designs: 60g, Ski meet stamp of 1939. 1.35z, Design from 1860 issue. 1.55z, 1945 liberation stamp. 2.50z, 1957 stamp day stamp.

**1960, Mar. 21**    **Perf. 11½x11**
**Litho. (40g, 1.35z); Litho. and Photo.**

| | | | | |
|---|---|---|---|---|
| 909 | A345 | 40g multicolored | .20 | .20 |
| 910 | A345 | 60g violet, ultra & blk | .30 | .20 |
| 911 | A345 | 1.35z gray, red & bl | .75 | .40 |
| 912 | A345 | 1.55z green, car & blk | .75 | .25 |
| 913 | A345 | 2.50z ap grn, dk grn & blk | | |

a. Block of 4, #918-921 | 1.00 | .45
Nos. 909-913 (5) | 3.00 | 1.50

Centenary of Polish stamps. Nos. 909-913 were also issued in sheets of 4. Value, $275. For overprint see No. 934.

Discus Thrower, Amsterdam
1928 — A346

**1960, June 15**    **Perf. 12½x12½**
**Lithographed and Embossed**

**Wmk. 326**    **Unwmk.**

| | | | | |
|---|---|---|---|---|
| 914 | A346 | 60g blue & blk | .20 | .20 |
| 915 | A346 | 60g car rose & blk | .20 | .20 |
| 916 | A346 | 60g violet & blk | .20 | .20 |
| 917 | A346 | 60g blue grn & blk | .20 | .20 |

a. Block of 4, #914-917 | .80 | .40
| 918 | A346 | 2.50z ultra & blk | .55 | .25 |
| 919 | A346 | 2.50z chestnut & blk | .55 | .25 |
| 920 | A346 | 2.50z red & blk | .55 | .25 |
| 921 | A346 | 2.50z emerald & blk | .55 | .25 |

a. Block of 4, #918-921 | 2.50 | 1.00
Nos. 914-921 (8) | 3.00 | 1.80

17th Olympic Games, Rome, 8/25-9/11. Nos. 917a and 921a have continuous design forming the stadium oval. Nos. 914-921 exist imperf. Value, set $5.

Polish Olympic Victories: No. 915, Runner. No. 916, Bicyclist. No. 917, Steeplechase. No. 918, Trumpeters. No. 919, Boxers. No. 920, Olympic flame. No. 921 Woman jumper.

Tomb of King Wladyslaw II Jagiello — A347

**1960**
| 922 | A347 | 60g violet brown | .35 | .20 |
| 923 | A347 | 90g olive gray | .70 | .35 |

90g, Detail from Grunwald monument.

Battle of Grunwald by Jan Matejko — A348

**1960**    **Perf. 11x11½**
**Wmk. 326**    **Engr.**

924 A348 2.50z dark gray | 2.00 | 1.10
Nos. 922-924 (3) | 3.05 | 1.65

**Size: 78x37mm**

550th anniversary, Battle of Grunwald.

The Annunciation — A349

Carvings by Veit Stoss, St. Mary's Church, Cracow: 30g, Nativity. 40g, Adoration of the Kings. 60g, The Resurrection. 2.50z, The Ascension. 5.60z, Descent of the Holy Ghost. 10z, The Assumption of the Virgin, vert.

**1960**    **Wmk. 326**    **Engr. Perf. 12**

| 925 | A349 | 20g Prus blue | .25 | .20 |
| 926 | A349 | 30g lt red brown | .25 | .20 |
| 927 | A349 | 40g violet | .25 | .20 |
| 928 | A349 | 60g dull green | .25 | .20 |
| 929 | A349 | 5.60z rose lake | .80 | .20 |
| 930 | A349 | 5.60z dark brown | .55 | .20 |
Nos. 925-930 (6) | 2.75 | .75

**Miniature Sheet**
**Imperf**

931 A349 10z black | 6.00 | 5.00
No. 931 contains one vertical stamp which measures 72x95mm.

A351

**1960, Sept. 26**    **Perf. 12½**

932 A350 2.50z black | .35 | .20

Birth cent. of Ignacy Jan Paderewski, statesman and musician.

A350

**1960, Sept. 14**    **Perf. 11**
**Engr. & Photo.**

933 A351 60g citron & black | .20 | .20

5th Pharmaceutical Congress; Ignacy Lukasiewicz, chemist-pharmacist.
Lukasiewicz and kerosene lamp.

**No. 909 Overprinted: "DZIEN ZNACZKA 1960"**

**1960**    **Litho.**    **Perf. 11½x11**

934 A345 40g multicolored | 1.25 | .60

Issued for Stamp Day, 1960.

Great Bustard A352

**1960**    **Unwmk. Photo. Perf. 11½**
**Birds in Natural Colors**

| 935 | A352 | 10g gray & blk | .20 | .20 |
| 936 | A352 | 20g gray & blk | .20 | .20 |
| 937 | A352 | 30g gray & blk | .20 | .20 |
| 938 | A352 | 40g gray & blk | .25 | .20 |
| 939 | A352 | 60g pale grn & blk | .30 | .20 |
| 940 | A352 | 60g pale grn & blk | .30 | .20 |
| 941 | A352 | 75g pale grn & blk | .40 | .20 |
| 942 | A352 | 90g pale grn & blk | .55 | .20 |
| 943 | A352 | 2.50z pale ol gray & blk | | |
| 944 | A352 | 4z pale ol gray & blk | 3.50 | 1.25 |
| 945 | A352 | 5.60z pale ol gray & blk | 2.50 | .55 |
| 946 | A352 | 6.50z pale ol gray & blk | 4.25 | .60 |
Nos. 935-946 (12) | 18.75 | 6.00

Birds: 20g, Raven. 30g, Great cormorant. 40g, Black stork. 50g, Eagle owl. 60g, White-tailed sea eagle. 75g, Golden eagle. 90g, Short-toed eagle. 2.50z, Rock thrush. 4z, European kingfisher. 5.60z, Wall creeper. 6.50z, European roller.

Ice Hockey A355

Part of Cogwheel A356

Front Page of "Merkuriusz" A354

**1960**    **Engr. Perf. 11½, 13x12½**

| 947 | A353 | 5g red brown | .20 | .20 |
| 948 | A353 | 10g green | .20 | .20 |
| 949 | A353 | 20g dark brown | .20 | .20 |
| 950 | A353 | 40g vermilion | .20 | .20 |
| 951 | A353 | 50g violet | .20 | .20 |
| 952 | A353 | 60g rose claret | .30 | .20 |
| 952A | A353 | 60g lt ultra ('61) | .30 | .20 |
| 953 | A353 | 80g blue | .30 | .20 |
| 954 | A353 | 90g brown ('61) | .30 | .20 |
| 955 | A353 | 95g olive gray | .20 | .20 |

**Engraved and Lithographed**

| 956 | A353 | 1z orange & gray | .40 | .20 |
| 957 | A353 | 1.15z slate grn & sal | .20 | .20 |
| 958 | A353 | 1.35z lil rose & lt grn | .20 | .20 |
| 959 | A353 | 1.50z sep & pale grn | .20 | .20 |
| 960 | A353 | 2z car lake & buff | .30 | .20 |
| 961 | A353 | 1.55z sepia & yel | .30 | .25 |
| 962 | A353 | 2.10z dk blue & pink | .25 | .25 |
| 963 | A353 | 2.50z di vio & pale | | |
| 964 | A353 | 3.10z ver & gray | .45 | .20 |
| 965 | A353 | 5.60z sl grn & lt grn | 1.10 | |
Nos. 947-965 (20) | 5.70 | 4.00

Historic Towns: 10g, Cracow. 20g, Warsaw. 40g, Poznan. 50g, Plock. 60g, Kalisz. No. 952A, Tczew. 80g, Frombork. 90g, Torun. 95g, Puck (ships). 1z, Slupsk. 1.15z, Gdansk (Danzig). 1.35z, Wroclaw. 1.50z, Szczecin. 1.55z, Opole. 2z, Kolobrzeg. 2.10z, Legnica. 2.50z, Katowice. 3.10z, Lodz. 5.60z, Welbrzych.

**1960-61**

Emblem of Poznan Fair — A358

**1961, May 25**    **Litho. Perf. 12½x12**

977 A358 40g brt bl, blk & red org | .20 | .20
978 A358 1.50z red org, blk & brt | .20 | .20

a. Souvenir sheet of 2 | 2.00 | 1.90

30th Int. Fair at Poznan.
No. 978a contains two of No. 978 with simulated perforation and blue marginal inscriptions. Sold for 4.50z. Issued July 29, 1961.

Famous Poles A359

| 979 | A359 | 60g chalky blue | .20 | .20 |
| 980 | A359 | 60g deep rose | .20 | .20 |
| 981 | A359 | 60g slate | .20 | .20 |
| 982 | A359 | 60g dull violet | .65 | .20 |
| 983 | A359 | 60g lt brown | .20 | .20 |
| 984 | A359 | 60g olive gray | .20 | .20 |
Nos. 979-984 (6) | 1.65 | 1.20

No. 979, Mieszko I. No. 980, Casimir Wielki. No. 981, Casimir Jagiello. No. 982, Nicolaus Copernicus. No. 983, Andrzej Frycz-Modrzewski. No. 984, Tadeusz Kosciuszko.

See Nos. 1059-1064, 1152-1155.

Maj. Yuri A. Gagarin A357

**1961, Apr. 27**    **Photo. Perf. 12**

| 969 | A357 | 40g lt violet, blk & yel | .40 | .20 |
| 970 | A357 | 60g lt ultra, blk & car | .40 | .30 |
| 971 | A357 | 1z lt blue, lt & red | 6.00 | 2.00 |
| 972 | A357 | 1.50z grnsh bl, blk & blk yel | | |
Nos. 969-972 (4) | 7.45 | 2.90

1st man in space, Yuri A. Gagarin, Apr. 12, 1961.

Design: 60g, Globe and path of rocket.

Trawler — A360

**1961, June 24**    **Unwmk.**
**Litho.**    **Perf. 11**

| 985 | A360 | 60g multicolored | .20 | .20 |
| 986 | A360 | 60g multicolored | .20 | .20 |
| 987 | A360 | 1.55z multicolored | .35 | .20 |
| 988 | A360 | 2.50z multicolored | .50 | .20 |
| 989 | A360 | 3.40z multicolored | .80 | .30 |

Designs: Various Polish Cargo Ships.

**1961, June 15**
**Photogravure and Engraved**
**Black Inscriptions and Designs**

**1961, Feb. 11**    **Perf. 12½**
973 A356 60g red & black | .20 | .20

Fourth Congress of Polish Engineers.

**1961, Feb. 1**    **Wmk. 326**
**Litho.**    **Perf. 12½**
974 A357 60g dark red & black | .75 | .35
975 A357 60g ultra, black & car | .45 | .20

1st Winter Spartacist Games of Friendly Armies.

60g, Ski jump. 1z, Soldiers on skis. 1.50z, Slalom.

Black Apollo Butterfly A375

## Insects in Natural Colors

Insects: 30g, Violet runner. 40g, Alpine longicorn beetle. 50g, Great oak capricorn beetle. 60g, Gold runner. 80g, Stag-horned beetle. 1.35z, Death's-head moth. 1.50z, Tiger-striped swallowtail butterfly. 1.55z, Apollo butterfly. 2.50z, Red ant. 5.60z, Bumble bee.

**1961, Dec. 30  Photo.  Perf. 12½x12  Unwmk.**

| | | | | |
|---|---|---|---|---|
| 1029 | A374 | 20g bister brown | .20 | .20 |
| 1030 | A374 | 30g pale gray grn | .20 | .20 |
| 1031 | A374 | 40g pale yellow grn | .20 | .20 |
| 1032 | A374 | 50g blue green | .20 | .20 |
| 1033 | A374 | 60g dull rose lilac | .20 | .20 |
| 1034 | A374 | 80g pale green | .25 | .20 |

**Perf. 11½**

| | | | | |
|---|---|---|---|---|
| 1035 | A375 | 1.15z ultra | .30 | .20 |
| 1036 | A375 | 1.35z sapphire | .30 | .20 |
| 1037 | A375 | 1.50z bluish green | .55 | .20 |
| 1038 | A375 | 1.55z brt purple | .45 | .45 |
| 1039 | A375 | 2.50z brt green | 1.40 | .45 |
| 1040 | A375 | 5.60z orange brown | 7.25 | 2.75 |
| | | Nos. 1029-1040 (12) | 11.50 | 5.20 |

Worker with Gun — A376

Women Skiers A377

#1042, Worker with trowel and gun. #1043, Worker with hammer. #1044, Worker at helm. #1045, Worker with dove and banner.

**1962, Jan. 5  Litho.  Unwmk.**

**Perf. 12½x12**

| | | | | |
|---|---|---|---|---|
| 1041 | A376 | 60g red, blk & green | .20 | .20 |
| 1042 | A376 | 60g red, blk & slate | .20 | .20 |
| 1043 | A376 | 60g blk & vio bl, red | .20 | .20 |
| 1044 | A376 | 60g blk & bis, red | .20 | .20 |
| 1045 | A376 | 60g blk & gray, red | 1.00 | 1.00 |
| | | Nos. 1041-1045 (5) | 1.00 | 1.00 |

Polish Workers' Party, 20th anniversary.

## Lithographed and Embossed

**1962, Feb. 14  Perf. 12**

Designs: 60g, Long distance skier. 1.50z, Ski jump, vert. 10z, FIS emblem, vert.

| | | | | |
|---|---|---|---|---|
| 1046 | A377 | 40g gray, red & gray | .20 | .20 |
| 1047 | A377 | 40g sepia, red & dull blue | .45 | .20 |
| 1048 | A377 | 60g sepia, red & dull blue | .20 | .20 |
| | | 1.50z gray, red & gray | .55 | .30 |
| a. | | 1.50z gray lilac & red | .30 | .20 |
| | | 1046-1048 (3) | 1.65 | .80 |
| | | | .70 | .60 |

## Souvenir Sheet

**Imperf**

| | | | | |
|---|---|---|---|---|
| 1049 | A377 | 10z gray, red & gray | 3.00 | 2.50 |

World Ski Championships at Zakopane (FIS). No. 1049 contains one stamp with simulated perforation. The sheet sold for 15z. Each of Nos. 1046-1048 exists in a souvenir sheet of 3, with vert. label. Value, set of 3, $57.50.

---

**1961, Oct. 9  Engr.  Perf. 12x12½**

| | | | | |
|---|---|---|---|---|
| 1018 | A369 | 60g deep green | .25 | .20 |
| 1019 | A369 | 60g violet brown | .25 | .20 |

Polish Postal Museum, 40th anniv.; Stamp Day.

Congress Emblem A370

**1961, Nov. 20  Wmk. 326  Perf. 12**

| | | | | |
|---|---|---|---|---|
| 1020 | A370 | 60g black | .20 | .20 |

Issued to publicize the Fifth World Congress of Trade Unions, Moscow, Dec. 4-16.

Child and Syringe — A372

Seal of Kopasyni Family, 1284 — A371

60g, Seal of Bytom, 14th century. 2.50z, Emblem of International Miners Congress, 1958.

**1961, Dec. 4  Litho.  Perf. 11x11½**

| | | | | |
|---|---|---|---|---|
| 1021 | A371 | 40g multicolored | .20 | .20 |
| 1022 | A371 | 60g bl, gray bl & vio bl | .20 | .20 |
| 1023 | A371 | 2.50z yel grn, grn & blk | .45 | .25 |
| | | Nos. 1021-1023 (3) | .85 | .65 |

1,000 years of the Polish mining industry.

**1961, Dec. 11  Perf. 12½x12, 12x12½**

| | | | | |
|---|---|---|---|---|
| 1024 | A372 | 40g lt blue & blk | .20 | .20 |
| 1025 | A372 | 60g orange & blk | .20 | .20 |
| 1026 | A372 | 2.50z brt bl grn & blk | .50 | .65 |
| | | Nos. 1024-1026 (3) | .90 | .65 |

15th anniversary of UNICEF.

Emblem A373

**1961, Dec. 12  Wmk. 326  Perf. 12**

| | | | | |
|---|---|---|---|---|
| 1027 | A373 | 40g dk red, yel & vio bl | .20 | .20 |
| 1028 | A373 | 60g vio bl, bl & red | .20 | .20 |

Design: 60g, Map with oil pipe line from Siberia to Central Europe.

15th session of the Council of Mutual Economic Assistance of the Communist States.

Ground Beetle — A374

---

| | | | | |
|---|---|---|---|---|
| 989 | A360 | 4z multicolored | 1.40 | .60 |
| 990 | A360 | 5.60z multicolored | 3.75 | 1.50 |
| | | | 7.00 | 3.00 |
| | | Nos. 985-990 (6) | | |

Polish ship industry. Sizes (width): 60g, 2.50z, 54mm; 1.55z, 3.40z, 4z, 80mm; 5.60z, 108mm.

Post Horn and Telephone Dial — A361

**Wmk. 326  Litho.  Perf. 12½**

**1961, June 26**

| | | | | |
|---|---|---|---|---|
| 991 | A361 | 40g sl, gray & red org | .20 | .20 |
| 992 | A361 | 60g gray, yel & vio | .20 | .20 |
| 993 | A361 | 2.50z ol bis, brt bl & vio bl | .35 | .25 |
| | | Souvenir sheet of 3, #991-993 | 2.75 | 1.50 |
| a. | | | .75 | .65 |

Post horn and dial: 60g, Radar screen. 2.50z, Conference emblem, globe.

Conference of Communications Ministers of Communist Countries, Warsaw. No. 993a sold for 5z.

Maj. Gherman Titov, Star, Globe, Orbit A365

Dove and Earth A366

**1961, Aug. 18**

| | | | | |
|---|---|---|---|---|
| 1006 | A364 | 40g bl grn, yel & red | .20 | .20 |
| 1007 | A364 | 60g multicolored | .90 | .35 |
| 1008 | A364 | 2.50z multicolored | 1.30 | .75 |
| | | Nos. 1006-1008 (3) | | |

6th European Canoe Championships, Poznan, Aug. 18-20. Exist imperf. Value, set $2.

**Perf. 12½x12½  Photo.  Unwmk.**

**1961, Aug. 24**

| | | | | |
|---|---|---|---|---|
| 1009 | A365 | 40g pink, blk & red | .30 | .20 |
| 1010 | A366 | 60g blue & black | .30 | .20 |

Manned space flight of Vostok 2, Aug. 6-7, in which Russian Maj. Gherman Titov orbited the earth 17 times.

Seal of Opole, 13th Century — A362

Cement Works, Opole A363

"PKO" Initials of Polish Savings Bank A368

**Wmk. 326**

**1961, Sept. 15  Litho.  Perf. 12**

| | | | | |
|---|---|---|---|---|
| 1011 | A368 | 40g gray & multicolored | .20 | .20 |
| 1012 | A368 | 1.55z gray & blue | .20 | .20 |

40th anniv. of the third Silesian uprising.

Insurgents' Monument, St. Ann's Mountain A367

Design: 1.55z, Cross of Silesian Insurgents.

**1961, Oct. 2  Wmk. 326  Perf. 12**

| | | | | |
|---|---|---|---|---|
| 1013 | A368 | 40g ver, blk & org | .20 | .20 |
| 1014 | A368 | 60g blue, blk & brt pink | .20 | .20 |
| 1015 | A368 | 60g bis brn, blk & ocher | .20 | .20 |
| 1016 | A368 | 60g brt grn, blk & dl red | .20 | .20 |
| 1017 | A368 | 2.50z car rose, gray & blk | 1.75 | 1.40 |
| | | Nos. 1013-1017 (5) | 2.55 | 2.20 |

Initials and: #1014, Boc and clover. #1015, Ant. #1016, Squirrel. 2.50z, Savings bankbook.

Issued to publicize Savings Month.

Mail Cart, by Jan Chelminski — A369

**1961-62  Wmk. 326  Engr.  Perf. 11**

**Western Territories**

| | | | | |
|---|---|---|---|---|
| 994 | A362 | 40g brown, grysh | .20 | .20 |
| 995 | A363 | 40g brown, grysh | .20 | .20 |
| a. | | "Block," #994-995 + label | .20 | |
| 996 | A362 | 60g violet, pink | .20 | .20 |
| 997 | A363 | 60g violet, pink | .20 | .20 |
| a. | | "Block," #996-997 + label | .20 | |
| 998 | A362 | 95g green, bluish | .30 | .25 |
| 999 | A363 | 95g green, bluish | .30 | .25 |
| a. | | "Block," #998-999 + label | .30 | |

**Northern Territories**

| | | | | |
|---|---|---|---|---|
| 1000 | A362 | 2.50z ol grn, grnsh | .30 | .30 |
| 1001 | A363 | 2.50z ol grn, grnsh | .30 | .30 |
| a. | | "Block," #1000-1001 + label | .65 | |

| | | | | |
|---|---|---|---|---|
| 1002 | A362 | 40g vio bl, bluish | .20 | .20 |
| 1003 | A363 | 40g vio bl, bluish | .20 | .20 |
| a. | | "Block," #1002-1003 + label | .40 | |
| 1004 | A362 | 1.55z brown, buff | .20 | .20 |
| 1005 | A363 | 1.55z brown, buff | .20 | .20 |
| a. | | "Block," #1004-1005 + label | .50 | |
| 1005A | A362 | 2.50z slate bl, grysh | .30 | .30 |
| 1005B | A363 | 2.50z slate bl, grysh | .30 | .30 |
| d. | | "Block," #1005A-1005B label | .65 | .40 |
| | | Nos. 994-1005B (14) | 3.20 | 2.80 |

Issued: #994-997, 1000-1001, 7/21; 95g, 2/23/62; #1002-1005B, 7/21/62.

Kayak Race Start and "E" — A364

Designs: 60g, Four-man canoes and "E." 2.50z, Paddle, Polish flag and "E," vert.

Designs: No. 996, Tombstone of Henry IV and seal, Wroclaw. No. 997, Apartment houses, Wroclaw. No. 998, Seal of Conrad II and Silesian eagle. No. 999, Steel works, Gliwice. No. 1000, Seal of Prince Barnim I. No. 1001, Seaport, Szczecin. No. 1002, Seal of Princess Elizabeth. No. 1003, Factory, Szczecinek. No. 1004, Seal of Unislaw. No. 1005, Shipyard, Gdansk. No. 1005A, Tower, Frombork Cathedral. No. 1005B, Chemical Laboratory, Kortowo.

## Broken Flower and Prison Cloth (Auschwitz) — A378

## Majdanek Concentration Camp — A379

Design: 1.50z, Proposed memorial, Treblinka concentration camp.

**1962, Apr. 3    Engr.    Perf. 11½**

| 1050 | A378 | 40g slate blue | .20 | .20 |
| 1051 | A378 | 60g dark gray | .30 | .20 |
| 1052 | A378 | 1.50z dark violet | .50 | .25 |
| Nos. 1050-1052 (3) | | | 1.00 | .65 |

International Resistance Movement Month to commemorate the millions who died in concentration camps, 1940-45.

---

## Bicyclist A380

2.50z, Cyclists in race. 3.40z, Wheel & arms of Berlin, Prague & Warsaw.

**1962, Apr. 27    Litho.    Unwmk.**

| 1053 | A380 | 60g blue & blk | .20 | .20 |
| 1054 | A380 | 2.50z yellow & blk | .35 | .20 |
| 1055 | A380 | 3.40z lilac & blk | .50 | .20 |
| Nos. 1053, 1055 (3) | | | 1.05 | .60 |

15th Intl. Peace Bicycle Race, Warsaw-Berlin-Prague. Size of #1053, 1055: 36x22mm, #1054: 74x22mm.

---

## Lenin in Bialy Dunajec A381

## Karol Swierczewski-Walter A382

Designs: 60g, Lenin, 2.50z, Lenin and Cracow fortifications.

### Engraved and Photogravure

**1962, May 25    Perf. 11x11½    Wmk. 326**

| 1056 | A381 | 40g pale grn & Prus grn | .20 | .20 |
| 1057 | A381 | 60g pink & dp claret | .50 | .20 |
| 1058 | A381 | 2.50z yellow & dk brn | .30 | .20 |
| Nos. 1056-1058 (3) | | | 1.00 | .60 |

50th anniv. of Lenin's arrival in Poland.

---

**1962, June 20    Engr. & Photo.**

### Black Inscriptions and Designs

| 1059 | A359 | 60g dull green | .20 | .20 |
| 1060 | A359 | 60g brown orange | .20 | .20 |

Famous Poles: No. 1060, Adam Mickiewicz. No. 1059, Juliusz Slowacki; No. 1061, Frederic Chopin. No. 1062, Romuald Traugutt. No. 1063, Jaroslaw Dabrowski; No. 1064, Maria Konopnicka.

### Famous Poles Type of 1961

**Perf. 12x12½    Litho.**

| 1061 | A359 | 60g dull blue | .20 | .20 |
| 1062 | A359 | 60g brown olive | .20 | .20 |
| 1063 | A359 | 60g rose lilac | .20 | .20 |
| 1064 | A359 | 60g blue green | .20 | .20 |
| Nos. 1059-1064 (6) | | | 1.20 | 1.20 |

**1962, July 14    Perf. 11x11½    Engr.    Unwmk.**

| 1065 | A382 | 60g black | .20 | .20 |

15th death anniv. of General Karol Swierczewski-Walter, organizer of the new Polish army.

---

## Crocus — A383

Flowers: No. 1067, Orchid. No. 1068, Monkshood. No. 1069, Gas plant. No. 1070, Water lily. No. 1071, Gentian. No. 1072, Daphne mezereum. No. 1073, Cowbell. No. 1074, Anemone. No. 1075, Globeflower. No. 1076, Snowdrop. No. 1077, Adonis vernalis.

**1962, Aug. 8    Photo.    Perf. 12**

### Flowers in Natural Colors    Unwmk.

| 1066 | A383 | 60g dull red & red | .20 | .20 |
| 1067 | A383 | 60g ol blk & red | | .45 |
| 1068 | A383 | 60g redsh brn & vio | | .75 |
| 1069 | A383 | 60g pink & lilac | | .20 |
| 1070 | A383 | 90g olive & green | | .20 |
| 1071 | A383 | 90g yel grn & red | | .20 |
| 1072 | A383 | 90g lt ol grn & red | | .20 |
| 1073 | A383 | 1.50z yel grn & bl | | .25 |
| 1074 | A383 | 1.50z gray bl & bl Prus grn & dk grn | | .60 |
| 1075 | A383 | 2.50z gray grn & dk grn | .30 | .20 |
| 1076 | A383 | 2.50z ol blk & dk grn bl | .80 | .45 |
| 1077 | A383 | 2.50z gray bl & grn bl & dk | 1.25 | .55 |
| Nos. 1066-1077 (12) | | | 5.75 | 3.50 |

Exist imperf. Value, set $4.

---

## The Poisoned Well by Jacek Malczewski — A384

**1962, Aug. 15    Engr.    Wmk. 326**

| 1078 | A384 | 60g black, buff | .30 | .20 |

Issued in sheets of 40 with alternating label for FIP Day (Federation Internationale de Philatelie), Sept. 1. Also issued in miniature sheet of 4. Value, $40.

---

## Pole Vault — A385

**1962, Sept. 12    Litho.    Unwmk.    Perf. 11**

| 1079 | A385 | 40g multicolored | .20 | .20 |
| 1080 | A385 | 60g multicolored | .20 | .20 |
| 1081 | A385 | 90g multicolored | .20 | .20 |
| 1082 | A385 | 1z multicolored | .20 | .20 |
| 1083 | A385 | 1.50z multicolored | .20 | .20 |
| 1084 | A385 | 1.55z multicolored | .20 | .20 |
| 1085 | A385 | 2.50z multicolored | .35 | .20 |
| 1086 | A385 | 3.40z multicolored | .90 | .25 |
| Nos. 1079-1086 (8) | | | 2.45 | 1.65 |

Designs: 60g, Relay race. 90g, Javelin. 1z, Hurdles. 1.50z, High jump. 1.55z, Discus. 2.50z, 100m. dash. 3.40z, Hammer throw.

7th European Athletic Championships, Belgrade, Sept. 12-16.

---

## Anopheles Mosquito A386

## Pavel R. Popovich and Andrian G. Nikolayev A387

Designs: 1.50z, Malaria blood cells, 2.50z, Cinchona flowers; 3.2z, Anopheles mosquito.

**1962, Oct. 1    Wmk. 326    Perf. 13x12**

| 1087 | A386 | 60g ol blk, dk brn & bl grn | .20 | .20 |
| 1088 | A386 | 1.50z red, gray & brt vio | .40 | .20 |
| 1089 | A386 | 2.50z multicolored | .80 | .60 |
| Nos. 1087-1089 (3) | | | | |

**Miniature Sheet    Imperf**

| 1090 | A386 | 3z multicolored | 1.00 | .60 |

WHO drive to eradicate malaria.

**1962, Oct. 6    Perf. 12x12**

| 1091 | A387 | 60g violet, blk & citron | .20 | .20 |
| 1092 | A387 | 2.50z Prus bl, blk & red | .25 | .20 |

**Souvenir Sheet    Perf. 12x11**

| 1093 | A387 | 10z sl bl, blk & red | 2.25 | 1.50 |

Design: 2.50z, Two stars around earth. 10z, Two stars in orbit.

1st Russian group space flight, Vostoks III and IV, Aug. 11-15, 1962.

---

## Woman Mailing Letter Warsaw — A388

**1962, Oct. 9    Engr.    Perf. 12½x12**

| 1094 | A388 | 60g black | .50 | .20 |
| 1095 | A388 | 2.50z red brown | .50 | .20 |

"Stamp Day. The design is from the painting "A Moment of Decision," by Anthony Kamienski.

---

## Mazovian Princes' Mansion A389

**1962, Oct. 13    Litho.**

| 1096 | A389 | 60g red & black | .20 | .20 |

25th anniversary of the founding of the Polish Democratic Party.

---

## Cruiser "Aurora" — A390

**1962, Nov. 3    Photo. & Engr.    Perf. 11**

| 1097 | A390 | 60g red & dk blue | .20 | .20 |

Russian October revolution, 45th anniv.

---

## Janusz Korczak by K. Dunikowski A391

## King on Horseback A392

Illustrations from King Matthew books: 90g, King giving fruit to island girl. 1z, King handcuffed and soldier with sword. 2.50z, King with dead bird. 5.60z, King ice skating in moonlight.

20th anniversary of the death of Dr. Janusz Korczak (Henryk Goldszmit), physician, pedagogue and writer, in the Treblinka concentration camp, Aug. 5, 1942.

**1962, Nov. 12    Unwmk.    Perf. 13x12    Litho.**

| 1098 | A391 | 40g blk, bis & sep | .55 | .20 |
| 1099 | A391 | 60g multicolored | .20 | .20 |
| 1100 | A391 | 90g multicolored | .35 | .20 |
| 1101 | A392 | 1z multicolored | .35 | .20 |
| 1102 | A392 | 2.50z brn, yel & brt | | .20 |
| 1103 | A392 | 5.60z brn, dk bl & grn | 1.60 | .75 |
| Nos. 1098-1103 (6) | | | 3.25 | 2.00 |

---

## View of Old Warsaw — A393

**1962, Nov. 26    Wmk. 326    Perf. 11**

| 1104 | A393 | 3.40z multicolored | .40 | .25 |
| a. | | Sheet of 4 | 3.00 | 3.00 |

5th Trade Union Cong., Warsaw, 11/26-12/1.

---

## Orphan Mary and the Dwarf — A394

Various Scenes from "Orphan Mary and the Dwarfs" by Maria Konopnicka.

**1962, Dec. 31    Perf. 13x12    Unwmk.    Litho.**

| 1105 | A394 | 40g multicolored | .30 | .20 |
| 1106 | A394 | 60g multicolored | .20 | .20 |
| 1107 | A394 | 1.50z multicolored | 2.00 | 1.00 |
| 1108 | A394 | 1.55z multicolored | .45 | .20 |

1109 A394 2.50z multicolored .55 .30
1110 A394 3.40z multicolored 2.00 1.10
Nos. 1105-1110 (6) 5.75 3.00

120th anniversary of the birth of Maria Konopnicka, poet and fairy tale writer.

Romuald Traugutt A395

**Perf. 11½x11 Wmk. 326**
**1963, Jan. 31**
1111 A395 60g aqua, blk & pale pink .20 .20

Centenary of the 1863 insurrection and to honor its leader, Romuald Traugutt.

Tractor and Wheat A396

Designs: 60g, Man reaping and millet. 2.50z, Combine and rice.

**Perf. 12x12½ Wmk. 326**
**1963, Feb. 25 Litho.**
1112 A396 40g gray, bl, blk & ocher .20 .20
1113 A396 60g brn red, blk, brn .50 .25
1114 A396 2.50z yel, buff, blk & grn .40 .20
Nos. 1112-1114 (3) 1.10 .65

FAO "Freedom from Hunger" campaign.

Cocker Spaniel — A397

30g, Polish sheep dog. 40g, Boxer. 50g, Airedale terrier, vert. 60g, French bulldog, vert. 1z, Poodle, vert. 1.55z, Hunting dog, vert. 3.40z, Sheep dog, vert. 6.50z, Great Dane.

**1963, Mar. 25 Unwmk. Perf. 12½**
1115 A397 20g lil, blk & org brn .20 .20
1116 A397 30g rose car & blk .20 .20
1117 A397 40g lil, blk & yel grn .20 .20
1118 A397 50g multicolored .25 .20
1119 A397 60g lt blue & blk .40 .40
1120 A397 1z yel grn & blk .70 .35
1121 A397 2.50z org, blk & brn 1.00 .50
1122 A397 3.40z red org & blk 2.25 1.00
1123 A397 6.50z brt yel & blk 4.25 2.75
Nos. 1115-1123 (9) 9.45 5.60

Ancient Ships: 10g, Phoenician merchant ship. 20g, Greek trireme. 30g, 3rd century merchantman. 40g, Scandinavian "Gokstad." 60g, Frisian "Kogge." 1z, 14th century "Holk." 1.15z, 15th century "Caraca."

**Photo. (Background) & Engr.**
**Perf. 11½**
**1963, Apr. 5**
1124 A398 5g brown, tan .20 .20
1125 A398 10g green, gray grn .20 .20
1126 A398 20g ultra, gray .20 .20
1127 A398 30g black, gray ol .20 .20
1128 A398 40g lt bl, bluish .20 .20
1129 A398 60g claret, gray .20 .20
1130 A398 1z black, bl .35 .20
1131 A398 1.15z grn, pale rose 1.75 1.60
Nos. 1124-1131 (8)

See Nos. 1206-1213, 1299-1306.

Egyptian Ship — A398

Fighter and Ruins of Warsaw Ghetto — A399

**Perf. 11½x11 Wmk. 326**
**1963, Apr. 19**
1132 A399 2.50z gray brn & gray .35 .20

Warsaw Ghetto Uprising, 20th anniv.

Centenary Emblem — A400

**Perf. 12½x12 Litho. Unwmk.**
**1963, May 8**
1133 A400 2.50z blue, yel & red .40 .20

Intl. Red Cross, cent. Every other stamp in sheet inverted.

Sand Lizard A401

40g, Smooth snake. 50g, European pond turtle. 60g, Grass snake. 90g, Slow worm. 1.15z, European tree frog. 1.55z, Alpine newt. 1.50z, Crested newt. 1.55z, Green toad. 2.50z, Firebellied toad. 3z, Fire salamander. 3.40z, Natterjack.

**1963, June 1 Unwmk. Photo.**
**Reptiles and Amphibians in Natural Colors**
**Perf. 11½**
1134 A401 30g grnsh gray & blk .20 .20
1135 A401 40g gray ol & blk .20 .20
1136 A401 50g bis brn & blk .20 .20
1137 A401 60g tan & blk .20 .20
1138 A401 90g gray grn & blk .20 .20
1139 A401 1.15z gray & blk .35 .35
1140 A401 1.35z gray bl & dk bl .40 .20
1141 A401 1.50z bluish grn & blk .35 .35
1142 A401 1.55z bluish gray & blk .75 .35
1143 A401 2.50z gray vio & blk 2.25 1.50
1144 A401 3z grn & blk
1145 A401 3.40z gray & blk 5.65 3.85
Nos. 1134-1145 (12)

Foil, Saber, Sword and Helmet A402

Designs: 40g, Fencers and knights in armor. 60g, Fencers and dragoons. 1.15z, Contemporary and 18th cent. fencers. 1.55z, Fencers and old houses, Gdansk. 6.50z, Arms of Gdansk, vert.

**Perf. 12x12½, 12½x12 Litho. Unwmk.**
**1963, June 29**
1146 A402 20g brown & orange .20 .20
1147 A402 40g dk blue & blue .20 .20
1148 A402 60g red & dp org .20 .20
1149 A402 1.15z green & emer .35 .20
1150 A402 1.55z violet & lilac 1.25 .45
1151 A402 6.50z yel brn, mar & yel 2.40 1.45
Nos. 1146-1151 (6)

28th World Fencing Championships, Gdansk, July 15-28. A souvenir sheet exists containing one each of Nos. 1147-1150. Value, $40.

Famous Poles Type of 1961

No. 1152, Ludwik Warynski. No. 1153, Ludwik Krzywicki. No. 1154, Marie Skiodowska-Walter. No. 1155, Karol Swierczewski-Walter.

**Perf. 12x12½ Wmk. 326**
**1963, July 20**
**Black Inscriptions and Designs**
1152 A359 60g red brown .20 .20
1153 A359 60g gray brown .20 .20
1154 A359 60g blue .30 .20
1155 A359 60g green .90 .80
Nos. 1152-1155 (4)

Valeri Bykovski — A403

**Perf. 11 Litho. Unwmk.**
**1963, Aug. 26**
1156 A403 40g ultra, emer & blk .20 .20
1157 A403 60g green, ultra & blk .20 .20
1158 A403 6.50z multicolored 1.25 .40
Nos. 1156-1158 (3) 1.65 .80

Space flights of Valeri Bykovski June 14-19, and Valentina Tereshkova, first woman cosmonaut, June 16-19, 1963. For overprints see Nos. 1175-1177.

Basketball A404

Designs: Various positions of ball, hands and players. 10z, Town Hall, People's Hall and Arms of Wroclaw.

**Perf. 11½ Unwmk.**
**1963, Sept. 16**
1159 A404 40g multicolored .20 .20
1160 A404 50g fawn, grn & blk .20 .20
1161 A404 60g red, grn & blk .20 .20
1162 A404 90g multicolored .20 .20
1163 A404 2.50z multicolored .25 .25
1164 A404 5.60z multicolored 1.25 1.25
Nos. 1159-1164 (6) 2.30

**Souvenir Sheet**
**Imperf**
1165 A404 10z multicolored 2.50 1.25

13th European Men's Basketball Championship, Wroclaw, Oct. 4-13. No. 1165 contains one stamp; inscription on margin also commemorates the simultaneous European Sports Stamp Exhibition. Sheet sold for 15z.

Eagle and Ground-to-Air Missile — A405

Eagle and: 40g, Destroyer. 60g, Jet fighter plane. 1.15z, Radar. 1.35z, Tank. 1.55z, Self-propelled rocket launcher. 2.50z, Amphibious troop carrier, 3z. Swords and medieval and modern soldiers.

Polish People's Army, 20th anniversary.

**Perf. 12x12½**
**1963, Oct. 1**
1166 A405 20g multicolored .20 .20
1167 A405 40g violet, grn & red .20 .20
1168 A405 60g multicolored .20 .20
1169 A405 1.15z multicolored .20 .20
1170 A405 1.35z multicolored .20 .20
1171 A405 1.55z multicolored .25 .20
1172 A405 2.50z multicolored .25 .20
1173 A405 3z multicolored .55 .55
Nos. 1166-1173 (8) 2.00 1.60

"Love Letter" by Wladyslaw Czachórski— A406

**Perf. 11½ Unwmk. Engr.**
**1963, Oct. 9**
1174 A406 60g dark red brown .20 .20

Issued for Stamp Day.

Nos. 1156-1158 Overprinted: "23-28 X. 1963" and name of astronaut.

**Perf. 11**
**1963 Litho.**
1175 A403 40g multicolored .25 .20
1176 A403 60g multicolored .30 .30
1177 A403 6.50z multicolored 1.50 .80
Nos. 1175-1177 (3) 2.05 1.20

Visit of Valentina Tereshkova and Valeri Bykovski to Poland, Oct. 23-28. The overprints are: 40g, W. F. Bykowski / w Polsce; 60g, W. W. Tierieszkowa / w Polsce; 6.50z, W. F. BYKOWSKI I W. W. TIERIESZKOWA W POLSCE.

Konstantin E. Tsiolkovsky's Rocket and Rocket Speed Formula — A407

**Perf. 11½x12 Litho. Unwmk.**
**Black Inscriptions**
**1963, Nov. 11**
1178 A407 30g dull bl grn & .20 .20
1179 A407 40g lt org & gray .20 .20
1180 A407 50g violet bl & gray .20 .20
1181 A407 60g brn org & gray .20 .20
1182 A407 1z brn & gray .20 .20
1183 A407 1.50z org red & gray .20 .20
1184 A407 1.55z blue & gray .20 .20
1185 A407 2.50z lilac & gray .50 .50
1186 A407 5.60z brt yel grn & gray .90 .90
1187 A407 6.50z grnsh bl & gray 3.00 2.00
Nos. 1178-1187 (10)

Conquest of space. A souvenir sheet contains 2 each of Nos. 1186-1187. Value $40.

Arab Stallion "Comet" — A408

Horses: 30g, Tarpans (wild horses). 40g, foals, horiz. 90g. Steeplechasers, horiz. 1.55z, Arab stallion "Witez II." 2.50z, Head of Arab horse, facing right. 4z, Mixed breeds, horiz. 6.50z, Head of Arab horse, facing left.

Horse from Sokolka. 50g, Arab mares and foals, horiz. 90g. Steeplechasers, horiz. 1.55z, Arab stallion "Witez II." 2.50z, Head of Arab horse, facing right. 4z, Mixed breeds, horiz. 6.50z, Head of Arab horse, facing left.

**Horses from Mazury Region — A409**

**1963, Dec. 30    Photo.**
**Perf. 11½x11 (A408); 12½x12, 12**
Sizes: 75x26mm (60g, 90g, 4z); 28x38mm (60g, 1.55z, 2.50z, 6.50z)

| | | | | |
|---|---|---|---|---|
| 1188 | A408 | 20g | black, yel & car | .20 .20 |
| 1189 | A408 | 30g | multicolored | .20 .20 |
| 1190 | A408 | 40g | multicolored | .20 .20 |
| 1191 | A409 | 20g | multicolored | .20 .20 |
| 1192 | A409 | 30g | multicolored | .20 .20 |
| 1193 | A409 | 40g | multicolored | .20 .20 |
| 1194 | A409 | 60g | multicolored | .50 .20 |
| 1195 | A409 | 90g | multicolored | .25 .20 |
| 1196 | A409 | 1.55z | multicolored | .60 .20 |
| 1197 | A409 | 2.50z | multicolored | .60 .20 |
| 1195 | A409 | 4z | multicolored | 1.40 1.50 |
| 1197 | A409 | 6.50z | yel, dl bl & blk | 6.25 3.60 |

Nos. 1188-1197 (10)

Issued to publicize Polish horse breeding.

**Ice Hockey A410**

Sports: 30g, Slalom. 40g, Skiing. 60g, Speed skating. 1z, Ski jump. 2.50z, Tobogganing. 5.60z, Cross-country skiing. 6.50z, Figure skating pair.

9th Winter Olympic Games, Innsbruck, Jan. 29-Feb. 9. A souvenir sheet contains 2 each of Nos. 1203, 1205. Value $35.

**1964, Jan. 25    Litho.    Perf. 12x12½**

| | | | | |
|---|---|---|---|---|
| 1199 | A410 | 20g | multicolored | .20 .20 |
| 1200 | A410 | 30g | multicolored | .20 .20 |
| 1201 | A410 | 40g | multicolored | .20 .20 |
| 1202 | A410 | 1z | multicolored | .25 .20 |
| 1203 | A410 | 2.50z | multicolored | .45 .20 |
| 1204 | A410 | 5.60z | multicolored | .75 .35 |
| 1205 | A410 | 6.50z | multicolored | 3.50 2.25 |

Nos. 1199-1205 (7)

**European Cat — A411**

40g, 60g, 1.55z, 2.50z, 6.50z, Various European cats. 50g, Siamese cat. 90g, 1.35z,

**Ship Type of 1963**

Sailing Ships: 1.35z, Caravel of Columbus, vert. 1.50z, Galleon. 1.55z, Polish warship, 1627, vert. 2z, Dutch merchant ship. 2.10z, Line ship. 2.50z, Frigate. 3z, 19th century merchantman. 3.40z, "Dar Pomorza," 20th century school ship, vert.

**1964, Mar. 19    Engr.    Perf. 12½**

| | | | | |
|---|---|---|---|---|
| 1206 | A398 | 1.35z | ultra | .20 .20 |
| 1207 | A398 | 1.50z | claret | .20 .20 |
| 1208 | A398 | 1.55z | black | .20 .20 |
| 1209 | A398 | 2z | violet | .20 .20 |
| 1210 | A398 | 2.10z | green | .20 .20 |
| 1211 | A398 | 2.50z | carmine rose | .25 .20 |
| 1212 | A398 | 3z | olive green | .40 .20 |
| 1213 | A398 | 3.40z | brown | .55 .20 |

Nos. 1206-1213 (8)

3.40z, Various Persian cats. 60g, 90g, 1.35z, 1.55z horiz.

**Cats in Natural Colors; Black Inscriptions**

**1964, Apr. 30    Litho.    Perf. 12½**

| | | | | |
|---|---|---|---|---|
| 1216 | A411 | 30g | yellow | .20 .20 |
| 1217 | A411 | 40g | orange | .20 .20 |
| 1218 | A411 | 50g | yellow | .20 .20 |
| 1219 | A411 | 60g | brt green | .40 .20 |
| 1220 | A411 | 90g | lt brown | .20 .20 |
| 1221 | A411 | 1.55z | emerald | .55 .20 |
| 1222 | A411 | 1.55z | violet blue | .55 .20 |
| 1223 | A411 | 2.50z | lilac | .90 .50 |
| 1224 | A411 | 3.40z | rose | 1.90 1.00 |
| 1225 | A411 | 6.50z | violet | 3.50 1.65 |

Nos. 1216-1225 (10)

**King Casimir III, the Great — A412**

**1964, May 5    Engr.    Perf. 11x11½**
Size: 22x35mm

| | | | | |
|---|---|---|---|---|
| 1226 | A412 | 40g | dull claret | .20 .20 |
| 1227 | A412 | 40g | green | .20 .20 |
| 1228 | A412 | 60g | violet | .20 .20 |
| 1229 | A412 | 60g | dark blue | .20 .20 |

Designs: No. 1227, Hugo Kollataj. No. 1228, Jan Dlugosz. No. 1229, Nicolaus Copernicus. 2.50z, King Wladyslaw II Jagiello and Queen Jadwiga.

| | | | | |
|---|---|---|---|---|
| 1230 | A412 | 2.50z | gray brown | .35 .20 |

Nos. 1226-1230 (5)    1.15 1.00

Jagiellonian University, Cracow, 600th anniv.

**Lapwing A413**

Waterfowl: 40g, White-spotted bluethroat. 50g, Black-tailed godwit. 60g, Osprey. 90g, Gray heron. 1.35z, Little gull. 1.55z, Shoveler. 5.60z, Arctic loon. 6.50z, Great crested grebe.

**1964, June 5    Photo.    Unwmk.**
**Birds in Natural Colors; Inscriptions**
Size: 34x34mm

| | | | | |
|---|---|---|---|---|
| 1231 | A413 | 30g | chalky blue | .20 .20 |
| 1232 | A413 | 40g | bister | .20 .20 |
| 1233 | A413 | 50g | brt yellow grn | .20 .20 |

**Perf. 11½x11**
Size: 34x48mm

| | | | | |
|---|---|---|---|---|
| 1234 | A413 | 60g | blue | .20 .20 |
| 1235 | A413 | 90g | lemon | .20 .20 |
| 1236 | A413 | 1.35z | green | .30 .20 |

**Perf. 11½**
Size: 34x34mm

| | | | | |
|---|---|---|---|---|
| 1237 | A413 | 1.55z | olive | .30 .30 |
| 1238 | A413 | 5.60z | brt green | .90 .40 |
| 1239 | A413 | 6.50z | brt green | 4.00 2.40 |

Nos. 1231-1239 (9)

**Hands Holding Red Flag — A414**

Designs: No. 1241, Red and white ribbon around hammer. No. 1242, Hammer and rye. No. 1243, Brick wall under construction and red flag.

**1964, June 15    Litho.    Perf. 11**

| | | | | |
|---|---|---|---|---|
| 1240 | A414 | 60g | ol bl, red, blk & pink | .20 .20 |
| 1241 | A414 | 60g | red, gray & black | .20 .20 |
| 1242 | A414 | 60g | magenta, blk & yel | .20 .20 |
| 1243 | A414 | 60g | gray, red, sal & blk | .80 .80 |

Nos. 1240-1243 (4)

4th congress of the Polish United Workers Party.

**Symbols of Peasant-Worker Alliance — A415**

**Atom Symbol and Book — A416**

**Shipyard, Gdansk — A417**

**1964    Litho.    Perf. 12x12½**

| | | | | |
|---|---|---|---|---|
| 1244 | A415 | 60g | red, org & blk | .20 .20 |
| 1245 | A415 | 60g | grn, red, ocher, bl & blk | .20 .20 |

Designs: No. 1245, Stylized oak. No. 1247, Factory and cogwheel. No. 1248, Tractor and grain. No. 1249, Pen, brush, mask and ornament. No. 1251, Lenin Metal Works, Nowa Huta. No. 1252, Cement factory, Chelm. No. 1253, Power Station, Turoszow. No. 1254, Oil refinery, Plock. No. 1255, Sulphur mine, Tarnobrzeg.

**1964    Photo.    Perf. 11**

| | | | | |
|---|---|---|---|---|
| 1246 | A416 | 60g | gray & blk | .20 .20 |
| 1247 | A416 | 60g | brt blue & blk | .20 .20 |
| 1248 | A416 | 60g | emerald & blk | .20 .20 |
| 1249 | A416 | 60g | orange & red | .20 .20 |

**Photogravure and Engraved**

| | | | | |
|---|---|---|---|---|
| 1250 | A417 | 60g | dl bl grn & ultra | .20 .20 |
| 1251 | A417 | 60g | brt pink & pur | .20 .20 |
| 1252 | A417 | 60g | gray & gray brn | .20 .20 |
| 1253 | A417 | 60g | grn & slate grn | .20 .20 |
| 1254 | A417 | 60g | salmon & claret | .20 .20 |
| 1255 | A417 | 60g | citron & sepia | .20 .20 |

Nos. 1244-1255 (12)    2.40 2.40

Polish People's Republic, 20 anniv.

**Warsaw Fighters, 1944 — A418**

**1964, Aug. 1    Litho.    Perf. 12½x12**

| | | | | |
|---|---|---|---|---|
| 1256 | A418 | 60g | multicolored | .20 .20 |

20th anniv. of the Warsaw insurrection against German occupation.

**Olympic Sports — A421**

**Women's High Jump — A420**

**Running — A419**

**1964, Aug. 17    Litho.    Unwmk.    Perf. 11**

| | | | | |
|---|---|---|---|---|
| 1257 | A419 | 20g | multicolored | .20 .20 |
| 1258 | A419 | 40g | grnsh bl, bl & yel | .20 .20 |
| 1259 | A419 | 60g | vio bl, red & yel | .20 .20 |
| 1260 | A419 | 90g | dk brown, red & yel | .20 .20 |
| 1261 | A419 | 1z | dk violet, lil & gray | .20 .20 |
| 1262 | A419 | 2.50z | multicolored | .40 .20 |
| 1263 | A419 | 5.60z | multicolored | .95 .80 |
| 1264 | A420 | 6.50z | multicolored | 1.50 .80 |

**Souvenir Sheet**
**Imperf**

| | | | | |
|---|---|---|---|---|
| 1265 | A421 | | Sheet of 4 | 3.50 1.65 |
| | a. | 2.50z | Sharpshooting | .45 .25 |
| | b. | 2.50z | Canoeing | .45 .25 |
| | c. | 5z | Fencing | .45 .25 |
| | d. | 5z | Basketball | .45 .25 |

Sports: 40g, Rowing (single). 60g, Weight lifting. 90g, Relay race (square). 1z, Boxing (square). 2.50z, Soccer (square). 6.50z, Diving.

18th Olympic Games, Tokyo, Oct. 10-25. Size of stamps in No. 1265: 24x24mm. A souvenir sheet containing 1 each of Nos. 1263-1264 with black marginal inscription exists. Value $45.

Nos. 1257-1264 (8)

POLAND

**Warsaw Mermaid and Stars**
A422

**1964, Sept. 7      Perf. 12½x12**
1266 A422 2.50z violet & black ....... .40 .20

15th Astronautical Congress, Warsaw, Sept. 7-12.

**Stefan Zeromski by Monika Zeromska**
A423

**1964, Sept. 21      Photo.    Perf. 12½**
1267 A423 60g olive gray ....... .20 .20

Stefan Zeromski (1864-1925), writer.

**Gun and Hand Holding Hammer — A424**

**1964, Sept. 21      Litho.    Perf. 11**
1268 A424 60g brt grn, blk & red ....... .20 .20

3rd Miners' Militia Cong., Warsaw, 9/24-26.

**1964, Sept. 28      Photo.    Perf. 12½**
1269 A425 60g black & red orange ....... .20 .20

First Socialist International, centenary.

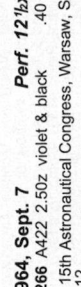

**Globe and Red Flag — A425**

**Stagecoach by Jozef Brodowski — A426**

**1964, Oct. 9      Engr.    Perf. 11½**
1270 A426 60g green ....... .20 .20
1271 A426 60g lt brown ....... .20 .20

Issued for Stamp Day.

**Eleanor Roosevelt (1884-1962) — A427**

**1964, Oct. 10      Perf. 12½**
1272 A427 2.50z black ....... .20 .20

---

**Proposed Monument for Defenders of Westerplatte, 1939 — A428**

**Polish Soldiers Crossing Oder River, 1945**
A429

Designs: No. 1274, Virtuti Military Cross. No. 1275, Nike, proposed monument for the martyrs of Bydgoszcz (woman with sword and torch). No. 1277, Battle of Studzianki, 1944.

**Perf. 12x11, 11x12**

**1964, Nov. 16      Engr.    Unwmk.**
1273 A428 40g blue violet ....... .20 .20
1274 A428 40g slate ....... .20 .20
1275 A428 60g dark blue ....... .20 .20
1276 A428 60g dark blue grn ....... .20 .20
1277 A429 60g grnsh black ....... .20 1.00

*Nos. 1273-1277 (5)* ....... 1.00 1.00

Struggle and martyrdom of the Polish people, 1939-45. The vertical stamps are printed in sheets of 56 stamps (8x7) with / labels in each outside vertical row. The horizontal stamps are printed in sheets of 50 stamps (5x10) with 10 labels in each outside vertical row. See Nos. 1366-1368.

**Souvenir Sheet**

**Col. Vladimir M. Komarov, Boris B. Yegorov and Dr. Konstantin Feoktistov — A430**

**1964, Nov. 21      Litho.    Perf. 11½x11**
1278 A430   Sheet of 3 ....... 1.25 .70
  a. 60g red & black (Komarov) ....... .35 .20
  b. 60g brt grn & blk (Feoktistov) ....... .35 .20
  c. 60g ultra & blk (Yegorov) ....... .35 .20

Russian three-manned space flight in space ship Voskhod, Oct. 12-13, 1964. Size of stamps: 27x36mm.

**Cyclamen**
A431

Garden Flowers: 30g, Freesia. 40g, Monique rose. 50g, Peony. 60g, Royal lily. 90g, Oriental poppy. 1.35z, Tulip. 1.50z, Narcissus. 1.55z, Begonia. 2.50z, Carnation. 3.40z, Iris. 5.60z, Camellia.

**1964, Nov. 30      Photo.    Perf. 11**
**Size: 35½x35½mm**
**Flowers in Natural Colors**
1279 A431 20g violet ....... .20 .20
1280 A431 30g deep lilac ....... .20 .20
1281 A431 40g blue ....... .20 .20
1282 A431 50g violet blue ....... .20 .20
1283 A431 60g lilac ....... .20 .20
1284 A431 90g deep green ....... .20 .20

**Size: 26x37½mm**
1285 A431 1.35z dark blue ....... .20 .20
1286 A431 1.50z deep carmine ....... .40 .20
1287 A431 1.52z green ....... .35 .20
1288 A431 2.50z ultra ....... .35 .25
1289 A431 3.40z redsh brown ....... .75 .50
1290 A431 5.60z olive gray ....... 1.40 .50

*Nos. 1279-1290 (72)* ....... 4.50 2.75

---

**Future Interplanetary Spacecraft**
A432

Designs: 30g, Launching of Russian rocket. 40g, Dog Laika and launching tower. 60g, Lunik 3 photographing far side of the Moon. 1.55z, Satellite exploring the ionosphere. 2.50z, Satellite "Elektron 2" exploring radiation belt. 5.60z, "Mars 1" between Mars and Earth.

**Perf. 12½x12**

**1964, Dec. 30      Litho.    Unwmk.**
1291 A432 20g multicolored ....... .20 .20
1292 A432 30g multicolored ....... .20 .20
1293 A432 40g ol grn, blk & bl ....... .20 .20
1294 A432 60g dk bl, blk & dk red ....... .20 .20
1295 A432 1.55z gray & multi ....... .25 .20
1296 A432 2.50z multicolored ....... .55 .20
1297 A432 5.60z multicolored ....... .90 .40

*Nos. 1291-1297,B108 (8)* ....... 4.00 2.25

Issued to publicize space research.

**Warsaw Mermaid, Ruins and New Buildings**
A433

**1965, Jan. 15      Engr.    Perf. 11x11½**
1298 A433 60g slate green ....... .20 .20

Liberation of Warsaw, 20th anniversary.

**Ship Type of 1963**

Designs as before.

**1965, Jan. 25      Engr.    Perf. 12½**
1299 A398 5g dark brown ....... .20 .20
1300 A390 10g slate green ....... .20 .20
1301 A398 20g slate blue ....... .20 .20
1302 A398 30g gray olive ....... .20 .20
1303 A398 40g dark blue ....... .20 .20
1304 A398 60g claret ....... .20 .20
1305 A398 1z red brown ....... .20 .20
1306 A398 1.15z dk red brown ....... 1.60 1.60

*Nos. 1299-1306 (8)* ....... 1.60 1.60

**Edaphosaurus — A434**

Dinosaurs: 30g, Cryptocleidus, vert. 40g, Brontosaurus. 60g, Mesosaurus, vert. 90g, Stegosaurus. 1.15z, Brachiosaurus, vert. 1.35z, Styracosaurus. 3.40z, Corythosaurus, vert. 5.60z, Rhamphorhynchus, vert. 6.50z, Tyrannosaurus.

**1965, Mar. 5      Litho.    Perf. 12½**
1307 A434 20g multicolored ....... .20 .20
1308 A434 30g multicolored ....... .20 .20
1309 A434 40g multicolored ....... .20 .20
1310 A434 60g multicolored ....... .25 .20
1311 A434 90g multicolored ....... .30 .20
1312 A434 1.15z multicolored ....... .30 .20
1313 A434 1.35z multicolored ....... .75 .20
1314 A434 3.40z multicolored ....... .75 .35
1315 A434 5.60z multicolored ....... 1.50 .90
1316 A434 6.50z multicolored ....... 2.25 .90
  6.15 2.85

*See Nos. 1395-1403.*

---

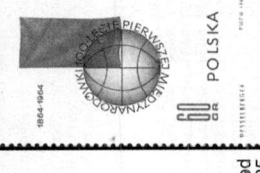

**Symbolic Wax Seal — A435**

**Russian and Polish Flags, Oil Refinery-Chemical Plant, Plock — A436**

**1965, Apr. 21      Perf. 12½x12, 12½**
1317 A435 60g multicolored ....... .20 .20
1318 A436 60g multicolored ....... .20 .20

20th anniversary of the signing of the Polish-Soviet treaty of friendship, mutual assistance and postwar cooperation.

**Polish Eagle and Town Coats of Arms**
A437

**1965, May 8      Engr.    Perf. 11½**
1319 A437 60g carmine rose ....... .20 .20

20th anniversary of regaining the Western and Northern Territories.

**Dove**
A438

**1965, May 8      Litho.    Perf. 12x12½**
1320 A438 60g red & black ....... .20 .20

Victory over Fascism, 20th anniversary.

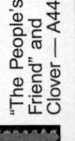

**ITU Emblem — A439**

**"The People's Friend" and Clover — A440**

**Factory and Rye**
A441

POLAND

## 1965, May 17 — Perf. 12½x12
**Litho.  Unwmk.**

1321 A439 2.50z brt bl, lil, yel & blk .45 .20

ITU. cent.

## 1965, June 5 — Perf. 11

1322 A440 40g multicolored .20 .20
1323 A441 60g multicolored .20 .20

"Popular Movement" in Poland, 70th anniv.

Finn Class Yachts — A442

## 1965, June 14 — Litho.  Perf. 12½

1324 A442 30g multicolored .20 .20
1325 A442 40g multicolored .20 .20
1326 A442 50g multicolored .20 .20
1327 A442 60g multicolored .20 .20
1328 A442 1.35z multicolored .20 .25
1329 A442 4z multicolored .55 .25
1330 A442 5.60z multicolored 1.00 .40
1331 A442 6.50z multicolored 1.65 .70
Nos. 1324-1331 (8) 4.20 2.35

Yachts: 30g, Dragon class. 40g, 5.5-m. class. 50g, Group of Finn class. 60g, V-class. 1.35z, Group of Cadet class. 4z, Group of Star class. 5.60z, Two Flying Dutchmen. 6.50z, Two Amethyst class. 15z, Finn class race. (30g, 40g, 60g, 5.60z vertical.)

### Miniature Sheet
**Perf. 11**

1332 A442 15z multicolored 2.00 1.25

World Championships of Finn Class Yachts, Gdynia, July 22-29. No. 1332 contains one stamp 48x22mm.

Marx and Lenin — A443

## 1965, June 14 — Photogravure and Engraved
**Perf. 11½x11**

1333 A443 60g black, ver .20 .20

6th Conference of Ministers of Post of Communist Countries, Peking, June 21-July 15.

Warsaw's Coat of Arms, 17th Cent. — A444

Old Town Hall, 18th Cent. — A445

## 1965, July 21 — Perf. 11x11, 11½x11, 12x12½, 12x12
**Engr.  Unwmk.**

1334 A444 5g carmine rose .20 .20
1335 A444 10g green .20 .20
1336 A445 20g violet blue .20 .20
1337 A445 40g brown .20 .20
1338 A445 60g orange .20 .20
1339 A444 1.50z black .20 .20
1340 A445 1.50z gray blue .20 .20
1341 A445 2.50z lilac .25 .20

### Photogravure and Engraved
**Perf. 11½**

1342 A444 3.40z citron & blk .90 .60
Nos. 1334-1342 (9) 2.55 2.20

Designs: 10g, Artifacts, 13th century. 20g, Tombstone of last Duke of Mazovia. 60g, Barbican. Gothic-Renaissance castle. 1.50z, Arsenal, 19th century. 1.55z, National Theater. 2.50z, Staszic Palace. 3.40z, Woman with sword from Heroes' Memorial and Warsaw Mermaid seal.

700th anniversary of Warsaw.

No. 1342 is perforated all around, with lower right quarter perforated or perforated to form a 21x26mm stamp within a stamp. It was issued in sheets of 25 (5x5). For surcharges see Nos. 1919-1926.

IQSY Emblem — A446

## 1965, Aug. 9 — Litho.

1343 A446 60g vio, ver, brt grn & blk .20 .20
a. 60g ultra, org, yel, bl & blk .25 .20
1344 A446 2.50z red, yel, bl & blk .20 .20
a. 2.50z red, brn, gray & blk .35 .20
1345 A446 3.40z, orange & multi .35 .20
a. 3.40z ultra & multi .80 .20
Nos. 1343-1345 (3) .80 .60

Designs: 2.50z, Radio telescope dish, Torun. 3.40z, Solar system.

International Quiet Sun Year, 1964-65.

Odontoglossum Grande — A447

Orchids: 30g, Cypripedium hibridum. 40g, Lycaste skinneri. 50g, Cattleya. 60g, Vanda sanderiana. 1.35z, Cypripedium hibridum. 4z, Sobralia. 5.60z, Disa grandiflora. 6.50z, Cattleya labiata.

## 1965, Sept. 6 — Photo.  Perf. 12½x12

1346 A447 20g multicolored .20 .20
1347 A447 30g multicolored .20 .20
1348 A447 40g multicolored .20 .20
1349 A447 50g multicolored .20 .20
1350 A447 60g multicolored .20 .25
1351 A447 1.35z multicolored .25 .20
1352 A447 4z multicolored .60 .30
1353 A447 5.60z multicolored 1.10 .40
1354 A447 6.50z multicolored 1.75 .75
Nos. 1346-1354 (9) 4.70 2.65

Weight Lifting — A448

## 1965, Oct. 8 — Photo.  Unwmk.

1355 A448 30g gold & multi .20 .20
1356 A448 40g gold & multi .20 .20
1357 A448 50g gold & multi .20 .20
1358 A448 60g gold & multi .20 .25
1359 A448 90g silver & multi .25 .20
1360 A448 3.40z gold & multi .50 .20
1361 A448 6.50z gold & multi 1.60 .40
1362 A448 7.10z bronze & multi 3.35 2.20
Nos. 1355-1362 (8)

Sport: 40g, Boxing. 50g, Relay race, men. 60g, Fencing. 90g, Women's 80-meter hurdles. 3.40z, Relay race, women. 6.50z, Hop, step and jump. 7.10z, Volleyball, women.

Victories won by the Polish team in 1964 Olympic Games. Each denomination printed in sheets of eight stamps and two center labels showing medals.

Mail Coach, by Piotr Michalowski — A449

## 1965, Oct. 9 — Engr.  Perf. 11x11½

1363 A449 60g brown .25 .20

Design: 2.50z, Departure of Coach, by Piotr Michalowski.

Issued for Stamp Day, 1965. Sheets of 50 with labels se-tenant inscribed "Dzien Znaczka 1965 R."

UN Emblem — A450

## 1965, Oct. 24 — Litho.  Perf. 12½x12

1364 A450 2.50z ultra .35 .20

20th anniversary of United Nations.

Plaszow Memorial — A451

## 1965, Nov. 29 — Engr.  Perf. 12x11, 11x12

1365 A451 60g gmsh gray .20 .20
1366 A451 60g brown .20 .20
1367 A451 60g chocolate .20 .20
1368 A451 60g black, horiz. .20 .20
Nos. 1366-1368 (3) .60 .60

#1367, Kielce Memorial. #1368, Chelm Memorial.

Note after #1277 applies also to #1366-1368.

Wolf A452

## 1965, Nov. 30 — Photo.  Perf. 11½

1369 A452 20g shown .20 .20
1370 A452 30g Lynx .20 .20
1371 A452 40g Red fox .20 .20
1372 A452 50g Badger .20 .20
1373 A452 60g Brown bear .20 .20
1374 A452 1.52z Wild Boar .50 .50
1375 A452 2.50z Red deer .50 .30
1376 A452 5.60z European bison 1.00 .35
1377 A452 7.10z Moose 4.25 2.50
Nos. 1369-1377 (9)

Gig — A453

Horse-drawn carriages, Lancut Museum: 40g, Coupé. 50g, Lady's basket. 60g, Vis-a-vis. 90g, Cab. 1.15z, Berlina. 2.50z, Hunting break. 6.50z, Caleche à la Daumont. 7.10z, English break.

## 1965, Dec. 30 — Litho.  Perf. 11
**Size: 50x23mm**

1378 A453 20g multicolored .20 .20
1379 A453 40g multicolored .20 .20
1380 A453 50g orange & multi .20 .20
1381 A453 60g fawn & multi .20 .20
1382 A453 90g yellow & multi .20 .20

**Size: 76x23mm**

1383 A453 1.15z multicolored .20 .20
1384 A453 2.50z olive & multi .45 .20
1385 A453 6.50z multicolored 1.25 .45

**Size: 103x23mm**

1386 A453 7.10z blue & multi .90
Nos. 1378-1386 (9) 4.65 2.75

Cargo Ship (No. 1389) — A454

## 1966 — Litho.  Perf. 11

1387 A454 60g multicolored .20 .20
1388 A454 60g multicolored .20 .20
1389 A454 60g multicolored .20 .20
1390 A454 60g multicolored .20 .20
1391 A454 60g multicolored .20 .20
1392 A454 60g multicolored .20 .20
1393 A454 60g multicolored .20 .20
1394 A454 60g multicolored .20 .20
Nos. 1387-1394 (8) 1.60 1.60

#1387, Supervising Technical Organization (NOT) emblem, symbols of industry. #1388, Pit head & miners' badge, vert. #1390, Chemical plant, Plock. #1391, Combine, vert. #1392, Railroad train. #1393, Building crane, vert. #1394, Pavilion & emblem of 35th Intl. Poznan Fair.

20th anniversary of the nationalization of Polish industry. No. 1394 also commemorates the 35th International Poznan Fair. Nos. 1387-1388 issued in connection with the 5th Congress of Polish Technicians, Katowice. Printed in sheets of 20 stamps and 20 labels with commemorative inscription within cogwheel on each label.

Issued: #1387-1388, 2/10; others, 5/21.

### Dinosaur Type of 1965

Prehistoric Vertebrates: 20g, Dinichthys. 30g, Eusthenopteron. 40g, Ichthyostega. 50g, Mastodonsaurus. 40g, Cynognathus. 2.50z, Archaeopteryx, vert. 3.40z, Brontotherium. 6.50z, Machairodus. 7.10z, Mammoth.

## 1966, Mar. 5 — Litho.  Perf. 12½

1395 A434 20g multicolored .20 .20
1396 A434 30g multicolored .20 .20
1397 A434 40g multicolored .20 .20
1398 A434 50g multicolored .20 .30
1399 A434 60g multicolored .30 .20
1400 A434 90g multicolored .55 .20
1401 A434 2.50z multicolored .35 .20
1402 A434 3.40z multicolored 1.25 .90
1403 A434 7.10z multicolored 5.25 2.75
Nos. 1395-1403 (9)

Henryk Sienkiewicz A455

## 1966, Mar. 30 — Photogravure and Engraved
**Perf. 11½**

1404 A455 60g black, dl yel .20 .20

Henryk Sienkiewicz (1846-1916), author and winner of 1905 Nobel Prize.

Soccer Game A456

Designs: Various phases of soccer. Each stamp inscribed with the place and the result of final game in various preceding soccer championships.

Peace Dove and War Memorial A457

## 1966, May 6  Photo.  Perf. 13x12

| | | | |
|---|---|---|---|
| 1405 | A456 | 20g multicolored | .20 .20 |
| 1406 | A456 | 40g multicolored | .20 .20 |
| 1407 | A456 | 60g multicolored | .20 .20 |
| 1408 | A456 | 90g multicolored | .25 .20 |
| 1409 | A456 | 1.50z multicolored | .35 .25 |
| 1410 | A456 | 3.40z multicolored | .60 .25 |
| 1411 | A456 | 6.50z multicolored | 1.25 .60 |
| 1412 | A456 | 7.10z multicolored | 1.65 .95 |
| | | Nos. 1405-1412 (8) | 4.65 2.80 |

World Cup Soccer Championship. Wembley, England, July 11-30. Each denomination printed in sheets of 10 (5x2).
See No. B109.

## 1966, May 9  Typo. & Engr.  Perf. 11½

| | | | |
|---|---|---|---|
| 1413 | A457 | 60g silver & multi | .20 .20 |

21st anniversary of victory over Fascism.

### Women's Relay Race A458

20g, Start of men's short distance race. 60g, Javelin. 90g, Women's 80-meter hurdles. 1.35z, Discus. 3.40z, Finish of men's medium distance race. 6.50z, Hammer throw. 7.10z, High jump.

## 1966, June 18  Perf. 11½x11, 11x11½  Litho.

| | | | |
|---|---|---|---|
| 1414 | A458 | 20g multi, vert. | .20 .20 |
| 1415 | A458 | 40g multi | .20 .20 |
| 1416 | A458 | 60g multi, vert. | .20 .20 |
| 1417 | A458 | 90g multi | .20 .20 |
| 1418 | A458 | 1.35z multi | .20 .20 |
| 1419 | A458 | 3.40z multi | .50 .30 |
| 1420 | A458 | 6.50z multi, vert. | .65 .30 |
| 1421 | A458 | 7.10z multi, vert. | .85 .50 |
| | | Nos. 1414-1421 (8) | 3.00 2.00 |

### Souvenir Sheet

#### Imperf

| | | | |
|---|---|---|---|
| 1422 | A458 | 5z multicolored | 1.75 .90 |

European Athletic Championships, Budapest, August, 1966. No. 1422 contains one 57x27mm stamp.

### Polish Eagle — A459

## 1966, July 21  Photogravure and Embossed  Perf. 12½x12  Unwmk.

| | | | |
|---|---|---|---|
| 1423 | A459 | 60g gold, red & blk | .20 .20 |
| 1424 | A459 | 60g gold, red & blk | .20 .20 |
| 1425 | A459 | 2.50z gold, red & blk | .25 .20 |
| 1426 | A459 | 2.50z gold, red & blk | .90 .80 |
| | | Nos. 1423-1426 (4) | |

1000th anniversary of Poland. Nos. 1423-1424 and 1425-1426 printed in 2 sheets of 10 (5x2); top row in each sheet in eagle design, bottom row in flag design.

Designs: Nos. 1424, 1426, Flag of Poland. No. 1425, Polish Eagle.

### Flowers and Farm Produce — A460

## 1966, Aug. 15  Photo.  Perf. 11

Designs: 60g, Woman holding loaf of bread. 3.40z, Farm girls holding harvest wreath.

**Size: 22x50mm**

| | | | |
|---|---|---|---|
| 1427 | A460 | 40g gold & multi | .25 .20 |
| 1428 | A460 | 60g gold & multi | .25 .20 |

**Size: 48x50mm**

| | | | |
|---|---|---|---|
| 1429 | A460 | 3.40z violet bl & multi | .55 .35 |
| | | Nos. 1427-1429 (3) | 1.05 .75 |

Issued to publicize the harvest festival.

### Chrysanthemum — A461

Flowers: 20g, Poinsettia. 30g, Centaury. 40g, Rose. 60g, Zinnias. 90g, Nasturtium. 5.60z, Dahlia. 6.50z, Sunflower. 7.10z, Magnolia.

## 1966, Sept. 1  Perf. 11½  Flowers in Natural Colors

| | | | |
|---|---|---|---|
| 1430 | A461 | 10g gold & black | .20 .20 |
| 1431 | A461 | 20g gold & black | .20 .20 |
| 1432 | A461 | 30g gold & black | .20 .20 |
| 1433 | A461 | 40g gold & black | .20 .20 |
| 1434 | A461 | 60g gold & black | .20 .20 |
| 1435 | A461 | 90g gold & black | .60 .20 |
| 1436 | A461 | 5.60z gold & black | .75 .35 |
| 1437 | A461 | 6.50z gold & black | 1.10 .50 |
| 1438 | A461 | 7.10z gold & black | .85 .60 |
| | | Nos. 1430-1438 (9) | 4.30 2.65 |

### Map Showing Tourist Attractions A462

Designs: 20g, Lighthouse, Hel. 40g, Amethyst yacht on Masurian Lake. No. 1442, Poniatowski Bridge, Warsaw, and sailboat. No. 1440, Mining Academy, Kielce. 1.15z, Dunajec Gorge. 1.35z, Old oaks, Rogalin. 1.55z, Planetarium, Katowice. 2z, M.S. Batory and globe.

#### Perf. 12½x12, 11½x12  Engr.

| | | | |
|---|---|---|---|
| 1439 | A462 | 10g carmine rose | .20 .20 |
| 1440 | A462 | 20g olive grn | .20 .20 |
| 1441 | A462 | 40g grysh blue | .20 .20 |
| 1442 | A462 | 60g redsh brown | .20 .20 |
| 1443 | A462 | 60g black | .20 .20 |
| 1444 | A462 | 1.15z green | .40 .20 |
| 1445 | A462 | 1.35z vermillion | .40 .45 |
| 1446 | A462 | 1.55z violet | 1.10 .75 |
| 1447 | A462 | 2z dark gray | 1.80 1.80 |
| | | Nos. 1439-1447 (9) | |

### Stableman with Percherons, by Piotr Michalowski — A463

2.50z, "Horses and Dogs" by Michalowski.

## 1966, Sept. 8  Perf. 11x11½

| | | | |
|---|---|---|---|
| 1448 | A463 | 60g gray brown | .20 .20 |
| 1449 | A463 | 2.50z green | .20 .20 |

Issued for Stamp Day, 1966.

### Capital of Romanesque Column from Tyniec and Polish Flag — A464

### Engraved and Photogravure

## 1966, Oct. 7  Perf. 11½

| | | | |
|---|---|---|---|
| 1450 | A464 | 60g dark brn & rose | .20 .20 |

Polish Cultural Congress.

### Soldier A465

## 1966, Oct. 20  Litho.  Perf. 11x11½

| | | | |
|---|---|---|---|
| 1451 | A465 | 60g blk, ol grn, & dl red | .20 .20 |

Participation of the Polish Jaroslawski Dabrowski Brigade in the Spanish Civil War.

### Green Woodpecker — A466

Forest Birds: 10g, The eight birds of the set combined. 30g, Eurasian jay. 40g, European golden oriole. 60g, Hoopoe. 2.50z, European redstart. 4z, Siskin (finch). 6.50z, Chaffinch. 7.10z, Great tit.

## 1966, Nov. 17  Photo.  Perf. 11½  Birds in Natural Colors; Black Inscription

| | | | |
|---|---|---|---|
| 1452 | A466 | 10g lt green | .20 .20 |
| 1453 | A466 | 20g dull violet bl | .20 .20 |
| 1454 | A466 | 30g dull green | .20 .20 |
| 1455 | A466 | 40g dull green | .20 .20 |
| 1456 | A466 | 60g gray green | .20 .20 |
| 1457 | A466 | 2.50z lt olive grn | .40 .20 |
| 1458 | A466 | 4z dull violet | 1.40 .45 |
| 1459 | A466 | 6.50z green | 1.10 .75 |
| 1460 | A466 | 7.10z gray blue | 2.00 2.80 |
| | | Nos. 1452-1460 (9) | 5.90 |

### Ceramic Ram, c. 4000 B.C. — A467

Designs: No. 1462, Bronze weapons and ornaments, c. 3500 B.C.; horiz. No. 1463, Biskupin, settlement plan, 2500 B.C.

## 1966, Dec. 10  Engr.  Perf. 11x11½

| | | | |
|---|---|---|---|
| 1461 | A467 | 60g dull violet blue | .20 .20 |
| 1462 | A467 | 60g brown | .20 .20 |
| 1463 | A467 | 60g green | .60 .60 |
| | | Nos. 1461-1463 (3) | |

### Polish Eagle, Hammer and Grain — A468

Designs: 60g, Eagle and map of Poland.

## 1966, Dec. 20  Litho.  Perf. 11

| | | | |
|---|---|---|---|
| 1464 | A468 | 40g brn, red & bluish lil | .20 .20 |
| 1465 | A468 | 60g brn, red & ol grn | .20 .20 |

Millenium of Poland.

### Vostok (USSR) — A469

Spacecraft: 40g, Gemini, American Spacecraft. 60g, Ariel 2 (Great Britian). 1.35z, Proton 1 (USSR). 1.50z, FR 1 (France). 3.40z, Alouette (Canada). 6.50z, San Marco 1 (Italy). 7.10z, Luna 9 (USSR).

## 1966, Dec. 20  Perf. 11½x11

| | | | |
|---|---|---|---|
| 1466 | A469 | 20g tan & multi | .20 .20 |
| 1467 | A469 | 40g brown & multi | .20 .20 |
| 1468 | A469 | 60g gray & multi | .20 .20 |
| 1469 | A469 | 1.35z multicolored | .20 .20 |
| 1470 | A469 | 1.50z multicolored | .20 .20 |
| 1471 | A469 | 3.40z multicolored | .50 .25 |
| 1472 | A469 | 6.50z multicolored | 1.10 .25 |
| 1473 | A469 | 7.10z multicolored | 1.40 .50 |
| | | Nos. 1466-1473 (8) | 4.00 1.95 |

### Dressage — A470

Horses: 20g, Horse race. 40g, Jump. 60g, Steeplechase. 90g, Trotting. 5.90z, Polo. 6.60z, Stallion "Ofir." 7z, Stallion "Skowronek."

## 1967, Feb. 25  Photo.  Perf. 12½

| | | | |
|---|---|---|---|
| 1474 | A470 | 10g ultra & multi | .20 .20 |
| 1475 | A470 | 20g orange & multi | .20 .20 |
| 1476 | A470 | 40g ver & multi | .20 .20 |
| 1477 | A470 | 60g multicolored | .20 .20 |
| 1478 | A470 | 90g green & multi | .25 .20 |
| 1479 | A470 | 5.90z multicolored | .95 .20 |
| 1480 | A470 | 6.60z multicolored | 1.25 .45 |
| 1481 | A470 | 7z violet & multi | 2.25 1.00 |
| | | Nos. 1474-1481 (8) | 5.50 2.65 |

Janov Podlaski stud farm, 150th anniv.

### Memorial at Auschwitz (Oswiecim) A471

### Emblem of Memorials Administration A472

**1967   Engr.   Perf. 11½x11, 11x11½**

| | | | | |
|---|---|---|---|---|
| 1482 | A471 | 40g brown olive | .20 | .20 |
| 1483 | A472 | 40g dull violet | .20 | .20 |
| 1484 | A472 | 40g black | .20 | .20 |
| 1485 | A472 | 40g green | .20 | .20 |
| 1486 | A472 | 40g black | .20 | .20 |
| 1487 | A472 | 40g ultra | .20 | .20 |
| 1488 | A471 | 40g brown | .20 | .20 |
| 1489 | A472 | 40g deep plum | 1.60 | 1.60 |
| Nos. 1482-1489 (8) | | | | |

Memorials at: No. 1484, Oswiecim-Monowice, No. 1485, Westerplatte, No. 1486, Lodz-Radugoszcz (Walcz). Stutthof. No. 1488, Lambinowice-Jencom. No. 1489, Zagan.

Issued to commemorate the martyrdom and fight of the Polish people, 1939-45. Issue dates: Nos. 1482-1484, Oct. 10. Nos. 1485-1487, Oct. 9. Nos. 1488-1489, Dec. 28. See Nos. 1620-1624.

**Striped Butterflyfish — A473**

**1967, Apr. 1   Litho.   Perf. 11x11½**

| | | | | |
|---|---|---|---|---|
| 1492 | A473 | 5g multicolored | .20 | .20 |
| 1493 | A473 | 10g multicolored | .20 | .20 |
| 1494 | A473 | 60g multicolored | .20 | .20 |
| 1495 | A473 | 60g multicolored | .20 | .20 |
| 1496 | A473 | 90g multicolored | .20 | .20 |
| 1497 | A473 | 90g multicolored | .20 | .20 |
| 1498 | A473 | 1.50z multicolored | .70 | .20 |
| 1499 | A473 | 4.50z multicolored | .80 | .70 |
| 1500 | A473 | 7z multicolored | .85 | .80 |
| Nos. 1492-1500 (9) | | | 4.25 | 2.55 |

Tropical fish: 10g, Imperial angelfish. 90g, Undulate triggerfish. 1.50z, Striped triggerfish. 4.50z, Black-eye butterflyfish. 7z, Saddleback butterflyfish.

Barred butterflyfish. 60g, Spotted triggerfish. 90g, Undulate triggerfish. Blue angelfish.

**Bicyclists — A474**

**1967, May 5   Litho.   Perf. 11**

| | | | | |
|---|---|---|---|---|
| 1501 | A474 | 60g multicolored | .20 | .20 |

20th Warsaw-Berlin-Prague Bicycle Race.

**Men's 100-meter Race — A475**

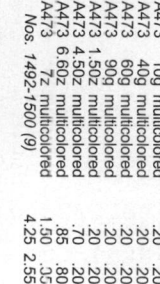

**1967, May 24   Litho.   Perf. 11**

| | | | | |
|---|---|---|---|---|
| 1502 | A475 | 20g multicolored | .20 | .20 |
| 1503 | A475 | 40g multicolored | .20 | .20 |
| 1504 | A475 | 60g multicolored | .20 | .20 |
| 1505 | A475 | 90g multicolored | .20 | .20 |
| 1506 | A475 | 1.35z multicolored | .20 | .20 |
| 1507 | A475 | 3.40z multicolored | .35 | .20 |
| 1508 | A475 | 6.60z multicolored | .75 | .25 |
| 1509 | A475 | 7z multicolored | .90 | .55 |
| Nos. 1502-1509 (8) | | | 3.00 | 2.00 |

Sports and Olympic Rings: 40g, Steeplechase. 60g, Women's relay race. 90g, Weightlifter. 1.35z, Hurdler. 3.40z, Gymnast on vaulting horse. 6.60z, High jump. 7z, Boxing.

19th Olympic Games, Mexico City, 1968. Nos. 1502-1509 printed in sheets of 8, (2x4) with label showing emblem of Polish Olympic Committee between each two horizontal stamps. See No. B110.

**Badge of Socialist Working Brigade A476**

**1967, June 2**

| | | | | |
|---|---|---|---|---|
| 1510 | A476 | 60g multicolored | .20 | .20 |

6th Congress of Polish Trade Unions. Printed in sheets of 20 stamps and 20 labels and in miniature sheets of 4 stamps and 4 labels.

**Mountain Arnica — A477**

**1967, June 14   Perf. 11½x11**

**Flowers in Natural Colors**

| | | | | |
|---|---|---|---|---|
| 1511 | A477 | 40g black & brn org | .20 | .20 |
| 1512 | A477 | 60g black & lt blue | .20 | .20 |
| 1513 | A477 | 3.40z black & dp org | .35 | .20 |
| 1514 | A477 | 4.50z black & lt vio | .20 | .20 |
| 1515 | A477 | 5z black & maroon | .40 | .20 |
| 1516 | A477 | 10z black & bister | .40 | .40 |
| Nos. 1511-1516 (6) | | | 2.50 | 1.40 |

Medicinal Plants: 60g, Columbine. 3.40z, Gentian. 4.50z, Ground pine. 5z, Iris sibirica. 10z, Azalea pontica.

**Monument for Silesian Insurgents A478**

**1967, July 21   Litho.   Perf. 11½**

| | | | | |
|---|---|---|---|---|
| 1517 | A478 | 60g multicolored | .20 | .20 |

Unveiling of the monument for the Silesian Insurgents of 1919-21 at Katowice, July, 1967.

**Marie Curie — A479**

**1967, Aug. 1   Engr.   Perf. 11½x11**

| | | | | |
|---|---|---|---|---|
| 1518 | A479 | 60g dk carmine rose | .20 | .20 |
| 1519 | A479 | 60g violet | .20 | .20 |
| 1520 | A479 | 60g sepia | .20 | .20 |
| Nos. 1518-1520 (3) | | | .60 | .60 |

Marie Skłodowska Curie (1867-1934), discoverer of radium and polonium.

**Sign Language and Emblem A480**

**1967, Aug. 1   Litho.   Perf. 11x11½**

| | | | | |
|---|---|---|---|---|
| 1521 | A480 | 60g brt blue & blk | .20 | .20 |

5th Congress of the World Federation of the Deaf, Warsaw, Aug. 10-17.

**Flowers of the Meadows A481**

**1967, Sept. 5   Photo.   Perf. 11½**

| | | | | |
|---|---|---|---|---|
| 1522 | A481 | 40g multicolored | .20 | .20 |
| 1523 | A481 | 40g multicolored | .20 | .20 |
| 1524 | A481 | 60g multicolored | .20 | .20 |
| 1525 | A481 | 90g multicolored | .20 | .20 |
| 1526 | A481 | 1.15z multicolored | .20 | .20 |
| 1527 | A481 | 1.35z multicolored | .50 | .20 |
| 1528 | A481 | 2.50z multicolored | .35 | .20 |
| 1529 | A481 | 3.40z multicolored | .50 | .20 |
| 1530 | A481 | 4.50z multicolored | 1.00 | .20 |
| Nos. 1522-1530 (9) | | | 4.10 | 1.90 |

Flowers: 40g, Poppy. 60g, Morning glory. 90g, Pansy. 1.15z, Common pansy. 2.50z, Corn cockle. 3.40z, Wild aster. 4.50z, Common pimpernel. 7.90z, Chicory.

**Wilanow Palace, by Wincenty Kasprzycki — A482**

**1967, Oct. 9   Engraved and Photogravure   Perf. 11½**

| | | | | |
|---|---|---|---|---|
| 1531 | A482 | 60g olive blk & lt bl | .20 | .20 |

Issued for Stamp Day, 1967.

**Cruiser Aurora — A483**

**1967, Oct. 9   Litho.   Perf. 11**

| | | | | |
|---|---|---|---|---|
| 1532 | A483 | 60g gray, red & blk | .20 | .20 |
| 1533 | A483 | 60g gray, dull red & blk | .20 | .20 |
| 1534 | A483 | 60g gray, red & blk | .20 | .20 |
| Nos. 1532-1534 (3) | | | .60 | .60 |

Designs: No. 1533, Lenin and library. No. 1534, Luna 10, earth and moon.

Russian Revolution, 50th anniv.

**Tadeusz Kosciusko — A485**

**1967, Oct. 14   Engraved and Photogravure   Perf. 12x11**

| | | | | |
|---|---|---|---|---|
| 1540 | A485 | 60g choc & ocher | .20 | .20 |
| 1541 | A485 | 2.50z sl grn & rose car | .20 | .20 |

Tadeusz Kosciusko (1746-1817), Polish patriot and general in the American Revolution.

**Vanessa Butterfly A486**

**1967, Oct. 14   Litho.   Perf. 11½**

**Butterflies in Natural Colors**

| | | | | |
|---|---|---|---|---|
| 1542 | A486 | 10g green | .20 | .20 |
| 1543 | A486 | 10g green | .20 | .20 |
| 1544 | A486 | 20g lt violet bl | .20 | .20 |
| 1545 | A486 | 40g yellow green | .20 | .20 |
| 1546 | A486 | 60g gray | .20 | .20 |
| 1547 | A486 | 90g lemon | .25 | .20 |
| 1548 | A486 | 2.50z blue | .30 | .20 |
| 1549 | A486 | 4.50z rose lilac | 1.25 | .60 |
| 1550 | A486 | 7.90z bister | 2.00 | .60 |
| Nos. 1542-1550 (9) | | | 5.00 | 2.60 |

Designs: Various Butterflies.

**Polish Woman, by Antoine Watteau A487**

**1967, Nov. 15   Photo.   Perf. 11½x11, 11x11½**

| | | | | |
|---|---|---|---|---|
| 1551 | A487 | 20g gold & multi | .20 | .20 |
| 1552 | A487 | 40g gold & multi | .20 | .20 |
| 1553 | A487 | 60g gold & multi | .20 | .20 |
| 1554 | A487 | 2z gold & multi | .25 | .20 |
| 1555 | A487 | 2.50z gold & multi | .40 | .20 |
| 1556 | A487 | 3.40z gold & multi | .40 | .20 |
| 1557 | A487 | 4.50z gold & multi | .95 | .45 |
| 1558 | A487 | 6.60z gold & multi | 1.10 | .45 |
| Nos. 1551-1558 (8) | | | 3.50 | 2.35 |

Printed in sheets of 5 + label.

Paintings from Polish Museums: 20g, Lady with the Ermine, by Leonardo da Vinci. 60g, Dog Fighting Heron, by Abraham Hondius. 2z, Guitarist after the Hunt, by J. Baptiste Greuze. 2.50z, Tax Collectors, by Marinus van Reymerswaele. 3.40z, Portrait of Daria Flodorowna, by Fiodor St. Rokotov. 4.50z, Still Life with Lobster, by Jean de Heem, horiz. 6.60z, Landscape (from the Good Samaritan), by Rembrandt, horiz.

**Ossolinski Medal, Book and Flags — A488**

**1967, Dec. 12   Litho.   Perf. 11**

| | | | | |
|---|---|---|---|---|
| 1559 | A488 | 60g lt bl, red & lt brn | .20 | .20 |

150th anniversary of the founding of the Ossolineum, a center for scientific and cultural activities, by Count Josef Maximilian Ossolinski.

**Wladyslaw S. Reymont (1867-1924), Writer, Nobel Prize Winner — A489**

**1967, Dec. 12   Engr.   Perf. 11**

| | | | | |
|---|---|---|---|---|
| 1560 | A489 | 60g dk brn, ocher & red | .20 | .20 |

Ice Hockey A490

Designs: 60g, Skiing. 90g, Slalom. 1.35z, Speed skating. 1.55z, Long-distance skiing. 2z, Sledding. 7z, Biathlon. 7.90z, Ski jump.

**1968, Jan. 10**

| | | | | | |
|---|---|---|---|---|---|
| **1561** | A490 | 40g multicolored | .20 | .20 |
| **1562** | A490 | 60g multicolored | .20 | .20 |
| **1563** | A490 | 90g multicolored | .20 | .20 |
| **1564** | A490 | 1.35z multicolored | .20 | .20 |
| **1565** | A490 | 1.55z multicolored | .20 | .20 |
| **1566** | A490 | 2z multicolored | .20 | .20 |
| **1567** | A490 | 7z multicolored | .45 | .35 |
| **1568** | A490 | 7.90z multicolored | .85 | .55 |
| | | *Nos. 1561-1568 (8)* | 2.50 | 2.10 |

10th Winter Olympic Games, Grenoble, France, Feb. 6-18, 1968.

Puss in Boots — A491

Fairy Tales: 40g, The Fox and the Raven. 60g, Mr. Twardowski (man flying on a cock). 2z, The Fisherman and the Fish. 2.50z, Little Red Riding Hood. 3.40z, Cinderella. 5.50z, Thumbelina. 7z, Snow White.

**1968, Mar. 15 Litho. *Perf. 12½***

| | | | | |
|---|---|---|---|---|
| **1569** | A491 | 20g multicolored | .20 | .20 |
| **1570** | A491 | 40g lt violet & multi | .20 | .20 |
| **1571** | A491 | 60g multicolored | .20 | .20 |
| **1572** | A491 | 2z olive & multi | .25 | .20 |
| **1573** | A491 | 2.50z ver & multi | .35 | .20 |
| **1574** | A491 | 3.40z multicolored | .65 | .20 |
| **1575** | A491 | 5.50z multicolored | .90 | .45 |
| **1576** | A491 | 7z multicolored | 1.50 | .60 |
| | | *Nos. 1569-1576 (8)* | 4.25 | 2.25 |

Bird-of-Paradise Flower — A492

Exotic Flowers: 10g, Clianthus dampieri. 20g, Passiflora quadrangularis. 40g, Coryphanta vivipara. 60g, Odontonia. 90g, Protea cynaroides.

**1968, May 15 Litho. *Perf. 11½***

| | | | | |
|---|---|---|---|---|
| **1577** | A492 | 10g sepia & multi | .20 | .20 |
| **1578** | A492 | 20g multicolored | .20 | .20 |
| **1579** | A492 | 30g brown & multi | .20 | .20 |
| **1580** | A492 | 40g ultra & multi | .20 | .20 |
| **1581** | A492 | 60g multicolored | .20 | .20 |
| **1582** | A492 | 90g multicolored | .20 | .20 |
| | | *Nos. 1577-1582,B111-B112 (8)* | 3.65 | 2.50 |

"Peace" by Henryk Tomaszewski A493

2.50z, Poster for Gounod's Faust, by Jan Lenica.

**1968, May 29 Litho. *Perf. 11½x11***

| | | | | |
|---|---|---|---|---|
| **1583** | A493 | 60g gray & multi | .20 | .20 |
| **1584** | A493 | 2.50z gray & multi | .20 | .20 |

2nd Intl. Poster Biennial Exhibition, Warsaw.

Zephyr Glider — A494

Polish Gliders: 90g, Storks. 1.50z, Swallow. 3.40z, Flies. 4z, Seal. 5.50z, Pirate.

**1968, May 29 *Perf. 12½***

| | | | | |
|---|---|---|---|---|
| **1585** | A494 | 60g multicolored | .20 | .20 |
| **1586** | A494 | 90g multicolored | .20 | .20 |
| **1587** | A494 | 1.50z multicolored | .20 | .20 |
| **1588** | A494 | 3.40z multicolored | .55 | .20 |
| **1589** | A494 | 4z multicolored | .80 | .30 |
| **1590** | A494 | 5.50z multicolored | .95 | .40 |
| | | *Nos. 1585-1590 (6)* | 2.90 | 1.50 |

11th Intl. Glider Championships, Leszno.

Child Holding Symbolic Stamp — A495

Sosnowiec Memorial — A496

No. 1592, Balloon over Poznan Town Hall.

**1968, July 2 Litho. *Perf. 11½x11***

| | | | | |
|---|---|---|---|---|
| **1591** | A495 | 60g multicolored | .20 | .20 |
| **1592** | A495 | 60g multicolored | .20 | .20 |

75 years of Polish philately; "Tematica 1968" stamp exhibition in Poznan. Printed in sheets of 12 (4x3) se-tenant, arranged checkerwise.

**Photogravure and Engraved**

**1968, July 20 *Perf. 11x11½***

| | | | | |
|---|---|---|---|---|
| **1593** | A496 | 60g brt rose lilac & blk | .20 | .20 |

The monument by Helena and Roman Husarski and Witold Ceckiewicz was unveiled Sept. 16, 1967, to honor the revolutionary deeds of Silesian workers and miners.

Relay Race and Sculptured Head A497

Sports and Sculptures: 40g, Boxing. 60g. Basketball. 90g, Long jump. 2.50z, Women's javelin. 3.40z, Athlete on parallel bars. 4z, Bicycling. 7.90z, Fencing.

**1968, Sept. 2 Litho. *Perf. 11x11½***
**Size: 35x26mm**

| | | | | |
|---|---|---|---|---|
| **1594** | A497 | 30g sepia & multi | .20 | .20 |
| **1595** | A497 | 40g brn org, brn & blk | .20 | .20 |
| **1596** | A497 | 60g gray & multi | .20 | .20 |
| **1597** | A497 | 90g violet & multi | .20 | .20 |
| **1598** | A497 | 2.50z multicolored | .20 | .20 |
| **1599** | A497 | 3.40z brt grn, blk & lt ultra | .35 | .20 |
| **1600** | A497 | 4z multicolored | .35 | .35 |
| **1601** | A497 | 7.90z multicolored | .65 | .40 |
| | | *Nos. 1594-1601,B113 (9)* | 4.25 | 2.75 |

19th Olympic Games, Mexico City, 10/12-27.

Jewish Woman with Lemons, by Aleksander Gierymski A498

Polish Paintings: 40g, Knight on Bay Horse, by Piotr Michalowski. 60g, Fisherman, by Leon Wyczolkowski. 1.35z, Eliza Parenska, by Stanislaw Wyspianski. 1.50z, "Manifest," by Wojciech Weiss. 4.50z, Stancyk (Jester), by Jan Matejko, horiz. 5z, Children's Band, by Tadeusz Makowski, horiz. 7z, Feast II, by Zygmunt Waliszewski, horiz.

***Perf. 11½x11, 11x11½***

**1968, Oct. 10 Litho.**

| | | | | |
|---|---|---|---|---|
| **1602** | A498 | 40g gray & multi | .20 | .20 |
| **1603** | A498 | 60g gray & multi | .20 | .20 |
| **1604** | A498 | 1.15z gray & multi | .20 | .20 |
| **1605** | A498 | 1.35z gray & multi | .35 | .20 |
| **1606** | A498 | 1.50z gray & multi | .50 | .30 |
| **1607** | A498 | 4.50z gray & multi | .50 | .25 |
| **1608** | A498 | 5z gray & multi | .80 | .60 |
| **1609** | A498 | 7z gray & multi | 1.25 | .60 |
| | | *Nos. 1602-1609 (8)* | 4.00 | 2.55 |

Issued in sheets of 4 stamps and 2 labels inscribed with painter's name.

"September, 1939" by M. Bylina — A499

Paintings: No. 1611, Partisans, by L. Maciag. No. 1612, Tank in Battle, by M. Bylina. No. 1613, Monte Cassino, by A. Boratynski. No. 1614, Tanks Approaching Warsaw, by S. Garwatowski. No. 1615, Battle on the Neisse, by M. Bylina. No. 1616, On the Oder, by K. Mackiowicz. No. 1617, "In Berlin," by M. Bylina. No. 1618, Warship "Blyskawica" by M. Mokwa. No. 1619, "Pursuit" (fighter planes), by T. Kulisiewicz.

**Litho., Typo. & Engr.**

**1968, Oct. 12 *Perf. 11½***

| | | | | |
|---|---|---|---|---|
| **1610** | A499 | 40g pale yel, ol & vio | .20 | .20 |
| **1611** | A499 | 40g lil, red lil & ind | .20 | .20 |
| **1612** | A499 | 40g gray, dk bl & ol | .20 | .20 |
| **1613** | A499 | 40g pale sal, org brn & blk | .20 | .20 |
| **1614** | A499 | 40g pale grn, dk grn & plum | .20 | .20 |
| **1615** | A499 | 60g gray, vio bl & blk | .20 | .20 |
| **1616** | A499 | 60g pale grn, ol grn & vio brn | .20 | .20 |
| **1617** | A499 | 60g pink, car & grnsh blk | .20 | .20 |
| **1618** | A499 | 60g pink, brn & grn | .20 | .20 |
| **1619** | A499 | 60g lt bl, grnsh bl & blk | .20 | .20 |
| | | *Nos. 1610-1619 (10)* | 2.00 | 2.00 |

Polish People's Army, 25th anniversary.

Memorial Types of 1967

Designs: No. 1620, Tomb of the Unknown Soldier, Warsaw. No. 1621, Nazi War Crimes Memorial, Zamosc. No. 1622, Guerrilla Memorial, Plichno. No. 1623, Guerrilla Memorial, Kartuzy. No. 1624, Polish Insurgents' Memorial, Poznan.

***Perf. 11½x11, 11x11½***

**1968, Nov. 15 Engr.**

| | | | | |
|---|---|---|---|---|
| **1620** | A471 | 40g slate | .20 | .20 |
| **1621** | A472 | 40g dull red | .20 | .20 |
| **1622** | A472 | 40g dark blue | .20 | .20 |
| **1623** | A471 | 40g sepia | .20 | .20 |
| **1624** | A472 | 40g sepia | .20 | .20 |
| | | *Nos. 1620-1624 (5)* | 1.00 | 1.00 |

Martyrdom & fight of the Polish people, 1939-45.

Strikers, S. Lentz A500

No. 1626, "Manifesto," by Wojciech Weiss. No. 1627, Party members, by F. Kowarski, horiz.

***Perf. 11½x11, 11x11½***

**1968, Nov. 11 Litho.**

| | | | | |
|---|---|---|---|---|
| **1625** | A500 | 60g dark red & multi | .20 | .20 |
| **1626** | A500 | 60g dark red & multi | .20 | .20 |
| **1627** | A500 | 60g dark red & multi | .20 | .20 |
| | | *Nos. 1625-1627 (3)* | .60 | .60 |

5th Cong. of the Polish United Workers' Party.

Departure for the Hunt, by Wojciech Kossak — A501

Hunt Paintings: 40g, Hunting with Falcon, by Juliusz Kossak. 60g, Wolves' Raid, by A. Wierusz-Kowalski. 1.50z, Bear Hunt, by Julian Falat. 2.50z, Fox Hunt, by T. Sutherland. 3.40z, Boar Hunt, by Frans Snyders. 4.50z, Hunters' Rest, by W. G. Pierow. 8.50z, Lion Hunt in Morocco, by Delacroix.

**1968, Nov. 20 *Perf. 11***

| | | | | |
|---|---|---|---|---|
| **1628** | A501 | 20g multicolored | .20 | .20 |
| **1629** | A501 | 40g multicolored | .20 | .20 |
| **1630** | A501 | 60g multicolored | .20 | .20 |
| **1631** | A501 | 1.50z multicolored | .20 | .20 |
| **1632** | A501 | 2.50z multicolored | .20 | .20 |
| **1633** | A501 | 3.40z multicolored | .40 | .20 |
| **1634** | A501 | 4.50z multicolored | .80 | .40 |
| **1635** | A501 | 8.50z multicolored | 1.40 | .80 |
| | | *Nos. 1628-1635 (8)* | 3.60 | 2.40 |

Afghan Greyhound A502

Dogs: 20g, Maltese. 40g, Rough-haired fox terrier, vert. 1.50z, Schnauzer. 2.50z, English setter. 3.40z, Pekinese. 4.50z, German shepherd. 8.50z, Pointer.

**1969, Feb. 2 *Perf. 11x11½, 11½x11***

**Dogs in Natural Colors**

| | | | | |
|---|---|---|---|---|
| **1636** | A502 | 20g gray & brt grn | .20 | .20 |
| **1637** | A502 | 40g gray & orange | .30 | .20 |
| **1638** | A502 | 60g gray & lilac | .30 | .20 |
| **1639** | A502 | 1.50z gray & black | .30 | .20 |
| **1640** | A502 | 2.50z gray & brt pink | .45 | .25 |
| **1641** | A502 | 3.40z gray & dk grn | .75 | .30 |
| **1642** | A502 | 4.50z gray & ver | 1.40 | .55 |
| **1643** | A502 | 8.50z gray & violet | 2.75 | 1.25 |
| | | *Nos. 1636-1643 (8)* | 6.45 | 3.15 |

General Assembly of the Intl. Kennel Federation, Warsaw, May 1969.

**Eagle-on-Shield House Sign — A503**

**1969, Feb. 23    Litho.    Perf. 11½x11**
1644 A503 60g gray, red & blk    .20 .20
9th Congress of Democratic Movement.

**Sheaf of Wheat A504**

**1969, Mar. 29    Litho.    Perf. 11½x11**
1645 A504 60g multicolored    .20 .20
5th Congress of the United Peasant Party, Warsaw, March 29-31.

**Runner — A505**

**1969, Apr. 25    Litho.    Perf. 11½x11**
1646 A505 10g orange & multi    .20 .20
1647 A505 20g ultra & multi    .20 .20
1648 A505 40g yellow & multi    .20 .20
1649 A505 60g red & multi    .20 .20
Nos. 1646-1649,B114-B117 (8)    3.10 1.65

Olympic Rings and; 20g, Woman gymnast. 40g, Weight lifting. 60g, Women's javelin.

50th anniv. of the Polish Olympic Committee, and the 75th anniv. of the Intl. Olympic Committee.

**Sailboat and Lighthouse, Kolobrzeg Harbor — A506**

**1969, May 20    Litho.    Perf. 11**
1650 A506 40g multicolored    .20 .20
1651 A506 60g multicolored    .20 .20
1652 A506 1.35z multicolored    .20 .20
1653 A506 1.50z multicolored    .20 .20
1654 A506 2.50z multicolored    .20 .20
1655 A506 3.40z multicolored    .25 .20
1656 A506 4z multicolored    .35 .20
1657 A506 4.50z multicolored    .60 .25
Nos. 1650-1657 (8)    2.20 1.65

40g, Tourist map of Swietokrzyski National Park. 60g, Ruins of 16th cent. castle, Niedzica, vert. 1.50z, Castle of the Dukes of Pomerania & ship, Szczecin. 2.50z, View of Torun & Vistula. 3.40z, View of Klodzko, vert. 4z, View of Sulejow. 4.50z, Market Place, Kazimierz Dolny, vert.

Issued for tourist publicity. Printed in sheets of 15 stamps and 15 labels. Domestic plants on labels of 40g, 60g and 1.35z, coats of arms on others.
See Nos. 1731-1735.

**World Map and Sailboat Opty A507**

**1969, June 21    Litho.    Perf. 11x11½**
1658 A507 60g multicolored    .20 .20
Leonid Teliga's one-man voyage around the world, Casablanca, Jan. 21, 1967, to Las Palmas, Apr. 16, 1969.

**Nicolaus Copernicus, Woodcut by Tobias Stimer — A508**

**1969, June 26    Photo., Engr. & Litho.    Perf. 11½**
1659 A508 40g dl yel, sep & dp    .20 .20
1660 A508 60g grnsh gray, blk & dp car    .20 .20
1661 A508 2.50z lt vio brn, bl & dp car    .40 .20
Nos. 1659-1661 (3)    .80 .60

Designs: 60g, Copernicus, by Jeremias Falck. 15th century globe and map of constellations. 2.50z, Copernicus, painting by Jan Matejko and map of heliocentric system.

**"Memory" Pathfinders' Cross and Protectors' Badge A509**

**1969, July 19    Photo., Engr. & Litho.    Perf. 11x11½**
1662 A509 60g ultra, blk & red    .20 .20
1663 A509 60g green, blk & red    .20 .20
1664 A509 60g carmine, blk & grn    .60 .60
Nos. 1662-1664 (3)    .20 .60

#1663, "Defense," military eagle and Pathfinders' cross. #1664, "Labor," map of Poland and Pathfinders' cross.

5th Natl. Alert of Polish Pathfinders' Union.

**Frontier Guard and Embossed Arms of Poland A510**

**Coal Miner — A511**

**1969, July 21    Litho. & Embossed    Perf. 11x11½**
1665 A510 60g red & multi    .20 .20
1666 A510 60g red & multi    .20 .20
1667 A510 60g red & multi    .20 .20

**1969,    Litho.    Perf. 11½x11**
1668 A510 60g red & multi    .20 .20
1669 A510 60g red & multi    .20 .20
  a. Strip of 3, #1005-1669    .40 .40
1670 A510 60g gray & multi    .20 .20
1671 A511 60g gray & multi    .20 .20
1672 A511 60g gray & multi    .20 .20
1673 A511 60g gray & multi    .20 .20
  a. Strip of 4, #1670-1673    .35 .35
Nos. 1669a,1673a (2)    .75 .75

25th anniv. of the Polish People's Republic.

**Landing Module on Moon, and Earth A512**

**1969, Aug. 21    Litho.    Perf. 12x12½**
1674 A512 2.50z multicolored    .80 .40

Man's first landing on the moon, July 20, 1969. US astronauts Neil A. Armstrong and Col. Edwin E. Aldrin, Jr., with Lieut. Col. Michael Collins piloting Apollo 11. Issued in sheets of 8 stamps and 2 tabs with decorative border. One tab shows Apollo 11 with lunar module, the other shows module's take-off from moon. Value, sheet, $20.

**"Hamlet," by Jacek Malczewski — A513**

**1969, Sept. 4    Photo.    Perf. 11x11½, 11½x11**
1675 A513 20g gold & multi    .20 .20
1676 A513 40g gold & multi    .20 .20
1677 A513 60g gold & multi    .20 .20
1678 A513 2z gold & multi    .20 .20
1679 A513 2.50z gold & multi    .20 .20
1680 A513 3.40z gold & multi    .30 .20
1681 A513 5.50z gold & multi    .80 .30
1682 A513 7z gold & multi    1.25 .50
Nos. 1675-1682 (8)    3.35 2.00

Polish Paintings: 20g, Motherhood, by Stanislaw Wyspianski. 60g, Indian Summer (sleeping woman), by Jozef Chelmonski. 2z, Two Girls, by Olga Boznanska, vert. 2.50z, "The Sun of May" (Breakfast on the Terrace), by Jozef Mehoffer, vert. 3.40z, Woman Combing her Hair, by Wladyslaw Slewinski. 5.50z, Still Life, by Jozef Pankiewicz. 7z, The Abduction of the King's Daughter, by Witold Wojtkiewicz.

Issued in sheets of 4 stamps and 2 labels inscribed with painter's name.

**Nike — A514**

**1969, Sept. 19    Litho.    Perf. 11½x11**
1683 A514 60g gray, red & bister    .20 .20
4th Congress of the Union of Fighters for Freedom and Democracy.

**Details from Memorial, Majdanek Concentration Camp — A515**

**1969, Sept. 20    Litho.    Perf. 11**
1684 A515 40g brt lil gray & blk    .20 .20
Unveiling of a monument to the victims of the Majdanek concentration camp. The monument was designed by the sculptor Wiktor Tolkin.

**Costumes from Krzczonow, Lublin — A516**

**1969, Sept. 30    Litho.    Perf. 11½x11**
1685 A516 40g multicolored    .20 .20
1686 A516 60g multicolored    .20 .20
1687 A516 1.15z multicolored    .20 .20
1688 A516 1.35z multicolored    .20 .20
1689 A516 1.50z multicolored    .25 .20
1690 A516 4.50z multicolored    .55 .20
1691 A516 5z multicolored    .80 .45
1692 A516 7z multicolored    .65 .30
Nos. 1685-1692 (8)    3.00 2.00

Regional Costumes: 60g, Lowicz, Lodz. 1.15z, Rozbark, Katowice. 1.35z, Wroclaw. 1.50z, Opoczno. 4.50z, Sacz, Cracow. 5z, Highlanders, Cracow. 7z, Kurpiow, Warsaw.

**Walk at Left — A517**

**1969, Oct. 4    Perf. 11**
1693 A517 40g multicolored    .20 .20
1694 A517 60g multicolored    .20 .20
1695 A517 2.50z multicolored    .60 .60
Nos. 1693-1695 (3)    .20 .60

Traffic safety: 60g, "Drive Carefully" (horses on road). 2.50z, "Lower your Lights" (automobile on road).

**ILO Emblem and Welder's Mask — A518**

**1969, Oct. 20    Perf. 11x11½**
1696 A518 2.50z violet bl & ol    .20 .20
ILO, 50th anniversary.

**Bell Foundry A519**

Miniatures from Behem's Code, completed 1505: 60g, Painter's studio. 1.35z, Wood carvers. 1.55z, Shoemaker. 2.50z, Cooper. 3.40z, Bakery. 4.50z, Tailor. 7z, Bowyer's shop.

**1969, Nov. 12   Litho.   Perf. 12½**

| | | | | |
|---|---|---|---|---|
| 1697 | A519 | 40g gray & multi | .20 | .20 |
| 1698 | A519 | 60g gray & multi | .20 | .20 |
| 1699 | A519 | 1.35z gray & multi | .20 | .20 |
| 1700 | A519 | 1.55z gray & multi | .20 | .20 |
| 1701 | A519 | 2.50z gray & multi | .25 | .20 |
| 1702 | A519 | 3.40z gray & multi | .25 | .25 |
| 1703 | A519 | 4.50z gray & multi | .40 | .25 |
| 1704 | A519 | 7z gray & multi | .85 | .40 |
| | | Nos. 1697-1704 (8) | 2.50 | 1.85 |

Angel — A520

Folk Art (Sculptures): 40g, Sorrowful Christ (head). 60g, Sorrowful Christ (seated figure). 2z, Crying woman. 2.50z, Adam and Eve. 3.40z, Woman with birds.

**1969, Dec. 19   Litho.   Perf. 12½**

Size: 21x36mm

| | | | | |
|---|---|---|---|---|
| 1705 | A520 | 20g lt blue & multi | .20 | .20 |
| 1706 | A520 | 40g lilac & multi | .20 | .20 |
| 1707 | A520 | 60g multicolored | .20 | .20 |
| 1708 | A520 | 2z multicolored | .20 | .20 |
| 1709 | A520 | 2.50z multicolored | .20 | .20 |
| 1710 | A520 | 3.40z multicolored | .30 | .20 |
| | | Nos. 1705-1710,B118-B119 (8) | 2.50 | 1.75 |

Leopold Staff (1878-1957) A521

Polish Writers: 60g, Wladyslaw Broniewski (1897-1962). 1.35z, Leon Kruczkowski (1900-1962). 1.50z, Julian Tuwim (1894-1953). 1.55z, Konstanty Ildefons Galczynski (1905-1953). 2.50z, Maria Dabrowska (1889-1965). 3.40z, Zofia Nalkowska (1885-1954).

**1969, Dec. 30   Litho., Typo. & Engr.   Perf. 11x11½**

| | | | | |
|---|---|---|---|---|
| 1711 | A521 | 40g nl grn & blk, *yllsh* | .20 | .20 |
| 1712 | A521 | 60g dp car & blk, *pink* | .20 | .20 |
| 1713 | A521 | 1.35z vio bl & blk, *grysh* | .20 | .20 |
| 1714 | A521 | 1.50z pur & blk, *pink* | .20 | .20 |
| 1715 | A521 | 1.55z dp grn & blk, *grnsh* | .20 | .20 |
| 1716 | A521 | 2.50z ultra & blk, *gray* | .30 | .20 |
| 1717 | A521 | 3.40z red brn & ylk, *pink* | 1.50 | 1.40 |
| | | Nos. 1711-1717 (7) | | |

Statue of Nike and Polish Colors A522

**1970, Jan. 17   Photo.   Perf. 11½**

| | | | | |
|---|---|---|---|---|
| 1718 | A522 | 60g sil, gold, red & blk | .20 | .20 |

Warsaw liberation, 25th anniversary.

Medieval Print Shop and Modern Color Proofs — A523

**1970, Jan. 20   Litho.   Perf. 11½x11**

| | | | | |
|---|---|---|---|---|
| 1719 | A523 | 60g multicolored | .20 | .20 |

Centenary of Polish printers' trade union.

Ringnecked Pheasant — A524

Game Birds: 40g, Mallard drake. 1.15z, Woodcock. 1.35z, Ruffs (males). 1.50z, Wood pigeon. 3.40z, Black grouse. 7z, Gray partridges (cock and hen). 8.50z, Capercaillie cock giving mating call.

**1970, Feb. 28   Litho.   Perf. 11½**

| | | | | |
|---|---|---|---|---|
| 1720 | A524 | 40g multicolored | .20 | .20 |
| 1721 | A524 | 60g multicolored | 1.25 | .20 |
| 1722 | A524 | 1.15z multicolored | .20 | .20 |
| 1723 | A524 | 1.35z multicolored | .20 | .20 |
| 1724 | A524 | 1.50z multicolored | .20 | .20 |
| 1725 | A524 | 3.40z multicolored | .35 | .35 |
| 1726 | A524 | 7z multicolored | 1.65 | .65 |
| 1727 | A524 | 8.50z multicolored | 1.90 | .65 |
| | | Nos. 1720-1727 (8) | 6.10 | 2.50 |

Lenin in his Kremlin Study, Oct. 1918, and Polish Lenin Steel Mill — A525

Designs: 60g, Lenin addressing 3rd International Congress in Leningrad, 1920, and Luna 13. 2.50z, Lenin with delegates to 10th Russian Communist Party Congress, Moscow, 1921, dove and globe.

**1970, Apr. 22   Engr. & Typo.   Perf. 11**

| | | | | |
|---|---|---|---|---|
| 1728 | A525 | 40g grnsh blk & dl red | .20 | .20 |
| 1729 | A525 | 60g sep & dp lil rose | .20 | .20 |
| a. | | Souvenir sheet of 4 | 1.25 | .50 |
| 1730 | A525 | 2.50z bluish blk & ver | .60 | .60 |
| | | Nos. 1728-1730 (3) | | |

Lenin (1870-1924), Russian communist leader. No. 1729a commemorates the Cracow Intl. Phil. Exhib.

**Tourist Type of 1969**

#1731, Townhall, Wroclaw, vert. #1732, Cathedral, Piast Castle tower and church towers, Opole. #1733, Castle, Legnica. #1734, Castle Tower, Bolkow. #1735, Town Hall, Brzeg.

**1970, May 9   Litho.   Perf. 11**

| | | | | |
|---|---|---|---|---|
| 1731 | A506 | 60g Wroclaw | .20 | .20 |
| 1732 | A506 | 60g Opole | .20 | .20 |
| 1733 | A506 | 60g Legnica | .20 | .20 |
| 1734 | A506 | 60g Bolkow | .20 | .20 |
| 1735 | A506 | 60g Brzeg | 1.00 | 1.00 |
| | | Nos. 1731-1735 (5) | | |

Issued for tourist publicity. Printed in sheets of 15 stamps and 15 labels, showing coats of arms.

Polish and Russian Soldiers before Brandenburg Gate — A526

Flower, Eagle and Arms of 7 Cities — A527

**Lithographed and Engraved**

**1970, May 9   Perf. 11**

| | | | | |
|---|---|---|---|---|
| 1736 | A526 | 60g tan & multi | .20 | .20 |

**Perf. 11½**

| | | | | |
|---|---|---|---|---|
| 1737 | A527 | 60g sil, red & sl grn | .20 | .20 |

25th anniv. of victory over Germany and of Polish administration of the Oder-Neisse border area.

Peasant Movement Flag A528

**1970, May 15   Litho.   Perf. 11½**

| | | | | |
|---|---|---|---|---|
| 1738 | A528 | 60g olive & multi | .20 | .20 |

Polish peasant movement, 75th anniv.

A529

**1970, May 20   Perf. 11½x11**

| | | | | |
|---|---|---|---|---|
| 1739 | A529 | 2.50z blue & vio bl | .25 | .20 |

Inauguration of new UPU headquarters, Bern.

A530

**1970, May 30   Litho.   Perf. 11½x11**

| | | | | |
|---|---|---|---|---|
| 1740 | A530 | 60g multicolored | .20 | .20 |

European Soccer Cup Finals. Printed in sheets of 15 stamps and 15 se-tenant labels inscribed with the scores of the games.

Lamp of Learning A531

**1970, June 3   Perf. 11½**

| | | | | |
|---|---|---|---|---|
| 1741 | A531 | 60g black, bis & red | .20 | .20 |

Plock Scientific Society, 150th anniversary.

Cross-country Race — A532

#1743, Runners from ancient Greek vase. #1744, Archer, drawing by W. Skoczylas.

**1970, June 16   Photo.   Perf. 11x11½**

| | | | | |
|---|---|---|---|---|
| 1742 | A532 | 60g yellow & multi | .20 | .20 |
| 1743 | A532 | 60g black & multi | .20 | .20 |
| 1744 | A532 | 60g dark blue & multi | .60 | .60 |
| | | Nos. 1742-1744 (3) | | |

10th session of the Intl. Olympic Academy. See No. B120.

Copernicus, by Bacciarelli and View of Bologna — A533

Designs: 60g, Copernicus, by W. Lesseur and view of Padua. 2.50z, Copernicus, by Zinck Nora and view of Ferrara.

**1970, June 26   Photo., Engr. & Typo.   Perf. 11½**

| | | | | |
|---|---|---|---|---|
| 1745 | A533 | 40g orange & multi | .20 | .20 |
| 1746 | A533 | 60g olive & multi | .20 | .20 |
| 1747 | A533 | 2.50z multicolored | .35 | .60 |
| | | Nos. 1745-1747 (3) | .75 | |

Aleksander Orlowski (1777-1832), Self portrait — A534

Miniatures: 40g, Jan Matejko (1838-1893), self-portrait. 60g, King Stefan Batory (1533-1586), anonymous painter. 2z, Maria Leszczynska (1703-1768), anonymous French painter. 2.50z, Maria Walewska (1789-1817), by Jacquotot Marie-Victoire. 3.40z, Tadeusz Kosciuszko (1746-1817), by Jan Rustem. 5.50z, Samuel Bogumil Linde (1771-1847), by G. Landolfi. 7z, Michal Oginski (1728-1800), by Windisch Nanette.

**1970, Aug. 27   Litho. & Photo.   Perf. 11½**

| | | | | |
|---|---|---|---|---|
| 1748 | A534 | 20g gold & multi | .20 | .20 |
| 1749 | A534 | 40g gold & multi | .20 | .20 |
| 1750 | A534 | 60g gold & multi | .20 | .20 |
| 1751 | A534 | 2z gold & multi | .25 | .25 |
| 1752 | A534 | 2.50z gold & multi | .25 | .25 |
| 1753 | A534 | 3.40z gold & multi | .65 | .35 |
| 1754 | A534 | 5.50z gold & multi | 1.10 | .50 |
| 1755 | A534 | 7z gold & multi | 3.15 | 2.10 |
| | | Nos. 1748-1755 (8) | | |

Nos. 1748-1755 printed in sheets of 4 stamps and 2 labels. The miniatures show famous Poles and are from collections in the National Museums in Warsaw and Cracow.

**Poster for Chopin Competition — A535**

**1970, Sept. 8 Photogravure and Engraved Perf. 11x11½**
1756 A535 2.50z black & vio .25 .20

8th Int'l Chopin Piano Competition, Warsaw, Oct. 7-25.

---

**UN Emblem — A536**

**1970, Sept. 8 Photo. Perf. 11½**
1757 A536 2.50z multicolored .25 .20

United Nations, 25th anniversary.

---

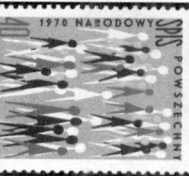

**Poles — A537**

Design: 60g, Family, home and Polish flag.

**1970, Sept. 15 Litho. Perf. 11½x11**
1758 A537 40g gray & multi .20 .20
1759 A537 60g multicolored .20 .20

National Census, Dec. 8, 1970.

---

**Cellist, by Jerzy Nowosielski A539**

Paintings: 40g, View of Lodz, by Benon Liberski. 60g, Studio Concert, by Waclaw Taranczewski. 1.50z, Still Life, by Zbigniew Pronaszko. 2z, Woman Hanging up Laundry, by Andrzej Wroblewski. 3.40z, "Expressions,"

---

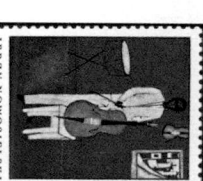

**Grunwald Cross and Warship Piorun (Thunderbolt) — A538**

Grunwald Cross and Warship: 60g, Orzel (Eagle). 2.50z, Garland.

**1970, Sept. 25 Engr. Perf. 11½x11**
1760 A538 40g sepia .20 .20
1761 A538 60g black .45 .20
1762 A538 2.50z deep brown .85 .60

Polish Navy during World War II.

---

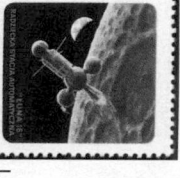

**Stag — A541**

**1970, Nov. 20 Litho. Perf. 11½x11**
1771 A540 2.50z multicolored .38 .20

**1970, Dec. 23 Photo. Perf. 11½x12**
1772 A541 60g multicolored .20 .20
1773 A541 1.15z purple & multi .20 .20
1774 A541 1.35z multicolored .20 .20
1775 A541 2z multicolored .20 .20
1776 A541 2.50z dk blue & multi .25 .20
1777 A541 4z green & multi .60 .35
1778 A541 4.50z multicolored .75 .60

*a.* Souvenir sheet of 8

Nos. 1772-1778 (7) 2.40 1.60

16th Cent. Tapestries in Wawel Castle: 1.15z, Stork. 1.35z, Leopard fighting dragon. 2z, Man's head. 2.50z, Child holding bird. 4z, God, Adam & Eve. 4.50z, Panel with monogram of King Sigismund Augustus. 5.50z, Poland's coat of arms.

---

**Souvenir Sheet Imperf**

1779 A541 5.50z black & multi 1.00 .75

No. 1779 contains one 48x57mm stamp. See No. B121.

---

**Luna 16 Landing on Moon — A540**

**1970, Oct. 9 Photo. Perf. 11½**
1763 A539 20g multicolored .20 .20
1764 A539 40g multicolored .20 .20
1765 A539 60g multicolored .20 .20
1766 A539 1.50z multicolored .20 .20
1767 A539 2z multicolored .30 .20
1768 A539 2.50z multicolored .20 .20
1769 A539 4z multicolored .45 .20
1770 A539 4.50z multicolored 1.00 .35

Nos. 1763-1770 (8) 2.75 1.75

Issued for Stamp Day.

by Maria Jarema, horiz. 4z, Canal in the Forest, by Piotr Potworowski, horiz. 8.50z, The Sun," by Wladyslaw Strzeminski, horiz.

---

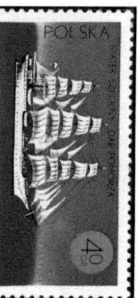

**School Sailing Ship Dar Pomorza — A542**

**1971, Jan. 30 Photo. Perf. 11**
1780 A542 40g ver & multi .20 .20
1781 A542 60g multicolored .20 .20
1782 A542 1.15z blue & multi .20 .20
1783 A542 1.35z yellow & multi .20 .20
1784 A542 1.50z multicolored .20 .20
1785 A542 2.50z violet & multi .20 .20
1786 A542 5z multicolored .50 .25
1787 A542 8.50z blue & multi .85 .45

Nos. 1780-1787 (8) 2.60 1.90

Polish Ships: 60g, Transatlantic Liner Stefan Batory. 1.15z, Ice breaker Perkun. 1.35z, Rescue ship R-1. 1.50z, Tanker Ziemia Szczecinska. 2.50z, Tanker Beskidy. 5z, Express freighter Hel. 8.50z, Ferry Gryf.

---

**Checiny Castle A543**

**1971, Mar. 5 Litho. Perf. 11**
1788 A543 20g multicolored .20 .20
1789 A543 40g multicolored .20 .20
1790 A543 60g multicolored .20 .20
1791 A543 2z multicolored .20 .20
1792 A543 2.50z multicolored .20 .20
1793 A543 3.40z multicolored .30 .20
1794 A543 4z multicolored .35 .20
1795 A543 8.50z multicolored .75 .40

Nos. 1788-1795 (8) 2.40 1.80

Polish Castles: 40g, Wisnicz. 60g, Bedzin. 2z, Ogrodzieniec. 2.50z, Niedzica. 3.40z, Kwidzyn. 4z, Pieskowa Skala. 8.50z, Lidzbark Warminski.

---

**Bishop Marianos A546**

**1971, Mar. 30 Photo. Perf. 11½x11**
Sizes: 26x34mm (40g, 1.50z); 26x47mm (60g)
1797 A545 40g shown .20 .20
1798 A545 60g Forest .20 .20
1799 A545 1.50z Cleaning .65 .60

Nos. 1797-1799 (3)

Proper forest management.

---

**Seedlings A545**

**1971, Mar. 3 Perf. 12½x12½**
1796 A544 60g vio bl, brn & red .20 .20

Centenary of the Paris Commune.

Fighting in Pouilly Castle, Jaroslaw Dabrowski and Walery Wroblewski — A544

---

**1971, Apr. 20**
1800 A546 40g gold & multi .20 .20
1801 A546 60g gold & multi .20 .20
1802 A546 1.15z gold & multi .20 .20
1803 A546 1.35z gold & multi .20 .20
1804 A546 1.50z gold & multi .20 .20
1805 A546 4.50z gold & multi .50 .20
1806 A546 5z gold & multi .50 .25
1807 A546 7z gold & multi .65 .30

Nos. 1800-1807 (8) 2.65 1.75

Frescoes from Faras Cathedral, Nubia, 8th-12th centuries: 60g, St. Anne. 1.15z, 1.50z, 7z, Archangel Michael (diff. frescoes). 1.35z, Hermit Anianun of Tuna cl Gabel. 4.50z, Cross with symbols of four Evangelists. 5z, Christ protecting Nubian dignitary.

Polish archaeological excavations in Nubia.

---

**Fair Emblem — A549**

**1971, June 1 Photo. Perf. 11½x11**
1817 A549 60g ultra, blk & dk car .20 .20

40th International Poznan Fair, June 13-22.

---

**Collegium Maius, Cracow — A550**

**1971, June Litho. Perf. 11**
1818 A550 40g multicolored .20 .20
1819 A550 60g blk, red brn & sep .20 .20
1820 A550 2.50z multicolored .25 .20
1821 A550 4z multicolored .45 .20

Nos. 1818-1821 (4) 1.10 .80

Nicolaus Copernicus (1473-1543), astronomer. Printed in sheets of 15 with labels showing portrait of Copernicus, page from "Euclid's Geometry," astrolabe or drawing of heliocentric system, respectively.

40g, Copernicus House, Torun, vert. 2.50z, Olsztyn Castle. 4z, Frombork Cathedral, vert.

---

**Silesian Insurrectionists — A547**

**1971, May 3 Photo. Perf. 11**
1808 A547 60g dk red brn & gold .20 .20
*a.* Souv. sheet of 3+3 labels 1.65 .60

50th anniversary of the 3rd Silesian uprising. Printed in sheets of 15 stamps and 15 labels showing Silesian Insurrectionists monument in Katowice.

---

**Peacock on the Lawn, by Dorota, 4 years old — A548**

**1971, May 20 Perf. 11½x11, 11x11½**
1809 A548 20g multicolored .20 .20
1810 A548 40g multicolored .20 .20
1811 A548 60g multicolored .20 .20
1812 A548 2z multicolored .20 .20
1813 A548 2.50z multicolored .30 .20
1814 A548 3.40z multicolored .30 .20
1815 A548 5.50z multicolored .50 .35
1816 A548 7z multicolored .80 .35

Nos. 1809-1816 (8) 2.60 1.80

Children's Drawings and UNICEF Emblem: 40g, Our Army. 60g, Spring. 2z, Cat with Ball, horiz. 2.50z, Flowers in Vase. 3.40z, Friendship, horiz. 5.50z, Clown. 7z, The Unknown Planet, horiz.

25th anniversary of UNICEF.

## Paper Cut-out — A551

Designs: Various paper cut-outs (folk art).

**1971, July 12** Photo., Engr. & Typo. **Perf. 12x11½**
| | | | | |
|---|---|---|---|---|
| 1822 | A551 | 20g blk & brt grn, bluish | .20 | .20 |
| 1823 | A551 | 40g sl grn & dk ol, lt gray | .20 | .20 |
| 1824 | A551 | 60g brn & bl, gray | .20 | .20 |
| 1825 | A551 | 1.15z plum & brn, buff | .20 | .20 |
| 1826 | A551 | 1.35z dk grn & ver, yel grn | 1.00 | 1.00 |

## Worker, by Xawery Dunikowski — A552

Sculptures: No. 1828, Founder, by Xawery Dunikowski. No. 1829, Miners, by Magdalena Wiecek. No. 1830, Woman harvester, by Stanisław Horno-Popławski.

**1971, July 21** Photo. **Perf. 11½x12**
| | | | | |
|---|---|---|---|---|
| 1827 | A552 | 40g silver & multi | .20 | .20 |
| 1828 | A552 | 40g silver & multi | .20 | .20 |
| 1829 | A552 | 60g silver & multi | .20 | .20 |
| 1830 | A552 | 60g silver & multi | .20 | .20 |
| a. | | Souv. sheet of 4, #1827-1830 | 2.50 | .85 |

Nos. 1827-1830 (4) .80 .80

## Punched Tape and Cogwheel — A553

**1971, Sept. 2** Litho. **Perf. 11½x11**
| | | | | |
|---|---|---|---|---|
| 1831 | A553 | 60g purple & red | .20 | .20 |

6th Congress of Polish Technicians, held at Poznan, February, 1971.

## Angel, by Jozef Mehoffer 1901 — A554
## Water Lilies, by Wyspianski A555

Stained Glass Windows: 60g, Detail from "The Elements" by Stanisław Wyspianski. 1.35z, Apollo, 14th century. 1.55z, Two Kings, 14th century. 3.40z, Flight into Egypt, 14th century. 5.50z, St. Jacob the Elder, 14th century.

**1971, Sept. 15** Photo. **Perf. 11½x11**
| | | | | |
|---|---|---|---|---|
| 1832 | A554 | 20g gold & multi | .20 | .20 |
| 1833 | A555 | 40g gold & multi | .20 | .20 |
| 1834 | A555 | 1.35z gold & multi | .20 | .20 |
| 1835 | A555 | 1.55z gold & multi | .25 | .20 |
| 1836 | A554 | 1.55z gold & multi | .30 | .20 |
| 1837 | A554 | 3.40z gold & multi | .50 | .25 |
| 1838 | A554 | 5.50z gold & multi | .50 | .25 |

Nos. 1832-1838,B122 (8) 2.70 1.90

## Mrs. Fedorowicz, by Witold Pruszkowski (1846-1896) — A556

Paintings of Women: 50g, Woman with Book, by Tytus Czyzewski (1885-1945). 60g, Girl with Chrysanthemums, by Olga Boznanska (1865-1940). 2.50z, Girl in Red Dress, by Jozef Pankiewicz (1866-1940), horiz. 3.40z, Nude, by Leon Chwistek (1884-1944), horiz. 4.50z, Strange Garden (woman), by Jozef Mehoffer (1869-1946). 5z, Artist's Wife with White Hat, by Zbigniew Pronaszko (1885-1958).

**1971, Oct. 9** Litho. **Perf. 11½x11, 11x11½**
| | | | | |
|---|---|---|---|---|
| 1839 | A556 | 40g gray & multi | .20 | .20 |
| 1840 | A556 | 50g gray & multi | .20 | .20 |
| 1841 | A556 | 60g gray & multi | .20 | .20 |
| 1842 | A556 | 2.50z gray & multi | .20 | .20 |
| 1843 | A556 | 3.40z gray & multi | .30 | .20 |
| 1844 | A556 | 4.50z gray & multi | .40 | .25 |
| 1845 | A556 | 4.50z gray & multi | .55 | .30 |

Nos. 1839-1845,B123 (8) 2.75 1.90

Stamp Day, 1971. Printed in sheets of 4 stamps and 2 labels inscribed "Women in Polish Paintings."

## Royal Castle, Warsaw A557

**1971, Oct. 14** Photo. **Perf. 11x11½**
| | | | | |
|---|---|---|---|---|
| 1846 | A557 | 60g gold, blk & brt red | .20 | .20 |

## P-11C Dive Bombers A558

Planes and Polish Air Force Emblem: 1.50z, PZL 23-A Karas fighters. 3.40z, PZL Los bomber.

**1971, Oct. 14** Photo. **Perf. 11x11½**
| | | | | |
|---|---|---|---|---|
| 1847 | A558 | 90g multicolored | .20 | .20 |
| 1848 | A558 | 1.50z blue, red & blk | .20 | .20 |
| 1849 | A558 | 3.40z multicolored | .35 | .20 |

Nos. 1847-1849 (3) .75 .60

Martyrs of the Polish Air Force, 1939.

## Lunokhod 1 on Moon — A559

No. 1850, Lunar Rover and Astronauts.

**1971, Nov. 17** **Perf. 11x11½, 11½x11**
| | | | | |
|---|---|---|---|---|
| 1850 | A559 | 2.50z multicolored | .50 | .20 |
| 1851 | A559 | 2.50z multicolored | .50 | .20 |

Apollo 15 US moon exploration mission, July 26-Aug. 7 (No. 1850); Luna 17 unmanned automated USSR moon mission, Nov. 10-17 (No. 1851). Printed in sheets of 6 stamps and 2 labels, with marginal inscriptions.

## Worker at Helm — A560
## Shipbuilding A561

No. 1853, Worker. No. 1855, Apartment houses under construction. No. 1856, "Bison" combine harvester. No. 1857, Polish Fiat 125. No. 1858, Mining tower. No. 1859, Chemical plant.

**1971, Dec. 8** **Perf. 11½x11**
| | | | | |
|---|---|---|---|---|
| 1852 | A560 | 60g gray, ultra & red | .20 | .20 |
| 1853 | A560 | 60g red & gray | .20 | .20 |
| a. | | Pair, #1852-1853 + label | | |

**Perf. 11x11½**
| | | | | |
|---|---|---|---|---|
| 1854 | A561 | 60g red, gold & blk | .20 | .20 |
| 1855 | A561 | 60g red, gold & blk | .20 | .20 |
| 1856 | A561 | 60g red, gold & blk | .20 | .20 |
| 1857 | A561 | 60g red, gold & blk | .20 | .20 |
| 1858 | A561 | 60g red, gold & blk | .50 | .50 |
| 1859 | A561 | 60g red, gold & blk | .60 | .50 |
| a. | | Souv. sheet of 6, #1854-1859 | | .90 |
| b. | | Block of 6, #1854-1859 | | .60 |

Nos. 1853a, 1859b (2) .80 .70

6th Congress of the Polish United Worker's Party. No. 1859b has outline of map of Poland extending over the block.

## Cherry Blossoms — A562

Blossoms: 20g, Niodzwiecki's apple. 40g, Pear. 60g, Peach. 1.15z, Japanese magnolia. 1.35z, Red hawthorne. 2.50z, Apple. 3.40z, Red chestnut. 5z, Acacia robinia. 8.50z, Cherry.

**1971, Dec. 28** Litho. **Perf. 12½**
**Blossoms in Natural Colors**
| | | | | |
|---|---|---|---|---|
| 1860 | A562 | 10g dull blue & blk | .20 | .20 |
| 1861 | A562 | 20g grnsh blue & blk | .20 | .20 |
| 1862 | A562 | 40g lt violet & blk | .20 | .20 |
| 1863 | A562 | 60g green & blk | .20 | .20 |
| 1864 | A562 | 1.15z Prus bl & blk | .20 | .20 |
| 1865 | A562 | 1.35z ocher & blk | .25 | .20 |
| 1866 | A562 | 2.50z green & blk | .40 | .20 |
| 1867 | A562 | 3.40z ocher & blk | .40 | .20 |
| 1868 | A562 | 5z tan & blk | .55 | .25 |
| 1869 | A562 | 8.50z bister & blk | 1.10 | .55 |

Nos. 1860-1869 (10) 3.45 2.40

## Fighting Worker, by J. Jarnuszkiewicz — A563

Photogravure and Engraved

**1972, Jan. 5** **Perf. 11½**
| | | | | |
|---|---|---|---|---|
| 1870 | A563 | 60g red & black | .20 | .20 |

Polish Workers' Party, 30th anniversary.

## Luge and Sapporo '72 Emblem — A564

Sapporo '72 Emblem and: 60g, Women's slalom, vert. 1.65z, Biathlon, vert. 2.50z, Ski jump.

**1972, Jan. 12** Photo. **Perf. 11**
| | | | | |
|---|---|---|---|---|
| 1871 | A564 | 40g silver & multi | .20 | .20 |
| 1872 | A564 | 60g silver & multi | .20 | .20 |
| 1873 | A564 | 1.65z silver & multi | .25 | .25 |
| 1874 | A564 | 2.50z silver & multi | .45 | .25 |

Nos. 1871-1874 (4) 1.10 .85

11th Winter Olympic Games, Sapporo, Japan, Feb. 3-13. See No. B124.

## Heart and Electro-cardiogram — A565

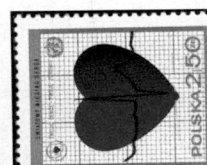

**1972, Mar. 28** Photo. **Perf. 11½x11**
| | | | | |
|---|---|---|---|---|
| 1875 | A565 | 2.50z blue, red & blk | .20 | .20 |

"Your heart is your health," World Health Day.

## Bicyclists Racing — A566

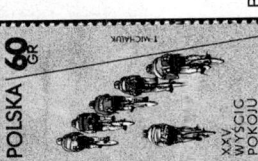

**1972, May 2** Photo. **Perf. 11½x11**
| | | | | |
|---|---|---|---|---|
| 1876 | A566 | 60g silver & multi | .20 | .20 |

25th Warsaw-Berlin-Prague Bicycle Race.

## Berlin Monument A567

**1972, May 9** Engr. **Perf. 11**
| | | | | |
|---|---|---|---|---|
| 1877 | A567 | 60g grnsh black | .20 | .20 |

Unveiling of monument for Polish soldiers and German anti-Fascists in Berlin, May 14.

## Olympic Runner — A568

**1972, May 20** Photo. **Perf. 11½x11**

Olympic Rings and "Motion" Symbol and: 30g, Archery. 40g, Boxing. 60g, Fencing.

2.50z, Wrestling. 3.40z, Weight lifting. 5z, Bicycling. 8.50z, Sharpshooting.

| 1878 | A568 | 20g multicolored | .20 | .20 |
|---|---|---|---|---|
| 1879 | A568 | 30g multicolored | .20 | .20 |
| 1880 | A568 | 40g multicolored | .20 | .20 |
| 1881 | A568 | 2z gray & multi | .20 | .20 |
| 1882 | A568 | 2.50z multicolored | .25 | .20 |
| 1883 | A568 | 3.40z multicolored | .40 | .25 |
| 1884 | A568 | 5z blue & multi | .50 | .25 |
| 1885 | A568 | 8.50z multicolored | .90 | .50 |
| | | Nos. 1878-1885 (8) | 2.85 | 1.95 |

20th Olympic Games, Munich, Aug. 26-Sept. 10. See No. B125.

Vistula and Cracow — A569

**1972, May 28 Photo. Perf. 11½x11**

1886 A569 60g red, grn & ocher .20 .20

50th anniversary of Polish Immigrants Society in Germany (Rodło).

Knight of King Mieszko I — A570

**1972, June 12**

1887 A570 60g gold, red brn, yel & blk .20 .20

Millennium of the Battle of Cedynia (Cidyny).

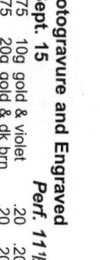

Zoo Animals — A571

**1972, Aug. 20 Litho. Perf. 12½**

| 1888 | A571 | 20g Cheetah | .20 | .20 |
|---|---|---|---|---|
| 1889 | A571 | 40g Giraffe, vert | .20 | .20 |
| 1890 | A571 | 60g Toco toucan | .20 | .20 |
| 1891 | A571 | 1.35z Chimpanzee | .25 | .20 |
| 1892 | A571 | 1.65z Gibbon | .30 | .20 |
| 1893 | A571 | 3.40z Crocodile | .35 | .20 |
| 1894 | A571 | 4z Kangaroo | 1.25 | .55 |
| 1895 | A571 | 7z Tiger, vert | 2.75 | 1.25 |
| 1896 | A571 | 4.50z Zebra | 7.75 | 4.00 |
| | | Nos. 1888-1896 (9) | | |

Ludwik Warynski — A572

**1972, Sept. 1 Photo. Perf. 11**

1897 A572 60g multicolored .20 .20

90th anniversary of Proletariat Party, founded by Ludwik Warynski. Printed in sheets of 25 stamps each se-tenant with label showing masthead of party newspaper "Proletariat."

---

**1972, Sept. 11 Litho. Perf. 11½**

1898 A573 60g red & black .20 .20

Feliks Dzerzhinski (1877-1926), Russian politician of Polish descent.

Feliks Dzerzhinski A573

Congress Emblem — A574

**1972, Sept. 15 Photo. Perf. 11½x11**

1899 A574 60g multicolored .20 .20

25th Congress of the International Cooperative Union, Warsaw, Sept. 1972.

"in the Barracks," by Moniuszko A575

**1972, Sept. 15**
**Photogravure and Engraved**
**Perf. 11½**

| 1900 | A575 | 10g gold & violet | .20 | .20 |
|---|---|---|---|---|
| 1901 | A575 | 20g gold & dk brn | .20 | .20 |
| 1902 | A575 | 40g gold & slate grn | .20 | .20 |
| 1903 | A575 | 60g gold & indigo | .20 | .20 |
| 1904 | A575 | 1.15z gold & dk blue | .20 | .20 |
| 1905 | A575 | 1.35z gold & dk blue | .20 | .20 |
| 1906 | A575 | 1.55z gold & grnsh blk | .20 | .20 |
| 1907 | A575 | 2.50z gold & dk brown | .35 | .20 |
| | | Nos. 1900-1907 (8) | 1.75 | 1.60 |

Scenes from Operas or Ballets by Moniuszko: 20g, The Countess. 40g, Halka. 1.15z, A New Don Quixote. 1.35z, Verbum Nobile. 1.55z, Ideal. 2.50z, Paria.

Stanislaw Moniuszko (1819-72), composer.

---

**1972, Sept. 28 Photo. Perf. 10½x11**

| 1908 | A576 | 30g gold & multi | .20 | .20 |
|---|---|---|---|---|
| 1909 | A576 | 40g gold & multi | .20 | .20 |
| 1910 | A576 | 60g gold & multi | .20 | .20 |
| 1911 | A576 | 2z gold & multi | .20 | .20 |
| 1912 | A576 | 2.50z gold & multi | .35 | .20 |
| 1913 | A576 | 3.40z gold & multi | .35 | .20 |
| 1914 | A576 | 4z gold & multi | .75 | .25 |
| | | Nos. 1908-1914,B126 (8) | 3.60 | 2.00 |

Stamp Day.

Copernicus, by Jacob van Meurs, 1654, Heliocentric System — A577

**1972, Sept. 28 Litho. Perf. 11x11½**

| 1915 | A577 | 40g brt blue & blk | .20 | .20 |
|---|---|---|---|---|
| 1916 | A577 | 60g ocher & blk | .20 | .20 |
| 1917 | A577 | 2.50z red & blk | .25 | .20 |
| 1918 | A577 | 3.40z yellow, grn & blk | .55 | .25 |
| | | Nos. 1915-1918 (4) | 1.20 | .85 |

Portraits of Copernicus: 60g, 16th century etching and Prussian coin. 1530. 2.50z, by Jeremiah Falck, 1645, and coat of arms of King of Prussia, 1520. 3.40z, Copernicus with lily of the valley and page from Theophilactus Simocatta's "Letters on Customs."

**Nos. 1337-1338 Surcharged in Red or Black**

a

b

**Engr. Perf. 11½x11**

**1972**

| 1919 | A445(a) | 50g on 40g (R) | .20 | .20 |
|---|---|---|---|---|
| 1920 | A445(a) | 90g on 40g (R) | .20 | .20 |
| 1921 | A445(a) | 1z on 40g (R) | .20 | .20 |
| 1922 | A445(b) | 1.50z on 60g | .20 | .20 |
| 1923 | A445(b) | 1.70z on 60g | .20 | .20 |
| 1924 | A445(b) | 4z on 60g | .30 | .20 |
| 1925 | A445(b) | 4.50z on 60g | .35 | .20 |
| 1926 | A445(b) | 4.90z on 60g | .45 | .20 |
| | | Nos. 1919-1926 (8) | 2.10 | 1.60 |

Issued: #1919-1920, 11/17; others, 10/2.

---

**1972, Oct. 16 Litho. Perf. 11½**

1927 A578 60g rose & black .20 .20

Children's health center (Centrum Zdrowia Dzieck), to be built as memorial to children killed during Nazi regime.

The Little Soldier, by E. Piwowarski A578

Warsaw Royal Castle, 1656, by Erik J. Dahlbergh — A579

**1972, Oct. 16 Photo. Perf. 11x11½**

1928 A579 60g violet, bl & blk .20 .20

Rebuilding of Warsaw Castle, destroyed during World War II.

**"Amazon," by Piotr Michalowski — A576**

Paintings: 40g, Ostafi Daszkiewicz, by Jan Matejko. 60g, "Summer Rain" (dancing woman), by Wojciech Gerson. 2z, Woman from Naples, by Aleksander Kotsis. 2.50z, Girl Taking Bath, by Pantaleon Szyndler. 3.40z, Count of Thun (old man), by Artur Grottger. 4z, Rhapsodist (old man), by Stanislaw Wyspianski. 60g and 2.50z inscribed "DZIEN ZNACZKA 1972."

---

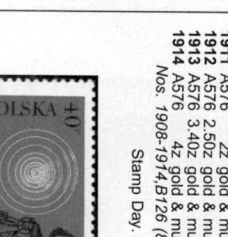

Mountain Lodge, Chocholowska Valley — A581

**1972, Nov. 13 Perf. 11½x11**

1929 A580 60g multicolored .20 .20

7th and 13th Polish Trade Union congresses, Nov. 13-15.

Ribbons with Symbols of Trade Union Activities — A580

**1972, Nov. 13 Perf. 11**

| 1930 | A581 | 40g multicolored | .20 | .20 |
|---|---|---|---|---|
| 1931 | A581 | 60g multicolored | .20 | .20 |
| 1932 | A581 | 1.55z multicolored | .20 | .20 |
| 1933 | A581 | 1.65z multicolored | .30 | .20 |
| 1934 | A581 | 2.50z multicolored | .60 | .25 |
| | | Nos. 1930-1934 (5) | 1.10 | 1.00 |

Mountain Lodges in Tatra National Park: 60g, Hala Ornak, West Tatra, horiz. 1.55z, Hala Gasienicowa. 1.65z, Pieciu Stawow Valley, horiz. 2.50z, Morskie Oko, Rybiego Potoku Valley.

---

**1972, Dec. 15 Litho. Perf. 12½**

| 1935 | A582 | 40g gray & multi | .20 | .20 |
|---|---|---|---|---|
| 1936 | A582 | 50g blue & multi | .20 | .20 |
| 1937 | A582 | 60g ocher & multi | .20 | .20 |
| 1938 | A582 | 1.65z ultra & multi | .25 | .20 |
| 1939 | A582 | 2.50z ocher & multi | .25 | .20 |
| 1940 | A582 | 3.40z multicolored | .30 | .20 |
| 1941 | A582 | 4z multicolored | .60 | .25 |
| 1942 | A582 | 8.50z multicolored | 1.25 | .55 |
| | | Nos. 1935-1942 (8) | 3.25 | 2.00 |

Flowering Shrubs: 50g, Alpine rose. 60g, Pomeranian honeysuckle. 1.65z, Viburnum. 2.50z, Mock orange. 3.40z, Rhododendron. 4z, Mock orange. 8.50z, Lilac.

Japanese Azalea — A582

Emblem A583

**1972, Dec. 15 Photo. Perf. 11½**

1943 A583 60g red & multi .20 .20

5th Congress of Socialist Youth Union.

**Coil Stamps**
Copernicus A584

**1972, Dec. 28 Photo. Perf. 14**

1944 A584 1z deep claret .20 .20
1945 A584 1.50z yellow brown .20 .20

Nicolaus Copernicus (1473-1543), astronomer. Black control number on back of every 5th stamp.

**Piast Knight, 10th Century A585**

Polish Cavalry: 40g, Knight, 13th century. 60g, Knight of Ladislas Jagello, 15th century, horiz. 1.35z, Hussar, 17th century. 4z, National Guard Uhlan, 18th century. 4.50z, Congress Kingdom Period, 1831. 5z, Light cavalry, 1939, horiz. 7z, Light cavalry, People's Army, 1945.

**1972, Dec. 28**     *Perf. 11*

| | | | | |
|---|---|---|---|---|
| 1946 | A585 | 20g | violet & multi | .20 .20 |
| 1947 | A585 | 40g | multicolored | .20 .20 |
| 1948 | A585 | 60g | orange & multi | .20 .20 |
| 1949 | A585 | 1.35z | orange & multi | .20 .20 |
| 1950 | A585 | 4z | orange & multi | .35 .20 |
| 1951 | A585 | 4.50z | orange & multi | .45 .20 |
| 1952 | A585 | 5z | brown & multi | .80 .30 |
| 1953 | A585 | 7z | multicolored | 1.10 .50 |
| | | Nos. 1946-1953 (8) | | 3.50 2.00 |

**Man and Woman, Sculpture by Wiera Muchina — A586**

**1972, Dec. 30**

| | | | | |
|---|---|---|---|---|
| 1954 | A586 | 40g | gray & multi | .20 .20 |
| 1955 | A586 | 60g | blk, red & vio bl | .20 .20 |

50th anniversary of the Soviet Union.

Design: 60g, Globe with Red Star.

**Nicolaus Copernicus, by M. Bacciarelli A587**

**1973, Feb. 18**    *Perf. 11½x11, 11x11½*    *Photo.*

| | | | | |
|---|---|---|---|---|
| 1956 | A587 | 1z | brown & multi | .20 .20 |
| 1957 | A587 | 1.50z | multicolored | .20 .20 |
| 1958 | A587 | 2.70z | multicolored | .20 .20 |
| 1959 | A587 | 4z | multicolored | .35 .20 |
| 1960 | A587 | 4.90z | multicolored | .50 .30 |
| | | Nos. 1956-1960 (5) | | 1.45 1.10 |

Portraits of Copernicus: 1.50z, painted in Torun, 16th century. 2.70z, by Zinck Nor. 4z, from Strasbourg clock. 4.90z, Copernicus in his Observatory, by Jan Matejko, horiz.

**Piast Coronation Sword, 12th Century — A588**

---

**Lenin Monument, Nowa Huta — A589**

Polish Art: No. 1962, Kruziowa Madonna, c. 1410. No. 1963, Hussar's armor, 17th century. No. 1964, Wawel head, wood, 16th century. No. 1965, Cock, sign of Rifle Fraternity, 16th century. 2.70z, Cover of Queen Anna Jagiellonka's prayer book (eagle), 1582. 4.90z, Skarbimierz Madonna, wood, c. 1340. 8.50z, The Nobleman Tenczynski, portrait by unknown artist, 17th century.

**1973, Mar. 28**    *Perf. 11½x11*    *Photo.*

| | | | | |
|---|---|---|---|---|
| 1961 | A588 | 50g | violet & multi | .20 .20 |
| 1962 | A588 | 1z | lt blue & multi | .20 .20 |
| 1963 | A588 | 1z | ultra & multi | .20 .20 |
| 1964 | A588 | 1.50z | blue & multi | .20 .20 |
| 1965 | A588 | 1.50z | green & multi | .20 .20 |
| 1966 | A588 | 2.70z | multicolored | .20 .20 |
| 1967 | A588 | 4.90z | multicolored | .40 .40 |
| 1968 | A588 | 8.50z | black & multi | 1.00 .35 |
| | | Nos. 1961-1968 (8) | | 2.60 1.75 |

**1973, Apr. 28**    *Perf. 11x11½*    *Litho.*

| | | | | |
|---|---|---|---|---|
| 1969 | A589 | 1z | multicolored | .20 .20 |

Unveiling of Lenin Monument at Nowa Huta.

**Envelope Showing Postal Code A590**

**1973, May 5**    *Perf. 11x11½*

| | | | | |
|---|---|---|---|---|
| 1970 | A590 | 1.50z | multicolored | .20 .20 |

Introduction of postal code system in Poland.

**Wolf — A591**

**1973, May 21**    *Perf. 11*    *Photo.*

| | | | | |
|---|---|---|---|---|
| 1971 | A591 | 50g | shown | .20 .20 |
| 1972 | A591 | 1z | Mouflon | .20 .20 |
| 1973 | A591 | 1.50z | Moose | .20 .20 |
| 1974 | A591 | 2.70z | Capercaillie | .30 .20 |
| 1975 | A591 | 3z | Deer | .40 .20 |
| 1976 | A591 | 4.50z | Lynx | .55 .40 |
| 1977 | A591 | 4.90z | European hart | 1.50 .65 |
| 1978 | A591 | 4.90z | Wild boar | 1.65 2.25 |
| | | Nos. 1971-1978 (8) | | 5.00 2.25 |

Intl. Hunting Committee Congress and 50th anniv. of Polish Hunting Assoc.

**US Satellite "Copernicus" over Earth — A592**

**1973, June 20**

| | | | | |
|---|---|---|---|---|
| 1979 | A592 | 4.90z | multicolored | .45 .25 |
| 1980 | A592 | 4.90z | multicolored | .45 .25 |

American and Russian astronomical observatories in space. No. 1979 and No. 1980 issued in sheets of 6 stamps and 2 labels.

---

**Flame Rising from Book — A593**    *Litho.*

**1973, June 26**

| | | | | |
|---|---|---|---|---|
| 1981 | A593 | 1.50z | blue & multi | .20 .20 |

2nd Polish Science Cong., Warsaw, June 26-29.

**Marceli Nowotko — A595**

**Arms of Poznan on 14th Century Seal — A594**

Polska '73 Emblem and: 1.50z, Tombstone of Nicolaus Tomicki, 1524. 2.70z, Kalisz paten, 12th century, 4z, Lion knocker from bronze gate, Gniezno, 12th century, horiz.

**1973, June 30**    *Perf. 11½x11, 11x11½*

| | | | | |
|---|---|---|---|---|
| 1982 | A594 | 1z | pink & multi | .20 .20 |
| 1983 | A594 | 1.50z | orange & multi | .20 .20 |
| 1984 | A594 | 2.70z | buff & multi | .20 .20 |
| 1985 | A594 | 4z | yellow & multi | .40 .80 |
| | | Nos. 1982-1985 (4) | | 1.00 |

POLSKA '73 Intl. Phil. Exhib., Poznan, Aug. 19-Sept. 2. See No. B128.

**1973, Aug. 8**    *Perf. 11½x11*    *Litho.*

| | | | | |
|---|---|---|---|---|
| 1986 | A595 | 1.50z | red & black | .20 .20 |

Marceli Nuwotko (1893-1942), labor leader, member of Central Committee of Communist Party of Poland.

**Emblem and Orchard — A596**

Human Environment Emblem and: 90g, Grazing cows. 1z, Stork's nest. 1.50z, Pond with fish and water lilies. 2.70z, Flowers on meadow. 4.90z, Underwater fauna and flora. 5z, Forest scene. 6.50z, Still life.

**1973, Aug. 30**    *Perf. 11*    *Photo.*

| | | | | |
|---|---|---|---|---|
| 1987 | A596 | 50g | black & multi | .20 .20 |
| 1988 | A596 | 90g | black & multi | .20 .20 |
| 1989 | A596 | 1z | black & multi | .20 .20 |
| 1990 | A596 | 1.50z | black & multi | .20 .20 |
| 1991 | A596 | 2.70z | black & multi | .20 .20 |
| 1992 | A596 | 4.90z | black & multi | .60 .25 |
| 1993 | A596 | 5z | black & multi | .90 .90 |
| 1994 | A596 | 6.50z | black & multi | 4.00 1.85 |
| | | Nos. 1987-1994 (8) | | |

Protection of the environment.

---

**Motorcyclist — A597**    *Perf. 11½*

**1973, Sept. 2**

| | | | | |
|---|---|---|---|---|
| 1995 | A597 | 1.50z | silver & multi | .20 .20 |

Finals in individual world championship motorcycle race on cinder track, Chorzów, Sept. 2.

**Tank — A598**    *Perf. 12½*    *Litho.*

**1973, Oct. 12**

| | | | | |
|---|---|---|---|---|
| 1996 | A598 | 1z | shown | .20 .20 |
| 1997 | A598 | 1z | Fighter plane | .20 .20 |
| 1998 | A598 | 1.50z | Missile | .20 .20 |
| 1999 | A598 | 1.50z | Warship | .80 .80 |
| | | Nos. 1996-1999 (4) | | |

Polish People's Army, 30th anniversary.

**Grzegorz Piramowicz — A599**

KOMISJA EDUKACJI NARODOWEJ 1773

**Photogravure and Engraved**

**1973, Oct. 13**    *Perf. 11½x11*

| | | | | |
|---|---|---|---|---|
| 2000 | A599 | 1z | huff & dk brn | .20 .20 |
| 2001 | A599 | 1.50z | gray & sl grn | .20 .20 |

Natl. Education Commission, bicent.

Design: 1.50z, J. Sniadecki, Hugo Kollataj and Julian Ursyn Niemcewicz.

**Henryk Arctowski, and Penguins A600**

**1973, Nov. 30**    *Perf. 10½x11*    *Photo.*

| | | | | |
|---|---|---|---|---|
| 2002 | A600 | 1z | gold & multi | .20 .20 |
| 2003 | A600 | 1z | gold & multi | .20 .20 |
| 2004 | A600 | 1.50z | gold & multi | .20 .20 |
| 2005 | A600 | 1.50z | gold & multi | .20 .20 |
| 2006 | A600 | 2.70z | gold & multi | .20 .20 |
| 2007 | A600 | 3z | gold & multi | .20 .20 |
| 2008 | A600 | 8z | gold & multi | .80 .35 |
| 2009 | A600 | | gold & multi | 2.25 1.75 |
| | | Nos. 2002-2009 (8) | | |

Polish Scientists: No. 2003, Pawel Edmund Strzelecki and Kangaroo. No. 2004, Benedykt Tadeusz Dybowski and Lake Baikal. No. 2005, Stefan Rogozinski, sailing ship "Lucia-Malgorzata. 2z, Bronislaw Malinowski, Trobriand Island drummers. 2.70z, Stefan Drzewiecki and submarine. 3z, Edward Adolf Strasburger and plants. 8z, Ignacy Domeyko, geological strata.

**1973, Dec. 15  Photo.  Perf. 11½x11**
2010 A601 1.50z dp ultra, red & gold  .20  .20

Polish United Workers' Party, 25th anniv.

Polish
Flag — A601

Jelcz-Berliet Bus — A602

Designs: Polish automotives.

**1973, Dec. 28  Photo.  Perf. 11½x11½**
2011 A602 50g Jelcz shown  .20  .20
2012 A602 90g Jelcz 316  .20  .20
2014 A602 1.50z Polski Fiat 126p  .20  .20
2015 A602 1.50z Polski Fiat 125p  .20  .20
2016 A602 4z Nysa M-521 bus  .40  .20
  A602 4.50z Star 660 truck  .50  .25
Nos. 2011-2016 (6)  1.70  1.25

Iris — A603

Flowers: 1z, Dandelion. 1.50z, Rose. 3z, Thistle. 4z, Cornflowers. 4.50z, Clover. (Paintings by Stanislaw Wyspianski.)

**1974, Jan. 22  Engr.  Perf. 12x11½**
2017 A603 50g lilac  .20  .20
2018 A603 1z green  .20  .20
2019 A603 1.50z red orange  .20  .20
2020 A603 3z deep violet  .25  .20
2021 A603 4z violet blue  .40  .20
2022 A603 4.50z emerald  .45  .20
Nos. 2017-2022 (6)  1.70  1.20

Cottage,
Kurpie
A604

Designs: 1.50z, Church, Sekowa. 4z, Town Hall, Sulmierzyce. 4.50z, Church, Lachowice. 4.90z, Windmill, Sobienie-Jeziory. 5z, Orthodox Church, Ulucz.

**1974, Mar. 5  Photo.  Perf. 11x11½**
2023 A604 1z multicolored  .20  .20
2024 A604 1.50z yellow & multi  .30  .20
2025 A604 4z pink & multi  .30  .20
2026 A604 4.50z lt blue & multi  .30  .20
2027 A604 4.90z multicolored  .45  .20
2028 A604 5z pink & multi  .35  .20
Nos. 2023-2028 (6)  1.80  1.20

Mail Coach and
UPU
Emblem — A605

**1974, Mar. 30  Perf. 11½x12**
2029 A605 1.50z multicolored  .20  .20

Centenary of Universal Postal Union.

Embroidery from
Cracow — A606

Embroideries from: 1.50z, Lowicz. 4z, Slask.

**1974, May 7  Photo.  Perf. 11½x11**
2030 A606 50g multicolored  .20  .20
2031 A606 1.50z multicolored  .20  .20
2032 A606 4z multicolored  .40  .20
 a. Souvenir sheet of 3 #2032, imperf.  1.75  1.25
 b. As "a," perf. 11½x11  6.00  4.50
Nos. 2030-2032 (3)  .80  .60

SOCPHILEX IV International Philatelic Exhibition, Katowice, May 18-June 2. No. 2032a sold for 17z. No. 2032b sold for 17z plus 15z for 4 envelopes.

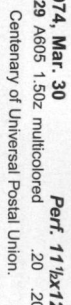

Association
Emblem — A607

**1974, May 8  Litho.  Perf. 12x11½**
2033 A607 1.50z gray & red  .20  .20

5th Congress of the Assoc. of Combatants for Liberty & Democracy, Warsaw, May 8-9.

Soldier and
Dove — A608

**1974, May 9**
2034 A608 1.50z org, lt bl & blk  .20  .20

29th anniversary of victory over Fascism.

Comecon
Building,
Moscow
A609

**1974, May 15  Litho.  Perf. 11½x11**
2035 A609 1.50z gray bl, bis & red  .20  .20

25th anniv. of the Council of Mutual Economic Assistance.

Soccer
Ball and
Games'
Emblem
A610

Design: No. 2037, Soccer players, Olympic rings and 1972 medal.

**1974, June 15  Photo.  Perf. 11x11½**
2036 A610 4.90z olive & multi  .50  .20
 a. Souv. sheet of 4 + 2 labels  4.50  2.00
2037 A610 4.90z olive & multi  .50  .20
 a. Souv. sheet, 2 each #2036-2037  12.00  7.00

World Cup Soccer Championship, Munich, June 13-July 7. No. 2036a issued to commemorate Poland's silver medal in 1974 Championship.

Sailing Ship,
16th
Century — A611

Chess, by Jan
Kochanowski
A612

**1974, June 29  Litho.  Perf. 11½x11**
2038 A611 1z multicolored  .20  .20
2039 A611 1.50z multicolored  .20  .20
2040 A611 2.70z multicolored  .20  .20
2041 A611 4z green & multi  .40  .25
2042 A611 4.90z dp blue & multi  .60  .30
Nos. 2038-2042 (5)  1.60  1.15

Polish Sailing Ships: 1.50z, "Dal," 1934. 2.70z, "Opty," sailed around the world, 1969. 4z, "Dar Pomorza," winner "Operation Sail," 1972. 4.90z, "Polonez," sailed around the world, 1973.

Man and Map of
Poland — A613

**1974, July 15  Litho.  Perf. 11½x11**
2043 A612 1z multicolored  .20  .20
2044 A612 1.50z multicolored  .25  .20

Design: 1.50z, "Education," etching by Daniel Chodowiecki.

10th International Chess Festival, Lublin.

Polish
Eagle — A614

**1974, July 21  Photo.  Perf. 11½x11**
2045 A613 1.50z black, gold & red  .20  .20

**1974, July 21**
2046 A614 1.50z silver & multi  .20  .20
2047 A614 1.50z red & multi  .20  .60
Nos. 2045-2047 (3)  .60

People's Republic of Poland, 30th anniv.

Lazienkowska Bridge Road — A615

**1974, July 21  Perf. 11x11½**
2048 A615 1.50z multicolored  .20  .20

Opening of Lazienkowska Bridge over Vistula south of Warsaw.

Strawberries and
Congress
Emblem — A616

**1974, Sept. 10  Photo.  Perf. 11½**
2049 A616 50g shown  .20  .20
2050 A616 90g Black currants  .20  .20
2051 A616 1z Apples  .20  .20
2052 A616 1.50z Cucumbers  .20  .20
2053 A616 2.70z Tomatoes  .20  .20
2054 A616 4z Peas  .40  .20
2055 A616 4.50z Pansies  .60  .25
2056 A616 5z Nasturtiums  1.25  .40
Nos. 2049-2056 (8)  3.25  1.85

19th Int'l. Horticultural Cong., Warsaw, Sept.

Civic Militia and
Security Service
Badge — A617

**1974, Oct. 3  Photo.  Perf. 11½x11**
2057 A617 1.50g multicolored  .20  .20

30th anniv. of the Civic Militia and the Security Service.

Polish Child, by
Lukasz
Orlowski — A618

**1974, Oct. 9**
2058 A618 50g multicolored  .20  .20
2059 A618 90g multicolored  .20  .20
2060 A618 1z multicolored  .20  .20
2061 A618 1.50z multicolored  .20  .20
2062 A618 4z multicolored  .30  .20
2063 A618 4.50z multicolored  .40  .20
2064 A618 4.90z multicolored  .45  .20
2065 A618 6.50z multicolored  .50  .30
Nos. 2058-2065 (8)  2.25  1.75

Polish paintings of Children: 90g, Girl with Pigeon, Anonymous artist, 19th century. 1z, Girl, by Stanislaw Wyspianski. 1.50z, The Orphan from Poronin, by Wladyslaw Slewinski. 3z, Peasant Boy, by Kazimierz Sichulski. 4.50z, Florentine Page, by Aleksander Gierymski. 4.90z, The Artist's Son Tadeusz, by Piotr Michalowski. 6.50z, Boy with Doe, by Aleksander Kotsis.

Children's Day. The 1z and 1.50z are inscribed "Dzien Znaczka (Stamp Day) 1974."

Cracow
Manger — A619

## Apollo and Soyuz Linked in Space A633

**1975, July 15**    *Perf. 11½x11½*
| | | | | |
|---|---|---|---|---|
| 2105 | A633 | 1.50z shown | .20 | .20 |
| 2106 | A633 | 4.90z Apollo | .50 | .25 |
| 2107 | A633 | 4.90z Soyuz | .50 | .25 |
| a. | | Souv. sheet, 2 each #2106-2107 + 2 labels | 7.50 | 3.50 |
| b. | | Pair, #2106-2107 | 7.00 | 3.50 |
| | | Nos. 2105-2107 (3) | 1.20 | .70 |

Apollo Soyuz space test project (Russo-American cooperation), launching July 15; link-up, July 17.

## Health Fund Emblem — A634

**1975, July 12**
2108 A634 1.50z silver, blk & bl   .20 .20
National Fund for Health Protection.

## "E" and Polish Flag A635

*Perf. 11x11½*
**1975, July 30 Litho.**
2109 A635 4z lt blue, red & blk   .30 .20
European Security and Cooperation Conference, Helsinki, July 30-Aug. 1.

## UN Emblem and Sunburst A636

**1975, July 25**
2110 A636 4z blue & multi   .30 .20
30th anniversary of the United Nations.

## Bolek and Lolek A637

*Perf. 11½x11½*
**1975, Aug. 30 Photo.**
| | | | | |
|---|---|---|---|---|
| 2111 | A637 | 50g violet bl & multi | .20 | .20 |
| 2112 | A637 | 1z multicolored | .20 | .20 |
| 2113 | A637 | 1.50z multicolored | .20 | .20 |
| 2114 | A637 | 4z multicolored | .45 | .20 |
| | | Nos. 2111-2114 (4) | 1.05 | .80 |

Cartoon Characters and Children's Health Center Emblem: 1z, Jacek and Agatka. 1.50z, Reksio, the dog. 4z, Telesfor, the dragon.
Children's television programs.

## Mountain Guides' Badge and Sudetic Mountains — A629

*Perf. 11*
**1975, Apr. 30 Photo.**
| | | | | |
|---|---|---|---|---|
| 2089 | A629 | 1z multicolored | .20 | .20 |
| 2090 | A629 | 1z multicolored | .20 | .20 |
| a. | | Pair, #2089-2090 | .20 | .20 |
| 2091 | A629 | 1.50z multicolored | .20 | .20 |
| 2092 | A629 | 1.50z multicolored | .20 | .20 |
| a. | | Pair, #2091-2092 | .30 | .20 |
| 2093 | A629 | 4z multicolored | .40 | .40 |
| 2094 | A629 | 4z multicolored | .40 | .40 |
| a. | | Pair, #2093-2094 | .80 | .40 |
| | | Nos. 2090a,2092a,2094a (3) | 1.30 | .80 |

Designs: #2089, Pine, badge and Tatra Mountains, vert. #2090, Gentian and Tatra Mountains, vert. #2092, Yew branch with berries, and Sudetic Mountains. #2093, River, Beskids Mountains and badge, vert. #2094, Arnica and Beskids Mountains, vert.
Centenary of Polish Mountain Guides Organizations. Pairs have continuous design.

## Hands Holding Tulips and Rifle — A630

**1975, May 9**
2095 A630 1.50z blue & multi   .20 .20
End of WWII, 30th anniv.; victory over Fascism.

## Warsaw Treaty Members' Flags — A631

*Perf. 11½x11*
**1975, May 14**
2096 A631 1.50z blue & multi   .20 .20
20th anniversary of the signing of the Warsaw Treaty (Bulgaria, Czechoslovakia, German Democratic Rep., Hungary, Poland, Romania, USSR).

## Cock and Hen, Congress Emblem — A632

*Perf. 12x11½*
**1975, June 23 Photo.**
| | | | | |
|---|---|---|---|---|
| 2097 | A632 | 50g shown | .20 | .20 |
| 2098 | A632 | 1z Geese | .20 | .20 |
| 2099 | A632 | 1.50z Cattle | .30 | .20 |
| 2100 | A632 | 2z Cow | .30 | .20 |
| 2101 | A632 | 3z Arabian stallion | .40 | .20 |
| 2102 | A632 | 4z Wielkopolska horses | .50 | .20 |
| 2103 | A632 | 4.50z Pigs | .85 | .30 |
| 2104 | A632 | 4.50z Sheep | 1.75 | .50 |
| | | Nos. 2097-2104 (8) | 4.40 | 2.00 |

20th Congress of the European Zootechnical Federation, Warsaw.

## "Auschwitz" A625

*Perf. 11½x12*
**1975, Jan. 23**
| | | | | |
|---|---|---|---|---|
| 2074 | A624 | 1z Lesser kestrel, male | .20 | .20 |
| a. | | Pair, #2074-2075 | .25 | .20 |
| 2075 | A624 | 1z same, female | .20 | .20 |
| 2076 | A624 | 1.50z Red-footed falcon, male | .20 | .25 |
| a. | | Pair, #2076-2077 | .35 | .25 |
| 2077 | A624 | 1.50z same, female | .20 | .25 |
| 2078 | A624 | 2z shown | .40 | .20 |
| 2079 | A624 | 3z Kestrel | .50 | .40 |
| 2080 | A624 | 4z Merlin | 1.50 | .75 |
| 2081 | A624 | 8z Peregrine | 2.25 | 2.35 |
| | | Nos. 2074-2081 (8) | 5.45 | |

Falcons.

### Photogravure and Engraved
**1975, Jan. 27**
2082 A625 1.50z red & black   .25 .20
30th anniversary of the liberation of Auschwitz (Oswiecim) concentration camp.

## Women's Hurdle Race A626

*Perf. 11x11½*
**1975, Mar. 8 Litho.**
| | | | | |
|---|---|---|---|---|
| 2083 | A626 | 1z multicolored | .20 | .20 |
| 2084 | A626 | 1.50z olive & multi | .20 | .20 |
| 2085 | A626 | 4z multicolored | .35 | .20 |
| 2086 | A626 | 4.90z green & multi | .40 | .25 |
| | | Nos. 2083-2086 (4) | 1.15 | .85 |

Designs: 1.50z, Pole vault. 4z, Hop, step and jump. 4.90z, Sprinting.
6th European Indoor Athletic Championships, Katowice, Mar 1975.

## St. Anne, by Veit Stoss, Arphila Emblem A627

*Perf. 11x11½*
**1975, Apr. 15 Photo.**
2087 A627 1.50z multicolored   .20 .20
ARPHILA 75, International Philatelic Exhibition, Paris, June 6-10.

## Amateur Radio Union Emblem, Globe A628

*Perf. 11½*
**1975, Apr. 15 Litho.**
2088 A628 1.50z multicolored   .20 .20
International Amateur Radio Union Conference, Warsaw, Apr. 1975.

## King Sigismund Vasa — A620

*Perf. 11½x11*
**1974, Dec. 2 Litho.**
| | | | | |
|---|---|---|---|---|
| 2066 | A619 | 1z multicolored | .20 | .20 |
| 2067 | A620 | 1.50z multicolored | .20 | .20 |
| 2068 | A619 | 4z multicolored | .25 | .20 |
| 2069 | A619 | 4z multicolored | .60 | .20 |
| | | Nos. 2066-2069 (4) | 1.25 | .80 |

Masterpieces of Polish art: 1.50z, Flight into Egypt, 1465. 4z, King Jan Olbracht.
Designs from 16th century woodcuts.

## Angler — A621

**1974-77**
   *Engr.*    *Perf. 11½x11*
| | | | | |
|---|---|---|---|---|
| 2070 | A621 | 1z black | .20 | .20 |
| 2071 | A621 | 1.50z indigo | .20 | .20 |
| 2071A | A621 | 4z slate green | .25 | .20 |
| 2071B | A621 | 4.50z dark brown | .90 | .80 |

Designs: 1.50z, Hunter with bow and arrow. 4z, Boy snaring geese. 4.50z, Beekeeper. Designs from 16th century woodcuts.
Issued: 1z-1.50z, 12/30; 4z-4.50z, 12/12/77.

## Pablo Neruda, by Osvaldo Guayasamin A622

*Perf. 11 11x11*
**1974, Dec. 31 Litho.**
2072 A622 1.50z multicolored   .20 .20
Pablo Neruda (1904-1973), Chilean poet.

## Nike Monument and Opera House, Warsaw — A623

*Perf. 11*
**1975, Jan. 17 Photo.**
2073 A623 1.50z multicolored   .20 .20
30th anniversary of the liberation of Warsaw.

## Hobby Falcon — A624

Circular Bar Graph and Institute's Emblem — A638

**1975, Sept. 1   Litho.   Perf. 11½x11**
2115  A638  1.50z multicolored   .20   .20
International Institute of Statistics, 40th session, Warsaw, Sept. 1975.

IWY Emblem, White, Yellow and Brown Women — A639

**1975, Sept. 8   Photo.   .20   .20**
2116  A639  1.50z multicolored
International Women's Year.

First Poles Arriving on "Mary and Margaret" 1608 A640

George Washington A641

Designs: 1.50z, Polish glass blower and glass works, Jamestown, 1608. 2.70z, Helena Modrzejewska (1840-1909), Polish actress, came to US in 1877. 4z, Casimir Pulaski (1747-1779), and Tadeusz Kosciusko (1748-1817), heroes of American War of Independence.

Nos. 2117-2121 (5)

2117  A640  1z black & multi      .20   .20
2118  A640  1.50z black & multi   .20   .20
2119  A640  2.70z black & multi   .20   .20
2120  A640  4z black & multi      .25   .20
2121  A640  6.40z black & multi   .40   .30
                                 1.25  1.10

**1975, Sept. 24   Litho.   Perf. 11x11½**

2122   Souvenir Sheet   Perf. 12
       Sheet of 3+3 labels         1.50  1.25
   a.  A641  4.90z shown            .40   .25
   b.  A641  4.90z Kosciusko        .40   .25
   c.  A641  4.90z Pulaski          .40   .25
American Revolution, bicentenary.

Albatross Biplane, 1918-1925 A642

**1975, Sept. 25   Perf. 11x11½**

2123  A642  2.40z buff & multi    .20   .20
2124  A642  4.90z gray & multi    .40   .20
Design: 4.90z, IL 62 jet, 1975.
50th anniversary of Polish air post stamps.

---

Frederic Chopin — A643

**1975, Oct. 7   Photo.**
2125  A643  1.50z gold, lt vio & blk   .20   .20
9th International Chopin Piano Competition, Warsaw, Oct. 7-28. Printed in sheets of 50 stamps with alternating labels with commemorative inscription.

Dunikowski, Self-portrait A644

**1975, Oct. 9   Perf. 11½x11**
Sculptures: 1z, "Breath." 1.50z, "Maternity."
2126  A644  50g silver & multi    .20   .20
2127  A644  1z silver & multi     .20   .20
2128  A644  1.50z silver & multi  .60   .60
Nos. 2126-2128 (3)
Stamp Day. Xawery Dunikowski (1875-1964), sculptor. See No. B131.

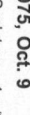

Town Hall, Zamosc — A645

**1975, Nov. 11   Photo.   Perf. 14**
2129  A645  1z olive green        .20   .20
2130  A645  1.50z rose brown      .20   .20
European Architectural Heritage Year. Black control number on back of every fifth stamp of Nos. 2129-2130.

Coil Stamps
1z, Arcades, Kazimierz Dolny, horiz.

Lodz, by Wladyslaw Strzeminski A646

**1975, Nov. 22   Litho.   Perf. 12½**
2131  A646  4.50z multicolored    .45   .20
   a. Souvenir sheet              .90   .50
Lodz 75, 12th Polish Philatelic Exhibition, for 25th anniv. of Polish Philatelists Union.

Piast Family Eagle A647

1.50z, Seal of Prince Boleslaw of Legnica. 4z, Coin of Prince Jerzy Wilhelm (1660-1675).

---

**1975, Nov. 29   Engr.   Perf. 11x11½**
2132  A647  1z green              .20   .20
2133  A647  1.50z brown           .30   .20
2134  A647  4z dull violet        .70   .60
Nos. 2132-2134 (3)
Piast dynasty's influence on the development of Silesia.

"7" Inscribed "ZJAZD" and "PZPR" — A648

**1975, Dec. 8   Photo.   Perf. 11½x11**
2135  A648  1t blue & multi       .20   .20
2136  A649  1.50z silver, red & ultra   .20   .20
7th Cong. of Polish United Workers' Party.

"VII ZJAZD PZPR" — A649

Ski Jump A650

**1976, Jan. 10   Perf. 11x11½**
Designs (Winter Olympic Games Emblem and): 1z, Ice hockey. 1.50z, Slalom. 2z, Speed skating. 4z, Luge. 6.40z, Biathlon.
2137  A650  50g silver & multi    .20   .20
2138  A650  1z silver & multi     .20   .20
2139  A650  1.50z silver & multi  .20   .20
2140  A650  2z silver & multi     .40   .20
2141  A650  4z silver & multi     .65   .20
2142  A650  6.40z silver & multi  1.85  1.25
Nos. 2137-2142 (6)
12th Winter Olympic Games, Innsbruck, Austria, Feb. 4-15.

Engine by Richard Trevithick, 1803 — A651

**1976, Feb. 13   Photo.   Perf. 11½x12**
Locomotives by: 1z, M. Murray and J. Blenkinsop, 1810. No. 2145, George Stephenson's Rocket, 1829. No. 2146, Polish electric locomotive, 1969. 2.70z, Stephenson, 1837. 3z, Joseph Harrison, 1840. 4.50z, Thomas Rogers, 1855. 4.90z, Chrzanow (Polish), 1922.
2143  A651  50g multicolored      .20   .20
2144  A651  1z multicolored       .20   .20
2145  A651  1.50z multicolored    .20   .20
2146  A651  1.50z multicolored    .20   .20
2147  A651  2z multicolored       .20   .20
2148  A651  3z multicolored       .20   .20
2149  A651  4.50z multicolored    .75   .20
2150  A651  4.90z multicolored    .80
Nos. 2143-2150 (8)                2.75  1.60
History of the locomotive.

---

Telephone, Radar and Satellites, ITU Emblem — A652

**1976, Mar. 10   Perf. 11**
2151  A652  1.50z multicolored    .20   .20
Centenary of first telephone call by Alexander Graham Bell, Mar. 10, 1876.

Atom Symbol and Flags of Communist Countries A653

**1976, Mar. 10   Litho.   Perf. 11½**
2152  A653  1.50z multicolored    .20   .20
Joint Institute of Nuclear Research, Dubna, USSR, 20th anniversary.

Ice Hockey — A654

**1976, Apr. 8   Photo.   Perf. 11½x11**
2153  A654  1z multicolored       .20   .20
2154  A654  1.50z multicolored    .20   .20
Ice Hockey World Championship 1976, Katowice.

Design: 1.50z, like 1z, reversed.

Soldier and Map of Sinai A655

**1976, Apr. 30   Photo.   Perf. 11x11½**
2155  A655  1.50z multicolored    .20   .20
Polish specialist troops serving with UN Forces in Sinai Peninsula.
No. 2155 printed se-tenant with label with commemorative inscription.

Sappers' Monument, by Stanislaw Kulow, Warsaw — A656

Civilian Defense
Medal — A671

**1977, Jan. 24    Litho.    Perf. 11½x11**
2196  A670  1.50z multicolored    .20    .20
Polish Red Cross.

**1977, Feb. 26    Litho.    Perf. 11**
2197  A671  1.50z multicolored    .20    .20
Civilian Defense.

Ball on the Road — A672

**1977, Mar. 12    Photo.**
2198  A672  1.50z olive & multi    .20    .20
Social Action Committee (founded 1966),
"Stop, Child on the Road!"

Forest
Fruits — A673

**1977, Mar. 17    Perf. 11½x11**
2199  A673  50g  Dewberry    .20    .20
2200  A673  90g  Cranberry    .20    .20
2201  A673  1z   Wild strawberry    .20    .20
2202  A673  1.50z Bilberry    .20    .20
2203  A673  2z   Raspberry    .20    .20
2204  A673  4z   Blueberry    .40    .40
2205  A673  6z   Dog rose    .70    .25
2206  A673  6.90z Hazelnut    2.50  1.65
Nos. 2199-2206 (8)

Flags of USSR
and Poland as
Computer
Tape — A674

Emblem and
Graph — A675

**1977, Apr. 4    Litho.    Perf. 11½x11**
2207  A674  1.50z red & multi    .20    .20
Scientific and technical cooperation
between Poland and USSR, 30th anniversary.

**1977, Apr. 22**
2208  A675  1.50z red & multi    .20    .20
7th Congress of Polish Engineers.

---

Pouring
Ladle — A666

Virgin and Child,
Epitaph,
1425 — A667

**1976, Nov. 26    Litho.    Perf. 11**
2184  A666  1.50z multicolored    .20    .20
First steel production at Katowice Foundry.

**1976, Dec. 15**
6z, The Beautiful Madonna, sculpture, c.
1410.
2185  A667  1z multicolored    .20    .20
2186  A667  6z multicolored    .40    .20

Polish Trade Union
Emblem — A668

**1976, Dec. 29**
2187  A668  1.50z multicolored    .20    .20
8th Polish Trade Union Congress.

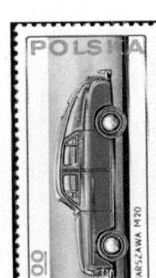

Tanker Zawrat Unloading,
Gdansk — A669

Polish Ports: No. 2189, Ferry "Gryf" and
cars at pier, Gdansk. No. 2190, Loading con-
tainers, Gdynia. No. 2191, "Stefan Batory" and
"People of the Sea" monument, Gdynia. 2z,
Barge and cargoship "Ziemia Szczecinska",
Szczecin. 4.20z, Coal loading installations,
Swinoujscie. 6.90z, Linor, hydrofoil and light-
house, Kolobrzeg. 8.40z, Map of Polish Coast
with ports, ships and emblem of Union of
Polish Ports.

**1976, Dec. 29    Photo.    Perf. 11**
2188  A669  1z multicolored    .20    .20
2189  A669  1z multicolored    .20    .20
2190  A669  1.50z multicolored    .20    .20
2191  A669  1.50z multicolored    .20    .20
2192  A669  ??  multicolored    .20    .20
2193  A669  4.20z multicolored    .30    .25
2194  A669  6.90z multicolored    .55    .30
2195  A669  8.40z multicolored    .60    .30
Nos. 2188-2195 (8)    2.45  1.75

Nurse Helping
Old
Woman — A670

---

Polish Theater,
Poznan — A662

**1976, July 12    Litho.    Perf. 11x11½**
2173  A662  1.50z gray olive & org    .20    .20
Polish Theater in Poznan, centenary.

Czekanowski, Lake Baikal — A663

**1976, Sept. 3    Photo.    Perf. 11x11½**
2174  A663  1.50z silver & multi    .20    .20
Aleksander Czekanowski (1833-1876),
geologist, death centenary.

Siren
A664

Designs: 1z, Sphinx, vert. 2z, Lion. 4.20z,
Bull. 4.50z, Goat. Designs from Corinthian
vases, 7th century B.C.

**Perf. 11x11½, 11½x11    Photo.**
2175  A664  1z gold & multi    .20    .20
2176  A664  1.50z gold & multi    .20    .20
2177  A664  2z gold & multi    .20    .20
2178  A664  4.20z gold & multi    .20    .20
2179  A664  4.50z gold & multi    .30    .20
Nos. 2175-2179,B133 (6)    2.30  1.50

Stamp Day.

Warszawa M20 — A665

Automobiles: 1.50z, Warszawa 223. 2z,
Syrena 104. 4.90z, Polski Fiat 125.

**1976, Nov. 6    Photo.    Perf. 11**
2180  A665  1z multicolored    .20    .20
2181  A665  1.50z multicolored    .20    .20
2182  A665  2z multicolored    .20    .20
2183  A665  4.90z multicolored    .35    .20
a.    Souvenir sheet of 4, #2180-2183    1.25  .55
      + 2 labels    .95  .80
Nos. 2180-2183 (4)

Zeran Automobile Factory, Warsaw, 25th
anniv.

---

Interphil 76,
Philadelphia — A657

Design: No. 2157, First Polish Army Monument, by Bronislaw Koniuszy, Warsaw.

**1976, May 8    Perf. 11½**
2156  A656  1z gold & multi    .20    .20
2157  A656  1z silver & multi    .20    .20
Memorials unveiled on 30th anniv. of WWII
victory.

**1976, May 20    Litho.    Perf. 11½x11**
2158  A657  8.40z gray & multi    .70    .35
Interphil 76, Intl. Phil. Exhib., Philadelphia,
May 29-June 6.

Wielkopolski Park and Owl — A658

National Parks: 1z, Wolinski Park and eagle.
1.50z, Slowinski Park and sea gull. 4.50z,
Bieszczadzki Park and lynx. 5z, Ojcowski Park
and bat. 6z, Kampinoski Park and elk.

**1976, May 22    Photo.    Perf. 12x11½**
2159  A658  90g multicolored    .20    .20
2160  A658  1z multicolored    .20    .20
2161  A658  1.50z multicolored    .20    .20
2162  A658  4.50z multicolored    .35    .20
2163  A658  5z multicolored    .40    .25
2164  A658  6z multicolored    .50    .25
Nos. 2159-2164 (6)    1.85  1.25

UN Headquarters, Dove-shaped
Globe — A659

**1976, June 29    Litho.    Perf. 11x11½**
2165  A659  8.40z multicolored    .70    .35
UN postage stamps, 25th anniversary

Fencing
and
Olympic
Rings — A660

**1976, June 30    Photo.**
2166  A660  50g  shown    .20    .20
2167  A660  50g  Bicycling    .20    .20
2168  A660  1.50z Soccer    .20    .20
2169  A660  4.20z Boxing    .35    .20
2170  A660  6.90z Weight lifting    .55    .35
2171  A660  8.40z Running    .35    .35
Nos. 2166-2171 (6)    2.15  1.45
21st Olympic Games, Montreal, Canada,
July 17-Aug. 1. See No. B132.

Venus, by
Rubens
A676

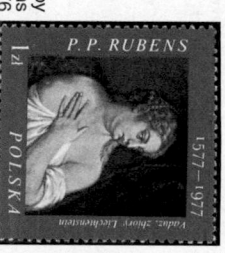

Paintings by Flemish painter Peter Paul Rubens (1577-1640): 1.50z, Bathsheba. 5z, Helene Fourment. 6z, Self-portrait.

**1977, Apr. 30** **Perf. 11½**

| | | | | | |
|---|---|---|---|---|---|
| 2209 | A676 | 1z | multicolored | .20 | .20 |
| 2210 | A676 | 1.50z | multicolored | .25 | .20 |
| 2211 | A676 | 5z | multicolored | .75 | .20 |
| 2212 | A676 | 6z | multicolored | .80 | .25 |
| | | Nos. 2209-2212 (4) | | 2.00 | .85 |

See No. B134.

**1977, May 6**
2213 A677 1.50z black, ultra & yel .20 .20
Congress of World Council of Peace, Warsaw, May 6-11.

Peace
Dove
A677

Frame in Gray Brown

**1977, May 6** **Perf. 11½**
2214 A678 1.50z gray & multi .20 .20
30th International Peace Bicycling Race, Warsaw-Berlin-Prague.

Bicyclist
A678

Wolf — A679

Violinist, by
Jacob
Toorenvliet
A680

**1977, May 12** **Photo. Perf. 11½x11**
2215 A679 1z silver & multi .20 .20
2216 A679 1.50z silver & multi .20 .20
2217 A679 5z silver & multi .20 .20
2218 A679 6z silver & multi .50 .20
Nos. 2215-2218 (4) 1.10 .80

Wildlife protection.

**1977, May 16**
2219 A680 6z gold & multi .40 .25
AMPHILEX '77 Int. Phil. Exhib., Amsterdam, May 26-June 5. No. 2219 issued in sheets of 6.

---

Midsummer Bonfire — A681

**1977, June 13** **Perf. 11½x11, 11½x11**
| | | | | | |
|---|---|---|---|---|---|
| 2220 | A681 | 90g | multicolored | .20 | .20 |
| 2221 | A681 | 1z | multicolored | .20 | .20 |
| 2222 | A681 | 1.50z | multicolored | .20 | .20 |
| 2223 | A681 | 3z | multicolored | .25 | .20 |
| 2224 | A681 | 6z | multicolored | .50 | .25 |
| 2225 | A681 | 8.40z | multicolored | .65 | .25 |
| | | Nos. 2220-2225 (6) | | 2.00 | 1.25 |

Folk Customs: 1z, Easter cock. 1.50z, Dousing the women on Easter Monday. 3z, Harvest festival. 6z Christmas procession with crèche. 8.40z, Wedding dance. 1z, 1.50z, 3z, 6z vertical.

Henryk Wieniawski and Musical Symbol — A682

Parnassius Apollo — A683

**1977, June 30** **Litho. Perf. 11½x11**
2226 A682 1.50z gold, blk & red .20 .20
Wieniawski Music Festivals, Poznan: 5th Intl. Lute Competition, June 30-July 10, and 7th Intl. Violin Competition, Nov. 13-27.

Butterflies: No. 2228, Nymphalis polychloros. No. 2229, Papilio machaon. No. 2230, Nymphalis antiopa. 1.50z, Fabriciana adippe. 6.90z, Argynnis paphia.

**1977, Aug. 22** **Photo. Perf. 11**
| | | | | | |
|---|---|---|---|---|---|
| 2227 | A683 | 1z | multicolored | .20 | .20 |
| 2228 | A683 | 1z | multicolored | .20 | .20 |
| 2229 | A683 | 1z | multicolored | .20 | .20 |
| 2230 | A683 | 1.50z | multicolored | .20 | .20 |
| 2231 | A683 | 5z | multicolored | .95 | .25 |
| 2232 | A683 | 6.90z | multicolored | 2.00 | .85 |
| | | Nos. 2227-2232 (6) | | 3.75 | 1.90 |

---

Arms of Slupsk,
Keyboard
A684

**1977, Sept. 3**
2233 A684 1.50z multicolored .20 .20
Slupsk Piano Festival.

Feliks Dzerzhinski
A685

**1977, Sept. 10** **Litho. Perf. 11½x11**
2234 A685 1.50z olive bis & sepia .20 .20
Feliks E. Dzerzhinski (1877-1926), organizer and head of Russian Secret Police (Cheka).

Monastery, Przasnysz — A688

Architectural landmarks: No. 2242, Wolin Gate, vert. No. 2243, Church, Debno, vert. No. 2245, Cathedral, Plock. 6z, Castle, Kornik. 6.90z, Palace and Garden, Wilanow.

**1977, Nov. 21** **Perf. 11½x11, 11x11½**
| | | | | | |
|---|---|---|---|---|---|
| 2242 | A688 | 1z | multicolored | .20 | .20 |
| 2243 | A688 | 1z | multicolored | .20 | .20 |
| 2244 | A688 | 1.50z | multicolored | .20 | .20 |
| 2245 | A688 | 1.50z | multicolored | .20 | .20 |
| 2246 | A688 | 6z | multicolored | .40 | .20 |
| 2247 | A688 | 6.90z | multicolored | .55 | .25 |
| | | Nos. 2242-2247 (6) | | 1.75 | 1.25 |

Vostok (USSR) and Mercury (USA) A689

**1977, Dec. 28** **Photo. Perf. 11½x11½**
2248 A689 6.90z ultra & multi .50 .30
a. Souvenir sheet of 6 4.25 3.00

20 years of space conquest. No. 2248a contains 6 No. 2248 (2 tete-beche pairs) and 2 labels, one showing Sputnik 1 and "4.X.1957," the other Explorer 1 and "31.1.1958."

Silver Coins: 1z, King Kazimierz Wielki's Cracow groszy, 14th century. 1.50z, Legnica-Brzeg-Wolow thaler, 17th century. 4.20z, King Augustus III guilder, Gdansk, 18th century. 4.50z, 5z (ship), 1936. 6z, 100z, Poland's millenium, 1966.

**1977, Oct. 9** **Photo. Perf. 11½x11**
| | | | | | |
|---|---|---|---|---|---|
| 2236 | A687 | 50g | silver & multi | .20 | .20 |
| 2237 | A687 | 1z | silver & multi | .20 | .20 |
| 2238 | A687 | 1.50z | silver & multi | .20 | .20 |
| 2239 | A687 | 4.20z | silver & multi | .30 | .20 |
| 2240 | A687 | 4.50z | silver & multi | .40 | .20 |
| 2241 | A687 | 4.50z | silver & multi | .70 | .25 |
| | | Nos. 2236-2241 (6) | | 2.00 | 1.25 |

Stamp Day.

Earth and Sputnik A686

**1977, Oct. 1** **Litho. Perf. 11½x11½**
2235 A686 1.50z ultra & car .20 .20
a. Souvenir sheet of 3+3 labels .90 .60

60th anniv. of the Russian Revolution and 20th anniv. of Sputnik space flight. Printed in sheets of 15 stamps and 15 carmine labels showing Winter Palace, Leningrad.

Boleslaw Chrobry's Denarius, 11th Century — A687

---

DN Class Iceboats — A690

**1978, Feb. 6** **Litho. Perf. 11**
2249 A690 1.50z lt ultra & blk .20 .20
2250 A690 1.50z lt ultra & blk .30 .20
a. Pair, #2249-2250 + label

6th World Iceboating Championships, Feb. 6-11.

Design: No. 2250. One iceboat.

Electric Locomotive, Katowice Station, 1957 — A691

Locomotives in Poland: No. 2252, Narrow-gauge engine and Gothic Tower, Znin. No. 2253, Pm36 engine and Cegielski factory, Poznan. No. 2254, Electric train and Olwock Station, 1936. No. 2255, Markl Train and Warsaw-Stalow Station, 1907. 4.50z, Ty51 coal train and Gdynia Station, 1933. 5z, Tr21 and Chrzanow factory, 1920. 6z, "Cockerill and Vienna Station, 1848.

**1978, Feb. 28** **Photo. Perf. 12x11½**
| | | | | | |
|---|---|---|---|---|---|
| 2251 | A691 | 50g | multicolored | .20 | .20 |
| 2252 | A691 | 1z | multicolored | .20 | .20 |
| 2253 | A691 | 1z | multicolored | .20 | .20 |
| 2254 | A691 | 1.50z | multicolored | .20 | .20 |
| 2255 | A691 | 1.50z | multicolored | .20 | .20 |
| 2256 | A691 | 4.50z | multicolored | .40 | .20 |
| 2257 | A691 | 5z | multicolored | .40 | .20 |
| 2258 | A691 | 6z | multicolored | .50 | .25 |
| | | Nos. 2251-2258 (8) | | 2.30 | 1.65 |

Pierwsze Wzloty, 1896, and Czeslaw Tanski A692

Polish Sport Planes: 1z, Zwyciezcy-Challenge, 1932. F. Zwirko and S. Wigura, vert. 1.50z, RWD-5 bis over South Atlantic, 1933, and S. Skarzynski, vert. 4.20z, MI-2 helicopter over mountains, Pezetel emblem, vert. 6.90z, PZL-104 Wilga 35, Pezetel emblem, vert. Motoszybowiec SZD-45 Ogar.

**1978, Apr. 15** **Perf. 11½x11½, 11½x11**
| | | | | | |
|---|---|---|---|---|---|
| 2259 | A692 | 50g | multicolored | .20 | .20 |
| 2260 | A692 | 1z | multicolored | .20 | .20 |
| 2261 | A692 | 1.50z | multicolored | .20 | .20 |
| 2262 | A692 | 4.20z | multicolored | .40 | .20 |
| 2263 | A692 | 6.90z | multicolored | .75 | .20 |
| 2264 | A692 | 8.40z | multicolored | .50 | .20 |
| | | Nos. 2259-2264 (6) | | 2.25 | 1.30 |

Soccer — A693

**1978, May 12** **Perf. 11½x11, 11x11½**
2265 A693 1.50z multicolored .20 .20
2266 A693 6.90z multicolored .50 .25

Design: 6.90z, Soccer ball, horiz.

11th World Cup Soccer Championships, Argentina, June 1-25.

Poster — A694

**1978, June 1** **Perf. 12x11½**
2267 A694 1.50z multicolored .20 .20
7th International Poster Biennale, Warsaw.

## Polish Combatants Monument, and Eiffel Tower, Paris — A710

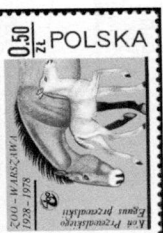

**1978, Nov. 2   Photo.   Perf. 11x11½**

| | | | | |
|---|---|---|---|---|
| 2300 | A710 | 1.50z | brown, red & bl | .20 .20 |

## Przewalski Mare and Colt — A711

Animals: 1z, Polar bears. 1.50z, Indian elephants. 2z, Jaguars. 4.20z, Gray seals. 4.50z, Hartebeests. 6z, Mandrills.

**1978, Nov. 10**

| | | | | |
|---|---|---|---|---|
| 2301 | A711 | 50g | multicolored | .20 .20 |
| 2302 | A711 | 1z | multicolored | .20 .20 |
| 2303 | A711 | 1.50z | multicolored | .20 .20 |
| 2304 | A711 | 2z | multicolored | .20 .20 |
| 2305 | A711 | 4.20z | multicolored | .30 .20 |
| 2306 | A711 | 4.50z | multicolored | .40 .20 |
| 2307 | A711 | 6z | multicolored | .50 1.40 |
| | | | Nos. 2301-2307 (7) | 2.00 1.40 |

Warsaw Zoological Gardens, 50th anniv.

## Adolf Warski (1868-1937) A712

## Party Emblem A713

#2309, Julian Lenski (1889-1937). #2310, Aleksander Zawadzki (1899-1964). #2311, Stanislaw Dubois (1901-1942).

**1978, Dec. 15   Photo.**

| | | | | |
|---|---|---|---|---|
| 2308 | A712 | 50g | red & brown | .20 .20 |
| 2309 | A712 | 1.50z | red & black | .20 .20 |
| 2310 | A712 | 1.50z | red & dk vio | .20 .20 |
| 2311 | A712 | 1.50z | red & dk blue | .20 .20 |
| 2312 | A713 | 1.50z | black, red & gold | .20 .20 |
| | | | Nos. 2308-2312 (5) | 1.00 1.00 |

Polish United Workers' Party, 30th anniv.

## LOT Planes 1929 and 1979 A714

**1979, Jan. 2   Photo.   Perf. 11x11½**

| | | | | |
|---|---|---|---|---|
| 2313 | A714 | 6.90g | gold & multi | .45 .20 |

LOT, Polish airline, 50th anniversary.

---

**1978-79   Litho.   Perf. 11½ (1z), 12½**

| | | | | |
|---|---|---|---|---|
| 2284 | A704 | 1z | violet | .20 .20 |
| 2285 | A704 | 1.50z | steel blue ('79) | .20 .20 |
| 2286 | A704 | 2z | brown ('79) | .20 .20 |
| 2287 | A704 | 2.50z | ultra ('79) | .80 .80 |
| | | | Nos. 2284-2287 (4) | |

## Polish Unit, UN Middle East Emergency Force — A706

Designs: No. 2289, Color Guard, Kosziusko Division (4 soldiers). No. 2290, Color Guard, field training (3 soldiers).

**1978, Oct. 6   Photo.   Perf. 12x11½**

| | | | | |
|---|---|---|---|---|
| 2289 | A706 | 1.50z | multicolored | .20 .20 |
| 2290 | A706 | 1.50z | multicolored | .20 .20 |
| 2291 | A706 | 1.50z | multicolored | .60 .60 |
| | | | Nos. 2289-2291 (3) | |

35th anniversary of People's Army.

## Young Man, by Raphael A707

**1978, Oct. 9   Perf. 11   .40 .20**

| | | | |
|---|---|---|---|
| 2292 | A707 | 6z | multicolored |

Stamp Day.

## Dr. Korczak and Children — A708

**1978, Oct. 11   Litho.   Perf. 11½x11**

| | | | | |
|---|---|---|---|---|
| 2293 | A708 | 1.50z | multicolored | .20 .20 |

Dr. Janusz Korczak, physician, educator, writer, birth centenary.

## Wojciech Boguslawski (1757-1829) — A709

Polish dramatists: 1z, Aleksander Fredro (1793-1878). 1.50z, Juliusz Slowacki (1809-1849). 2z, Adam Mickiewicz (1798-1855). 4.50z, Stanislaw Wyspianski (1869-1907). 6z, Gabriela Zapolska (1857-1921).

**1978, Nov. 11   Litho.   Perf. 11½**

| | | | | |
|---|---|---|---|---|
| 2294 | A709 | 50g | multicolored | .20 .20 |
| 2295 | A709 | 1z | multicolored | .20 .20 |
| 2296 | A709 | 1.50z | multicolored | .20 .20 |
| 2297 | A709 | 2z | multicolored | .35 .20 |
| 2298 | A709 | 4.50z | multicolored | .50 .20 |
| 2299 | A709 | 6z | multicolored | 1.65 1.20 |
| | | | Nos. 2294-2299 (6) | |

---

## Anopheles Mosquito and Blood Cells — A700

Design: 6z, Tsetse fly and blood cells.

**1978, Aug. 19   Litho.   Perf. 11½x11**

| | | | | |
|---|---|---|---|---|
| 2274 | A700 | 1.50z | multicolored | .20 .20 |
| 2275 | A700 | 6z | multicolored | .45 .20 |

4th International Parasitological Congress.

## Norway Maple, Environment Emblem — A701

Human Environment Emblem and: 1z, English oak. 1.50z, White poplar. 4.20z, Scotch pine. 4.50z, White willow. 6z, Birch.

**1978, Sept. 6   Photo.   Perf. 14**

| | | | | |
|---|---|---|---|---|
| 2276 | A701 | 50g | gold & multi | .20 .20 |
| 2277 | A701 | 1z | gold & multi | .20 .20 |
| 2278 | A701 | 1.50z | gold & multi | .20 .20 |
| 2279 | A701 | 4.20z | gold & multi | .35 .20 |
| 2280 | A701 | 4.50z | gold & multi | .35 .20 |
| 2281 | A701 | 6z | gold & multi | 1.80 1.20 |
| | | | Nos. 2276-2281 (6) | |

Protection of the environment.

## Souvenir Sheet

## Jan Zizka, Battle of Grunwald, by Jan Matejko — A702

**1978, Sept. 8   Perf. 11½x11**

| | | | | |
|---|---|---|---|---|
| 2282 | A702 | 6z | gold & multi | .90 .35 |

PRAGA '78 Intl. Phil. Exhib., Prague, Sept. 8-17.

## Letter, Telephone and Satellite — A703

**1978, Sept. 20   Litho.   Perf. 11**

| | | | | |
|---|---|---|---|---|
| 2283 | A703 | 1.50z | multicolored | .20 .20 |

20th anniversary of the Organization of Ministers of Posts and Telecommunications of Warsaw Pact countries.

## Peace, by Andre le Brun — A704

---

## Fair Emblem — A695

**1978, June 10   Perf. 11   .20 .20**

| | | | |
|---|---|---|---|
| 2268 | A695 | 1.50z | multicolored |

50th International Poznan Fair.

## Polonez Passenger Car — A696

**1978, June 10   Photo.   Perf. 11**

| | | | | |
|---|---|---|---|---|
| 2269 | A696 | 1.50z | multicolored | .20 .20 |

## Maj. Miroslaw Hermaszewski A697

1st Polish cosmonaut on Russian space mission. Nos. 2270a, 2271a printed in sheets of 6 stamps and 2 labels.

**1978, June 27   Perf. 11½x11, 11x11½   Photo.**

| | | | | |
|---|---|---|---|---|
| 2270 | A697 | 1.50z | multi | .20 .20 |
| a. | | Without date | | .30 .30 |
| 2271 | A697 | 6.90z | multi, horiz. | .50 .25 |
| a. | | Without date | | 1.00 1.00 |

6.90z, Hermaszewski, globe & trajectory.

## Youth Festival Emblem A698

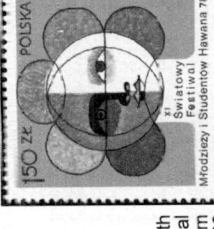

**1978, July 12   Litho.   Perf. 11½**

| | | | | |
|---|---|---|---|---|
| 2272 | A698 | 1.50z | multicolored | .20 .20 |

11th Youth Festival, Havana, July 28-Aug. 5.

## Souvenir Sheet

## Flowers — A699

Illustration reduced.

**1978, July 20   Perf. 11½x11**

| | | | | |
|---|---|---|---|---|
| 2273 | A699 | 1.50z | gold & multi | .30 .20 |

30th anniv. of Polish Youth Movement.

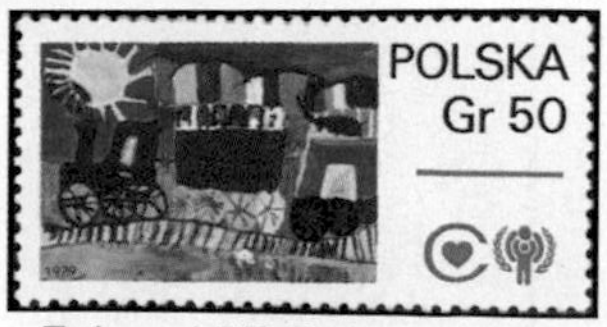

Train and IYC Emblem — A715

Children's Paintings: 1z, Children with toys. 1.50z, Children in meadow. 6z, Family.

**1979, Jan. 13** *Perf. 11*
**2314** A715 50g multicolored .20 .20
**2315** A715 1z multicolored .20 .20
**2316** A715 1.50z multicolored .20 .20
**2317** A715 6z multicolored .50 .20
*Nos. 2314-2317 (4)* 1.10 .80

International Year of the Child.

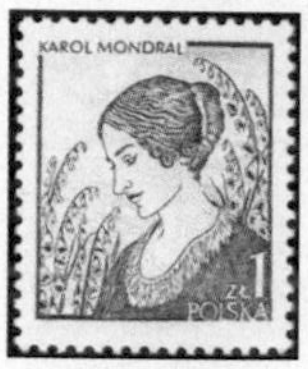

Artist's Wife, by Karol Mondral — A716

Modern Polish Graphic Arts: 50g, "Lightning," by Edmund Bartlomiejcyk, horiz. 1.50z, Musicians, by Tadeusz Kulisiewicz. 4.50z, Portrait of a Brave Man, by Wladyslaw Skoczylas.

*Perf. 11½x12, 12x11½*
**1979, Mar. 5** **Engr.**
**2318** A716 50g brt violet .20 .20
**2319** A716 1z slate green .20 .20
**2320** A716 1.50z blue gray .20 .20
**2321** A716 4.50z violet brown .40 .20
*Nos. 2318-2321 (4)* 1.00 .80

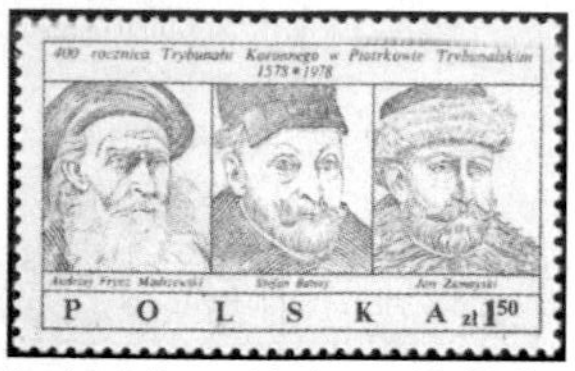

Andrzej Frycz-Modrzewski, Stefan Batory, Jan Zamoyski — A717

**Photogravure and Engraved**
**1979, Mar. 12** *Perf. 12x11½*
**2322** A717 1.50z cream & sepia .20 .20

Royal Tribunal in Piotrkow Trybunalski, 400th anniversary.

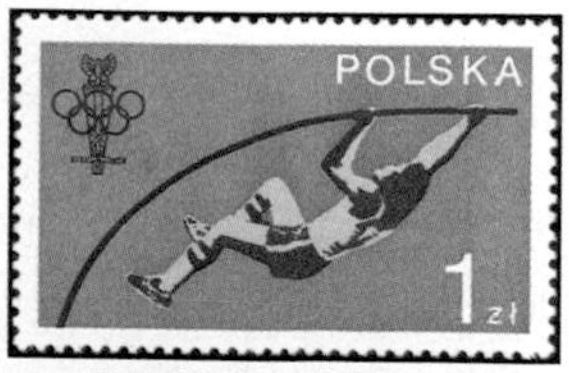

Pole Vault and Olympic Emblem — A718

Olympic Emblem and: 1.50z, High jump. 6z, Cross-country skiing. 8.40z, Equestrian.

**1979, Mar. 26 Photo.** *Perf. 12x11½*
**2323** A718 1z multicolored .20 .20
**2324** A718 1.50z multicolored .20 .20
**2325** A718 6z multicolored .40 .20
**2326** A718 8.40z multicolored .60 .20
*Nos. 2323-2326 (4)* 1.40 .80

1980 Olympic Games.

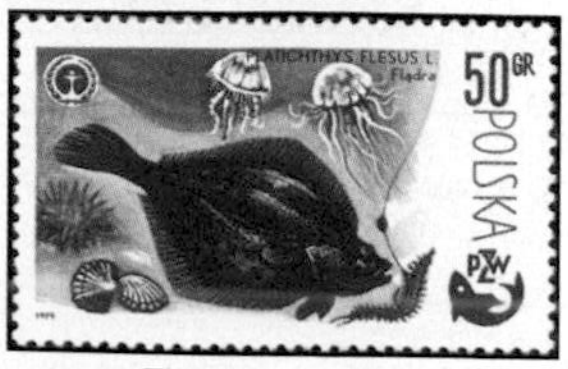

Flounder — A720

Fish and Environmental Protection Emblem: 90g, Perch. 1z, Grayling. 1.50z, Salmon. 2z, Trout. 4.50z, Pike. 5z, Carp. 6z, Catfish and frog.

**1979, Apr. 26 Photo.** *Perf. 11½x11*
**2327** A720 50g multicolored .20 .20
**2328** A720 90g multicolored .20 .20
**2329** A720 1z multicolored .20 .20
**2330** A720 1.50z multicolored .20 .20
**2331** A720 2z multicolored .20 .20
**2332** A720 4.50z multicolored .25 .20
**2333** A720 5z multicolored .35 .20
**2334** A720 6z multicolored .40 .20
*Nos. 2327-2334 (8)* 2.00 1.60

Polish angling, centenary, and protection of the environment.

A721

**1979, Apr. 30 Litho.** *Perf. 11x11½*
**2335** A721 1.50z multicolored .20 .20

Council for Mutual Economic Aid of Socialist Countries, 30th anniversary.

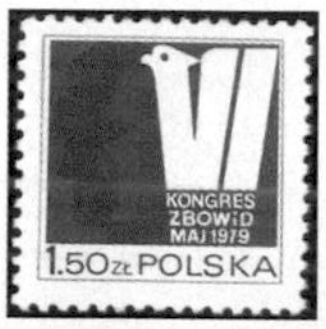

Faces and Emblem — A722

**1979, May 7** *Perf. 11*
**2336** A722 1.50z red & black .20 .20

6th Congress of Association of Fighters for Liberty and Democracy, Warsaw, May 7-8.

St. George's Church, Sofia A722a

**1979, May 15 Photo.** *Perf. 11x11½*
**2337** A722a 1.50z multicolored .20 .20

Philaserdica '79 Phil. Exhib., Sofia, Bulgaria, May 18-27.

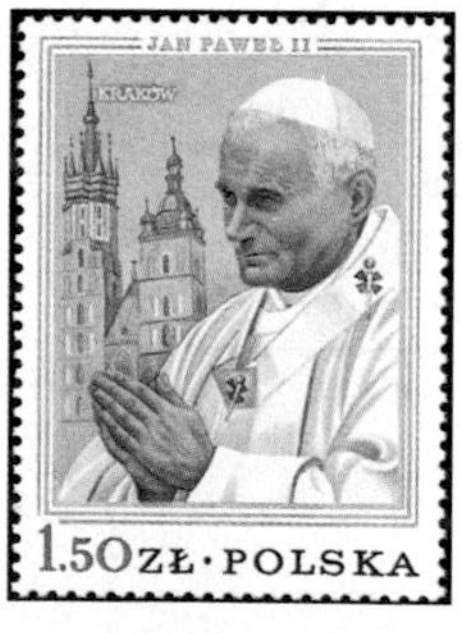

Pope John Paul II, Cracow Cathedral A723

Designs: 8.40z, Pope John Paul II, Auschwitz-Birkenau Memorial. 50z, Pope John Paul II.

**1979, June 2 Photo.** *Perf. 11x11½*
**2338** A723 1.50z multicolored .20 .20
**2339** A723 8.40z multicolored .80 .20

**Souvenir Sheet**
*Perf. 11½x11*
**2340** A723 50z multicolored & gold 9.00 6.00

Visit of Pope John Paul II to Poland, June 2-11. No. 2340 contains one 26x35mm stamp.
A variety of #2340 with silver margin exists. Values, unused $30, used $22.50.

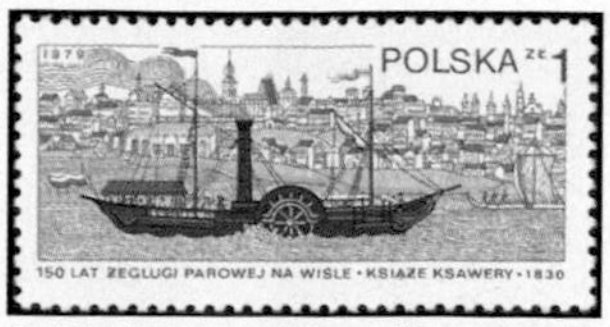

Paddle Steamer Prince Ksawery and Old Warsaw — A724

Designs: 1.50z, Steamer Gen. Swierczewski and Gdansk, 1914. 4.50z, Tug Aurochs and Plock, 1960. 6z, Motor ship Mermaid and modern Warsaw, 1959.

**1979, June 15 Litho.** *Perf. 11*
**2341** A724 1z multicolored .20 .20
**2342** A724 1.50z multicolored .20 .20
**2343** A724 4.50z multicolored .35 .20
**2344** A724 6z multicolored .50 .20
*Nos. 2341-2344 (4)* 1.25 .80

Vistula River navigation, 150th anniversary.

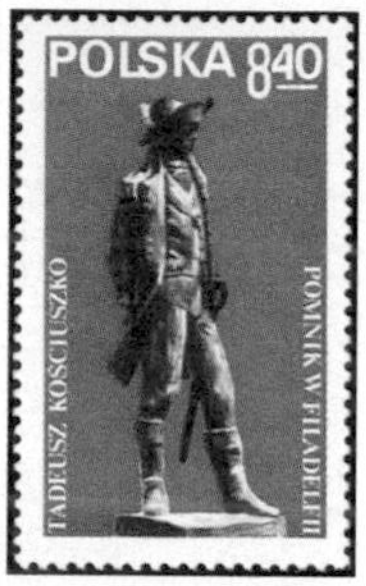

Kosciuszko Monument, Philadelphia A725

**1979, July 1 Photo.** *Perf. 11½*
**2345** A725 8.40z multicolored .60 .25

Gen. Tadeusz Kosziuszko (1746-1807), Polish soldier and statesman who served in American Revolution.

Mining Machinery A726

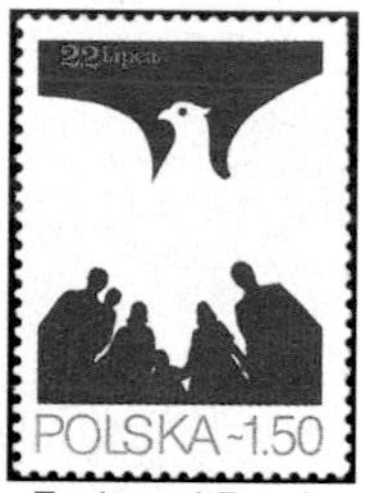

Eagle and People A727

Design: 1.50z, Salt crystals.

**1979, July 14 Photo.** *Perf. 14*
**2346** A726 1z lt brown & blk .20 .20
**2347** A726 1.50z blue grn & blk .20 .20

Wieliczka ancient rock-salt mines.

**1979, July 21** *Perf. 11½x11*

No. 2349, Man with raised hand and flag.

**2348** A727 1.50z red, blue & gray .20 .20
**2349** A727 1.50z silver, red & blk .20 .20

35 years of Polish People's Republic.

**Souvenir Sheet**
**1979, Sept. 2 Photo.** *Perf. 11½x11*
**2350** A727 Sheet of 2, #2348-2349 + label .50 .45

13th National Philatelic Exhibition.

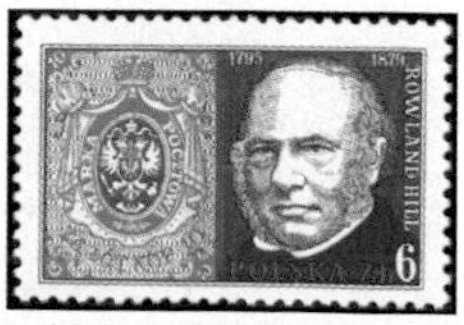

Poland No. 1, Rowland Hill (1795-1879), Originator of Penny Postage — A728

**1979, Aug. 16 Litho.** *Perf. 11½x11*
**2351** A728 6z multicolored .40 .20

Souvenir Sheet

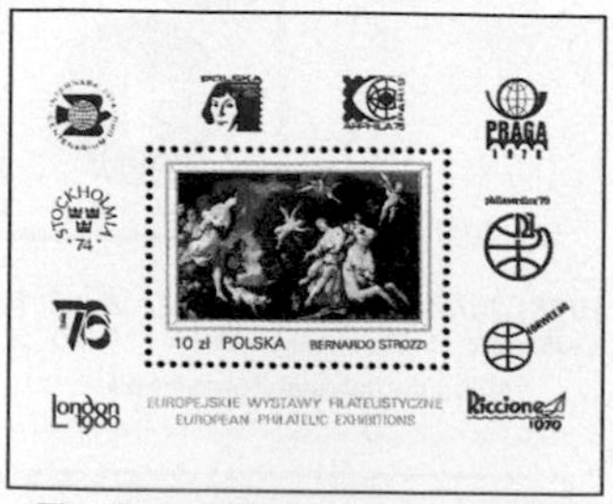

The Rape of Europa, by Bernardo Strozzi — A729

**1979, Aug. 20 Photo.** *Perf. 11x11½*
**2352** A729 10z multicolored .75 .50

Europhil '79, Intl. Phil. Exhib.

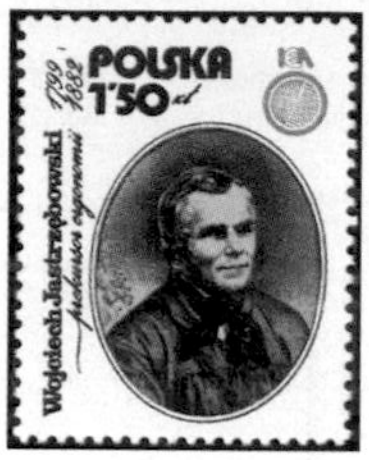

Wojciech Jastrzebowski A730

**1979, Aug. 27** *Perf. 11½x11*
**2353** A730 1.50z multicolored .20 .20

Economic Congress.

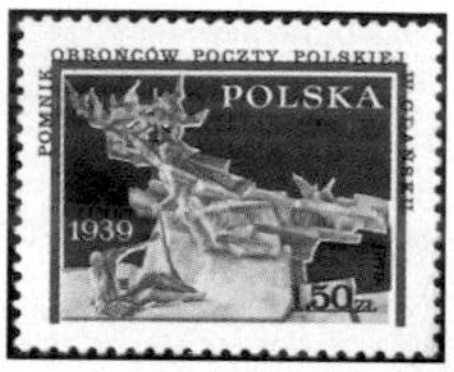

Postal Workers' Monument A731

**1979, Sept. 1** *Perf. 11x11½*
**2354** A731 1.50z multicolored .20 .20

40th anniversary of Polish postal workers' resistance to Nazi invaders. See No. B137.

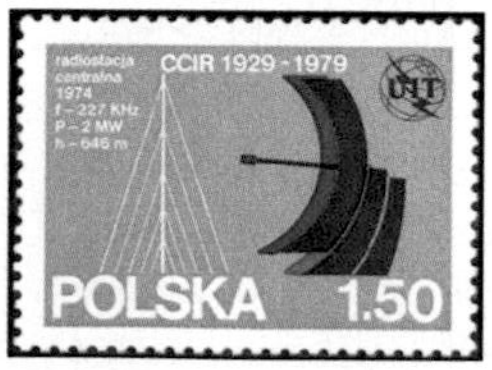

ITU Emblem, Radio Antenna A732

**1979, Sept. 24** *Perf. 11x11½*
**2355** A732 1.50z multicolored .20 .20

Intl. Radio Consultative Committee (CCIR) of the ITU, 50th anniv.

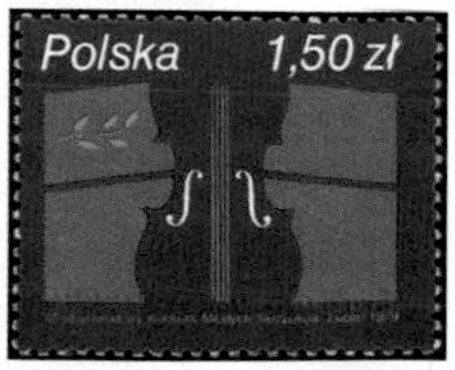

Violin A733

**1979, Sept. 25** **Litho.**
**2356** A733 1.50z dk blue, org, grn .20 .20

Henryk Wieniawski Young Violinists' Competition, Lublin.

**Pulaski Monument, Buffalo — A734**

**1979, Oct. 1**    Photo.    Perf. 11½x12
2357 A734 8.40z multicolored   .50   .25

Gen. Casimir Pulaski (1748-1779), Polish nobleman who served in American Revolutionary War.

**Gen. Franciszek Jozwiak — A735**

**1979, Oct. 3**
2358 A735 1.50z gray blue, dk blue & gold   .20   .20   Perf. 11½x11

35th anniv. of Civil and Military Security Service, founded by Gen. Franciszek Jozwiak (1895-1966).

**Drive-in Post Office — A736**

Designs: 1.50z, Parcel sorting. 4.50z, Loading mail train 6z, Mobile post office.

**1979, Oct. 9**    Perf. 11½
2359 A736 1z multicolored   .20   .20
2360 A736 1.50z multicolored   .20   .20
2361 A736 4.50z multicolored   .35   .20
2362 A736 6z multicolored   .50   .80
Nos. 2359-2362 (4)   1.25   .80

Stamp Day.

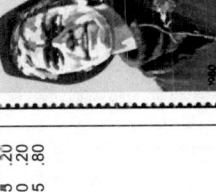

**Holy Family — A737**

Design: 6.90z, Nativity, horiz.

**1979, Dec. 4**    Photo.    Perf. 11½x11, 11x11½
2363 A737 2z multicolored   .20   .20
2364 A737 6.90z multicolored   .45   .20

**A738**

Space Achievements: 1z, Soyuz 30 and Salyut 6. 1.50z, Kopernik 500 and Copernicus satellite. 2z, Lunik 2 and Ranger 7. 4.50z, Yuri Gagarin and Vostok. 6.90z, Neil Armstrong and Apollo 11.

**1979, Dec. 28**    Photo.    Perf. 11½x11
2365 A738 1z multi   .20   .20
2366 A738 1.50z multi   .20   .20
2367 A738 2z multi   .20   .20
2368 A738 4.50z multi   .25   .20
2369 A738 6.90z multi   .40   1.25
   a. Souvenir sheet of 5   1.60   1.25
Nos. 2365-2369 (5)   1.25   1.00

No. 2369a contains Nos. 2365-2369, tete beche plus label.

**A739**

**1980, Jan. 31**    Photo.    Perf. 11½x12

Designs: Horse Paintings.
2370 A739 1z Stagecoach   .20   .20
2371 A739 2z Horse, trainer   .20   .20
2372 A739 2.50z Trotters   .25   .20
2373 A739 3z Fox hunt   .25   .20
2374 A739 4z Sled   .30   .20
2375 A739 6z Hay cart   .50   .20
2376 A739 6.50z Pairs   .55   .20
2377 A739 6.90z Hurdles   .55   .20
Nos. 2370-2377 (8)   2.75   1.60

Sierakov horse stud farm, 150th anniv.

**Party Slogan on Map of Poland — A740**

**Worker, by Janusz Stanny — A741**

**1980, Feb. 11**    Photo.    Perf. 11½x11
2378 A740 2.50z multi   .20   .20
2379 A741 2.50z multi   .20   .20

Polish United Workers' Party, 8th Congress.

**Equestrian, Olympic Rings — A742**

**1980, Mar. 31**    Perf. 12x11½
2380 A742 2z shown   .20   .20
2381 A742 2.50z Archery   .25   .20
2382 A742 6.50z Biathlon   .50   .20
2383 A742 8.40z Volleyball   .65   .65
Nos. 2381-2383 (3)   1.35   .65

13th Winter Olympic Games, Lake Placid, N.Y., Feb. 12-24 (6.50z); 22nd Summer Olympic Games, Moscow, July 19-Aug. 3. See No. B138.

**Map and Old Town Hall, 1591, Zamosc A743**

**1980, Apr. 3**    Litho.    Perf. 11½
2384 A743 2.50z multi   .20   .20

Zamosc, 400th anniversary.

**Arms of Poland and Russia A744**

**1980, Apr. 21**    Litho.    Perf. 11½
2385 A744 2.50z multi   .20   .20

Treaty of Friendship, Cooperation and Mutual Assistance between Poland and USSR, 35th anniversary.

**Lenin, 110th Birth Anniversary A745**

**1980, Apr. 22**    Photo.    Perf. 11
2386 A745 2.50z multi   .25   .20

**Workers Marching A746**

**Dove Over Liberation Date — A747**

**1980, May 1**    Perf. 11½x11
2387 A746 2.50z multi   .20   .20
Revolution of 1905, 75th anniversary.

**1980, May 9**    Perf. 11½x12
2388 A747 2.50z multi   .20   .20
Victory over fascism, 35th anniversary.

**Arms of Treaty-signing Countries A748**

**1980, May 14**    Litho.    Perf. 11½x11
2389 A748 2z red & blk   .20   .20

Signing of Warsaw Pact (Bulgaria, Czechoslovakia, German Democratic Rep., Hungary, Poland, Romania, USSR), 25th anniversary.

**Caverns, (1961 Expedition) Map of Cuba — A749**

**1980, May 22**    Photo.    Perf. 14
2390 A749 2z shown   .20   .20
2391 A749 2z Seals, Antarctica, 1959   .20   .20
2392 A749 2.50z Ethnology, Mongolia, 1963   .25   .20
2393 A749 2.50z Archaeology, Syria, 1959   .25   .20
2394 A749 6.50z Mountain climbing, Nepal, 1978   .50   .20
2395 A749 8.40z Paleontology, Mongolia, 1963   .65   .25
Nos. 2390-2395 (6)   2.05   1.25

**Malachowski Lyceum, Arms of Polish Order of Labor — A750**

**1980, June 7**    Photo.    Perf. 11x12
2396 A750 2z blk & dl grn   .20   .20

Malachowski Lyceum (oldest school in Plock), 800th anniversary.

**Xerocomus Parasiticus — A751**

**1980, June 30**    Photo.    Perf. 11½x11
2397 A751 2z shown   .20   .20
2398 A751 2z Clathrus ruber   .20   .20
2399 A751 2.50z Phallus hadriani   .25   .20
2400 A751 2.50z Strobilomyces floccopus   .25   .20
2401 A751 8z Sparassis crispa   .60   .25
2402 A751 10.50z Langermannia gigantea   .80   .30
Nos. 2397-2402 (6)   2.30   1.35

**Sandomierz Millenium — A752**

**1980, July 12**    Photo.    Perf. 11x11½
2403 A752 2.50z dk brown   .22   .20

## "Lwow", T. Ziolkowski — A753

**1980, July 21      Litho.      Perf. 11**

Ships and Teachers: 2.50z, Antoni Garnuszewski; A. Garnuszewski, 6z, Zenit, A.
Ledochowski, 6.50z, Jan Turlejski, K. Poreb-
ski, 6.90z, Horyzon, G. Kanski, 8.40z, Dar
Pomorza, K. Maciejewicz.

| | | | | |
|---|---|---|---|---|
| 2404 | A753 | 2z multi | .20 | .20 |
| 2405 | A753 | 2.50z multi | .25 | .20 |
| 2406 | A753 | 6z multi | .50 | .20 |
| 2407 | A753 | 6.50z multi | .60 | .20 |
| 2408 | A753 | 6.90z multi | .60 | .25 |
| 2409 | A753 | 8.40z multi | .70 | .30 |
| Nos. 2404-2409 (6) | | | 2.85 | 1.40 |

Marize Maritime High School.

A754

A755

Designs: Medicinal plants.

**1980, Aug. 15      Litho.      Perf. 11½x11**

| | | | | |
|---|---|---|---|---|
| 2410 | A754 | 2z Atropa bella-donna | .20 | .20 |
| 2411 | A754 | 2.50z Datura innoxia | .25 | .20 |
| 2412 | A754 | 3.42z Valeriana | .45 | .20 |
| 2413 | A754 | 5z Mentha piperita | .55 | .25 |
| 2414 | A754 | 6.50z Calendula | .55 | .30 |
| 2415 | A754 | 8z Salvia officinalis | .60 | .30 |
| Nos. 2410-2415 (6) | | | 2.30 | 1.35 |

**1980, Aug. 20      Perf. 11**

Jan Kochanowski (1530-1584), poet.

| 2416 | A755 | 2.50z multi | .25 | .20 |
|---|---|---|---|---|

**1980, Sept. 19      Photo.      Perf. 11x11½**

United Nations, 35th Anniversary — A756

| 2417 | A756 | 8.40z multi | .75 | .30 |
|---|---|---|---|---|

---

## Chopin Piano Competition — A757

**1980, Oct. 2      Litho.      Perf. 11**

| 2418 | A757 | 6.90z blk & tan | .60 | .30 |
|---|---|---|---|---|

## Mail Pick-up — A758

**1980, Oct. 9      Photo.      Perf. 12x11½**

| | | | | |
|---|---|---|---|---|
| 2419 | A758 | 2z shown | .20 | .20 |
| 2420 | A758 | 2.50z Letter sorting | .20 | .20 |
| 2421 | A758 | 6z Loading mail plane | .55 | .25 |
| 2422 | A758 | 6.50z Mail boxes | .55 | .25 |
| a. | | Souvenir sheet of 4, #2419-2422 | 3.75 | 2.50 |
| Nos. 2419-2422 (4) | | | 1.50 | .90 |

Stamp Day.

Girl Embracing Dove, UN Emblem — A759

**1980, Nov. 21      Litho.      Perf. 11x11½**

| 2423 | A759 | 8.40z multicolored | .75 | .35 |
|---|---|---|---|---|

UN Declaration on the Preparation of Societies for Life in Peace.

Battle of Olzynska Grochowska, by W.
Kossak — A760

**1980, Nov. 29      Photo.      Perf. 11**

| 2424 | A760 | 2.50z multicolored | .25 | .20 |
|---|---|---|---|---|

Battle of Olzynska Grochowska, 1830.

Horse-drawn Fire Engine — A761

Designs: Horse-drawn vehicles.

**1980, Dec. 16**

| | | | | |
|---|---|---|---|---|
| 2425 | A761 | 2z shown | .20 | .20 |
| 2426 | A761 | 2.50z Passenger coach | .25 | .20 |
| 2427 | A761 | 3z Beer wagon | .25 | .20 |
| 2428 | A761 | 5z Sled | .45 | .20 |
| 2429 | A761 | 6z Bus | .50 | .25 |
| 2430 | A761 | 6.50z Two-seater | .55 | .25 |
| Nos. 2425-2430 (6) | | | 2.20 | 1.30 |

---

## Honor to the Silesian Rebels, by Jan Borowczak — A762

**1981, Jan. 22      Engr.      Perf. 11½**

| 2431 | A762 | 2.50z gray grn | .20 | .20 |
|---|---|---|---|---|

Silesian uprising, 60th anniversary.

## Pablo Picasso — A763

**1981, Mar. 10      Photo.      Perf. 11½x11**

Pablo Picasso (1881-1973), artist, birth centenary. No. 2432 se-tenant with label showing
A Crying Woman. Sold for 20.80z.

| 2432 | A763 | 8.40z multi | .55 | .35 |
|---|---|---|---|---|
| a. | | Miniature sheet of 2 + 2 labels | 2.50 | 1.25 |

Balloon Flown by Pilatre de Rozier, 1783 — A764

**1981, Mar. 25      Photo.      Perf. 11½x12**

Gordon Bennett Cup (Balloons): No. 2434,
J. Blanchard, J. Jeffries, 1875, 2.50z, F.
Godard, 1850, 3z, F. Hynek, Z. Burzynski,
1933, 6z, Z. Burzynski, N. Wysocki, 1935,
6.50z, B. Abruzzo, M. Anderson, P. Newman,
1978, 10.50z, Winners' names, 1933-1935,
1938.

| | | | | |
|---|---|---|---|---|
| 2433 | A764 | 2z multi | .20 | .20 |
| 2434 | A764 | 2.50z multi | .25 | .20 |
| 2435 | A764 | 2.50z multi | .25 | .20 |
| 2436 | A764 | 6z multi | .55 | .20 |
| 2437 | A764 | 6.50z multi | .55 | .25 |
| 2438 | A764 | 6.50z multi | .60 | .25 |
| Nos. 2433-2438 (6) | | | 2.05 | 1.30 |

**Souvenir Sheet**

**Imperf**

| 2439 | A764 | 10.50z multi | .95 | .70 |
|---|---|---|---|---|

---

## Ipheigenia, by Franz Anton Maulbertsch (1724-1796), WIPA '81 Emblem — A765

**1981, May 11      Litho.      Perf. 11½**

| 2440 | A765 | 10.50z multi | 1.00 | .48 |
|---|---|---|---|---|

WIPA '81 Intl. Phil. Exhib., Vienna, 5/22-31.

Wroclaw, 1493 — A766

**1981, May 15      Photo.      Perf. 14**

| 2441 | A766 | 6.50z brown | .50 | .25 |
|---|---|---|---|---|

See #2456-2459. For surcharge see #2526.

Gen. Wladyslaw Sikorski (1881-1943) — A767

**1981, May 20      Photo.      Perf. 11½x11**

| 2442 | A767 | 6.50z multi | .40 | .25 |
|---|---|---|---|---|

Kwan Vase, 18th Cent. — A768

Intl. Architects Union, 14th Congress, Warsaw — A769

**1981, June 15**

| | | | | |
|---|---|---|---|---|
| 2443 | A768 | 1z shown | .20 | .20 |
| 2444 | A768 | 2z Cup, saucer, 1820 | .20 | .20 |
| 2445 | A768 | 2.50z Jug, 1820 | .25 | .20 |
| 2446 | A768 | 5z Portrait plate, 1880 | .50 | .20 |
| 2447 | A768 | 6.50z Vase, 1900 | .65 | .20 |
| 2448 | A768 | 8.40z Basket, 1840 | .75 | .25 |
| Nos. 2443-2448 (6) | | | 2.60 | 1.25 |

**1981, July 15      Litho.**

| 2449 | A769 | 2.50z multi | .20 | .20 |
|---|---|---|---|---|

Moose, Rifle and Pouch — A770

A770a

**1981, July 30**

| | | | | |
|---|---|---|---|---|
| 2450 | A770 | 2z shown | .20 | .20 |
| 2451 | A770 | 2z Boar | .20 | .20 |
| 2452 | A770 | 2.50z Fox | .25 | .20 |
| 2453 | A770 | 2.50z Elk | .25 | .20 |
| 2454 | A770 | 6.50z Greylag goose, horiz. | .65 | .20 |
| 2455 | A770 | 6.50z Fen duck | .65 | .20 |
| Nos. 2450-2455 (6) | | | 2.20 | 1.20 |

Ignacy Łukasiewicz (1822-1882), Oil Lamp Inventor — A784

Designs: Various oil lamps.

**1982, Mar. 22   Photo.   Perf. 11½x11**
| | | | |
|---|---|---|---|
| 2508 | A784 | 1z multi | .20 .20 |
| 2509 | A784 | 2z multi | .20 .20 |
| 2510 | A784 | 2.50z multi | .25 .25 |
| 2511 | A784 | 3.50z multi | .30 .30 |
| 2512 | A784 | 8z multi | .85 .35 |
| 2513 | A784 | 10z multi | .90 .40 |
| | | Nos. 2508-2513 (6) | 2.70 1.55 |

Karol Szymanowski (1882-1937), Composer A785

**1982, Apr. 8**
2514 A785 2.50z dk brn & gold .25 .20

Victory in Challenge Trophy Flights A786

**1982, May 5   Photo.   Perf. 11x11½**
2515 A786 27z RWD 6 monoplane 1.25 .65
2516 A786 31z RWD-9 1.75 .85
a. Souv. sheet of 2, #2515-2516 3.00 1.75

Henryk Sienkiewicz (1846-1916), Writer — A787

1982 World Cup — A788

Polish Nobel Prize Winners: 1.5z Wladyslaw Reymont (1867-1925), writer, 1924. 25z, Marie Curie (1867-1934), physicist, 1903, 1911. 3z, Czeslaw Milosz (b. 1911), poet, 1980.

**1982, May 10   Litho.   Perf. 11½x11**
2517 A787 3z black & dk grn .20 .20
2518 A787 15z black & brown .65 .25
2519 A787 25z black 1.10 .40
2520 A787 31z black & gray 1.25 .50
Nos. 2517-2520 (4) 3.20 1.35

**Perf. 11½x11, 11x11½   Photo.**
**1982, May 28**
2521 A788 25z Ball 1.25 .60
2522 A788 27z Bull, ball, horiz. 1.50 .65

---

Souvenir Sheet

Vistula River Project — A780

**1981, Dec. 20   Litho.   Perf. 11½x12**
2492 A780 10.50z multi 1.25 .75

Flowering Succulent Plants A781

**1981, Dec. 22   Photo.   Perf. 13**
2493 A781 90g Epiphyllopsis gaertneri .20 .20
2494 A781 1z Cereus tonduzii .20 .20
2495 A781 2z Cylindropuntia leptocaulis .20 .20
2496 A781 2.50z Cylindroppuntia fulgida .20 .20
2497 A781 2.50z Caralluma lugardi .25 .25
2498 A781 6.50z Nopalea cochenillifera .25 .25
2499 A781 6.50z Lithopsps helmutii .50 .50
2500 A781 10.50z Cylindropuntia spinosior .75 .35
Nos. 2493-2500 (8) 2.85 1.80

Polish Workers' Party, 40th Anniv. — A782

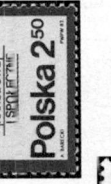

**1982, Jan. 5   Photo.   Perf. 11½x11**
2501 A782 2.50z multi .25 .20

Stoneware Plate, 1890 — A783

**1982, Jan. 20**

Porcelain or Stoneware: 2z, Plate, mug, 1790. 2.50z, Soup tureen, gravy dish, 1830. 6z, Salt and pepper dish, 1844. 8z, Stoneware jug, 1840. 10.50z, Stoneware figurine, 1740.
2502 A783 1z multi .20 .20
2503 A783 2z multi .20 .20
2504 A783 2.50z multi .20 .25
2505 A783 6z multi .60 .25
2506 A783 8z multi .80 .30
2507 A783 10.50z multi 1.00 .40
Nos. 2502-2507 (6) 3.05 1.55

---

A776

A777

**1981, Oct. 10   Perf. 11½x12**
2482 A776 2.50z multi .25 .20

Henryk Wieniawski (1835-1880), violinist and composer.

**1981, Oct. 15   Litho.**

Working Movement Leaders: 50g, Bronislaw Wesolowski (1870-1919). 2z, Malgorzata Fornalska (1902-1944). 2.50z, Maria Koszutska (1876-1939). 6.50z, Marcin Kasprzak (1860-1905).
2483 A777 50g grn & blk .20 .20
2484 A777 2z hl & blk .20 .20
2485 A777 2.50z brn & blk .20 .20
2486 A777 6.50z lil rose & blk .45 .80
Nos. 2483-2486 (4) 1.05 .80

World Food Day — A778

**1981, Oct. 16   Perf. 11x11½**
2487 A778 6.90z multi .65 .25

Old Theater, Cracow, 200th Anniv. — A779

Theater Emblem and: 2z, Helena Modrzejewska (1840-1909), actress. 2.50z, Stanislaw Kozmian (1836-1922), theater director, 1865-1885, founder of Cracow School. 6.50z, Konrad Swinarski (1929-1975), stage manager.

**1981, Oct. 17   Photo. & Engr.   Perf. 12x11½**
2488 A779 2z multi .20 .20
2489 A779 2.50z multi .30 .20
2490 A779 6.50z multi .60 .25
2491 A779 8z multi .75 .85
Nos. 2488-2491 (4) 1.90 .85

---

City Type of 1981

**Perf. 11x11½, 11½x13   Photo.**
**1981, July 28**
2456 A766 4z Gdansk, 1652, vert. .30 .20
2457 A766 5z Krakow, 1493, vert. .40 .25
2458 A766 6z Legnica, 1744 .50 .30
2459 A766 8z Warsaw, 1618 .65 .95
Nos. 2456-2459 (4) 1.85 .95
For surcharge see #2939.

**1982, Nov. 2   Photo.   Perf. 11½**
2461 A770a 1z Vistula River .25 .20
2463 A770a 17z Kasimierz Dolny .30 .20
2466 A770a 25z Gdansk .45 .65
Nos. 2461-2466 (3) 1.00 .65

Wild Bison — A771

**1981, Aug. 27   Perf. 11½x11**
2471 Strip of 5 3.50 1.50
a.-e. A771 6.50z, any single .65 .25

60th Anniv. of Polish Tennis Federation — A772

**1981, Sept. 17   Photo.   Perf. 11x11½**
2472 A772 6.50z multi .60 .25

Model Airplane — A773

**1981, Sept. 24   Perf. 14**
2473 A773 1z shown .20 .20
2474 A773 2z Boats .30 .20
2475 A773 2.50z Racing cars .25 .20
2476 A773 4.20z Gliders .45 .20
2477 A773 6.50z Radio-controlled racing cars .65 .20
2478 A773 8z Yachts .70 .25
Nos. 2473-2478 (6) 2.55 1.25

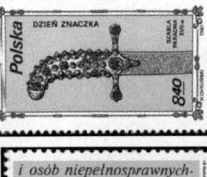

Intl. Year of the Disabled — A774

Stamp Day — A775

**1981, Sept. 25   Litho.   Perf. 11½x11**
2479 A774 8.40z multi .75 .30

**1981, Oct. 9   Photo.   Perf. 14**
2480 A775 2.50z Pistol, 18th cent., horiz. .25 .20
2481 A775 8.40z Sword, 18th cent. .75 .25

## Souvenir Sheet

MARIA KAZMIERA SOBIESKA de la Grange d'Arquien — MIĘDZYNARODOWA WYSTAWA FILATELISTYCZNA — PARYŻ

Maria Kaziera Sobieska — A789

**1982, June 11 Photo. Perf. 11½x11**
2523 A789 65z multi .......... 3.25 2.25
PHILEXFRANCE '82 Intl. Stamp Exhibition, Paris, June 11-21.

Assoc. Presidents Stanislaw Sierakowski and Boleslaw Domanski — A790

**1982, July 20**
2524 A790 4.50z. multi .......... .45 .20
Assoc. of Poles in Germany, 60th anniv.

2nd UN Conference on Peaceful Uses of Outer Space, Vienna, Aug. 9-21 — A791

POLSKA 31z UNISPACE-82

**1982, Aug. 9 Photo.**
2525 A791 31z Globe .......... 1.25 .65

**1982, Aug. 20**
2526 A766 1oz on 6.50z brn .......... .40 .20
No. 2441 Surcharged

POLSKA 65 Zl — MADONNA CZESTOCHOWSKA

Black Madonna of Jasna Gora, 600th Anniv. A792

**1982, Aug. 26 Perf. 11**
2527 A792 2.50z multi .......... .20 .20
2528 A792 25z multi .......... .50 .25
2529 A792 65z multi, horiz. .......... 2.20 .85
Nos. 2527-2529 (3) .......... 1.50 .40

2.50z., Father Augustin Kordecki (1603-1673), 25z, Siege of Jasna Gora by Swedes, 1655, horiz.
A souvenir sheet of 2 No. 2529 exists. Value $10.

---

STANISLAW ZAREMBA 1863-1940 — POLSKA 5.00

POLSKA 6 — Workers' Movement

**1982, Sept. 3 Perf. 11½x11**
2530 A793 6z multicolored .......... .35 .20
Workers' Movement A793

Norbert Barlicki (1880-1941) A794

**1982, Sept. 10 Perf. 12x11½**
2531 A794 5z multi .......... .30 .20
2532 A794 6z multi .......... .30 .20
2533 A794 15z multi .......... .75 .30
2534 A794 20z multi .......... .95 .30
2535 A794 100z multi .......... 3.40 1.40
Nos. 2531-2535 (5) .......... 1.10 .40

Workers' Activists: 6z, Pawel Finder (1904-1944), 15z, Marian Buczek (1896-1939), 20z, Cezaryna Wojnarowska (1861-1911), 29z, Ignacy Daszynski (1866-1936).

Carved Head, Wawel Castle A795

**1982, Sept. 25**
2536 A795 60z Woman's head .......... 2.25 1.00
2537 A795 100z Man's head .......... 3.25 1.75

O. MAKSYMILIAN KOLBE 1894-1941 — POLSKA 27zl

TB Bacillus Centenary A796

POLSKA 10.00 — Robert Koch 1843-1910

**1982, Sept. 22 Perf. 11½x11**
2538 A796 10z Koch .......... .40 .20
2539 A796 25z Oko Bujwid .......... 1.00 .40

10z, Robert Koch (1843-1910), bacteriologist. 25z, Oko Bujwid (1857-1942), bacteriologist.

St. Maximilian Kolbe (1894-1941) A797

**1982, Sept. Photo. Perf. 11½x11**
2540 A797 27z multi .......... 1.00 .40

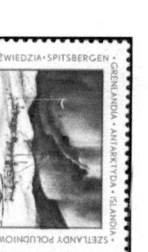
WYSPA NIEDŹWIEDZIA · SPITSBERGEN — POLSKA 27zl — POLSKICH BADAN POLARNYCH 1932-1982

50th Anniv. of Polar Research A798

**1982, Oct. 25 Litho. Perf. 11½**
2541 A798 27z multi .......... 1.00 .45

---

Stanislaw Zaremba (1863-1942), Mathematician — A799

First Anniv. of Military Rule — A800

POLSKA 2.50

**1982, Dec. 13 Perf. 12x11½**
2546 A800 2.50z Medal obverse and reverse .......... .20 .20

Mathematicians A799

**1982, Nov. 23 Photo. Perf. 11x11½**
2542 A799 6z multicolored .......... .20 .20
2543 A799 6z multicolored .......... .25 .20
2544 A799 15z multicolored .......... .50 .30
2545 A799 15z multicolored .......... .60 .25
Nos. 2542-2545 (4) .......... 1.55 .95

Mathematicians: 6z, Waclaw Sierpinski (1882-1969), 12z, Zygmunt Janiszewski (1888-1920), 15z, Stefan Banach (1892-1945).

Cracow Monuments Restoration A801

POLSKA 15zl

**1982, Dec. 20 Litho. Perf. 11½x11**
2547 A801 15z Deanery portal .......... .50 .25
2548 A801 25z Law College portal .......... .80 .40

### Souvenir Sheet
Lithographed and Engraved
**Imperf**
2549 A801 65z City map .......... 1.25 1.00

No. 2549 contains one stamp 22x27mm. See Nos. 2593-2594, 2656-2657, 2717-2718, 2809, 2847.

Map of Poland, by Bernard Wapowski, 1526 A802

POLSKA zl 5.00

**1982, Dec. 28 Litho. Perf. 11½**
2550 A802 5z multicolored .......... .20 .20
2551 A802 6z multicolored .......... .20 .20
2552 A802 8z multicolored .......... .30 .20
2553 A802 25z multicolored .......... .85 .40
Nos. 2550-2553 (4) .......... 1.55 1.00

Maps: 6z, Warsaw, Polish Kingdom Quartermaster, 1839, 8z, Poland, Romer's Atlas, 1908, 25z, Krakow, by A. Buchowiecki, 1703, 17th cent.

---

Warsaw Theater Sesquicentennial — A804

150 LAT TEATRU WIELKIEGO — POLSKA 6

**1983, Feb. 24 Photo.**
2555 A804 6z multicolored .......... .25 .20

120th Anniv. of 1863 Uprising — A803

POLSKA 6 zl — 1863 — Powstanie Styczniowe

**1983, Jan. 22 Photo. Perf. 12x11½**
2554 A803 6z The Battle, by Arthur Grottger (1837-67) .......... .25 .20

10th Anniv. of UN Conference on Human Environment, Stockholm — A805

5 ZL POLSKA

**1983, Mar. 24 Litho. Perf. 11½**
2556 A805 5z Wild flowers .......... .20 .20
2557 A805 5z Swan, carp, eel .......... .25 .20
2558 A805 17z Hoopoe .......... .55 .30
2559 A805 30z Fish .......... .55 .30
2560 A805 30z Deer, fawn, buffalo .......... .95 .45
2561 A805 38z Fruit .......... 1.10 .55
Nos. 2556-2561 (6) .......... 4.10 2.30

Karol Kurpinski (1785-1857), Composer A806

Polska 5 zl — KAROL KURPINSKI 1785-1857

**1983, Mar. 25 Photo. Perf. 11½x11**
2562 A806 5z tan & brn .......... .20 .20
2563 A806 6z pink & vio .......... .20 .20
2564 A806 17z dk grn & lt grn .......... .55 .30
2565 A806 20z bister & brn .......... .85 .40
2566 A806 27z tt bl & dk bl .......... .95 .45
2567 A806 31z violet & pur .......... 1.10 .55
Nos. 2562-2567 (6) .......... 3.90 2.10

Famous People: 6z, Maria Jasnorzewska Pawlikowska (1891-1945), poet, 17z, Stanislaw Szober (1879-1938), linguist, 25z, Tadeusz Banachiewicz (1882-1954), astronomer, 27z, Jaroslaw Iwaszkiewicz (1894-1980), writer, 31z, Wladyslaw Tatarkiewicz (1886-1980), philosopher, art historian.

Polish Medalists in 22nd Olympic Games, 1980 A807

5 zl POLSKA

**1983, Apr. 5 Perf. 11x11½**
2568 A807 5z Steeplechase .......... .20 .20
2569 A807 6z Equestrian .......... .20 .20
2570 A807 15z Soccer, 1982 World Cup .......... .50 .25
2571 A807 27z + 5z Pole vault .......... 1.90 1.15
Nos. 2568-2571 (4)

## 1983 — 1984

**Warsaw Ghetto Uprising, 40th Anniv. — A808**

1983, Apr. 19  Photo.  Perf. 11½x11
2572 A808 6z Heroes' Monument, by Natan Rappaport  .25 .20
Se-tenant with label showing anniversary medal.

**Customs Cooperation Council, 30th Anniv. — A809**

1983, Apr. 28
2573 A809 5z multicolored  .20 .20

**Second Visit of Pope John Paul II — A810**

Portraits of Pope. 31z vert.
1983, June 10  Photo.  Perf. 11
2574 A810 31z multicolored  1.10 .50
2575 A810 65z multicolored  2.25 1.10
a. Souvenir sheet  2.25 1.75

**Army of King John III Sobieski — A811**

1983, July 5  Perf. 11½x11
2576 A811 5z Dragoons  .20 .20
2577 A811 5z Knight in armor  .20 .20
2578 A811 6z Non-commissioned infantry officers  .50 .25
2579 A811 15z Light cavalryman  .90 .45
2580 A811 27z Hussars  2.00 1.30
Nos. 2576-2580 (5)

**750th Anniv. of Torun Municipality — A812**

1983, Aug. 25  Photo.  Perf. 11
2581 A812 6z multicolored  .25 .20
a. Souvenir sheet of 4  3.00 2.75
No. 2581a had limited distribution.

**60th Anniv. of Polish Boxing Union A813**

1983, Nov. 4  Litho.  Perf. 11½x11
2582 A813 6z multicolored  .25 .20

**Enigma Decoding Machine, 50th Anniv. — A813a**
**Girl Near House — A813b**

1983, Aug. 16  Litho.  Perf. 11½x11
2582A A813a 5z multicolored  .20 .20
1983  Photo.  Perf. 11½x12
2582B A813b 6z multicolored  .25 .20
Public courtesy campaign.

**Portrait of King John III Sobieski A814**

King's Portraits by: #2584, Unknown court painter. #2585, Sobieski on Horseback, by Francesco Trevisani (1656-1746). 25z, Jerzy Eleuter Szymonowicz-Siemiginowski (1660-1711), 65z+10z, Sobieski at Vienna, by Jan Matejko (1838-1893).
1983, Sept. 12  Perf. 11
2583 A814 5z multicolored  .20 .20
2584 A814 6z multicolored  .25 .20
2585 A814 6z multicolored  .25 .20
2586 A814 25z multicolored  .95 .40
1.65 1.00
Nos. 2583-2586 (4)
Souvenir Sheet  Imperf
2587 A814 65z + 10z multi  2.50 2.00
Victory over the Turks in Vienna, 300th anniv.

**Polish Peoples' Army, 40th Anniv. — A815**

#2588, General Zygmunt Berling (1896-1980). #2589, Wanda Wasilewska (1905-64). #2591, Troop formation.
1983, Oct. 12  Photo.  Perf. 11
2588 A815 5z multicolored  .20 .20
2589 A815 5z multicolored  .20 .20
2590 A815 6z multicolored  .20 .20
2591 A815 6z multi, horiz.  .80 .80
Nos. 2588-2591 (4)

**World Communications Year — A816**

1983, Oct. 18  Photo.  Perf. 11
2592 A816 15z multicolored  .50 .25

**Cracow Restoration Type of 1982**

1983, Nov. 25  Litho.  Perf. 11
2593 A801 5z Cloth Hall, horiz.  .30 .20
2594 A801 6z Town Hall Tower  .20 .20

**Traditional Hats — A818**

1983, Dec. 16  Photo.  Perf. 11½x11
2595 A818 5z Biskupianski  .20 .20
2596 A818 5z Rozbarski  .20 .20
2597 A818 6z Warminsko-Mazurki  .20 .20
2598 A010 6z Cleszynski  .75 .40
2599 A818 25z Kurpiowski  1.10 .55
2600 A818 38z Lubuski  2.65 1.75
Nos. 2595-2600 (6)

**Natl. People's Council, 40th Anniv. — A819**

1983, Dec. 31
2601 A819 6z Hand holding sword (poster)  .25 .20

**People's Army, 40th Anniv. — A820**

**Musical Instruments A821**

1984, Jan. 1  Litho.  Perf. 11½x11
2602 A820 5z Gen. Bem Brigade badge  .20 .20

1984, Feb. 10  Photo.
2603 A821 5z Dulcimer  .20 .20
2604 A821 6z Drum, tambourine  .20 .20
2605 A821 10z Accordion  .35 .25
2606 A821 15z Double bass  .40 .25
2607 A821 17z Bagpipes  .60 .25
2608 A821 29z Figurines by Tadeusz Zak  1.10 .40
2.85 1.45
Nos. 2603-2608 (6)

**Wincenty Witos (1874-1945), Prime Minister — A822**

1984, Mar. 2  Litho.  Perf. 11½x11
2609 A822 6z green & sepia  .20 .20

**Local Flowers (Clematis Varieties) A823**

Perf. 11x11½
1984, Mar. 26  Photo.
2610 A823 5z Lanuginosa  .20 .20
2611 A823 6z Tangutica  .25 .20
2612 A823 10z Texensis  .30 .25
2613 A823 15z Alpina  .65 .25
2614 A823 25z Vitalba  .90 .35
2615 A823 27z Montana  .40 .40
3.30 1.60
Nos. 2610-2615 (6)

**The Ecstasy of St. Francis, by El Greco A824**

1984, Apr. 21  27z multicolored  Perf. 11  1.00 .30

**1984 Olympics A825**

1984, Apr. 25  Perf. 11x11½
2617 A825 5z Handball  .20 .20
2618 A825 6z Fencing  .25 .20
2619 A825 12z Bicycling  .55 .25
2620 A825 16z Running  .60 .25
2621 A825 17z Running diff.  .65 .25
a. Souv. sheet of 2, #2620-2621  1.50 1.25
2622 A825 31z Skiing  1.00 .45
Souv. sheet of 2, 2617-2622 (6)  3.25 1.55
No. 2621a sold for 43z.

**1984, May 18    Photo.    Perf. 11½x11**

2623  A826  15z  Memorial Cross  .50  .20

Battle of Monte Cassino, 40th Anniv. — A826

View of Warsaw from the Praga Bank, by Bernardo Belotto Canaletto — A827

**1984, June 20    Photo.    Perf. 11**

2624  A827  5z  multicolored  .20  .20
2625  A827  6z  multicolored  .20  .20
2626  A827  25z  multicolored  .80  .35
2627  A827  27z  multicolored  .80  .40
Nos. 2624-2627 (4)  2.00  1.15

Paintings of Vistula River views: 6z, Trumpet Festivity, by Aleksander Gierymski. 25z, The Vistula near the Bielany District, by Jozef Rapacki. 27z, Steamship Harbor in the Powisle District, by Franciszek Kostrzewski.

Eastern Ruler — A828

**1984-85    Photo.    Perf. 11½x12**

2628  A828  3.50z  brown  .20  .20
2628A  A828  5z  dark claret  .30  .20
2628B  A828  10z  brt ultra  .70  .60
Nos. 2628-2628B (3)

Sculptures: 3.50z, Eastern ruler. No. 2628A, Woman wearing wreath. 10z, Man wearing hat. No. 2629, Warrior's Head, Wawel Castle.

**Coil Stamp**
**Perf. 13½x14**

2629  A828  5z  dark blue green  .20  .20

Issued: 3.50z, 1/24/85, #2628A, 10z, 7/8/85; No. 2629, 7/10/84.

No. 2629 has black control number on back of every fifth stamp.

See Nos. 2738-2744.

Order of Grunwald Cross — A829

**1984, July 21    Photo.    Perf. 11½**

2630  A829  5z  multicolored  .20  .20
2631  A829  6z  multicolored  .20  .20
2632  A829  10z  multicolored  .20  .20
2633  A829  16z  multicolored  .50  .25
a.  Sheet of 4, #2630-2633, perf. 11½x12  3.25  3.00
Nos. 2630-2633 (4)  1.20  .85

Designs: 6z, Order of Revival of Poland. 10z, Order of the Banner of Labor, First Class. 16z, Order of Builders of People's Poland.

40th anniversary of July Manifesto (Origin of Polish People's Republic).

---

**1984, Aug. 1**

2634  A830  4z  multicolored  .20  .20
2635  A830  5z  multicolored  .20  .20
2636  A830  5z  multicolored  .75  .35
2637  A830  25z  multicolored  .95
Nos. 2634-2637 (4)  1.35  .95

Warsaw Uprising, 40th Anniv. A830

**1984, Aug. 31**

2638  A831  16z  multicolored  .50  .25

Broken Heart Monument, Lodz — A831

Defense of Oksywie Holm, Col. S. Dahek — A832

**1984, Sept. 1**

2639  A832  5z  shown  .20  .20
2640  A832  6z  Bzura River battle, Gen. T. Kutrzeba  .25  .20

Invasion of Poland, 45th anniversary.
See Nos. 2692-2693, 2757, 2824-2826, 2864-2866, 2922-2925.

Polish Militia, 40th Anniv. A833

**1984, Sept. 29    Photo.    Perf. 11½**

2641  A833  5z  shown  .20  .20
2642  A833  6z  Militiaman at Control Center  .25  .20

Polish Aviation A834

**1984, Nov. 6    Photo.    Perf. 11x11½**

2643  A834  5z  Balloon ascent, 1784  .20  .20
2644  A834  5z  Powered flight, 1911  .20  .20
2645  A834  6z  Balloon Polonez, 1983  .20  .20
2646  A834  10z  Modern gliders  .20  .20
2647  A834  18z  Wilga, 1983  .30  .20
2648  A834  27z  Farman, 1914  .50  .25
2649  A834  31z  Los and PZL P-7  .90  .40
Nos. 2643-2649 (7)  3.25  1.85

---

Protected Animals A835

**1984, Dec. 4    Photo.    Perf. 11x11½**

2650  A835  4z  Mustela nivalis  .20  .20
2651  A835  5z  Martes foina  .20  .20
2652  A835  5z  Mustela erminea  .20  .20
2653  A835  10z  Castor fiber, vert.  .30  .20
2654  A835  35z  Lutra lutra, vert.  .30  .20
2655  A835  65z  Marmota marmota, vert.  1.90  .70
Nos. 2650-2655 (6)  3.10  1.70

Cracow Restoration Type of 1982

**1984, Dec. 10    Perf. 11½x11, 11x11½**

2656  A801  5z  Royal Cathedral, Wawel  .20  .20
**Litho.**
2657  A801  15z  Royal Castle, Wawel, horiz.  .30  .20

Religious Buildings A837

**1984, Dec. 28    Photo.    Perf. 11½x12, 12x11½**

2658  A837  5z  Protestant Church, Warsaw  .20  .20
2659  A837  10z  Saint Andrew Church, Cracow  .20  .20
2660  A837  15z  Greek Orthodox Church, Rychwald  .30  .20
2661  A837  20z  Orthodox Church, Warsaw  .45  .20
2662  A837  25z  Tykocin Synagogue, horiz.  .55  .20
2663  A837  31z  Tartar Mosque, Kruszyniany, horiz.  .70  .25
Nos. 2658-2663 (6)  3.00  1.35

Classic and Contemporary Fire Engines — A838

**1985, Feb. 25    Photo.    Perf. 11x11½**

2664  A838  4z  multicolored  .20  .20
2665  A838  5z  multicolored  .30  .20
2666  A838  12z  multicolored  .30  .20
2667  A838  12z  multicolored  .40  .20
2668  A838  20z  multicolored  .55  .25
2669  A838  30z  multicolored  .85  .35
Nos. 2664-2669 (6)  2.60  1.40

Designs: 4z, Horse-drawn fire pump, 19th cent. 10z, Polski Fiat, c. 1930. 12z, Jelcz 315, 1970s. 15z, Horse-drawn hand pump, 1899. 20z, Jelcz engine, Magirus power ladder, 1970s. 30z, Hand pump, 18th cent.

---

Battle of Raclawice, April, 1794, by Jan Styka — A839

**1985, Apr. 4**

2670  A839  27z  multicolored  .75  .30

Kosciuszko Insurrection cent.

Wincenty Rzymowski (1883-1950), Democratic Party founder.

**1985, Apr. 11    Litho.    Perf. 11½**

2671  A840  10z  sal rose & dk vio  .25  .20

A840

**1985, Apr. 25    Photo.    Perf. 11½x11**

2672  A841  15z  Blue jeans, badge  .35  .20

Int. Youth Year.

A841

Prince Boleslaw Krzywousty (1085-1138) — A842

**1985, May 8    Litho.    Perf. 11½**

2673  A842  5z  multicolored  .20  .20
2674  A842  10z  multicolored  .25  .20
2675  A842  20z  multicolored  1.00  .60
Nos. 2673-2675 (3)

Regional maps and: 10z, Wladyslaw Gomulka (1905-82), sec.-gen. of the Polish Workers Party, prime minister 1945-49. 20z, Piotr Zaremba (b. 1910), president of Gdansk Province 1945-50.

Restoration of the Western & Northern Territories to Polish control, 40th anniv.

Victory Berlin 1945, by Jozef Mlynarski (b. 1925) — A843

**Halley's Comet — A857**

**1986, Jan. 16**　　**Perf. 11½x11**
2713 A856 10z lt ultra, brt ultra & ultra　.25　.20

Congress of Intellectuals for World Peace, Warsaw.

**1986, Feb. 7**　**Photo.**　**Perf. 11½**
Designs: No. 2714. Michal Kamienski (1879-1973), astronomer, orbit diagram. No. 2715, Comet, Vega, Giotto, Planet-A, ICE-3 space probes.
2714 A857 25z multicolored　.60　.30
2715 A857 25z multicolored　.60　.30
　a. Pair, #2714-2715　1.20　.60

**1986, Mar. 20**　**Photo.**　**Perf. 11½x11**
2716 A858 25z turq bl, yel & ultra　.60　.40

**Cracow Restoration Type of 1982**
Designs: 5z, Collegium Maius, Jagiellonian Museum. 10z, Town Hall, Kazimierz.
**1986, Mar. 20**　**Litho.**　**Perf. 11½**
2717 A801 5z multicolored　.20　.20
2718 A801 10z multicolored　.25　.20

**Wildlife A859**

**1986, Apr. 15**　**Photo.**　**Perf. 11½x11**
2719 A859 5z Perdix perdix　.20　.20
2720 A859 5z Oryctolagus cuniculus　.20　.20
2721 A859 10z Dama dama　.20　.20
2722 A859 10z Phasianus colchicus　.20　.20
2723 A859 20z Lepus europaeus　.40　.20
2724 A859 40z Ovis ammon　.80　.35
　a. Pair, #2719-2724　2.00　1.35
Nos. 2719-2720, 2723-2724 vert.

Stanislaw Kulczynski (1895-1975), Scientist, Party Leader — A860

**Photogravure and Engraved**
**1986, May 3**　**Perf. 11½x11**
2725 A860 10z buff & choc　.25　.20

Warsaw Fire Brigade, 150th Anniv. — A861

Painting detail: The Fire Brigade on the Cracow Outskirts on Their Way to a Fire, 1871, by Josef Brodowski (1828-1900).

**1986, May 16**　**Perf. 11**
2726 A861 10z dl brn & dk brn　.25　.20

---

Polish Ballet, 200th Anniv. — A853

**1985, Dec. 4**
2705 A853 5z Prima ballerina　.20　.20
2706 A853 15z Male dancer　.40　.20

**Paintings by Stanislaw Ignacy Witkiewicz (1885-1939) — A854**
5z, Marysia and Burek in Ceylon. No. 2708, Woman with a Fox. No. 2709, Self-portrait, 1931. 20z, Compositions, 1917. 25z, Portrait of Nena Stachurska, 1929. Nos. 2707, 2709-2711 vert.

**1985, Dec. 6**　**Perf. 11½x11, 11x11½**　**Photo.**
2707 A854 5z multicolored　.20　.20
2708 A854 10z multicolored　.30　.20
2709 A854 10z multicolored　.30　.25
2710 A854 20z multicolored　.55　.30
2711 A854 25z multicolored　.70　.30
Nos. 2707-2711 (5)　2.05　1.15

**Souvenir Sheet**

Johann Sebastian Bach — A855

**1985, Dec. 30**　**Perf. 11½x11**
2712 A855 65z multicolored　1.75　1.75
　a. With inscription　7.00　7.00
No. 2712a inscribed "300 Rocznica Urodzin Jana Sebastiana Bacha." Distribution was limited.

Profile, Emblem, Sigismond III Column, Royal Castle Tower — A856

Intl. Peace Year — A858

---

Tomasz Nocznicki (1862-1944) — A848

Polish Labor Movement founders: 20z, Maciej Rataj (1884-1940).
**1985, July 26**　**Engr.**　**Perf. 11x11½**
2689 A848 10z grnsh black　.30　.20
2690 A848 20z brown black　.50　.25
Natl. labor movement, 90th anniv.

Polish Field Hockey Assn., 50th Anniv. A849

**1985, Aug. 22**　**Litho.**　**Perf. 11½x11**
2691 A849 5z multicolored　.25　.20

**World War II Battles Type of 1984**
Designs: 5z, Defense of Wizny, Capt. Wladyslaw Raginis. 10z, Attack on Mlawa, Col. Wilhelm Andrzej Liszka-Lawicz.
**1985, Sept. 1**　**Photo.**　**Perf. 12x11½**
2692 A832 5z multicolored　.25　.20
2693 A832 10z multicolored　.35　.20

Pafawag Railway Rolling Stock Co. A850

**1985, Sept. 18**　**Litho.**　**Perf. 11½**
2694 A850 5z Box car　.20　.20
2695 A850 10z 201 E locomotive　.30　.20
2696 A850 1/z Two-axle coal car　.50　.25
2697 A850 20z Passenger car　.60　.30
Nos. 2694-2697 (4)　1.60　.95

Wild Ducks A851

**1985, Oct. 21**　**Photo.**　**Perf. 11½x11**
2698 A851 5z Anas crecca　.20　.20
2699 A851 5z Anas querquedula　.20　.20
2700 A851 10z Aythya fuligula　.20　.20
2701 A851 15z Bucephala clangula　.40　.20
2702 A851 25z Somateria mollissima　.65　.30
2703 A851 29z Netta rufina　.80　.35
Nos. 2698-2703 (6)　2.55　1.45

UN, 40th Anniv. A852

**1985, Oct. 24**　**Litho.**　**Perf. 11½x11**
2704 A852 27z multicolored　.75　.30

---

Painting: Polish and Soviet soldiers at Brandenburg Gate, May 9, 1945.
**1985, May 9**　**Photo.**　**Perf. 12x11½**
2676 A843 5z multicolored　.20　.20
Liberation from German occupation, 40th anniv.

Warsaw Treaty Org., 30th Anniv. — A844

**1985, May 14**　**Litho.**　**Perf. 11x11**
2677 A844 5z Emblem, member flags　.20　.20

World Wildlife Fund A845

Endangered Wildlife: Canis lupus.
**1985, May 25**　**Photo.**　**Perf. 11x11½**
2678 A845 5z Wolves, winter landscape　.90　.25
2679 A845 10z Female, cubs　1.25　.50
2680 A845 20z Wolf　1.25　.50
2681 A845 20z Wolves, summer landscape　2.50　1.25
Nos. 2678-2681 (4)　5.90　2.50

A847　　A846

Folk instruments.
**1985, June 25**　**Perf. 11½x11**
2682 A846 5z Wooden rattle　.20　.20
2683 A846 10z Jingle　.25　.20
2684 A846 12z Clay whistles　.35　.20
2685 A846 20z Wooden fiddles　.60　.20
2686 A846 25z Tuned bells　.70　.25
2687 A846 31z Shepherd's flutes, ram's horn, ocarina　.90　.35
Nos. 2682-2687 (6)　3.00　1.40

**Photogravure and Engraved**
**1985, June 29**
Design: O.R.P. Iskra and emblem.
2688 A847 5z bluish blk & yel　.20　.20
Polish Navy, 40th anniv.

**1986, May 22**    *Perf. 11½x11*
2727 A862 65z multicolored    1.50 .70

Paderewski
A862

AMERIPEX'86.

---

1986 World Cup Soccer
Championships, Mexico — A863

**1986, May 26**    *Perf. 11½*
2728 A863 25z multicolored    .50 .25

---

**Engr., Photo. (15z, No. 2740, 60z)**

**1986-89**
| | | | | |
|---|---|---|---|---|
| 2738 | A828 | 15z rose brown | .20 | .20 |
| 2739 | A828 | 20z green | .35 | .20 |
| 2740 | A828 | 20z peacock blue | .75 | .35 |
| 2742 | A828 | 40z gray | .25 | .35 |
| 2743 | A828 | 60z dark green | .25 | .20 |
| 2744 | A828 | 200z dark gray | 5.50 | 2.90 |

Nos. 2738-2744 (6)

Issued: 15z, 9/22/88; 20z, #2739, 2742, 7/30/86; 20z, #2740, 3/31/89; 60z, 12/18/89; 200z, 11/11/86.

No. 2740 and 60z are coil stamps, have black control number on back of every 5th stamp. For surcharge see No. 2954.

This is an expanding set. Numbers will change if necessary.

---

Ferryboats — A864

**1986, June 18**    **Photo.**    *Perf. 11*
| | | | | |
|---|---|---|---|---|
| 2729 | A864 | 10z Wilanow | .20 | .20 |
| 2730 | A864 | 10z Wawel | .20 | .20 |
| a. | Souv. sheet of 2, #2729-2730 | | 1.65 | 1.65 |
| 2731 | A864 | 15z Pomerania | .30 | .20 |
| 2732 | A864 | 25z Rogalin | .55 | .20 |
| a. | Souv. sheet of 2, #2731-2732 | | 3.25 | 3.25 |

Nos. 2729-2732 (4)    1.25 .85

Nos. 2729-2732 printed se-tenant with labels picturing historic sites from the names of cities serviced. No. 2730a sold for 30z; No. 2732a for 55z. Surtax for the Natl. Assoc. of Philatelists.

---

Antarctic Agreement, 25th
Anniv. — A865

**1986, June 23**    **Litho.**    *Perf. 11½x11*
| | | | | |
|---|---|---|---|---|
| 2733 | A865 | 5z ver, pale grn & blk | .20 | .20 |
| 2734 | A865 | 40z org, pale vio & dk vio | 1.10 | .40 |

Map of Antarctica and: 5z, A. B. Dobrowolski, Kopernik research ship; 40z, H. Arctowski, Professor Siedlecki research ship.

---

**1986, July 29**    **Photo.**    *Perf. 11x11½*
2735 A866 10z red & dk gray bl    .25 .20

Polish
United
Workers'
Party,
10th
Congress
A866

Wawel Heads Type of 1984-85

Designs: 15z, Woman wearing a wreath (like No. 2628A). No. 2739, Thinker. No. 2740, Youth wearing beret. 60z, Warrior. 200z, Man's head.

Eastern ruler. 40z,

---

Jasna Gora
Monastery
Collection
A867

**1986, Aug. 15**    **Photo.**    *Perf. 11½x11*
| | | | | |
|---|---|---|---|---|
| 2746 | A867 | 5z multicolored | .20 | .20 |
| 2747 | A867 | 5z multicolored | .20 | .20 |
| 2748 | A867 | 20z multicolored | .40 | .20 |
| 2749 | A867 | 40z multicolored | .80 | .40 |

Nos. 2746-2749 (4)    1.60 1.00

Designs: No. 2746. The Paulinite Church on Skalka in Cracow, oil painting detail, circa 1627. No. 2747, Jesse's Tree, oil on wood, 17th cent. No. 2748, Gilded chalice, 15th cent. No. 2749, Virgin Mary embroidery, 15th cent.

---

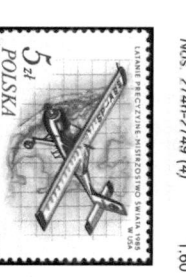

Victories of Polish Athletes at 1985
World Championships — A868

**1986, Aug. 21**    *Perf. 11½*
| | | | | |
|---|---|---|---|---|
| 2750 | A868 | 5z multicolored | .20 | .20 |
| 2751 | A868 | 5z multicolored | .20 | .20 |
| 2752 | A868 | 10z multicolored | .25 | .20 |
| 2753 | A868 | 15z multicolored | .35 | .20 |
| 2754 | A868 | 20z multicolored | .55 | .20 |
| 2755 | A868 | 30z multicolored | .70 | .30 |

Nos. 2750-2755 (6)    2.30 1.30

Designs: No. 2750, Precision Flying, Kissimmee, Florida, won by Waclaw Nycz. No. 2751, Wind Sailing, Tallinn, USSR, won by Malgorzata Palasz-Piasecka. No. 2752, Acrobatics, Vienna, won by Jerzy Makula. No. 2753, Greco-Roman Wrestling (82kg), Kolbolen, Norway, won by Bogdan Daras. No. 2754, Road Cycling, Giavera del Montello, Italy, won by Lech Piasecki. No. 2755, Women's Modern Pentathlon, Montreal, won by Barbara Kotowska.

---

Prof. Tadeusz
Kotarbinski (1886-
1981) — A873

**1986, Nov. 19**    **Litho.**    *Perf. 11½*
2766 A873 10z sepia, buff & brn blk    .30 .20

---

STOCKHOLMIA '86 — A869

**1986, Aug. 28**
2756 A869 65z multicolored    *Perf. 11x11½*    1.50 .75
a.    Souvenir sheet    1.50 .75

---

**1986, Sept. 1**
2757 A832 10z multicolored    *Perf. 12x11½*    .25 .20

World War II Battles Type of 1984

Design: Battle of Jordanow, Col. Stanislaw Maczek, motorized cavalry 10th brigade commander-in-chief.

---

17th-20th Cent. Architecture — A874

**1986, Nov. 26**    **Photo.**
    *Perf. 11x11½, 11½x11*
| | | | | |
|---|---|---|---|---|
| 2767 | A874 | 5z multicolored | .20 | .20 |
| 2768 | A874 | 5z multi. vert. | .20 | .20 |
| 2769 | A874 | 10z multicolored | .20 | .20 |
| 2770 | A874 | 15z multicolored | .30 | .25 |
| 2771 | A874 | 25z multicolored | .50 | .30 |
| 2772 | A874 | 30z multicolored | .55 | .30 |

Nos. 2767-2772 (6)    1.95 1.35

Designs: No. 2767, Church, Baczal Dolny. No. 2768, Windmill, Zygmuntow. 10z, Oravian cottage, Zubrzyca Gorna. 15z, Kashubian Arcade cottage, Wazydze. 25z, Barn, Grzawa. 30z, Water mill, Molkowice Stare.

---

Albert
Schweitzer
A870

World Post Day
A871

**1986, Sept. 26**
2758 A870 5z bl vio, sep & buff    *Perf. 12x11½*    .20 .20

**Photogravure and Engraved**

**1986, Oct. 9**    **Litho.**    *Perf. 11x11½*
2759 A871 40z org, ultra & sep    .75 .35
a.    Souvenir sheet of 2    11.50 11.50

No. 2759a sold for 120z.

---

Folk and
Fairy
Tale
Legends
A872

**1986, Oct. 28**    **Photo.**    *Perf. 11½x11*
| | | | | |
|---|---|---|---|---|
| 2760 | A872 | 5z multicolored | .20 | .20 |
| 2761 | A872 | 5z multicolored | .20 | .20 |
| 2762 | A872 | 10z multicolored | .20 | .20 |
| 2763 | A872 | 10z multicolored | .20 | .20 |
| 2764 | A872 | 20z multicolored | .35 | .20 |
| 2765 | A872 | 50z multicolored | .95 | .50 |

Nos. 2760-2765 (6)    2.10 1.50

Designs: No. 2760, Basilisk. No. 2761, Duke Popiel. No. 2762, Golden Duck. No. 2763, Boruta, the Devil, vert. No. 2764, Janosik the Thief, vert. No. 2765, Lajkonik, conqueror of the Tartars, 13th cent., vert.

---

New Year
A876

**1986, Dec. 12**    **Photo.**    *Perf. 11x11½*
2775 A876 25z multicolored    .50 .30

---

Warsaw
Cyclists
Soc.,
Cent.
A877

**1986, Dec. 19**    *Perf. 13x12½, 12½x13*
| | | | | |
|---|---|---|---|---|
| 2776 | A877 | 5z multi | .20 | .20 |
| 2777 | A877 | 5z multi. vert. | .20 | .20 |
| 2778 | A877 | 10z multi. | .20 | .20 |
| 2779 | A877 | 10z multi. vert. | .20 | .20 |
| 2780 | A877 | 10z multi. vert. | .20 | .20 |
| 2781 | A877 | 50z multi, vert. | .95 | .45 |

Nos. 2776-2781 (6)    2.30 1.55

#2776, First trip to Bielany, uniformed escort, 1887. #2777, Jan Stanislaw Skrodzki (1867-1957), 1895 record-holder. #2778, Dynasy Society building. 1892-1937. #2779, Mieczyslaw Baranski, champion, 1896. #2780, Karolina Kociecka (b. 1875), female competitor. #2781, Henryk Weiss (d. 1912), Dynasy champion, 1904-1908.

---

**1987, Feb. 13**    **Litho.**    *Perf. 11½*
| | | | | |
|---|---|---|---|---|
| 2782 | A878 | 5z multicolored | .20 | .20 |
| 2783 | A878 | 5z multicolored | .20 | .20 |
| 2784 | A878 | 10z multicolored | .20 | .20 |
| 2785 | A878 | 10z multicolored | .20 | .20 |
| 2786 | A878 | 30z multicolored | .60 | .30 |
| 2787 | A878 | 40z multicolored | .85 | .40 |

Nos. 2782-2787 (6)    2.25 1.50

Wildlife and ships: No. 2782, Euphausia superba, training freighter Antoni Garnuszewski. No. 2783, Notothenia rossi, Dissostichus mawsoni, Zulawy transoceanic ship. No. 2784, Fulmarus glacialoides, yacht Pogoria. No. 2785, Pigoscelis adeliae, yacht Gedania. 30z, Arctocephalus, research boat Dziunia. 40z, Hydruga leptonyx, ship Kapitan Ledochowski.

Henryk
Arctowski
Antarctic
Station,
10th Anniv.
A878

---

Royalty
A875

**Photogravure and Engraved**

**1986, Dec. 4**    *Perf. 11*
| | | | | |
|---|---|---|---|---|
| 2773 | A875 | 10z Mieszko I | .20 | .20 |
| 2774 | A875 | 25z Dobrawa | .50 | .25 |

See Nos. 2838-2839, 2884-2885, 2932-2933, 3033-3034, 3068-3069, 3141-3144, 3191-3192, 3222-3225, 3309-3312, 3366-3369, 3394-3397, 3479-3482. For surcharges see Nos. 3016-3017.

## Souvenir Sheet

XXX LAT BADANIA KOSMOSU

1st Artificial Satellite, Sputnik, 30th Anniv. — A896

**1987, Oct. 2  Photo.  Perf. 11½x11**
2829  A896  40z  Stacionar 4 satel-lite  1.00  1.00

SWIATOWY DZIEŃ POCZTY POLSKA

World Post Day A897

Design: Ignacy Franciszek Przebendowski (1730-1791), postmaster general, and post office building, 19th cent., Krakowskie Przedmiescie, Warsaw.

**1987, Oct. 9  Litho.**
2830  A897  15z  lt olive grn & rose claret  .25  .20

Col. Stanislaw Wieckowski — A898

**1987, Oct. 16  Photo. & Engr.  Perf. 12x11½**
2831  A898  15z  deep blue & blk  .25  .20

Col. Wieckowski (1884-1942), physician and social reformer executed by the Nazis at Auschwitz.

Baśnie

Polska 10 zł

HAFNIA '87 — A899

Fairy tales by Hans Christian Andersen (1805-1875): No. 2832, The Little Mermaid. No. 2833, The Nightingale. No. 2834, The Wild Swan. No. 2835, The Match Girl. 30z, The Snow Queen. 40z, The Brave Toy Soldier.

**1987, Oct. 16  Photo.  Perf. 11x11½**
| 2832 | A899 | 10z | multicolored | .20 | .20 |
| 2833 | A899 | 10z | multicolored | .20 | .20 |
| 2834 | A899 | 20z | multicolored | .40 | .20 |
| 2835 | A899 | 20z | multicolored | .40 | .20 |
| 2836 | A899 | 30z | multicolored | .60 | .30 |
| 2837 | A899 | 40z | multicolored | .80 | .40 |

Nos. 2832-2837 (6)  2.60  1.50

Royalty Type of 1986

**Photo. & Engr.**
**1987, Dec. 4  Perf. 11**
| 2838 | A875 | 10z | Boleslaw I Chrobry | .20 | .20 |
| 2839 | A875 | 15z | Mieszko II | .30 | .20 |

No. 2838 exists with label.

---

**1987, July 25  Litho.  Perf. 11½**
2811  A890  45z  Ludwig L. Zamenhof  .80  .40

POLSKA · 15 zł

Stanisław Wyspiański Poznań

A891

10 zł Polska

A892

Poznan and Town Hall, by Stanislaw Wyspianski.

**1987, Aug. 3**
2812  A891  15z  blk & pale salmon  .25  .20
POZNAN '87, Aug. 8-16.

**1987, Aug. 20  Photo.  Perf. 11½x11**
| 2813 | A892 | 10z | Queen | .20 | .20 |
| 2814 | A892 | 10z | Worker | .20 | .20 |
| 2815 | A892 | 15z | Drone | .30 | .20 |
| 2816 | A892 | 15z | Box hive, orchard | .30 | .20 |
| 2817 | A892 | 40z | Bee collecting pollen | .75 | .35 |
| 2818 | A892 | 50z | Beekeeper collecting honey | .90 | .45 |

Nos. 2813-2818 (6)  2.85  1.60

31st World Apiculture Congress, Warsaw.

Polska  SKOK  10 zł

Success of Polish Athletes at World Championship Events — A894

**1987, Sept. 24  Litho.  Perf. 14**
2820  A894  10z  Acrobatics, France  .20  .20
| 2821 | A894 | 15z | Kayak, Canada | .25 | .20 |
| 2822 | A894 | 20z | Marksmanship, E. Germany | .30 | .20 |
| 2823 | A894 | 25z | Wrestling, Hungary | .40 | .20 |

Nos. 2820-2823 (4)  1.15  .80

**World War II Battles Type of 1984**

Designs: No. 2824, Battle of Mokra; Julian Filipowicz. No. 2825, Battle scene near Oleszycami, Brig.-Gen. Josef Rudolf Kustron. 15z, Air battles over Warsaw, pilot Stefan Pawilkowlski.

**1987, Sept. 1  Photo.  Perf. 12x11½**
| 2824 | A832 | 10z | multicolored | .20 | .20 |
| 2825 | A832 | 10z | multicolored | .20 | .20 |
| 2826 | A832 | 15z | multicolored | .70 | .60 |

Nos. 2824-2826 (3)

Jan Hevelius (1611-1687)

40 zł

Jan Hevelius (1611-1687), Astronomer, and Constellations — A895

**1987, Sept. 15  Litho.  Perf. 11½**
2827  A895  15z  Hevelius, sextant, vert.  .25  .20
2828  A895  40z  shown  .65  .35

---

POLSKA 10 zł  SAUER ZAWRAT 1936

Motor Vehicles — A884

**1987, May 19  Photo.  Perf. 12x11½**
| 2798 | A884 | 10z | 1936 Saurer-Zawrat | .20 | .20 |
| 2799 | A884 | 10z | 1928 CWS T-1 | .20 | .20 |
| 2800 | A884 | 15z | 1928 Ursus-A | .30 | .20 |
| 2801 | A884 | 15z | 1936 Lux-Sport | .30 | .25 |
| 2802 | A884 | 25z | 1939 Podkowa | .50 | .25 |
| 2803 | A884 | 45z | 1935 Sokol 600 RT | .90 | .45 |

Nos. 2798-2803 (6)  2.40  1.50

Royal Castle, Warsaw — A885

**1987, June 5**
2804  A885  50z  multicolored  .90  .50

A souvenir sheet of 1 exists. Value $50.

Jan Paweł pp.II

15 zł Polska

A886

III Wizyta Papieża Jana Pawła II w Polsce

State Visit of Pope John Paul II — A887

**1987, June 8  Perf. 11**
2805  A886  15z  shown  .30  .30
2806  A886  45z  Portrait, diff.  .90  .45
a.  Pair. #2805-2806  1.20  .60

**Souvenir Sheet**
**Perf. 12x11½**
2807  A887  50z  shown  1.00  1.00

No. 2806a has continuous design.

Cracow Restoration Type of 1982

**1987, July 6  Litho.  Perf. 11½**
2809  A801  10z  Barbican Gate, Wawel, horiz.  .20  .20

POLSKA 45 zł

Esperanto Language, Cent. — A890

---

L.WYCZOŁKOWSKI 1852-1936

5 zł  POLSKA

Paintings by Leon Wyczolkowski (1852-1936) — A879

**1987, Mar. 20  Photo.  Perf. 11**
| 2788 | A879 | 5z | Cineraria Flowers, 1924 | .20 | .20 |
| 2789 | A879 | 10z | Portrait of a Woman, 1883 | .20 | .20 |
| 2790 | A879 | 10z | Wood Church, 1910 | .20 | .20 |
| 2791 | A879 | 25z | Harvesting Beetroot, 1910 | .50 | .25 |
| 2792 | A879 | 30z | Wading Fishermen, 1891 | .60 | .30 |
| 2793 | A879 | 40z | Self-portrait, 1912 | .80 | .40 |

Nos. 2788-2793 (6)  2.50  1.55

Nos. 2789 and 2791 vert.

ARTUR GROTTGER 1837-1867

15 zł  POLSKA

The Ravage, 1866, by Artur Grottger (1837-1867) — A880

**1987, Mar. 26  Photo.  Perf. 11**
2794  A880  15z  dk brown & buff  .25  .20

Gen. Karol Swierczewski-Walter

15  POLSKA

Gen. Karol Swierczewski-Walter (1897-1947) — A881

**1987, Mar. 27  Engr.  Perf. 11½x12**
2795  A881  1z  olive green  .25  .20

65 zł  Polska

Pawel Edmund Strzelecki (1797-1873), Explorer — A882

**1987, Apr. 23  Photo.  Perf. 11½x11**
2796  A882  65z  olive black  1.10  .65

Colonization of Australia, bicentennial.

POLSKA 10 zł  PRON

2nd PRON Congress A883

**1987, May 8  Litho.  Perf. 11½**
2797  A883  10z  pale gray, brn, red & brt ultra  .20  .20

Patriotic Movement of the National Renaissance Congress.

**1987, Dec. 14 Photo. Perf. 11x11½**
2840 A900 15z multicolored .25 .20

New Year
1988
A900

Dragonflies — A901

**1988, Feb. 23 Perf. 11x11½, 11½x11**
Photo.
2841 A901 10z Anax imperator .20 .20
2842 A901 15z Libellula
quadrimaculata,
vert. .20 .20
2843 A901 15z Calopteryx
splendens .25 .20
2844 A901 20z Cordulegaster annulatus, vert. .35 .20
2845 A901 30z Sympetrum .50 .25
2846 A901 50z Aeschna viridis,
pedemontanum .90 .45
Nos. 2841-2846 (6) 2.45 1.50

Cracow Restoration Type of 1982
**1988, Mar. 8 Litho. Perf. 11½x11**
2847 A801 15z Florianska Gate,
1300 .25 .20
2848 A903 40z multicolored .50 .25

Int'l. Year
of
Graphic
Design
A903

**1988, Apr. 28 Photo. Perf. 11x11½**
2848 A903 40z multicolored .50 .25

Antique Clocks — A904

Clocks in the Museum of Artistic and Precision Handicrafts, Warsaw, and clockworks;
No. 2849, Frisian wall clock, 17th cent., vert.
No. 2850, Anniversary clock and rotary pendulum, 20th cent. No. 2851, Carriage clock, 18th
cent., vert. No. 2852, Louis XV rococo bracket
clock, 18th cent., vert. 20z, Pocket watch, 19th
cent. 40z, Gdansk six-sided clock signed by
Benjamin Zoll, 17th cent.

**1988, May 19 Photo.**
2849 A904 10z lt green & multi .20 .20
2850 A904 10z purple & multi .20 .20
2851 A904 15z dull org & multi .20 .20
2852 A904 15z brown & multi .20 .20
2853 A904 20z multicolored .30 .20
2854 A904 40z multicolored .65 .30
Nos. 2849-2854 (6) 1.85 1.30

1988
Summer
Olympics,
Seoul
A905

**1988, May 19 Perf. 11½x12, 12½x11½**
Photo.

**1988, June 27 Photo. Perf. 11x11½**
2855 A905 15z Triple jump .20 .20
2856 A905 20z Wrestling .20 .20
2857 A905 20z Two-man kayak .20 .20
2858 A905 25z Judo .35 .20
2859 A905 40z Shooting .50 .20
2860 A905 55z Swimming .75 .20
Nos. 2855-2860 (6) 2.30 1.20

Natl.
Industry
A906

**1988, Aug. 23 Photo. Perf. 11x11½**
2861 A906 45z Los "Elk" aircraft .75 .40
See Nos. 2867, 2871, 2881-2883.

16th European
Regional FAO
Conference,
Cracow — A907

15z, Computers and agricultural growth,
40z, Balance between industry and nature.

**1988, Aug. 22 Perf. 11½x11**
2862 A907 15z multicolored .25 .20
2863 A907 40z multicolored .60 .30

World War II Battles Type of 1984
Battle scenes and commanders: 15z, Mod-
lin, Brig.-Gen. Wiktor Thommee, No. 2865,
Warsaw, Brig.-Gen. Walerian Czuma, No.
2866, Tomaszow Lubelski, Brig.-Gen. Antoni
Szyling.

**1988, Sept. 1 Photo. Perf. 12½x11½**
2864 A832 15z multicolored .25 .20
2865 A832 20z multicolored .30 .20
2866 A832 20z multicolored .30 .20
Nos. 2864-2866 (3) .85 .60

Natl. Industries Type of 1988
**1988, Sept. 5 Size: 35x27mm**
2867 A906 15z multicolored .25 .20

World Post
Day
A909

Design: Postmaster Tomasz Arciszewski
(1877-1955), Post and Telegraph Administration emblem used from 1919 to 1927.

**1988, Oct. 9 Litho. Perf. 11½x11**
2868 A909 20z multicolored .25 .20
Also printed in sheet of 12 plus 12 labels.

World War II
Combat
Medals — A910

**1988, Oct. 12 Photo.**
2869 A910 20z Battle of Lenino
Cross .30 .20
2870 A910 20z multicolored .30 .20

Natl. Industries Type of 1988
Air Force Medical Institute, 60th anniv.
See Nos. 2930-2931.

**1988, Oct. 12 Size: 38x27mm Perf. 11x11½**
2871 A906 20z multicolored .25 .20

Stanisław Małachowski, Kazimierz
Nestor Sapieha — A912

Four Years' Sejm (Parliament) (1788-1792),
bicent.

**1988, Oct. 16 Perf. 11**
2872 A912 20z multicolored .25 .20

National
Leaders — A913

**1988, Nov. 11 Perf. 12x11½**
2873 A913 15z Wincenty
Witos .25 .20
2874 A913 15z Ignacy Das-
zynski .25 .20
2875 A913 20z Wojciech
Korfanty .25 .20
2876 A913 20z Stanisław
Wojciechow-
ski .25 .20
2877 A913 20z Julian Mar-
chlewski .25 .20
2878 A913 200z Ignacy Paderewski .25 .20
2879 A913 200z Józef Piłsudski 2.25 1.00
2880 A913 200z Gabriel
Narutowicz 2.25 1.00
a. Souvenir sheet of 3, #2878-
2880 8.00 4.00
Nos. 2873-2880 (8) 17.50 8.00

15z, Wharf, Gdynia, 20z, Industrialist Hipolit
Cegielski, 1883 steam locomotive, 40z, Poznan fair grounds, Upper Silesia Tower.

**1988 Photo. Perf. 11x11½**
Size: 39x27mm
2881 A906 15z multicolored .30 .20
2882 A906 20z multicolored .40 .20

Size: 35x27mm
2883 A906 40z multicolored .80 .40
Nos. 2881-2883 (3) 1.50 .80
70th anniv. of Polish independence. Gdynia
Port, 65th anniv. (15z); Metal Works in Poznan,
142nd anniv. (20z); and Poznan Int'l Fair 60th
anniv. (40z).
Issued: 15z, 12/12; 20z, 11/28; 40z, 12/21.

Royalty Type of 1986
**1988, Dec. 4 Photo. & Engr. Perf. 11**
2884 A875 10z Rycheza .20 .20
2885 A875 15z Kazimierz I
Odnowiciel .30 .20

Krzyż Bitwy pod Lenino

**1988, Dec. 9 Photo. Perf. 11x11½**
2886 A914 20z multicolored .30 .20

New Year
1989
A914

Unification of
Polish Workers'
Unions, 40th
Anniv. — A915

**1988, Dec. 15 Perf. 11½x12**
2887 A915 20z black & ver .25 .20

Fire
Boats — A916

**1988, Dec. 29 Litho. Perf. 14**
2888 A916 10z Błysk .20 .20
2889 A916 15z Żar .25 .20
2890 A916 15z Strażak 4 .30 .20
2891 A916 20z Płomień .35 .20
2892 A916 20z Strażak 11 .30 .20
2893 A916 45z Śmiałek 25 .75 .40
Nos. 2888-2893 (6) 2.05 1.40

Światowy Dzień Poczty

Horses — A917

**1989, Mar. 6 Photo. Perf. 11**
2894 A917 15z Lippizaner .25 .20
2895 A917 15z Arden, vert. .25 .20
2896 A917 20z English .35 .20
2897 A917 20z Arabian, vert. .35 .20
2898 A917 30z Wielkopolski .55 .20
2899 A917 70z Polish, vert. 1.00 .25
Nos. 2894-2899 (6) 2.75 1.30

Dogs — A918

**1989, May 3 Photo. Perf. 11½x11**
2900 A918 15z Wire-haired
dachshund .20 .20
2901 A918 15z Cocker spaniel .20 .20
2902 A918 20z Czech fousek
pointer .20 .20

Battle of Monte
Cassino, 45th
Anniv. — A919

**2903** A918 20z Welsh terrier .20 .20
**2904** A918 25z English setter .20 .20
**2905** A918 45z Pointer .40 .20
*Nos. 2900-2905 (6)* 1.40 1.20

**1989, May 18** *Perf. 11½x12*

Design: 165z, Battle of Falaise, General Stanislaw Maczek, horiz. 210z, Battle of Arnhem, Gen. Stanislaw Sosabowski, vert.

**2906** A919 80z Gen. W. Anders .45 .25
**2907** A919 165z multicolored .85 .40
**2907A** A919 210z multicolored 1.20 .60
*Nos. 2906-2907A (3)* 2.50 1.25

1st Armored Division at the Battle of Falaise, 45th anniv. Battle of Arnhem, 45th anniv.

See No. 2968.

A 50z stamp for Gen. Grzegorz Korczynski was prepared but not released.

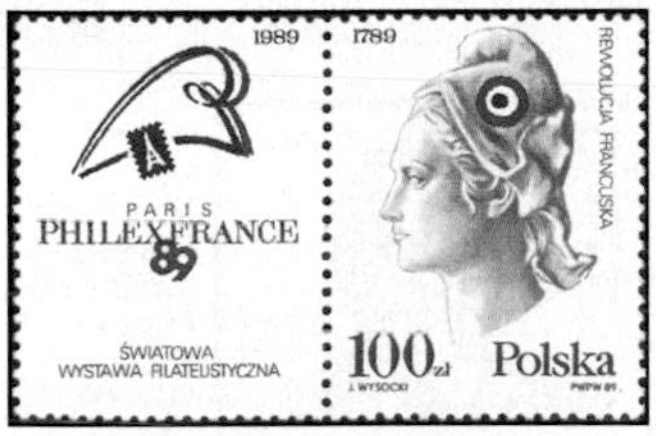


Woman Wearing a Phrygian Cap — A920

**1989, July 3** **Litho.** *Perf. 11½x11*
**2908** A920 100z blk, dark red & dark ultra .70 .30
*a.* Souv. sheet of 2+2 labels 2.00 2.00

French revolution bicent., PHILEXFRANCE '89. No. 2908 printed se-tenant with inscribed label picturing exhibition emblem. No. 2908a sold for 270z. Surcharge benefited the Polish Philatelic Union.

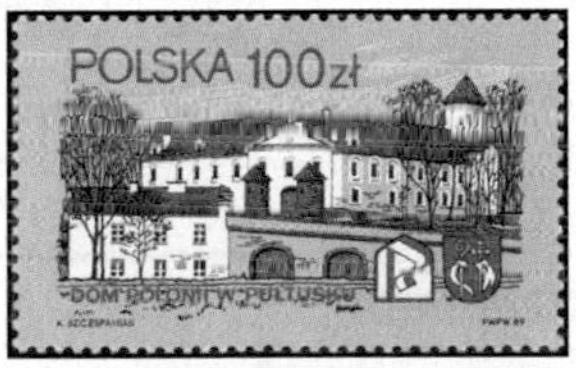


Polonia House, Pultusk — A921

**1989, July 16** **Photo.** *Perf. 11½*
**2909** A921 100z multicolored .70 .30

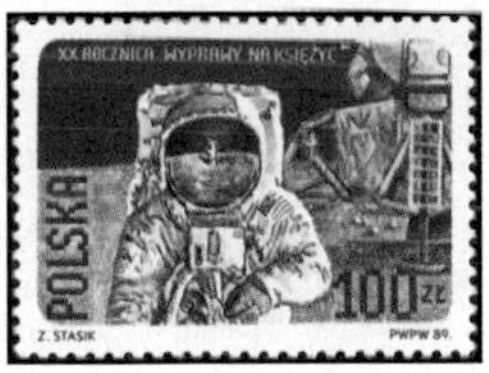


First Moon Landing, 20th Anniv. A922

**1989, July 21** *Perf. 11x11½*
**2910** A922 100z multicolored .70 .30
*a.* Souvenir sheet of 1 2.00 1.00

No. 2910a exists imperf. Value $20.

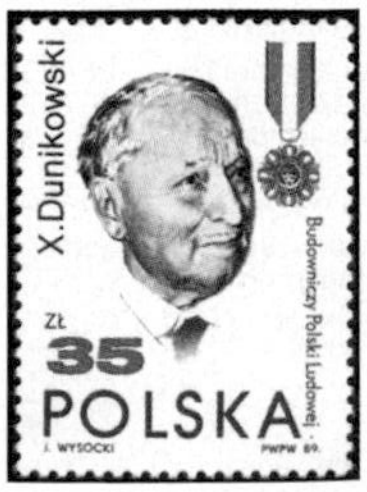


Polish People's Republic, 45th Anniv. — A923

Winners of the Order of the Builders of People's Poland: No. 2911, Ksawery Dunikowski (1875-1964), artist. No. 2912, Stanislaw Mazur (1897-1964), agriculturist. No. 2913, Natalia Gasiorowska (1881-1964), historian. No. 2914, Wincenty Pstrowski (1904-1948), coal miner.

**1989, July 21** *Perf. 11½x11*
**2911** A923 35z multicolored .25 .20
**2912** A923 35z multicolored .25 .20
**2913** A923 35z multicolored .25 .20
**2914** A923 35z multicolored .25 .20
*Nos. 2911-2914 (4)* 1.00 .80

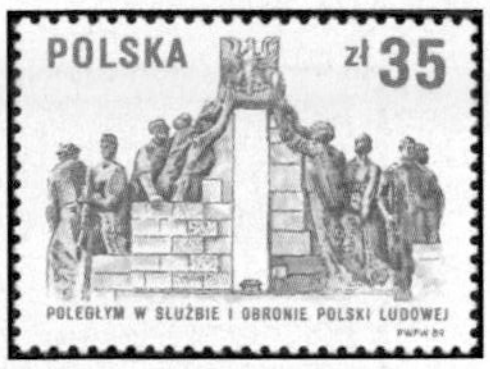


Security Service and Militia, 45th Anniv. A924

**1989, July 21** *Perf. 11x11½*
**2915** A924 35z dull brn & slate blue .35 .20

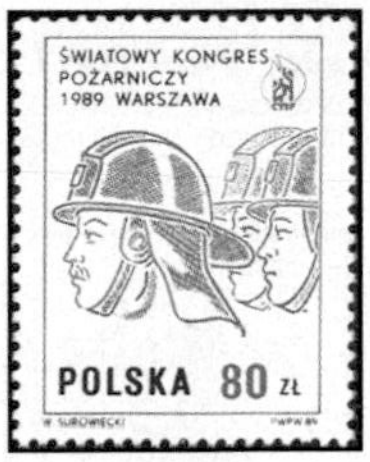


World Fire Fighting Congress, July 25-30, Warsaw — A925

**1989, July 25** *Perf. 11½x11*
**2916** A925 80z multicolored .55 .30

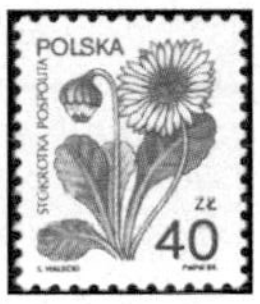


Daisy — A926

Designs: 60z, Juniper. 150z, Daisy. 500z, Wild rose. 1000z, Blue corn flower.

**1989** **Photo.** *Perf. 11x12*
**2917** A926 40z slate green .20 .20
**2918** A926 60z violet blue .20 .20
**2919** A926 150z rose lake .20 .20
**2920** A926 500z bright violet .55 .25
**2921** A926 1000z bright blue 1.10 .50
*Nos. 2917-2921 (5)* 2.25 1.35

Issue dates: 40z, 60z, Aug. 25. 150z, Dec. 4; 500z, 1000z, Dec. 19.

See Nos. 2978-2979, 3026. For surcharge see No. 2970.

World War II Battles Type of 1984

Battle scenes and commanders: No. 2922, Westerplatte, Capt. Franciszek Dabrowski. No. 2923, Hel, Artillery Capt. B. Przybyszewski. No. 2924, Kock, Brig.-Gen. Franciszek Kleeberg. No. 2925, Lwow, Brig.-Gen. Wladyslaw Langner.

**1989, Sept. 1** *Perf. 12x11½*
**2922** A832 25z multicolored .20 .20
**2923** A832 25z multicolored .20 .20
**2924** A832 35z multicolored .25 .20
**2925** A832 35z multicolored .25 .20
*Nos. 2922-2925 (4)* .90 .80

Nazi invasion of Poland, 50th anniv.

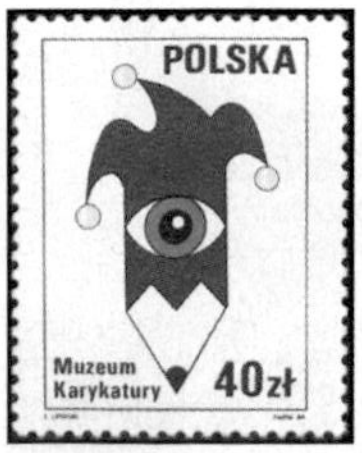


Caricature Museum — A927

**1989, Sept. 15** **Photo.** *Perf. 11½x11*
**2926** A927 40z multicolored .20 .20

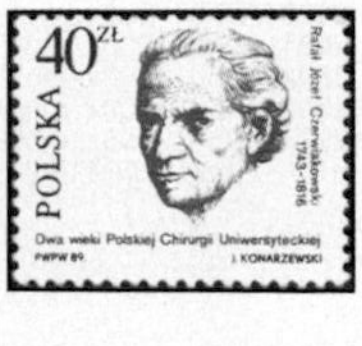


Teaching Surgery at Polish Universities, Bicent., and Surgeon's Soc. Cent. — A928

Surgeons: 40z, Rafal Jozef Czerwiakowski (1743-1813), 1st professor of surgery and founder of the 1st surgical department, Jagellonian University, Cracow. 60z, Ludwik Rydygier (1850-1920), founder of the Polish Surgeons Society.

**1989, Sept. 18** *Perf. 11½x12*
**2927** A928 40z black & brt ultra .20 .20
**2928** A928 60z black & brt green .30 .20

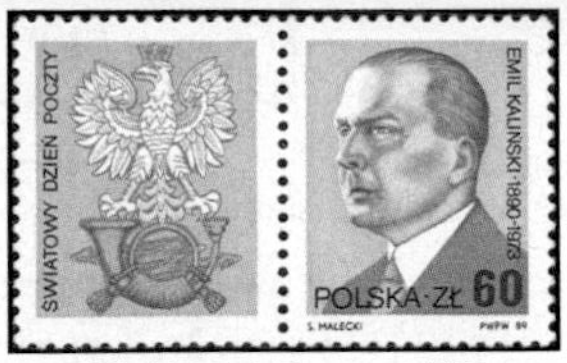


World Post Day — A929

Design: Emil Kalinski (1890-1973), minister of the Post and Telegraph from 1933-1939.

**1989, Oct. 9** *Perf. 12x11½*
**2929** A929 60z multicolored .30 .20

Printed se-tenant with label picturing postal emblem of the second republic.

WWII Decorations Type of 1988

Medals: No. 2930, Participation in the Struggle for Control of the Nation. No. 2931, Defense of Warsaw, 1939-45.

**1989, Oct. 12** **Photo.** *Perf. 11½x11*
**2930** A910 60z multicolored .25 .20
**2931** A910 60z multicolored .25 .20

Royalty Type of 1986

**Photo. & Engr.**

**1989, Oct. 18** *Perf. 11*
**2932** A875 20z Boleslaw II Szczodry .20 .20
**2933** A875 30z Wladyslaw I Herman .20 .20

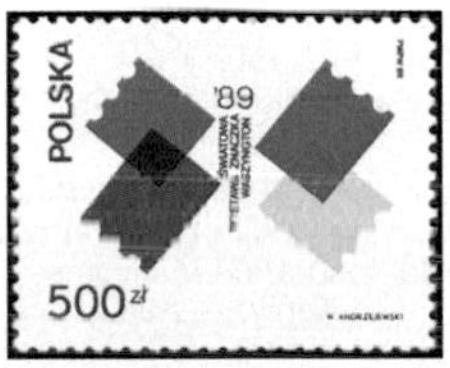


World Stamp Expo '89, Washington, DC, Nov. 17-Dec.3 — A930

**1989, Nov. 14** **Photo.** *Perf. 11x11½*
**2934** A930 500z multicolored 1.65 .80

Exists imperf. Value $5.

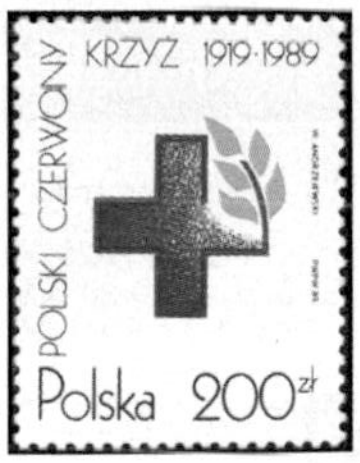


Polish Red Cross Soc., 70th Anniv. — A931

**1989, Nov. 17** *Perf. 11½x11*
**2935** A931 200z blk, brt yel grn & scar .75 .30

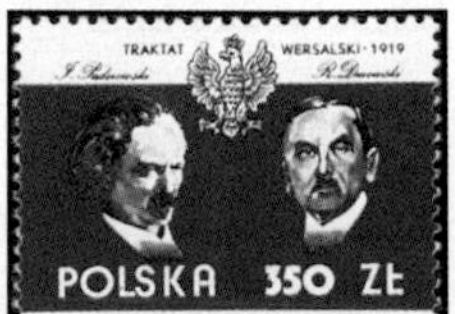


Treaty of Versailles, 70th Anniv. A932

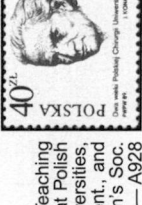

Design: State arms and representatives of Poland who signed the treaty, including Ignacy Jan Paderewski (1860-1941), pianist, composer, statesman, and Roman Dmowski (1864-1939), statesman.

**1989, Nov. 21** *Perf. 11x11½*
**2936** A932 350z multicolored 1.25 .50

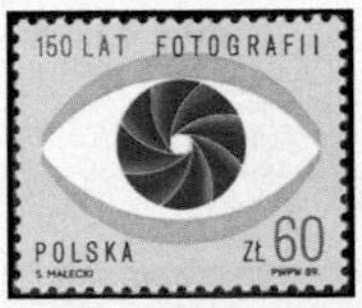


Camera Shutter as the Iris of the Eye — A933

Designs: 40z, Photographer in silhouette, Maksymilian Strasz (1804-1870), pioneer of photography in Poland.

*Perf. 11½x12, 12x11½*

**1989, Nov. 27**
**2937** A933 40z multicolored .20 .20
**2938** A933 60z shown .20 .20

Photography, 150th anniv.

No. 2456 Surcharged

**1989, Nov. 30** **Photo.** *Perf. 11x11½*
**2939** A766 500z on 4z dark violet 1.25 .50

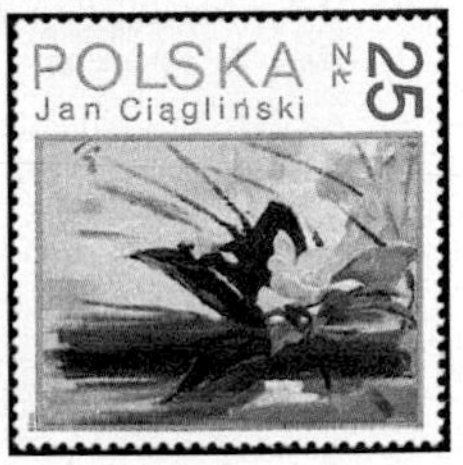


Flowers, Still-life Paintings in the National Museum, Warsaw A934

**1989, Dec. 18** *Perf. 13*
**2940** A934 25z Jan Ciaglinski .20 .20
**2941** A934 30z Wojciech Weiss .20 .20
**2942** A934 35z Antoni Kolasinski .20 .20
**2943** A934 50z Stefan Nacht-Samborski .20 .20
**2944** A934 60z Jozef Pankiewicz .20 .20
**2945** A934 85z Honryka Beyer .25 .20
**2946** A934 110z Wladyslaw Slewinski .30 .20
**2947** A934 190z Czeslaw Wdowiszewski .50 .30
*Nos. 2940-2947 (8)* 2.05 1.70

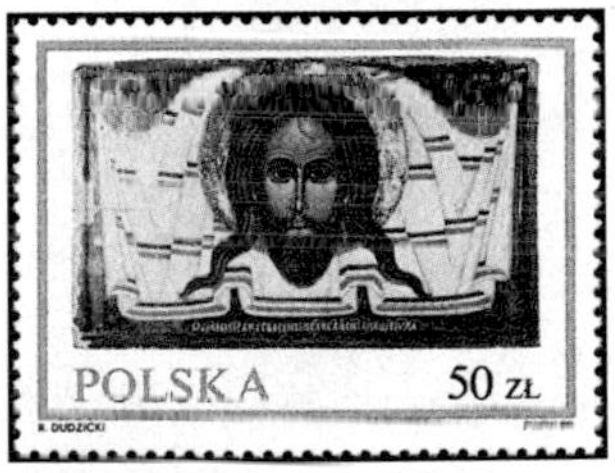


Religious Art — A935

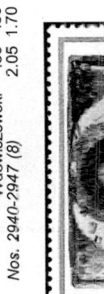

**1989, Dec. 21** *Perf. 11½x11*
**2948** A935 50z Jesus, shroud .25 .20
**2949** A935 60z Two saints .25 .20
**2950** A935 90z Three saints .25 .20

*Perf. 11x11½*

**2951** A935 150z Jesus, Mary, Joseph .45 .25
**2952** A935 200z Madonna and Child Enthroned .60 .30
**2953** A935 350z Holy Family with angels 1.25 .50
*Nos. 2948-2953 (6)* 3.05 1.65

Nos. 2951-2953 vert.

**Republic of Poland**

No. 2738 Surcharged

**1990, Jan. 31** **Photo.** *Perf. 11½x12*
**2954** A828 350z on 15z rose brn .25 .20

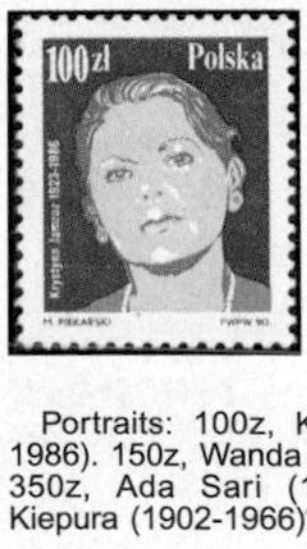


Opera Singers — A936

Portraits: 100z, Krystyna Jamroz (1923-1986). 150z, Wanda Werminska (1900-1988). 350z, Ada Sari (1882-1968). 500z, Jan Kiepura (1902-1966).

**POLAND**

**1990, Feb. 9**  Perf. 12x11½
| | | | |
|---|---|---|---|
| 2955 | A936 | 100z multicolored | .20 .20 |
| 2956 | A936 | 150z multicolored | .20 .20 |
| 2957 | A936 | 350z multicolored | .30 .20 |
| 2958 | A936 | 500z multicolored | .90 .80 |

Nos. 2955-2958 (4)

**1990, Mar. 29**  Perf. 11x11½
Yachting — A937

| | | | |
|---|---|---|---|
| 2959 | A937 | 100z shown | .20 .20 |
| 2960 | A937 | 200z Rugby | .20 .20 |
| 2961 | A937 | 400z High jump | .20 .20 |
| 2962 | A937 | 500z Figure skating | .25 .20 |
| 2963 | A937 | 500z Diving | .25 .20 |
| 2964 | A937 | 1000z Rhythmic gymnastics | .50 .50 |

Nos. 2959-2964 (6)   1.60 1.25

**1990, Apr. 17**  Photo. Perf. 11x11½
Roman Kozlowski (1889-1977), Paleontologist — A938

2965 A938 500z red & olive bis   .30 .20

**1990, May 18**  Perf. 11
Pope John Paul II, 70th Birthday A939

2966 A939 1000z multicolored   .55 .25

First Polish Postage Stamp, 130th Anniv. — A940
Souvenir Sheet

BO LAT POLSKIEGO ZNACZKA POCZTOWEGO

Design includes No. 1 separated by simulated perforations from 1000z commemorative version at right.

**1990, May 25**  Perf. 11½
2967 A940 1000z multicolored   .55 .25

Battle Type of 1989
Design: Battle of Narvik, 1940, General Z.

**1990, May 28**
2968 A919 1500z multicolored   .60 .25

Design: Bohusz-Szyszko.

**1990, June 8**  Perf. 11½x11
World Cup Soccer Championships, Italy — A941

2969 A941 1000z multicolored   .60 .30

No. 2918 Surcharged in Vermilion

**1990, June 18**  Photo. Perf. 11x12
2970 A926 70z on 60z vio bl   .40 .20

**1990, June 28**  Photo. Perf. 12x10
Memorial to Victims of June 1956 Uprising, Poznan — A942

2971 A942 1500z multicolored   .70 .30

**1990, July 5**
Social Insurance Institution, 70th Anniv. — A943

2972 A943 1500z multicolored   .75 .35
Perf. 11x11½

**1990, July 16**  Perf. 11½, 14 (#2974)
Shells — A944

| | | | |
|---|---|---|---|
| 2973 | A944 | B (500z) dk pur | .20 .20 |
| 2974 | A944 | A (700z) olive grn | .35 .20 |

#2973, Mussel. #2974, Fresh water snail.

**1990, July 20**  Perf. 11½x11
Katyn Forest Massacre, 50th Anniv. — A945

2975 A945 1500z gray, red & blk   .75 .35

**1990, July 27**  Perf. 11½x11
Polish Meteorological Service — A946

| | | | |
|---|---|---|---|
| 2976 | A946 | 500z shown | .25 .20 |
| 2977 | A946 | 700z Water depth gauge | .40 .20 |

**1990, Aug. 13**   Self Adhesive   Die Cut
Flower Type of 1989

| | | | |
|---|---|---|---|
| 2978 | A926 | 2000z olive grn | .75 .55 |
| 2979 | A926 | 5000z violet | 2.00 .95 |

Designs: 2000z, Nuphar. 5000z, German iris.

**1990, Aug. 22**  Photo. Perf. 11x11½
World Kayaking Championships, Poznan — A947

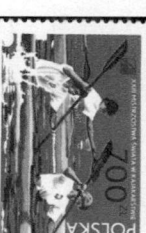

| | | | |
|---|---|---|---|
| 2980 | A947 | 700z multicolored | .40 .20 |
| 2981 | A947 | 1000z multicolored | .60 .30 |
| a. | | Souv. sheet of 1 + label | 4.50 4.50 |

Design: 1000z, One-man kayak.

**1990, Aug. 31**  Perf. 11½x11
2982 A948 1500z blk, red & gray   .75 .35

Solidarity, 10th anniv.

A948

**1990, Sept. 24**  Photo. Perf. 11½x11
Flowers. — A949

A949

| | | | |
|---|---|---|---|
| 2983 | A949 | 200z Polemonium coeruleum | .20 .20 |
| 2984 | A949 | 700z Nymphoides peltata | .20 .20 |
| 2985 | A949 | 700z Dracocephalum ruyschiana | .35 .20 |
| 2986 | A949 | 1000z Helleborus purpurascens | .55 .25 |
| 2987 | A949 | 1500z Daphne cneorum | .80 .30 |
| 2988 | A949 | 1700z Dianthus superbus | .90 .40 |

Nos. 2983-2988 (6)   3.15 1.55

**1990, Oct. 31**  Photo. Perf. 11
Cmielow Porcelain Works, Bicentennial — A950

| | | | |
|---|---|---|---|
| 2989 | A950 | 700z multicolored | .20 .20 |
| 2990 | A950 | 800z multicolored | .20 .20 |
| 2991 | A950 | 1000z multicolored | .20 .20 |
| 2992 | A950 | 1000z multicolored | .35 .20 |
| 2993 | A950 | 1500z multicolored | .60 .20 |
| 2994 | A950 | 2000z multicolored | 1.00 .40 |

Nos. 2989-2994 (6)   2.70 1.50

Designs: 700z, Platter, 1887. 800z, Plate, 1870-1887. 800z, vert. No. 2991, Figurine, 1887-1944, vert. No. 2992, Cup, saucer, c. 1887. 1500z, Candy box, 1930-1990. 2000z, Vase, 1979, vert.

**1990, Nov. 6**  Litho. Perf. 14
Owls — A951

| | | | |
|---|---|---|---|
| 2995 | A951 | 20z Athene noctua | .20 .20 |
| 2996 | A951 | 50z Strix aluco, shown | .30 .20 |
| 2997 | A951 | 500z Strix aluco, winter | .30 .20 |
| 2998 | A951 | 1000z Asio flammeus | .60 .25 |
| 2999 | A951 | 1500z Asio otus | .90 .40 |
| 3000 | A951 | 2000z Tyto alba | 2.45 1.75 |

Nos. 2995-3000 (6)   3.55 1.75

**1990, Dec. 12**  Litho. Perf. 11½x11
Pres. Lech Walesa, 1983 Nobel Peace Prize Winner A952

3001 A952 1700z multicolored   1.00 .45

**1990, Dec. 21**  Photo. Perf. 11½x11
3002 A953 1500z multicolored   .75 .35

Polish participation in Battle of Britain, 50th anniv.

A953

**1990, Dec. 28**  Litho. Perf. 11½
Architecture: 700z, Collegiate Church, 12th cent., Leczyca. 800z, Castle, 14th cent., Reszel. 1500z, Town Hall, 16th cent., Chelmno. 1700z, Church of the Nuns of the Visitation, 18th cent., Warsaw.

A954

| | | | |
|---|---|---|---|
| 3003 | A954 | 700z multicolored | .35 .20 |
| 3004 | A954 | 800z multicolored | .40 .20 |
| 3005 | A954 | 1500z multicolored | .80 .30 |
| 3006 | A954 | 1700z multicolored | .90 .35 |

Nos. 3003-3006 (4)   2.45 1.05

No. 3006 printed with se-tenant label for World Philatelic Exhibition, Poland '93.

POLSKA 500 zł
PORTRET ZYGMUNTA AUGUSTA w XVI/XVII

Art Treasures of the Natl. Gallery, Warsaw
A955

Paintings: 500z, King Sigismund Augustus. 700z, The Adoration of the Magi, Pultusk Codex. 1000z, St. Matthew, Pultusk Codex. 1500z, Christ Removing the Moneychangers by Mikolaj Haberschrack. 1700z, The Annunciation. 2000z, The Three Marys by Haberschrack.

**1991, Jan. 11** **Photo.** ***Perf. 11***

| | | | | | |
|---|---|---|---|---|---|
| **3007** | A955 | 500z multicolored | .20 | .20 |
| **3008** | A955 | 700z multicolored | .30 | .20 |
| **3009** | A955 | 1000z multicolored | .35 | .20 |
| **3010** | A955 | 1500z multicolored | .50 | .20 |
| **3011** | A955 | 1700z multicolored | .55 | .25 |
| **3012** | A955 | 2000z multicolored | .65 | .30 |
| | | *Nos. 3007-3012 (6)* | 2.55 | 1.35 |

700
Polska

Pinecones — A956

**1991, Feb. 22** ***Perf. 12x11½***

| | | | | |
|---|---|---|---|---|
| **3013** | A956 | 700z Ables alba | .20 | .20 |
| **3014** | A956 | 1500z Pinus strobus | .40 | .20 |

See Nos. 3163-3164, 3231-3232.

POLSKA PRZYJĘCIE DO CEPT
1500zł
Urząd Rady Ministrów / Pałac Radziwiłłów

Radziwill Palace
A957

**1991, Mar. 3** **Photo.** ***Perf. 11x12***

**3015** A957 1500z multicolored .40 .20

Admission to CEPT.

Royalty Type of 1986 Surcharged in Red

BOLESŁAW III KRZYWOUSTY
1000 zł
POLSKA

Designs: 1000z, Boleslaw III Krzywousty. 1500z, Wladyslaw II Wygnaniec.

**Photo. & Engr.**

**1991, Mar. 25** ***Perf. 11***

| | | | | |
|---|---|---|---|---|
| **3016** | A875 | 1000z on 40z, grn & blk | .30 | .20 |
| **3017** | A875 | 1500z on 50z, red vio & gray blk | .50 | .25 |

Not issued without surcharge.

2000 zł Polska

Brother Albert (Adam Chmielowski, 1845-1916) — A958

**1991, Mar. 29** **Photo.** ***Perf. 12x11½***

**3018** A958 2000z multicolored .50 .25

POLSKA
1500 zł
BITWA POD LEGNICA 9 KWIETNIA 1241

Battle of Legnica, 750th Anniv.
A959

**Photo. & Engr.**

**1991, Apr. 9** ***Perf. 14½x14***

**3019** A959 1500z multicolored .45 .25

See Germany No. 1635.

POLSKA 500 zł

Polish Icons
A960

Designs: 500z, 1000z, 1500z, Various paintings of Madonna and Child. 700z, 2000z, 2200z, Various paintings of Jesus.

**1991, Apr. 22** **Photo.** ***Perf. 11***

| | | | | |
|---|---|---|---|---|
| **3020** | A960 | 500z multicolored | .20 | .20 |
| **3021** | A960 | 700z multicolored | .25 | .20 |
| **3022** | A960 | 1000z multicolored | .35 | .20 |
| **3023** | A960 | 1500z multicolored | .50 | .25 |
| **3024** | A960 | 2000z multicolored | .70 | .30 |
| **3025** | A960 | 2200z multicolored | .75 | .35 |
| | | *Nos. 3020-3025 (6)* | 2.75 | 1.60 |

Flower Type of 1989

Design: 700z, Lily of the Valley.

**1991, Apr. 26** **Litho.** ***Perf. 14***

**3026** A926 700z dk blue green .25 .20

Royalty Type of 1986

Designs: 1000z, Boleslaw IV Kedzierzawy. 1500z, Mieszko III Stary.

**Photo. & Engr.**

**1991, Apr. 30** ***Perf. 11x11½***

| | | | | |
|---|---|---|---|---|
| **3033** | A875 | 1000z brn red & black | .35 | .20 |
| **3034** | A875 | 1500z brt bl & bluish blk | .60 | .20 |

2000 ZŁ
USTAWA RZĄDOWA
3 MAJA 1791-1991
POLSKA

A961

Europa
1000 zł
POLSKA
ACTIVE

A962

2000z, Title page of act. 2500z, Debate in the Sejm. 3000z, Adoption of Constitution, May 3, 1791, by Jan Matejko (1838-1893).

**1991, May 2** **Litho.** ***Perf. 11½***

| | | | | |
|---|---|---|---|---|
| **3035** | A961 | 2000z brown & ver | .50 | .20 |
| **3036** | A961 | 2500z brown & ver | .70 | .40 |

**Souvenir Sheet**

**3037** A961 3000z multicolored 1.00 1.00

May 3, 1791 Polish constitution, bicent.

**1991, May 6** **Litho.** ***Perf. 11½x11***

**3038** A962 1000z multicolored *1.25* .20

Europa.

2000 zł · POLSKA
KRAKÓW · 1991

European Conference for Protection of Cultural Heritage, Cracow — A963

**1991, May 27** **Litho.** ***Perf. 11½***

**3039** A963 2000z blue & lake .65 .25

POLSKA
ATLANTYK
2000 zł
OPERACJA „PIORUNA" PRZECIWKO „BISMARCKOWI"

Sinking of the Bismarck, 50th Anniv. — A964

**1991, May 27**

**3040** A964 2000z multicolored .65 .25

Jan Paweł II
Polska
1000 zł

A965

2000 zł · POLSKA
UKŁAD W SPRAWIE ANTARKTYKI 1961 - 1991

A966

Designs: 1000z, Pope John Paul II. 2000z, Pope wearing white.

**1991, June 1** **Litho.** ***Perf. 11½x11***

| | | | | |
|---|---|---|---|---|
| **3041** | A965 | 1000z multicolored | .30 | .20 |
| **3042** | A965 | 2000z multicolored | .70 | .30 |

**1991, June 21** **Litho.** ***Perf. 11½***

**3043** A966 2000z multicolored .60 .25

Antarctic Treaty, 30th anniv.

2500 zł POLSKA
500 LAT PAPIERNICTWA W POLSCE

Polish Paper Industry, 500th Anniv.
A967

**1991, July 8**

**3044** A967 2500z lake & gray .75 .30

Polska 2500 zł
OFIAROM STALINIZMU

Victims of Stalin — A968

**1991, July 29** **Litho.** ***Perf. 11½x12***

**3045** A968 2500z black & red .65 .25

Souvenir Sheet

Polska
Jan Paweł II
3500 zł
VI ŚWIATOWY DZIEŃ MŁODZIEŻY CZĘSTOCHOWA 1991

Pope John Paul II — A969

**1991, Aug. 15** **Photo.** ***Perf. 11½x11***

**3046** A969 3500z multicolored 1.00 1.00

POLSKA
2500 zł

Basketball, Cent. — A970

**1991, Aug. 19** **Litho.** ***Perf. 11x11½***

**3047** A970 2500z multicolored .65 .25

3000 ZŁ
XVI OGÓLNOPOLSKA WYSTAWA FILATELISTYCZNA BYDGOSZCZ '91
POLSKA

Leon Wyczolkowski (1852-1936), painter — A971

**1991, Sept. 7** **Photo.** ***Perf. 11½x12***

| | | | | |
|---|---|---|---|---|
| **3048** | A971 | 3000z olive brown | .80 | .40 |
| *a.* | | Sheet of 4 | 3.50 | 3.50 |

16th Polish Philatelic Exhibition, Bydgoszcz '91.

Polska
2500 zł
KAZIMIERZ TWARDOWSKI
1866-1938

Kazimierz Twardowski (1866-1938) — A972

**1991, Oct. 10** ***Perf. 11x11½***

**3049** A972 2500z sepia & blk .85 .30

Butterflies — A973

| | | |
|---|---|---|
| **1991, Nov. 16** | | **Litho.** | **Perf. 12½** |
| 3050 A973 | 1000z Papilio | | |
| | machaon | .20 | .20 |
| 3051 A973 | 1000z Mormonia | .20 | .20 |
| 3052 A973 | 1500z Vanessa | | |
| | sponsa | .30 | .20 |
| 3053 A973 | 1500z cardui | .30 | .20 |
| 3054 A973 | 1500z iphiclides | | |
| | podalirius | .30 | .20 |
| 3055 A973 | 2500z Panaxia | | |
| | dominula | .50 | .30 |
| a. | Block of 6, #3050-3055 | 2.75 | 2.00 |

Nativity
Scene, by
Francesco
Solimena
A974

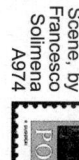

**1991, Nov. 25** **Photo.** **Perf. 11**
3057 A974 1000z multicolored .40 .20

**Souvenir Sheet**
3056 A973 15,000z Aporia
crataegi 2.75 2.75

No. 3056 has a holographic image on the stamp and comes se-tenant with a Phila Nippon '91 label. The image may be affected by soaking in water. Varieties such as missing hologram, double and shifted images, and imperfs exist.
On Jan. 15, 1994, the Polish postal administration demonetized No. 3056.

Polish Armed Forces at Tobruk, 50th Anniv. — A975

**1991, Dec. 10** **Photo.**
3058 A975 2000z Gen. Stanislaw
Kopanski .85 .30

World War II Commanders: 2000z, Brig. Gen. Michal Tokarzowski-Karaszewicz (1093-1964). 2500z, Gen. Kazimierz Sosukowski (1885-1969). 3000z, Gen. Stefan Rowecki (1895-1944). 5000z, Gen. Tadeusz Komorowski (1895-1966). 6500z, Brig. Gen. Leopold Okulicki (1898-1946).

**1991, Dec. 20** **Litho.**
3059 A976 2000z vermilion & blk .75 .40
3060 A976 2500z violet bl & lake .40 .20
3061 A976 3000z magenta & dk
bl .60 .30
3062 A976 5000z olive & brn 1.25 .60
3063 A976 6500z brn org & brn 1.00 .50
Nos. 3059-3063 (5) 4.75 2.50

**1992, Mar. 5** **Photo.** **Perf. 11½x11**
3078 A980 2500z brown .95 .40

Tadeusz
Manteuffel
(1902-1970),
Historian
A980

Famous
Poles
A981

Designs: 1500z, Nicolaus Copernicus, astronomer. 2000z, Frederic Chopin, composer. 2500z, Henryk Sienkiewicz, novelist. 3500z, Marie Sklodowska Curie, scientist. 5000z, Casimir Funk, biochemist.

**1991, Dec. 30** **Photo.** **Perf. 12x11½**
Boy Scouts in Poland, 80th anniv.: 1500z, Lord Robert Baden-Powell, founder of Boy Scouts. 2000z, Andrzej Malkowski (1889-1919), founder of Boy Scouts in Poland. 2500z, Scout standing guard, 1920. 3500z, Soldier scout, 1944.

1992
Winter
Olympics,
Albertville
A979

**1992, Feb. 8** **Litho.** **Perf. 11x11½**
3076 A979 1500z Skiing .35 .20
3077 A979 2500z Hockey .55 .20
See Nos. 3095-3098.

Paintings (self-portraits except for 2200z) by: 700z, Sebastien Bourdon. 1000z, Sir Joshua Reynolds. 1500z, Sir Gottfried Kneller. 2000z, Murillo. 2200z, Rubens. 3000z, Diego de Silva y Velazquez.

**1992, Jan. 16** **Photo.**
3070 A978 700z multicolored .20 .20
3071 A978 1000z multicolored .20 .20
3072 A978 1500z multicolored .25 .20
3073 A978 1500z multicolored .25 .20
3074 A978 2200z multicolored .50 .20
3075 A978 3000z multicolored .75 .25
Nos. 3070-3075 (6) 2.35 1.25

Royalty Type of 1986

**1992, Jan. 15** **Photo. & Engr.** **Perf. 11**
3068 A875 1500z olive green &
brn .45 .20
3069 A875 2000z gray blue & blk .60 .30

Designs: 1500z, Kazimierz II Sprawiedliwy. 2000z, Leszek Bialy.

Paintings
A978

| | | |
|---|---|---|
| 3064 A977 | 1500z multicolored | .45 | .20 |
| 3065 A977 | 2000z multicolored | .55 | .25 |
| 3066 A977 | 2500z multicolored | .70 | .35 |
| 3067 A977 | 3500z multicolored | 1.00 | .55 |
| | Nos. 3064-3067 (4) | 2.70 | 1.35 |

Famous
Poles
A981

**1992, Mar. 5** **Litho.** **Perf. 11x11½**
3079 A981 1500z multicolored .20 .25
3080 A981 2000z multicolored .30 .25
3081 A981 2500z multicolored .30 .40
3082 A981 3500z multicolored .50 .50
a. Pair, #3081-3082 1.00 1.35

**Souvenir Sheet**
3083 A981 5000z multicolored 1.10 1.10
Expo '92, Seville (#3083).

Discovery of America, 500th Anniv. — A982

**1992, May 5**
3084 A982 1500z Columbus,
chart .25 .20
3085 A982 3000z Chart, Santa
Maria .75 .30
a. Pair, #3084-3085 1.25 1.00
Europa.

Waterfalls
A983

**1992, June 1** **Litho.** **Perf. 11½**
3086 A983 2000z Pstrag (trout) .35 .20
3087 A983 2500z Zimorodek
(kingfisher) .45 .25
3088 A983 3000z Jelec (whiting) .70 .90
3089 A983 3500z Pluszcz .90 .25
Nos. 3086-3089 (4) 2.40 .90

Order of
Virtuti
Militari,
Bicent.
A984

Designs: 1500z, Prince Jozef Poniatowski (1763-1813). 3000z, Marshal Jozef Pilsudski (1867-1935). No. 3092, Black Madonna of Czestochowa.

**1992, June 18**
3090 A984 1500z multi .25 .20
3091 A984 3000z multi .50 .25

**Souvenir Sheet** **Imperf**
3092 A984 20,000z multi 4.25 4.25
No. 3092 contains one 39x60mm stamp.

Children's
Drawings of
Love — A985

**1992, July 25** **Litho.** **Perf. 11½x11**
3093 A985 1500z multicolored .25 .20
3094 A985 3000z multicolored .50 .35
a. Pair, #3093-3094

1500z, Heart between woman and man. 3000z, Butterfly, animals with sun and rain.

OLYMPHILEX '92, Barcelona — A986

**1992, July 29**
3099 A986 20,000z Runners 4.25 4.25
Exists imperf. Value $9.50.

Olympics Type of 1992
**1992, June 26** **Litho.** **Perf. 11½x11**
3095 A979 1500z Fencing .20 .20
3096 A979 1500z Boxing .20 .20
3097 A979 2500z Sprinting .45 .20
3098 A979 3000z Cycling .75 .40
Nos. 3095-3098 (4) 1.60 1.05

**Souvenir Sheet**
1992 Summer Olympics, Barcelona.

**1992, Aug. 5** **Photo.** **Perf. 11x11½**
3100 A987 1500z multicolored .40 .20
Janusz Korczak (1879-1942), Physician, Concentration Camp Victim — A987

**1992, Aug. 19**
3101 A988 3000z multicolored .70 .35
Polish Emigrants Assoc. World Meeting — A988

**1992, Aug. 14** **Perf. 11½x11**
3102 A989 3000z multicolored .75 .40
World War II Combatants World Meeting — A989

## Stefan Cardinal Wyszynski (1901-1981) — A990

3000z, Pope John Paul II embracing person.

Litho.
1992, Aug. 15
3103  A990  1500z multicolored  .40  .20
3104  A990  3000z multicolored  .85  .40
a.  Block of 2, #3103-3104 + 2 labels  1.25

6th World Youth Cong., Czestochowa (#3104).

## Adampol, Polish Village in Turkey, 150th Anniv. A991

1992, Sept. 15  Photo.  Perf. 11x11½
3105  A991  3500z multicolored  .85  .40

## World Post Day — A992

Perf. 11½x11
1992, Oct. 9
3106  A992  3500z multicolored  .85  .40

## Bruno Schulz (1892-1942), Author — A993

Perf. 11x11½
1992, Oct. 26  Litho.
3107  A993  3000z multicolored  .70  .35

## Polish Sculptures, Natl. Museum, Warsaw A994

Designs: 2000z, Seated Girl, by Henryk Wicinski. 2500z, Portrait of Tytus Czyzewski, by Zbigniew Pronaszko. 3000z, Polish Nike, by Edward Wittig. 3500z, The Nude, by August Zamoyski.

1992, Oct. 29  Perf. 11½
3108  A994  2000z multicolored  .55  .35
3109  A994  2500z multicolored  .70  .35
3110  A994  3000z multicolored  .80  .40
3111  A994  3500z multicolored  .95  .50
a.  Souvenir sheet of 4, #3108-3111  3.00  1.50
Nos. 3108-3111 (4)  3.00  1.55

Polska '93 (#3111a).

## Posters — A995

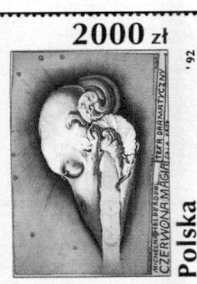

Designs: 1500z, 10th Theatrical Summer in Zamosc, by Jan Mlodozeniec, vert. 2000z, Red Magic, by Franciszek Starowieyski. 2500z, Circus, by Waldemar Swierzy, vert. 3500z, Mannequins, by Henryk Tomaszewski.

1992, Oct. 30  Perf. 13½
3112  A995  1500z multicolored  .35  .20
3113  A995  2000z multicolored  .45  .25
3114  A995  2500z multicolored  .60  .30
3115  A995  3500z multicolored  .80  .40
Nos. 3112-3115 (4)  2.20  1.15

## Illustrations by Edward Lutczyn — A996

Designs: 1500z, Girl using snake as jump rope. 2000z, Boy on rocking horse with rocker reversed. 2500z, Boy using bird as arrow. 3500z, Girl with ladder, wind-up giraffe with keys on back.

1992, Nov. 16  Photo.  Perf. 11
3116  A996  1500z multicolored  .30  .20
3117  A996  2000z multicolored  .40  .25
3118  A996  2500z multicolored  .50  .25
3119  A996  3500z multicolored  .65  .30
Nos. 3116-3119 (4)  1.85  .95

Polska '93.

## Home Army A997

1992, Nov. 20  Litho.  Perf. 13½
3120  A997  1500z shown  .30  .20
3121  A997  3500z Soldiers, diff.  .65  .30
a.  Pair, #3120-3121  .95  .50

Souvenir Sheet
3122  A997  20,000z +500z "WP AK," vert.  4.00  4.00

## Christmas A998

Perf. 11½
1992, Nov. 25  Photo.
3123  A998  1000z multicolored  .20  .20

## A999

Photo.  Perf. 11½x11
Litho.
1992, Dec. 5
3124  A999  1500z Wheat stalks  1.00  .50
3125  A999  3500z Food products  .70  .35

Intl. Conference on Nutrition, Rome.

## A1000

1992, Dec. 10  Litho.
3126  A1000  3000z multicolored  .70  .35

Postal Agreement with the Sovereign Military Order of Malta, Aug. 1, 1991.

## Natl. Arms — A1001

Perf. 12x11½
1992, Dec. 14  Photo.
3127  A1001  2000z 1295  .55  .30
3128  A1001  2500z 15th cent.  .70  .35
3129  A1001  3000z 18th cent.  .85  .40
3130  A1001  3500z 1919  1.00  .45
3131  A1001  5000z 1990  1.40  .65
Nos. 3127-3131 (5)  4.50  2.15

## Polish Philatelic Society, Cent. A1002

Perf. 11½
1993, Jan. 6  Photo.
3132  A1002  1500z multicolored  .50  .25

## 1993 Winter University Games, Zakopane. A1003

Perf. 11½x11
1993, Feb. 5
3133  A1003  3000z multicolored  1.00  .50

## A1004

Design: I Love You.

1993, Feb. 14
3134  A1004  1500z shown  .50  .25
3135  A1004  3000z Heart on envelope  1.00  .50

## Amber — A1005

Various pieces of amber.

Litho.  Perf. 13½
1993, Jan. 29
3136  A1005  1500z multicolored  .40  .20
3137  A1005  2000z multicolored  .55  .30
3138  A1005  2500z multicolored  .70  .35
3139  A1005  3000z multicolored  .85  .40
Nos. 3136-3139 (4)  2.50  1.25

Souvenir Sheet
3140  A1005  20,000z Necklace, map, horiz.  3.50  3.50

Polska '93 (#3140).

## Royalty Type of 1986

Designs: 1500z, Wladyslaw Laskonogi. 2000z, Henryk I Brodaty (1201-38). 2500z, Konrad I Mazowiecki. 3000z, Boleslaw V Wstydliwy.

Photo. & Engr.  Perf. 11
1993, Mar. 25
3141  A875  1500z yel grn & brn  .40  .20
3142  A875  2000z red vio & ind  .55  .30
3143  A875  2500z gray & black  .70  .35
3144  A875  3000z yel brn & brn  .85  .40
Nos. 3141-3144 (4)  2.50  1.25

#3144 printed with se-tenant label for Polska '93.

## Battle of the Arsenal, 50th Anniv. — A1006

Photo.  Perf. 11½
1993, Mar. 26
3145  A1006  1500z multicolored  .40  .20

## Intl. Medieval Knights' Tournament, Golub-Dobrzyn — A1007

Various knights on horseback.

Perf. 11x11½
1993, Mar. 29
3146  A1007  1500z multicolored  .40  .20
3147  A1007  2000z multicolored  .55  .30
3148  A1007  2500z multicolored  .70  .35
3149  A1007  3500z multicolored  .90  .45
Nos. 3146-3149 (4)  2.55  1.30

## City of Szczecin, 750th Anniv. A1008

1993, Apr. 3  Litho.  Perf. 11½x11
3150  A1008  1500z multicolored  .40  .20

**Warsaw Ghetto Uprising, 50th Anniv. — A1009**

**1993, Apr. 19      Litho.      Perf. 14**
3151 A1009 4000z gray, blk & yel    .95   .60
See Israel No. 1163.

**Europa — A1010**

**1993, Apr. 30      Photo.      Perf. 11x11½**
3152 A1010 1500z multicolored    .30   .20
3153 A1010 4000z multicolored    .70   .40
a.   Pair, #3152-3153    1.00   .60
Contemporary art by: No. 3152, A. Szapocznikow and J. Lebenstein. No. 3153, S. Gierowski and B. Linke.

**Polish Parliament (Sejm), 500th Anniv. — A1011**

**1993, May 2      Photo.      Perf. 11**
3154 A1011 2000z multicolored    .55   .30

**Death of Francesco Nullo, 130th Anniv. — A1012**

**1993, May 5      Litho.      Perf. 11x11½**
3155 A1012 2500z multicolored    .70   .35

**Legend of the White Eagle — A1013**

**1993, May 7      Engr.      Perf. 13½**
3156 A1013 50,000z dark brn    9.00   9.00
Polska '93.

**Cadets of Second Polish Republic — A1014**

**1993, May 21      Litho.      Perf. 11x11½**
3157 A1014 2000z multicolored    .55   .30

**Nicolaus Copernicus (1473-1543) — A1015**

**1993, May 24**
3158 A1015 2000z multicolored    .55   .30

**Kornel Makuszynski, 40th Death Anniv. — A1016**

**1993, June 1**
3159 A1016 1500z multicolored    .40   .20
3160 A1016 2000z multicolored    .55   .30
3161 A1016 3000z multicolored    .85   .40
3162 A1016 5000z multicolored    1.40   .70
Nos. 3159-3162 (4)    3.20   1.60
Illustrations: 1500z, Lion, monkey. 2000z, Goat walking. 3000z, Monkey. 5000z, Goat riding bird.

**Pine Cone Type of 1991**

**1993, June 30      Photo.      Perf. 12x11½**
3163 A956 10,000z Pinus cembra    1.75   .75
3164 A956 20,000z Pinus sylves-tris    2.75   1.75

**Birds — A1017**

**1993, July 15      Litho.      Perf. 11**
3165 A1017 1500z Passer montanus    .25   .20
3166 A1017 2000z Motacilla alba    .30   .20
3167 A1017 3000z Dendrocopos syriacus    .50   .25
3168 A1017 4000z Carduelis carduelis    .65   .30
3169 A1017 5000z Sturnus vul-garis    .80   .40
3170 A1017 6000z Pyrrhula pyr-rhula    .95   .50
Nos. 3165-3170 (6)    3.45   1.85

**Polish Natl. Anthem, Bicent. — A1018**

**1993, July 20      Photo.      Perf. 11x11½**
3171 A1018 1500z multicolored    .25   .20
See No. 3206.

**Madonna and Child A1019**

Designs: 1500z, Stone carving from Basil-ica, Lesna Podlaska. 2000z, Statue, Swieta Lipska.

**Perf. 11x11½ Syncopated Type A**

**1993, Aug. 15**
3172 A1019 1500z multicolored    .20   .20
3173 A1019 2000z multicolored    .25   .20

**World Post Day — A1020**

**1993, Oct. 9      Photo. & Engr.      Perf. 11½x11**
3174 A1020 2500z multicolored    .30   .20

**Polish Parachute Brigade A1021**

**Perf. 11x11½, Syncopated Type A**

**1993, Sept. 25**
3175 A1021 1500z multicolored    .25   .20

**Death of St. Hedwig (Jadwiga), 750th Anniv. — A1022**

**1993, Oct. 14      Litho.      Perf. 14**
3176 A1022 2500z multicolored    .35   .20
See Germany No. 1816.

**35th Intl. Jazz Jamboree — A1023**

**1993, Sept. 27      Litho.**
**Perf. 11½ Syncopated Type A**
3177 A1023 2000z multicolored    .25   .20

**Election of Pope John Paul II, 15th Anniv. — A1024**

**Souvenir Sheet**

**1993, Oct. 16**
3178 A1024 20,000z multicolored    3.00   2.00

**1993, Nov. 11**
3179 A1025 4000z Eagle, crown    .50   .25
A1025

**Souvenir Sheet**
3180 A1025 20,000z Dove    4.00   4.00
Independence, 75th anniv. No. 3180 has a continuous design.

**1993, Nov. 25**
3181 A1026 1500z multicolored    .25   .20
Christmas.
A1026

**Posters A1027**

**1993, Dec. 10**
3182 A1027 2000z multicolored    .30   .20
3183 A1027 5000z multicolored    .65   .30
Designs: 2000z, "Come and see Polish mountains." 5000z, Alban Berg Wozzeck.
See Nos. 3203-3204, 3259-3260.

**"I Love You" — A1028**

Basilica of St. Brigida, Gdansk A1044

**1994, Aug. 28**
3209 A1044 4000z multicolored .50 .25

Modern Olympic Games, Cent. A1045

*Perf. 11x11½ Syncopated Type A*
**1994, Sept. 5**
3210 A1045 4000z multicolored .70 .35

Krzysztof Komeda (1931-69), Jazz Musician — A1046

*Perf. 11½ Syncopated Type A*    Litho.
**1994, Sept. 22**
3211 A1046 6000z multicolored .70 .35

Aquarium Fish — A1047

Designs: No. 3212a, Ancistrus dolichopterus. b. Pterophyllum scalare. c, Xiphophorus helleri, paracheirodon innesi. d, Poecilia reticulata.

*Perf. 11½x11 Syncopated Type A*    Litho.
**1994, Sept. 28**
3212   Strip of 4    2.00 1.50
a.-d. A1047 4000z any single .50 .40

World Post Day — A1048

**1994, Oct. 9**
3213 A1048 4000z Postal Arms, 1858 .50 .25

---

1994 World Soccer Cup Championships, U.S. — A1039

*Perf. 11½x11 Syncopated Type A*
**1994, June 17**
3202 A1039 6000z multicolored .75 .40

Poster Art Type of 1993

4000z, Mr. Fabre, by Wiktor Gorka. 6000z, VIII OISTAT Congress, by Hubert Hilscher, horiz.

*Perf. 11x11½, 11½x11½ Syncopated Type A*
**1994, July 4**
3203 A1027 4000z multicolored .60 .30
3204 A1027 6000z multicolored .90 .45

Florian Znaniecki (1882-1958), Sociologist A1040

*Perf. 11½ Syncopated Type A*    Litho.
**1994, July 15**
3205 A1040 9000z multicolored 1.10 .55

Polish Natl. Anthem Type of 1993

Design: 2500z, Battle of Raclawice, 1794.

*Perf. 11x11½*    Photo.
**1994, July 20**
3206 A1018 2500z multicolored .35 .20

A1041

A1042

A1043

*Perf. 11½x11 Syncopated Type A*    Litho.
**1994, Aug. 1**
3207 A1042 2500z Natl. arms .35 .20
Warsaw Uprising, 50th anniv.

**1994, Aug. 16**
3208 A1043 4000z PHILAKOREA '94 .50 .25
Stamp Day.

---

sighting device, with profile of Copernicus (1473-1543).

*Perf. 11½x11 Syncopated Type A*    Litho.
**1994, Apr. 30**
3193 A1033 2500z multicolored .45 .25
3194 A1033 6000z multicolored 1.10 .60

St. Mary's Sanctuary A1034

*Perf. 11½x11½ Syncopated Type A*    Litho.
**1994, May 16**
3195 A1034 4000z multicolored .85 .40

Battle of Monte Cassino, 50th Anniv. A1035

*Perf. 11x11½ Syncopated Type A*
**1994, May 18**
3196 A1035 6000z multicolored .80 .40

Traditional Dances A1036

*Perf. 11½ Syncopated Type A*
**1994, May 25**
3197 A1036 3000z Mazurka .35 .20
3198 A1036 4000z Goralski .50 .25
3199 A1036 9000z Krakowiak 1.25 .65
Nos. 3197-3199 (3) 2.10 1.05

ILO, 75th Anniv. A1037

*Perf. 11½x11 Syncopated Type A*    Litho.
**1994, June 7**
3200 A1037 6000z multicolored .75 .35

Polish Electricians Assoc., 75th Anniv. A1038

*Perf. 11x11½ Syncopated Type A*
**1994, June 10**
3201 A1038 4000z multicolored .55 .30

---

A1029

*Perf. 11½x11 Syncopated Type A*    Litho.
**1994, Jan. 14**
3184 A1028 1500z multicolored .25 .20

*Perf. 11½x11*    Photo.    *Perf. 11½x11*
**1994, Feb. 12**
3185 A1029 2500z Cross-country skiing .30 .20
3186 A1029 5000z Ski jumping .60 .30

**Souvenir Sheet**
3187 A1029 10,000z Downhill skiing 1.50 1.50
1994 Winter Olympics, Lillehammer. Intl. Olympic Committee, cent. (#2187).

Kosciuszko Insurrection, Bicent. — A1030

*Perf. 11½x11 Syncopated Type A*    Photo.
**1994, Mar. 24**
3188 A1030 2000z multicolored .30 .20

Zamosc Academy, 400th Anniv. — A1031

*Perf. 11½ Syncopated Type A*
**1994, Mar. 15**
3189 A1031 5000z brn, blk & gray .65 .30

Gen. Jozef Bem (1794-1850) — A1032

Royalty Type of 1986 with Denomination at Bottom

**Photo. & Engr.**
*Perf. 11*
**1994, Mar. 14**
3190 A1032 5000z multicolored .65 .30

**1994, Apr. 15**
3191 A875 2500z Leszek Czarny .30 .20
3192 A875 5000z Przemysl II .60 .30

Inventions A1033

Europa: 2500z, Petroleum lamp, invented by I. Lukasiewicz (1822-82). 6000z, Astronomical

**1994, Oct. 24 Photo. Perf. 11x11½**
St. Maximilian Kolbe (1894-1941), Concentration Camp Victim — A1049
3214 A1049 2500z multicolored .35 .20

Pigeons
A1050
**1994, Oct. 28 Perf. 11x11½**
3215 A1050 Block of 4 2.25 1.10
a.-b. A1050 4000z any single .45 .20
c.-d. A1050 6000z any single .65 .30
a. Mewka polska b. Krymka białostacka. c. Srebniak polski d. Sokot gdański. 10,000z, Polski gołąb pocztowy.

Souvenir Sheet
3216 A1050 10,000z multicolored 1.25 .60

European Union A1052
**1994, Nov. 25 Perf. 11x11½ Syncopated Type A**
3217 A1051 2500z multicolored .35 .20

Christmas
A1051
**1994, Dec. 15**
3218 A1052 6000z multicolored .75 .35

Love Stamp — A1053
**1995, Jan. 31 Perf. 11½x11 Syncopated Type A**
3219 A1053 35g dk bl & rose car .40 .20

Hydro-Meteorological Service, 75th Anniv. — A1054
**Perf. 11x11½ Syncopated Type A**
**1995, Jan. 31**
3220 A1054 60g multicolored .50 .25

**1995, Feb. 10**
3221 A1055 45g multicolored .50 .25
Poland's Renewed Access to the Sea, 75th Anniv. A1055

Polish Royalty Type of 1986 with Denomination at Bottom
**Photo. & Engr. Perf. 11**
**1995, Feb. 28**
3222 A875 35g Wacław II .40 .20
3223 A875 45g Władysław I Lo-tiek .45 .25
3224 A875 60g Kazimierz III, the Great .65 .30
3225 A875 80g Ludwik Wegierski .80 .40
Nos. 3222-3225 (4) 2.30 1.15

St. John of God (1495-1550), Initiator of Order — A1056
**1995, Mar. 8 Perf. 12x11½ Syncopated Type A**
3226 A1056 60g multicolored .70 .35

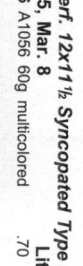

Easter Eggs A1057
Each stamp showing various designs on 3 eggs.
**1995, Mar. 16 Perf. 11½ Syncopated Type A**
**Background Color**
3227 A1057 35g dull red .35 .20
3228 A1057 35g violet .35 .20
3229 A1057 45g bright blue .45 .25
3230 A1057 45g blue green .45 .25
Nos. 3227-3230 (4) 1.60 .90

Pinecone Type of 1991 **Photo. Perf. 11½**
**1995, Mar. 27**
3231 A956 45g Larix decidua .45 .25
3232 A956 80g Pinus mugo .80 .40

Katyn Forest Massacre, 55th Anniv. A1058
**1995, Mar. 27 Photo. Perf. 11½**
**1995, Apr. 13 Perf. 11½ Syncopated Type A**
3233 A1058 80g multicolored .85 .45

Europa A1060
**1995, Apr. 28 Perf. 11x11½ Syncopated Type A Litho.**
3234 A1060 35g shown .35 .25
3235 A1060 80g Flowers in hel-met .85 .50

Return of Western Polish Territories, 50th Anniv. — A1061
**1995, May 6 Perf. 11½ Syncopated Type A Litho.**
3236 A1061 45g multicolored .50 .25

Pope John Paul II, 75th Birthday A1062
**1995, May 18 Perf. 11½ Syncopated Type A Litho.**
3237 A1062 80g multicolored .85 .45

Groteska Theatre of Fairy Tales, 50th Anniv. — A1063
Designs: No. 3238, Stage scene. No. 3239, on barrel, vert. No. 3240, Puppet leaning flower, vert. No. 3241, Character holding flower, vert. Two performing.
**1995, May 25**
3238 A1063 35g multicolored .35 .20
3239 A1063 35g multicolored .35 .20
3240 A1063 45g multicolored .50 .25
3241 A1063 45g multicolored .50 .25
a. A1063 Pair, #3240-3241 1.00 .50
Nos. 3238-3241 (4) 1.70 .90

Polish Railways, 150th Anniv. A1064
Designs: 35g, Warsaw-Vienna steam train, 1945. 60g, Combustion fuel powered train, 1927. 80g, Electric train, 1936. 1z, Euro City Sobieski, Warsaw-Vienna, 1992.
**1995, June 9**
3242 A1064 35g multicolored .35 .20
3243 A1064 60g multicolored .65 .30
a. A1064 Pair, #3242-3243 1.00 .50
3244 A1064 80g multicolored .85 .45
3245 A1064 1z multicolored 1.10 .55
a. A1064 Pair, #3244-3245 2.00 1.00
Nos. 3242-3245 (4) 2.95 1.50

UN, 50th Anniv. A1065
**1995, June 26 Perf. 11½ Syncopated Type A Litho.**
3246 A1065 80g multicolored .90 .45

Handlowy Bank, Warsaw, 125th Anniv. — A1066
**1995, June 30 Perf. 11½ Syncopated Type A Litho.**
3247 A1066 45g multicolored .50 .25

Polish Peasants' Movement, Cent. A1067
**1995, July 13 Perf. 11½ Syncopated Type A Litho.**
3248 A1067 45g multicolored .50 .25

Polish Natl. Anthem, Bicent. A1068
**1995, July 20 Photo. Perf. 11½**
3249 A1068 35g multicolored .40 .20

Deciduous Trees — A1069
**1995, July 31 Perf. 12x11½**
3250 A1069 B Quercus petraea .40 .20
3251 A1069 A Sorbus aucuparia .50 .25
On day of issue #3250 was valued at 35g; #3551 at 45g.

St. Mary of Consolation, Holy Trinity and All Saints Basilica, Leżajsk A1070
**1995, Aug. 2 Perf. 11½ Syncopated Type A Litho.**
3252 A1070 45g multicolored .45 .20

Design: 45g, Józef Piłsudski (1867-1935)
Battle of Warsaw, 75th Anniv. A1071
**1995, Aug. 14 Perf. 11½ Syncopated Type A Litho.**
3253 A1071 45g multicolored .45 .20

# POLAND

Horse-Equipage Driving World Championships, Poznan — A1072

Designs: 60g, Horses pulling carriage, men in formal attire. 80g, Marathon race through water, around pylons.

**1995, Aug. 23**   *Perf. 11½ Syncopated Type A*   *Litho.*
| | | | |
|---|---|---|---|
| 3254 | A1072 | 60g multicolored | .65 .30 |
| 3255 | A1072 | 80g multicolored | .85 .45 |
| a. | | Pair, #3254-3255 | 1.50 .75 |

18th All Polish Philatelic Exhibition, Warsaw A1073

Designs: 35g, Warsaw Technical University, School of Architecture. 1z, Warsaw Castle Place, Old Town, horiz.

**1995, Aug. 30**   *Perf. 11½ Syncopated Type A*   *Litho.*
| | | | |
|---|---|---|---|
| 3256 | A1073 | 35g multicolored | .35 .20 |

**Souvenir Sheet**
| | | | |
|---|---|---|---|
| 3257 | A1073 | 1z multicolored | 1.10 .55 |

11th World Congress of Space Flight Participants, Warsaw A1074

**1995, Sept. 10**   *Perf. 11½ Syncopated Type A*   *Litho.*
| | | | |
|---|---|---|---|
| 3258 | A1074 | 80g multicolored | .80 .40 |

**Poster Art type of 1993**

35g, The Crazy Locomotive, by Jan Sawka. 45g, The Wedding, by Eugeniusz Get Stankiewicz.

**1995, Sept. 27**   *Perf. 11½ Syncopated Type A*   *Litho.*
| | | | |
|---|---|---|---|
| 3259 | A1027 | 35g multicolored | .35 .20 |
| 3260 | A1027 | 45g multicolored | .50 .25 |

13th Intl. Chopin Piano Festival A1076

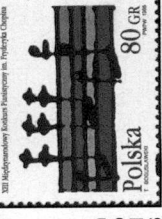

**1995, Oct. 1**   *Perf. 11½ Syncopated Type A*   *Litho.*
| | | | |
|---|---|---|---|
| 3261 | A1076 | 80g Polonaise score | .80 .40 |

World Post Day 45g, Postman in uniform, Polish Kingdom. 80g, Feather, wax seal of Stanislaw II Poniatowski.

**1995, Oct. 9**
| | | | |
|---|---|---|---|
| 3262 | A1077 | 45g multicolored | .45 .20 |
| 3263 | A1077 | 80g multicolored | .80 .40 |

**1995, Oct. 26**
| | | | |
|---|---|---|---|
| 3264 | A1078 | 45g multicolored | .45 .20 |

Acrobatic Sports World Championships, Wroclaw.

Janusz Groszkowski (1898-1984), Physicist — A1079

**1995, Nov. 10**   *Perf. 11½ Syncopated Type A*   *Litho.*
| | | | |
|---|---|---|---|
| 3265 | A1079 | 45g multicolored | .50 .25 |

Christmas — A1080

**1995, Nov. 27**
| | | | |
|---|---|---|---|
| 3266 | A1080 | 35g Nativity | .35 .20 |
| 3267 | A1080 | 45g Magi, tree | .50 .25 |
| a. | A1080 | Pair, Nos. 3266-3267 | .86 .46 |

No. 3267a is a continuous design.

Songbird Chicks — A1081

Designs: a, 35g, Parus caeruleus. b, 45g, Aegithalos caudatus. c, 60g, Lanius excubitor. d, 80g, Coccothraustes.

**1995, Dec. 15**
| | | | |
|---|---|---|---|
| 3268 | A1081 | Block of 4, #a.-d. | 2.25 1.10 |

See No. 3377.

Krzysztof Kamil Baczynski (1921-44), Poet A1082

**1996, Jan. 22**   *Perf. 11½ Syncopated Type A*   *Litho.*
| | | | |
|---|---|---|---|
| 3269 | A1082 | 35g multicolored | .35 .20 |

Love — A1083

**1996, Jan. 31**
| | | | |
|---|---|---|---|
| 3270 | A1083 | 40g Cherries | .40 .20 |

Architecture A1084

40g, Romanesque style church, Inowlodz, 11-12th cent. 55g, Gothic syle, St. Virgin Mary's Church, Cracow, 14th cent. 70g, Renaissance period, St. Sigismundus Chapel of Cracow, Wawel Castle, 1519-33. 1z, Order of Holy Sacrament Nuns Baroque Church, Warsaw, 1688-92.

**1996, Feb. 27**   *Perf. 11½ Syncopated Type A*   *Litho.*
| | | | |
|---|---|---|---|
| 3271 | A1084 | 40g multicolored | .35 .20 |
| 3272 | A1084 | 55g multicolored | .50 .25 |
| 3273 | A1084 | 70g multicolored | .65 .30 |
| 3274 | A1084 | 1z multicolored | .90 .45 |
| | | Nos. 3271-3274 (4) | 2.40 1.20 |

Polish Sailing Ships A10bb

Designs: a, 40g, Topmast schooner, "Oceania," 1985. b, 55c, Staysail schooner, "Zawisza Czarny," 1961. c, 70g, Schooner, "General Zaruski," 1939. d, 75g, Brig, "Fryderyk Chopin," 1992.

**1996, Mar. 11**
| | | | |
|---|---|---|---|
| 3275 | A1085 | Strip of 4, #a.-d. | 2.20 1.10 |

Warsaw, Capital of Poland, 400th Anniv. A1086

**1996, Mar. 18**
| | | | |
|---|---|---|---|
| 3276 | A1086 | 55g multicolored | .55 .25 |

Signs of the Zodiac — A1087

**1996**   *Photo.*   *Perf. 12x11½*
| | | | |
|---|---|---|---|
| 3277 | A1087 | 5g Aquarius | .20 .20 |
| 3278 | A1087 | 10g Pisces | .20 .20 |
| 3279 | A1087 | 20g Taurus | .20 .20 |
| 3280 | A1087 | 25g Gemini | .25 .20 |
| 3281 | A1087 | 30g Cancer | .30 .20 |
| 3282 | A1087 | 40g Virgo | .40 .20 |
| 3283 | A1087 | 50g Leo | .50 .20 |
| 3284 | A1087 | 55g Libra | .55 .20 |
| 3285 | A1087 | 70g Aries | .65 .50 |
| 3286 | A1087 | 1z Scorpio | .95 .50 |
| 3287 | A1087 | 2z Sagittarius | 1.90 .95 |
| 3288 | A1087 | 5z Capricorn | 4.75 2.40 |
| | | Nos. 3277-3288 (12) | 10.85 5.85 |

Design will dissolve when soaked on at least three denominations, 5g, 20g and 25g, from the second printing which is on fluorescent paper.

Issued: 70g, 3/21; 20g, 4/21; 25g, 5/10; 30g, 5/20; 40g, 50g, 5/31; 55g, 6/10; 1z, 6/20; 2z, 6/28; 5z, 7/10; 5g, 7/19; 10g, 7/31.

Famous Women A1088

Europa: 40g, Hanka Ordonowa (1902-50), singer. 1z, Pola Negri (1896-1987), actress.

**1996, Apr. 30**   *Perf. 11½ Syncopated Type A*   *Litho.*
| | | | |
|---|---|---|---|
| 3289 | A1088 | 40g multicolored | .40 .25 |
| 3290 | A1088 | 1z multicolored | 1.00 .50 |

3rd Silesian Uprising, 75th Anniv. A1089

**1996, May 2**   *Perf. 11 ½ Syncopated Type A*   *Litho.*
| | | | |
|---|---|---|---|
| 3291 | A1089 | 55g multicolored | 60 .30 |

UNICEF, 50th Anniv. — A1090

Illustrations from tales of Jan Brzechwa. No. 3292, Cat and mouse. No. 3293, Man at table, waiters. No. 3294, People with "onion heads." No. 3295, Chef, duck, vegetables at table. No. 3296, Man talking to bird with human head. No. 3297, Fox standing in front of bears.

**1996, May 31**
| | | | |
|---|---|---|---|
| 3292 | A1090 | 40g multicolored | .35 .20 |
| 3293 | A1090 | 40g multicolored | .35 .25 |
| 3294 | A1090 | 55g multicolored | .50 .25 |
| 3295 | A1090 | 55g multicolored | .50 .30 |
| 3296 | A1090 | 70g multicolored | .65 .30 |
| 3297 | A1090 | 70g multicolored | .65 .30 |
| | | Nos. 3292-3297 (6) | 3.00 1.50 |

Drawings by Stanislaw Noakowski (1867-1928) A1091

Designs: 40g, Renaissance building. 55g, Renaissance bedroom. 70g, Gothic village church. 1z, Stanislaw August Library, 18th cent.

**1996, June 28**
| | | | |
|---|---|---|---|
| 3298 | A1091 | 40g multicolored | .35 .20 |
| 3299 | A1091 | 55g multicolored | .50 .25 |
| 3300 | A1091 | 70g multicolored | .65 .30 |
| 3301 | A1091 | 1z multicolored | .90 .45 |
| | | Nos. 3298-3301 (4) | 2.40 1.20 |

## 1996 Summer Olympic Games, Atlanta A1092

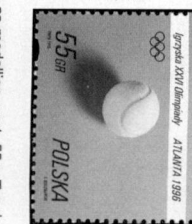

40g, Discus as medallion, vert. 55g, Tennis ball. 70g, Polish flag, Olympic rings. 1z, Tire & wheel of mountain bicycle, vert.

1996, July 5
| 3302 | A1092 | 40g multicolored | .35 | .20 |
| 3303 | A1092 | 55g multicolored | .50 | .25 |
| 3304 | A1092 | 70g multicolored | .65 | .30 |
| 3305 | A1092 | 1z multicolored | .90 | .45 |
| | | Nos. 3302-3305 (4) | 2.40 | 1.20 |

## OLYMPHILEX '96, Atlanta — A1093

1996, July 5
| 3306 | A1093 | 1z multicolored | .90 | .45 |

## National Anthem, Bicent. A1094

1996, July 20  Photo.  Perf. 11x11½
| 3307 | A1094 | 40g multicolored | .35 | .20 |

## Madonna and Child, St. Mary's Ascension Church, Przeczyce A1095

1996, Aug. 2
| 3308 | A1095 | 40g multicolored | .40 | .20 |

## Royalty Type of 1986

Designs: 40g, Jadwiga. 55g, Wladyslaw II Jagiello. 70g, Wladyslaw II Warnenczyk. 1z, Kazimierz Jagiellonczyk.

1996, Aug. 29  Engr.  Perf. 11
| 3309 | A875 | 40g olive brown & brown | .40 | .20 |
| 3310 | A875 | 55g red violet & violet | .55 | .25 |
| 3311 | A875 | 70g gray & black | .65 | .30 |
| 3312 | A875 | 1z yellow green & green | .95 | .50 |
| | | Nos. 3309-3312 (4) | 2.55 | 1.25 |

## Mountain Scenes, Tatra Natl. Park A1096

Perf. 11½x11 Syncopated Type A
1996, Sept. 5  Litho.
| 3313 | A1096 | 40g Giewont | .35 | .20 |
| 3314 | A1096 | 40g Krzesanica | .35 | .20 |
| 3315 | A1096 | 55g Swinica | .50 | .25 |
| 3316 | A1096 | 55g Koscielec | .50 | .25 |
| 3317 | A1096 | 70g Rysy | .65 | .30 |
| 3318 | A1096 | 70g Miguszowieckie Szczyty | .65 | .30 |
| | | Nos. 3313-3318 (6) | 3.00 | 1.50 |

## Zbigniew Seifert (1946-79), Jazz Musician A1097

1996, Sept. 25
| 3319 | A1097 | 70g multicolored | .65 | .30 |

## Post and Telecommunications Museum, Wroclaw, 75th Anniv. — A1098

ŚWIATOWY DZIEŃ POCZTY

Paintings: 40g, Horse Exchange and Post Station, by M. Walorski. 12+20g, Stagecoach in Jagniatkowo, by Prof. Tager.

1996, Oct. 9  Photo.  Perf. 12x11½
| 3320 | A1098 | 40g multicolored | .35 | .20 |

Souvenir Sheet
Perf. 11x11½
| 3321 | A1098 | 1z +20g multi | 1.15 | .60 |

Nos. 3321 contains one 43x31mm stamp.

## Christmas A1099

Perf. 11½x11½ Syncopated Type A
1996, Nov. 27  Litho.
| 3322 | A1099 | 40g Santa in sleigh | .40 | .20 |
| 3323 | A1099 | 55g Carolers | .50 | .25 |

## Bison Bonasus A1100

1996, Dec. 4
| 3324 | A1100 | 55g shown | .50 | .25 |
| 3325 | A1100 | 55g Facing | .50 | .25 |
| 3326 | A1100 | 55g Two animals | .50 | .25 |
| 3327 | A1100 | 55g Adult male | .50 | .25 |
| a. | | Strip of 4, #3324-3327 | 2.00 | 1.00 |

## Wislawa Szymborska, 1996 Nobel Laureate in Literature A1101

1996, Dec. 10
| 3328 | A1101 | 1z multicolored | .95 | .50 |

## Queen of Hearts A1102

Perf. 11½x11½ Syncopated Type A
1997, Jan. 14  Litho.
| 3329 | A1102 | B King of Hearts | .40 | .20 |
| 3330 | A1102 | A Queen of Hearts | .90 | .25 |
| a. | | Pair, #3329-3330 | 3.60 | |
| | | Complete booklet, 4 #3330a | |

Nos. 3329-3330 sold for 40g and 55g, respectively, on day of issue.

## Easter Traditions A1103

50g, Man, woman in traditional costumes holding palms. 60g, Decorating eggs. 80g, Blessing the Easter meal. 1.10z, Man pouring water on woman.

Perf. 11½x11½ Syncopated Type A
1997, Mar. 14  Litho.
| 3331 | A1103 | 50g multicolored | .40 | .20 |
| 3332 | A1103 | 60g multicolored | .50 | .25 |
| 3333 | A1103 | 80g multicolored | .65 | .30 |
| 3334 | A1103 | 1.10z multicolored | .90 | .45 |
| | | Nos. 3331-3334 (4) | 2.45 | 1.20 |

## St. Adalbert (956-97) A1105

A1104

50g, St. Adalbert among heathen, horiz.

1997  Engr.  Perf. 11x11½, 11½x11
| 3335 | A1104 | 50g brown | .50 | .25 |
| 3336 | A1104 | 60g slate | .60 | .30 |
| 3337 | A1105 | 1.10z purple | 1.00 | .50 |
| | | Nos. 3335-3337 (3) | 2.10 | 1.05 |

See Czech Republic No. 3012, Germany No. 1964, Hungary No. 3569, Vatican City No. 1040.
Issued: #3335-3336, 4/19; #3337, 4/23.

## Stories and Legends A1106

Europa: 50g, shown. 1.10z, Mermaid.
Perf. 11½ Syncopated Type A
1997, May 5
| 3338 | A1106 | 50g multicolored | .50 | .40 |
| 3339 | A1106 | 1.10z multicolored | 1.25 | .60 |

## 46th Eucharistic Congress — A1107

1997, May 6
| 3340 | A1107 | 50g multicolored | .50 | .25 |

## Pope John Paul II — A1108

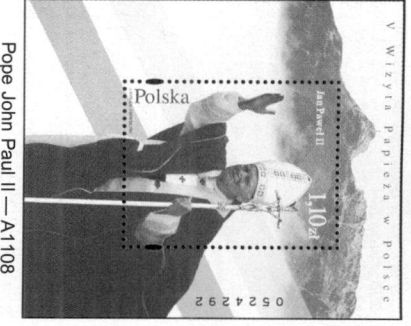

1997, May 28  Souvenir Sheet
| 3341 | A1108 | 1.10z multicolored | 1.25 | 1.25 |

## City of Gdansk, 1000th Anniv. — A1109

Design: 1.10z, View of city, horiz.
1997, Apr. 18
| 3342 | A1109 | 50g multicolored | .50 | .25 |

Souvenir Sheet
| 3343 | A1109 | 1.10z multicolored | 2.00 | 1.00 |

## Polish Country Estates — A1110

1997  Photo.  Perf. 11½x11, 11x11½
| 3344 | A1110 | 50g Lopusznej | .40 | .30 |
| 3345 | A1110 | 60g Zyrzyna | .50 | .40 |
| 3346 | A1110 | 1.10z Ozarowie | .75 | .60 |
| 3347 | A1110 | 1.70z Tulowicach | 1.10 | 1.00 |
| 3348 | A1110 | 2.20z Kuznocinie | 1.40 | 1.20 |
| 3349 | A1110 | 10z Koszutach | 6.50 | 5.00 |
| | | Nos. 3344-3349 (6) | 10.65 | 8.55 |

Issued: 50g, 60g, 4/26/97; 1.10z, 1.70z, 2.20z, 10z, 5/23/97.
See Nos. 3385-3390, 3463-3467, 3511-3514.

## PACIFIC 97 — A1111

Design: San Francisco-Oakland Bay Bridge.

*Easter — A1127*

WIELKANOC / POLSKA 55gr

3389 A1110 90g multicolored .55 .25
3390 A1110 1.20z multicolored .70 .35
2.75 1.40
*Nos. 3385-3390 (6)*
No. 3385 was valued at 55g, and No. 3387 was valued at 65g on day of issue.
Issued: B, A, 1/15; 55g, 65g, 90g, 1.20z, 3/3.

**Perf. 11½ Syncopated Type A**
**1998, Mar. 12** Litho.
3391 A1127 55g shown .35 .20
3392 A1127 65g Image of Christ .40 .20

**European Revolutionary Movements of 1848, 150th Anniv. — A1128**

POLSKA 55 GR

**1998, Mar. 20** Engr. **Perf. 11x11½**
3393 A1128 55g gray violet .35 .20

**Royalty Type of 1986**
Designs: 55g, Henryk Walezy. 65g, Anna Jagiellonka. 80g, Stefan Batory. 90g, Zygmunt III.
**1998, Mar. 31** **Perf. 11**
3394 A875 55g multicolored .35 .20
3395 A875 65g multicolored .40 .20
3396 A875 80g multicolored .45 .25
3397 A875 90g multicolored .55 .35
1.75 .90
*Nos. 3394-3397 (4)*

**Protection of the Baltic Sea — A1129**

POLSKA 65g

Marine life: #3398, Halichoerus grypus. #3399, Pomatoschistus microps. #3400, Alosa fallax, syngnathus typhle. #3401, Acipenser sturio. #3402, Salmo salar. #3403, Phocoena phocoena.
1.20z, Halichoerus grypus.

**Perf. 11½ Syncopated Type B**
**1998, Apr. 28** Litho.
3398 A1129 65g multicolored .40 .20
3399 A1129 65g multicolored .40 .20
3400 A1129 65g multicolored .40 .20
3401 A1129 65g multicolored .40 .20
3402 A1129 65g multicolored .40 .20
3403 A1129 65g multicolored .40 .20
a. Strip of 6, #3398-3403 3.25 3.25

**Souvenir Sheet**
3404 A1129 1.20z multicolored 1.10 1.10

**Israel '98 World Philatelic Exhibition, Tel Aviv — A1130**

ISRAEL'98 POLSKA 90 GR

**Perf. 11½ Syncopated Type A**
**1998, Apr. 30**
3405 A1130 90g Israel No. 8, logo .90 .90

---

**Theater Poster Art — A1123**

50 gr RADIO Polska

#3373, "Sam Pierze Radion," black cat becoming white cat, by T. Gronowski, 1926. #3374, "Szewcy" (Bootmakers), by R. Cieslewicz, 1971. #3375, "Goya," by W. Sadowski, 1983. #3376, "Maz i zona," by A. Pagowski, 1977.

**Perf. 11x11½, 11½x11 Syncopated Type A**
**1997, Nov. 14** Litho.
3373 A1123 50g multi .55 .30
3374 A1123 50g multi, vert. .55 .30
3375 A1123 60g multi, vert. .65 .35
3376 A1123 60g multi, vert. .65 .35
2.40 1.30
*Nos. 3373-3376 (4)*

**Chick Type of 1995**
Designs: a, Tadorna tadorna. b, Mergus merganser. c, Gallinago gallinago. d, Gallinula chloropus.
**Perf. 11½ Syncopated Type A**
**1997, Dec. 5**
3377 A1081 50g Block of 4, #a.- d. 1.60 .80

**Christmas A1124**

WIGILIA / POLSKA 60 GR

50g, Nativity. 60g, Food, candles. 80g, Outdoor winter scene, star, church. 1.10z, Carolers.

**Perf. 11½x11, 11½x11 Syncopated Type A**
**1997, Nov. 27**
3378 A1124 50g multi, vert. .35 .25
3379 A1124 60g multi .50 .36
3380 A1124 80g multi .75 .45
3381 A1124 1.10z multi, vert. 1.00 .60
2.60 1.65
*Nos. 3378-3381 (4)*

---

B POLSKA / A1126

A1125

**Perf. 11½ Syncopated Type A**
**1998, Jan. 5** Litho.
3382 A1125 1.40z multicolored .85 .50
1998 Winter Olympic Games, Nagano.

POLSKA 1.40zl — XVIII Zimowe Igrzyska Olimpijskie NAGANO 1998

**Perf. 12x11½ Syncopated Type A**
**1998, Jan. 14**
Love Stamps: B, Face of dog, cat on shirt. A, Face of cat, dog on shirt.
3383 A1126 B multicolored .35 .20
3384 A1126 A multicolored .40 .20
Nos. 3383-3384 were valued at 55g and 65g, respectively, on day of issue.

**Polish Country Estates Type of 1997**
Designs: B, Gluchach. 55g, Oblegorku. A, Czarnolesie. 65g, Bronowicach. 90g, Oborach. 1.20z, Romanowie.
**1998** Photo. **Perf. 11½x12**
3385 A1110 B multicolored .35 .20
3386 A1110 55g multicolored .35 .20
3387 A1110 A multicolored .40 .20
3388 A1110 65g multicolored .40 .20

---

**Perf. 11½ Syncopated Type A**
**1997, May 20** Litho.
3350 A1111 1.30z multicolored 1.25 .50

Polska 50 GR

**Bats A1113**
50g, Plecotus auritus. 60g, Nyctalus noctula. 80g, Myotis myotis. 1.30z, Vespertilio murinus.
**1997, May 30**
3352 A1113 50g multicolored .45 .20
3353 A1113 60g multicolored .55 .25
3354 A1113 80g multicolored .70 .35
3355 A1113 1.30z multicolored 1.15 .60
2.85 1.40
*Nos. 3352-3355 (4)*

Designs: 50g, People in city waving hats at Gen. Jan Henryk Dabrowski. 1.10z, Words to Natl. Anthem, Dabrowski.
**1997, July 18**
3362 A1117 50g multicolored .45 .20
**Souvenir Sheet**
3363 A1117 1.10z multicolored .95 .50

POLSKA 1,50z (A1118) — (1797-1873)

*August 1997 Semposta|*

**Perf. 11x11½**
**1997, July ...**
3364 A1118 1.50z mul... .95 .50

**Virgin of Consolation, Church of the Virgin of Consolation and St. Michael Archangel, Gorka Duchowna A1119**

50 gr POLSKA / Matka Boza Pocieszenia

**Perf. 11½x11 Syncopated Type A**
**1997, Aug. 28**
3365 A1119 50g multicolored .45 .20

**Royalty Type of 1986**
Kings: 50g, Jan I Olbracht (1459-1501). 60g, Aleksander (1461-1506). 80g, Sigismundus I Stary (1467-48). 1.10z, Sigismundus II Augustus (1520-72).
**1997, Sept. 22** Engr.
3366 A875 50g brn & dk brn .40 .20
3367 A875 60g blue & dp brn .50 .25
3368 A875 80g grn & dk brn .65 .35
3369 A875 1.10z brn & dk slate .90 .45
2.45 1.25
*Nos. 3366-3369 (4)*

**World Post Day A1121**

Swiatowy Dzien Poczty / POLSKA 50 gr

**Perf. 11½ Syncopated Type A**
**1997, Oct. 3** Litho.
3370 A1120 80g multicolored .65 .35
**1997, Oct. 9**
3371 A1121 50g multicolored .45 .20

**Moscow '97 Intl. Philatelic Exhibition A1122**

SWIATOWA WYSTAWA FILATELISTYCZNA Moskwa '97 / 80 gr Polska

**Perf. 11½ Syncopated Type B**
**1997, Oct. 13**
3372 A1122 80g multicolored .70 .35

---

**Jagiellon University School of Theology, 600th Anniv. A1114**
Painting by Jan Matejko
**1997, June 6**
3356 A1114 80g multicolored .70 .35

WYDZIALU TEOLOGICZNEGO UJ — POLSKA 80 gr / KROLOWA JADWIGA FUNDATORKA

**Polish Settlement in Argentina, Cent. — A1115**

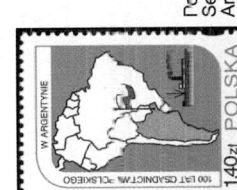

140 zl POLSKA — W ARGENTYNIE / 100 LAT OSADNICTWA POLSKIEGO

**Perf. 11½ Syncopated Type A**
**1997, June 6**
3357 A1115 1.40z multicolored 1.25 .60

**Paintings, by Juliusz Kossak (1824-99) — A1116**

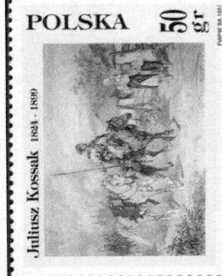

Juliusz Kossak 1824-1899 — POLSKA 50 gr

Designs: 50g, Man on horse, woman, child. 60g, Men on galloping horses, carriage. 80g, Feeding horses in stable. 1.10z, Man with horses.
**1997, July 4** Photo. **Perf. 11**
3358 A1116 50g multicolored .45 .20
3359 A1116 60g multicolored .50 .25
3360 A1116 80g multicolored .70 .35
3361 A1116 1.10z multicolored .95 .50
2.60 1.30
*Nos. 3358-3361 (4)*

**Polish Natl. Anthem, Bicent. A1117**

POLSKA 50 GR

**Nat'l Holidays and Festivals A1131**

**1998, May 5**

| | | | | |
|---|---|---|---|---|
| 3406 | A1131 | 55g multicolored | .45 | .30 |
| 3407 | A1131 | 1.20z multicolored | 1.25 | .70 |
| a. | | Pair, #3406-3407 | 1.75 | 1.75 |

Europa, 55g, Logo of Warwaw Autumn, Intl. Festival of Contemporary Music. 1.20z, First bars of song, "Welcome the May Dawn," 3rd of May Constitution Day.

**Coronation of Longing Holy Mother—A1132**

**1998, June 28**

| 3408 | A1132 | 55g multicolored | .40 | .20 |
|---|---|---|---|---|

**Perf. 11½x12 Syncopated Type A**
**Litho.**

**Nikifor (Epifan Drowniak) (1895-1968), Artist—A1133**

**1998, July 10**

| | | | | |
|---|---|---|---|---|
| 3409 | A1133 | 55g multicolored | .40 | .30 |
| 3410 | A1133 | 65g multicolored | .45 | .35 |
| 3411 | A1133 | 1.20z multicolored | .85 | .60 |
| 3412 | A1133 | 2.35z multicolored | 1.60 | 1.25 |
| | | Nos. 3409-3412 (4) | 3.30 | 2.50 |

**Perf. 11x11½ Syncopated Type A**

Paintings: 55g, "Triple Self-portrait." 65g, "Cracow Office." 1.20z, "Orthodox Church." 2.35z, "Ucrybow Station."

**80 lat / Głównego / Urzędu / Statystycznego / 55 gr / Polska**

**Main Board of Statistics, 80th Anniv. A1134**

**1998, July 13**

| 3413 | A1134 | 55g multicolored | .40 | .20 |
|---|---|---|---|---|

**Perf. 11x11½ Syncopated Type A**

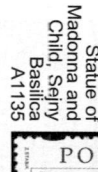

**15th Cent. Statue of Madonna and Child, Sejny Basilica A1135**

**1998, Aug. 14**

| 3414 | A1135 | 55g multicolored | .40 | .20 |
|---|---|---|---|---|

**Perf. 11½ Syncopated Type A**

---

**1998, Aug. 28**

| 3415 | A1136 | 65g multicolored | .50 | .25 |
|---|---|---|---|---|

**Warsaw Diocese, Bicent. A1136**

**Souvenir Sheet**

**17th Polish Philatelic Exhibition, Szczecin — A1137**

**1998, Sept. 18**

| 3416 | A1137 | 65g multicolored | 1.10 | .75 |
|---|---|---|---|---|

View of city, 1624: a, People on raft, pier. b, Sailing ships, pier.

Sheet of 2, #a.-

**Engr. Perf. 11x11½**

**Discovery of Radium and Polonium, Cent. A1138**

**1998, Sept. 18**

| 3417 | A1138 | 1.20z Pierre, Marie Curie | .90 | .50 |
|---|---|---|---|---|

**Perf. 11x11½ Syncopated Type A**
**Litho.**

**Mazowsze Song and Dance Ensemble, 50th Anniv. — A1139**

**1998, Sept. 22**

| | | | | |
|---|---|---|---|---|
| 3418 | A1139 | 65g multicolored | .45 | .25 |
| 3419 | A1139 | 65g multicolored | .45 | .25 |
| a. | | Pair, #3418-3419 | .90 | .50 |

**Perf. 11½ Syncopated Type A**

Couple dancing, denomination at: No. 3418, LL. No. 3419, LR.

**Mniszech Palace (Belgian Embassy), Warsaw, Bicent. A1140**

**1998, Sept. 28**

| 3420 | A1140 | 1.20z multicolored | .90 | .45 |
|---|---|---|---|---|

See Belgium No. 1706.

**Photo. & Engr. Perf. 11½**

---

**Sigismund III Vasa (1566-1632), King of Sweden and Poland—A1141**

**1998, Oct. 3   Engr.   Perf. 11½x11**

| 3421 | A1141 | 1.20z deep claret | .90 | .45 |
|---|---|---|---|---|

See Sweden No. 2312.

**World Stamp Day—A1142**

**1998, Oct. 9**

| 3422 | A1142 | 65g multicolored | .45 | .25 |
|---|---|---|---|---|

**Perf. 11½x11 Syncopated Type A**
**Litho.**

**Pontificate of John Paul II, 20th Anniv. — A1143**

**1998, Oct. 16**

| 3423 | A1143 | 65g multicolored | .45 | .25 |
|---|---|---|---|---|

**Perf. 11½x12 Syncopated Type A**

**Independence, 80th Anniv. — A1144**

**1998, Nov. 11**

| 3424 | A1144 | 65g multicolored | .45 | .25 |
|---|---|---|---|---|

**Perf. 12x11½ Syncopated Type A**

**Christmas A1145**

**1998, Nov. 27   Photo.   Perf. 11½x11**

| 3425 | A1145 | 55g multicolored | .40 | .20 |
|---|---|---|---|---|
| 3426 | A1145 | 65g multicolored | .45 | .25 |

Paintings: 55g, Nativity scene. 65g, Adoration of the Magi.

**Universal Declaration of Human Rights, 50th Anniv. A1146**

**1998, Dec. 10**

| 3427 | A1146 | 1.20z blue & dark blue | .90 | .45 |
|---|---|---|---|---|

**Perf. 11x11½ Syncopated Type A**
**Litho.**

---

**Adam Mickiewicz (1798-1855), Poet—A1147**

**1998, Dec. 24**

| | | | | |
|---|---|---|---|---|
| 3428 | A1147 | 55g multicolored | .40 | .20 |
| 3429 | A1147 | 65g multicolored | .45 | .25 |
| 3430 | A1147 | 90g multicolored | .65 | .35 |
| 3431 | A1147 | 1.20z multicolored | .90 | .45 |
| | | Nos. 3428-3431 (4) | 2.40 | 1.25 |

**Perf. 12x11½ Syncopated Type A**

**Souvenir Sheet**

| 3432 | A1147 | 2.45z multicolored | 1.75 | .90 |
|---|---|---|---|---|

No. 3432 contains one 27x35mm stamp.

Scenes, quotations from poems: 55g, Maryla Wereszczakówna, flower, night landscape. 65g, Cranes flying over tomb of Maria Potocka. 90g, Burning candles, cross. 1.20z, Nobleman's house, flowers, uhlan's cap. 2.45z, Bust of Mickiewicz, by Jean David d'Angers.

**Polish Navy, 80th Anniv. (in 1998) A1148**

**1999, Jan. 4**

| | | | | |
|---|---|---|---|---|
| 3433 | A1148 | 55g multicolored | .35 | .20 |
| 3434 | A1148 | 65g multicolored | .35 | .20 |
| a. | | Pair, #3433-3434 | .70 | .40 |

**Perf. 11½x11½ Syncopated Type A**
**Litho.**

No. 3433, Destroyer ORP Piorun, 1942-46. No. 3434, Frigate ORP Piorun, 1994.

**Love Stamps A1149**

**1999, Feb. 5**

| 3435 | A1149 | B Dominoes | .40 | .20 |
|---|---|---|---|---|
| 3436 | A1149 | A Dominoes, diff. | .50 | .25 |

Nos. 3535-3436 were valued at 55g and 65g, respectively, on day of issue.

**Perf. 11½x11½ Syncopated Type A**

**Famous Polish Men A1150**

**1999, Feb. 12**

| 3437 | A1150 | 1z multicolored | .65 | .35 |
|---|---|---|---|---|
| 3438 | A1150 | 1.60z multicolored | 1.10 | .55 |

**Perf. 11½ Syncopated Type A**

Designs: 1z, Ernest Malinowski (1818-99), constructor of Central Trans-Andean Railway, Peru. 1.60z, Rudolf Modrzejewski (Ralph Modjeski) (1861-1940), bridge builder.

Easter — A1151

Scenes from Srudziadz Polyptych: 60g, Prayer in Ogrójec. 65g, Carrying cross. 1.40z, Resurrection. 1z, Tubadzin Pieta, 15th cent.

**Perf. 11½x11¼**
**1999, Mar. 5**
3439 A1151 60g multicolored .40 .20
3440 A1151 65g multicolored .45 .20
3441 A1151 1z multicolored .65 .35
3442 A1151 1.40z multicolored .90 .45
Nos. 3439-3442 (4) 2.40 1.20

**Souvenir Sheet**

China 1999, World Philatelic Exhibition — A1152

Illustration reduced.

**Perf. 11½x11¾ Syncopated Type A**
**1999, Mar. 31**
3443 A1152 1.70z Ideogram, dragon 1.25 .65

Virgin Mary, Patron Saint of Soldiers A1153

**Perf. 11½x11¾ Syncopated Type A    Litho.**
**1999, Apr. 2**
3444 A1153 60g shown .50 .25
3445 A1153 70g Katyn .60 .30

Characters from Works by Henryk Sienkiewicz — A1154

**Perf. 11¾x11½ Syncopated Type B    Litho.**
**1999, Apr. 6**
3446 A1154 70g Jan Skrzetuski .45 .25
3447 A1154 70g Onufry Zagloba .45 .25
3448 A1154 70g Longin Podbipieta .45 .25
3449 A1154 70g Bohun .45 .25
3450 A1154 70g Andrzej Kmicic .45 .25
3451 A1154 70g Michal Jerzy Wolodyjowski .45 .25
a. Block of 6, # 3446-3451 2.75 1.50

Poland's Admission to NATO — A1155

**Perf. 11½ Syncopated Type B    Litho.**
**1999, Apr. 22**
3452 A1155 70g multicolored .60 .30

Council of Europe, 50th Anniv. — A1156

**Perf. 11½x11 Syncopated Type A    Litho.**
**1999, May 5**
3453 A1156 1z multicolored .65 .35

Europa A1157

**Perf. 11½ Syncopated Type A    Litho.**
**1999, May 5**
3454 A1157 1.40z multicolored 1.10 .75

Sports A1158

Designs: 60g, Cycling. 70g, Snowboarding. 1z, Skateboarding. 1.40z, Roller blading.

**Perf. 11½ Syncopated Type B    Litho.**
**1999, June 1**
3455 A1158 60g Cycling .40 .20
3456 A1158 70g Snowboarding .45 .25
3457 A1158 1z Skateboarding .65 .45
3458 A1158 1.40z Roller blading .90 .45
Nos. 3455-3458 (4) 2.40 1.25

Visit of Pope John Paul II — A1159

Pope and: 60g, Church of the Virgin Mary, Cracow, crowd with Solidarity banners. 70g, Crowd with crosses. 1z, Crowd with flags. 1.40z, Eiffel Tower, Monument to Christ the Redeemer, Rio, Shrine of Our Lady of Fatima.

**Perf. 11½x11½ Syncopated Type A    Litho.**
**1999, June 5**
3459 A1159 60g multicolored .40 .20
a. Complete booklet, 10 #3459 4.00
3460 A1159 70g multicolored .45 .25
a. Complete booklet, 10 #3460 4.50
3461 A1159 1z multicolored .65 .45
3462 A1159 1.40z multicolored .90 .45
Nos. 3459-3462 (4) 2.40 1.25

**Country Estates Type of 1997**
**Perf. 11½x11¾    Photo.**
**1999, June 15**
3463 A1110 70g Modlnicy .45 .35
3464 A1110 1z Krzeslawicach .65 .50
3465 A1110 1.40z Winnej Gorze .90 .65

3466 A1110 1.60z Potoku Zlotym 1.10 .75
3467 A1110 1.85z Kasnej Dolnej 1.25 .90
Nos. 3463-3467 (5) 4.35 3.15

Versailles Treaty, 80th Anniv. A1159a

**Perf. 11½x11½ Syncopated Type A    Litho.**
**1999, June 29**
3467A A1159a 1.40z multi .90 .45

Depictions of the Virgin Mary — A1160

Designs: 60g, Painting from church in Rokitno. 70g, Crowned statue.

**Perf. 11½x11½ Syncopated Type A    Litho.**
**1999, July 9**
3468 A1160 60g multi .40 .20
3469 A1160 70g multi .45 .25

Insects — A1161

Designs: No. 3470, Corixa punctata. No. 3471, Dytiscus marginalis. No. 3472, Perla marginata. No. 3473, Limnophilus. No. 3474, Anax imperator. No. 3475, Ephemera vulgata.

**Perf. 11½x11¾ Syncopated Type B    Litho.**
**1999, July 16**
3470 A1161 60g multi .40 .30
3471 A1161 60g multi .40 .30
3472 A1161 70g multi .40 .30
3473 A1161 70g multi .45 .30
3474 A1161 70g multi .90 .60
3475 A1161 1.40z multi .90 .60
Nos. 3470-3475 (6) 3.50 2.40

**Souvenir Sheet**

Ksiaz Castle — A1162

1001.znaczek Czeslawa Slani

**Engr. (Margin Photo.)    Perf. 11½x11**
**1999, Aug. 14**
3476 A1162 1z blue .80 .40
Natl. Philatelic Exhibition, Walbrzych, Czeslaw Slania's 1001st stamp design.

Polish-Ukrainian Cooperation in Nature Conservation — A1163

Designs: No. 3477, Cervus elaphus. No. 3478, Felis silvestris.

**Perf. 11x11½ Syncopated Type A    Litho.**
**1999, Sept. 22**
3477 A1163 1.40z multi .90 .45
3478 A1163 1.40z multi .90 .45
a. Pair, #3477-3478 1.80 .90
See Ukraine No. 354.

**Royalty Type of 1986 with Denomination at Bottom**

Designs: 60g, Wladyslaw IV. 70g, Jan II Kazimierz. 1z, Michal Korybut Wisniowiecki. 1.40z, Jan III Sobieski.

**Photo. & Engr.**
**1999, Sept. 25**
3479 A875 60g olive & black .45 .25
3480 A875 70g brn & dk brn .45 .25
3481 A875 1z blue & black .65 .30
3482 A875 1.40z lilac & claret .90 .45
Nos. 3479-3482 (4) 2.40 1.20

UPU, 125th Anniv., World Post Day A1164

**Perf. 11½x11½ Syncopated Type A    Litho.**
**1999, Oct. 9**
3483 A1164 1.40z multi .90 .45

Frédéric Chopin (1810-49), Composer — A1165

**Perf. 11x11½    Engr.**
**1999, Oct. 17**
3484 A1165 1.40z dark green .90 .45
See France No. 2744.

Jerzy Popieluszko (1947-84), Priest Murdered by Secret Police — A1166

**Perf. 11½x11½ Syncopated Type A    Litho.**
**1999, Oct. 19**
3485 A1166 70g multi .45 .20

POLAND

Souvenir Sheet

## Memorial to Heroes of World War II — A1167

**1999, Oct. 21**
3486 A1167 1z multi .60 .30

Illustration reduced.

## Christmas A1168

Various angels.

**1999, Nov. 26**
**Perf. 11½x11½ Syncopated Type A**
Litho.
3487 A1168 60g orange .40 .20
3488 A1168 70g blue .45 .25
3489 A1168 1z red .65 .30
3490 A1168 1.40z olive green .90 .45
Nos. 3487-3490 (4) 2.40 1.20

## Polish Cultural Buildings in Foreign Countries A1169

Designs: 1z, Polish Museum, Rapperswil, Switzerland. 1.40z, Marian Fathers Museum at Fawley Court Historic House, United Kingdom. 1.60z, Polish History and Literary Society Library, Paris. 1.80z, Polish Institute and Sikorski Museum, London.

Panel Color

**1999, Dec. 6**
**Perf. 11½x11½ Syncopated Type A**
Litho.
3491 A1169 1z multi .60 .30
3492 A1169 1.40z multi .85 .40
3493 A1169 1.60z multi .95 .50
3494 A1169 1.80z multi 1.10 .55
Nos. 3491-3494 (4) 3.50 1.75

## New Year 2000 — A1170

**2000, Jan. 2**
**Perf. 11½x11¾ Syncopated Type A**
Litho.
3495 A1170 A multi .45 .25
No. 3495 sold for 70g on day of issue.

## Famous Poles A1171

Designs: 1.55z, Bronislaw Malinowski (1884-1942), ethnologist. 1.95z, Józef Zwierzycki (1888-1961), geologist.

**2000, Feb. 22**
**Perf. 11¾x11½ Syncopated Type A**
3496 A1171 1.55z multi .90 .45
3497 A1171 1.95z multi 1.10 .55

## Gniezno Summit, 1000th Anniv. — A1172

Designs: 70g, Holy Roman Emperor Otto III granting crown to Boleslaw Chroby. 80g, Four bishops. 1.55z, Sclaunia, Germania, Gallia, Roma and Otto III, horiz.

**2000, Mar. 12**
3498 A1172 70g multi .40 .20
3499 A1172 80g multi .45 .25

Souvenir Sheet
**Perf. 11½x11½**
3500 A1172 1.55z multi .90 .45

Organization of Roman Catholic Church in Poland, 1000th anniv.

## Easter A1173

Designs: 70g, Christ in tomb. 80g, Resurrected Christ.

**2000, Mar. 24**
**Perf. 11½x11½ Syncopated Type B**
Litho.
3501 A1173 70g multi .40 .20
3502 A1173 80g multi .45 .25

## Dinosaurs — A1174

Designs: 70g, Saurolophus. #3504, Gallimimus. #3505, Saichania. #3506, Protoceratops. #3507, Prenocephale. #3508, Velociraptor.

**2000, Mar. 24**
**Perf. 11½x11¾ Syncopated Type A**
Litho.
3503 A1174 70g multi .40 .20
3504 A1174 70g multi .40 .20
3505 A1174 70g multi .40 .20
3506 A1174 80g multi .45 .25
3507 A1174 1.55z multi .90 .45
3508 A1174 1.55z multi .90 .45
Nos. 3503-3508 (6) 3.50 1.80
a. Souvenir sheet, #3503-3508 7.50 3.75

## Awarding of Honorary Academy Award to Director Andrzej Wajda A1175

**2000, Mar. 26**
3509 A1175 1.10z blk & gray .60 .30
a. Tete beche pair 1.25 .60

## Holy Year 2000 — A1176

**2000, Apr. 7**
**Perf. 11½x11¾ Syncopated Type B**
3510 A1176 80g multi .45 .25

## Country Estates Type of 1997

**2000, Apr. 14**
**Perf. 11½x11¾**
Photo.
3511 A1110 80g Grabonog .45 .25
3512 A1110 1.55z Zelazowa Wola .90 .45
3513 A1110 1.65z Sucha .95 .50
3514 A1110 2.55z Liwia, Węgrów 1.60 .80
Nos. 3511-3514 (4) 3.90 2.00

## Cracow, 2000 European City of Culture — A1177

70g, Jan Matejko, Franciszek Joseph, Stanislaw Wyspianski, Konstanty Ildefons Galczynski, Stanislaw Lem, Slawomir Mrozek, Piotr Skrzynecki and Cloth Hall. 1.55z, Queen Jadwiga, Jozef Dietl, Krzysztof Penderecki, Casimir the Great, Pope John Paul II, Jerzy Turowicz, Brother Albert, Copernicus, Collegium Maius and St. Mary's Church. 1.75z, Panorama of Cracow from 1493, wood engraving.

**2000, Apr. 24**
**Perf. 11½x11¾ Syncopated Type A**
Litho.
3515 A1177 70g multi .40 .20
3516 A1177 1.55z multi .90 .45

Souvenir Sheet
Engr.
3517 A1177 1.75z blue 1.50 1.00
No. 3517 contains one 39x31mm stamp. No. 3517 exists imperf. Value $9.

## Fight Against Drug Addiction A1178

**2000, Apr. 28**
**Perf. 11½x11¾ Syncopated Type B**
Litho.
3518 A1178 70g multi .40 .20

## Pope John Paul II, 80th Birthday A1179

Designs: 80g, Pope. 1.10z, Black Madonna of Jasna Gora. 1.55z, Pope's silver cross.

**2000, May 9**
**Engr., Litho. & Engr. (1.10z)**
**Perf. 12¾**
3520 A1179 80g purple .45 .25
3521 A1179 1.10z multi .65 .30
3522 A1179 1.55z green .90 .45
Nos. 3520-3522 (3) 2.00 1.00
See Vatican City Nos. 1153-1155.

## Europa, 2000 Common Design Type

**2000, May 9**
**Perf. 11½x11¾ Syncopated Type B**
3519 CD17 1.55z multi 1.50 .75

## España 2000 Intl. Philatelic Exhibition A1180

**2000, May 26**
**Perf. 11½x11¾ Syncopated Type A**
3523 A1180 1.55z multi 1.50 .75

## Parenthood A1181

**2000, May 31**
**Perf. 11½x11¾ Syncopated Type B**
3524 A1181 70g multi .55 .20

## Wroclaw, 1000th Anniv. — A1182

**2000, June 15**
**Perf. 11½x11½ Syncopated Type A**
3525 A1182 1.55z multi 1.50 1.00

Illustration reduced.

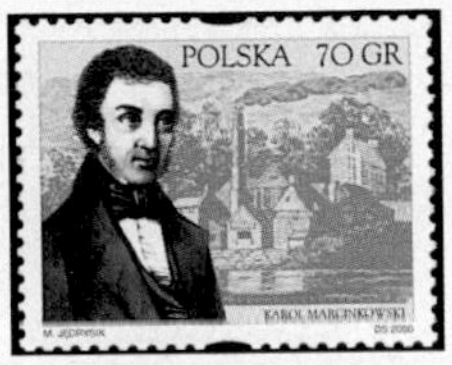

Social Activists A1183

70g, Karol Marcinkowski (1800-46), philantropist. 80g, Blessed Josemaría Escrivá de Balaguer, (1902-75), founder of Opus Dei.

***Perf. 11¼x11½ Suncopated Type B***

**2000, June 23**
**3526-3527** A1183 Set of 2 .80 .40

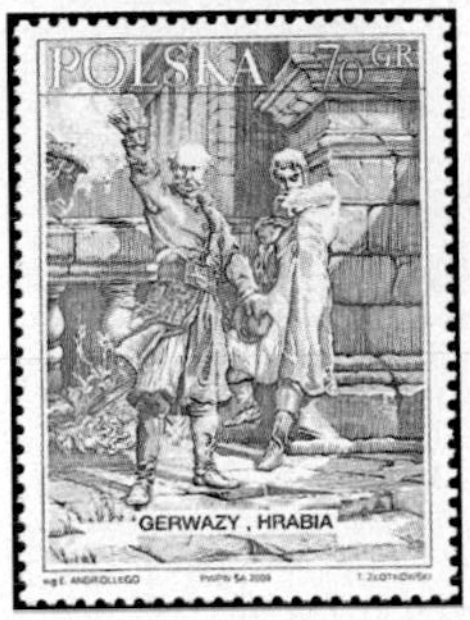

Illustrations of Characters from Pan Tadeusz, by Adam Mickiewicz A1184

#3528, 70g, Gerwazy & Count. #3529, 70g, Telimena & Judge. #3530, 80g, Father Robak, Judge &Gerwazy. #3531, 80g, Wojski. #3532, 1.10z, Jankiel. #3533, 1.10z, Zofia & Tadeusz.

**2000, June 30 Engr. *Perf. 11x11¼***
**3528-3533** A1184 Set of 6 4.00 2.50

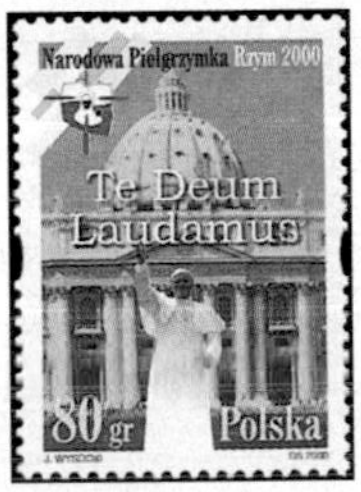

National Pilgrimage to Rome — A1185

Designs: 80g, Pope John Paul II, St. Peter's Basilica. 1.55z, Cross, Colosseum.

***Perf. 11½x11¾ Syncopated Type B***

**2000, July 1 Litho.**
**3534-3535** A1185 Set of 2 1.10 .55

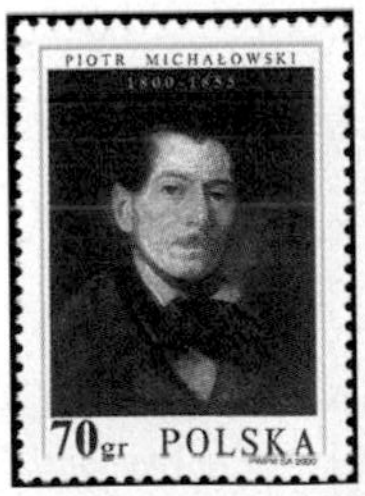

Piotr Michalowski (1800-55), Artist — A1186

70g, Self-portrait, vert. 80g, Portrait of Boy in a Hat, vert. 1.10z, Stableboy Bridling Percherons. 1.55z, Horses & a Horse Cart.

***Perf. 11½x11¼ (no syncopation), 11¾x11½ Syncopated Type A***

**2000, July 2**
**3536-3539** A1186 Set of 4 2.25 1.10

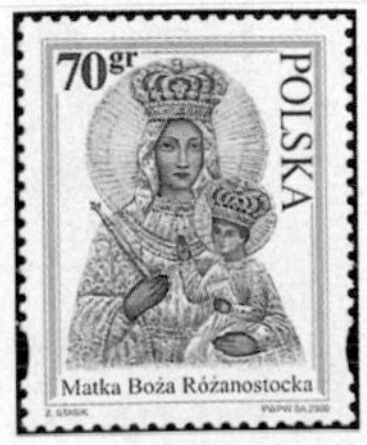

Depictions of the Virgin Mary — A1187

Designs: 70g, Rózanostok. 1.55z, Lichen.

***Perf. 11½x11¼ Syncopated Type A***

**2000, Aug. 14**
**3540-3541** A1187 Set of 2 1.25 .60

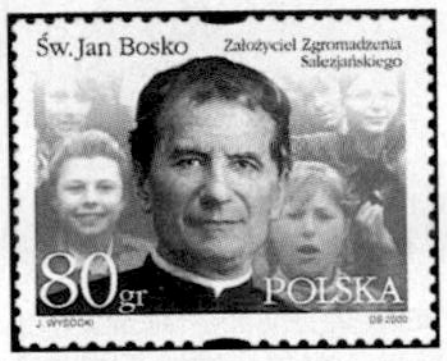

St. John Bosco and Adolescents A1188

***Perf. 11¼x11½ Syncopated Type B***

**2000, Aug. 25**
**3542** A1188 80g multi .45 .20

Educational work of Salesian order.

Souvenir Sheet

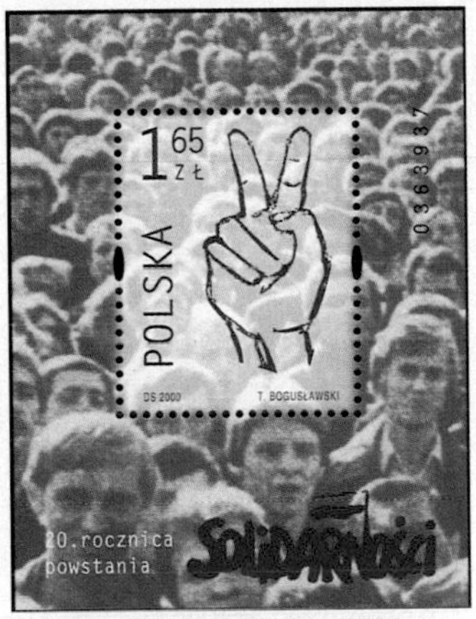

Solidarity Labor Union, 20th Anniv. — A1189

Illustration reduced.

***Perf. 11½x11¼ Syncopated Type B***

**2000, Aug. 31**
**3543** A1189 1.65z multi .90 .45

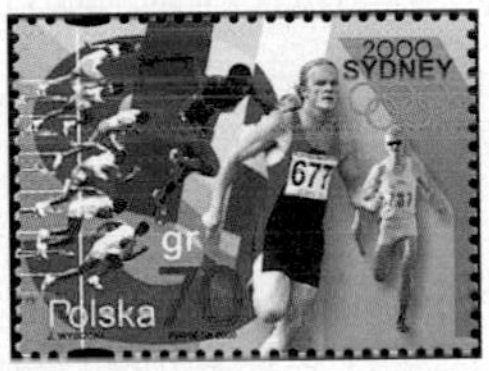

2000 Summer Olympics, Sydncy A1190

Designs: 70g, Runners. 80g, Diving, sailing, rowing. 1.10z, High jump, weight lifting, fencing. 1.55z, Basketball, judo, runner.

***Perf. 11¾x11½ Syncopated Type A***

**2000, Sept. 1**
**3544-3547** A1190 Set of 4 2.25 1.10

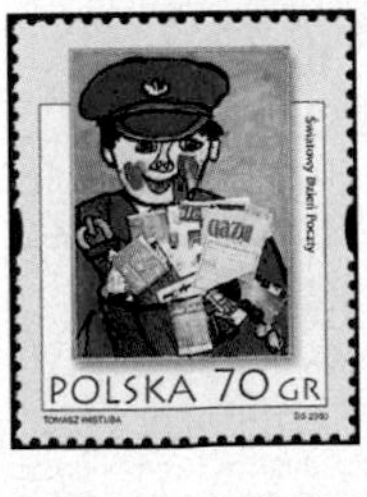

World Post Day — A1191

Children's art by: 70g, Tomasz Wistuba, vert. 80g, Katarzyna Chrzanowska. 1.10z, Joanna Zbik. 1.55z, Katarzyna Lonak.

***Perf. 11½x11¼, 11¼x11½ All Sync. Type B***

**2000, Oct. 9 Litho.**
**3548-3551** A1191 Set of 4 2.60 1.25

Souvenir Sheet

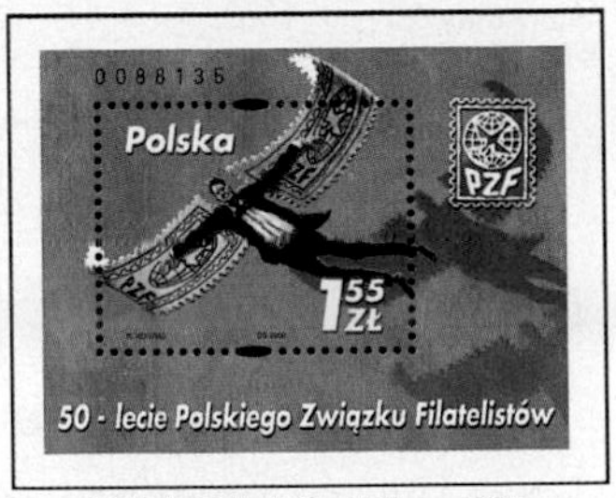

Polish Philatelic Union, 50th Anniv. — A1192

***Perf. 11¼x11½ Sync. Type B***

**2000, Oct. 12**
**3552** A1192 1.55z multi 1.50 1.00

**Royalty Type of 1986 With Denominations at Bottom**

Designs: 70g, August II. 80g, Stanislaw Leszczynski. 1.10z, August III. 1.55z, Stanislaw August Poniatowski.

**2000, Oct. 23 Engr. *Perf. 10¾x11***
**3553-3556** A875 Set of 4 2.60 1.25

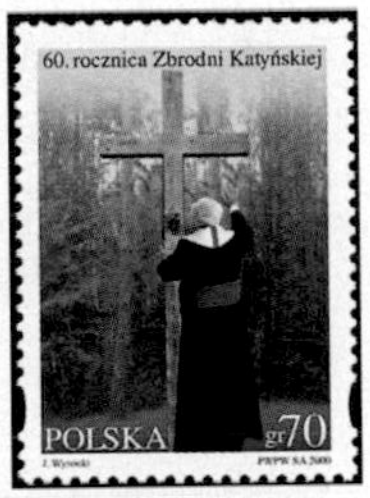

Katyn Massacre, 60th Anniv. — A1193

Designs: 70g, Priest and cross. 80g, Pope John Paul II at monument in Warsaw.

***Perf. 11½x11¾ Sync. Type A***

**2000, Nov. 15 Litho.**
**3557-3558** A1193 Set of 2 .90 .45

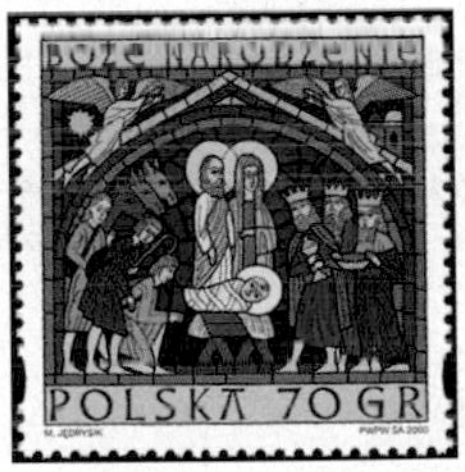

Christmas A1194

Scenes from the life of Jesus: 70g, Nativity. 80g, Wedding at Cana. 1.10g, Last Supper. 1.55z, Ascension.

***Perf. 11½ Sync. Type A***

**2000, Nov. 27**
**3559-3562** A1194 Set of 4 2.60 1.25

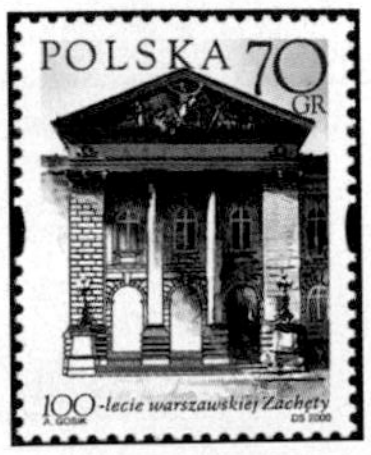

Zacheta Art Museum, Warsaw, Cent. — A1195

***Perf. 11½x11¼ Sync. Type B***

**2000, Dec. 4**
**3563** A1195 70g multi .45 .20

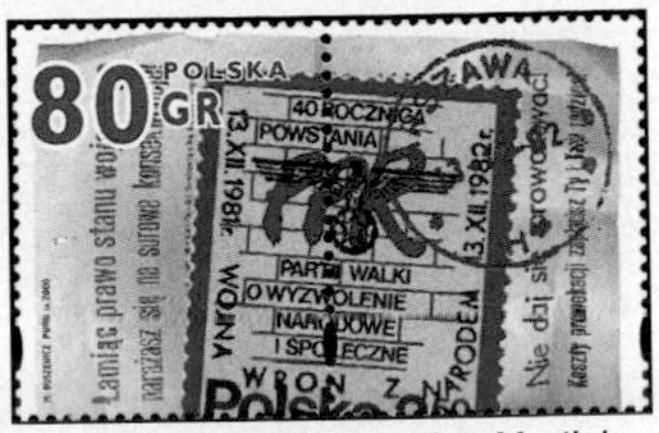

Underground Post During Martial Law — A1196

Illustration reduced.

***Perf. 11½x11¼ Sync. Type A***

**2000, Dec. 13**
**3564** A1196 80g multi + label .50 .25
*a.* Tete beche block of 2 stamps + 2 labels 1.00 .50

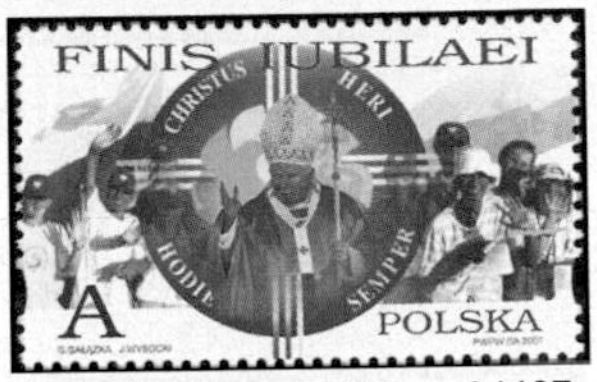

End of Holy Year 2000 — A1197

Type C Syncopation (1st stamp #3565): Like Type A Syncopation but with oval hole on shorter sides rather than longer sides.

***Perf. 11¾x11½ Sync. Type C***

**2001, Jan. 6 Litho.**
**3565** A1197 A multi .55 .25

Sold for 1z on day of issue.

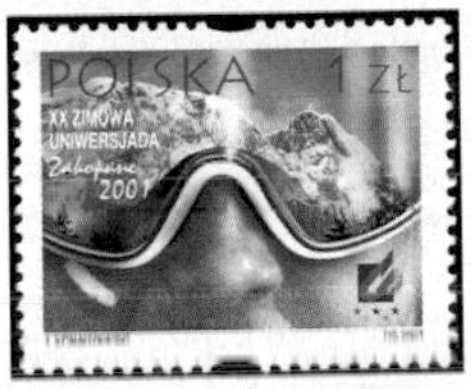

20th Winter Universiade, Zakopane — A1198

***Perf. 11¼x11½ Sync. Type B***

**2001, Feb. 7**
**3566** A1198 1z multi .55 .25

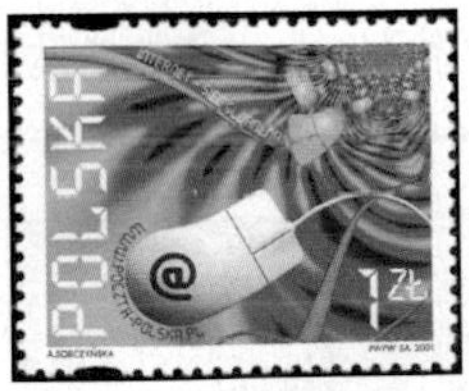

Internet A1199

***Perf. 11¼x11½ Sync. Type A***

**2001, Feb. 22**
**3567** A1199 1z multi .55 .25

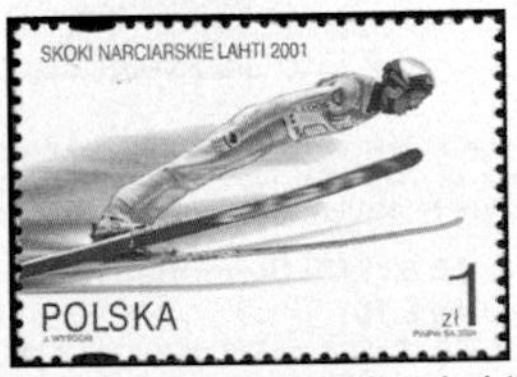

World Ski Championships, Lahti, Finland — A1200

***Perf. 11½ Sync. Type A***

**2001, Feb. 23**
**3568** A1200 1z shown .55 .25

**With Inscription "Adam Malysz" in Black**

**3569** A1200 1z multi .55 .25

**As #3569, With Inscription "Mistrzem Swiata" in Red**

**3570** A1200 1z multi .55 .25
*Nos. 3568-3570 (3)* 1.65 .75

**Country Estates Type of 1997**

*Perf. 11½x11¾*

**2001, Feb. 28** **Photo.**

**3571** A1110 10g Lipków .20 .20
**3572** A1110 1.50z Sulejówek .95 .50
**3573** A1110 1.90z Petrykozy 1.10 .55
**3574** A1110 3z Janowiec 1.75 .85

Issued: 1.90z, 3z, 2/28. 10g, 1.50z, 6/20.

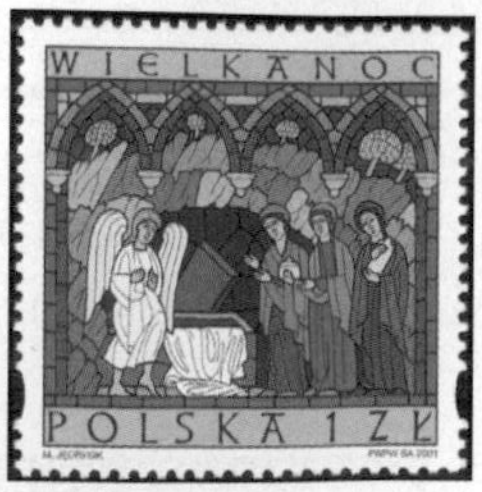


Easter A1201

Designs: 1z, Women at empty tomb. 1.90z, Resurrected Christ with apostles.

*Perf. 11½ Sync. Type A*

**2001, Mar. 16** **Litho.**

**3575-3576** A1201 Set of 2 1.60 .80

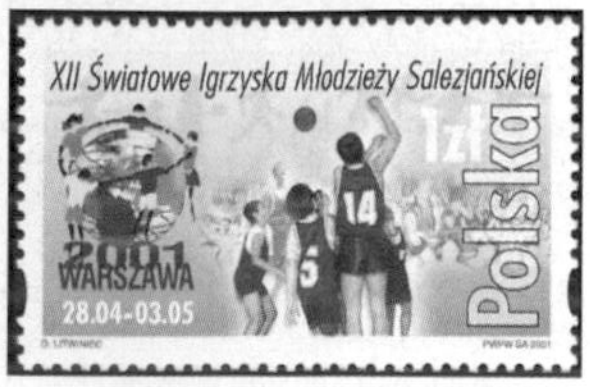


12th Salesian Youth World Championships — A1202

*Perf. 11¾x11½ Sync. Type C*

**2001, Apr. 28**

**3577** A1202 1z multi .55 .25

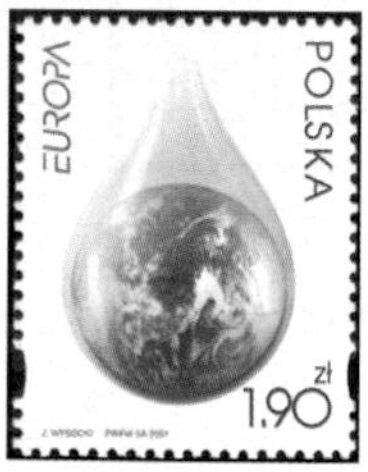


Europa — A1203

*Perf. 11½x11¼ Sync. Type A*

**2001, May 5**

**3578** A1203 1.90z multi 1.50 1.00

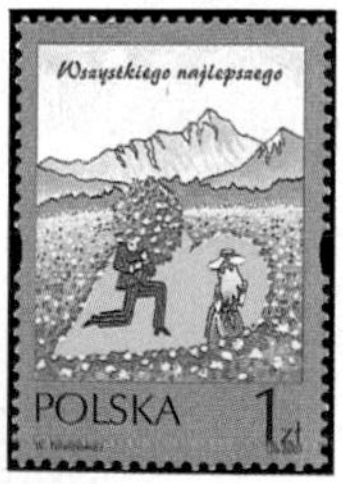


Greetings A1204

Designs: No. 3579, 1z, All the best (couple in field of flowers). No. 3580, 1z, Vacation greetings (merman and mermaid at beach).

*Perf. 11½x11¾ Syncopated Type B*

**2001, May 10** **Litho.**

**3579-3580** A1204 Set of 2 1.25 .65

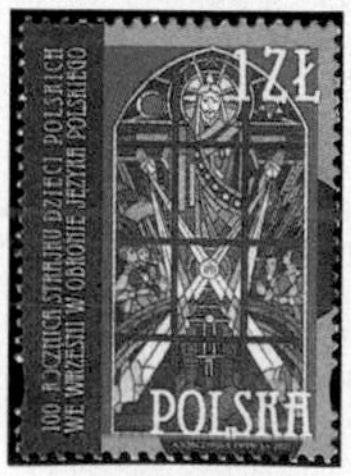


Wrzesnia Children's Strike Against German Language, Cent. — A1205

*Perf. 11½x11¾ Syncopated Type A*

**2001, May 20**

**3581** A1205 1z multi .65 .30

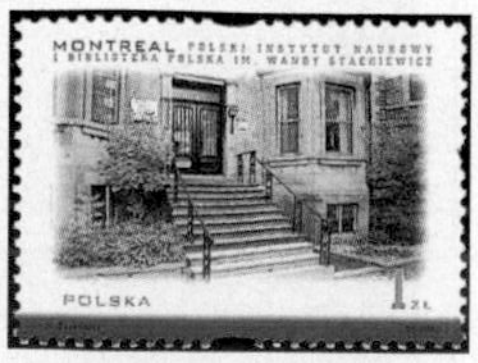


Polish Cultural Buildings in North America A1206

Designs: 1z, Poland Scientific Institute and Wanda Stachiewicz Polish Library, Montreal. 1.90z, Josef Pilsudski Institute, New York. 2.10z, Polonia Archives, Library and Museum, Orchard Lake, Mich. 2.20z, Polish Museum, Chicago.

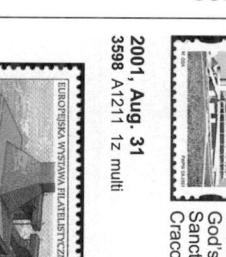

*Perf. 11½ Syncopated Type B*

**2001, June 29**

**3582** A1206 1z multi .65 .30
*a.* Tete beche pair 1.30 .60
**3583** A1206 1.90z multi 1.25 .60
*a.* Tete beche pair 2.50 1.20
**3584** A1206 2.10z multi 1.40 .70
*a.* Tete beche pair 2.80 1.40
**3585** A1206 2.20z multi 1.40 .70
*a.* Tete beche pair 2.80 1.40
*Nos. 3582-3585 (4)* 4.70 2.30

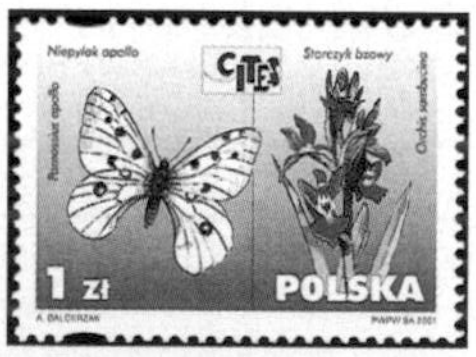


Endangered Flora and Fauna — A1207

Convention on Intl. Trade in Endangered Species emblem and: No. 3586, 1z, Parnassius apollo, Orchis sambucina. No. 3587, 1z, Bubo bubo, Adonis vernalis. No. 3588, 1z, Galanthus nivalis, Lynx lynx. No. 3589, 1.90z, Orchis latifolia, Lutra lutra. No. 3590, 1.90z, Falco peregrinus, Orchis pallens. No. 3591, 1.90z, Cypripedium calceolus, Ursus arctos. 2z, World map.

*Perf. 11½ Syncopated Type A*

**2001, July 10**

**3586-3591** A1207 Set of 6 7.00 5.00

**Souvenir Sheet**

*Perf. 11¼x11½ Syncopated Type A*

**3592** A1207 2z multi 1.25 .65

No. 3592 contains one 39x30mm stamp.

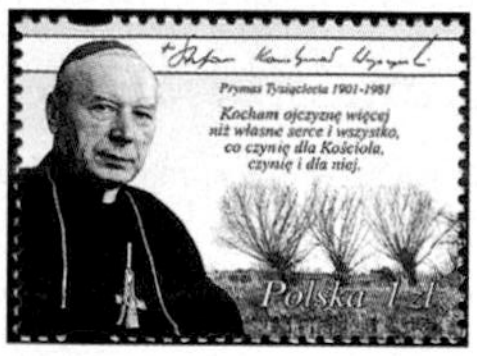


Stefan Cardinal Wyszynski (1901-81) A1208

*Perf. 11¾x11½ Syncopated Type A*

**2001, Aug. 3**

**3593** A1208 1z multi .65 .30

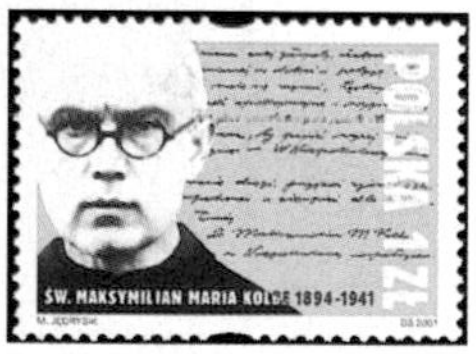


St. Maximilian Kolbe (1894-1941) — A1209

*Perf. 11¾x11½ Syncopated Type B*

**2001, Aug. 14**

**3594** A1209 1z multi .65 .30

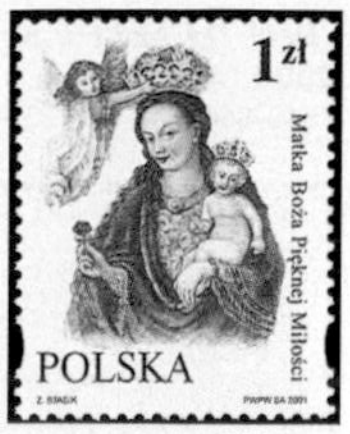


Depictions of the Virgin Mary — A1210

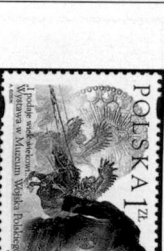

Designs: No. 3595, 1z, Pieknej Milosci, Bydgoszcz. No. 3596, 1z, Królowa Podhala, Ludzmierz. 1.90z, Mariampol, Wroclaw.

*Perf. 11½x11¼ Syncopated Type A*

**2001, Aug. 14**

**3595-3597** A1210 Set of 3 2.50 1.25

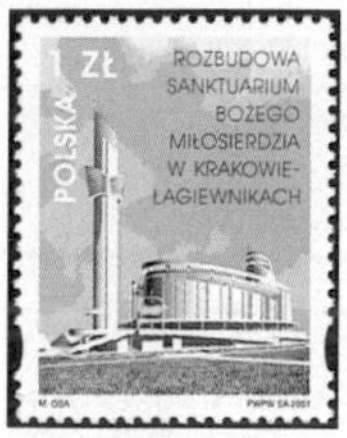


Extension of God's Mercy Sanctuary, Cracow — A1211

**2001, Aug. 31**

**3598** A1211 1z multi .65 .30

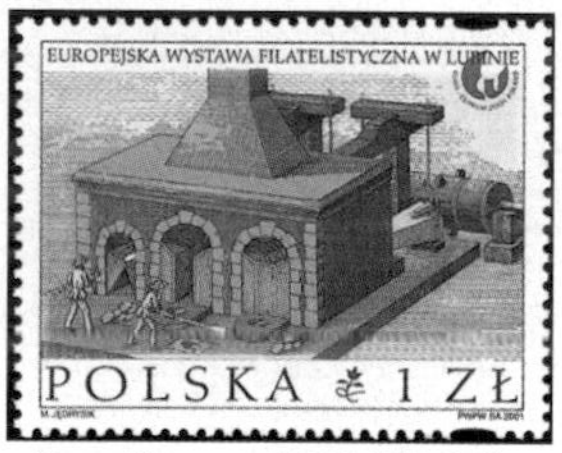


Euro Cuprum 2001 Philatelic Exhibition, Lubin — A1212

Designs: 1z, Copper smelter. 1.90z, Copper engravers at work. 2z, Copying with a copper engraving press.

3z, Engraver's burin, view of Lubin, 18th cent.

*Perf. 11½x11¼ Syncopated Type A*

**2001, Sept. 1** **Litho. & Engr.**

**3599-3601** A1212 Set of 3 4.25 1.75

**Souvenir Sheet**

**Litho.**

**3602** A1212 3z multi 2.75 2.00

No. 3602 exists imperf. Value $8.50.

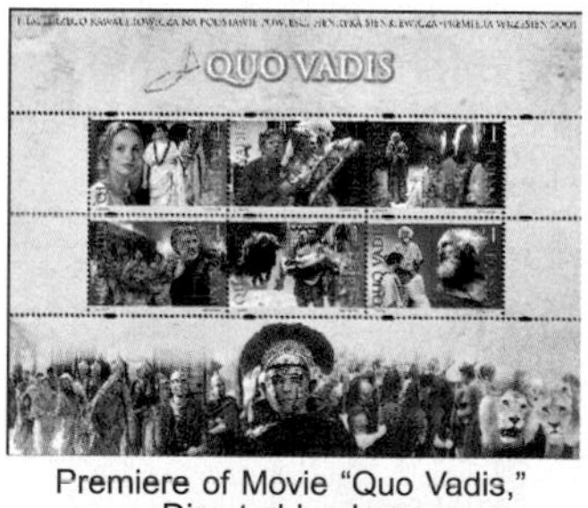


Premiere of Movie "Quo Vadis," Directed by Jerzy Kawalerowicz — A1213

No. 3603: a, Ligia, Vinicius, Petrinius (red and light yellow inscriptions). b, Nero singing (blue and red inscriptions). c, Apostle Peter in catacombs, baptism of Chilon Chilonides (orange and yellow inscriptions). d, Chilon Chilonides, fire in Rome (white and yellow inscriptions). e, Ligia tied to back of aurochs, Ursus holding Ligia (red and white inscriptions). f, Apostle Peter blessing Vinicius and Ligia, close-up of Peter (purple and pink inscriptions).

*Perf. 11¾x11½ Syncopated Type A*

**2001, Sept. 1** **Litho.**

**3603** A1213 1z Sheet of 6, #a-f 5.00 3.00

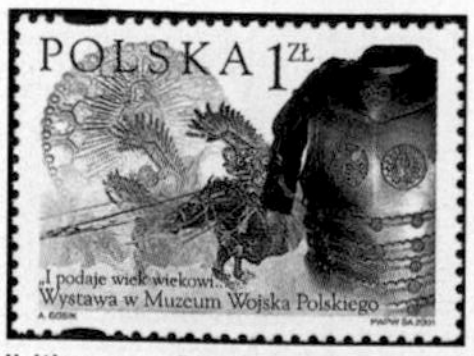


Exhibition on Christian Traditions in Military at Polish Army Museum A1214

*Perf. 11¾x11½ Syncopated*

**2001, Sept. 10** **Litho.**

**3604** A1214 1z multi .65 .30

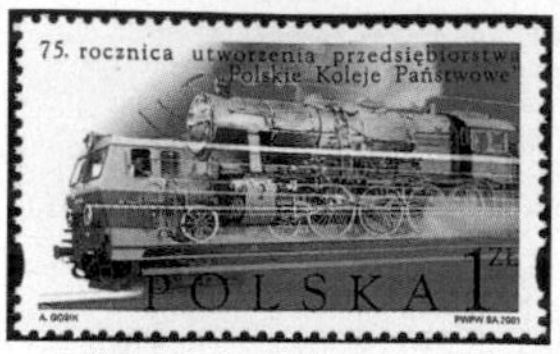


Polish State Railways, 75th Anniv. — A1215

**2001, Sept. 24**

**3605** A1215 1z multi .65 .30

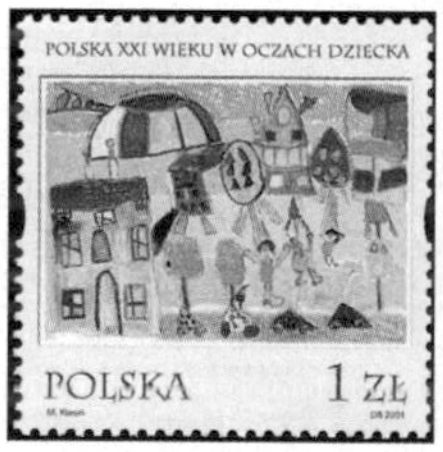


Children's Stamp Design Contest Winners A1216

Art by: 1z, Marcin Kuron. 1.90z, Agata Grzyb, vert. 2z, Joanna Sadrakula.

*Perf. 11½ Syncopated*

**2001, Sept. 28**

**3606-3608** A1216 Set of 3 3.25 1.60

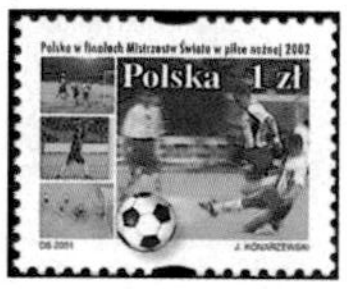


Poland's Advancement to 2002 World Cup Soccer Championships A1217

*Perf. 11½x11¾ Syncopated*

**2001, Oct. 6**

**3609** A1217 1z multi .65 .30

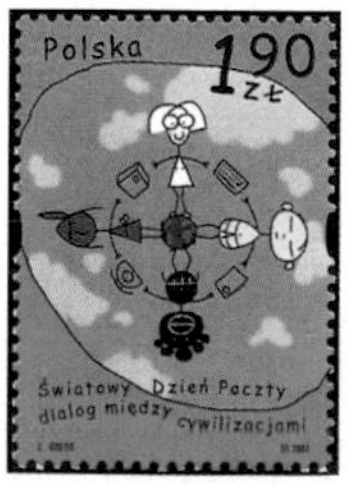


Year of Dialogue Among Civilizations A1218

**2001, Oct. 9**

**3610** A1218 1.90z multi 1.25 .60
*a.* Tete beche pair 2.50 1.20

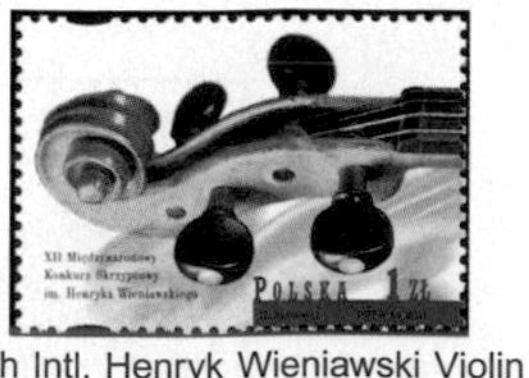


12th Intl. Henryk Wieniawski Violin Competition — A1219

*Perf. 11¾x11½ Syncopated*

**2001, Oct. 13**

**3611** A1219 1z multi .65 .30

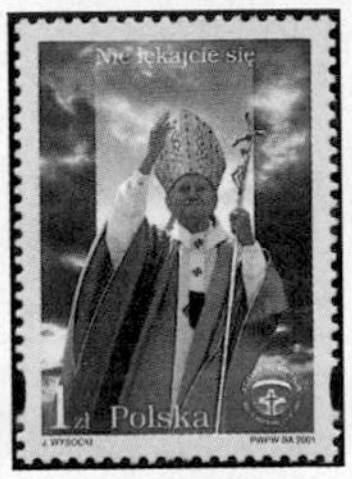

Papal Day — A1220

*Perf. 11½x11¾ Syncopated*

**2001, Oct. 14**

**3612** A1220 1z multi .65 .30

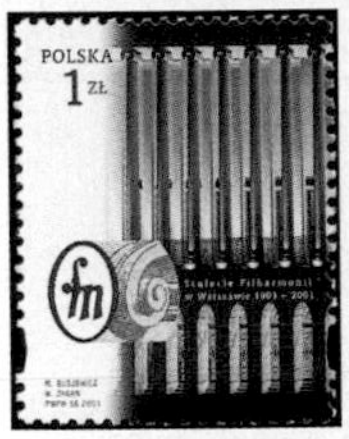

Warsaw Philharmonic, Cent. — A1221

*Perf. 11½x11¼ Syncopated*

**2001, Nov. 5**

**3613** A1221 1z multi .65 .30
*a.* Tete beche pair 1.30 .60

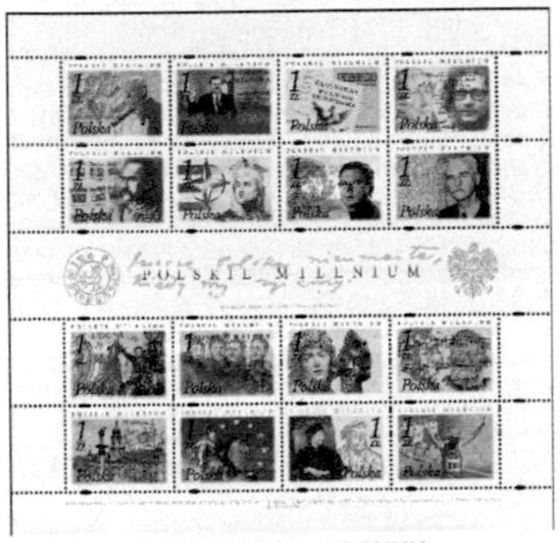

Millennium A1222

No. 3614: a, Pope John Paul II, Gniezno Doors. b, Pres. Lech Walesa taking oath, cover of May 1791 Constitution. c, Covers of three magazines. d, Playwright Wojciech Boguslawski and Director Jerzy Grotowski, manuscript by Adam Mickiewicz. e, Marshal Józef Pilsudski, Solidarity posters. f, NATO emblem, Gen. Casimir Pulaski. g, Astronomers Nicolaus Copernicus and Aleksander Wolszczan, text from De Revolutionibus Orbium Coelestium, by Copernicus. h, Woodcut of mathematician Jan of Glogow, physicist Tadeusz Kotarbinski. i, Detail from 1920 poster and painting, Battle of Grunwald, by Jan Matejko. j, Four members of the Belvedere Group, masthead of Warszawa Walczy newspaper, soldiers at Warsaw Uprising of 1944, seal of Marian Langiewicz. k, Head of John the Apostle, by Veit Stoss, and self-sculpture, by Magdalena Abakanowicz. l, Composers Krzysztof Penderecki and Frederic Chopin, Mazurka No. 10, Opus 50, by Karol Szymanowski. m, Engraving of Cracow and Royal Castle, Warsaw. n, Portrait of Jan III Sobieski, flag of European Union. o, Writers Wislawa Szymborska and Mikolaj Rej. p, Runners Janusz Kusocinski and Robert Korzeniowski.

*Perf. 11¼x11½ Syncopated*

**2001, Nov. 11**

**3614** A1222 1z Sheet of 16, #a-p 11.50 6.75

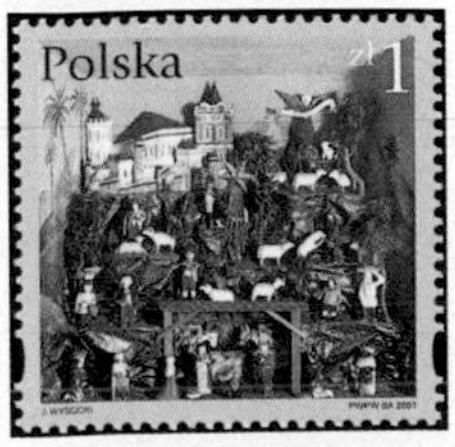

Christmas A1223

Creches from Lower Silesia: 1z, 1.90z.

**2001, Nov. 27**

**3615-3616** A1223 Set of 2 1.90 .95

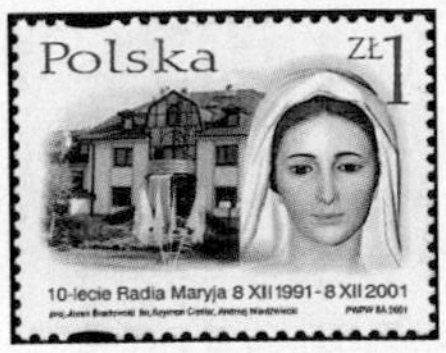

Radio Maryja, 10th Anniv. A1224

Designs: No. 3617, 1z, Head of Virgin Mary statue, building.

No. 3618: a, 1z, Statue of Virgin Mary praying, crowd with flag. b, 1z, Statue of crowned Virgin Mary, crowd with flag.

**2001, Dec. 7**

**3617** A1224 1z multi .65 .30

**Souvenir Sheet**

**3618** A1224 1z Sheet, #a-b, 3617 2.25 1.25

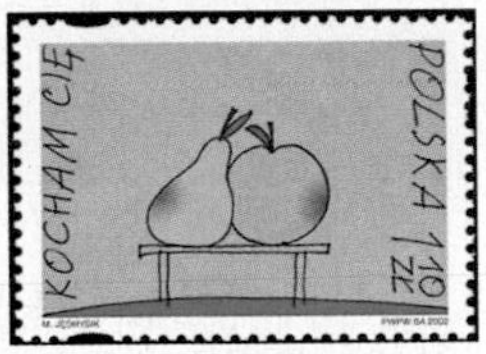

Love A1225

*Perf. 11¾x11½ Syncopated*

**2002, Feb. 4** **Litho.**

**3619** A1225 1.10z multi .65 .30

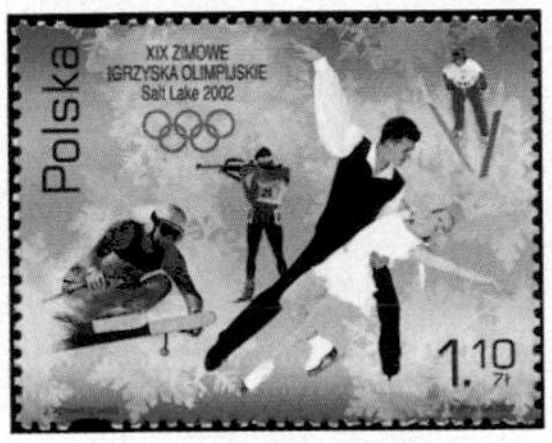

2002 Winter Olympics, Salt Lake City — A1226

*Perf. 11½x11¼ Syncopated*

**2002, Feb. 8**

**3620** A1226 1.10z multi .65 .30
*a.* Stamp + label .65 .30

No. 3620a was issued 2/22, and lists medals won by Adam Malysz.

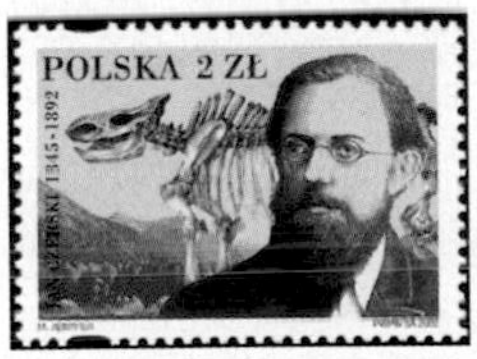

Famous Poles A1227

Designs: No. 3621, 2z, Jan Czerski (1845-92), geologist. No. 3622, 2z, Bronislaw Pilsudski (1866-1918), linguist.

*Perf. 11¾x11½ Syncopated*

**2002, Feb. 22**

**3621-3622** A1227 Set of 2 2.00 1.00

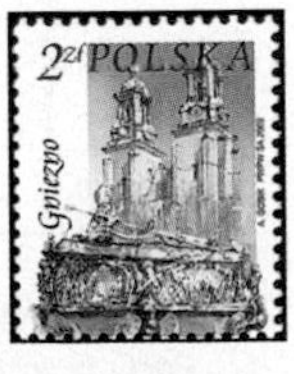

City Landmarks — A1228

Designs: 2z, Cathedral, St. Adalbert's coffin, Gniezno. 2.10z, Wawel Cathedral, St. Mary's Church, Lajkonik, Cracow. 3.20z, Mermaid monument, Royal Palace, Warsaw.

**2002, Mar. 1** **Photo.** *Perf. 11¾x11½*

**3623** A1228 2z multi 1.00 .50
**3624** A1228 2.10z multi 1.00 .50
**3625** A1228 3.20z multi 1.60 .80
*Nos. 3623-3625 (3)* 3.60 1.80

See Nos. 3643-3644.

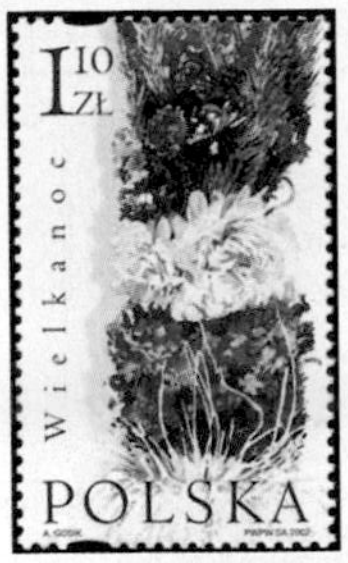

Easter — A1229

Designs: 1.10z, Flowers. 2z, Chicks.

*Perf. 11½x11¾ Syncopated*

**2002, Mar. 8** **Litho.**

**3626-3627** A1229 Set of 2 1.60 .80

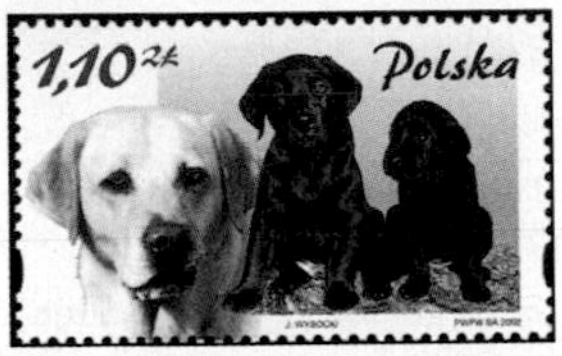

Mammals and Their Young — A1230

No. 3628: a, Dog (purple denomination). b, Cat (brown denomination). c, Wolf (red denomination). d, Lynx (blue denomination).

*Perf. 11¾x11½ Syncopated*

**2002, Mar. 25**

**3628** Horiz. strip of 4 3.50 2.50
*a.-d.* A1230 1.10z Any single .85 .30

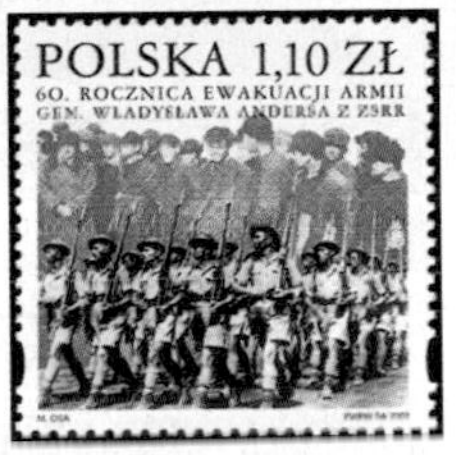

Evacuation of Gen. Wladyslaw Anders' Army from USSR, 60th Anniv. A1231

*Perf. 11½ Syncopated*

**2002, Mar. 26**

**3629** A1231 1.10z multi .60 .30

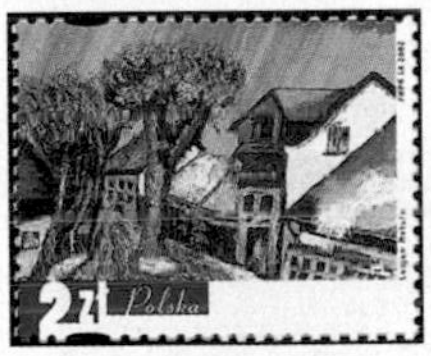

Paintings by Disabled Artists A1232

Unnamed works by: No. 3630, 1.10z, Henryk Paraszczuk, vert. No. 3631, 1.10z, Amanda Zejmis, vert. 2z, Lucjan Matula. 3.20z, Józefa Laciak.

*Perf. 11½x11¼ Sync., 11¼x11½ Sync.*

**2002, Apr. 7** **Litho.**

**3630-3633** A1232 Set of 4 6.00 3.00

Census A1233

**2002, Apr. 30** *Perf. 11¼x11½ Sync.*

**3634** A1233 1.10z multi .55 .25

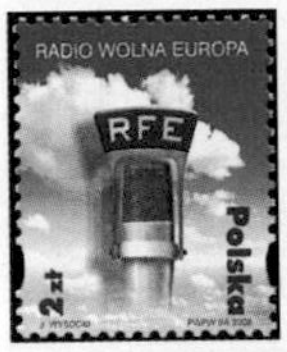

Radio Free Europe, 50th Anniv. — A1234

**2002, May 2** *Perf. 11¾x11½ Sync.*

**3635** A1234 2z multi 1.00 .50

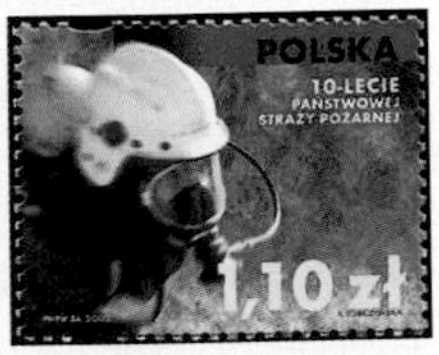

State Fire Brigade, 10th Anniv. A1235

**2002, May 4** *Perf. 11¼x11½ Sync.*

**3636** A1235 1.10z multi .55 .25

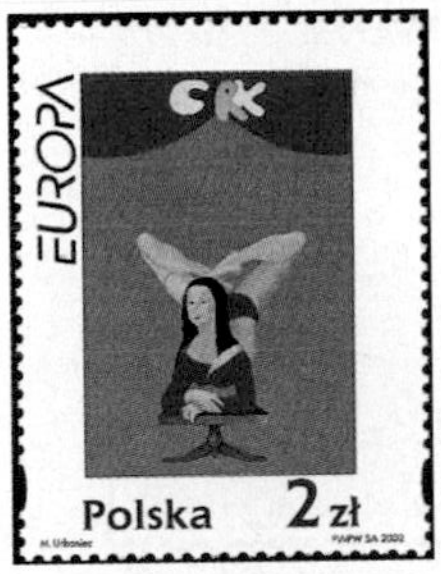

Europa A1236

**2002, May 5**

**3637** A1236 2z multi 1.00 .50

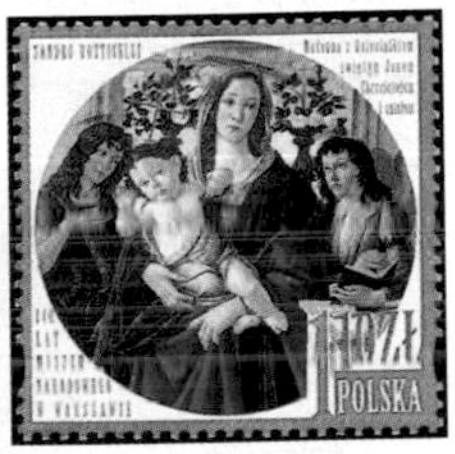

Madonna With Child, St. John the Baptist and Angel, by Sandro Botticelli A1237

**2002, May 18** *Perf. 11½ Sync.*

**3638** A1237 1.10z multi .55 .25

National Gallery, Warsaw, 140th anniv.

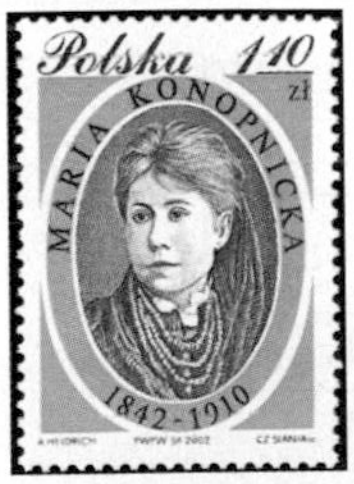

Maria Konopnicka (1842-1910), Poet — A1238

**Photo. & Engr.**

**2002, May 23** *Perf. 11½x11¼*

**3639** A1238 1.10z multi .85 .50

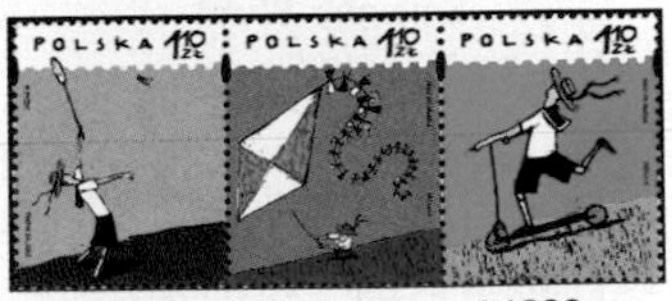

Children's Activities — A1239

No. 3640: a, Child playing badminton. b, Child flying kite. c, Child riding scooter. Illustration reduced.

*Perf. 11½x11¼ Syncopated*

**2002, May 31** **Litho.**

**3640** A1239 1.10z Horiz. strip of 3, #a-c 2.50 1.25

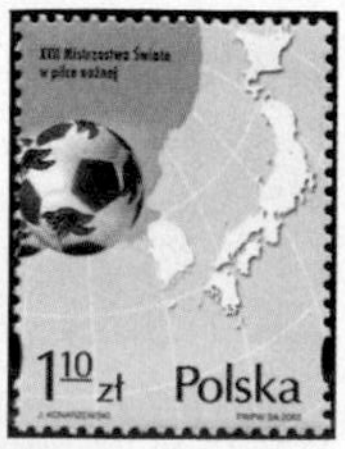


2002 World Cup Soccer Championships, Japan and Korea — A1240

Soccer ball and: 1.10z, Map. 2z, Players.

**2002, June 1**
**3641-3642** A1240 Set of 2 2.50 1.25

**Soccer World Cup Type of 2002**

***Perf. 11½x11¼ Syncopated***

**2002, June 1** **Litho.**
*3642a* Souvenir sheet, 2 each #3641-3642 5.00 2.50

**City Landmarks Type of 2002**

Designs: 1.80z, Roman paten, St. Joseph's Sanctuary, Kalisz. 2.60z, Castle, reliquary of St. Sigismund, Plock, horiz.

***Perf. 11¾x11½, 11½x11¾***

**2002, July 1** **Photo.**
**3643** A1228 1.80z multi 1.00 .60
**3644** A1228 2.60z multi 1.75 .80

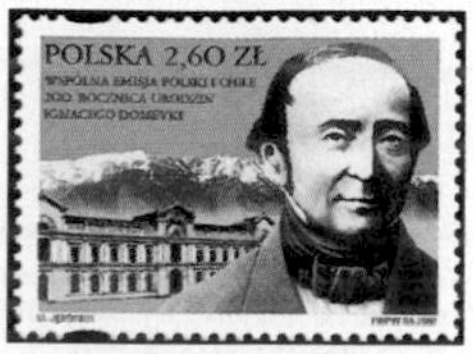


Ignacy Domeyko (1802-89), Mineralogist — A1241

***Perf. 11¾x11½ Syncopated***

**2002, July 3** **Litho.**
**3645** A1241 2.60z multi 1.75 1.00

See Chile No. 1389.

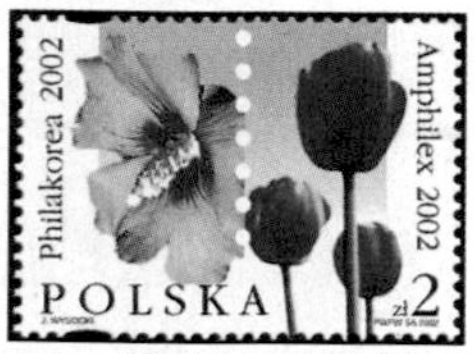


Philakorea 2002 and Anphilex 2002 Stamp Exhibitions — A1242

**2002, July 12**
**3646** A1242 2z multi 1.60 1.00

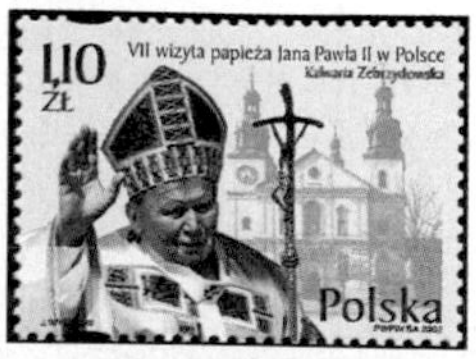


Seventh Visit of Pope John Paul II
A1243

Pope at: 1.10z, Kalwaria Zebrzydowska. 1.80z, Lagiewniki, Cracow. 3.20z, Wawel Castle, Cracow.

***Perf. 11¾x11½ Syncopated***

**2002** **Litho.**
**3647-3648** A1243 Set of 2 2.25 1.50

**Souvenir Sheet**

**Engr.**

***Perf. 11x11½***

**3649** A1233 3.20z blue 2.50 2.00

Issued: 1.10z, 1.80z, 8/5; 3.20z, 8/16.

**Depictions of the Virgin Mary Type of 2001**

Designs: No. 3650, 1.10z, Holy Lady of Incessant Assistance (Matka Boza Nieustajacej Pomocy), Jaworzno. No. 3651, 1.10z, Holy Lady of Opole. 2z, Holy Lady of Trabki, Trabki Wielkie.

***Perf. 11½x11¼ Syncopated***

**2002, Aug. 14** **Litho.**
**3650-3652** A1210 Set of 3 3.00 1.50

Souvenir Sheet

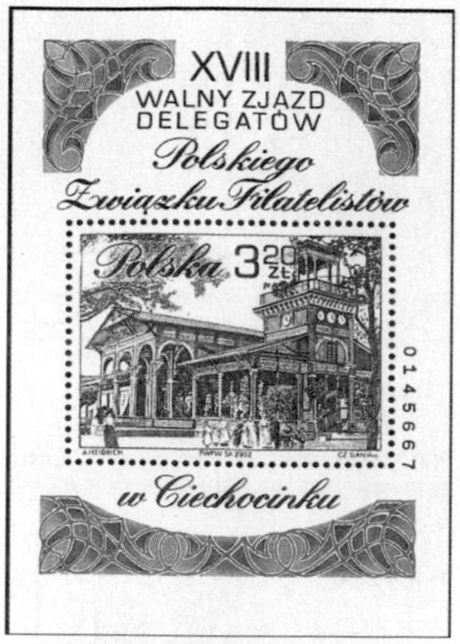


23rd Polish Philatelic Association Convention, Ciechocinek — A1244

**Engr. (Margin Photo. & Engr.)**

**2002, Sept. 1** ***Perf. 11x10¾***
**3653** A1244 3.20z brown 2.50 1.25

Exists imperf. Value $6.50.

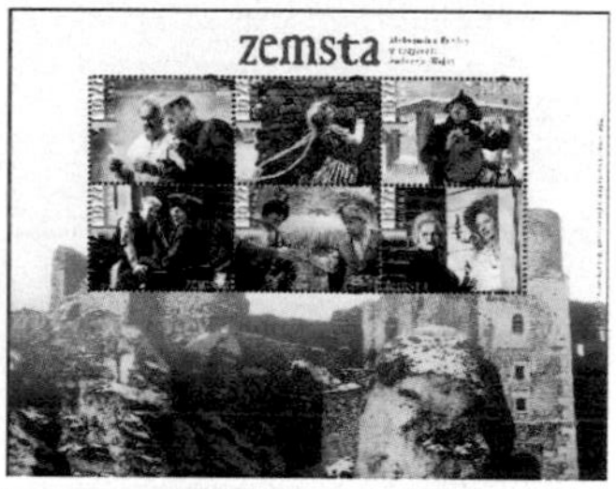


Premiere of Film "Zemsta," Directed by Andrzej Wajda — A1245

No. 3654: a, Czesnik and Dyndalski reading letter. b, Klara and Waclaw kissing. c, Papkin with mandolin. d, Rejent and Papkin, in chair. e, Rejent and Czesnik shaking hands. f, Attendant and Klara.

***Perf. 11¾x11½ Syncopated***

**2002, Sept. 12** **Litho.**
**3654** A1245 1.10z Sheet of 6, #a-f 5.00 2.50

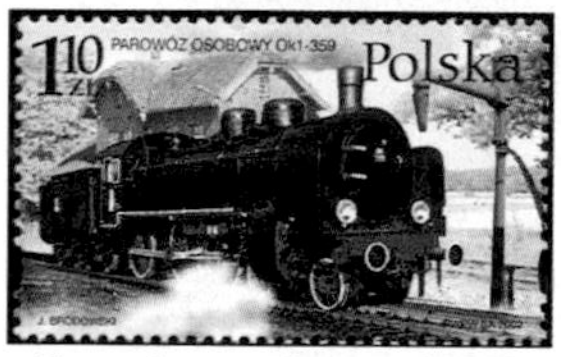


Steam Locomotives — A1246

Designs: No. 3655, 1.10z, Ok1-359. No. 3656, 1.10z, Ol49-7. No. 3657, 2z, TKi3-87. No. 3658, 2z, Pm36-2.

***Perf. 11¾x11½ Syncopated***

**2002, Sept. 21** **Litho.**
**3655-3658** A1246 Set of 4 3.00 1.50
*a.* Horiz. strip of 4, #3655-3658 4.75 3.75

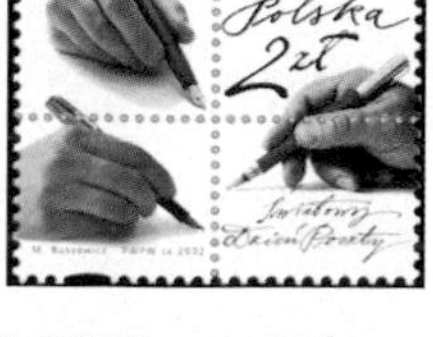


World Post Day
A1247

***Perf. 11¼x11½ Syncopated***

**2002, Oct. 9**
**3659** A1247 2z multi 1.00 .50

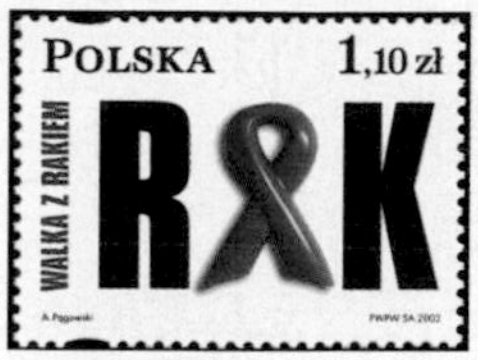


Fight Against Cancer
A1248

***Perf. 11¾x11½ Syncopated***

**2002, Oct. 25**
**3660** A1248 1.10z multi .55 .30

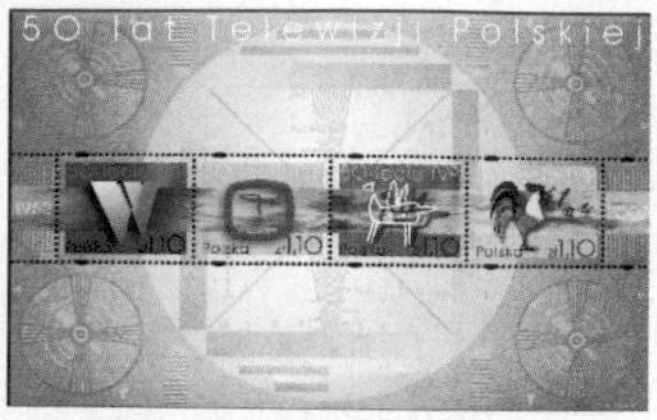


Polish Television, 50th Anniv. — A1249

No. 3661 — Programs: a, Wiadomosci (News, red background). b, Teatru Televizji (Television theater, green background). c, Pegaz (Cultural program). d, Teleranek (children's program).

***Perf. 11¼x11½ Syncopated***

**2002, Oct. 25**
**3661** A1249 1.10z Sheet of 4, #a-d 3.00 1.50

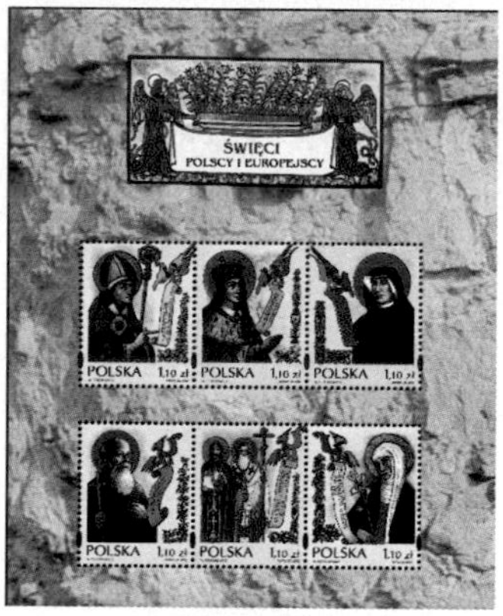


Saints — A1250

No. 3662: a, St. Stanislaw of Szczepanow (1030-79). b, St. Kazimierz (1458-84). c, St. Faustyna Kowalska (1905-38). d, St. Benedict (480-547). e, Sts. Cyril (826-869) and Methodius (815-85). f, St. Catherine of Siena (1347-80).

***Perf. 11½x11¼ Syncopated***

**2002, Nov. 8**
**3662** A1250 1.10z Sheet of 6, #a-f 4.00 2.00

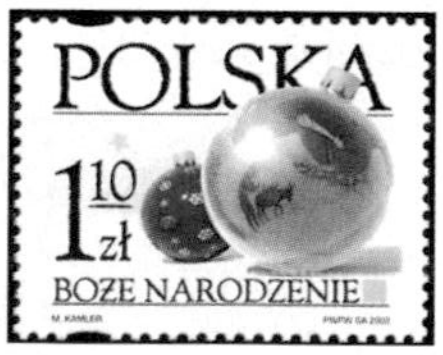


Christmas
A1251

Ornaments: 1.10z, 2z.

***Perf. 11¼x11½ Syncopated***

**2002, Nov. 27**
**3663-3664** A1251 Set of 2 1.60 .80
Booklet, 10 #3663 5.50

**City Landmarks Type of 2002**

Designs: 1.20z, Towers of Old City Hall, Statue of Nicolaus Copernicus, Torun, horiz. 3.40z, Church and well, Kazimierz Dolny, horiz.

**2003** **Photo.** ***Perf. 11½x11¾***
**3665** A1228 1.20z multi .65 .30
**3666** A1228 3.40z multi 1.75 .85

Issued: 1.20z, 1/31; 3.40z, 4/10.

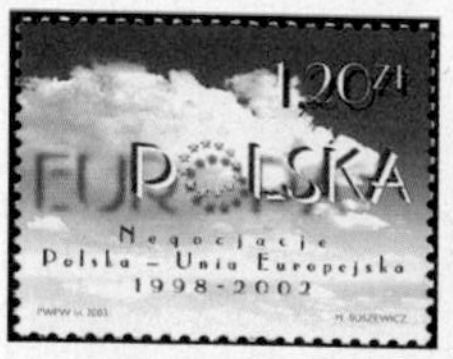


1998-2002 Negotiations to Join European Union
A1252

**2003, Feb. 18** ***Perf. 11x11½***
**3667** A1252 1.20z multi .65 .30

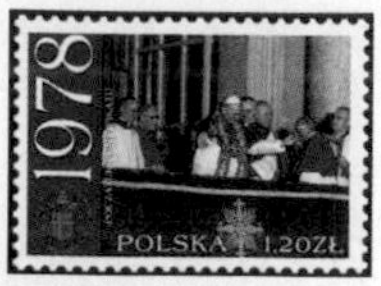


A1253

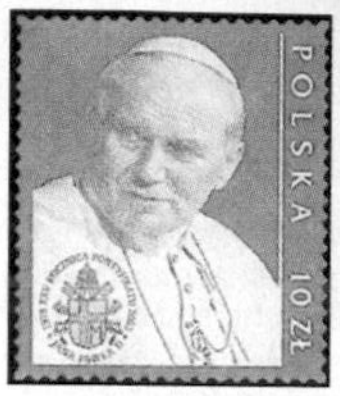


Pontificate of John Paul II, 25th Anniv. — A1254

No. 3668: a, Election as Pope, 1978. b, In Poland, 1979. c, In France, 1980. d, Assassination attempt, 1981. e, At Fatima, Portugal, 1982. f, Extraordinary Holy Year, 1983. g, At Quirinale Palace, Rome, 1984. h, World Youth Day, 1985. i, At synagogue, Rome, 1986. j, Pentecost vigil, 1987. k, At European Parliament, Strasbourg, France, 1988. l, Meeting with Mikhail Gorbachev, 1989. m, At Guinea-Bissau leper colony, 1990. n, At European Bishops' Synod, 1991. o, Publication of Catechism of the Catholic Church, 1992. p, Praying for the Balkans in Assisi, 1993. q, At Sistine Chapel, 1994. r, At UN Headquarters for 50th anniv. celebrations, 1995. s, In Germany, 1996. t, In Sarajevo, Bosnia & Herzegovina, 1997. u, In Cuba, 1998. v, Opening Holy Doors, 1999. w, World Youth Day, 2000. x, Closing Holy Doors, 2001. y, Addressing Italian Parliament, 2002.

**2003, Mar. 20** **Litho.** ***Perf. 13x13¼***
**3668** Sheet of 25 24.50 20.00
*a.-y.* A1253 1.20z Any single .90 .30

**Etched on Silver Foil**

***Die Cut Perf. 12½x13***

**Self-Adhesive**

**3669** A1254 10z Pope John Paul II 8.50 8.50

Cancels can be easily removed from No. 3669. See Vatican City Nos. 1236-1237.

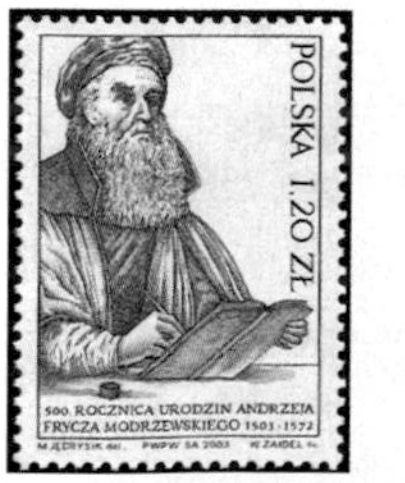


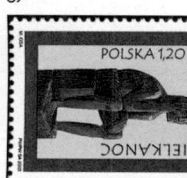

Andrzej Frycz-Modrzewski (1503-72), Writer — A1255

**2003, Mar. 28** **Engr.** ***Perf. 11½x11***
**3670** A1255 1.20z brown .65 .30

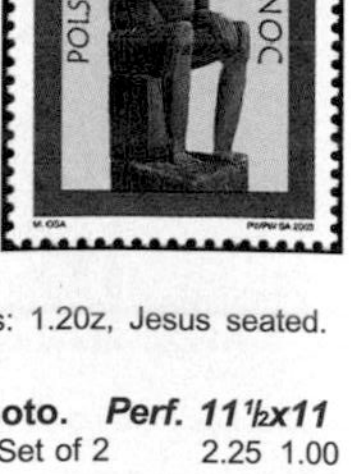


Easter — A1256

Folk representations: 1.20z, Jesus seated. 2.10z, Jesus standing.

**2003, Mar. 28** **Photo.** ***Perf. 11½x11***
**3671-3672** A1256 Set of 2 2.25 1.00

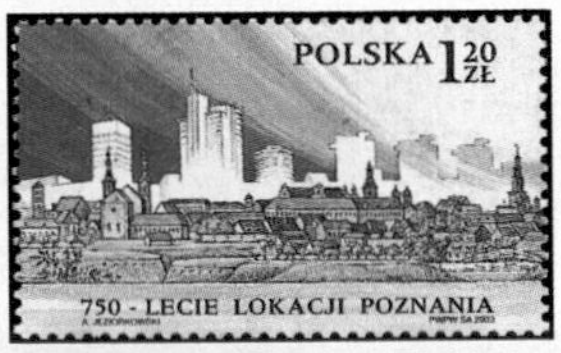


Granting of Municipal Rights to Poznan, 750th Anniv. — A1257

Designs: 1.20z, Old and modern skylines of Poznan.
3.40z, View of Poznan, 1626.

*Perf. 11¾x11½*

**2003, Apr. 15** **Photo.**
**3673** A1257 1.20z multi .65 .30

**Souvenir Sheet**
**Photo. & Engr.**
*Perf. 11¼x11½*

**3674** A1257 3.40z brown & lt brown 2.25 1.00

No. 3674 contains one 39x31mm stamp.

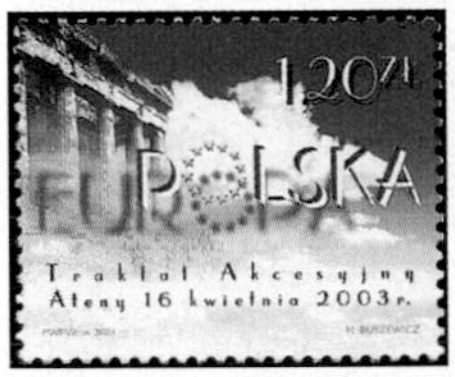


Signing of European Union Accession Treaty — A1257a

**2003, Apr. 16** **Photo.** *Perf. 11x11½*
**3674A** A1257a 1.20z multi .65 .30

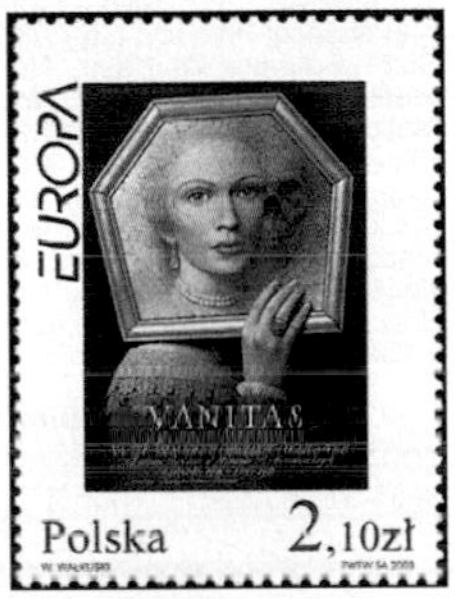


Europa A1258

**2003, May 5** **Photo.** *Perf. 11*
**3675** A1258 2.10z multi 1.10 .55

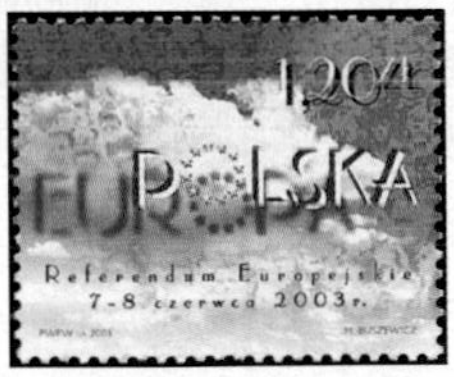


European Union Referendum — A1258a

**2003, May 26** **Photo.** *Perf. 11x11½*
**3675A** A1258a 1.20z multi .65 .30

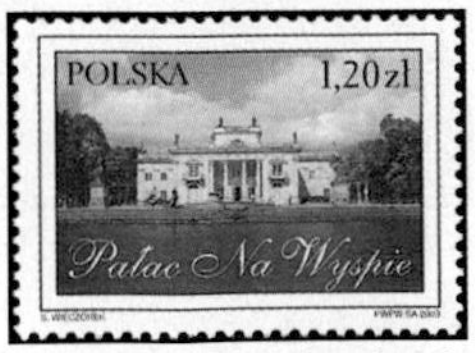


Lazienkowski Park Landmarks, Warsaw — A1259

Designs: 1.20z, Palac Na Wyspie. 1.80z, Palac Na Wyspie, diff. 2.10z, Palac Myslewicki. 2.60z, Amphitheater.

*Perf. 11¼x11½*

**2003, May 30** **Photo.**
**3676-3679** A1259 Set of 4 5.00 3.50

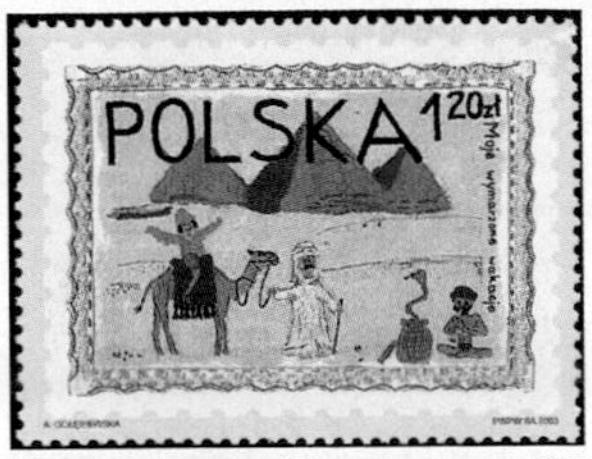


Children's Dream Vacations — A1260

Children's art by: 1.20z, Anna Golebiewska. 1.80z, Marlena Krejpcio, vert. 2.10z, Michal Korzen. 2.60z, Ewa Zajdler.

**2003, June 20** *Perf. 11*
**3680-3683** A1260 Set of 4 5.00 3.50

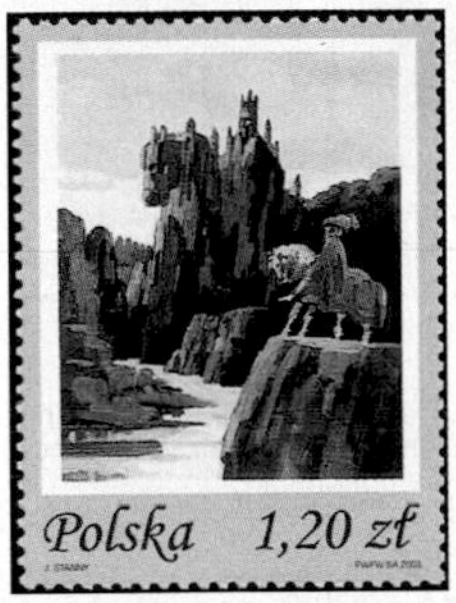


Fairy Tales A1261

Designs: 1.20z, Krak, traditional tale. 1.80z, Stupid Mateo, by Jozef Ignacy Kraszewski. 2.10z, The Princess Enchanted Into a Frog, by Antoni Jozef Glinski. 2.60z, The Crock of Gold, by Kraszewski.

**2003, June 30**
**3684-3687** A1261 Set of 4 5.00 3.50

Souvenir Sheet

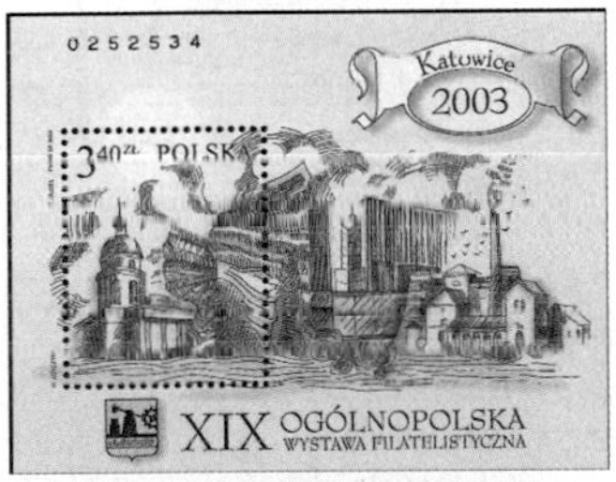


19th National Philatelic Exhibition, Katowice — A1262

**Photo. & Engr.**

**2003, Aug. 18** *Perf. 11½x11¼*
**3688** A1262 3.40z multi 2.25 1.00

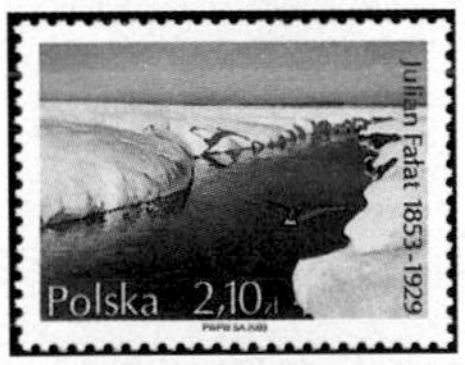


Paintings of Julian Falat (1853-1929) — A1263

Designs: 1.20z, Self-portrait, vert. 1.80z, Spearsmen, vert. 2.10z, Winter Landscape with River and Bird. 2.60z, On the Ship — Merchants at Ceylon.

*Perf. 11½x11¼, 11¼x11½*

**2003, Sept. 30** **Photo.**
**3689-3692** A1263 Set of 4 5.00 3.00

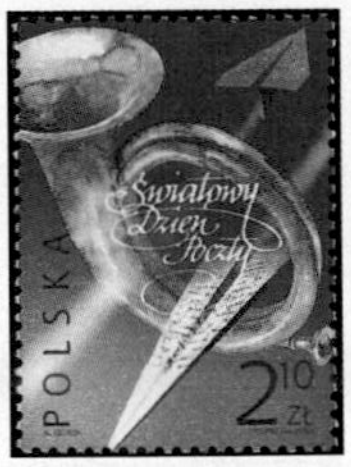


World Post Day — A1264

**2003, Oct. 9** *Perf. 11½x11¼*
**3693** A1264 2.10z multi 1.10 .55

**Depictions of the Virgin Mary Type of 2001**

Designs: 1.20z, Mother of the Redeemer. 1.80z, Holy Mother Benevolent, Krzeszowice. 2.10z, Holy Mother, Zieleniec.

**2003, Oct. 14**
**3694-3696** A1210 Set of 3 2.60 1.25

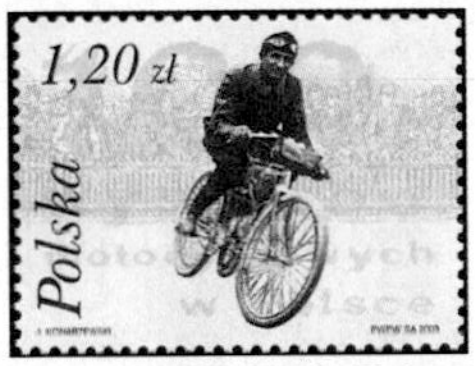


Motorcycle Racing in Poland, Cent. — A1265

No. 3697 — Motorcycles of various eras with text in: a, Yellow. b, Green. c, Pink.

**2003, Oct. 20** *Perf. 11¼x11½*
**3697** Horiz. strip of 3 2.50 1.00
*a.-c.* A1265 1.20z Any single .75 .30

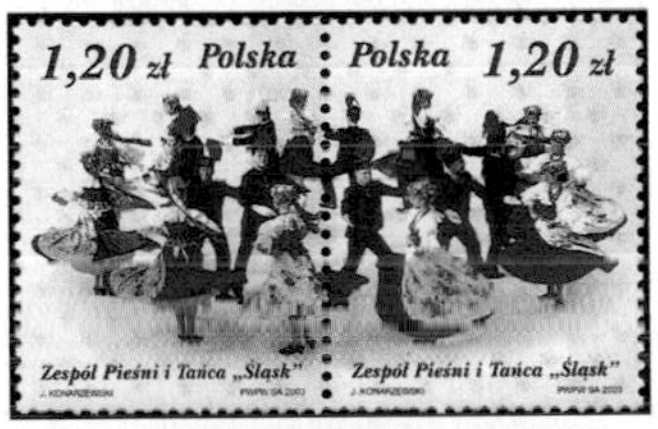


Silesian Folk Ensemble — A1266

No. 3698: a, Denomination at left. b, Denomination at right.
Illustration reduced.

**2003, Oct. 29** *Perf. 11½x11¼*
**3698** A1266 1.20z Horiz. pair, #a-b 1.50 .75

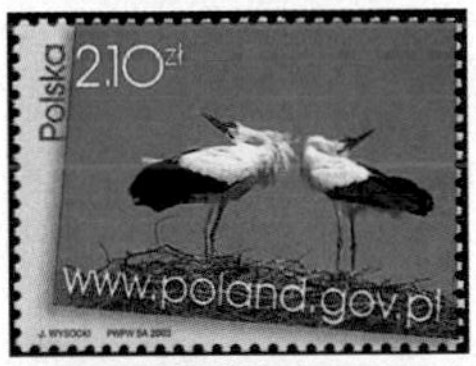


Cranes and Polish Government Internet Address — A1267

**2003, Oct. 31** *Perf. 11¼x11½*
**3699** A1267 2.10z multi 1.50 .75

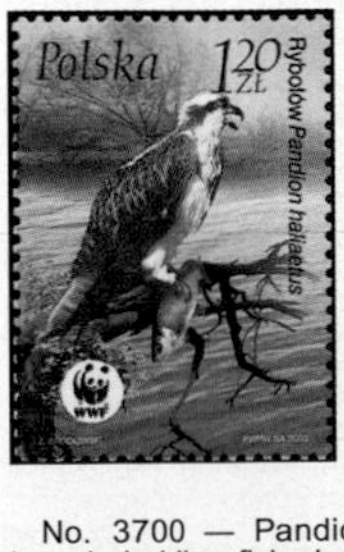


Worldwide Fund for Nature (WWF) — A1268

No. 3700 — Pandion haliaetus: a, On branch holding fish. b, Adult and young at nest. c, Adult hunting for prey. d, Adult flying with fish in talons.

**2003, Oct. 31** *Perf. 11½x11¼*
**3700** Horiz. strip of 4 3.75 2.75
*a.-d.* A1268 1.20z Any single .90 .30

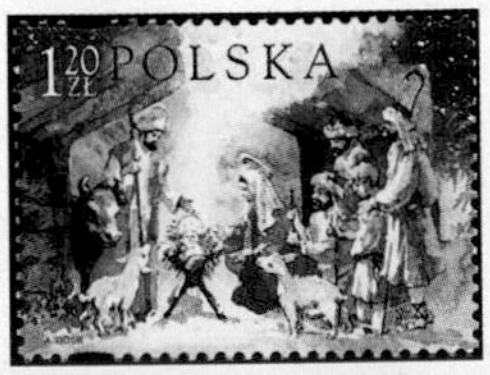


Christmas — A1269

Designs: 1.20z, Nativity. 1.80z, The Magi. 2.10z, The Annunciation, vert. 2.60z, Holy Family, vert.

*Perf. 11½ Syncopated*

**2003, Nov. 27** **Litho.**
**3701-3704** A1269 Set of 4 5.50 2.50

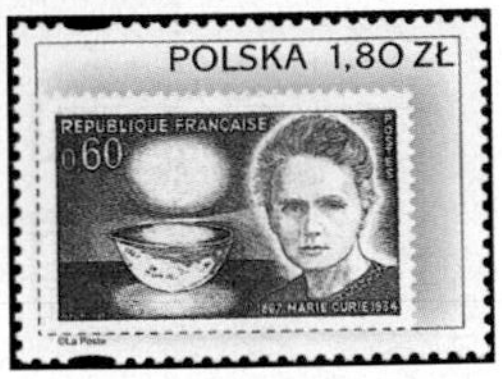


Foreign Stamps Depicting Polish Subjects A1270

Designs: 1.20z, Sweden #2399a (Wislawa Szymborska), vert. 1.80z, France #1195 (Marie Curie). 2.10z, Sweden #1598 (Czeslaw Milosz), vert. 2.60z, Vatican City #437 (Black Madonna of Czestochowa).

**2003, Dec. 12**
**3705-3708** A1270 Set of 4 5.75 5.00

**City Landmarks Type of 2002**

Designs: 5g, Town Hall, church archway, Sandomierz, horiz. 1.25z, Town Hall, Neptune Fountain, Gdansk. 1.90z, Church of the Descent of the Holy Ghost, Israel Poznanski House, Lódz, horiz. 3.45z, Union Monument, Lublin Castle, Lublin, horiz.

*Perf. 11½x11¾, 11¾x11½*

**2004** **Photo.**
**3709** A1228 5g multi .20 .20
**3710** A1228 1.25z multi .70 .35
**3711** A1228 1.90z multi .95 .50
**3712** A1228 3.45z multi 1.75 .90
*Nos. 3709-3712 (4)* 3.60 1.95

Issued: 5g, 1/1; 1.25z, 1/0; 1.00z, 5/11; 3.45z, 2/23. Sheet margins of No. 3711 served as etiquettes.

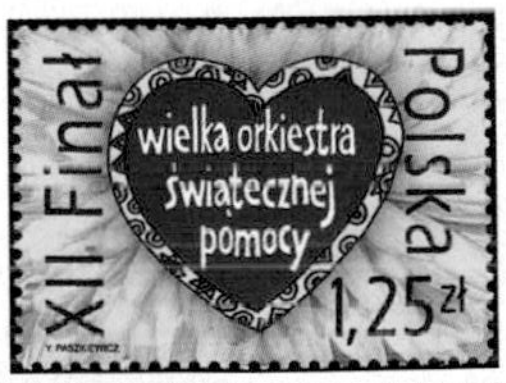


12th Concert of the Great Holiday Help Orchestra — A1271

**2004, Jan. 5** *Perf. 11x11½*
**3713** A1271 1.25z multi .70 .35

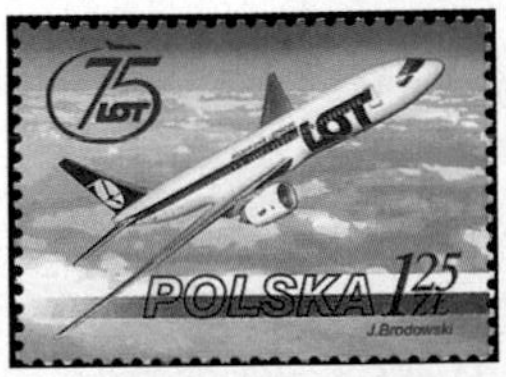


LOT (Polish National Airlines), 75th Anniv. A1272

**2004, Jan. 21**
**3714** A1272 1.25z multi .65 .35

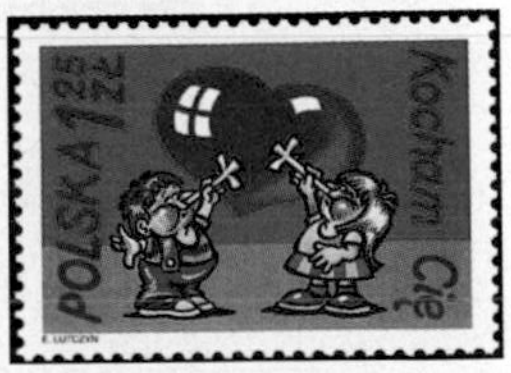


Love A1273

**2004, Feb. 2**
**3715** A1273 1.25z multi .70 .35

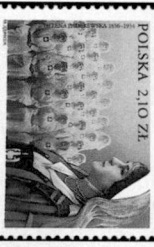

**2004, Feb. 27**
3716-3717 A1274    Set of 2
3716    2.10z    2.25    1.10
3717    2.10z

Famous
Poles
A1274

Designs: No. 3716, 2.10z, Helena Paderew-
ska (1856-1934), chairwoman of Polish White
Cross. No. 3717, 2.10z, Father Lucjan
Bójnowski (1868-1960), Polish Army recruiter
in US.

**2004, Mar. 12**
3718-3719 A1275    Set of 2
Easter — A1275

**Perf. 11½x11¾**
Designs: 1.25z, Rabbit. 2.10z, Lamb.
3718    1.25z    1.75    .90
3719    2.10z

No. 3720: a. Beaver, frog, flowers, b. Kingfisher holding fish, crawfish holding fish, snail,
beetle and water lilies. c. Grayling, leech, mus-
sel, snail. d. Pike chasing smaller fish, grebe,
snail.

**2004, Mar. 30**
3720    Horiz. strip of 4
3720    A1276    1.25z Any single

Flora and Fauna in
Reservoirs — A12/6

**Perf. 11¾x11½ Syncopated**
        Litho.
a.-d.    3.25    3.00
        .80    .35

RZECZPOSPOLITA
POLSKA

**2004, May 1**
3721 A1277  2.10z multi + label
Admission to
European
Union — A1277
    1.10    .55

**Perf. 11½x11¾ Syncopated**

**2004, May 5**
3722 A1278  2.10z multi
Europa
A1278
    1.10    .55

**2004, May 7**    **Perf. 11½x11¾**
3723 A1279  3.45z multi + label
Tenth
Government
Postage Stamp
Printers'
Conference,
Krakow
A1279
    2.00    1.00

Photo. & Engr.

WIZYTY DUSZPASTERSKIE OJCA ŚWIĘTEGO
POLSKI I WATYKANU
WSPÓLNA EMISJA
JANA PAWŁA II W POLSCE

WIZYTY DUSZPASTERSKIE OJCA ŚWIĘTEGO
POLSKI I WATYKANU
WSPÓLNA EMISJA
A1280
JANA PAWŁA II W POLSCE

Visits to Poland by Pope John Paul
II — A1281

No. 3724: a. Wearing red stole, hand on
chin. b. Wearing red stole, praying. c. Holding
crucifix with rays. d. Holding crucifix.
No. 3725: a. Wearing gold stole, holding
crucifix. b. With arm raised. c. Wearing white
vestments, seated. d. Wearing red stole,
seated.

**2004, June 2**    **Perf. 13¼x13**
3724 A1280  1.25z Sheet of 4,
        #a-d, + 8 la-
        bels        3.50    2.50

Litho. (Embossed Labels)
Country Name in Blue

Paintings by Jacek Malczewski (1854-
1929) — A1283

Jacek Malczewski 1854-1929

Polska 2,10z

**2004, July 15**    **Perf. 11½x11¾,**
3727-3730 A1283    **11½x11½**
Souvenir Sheet    **Photo.**
        Set of 4    5.50    3.50

Designs: 1.20z, Self-portrait, vert. 1.90z,
Ellenai, vert. 2.10z, Tobias and Harpy. 2.60z,
The Unknown Note.

No. 3726: a. Platycercus elegans. b.
Platycercus eximius. c. Nymphicus hollandicus. d. Melopsittacus undulatus. d.
Chloebia gouldiae. Poephila guttata. Padda
oryzivora.

**2004, June 30**    **Perf. 11¾x11¾ Syncopated**
3726 A1282  1.25z Block of 4, #a-    **Litho.**
        d        7.00    3.00

Birds — A1282

POLSKA 1.25z
Bendia trifolium Porsycrocius arghanus
Zebelka Poephila guttata
POLSKA 1.25z
Nimla Nymphicus hollandicus

Country Name in Red
3725 A1281  1.25z Sheet of 4,
        #a-d, + 8 la-
        bels        3.50    2.50

**2004 Summer Olympics,
Athens — A1285**

No. 3732: a. Boxing. b. Women's track. c.
Equestrian. d. Wrestling.

**2004, July 30**    **Perf. 11½x11¾ Syncopated**
3731 A1284  3.45z multi    **Litho.**
    a.    Imperf.        2.25    1.25
                    6.25    6.25

Singapore World Stamp Championship
2004 — A1284
Miniature Sheet

POLSKA 1,25 zł

Motor
Sports
A1290

**2004, Sept. 3**
3752 A1289  2.10z multi
Dunajec River Raftsmen — A1289
    1.25    .60

See Slovakia No. 463.

Czeslaw Niemen

Polska 1,25 zł

Czeslaw Niemen (1939-2004),
Musician — A1288

**2004, Aug. 30**    **Perf. 11¾x11½ Syncopated**
3751 A1288  1.25z black & gray    **Litho.**
    .70    .35

Matka Boża Dzikowska

POLSKA

1.25 zł

Inscriptions: No. 3734, 1.25z, Matka Boża
Dzikowska. No. 3735, 1.25z, Matka Boża
Fatimska. No. 3736, 1.25z, Matka Boża Jas-
nogórska. No. 3737, 1.25z, Matka Boża Las-
kawa. No. 3738, 1.25z, Matka Boża Łomżyn-
ska. No. 3739, 1.25z, Matka Boża Lomzyn-
ska. No. 3740, 1.25z, Matka Boża
Nieustającej Pomocy. No. 3741, 1.25z, Matka
Boża Bolesna Oborska. No. 3742, 1.25z, Matka
Boża Piekarska. No. 3743, 1.25z, Matka
Boża Pocieszenia. No. 3744, 1.25z, Matka
Boża Pokorna Rudzka. No. 3745, 1.25z, Matka
Boża Rychwałdzka. No. 3746, 1.25z, Matka
Boża Rywałdzka. No. 3747, 1.25z, Matka
Boża Rzeszowska. No. 3748, 1.25z, Matka
Boża Sianowska. No. 3749, 1.25z, Matka
Boża Skrzatuska. No. 3750, 1.25z, Matka
Boża Swierodzinna.

**2004, Aug. 14**    **Perf. 11½x11¾ Syncopated**
3734-3750 A1287    **Litho.**
        Set of 17    14.00    8.00

Depictions of the
Virgin
Mary — A1287

WITOLD GOMBROWICZ 1904-1969

POLSKA    1.25 zł

**2004, Aug. 2**
3732 A1285  1.25z Sheet of 4,
        #a-d        3.00    1.50

**Perf. 11¾x11¾ Syncopated**

Witold
Gombrowicz
(1904-69),
Writer — A1286

**2004, Aug. 4**    **Perf. 11¾x11¾ Syncopated**
3733 A1286  1.25z blue    .70    .35

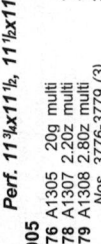

All Saints Collegiate Church, Sieradz — A1305

Baltic Shore, Sopot — A1307

Buildings, Szczecin A1308

**Perf. 11¼x11½, 11½x11¾ Photo.**

| | | |
|---|---|---|
| | .20 | .20 |
| 3776 A1305 | 20g multi | .20 | .20 |
| 3778 A1307 | 2.20z multi | 1.40 | .70 |
| 3779 A1308 | 2.80z multi | 1.75 | .85 |
| | | 3.35 | 1.75 |

Nos. 3776-3779 (3)

**2005**

Issued: 20g, 7/29; 2.20z, 6/15; 2.80z, 5/30.

Europa A1310

Europa — A1310

**Perf. 11¼x11½ Syncopated Litho. & Embossed**

2005, May 5 3781 A1310 2.20z multi 1.40 .70

Youth Literature — A1312

No. 3783: a, 1.30z, *Hour of the Crimson Rose,* by Maria Krüger. b, 2z, *The Little Prince,* by Antoine de Saint-Exupery. c, 2.20z, 20,000 Leagues Under the Sea, by Jules Verne. d, 2.80z, In Desert and Wilderness, by Henryk Sienkiewicz.

**Perf. 11½ Syncopated Litho.**

2005, June 1 3783 A1312 Sheet of 4, #a-d 5.00 2.50

Pope John Paul II (1920-2005) A1301

Pope John Paul II (1920-2005) — A1301

**Perf. 11¼x11¾ Syncopated Litho.**

.85 .40

2005, Apr. 8 3772 A1301 1.30z multi

Extreme Sports — A1302

No. 3773: a, Parachuting. b, Bungee jumping. c, Rock climbing. d, White water rafting. Illustration reduced.

**Perf. 11¼x11½ Syncopated Litho.**

3.25 1.60

2005, Apr. 15 3773 A1302 1.30z Block of 4, #a-d

Pacific Explorer 2005 World Stamp Expo, Sydney — A1303

Souvenir Sheet

**Perf. 11¼x11½ Syncopated Litho.**

2.10 1.10

2005, Apr. 21 3774 A1303 3.50z multi

Pope John Paul II (1920-2005) — A1304

Souvenir Sheet

**Perf. 11¾x11¼ Syncopated Litho.**

2.10 1.10

2005, Apr. 22 3775 A1304 3.50z multi

13th Concert of the Great Holiday Help Orchestra — A1295

**Perf. 11¼x11½ Litho.**

.85 .40

2005, Jan. 6 3764 A1295 1.30z multi

Konstanty Ildefons Galczynski (1905-53) Poet — A1296

**Perf. 11½x11¼ Litho.**

.85 .40

2005, Jan. 14 3765 A1296 1.30z multi

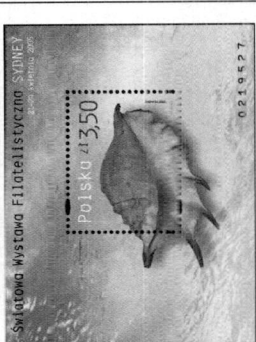

Mikolaj Rej (1505-69), Writer A1297

**Perf. 11¼x11½ Litho.**

.85 .40

2005, Jan. 26 3766 A1297 1.30z black & red

Love A1298

**Perf. 11¼x11½ Litho.**

.85 .40

2005, Feb. 1 Photo. 3767 A1298 1.30z multi

Easter — A1299

Flowers and: 1.30z, Rabbit. 2.20z, Chick.

**Perf. 11¾x11¼ Litho.**

2005, Mar. 1 2.40 1.25 3768-3769 A1299 Set of 2

Hans Christian Andersen (1805-75), Author — A1300

Designs: No. 3770, 1.30z, The Little Mermaid (Mala Syrenka). No. 3771, 1.30z, The Snow Queen (Królowa Sniegu).

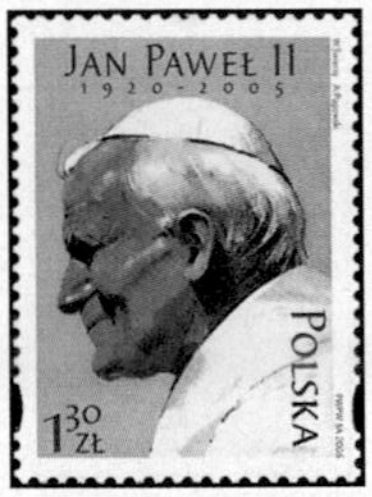

**Perf. 11½x11¾ Syncopated Litho.**

1.75 .85

2005, Mar. 15 3770-3771 A1300 Set of 2

No. 3753: a. Cinder track motorcycle racing (four motorcycles). b, Auto racing. c, Go-kart racing. d, Motorcycle racing (one motorcycle).

**Perf. 11¼x11½ Syncopated**

3.50 2.00 .85 .40

2004, Sept. 11 3753 Horiz. strip of 4 a.-d. A1290 1.25z Any single

World Post Day A1291

**Perf. 11¼x11½ Syncopated Litho.**

1.25 .60

2004, Oct. 9 3754 A1291 2.10z multi

UNESCO World Heritage Sites — A1292

Designs: No. 3755, 1.25z, Castle of the Teutonic Order, Malbork. No. 3756, 1.25z, Historic Center of Warsaw. No. 3757, 1.25z, Historic Center of Cracow, vert. No. 3758, 1.25z, Medieval Town of Torun, vert. No. 3759, 1.25z, Old City of Zamosc.

**Perf. 11½ Syncopated**

3.75 1.90

2004, Oct. 22 3755-3759 A1292 Set of 5

Christmas A1293

Designs: 1.25z, Worshippers at shrine. 2.10z, Window, ornaments, candle, poinsettia.

**Perf. 11¾x11¼**

2.10 1.10

2004, Nov. 5 Photo. 3760-3761 A1293 Set of 2

History of the Earth — A1294

No. 3762: a, 1.25z, Birth (narodziny). b, Infancy (dziecinstwo). c, Youth (mlodosc). d, Maturity (dojrzalosc).

**Perf. 11½ Syncopated Litho.**

3.25 1.60

2004, Dec. 3 3762 A1294 1.25z Block of 4, #a-d

City Landmarks Type of 2002

Design: Monument of Hygea, Raczynski Library, Poznan.

**Perf. 11½x11¾**

.85 .40

2005, Jan. 3 Photo. 3763 A1228 1.30z multi

POLAND

## Souvenir Sheet

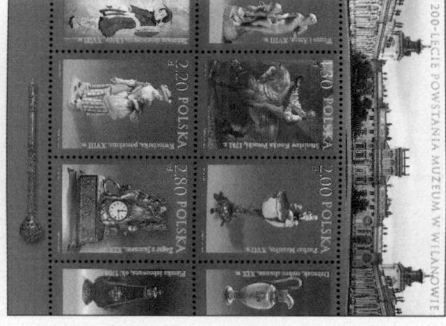 

Items in the Wilanow Museum — A1313

**2005, June 21**
3784 A1313 Sheet of 4, #a-d **Photo.**
5.00 2.50

No. 3784: a, 1.30z. Portrait of Stanislaw Kostka Potocki, by Jacques Louis David, 1781. b, 2z. Nautilus wine cup, 17th cent. c, 2.20z. Porcelain figurine of flower girl, 18th cent. d, 2.80z. Decorative clock, 19th cent.

Embroidered Roses — A1314

**2005, July 15** **Litho.**
3785-3788 A1314 Set of 4 5.00 2.50

Embroidered roses from: 1.30z, Lowicz region. 2z, Lowicz region. 2.20z, Podhale region, diff. 2.80z, Lowicz region, diff.

World Track and Field Championships, Helsinki — A1315

**2005, Aug. 8** **Perf. 11¾x11½ Syncopated**
3789 A1315 Sheet of 4, #a-d 4.25 2.10

No. 3789: a, 1.30z, Hurdles. b, 1.30z, Shot put. c, 2z, Long jump. d, 2z, Pole vault.

## Souvenir Sheet

Polish Eagle and Józef Piłsudski — A1316

**2005, Aug. 12** **Perf. 11½x11½**
3790 A1316 3.50z. multi **Photo.**
2.25 1.10

"Miracle on the Vistula," repulse of Red Army counter-offensive, 85th anniv.

Lech Walesa and Solidarity Emblem — A1317

**2005, Aug. 17** **Perf. 11½x11¾ Syncopated**
3791 A1317 2.20z red & gray 1.40 .70

Solidarity Trade Union, 25th anniv.

Polish Radio, 80th Anniv. — A1318

**2005, Sept. 1** **Perf. 11½x11¾ Syncopated**
3792 A1318 1.30z multi **Photo.**
.85 .40

15th Frederic Chopin Piano Competition A1319

**2005, Sept. 16** **Perf. 11½x11¾ Syncopated**
3793 A1319 2.20z multi **Litho.**
1.40 .70

Zoo Animals A1320

**2005, Sept. 30** **Perf. 11¾x11¾ Syncopated**
3794-3797 A1320 Set of 4 5.25 2.60

Designs: 1.30z, Lemuridae, Opole Zoo. 2z, Panthera tigris altaica, Wroclaw Zoo. 2.20z, Ceratotherium simum, Poznan Zoo. 2.80z, Myrmecophagidae, Warsaw Zoo.

Main Post Office, Cracow A1321

**2005, Oct. 7** **Perf. 11¾x11¾ Syncopated**
3798 A1321 1.30z multi .85 .40

World Post Day.

United Nations, 60th Anniv. A1322

**2005, Oct. 14** **Perf. 11½x11½ Syncopated**
3799 A1322 2.20z multi 1.40 .70

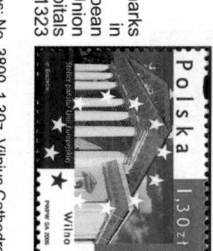

Landmarks in European Union Capitals A1323

**2005, Oct. 24** **Perf. 11½x11½ Syncopated**
3800-3804 A1323 Set of 5 6.00 3.00

Designs: No. 3800, 1.30z, Vilnius Cathedral, Vilnius, Lithuania. No. 3801, 1.30z, St. Matthias's Church, Statue of St. Stephen, Budapest, Hungary. No. 3802, 2.20z, Government building, Dublin, Ireland. No. 3803, 2.20z, Monument, Lisbon, Portugal. 2.80z, Arc de Triomphe, Paris, France.

## Souvenir Sheet

Paintings by Polish Impressionists — A1324

**2005, Nov. 3** **Photo.**
3805 A1324 Sheet of 4, #a-d, + 2 labels 4.00 4.00

No. 3805: a, 1.30z, Plowing in the Ukraine, by L. J. Wyczolkowski. b, 1.30z, Still Life, by J. Pankiewicz. c, 2z, Flower Sellers, by O. Boznanska. d, 2z, Gooseberry Bushes, by W. Podkowinski.

Polish Doctors' Association, Bicent. — A1325

**2005, Nov. 24** **Perf. 11½x11½ Syncopated**
3806 A1325 1.30z. multi **Litho.**
.80 .40

Christmas — A1326

**2005, Nov. 28** **Perf. 11¾x11½ Syncopated**
3807-3808 A1326 Set of 2 **Photo.**
2.25 1.10

Christmas trees and angel in: 1.30z, Blue. 2.20z, Rose pink.

## SEMI-POSTAL STAMPS

Regular Issue of 1919 Surcharged in Violet

a

b

First Polish Philatelic Exhibition. The surtax benefited the Polish White Cross Society.

| | | | **1919, May 3** **Unwmk.** | | **Imperf.** |
|---|---|---|---|---|---|
| B1 | A10(a) | 5f + 5f grn | .20 | .20 | |
| B2 | A10(a) | 10f + 5f red vio | 2.00 | 1.40 | |
| B3 | A10(a) | 15f + 5f dp red | .40 | .20 | |
| B4 | A11(b) | 25f + 5f ol grn | .40 | .20 | |
| B5 | A11(b) | 50f + 5f bl grn | .60 | .30 | |
| | | | **Perf. 11½** | | |
| B6 | A10(a) | 5f + 5f grn | .25 | .20 | |
| B7 | A10(a) | 10f + 5f red vio | .50 | .20 | |
| B8 | A10(a) | 15f + 5f dp red | .30 | .20 | |
| B9 | A11(b) | 25f + 5f ol grn | .30 | .20 | |
| B10 | A11(b) | 50f + 5f bl grn | 1.00 | .40 | |
| | | | Nos. B1-B10 (10) | | 5.90 3.50 |

Regular Issue of 1920 Surcharged in Carmine

**1921, Mar. 5** **Thin Laid Paper** **Perf. 9**
| B11 | A14 | 5m + 30m red vio | 5.00 | 7.00 |
|---|---|---|---|---|
| B12 | A14 | 6m + 30m dp rose | 5.00 | 7.00 |
| B13 | A14 | 8m + 30m lt red | 12.00 | 19.00 |
| B14 | A14 | 20m + 30m gray grn | 37.50 | 65.00 |
| | | Nos. B11-B14 (4) | 59.50 | 98.00 |

Counterfeits, differently perforated, exist of Nos. B11-B14.

SP1

POLAND

## Polish Volunteers in Spain — SP14

**1946, Mar. 10**

B43 SP14 3z + 5z red — 3.00 4.25 / 4.00
Never hinged

Participation of the Jaroslaw Dabrowski Brigade in the Spanish Civil War.

## 14th Century Piast Eagle and Soldiers — SP15

## "Death" Spreading Poison Gas over Majdanek Prison Camp — SP16

**1946, May 2**

B44 SP15 3z + 7z brn — .60 .50 / 1.00
Never hinged

Silesian uprisings of 1919-21, 1939-45.

**1946, Apr. 29**

B45 SP16 3z + 5z Prus grn — 2.00 3.00 / 3.00
Never hinged

Issued to recall Majdanek, a concentration camp of World War II near Lublin.

## Map of Polish Coast and Baltic Sea — SP18

## Bydgoszcz (Bromberg) Canal — SP17

**1946, Apr. 19   Unwmk.   Perf. 11**

B46 SP17 3z + 2z ol blk — 2.25 6.00 / 3.75
Never hinged

600th anniv. of Bydgoszcz (Bromberg).

**1946, July 21**

B47 SP18 3z + 7z dp bl — 1.25 2.00 / 2.00
Never hinged

Maritime Holiday of 1946. The surtax was for the Polish Maritime League.

---

## Polish People's Republic

 Polish Warship SP7

## Polish Naval Ensign and Merchant Flag — SP9

2 + 4z!

Sailing Vessel — SP8

1 + 3z!

## Crane and Crane Tower, Gdansk SP10

**1945, Apr. 24   Typo.   Perf. 11**

B36 SP7 50g + 2z red — 2.50 4.25
B37 SP8 1z + 3z dp bl — 2.50 4.25
B38 SP9 2z + 4z dk car — 2.50 4.25
B39 SP10 3z + 5z ol grn — 10.00 17.00
Set, never hinged — 13.00
Nos. B36-B39 (4)

Polish Maritime League, 25th anniv.

## City Hall, Poznan — SP11

**1945, June 16   Photo.**

B40 SP11 1z + 5z green — 15.00 20.00 / 20.00
Never hinged

Postal Workers' Convention, Poznan, June 16, 1945. Exists imperf. Value, $35.

## Last Stand at Westerplatte — SP12

**1945, Sept. 1**

B41 SP12 1z + 9z steel blue — 12.00 20.00 / 15.00

Polish army's last stand at Westerplatte, Sept. 1, 1939. Exists imperf. Value, $21.

## "United Industry" — SP13

**1945, Nov. 18   Unwmk.   Perf. 11**

B42 SP13 1.50z + 8.50z sl blk — 5.00 7.50 / 7.00
Never hinged

Trade Unions Congress, Warsaw, Nov. 18.

---

## Souvenir Sheet

Cena 2 zl

## Stratosphere Balloon over Mountains — SP4

**1938, Sept. 15   Perf. 12½**

B31 SP4 75g dp vio, sheet — 55.00 60.00 / 75.00
Never hinged

Issued in advance of a proposed Polish stratosphere flight. Sold for 2z.

## Winterhelp Issue

SP5

**1938-39**

B32 SP5 5g + 5g red org — .55 .95
B33 SP6 25g + 10g dk vio ('39) — .90 1.40
B34 SP5 55g + 15g brt ultra ('39) — 1.75 2.25
Nos. B32-B34 (3) — 3.20 4.60
Set, never hinged — 5.00

For surcharges see Nos. N48-N50.

## Souvenir Sheet

SP6

1914 6. VIII 1939

**1939, Aug. 1**

B35 SP6   Sheet of 3, dark blue gray — 27.50 20.00 / 32.50
Never hinged
a. 25g Marshal Pilsudski Reviewing Troops — 4.75 3.50
b. 25g Marshal Pilsudski — 4.75 3.50
c. 25g Marshal Smigly-Rydz — 4.75 3.50

25th anniv. of the founding of the Polish Legion. The sheets sold for 1.75z, the surtax going to the National Defense fund. See types A64, A80, A99.

---

## Light of Knowledge — SP2

**1925, Jan. 1   Typo.   Perf. 12½**

B15 SP1 1g orange brn — 12.00 14.00
B16 SP1 2g dk brown — 12.00 14.00
B17 SP1 3g orange — 12.00 14.00
B18 SP1 5g olive grn — 12.00 14.00
B19 SP1 10g blue grn — 12.00 14.00
B20 SP1 15g red — 12.00 14.00
B21 SP1 20g blue — 12.00 14.00
B22 SP1 25g red brown — 12.00 14.00
B23 SP1 30g dp violet — 12.00 14.00
B24 SP1 40g indigo — 35.00 14.00
B25 SP1 50g magenta — 155.00 154.00
Nos. B15-B25 (11) — 155.00 200.00
Set, never hinged

"Na Skarb" means "National Funds." These stamps were sold at a premium of 50 groszy each, for charity.

**1927, May 3   Perf. 11½**

B26 SP2 10g + 5g choc & grn — 7.00 4.50
B27 SP2 20g + 5g dk bl & buff — 7.00 4.50
Set, never hinged — 24.00

"NA OSWIATE" means "For Public Instruction." The surtax aided an Association of Educational Societies.

## Torun Type of 1933   Engr.

**1933, May 21**

B28 A59 60g (+40g) red brn. — 16.00 12.00 / 21.00
buff
Never hinged

Philatelic Exhibition at Torun, May 21-28, 1933, and sold at a premium of 40g to aid the exhibition funds.

## Souvenir Sheet

## Stagecoach and Wayside Inn — SP3

**1938, May 3   Engr.   Perf. 12, Imperf.**

B29 SP3   Sheet of 4 — 72.50 65.00 / 90.00
Never hinged
a. 45g green — 7.50 7.50
b. 55g blue — 7.50 7.50

5th Phil. Exhib., Warsaw, May 3-8. The sheet contains two 45g and two 55g stamps. Sold for 3z.

## 1946, Sept. 14
B48 SP19 3z + 12z slate
Never hinged

Polish postal employees killed in the German attack on Danzig (Gdansk), Sept. 1939.

Salute to P.T.T. Casualty and Views of Gdansk — SP19

## 1946, Oct. 10   Unwmk.   Perf. 11½
| | | | |
|---|---|---|---|
| B49 SP20 3z + 22z dk red | | 22.50 | 35.00 |
| Never hinged | | 22.50 | 35.00 |
| B49A SP20 6z + 24z dk bl | | 400.00 | 375.00 |
| B49B SP20 11z + 19z dk grn | | 22.50 | 35.00 |
| Never hinged | | 22.50 | 35.00 |
| c. Souv. sheet of 3, #B49-B49B | | 315.00 | 375.00 |
| Never hinged | | 400.00 | |
| Nos. B49-B49B (3) | | 67.50 | 105.00 |
| | | 77.50 | |

Designs: 6z+24z, Courtyard of Jagiellon University, Cracow. 11z+19z, Gregor Piramowicz (1735-1801), founder of Education Commission.

School Children — SP20

Polish educational work. International Bureau of Education. No. B49Bc sold for 100z.

## 1946, Dec. 1
| | | | |
|---|---|---|---|
| B50 SP21 5z + 10z bl grn | | 1.00 | 1.40 |
| B51 SP21 5z + 10z dull blue | | 1.00 | 1.40 |
| B52 SP21 5z + 10z olive | | 1.00 | 1.40 |
| Never hinged | | 3.00 | 4.20 |
| Nos. B50-B52 (3) | | 3.00 | 4.00 |

Stanislaw Stojalowski, Jakob Bojko, Jan Stapinski and Wincenty Witos — SP21

50th anniv. of the Peasant Movement. The surtax was for education and cultural improvement among the Polish peasantry.

## 1947, Feb. 4
| | | | |
|---|---|---|---|
| B53 A127 3z + 7z purple | | 5.50 | 8.00 |
| Never hinged | | 6.75 | |

Opening of the Polish Parliament, 1/19/47.

No. 391 Surcharged in Red

## 1947, Feb. 21
| | | | |
|---|---|---|---|
| B54 A103 5z + 15z on 25g | | 1.25 | 2.00 |
| Never hinged | | 2.50 | 3.50 |

Ski Championship Meet, Zakopane. Counterfeits exist.

---

No. 344 Surcharged in Blue

Catalogue values for unused stamps in this section, from this point to the end of the section, are for Never Hinged items.

## 1947, Mar. 1   Photo.   Perf. 12½
| | | | |
|---|---|---|---|
| B55 SP22 5z + 15z dl gray grn | | 1.25 | 3.50 |
| Never hinged | | 2.50 | 3.50 |

Emil Zegadlowicz — SP22

## 1947, June 1
| | | | |
|---|---|---|---|
| B56 SP23 5z + 5z ol blk & red | | 2.50 | 3.50 |
| Never hinged | | | 3.25 |

The surtax was for the Red Cross.

Nurse and War Victims SP23

## 1947, Dec. 21
| | | | |
|---|---|---|---|
| B57 SP24 2z + 18z dk vio | | .30 | .25 |
| Never hinged | | | .50 |

Adam Chmielowski SP24

## 1948, Nov. 1   Perf. 10½
| | | | |
|---|---|---|---|
| B58 SP25 15z + 5z green | | 1.25 | 2.25 |
| Never hinged | | | 1.65 |

The surtax was to aid in the reconstruction of Warsaw.

Zamkowy Square and Proposed Highway SP25

## 1948, Dec. 16   Perf. 11½
| | | | |
|---|---|---|---|
| B59 SP26 3z + 2z dl grn | | 2.00 | 2.50 |
| B60 SP26 5z + 5z bre | | 2.00 | 2.50 |
| B61 SP26 6z + 4z vio | | 1.65 | 2.50 |
| B62 SP26 15z + 10z car lake | | 2.50 | 2.50 |
| Never hinged | | | |
| Nos. B59-B62 (4) | | 7.30 | 10.00 |
| | | 9.00 | |

Infant and TB Crosses — SP26

Various Portraits of Children

---

Workers Party Type of 1952

## 1952, Jan. 18   Engr.   Unwmk.   Perf. 12½
| | | | |
|---|---|---|---|
| B63 A195 45z + 15z Marceli Nowotko | | .20 | .20 |

## 1952, Mar. 8   Perf. 12½x12
| | | | |
|---|---|---|---|
| B64 A196 45g + 15g chocolate | | .30 | .20 |

Women's Day Type of 1952

Swierczewski-Walter Type of 1952

## 1952, Mar. 28   Perf. 12½
| | | | |
|---|---|---|---|
| B65 A197 45g + 15g chocolate | | .40 | .20 |

Bierut Type of 1952

## 1952, Apr. 18
| | | | |
|---|---|---|---|
| B66 A198 45g + 15g red | | .50 | .20 |
| B67 A198 15g + 15g ultra | | .50 | .20 |

## 1952
Type of Regular issue of 1951-52
Inscribed "Plan 6," etc.

Design: 45g+15g, Electrical installation.

| | | | |
|---|---|---|---|
| B68 A193 30g + 15g brn red | | .35 | .20 |
| B69 A193 45g + 15g chocolate | | .60 | .30 |
| B69A A194 1.20z + 15g red org | | .30 | .25 |
| Nos. B68-B69A (3) | | 1.25 | .75 |

Labor Day Type of Regular Issue of 1952

## 1952, May 1
| | | | |
|---|---|---|---|
| B70 A200 45g + 15g car rose | | .30 | .20 |

Similar to Regular issue of 1952
#B71, Maria Konopnicka. #B72, Hugo Kollataj.

## 1952, May
### Different Frames
| | | | |
|---|---|---|---|
| B71 A201 30g + 15g blue green | | .50 | .20 |
| B72 A201 45g + 15g brown | | .25 | .20 |

Issued: No. B71, May 10. No. B72, May 20.

## 1952, May 1
| | | | |
|---|---|---|---|
| B73 SP28 30g + 15g ultra | | .85 | .50 |

500th birth anniv. of Leonardo da Vinci.

Leonardo da Vinci — SP28

---

## 1952, June 1   Photo.   Perf. 13½x14
| | | | |
|---|---|---|---|
| B74 SP29 45g + 15g blue | | 2.50 | .60 |

Intl. Children's Day, June 1.

Pres. Bierut and Children — SP29

Sports Type

## 1952, June 21   Perf. 13
| | | | |
|---|---|---|---|
| B75 A203 30g + 15g blue | | 3.75 | 1.40 |
| B76 A203 45g + 15g purple | | 1.75 | .35 |

45g+15g, Soccer players and trophy.

## 1952, June 28   Engr.   Perf. 12½
| | | | |
|---|---|---|---|
| B77 SP31 30g + 15g dp bl grn | | 2.75 | .90 |
| B78 SP32 45g + 15g dp ultra | | .70 | .25 |

Shipbuilders' Day, 1952.

Yachts SP31
"Dar Pomorza" SP32

## 1952, July 17   Perf. 12½x12, 12½x12½
| | | | |
|---|---|---|---|
| B79 SP33 30g + 15g dp grn | | .30 | .20 |
| B80 SP34 45g + 16g red | | .70 | .20 |

Issued to publicize the Youth Festival, 1952.

Workers on Holiday — SP33
Students SP34

Constitution Type of Regular Issue

## 1952, July 22   Photo.   Perf. 11
| | | | |
|---|---|---|---|
| B81 A208 45g + 15g tl bl grn & dk brn | | 1.10 | .25 |

Power Plant Type of Regular issue

## 1952, Aug. 7   Engr.   Perf. 12½
| | | | |
|---|---|---|---|
| B82 A209 45g + 15g red | | .65 | .20 |

## 1952, July 31
| | | | |
|---|---|---|---|
| B83 SP36 30g + 15g dk red | | .40 | .20 |
| B84 SP36 45g + 15g blk brn | | .40 | .20 |

70th birth anniv. of Ludwik Warynski, political organizer.

Ludwik Warynski SP36
Church of Frydman SP37

## 1952, Aug. 18
| | | | |
|---|---|---|---|
| B85 SP37 45g + 15g vio brn | | .90 | .20 |

Aviator Watching Glider SP38

Henryk Sienkiewicz SP39

Design: 45g+15g, Pilot entering plane.

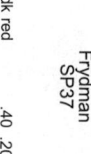

**1952, Aug. 23**
| | | |
|---|---|---|
| B86 SP38 30g + 15g grn | .55 | .30 |
| B87 SP38 45g + 15g brn red | 2.25 | .90 |

Aviation Day, Aug. 23.

**1952, Oct. 25**
| | | |
|---|---|---|
| B88 SP39 45g + 15g vio brn | .35 | .25 |

Henryk Sienkiewicz (1846-1916), author of "Quo Vadis" and other novels, Nobel prizewinner (literature, 1905).

**Revolution Type of Regular Issue**

**1952, Nov. 7      Perf. 12x12½**
| | | |
|---|---|---|
| B92 A214 45g + 15g red brn | .70 | .20 |

Exists imperforate. See #562.

Miner — SP43

Lenin — SP42

**1952, Nov. 7      Perf. 12½**
| | | |
|---|---|---|
| B93 SP42 30g + 15g vio brn | .30 | .20 |
| B94 SP42 45g + 15g brn | .70 | .30 |
| a.  "LENIN" omitted | 20.00 | |

Month of Polish-Soviet friendship, Nov. 1952.

**1952, Dec. 4**
| | | |
|---|---|---|
| B95 SP43 45g + 15g blk brn | .20 | .20 |
| B96 SP43 1.20z + 15g brn | .50 | .20 |

Miners' Day, Dec. 4.

Henryk Wieniawski and Violin — SP44

**1952, Dec. 5      Photo.**
| | | |
|---|---|---|
| B97 SP44 30g + 15g dk grn | .55 | .30 |
| B98 SP44 45g + 15g purple | 2.75 | .60 |

Henryk Wieniawski; 2nd Intl. Violin Competition.

**Type of Regular Issue of 1952**

**1952, Dec. 12      Engr.**
| | | |
|---|---|---|
| B99 A215 45g + 15g dp grn | .30 | .20 |

Truck Factory, Lublin — SP45

**1953, Feb. 20**
| | | |
|---|---|---|
| B100 SP45 30g + 15g dp bl | .20 | .20 |
| B101 SP45 60g + 20g vio brn | .40 | .20 |

**Souvenir Sheet**

Town Hall in Poznan — SP46

---

**Souvenir Sheet**

"Peace" (POKOJ) and Warsaw Mermaid — SP47

**1955, July 7      Photo. & Litho.      Imperf.**
| | | |
|---|---|---|
| B102 SP46 2z pck grn & ol grn | 3.50 | 2.00 |
| B103 SP46 3z car rose & ol blk | 19.00 | 10.50 |

6th Polish Philatelic Exhibition in Poznan. Sheets sold for 3z and 4.50z respectively.

Design: 1z, Pansies (A266) and inscription on map of Europe, Africa and Asia.

**1955, Aug. 3**
| | | |
|---|---|---|
| B104 SP47 1z bis, rose vio & yel | 4.25 | 1.50 |
| B105 SP47 2z ol of gray, ultra & lt bl | 20.00 | 7.50 |

Intl. Phil. Exhib. Warsaw, Aug. 1-14, 1955. Sheets sold for 2z and 3z respectively.

**Souvenir Sheet**

Chopin and Liszt — SP48

**1956, Oct. 25      Photo.      Imperf.**
| | | |
|---|---|---|
| B106 SP48 4z dk blue grn | 30.00 | 16.00 |

Day of the Stamp; Polish-Hungarian friendship. The sheet sold for 6z.

---

**Souvenir Sheet**

Stamp of 1860 — SP49

**Wmk. 326**

**1960, Sept. 4      Litho.      Perf. 11**
| | | |
|---|---|---|
| B107 SP49  Sheet of 4 | 40.00 | 35.00 |
| a.  10z + 10z blue, red & black | 9.00 | 9.00 |

Intl. Phil. Exhib. "POLSKA 60," Warsaw, 9/3-11.
Sold only with 5z ticket to exhibition.

**Type of Space Issue, 1964**
Design: Yuri A. Gagarin in space capsule.

**Perf. 12½x12**

**1964, Dec. 30      Unwmk.**
| | | |
|---|---|---|
| B108 A432 6.50z + 2z Prus grn & multi | 1.50 | .65 |

**Souvenir Sheet**

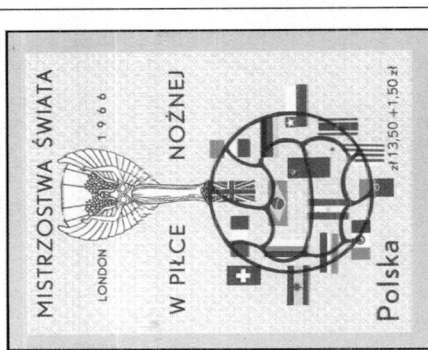

Jules Rimet Cup and Flags of Participating Countries — SP50

**1966, May 9      Litho.      Imperf.**
| | | |
|---|---|---|
| B109 SP50 13.50z + 1.50z multi | 2.50 | 1.50 |

World Cup Soccer Championship, Wembley, England, July 11-30.

---

**Souvenir Sheet**

J. Kusocinski, Olympic Winner 10,000-Meter Race, 1932 — SP51

**1967, May 24      Litho.      Imperf.**
| | | |
|---|---|---|
| B110 SP51 10z + 5z multi | 1.50 | 1.00 |

19th Olympic Games, Mexico City, 1968. Simulated perforations.

**Flower Type of Regular Issue**
Flowers: 4z+2z, Abutilon; 8z+4z, Rosa polyantha hybr.

**1968, May 15      Litho.      Perf. 11½**
| | | |
|---|---|---|
| B111 A492 4z + 2z vio & multi | .80 | .40 |
| B112 A492 8z + 4z lt vio & multi | 1.65 | .90 |

**Olympic Type of Regular Issue, 1968**
Design: 10z+5z, Runner with Olympic torch and Chin cultic carved stone disc showing Mayan ball player and game's scoreboard.

**1968, Sept. 2      Litho.      Perf. 11½**

Size: 56x45mm
| | | |
|---|---|---|
| B113 A497 10z + 5z multi | 1.90 | .80 |

19th Olympic Games, Mexico City, Oct. 12-27. The surtax was for the Polish Olympic Committee.

**Olympic Type of Regular Issue, 1969**
Olympic Rings and: 2.50z+50g, Women's discus, 3.40z+1z, Running; 4z+1.50z, Boxing, 7z+2z, Fencing.

**1969, Apr. 25      Litho.      Perf. 11½x11**
| | | |
|---|---|---|
| B114 A505 2.50z + 50g multi | .30 | .20 |
| B115 A505 3.40z + 1z multi | .40 | .20 |
| B116 A505 4z + 1.50z multi | .60 | .20 |
| B117 A505 7z + 2z multi | 1.00 | .25 |
| Nos. B114-B117 (4) | 2.30 | .85 |

**Folk Art Type of Regular Issue**
5.50z+1.50z, Choir. 7z+1.50z, Organ grinder.

**1969, Dec. 19      Litho.      Perf. 11½x11**

Size: 24x36mm
| | | |
|---|---|---|
| B118 A520 5.50z + 1.50z multi | .50 | .25 |
| B119 A520 7z + 1.50z multi | .70 | .30 |

**Sports Type of Regular Issue**

**Souvenir Sheet**

Design: "Horse of Glory," by Z. Kaminski.

**1970, June 16      Photo.      Imperf.**
| | | |
|---|---|---|
| B120 A532 10z + 5z multi | 1.75 | 1.00 |

The surtax was for the Polish Olympic Committee. No. B120 contains one imperf. stamp with simulated perforations.

**Tapestry Type of Regular Issue**

**Souvenir Sheet**

Design: 7z+3z, Satyrs holding monogram of King Sigismund Augustus.

**1970, Dec. 23      Photo.      Imperf.**
| | | |
|---|---|---|
| B121 A541 7z + 3z multi | 1.75 | 1.00 |

**Type of Regular Issue**

Design: 8.50z+4z, Virgin Mary, 15th century stained glass window.

**1971, Sept. 15      Photo.      Perf. 11½x11**
| | | |
|---|---|---|
| B122 A555 8.50z + 4z multi | .90 | .45 |

**Painting Type of Regular Issue**

7z+1z, Nude, by Wojciech Weiss (1875-1950).

**1971, Oct. 9**    **Litho.**
B123 A556 7z + 1z multi    .70 .35

**1972, Jan. 12**   **Photo.**
B124 A564 10z + 5z multi    2.00 1.25
No. B124 contains one stamp with simulated perforations, 27x52mm.

**Winter Olympic Type of Regular Issue**
Souvenir Sheet
Slalom and Sapporo '72 emblem, vert.

**1972, May 20**   **Photo.**   **Imperf.**
B125 A568 10z + 5z multi    1.75 1.00

**Summer Olympic Type of Regular Issue**
Souvenir Sheet
Design: 10z+5z, Archery (like 30g).

**1972, Sept. 28**   **Photo.**   **Perf. 11½x10½**
B126 A576 8.50z + 4z multi    1.50 .55

**Painting Type of Regular Issue, 1972**
Design: 8.50z+4z, Portrait of a Young Lady, by Jacek Malczewski, horiz.

Souvenir Sheet

Copernicus — SP52

**1972, Sept. 28**
B127 SP52 10z + 5z vio bl, gray & car    1.50 .85
Engraved and Photogravure   **Perf. 11½**

Nicolaus Copernicus (1473-1543), astronomer. No. B127 shows the Ptolemaic and Copernican concepts of solar system from L'Harmonica Microcosmica, by Cellarius, 1660.

Poznan, 1740, by F. B. Werner — SP53

**1973, Aug. 19**    **Imperf.**
B128 SP53 10z + 5z ol & dk brn    2.00 .90
a.   10z + 5z pale lilac & dk brn    6.00 4.00
POLSKA 73 Intl. Phil. Exhib., Poznan, Aug. 19-Sept. 2. No. B128 contains one stamp with simulated perforations.
No. B128a was sold only in combination with an entrance ticket.

Souvenir Sheet

**1973, Sept. 27**   **Photo.**   **Perf. 11x11½**
B129 SP54 4z + 2z multi    .50 .30
Stamp Day. The surtax was for the reconstruction of the Royal Castle in Warsaw.

Souvenir Sheet
Copernicus, by Marcello Baciarelli — SP54

**Montreal Olympic Games Emblem — SP55**

**1975, Mar. 8**    **Photo. & Engr.**
B130 SP55 10z + 5z sil & grn    1.50 1.00
21st Olympic Games, Montreal, Canada, July 17-Aug. 1, 1976.

Souvenir Sheet

**Dunikowski Type of 1975**
Design: 8z+4z, Mother and Child, from Silesian Insurrectionist Monument, by Dunikowski.

**1975, Oct. 9**   **Photo.**   **Perf. 11x11½**
B131 A644 8z + 4z multi    1.00 .45
Outer edge of souvenir sheet is perforated.

Volleyball — SP56

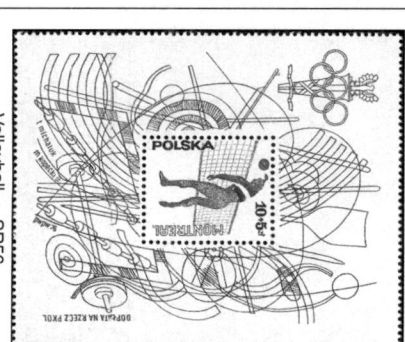

**1976, June 30**
B132 SP56 10z + 5z blk & car    1.40 .70
Engraved and Photogravure   **Perf. 11½**
21st Olympic Games, Montreal, Canada, July 17-Aug. 1. No. B132 contains one perf. 11½ stamp and is perf. 11½ all around.

**Corinthian Art Type 1976**
Design: 8z+4z, Winged Sphinx, vert.

**1976, Oct. 30**   **Photo.**   **Perf. 11½x11**
B133 A664 8z + 4z multi    1.10 .50

**1977, Apr. 30**   **Engr.**   **Perf. 12x11½**
B134 SP57 8z + 4z sepia    1.10 .65
Peter Paul Rubens (1577-1640), Flemish painter. Outer edge of souvenir sheet is perforated.

Souvenir Sheet
Stoning of St. Stephen, by Rubens — SP57

**1978, June 6**   **Photo.**   **Perf. 11½x11**
B135 SP58 8.40z + 4z multi    1.10 .55
CAPEX '78 Canadian Intl. Phil. Exhib., Toronto, June 9-18. K. S. Gzowski (1813-1898), Polish engineer and lawyer living in Canada, built International Bridge over Niagara River.

Souvenir Sheet
Kazimierz Gzowski — SP58

Olympic Rings — SP59

**1979, May 19**   **Engr.**   **Imperf.**
B136 SP59 10z + 5z black    1.00 .75
1980 Olympic Games.

**Monument Type of 1979**
Souvenir Sheet

**1979, Sept. 1**   **Photo.**   **Imperf.**
B137 A731 10z + 5z multi    1.25 .75
Surtax was for monument.

**Summer Olympic Type of 1980**
Souvenir Sheet

**1980, Mar. 31**   **Photo.**   **Perf. 11½x11**
B138 A742 10.50z + 5z Kayak    1.00 .75
No. B138 contains one stamp measuring 42x30mm.

**1980, Apr. 12**    **Perf. 11½x11**
B139 SP60 6.90z + 3z multi    .85 .75

Intercosmos Cooperative Space Program — SP60
Souvenir Sheet

**1981, Dec. 16**   **Photo.**   **Perf. 11½x12**
B140 SP61 2.50 + 1z blk & red    .70 .30
B141 SP61 6.50 + 1z blk & lil    1.00 .70
1970 Uprising Memorial: 2.50z + 1z, Triple Crucifix, Gdansk (27x46mm). 6.50z + 1z, Monument, Gdynia.

SP61

**1984, May 15**   **Photo.**   **Perf. 11½x12**
B142 SP62 27z + 10z multi    1.50 .80
Portrait of a German Princess, by Lucas Cranach
1984 UPU Congress, Hamburg. No. B142 issued se-tenant with multicolored label showing UPU emblem and text.

SP62

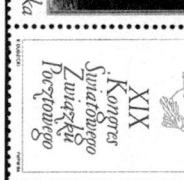

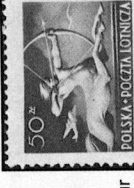

**Souvenir Sheet**

Madonna with Child, St. John and the Angel, by Sandro Botticelli (1445-1510), Natl. Museum, Warsaw — SP63

**1985, Sept. 25    Photo.    Perf. 11**
B143  SP63  65z + 15z multi       2.25  1.25
a.    Inscribed "35 LAT POL-
      SKIEGO . . . .                4.50  4.50
ITALIA '85. Surtax for Polish Association of Philatelists.
No. B143a was for the 35th anniv. of the Polish Philatelic Union. Distribution was limited.

Joachim Lelewel (1786-1861), Historian — SP64

**1986, Dec. 22    Photo.    Perf. 11½x12**
B144  SP64  10z + 5z multi        .30  .20
Surtax for the Natl. Committee for School Aid.

Polish Immigrant Settling in Kasubia, Ontario — SP65

**1987, June 13    Photo.    Perf. 12x11½**
B145  SP65  50z + 20z multi      1.40  .70
CAPEX '87, Toronto, Canada. Surtaxed for the Polish Philatelists' Union.

**Souvenir Sheet**

OLYMPHILEX '87, Rome — SP66

**1987, Aug. 28    Litho.    Perf. 14**
B146  SP66  45z + 10z like #2617  1.10  1.10

---

FINLANDIA '88 — SP67

**1988, June 1    Photo.    Perf. 12x11½**
B147  SP67  45z +20z Salmon,
            reindeer             1.25  .65

**Souvenir Sheet**

Jerzy Kukuczka, Mountain Climber Awarded Medal by the Intl. Olympic Committee for Climbing the Himalayas — SP68

**1988, Aug. 17    Photo.    Perf. 11x11½**
B148  SP68  70z +10z multi       1.50  .80
Surtax for the Polish Olympic Fund.

Aid for Victims of 1997 Oder River Flood — SP69

**1007, Aug. 18    Photo.    Porf. 11½x12**
B149  SP69  60g +30g multi        .80  .40

**Souvenir Sheet**

Museum of Posts and Telecommunications, 80th Anniv. — SP70

**2001, Oct. 9    Photo.    Perf. 11¼x11½**
B150  SP70  3z +75g multi        2.40  1.25

**AIR POST STAMPS**

Biplane — AP1

**1925, Sept. 10    Typo.    Unwmk.**
**Perf. 12½**
C1  AP1  1g  lt blue              .65  2.25
C2  AP1  2g  orange               .65  2.25
C3  AP1  3g  yellow brn           .65  1.75
C4  AP1  5g  dk brown            1.90  1.75
C5  AP1  10g dk green            1.65  .75
C6  AP1  15g red violet          2.50  .85
C7  AP1  20g olive grn          10.50  4.25

---

**1948**
C21  AP4  15z  dk violet         1.50  .25
C22  AP4  25z  deep blue          .80  .20
C23  AP4  30z  brown              .65  .45
C24  AP4  50z  dk green          1.25  .45
C25  AP4  75z  gray black        1.50  .55
C26  AP4  100z red orange        1.50  .45
                                 7.20  2.35
      Nos. C21-C26 (6)           9.50
Set, never hinged

Centaur AP4

Pres. F. D. Roosevelt AP5

**Perf. 11½ to 12½ and Compound**
Capt. Franciszek Zwirko and Stanislaus Wigura — AP2

**1933, Apr. 15    Engr.    Wmk. 234**
C10  AP2  30g gray green        14.00  1.00
Never hinged
Winning of the circuit of Europe flight by two Polish aviators in 1932. The stamp was available for both air mail and ordinary postage.
For overprint see No. C12.

**1934, Aug. 28    Unwmk.    Perf. 12½**
C11  AP1  20g olive green       12.50  6.75

**Wmk. 234**
**Perf. 11½**
C12  AP2  30g gray green         7.00  2.25
Set, never hinged               26.00

**Polish People's Republic**

Douglas Plane over Ruins of Warsaw — AP3

**Unwmk.**
**1946, Mar. 5    Photo.    Perf. 11**
C13  AP3  5z  grnsh blk          .40  .70
a.    Without control number    4.00  .40
     Never hinged               6.00
C14  AP3  10z dk violet          .40  .20
C15  AP3  15z blue              1.25  .25
C16  AP3  20z rose brn           .80  .40
C17  AP3  25z dk bl grn         1.65  .40
C18  AP3  30z red               2.50  .55
      Nos. C13-C18 (6)          7.00  1.80
Set, never hinged              10.00

The 10z, 20z and 30z were issued only with control number in lower right stamp margin.
The 15z and 25z exist only without number.
Nos. C13-C18 exist imperforate.

Nos. 345, 344 and 344a Surcharged in Red or Black

---

Airplane Mechanic and Propeller — AP5a

100z, Casimir Pulaski. 120z, Tadeusz Kosciusko.

**1948, Dec. 30    Photo.**
**Granite Paper**
C26A  AP5  80z  blue blk        13.00  22.50
C26B  AP5  90z  purple         14.00  19.00
C26C  AP5  120z deep blue      14.00  19.00
d.    Souvenir sheet of 3     140.00  250.00
      Never hinged            250.00
      Nos. C26A-C26C (3)       41.00  60.50
Set, never hinged              50.00

Nos. C26A-C26C were issued in panes containing 16 stamps and 4 labels.
No. C26Cd contains stamps similar to Nos. C26A-C26C, with colors changed; 80z ultramarine, 100z carmine rose, 120z dark green. Sold for 500z.

**1950, Feb. 6    Engr.    Perf. 12½**
C27  AP5a  500z rose lake       3.25  3.50
Never hinged                    5.00

---

**Catalogue values for unused stamps in this section, from this point to the end of the section, are for Never Hinged items.**

Seaport AP6

Designs: 90g, Mechanized farm. 1.40z, Warsaw. 5z, Steel mill.

**1952, Apr. 10    Perf. 12x12½**
C28  AP6  55g intense blue        .20  .20
C29  AP6  90g dull green          .30  .20
C30  AP6  1.40z violet brn        .45  .20
C31  AP6  5z  gray black         1.65  .60
      Nos. C28-C31 (4)          2.60  1.20
Nos. C28-C31 exist imperf. Value $15.

Congress Badge — AP7

---

**Perf. 11**
C8  AP1  30g dull rose          6.75  1.50
C9  AP1  45g dk violet          8.50  4.25
      Nos. C7-C9 (9)           32.50  19.20
Set, never hinged              45.00
Counterfeits exist.
For overprint see No. C11.

**Challenge 1934**

Nos. C7 and C10 Overprinted in Red

**LOTNICZA zł 50 zł**
**POCZTA POLSKA**
**b**

**LOTNICZA zł 40 ZŁ**
**POCZTA POLSKA**
**a**

**Perf. 12½**
**1947, Sept. 10**
C19  A104(a)  40z on 50g (R)    1.65  .90
C20  A103(b)  40z on 25g dl red 1.90  1.75
a.    50z on 25g deep red      2.75  2.50
b.    40z on 25g red, #c20a    3.50
Set, never hinged              5.50
Counterfeits exist.

POLSKA POCZTA LOTNICZA

POLAND

## 1953, Aug. 24
**Photo.** **Imperf.**
C32 AP7 55g brown lilac 1.00 1.00
C33 AP7 75g brown org 1.50 1.00
3rd World Congress of Students, Warsaw, 1953.

Souvenir Sheet

AP8

## 1954, May 23
**Engr.** **Perf. 12x12½**
C34 AP8 5z gray green 30.00 20.00
3rd congress of the Polish Phil. Assoc., Warsaw, 1954. Sold for 7.50 zlotys. A similar sheet, imperf. and in dark blue, was issued but had no postal validity.

80g Kazimierz Dolny, 1.15z Wawel castle, Cracow, 1.50z, City Hall, Wroclaw, 1.55z, Lazlersky Square, Warsaw, 1.95z, Cracow gate, Lublin.

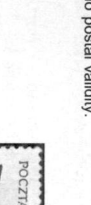

## 1954, July 9
**Perf. 12½**
C35 AP9 60g dk gray grn .20 .20
C36 AP9 80g red .20 .20
C37 AP9 1.15z black 1.00 .40
C38 AP9 1.50z rose lake .40 .20
C39 AP9 1.55z dp gray bl .40 .20
C40 AP9 1.95z chocolate 3.00 1.55
Nos. C35-C40 (6)

Paczkow Castle, Luban AP9

Plane over "Peace" Steelworks AP10

## Wmk. 326 ('58 Values); Unwmkd.
## 1957-58 Engr. & Photo. Perf. 12½
Plane over: 1.50z, Castle Square, Warsaw, 3.40z, Old Market, Cracow, 3.92z, King Boleslaw Chrobry Wall, Szczecin, 4z, Karkonosze mountains, 15z, Old City, Lublin, 20z, Kasprowy Wierch Peak and cable car, 30z, Poraba dam, 50z, M. S. Batory and Gdynia harbor.

C41 AP10 90g black & pink .20 .20
C43 AP10 1.50z brn & salmon .20 .20
C43 AP10 3.40z sep & buff .35 .20
C44 AP10 3.92z dk brn & cit .60 .45
C45 AP10 4z ind & lt grn .30 .20
C46 AP10 15z maroon & gray .55 .20
C47 AP10 10z sepia & grn 1.10 .25
C48 AP10 20z vio bl & pale bl 1.40 .45
C49 AP10 20z vio blk & lem 2.75 .60
C50 AP10 30z ol gray & bis 3.75 1.25
C51 AP10 50z dk bl & gray 6.00 1.65
Nos. C41-C51 (11) 17.20 5.65

## 1959, May 23 Litho. Wmk. 326
C52 AP10 10z sepia 1.75 1.50
a. With 5z label 2.00 2.00

Issue dates: 5z, 10z, 20z, 30z, 50z, Dec. 15, 1958. Others, Dec. 6, 1957.

D6

5z for a fund to build a Society clubhouse in Warsaw.

Contemporary aviation: 10z, Mi6 transport helicopter, 20z, PZL-106 Kruk, crop spraying plane, 50z, Plane over Warsaw Castle.

## 1976-78 Unwmk. Engr. Perf. 11½
C53 AP11 5z dk blue grn .40 .25
C54 AP11 10z dk brown .80 .75
C55 AP11 20z grnsh black 1.50 1.90
C56 AP11 50z claret 5.70 3.40
Nos. C53-C56 (4)
Issued: 5z, 10z, 3/27/76; 20z, 2/15/77; 50z, 2/2/78.

Jantar Glider — AP11

---

## AIR POST SEMI-POSTAL STAMP

Catalogue values for unused stamps in this section are for Never Hinged items.

Polish People's Republic

Wing of Jet Plane and Letter — SPAP1

## 1957, Mar. 28 Unwmk. Perf. 11½
CB1 SPAP1 4z + 2z blue 3.00 3.50
a. Souv. sheet of 1, ultra, imperf. 10.00 4.50

7th Polish National Philatelic Exhibition, Warsaw. Sheet of 12 with 4 diagonally arranged gray labels.

---

## POSTAGE DUE STAMPS

### Cracow Issues

Postage Due Stamps of Austria, 1916. Overprinted in Black or Red.

## 1919, Jan. 10 Unwmk. Perf. 12½
J1 D4 5h rose red 7.00 6.00
J2 D4 10h rose red 2.500 1,750.
J3 D4 15h rose red 3.75
J4 D4 20h rose red 150.00
**Inverted overprint.**
J5 D4 25h rose red 275.00
J6 D4 30h rose red 17.50 25.00
J7 D4 40h rose red 800.00 700.00
J8 D4 50h rose red 700.00 600.00
J9 D4 1k ultra (R) 2,400. 2,400.
J10 D5 5k ultra (R) 2,400. 2,400.
J10 D5 10k ultra (R) 10,000. 10,000.
a. Black overprint 42,500.
Nos. J1-J10

Overprint on Nos. J1-J7, J10a is type. Overprint on Nos. J8-J10 is slightly larger than illustration, has a different ornament between lines of type and is litho.

### Regular Issue of 1919 Surcharged

## 1921, Jan. 25 Wove Paper
J35 A9 20f on 15h brown .75 .50
J36 A9 6m on 25h car .35 .25
J37 A9 20m on 10h lake .75 .40
J38 A9 20m on 50h red 1.50 1.10
J39 A9 35m on 70h dp bl 2.00 1.40
Nos. J35-J39 (4)

### Perf. 9 to 14½ and Compound
## 1921-22 Thin Laid or Wove Paper Typo.
Size: 17x22mm
J40 D8 1m indigo .30 .30
J41 D8 2m indigo .30 .30
J42 D8 4m indigo .30 .30
J43 D8 6m indigo .30 .30
J44 D8 8m indigo .30 .30
J45 D8 20m indigo .30 .30
J46 D8 50m indigo .30 .30
J47 D8 100m indigo .60 .30
Nos. J40-J47 (8)

### Perf. 9 to 14½ and Compound
## 1923, Nov.
J48 D8 10.000m on 8m indi- .30 .30
J49 D8 20,000(m) on 20m indi- 1.50 .20
J50 D8 50,000(m) on 2m indi- .70 .20
Nos. J48-J50 (3) 10.00 1.10

---

### Regular Issues

Numerals of Value D7

## 1919 Typo. Perf. 11½
### For Northern Poland
J13 D7 2f red orange .40 .30
J14 D7 4f red orange .30 .25
J15 D7 5f red orange .20 .20
J16 D7 10f red orange .20 .20
J17 D7 20f red orange .20 .20
J18 D7 30f red orange .20 .20
J19 D7 50f red orange .45 .45
J20 D7 100f red orange 1.10 .25
J21 D7 500f red orange 1.75 1.25

### For Southern Poland
J22 D7 2h dark blue .20 .20
J23 D7 4h dark blue .20 .20
J24 D7 5h dark blue .20 .20
J25 D7 10h dark blue .20 .20
J26 D7 20h dark blue .20 .20
J27 D7 30h dark blue .20 .20
J28 D7 50h dark blue .25 .20
J29 D7 100h dark blue 1.40 .30
J30 D7 500h dark blue 7.20 5.95
Nos. J13-J30 (18)

Counterfeits exist.

## 1920 Thin Laid Paper Perf. 9, 10, 11½
J31 D7 20f dark blue .70 .50
J32 D7 100f dark blue .35 .25
J33 D7 200f dark blue .60 .50
J34 D7 500f dark blue .35 .25
Nos. J31-J34 (4) 2.00 1.50
Counterfeits exist.

Type of Austria, 1916-18, Surcharged in Black

## 1919, Jan. 10 Perf. 11½
J11 D6 15h on 36h vio 300.00 200.00
J12 D6 50h on 42h choc 30.00 50.00
a. Double surcharge 8,000.

See note above No. 41.
Counterfeits exist of Nos. J1-J12.

---

D9

Type of 1921-22 Issue Typo.
## 1923 Size: 19x24mm Perf. 12½
J51 D8 50m indigo .20 .20
J52 D8 100m indigo .20 .20
J53 D8 500m indigo .25 .20
J54 D8 1000m indigo .25 .20
J55 D8 2000m indigo .25 .20
J56 D8 5000m indigo .30 .20
J57 D8 10,000m indigo .35 .20
J58 D8 20,000m indigo .45 .20
J59 D8 30,000m indigo .45 .20
J60 D8 50,000m indigo .45 .20
J61 D8 100,000m indigo .45 .20
J62 D8 200,000m indigo .45 .30
J63 D8 500,000m indigo .65 .20
J64 D8 1,000,000m indigo 1.50 .60
J65 D8 2,000,000m indigo 2.75 .60
J66 D8 3,000,000m indigo 3.00 .20
J67 D8 5,000,000m indigo 11.40 4.95
Nos. J51-J67 (17)

D10

## 1923 Typo. Size: 20x25½mm
### Perf. 10 to 13½ and Compound
## 1924
For surcharges see Nos. J68-J91.
J68 D9 1g brown .30 .25
J69 D9 2g brown .30 .25
J70 D9 4g brown .55 .25
J71 D9 6g brown .55 .25
J72 D9 10g brown 3.25 .25
J73 D9 15g brown 2.50 .40
J74 D9 20g brown 2.50 .40
J75 D9 25g brown 2.50 .40
J76 D9 30g brown 6.00 .40
J77 D9 40g brown 6.00 .40
J78 D9 50g brown 1.10 .40
J79 D9 1z brown 1.10 .40
J80 D9 2z brown 1.00 .55
J81 D9 3z brown 1.90 .55
J82 D9 5z brown 27.30 7.85
Nos. J68-J82 (15)

Nos. J68-J69 and J72-J75 exist measuring 19½x24 ½mm.
For surcharges see Nos. J84-J91.

## 1930, July
J83 D10 5g olive brown .70 .20
Never hinged .20

## Perf. 12½
J83 D10 5g olive brown .70 .20

## 1934-36
### Perf. 10 to 13½ and Compound
J84 D9 1g on 2z brown ('38) .40 .30
J85 D9 1g on 2z brown .40 .30
J86 D9 15g on 1z brown ('38) .40 .30
J87 D9 20g on 1z brown 2.00 .30
J88 D9 20g on 1z brown .55 .55
J89 D9 25g on 40g brown .85 .55
J90 D9 50g on 40g brown .85 .70
J91 D9 50g on 3z brown ('35) .70 .70
Nos. J84-J91 (8) 7.90 4.25

## 1934-36
J92 A50 10g on 1z ('36) .80 .20
J93 A50 20g on 1z (R) ('36) .80 .20
J94 A50 50g on 1z (R) ('36) 1.75 1.00
a. Vertically laid paper (No. J92-J94) .40 .30
Nos. J92-J94 (3)
Set, never hinged

No. 255a Surcharged in Red or Indigo
No. 255 Surcharged

### Laid Paper
80 .20
25.00 18.00
1.50 .20
30.00 18.00
4.10 .90
8.00 1.30

## Postage Due — Polish People's Republic

**D11**

**1938-39 Typo. Perf. 12½x12 Unwmk.**
- J95 D11 5g dark blue green .20 .20
- J96 D11 10g dark blue green .20 .20
- J97 D11 15g dark blue green .60 .20
- J98 D11 20g dark blue green .20 .20
- J99 D11 25g dark blue green .40 .20
- J100 D11 30g dark blue green .80 1.25
- J101 D11 50g dark blue green 2.50 1.65
- J102 D11 1z dark blue green 5.10 4.10
- Nos. J95-J102 (8) 12.00
- Set, never hinged

For surcharges see Nos. N51-N55.

### Polish People's Republic

Post Horn with Thunderbolts — D12
Polish Eagle — D13 

**1945, May 20 Litho. Size: 25½x19mm**
- J103 D12 1z orange brown .20 .20
- J104 D12 2z orange brown .20 .20
- J105 D12 3z orange brown .25 .20
- J106 D12 5z orange brown .35 .30
- 1.00 .90
- Nos. J103-J106 (4) 2.00

**Type of 1945**
**1946-49 Perf. 11, 11½ (P) or Imperf. (I) Photo.**
Size: 29x21½mm
- J106A D12 1z org brn (P) ('49) .20 .20
- J107 D12 2z org brn (P,I) .20 .20
- J108 D12 3z org brn (I) .30 .30
- J109 D12 5z org brn (I) .25 .30
- J110 D12 6z org brn (I) .25 .35
- J111 D12 10z org brn (I)
- J112 D12 15z org brn (P,I) .55 .90
- J113 D12 20z org brn (P,I) .75 .60
- J114 D12 25z org brn (P,I) .90 .90
- J115 D12 50z brn (P) ('49) 2.00 1.00
- 6.00 6.00
- Nos. J106A-J115 (10) 8.00

**1950 Engr.**
- J116 D13 5z red brown .20 .20
- J117 D13 10z red brown .20 .20
- J118 D13 15z red brown .20 .30
- J119 D13 20z red brown .25 .30
- J120 D13 25z red brown .45 .45
- J121 D13 50z red brown .70 .60
- J122 D13 100z red brown .90 3.00
- 3.00 6.00
- Nos. J116-J122 (7)

**1951-52**
- J123 D13 5g red brown .20 .20
- J124 D13 10g red brown .20 .20
- J125 D13 15g red brown .20 .30
- J126 D13 20g red brown .25 .25
- J127 D13 25g red brown .25 .30
- J128 D13 30g red brown .35 .30
- J129 D13 40g red brown .50 .45
- J130 D13 60g red brown .50 .45
- J131 D13 90g red brown .60 .55
- J132 D13 1z red brown 1.25 .95
- J133 D13 2z red brown 2.75 2.25
- J134 D13 5z brown violet 6.95 6.00
- Nos. J123-J134 (12) 9.00
- Set, never hinged

**1953, Apr. Without imprint Photo.**
- J135 D13 5g red brown .25 .25
- J136 D13 10g red brown .25 .25
- J137 D13 15g red brown .25 .25
- J138 D13 20g red brown .25 .25
- J139 D13 25g red brown .25 .25
- J140 D13 30g red brown .50 .40
- J141 D13 40g red brown .70 .60
- J142 D13 60g red brown .95 .75
- J143 D13 90g red brown

- J144 D13 1z red brown 1.10 1.00
- J145 D13 2z red brown 2.25 1.75
- 7.00 6.00
- Nos. J135-J145 (11) 9.00
- Set, never hinged

> Catalogue values for unused stamps in this section, from this point to the end of the section, are for Never Hinged items.

**1980, Sept. 2 Litho. Perf. 12½**
- J146 D14 1z lt red brown .20 .20
- J147 D14 2z gray olive .20 .20
- J148 D14 3z dull violet .30 .20
- J149 D14 5z brown .45 .20
- 1.15 .80
- Nos. J146-J149 (4)

**5 groszy — DOPLATA — POCZTA POLSKA — D14**

**1998, June 18 Litho. Perf. 14**
- J150 D14 5g lilac, blk & yel .20 .20
- J151 D14 10g green blue, blk & yel .20 .20
- J152 D14 20g green, blk & black .20 .20
- J153 D14 50g yellow & black .35 .20
- J154 D14 80g orange, blk & yel .60 .30
- J155 D14 1z red, blk & yel .75 .40
- 2.30 1.50
- Nos. J150-J155 (6)

## OFFICIAL STAMPS

O1

**Perf. 10, 11½, 10x11½, 11½x10 Unwmk.**
**1920, Feb. 1 Litho.**
- O1 O1 3f vermilion .35 .45
- O2 O1 5f vermilion .35 .45
- O3 O1 10f vermilion .35 .45
- O4 O1 15f vermilion .35 .45
- O5 O1 25f vermilion .35 .45
- O6 O1 50f vermilion .35 .45
- O7 O1 100f vermilion .65 .45
- O8 O1 150f vermilion .65 .45
- O9 O1 200f vermilion .65 .45
- O10 O1 300f vermilion .50 .45
- O11 O1 600f vermilion .75 .45
- 5.00 4.95
- Nos. O1-O11 (11)

The stars on either side of the denomination do not appear on Nos. O7-O11.

**Numerals Larger**
**Stars inclined outward**
**1920, Nov. 20 Thin Laid Paper Perf. 11½**
- O12 O1 5f red .25 .40
- O13 O1 10f red .75 .70
- O14 O1 15f red .50 .95
- O15 O1 25f red 1.10 .95
- O16 O1 50f red 4.00 4.00
- 6.00
- Nos. O12-O16 (5)

**Polish Eagle — O3 / O4**

**1933, Aug. 1 Typo. Wmk. 234**
- O17 O3 (30g) vio (Zwyczajna) .95 .20
- O18 O3 (80g) red (Polecona) 2.25 .30
- 4.00
- Set, never hinged

**1935, Apr. 1 Perf. 12x12½**
- O19 O4 (25g) bl vio (Zwyczajna) .20 .20
- O20 O4 (55g) car (Polecona) .30 .20
- .75
- Set, never hinged

Stamps inscribed "Zwyczajna" or "Zwykla" were for ordinary official mail. Those with "Polecona" were for registered official mail.

### Polish People's Republic

Polish Eagle — O5

**Perf. 11, 14 Photo.**
**1945, July 1 Unwmk.**
- O21 O5 (5z) bl vio (Zwykla) .35 1.00
  - a. Imperf. 1.00 1.00
- O22 O5 (10z) red (Polecona) .65 1.25
  - a. Imperf. 1.65 2.00
- O22a 4.00

Set, never hinged, #O21, O22  M-01705
Set, never hinged, #O21a, O22a
Control number at bottom right: M-01706 on No. O22.
on No. O21; M-01705 on No. O22a.

**Type of 1945 Redrawn**
**1946, July 31**
- O23 O5 (5z) dl bl vio (Zwykla) .30 .20
- O24 O5 (10z) dl rose red (Polecona) .50 .25
- 1.50
- Set, never hinged

The redrawn stamps appear blurred and the eagle contains fewer lines of shading. Control number at bottom right: M-01709 on Nos. O23-O26.

**Redrawn Type of 1946 Imperf.**
**1946, July 31**
- O25 O5 (60g) dl bl vio (Zwykla) .40 .20
- O26 O5 (1.552) dl rose red (Polecona) .40 .20
- 1.25
- Set, never hinged

**Type of 1945, 2nd Redrawing**
**No Control Number at Lower Right**
**Perf. 11, 11½, 11x12½ Unwmk.**
**1950-53**
- O27 O5 (60g) blue (Zwykla) .25 .20
- O28 O5 (1.552) red (Polecona) .40 .20
- .80
- Set, never hinged

**Redrawn Type of 1952**
**Perf. 13x11, 11½, 14 Engr.**
**1954**
- O29 O5 (6Ug) slate gray (Zwykla) 3.00 1.00
- Never hinged 5.00

O6

**Perf. 11x11½, 12x12½ Engr.**
**1954, Aug. 15**
- O30 O6 (60g) dark blue (Zwykla) .25 .20
- O31 O6 (1.552) red (Polecona) .45 .25
- 1.00
- Set, never hinged

Polish People's Republic, 10th anniversary.

## NEWSPAPER STAMPS

Austrian Newspaper Stamps of 1916 Overprinted

**Perf. 12½ Unwmk.**
**1919, Jan. 10 Imperf.**
- P1 N9 2h brown 9.50 15.75
- P2 N9 4h green 2.75 5.25
- P3 N9 6h dark blue 67.50 62.50
- P4 N9 10h orange 7.50 11.25
- P5 N9 30h claret 90.00 100.00
- Nos. P1-P5 (5)

See note above No. 41.
Counterfeits exist of Nos. P1-P5.

## OCCUPATION STAMPS

### Issued under German Occupation

German Stamps of 1905 Overprinted

**Perf. 14, 14½ Wmk. 125**
**1915, May 12**
- N1 A16 3pf brown .60 .50
- N2 A16 5pf green 1.25 .50
- N3 A16 10pf carmine 1.25 .50
- N4 A16 20pf ultra 2.50 .75
- N5 A16 40pf lake & blk 7.50 3.75
- 13.10 6.00
- Nos. N1-N5 (5) 35.00
- Set, never hinged

German Stamps of 1905-17 Overprinted

**1916-17**
- N6 A22 2½pf gray 1.25 2.50
- N7 A16 3pf green 1.25 2.50
- N8 A16 5pf green 1.25 2.50
- N9 A22 7½pf orange 1.25 2.50
- N10 A16 10pf carmine 3.50 3.50
- N11 A22 15pf yel brn 3.50 2.50
- N12 A22 15pf dk vio ('17) 1.75 2.50
- N13 A16 20pf ultra 7.00 15.00
- N14 A16 30pf org & blk, buff 2.50 2.50
- N15 A16 40pf lake & blk 3.00 3.50
- N16 A16 60pf magenta 25.25 42.00
- 60.00
- Nos. N6-N16 (11)
- Set, never hinged

For overprints and surcharges see #15-26.

German Stamps of 1934 Surcharged in Black

**6 Groschen 6 — Deutsche Post OSTEN**

**Perf. 14 Wmk. 237**
**1939, Dec. 1**
- N17 A64 6g on 3pf bister .20 .40
- N18 A64 8g on 4pf dl bl .20 .40
- N19 A61 12g on 6pf dk grn .40 1.00
- N20 A64 16g on 8pf vermilion .20 .40
- N21 A64 20g on 6pf vermilion .20 .40
- N22 A64 24g on 12pf dp car .50 .90
- N23 A64 30g on 15pf maroon .50 .40
- N24 A64 40g on 20pf brt bl .40 .75
- N25 A64 50g on 25pf ultra .40 .75
- N26 A64 60g on 30pf ol grn .40 .80
- N27 A64 80g on 40pf red vio .50 .80
- N28 A64 2z on 50pf dk grn & blk 1.00 1.25
- N29 A64 2z on 100(pf) org & blk 2.00 3.50
- 6.60 10.80
- Nos. N17-N29 (13) 17.50
- Set, never hinged

Stamps of Poland 1937, Surcharged in Black or Brown

**General Gouvernement — 24 GR 24**

**1940 Unwmk. Perf. 12½, 12½x13**
- N30 A80 24g on 25g sl grn 1.25 3.25
- N31 A81 40g on 30g rose vio 1.25
- N32 A80 50g on 55g blue .40 .65 .25

Similar Surcharge on Stamps of 1938-39
- N33 A83 2g on 5g red org .40
- N34 A83 4(g) on 5g red org .40
- N35 A83 6(g) on 10g grn org .20
- N36 A83 8(g) on 10g grn .20
- N37 A83 10(g) on 15g redsh brn (Br) .20
- N38 A83 12(g) on 15g redsh brn (#339) .20 .40

N39 A83 16(g) on 15g redsh brn (#339) .20 .40
N40 A83 24g on 25g dl vio .20 .40
N41 A83 30(g) on 30g rose red .20 .40
N42 A83 50(g) on 50g brt red vio .25 .65
N43 A83 60(g) on 55g ultra 6.00 17.00
N44 A83 80(g) on 75g dl grn 6.00 17.00
N45 A83 1z on 1z org 6.00 17.00
N46 A83 2z on 2z car rose 3.00 7.50
N47 A95 3z on 3z gray blk 4.00 10.00

**Similar Surcharge on Nos. B32-B34**

N48 SP5 30g on 5g+5g .25 .65
N49 SP5 40g on 25g+10g .25 .65
N50 SP5 1z on 55g+15g 4.00 10.00

**Similar Surcharge on Nos. J98-J102**

*Perf. 12½x12*

N51 D11 50(g) on 20g 1.25 3.25
N52 D11 50(g) on 25g 6.00 17.50
N53 D11 50(g) on 30g 14.00 37.50
N54 D11 50(g) on 50g .75 2.40
N55 D11 50(g) on 1z 1.75 4.75
*Nos. N30-N55 (26)* 57.20 154.60
Set, never hinged 140.00

The surcharge on Nos. N30 to N55 is arranged to fit the shape of the stamp and obliterate the original denomination. On some values, "General Gouvernement" appears at the bottom. Counterfeits exist.

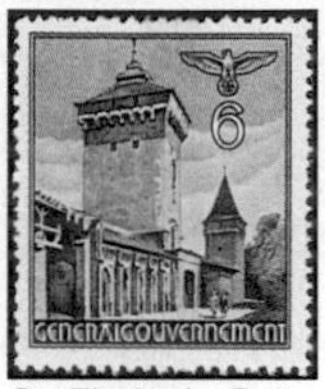

St. Florian's Gate, Cracow — OS1

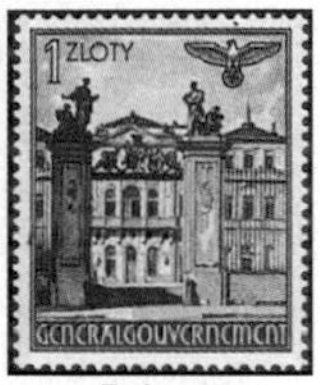

Palace, Warsaw — OS13

Designs: 8g, Watch Tower, Cracow. 10g, Cracow Gate, Lublin. 12g, Courtyard and statue of Copernicus. 20g, Dominican Church, Cracow. 24g, Wawel Castle, Cracow. 30g, Church, Lublin. 40g, Arcade, Cloth Hall, Cracow. 48g, City Hall, Sandomierz. 50g, Court House, Cracow. 60g, Courtyard, Cracow. 80g, St. Mary's Church, Cracow.

**1940-41 Unwmk. Photo. *Perf. 14***

N56 OS1 6g brown .20 .75
N57 OS1 8g brn org .20 .75
N58 OS1 8g bl blk ('41) .20 .50
N59 OS1 10g emerald .20 .25
N60 OS1 12g dk grn 1.75 .70
N61 OS1 12g dp vio ('41) .20 .25
N62 OS1 20g dk ol brn .20 .20
N63 OS1 24g henna brn .20 .20
N64 OS1 30g purple .20 .20
N65 OS1 30g vio brn ('41) .20 .25
N66 OS1 40g slate blk .20 .20
N67 OS1 48g chnt brn ('41) .50 1.50
N68 OS1 50g brt bl .20 .20
N69 OS1 60g slate grn .20 .25
N70 OS1 80g dull pur .20 .50
N71 OS13 1z rose lake 1.25 1.25
N72 OS13 1z Prus grn ('41) .55 1.00
*Nos. N56-N72 (17)* 6.65 8.95
Set, never hinged 14.50

For surcharges see Nos. NB1-NB4.

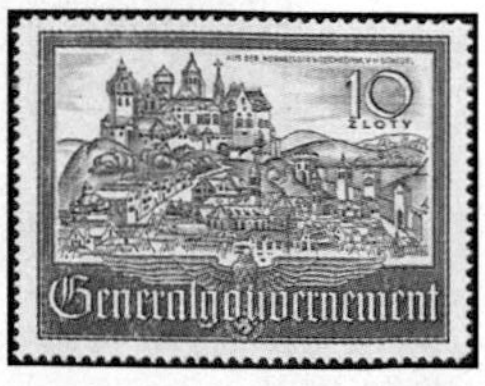

Cracow Castle and City, 15th Century OS14

**1941, Apr. 20 Engr. *Perf. 14½***

N73 OS14 10z red & ol blk .85 2.75
Never hinged 2.50

Printed in sheets of 8.

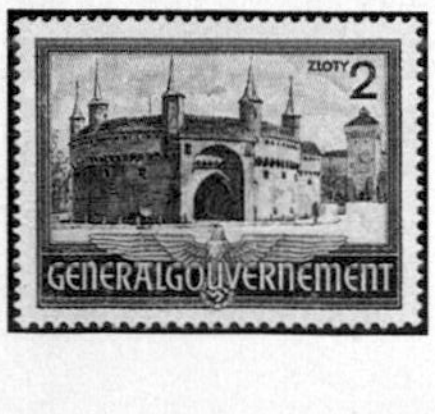

Rondel and Florian's Gate, Cracow OS15

Design: 4z, Tyniec Monastery, Vistula River.

**1941 *Perf. 13½x14***

N74 OS15 2z dk ultra .35 1.00
N75 OS15 4z slate grn .35 1.40
Set, never hinged 2.00

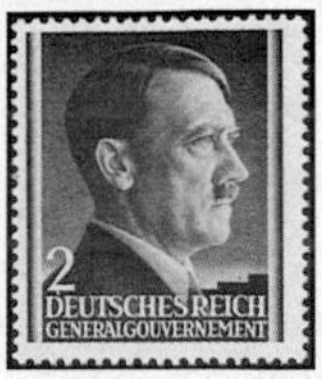

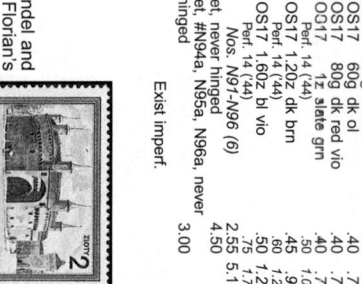

Adolf Hitler — OS17

**1941-43 Unwmk. Photo. *Perf. 14***

N76 OS17 2g gray blk .20 .20
N77 OS17 6g golden brn .20 .20
N78 OS17 8g slate blue .20 .20
N79 OS17 10g green .20 .20
N80 OS17 12g purple .20 .20
N81 OS17 16g org red .20 .60
N82 OS17 20g blk brn .20 .20
N83 OS17 24g henna .20 .20
N84 OS17 30g rose vio .20 .20
N85 OS17 32g dk bl grn .20 .50
N86 OS17 40g brt blue .20 .20
N87 OS17 48g chestnut .25 .50
N88 OS17 50g vio bl ('43) .20 .20
N89 OS17 60g dk olive ('43) .20 .20
N90 OS17 80g dk vio ('43) .20 .20
*Nos. N76-N90 (15)* 3.05 4.00
Set, never hinged 3.50

A 20g black brown exists with head of Hans Frank substituted for that of Hitler. It was printed and used by Resistance movements.
Nos. N76-N80, N82-N90 exist imperf.

**1942-44 Engr. *Perf. 12½***

N91 OS17 50g vio bl .40 .75
N92 OS17 60g dk ol .40 .75
N93 OS17 80g dk red vio .40 .75
N94 OS17 1z slate grn .40 .75
a. Perf. 14 ('44) .50 1.00
N95 OS17 1.20z dk brn .45 .90
a. Perf. 14 ('44) .60 1.25
N96 OS17 1.60z bl vio .50 1.25
a. Perf. 14 ('44) .75 1.75
*Nos. N91-N96 (6)* 2.55 5.15
Set, never hinged 4.50
Set, #N94a, N95a, N96a, never hinged 3.00

Exist imperf.

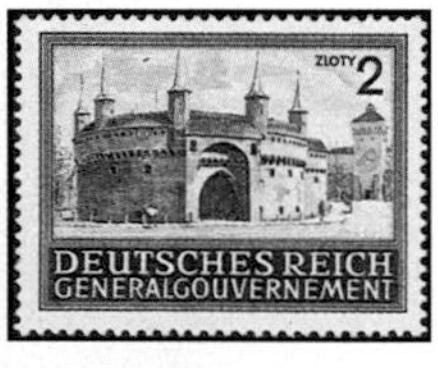

Rondel and Florian's Gate, Cracow OS18

Designs: 4z, Tyniec Monastery, Vistula River. 6z, View of Lwow. 10z, Cracow Castle and City, 15th Century.

**1943-44 *Perf. 13½x14***

N100 OS18 2z slate grn .20 .20
N101 OS18 4z dk gray vio .20 .35
N102 OS18 6z sepia ('44) .25 .50
N103 OS18 10z org brn & gray blk .25 .60
*Nos. N100-N103 (4)* .90 1.65
Set, never hinged 1.25

---

## OCCUPATION SEMI-POSTAL STAMPS

### Issued under German Occupation

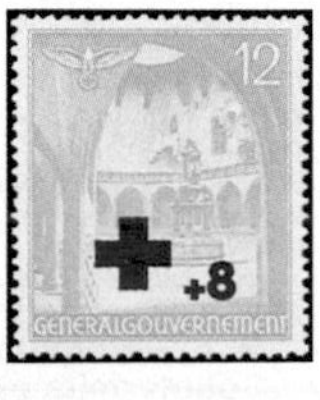

Types of 1940 Occupation Postage Stamps Surcharged in Red

**Unwmk.**

**1940, Aug. 17 Photo. *Perf. 14***

NB1 OS1 12g + 8g olive gray 1.25 3.50
NB2 OS1 24g + 16g olive gray 1.25 3.50
NB3 OS1 50g + 50g olive gray 1.50 4.00
NB4 OS1 80g + 80g olive gray 1.50 4.00
*Nos. NB1-NB4 (4)* 5.50 15.00
Set, never hinged 15.00

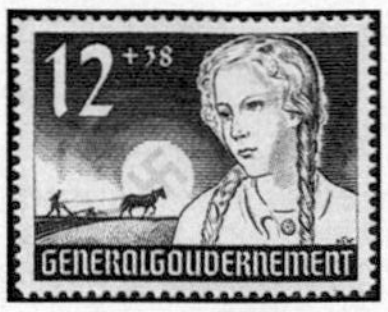

German Peasant Girl in Poland OSP1

Designs: 24g+26g, Woman wearing scarf. 30g+20g, Similar to type OSP4.

**1940, Oct. 26 Engr. *Perf. 14½***
**Thick Paper**

NB5 OSP1 12g + 38g dk sl grn .85 2.75
NB6 OSP1 24g + 26g cop red .85 2.75
NB7 OSP1 30g + 20g dk pur 1.50 5.00
*Nos. NB5-NB7 (3)* 3.20 10.50
Set, never hinged 8.50

1st anniversary of the General Government.

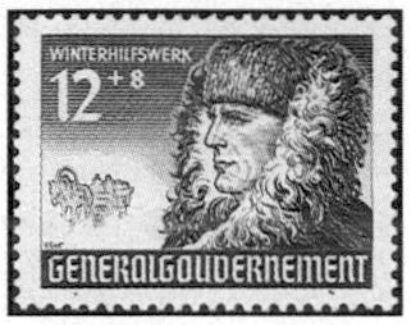

German Peasant OSP4

**1940, Dec. 1 *Perf. 12***

NB8 OSP4 12g + 8g dk grn .35 .90
NB9 OSP4 24g + 16g rose red .40 1.75
NB10 OSP4 30g + 30g vio brn 1.00 2.50
NB11 OSP4 50g + 50g ultra 1.00 3.00
*Nos. NB8-NB11 (4)* 2.75 8.15
Set, never hinged 7.00

The surtax was for war relief.

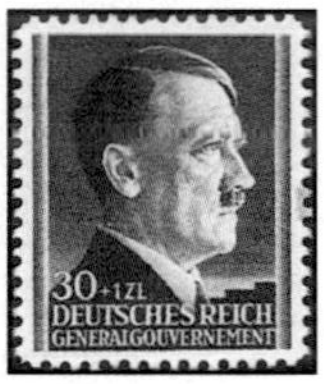

Adolf Hitler — OSP5

**Unwmk.**

**1942, Apr. 20 Engr. *Perf. 11***
**Thick Cream Paper**

NB12 OSP5 30g + 1z brn car .30 .60
NB13 OSP5 50g + 1z dk ultra .30 .60
NB14 OSP5 1.20z + 1z brown .30 .60
*Nos. NB12-NB14 (3)* .90 1.80
Set, never hinged 1.60

To commemorate Hitler's 53rd birthday. Printed in sheets of 25.

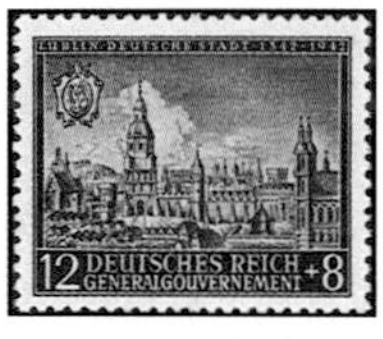

Ancient Lublin — OSP6

Designs: 24g+6g, 1z+1z, Modern Lublin.

**1942, Aug. 15 Photo. *Perf. 12½***

NB15 OSP6 12g + 8g rose vio .20 .35
NB16 OSP6 24g + 6g henna .20 .35
NB17 OSP6 50g + 50g dp bl .20 .45
NB18 OSP6 1z + 1z dp grn .40 .80
*Nos. NB15-NB18 (4)* 1.00 1.95
Set, never hinged 1.50

600th anniversary of Lublin.

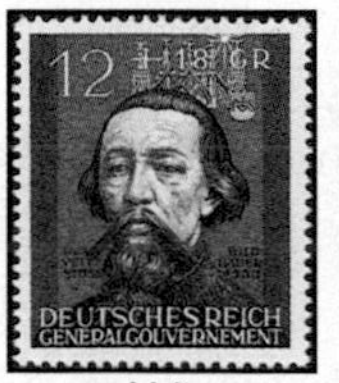

Veit Stoss — OSP8

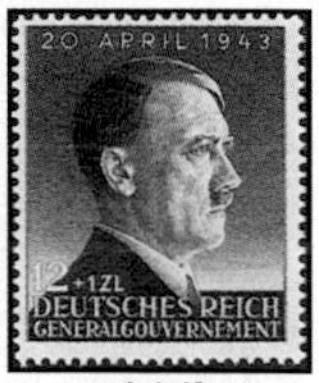

Adolf Hitler — OSP13

Designs: 24g+26g, Hans Durer. 30g+30g, Johann Schuch. 50g+50g, Joseph Elsner. 1z+1z, Nicolaus Copernicus.

**1942, Nov. 20 Engr. *Perf. 13½x14***

NB19 OSP8 12g + 18g dl pur .20 .20
NB20 OSP8 24g + 26g dl henna .20 .20
NB21 OSP8 30g + 30g dl rose vio .20 .20
NB22 OSP8 50g + 50g dl bl vio .20 .20
NB23 OSP8 1z + 1z dl myr grn .20 .40
*Nos. NB19-NB23 (5)* 1.00 1.20
Set, never hinged 1.40

For overprint see No. NB27.

**1943, Apr. 20**

NB24 OSP13 12g + 1z purple .20 .40
NB25 OSP13 24g + 1z rose car .20 .40
NB26 OSP13 84g + 1z myrtle grn .25 .40
*Nos. NB24-NB26 (3)* .65 1.20
Set, never hinged 1.20

To commemorate Hitler's 54th birthday.

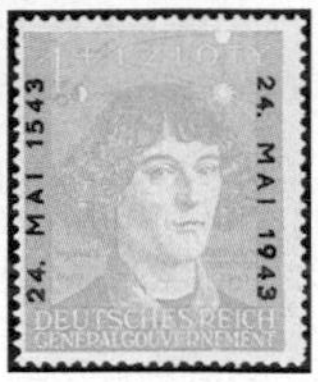

Type of 1942 Overprinted in Black

**1943, May 24**

NB27 OSP8 1z + 1z rose lake .55 .90
Never hinged .90

Nicolaus Copernicus. Printed in sheets of 10, with marginal inscription.

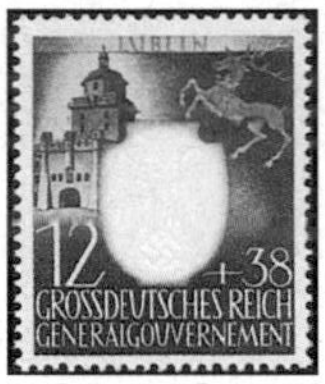

Cracow Gate, Lublin — OSP14

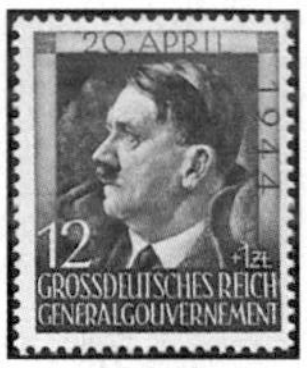

Adolf Hitler — OSP19

Designs: 24g+76g, Cloth Hall, Cracow. 30g+70g, New Government Building, Radom. 50g+1z, Bruhl Palace, Warsaw. 1z+2z, Town Hall, Lwow.

The center of the designs is embossed with the emblem of the National Socialist Party.

**1943 Photogravure, Embossed**

NB28 OSP14 12g + 38g dk grn .20 .20
NB29 OSP14 24g + 76g red .20 .20
NB30 OSP14 30g + 70g rose vio .20 .20
NB31 OSP14 50g + 1z brt bl .20 .20
NB32 OSP14 1z + 2z bl blk .20 .20
*Nos. NB28-NB32 (5)* 1.00 1.00
Set, never hinged .90

3rd anniversary of the National Socialist Party in Poland.

**1944, Apr. 20 Photo. *Perf. 14x13½***

NB33 OSP19 12g + 1z green .20 .20
NB34 OSP19 24g + 1z brn red .20 .20
NB35 OSP19 84g + 1z dk vio .20 .20
*Nos. NB33-NB35 (3)* .60
Set, never hinged .60

To commemorate Hitler's 55th birthday. Printed in sheets of 25.

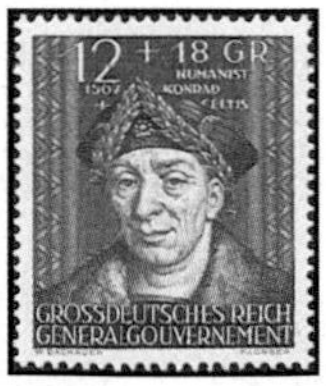

Conrad Celtis — OSP20

Designs: 24g+26g, Andreas Schluter. 30g+30g, Hans Boner. 50g+50g, Augustus II. 1z+1z, Georg Gottlieb Pusch.

**1944, July 15 Engr. *Perf. 13½x14***

NB36 OSP20 12g + 18g dk grn .20 .20
NB37 OSP20 24g + 26g dk red .20 .20
NB38 OSP20 30g + 30g rose vio .20 .20
NB39 OSP20 50g + 50g ultra .20 .20
NB40 OSP20 1z + 1z dl red brn .20 .20
*Nos. NB36-NB40 (5)* 1.00 1.00
Set, never hinged .85

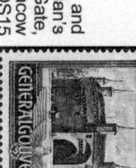

## OFFICES IN THE TURKISH EMPIRE

### 1919, May — Unwmk. Wove Paper — Perf. 11½

| | | | | |
|---|---|---|---|---|
| 2K1 | A10 | 3f bister brn | 42.50 | 75.00 |
| 2K2 | A10 | 5f green | 42.50 | 75.00 |
| 2K3 | A10 | 10f red vio | 42.50 | 75.00 |
| 2K4 | A10 | 15f red | 42.50 | 75.00 |
| 2K5 | A11 | 20f dp blue | 42.50 | 75.00 |
| 2K6 | A11 | 25f olive grn | 42.50 | 75.00 |
| 2K7 | A11 | 50f blue grn | 42.50 | 75.00 |

Overprinted

| | | | | |
|---|---|---|---|---|
| 2K8 | A12 | 1m violet | 42.50 | 75.00 |
| 2K9 | A12 | 1.50m dp green | 42.50 | 75.00 |
| 2K10 | A12 | 2m dk brown | 42.50 | 75.00 |
| 2K11 | A13 | 2.50m orange brn | 42.50 | 75.00 |
| 2K12 | A14 | 5m red violet | 510.00 | 900.00 |
| | | Nos. 2K1-2K12 (12) | | |

Counterfeit cancellations are plentiful. Counterfeits exist of Nos. 2K1-2K12. Reissues are lighter, shiny red. Value, set $17.50.

Polish stamps with "P.P.C." overprint (Poste Polonaise Constantinople) were used on consular mail for a time.

Seven stamps with these overprints were not issued. Value, set $20.

## EXILE GOVERNMENT IN GREAT BRITAIN

These stamps were issued by the Polish government in exile for letters posted from Polish merchant ships and warships.

G.10 Polish Ministry of Finance Ruins, Warsaw — A2

G.5 United States Embassy Ruins, Warsaw — A1

Z1 G.50 Polish Submarine "Orzel" — A8

G.25 Destruction of Mickiewicz Monument, Cracow — A3

G.55 Ruins of Warsaw A4

G.75 Polish Machine Gunners A5

---

## OFFICES IN DANZIG (continued)

### 1929-30 — Perf. 12x12½

| | | | | |
|---|---|---|---|---|
| 1K20 | A53 | 5g dk violet | 1.65 | 1.40 |
| 1K21 | A53 | 10g green ('30) | 1.65 | 1.40 |
| 1K22 | A53 | 25g red brown | 2.75 | 1.40 |
| | | Nos. 1K20-1K22 (3) | 6.05 | 4.20 |
| | | | 8.00 | |

Same Overprint on Poland No. 257 — Perf. 12½

### 1931, Jan. 5

| | | | | |
|---|---|---|---|---|
| 1K23 | A52 | 15g ultra | 3.50 | 4.00 |
| | | Never hinged | 5.00 | |

Poland No. 255 Overprinted in Dark Blue

### 1933, July 1 — Laid Paper — Perf. 11½

| | | | | |
|---|---|---|---|---|
| 1K24 | A50 | 1z black, cream | 82.50 | 100.00 |
| | | Never hinged | 110.00 | |

Poland Nos. 268-270 Overprinted in Black

### 1934-36 — Wmk. 234 — Perf. 12x12½

| | | | | |
|---|---|---|---|---|
| 1K25 | A58 | 5g dl violet | 3.25 | 3.75 |
| 1K26 | A58 | 10g green ('36) | 35.00 | 72.50 |
| 1K27 | A58 | 25g red brown | 41.50 | 80.00 |
| | | Nos. 1K25-1K27 (3) | 60.00 | |

Poland Nos. 294, 296, 298 Overprinted in Black in one or two lines

### 1935-36 — Unwmk — Perf. 12½x13

| | | | | |
|---|---|---|---|---|
| 1K28 | A65 | 5g violet blue | 3.25 | 3.75 |
| 1K29 | A65 | 15g Prus green | 3.50 | 4.75 |
| 1K30 | A65 | 25g myrtle green | 3.50 | 2.00 |
| | | Nos. 1K28-1K30 (3) | 10.50 | 9.75 |
| | | | 14.00 | |

Same Overprint in Black on Poland Nos. 308, 310

### 1937, June 5

| | | | | |
|---|---|---|---|---|
| 1K31 | A65 | 5g violet blue | 1.10 | 1.75 |
| 1K32 | A65 | 15g red brown | 1.10 | 1.75 |
| | | | 3.25 | |

Polish Merchants Selling Wheat in Danzig, 16th Century — A2

### 1938, Nov. 11 — Engr. — Perf. 12½

| | | | | |
|---|---|---|---|---|
| 1K33 | A2 | 5g red orange | .65 | .95 |
| 1K34 | A2 | 15g red brown | .65 | .95 |
| 1K35 | A2 | 25g dull violet | 1.65 | |
| 1K36 | A2 | 55g brt ultra | 3.00 | |
| | | Nos. 1K33-1K36 (4) | 3.60 | 6.55 |
| | | | 9.75 | |

## OFFICES IN THE TURKISH EMPIRE

Stamps of Poland 1919, Overprinted in Carmine

---

## POLISH OFFICES ABROAD

## OFFICES IN DANZIG

Poland Nos. 215-225 Overprinted

### 1925, Jan. 5 — Unwmk. — Perf. 11½x12

| | | | | |
|---|---|---|---|---|
| 1K1 | A36 | 1g orange brn | .45 | 1.10 |
| 1K2 | A36 | 2g dk brown | .60 | 3.25 |
| 1K3 | A36 | 3g orange | .60 | 1.10 |
| 1K4 | A36 | 5g blue grn | .60 | 7.50 |
| 1K5 | A36 | 10g blue grn | 15.00 | 2.25 |
| 1K6 | A36 | 15g red | 5.00 | 5.75 |
| 1K7 | A36 | 20g blue | 1.75 | 1.10 |
| 1K8 | A36 | 25g dp brown | 1.75 | 1.10 |
| 1K9 | A36 | 40g red violet | 2.00 | 1.10 |
| 1K10 | A36 | 40g indigo | 2.00 | 1.10 |
| 1K11 | A36 | 50g magenta | 5.50 | 1.65 |
| | | Nos. 1K1-1K11 (11) | 64.65 | 27.00 |

Same Ovpt. on Poland Nos. 230,231 — Perf. 11½, 12

### 1926

| | | | | |
|---|---|---|---|---|
| 1K11A | A39 | 5g yellow grn | 52.50 | 37.50 |
| 1K12 | A40 | 10g violet | 12.50 | 15.00 |

Counterfeit overprints are known on Nos. 1K1-1K32.

No. 232 Overprinted

### 1926-27

| | | | | |
|---|---|---|---|---|
| 1K13 | A41 | 15g rose red | 45.00 | 40.00 |

Same Overprint on Redrawn Stamps of 1926-27 — Perf. 13

| | | | | |
|---|---|---|---|---|
| 1K14 | A39 | 5g yellow grn | 2.00 | 1.75 |
| 1K15 | A40 | 10g violet | 2.00 | 1.75 |
| 1K16 | A41 | 15g red orange | 4.00 | 3.75 |
| 1K17 | A42 | 25g dull red | 3.25 | 2.25 |
| | | Nos. 1K14-1K17 (4) | 11.25 | 9.50 |

Same Ovpt. on Poland Nos. 250, 255a — Perf. 12½

### 1928-30

| | | | | |
|---|---|---|---|---|
| 1K18 | A44 | 25g yellow brn | 4.75 | 1.50 |

Laid Paper — Perf. 11½x12, 12½x11½

| | | | | |
|---|---|---|---|---|
| 1K19 | A50 | 1z blk, cr ('30) | 30.00 | 30.00 |
| | | Set, never hinged | 47.50 | |

Poland Nos. 258-260 Overprinted

---

## Cracow Castle OSP25

### 1944, Oct. 26 — Perf. 14½

| | | | | |
|---|---|---|---|---|
| NB41 | OSP25 | 10z + 10z red & blk | 7.50 | 17.00 |
| a. | | Never hinged | 13.00 | |
| | | Imperf. | 9.00 | |
| b. | | 10z + 10z car & greenish blk | 12.50 | 18.00 |
| | | Never hinged | 12.00 | |

5th anniv. of the General Government, Oct. 26, 1944. Printed in sheets of 8.

## OCCUPATION RURAL DELIVERY STAMPS

Issued under German Occupation

OSD1

### 1940, Dec. 1 — Perf. 13½ — Photo.

| | | | | |
|---|---|---|---|---|
| NL1 | OSD1 | 10g red orange | .45 | 1.00 |
| NL2 | OSD1 | 20g red orange | .45 | 1.25 |
| NL3 | OSD1 | 30g red orange | .45 | 1.25 |
| NL4 | OSD1 | 50g red orange | 1.10 | 3.00 |
| | | Nos. NL1-NL4 (4) | 2.45 | 6.50 |
| | | Set, never hinged | 4.00 | |

## OCCUPATION OFFICIAL STAMPS

Issued under German Occupation

Eagle and Swastika OOS1

### 1940, Apr. — Perf. 12, 13½x14 — Photo. Size: 31x23mm — Unwmk.

| | | | | |
|---|---|---|---|---|
| NO1 | OOS1 | 6g lt brown | .50 | 2.00 |
| NO2 | OOS1 | 8g gray | .50 | 2.00 |
| NO3 | OOS1 | 10g green | .50 | 2.00 |
| NO4 | OOS1 | 12g dk green | .50 | 1.75 |
| NO5 | OOS1 | 20g dk brown | .50 | 2.50 |
| NO6 | OOS1 | 24g henna brn | 8.00 | 1.75 |
| NO7 | OOS1 | 30g rose lake | .60 | 2.75 |
| NO8 | OOS1 | 40g dl violet | .60 | 5.00 |
| NO9 | OOS1 | 48g dl olive | .60 | 5.00 |
| NO10 | OOS1 | 50g royal red | 6.50 | 5.00 |
| NO11 | OOS1 | 60g dk ol grn | .50 | 2.00 |
| NO12 | OOS1 | 80g rose vio | .50 | 2.00 |

Size: 35x26mm

| | | | | |
|---|---|---|---|---|
| NO13 | OOS1 | 1z gray blk & brn vio | 1.25 | 4.75 |
| NO14 | OOS1 | 3z gray blk & chmt | 1.25 | 4.75 |
| NO15 | OOS1 | 5z gray blk & org brn | | 11.25 |
| | | Nos. NO1-NO15 (15) | 24.20 | 46.50 |
| | | | 65.00 | |

### 1940 — Perf. 12 — Size: 21¼x16¼/4mm

| | | | | |
|---|---|---|---|---|
| NO16 | OOS1 | 6g brown | .35 | 1.10 |
| NO17 | OOS1 | 8g slate | .85 | 1.75 |
| NO18 | OOS1 | 10g dp gray | .85 | 2.00 |
| NO19 | OOS1 | 12g slate grn | .50 | 1.10 |
| NO20 | OOS1 | 20g dk brown | .85 | 1.10 |
| NO21 | OOS1 | 24g cop brn | .35 | 1.75 |
| NO22 | OOS1 | 30g rose lake | .85 | 2.00 |
| NO23 | OOS1 | 40g dl pur | .85 | 2.00 |
| NO24 | OOS1 | 50g royal blue | 5.60 | 14.80 |
| | | Nos. NO16-NO24 (9) | | 16.00 |

Nazi Emblem and Cracow Castle — OOS2

### 1943 — Photo. — Perf. 14

| | | | | |
|---|---|---|---|---|
| NO25 | OOS2 | 6g brown | .20 | .35 |
| NO26 | OOS2 | 8g slate blue | .20 | .35 |
| NO27 | OOS2 | 10g green | .20 | .35 |
| NO28 | OOS2 | 12g dk vio | .20 | .35 |
| NO29 | OOS2 | 16g red org | .20 | .35 |
| NO30 | OOS2 | 20g dk brn | .20 | .35 |
| NO31 | OOS2 | 24g dk red | .20 | .35 |
| NO32 | OOS2 | 30g rose vio | .20 | .35 |
| NO33 | OOS2 | 40g blue | .20 | .35 |
| NO34 | OOS2 | 60g olive grn | .20 | .35 |
| NO35 | OOS2 | 80g dull claret | .20 | .35 |
| NO36 | OOS2 | 100g slate blk | 2.40 | 4.20 |
| | | Nos. NO25-NO36 (12) | | 3.00 |
| | | Set, never hinged | | |

## Polish Planes in Great Britain A7

## Armored Tank A6

## Polish Air Force in Battle of the Atlantic — A9

## Polish Merchant Navy A10

## Polish Army in France, 1939-40 — A11

## Polish Army in Narvik, Norway, 1940 — A12

## The Homeland Fights On — A15

## Polish Army in Libya, 1941-42 A13

## General Sikorsky and Polish Soldiers in the Middle East, 1943 A14

## The Secret Press in Poland A16

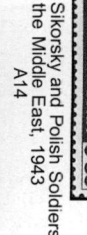

**1941, Dec. 15**   **Perf. 12½, 11½x12 Engr.**   **Unwmk.**

| | | | | |
|---|---|---|---|---|
| 3K1 | A1 | 5g rose violet | .50 | 1.25 |
| 3K2 | A2 | 10g dk bl grn | .75 | 1.25 |
| 3K3 | A3 | 25g black | 2.25 | 2.00 |
| 3K4 | A4 | 55g dark blue | 3.75 | 6.50 |
| 3K5 | A5 | 75g dk car grn | 3.75 | 6.50 |
| 3K6 | A6 | 80g olive grn | 3.75 | 6.50 |
| 3K7 | A7 | 1z slate blue | 3.75 | 6.50 |
| 3K8 | A8 | 1.50z copper brn | 19.75 | 30.25 |
| | | Nos. 3K1-3K8 (8) | 30.00 | |

These stamps were used for correspondence carried on Polish ships and, on certain days, in Polish Military camps in Great Britain. For surcharges see Nos. 3K17-3K20.

**1943, Nov. 1**

| | | | | |
|---|---|---|---|---|
| 3K9 | A9 | 5g rose lake | .40 | 1.00 |
| 3K10 | A10 | 10g dk bl grn | .65 | 1.10 |
| 3K11 | A11 | 25g dk vio | .65 | 1.10 |
| 3K12 | A12 | 55g dk blue | 1.00 | 1.65 |
| 3K13 | A13 | 75g sapphire | 1.65 | 3.00 |
| 3K14 | A14 | 75g brn car | 1.65 | 3.00 |
| 3K15 | A15 | 80g rose car | 2.25 | 3.50 |
| 3K16 | A16 | 1z olive blk | 3.00 | 3.50 |
| | | Nos. 3K9-3K16 (8) | 11.85 | 21.35 |
| | | Set, never hinged | 15.00 | |

**Nos. 3K5 to 3K8 Surcharged in Blue**

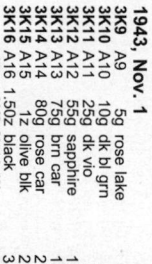

MONTE CASSINO 18. V. 1944

**1944, June 27**   **Perf. 12½, 11½x12**   **Unwmk.**

| | | | | |
|---|---|---|---|---|
| 3K17 | A5 | 45g on 75g | 6.00 | 17.50 |
| 3K18 | A6 | 55g on 80g | 6.00 | 17.50 |
| 3K19 | A7 | 55g on 1z | 6.00 | 17.50 |
| 3K20 | A8 | 1.20z on 1.50z | 6.00 | 17.50 |
| | | Nos. 3K17-3K20 (4) | 24.00 | 70.00 |
| | | Set, never hinged | 52.50 | |

Capture of Monte Cassino by the Poles, May 18, 1944.

## EXILE GOVERNMENT IN GREAT BRITAIN SEMI-POSTAL STAMP

WARSZAWA 1.VIII — 3.X.1944

Heroic Defenders of Warsaw — SP1

**1945, Feb. 3**   **Perf. 11½**   **Unwmk.**   **Engr.**

| | | | | |
|---|---|---|---|---|
| 3KB1 | SP1 | 1z + 2z slate green | 3.75 | 10.00 |
| | | Never hinged | 7.25 | |

Warsaw uprising, Aug. 1-Oct. 3, 1944.

| | | | | |
|---|---|---|---|---|
| 11 | A1 | 200r dk bl, bl | 62.50 | 45.00 |
| 12 | A1 | 300r dk bl, salmon | 47.50 | |

Nos. 1, 4 and 9-12 were reprinted in 1900 (perf. 11½). Value, each $50. All values were reprinted in 1905 (perf. 13½). Value, each $25. The reprints are on paper slightly thinner than that of the originals, and unsurfaced. They have white gum and clean-cut perfs. See the Scott Classic Specialized Catalogue for listings by perforation.

**1897-1905**   **Name and Value in Black except Nos. 25 and 34**   **Perf. 11½**

| | | | | |
|---|---|---|---|---|
| 13 | A2 | 2½r gray | .60 | .35 |
| 14 | A2 | 5r orange | .60 | .35 |
| 15 | A2 | 10r lt green | .80 | .35 |
| 16 | A2 | 15r brown | 6.50 | 4.50 |
| 17 | A2 | 15r gray grn ('99) | 2.25 | 1.10 |
| 18 | A2 | 20r dull violet | 2.25 | 1.25 |
| 19 | A2 | 25r sea green | 3.00 | 2.25 |
| 20 | A2 | 25r rose red ('99) | 2.25 | 1.40 |
| 21 | A2 | 50r rose | 3.00 | 1.25 |
| 22 | A2 | 50r ultra ('05) | 18.50 | 11.00 |
| 23 | A2 | 65r slate blue ('98) | 1.40 | 1.25 |
| 24 | A2 | 75r blue | 7.00 | 1.25 |
| 25 | A2 | 75r brn & car, yel ('05) | | |
| 26 | A2 | 80r violet | 15.00 | 8.75 |
| 27 | A2 | 100r dk bl, bl | 1.90 | 1.25 |
| 28 | A2 | 115r org brn, rose | 4.25 | 1.25 |
| 29 | A2 | 130r gray brn, buff ('98) | 3.25 | 1.60 |
| 30 | A2 | 150r gray brn, buff ('98) | 3.75 | 1.60 |
| 31 | A2 | 150r lt brn, buff | 3.75 | 2.25 |
| 32 | A2 | 180r sl, pnksh ('98) | 7.75 | 5.50 |
| 33 | A2 | 200r red vio, pnksh | 9.00 | 5.50 |
| 34 | A2 | 300r blue, rose | 45.00 | 10.00 |
| | a. | Perf. 12½ | 16.50 | 10.00 |
| | a. | Perf. 12½ | 22.50 | 10.00 |
| | | 500r blk & red, bl | | |
| | | Nos. 13-34 (22) | 116.85 | 63.45 |

Imperfs are proofs.

# PONTA DELGADA

,pän-ta del-gä-da

LOCATION — Administrative district of the Azores comprising the islands of Sao Miguel and Santa Maria
GOVT. — A district of Portugal
AREA — 342 sq. mi.
POP. — 124,000 (approx.)
CAPITAL — Ponta Delgada

1000 Reis = 1 Milreis

The stamps of Ponta Delgada were superseded by those of the Azores, which in 1931 were replaced by those of Portugal.

## King Carlos

A1    A2

**1892-93**   **Perf. 12½, 11½ (25r), 13½ (75r, 150r)**   **Typo.**   **Unwmk.**

| | | | | |
|---|---|---|---|---|
| 1 | A1 | 5r yellow | 2.75 | 1.60 |
| | c. | Diagonal half used as 2½r on piece | 17.50 | |
| 2 | A1 | 10r reddish vio | 2.75 | 1.60 |
| 3 | A1 | 15r chocolate | 3.50 | 2.25 |
| 4 | A1 | 20r lavender | 3.50 | 2.25 |
| | a. | Perf. 13½ | | |
| 5d | A1 | 25r deep green | 7.50 | 1.10 |
| 6 | A1 | 50r ultra | 7.50 | 3.25 |
| 7 | A1 | 75r carmine | 7.75 | 5.25 |
| 8 | A1 | 80r yellow grn | 11.00 | 5.50 |
| 9 | A1 | 100r brn, yel | 11.00 | 9.00 |
| 10 | A1 | 150r car, rose | 70.00 | 32.50 |

# PORTUGAL

'pōr-chi-gəl

LOCATION — Southern Europe, on the western coast of the Iberian Peninsula
GOVT. — Republic
AREA — 35,516 sq. mi.
POP. — 9,918,040 (1999 est.)
CAPITAL — Lisbon

Figures for area and population include the Azores and Madeira, which are integral parts of the republic. The republic was established in 1910. See Azores, Funchal, Madeira.

1000 Reis = 1 Milreis
10 Reis = 1 Centimo
100 Centavos = 1 Escudo (1912)
100 Cents = 1 Euro (2002)

**Catalogue values for unused stamps in this country are for Never Hinged items, beginning with Scott 662 in the regular postage section, Scott C11 in the air-post section, Scott J65 in the postage due section, and Scott O2 in the officials section.**

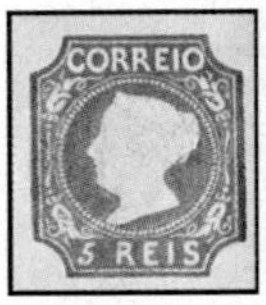
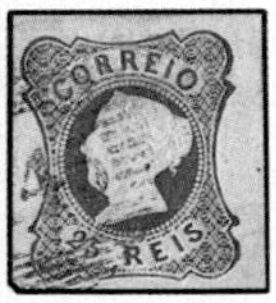

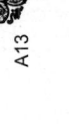

Queen Maria II
A1 A2

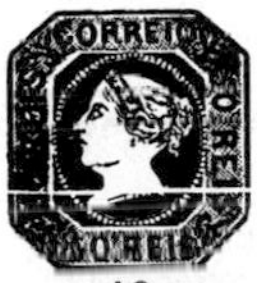
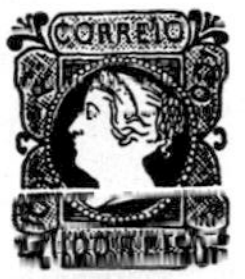

A3 A4

### Typo. & Embossed

**1853** **Unwmk.** ***Imperf.***

| | | | | |
|---|---|---|---|---|
| **1** | A1 | 5r reddish brown | 2,850. | 850.00 |
| **2** | A2 | 25r blue | 925.00 | 19.00 |
| **3** | A3 | 50r dp yellow grn | 3,400. | 875.00 |
| *a.* | | 50r blue green | 6,750. | 1,660. |
| **4** | A4 | 100r lilac | 31,000. | 1,900. |

*The stamps of the 1853 issue were reprinted in 1864, 1885, 1905 and 1953. Many stamps of subsequent issues were reprinted in 1885 and 1905. The reprints of 1864 are on thin white paper with white gum. The originals have brownish gum which often stains the paper. The reprints of 1885 are on a stout, very white paper. They are usually ungummed, but occasionally have a white gum with yellowish spots. The reprints of 1905 are on creamy white paper of ordinary quality with shiny white gum.*

*When perforated the reprints of 1885 have a rather rough perforation 13½ with small holes; those of 1905 have a clean-cut perforation 13½ with large holes making sharp pointed teeth.*

*The colors of the reprints usually differ from those of the originals, but actual comparison is necessary.*

*The reprints are often from new dies which differ slightly from those used for the originals.*

*5 reis: There is a defect in the neck which makes the Adam's apple appear very large in the first reprint. The later ones can be distinguished by the paper and the shades and by the absence of the pendant curl.*

*25 reis: The burelage of the ground work in the original is sharp and clear, while in the 1864 reprints it is blurred in several places; the upper and lower right hand corners are very thick and blurred. The central oval is less than ½mm from the frame at the sides in the originals and fully ¾mm in the 1885 and 1905 reprints.*

*50 reis: In the reprints of 1864 and 1885 there is a small break in the upper right hand diagonal line of the frame, and the initials of the engraver (F. B. F.), which in the originals are plainly discernible in the lower part of the bust, do not show. The reprints of 1905 have not the break in the frame and the initials are distinct.*

*100 reis: The small vertical lines at top and bottom at each side of the frame are heavier in the reprints of 1864 than in the originals. The reprints of 1885 and 1905 can be distinguished only by the paper, gum and shades.*

*Reprints of 1953 have thick paper, no gum and dates "1853/1953" on back. Value $55 each.*

*Values of lowest-cost earlier reprints (1905) of Nos. 1, $100; No. 2, $120; Nos. 3, 4, $150.*

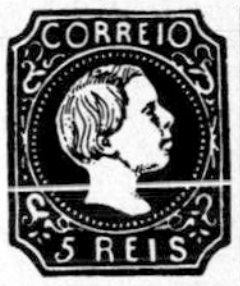
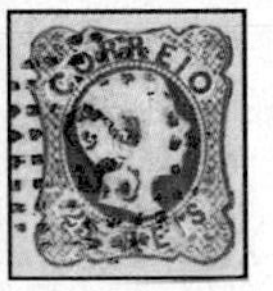

King Pedro V
A5 A6

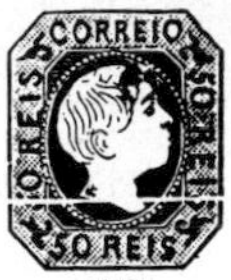
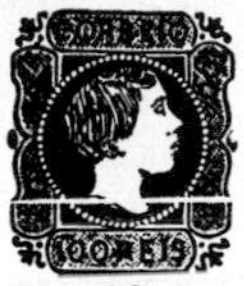

A7 A8

**1855** **With Straight Hair**

TWENTY-FIVE REIS:
Type I — Pearls mostly touch each other and oval outer line.
Type II — Pearls are separate from each other and oval outer line.

| | | | | |
|---|---|---|---|---|
| **5** | A5 | 5r red brown | 8,250. | 900.00 |
| **6** | A6 | 25r blue, type II | 950.00 | 25.00 |
| *a.* | | 25r blue, type I | 1,150. | 30.00 |
| **7** | A7 | 50r green | 500.00 | 70.00 |
| **8** | A8 | 100r lilac | 750.00 | 90.00 |

Several types of No. 5 exist, differing in number of pearls encircling head (74 to 89) and other details.

*All values were reprinted in 1885 and 1905. Value for lowest-cost, $60 each.*

*See note after No. 4.*

**1856** **With Curled Hair**

TWENTY-FIVE REIS:
Type I — The network is fine (single lines).
Type II — The network is coarse (double lines).

| | | | | |
|---|---|---|---|---|
| **9** | A5 | 5r brown (shades) | 375.00 | 70.00 |
| **10** | A6 | 25r blue, type II | 375.00 | 13.50 |
| *a.* | | 25r blue, type I | 9,500. | 55.00 |

**1858**

| | | | | |
|---|---|---|---|---|
| **11** | A6 | 25r rose, type II | 275.00 | 6.50 |

*The 5r dark brown, formerly listed and sold at about $1, is now believed by the best authorities to be a reprint made before 1866. It is printed on thin yellowish white paper with yellowish white gum and is known only unused. The same remarks will apply to a 25r blue which is common unused but not known used. It is printed from a die which was not used for the issued stamps but the differences are slight and can only be told by expert comparison.*

*Nos. 9 and 10, also 10a in rose, were reprinted in 1885 and Nos. 9, 10, 10a and 11 in 1905. Value of lowest-cost reprints, $40 each.*

*See note after No. 4.*

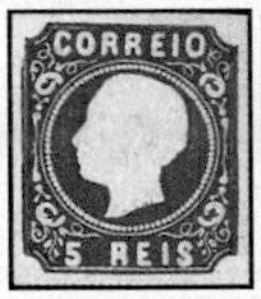
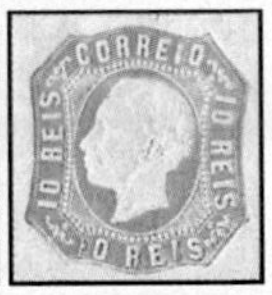

King Luiz
A9 A10

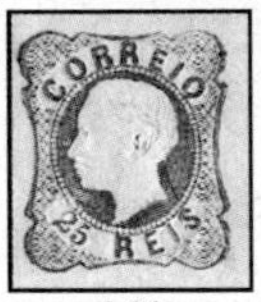
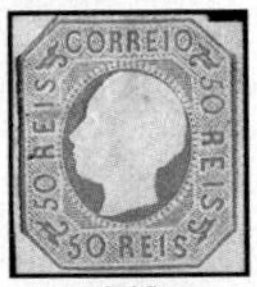

A11 A12

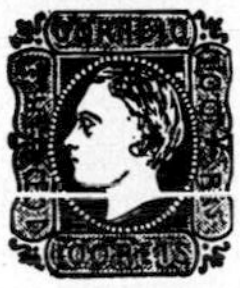

A13

**1862-64**

FIVE REIS:
Type I — The distance between "5" and "reis" is 3mm.
Type II — The distance between "5" and "reis" is 2mm.

| | | | | |
|---|---|---|---|---|
| **12** | A9 | 5r brown, type I | 125.00 | 10.00 |
| *a.* | | 5r brown, type II | 160.00 | 25.00 |
| *b.* | | Double impression, type II | 650.00 | 350.00 |
| *d.* | | Double embossing, type I | — | 275.00 |
| **13** | A10 | 10r orange | 140.00 | 47.50 |
| **14** | A11 | 25r rose | 100.00 | 4.75 |
| *a.* | | Double impression | 1,350. | 375.00 |
| *b.* | | Double embossing, type I | 1,350. | 375.00 |
| **15** | A12 | 50r yellow green | 725.00 | 77.50 |
| **16** | A13 | 100r lilac ('64) | 825.00 | 90.00 |
| | | *Nos. 12-16 (5)* | 1,915. | 229.75 |

*All values were reprinted in 1885 and all except the 25r in 1905. Value of lowest-cost reprints, $10 each.*

*See note after No. 4.*

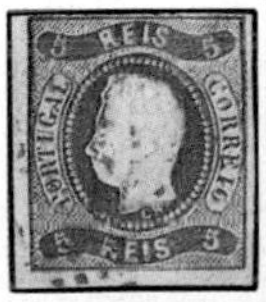
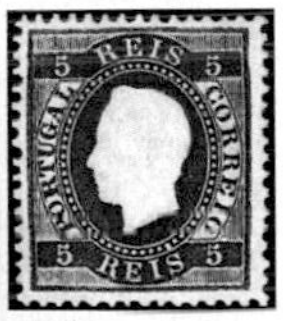

King Luiz
A14 A15

**1866-67** ***Imperf.***

| | | | | |
|---|---|---|---|---|
| **17** | A14 | 5r black | 110.00 | 10.00 |
| *a.* | | Double impression | 275.00 | 190.00 |
| **18** | A14 | 10r yellow | 225.00 | 140.00 |
| **19** | A14 | 20r bister | 190.00 | 67.50 |
| **20** | A14 | 25r rose ('67) | 225.00 | 8.00 |
| *a.* | | Double impression | | 200.00 |
| **21** | A14 | 50r green | 250.00 | 67.50 |
| **22** | A14 | 80r orange | 250.00 | 67.50 |
| **23** | A14 | 100r dk lilac ('67) | 300.00 | 97.50 |
| **24** | A14 | 120r blue | 325.00 | 70.00 |
| *a.* | | Double impression | 725.00 | 450.00 |
| | | *Nos. 17-24 (8)* | 1,875. | 528.00 |

Some values with unofficial percé en croix (diamond) perforation were used in Madeira.

*All values were reprinted in 1885 and 1905. Value: Nos. 17-23, each $30-$40; No. 24, $100.*

*See note after No. 4.*

### Typographed & Embossed

**1867-70** ***Perf. 12½***

| | | | | |
|---|---|---|---|---|
| **25** | A14 | 5r black | 125.00 | 42.50 |
| *a.* | | Double impression | 225.00 | 110.00 |
| **26** | A14 | 10r yellow | 250.00 | 110.00 |
| **27** | A14 | 20r bister ('69) | 300.00 | 110.00 |
| **28** | A14 | 25r rose | 65.00 | 6.75 |
| *a.* | | Double impression | 550.00 | 200.00 |
| **29** | A14 | 50r green ('68) | 250.00 | 110.00 |
| **30** | A14 | 80r orange ('69) | 350.00 | 110.00 |
| **31** | A14 | 100r lilac ('69) | 250.00 | 110.00 |
| **32** | A14 | 120r blue | 300.00 | 67.50 |
| *a.* | | Double impression | 625.00 | 160.00 |
| **33** | A14 | 240r pale vio ('70) | 1,000. | 475.00 |
| | | *Nos. 25-33 (9)* | 2,890. | 1,141. |

Nos. 25-33 frequently were separated with scissors. Slightly blunted perfs on one or two sides are to be expected for stamps of this issue.

Two types each of 5r and 100r differ in the position of the "5" at upper right and the "100" at lower right in relation to the end of the label.

*Nos. 25-33 were reprinted in 1885 and 1905. Some of the 1885 reprints were perforated 12½ as well as 13½. Value of the lowest-cost reprints, $10 each.*

*See note after No. 4.*

**1870-84** ***Perf. 12½, 13½***

| | | | | |
|---|---|---|---|---|
| **34** | A15 | 5r black | 55.00 | 5.25 |
| *a.* | | Imperf. | 500.00 | |
| *f.* | | Double impression | 275.00 | 67.50 |
| **35** | A15 | 10r yellow ('71) | 77.50 | 27.50 |
| *a.* | | Imperf. | 500.00 | |
| **36** | A15 | 10r bl grn ('79) | 385.00 | 175.00 |
| **37b** | A15 | 10r yellow grn ('80) | 110.00 | 24.00 |
| *d.* | | Double impression | 250.00 | 130.00 |
| **38** | A15 | 15r lilac brn ('75) | 110.00 | 29.00 |
| *d.* | | Double impression | 500.00 | 250.00 |
| **39** | A15 | 20r bister | 72.50 | 25.00 |
| *a.* | | Imperf. | 500.00 | |
| **40** | A15 | 20r rose ('84) | 325.00 | 55.00 |
| **41** | A15 | 25r rose | 30.00 | 3.75 |
| *a.* | | Imperf. | 500.00 | |
| **42** | A15 | 50r pale green | 140.00 | 37.50 |
| **43** | A15 | 50r blue ('79) | 350.00 | 50.00 |
| **44e** | A15 | 80r orange | 125.00 | 19.00 |
| **45e** | A15 | 100r pale lil ('71) | 65.00 | 12.00 |
| **46** | A15 | 120r bl, perf. 12½ ('71) | 300.00 | 62.50 |
| **47** | A15 | 150r pale bl ('76) | 375.00 | 110.00 |
| **48b** | A15 | 150r yellow ('80) | 125.00 | 13.50 |
| **49** | A15 | 240r pale vio ('73) | 1,700. | 1,050. |
| **50a** | A15 | 300r dull vio ('76) | 110.00 | 27.50 |
| **51a** | A15 | 1000r black ('84) | 275.00 | 77.50 |

Nos. 34-51 were printed on three types of paper, plain, ribbed and enamel surfaced, and with perfs gauging 11, 12½, 13½, or 14¼. Values are for the least expensive varieties. For detailed listings, see the *Scott Classic Specialized Catalogue.*

Two types each of 15r, 20r and 80r differ in the distance between the figures of value.

Imperfs probably are proofs.

For overprints and surcharges see Nos. 86-87, 94-96.

*All values of the issues of 1870-84 were reprinted in 1885 and 1905. Value of the low cst-cost reprints, $10 each.*

*See note after No. 4.*

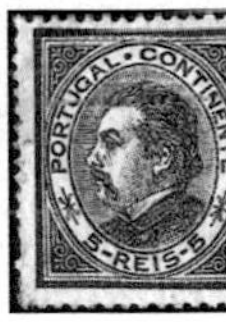
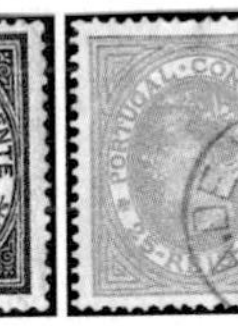

King Luiz
A16 A17

372 PORTUGAL

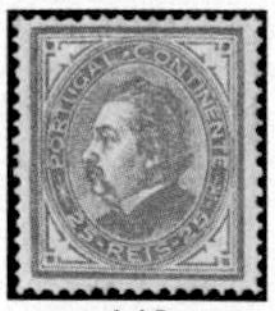
A18

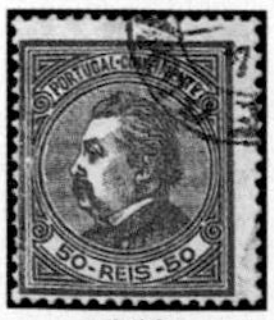
A19

**1880-81** **Typo.** ***Perf. 12½, 13½***

| | | | | |
|---|---|---|---|---|
| **52** | A16 | 5r black | 27.50 | 4.00 |
| **53** | A17 | 25r bluish gray | 300.00 | 29.00 |
| **54** | A18 | 25r gray | 30.00 | 3.50 |
| **55** | A18 | 25r brown vio ('81) | 30.00 | 3.50 |
| **56** | A19 | 50r blue ('81) | 300.00 | 15.00 |
| | | *Nos. 52-56 (5)* | 687.50 | 55.00 |

*All values were reprinted in 1885 and 1905. Value of the lowest-cost reprints, $5 each.*
*See note after No. 4.*

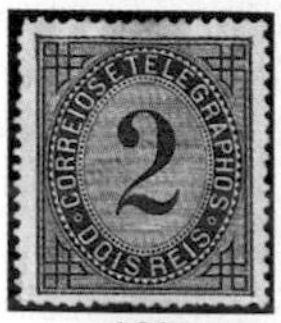
A20

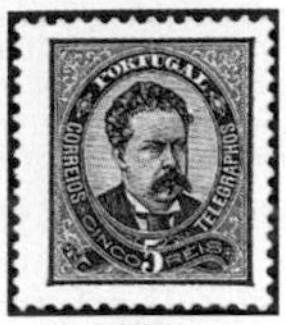
A21

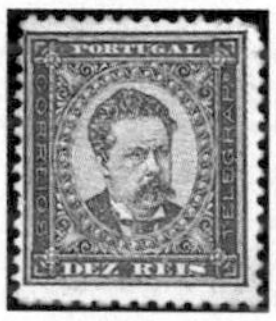

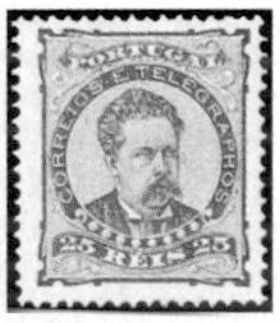
King Luiz
A22 A23

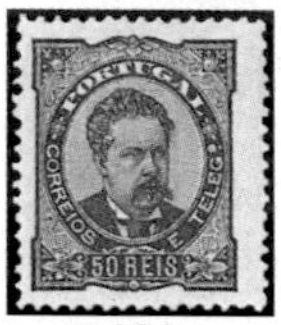
A24

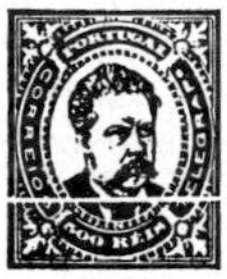
A24a

**1882-87** ***Perf. 11½, 12½, 13½***

| | | | | |
|---|---|---|---|---|
| **57** | A20 | 2r black ('84) | 24.00 | 17.50 |
| **58** | A21 | 5r black ('83) | 32.50 | 3.50 |
| **59** | A22 | 10r green ('84) | 35.00 | 4.00 |
| **60c** | A23 | 25r brown | 29.00 | 2.40 |
| **61** | A24 | 50r blue | 45.00 | 3.00 |
| **62** | A24a | 500r black ('84) | 500.00 | 300.00 |
| **63** | A24a | 500r violet ('87) | 275.00 | 52.50 |
| | | *Nos. 57-63 (7)* | 940.50 | 382.90 |

Nos. 57-63 were printed on both plain and enamel surfaced papers, with one or more perf varieties for each value. Values are for the least expensive varieties. For a detailed listing, see the *Scott Classic Specialized Catalogue.*
For overprints see Nos. 79-82, 85, 88-89, 93.
*The stamps of the 1882-87 issues were reprinted in 1885, 1893 and 1905. Value of the lowest-cost reprints, $5 each.*
*See note after No. 4.*

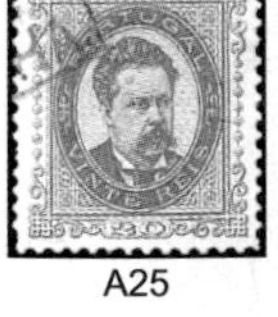
A25

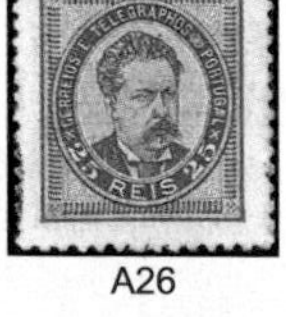
A26

**1887** ***Perf. 11½***

| | | | | |
|---|---|---|---|---|
| **64** | A25 | 20r rose | 42.50 | 17.00 |
| **65** | A26 | 25r violet | 27.50 | 3.00 |
| **66** | A26 | 25r lilac rose | 27.50 | 3.00 |
| | | *Nos. 64-66 (3)* | 97.50 | 23.00 |

For overprints see Nos. 83-84, 90-92.
*Nos. 64-66 were reprinted in 1905. Value $5 each. See note after No. 4.*

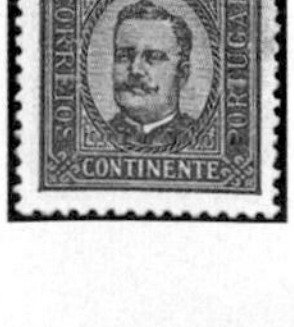
King Carlos — A27

**1892-93** ***Perf. 11½, 12½, 13½***

| | | | | |
|---|---|---|---|---|
| **67** | A27 | 5r orange | 12.00 | 2.00 |
| **68** | A27 | 10r redsh violet | 30.00 | 5.25 |
| **69b** | A27 | 15r chocolate | 27.50 | 6.00 |
| **70** | A27 | 20r lavender | 32.50 | 8.75 |
| **71a** | A27 | 25r dk green | 27.50 | 2.00 |
| **72** | A27 | 50r blue | 35.00 | 9.25 |
| **73** | A27 | 75r carmine ('93) | 67.50 | 8.00 |
| **74a** | A27 | 80r yellow grn | 85.00 | 42.50 |
| **75** | A27 | 100r brn, *buff* ('93) | 65.00 | 6.25 |
| **76** | A27 | 150r car, *rose* ('93) | 160.00 | 42.50 |
| **77** | A27 | 200r dk bl, *bl* ('93) | 160.00 | 35.00 |
| **78** | A27 | 300r dk bl, *sal* ('93) | 175.00 | 57.50 |
| | | *Nos. 67-78 (12)* | 877.00 | 225.00 |

Nos. 67-78 were printed on one or both of two types of paper, and appear with one of three perfs. Values are for the least expensive varieties. For a detailed listing, see the *Scott Classic Specialized Catalogue.*
*Nos. 76-78 were reprinted in 1900 (perf. 11½). Value, each $100. All values were reprinted in 1905 (perf. 13½). Value, each $50.*
*See note after No. 4.*

Stamps and Types of Previous Issues Overprinted in Black or Red:

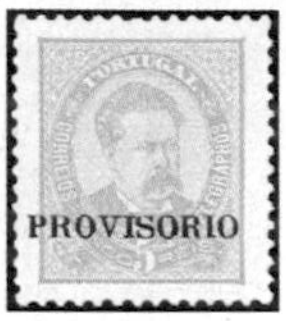
a

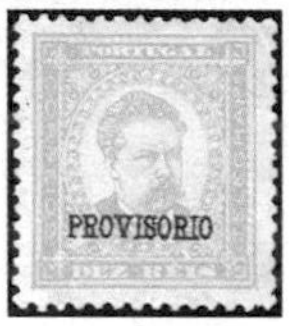
b

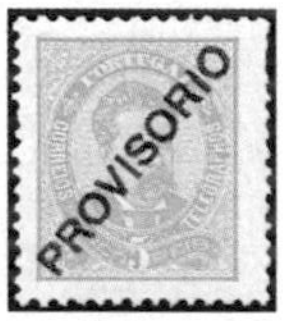
c

**1892**

| | | | | |
|---|---|---|---|---|
| **79** | A21 (a) | 5r gray blk | 16.00 | 8.75 |
| *a.* | | Double overprint | 650.00 | 450.00 |
| **80** | A22 (b) | 10r green | 16.00 | 8.75 |
| *a.* | | Inverted overprint | — | — |
| *b.* | | Double overprint | 650.00 | 450.00 |

**1892-93**

| | | | | |
|---|---|---|---|---|
| **81** | A21 (c) | 5r gray blk (R) | 13.50 | 6.75 |
| **82** | A22 (c) | 10r green (R) | 16.00 | 7.25 |
| *a.* | | Inverted overprint | 160.00 | 160.00 |
| **83** | A25 (c) | 20r rose | 42.50 | 22.50 |
| *a.* | | Inverted overprint | 225.00 | 225.00 |
| **84** | A26 (c) | 25r rose lilac | 14.50 | 5.25 |
| *a.* | | Perf. 12½ | 475.00 | 70.00 |
| **85** | A24 (c) | 50r bl (R; '93) | 77.50 | 62.50 |
| | | *Nos. 81-85 (5)* | 164.00 | 104.25 |

**1893**

| | | | | |
|---|---|---|---|---|
| **86** | A15 (c) | 15r bister brn (R) | 20.00 | 12.00 |
| **87** | A15 (c) | 80r yellow | 110.00 | 87.50 |

Nos. 86-87 are found in two types each. See note below No. 51.
*Some of Nos. 79-87 were reprinted in 1900 and all values in 1905. Value of lowest-cost reprint, $10.*
*See note after No. 4.*

Stamps and Types of Previous Issues Overprinted or Surcharged in Black or Red:

d

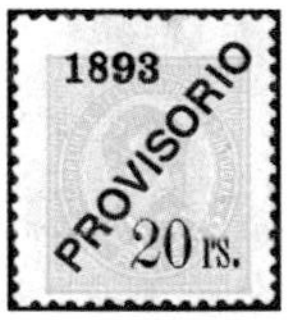
e

**1893** ***Perf. 11½, 12½***

| | | | | |
|---|---|---|---|---|
| **88** | A21 (d) | 5r gray blk (R) | 26.00 | 22.50 |
| **89** | A22 (d) | 10r green (R) | 24.00 | 20.00 |
| *a.* | | "1938" | 300.00 | 300.00 |
| *b.* | | "1863" | 300.00 | 300.00 |
| *c.* | | "1838" | 300.00 | 300.00 |
| *d.* | | Perf. 12½ | 1,650. | 1,100. |
| **90** | A25 (d) | 20r rose | 40.00 | 32.50 |
| *a.* | | Inverted overprint | 125.00 | 100.00 |
| *b.* | | "1938" | 300.00 | 300.00 |
| **91** | A26 (e) | 20r on 25r lil rose | 52.50 | 47.50 |
| **92** | A26 (d) | 25r lilac rose | 110.00 | 100.00 |
| *a.* | | Inverted overprint | 275.00 | 275.00 |
| **93** | A24 (d) | 50r blue (R) | 110.00 | 110.00 |

***Perf. 12½***

| | | | | |
|---|---|---|---|---|
| **94** | A15 (e) | 50r on 80r yel | 125.00 | 100.00 |
| **95** | A15 (e) | 75r on 80r yel | 75.00 | 72.50 |
| **96** | A15 (d) | 80r yellow | 110.00 | 95.00 |
| | | *Nos. 88-96 (9)* | 672.50 | 600.00 |

Nos. 94-96 are found in two types each. See note below No. 51.

*Some of Nos. 88-96 were reprinted in 1900 and all values in 1905. Value of lowest-cost reprint, $45 each.*
*See note after No. 4.*

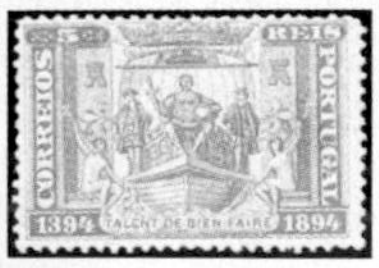
Prince Henry on his Ship — A46

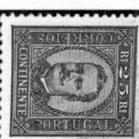

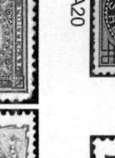

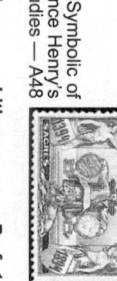

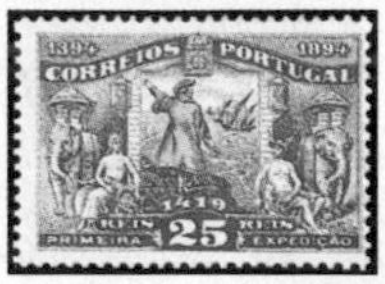
Prince Henry Directing Fleet Maneuvers A47

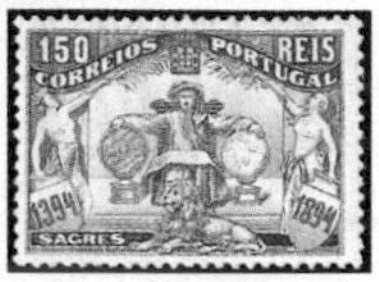
Symbolic of Prince Henry's Studies — A48

**1894** **Litho.** ***Perf. 14***

| | | | | |
|---|---|---|---|---|
| **97** | A46 | 5r orange | 3.75 | .65 |
| **98** | A46 | 10r magenta | 3.75 | .65 |
| **99** | A46 | 15r red brown | 11.00 | 3.25 |
| **100** | A46 | 20r dull violet | 11.00 | 4.00 |
| **101** | A47 | 25r gray green | 9.75 | 1.40 |
| **102** | A47 | 50r blue | 27.50 | 6.00 |
| **103** | A47 | 75r car rose | 52.50 | 11.50 |
| **104** | A47 | 80r yellow grn | 52.50 | 14.00 |
| **105** | A47 | 100r lt brn, *pale buff* | 40.00 | 10.00 |

**Engr.**

| | | | | |
|---|---|---|---|---|
| **106** | A48 | 150r lt car, *pale rose* | 125.00 | 32.50 |
| **107** | A48 | 300r dk bl, *sal buff* | 140.00 | 37.50 |
| **108** | A48 | 500r dp vio, *pale lil* | 325.00 | 77.50 |
| **109** | A48 | 1000r gray blk, *grysh* | 550.00 | 110.00 |
| | | *Nos. 97-109 (13)* | 1,351. | 308.95 |

5th centenary of the birth of Prince Henry the Navigator.

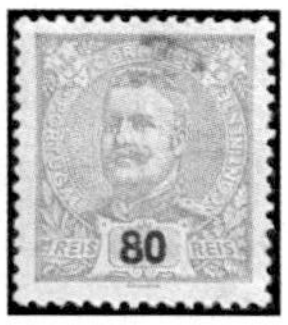
King Carlos — A49

**1895-1905** **Typo.** ***Perf. 11½***
**Value in Black or Red (#122, 500r)**

| | | | | |
|---|---|---|---|---|
| **110** | A49 | 2½r gray | .25 | .20 |
| **111** | A49 | 5r orange | .25 | .20 |
| **112** | A49 | 10r lt green | .50 | .25 |
| **113** | A49 | 15r brown | 90.00 | 3.50 |
| **114** | A49 | 15r gray grn ('99) | 47.50 | 2.40 |
| **115** | A49 | 20r gray violet | .85 | .35 |
| **116** | A49 | 25r sea green | 65.00 | .25 |
| **117** | A49 | 25r car rose ('99) | .40 | .20 |
| **118** | A49 | 50r blue | 82.50 | .40 |
| **119** | A49 | 50r ultra ('05) | .55 | .25 |
| **120** | A49 | 65r slate bl ('98) | .55 | .25 |
| **121** | A49 | 75r rose | 110.00 | 4.50 |
| **122** | A49 | 75r brn, *yel* ('05) | 1.75 | .65 |
| **123** | A49 | 80r violet | 2.10 | 1.25 |
| **124** | A49 | 100r dk bl, *bl* | 1.00 | .40 |
| **125** | A49 | 115r org brn, *pink* ('98) | 4.75 | 2.75 |
| **126** | A49 | 130r gray brn, *straw* ('98) | 3.75 | 1.40 |
| **127** | A49 | 150r lt brn, *straw* | 140.00 | 22.50 |
| **128** | A49 | 180r sl, *pnksh* ('98) | 15.00 | 9.00 |
| **129** | A49 | 200r red lil, *pnksh* | 5.00 | 1.25 |
| **130** | A49 | 300r blue, *rose* | 3.75 | 2.00 |
| **131** | A49 | 500r blk, *bl* ('96) | 9.75 | 4.50 |
| *a.* | | Perf. 12½ | 110.00 | 26.00 |
| | | *Nos. 110-131 (22)* | 585.20 | 58.45 |

Several values of the above type exist without figures of value, also with figures inverted or otherwise misplaced but they were not regularly issued.

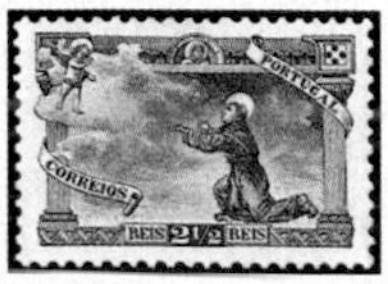
St. Anthony and his Vision — A50

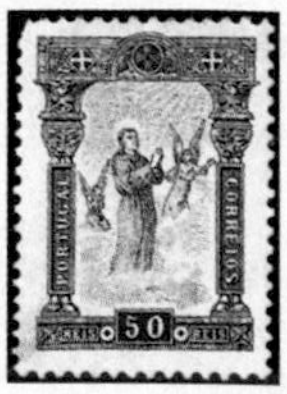
St. Anthony Ascends to Heaven — A52

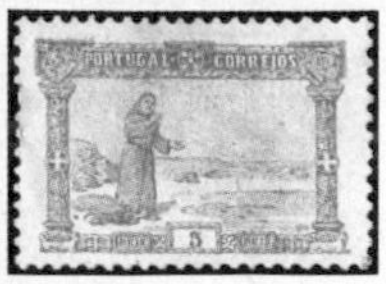
St. Anthony Preaching to Fishes — A51

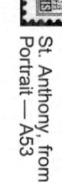

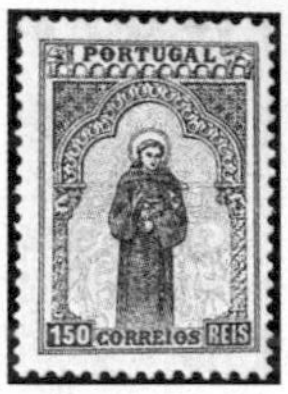
St. Anthony, from Portrait — A53

***Perf. 11½, 12½ and Compound***

**1895** **Typo.**

| | | | | |
|---|---|---|---|---|
| **132** | A50 | 2½r black | 4.00 | 1.10 |

**Litho.**

| | | | | |
|---|---|---|---|---|
| **133** | A51 | 5r brown org | 4.00 | 1.10 |
| **134** | A51 | 10r red lilac | 13.50 | 8.25 |
| **135** | A51 | 15r chocolate | 14.50 | 8.25 |
| **136** | A51 | 20r gray violet | 14.50 | 8.25 |
| **137** | A51 | 25r green & vio | 13.00 | 1.00 |
| **138** | A52 | 50r blue & brn | 32.50 | 22.50 |
| **139** | A52 | 75r rose & brn | 50.00 | 40.00 |
| **140** | A52 | 80r lt grn & brn | 62.50 | 60.00 |
| **141** | A52 | 100r choc & blk | 55.00 | 30.00 |
| **142** | A53 | 150r car & bis | 160.00 | 100.00 |
| **143** | A53 | 200r blue & bis | 150.00 | 125.00 |
| **144** | A53 | 300r slate & bis | 210.00 | 140.00 |
| **145** | A53 | 500r vio brn & grn | 375.00 | 300.00 |
| **146** | A53 | 1000r violet & grn | 625.00 | 375.00 |
| | | *Nos. 132-146 (15)* | 1,783. | 1,220. |

7th centenary of the birth of Saint Anthony of Padua. Stamps have eulogy in Latin printed on the back.

Common Design Types pictured following the introduction.

**Vasco da Gama Issue**
Common Design Types

**1898** **Engr.** ***Perf. 12½ to 16***

| | | | | |
|---|---|---|---|---|
| **147** | CD20 | 2½r blue green | 1.40 | .35 |
| **148** | CD21 | 5r red | 1.40 | .35 |
| **149** | CD22 | 10r red violet | 8.50 | 1.50 |
| **150** | CD23 | 25r yel grn | 5.00 | .50 |
| **151** | CD24 | 50r dark blue | 10.50 | 3.00 |
| **152** | CD25 | 75r violet brown | 45.00 | 10.50 |
| **153** | CD26 | 100r bis brn | 30.00 | 10.50 |
| **154** | CD27 | 150r bister | 67.50 | 27.50 |
| | | *Nos. 147-154 (8)* | 169.30 | 54.20 |

For overprints and surcharges see Nos. 185-192, 199-206.

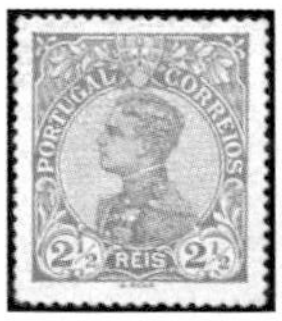

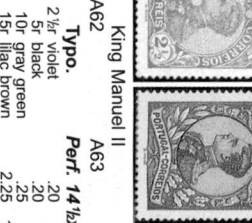

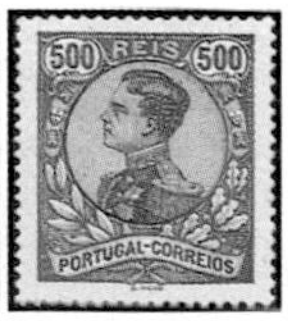
King Manuel II
A62 A63

**1910** **Typo.** ***Perf. 14½x15***

| | | | | |
|---|---|---|---|---|
| **156** | A62 | 2½r violet | .20 | .20 |
| **157** | A62 | 5r black | .20 | .20 |
| **158** | A62 | 10r gray green | .25 | .20 |
| **159** | A62 | 15r lilac brown | 2.25 | 1.40 |
| **160** | A62 | 20r carmine | .80 | .65 |
| **161** | A62 | 25r violet brn | .60 | .20 |
| **162** | A62 | 50r dark blue | 1.50 | .65 |
| **163** | A62 | 75r bister brn | 9.25 | 5.00 |
| **164** | A62 | 80r slate | 2.50 | 2.25 |
| **165** | A62 | 100r brn, *lt grn* | 10.00 | 3.00 |
| **166** | A62 | 200r dk grn, *sal* | 6.00 | 4.25 |
| **167** | A62 | 300r blk, *azure* | 6.75 | 5.00 |
| **168** | A63 | 500r ol grn & vio brn | 13.50 | 11.50 |
| **169** | A63 | 1000r dk bl & blk | 30.00 | 24.00 |
| | | *Nos. 156-169 (14)* | 83.80 | 58.50 |

For overprint see No. RA1.

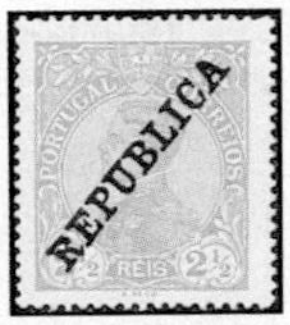

Preceding Issue Overprinted in Carmine or Green

**1910**

| | | | | |
|---|---|---|---|---|
| **170** | A62 | 2½r violet | .25 | .20 |
| **171** | A62 | 5r black | .25 | .20 |
| **172** | A62 | 10r gray green | 3.50 | 1.25 |
| **173** | A62 | 15r lilac brn | 1.25 | .85 |
| **174** | A62 | 20r carmine (G) | 4.25 | 1.50 |
| **175** | A62 | 25r violet brn | .80 | .25 |
| **176** | A62 | 50r dk blue | 6.00 | 2.00 |
| **177** | A62 | 75r bister brn | 9.00 | 3.75 |
| **178** | A62 | 80r slate | 3.25 | 2.40 |
| **179** | A62 | 100r brn, *lt grn* | 2.00 | .75 |
| **180** | A62 | 200r dk grn, *sal* | 2.50 | 1.60 |
| **181** | A62 | 300r blk, *azure* | 3.75 | 2.75 |
| **182** | A63 | 500r ol grn & vio brn | 9.50 | 8.25 |
| **183** | A63 | 1000r dk bl & blk | 24.00 | 20.00 |
| | | *Nos. 170-183 (14)* | 70.30 | 45.75 |

The numerous inverted and double overprints on this issue were unofficially and fraudulently made.

The 50r with blue overprint is a fraud.

Vasco da Gama Issue Overprinted or Surcharged:

a

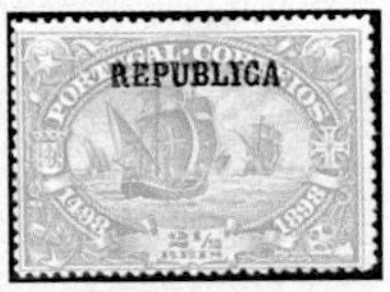

b

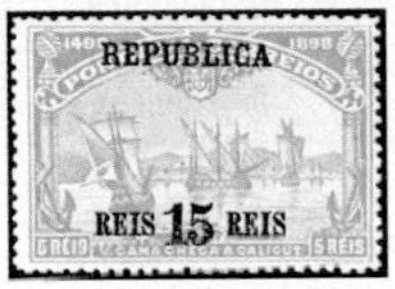

c

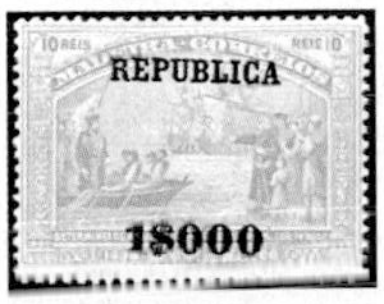

**1911** ***Perf. 12½ to 16***

| | | | | |
|---|---|---|---|---|
| **185** | CD20(a) | 2½r blue grn | .45 | .20 |
| *a.* | | Inverted overprint | 14.00 | 12.00 |
| **186** | CD21(b) | 15r on 5r red | .80 | .35 |
| *a.* | | Inverted surcharge | 10.50 | 9.00 |
| **187** | CD23(a) | 25r yel grn | .45 | .20 |
| **188** | CD24(a) | 50r dark blue | 3.25 | 1.60 |
| *a.* | | Inverted overprint | | |
| **189** | CD25(a) | 75r violet brn | 42.50 | 32.50 |
| **190** | CD27(b) | 80r on 150r bis | 6.75 | 4.75 |
| **191** | CD26(a) | 100r bister brn | 6.75 | 3.00 |
| *a.* | | Inverted overprint | 29.00 | 24.00 |
| **192** | CD22(c) | 1000r on 10r red vio | 62.50 | 37.50 |
| | | *Nos. 185-192 (8)* | 123.45 | 80.10 |

Postage Due Stamps of 1898 Overprinted or Surcharged for Regular Postage:

d

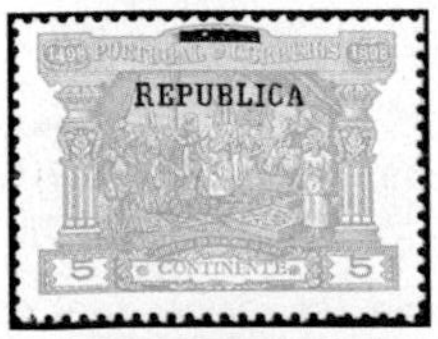

e

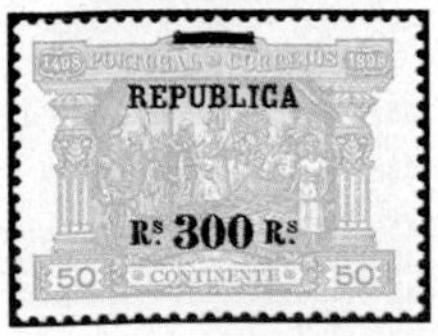

**1911** ***Perf. 12***

| | | | | |
|---|---|---|---|---|
| **193** | D1(d) | 5r black | .85 | .35 |
| *a.* | | Double ovpt., one inverted | 14.00 | 11.00 |
| **194** | D1(d) | 10r magenta | 1.50 | .65 |
| **195** | D1(d) | 20r orange | 5.75 | 3.00 |
| **196** | D1(d) | 200r brn, *buff* | 125.00 | 67.50 |
| **197** | D1(e) | 300r on 50r slate | 90.00 | 42.50 |
| **198** | D1(e) | 500r on 100r car, *pink* | 47.50 | 24.00 |
| *a.* | | Inverted surcharge | 125.00 | 87.50 |
| | | *Nos. 193-198 (6)* | 270.60 | 138.00 |

Vasco da Gama Issue of Madeira Overprinted or Surcharged Types "a," "b" and "c"

**1911** ***Perf. 12½ to 16***

| | | | | |
|---|---|---|---|---|
| **199** | CD20(a) | 2½r blue grn | 11.50 | 8.25 |
| *a.* | | Double overprint | | |
| **200** | CD21(b) | 15r on 5r red | 2.50 | 2.00 |
| *a.* | | Inverted surcharge | 12.50 | 11.00 |
| **201** | CD23(a) | 25r yel grn | 5.75 | 4.75 |
| **202** | CD24(a) | 50r dk blue | 11.00 | 8.25 |
| *a.* | | Inverted overprint | | |
| **203** | CD25(a) | 75r violet brn | 11.00 | 5.50 |
| *a.* | | Inverted overprint | 35.00 | 30.00 |
| **204** | CD27(b) | 80r on 150r bis | 12.50 | 11.00 |
| *a.* | | Inverted surcharge | 47.50 | 40.00 |
| **205** | CD26(a) | 100r bister brn | 37.50 | 8.25 |
| *a.* | | Inverted overprint | 125.00 | 100.00 |
| **206** | CD22(c) | 1000r on 10r red vio | 37.50 | 50.00 |
| | | *Nos. 199-206 (8)* | 129.25 | 98.00 |

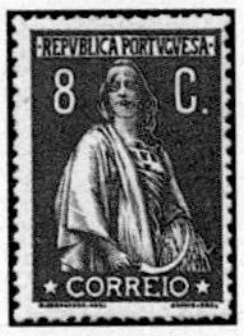

Ceres — A64

With Imprint

**1912-31** **Typo.** ***Perf. 15x14, 12x11½***

| | | | | |
|---|---|---|---|---|
| **207** | A64 | ¼c dark olive | .40 | .25 |
| **208** | A64 | ½c black | .40 | .25 |
| **209** | A64 | 1c deep green | .65 | .20 |
| **210** | A64 | 1c choc ('18) | .20 | .20 |
| **211** | A64 | 1½c chocolate | 5.50 | 2.50 |
| **212** | A64 | 1½c dp green ('18) | .20 | .20 |
| **213** | A64 | 2c carmine | 5.50 | 2.50 |
| **214** | A64 | 2c orange ('18) | .20 | .20 |
| **215** | A64 | 2c yellow ('24) | .55 | .25 |
| **216** | A64 | 2c choc ('26) | 1.40 | 1.40 |
| **217** | A64 | 2½c violet | .20 | .20 |
| **218** | A64 | 3c car rose ('17) | .20 | .20 |
| **219** | A64 | 3c ultra ('21) | .50 | .25 |
| **220** | A64 | 3½c lt grn ('18) | .20 | .20 |
| **221** | A64 | 4c lt grn ('19) | .20 | .20 |
| **222** | A64 | 4c orange ('26) | 1.40 | 1.60 |
| **223** | A64 | 5c deep blue | 5.50 | .55 |
| **224** | A64 | 5c yel brn ('18) | 1.00 | .40 |
| **225** | A64 | 5c ol brn ('23) | .25 | .25 |
| **226** | A64 | 5c blk brn ('31) | .20 | .20 |
| **227** | A64 | 6c pale rose ('20) | .20 | .20 |
| **228** | A64 | 6c brown ('24) | .55 | .25 |
| **229** | A64 | 6c red brn ('30) | .20 | .20 |
| **230** | A64 | 7½c yellow brn | 12.00 | 2.50 |
| **231** | A64 | 7½c dp bl ('18) | .20 | .20 |
| **232** | A64 | 8c slate | .20 | .20 |
| **233** | A64 | 8c bl grn ('22) | .45 | .25 |
| **234** | A64 | 8c orange ('24) | .45 | .45 |
| **235** | A64 | 10c orange brn | .45 | .25 |
| **236** | A64 | 10c red ('31) | .45 | .25 |
| **237** | A64 | 12c bl gray ('20) | 1.25 | .65 |
| **238** | A64 | 12c dp grn ('21) | .15 | .40 |
| **239** | A64 | 13½c chlky bl ('20) | 1.40 | .45 |
| **240** | A64 | 14c dk bl, *yel* ('20) | 3.25 | 1.25 |
| **241** | A64 | 14c brt vio ('21) | 1.10 | .55 |
| **242** | A64 | 15c plum | 3.25 | .85 |
| **243** | A64 | 15c black ('23) | .40 | .25 |
| **244** | A64 | 16c brt ultra ('24) | .90 | .65 |
| **245** | A64 | 20c vio brn, *grn* | 13.00 | 1.50 |
| **246** | A64 | 20c brn, *buff* ('20) | 15.00 | 3.50 |
| **247** | A64 | 20c dk brn ('21) | .50 | .25 |
| **248** | A64 | 20c dp grn ('23) | .45 | .25 |
| **249** | A64 | 20c gray ('24) | .20 | .20 |
| **250** | A64 | 24c grnsh bl ('21) | .45 | .25 |
| **251** | A64 | 25c sal pink ('23) | .45 | .25 |
| **252** | A64 | 25c lt gray ('26) | .45 | .25 |
| **253** | A64 | 25c bl grn ('30) | .90 | .25 |
| **254** | A64 | 30c brn, *pink* | 100.00 | 9.50 |
| **255** | A64 | 30c lt brn, *yel* ('17) | 8.75 | 1.60 |
| **256** | A64 | 30c gray brn ('21) | .50 | .25 |
| **257** | A64 | 30c dk brn ('24) | 6.50 | 1.60 |
| **258** | A64 | 32c dp grn ('24) | 1.10 | .40 |
| **259** | A64 | 36c red ('21) | 1.75 | .45 |
| **260** | A64 | 40c dk bl ('23) | .90 | .55 |
| **261** | A64 | 40c choc ('24) | .45 | .45 |
| **262** | A64 | 40c green ('26) | .20 | .20 |
| **263** | A64 | 48c rose ('24) | 5.50 | 3.25 |
| **264** | A64 | 50c org, *sal* | 12.00 | 1.10 |
| **265** | A64 | 50c yellow ('21) | 1.90 | .70 |
| **266** | A64 | 50c bister ('30) | 2.25 | 1.40 |
| **267** | A64 | 50c red brn ('30) | 2.25 | 1.40 |
| **268** | A64 | 60c blue ('21) | 1.40 | .60 |
| **269** | A64 | 64c pale ultra ('24) | 6.50 | 4.50 |
| **270** | A64 | 75c dull rose ('23) | 12.00 | 5.50 |
| **271** | A64 | 75c car rose ('30) | 2.25 | 1.10 |
| **272** | A64 | 80c brn rose ('21) | 1.40 | 1.10 |
| **273** | A64 | 80c violet ('24) | 1.00 | .55 |
| **274** | A64 | 80c dk grn ('30) | 2.25 | 1.10 |
| **275** | A64 | 90c chalky bl ('21) | 1.60 | .85 |
| **276** | A64 | 96c dp rose ('26) | 27.50 | 25.00 |
| **277** | A64 | 1e dp grn, *bl* | 19.00 | 1.40 |
| **278** | A64 | 1e violet ('21) | 4.50 | 1.90 |
| *a.* | | Perf. 15x14 | 140.00 | 77.50 |
| **279** | A64 | 1e dk bl ('23) | 5.00 | 2.25 |
| **280** | A64 | 1e gray vio ('24) | 1.50 | 1.10 |
| **281** | A64 | 1e brn lake ('30) | 6.50 | 1.10 |
| **282** | A64 | 1.10e yel brn ('21) | 4.50 | 1.60 |
| **283** | A64 | 1.20e yel grn ('21) | 2.50 | 1.40 |
| **284** | A64 | 1.20e buff ('24) | 50.00 | 32.50 |
| **285** | A64 | 1.20e pur brn ('31) | 4.50 | 1.10 |
| **286** | A64 | 1.25e dk bl ('31) | 4.50 | 1.10 |
| **287** | A64 | 1.50e blk vio ('23) | 13.00 | 3.25 |
| **288** | A64 | 1.50e lilac ('24) | 30.00 | 5.00 |
| **289** | A64 | 1.60e dp bl ('24) | 19.00 | 5.00 |
| **290** | A64 | 2e sl grn ('21) | 37.50 | 5.50 |
| **291** | A64 | 2e red vio ('31) | 19.00 | 6.50 |
| **292** | A64 | 2.40e ap grn ('26) | 160.00 | 110.00 |
| **293** | A64 | 3e pink ('26) | 160.00 | 100.00 |
| **294** | A64 | 3.20e gray grn ('24) | 32.50 | 12.00 |
| **295** | A64 | 4.50e org ('31) | 65.00 | 45.00 |
| **296** | A64 | 5e emer ('24) | 35.00 | 9.00 |
| **297** | A64 | 10e pink ('24) | 140.00 | 50.00 |
| **298** | A64 | 20e pale turq ('24) | 275.00 | 160.00 |
| | | *Nos. 207-298 (92)* | 1,371. | 648.35 |

See design A85. For surcharges & overprints see #453-495, RA2.

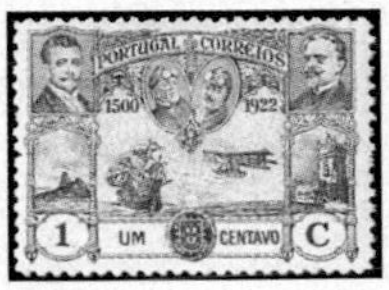

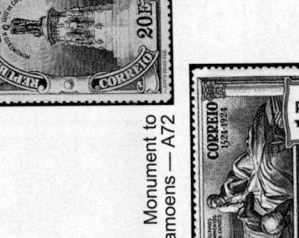

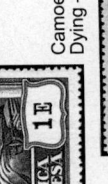

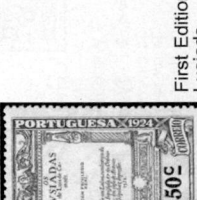

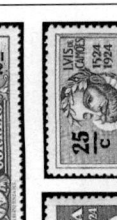

Presidents of Portugal and Brazil and Aviators Cabral and Coutinho A65

**1923** **Litho.** ***Perf. 14***

| | | | | |
|---|---|---|---|---|
| **299** | A65 | 1c brown | .20 | .65 |
| **300** | A65 | 2c orange | .20 | .65 |
| **301** | A65 | 3c ultra | .20 | .65 |
| **302** | A65 | 4c yellow grn | .20 | .65 |
| **303** | A65 | 5c bister brn | .20 | .65 |
| **304** | A65 | 10c brown org | .20 | .65 |
| **305** | A65 | 15c black | .20 | .65 |
| **306** | A65 | 20c blue grn | .20 | .65 |
| **307** | A65 | 25c rose | .20 | .65 |
| **308** | A65 | 30c olive brn | .60 | 1.90 |
| **309** | A65 | 40c chocolate | .20 | .65 |
| **310** | A65 | 50c yellow | .35 | .85 |
| **311** | A65 | 75c violet | .35 | 1.00 |
| **312** | A65 | 1e dp blue | .35 | 2.00 |
| **313** | A65 | 1.50e olive grn | .65 | 2.50 |
| **314** | A65 | 2e myrtle grn | .65 | 6.00 |
| | | *Nos. 299-314 (16)* | 4.95 | 20.75 |

Flight of Sacadura Cabral and Gago Coutinho from Portugal to Brazil.

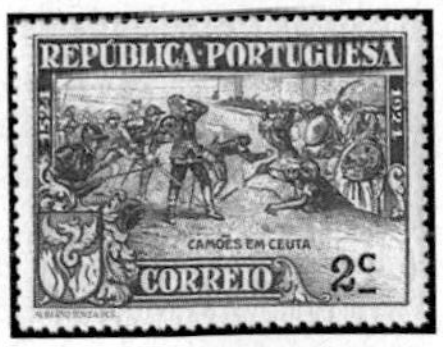

Camoens at Ceuta A66

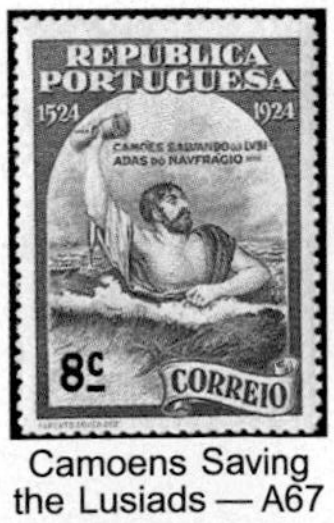

Camoens Saving the Lusiads — A67

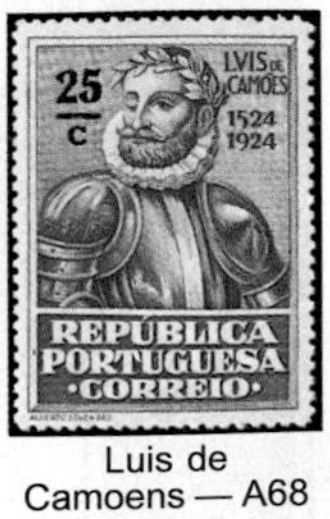

Luis de Camoens — A68

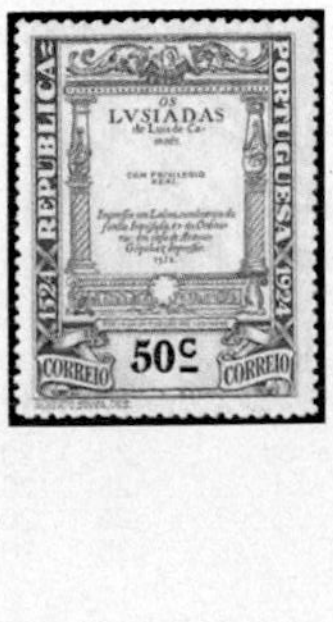

First Edition of the Lusiads — A69

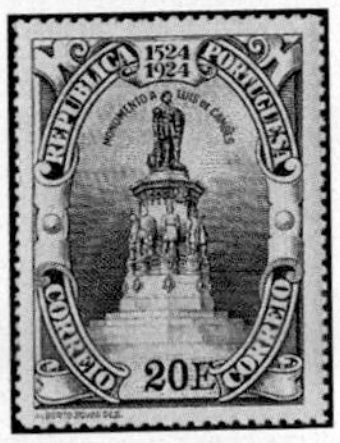

Monument to Camoens — A72

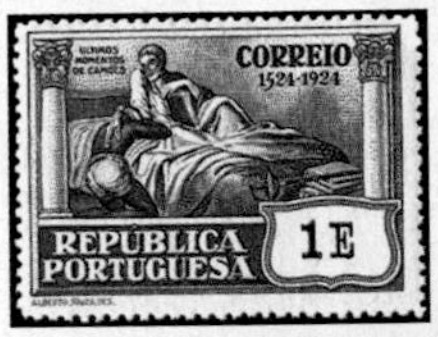

Camoens Dying — A70

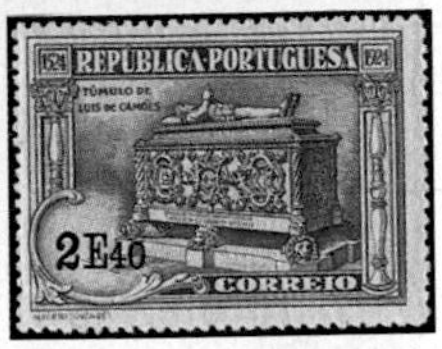

Tomb of Camoens A71

**Engr.; Values Typo. in Black**

**1924, Nov. 11** ***Perf. 14, 14½***

| | | | | |
|---|---|---|---|---|
| **315** | A66 | 2c lt blue | .20 | .20 |
| **316** | A66 | 3c orange | .20 | .20 |
| **317** | A66 | 4c dk gray | .20 | .20 |
| **318** | A66 | 5c yellow grn | .20 | .20 |
| **319** | A66 | 6c lake | .20 | .20 |
| **320** | A67 | 8c orange brn | .20 | .20 |
| **321** | A67 | 10c gray vio | .20 | .20 |
| **322** | A67 | 15c olive grn | .20 | .20 |
| **323** | A67 | 16c violet brn | .20 | .20 |
| **324** | A67 | 20c dp orange | .30 | .20 |
| **325** | A68 | 25c lilac | .30 | .20 |
| **326** | A68 | 30c dk brown | .30 | .20 |
| **327** | A68 | 32c dk green | .90 | 1.00 |
| **328** | A68 | 40c ultra | .30 | .25 |
| **329** | A68 | 48c red brown | 1.25 | 1.25 |
| **330** | A69 | 50c red orange | 1.40 | .90 |
| **331** | A69 | 64c green | 1.40 | .90 |
| **332** | A69 | 75c dk violet | 1.40 | .90 |
| **333** | A69 | 80c bister | 1.10 | .90 |
| **334** | A69 | 96c lake | 1.10 | .90 |
| **335** | A70 | 1e slate | 1.10 | .80 |
| **336** | A70 | 1.20e lt brown | 5.25 | 4.75 |
| **337** | A70 | 1.50e red | 1.25 | .90 |
| **338** | A70 | 1.60e dk blue | 1.25 | .90 |
| **339** | A70 | 2e apple grn | 5.25 | 4.75 |
| **340** | A71 | 2.40e green, *grn* | 3.75 | 2.75 |
| **341** | A71 | 3e dk bl, *bl* | 1.60 | 1.00 |
| *a.* | | Value double | 125.00 | 125.00 |
| *b.* | | Value omitted | | |
| **342** | A71 | 3.20e blk, *green* | 1.60 | 1.00 |
| **343** | A71 | 4.50e blk, *orange* | 4.25 | 2.75 |
| **344** | A71 | 10e dk brn, *pnksh* | 9.25 | 8.00 |
| **345** | A72 | 20e dk vio, *lil* | 9.25 | 7.00 |
| | | *Nos. 315-345 (31)* | 55.35 | 44.00 |

Birth of Luis de Camoens, poet, 400th anniv.

For overprints see Nos. 1S6-1S71.

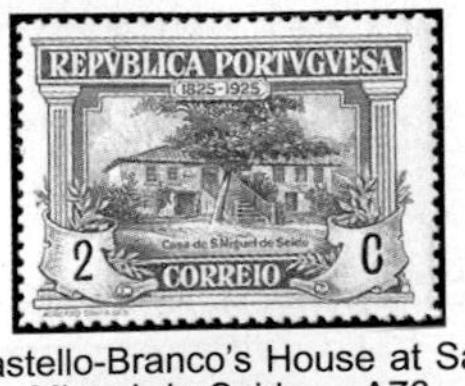

Castello-Branco's House at Sao Miguel de Seide — A73

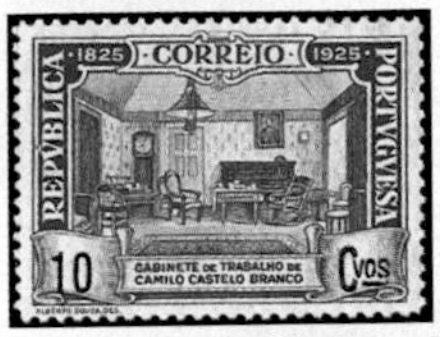

Castello-Branco's Study — A74

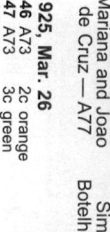

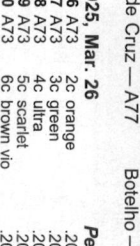

Camillo Castello-
Branco
A75

Teresa de
Albuquerque
A76

**1925, Mar. 26**

Mariana and Joao
de Cruz — A77

Simao de
Botelho — A78

Alfonso the
Conqueror, First
King of
Portugal — A79

**First Independence Issue**

**Perf. 12½**

| | | | |
|---|---|---|---|
| 346 | A73 | 2c orange | .20 |
| 347 | A73 | 3c green | .20 |
| 348 | A73 | 4c | .20 |
| 349 | A73 | 5c scarlet | .20 |
| 350 | A73 | 6c brown vio | .20 |
| a. | "6" and "C" omitted | | |
| 351 | A73 | 8c black brn | .20 |
| 352 | A73 | 10c pale blue | .20 |
| 353 | A73 | 15c olive grn | .20 |
| 354 | A73 | 16c red orange | .30 |
| 355 | A73 | 20c dk violet | .30 |
| 356 | A73 | 25c car rose | .30 |
| 357 | A73 | 30c bister brn | .30 |
| 358 | A73 | 80c brown | .30 |
| 359 | A73 | 96c car rose | .60 |
| 360 | A75 | 1e gray vio | 1.10 |
| 361 | A75 | 1.20e yellow grn | .65 |
| 362 | A75 | 1.50e red brn | .65 |
| 363 | A75 | 1.60e indigo | 4.75 |
| 364 | A75 | 2e blue green | 3.00 |
| 365 | A75 | 40c groon & blk | 3.00 |
| 366 | A76 | 48c red brn | 3.00 |
| 367 | A76 | 50c blue green | 3.00 |
| 368 | A76 | 64c orange brn | 3.00 |
| 369 | A76 | 75c gray blk | 3.00 |
| 370 | A77 | 2c dk grn, org | 6.25 |
| 371 | A77 | 2.40e red, org | 52.50 |
| 372 | A77 | 3e lake, bl | 67.50 |
| 373 | A77 | 3.20e green | 32.50 |
| 374 | A75 | 4.50e red & blk | 12.50 |
| 375 | A78 | 10e brn, yel | 13.50 |
| 376 | A78 | 20e orange | 375.00 |

Set, never hinged
Nos. 346-376 (31) 151.80

Centenary of the birth of Camillo Castello-
Branco, novelist.

---

REPUBLICA PORTUGUESA 1825-1925 1E50 CORREIO

REPUBLICA PORTUGUESA 20E PTAS. CORREIO

1825-1925 50C CORREIO

Filipa de
Vilhena Arming
her Sons
A82

King John IV
(The Duke of
Braganza)
A83

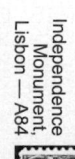

Independence
Monument,
Lisbon — A84

**1926, Aug. 13**   **Perf. 14, 14½**

**Center in Black**

| | | | |
|---|---|---|---|
| 377 | A79 | 2c orange | .20 |
| 378 | A79 | 3c ultra | .20 |
| 379 | A79 | 4c yellow grn | .20 |
| 380 | A79 | 5c black brn | .20 |
| 381 | A79 | 6c ocher | .20 |
| 382 | A80 | 15c dk green | .20 |
| 383 | A79 | 16c dp blue | .70 |
| 384 | A81 | 20c dull violet | .70 |
| 385 | A81 | 25c scarlet | .65 |
| 386 | A81 | 32c dp green | .90 |
| 387 | A81 | 40c yellow brn | .55 |
| 388 | A82 | 46c carmine | .55 |
| 389 | A82 | 50c olive bis | 3.25 |
| 390 | A83 | 75c blue green | 3.25 |
| 391 | A82 | 80c red brown | 4.50 |
| 392 | A84 | 96c black vio | 4.50 |
| 393 | A83 | 1e dull red | 6.75 |
| 394 | A81 | 1.60e myrtle grn | 7.00 |
| 395 | A83 | 3e plum | 27.50 |
| 396 | A84 | 4.50e olive grn | 35.00 |
| 397 | A81 | 10e carmine | 150.00 |

Set, never hinged
Nos. 377-397 (21) 240.00

The use of these stamps instead of the regular issue was obligatory on Aug. 13th and
14th, Nov. 30th and Dec. 1st, 1926.

---

**1926**

Surcharged with Bars and

※2 C.※

Surcharged with Bars and
these surcharges.

There are two styles of the ornaments in

**Center in Black**

| | | | |
|---|---|---|---|
| 397A | A80 | 2c on 5c blk brn | 1.10 |
| 397B | A79 | 3c on 46c car | 1.10 |
| 397C | A80 | 2c on 64c bl grn | 1.50 |
| 397D | A82 | 3c on 75c red brn | 1.50 |
| 397E | A84 | 3c on 96c dull rod | 2.00 |
| 397F | A81 | 3c on 1e blk vio | 1.60 |
| 397G | A81 | 4c on 1.60e myr | |
| 397H | A84 | 4c on 3e plum | 11.50 |
| 397J | A81 | 6c on 4.50e ol grn | 4.00 |
| 397K | A81 | 6c on 10e carmine | 47.50 |

Set, never hinged
Nos. 397A-397K (10)

---

Ceres — A85

**1926, Dec. 2**   **Typo.**   **Perf. 13½x14**

Without Imprint

| | | | |
|---|---|---|---|
| 398 | A85 | 2c chocolate | .20 |
| 399 | A85 | 3c brt blue | .20 |
| 400 | A85 | 4c orange | .20 |
| 401 | A85 | 5c dp orange | .20 |
| 402 | A85 | 6c dp brown | .20 |
| 403 | A85 | 10c orange red | .20 |
| 404 | A85 | 15c black | .20 |
| 405 | A85 | 16c ultra | .20 |
| 406 | A85 | 25c gray | .20 |

---

Gonçalo
Mendes da
Maia — A86

Dr. Joao das
Regras — A88

Guimaraes
Castle — A87

Battle of
Montijo — A89

Brites de
Almeida — A90

Joao Pinto
Ribeiro — A91

**Second Independence Issue**

See design A64.

| | | | |
|---|---|---|---|
| 407 | A85 | 32c dp green | .35 |
| 408 | A85 | 40c blue green | .55 |
| 409 | A85 | 48c rose | .90 |
| 410 | A85 | 50c ocher | 1.10 |
| 411 | A85 | 64c deep blue | 1.60 |
| 412 | A85 | 80c violet | 1.55 |
| 413 | A85 | 96c car rose | 2.10 |
| 414 | A85 | 1e red brown | 3.75 |
| 415 | A85 | 1.20e yellow brn | 1.10 |
| 416 | A85 | 1.60e dark blue | .55 |
| 417 | A85 | 2e green | 1.00 |
| 418 | A85 | 4.50e olive grn | 14.50 |
| 419 | A85 | 3.20e yellow | 5.50 |
| 420 | A85 | 5e brown olive | 1.00 |
| 421 | A85 | 10e red | 3.75 |

Set, never hinged
Nos. 398-421 (24) 19.40

---

**1927, Nov. 29**   **Engr.**

**Center in Black**   **Perf. 14**

| | | | |
|---|---|---|---|
| 422 | A86 | 2c brown | .20 |
| 423 | A87 | 3c ultra | .20 |
| 424 | A86 | 4c orange | .20 |
| 425 | A88 | 5c olive brn | .20 |
| 426 | A89 | 6c orange brn | .20 |
| 427 | A87 | 15c black brn | .45 |
| 428 | A88 | 16c deep blue | 1.00 |
| 429 | A89 | 25c green | 1.25 |
| 430 | A89 | 32c blue grn | 2.50 |
| 431 | A90 | 40c yellow grn | .65 |
| 432 | A86 | 48c brown red | .50 |
| 433 | A87 | 80c dk violet | 8.25 |
| 434 | A90 | 96c dull red | 14.50 |
| 435 | A88 | 1.60e bister | 15.00 |
| 436 | A91 | 4.50e bister | 78.60 |

Set, never hinged
Nos. 422-436 (15) 125.00

The use of these stamps instead of the regular issue was compulsory on Nov. 29-30,
Dec. 1-2, 1927. The money derived from their
sale was used for the purchase of a palace for
a war museum, the organization of an international exposition in Lisbon in 1940, and for
fêtes to be held in that year in commemoration
of the 8th cent. of the founding of Portugal and
the 3rd cent. of its restoration.

---

Type and Stamps of
1912-28 Surcharged in
Black

4 C.

| | | | |
|---|---|---|---|
| 453 | A64 | 4c orange | .40 |
| 454 | A64 | 4c on 30c dk | .35 |

**1928-29**

| | | | |
|---|---|---|---|
| 455 | A64 | 10c on ¼c dk ol | .40 |
| a. | 10c on ½c blk | 110.00 |
| 456 | A64 | 10c on ½c blk | .35 |

---

Joana de
Gouveia
A97

Matias de
Albuquerque
A96

Battle of
Rolica — A95

Battle of
Atoleiros
A96

Gualdim
Paes — A93

The Siege of
Santarem — A94

**Third Independence Issue**

**1928, Nov. 28**

**Center in Black**

| | | | |
|---|---|---|---|
| 437 | A93 | 2c lt blue | .20 |
| 438 | A94 | 3c lt green | .20 |
| 439 | A95 | 4c lake | .20 |
| 440 | A96 | 5c olive grn | .20 |
| 441 | A97 | 6c orange brn | .20 |
| 442 | A94 | 15c slate | .75 |
| 443 | A94 | 16c dk violet | .75 |
| 444 | A93 | 25c ultra | .75 |
| 445 | A95 | 32c dk green | 3.75 |
| 446 | A96 | 40c olive brn | .75 |
| 447 | A94 | 48c yellow brn | 3.75 |
| 448 | A96 | 80c it gray | 9.75 |
| 449 | A97 | 96c carmine | 7.00 |
| 450 | A94 | 1e claret | 17.50 |
| 451 | A93 | 1.60e dk gray | 14.00 |
| 452 | A93 | 4.50e yellow | 98.75 |

Set, never hinged
Nos. 437-452 (16) 150.00

Obligatory 11/27-30. See note after #436.

| | | | |
|---|---|---|---|
| 457 | A64 | 10c on 1c choc | .45 |
| a. | Perf. 15x14 | | .60 |
| 458 | A64 | 10c on 4c grn | .45 |
| 459 | A64 | 10c on 4c orange | .45 |
| 460 | A64 | 10c on 6c brn | .45 |
| a. | Perf. 15x14 | | 87.50 |
| 461 | A64 | 15c on 16c blue | 1.00 |
| 462 | A64 | 15c on 16c ultra | .80 |
| 463 | A64 | 15c on 20c grn | .80 |
| 464 | A64 | 15c on 24c gray | .45 |
| a. | Perf. 15x14 | | 32.50 |
| 465 | A64 | 15c on 24c grnsh | .35 |

**Perf. 12x11½, 15x14**

| | | | |
|---|---|---|---|
| 466 | A64 | 15c on 25c gray | 2.10 |
| 467 | A64 | 15c on 25c sal pink | .45 |
| 468 | A64 | 16c on 32c dp pink | .90 |
| 469 | A64 | 40c on 32c dp grn | .80 |
| 470 | A64 | 40c on 2c yellow | 4.50 |
| 471 | A64 | 40c on 2c choc | 3.25 |

---

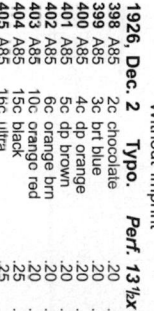

Battle of
Aljubarrota
A81

Batalha
Monastery and
King John
I — A80

**1925, Mar. 26**

Set, never hinged

Nos. 346-376 (31) 151.80

PORTUGAL

Rod and Bowl of Aesculapius A116

Queen Maria A115

**Typographed, Head Embossed**

1935, June 1 — Perf. 11½
570 A115 40c scarlet — 1.40 .25
  Never hinged — 1.90

1937, July 24 — Typo. — Perf. 11½x12
571 A116 25c blue — 10.50 .85
  Never hinged — 15.00

First Portuguese Philatelic Exhibition.

Centenary of the establishment of the School of Medicine in Lisbon and Oporto.

Grapes A118

Gil Vicente A117

1937
572 A117 40c dark brown — 19.00 .20
573 A117 1e rose red — 2.50 .20
      — 32.50

400th anniversary of the death of Gil Vicente (1465-1536). Portuguese playwright. Design shows him in cowherd role in his play, "Auto do Vaqueiro."

1938 — Perf. 11½
575 A118 15c brt purple — 1.40 .55
576 A118 25c brt blue — 3.00 1.60
577 A118 40c dp red lilac — 10.00 .35
578 A118 1.75e dp blue — 30.00 15.00
      — 44.40 17.50
  Nos. 575-578 (4) — 65.00
  Set, never hinged

International Vineyard and Wine Congress.

Emblem of Portuguese Legion — A119

1940, Jan. 27 — Unwmk. — Perf. 11½
579 A119 5c dull yellow — .35 .20
580 A119 10c violet — .35 .20
581 A119 15c brt blue — .35 .20
582 A119 25c brown — 22.50 1.10
583 A119 40c dk green — 37.50 .40
584 A119 80c yellow grn — 2.40 .55
585 A119 1e brt red — 57.50 3.50
586 A119 1.75e dark blue — 8.00 2.75
a. Souv. sheet of 8, #579-586 — 300.00 350.00
   Never hinged — 600.00
   Nos. 579-586 (8) — 128.95 8.90
   Set, never hinged — 190.00

Issued in honor of the Portuguese Legion. No. 586a sold for 5.50e, the proceeds going to various charities.

Portuguese World Exhibition A120

546 A105 40c on 75c — 8.00 5.25
547 A106 40c on 1.25e — 8.00 5.25
548 A107 40c on 4.50e — 8.00 5.25
  Nos. 543-548 (6) — 29.10 17.70
  Set, never hinged — 40.00

Nos. 534-539 Surcharged

1933 — Perf. 12x11½
549 A108 15c on 40c — .65 .35
550 A108 40c on 15c — 3.75 2.40
551 A108 40c on 25c — 1.00 .80
552 A108 40c on 75c — 8.00 4.00
553 A108 40c on 1.25e — 8.00 4.00
554 A108 40c on 4.50e — 8.00 4.00
  Nos. 549-554 (6) — 29.40 15.55
  Set, never hinged — 40.00

Head of a Colonial A110

President Carmona A109

1934, May 28 — Typo.
556 A109 40c brt violet — 18.00 .35
  Never hinged — 29.00

1934, July — Perf. 11½x12
558 A110 25c dk brown — 3.00 1.60
559 A110 40c scarlet — 19.00 .40
560 A110 1.60e dk blue — 29.00 10.00
  Nos. 558-560 (3) — 51.00 12.00
  Set, never hinged — 110.00

Colonial Exposition.

Prince Henry the Navigator A112

Coimbra Cathedral A114

Roman Temple, Evora A111

"All for the Nation" A113

1935-41 — Perf. 11½, 12x11½ (1.75e)
561 A111 4c black — .45 .20
562 A111 5c blue — .50 .20
563 A111 6c choc ('36) — .75 .35

Perf. 11½, 12x11½
564 A112 10c turq grn — .65 .20
565 A112 15c red brown — .35 .20
  a. Booklet pane of 4 — 6.00
566 A112 25c dp blue — 6.00 .45
  a. Booklet pane of 4
567 A113 40c brown — 2.00 .20
  a. Booklet pane of 4
568 A113 1e rose red — 9.25 .50
568A A114 1.75e blue — 75.00 1.25
568B A113 10e gray blk — 30.00 2.50
   (41)
569 A113 20e turq grn — 40.00 2.10
   (41) — 164.95 8.15
  Nos. 561-569 (11) — 250.00
  Set, never hinged

For overprint see No. O1.

---

472 A64 40c on 3c ultra — .45 .35
473 A64 40c on 50c yel — .40 .25
474 A64 40c on 60c dull bl — .90 .65
a.   Perf. 15x14 — 10.00 8.00
475 A64 40c on 64c pale
       ultra — .90 .80
476 A64 40c on 75c dl
       rose — .90 .55
477 A64 40c on 80c violet — 4.50 3.25
478 A64 40c on 90c chlky
       bl — 11.50 8.75
a.   Perf. 15x14
479 A64 40c on 1e gray — .85 .85
480 A64 40c on 1.10e yel
       vio — .90 .80
481 A64 80c on 6c pale
       rose — .85 .70
482 A64 80c on 6c choc — .85 .70
483 A64 80c on 48c rose — 1.25 1.10
484 A64 80c on 1.50e lil — 3.00 1.25
485 A64 96c on 1.20e yel
       grn — 3.50 2.40
486 A64 96c on 1.20e buff — 3.50 2.75
487 A64 1.60e on 2e slate
       grn — 35.00 27.50
488 A64 1.60e on 3.20e
       gray grn — 10.00 7.25
489 A64 1.60e on 20e pale
       turq — 14.00 10.00
       — 130.55 106.55
   Nos. 453-489 (37)
   Set, never hinged

Stamps of 1912-26 Overprinted in Black or Red

1929 — Perf. 12x11½
490 A64 10c orange brn — .45 .35
       — 275.00 275.00
   Never hinged
   Perf. 15x14
491 A64 40c black (R) — 275.00 425.00
492 A64 40c green — .40 .35
493 A64 40c chocolate — .55 .45
494 A64 96c rose — 5.50 4.50
495 A64 1.60e brt blue — 22.50 17.50
a.   Double overprint — 160.00 100.00
   Never hinged — 30.05 23.70
   Nos. 490-495 (6) — 45.00

Liberty A100

1929, May — Perf. 11½x12
496 A100 1.60e on 5c red brn — 11.50 7.00

---

Font where St. Anthony was Baptized A103

Lisbon Cathedral A104

St. Anthony with Infant Jesus A105

Santa Cruz Cathedral A106

St. Anthony's Tomb at Padua A107

"Portugal" Holding Volume of "Lusiade" A101

1931, June — Typo.
528 A102 15c plum — .65 .25

   Litho.
529 A103 25c gray & pale
       grn — 1.00 .25
530 A104 40c gray brn &
       buff — .65 .25
531 A105 75c dl rose &
       pale rose — 22.50 14.00
532 A106 1.25e gray & pale
       bl — 52.50 30.00
533 A107 4.50e gray vio & lll — 102.30 40.25
a.   Nos. 528-533 (b)
   Nos. 528-533 (6) — 190.00
   Set, never hinged

7th centenary of the death of St. Anthony of Padua and Lisbon.
For surcharges see Nos. 543-548.

Nuno Alvares Pereira (1360-1431), Portuguese Warrior and Statesman — A108

1931, Nov. 1 — Typo.
534 A108 15c black — 1.00 1.10
535 A108 25c gray grn &
       blk — 1.10
536 A108 40c orange — 10.50 .50
a.   Value omitted — 2.75
537 A108 75c car rose — 150.00 150.00
538 A108 1.25e dk bl & pale — 150.00 21.00
539 A108 4.50e choc & lt
       grn — 26.00 20.00
a.   Value omitted
   Nos. 534-539 (6) — 186.25 96.20
   Set, never hinged — 325.00

For surcharges see Nos. 549-554.

Nos. 528-533 Surcharged

1933 — Perf. 12
543 A104 15c on 40c — .80 .35
544 A102 40c on 15c — 2.40 1.25
545 A103 40c on 25c — 1.90 .35

---

1931-38, May — Typo. — Perf. 14
497 A101 4c bister brn — .25 .20
498 A101 5c olive gray — .25 .20
499 A101 6c lt gray — .25 .20
500 A101 6c dk violet — .25 .20
501 A101 15c gray blk — .25 .45
502 A101 15c brt blue — 1.25 .65
503 A101 25c deep green — 3.00 .35
504 A101 25c brt bl ('33) — 1.90 .40
505 A101 30c dk grn ('33) — 1.90 .90
506 A101 40c orange red — 6.25 .95
508 A101 48c fawn — 6.25 .30
509 A101 50c lt brown — .30 .20
510 A101 75c car rose — 1.25 1.10
511 A101 80c emerald — .40 .20
512 A101 95c car rose ('33) — 16.00 6.75
513 A101 1e claret — 30.00 .20
514 A101 1.20e olive grn — 2.10 .95
515 A101 1.25e dk blue — 1.90 .20
516 A101 1.60e dk blue ('33) — 32.50 4.25
517 A101 1.75e dk blue ('38) — .65 .25
518 A101 2e dull violet — .75 .25
519 A101 4.50e orange — 1.50 .25
       — 111.00 18.80
   Nos. 497-519 (23) — 175.00
   Set, never hinged

Birthplace of St. Anthony A102

King John IV — A121

Discoveries Monument, Belém — A122

King Alfonso I — A123

## 1940    Engr.    Perf. 12x11½, 11½x12

| | | | | |
|---|---|---|---|---|
| 587 | A120 | 10c brown violet | .35 | .20 |
| 588 | A121 | 15c dk grnsh bl | .25 | .20 |
| 589 | A122 | 25c dk slate grn | .20 | .20 |
| 590 | A121 | 35c yellow | 1.10 | .35 |
| 591 | A123 | 40c olive bister | 2.75 | .20 |
| 592 | A120 | 80c dk violet | 5.25 | .35 |
| 593 | A121 | 1e dark red | 12.00 | 1.60 |
| 594 | A123 | 1.75e ultra | 7.00 | 2.75 |
| a. | | Souv. sheet of 6, #587-594 | | |

Never hinged ..... 140.00
Souv. sheet of 6, #587-594 ..... 110.00
Never hinged ..... 275.00
Nos. 587-594 (8) ..... 30.00
Set, never hinged ..... 47.50 ..... 5.85

Portuguese Intl. Exhibition, Lisbon (10c, 15c, 35c); restoration of the monarchy, 300th anniv (80c); Portuguese independence, 800th anniv (40c, 1.75e).
No. 594a sold for 10e.

Fisherwoman of Nazare A126

Native of Coimbra A127

Sir Rowland Hill — A124

## 1940, Aug. 12    Typo.    Perf. 11½x12

| | | | | |
|---|---|---|---|---|
| 595 | A124 | 15c dk violet brn | .25 | .20 |
| 596 | A124 | 25c dp org brn | .30 | .20 |
| 597 | A124 | 35c green | .30 | .20 |
| 598 | A124 | 40c brown violet | .50 | .20 |
| 599 | A124 | 50c turq green | 18.00 | 4.25 |
| 600 | A124 | 80c lt blue | 2.10 | 1.10 |
| 601 | A124 | 1e crimson | 3.50 | .20 |
| 602 | A124 | 1.75e dk blue | 6.75 | 3.50 |
| a. | | Souv. sheet of 8, #595-602 | | |

Souv. sheet of 8, #595-602 ..... 75.00
Never hinged (41) ..... 125.00
Nos. 595-602 (8) ..... 49.20 ..... 13.15
Set, never hinged ..... 75.00

Postage stamp centenary.
No. 602a sold for 10e.

---

Rancher of Ribatejo A134

Native of Madeira A132

Native of Olhao — A130

Native of Saloio — A128

Fisherwoman of Lisbon — A129

Native of Viana do Castelo A133

Native of Aveiro — A131

Peasant of Alentejo A135

## 1941, Apr. 4    Typo.    Perf. 11½

| | | | | |
|---|---|---|---|---|
| 605 | A126 | 4c sage green | .20 | .20 |
| 606 | A127 | 5c orange brn | .20 | .20 |
| 607 | A126 | 10c red violet | 3.50 | 1.25 |
| 608 | A129 | 15c lt yel grn | .20 | .20 |
| 609 | A126 | 20c rose violet | 2.50 | .70 |
| 610 | A136 | 30c brown grn | .20 | .20 |
| 611 | A131 | 40c yellow grn | 3.75 | .20 |
| 612 | A132 | 80c lt blue | 10.00 | 1.60 |
| 613 | A133 | 1e rose red | 42.50 | 2.25 |
| 614 | A134 | 1.75e dull blue | 125.00 | 4.75 |
| a. | A135 | 2e red orange | 125.00 | |

Sheet of 10, #605-614 ..... 210.00 ..... 125.00
Never hinged ..... 74.05 ..... 110.00
Nos. 605-614 (10) ..... 31.35
Set, never hinged

No. 614a sold for 10e.

Ancient Sailing Vessel — A136

## 1943

| | | | | |
|---|---|---|---|---|
| 615 | A136 | 5c black | .20 | .20 |
| 616 | A136 | 10c fawn | .20 | .20 |
| 617 | A136 | 15c lilac gray | .20 | .20 |
| 618 | A136 | 25c dull violet | .20 | .20 |
| 619 | A136 | 30c brown violet | .20 | .20 |
| 620 | A136 | 40c rose red | .20 | .20 |
| 621 | A136 | 50c plum | .20 | .20 |
| 622 | A136 | 80c lt blue | .20 | .20 |
| 623 | A136 | 1e deep rose | 7.25 | .20 |
| 624 | A136 | 1.75e indigo | 22.50 | .20 |
| 625 | A136 | 2e dull claret | 1.60 | .20 |
| 626 | A136 | 2.50e grnsh blue | 11.00 | .20 |
| 627 | A136 | 3e dp orange | 3.00 | 1.40 |
| 628 | A136 | 3.50e crim rose | 2.75 | .20 |
| 629 | A136 | 10e blue gray | .50 | .20 |
| 630 | A136 | 15e olive green | 87.50 | .60 |
| 631 | A136 | 50e salmon | 415.90 | 1.00 |

Nos. 615-631 (17) ..... 250.00
Set, never hinged ..... 850.00 ..... 5.80

See Nos. 702-710.

---

Portrait of Avellar Brotero — A139

Statue of Brotero — A140

## 1944, Nov. 23    Typo.    Perf. 11½x12

| | | | | |
|---|---|---|---|---|
| 638 | A139 | 10c chocolate | .25 | .20 |
| 639 | A140 | 50c dull green | 1.40 | .20 |
| 640 | A140 | 1e carmine | 7.50 | 1.60 |
| 641 | A139 | 1.75e dark blue | 6.75 | 2.75 |
| a. | | Sheet of 4, #638-641 | 37.50 | 40.00 |

Nos. 638-641 (4) ..... 15.90 ..... 4.75
Set, never hinged ..... 21.00

Avellar Brotero, botanist, 200th birth anniv.
No. 641a sold for 7.50e.

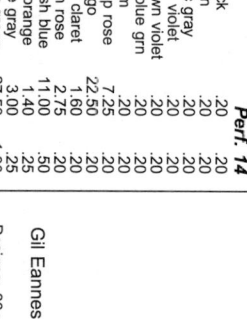

Gil Eannes — A141

## 1945, July 29    Engr.    Perf. 13½

| | | | | |
|---|---|---|---|---|
| 642 | A141 | 10c violet brn | .20 | .20 |
| 643 | A141 | 30c yellow brn | .20 | .20 |
| 644 | A141 | 35c olive green | .20 | .20 |
| 645 | A141 | 50c dk olive grn | 1.25 | .25 |
| 646 | A141 | 1e vermilion | .65 | .25 |
| 647 | A141 | 1.75e slate blue | 3.05 | .20 |
| 648 | A141 | 2e black | 2.40 | .20 |
| a. | | Sheet of 8, #642-649 | 8.75 | 5.75 |
| 649 | A141 | 3.50e carmine rose | 4.50 | 4.25 |

Sheet of 8, #642-649 ..... 22.00 ..... 10.25
Nos. 642-649 (8) ..... 32.50
Set, never hinged ..... 40.00

Designs: 30c, Joao Goncalves Zarco. 35c, Bartolomeu Dias. 1e, Vasco da Gama. 1.75e, Pedro Alvares Cabral. 2e, Fernando Magellan. 2.50e, Goncalo Velho. 3.50e, Diogo Cao.
Portuguese navigators of 15th and 16th centuries.
No. 649a sold for 15e.

---

Farmer A137

## 1943, Oct.    Perf. 11½

| | | | | |
|---|---|---|---|---|
| 632 | A137 | 10c dull blue | .80 | .30 |
| 633 | A137 | 50c red | 1.25 | .35 |

Set, never hinged ..... 2.75
Congress of Agricultural Science.

Postrider A138

## 1944, May    Unwmk.

| | | | | |
|---|---|---|---|---|
| 634 | A138 | 10c dk violet brn | .25 | .20 |
| 635 | A138 | 50c purple | .25 | .20 |
| 636 | A138 | 1e cerise | 3.50 | .65 |
| 637 | A138 | 1.75e brt blue | 3.50 | 1.90 |
| a. | | Sheet of 4, #634-637 | 32.50 | 35.00 |

Never hinged ..... 50.00
Nos. 634-637 (4) ..... 7.50 ..... .70
Set, never hinged ..... 10.00

3rd Philatelic Exhibition, Lisbon.
No. 637a sold for 7.50e.

## 1945, Nov. 12    Photo.    Perf. 11½

| | | | | |
|---|---|---|---|---|
| 650 | A149 | 10c bright violet | .25 | .20 |
| 651 | A149 | 30c copper brown | | .20 |

Unwmk.

## 1945, Dec. 27    Litho.

| | | | | |
|---|---|---|---|---|
| 652 | A149 | 35c dark green | .40 | .25 |
| 653 | A149 | 50c dark olive | .25 | .20 |
| 654 | A149 | 1e dark red | 1.40 | .75 |
| 655 | A149 | 1.75e dark red | 4.00 | 2.75 |
| 656 | A149 | 2e deep claret | 45.00 | 5.00 |
| 657 | A149 | 3.50e slate black | 110.00 | 7.50 |
| a. | | Sheet of 8, #650-657 | 110.00 | |

Never hinged ..... 210.00
Nos. 650-657 (8) ..... 96.90 ..... 150.00
Set, never hinged ..... 18.70

No. 657a sold for 15e.

Pres. Antonio Oscar de Fragoso Carmona A149

Astrolabe A150

| | | | | |
|---|---|---|---|---|
| 658 | A150 | 10c light brown | .25 | .20 |
| 659 | A150 | 50c gray green | .25 | .20 |
| 660 | A150 | 1e brown red | 3.00 | .75 |
| 661 | A150 | 1.75e dull chalky bl | 3.50 | 2.75 |
| a. | | Sheet of 4, #658-661 ('46) | 26.00 | 27.50 |

Never hinged ..... 42.50
Nos. 658-661 (4) ..... 7.00 ..... 3.90
Set, never hinged ..... 10.00

Centenary of the Portuguese Naval School.
No. 661a, issued Apr. 29, sold for 7.50e.

> **Catalogue values for unused stamps in this section, from this point to the end of the section, are for Never Hinged items.**

Almourol Castle A152

Silves Castle A151

Figure with Tablet and Arms — A153

## 1946, June 1    Engr.

| | | | | |
|---|---|---|---|---|
| 662 | A152 | 10c brown vio | .20 | .20 |
| 663 | A151 | 30c brown red | .20 | .20 |
| 664 | A151 | 35c olive grn | .20 | .20 |
| 665 | A151 | 50c gray blk | .55 | .20 |
| 666 | A152 | 1e brt carmine | 2.00 | 1.00 |
| 667 | A152 | 1.75e dull chalky bl | 62.55 | 2.40 |
| a. | | Sheet of 4 | 19.00 | 90.00 |
| 668 | A152 | 2e dk gray grn | 91.00 | 4.50 |
| 669 | A152 | 3.50e orange brn | 62.50 | 5.75 |

Hinged ..... 142.65 ..... 14.45
Nos. 662-669 (8)

Castles: 30c, Leiria. 35c, Feira. 50c, Guimaraes. 1.75e, Lisbon. 2e, Braganca. 3.50e, Ourem.
No. 667a printed on buff granite paper, size 135x102mm, sold for 12.50e.

$.04 PORTUGAL    $.05 PORTUGAL

## Madonna and Child — A154

**1946, Nov. 19** — Perf. 12x11½
| 670 A153 | 50c dark blue | .75 | .25 |
|---|---|---|---|
| a. Sheet of 4 | | 140.00 | 100.00 |
| | | 80.00 | |

Establishment of the Bank of Portugal, cent. No. 670a measures 155x143½mm and sold for 7.50e.

**1946, Dec. 8** — Unwmk. — Perf. 13½
| 671 A154 | 30c gray black | .30 | .20 |
|---|---|---|---|
| 672 A154 | 50c deep green | .30 | .20 |
| 673 A154 | 1e rose car | 3.25 | 1.10 |
| 674 A154 | 1.75e brt blue | 5.25 | 2.25 |
| a. Sheet of 4, #671-674 (47) | | 67.50 | 52.50 |
| Nos. 671-674 (4) | | 9.10 | 3.75 |

300th anniv. of the proclamation making the Virgin Mary patroness of Portugal. No. 674a sold for 7.50e.

## Shepherdess, Caramullo — A155

30c, Timbrel player, Malpique. 35c, Flute player, Monsanto. 50c, Woman of Avintes. 1e, Field laborer, Maia. 1.75e, Woman of Algarve. 2e, Bastonet player, Miranda. 3.50e, Woman of the Azores.

**1947, Mar. 1** — Photo. — Perf. 11½
| 675 A155 | 10c rose violet | .20 | .20 |
|---|---|---|---|
| 676 A155 | 30c dark red | .20 | .20 |
| 677 A155 | 35c dk olive grn | .20 | .20 |
| 678 A155 | 50c dark brown | .35 | .20 |
| 679 A155 | 1e red | .60 | .55 |
| 680 A155 | 1.75e slate blue | 19.00 | 4.00 |
| 681 A155 | 2e peacock bl | 65.00 | 4.50 |
| 682 A155 | 3.50e slate blk | 150.00 | 7.50 |
| a. Sheet of 8, #675-682 | | 210.00 | |
| Nos. 675-682 (8) | | 155.35 | 17.35 |

No. 682a sold for 15e.

## Surrender of the Moors, 1147 — A163

**1947, Oct. 13** — Engr. — Perf. 12½
| 683 A163 | 5c blue green | .20 | .20 |
|---|---|---|---|
| 684 A163 | 20c dk carmine | .20 | .20 |
| 685 A163 | 25c violet | .30 | .20 |
| 686 A163 | 1.75e dark blue | 7.25 | 5.00 |
| 687 A163 | 2.50e chocolate | 11.00 | 6.50 |
| 688 A163 | 3.50e slate black | 19.00 | 10.50 |
| Nos. 683-688 (6) | | 37.95 | 22.60 |

Conquest of Lisbon from the Moors, 800th anniv.

## St. John de Britto — A164 / A165

**1948, May 28** — Perf. 11½x12
| 689 A164 | 30c green | .20 | .20 |
|---|---|---|---|
| 690 A164 | 50c dark brown | .25 | .20 |
| 691 A164 | 1e rose carmine | 10.50 | 1.60 |
| 692 A165 | 1.75e blue | 13.00 | 2.75 |
| Nos. 689-692 (4) | | 23.95 | 4.75 |

Birth of St. John de Britto, 300th anniv.

## Architecture and Engineering A166

**1948, May 28** — Perf. 13x12½
| 693 A166 | 50c violet brn | .65 | .25 |
|---|---|---|---|

Exposition of public Works and Natl. Congress of Engineering and Architecture, 1948.

## King John I — A167

**1949, May 6** — Photo. — Perf. 11½ — Unwmk.

Designs: 30c, Philippa of Lancaster. 35c, Prince Ferdinand. 50c, Prince Henry the Navigator. 1e, Nuno Alvarez Pereira. 1.75e, John das Regras. 2e, Fernao Lopes. 3.50e, Affonso Domingues.

| 694 A167 | 10c brn vio & cr | .30 | .20 |
|---|---|---|---|
| 695 A167 | 30c dk bl grn & cr | .30 | .20 |
| 696 A167 | 35c dk ol grn & cr | .55 | .20 |
| 697 A167 | 50c dp blue & cr | 1.60 | .20 |
| 698 A167 | 1e dk red & cr | 1.60 | .20 |
| 699 A167 | 1.75e dk gray & cr | 30.00 | 15.00 |
| 700 A167 | 2e dk gray bl & cr | 16.00 | 2.00 |
| 701 A167 | 3.50e dk brn & gray | 57.50 | 17.00 |
| a. Sheet of 8, #694-701 | | 72.50 | 75.00 |
| Nos. 694-701 (8) | | 107.85 | |

No. 701a sold for 15e. Stamps from No. 701a differ from Nos. 694-701 in that they do not have "P. GUEDES" and "COURVOISIER S.A." below the design. Each stamp from the sheet of 8 has the same retail value.

## Ship Type of 1942

Typo. — Perf. 14

**1948-49**
| 702 A100 | 80c dp green | 4.75 | .45 |
|---|---|---|---|
| 703 A136 | 1e dp claret (48) | 3.25 | .25 |
| 704 A136 | 1.20e dp carmine | 4.75 | .40 |
| 705 A136 | 1.50e olive | 55.00 | 2.00 |
| 706 A136 | 1.8ue yellow org | 47.50 | 7.00 |
| 707 A136 | 2e deep blue | 7.00 | 3.25 |
| 708 A136 | 4e orange | 75.00 | 3.75 |
| 709 A136 | 6e yellow grn | 140.00 | 3.50 |
| 710 A136 | 7.50e grnsh gray | 42.50 | 14.25 |
| Nos. 702-710 (9) | | 379.75 | |
| Set, hinged | | 250.00 | |

## Angel, Coimbra Museum A168 / Symbols of the UPU A169

**1949, Dec. 20** — Engr. — Perf. 13x14
| 711 A168 | 1e red brown | 11.00 | .20 |
|---|---|---|---|
| 712 A168 | 5e olive brown | 2.75 | .25 |

16th Intl. Congress of History and Art.

**1949, Dec. 29**
| 713 A169 | 1e brown violet | .35 | .25 |
|---|---|---|---|
| 714 A169 | 2e deep blue | 1.10 | .25 |
| 715 A169 | 2.50e deep green | 5.75 | 1.25 |
| 716 A169 | 4e brown red | 15.00 | 3.50 |
| Nos. 713-716 (4) | | 22.20 | 5.20 |

75th anniv. of the UPU.

## Madonna of Fatima — A170 / St. John of God Helping Ill Man — A171

**1950, May 13** — Perf. 11½x12
| 717 A170 | 50c dark green | .65 | .25 |
|---|---|---|---|
| 718 A170 | 1e dark brown | 3.25 | .25 |
| 719 A170 | 2e blue | 7.25 | 1.60 |
| 720 A170 | 5e lilac | 100.00 | 29.00 |
| Nos. 717-720 (4) | | 111.15 | 31.05 |

Holy Year, 1950, and to honor "Our Lady of the Rosary" at Fatima.

Unwmk.
**1950, Oct. 30**
| 721 A171 | 20c gray violet | .30 | .20 |
|---|---|---|---|
| 722 A171 | 50c cerise | .50 | .20 |
| 723 A171 | 1e olive grn | 2.00 | .45 |
| 724 A171 | 1.50e deep orange | 17.00 | 3.00 |
| 725 A171 | 2e blue | 14.50 | 2.25 |
| 726 A171 | 4e chocolate | 57.50 | 8.75 |
| Nos. 721-726 (6) | | 91.80 | 14.85 |

400th anniv. of the death of St. John of God.

## Guerra Junqueiro A172

**1951, Mar. 2** — Perf. 13½
| 727 A172 | 50c dark brown | 5.00 | .35 |
|---|---|---|---|
| 728 A172 | 1e dk slate gray | 1.25 | .30 |

Birth centenary of Guerra Junqueiro, poet.

## Fisherman and Catch — A173

**1951, Mar. 9** — Litho.
| 729 A173 | 50c gray grn, buff | 4.00 | .50 |
|---|---|---|---|
| 730 A173 | 1e rose lake, buff | 1.00 | .20 |

3rd National Congress of Fisheries.

## Dove — A174 / Pope Pius XII — A175

**1951, Oct. 11**
| 731 A174 | 20c dk brn & buff | .40 | .20 |
|---|---|---|---|
| 732 A174 | 50c dk grn & cr | 1.00 | 1.75 |
| 733 A175 | 1e dp cl & pink | 11.00 | .25 |
| 734 A175 | 2.30e dk bl grn & bl | 15.00 | 2.10 |
| Nos. 731-734 (4) | | 37.40 | 4.30 |

End of the Holy Year.

## 15th Century Colonists, Terceira A176

**1951, Oct. 24** — Perf. 13x13½
| 735 A176 | 50c dk bl, salmon | 2.10 | .45 |
|---|---|---|---|
| 736 A176 | 1e dk brn, cream | 1.25 | .35 |

500th anniversary (in 1950) of the colonizing of the island of Terceira.

## Student, Soldiers and Workers A177

**1951, Nov. 22** — Perf. 13½x13
| 737 A177 | 1e violet brown | 9.50 | .20 |
|---|---|---|---|
| 738 A177 | 2.30e dark blue | 5.50 | 1.40 |

25th anniversary of the national revolution.

## 16th Century Coach A178

Designs: Various coaches.

**1952, Jan. 8** — Perf. 13x13½ — Engr. — Unwmk.
| 739 A178 | 10c purple | .20 | .20 |
|---|---|---|---|
| 740 A178 | 20c olive gray | .20 | .20 |
| 741 A178 | 50c steel blue | .80 | .20 |
| 742 A178 | 90c green | 1.50 | |
| 743 A178 | 1e red orange | 3.00 | .20 |
| 744 A178 | 1.40e rose pink | 1.10 | .20 |
| 745 A178 | 1.50e rose brown | 6.50 | 2.25 |
| 746 A178 | 2.30e deep ultra | 6.50 | 2.25 |
| | | 4.00 | 2.00 |
| Nos. 739-746 (8) | | 22.30 | 11.06 |

National Museum of Coaches.

## Symbolical of NATO — A179

**1952, Apr. 4** — Perf. 12½ — Litho.
| 747 A179 | 1e green & blk | 13.00 | .20 |
|---|---|---|---|
| 748 A179 | 3.50e gray & vio bl | 325.00 | 21.00 |
| Set, hinged | | 200.00 | |

North Atlantic Treaty signing, 3rd anniv.

## Hockey Players on Roller Skates A180

**1952, June 28** — Perf. 13x13½
| 749 A180 | 1e dk blue & gray | 4.25 | .20 |
|---|---|---|---|
| 750 A180 | 3.50e dk red brown | 5.75 | 2.25 |

Issued to publicize the 8th World Championship Hockey-on-Skates matches.

Francisco Gomes Teixeira — A181

St. Francis and Two Boys — A182

**1952, Nov. 25** *Perf. 14x14½*
751 A181 1e cerise .65 .20
752 A181 2.30e deep blue 6.00 4.25

Centenary of the birth of Francisco Gomes Teixeira (1851-1932), mathematician.

**1952, Dec. 23** *Perf. 13½*
753 A182 1e dark green .55 .20
754 A182 2e dp claret 1.90 .35
755 A182 3.50e chalky blue 24.00 11.50
756 A182 5e dark purple 45.00 4.00
*Nos. 753-756 (4)* 71.45 16.05

400th anniv. of the death of St. Francis Xavier.

Marshal Carmona Bridge A183

Designs: 1.40e, "28th of May" Stadium. 2e, University City, Coimbra. 3.50e, Salazar Dam.

**1952, Dec. 10 Unwmk.** *Perf. 12½*
**Buff Paper**
757 A183 1e red brown .70 .25
758 A183 1.40e dull purple 13.00 5.00
759 A183 2e dark green 7.00 2.50
760 A183 3.50e dark blue 13.50 4.00
*Nos. 757-760 (4)* 34.20 11.75

Centenary of the foundation of the Ministry of Public Works.

Equestrian Seal of King Diniz — A184

**1953-56** **Litho.**
761 A184 5c green, *citron* .20 .20
762 A184 10c ind, *salmon* .20 .20
763 A184 20c org red, *citron* .20 .20
763A A184 30c rose lil, *cr* ('56) .25 .20
764 A184 50c gray .20 .20
765 A184 90c dk grn, *cit* 17.50 .60
766 A184 1e vio brn, *rose* .45 .20
767 A184 1.40e rose red 18.00 1.25
768 A184 1.50e red, *cream* .65 .20
769 A184 2e gray 1.25 .20
770 A184 2.30e blue 24.00 .85
771 A184 2.50e gray blk, *sal* 1.60 .20
772 A184 5e rose vio, *cr* 1.60 .20
773 A184 10e blue, *citron* 10.00 .25
774 A184 20e bis brn, *cit* 20.00 .30
775 A184 50e rose violet 5.75 .45
*Nos. 761-775 (16)* 101.85 5.70

St. Martin of Braga A185

Guilherme Gomes Fernandes A186

*Perf. 13x13½*
**1953, Feb. 26** **Unwmk.**
776 A185 1e gray blk & gray 1.60 .20
777 A185 3.50e dk brn & yel 12.50 5.50

14th centenary of the arrival of St. Martin of Dume on the Iberian peninsula.

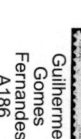

**1953, Mar. 28** *Perf. 13*
778 A186 1e red violet 1.10 .20
779 A186 2.30e deep blue 11.00 5.50

Birth of Guilherme Gomes Fernandes, General Inspector of the Firemen of Porto.

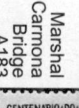

Emblems of Automobile Club — A187

**1953, Apr. 15** *Perf. 12½*
780 A187 1e dk grn & yel grn .80 .20
781 A187 3.50e dk brn & buff 13.50 5.25

Portuguese Automobile Club, 50th anniv.

Princess St. Joanna — A188

Queen Maria II — A189

*Perf. 14½x14*
**1953, May 14 Litho. Unwmk.**
782 A188 1e blk & gray grn 2.00 .20
783 A188 3.50e dk blue & blue 13.50 6.50

Birth of Princess St. Joanna, 500th anniv.

**1953, Oct. 3 Photo.** *Perf. 13½*
**Background of Lower Panel in Gold**
784 A189 50c red brown .20 .20
785 A189 1e claret brn .20 .20
786 A189 1.40e dk violet 2.10 .65
787 A189 2.30e dp blue 5.00 2.00
788 A189 3.50e violet blue 5.00 2.10
789 A189 4.50e dk blue grn 3.50 1.40
790 A189 5e dk ol grn 8.00 1.40
791 A189 20e red violet 72.50 8.25
*Nos. 784-791 (8)* 96.50 16.20

Centenary of Portugal's first postage stamp.

Allegory A190

**1954, Sept. 22** *Perf. 13*
792 A190 1e bl & dk grnsh bl .60 .20
793 A190 1.50e buff & dk brn 3.25 .65

150th anniversary of the founding of the State Secretariat for Financial Affairs.

Open Textbook A191

Cadet and College Arms — A192

**1954, Oct. 15** **Litho.**
794 A191 50c blue .40 .20
795 A191 1e red .40 .20
796 A191 2e dk green 35.00 1.40
797 A191 2.50e orange brn 29.00 1.25
*Nos. 794-797 (4)* 64.80 3.05

National literacy campaign.

**1954, Nov. 17**
798 A192 1e choc & lt grn 1.60 .20
799 A192 3.50e dk bl & gray grn 6.50 2.50

150th anniversary of the Military College.

Manuel da Nobrega and Crucifix — A193

King Alfonso I — A194

**1954, Dec. 17 Engr.** *Perf. 14x13*
800 A193 1e brown .80 .25
801 A193 2.30e deep blue 60.00 22.50
802 A193 3.50e gray green 17.00 3.25
803 A193 5e green 50.00 4.75
*Nos. 800-803 (4)* 127.80 30.75

Founding of Sao Paulo, Brazil, 400th anniv.

**1955, Mar. 17** *Perf. 13½x13*

Kings: 20c, Sancho I. 50c, Alfonso II. 90c, Sancho II. 1e, Alfonso III. 1.40e, Diniz. 1.50e, Alfonso IV. 2e, Pedro I. 2.30e, Ferdinand I.

804 A194 10c rose violet .25 .20
805 A194 20c dk olive grn .25 .20
806 A194 50c dk blue grn .40 .20
807 A194 90c green 3.25 1.40
808 A194 1e red brown 1.40 .20
809 A194 1.40e carmine rose 9.00 3.50
810 A194 1.50e olive brn 3.75 1.10
811 A194 2e deep orange 11.00 3.00
812 A194 2.30e violet blue 9.75 2.50
*Nos. 804-812 (9)* 39.05 12.30

Telegraph Pole — A195

A. J. Ferreira da Silva — A196

**1955, Sept. 16 Litho.** *Perf. 13½*
813 A195 1e ocher & hn brn .65 .20
814 A195 2.30e gray grn & Prus bl 26.00 3.75
815 A195 3.50e lemon & dp grn 25.00 3.25
*Nos. 813-815 (3)* 51.65 7.20

Centenary of the telegraph system in Portugal.

**1956, May 8 Photo. Unwmk.**
816 A196 1e blue & dk blue .45 .20
817 A196 2.30e grn & dk grn 16.00 5.00

Centenary of the birth of Prof. Antonio Joaquim Ferreira da Silva, chemist.

Steam Locomotive, 1856 — A197

Madonna, 15th Century — A198

Design: 1.50e, 2e, Electric train, 1956.

**1956, Oct. 28 Litho.** *Perf. 13*
818 A197 1e lt & dk ol grn .65 .20
819 A197 1.50e Prus bl & lt grnsh bl 4.75 .35
820 A197 2e dk org brn & bis 35.00 1.40
821 A197 2.50e choc & brn 47.50 2.25
*Nos. 818-821 (4)* 87.90 4.20

Centenary of the Portuguese railways.

**1956, Dec. 8** **Photo.**
822 A198 1e dp grn & lt ol grn .40 .20
823 A198 1.50e dk red brn & ol bis 1.00 .25

Mothers' Day, Dec. 8.

J. B. Almeida Garrett A199

**1957, Mar. 7 Engr.** *Perf. 13½x14*
824 A199 1e sepia .75 .20
825 A199 2.30e lt purple 47.50 11.00
826 A199 3.50e dull green 10.00 1.10
827 A199 5e rose carmine 80.00 10.50
*Nos. 824-827 (4)* 138.25 22.80

Issued in honor of Joao Baptista da Silva Leitao de Almeida Garrett, poet.

Cesarío Verde A200

Exhibition Emblems A201

**1957, Dec. 12 Litho.** *Perf. 13½*
828 A200 1e citron & brown .40 .20
829 A200 3.30e gray grn, yel grn & dk ol 1.90 1.10

Jose Joaquim de Cesario Verde (1855-86), poet.

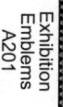

**1958, Apr. 7**
830 A201 1e multicolored .35 .20
831 A201 3.30e multicolored 1.90 1.40

Universal & Intl. Exposition at Brussels.

Queen St. Isabel — A202

Institute for Tropical Medicine A203

Design: 2e, 5e, St. Teotonio.

*Perf. 14½x14*
**1958, July 10 Photo. Unwmk.**
832 A202 1e rose brn & buff .25 .20
833 A202 2e dk green & buff .65 .35
834 A202 2.50e purple & buff 5.50 .85
835 A202 5e brown & buff 7.00 1.00
*Nos. 832-835 (4)* 13.40 2.40

**1958, Sept. 4 Litho.** *Perf. 13*
836 A203 1e dk grn & lt gray 2.50 .20
837 A203 2.50e bl & pale bl 7.75 1.50

6th Intl. Cong. for Tropical Medicine and Malaria, Lisbon, Sept. 1958, and opening of the new Tropical Medicine Institute.

## Cargo Ship and Loading Crane — A204

**1958, Nov. 27　Unwmk.　Perf. 13**

| | | | |
|---|---|---|---|
| 838 | A204 | 1e brn & dk brn | 6.50 .20 |
| 839 | A204 | 4.50e vio bl & dk bl | 5.00 2.25 |

2nd Natl. Cong. of the Merchant Marine, Porto.

## Queen Leonor A205

**1958, Dec. 17**

| | | | |
|---|---|---|---|
| 840 | A205 | 1e multi | .20 .20 |
| 841 | A205 | 1.50e bis, blk, bl & dk bis brn | .50 .70 |
| a. | | Dark bister brown omitted | |
| 842 | A205 | 2.30e multi | 3.75 1.10 |
| 843 | A205 | 4.10e multi | 3.75 1.60 |
| | | | 11.70 3.60 |

Nos. 840-843 (4)

500th anniv. of the birth of Queen Leonor.

## Arms of Aveiro — A206

**1959, Aug. 30　Litho.**

| | | | |
|---|---|---|---|
| 844 | A206 | 1e ol bis, brn, gold & sil | 1.75 .20 |
| 845 | A206 | 5e grnsh gray, gold & sil | 14.00 1.90 |

Millenium of Aveiro.

## Symbols of Hope and Peace — A207

**1960, Mar. 2　Perf. 12½**

| | | | |
|---|---|---|---|
| 846 | A207 | 1e violet & blk | .35 .20 |
| 847 | A207 | 3.50e gray & dk grn | 3.25 1.75 |

10th anniversary (in 1959) of NATO.

## Open Door to "Peace" and WRY Emblem — A208

## Glider — A209

**1960, Apr. 7　Unwmk.　Perf. 13**

| | | | |
|---|---|---|---|
| 848 | A208 | 20c multi | .20 .20 |
| 849 | A208 | 1e multi | .50 .20 |
| 850 | A208 | 1.80e yel grn, org & blk | 1.10 .95 |
| | | | 1.80 1.35 |

Nos. 848-850 (3)

World Refugee Year, 7/1/59-6/30/60.

## Father Cruz — A210

**1960, May 2**

Designs: 1.50e, Plane and parachutes. 2.50e, Model plane.

| | | | |
|---|---|---|---|
| 851 | A209 | 1e yel, gray & bl | .20 .20 |
| 852 | A209 | 1.50e multicolored | .65 .25 |
| 853 | A209 | 2.50e grn, yel & blk | 1.25 .60 |
| 854 | A209 | 2.50e grnsh bl, ocher & red | 2.50 1.10 |
| | | | 4.60 2.15 |

Nos. 851-854 (4)

Aero Club of Portugal, 50th anniv. (in 1959).

**1960, July 18　Unwmk.　Perf. 13**

| | | | |
|---|---|---|---|
| 855 | A210 | 1e deep brown | .25 .20 |
| 856 | A210 | 4.30e Prus blue & blk | 8.75 6.25 |

Father Cruz, "father of the poor."

## University of Evora Seal — A211

**1960, July 18　Litho.**

| | | | |
|---|---|---|---|
| 857 | A211 | 50c violet blue | .20 .20 |
| 858 | A211 | 1e red brn & yel | .40 .20 |
| 859 | A211 | 1.40e rose cl & rose | 2.75 1.50 |
| | | | 3.35 1.90 |

Nos. 857-859 (3)

Founding of the University of Evora, 400th anniv.

## Arms of Prince Henry — A212

## Arms of Lisbon and Symbolic Ship — A213

**1960, Aug. 4　Photo.　Perf. 12x12½**

| | | | |
|---|---|---|---|
| 860 | A212 | 1e gold & multi | .35 .20 |
| 861 | A212 | 2.50e gold & multi | 3.50 .30 |
| 862 | A212 | 3.50e gold & multi | 5.00 1.40 |
| 863 | A212 | 5e gold & multi | 8.25 .80 |
| 864 | A212 | 8e gold & multi | 2.00 .75 |
| 865 | A212 | 10e gold & multi | 14.00 1.90 |
| | | | 33.10 5.35 |

Nos. 860-865 (6)

500th anniversary of the death of Prince Henry the Navigator.

### Europa Issue, 1960
### Common Design Type

**1960, Sept. 16　Litho.　Perf. 13**

Size: 31x21mm

| | | | |
|---|---|---|---|
| 866 | CD3 | 1e ultra & gray blue | .20 .20 |
| 867 | CD3 | 3.50e brn red & rose | 3.50 1.40 |

**1960, Nov. 17　Perf. 13**

| | | | |
|---|---|---|---|
| 868 | A213 | 1e gray ol, blk & vio bl | .40 .20 |
| 869 | A213 | 3.30e bl, blk & ultra | 5.25 3.25 |

5th Natl. Philatelic Exhibition, Lisbon, part of the Prince Henry the Navigator festivities. (The ship in the design is in honor of Prince Henry).

## Flag and Laurel — A214

**1960, Dec. 20　Litho.**

| | | | |
|---|---|---|---|
| 870 | A214 | 1e multicolored | .25 .20 |

50th anniversary of the Republic.

## King Pedro V A215

**1961, Aug. 3　Engr.　Perf. 13**

| | | | |
|---|---|---|---|
| 871 | A215 | 1e gray brn & dk grn | .30 .20 |
| 872 | A215 | 6.50e dk blue & blk | 3.50 .65 |

Centenary of the founding of the Faculty of Letters, Lisbon University.

## Setubal Sea Gate and Ships A216

**1961, Aug. 24　Litho.　Perf. 12x11½**

| | | | |
|---|---|---|---|
| 873 | A216 | 1e gold & multi | .35 .20 |
| 874 | A216 | 4.30e gold & multi | 17.50 5.00 |

Centenary of the city of Setubal.

## Clasped Hands and CEPT Emblem — A217

### Europa Issue, 1961

**1961, Sept. 18　Perf. 13½x13**

| | | | |
|---|---|---|---|
| 875 | A217 | 1e blue & lt blue | .20 .20 |
| 876 | A217 | 1.50e green & brt green | 2.00 1.00 |
| 877 | A217 | 3.50e brown, pink & red | 2.40 1.25 |
| | | | 4.60 2.45 |

Nos. 875-877 (3)

## Tomar Castle and River Nabao — A218

**1962, Jan. 26　Perf. 11½x12**

| | | | |
|---|---|---|---|
| 878 | A218 | 1e gold & multi | 1.40 .85 |
| 879 | A218 | 3.50e gold & multi | |

800th anniversary of the city of Tomar.

## National Guardsman A219

Republican National Guard, 50th anniv.

**1962, Feb. 20　Unwmk.　Perf. 13½**

| | | | |
|---|---|---|---|
| 880 | A219 | 1e multi | .20 .20 |
| 881 | A219 | 2e multi | .60 .60 |
| 882 | A219 | 2.50e multi | 2.00 .50 |
| | | | 4.20 1.30 |

Nos. 880-882 (3)

## Archangel Gabriel A220

**1962, Mar. 24　Perf. 13**

| | | | |
|---|---|---|---|
| 883 | A220 | 1e ol, pink & red brn | .70 .20 |
| 884 | A220 | 3.50e ol, pink & dk grn | .50 .40 |

Issued for St. Gabriel's Day. St. Gabriel is patron of telecommunications.

## Tents and Scout Emblem A221

**1962, June 11　Unwmk.　Perf. 13**

| | | | |
|---|---|---|---|
| 885 | A221 | 20c gray, bis, yel & blk | .20 .20 |
| a. | | Double impression of gray frame lettering | |
| 886 | A221 | 50c multi | .20 .20 |
| 887 | A221 | 1e multi | .60 .20 |
| 888 | A221 | 2.50e multi | 4.00 .50 |
| 889 | A221 | 3.50e multi | .90 .50 |
| 890 | A221 | 6.50e multi | 1.25 .65 |
| | | | 7.15 2.25 |

Nos. 885-890 (6)

50th anniv. of the Portuguese Boy Scouts and the 18th Boy Scout World Conf., Sept. 19-24, 1961.

## Children Reading A222

Designs: 1e, Vaccination. 2.80e, Children playing ball. 3.50e, Guarding sleeping infant.

**1962, Sept. 10　Litho.　Perf. 13½**

| | | | |
|---|---|---|---|
| 891 | A222 | 50c bluish grn, yel & blk | .20 .20 |
| 892 | A222 | 1e pale bl, yel & blk | .90 .20 |
| 893 | A222 | 2.80e dp org yel & blk | 2.50 .90 |
| 894 | A222 | 3.50e dl rose, yel & blk | 5.00 1.40 |
| | | | 8.60 2.70 |

Nos. 891-894 (4)

10th Intl. Cong. of Pediatrics, Lisbon, Sept. 9-15.

## 19-Cell Honeycomb A223

**1962, Sept. 17**

| | | | |
|---|---|---|---|
| 895 | A223 | 1e bl, dk bl & gold | .20 .20 |
| 896 | A223 | 1.50e lt & dk grn & gold | 2.00 .55 |
| 897 | A223 | 3.50e dp rose, mar & gold | 2.50 1.10 |
| | | | 4.70 1.85 |

Nos. 895-897 (3)

Europa. The 19 cells represent the 19 original members of the Conference of European Postal and Telecommunications Administrations, C.E.P.T.

## St. Zenon, the Courier — A224

## European Soccer Cup and Emblem — A225

**1962, Dec. 1　Unwmk.　Perf. 13½**

| | | | |
|---|---|---|---|
| 898 | A224 | 1e multi | .20 .20 |
| 899 | A224 | 2e multi | 1.00 .55 |
| 900 | A224 | 2.80e multi | 1.90 1.40 |
| | | | 3.10 2.15 |

Nos. 898-900 (3)

Issued for Stamp Day.

PORTUGAL

**1963, Feb. 5**    **Perf. 13½**
901 A225   1e multi    .80   .20
902 A225   4.30e multi    1.10   .90

Victories of the Benfica Club of Lisbon in the
1961 and 1962 European Soccer
Championships.

**1963, Mar. 21**    **Litho.**
903 A226   1e multi    .20   .20
904 A226   3.30e multi    1.40   .80
905 A226   3.50e multi    1.75   .75

*Nos. 903-905 (3)*    2.85 1.75

FAO "Freedom from Hunger" campaign.

Wheat
Emblem
A226

St. Vincent de Paul
by
Monsaraz — A228

**1963, May 7**    **Perf. 12x11½**
906 A227   1e gray, lt & dk bl    .20   .20
907 A227   1.50e bis, dk brn & lil   
908 A227   5e org brn, dk brn & .20
   rose    2.10   .40
a.   5e dp rose car &    .60   .30
   blk    .90   .90

*Nos. 906-908 (3)*    2.90   .90

1st Intl. Postal Conference, Paris, 1863.

**1963, July 10**    **Photo. Perf. 13½x14**
         **Gold Inscription**
909 A228   20c lt blue & ultra    .20   .20
a.   Gold inscription omitted    60.00
910 A228   1e gray & slate    .35   .20
911 A228   2.80e green & slate    4.50   1.40
912 A228   5e dp rose car & .20
a.   Gold inscription omitted    70.00

*Nos. 909-912 (4)*    3.50 1.00
            8.55 2.80

Tercentenary of the death of St. Vincent de
Paul.

**1963, Aug. 13**    **Litho. Perf. 11½**
913 A229   1e multi    .20   .20
914 A229   1.50e multi    .55   .25
915 A229   2.50e multi    1.40   .70

*Nos. 913-915 (3)*    2.15 1.15

800th anniv. of the Military Order of Avis.

Emblem of
Order and
Knight
A229

Europa Issue, 1963

**1963, Sept. 16**    **Perf. 13½**
916 A230   1e lt bl, gray & blk    .80   .20
917 A230   1.50e grn, green & blk    .75   .20
918 A230   3.50e red, gray & blk    12.50 1.50

*Nos. 916-918 (3)*    20.00 2.60

Stylized
Bird — A230

---

Stagecoach — A227

**1963, Dec. 1**    **Litho.**
919 A231   1e dk bl & lt bl    .20   .20
920 A231   2.50e dk grn & yel grn    1.25   .50
921 A231   3.50e org brn & org    1.60   .85

*Nos. 919-921 (3)*    3.05 1.55

Transportes Aéreos Portugueses, TAP, 10th
anniv.

Plane — A231

Jet
Apothecary
Jar — A232

**1964, Apr. 9**    **Unwmk. Perf. 13½**
922 A232   50c brn ol, dk brn & .20   .20
   blk    .50
923 A232   1e rose brn, dp cl & .35   .20
   blk
924 A232   4.30e dk gray, sl & blk    4.50 2.75

*Nos. 922-924 (3)*    5.20 3.15

4th centenary of the publication (in Goa,
Apr. 10, 1563) of "Coloquios Dos Simples e
Drogas" (Herbs and Drugs in India) by Garcia
D'Orta.

Emblem of
National
Overseas
Bank — A233

**1964, May 19**    **Unwmk. Perf. 13½**
925 A233   1e bister, yel & dk    .20   .20
   bl
926 A233   2.50e ocher, yel & grn    .75   .20
927 A233   3.50e bister, yel & brn    2.50   .90

*Nos. 925-927 (3)*    3.45 1.30

Centenary of National Overseas Bank.

**1964, June 5**    **Litho.**
928 A234   1e red brn, bis & dl brn    .20   .20
929 A234   2e brn, bis & dl brn    1.75   .60
930 A234   5e dk vio bl, bis & gray    2.25   .80

*Nos. 928-930 (3)*    4.20 1.60

Centenary of the Shrine of Our Lady of Mt.
Sameiro, Braga.

Mt. Sameiro
Church — A234

**1964, Sept. 14**    **Unwmk. Perf. 13½**
     **Size: 19x32mm.**
931 A235   1e bl, lt bl & dk bl    .20   .20
932 CD7   3.50e rose brn, buff
   & dk brn    12.00   .80
933 CD7   4.30e grn, yel grn & .85
   dk grn

*Nos. 931-933 (3)*    17.00 2.50
             30.00 3.55

Europa Issue, 1964
Common Design Type

Partial Eclipse
of
Sun — A235

Sun — A235

**1964** 
934 A235   1e multicolored    .25   .20
935 A235   8e multicolored    1.40   .85

International Quiet Sun Year, 1964-65.

---

PORTUGAL

Jet — A231 Plane — A231

Eduardo
Coelho — A237

Traffic Signs
and Signals
A238

**1964, Dec. 1**    **Unwmk. Perf. 13½**
     **Black Inscriptions; Olympic Rings**
         **in Pale Yellow**
936 A236   20c tan, red & vio bl    .20   .20
937 A236   1e ultra, red & vio bl    .20   .20
938 A236   1.50e yel grn, red &    .20
   vio bl
939 A236   6.50e rose lil, red & vio    1.60   .75
   bl

*Nos. 936-939 (4)*    2.40 1.40
            4.40 2.55

18th Olympic Games, Tokyo, Oct. 10-25.

**1964, Dec. 28**    **Litho. Perf. 13½**
940 A237   1e multicolored    .50   .20
941 A237   5e multicolored    7.00   .75

Centenary of the founding of Portugal's first
newspaper, "Diario de Noticias," and to honor
the founder, Eduardo Coelho, journalist.

**1965, Feb. 15**    **Litho.**
942 A238   1e yellow, red & .20   .20
943 A238   3.30e multicolored    6.00 3.00
944 A238   3.50e red, yellow & .20

*Nos. 942-944 (3)*    3.75 1.10
            9.95 4.30

1st National Traffic Cong., Lisbon, 2/15-19.

Ferdinand I, Duke
of
Braganza — A239

**1965, Mar. 16**    **Unwmk. Perf. 13½**
945 A239   1e rose brown & blk    .20   .20
946 A239   10e Prus green & blk    2.40   .65

500th anniv. of the city of Braganza (in
1964).

Coimbra Gate,
Angel with Censer
and
Sword — A240

**1965, Apr. 27**    **Perf. 11½x12**
947 A240   1e blue & multi    .20   .20
948 A240   2.50e multi    2.10 1.10
949 A240   5e multi    2.10 1.40

*Nos. 947-949 (3)*    4.40 2.70

9th centenary (in 1964) of the capture of the
city of Coimbra from the Moors.

ITU
Emblem — A241

**1965, May 17**    **Perf. 13½**
950 A241   1e bis brn, ol grn & .20
951 A241   3.50e ol, rose cl & dp    1.60 1.00
   bl
952 A241   6.50e ol grn, dl bl & sl    1.40   .90

*Nos. 950-952 (3)*    3.20 2.10

International Telecommunication Union, cent.

---

Calouste
Gulbenkian
A242

Red
Cross — A243

**1965, July 20**    **Litho.**
953 A242   1e multicolored    .60   .20
954 A242   8e multicolored    .55   .40

Gulbenkian (1869-1955), oil industry pioneer and sponsor of the Gulbenkian
Foundation.

**1965, Aug. 17**    **Unwmk. Perf. 13½**
955 A243   1e grn, red & blk    .20   .20
956 A243   4e ol, red & blk    2.25   .90
957 A243   4.30e lt rose brn,   
         12.50   6.00
         14.95   7.10

*Nos. 955-957 (3)*

Centenary of the Portuguese Red Cross.

Europa Issue, 1965
Common Design Type

**1965, Sept. 27**    **Litho. Perf. 13**
     **Size: 31x24mm.**
958 CD8   1e saph, grnsh bl & .20
   dk bl
959 CD8   3.50e rose brn, sal & .20
   brn
960 CD8   4.30e grn, yol grn & .20
   dk grn

*Nos. 958-960 (3)*    12.50   .20
           12.50 1.10
           32.50 5.25
           57.50 6.55

Military
Plane — A244

**1965, Oct. 20**    **Perf. 13½**
961 A244   1e ol grn, red & dk grn    .20   .20
962 A244   2e sepia, red & dk grn    1.40   .55
963 A244   5e chky bl, red & dk   
   grn

*Nos. 961-963 (3)*    2.25 1.10
           3.85 1.85

Portuguese Air Force founding, 50th anniv.

Woman — A245

**1965, Dec. 1**    **Litho. Perf. 13½**
964 A245   20c ol, pale yel & blk    .20   .20
965 A245   1e grn, pale yel & .20
   blk
966 A245   2.50e dk red, buff & blk    .35   .20
967 A245   6.50e blue, gray & blk    3.25   .45

*Nos. 964-967 (4)*    1.10   .55
           4.90 1.40

Gil Vicente (1465?-1536?).

**1966, Mar. 28**    **Litho. Perf. 13½**
968 A246   1e ol bis, gold & .25   .20
   blk
969 A246   3.30e gray, gold & blk    6.25 2.75

Designs: Characters from Gil Vicente Plays.

Chrismon with
Alpha and
Omega
A246

PORTUGAL

970 A246 5e rose cl, gold & blk  4.00  .90  
                     10.50  3.85  
Nos. 968-970 (3)  
Congress of the International Committee for the Defense of Christian Civilization, Lisbon.

Symbols of Peace and Labor — A247

**1966, May 28  Litho.  Perf. 13½**  
971 A247 1e dk bl, sl bl & lt sl bl  .20  .20  
972 A247 3.50e ol, ol brn, & lt ol  2.75  1.10  
973 A247 4e dk brn, brn car & dl rose  2.75  .80  
                     5.70  2.10  
Nos. 971-973 (3)  
40th anniversary of National Revolution.

Knight Giraldo on Horseback A248

**1966, June 8**  
974 A248 1e multicolored  .30  .20  
975 A248 8e multicolored  1.10  .55  
Conquest of Evora from the Moors, 800th anniv.

Salazar Bridge — A249

Designs: 2.80e, 4.30e, View of bridge, vert.

**1966, Aug. 6  Litho.  Perf. 13½**  
976 A249 1e gold & red  .20  .20  
977 A249 2.50e gold & ultra  1.40  .50  
978 A249 2.80e silver & dp ultra  2.10  1.10  
979 A249 4.30e silver & dk grn  2.25  1.25  
                     5.95  3.05  
Nos. 976-979 (4)  
Issued to commemorate the opening of the Salazar Bridge over the Tejo River, Lisbon.

**Europa Issue, 1966**  
Common Design Type  Perf. 11½x12  
Size: 26x32mm  
**1966, Sept. 26  Litho.**  
980 CD9 1e blue & blk  .75  .20  
981 CD9 3.50e red brn & blk  24.00  1.40  
982 CD9 4.30e yel grn & blk  25.00  2.25  
                     49.75  3.85  
Nos. 980-982 (3)

Pestana A250

Bocage A251

**1966, Dec. 1  Litho.  Perf. 13½**  
**Portrait and Inscription in Dark Brown and Bister**  
983 A250 20c gray green  .20  .20  
984 A250 50c orange  .20  .20  
985 A250 1e lemon  .25  .20  
986 A250 1.50e bister brn  .35  .20

Portraits: 20c, Camara Pestana (1863-1899), bacteriologist. 50c, Egas Moniz (1874-1955), neurologist. 1e, Antonio Pereira Coutinho (1851-1939), botanist. 1.50e, José Corrêa da Serra (1750-1823), botanist. 2e, Ricardo Jorge (1858-1938), hygienist and anthropologist. 2.50e, J. Liete de Vasconcelos (1858-1941), ethnologist. 2.80e, Maximiano Lemos (1860-1923), medical historian. 4.30e, José Antonio Serrano, anatomist.

987 A250 2e brown org  1.75  .20  
988 A250 2.50e pale green  2.00  .40  
989 A250 2.80e salmon  2.10  1.25  
990 A250 4.30e Prus blue  3.75  2.10  
                     10.60  4.75  
Nos. 983-990 (8)  
Issued to honor Portuguese scientists.

**1966, Dec. 28  Litho.  Perf. 11½x12**  
991 A251 1e bis, grnsh gray & blk  .20  .20  
992 A251 2e brn org, grnsh gray & blk  .90  .30  
993 A251 6e gray, grnsh gray & blk  1.40  .60  
                     2.50  1.10  
Nos. 991-993 (3)  
200th anniversary of the birth of Manuel Maria Barbosa du Bocage (1765-1805), poet.

**Europa Issue, 1967**  
Common Design Type  Perf. 13  
Litho.  Size: 21½x31mm  
**1967, May 2**  
994 CD10 1e lt bl, Prus bl & blk  .60  .20  
995 CD10 3.50e sal, brn red & blk  15.00  .95  
996 CD10 4.30e yel grn, ol grn & blk  25.00  1.75  
                     40.60  2.90  
Nos. 994-996 (3)

Apparition of Our Lady of Fatima — A252

**1967, May 13  Perf. 11½x12  Litho.**  
997 A252 1e multicolored  .20  .20  
998 A252 2.80e multicolored  .55  .40  
999 A252 3.50e multicolored  .35  .25  
1000 A252 4e multicolored  .50  .25  
                     1.60  1.10  
Nos. 997-1000 (4)  
50th anniversary of the apparition of the Virgin Mary to 3 shepherd children at Fatima.

Statues of Roman Senators — A253

Designs: 2.80e, Church and Golden Rose. 3.50e, Statue of the Pilgrim Virgin, with lilies and doves. 4e, Doves holding crown over Chapel of the Apparition.

**1967, June 1  Perf. 13  Litho.**  
1001 A253 1e gold & rose claret  .20  .20  
1002 A253 2.50e gold & dull blue  2.10  .85  
1003 A253 4.30e gold & gray green  1.25  .85  
                     3.55  1.90  
Nos. 1001-1003 (3)  
Introduction of a new civil law code.

Shipyard, Margueira, Lisbon — A254

**1967, June 23**  
1004 A254 1e aqua & multi  .20  .20  
1005 A254 2.80e multicolored  2.25  .95  
1006 A254 3.50e multicolored  1.60  .85  
1007 A254 4.30e multicolored  2.50  .95  
                     6.55  2.95  
Nos. 1004-1007 (4)  
Issued to commemorate the inauguration of the Lisnave Shipyard at Margueira, Lisbon.

Symbols of Healing — A255

**1967, Oct. 8  Litho.  Perf. 13½**  
1008 A255 1e multicolored  .20  .20  
1009 A255 2e multicolored  1.10  .50  
1010 A255 5e multicolored  1.75  .95  
                     3.05  1.65  
Nos. 1008-1010 (3)  
Issued to publicize the 6th European Congress of Rheumatology, Lisbon, Oct. 8-13.

Flags of EFTA Nations — A256

**1967, Oct. 24  Litho.  Perf. 13½**  
1011 A256 1e bister & multi  .20  .20  
1012 A256 3.50e buff & multi  1.10  .85  
1013 A256 4.30e gray & multi  3.00  2.25  
                     4.30  3.30  
Nos. 1011-1013 (3)  
Issued to publicize the European Free Trade Association. See note after Norway No. 501.

Tables of the Law — A257

**1967, Dec. 27  Litho.  Perf. 13½**  
1014 A257 1e olive  .20  .20  
1015 A257 2e red brown  1.25  .65  
1016 A257 5e green  2.10  1.25  
                     3.55  2.10  
Nos. 1014-1016 (3)  
Centenary of abolition of death penalty.

Bento de Goes — A258

**1968, Feb. 14  Engr.  Perf. 12x11½**  
1017 A258 1e olive, indigo & dk grn  .70  .20  
1018 A258 8e org brn, dl pur & ol grn  1.40  .50  
360th anniversary (in 1967) of the death of Bento de Goes (1562-1607), Jesuit explorer of the route to China.

**Europa Issue, 1968**  
Common Design Type  Perf. 13  
**1968, Apr. 29  Litho.  Size: 31x21mm**  
1019 CD11 1e multicolored  .85  .85  
1020 CD11 3.50e multicolored  20.00  1.25  
1021 CD11 4.30e multicolored  37.50  2.75  
                     58.35  4.20  
Nos. 1019-1021 (3)

Mother's and Child's Hands — A259

**1968, May 26  Litho.  Perf. 13½**  
1022 A259 1e lt gray, blk & red  .85  .20  
1023 A259 2e salmon, blk & red  1.60  .50  
1024 A259 5e lt bl, blk & red  3.00  1.10  
                     4.80  1.80  
Nos. 1022-1024 (3)  
Mothers' Organization for Natl. Education. 30th anniv.

"Victory over Disease" and WHO Emblem A260

**1968, July 10  Litho.  Perf. 12½**  
1025 A260 1e multicolored  .20  .20  
1026 A260 3.50e multicolored  1.40  .50  
1027 A260 4.30e tan & multi  7.50  4.00  
                     9.10  4.70  
Nos. 1025-1027 (3)  
20th anniv. of WHO.

Madeira Grapes and Wine A261

Joao Fernandes Vieira — A262

Designs: 1e, Fireworks on New Year's Eve. 1.50e, Mountains and valley. 3.50e, Woman doing Madeira embroidery. 4.30e, Joao Gonçalves Zarco. 20e, Muschia aurea (flower).

**1968, Aug. 17  Perf. 12x11½, 11½x12  Litho.**  
1028 A261 50c multi  .20  .20  
1029 A261 1e multi  .20  .20  
1030 A261 1.50e multi  .35  .20  
1031 A261 2.80e multi  2.40  1.25  
1032 A262 3.50e multi  1.50  .85  
1033 A262 4.30e multi  0.25  5.00  
1034 A262 20e multi  16.90  8.65  
Nos. 1028-1034 (7)

Issued to publicize Madeira and the Lubrapex 1968 stamp exhibition. Design descriptions in Portuguese, French and English printed on back of stamps.

Pedro Alvares Cabral A263

Cabral's Fleet A264

Design: 3.50e, Cabral's coat of arms, vert.

**1969, Jan. 30  Perf. 12x12½, 12½x12  Engr.**  
1035 A263 1e vio bl, bl & gray  .20  .20  
1036 A263 3.50e deep claret  4.25  1.75  
                  Litho.  
1037 A264 6.50e green & multi  2.50  1.60  
                     6.95  3.55  
Nos. 1035-1037 (3)

5th cent. of the birth of Pedro Alvarez Cabral (1468-1520), navigator, discoverer of Brazil. Nos. 1035-1037 have separate description of the designs printed on the back in Portuguese, French and English.

## Europa Issue, 1969
### Common Design Type

**1969, Apr. 28**    **Litho.**    **Perf. 13**
Size: 31x22½mm
| | | | |
|---|---|---|---|
| 1038 | CD12 | 1e dp blue & multi | 1.00 .20 |
| 1039 | CD12 | 3.50e multicolored | 26.00 1.40 |
| 1040 | CD12 | 4.30e green & multi | 50.00 3.00 |
| | | Nos. 1038-1040 (3) | 77.00 4.60 |

King José I and Arms of National Press — A265

**1969, May 14**    **Litho.**    **Perf. 11½x12**
| | | | |
|---|---|---|---|
| 1041 | A265 | 1e multicolored | .20 .20 |
| 1042 | A265 | 2e multicolored | 1.10 .45 |
| 1043 | A265 | 8e multicolored | 2.30 1.25 |
| | | Nos. 1041-1043 (3) | |

Bicentenary of the National Press.

ILO Emblem A266

**1969, May 28**    **Perf. 13**
| | | | |
|---|---|---|---|
| 1044 | A266 | 1e bluish grn, blk & sil | .20 .20 |
| 1045 | A266 | 3.50e red, blk & sil | 1.75 .60 |
| 1046 | A266 | 4.30e brt bl, blk & sil | 2.25 1.40 |
| | | Nos. 1044-1046 (3) | 4.20 2.20 |

50th anniversary of the ILO.

Juan Cabrillo Rodriguez A267

**1969, July 16**    **Litho.**    **Perf. 11½x12**
| | | | |
|---|---|---|---|
| 1047 | A267 | 1e multi | .20 .20 |
| 1048 | A267 | 2.50e multi | 1.60 .45 |
| 1049 | A267 | 6.50e multi | 3.55 1.55 |
| | | Nos. 1047-1049 (3) | |

Bicent. of San Diego, Calif., & honoring Juan Cabrillo Rodriguez, explorer of California coast.
Backs inscribed. See note below No. 1034.

Vianna da Motta by Columbano Bordalo Pinheiro — A268

**1969, Sept. 24**    **Litho.**    **Perf. 12**
| | | | |
|---|---|---|---|
| 1050 | A268 | 1e multicolored | .90 .20 |
| 1051 | A268 | 9e gray & multi | .90 .60 |

Centenary of the birth of Vianna da Motta (1868-1948), pianist and composer.

Gago Coutinho and 1922 Seaplane A269

**1969, Oct. 22**    **Litho.**    **Perf. 11½x12**
| | | | |
|---|---|---|---|
| 1052 | A269 | 1e grnsh gray, dk & lt brn | .20 .20 |
| 1053 | A269 | 2.80e yel bis, dk & lt brn | 2.25 1.00 |
| 1054 | A269 | 3.30e gray bl, dk & lt brn | 2.10 1.00 |
| 1055 | A269 | 4.30e lt rose brn, dk & lt brn | 2.10 1.25 |
| | | Nos. 1052-1055 (4) | |

Designs: 2.80e, 4.30e, Adm. Coutinho and Coutinho sextant.
Admiral Carlos Viegas Gago Coutinho (1869-1959), explorer and aviation pioneer.

Vasco da Gama A270

**1969, Dec. 30**    **Perf. 12x11½, 11½x12**    **Litho.**
| | | | |
|---|---|---|---|
| 1056 | A270 | 1e multi | .25 .20 |
| 1057 | A270 | 2.80e multi | 3.00 1.75 |
| 1058 | A270 | 3.30e multi | 2.25 .60 |
| 1059 | A270 | 3.50e multi | 1.60 .30 |
| | | Nos. 1056-1059 (4) | 7.60 3.30 |

Designs: 2.80e, Da Gama's coat of arms. 3.50e, Map showing route to India and compass rose, horiz. 4e, Da Gama's fleet, horiz.

Vasco da Gama (1469-1525), navigator who found sea route to India.
Design descriptions in Portuguese, French and English printed on back of stamps.

## Europa Issue, 1970
### Common Design Type

**1970, May 4**    **Litho.**    **Perf. 13½**
Size: 31x22mm
| | | | |
|---|---|---|---|
| 1060 | CD13 | 1e multicolored | 1.00 .20 |
| 1061 | CD13 | 3.50e multicolored | 47.50 3.00 |
| 1062 | CD13 | 4.30e multicolored | 74.50 4.20 |
| | | Nos. 1060-1062 (3) | |

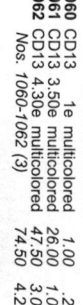

Distillation Plant — A271

**1970, June 5**    **Litho.**    **Perf. 13**
| | | | |
|---|---|---|---|
| 1063 | A271 | 1e dk bl & dl bl | .20 .20 |
| 1064 | A271 | 2.80e sl grn & pale grn | 2.50 1.40 |

Opening of the Oporto Oil Refinery.

Marshal Carmona and Oak Leaves A272

**1970, July 1**    **Litho. & Engr.**    **Perf. 12x12½**
| | | | |
|---|---|---|---|
| 1065 | A271 | 3.30e dk ol grn & ol ocher | 1.60 1.00 |
| 1066 | A271 | 6e dk brn & dl ocher | 1.40 .85 |
| | | Nos. 1063-1066 (4) | 5.70 3.45 |

| | | | |
|---|---|---|---|
| 1067 | A272 | 1e ol grn & blk | .20 .20 |
| 1068 | A272 | 2.50e red, ultra & blk | 1.90 .60 |
| 1069 | A272 | 7e slate bl & blk | 3.70 1.70 |
| | | Nos. 1067-1069 (3) | |

Designs: 2.50e, Carmona, Portuguese coat of arms and laurel. 7e, Carmona and ferns.
Centenary of the birth of Marshal Antonio Oscar de Fragoso Carmona (1869-1951), President of Portugal, 1926-1951.

Emblem of Plant Research Station A273

**1970, July 29**    **Litho.**
| | | | |
|---|---|---|---|
| 1070 | A273 | 1e multi | .20 .20 |
| 1071 | A273 | 2.50e multi | 1.90 .55 |
| 1072 | A273 | 5e multi | 3.50 1.15 |
| | | Nos. 1070-1072 (3) | |

25th anniv. of the Plant Research Station at Elvas.

Compass Rose and EXPO Emblem — A274

**1970, Sept. 16**    **Litho.**    **Perf. 13**
| | | | |
|---|---|---|---|
| 1073 | A274 | 1e gold & multi | .20 .20 |
| 1074 | A274 | 5e silver & multi | 1.50 .90 |
| 1075 | A274 | 6.50e multicolored | 3.75 2.25 |
| C11 | A274 | | 6.15 3.75 |
| | | Nos. 1073-1075,C11 (4) | |

Designs: 5e, Monogram of Christ (IHS) and EXPO emblem. 6.50e, "Portugal and Japan" emblem.
Designs as written in old manuscripts, and EXPO.
EXPO '70 International Exhibition, Osaka, Japan, Mar. 15-Sept. 13.

Castle (from Arms of Santarem) A275

**1970, Oct. 7**    **Litho.**    **Perf. 12x11½**
| | | | |
|---|---|---|---|
| 1076 | A275 | 1e multicolored | .20 .20 |
| 1077 | A275 | 1e ultra & multi | .20 .20 |
| 1078 | A275 | 2.80e red & multi | 3.00 1.25 |
| 1079 | A275 | 4e gray & multi | 1.60 .70 |
| | | Nos. 1076-1079 (4) | 5.00 2.35 |

#1077, Star & wheel, from Covilha coat of arms. 2.80e, Ram & Covilha coat of arms. 4e, Knights on horseback & Santarem coat of arms.
City of Santarem, cent. (#1076, 1079); City of Covilha, cent. (#1077-1078).

Paddlesteamer Great Eastern Laying Cable — A276

**1970, Nov. 21**    **Litho.**    **Perf. 14**
| | | | |
|---|---|---|---|
| 1080 | A276 | 1e multicolored | 1.00 .20 |
| 1081 | A276 | 2.50e multi | 1.90 .40 |
| 1082 | A276 | 2.80e multi | 3.50 2.00 |
| 1083 | A276 | 4e multi | 1.60 .90 |
| | | Nos. 1080-1083 (4) | 7.20 3.20 |

Designs: 2.80e, 4e, Cross section of cable.
Centenary of the Portugal-Great Britain submarine telegraph cable.

Grapes and Woman Filling Baskets A277

Designs: 1e, Worker carrying basket of grapes, and jug. 3.60e, Glass of wine, and barge with barrels on River Douro. 7e, Wine bottle and barrels.
Publicity for port wine export.

**1970, Dec. 20**    **Litho.**    **Perf. 12x11½**
| | | | |
|---|---|---|---|
| 1084 | A277 | 50c multi | .20 .20 |
| 1085 | A277 | 1e multi | .20 .20 |
| 1086 | A277 | 3.50e multi | 1.00 .50 |
| 1087 | A277 | 7e multi | 2.40 1.10 |
| | | Nos. 1084-1087 (4) | |

Mountain Windmill, Bussaco Hills — A278

**1971, Feb. 24**    **Litho.**    **Perf. 13**
| | | | |
|---|---|---|---|
| 1088 | A278 | 20c multicolored | .20 .20 |
| 1089 | A278 | 50c lt blue & multi | .25 .25 |
| 1090 | A278 | 1e gray & multi | .25 .20 |
| 1091 | A278 | 2e multicolored | .90 .20 |
| 1092 | A278 | 3.30e ocher & multi | 2.75 1.60 |
| 1093 | A278 | 5e olive & multi | 6.70 2.95 |
| | | Nos. 1088-1093 (6) | |

Windmills: 50c, Beira Litoral Province. 1e, Estremadura Province. 2e, St. Miguel, Azores. 3.30e, Porto Santo, Madeira. 5e, Pico, Azores.
Backs inscribed. See note below No. 1034.

Francisco Franco (1885-1955) A279

## Europa Issue, 1971
### Common Design Type

**1971, May 3**    **Photo.**    **Perf. 14**
Size: 32x22mm
| | | | |
|---|---|---|---|
| 1094 | CD14 | 1e dk bl, lt grn & blk | .20 .20 |
| 1095 | CD14 | 3.50e red brn, yel & blk | .80 .20 |
| 1096 | CD14 | 7.50e olive, yel & blk | 17.50 .65 |
| | | Nos. 1094-1096 (3) | |

Portuguese Sculptors: 1e, Antonio Teixeira Lopes (1866-1942). 1.50e, Antonio Augusto da Costa Mota (1862-1930). 2.50e, Rui Roque Gameiro (1906-1935). 3.50e, José Simoes de Almeida (nephew; 1880-1950). 4e, Francisco dos Santos (1878-1930).

**1971, July 7**    **Engr.**
| | | | |
|---|---|---|---|
| 1097 | A279 | 20c black | .20 .20 |
| 1098 | A279 | 1e claret | .60 .40 |
| 1099 | A279 | 1.50e sepia | .60 .40 |
| 1100 | A279 | 2.50e dark blue | 1.00 .30 |
| 1101 | A279 | 3.50e carmine rose | 1.40 .45 |
| 1102 | A279 | 4e gray green | 2.50 1.50 |
| | | Nos. 1097-1102 (6) | 6.00 3.05 |

Perf. 11½x12½, 13½ (2.50e, 4e)

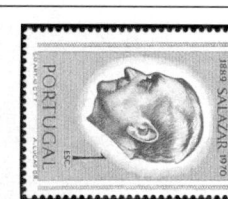

Pres. Antonio Salazar A280

**1971, July 27**    **Engr.**
| | | | |
|---|---|---|---|
| 1103 | A280 | 1e multicolored | .20 .20 |
| a. | | Perf. 12½x12 | 100.00 2.75 |
| 1104 | A280 | 5e multicolored | 1.75 .35 |
| a. | | Perf. 12½x12 | 2.75 .95 |
| 1105 | A280 | 50 multicolored | 18.00 1.75 |
| a. | | Perf. 12x12 | 4.70 1.50 |
| | | Nos. 1103-1105 (3) | |

Wolframite Crystals A281

Minerals: 2.50e, Arsenopyrite (gold), 3.50e, Beryllium, 6.50e, Chalcopyrite (copper).

| 1971, Sept. 24 | Litho. | Perf. 12 | | |
|---|---|---|---|---|
| 1106 | A281 | 1e multicolored | .20 | .20 |
| 1107 | A281 | 2.50e carmine & multi | 2.00 | .40 |
| 1108 | A281 | 3.50e green & multi | .65 | .30 |
| 1109 | A281 | 6.50e blue & multi | 1.25 | 1.35 |
| | | Nos. 1106-1109 (4) | 4.10 | 1.35 |

Spanish-Portuguese-American Economic Geology Congress.

Town Gate, Castelo Branco — A282

Weather Recording Station and Barograph Charts — A283

| 1971, Oct. 7 | | Perf. 14 | | |
|---|---|---|---|---|
| 1110 | A282 | 3e multi | .20 | .20 |
| 1111 | A282 | 3e multi | 1.40 | .50 |
| 1112 | A282 | 12.50e multi | 1.10 | .50 |
| | | Nos. 1110-1112 (3) | 2.70 | 1.20 |

Bicentenary of Castelo Branco as a town.

1971, Oct. 29   Perf. 13½

Designs: 4e, Stratospheric weather balloon and weather map of southwest Europe and North Africa. 6.50e, Satellite and aerial map of Atlantic Ocean off Portugal.

| 1113 | A283 | 4e buff & multi | .20 | .20 |
|---|---|---|---|---|
| 1114 | A283 | 4e multicolored | 2.25 | .85 |
| 1115 | A283 | 6.50e blk, dl red brn & org | 1.50 | .45 |
| | | Nos. 1113-1115 (3) | 3.95 | 1.50 |

25 years of Portuguesa meteorological service.

Missionaries and Ship — A284

1971, Nov. 24

| 1116 | A284 | 1e gray, ultra & blk | .20 | .20 |
|---|---|---|---|---|
| 1117 | A284 | 3.30e dp bis, lil & blk | 2.00 | 1.00 |
| 1118 | A284 | 4.80e olive, grn & blk | 2.10 | 1.10 |
| | | Nos. 1116-1118 (3) | 4.30 | 2.30 |

400th anniv. of the martyrdom of a group of Portuguese missionaries on the way to Brazil.

"Man" A285

| 1971, Dec. 22 | Litho. | Perf. 12 | | |
|---|---|---|---|---|

Nature Conservation: 3.30e, "Earth" (animal, vegetable, mineral). 3.50e, "Air" (birds). 4.50e, "Water" (fish).

| 1119 | A285 | 1e brown & multi | .20 | .20 |
|---|---|---|---|---|
| 1120 | A285 | 3.30e lt bl, yel & grn | .55 | .30 |
| 1121 | A285 | 3.50e lt bl, rose & vio | .65 | .25 |
| 1122 | A285 | 4.50e lt bl, grn & ultra | 1.25 | 1.25 |
| | | Nos. 1119-1122 (4) | 3.65 | 2.00 |

City Hall, Sintra — A286

Designs: 5c, Aqueduct, Lisbon. 50c, University, Coimbra. 1e, Torre dos Clerigos, Porto. 1.50e, Belem Tower, Lisbon. 2.50e, Castle, Vila da Feira. 3e, Misericordia House, Viana do Castelo. 3.50e, Window, Tomar Convent. 8e, Ducal Palace, Guimaraes. 10e, Cape Girao, Madeira. 20e, Episcopal Garden, Castelo Branco. 100e, Lakes of Seven Cities, Azores.

| 1972-73 | Litho. | Size: 22x17½mm | Perf. 12½ | |
|---|---|---|---|---|
| 1123 | A286 | 5c gray, grn & blk | .20 | .20 |
| 1124 | A286 | 50c gray bl, blk & org | .20 | .20 |
| 1125 | A286 | 1e green, blk & org | .20 | .20 |
| 1126 | A286 | 1.50e blue, bis & blk | .20 | .20 |
| 1127 | A286 | 2.50e brn, dk brn & gray | .20 | .20 |
| 1128 | A286 | 3e yellow, blk & brn | .20 | .20 |
| 1129 | A286 | 3.50e dp org, sl & brn | .20 | .20 |
| 1130 | A286 | 8e blk, ol & grn | 1.40 | .30 |
| | | Perf. 13½ | | |
| 1131 | A286 | 10e gray & multi | .50 | .20 |
| 1132 | A286 | 20e green & multi | 3.75 | |
| 1133 | A286 | 50e gray bl, ocher & blk | 1.90 | .25 |
| | | | 5.50 | .45 |
| | | Size: 31x22mm | | |
| 1134 | A286 | 100e green & multi | 14.45 | 2.80 |
| | | Nos. 1123-1134 (12) | | |

"CTT" and year date printed in minute gray multiple rows on back of stamps. Values are for most common dates.

Issue dates: 1e, 1.50e, 50e, 100e, Mar. 1; 50c, 3e, 10e, 20e, Dec. 6, 1972; 5c, 2.50e, 3.50e, 8e, Sept. 5, 1973.

See Nos. 1207-1214.

**Tagging**

Starting in 1975, phosphor (bar or L-shape) was applied to the face of most definitives and commemoratives. Stamps issued both with and without tagging include Nos. 1124-1125, 1128, 1130-1131, 1209, 1213-1214, 1250, 1253, 1257, 1260, 1263.

Window, Pinhel Church — A287

| 1972, Mar. 29 | | Perf. 13½ | | |
|---|---|---|---|---|
| 1135 | A287 | 1e blue & multi | .20 | .20 |
| | a. | Perf. 11½x12½ | 3.00 | 3.00 |
| 1136 | A287 | 2.50e multicolored | 1.75 | .30 |
| 1137 | A287 | 7.50e blue & multi | 1.40 | .50 |
| | | Nos. 1135-1137 (3) | 3.35 | 1.00 |

Bicentenary of Pinhel as a town.

1e, Arms of Pinhel, horiz. 7.50e, Stone lantern.

Heart and Pendulum A288

1972, Apr. 24

Designs: 4e, Heart and spiral pattern. 9e, Heart and continuing coil pattern.

| 1138 | A288 | 1e violet & red | .20 | .20 |
|---|---|---|---|---|
| 1139 | A288 | 4e green & red | 3.00 | .90 |
| 1140 | A288 | 9e brown & red | 1.60 | .60 |
| | | Nos. 1138-1140 (3) | 4.80 | 1.70 |

"Your heart is your health," World Health Day.

**Europa Issue 1972**
Common Design Type

| 1972, May 1 | Size: 21x31mm | | Perf. 13½ | |
|---|---|---|---|---|
| 1141 | CD15 | 1e gray & multi | 1.00 | .20 |
| 1142 | CD15 | 3.50e salmon & multi | 10.00 | .40 |
| 1143 | CD15 | 6e green & multi | 29.00 | 1.40 |
| | | Nos. 1141-1143 (3) | 40.00 | 2.00 |

Trucks — A289

| 1972, May 17 | | Litho. | | |
|---|---|---|---|---|
| 1144 | A289 | 1e shown | .20 | .20 |
| 1145 | A289 | 4.50e Taxi | 2.10 | .90 |
| 1146 | A289 | 8e Autobus | 1.75 | .70 |
| | | Nos. 1144-1146 (3) | 4.05 | 1.80 |

13th Congress of International Union of Road Transport (I.R.U.), Estoril, May 15-18.

Soccer, Olympic Rings A290

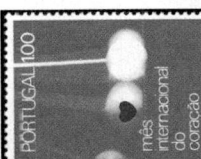

| 1972, July 26 | | Litho. | Perf. 14 | |
|---|---|---|---|---|
| 1147 | A290 | 50c Soccer | .20 | .20 |
| 1148 | A290 | 1e Running | .20 | .20 |
| 1149 | A290 | 1.50e Equestrian | .45 | .20 |
| 1150 | A290 | 3.50e Swimming, women's | 1.10 | .30 |
| 1151 | A290 | 4.50e Yachting | 1.50 | .85 |
| 1152 | A290 | 8e Gymnastics, women's | 2.75 | .80 |
| | | Nos. 1147-1152 (6) | 6.20 | 2.55 |

20th Olympic Games, Munich, 8/26-9/11.

Marquis of Pombal — A291

| 1972, Aug. 28 | | Perf. 13½ | | |
|---|---|---|---|---|
| 1153 | A291 | 1e shown | .20 | .20 |
| 1154 | A291 | 2.50e Scientific apparatus | 1.60 | .60 |
| 1155 | A291 | 8e Seal of Univ. of Coimbra | 1.75 | .95 |
| | | Nos. 1153-1155 (3) | 3.55 | 1.75 |

Bicentenary of the Pombaline reforms of University of Coimbra.

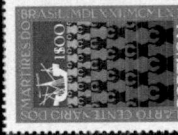

Tomé de Sousa — A292

| 1972, Oct. 5 | Litho. | | Perf. 13½ | |
|---|---|---|---|---|

Designs: 2.50e, José Bonifacio. 3.50e, Dom Pedro IV. 6e, Allegory of Portuguese-Brazilian Community.

| 1156 | A292 | 1e gray & multi | .20 | .20 |
|---|---|---|---|---|
| 1157 | A292 | 2.50e green & multi | .75 | .25 |
| 1158 | A292 | 3.50e multicolored | .75 | .30 |
| 1159 | A292 | 6e blue & multi | 1.60 | .65 |
| | | Nos. 1156-1159 (4) | 3.30 | 1.40 |

150th anniv. of Brazilian independence.

Sacadura Cabral, Gago Coutinho and Plane — A293

2.50e, 3.80e, Map of flight from Lisbon to Rio.

| 1972, Nov. 15 | | Perf. 11½x12½ | | |
|---|---|---|---|---|
| 1160 | A293 | 1e blue & multi | .20 | .20 |
| | a. | Perf. 13½ | 40.00 | .95 |
| 1161 | A293 | 2.50e multi | .80 | .30 |
| 1162 | A293 | 2.80e multi | 1.00 | .60 |
| 1163 | A293 | 3.80e multi | 1.60 | 1.00 |
| | a. | Perf. 13½ | 125.00 | 37.50 |
| | | Nos. 1160-1163 (4) | 3.60 | 2.10 |

50th anniv. of the Lisbon to Rio flight by Commander Arturo de Sacadura Cabral and Adm. Carlos Viegas Gago Coutinho, Mar. 30-June 5, 1922.

Luiz Camoens A294

Designs: 3e, Hand saving manuscript from sea. 10e, Symbolic of man's questioning and discovering the unknown.

| 1972, Dec. 27 | Litho. | | Perf. 13 | |
|---|---|---|---|---|
| 1164 | A294 | 1e org brn, buff & blk | .20 | .20 |
| 1165 | A294 | 3e dull bl, lt grn & blk | 1.40 | .50 |
| 1166 | A294 | 10e red brn, buff & yel | 1.60 | .65 |
| | | Nos. 1164-1166 (3) | 3.20 | 1.35 |

4th centenary of the publication of The Lusiads by Luiz Camoens (1524-1580).

Graphs and Sequence Count — A295

| 1973, Apr. 11 | Litho. | | Perf. 14½ | |
|---|---|---|---|---|
| 1167 | A295 | 1e shown | .20 | .20 |
| 1168 | A295 | 4e Odometer | 1.40 | .50 |
| 1169 | A295 | 9e Graphs | 1.25 | .45 |
| | | Nos. 1167-1169 (3) | 2.85 | 1.15 |

Productivity Conference '72, 1/17-22/72.

**Europa Issue 1973**
Common Design Type

| 1973, Apr. 30 | Size: 31x29mm | | Perf. 13 | |
|---|---|---|---|---|
| 1170 | CD16 | 1e multicolored | 2.00 | .20 |
| 1171 | CD16 | 4e brn red & multi | 42.50 | .90 |
| 1172 | CD16 | 6e green & multi | 50.00 | 1.90 |
| | | Nos. 1170-1172 (3) | 94.50 | 3.00 |

Gen. Medici, Arms of Brazil and Portugal A296

**Lithographed and Engraved**

| 1973, May 16 | | Perf. 12x11½ | | |
|---|---|---|---|---|

2.80e, 4.80e, Gen. Medici and world map.

| 1173 | A296 | 1e dk grn, blk & multi | .20 | .20 |
|---|---|---|---|---|
| 1174 | A296 | 2.80e olive & multi | .75 | .50 |
| 1175 | A296 | 3.50e olive bl, blk & buff | .85 | .45 |
| 1176 | A296 | 4.80e multicolored | .50 | .50 |
| | | Nos. 1173-1176 (4) | 2.70 | 1.65 |

Visit of Gen. Emilio Garrastazu Medici, President of Brazil, to Portugal.

## Child and Birds — A297

**1973, May 28  Litho.  Perf. 13**

| | | | | |
|---|---|---|---|---|
| 1177 | A297 | 1e ultra & multi | .20 | .20 |
| 1178 | A297 | 4e multicolored | 1.50 | .80 |
| 1179 | A297 | 7.50e bister & multi | 3.30 | 1.50 |

Nos. 1177-1179 (3)

To pay renewed attention to children.

Designs: 4e, Child and flowers. 7.50e, Child.

## Transportation, Weather Map — A298

**1973, June 25  Litho.  Perf. 13**

| | | | | |
|---|---|---|---|---|
| 1180 | A298 | 1e multi | .20 | .20 |
| 1181 | A298 | 3.80e multi | 1.10 | .50 |
| 1182 | A298 | 6e multi | 1.75 | 1.00 |

Nos. 1180-1182 (3)

Ministry of Communications, 25th anniv.

3.80e, Communications: telephone, radio, satellite. 6e, Postal service: mailbox, truck, mail distribution diagram.

## Pupil and Writing Exercise — A299

**1973, Oct. 24  Litho.  Perf. 13**

| | | | | |
|---|---|---|---|---|
| 1183 | A299 | 1e blue & multi | .20 | .20 |
| 1184 | A299 | 4.50e brown & multi | 1.60 | .40 |
| 1185 | A299 | 5.30e lt blue & multi | 1.25 | .50 |
| 1186 | A299 | 8e green & multi | 2.75 | 1.10 |

Nos. 1183-1186 (4)  5.80  2.20

Primary state school education, bicent.

Designs: 4.50e, Illustrations from 18th century primer. 5.30e, School and children, by 9-year-old Marie de Luz, horiz. 8e, Symbolic chart of teacher-pupil link, horiz.

## Oporto Streetcar, 1910 — A300

**1973, Nov. 7**

**Size: 31½x34mm**

| | | | | |
|---|---|---|---|---|
| 1187 | A300 | 1e brn, yel & blk | .20 | .20 |
| 1188 | A300 | 3.50e choc & multi | 2.10 | 1.00 |

**Size: 37½x27mm  Perf. 12½**

| | | | | |
|---|---|---|---|---|
| 1189 | A300 | 7.50e buff & multi | 4.70 | 2.10 |

Nos. 1187-1189 (3)

Cent. of public transportation in Oporto.

Designs: 1e, Horse-drawn streetcar, 1872. 3.50e, Double-decker Leyland bus, 1972.

## Servicemen's League Emblem — A301

**1973, Nov. 28  Litho.  Perf. 13**

| | | | | |
|---|---|---|---|---|
| 1190 | A301 | 1e multi | .20 | .20 |
| 1191 | A301 | 2.50e multi | 2.10 | .55 |
| 1192 | A301 | 11e dk blue & multi | 4.05 | 1.20 |

Nos. 1190-1192 (3)

50th anniv. of the Servicemen's League.

Designs: 2.50e, Sailor, soldier and aviator. 11e, Military medals.

## Death of Nuño Gonzalves — A302

**1973, Dec. 19  Litho.  Perf. 13**

| | | | | |
|---|---|---|---|---|
| 1193 | A302 | 1e slate blue & org | .30 | .20 |
| 1194 | A302 | 10e violet brn & org | 2.10 | .85 |

600th anniv. of the heroism of Nuno Gonzalves, alcaide of Faria Castle.

## Damião de Goís, by Dürer (?) — A303

**1974, Apr. 5  Litho.  Perf. 12**

| | | | | |
|---|---|---|---|---|
| 1195 | A303 | 1e multi | .20 | .20 |
| 1196 | A303 | 4.50e multi | 2.40 | .45 |
| 1197 | A303 | 7.50e multi | 4.00 | 1.05 |

Nos. 1195-1197 (3)

400th anniversary of the death of Damião de Gois (1502-1574), humanist, writer, composer.

Designs: 4.50e, Title page of Cronica de Principe D. Joao. 7.50e, Lute and score of Dodecachordon.

## "The Exile," by Soares dos Reis — A304

**Europa Issue 1974**

**1974, Apr. 29  Litho.  Perf. 13**

| | | | | |
|---|---|---|---|---|
| 1198 | A304 | 1e multicolored | 1.60 | .20 |
| 1199 | A304 | 4e dk red & multi | 42.50 | .75 |
| 1200 | A304 | 6e dk grn & multi | 52.50 | 1.40 |

Nos. 1198-1200 (3)  96.60  2.35

## Pattern of Light Emission — A305

**1974, June 26  Litho.  Perf. 14**

| | | | | |
|---|---|---|---|---|
| 1201 | A305 | 1e gray olive | .20 | .20 |
| 1202 | A305 | 4.50e dark blue | 1.25 | .50 |
| 1203 | A305 | 5.30e brt rose lilac | 2.00 | .75 |

Nos. 1201-1203 (3)  3.45  1.45

Establishment of satellite communications network via Intelsat among Portugal, Angola and Mozambique.

Designs: 4.50e, Spiral wave radiation pattern. 5.30e, Satellite and earth.

## Diffusion of Hertzian Waves — A306

Guglielmo Marconi (1874-1937), Italian electrical engineer and inventor.

**1974, Sept. 4  Litho.  Perf. 12**

| | | | | |
|---|---|---|---|---|
| 1204 | A306 | 1.50e multi | .20 | .20 |
| 1205 | A306 | 3.30e multi | 2.00 | .60 |
| 1206 | A306 | 10e multi | 3.45 | 1.20 |

Nos. 1204-1206 (3)

Designs (Symbolic): 3.30e, Navigation help. 10e, Messages through space.

## Buildings Type of 1972-73

**1974, Sept. 18  Litho.  Perf. 12½**

**Size: 22x17½mm**

| | | | | |
|---|---|---|---|---|
| 1207 | A286 | 10c multi | .20 | .20 |
| 1208 | A286 | 30c multi | .20 | .20 |
| 1209 | A286 | 2e multi | .55 | .20 |
| 1210 | A286 | 4e multi | .55 | .20 |
| 1211 | A286 | 4.50e multi | .90 | .20 |
| 1212 | A286 | 5e multi | 5.75 | .20 |
| 1213 | A286 | 6e multi | 2.10 | .20 |
| 1214 | A286 | 7.50e multi | 11.00 | 1.00 |

Nos. 1207-1214 (8)

Designs: 10c, Ponte do Lima (Roman bridge). 30c, Alcobaça Monastery, interior. 2e, City Hall, Bragança. 4e, New Gate, Braga. 4.50e, Dolmen of Carrazeda. 5e, Roman Temple, Évora. 6e, Leça do Balio Monastery. 7.50e, Almoural Castle.

"CTT" and year date printed in minute gray multiple rows on back of stamps. Values are for most common dates.

## Postillion, Truck and Letter — A307

**1974, Oct. 9  Litho.  Perf. 13**

| | | | | |
|---|---|---|---|---|
| 1220 | A307 | 1.50e brown & multi | .20 | .20 |
| 1221 | A307 | 2e multicolored | .75 | .20 |
| 1222 | A307 | 3.30e olive & multi | .40 | .20 |
| 1223 | A307 | 4.50e multicolored | 1.40 | .50 |
| 1224 | A307 | 5.30e multicolored | .55 | .30 |
| 1225 | A307 | 20e multicolored | 6.25 | .95 |
| a. | | Souvenir sheet of 6 | 5.80 | 6.25 |

Nos. 1220-1225 (6)  ...  2.30

Centenary of UPU. No. 1225a contains one each of Nos. 1220-1225, arranged to show a continuous design with a globe in center. Sold for 50e.

Designs: 2e, Hand holding letter. 3.30e, Packet and steamship. 4.50e, Pigeon and letters. 5.30e, Hand holding sealed letter. 20e, Old and new locomotives.

## Luisa Todi, Singer (1753-1833) — A308

## Marcos Portugal, Composer (1762-1838) — A309

**1974, Oct. 30  Litho.  Perf. 12**

| | | | | |
|---|---|---|---|---|
| 1226 | A308 | 1.50e brt pink | .20 | .20 |
| 1227 | A308 | 2e vermilion | 1.10 | .25 |
| 1228 | A308 | 2.50e brown | .75 | .25 |
| 1229 | A308 | 3e bluish black | 1.25 | .30 |
| 1230 | A308 | 5.30e slate green | .75 | .30 |
| 1231 | A309 | 11e rose lake | 4.95 | 1.80 |

Nos. 1226-1231 (6)

Portuguese Musicians: 2e, Joao Domingos Bontempo (1775-1842). 2.50e, Carlos Seixas (1704-1742). 3e, Duarte Lobo (1565-1646). 5.30e, Joao de Sousa Carvalho (1745-1798).

## Coat of Arms of Beja — A310

**1974, Nov. 13**

| | | | | |
|---|---|---|---|---|
| 1232 | A310 | 1.50e multi | .20 | .20 |
| 1233 | A310 | 3.50e multi | 2.25 | .80 |
| 1234 | A310 | 7e multi | 2.50 | .95 |

Nos. 1232-1234 (3)  4.95  1.95

2,000th Anniv. of Beja. 3.50e, Men of Beja in costumes from Roman times to date. 7e, Moorish Arches and view across plains.

## Annunciation — A311  Rainbow and Dove — A312

**1974, Dec. 18  Litho.  Perf. 13**

| | | | | |
|---|---|---|---|---|
| 1235 | A311 | 1.50e red & multi | .20 | .20 |
| 1236 | A311 | 4.50e multicolored | 3.25 | .45 |
| 1237 | A311 | 10e blue & multi | 5.95 | 1.25 |

Nos. 1235-1237 (3)

Christmas: 4.50e, Adoration of the Shepherds. 10e, Flight into Egypt. Designs show Portuguese costumes from Nazare township.

**1974, Dec. 18  Litho.  Perf. 12**

| | | | | |
|---|---|---|---|---|
| 1238 | A312 | 1.50e multi | .20 | .20 |
| 1239 | A312 | 3.50e multi | 1.40 | .40 |
| 1240 | A312 | 5e multi | 1.90 | .60 |

Nos. 1238-1240 (3)  5.35  2.10

Armed Forces Movement of Apr. 25, 1974.

## Egas Moniz — A313

**1974, Dec. 27  Engr.  Perf. 11½x12**

| | | | | |
|---|---|---|---|---|
| 1241 | A313 | 1.50e yellow & multi | .25 | .20 |
| 1242 | A313 | 3.30e brown & ocher | 1.40 | .35 |
| 1243 | A313 | 10e gray & ultra | 5.00 | .60 |

Nos. 1241-1243 (3)  6.65  1.15

Egas Moniz (1874-1955), brain surgeon.

3.30e, Lobotomy probe and Nobel Prize medal, 1949. 10e, Cerebral angiograph, 1927.

## Soldier as Farmer, Farmer as Soldier — A314

**1975, Mar. 21  Litho.  Perf. 12**

| | | | | |
|---|---|---|---|---|
| 1244 | A314 | 1.50e green & multi | .20 | .20 |
| 1245 | A314 | 3e gray & multi | 1.90 | .90 |
| 1246 | A314 | 4.50e multicolored | 4.35 | 1.45 |

Nos. 1244-1246 (3)

Cultural progress and citizens' guidance campaign.

King Ferdinand I — A330

Designs: 5e, Plowshare, farmers chasing off hunters. 10e, Harvest.

**1976, July 2      Litho.      *Perf. 12***
| | | | |
|---|---|---|---|
| 1288 | A330 | 3e lt bl & multi | .20 | .20 |
| 1289 | A330 | 5e yel grn & multi | 1.60 | .30 |
| 1290 | A330 | 10e multicolored | 1.90 | .60 |
| | | | 1.50 | .90 |
| | | Souv. sheet of 3, #1288-1290 | 4.50 | 4.50 |
| *a.* | | Nos. 1288-1290 (3) | 3.70 | 1.10 |

Agricultural reform law (compulsory cultivation of uncultivated lands), 600th anniversary. No. 1290a sold for 30e.

Torch Bearer A331

7e, Women's relay race. 10.50e, Olympic flame.

**1976, July 16      *Perf. 13½***
| | | | |
|---|---|---|---|
| 1291 | A331 | 3e red & multi | .20 | .20 |
| 1292 | A331 | 7e red & multi | 1.50 | .90 |
| 1293 | A331 | 10.50e red & multi | 2.10 | .80 |
| | | Nos. 1291-1293 (3) | 3.80 | 1.90 |

21st Olympic Games, Montreal, Canada, July 17-Aug. 1.

Farm A332

**1976, Sept. 15      Litho.      *Perf. 12***
| | | | |
|---|---|---|---|
| 1294 | A332 | 3e as shown | .55 | .20 |
| 1295 | A332 | 3e Ship | .55 | .20 |
| 1296 | A332 | 3e City | .55 | .20 |
| 1297 | A332 | 3e Factory | 1.10 | .20 |
| | | Souv. sheet of 4, #1294-1297 | 12.50 | 12.50 |
| *b.* | | | 2.75 | .80 |
| | | Nos. 1294-1297 (4) | | |

Flight against illiteracy. #1297b sold for 25e.

**      *Perf. 13½***
| | | | |
|---|---|---|---|
| 1294a | A332 | 3e | .50 | .50 |
| 1295a | A332 | 3e | .80 | |
| 1296a | A332 | 3e | 24.00 | |
| 1297a | A332 | 3e | .80 | |
| | | | 24.00 | |
| | | Nos. 1294a-1297a (4) | 49.60 | 1.40 |

Azure-winged Magpie A333

Designs: 5e, Lynx. 7e, Portuguese laurel cherry. 10.50e, Little wild carnations.

**1976, Sept. 30      Litho.      *Perf. 12***
| | | | |
|---|---|---|---|
| 1298 | A333 | 3e multi | .25 | .20 |
| 1299 | A333 | 5e multi | 1.10 | .25 |
| 1300 | A333 | 7e multi | 1.25 | .65 |
| 1301 | A333 | 10.50e multi | 1.40 | .85 |
| | | Nos. 1298-1301 (4) | 4.00 | 1.95 |

Portucale 77, 2nd International Thematic Exhibition, Oporto, Oct. 29-Nov. 6, 1977.

---

**1975, Dec. 30      Litho.      *Perf. 13½***
| | | | |
|---|---|---|---|
| 1273 | A324 | 50c multicolored | .20 | .20 |
| 1274 | A324 | 2e multicolored | 1.00 | .25 |
| 1275 | A324 | 3.50e multicolored | 1.00 | .45 |
| 1276 | A324 | 8e multicolored | 1.50 | .90 |
| | | Souvenir sheet of 4 | 4.00 | 4.00 |
| *a.* | | | 3.70 | 1.80 |
| | | Nos. 1273-1276 (4) | | |

International Women's Year 1975. No. 1276a contains 4 stamps similar to Nos. 1273-1276 in slightly changed colors. Sold for 25e.

Pen Nib as Plowshare A325

**1976, Feb. 6      Litho.      *Perf. 12***
| | | | |
|---|---|---|---|
| 1277 | A325 | 3e dk bl & red org | .40 | .20 |
| 1278 | A325 | 20e org, ultra & red | 4.00 | .90 |

Portuguese Soc. of Writers, 50th anniv.

Telephones, 1876, 1976 — A326

10.50e, Alexander Graham Bell & telephone.

**1976, Mar. 10      Litho.      *Perf. 12x12½***
| | | | |
|---|---|---|---|
| 1279 | A326 | 3e yel grn, grn & blk | .90 | .20 |
| 1280 | A326 | 10.50e rose, red & blk | 3.25 | .65 |

Centenary of first telephone call by Alexander Graham Bell, March 10, 1876.

Industry and Shipping — A327

1e, Garment, food and wine industries.

**1976, Apr. 7      Litho.      *Perf. 12½***
| | | | |
|---|---|---|---|
| 1281 | A327 | 3e red brown | .20 | .20 |
| 1282 | A327 | 1e slate | .45 | .20 |

Support of national production.

Carved Spoons, Olive Wood A328

Europa: 20e, Gold filigree pendant, silver box and CEPT emblem.

**1976, May 3      Litho.      *Perf. 12x12½***
| | | | |
|---|---|---|---|
| 1283 | A328 | 3e olive & multi | 6.25 | .20 |
| 1284 | A328 | 20e tan & multi | 100.00 | 4.50 |

Stamp Collectors A329

Designs: 7.50e, Stamp exhibition and hand canceler. 10e, Printing and designing stamps.

**1976, May 29      Litho.      *Perf. 14½***
| | | | |
|---|---|---|---|
| 1285 | A329 | 3e multicolored | .20 | .20 |
| 1286 | A329 | 7.50e multicolored | 1.10 | .45 |
| 1287 | A329 | 10e multicolored | 1.60 | .50 |
| | | Nos. 1285-1287 (3) | 2.90 | 1.15 |

Interphil 76, International Philatelic Exhibition, Philadelphia, Pa., May 29-June 6.

---

People and Sapling A320

4.50e, Brown hands reaching for dove. 10e, Dove with olive branch and arms of Portugal.

**1975, Sept. 17      Litho.      *Perf. 13½***
| | | | |
|---|---|---|---|
| 1260 | A320 | 2e green & multi | .45 | .20 |
| 1261 | A320 | 4.50e vio & multi | 1.60 | .40 |
| 1262 | A320 | 20e multicolored | 3.50 | 1.60 |
| | | Nos. 1260-1262 (3) | 5.55 | 1.60 |

United Nations, 30th anniversary.

Icarus and Rocket — A321

Designs: 4.50e, Apollo and Soyuz in space. 5.30e, Robert H. Goddard, Robert Esnault-Pelterie, Hermann Oberth and Konstantin Tsiolkovski. 10e, Sputnik, man in space, moon landing module.

**1975, Sept. 26      Litho.      *Size: 30½x26½mm***
| | | | |
|---|---|---|---|
| 1263 | A321 | 2e green & multi | .40 | .20 |
| 1264 | A321 | 4.50e brown & multi | 2.00 | .60 |
| 1265 | A321 | 5.30e lilac & multi | .95 | .95 |

**      *Size: 65x28mm***
| | | | |
|---|---|---|---|
| 1266 | A321 | 10e blue & multi | 4.25 | 1.00 |
| | | Nos. 1263-1266 (4) | 7.60 | 2.40 |

26th Congress of International Astronautical Federation, Lisbon, Sept. 1975.

Land Survey A322

Designs: 8e, Ocean survey. 10e, People of many races and globe.

**1976, Nov. 19      Litho.      *Perf. 12x12½***
| | | | |
|---|---|---|---|
| 1267 | A322 | 2e ocher & multi | .20 | .20 |
| 1268 | A322 | 8e blue & multi | 1.40 | .55 |
| 1269 | A322 | 10e uk vlu & multi | 3.00 | .85 |
| | | Nos. 1267-1269 (3) | 4.60 | 1.60 |

Centenary of Lisbon Geographical Society.

Arch and Trees — A323

Designs: 8e, Plan, pencil and ruler. 10e, Hand, old building and brick tower.

**1975, Nov. 28      *Perf. 13½***
| | | | |
|---|---|---|---|
| 1270 | A323 | 8e dk bl & gray | .30 | .20 |
| 1271 | A323 | 8e dk car & gray | 3.25 | .65 |
| 1272 | A323 | 10e ocher & multi | 3.50 | .90 |
| | | Nos. 1270-1272 (3) | 7.05 | 1.75 |

European Architectural Heritage Year 1975.

Nurse and Hospital Ward — A324

Designs (IWY Emblem and): 2e, Farm workers. 3.50e, Secretary. 8e, Factory worker.

---

Hands and Dove — A315

4.50e, Brown hands reaching for dove. 10e, Dove with olive branch and arms of Portugal.

**1975, Apr. 23      Litho.      *Perf. 13½***
| | | | |
|---|---|---|---|
| 1247 | A315 | 1.50e red & multi | .20 | .20 |
| 1248 | A315 | 4.50e brown & multi | 2.25 | .55 |
| 1249 | A315 | 10e green & multi | 3.25 | .85 |
| | | Nos. 1247-1249 (3) | 5.70 | 1.55 |

Movement of April 25th, first anniversary. Slogans in Portuguese, French and English printed on back of stamps.

God's Hand Reaching Down — A316

Designs: 4.50e, Jesus' hand holding up cross. 10e, Dove (Holy Spirit) descending.

**1975, May 13      Litho.      *Perf. 13½***
| | | | |
|---|---|---|---|
| 1250 | A316 | 1.50e multicolored | .20 | .20 |
| 1251 | A316 | 4.50e plum & multi | 3.25 | .75 |
| 1252 | A316 | 10e blue & multi | 4.25 | .80 |
| | | Nos. 1250-1252 (3) | 7.70 | 1.75 |

Holy Year 1975.

Horseman of the Apocalypse, 12th Century — A317

Europa: 10e, The Poet Fernando Pessoa, by Almada Negreiros (1893-1970).

**1975, May 26      Litho.**
| | | | |
|---|---|---|---|
| 1253 | A317 | 1.50e multi | 3.00 | .25 |
| 1254 | A317 | 10e multi | 110.00 | 2.00 |

Assembly Building A318

**1975, June 2      Litho.      *Perf. 13½***
| | | | |
|---|---|---|---|
| 1255 | A318 | 2e red, blk & yel | .30 | .20 |
| 1256 | A318 | 20e emer, blk & yel | 5.75 | 1.00 |

Opening of Constituent Assembly.

Hikers — A319

Designs: 4.50e, Campsite on lake. 5.30e, Mobile homes on the road.

**1975, Aug. 4      Litho.      *Perf. 13½***
| | | | |
|---|---|---|---|
| 1257 | A319 | 2e multicolored | .95 | .20 |
| 1258 | A319 | 4.50e multicolored | 2.75 | .80 |
| 1259 | A319 | 5.30e multicolored | 1.60 | .75 |
| | | Nos. 1257-1259 (3) | 5.30 | 1.75 |

36th Rally of the International Federation of Camping and Caravanning, Santo Andre Lake.

Exhibition Hall — A334

Design: 20e, Symbolic stamp and emblem.

**1976, Oct. 9 Litho. *Perf. 13½***
**1302** A334 3e bl & multi .35 .20
**1303** A334 20e ocher & multi 2.25 1.10
*a.* Souv. sheet of 2, #1302-1303 3.75 3.75

6th Luso-Brazilian Phil. Exhib., LUBRAPEX 76, Oporto, Oct. 9. #1303a sold for 30e.

Bank Emblem and Family A335

7e, Grain. 15e, Cog wheels.

**1976, Oct. 29 *Perf. 12***
**1304** A335 3e org & multi .20 .20
**1305** A335 7e grn & multi 2.10 .60
**1306** A335 15e bl & multi 2.75 .85
*Nos. 1304-1306 (3)* 5.05 1.65

Trust Fund Bank centenary.

Sheep Grazing on Marsh A336

Designs: 3e, Drainage ditches. 5e, Fish in water. 10e, Ducks flying over marsh.

**1976, Nov. 24 Litho. *Perf. 14***
**1307** A336 1e multicolored .20 .20
**1308** A336 3e multicolored .90 .20
**1309** A336 5e multicolored 2.00 .30
**1310** A336 10e multicolored 3.75 .75
*Nos. 1307-1310 (4)* 6.85 1.45

Protection of wetlands.

"Liberty" — A337

**1976, Nov. 30 Litho. *Perf. 13½***
**1311** A337 3e gray, grn & ver .65 .20

Constitution of 1976.

Mother Examining Child's Eyes A338

Designs: 5e, Welder with goggles. 10.50e, Blind woman reading Braille.

**1976, Dec. 13**
**1312** A338 3e multicolored .20 .20
**1313** A338 5e multicolored 2.00 .25
**1314** A338 10.50e multicolored 1.60 .80
*Nos. 1312-1314 (3)* 3.80 1.25

World Health Day and campaign against blindness.

Hydroelectric Energy — A339

Abstract Designs: 4e, Fossil fuels. 5e, Geothermal energy. 10e, Wind power. 15e, Solar energy.

**1976, Dec. 30**
**1315** A339 1e multicolored .20 .20
**1316** A339 4e multicolored .55 .20
**1317** A339 5e multicolored .70 .25
**1318** A339 10e multicolored 1.50 .60
**1319** A339 15e multicolored 2.40 1.10
*Nos. 1315-1319 (5)* 5.35 2.35

Sources of energy.

Map of Council of Europe Members A340

**1977, Jan. 28 Litho. *Perf. 12***
**1320** A340 8.50e multicolored 1.25 .95
**1321** A340 10e multicolored 1.25 .85

Portugal's joining Council of Europe.

Alcoholic and Bottle — A341

Designs (Bottle and): 5e, Symbolic figure of broken life. 15e, Bars blotting out the sun.

**1977, Feb. 4 *Perf. 13***
**1322** A341 3e multicolored .20 .20
**1323** A341 5e ocher & multi .95 .30
**1324** A341 15e org & multi 2.25 .95
*Nos. 1322-1324 (3)* 3.40 1.45

Anti-alcoholism Day and 10th anniversary of Portuguese Anti-alcoholism Society.

Trees Tapped for Resin — A342

Designs: 4e, Trees stripped for cork. 7e, Trees and logs. 15e, Trees at seashore as windbreakers.

**1977, Mar. 21 Litho. *Perf. 13½***
**1325** A342 1e multicolored .20 .20
**1326** A342 4e multicolored .70 .25
**1327** A342 7e multicolored 1.50 .95
**1328** A342 15e multicolored 1.50 .95
*Nos. 1325-1328 (4)* 3.90 2.35

Forests, a natural resource.

"Suffering" A343

6e, Man exercising. 10e, Group exercising. All designs include emblems of WHO & Portuguese Institute for Rheumatology.

**1977, Apr. 13 Litho. *Perf. 12x12½***
**1329** A343 4e blk, brn & ocher .20 .20
**1330** A343 6e blk, bl & vio 1.10 .75
**1331** A343 10e blk, pur & red 1.00 .50
*Nos. 1329-1331 (3)* 2.30 1.45

International Rheumatism Year.

Southern Plains Landscape A344

Europa: 8.50e, Northern mountain valley.

**1977, May 2**
**1332** A344 4e multi .75 .20
**1333** A344 8.50e multi 4.25 .60
*a.* Min. sheet, 2 each #1332-1333 52.50 30.00

Pope John XXI Enthroned A345

Petrus Hispanus, the Physician A346

**1977, May 20 Litho. *Perf. 13½***
**1334** A345 4e multicolored .25 .20
**1335** A346 15e multicolored .60 .35

Pope John XXI (Petrus Hispanus), only Pope of Portuguese descent, 7th death centenary.

Compass Rose, Camoens Quotation A347

**1977, June 8 *Perf. 12***
**1336** A347 4e multi .20 .20
**1337** A347 8.50e multi 1.10 .80

Camoens Day and to honor Portuguese overseas communities.

Student, Computer and Book — A348

Designs (Book and): No. 1339, Folk dancers, flutist and boat. No. 1340, Tractor drivers. No. 1341, Atom and people.

**1977, July 20 Litho. *Perf. 12x12½***
**1338** A348 4e multicolored .40 .20
**1339** A348 4e multicolored .40 .20
**1340** A348 4e multicolored .40 .20
**1341** A348 4e multicolored .40 .20
*a.* Souv. sheet of 4, #1338-1341 4.50 4.50
*Nos. 1338-1341 (4)* 1.60 .80

Continual education. #1341a sold for 20e.

Pyrites, Copper, Chemical Industry A349

Designs: 5e, Marble, statue, public buildings. 10e, Iron ore, girders, crane. 20e, Uranium ore, atomic diagram.

**1977, Oct. 4 Litho. *Perf. 12x11½***
**1342** A349 4e multicolored .25 .20
**1343** A349 5e multicolored .95 .25
**1344** A349 10e multicolored 1.00 .35
**1345** A349 20e multicolored 2.40 .90
*Nos. 1342-1345 (4)* 4.60 1.70

Natural resources from the subsoil.

Alexandre Herculano — A350

**1977, Oct. 19 Engr. *Perf. 12x11½***
**1346** A350 4e multicolored .25 .20
**1347** A350 15e multicolored 1.60 .50

Alexandre Herculano de Carvalho Araujo (1810-1877), historian, novelist, death centenary.

Maria Pia Bridge A351

4e, Arrival of first train, ceramic panel by Jorge Colaco, St. Bento railroad station.

**1977, Nov. 4 Litho. *Perf. 12x11½***
**1348** A351 4e multicolored .25 .20
**1349** A351 10e multicolored 2.25 1.25

Centenary of extension of railroad across Douro River.

Povoiro Bark A352

Coastal Fishing Boats: 3e, Do Mar bark. 4e, Nazaré bark. 7e, Algarve skiff. 10e, Xavega bark. 15e, Bateira de Buarcos.

**1977, Nov. 19 *Perf. 12***
**1350** A352 2e multicolored .40 .20
**1351** A352 3e multicolored .25 .20
**1352** A352 4e multicolored .25 .20
**1353** A352 7e multicolored .50 .20
**1354** A352 10e multicolored .80 .40
**1355** A352 15e multicolored 1.25 .65
*a.* Souv. sheet of 6, #1350-1355 4.25 4.25
*Nos. 1350-1355 (6)* 3.45 1.85

PORTUCALE 77, 2nd International Topical Exhibition. Oporto, Nov. 19-20. No. 1355a sold for 60e.

Nativity A353

Children's Drawings: 7e, Nativity. 10e, Holy Family, vert. 20e, Star and Christ Child, vert.

***Perf. 12x11½, 11½x12***
**1977, Dec. 12 Litho.**
**1356** A353 4e multicolored .20 .20
**1357** A353 7e multicolored 1.10 .30
**1358** A353 10e multicolored 1.25 .45
**1359** A353 20e multicolored 2.75 .80
*Nos. 1356-1359 (4)* 5.30 1.75

Christmas 1977.

Old Desk and Computer — A354

Designs: Work tools, old and new.

PORTUGAL

Automobile Traffic — A368

Combat noise pollution: 5e, Pneumatic drill. 14e, Man with bull horn.

**1979, Mar. 14**    **Perf. 13½**
| | | | |
|---|---|---|---|
| 1418 | A368 | 4e multicolored | .20 .20 |
| 1419 | A368 | 5e multicolored | .70 .50 |
| 1420 | A368 | 14e multicolored | 1.60 .90 |
| | | Nos. 1418-1420 (3) | 2.50 |

NATO Emblem A369

**1979, Apr. 4**    **Litho.**    **Perf. 12**
| | | | |
|---|---|---|---|
| 1421 | A369 | 5e multicolored | .30 .20 |
| 1422 | A369 | 50e multicolored | 2.75 1.60 |
| a. | Souv. sheet, 2 ea #1421-1422 | | 6.50 6.50 |

NATO, 30th anniv.

Mail Delivery, 16th Century A370

Europa: 40e, Mail delivery, 19th century.

**1979, Apr. 30**    **Litho.**    **Perf. 12**
| | | | |
|---|---|---|---|
| 1423 | A370 | 14e multicolored | .75 .30 |
| 1424 | A370 | 40e multicolored | 2.00 1.60 |
| a. | Souv. sheet, 2 ea #1423-1424 | | 22.50 14.00 |

Mother, Infant, Dove A371

Designs (IYC Emblem and): 5.50e, Children playing ball. 10c, Child in nursery school. 14e, Black and white boys.

**1979, June 1**    **Litho.**    **Perf. 12x12½**
| | | | |
|---|---|---|---|
| 1425 | A371 | 5.50e multi | .30 .20 |
| 1426 | A371 | 6.50e multi | .30 .25 |
| 1427 | A371 | 10e multi | .45 .25 |
| 1428 | A371 | 14e multi | 1.00 .65 |
| a. | Souv. sheet of 4, #1425-1428 | | 3.75 3.75 |
| | Nos. 1425-1428 (4) | | 1.95 1.30 |

Intl. Year of the Child. No. 1428a sold for 40e.

Salute to the Flag — A372

**1979, June 8**
| | | | |
|---|---|---|---|
| 1429 | A372 | 6.50e multicolored | .35 .20 |
| a. | Souvenir sheet of 9 | | 4.50 4.50 |

Portuguese Day.

---

Designs: No. 1405, Carrier pigeon. No. 1406, Envelopes. No. 1407, Pen.

**1978, Oct. 30**    **Litho.**    **Perf. 12**
| | | | |
|---|---|---|---|
| 1404 | A363 | 5e yel & multi | .35 .20 |
| 1405 | A363 | 5e bl gray & multi | .35 .20 |
| 1406 | A363 | 5e grn & multi | .35 .20 |
| 1407 | A363 | 5e red & multi | .35 .20 |
| | Nos. 1404-1407 (4) | | 1.40 .80 |

Introduction of Postal Code.

Human Figure, Flame Emblem A364

Design: 40e, Human figure pointing the way and flame emblem.

**1978, Dec. 7**    **Litho.**    **Perf. 12**
| | | | |
|---|---|---|---|
| 1408 | A364 | 14e multicolored | .65 .30 |
| 1409 | A364 | 40e multicolored | 1.90 .90 |
| a. | Souv. sheet, 2 ea #1408-1409 | | 6.25 6.25 |

Universal Declaration of Human Rights, 30th anniv. and 25th anniv. of European Declaration.

Sebastião Magalhães Lima — A365

**1978, Dec. 7**
| | | | |
|---|---|---|---|
| 1410 | A365 | 5e multicolored | .25 .20 |

Sebastião Magalhães Lima (1850-1928), lawyer, journalist, statesman.

Mail Boxes and Scale A366

Designs: 5e, Telegraph and condenser lens. 10e, Portugal Nos. 2-3 and postal card printing press, 1879. 14e, Book and bookcases, 1879, 1979.

**1978, Dec. 20**
| | | | |
|---|---|---|---|
| 1411 | A366 | 4e multicolored | .30 .20 |
| 1412 | A366 | 5e multicolored | .30 .20 |
| 1413 | A366 | 10e multicolored | 1.10 .20 |
| 1414 | A366 | 14e multicolored | 2.50 1.25 |
| a. | Souv. sheet of 4, #1411-1414 | | 4.20 1.85 |
| | Nos. 1411-1414 (4) | | 5.50 |

Centenary of Postal Museum and Postal Library; 125th anniversary of Portuguese stamps (10e). No. 1414a sold for 40e.

Emigrant at Railroad Station A367

Designs: 14e, Farewell at airport. 17e, Emigrant greeting child at railroad station.

**1979, Feb. 21**    **Litho.**    **Perf. 12**
| | | | |
|---|---|---|---|
| 1415 | A367 | 5e multicolored | .20 .20 |
| 1416 | A367 | 14e multicolored | .70 .35 |
| 1417 | A367 | 17e multicolored | 1.00 .80 |
| | Nos. 1415-1417 (3) | | 1.90 1.35 |

Portuguese emigration.

---

Trajan's Bridge — A358

Roman Tablet from Bridge — A359

**1978, June 14**    **Litho.**    **Perf. 13½**
| | | | |
|---|---|---|---|
| 1392 | A358 | 5e multicolored | .40 .20 |
| 1393 | A359 | 20e multicolored | 2.50 .80 |

1900th anniv. of Chaves (Aquae Flaviae).

Running A360

**1978, July 24**    **Litho.**
| | | | |
|---|---|---|---|
| 1394 | A360 | 5e shown | .20 .20 |
| 1395 | A360 | 10e Bicycling | .40 .20 |
| 1396 | A360 | 12.50e Watersport | .95 .65 |
| 1397 | A360 | 15e Soccer | 2.50 1.55 |
| | Nos. 1394-1397 (4) | | |

Sport for all the people.

Pedro Nunes A361

Design: 20e, "Nonio" navigational instrument and diagram from Tratado da Rumação do Globo.

**1978, Aug. 9**    **Litho.**    **Porf. 12x11½**
| | | | |
|---|---|---|---|
| 1398 | A361 | 5e multicolored | .20 .20 |
| 1399 | A361 | 20e multicolored | 1.40 .35 |

Pedro Nunes (1502-78), navigator and cosmographer.

Trawler, Frozen Fish Processing, Can of Sardines — A362

Fishing: 9e, Deep-sea trawler, loading and unloading at dock. 12.50e, Trawler with radar and instruction in use of radar. 15e, Trawler with echo-sounding equipment, microscope and test tubes.

**1978, Sept. 16**    **Litho.**    **Perf. 12x11½**
| | | | |
|---|---|---|---|
| 1400 | A362 | 5e multi | .20 .20 |
| 1401 | A362 | 9e multi | .65 .20 |
| 1402 | A362 | 12.50e multi | 1.25 .70 |
| 1403 | A362 | 15e multi | 1.90 .90 |
| | Nos. 1400-1403 (4) | | 4.00 2.00 |

Natural resources.

Postrider A363

---

**1978-83**    **Litho.**    **Perf. 12½**    **Size: 22x17mm**
| | | | |
|---|---|---|---|
| 1360 | A354 | 50c Medical | .20 .20 |
| 1361 | A354 | 1e Household | .20 .20 |
| 1362 | A354 | 2e Communications | .20 .20 |
| 1363 | A354 | 3e Garment making | .20 .20 |
| 1364 | A354 | 4e Office | .20 .20 |
| 1365 | A354 | 5e Fishing craft | .20 .20 |
| 1366 | A354 | 5.50e Weaving | .20 .20 |
| 1367 | A354 | 6e Plows | .20 .20 |
| 1368 | A354 | 6.50e Aviation | .20 .20 |
| 1369 | A354 | 7e Printing | .20 .20 |
| 1370 | A354 | 8e Carpentry | .20 .20 |
| 1371 | A354 | 8.50e Potter's wheel | .20 .20 |
| 1372 | A354 | 9e Photography | .25 .25 |
| 1373 | A354 | 10e Saws | .25 .25 |
| 1373A | A354 | 12.50e Compasses ('83) | .30 .20 |
| 1373B | A354 | 16e Mail processing ('83) | .30 .20 |

**Perf. 13½**    **Size: 31x22mm**
| | | | |
|---|---|---|---|
| 1374 | A354 | 20e Construction | .55 .20 |
| 1375 | A354 | 30e Steel industry | .65 .30 |
| a. | Incomplete arch | | 1.00 .30 |
| 1376 | A354 | 40e Transportation | .75 .25 |
| 1377 | A354 | 50e Chemistry | 1.10 .20 |
| 1378 | A354 | 100e Shipbuilding | 1.75 .60 |
| 1379 | A354 | 250e Telescopes | 4.25 .60 |
| | Nos. 1360-1379 (22) | | 12.60 5.05 |

Red Mediterranean Soil — A355

Designs: 5e, Stone formation. 10e, Alluvial soil. 20e, Black soil.

**1978, Mar. 6**    **Litho.**
| | | | |
|---|---|---|---|
| 1380 | A355 | 4e multicolored | .25 .20 |
| 1381 | A355 | 5e multicolored | .50 .20 |
| 1382 | A355 | 10e multicolored | 1.00 .45 |
| 1383 | A355 | 20e multicolored | 2.50 .60 |
| | Nos. 1380-1383 (4) | | 4.25 1.45 |

Soil, a natural resource.

Street Crossing A356

Designs: 2e, Motorcyclist. 2.50e, Children in back seat of car. 5e, Hands holding steering wheel. 9e, Driving on country road. 12.50e, "Avoid drinking and driving."

**1978, Apr. 19**    **Litho.**
| | | | |
|---|---|---|---|
| 1384 | A356 | 1e multi | .20 .20 |
| 1385 | A356 | 2e multi | .30 .20 |
| 1386 | A356 | 2.50e multi | .70 .20 |
| 1387 | A356 | 5e multi | 1.40 .20 |
| 1388 | A356 | 9e multi | 2.25 .50 |
| 1389 | A356 | 12.50e multi | 3.50 1.25 |
| | Nos. 1384-1389 (6) | | 8.35 2.55 |

Road safety campaign.

Roman Tower, Belmonte A357

Europa: 40e, Belém Monastery of Hieronymite monks (inside).

**1978, May 2**
| | | | |
|---|---|---|---|
| 1390 | A357 | 10e multicolored | 2.25 .20 |
| 1391 | A357 | 40e multicolored | 6.25 .90 |
| a. | Souv. sheet, 2 each #1390-1391 | | 37.50 25.00 |

No. 1391a sold for 120e.

**1979, June 6**

Pregnant Woman A373

Designs: 17e, Boy sitting in a cage. 20e, Face, and hands using hammer.

| | | | | |
|---|---|---|---|---|
| 1430 | A373 | 6.50e | multi | .35 | .20 |
| 1431 | A373 | 17e | multi | .80 | .60 |
| 1432 | A373 | 20e | multi | 1.10 | .60 |
| | | | Nos. 1430-1432 (3) | 2.25 | 1.30 |

Help for the mentally retarded.

**1979**

Children Reading Book, UNESCO Emblem A374

17e, Teaching deaf child, and UNESCO emblem.

**1979, June 25** **Litho.** **Perf. 12x12½**

| 1433 | A374 | 0.30e | multi | .95 | .20 |
|---|---|---|---|---|---|
| 1434 | A374 | 17e | multi | 1.75 | .70 |

Int. Bureau of Education, 50th anniv.

Water Cart, Brasiliana '79 Emblem A375

Brasiliana '79 Philatelic Exhibition: 5.50e, Wine sledge. 6.50e, Wine cart. 16e, Covered cart. 19e, Mogadouro cart. 20e, Sand cart.

**1979, Sept. 15** **Litho.** **Perf. 12**

| 1435 | A375 | 2.50e | multi | .20 | .20 |
|---|---|---|---|---|---|
| 1436 | A375 | 5.50e | multi | .20 | .20 |
| 1437 | A375 | 6.50e | multi | .35 | .20 |
| 1438 | A375 | 16e | multi | .85 | .55 |
| 1439 | A375 | 19e | multi | .95 | .45 |
| 1440 | A375 | 20e | multi | 1.10 | .75 |
| | | | Nos. 1435-1440 (6) | 3.80 | 2.20 |

Antonio Jose de Almeida (1866-1929) A376

Republican Leaders: 6.50e, Afonso Costa (1871-1937). 10e, Teofilo Braga (1843-1924). 16e, Bernardino Machado (1851-1944). 19.50e, Joao Chagas (1863-1925). 20e, Elias Garcia (1830-1891).

**1979, Oct. 4** **Perf. 12½x12**

| 1441 | A376 | 5.50e | multi | .35 | .20 |
|---|---|---|---|---|---|
| 1442 | A376 | 6.50e | multi | .35 | .20 |
| 1443 | A376 | 10e | multi | .55 | .20 |
| 1444 | A376 | 16e | multi | .95 | .45 |
| 1445 | A376 | 19.50e | multi | 1.60 | .80 |
| 1446 | A376 | 20e | multi | 1.40 | .35 |
| | | | Nos. 1441-1446 (6) | 5.20 | 2.20 |

See Nos. 1454-1459.

Red Cross and Family A377

20e, Doctor examining elderly man.

17e, Teaching deaf child, and UNESCO emblem.

---

**1979, Oct. 26** **Perf. 12x12½**

| 1447 | A377 | 6.50e | multi | .35 | .20 |
|---|---|---|---|---|---|
| 1448 | A377 | 20e | multi | 1.40 | .40 |

National Health Service Campaign.

Holy Family, 17th Century Mosaic A378

Mosaics, Lisbon Tile Museum: 6.50e, Nativity, 16th century. 16e, Flight into Egypt, 18th century.

**1979, Dec. 5** **Litho.** **Perf. 12x12½**

| 1449 | A378 | 5.50e | multi | .40 | .25 |
|---|---|---|---|---|---|
| 1450 | A378 | 6.50e | multi | .40 | .20 |
| 1451 | A378 | 16e | multi | 1.10 | .70 |
| | | | Nos. 1449-1451 (3) | 1.90 | 1.15 |

Christmas 1979.

Rotary International, 75th Anniversary — A379

**1980, Feb. 22** **Perf. 12x11½**

| 1452 | A379 | 16e shown | 1.00 | .45 |
|---|---|---|---|---|
| 1453 | A379 | 50e | Emblem, torch | 2.75 | 1.25 |

Portrait Type of 1979

Leaders of the Republican Movement: 3.50e, Alvaro de Castro (1878-1928). 5.50e, Antonio Sergio (1883-1969). 6.50e, Norton de Matos (1867-1955). 10e, Jose Domingues dos Santos (1885-1958). 11e, Jaime Cortesao (1884-1960). 16e, Teixeira Gomes (1860-1941). 20e, Jose Domingues dos Santos (1885-1958). Nos. 1454-1459 horizontal.

**1980, Mar. 19**

| 1454 | A376 | 3.50e | multi | .20 | .20 |
|---|---|---|---|---|---|
| 1455 | A376 | 5.50e | multi | .20 | .20 |
| 1456 | A376 | 6.50e | multi | .30 | .20 |
| 1457 | A376 | 11e | multi | .75 | .30 |
| 1458 | A376 | 16e | multi | 1.00 | .50 |
| 1459 | A376 | 20e | multi | 1.00 | .50 |
| | | | Nos. 1454-1459 (6) | 4.30 | 2.15 |

Luiz Camoens (1524-80) A382

**1980, June 9** **Lithographed & Engraved**

Perf. 11½x12

| 1465 | A381 | 20e Golden eagle | 1.10 | .35 |
|---|---|---|---|---|
| a. | Souv. sheet of 4, #1462-1465 | 3.75 | 3.75 |
| | Nos. 1462-1465 (4) | 3.30 | 1.25 |

European Campaign for the Protection of Species and their Habitat (Lisbon Zoo animals); London 1980 International Stamp Exhibition, May 6-14.

---

Barn Owl A381

**1980, May 6** **Litho.** **Perf. 12x11½**

| 1462 | A381 | 6.50e | shown | .30 | .20 |
|---|---|---|---|---|---|
| 1463 | A381 | 16e | Red fox | .80 | .30 |
| 1464 | A381 | 19.50e | Timber wolf | 1.10 | .40 |

Europa Issue

**1980, Apr. 14**

| 1460 | A380 | 16e shown | 1.25 | .30 |
|---|---|---|---|---|
| 1461 | A380 | 60e Vasco da Gama | 4.25 | .75 |
| a. | Souv. sheet, 2 each #1460-1461 | 10.00 | 9.00 |

Serpa Pinto (1864-1900), Explorer of Africa A380

St. Vincent and Old Lisbon A384

**1980, June 30** **Litho.** **Perf. 12x12½**

| 1466 | A382 | 6.50e | multi + label | .35 | .20 |
|---|---|---|---|---|---|
| 1467 | A382 | 20e | multi + label | 1.10 | .75 |

Mendes Pinto and Chinese Men A383

**1980, June 30** **Litho.**

| 1468 | A383 | 6.50e shown | .35 | .20 |
|---|---|---|---|---|
| 1469 | A383 | 10e Battle at sea | 1.00 | .40 |

A Peregrinacao (The Peregrination) by Fernao Mendes Pinto (1509-1583), written in 1580, published in 1614.

Caravel, Lubrapex '80 Emblem A385

**1980, Oct. 18** **Litho.** **Perf. 12x11½**

| 1476 | A385 | 6.50e shown | .35 | .20 |
|---|---|---|---|---|
| 1477 | A385 | 8e | Three-master Nau | .70 | .30 |
| 1478 | A385 | 16e | Galleon | 1.40 | .45 |
| 1479 | A385 | 19.50e | Paddle steam | 1.90 | .50 |
| a. | Souv. sheet of 4, #1476-1479 | 6.50 | 6.50 |
| | Nos. 1476-1479 (4) | 4.35 | 1.45 |

Lubrapex '80 Stamp Exhib., Lisbon, Oct. 18-26.

World Tourism Conf., Manila, Sept. 27.

**1980, Sept. 17** **Litho.** **Perf. 12x12½**

| 1470 | A384 | 6.50e | multi | .30 | .20 |
|---|---|---|---|---|---|
| 1471 | A384 | 8e | multi | .35 | .25 |
| 1472 | A384 | 11e | multi | .55 | .20 |
| 1473 | A384 | 16e | multi | .80 | .55 |
| 1474 | A384 | 19.50e | multi | 1.75 | .65 |
| 1475 | A384 | 20e | multi | 1.60 | .40 |
| | | | Nos. 1470-1475 (6) | 6.20 | 2.40 |

Designs: 8e, Lantern Tower, Evora Cathedral. 11e, Jesus with top hat, Miranda do Douro Cathedral, and mountain. 16e, Our Lady of the Milk, Braga Cathedral, and Canicada Dam. 19.50e, Pulpit, Santa Cruz Monastery, Coimbra, and Aveiro River. 20e, Algarve chimney, and Rocha Beach.

---

Student, School and Sextant A387

**1980, Oct. 31**

| 1481 | A386 | 16e shown | .30 | .20 |
|---|---|---|---|---|
| 1482 | A387 | 6.50e Founder, book, emblem | 1.40 | .50 |
| 1483 | A387 | 19.50e shown | 2.00 | .55 |

Lisbon Academy of Science bicentennial.

Energy conservation.

Man with Diseased Heart and Lungs, Hand Holding Cigarette A388

**1980, Dec. 19** **Litho.** **Perf. 13½**

| 1484 | A388 | 6.50e shown | 5.00 | .50 |
|---|---|---|---|---|
| 1485 | A388 | 19.50e Healthy man rejecting cigarette | 1.75 | .80 |

Anti-smoking campaign.

Fragata on Tejo River A390

**1981, Feb. 23** **Litho.** **Perf. 12x12½**

| 1488 | A390 | 8e shown | .25 | .20 |
|---|---|---|---|---|
| 1489 | A390 | 8.50e Rabelo, Douro | .25 | .20 |
| 1490 | A390 | 10e Moliceiro, Aveiro River | .50 | .20 |
| 1491 | A390 | 16e Barco, Lima River | .70 | .45 |
| 1492 | A390 | 19.50e Caracho, Minho River | .85 | .45 |
| 1493 | A390 | 20e Varino, Tejo River | .85 | .35 |
| | | Nos. 1488-1493 (6) | 3.40 | 1.85 |

Census Form and Houses A389

**1981, Jan. 28** **Litho.**

| 1486 | A389 | 6.50e multi | .35 | .20 |
|---|---|---|---|---|
| 1487 | A389 | 16e Form, head | 1.40 | .95 |

Census

Rajola Tile, Valencia, 15th Century A391

**1981** **Litho.** **Perf. 11½x12**

| 1494 | A391 | 8.50e | multi | .75 | .20 |
|---|---|---|---|---|---|
| a. | Miniature sheet of 6 | 5.00 | 5.00 |
| 1495 | A391 | 8.50e | multi | .75 | .20 |
| a. | Miniature sheet of 6 | 4.50 | 4.50 |
| 1496 | A391 | 8.50e | multi | .75 | .20 |
| a. | Miniature sheet of 6 | 4.50 | 4.50 |

Designs: No. 1495, Moresque tile, Coimbra, 16th cent. No. 1496, Arms of Duke of Braganza, 1510. No. 1497, Pisanos design, 1596.

Car Emitting Gas Fumes A386

POUPE ENERGIA 16.00

**1982, May 13**    **Perf. 14**
1539 A406 10e Fatima    .45 .20
1540 A406 27e Sameiro    2.00 1.10
1541 A406 33.50e Lisbon    2.25 1.00
     a.   Min. sheet, 2 each #1539-1541   9.00 9.00
     Nos. 1539-1541 (3)   4.70 2.30

Tejo Estuary
Nature Reserve
Birds — A407

**1982, June 11**    **Perf. 11½x12**
1542 A407 10e Dunlin    .50 .20
1543 A407 19e Red-crested pochard    1.60 .55
1544 A407 27e Greater flamingo    2.00 .80
1545 A407 33.50e Black-winged stilt    2.10 .90
     Nos. 1542-1545 (4)   6.20 2.45

PHILEXFRANCE '82 Stamp Exhibition, Paris, June 11-21.

TB Bacillus Centenary — A408

**1982, July 27**    **Perf. 12½x11½**
1546 A408 27e Koch    1.50 1.10
1547 A408 33.50e Virus, lungs    1.60 1.10

Don't Drink and Drive! — A409

**1982, Sept. 22**    **Perf. 12**
1548 A409 10e multicolored    .55 .20

Boeing 747 A410

Lubrapex '82 Stamp Exhibition (Historic Flights): 10e, South Atlantic crossing, 1922. 19e, South Atlantic night crossing, 1927. 33.50e, Lisbon-Rio de Janeiro discount fare flights, 1960-1967. 50e, Portugal-Brazil service, 10th anniv.

**1982, Oct. 15**    **Perf. 12x11½**
1549 A410 10e Fairey III D    .30 .20
1550 A410 19e Dornier DO MK2    1.25 .70
1551 A410 33.50e DC-7C    1.90 1.00
1552 A410 50e shown    2.40 1.00
     a.   Souv. sheet of 4, #1549-1552   6.00 6.00
     Nos. 1549-1552 (4)   5.85 2.60

Marques de Pombal, Statesman, 200th Anniv. of Death — A411

**1982, Nov. 24**    **Litho.**    **Perf. 12x11½**
1553 A411 10e multicolored    .50 .20

---

25th Anniv. of European Economic Community A402

**1982, Feb. 24**    **Perf. 12x11½**
1527 A402 27e multi    1.25 .65
     a.   Souvenir sheet of 4   5.00 5.00

Tile Type of 1981

Designs: No. 1528, Italo-Flemish pattern, 17th cent. No. 1529, Oriental fabric pattern altar frontal, 17th cent. No. 1530, Greek cross, 1630-1640. No. 1531, Blue and white design, Mother of God Convent, Lisbon, 1670.

**1982**    **Litho.**    **Perf. 12x11½**
1528 A391 10e multi    .75 .20
     a.   Miniature sheet of 6   5.00 5.00
1529 A391 10e multi    .75 .20
     a.   Miniature sheet of 6   4.50 4.50
1530 A391 10e multi    .75 .20
     a.   Miniature sheet of 6   4.50 4.50
1531 A391 10e red & blue    .75 .20
     a.   Souv. sheet of 4, #1528-1531   4.50 4.50
     b.   Miniature sheet of 6   3.00 .80

Issued: No. 1528, Mar. 24; No. 1529, June 11; No. 1530, Sept. 22; No. 1531, Dec. 15.

A404

Major Sporting Events of 1982: 27e, Lisbon Sail. 33.50e, 25th Roller-hockey Championships, Lisbon and Barcelos, May 1-16. 50e, Intl 470 Class World Championships, Cascais Bay. 75e, Espana '82 World Cup Soccer.

**1982, Mar. 24**    **Perf. 12x12½**
1532 A403 27e multi    1.50 .80
1533 A403 33.50e multi    2.00 1.10
1634 A403 50e multi    3.00 1.25
1635 A403 75e multi    4.75 1.50
     Nos. 1532-1535 (4)   11.25 4.65

**1982, Apr. 14**    **Litho.**    **Perf. 11½x12**
1536 A404 10e Phone, 1882    .45 .20
1537 A404 27e 1887    1.25 1.00

Telephone centenary.

Europa 1982 A405

**1982, May 3**    **Perf. 12x11½**
1538 A405 33.50e multi    2.00 .75
     a.   Miniature sheet of 4   19.00 19.00

Embassy of King Manuel to Pope Leo X, 1514.

Visit of Pope John Paul II — A406

Designs: Pope John Paul and cathedrals.

---

125th Anniv. of Portuguese Railroads — A397

Designs: Locomotives.

**1981, Oct. 28**    **Litho.**    **Perf. 12x11½**
1512 A397 8.50e Dom Luis, 1862    .65 .20
1513 A397 19e Pacific 500, 1925    2.00 .90
1514 A397 27e ALCO 1500, 1948    2.10 1.00
1515 A397 33.50e BB 2600 ALSTHOM, '74    2.75 .85
     Nos. 1512-1515 (4)   7.50 2.95

Pearier Pump Fire Engine, 1856 — A398

**1981, Nov. 18**    **Litho.**    **Perf. 12x12½**
1516 A398 7e shown    .45 .20
1517 A398 8.50e Ford, 1927    .65 .20
1518 A398 27e Renault, 1914    2.25 .95
1519 A398 33.50e Snorkel, Ford 1978    2.90 .90
     Nos. 1516-1519 (4)   6.25 2.25

A399

A400

Christmas: Clay creches.

**1981, Dec. 16**    **Perf. 12½x12**
1520 A399 7e multi    .55 .30
1521 A399 8.50e multi    .75 .20
1522 A399 27e multi    2.25 1.40
     Nos. 1520-1522 (3)   3.55 1.90

**1982, Jan. 20**    **Litho.**    **Perf. 12½x12**
1523 A400 8.50e With animals    .40 .20
1524 A400 27e Building church    2.00 1.40

800th birth anniv. of St. Francis of Assisi.

Centenary of Figueira da Foz A401

**1982, Feb. 24**    **Litho.**    **Perf. 13½**
1525 A401 10e St. Catherine Fort    .55 .20
1526 A401 19e Tagus Bridge, ships    1.60 .85

---

1497 A391 8.50e multi    .75 .20
     a.   Miniature sheet of 6   4.50 4.50
     b.   Souv. sheet of 4, #1494-1497 (4)   5.00 5.00
     Nos. 1494-1497 (4)   3.00 .80

Issued: #1494, 3/16; #1495, 6/13; #1496, 8/28; #1497, 12/16. See #1528-1531, 1563-1566, 1593-1596, 1617-1620.

Perdigueiro A392

**1981, Mar. 16**    **Perf. 12**
1498 A392 7e Cao de agua    .45 .20
1499 A392 8.50e Serra de aires    .45 .20
1500 A392 15e shown    .80 .20
1501 A392 22e Podengo    1.10 .65
1502 A392 25.50e Castro laboreiro    1.75 1.00
1503 A392 33.50e Serra da estrela    2.25 .65
     Nos. 1498-1503 (6)   6.80 2.90

Portuguese Kennel Club, 50th anniversary.

Workers and Rainbow A393

**Europa Issue**

**1981, Apr. 30**    **Litho.**    **Perf. 12x12½**
1504 A393 8.50e shown    .30 .20
1505 A393 25.50e Rainbow, demonstration    1.40 .85

International Workers' Day.

Dancer in National Costume — A394

**1981, May 11**    **Perf. 13½**
1506 A394 22e shown    1.25 .50
1507 A394 48e Painted boat, horiz.    2.75 1.25
     a.   Souv. sheet, 2 ea #1506-1507   19.00 19.00

St. Anthony Writing A395

St. Anthony of Lisbon, 750th Anniversary of Death: 70e, Blessing people.

**1981, June 13**    **Perf. 12x11½**
1508 A395 8.50e multi    .45 .20
1509 A395 70e multi    3.50 1.75

500th Anniv. of King Joao II A396

**1981, Aug. 28**    **Perf. 12x11½**
1510 A396 8.50e shown    .45 .20
1511 A396 27e Joao II leading army    2.40 .95

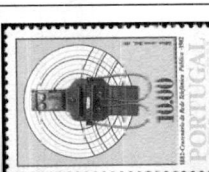

**1983, Jan. 5**
1554 A412 10e Ships .50 .20

75th Anniv. of Port Authority of Lisbon — A412

*Perf. 12½*

**1983, Jan. 5**
1555 A413 27e multicolored 1.50 .70

French Alliance Centenary A413

*Perf. 12x11½*

**1983, Jan. 28**
1556 A414 10e multicolored 1.60 1.00

Export Effort A414

**1983, Feb. 23  Litho.    Perf. 11½x12**
1557 A415 10e blue & multi .50 .20
1558 A415 33.50e It brown & multi 1.60 1.00

World Communications Year — A415

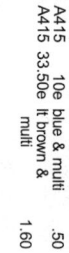

**1983, Feb. 23    Perf. 13½**
1559 A416 12.50e multi

| | | |
|---|---|---|
| 1560 A416 25e Sailor, 1845. | .55 | .20 |
| 1561 A416 30e Sergeant, 1900. | 1.40 | .35 |
| 1562 A416 37.50e Midshipman, 1892, Co- mandante Joao Belo | 1.60 | .50 |
| a. Bklt. pane of 4, #1559-1562 | 2.00 | .70 |

Midshipman, 1782; Vasco da Gama; Estefania; Sailor, 1845; Adamastor; Midshipman, 1892, Co- mandante Joao Belo

See Nos. 1559-1592.

*Perf. 13½*

**1983**
1563 A391 12.50e multi .80 .20
1564 A391 12.50e multi .80 .25
a. Miniature sheet of 6 5.25 5.25
1565 A391 12.50e multi .80 .20
a. Miniature sheet of 6 5.00 5.00

No. 1563, Hunting scene, 1680. No. 1564, Birds, 18th cent. No. 1565, Flowers and Birds, 18th cent. No. 1566, Figurative tile, 18th cent.

*Perf. 12x11½*

Tile Type of 1981

a. Miniature sheet of 6 5.00 5.00
a. Miniature sheet of 6 .80 .20

---

**1983, May 16**
1574 A419 30e multi 2.25 .65

European Conference of Ministers of Transport — A419

**1983, July 29    Litho.    Perf. 12x11½**

| | | |
|---|---|---|
| 1575 A420 12.50e Sea wolf | .85 | .20 |
| 1576 A420 30e Dolphin | 2.00 | .45 |
| 1577 A420 37.50e Killer whale | 2.75 | 1.10 |
| 1578 A420 80e Humpback whale | 4.50 | 1.00 |
| a. Souv. sheet of 4, #1575-1578 | 10.00 | 10.10 |

Endangered Sea Mammals — A420

Nos. 1575-1578 (4) 10.10 2.75

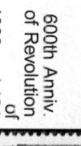

BRASILIANA '83 Intl. Stamp Exhibition, Rio de Janeiro, July 29-Aug. 7.

600th Anniv. of Revolution of 1383 — A421

**1983, May 5    Litho.**
1573 A418 37.50e multi 2.75 .60
a. Souvenir sheet of 4 20.00 20.00

Antonio Egas Moniz (1874-1955), Cerebral Angiography and Pre-frontal Leucotomy Pioneer — A418

**Europa Issue**

| | | |
|---|---|---|
| 1567 A417 11e multi | .55 | .20 |
| 1568 A417 12.50e multi | .75 | .20 |
| 1569 A417 25e multi | 1.50 | .55 |
| 1570 A417 30e multi | 2.25 | .85 |
| 1571 A417 37.50e multi | 2.25 | .80 |
| 1572 A417 40e multi | .80 | |
| a. Souv. sheet of 6, #1567- 1572 | 9.30 | 3.15 |

Portuguese Discoveries and Renaissance Europe: 11e, Helmet, 16th cent. 12.50e, Astrolabe. 25e, Ships, Flemish tapestry. 30e, Column capital, 12th cent. 37.50e, Hour glass. 40e, Chinese panel painting.

Nos. 1567-1572 (6) 13.00 3.00

**1983, Apr. 6**

17th European Arts and Sciences Exhibition, Lisbon — A417

PORTUGAL EXPO XVII

1566 A391 12.50e multi .80 .20
a. Miniature sheet of 6 4.50 4.50
b. Souv. sheet of 4, #1563-1566 3.20 .80

Issued: No. 1563, Mar. 16; Nos. 1563-1566 (4) No. 1564, June 16; No. 1565, Oct. 19; No. 1566, Nov. 23.

---

**1984, Feb. 5    Litho.    Perf. 13½**

| | | |
|---|---|---|
| 1589 A416 16e multi | .50 | .20 |
| 1590 A416 35e multi | 2.00 | .55 |
| 1591 A416 40e multi | 1.75 | .60 |
| 1592 A416 51e multi | 2.40 | .85 |
| a. Bklt. pane of 4, #1589-1592 | 6.65 | 2.20 |

Air Force Dress Uniforms and Planes: 16e, Hawker Hurricane II, 1943. 35e, 1960; Republic F-84G Thunderjet. 40e, Paratrooper; 1966; 2502 Nord Noratlas, 1960. 51e, 1966; Corsair II, 1982.

Nos. 1589-1592 (4)

Military Type of 1983

**1984, Jan. 18    Litho.    Perf. 12x11½**

| | | |
|---|---|---|
| 1585 A424 16e Siberian tigers | 1.60 | .20 |
| 1586 A424 16e White rhinoceros | 1.60 | .20 |
| 1587 A424 16e Damalisco Al- bifronte | 1.60 | .20 |
| 1588 A424 16e Cheetahs | 1.60 | .20 |
| a. Strip of 4, #1585-1588 | 6.50 | 2.50 |

Lisbon Zoo Centenary — A424

**1984**
1593 A391 16e multi .85 .20
1594 A391 16e multi .85 .25
a. Miniature sheet of 6 5.25 5.25
1595 A391 16e multi .85 .20
a. Miniature sheet of 6 5.00 5.00
1596 A391 16e multi .85 .20
a. Miniature sheet of 6 5.00 5.00
b. Souv. sheet of 4, #1593-1596 3.40 .80

Design: 16e, Royal arms, 19th cent. No. 1594, Pombal Palace wall tile, 19th cent. No. 1595, Facade covering, 19th cent. No. 1596, Grasshoppers, by Rafael Bordalo Pinheiro, 19th cent.

Tile Type of 1983

Issued: No. 1593, Mar. 8; No. 1594, July 18; Nos. 1593-1596 (4) No. 1595, Aug. 3; No. 1596, Oct. 17.

**1984, Mar. 8    Litho.    Perf. 12x11½**

---

**1983, Nov. 23    Perf. 12½**
1583 A423 12.50e multi .65 .20
1584 A423 30e multi 2.25 .85

Stained Glass Windows, Monastery at Batalha: 12.50e, Adoration of the Magi. 30e, Flight to Egypt.

Christmas 1983 — A423

**1983, Nov. 9    Litho.    Perf. 12x11½**
1581 A422 16e multicolored .75 .20
1582 A422 51e multicolored 1.75 .85

Designs: 16e, Bartolomeu Lourenco de Gusmao, Passarola flying machine. 51e, Montgolfier Balloon, first flight.

First Manned Balloon Flight A422

**1983, Sept. 14    Perf. 13½**
1579 A421 12.50e Death of Joao Fernandes Andeiro .75 .20
1580 A421 30e Rebellion 2.50 1.10

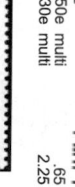

PORTUGAL EUROPA 1984

**1984, May 2    Perf. 12x11½**
1001 A427 51e multicolored 2.50 1.00
a. Souvenir sheet of 4 17.50 15.00

Europa (1959-84) A427

PORTUGAL 16.

**1984, May 9    Litho.    Perf. 12x11½**

| | | |
|---|---|---|
| 1602 A428 16e multicolored | .65 | .20 |
| 1603 A428 40e multicolored | 2.00 | .55 |
| 1604 A428 51e multicolored | 2.75 | .95 |
| 1605 A428 66e multicolored | 3.25 | 1.10 |
| a. Souv. sheet of 4, #1602-1605 | 9.15 | 2.75 |

Paintings: 16e, Nun, 15th cent. 40e, St. John, by Master of the Retable of Santiago, 16th cent. 51e, View of Lisbon, 17th cent. 66e, Cabeca de Jovem, by Domingos Sesqueira, 19th cent.

LUBRAPEX '84 and Natl. Early Art Museum Centenary — A428

Nos. 1602-1605 (4) 9.00 9.00

**1984, Apr. 3    Perf. 13½**
1597 A425 36e multicolored 1.60 .50
1598 A425 40e multicolored 1.75 .65
1599 A425 51e multicolored 2.25 .85
Nos. 1597-1599 (3) 5.60 2.00

Events: 40e, World Food Day. 51e, 15th Rehabilitation Intl. World Congress, Lisbon, June 4-8, vert.

**1984, Apr. 25**
1600 A426 16e multicolored 1.10 .20

April 25th Revolution, 10th Anniv. — A426

25th Lisbon Intl. Fair, May 9-13 A425

PORTUGAL 35.00

**1984 Summer Olympics A429**

**1984, June 5    Souvenir Sheet**

| | | |
|---|---|---|
| 1606 A429 35e Fencing | 1.50 | .30 |
| 1607 A429 40e Gymnastics | 2.00 | .55 |
| 1608 A429 51e Running | 2.75 | .95 |
| 1609 A429 80e Pole vault | 3.00 | 1.00 |
| Nos. 1606-1609 (4) | 9.25 | 2.80 |

1610 A429 100e Hurdles 7.00 7.00

## Historical Events — A430

Designs: 16e, Gil Eanes, explorer who reached west coast of Africa, 1434. 51e, King Peter I of Brazil and IV of Portugal.

**1984, Sept. 24**   **Perf. 12x11½**
| | | | | |
|---|---|---|---|---|
| 1611 | A430 | 16e multicolored | .45 | .20 |
| 1612 | A430 | 51e multicolored | 2.40 | .90 |

See Brazil No. 1954.

## Infantry Grenadier, 1740 — A431

**1985, Jan. 23   Litho.   Perf. 13½**
| | | | | |
|---|---|---|---|---|
| 1613 | A431 | 20e shown | .50 | .20 |
| 1614 | A431 | 46e 5th Cavalry Regiment Officer, 1810 | 2.40 | .55 |
| 1615 | A431 | 60e Artillery Corporal, 1892 | 2.50 | .70 |
| 1616 | A431 | 100e Engineering Soldier, 1985 | 3.00 | 1.10 |
| a. | | Bkit. pane of 4, #1613-1616 | 8.50 | |
| | | Nos. 1617-1620 (4) | 8.40 | 2.55 |

## Tile Type of 1981

Designs: No. 1617, Tile from entrance hall of Lisbon's Faculdade de Letras, by Jorge Barradas, 20th cent.; No, 1618, Explorer and sailing ship, detail from tile panel by Maria Keil, Avenida Infante Santo, Lisbon; No. 1619, Profile and key, detail from a 20th century tile mural by Querubim Lapa; No. 1620, Geometric designs and flowers, by Manuel Cargaleiro.

**1985   Litho.   Perf. 12x11½**
| | | | | |
|---|---|---|---|---|
| 1017 | A391 | 27e multicolored | | .20 |
| 1618 | A391 | 20e multicolored | .85 | .20 |
| 1619 | A391 | 20e multicolored | .85 | .20 |
| 1620 | A391 | 20e multicolored | .85 | .20 |
| a. | | Miniature sheet of 6 | 5.00 | 5.00 |
| b. | | Souv. sheet of 4, #1617-1620 | 5.00 | 5.00 |
| | | Nos. 1617-1620 (4) | 3.40 | .80 |

Issued: Nu, 1617, Feb. 13; No. 1617, Nov. 15.

## Kiosks — A432

**1985, Mar. 19   Litho.   Perf. 11½x12**
| | | | | |
|---|---|---|---|---|
| 1621 | A432 | 20e Green kiosk | 1.00 | .20 |
| 1622 | A432 | 20e Red kiosk | 1.00 | .20 |
| 1623 | A432 | 20e Gray kiosk | 1.00 | .20 |
| 1624 | A432 | 20e Blue kiosk | 1.00 | .20 |
| a. | | Strip of 4, #1621-1624 | 6.00 | |

## 25th Anniv., European Free Trade Association — A433

**1985, Apr. 10   Litho.   Perf. 12x11½**
| | | | | |
|---|---|---|---|---|
| 1625 | A433 | 46e Flags of members | 1.40 | .55 |

## Intl. Youth Year A434

**1985, Apr. 10   Litho.**
| | | | | |
|---|---|---|---|---|
| 1626 | A434 | 60e Heads of boy and girl | 1.75 | .80 |

## Europa 1985-Music A435

**1985, May 6   Litho.   Perf. 11½x12**
| | | | | |
|---|---|---|---|---|
| 1627 | A435 | 60e Woman playing tambourine | 1.00 | |
| a. | | Souvenir sheet of 4 | 4.00 | 6.00 |
| | | | 24.00 | |

## Historic Anniversaries — A436

20e, King John I at the Battle of Aljubarrota, 1385. 46e, Queen Leonor (1458-1525) founding the Caldas da Rainha Hospital. 60e, Cartographer Pedro Reinel, earliest Portuguese map, c. 1483.

**1985, July 5   Litho.   Perf. 12x11½**
| | | | | |
|---|---|---|---|---|
| 1628 | A436 | 20e multicolored | .65 | .20 |
| 1629 | A436 | 46e multicolored | 2.10 | .70 |
| 1630 | A436 | 60e multicolored | 2.25 | .95 |
| | | Nos. 1628-1630 (3) | 5.00 | 1.85 |

See Nos. 1678-1680.

## Traditional Architecture A437

**1985-89   Litho.   Perf. 12**
| | | | | |
|---|---|---|---|---|
| 1631 | A437 | 50c Saloia, Estremadura | .20 | .20 |
| 1632 | A437 | 1e Beira interior | .20 | .20 |
| 1633 | A437 | 1.50e Ribatejo | .20 | |
| 1634 | A437 | 2.50e Transmontanas | .20 | |
| 1635 | A437 | 10e Minho and Douro Litoral | .20 | |
| 1636 | A437 | 20e Farm house, Minho | .20 | |
| 1637 | A437 | 22.50e Alentejo | .30 | .20 |
| 1638 | A437 | 25e African Sitio, Algarve | .30 | |
| 1639 | A437 | 27e Beira Interior | .35 | .20 |
| 1640 | A437 | 29e Hill country | .45 | |
| 1641 | A437 | 30e Algarve | .45 | |
| 1642 | A437 | 40e Beira Interior | .45 | |
| 1643 | A437 | 50e Private home, Beira Litoral | .75 | .20 |
| 1644 | A437 | 55e Tras-os-Montes | .75 | .20 |
| 1645 | A437 | 60e Beira Litoral | 1.00 | .25 |
| 1646 | A437 | 70e Estremadura Sul and Alentejo | 1.10 | |
| 1647 | A437 | 80e Estremadura | 1.10 | .25 |
| 1648 | A437 | 90e Minho | 1.10 | .35 |
| 1649 | A437 | 100e Adobe Monte, Alentejo | 1.25 | .35 |
| 1650 | A437 | 500e Algarve | 6.25 | .75 |
| | | Nos. 1631-1650 (20) | 17.60 | 5.10 |

Issued: 20e, 25e, 50e, 100e, 8/20; 2.50e, 22.50e, 80e, 90e, 3/10/86; 10e, 40e, 60e, 70e, 3/6/87; 1.50e, 27e, 30e, 55e, 3/15/88; 50c, 1e, 29e, 500e, 3/8/89.

## Aquilino Ribeiro (1885-1963) Author — A438

46e, Fernando Pessoa (1888-1935), poet.

**1985, Oct. 2   Litho.   Perf. 12**
| | | | | |
|---|---|---|---|---|
| 1651 | A438 | 20e multicolored | .65 | .20 |
| 1652 | A438 | 46e multicolored | 1.75 | .60 |

## Natl. Parks and Reserves A439

**1985, Oct. 25**
| | | | | |
|---|---|---|---|---|
| 1653 | A439 | 20e Berlenga Island | .45 | .20 |
| 1654 | A439 | 40e Estrela Mountain Chain | 1.60 | .55 |
| 1655 | A439 | 46e Boquilobo Marsh | 2.40 | .80 |
| 1656 | A439 | 80e Formosa Lagoon | 2.50 | .85 |
| | | Nos. 1653-1656 (4) | 6.95 | 2.40 |

### Souvenir Sheet

| | | | | |
|---|---|---|---|---|
| 1657 | A439 | 100e St. Jacinto Dunes | 5.50 | 2.25 |

"ITALIA '85."

## Christmas 1985 — A440

Illuminated codices from The Prayer Times Book, Book of King Manuel, 1517-1538.

**1985, Nov. 15   Litho.   Perf. 11½x12**
| | | | | |
|---|---|---|---|---|
| 1658 | A440 | 20e The Nativity | .50 | .20 |
| 1659 | A440 | 46e Adoration of the Magi | 1.75 | .65 |

## Postrider A441

**1985, Dec. 13   Litho.   Perf. 13½**
| | | | | |
|---|---|---|---|---|
| 1660 | A441 | A(22.50e) lt yel grn & dp yel grn | .75 | .20 |

See No. 1938 for another stamp with postrider inscribed "Serie A."

## Flags of EEC Member Nations A442

Design: 57.50e, Map of EEC, flags.

**1986, Jan. 7   Litho.   Perf. 12**
| | | | | |
|---|---|---|---|---|
| 1661 | A442 | 20e multi | .60 | .20 |
| 1662 | A442 | 57.50e multi | 2.25 | .80 |
| a. | | Souv. sheet, 2 ea #1661-1662 | 6.00 | 6.00 |

Admission of Portugal and Spain to the European Economic Community, Jan. 1. See Spain Nos. 2463-2466.

No. 1662a contains 2 alternating pairs of Nos. 1661-1662.

## Castles A443

**1986, Feb. 18   Litho.   Perf. 12**
| | | | | |
|---|---|---|---|---|
| 1663 | A443 | 22.50e Beja | .85 | .20 |
| a. | | Booklet pane of 4 | 3.50 | |
| 1664 | A443 | 22.50e Feira | .85 | .20 |
| a. | | Booklet pane of 4 | 3.50 | |

**1986, Apr. 10**
| | | | | |
|---|---|---|---|---|
| 1665 | A443 | 22.50e Guimaraes | .85 | .20 |
| a. | | Booklet pane of 4 | 3.50 | |
| 1666 | A443 | 22.50e Braganca | .85 | .20 |
| a. | | Booklet pane of 4 | 3.50 | |

**1986, Sept. 18**
| | | | | |
|---|---|---|---|---|
| 1667 | A443 | 22.50e Montemor-o-Velho | .85 | .20 |
| a. | | Booklet pane of 4 | 3.50 | |
| 1668 | A443 | 22.50e Belmonte | .85 | .20 |
| a. | | Booklet pane of 6 | 5.10 | 1.20 |
| | | Nos. 1663-1668 (6) | | |

See Nos. 1688-1695, 1723-1726.

## Intl. Peace Year A445

**1986, Feb. 18   Litho.   Perf. 12**
| | | | | |
|---|---|---|---|---|
| 1669 | A445 | 75e multicolored | 2.50 | 1.00 |

## Automobile Centenary — A446

**1986, Apr. 10   Litho.   Perf. 12**
| | | | | |
|---|---|---|---|---|
| 1670 | | 22.50e 1886 Benz | 1.10 | .20 |
| 1671 | | 22.50e 1886 Daimler | 1.10 | .20 |
| | A446 | Pair, #1670-1671 | 2.25 | 2.25 |

## Europa 1900 A447

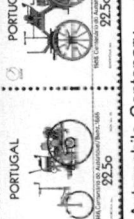

**1986, May 5   Litho.**
| | | | | |
|---|---|---|---|---|
| 1672 | A447 | 68.50e Shad | 3.75 | 1.00 |
| a. | | Souvenir sheet of 4 | 24.00 | 6.00 |

## Horse Breeds A448

**1986, May 22   Litho.**
| | | | | |
|---|---|---|---|---|
| 1673 | A448 | 22.50e Alter | .60 | .20 |
| 1674 | A448 | 47.50e Lusitano | 1.75 | .70 |
| 1675 | A448 | 52.50e Garrano | 2.40 | .90 |
| 1676 | A448 | 68.50e Sorraia | 2.75 | .95 |
| | | Nos. 1673-1676 (4) | 7.50 | 2.75 |

PORTUGAL

## Souvenir Sheet

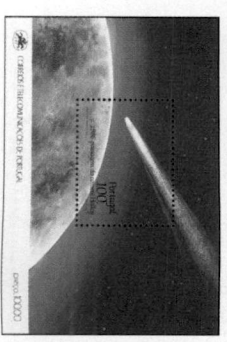

**Halley's Comet — A449**

**Anniversaries Type of 1985**

**1986, June 24**
1677 A449 100e multi .......... 12.00 8.00

**1986, Aug. 28**
1678 A436 22.50e multi ........ .55 .20
1679 A436 52.50e multi ........ 1.60 .70
1680 A436 52.50e multi ........ 1.60 .70
Nos. 1678-1680 (3) ............ 3.75 1.60

Designs: 22.50e, Diogo Cao, explorer, expedition. No. 1679, Manuel Passos, Corinthian column. No. 1680, Joao Baptista Ribeiro, painter, Oporto Academy director, c. 1836, and musicians.

Diogo Cao's voyages, 500th anniv. Academies of Fine Art, 150th anniv.

**Natl. Guard, 75th Anniv. — A451**

**Order of Engineers, 50th Anniv. — A452**

**Stamp Day — A450**

**1986, Oct. 24 Litho.**
1681 A450 22.50e multi ........ .85 .20
1682 A451 47.50e multi ........ 1.50 .65
1683 A452 52.50e multi ........ 1.60 .70
Nos. 1681-1683 (3) ............ 3.95 1.55

No. 1681, Postal card, 100th anniv.

**Watermills A453**

**1986, Nov. 7**
1684 A453 22.50e Duoro ........ .50 .20
1685 A453 47.50e Coimbra ...... 1.25 .85
1686 A453 52.50e Gerez ........ 1.75 .80
1687 A453 90e Braga ........... 2.50 .90
a. Souv. sheet of 4, #1684-1687 6.00 2.75

LUBRAPEX '86 #1687a issued Nov. 21.

---

## Castle Type of 1986

**1987-88 Litho.**
1688 A443 25e Silves .......... .85 .20
1689 A443 25e Evora Monte ..... .85 .20
1690 A443 25e Leiria .......... .85 .20
1691 A443 25e Trancoso ........ .85 .20
1692 A443 25e St. George ...... .90 .20
1693 A443 25e Marvao ......... .90 .20
1694 A443 27e Fernando's Walls
of Oporto .................... 3.50 .20
  a. Booklet pane of 4 ........ 3.50
1695 A443 27e Almourol ........ 3.50 .25
  a. Booklet pane of 4 ........ 3.50
1696 A443 27e Almourol ........ 6.90 1.70

Issued: #1688-1689, 1/16; #1690-1691, 4/10; #1692-1693, 9/15; #1694-1695, 1/19/88.

**Natl. Tourism Organization, 75th Anniv. — A454**

**1987, Feb. 10 Litho.**
1696 A454 25e Beach houses,
Tocha ........................ .50 .20
1697 A454 57e Boats, Espinho .. 2.10 .90
1698 A454 98e Chafariz Fountain, Arraioles ..................... 2.75 .85
Nos. 1696-1698 (3) ........... 5.35 1.95

**European Nature Conservation Year — A455**

**1987, Mar. 20 Perf. 12x12½**
1699 A455 25e shown ........... .50 .20
1700 A455 57e Hands, flower,
map .......................... 1.50 .75
1701 A455 74.50e Hands, star, rainbow ....................... 2.50 .85
Nos. 1699-1701 (3) ........... 4.50 1.80

**Europa 1987 A456**

**1987, May 5 Perf. 12**
1702 A456 74.50e multi ........ 3.75 1.00
a. Souvenir sheet of 4 ........ 22.50 7.50

Modern architecture: Bank Borges and Irmao Agency, 1986, Vila do Conde.

A457

---

## Lighthouses A458

**1987, June 12 Perf. 11½x12**
1703 A457 25e Aveiro ......... .85 .20
1704 A457 25e Berlenga ....... .85 .20
1705 A457 25e Cape Mondego ... .85 .20
1706 A457 25e Cape St.
Vincente ..................... .85 .20
a. Strip of 4, #1703-1706 .... 4.50

A458

**1987, Aug. 27 Litho.**
1707 A458 74.50e multi ....... 1.75 .75

Amadeo de Souza-Cardoso (1887-1919), painter.

**Portuguese Royal Library, Rio de Janeiro, 150th anniv. A459**

**1987, Aug. 27 Perf. 12**
1708 A459 125e multicolored .. 2.75 1.00

**Paper Currency of Portugal, 300th Anniv. A460**

**1987, Aug. 27 Perf. 12x11½**
1709 A460 100e multicolored .. 2.50 .75

**Voyages of Bartolomeu Dias (d. 1499), 500th Anniv. — A461**

**1987, Aug. 27 Perf. 12x11½**
1710 A461 25e Departing from Lisbon, 1487 ................... .90 .20
1711 A461 25e Discovering the African Coast, 1488 .......... .90 .20
a. A461 Pair, #1710-1711 ..... 2.00 2.00

No. 1711a has continuous design. See Nos. 1721-1722.

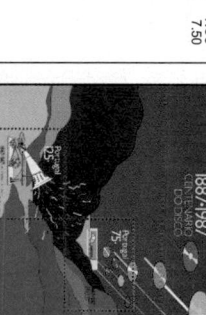

## Souvenir Sheet

**1987, Oct. 9 Litho.**
1712 A462 75e multi .......... 9.00 7.50
a. 75e Compact-disc player ... 3.25 2.90
b. 125e Gramophone ........... 5.25 4.50

**Phonograph Record, 100th Anniv. — A462**

---

**Christmas A463**

**1987, Nov. 6 Perf. 12**
1713 A463 25e Angels, magi,
tree ......................... .60 .20
1714 A463 57e Friendship circle .................... 1.60 .70
1715 A463 74.50e Santa riding dove ......................... 2.00 1.00
a. Souv. sheet of 3, #1713-1715 ... 5.00 5.00
Nos. 1713-1715 (3) .......... 4.20 1.90

Various children's drawings. Intl. Year of the Child emblem.

**Journey of Pero da Covilha to the East, 500th Anniv. A465**

**1988, Feb. 3 Perf. 12**
1720 A465 105e multi ......... 2.50 .95

**World Wildlife Fund A464**

Lynx, Lynx pardina.

**1988, Feb. 3 Litho. Perf. 12**
1716 A464 27e Stalking ....... 1.00 .20
1717 A464 27e Carrying prey .. 1.00 .20
1718 A464 27e Two adults ..... 1.00 .20
1719 A464 27e Adult, young ... 1.00 .20
a. Strip of 4, Nos. 1716-1719 6.00 6.00

Printed in a continuous design.

**Bartolomeu Dias Type of 1987**

**1988, Feb. 3**
1721 A461 27e multi .......... .85 .25
1722 A461 27e multi .......... .85 .25
a. Bkt. pane of 4, Nos. 1710-1711, 1721-1722 ............ 6.00
b. Pair, #1721-1722 .......... 1.75 1.75

No. 1722b has continuous design.

Discovery of the link between the Atlantic and Indian Oceans by Dias, 500th Anniv.: No. 1721, Tidal wave, ship. No. 1722, Henricus Martelus Germanus's map (1489), picturing the African coast and linking the two oceans.

**Castle Type of 1986**

**1988, Mar. 15 Litho. Perf. 12**
1723 A443 27e Vila Nova de
Cerveira ..................... .85 .25
1724 A443 27e Palmela ........ .85 .20
a. Bkt. pane of 4 ............ 3.50
1725 A443 27e Chaves ......... .85 .20
1726 A443 27e Penedono ....... .85 .20
a. Bkt. pane of 4 ............ 3.50
b. Bkt. pane of 4 ............ 3.40 .80
Nos. 1723-1726 (4)

**Europa 1988 A466**

**1988, Apr. 21 Litho. Perf. 12**
1735 A466 80e multi .......... 7.00 1.00
a. Souv. sheet of 4 .......... 22.50 7.50

Transportation: Mail coach, Lisbon-Oporto route, 1855-1864.

## Souvenir Sheet

French Revolution, 200th
Anniv. — A479

**1989, July 7**    Litho.    *Perf. 11½x12*
1786 A479 250e Drummer    8.00 6.50

No. 1786 has multicolored inscribed margin
picturing the PHILEXFRANCE '89 emblem
and the storming of the Bastille.

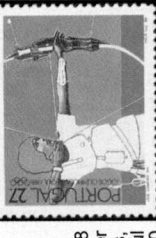

Natl.
Palaces
A480

**1989, Oct. 18**   Litho.   *Perf. 12*
1787 A480 29e Ajuda, Lisbon,   .35   .20
   and King Luiz I
1788 A480 60e Queluz    1.40   .80

Death cent. of King Luiz.

Exhibition
Emblem and
Wildflowers
A481

**1989, Nov. 17**    Litho.
1789 A481 29e *Armeria*    .40   .20
   *santolina im-*
1790 A481 60e *pressa*    1.10   .60
1791 A481 87e *Linaria lamarckii*   1.60   .85
1792 A481 100e *Limonium mul-*   2.25 1.10
   *tiforum*
  a.   Bkt. pane of 4, #1789-1792   5.50 2.75
     1789-1792 (4)    5.35 2.75

World Stamp Expo '89, Washington, DC.

Portuguese
Faience,
17th Cent.
A482

**1990, Jan. 24**    Litho.    *Perf. 12x11½*
1793 A482 33e shown    .50   .25
1794 A482 33e Nobleman    .50   .25
   (plate)
1795 A482 35e Urn    .70   .25
1796 A482 60e Fish (pitcher)   1.25   .70
1797 A482 60e Crown, shield   1.25   .70
   (plate)
1798 A482 60e Lidded bowl   1.25   .70
  a.   Bkt. pane of 6,   5.45 2.85
     Nos. 1793-1798 (6)

## Souvenir Sheet

*Perf. 12*
1799 A482 250e Plate    6.00 5.00

No. 1799 contains one 52x45mm. stamp.
See Nos. 1829-1835, 1890-1896.

---

**1990, Sept. 21**

Paintings by Portuguese artists: 32e, *Costa Pinheiro.* 60e, *Paula Rego.* 95e, *Jose De Guimaraes.*

1763 A469 32e multicolored    .40   .20
1764 A469 60e multicolored   1.00   .55
1765 A469 95e multicolored   1.75   .85
  a.   Min. sheet of 3, #1763-1765   5.50 5.00
  b.   Min. sheet of 6, #1760-1765   9.00 9.00
     Nos. 1763-1765 (3)    3.15 1.60

A475

**1989, Feb. 15**    Litho.    *Perf. 12*
1772 A474 29e multi    .50   .20
  a.   Bkt. pane of 8    4.00
1773 A474 60e With love   1.00   .50
  a.   Bkt. pane of 8    8.00

A474

Special occasions.

**1989, Mar. 8**    Litho.    *Perf. 11½x12*
1774 A475 60e multi    1.25   .60

European Parliament elections.

Europa
1989
A476

Children's toys.

**1989, Apr. 26**    Litho.    *Perf. 12*
1775 A476 80e Top    1.75 1.00

## Souvenir Sheet

1776    Sheet of 4, 2 each   24.00 6.00
   #1775, 1776a    2.75 1.25
  a.   A476 80e top tops

Surface
Transportation,
Lisbon — A477

29e, Carris Co. elevated railway, Bica Street. 65e, Carris electric tram. 87e, Carmo Elevator, Santa Justa Street. 100e, Carris doubledecker bus. 250e, Transtejo Co. riverboat *Cacilheiro,* horiz.

**1989, May 22**    Litho.
1777 A477 29e multi    .50   .20
1778 A477 65e multi    1.60   .75
1779 A477 87e multi    1.75 1.00
1780 A477 100e multi    2.25   .75
  a.   Bkt. pane of 4,   6.10 2.70
     Nos. 1777-1780 (4)

## Souvenir Sheet

1781 A477 250e multi    7.50 6.50

Windmills
A478

**1989, June 14**    Litho.    .50   .20
1782 A478 29e Ansiao    .50   .20
1783 A478 60e Santiago do   1.60   .75
   Cacem
1784 A478 87e Affife    1.75   .90
1785 A478 100e Caldas da   2.00   .85
   Rainha
  a.   Bkt. pane of 4, #1782-1785   7.00
     Nos. 1782-1785 (4)    5.85 2.70

---

Remains of
the Roman
Civilization
in Portugal
A471

Mozaics. 27e, *"Winter Image,"* detail of *Mosaic of the Four Seasons,* limestone and glass, 3rd cent., House of the Waterworks, Coimbra. 80e, *Fish in Marine Water,* limestone, 3rd-4th cent., cover of a tank wall, public baths, Faro.

**1988, Oct. 18**    Litho.    *Perf. 12*
1746 A471 27e multi    .55   .20
1747 A471 80e multi    1.75   .75

20th Cent. Art Type of 1988

Paintings by Portuguese artists: 27e, *Burial,* 1938, by Mario Eloy. 60e, *Lisbon Roofs,* c. 1936, by Carlos Botelho. 80e, *Avejao Lirico,* 1939, by Antonio Pedro.

**1988, Nov. 18**    Litho.    *Perf. 11½x12*
1748 A469 27e multi    .45   .20
1749 A469 60e multi    1.40   .65
1750 A469 80e multi    1.75   .75
  a.   Souv. sheet of 3, #1748-   5.50 5.50
     1750
  b.   Min. sheet of 6, #1738-   10.00 10.00
     1740, 1748-1750
     Nos. 1748-1750 (3)    3.60 1.60

Braga
Cathedral,
900th
Anniv.
A472

**1989, Jan. 20**    *Perf. 12*
1751 A472 30e multi    .75   .25

INDIA
'89 — A473

55e, Caravel, Sao Jorge da Mina Fort, 1482. 60e, Navigator using astrolabe, 16th cent.

**1989, Jan. 20**
1752 A473 55e multi    1.25   .65
1753 A473 60e multi    1.75   .80

20th Cent. Art Type of 1988

Paintings by Portuguese artists: 29e, *Antithesis of Calm,* 1940, by Antonio Dacosta. 60c, *Lunch of the Unskilled Mason,* c. 1926, by Julio Pomar. 87e, *Simums,* 1949, by Vespeira.

**1989, Feb. 15**    Litho.    *Perf. 11½x12*
1754 A469 29e multi    .45   .20
1755 A469 60e multi    1.40   .60
1756 A469 87e multi    1.75   .90
  a.   Souv. sheet of 3, #1754-1756   5.50 5.50
     Nos. 1754-1756 (3)    3.60 1.70

**1989, July 7**

Paintings by Portuguese artists: 29e, *046-72,* 1972, by Fernando Lanhas. 60e, *Les Spirales,* 1954, by Nadir Afonso. 87e, *Sim,* 1987, by Carlos Calvet.

1757 A469 29e multi    .45   .20
1758 A469 60e multi    1.40   .55
1759 A469 87e multi    1.75   .90
  a.   Souv. sheet of 3, #1757-1759   5.50 5.50
  b.   Min. sheet of 6, #1754-1759   9.00 9.00
     Nos. 1757-1759 (3)    3.60 1.65

**1990, Feb. 14**

Paintings by Portuguese artists: 32e, *Aluenda-Tordesillas* by Joaquim Rodrigo. 60e, *Pintura* by Noronha da Costa. 95e, *Pintura* by Vasco Costa (1917-1985).

1760 A469 32e multicolored    .40   .20
1761 A469 60e multicolored   1.10   .60
1762 A469 95e multicolored   1.75   .85
  a.   Souv. sheet of 3, #1760-1762   5.50 5.50
     Nos. 1760-1762 (3)    3.25 1.55

---

Jean Monnet (1888-1979),
Economist — A467

**1988, May 9**    Litho.    1.40   .55
1736 A467 60e multi

## Souvenir Sheet

National Heritage (Patrimony) — A468

Design: 150e, Belvedere of Cordovil House and Fountain of Porta de Moura reflected in the Garcia de Resende balcony window, Evora, 16th cent.

**1988, May 13**    *Perf. 13½x12½*
1737 A468 150e multi    7.50 7.50

No. 1737 has inscribed margin picturing LUBRAPEX '88 and UNESCO emblems.

20th Cent.
Paintings by
Portuguese
Artists — A469

Designs: 27e, *Viola,* c. 1916, by Amadeo de Souza-Cardoso, (1887-1918). 60e, *Jugglers and Tumblers Do Not Fall,* 1949, by Jose de Almada Negreiros (1893-1970). 80e, *Still-life with Guitar,* c. 1940, by Eduardo Viana (1881-1967).

**1988, Aug. 23**    Litho.    *Perf. 11½x12*
1738 A469 27e multi    .50   .20
1739 A469 60e multi    1.50   .70
1740 A469 80e multi    1.75   .85
  a.   Min. sheet of 3, #1738-1740   5.50 5.50
     Nos. 1738-1740 (3)    3.75 1.75

See Nos. 1748-1750, 1754-1765.

1988
Summer
Olympics,
Seoul
A470

**1988, Sept. 16**    Litho.    *Perf. 12x11½*
1741 A470 27e Archery    .45   .20
1742 A470 55e Weight lifting   1.40   .75
1743 A470 60e Judo    1.50   .80
1744 A470 80e Tennis    2.25   .80
  a.   Nos. 1741-1744 (4)    5.60 2.55

## Souvenir Sheet

1745 A470 200e Yachting    9.00 7.00

**1990, Mar. 6**
1804 A483 32e multicolored .45 .20
A Portuguesa, the Natl. Anthem, cent. (32e).

Score,
Alfred Keil
and
Henrique
Lopes de
Mondonca
A483

**1990, Mar. 6** Perf. 12x11½
1805 A484 70e multicolored
A Portuguesa, the Natl. Anthem, cent. (32e).

University
Education in
Portugal, 700th
Anniv. — A484

**1990, Apr. 11** Perf. 11½x12
1806 A485 80e Santo Tirso 1.60 .70
P.O.

Europa
1990
A485

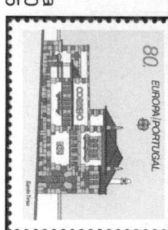

**Souvenir Sheet**
1807 Perf. 12x11½
Sheet of 4, 2 each
#1806, 1807a
a. A485 80e Mala Posta P.O. 1.25 1.00

Souvenir Sheet
25.00
2.00
6.00
1.25

150 anos do Selo postal

**1990, May 3**
1808 A486 250e multicolored 8.00 5.50
Stamp World London '90 and 150th anniv.
of the Penny Black.

Gentleman Using Postage Stamp,
1840 — A486

"FELICITAÇOES" and street scenes.

**1990, June 5** Litho. Perf. 12
1809 A487 60e Stairway 1.00 .45
1810 A487 60e Automobile 1.00 .45
1811 A487 60e Man in street 1.00 .45
1812 A487 60e shown 1.00 .45
Nos. 1809-1812 (4) 4.00 1.80

Greetings
Issue
A487

---

**1990, Sept. 21** Litho. Perf. 12
1815 A489 32e Barca .40 .20
1816 A489 60e Caravela Pes- 1.10 .50

Ships
A489

1817 A489 70e Barinel 1.25 .75
1818 A489 95e Caravela 1.75 1.00
Nos. 1815-1818 (4) 4.50 2.45

**Perf. 13½ Vert.**
1819a A489 32e 1.25 1.25
1816a A489 60e 1.25 1.25
1817a A489 70e 1.25 1.25
1818a A489 95e 1.25 1.25
b. Bklt. pane of 4, #1815a-
1818a 5.00

**1990, Oct. 11** Litho. Perf. 12
1819 A490 32e Pena .45 .20
1820 A490 60e Vila 1.10 .50
1821 A490 70e Mafra 1.25 .75
1822 A490 120e Guimaraes 4.55 1.00
Nos. 1819-1822 (4) 4.55 2.45

National
Palaces — A490

**1990, Nov. 7**
1823 A491 32e ol brn & blk .55 .25
Francisco Sa Carneiro (1934-1980),
Politician — A491

Rossio
Railway
Station,
Cent.
A492

Various locomotives.

**1990 Nov 5** (Railway)

---

**1990, July 11** Litho. Perf. 12x11½
1813 A488 65e multicolored 1.10 .65
1814 A488 70e multicolored 1.25 .70
Designs: 70e, Friar Bartolomeu dos Mar-
tires (1514-1590), theologian.

Camilo Castelo Branco (1825-1890),
Writer — A488

**1990-94** Litho. Perf. 12x11½
1839 A495 2e Joao Gon- .20 .20
calves Zarco
1840 A495 3e Pedro Lopes .20 .20
de Sousa
1841 A495 4e Duarte .20 .20
Pacheco
Pereira
1842 A495 5e Tristao Vaz .20 .20
Teixeira
1843 A495 6e Pedro Alvares .20 .20
Cabral
1844 A495 10e Joao de Cas- .20 .20
tro
1845 A495 32e Bartolomeu .45 .20
Perestrelo
1846 A495 35e Gil Eanes .40 .20
1847 A495 38e Vasco da .35 .20
Gama
1848 A495 42e Joao de Lis- .35 .20
boa
1849 A495 45e Joaoa Rodri- .45 .20
ques Cabril-
lo
1850 A495 60e Nuno Tristao .45 .20
1851 A495 65e Joao da Nova .90 .30
1852 A495 70e Ferdinand .90 .20
Magellan
1853 A495 75e Pedro Fer- .90 .20
nandes de
Queiros
1854 A495 80e Diogo Gomes .85 .45
1855 A495 100e Diogu de .85 .50
Silves
1856 A495 200e Estevao 1.75 .65
Gomes
1857 A495 250e Diogo Cao 2.50 .60
1858 A495 350e Bartolomeu 4.00 1.25
Dias

Portuguese
Navigators
A495

Issued: 2e, 5e, 32e, 100e, 3/6/91; 6e, 38e, 65e,
350e, 3/6/91; 35e, 60e, 80e, 250e, 3/6/92; 4e,
42e, 70e, 200e, 4/6/93; 3e, 10e, 45e, 75e,
4/29/94.
Nos. 1839-1858 (20) 21.10 7.85

**1991, Feb. 7** Litho. Perf. 12
1829 A492 32e Steam, 1887 .45 .20
1829 A492 35e Lavabo .50 .25
1830 A492 35e Tureen and .50 .25
plate
1831 A482 35e Flower vase .50 .25
1832 A482 60e Finger bowl 1.00 .50
1833 A482 60e Coffee pot 1.00 .50
1834 A482 60e Mug 1.00 .50
Nos. 1829-1834 (6) 4.50 2.25

Ceramics Type of 1990

---

**1991, Mar. 6** Litho. Perf. 12
1836 A494 60e Flamingos .95 .50
1837 A494 110e Chameleon 1.70 .85

European
Tourism
Year
A494

**1991, May 27** Litho. Perf. 12
1862 A498 35e Caravel .45 .20
1863 A498 75e Nau 1.25 .55
1864 A498 80e Nau, stern 1.25 .60
1865 A498 110e Galleon 1.75 .65
Nos. 1862-1865 (4) 4.70 2.10

Discovery
Ships
A498

**Perf. 13½ Vert.**
1862a A498 35e 1.25 1.25
1863a A498 75e 1.25 1.25
1864a A498 80e 1.25 1.25
1865a A498 110e 1.25 1.25
b. Bklt. pane of 4, #1862a-
1865a 5.00

Portuguese
Crown
Jewels — A499

Designs: 35e, Running knot, diamonds &
emeralds, 18th cent. 60e, Royal scepter, 19th
cent. 70e, Sash of the Grand Cross, ruby &
diamonds, 18th cent. 80e, Court saber, gold &
diamonds in hilt, 19th cent. 140e, Royal crown,
19th cent.

**1991, July 8** Litho. Perf. 13½ Vert.
1866 A499 35e multicolored .45 .20
1867 A499 60e multicolored 1.00 .50
1868 A499 80e multicolored 1.40 .60
1869 A499 140e multicolored 2.10 .85
Nos. 1866-1869 (4) 4.95 2.15

a. Booklet pane of 5
See Nos. 1898-1902.

---

**1990, Nov. 7** Souvenir Sheet
1828 A492 200e Railway station 6.00 5.00

No. 1835 250e Plate 6.00 5.00
No. 1835 contains one 52x44mm stamp.

Souvenir Sheet
1835 A482 250e Plate
Princess Isabel & Philip le
Bon — A497

**1991, May 27** Litho. Perf. 12½
1861 A497 300e multicolored 7.50 6.00
Europalia '91. See Belgium No. 1402.

Europa
A496

**1991, Apr. 11** Litho. Perf. 12
1859 A496 80e Eutelsat II 1.50 1.00

**Souvenir Sheet**
1860 Sheet, 2 ea #1859,
1860a 24.00 7.50
a. A496 80e Olympus I 2.50 1.75

PORTUGAL

Europa A515

Voyages of Columbus — A515

Designs: 85e, King John II with Columbus. No. 1918, Columbus in sight of land. No. 1919, Landing of Columbus. No. 1920, Columbus soliciting aid from Queen Isabella. No. 1921, Columbus welcomed at Barcelona. No. 1922, Columbus presenting natives. No. 1923, Columbus.
Nos. 1918-1923 are similar in design to US Nos. 230-231, 234-235, 237, 245.

**1992, May 22   Litho.   Perf. 12x11½**
1917   A514   85e gold & multi   3.00   .60

**Souvenir Sheets**
**Perf. 12**
| | | | | |
|---|---|---|---|---|
| 1918 | A515 | 260e blue | 7.00 | 4.50 |
| 1919 | A515 | 260e brown violet | 7.00 | 4.50 |
| 1920 | A515 | 260e brown | 7.00 | 4.50 |
| 1921 | A515 | 260e violet black | 7.00 | 4.50 |
| 1922 | A515 | 260e black | 7.00 | 4.50 |
| 1923 | A515 | 260e black | 7.00 | 4.50 |

Europa.
See US Nos. 2624-2629, Italy Nos. 1883-1888, and Spain Nos. 2677-2682.

UN Conference on Environmental Development — A516

70e, Bird flying over polluted water system. 120e, Clean water system, butterfly, bird, flowers.

**1992, June 12   Litho.   Perf. 12x11½**
| | | | | |
|---|---|---|---|---|
| 1924 | A516 | 70e multicolored | 1.10 | .55 |
| 1925 | A516 | 120e multicolored | 2.00 | 1.00 |
| a. | | A516 Pair, #1924-1925 | 4.00 | 2.00 |

1992 Summer Olympics, Barcelona A517

**1992, July 29   Litho.   Perf. 11½x12**
| | | | | |
|---|---|---|---|---|
| 1926 | A517 | 38e Women's running | | .30 |
| 1927 | A517 | 70e Soccer | .65 | .30 |
| 1928 | A517 | 85e Hurdles | 1.15 | .60 |
| 1929 | A517 | 120e Roller hockey | 1.40 | .70 |
| | | | 2.00 | 1.00 |
| | | Nos. 1926-1929 (4) | 5.20 | 2.60 |

**Souvenir Sheet**
**Perf. 12**
1930   A517   250e Basketball   9.00   6.00

Olymphilex '92 (#1930).

Campo Pequeno Bull Ring, Lisbon, Cent. A518

Various scenes of picadors.

**1992, Aug. 18   Perf. 12x11½**
| | | | | |
|---|---|---|---|---|
| 1931 | A518 | 38e multicolored | .65 | .30 |
| 1932 | A518 | 65e multicolored | 1.10 | .55 |
| 1933 | A518 | 70e multicolored | 1.25 | .60 |
| 1934 | A518 | 155e multicolored | 2.50 | 1.25 |
| | | Nos. 1931-1934 (4) | 5.50 | 2.70 |

---

Granada '92: 120e, Three men with gifts, Japanese.

**1992, Apr. 24   Litho.   Perf. 12**
1907   A508   38e shown   .45   .20
1908   A508   120e multicolored   1.60   .75

Portuguese Pavilion, Expo '92, Seville — A509

**1992, Apr. 24   Litho.   Perf. 11½x12**
1909   A509   65e multicolored   .80   .40

Instruments of Navigation — A510

**1992, May 9   Litho.   Perf. 12x11½**
| | | | | |
|---|---|---|---|---|
| 1910 | A510 | 60e Cross staff | .80 | .25 |
| 1911 | A510 | 70e Quadrant | .95 | .50 |
| 1912 | A510 | 100e Astrolabe | 1.40 | .50 |
| 1913 | A510 | 120e Compass | 1.50 | .70 |
| a. | | Souv. sheet of 4, #1910-1913 | 4.50 | 4.65 | 2.00 |

Lubrapex '92 (#1913a).
Nos. 1910-1913 (4)

Royal Hospital of All Saints, 500th Anniv. A511

**1992, May 11**
1914   A511   38e multicolored   .90   .40

Apparitions of Fatima, 75th Anniv. A512

**1992, May 11**
1915   A512   70e multicolored

Port of Leixoes, Cent. A513

**1992, May 11**
1916   A513   120e multicolored   1.50   .65

A514

---

Automobile Museum, Caramulo A505

**1991, Nov. 15**
| | | | | |
|---|---|---|---|---|
| 1885 | A505 | 35e Peugeot, 1899 | .45 | .20 |
| 1886 | A505 | 60e Rolls Royce, 1911 | .90 | .45 |
| 1887 | A505 | 80e Bugatti 35B, 1930 | 1.25 | .65 |
| 1888 | A505 | 110e Ferrari 195 Inter, 1950 | 1.60 | .70 |
| | | Nos. 1885-1888 (4) | 4.20 | 2.00 |

**Souvenir Sheet**
1889
| | | | |
|---|---|---|---|
| a.-b. | | Sheet 2 each #1889a-1889b | 4.50 | 4.50 |
| | | A505 70e any single | 1.10 | .55 |

Phila Nippon '91 (#1889). See #1903-1906A.

Designs: No. 1889a, Mercedes 380K, 1934. b, Hispano-Suiza, 1924.

**Ceramics Type of 1990**
**1992, Jan. 24   Litho.   Perf. 12**
| | | | | |
|---|---|---|---|---|
| 1890 | A482 | 40e Tureen with lid | .60 | .30 |
| 1891 | A482 | 40e Plate | .60 | .30 |
| 1892 | A482 | 40e Pitcher with lid | .60 | .30 |
| 1893 | A482 | 65e Violin | .95 | .50 |
| 1894 | A482 | 65e Bottle in form of woman | .95 | .50 |
| 1895 | A482 | 65e Man seated on barrel | .95 | .50 |
| | | Nos. 1890-1895 (6) | 4.65 | 2.40 |

**Souvenir Sheet**
1896   A482   260e Political caricature   4.00   3.00

No. 1896 contains one 51x44mm stamp.

Portuguese Presidency of the European Community Council of Ministers A506

PORTUGAL 65.

**1992, Jan. 24**
1907   A506   65e multicolored   .95   .45

**Crown Jewels Type of 1991**

Designs: 38e, Coral flowers, 19th cent. 65e, Clock of gold, enamel, ivory and diamonds, 20th cent. 70e, Tobacco box encrusted with diamonds and emeralds, 1755. 85e, Royal scepter, 1828. 125e, Eighteen star necklace with diamonds, 1863.

**1992, Feb. 7   Litho.   Perf. 11½x12**
| | | | | |
|---|---|---|---|---|
| 1898 | A499 | 38e multicolored | .45 | .20 |
| 1899 | A499 | 70e multicolored | .85 | .40 |
| 1900 | A499 | 85e multicolored | 1.10 | .65 |
| 1901 | A499 | 125e multicolored | 1.50 | .80 |

**Perf. 13½ Vert.**
1902   A499   65e multicolored   1.10   .50
a.   Booklet pane of 5   5.00   2.55
Nos. 1898-1902 (5)

**Automobile Museum Type of 1991**

Designs: 38e, Citroen Torpedo, 1922. 65e, Rochet Schneider, 1914. 85e, Austin Seven, 1933. 120e, Mercedes Benz 770, 1938. No. 1906b, Renault, 1911. c, Ford Model T, 1927.

**1992, Mar. 6   Litho.   Perf. 12**
| | | | | |
|---|---|---|---|---|
| 1903 | A505 | 38e multicolored | .45 | .20 |
| 1904 | A505 | 65e multicolored | 1.00 | .50 |
| 1905 | A505 | 85e multicolored | 1.25 | .65 |
| 1906 | A505 | 120e multicolored | 1.50 | .75 |
| | | Nos. 1903-1906 (4) | 4.20 | 2.10 |

**Souvenir Sheet**
1906A   A505 Sheet of 2 each, #b-c.   4.50   4.50
b.-c.   A505 70e any single   1.10   .55

Automobile Museum, Oeiras.

Portuguese Arrival in Japan, 450th Anniv. A508

---

Antero de Quental (1842-1891), Poet — A500

First Missionaries to Congo, 500th Anniv. — A501

**1991, Aug. 2   Perf. 12**
1871   A500   35e multicolored   .45   .20
1872   A501   110e multicolored   1.70   .85

Architectural Heritage — A502

Designs: 35e, School of Architecture, Oporto University, by Siza Vieira. 60e, Torre do Tombo, by Ateliers Associates of Arsenio Cordeiro. 80e, Railway Bridge over Douro River, by Edgar Cardoso. 110e, Setubal-Braga highway bridge.

**1991, Sept. 4   Litho.   Perf. 12**
| | | | | |
|---|---|---|---|---|
| 1873 | A502 | 35e multicolored | .50 | .25 |
| 1874 | A502 | 60e multicolored | .80 | .45 |
| 1875 | A502 | 80e multicolored | 1.25 | .60 |
| 1876 | A502 | 110e multicolored | 1.70 | .75 |
| | | Nos. 1873-1876 (4) | 4.25 | 2.05 |

1992 Summer Olympics, Barcelona A503

**1992, Oct. 9   Litho.   Perf. 12**
| | | | | |
|---|---|---|---|---|
| 1877 | A503 | 35e Equestrian | .45 | .20 |
| 1878 | A503 | 60e Fencing | .85 | .40 |
| 1879 | A503 | 80e Shooting | 1.25 | .60 |
| 1880 | A503 | 110e Sailing | 1.70 | .75 |
| | | Nos. 1877-1880 (4) | 4.25 | 1.95 |

History of Portuguese Communications — A504

Designs: 35e, King Manuel I appointing first Postmaster, 1520. 60e, Mailbox, telegraph, 1880. 80e, Automobile, telephone, 1911. 110e, Airplane, mail truck, 1991.

**1991, Oct. 9**
| | | | | |
|---|---|---|---|---|
| 1881 | A504 | 35e multicolored | .45 | .20 |
| 1882 | A504 | 60e multicolored | .90 | .45 |
| 1883 | A504 | 80e multicolored | 1.25 | .60 |
| | | Nos. 1881-1883 (3) | 2.60 | 1.25 |

**Souvenir Sheet**
1884   A504   110e multicolored   1.90   1.40

## Souvenir Sheet

**Perf. 13½x12½**
1935 A518 250e Bull ring, vert. 7.50 5.00
No. 1935 contains one 35x50mm stamp.
1936 A519 65e multicolored .95 .50

**1992, Nov. 4**   **Litho.**   **Perf. 12x11½**

Single European Market
A519

European Year for Security, Hygiene and Health at Work
A520

1937 A520 120e multicolored .95 .50

**1992, Nov. 4**
1938 A521 (A) henna brown, gray & black 1.75 .90

No. 1938 sold for 42e on date of issue. See No. 2276A.

**1993, Mar. 9**   **Litho.**   **Perf. 12x12½**

Postrider
A521

  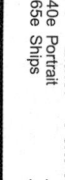

Almada Negreiros (1893-1970), Artist — A522

**1993, Mar. 9**   **Litho.**   **Perf. 11½x12**
1939 A522 40e Portrait .60 .30
1940 A522 65e Ships .95 .50

Instruments of Navigation — A523

**1993, Apr. 6**   **Perf. 12x11½**
1941 A523 42e Hourglass .60 .30
1942 A523 70e Nocturlabe 1.00 .60
1943 A523 90e Kamal 1.30 .65
1944 A523 130e Backstaff 1.90 .95
Nos. 1941-1944 (4) 4.80 2.40

Contemporary Paintings by Jose Escada (1934-1980) — A524

**1993, Apr. 6**   **Perf. 12x11½**
Europa. No. 1945, Cathedral, 1979. No. 1946a, Abstract shapes, 1966.
1945 A518 250e Bull ring, vert. 7.50 5.00
**1993, May 5**   **Litho.**   **Perf. 12x11½**
1945 A524 90e multicolored 1.25 .60

---

**1946**   Sheet, 2 each #1945,
a. A524 90e multicolored 1.75 1.25

Assoc. of Volunteer Firemen of Lisbon, 125th Anniv.
A525

**1993, June 21**   **Litho.**   **Perf. 12x11½**
1947 A525 70e multicolored .90 .45

Sao Carlos Natl. Theatre, Bicent.
A526

**1993, June 21**
1948 A526 42e Rossini .50 .25
1949 A526 70e Verdi .90 .45
1950 A526 90e Wagner 1.15 .55
1951 A526 130e Mozart 1.65 .80
Nos. 1948-1951 (4) 4.20 2.05

**Souvenir Sheet**
1952 A526 300e Theatre 6.00 5.00

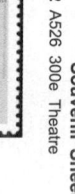 

Union of Portuguese Speaking Capitals — A527

**1993, July 30**   **Litho.**   **Perf. 11½x12**
1953 A527 130e multicolored 1.60 .80
a. Miniature sheet of 4 + 2 labels 9.00 6.00
Brasiliana '93 (#1953a).

Sculpture — A528

**1993, Aug. 18**   **Perf. 11½x12, 12x11½**
1954 A528 42e multicolored .55 .30
1955 A528 70e multicolored .90 .45
1956 A528 75e multicolored .95 .45
1957 A528 90e multicolored 1.10 .50
1958 A528 130e multicolored 1.60 .80
1959 A528 170e multicolored 2.25 1.10
Nos. 1954-1959 (6) 7.35 3.75

**Souvenir Sheet**
1960 A528 Sheet of 4
a.-d. A528 75e any single .95 .95
See Nos. 2001-2007, 2067-2073.

Designs: 42e, Annunciation Angel, 12th cent. 70e, St. Mark, 16th cent., horiz. No. 1956, Virgin and Child, 17th cent. 90e, Archangel St. Michael, 18th cent. 130e, Conde de Ferreira, 19th cent. 170e, Modern sculpture, 20th cent.
No. 1960a, Head of Agrippina, the Elder, 1st cent. No. 1960b, Virgin of the Annunciation, 16th cent. No. 1960c, The Widow, 19th cent. No. 1960d, Love Ode, 20th cent.

---

A532

**1993, Oct. 1**   **Litho.**   **Perf. 12x11½**
1967 A531 42e Twin-mast .55 .30
1968 A531 70e Single-mast .90 .45
1969 A531 90e SS Germano 3 1.10 .55
1970 A531 130e Steam-powered 1.75 .85
Nos. 1967-1970 (4) 4.30 2.15
**Perf. 11½**
1967a A531 42e .55 .30
1968a A531 70e .90 .45
1969a A531 90e 1.10 .55
1970a A531 130e 1.75 .85
b. Booklet pane of 4, #1967a-1970a 5.00

Trawlers
A531

Designs: 42e, Japanese using musket. 130e, Catholic priests. 350e, Exchanging items of trade.

**1993, Sept. 22**   **Litho.**   **Perf. 12**
1964 A530 42e multicolored .55 .30
1965 A530 130e multicolored 1.60 .80
1966 A530 350e multicolored 4.50 2.25
Nos. 1964-1966 (3) 6.65 3.40
See Macao Nos. 704-706.

Portuguese Arrival in Japan, 450th Anniv.
A530

90e, Cars on railway overpass, train, 130e, Traffic jam, train, 300e, Train, track skirting tree.

**1993, Sept. 6**   **Perf. 12x11½**
1961 A529 90e multicolored 1.10 .55
1962 A529 130e multicolored 1.60 .80

**Souvenir Sheet**
1963 A529 300e multicolored 6.00 5.00

Railway World Congress
A529

**1993, Oct. 9**   **Litho.**
1971 A532 42e multicolored .50 .25
1972 A532 70e multicolored .80 .40
1973 A532 90e multicolored 1.00 .50
1974 A532 130e multicolored 1.50 .75
Nos. 1971-1974 (4) 3.80 1.90

**Souvenir Sheet**
1975 A532 300e multicolored 6.00 5.00
No. 1975 has continuous design.

---

Mailboxes: 42e, Rural mail bag, 1880. 70e, Railroad wall-mounted mailbox, 19th cent. 90e, Free-standing mailbox, 19th cent. 130e, Modern mailbox, 1992. 300e, Mailbox from horse-drawn postal vehicle, 19th cent.

A533

A536

**1994, Jan. 27**
1982 A536 85e multicolored

West European Union, 40th Anniv.
A536

**1994, Jan. 27**   **Litho.**   **Perf. 12**
1983 A537 100e multicolored 1.25 .65
1984 A537 100e multicolored 1.25 .65

Design: No. 1984, Olympic torch, rings.

Issued in sheets of 8, 4 each + label.

Intl. Olympic Committee, Cent.
A537

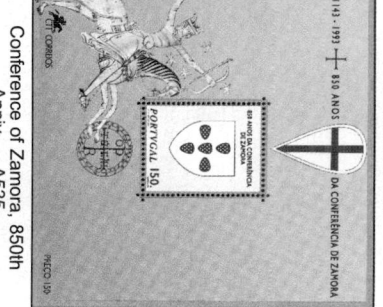

**1993, Dec. 9**
1981 A535 150e multicolored 3.00 2.00

Conference of Zamora, 850th Anniv. — A535

**1993, Oct. 9**   **Perf. 12**
Endangered birds of prey.
1976 A533 42e Imperial eagle .50 .25
1977 A533 70e Royal eagle owl .80 .40
1978 A533 130e Peregrine falcon 1.50 .75
1979 A533 350e Hen harrier 4.00 2.00
Nos. 1976-1979 (4) 6.80 3.40

Brazil-Portugal Treaty of Consultation and Friendship, 40th Anniv. — A534

**1993, Nov. 3**
1980 A534 130e multicolored 1.50 .75
See Brazil No. 2430.

## Historical Inns A552

45e, S. Filipe Fort, Setubal. 75e, Obidos Castle. 100e, Dos Loios Convent, Evora. 140e, St. Marinha Guimaraes Monastery.

**1994, Nov. 7**

| | | | | |
|---|---|---|---|---|
| 2028 | A552 | 45e multicolored | .55 | .30 |
| 2029 | A552 | 75e multicolored | .90 | .45 |
| 2030 | A552 | 100e multicolored | 1.25 | .60 |
| 2031 | A552 | 140e multicolored | 1.75 | .90 |
| | | Nos. 2028-2031 (4) | 4.45 | 2.25 |

## Evangelization and Meeting of Cultures — A553

45e, Carving of missionary, Mozambique, 19th cent., vert. 75e, Sculpture, young Jesus ministering to the people, India, 17th cent., vert. 100e, Chalice, Macao, 17th cent. vert. 140e, Carving of native, Angola, 19th cent.

**1994, Nov. 17     Litho.     Perf. 12**

| | | | | |
|---|---|---|---|---|
| 2032 | A553 | 45e multicolored | .55 | .30 |
| 2033 | A553 | 75e multicolored | .95 | .45 |
| 2034 | A553 | 100e multicolored | 1.25 | .60 |
| 2035 | A553 | 140e multicolored | 1.75 | .90 |
| | | Nos. 2032-2035 (4) | 4.50 | 2.25 |

## Arrival of Portuguese in Senegal, 550th Anniv. A554

**1994, Nov. 17**

| | | | | |
|---|---|---|---|---|
| 2036 | A554 | 140e multicolored | 1.75 | .90 |

See Senegal No. 1083.

### Souvenir Sheet

Battle of Montijo, 350th Anniv. — A555

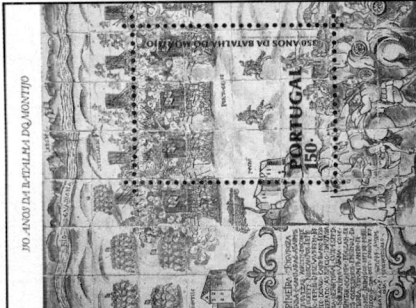

Illustration reduced.

**1994, Dec. 1**

| | | | | |
|---|---|---|---|---|
| 2037 | A555 | 150e multicolored | 4.00 | 3.00 |

## Trawlers A547

**1994, Sept. 16     Perf. 12x11½**

| | | | | |
|---|---|---|---|---|
| 2013 | A547 | 45e Maria Arminda | .60 | .30 |
| 2014 | A547 | 75e Bom Pastor | .95 | .50 |
| 2015 | A547 | 100e With triplex haulers | 1.25 | .60 |
| 2016 | A547 | 140e Sueste | 1.75 | .85 |
| | | Nos. 2013-2016 (4) | 4.55 | 2.25 |

**Perf. 11½ Vert.**

| | | | | |
|---|---|---|---|---|
| 2013a | A547 | 45e | .60 | .30 |
| 2014a | A547 | 75e | .95 | .50 |
| 2016a | A547 | 140e | 1.75 | .85 |
| b. | | Booklet pane of 4, #2013a-2016a | 6.00 | |

## Modern Railway Transport — A548

45e, Sintra Railway, electric multiple car unit. 75e, 5600 series locomotives. 140e, Lisbon subway cars. Illustration reduced.

**1994, Oct. 10     Litho.     Perf. 12**

| | | | | |
|---|---|---|---|---|
| 2017 | A548 | 45e multicolored | .55 | .30 |
| 2018 | A548 | 75e multicolored | .90 | .45 |
| 2019 | A548 | 140e multicolored | 1.75 | .90 |
| | | Nos. 2017-2019 (3) | 3.20 | 1.65 |

## Vehicles of Postal Transportation — A549

45e, Horse-drawn mail coach, 19th cent. 75e, Railway postal ambulance, 19th cent. 100e, Mercedes station wagon, No. 222, 1950. 140e, Volkswagen van, 1952. 250e, DAF 2500 truck, 1983.

**1994, Oct. 10     Litho.**

| | | | | |
|---|---|---|---|---|
| 2020 | A549 | 45e multicolored | .55 | .30 |
| 2021 | A549 | 75e multicolored | .90 | .45 |
| 2022 | A549 | 100e multicolored | 1.25 | .65 |
| 2023 | A549 | 140e multicolored | 1.75 | .90 |
| | | Nos. 2020-2023 (4) | 4.45 | 2.30 |

### Souvenir Sheet

| | | | | |
|---|---|---|---|---|
| 2024 | A549 | 250e multicolored | 6.00 | 5.00 |

## First Savings Bank in Portugal, 150th Anniv. A550

**1994, Oct. 31**

| | | | | |
|---|---|---|---|---|
| 2025 | A550 | 45e Pelican medal-lion | .55 | .30 |
| 2026 | A550 | 100e Modern coins | 1.25 | .65 |

World Wide Savings Day (#2026).

## American Society of Travel Agents, 64th Congress, Lisbon A551

**1994, Nov. 7**

| | | | | |
|---|---|---|---|---|
| 2027 | A551 | 140e multicolored | 1.75 | .90 |

## 1994 World Cup Soccer Championships, US — A544

**1994, June 7**

| | | | | |
|---|---|---|---|---|
| 1994 | A544 | 100e shown | 1.25 | .60 |
| 1995 | A544 | 140e Ball, 4 shoes | 1.90 | .95 |

## Lisbon '94, European Capital of Culture A545

Birds and: 45e, Music. 75e, Photography. 100e, Theater and ballet. 145e, Art.

**1994, July 1**

| | | | | |
|---|---|---|---|---|
| 1996 | A545 | 45e multicolored | .55 | .30 |
| 1997 | A545 | 75e multicolored | .95 | .50 |
| 1998 | A545 | 100e multicolored | 1.25 | .60 |
| 1999 | A545 | 145e multicolored | 1.90 | .95 |
| a. | | Souvenir sheet of 4, #1996-1999 | 4.65 | 2.35 |
| | | Nos. 1996-1999 (4) | | |

## Year of Road Safety — A545a

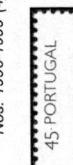

**1994, Aug. 16     Litho.     Perf. 11½x12**

| | | | | |
|---|---|---|---|---|
| 2000 | A545a | 45e blk, red & grn | .60 | .30 |

## Sculpture Type of 1993

Designs: 45e, Pedra Formosa, Castreja culture. No. 2002, Carved pilaster, 7th cent., vert. 80e, Capital carved with figures, 12th cent. 100e, Laying Christ in the Tomb, 16th cent. 140e, Reliquary chapel, 17th cent. 180e, Bas relief, 20th cent. No. 2007: a, Sarcophagus of Queen Urraca, 13th cent. b, Sarcophagus of Dom Afonso. c, Tomb of Dom Joao de Noronha and Dona Isabel de Sousa, 16th cent. d, Mausoleum of Adm. Machado Santos, 20th cent.

**1994, Aug. 16     Perf. 12x11½, 11½x12**

| | | | | |
|---|---|---|---|---|
| 2001 | A528 | 45e multicolored | .60 | .30 |
| 2002 | A528 | 45e multicolored | .95 | .50 |
| 2003 | A528 | 80e multicolored | 1.00 | .50 |
| 2004 | A528 | 100e multicolored | 1.25 | .60 |
| 2005 | A528 | 140e multicolored | 1.75 | .85 |
| 2006 | A528 | 180e multicolored | 2.25 | 1.10 |
| | | Nos. 2001-2006 (6) | 7.80 | 3.85 |

### Souvenir Sheet     Perf. 12x11½

| | | | | |
|---|---|---|---|---|
| 2007 | | Sheet of 4 | 6.00 | 5.00 |
| a.-d. | A528 | 75e any single | .95 | .95 |

## Falconry A546

Designs: 45e, Falconer, hooded bird, dog. 75e, Falcon flying after prey. 100e, Falcon, perched. 140e, Three falcons on perches. 250e, Hooded falcon.

**1994, Sept. 16     Litho.**

| | | | | |
|---|---|---|---|---|
| 2008 | A546 | 45e multicolored | .60 | .30 |
| 2009 | A546 | 75e multicolored | .95 | .50 |
| 2010 | A546 | 100e multicolored | 1.25 | .60 |
| 2011 | A546 | 140e multicolored | 1.75 | .85 |
| | | Nos. 2008-2011 (4) | 4.55 | 2.25 |

### Souvenir Sheet

| | | | | |
|---|---|---|---|---|
| 2012 | A546 | 250e multicolored | 6.00 | 5.00 |

## Oliveira Martins (1845-94), Historian A538

100e, Florbela Espanca (1894-1930), poet.

**1994, Feb. 21**

| | | | | |
|---|---|---|---|---|
| 1985 | A538 | 45e multicolored | .60 | .30 |
| 1986 | A538 | 100e multicolored | 1.25 | .65 |

## Prince Henry the Navigator (1394-1460) — A539

See Brazil No. 2463, Cape Verde No. 664, Macao No. 719.

Illustration reduced.

**1994, Mar. 4**

| | | | | |
|---|---|---|---|---|
| 1987 | A539 | 140e multicolored | 1.75 | .85 |

## Transfer of Power, 20th Anniv. A540

**1994, Apr. 22     Litho.     Perf. 12x11½**

| | | | | |
|---|---|---|---|---|
| 1988 | A540 | 75e multicolored | .90 | .45 |

## Europa A541

**1994, May 5     Litho.     Perf. 12x11½**

| | | | | |
|---|---|---|---|---|
| 1989 | A541 | 100e People of Ormuz | 1.25 | .65 |

### Souvenir Sheet

| | | | | |
|---|---|---|---|---|
| 1990 | | Sheet of 4, 2 each #1989, 1990a | 6.00 | 4.50 |
| a. | A541 | 100e Ears of corn | 1.25 | 1.25 |

## Intl. Year of the Family A542

## Treaty of Tordesillas, 500th Anniv. — A543

**1994, May 15     Litho.     Perf. 12x11½**

| | | | | |
|---|---|---|---|---|
| 1991 | A542 | 45e blk, red & brn | .55 | .30 |
| 1992 | A542 | 140e blk, red & grn | 1.75 | .85 |

Illustration reduced.

**1994, June 7     Litho.     Perf. 12x11½**

| | | | | |
|---|---|---|---|---|
| 1993 | A543 | 140e multicolored | 1.75 | .90 |

Souvenir Sheet

**1994, Dec. 8**
**Christmas — A556**
2038 A556 150e Magi ... 1.90 .95

**Nature Conservation in Europe — A557**

Designs: 42e, Otis tarda. 90e, Pandion haliaetus. 130e, Lacerta schreiberi.

| | | | | |
|---|---|---|---|---|
| **1995, Feb. 22** | | **Litho.** | **Perf. 12** | |
| 2039 | A557 | 42e multicolored | .60 | .30 |
| 2040 | A557 | 90e multicolored | 1.25 | .85 |
| 2041 | A557 | 130e multicolored | 1.75 | .85 |
| a. | | Souvenir sheet of 3, #2039-2041 | 3.60 | 1.75 |
| | | Nos. 2039-2041 (3) | 6.00 | 5.00 |

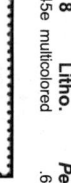

**St. Joao de Deus (1495-1550), Founder of Order of Hospitalers A558**

| | | | | |
|---|---|---|---|---|
| **1995, Mar. 8** | | **Litho.** | **Perf. 12** | |
| 2042 | A558 | 45e multicolored | .60 | .30 |

**Trams & Automobiles in Portugal, Cent. — A559**

Designs: 90e, 1895 Electric tram. 130e, 1895 Panhard & Levassor automobile.

| | | | | |
|---|---|---|---|---|
| **1995, Mar. 8** | | | | |
| 2043 | A559 | 90e multicolored | 1.25 | .60 |
| 2044 | A559 | 130e multicolored | 1.90 | .95 |

**19th Century Professions A560**

Designs: 1e, Baker woman. 20e, Spinning wheel and spoon vendor. 45e, Junk dealer. 50e, Fruit vendor. 75e, Whitewasher.

| | | | | |
|---|---|---|---|---|
| **1995, Apr. 20** | | **Litho.** | **Perf. 12** | |
| 2045 | A560 | 1e multicolored | .20 | .20 |
| 2046 | A560 | 20e multicolored | .20 | .20 |
| 2047 | A560 | 45e multicolored | .60 | .30 |
| a. | | Complete booklet, 10 #2047 | 6.00 | |

---

## PORTUGAL

**Peace & Freedom — A561**

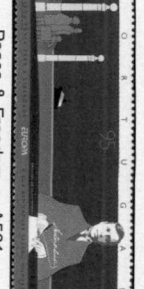

Europa: No. 2050, People awaiting ships for America. Aristides de Sousa Mendes signing entrance visas, 1940. No. 2051, Transportation of refugees from Gibraltar to Madeira, 1940. Illustration reduced.

| | | | | |
|---|---|---|---|---|
| **1995, May 5** | | **Litho.** | **Perf. 12** | |
| 2050 | A561 | 95e multicolored | 1.25 | .50 |
| 2051 | A561 | 95e multicolored | 1.25 | .50 |
| 2048 | A560 | 50e multicolored | .70 | .35 |
| 2049 | A560 | 75e multicolored | 1.00 | .50 |
| a. | | Complete booklet, 10 #2049 | 10.00 | |
| | | Nos. 2045-2049 (5) | 2.80 | 1.55 |

See Nos. 2088-2092, 2147-2151, 2210-2214, 2277-2281B.

**UN, 50th Anniv. A562**

| | | | | |
|---|---|---|---|---|
| **1995, May 5** | | | | |
| 2052 | A562 | 135e multicolored | 1.00 | .90 |
| 2053 | A562 | 135e multicolored | 1.75 | .90 |
| a. | | Souv. sheet, 2 ea #2052-2053 | 8.00 | 6.00 |

135e, like #2052, clouds in background.

**St. Anthony of Padua (1195-1231) A564**

| | | | | |
|---|---|---|---|---|
| **1995, June 13** | | **Litho.** | **Perf. 12** | |
| 2054 | A563 | 45e shown | .60 | .30 |
| 2055 | A564 | 75e shown | 1.00 | .50 |
| | | Christ | | |
| | | **Souvenir Sheet** | | |
| 2056 | A564 | 135e Statue holding | 1.90 | .95 |
| 2057 | A563 | 250e Statue holding Christ | 7.00 | 5.00 |
| | | Nos. 2054-2056 (3) | 3.50 | 1.75 |

See Italy Nos. 2040-2041, Brazil No. 2539.

**Firemen in Portugal, 600th Anniv. A565**

Designs: No. 2058, Carpenters with axes, women with pitchers, firemen. 1395. No. 2059, Dutch firemen, water pumper. 1701. 75e, Fireman of Lisbon, water wagon. 1780. firemen. 1782. 80e, Firemen pulling pumper, carrying water kegs. 1834. 95e, Fire chief directing firemen on Merryweather steam pumper. 1867. 135e, Firemen, hydrant, early fire truck. 1908.

| | | | | |
|---|---|---|---|---|
| **1995, July 4** | | **Litho.** | **Perf. 12** | |
| 2058 | A565 | 45e multicolored | .60 | .30 |
| 2059 | A565 | 45e multicolored | 2.00 | .30 |
| 2060 | A565 | 75e multicolored | 2.00 | 1.25 |
| a. | | Miniature sheet of 4 | 2.50 | .50 |
| | | | 10.00 | 2.00 |

**Dom Manuel I, 500th Anniv. of Acclamation — A566**

| | | | | |
|---|---|---|---|---|
| **1995, Aug. 4** | | **Litho.** | **Perf. 12** | |
| 2061 | A565 | 80e multicolored | 1.10 | .55 |
| 2062 | A565 | 95e multicolored | 1.25 | .65 |
| 2063 | A565 | 135e multicolored | 1.90 | .90 |
| | | Nos. 2058-2063 (6) | 9.35 | 3.20 |
| 2064 | A566 | 45e buff, brown & red | .60 | .30 |
| a. | | Miniature sheet of 4 | 5.00 | 4.00 |

**New Electric Railway Tram — A567**

| | | | | |
|---|---|---|---|---|
| **1995, Sept. 1** | | | | |
| 2066 | A567 | 80e multicolored | 1.10 | .55 |
| a. | | Complete booklet, No. 2066a | 4.50 | |

Illustration reduced.

**Sculpture Type of 1993**

Designs: 45e, Warrior, Castreja culture. 75e, Two-headed fountain. 80e, Statue, "The Truth," by Teixeira Lopes. 95e, Monument to the war dead. 135e, Statue of Fernão Lopes, by Martins Correia. 190e, Monument to Fernando Pessoa, by Lagoa Henriques. Equestrian statues: No. 2073: a, Medieval cavalryman. b, D. José I. c, D. João IV. d, Vimara Peres.

| | | | | |
|---|---|---|---|---|
| **1995, Sept. 27** | | **Litho.** | **Perf. 11½x12** | |
| 2067 | A528 | 45e multicolored | .60 | .30 |
| 2068 | A528 | 75e multicolored | 1.00 | .50 |
| 2069 | A528 | 80e multicolored | 1.10 | .55 |
| 2070 | A528 | 95e multicolored | 1.25 | .65 |
| 2071 | A528 | 135e multicolored | 1.80 | .90 |
| 2072 | A528 | 190e multicolored | 2.50 | 1.25 |
| | | Nos. 2067-2072 (6) | 8.25 | 4.15 |
| | | **Souvenir Sheet** | | |
| 2073 | A528 | 75e any single | 1.00 | 1.00 |
| a.-d. | | Sheet of 4 | 7.00 | 5.00 |

**Portuguese Expansion Period Art — A568**

45e, Statue of the Guardian Angel of Portugal. 75e, Reliquary of Queen D. Leonor. 80e, Statue of Dom Manuel. 95e, Painting, St. Anthony, by Nuno Goncalves. 135e, Adoration of the Magi, by Nuno Goncalves. 190e, Painting, Christ on the Way to Mount Calvary, by Jorge Afonso. 200e, Altarpiece for Convent of St. Vincent, by Nuno Goncalves.

| | | | | |
|---|---|---|---|---|
| **1995, Oct. 9** | | **Litho.** | **Perf. 12** | |
| 2074 | A568 | 45e multicolored | .60 | .25 |
| 2075 | A568 | 75e multicolored | 1.00 | .50 |
| 2076 | A568 | 80e multicolored | 1.00 | .50 |
| 2077 | A568 | 95e multicolored | 1.25 | .60 |
| 2078 | A568 | 135e multicolored | 1.75 | .90 |
| 2079 | A568 | 190e multicolored | 2.50 | 1.25 |
| | | Nos. 2074-2079 (6) | 8.10 | 4.00 |
| | | **Souvenir Sheet** | | |
| 2080 | A568 | 200e multicolored | 6.00 | 4.00 |

No. 2080 contains one 76x27mm stamp.

---

**José Maria Eça de Queiroz (1845-1900), Writer — A569**

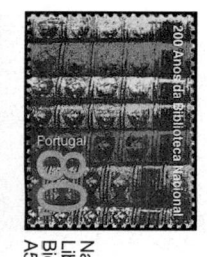

| | | | | |
|---|---|---|---|---|
| **1995, Oct. 27** | | **Litho.** | **Perf. 12** | |
| 2081 | A569 | 135e multicolored | 1.75 | .90 |

**Christmas A570**

| | | | | |
|---|---|---|---|---|
| **1995, Nov. 14** | | | | |
| 2082 | A570 | 80e Annunciation an- | 1.00 | .50 |
| a. | | "PORTUGAL" omitted | 1.00 | .50 |
| b. | | Miniature sheet, 4 #2082 | 4.00 | 4.00 |
| c. | | Miniature sheet, 4 #2082a | 4.00 | 4.00 |

**IAP Air Portugal, 50th Anniv. A571**

| | | | | |
|---|---|---|---|---|
| **1995, Nov. 14** | | | | |
| 2083 | A571 | 135e Airbus A340/300 | 1.75 | .90 |

**Oceanographic Voyages of King Charles I of Portugal and Prince Albert I of Monaco, Cent. — A572**

95e, Ship, King Charles I holding sextant, microscope, sea life. 135e, Fish in sea, net, Prince Albert I holding binoculars, ship. Illustration reduced.

| | | | | |
|---|---|---|---|---|
| **1996, Feb. 1** | | | | |
| 2084 | A572 | 95e multicolored | 1.25 | .60 |
| 2085 | A572 | 135e multicolored | 1.75 | .90 |

See Monaco Nos. 1992-1993.

**Natl. Library, Bicent. A573**

| | | | | |
|---|---|---|---|---|
| **1996, Feb. 29** | | | | |
| 2086 | A573 | 80e multicolored | 1.00 | .50 |

**Use of Portuguese as Official Language, 700th Anniv. — A574**

| | | | | |
|---|---|---|---|---|
| **1996, Feb. 29** | | | | |
| 2087 | A574 | 200e multicolored | 2.50 | 1.25 |

**Bank of Portugal, 150th Anniv. A591**

*Perf. 12*
**1996, Nov. 12** Litho.
2134 A591 78e multicolored 1.00 .50

**Rights of the People of East Timor A592**

**1996, Nov. 12**
2135 A592 140e black & red 1.75 .90

**Discovery of Maritime Route to India, 500th Anniv. — A593**

Voyage of Vasco da Gama: 47e, Visit of D. Manuel I to shipyards. 78e, Departure from Lisbon, July 8, 1497. 98e, Trip over Atlantic Ocean. 140e, Passing Cape of Good Hope. 315e, Dream of Manuel.

*Perf. 13½*
**1996, Nov. 12**
2136 A593 47e multicolored .60 .30
2137 A593 78e multicolored 1.00 .50
2138 A593 98e multicolored 1.25 .65
2139 A593 140e multicolored 1.75 .85
**Souvenir Sheet**
2140 A593 315e multicolored 4.00 4.00
See Nos. 2191-2195, 2265-2270.

**1996 Organization for Security and Cooperation in Europe Summit, Lisbon — A594**

**Souvenir Sheet**
Illustration reduced.
**1996, Dec. 2**
2141 A594 200e multicolored 2.50 2.50

**Ships of the Indian Shipping Line A595**

*Perf. 12*
Designs: 49e, Portuguese galleon, 16th cent. 80e, "Principe da Beira", 1780. 100e, ...

---

**Azeredo Perdigao (1896-1993), Lawyer, Chairman of Calouste Gulbenkian Foundation — A586**

*Perf. 12*
**1996, Sept. 19** Litho.
2115 A586 47e multicolored .60 .30

**Arms of the Districts of Portugal A587**

**1996, Sept. 27**
2116 A587 47e Aveiro .60 .30
2117 A587 78e Beja 1.00 .50
2118 A587 80e Braga 1.00 .50
a. Souvenir sheet, #2116-2118 2.60 2.60
2119 A587 98e Branganca 1.25 .65
2120 A587 100e Castelo Branco 1.25 .65
2121 A587 140e Coimbra 1.75 .90
a. Souvenir sheet, #2119-2121 4.50 4.50
Nos. 2116-2121 (6) 6.85 3.50

**County of Portucale, 900th Anniv. A588**

**1996, Oct. 9**
2122 A588 47e multicolored .60 .30

**Home Mail Delivery, 175th Anniv. — A589**

Designs: 47e, Mail carrier, 1821. 78e, Postman, 1854. 98e, Rural mail distrubutor, 1893. 100e, Postman, 1939. 140e, Postman, 1992.
**1996, Oct. 9**
2123 A589 47e multicolored .60 .30
2124 A589 78e multicolored 1.00 .50
2125 A589 98e multicolored 1.25 .65
2126 A589 100e multicolored 1.25 .65
2127 A589 140e multicolored 1.75 .90
Nos. 2123-2127 (5) 5.85 3.00

**Traditional Food A590**

47e, Minho-style pork. 78e, Trout, Boticas. 80e, Tripe, Oporto. 98e, Baked codfish, potatoes. 100e, Eel chowder, Aveiro. 140e, Lobster, Peniche.
**1996, Oct. 9**
2128 A590 47e multicolored .60 .30
2129 A590 78e multicolored 1.00 .50
2130 A590 80e multicolored 1.00 .50
2131 A590 98e multicolored 1.25 .65
2132 A590 100e multicolored 1.25 .65
2133 A590 140e multicolored 1.75 .90
Nos. 2128-2133 (6) 6.85 3.50
See Nos. 2170-2175.

---

**Joao Vaz Corte-Real, Explorer, 500th Death Anniv. — A581**

Illustration reduced.
**1996, June 7**
2100 A581 140e multicolored 1.75 .90
**Souvenir Sheet**
2101 A581 315e like #2100 4.00 4.00
No. 2101 contains one 40x31 stamp with a continuous design.

**1996 Summer Olympics, Atlanta A582**

**1996, June 24**
2102 A582 47e Wrestling .60 .30
2103 A582 78e Equestrian 1.00 .50
2104 A582 98e Boxing 1.25 .65
2105 A582 140e Running 1.75 .90
**Souvenir Sheet**
2106 A582 300e Early track event 4.00 4.00
Olymphilex '96 (#2106).

**Augusto Hilário (1864-96), Singer A583**

*Perf. 12x11½*
**1996, July 1** Litho.
2107 A583 00e multicolored 1.00 .50

**Alphonsine Condification of Statutes, 550th Anniv. — A584**

**1996, Aug. 7**
2108 A584 350e multicolored 4.50 2.25

**Motion Pictures, Cent. A585**

Directors, stars of motion pictures: 47e, António Silva. 78e, Vasco Santana. 80e, Laura Alves. 98e, Aurélio Pais dos Reis. 100e, Leitao de Barros. 140e, António Lopes Ribeiro.
**1996, Aug. 7**
2109 A585 47e multicolored .60 .30
2110 A585 78e multicolored 1.00 .50
2111 A585 80e multicolored 1.00 .50
a. Souvenir sheet, #2109-2111 2.60 2.60
2112 A585 98e multicolored 1.25 .65
2113 A585 100e multicolored 1.25 .65
2114 A585 140e multicolored 1.75 .90
a. Souvenir sheet, #2112-2114 4.50 4.50
b. Souvenir sheet, #2109-2114 7.00 7.00
Nos. 2109-2114 (6) 6.85 3.50

---

**Type of 1995**

Designs: 3e, Exchange broker. 47e, Woman selling chestnuts. 78e, Cloth seller. 100e, Black woman selling mussels. 250e, Water seller.

*Perf. 11½x12*
**1996, Mar. 20** Litho.
2088 A560 3e multicolored .20 .20
2089 A560 47e multicolored .20 .30
a. Booklet pane, 10 #2089 6.00
2090 A560 78e multicolored 1.00 .50
a. Booklet pane, 10 #2090 10.00
2091 A560 100e multicolored 1.25 .65
2092 A560 250e multicolored 3.20 1.60
Nos. 2088-2092 (5) 6.25 3.25

**Joao de Deus (1830-96), Founder of New Method to Teach Reading A576**

*Perf. 12*
**1996, Apr. 12**
2093 A576 78e multicolored 1.00 .50

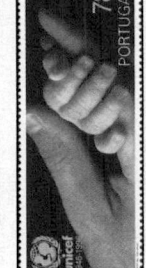

**UNICEF, 50th Anniv. — A577**

Illustration reduced.
**1996, Apr. 12**
2094 A577 78e shown 1.00 .50
2095 A577 140e Children 1.75 .90
a. Bkt. pane, 2 ea #2094-2095 5.50
Complete booklet, #2095a 5.50

**Joao de Barros (1496-1570), Writer — A578**

**1996, Apr. 12**
2096 A578 140e multicolored 1.75 .90

**Helena Vieira da Silva (1908-92), Painter — A579**

**1996, May 3**
2097 A579 98e multicolored 1.25 .60
a. Souvenir sheet of 3 3.75 3.75
Europa.

**Euro '96, European Soccer Championships, Great Britain — A580**

*Perf. 12*
**1996, June 7** Litho.
2098 A580 78e Soccer players 1.00 .50
2099 A580 140e Soccer players, diff. 1.75 .90
a. Souvenir sheet, #2098-2099 2.75 2.75

Bow of Frigate "D. Fernando II e Gloria," 1843.
140e, Stern of "D. Fernando II e Gloria."

**1997, Feb. 12** *Litho.* *Perf. 12*
| 2142 | A595 | 49e | multicolored | .60 | .30 |
| 2143 | A595 | 80e | multicolored | 1.00 | .50 |
| 2144 | A595 | 100e | multicolored | 1.25 | .65 |
| 2145 | A595 | 140e | multicolored | 1.75 | .90 |
| | | | Nos. 2142-2145 (4) | 4.60 | 2.35 |

Project
Life — A596

**1997, Feb. 20**
2146 A596 80e multicolored 5.00 .50
a. Booklet pane of 5 5.00
b. Complete booklet, #2146a 5.00

19th Cent. Professions Type of 1995

Designs: 2e, Laundry woman. 5e, Broom seller. 30e, Olive oil seller. 49e, Woman with cape. 80e, Errand boy.

**1997, Mar. 12** *Litho.* *Perf. 11½x12*
| 2147 | A560 | 2e | multicolored | .20 | .20 |
| 2148 | A560 | 5e | multicolored | .20 | .20 |
| 2149 | A560 | 30e | multicolored | .35 | .20 |
| 2150 | A560 | 49e | multicolored | .60 | .30 |
| | | | Complete booklet, #2150a | 6.00 | |
| a. | | | Booklet pane of 10 | 6.00 | |
| 2151 | A560 | 80e | multicolored | 1.00 | .50 |
| | | | Complete booklet, #2151a | 10.00 | |
| a. | | | Booklet pane of 10 | 10.00 | |
| | | | Nos. 2147-2151 (5) | 2.35 | 1.40 |

Managing Institute of Public Credit, Bicent. A597

**1997, Mar. 12** *Litho.* *Perf. 12*
2152 A597 49e multicolored .60 .30

World Wildlife Fund — A598

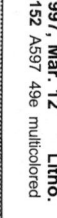

Galemys pyrenaicus: No. 2153. Looking upward. No. 2154. Paws around nose. No. 2155. Eating earthworm. No. 2156. Heading downward.

**1997, Mar. 12** *Litho.* *Perf. 12*
| 2153 | A598 | 49e | multicolored | .65 | .30 |
| 2154 | A598 | 49e | multicolored | .65 | .30 |
| 2155 | A598 | 49e | multicolored | .65 | .30 |
| 2156 | A598 | 49e | multicolored | .65 | .30 |
| a. | | | A598 Strip of 4, #2153-2156 | 2.75 | 1.50 |

Stories and Legends — A599

**1997, May 5** *Litho.* *Perf. 12*
2157 A599 100e multicolored 1.25 .65
a. Souvenir sheet of 3 4.50 3.25

Europa: Moorish girl watching over treasures.

---

Sports A600

**1997, May 29** *Perf. 12*
| 2158 | A600 | 49e | Surfing | .60 | .30 |
| 2159 | A600 | 80e | Skate board- ing | 1.00 | .50 |
| 2160 | A600 | 100e | Roller blading | 1.25 | .65 |
| 2161 | A600 | 140e | Parasailing | 1.75 | .90 |
| | | | Nos. 2158-2161 (4) | 4.60 | 2.35 |

#2162: a, BMX bike riding. b, Hang gliding.

2162 **Souvenir Sheet**
a.-b. A600 150e any single 1.60 1.60
Sheet of 2 5.00 4.00

Capture of Lisbon and Santarém from the Moors, 850th Anniv. — A601

Designs: No. 2163, Soldier on horse, front of fortress of Lisbon. No. 2164, Soldiers climbing ladders into Santareém at night.

**1997, June 9** *Perf. 12*
| 2163 | A601 | 80e | multicolored | 1.00 | .50 |
| 2164 | A601 | 80e | multicolored | 1.00 | .50 |
| a. | | | Pair, #2163-2164 | 2.00 | 2.00 |
| b. | | | Souvenir sheet, 2 #2164a | 4.00 | 4.00 |

Fr. Luís Frois (1532-97), Missionary, Historian — A602

Design: No. 2169, Fr. António Vieira (1608-97), missionary in Brazil, diplomat.

**1997, June 9**
| 2165 | A602 | 80e | multi, horiz. | 1.00 | .90 |
| 2166 | A602 | 140e | multi | 1.75 | .90 |
| 2167 | A602 | 140e | multi | 1.75 | .90 |
| | | | Nos. 2165-2167 (3) | 4.50 | 2.30 |

See Macao 878-879.

Fr. José de Anchieta (1534-97), Missionary in Brazil — A603

80e, Frois on mission in Orient. #2166, Frois holding hands across chest. #2167, Frois, church.

**1997, June 9** *Litho.*
2168 A603 140e multicolored 1.75 .90
2169 A603 350e multicolored 4.50 2.25

See Brazil Nos. 2639-2640.

---

City of Oporto, UNESCO World Heritage Site — A605

Illustration reduced.

**1997, July 5** *Litho.* *Perf. 12*
2174 A590 140e multicolored 1.75 .85
2175 A590 200e multicolored 2.50 1.25
**Souvenir Sheet**
2176 A605 350e multicolored 4.50 4.50
Nos. 2170-2175 (6) 7.30 3.75

A606

**1997, July 19** *Litho.* *Perf. 12*
2177 A606 100e multicolored 1.25 .65

Brotherhood of the Yeoman of Beja, 700th anniv.

**1997, Aug. 29** *Litho.* *Perf. 12*
2178 A607 50e multicolored .65 .30

Natl. Laboratory of Civil Engineering, 50th anniv.

A607

Treaty of Alcanices, 700th Anniv. A608

**1997, Sept. 12**
2179 A608 80e multicolored 1.00 .50

Traditional Food Type of 1996

10e, Roasted kid, Beira Baixa. 49e, Fried shad. 80e, Lamb stew. 100e, Fish chowder, 140e, Swordfish fillets with corn. 200e, Stewed octopus, Azores.

**1997, July 5** *Litho.* *Perf. 12*
| 2170 | A590 | 10e | multicolored | .20 | .20 |
| 2171 | A590 | 49e | multicolored | .60 | .30 |
| 2172 | A590 | 80e | multicolored | 1.00 | .50 |
| 2173 | A590 | 100e | multicolored | 1.25 | .65 |

Arms of the Districts of Portugal A609

**1997, Sept. 17**
| 2180 | A609 | 10e | Evora | .20 | .20 |
| 2181 | A609 | 49e | Faro | .60 | .30 |
| 2182 | A609 | 80e | Guarda | 1.00 | .50 |
| 2183 | A609 | 100e | Leiria | 1.25 | .65 |
| 2184 | A609 | 140e | Lisboa | 1.75 | .90 |
| 2185 | A609 | 200e | Portalegre | 2.50 | 1.25 |
| a. | | | Souv. sheet, #2180, 2182, 2184 | 3.00 | 3.00 |
| b. | | | Souv. sheet, #2181, 2183, 2185 | 4.50 | 4.50 |
| | | | Nos. 2180-2185 (6) | 7.30 | 3.80 |

See Nos. 2249-2254.

---

Incorporation of Postal Service in State Administration, Bicent. — A610

**1997, Oct. 9**
2186 A610 80e multicolored 1.00 .50

Portuguese Cartography — A611

Designs: 49e, Map from atlas of Lopo Homen-Reineis, 1519. 80e, Map from atlas of Joao Freire, 1546. 100e, Chart by Diogo Ribeiro, 1529. 140e, Anonymous map, 1630.

**1997, Oct. 9**
| 2187 | A611 | 49e | multicolored | .60 | .30 |
| 2188 | A611 | 80e | multicolored | 1.00 | .50 |
| 2189 | A611 | 100e | multicolored | 1.25 | .65 |
| 2190 | A611 | 140e | multicolored | 1.75 | .90 |
| a. | | | Souvenir sheet #2187-2190 | 4.60 | 2.30 |
| | | | Nos. 2187-2190 (4) | 4.75 | 4.75 |

Discovery of Maritime Route to India Type of 1996

Voyage of Vasco da Gama: 49e, St. Gabriel's cross, Quelimane. 80e, Stop at island off Mozambique. 100e, Arrival in Mombasa. 140e, Reception for king of Molinda. 315e, Trading with natives, Natal.

**1997, Nov. 5** *Perf. 13½*
| 2191 | A593 | 49e | multicolored | .60 | .30 |
| 2192 | A593 | 80e | multicolored | 1.00 | .50 |
| 2193 | A593 | 100e | multicolored | 1.25 | .65 |
| 2194 | A593 | 140e | multicolored | 1.75 | .90 |
| a. | | | Souvenir sheet #2191-2194 | 4.60 | 2.30 |
| | | | Nos. 2191-2194 (4) | 4.60 | 2.30 |
| 2195 | A593 | 315e | multicolored | 4.00 | 4.00 |

Expo '98 — A612

Plankton: 49e, Loligo vulgaris. 80e, Scylarus arctus. 100e, Pontellina plumata. 140e, Solea senegalensis. 200e, Calcidiscus leptoporus. b, Tabellaria.

No. 2200: a, Calcidiscus leptoporus. b, Solea senegalensis.

**1997, Nov. 5** *Perf. 12*
| 2196 | A612 | 49e | multicolored | .60 | .30 |
| 2197 | A612 | 80e | multicolored | 1.00 | .50 |
| 2198 | A612 | 100e | multicolored | 1.25 | .65 |
| 2199 | A612 | 140e | multicolored | 1.75 | .90 |
| | | | Nos. 2196-2199 (4) | 4.60 | 2.35 |
| | | | **Souvenir Sheet** | | |
| | | | *Perf. 12½* | | |
| 2200 | | | Sheet of 2 | 2.50 | 2.50 |
| a.-b. | | | A612 100e any single | 1.25 | 1.25 |

See Nos. 2215-2219, 2226-2244.

Souvenir Sheet

Sintra, UNESCO World Heritage Site — A613

**1997, Dec. 5**      *Perf. 12*
2201 A613 350e multicolored    4.50 4.50

Portuguese Military Engineering, 350th Anniv. — A614

Engineering officer, map of fortress: 50e, Almeida, 80e, Miranda do Douro. 100e, Moncan. 140e, Elvas.

**1998, Jan. 28**    *Litho.*      *Perf. 12*
2202 A614 50e multicolored       .60 .30
2203 A614 80e multicolored      1.00 .50
2204 A614 100e multicolored    1.25 .65
2205 A614 140e multicolored    1.75 .90
a. Booklet pane, #2202-2205, perf. 12 vert.      4.75
Complete booklet, #2206a    4.75
*Nos. 2202-2205 (4)*      4.60 2,35

Roberto Ivens (1850-98), Naturalist A615

**1998, Jan. 28**
2206 A615 140e multicolored      1.75 .90

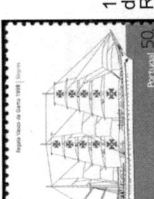

Misericórdias (Philanthropic Organizations), 500th Anniv. — A616

Sculptures: 80e, Madonna wearing crown surrounded by angels, people kneeling in praise, vert. 100e, People of antiquity gathered around another's bedside.

**1998, Feb. 20**
2207 A616 80e multicolored      1.00 .50
2208 A616 100e multicolored    1.25 .65

---

Souvenir Sheet

Aqueduct of the Free Waters, 250th Anniv. — A617

**1998, Feb. 20**
2209 A617 350e multicolored    4.50 2.25

**19th Cent. Professions Type of 1995**

10e, Fish seller. 40e, Collector of alms. 50e, Ceramics seller. 85e, Duck and eggs vendor. 250e, Quejjadas (small cakes made of cheese) seller.

**1998, Mar. 20**      *Perf. 11½x12*
2210 A560 10e multicolored      .20 .20
2211 A560 40e multicolored      .50 .25
2212 A560 50e multicolored      .60 .30
a. Booklet pane of 10      6.25
2212a Complete booklet, #2212a    6.25
2213 A560 85e multicolored    1.10 .55
a. Booklet pane of 10    10.50
2214 A560 250e multicolored    3.25 1.60
a. Complete booklet, #2213a    10.50
*Nos. 2210-2214 (5)*      5.65 2.90

**Expo '98 Type of 1997**

Plankton: 50e, Pilumnus hirtellus. 85e, Lophius piscatorius. 100e, Sparus aurata. 140e, Cladonema radiatum.
No. 2219: a, Noctiluca miliaris. b, Dinophysis acuta.

**1998, Mar. 20**      *Perf. 12*
2215 A612 50e multicolored      .60 .30
2216 A612 85e multicolored    1.00 .50
2217 A612 100e multicolored    1.25 .65
2218 A612 140e multicolored    1.75 .90
*Nos. 2215-2218 (4)*      4.60 2.35

**Souvenir Sheet**

2219 A612 100e Sheet of 2, #a.-b.    2.50 2.50
c. Sheet of 12, #2106-2199, 2200a-2200b, 2215-2210, 2219a-2219b)    15.00 16.00

Opening of the Vasco Da Gama Bridge A618

**1998, Mar. 29**    *Litho.*      *Perf. 12*
2220 A618 200e multicolored    2.50 1.25

**Souvenir Sheet**

2221 A618 200e like #2220    2.50 2.50
Stamp in No. 2221 is a continuous design and shows bridge cables overlapping at far left.

Oporto Industrial Assoc., 150th Anniv. A619

**1998, Apr. 30**
2222 A619 80e multicolored    1.00 .50

Vasco da Gama Aquarium, Cent. A620

**1998, May 13**
2223 A620 50e Seahorse      .60 .30
2224 A620 80e Fish    1.00 .50

---

National Festivals A621

**1998, May 21**
2225 A621 100e People's Saints    1.25 .65
a. Souvenir sheet of 3    3.75 3.75

Europa.

**Expo '98 Type of 1997**

Designs: No. 2226. Portuguese sailing ship, face on stone cliff. No. 2227, Diver, astrolabe. No. 2228, Various fish. No. 2230, Mermaid swimming, fish. No. 2231, Children under water holding globe.
No. 2232: a, Portuguese Pavilion. b, Pavilion of the Future. c, Oceans Pavilion. d, Knowledge of the Seas Pavilion. e, Pavilion of Utopia. f, Mascot putting letter into mailbox.
No. 2233, like #2216. No. 2234, like #2219a. No. 2235, like #2215. No. 2236, like #2217. No. 2237, like #2218. No. 2238, like #2218. No. 2239, like #2227. No. 2240, like #2229. No. 2241, like #2231. No. 2242, like #2226. No. 2243, like #2228. No. 2244, like #2230.

**1998, May 21**
2226 A612 50e multicolored      .60 .30
2227 A612 50e multicolored      .60 .50
2228 A612 85e multicolored    1.00 .50
2229 A612 85e multicolored    1.75 .90
2230 A612 140e multicolored    1.75 .90
2231 A612 140e multicolored    1.75 .90
2232    Sheet of 6    6.75 6.75
a.-f.       #a.-f.    6.75 6.75
a. A612 50e multicolored      .60 .30
b.-c. A612 85e any single    1.00 .50
d.-e. A612 140e any single    1.75 .90
g. A612 80e multicolored    1.25 .6b
a. Souvenir sheet, #2232a-2232e    6.25 6.25

**Die Cut 11½**

**Self-Adhesive Coil Stamps**

**Size: 29x24mm**

2233 A612 50e multicolored      .60 .30
2234 A612 50e multicolored      .60 .30
2235 A612 50e multicolored      .60 .30
2236 A612 50e multicolored      .60 .30
2237 A612 50e multicolored      .60 .30
2238 A612 50e multicolored      .60 .30
a. Strip of 6, #2233-2238    3.75
2239 A612 85e multicolored    1.00 .45
2240 A612 85e multicolored    1.00 .45
2241 A612 85e multicolored    1.00 .45
2242 A612 85e multicolored    1.00 .45
2243 A612 85e multicolored    1.00 .45
2244 A612 85e multicolored    1.00 .45
a. Strip of 6, #2239-2244    6.00
Nos. 2233-2238 are not inscribed with Latin names.

Discovery of Radium, Cent. — A622

**1998, June 1**
2245 A622 140e Marie Curie    1.75 .90

Ferreira de Castro (1898-1974), Writer — A623

**1998, June 10**
2246 A623 50e multicolored      .60 .30

---

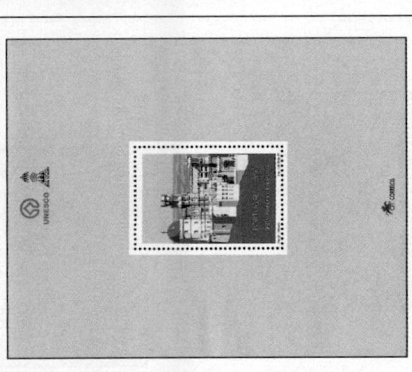

Bernardo Marques, Writer, Birth Cent. — A624

**1998, June 10**
2247 A624 85e multicolored    1.00 .50

**Souvenir Sheet**

Universal Declaration of Human Rights, 50th Anniv. — A625

Illustration reduced.

**District Arms Type of 1997**

**1998, June 18**
2248 A625 315e multicolored    4.00 2.00

**1998, June 23**
2249 A609 50e Vila Real      .60 .30
2250 A609 85e Setubal    1.00 .50
2251 A609 85e Viana do Castelo    1.00 .65
2252 A609 100e Santarem    1.25 .65
2253 A609 100e Viseu    1.25 .6b
a. Souvenir sheet of 3, #2250, 2252-2253    3.50 3.50
2254 A609 200e Porto    2.50 1.25
a. Souvenir sheet of 3, #2249, 2251, 2254    4.25 4.25
*Nos. 2249-2254 (6)*    7.60 3.85

Marinha Grande Glass Industry, 250th Anniv. A626

Designs. 50e, Blowing glass, furnace. 80e, Early worker heating glass, ornament. 100e, Factory, bottles. 140e, Modern worker heating glass, vases.

**1998, July 7**
2255 A626 50e multicolored      .60 .30
2256 A626 80e multicolored    1.00 .50
2257 A626 100e multicolored    1.25 .65
2258 A626 140e multicolored    1.75 .90
*Nos. 2255-2258 (4)*    4.60 2.35

1998 Vasco da Gama Regatta A627

Sailing ship, country represented: 50e, Sagres, Portugal. No. 2260, Asgard II, Ireland. 80e, Rose, US. No. 2262, Kruzenshtern, Russia. No. 2263, Amerigo Vespucci, Italy. 140e, Creoula, Portugal.

**1998, July 31**
2259 A627 50e multicolored      .60 .30
2260 A627 50e multicolored      1.00 .50
2261 A627 85e multicolored    1.00 .65
2262 A627 100e multicolored    1.25 .65
2263 A627 100e multicolored    1.75 .65
2264 A627 140e multicolored    1.75 .90
*Nos. 2259-2264 (6)*    6.85 3.50

**Discovery of Maritime Route to India Type of 1996**

Voyage of Vasco da Gama: No. 2265, Meeting with pilot, Ibn Madjid. 80e, Storm in the Indian Ocean. 100e, Arrival in Calicut. 140e, Meeting with the Samorin of Calicut.
No. 2269: a, like #2136. b, like #2137. c, like #2138. d, like #2139. e, like #2191. f, like #2191.

#2192, g, like #2193, h, like #2194, i, like #2266, j, like #2267, k, like #2268, 315e, King of Melinde listening to narration of the history of Portugal.

**1998, Sept. 4**    *Perf. 13½*

| | | | | |
|---|---|---|---|---|
| 2265 | A593 | 50e | multicolored | .60 .30 |
| 2266 | A593 | 80e | multicolored | 1.00 .50 |
| 2267 | A593 | 100e | multicolored | 1.25 .65 |
| 2268 | A593 | 140e | multicolored | 1.75 .90 |

Nos. 2265-2268 (4)   4.60 2.35

**Sheet of 12**
2269 A593 50e #a.-k. + #2265  7.50 7.50

**Souvenir Sheet**
2270 A593 315e multicolored  4.00 4.00

**1998, Oct. 9**    *Perf. 12x11½*
2271 A628 50e multicolored  .60 .30
2272 A628 140e multicolored  1.75 .90
See Brazil No. 2691.

Lisbon-Coimbra Mail Coach, Decree to Reorganize Maritime Mail to Brazil, Bicent. — A628

50e, Modern van delivering mail, postal emblm. 140e, Sailing ship, Postilhao da America, mail coach.

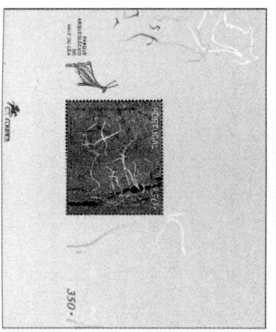

**Souvenir Sheet**

8th Iberian-American Summit, Oporto — A629

Illustration reduced.

**1998, Oct. 18**    *Perf. 12½*
2273 A629 140e multicolored  1.75 .90

Coa Valley Archaeological Park — A630

**1998, Nov. 5**
2274 A630 350e multicolored  4.50 2.25

Health in Portugal — A631

**1998, Nov. 5**    *Perf. 12*
2275 A631 100e multicolored  1.25 .65

---

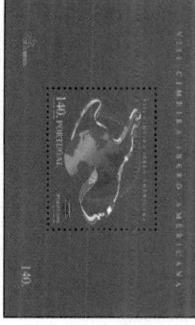
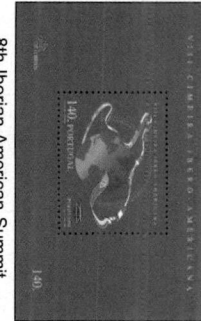

**Souvenir Sheet**

**1998, Dec. 15**    **Litho.**    *Perf. 12*
2276 A632 200e multicolored  2.50 1.25

José Saramago, 1998 Nobel Prize Winner for Literature — A632

**1999, Jan. 11**    **Litho.**    *Perf. 13¼*
2276A A521 A brown, gray & black  1.00 .50

No. 2276A sold for 51e on date of issue. Inscription at LR reads "Imp : Lito Maia 99."

Postrider Type of 1993

**19th Cent. Professions Type**

**1999, Feb. 26**    **Litho.**    *Perf. 11½x12*
2277 A560 51e multicolored  .65 .35
2278 A560 86e multicolored  1.10 .55
2279 A560 95e multicolored  1.25 .65
2280 A560 100e multicolored  1.25 .65
2281 A560 210e multicolored  2.75 1.40
Nos. 2277-2281 (5)  7.00 3.60

Designs: 51e, Knife grinder. 86e, Female bread seller. 95e, Coachman. 100e, Milkmaid. 210e, Basket seller.

**Booklet Stamps**
**Self-Adhesive**
*Serpentine Die Cut 11¼*
2281A A560 51e like #2277  .65 .35
  c. Booklet pane of 10  6.50
2281B A560 95e like #2279  1.25 .65
  d. Booklet pane of 10  12.50
Nos. 2281Ac, 2281Bd are complete booklets. The peelable backing serves as a booklet cover.

Beginning with No. 2282 denominations are on the stamps in both escudos and euros. Listings show the value in escudos.

Introduction of the Euro — A633
**1999, Mar. 15**    *Perf. 12*
2282 A633 95e multicolored  1.25 .65

Australia '99, World Stamp Expo — A634

**1999, Mar. 19**
2283 A634 140e multicolored  1.75 .90
2284 A634 140e multicolored  1.75 .90
  a. Pair, #2283-2284.  3.50 3.50
Portuguese in Australia: No. 2283, Sailing ship offshore, kangaroos. No. 2284, Sailing ship, natives watching. 350e, like #2783-2784.

**Souvenir Sheet**
**1999, Mar. 19**
2285 A634 350e multicolored  4.25 4.25
No. 2285 contains one 80x30mm stamp and is a continuous design.

---

Joao Almeida Garrett (1799-1854), Writer — A636
**1999, Mar. 24**
2287 A636 95e multicolored  1.25 .65

**Souvenir Sheet**
2288 A636 210e like #2287  2.75 1.40

Flight Between Portugal and Macao, 75th Anniv. — A637
Airplanes: No. 2289, "Patria". No. 2290, DH9.
**1999, Apr. 19**
2289 A637 140e multicolored  1.75 .90
2290 A637 140e multicolored  1.75 .90
  a. Souvenir sheet, #2289-2290.  3.50 3.50
See Macao 979-980.

Presidential Campaign of José Norton de Matos, 50th Anniv. — A635
**1999, Mar. 24**
2286 A635 80e multicolored  1.00 .50

**1999, Apr. 25**
2291 A638 51e Carnation  .65 .30
2292 A639 80e Assembly building  1.00 .50
  a. Souvenir sheet, #2291-2292  1.75 1.75

Revolution, 25th Anniv. — A639
Illustration reduced (#2292).

Council of Europe, 50th Anniv. — A640

A638

---

Marquis de Pombal (1699-1782), Statesman — A642
**1999, May 13**
2295 A642 80e multicolored  1.00 1.00

**Souvenir Sheet**
2296 A642 80e multicolored  3.00 3.00
Souvenir Sheet of 2, #a.-b.

No. 2295: 80e Portrait. No. 2296: a. 80e, Portrait and portion of statue. b. 210e, Hand, quill pen.

Europa A641
**1999, May 5**
2294 A641 100e Wolf, iris, Peneda-Gerês Natl. Park  1.25 .65
  a. Souvenir sheet of 3  3.75 3.75

Meeting of Portuguese and Chinese Cultures in Macao — A643
Designs: 51e, Ship, junk, bridge. 80e, Macao dancers in Portuguese outfits. 95e, Virgin Mary statue, dragon heads. 140e, Church, temple. 140e, Statues in park, horiz.
**1999, June 24**    *Perf. 11¾x12, 12x11¾*    **Litho.**
2297 A643 51e multicolored  .60 .30
2298 A643 80e multicolored  1.00 .50
2299 A643 95e multicolored  1.25 .60
2300 A643 100e multicolored  1.25 .65
2301 A643 140e multicolored  1.75 .90
Nos. 2297-2301 (5)  5.85 2.95

Portuguese Air Force, 75th Anniv. — A644
Designs: No. 2302, De Havilland DH 82A Tiger Moth. No. 2303, Supermarine Spitfire Vb. No. 2304, Breguet Bre XIV A2. No. 2305, Spad S. VII-C1. No. 2306, Caudron G.III. No. 2307, Junkers Ju-52/3m g3e.
**1999, July 1**    *Perf. 12x11¾*
2302 A644 51e multicolored  .60 .30
2303 A644 51e multicolored  .60 .30
2304 A644 85e multicolored  1.10 .55
2305 A644 85e multicolored  1.10 .55
2306 A644 95e multicolored  1.25 .65
2307 A644 95e multicolored  1.25 .65
  a. Souv. sheet of 6, #2302-2307  6.00 6.00
Nos. 2302-2307 (6)  5.90 3.00

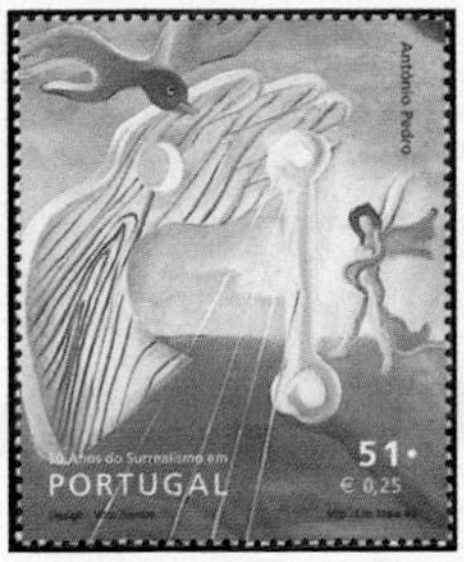

Surrealist Group of Lisbon, 50th Anniv. A645

Sections of Painting "Cadavre Exquis" by: 51e, António Pedro (1909-66). 80e, Marcellino Vespeira (b. 1926). 95e, Joao Moniz Pereira (1920-89). 100e, Fernando de Azevedo (b. 1923). 140e, António Domingues (b. 1921).

**1999, July 2 Litho.** ***Perf. 13¼***
**2308** A645 51e multicolored .60 .30
**2309** A645 80e multicolored 1.00 .50
**2310** A645 95e multicolored 1.25 .60
**2311** A645 100e multicolored 1.25 .65
**2312** A645 140e multicolored 1.75 .90
*a.* Souv. sheet of 5, #2308-2312 5.75 5.75
*Nos. 2308-2312 (5)* 5.85 2.95

PhilexFrance 99, No. 2312a.

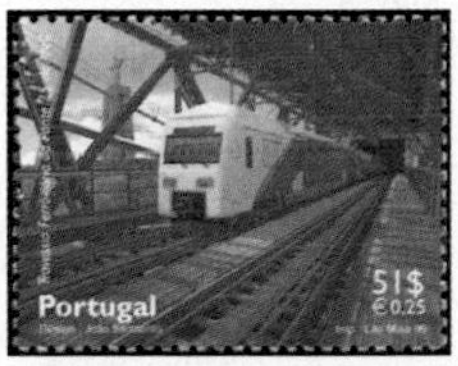

Inauguration of Rail Link Over 25th of April Bridge — A646

51e, No. 2315, Train, tunnel entrance. 95e, No. 2316, Train, viaduct, Tagus River.

**1999, July 29 Litho.** ***Perf. 12x11¾***
**2313** A646 51e multicolored .60 .30
**2314** A646 95e multicolored 1.25 .60

**Souvenir Sheets**

**2315** A646 350e multicolored 4.50 4.50
**2316** A646 350e multicolored 4.50 4.50

Nos. 2315-2316 each contain one 80x30mm stamp.

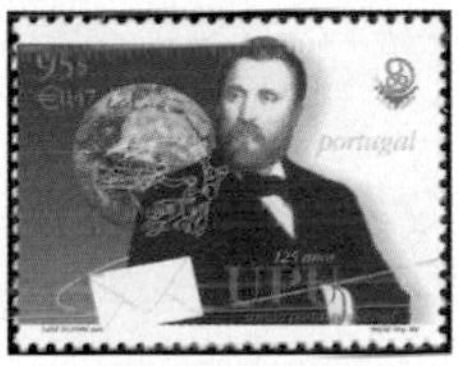

UPU, 125th Anniv. A647

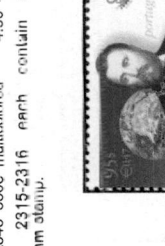

Designs: 95e, Heinrich von Stephan, earth, letter. 140e, Computer, earth, letter. 315e, Von Stephan, computer, earth, letters.

**1999, Aug. 21**
**2317** A647 95e multicolored 1.25 .65
**2318** A647 140e multicolored 1.75 .90

**Souvenir Sheet**

**2319** A647 315e multicolored 4.00 4.00

No. 2319 contains one 80x30mm stamp.

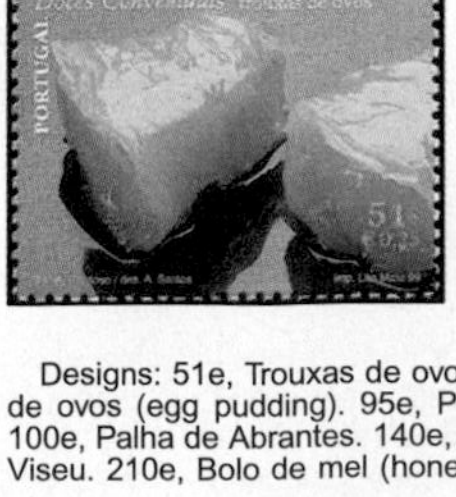

Desserts Originating in Convents A648

Designs: 51e, Trouxas de ovos. 80e, Pudim de ovos (egg pudding). 95e, Papos de anjo. 100e, Palha de Abrantes. 140e, Castanhas de Viseu. 210e, Bolo de mel (honey cake).

**1999, Aug. 30**
**2320** A648 51e multicolored .60 .30
**2321** A648 80e multicolored 1.00 .50
**2322** A648 95e multicolored 1.25 .60
**2323** A648 100e multicolored 1.25 .65
**2324** A648 140e multicolored 1.75 .90
**2325** A648 210e multicolored 2.75 1.40
*Nos. 2320-2325 (6)* 8.60 4.35

See Nos. 2366-2371.

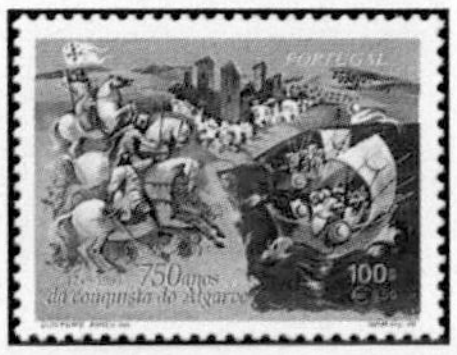

Conquest of Algarve, 750th Anniv. A649

**1999, Sept. 3 Litho.** ***Perf. 12x11¾***
**2326** A649 100e multi 1.25 .65

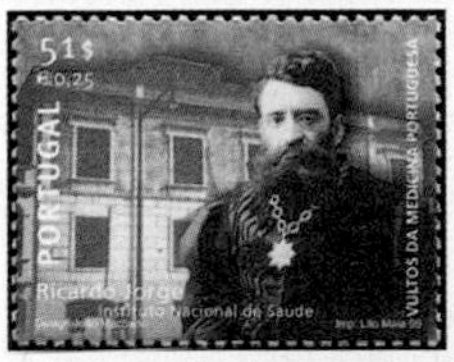

Medical Pioneers A650

#2327, Ricardo Jorge (1858-1939), Natl. Health Inst. #2328, Camara Pestana (1863-99), microscope, Pestana Bacteriological Inst. #2329, Francisco Gentil (1878-1964), Portuguese Inst. of Oncology. #2330, Egas Moniz (1874-1955), cerebral angiogram. #2331, Reynaldo dos Santos (1880-1970), arteriogram. #2332, Joao Cid dos Santos (1907-76), performer of 1st endarterectomy.

**1999, Sept. 20**
**2327** A650 51e multi .60 .30
**2328** A650 51e multi .60 .30
**2329** A650 80e multi 1.00 .50
**2330** A650 80e multi 1.00 .50
**2331** A650 95e multi 1.25 .60
**2332** A650 95e multi 1.25 .60
*Nos. 2327-2332 (6)* 5.70 2.80

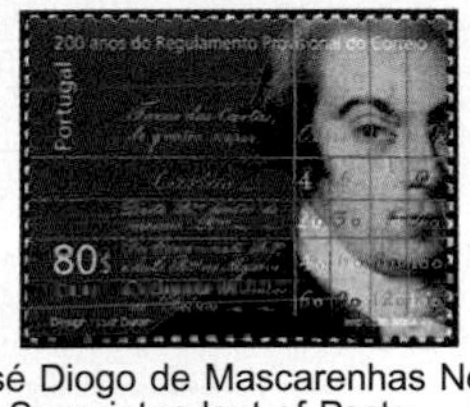

José Diogo de Mascarenhas Neto, First Superintendent of Posts — A651

**1999, Oct. 9**
**2333** A651 80e multi 1.00 .50

Postal reorganization and provisional mail regulations, bicent.

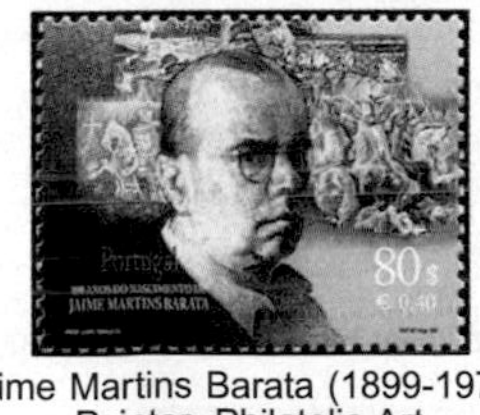

Jaime Martins Barata (1899-1970), Painter, Philatelic Art Consultant — A652

**1999, Oct. 9**
**2334** A652 80e multi 1.00 .50

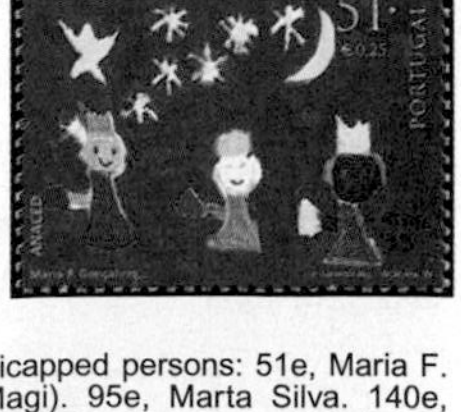

Christmas A653

Art by handicapped persons: 51e, Maria F. Gonçalves (Magi). 95e, Marta Silva. 140e, Luis F. Farinha. 210e, Gonçalves (Nativity).

**1999, Nov. 19**
**2335** A653 51e multi .60 .30
**2336** A653 95e multi 1.25 .60
**2337** A653 140e multi 1.75 .90
**2338** A653 210e multi 2.75 1.40
*Nos. 2335-2338 (4)* 6.35 3.20

**Souvenir Sheet**

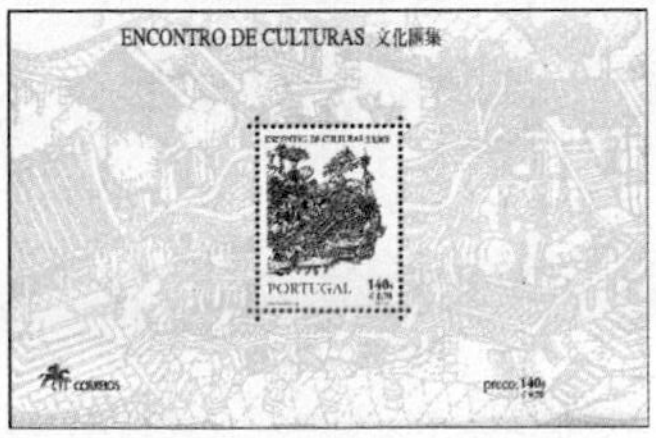

Meeting of Portuguese and Chinese Cultures — A654

**1999, Nov. 19** ***Perf. 11¾x12***
**2339** A654 140e multi 1.75 .90

See Macao No. 1009.

**Souvenir Sheet**

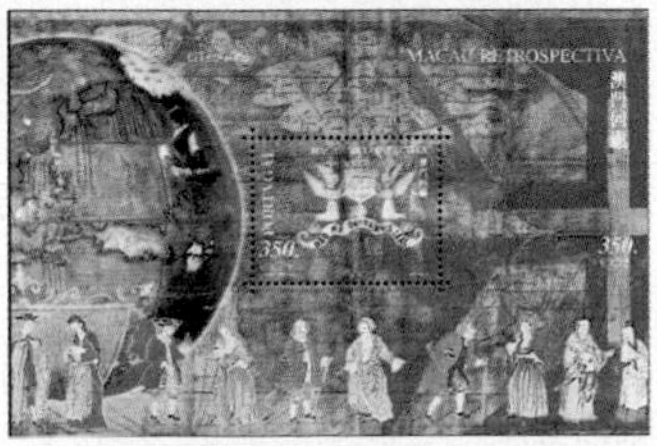

Retrospective of Macao's Portuguese History — A655

**1999, Dec. 19 Litho.** ***Perf. 12x11¾***
**2340** A655 350e multi 4.50 4.50

See Macao No. 1011.

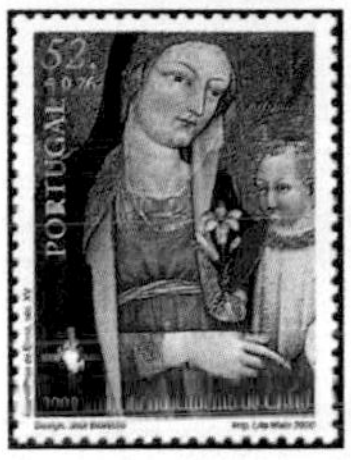

Birth of Jesus Christ, 2000th Anniv. — A656

**2000, Feb. 15 Litho.** ***Perf. 11¾x12***
**2341** A656 52e multi .60 .30

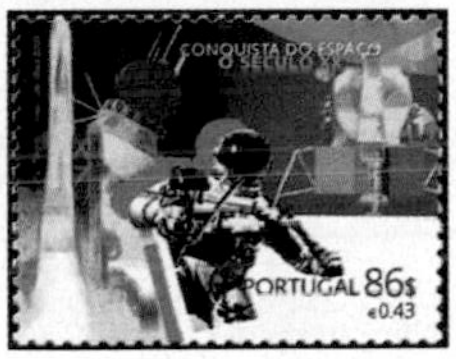

The 20th Century A657

Designs: 86e, Astronaut and spacecraft.

No. 2343: a, Human rights. b, Fashions (60x30mm). c, Ecology (60x30mm). d, Transportation (old). e, Transportation (modern). f, Like No. 2342. g, Space shuttle.

No. 2344: a, Authors Marcel Proust, Thomas Mann, James Joyce, Franz Kafka, Fernando Pessoa, Jorge Luis Borges, Samuel Beckett (50x30mm). b, Musicians and composers Claude Debussy, Igor Stravinsky, Arnold Schoenberg, Béla Bartók, George Gershwin, Charlie Parker, Bill Evans (50x30mm). c, Stage. d, Stage, diff. (60x30mm). e, Art (50x30mm). f, Art (30x30mm). g. Cinema (50x30mm). h, Cinema and television (30x30mm). i, Architecture (denomination at LL). j, Architecture (denomination at LR). k, Architecture (denomination at center).

No. 2345: a, Philosophers Edmund Husserl, Ludwig Wittgenstein, Martin Heidegger. b, Mathematicians Jules-Henri Poincaré, Kurt Gödel, Andrei Kolmogorov. c, Physicists Max Planck, Albert Einstein, Niels Bohr (50x30mm). d, Anthropologists Franz Boas, Claude Lévi-Strauss, Margaret Mead. e, Psychoanalyst Sigmund Freud and medical researcher Sir Alexander Fleming (30x30mm). f, Transplant pioneer Dr. Christiaan Barnard. g, Economists Joseph Schumpeter, John Maynard Keynes. h, Technology. i, Technology (30x30mm). j, Computer pioneers Alan Turing, John von Neumann. k, Radio pioneer Guglielmo Marconi. l, Information and communications (30x30mm).

**2000, Feb. 18** ***Perf. 12x11¾***
**2342** A657 86e multi 1.10 .55

**Souvenir Sheets of 7, 11, 12**

**2343** A657 52e #a.-g. 4.50 4.50
**2344** A657 52e #a.-k. 7.00 7.00
**2345** A657 52e #a.-l. 7.75 7.75

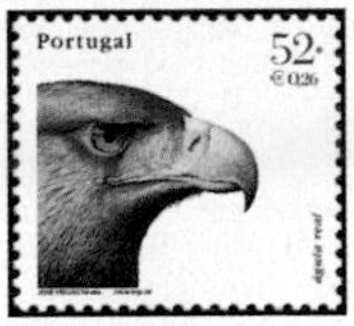

Birds — A658

Designs: 52e, Golden eagle. 85e, Great crested grebe. 90e, Flamingo. 100e, Gannet. 215e, Teal.

**2000, Mar. 2 Litho.** ***Perf. 11¾x11½***
**2346** A658 52e multi .60 .30
**2347** A658 85e multi 1.10 .55
**2348** A658 90e multi 1.10 .55
**2349** A658 100e multi 1.25 .65
**2350** A658 215e multi 2.75 1.40
*Nos. 2346-2350 (5)* 6.80 3.45

**Booklet Stamps**

***Serpentine Die Cut 11¼***

**Self-Adhesive**

**2351** A658 52e Like #2346 .60 .30
*a.* Booklet, 10 #2351 6.00
**2352** A658 100e Like #2349 1.25 .65
*a.* Booklet, 10 #2352 12.50

See Nos. 2401-2407.

Portuguese Presidency of Council of Europe A659

**2000, Mar. 23** ***Perf. 12x11¾***
**2353** A659 100e multi 1.25 .65

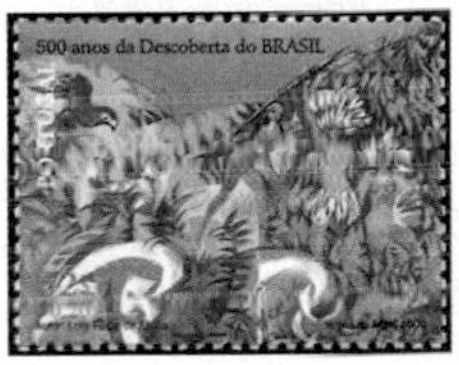

Discovery of Brazil, 500th Anniv. A660

Designs: 52e, Two sailors, three natives, parrot. 85e, Sailor, ships, four natives. 100e, Sailors, natives, sails. 140e, Sailor and natives inspecting tree.

**2000, Apr. 11 Litho.** ***Perf. 12x11¾***
**2354** A660 52e multi .60 .30
**2355** A660 85e multi 1.10 .55
**2356** A660 100e multi 1.25 .65
**2357** A660 140e multi 1.25 .60
*a.* Souvenir sheet, #2354-2357 3.50 1.75
*Nos. 2354-2357 (4)* 4.20 2.10

Lubrapex 2000 (#2357a). See Brazil No. 2738.

**Europa, 2000**

Common Design Type

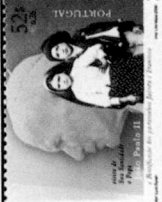

**2000, May 9** ***Perf. 11¾x12***
**2358** CD17 100e multi 1.25 .65
*a.* Souvenir sheet of 3 3.75 3.75

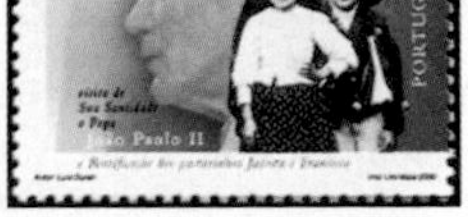

Visit of Pope John Paul II A661

**2000, May 12** ***Perf. 12x11¾***
**2359** A661 52e multi .60 .30

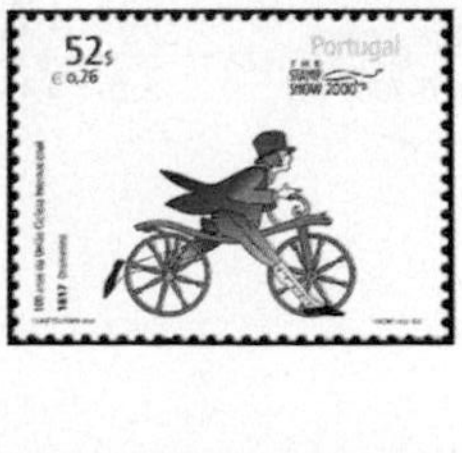

Intl. Cycling Union, Cent. and The Stamp Show 2000, London A662

**Bicycles: 52e., Draisenne, 1817, 85e.,**
Michaux, 1868. 100e. Ariel, 1871, 140e.,
Rover, 1888. BTX, 2000. 350e, GT,
2000.

## 2000, May 22

| | | | |
|---|---|---|---|
| 2360 | A662 | 52e | multi | .60 |
| 2361 | A662 | 85e | multi | 1.10 |
| 2362 | A662 | 100e | multi | 1.25 |
| 2363 | A662 | 140e | multi | 1.75 |
| 2364 | A662 | 215e | multi | 2.75 |
| 2365 | A662 | 350e | multi | 4.50 |
| a. | Souvenir sheet #2360-2365 | | | 11.95 |

Nos. 2360-2365 (6) 12.00

**Desserts Type of 1999**

Designs: 52e., Fatias de Tomar. 85e., Dom
rodrigos, 100e., Sericaia, 140e., Pao-de-ló,
215e., Pao de rala. 350e, Bolo real paraiso,
2000.

## 2000, May 30

| | | | |
|---|---|---|---|
| 2366 | A648 | 52e | multi | .60 |
| 2367 | A648 | 85e | multi | 1.10 |
| 2368 | A648 | 100e | multi | 1.25 |
| 2369 | A648 | 140e | multi | 1.75 |
| 2370 | A648 | 215e | multi | 2.75 |
| 2371 | A648 | 350e | multi | 4.50 |
| a. | Souvenir sheet #2366-2371 | | | 11.95 |

Nos. 2366-2371 (6) 6.05

## 2000, May 31
Fishermen's Day — A663

2372 A663 52e multi .60 .30

## 2000, Aug. 16 Litho. Perf. 12x11¾
Eça de Queiroz (1845-1900),
Writer — A667

2382 A667 85e multi 1.10 .55

## 2000, June 1

2373 A664 100e multi 1.25 .65

**Souvenir Sheet**

2374 A664 350e multi 4.50 4.50

Illustration reduced.
Designs: 100e, Portuguese landscapes.
350e, Portuguese pavilion.

No. 2374 contains one 40x31mm stamp.

Expo 2000, Hanover — A664

## 2000, June 2

2375 A665 85e multi 1.10 .55

Constituent
Assembly,
25th Anniv.
A665

## 2000, June 24
Color of Denominations
Perf. 12x11¾

| | | | |
|---|---|---|---|
| 2376 | A666 | 52e | rose | .60 | .30 |
| 2377 | A666 | 85e | claret | 1.10 | .55 |
| 2378 | A666 | 100e | green | 1.25 | .65 |
| 2379 | A666 | 100e | red | 1.25 | .65 |
| 2380 | A666 | 140e | yellow | 1.75 | .90 |
| 2381 | A666 | 215e | brown | 2.75 | 1.40 |
| a. | Souvenir sheet #2376-2381 | | | 8.75 | 8.75 |

Nos. 2376-2381 (6) 8.70 4.45

Cod, various fishermen and boats.

Cod
Fishing
A666

---

**Designs: 52e., Runner, 85e., Diving,**
100e, Yachting, 140e, Show jumping,
No. 2387, a, 85e, Fencing, b, 215e, Beach
volleyball.

## 2000, Sept. 15
2383-2386 A668 Set of 4 4.75 2.40

**Souvenir Sheet**

2387 A668 Sheet of 2, #a-b 3.75 3.75
Olymphilex 2000, Sydney (No. 2387).

2000
Summer
Olympics,
Sydney
A668

## 2000, Oct. 6
2388-2393 A669 Set of 6 7.75 7.75
2393a Souvenir sheet, #2393a 7.75 7.75

**Snoopy: No. 2388, 52e, At computer on dog
house No. 2389, 52e, Mailing letter, 85e, Driving mail truck. 100e, At letter sorting machine.
140e, Delivering mail, 215e, Reading letter.**

Snoopy
A669

## 2000, Nov. 10

2394 A670 Horiz. pair, #a-b 2.25 1.10

No. 2394: a, 85e, African native, geographer, theodolite, sextant. b, 100e, Sextant,
society emblem; map, zebras.
Illustration reduced.

Lisbon Geographic Society, 125th
Anniv. — A670

## 2001, Feb. 20 Litho. Perf. 12x11¾
2395 A671 85e Any single 1.10 .55

Sheet of 8 + 4 labels 8.75 0.75

**No. 2395: a, Carolina Michaelis de Vascon-
cellos (1851-1925), teacher. b, Miguel
Bombarda (1851-1910), doctor, politician. c,
Bernardino Machado (1851-1944), politician.
d, Tomás Alcaide (1901-1967), singer. e, José
Régio (1901-69), writer. f, José Rodrigues
Miguéis (1901-80), writer. g, Vitorino Nemésio
(1901-78), writer. h, Bento de Jesus Caraça
(1901-48), writer.**

Famous People — A671

---

**World Indoor Track and Field
Championships — A672**

Designs: 85e, Runners, 90e, Pole vault.
105e, Shot put. 250e, High jump.

## 2001, Mar. 1
2396-2399 A672 Set of 4 6.50 3.25

**Souvenir Sheet**
Bird Type of 2000 and

2400 A672 350e Hurdles 4.25 2.10

A672a

**Designs: 53e, Sisao. 105e, Perdiz-do-mar.
140e, Caimao. cinzento. 225e, Abutre do
Egipto.**

## 2001, Mar. 6 Litho. Perf. 11¾x11½

| | | | |
|---|---|---|---|
| 2401 | A658 | 53e | multi | .65 | .35 |
| 2402 | A658 | 85e | multi | 1.10 | .55 |
| 2403 | A658 | 105e | multi | 1.25 | .65 |
| 2404 | A658 | 140e | multi | 1.75 | .90 |
| 2405 | A658 | 225e | multi | 2.75 | 1.40 |

Nos. 2401-2405 (5) 7.50 3.85

**Serpentine Die Cut 11½x12
Self-Adhesive**

| | | | |
|---|---|---|---|
| 2406 | A658 | 53e | multi | .65 | .35 |
| 2406B | A672a | 85e | shown | 1.10 | .55 |
| a. | Booklet of 10 | | | 6.50 | |
| 2407 | A658 | 105e | multi | 1.25 | .65 |
| a. | Booklet of 10 | | | 12.50 | |

Arab
Heritage in
Portugal
A673

**Designs: 53e, Plate with ship design, 15th
cent. 90e, Tiles, 16th cent. 105e, Tombstone,
14th cent. 140e, Gold dinar, 12th cent. 225e,
container; 11th cent. 350e, Ceramic jug, 12th-
13th cent.**

## 2001, Mar. 28 Litho. Perf. 12x11¾
2408-2413 A673 Set of 6 12.00 6.00

Stampin'
the Future
Children's
Stamp
Design
Contest
Winners
A674

Art by: 85e, Angela M. Lopes. 90e, Maria G.
Silva, vert. 105e, Joao A. Ferreira.

## 2001, Apr. 10 Litho.
2414-2416 A674 Set of 3 3.50 1.75

Natl. Fine
Arts
Society,
Cent.
A675

**Designs: 85e, Sculpture, building, stained
glass window. 105e, Artist, painting.
350p, Hen and Chicks, by Girao.**

---

## 2001, Apr. 19 Perf. 12x11¾
2417-2418 A675 Set of 2 2.40 1.25
2419 A675 350e multi 4.25

**Constitution, 25th Anniv. — A676**

**Souvenir Sheet**

## 2001, Apr. 25
2420 A676 85e multi 1.10 .55
a. Souvenir sheet of 3

Europa
A677

## 2001, May 9
2421 A677 105e multi 1.25 .65

**Congratulations
A678**

Designs: No. 2422, 85e, Couple, hearts. No.
2423, 85e, Birthday cake. No. 2424, 85e,
Drinks. No. 2425, 85e, Flowers.

## 2001, May 16 Perf. 11¾x12
2422-2425 A678 Set of 4 4.25 2.10
2425a Souvenir sheet, #2422-
2425 4.25 4.25

Porto,
European
City of
Culture
A679

**Bridge and: 53e, Open book, 85e, Globe,
binary code, 105e, Piano. 140e, Stage curtain.
225e, Picture frame, 350e, Fireworks.**

## 2001, May 23 Perf. 12x11¾
2426-2431 A679 Set of 6 12.00 6.00
2431a Souvenir sheet, #2426-
2431 12.00 12.00

Military
Museum,
150th
Anniv.
A680

**Designs: 85e, Shell, 1773. 105e, Suit of
armor, 16th cent. No. 2434: a, 53e, Pistol of
King Joseph I, 1757. b, 53e, Cannon, 1797. c, 140e, Cannon,
1533. d, 140e, Helmet, 14th-15th cent.**

## 2001, June 7
2432-2433 A680 Set of 2 2.40 1.25

**Souvenir Sheet**

2434 A680 Sheet of 4, #a-d 4.75 4.75

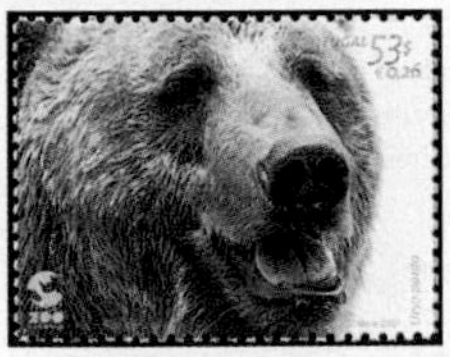

Animals at Lisbon Zoo
A681

Designs: 53e, Bear. 85e, Monkey. 90e, Iguana. 105e, Penguin. 225e, Toucan. 350e, Giraffe.

No. 2441, vert.: a, 85e, Elephant. b, 85e, Zebra. c, 225e, Lion. d, 225e, Rhinoceros.

**2001, June 11** *Perf. 12x11¾*
**2435-2440** A681 Set of 6 11.50 5.75

**Souvenir Sheet**

**2441** A681 Sheet of 4, #a-d 7.75 7.75

Belgica 2001 Intl. Stamp Exhibition, Brussels (#2441).

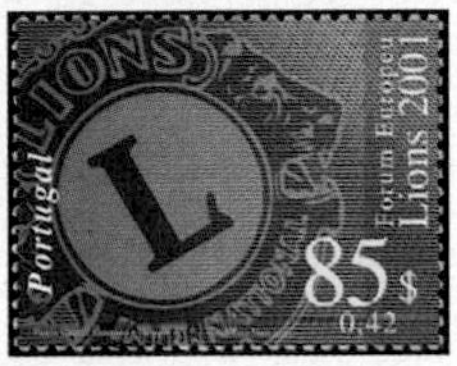

2001 Lions Intl. European Forum
A682

**2001, Sept. 6 Litho.** *Perf. 12x11¾*
**2442** A682 85e multi 1.10 .55

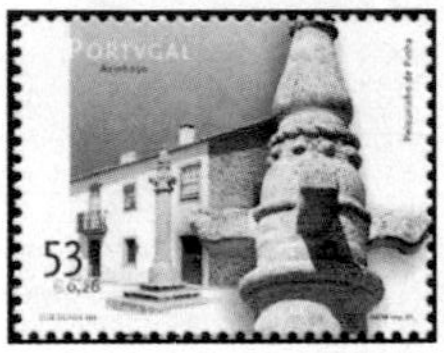

Pillars
A683

No. 2443: a, Azinhoso. b, Soajo. c, Bragança. d, Linhares. e, Arcos de Valdevez. f, Vila de Rua. g, Sernancelhe. h, Frechas.

**2001, Sept. 19**
**2443** Block of 8 5.25 2.75
*a.-h.* A683 53e Any single .65 .35

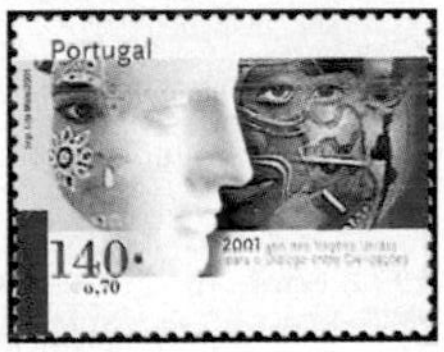

Year of Dialogue Among Civilizations
A684

**2001, Oct. 9**
**2444** A684 140e multi 1.75 .90

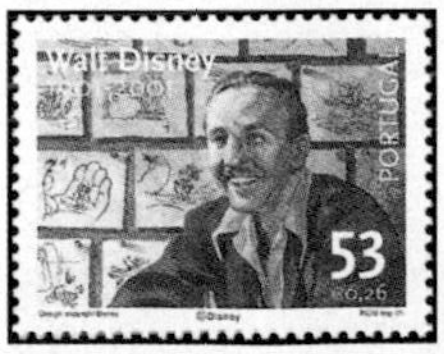

Walt Disney (1901-66)
A685

Designs: No. 2445, Disney and sketches.

No. 2446 — Various tiles and: a, Huey, Dewey and Louie. b, Mickey Mouse. c, Minnie Mouse. d, Goofy. e, Pluto. f, Donald Duck. g, Scrooge McDuck. h, Daisy Duck.

**2001, Oct. 18 Litho.** *Perf. 12x11¾*
**2445** A685 53e multi .65 .35

**Souvenir Sheet**

**2446** Sheet of 9, #a-h, 2445 6.00 6.00
*a.-h.* A685 53e Any single .65 .35

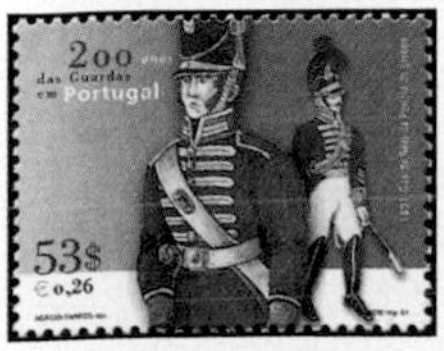

Security Services, 200th Anniv.
A686

Designs: 53e, Royal police guards, Lisbon, 1801. 85e, Municipal guard, Lisbon, 1834. 90e, National infantry guard, 1911. 105e, National cavalry guard, 1911. 140e, Transit brigade guard, 1970. 350e, Fiscal brigade guard, 1993.

225e, National cavalry guard, 1911, diff.

**2001, Oct. 22**
**2447-2452** A686 Set of 6 10.00 5.00

**Souvenir sheet**

**2453** A686 225e multi 2.75 2.75

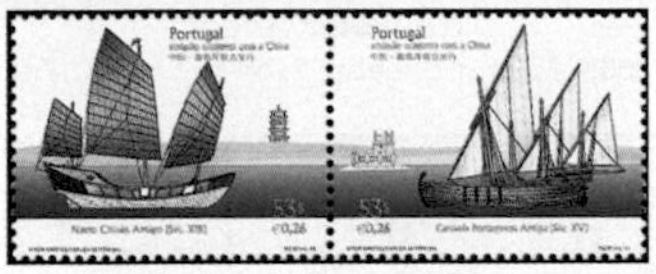

Sailing Ships — A687

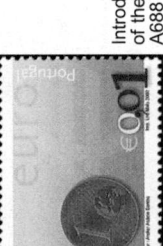

No. 2454: a, Chinese junk, 13th cent. b, Portuguese caravel, 15th cent.

Illustration reduced.

**2001, Nov. 8**
**2454** A687 53e Horiz. pair, #a-b 1.25 1.25

See People's Republic of China No. 3146.

100 Cents = 1 Euro (€)

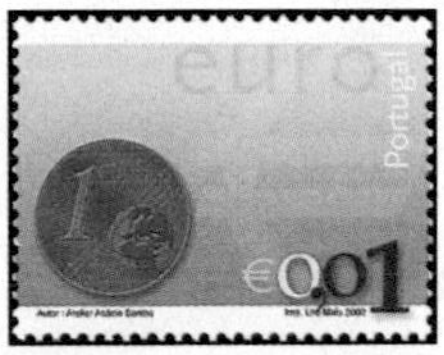

Introduction of the Euro
A688

**2002, Jan. 2 Litho.** *Perf. 12x11¾*

| | | | | | |
|---|---|---|---|---|---|
| **2455** | A688 | 1c | 1c coin | .20 | .20 |
| **2456** | A688 | 2c | 2c coin | .20 | .20 |
| **2457** | A688 | 5c | 5c coin | .20 | .20 |
| **2458** | A688 | 10c | 10c coin | .25 | .20 |
| **2459** | A688 | 20c | 20c coin | .50 | .25 |
| **2460** | A688 | 50c | 50c coin | 1.25 | .60 |
| **2461** | A688 | €1 | €1 coin | 2.50 | 1.25 |
| **2462** | A688 | €2 | €2 coin | 5.00 | 2.50 |
| | *Nos. 2455-2462 (8)* | | | 10.10 | 5.40 |

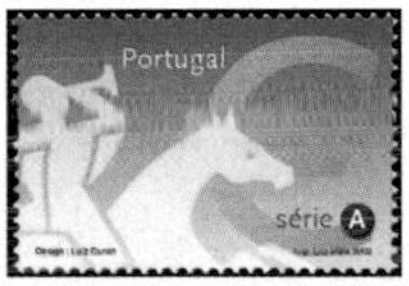

Postrider
A689

**2002, Jan. 2** *Perf. 13¼*
**2463** A689 A multi .80 .40

No. 2463 sold for 28c on day of issue.

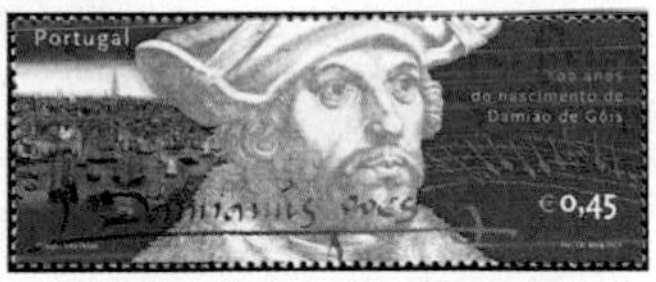

Damiao de Góis (1502-74), Diplomat and Historian — A690

Illustration reduced.

**2002, Feb. 26** *Perf. 12x11¾*
**2464** A690 45c multi 1.10 .55

**Bird Type of 2000 with Euro Denominations Only and**

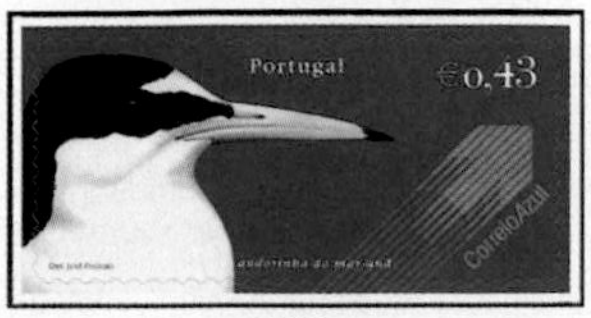

A690a

Designs: 2c, Abelharuco. No. 2466, 28c, Andorinha do mar ana. No. 2467, 43c, Bufo real. No. 2468, 54c, Cortiçol de barriga branca. 60c, Noitibó de nuca vermelha. 70c, Cuco rabilongo. Nos. , 2472A, 28c, Cuco-rabilongo. No. 2471A, 43c, Andorinha do mar ana. Nos. 2472, 2473, 54c, Bufo real.

**2002, Feb. 26** *Perf. 11¾x11½*

| | | | | | |
|---|---|---|---|---|---|
| **2465** | A658 | 2c | multi | .20 | .20 |
| **2466** | A658 | 28c | multi | .70 | .35 |
| **2467** | A658 | 43c | multi | 1.10 | .55 |
| **2468** | A658 | 54c | multi | 1.40 | .70 |
| **2469** | A658 | 60c | multi | 1.50 | .75 |
| **2470** | A658 | 70c | multi | 1.75 | .90 |

**Serpentine Die Cut 11½x12, 11x11½ (#2471A)**

| | | | | | |
|---|---|---|---|---|---|
| **2471** | A658 | 28c | multi | .70 | .35 |
| **2471A** | A690a | 43c | multi | 1.10 | .55 |
| **2472** | A658 | 54c | multi | 1.40 | .70 |

**Booklet Stamps**

***Serpentine Die Cut 11¼x11***

| | | | |
|---|---|---|---|
| **2472A** A658 28c multi | | .70 | .35 |
| *b.* | Booklet pane of 10 | 7.00 | |
| **2473** A658 54c multi | | 1.40 | .70 |
| *a.* | Booklet pane of 10 | 14.00 | |
| | *Nos. 2465-2473 (11)* | 11.95 | 6.10 |

No. 2472A has thicker numerals than No. 2471. No. 2473 lacks dot between "bufo" and "real" found on No. 2472. No. 2472A lacks dot between "cuco" and "rebilongo" found on No. 2471.

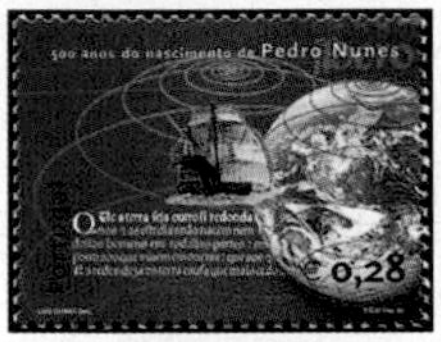

Pedro Nunes (1502-78), Mathematician and Geographer — A691

Designs: No. 2474, 28c, Ship, Earth. No. 2475, 28c, Ship, sextant. €1.15, Nunes.

**2002, Mar. 6** *Perf. 12x11¾*
**2474-2476** A691 Set of 3 4.25 2.10
*2476a* Souvenir sheet, #2474-2476 4.25 4.25

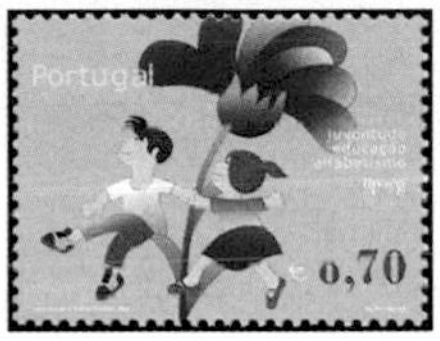

America Issue — Youth, Education and Literacy
A692

Children and: No. 2477, 70c, Flower. No. 2478, 70c, Pencil. No. 2479, 70c, Book.

**2002, Mar. 12**
**2477-2479** A692 Set of 3 5.25 2.75

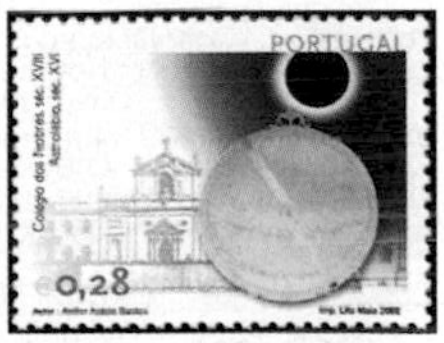

Astronomy
A693

Designs: No. 2480, 28c, Nobres College, 16th cent. astrolabe, solar eclipse. No. 2481, Polytechnic Observatory, Lisbon, telescope, Jupiter. 43c, Coimbra Observatory, quadrant, stars. No. 2483, 45c, King Pedro V, telescope, sun. No. 2484, 45c, King Luis, Cassegrain telescope, comet. 54c, Ajuda Observatory, telescope, Moon. €1.15, Porto Observatory Cassegrain telescope, Saturn. €1.75 Projector of C. Gulbenkian Planetarium, planets.

No. 2488: a, 18th cent. armillary sphere. b, 19th cent. theodolite.

**2002, Apr. 23 Litho.** *Perf. 12x11¾*
**2480-2487** A693 Set of 8 13.00 6.50

**Souvenir Sheet**

**2488** A693 70c Sheet of 2, #a-b 3.50 3.50

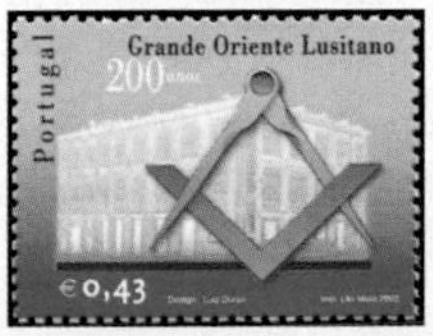

Grande Oriente Lusitano Masonic Organization, Bicent. — A694

**2002, May 9**
**2489** A694 43c multi 1.10 .55

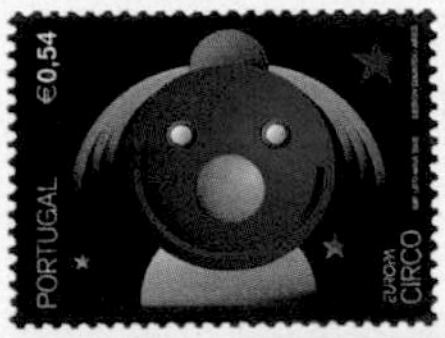

Europa
A695

**2002, May 9**
**2490** A695 54c multi 1.40 .70
*a.* Souvenir sheet of 3, perf. 12½ 4.25 4.25

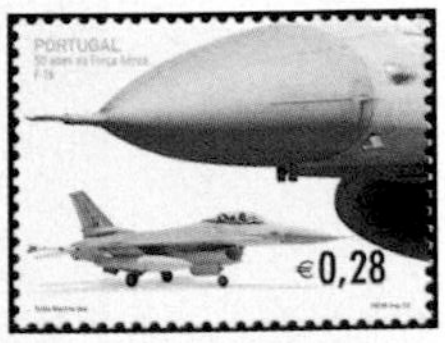

Portuguese Air Force, 50th Anniv.
A696

Designs: 28c, F-16. 43c, SA-300 Puma helicopter. 54c, A-Jet. 70c, C-130. €1.25, P-3P. No. 2496, €1.75, Fiat G91.

No. 2497: a, €1.15, Asas de Portugal. b, €1.75, Epsilon.

**2002, July 1 Litho.** *Perf. 12x11¾*
**2491-2496** A696 Set of 6 12.00 6.00

**Souvenir Sheet**

**2497** A696 Sheet of 2, #a-b 7.25 7.25

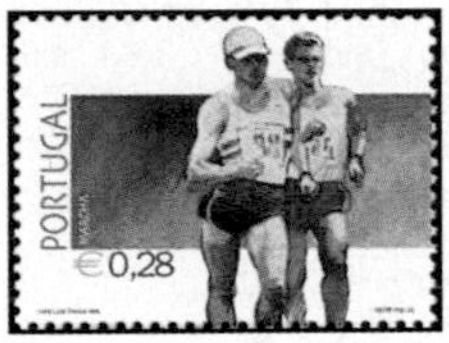

Sports
A697

Designs: No. 2498, 28c, Race walking. No. 2499, 28c, Gymnastics. No. 2500, 45c, Basketball. No. 2501, 45c, Handball. No. 2502, 54c, Fencing. No. 2503, 54c, Women's roller hockey. No. 2504, €1.75, Golf. No. 2505, €1.75, Soccer.

No. 2506: a, €1, Soccer players. b, €2, Soccer players, diff.

**2002, Aug. 2**
**2498-2505** A697 Set of 8 15.00 7.50

**Souvenir Sheet**

**2506** A697 Sheet of 2, #a-b 7.25 7.25

Portuguese Gymnastics Federation, 50th anniv. (#2499), World Fencing Championships (#2502), 6th Women's Roller Hockey Championships (#2503), 2002 World Cup Soccer Championships, Japan and Korea (#2505-2506), PhilaKorea 2002 World Stamp Exhibition (#2506).

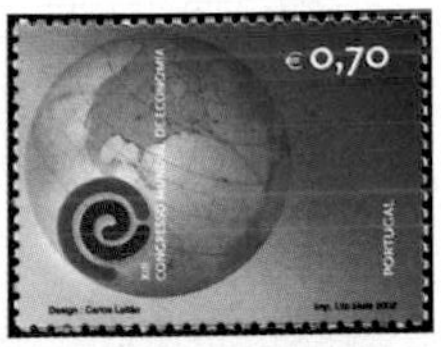

13th World Economics Congress
A698

**2002, Sept. 9**
**2507** A698 70c multi 1.75 .90

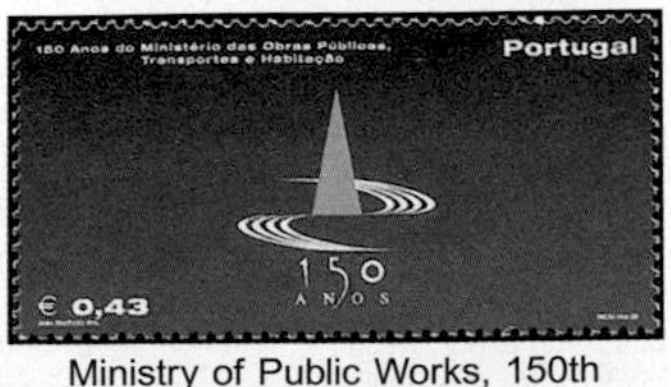

Ministry of Public Works, 150th Anniv. — A699

Designs: No. 2508, Anniversary emblem.

No. 2509: a, Port administration. b, Rail transportation. c, Air transportation. d, Infrastructure. e, Public buildings. f, Housing.

**2002, Sept. 30 Litho.** *Perf. 12x12½*
**2508** A699 43c shown 1.10 .85

**Miniature Sheet**

**2509** Sheet of 6 6.75 6.75
*a.-f.* A699 43c Any single 1.10 .85

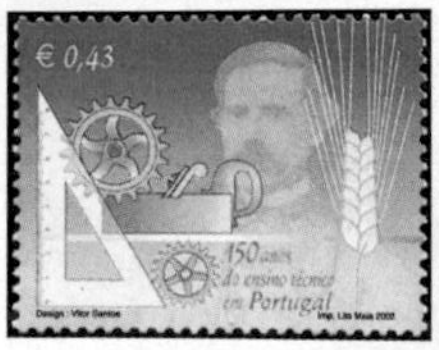

Technical Education in Portugal, 150th Anniv. A700

**2002, Oct. 9** *Perf. 12x11¾*
**2510** A700 43c multi 1.10 .85

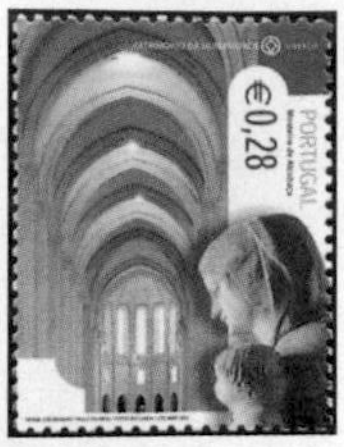

UNESCO World Heritage Sites — A701

Various views of: No. 2511, 28c, No. 2518, 70c, No. 2519, €1.25, Alcobaça Monastery. No. 2512, 28c, No. 2517, 70c, No. 2520, €1.25, Monastery of the Hieronymites. No. 2513, 43c, No. 2516, 54c, No. 2521, €1.25, Historic Center of Guimaraes. No. 2514, 43c, No. 2515, 54c, No. 2522, €1.25, Alto Douro Wine Region.

**2002, Nov. 7** *Perf. 11¾x12, 12x11¾*
**2511-2518** A701 Set of 8 9.50 8.00

**Souvenir Sheets**

**2519-2522** A701 Set of 4 12.50 12.50

Size of Nos. 2515-2518: 80x30mm.

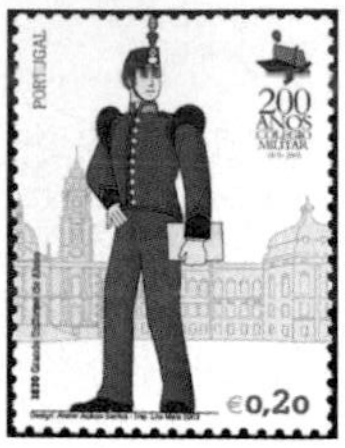

Portuguese Military College, Bicent. — A702

Military uniforms from: 20c, 1870. 30c, 1806. 43c, 1837. 55c, 1861. 70c, 1866. €2, 1912.
No. 2529: a, 1802. b, 1948.

**2003, Feb. 22** **Litho.** *Perf. 11¾x12*
**2523-2528** A702 Set of 6 9.00 4.50

**Souvenir Sheet**

**2529** A702 €1 Sheet of 2, #a-b 4.25 4.25

**Bird Type of 2000 With Euro Denominations Only and**

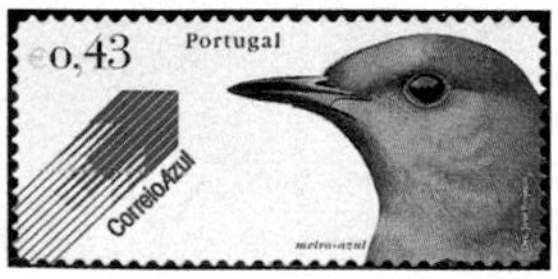

A703

Designs: 1c, Peto verde. 30c, Pombo das rochas. 43c, Melro azul. 55c, Toutinegra carrasqueira. 70c, Chasco ruivo.

**2003, Mar. 7** *Perf. 11¾x11½*
**2530** A658 1c multi .20 .20
**2531** A658 30c multi .65 .30
**2532** A658 43c multi .95 .45
**2533** A658 55c multi 1.25 .60
**2534** A658 70c multi 1.50 .75

**Self-Adhesive**

***Serpentine Die Cut 11¾***

**2535** A658 30c multi .65 .30
**2536** A703 43c multi .95 .45
**2537** A658 55c multi 1.25 .60
*Nos. 2530-2537 (8)* 7.40 3.65

Position of country name is at UL on No. 2531 but at LR on No. 2535; UR on No. 2533 but LL on No. 2537.

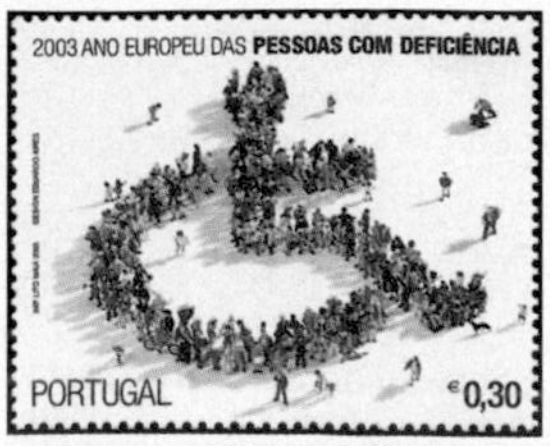

European Year of Disabled People — A704

Crowd of people in design of: 30c, Person in wheelchair. 55c, Head with blue brain. 70c, Head with pink ear, eye and mouth.

**2003, Mar. 12** *Perf. 13¼*
**2538-2540** A704 Set of 3 3.50 1.75

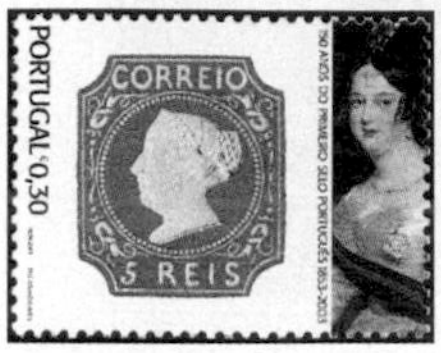

Portuguese Postage Stamps, 150th Anniv. A705

Designs: 30c, #1. 43c, #2. 55c, #3. 70c, #4.

**2003, Mar. 13** *Perf. 12x11¾*
**2541-2544** A705 Set of 4 4.25 2.10

See No. 2578.

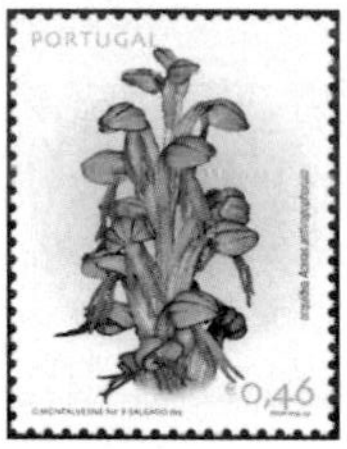

Orchids — A706

Designs: No. 2545, 46c, Aceras anthropophorum. No. 2546, 46c, Dactylorhiza maculata.
No. 2547, 30c: a, Orchis champagneuxii. b, Orchis morio. c, Serapias cordigera. d, Orchis coriophora. e, Ophrys bombyliflora. f, Ophrys vernixia. g, Ophrys speculum. h, Ophrys scolopax. i, Anacamptis pyramidalis.
No. 2548, 30c: a, Orchis italica. b, Ophrys tenthredinifera. c, Ophrys fusca fusca. d, Orchis papilionacea. e, Barlia robertiana. f, Ophrys lutea. g, Ophrys fusca. h, Ophrys apifera. i, Dactylorhiza ericetorum.

**2003, Apr. 29** **Litho.** *Perf. 11¾x12*
**2545-2546** A706 Set of 2 2.10 1.10

**Sheets of 9, #a-i**

**2547-2548** A706 Set of 2 12.50 12.50

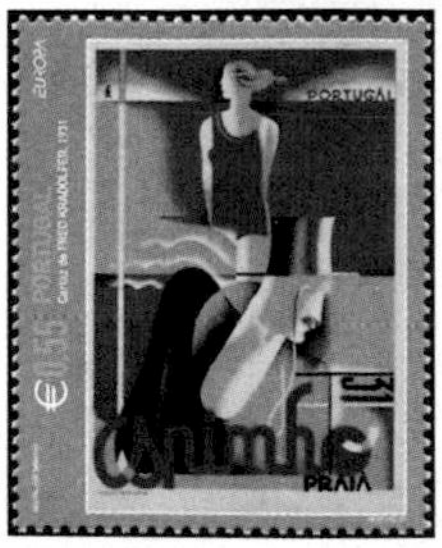

Europa A707

Poster art by: No. 2549, 55c, Fred Kradolfer, 1931. No. 2550, 55c, Joao Machado, 1997.

**2003, May 5** *Perf. 12x12½*
**2549-2550** A707 Set of 2 2.50 1.25
*2550a* Souvenir sheet, #2549-2550 2.50 2.50

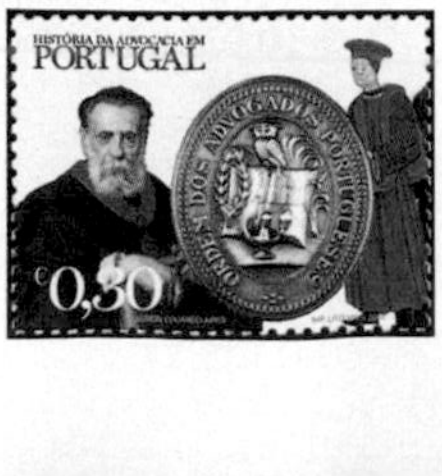

History of Law A708

Designs: 30c, Lawyer in black robe, lawyer in red robe, order of Portuguese lawyers. 43c, Two lawyers in black robes, national arms. 55c, Lawyer, bishop, manuscript. 70c, Lawyer in black robe, order of Portuguese lawyers, diff.
No. 2555: a, €1, Lawyer in red robe, left half of order of Portuguese lawyers. b, €2, Right half of order of Portuguese lawyers, bishop.

**2003, May 13** *Perf. 12x11¾*
**2551-2554** A708 Set of 4 4.75 2.40

**Souvenir Sheet**

**2555** A708 Sheet of 2, #a-b 7.00 7.00

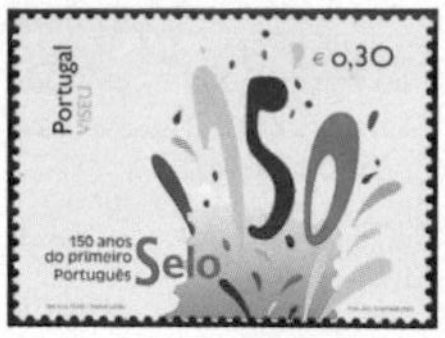

Traveling Exhibition on the 150th Anniv. of the First Portuguese Stamp A709

Exhibition stops: No. 2556, Viseu. No. 2557, Faro. No. 2558, Porto.

**2003** *Perf. 14x13½*

**Background Color**

**2556** A709 30c yellow .70 .35
**2557** A709 30c white .70 .35
**2558** A709 30c blue .70 .35
*Nos. 2556-2558 (3)* 2.10 1.05

Issued: No. 2556, 5/23; No. 2557, 7/21.

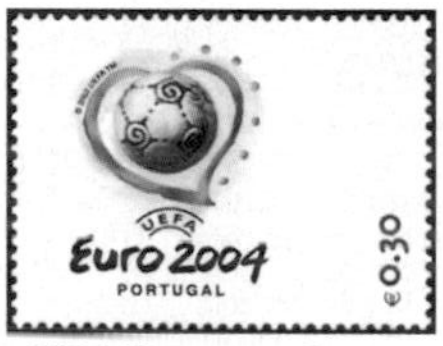

2004 European Soccer Championships, Portugal — A710

Emblem with background color of: 30c, White. 43c, Dark blue. 47c, Brown carmine. 55c, Green. 70c, Brown orange.
No. 2564 — Emblem and quadrant of emblem with denomination at: a, LL. b, LR. c, UL. d, UR.

**2003, May 28** **Litho.** *Perf. 14x13½*
**2559-2563** A710 Set of 5 5.75 2.75

**Souvenir Sheet**

**2564** A710 Sheet of 4 5.25 5.25
*a.-d.* 55c Any single 1.25 1.25
*e.* Souvenir sheet, #2559-2563, 2564a-2564d 11.00 11.00

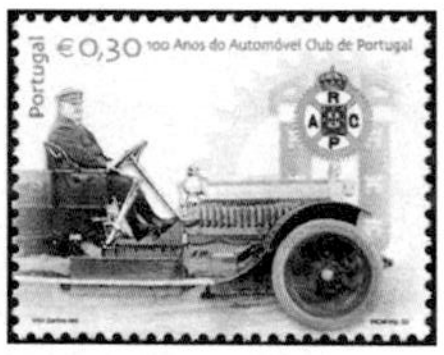

Portuguese Automobile Club, Cent. A711

Emblems and: 30c, Driver in old automobile. 43c, Motorcyclist. €2, Driver in old automobile, blurred race car.

**2003, June 24** *Perf. 12x11¾*
**2565-2567** A711 Set of 3 6.25 3.25

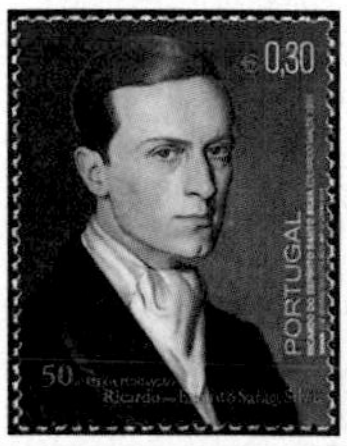

Ricardo do Espírito Santo Silva Foundation, 50th Anniv. — A712

Designs: No. 2568, 30c, Portrait of Ricardo do Espírito Santo Silva, by Eduardo Malta. No. 2569, 30c, Chess table, 18th cent. No. 2570, 43c, Cutlery in decorated case, c. 1720-1750. No. 2571, 43c, Salver, 15th cent. No. 2572, 55c, Chinese cutlery case, c, 1700-1722. No. 2573, 55c, Wooden tub, 18th cent.
No. 2574: a, €1, Chest with drawers, 17th cent. b, €2, Carpet, 18th cent.

**2003, July 9** *Perf. 11¾x12*
**2568-2573** A712 Set of 6 5.75 3.00

**Souvenir Sheet**

**2574** A712 Sheet of 2, #a-b 6.75 6.75

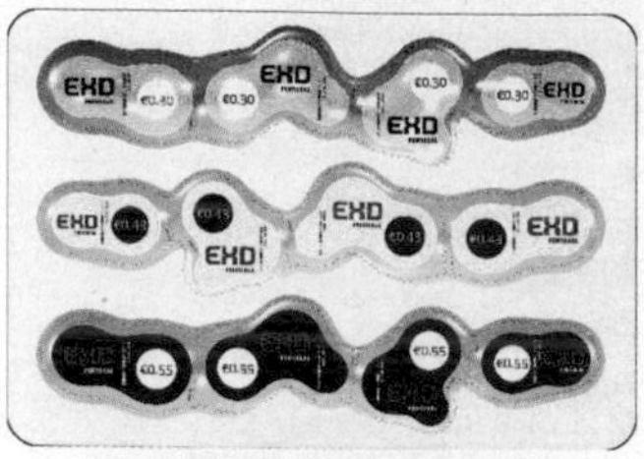

Experimental Design — A713

No. 2575: a, 2 lobes, black "EXD," white denomination circle to right. b, 3 lobes, black "EXD," white denomination circle below and to left. c, 3 lobes, black "EXD," white denomination circle above. d, 2 lobes, black "EXD," white denomination circle to left. e, 2 lobes, red "EXD," black denomination circle to right. f, 3 lobes, red "EXD," black denomination circle above. g, 3 lobes, red "EXD," black denomination circle below and to right. h, 2 lobes, red "EXD," black denomination circle to left. i, 2 lobes, red "EXD," white denomination circle to right. j, 3 lobes, red "EXD," white denomination circle below and to left. k, 3 lobes, red "EXD," white denomination circle above. l, 2 lobes, red "EXD," white denomination circle to left.

***Serpentine Die Cut***

**2003, Sept. 17** **Litho.**

**Self-Adhesive**

**2575** A713 Sheet of 12 12.00
*a.-d.* 30c Any single .70 .35
*e.-h.* 43c Any single 1.00 .50
*i.-l.* 55c Any single 1.25 .60

Souvenir Sheet

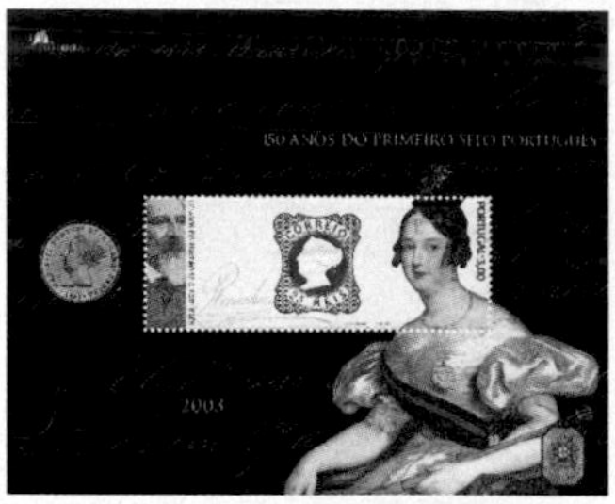

Portuguese Stamps, 150th Anniv. — A714

**Litho. & Embossed**

**2003, Sept. 19** *Perf. 12x11¾*
**2576** A714 €3 Queen Maria II, Type A2 6.75 6.75

Souvenir Sheet

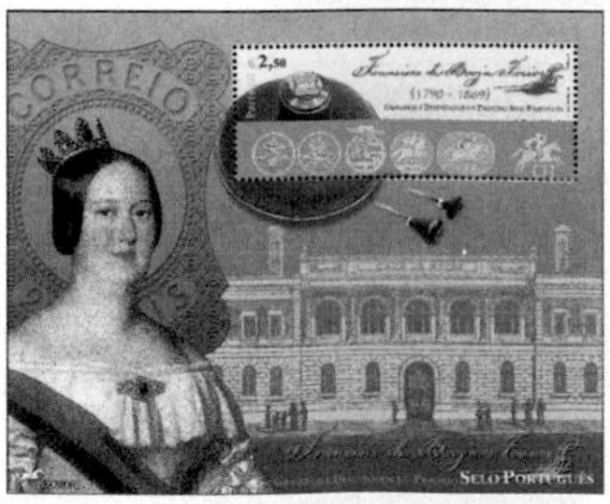

Francisco de Borja Freire (1790-1869), Designer and Engraver of First Portuguese Stamp — A715

**Litho. With Hologram Applied**

**2003, Sept. 23** *Perf. 12x12½*
**2577** A715 €2.50 multi 6.00 6.00

Souvenir Sheet

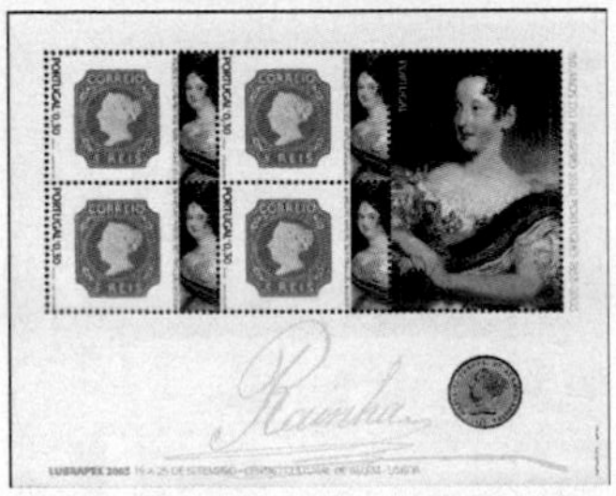

Lubrapex 2003 Philatelic Exhibition, Lisbon — A716

**2003, Sept. 25 Litho.** ***Perf. 12x11¾***
**2578** A716 Sheet, #2578a, 4 #2541 3.50 3.50
*a.* 30c Queen Maria II .70 .70

Size of No. 2578a: 40x60mm.

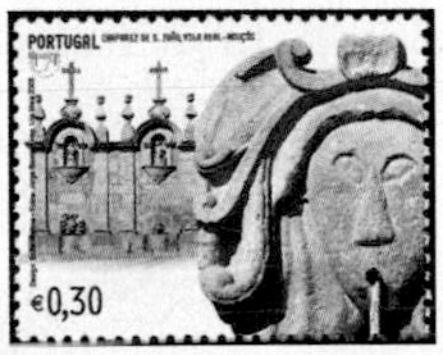

Fountains A717

Designs: 30c, Sao Joao Fountain, Moucós. 43c, Fountain of Virtues, Porto. 55c, Giraldo Square Fountain, Evora. 70c, Blessed Woman Fountain, Sao Marcos de Tavira. €1, Town Fountain, Castelo de Vide. €2, Santo André Fountain, Guarda.

**2003, Oct. 1** ***Perf. 12x11¾***
**2579-2584** A717 Set of 6 12.00 6.00

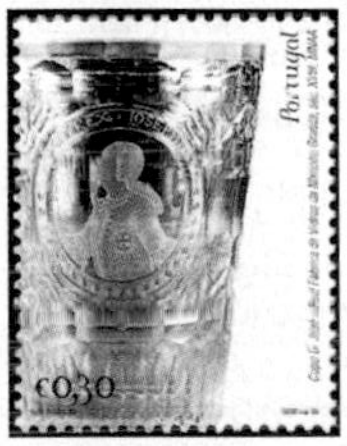

Glass — A718

Designs: 30c, Glass of King José I, 18th cent. 55c, Glass of Queen Maria II, 19th cent. 70c, Glass by Carmo Valente, 20th cent. €2, Glass by M. Helena Matos, 20th cent.

€1.50, Stained glass by Fernando Santos, 19th cent.

**2003, Oct. 9** ***Perf. 11¾x12***
**2585-2588** A718 Set of 4 8.50 4.25

**Souvenir Sheet**

**2589** A718 €1.50 multi 3.50 3.50

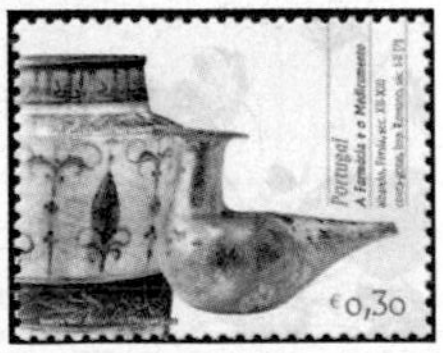

Apothecary Items A719

Designs: 30c, Persian jar, 12th-13th cent., Roman Empire medicine dropper, 1st-2nd cent. 43c, Bottle and bowl, 17th cent. 55c, Mortars and pestle, 16th and 17th cent. 70c, Alembic, 1910, and flask, 1890-1930.

**2003, Oct. 23** ***Perf. 12x11¾***
**2590-2593** A719 Set of 4 4.75 2.40

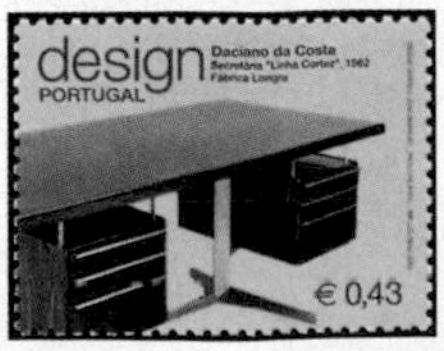

Portuguese Design A720

Designs: No. 2594, 43c, Secretary, by Daciano da Costa, 1962. No. 2595, 43c, Chair, by António Garcia, 1970, vert. No. 2596, 43c, Drawing table, by José Espinho, 1970. No. 2597, 43c, Chairs by Leonor and António Sena da Silva, 1973. No. 2598, 43c, Telephone booth, by Pedro Silva Dias, 1998, vert. No. 2599, 43c, Cutlery, by Eduardo Afonsa Dias, 1976. No. 2600, 43c, Faucet, by Carlos Aguiar, 1998. No. 2601, 43c, Thermos bottle, by Carlos Rocha, 1982, vert. No. 2602, 43c, Tea cart, by Cruz de Carvalho, 1957.

**2003, Oct. 31** ***Perf. 12x11¾, 11¾x12***
**2594-2602** A720 Set of 9 9.00 4.50

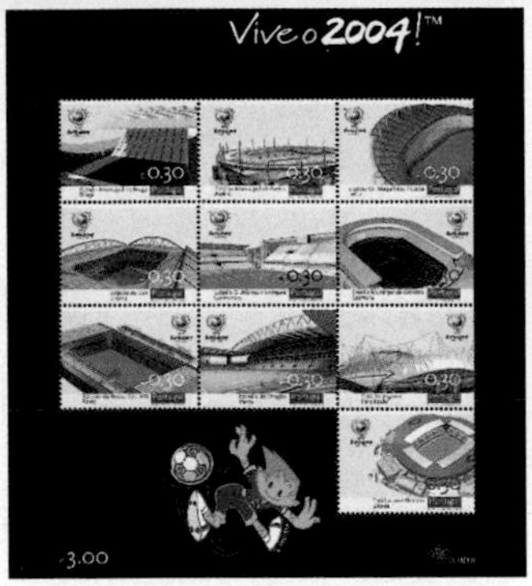

Stadiums for 2004 European Soccer Championships — A721

No. 2603: a, Braga Municipal Stadium, Braga. b, Aveiro Municpal Stadium, Aveiro. c, Dr. Magalhaes Pessoa Stadium, Leiria. d, Luz Stadium, Lisbon. e, D. Afonso Henriques Stadium, Guimaraes. f, Coimbra Municipal Stadium, Coimbra. g, Bessa 21st Century Stadium, Porto. h, Dragao Stadium, Porto. i, Algarve Stadium, Faro-Loulé. j, José Alvalade Stadium, Lisbon.

**2003, Nov. 28 Litho.** ***Perf. 14x13½***
**2603** A721 Sheet of 10 7.50 7.50
*a.-j.* 30c Any single .75 .75

Souvenir Sheet

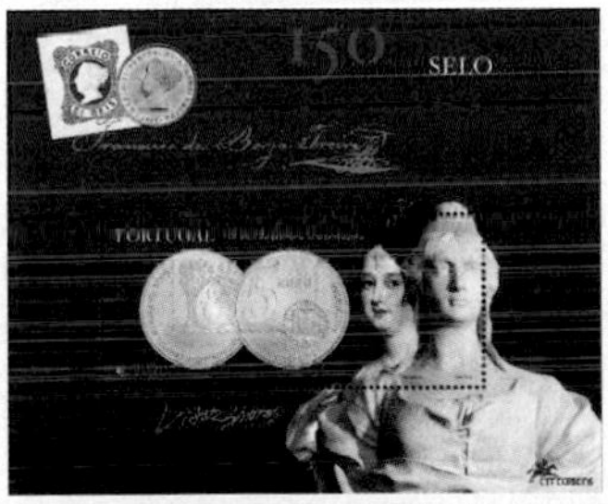

Coin Commemorating 150th Anniv. of First Portuguese Stamps, Bust and Portrait of Queen Maria II — A722

**2003, Dec. 12** ***Perf. 12***
**2604** A722 €1 multi 2.50 2.50

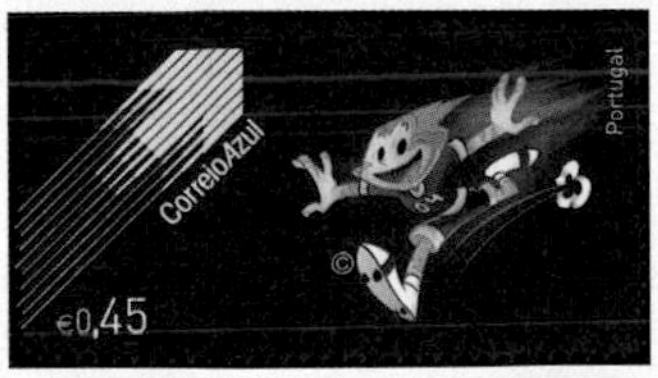

Mascot of 2004 European Soccer Championships — A723

Mascot and: 45c, CorreioAzul emblem. €1.75, Priority air mail emblem.

***Serpentine Die Cut 11½***

**2004, Mar. 16 Litho.**

**Self-Adhesive**

**2605** A723 45c multi 1.10 .55
**2606** A723 €1.75 multi 4.25 2.10

No. 2606 is airmail.

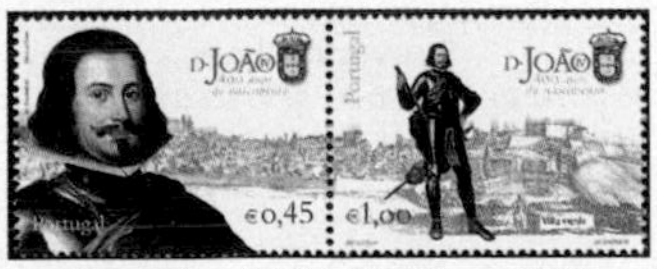

King John IV (1604-56) — A724

No. 2607 — Vila Viçosa, birthplace and: a, 45c, Head of King. b, €1, King with sword. Illustration reduced.

**2004, Mar. 19** ***Perf. 14x13½***
**2607** A724 Horiz. pair, #a-b 3.50 1.75

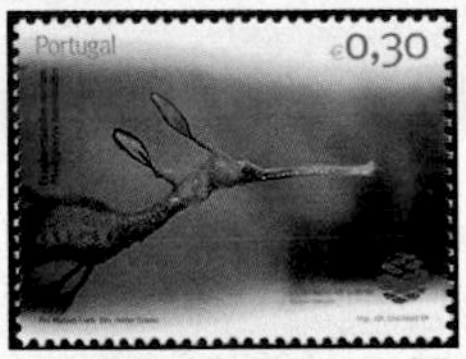

Lisbon Oceanarium — A725

Designs: 30c, Phyllopteryx taeniolatus. 45c, Spheniscus magellanicus. 56c, Hypsypops rubicundus. 72c, Enhydra lutris. €1, Carcharias taurus. €2, Fratercula arctica.

€1.50, Eudyptes chysolophus, people at Oceanarium.

**2004, Mar. 22**
**2608-2613** A725 Set of 6 12.50 6.25

**Souvenir Sheet**

**2614** A725 €1.50 multi 3.75 3.75

No. 2614 contains one 80x30mm stamp.

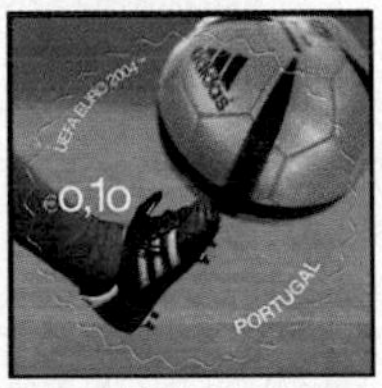

2004 European Soccer Championships A726

Designs: Nos. 2615a, 2616, 10c, Foot kicking soccer ball. Nos. 2615b, 2617, 20c, Soccer ball in air. Nos. 2615c, 2618, 30c, Soccer ball on chalk line. Nos. 2615d, 2619, 50c, Soccer ball, corner of goal.

**2004, Mar. 30** ***Perf.***

**Souvenir Sheet**

**2615** A726 Sheet of 4, #a-d 2.75 2.75

**Self-Adhesive**

***Serpentine Die Cut***

**2616-2619** A726 Set of 4 2.75 1.40

No. 2615 contains four 24mm diameter stamps.

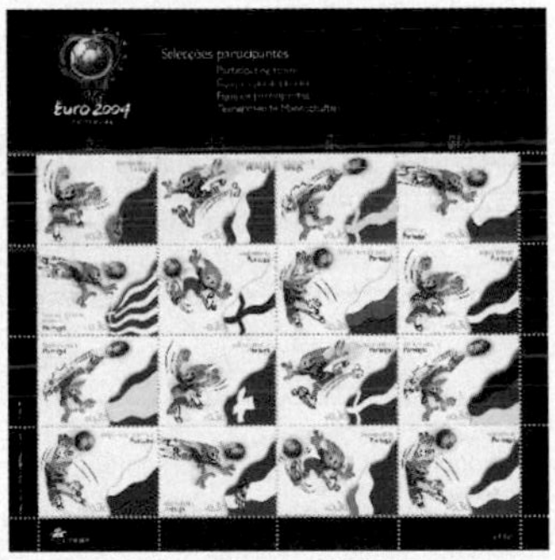

Flags of Countries in 2004 European Soccer Championships and Mascot — A727

No. 2620: a, Portugal. b, France. c, Sweden. d, Czech Republic. e, Greece. f, England. g, Bulgaria. h, Latvia. i, Spain. j, Switzerland. k, Denmark. l, Germany. m, Russia. n, Croatia. o, Italy. p, Netherlands.

**2004, Apr. 6** ***Perf. 13x13¼***
**2620** A727 Sheet of 16 12.00 12.00
*a.-p.* 30c Any single .75 .40

**Bird Type of 2000 With Euro Denominations Only and**

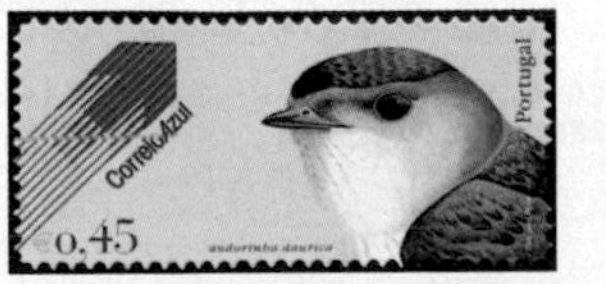

Andorinha Daurica — A728

Designs: 30c, Cruza bico comun. No. 2622, Andorinha daurica, diff. 56c, Papa figos. 58c, Cotovia montesina. 72c, Chapim de poupa.

**2004, Apr. 15** ***Perf. 11¾x11½***
**2621** A658 30c multi .70 .35
**2622** A658 45c multi 1.10 .55
**2623** A658 56c multi 1.25 .65
**2624** A658 58c multi 1.40 .70
**2625** A658 72c multi 1.75 .85

**Self-Adhesive**

**Size: 26x21mm (#2626, 2628)**

***Serpentine Die Cut 11½, 11½x11¾ (#2627)***

**2626** A658 30c multi .70 .35
**2627** A728 45c multi 1.10 .55
**2628** A658 56c multi 1.25 .65
*Nos. 2621-2628 (8)* 9.25 4.65

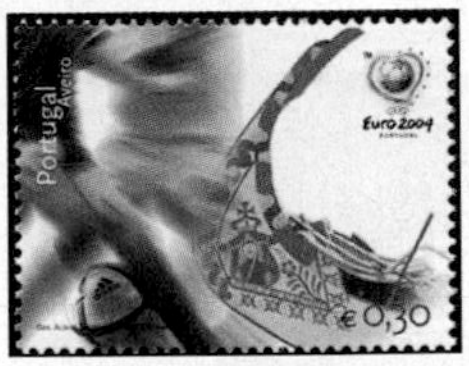

Landmarks in Host Cities of 2004 European Soccer Championships and Players — A729

Host city: No. 2629, 30c, Aveiro. No. 2630, 30c, Braga. No. 2631, 30c, Coimbra. No. 2632, 30c, Faro-Loulé. No. 2633, 30c, Guimaraes. No. 2634, 30c, Leiria. No. 2635, 30c, Lisbon. No. 2636, 30c, Porto.

**2004, Apr. 20** ***Perf. 14x13¼***
**2629-2636** A729 Set of 8 5.75 3.00

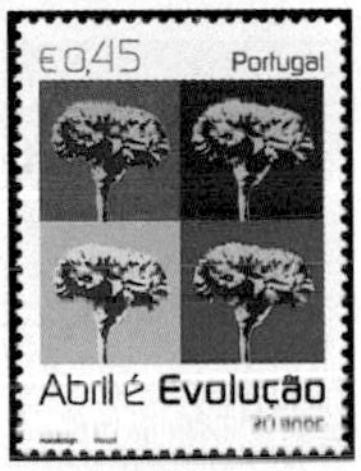

Coup of Apr. 25, 1974, 30th Anniv. — A730

**2004, Apr. 25** ***Perf. 13¼x13***
**2637** A730 45c multi 1.10 .55

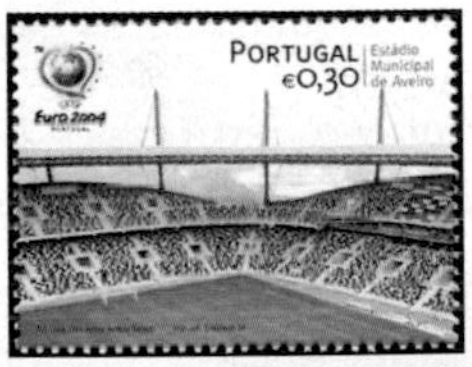

Stadiums for 2004 European Soccer Championships — A731

Designs: No. 2638, 30c, Aveiro Municipal Stadium, Aveiro. No. 2639, 30c, Braga Municipal Stadium, Braga. No. 2640, 30c, Coimbra Municipal Stadium, Coimbra. No. 2641, 30c, D. Afonso Henriques Stadium, Guimaraes. No. 2642, 30c, Algarve Stadium, Faro-Loulé. No. 2643, 30c, Dr. Magalhaes Pessoa Stadium, Leiria. No. 2644, 30c, José Alvalade Stadium, Lisbon. No. 2645, 30c, Luz Stadium, Lisbon. No. 2646, 30c, Bessa 21st Century Stadium, Porto. No. 2647, 30c, Dragao Stadium, Porto.

**2004, Apr. 28** ***Perf. 14x13¼***
**2638-2647** A731 Set of 10 7.25 3.50

2004 European Parliament Elections A732

**2004, May 3**
**2648** A732 30c multi .70 .35

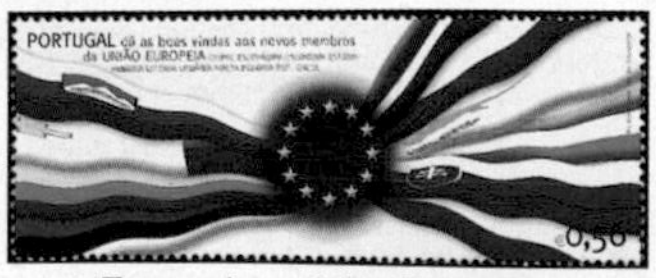

Expansion of the European Union — A733

Designs: 56c, Flags of newly-added nations, stars. €2, Flags of newly-added nations, flags of previous members.
Illustration reduced.

**2004, May 3** **Litho.**
**2649** A733 56c multi 1.25 .65

**Souvenir Sheet**

**2650** A733 €2 multi 4.75 4.75

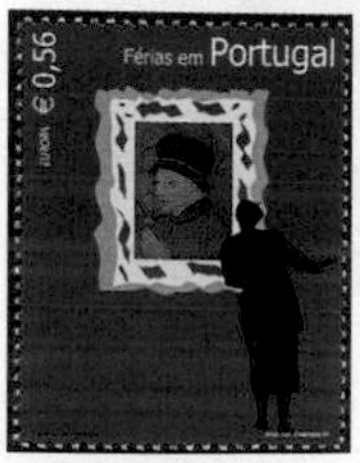

Europa — A734

Designs: No. 2651, 56c, Woman looking at painting. No. 2652, 56c, Vacationer with gear on beach.

**2004, May 10** ***Perf. 13¼x14***
**2651-2652** A734 Set of 2 2.75 1.40
*2652a* Souvenir sheet, #2651-2652 2.75 2.75

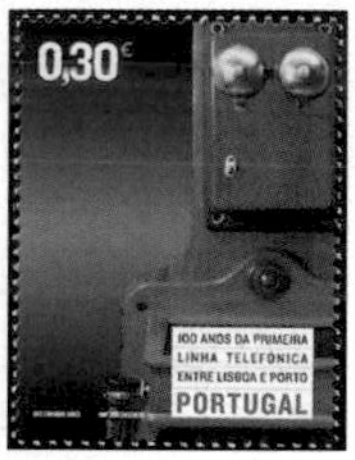

First Telephone Line Between Lisbon and Porto, Cent. — A735

Designs: 30c, Old telephone. 45c, Telephone pole. 56c, Fiber-optic cables. 72c, Picture phone.
No. 2657: a, Old telephone, diff. b, Like 72c.

**2004, May 17**
**2653-2656** A735 Set of 4 5.00 2.50

**Souvenir Sheet**

**2657** A735 €1 Sheet of 2, #a-b 4.75 4.75

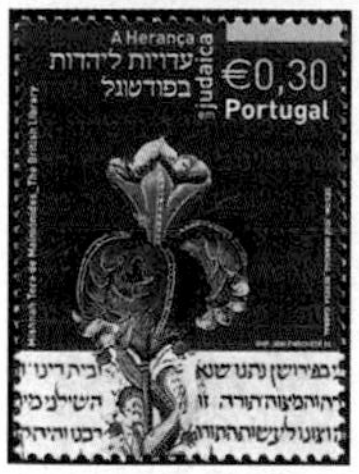

Jewish Heritage of Portugal — A736

Designs: 30c, Mishnah Torah of Maimonides, British Library. 45c, Star of David with lion, Cervera Bible, National Library. 56c, Menorah, Cervera Bible, National Library. 72c, Menorah carved on rock, Mértola Museum. €1, Abravanel Bible, Coimbra University Library. €2, Statue of prophet, Christ Convent, Tomar.
€1.50, Interior of Shaare Tikva Synagogue.

**2004, May 20**
**2658-2663** A736 Set of 6 12.00 6.00

**Souvenir Sheet**

**2664** A736 €1.50 multi 3.75 3.75
Shaare Tikva Synagogue, Cent.

**Souvenir Sheet**

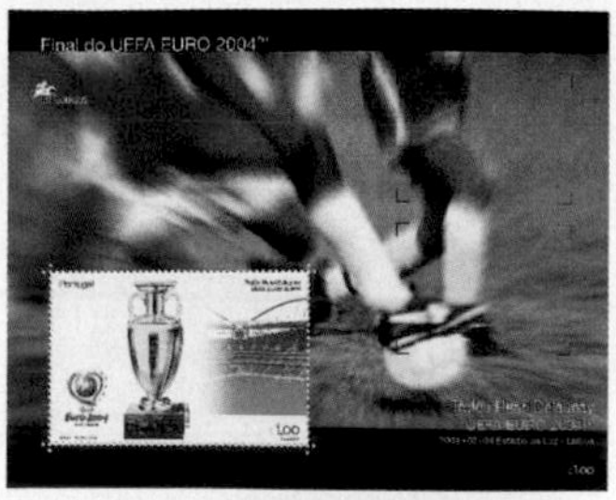

Final Match of 2004 European Soccer Championships — A737

**2004, May 27** ***Perf. 13¼x13***
**2665** A737 €1 multi 2.40 2.40

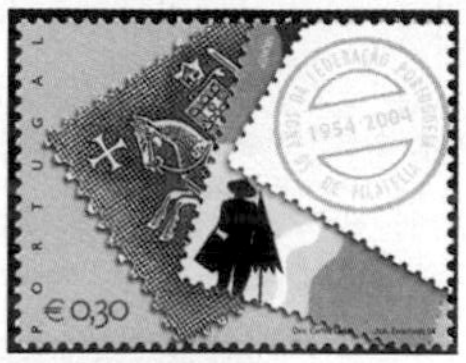

Portuguese Philatelic Federation, 50th Anniv. — A738

Designs: 30c, Anniversary emblem, #761, 2652. €1.50, Handstamp and letter.

**2004, June 18** ***Perf. 14x13¼***
**2666** A738 30c multi .75 .35

**Souvenir Sheet**

**2667** A738 €1.50 multi 3.75 3.75

**Souvenir Sheet**

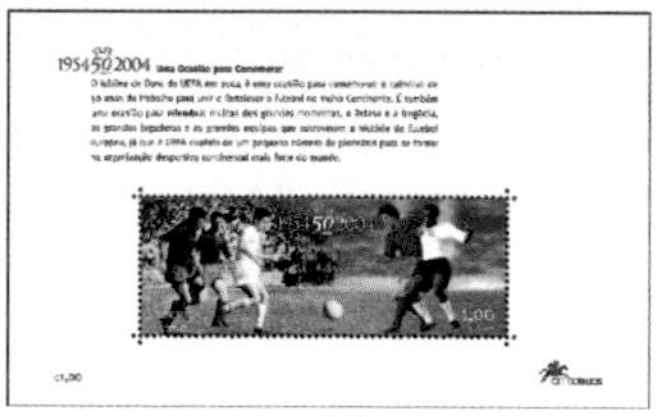

UEFA (European Football Union), 50th Anniv. — A739

**2004, July 29** **Litho.** ***Perf. 13x13¼***
**2668** A739 €1 multi 2.40 2.40

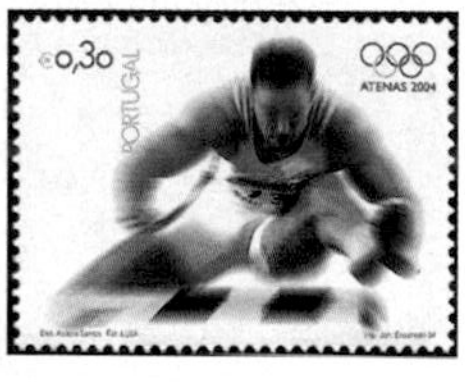

2004 Summer Olympics, Athens A740

Designs: 30c, Hurdles. 45c, High jump.

**2004, Aug. 13** ***Perf. 14x13¼***
**2669-2670** A740 Set of 2 1.90 .95

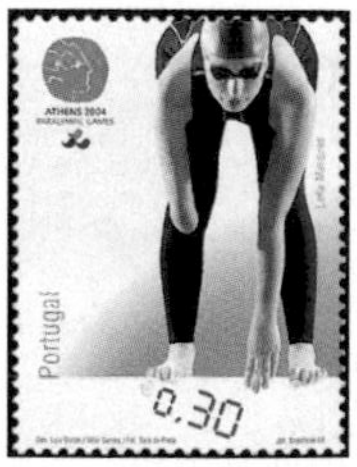

2004 Paralympics, Athens — A741

Designs: 30c, Swimming. 45c, Wheelchair racing. 56c, Cycling. 72c, Running.

**2004, Sept. 2** ***Perf. 13¼x14***
**2671-2674** A741 Set of 4 5.00 2.50

**Souvenir Sheet**

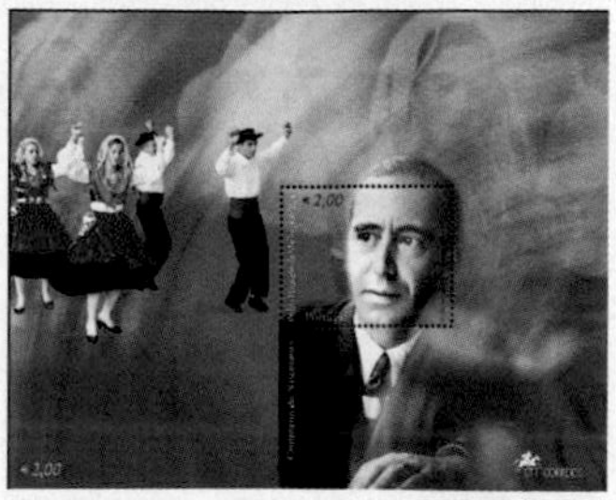

Pedro Homem de Mello (1904-84), Poet — A742

**2004, Sept. 6** ***Perf. 14x13¼***
**2675** A742 €2 multi 5.00 5.00

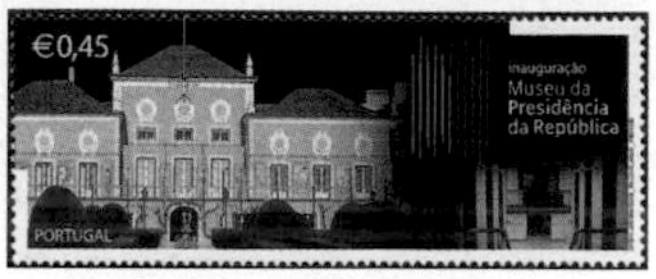

Opening of Presidential Museum — A743

Designs: 45c, Museum exterior. €1, Museum interior.
Illustration reduced.

**2004, Oct. 5**
**2676** A743 45c multi 1.10 .55

**Souvenir Sheet**

**2677** A743 €1 multi 2.50 2.50

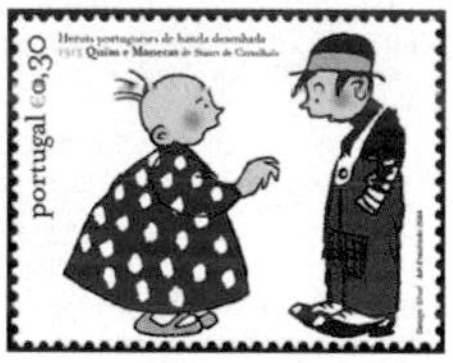

Comic Strips A744

Designs: 30c, Quim e Manecas, by Stuart de Carvalhais. 45c, Guarda Abília, by Júlio Pinto and Nuno Saraiva. 56c, Simao Infante, by Raul Correia and Eduardo Teixeira Coelho. 72c, A Pior Bando do Mundo, by José Carlos Fernandes.
No. 2682: a, O Espiao Acácio, by Relvas. b, Jim del Monaco, by Louro and Simoes. c, Tomahawk Tom, by Vitor Péon. d, Pitanga, by Arlindo Fagundes.

**2004, Oct. 8**
**2678-2681** A744 Set of 4 5.00 2.50

**Souvenir Sheet**

**2682** A744 50c Sheet of 4, #a-d 5.00 5.00

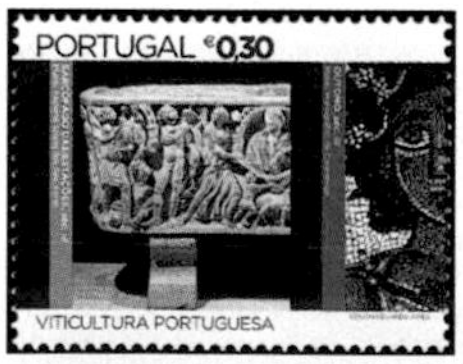

Viticulture A745

Designs: 30c, Sarcophagus depicting seasonal scenes, detail of mosaic of Autumn, 3rd cent. 45c, Detail of mosaic of Autumn, Apocalypse of Lorvao, 12th cent. 56c, Lorvao Missal illustration, 14th cent., detail of illustration from Book of Hours, by D. Fernando, 15th-16th cent. 72c, Detail of illustration from Book of Hours, detail of Group of the Lion, Columbano, 19th cent. €1, Detail of Group of the Lion, stained glass window, by Lino António, 20th cent.
No. 2688: a, Grapes, harvester. b, Harvester, wine jugs. c, Winery. d, Wine barrels, bottles and glasses.

**2004, Oct. 15**
**2683-2687** A745 Set of 5 7.50 3.75

**Souvenir Sheet**

**2688** A745 50c Sheet of 4, #a-d 5.00 5.00

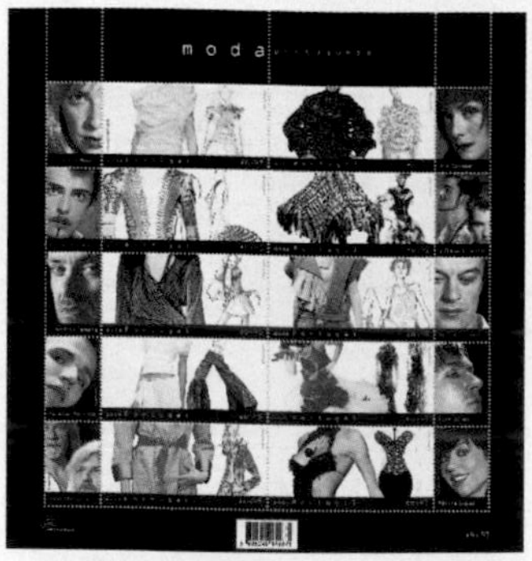

Women's Fashion — A746

No. 2689 — Clothing designed by: a, Alexandra Moura. b, Ana Salazar. c, Filipe Faisca. d, J. Branco and L. Sanchez. e, J. António Tenente. f, Luís Buchinho. g, Osvaldo Martins. h, Dino Alves. i, Alves and Gonçalves, j, Fátima Lopes. Designers names and pictures are on labels adjacent to stamps showing their clothing.

**2004, Nov. 10** ***Perf. 13¾x14¼***
**2689** A746 45c Sheet of 10 + 10 labels 12.00 12.00

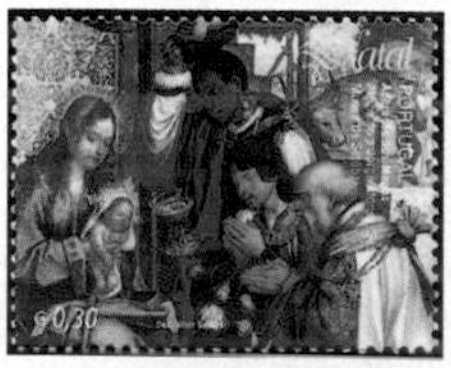

Christmas A747

Paintings: 30c, Adoration of the Magi, attributed to Jorge Afonso. 45c, Adoration of the Magi, by Flemish School. 56c, Flight into Egypt, by Francisco Vieira. 72c, Nativity, by Portuguese School.
€3, Nativity, by Josefa de Obidos.

**2004, Nov. 19** ***Perf. 13x13¼***
**2690-2693** A747 Set of 4 5.50 2.75

**Souvenir Sheet**
***Perf. 13½x13¼***

**2694** A747 €3 multi 8.25 8.25

No. 2694 contains one 50x35mm stamp.

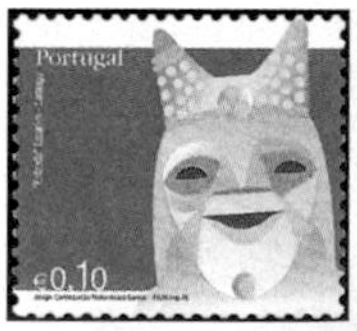

Masks — A748

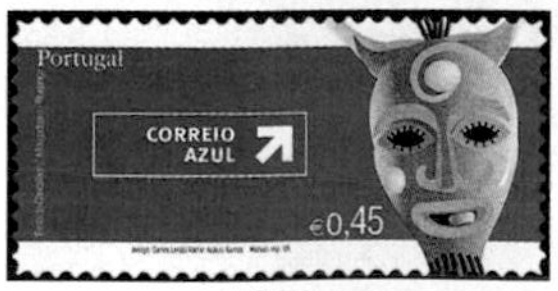

A748a

Designs: 10c, Entrudo, Lazarim. 30c Festa dos Rapazes, Salsas. 45c, Festa do Chocalheiro, Mogadouro. 57c, Cardador, Vale de Ilhavo. 74c, Festa dos Rapazes, Aveleda.

***Perf. 11¾x11½***

**2005, Feb. 17** **Litho.**

| | | | | | |
|---|---|---|---|---|---|
| **2695** | A748 | 10c multi | .25 | .20 |
| **2696** | A748 | 30c multi | .75 | .20 |
| **2697** | A748 | 45c multi | 1.20 | .60 |
| **2698** | A748 | 57c multi | 1.50 | .75 |
| **2699** | A748 | 74c multi | 2.00 | 1.00 |
| | | *Nos. 2695-2699 (5)* | 5.70 | 2.75 |

**Self-Adhesive**

***Serpentine Die Cut 11½, 11 (45c)***

| | | | | |
|---|---|---|---|---|
| **2699A** | A748 | 30c multi | .80 | .40 |
| **2699B** | A748a | 45c multi | 1.25 | .60 |
| **2699C** | A748 | 57c multi | 1.50 | .75 |
| | | *Nos. 2699A-2699C (3)* | 3.55 | 1.75 |

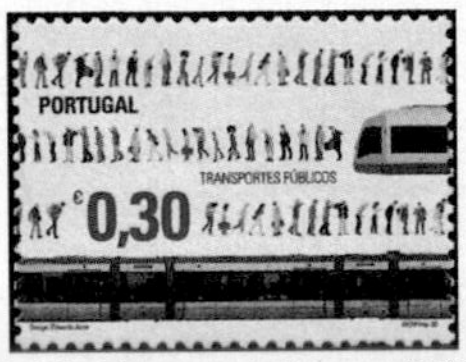

Public Transportation — A749

Lines of people and: 30c, Train, front of trolley. 50c, Trolley, rear of train. 57c, Ferry, rear of trolley. €1, Rear of articulated bus, front of train. €2, Front of articulated bus, rear of train.

**2005, Mar. 17** *Perf. 12x11¾*
**2700-2704** A749 Set of 5 11.50 11.50

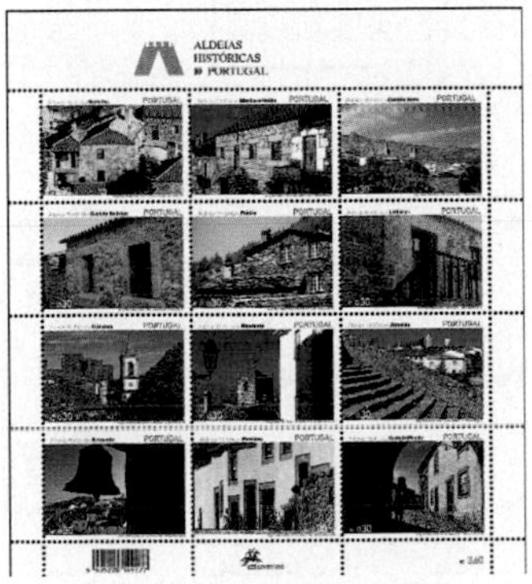

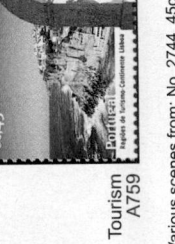

Historic Villages — A750

No. 2705: a, Sortelha. b, Idanha-a-Velha. c, Castelo Novo. d, Castelo Rodrigo. e, Piódao. f, Linhares. g, Trancoso. h, Monsanto. i, Almeida. j, Belmonte. k, Marialva. l, Castelo Mendo.

**2005, Apr. 28 Litho.** *Perf. 14x13¼*
**2705** A750 Sheet of 12 9.25 9.25
*a.-l.* 30c Any single .75 .40

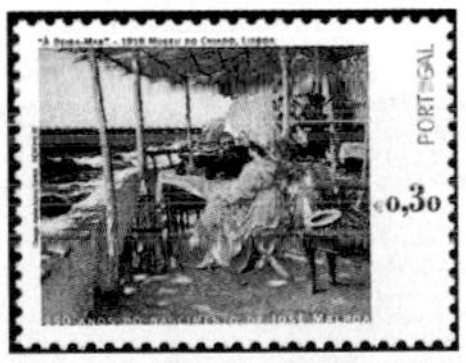

Paintings by José Malhoa (1855-1933) — A751

Designs: 30c, A Beira-Mar. 45c, As Promessas.
€1.77, Conversa com o Vizinho.

**2005, Apr. 28** *Perf. 12x11¾*
**2706-2707** A751 Set of 2 2.00 2.00

**Souvenir Sheet**

**2708** A751 €1.77 multi 4.50 4.50

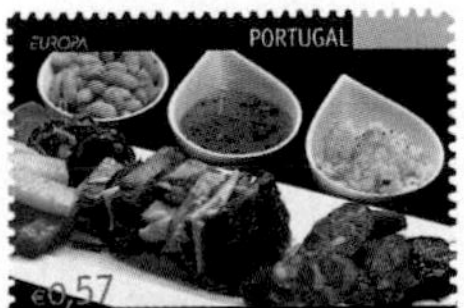

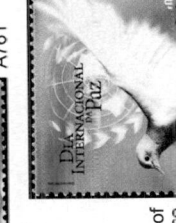

Europa A752

Designs: No. 2709, Cozido à Portuguesa. No. 2710a, Bacalhau Assado com Batatas a Murro (dried cod and baked potatoes).

**2005, May 5** *Perf. 14x13¼*
**2709** A752 57c multi 1.50 .75

**Souvenir Sheet**

**2710** Sheet of 2 #2710a 3.00 3.00
*a.* A752 57c multi 1.50 1.50

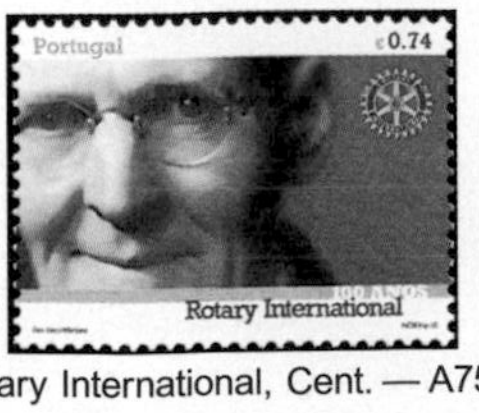

Rotary International, Cent. — A753

**2005, May 20** *Perf. 12x11¾*
**2711** A753 74c Paul Harris 1.90 .95

**Souvenir Sheet**

**2712** A753 €1.75 Harris, diff. 4.25 4.25

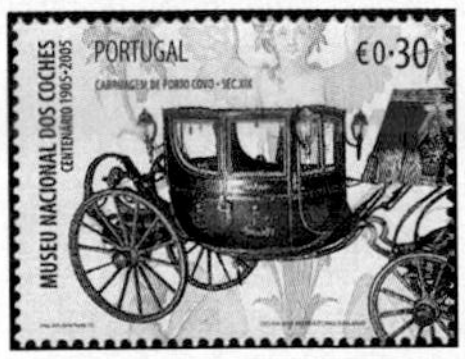

National Coach Museum, Cent. A754

Designs: No. 2713, 30c, Porto Covo carriage, 19th cent. No. 2714, 30c, Carriage, 19th cent. No. 2715, 45c, Coach of Francisca Sabóia, 17th cent. No. 2716, 45c, Sege "Das Plumas," 18th cent. 57c, Palanquin, 18th cent. 74c, Coche Dos Oceanos, 18th cent.
€1.75, Coaches and Queen Amelia.

**2005, May 23** *Perf. 14x13¼*
**2713-2718** A754 Set of 6 7.00 3.50

**Souvenir Sheet**

**2719** A754 €1.75 multi 4.25 4.25

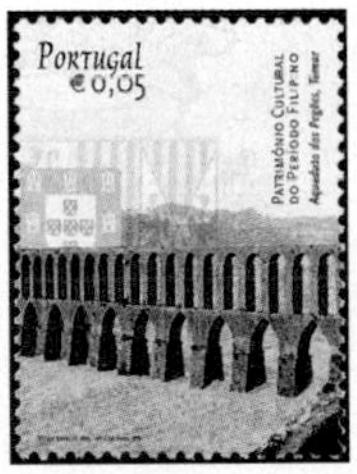

Era of Kings Philip I to Philip III — A755

Arms and: 5c, Pegoes Aqueduct, Tomar. 30c, Chalice from Elvas Cathedral. 45c, Tile panel of cross from Christ Convent, Tomar. 57c, Fort St. John the Baptist, Angra.€1, Armada. €2, St. Vincent of Fora Church, Lisbon.
€1.20, Cross and reliquary from Lisbon Cathedral.

**2005, June 7** *Perf. 11¾x12*
**2720-2725** A755 Set of 6 11.00 5.50

**Souvenir Sheet**

**2726** A755 €1.20 multi 3.00 3.00

Miniature Sheet

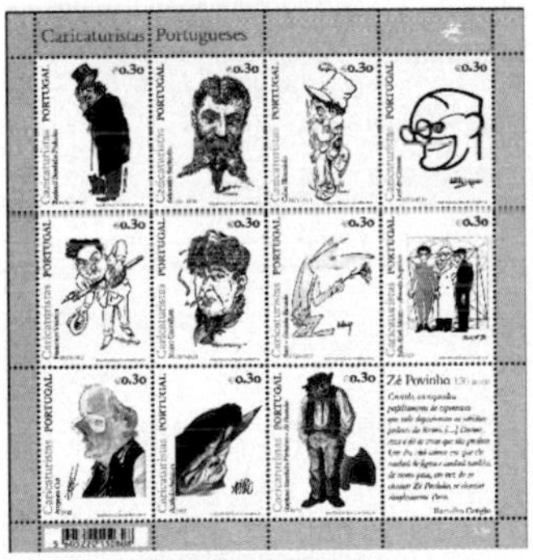

Caricatures — A756

No. 2727 — Caricatures by: a, Raphael Bordallo Pinheiro. b, Sebastiao Sanhudo. c, Celso Herminio. d, Leal da Camara. e, Francisco Valença. f, Stuart Carvalhais. g, Sam. h, Joao Abel Manta. i, Augusto Cid. j, António Antunes. k, Pinheiro (Zé Povinho).

**2005, June 12** *Perf. 13¼x14*
**2727** A756 Sheet of 11 + label 8.00 8.00
*a.-k.* 30c Any single .70 .35

Souvenir Sheets

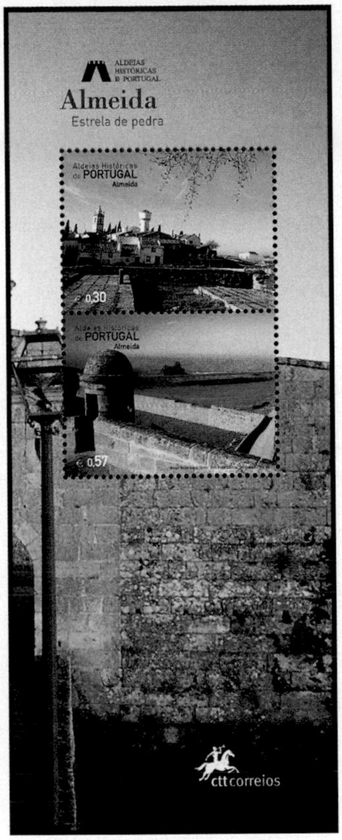

Historic Villages — A757

Various views of named villages.

**2005, June 8 Litho.** *Perf. 14x13¼*

**Sheets of 2, #a-b**

| | | | |
|---|---|---|---|
| **2728** A757 | Almeida | 2.25 | 2.25 |
| *a.* | 30c multi | .75 | .35 |
| *b.* | 57c multi | 1.40 | .70 |
| **2729** A757 | Belmonte | 2.25 | 2.25 |
| *a.* | 30c multi | .75 | .35 |
| *b.* | 57c multi | 1.40 | .70 |
| **2730** A757 | Castelo Mendo | 2.25 | 2.25 |
| *a.* | 30c multi | .75 | .35 |
| *b.* | 57c multi | 1.40 | .70 |
| **2731** A757 | Castelo Novo | 2.25 | 2.25 |
| *a.* | 30c multi | .75 | .35 |
| *b.* | 57c multi | 1.40 | .70 |
| **2732** A757 | Castelo Rodrigo | 2.25 | 2.25 |
| *a.* | 30c multi | .75 | .35 |
| *b.* | 57c multi | 1.40 | .70 |
| **2733** A757 | Idanha-a-Velha | 2.25 | 2.25 |
| *a.* | 30c multi | .75 | .35 |
| *b.* | 57c multi | 1.40 | .70 |
| **2734** A757 | Linhares da Beira | 2.25 | 2.25 |
| *a.* | 30c multi | .75 | .35 |
| *b.* | 57c multi | 1.40 | .70 |
| **2735** A757 | Marialva | 2.25 | 2.25 |
| *a.* | 30c multi | .75 | .35 |
| *b.* | 57c multi | 1.40 | .70 |
| **2736** A757 | Monsanto | 2.25 | 2.25 |
| *a.* | 30c multi | .75 | .35 |
| *b.* | 57c multi | 1.40 | .70 |
| **2737** A757 | Piodao | 2.25 | 2.25 |
| *a.* | 30c multi | .75 | .35 |
| *b.* | 57c multi | 1.40 | .70 |
| **2738** A757 | Sortelha | 2.25 | 2.25 |
| *a.* | 30c multi | .75 | .35 |
| *b.* | 57c multi | 1.40 | .70 |
| **2739** A757 | Trancoso | 2.25 | 2.25 |
| *a.* | 30c multi | .75 | .35 |
| *b.* | 57c multi | 1.40 | .70 |
| | *Nos. 2728-2739 (12)* | 27.00 | 27.00 |

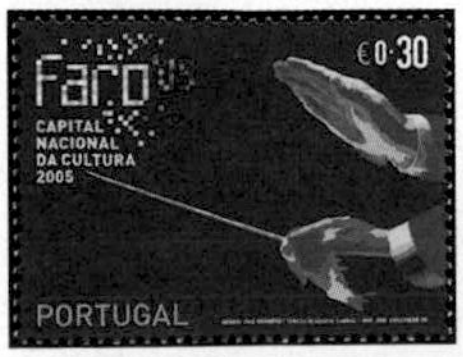

Faro, 2005 National Cultural Capital A758

Designs: 30c, Conductor's hands and baton. 45c, Broken pot. 57c, Shell. 74c, Hands applauding.

**2005, June 15**
**2740-2743** A758 Set of 4 5.00 2.50

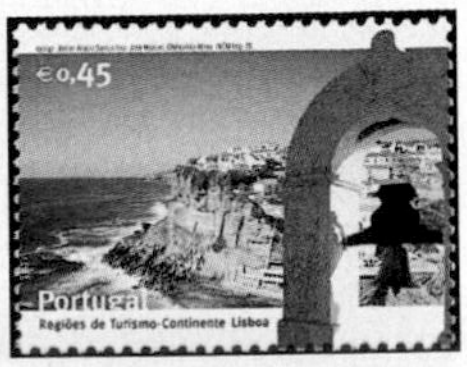

Tourism A759

Various scenes from: No. 2744, 45c, Lisbon. No. 2745, 45c, Porto e Norte. No. 2746, 48c, Lisbon, diff. No. 2747, 48c, Porto e Norte, diff. No. 2748, 57c, Lisbon, diff. No. 2749, 57c, Porto e Norte, diff.

**2005, July 8** *Perf. 12x11¾*
**2744-2749** A759 Set of 6 7.25 3.50

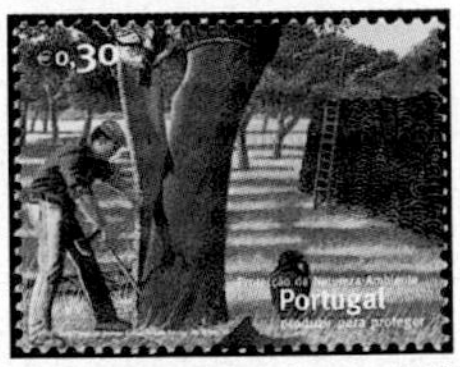

Nature Conservation — A760

Designs: 30c, Man with hatchet inspecting tree. 45c, Forest fire prevention squad. 57c, Bird on branch, building in forest.
€2, Bird on fence, large trees.

**2005, Aug. 19** *Perf. 12x11¾*
**2750-2752** A760 Set of 3 3.50 1.75

**Souvenir Sheet**

*Perf. 12x12½*

**2753** A760 €2 multi 5.00 5.00

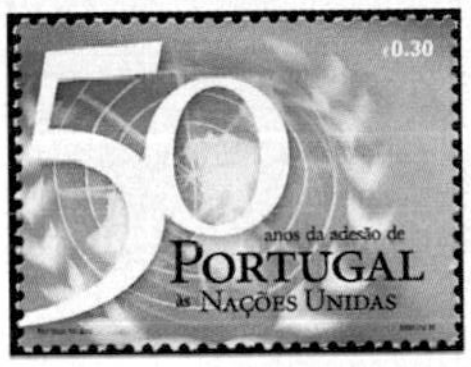

United Nations, 60th Anniv. A761

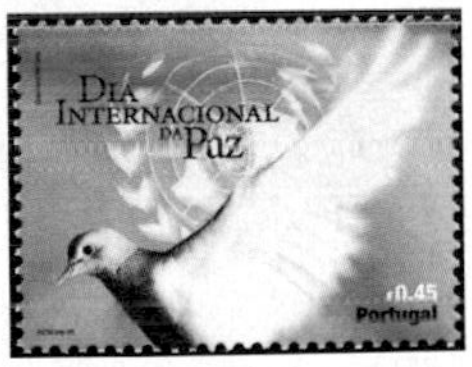

Intl. Day of Peace A762

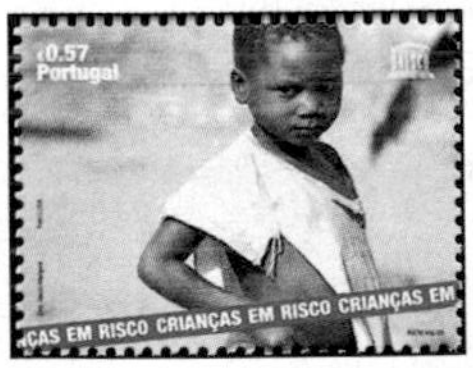

Children at Risk A763

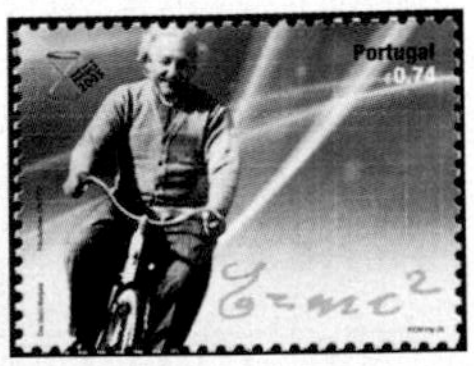

Intl. Year of Physics A764

**2005, Sept. 21** *Perf. 12x11¾*

| | | | |
|---|---|---|---|
| **2754** | A761 30c multi | .75 | .35 |
| **2755** | A762 45c multi | 1.10 | .55 |
| **2756** | A763 57c multi | 1.40 | .70 |
| **2757** | A764 74c multi | 1.90 | .95 |
| | *Nos. 2754-2757 (4)* | 5.15 | 2.55 |

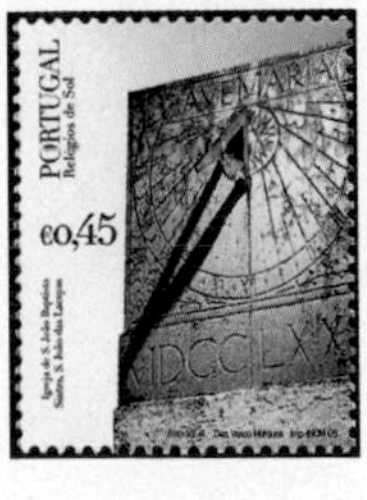

Sundials — A765

## Annular Solar Eclipse, Oct. 3, 2005 — A766

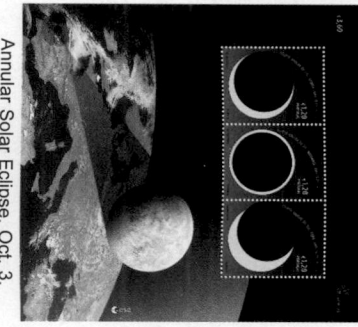

**2005, Oct. 3**   **Perf. 12½x12**
2758-2759 A765   Set of 2
2760 A766   Sheet of 3   3.50 1.75
  a.-c.            2.75 1.40

Sundial from: 45c, St. John the Baptist Church, Sintra. €1, Maritime Museum, Lisbon. €1.20, view of eclipsed Sun from: a, Lisbon at 9:53. b, Bragança at 9:55. c, Faro at 9:55.

## Communications Media — A768

**2005, Oct. 3**   **Souvenir Sheet**
  **Perf. 12**
2760 A766   Sheet of 3   8.75 8.75
  a.-c.            2.75 1.40

Designs: 30c, Press (fountain pen); 45c, Radio (microphone); 57c, Television (portable camera). 74c, Internet (globe and "@" studio). €1, Press (newspaper); a, Radio (studio).
No. 2765: a, Press (newspaper); a, Radio (studio). No. 2766: a, Television (studio). b, Internet (beginning of website address).

## Fishing Villages — A769

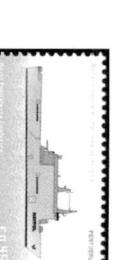

**2005, Oct. 13**   **Souvenir Sheets**
2761-2764 A767   **Perf. 12x12½**   Set of 4   5.00 2.50
2765 A768   Set of 2
  a.  €1.10 multi   6.50 6.50
      3.75 1.40
2766 A768   Sheet of 2
  a.  €1.55 multi   6.50 6.50
  b.  €1.10 multi   3.75 1.90
      €1.55 multi   6.50 6.50
                    3.75 1.90

Designs: 45c, Radio. €1.10, €1.55 multi.

**2005, Oct. 18**   **Horiz. Pairs, #a-b**
2767-2768 A769   **Perf. 13½x13¾**   Set of 2
  a.            3.00 1.50
2767-2768

See Hong Kong Nos. 1160-1163.

No. 2767, 30c — Aldeia da Carrasquiera, Portugal. a: Denomination at R. b: Denomination at L. No. 2768, 30c — Tai O, Hong Kong. a: Denomination at R. b: Denomination at L. Illustration reduced.

## Serralves Foundation A771

**2005, Nov. 10**   **Perf. 12x12½**
2769 A770   30c multi   .70  .35
2770 A770   €1 multi   **Souvenir Sheet**
                        2.40 2.40

Designs: 30c, Cunhal in crowd. €1, Cunhal with young girl.

## Álvaro Cunhal (1913-2005), Communist Politician — A770

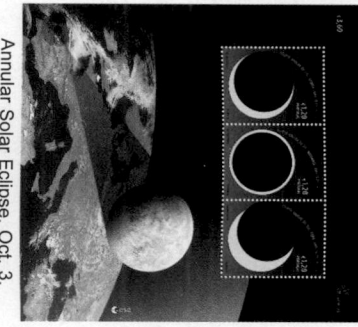

## Lisbon Earthquake, 250th Anniv. — A772

**2005, Nov. 15**   **Souvenir Sheets**
2771-2776 A771   **Perf. 13½x14**   Set of 6   8.50 4.25
2777 A771   Sheet of 5   5.00 5.00
  a.  30c multi   .70  .35
  b.-e.  45c Any single   1.00  .50
2778 A771   €1 Any single   **Perf. 14x13½**
2778   Sheet of 3   7.00 7.00
  a.-c.            2.25 1.10

Designs: No. 2771, 30c, White building. No. 2772, 45c, Silhouette of seated person. 48c, Red brown building entrance, diff. 57c, Sculpture of garden shovel. 74c, Person painting. No. 2776, €1, Walkway and hedges.
No. 2777: a, 30c, Red brown building entrance, horiz. b, 45c, Walkway and trees. c, 45c, Columns in building, diff. d, 45c, Tower. e, 45c, Walkway and hedges, diff. No. 2778: a, €1, White building, horiz. b, €1, Art in gallery, horiz. c, €1, Trees and lawn.

## Modernization of the Navy — A773

**2005, Nov. 25**   **Souvenir Sheet**
2779-2780 A772   Set of 2
2781 A772   €2.65 multi   **Perf. 14x13½**
                          6.25 6.25
                          5.75 2.75

Designs: 45c, Navpol ship. 74c, Ocean patrol boat and helicopter. €2 Submarine.
No. 2781 contains one 40x30mm stamp.

## Soccer Teams A774

**2005, Nov. 25**   **Souvenir Sheets**
2782-2785 A773   **Perf. 12x12½**   Set of 4   9.00 4.50
2786-2788 A774   Set of 3
  **Perf. 12x11¾**
  a.  Souvenir Sheets   7.00 7.00
                        2.10 1.10
2789-2791 A774   Set of 3

Players and team emblems: No. 2786, N, Sporting Clube de Portugal. No. 2787, N, Sport Lisboa e Benfica. No. 2788, N, Futebol Clube do Porto.
No. 2789, €1, Sporting Clube de Portugal, diff. No. 2790, €1, Sport Lisboa e Benfica, diff. No. 2791, €1, Player lifting trophy, Futebol Clube do Porto.
Nos. 2786-2788 each sold for 30c on day of issue.

## Greetings A775

**2006, Feb. 7**   **Perf. 12x12½**
2792 A775   N multi   .75  .35
  a.  Perf. 12 vert. (from booklet pane)   .75  .35
2793 A775   N multi   .75  .35
  a.  Perf. 12 vert. (from booklet pane)   .75  .35
2794 A775   N multi   .75  .35
  a.  Perf. 12 vert. (from booklet pane)   .75  .35
2795 A775   N multi   .75  .35
  a.  Perf. 12 vert. (from booklet pane)   .75  .35
2796 A775   N multi   .75  .35
  a.  Perf. 12 vert. (from booklet pane)   .75  .35
  b.  Booklet pane, 5   3.75
      Complete booklet, #2792a-2796a   —
      Nos. 2792-2796 (5)   3.75 1.75

Designs: No. 2792, Parabéns (birthday party). No. 2793, Amote (men and women dancing and exchanging gifts, child). No. 2794, Parabéns (man, woman and two children, stork with baby). No. 2795, Parabéns (conductor, cocktail party). No. 2796, Parabéns (man, woman, fairy, Cupid).

## Masks Type of 2005

**2006, Mar. 1**   **Serpentine Die Cut 11½**
  **Self-Adhesive**
2797 A748   N multi   .75  .35
2798 A748   N multi   1.10  .55
2799 A748   A multi   .70
  Nos. 2797-2799 (3)   3.25 1.60

Designs: N, Like No. 2696. A, "Carnaval" Lazarim, Bragança. E, "Dia de Ano Novo" Mogadouro, Bragança.
No. 2797 sold for 30c, No. 2798 sold for 57c, and No. 2799 sold for 57c on day of issue.

## Symbol of Aviation AP1

## AIR POST STAMPS

**1936-41**   **Perf. 12x11½**
  **Unwmk.**   **Typo.**
C1 AP1   1.50e dark blue   .45  .30
C2 AP1   1.75e red orange   .75  .35
C3 AP1   1.75e red orange   .85  .35
C4 AP1   2.50e rose red   14.00 12.00
C5 AP1   4e dp yel grn (41)
C6 AP1   5e car lake   18.00 18.00
C7 AP1   10e brown lake   1.75 1.25
C8 AP1   15e orange (41)   3.00 1.25
C9 AP1   20e black brn (41)   11.50 2.00
C10 AP1   50e blu vio (41)   9.00 2.00
  Nos. C1-C10 (10)   220.00 75.00
                     390.00 118.25

Never hinged
Nos. C1-C10 exist imperf.

## POSTAGE DUE STAMPS

## Vasco da Gama Issue

The Zamorin of Calicut Receiving Vasco da Gama — D1

**1898, May 1**   **Unwmk.**   **Typo.**   **Perf. 12**
  **Denomination in Black**
D1 D1   5r black   2.40  1.25
  a.  Value and "Continente" omitted
D2 D1   10r lilac & blk   5.00
D3 D1   20r orange & blk   4.00  1.75
D4 D1   50r slate & blk   6.50  2.75
D5 D1   100r car & blk, pink   50.00 11.00
D6 D1   200r brn & blk, buff   87.50 60.00
  Nos. J1-J6 (6)   92.50 60.00
                   242.90 116.50

For overprints and surcharges see Nos. 193-198.

**1904**   **Perf. 11½x12**
D2
J7 D2   5r brown   .45  .40
J8 D2   10r orange   2.75  .90
J9 D2   20r lilac   8.00  3.75
J10 D2   30r gray green   5.75  2.75
J11 D2   40r gray violet   7.00  2.75
J12 D2   50r carmine   52.50  4.50
  a.  Imperf.
J13 D2   100r dull blue   8.75  6.50
  a.  Imperf.
  Nos. J7-J13 (7)   85.20 21.55

**1910**
D3
J14 D2   5r brown   .40  .25
J15 D2   10r orange   .40  .40
J16 D2   20r lilac   1.40  1.00
J17 D2   30r gray green   1.40  .25
J18 D2   40r gray violet   1.25  .25
J19 D2   50r carmine (G)   6.00  4.50
J20 D2   100r dull blue   6.50  5.25
  Nos. J14-J20 (7)   17.35 11.75

See note after No. 183.

## Preceding Issue Overprinted in Carmine or Green

**1915, Mar. 18**   **Typo.**
J21 D3   ½c brown   .45  .40
J22 D3   1c orange   .60  .60
J23 D3   2c claret   .60  .60
J24 D3   3c green   .60  .60
J25 D3   4c dl green   .60  .60
J26 D3   5c carmine   .60  .60
J27 D3   10c dark blue   4.20  4.20
  Nos. J21-J27 (7)   4.20 4.20

## Vasco da Gama — D1

## EXPO Type of Regular Issue

**1970, Sept. 21**   **Litho.**   **Perf. 12½x11½**
C11 A274   3.50e silver & multi   1.10  .55
                                  1.25  .80

**1979, Sept. 21**   **Litho.**   **Perf. 13**
C12 AP2   16e multicolored   .70  .40
C13 AP2   19e multicolored

TAP-Airline of Portugal 35th Anniversary AP2

Design: 19e, Jet flying past sun.

## PORTUGAL

**1921-27** (Perf. 12x11½)

| | | | | |
|---|---|---|---|---|
| J28 | D3 | ½c gray green ('22) | .35 | .35 |
| J29 | D3 | 4c gray green ('27) | .35 | .35 |
| J30 | D3 | 8c gray green ('23) | .35 | .35 |
| J31 | D3 | 10c gray green ('22) | .35 | .35 |
| J32 | D3 | 12c gray green | .50 | .50 |
| J33 | D3 | 16c gray green ('23) | .50 | .50 |
| J34 | D3 | 20c gray green | .50 | .50 |
| J35 | D3 | 24c gray green ('23) | .50 | .50 |
| J36 | D3 | 32c gray green ('23) | .50 | .75 |
| J37 | D3 | 40c gray green ('23) | 1.50 | 1.50 |
| J38 | D3 | 40c gray green ('23) | .65 | .65 |
| J39 | D3 | 48c gray green ('23) | .65 | .65 |
| J40 | D3 | 50c gray green | .65 | .65 |
| J41 | D3 | 60c gray green | .65 | .65 |
| J42 | D3 | 72c gray green ('23) | .65 | 7.50 |
| J43 | D3 | 80c gray green ('23) | 7.50 | 7.50 |
| J44 | D3 | 1.20e gray green | 3.00 | 18.50 |

Nos. J28-J44 (17) 20.00

D4

**1932-33** Unwmk. Perf. 12½

| | | | | |
|---|---|---|---|---|
| J45 | D4 | 5c buff | .50 | .50 |
| J46 | D4 | 10c lt blue | .50 | .50 |
| J47 | D4 | 10c pink | 1.25 | 1.00 |
| J48 | D4 | 30c blue green | 1.50 | 1.00 |
| J49 | D4 | 20c dk car rose | 1.50 | 1.00 |
| J50 | D4 | 40c purple | 1.60 | 1.00 |
| J51 | D4 | 40c cerise | 4.25 | 2.00 |
| J52 | D4 | 60c yellow grn | 8.00 | 4.00 |
| J53 | D4 | 1.20e violet brn | 13.00 | 12.00 |

Nos. J45-J53 (9) 32.10 22.90

**1940, Feb. 1** Unwmk. Perf. 12½

| | | | | |
|---|---|---|---|---|
| J54 | D5 | 5c bister, perf. 14 | .50 | .35 |
| J55 | D5 | 10c rose lilac | .50 | .35 |
| J56 | D5 | 20c blue green | 1.50 | 1.00 |
| J57 | D5 | 30c dk car rose | 1.50 | 1.00 |
| J58 | D5 | 40c purple | 1.60 | 1.00 |
| J59 | D5 | 50c brt green | .30 | .30 |
| J60 | D5 | 60c yellow grn | .30 | .30 |
| J61 | D5 | 80c scarlet | .30 | .30 |
| J62 | D5 | 1e brown | .55 | .45 |
| J63 | D5 | 2e dk rose vio | 11.00 | 9.00 |
| a. | | Perf. 12½ | 175.00 | 125.00 |
| J64 | D5 | 5e org red, perf. 14 | 14.45 | 11.40 |

Nos. J54-J64 were first issued perf. 14. In 1955 all but the 5c were reissued in purf. 12½.

D5

**1967-84** Litho. Perf. 11½

| | | | | |
|---|---|---|---|---|
| J65 | D6 | 10c dp org, red brn & yel | .20 | .20 |
| J66 | D6 | 20c bis, dk brn & yel | .20 | .20 |
| J67 | D6 | 30c org, red brn & yel | .20 | .20 |
| J68 | D6 | 40c ol bis, dk car rose | .20 | .20 |
| J69 | D6 | 50c ultra, dk bl & bl | .20 | .20 |
| J70 | D6 | 60c grnsh bl, dk grn & lt bl | .20 | .20 |
| J71 | D6 | 80c bl, dk bl & lt bl | .20 | .20 |
| J72 | D6 | 1e vio bl, dk bl & lt grn | .20 | .20 |
| J73 | D6 | 2e grn, dk grn & lt grn ('75) | .20 | .20 |
| J74 | D6 | 3e lt grn, grn & yel ('75) | .20 | .20 |
| J75 | D6 | 4e bl grn, dk grn & lt bl ('75) | .20 | .20 |
| J76 | D6 | 5e cl, dp cl & pink | .20 | .20 |
| J77 | D6 | 9e vio, dk vio & pink ('75) | .20 | .20 |
| J78 | D6 | 10e lil, pur & pale vio ('75) | .20 | .20 |
| J79 | D6 | 20e red, brn & pale vio ('75) | .70 | .20 |
| J80 | D6 | 40e dp red lil, rose vio & bluish lil ('84) | 1.50 | .50 |
| J81 | D6 | 50e lil, brn & pale gray ('84) | 1.60 | .80 |

Nos. J65-J81 (17) 6.60 4.30

D6

Catalogue values for unused stamps in this section, from this point to the end of the section, are for Never Hinged items.

**1992-93** Litho. Perf. 12x11½

| | | | | |
|---|---|---|---|---|
| J82 | D7 | 1e multicolored | .20 | .20 |
| J83 | D7 | 2e multicolored | .20 | .20 |
| J84 | D7 | 5e multicolored | .20 | .20 |
| J85 | D7 | 10e multicolored | .20 | .25 |
| J86 | D7 | 20e multicolored | .55 | .25 |
| J87 | D7 | 50e multicolored | 1.00 | .55 |
| J88 | D7 | 100e multicolored | 2.00 | 1.25 |
| J89 | D7 | 200e multicolored | 4.60 | 3.05 |

Nos. J82-J89 (8)

Issued: 1e, 2e, 5e, 200e, 10/7/92; 10e, 20e, 50e, 100e, 3/9/93.

Type D7 Inscribed "CTT CORREIOS"
**1995-96**

| | | | | |
|---|---|---|---|---|
| J90 | D7 | 3e multicolored | .20 | .20 |
| J91 | D7 | 4e multicolored | .20 | .20 |
| J92 | D7 | 9e multicolored | .20 | .20 |
| J93 | D7 | 20e multicolored | .35 | .25 |
| J94 | D7 | 40e multicolored | .55 | .45 |
| J95 | D7 | 50e multicolored | .85 | .45 |
| J96 | D7 | 100e multicolored | 2.95 | 2.10 |

Nos. J90-J98 (9)

Issued: 3e, 4e, 9e, 40e, 4/20/95; 5e, 10e, 20e, 100e, 5/24/96.

Numerals — D8

**2002, Jan. 2** Litho. Perf. 11¾x11½

| | | | | |
|---|---|---|---|---|
| J99 | D8 | 1c multi | .20 | .20 |
| J100 | D8 | 2c multi | .20 | .20 |
| J101 | D8 | 5c multi | .20 | .20 |
| J102 | D8 | 10c multi | .60 | .20 |
| J103 | D8 | 25c multi | 1.20 | .70 |
| J104 | D8 | 50c multi | 2.40 | .70 |
| J105 | D8 | €1 multi | 5.00 | 2.05 |

Nos. J99-J105 (7)

### OFFICIAL STAMPS

No. 567 Overprinted in Black
**1938** Unwmk. Perf. 11½
O1 A113 40c brown .45 .20

Catalogue values for unused stamps in this section, from this point to the end of the section, are for Never Hinged items.

### NEWSPAPER STAMPS

| | | | | |
|---|---|---|---|---|
| **1952, Sept.** | Litho. | | | |
| O2 | O1 | black & cream | .45 | .20 |
| **1975, June** | | | | |
| O3 | O1 | black & yellow | .60 | .20 |

N1

---

### PARCEL POST STAMPS

**1876** Typo. Perf. 11½, 12½, 13½
P1 N1 2½r olive green 14.00 1.40
a. 2½r olive green 14.00 1.40

Various shades.

Mercury and Commerce PP1

**1920-22** Unwmk. Typo. Perf. 12

| | | | | |
|---|---|---|---|---|
| Q1 | PP1 | 1c lilac brown | .20 | .20 |
| Q2 | PP1 | 2c orange | .20 | .20 |
| Q3 | PP1 | 5c lt brown | .20 | .20 |
| Q4 | PP1 | 10c red brown | .30 | .25 |
| Q5 | PP1 | 20c gray blue | .30 | .25 |
| Q6 | PP1 | 40c carmine rose | .35 | .45 |
| Q7 | PP1 | 50c black | .50 | .45 |
| Q8 | PP1 | 60c dk blue ('21) | 3.00 | 2.00 |
| Q9 | PP1 | 70c gray brn ('21) | 3.50 | 3.25 |
| Q10 | PP1 | 80c ultra ('21) | 3.50 | 3.25 |
| Q11 | PP1 | 90c lt vio ('21) | 4.00 | 2.25 |
| Q12 | PP1 | 1e green | 3.50 | 3.50 |
| Q13 | PP1 | 2e pale lilac ('22) | 11.00 | 4.00 |
| Q14 | PP1 | 3e olive ('22) | 21.00 | 7.00 |
| Q15 | PP1 | 4e ultra ('22) | 42.50 | 7.00 |
| Q16 | PP1 | 5e gray green ('22) | 55.00 | 9.25 |
| Q17 | PP1 | 10e chocolate ('22) | 82.50 | 9.25 |

Nos. Q1-Q17 (17) 228.45 40.45

Parcel Post Package PP2

**1936**

| | | | | |
|---|---|---|---|---|
| Q18 | PP2 | 50c olive brown | .65 | .50 |
| Q19 | PP2 | 1e bister brown | .65 | .50 |
| Q20 | PP2 | 1.50e purple | .65 | .60 |
| Q21 | PP2 | 2e carmine lake | 2.75 | .60 |
| Q22 | PP2 | 2.60e olivo groon | 5.75 | .65 |
| Q23 | PP2 | 4.50e olive lake | 5.75 | .65 |
| Q24 | PP2 | 5e violet | 9.00 | .75 |
| Q25 | PP2 | 10e orange | 12.00 | 1.75 |

Nos. Q18-Q25 (8) 34.20 5.85

### POSTAL TAX STAMPS

These stamps represent a special fee for the delivery of postal matter on certain days in each year. The money derived from their sale is applied to works of public charity.

Regular Issues Overprinted in Carmine

**1911, Oct. 4** Unwmk. Perf. 14½x15
RA1 A62 10r gray green 8.50 2.25

The 20r carmine of this type was for use on telegrams.

**1912, Oct. 4** Perf. 15x14½
RA2 A64 1c deep green 6.00 1.75

The 2c carmine of this type was for use on telegrams.

"Lisbon" — PT1

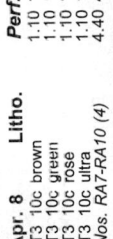

"Charity" — PT2

**1913, June 8** Litho. Perf. 12x11½
RA3 PT1 1c dark green .95 .70

The 2c dark brown of this type was for use on telegrams.

**1915, Oct. 4** Typo.
RA4 PT2 1c carmine .35 .30

The 2c plum of this type was for use on telegrams. See No. RA6.

No. RA4 Surcharged

**1924, Oct. 4**
RA5 PT2 15c on 1c dull red 1.25 .70

The 30c on 2c claret of this type was for use on telegrams.

Charity Type of 1915 Issue
**1925, Oct. 4** Perf. 12½
RA6 PT2 15c carmine .35 .35

The 30c brown violet of this type was for use on telegrams.

### Comrades of the Great War Issue

Muse of History with Tablet — PT3

**1925, Apr. 8** Litho. Perf. 11

| | | | | |
|---|---|---|---|---|
| RA7 | PT3 | 10c brown | 1.10 | 1.10 |
| RA8 | PT3 | 10c green | 1.10 | 1.10 |
| RA9 | PT3 | 10c red | 1.10 | 1.10 |
| RA10 | PT3 | 10c ultra | 4.40 | 4.40 |

Nos. RA7-RA10 (4)

The use of these stamps, in addition to the regular postage, was obligatory on certain days of the year. If the tax represented by these stamps was not prepaid, it was collected by means of Postal Tax Due Stamp No. RAJ1.

Pombal Issue
Common Design Types
Engraved; Value and "Continente" Typographed in Black

**1925, May 8** Perf. 12½

| | | | | |
|---|---|---|---|---|
| RA11 | CD28 | 15c ultra | .50 | .40 |
| RA12 | CD29 | 15c ultra | 1.00 | .75 |
| RA13 | CD30 | 15c ultra | 2.50 | 1.90 |

Nos. RA11-RA13 (3)

### Olympic Games Issue

Hurdler — PT7

**1928** Litho. Perf. 12
RA14 PT7 15c dull red & blk 4.00 2.75

The use of this stamp, in addition to the regular postage, was obligatory on May 22-24, 1928. 10% of the money thus obtained was

## POSTAL TAX DUE STAMPS

retained by the Postal Administration; the balance was given to a Committee in charge of Portuguese participation in the Olympic games at Amsterdam.

 PTD1     PTD2

**Comrades of the Great War Issue**
**1925 Unwmk. Typo. Perf. 11x11½**
RAJ1 PTD1 20c brown orange .55 .45
See Note after No. RA10.

**1925**
**Pombal Issue**
Common Design Types
**Perf. 12½**
| | | | |
|---|---|---|---|
| RAJ2 | CD28 | 30c ultra | 1.10 1.10 |
| RAJ3 | CD29 | 30c ultra | 1.10 1.10 |
| RAJ4 | CD30 | 30c ultra | 1.10 1.10 |
| Nos. RAJ2-RAJ4 (3) | | | 3.30 3.30 |

When the compulsory tax was not paid by the use of stamps #RA11-RA13, double the amount was collected by means of #RAJ2-RAJ4.

**Olympic Games Issue**
**1928 Litho. Perf. 11½**
RAJ5 PTD2 30c lt red & blk 1.75 1.75

## FRANCHISE STAMPS

These stamps are supplied by the Government to various charitable, scientific and military organizations for franking their correspondence. This franking privilege was withdrawn in 1938.

### FOR THE RED CROSS SOCIETY

 F1  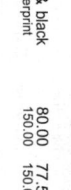

**1889-1915 Unwmk. Typo. Perf. 11½**
1S1 F1 rose & blk .45 .40
  **Perf. 12½**
a. rose & blk ('15) 5.75 5.00
b. Red & black, perf 12½ 65.00 6.25

**1917**
1S3 F1 rose & black 80.00 77.50
a. Inverted overprint 150.00 150.00

"Charity" Extending Hope to Invalid — F1a

**No. 1S1 Overprinted in Green**
**1928**
1S1 Overprinted in Green 96c lake

**Camoens Issue of 1924 Overprinted in Black or Red**
**1926 Litho. Perf. 14**
Inscribed "LISBOA"
1S4 F1a black & red 7.00 7.00
Inscribed "DELEGACOES"
1S5 F1a black & red 7.00 7.00
No. 1S4 was for use in Lisbon. No. 1S5 was for the Red Cross chapters outside Lisbon. For overprints see Nos. 1S72-1S73.

**Camoens Issue of 1924 Overprinted in Black or Red**

**1927**
| | | | |
|---|---|---|---|
| 1S6 | A68 | 40c ultra | 1.10 1.00 |
| 1S7 | A68 | 48c red brown | 1.10 1.00 |
| 1S8 | A69 | 64c green | 1.10 1.00 |
| 1S9 | A69 | 75c dk violet | 1.10 1.00 |
| 1S10 | A71 | 4.50e blk, org (R) | 1.10 1.00 |
| 1S11 | A71 | 10e dk brn, pnksh | 6.60 6.00 |
| Nos. 1S6-1S11 (6) | | | |

**1928**
| | | | |
|---|---|---|---|
| 1S12 | A67 | 15c olive grn | 1.10 1.00 |
| 1S13 | A67 | 16c violet brn | 1.10 1.00 |
| 1S14 | A68 | 25c lilac | 1.10 1.00 |
| 1S15 | A68 | 40c brown | 1.10 1.00 |
| 1S16 | A70 | 2e apple green | 1.10 1.00 |
| 1S17 | A70 | 2e lt brown | 6.60 6.00 |
| Nos. 1S12-1S17 (6) | | | |

**1929**
| | | | |
|---|---|---|---|
| 1S18 | A68 | 30c dk brown | 1.10 1.00 |
| 1S19 | A68 | 40c ultra | 1.10 1.00 |
| 1S20 | A69 | 80c bister | 1.10 1.00 |
| 1S21 | A69 | 96c blue | 1.10 1.00 |
| 1S22 | A70 | 1.60e dark blue | 1.10 1.00 |
| 1S23 | A70 | 2.40e green, grn | 6.60 6.00 |
| Nos. 1S18-1S23 (6) | | | |

**Same Overprint Dated "1930"**
**1930**
| | | | |
|---|---|---|---|
| 1S24 | A68 | 30c dk brown | 1.10 1.00 |
| 1S25 | A68 | 40c ultra | 1.10 1.00 |
| 1S26 | A69 | 50c red orange | 1.10 1.00 |
| 1S27 | A69 | 96c blue | 1.10 1.00 |
| 1S28 | A70 | 1.60e dk blue | 1.10 1.00 |
| 1S29 | A72 | 2.40e dk violet, lil | 6.60 6.00 |
| Nos. 1S24-1S29 (6) | | | |

**Camoens Issue of 1924 Overprinted in Red**

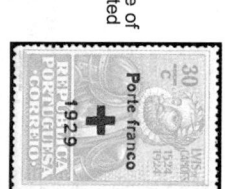 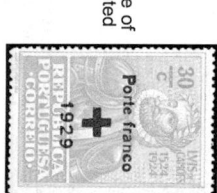  

**1931**
| | | | |
|---|---|---|---|
| 1S30 | A68 | 25c lilac | 1.25 1.10 |
| 1S31 | A68 | 32c dk green | 1.25 1.10 |
| 1S32 | A68 | 40c dk green | 1.25 1.10 |
| 1S33 | A69 | 96c lake | 1.25 1.10 |

**Same Overprint Dated "1932"**
**1931**
| | | | |
|---|---|---|---|
| 1S34 | A70 | 1.60e dark blue | 1.25 1.10 |
| 1S35 | A71 | 3.20e black, green | 7.50 6.60 |
| Nos. 1S30-1S35 (6) | | | |

**Nos. 1S6-1S11 Overprinted in Red**
**1932**
| | | | |
|---|---|---|---|
| 1S36 | A70 | 20c dp orange | 1.75 1.75 |
| 1S37 | A68 | 40c ultra | 1.75 1.75 |
| 1S38 | A68 | 48c red brown | 1.75 1.75 |
| 1S39 | A68 | 64c green | 1.75 1.75 |
| 1S40 | A70 | 1.60e dark blue | 1.75 1.75 |
| 1S41 | A71 | 10e dk brown, pnksh | 10.50 10.50 |
| Nos. 1S36-1S41 (6) | | | |

**1932**
| | | | |
|---|---|---|---|
| 1S42 | A70 | 40c ultra | 1.75 1.75 |
| 1S43 | A68 | 48c red brown | 1.75 1.75 |
| 1S44 | A68 | 64c green | 1.75 1.75 |
| 1S45 | A69 | 75c dk violet | 1.75 1.75 |
| 1S46 | A71 | 4.50e blk, orange | 1.75 1.75 |
| 1S47 | A71 | 10e dk brn, pnksh | 10.50 10.50 |
| Nos. 1S42-1S47 (6) | | | |

**1933 Dated "1934"**
| | | | |
|---|---|---|---|
| 1S48 | A68 | 40c ultra | 2.25 2.25 |
| 1S49 | A68 | 48c red brown | 2.25 2.25 |
| 1S50 | A69 | 64c green | 2.25 2.25 |
| 1S51 | A69 | 75c dk violet | 2.25 2.25 |
| 1S52 | A71 | 4.50e blk, orange | 2.25 2.25 |
| 1S53 | A71 | 10e dk brn, orange, pnksh | 13.50 13.50 |
| Nos. 1S48-1S53 (6) | | | |

**1935 Dated "1935"**
| | | | |
|---|---|---|---|
| 1S54 | A68 | 40c ultra | 2.60 2.60 |
| 1S55 | A68 | 48c red brown | 2.60 2.60 |
| 1S56 | A69 | 64c green | 2.60 2.60 |
| 1S57 | A69 | 75c dk violet | 2.60 2.60 |
| 1S58 | A71 | 4.50e black, orange | 2.60 2.60 |
| 1S59 | A71 | 10e dk brn, orange, pnksh | 15.60 15.60 |
| Nos. 1S54-1S59 (6) | | | |

**Camoens Issue of 1924 Overprinted in Red**
**1935**
| | | | |
|---|---|---|---|
| 1S60 | A68 | 25c lilac | 1.10 1.00 |
| 1S61 | A68 | 40c ultra (R) | 1.10 1.00 |
| 1S62 | A69 | 50c red orange | 1.10 1.00 |
| 1S63 | A70 | 1e slate | 1.10 1.00 |
| 1S64 | A70 | 2e apple green | 1.10 1.00 |
| 1S65 | A72 | 2.40e dk violet, lilac | 6.50 6.10 |
| Nos. 1S60-1S65 (6) | | | |

**1936**
| | | | |
|---|---|---|---|
| 1S66 | A68 | 30c dk brown | 1.10 1.10 |
| 1S67 | A68 | 32c dk green | 1.10 1.10 |
| 1S68 | A68 | 80c bister | 1.10 1.10 |
| 1S69 | A70 | 1.20e lt brown | 1.10 1.10 |
| 1S70 | A71 | 3e dk blue, bl | 1.10 1.10 |
| 1S71 | A71 | 4.50e blue & red, bl | 6.60 6.60 |
| Nos. 1S66-1S71 (6) | | | |

**Camoens Issue of 1924 Overprinted in Black or Red**
**No. 1S4 Overprinted "1935"**
**1936 Unwmk. Perf. 14**
1S72 F1a black & red 8.25 8.25

### FOR CIVILIAN RIFLE CLUBS

**Same Stamp with Additional Overprint "Delegacoes"**
1S73 F1a black & red 8.25 8.25

After the government withdrew the franking privilege in 1938, the Portuguese Red Cross Society distributed charity labels which lacked postal validity.

Rifle Club
Emblem — F2

**1899-1910 Typo. Perf. 11½x12 Unwmk.**
| | | | |
|---|---|---|---|
| 2S1 | F2 | bl grn & car ('99) | 10.00 10.00 |
| 2S2 | F2 | brn & yel grn ('00) | 10.00 10.00 |
| 2S3 | F2 | car & buff ('01) | 1.00 1.00 |
| 2S4 | F2 | bl & org ('02) | 1.00 1.00 |
| 2S5 | F2 | bl & org ('03) | 1.00 1.00 |
| 2S6 | F2 | lt brn & blue ('04) | 1.60 1.60 |
| 2S7 | F2 | mar & ultra ('05) | 4.25 4.25 |
| 2S8 | F2 | mar & ultra ('06) | 4.25 4.25 |
| 2S9 | F2 | choc & car ('07) | 4.25 4.25 |
| 2S10 | F2 | car & ultra ('08) | 1.00 1.00 |
| 2S11 | F2 | bl & yel grn ('09) | 1.60 1.60 |
| 2S12 | F2 | grn & brn, pink ('10) | 1.00 1.00 |
| Nos. 2S1-2S12 (12) | | | 37.45 37.45 |

### FOR THE GEOGRAPHICAL SOCIETY OF LISBON

Coat of Arms
F3    F4

**1903-34 Unwmk. Litho. Perf. 11½**
| | | | |
|---|---|---|---|
| 3S1 | F3 | bl, rose, bl & red | 9.00 5.00 |
| 3S2 | F3 | bl, yel, red & grn | 12.00 5.00 |
| 3S3 | F4 | blk, org, bl & red | 5.50 4.00 |
| 3S4 | F4 | blk & brn org ('22) | 4.75 4.00 |
| 3S5 | F4 | blk & bl ('24) | 15.00 8.50 |
| 3S6 | F4 | blk & rose ('26) | 8.50 4.75 |
| 3S7 | F4 | blk & grn ('27) | 6.75 4.75 |
| 3S8 | F4 | bl, yel & red ('29) | 6.75 4.75 |
| 3S9 | F4 | dp bl, lil & red ('30) | 4.75 3.50 |
| 3S10 | F4 | blk, red & vio ('31) | 4.75 3.50 |
| 3S11 | F4 | bis brn & red ('32) | 4.75 3.50 |
| 3S12 | F4 | lt grn & red ('33) | 4.75 3.50 |
| 3S13 | F4 | blue & red ('34) | 90.25 57.75 |
| Nos. 3S1-3S13 (13) | | | |

No. 3S12 with three-line overprint "C.I.C.I. Portugal 1933" was not valid for postage and was sold only to collectors.
No. 3S2 was reprinted in 1933. Green vertical lines behind "Porte Franco" omitted. Value $7.50.

 F5

**1934**
3S15 F5 blue & red 5.00 3.50

**1935-38 Litho. Perf. 11**
| | | | |
|---|---|---|---|
| 3S16 | F5 | blue | 6.50 6.50 |
| 3S17 | F5 | blk bl & red ('36) | 5.25 5.25 |
| 3S18 | F5 | lil & red ('37) | 3.50 2.75 |
| 3S19 | F5 | blk, grn & car ('38) | 2.75 2.75 |
| Nos. 3S16-3S19 (4) | | | 18.25 15.00 |

The inscription in the inner circle is omitted on Nos. 3S16-3S19.

## FOR THE NATIONAL AID SOCIETY FOR CONSUMPTIVES

F10

**Perf. 11½x12 Typo. Unwmk.**

**1904, July**
| | | | | |
|---|---|---|---|---|
| 451 | F10 | brown & green | 5.00 | 5.00 |
| 452 | F10 | carmine & yellow | 5.00 | 5.00 |

---

# AZORES

Starting in 1980, stamps inscribed Azores and Madeira were valid and sold in Portugal. See Vols. 1 and 4 for prior issues.

Azores No. 2 — A33

Design: 19.50e, Azores No. 6.

**1980, Jan. 2 Litho. Perf. 12**
| | | | | |
|---|---|---|---|---|
| 314 | A33 | 6.50e multi | .20 | .20 |
| 315 | A33 | 19.50e multi | .05 | .50 |
| a. | | Souvenir sheet of 2, #314-315 | 3.75 | 3.75 |

No. 315a exists overprinted for Capex 87.

Map of Azores A34

**1980, Sept. 17 Litho. Perf. 12x11½**
| | | | | |
|---|---|---|---|---|
| 316 | A34 | 50c shown | .20 | .20 |
| 317 | A34 | 1e Cathedral | .20 | .20 |
| 318 | A34 | 5c Windmill | .40 | .20 |
| 319 | A34 | 6.50e Local women | .50 | .20 |
| 320 | A34 | 6e Coastline | .70 | .25 |
| 321 | A34 | 30e Ponta Delgada | 3.60 | 1.50 |
| | | Nos. 316-321 (6) | | |

World Tourism Conf., Manila, Sept. 27.

## Europa Issue 1981

St. Peter's Cavalcade, St. Miguel Island A35

**1981, May 11 Litho. Perf. 12**
| | | | | |
|---|---|---|---|---|
| 322 | A35 | 22e multicolored | 1.25 | .60 |
| a. | | Souvenir sheet of 2 | 7.00 | 2.00 |

Bulls Attacking Spanish Soldiers A36

Battle of Salga Valley, 400th Anniv.: 33.50e, Friar Don Pedro leading citizens.

**1981, July 24 Litho. Perf. 12½x11½**
| | | | | |
|---|---|---|---|---|
| 323 | A36 | 8.50e multi | .45 | .20 |
| 324 | A36 | 33.50e multi | 1.60 | .75 |

---

Tolpis Azorica — A37

Designs: Local flora.

**1981, Sept. 21 Litho. Perf. 12½x12**
| | | | | |
|---|---|---|---|---|
| 325 | A37 | 7e shown | .20 | .20 |
| 326 | A37 | 8.50e Ranunculus azoricus | .35 | .20 |
| 327 | A37 | 20e Platanthera micrantha | .65 | .35 |
| 328 | A37 | 50e Laurus azorica | 1.40 | .75 |
| a. | | Booklet pane of 4, #325-328 | 5.00 | |
| | | Nos. 325-328 (4) | 2.60 | 1.50 |

**1982, Jan. 29**
| | | | | |
|---|---|---|---|---|
| 329 | A37 | 4e Myosotis azorica | .20 | .20 |
| 330 | A37 | 10e Lactuca watsoniana | .50 | .20 |
| 331 | A37 | 27e Vicia dennesiana | 1.10 | .60 |
| 332 | A37 | 33.50e Azorina vidalii | 1.10 | .75 |
| a. | | Booklet pane of 4 | 5.00 | |
| | | Nos. 329-332 (4) | 2.90 | 1.75 |

See Nos. 338-341.

## Europa Type of Portugal

Heroes of Mindelo embarkation, 1832.

**1982, May 3 Litho. Perf. 12x11½**
| | | | | |
|---|---|---|---|---|
| 333 | A405 | 33.50e multi | 1.75 | .65 |
| a. | | Souvenir sheet of 3 | 18.00 | 4.00 |

Chapel of the Holy Ghost — A39

Various Chapels of the Holy Ghost

**1982, Nov. 24 Litho. Perf. 12½x12**
| | | | | |
|---|---|---|---|---|
| 334 | A39 | 27e multi | 1.10 | .60 |
| 335 | A39 | 33.50e multi | 1.50 | .80 |

Europa 1983 A40

**1983, May 5 Litho. Perf. 12½**
| | | | | |
|---|---|---|---|---|
| 336 | A40 | 37.50e Geothermal energy | 2.00 | .55 |
| a. | | Souvenir sheet of 3 | 20.00 | 5.00 |

Flag of the Autonomous Region — A41

**1983, May 23 Litho. Perf. 12x11½**
| | | | | |
|---|---|---|---|---|
| 337 | A41 | 12.50e multi | .65 | .20 |

## Flower Type of 1981

**1983, June 16 Perf. 12½x12**
| | | | | |
|---|---|---|---|---|
| 338 | A37 | 12.50e St. John's wort | .25 | .20 |
| 339 | A37 | 30e Prickless bramble | .70 | .30 |
| 340 | A37 | 37.50e Romania bush | .90 | .55 |
| 341 | A37 | 100e Common juniper | 1.90 | 1.00 |
| a. | | Booklet pane of 4, #338-341 | 6.00 | |
| | | Nos. 338-341 (4) | 3.85 | 2.05 |

---

Woman Wearing Terceira Cloaks — A42

**1984, Mar. 8 Litho. Perf. 13½**
| | | | | |
|---|---|---|---|---|
| 342 | A42 | 16e Jesters costumes, 18th cent. | .50 | .20 |
| 343 | A42 | 51e shown | 1.75 | 1.00 |

## Europa Type of Portugal

**1984, May 2 Perf. 12x11½**
| | | | | |
|---|---|---|---|---|
| 344 | A427 | 51e multicolored | 2.50 | .95 |
| a. | | Souvenir sheet of 3 | 20.00 | 5.00 |

Megabombus Ruderatus — A44

**1984, Sept. 3 Litho. Perf. 12x11½**
| | | | | |
|---|---|---|---|---|
| 345 | A44 | 16e shown | .30 | .20 |
| 346 | A44 | 35e Pieris brassicae azorensis | .50 | .50 |
| 347 | A44 | 40e Chrysomela banksi | 1.25 | .50 |
| 348 | A44 | 51e Phlogophora interrupta | 1.50 | .80 |
| | | Nos. 345-348 (4) | 3.95 | 2.00 |

**Perf. 12 Vert.**
| | | | | |
|---|---|---|---|---|
| 345a | A44 | 16e | 1.50 | 1.50 |
| 346a | A44 | 35e | 1.50 | 1.50 |
| 347a | A44 | 40e | 1.50 | 1.50 |
| 348a | A44 | 51e | 1.50 | 1.50 |
| b. | | Bklt. pane of 4, #345a-348a | 9.00 | |

**1985, Feb. 13 Perf. 12x11½**
| | | | | |
|---|---|---|---|---|
| 349 | A44 | 20e Polyspilla polyspila | .30 | .20 |
| 350 | A44 | 40e Sphaerophoria nigra | .90 | .40 |
| 351 | A44 | 46e Colias croceus | 1.25 | .60 |
| 352 | A44 | 60e Ilipparchia azorina | 1.40 | .85 |
| | | Nos. 349-352 (4) | 3.85 | 1.85 |

**Perf. 12 Vert.**
| | | | | |
|---|---|---|---|---|
| 349a | A44 | 20e | 1.50 | 1.50 |
| 350a | A44 | 46e | 1.50 | 1.50 |
| 351a | A44 | 46e | 1.50 | 1.50 |
| 352a | A44 | 60e | 1.50 | 1.50 |
| b. | | Bklt. pane of 4, #349-352a | 9.00 | |

## Europa Type of Portugal

**1985, May 6 Litho. Perf. 11½x12**
| | | | | |
|---|---|---|---|---|
| 353 | A435 | 61e Man playing folia drum | 2.75 | .80 |
| a. | | Souvenir sheet of 3 | 24.00 | 6.00 |

Native Boats — A46

**1985, June 19 Litho. Perf. 12x12½**
| | | | | |
|---|---|---|---|---|
| 354 | A46 | 40e Jeque | 1.10 | .60 |
| 355 | A46 | 60e Bote | 1.60 | .70 |

## Europa Type of Portugal

**1986, May Litho.**
| | | | | |
|---|---|---|---|---|
| 356 | A447 | 68.50e Pyrrhula murina | 2.75 | .90 |
| a. | | Souvenir sheet of 3 | 24.00 | 6.00 |

Regional Architecture A48

**1986, Sept. 18 Litho. Perf. 12**
| | | | | |
|---|---|---|---|---|
| 357 | A48 | 22.50e multi | .50 | .20 |
| 358 | A48 | 52.50e multi | 1.50 | .70 |
| 359 | A48 | 68.50e multi | 2.25 | .90 |
| 360 | A48 | 100e multi | 3.00 | .75 |
| a. | | Booklet pane of 4, #357-360 | 9.00 | |
| | | Nos. 357-360 (4) | 7.25 | 2.55 |

---

Traditional Modes of Transportation — A49

**1986, Nov. 7 Litho.**
| | | | | |
|---|---|---|---|---|
| 361 | A49 | 25e Isle of Santa Maria ox cart | .50 | .20 |
| 362 | A49 | 75e Ram cart | 2.25 | 1.10 |

## Europa Type of Portugal

Modern architecutre: Regional Assembly, Horta, designed by Manuel Correia Fernandes and Luis Miranda.

**1987, May 5 Litho. Perf. 12**
| | | | | |
|---|---|---|---|---|
| 363 | A456 | 74.50e multicolored | 3.00 | .90 |
| a. | | Souvenir sheet of 4 | 22.50 | 5.00 |

Windows and Balconies A51

**1987, July 1**
| | | | | |
|---|---|---|---|---|
| 364 | A51 | 51e Santa Cruz, Graciosa | 1.40 | .70 |
| 365 | A51 | 74.50e Ribiera Grande, San Miguel | 1.75 | .70 |

Aviation History A52

Seaplanes.

**1987, Oct. 9 Perf. 12x11½**
| | | | | |
|---|---|---|---|---|
| 366 | A52 | 25e NC-4 Curtiss Flyer, 1919 | .40 | .20 |
| 367 | A52 | 57e Dornier DO-X, 1932 | 1.50 | .90 |
| 368 | A52 | 74.50e Savoia-Marchetti S 55-X, 1933 | 2.25 | .85 |
| 369 | A52 | 125e Lockheed Sirius, 1933 | 2.60 | 1.10 |
| | | Nos. 366-369 (4) | 6.75 | 3.05 |

**Perf. 12 Vert.**
| | | | | |
|---|---|---|---|---|
| 366a | A52 | 25e | 2.25 | 2.25 |
| 367a | A52 | 57e | 2.25 | 2.25 |
| 368a | A52 | 74.50e | 2.25 | 2.25 |
| 369a | A52 | 125e | 2.25 | 2.25 |
| b. | | Bklt. pane of 4, #366a-369a | 9.00 | |

## Europa Type of Portugal

**1988, Apr. 21 Litho. Perf. 12**
| | | | | |
|---|---|---|---|---|
| 370 | A466 | 80e multicolored | 18.00 | 1.20 |
| a. | | Souvenir sheet of 4 | 24.00 | 5.50 |

Birds — A54

**1988, Oct. 18 Litho.**
| | | | | |
|---|---|---|---|---|
| 371 | A54 | 27e Columba palambus azorica | .50 | .20 |
| 372 | A54 | 60e Scolopax rusticola | 1.50 | .70 |
| 373 | A54 | 80e Sterna dougalli | 1.75 | .75 |

19th Century fountains: 22.50e, Alto das Covas, Angra do Heroismo; 52.50e, Faja de Baixo, San Miguel; 68.50e, Gates of St. Peter, Terceira; 100e, Agua d'Alto, San Miguel.

**1988, Nov. 18**
374 A54 100e Buteo buteo 2.10 .80
a. Booklet pane of 4, #371-374 9.00
Nos. 371-374 (4) 5.85 2.45

**Coats of Arms A55**
Litho.
375 A55 55e Dominion of Azores 1.25 .60
376 A55 80e Bettencourt family 1.75 .80

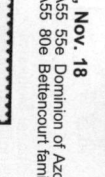

Wildlife Conservation A56

**1989, Jan. 20**
Various kinglets, *Regulus regulus*.
Litho.
377 A56 30e Adult on branch .75 .25
378 A56 30e Two adults .75 .25
379 A56 30e Adult, nest .75 .25
380 A56 30e Bird in flight .75 .25
a. Strip of 4, Nos. 377-380 3.25 3.25
See Nos. 385-388.

**Europa Type of Portugal**
Children's toys.
**1989, Apr. 26** Litho.
381 A476 80e Tin boat 2.50 .80

**Souvenir Sheet**
382 Sheet, 2 each #381, 382a 25.00 6.00
a. A476 80e Tin boat, diff. 2.50 2.50

**1989, Sept. 20**
Settlement of the Azores, 550th Anniv. A58
Litho.
383 A58 29e Friar Goncalho Velho .45 .20
384 A58 87e Settlers farming 2.00 .90

**Bird Type of 1989 With World Wildlife Fund Emblem**
Various *Pyrrhula murina*.
**1990, Feb. 14** Litho. Perf. 12
385 A56 32e Adult on branch .90 .25
386 A56 32e Two adults .90 .25
387 A56 32e Brooding .90 .25
388 A56 32e Bird in flight .90 .25
a. Strip of 4, Nos. 385-388 4.00 4.00
No. 388a has continuous design.

**Europa Type of Portugal**
P.O. A61
**1990, Apr. 11** Litho. Perf. 12
389 A466 80e Vasco da Gama P.O. 2.25 .55

**Souvenir Sheet**
390 Sheet of 4, 2 each #389, 390a 25.00 5.00
a. A406 80e Maia P.O. 2.25 2.25

Professions A61

**1990, July 11** Litho. Perf. 12
391 A61 5e Cart maker .20 .20
392 A61 32e Potter .45 .20
393 A61 60e Metal worker .85 .55
394 A61 100e Cooper 1.75 .85
391a A61 5e 1.50 1.50
392a A61 32e 1.50 1.50
393a A61 60e 1.50 1.50
394a A61 100e 1.50 1.50
a. Bklt. pane of 4, #391a-394a 6.00
Nos. 391-394 (4) 3.65 1.80
See Nos. 397-400, 406-409.

**Europa A62**
**1991, Apr. 11** Litho. Perf. 13½ Vert.
395 A62 80e Hermes space shuttle 3.65 1.80

**Souvenir Sheet**
396 Sheet, 2 each #395, 396a 25.00 5.00
a. A62 80e Sanger 2.25 2.25

**Professions Type of 1990**
**1991, Aug. 2** Litho. Perf. 12x11½
397 A61 35e Tile makers .45 .20
398 A61 65e Mosaic artists 1.00 .55
399 A61 70e Quarrymen 1.10 .65
400 A61 110e Stonemasons 1.75 .95
397a A61 35e 1.25 1.25
398a A61 65e 1.25 1.25
399a A61 70e 1.25 1.25
400a A61 110e 1.25 1.25
a. Bklt. pane of 4, #397a-400a 4.30 1.95
Nos. 397-400 (4)

Ships and Planes: 35e, Schooner Helena, 1918. 60e, Beechcraft C5, 1947. 80e, Yacht, Cruzeiro do Canal, 1987. 110e, British Aerospace ATP, 1991.

**Transportation in the Azores — A63**
**1991, Nov. 15** Litho. Perf. 12x11½
401 A63 35e multicolored .45 .20
402 A63 60e multicolored .90 .45
403 A63 80e multicolored 1.25 .60
404 A63 110e multicolored 1.60 .80
Nos. 401-404 (4) 4.20 2.05

**Transportation Type of 1991**
85e, Columbus aboard Santa Maria.
**1992, May 22** Litho. Perf. 12x11½
405 A514 85e gold & multi 6.00 .70

**Europa Type of Portugal**
**1992, June 12** Litho. Perf. 12x11½
406 A61 10e Guitar maker .45 .20
407 A61 38e Carpenter .45 .20
408 A61 85e Basket maker 1.10 .50
409 A61 120e Boat builders 1.40 .75
Nos. 406-409 (4) 3.15 1.65

**Professions Type of 1990**
**1992, June 12** Litho. Perf. 13½ Vert.
406a A61 10e 1.50 1.50
407a A61 38e 1.50 1.50
408a A61 85e 1.50 1.50
409a A61 120e 1.50 1.50
a. Bklt. pane of 4, #406a-409a 6.00
Nos. 406-409 (4)

Ships.
**1992, Oct. 7** Litho. Perf. 12x11½
410 A63 38e Insulano .45 .20
411 A63 65e Carvalho Araujo .85 .50
412 A63 85e Funchal 1.10 .55
413 A63 120e Terceirense 1.40 .65
Nos. 410-413 (4) 3.80 1.90

**Contemporary Paintings by Antonio Dacosta (1914-90) — A64**
**1993, May 5** Litho. Perf. 12x11½
414 A64 90e multicolored 1.25 .60

**Souvenir Sheet**
415 Sheet, 2 each #414, 415a 8.00 6.00
a. A64 90e multicolored 1.25 .60

**Grinding Stones A64a**
Designs: 42e, Animal-powered mill. 130e, Woman using hand-driven mill.
**1993, May 5** Litho. Perf. 12x11
416 A64a 42e multicolored .45 .20
417 A64a 130e multicolored 1.75 .75

Church of Praia da Vitoria: 42e, Main entry. 70e, South entry. 130e, South entry. Church of Ponta Delgada: 90e, Main entry.

**Architecture A65**
**1993, Nov. 3** Litho. Perf. 12
418 A65 42e multicolored .45 .20
419 A65 70e multicolored .80 .40
420 A65 90e multicolored 1.00 .50
421 A65 130e multicolored 1.50 .75
Nos. 418-421 (4) 3.75 1.85

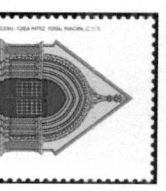

**Tile Used in Religious Architecture A66**
Designs: 40e, Blue and white pattern, Caloura church, Sao Miguel. 70e, Blue, white and yellow pattern, Caloura church, Sao Miguel. 100e, Drawing of Adoration of the Wise Men, by Bartolomeu Anfunco, Caloura monastery, Ponta Delgada. 150e, Drawing, frontal altar, Nossa Senhora dos Anjos chapel.
**1994, Mar. 28** Litho. Perf. 12
422 A66 40e multicolored .40 .20
423 A66 70e multicolored .80 .35
424 A66 100e multicolored 1.10 .55
425 A66 150e multicolored 1.50 .75
Nos. 422-425 (4) 3.80 1.85
422a A66 40e
423a A66 70e
424a A66 100e
425a A66 150e
a. .
b. Bklt. pane of 4, #422a-425a

**Europa Type of Portugal**
Wildlife, country: No. 426, Monkey, Brazil. No. 427a, Armadillo, Africa.

**Architecture Type of 1993**
Designs: 45e, Church of Santa Barbara, Manueline Entry, Cedros. 140e, Railed window, Ribeira Grande.
**1994, May 5** Litho. Perf. 12
426 A541 100e multicolored 1.25 .60

**Souvenir Sheet**
427 Sheet, 2 each #426, 427a 8.00 6.00
a. A541 100e multicolored 1.25 .60

**Architecture Type of 1993**
**1994, Sept. 16** Litho. Perf. 12
428 A65 45e multicolored .60 .30
429 A65 140e multicolored 1.75 .85

**Advocates of Local Autonomy A67**
42e, Aristides Moreira da Motta (1855-1942). 130e, Gil Mont/Alverne de Sequeira (1859-1931).
**1995, Mar. 2** Litho. Perf. 12
430 A67 42e multicolored .60 .30
431 A67 130e multicolored 1.90 .95

**19th Century Architecture A68**
Designs: 45e, Santana Palace, Ponta Delgada. 80e, Our Lady of Victories Chapel, Furnas Lake. 95e, Hospital of the Santa Casa da Misericórdia, Ponta Delgada. 135e, Residence of Ernesto do Canto, Myrthes Park, Furnas Lake.
**1995, Sept. 1** Litho. Perf. 12
432 A68 45e multicolored .60 .30
433 A68 80e multicolored 1.00 .50
434 A68 95e multicolored 1.25 .60
435 A68 135e multicolored 1.75 .90
Nos. 432-435 (4) 4.60 2.30
432a A68 45e
433a A68 80e
434a A68 95e
435a A68 135e
a. Bklt. pane, #432a-435a 4.75
b. Complete booklet, No. 435b 6.00

Natália Correia (1923-93), Writer A69

**1996, May 3** Litho. Perf. 12
436 A69 98e multicolored 1.50 .60
a. Souvenir sheet of 3 6.00
Europa.

**Lighthouses — A70**
Designs: 47e, Contendas, Terceira Island. 78e, Mohte, Port of Ponta Delgada, San Miguel Island. 98e, Arnel, San Miguel. 140e, Santa Clara, San Miguel. 200e, Ponta da Barca, Graciosa Island. Illustration reduced.

## PORTUGAL — AZORES

**1996, May 3**
Souvenir Sheet
437 A70 47e multicolored .60 .30
438 A70 78e multicolored .90 .45
439 A70 98e multicolored 1.25 .60
440 A70 140e multicolored 1.75 .90
Nos. 437-440 (4) 4.50 2.25
441 A69 200e multicolored 4.00 3.00

Carved Work from Church Altar Pieces — A71

**1997, Apr. 16   Litho.   Perf. 12**
442 A71 49e multicolored .55 .30
443 A71 80e multicolored .90 .45
444 A71 100e multicolored 1.10 .60
445 A71 140e multicolored 4.15 2.15
Nos. 442-445 (4)

*Perf. 11½ Vert.*
442a A71 49e .55
443a A71 80e .90
444a A71 100e 1.10
445a A71 140e 1.60
b. Bkt. pane, #442a-445a 5.25
Complete booklet, #445b

Stories and Legends Type of Portugal
Europa: Man on ship from "Legend of the Island of Seven Cities," horiz.

**1997, May 5   Litho.   Perf. 12**
446 A599 100e multicolored 1.25 .55
5.00 1.75

Natl. Festivals Type of Portugal
**1998, May 21   Litho.   Perf. 12**
447 A621 100e Holy Spirit 1.25 .55
5.00 1.75

**1998, Aug. 4   Perf. 12**
448 A72 50e multicolored .60 .30

*Size: 80x30mm*
449 A72 140e multicolored 1.75 .80

*Perf. 11½ Vert.*
448a A72 50e .60 .30
449a A72 140e 1.75 .80
b. Booklet pane, #448a-449a + label 3.00
Complete booklet, #449b 3.00

Europa Type of Portugal
**1999, May 5   Litho.   Perf. 12x11¾**
450 A641 100e Flowers, Pico Mountain Natural Reserve 1.25 .50
a. Souvenir sheet of 3 3.75 3.75

Ocean Creatures — A/2

Designs: 50e, Stenella frontalis. 140e, Physeter macrocephalus.

**1999, Sept. 3   Litho.   Perf. 12x11¾, 11¾x12**
451 A73 51e multi .60 .25
452 A73 95e multi .90 .45
453 A73 100e multi 1.10 .50
454 A73 140e multi 1.75 .70

*Perf. 11¾ Vert., 11¾ Horiz. (#452a)*
451a A73 51e multi .60 .25
452a A73 95e multi 1.10 .50
453a A73 100e multi 1.25 .50
454a A73 140e multi 1.75 .70
b. Bklt. pane of 4, #451a-454a 4.00
Complete booklet, #454b 4.75

Europa, 2000
Common Design Type
**2000, May 9   Perf. 11¾x12**
455 CD17 100e multi 1.25 .50
a. Souvenir sheet of 3 3.75 1.50

Mail Delivery Systems of the Past — A74

Designs: 85e, Buoy mail. 140e, Zeppelin mail, vert.

**2000, Oct. 9   Perf. 12x11¾, 11¾x12**
456-457 A74 Set of 2 2.75 1.10

Europa Type of Portugal
**2001, May 9   Litho.   Perf. 12x11¾**
458 A677 105e Marine life 1.25 .45
a. Souvenir sheet of 3 3.75 3.75

Angra do Heroismo World Heritage Site — A75

Designs: Vluw of town, ooa and: 63o, Arohway, Uuo, Monument. 140e, Window.

**2001, June 4**
459-461 A75 Set of 3 3.25 1.25
Souvenir Sheet
462 A75 350e Map 4.25 4.25

Europa Type of Portugal
**2002, May 9   Litho.   Perf. 12x11¾**
463 A695 54c Clown, diff. 1.25 .55
a. Souvenir sheet of 3, perf. 12½ 3.75 3.75

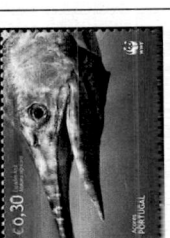

Designs: 28c, Scabiosa nitens. 45c, Viburnum tinus. 54c, Euphorbia azorica. 70c, Lysimachia nemorum. No. 468, €1.15, Bellis azorica. No. 469, €1.75, Spergularia azorica. No. 470: a, €1.15, Azorina vidalli. b, €1.75, Senecio malvifolius.

Flowers — A76
**2002, May 20   Litho.   Perf. 12x11¾**
464-469 A76 Set of 6 11.50 4.50
Souvenir Sheet
470 A76 Sheet of 2, #a-b 7.00 7.00

Windmills — A77
**2002, July 12   Litho.   Perf. 11¾x12**
471-472 A77 Set of 2 2.75 .95
See Belgium Nos. 1925-1926.

Europa Type of Portugal
Design: Poster art by Sebastiao Rodrigues, 1983.
**2003, May 5   Litho.   Perf. 12x12½**
473 A707 55c multi 1.25 .65
a. Souvenir sheet of 2 2.50 2.50

Designs: 30c, Pineapple and plants. 43c, Grapes, vines. 55c, Tea leaves and plants. 70c, Tobacco leaf and plants. Terceira Island. b, €2, Festival of the Holy Spirit.

Heritage of the Azores — A78
**2003, June 6   Litho.   Perf. 12x11¾**
474-477 A78 Set of 4 4.75 2.40
Souvenir Sheet
478 A78 Sheet of 2, #a-b 7.00 7.00

Europa Type of Portugal
Design: People in flower garden.
**2004, May 10   Litho.   Perf. 13¼x14**
479 A734 56c multi 1.40 .70
a. Souvenir sheet of 2 2.80 2.80

Worldwide Fund for Nature (WWF) — A79

No. 480: a, Front of Makaira nigricans. b, Rear of Makaira nigricans, fish in background. c, Front of Tetrapturus albidus. d, Rear of tetrapturus albidus, fish in background.

**2004, June 28   Litho.   Perf. 13x13¼**
480 A79 30c Any single 3.00 1.50
.75 .35
a.-d. Horiz. strip of 4

Europa Type of Portugal
Designs: No. 481, Iorresmos. No. 482a, Polvo Guisado (stewed octopus).
**2005, May 5   Litho.   Perf. 14x13¼**
481 A752 57c multi 1.50 .75
Souvenir Sheet
482 Sheet of 2 #482a 3.00 3.00
a. A752 57c multi 1.50 1.50

Tourism — A80
**2005, May 13   Litho.   Perf. 12x11¾**
483-488 A80 Set of 6 7.00 3.50
Souvenir Sheet
489 A80 Sheet of 2, #a-b 4.50 4.50
Designs: No. 483, 30c. No. 484, 30c, Arch. No. 485, 45c, Building. No. 486, 45c, Windmill. 57c, Arm of windmill, whale, pineapple. 74c, Pineapple, volcanic lake. No. 489: a, 30c, Statue of Jesus. b, €1.55, Embroidered dove.

## MADEIRA

Type of Azores, 1980
6.50e, Madeira #2. 19.50e, Madeira #5.

**1980, Jan. 2   Litho.**
66 A33 6.50e multi .20 .20
67 A33 19.50e multi .85 .55
a. Souvenir sheet of 2, #66-67 3.75 3.75
No. 67a exists overprinted for Capex 87.

Grapes and Wine — A7

**1980, Sept. 17   Litho.   Perf. 11¾x12**
68 A7 50c Bullock cart .20 .20
69 A7 1e shown .20 .20
70 A7 5e Produce map of Madeira .40 .20
71 A7 6.50e Basket and lace .50 .20
72 A7 8e Orchid .80 .25
73 A7 30e Madeira boat 1.60 .45
Nos. 68-73 (6) 3.70 1.50

Europa Issue 1981

O Bailinho Folk Dance — A8

**1981, May 11   Litho.   Perf. 12**
74 A8 22e multi 1.25 .65
a. Souvenir sheet of 2 7.50 1.50

**1981, July 1   Litho.   Perf. 12x11½**
75 A9 8.50e shown .45 .20
76 A9 33.50e Map 1.60 .55

Explorer Ship — A9

Discovery of Madeira anniv.

A10

A12

Designs: Local flora.
**1981, Oct. 6   Litho.   Perf. 12½x12**
77 A10 7e Dactylorhiza foliosa .30 .20
78 A10 8.50e Echium candicans .35 .20
79 A10 20e Geranium maderense .65 .35
80 A10 50e Isoplexis sceptrum 1.40 .75
Nos. 77-80 (4) 2.70 1.50
a. Booklet pane of 4, #77-80 5.00
See Nos. 82-85, 90-93.

Europa Type of Portugal
**1982, May 3   Litho.   Perf. 12x11½**
81 A4b5 33.50e Sugar mills, 15th cent. 1.75 .65
a. Souvenir sheet of 3 18.00 3.00

**1982, Aug. 31   Litho.   Perf. 12½x12**
82 A10 9e Goodyera macrophylla .40 .20
83 A10 10e Armeria maderensis .45 .20

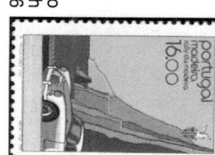

84 A10 27e Viola paradoxa 1.10 .50
85 A10 33.50e Scilla maderensis
a. Booklet pane of 4, #82-85
Nos. 82-85 (4) 3.05 1.60

**1982, Dec. 15** Litho. Perf. 13½
86 A12 27e Brinco dancing dolls 1.10 .70
87 A12 33.50e Dancers 5.00 1.60

Europa 1983 — A13

**1983, May 5** Litho. Perf. 12½
88 A13 37.50e Levadas irrigation system 1.60 .80
a. Souvenir sheet of 3 2.00 .55
20.00 4.00

Flag of the Autonomous Region — A14

**1983, July 1** Litho. Perf. 12x11½
89 A14 12.50e multi .65 .20

Flower Type of 1981
**1983, Oct. 19** Litho. Perf. 12½x12
90 A10 12.50e Matthiola maderensis .20 .20
91 A10 30e Erica maderensis .75 .25
92 A10 37.50e Cirsium latifolium .85 .55
93 A10 100e Clethra arborea 2.00 .80
a. Booklet pane of 4, #90-93
Nos. 90-93 (4) 3.80 1.80

**1984, May 2** Litho. Perf. 12½x12
Europa Type of Portugal
94 A427 51e multi 3.00 .95
a. Souvenir sheet of 3 20.00 5.00

Various cars.
Madeira Rally (Auto Race), 25th Anniv. — A16

**1984, Aug. 3** Litho. Perf. 12
95 A16 16e multicolored .45 .20
96 A16 51e multicolored 1.60 .60

Traditional Means of Transportation — A17

**1984, Nov. 22**
97 A17 16e Mountain sledge .30 .20
98 A17 35e Hammock .85 .50
99 A17 40e Winebag carriers' procession 1.25 .50
100 A17 51e Carreira Boat 1.25 .50
a. Booklet pane of 4, Nos. 97-100
Nos. 97-100 (4) 3.90 1.85
See Nos. 104-107.

Europa Type of Portugal
**1985, May 6** Litho. Perf. 11½x12
101 A435 60e Man playing guitar 2.75 .80
a. Souvenir sheet of 3 24.00 4.00

---

Marine Life — A19

**1985, July 5** Litho. Perf. 12½
102 A19 40e Aphanopus carbo 1.10 .55
103 A19 60e Lampris guttatus 1.60 .65
See Nos. 108-109.

Transportation type of 1984
**1985, Sept. 11** Litho. Perf. 12x11½
104 A17 20e Ox-drawn sledge .35 .20
105 A17 40e Mountain train .90 .40
106 A17 46e Fish vendors 1.00 .45
107 A17 60e Coastal steamer 1.50 .70
a. Booklet pane of 4, Nos. 104-107
Nos. 104-107 (4) 4.00 2.10

Europa Type of Portugal
**1986, Jan. 7** Litho.
110 A447 68.50e Great Shearwater 2.75 .90
a. Souvenir sheet of 3 24.00 4.00

Marine Life Type of 1985
**1986, May 5** Litho.
108 A19 20e Thunnus obesus .55 .20
109 A19 75e Beryx decadactylus 2.50 .75

Forts in Funchal and Machico — A21

**1986, July 1** Litho. Perf. 12
111 A21 22.50e Sao Lourenco, 1583 .50 .20
112 A21 52.50e Sao Joao do Pico, 1611 1.50 .70
113 A21 68.50e Sao Tiago, 1614 2.25 .90
114 A21 100e Sao do Amparo, 1706 3.00 .75
a. Booklet pane of 4, #111-114
Nos. 111-114 (4) 7.25 2.55

Indigenous birds.
A22

**1987, Mar. 6** Litho. Perf. 12
115 A22 25e Regulus ignicapillus .50 .20
116 A22 57e Columba trocaz maderensis 1.60 .80
117 A22 74.50e Tyto alba schmitzi 2.25 1.10
118 A22 125e Pterodroma madeira 3.00 1.25
a. Booklet pane of 4, #115-118
Nos. 115-118 (4) 7.35 3.35

Europa Type of Portugal
Modern Architecture: Social Services Center, Funchal, designed by Raul Chorao Ramalho.

---

**1987, May 5** Perf. 12x12½
Natl. monuments.
120 A24 51e Funchal Castle, 15th cent., Santa Cruz 1.40 .70
121 A24 74.50e Old Town Hall, 16th cent. 1.75 .70

Europa Type of Portugal
Transportation Modern mail boat PS 13 TL.
**1987, July 1** Litho. Perf. 12x12½
119 A456 74.50e multicolored 3.00 .90
a. Souvenir sheet of 4 22.50 5.00

**1988, Apr. 21** Litho. Perf. 12
122 A466 80e multicolored 18.00 1.20
a. Souvenir sheet of 4 24.00 5.50

Bird Type of 1987
**1988, June 15** Litho.
123 A22 27e Erithacus rubecula 1.40 .20
124 A22 60e Petronia petronia 2.00 .75
125 A22 80e Fringilla coelebs 2.25 .80
126 A22 100e Accipiter nisus 6.00 2.00
a. Booklet pane of 4, #123-126
Nos. 123-126 (4) 6.10 2.55

Portraits of Christopher Columbus and Purported Residences on Madeira — A27
**1988, July 1** Litho. Perf. 12
127 A27 55e Funchal, 1480-1481, vert. 1.50 .60
128 A27 80e Porto Santo 1.75 .70

Europa Type of Portugal
Children's toys.
**1989, Apr. 26** Litho.
129 A476 80e Kite 2.50 .80

Souvenir Sheet
130 Sheet, 2 each #129, 130a 25.00 6.00
a. A476 80e Kite, diff. 2.50 2.50

Monuments — A29
Churches: 29e, Church of the Colegio (St. John the Evangelist Church); 87e, Santa Clara Church and convent.
**1989, Sept. 20** Litho.
131 A29 29e multi .45 .20
132 A29 87e multi 1.90 .90

Fish — A30
**1989, July 28** Litho. Perf. 13½
133 A30 29e Argyropelecus aculeatus .45 .20
134 A30 60e Pseudolepidaplois scrofa 1.25 .65
135 A30 87e Coris julis 1.60 .80
136 A30 100e Scorpaena maderensis 2.00 .85
a. Booklet pane of 4, #133-136
Nos. 133-136 (4) 5.70 2.95

Europa Type of Portugal
**1990, Apr. 11** Litho. Perf. 12x11½
137 A486 80e Zarco P.O. 2.75 .55

Souvenir Sheet
138 Sheet, 2 ea #137, 138a 25.00 5.00
a. A486 80e Porto da Cruz P.O. 2.25 2.25

---

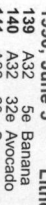

Subtropical Fruits and Plants — A32
**1990, June 5** Litho. Perf. 13½ Vert.
139 A32 32e Banana 1.50 .20
140 A32 5e Avocado 1.25 .45
141 A32 60e Sugar apple 1.50 .55
142 A32 100e Passion fruit 3.80 1.80
a. Bklt. pane of 4, #139-142a
See Nos. 153-160.

Boats of Madeira — A33
**1990, Aug. 24** Litho. Perf. 12
143 A33 32e Tuna 1.00 .45
144 A33 60e Desert islands 1.00 .45
145 A33 70e Maneiro 1.75 .90
146 A33 95e Chavelha 4.45 2.20
Nos. 143-146 (4)

Columba Trocaz Heineken — A34
**1991, Jan. 23** Litho. Perf. 12
147 A34 35e shown .65 .20
148 A34 35e On branch .65 .20
149 A34 35e In flight 1.25 .60
150 A34 35e On nest 1.30 .65
a. Strip of 4, #147-150 4.35 2.00

Europa — A35
**1991, Apr. 11** Litho. Perf. 12
151 A35 80e ERS-1 1.25 .75

Souvenir Sheet
152 Sheet, 2 each #151, 152a 25.00 5.00
a. A35 80e SPOT 2.25 2.25

Subtropical Fruits Type of 1990
**1991, June 7** Litho. Perf. 12
153 A32 35e Mango .50 .25
154 A32 65e Surinam cherry 1.00 .50
155 A32 70e Brazilian guava 1.25 .60
156 A32 110e Papaya 1.60 .65
a. Bklt. pane of 4, #153-156
Nos. 153-156 (4) 4.35 2.00

**1992, Feb. 21** Litho. Perf. 11½x12
157 A32 10e Prickly pear 1.10 1.10
158 A32 36e Tree tomato 1.10 1.10
159 A32 85e Ceriman 1.90 1.10
160 A32 125e Guava 5.00 5.00
a. Perf. 13½ Vert.
157a A32 10e .20 .20
158a A32 36e .45 .25
159a A32 85e 1.30 .65
160a A32 125e 1.90 .95
b. Bklt. pane of 4, #157a-160a
Nos. 157-160 (4) 3.85 2.00

## Plants from Laurissilva Forest A45

52e, Purple orchid. 85e, White orchid. No. 211, 100e, Folhado. No. 212, 100e, Laurel tree. 140e, Barbusano. 350e, Visco.

**2000, July 4**  A45  Litho.  *Perf. 12x11¾*
| 209-214 | Set of 6 | 10.00 | 10.00 |
|---|---|---|---|
| 214a | Souvenir sheet #209-214 | 4.00 | 10.00 |

## Expansion of Madeira Airport A46

**2000, Sept. 15**
| 215 | A46 | 140e | multi | .70 | .70 |
|---|---|---|---|---|---|
| a. | Souvenir sheet of 1 | | | | |

## Europa Type of Portugal

**2001, May 9**  Litho.  *Perf. 12x11¾*
| 216 | A677 | 105e | Signals | 1.25 | .45 |
|---|---|---|---|---|---|
| a. | Souvenir sheet of 3 | | | 3.75 | 3.75 |

## Scenes of Traditional Life — A47

Designs: 53e, People returning home. 85e, On the road to the marketplace. 105e, Traditional clothes. 350e, Leisure time.

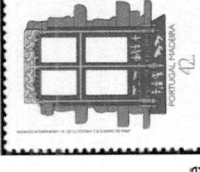

**2001, July 19**  Litho.
| 217-219 | A47 | Set of 3 | 3.00 | 1.10 |
|---|---|---|---|---|

Souvenir Sheet
| 220 | A47 | 350c | multi | 4.26 | 4.26 |
|---|---|---|---|---|---|

## Europa Type of Portugal

**2002, May 9**  Litho.  *Perf. 12x11¾*
| 221 | A695 | 54c | Clown, diff | 1.25 | .50 |
|---|---|---|---|---|---|
| a. | Souvenir sheet of 3, perf. 12½ | | | 3.00 | 3.00 |

## Worldwide Fund for Nature (WWF) — A48

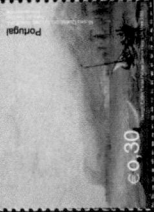

Streptopelia turtur: a, On nest with chicks. b, On branch, with wings extended. c, Pair on branch. d, One on branch. Illustration reduced.

**2002, Aug. 30**  Litho.  *Perf. 12x12½*
| 222 | A48 | 28c | Horiz. strip or block of 4, #a.-d. | 2.75 | 1.10 |
|---|---|---|---|---|---|

## Europa Type of Portugal

**2003, May 5**  Litho.  *Perf. 11¾x12*
| 223 | A707 | 55c | multi | 1.25 | .65 |
|---|---|---|---|---|---|
| a. | Souvenir sheet of 2 | | | 2.50 | 2.50 |

## Items in Madeira Museums A49

Designs: 30c, Funchal Bay, by W. G. James. 43c, Creche, by Manuel Orlando Noronha Gois. 55c, O Largo da Fonte, by Andrew Picken. 70c, Le Depart, by Martha Teles.

---

## Moths & Butterflies A43

Designs: 49e, Eumichtis albostigmata. 80e, Menophra maderea. 100e, Vanessa indica vulcania. 140e, Pieris brassicae wollastoni.

**1997, Feb. 12**  Litho.  *Perf. 12*
| 191 | A43 | 49e | multicolored | .60 | .30 |
|---|---|---|---|---|---|
| 192 | A43 | 80e | multicolored | .95 | .45 |
| 193 | A43 | 100e | multicolored | 1.25 | .60 |
| 194 | A43 | 140e | multicolored | 1.60 | .80 |
| | | *Nos. 191-194 (4)* | | 4.40 | 2.15 |

*Perf. 11½ Vert.*
| 191a | A43 | 49e | multicolored | .60 | .30 |
|---|---|---|---|---|---|
| 192a | A43 | 80e | multicolored | .95 | .45 |
| 193a | A43 | 100e | multicolored | 1.25 | .60 |
| 194a | A43 | 140e | multicolored | 1.60 | .80 |
| b. | Booklet pane, #191a-194a | | | 6.00 | 6.00 |
| | Complete booklet, #194b | | | 6.00 | |

See Nos. 197-200.

## Stories and Legends Type of Portugal

Europa: Man holding woman from "Legend of Machico," horiz.

**1997, May 5**  Litho.  *Perf. 12*
| 195 | A599 | 100e | multicolored | 1.25 | .55 |
|---|---|---|---|---|---|
| a. | Souvenir sheet of 3 | | | 5.00 | 3.00 |

Europa.

## Natl. Festivals Type of Portugal

**1998, May 21**  Litho.  *Perf. 12*
| 196 | A621 | 100e | New Year's Eve | 1.25 | .55 |
|---|---|---|---|---|---|
| a. | Souvenir sheet of 3 | | | 5.00 | 3.00 |

## Moths and Butterflies Type of 1997

Designs: 50e, Gonepteryx cleopatra. 85e, Xanthorhoe rupicola. 100e, Noctua teixeirai. 140e, Xenochlorodes nubigena.

**1998, Sept. 6**  Litho.  *Perf. 12*
| 197 | A43 | 50e | multicolored | .60 | .30 |
|---|---|---|---|---|---|
| 198 | A43 | 85e | multicolored | 1.00 | .45 |
| 199 | A43 | 100e | multicolored | 1.25 | .55 |
| 200 | A43 | 140e | multicolored | 1.60 | .80 |
| a. | Booklet pane, #197-200, perf. 12 vert. | | | 6.00 | |
| | Complete booklet, #200a | | | 6.00 | |
| | *Nos. 197-200 (4)* | | | 4.45 | 2.10 |

## Europa Type of Portugal

**1999, May 5**  Litho.  *Perf. 12x11¾*
| 201 | A641 | 100e | Flowers, Madeira Island Natural Park | 1.25 | .50 |
|---|---|---|---|---|---|
| a. | Souvenir sheet of 3 | | | 3.75 | 3.75 |

## Glazed Tiles From Frederico de Freitas Museum, Funchal A44

Designs: 51e, Griffin, from Middle East, 13th-14th cent. 80e, Flower, from England, 19th-20th cent. 95e, Bird, from Persia, 14th cent. 100e, Geometric, from Moorish Spain, 13th cent. 140e, Ship, from Holland, 18th cent. 210e, Flowers from Syria, 13th-14th cent.

**1999, July 1**
| 202 | A44 | 51e | multicolored | .60 | .25 |
|---|---|---|---|---|---|
| 203 | A44 | 80e | multicolored | .95 | .40 |
| 204 | A44 | 95e | multicolored | 1.10 | .50 |
| 205 | A44 | 100e | multicolored | 1.25 | .50 |
| 206 | A44 | 140e | multicolored | 1.75 | .75 |
| 207 | A44 | 210e | multicolored | 2.50 | 1.10 |
| | | *Nos. 202-207 (6)* | | 8.15 | 3.50 |
| a. | Souvenir sheet of 6, #202-207 | | | 8.50 | 8.50 |

## Europa, 2000
### Common Design Type

**2000, May 9**  *Perf. 11¾x12*
| 208 | CD17 | 100e | multi | 1.25 | .50 |
|---|---|---|---|---|---|
| a. | Souvenir sheet of 3 | | | 3.75 | 3.75 |

---

## Europa Type of Portugal

Europa: 85e, Columbus at Funchal.

**1992, May 22**  Litho.  *Perf. 12x11½*
| 161 | A514 | 85e | gold & multi | 4.50 | .70 |
|---|---|---|---|---|---|

## Ships Type of 1990

**1992, Sept. 18**  Litho.  *Perf. 12x11½*
| 162 | A33 | 38e | Gaviao | .65 | .30 |
|---|---|---|---|---|---|
| 163 | A33 | 65e | Independencia | 1.10 | .55 |
| 164 | A33 | 85e | Madeirense | 1.40 | .70 |
| 165 | A33 | 120e | Funchalense | 2.00 | 1.00 |
| | | *Nos. 162-165 (4)* | | 5.15 | 2.55 |

## Contemporary Paintings by Lourdes Castro — A36

Europa: No. 166, Shadow Projection of Christa Maar, 1968. No. 167a, Shadow Projection of a Dahlia, c. 1970.

**1993, May 5**  Litho.  *Perf. 11½x12*
| 166 | A36 | 90e | multicolored | 1.25 | .60 |
|---|---|---|---|---|---|

Souvenir Sheet
| 167 | | Sheet, 2 each #166, 167a | 8.00 | 5.00 |
|---|---|---|---|---|
| a. | A36 | 90e multicolored | 1.25 | .60 |

## Nature Preservation — A37

Monachus monachus: No. 168, Adult on rock. No. 169, Swimming. No. 170, Mother nursing pup. No. 171, Two on rocks.

**1993, June 30**  Litho.  *Perf. 11½x12*
| 168 | A37 | 42e | multicolored | 1.00 | .50 |
|---|---|---|---|---|---|
| 169 | A37 | 42e | multicolored | 1.00 | .50 |
| 170 | A37 | 42e | multicolored | 1.00 | .50 |
| 171 | A37 | 42e | multicolored | 1.00 | .50 |
| a. | A37 | Strip of 4, #168-171 | | 4.50 | 2.00 |

## Architecture A38

Designs: 42e, Window from Sao Francisco Convent, Funchal. 130e, Window of Mercy (Old Hospital), Funchal.

**1993, July 30**  *Perf. 11½x12*
| 172 | A38 | 42e | multicolored | .50 | .25 |
|---|---|---|---|---|---|
| 173 | A38 | 130e | multicolored | 1.60 | .80 |

## Europa Type of Portugal

Discoveries: No. 174, Native with bow and arrows. No. 175a, Palm tree.

**1994, May 5**  Litho.  *Perf. 12*
| 174 | A541 | 100e | multicolored | 1.25 | .60 |
|---|---|---|---|---|---|

Souvenir Sheet
| 175 | A541 | 100e multicolored | 7.50 | 5.00 |
|---|---|---|---|---|
| a. | Sheet, 2 each #174-175a | | 1.25 | |

## Native Handicrafts A39

**1994, May 5**  Litho.  *Perf. 12x11½*
| 176 | A39 | 45e | Embroidery | .55 | .30 |
|---|---|---|---|---|---|
| 177 | A39 | 75e | Tapestry | .90 | .45 |
| 178 | A39 | 100e | Shoes | 1.25 | .60 |
| 179 | A39 | 140e | Wicker work | 1.60 | .85 |
| | | *Nos. 176-179 (4)* | | 4.30 | 2.20 |

*Perf. 11½ Vert.*
| 176a | A39 | 45e | .55 | .30 |
|---|---|---|---|---|
| 177a | A39 | 75e | .90 | .45 |
| 178a | A39 | 100e | 1.25 | .60 |
| 179a | A39 | 140e | 1.60 | .85 |
| b. | Bkt. pane of 4, #176a-179a | | 6.00 | |

## Arms of Madeira Districts — A40

**1994, July 1**  Litho.  *Perf. 11½x12*
| 180 | A40 | 45e | Funchal | .55 | .30 |
|---|---|---|---|---|---|
| 181 | A40 | 140e | Porto Santo | 1.90 | .95 |

## Traditional Arts & Crafts — A41

Designs: 45e, Chicken puppets made of flour paste. 80e, Inlaid wood furniture piece. 95e, Wicker bird cage. 135e, Knitted wool bonnet.

**1995, June 30**  Litho.  *Perf. 11½x12*
| 182 | A41 | 45e | multicolored | .60 | .30 |
|---|---|---|---|---|---|
| 183 | A41 | 80e | multicolored | 1.10 | .55 |
| 184 | A41 | 95e | multicolored | 1.25 | .65 |
| 185 | A41 | 135e | multicolored | 1.90 | .95 |
| | | *Nos. 182-185 (4)* | | 4.85 | 2.45 |

*Perf. 11½ Vert.*
| 182a | A41 | 45e | .60 | .30 |
|---|---|---|---|---|
| 183a | A41 | 80e | 1.10 | .55 |
| 184a | A41 | 95e | 1.25 | .65 |
| 185a | A41 | 135e | 1.90 | .95 |
| a. | Booklet pane, #182a-185a | | 6.00 | |
| | Complete booklet, #185b | | | |

## Famous Woman Type of Azores, 1996

Europa: Guiomar Vilhena, entrepreneur.

**1996, May 3**  Litho.  *Perf. 12*
| 186 | A69 | 98e | multicolored | 1.25 | .60 |
|---|---|---|---|---|---|
| a. | Souvenir sheet of 3 | | | 3.75 | 1.90 |

## Paintings from Flemish Group, Museum of Sacred Paintings of Funchal (Madeira) A42

Designs: 47e, The Adoration of the Magi, vert. 78e, St. Mary Magdalene, vert. 98e, Annunciation. 140e, St. Peter, St. Paul and St. Andrew.

**1996, July 1**  *Perf. 11½x12, 12x11½*
| 187 | A42 | 47e | multicolored | .60 | .30 |
|---|---|---|---|---|---|
| 188 | A42 | 78e | multicolored | 1.00 | .50 |
| 189 | A42 | 98e | multicolored | 1.40 | .65 |
| 190 | A42 | 140e | multicolored | 1.90 | .90 |
| | | *Nos. 187-190 (4)* | | 4.90 | 2.35 |

*Perf. 11½ on 2 Sides*
| 187a | A42 | 47e | .60 | .30 |
|---|---|---|---|---|
| 188a | A42 | 78e | 1.00 | .50 |
| 189a | A42 | 98e | 1.40 | .65 |
| 190a | A42 | 140e | 1.90 | .90 |
| b. | Booklet pane, #187a-190a | | 6.00 | |
| | Complete booklet, #190b | | 6.00 | |

No. 228: a, €1, Photograph of Vicente Gomes da Silva. b, €2, Photograph of Jorge Bettencourt.

**2003, Aug. 30 Litho.** ***Perf. 12x11¾***
**224-227** A49 Set of 4 4.50 2.25

**Souvenir Sheet**

**228** A49 Sheet of 2, #a-b 6.75 6.75

**Europa Type of Portugal**

Design: Hiker in flower garden.

**2004, May 10 Litho.** ***Perf. 13¼x14***
**229** A734 56c multi 1.40 .70
*a.* Souvenir sheet of 2 2.80 2.80

Flora and Fauna of the Selvagens Islands
A50

Designs: 30c, Pelagodroma marina hypoleuca. 45c, Monanthes lowei. 72c, Tarentola bischoffi.

**2004, May 24** ***Perf. 13x13¼***
**230-232** A50 Set of 3 3.50 1.75
*232a* Souvenir sheet, #230-232 3.50 3.50

**Europa Type of Portugal**

Designs: No. 233, Espetada em pau de louro. No. 234a, Filete de espada (Scabbard fish filet).

**2005, May 5** ***Perf. 14x13¼***
**233** A752 57c multi 1.50 .75

**Souvenir Sheet**

**234** Sheet of 2 #234a 3.00 3.00
*a.* A752 57c multi 1.50 1.50

Tourism
A51

Designs: No. 235, 30c, Coastal village, offshore rocks, flowers. No. 236, 30c, Flowers, bird, waterfall. No. 237, 45c, Man and woman on footpath, golf course. No. 238, 45c, Windmill on beach. 57c, Horses and riders, scuba diver. 74c, Flowers, fireworks.

No. 241: a, 30c, Wicker chair, girls with flower baskets, lace. b, €1.55, Lace, clock tower.

**2005, July 1 Litho.** ***Perf. 14x13¼***
**235-240** A51 Set of 6 6.75 3.50

**Souvenir Sheet**

**241** A51 Sheet of 2, #a-b 4.50 4.50

Flowers
A52

Designs: 30c, Euphorbia pulcherrima. No. 243, 45c, Aloe arborescens. 57c, Senna didymobotrya. 74c, Anthurium andraeanum. €1, Strelitzia reginae. €2, Hydrangea macrophylla.

No. 248, 45c: a, Rosa cultivar. b, Leucospermum nutans. c, Paphiopedilum insigne. d, Hippeastrum vittatum.

No. 249, 45c: a, Bougainvillea cultivar. b, Cymbidium cultivar. c, Hibiscus rosa-sinensis. d, Erythrina crista-galli.

**2006, Mar. 7 Litho.** ***Perf. 12x11¾***
**242-247** A52 Set of 6 12.50 6.25

**Souvenir Sheets**

**248** Sheet of 4 4.50 4.50
*a.-d.* A52 45c Any single 1.10 .55
**249** Sheet of 4 4.50 4.50
*a.-d.* A52 45c Any single 1.10 .55

## PORTUGUESE AFRICA

'pōr-chə-,gēz 'a-fri-kə

For use in any of the Portuguese possessions in Africa.

1000 Reis = 1 Milreis
100 Centavos = 1 Escudo

Common Design Types pictured following the introduction.

**Vasco da Gama Issue**
Common Design Types
Inscribed "Africa - Correios"
***Perf. 13½ to 15½***

**1898, Apr. 1 Engr. Unwmk.**

| | | | | |
|---|---|---|---|---|
| **1** | CD20 | 2½r blue green | .90 | .90 |
| **2** | CD21 | 5r red | .90 | .90 |
| **3** | CD22 | 10r red violet | .90 | .90 |
| **4** | CD23 | 25r yellow green | .90 | .90 |
| **5** | CD24 | 50r dark blue | 1.10 | 1.10 |
| **6** | CD25 | 75r violet brown | 6.25 | 6.25 |
| **7** | CD26 | 100r bister brown | 5.00 | 4.50 |
| **8** | CD27 | 150r bister | 8.00 | 6.25 |
| | | *Nos. 1-8 (8)* | 23.95 | 21.70 |
| | | Set, never hinged | 32.50 | |

Vasco da Gama's voyage to India.

**POSTAGE DUE STAMPS**

D1

**1945 Unwmk. Typo.** ***Perf. 11½x12***
**Denomination in Black**

| | | | | |
|---|---|---|---|---|
| **J1** | D1 | 10c claret | .70 | .70 |
| **J2** | D1 | 20c purple | .70 | .70 |
| **J3** | D1 | 30c deep blue | .70 | .70 |
| **J4** | D1 | 40c chocolate | .70 | .70 |
| **J5** | D1 | 50c red violet | 1.00 | *1.25* |
| **J6** | D1 | 1e orange brown | 2.00 | *4.00* |
| **J7** | D1 | 2e yellow green | 7.50 | 7.00 |
| **J8** | D1 | 3e bright carmine | 12.00 | 12.00 |
| **J9** | D1 | 5e orange yellow | 25.00 | 25.00 |
| | | *Nos. J1-J9 (9)* | 50.30 | 52.05 |
| | | Set, never hinged | 62.50 | |

**WAR TAX STAMPS**

Liberty
WT1

***Perf. 12x11½, 15x14***
**1919 Typo. Unwmk.**
**Overprinted in Black, Orange or Carmine**

| | | | | |
|---|---|---|---|---|
| **MR1** | WT1 | 1c green (Bk) | .75 | .75 |
| *a.* | | Figures of value omitted | 25.00 | |
| **MR2** | WT1 | 4c green (O) | 1.00 | |
| **MR3** | WT1 | 5c green (C) | .75 | .75 |
| | | *Nos. MR1-MR3 (3)* | 2.50 | |

Values the same for either perf.

No. MR2 used is known only with fiscal cancelation. Some authorities consider No. MR2 a revenue stamp.

## PORTUGUESE CONGO

'pōr-chi-gēz 'käŋ-,gō

LOCATION — The northernmost district of the Portuguese Angola Colony on the southwest coast of Africa
CAPITAL — Cabinda

Stamps of Angola replaced those of Portuguese Congo.

1000 Reis = 1 Milreis
100 Centavos = 1 Escudo (1913)

King Carlos
A1 A2

***Perf. 12½***
**1894, Aug. 5 Typo. Unwmk.**

| | | | | |
|---|---|---|---|---|
| **1** | A1 | 5r yellow | .90 | .75 |
| *b.* | | 5r orange yellow, perf. 13½ | 17.00 | 12.50 |
| **2** | A1 | 10r redsh violet | 1.60 | .80 |
| *a.* | | Perf. 13½ | 17.50 | 12.50 |
| **3** | A1 | 15r chocolate | 2.75 | 2.00 |
| **4** | A1 | 20r lavender | 2.50 | 2.00 |
| **5** | A1 | 25r green | 1.50 | .80 |
| | | ***Perf. 13½*** | | |
| **6** | A1 | 50r light blue | 2.75 | 2.00 |
| | | ***Perf. 11½*** | | |
| **7** | A1 | 75r rose | 5.00 | 3.75 |
| *a.* | | Perf. 12½ | 20.00 | 15.00 |
| **8** | A1 | 80r yellow green | 7.00 | 6.00 |
| *a.* | | Perf. 12½ | 60.00 | 37.50 |
| **9** | A1 | 100r brown, *yel* | 5.50 | 3.75 |
| *a.* | | Perf. 13½ | 32.50 | 19.00 |
| | | ***Perf. 12½*** | | |
| **10** | A1 | 150r carmine, *rose* | 10.50 | 9.00 |
| **11** | A1 | 200r dk blue, *bl* | 10.50 | 9.00 |
| **12** | A1 | 300r dk blue, *salmon* | 13.00 | 11.00 |
| | | *Nos. 1-12 (12)* | 63.50 | 50.85 |

For surcharges and overprints see Nos. 36-47, 127-131.

**1898-1903** ***Perf. 11½***
**Name & Value in Black except 500r**

| | | | | |
|---|---|---|---|---|
| **13** | A2 | 2½r gray | .35 | .30 |
| **14** | A2 | 5r orange | .35 | .30 |
| **15** | A2 | 10r lt green | .55 | .30 |
| **16** | A2 | 15r brown | 1.50 | 1.25 |
| **17** | A2 | 15r gray grn ('03) | 1.00 | .55 |
| **18** | A2 | 20r gray violet | 1.00 | .70 |
| **19** | A2 | 25r sea green | 1.40 | .90 |
| **20** | A2 | 25r car rose ('03) | .90 | .45 |
| **21** | A2 | 50r deep blue | 1.65 | 1.25 |
| **22** | A2 | 50r brown ('03) | 2.75 | 1.75 |
| **23** | A2 | 65r dull blue ('03) | 7.50 | 6.50 |
| **24** | A2 | 75r rose | 4.00 | 2.25 |
| **25** | A2 | 75r red lilac ('03) | 2.75 | 2.25 |
| **26** | A2 | 80r violet | 3.00 | 2.50 |
| **27** | A2 | 100r dk bl, *bl* | 2.40 | 1.75 |
| **28** | A2 | 115r org brn, *pink* ('03) | 6.50 | 5.00 |
| **29** | A2 | 130r brn, *straw* ('03) | 17.00 | 11.00 |
| **30** | A2 | 150r brown, *buff* | 4.00 | 2.50 |
| **31** | A2 | 200r red lilac, *pnksh* | 5.00 | 3.00 |
| **32** | A2 | 300r dk blue, *rose* | 6.00 | 3.25 |
| **33** | A2 | 400r dl bl, *straw* ('03) | 11.00 | 9.50 |
| **34** | A2 | 500r blk & red, *bl* ('01) | 15.00 | 9.00 |
| **35** | A2 | 700r vio, *yelsh* ('01) | 25.00 | 17.50 |
| | | *Nos. 13-35 (23)* | 120.60 | 83.75 |

For overprints and surcharges see Nos. 49-53, 60-74, 117-126, 136-138.

Surcharged in Black

**1902** ***Perf. 11½, 12½, 13½***
**On Issue of 1894**

| | | | | |
|---|---|---|---|---|
| **36** | A1 | 65r on 15r choc | 3.50 | 3.00 |
| *a.* | | Perf. 11½ | 17.00 | 9.00 |
| **37** | A1 | 65r on 20r lav | 4.00 | 3.00 |
| **38** | A1 | 65r on 25r green | 4.00 | 3.00 |
| *a.* | | Perf. 11½ | 17.00 | 12.50 |
| **39** | A1 | 65r on 300r bl, *sal* | 4.75 | 4.50 |
| **40** | A1 | 115r on 10r red vio | 4.00 | 3.00 |
| **41** | A1 | 115r on 50r lt bl | 3.75 | 2.50 |
| **42** | A1 | 130r on 5r yellow | 4.00 | 2.75 |
| *a.* | | Inverted surcharge | 27.50 | 27.50 |
| **43** | A1 | 130r on 75r rose | 3.50 | 3.00 |
| *a.* | | Perf. 12½ | 7.00 | 6.00 |
| **44** | A1 | 130r on 100r brn, *yel* | 3.75 | 3.75 |
| *a.* | | Inverted surcharge | 40.00 | 35.00 |
| *b.* | | Perf. 11½ | 20.00 | 12.50 |
| **45** | A1 | 400r on 80r yel grn | 1.75 | 1.25 |
| **46** | A1 | 400r on 150r car, *rose* | 2.25 | 1.90 |
| **47** | A1 | 400r on 200r bl, *bl* | 2.25 | 1.90 |

**On Newspaper Stamp of 1894**

| | | | | |
|---|---|---|---|---|
| **48** | N1 | 115r on 2½r brn | 3.75 | 2.50 |
| *a.* | | Inverted surcharge | 25.00 | 25.00 |
| | | *Nos. 36-48 (13)* | 45.25 | 36.05 |

Nos. 16, 19, 21 and 24 Overprinted in Black

**1902** ***Perf. 11½***

| | | | | |
|---|---|---|---|---|
| **49** | A2 | 15r brown | 2.00 | 1.25 |
| **50** | A2 | 25r sea green | 2.00 | 1.40 |
| **51** | A2 | 50r blue | 2.00 | 1.40 |
| **52** | A2 | 75r rose | 4.00 | 2.75 |
| | | *Nos. 49-52 (4)* | 10.00 | 6.80 |

No. 23 Surcharged

**1905**
**53** A2 50r on 65r dull blue 4.00 2.50

Angola Stamps of 1898-1903 (Port. Congo type A2) Overprinted or Surcharged:

a

b

**1911**

| | | | | |
|---|---|---|---|---|
| **54** | (a) | 2½r gray | 1.10 | .90 |
| **55** | (a) | 5r orange | 1.60 | 1.25 |
| **56** | (a) | 10r lt green | 1.60 | 1.25 |
| *a.* | | "REPUBLICA" inverted | 17.50 | 17.50 |
| **57** | (a) | 15r gray green | 1.60 | 1.25 |
| *a.* | | "REPUBLICA" inverted | 17.50 | 17.50 |
| **58** | (b) | 25r on 200r red vio, *pnksh* | 2.50 | 2.00 |
| *a.* | | "REPUBLICA" inverted | 17.50 | 17.50 |
| *b.* | | "CONGO" double | 17.50 | 17.50 |

**Thin Bar and "CONGO" as Type "b"**

| | | | | |
|---|---|---|---|---|
| **59** | (a) | 2½r gray | 1.10 | .90 |
| | | *Nos. 54-59 (6)* | 9.50 | 7.55 |

Issue of 1898-1903 Overprinted in Carmine or Green —
c

**1911**

| | | | | |
|---|---|---|---|---|
| **60** | A2 | 2½r gray | .20 | .20 |
| **61** | A2 | 5r orange | .25 | .20 |
| **62** | A2 | 10r lt green | .25 | .20 |
| **63** | A2 | 15r gray grn | .25 | .25 |
| **64** | A2 | 20r gray vio | .45 | .25 |
| **65** | A2 | 25r car rose (G) | .55 | .25 |
| **66** | A2 | 50r brown | .65 | .35 |
| **67** | A2 | 75r red lilac | 1.10 | .55 |
| **68** | A2 | 100r dk bl, *bl* | .80 | .60 |
| **69** | A2 | 115r org brn, *pink* | 2.10 | 1.40 |
| **70** | A2 | 130r brown, *straw* | 2.10 | 1.40 |
| **71** | A2 | 200r red vio, *pnksh* | 3.00 | 1.90 |
| **72** | A2 | 400r dull bl, *straw* | 3.00 | 2.50 |
| **73** | A2 | 500r blk & red, *bl* | 4.25 | 2.25 |
| **74** | A2 | 700r violet, *yelsh* | 4.25 | 2.25 |
| | | *Nos. 60-74 (15)* | 23.20 | 14.55 |

Numerous inverts and doubles exist. These are printer's waste or made to order.

Common Design Types pictured following the introduction.

Vasco da Gama Issue of Various Portuguese Colonies Surcharged

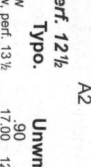

**1913**

**On Stamps of Macao**

| | | | | |
|---|---|---|---|---|
| 75 | CD20 | ¼c on ½a bl grn | 1.25 | 1.25 |
| 76 | CD21 | ½c on 1a red | 1.25 | 1.25 |
| 77 | CD22 | 1c on 2a red vio | 1.25 | 1.25 |
| 78 | CD23 | 2½c on 4a yel grn | 1.25 | 1.25 |
| 79 | CD24 | 5c on 8a dk blue | 1.25 | 1.25 |
| 80 | CD25 | 7½c on 12a vio brn | 2.50 | 2.50 |
| 81 | CD26 | 10c on 16a bis brn | 1.75 | 1.75 |
| 82 | CD27 | 15c on 24a bister | 1.75 | 1.75 |
| | | *Nos. 75-82 (8)* | 12.25 | 12.25 |

**On Stamps of Portuguese Africa**

| | | | | |
|---|---|---|---|---|
| 83 | CD20 | ¼c on 2½r bl grn | .80 | .80 |
| 84 | CD21 | ½c on 5r red | .80 | .80 |
| 85 | CD22 | 1c on 10r red vio | .80 | .80 |
| 86 | CD23 | 2½c on 25r yel grn | .80 | .80 |
| 87 | CD24 | 5c on 50r dk bl | 1.10 | 1.10 |
| 88 | CD25 | 7½c on 75r vio brn | 1.90 | 1.90 |
| 89 | CD26 | 10c on 100r bis brn | 1.25 | 1.25 |
| a. | | Inverted surcharge | 25.00 | 25.00 |
| 90 | CD27 | 15c on 150r bister | 1.50 | 1.50 |
| | | *Nos. 83-90 (8)* | 8.95 | 8.95 |

**On Stamps of Timor**

| | | | | |
|---|---|---|---|---|
| 91 | CD20 | ¼c on ½a bl grn | 1.25 | 1.25 |
| 92 | CD21 | ½c on 1a red | 1.25 | 1.25 |
| 93 | CD22 | 1c on 2a red vio | 1.25 | 1.25 |
| 94 | CD23 | 2½c on 4a yel grn | 1.25 | 1.25 |
| 95 | CD24 | 5c on 8a dk blue | 1.25 | 1.25 |
| a. | | Double surcharge | 25.00 | 25.00 |
| 96 | CD25 | 7½c on 12a vio brn | 2.50 | 2.50 |
| 97 | CD26 | 10c on 16a bis brn | 2.25 | 2.25 |
| 98 | CD27 | 15c on 24a bister | 2.25 | 2.25 |
| | | *Nos. 91-98 (8)* | 13.25 | 13.25 |
| | | *Nos. 75-98 (24)* | 34.45 | 34.45 |

Ceres — A3

**1914 Typo. Perf. 15x14**

**Name and Value in Black**

| | | | | |
|---|---|---|---|---|
| 99 | A3 | ¼c olive brn | .35 | *.50* |
| a. | | Inscriptions inverted | | |
| 100 | A3 | ½c black | .65 | *1.00* |
| 101 | A3 | 1c blue grn | 3.00 | *4.25* |
| 102 | A3 | 1½c lilac brn | 1.25 | *1.40* |
| 103 | A3 | 2c carmine | 1.25 | *1.40* |
| 104 | A3 | 2½c lt violet | .40 | *.90* |
| 105 | A3 | 5c dp blue | .70 | *1.40* |
| 106 | A3 | 7½c yellow brn | 1.00 | *1.40* |
| 107 | A3 | 8c slate | 1.00 | *3.25* |
| 108 | A3 | 10c orange brn | 1.60 | *3.25* |
| 109 | A3 | 15c plum | 1.90 | *3.25* |
| 110 | A3 | 20c yellow grn | 2.25 | *3.25* |
| 111 | A3 | 30c brown, *grn* | 2.75 | *5.00* |
| 112 | A3 | 40c brown, *pink* | 4.50 | *6.50* |
| 113 | A3 | 50c orange, *salmon* | 4.50 | *6.50* |
| 114 | A3 | 1e green, *blue* | 5.50 | *8.75* |
| | | *Nos. 99-114 (16)* | 33.20 | *52.00* |

Issue of 1898-1903 Overprinted Locally in Green or Red

**1914-18 Perf. 11½**

| | | | | |
|---|---|---|---|---|
| 117 | A2 | 50r brown (G) | .95 | .65 |
| 118 | A2 | 75r rose (G) | *450.00* | |
| 119 | A2 | 75r red lilac (G) | 2.25 | 1.50 |
| 120 | A2 | 100r blue, *bl* (R) | .95 | .80 |
| 121 | A2 | 200r red vio, *pink* (G) | 1.90 | 1.25 |
| 122 | A2 | 400r dl bl, *straw* (R) ('18) | 80.00 | 55.00 |
| 123 | A2 | 500r blk & red, *bl* (R) | 65.00 | 42.50 |

**Same on Nos. 51-52**

| | | | | |
|---|---|---|---|---|
| 124 | A2 | 50r blue (R) | .95 | .70 |
| 125 | A2 | 75r rose (G) | 1.50 | 1.10 |

**Same on No. 53**

| | | | | |
|---|---|---|---|---|
| 126 | A2 | 50r on 65r dl bl (R) | 1.25 | 1.10 |
| | | *Nos. 117,119-126 (9)* | 154.75 | 104.60 |

No. 118 was not regularly issued.

Provisional Issue of 1902 Overprinted Type "c" in Red

**1915 Perf. 11½, 12½, 13½**

| | | | | |
|---|---|---|---|---|
| 127 | A1 | 115r on 10r red vio | .25 | .20 |
| a. | | Perf. 13½ | 17.00 | 14.00 |
| 128 | A1 | 115r on 50r lt bl | .25 | .20 |
| a. | | Perf. 11½ | 1.90 | .65 |
| 129 | A1 | 130r on 5r yellow | .35 | .25 |
| 130 | A1 | 130r on 75r rose | 1.50 | .65 |
| 131 | A1 | 130r on 100r brn, *buff* | .45 | .40 |
| 135 | N1 | 115r on 2½r brn | .45 | .40 |

**Nos. 49, 51 Overprinted Type "c"**

| | | | | |
|---|---|---|---|---|
| 136 | A2 | 15r brown | .65 | .55 |
| 137 | A2 | 50r blue | .45 | .40 |

**No. 53 Overprinted Type "c"**

| | | | | |
|---|---|---|---|---|
| 138 | A2 | 50r on 65r dull blue | .55 | .40 |
| | | *Nos. 127-138 (9)* | 4.90 | 3.45 |

**NEWSPAPER STAMP**

N1

**Perf. 12½, 13½**

**1894, Aug. 5 Typo. Unwmk.**

| | | | | |
|---|---|---|---|---|
| P1 | N1 | 2½r brown | 1.00 | .60 |

For surcharge and overprint see Nos. 48, 135.

## PORTUGUESE GUINEA

'pōr-chi-gēz 'gi-nē

LOCATION — On the west coast of Africa between Senegal and Guinea
GOVT. — Portuguese Overseas Territory
AREA — 13,944 sq. mi.
POP. — 560,000 (est. 1970)
CAPITAL — Bissau

The territory, including the Bissagos Islands, became an independent republic on Sept. 10, 1974. See Guinea-Bissau in Vol. 3.

1000 Reis = 1 Milreis
100 Centavos = 1 Escudo (1913)

**Catalogue values for unused stamps in this country are for Never Hinged items, beginning with Scott 273 in the regular postage section, Scott J40 in the postage due section, and Scott RA17 in the postal tax section.**

Nos. 1-7 are valued with small faults such as short perfs or small thins. Completely fault-free examples of any of these stamps are very scarce and are worth more than the values given.

Stamps of Cape Verde, 1877-85 Overprinted in Black

**1881 Unwmk. Perf. 12½**

**Without Gum (Nos. 1-7)**

| | | | | |
|---|---|---|---|---|
| 1 | A1 | 5r black | *1,000.* | *800.* |
| 1A | A1 | 10r yellow | *1,750.* | *800.* |
| 2 | A1 | 20r bister | *475.* | *250.* |
| 3 | A1 | 25r rose | *1,400.* | *775.* |
| 4 | A1 | 40r blue | *1,250.* | *800.* |
| a. | | Cliché of Mozambique in Cape Verde plate | *16,500.* | *15,250.* |
| 4B | A1 | 50r green | *2,000.* | *725.* |
| 5 | A1 | 100r lilac | *275.* | *175.* |
| 6 | A1 | 200r orange | *575.* | *475.* |
| 7 | A1 | 300r brown | *575.* | *475.* |

Excellent forgeries exist of Nos. 1-7.

Overprinted in Red or Black

**1881-85 Perf. 12½, 13½**

| | | | | |
|---|---|---|---|---|
| 8 | A1 | 5r black (R) | 4.00 | 2.75 |
| 9 | A1 | 10r yellow | 160.00 | 160.00 |
| 10 | A1 | 10r green ('85) | 6.00 | 5.50 |
| 11 | A1 | 20r bister | 3.00 | 2.25 |
| 12 | A1 | 20r rose ('85) | 6.75 | 5.00 |
| a. | | Double overprint | | |
| 13 | A1 | 25r carmine | 2.40 | 1.75 |
| a. | | Perf. 13½ | 67.50 | 37.50 |
| 14 | A1 | 25r violet ('85) | 3.00 | 1.90 |
| a. | | Double overprint | | |
| 15 | A1 | 40r blue | 175.00 | 110.00 |
| a. | | Cliché of Mozambique in Cape Verde plate | *1,250.* | *875.00* |
| 16 | A1 | 40r yellow ('85) | 1.90 | 1.60 |
| a. | | Cliché of Mozambique in Cape Verde plate | 50.00 | 45.00 |
| b. | | Imperf. | | |
| c. | | As "a," imperf. | | |
| d. | | Double overprint | | |
| 17 | A1 | 50r green | 175.00 | 110.00 |
| 18 | A1 | 50r blue ('85) | 5.75 | 2.75 |
| a. | | Imperf. | | |
| b. | | Double overprint | | |
| 19 | A1 | 100r lilac | 7.75 | 6.00 |
| a. | | Inverted overprint | | |
| 20 | A1 | 200r orange | 11.50 | 8.00 |
| 21 | A1 | 300r yellow brn | 14.00 | 11.00 |
| a. | | 300r lake brown | 16.00 | 12.50 |

Varieties of this overprint may be found without accent on "E" of "GUINE," or with grave instead of acute accent.

*Stamps of the 1879-85 issues were reprinted on a smooth white chalky paper, ungummed, and on thin white paper with shiny white gum and clean-cut perforation 13½.*

*See Scott Classic Catalogue for listings by perforation.*

King Luiz — A3

**1886 Typo. Perf. 12½, 13½**

| | | | | |
|---|---|---|---|---|
| 22 | A3 | 5r gray black | 6.00 | 5.50 |
| a. | | Imperf. | | |
| 23 | A3 | 10r green | 7.25 | 4.00 |
| a. | | Perf. 13½ | 8.25 | 6.75 |
| b. | | Imperf. | | |
| 24 | A3 | 20r carmine | 10.50 | 4.00 |
| 25 | A3 | 25r red lilac | 10.50 | 6.25 |
| a. | | Imperf. | | |
| 26 | A3 | 40r chocolate | 8.50 | 6.25 |
| a. | | Perf. 12½ | 82.50 | 60.00 |
| 27 | A3 | 50r blue | 17.00 | 8.75 |
| a. | | Imperf. | | |
| 28 | A3 | 80r gray | 16.00 | 11.00 |
| a. | | Perf. 12½ | 82.50 | 60.00 |
| 29 | A3 | 100r brown | 16.00 | 11.00 |
| a. | | Perf. 12½ | 37.50 | 22.60 |
| 30 | A3 | 200r gray lilac | 37.50 | 22.50 |
| 31 | A3 | 300r orange | 47.50 | 35.00 |
| a. | | Perf. 13½ | 210.00 | 210.00 |
| | | *Nos. 22-31 (10)* | 176.75 | 111.75 |

For surcharges and overprints see Nos. 67-76, 180-183.

*Reprinted in 1905 on thin white paper with shiny white gum and clean-cut perforation 13½.*

King Carlos
A4 A5

**1893-94 Perf. 11½**

| | | | | |
|---|---|---|---|---|
| 32 | A4 | 5r yellow | 1.90 | 1.10 |
| a. | | Perf. 12½ | 2.00 | 1.25 |
| 33 | A4 | 10r red violet | 1.90 | 1.10 |
| 34 | A4 | 15r chocolate | 2.40 | 1.60 |
| 35 | A4 | 20r lavender | 2.40 | 1.60 |
| 36 | A4 | 25r blue green | 2.40 | 1.60 |
| 37 | A4 | 50r lt blue | 4.25 | 3.75 |
| a. | | Perf. 12½ | 17.00 | 12.50 |
| 38 | A4 | 75r rose | 11.50 | 7.50 |
| 39 | A4 | 80r lt green | 11.50 | 7.50 |
| 40 | A4 | 100r brn, *buff* | 11.50 | 7.50 |
| 41 | A4 | 150r car, *rose* | 11.50 | 8.00 |
| 42 | A4 | 200r dk bl, *bl* | 19.00 | 15.00 |
| 43 | A4 | 300r dk bl, *sal* | 18.00 | 15.00 |
| | | *Nos. 32-43 (12)* | 98.25 | 71.25 |

Almost all of Nos. 32-43 were issued without gum.

For surcharges and overprints see #77-88, 184-188, 203-205.

**1898-1903 Perf. 11½**

**Name & Value in Black except 500r**

| | | | | |
|---|---|---|---|---|
| 44 | A5 | 2½r gray | .40 | .35 |
| 45 | A5 | 5r orange | .40 | .35 |
| 46 | A5 | 10r lt green | .40 | .35 |
| 47 | A5 | 15r brown | 3.25 | 2.25 |
| 48 | A5 | 15r gray grn ('03) | 1.75 | 1.25 |
| 49 | A5 | 20r gray violet | 1.40 | 1.10 |
| 50 | A5 | 25r sea green | 1.75 | .90 |
| 51 | A5 | 25r carmine ('03) | 1.00 | .55 |
| 52 | A5 | 50r dark blue | 2.75 | 1.40 |
| 53 | A5 | 50r brown ('03) | 3.25 | 2.25 |
| 54 | A5 | 65r dl blue ('03) | 11.00 | 8.75 |
| 55 | A5 | 75r rose | 17.00 | 8.00 |
| 56 | A5 | 75r lilac ('03) | 4.00 | 2.25 |
| 57 | A5 | 80r brt violet | 3.00 | 1.90 |
| 58 | A5 | 100r dk bl, *bl* | 2.75 | 1.90 |
| a. | | Perf. 12½ | 52.50 | 22.50 |
| 59 | A5 | 115r org brn, *pink* ('03) | 8.50 | 6.00 |
| a. | | 115r orange brown, *yellowish* | 8.25 | 5.00 |
| 60 | A5 | 130r brn, *straw* ('03) | 10.00 | 7.50 |
| 61 | A5 | 150r lt brn, *buff* | 11.00 | 3.25 |
| 62 | A5 | 200r red lilac, *pnksh* | 10.00 | 3.25 |
| 63 | A5 | 300r blue, *rose* | 11.00 | 4.25 |
| 64 | A5 | 400r dl bl, *straw* ('03) | 13.00 | 10.00 |
| 65 | A5 | 500r blk & red, *bl* ('01) | 14.50 | 7.75 |
| 66 | A5 | 700r vio, *yelsh* ('01) | 17.00 | 10.00 |
| | | *Nos. 44-66 (23)* | 149.10 | 85.55 |

Stamps issued in 1903 were without gum.

For overprints and surcharges see Nos. 90-115, 190-194, 197.

Issue of 1886 Surcharged in Black or Red

**1902, Oct. 20 Perf. 12½, 13½**

| | | | | |
|---|---|---|---|---|
| 67 | A3 | 65r on 10r green | 6.50 | 5.50 |
| 68 | A3 | 65r on 20r car | 6.50 | 5.00 |
| 69 | A3 | 65r on 25r red lilac | 6.50 | 5.00 |
| 70 | A3 | 115r on 40r choc | 5.75 | 4.50 |
| a. | | Perf. 13½ | 13.00 | 9.50 |
| 71 | A3 | 115r on 50r blue | 5.75 | 4.50 |
| 72 | A3 | 115r on 300r orange | 7.25 | 5.75 |
| 73 | A3 | 130r on 80r gray | 7.25 | 5.00 |
| a. | | Perf. 13½ | 14.00 | 5.75 |
| 74 | A3 | 130r on 100r brown | 7.75 | 5.75 |
| a. | | Perf. 13½ | 20.00 | 14.00 |
| 75 | A3 | 400r on 200r gray lil | 13.00 | 8.75 |
| 76 | A3 | 400r on 5r gray blk (R) | 32.50 | 24.00 |
| | | *Nos. 67-76 (10)* | 98.75 | 73.75 |

*Reprints of No. 76 are in black and have clean-cut perforation 13½.*

**Same Surcharge on Issue of 1893-94**

**Perf. 11½, 12½, 13½**

| | | | | |
|---|---|---|---|---|
| 77 | A4 | 65r on 10r red vio | 5.75 | 3.50 |
| 78 | A4 | 65r on 15r choc | 5.75 | 3.50 |
| 79 | A4 | 65r on 20r lav | 5.75 | 3.50 |
| 80 | A4 | 65r on 50r lt bl | 3.00 | 2.25 |
| a. | | Perf. 13½ | 3.25 | 2.50 |
| 81 | A4 | 115r on 5r yel | 5.50 | 3.00 |
| a. | | Inverted surcharge | 45.00 | 45.00 |
| b. | | Perf. 12½ | 55.00 | 40.00 |
| 82 | A4 | 115r on 25r bl grn | 6.00 | 3.25 |
| 83 | A4 | 130r on 150r car, *rose* | 6.00 | 3.25 |
| 84 | A4 | 130r on 200r dk bl, *bl* | 6.50 | 4.50 |
| 85 | A4 | 130r on 300r dk bl, *sal* | 6.50 | 4.50 |
| 86 | A4 | 400r on 75r rose | 4.50 | 3.00 |
| 87 | A4 | 400r on 80r lt grn | 3.00 | 1.60 |
| 88 | A4 | 400r on 100r brn, *buff* | 4.00 | 1.60 |

**Same Surcharge on No. P1**

| | | | | |
|---|---|---|---|---|
| 89 | N1 | 115r on 2½r brn | 4.50 | 3.25 |
| a. | | Perf. 13½ | 5.25 | 4.00 |
| | | *Nos. 77-89 (13)* | 66.75 | 40.70 |

Issue of 1898 Overprinted in Black

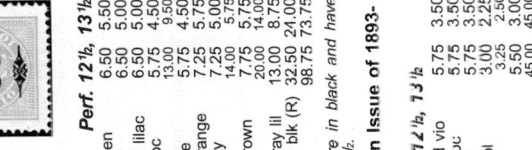

**1902, Oct. 20 Perf. 11½**

| | | | | |
|---|---|---|---|---|
| 90 | A5 | 15r brown | 2.50 | 1.25 |
| 91 | A5 | 25r sea green | 2.50 | 1.60 |
| 92 | A5 | 50r dark blue | 3.00 | 1.60 |
| 93 | A5 | 75r rose | 5.75 | 4.00 |
| | | *Nos. 90-93 (4)* | 13.75 | 8.45 |

No. 54 Surcharged in Black

**1905**

| | | | | |
|---|---|---|---|---|
| 94 | A5 | 50r on 65r dull blue | 4.50 | 2.50 |

Issue of 1898-1903 Overprinted in Carmine or Green

**1911** *Perf. 11½*

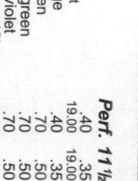

**95** A5 2½r gray .40 .35
*a.* Inverted overprint 19.00 19.00
**96** A5 5r orange .40 .35
**97** A5 10r lt green .70 .50
**98** A5 15r gray green .70 .50
**99** A5 20r gray violet .70 .50
**100** A5 25r carmine (G) .70 .50
*a.* Double overprint 15.00 15.00
**101** A5 50r brown .45 .40
**102** A5 75c lilac .45 .40
**103** A5 100r dk bl, *bl* 1.50 .75
**104** A5 115r org brn, *pink* 1.50 1.00
**105** A5 130r brn, *straw* 1.50 1.00
**106** A5 200r red lil, *pink* 6.50 3.25
**107** A5 400r dl bl, *straw* 2.50 1.50
**108** A5 500r blk & red, *bl* 2.75 1.50
**109** A5 700r vio, *yelsh* 4.25 2.25
*Nos. 95-109 (15)* 25.00 14.75

Issued without gum: #101-102, 104-105, 107.

Issue of 1898-1903 Overprinted in Red

**1913** *Perf. 11½*

**Without Gum (Nos. 110-115)**

**110** A5 15r gray grn 10.00 6.50
**111** A5 75r lilac 10.00 6.50
*a.* Inverted overprint 35.00 35.00
**112** A5 100r bl, *bl* 6.00 4.50
*a.* Inverted overprint 35.00 35.00
**113** A5 200r red lil, *pnksh* 30.00 25.00
*a.* Inverted overprint 82.50 82.50

**Same Overprint on Nos. 90, 93 in Red**

**114** A5 15r brown 10.00 7.25
*a.* "REPUBLICA" double *35.00 35.00*
*b.* "REPUBLICA" inverted *30.00 30.00*
**115** A5 75r rose 10.00 7.25
*a.* "REPUBLICA" inverted 35.00 35.00
*Nos. 110-115 (6)* 76.00 57.00

Vasco da Gama Issue of Various Portuguese Colonies Surcharged

**1913**

**On Stamps of Macao**

**116** CD20 ¼c on ½a bl grn 1.60 1.60
**117** CD21 ½c on 1a red 1.60 1.60
**118** CD22 1c on 2a red vio 1.60 1.60
**119** CD23 2½c on 4a yel grn 1.60 1.60
**120** CD24 5c on 8a dk bl 1.60 1.60
**121** CD25 7½c on 12a vio brn 3.25 3.25
**122** CD26 10c on 16a bis brn 1.60 1.60
*a.* Inverted surcharge 30.00 30.00
**123** CD27 15c on 24a bis 2.75 2.75
*Nos. 116-123 (8)* 15.60 15.60

**On Stamps of Portuguese Africa**

**124** CD20 ¼c on 2½c bl grn 1.40 1.40
**125** CD21 ½c on 5r red 1.40 1.40
**126** CD22 1c on 10r red vio 1.40 1.40
**127** CD23 2½c on 25r yel grn 1.40 1.40
**128** CD24 5c on 50r dk bl 1.40 1.40
**129** CD25 7½c on 75r vio brn 3.00 3.00
**130** CD26 10c on 100r bis brn 1.40 1.40
**131** CD27 15c on 150r bis 4.00 4.00
*Nos. 124-131 (8)* 15.40 15.40

**On Stamps of Timor**

**132** CD20 ¼c on ½a bl grn 1.60 1.60
**133** CD21 ½c on 1a red 1.60 1.60
**134** CD22 1c on 2a red vio 1.60 1.60
**135** CD23 2½c on 4a yel grn 1.60 1.60
**136** CD24 5c on 8a dk blue 1.60 1.60
**137** CD25 7½c on 12a vio brn 3.00 3.00
**138** CD26 10c on 16a bis brn 1.60 1.60
**139** CD27 15c on 24a bister 3.00 3.00
*Nos. 132-139 (8)* 15.60 15.60
*Nos. 116-139 (24)* 46.60 46.60

Ceres — A6

**1914-26** *Perf. 15x14, 12x11½*

**Name and Value in Black**

**140** A6 ¼c olive brown .20 .20
**141** A6 ½c black .20 .20
**142** A6 1c blue green 1.40 1.40
**143** A6 1c yel grn ('22) .20 .20
**144** A6 1½c lilac brn .20 .20
**145** A6 2c carmine .20 .20
**146** A6 2c gray ('25) .20 *1.60*
**147** A6 2½c lt violet .20 .20
**148** A6 3c orange ('22) .20 *1.60*
**149** A6 4c deep red ('22) .20 *1.60*
**150** A6 4½c gray ('22) .20 *1.60*
**151** A6 5c deep blue .65 .55
**152** A6 5c brt blue ('22) .20 .20
**153** A6 6c lilac ('22) .20 *1.60*
**154** A6 7c ultra ('22) .30 *1.60*
**155** A6 7½c yellow brn .20 .20
**156** A6 8c slate .20 .20
**157** A6 10c orange brn .20 .20
**158** A6 12c blue grn ('22) .65 .50
**159** A6 15c plum 8.25 7.25
**160** A6 15c brn rose ('22) .50 .35
**161** A6 20c yellow grn .20 .20
**162** A6 24c ultra ('25) 1.90 1.60
**163** A6 25c brown ('25) 2.50 2.25
**164** A6 30c brown, *grn* 7.00 6.00
**165** A6 30c gray grn ('22) .90 .25
**166** A6 40c brown, *pink* 3.50 3.25
**167** A6 40c turq bl ('22) .90 .40
**168** A6 50c orange, *salmon* 3.50 3.25
**169** A6 50c violet ('25) 1.90 .90
**170** A6 60c dk blue ('22) 1.90 .95
**171** A6 60c dp rose ('26) 2.50 1.75
**172** A6 80c brt rose ('22) 1.60 1.00
**173** A6 1e green, *blue* 4.00 3.50
**174** A6 1e pale rose ('22) 2.75 1.50
**175** A6 1e indigo ('26) 3.50 2.75
**176** A6 2e dk violet ('22) 3.00 1.60
**177** A6 5e buff ('25) 13.00 10.50
**178** A6 10e pink ('25) 27.50 17.50
**179** A6 20e pale turq ('25) 60.00 35.00
*Nos. 140-179 (40)* 156.80 115.70

For surcharges see Nos. 195-196, 211-213.

Provisional Issue of 1902 Overprinted in Carmine

**1915** *Perf. 11½, 12½, 13½*

**180** A3 115r on 40r choc 1.10 .65
*a.* Perf. 13½ 13.00 8.50
**181** A3 115r on 50r blue 1.40 .75
**182** A3 130r on 80r gray 4.50 1.90
*a.* Perf. 12½ 27.50 22.50
**183** A3 130r on 100r brn 3.50 1.90
*a.* Perf. 13½ 14.50 11.00
**184** A4 115r on 5r yellow .80 .65
*a.* Perf. 11½ 5.00 4.50
**185** A4 115r on 25r bl grn .75 .65
**186** A4 130r on 150r car, *rose* 1.25 .80
**187** A4 130r on 200r bl, *bl* .80 .70
**188** A4 130r on 300r dk bl, *sal* 1.10 .80
**189** N1 115r on 2½r brn 1.25 .90
*a.* Perf. 13½ 13.00 11.00
*b.* Inverted overprint 22.50 22.50

**On Nos. 90, 92, 94**

*Perf. 11½*

**190** A5 15r brown .80 .70
**191** A5 50r dark blue .80 .70
**192** A5 50r on 65r dl bl .80 .70
*Nos. 180-192 (13)* 18.85 11.80

Nos. 64, 66 Overprinted

**1919** **Without Gum** *Perf. 11½*

**193** A5 400r dl bl, *straw* 50.00 21.00
**194** A5 700r vio, *yelsh* 11.00 6.25

Nos. 140, 141 and 59 Surcharged:

= =
$04
centavos
a

b

**1920, Sept.** *Perf. 15x14, 11½*

**Without Gum**

**195** A6(a) 4c on ¼c 3.25 2.75
**196** A6(a) 6c on ½c 4.00 2.75
**197** A5(b) 12c on 115r 5.50 4.50
*Nos. 195-197 (3)* 12.75 10.00

Nos. 86-88 Surcharged

**1925** *Perf. 11½*

**203** A4 40c on 400r on 75r .95 .75
**204** A4 40c on 400r on 80r .70 .55
**205** A4 40c on 400r on 100r .70 .55
*Nos. 203-205 (3)* 2.35 1.85

Nos. 171-172, 176 Surcharged

**1931** *Perf. 12x11½*

**211** A6 50c on 60c dp rose 3.25 1.60
**212** A6 70c on 80c pink 3.25 1.90
**213** A6 1.40e on 2e dk vio 6.50 4.00
*Nos. 211-213 (3)* 13.00 7.50

Ceres — A7

**1933** **Wmk. 232** *Perf. 12 x 11½*

**214** A7 1c bister .20 .20
**215** A7 5c olive brn .20 .20
**216** A7 10c violet .20 .20
**217** A7 15c black .20 .20
**218** A7 20c gray .20 .20
**219** A7 30c dk green .25 .20
**220** A7 40c red orange .45 .20
**221** A7 45c lt blue 1.10 .80
**222** A7 50c lt brown 1.10 .55
**223** A7 60c olive grn 1.40 .55
**224** A7 70c orange brn 2.75 .65
**225** A7 80c emerald 1.50 .80
**226** A7 85c deep rose 3.00 1.40
**227** A7 1e red brown 1.40 .90
**228** A7 1.40e dk blue 6.50 2.25
**229** A7 2e red violet 4.50 1.90
**230** A7 5e apple green 10.00 5.75
**231** A7 10e olive bister 17.50 9.50
**232** A7 20e orange 55.00 25.00
*Nos. 214-232 (19)* 107.45 51.45

Common Design Types pictured following the introduction.

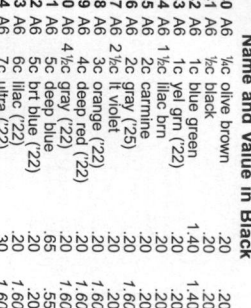

Common Design Types

**Engr.; Name & Value Typo. in Black**

**1938** **Unwmk.** *Perf. 13½x13*

**233** CD34 1c gray grn .20 .20
**234** CD34 5c orange brn .20 .20
**235** CD34 10c dk carmine .20 .20
**236** CD34 15c dk vio brn .20 .20
**237** CD34 20c slate .40 .20
**238** CD35 30c rose violet .60 .25
**239** CD35 35c brt green .65 .35
**240** CD35 40c brown 1.10 .35
**241** CD35 50c brt red vio 1.10 .35
**242** CD36 60c gray black 1.60 .35
**243** CD36 70c brown vio 1.60 .35
**244** CD36 80c orange 1.90 .70
**245** CD36 1e red 1.50 .50
**246** CD37 1.75e blue 2.10 1.00
**247** CD37 2e brown car 5.00 1.40
**248** CD37 5e olive grn 5.50 2.25
**249** CD38 10e blue vio 7.50 2.75
**250** CD38 20e red brown 22.50 4.50
*Nos. 233-250 (18)* 53.85 16.10

Fort of Cacheu A8

Nuno Tristam — A9

Ulysses S. Grant — A10

Designs: 3.50e, Teixeira Pinto. 5e, Honorio Barreto. 20e, Bissau Church.

**Unwmk.**

**1946, Jan. 12** **Litho.** *Perf. 11*

**251** A8 30c gray & lt gray .80 .70
**252** A9 50c black & pink .80 .40
**253** A9 50c gray grn & lt grn .80 .40
**254** A10 1.75e blue & lt blue 3.25 1.60
**255** A10 3.50e red & pink 4.75 2.75
**256** A10 5e lt brn & buff 10.00 5.50
**257** A8 20e vio & lt vio 14.50 7.50
*a.* Sheet of 7, #251-257 ('47) 72.50 72.50
*Nos. 251-257 (7)* 34.90 18.85

Discovery of Guinea, 500th anniversary. No. 257a sold for 40 escudos.

Guinea Village — A11

UPU Symbols — A12

Designs: 10c, Crowned crane. 20c, 3.50e, Tribesman. 35c, 5e, Woman in ceremonial dress. 50c, Musician. 70c, Man. 80c, 20e, Girl. 1e, 2e, Drummer. 1.75e, Antelope.

**1948, Apr.** **Photo.** *Perf. 11½*

**258** A11 5c chocolate .20 .20
**259** A11 10c lt violet .65 .65
**260** A11 20c dull rose .45 .25
**261** A11 35c green .40 .25
**262** A11 50c dp orange .40 .20
**263** A11 70c dp gray bl .45 .25
**264** A11 80c dk ol grn .95 .35
**265** A11 1e rose red .95 .45
**266** A11 1.75e ultra 4.00 2.25
**267** A11 2e blue 8.25 1.10
**268** A11 3.50e orange brn 2.75 .90
**269** A11 5e slate 5.00 1.40
**270** A11 20e violet 11.00 3.25
*a.* Sheet of 13, #258-270 + 2 labels 67.50 67.50
*Nos. 258-270 (13)* 35.45 11.50

No. 270a sold for 40 escudos.

**Lady of Fatima Issue**

Common Design Type

**1948, Oct.** **Litho.** *Perf. 14½*

**271** CD40 50c deep green 3.25 3.00

**1949, Oct.** *Perf. 14*

**272** A12 2e dp org & cream 4.50 2.50

Universal Postal Union, 75th anniversary.

**Catalogue values for unused stamps in this section, from this point to the end of the section, are for Never Hinged items.**

**Holy Year Issue**

Common Design Types

**1950, May** *Perf. 13x13½*

**273** CD41 1e brown lake 1.40 1.10
**274** CD42 3e blue green 2.10 1.50

## Holy Year Extension Issue
Common Design Type

1951, Oct. Perf. 14
275 CD43 1e choc & pale brn 1.00 .65

## Medical Congress Issue
Common Design Type

Design: Physical examination.

1952 Perf. 13½
276 CD44 50c purple & choc + label .45 .35

Stamps without label attached sell for less.

Exhibition Entrance — A13

1953, Jan. Litho. Perf. 13
277 A13 10c brn lake & ol .20 .20
278 A13 50c dk blue & bister .80 .25
279 A13 3e blk, dk brn & sal 2.25 1.00
  Nos. 277-279 (3) 3.25 1.45

Exhibition of Sacred Missionary Art held at Lisbon in 1951.

1953 Photo. Unwmk.
280 A14 50c multicolored .65 .55

Centenary of Portugal's first postage stamps.

Stamp of Portugal and Arms of Colonies — A14

Anopheles Trifasciata — A15

## Various Beetles in Natural Colors

1953 Perf. 11½
281 A15 5c yellow .20 .20
282 A15 10c blue .20 .20
283 A15 30c org vermilion .20 .20
284 A15 50c .20 .20
285 A15 70c gray brn .45 .25
286 A15 1e orange .45 .25
287 A15 2e pale ol grn 1.10 .25
288 A15 3e lilac rose 1.60 .70
289 A15 5e lt blue grn 2.75 .90
290 A15 10e lilac 4.50 1.10
  Nos. 281-290 (10) 11.65 4.25

## Sao Paulo Issue
Common Design Type

1954 Litho. Perf. 13½
291 A16 1e lil rose, bl gray & blk .35 .20

Belem Tower, Lisbon, and Colonial Arms — A16

1955, Apr. 14
292 A16 1e blue & multi .20 .20
293 A16 2.50e gray & multi .50 .20

Visit of Pres. Francisco H. C. Lopes.

Fair Emblem, Globe and Arms — A17

1958 Unwmk. Perf. 12x11½
294 A17 2.50e multicolored .65 .55

World's Fair at Brussels.

## Tropical Medicine Congress Issue
Common Design Type

Design: Maytenus senegalensis.

1958 Perf. 13½
295 CD47 5e multicolored 2.10 1.10

Nautical Astrolabe — A19

Honorio Barreto — A18

1959, Apr. 29 Litho. Perf. 13½
296 A18 2.50e multicolored .40 .20

Centenary of the death of Honorio Barreto, governor of Portuguese Guinea.

1960, June 25 Perf. 13½
297 A19 2.50e multicolored .40 .20

500th anniversary of the death of Prince Henry the Navigator.

Traveling Medical Unit — A20

1960 Unwmk. Perf. 14½
298 A20 1.50e multicolored .40 .20

10th anniv. of the Commission for Technical Cooperation in Africa South of the Sahara (C.C.T.A.).

## Sports Issue
Common Design Type

1962, Jan. 18 Litho. Perf. 13½
299 CD48 50c Automobile race .25 .20
300 CD48 1e Tennis 1.00 .25
301 CD48 1.50e Shot put .70 .20
302 CD48 2.50e Wrestling .70 .20
303 CD48 3.50e Trapshooting .70 .20
304 CD48 15e Volleyball 1.60 .90
  Nos. 299-304 (6) 4.95 1.95

## Anti-Malaria Issue
Common Design Type

Design: Anopholes gambiae.

1962 Unwmk. Perf. 13½
305 CD49 2.50e multicolored .65 .35

African Spitting Cobra — A21

Snakes: 35c, African rock python. 70c, Boomslang. 80c, West African mamba. 1.50e, Smythe's water snake. 2e, Common night adder, horiz. 2.50e, Green swamp snake. 3.50e, Brown house snake. 4e, Spotted wolf snake. 5e, Common puff adder. 15e, Striped beauty snake. 20e, African egg-eating snake, horiz.

1963, Jan. 17 Litho. Perf. 13½
306 A21 20c multicolored .25 .20
307 A21 35c multicolored .25 .20
308 A21 50c multicolored .45 .35
309 A21 80c multicolored .55 .35
310 A21 1.50e multicolored .80 .35
311 A21 2e multicolored .65 .20
312 A21 2.50e multicolored .80 .45
313 A21 3.50e multicolored .80 .45
314 A21 4e multicolored .80 .45
315 A21 5e multicolored .80 .70
316 A21 15e multicolored 2.25 .80
317 A21 20e multicolored 2.75 .80
  Nos. 306-317 (12) 12.60 5.30

For overprints see Guinea-Bissau Nos. 696-703.

## Airline Anniversary Issue
Common Design Type

1963 Litho. Perf. 14½
318 CD50 2.50e lt brown & multi .65 .35

## National Overseas Bank Issue
Common Design Type

Design: 2.50e, Joao de Andrade Córvo.

1964, May 16 Perf. 13½
319 CD51 2.50e multicolored .65 .40

## ITU Issue
Common Design Type

1965, May 17 Unwmk. Perf. 14½
320 CD52 2.50e lt blue & multi 1.90 .75

Sacred Heart of Jesus Monument and Chapel of the Apparition A23

Soldier, 1548 A22

40c, Rifleman, 1578. 60c, Rifleman, 1640. 1.50e, Grenadier, 1721. 2.50e, Fusiliers captain, 1740. 4.50e, Infantryman, 1740. 7.50e, Sergeant major, 1762. 10e, Engineers' officer, 1806.

1966, Jan. 8 Litho. Perf. 13½
321 A22 25c multicolored .20 .20
322 A22 40c multicolored .20 .20
323 A22 60c multicolored .35 .20
324 A22 1e multicolored .45 .20
325 A22 2.50e multicolored 1.25 .40
326 A22 4.50e multicolored 2.10 1.10
327 A22 7.50e multicolored 2.10 1.40
328 A22 10e multicolored 2.75 1.60
  Nos. 321-328 (8) 9.40 5.30

## National Revolution Issue
Common Design Type

2.50e, Berta Craveiro Lopes School and Central Pavilion of Bissau Hospital.

1966, May 28 Litho. Perf. 11½
329 CD53 2.50e multicolored .55 .35

## Navy Club Issue
Common Design Type

Designs: 50c, Capt. Oliveira Muzanty and cruiser Republica. 1e, Capt. Afonso de Cerqueira and torpedo boat Guadiana.

1967, Jan. 31 Litho. Perf. 13
330 CD54 50c multicolored .40 .25
331 CD54 1e multicolored .80 .65

1967, May 13 Perf. 12½x13
332 A23 50c multicolored .35 .35

50th anniv. of the appearance of the Virgin Mary to three shepherd children at Fatima.

Cabral's Coat of Arms — A25

Pres. Rodrigues Thomaz — A24

1968, Feb. 2 Litho. Perf. 13½
333 A24 1e multicolored .20 .20

Issued to commemorate the 1968 visit of Pres. Americo de Deus Rodrigues Thomaz.

1968, Apr. 22 Litho. Perf. 14
334 A25 2.50e multicolored .55 .20

Pedro Alvares Cabral, navigator who took possession of Brazil for Portugal, 500th birth anniv.

## Admiral Coutinho Issue
Common Design Type

Design: 1e, Adm. Coutinho and astrolabe.

1969, Feb. 17 Litho. Perf. 14
335 CD55 1e multicolored .35 .20

Arms of King Manuel I — A27

Da Gama Coat of Arms — A26

## Vasco da Gama Issue

1969, Aug. 29 Litho. Perf. 14
336 A26 2.50e multicolored .35 .20

Vasco da Gama (1469-1524), navigator.

## Administration Reform Issue
Common Design Type

1969, Sept. 25 Litho. Perf. 14
337 CD56 50c multicolored .20 .20

## King Manuel I Issue

1969, Dec. 1 Litho. Perf. 14
338 A27 2e multicolored .35 .20

Pres. Ulysses S. Grant and View of Bolama — A28

1970, Oct. 25 Litho. Perf. 13½
339 A28 2.50e multicolored .45 .20

Centenary of Pres. Grant's arbitration in 1868 of Portuguese-English dispute concerning Bolama.

## Marshal Carmona Issue
Common Design Type

Design: 1.50e, Antonio Oscar Carmona in general's uniform.

1970, Nov. 15 Litho. Perf. 14
340 CD57 1.50e multicolored .35 .20

## Olympic Games Issue

**1972, May 25   Litho.   Perf. 13**
Common Design Type

| | | | |
|---|---|---|---|
| 341 | A29 | 50c brn org & multi | .20 .20 |

Design: 2.50e. Weight lifting, hammer throw and Olympic emblem.

4th centenary of publication of The Lusiads by Luiz Camoens (1524-1580).

Luiz Camoens — A29

### Lisbon-Rio de Janeiro Flight Issue

Common Design Type

**1972, June 20   Perf. 14x13½**

| 342 | CD59 | 2.50e multicolored | .45 .20 |
|---|---|---|---|

1e., "Lusitania" taking off from Lisbon.

**1972, Sept. 20   Litho.   Perf. 13½**
Common Design Type

| 343 | CD60 | 1e multicolored | .20 .20 |
|---|---|---|---|

### WMO Centenary Issue

**1973, Dec. 15   Litho.   Perf. 13**
Common Design Type

| 344 | CD61 | 2e lt brown & multi | .45 .35 |
|---|---|---|---|

## AIR POST STAMPS

**1938, Sept. 19   Engr.   Perf. 13½x13**
Name and Value in Black
Common Design Type

| | | | Unwmk. |
|---|---|---|---|
| C1 | CD39 | 10c red orange | .45 .35 |
| C2 | CD39 | 20c purple | .50 .35 |
| C3 | CD39 | 50c orange | .50 .35 |
| C4 | CD39 | 1e ultra | .50 .45 |
| C5 | CD39 | 2e lilac brown | 5.25 3.50 |
| C6 | CD39 | 3e dark green | 1.40 .95 |
| C7 | CD39 | 5e rose carmine | 4.00 1.00 |
| C8 | CD39 | 9e red brown | 4.00 4.00 |
| C9 | CD39 | 10e rose carmine | 25.95 12.20 |
| | | Nos. C1-C9 (9) | 34.90 23.50 |

No. C7 exists with overprint "Exposicao Internacional de Nova York, 1939-1940" and Trylon and Perisphere.

## POSTAGE DUE STAMPS

D1    D2

**1904   Unwmk.   Typo.   Perf. 12**
**Without Gum**

| J1 | D1 | 5r yellow green | .60 .45 |
|---|---|---|---|
| J2 | D1 | 10r slate | .60 .45 |
| J3 | D1 | 20r yellow brown | .65 .45 |
| J4 | D1 | 30r red orange | .65 .55 |
| J5 | D1 | 50r gray brown | 1.90 1.60 |
| J6 | D1 | 60r red brown | 1.90 1.60 |
| J7 | D1 | 100r brown | 4.25 2.75 |
| J8 | D1 | 130r dull blue | 6.50 5.25 |
| J9 | D1 | 200r carmine | 11.00 6.00 |
| J10 | D1 | 500r violet | 34.90 23.50 |
| | | Nos. J1-J10 (10) | |

Same Overprinted in Carmine or Green

**1911   Without Gum**

| J11 | D1 | 5r yellow green | .25 .20 |
|---|---|---|---|
| J12 | D1 | 10r slate | .25 .20 |
| J13 | D1 | 20r yellow brown | .35 .35 |
| J14 | D1 | 30r red orange | .35 .35 |
| J15 | D1 | 50r gray brown | .80 .35 |
| J16 | D1 | 60r red brown | 1.00 .80 |
| J17 | D1 | 100r lilac | 1.40 1.00 |
| J18 | D1 | 130r dull blue | 1.90 1.00 |
| J19 | D1 | 200r carmine (G) | 1.50 1.50 |
| J20 | D1 | 500r violet | 9.35 7.15 |
| | | Nos. J11-J20 (10) | |

**1919   Overprinted**
Nos. J2-J10

**1919   Without Gum**

| J21 | D1 | 10r slate | 8.25 8.25 |
|---|---|---|---|
| J22 | D1 | 20r yellow brown | 9.00 9.00 |
| J23 | D1 | 30r red orange | 6.50 5.75 |
| J24 | D1 | 50r gray brown | 2.50 2.10 |
| J25 | D1 | 60r red brown | 550.00 450.00 |
| J26 | D1 | 100r lilac | 2.25 1.90 |
| J27 | D1 | 130r dull blue | 22.50 19.00 |
| J28 | D1 | 200r carmine | 2.50 2.50 |
| J29 | D1 | 500r violet | 68.50 68.00 |
| | | Nos. J21-J24,J26-J29 (8) | 77.75 24.00 |

No. J25 was not regularly issued but exists on genuine covers.

**1921**

| J30 | D2 | ½c yellow green | .20 .20 |
|---|---|---|---|
| J31 | D2 | 1c slate | .20 .20 |
| J32 | D2 | 2c orange brown | .20 .20 |
| J33 | D2 | 3c orange | .20 .20 |
| J34 | D2 | 6c light brown | .20 .20 |
| J35 | D2 | 6c red violet | .20 .20 |
| J36 | D2 | 10c dull blue | .25 .25 |
| J37 | D2 | 13c dull brown | .25 .25 |
| J38 | D2 | 20c carmine | .35 .35 |
| J39 | D2 | 50c gray | .35 .35 |
| | | Nos. J30-J39 (10) | 2.40 2.40 |

Catalogue values for unused stamps in this section, from this point to the end of the section, are for Never Hinged items.

Common Design Type
**1952   Unwmk.   Perf. 14**
Numeral in Red, Frame Multicolored
Photogravure and Typographed

| J40 | CD45 | 10c olive green | .20 .20 |
|---|---|---|---|
| J41 | CD45 | 20c purple | .20 .20 |
| J42 | CD45 | 30c dark green | .20 .20 |
| J43 | CD45 | 1e violet blue | .50 .50 |
| J44 | CD45 | 2e olive black | .50 .50 |
| J45 | CD45 | 5e brown red | 1.00 1.00 |
| | | Nos. J40-J45 (6) | 2.40 2.40 |

## WAR TAX STAMPS

WT1

**1919, May 20   Typo.   Perf. 11½x12**
**Unwmk.**

| MR1 | WT1 | 10r brn, buff & blk | 45.00 20.00 |
|---|---|---|---|
| MR2 | WT1 | 40r brn, buff & blk | 40.00 22.50 |
| MR3 | WT1 | 50r brn, buff & blk | 42.50 27.50 |
| | | Nos. MR1-MR3 (3) | 127.50 75.00 |

The 40r is not overprinted "REPUBLICA." Some authorities consider Nos. MR2-MR3 to be revenue stamps.

## NEWSPAPER STAMP

N1

**1893   Typo.   Perf. 12½, 13½   Unwmk.**

| P1 | N1 | 2½r brown | 1.25 .75 |
|---|---|---|---|
| a. | | Perf. 13½ | 1.25 .90 |

For surcharge & overprint see #89, 189.

## POSTAL TAX STAMPS

**1925   Pombal Issue**
Common Design Types
Unwmk. Engr. Perf. 12½

| RA1 | CD28 | 15c red & black | .55 .45 |
|---|---|---|---|
| RA2 | CD29 | 15c red & black | .55 .45 |
| RA3 | CD30 | 15c red & black | .55 .45 |
| | | Nos. RA1-RA3 (3) | 1.65 1.35 |

Coat of Arms — PT7

**1934, Apr. 1   Typo.   Perf. 11½**
**Without Gum**

| RA4 | PT7 | 50c red brn & grn | 6.25 4.00 |
|---|---|---|---|
| a. | | Tête bêche pair | 450.00 |

Coat of Arms
PT8    PT9

**1938-40   Without Gum**

| RA5 | PT8 | 50c ol bis & citron | 6.00 3.25 |
|---|---|---|---|
| RA6 | PT8 | 50c lt grn & ol brn ('40) | 6.00 3.25 |

**1942   Without Gum   Perf. 11**

| RA7 | PT9 | 50c black & yellow | 1.60 1.00 |
|---|---|---|---|

**1959, July   Without Gum   Unwmk.**

| RA8 | PT9 | 30c dark ocher & blk | .20 .20 |
|---|---|---|---|

See Nos. RA24-RA26.

Lusignian Cross
PT10    PT11

**1967   Typo.   PT10   Perf. 11x11½**
**Without Gum**

| RA9 | PT10 | 50c pink, red & blk | .80 .80 |
|---|---|---|---|
| RA10 | PT10 | 1e grn, red & blk | .80 .80 |
| RA11 | PT10 | 5e gray, red & blk | 1.10 1.10 |
| RA12 | PT10 | 10e lt grn, red & blk | 1.25 2.25 |
| | | Nos. RA9-RA12 (4) | 4.95 4.95 |

The tax was for national defense.

Carved Figurine — PT12

**1967, Aug.   Typo.   Perf. 11**
**Without Gum**

| RA13 | PT11 | 50c pink, blk & red | .55 .55 |
|---|---|---|---|
| RA14 | PT11 | 1e pale grn, blk & red | .55 .55 |
| RA15 | PT11 | 5e gray, blk & red | 1.10 1.10 |
| RA16 | PT11 | 10e lt blk, blk & red | 2.25 2.25 |
| | | Nos. RA13-RA16 (4) | 4.45 4.45 |

The tax was used for national defense.

A 50e was used for revenue only.

Catalogue values for unused stamps in this section, from this point to the end of the section, are for Never Hinged items.

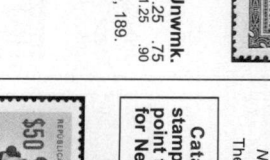

**1968   Litho.   Perf. 13½**

| RA17 | PT12 | 50c gray & multi | .20 .20 |
|---|---|---|---|
| a. | | Yellow paper | .80 .80 |
| RA18 | PT12 | 1e multi | .25 .25 |
| RA19 | PT12 | 2e (Vaca Bruto) | .20 .20 |
| RA20 | PT12 | 2e (Tocador de Bombolon) | .20 .20 |
| RA21 | PT12 | 2.50e multi | .25 .25 |
| RA22 | PT12 | 5e multi | .35 .35 |
| RA23 | PT12 | 10e multi | .75 .75 |
| | | Nos. RA17-RA19,RA21-RA23 (6) | 1.95 1.95 |

Art from Bissau Museum: 1e. Tree of Life, with 2 birds, horiz.; #RA19, Man wearing horned headgear ("Vaca Bruto"). #RA20, inscribed "Tocador de Bombolon," 2.50e. The Magistrate, 5e. Man bearing burden on head. 10e. Stylized pelican.

Obligatory on all inland mail Mar. 15-Apr. 15 and Dec. 15-Jan. 15, and all year on parcels. A souvenir sheet embracing Nos. RA17-RA19 and RA21-RA23 exists. The stamps have simulated perforations. Value $3.50. For surcharges see Nos. RA27-RA28.

**1968**
**Typo.   Perf. 11**
**Without Gum**
Arms Type of 1942

| RA24 | PT9 | 2.50e lt blue & blk | .45 .45 |
|---|---|---|---|
| RA25 | PT9 | 5e green & blk | .80 .80 |
| RA26 | PT9 | 10e dp blue & blk | 1.60 1.60 |
| | | Nos. RA24-RA26 (3) | 2.85 2.85 |

No. RA20 Surcharged

**1968**

| RA27 | PT12 | 50c on 2e multi | .35 .35 |
|---|---|---|---|
| RA28 | PT12 | 1e on 2e multi | .35 .35 |

Black and White Hands Holding Sword — PT13

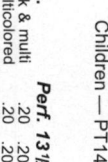

Mother and Children — PT14

**1968   Litho.   Perf. 13½**

| RA29 | PT13 | 50c pink & multi | .20 .20 |
|---|---|---|---|
| RA30 | PT13 | 1e multicolored | .20 .20 |
| RA31 | PT13 | 2e yellow & multi | .20 .20 |
| RA32 | PT13 | 2.50e buff & multi | .25 .25 |
| RA33 | PT13 | 3e multicolored | .35 .35 |
| RA34 | PT13 | 4e gray multi | .40 .40 |

| | | | | |
|---|---|---|---|---|
| **RA35** | PT13 | 5e multicolored | .45 | .45 |
| **RA36** | PT13 | 10e multicolored | .90 | .90 |
| | | *Nos. RA29-RA36 (8)* | 2.95 | 2.95 |

The surtax was for national defense. Other denominations exist: 8e, 9e, 15e. Value, $1 each.

**1971, June** **Litho.** ***Perf. 13½***

| | | | | |
|---|---|---|---|---|
| **RA37** | PT14 | 50c multicolored | .20 | .20 |
| **RA38** | PT14 | 1e multicolored | .20 | .20 |
| **RA39** | PT14 | 2e multicolored | .20 | .20 |
| **RA40** | PT14 | 3e multicolored | .25 | .20 |
| **RA41** | PT14 | 4e multicolored | .35 | .25 |
| **RA42** | PT14 | 5e multicolored | .45 | .40 |
| **RA43** | PT14 | 10e multicolored | .90 | .55 |
| | | *Nos. RA37-RA43 (7)* | 2.55 | 2.00 |

A 20e exists. Value $2.

## POSTAL TAX DUE STAMPS

### Pombal Issue

Common Design Types

**1925** **Unwmk.** ***Perf. 12½***

| | | | | |
|---|---|---|---|---|
| **RAJ1** | CD28 | 30c red & black | .55 | .45 |
| **RAJ2** | CD29 | 30c red & black | .55 | .45 |
| **RAJ3** | CD30 | 30c red & black | .55 | .45 |
| | | *Nos. RAJ1-RAJ3 (3)* | 1.65 | 1.35 |

# PORTUGUESE INDIA

'pōr-chi-gēz 'in-dē-ə

LOCATION — West coast of the Indian peninsula
GOVT. — Portuguese colony
AREA — 1,537 sq. mi.
POP. — 649,000 (1958)
CAPITAL — Panjim (Nova-Goa)

The colony was seized by India on Dec. 18, 1961, and annexed by that republic.

1000 Reis = 1 Milreis
12 Reis = 1 Tanga (1881-82)
(Real = singular of Reis)
10 Tangas = 1 Rupia
100 Centavos = 1 Escudo (1959)

**Catalogue values for unused stamps in this country are for Never Hinged items, beginning with Scott 490 in the regular postage section, Scott J43 in the postage due section, and Scott RA6 in the postal tax section.**

Expect Nos. 1-55, 70-112 to have rough perforations. Stamps frequently were cut apart because of the irregular and missing perforations. Scissor separations that do not remove perfs do not negatively affect value.

Numeral of Value
A1 A2

A1: Large figures of value.
"REIS" in Roman capitals. "S" and "R" of "SERVICO" smaller and "E" larger than the other letters. 33 lines in background. Side ornaments of four dashes.
A2: Large figures of value.
"REIS" in block capitals. "S," "E" and "R" same size as other letters of "SERVICO." 44 lines in background. Side ornaments of five dots.

### Handstamped from a Single Die
***Perf. 13 to 18 & Compound***

**1871, Oct. 1** **Unwmk.**

**Thin Transparent Brittle Paper**

| | | | | |
|---|---|---|---|---|
| **1** | A1 | 10r black | 625.00 | 325.00 |
| **2** | A1 | 20r dk carmine | 1,350 | 300.00 |
| *a.* | | 20r orange vermilion | 1,350. | 300.00 |
| **3** | A1 | 40r Prus blue | 475.00 | 325.00 |
| **4** | A1 | 100r yellow grn | 550.00 | 375.00 |
| **5** | A1 | 200r ocher yel | 850.00 | 450.00 |

**1872**

**Thick Soft Wove Paper**

| | | | | |
|---|---|---|---|---|
| **5A** | A1 | 10r black | *1,500.* | 350.00 |
| **6** | A1 | 20r dk carmine | *1,650.* | 400.00 |
| **7** | A1 | 20r orange ver | *1,800.* | 400.00 |
| **7A** | A1 | 100r yellow grn | | — |
| **8** | A1 | 200r ocher yel | *1,700.* | 1,000. |
| **9** | A1 | 300r dp red violet | | *2,250.* |

The 600r and 900r of type A1 are bogus.
See Nos. 24-28. For surcharges see Nos. 70-71, 73, 83, 94, 99, 104, 108.

***Perf. 12½ to 14½ & Compound***

**1872**

| | | | | |
|---|---|---|---|---|
| **10** | A2 | 10r black | 260.00 | 100.00 |
| **11** | A2 | 20r vermilion | 225.00 | 85.00 |
| *a.* | | "20" omitted | | *1,000.* |
| **12** | A2 | 40r blue | 70.00 | 60.00 |
| *a.* | | Tête bêche pair | *5,750.* | *5,750.* |
| *b.* | | 40r dark blue | 85.00 | 60.00 |
| **13** | A2 | 100r deep green | 70.00 | 60.00 |
| **14** | A2 | 200r yellow | 275.00 | 250.00 |
| **15** | A2 | 300r red violet | 275.00 | 225.00 |
| *a.* | | Imperf. | | |
| **16** | A2 | 600r red violet | 175.00 | 140.00 |
| *a.* | | "600" double | *700.00* | |
| **17** | A2 | 900r red violet | 200.00 | 175.00 |
| | | *Nos. 10-17 (8)* | 1,550. | 1,095. |

An unused 100r blue green exists with watermark of lozenges and gray burelage on back. Experts believe it to be a proof.

**White Laid Paper**

| | | | | |
|---|---|---|---|---|
| **18** | A2 | 10r black | 37.50 | 32.50 |
| *a.* | | Tête bêche pair | *14,000.* | *8,500.* |
| *b.* | | 10r brownish black | 37.50 | 30.00 |
| **19** | A2 | 20r vermilion | 35.00 | 27.50 |
| **20** | A2 | 40r blue | 70.00 | 57.50 |
| *a.* | | "40" double | — | |
| *b.* | | Tête bêche pair | — | — |
| **21** | A2 | 100r green | 62.50 | 45.00 |
| *a.* | | "100" double | *450.00* | |
| **22** | A2 | 200r yellow | 175.00 | 175.00 |
| | | *Nos. 18-22 (5)* | 380.00 | 337.50 |

See No. 23. For surcharges see Nos. 72, 82, 95-96, 100-101, 105-106, 109-110.

**1873**

### Re-issues

**Thin Bluish Toned Paper**

| | | | | |
|---|---|---|---|---|
| **23** | A2 | 20r vermilion | 200.00 | 160.00 |
| **24** | A1 | 10r black | 14.00 | 8.50 |
| *a.* | | "1" inverted | 125.00 | 100.00 |
| *b.* | | "10" double | 400.00 | |
| **25** | A1 | 20r vermilion | 17.00 | 11.50 |
| *a.* | | "20" double | 400.00 | |
| *b.* | | "20" inverted | | |
| **26** | A1 | 300r dp violet | 110.00 | 85.00 |
| *a.* | | "300" double | 475.00 | |
| **27** | A1 | 600r dp violet | 140.00 | 100.00 |
| *a.* | | "600" double | 575.00 | |
| *b.* | | "600" inverted | 575.00 | |
| **28** | A1 | 900r dp violet | 140.00 | 100.00 |
| *a.* | | "900" double | 675.00 | |
| *b.* | | "900" triple | 1,000. | |
| | | *Nos. 23-28 (6)* | 621.00 | 465.00 |

Nos. 23 to 26 are re-issues of Nos. 11, 5A, 7, and 9. The paper is thinner and harder than that of the 1871-72 stamps and slightly transparent. It was originally bluish white but is frequently stained yellow by the gum.

A3

A4

A3: Same as A1 with small figures.
A4: Same as A2 with small figures.

**1874**

**Thin Bluish Toned Paper**

| | | | | |
|---|---|---|---|---|
| **29** | A3 | 10r black | 35.00 | 27.50 |
| *a.* | | "10" and "20" superimposed | 475.00 | *450.00* |
| **30** | A3 | 20r vermilion | 550.00 | 350.00 |
| *a.* | | "20" double | | *625.00* |

For surcharge see No. 84.

**1875**

| | | | | |
|---|---|---|---|---|
| **31** | A4 | 10r black | 37.50 | 22.50 |
| *a.* | | Value sideways | | 550.00 |
| **32** | A4 | 15r rose | 12.50 | 9.00 |
| *a.* | | "15" inverted | 475.00 | |
| *b.* | | "15" double | | |
| *c.* | | Value omitted | 1,150. | |
| **33** | A4 | 20r vermilion | 70.00 | 42.50 |
| *a.* | | "0" missing | 850.00 | 575.00 |
| *b.* | | "20" sideways | *850.00* | |
| *c.* | | "20" double | | |
| | | *Nos. 31-33 (3)* | 120.00 | 74.00 |

For surcharges see Nos. 74, 78, 85.

A5

A6

A5: Re-cutting of A1.
Small figures. "REIS" in Roman capitals. Letters larger. "V" of "SERVICO" barred. 33 lines in background. Side ornaments of five dots.
A6: First re-cutting of A2.
Small figures. "REIS" in block capitals. Letters re-cut. "V" of "SERVICO" barred. 41 lines above and 43 below "REIS." Side ornaments of five dots.

***Perf. 12½ to 13½ & Compound***

**1876**

| | | | | |
|---|---|---|---|---|
| **34** | A5 | 10r black | 20.00 | 14.00 |
| **35** | A5 | 20r vermilion | 16.00 | 11.50 |
| *a.* | | "20" double | | — |
| **36** | A6 | 10r black | 6.25 | 4.25 |
| *a.* | | Double impression | 525.00 | |
| *b.* | | "10" double | 525.00 | |
| **37** | A6 | 15r rose | 425.00 | 325.00 |
| *a.* | | "15" omitted | — | *1,000.* |
| **38** | A6 | 20r vermilion | 22.50 | 17.00 |
| **39** | A6 | 40r blue | 110.00 | 85.00 |
| **40** | A6 | 100r green | 160.00 | 150.00 |
| *a.* | | Imperf. | | |
| **41** | A6 | 200r yellow | 950.00 | 675.00 |
| **42** | A6 | 300r violet | 550.00 | 450.00 |
| *a.* | | "300" omitted | | |
| **43** | A6 | 600r violet | *800.00* | *675.00* |
| **44** | A6 | 900r violet | *1,000.* | *750.00* |
| *a.* | | "900" omitted | | |

For surcharges see Nos. 75-76, 78C-80, 86-87, 91-92, 98, 102, 107, 111.

A7

A8

A9

A7: Same as A5 with addition of a star above and a bar below the value.
A8: Second re-cutting of A2. Same as A6 but 41 lines both above and below "REIS." Star above and bar below value.
A9: Third re-cutting of A2. 41 lines above and 38 below "REIS." Star above and bar below value. White line around central oval.

**1877**

| | | | | |
|---|---|---|---|---|
| **45** | A7 | 10r black | 30.00 | 25.00 |
| **46** | A8 | 10r black | 42.50 | 37.50 |
| **47** | A9 | 10r black | 29.00 | 25.00 |
| *a.* | | "10" omitted | | |
| **48** | A9 | 15r rose | 32.50 | 27.50 |
| **49** | A9 | 20r vermilion | 8.50 | 8.00 |
| **50** | A9 | 40r blue | 17.00 | 16.00 |
| *a.* | | "40" omitted | 42.50 | 35.00 |
| **51** | A9 | 100r green | 70.00 | 60.00 |
| *a.* | | "100" omitted | | |
| **52** | A9 | 200r yellow | 75.00 | 70.00 |
| **53** | A9 | 300r violet | 100.00 | 85.00 |
| **54** | A9 | 600r violet | 100.00 | 85.00 |
| **55** | A9 | 900r violet | 100.00 | 85.00 |
| | | *Nos. 45-55 (11)* | 604.50 | 524.00 |

No. 47, 20r, 40r and 200r exist imperf.
For surcharges see Nos. 77, 81, 88-90, 93, 112.

Portuguese Crown — A10

**1877, July 15** **Typo.** ***Perf. 12½, 13½***

| | | | | |
|---|---|---|---|---|
| **56** | A10 | 5r black | 5.00 | 3.50 |
| **57** | A10 | 10r yellow | 9.00 | 7.25 |
| *a.* | | Imperf. | | |
| **58** | A10 | 20r bister | 9.50 | 7.00 |
| **59** | A10 | 25r rose | 10.00 | 8.00 |
| **60** | A10 | 40r blue | 14.00 | 11.00 |
| *a.* | | Perf. 12½ | 175.00 | 140.00 |
| **61** | A10 | 50r yellow grn | 32.50 | 20.00 |
| **62** | A10 | 100r lilac | 16.00 | 11.50 |
| **63** | A10 | 200r orange | 22.50 | 17.00 |
| **64** | A10 | 300r yel brn | 29.00 | 25.00 |
| | | *Nos. 56-64 (9)* | 147.50 | 110.25 |

**1880-81**

| | | | | |
|---|---|---|---|---|
| **65a** | A10 | 10r green | 10.00 | 8.50 |
| **66** | A10 | 25r slate | 37.50 | 27.50 |
| **67a** | A10 | 25r violet | 27.50 | 20.00 |
| **68a** | A10 | 40r yellow | 32.50 | 25.00 |
| **69a** | A10 | 50r dk blue | 17.00 | 15.00 |
| | | *Nos. 65a-69a (5)* | 124.50 | 96.00 |

The 1880-81 issue exists perf 12½ and 13½ on thin paper, and 13½ on medium paper. Nos. 65a-69a above are the most common varieties. For detailed listings, see the *Scott Classic Specialized Catalogue.*

*The stamps of the 1877-81 issues were reprinted in 1885, on stout very white paper, ungummed and with rough perforation 13½. They were again reprinted in 1905 on thin white paper with shiny white gum and clean-cut perforation 13½ with large holes. Value of the lowest-cost reprint, $3 each.*

For surcharges see Nos. 113-161.

### Stamps of 1871-77 Surcharged with New Values

Black Surcharge

**1881**

| | | | | |
|---|---|---|---|---|
| **70** | A1 | 1½r on 20r (#2) | | *1,000.* |
| **71** | A1 | 1½r on 20r (#7) | | *900.00* |
| **72** | A2 | 1½r on 20r (#11) | | *600.00* |
| **73** | A1 | 1½r on 20r (#25) | 225.00 | 200.00 |
| **74** | A4 | 1½r on 20r (#33) | 140.00 | 125.00 |
| *a.* | | Inverted surcharge | | 250.00 |
| **75** | A5 | 1½r on 20r (#35) | 110.00 | 85.00 |
| **76** | A6 | 1½r on 20r (#38) | 125.00 | 110.00 |
| **77** | A9 | 1½r on 20r (#49) | 200.00 | 140.00 |
| **78** | A4 | 5r on 15r (#32) | 2.50 | 2.50 |
| *a.* | | Double surcharge | 10.00 | |
| *b.* | | Inverted surcharge | 10.00 | |
| **78C** | A6 | 5r on 15r (#37) | 2.50 | 2.50 |
| **79** | A5 | 5r on 20r (#35) | 2.50 | |
| *a.* | | Double surcharge | 14.00 | |
| *b.* | | Inverted surcharge | — | |
| **80** | A6 | 5r on 20r (#38) | 2.75 | 2.50 |
| *a.* | | Double surcharge | — | |
| *b.* | | Inverted surcharge | — | |
| **81** | A9 | 5r on 20r (#49) | 5.00 | 4.00 |
| *a.* | | Double surcharge | — | |
| *b.* | | Invtd. surcharge | — | |

**Red Surcharge**

| | | | | |
|---|---|---|---|---|
| **82** | A2 | 5r on 10r (#18) | *175.00* | *350.00* |
| **83** | A1 | 5r on 10r (#24) | *525.00* | *300.00* |
| **84** | A3 | 5r on 10r (#29) | *1,750.* | |
| **85** | A4 | 5r on 10r (#31) | *125.00* | *125.00* |
| **86** | A5 | 5r on 10r (#34) | 6.00 | 6.00 |
| *a.* | | Double surcharge | 17.00 | |
| **87** | A6 | 5r on 10r (#36) | 9.50 | 7.75 |
| *a.* | | Inverted surcharge | | |
| **88** | A7 | 5r on 10r (#45) | 90.00 | 50.00 |
| *a.* | | Inverted surcharge | 175.00 | |
| **89** | A8 | 5r on 10r (#46) | 190.00 | 82.50 |
| **90** | A9 | 5r on 10r (#47) | 40.00 | 35.00 |
| *a.* | | Inverted surcharge | 82.50 | |
| *b.* | | Double surcharge | 82.50 | |

### Similar Surcharge, Handstamped

Black Surcharge

**1883**

| | | | | |
|---|---|---|---|---|
| **91** | A5 | 1½r on 10r (#34) | 1,650. | *825.00* |
| **92** | A6 | 1½r on 10r (#36) | 1,100. | *825.00* |
| **93** | A9 | 1½r on 10r (#47) | *825.00* | *600.00* |
| **94** | A1 | 4½r on 40r (#3) | 2,200. | *775.00* |
| **95** | A2 | 4½r on 40r (#12) | 35.00 | 35.00 |
| **96** | A2 | 4½r on 40r (#20) | 35.00 | 35.00 |
| **98** | A6 | 4½r on 40r (#39) | 35.00 | 35.00 |
| **99** | A1 | 4½r on 100r (#4) | 2,200. | *775.00* |
| **100** | A2 | 4½r on 100r (#13) | 45.00 | 42.50 |
| **101** | A2 | 4½r on 100r (#21) | 45.00 | 42.50 |
| **102** | A6 | 4½r on 100r (#40) | 40.00 | 42.50 |
| **104** | A1 | 6r on 100r (#4) | 2,200. | *1,200.* |
| **105** | A2 | 6r on 100r (#13) | 375.00 | *275.00* |
| **106** | A2 | 6r on 100r (#21) | *275.00* | *225.00* |
| **107** | A6 | 6r on 100r (#40) | *350.00* | *275.00* |
| **108** | A1 | 6r on 200r (#5) | *825.00* | *600.00* |
| **109** | A2 | 6r on 200r (#14) | | *275.00* |
| **110** | A2 | 6r on 200r (#22) | *275.00* | *275.00* |
| **111** | A6 | 6r on 200r (#41) | | *450.00* |
| **112** | A9 | 6r on 200r (#52) | *550.00* | *500.00* |

### Stamps of 1877-81 Surcharged in Black

**1881-82**

| | | | | |
|---|---|---|---|---|
| **113** | A10 | 1½r on 5r blk | 1.40 | 1.10 |
| *a.* | | With additional surcharge "4½" in blue | 125.00 | 110.00 |
| **114** | A10 | 1½r on 10r grn | 1.40 | 1.10 |
| *a.* | | With additional surch. "6" | 160.00 | 110.00 |
| **115** | A10 | 1½r on 20r bis | 11.50 | 8.75 |
| *a.* | | Inverted surcharge | 27.50 | |
| *b.* | | Double surcharge | 27.50 | |
| *c.* | | Pair, one without surcharge | — | |
| **116** | A10 | 1½r on 25r slate | 40.00 | 35.00 |
| **117** | A10 | 1½r on 100r lil | 60.00 | 47.50 |
| **118** | A10 | 4½r on 10r grn | 190.00 | 160.00 |
| **119** | A10 | 4½r on 20r bis | 4.00 | 2.75 |
| *a.* | | Inverted surcharge | 82.50 | 65.00 |

**120** A10 4½r on 25r vio 11.50 11.00
**121** A10 4½r on 100r lil 225.00 160.00
**122** A10 6r on 10r yel 47.50 45.00
**123** A10 6r on 10r grn 10.00 8.00
**124** A10 6r on 20r bis 17.00 15.00
**125** A10 6r on 25r slate 35.00 27.50
**126** A10 6r on 25r vio 2.25 1.75
**127** A10 6r on 40r blue 82.50 70.00
**128** A10 6r on 40r yel 42.50 35.00
**129** A10 6r on 50r grn 47.50 38.50
**130** A10 6r on 50r blue 110.00 90.00
*Nos. 113-130 (18)* 939.05 757.95

Surcharged in Black

**131** A10 1t on 10r grn 450.00 325.00
*a.* With additional surch. "6" 875.00 775.00
**132** A10 1t on 20r bis 47.50 42.50
**133** A10 1t on 25r slate 35.00 30.00
**134** A10 1t on 25r vio 13.00 9.00
**135** A10 1t on 40r blue 19.00 17.50
**136** A10 1t on 50r grn 55.00 47.50
**137** A10 1t on 50r blue 25.00 19.00
**138** A10 1t on 100r lil 24.00 13.00
**139** A10 1t on 200r org 47.50 42.50
**140** A10 2t on 25r slate 35.00 35.00
*a.* Small "T" 55.00 40.00
**141** A10 2t on 25r vio 14.00 11.50
**142** A10 2t on 40r blue 42.50 35.00
**143** A10 2t on 40r yel 52.50 42.50
**144** A10 2t on 50r grn 15.00 13.00
*a.* Inverted surcharge 110.00 100.00
**145** A10 2t on 50r blue 90.00 75.00
**146** A10 2t on 100r lil 11.50 9.25
**147** A10 2t on 200r org 40.00 35.00
**148** A10 2t on 300r brn 35.00 30.00
**149** A10 4t on 10r grn 14.00 11.50
*a.* Inverted surcharge 45.00 45.00
**150** A10 4t on 50r grn 13.00 10.00
*a.* With additional surch. "2" 160.00 110.00
**151** A10 4t on 200r org 40.00 36.00
**152** A10 8t on 20r bis 35.00 24.00
**153** A10 8t on 25r rose 190.00 160.00
**154** A10 8t on 40r blue 47.50 40.00
**155** A10 8t on 100r lil 40.00 35.00
**156** A10 8t on 200r org 35.00 30.00
**157** A10 8t on 300r brn 47.50 40.00
*Nos. 131-157 (27)* 1,513. 1,217.

**1882**

**Blue Surcharge**

**158** A10 4½r on 5r black 12.00 10.50

Similar Surcharge, Handstamped

**1883**

**159** A10 1½r on 5r black 55.00 35.00
**160** A10 1½r on 10r grn 82.50 45.00
**161** A10 4½r on 100r lil *400.00 325.00*

The "2" in "½" is 3mm high, instead of 2mm as on Nos. 113, 114 and 121.

The handstamp is known double on #159-161.

A12

**1882-83** **Typo.**

**With or Without Accent on "E" of "REIS"**

**162** A12 1½r black .55 .45
*a.* "½" for "1½"
**163** A12 4½r olive bister .95 .45
**164** A12 6r green .80 .45
**165** A12 1t rose .80 .45
**166** A12 2t blue .80 .45
**167** A12 4t lilac 3.25 2.75
**168** A12 8t orange 3.25 2.75
*Nos. 162-168 (7)* 10.40 7.75

There were three printings of the 1882-83 issue. The first had "REIS" in thick letters with acute accent on the "E." The second had "REIS" in thin letters with accent on the "E." The third had the "E" without accent. In the first printing the "E" sometimes had a grave or circumflex accent.

The third printing may be divided into two sets, with or without a small circle in the cross of the crown.

Stamps doubly printed or with value omitted, double, inverted or misplaced are printer's waste.

*Nos. 162-168 were reprinted on thin white paper, with shiny white gum and clean-cut perforation 13½. Value of lowest-cost reprint, $1 each.*

"REIS" no serifs — A13

"REIS" with serifs — A14

**1883** **Litho.** ***Imperf.***

**169** A13 1½r black 1.40 1.10
*a.* Tête bêche pair
*b.* "1½" double *425.00 325.00*
**170** A13 4½r olive grn 14.00 11.00
*a.* "4½" omitted 350.00 275.00
**171** A13 6r green 14.00 11.00
*a.* Tête bêche pair 1,200.
*b.* "6" omitted 400.00 300.00
**172** A14 1½r black 95.00 55.00
*a.* "1½" omitted 350.00 325.00
**173** A14 6r green 62.50 47.50
*a.* "6" omitted 425.00 350.00
*Nos. 169-173 (5)* 186.90 125.60

Nos. 169-171 exist with unofficial perf. 12.

King Luiz — A15

King Carlos — A16

***Perf. 12½, 13½***

**1886, Apr. 29** **Embossed**

**174** A15 1½r black 2.50 1.40
*a.* Perf. 13½ 110.00 70.00
**175** A15 4½r bister 3.25 1.50
*a.* Perf. 13½ 30.00 14.00
**176** A15 6r dp green 4.50 1.75
*a.* Perf. 13½ 35.00 15.00
**177** A15 1t brt rose 6.50 3.00
**178** A15 2t deep blue 8.75 4.50
**179** A15 4t gray vio 11.00 4.50
**180** A15 8t orange 10.00 4.75
*Nos. 174-180 (7)* 46.50 21.40

For surcharges and overprints see Nos. 224-230, 277-278, 282, 317-323, 354, 397.

*Nos. 178-179 were reprinted. Originals have yellow gum. Reprints have white gum and clean-cut perforation 13½. Value, $4 each.*

**1895-96** **Typo.** ***Perf. 11½, 12½, 13½***

**181** A16 1½r black 1.40 .65
**182** A16 4½r pale orange 1.40 .65
*a.* Perf. 13½ 8.00 1.60
**183** A16 6r green 1.40 .65
*a.* Perf. 12½ 3.00 1.10
**184** A16 9r gray lilac 4.25 3.00
**185** A16 1t lt blue 1.40 .55
*a.* Perf. 12½ 5.50 2.50
**186** A16 2t rose 1.00 .65
*a.* Perf. 12½ 4.25 2.25
**187** A16 4t dk blue 1.60 .80
*a.* Perf. 12½ 5.25 3.25
**188** A16 8t brt violet 3.25 2.75
*Nos. 181-188 (8)* 15.70 9.70

For surcharges and overprints see Nos. 231-238,275-276, 279-281, 324-331, 352.

*No. 184 was reprinted. Reprints have white gum, and clean-cut perforation 13½. Value $10.*

Common Design Types pictured following the introduction.

**Vasco da Gama Issue**

Common Design Types

**1898, May 1** **Engr.** ***Perf. 14 to 15***

**189** CD20 1½r blue green 1.00 .90
**190** CD21 4½r red 1.00 .90
**191** CD22 6r red violet 1.00 .75
**192** CD23 9r yellow green 1.00 1.00
**193** CD24 1t dk blue 1.60 1.60
**194** CD25 2t violet brn 2.25 1.90
**195** CD26 4t bister brn 2.25 1.90
**196** CD27 8t bister 4.50 4.00
*Nos. 189-196 (8)* 14.60 12.95

For overprints and surcharges see Nos. 290-297, 384-389.

King Carlos — A17

**1898-1903** **Typo.** ***Perf. 11½***

**Name and Value in Black except No. 219**

**197** A17 1r gray ('02) .35 .20
**198** A17 1½r orange .35 .25
**199** A17 1½r slate ('02) .45 .25
**200** A17 2r orange ('02) .35 .25
**201** A17 2½r yel brn ('02) .45 .25
**202** A17 3r dp blue ('02) .45 .25
**203** A17 4½r lt green .70 .55
**204** A17 6r brown .70 .55
**205** A17 6r gray grn ('02) .45 .25
**206** A17 9r dull vio .80 .55
*a.* 9r gray lilac 1.75 1.75
**208** A17 1t sea green .80 .50
**209** A17 1t car rose ('02) .60 .25
**210** A17 2t blue 1.40 .55
*a.* Perf. 13½ 30.00 7.75
**211** A17 2t brown ('02) 3.25 2.10
**212** A17 2½t dull bl ('02) 11.00 6.50
**213** A17 4t blue, *blue* 3.25 2.25
**214** A17 5t brn, *straw* ('02) 4.50 2.10
**215** A17 8t red lil, *pnksh* 5.50 1.40
**216** A17 8t red vio, *pink* ('02) 5.00 3.00
**217** A17 12t blue, *pink* 6.50 2.25
**218** A17 12t grn, *pink* ('02) 5.00 3.25
**219** A17 1rp blk & red, *bl* 10.00 6.50
**220** A17 1rp dl bl, *straw* ('02) 11.00 7.25
**221** A17 2rp vio, *yelsh* 14.50 8.25
**222** A17 2rp gray blk, *straw* ('03) 17.00 12.00
*Nos. 197-222 (25)* 104.35 61.50

Several stamps of this issue exist without value or with value inverted but they are not known to have been issued in this condition. The 1r and 6r in carmine rose are believed to be color trials.

For surcharges and overprints see Nos. 223, 239-259, 260C-274, 283-289, 300-316, 334-350, 376-383, 390-396, 398-399.

No. 210 Surcharged in Black

**1900**

**223** A17 1½r on 2t blue 4.50 1.10
*a.* Inverted surcharge
*b.* Perf. 13½ 35.00 22.50

Stamps of 1885-96 Surcharged in Black or Red

On Stamps of 1886

**1902** ***Perf. 12½, 13½***

**224** A15 1r on 2t blue 1.10 .50
**225** A15 2r on 4½r bis .65 .50
*a.* Inverted surcharge *22.50 22.50*
*b.* Double surcharge
**226** A15 2½r on 6r green .55 .25
**227** A15 3r on 1t rose .55 .25
**228** A15 2½t on 1½r blk (R) 2.25 1.40
**229** A15 2½t on 4t gray vio 3.25 1.40
**230** A15 5t on 8t orange 2.25 .65
*a.* Perf. 12½ 27.50 17.00

**On Stamps of 1895-96**

***Perf. 11½, 12½, 13½***

**231** A16 1r on 6r green .50 .25
**232** A16 2r on 8t brt vio .35 .25
**233** A16 2½r on 9r gray vio .35 .35
**234** A16 3r on 4½r yel 1.75 1.00
*a.* Inverted surcharge 24.00 24.00
**235** A16 3r on 1t bl 1.40 .90
**236** A16 2½t on 1½r blk (R) 2.25 .80
**237** A16 5t on 2t rose 2.25 .80
*a.* Perf. 12½ 35.00 22.50
**238** A16 5t on 4t dk bl 2.25 .80
*a.* Perf. 12½ 35.00 22.50
*Nos. 224-238 (15)* 21.70 10.10

*Nos. 224, 229, 231, 233, 234, 235 and 238 were reprinted in 1905. They have whiter gum than the originals and very clean-cut perf. 13½. Value $2.50 each.*

Nos. 204, 208, 210 Overprinted

**1902** ***Perf. 11½***

**239** A17 6r brown 2.25 1.40
*a.* Inverted overprint

**240** A17 1t sea green 3.25 1.40
**241** A17 2t blue 2.75 1.40
*a.* Perf. 13½ 150.00 100.00
*Nos. 239-241 (3)* 8.25 4.20

No. 212 Surcharged in Black

**1905**

**243** A17 2t on 2½t dull blue 2.25 1.60

Stamps of 1898-1903 Overprinted in Lisbon in Carmine or Green

**1911**

**244** A17 1r gray .20 .20
*a.* Inverted overprint 11.00 11.00
**245** A17 1½r slate .20 .20
*a.* Double overprint 11.00 11.00
**246** A17 2r orange .25 .20
*a.* Double overprint 15.00 15.00
*b.* Inverted overprint 11.00 11.00
**247** A17 2½r yellow brn .25 .20
**248** A17 3r deep blue .25 .20
**249** A17 4½r light green .35 .20
**250** A17 6r gray green .20 .20
**251** A17 9r gray lilac .35 .20
**252** A17 1t car rose (G) .35 .20
**253** A17 2t brown .35 .20
**254** A17 4t blue, *blue* 1.40 1.00
**255** A17 5t brn, *straw* 1.40 1.00
**256** A17 8t vio, *pink* 4.25 2.50
**257** A17 12t grn, *pink* 4.50 2.50
**258** A17 1rp dl bl, *straw* 5.75 4.75
**259** A17 2rp gray blk, *straw* 8.75 7.50
*Nos. 244-259 (16)* 28.80 21.25

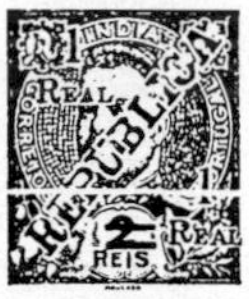

A18

Values are for pairs, both halves.

**1911** **Perforated Diagonally**

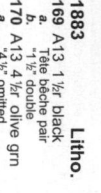

**260** A18 1r on 2r orange .80 .70
*a.* Without diagonal perf. 4.50 4.00
*b.* Cut diagonally instead of perf. 3.50 3.25

Stamps of Preceding Issues Perforated Vertically through the Middle and Each Half Surcharged with New Value:

a

b

Values are for pairs, both halves of the stamp.

**1912-13**

**On Issue of 1898-1903**

**260C** A17(a) 1r on 2r org .25 .20
**261** A17(a) 1r on 1t car .25 .20
**262** A17(a) 1r on 5t brn, *straw* 275.00 225.00
**263** A17(b) 1r on 5t brn, *straw* 7.75 6.00
**264** A17(a) 1½r on 2½r yel brn .75 .65
**264C** A17(a) 1½r on 4½r lt grn 12.00 7.75
**265** A17(a) 1½r on 9r gray lil .55 .45
**266** A17(a) 1½r on 4t bl, *bl* .55 .45
**267** A17(a) 2r on 2½r yel brn .70 .45
**268** A17(a) 2r on 4t bl, *bl* 1.00 .70
**269** A17(a) 3r on 2½r yel brn .70 .45
**270** A17(a) 3r on 2t brown .70 .50
**271** A17(a) 6r on 4½r lt grn .70 .60
**272** A17(a) 6r on 9r gray lil .70 .55
**273** A17(a) 6r on 9r dull vio 4.50 3.50
**274** A17(b) 6r on 8t red vio, *pink* 1.60 1.00

**Vasco da Gama and Flagship — A22**

## 1925, Jan. 30    Litho.    Without Gum
411 A22 6r brown — 5.00 3.25
412 A22 1t red violet — 7.00 5.00

400th anniv. of the death of Vasco da Gama (1469?-1524), Portuguese navigator.

Image of St. Francis — A25

Monument to St. Francis — A23

Autograph of St. Francis A24

Image of St. Francis — A26

Tomb of St. — A28

Church of Bom Jesus at Goa — A27

## 1931, Dec. 3    *Perf. 14*
| | | | |
|---|---|---|---|
| 414 | A23 | 1r gray green | .55 .50 |
| 415 | A24 | 2r brown | .55 .50 |
| 416 | A25 | 2r red violet | 1.60 .65 |
| 417 | A26 | 1½t yellow brn | 5.75 3.50 |
| 418 | A27 | 2t deep blue | 7.00 4.25 |
| 419 | A28 | 2½t light red | 11.50 4.25 |
| | | *Nos. 414-419 (6)* | 26.95 13.55 |

Exposition of St. Francis Xavier at Goa, in December, 1931.

**Nos. 371 and 404 Surcharged**

## 1931-32    *Perf. 15x14, 12x11½*
420 A21 1½r on 8t plum (32) 1.50 1.10
423 A21 2t on 3t4r yel brn 65.00 50.00

"Portugal" and Vasco da Gama's Flagship "San Gabriel" — A29

---

**382 A17 3r on 4½r yel** — 82.50 55.00
**383 A17 3r on 2rp rose (G)** 82.50 55.00
     straw 7.75 3.00
     3r on 2rp gray blk, 7.75 4.25

There are 3 varieties of the "2" in "1½." Nos. 376-377 exist with inverted surcharge.

**Vasco da Gama Issue Surcharged in Black**

## 1913-15
334 A17 1t sea green 15.00 5.00
335 A17 2t blue 15.00 6.00

This overprint was applied to No. 239 without official authorization.

**On Issue of 1912-13 Perforated through the Middle**

Values are for pairs, both halves of the stamp.

| | | | |
|---|---|---|---|
| 336 | A17(a) | 1r on 2r org | 17.00 11.00 |
| 340 | A17(a) | 1r on 4½r lt grn | 17.00 11.00 |
| 341 | A17(a) | 1½r on 9r gray lil | 20.00 |
| 342 | A17(a) | 1½r on 4t bl, *bl* | 27.50 |
| 343 | A17(a) | 2r on 2½r yel brn | |
| 344 | A17(a) | 2r on 4t, bl, *bl* | 20.00 |
| 345 | A17(a) | 3r on 2½r yel brn | 27.50 7.25 |
| 346 | A17(a) | 3r on 2t brn | 22.50 |
| 347 | A17(a) | 6r on 4t lt grn | 17.00 5.25 |
| 348 | A17(b) | 6r on 9r gray lil | 1.10 .90 |
| 350 | A17(b) | 6r on 8t red vio, *pink* | 1.60 1.60 |
| 352 | A16(b) | 1r on 5t on 4t bl | 1.60 |
| 354 | A15(a) | 2r on 2½r on 6r grn | 110.00 |
| | | | 325.80 49.60 |
| | | *Nos. 334-354 (15)* | 13.00 |

The 1r on 5t (A15), 1r on 1t (A17), 1½r on 2½r (A17), 3r on 5t on 8t (A15), and 6r on 9r (A17) were clandestinely printed. Nos. 336, 347 exist with inverted surcharge. Some authorities question the status of Nos. 341-345, 352 and 354.

Ceres — A21

## 1913-21    Typo.    *Perf. 12x11½, 15x14*
**Name and Value in Black**
| | | | |
|---|---|---|---|
| 357 | A21 | 1r olive brn | .35 .25 |
| 358 | A21 | 1½r yellow grn | .35 .25 |
| a. | | *imperf.* | |
| 359 | A21 | 2r black | .40 .35 |
| 360 | A21 | 2½r olive grn | .40 .45 |
| 361 | A21 | 3r lilac | .40 .20 |
| 362 | A21 | 4½r orange brn | .40 .20 |
| 363 | A21 | 5r blue green | .70 .50 |
| 364 | A21 | 6r lilac brown | .60 .25 |
| 365 | A21 | 9r ultra | .95 .55 |
| 366 | A21 | 10r carmine | .45 .25 |
| 367 | A21 | 1t violet | .95 .45 |
| 368 | A21 | 2t deep blue | 1.90 .95 |
| 369 | A21 | 3t yellow brown | .95 .95 |
| 370 | A21 | 4t slate | 2.25 1.25 |
| 371 | A21 | 8t plum | 4.50 4.00 |
| 372 | A21 | 12t brown, *green* | 4.00 3.25 |
| 373 | A21 | 1rp brown, *pink* | 24.00 17.50 |
| 374 | A21 | 2rp org, *salmon* | 15.00 12.00 |
| 375 | A21 | 3rp green, *blue* | 22.50 17.00 |
| | | *Nos. 357-375 (19)* | 80.50 59.75 |

The 1, 2, 2½, 3, 4½r, 1, 2, and 4t exist with the black inscriptions inverted and the 2½t with them double, one inverted, but it is not known that any of these were regularly issued. For surcharges see Nos. 400, 420, 423.

**390 A17 1½r on 4½r grn** — 45.00 22.50
**a. "REPUBLICA" omitted** 77.50 47.50
**b. "REPUBLICA" inverted** 82.50
**391 A17 1½r on 9r gray lil** 14.00 8.25
**a. "REPUBLICA" omitted** 35.00
**392 A17 1½r on 12t grn, *pink*** 1.40 1.10
**396 A17 3r on 2½t gray blk,**
     *straw* 55.00 22.50
     *Nos. 390-396 (4)* 115.40 54.35

Nos. 390, 390a, 390b, 391, and 391a were not regularly issued. The 3r on 2½r (A17) was surcharged without official authorization.

**Preceding Issues Overprinted in Carmine**

## 1915
397 A15 5t on 8t org — 2.75 1.50

**On No. 230**
398 A17 2t blue 2.25 1.40
399 A17 2t on 2½t dl bl 2.75 1.40
     *Nos. 397-399 (3)* 7.75 4.30

**No. 359 Surcharged in Carmine**

## 1922
400 A21 1½r on 2r black .55 .45

## 1922-25    Ceres Type of 1913-21    Typo.    *Perf. 12x11½*
**Name and Value in Black**
| | | | |
|---|---|---|---|
| 401 | A21 | 4r blue | 1.40 1.25 |
| 402 | A21 | 1½t gray green | 1.40 .95 |
| 403 | A21 | 2t turq blue | 1.50 1.25 |
| 404 | A21 | 3t yellow brn | |
| 405 | A21 | 4t gray (25) | 5.50 4.50 |
| 406 | A21 | 4t dull rose | 2.25 1.25 |
| 407 | A21 | 1rp gray brn | 7.75 5.50 |
| 408 | A21 | 2rp deep grn | 17.50 17.00 |
| 409 | A21 | 3rp bluish grn | 25.00 45.00 |
| 410 | A21 | 5rp carmine rose | 35.00 65.00 |
| | | *Nos. 401-410 (10)* | 137.30 251.70 |

**Nos. 249, 251-253, 256-259 Surcharged in Black**

## 1914
| | | | |
|---|---|---|---|
| 376 | A17 | 1½r on 4½r grn | .35 .25 |
| 377 | A17 | 1½r on 9r gray lil | .45 .35 |
| 378 | A17 | 1½r on 12t grn, *pink* | .45 .40 |
| 379 | A17 | 3r on 2t brn | |
| 380 | A17 | 3r on 8t red vio, *pink* | 3.25 2.75 |
| 381 | A17 | 3r on 8t red vio, *pink* | 2.50 2.25 |

---

## On Nos. 237-238, 230, 226, 233
| | | | |
|---|---|---|---|
| 275 | A16(b) | 1r on 5t on 4t | 20.00 17.00 |
| 291 | CD21 | 1r on 5t on 4t | 9.25 |
| | | 1r on 5t on 8t | 5.00 3.25 |
| 277 | A15(b) | 1r on 5t on 8t | 4.25 3.25 |
| 278 | A15(a) | 2r on 2½r on 6r | 25.00 24.00 |
| 279 | A16(a) | 2r on 2½r on 9r | 7.75 6.25 |
| 280 | A16(b) | 3r on 5t on 4t | 7.75 6.25 |
| 281 | A16(b) | 3r on 5t on 4t | 2.50 1.60 |
| 282 | A15(b) | 3r on 5t on 8t | |

The 2½r on 1½r on 1½r and A16, the 3r on 1t (A15) and 2½r on 9r (A16) were clandestinely printed.

## On Issue of 1911
| | | | |
|---|---|---|---|
| 283 | A17(a) | 1r on 1r gray | .25 .25 |
| 283B | A17(a) | 1r on 2r org | .25 .25 |
| 284 | A17(a) | 1r on 1t car | .35 .25 |
| 285 | A17(a) | 1r on 5t brn, *straw* | .35 .25 |
| 285A | A17(b) | 1r on 4½r lt grn | 825.00 550.00 |
| 286 | A17(b) | 1½r on 4½r lt grn | .65 .50 |
| 289 | A17(a) | 3r on 2t brn | 11.50 8.50 |
| | | 3r on 9r gray | .55 .45 |

There are several settings of these surcharges and many minor varieties of the letters and figures, notably a small "6." Nos. 260-289 were issued mostly without gum. More than half of Nos. 260C-289 exist with inverted double surcharge, or with bisecting perforation omitted. The legitimacy of these varieties is questioned. Price of inverted surcharges, $3-$15; double surcharges, $1-$4; perf. omitted, $1.50-$15. Similar surcharges made without official authorization on stamps of type A17 are: 2r on 2½r, 3r on 2½r, 3r on 5t, and 6r on 4½r.

**Vasco da Gama Issue Overprinted**

## 1913
| | | | |
|---|---|---|---|
| 290 | CD20 | 1½r blue green | .25 .25 |
| 291 | CD21 | 1½r red | .35 .25 |
| a. | | Double overprint | 22.50 |
| 292 | CD22 | 6r red violet | .45 .40 |
| a. | | Double overprint | 22.50 |
| 293 | CD23 | 9r yellow grn | .45 .40 |
| 294 | CD24 | 1t dark blue | 1.00 .55 |
| 295 | CD25 | 2t violet brown | 2.25 1.25 |
| 296 | CD26 | 4t orange brn | 2.25 1.00 |
| 297 | CD27 | 8t bister | 1.40 5.50 |
| | | *Nos. 290-297 (8)* | 0.55 |

**Issues of 1898-1913 Overprinted Locally in Red**

## 1913-15
**On Issues of 1898-1903**
| | | | |
|---|---|---|---|
| 300 | A17 | 2r orange | 10.00 10.00 |
| 301 | A17 | 2r orange | .95 .80 |
| 302 | A17 | 3r dp blue | 19.00 17.00 |
| 303 | A17 | 4½r lt green | 1.90 1.60 |
| 304 | A17 | 6r gray grn | 25.00 20.00 |
| 305 | A17 | 9r gray lilac | 1.90 1.40 |
| 306 | A17 | 1t sea green | 45.00 35.00 |
| 307 | A17 | 2t blue | 40.00 35.00 |
| 309 | A17 | 4t blue, *blue* | 45.00 27.50 |
| 310 | A17 | 5t brn, *straw* | 55.00 35.00 |
| 311 | A17 | 8t red vio, *pink* | 65.00 45.00 |
| 312 | A17 | 12t grn, *pink* | 3.50 2.50 |
| 313 | A17 | 1rp blk, *straw* | 100.00 82.50 |
| 314 | A17 | 1rp dl bl, *straw* | 65.00 45.00 |
| 315 | A17 | 2rp gray blk, *straw* | 82.50 55.00 |
| 316 | A17 | 2rp vio, *yelsh* | 77.50 45.00 |
| | | *Nos. 300-316 (16)* | 642.25 458.30 |

Inverted or double overprints exist on 2½r, 4½r, 9r, 1rp and 2rp. Nos. 300-316 were issued without gum except 4½r and 9r. Nos. 302, 304, 306, 307, 310, 311 and 313 were not regularly issued. Nor were the 1½r, 2t brown and 12t blue on pink with preceding overprint.

**Same Overprint in Red or Green**
**On Provisional Issue of 1902**
| | | | |
|---|---|---|---|
| 317 | A15 | 1r on 2t blue | 45.00 27.50 |
| a. | | "REPUBLICA" inverted | 140.00 |
| 318 | A15 | 2r on 4½r bis | 45.00 27.50 |
| a. | | "REPUBLICA" inverted | 140.00 |
| 319 | A15 | 2½r on 6r grn | .75 .65 |
| 320 | A15 | 1t rose (R) | 19.00 8.75 |
| 321 | A15 | 2½t gray vio | 11.00 45.00 |
| 323 | A15 | 5t on 8t org (G) | 11.00 22.50 |
| | | | 27.50 |
| 324 | A16 | 1r on 6r grm | 35.00 22.50 |
| 325 | A16 | 1r on 8t org | 35.00 22.50 |
| a. | | Inverted surcharge | 110.00 |

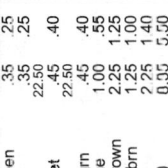

**REPUBLICA 1½ REIS**

## 1913-15
**Same Overprint on Nos. 240-241**
| | | | |
|---|---|---|---|
| 334 | A17 | 1t sea green | 5.00 |
| 335 | A17 | 2t blue | 6.00 |
|     | | *straw* | 11.50 |

**Vasco da Gama Issue Surcharged in Black**
| | | | |
|---|---|---|---|
| 384 | CD21 | 1½r on 4½r red | .40 .35 |
| 385 | CD23 | 1½r on 9r yel grn | .50 .35 |
| 386 | CD24 | 3r on 2t vio brn | .40 .50 |
| 387 | CD25 | 3r on 2t vio brn | .60 .50 |
| 388 | CD26 | 3r on 4t org brn | .35 1.25 |
| 389 | CD27 | 3r on 8t bister | 1.40 10.95 |
| | | *Nos. 376-389 (14)* | 13.30 |

Double, inverted and other surcharge varieties exist on Nos. 384-386, 389.

**Stamps of 1898-1903 Surcharged in Red**

**1933** *Perf. 11½x12* **Typo.** **Wmk. 232**

| | | | | |
|---|---|---|---|---|
| **424** | A29 | 1r bister | .20 | .20 |
| **425** | A29 | 2r olive brn | .20 | .20 |
| **426** | A29 | 4r violet | .20 | .20 |
| **427** | A29 | 6r dk green | .20 | .20 |
| **428** | A29 | 8r black | .20 | .20 |
| **429** | A29 | 1t gray | .25 | .20 |
| **430** | A29 | 1½t dp rose | .35 | .20 |
| **431** | A29 | 2t brown | .40 | .20 |
| **432** | A29 | 2½t dk blue | 2.25 | .45 |
| **433** | A29 | 3t brt blue | 2.50 | .45 |
| **434** | A29 | 5t red orange | 2.50 | .45 |
| **435** | A29 | 1rp olive grn | 11.00 | 3.25 |
| **436** | A29 | 2rp maroon | 27.50 | 7.50 |
| **437** | A29 | 3rp orange | 40.00 | 8.75 |
| **438** | A29 | 5rp apple grn | 55.00 | 25.00 |
| | | *Nos. 424-438 (15)* | 142.75 | 47.45 |

For surcharges see Nos. 454-463, 472-474, J34-J36.

Common Design Types

*Perf. 13½x13*

**1938, Sept. 1** **Engr.** **Unwmk.**

**Name and Value in Black**

| | | | | |
|---|---|---|---|---|
| **439** | CD34 | 1r gray grn | .20 | .20 |
| **440** | CD34 | 2r orange brn | .20 | .20 |
| **441** | CD34 | 3r dk vio brn | .20 | .20 |
| **442** | CD34 | 6r brt green | .20 | .20 |
| **443** | CD35 | 10r dk carmine | .35 | .25 |
| **444** | CD35 | 1t brt red vio | .55 | .25 |
| **445** | CD35 | 1½t red | .90 | .25 |
| **446** | CD37 | 2t orange | .90 | .25 |
| **447** | CD37 | 2½t blue | .90 | .25 |
| **448** | CD37 | 3t slate | 1.75 | .35 |
| **449** | CD36 | 5t rose vio | 2.75 | .50 |
| **450** | CD36 | 1rp brown car | 4.50 | .90 |
| **451** | CD36 | 2rp olive grn | 7.75 | 2.75 |
| **452** | CD38 | 3rp blue vio | 13.00 | 6.50 |
| **453** | CD38 | 5rp red brown | 22.50 | 3.50 |
| | | *Nos. 439-453 (15)* | 56.65 | 16.55 |

For surcharges see Nos. 492-495, 504-505.

Stamps of 1933 Surcharged in Black

1 tanga

**1941, June** **Wmk. 232** *Perf. 11½x12*

| | | | | |
|---|---|---|---|---|
| **454** | A29 | 1t on 1½t dp rose | 2.25 | 1.50 |
| **455** | A29 | 1t on 1rp olive grn | 2.25 | 1.50 |
| **456** | A29 | 1t on 2rp maroon | 2.25 | 1.50 |
| **457** | A29 | 1t on 5rp apple grn | 2.25 | 1.50 |
| | | *Nos. 454-457 (4)* | 9.00 | 6.00 |

Nos. 430-431 Surcharged

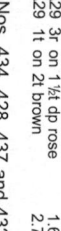

3
RÉIS

**1943**

| | | | | |
|---|---|---|---|---|
| **458** | A29 | 3r on 1½t dp rose | 1.60 | .80 |
| **459** | A29 | 1t on 2t brown | 2.75 | 2.25 |

Nos. 434, 428, 437 and 432 Surcharged in Dark Blue or Carmine

1
REAL

a

6
Réis

b

**1945-46** **Wmk. 232** *Perf. 11½x12*

| | | | | |
|---|---|---|---|---|
| **460** | A29(a) | 1r on 5t red org (DB) | .70 | .50 |
| **461** | A29(b) | 2r on 8r blk (C) | .55 | .45 |
| **462** | A29(b) | 3r on 3rp org (DB) ('46) | 1.50 | 1.40 |
| **463** | A29(b) | 6r on 2½t dk bl (C) | 1.60 | 1.60 |
| | | *Nos. 460-463 (4)* | 4.35 | 3.95 |

St. Francis Xavier A30

Luis de Camoens A31

Garcia de Orta — A32

St. John de Britto — A33

Arch of the Viceroy A34

Affonso de Albuquerque A35

Vasco da Gama — A36

Francisco de Almeida — A37

*Perf. 11½*

**1946, May 28** **Litho.** **Unwmk.**

| | | | | |
|---|---|---|---|---|
| **464** | A30 | 1r black & gray blk | .50 | .25 |
| **465** | A31 | 2r rose brn & pale rose brn | .50 | .25 |
| **466** | A32 | 6r ocher & dl yel | .50 | .25 |
| **467** | A33 | 7r vio & pale vio | 2.25 | *6.50* |
| **468** | A34 | 9r sepia & buff | 2.25 | .55 |
| **469** | A35 | 1t dk sl grn & sl grn | 2.25 | .55 |
| **470** | A36 | 3½t ultra & pale ultra | 2.50 | 1.25 |
| **471** | A37 | 1rp choc & bis brn | 5.50 | 1.50 |
| *a.* | | Miniature sheet of 8, #464-471 | 21.00 | 21.00 |
| | | *Nos. 464-471 (8)* | 16.25 | 11.10 |

No. 471a sold for 1½ rupias.

See #476. For surcharges see #595, J43-J46.

No. 428, 431 and 433 Surcharged in Carmine or Black

1
Real

**1946** **Wmk. 232** *Perf. 11½x12*

| | | | | |
|---|---|---|---|---|
| **472** | A29 (c) | 1r on 8r blk (C) | .65 | .55 |
| **473** | A29 (b) | 3r on 2t brn | .65 | .60 |
| **474** | A29 (b) | 6r on 3t brt bl | 2.25 | 1.90 |
| | | *Nos. 472-474 (3)* | 3.55 | 3.05 |

Type of 1946 and

Joao de Castro — A38

José Vaz — A39

Luis de Ataide — A40

Duarte Pacheco Pereira — A41

**1948** **Unwmk.** **Litho.** *Perf. 11½*

| | | | | |
|---|---|---|---|---|
| **475** | A38 | 3r brt ultra & lt bl | 1.00 | .55 |
| **476** | A30 | 1t dk grn & yel grn | 1.40 | .65 |
| **477** | A39 | 1½t dk pur & dl vio | 2.25 | 1.25 |
| **478** | A40 | 2½t brt ver | 2.50 | 1.75 |
| **479** | A41 | 7½t dk brn & org brn | 4.50 | 2.50 |
| *a.* | | Miniature sheet of 5 | 21.00 | 21.00 |
| | | *Nos. 475-479 (5)* | 11.65 | 6.70 |

No. 476 measures 21x31mm.

No. 479a measures 106x146mm. and contains one each of Nos. 475-479. Marginal inscriptions in gray. The sheet sold for 16 tangas (1 rupia).

For surcharge see No. 591.

**Lady of Fatima Issue**

Common Design Type

**1948** *Perf. 14½*

| | | | | |
|---|---|---|---|---|
| **480** | CD40 | 1t dk blue green | 2.50 | 2.25 |

Our Lady of Fatima A42

UPU Symbols A42a

**1949** **Litho.** *Perf. 14*

| | | | | |
|---|---|---|---|---|
| **481** | A42 | 1r blue | .80 | .55 |
| **482** | A42 | 3r orange yel | .80 | .55 |
| **483** | A42 | 9r dk car rose | 1.40 | .75 |
| **484** | A42 | 2t green | 3.50 | 1.90 |
| **485** | A42 | 9t orange red | 4.25 | 1.40 |
| **486** | A42 | 2rp dk vio brn | 7.00 | 3.00 |
| **487** | A42 | 5rp olive grn | 15.00 | 5.00 |
| **488** | A42 | 8rp violet blue | 35.00 | 13.00 |
| | | *Nos. 481-488 (8)* | 67.75 | 26.15 |

Our Lady of the Rosary at Fatima, Portugal.

**1949, Oct.**

| | | | | |
|---|---|---|---|---|
| **489** | A42a | 2½t scarlet & pink | 2.50 | 1.60 |

UPU, 75th anniversary.

**Catalogue values for unused stamps in this section, from this point to the end of the section, are for Never Hinged items.**

**Holy Year Issue**

Common Design Types

**1950, May** *Perf. 13x13½*

| | | | | |
|---|---|---|---|---|
| **490** | CD41 | 1r olive bister | .65 | .60 |
| **491** | CD42 | 2t dk gray green | 1.10 | .60 |

See Nos. 496-503.

No. 443 Surcharged in Black

1 Real

**1950** *Perf. 13½x13*

| | | | | |
|---|---|---|---|---|
| **492** | CD35 | 1r on 10r dk car | .25 | .25 |
| **493** | CD35 | 2r on 10r dk car | .25 | .25 |

**Similar Surcharge on No. 447 in Black or Red**

| | | | | |
|---|---|---|---|---|
| **494** | CD37 | 1r on 2½t blue | .25 | .25 |
| **495** | CD37 | 3r on 2½t blue (R) | .25 | .25 |
| | | *Nos. 492-495 (4)* | 1.00 | 1.00 |

Letters with serifs, small (lower case) "r" in "real" and "réis."

**Holy Year Issue**

Common Design Types

**1951** **Litho.** *Perf. 13½*

| | | | | |
|---|---|---|---|---|
| **496** | CD41 | 1r dp car rose | .25 | .25 |
| **497** | CD41 | 2r emerald | .35 | .25 |
| **498** | CD42 | 3r red brown | .35 | .25 |
| **499** | CD41 | 6r gray | .40 | .40 |
| **500** | CD42 | 9r brt pink | .80 | .70 |
| **501** | CD41 | 1t blue violet | .55 | .50 |
| **502** | CD42 | 2t yellow | .95 | .60 |
| **503** | CD41 | 4t violet brown | .95 | .60 |
| | | *Nos. 496-503 (8)* | 4.60 | 3.55 |

No. 447 with Surcharge Similar to Nos. 492-493 in Red

**1951** *Perf. 13½x13*

| | | | | |
|---|---|---|---|---|
| **504** | CD37 | 6r on 2½t blue | .35 | .35 |
| **505** | CD37 | 1t on 2½t blue | .25 | .25 |

Letters with serifs, small (lower case) "r" in "réis."

**Holy Year Extension Issue**

Common Design Type

**1951** **Litho.** *Perf. 14*

| | | | | |
|---|---|---|---|---|
| **506** | CD43 | 1rp bl vio & pale vio + label | 1.60 | .65 |

Stamp without label sells for less.

José Vaz — A43

Ruins of Sancoale Church — A44

Design: 12t, Altar.

**1951** **Litho.** *Perf. 14½*

**Dated: "1651-1951"**

| | | | | |
|---|---|---|---|---|
| **507** | A43 | 1r Prus bl & pale bl | .25 | .20 |
| **508** | A44 | 2r ver & red brn | .25 | .20 |
| **509** | A43 | 3r gray blk & gray | .55 | .25 |
| **510** | A44 | 1t vio bl & ind | .25 | .20 |
| **511** | A43 | 2t dp cl & cl | .40 | .20 |
| **512** | A44 | 3t ol grn & blk | .55 | .20 |
| **513** | A43 | 9t indigo & ultra | .70 | .45 |
| **514** | A44 | 10t lilac & vio | 1.10 | .55 |
| **515** | A44 | 12t blk brn & brn | 1.90 | .80 |
| | | *Nos. 507-515 (9)* | 5.95 | 3.05 |

300th anniversary of the birth of José Vaz.

**Medical Congress Issue**

Common Design Type

Design: Medical School, Goa.

**1952** **Unwmk.** *Perf. 13½*

| | | | | |
|---|---|---|---|---|
| **516** | CD44 | 4½t blk & lt blue | 3.25 | 1.75 |

## St. Francis Xavier Issue

Statue of Saint Francis Xavier — A44a

**1952, Oct. 25  Litho.  Perf. 14**
| | | | |
|---|---|---|---|
| 517 | A44a | 6r aqua & multi | .25 .20 |
| 518 | A44a | 2t cream & multi | 2.25 .60 |
| 519 | A44a | 5t pink & silver | 4.00 1.40 |
| | | Nos. 517-519 (3) | 6.50 2.20 |

### Souvenir Sheets
**Perf. 13**
| | | | |
|---|---|---|---|
| 520 | A45 | 9t brn & dk brn | 11.00 11.00 |
| 521 | A46 | 12t Sheet of 2 | 11.00 11.00 |
| a. | | 4t orange buff & black | 3.25 3.25 |
| b. | | 8t slate & black | 3.25 3.25 |

A45

St. Francis Xavier and his Tomb, Goa — A46

Designs: 2t, Miraculous Arm of St. Francis. 4t, 5t, Tomb of St. Francis.

400th anniv. of the death of St. Francis Xavier.

Numeral A47

**1952, Dec. 4  Litho.  Perf. 13½**
| | | | |
|---|---|---|---|
| 522 | A47 | 3t black | 8.75 8.75 |
| 523 | A48 | 5t dk violet & blk | 8.75 8.75 |
| a. | | Strip of 2 + label | 19.00 19.00 |

Issued to publicize Portuguese India's first stamp exhibition, Goa, 1952.
No. 523a consists of a tête bêche pair of Nos. 522-523 separated by a label publicizing the exhibition.

---

Statue of Virgin Mary — A49

**1953, Jan.**
| | | | |
|---|---|---|---|
| 524 | A49 | 6r dk & lt blue | .20 .20 |
| 525 | A49 | 1t brown & buff | .80 .55 |
| 526 | A49 | 3t dk pur & pale ol | 3.75 2.15 |
| | | Nos. 524-526 (3) | |

Exhibition of Sacred Missionary Art held at Lisbon in 1951.
For surcharge see No. 594.

### Stamp Centenary Issue
**1953  Typo.**
| | | | |
|---|---|---|---|
| 527 | A49a | 1t multicolored | .90 .70 |

Centenary of Portugal's first postage stamps.

Stamp of Portugal and Arms of Colonies — A49a

---

Map of Bassein by Pedro Barreto de Resendo, 1635 — A55

Portraits: 9r, Affonso de Albuquerque. 1t, Vasco da Gama. 1½t, Filipe Nery Xavier. 3t, Nuno da Cunha. 4t, Agostino Vicente Lourenco. 8t, Jose Vaz. 9t, Manuel Godinho de Heredia. 10t, Joao de Castro. 2rp, Antonio Caetano Pacheco. 3rp, Constantino de Braganca.
Maps of ancient forts, drawn in 1635: 2½t, Mombaim (Bombay). 3½t, Damao (Daman). 5t, Diu. 12t, Cochin. 1rp, Goa.

Inscribed: "450 Aniversario da Fundacao do Estado da India 1505-1955."

**Perf. 11½x12 (A53), 14½ (A54), 12½ (A55)**

**1956, Mar. 24**

Unwmk.
| | | | |
|---|---|---|---|
| 534 | A54 | 3r multicolored | .20 .20 |
| 535 | A54 | 6r multicolored | .20 .20 |
| 536 | A53 | 6r multicolored | .35 .35 |
| 537 | A53 | 1t multicolored | .35 .35 |
| 538 | A54 | 1½t multicolored | .20 .20 |
| 539 | A54 | 2t multicolored | 2.10 1.50 |
| 540 | A54 | 2½t multicolored | 1.40 1.00 |
| 541 | A55 | 3t multicolored | .35 .35 |
| 542 | A54 | 3½t multicolored | 1.50 1.00 |
| 543 | A54 | 4t multicolored | .45 .45 |
| 544 | A54 | 5t multicolored | .65 .45 |
| 545 | A54 | 8t multicolored | .55 .45 |
| 546 | A54 | 9t multicolored | .55 .45 |
| 547 | A53 | 10t multicolored | .55 .45 |
| 548 | A55 | 1rp multicolored | 1.25 .90 |
| 549 | A55 | 1rp multicolored | 1.50 1.50 |
| 550 | A54 | 2rp multicolored | 2.10 1.25 |
| 551 | A53 | 3rp multicolored | 2.75 1.60 |
| | | Nos. 534-551 (18) | 17.50 12.20 |

Portuguese settlements in India, 450th anniv.
For surcharges see Nos. 575-577, 579-581, 592.

---

C. A. da Gama Pinto, Ophthalmologist and Author, Birth Cent. — A50

**1954, Apr. 10  Litho.  Perf. 11½**
| | | | |
|---|---|---|---|
| 528 | A50 | 3r gray & ol grn | .25 .20 |
| 529 | A50 | 2t black & gray blk | .20 .20 |

### São Paulo Issue
Common Design Type
**1954, Oct. 2  Unwmk.  Perf. 13½**
| | | | |
|---|---|---|---|
| 530 | CD46 | 2t dk Prus bl, bl & blk | .25 .25 |

For surcharge see No. 593.

Affonso de Albuquerque School — A51

**1955, Feb. 26**
| | | | |
|---|---|---|---|
| 531 | A51 | 9t multicolored | .95 .65 |

Centenary (in 1954) of the founding of the Affonso de Albuquerque National School.

Msgr. Sebastiao Rodolfo Dalgado — A52

**1955, Nov. 15  Unwmk.  Perf. 13½**
| | | | |
|---|---|---|---|
| 532 | A52 | 1r multicolored | .20 .20 |
| 533 | A52 | 1t multicolored | .55 .25 |

Birth cent. of Msgr. Sebastiao Rodolfo Dalgado.

St. Francis Xavier A48

---

Arms of Vasco da Gama — A57

Map of Damao and Nagar Aveli — A56

**1957  Litho.  Perf. 11½**
### Map and Inscriptions in Black, Red, Ocher and Blue
| | | | |
|---|---|---|---|
| 552 | A56 | 3r gray & buff | .20 .20 |
| 553 | A56 | 6r bl grn & pale lem | .20 .20 |
| 554 | A56 | 3t pink & lt gray | .20 .20 |
| 555 | A56 | 6t blue | .40 .40 |
| 556 | A56 | 1t ol bis & lt vio gray | .80 .60 |
| 557 | A56 | 2rp lt vio & pale gray | 1.90 1.25 |
| 558 | A56 | 3rp citron & pink | 2.25 1.60 |
| 559 | A56 | 5rp magenta & pink | 2.50 1.90 |
| | | Nos. 552-559 (8) | 8.45 6.35 |

For surcharges see Nos. 571, 578, 584-585, 588-590.

### Arms in Original Colors
Inscriptions in Black and Red
**1958, Apr. 3  Unwmk.  Perf. 13x13½**
| | | | |
|---|---|---|---|
| 560 | A57 | 2r buff & ocher | .20 .20 |
| 561 | A57 | 6r gray & ocher | .20 .20 |
| 562 | A57 | 9r pale blue & emer | .20 .20 |
| 563 | A57 | 1t pale citron & brn | .40 .20 |
| 564 | A57 | 4t pale bl grn & lil | .45 .25 |
| 565 | A57 | 5t buff & blue | .55 .35 |
| 566 | A57 | 11t pink & lt brn | .70 .45 |
| 567 | A57 | 1rp pale grn & maroon | 1.10 .65 |
| | | Nos. 560-567 (8) | 3.80 2.45 |

For surcharges see Nos. 570, 572-574, 582-583, 586-587.

---

Exhibition Emblem and View — A58

**1958, Dec. 15  Litho.  Perf. 14½**
| | | | |
|---|---|---|---|
| 568 | A58 | 1rp multicolored | .55 .55 |

World's Fair, Brussels, Apr. 17-Oct. 19.
For surcharge see No. 597.

### Tropical Medicine Congress Issue
Common Design Type
Design: Holarrhena antidysenterica.
**1958, Dec. 15  Perf. 13½**
| | | | |
|---|---|---|---|
| 569 | CD47 | 5t gray, brn, grn & red | 1.10 .75 |

For surcharge see No. 596.

### Stamps of 1955-58 Surcharged with New Values and Bars

**1959, Jan. 1  Litho.  Unwmk.**
| | | | |
|---|---|---|---|
| 570 | A57 | 5c on 2r | .20 .20 |
| 571 | A56 | 10c on 3r multi | .20 .20 |
| 572 | A57 | 15c on 6r | .20 .20 |
| 573 | A57 | 20c on 9r | .20 .20 |
| 574 | A57 | 30c on 1t | .20 .20 |
| 575 | A55 | 40c on 2½t | .80 .35 |
| 576 | A55 | 40c on 2½t (#540) | .80 .35 |
| 577 | A55 | 40c on 3½t (#542) | .35 .20 |
| 578 | A56 | 50c on 3t | .20 .20 |
| 579 | A53 | 80c on 3t (#541) | .80 .80 |
| 580 | A53 | 80c on 3rp (#551) | 1.60 .95 |
| 581 | A53 | 80c on 3rp (#551) | 1.60 .35 |
| 582 | A57 | 1e on 4t | .25 .25 |
| 583 | A57 | 1.50e on 5t | .65 .90 |
| 584 | A56 | 2e on 6t | .65 .35 |
| 585 | A56 | 2.50e on 11t | .90 .90 |
| 586 | A57 | 4e on 11t | 1.10 1.10 |
| 587 | A57 | 4.50e on 1rp | 1.10 .55 |
| 588 | A56 | 10e on 2rp (#557) | 2.25 1.60 |
| 589 | A56 | 10e on 3rp (#558) | 2.25 1.60 |
| 590 | A56 | 30e on 5rp (#559) | 5.00 2.70 |
| | | Nos. 570-590 (21) | 18.05 10.40 |

Arms of Prince Henry — A60

### Types of 1946-1958 Surcharged with New Values, Old Values Obliterated
**1959  Litho.  Unwmk.**
| | | | |
|---|---|---|---|
| 591 | A39 | 40c on 1½t dl pur | .65 .20 |
| 592 | A54 | 40c on 1½t multi | .65 .20 |
| 593 | CD46 | 80c on 2t bl & gray | 1.10 .80 |
| 594 | A49 | 80c on 3t blk & pale clt | |
| 595 | A36 | 80c on 3½t blk bl | .65 .20 |
| 596 | CD47 | 80c on 5t gray, brn, grn & red | .80 .20 |
| 597 | A58 | 80c on 1rp multi | .80 .45 |
| | | Nos. 591-597 (7) | |

Coin, Manuel I — A59

Various Coins from the Reign of Manuel I (1495-1521) to the Republic.

**1959, Dec. 1  Litho.  Unwmk.**
### Inscriptions in Black and Red
| | | | |
|---|---|---|---|
| 598 | A59 | 5c lt bl & gold | .20 .20 |
| 599 | A59 | 10c pale brn & gold | .20 .20 |
| 600 | A59 | 15c pale grn & gray | .20 .20 |
| 601 | A59 | 30c salmon & gray | .20 .20 |
| 602 | A59 | 40c pale yel & gray | .20 .20 |
| 603 | A59 | 50c lilac & gray | .20 .20 |
| 604 | A59 | 60c pale yel grn & gray | .25 .20 |
| 605 | A59 | 80c lt bl & gray | .20 .20 |
| 606 | A59 | 1e ocher & gray | .20 .20 |
| 607 | A59 | 1.50e blue & gray | .20 .20 |
| 608 | A59 | 2e pale bl & gold | .20 .20 |
| 609 | A59 | 2.50e pale gray & gold | .25 .20 |
| 610 | A59 | citron & gray | .35 .20 |
| 611 | A59 | 4e pink & gray | .50 .20 |
| 612 | A59 | 4.40e pale bis & vio brn | .60 .35 |
| 613 | A59 | 5e pale dl vio & gray | .75 .45 |
| 614 | A59 | 10e brt yel & gray | 1.10 .75 |
| 615 | A59 | 20e beige & gray | 2.50 1.75 |

| | | Unused | Used |
|---|---|---|---|
| 616 | A59 | 30e brt yel grn & lt cop brn | 2.75 | 2.75 |
| 617 | A59 | 50e lt gray & gray | 4.50 | 4.50 |
| 618 | A60 | 3e multicolored | .55 | .55 |
| | | Nos. 598-617 (20) | 15.65 | 13.35 |

**1960, June 25**  Perf. 13½

500th anniversary of the death of Prince Henry the Navigator.

Portugal continued to print special-issue stamps for its lost colony after its annexation by India Dec. 18, 1961. Stamps of India were first used on Dec. 29. Stamps of Portuguese India remained valid until Jan. 5, 1962.

## AIR POST STAMPS

Common Design Type

**1938, Sept. 1   Engr.   Perf. 13½x13**
Name and Value in Black    Unwmk.

| | | | Unused | Used |
|---|---|---|---|---|
| C1 | CD39 | 1t red orange | .55 | .25 |
| C2 | CD39 | 2½t purple | .65 | .25 |
| C3 | CD39 | 3½t orange | .65 | .25 |
| C4 | CD39 | 4½t orange | 1.60 | .45 |
| C5 | CD39 | 7t ultra | 1.75 | .80 |
| C6 | CD39 | 7½t lilac brown | 2.50 | .80 |
| C7 | CD39 | 9t dark green | 4.50 | 1.25 |
| C8 | CD39 | 11t magenta | 5.00 | 1.25 |
| | | Nos. C1-C8 (8) | 17.20 | 5.05 |

No. C4 exists with overprint "Exposicao Internacional de Nova York, 1939-1940" "Esposicao" and Periphere. Value, unused $90, never hinged $125.

## POSTAGE DUE STAMPS

D1 — 2 REIS

**1904    Name and Value in Black**
Unwmk.    Typo.    Perf. 11½

| | | | Unused | Used |
|---|---|---|---|---|
| J1 | D1 | 2r gray green | .50 | .35 |
| J2 | D1 | 3r yellow grn | .50 | .35 |
| J3 | D1 | 4r orange | .50 | .45 |
| J4 | D1 | 5r slate | .50 | .50 |
| J5 | D1 | 6r gray | .50 | .50 |
| J6 | D1 | 6r yellow brn | .80 | .50 |
| J7 | D1 | 9r yellow brn | .55 | .55 |
| J8 | D1 | 1t red orange | 2.25 | .80 |
| J9 | D1 | 2t gray brown | 3.25 | 1.60 |
| J10 | D1 | 5t dull blue | 7.75 | 3.50 |
| J11 | D1 | 1rp carmine | 13.00 | 3.50 |
| | | Nos. J1-J11 (11) | 33.85 | 19.15 |

**1911    Overprinted**
Nos. J1-J11 Overprinted in Carmine or Green

| | | | Unused | Used |
|---|---|---|---|---|
| J12 | D1 | 2r gray grn | .20 | .20 |
| J13 | D1 | 3r yellow grn | .20 | .20 |
| J14 | D1 | 4r orange | .20 | .20 |
| J15 | D1 | 5r slate | .20 | .20 |
| J16 | D1 | 6r gray | .45 | .20 |
| J17 | D1 | 9r yellow brn | .55 | .35 |
| J18 | D1 | 1t red org | .65 | .35 |
| J19 | D1 | 2t gray brn | .90 | .55 |
| J20 | D1 | 5t dull blue | 2.25 | 1.40 |
| J21 | D1 | 1t carmine (G) | 7.75 | 3.25 |
| J22 | D1 | 1rp dull violet | 16.60 | 8.80 |
| | | Nos. J12-J22 (11) | | |

**1914**
Nos. J1-J11 Overprinted in Carmine or Green

| | | | Unused | Used |
|---|---|---|---|---|
| J23 | D1 | 2r gray grn | 1.10 | 1.10 |
| J24 | D1 | 3r yellow grn | 1.10 | 1.10 |
| J25 | D1 | 4r orange | 1.10 | 1.10 |
| J26 | D1 | 5r slate | 1.10 | 1.10 |
| J27 | D1 | 6r gray | 1.40 | 1.10 |
| J28 | D1 | 9r yellow brn | 3.25 | 1.10 |
| J29 | D1 | 1t red org | 1.10 | 1.10 |
| J30 | D1 | 2t gray brn | 3.25 | 1.10 |
| J31 | D1 | 5t dull blue | 4.50 | 2.00 |
| J32 | D1 | 10t carmine | 8.75 | 4.50 |
| J33 | D1 | 1rp dull violet | 35.00 | 8.75 |
| | | Nos. J23-J33 (11) | 95.95 | 30.70 |

D2

**1943    Wmk. 232    Perf. 11½x12**
Nos. 432, 433 and 434 Surcharged in Red or Black

| | | | Unused | Used |
|---|---|---|---|---|
| J34 | A29 | 3r on 2½t dk bl (R) | .65 | .45 |
| J35 | A29 | 6r on 3t brt bl (R) | .90 | .90 |
| J36 | A29 | 1t on 5t red org (Bk) | 1.60 | 1.60 |
| | | Nos. J34-J36 (3) | 3.45 | 2.95 |

**1945    Country Name and Denomination in Black**
Unwmk.    Typo.

| | | | Unused | Used |
|---|---|---|---|---|
| J37 | D2 | 2r brt carmine | 1.90 | 1.90 |
| J38 | D2 | 3r blue | 1.90 | 1.90 |
| J39 | D2 | 4r orange yel | 1.90 | 1.90 |
| J40 | D2 | 6r yellow grn | 1.90 | 1.90 |
| J41 | D2 | 1t bister brn | 1.90 | 1.90 |
| J42 | D2 | 2t chocolate | 11.40 | 11.40 |
| | | Nos. J37-J42 (6) | 11.40 | 11.40 |

Catalogue values for unused stamps in this section, from this point to the end of the section, are for Never Hinged items.

**1951, Jan. 1    Perf. 11½**
Nos. 467 and 471 Surcharged in Carmine or Black

| | | | Unused | Used |
|---|---|---|---|---|
| J43 | A33 | 2r on 7r vio & pale vio | .60 | .60 |
| J44 | A33 | 3r on 7r vio & pale vio | .60 | .60 |
| | | (C) | | |
| J45 | A37 | 1t on 1rp choc & bis brn | .60 | .60 |
| J46 | A37 | 2t on 1rp choc & bis brn | 2.40 | 2.40 |
| | | Nos. J43-J46 (4) | | |

Porteado 3 Reis

**1952    Numeral in Red; Frame Multicolored    Perf. 14**
Photogravure and Typographed
Common Design Type

| | | | Unused | Used |
|---|---|---|---|---|
| J47 | CD45 | 2r olive | .25 | .25 |
| J48 | CD45 | 3r black | .40 | .40 |
| J49 | CD45 | 6r dark blue | .55 | .55 |
| J50 | CD45 | 6r dk carmine | .80 | .80 |
| J51 | CD45 | 2t orange | 1.10 | 1.10 |
| J52 | CD45 | 10t violet brn | 3.00 | 3.00 |
| | | Nos. J47-J52 (6) | 6.10 | 6.10 |

**1959, Jan.    Numeral in Red; Frame Multicolored**

| | | | Unused | Used |
|---|---|---|---|---|
| J53 | CD45 | 5c on 2r olive | .20 | .20 |
| J54 | CD45 | 10c on 3r black | .35 | .45 |
| J55 | CD45 | 15c on 6r dk blue | .65 | 1.00 |
| J56 | CD45 | 60c on 2t orange | 2.25 | 2.25 |
| J57 | CD45 | 60c on 10t vio blue | 4.45 | 5.15 |
| | | Nos. J53-J57 (5) | | |

## WAR TAX STAMPS

WT1

**1919, Apr. 15    Typo.    Perf. 15x14**
Overprinted in Black or Carmine
Denomination in Black    Unwmk.

| | | | Unused | Used |
|---|---|---|---|---|
| MR1 | WT1 | 0:00:05,48p grn | 1.50 | 1.25 |
| MR2 | WT1 | 0:01:09,94p grn | 1.50 | 1.25 |
| MR3 | WT1 | 0:02:03,43p grn | 4.50 | 3.00 |
| | | (C) | | |
| MR1 | WT1 | | 4.50 | 3.00 |
| MR2 | WT1 | | 10.50 | 7.25 |
| MR3 | WT1 | | 22.50 | |
| | | Nos. MR1-MR3 (3) | | |

Some authorities consider No. MR2 a revenue stamp.

## POSTAL TAX STAMPS

Pombal Issue
Common Design Types

**1925    Unwmk.    Perf. 12½**

| | | | Unused | Used |
|---|---|---|---|---|
| RA1 | CD28 | 6r rose & black | .50 | .50 |
| RA2 | CD29 | 6r rose & black | .50 | .50 |
| RA3 | CD30 | 6r rose & black | .50 | .50 |
| | | Nos. RA1-RA3 (3) | 1.50 | 1.50 |

Mother and Child — PT1

**1948    Litho.    Perf. 11**

| | | | Unused | Used |
|---|---|---|---|---|
| RA4 | PT1 | 6r yellow green | 3.00 | 2.75 |
| RA5 | PT1 | 1t carmine | 3.00 | 2.75 |

See Nos. RA7-RA7A, RA9, RA12. For surcharge and overprint see Nos. RA6, RA8.

Catalogue values for unused stamps in this section, from this point to the end of the section, are for Never Hinged items.

**1951**

| | | | Unused | Used |
|---|---|---|---|---|
| RA6 | PT1 | 1t on 6r carmine | 3.25 | 2.25 |

Type of 1948 Surcharged with New Value and Bar in Black

**1952-53**

| | | | Unused | Used |
|---|---|---|---|---|
| RA7 | PT1 | 1t gray | 2.75 | 1.75 |
| RA7A | PT1 | 1t red orange ('53) | 3.00 | 2.10 |

Type of 1948

**1953**

| | | | Unused | Used |
|---|---|---|---|---|
| RA8 | PT1 | 1t carmine | 8.00 | 6.50 |

Type of 1948

**1954    Typo.**

| | | | Unused | Used |
|---|---|---|---|---|
| RA9 | PT1 | 6r pale bister | 4.50 | 4.25 |

No. RA5 Overprinted in Black

P.A.P.

Umā Tanga — PT2

**1956    Typo.    Perf. 11**
Mother and Child — PT2 / PT3
Surcharged in Black

| | | | Unused | Used |
|---|---|---|---|---|
| RA10 | PT2 | 1t on 4t lt blue | 12.00 | 11.00 |

**1956    Litho.    Perf. 13**
Type of 1948 Redrawn — Without Gum

| | | | Unused | Used |
|---|---|---|---|---|
| RA11 | PT3 | 1t blk, pale grn & red | 1.40 | 1.00 |
| RA12 | PT1 | 1t bluish green | 3.50 | 3.25 |

Denomination in white oval at left.
See No. RA14. For surcharges see Nos. RA13, RA15-RA16.

**1957    Perf. 13½**

| | | | Unused | Used |
|---|---|---|---|---|
| RA13 | PT3 | 6r on 1t | 1.00 | .80 |

No. RA11 Surcharged with New Value and Bars in Red

**1958    Unwmk.    Perf. 13**
Type of 1956

| | | | Unused | Used |
|---|---|---|---|---|
| RA14 | PT3 | 1t dk bl, sal & grn | .80 | .65 |

**1959, Jan.    Litho.    Perf. 13**

| | | | Unused | Used |
|---|---|---|---|---|
| RA15 | PT3 | 20c on 1t | .60 | .60 |
| RA16 | PT3 | 40c on 1t | .60 | .60 |

No. RA14 Surcharged with New Values and Four Bars

**1960    Perf. 13½**

| | | | Unused | Used |
|---|---|---|---|---|
| RA17 | PT4 | 20c brown & red | .25 | .25 |

Arms and People Seeking Help — PT4

## POSTAL TAX DUE STAMPS

Pombal Issue
Common Design Types

**1925    Unwmk.    Perf. 12½**

| | | | Unused | Used |
|---|---|---|---|---|
| RAJ1 | CD28 | 1t rose & black | .65 | .65 |
| RAJ2 | CD29 | 1t rose & black | .65 | .65 |
| RAJ3 | CD30 | 1t rose & black | 1.95 | 1.95 |
| | | Nos. RAJ1-RAJ3 (3) | | |

See note after Portugal No. RAJ4.

# PUERTO RICO

ˌpwer-tə-ˈrē-ˌkō

(Porto Rico)

LOCATION — A large island in the West Indies, east of Hispaniola
GOVT. — Former Spanish Colony
AREA — 3,435 sq. mi.
POP. — 953,243 (1899)
CAPITAL — San Juan

The island was ceded to the United States by the Treaty of 1898.

100 Centimes = 1 Peseta
1000 Milesimas = 100 Centavos = 1 Peso (1881)
100 Cents = 1 Dollar (1898)

Values for unused stamps are for examples with original gum as defined in the catalogue introduction. Very fine examples of Nos. 1-170, MR1-MR13 will have perforations clear of the design but will be noticeably poorly centered. Extremely fine examples will be well centered; these are scarce and command substantial premiums.

## Issued under Spanish Dominion

Puerto Rican stamps of 1855-73, a part of the Spanish colonial period, were also used in Cuba. They are listed as Cuba Nos. 1-4, 9-14, 18-21, 31-34, 39-41, 47-49, 51-53, 55-57.

Stamps of Cuba Overprinted in Black:

a

b

c

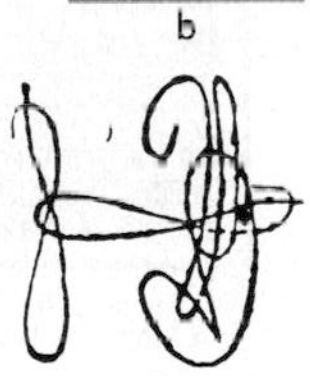
d

**1873** **Unwmk.** *Perf. 14*

| | | | | |
|---|---|---|---|---|
| 1 | A10 (a) | 25c gray | 45.00 | 1.90 |
| 2 | A10 (a) | 50c brown | 115.00 | 5.75 |
| 3 | A10 (a) | 1p red brown | 300.00 | 19.00 |
| | | *Nos. 1-3 (3)* | 460.00 | 26.65 |

**1874**

| | | | | |
|---|---|---|---|---|
| 4 | A11 (b) | 25c ultra | 37.50 | 2.50 |
| a. | | Double overprint | 210.00 | |
| b. | | Inverted overprint | 210.00 | |

**1875**

| | | | | |
|---|---|---|---|---|
| 5 | A12 (b) | 25c ultra | 27.50 | 2.75 |
| a. | | Inverted overprint | 75.00 | 45.00 |
| 6 | A12 (b) | 50c green | 35.00 | 3.00 |
| a. | | Inverted overprint | *175.00* | *87.50* |
| 7 | A12 (b) | 1p brown | 140.00 | 14.50 |
| | | *Nos. 5-7 (3)* | 202.50 | 20.25 |

**1876**

| | | | | |
|---|---|---|---|---|
| 8 | A13 (c) | 25c pale violet | 4.25 | 1.90 |
| 9 | A13 (c) | 50c ultra | 10.50 | 3.25 |
| 10 | A13 (c) | 1p black | 42.50 | 12.00 |
| 11 | A13 (d) | 25c pale vio | 35.00 | 1.40 |
| 12 | A13 (d) | 1p black | 75.00 | 11.00 |
| | | *Nos. 8-12 (5)* | 167.25 | 29.55 |

Varieties of overprint on Nos. 8-11 include: inverted, double, partly omitted and sideways. Counterfeit overprints exist.

King Alfonso XII
A5 A6

**1877** **Typo.**

| | | | | |
|---|---|---|---|---|
| 13 | A5 | 5c yellow brown | 7.25 | 2.60 |
| a. | | 5c carmine (error) | 225.00 | — |
| 14 | A5 | 10c carmine | 24.00 | 6.75 |
| a. | | 10c brown (error) | 225.00 | — |
| 15 | A5 | 15c deep green | 35.00 | 14.00 |
| 16 | A5 | 25c ultra | 15.00 | 2.40 |
| 17 | A5 | 50c bister | 24.00 | 6.00 |
| | | *Nos. 13-17 (5)* | 105.25 | 31.75 |

Dated "1878"

**1878**

| | | | | |
|---|---|---|---|---|
| 18 | A5 | 5c ol bister | 15.00 | 15.00 |
| 19 | A5 | 10c red brown | 250.00 | 85.00 |
| 20 | A5 | 25c deep green | 1.90 | 1.20 |
| 21 | A5 | 50c ultra | 6.75 | 2.60 |
| 22 | A5 | 1p bister | 12.50 | 5.75 |
| | | *Nos. 18-22 (5)* | 286.15 | 109.55 |

Dated "1879"

**1879**

| | | | | |
|---|---|---|---|---|
| 23 | A5 | 5c lake | 12.00 | 5.50 |
| 24 | A5 | 10c dark brown | 12.00 | 5.50 |
| 25 | A5 | 15c dk olive grn | 12.00 | 5.50 |
| 26 | A5 | 25c blue | 4.00 | 1.75 |
| 27 | A5 | 50c dark green | 12.00 | 5.50 |
| 28 | A5 | 1p gray | 57.50 | 25.00 |
| | | *Nos. 23-28 (6)* | 109.50 | 48.75 |

Imperforates of type A5 are from proof or trial sheets.

**1880**

| | | | | |
|---|---|---|---|---|
| 29 | A6 | ¼c deep green | 27.50 | 20.00 |
| 30 | A6 | ½c brt rose | 6.75 | 2.50 |
| 31 | A6 | 1c brown lilac | 12.00 | 10.00 |
| 32 | A6 | 2c gray lilac | 6.25 | 4.25 |
| 33 | A6 | 3c buff | 7.00 | 4.75 |
| 34 | A6 | 4c black | 7.00 | 4.75 |
| 35 | A6 | 5c gray green | 3.50 | 1.90 |
| 36 | A6 | 10c rose | 4.00 | 2.30 |
| 37 | A6 | 15c yellow brn | 7.00 | 3.50 |
| 38 | A6 | 25c gray blue | 3.50 | 1.60 |
| 39 | A6 | 40c gray | 14.00 | 1.75 |
| 40 | A6 | 50c dark brown | 29.00 | 15.50 |
| 41 | A6 | 1p olive bister | 97.50 | 21.00 |
| | | *Nos. 29-41 (13)* | 225.00 | 93.80 |

Dated "1881"

**1881**

| | | | | |
|---|---|---|---|---|
| 42 | A6 | ½m lake | .40 | .40 |
| 43 | A6 | 1m violet | .40 | .20 |
| 44 | A6 | 2m pale rose | .60 | .40 |
| 45 | A6 | 4m brt yellowish grn | 1.00 | .20 |
| 46 | A6 | 6m brown lilac | 1.00 | .60 |
| 47 | A6 | 8m ultra | 2.50 | 1.40 |
| 48 | A6 | 1c gray green | 3.25 | 1.20 |
| 49 | A6 | 2c lake | 4.50 | 3.75 |
| 50 | A6 | 3c dark brown | 10.00 | 6.25 |
| 51 | A6 | 5c grayish ultra | 3.50 | .45 |
| 52 | A6 | 8c brown | 3.50 | 1.80 |
| 53 | A6 | 10c slate | 32.50 | 9.50 |
| 54 | A6 | 20c olive bister | 37.50 | 17.50 |
| | | *Nos. 42-54 (13)* | 100.65 | 43.65 |

Alfonso XII
A7

Alfonso XIII
A8

**1882-86**

| | | | | |
|---|---|---|---|---|
| 55 | A7 | ½m rose | .30 | .20 |
| a. | | ½m salmon rose | .55 | .35 |
| 56 | A7 | ½m lake ('84) | .55 | .40 |
| 57 | A7 | 1m pale lake | .85 | 1.10 |
| 58 | A7 | 1m brt rose ('84) | .30 | .20 |
| 59 | A7 | 2m violet | .30 | .20 |
| 60 | A7 | 4m brown lilac | .30 | .20 |
| 61 | A7 | 6m brown | .45 | .20 |
| 62 | A7 | 8m yellow green | .45 | .20 |
| 63 | A7 | 1c gray green | .30 | .20 |
| 64 | A7 | 2c rose | 1.10 | .20 |
| 65 | A7 | 3c yellow | 4.00 | 2.10 |
| a. | | Cliché of 8c in plate of 3c | 120.00 | |
| 66 | A7 | 3c yellow brn ('84) | 4.00 | .85 |
| a. | | Cliché of 8c in plate of 3c | 25.00 | |
| 67 | A7 | 5c gray blue | 14.50 | 1.20 |
| 68 | A7 | 5c gray bl, 1st retouch ('84) | 14.50 | 2.75 |
| 69 | A7 | 5c gray bl, 2nd retouch ('86) | 110.00 | 5.50 |
| 70 | A7 | 8c gray brown | 3.50 | .20 |
| 71 | A7 | 10c dark green | 3.50 | .30 |
| 72 | A7 | 20c gray lilac | 5.25 | .30 |
| a. | | 20c olive brown (error) | *110.00* | |
| 73 | A7 | 40c blue | 40.00 | 14.50 |
| 74 | A7 | 80c olive bister | 55.00 | 20.00 |
| | | *Nos. 55-74 (20)* | 259.15 | 50.80 |

For differences between the original and the retouched stamps see note on the 1883-86 issue of Cuba.

**1890-97**

| | | | | |
|---|---|---|---|---|
| 75 | A8 | ½m black | .30 | .20 |
| 76 | A8 | ½m olive gray ('92) | .20 | .20 |
| 77 | A8 | ½m red brn ('94) | .20 | .20 |
| 78 | A8 | ½m dull vio ('96) | .20 | .20 |
| 79 | A8 | 1m emerald | .25 | .20 |
| 80 | A8 | 1m dk violet ('92) | .20 | .20 |
| 81 | A8 | 1m ultra ('94) | .20 | .20 |
| 82 | A8 | 1m dp brown ('96) | .20 | .20 |
| 83 | A8 | 2m lilac rose | .20 | .20 |
| 84 | A8 | 2m violet brn ('92) | .20 | .20 |
| 85 | A8 | 2m red org ('94) | .20 | .20 |
| 86 | A8 | 2m yel grn ('96) | .20 | .20 |
| 87 | A8 | 4m dk olive grn | 11.00 | 5.50 |
| 88 | A8 | 4m ultra ('92) | .20 | .20 |
| 89 | A8 | 4m yel brn ('94) | .20 | .20 |
| 90 | A8 | 4m blue grn ('96) | 1.00 | .35 |
| 91 | A8 | 6m dk brown | 35.00 | 14.00 |
| 92 | A8 | 6m pale rose ('92) | .20 | .20 |
| 93 | A8 | 8m olive bister | 27.50 | 21.00 |
| 94 | A8 | 8m yel grn ('92) | .20 | .20 |
| 95 | A8 | 1c yellow brown | .30 | .20 |
| 96 | A8 | 1c blue grn ('91) | .55 | .20 |
| 97 | A8 | 1c violet brn ('94) | 5.75 | .45 |
| 98 | A8 | 1c claret ('96) | .65 | .20 |
| 99 | A8 | 2c brownish violet | 1.00 | .85 |
| 100 | A8 | 2c red brn ('92) | .95 | .20 |
| 101 | A8 | 2c lilac ('94) | 2.25 | .45 |
| 102 | A8 | 2c org brn ('96) | .65 | .20 |
| 103 | A8 | 3c slate blue | 7.25 | 1.00 |
| 104 | A8 | 3c orange ('92) | .90 | .20 |
| 105 | A8 | 3c ol gray ('94) | 5.75 | .45 |
| 106 | A8 | 3c blue ('96) | 21.00 | .35 |
| 107 | A8 | 3c claret brn ('97) | .30 | .20 |
| 108 | A8 | 4c slate bl ('94) | 1.40 | .45 |
| 109 | A8 | 4c gray brn ('96) | .70 | .20 |
| 110 | A8 | 5c brown violet | 12.50 | .45 |
| 111 | A8 | 5c yel grn ('94) | 5.50 | 1.10 |
| 112 | A8 | 5c bl grn ('92) | .90 | .20 |
| 113 | A8 | 5c blue ('96) | .30 | .20 |
| 114 | A8 | 6c orange ('94) | .45 | .20 |
| 115 | A8 | 6c violet ('96) | .35 | .20 |
| 116 | A8 | 8c ultra | 15.00 | 1.60 |
| 117 | A8 | 8c gray brn ('92) | .20 | .20 |
| 118 | A8 | 8c dull vio ('94) | 12.00 | 4.75 |
| 119 | A8 | 8c car rose ('96) | 2.75 | 1.40 |
| 120 | A8 | 10c rose | 4.50 | 1.10 |
| a. | | 10c salmon rose | 11.00 | 2.50 |
| 121 | A8 | 10c lilac rose ('92) | 1.40 | .35 |
| 122 | A8 | 20c red orange | 5.00 | 4.50 |
| 123 | A8 | 20c lilac ('92) | 2.25 | .55 |
| 124 | A8 | 20c car rose ('94) | 1.50 | .45 |
| 125 | A8 | 20c olive gray ('96) | 6.50 | 1.40 |
| 126 | A8 | 40c orange | 160.00 | 47.50 |
| 127 | A8 | 40c slate blue ('92) | 5.50 | 3.75 |
| 128 | A8 | 40c claret ('94) | 7.25 | 12.50 |
| 129 | A8 | 40c salmon ('96) | 6.75 | 1.60 |
| 130 | A8 | 80c yellow green | 600.00 | 200.00 |
| 131 | A8 | 80c orange ('92) | 14.00 | 11.00 |
| 132 | A8 | 80c black ('97) | 26.00 | 22.50 |

Imperforates of type A8 were not issued and are variously considered to be proofs or printer's waste.

Shades of No. 129 are often mistaken for No. 120. Value for No. 120 is for expertized copies.

For overprints see Nos. 154A-170, MR1-MR13.

PUERTO - RICO
19 NOVIEMBRE
1493-1893
CENTAVOS DE PESO
Landing of Columbus on Puerto Rico — A9

Alfonso XIII — A10

**1893, Nov. 19** **Litho.** *Perf. 12*

| | | | | |
|---|---|---|---|---|
| 133 | A9 | 3c dark green | 200.00 | 50.00 |

400th anniversary, landing of Columbus on Puerto Rico.

This stamp was valid for postage for only one day and for internal use only..

Counterfeits exist.

**1898** **Typo.**

| | | | | |
|---|---|---|---|---|
| 135 | A10 | 1m orange brown | .20 | .20 |
| 136 | A10 | 2m orange brown | .20 | .20 |
| 137 | A10 | 3m orange brown | .20 | .20 |
| 138 | A10 | 4m orange brown | 1.60 | .65 |
| 139 | A10 | 5m orange brown | .20 | .20 |
| 140 | A10 | 1c black violet | .20 | .20 |
| a. | | Tête bêche pair | *1,500.* | |
| 141 | A10 | 2c dk blue green | .20 | .20 |
| 142 | A10 | 3c dk brown | .20 | .20 |
| 143 | A10 | 4c orange | 1.60 | 1.30 |
| 144 | A10 | 5c brt rose | .20 | .20 |
| 145 | A10 | 6c dark blue | .65 | .20 |
| 146 | A10 | 8c gray brown | .20 | .20 |
| 147 | A10 | 10c vermilion | .20 | .20 |
| 148 | A10 | 15c dull olive grn | .20 | .20 |
| 149 | A10 | 20c maroon | 1.90 | .60 |
| 150 | A10 | 40c violet | 1.50 | 1.60 |
| 151 | A10 | 60c black | 1.50 | 1.60 |
| 152 | A10 | 80c red brown | 5.50 | 6.00 |
| 153 | A10 | 1p yellow green | 12.00 | 12.00 |
| 154 | A10 | 2p slate blue | 27.50 | 17.50 |
| | | *Nos. 135-154 (20)* | 55.95 | 43.65 |

Nos. 135-154 exist imperf. Value, set $900.

Habilitado
PARA

Stamps of 1890-97 Handstamped in Rose or Violet

**1898**

| | | | | |
|---|---|---|---|---|
| 154A | A8 | ½m dull violet | 16.00 | 9.00 |
| 155 | A8 | 1m deep brown | 1.40 | 1.40 |
| 156 | A8 | 2m yellow green | .40 | .40 |
| 157 | A8 | 4m blue green | .40 | .40 |
| 158 | A8 | 1c claret | 4.00 | 4.00 |
| 159 | A8 | 2c orange brown | .55 | .80 |
| 160 | A8 | 3c blue | 35.00 | 15.00 |
| 161 | A8 | 3c claret brn | 2.75 | 2.75 |
| 162 | A8 | 4c gray brn | .65 | .65 |
| 163 | A8 | 4c slate blue | 19.00 | 13.50 |
| 164 | A8 | 5c yellow grn | 9.00 | 7.00 |
| 165 | A8 | 5c blue | .65 | .65 |
| 166 | A8 | 6c violet | .65 | .45 |
| 167 | A8 | 8c car rose (V) | 1.10 | .80 |
| a. | | Rose overprint | 17.50 | 17.50 |
| 168 | A8 | 20c olive gray | 1.10 | 1.10 |
| 169 | A8 | 40c salmon | 2.75 | 2.75 |
| 170 | A8 | 80c black | 35.00 | 22.50 |
| | | *Nos. 154A-170 (17)* | 130.40 | 83.15 |

As usual with handstamps there are many inverted, double and similar varieties. Counterfeits of Nos. 154A-170 abound.

## Issued under US Administration

POSTAGES
5 cts.
CORREOS
A11

CORREOS
5 CTS.
COAMO
A12

### Ponce Issue

**1898** **Unwmk.** *Imperf.*

| | | | |
|---|---|---|---|
| 200 | A11 5c vio, *yelsh* | *7,500.* | |

The only way No. 200 is known used is handstamped on envelopes. Both unused stamps and used envelopes have a violet control mark. Counterfeits exist of Nos. 200-201.

### Coamo Issue

**1898** **Unwmk.** *Imperf.*

| | | | |
|---|---|---|---|
| 201 | A12 5c black | 650.00 | 1,050. |

There are ten varieties in the setting (See the Scott United States Specialized Catalogue). The stamps bear the control mark "F. Santiago" in violet.

PORTO RICO

United States Nos. 279, 279Bf, 281, 272 and 282C Overprinted in Black at 36 degree angle

**1899** **Wmk. 191** *Perf. 12*

| | | | | |
|---|---|---|---|---|
| 210 | A87 | 1c yellow green | 5.00 | 1.40 |
| a. | | Ovpt. at 25 degree angle | 7.50 | 2.25 |
| 211 | A88 | 2c reddish car, type IV | 4.25 | 1.25 |
| a. | | Ovpt. at 25 degree angle | 5.50 | 2.25 |
| 212 | A91 | 5c blue | 12.50 | 2.50 |
| 213 | A93 | 8c violet brown | 35.00 | 17.50 |
| a. | | Ovpt. at 25 degree angle | 40.00 | 19.00 |
| c. | | "PORTO RIC" | 150.00 | 110.00 |
| 214 | A94 | 10c brown, type I | 25.00 | 6.00 |
| | | *Nos. 210-214 (5)* | 81.75 | 28.65 |

Misspellings of the overprint, actually broken letters (PORTO RICU, PORTU RICO, FORTO RICO), are found on 1c, 2c, 8c and 10c.

PUERTO RICO

United States Nos. 279 and 279B Overprinted Diagonally in Black

## POSTAGE DUE STAMPS

Stamps of Puerto Rico were replaced by those of the United States.

United States Nos. J38, J39 and J42 Overprinted in Black at 36 degree angle

**1899    Wmk. 191    Perf. 12**

| | | | | |
|---|---|---|---|---|
| J1 | D2 | 1c deep claret | 25.00 | 6.00 |
| a. | | Overprinted at 25 degree angle | 25.00 | 4.75 |
| J2 | D2 | 2c deep claret | 22.50 | 8.25 |
| a. | | Overprinted at 25 degree angle | 22.50 | 7.75 |
| J3 | D2 | 10c deep claret | 200.00 | 65.00 |
| a. | | Overprinted at 25 degree angle | 190.00 | 90.00 |
| | | Nos. J1-J3 (3) | 247.50 | 77.50 |

**1900**

| | | | | |
|---|---|---|---|---|
| 215 | A87 | 1c yellow green | 6.50 | 1.40 |
| a. | | Inverted overprint | | |
| 216 | A88 | 2c red, type IV | 4.75 | 2.00 |
| b. | | Inverted overprint | | 8,250. |

## WAR TAX STAMPS

*IMPUESTO DE GUERRA*

Stamps of 1890-94 Overprinted or Surcharged by Handstamp

**1898    Unwmk.    Perf. 14**

Purple Overprint or Surcharge

| | | | | |
|---|---|---|---|---|
| MR1 | A8 | 1c yellow brn | 6.00 | 4.50 |
| MR2 | A8 | 2c on 2m orange | 2.75 | 2.25 |
| MR3 | A8 | 2c on 5c blue grn | 3.60 | 2.75 |
| MR4 | A8 | 2c dark violet | .70 | .70 |
| MR5 | A8 | 2c lilac | .65 | .65 |
| MR6 | A8 | 2c red brown | .35 | .20 |
| MR7 | A8 | 5c blue green | 1.40 | 1.40 |
| MR8 | A8 | 5c br grn | 6.50 | 4.50 |

Rose Surcharge

| | | | | |
|---|---|---|---|---|
| MR9 | A8 | 2c on 2m orange | 1.40 | 1.40 |
| MR10 | A8 | 2c on 5c vio | .20 | .20 |
| MR11 | A8 | 2c on 1m dl bl | .60 | .60 |

Magenta Surcharge

| | | | | |
|---|---|---|---|---|
| MR12 | A8 | 5c on 1m dl bl | .35 | .20 |
| MR13 | A8 | 5c on 1m dl bl | 2.25 | 2.25 |
| | | Nos. MR1-MR13 (13) | 26.75 | 21.60 |

Nos. MR2-MR13 were issued as War Tax Stamps (2c on letters or sealed mail; 5c on telegrams) but, during the early days of American occupation, they were accepted for ordinary postage.

Double, inverted and similar varieties of overprints are numerous in this issue. Counterfeit overprints exist.

---

The market for Qatar stamps is extremely volatile, and dealer stocks are quite limited. All values for this country are tentative.

Wmk. 368 — JEZ Multiple

---

# QATAR
*Kát-ar*

**LOCATION**—A peninsula in eastern Arabia
**GOVT.**—Independent state
**AREA**—4,575 sq. mi.
**POP.**—580,000 (1998 est.)
**CAPITAL**—Doha

100 Naye Paise = 1 Rupee
100 Dirhams = 1 Riyal (1967)

Qatar was a British protected sheikdom until Sept. 1, 1971, when it declared its independence. Stamps of Muscat were used until 1957.

Catalogue values for all unused stamps in this country are for Never Hinged items.

Watermarks

Sheik Ahmad bin Ali al Thani—A1

Dhow—A2

Oil Derrick—A3

Stamps of Great Britain Nos. 317-325, 328, 332-333 and 309-311 Surcharged "QATAR" and New Value in Black

**1957, Apr. 1    Wmk. 308    Photo.    Perf. 14½x14**

| | | | | |
|---|---|---|---|---|
| 1 | A129 | 1np on 5p lt brn | .25 | .25 |
| 2 | A126 | 3np on 6p red org | .25 | .25 |
| 3 | A126 | 5np on 1p ultra | .25 | .25 |
| 4 | A126 | 9np on 1½p red brn | .25 | .25 |
| 5 | A127 | 15np on 2½p scarlet | .40 | .65 |
| 6 | A126 | 20np on 3p dp lil | .50 | .65 |
| 7 | A126 | 25np on 4p ultra | .45 | .30 |
| 8 | A128 | 40np on 5p brn | .80 | .80 |
| 9 | A126 | 50np on 6p dl pur | .55 | .40 |
| 10 | A130 | 75np on 9p dp grn | .80 | .55 |
| 11 | A131 | 1ru on 1sh6p dk gray | 1.40 | .80 |
| 12 | A131 | 1ru on 1sh6p dk bl | 10.50 | .65 |
| | | **Engr.** | | |
| 13 | A133 | 2ru on 2sh6p dk brn | 5.50 | 2.25 |
| 14 | A133 | 5ru on 5sh crimson | 7.75 | 4.50 |
| 15 | A133 | 10ru on 10sh brt ultra | 9.75 | 11.50 |
| | | Nos. 1-15 (15) | 38.70 | 23.30 |

Both typeset and stereotyped overprints were used on Nos. 13-15. The typeset bars close together and thick, bold letters. The stereotyped have bars wider apart and thinner letters.

**1957, Aug. 1    Perf. 14½x14**

Great Britain Nos. 334-336 Surcharged "QATAR," New Value and Square of Dots in Black

| | | | | |
|---|---|---|---|---|
| 16 | A138 | 15np on 2½p scarlet | .75 | .50 |
| 17 | A138 | 25np on 4p ultra | 1.50 | 1.10 |
| 18 | A138 | 75np on 1sh3p dk grn | 2.50 | 1.75 |
| | | Nos. 16-18 (3) | 4.75 | 3.35 |

50th anniv. of the Boy Scout movement and the World Scout Jubilee Jamboree, Aug. 1-12.

**1960    Wmk. 322    Perf. 14½x14**

Surcharged "QATAR" and New Value
Great Britain Nos. 353-358, 362

| | | | | |
|---|---|---|---|---|
| 19 | A126 | 3np on ½p red org | 1.10 | .70 |
| 20 | A126 | 6np on 1p ultra | 2.00 | 2.20 |
| 21 | A126 | 9np on 1½p green | 1.25 | 3.25 |
| 22 | A126 | 12np on 2p red brn | 1.50 | 1.75 |
| 23 | A126 | 15np on 2½p red brn | 6.00 | 8.25 |
| 24 | A127 | 20np on 3p dp lil | .55 | .20 |
| 25 | A129 | 40np on 6p lil rose | .95 | .40 |
| | | Nos. 19-25 (7) | 12.40 | 16.15 |

Column—A4

**1964, Nov. 22    Photo.    Perf. 14½**

| | | | | |
|---|---|---|---|---|
| 42 | A2 | 50np sepia | 1.50 | .95 |
| 43 | A2 | 75np ultra | 2.40 | 1.40 |
| | | **Engr.** | | |
| 44 | A3 | 1ru on 10ru blk | 4.75 | 2.75 |
| 45 | A3 | 2ru blue | 12.50 | 7.50 |
| 46 | A3 | 5ru ultra | 29.00 | 16.00 |
| | | Nos. 42-46 (5) | 50.15 | 28.60 |

Pres. John F. Kennedy (1917-63). For surcharges see Nos. 111-111D.

**1965, Jan. 17    Photo.    Perf. 14½x14    Unwmk.**

| | | | | |
|---|---|---|---|---|
| 47 | A4 | 1np multicolored | .60 | .60 |
| 48 | A4 | 2np multicolored | .60 | .60 |
| 49 | A4 | 3np multicolored | .60 | .60 |
| 50 | A4 | 1.50ru multicolored | 3.00 | .60 |
| 51 | A4 | 1.50ru multicolored | 8.25 | 1.25 |
| 52 | A4 | 2ru multicolored | 24.75 | 5.05 |
| | | Nos. 47-52 (6) | | |

Designs: 2np, 1.50r, Isis Temple and Colonnade, Philae. 3np, 1r, Trajan's Kiosk, Philae. UNESCO world campaign to save historic monuments in Nubia.

---

**1961, Sept. 2    Unwmk.    Perf. 13    Photo.**

Mosque.

| | | | | |
|---|---|---|---|---|
| 26 | A1 | 5np rose carmine | .45 | .45 |
| 27 | A1 | 15np brown black | .45 | .45 |
| 28 | A1 | 20np claret | .45 | .45 |
| 29 | A1 | 30np deep green | .45 | .45 |
| 30 | A1 | 40np red | .65 | .65 |
| 31 | A1 | 50np sepia | .75 | .55 |
| 32 | A1 | 75np ultra | .75 | 2.25 |
| | | **Engr.** | | |
| 33 | A3 | 1ru rose red | 1.10 | 1.75 |
| 34 | A3 | 2ru blue | 3.25 | 1.60 |
| 35 | A3 | 5ru green | 45.00 | 11.00 |
| 36 | A3 | 10ru black | 76.30 | 24.40 |
| | | Nos. 26-36 (11) | | |

Designs: 40np, Peregrine Falcon. 5r, 10r, Mosque.

**1964, Oct. 25    Photo.    Perf. 13**

Nos. 31-32, 34-36 Overprinted or Surcharged

| | | | | |
|---|---|---|---|---|
| 37 | A2 | 50np sepia | 2.00 | 1.75 |
| 38 | A2 | 75np ultra | 3.25 | 3.25 |
| | | **Engr.** | | |
| 39 | A3 | 1ru on 10r black | 4.25 | 1.50 |
| 40 | A3 | 2ru blue | 9.00 | 3.00 |
| 41 | A3 | 5ru green | 22.50 | 8.75 |
| | | Nos. 37-41 (5) | 41.00 | 17.50 |

18th Olympic Games, Tokyo, Oct. 10-25. For surcharges see Nos. 110-110D.

---

Qatar Scout Emblem, Tents and Sheik Ahmad—A5

Scouts Saluting and Sheik Ahmad—A6

**1965, May 22    Photo.    Perf. 14 (A5), 14½x14 (A6)**

| | | | | |
|---|---|---|---|---|
| 53 | A5 | 1np ol grn & dk red | 1.25 | .45 |
| 54 | A5 | 2np sal & dk vio bl | .40 | .40 |
| 55 | A5 | 3np dk vio bl & grn | .40 | .40 |
| 56 | A5 | 4np bl & dk red brn | .40 | .40 |
| 57 | A5 | 5np dk vio bl & grnsh | .40 | .40 |
| 58 | A6 | 30np multi | 3.00 | .40 |
| 59 | A6 | 40np multi | 3.50 | 1.25 |
| 60 | A6 | 1ru multi | 12.00 | 2.50 |
| | | Nos. 53-60 (8) | 20.50 | 6.65 |

Issued to honor the Qatar Boy Scouts. Perf. and imperf. souvenir sheets contain one each of Nos. 58-60 with red brown marginal inscription. Size: 108x76mm. Value, perf $15, imperf $25. For surcharges see Nos. 113-113G.

Eiffel Tower, Telstar, ITU Emblem and "Qatar" in Morse Code—A7

**1965, Oct. 16    Photo.    Perf. 13½x14    Unwmk.**

| | | | | |
|---|---|---|---|---|
| 61 | A7 | 1np dk bl & red brn | 1.25 | .45 |
| 62 | A7 | 2np bl & dk red brn | 1.25 | .45 |
| 63 | A7 | 3np dp yel grn & brt pur | .45 | .45 |
| 64 | A7 | 4np org brn & brt bl | 1.25 | .90 |
| 65 | A7 | 5np dl vio & dk ol bl | .45 | .45 |
| 66 | A7 | 40np dk car rose & bl | .90 | |
| 67 | A7 | 50np si grn & bls | 1.10 | |
| 68 | A7 | 1ru omor & car | 2.25 | |
| a. | | Souvenir sheet of 2 | 25.00 | |
| | | Nos. 61-68 (8) | 27.50 | 6.50 |

Designs: 2np, 1ru, Tokyo Olympic Games emblem and Syncom III. 3np, 40np, Radar tracking station and Relay satellite. 4np, 50np, Post Office Tower, London, and Echo II, Syncom III, Telstar and Relay satellites around globe.

Cent. of the ITU. #68a also exists imperf. Value $25. For overprints and surcharges see Nos. 91-98, 114-114G, 117-117G.

Triggerfish—A8

Various Fish, including: 2np, 50np, Clown grunt. 2np, 10ru, Saddleback butterflyfish. 4np, 5ru, Butterflyfish. 15np, 3ru, Paradisefish. 20np, 1ru, Rio Grande perch. 75np, Triggerfish.

## 1965, Oct. 18 — Perf. 14x14½

| | | | |
|---|---|---|---|
| 69 | A8 | 1np multi & black | .35 .35 |
| 70 | A8 | 2np multi & black | .35 .35 |
| 71 | A8 | 3np multi & black | .35 .35 |
| 72 | A8 | 4np multi & black | .35 .35 |
| 73 | A8 | 5np multi & black | 1.00 .35 |
| 74 | A8 | 15np multi & black | .75 .35 |
| 75 | A8 | 20np multi & black | 1.75 .35 |
| 76 | A8 | 30np multi & black | .65 .45 |
| 77 | A8 | 40np multi & gold | .90 .65 |
| 78 | A8 | 50np multi & gold | 2.75 .90 |
| 79 | A8 | 75np multi & gold | 4.75 1.25 |
| 80 | A8 | 1ru multi & gold | 12.00 2.25 |
| 81 | A8 | 2ru multi & gold | 18.00 3.50 |
| 82 | A8 | 3ru multi & gold | 4.50 |
| 83 | A8 | 4ru multi & gold | 25.00 6.25 |
| 84 | A8 | 5ru multi & gold | 80.00 11.50 |
| 85 | A8 | 10ru multi & gold | 194.25 34.05 |

*Nos. 69-85 (17)*

Basketball — A9

No. 87, Horse jumping. No. 88, Running. No. 89, Soccer. No. 90, Weight lifting.

## 1966, Jan. 10 — Photo.
### Granite Paper — Perf. 11½

| | | | |
|---|---|---|---|
| 86 | A9 | 1ru gray, blk & dk red | 4.00 1.25 |
| 87 | A9 | 1ru brn & ol grn | 4.00 1.25 |
| 88 | A9 | 1ru dull rose & blue | 4.00 1.25 |
| 89 | A9 | 1ru grn & blk | 4.00 1.25 |
| 90 | A9 | 1ru bl & brn | 4.00 1.25 |

*Nos. 86-90 (5)* — 20.00 6.25

4th Pan Arab Games, Cairo, Sept. 2-11. Nos. 86-90 are printed in one sheet of 25 in horizontal rows of five.

## Nos. 61-68 Overprinted in Black

## 1966, Feb. 9 — Photo., Perf. 13½x14

| | | | |
|---|---|---|---|
| 91 | A7 | 1np dk bl & red brn | 1.75 .40 |
| 92 | A7 | 2np bl & dk red brn | 1.75 .40 |
| 93 | A7 | 3np dp yel grn & brt pur | |
| 94 | A7 | 4np org brn & brt bl | 1.75 .40 |
| 95 | A7 | 5np dl vio & dk ol bis | 1.75 .40 |
| 96 | A7 | 10np dk car rose & blk | 6.25 .45 |
| 97 | A7 | 50np slate grn & bis | 7.25 .55 |
| 98 | A7 | 1ru emer & car | 21.00 1.10 |
| | | brn | 43.25 4.10 |

Issued to commemorate the rendezvous in space of Gemini 6 and 7, Dec. 15, 1965. Value, set $150. Nos. 96-98 also exist overprinted in blue, set $125.

For surcharges see Nos. 117-117G.

Sheik Ahmad — A9a

## Litho. & Embossed Gold or Silver Foil

Designs: 3np, 5np, 40np, 80np, 2ru, 10ru, Reverse of coin with Arabic inscription.

## 1966, Feb. 24 — Imperf.

| | | | |
|---|---|---|---|
| 99 | A9a | 1np ol & lll (S) | .40 .40 |
| 99A | A9a | 3np blk & red (S) | .40 .40 |
| 99B | A9a | 3np blk & org (S) | .40 .40 |
| 99C | A9a | 4np pur & red | .40 .40 |
| 99D | A9a | 5np grn & blk | .40 .40 |

**Diameter: 55mm**

| | | | |
|---|---|---|---|
| 99E | A9a | 10np brn & blt vio | 1.60 .40 |
| | | (S) | |
| | | 40np red & bl | 2.50 .75 |
| | | (S) | |

| | | | |
|---|---|---|---|
| 99F | A9a | 70np Prus bl & bl | 1.60 |
| | | vio | 1.60 |
| 99G | A9a | 80np car & grn | 5.25 2.10 |

**Diameter: 65mm**

| | | | |
|---|---|---|---|
| 99H | A9a | 1ru red vio & blk | 7.25 4.00 |
| | | (S) | |
| 99J | A9a | 2ru bl grn & cl (S) | 12.50 9.00 |
| 99K | A9a | 5ru red lll & ver | 30.00 |
| 99L | A9a | 10ru bl vio & brn | |
| | | car | 52.50 21.00 |
| | | | 118.45 42.05 |

*Nos. 99-99L (12)*

John F. Kennedy, UN Headquarters, NY, and ICY Emblem — A10

Designs (ICY emblem and): #100, UN emblem. #100B, Dag Hammarskjold and UN General Assembly. #100C, Jawaharlal Nehru and dove.

## 1966, Mar. 8 — Granite Paper — Perf. 11½

| | | | |
|---|---|---|---|
| 100 | A10 | 40np brt bl, vio bl & red brn | 5.00 2.00 |
| 100A | A10 | 40np brt grn, vio & brn | 5.00 2.00 |
| 100B | A10 | 40np red brn, brt bl & brn | 5.00 2.00 |
| 100C | A10 | 40np dk vio & brt grm | 5.00 2.00 |

d. Block of 4, #100-100C — 25.00 12.00

UN Intl. Cooperation Year, 1965. Printed in sheets of 16 + 9 labels in shape of a cross. An imperf. souvenir sheet of 4 contains one each of Nos. 100-100C. Value $40.

## Nos. 100-100C Overprinted in Black

U.N. 20th ANNIVERSARY

Designs: No. 101, John F. Kennedy, "In Memoriam / John F. Kennedy / 1917-1963." No. 101A, Olive branches, Churchill quote and "In Memoriam / 1874-1965." No. 101B, like #101 portrait facing left, no overprint. No. 101C, Eternal flame, Arabic inscription.

## 1966, Mar. 8 — Granite Paper

| | | | |
|---|---|---|---|
| 101 | A10a | 5np bl grn, car & blk | |
| 101A | A10a | 5np bl grn, rose & blk | |
| 101B | A10a | 5np bl grn & blk | |
| 101C | A10a | 5np bl grn, rose & blk | |
| 101D | A10a | 5np bl brn, car & blk | |
| 101E | A10 | 40np on No. 100 | |
| 101F | A10 | 40np on No. 100A | |
| 101G | A10 | 40np on No. 100B | |
| 101H | A10 | 40np on No. 100C | 80.00 |

*Nos. 101-101H (9)*

Nos. 101-101H were made from the sheets of Nos. 100-100C. The 4 outer labels and the center label were surcharged to create Nos. 101-101D. The other 4 labels were overprinted but have no denomination. Exists with red overprint. souvenir sheet exists with overprint in margin:"IN VICTORY / MAGNANIMITY / IN PEACE / GOODWILL / WINSTON CHURCHILL." The margin overprint overlaps onto No. 101A in an upper left quarter of stamp.
Nos. 101-101H exist imperf.
For surcharges see Nos. 118-118C.

John F. Kennedy (1917-1963) — A10b

Kennedy and: #102c, 10np, 70np, NYC. #102d, 80np, #102g, 80np, Rocket lifting off at Cape Kennedy. #102e, 60np, #102h, 1ru, Statue of Liberty. No. 102B, Statue of Liberty.

## 1966, July 18 — Perf. 13½

| | | | |
|---|---|---|---|
| 102 | A10b | Strip of 3, #c-e. | 2.75 1.50 |
| 102A | A10b | Strip of 3, #f-h. | 4.75 2.50 |

### Souvenir Sheet
### Imperf

| | | | |
|---|---|---|---|
| 102B | A10b | 50np multicolored | 30.00 |

Nos. 102-102A exist imperf. For surcharges see Nos. 119-119B.

1968 Summer Olympics, Mexico City — A10c

Designs: #103c, 1np, #103f, 70np, #103B, Equestrian. #103d, 4np, #103g, 80np, Running. #103e, 5np, #103h, 90np, Javelin.

## 1966, July 20 — Perf. 13½

| | | | |
|---|---|---|---|
| 103 | A10c | Strip of 3, #c-e. | 3.00 3.00 |
| 103A | A10c | Strip of 3, #f-h. | 12.00 8.00 |

### Souvenir Sheet
### Imperf

| | | | |
|---|---|---|---|
| 103B | A10c | 50np multicolored | 22.50 |

Nos. 103-103A exist imperf. For surcharges see Nos. 120-120B.

American Astronauts — A10e

Astronaut and space vehicle: No. 104c, 5np, James A. Lovell. d, 10np, Thomas P. Stafford. e, 15np, Alan B. Shepard.
No. 104f, 20np, John H. Glenn. g, 30np, M. Scott Carpenter. h, 40np, Walter M. Schirra. i, 50np, Virgil I. Grissom. j, 60np, L. Gordon Cooper, Jr.
No. 104d, 30np, Stafford, Schirra, Frank Borman, Lovell and diagram of space rendezvous.

## 1966, Aug. 20 — Perf. 12

| | | | |
|---|---|---|---|
| 104 | A10d | Strip of 3, #c-e. | 4.50 |
| 104A | A10e | Strip of 5, #f-j. | 13.50 |

### Souvenir Sheet
### Imperf — Size: 115x75mm

| | | | |
|---|---|---|---|
| 104B | A10e | 50np multicolored | 30.00 |

The name of James A. Lovell is spelled "Lovell" on No. 104c. No. 104-104A exist imperf. For surcharges see Nos. 121-121B.

## 1966 World Cup Soccer Championships, London — A10i

Designs: 1np-4np, Jules Rimet Cup. 60np, #107H, Hands holding Cup. soccer ball. 70np, #107J, Cup, soccer ball. 80np, #107K, Soccer players, ball. 90np, #107L, Wembley Stadium.

## 1966, Nov. 27 — Photo. — Perf. 13½

| | | | |
|---|---|---|---|
| 107 | A10i | 1np blue | — |
| 107A | A10i | 2np blue | — |
| 107B | A10i | 3np blue | — |
| 107C | A10i | 4np blue | 22.50 |
| m. | | Block of 4, #107-107C | |
| 107D | A10i | 60np multicolored | — |
| 107E | A10i | 70np multicolored | — |
| 107F | A10i | 80np multicolored | — |
| 107G | A10i | 90np multicolored | — |
| n. | | Block of 4, #107D-107G | |

Nos. 107-107C are airmail. Issued in sheets of 36 containing 5 #107m and 4 #107n. Nos. 107-107G exist imperf.

### Souvenir Sheets
### Imperf

| | | | |
|---|---|---|---|
| 107H | A10i | 25np multicolored | — 22.50 |
| 107J | A10i | 25np multicolored | — 22.50 |
| 107K | A10i | 25np multicolored | — 22.50 |
| 107L | A10i | 25np multicolored | — 22.50 |

## Nos. 37-41 Surcharged with New Currency in Gray or Red

### Photo. — Perf. 14½

| | | | |
|---|---|---|---|
| 110 | A2 | 50d on 75np #37 | — |
| 110A | A2 | 75d on 75np #38 | 200.00 |

### Engr. — Perf. 13

| | | | |
|---|---|---|---|
| 110B | A3 | 1r on 1ru on 10ru #44 | — |
| 110C | A3 | 2r on 2ru #45 | — |
| 110D | A3 | 5r on 5ru #46 | 300.00 |

*Set, #110-110D (5)*

## Nos. 42-46 Surcharged with New Currency in Gray or Red

### Photo. — Perf. 14½

| | | | |
|---|---|---|---|
| 111 | A2 | 50d on 50np #42 (G) | — |
| 111A | A2 | 75d on 75np #43 | — |

### Engr. — Perf. 13

| | | | |
|---|---|---|---|
| 111B | A3 | 1r on 1ru on 10ru #44 | — |
| 111C | A3 | 2r on 2ru #45 | — |
| 111D | A3 | 5r on 5ru #46 | 75.00 |

*Set, #111-111D (5)*

## Nos. 53-60 Surcharged with New Currency

### Perf. 14 (A5), 14½x14 (A6) — Photo.

| | | | |
|---|---|---|---|
| 113 | A5 | 1d on 1np #53 | — |
| 113A | A5 | 2d on 2np #54 | — |
| 113B | A5 | 3d on 3np #55 | — |
| 113C | A5 | 4d on 4np #56 | — |
| 113D | A5 | 5d on 5np #57 | — |
| 113E | A6 | 30d on 30np #58 | — |
| 113F | A6 | 40d on 40np #59 | — |
| 113G | A6 | 50d on 50np #60 | — |

*Set, #113-113G (8)*

Exist imperf. Perf and imperf souvenir sheets contain one each of #113E-113G surcharged with new currency.

## Nos. 61-68 Surcharged with New Currency in Black and Red

### Perf. 13½x14

| | | | |
|---|---|---|---|
| 114 | A7 | 1d on 1np #61 | — |
| 114A | A7 | 2d on 2np #62 | — |
| 114B | A7 | 3d on 3np #63 | — |
| 114C | A7 | 4d on 4np #64 | — |
| 114D | A7 | 5d on 5np #65 | — |
| 114E | A7 | 30d on 30np #66 | — |
| 114F | A7 | 40d on 50np #67 | — |
| 114G | A7 | 1r on 1ru #68 | 75.00 |

*Set, #114-114G (8)*

Exist imperf.

**1966**
**Nos. 91-98 Surcharged with New Currency**
Photo.   Perf. 13½x14
117 A7 1d on 1np #91
117A A7 2d on 2np #92
117B A7 3d on 3np #93
117C A7 4d on 4np #94
117D A7 5d on 5np #95
117E A7 40d on 40np #96
117F A7 50d on 50np #97
117G A7 1r on 1ru #98
Set, #117-117G (8)   60.00

**1966**
**Nos. 101E-101H with Red Overprint Surcharged with New Currency**
Photo.   Perf. 11½
118 A10a 40d on 40np #101E
118A A10a 40d on 40np #101F
118B A10a 40d on 40np #101G
118C A10a 40d on 40np #101H
Block of 4, #118-118C   100.00

Exist imperf. Imperf. souvenir sheets mentioned after Nos. 100C. 101H exist surcharged with new currency.

**1966**
**Nos. 102-102B Surcharged with New Currency**
Granite Paper   Photo.   Perf. 11½
119 A10b 50d on 50np #102   30.00

**Souvenir Sheet**
**Imperf.**
119A A10b 50d on 50np #102B   —   30.00

Nos. 119-119A exist imperf.

**1966**
**Nos. 103-103B Surcharged with New Currency**
Photo.   Perf. 13½
119B A10b 50d on 50np #103   45.00

**Souvenir Sheet**
**Imperf.**
119B A10b 50d on 50np #102B   —   20.00

Traffic Light and Intersection — A12

**1966**
**Nos. 104-104B Surcharged with New Currency**
120 A10c 50d on 50np #104   —   45.00
Nos. 120-120A exist imperf.

**Souvenir Sheet**
**Imperf.**
120B A10c 50d on 50np #104B   —   15.00

**1966**
**Nos. 104-104B Surcharged with New Currency**
121   Perf. 12

**Souvenir Sheet**
**Imperf**
121A A10e 50d on 50np #104B
121B A10e 50d on 50np #104B
Nos. 121-121A printed se-tenant with five labels showing Arabic inscription.

Arab Postal Union Emblem — A11

---

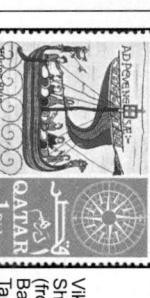

Viking Ship (from Bayeux Tapestry) — A14

Famous Ships: 2d, Santa Maria (Columbus). 3d, San Gabriel (Vasco da Gama). 75d, Victoria (Ferdinand Magellan). 1r, Golden Hind (Sir Francis Drake). 2r, Gipsy Moth IV (Sir Francis Chichester).

**1967, Nov. 27**   Litho.   Perf. 13½
126 A14 1d org & multi   .85   .35
126A A14 2d lt bl, tan & blk   .85   .35
126B A14 3d lt bl & multi   .85   .35
126C A14 75d fawn & multi   2.50   1.00

Boy Scouts and Sheik Ahmad — A13

Designs: 1d, First Boy Scout camp, Brownsea Island, 1907, and tents, Idaho, US, 1967. 2d, Lord Baden-Powell. 5d, Boy Scout canoeing. 15d, Swimming. 75d, Mountain climbing. 2r, Boy Scout saluting flag and emblem of 12th World Jamboree, Farragut State Park, Idaho, Aug. 1-9.

**1967, Sept. 15**   Litho. and Engr.   Perf. 11½x11
125 A13 3d rose & multi   .75   .45
125A A13 1d multicolored   .75   .45
125B A13 3d rose & multi   .75   .45
125C A13 5d lilac & multi   1.25   .55
125D A13 15d multicolored   1.50   .55
125E A13 75d green & multi   11.50   7.25
125F A13 2r sepia & multi   18.25   11.35
Nos. 125-125A for 60th anniv. of the Boy Scouts. Nos. 125B-125F for 12th Boy Scout World Jamboree, Farragut State Park, Idaho, Aug. 1-9.

**1967, May 24**   Litho.   Perf. 13½
124 A12 20d vio & multi   1.25   .40
124A A12 30d multi   .70   .65
124B A12 50d multi   3.50   2.20
124C A12 1r ultra & multi   4.60   2.75
Nos. 124-124C (4)   10.50   5.00
Issued for Traffic Day.

---

Apollo Project — A11a

**1967, Apr. 15**   Photo.   Perf. 11x11½
122 A11 70d magenta & sepia   4.00   1.25
122A A11 80d dull blue & sepia   6.00   1.60
Qatar's joining the Arab Postal Union.

Designs: 5d, 70d, Two astronauts on Moon. 10d, 80d, Command and lunar modules in lunar orbit. 20d, 1r, Lunar module on Moon. 30d, 1.20r, Lunar module ascending from Moon. 40d, 2r, Saturn 5 rocket.

**1967, May 1**
123 A11a 5d multicolored   .70   .35
123A A11a 10d multicolored   .70   .35
123B A11a 20d multicolored   .70   .35
123C A11a 30d multicolored   .85   .35
123D A11a 40d multicolored   1.25   .35
123E A11a 70d multicolored   2.40   .75
123F A11a 80d multicolored   3.00   1.00
123G A11a 1r multicolored   3.00   1.40
123H A11a 1.20r multicolored   5.00   2.10
123J A11a 2r multicolored   7.00   3.00
Nos. 123-123J (10)   24.60   10.00
#123J exists in an imperf. souv. sheet of one. Value $30.

---

**1967, Nov. 27** (cont.)
126D A14 1r gray, yel grn & red   5.00   2.10
126E A14 2r red   12.00   4.25
Nos. 126-126E (6)   22.05   8.40

Professional Letter Writer — A15

Human Rights Flame and Barbed Wire — A16

Designs: 2d, Carrier pigeon and man releasing pigeon, vert. 3d, Postrider, 60d, Mail transport by rowboat, vert. 1.25r, Mailman riding camel, jet plane and modern buildings. 2r, Qatar No. 1, hand holding pen, paper, envelopes and inkwell.

**1968, Feb. 14**   Photo.   Perf. 12½
127 A15 1d multicolored   .75   .40
127A A15 2d multicolored   .75   .40
127B A15 3d multicolored   .75   .40
127C A15 60d multicolored   3.25   1.25
127D A15 1.25r multicolored   5.75   2.50
127E A15 2r multicolored   10.50   4.25
Nos. 127-127E (6)   21.75   9.20
Ten years of Qatar postal service.

Designs: 2d, Arab refugee family leaving concentration camp. 3d, Scales of Justice. 60d, Hands opening gates to the sun. 1.25r, Family and sun, vert. 2r, Stylized family groups.

**1968, Apr. 10**
128 A16 1d gray & multi   .60   .30
129 A16 2d multicolored   .60   .30
130 A16 3d brt grn, org & blk   .60   .30
131 A16 60d org, brn & blk   3.25   3.00
132 A16 1.25r brt grn, blk & yel   8.25   3.00
133 A16 2r multicolored   11.50   4.25
Nos. 128-133 (6)   24.30   9.15
International Human Rights Year.

---

Olympic Rings and Gymnast — A18

Nurse Attending Premature Baby — A17

Designs (WHO Emblem and): 2d, Dentist. 60d, Operating room. 3d, X-ray examination. 1.25r, Medical laboratory. 2r, State Hospital.

**1968, June 20**
134 A17 1d multi   .40   .40
135 A17 3d multi   .40   .40
136 A17 3d multi   .40   .40
137 A17 60d multi   3.25   1.70
138 A17 1.25r multi   6.25   3.25
139 A17 2r multi   11.50   3.25
Nos. 134-139 (6)   22.20   7.40
20th anniv. of the World Health Organization.

Designs (Olympic Rings and): 1d, Discobolus and view of Mexico City. 2d, Runner and flaming torch. 60d, Weight lifting and torch. 1.25r, Olympic flame as a mosaic, vert. 2r, Mythological bird.

**1968, Aug. 24**
140 A18 1d multicolored   .50   .50
141 A18 3d multicolored   .50   .50
142 A18 3d multicolored   .50   .50
143 A18 60d multicolored   3.25   1.25
144 A18 1.25r multicolored   7.50   2.40
145 A18 2r multicolored   12.50   4.25
Nos. 140-145 (6)   24.75   9.25
19th Olympic Games, Mexico City, 10/12-27.

---

Sheik Ahmad bin Ali al Thani — A19
Dhow — A20
Rayyan — A21

**1968**   Litho.   Perf. 13½
146 A19 5d blue & green   2.25   .50
147 A19 10d brt bl & red brn   .50   .50
148 A19 20d blk & vermilion   .50   .50
149 A19 25d red brn & brt grn   .85   .50

**Lithographed and Engraved**
Designs: 40d, Desalination plant. 60d, Loading platform and oil tanker. 70d, Qatar Mosque. 1r, Clock Tower, Market Place, Doha. 1.25r, Doha Fort. 1.50r, Falcon.
150 A20 35d grn & brt pink   2.25   .50

**Perf. 11½**
151 A20 40d grn & brt green   3.00   .50
152 A20 60d lt bl, brn & lil   4.75   .85
153 A20 70d blk, lt bl & brt grn   5.50   1.10
154 A20 1r vio bl, yel & brt grn   6.50   1.40
155 A20 1.25r ind, brt bl & ocher   8.50   1.75
156 A20 1.50r lt bl, dk grn & rose lil   14.50   2.10

**Perf. 13**
157 A21 2r brn, ocher & bl   14.50   3.00
158 A21 5r grn, lt grn & gray   35.00   7.25
159 A21 10r ultra, lt bl & pur   60.00   13.50
Nos. 146-159 (14)   156.85   33.95

---

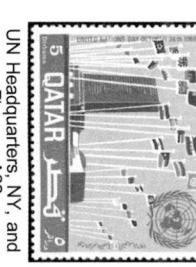

UN Headquarters, NY, and Flags — A22

Designs: 1d, Flags 4d, World map and dove. 60d, Classroom. 1.50r, Farmers, wheat and tractor. 2r, Soc. Gen. U Thant and General Assembly Hall.

**1968, Oct. 24**   Litho.   Perf. 13½x13
160 A22 1d multi   .50   .50
161 A22 4d multi   .50   .50
162 A22 5d multi   .50   .50
163 A22 60d multi   5.25   1.50
164 A22 1.50r multi   7.75   2.40
165 A22 2r multi   10.50   4.00
Nos. 160-165 (6)   25.00   9.40
United Nations Day, Oct. 24, 1968.

Fishing Vessel Ross Rayyan — A23

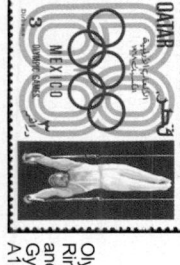

Al Jahiz and Old World Map A34

Designs: 2d, Sultan Saladin and palace. 3d, Al Farabi, sailboat and musical instruments. 35d, Iben al Haithum and palace. 1.50r, Al Motanabbi and camels. 2r, Avicenna and old world map.

**1971, Feb. 20**    **Perf. 13½x14**

| | | | |
|---|---|---|---|
| 232 | A34 | 1d brt pink & multi | .40 .40 |
| 233 | A34 | 2d pale bl & multi | .40 .40 |
| 234 | A34 | 3d dl yel & multi | .40 .40 |
| 235 | A34 | 35d lt bl & multi | 3.00 .65 |
| 236 | A34 | 1.50r yel grn & multi | 12.00 3.00 |
| 237 | A34 | 2r pale grn & multi | 19.00 4.25 |

*Nos. 232-237 (6)*    35.20 9.10

Famous men of Islam.

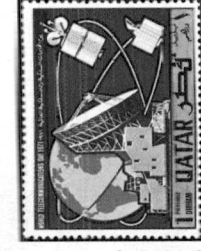

Cormorant — A35

Designs: 2d, Lizard and prickly pear. 3d, Flamingos and palms. 60d, Oryx and yucca. 1.25r, Gazelle and desert dandelion. 2r, Camel, palm and bronzed chenopod.

**1971, Apr. 14**    **Litho.**    **Perf. 11x12**

| | | | |
|---|---|---|---|
| 238 | A35 | 1d multi | .35 .35 |
| 239 | A35 | 2d multi | .35 .35 |
| 240 | A35 | 3d multi | .35 .35 |
| 241 | A35 | 60d multi | 6.75 1.00 |
| 242 | A35 | 1.25r multi | 10.00 1.90 |
| 243 | A35 | 2r multi | 17.00 3.00 |

*Nos. 238-243 (6)*    34.80 6.95

Goonhilly Satellite Tracking Station A36

Designs: 2d, Cable ship, and section of submarine cable. 3d, 35d, London Post Office Tower, and television control room. 4d, Various telephones. 5d, 75d, Video telephone. 3r, Telex machine and tape.

**1971, May 17**    **Perf. 13½x13**

| | | | |
|---|---|---|---|
| 244 | A36 | 1d vio bl & multi | .35 .35 |
| 245 | A36 | 2d multicolored | .35 .35 |
| 246 | A36 | 3d rose red & multi | .35 .35 |
| 247 | A36 | 4d magenta & multi | .35 .35 |
| 248 | A36 | 5d rose red & multi | .35 .35 |
| 249 | A36 | 35d multicolored | 2.00 .35 |
| 250 | A36 | 75d magenta & multi | 4.50 .65 |
| 251 | A36 | 3r ocher & multi | 16.00 2.75 |

*Nos. 244-251 (8)*    24.25 5.50

3rd World Telecommunications Day.

**State of Qatar**

Arab Postal Union Emblem — A37

**1971, Sept. 4**    **Perf. 13**

| | | | |
|---|---|---|---|
| 252 | A37 | 35d red & multi | 1.90 .50 |
| 253 | A37 | 55d blue & multi | 2.40 .90 |
| 254 | A37 | 75d brown & multi | 4.00 1.25 |
| 255 | A37 | 1.25r violet & multi | 6.50 1.90 |

*Nos. 252-255 (4)*    14.80 4.55

25th anniv. of the Conf. of Sofar, Lebanon, establishing the Arab Postal Union.

---

**1970, May 24**    **Perf. 13x12½**

| | | | |
|---|---|---|---|
| 212 | A30 | 35d blue & multi | 3.25 1.60 |
| 213 | A30 | 60d blue & multi | 6.75 1.40 |

Intl. Education Year. Translation of Koran quotation: "And say, O God, give me more knowledge."

Flowers — A31

**1970, July 2**    **Perf. 13x13½**

| | | | |
|---|---|---|---|
| 214 | A31 | 1d Freesia | .80 .45 |
| 215 | A31 | 2d Azalea | .80 .45 |
| 216 | A31 | 3d Ixia | 1.10 .45 |
| 217 | A31 | 60d Amaryllis | 4.50 1.60 |
| 218 | A31 | 1.25r Cineraria | 8.00 3.50 |
| 219 | A31 | 2r Rose | 11.50 4.50 |

*Nos. 214-219 (6)*    26.70 10.95

For surcharges see Nos. 287-289.

EXPO Emblem and Fisherman on Shikoku Beach — A32

1d, Toyahama fishermen honoring ocean gods. 2d, Map of Japan. 60d, Mt. Fuji. 1.50r, Camphorwood torii. 2r, Tower of Motherhood, EXPO Tower and Mt. Fuji.

**Perf. 13½x13, 13x13½**

**1970, Sept. 29**

| | | | |
|---|---|---|---|
| 220 | A32 | 1d multi, horiz. | .45 .45 |
| 221 | A32 | 2d multi, horiz. | .45 .45 |
| 222 | A32 | 3d multi | .45 .45 |
| 223 | A32 | 60d multi | 1.10 |
| | | Souvenir sheet of 4 | 2.75 9.25 |
| 224 | A32 | 1.50r multi, horiz. | 9.25 3.50 |
| 225 | A32 | 2r multi | 11.50 4.50 |

*Nos. 220-225 (6)*    24.85 10.45

EXPO '70 Intl. Exhib., Osaka, Japan, Mar. 15-Sept. 13. No. 223a contains 4 imperf. stamps similar to Nos. 220-223 with simulated perforations. Sold for 1r.

Globe and UN Emblem — A33

UN, 25th anniv.: 2d, Cannon used as flower vase. 3d, Birthday cake and dove. 35d, Emblems of UN agencies forming wall. 1.50r, Trumpet and emblems of UN agencies. 2r, Two men, black and white, embracing, and globe.

**1970, Dec. 7**    **Litho.**    **Perf. 14x13½**

| | | | |
|---|---|---|---|
| 226 | A33 | 1d blue & multi | .70 .35 |
| 227 | A33 | 2d multicolored | .70 .35 |
| 228 | A33 | 3d brt pur & multi | .70 .35 |
| 229 | A33 | 35d grn & multi | 1.75 .75 |
| 230 | A33 | 1.50r multi | 9.50 1.75 |
| 231 | A33 | 2r brn red & multi | 11.50 2.25 |

*Nos. 226-231 (6)*    24.85 5.40

---

Progress in Qatar: 4d, Elementary School and children playing. 5d, Doha Intl. Airport. 60d, Cement factory and road building. 1.50r, Power station. 2r, Housing development.

**1969, Jan. 13**

| | | | |
|---|---|---|---|
| 166 | A23 | 1d brt bl & multi | .40 .40 |
| 167 | A23 | 4d green & multi | .40 .40 |
| 168 | A23 | 5d dl org & multi | .40 .40 |
| 169 | A23 | 60d multicolored | 4.00 .80 |
| 170 | A23 | 1.50r brt lil & multi | 9.00 1.90 |
| 171 | A23 | 2r buff & multi | 11.00 2.75 |

*Nos. 166-171 (6)*    25.20 6.65

Armored Cars A24

Designs: 2d, Traffic police. 3d, Military helicopter. 60d, Oil rig, storage tanks. 1.50r, Oil refinery. 2r, Oil tankers, 1890-1968.

**1969, May 6**    **Litho.**    **Perf. 13½**

| | | | |
|---|---|---|---|
| 172 | A24 | 1d multicolored | .45 .45 |
| 173 | A24 | 2d lt blue & multi | .45 .45 |
| 174 | A24 | 3d gray & multi | .65 .45 |
| 175 | A24 | 60d multicolored | 2.75 .75 |
| 176 | A24 | 1.50r multicolored | 7.75 2.25 |
| 177 | A24 | 2r blue & multi | 12.00 3.25 |

*Nos. 172-177 (6)*    24.05 7.60

Issued to honor the public security forces.

Oil Tanker A25

2d, Research laboratory. 3d, Off-shore oil rig, helicopter. 60d, Oil rig, storage tanks. 1.50r, Oil refinery. 2r, Oil tankers.

**1969, July 4**

| | | | |
|---|---|---|---|
| 178 | A25 | 1d gray & multi | .40 .40 |
| 179 | A25 | 2d olive & multi | .40 .40 |
| 180 | A25 | 3d ultra & multi | .40 .40 |
| 181 | A25 | 60d lilac & multi | 3.50 1.75 |
| 182 | A25 | 1.50r red brn & multi | 8.50 4.25 |
| 183 | A25 | 2r brown & multi | 11.00 5.25 |

*Nos. 178-183 (6)*    24.20 12.45

Qatar oil industry.

Boy Scouts Building Boats A26

Designs: 2d, Scouts at work and 10 symbolic candles. 3d, Parade. 60d, Gate to camp interior. 1.25r, Main camp gate. 2r, Hoisting Qatar flag, and Sheik Ahmad.

**1969, Sept. 18**    **Litho.**    **Perf. 13½x13**

| | | | |
|---|---|---|---|
| 184 | A26 | 1d multicolored | .30 .30 |
| 185 | A26 | 2d multicolored | .30 .30 |
| 186 | A26 | 3d multicolored | .30 .30 |
| 187 | A26 | 60d multicolored | 3.50 1.10 |
| a. | | Souvenir sheet of 4, #184-187 | 25.00 16.00 |
| 188 | A26 | 1.25r multicolored | 8.00 3.50 |
| 189 | A26 | 2r multicolored | 12.00 3.75 |

*Nos. 184-189 (6)*    24.40 7.75

10th Qatar Boy Scout Jamboree. No. 187a sold for 1r.

---

Designs: 2d, Col. Edwin E. Aldrin, Jr. 3d, Lt. Col. Michael Collins. 60d, Astronaut walking on moon. 1.25r, Blast-off from moon. 2r, Capsule and raft in Pacific, horiz.

**1969, Dec. 6**    **Perf. 13x13½, 13½x13**

| | | | |
|---|---|---|---|
| 190 | A27 | 1d blue & multi | .50 .50 |
| 191 | A27 | 2d multicolored | .50 .50 |
| 192 | A27 | 3d grn & multi | .85 .50 |
| 193 | A27 | 60d multicolored | 3.00 1.25 |
| 194 | A27 | 1.25r pur & multi | 6.50 3.00 |
| 195 | A27 | 2r multicolored | 8.50 4.25 |

*Nos. 190-195 (6)*    19.85 10.00

See note after US No. C76.

UPU Emblem, Boeing Jet Loading in Qatar A28

2d, Transatlantic ocean liner. 3d, Mail truck and mail bags. 60d, Qatar Post Office. 1.25r, UPU Headquarters, Bern. 2r, UPU emblem.

**1970, Jan. 31**    **Litho.**    **Perf. 13½x13**

| | | | |
|---|---|---|---|
| 196 | A28 | 1d multi | .50 .50 |
| 197 | A28 | 2d multi | .50 .50 |
| 198 | A28 | 3d multi | 1.00 .50 |
| 199 | A28 | 60d multi | 4.00 1.50 |
| 200 | A28 | 1.25r multi | 7.25 3.25 |
| 201 | A28 | 2r brt yel grn, blk & lt brn | 11.00 5.75 |

*Nos. 196-201 (6)*    24.25 12.00

Qatar's admission to the UPU.

Map of Arab League Countries, Flag and Emblem — A28a

**1970, Mar.**    **Perf. 13x13½**

| | | | |
|---|---|---|---|
| 202 | A28a | 35d yellow & multi | 2.50 .70 |
| 203 | A28a | 60d blue & multi | 5.00 .90 |
| 204 | A28a | 1.25r multi | 10.00 2.00 |
| 205 | A28a | 1.50r vio & multi | 12.50 2.75 |

*Nos. 202-205 (4)*    30.00 6.35

25th anniversary of the Arab League.

VC10 Touching down for Landing A29

Designs: 2d, Hawk, and VC10 in flight. 3d, VC10 and airport. 60d, Map showing route Doha to London. 1.25r, VC10 over Gulftown. 2r, Tail of VC10 with emblem of Gulf Aviation.

**1970, Apr. 5**    **Perf. 13½x13**

| | | | |
|---|---|---|---|
| 206 | A29 | 1d multi | .45 .45 |
| 207 | A29 | 2d multi | .45 .45 |
| 208 | A29 | 3d multi | .45 .45 |
| 209 | A29 | 60d multi | 1.50 |
| 210 | A29 | 1.25r multi | 5.00 3.00 |
| 211 | A29 | 1.50r multi | 8.75 4.50 |

*Nos. 206-211 (6)*    31.10 10.35

Issued to publicize the first flight to London from Doha by Gulf Aviation Company.

Education Year Emblem, Spaceship Trajectory, Koran Quotation — A30

Neil A. Armstrong A27

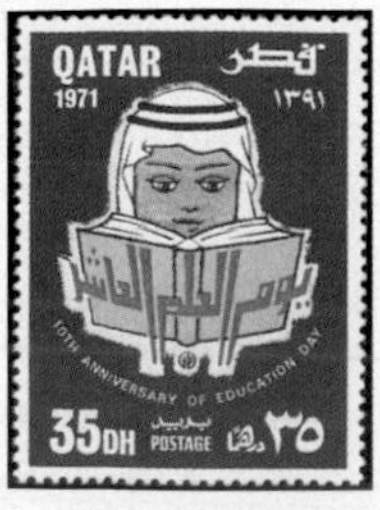

Boy Reading — A38

**1971, Aug. 10** *Perf. 13x13½*
**256** A38 35d brown & multi 3.75 .40
**257** A38 55d ultra & multi 5.25 .60
**258** A38 75d green & multi 6.00 .75
*Nos. 256-258 (3)* 15.00 1.75

International Literacy Day, Sept. 8.

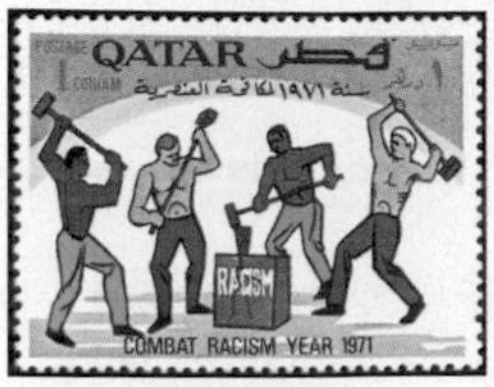

Men Splitting Racism A39

2d, 3r, People fighting racism. 3d, Soldier helping war victim. 4d, Men of 4 races rebuilding. 5d, Children on swing. 35d, Wave of racism engulfing people. 75d, like 1d.

*Perf. 13½x13, 13x13½*

**1971, Oct. 12** **Litho.**
**259** A39 1d multi .55 .55
**260** A39 2d multi .55 .55
**261** A39 3d multi .55 .55
**262** A39 4d multi, vert. .55 .55
**263** A39 5d multi, vert. .55 .55
**264** A39 35d multi 1.50 .55
**265** A39 75d multi 4.00 1.40
**266** A39 3r multi 16.00 6.75
*Nos. 259-266 (8)* 24.25 11.45

Intl. Year Against Racial Discrimination.

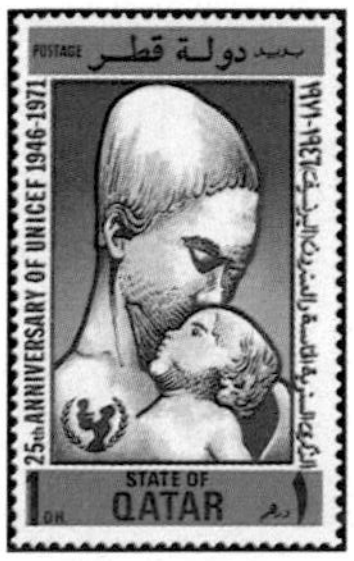

UNICEF Emblem, Mother and Child — A40

UNICEF, 25th anniv.: 2d, Child's head, horiz. 3d, 75d, Child with book. 4d, Nurse and child, horiz. 5d, Mother and child, horiz. 35d, Woman and daffodil. 3r, like 1d.

**1971, Dec. 6** *Perf. 14x13½, 13½x14*
**267** A40 1d blue & multi .50 .50
**268** A40 2d lil rose & multi .50 .50
**269** A40 3d blue & multi .50 .50
**270** A40 4d yellow & multi .50 .50
**271** A40 5d blue & multi .50 .50
**272** A40 35d lil rose & multi 2.25 .65
**273** A40 75d yellow & multi 4.00 1.00
**274** A40 3r multicolored 16.00 4.50
*Nos. 267-274 (8)* 24.75 8.65

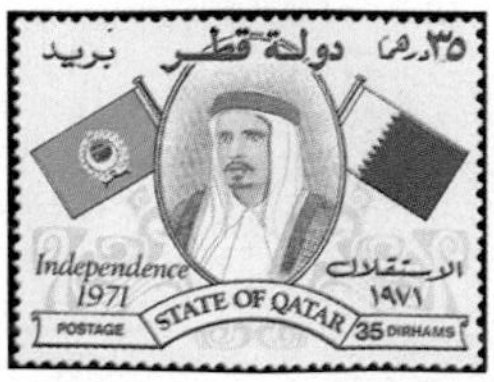

Sheik Ahmad, Flags of Arab League and Qatar A41

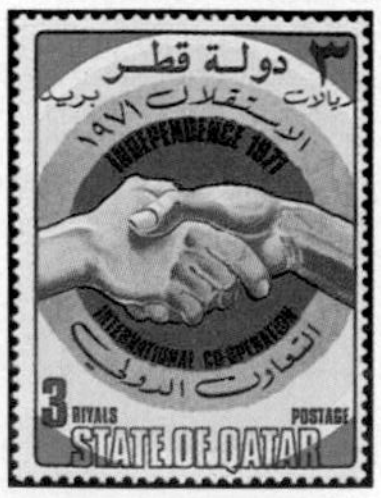

"International Cooperation" A42

75d, Sheik Ahmad, flags of UN and Qatar. 1.25r, Sheik Ahmad bin Ali al Thani.

**1972, Jan. 17** *Perf. 13½x13, 13x13½*
**275** A41 35d black & multi 2.50 .50
**276** A41 75d black & multi 4.50 1.25
**277** A42 1.25r lt brn & blk 6.50 1.75
**278** A42 3r multicolored 15.00 4.50
*a.* Souvenir sheet 40.00 9.00
*Nos. 275-278 (4)* 28.50 8.00

Independence 1971. No. 278a contains one stamp with simulated perforations.

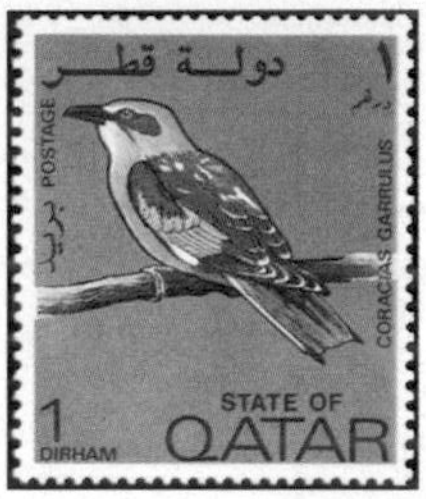

European Roller — A43

Birds: 2d, European kingfisher. 3d, Rock thrush. 4d, Caspian tern. 5d, Hoopoe. 35d, European bee-eater. 75d, European golden oriole. 3r, Peregrine falcon.

**1972, Mar. 1** **Litho.** *Perf. 12x11*
**279** A43 1d sepia & multi 1.75 .85
**280** A43 2d emerald & multi 1.75 .85
**281** A43 3d bister & multi 1.75 .85
**282** A43 4d lt blue & multi 1.75 .85
**283** A43 5d yellow & multi 1.75 .85
**284** A43 35d vio bl & multi 3.75 .85
**285** A43 75d pink & multi 9.25 2.10
**286** A43 3r blue & multi 37.50 8.50
*Nos. 279-286 (8)* 59.25 15.70

Nos. 217-219 Surcharged

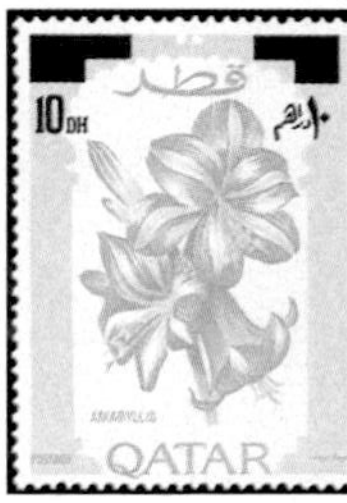

**1972, Mar. 7** *Perf. 13x13½*
**287** A31 10d on 60d multi .40 .40
**288** A31 1r on 1.25r multi 10.50 1.90
**289** A31 5r on 2r multi 52.50 8.50
*Nos. 287-289 (3)* 63.40 10.80

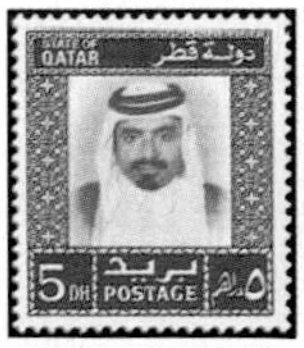

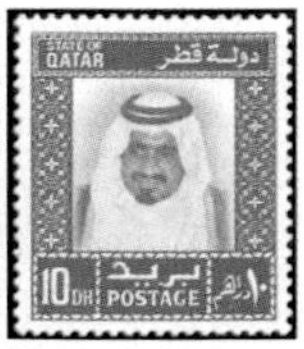

Sheik Khalifa bin Hamad al Thani
A44 A44a

**1972** *Perf. 14*

**Size: 23x27mm**

**290** A44 5d pur & ultra .60 .30
**291** A44 10d brn & rose red .60 .30
**291A** A44a 10d lt brown & lt red 175.00
**291B** A44a 25d violet & emerald 175.00
**292** A44 35d org & dl grn 2.25 .40
**293** A44 55d brt grn & lil 3.75 .60
**294** A44 75d vio & lil rose 4.50 .75

**Size: 26½x32mm**

**295** A44 1r bister & blk 7.50 1.10
**296** A44 1.25r olive & blk 9.00 1.25
**297** A44 5r blue & blk 45.00 5.25
**298** A44 10r red & blk 75.00 10.50
*Nos. 290-298 (11)* 498.20
*Nos. 290-291,292-298 (9)* 20.45

Issued: Type A44, Mar. 7.

Book Year Emblem A45

**1972, Apr. 23** *Perf. 13½x13*
**299** A45 35d lt ultra & blk 3.00 .45
**300** A45 55d lt brown & blk 4.50 .75
**301** A45 75d green & blk 6.00 1.10
**302** A45 1.25r violet & blk 9.00 1.50
*Nos. 299-302 (4)* 22.50 3.80

International Book Year 1972.

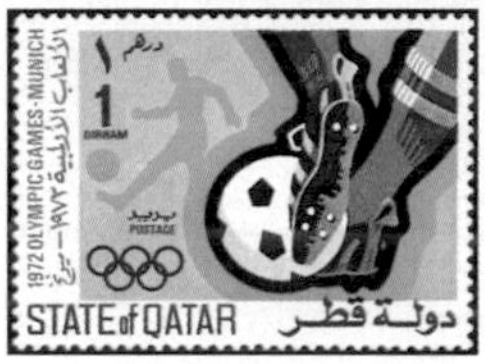

Olympic Rings, Soccer A46

2d, 3r, Running. 3d, Bicycling. 4d, Gymnastics. 5d, Basketball. 35d, Discus. 75d, Like 1d.

**1972, June 12** *Perf. 13½x13*
**303** A46 1d green & multi .80 .40
**304** A46 2d yel grn & multi .80 .40
**305** A46 3d blue & multi .80 .40
**306** A46 4d lilac & multi .80 .40
**307** A46 5d blue & multi .80 .40
**308** A46 35d gray & multi 1.60 .40
*a.* Souvenir sheet of 6 25.00 3.00
**309** A46 75d green & multi 3.25 .80
**310** A46 3r multicolored 13.50 2.75
*Nos. 303-310 (8)* 22.35 5.95

20th Olympic Games, Munich, Aug. 26-Sept. 10. No. 308a contains stamps with simulated perforations similar to Nos. 303-308.

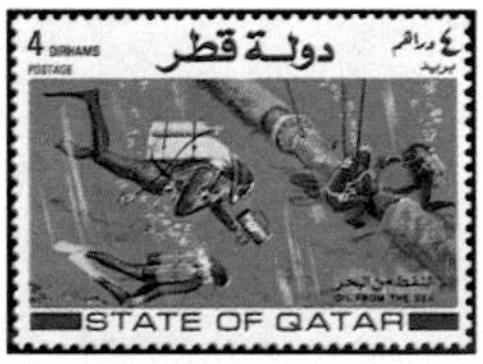

Installation of Underwater Pipe Line — A47

**1972, Aug. 8** **Litho.** *Perf. 13x13½*
**311** A47 1d Drilling for oil, vert. .40 .40
**312** A47 4d shown .40 .40
**313** A47 5d Drilling platform .40 .40
**314** A47 35d Ship searching for oil 1.90 .55
**315** A47 75d like 1d, vert. 4.25 1.10
**316** A47 3r like 5d 17.00 4.75
*Nos. 311-316 (6)* 24.35 7.60

Oil from the sea.

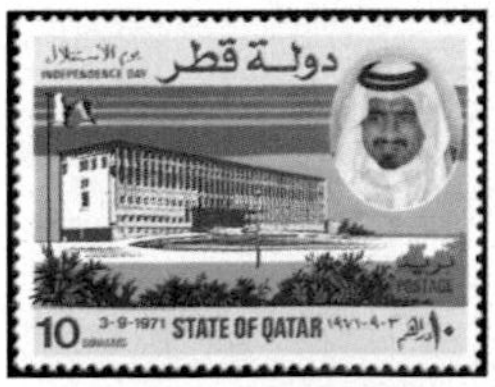

Government Palace — A48

Designs: 35d, Clasped hands, Qatar flag. 75d, Clasped hands, UN flag. 1.25r, Sheik Khalifa bin Hamad al-Thani, vert.

**1972, Sept. 3** *Perf. 13½x13, 13x13½*
**317** A48 10d yel & multi .50 .50
**318** A48 35d blk & multi 4.00 .65
**319** A48 75d blk & multi 7.00 1.25
**320** A48 1.25r gold & multi 13.00 1.90
*a.* Souvenir sheet of 1 35.00 26.00
*Nos. 317-320 (4)* 24.50 4.30

Independence Day, 1st anniv. of independence.

No. 320a contains one stamp with simulated perforations similar to No. 320.

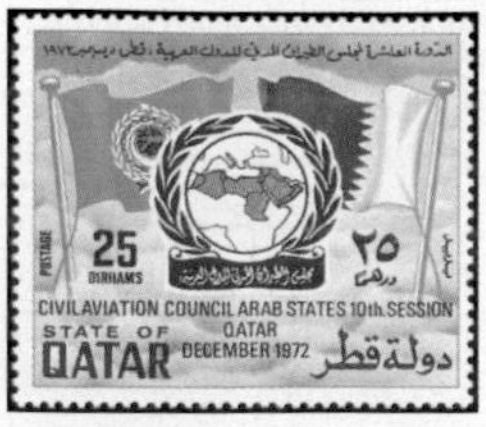

Qatar Flag, Council Emblem and Flag A49

**1972, Dec. 4** **Litho.** *Perf. 14x13½*
**321** A49 25d blue & multi 3.00 .95
**322** A49 30d vio bl & multi 3.75 1.25

Civil Aviation Council of Arab States, 10th session.

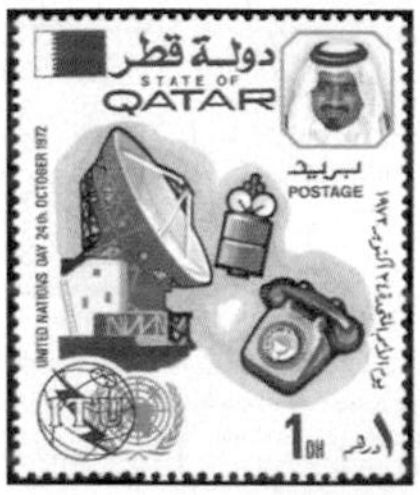

Tracking Station, Satellite, Telephone, ITU and UN Emblems A50

Designs (Agency and UN Emblems): 2d, Surveyor, artist; UNESCO. 3d, Tractor, helicopter, fish, grain and fruit; FAO. 4d, Reading children, teacher, UNICEF. 5d, Weather satellite and map; WMO. 25d, Workers and crane; ILO. 55d, Health clinic; WHO. 1r, Mail plane and post office; UPU.

**1972, Oct. 24** *Perf. 13½x14*
**323** A50 1d multicolored .60 .25
**324** A50 2d multicolored .60 .25
**325** A50 3d multicolored .60 .25
**326** A50 4d multicolored .60 .25
**327** A50 5d multicolored .60 .25
**328** A50 25d multicolored 6.25 .25
**329** A50 55d multicolored 16.00 .55
**330** A50 1r multicolored 25.00 .95
*Nos. 323-330 (8)* 50.25 3.00

United Nations Day, Oct. 24, 1972. Each stamp dedicated to a different UN agency.

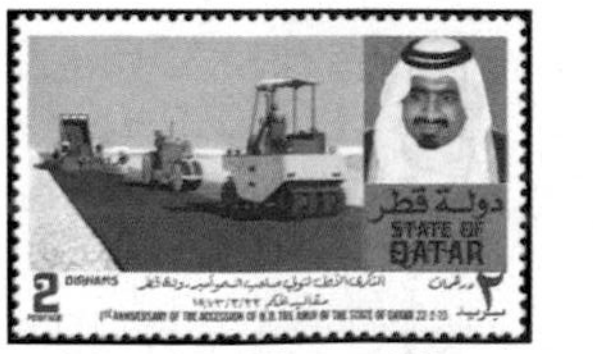

Road Building — A51

**1973, Feb. 22** **Litho.** *Perf. 13x13½*
**331** A51 2d shown .80 .40
**332** A51 3d Housing development .80 .40
**333** A51 4d Operating room .80 .40
**334** A51 5d Telephone operators .80 .40
**335** A51 15d School, classroom .80 .40
**336** A51 20d Television studio 1.40 .40
**337** A51 35d Sheik Khalifa 2.00 .50
**338** A51 55d New Gulf Hotel 4.00 .80
**339** A51 1r Fertilizer plant 6.00 1.60
**340** A51 1.35r Flour mill 12.00 2.25
*Nos. 331-340 (10)* 29.40 7.55

1st anniv. of the accession of Sheik Khalifa bin Hamad al Thani as Emir of Qatar.

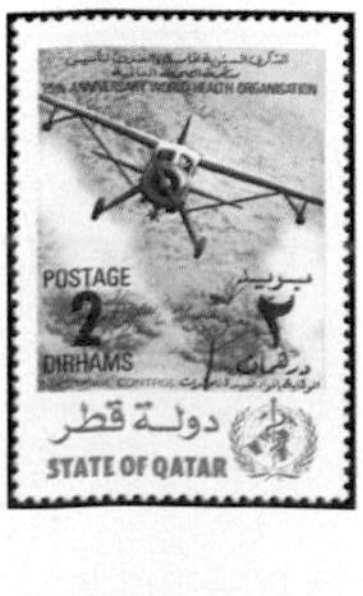

Aerial Post Control — A52

## Weather Ship A53 / WHO (A52)

WHO, 25th anniv.: 3d, Medicines. 4d, Poliomyelitis prevention. 5d, Malaria control. 55d, Mental health. 1r, Pollution control.

**Perf. 14**
**1973, May 14    Litho.**

| | | | | |
|---|---|---|---|---|
| 341 | A52 | 2d blue & multi | .60 | .30 |
| 342 | A52 | 3d blue & multi | .60 | .30 |
| 343 | A52 | 4d blue & multi | .60 | .30 |
| 344 | A52 | 5d blue & multi | .60 | .30 |
| 345 | A52 | 55d blue & multi | 9.75 | 1.10 |
| 346 | A52 | 1r blue & multi | 18.00 | 2.25 |
| | | Nos. 341-346 (6) | 30.15 | 4.55 |

**Weather Ship A53**

Designs (WMO Emblem and): 3d, Launching of radiosonde balloon. 4d, Plane and meteorological data checking. 5d, Cup anemometers and meteorological station. 10d, Weather plane in flight. 1r, Nimbus I weather satellite. 1.55r, Launching of rocket carrying weather satellite.

**Perf. 14x13**
**1973, July    Litho.**

| | | | | |
|---|---|---|---|---|
| 347 | A53 | 2d multicolored | .40 | .40 |
| 348 | A53 | 3d multicolored | .40 | .40 |
| 349 | A53 | 4d multicolored | .40 | .40 |
| 350 | A53 | 5d multicolored | .40 | .40 |
| 351 | A53 | 10d multicolored | .40 | .40 |
| 352 | A53 | 1r multicolored | 11.00 | 1.25 |
| 353 | A53 | 1.55r multicolored | 16.00 | 2.00 |
| | | Nos. 347-353 (7) | 29.00 | 5.25 |

Cent. of intl. meteorological cooperation.

## Sheik Khalifa — A54 / Clock Tower, Doha — A55

**1973-74    Litho.**
**Size: 18x27mm**

| | | | | |
|---|---|---|---|---|
| 354 | A54 | 5d green & multi | 1.10 | .40 |
| 355 | A54 | 10d lt bl & multi | 1.10 | .40 |
| 356 | A54 | 20d ver & multi | 1.10 | .40 |
| 357 | A54 | 25d orange & multi | 1.25 | .40 |
| 358 | A54 | 35d purple & multi | 2.10 | .60 |
| 359 | A54 | 55d dk gray & multi | 4.25 | .85 |

**Engr.**
**Perf. 13½**

| | | | | |
|---|---|---|---|---|
| 360 | A55 | 75d lil, bl & grn | 5.25 | 1.25 |

**Photo.**
**Perf. 13**
**Size: 27x32mm**

| | | | | |
|---|---|---|---|---|
| 360A | A54 | 1r multicolored | 8.50 | 4.25 |
| 360B | A54 | 5r multicolored | 42.50 | 16.00 |
| 360C | A54 | 10r multicolored | 167.15 | 77.05 |
| | | Nos. 354-360C (10) | | |

Issue dates: 20d, 75d, July 3, 1973; 1r-10r, July 1974; others, Jan. 27, 1973.

## Flag of Qatar, Handclasp, Sheik Khalifa — A56

Flag, Sheik and: 35d, Harvest. 55d, Government Building. 1.35r, Market and Clock Tower, Doha. 1.55r, Illuminated fountain.

**Perf. 13**
**1973, Oct. 4    Litho.**

| | | | | |
|---|---|---|---|---|
| 361 | A56 | 15d red & multi | .65 | .30 |
| 362 | A56 | 35d buff & multi | 1.10 | .30 |
| 363 | A56 | 55d multi | 3.00 | .50 |
| 364 | A56 | 1.35r vio & multi | 6.50 | 1.25 |
| 365 | A56 | 1.55r multi | 8.25 | 1.60 |
| | | | 19.50 | 3.95 |
| | | Nos. 361-365 (5) | | |

2nd anniversary of independence.

## Planting Tree, Qatar and UN Flags, UNESCO Emblem — A57

Qatar and UN Flags and: 4d, UN Headquarters and flags. 5d, Pipe laying, cement mixer, helicopter and ILO emblem. 35d, Nurse, patient and UNICEF emblem. 1.35r, Telecommunications and ITU emblem. 3r, Cattle, wheat disease analysis and FAO emblem.

**1973, Oct. 24    Litho.**

| | | | | |
|---|---|---|---|---|
| 366 | A57 | 2d multi | .50 | .50 |
| 367 | A57 | 4d multi | .50 | .50 |
| 368 | A57 | 5d multi | .60 | .50 |
| 369 | A57 | 35d multi | 1.90 | .50 |
| 370 | A57 | 1.35r multi | 7.50 | 2.25 |
| 371 | A57 | 3r multi | 19.00 | 6.25 |
| | | | 30.00 | 10.50 |
| | | Nos. 366-371 (6) | | |

United Nations Day.

## Prison Gates Opening — A58

4d, Marchers with flags. 5d, Scales of Justice. 35d, Teacher and pupils. 1.35r, UN General Assembly. 3r, Human Rights flame, vert.

**Perf. 13x13½**
**1973, Dec.    Litho.**

| | | | | |
|---|---|---|---|---|
| 372 | A58 | 2d yellow & multi | .40 | .40 |
| 373 | A58 | 4d pale lil & multi | .40 | .40 |
| 374 | A58 | 5d rose & multi | .40 | .40 |
| 375 | A58 | 35d lt bl & multi | 1.60 | .50 |
| 376 | A58 | 1.35r lt bl & multi | 6.25 | 2.10 |
| 377 | A58 | 3r citron & multi | 10.50 | 4.25 |
| | | | 19.55 | 8.05 |
| | | Nos. 372-377 (6) | | |

25th anniversary of the Universal Declaration of Human Rights.

## Highway Overpass — A59

**1974, Feb. 22    Litho.**
**Perf. 14x13½**

| | | | | |
|---|---|---|---|---|
| 378 | A59 | 2d shown | .70 | .35 |
| 379 | A59 | 3d Symbol of learning | .70 | .35 |
| 380 | A59 | 5d Oil field | .70 | .35 |
| 381 | A59 | 35d Gulf Hotel, Doha | 1.75 | 1.35 |
| 382 | A59 | 2.25r Radar station | 9.00 | 1.75 |
| 383 | A59 | 2.25r Sheik Khalifa | 11.50 | 2.75 |
| | | | 24.35 | 5.90 |
| | | Nos. 378-383 (6) | | |

Accession of Sheik Khalifa as Emir, 2nd, anniv.

## Mail Truck, Camel Caravan and UPU Emblem — A60

UPU cent.: 3d, Old and new trains, Arab Postal Union emblem. 10d, Old and new ships and Qatar coat of arms. 35d, Old and new planes. 75d, Mail sorting by hand and computer, and Arab Postal Union emblem. 1.25r, Old and new post offices, and Qatar coat of arms.

**1974, May 22    Litho.**
**Perf. 13½**

| | | | | |
|---|---|---|---|---|
| 384 | A60 | 2d brt yel & multi | .85 | .45 |
| 385 | A60 | 3d lt bl & multi | .85 | .45 |
| 386 | A60 | 10d dp org & multi | .85 | .45 |
| 387 | A60 | 35d slate & multi | 3.25 | .65 |
| 388 | A60 | 75d yellow & multi | 7.75 | 1.25 |
| 389 | A60 | 1.25r lt bl & multi | 11.00 | 2.25 |
| | | | 24.55 | 5.50 |
| | | Nos. 384-389 (6) | | |

## Doha Hospital — A61

5d shown. 10d WPY emblem and people. 15d WPY emblem. 35d World map. 75d Clock and infants. 1.75r Family.

**1974, July 13    Litho.**
**Perf. 13½**

| | | | | |
|---|---|---|---|---|
| 390 | A61 | 5d shown | 1.10 | .60 |
| 391 | A61 | 10d WPY emblem and people | 1.10 | .60 |
| 392 | A61 | 15d WPY emblem | 1.75 | .60 |
| 393 | A61 | 35d World map | 2.00 | .70 |
| 394 | A61 | 75d Clock and infants | 8.75 | 3.00 |
| 395 | A61 | 1.75r Family | 11.00 | 3.50 |
| | | | 24.80 | 8.90 |
| | | Nos. 390-395 (6) | | |

World Population Year 1974.

## Television Station — A62

**1974, Sept. 2    Litho.**
**Perf. 13½x13**

| | | | | |
|---|---|---|---|---|
| 399 | A62 | 5d shown | .45 | .45 |
| 400 | A62 | 10d Palace of Doha | .45 | .45 |
| 401 | A62 | 15d Teachers' College | .45 | .45 |
| 402 | A62 | 75d Clock Tower and Mosque | 5.25 | 1.10 |
| 403 | A62 | 1.55r Traffic circle, Doha | 8.50 | 1.75 |
| 404 | A62 | 2.25r Sheik Khalifa | 13.50 | 2.75 |
| | | | 28.60 | 6.95 |
| | | Nos. 399-404 (6) | | |

3rd anniversary of independence.

## Operating Room and WHO Emblem — A63

UN Day: 10d, Satellite earth station and ITU emblem. 20d, Tractor, UN and FAO emblems. 25d, School children, UN and UNESCO emblems. 1.75r, Open air court, UN Headquarters, emblems. 2r, UPU and UN emblems.

**1974, Oct. 24    Litho.**
**Perf. 13x13½**

| | | | | |
|---|---|---|---|---|
| 405 | A63 | 5d multi | .55 | .55 |
| 406 | A63 | 10d multi | .55 | .55 |
| 407 | A63 | 20d multi | .55 | .55 |
| 408 | A63 | 25d multi | 1.40 | 1.35 |
| 409 | A63 | 1.75r multi | 12.50 | 2.75 |
| 410 | A63 | 2r multi | 14.00 | 3.50 |
| | | | 29.55 | 8.45 |
| | | Nos. 405-410 (6) | | |

## VC-10, Gulf Aviation Airliner — A64 / Arab League and Qatar Flags, Civil Aviation Emblem — A65

Design: 25d, Doha Airport.

**1974, Dec. 1    Litho.**
**Perf. 13½**

| | | | | |
|---|---|---|---|---|
| 411 | A64 | 20d multi | 3.00 | .55 |
| 412 | A64 | 25d yel & dk bl | 4.50 | .70 |
| 413 | A65 | 30d multi | 5.75 | .85 |
| 414 | A65 | 50d multi | 11.50 | 1.40 |
| | | Nos. 411-414 (4) | 24.75 | 3.50 |

Arab Civil Aviation Day.

## Caspian Terns, Hoopoes and Shara'o Island — A66 / Dhow by Moonlight — A67

5d, Clock Tower, Doha, vert. 15d, Zubara Fort. 35d, Gulf Hotel & sailboats. 75d, Arabian oryx. 1.25r, Khor Al-Udein. 1.75r, Ruins, Wakrah.

**1974, Dec. 21    Litho.**
**Perf. 13½**

| | | | | |
|---|---|---|---|---|
| 415 | A66 | 5d multi | .40 | .40 |
| 416 | A66 | 10d multi | .40 | .40 |
| 417 | A66 | 15d multi | .40 | .40 |
| 418 | A66 | 35d multi | 1.00 | .40 |
| 419 | A67 | 75d multi | 2.00 | .70 |
| 420 | A66 | 75d multi | 3.50 | 1.00 |
| 421 | A67 | 1.75r multi | 11.00 | 1.75 |
| 422 | A66 | 2.25r multi | 15.00 | 2.50 |
| | | | 33.70 | 7.55 |
| | | Nos. 415-422 (8) | | |

## Traffic Circle, Doha A68 / Sheik Khalifa — A69

35d, Pipe line from offshore platform. 55d, Laying underwater pipe line. 1r, Refinery.

**1975, Feb. 22    Litho.**
**Perf. 13½**

| | | | | |
|---|---|---|---|---|
| 423 | A68 | 10d multi | .40 | .40 |
| 424 | A68 | 35d multi | 2.10 | .85 |
| 425 | A68 | 55d multi | 3.25 | 1.25 |
| 426 | A68 | 1r multi | 6.25 | 2.50 |
| 427 | A69 | 1.55r sil & multi | 7.25 | 3.25 |
| 428 | A69 | 1.55r gold & multi | 9.50 | 3.50 |
| | | | 28.75 | 11.75 |
| | | Nos. 423-428 (6) | | |

Accession of Sheik Khalifa, 3rd anniv.

## Qatar Flag and Arab Labor Charter Emblem — A70

**1975, May 28    Litho.    Perf. 13**

| | | | |
|---|---|---|---|
| 429 | A70 | 10d bl, red brn & blk | .55 .55 |
| 430 | A70 | 35d multicolored | 4.25 1.00 |
| 431 | A70 | 1r green & multi | 11.00 2.75 |
| | | Nos. 429-431 (3) | 15.80 4.30 |

Arab Labor Charter and Constitution, 10th anniversary.

## Flintlock Pistol with Ornamental Grip — A71

**1975, June 23    Perf. 13**

| | | | |
|---|---|---|---|
| 432 | A71 | 2d multi | .40 .40 |
| 433 | A71 | 3d ver blk & gold | .40 .40 |
| 434 | A71 | 15d lt blue & multi | 1.90 .50 |
| 435 | A71 | 75d ver & multi | 4.75 1.00 |
| 436 | A71 | 1.25r vio & multi | 8.50 1.75 |
| 437 | A71 | 3r fawn & multi | 19.00 3.75 |
| | | Nos. 432-437 (6) | 34.95 7.80 |

Opening of Qatar National Museum.

Designs: 3d, Ornamental mosaic. 35d, View of museum. 75d, Arch and museum, vert. 1.25r, Flint arrowheads and tool. 3r, Gold necklace, vert.

## Traffic Signs, Policeman, Doha — A72

**1975, June 24**

| | | | |
|---|---|---|---|
| 438 | A72 | 5d lt green & multi | .50 .50 |
| 439 | A72 | 15d lt blue & multi | 3.25 .50 |
| 440 | A72 | 35d lemon & multi | 7.75 1.90 |
| 441 | A72 | 55d lt violet & multi | 24.50 4.00 |
| | | Nos. 438-441 (4) | 13.00 1.90 |

Designs: 15d, 55d, Cars, arrows, traffic lights, Doha Clock Tower. 35d, like 5d.
Traffic Week.

## Constitution, Arabic Text — A73

**1975, Sept. 2    5d**

| | | | |
|---|---|---|---|
| 442 | A73 | 5d multi | .40 .40 |
| 443 | A73 | 15d multi | 2.10 .95 |
| 444 | A73 | 35d multi | 2.50 .65 |
| 445 | A73 | 75d multi | 4.25 1.25 |
| 446 | A73 | 1r multi | 5.75 1.25 |
| 447 | A73 | 1.25r multi | 7.50 1.75 |
| | | Nos. 442-447 (6) | 24.00 6.30 |

4th anniversary of independence.

Designs: 5d Government buildings, horiz. 15d, Museum & Clock Tower, horiz. 55d, Sheik Khalifa & Qatar flag. 75d, Constitution, English text.

## Satellite over Globe, ITU Emblem — A74

**1975, Oct. 25    Litho.    Perf. 13x13½**

| | | | |
|---|---|---|---|
| 448 | A74 | 5d multi | .55 .55 |
| 449 | A74 | 15d multi | 1.40 .55 |
| 450 | A74 | 35d multi | 2.10 .55 |
| 451 | A74 | 75d multi | 6.25 1.40 |
| 452 | A74 | 1r multi | 7.00 1.60 |
| 453 | A74 | 1.25r multi | 12.50 2.75 |
| | | Nos. 448-453 (6) | 29.80 7.35 |

UN, 30th anniv.: 15d, UN Headquarters, NY and UN emblem. 35d, UPU emblem over Eastern Arabia, UN emblem. 1.25r, Nurses and infant, WHO emblem. 1r, Road building, equipment, ILO emblem. 2r, Students, UNESCO emblem.

## Fertilizer Plant — A75

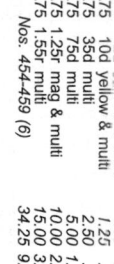
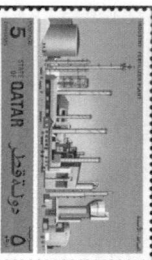
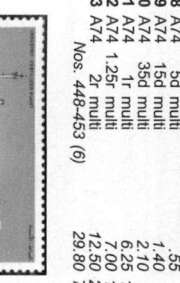

**1975, Dec. 6**

| | | | |
|---|---|---|---|
| 454 | A75 | 5d salmon & multi | .50 .50 |
| 455 | A75 | 10d yellow & multi | 1.25 .60 |
| 456 | A75 | 35d multi | 2.50 .60 |
| 457 | A75 | 75d multi | 10.00 1.50 |
| 458 | A75 | 1.25r mag & multi | 15.00 3.50 |
| 459 | A75 | 1.55r multi | 34.25 9.10 |

Designs: 10d, Flour mill, vert. 35d, Natural gas plant. 75d, Oil refinery. 1.25r, Cement works. 1.55r, Steel mill.

## Modern Building, Doha — A76

**1976, Feb. 22    Litho.    Perf. 13**

| | | | |
|---|---|---|---|
| 460 | A76 | 5d multi | .55 .55 |
| 461 | A76 | 10d multi | .55 .55 |
| 462 | A76 | 35d multi | 2.25 .85 |
| 463 | A76 | 55d multi | 4.25 .85 |
| 464 | A76 | 75d multi | 5.50 1.25 |
| 465 | A76 | 1.55r multi | 11.00 2.50 |
| | | Nos. 460-465 (6) | 24.10 6.25 |

Designs: 10d, 35d, 1.55r, Various modern buildings. 55d, 75d, Sheik Khalifa & Qatar flag, diff.
Accession of Sheik Khalifa, 4th anniv.

## Satellite Earth Station — A77

**1976, Mar. 1    Litho.**

| | | | |
|---|---|---|---|
| 466 | A77 | 35d multicolored | 2.50 .40 |
| 467 | A77 | 55d dp bis & multi | 3.25 1.00 |
| 468 | A77 | 75d vermilion & multi | 4.75 .70 |
| 469 | A77 | 1r violet & multi | 7.25 .95 |
| | | Nos. 466-469 (4) | 17.75 2.55 |

Designs: 55d, 1r, Satellite. 75d, Like 35d.
Inauguration of satellite earth station in Qatar.

## Telephones, 1876 and 1976 — A78

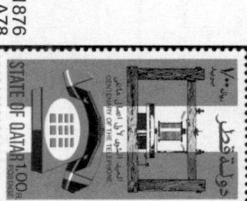

**1976, Mar. 10    Litho.    Perf. 13x13½**

| | | | |
|---|---|---|---|
| 470 | A78 | 1r rose & multi | 4.00 1.75 |
| 471 | A78 | 1.35r lt bl & multi | 5.75 2.25 |

Centenary of first telephone call by Alexander Graham Bell, Mar. 10, 1876.

## Arabian Soccer League Emblem — A79

**1976, Mar. 25    Litho.    Perf. 13½x13**

| | | | |
|---|---|---|---|
| 472 | A79 | 5d lil & multi | .45 .45 |
| 473 | A79 | 10d pink & multi | .45 .45 |
| 474 | A79 | 35d bl grn & multi | 1.75 .60 |
| 475 | A79 | 75d multi | 3.50 .90 |
| 476 | A79 | 1r multi | 8.25 2.40 |
| 477 | A79 | 1.25r multi | 19.15 6.25 |
| | | Nos. 472-477 (6) | |

Designs: 10d, Stadium, Doha. 35d, Like 5d. 55d, Players. 75d, One player.
4th Arabian Gulf Soccer Cup Tournament, Doha, Mar. 22-Apr.

## Dhow — A80

**1976, Apr. 19    Perf. 13½x14**

| | | | |
|---|---|---|---|
| 478 | A80 | 5d blue & multi | .35 .35 |
| 479 | A80 | 10d blue & multi | 2.75 .35 |
| 480 | A80 | 35d blue & multi | 5.50 .80 |
| 481 | A80 | 80d blue & multi | 10.00 1.40 |
| 482 | A80 | 1.50r blue & multi | 11.50 1.40 |
| 483 | A80 | 2r blue & multi | 18.00 2.50 |
| | | Nos. 478-483 (6) | 48.10 7.00 |

Designs: Various dhows.

## Soccer — A81

**1976, May 15    Litho.    Perf. 14x13½**

| | | | |
|---|---|---|---|
| 484 | A81 | 5d multicolored | .85 .40 |
| 485 | A81 | 10d blue & multi | .85 .40 |
| 486 | A81 | 35d orange & multi | .85 .40 |
| 487 | A81 | 80d bister & multi | 5.50 .85 |
| 488 | A81 | 80d lilac & multi | 9.50 1.60 |
| 489 | A81 | 1.50r rose & multi | 12.50 1.60 |
| | | Nos. 484-489 (6) | 30.05 5.75 |

Designs: 10d, Yachting. 35d, Steeplechase. 80d, Boxing. 1.25r, Weight lifting. 1.50, Basketball.
21st Olympic Games, Montreal, Canada, July 17-Aug. 1.

## Village and Emblems — A82

**1976, May 31    Perf. 13½x14**

| | | | |
|---|---|---|---|
| 490 | A82 | 10d orange & multi | .65 .30 |
| 491 | A82 | 35d yellow & multi | 2.50 .30 |
| 492 | A82 | 80d citron & multi | 5.75 .70 |
| 493 | A82 | 1.25r dp blue & multi | 9.00 2.55 |
| | | Nos. 490-493 (4) | 17.90 2.55 |

Designs: 35d, Emblems. 80d, Village. 1.25r, Sheik Khalifa.
Habitat, UN Conf. on Human Settlements, Vancouver, Canada, May 31-June 11.

## Snowy Plover — A83

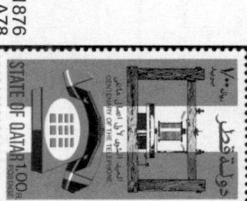

**1976, July 19    Perf. 13½x14, 14x13½    Litho.**

| | | | |
|---|---|---|---|
| 494 | A83 | 5d multi | 1.25 .30 |
| 495 | A83 | 10d multi | 2.75 .30 |
| 496 | A83 | 35d multi | 5.50 .40 |
| 497 | A83 | 80d multi | 12.00 1.00 |
| 498 | A83 | 1.25r multi | 17.50 2.50 |
| 499 | A83 | 2r multi | 20.00 1.60 |
| | | Nos. 494-499 (6) | 59.00 6.10 |

Birds: 10d, Great cormorant. 35d, Osprey. 80d, Flamingo. 1.25r, Rock thrush. 2r, Saker falcon. 35d, 80d, 1.25r, 2r, vertical.

## Sheik Khalifa and Qatar Flag — A84

**1976, Sept. 2    Perf. 14x13½, 13½x14**

| | | | |
|---|---|---|---|
| 500 | A84 | 5d gold & multi | .50 .50 |
| 501 | A84 | 10d silver & multi | .50 .50 |
| 502 | A84 | 40d multicolored | 1.90 .60 |
| 503 | A84 | 80d multicolored | 3.50 .90 |
| 504 | A84 | 1.25r multicolored | 5.50 1.90 |
| 505 | A84 | 1.50r multicolored | 7.00 2.25 |
| | | Nos. 500-505 (6) | 19.40 7.00 |

5th anniversary of independence.

## Government Building — A85

Designs: 10d, like 80d, Government building. 1.25r, Offshore oil platform. 1.50r, UN emblem and Qatar coat of arms.

## Qatar Flag and UN Emblem — A86

**1976, Oct. 24    Litho.    Perf. 13½x14**

| | | | |
|---|---|---|---|
| 506 | A86 | 2r multi | 5.00 1.75 |
| 507 | A86 | 3r multi | 6.75 2.50 |

United Nations Day 1976.

**A87**
**A88**
Sheik Khalifa

**1977, Feb. 22 Litho. Perf. 14x13½**
| 508 | A87 | 20d silver & multi | 1.50 | .40 |
| 509 | A87 | 1.80r gold & multi | 11.00 | 1.75 |

Accession of Sheik Khalifa, 5th anniv.

Sheik Khalifa

**1977, Mar. 1 Litho. Perf. 14x14½**
**Size: 22x27mm**
| 510 | A88 | 5d multicolored | .30 | .30 |
| 511 | A88 | 10d aqua & multi | .30 | .30 |
| 512 | A88 | 35d orange & multi | 1.10 | .30 |
| 513 | A88 | 80d multicolored | 2.25 | .45 |

**Perf. 13½**
**Size: 25x30mm**
| 514 | A88 | 1r vio bl & multi | 3.75 | .70 |
| 515 | A88 | 5r yellow & multi | 12.00 | 3.25 |
| 516 | A88 | 10r multicolored | 30.00 | 6.75 |
| | | Nos. 510-516 (7) | 49.70 | 12.05 |

Letter, APU Emblem, Flag — A89

**1977, Apr. 12 Perf. 14x13½**
| 517 | A89 | 35d blue & multi | 1.50 | .70 |
| 518 | A89 | 1.35r blue & multi | 4.50 | 2.00 |

Arab Postal Union, 25th anniversary.

Waves and Sheik Khalifa A90

**1977, May 17 Litho. Perf. 13½x14**
| 519 | A90 | 35d multi | .90 | .45 |
| 520 | A90 | 1.80r multi | 6.00 | 2.50 |

World Telecommunications Day.

Sheik Khalifa — A90a

**1977, June 29 Litho. Wmk. 368**
**Perf. 13½x13**
| 520A | A90a | 5d multi | .40 | .40 |
| 520B | A90a | 10d multi | .40 | .40 |
| 520C | A90a | 35d multi | .40 | .40 |
| 520D | A90a | 80d multi | 3.50 | .95 |
| | | Nos. 520A-520D (4) | 4.70 | 2.15 |
| e. | | Bkt. pane, 4 5d, 3 10d, 2 35d, 80d | 30.00 | 12.50 |

Issued in booklets only.

Parliament, Clock Tower, Minaret — A91

Designs: No. 522, Main business district, Doha. No. 523, Highway crossings, Doha.

**1977, Sept. 1 Litho. Perf. 13x13½**
| 521 | A91 | 80d multicolored | 4.00 | 1.25 |
| 522 | A91 | 80d multicolored | 4.00 | 1.25 |
| 523 | A91 | 80d multicolored | 12.00 | 3.75 |
| | | Nos. 521-523 (3) | | |

6th anniversary of independence.

UN Emblem, Flag — A92

**1977, Oct. 24 Litho. Perf. 13½x14**
| 524 | A92 | 20d green & multi | 1.00 | .40 |
| 525 | A92 | 1r blue & multi | 4.00 | 1.50 |

United Nations Day.

Surgery — A93

**1978, Feb. 22 Litho. Perf. 13½x14**
| 526 | A93 | 20d multicolored | .40 | .40 |
| 527 | A93 | 80d multicolored | 2.50 | .85 |
| 528 | A93 | 1r multicolored | 3.00 | 1.10 |
| 529 | A93 | 5r multicolored | 16.00 | 5.25 |
| | | Nos. 526-529 (4) | 21.90 | 7.60 |

Designs: 20d, Steel mill. 1r, Classroom. 5r, Sheik Khalifa.

Accession of Sheik Khalifa, 6th anniv.

Oil Refinery — A94

80d, Office buildings, Doha. 1.35r, Traffic Circle, Doha. 1.80r, Sheik Khalifa and flag.

**1978, Aug. 31 Litho. Perf. 13½x14**
| 530 | A94 | 35d multi | .95 | .40 |
| 531 | A94 | 80d multi | 2.40 | .95 |
| 532 | A94 | 1.35r multi | 3.75 | 1.90 |
| 533 | A94 | 1.80r multi | 4.75 | 1.90 |
| | | Nos. 530-533 (4) | 11.85 | 4.65 |

7th anniversary of independence.

Man Learning to Read — A95

**1978, Sept. 8 Litho. Perf. 13½x14**
| 534 | A95 | 35d multicolored | 1.25 | .30 |
| 535 | A95 | 80d multicolored | 3.50 | 1.40 |

International Literacy Day.

Flag and UN Emblem — A96

**Perf. 13x13½**
**1978, Oct. 14**
| 536 | A96 | 35d multi | 3.00 | 1.10 |
| 537 | A96 | 80d multi | | |

United Nations Day.

Human Rights Emblem — A97

IYC Emblem — A98

Designs: 80d, like 35d, 1.25r, 1.80r, Scales and Human Rights emblem.

**1978, Dec. 10 Litho. Perf. 14x13½**
| 538 | A97 | 35d multi | .60 | .35 |
| 539 | A97 | 80d multi | 1.75 | 1.00 |
| 540 | A97 | 1.25r multi | 2.10 | 1.40 |
| 541 | A97 | 1.80r multi | 4.25 | 2.10 |
| | | Nos. 538-541 (4) | 8.70 | 4.85 |

30th anniversary of Universal Declaration of Human Rights.

**Wmk. JEZ Multiple (368)**
**1979, Jan. 1 Litho. Perf. 13½x13**
| 542 | A98 | 35d multi | 1.00 | .65 |
| 543 | A98 | 1.80r multi | 4.00 | 3.25 |

International Year of the Child.

Sheik Khalifa — A100

A99

**Perf. 14 Unwmk.**
**1979, Jan. 15**
| 544 | A99 | 5d multi | .30 | .30 |
| 545 | A99 | 10d multi | .30 | .30 |
| 546 | A99 | 20d multi | .30 | .30 |
| 547 | A99 | 35d multi | .40 | .30 |
| 548 | A99 | 35d multi | .55 | .50 |
| 549 | A99 | 60d multi | 1.40 | .50 |
| 550 | A99 | 80d multi | 1.60 | .65 |

**Size: 27x32mm**
| 551 | A99 | 1r multi | 2.00 | .80 |
| 552 | A99 | 1.25r multi | 2.40 | 1.00 |
| 553 | A99 | 1.35r multi | 3.25 | 1.25 |
| 554 | A99 | 1.80r multi | 4.00 | 1.40 |
| 555 | A99 | 9r multi | 11.00 | 4.00 |
| 556 | A99 | 10r multi | 22.50 | 8.00 |
| | | Nos. 544-556 (13) | 50.00 | 19.10 |

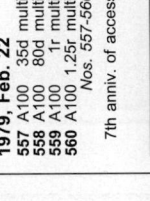

**Wmk. 368**
**1979, Feb. 22**
| 557 | A100 | 35d multi | .90 | .50 |
| 558 | A100 | 80d multi | 2.00 | 1.10 |
| 559 | A100 | 1r multi | 2.00 | 1.50 |
| 560 | A100 | 1.25r multi | 3.75 | 1.90 |
| | | Nos. 557-560 (4) | 9.65 | 5.00 |

7th anniv. of accession of Sheik Khalifa.

Cables and People — A101

**1979, May 17 Litho. Perf. 14x13½**
| 561 | A101 | 2r multi | 3.00 | 2.00 |
| 562 | A101 | 2.80r multi | 4.00 | 2.50 |

World Telecommunications Day.

Children Holding Globe, UNESCO Emblem — A102

**Perf. 13x13½ Litho. Unwmk.**
**1979, July 15**
| 563 | A102 | 35d multicolored | .90 | .45 |
| 564 | A102 | 80d multicolored | 4.00 | 1.40 |

International Bureau of Education, Geneva, 50th anniversary.

Rolling Mill — A103

UN Day — A104

**Wmk. 368**
**1979, Sept. 2 Litho. Perf. 13½**
| 565 | A103 | 5d shown | .75 | .40 |
| 566 | A103 | 10d Doha, aerial view | 4.25 | 1.60 |
| 567 | A103 | 1.25r Qatar flag | 6.25 | 2.10 |
| 568 | A103 | 2r Sheik Khalifa | 12.00 | 4.50 |
| | | Nos. 565-568 (4) | | |

Independence, 8th anniversary.

**1979, Oct. 24 Litho. Perf. 13½x13**
| 569 | A104 | 1.25r multi | 4.25 | 1.40 |
| 570 | A104 | 2r multi | 7.50 | 2.40 |

**1979, Nov. 24**
Conference Emblem — A105
Perf. 13x13½

571 A105 35d multi 2.75 .45
572 A105 1.80r multi 9.00 2.25
Hegira (Pilgrimage Year); 3rd World Conference on Prophets.

**1980, Feb. 22**
Sheik Khalifa, 8th Anniversary of Accession — A106
Litho. Perf. 13x13½

573 A106 20d multi .30 .30
574 A106 60d multi 2.40 .55
575 A106 1.25r multi 4.50 1.00
576 A106 2r multi 9.50 2.00
16.70 3.85
Nos. 573-576 (4)

**1980, Mar. 1**
Map of Arab Countries — A107
Litho. Perf. 13½x14

577 A107 2.35r multi 8.50 1.75
578 A107 2.80r multi 11.50 2.10
6th Congress of Arab Town Organization, Doha, Mar. 1-4.

Oil Refinery — A108

**1980, Sept. 2**
Litho. Perf. 14½
579 A108 10d shown .40 .40
580 A108 35d View of Doha 1.90 .40
581 A108 2r Oil ring 7.50 2.10
582 A108 2.35r Hospital 9.50 3.25
19.30 6.25
Nos. 579-582 (4)
9th anniversary of independence.

Men Holding OPEC Emblem — A109

**1980, Sept. 15**
OPEC, 20th anniversary.
583 A109 1.35r multi 4.00 1.40
584 A109 2r multi 5.75 2.10

**1980, Oct. 24**
United Nations Day 1980 — A110
Perf. 14x13½

585 A110 1.35r multi 3.00 1.25
586 A110 1.80r multi 4.50 1.60

**1980, Nov. 8**
Hegira (Pilgrimage Year) — A111
Litho. Perf. 14½

587 A111 10d multi .50 .50
588 A111 35d multi 1.00 .65
589 A111 1.25r multi 3.25 2.10
590 A111 2.80r multi 7.00 5.00
11.75 8.25
Nos. 587-590 (4)

**1981, Jan. 5**
International Year of the Disabled — A112
Granite Paper Photo. Perf. 11½

591 A112 2r multi 5.00 2.00
592 A112 3r multi 7.00 3.00

Education Day — A113
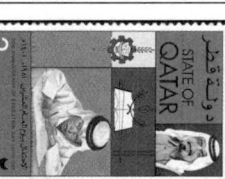

**1981, Feb. 22**
Perf. 14x13½
Litho. Wmk. 368
593 A113 2r multi 4.25 1.50
594 A113 3r multi 5.75 2.40

Sheik Khalifa, 9th Anniversary of Accession A114

**1981, Feb. 22**
595 A114 10d multi .40 .40
596 A114 35d multi 2.00 .40
597 A114 80d multi .70
598 A114 5r multi 15.00 4.50
17.80 6.00
Nos. 595-598 (4)

A115
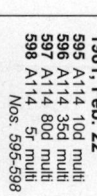
A116

**1981, May 17**
Litho. Perf. 13½x13
599 A115 2r multi 4.25 1.75
600 A115 2.80r multi 5.75 2.40
13th World Telecommunications Day.

**1981, June 11**
Championship emblem.
601 A116 1.25r multi 4.50 1.10
602 A116 2.80r multi 10.00 2.50
30th Intl. Military Soccer Championship, Doha.
Litho. Perf. 14x13½

**1981, Sept. 2**
10th Anniv. of Independence — A117
Perf. 13½x14
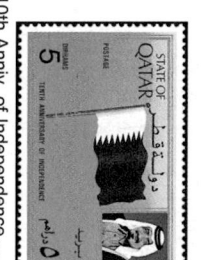
603 A117 5d multicolored .40 .40
604 A117 60d multicolored 1.90 .55
605 A117 80d multicolored 2.75 .75
606 A117 2r multicolored 14.50 5.25
19.55 6.95
Nos. 603-606 (4)
Litho. Wmk. 368

**1981, Oct. 16**
World Food Day — A118

607 A118 2r multi 6.25 2.75
608 A118 2.80r multi 8.00 4.00
Litho. Perf. 13

Red Crescent Society — A119

**1982, Jan. 16**
10th Anniv. of Sheik Khalifa's Accession — A120
Litho. Perf. 14x13½

609 A119 20d multi .80 .30
610 A119 2.80r multi 6.75 3.25

**1982, Feb. 22**
Litho. Wmk. 368 Perf. 13½x14
611 A120 10d multi .45 .45
612 A120 20d multi 1.10 .45
613 A120 1.25r multi 6.50 1.40
614 A120 2.80r multi 13.00 3.00
21.05 5.30
Nos. 611-614 (4)

Sheik Khalifa — A121

Oil Refinery — A122

**1982, Mar. 1**
Designs: 5r, 10r, 15r, Hoda Clock Tower.
Granite Paper Photo. Perf. 11½x12
615 A121 5d multi .30 .30
616 A121 10d multi .30 .30
617 A121 15d multi .30 .30
618 A121 20d multi .30 .30
619 A121 35d multi .30 .30
620 A121 80d multi .75 .40
621 A121 1r multi .50 .30
622 A121 1.25r multi .65 .40
623 A121 2r multi .90 .50
624 A121 5r multi 1.25 .65
625 A122 10r multi 2.50 1.40
626 A122 15r multi 6.75 3.25
627 A122 multi 13.50 6.75
628 A122 multi 19.00 9.75
49.00 25.40
Nos. 615-628 (14)

**1982, Mar.**
Hamad General Hospital — A123

629 A123 10d multi .40 .30
630 A123 2.35r multi 5.75 2.50
Litho. Perf. 13½x13½

**1982, Mar. 6**
6th Anniv. of United Arab Shipping Co. — A124

631 A124 20d multi .90 .35
632 A124 2.35r multi 8.00 2.50
Litho. Perf. 13½x13½

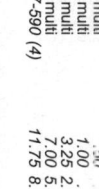

**1985, Sept. 2 Granite Paper Perf. 11½x12**

| | | | |
|---|---|---|---|
| 674 | A140 | 40d Doha | .85 .35 |
| 675 | A140 | 50d Earth satellite | 1.25 .40 |
| 676 | A140 | 1.50r Oil refinery | 3.75 1.25 |
| 677 | A140 | 4r Storage facility | 8.50 3.50 |
| | | *Nos. 674-677 (4)* | 14.35 5.50 |

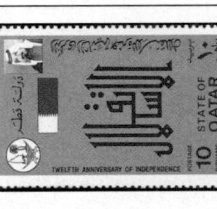

Org. of Petroleum Exporting Countries, 25th Anniv. — A141

**1985, Sept. 14 Perf. 13½x14**

| | | | |
|---|---|---|---|
| 678 | A141 | 1r brt yel grn & multi | 4.50 1.10 |
| 679 | A141 | 1r salmon rose & multi | 4.50 1.10 |

UN, 40th Anniv. A142

**1985, Oct. 24 Litho. Perf. 13½x14**

| | | | |
|---|---|---|---|
| 680 | A142 | 1r multi | 1.25 .75 |
| 681 | A142 | 3r multi | 3.75 2.25 |

Population and Housing Census — A143

**1986, Mar. 1 Photo. Perf. 11½x12**

| | | | |
|---|---|---|---|
| 682 | A143 | 1r multi | 2.25 1.00 |
| 683 | A143 | 3r multi | 5.00 3.00 |

United Arab Shipping Co., 10th Anniv. — A144

**1986, May 30 Litho. Perf. 13½x14**

| | | | |
|---|---|---|---|
| 684 | A144 | 1.50r Qatari ibn al Fuja'a | 2.00 1.40 |
| 685 | A144 | 4r Al Wajba | 5.25 3.50 |

Natl. Independence, 15th Anniv. — A145

**1986, Sept. 2 Litho. Unwmk. Perf. 13x13½**

| | | | |
|---|---|---|---|
| 686 | A145 | 40d multi | .65 .40 |
| 687 | A145 | 50d multi | .80 .40 |
| 688 | A145 | 1r multi | 1.60 .95 |
| 689 | A145 | 4r multi | 5.50 3.50 |
| | | *Nos. 686-689 (4)* | 8.55 5.25 |

---

Literacy Day, 1984 — A135

40th Anniv., ICAO — A136

**1984, Sept. 8 Litho. Perf. 14x13½**

| | | | |
|---|---|---|---|
| 664 | A135 | 1r lilac & multi | 3.50 1.00 |
| 665 | A135 | 1r orange & multi | 3.50 1.00 |

**1984, Dec. 7 Litho. Perf. 13½x13**

| | | | |
|---|---|---|---|
| 666 | A136 | 20d multi | .50 .40 |
| 667 | A136 | 3.50r multi | 9.50 3.50 |

League of Arab States, 40th Anniv. — A137

**1985, Mar. 22 Photo. Perf. 11½**

| | | | |
|---|---|---|---|
| 668 | A137 | 50d multi | 1.25 .40 |
| 669 | A137 | 4r multi | 8.50 3.25 |

Traffic Crossing — A139

Intl. Youth Year — A138

**1985, Mar. 4 Granite Paper Perf. 11½x12**

| | | | |
|---|---|---|---|
| 670 | A138 | 50d multi | 1.60 .40 |
| 671 | A138 | 1r multi | 3.25 .80 |

**1985, Mar. 9 Perf. 14x13½**

| | | | |
|---|---|---|---|
| 672 | A139 | 1r lt bl & multi | 3.00 1.00 |
| 673 | A139 | 1r pink & multi | 3.00 1.00 |

Gulf Cooperation Council Traffic Safety Week, Mar. 16-22.

Natl. Independence, 14th Anniv. — A140

---

A130

**1983, Sept. 2 Litho. Perf. 14**

| | | | |
|---|---|---|---|
| 643 | A129 | 10d multi | .45 .45 |
| 644 | A129 | 35d multi | .90 .45 |
| 645 | A129 | 80d multi | 2.00 .65 |
| 646 | A129 | 2.80r multi | 6.50 2.50 |
| | | *Nos. 643-646 (4)* | 9.85 4.05 |

12th anniv. of Independence.

**1983, Nov. 7 Litho. Perf. 13½x14**

| | | | |
|---|---|---|---|
| 647 | A130 | 35d multi | .80 .40 |
| 648 | A130 | 2.80r multi | 9.00 2.25 |

GCC Supreme Council, 4th regular session.

35th Anniv. of UN Declaration of Human Rights — A131

**1983, Dec. 10 Litho. Perf. 13½x14**

| | | | |
|---|---|---|---|
| 649 | A131 | 1.25r Globe, emblem | 4.50 1.50 |
| 650 | A131 | 2.80r Scale | 7.00 3.00 |

A132

A133

**1984, Mar. 1 Litho. Perf. 13½x13½**

| | | | |
|---|---|---|---|
| 651 | A132 | 15d multi | .25 .25 |
| 652 | A132 | 40d multi | .65 .30 |
| 653 | A132 | 50d multi | .80 .40 |

**Perf. 14x13½**

| | | | |
|---|---|---|---|
| 654 | A133 | 1r multi | 1.25 1.10 |
| 655 | A133 | 1.50r multi | 2.00 2.00 |
| 656 | A133 | 2.50r multi | 3.25 2.25 |
| 657 | A133 | 5r multi | 4.00 4.00 |
| 658 | A133 | 10r multi | 7.75 7.75 |
| 659 | A133 | 10r multi | 13.00 13.00 |
| | | *Nos. 651-659 (9)* | 32.95 18.80 |

See Nos. 707-709, 792-801.

13th Anniv. of Independence — A134

**1984, Sept. 2 Photo. Perf. 12**

| | | | |
|---|---|---|---|
| 660 | A134 | 15d multi | .45 .45 |
| 661 | A134 | 1r multi | 3.25 1.25 |
| 662 | A134 | 2.50r multi | 7.00 3.25 |
| 663 | A134 | 3.50r multi | 9.25 4.25 |
| | | *Nos. 660-663 (4)* | 19.95 9.20 |

---

A125

A126

**1982, Apr. 12 Litho. Perf. 13½x13**

| | | | |
|---|---|---|---|
| 633 | A125 | 35d yellow & multi | .90 .35 |
| 634 | A125 | 2.80r blue & multi | 8.00 2.50 |

30th anniv. of Arab Postal Union.

**1982, Sept. 2 Litho. Perf. 13½x13**

| | | | |
|---|---|---|---|
| 635 | A126 | 10d multi | .45 .30 |
| 636 | A126 | 80d multi | 1.90 .60 |
| 637 | A126 | 1.25r multi | 3.25 1.00 |
| 638 | A126 | 2.80r multi | 6.75 2.10 |
| | | *Nos. 635-638 (4)* | 12.35 4.00 |

11th anniv. of Independence.

World Communications Year — A127

**1983, Jan. 10 Litho. Perf. 13½x13**

| | | | |
|---|---|---|---|
| 639 | A127 | 35d multi | .85 .35 |
| 640 | A127 | 2.80r multi | 5.00 2.10 |

Gulf Postal Org., 2nd Conference, Doha, Apr. — A128

**1983, Apr. 9 Litho. Perf. 13½x14**

| | | | |
|---|---|---|---|
| 641 | A128 | 1r multi | 2.50 .95 |
| 642 | A128 | 1.35r multi | 3.25 1.40 |

A129

## Sheik Khalifa — A146

**1987, Jan. 1    Photo.    Perf. 11½x12**
Granite Paper
690 A146 15r multi — 15.00 10.50
691 A146 20r multi — 19.00 14.00
692 A146 30r multi — 35.00 21.00
Nos. 690-692 (3) — 69.00 45.50

15th Anniv. of Sheik Khalifa's Accession — A147

**1987, Feb. 22    Granite Paper    Perf. 12x11½**
693 A147 50d multi — .55 .50
694 A147 1r multi — 1.25 .95
695 A147 1.50r multi — 2.40 3.50
696 A147 4r multi — 5.50 3.50
Nos. 693-696 (4) — 9.70 6.35

Arab Postal Union, 35th Anniv. — A148

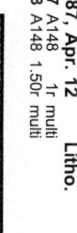

**1987, Apr. 12    Litho.    Perf. 13½x13½**
Unwmk.
697 A148 1r multi — 2.00 .95
698 A148 1.50r multi — 2.75 1.40

Natl. Independence, 16th Anniv. — A149

**1987, Sept. 2    Litho.    Perf. 13½x13½**
699 A149 25d Housing complex — .35 .35
700 A149 75d Water tower, city — 1.40 .80
701 A149 2r Modern office building — 3.50 2.25
702 A149 4r Oil refinery — 7.75 4.00
Nos. 699-702 (4) — 13.00 7.40

A150

---

A151

**1987, Apr. 24    Litho.    Perf. 13½x13**
703 A150 1.50r multicolored — 1.90 1.25
704 A150 4r multicolored — 4.50 3.25
Intl. Literacy Day.

**1987, Sept. 8    Litho.    Perf. 13½x13**
705 A151 1r multicolored — 1.50 .90
706 A151 4r multicolored — 5.75 3.25
Gulf Environment Day.

**1988, Jan. 1    Perf. 13½x13½**
Sheik Type of 1984
Size of 25d, 75d: 22x27mm
707 A133 25d multicolored — .30 .30
708 A133 75d multicolored — 1.25 .70
709 A133 2r multicolored — 3.25 1.90
This is an expanding set. Numbers will change if necessary.

WHO, 40th Anniv. — A152

**1988, Apr. 7    Litho.    Perf. 14x13½**
714 A152 1.50r multicolored — 1.60 1.10
715 A152 2r multicolored — 2.25 1.60

Independence, 17th Anniv. — A153

**1988, Sept. 2    Litho.    Perf. 11½x12**
Granite Paper
716 A153 50d multicolored — .80 .50
717 A153 75d multicolored — 1.25 .70
718 A153 1.50r multicolored — 2.40 1.40
719 A153 2r multicolored — 2.75 1.60
Nos. 716-719 (4) — 7.20 4.60
Unwmk.

Opening of the Doha General P.O. — A154

**1988, Sept. 3    Litho.    Perf. 13½x13½**
720 A154 1.50r multicolored — 1.40 1.00
721 A154 4r multicolored — 3.25 2.50

---

Arab Housing Day — A155

**1988, Oct. 3    Granite Paper    Perf. 11½x12**
722 A155 1.50r multicolored — 2.10 1.25
723 A155 4r multicolored — 5.25 3.25

A156

**1988, Dec. 10    Perf. 14x13½    Wmk. 368**
724 A156 1.50r multicolored — 1.60 1.10
725 A156 2r multicolored — 1.90 1.60
Declaration of Human Rights, 40th anniv.

A157

**1989, May 17    Granite Paper    Perf. 12x11½**
Unwmk.
726 A157 2r multicolored — 2.00 1.60
727 A157 4r multicolored — 4.00 3.00
World Telecommunications Day.

Qatar Red Crescent Soc., 10th Anniv. — A158

**1989, Aug. 8    Perf. 13½x14    Wmk. 368**
728 A158 4r multicolored — 8.50 4.25

Natl. Independence, 18th Anniv. — A159

**1989, Sept. 2    Perf. 13½x13½**
Unwmk.
729 A159 75d multicolored — .90 .65
730 A159 1r multicolored — 1.25 .90
731 A159 1.50r multicolored — 1.90 1.40
732 A159 2r multicolored — 2.00 1.40
Nos. 729-732 (4) — 6.30 4.85

---

Gulf Air, 40th Anniv. — A160

**1990, Mar. 24    Litho.    Perf. 13x13½**
733 A160 50d multicolored — 1.85 .35
734 A160 75d multicolored — 2.75 .50
735 A160 4r multicolored — 9.60 3.60
Nos. 733-735 (3)

Independence, 19th Anniv. — A161

Designs: 75d, Map. 1.50r, Swordsman, musicians.

**1990, Sept. 2    Perf. 14x13½**
736 A161 50d multicolored — .65 .35
737 A161 75d multicolored — 1.40 .55
738 A161 1.50r multicolored — 4.50 1.40
739 A161 2r multicolored — 9.55 3.40
Nos. 736-739 (4)

Organization of Petroleum Exporting Countries (OPEC), 30th Anniv. — A162

**1990, Sept. 14**
740 A162 50d shown — 1.40 .35
741 A162 1.50r Flags — 3.50 1.10
50d, Map. 1.50r, Flags shown

GCC Supreme Council, 11th Regular Session: 1r, Leaders of member nations. 1.50r, Flag, council emblem. 2r, State seal, emblem.

A163

A164

**1990, Dec. 22    Litho.    Wmk. 368**
Perf. 14x13½
742 A163 50d multicolored — 1.25 .40
743 A163 1r multicolored — 3.50 .80
744 A163 1.50r multicolored — 2.00 .80
745 A163 2r multicolored — 8.75 3.25
Nos. 742-745 (4)

QATAR

---

**1991, June 20   Perf. 12½x13½   Litho.   Wmk. 368**

Plants.

| | | | | |
|---|---|---|---|---|
| 747 | A164 | 10d | Glossonema edule | .25 | .25 |
| 748 | A164 | 25d | Lycium shawii | .25 | .35 |
| 749 | A164 | 50d | Acacia tortilis | .55 | .35 |
| 750 | A164 | 75d | Acacia ehrenbergiana | .85 | .55 |
| 751 | A164 | 1r | Capparis spinosa | 1.10 | .70 |
| 752 | A164 | 4r | Cymhopogon parkeri | 4.25 | 2.75 |
|  |  |  |  | 7.25 | 4.85 |

*Nos. 747-752 (6)*

World Health Day A169

**1992, Apr. 7   Perf. 14x13½, 13½x14**
785 A169 50d Heart with face, vert.   .60   .35
786 A169 1.50r shown   1.90 1.00

Children's Paintings A170

**1992, June 15   Unwmk.   Perf. 11½**
787 A170 25d Girls dancing   .40   .40
788 A170 50d Children playing   1.25   .40
789 A170 75d Ships   1.90   .50
790 A170 1.50r Fishing from boats   3.75 1.25
a. Souvenir sheet of 4, #787-790   250.00
*Nos. 787-790 (4)*   7.30 2.55

Type of 1984 with Smaller Arabic Inscription and

A171

**Independence, 20th Anniv.— A165**

**1991, Aug. 15   Litho.   Perf. 14x14½**
Granite Paper
762 A165 25d shown   .30   .30
763 A165 75d red vio & multi   1.00   .40

**Perf. 14½x14**
764 A165 1r Doha skyline, horiz.   1.40   .60
765 A165 1.50r Palace, horiz.   2.10   .90
*Nos. 762-765 (4)*   4.80 2.20

Fish A166

Various species of fish.

**1991, Dec. 1**   **Perf. 14x13½**
767 A166 10d multicolored   .40   .40
768 A166 15d multicolored   .40   .40
769 A166 25d multicolored   .40   .40
770 A166 50d multicolored   .65   .45
771 A166 75d multicolored   .95   .50
772 A166 1r multicolored   1.40   .75
773 A166 1.50r multicolored   2.40 1.10
774 A166 4r multicolored   3.25 1.50
  9.85 5.45
*Nos. 767-774 (8)*

A167

Sheik Khalifa, 20th Anniv. of Accession A168

**1992, Feb. 22   Litho.   Wmk. 368**
   **Perf. 14x13½**
781 A167 25d multicolored   .35   .35
782 A167 50d multicolored   .90   .45
783 A168 75d multicolored   1.40   .45
784 A168 1.50r multicolored   3.25 1.10
  5.90 2.25

---

A172

**1992   Litho.   Perf. 13x13½**
791 A171 10d multicolored   .25   .25
792 A132 25d multicolored   .25   .25
793 A132 50d multicolored   .40   .30

   **Perf. 13½x13**
794 A132 75d multicolored   .60   .45
795 A132 1r multicolored   .75   .65

   **Size: 25x32mm**
   **Perf. 14½x13, 13½x14½**
796 A132 1.50r multicolored   1.10   .50
797 A132 2r multicolored   1.60 1.25
798 A132 3r multicolored   2.50 2.00
799 A132 4r multicolored   3.25 2.50
800 A132 5r multicolored   4.00 3.25
801 A132 10r multicolored   8.00 6.50
802 A172 15r multicolored   11.50 9.75
803 A172 20r multicolored   13.00 13.00
804 A172 30r multicolored   75.20 60.65
*Nos. 791-804 (14)*

Issued: 10-50d, 1.50, 2, 5, 15, 30r, 5/14; others, 5/14.

1992 Summer Olympics, Barcelona A174

**1992, July 25   Litho.   Perf. 15**
805 A174 50d Running   .55   .30
806 A174 1.50r Soccer   2.50   .95

11th Persian Gulf Soccer Cup A175

---

**1992, Nov. 27   Litho.   Perf. 14½**
807 A175 50d shown   .70   .40
808 A175 1r Ball, net, vert.   1.50   .40

A176

**Independence, 21st Anniv.— A177**

Sheik Khalifa and: No. 810, "21" in English and Arabic. No. 811, Tree, dhow in harbor. No. 812, Natural gas well, pen, dhow.

**1992, Sept. 2   Litho.   Unwmk.**
Granite Paper
809 A176 50d shown   .60   .35
810 A176 50d multicolored   .60   .35
811 A177 1r multicolored   1.25   .70
812 A177 1r multicolored   1.25   .70
a. Strip of 8, 2 each #809-812   10.00 6.75
*Nos. 809-812 (4)*   3.70 2.10

Intl. Conference on Nutrition, Rome — A178

**1992, Dec. 12   Perf. 14½**
813 A178 50d Globe, emblems, vert.   .90   .35
814 A178 1r Cornucopia   3.25   .70

Qatar Broadcasting, Silver Jubilee — A179

Designs: 25d, Man at microphone, satellite dish. 50d, Rocket lift-off, satellite. 75d, Communications building. 1r, Technicians working on books.

**1993, June 25   Photo.   Perf. 12x11½**
Granite Paper
819 A179 25d multicolored   .40   .40
820 A179 50d multicolored   1.50 1.20
821 A179 75d multicolored   2.00   .60
822 A179 1r multicolored   2.50   .80
a. Souvenir sheet of 4, #819-822   150.00
*Nos. 819-822 (4)*   6.40 2.20

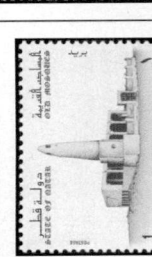

Ruins A180

Mosque with: a, Minaret (at left, shown). b, Minaret with side projections (at right). c, Minaret with catwalk, inside wall. d, Minaret at right, outside wall.

---

**Independence, 22nd Anniv. — A181**

**1993, May 10   Litho.   Perf. 12**
Granite Paper
823 A180 1r Strip of 4, #a.-d.   7.50 2.50

Intl. Literacy Day — A182

Designs: 25c, Oil pumping station. 50d, Flag, clock tower. 75d, Coat of arms, "22." 1.50r, Flag, fortress tower.

**1993, Sept. 2   Litho.   Perf. 11½**
Granite Paper
824 A181 25d multicolored   .30   .30
825 A181 50d multicolored   .50   .50
826 A181 75d multicolored   .70   .95
827 A181 1.50r multicolored   1.40 .95
  2.90 2.05
*Nos. 824-827 (4)*

**1993, Sept. 2   Litho.   Wmk. 368**

Designs: 25d, Quill, paper. 50d, Papers with English letters, pen. 75d, Papers with Arabic letters, pen. 1.50r, Scroll, Arabic letters, pen.

028 A182 25d multicolored   .30   .30
829 A182 50d multicolored   .50   .50
830 A182 75d multicolored   .70   .95
831 A182 1.50r multicolored   1.40 .95
  2.90 2.05
*Nos. 828-831 (4)*

Children's Games A183

Designs: 25d, Girls with thread and spinners. 50d, Boys with stick and disk, vert. 75r, Children guiding wheels with sticks, vert. 1.50r, Girls with jump rope.

**1993, Dec. 5   Litho.   Perf. 11½**
Granite Paper
832 A183 25d multicolored   .35   .35
833 A183 50d multicolored   1.10 .35
834 A183 75d multicolored   1.90 .50
835 A183 1.50r multicolored   4.00 1.00
a. Souvenir sheet, 2 each #832, #835   60.00
835. Souvenir sheet, 2 each #832, #835   60.00
  7.35 2.20
*Nos. 832-835 (4)*

Falcons — A184

**1993, Dec. 22   Granite Paper**
836 A184 25d Lanner   .40   .40
837 A184 50d Saker   .90   .40
838 A184 75d Barbary   1.60   .60

A185

**1994, May 6** Litho. Perf. 14
839 A184 1.50r Peregrine 3.50 1.25
a. Souvenir sheet, #836-839 125.00
Nos. 836-839 (4) 6.40 2.65

Society for Handicapped Welfare and Rehabilitation: 75d, Hands above and below handicapped symbol.
840 A185 25d shown .40 .40
841 A185 75d multi 1.60 .55

A186

Qatar Insurance Co. 30th Anniv.: 50d, Building. 1.50r, Co. arms, global tourist attractions.

**1994, Mar. 11** Litho. Perf. 14½ Unwmk.
842 A186 50d gold & multi .65 .30
843 A186 1.50r gold & multi 3.25 .95

A187

**1994, Mar. 22** Litho. Perf. 11½
World Day for Water: 1r, UN emblem, hands catching water drop, tower, grain.
844 A187 25d shown .35 .35
845 A187 1r multicolored 1.60 .65

A188

**1994, Mar. 22** Litho. Perf. 12x11½
Intl. Law Conference.
846 A188 75d shown .60 .30
847 A188 2r Scales, gavel 1.90 1.10

A189

**1994, July 16** Litho. Perf. 11½
Intl. Year of the Family.
848 A189 25d shown .30 .30
849 A189 1r Family, UN emblem 1.60 .65

A190

Independence, 23rd Anniv. — A190
25d, 2r, Text, 75d, Island, 1r, Oil drilling plant.

**1994, Sept. 2** Photo. Perf. 12
Granite Paper
850 A190 25d green & multi .35 .35
851 A190 75d multicolored .90 .50
852 A190 1r multicolored 1.25 .70
853 A190 2r pink & multi 6.00 2.95
Nos. 850-853 (4) 3.50 1.40

ILO, 75th Anniv. — A191

**1994, May 28** Perf. 14
854 A191 25d salmon & multi .35 .35
855 A191 2r green & multi, diff. 3.50 1.40

ICAO, 50th Anniv. A192

**1994, Dec. 7** Perf. 13½x14
856 A192 25d shown .40 .40
857 A192 75d Emblem, airplane 3.25 .55

Shells: No. 864a, Conus pennaceus, b, Cerithidea cingulata, c, Hexaplex kuesterianus, d, Epitonium scalare.
No. 865a, Murex, scolopax, b, Thais mutabilis, c, Fusinus arabicus, d, Lambis truncata sebae.

Gulf Environment Day — A198

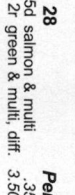

**1995, Apr. 24** Perf. 14
864 A198 75d Strip of 4, #a-d. 2.75 1.75
865 A198 1r Strip of 4, #a-d. 3.50 2.40

Int'l. Nursing Day — A199

Designs: 1r, Nurse adjusting IV for patient. 1.50r, Injecting shot into arm of infant.

**1995, May 12** Litho. Perf. 13½
866 A199 1r multicolored 1.10 .60
867 A199 1.50r multicolored 2.25 .80

Rock Carvings at Jabal Jusasiyah — A197

A193 A194 A195 A196

**1995, Mar. 18** Litho. Perf. 14¾x15
858 A193 1r multicolored 1.00 .55
859 A194 1r multicolored 1.00 .55
860 A195 1r multicolored 1.00 .55
861 A196 1r multicolored 1.00 .55
862 A197 1r multicolored 1.00 .55
863 A197 1r multi, diff. 1.00 .55
a. Vert. strip of 6, multi, #858-863 6.50 3.50

Independence, 24th Anniv. — A200
Designs: a, 1.50r, Shipping dock, city. b, 1r, Children in classroom. c, 1.50r, Aerial view of city. d, 1r, Palm trees.

**1995, Sept. 2** Litho. Perf. 13½x14
868 A200 Block of 4, #a-d. 7.50 2.40

UN, 50th Anniv. — A201

**1995, Oct. 24** Perf. 13½
869 A201 1.50r multicolored 1.50 .70

Gazelles A202

No. 870: a, 75c, Gazella dorcas pelzelni. b, 25d, Dorcatragus megalotis. c, 25d, Gazella dama. d, 1.50r, Gazella spekei. e, 2r, Gazella soemmerringi. f, 1r, Gazella dorcas pelzelni.
3r, Gazella soemmerringi.

**1996, Jan.** Litho. Perf. 11½
870 A202 Strip of 6, #a-f. 8.00 4.75

Fight Against Drug Abuse — A203

**1996, June 26** Litho. Perf. 14x13
872 A203 50d shown .55 .40
873 A203 1r "NO" needles, hand 1.10 .75

Size: 121x81mm Imperf
871 A202 3r multicolored 35.00 29.00

1996 Summer Olympic Games, Atlanta — A204

a, 10d, Olympic emblem, map of Qatar. b, 15d, Shooting. c, 25d, Bowling. d, 50d, Table tennis. e, 1r, Athletics. f, 1.50r, Yachting.

**1996, July 19** Litho. Perf. 14x13½
874 A204 Strip of 6, #a-f. 4.00 2.10

Independence, 25th Anniv. — A204a

**1996, Sept. 2** Litho. & Typo. Perf. 12
Granite Paper
875 A204a 1.50r silver & multi 1.75 .95
876 A204a 2r gold & multi 2.10 1.25

Forts A204b

**1997, Jan. 15** Litho. Perf. 14½
877 A204b 25d multicolored .25 .25
878 A204b 75d multicolored .60 .40
879 A204b 1r multicolored .80 .45
880 A204b 2r multicolored 2.25 1.60
Nos. 877-880 (4) 3.90 2.70
25d, Al-Wajbah, vert. 75d, Al-Zubarah. 1r, Al-Kout. 3r, Umm Salal Mohammed.

Sheik Khalifa

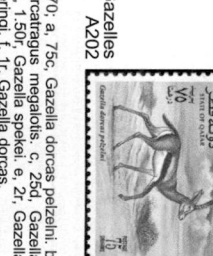

A205

A206

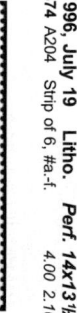

**1996, Nov. 16  Photo.  Perf. 11½x12**

**Granite Paper**

| | | | | |
|---|---|---|---|---|
| 881 | A205 | 25d pink & multi | .20 | .20 |
| 882 | A205 | 50d green & multi | .30 | .30 |
| 883 | A205 | 75d bl green & multi | .45 | .45 |
| 884 | A205 | 1r gray & multi | .60 | .60 |

**Perf. 11½**

| | | | | |
|---|---|---|---|---|
| 885 | A206 | 1.50r grn bl & multi | .85 | .50 |
| 886 | A206 | 2r green & multi | 1.25 | .80 |
| 887 | A206 | 4r ver & multi | 2.40 | 1.60 |
| 888 | A206 | 5r purple & multi | 3.00 | 2.00 |
| 889 | A206 | 10r brown & multi | 6.00 | 4.00 |
| 890 | A206 | 20r blue & multi | 12.00 | 8.00 |
| 891 | A206 | 30r orange & multi | 18.00 | 12.00 |
| | | Nos. 881-891 (11) | 45.05 | 30.00 |

A207

UNICEF, 50th Anniv.: No. 893, Children, open book emblem.

**1996, Dec. 11  Litho.  Perf. 14½**

| | | | | |
|---|---|---|---|---|
| 892 | A207 | 75d blue & multi | .60 | .40 |
| 893 | A207 | 75d violet & multi | .60 | .40 |

**1996, Dec. 7**

A208

17th Session of GCC Supreme Council: 1.50r, Emblem, dove with olive branch, Sheik Khalifa.

| | | | | |
|---|---|---|---|---|
| 894 | A208 | 1r multicolored | .90 | .60 |
| 895 | A208 | 1.50r multicolored | 1.10 | .80 |

**Opening of Port of Ras Laffan — A209**

Illustration reduced.

**1997, Feb. 24  Litho.  Perf. 13½**

| | | | | |
|---|---|---|---|---|
| 896 | A209 | 3r multicolored | 3.00 | 1.10 |

**Arabian Horses — A210**

**1997, Mar. 19  Photo.  Perf. 12x11½**

| | | | | |
|---|---|---|---|---|
| 897 | A210 | 25d Red horse with tan mane | .30 | .30 |
| 898 | A210 | 75d Black horse | .65 | .40 |
| 899 | A210 | 1r White horse | .75 | .40 |
| 900 | A210 | 1.50r Red brown horse | 1.25 | .65 |
| | | Nos. 897-900 (4) | 2.95 | 1.75 |

**Size: 115x75mm  Imperf**

| | | | | |
|---|---|---|---|---|
| 901 | A210 | 3r Mares, foals | 80.00 | |

**Independence, 26th Anniv. — A211**

**1997, Sept. 2  Photo.  Perf. 11½x12**

**Granite Paper**

| | | | | |
|---|---|---|---|---|
| 902 | A211 | 1r shown | .70 | .40 |
| 903 | A211 | 1.50r Oil refinery | 1.10 | .80 |

**Doha-Mena Economic Conference — A212**

Doha '97, Doha-Mena Economic Conference — A212

**1997, Nov. 16  Litho.  Perf. 11**

| | | | | |
|---|---|---|---|---|
| 904 | A212 | 2r multicolored | 1.50 | 1.00 |

**Insects — A213**

a, Nubian flower bee. b, Domino beetle. c, Seven-spot ladybird. d, Desert giant ant. e, Eastern death's-head hawkmoth. f, Arabian darkling beetle. g, Yellow digger. h, Mole cricket. i, Migratory locust. j, Elegant rhinoceros beetle. k, Oleander hawkmoth. l, American cockroach. m, Girdled skimmer. n, Sabre-toothed beetle. o, Arabian cicada. p, Pinstriped ground weevil. q, Praying mantis. r, Rufous bombardier beetle. s, Diardem t, Shore earwig.

**1998, July 20  Litho.  Perf. 11½x12**

**Granite Paper**

| | | | | |
|---|---|---|---|---|
| 905 | A213 | Sheet of 20, #a.-t. | 30.00 | 20.00 |
| | | u. Souvenir sheet, #905i | 15.00 | 15.00 |
| | | v. Souvenir sheet, #905s | 15.00 | 10.00 |

**Early Diving Equipment — A214**

**1998, Aug. 15  Litho.  Perf. 11½x12, 12x11½  Photo.**

**Granite Paper**

| | | | | |
|---|---|---|---|---|
| 906 | A214 | 25d Meflaja | .20 | .20 |
| 907 | A214 | 75d Mahar | .45 | .35 |
| 908 | A214 | 1r Dasta | .55 | .40 |
| 909 | A214 | 1.50r Deyen, vert. | .85 | .65 |
| | | Nos. 906-909 (4) | 2.05 | 1.60 |

**Souvenir Sheet**

| | | | | |
|---|---|---|---|---|
| 910 | A214 | 2r Man seated in boat | 9.00 | 7.00 |

**Qatar University, 25th Anniv. — A215**

**1998, Sept. 2  Litho.  Perf. 13½x13**

| | | | | |
|---|---|---|---|---|
| 911 | A215 | 1r blue & multi | 1.10 | .70 |
| 912 | A215 | 1.50r gray & multi | 1.75 | 1.10 |

**Independence, 27th Anniv. — A216**

**1998, Sept. 2  Litho.  Perf. 14**

| | | | | |
|---|---|---|---|---|
| 913 | A216 | 1r Sheik Khalifa, vert. | .70 | .50 |
| 914 | A216 | 1.50r Sheik Khalifa | 1.10 | .80 |

**Camels — A217**

**1999, Jan. 25  Litho.  Perf. 11½**

**Granite Paper**

| | | | | |
|---|---|---|---|---|
| 915 | A217 | 25d shown | .20 | .20 |
| 916 | A217 | 75d One standing | .45 | .35 |
| 917 | A217 | 1r Three standing | .60 | .45 |
| 918 | A217 | 1.50r Four standing, vert. | .85 | .65 |
| | | Nos. 915-918 (4) | 2.10 | 1.65 |

**Souvenir Sheet**

| | | | | |
|---|---|---|---|---|
| 919 | A217 | 2r Adult, juvenile | 14.00 | 10.50 |

**1999 FEI General Assembly Meeting, Doha — A218**

**Perf. 13½x13**

**1999  Litho.**

| | | | | |
|---|---|---|---|---|
| 920 | A218 | 1.50r multicolored | .85 | .65 |

**Ancient Coins — A219**

Obverse, reverse of dirhams — #921: a, Umayyad (shown). b, Umayyad. c, Abbasid (3 lines of text on obv.). d, Abbasid (6 lines of text obv.). e, Umayyad, diff. (small circles near edge at top of obv. & rev.).

Obverse, rev. of dinars — #922: a, Abbasid (3 lines of text obv.). b, Umayyad. c, Abbasid (5 lines of text obv.). d, Marabitid. e, Fatimid.

Obverse and reverse of: No. 923, Arab Sasanian dirham. 3r, Umayyad dinar, diff.

**1999  Litho.  Perf. 11½**

**Granite Paper**

| | | | | |
|---|---|---|---|---|
| 921 | A219 | 1r Strip of 5, #a.-e. | 3.25 | 2.75 |
| 922 | A219 | 2r Strip of 5, #a.-e. | 6.75 | 5.50 |

**Souvenir Sheets**

| | | | | |
|---|---|---|---|---|
| 923 | A219 | 2r multicolored | 8.00 | 8.00 |
| 924 | A219 | 3r multicolored | 10.00 | 10.00 |

**Independence, 28th Anniv. — A220**

**1999, Sept. 2  Litho.  Wmk. 368**

**Perf. 12¾x13¾**

| | | | | |
|---|---|---|---|---|
| 925 | A220 | 1r violet & multi | .70 | .70 |
| 926 | A220 | 1.50r yellow & multi | 1.00 | 1.00 |

A222

UPU, 125th anniv.: 1r, Tree with letters. 1.50r, Building, horiz.

**1999, Oct. 9  Litho.  Unwmk.**

**Perf. 11½**

**Granite Paper**

| | | | | |
|---|---|---|---|---|
| 927 | A221 | 1r multicolored | .70 | .70 |
| 928 | A221 | 1.50r multicolored | 1.00 | 1.00 |

**1999, Oct. 30  Granite Paper**

| | | | | |
|---|---|---|---|---|
| 929 | A222 | 1r multicolored | .70 | .70 |
| 930 | A222 | 1.50r multicolored | 1.00 | 1.00 |

A221

Fifth Stamp Exhibition for the Arab Gulf Countries: 1r, Emblem, stamps. 1.50r, Emblem, horiz.

**National Committee for Children with Special Needs — A223**

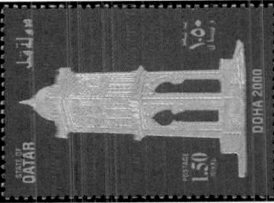

**Perf. 12¾x13¼  Litho.  Wmk. 368**

| | | | | |
|---|---|---|---|---|
| 931 | A223 | 1.50r multi | 1.00 | 1.00 |

Millennium
A224

**Photo. & Embossed  Perf. 11¾**

**2000, Jan. 1  Unwmk.  Granite Paper**

| | | | | |
|---|---|---|---|---|
| 932 | A224 | 1.50r red & gold | .80 | .80 |
| 933 | A224 | 2r blue & gold | 1.10 | 1.10 |

**Qatar Tennis Open — A225**

Trophy and: 1r, Stadium. 1.50r, Racquet.

**2000, Jan. 3  Litho.  Perf. 13¼x13½**

| | | | | |
|---|---|---|---|---|
| 934 | A225 | 1r multi | .60 | .60 |
| 935 | A225 | 1.50r multi | .90 | .90 |

**GCC Water Week — A226**

**2000, Mar. 1**

936 A226 1r. Map, water drop .60 .60
937 A226 1.50r Hands, water drop .90 .90

**2000, May 1 Photo. Perf. 11¾**
Granite Paper

15th Asian Table Tennis Championships, Doha — A227

938 A227 1.50r multi .85 .85

Independence, 29th Anniv. — A228

Sheik Khalifa and: 1r, Fort. 1.50r, Oil derrick, city skyline.

**2000, Sept. 2 Photo.**
Granite Paper Set of 2
939-940 A228 1.75 1.75

Monument, building and: 1.50r, Bird. 2r, Magnifying glass.

Post Office, 50th Anniv. A229

**2000, Oct. 9 Perf. 11½x11¾**
Photo. & Embossed
943 A230

No. 943: a. 1r, Emblem (size: 21x28mm), b. 1.50r, Emblem, olive branch (size: 45x28mm).

9th Islamic Summit Conference — A230

**2000, Nov. 12 Perf. 11¾**
Granite Paper Set of 2
941-942 A229 2.50 2.50

**2000, Nov. 12**
Granite Paper Photo.
943 A230 Pair, #a-b
1.75 1.75

**2001, Feb. 26 Photo. Perf. 11½**
Granite Paper

Clean Environment Day — A231

Designs: 1r, Qatar Gas emblem, tanker ship, coral reef. 1.50r, RasGas emblem, refinery, antelopes. 2r, Ras Laffan Industrial City emblem, flamingos near industrial complex. 3r, Qatar Petroleum emblem, view of Earth from space.

944-947 A231 Set of 4 4.75 4.75

---

Independence, 30th Anniv. — A232

**2001, Sept. 2 Litho. Perf. 14x14½**
Background colors: 1r, Olive. 1.50r, Blue.

948-949 A232 Set of 2 1.75 1.75

Designs: 1.50r, Shown. 2r, Branch with leaves of many colors.

Year of Dialogue Among Civilizations A233

**2001, Oct. 9 Perf. 13¼**
950-951 A233 Set of 2 2.50 2.50

4th World Trade Organization Ministerial Conference — A234

Background colors: 1r, Yellow brown. 1.50r, Blue.

**2001, Nov. 9**
952-953 A234 1.40 1.40

**2001, Dec. 30 Perf. 14½**
954-957 A235 Set of 4 3.25 3.25

Old Doors — A235

Various doors: 25d, 75d, 1.50r, 2r.

OLD DOORS

958 A235 3r multi 7.25 7.25

2002 World Cup Soccer Championships, Japan and Korea — A236

Souvenir Sheet

No. 959 — World Cup Posters (except for #959h) from: a. 1930. b. 1934 (Italian). c. 1938. d. 1950. e. 1954. f. 1958. g. 1962. h. 1966. i. 1970. j. 1974. k. 1978. l. 1982. m. 1986. n. 1990. o. 1994. p. 1998. q. 2002. r. World Cup Trophy.

**2002 Litho. Perf. 14**
959 Sheet of 18
a.-r. A236 2r Any single 22.50 22.50
s. Souvenir sheet #959g-959r 2.50 2.50

---

Asian Games Emblems — A237

No. 960: a. 1r, 2002 Asian Games emblem, Busan, South Korea. b. 3r, 2006 Asian Games emblem, Doha, Qatar.

SEE YOU IN DOHA — 2006

**2002, Sept. 29 Photo. Perf. 14½**
Granite Paper
960 A237 Sheet of 2, #a-b 2.25 2.25

Qatar General Postal Corporation, 1st Anniv. — A238

Background colors: 1r, White. 3r, Light blue.

**2002, Oct. 25 Litho. Perf. 12½**
961-962 A238 Set of 2 2.25 2.25

World No Tobacco Day — A239

**2003, May 31 Perf. 13¼**
963 A239 1.50r red .85 .85

Qatar Red Crescent, 25th Anniv. — A240

No. 964: a. Red crescent, boy (30mm diameter). b. Headquarters building.

**2003, July 1 Litho. With Foil Application Perf. 13¼**
964 A240 75d Horiz. pair, #a-b .85 .85

Jewelry — A241

AL MASHMOOM

Designs: No. 965, 25d, Al-mashmoom. No. 966, 25d, Al-mertash. No. 967, 50d, Khatim. No. 968, 50d, Ishqab. No. 969, 1.50r, Tassa. No. 970, 1.50r, Shmailat.

**2003, Oct. 1 Photo. & Embossed Perf. 14½x14¾**
965-970 A241 Set of 6 2.50 2.50

---

Powered Flight, Cent. — A242

No. 971: a. Wright Flyer. b. Man with winged glider. c. Qatar Airways jet. d. Plane with propellers.

Souvenir Sheet

**2003, Dec. 17 Litho. Perf. 13½**
971 A242 50d Sheet of 4, #a-d 1.10 1.10

Int'l. Year of the Family, 10th Anniv. — A243

**2004, Apr. 15 Perf. 14½**
972 A243 2.50r multi 1.40 1.40

FIFA (Fédération Internationale de Football Association), Cent. — A244

**2004, May 21 Perf. 13**
973 A244 50d multi .30 .30

Values are for stamps with selvage adjacent to diagonal sides.

Permanent Constitution — A245

**2004, June 8 Litho. Perf. 13½x13¾**
974 A245 75d multi .45 .45

2004 Summer Olympics, Athens — A246

XXVIII OLYMPIAD

Souvenir Sheet

No. 975: a. Denomination at left. b. Denomination at right.

**2004, Aug. 13 Litho. Perf. 13**
975 A246 3r Sheet of 2, #a-b 3.50 3.50

Souvenir Sheet

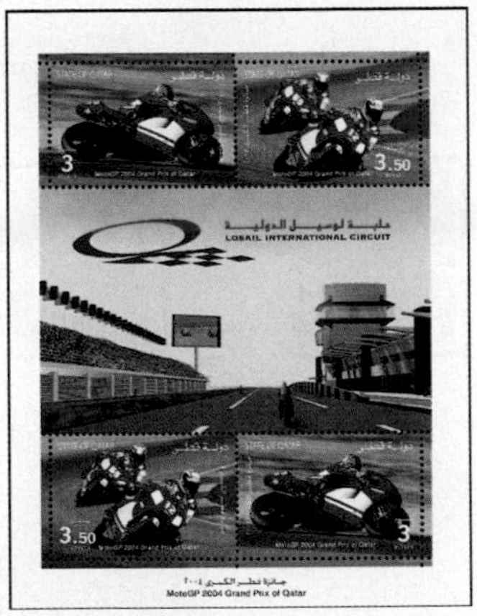

MotoGP 2004 Grand Prix Motorcycle Race — A247

No. 976: a, 3r, Motorcycle, denomination at left. b, 3.50r, Two motorcycles, denomination at right. c, 3.50r, Two motorcycles, denomination at left. d, 3r, Motorcycle, denomination at right

***Perf. 13x14x14x14, 14x14x13x14***

**2004, Sept. 30**

| | | | |
|---|---|---|---|
| **976** | A247 | Sheet of 4, #a-d | *7.25 7.25* |

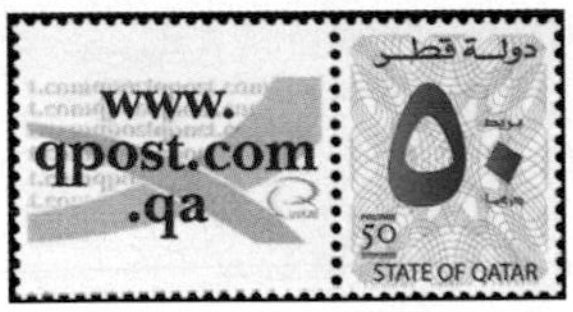
www.
qpost.com
.qa
STATE OF QATAR

Numeral — A248

**2004, Nov. 1 Litho. *Perf. 13½x12½***

**Stamp + Label**

| | | | | | |
|---|---|---|---|---|---|
| **977** | A248 | 50d | blue | .30 | .30 |
| **978** | A248 | 50d | red | .30 | .30 |
| **979** | A248 | 50d | orange | .30 | .30 |
| **980** | A248 | 50d | blue green | .30 | .30 |
| **981** | A248 | 50d | olive green | .30 | .30 |
| ***a.*** | | Vert. strip, #977-981, + 5 labels | | 1.50 | 1.50 |
| | | *Nos. 977-981 (5)* | | 1.50 | 1.50 |

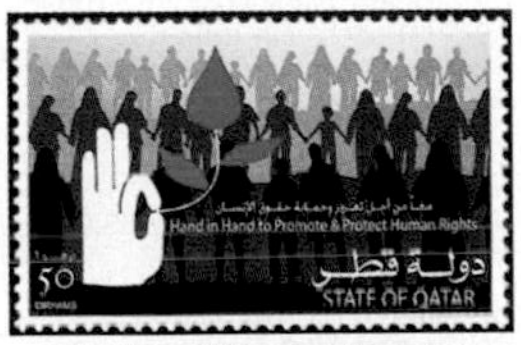

National Human Rights Committee — A249

**2004, Nov. 11 Litho. *Perf. 13¼x13***

| | | | |
|---|---|---|---|
| **982** | A249 | 50d multi | *.30 .30* |

Souvenir Sheet

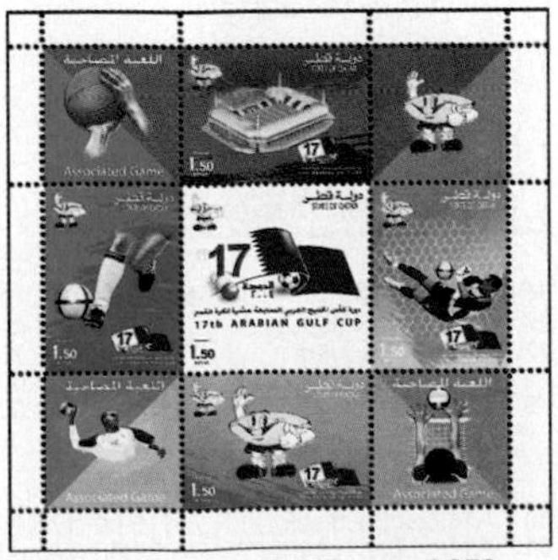

17th Arabian Gulf Cup — A250

No. 983: a, Mascot, emblem, stadium (35x25mm). b, Mascot, emblem, player kicking ball (25x35mm). c, Mascot, emblem (35x35mm). d, Mascot, emblem, goalie catching ball (25x35mm). e, Emblem, two mascots (35x25mm).

**2004, Dec. 10 *Perf. 12¾x13¼***

| | | | |
|---|---|---|---|
| **983** | A250 | 1.50r Sheet of 5, #a-e, + 4 labels | *4.25 4.25* |

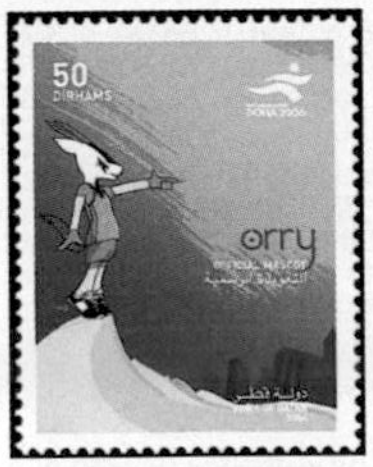

2006 Asian Games, Doha — A251

Mascot Orry: Nos. 984, 990a, 50d, Pointing to Doha. Nos. 985, 990b, 1r, On dhow in Doha harbor, horiz. Nos. 986, 990c, 1.50r, Counting down days on calendar, horiz. Nos. 987, 990d, 2r, Carrying torch. Nos. 988, 990e, 3r, Lighting flame. Nos. 989, 990f, Carrying Qatari flag.

***Perf. 13¼x13, 13x13¼***

**2004, Dec. 31 Litho.**

| | | | |
|---|---|---|---|
| **984-989** | A251 | Set of 6 | 6.50 6.50 |

**Self-Adhesive**

***Serpentine Die Cut 12½***

| | | | |
|---|---|---|---|
| **990** | A251 | Booklet pane of 6, #a-f | 6.50 6.50 |

Miniature Sheet

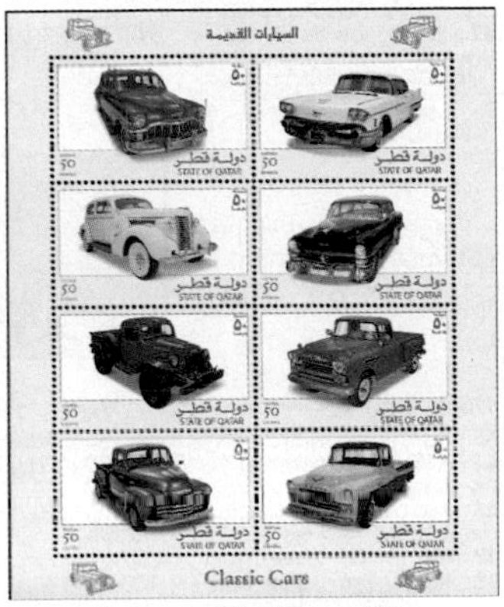
Classic Cars

Cars and Trucks — A252

No. 991: a, 1949 DeSoto (green car). b, 1958 Cadillac Sedan de Ville (white car facing left). c, 1938 Buick (white car facing right). d, 1953 Chrysler Windsor (black car). e, 1962 Dodge Powerwagon (red truck facing right). f, 1958 Chevrolet Pickup (orange red truck facing left). g, 1948 Chevrolet Pickup (green truck). h, 1957 Dodge Sweptside (white and red truck).

**2005, Feb. 1 *Perf. 13½x13¾***

| | | | |
|---|---|---|---|
| **991** | A252 | 50d Sheet of 8, #a-h | 2.25 2.25 |

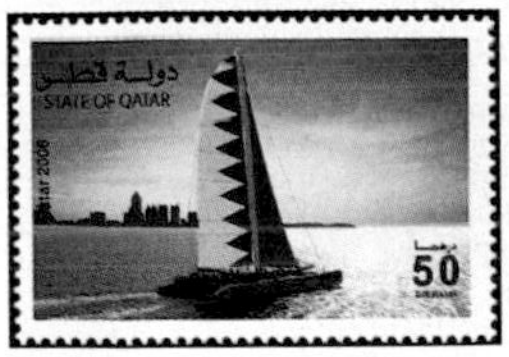

Oryx Quest 2005 Catamaran Race — A253

Designs: No. 992, 50d, Qatar 2006. No. 993, 50d, Daedalus. No. 994, 50d, Cheyenne, vert. No. 995, 50d, Geronimo, vert.

**2005, Feb. 1 *Perf. 14½***

| | | | |
|---|---|---|---|
| **992-995** | A253 | Set of 4 | 1.10 1.10 |

Souvenir Sheet

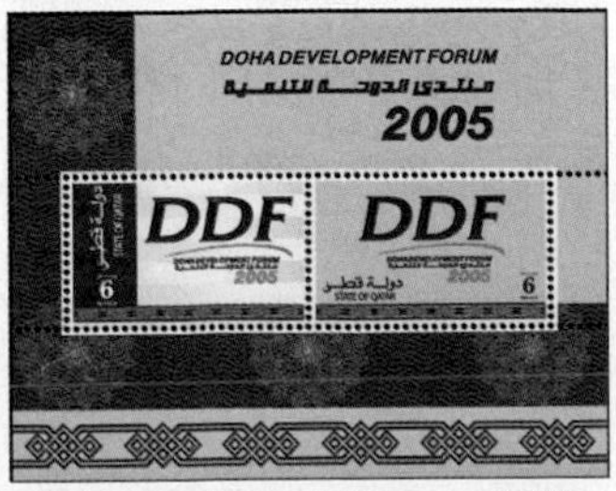
DOHA DEVELOPMENT FORUM
2005
DDF
DDF

Doha Development Forum — A255

No. 998: a, Denomination in white. b, Denomination in maroon.

**2005, Apr. 9 Litho. *Perf. 12¼x13¼***

| | | | |
|---|---|---|---|
| **998** | A255 | 6r Sheet of 2, #a-b | 6.75 6.75 |

Souvenir Sheet

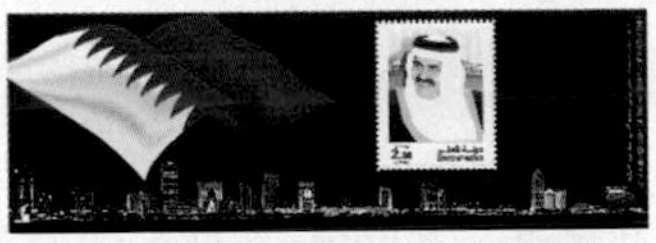

Accession of Emir Sheikh Hamad bin Khalifa Al Thani, 10th Anniv. — A256

**Litho. & Embossed with Foil Application**

**2005, June 27 *Perf. 13¼x13¾***

| | | | |
|---|---|---|---|
| **999** | A256 | 2.50r multi | 1.40 1.40 |

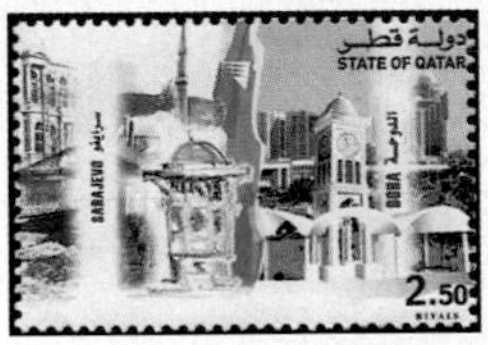

Friendship Between Doha, Qatar and Sarajevo, Bosnia and Herzegovina — A257

**2005, July 13 Litho. *Perf. 13***

| | | | |
|---|---|---|---|
| **1000** | A257 | 2.50r multi | 1.40 1.40 |

See Bosnia & Herzegovina No. 504.

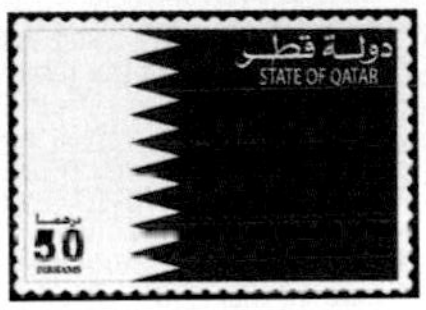
STATE OF QATAR
50

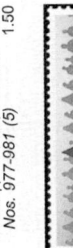

National Flag — A258

***Serpentine Die Cut 12¾***

**2005, Aug. 1**

**Self-Adhesive**

| | | | | |
|---|---|---|---|---|
| **1001** | | Booklet pane of 6 | 6.75 | |
| ***a.*** | A258 | 50d maroon | .30 | .30 |
| ***b.*** | A258 | 1r maroon | .55 | .55 |
| ***c.*** | A258 | 1.50r maroon | .85 | .85 |
| ***d.*** | A258 | 2.50r maroon | 1.40 | 1.40 |
| ***e.*** | A258 | 3r maroon | 1.75 | 1.75 |
| ***f.*** | A258 | 3.50r maroon | 1.90 | 1.90 |

Souvenir Sheet

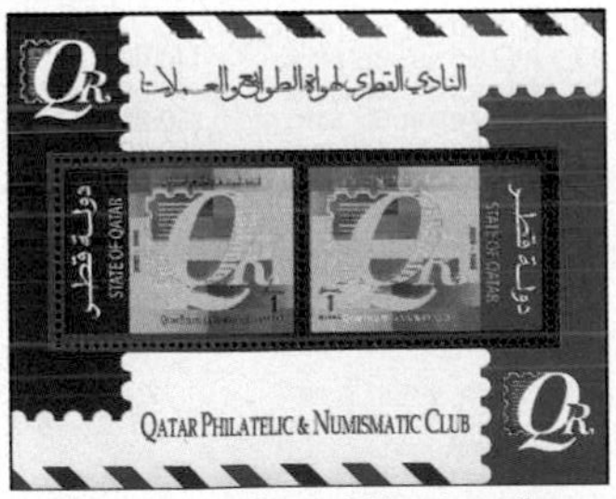
QATAR PHILATELIC & NUMISMATIC CLUB

Qatar Philatelic and Numismatics Club — A260

No. 1003: a, Denomination in maroon. b, Denomination in blue.

**Litho. & Embossed with Foil Application**

**2005, Dec. 16 *Perf. 12¾***

| | | | |
|---|---|---|---|
| **1003** | A260 | 1r Sheet of 2, #a-b | 1.10 1.10 |

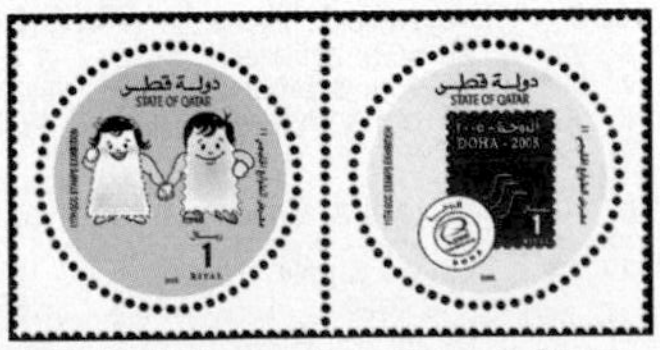

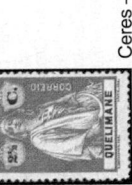

11th Gulf Cooperation Council Stamp Exhibition — A261

No. 1004: a, Mascots. b, Emblems of exhibition and Qatar General Postal Corporation.

Illustration reduced.

**2005, Dec. 21 Litho. *Perf. 13¾***

| | | | |
|---|---|---|---|
| **1004** | A261 | 1r Pair, #a-b | 1.10 1.10 |

## QUELIMANE

ˌkel-ə-ˈmän-ə

LOCATION — A district of the Mozambique Province in Portuguese East Africa

GOVT. — Part of the Portuguese East Africa Colony

AREA — 39,800 sq. mi.

POP. — 877,000 (approx.)

CAPITAL — Quelimane

This district was formerly a part of Zambezia. Quelimane stamps were replaced by those of Mozambique.

100 Centavos = 1 Escudo

Vasco da Gama Issue of Various Portuguese Colonies Surcharged as

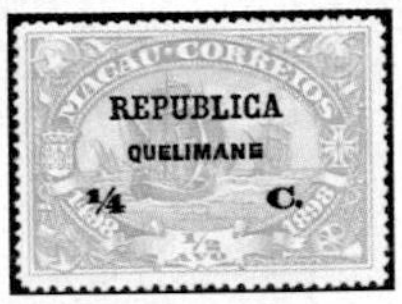
REPUBLICA
QUELIMANE
¼ C.

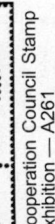

**1913 Unwmk. *Perf. 12½ to 16***

**On Stamps of Macao**

| | | | | |
|---|---|---|---|---|
| **1** | CD20 | ¼c on ½a bl grn | 6.00 | 6.00 |
| **2** | CD21 | ½c on 1a red | 3.00 | 3.00 |
| **3** | CD22 | 1c on 2a red vio | 3.00 | 3.00 |
| **4** | CD23 | 2½c on 4a yel grn | 3.00 | 3.00 |
| **5** | CD24 | 5c on 8a dk bl | 3.00 | 3.00 |
| **6** | CD25 | 7½c on 12a vio brn | 4.00 | *5.00* |
| **7** | CD26 | 10c on 16a bis brn | 3.00 | 3.00 |
| ***a.*** | | Inverted surcharge | 45.00 | |
| **8** | CD27 | 15c on 24a bister | 3.00 | 3.00 |
| | | *Nos. 1-8 (8)* | 28.00 | 29.00 |

**On Stamps of Portuguese Africa**

| | | | | |
|---|---|---|---|---|
| **9** | CD20 | ¼c on 2½r bl grn | 2.00 | *3.00* |
| **10** | CD21 | ½c on 5r red | 2.00 | *3.00* |
| **11** | CD22 | 1c on 10r red vio | 2.00 | *3.00* |
| **12** | CD23 | 2½c on 25r yel grn | 2.00 | *3.00* |
| **13** | CD24 | 5c on 50r dk bl | 2.00 | *3.00* |
| **14** | CD25 | 7½c on 75r vio brn | 2.50 | *4.50* |
| **15** | CD26 | 10c on 100r bister | 2.00 | *3.00* |
| **16** | CD27 | 15c on 150r bister | 2.00 | *3.00* |
| | | *Nos. 9-16 (8)* | 16.50 | 25.50 |

**On Stamps of Timor**

| | | | | |
|---|---|---|---|---|
| **17** | CD20 | ¼c on ½a bl grn | 2.50 | *3.00* |
| **18** | CD21 | ½c on 1a red | 2.50 | *3.00* |
| **19** | CD22 | 1c on 2a red vio | 2.50 | *3.00* |
| **20** | CD23 | 2½c on 4a yel grn | 2.50 | *3.00* |
| **21** | CD24 | 5c on 8a dk bl | 2.50 | *3.00* |
| **22** | CD25 | 7½c on 12a vio brn | 4.00 | *4.50* |
| **23** | CD26 | 10c on 16a bis brn | 2.50 | *3.00* |
| **24** | CD27 | 15c on 24a bister | 2.50 | *3.00* |
| | | *Nos. 17-24 (8)* | 21.50 | 25.50 |
| | | *Nos. 1-24 (24)* | 66.00 | 80.00 |

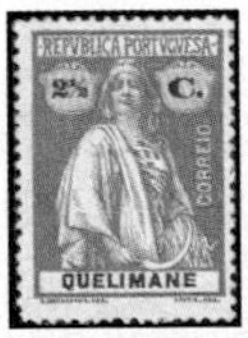
REPUBLICA PORTUGUESA
QUELIMANE
CORREIO

Ceres — A1

**1914 Typo. *Perf. 15x14***

**Name and Value in Black**

| | | | | |
|---|---|---|---|---|
| **25** | A1 | ¼c olive brown | .80 | *3.00* |
| **26** | A1 | ½c black | 1.25 | *3.00* |
| **27** | A1 | 1c blue green | 1.10 | *3.00* |
| ***a.*** | | Imperf. | | |
| **28** | A1 | 1½c lilac brown | 1.60 | *3.00* |
| **29** | A1 | 2c carmine | 1.75 | *3.00* |
| **30** | A1 | 2½c light violet | .50 | *1.50* |
| **31** | A1 | 5c deep blue | 1.25 | *3.00* |
| **32** | A1 | 7½c yellow brown | 1.25 | *3.00* |
| **33** | A1 | 8c slate | 2.00 | *3.00* |
| **34** | A1 | 10c orange brown | 1.75 | *3.00* |
| **35** | A1 | 15c plum | 3.00 | *5.00* |
| **36** | A1 | 20c yellow green | 2.50 | *2.50* |
| **37** | A1 | 30c brown, *green* | 5.00 | *8.50* |
| **38** | A1 | 40c brown, *pink* | 6.00 | *9.00* |
| **39** | A1 | 50c orange, *salmon* | 10.00 | *10.00* |
| **40** | A1 | 1e green, *blue* | 14.00 | *12.00* |
| | | *Nos. 25-40 (16)* | 53.75 | *75.50* |

# RAS AL KHAIMA
,räs al ki-ma

LOCATION — Oman Peninsula, Arabia, on Persian Gulf

GOVT. — Sheikdom under British protection

Ras al Khaima was the 7th Persian Gulf sheikdom to join the United Arab Emirates, doing so in Feb. 1972. See United Arab Emirates.

**100 Naye Paise = 1 Rupee**

Catalogue values for all unused stamps in this country are for **Never Hinged** items.

Sheik Saqr bin Mohammed al Qasimi — A1

Dhow A3

Seven Palm Trees — A2

## 1964, Dec. 21    Photo.    Perf. 14½x14    Unwmk.

| | | | |
|---|---|---|---|
| 1 | A1 | 5np brown & black | .20 .20 |
| 2 | A1 | 15np deep blue & blk | .20 .20 |
| 3 | A2 | 30np ocher & black | .20 .20 |
| 4 | A2 | 40np blue & black | .70 .50 |
| 5 | A2 | 75np brn red & blk | 3.00 1.00 |
| 6 | A3 | 1r lt grn & sepia | 3.00 2.00 |
| 7 | A3 | 2r brt vio & sepia | 8.50 5.00 |
| 8 | A3 | 5r blue gray & sepia | 22.50 9.30 |
| | | Nos. 1-8 (8) | 35.60 |

---

A1

A2

# RHODESIA
rō-'dē-zh ē-ə

(British South Africa)

LOCATION — Southeastern Africa

GOVT. — Administered by the British South Africa Company

AREA — 440,653 sq. mi.

POP. — 1,738,000 (estimated 1921)

CAPITAL — Salisbury

In 1923 the area was divided and the portion south of the Zambezi River became the British Crown Colony of Southern Rhodesia. In the following year the remaining territory was formed into the Protectorate of Northern Rhodesia. The Federation of Rhodesia and Nyasaland (comprising Southern Rhodesia, Northern Rhodesia and Nyasaland) was established Sept. 3, 1953.

**12 Pence = 1 Shilling**
**20 Shillings = 1 Pound**

Coat of Arms — A3

## Engr. (A1, A3); Engr., Typo. (A2)
### 1890-94    Unwmk.    Perf. 14, 14½
Thin Paper

| | | | |
|---|---|---|---|
| 1 | A1 | ½p blue & ver ('91) | 2.50 3.00 |
| 2 | A1 | 1p black | 10.50 2.75 |
| 3 | A2 | 2p gray grn & ver | |
| 4 | A2 | 3p gray & grn ('91) | 20.00 2.50 |
| 5 | A2 | 4p red brn & blk ('91) | 11.50 4.00 |
| 6 | A2 | 6p ultra | 22.50 2.50 |
| 7 | A1 | 8p deep blue | 52.50 25.00 |
| 8 | A1 | 8p rose & bl ('91) | 11.50 3.75 |
| 9 | A1 | 1sh gray brown | 11.50 9.00 |
| 10 | A1 | 2sh vermilion | 42.50 26.00 |
| 11 | A1 | 2sh6p dull lilac | 30.00 40.00 |
| 12 | A1 | 3sh brn & grn ('94) | 150.00 77.50 |
| a. | | Revenue cancellation | .75 |
| 13 | A2 | 4sh gray & ver ('93) | 37.50 22.50 |
| a. | | Revenue cancellation | 2.25 |
| 14 | A1 | 5sh yellow | 67.50 52.50 |
| a. | | Revenue cancellation | 1.00 |
| 15 | A1 | 10sh deep green | 82.50 100.00 |
| a. | | Revenue cancellation | 1.25 |
| 16 | A3 | £1 dark blue | 190.00 140.00 |
| a. | | Revenue cancellation | 6.75 |
| 17 | A3 | £2 rose | 400.00 160.00 |
| a. | | Revenue cancellation | 19.00 |
| 18 | A3 | £5 yellow grn | 1,650.00 450.00 |
| a. | | Revenue cancellation | 47.50 |
| 19 | A3 | £10 orange brn | 2,850.00 800.00 |
| a. | | Revenue cancellation | 800.00 |
| | | Nos. 1-16 (16) | 798.50 552.50 |

The paper of the 1891 issue has the trademark and initials of the makers in a monogram watermarked in each sheet. Some of the lower values were also printed on a slightly thicker paper without watermark.

Copies of #16-19 with cancellations removed are frequently offered as unused specimens.

See #24-25, 58. For surcharges see #20-23, 40-42. For overprints see British Central Africa #1-20.

## 1896, Apr.    Perf. 14

One Penny

| | | | |
|---|---|---|---|
| 37 | A4 | 4sh red & bl, grn | 55.00 |
| 38 | A4 | 5sh org red & grn | 3.25 |
| 39 | A4 | 10sh sl & car, rose | 100.00 |
| | | Nos. 26-39 (14) | 456.75 205.90 |

Three Pence

Nos. 4, 13-14 Surcharged in Black

| | | | |
|---|---|---|---|
| 40 | A2 | 1p on 3p | 525.00 550.00 |
| a. | | "P of "Penny" inverted | 26,500. |
| 41 | A2 | 2p on 4sh | 325.00 |
| a. | | Double surcharge | |
| b. | | "y" of "Penny" inverted | |
| 42 | A1 | 3p on 5s yellow | 200.00 250.00 |
| a. | | "T" of "THREE" inverted | |
| b. | | "R" of "THREE" inverted | |
| | | Nos. 40-42 (3) | 1,025. 1,125. |

The plates for this issue were made from two dies. Stamps of die I have a small dot at the right of the tail of the supporter at the right of the shield, and the body of die II is not fully shaded. Stamps of die II have not the dot and the lion is heavily shaded. See type A7.

## 1896, May 22    Wmk. 2

A6

| | | | |
|---|---|---|---|
| 43 | A6 | ½p slate | 11.50 18.00 |
| 44 | A6 | 1p carmine | 14.00 10.50 |
| 45 | A6 | 2p bister brown | 17.50 10.50 |
| 46 | A6 | 4p deep blue | 20.00 20.00 |
| a. | | "COMPANY" omitted | |
| 47 | A3 | 6p violet | 57.50 75.00 |
| 48 | A6 | 1sh yellow buff | 160.00 160.00 |
| 49 | A6 | 3p claret | 57.50 80.00 |
| | | Nos. 43-49 (7) | 338.00 383.50 |

Nos. 42-49 were used at Bulawayo during the Matabele Rebellion. Forgeries are known.

Cape of Good Hope Stamps Overprinted in Black

## 1898-1908

A8

| | | | |
|---|---|---|---|
| 58 | A3 | £2 bright red | 1,775. 450.00 |
| a. | | Revenue cancellation | 60.00 |

See note on remainders following No. 49.

Thick Paper
**Perf. 15**

| | | | |
|---|---|---|---|
| 59 | A8 | ½p yellow green | 2.50 1.00 |
| 60 | A8 | 1p rose | 3.75 .60 |
| a. | | Imperf. pair | 750.00 |
| b. | | Horiz. pair, imperf. vert. | 575.00 |
| 61 | A8 | 2p brown | 600.00 .70 |
| a. | | 1p red | |
| 62 | A8 | 2½p cobalt bl | 3.25 .70 |
| d. | | "R" of "THREE" inverted | |
| 63 | A8 | 3p claret | 5.25 1.00 |
| a. | | Horiz. pair, imperf. be-tween | |
| 64 | A8 | 4p olive | 5.00 .35 |
| a. | | Vert. pair, imperf. be-tween | |
| 65 | A8 | 6p lilac | 11.50 1.00 |
| a. | | 1sh olive bis-ter | |
| 66 | A9 | 8p olive green | 16.00 2.50 |
| 67 | A9 | 2sh6p bluish | 52.50 .85 |
| a. | | Vert. pair, imperf. be-tween | |
| b. | | Horiz. or vert. pair, im-perf. btwn. | |
| 68 | A8 | 3sh brown | 15.00 1.90 |
| 69 | A9 | 5sh orange | 42.50 11.00 |
| a. | | Imperf. pair | 575.00 |
| 70 | A9 | 7sh6p olive | 11.00 19.00 |
| 71 | A9 | 10sh bluish grn | 25.00 1.10 |
| 72 | A10 | £1 gray vio | 92.50 2.50 |
| 73 | A10 | £2 red brown | 85.00 7.50 |
| 74 | A10 | £5 dk blue | 3,500. 2,350. |
| 75 | A10 | £10 olive lil | 597.00 141.90 |

For overprints and surcharges see #82-100. See note on remainders following No. 49.

Victoria Falls — A11

## 1905, July 13    Perf. 13½ to 15

| | | | |
|---|---|---|---|
| 76 | A11 | 1p rose red | 3.75 6.20 |
| 77 | A11 | 2½p ultra | 9.25 6.25 |
| 78 | A11 | 1sh green | 25.00 55.00 |
| 79 | A11 | 1sh blue green | 26.00 40.00 |
| 80 | A11 | 5sh violet | 97.50 326.25 |
| 81 | A11 | £1 2sh6p black | 271.50 |
| | | Nos. 76-81 (6) | |

Opening of the Victoria Falls. See note on remainders following No. 49.

The Zambezi River.

---

## 1895
Nos. 6 and 9 Surcharged in Black

A4

| | | | |
|---|---|---|---|
| 24 | A2 | 2p green & red | 25.00 11.50 |
| 25 | A2 | 4p ocher & black | 25.00 14.00 |
| a. | | Imperf. pair | 2,000. |

Thick Soft Paper

**Perf. 12½**

Beware of forged surcharges.

## 1891, Mar.

| | | | |
|---|---|---|---|
| 20 | A1 | ½p on 6p ultra | 110.00 |
| 21 | A1 | 1p on 6p ultra | 110.00 |
| 22 | A1 | 4p on 6p ultra | 150.00 |
| 23 | A1 | 8p on 1sh brown | 520.00 |
| | | Nos. 20-23 (4) | |

Engraved, Typo.    Perf. 14

| | | | |
|---|---|---|---|
| 26 | A4 | ½p slate & violet | 3.00 3.75 |
| 27 | A4 | 1p scar & emer | 3.75 4.25 |
| 28 | A4 | 2p on 6p ultra | 19.00 4.50 |
| 29 | A4 | 3p red brn & ul-tra | |
| 30 | A4 | 4p blue & red lil | 4.25 2.00 |
| 31 | A4 | 1r lt grn & blk | 9.25 .60 |
| d. | | Horiz. pair, imperf. btwn. | |
| 32 | A4 | 8p dp grn & vio, rose | 7.25 .85 |
| 33 | A4 | Horiz. pair, imperf. btwn. | |
| 34 | A4 | 1sh brt grn & ultra buff | 17.50 3.25 |
| 35 | A4 | 2sh6p brn & vio, yel | 75.00 9.75 |
| 36 | A4 | 3sh dgrn & rod vio, bl | 80.00 55.00 |

## 1896
| | | | |
|---|---|---|---|
| a. | Imperf. pair | | 7,000. |
| a. | Imperf. pair | | 37.50 |

## 1897    Perf. 14

A7

| | | | |
|---|---|---|---|
| 50 | A7 | ½p slate & violet | 2.75 2.25 |
| 51 | A7 | 1p ver & gray grn | 3.50 3.00 |
| 52 | A7 | 2p brown & lil | |
| 53 | A7 | 3p red brn & gray | 7.25 1.75 |
| bl | | | |
| 54 | A7 | 4p blue & red li-lac | 3.00 .45 |
| 55 | A7 | 6p violet & salm-on | 10.50 1.75 |
| 56 | A7 | 8p dk grn & vio, buff | 7.50 4.00 |
| 57 | A7 | £1 black & red, buff | 400.00 250.00 |
| | | Nos. 50-56 (7) | |

Type A7 differs from type A4 in having the ends of the scroll which is below the shield curved between the hind legs instead of passing behind one leg of each. There are other minor differences.

Remainders

Rhodesian authorities made available remainders in large quantities of all stamps in 1897, 1898-1908, 1905, 1909 and 1910 issues, CTO. Some varieties exist only as remainders. See notes following Nos. 100 and 118.

Perf. 13½ to 16    Unwmk.    Engr.

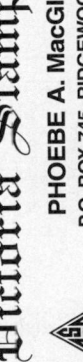

Stamps of 1898-1908 Overprinted or Surcharged:

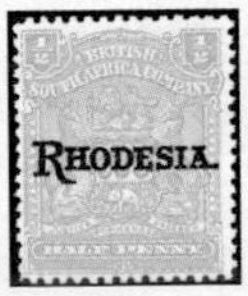
RHODESIA.

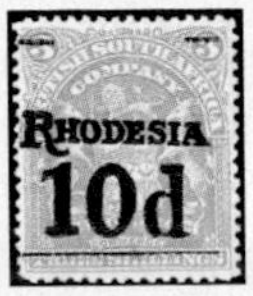
RHODESIA
10d

**1909** *Perf. 14, 15*

82 A8 ½p yellow green 2.00 1.40
83 A8 1p red 2.75 .85
a. Horiz. pair, imperf., vert. 475.00
84 A8 2p brown 1.90 3.75
85 A8 2½p cobalt blue 1.40 .80
86 A8 3p claret 1.90 .60
87 A8 4p olive green 3.25 1.10
88 A8 5p on 6p lilac 7.50 14.00
89 A8 6p lilac 5.75 4.25
90 A9 7½p on 2sh6p 4.00 4.25
91 A9 10p on 3sh pur 15.00 18.00
92 A9 1sh olive bis 9.75 3.50
93 A9 2sh on 5sh org 14.00 8.50
94 A9 2sh6p bluish gray 20.00 9.75
95 A9 3sh purple 17.50 9.75
96 A9 5sh orange 29.00 35.00
97 A9 7sh6p black 97.50 20.00
98 A9 10sh bluish grn 37.50 12.50
99 A10 £1 gray violet 160.00 85.00
a. Pair, one without overprint 28,750.
b. Violet overprint 400.00 210.00
100 A10 £2 red brown 3,750. 325.00
*Nos. 82-99 (18)* 430.70 233.00

See note on remainders following No. 49. The remainders included inverted overprints of the 3p ($35), 4p ($15) and 2s6p ($27.50).

Nos. 82-87, 89, 92, 94, 96 and 98 exist without period after "Rhodesia."

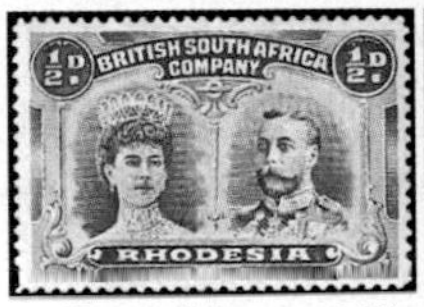
BRITISH SOUTH AFRICA COMPANY
RHODESIA

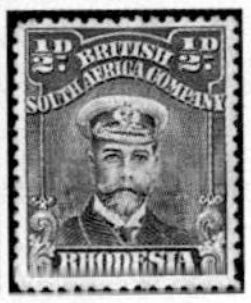
RHODESIA

Queen Mary and King George V
A12 A13

**1910 Engr.** *Perf. 14, 15x14, 14x15*

101 A12 ½p green 11.00 2.00
a. ½p olive green 30.00 3.00
b. Perf. 15 325.00 10.00
c. Imperf., pair 12,500. 5,250.
d. Perf. 13½ 325.00 45.00
102 A12 1p rose car 18.00 2.00
a. Vertical pair, imperf. btwn. 17,500. 11,500.
b. Perf. 15 325.00 9.75
c. Perf. 13½ 2,050. 55.00
103 A12 2p gray & blk 55.00 6.25
b. Perf. 15 975.00 35.00
104 A12 2½p ultramarine 22.50 6.25
a. 2½p light blue 22.50 15.00
b. Perf. 15 80.00 40.00
c. Perf. 13½ 40.00 70.00
105 A12 3p ol yel & vio 30.00 12.50
a. Perf. 15 2,900. 57.50
106 A12 4p org & blk 37.50 12.50
a. 4p orange & violet black 75.00 57.50
b. Perf. 15x14 475.00
c. Perf. 15 47.50 70.00
107 A12 5p ol grn & brn 27.50 45.00
a. 5p olive yel & brn (error) 625.00 175.00
b. Perf. 15 800.00 85.00
108 A12 6p claret & brn 32.50 14.00
a. Perf. 15 950.00 70.00
109 A12 8p brn vio & gray blk 150.00 100.00
a. Perf. 13½ 70.00 275.00
110 A12 10p plum & rose red 35.00 55.00
111 A12 1sh turq grn & black 40.00 19.00
b. Perf. 15 1,100. 62.50
112 A12 2sh gray bl & black 85.00 57.50
a. Perf. 15 2,100 375.00
113 A12 2sh6p car rose & blk 350.00 325.00
114 A12 3sh vio & bl grn 175.00 175.00
115 A12 5sh yel grn & brn red 250.00 225.00
116 A12 7sh6p brt bl & car 700.00 475.00
117 A12 10sh red org & bl grn 425.00 425.00
a. 10sh red org & myrtle grn 700.00 275.00
118 A12 £1 bluish sl & car 1,150. 550.00
a. £1 black & red 1,250. 400.00
c. Perf 15 17,500 3,500.
*Nos. 101-118 (18)* 3,594. 2,507.

See note on remainders following No. 49. The £1 in plum and red is from the remainders.

**1913-19** *Perf. 14*

119 A13 ½p green 5.00 1.75
a. Horiz. pair, imperf. vert. 800.00 750.00
b. Perf. 15 9.75 15.00
c. Perf. 14x15 5,750. 200.00
d. Perf. 15x14 5,750. 375.00
120 A13 1p brown rose 4.25 1.40
a. 1p bright rose 5.25 1.40
b. As "a," horiz. pair, imperf btwn. 800.00 575.00
c. Perf. 15, brown rose 3.25 5.50
d. Perf. 15, rose red 625.00 25.00
e. As "d," horiz. pair, imperf btwn. 12,500.
121 A13 1½p bister 3.75 1.40
a. Perf. 15 29.00 6.00
b. Perf. 15x14
c. Vert. pair, imperf. btwn. 1,850.
d. Horiz. pair, imperf. btwn. 625.00
122 A13 2p vio blk & blk 7.50 2.75
a. 2p gray & black 9.25 3.75
b. Perf. 15 7.50 7.50
c. Horiz. pair, imperf. btwn. 5,200.
123 A13 2½p ultra 4.50 26.00
a. Perf. 15 18.00 40.00
124 A13 3p org yel & blk 9.00 2.00
a. 3p yellow & black 9.00 2.00
b. Perf. 15 5.50 19.00
125 A13 4p org red & blk 11.00 7.50
a. Perf. 15 150.00 18.00
126 A13 5p yel grn & blk 4.25 11.50
127 A13 6p lilac & blk 5.50 3.25
a. Perf. 15 5.50 6.25
128 A13 8p gray grn & violet 11.50 55.00
a. Perf. 15 210.00 175.00
129 A13 10p car rose & bl, perf. 15 7.50 30.00
a. Perf. 14 14.00 50.00
130 A13 1sh turq bl & blk 7.50 6.50
a. Perf. 15 55.00 11.00
131 A13 1sh lt grn & blk ('19) 80.00 30.00
132 A13 2sh brn & blk, perf. 14 14.00 17.00
a. Perf. 15 11.00 35.00
133 A13 2sh6p ol gray & vio bl 35.00 60.00
a. 2sh6p gray & blue 50.00 32.50
b. Perf. 15 11.50 35.00
134 A13 3sh brt blue & red brown 85.00 110.00
a. Perf. 15 700.00 290.00
135 A13 5sh grn & bl 55.00 62.50
a. Perf. 15 125.00 140.00
136 A13 7sh6p black & vio, perf. 15 125.00 175.00
a. Perf. 14 260.00 290.00
137 A13 10sh yel grn & car 200.00 310.00
a. Perf. 15 200.00 425.00
138 A13 £1 violet & blk 400.00 625.00
a. £1 magenta & black 475.00 675.00
b. Perf. 15 1,400. 1,500.
*Nos. 119-138 (20)* 1,075. 1,538.

Three dies were used for the stamps of this issue: 1) Outline at top of cap absent or very faint and broken. Left ear not shaded or outlined and appears white; 2) Outline at top of cap faint and broken. Ear shaded all over, with no outline; 3) Outline at top of cap continuous. Ear shaded all over, with continuous outline.

The existence of #121b has been questioned.

No. 120 Surcharged in Dark Violet:

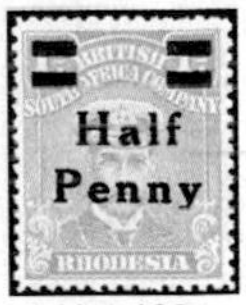
Half
Penny
No. 139

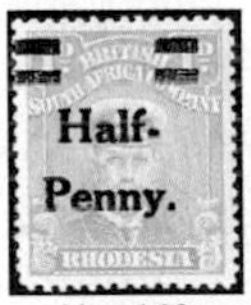
Half-
Penny.
No. 140

**1917**

139 A13 ½p on 1p 3.00 8.00
a. Inverted surcharge 1,600. 1,700.
140 A13 ½p on 1p 2.00 7.50

Nos. 141-190 are accorded to Rhodesia and Nyasaland.

## RHODESIA AND NYASALAND

rō-ˈdē-zhˌē-ˌə ənˌdˌ nī-ˈa-sə-ˌland

LOCATION — Southern Africa
GOVT. — Federal State in British Commonwealth
AREA — 486,973 sq. mi.
POP. — 8,510,000 (est. 1961)
CAPITAL — Salisbury, Southern Rhodesia

The Federation of Southern Rhodesia, Northern Rhodesia and Nyasaland was created in 1953, dissolved at end of 1963.

12 Pence = 1 Shilling
20 Shillings = 1 Pound

**Catalogue values for all unused stamps in this country are for Never Hinged items.**

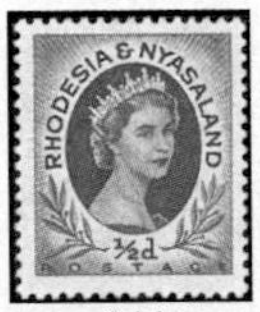
RHODESIA & NYASALAND
½d
A14

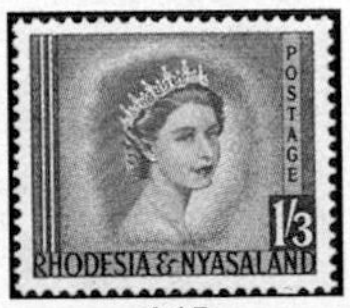
POSTAGE
1/3
RHODESIA & NYASALAND
A15

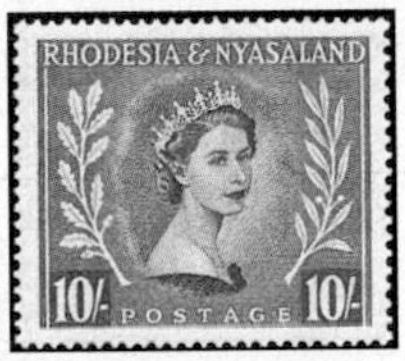
RHODESIA & NYASALAND
10/-
POSTAGE
10/-
Queen Elizabeth II
A16

*Perf. 13½x14 (A14), 13½x13 (A15), 14x13 (A16)*

**1954-56 Engr. Unwmk.**

141 A14 ½p vermilion .20 .20
a. Booklet pane of 6 1.25
b. Perf. 12½x14 .60 .40
142 A14 1p ultra .20 .20
a. Booklet pane of 6 1.25
b. Perf. 12½x14 .80 .50
143 A14 2p emerald .20 .20
a. Booklet pane of 6 1.60
143B A14 2½p ocher ('56) 2.75 .20
144 A14 3p carmine .20 .20
145 A14 4p red brown .50 .20
146 A14 4½p blue green .20 .20
147 A14 6p red lilac 1.60 .20
148 A14 9p purple 1.25 .35
149 A14 1sh gray 1.40 .20
150 A15 1sh3p ultra & ver 2.40 .20
151 A15 2sh brn & dp bl 6.00 .70
152 A15 2sh6p car & blk 4.75 .55
153 A15 5sh ol & pur 13.50 1.40
154 A16 10sh red org & aqua 15.00 7.00
155 A16 £1 brn car & ol 24.00 21.00
*Nos. 141-155 (16)* 74.15 33.00

Issue dates: 2½p, Feb. 15, others, July 1.
Nos. 141b and 142b are coils.

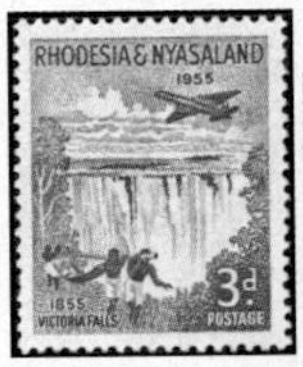
RHODESIA & NYASALAND
1955
3d
POSTAGE

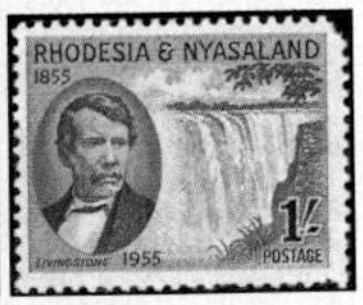
RHODESIA & NYASALAND
1855
1955
1/-
POSTAGE

Victoria Falls
A17 A18

**1955, June 15** *Perf. 13½*

156 A17 3p Plane .30 .20
157 A18 1sh David Livingstone .85 .55

Centenary of discovery of Victoria Falls.

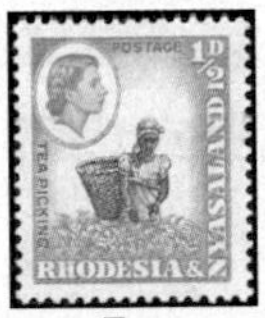
POSTAGE
RHODESIA &
Tea Picking — A19

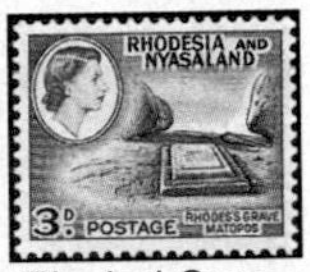
RHODESIA AND NYASALAND
3d POSTAGE
Rhodes' Grave, Matopos — A20

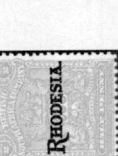

Designs: 1p, V. H. F. Mast. 2p, Copper mining. 2½p, Kingsley Fairbridge Memorial. 4p, Boat on Lake Bangweulu. 6p, Victoria Falls. 9p, Railroad trains. 1sh, Tobacco. 1sh3p, Ship on Lake Nyasa. 2sh, Chirundu Bridge, Zambezi River. 2sh6p, Salisbury Airport. 5sh, Cecil Rhodes statue, Salisbury. 10sh, Mlanje mountain. £1, Coat of arms.

**1959-63**
Size: 18½x22½mm, 22½x18½mm
Perf. 13½x14, 14x13½   Engr.   Unwmk.

Kariba Gorge, 1955 — A21

| | | | | |
|---|---|---|---|---|
| 158 | A19 | ½p emer & blk | .55 | .25 |
| a. | | Perf. 12½x13½ | 2.75 | 4.50 |
| 159 | A19 | 1p blk & rose | .20 | |
| a. | | Perf. 12½x13½ | 2.75 | |
| b. | | Rose red (center) omitted | 325.00 | |
| 160 | A19 | 2p ocher & vio | .20 | 4.50 |
| 161 | A19 | 2½p slate & lil. | 1.25 | |
| 162 | A20 | 3p blue & blk | .75 | .30 |
| a. | | 3p blue & black | .20 | |
| b. | | Black omitted | | |

Size: 24x27mm, 27x24mm
Perf. 14½

| | | | | |
|---|---|---|---|---|
| 163 | A19 | 4p olive & blk | .25 | .20 |
| 164 | A19 | 6p grn & ultra | .20 | |
| 164A | A20 | 9p pur & ocher (62) | 7.50 | |
| 165 | A19 | 1sh ultra & yel | 2.10 | .75 |
| 166 | A20 | 1sh3p sep & brt grn, perf. 14 | 2.75 | .20 |
| 167 | A20 | 2sh lake & grn | 3.00 | .50 |
| 168 | A20 | 2sh6p ocher & bl | 3.75 | .25 |

Size: 32x27mm
Perf. 11½

| | | | | |
|---|---|---|---|---|
| 169 | A20 | 5sh yel grn & blk | 7.50 | 2.10 |
| 170 | A20 | 10sh brt rose & choc | 8.00 | 2.00 |
| 171 | A20 | £1 violet & blk | 24.00 | 10.50 |
| | | Nos. 158-171 (15) | 99.35 | 50.00 |

Nos. 158a and 159a are coils.
Issue dates: 9p, May 15, others, Aug. 12.

**1960, May 17**   Photo.   Perf. 14½x14

| | | | | |
|---|---|---|---|---|
| 172 | A21 | 3p org & sl grn | .50 | .20 |
| 173 | A21 | 6p yel brn & blk | | |
| 174 | A21 | 1sh dull bl & ember | | |
| 175 | A21 | 1sh3p grnsh bl & ocher | 1.75 | 3.00 |
| 176 | A21 | 2sh6p org ver & blk | 1.90 | 2.00 |
| 177 | A21 | 5sh grnsh bl & lilac | 2.50 | 6.75 |
| | | Nos. 172-177 (6) | 13.15 | 21.90 |

Designs: 6p, Power lines. 1sh, View of dam. 1sh3p, View of dam and lake. 2sh6p, Power station. 5sh, Dam and Queen Mother Elizabeth.

Miner with Drill—A22

**1961, May 8**

| | | | | |
|---|---|---|---|---|
| 178 | A22 | 6p chnt brn & ol grn | .40 | .25 |
| 179 | A22 | 1sh3p lt blue & blk | .40 | .65 |

Design: 1sh3p, Mining surface installations.

7th Commonwealth Mining and Metallurgical Cong., Apr. 10-May 20.

---

## POSTAGE DUE STAMPS

D1

**1961, Apr. 19**   Perf. 12½   Unwmk.   Typo.

| | | | | |
|---|---|---|---|---|
| J1 | D1 | 1p vermilion | 2.25 | 3.00 |
| a. | | Horiz. pair, imperf. btwn. | 350.00 | |
| J2 | D1 | 2p dark blue | 2.25 | 3.00 |
| J3 | D1 | 4p emerald | 4.25 | 7.00 |
| J4 | D1 | 6p dark purple | 4.25 | 7.00 |
| a. | | Horiz. pair, imperf. btwn. | 550.00 | |
| | | Nos. J1-J4 (4) | 11.00 | 20.00 |

Nos. 142-143 exist with provisional "Postage Due" handstamp.

---

**1962, Feb. 6**

DH Hercules Biplane — A23

| | | | | |
|---|---|---|---|---|
| 180 | A23 | 6p ver & ol grn | .50 | .20 |
| 181 | A23 | 1sh3p bl, blk, grn & yel | 1.25 | .25 |
| 182 | A23 | 2sh6p dk pur & car rose | 6.50 | 4.75 |
| | | Nos. 180-182 (3) | 8.00 | 5.50 |

Designs: 1sh3p, Flying boat over Zambezi River. 2sh6p, DH Comet, Salisbury Airport.

30th anniv. of the inauguration of the Rhodesia-London airmail service.

Tobacco Plant — A24

**1963, Feb. 18**   Photo.   Perf. 14x14½

| | | | | |
|---|---|---|---|---|
| 184 | A24 | 3p gray brown & grn | .20 | .20 |
| 185 | A24 | 6p blue, grn & brn | .20 | .20 |
| 186 | A24 | 1sh3p slate & red brn | .35 | .35 |
| 187 | A24 | 2sh6p brown & org brn | 1.50 | 2.75 |
| | | Nos. 184-187 (4) | 2.25 | 3.50 |

Designs: 6p, Tobacco field. 1sh3p, Auction floor. 2sh6p, Cured tobacco.

3rd World Tobacco Scientific Cong., Salisbury, Feb. 18-26 and the 1st Intl. Tobacco Trade Cong., Salisbury, March 6-16.

Red Cross A25

**1963, Aug. 6**

| | | | | |
|---|---|---|---|---|
| 188 | A25 | 3p red | .80 | .20 |

Centenary of the International Red Cross.

"Round Table" Emblem A26

**1963, Sept. 11**

| | | | | |
|---|---|---|---|---|
| 189 | A26 | 6p multicolored | .45 | .80 |
| 190 | A26 | 1sh3p multicolored | .45 | .60 |

World Council of Young Men's Service Clubs at University College of Rhodesia and Nyasaland, Sept. 8-15.

---

## RHODESIA AND NYASALAND — RHODESIA

### Self-Governing State (formerly Southern Rhodesia)

**RHODESIA**
rō-dē-zhē,-a

LOCATION — Southeastern Africa, bordered by Zambia, Mozambique, South Africa and Botswana.
GOVT. — Self-governing member of British Commonwealth.
AREA — 150,333 sq. mi.
POP. — 4,670,000 (est. 1968)
CAPITAL — Salisbury

In Oct. 1964, Southern Rhodesia assumed the name Rhodesia. On Nov. 11, 1965, the white minority government declared Rhodesia independent. Rhodesia became Zimbabwe on Apr. 18, 1980. For earlier issues, see Southern Rhodesia and Rhodesia and Nyasaland.

12 Pence = 1 Shilling
20 Shillings = 1 Pound
100 Cents = 1 Dollar (1967)

> Catalogue values for all unused stamps in this country are for Never Hinged items.

ITU Emblem, Old and New Communication Equipment — A27

**1965, May 17**   Unwmk.   Photo.   Perf. 14

| | | | | |
|---|---|---|---|---|
| 200 | A27 | 6p apple grn & brt vio | .80 | .35 |
| 201 | A27 | 1sh3p brn vio & dk vio | 1.25 | 1.00 |
| 202 | A27 | 2sh6p org brn & dk vio | 4.25 | 4.25 |
| | | Nos. 200-202 (3) | 6.30 | 5.60 |

Cent. of the ITU.

Bangala Dam — A28

**1965, July 19**   Photo.   Perf. 14

| | | | | |
|---|---|---|---|---|
| 203 | A28 | 3p dull bl, grn & ocher | .25 | .20 |
| 204 | A28 | 4p blue, grn & brn | .75 | .70 |
| 205 | A28 | 2sh6p multicolored | 4.00 | 3.25 |
| | | Nos. 203-205 (3) | 5.00 | 4.15 |

Designs: 4p, Irrigation canal through sugar plantation. 2sh6p, Worker cutting sugar cane.

Issued to publicize Conservation Week of the Natural Resources Board.

Churchill, Parliament, Quill and Sword—A29

**1965, Aug. 16**

| | | | | |
|---|---|---|---|---|
| 206 | A29 | 1sh3p ultra & black | .60 | .35 |

Sir Winston Spencer Churchill (1874-1965), statesman and WWII leader.
For surcharge see No. 222.

---

### Issues of Smith Government

**1965, Dec. 8**   Photo.   Perf. 11

Arms of Rhodesia A30

| | | | | |
|---|---|---|---|---|
| 207 | A30 | 2sh6p violet & multi | .30 | .20 |
| a. | | Imperf., pair | 825.00 | |

Declaration of independence by the government of Prime Minister Ian Smith.

Southern Rhodesia Overprinted

Southern Rhodesia Nos. 95-108 Overprinted

**1965, Jan. 17**   Perf. 13½x13
Size: 27x23mm

| | | | | |
|---|---|---|---|---|
| 208 | A30 | ½p lt bl, yel & grn | .20 | .20 |
| 209 | A30 | 1p ocher & pur | .20 | .20 |
| 210 | A30 | 2p vio & org yel | .20 | .20 |
| 211 | A30 | 3p lt blue & choc | .20 | .20 |
| 212 | A30 | 4p sl grn & org | .20 | .20 |
| 213 | A30 | 6p dull grn, red & yel | .20 | .20 |
| 214 | A30 | 9p ol grn, yel & brn | .20 | |
| a. | | Pair, one without overprint | 200.00 | |
| 215 | A30 | 1sh ocher & brt grn | .20 | .20 |
| 216 | A30 | 1sh3p grn, vio & dk red | .30 | .25 |
| a. | | Double overprint | 250.00 | |
| 217 | A30 | 2sh dull bl & yel | .35 | .30 |
| 218 | A30 | 2sh6p ultra & red | .65 | .55 |
| a. | | Red omitted | | |
| 219 | A30 | 5sh bl, grn, ocher & lt brn | 8.00 | 9.25 |
| 220 | A30 | 10sh ocher, blk, red & bl | 2.50 | 2.00 |
| a. | | Double overprint | 425.00 | |
| 221 | A30 | £1 rose, sep, ocher & grn | 16.25 | 18.25 |
| | | Nos. 208-221 (14) | | |

Overprint 26mm Wide
Size: 32x27mm
Perf. 14½x14

No. 206 Surcharged in Red

**1965**

| | | | | |
|---|---|---|---|---|
| 222 | A29 | 5sh on 1sh3p | 20.00 | 30.00 |

---

Ansellia Orchid—A31

**1966, Feb. 9**   Photo.   Perf. 14½
Size: 23x19mm

| | | | | |
|---|---|---|---|---|
| 223 | A31 | 1p ocher & pur | .20 | .20 |
| 224 | A31 | 2p slate grn & org | .20 | .20 |
| a. | | Orange omitted | 1,000. | |
| 225 | A31 | 3p lt blue & choc | .20 | .20 |
| b. | | Queen's head omitted | | |
| c. | | Booklet pane of 4 | .85 | |
| d. | | Lt blue omitted | 1,500. | |
| 226 | A31 | 4p gray & brt grn | .50 | .20 |

Designs: 1p, Cape Buffalo. 2p, Oranges. 3p, Kudu. 4p, Emeralds. 6p, Flame lily. 9p, Tobacco. 1sh, Corn. 1sh3p, Lake Kyle. 2sh, Aloe. 2sh6p, Tigerfish. 5sh, Cattle. 10sh, Gray-breasted helmet guinea fowl. £1, Arms of Rhodesia.

Printed by Harrison & Sons, London.

*Perf. 13½x13*
**Size: 27x23mm**

227 A31 6p dull grn, red & yel .20 .20
228 A31 9p purple & ocher .20 .20
229 A31 1sh lt bl, yel & grn .20 .20
230 A31 1sh3p dull blue & yel .25 .20
*b.* Yellow omitted 1,850.
231 A31 1sh6p ol grn, yel & brn 1.25 .25
232 A31 2sh lt ol grn, vio & dk red .40 .70
233 A31 2sh6p brt grnsh bl, ultra & ver .50 .25

*Perf. 14½x14*
**Size: 32x27mm**

234 A31 5sh bl, grn, ocher & lt brn .55 .55
235 A31 10sh dl yel, blk, red & bl 3.25 3.25
236 A31 £1 sal pink, sep, ocher & grn 11.00 11.00
*Nos. 223-236 (14)* 18.90 17.60

Printed by Mardon Printers, Salisbury

**1966-68** **Litho.** *Perf. 14½*
*223a* A31 1p ocher & pur .20 .20
*224a* A31 2p sl grn & org ('68) .20 .20
*225a* A31 3p lt bl & choc ('68) .20 .20
*226a* A31 4p sep & brt grn .30 .30
*227a* A31 6p gray grn, red & yel .45 .45
*228a* A31 9p pur & ocher ('68) .60 .60
*230a* A31 1sh3p dl bl & yel .80 .80
*232a* A31 2sh lt ol grn, vio & dk red 3.75 4.00

*Perf. 14*

*234a* A31 5sh brt bl, grn, ocher & brn 8.25 6.00
*235a* A31 10sh ocher, blk, red & bl 25.00 27.50
*236a* A31 £1 sal pink, sep, ocher & grn 35.00 35.00
*Nos. 223a-236a (11)* 74.75 75.25

See Nos. 245-248A.

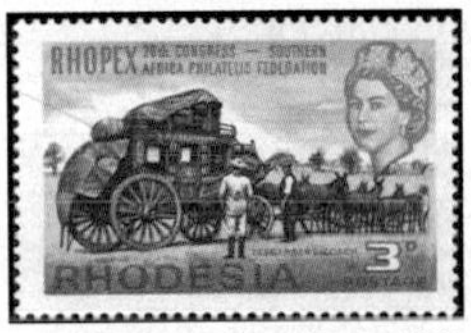

Zeederberg Coach — A32

Designs: 9p, Sir Rowland Hill. 1sh6p, Penny Black. 2sh6p, Rhodesia No. 18, £5.

*Perf. 14½*
**1966, May 2** **Litho.** **Unwmk.**
237 A32 3p blue, org & blk .20 .20
238 A32 9p beige & brown .20 .20
239 A32 1sh6p blue & black .40 .30
240 A32 2sh6p rose, yel grn & blk .70 .70
*a.* Souvenir sheet of 4, #237-240 13.50 *15.00*
*Nos. 237-240 (4)* 1.50 1.40

28th Cong. of the Southern Africa Phil. Fed. and the RHOPEX Exhib., Bulawayo, May 2-7.

No. 240a was printed in sheets of 12 and comes with perforations extending through the margins in four different versions. Many have holes in the top margin made when the sheet was cut into individual panes. Sizes of panes vary.

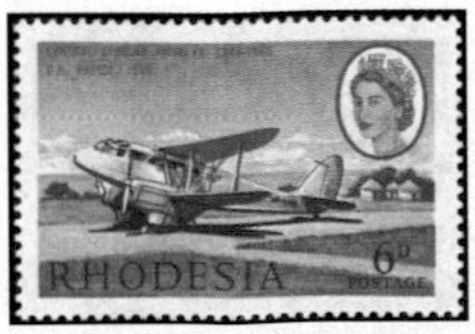

De Havilland Dragon Rapide A33

Planes: 1sh3p, Douglas DC-3. 2sh6p, Vickers Viscount. 5sh, Jet.

**1966, June 1**
241 A33 6p multicolored .80 .60
242 A33 1sh3p multicolored 1.40 .70
243 A33 2sh6p multicolored 3.50 2.75
244 A33 5sh blue & black 6.00 4.25
*Nos. 241-244 (4)* 11.70 8.30

20th anniv. of Central African Airways.

**Dual Currency Issue**

Type of 1966 with Denominations in Cents and Pence-Shillings

**1967-68** **Litho.** *Perf. 14½*
245 A31 3p/2½c lt blue & choc .60 .20
246 A31 1sh/10c multi .75 .45
247 A31 1sh6p/15c multi 4.00 .90
248 A31 2sh/20c multi 6.50 *7.50*
248A A31 2sh6p/25c multi 32.50 *45.00*
*Nos. 245-248A (5)* 44.35 *54.05*

These locally printed stamps were issued to acquaint Rhodesians with the decimal currency to be introduced in 1969-1970.

Issued: 3p, 3/15; 1sh, 11/1/67; 1sh6p, 2sh, 3/11/68; 2sh6p, 12/9/68.

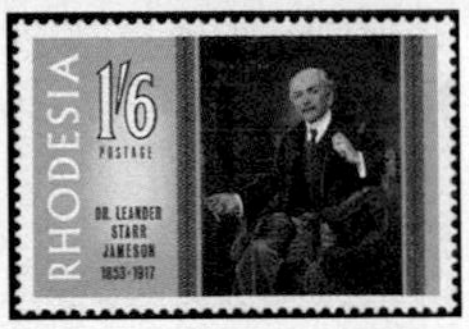

Leander Starr Jameson, by Frank Moss Bennett A34

**1967, May 17**
249 A34 1sh6p emerald & multi .40 .40

Dr. Leander Starr Jameson (1853-1917), pioneer with Cecil Rhodes and Prime Minister of Cape Colony. See No. 262.

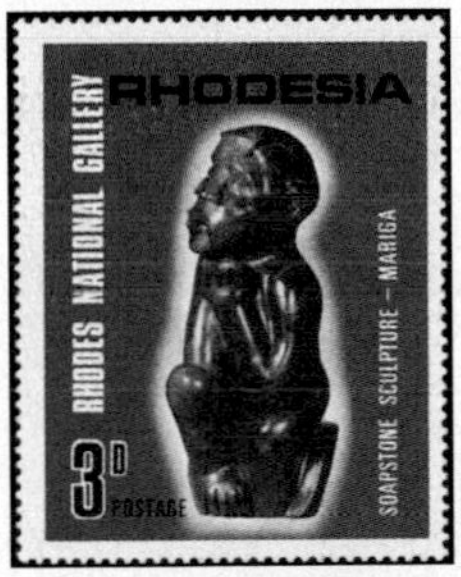

Soapstone Sculpture, by Joram Mariga A35

9p, Head of Burgher of Calais, by Auguste Rodin. 1sh3p, "Totem," by Roberto Crippa. 2sh6p, St. John the Baptist, by Michele Tosini.

**1967, July 12** **Litho.** *Perf. 14*
250 A35 3p brn, blk & ol grn .20 .20
251 A35 9p brt bl, blk & ol grn .20 .20
*a.* Perf. 13½ 11.00 17.50
252 A35 1sh3p multicolored .20 .20
253 A35 2sh6p multicolored .50 .45
*Nos. 250-253 (4)* 1.10 1.05

10th anniv. of the Rhodes Natl. Gallery, Salisbury.

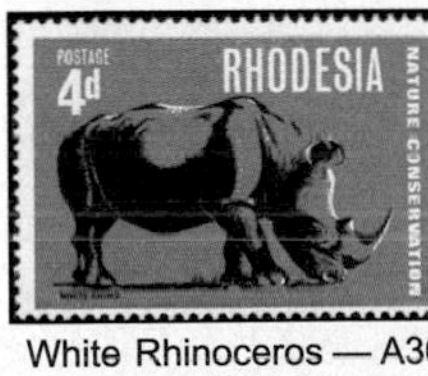

White Rhinoceros — A36

#255, Parrot's beak gladioli, vert. #256, Baobab tree. #257, Elephants.

**1967, Sept. 6** **Unwmk.** *Perf. 14½*
254 A36 4p olive & black .20 .20
255 A36 4p dp orange & blk .20 .20
256 A36 4p brown & blk .20 .20
257 A36 4p gray & blk .20 .20
*Nos. 254-257 (4)* .80 .80

Issued to publicize nature conservation.

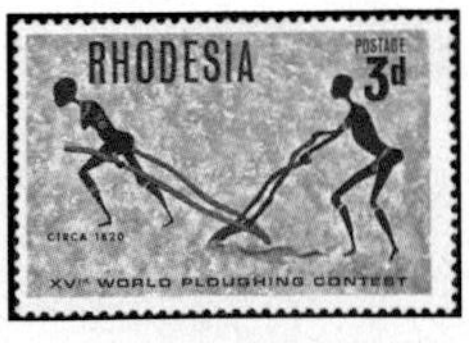

Wooden Hand Plow, c. 1820 A37

Designs: 9p, Ox-drawn plow, c. 1860. 1sh6p, Steam tractor and plows, c. 1905. 2sh6p, Tractor and moldboard plow, 1968.

**1968, Apr. 26** **Litho.** *Perf. 14½*
258 A37 3p multicolored .20 .20
259 A37 9p multicolored .20 .20
260 A37 1sh6p multicolored .25 .30
261 A37 2sh6p multicolored .35 .40
*Nos. 258-261 (4)* 1.00 1.10

15th world plowing contest, Kent Estate, Norton.

Portrait Type of 1967

Design: 1sh6p, Alfred Beit (portrait at left).

**1968, July 15** **Unwmk.** *Perf. 14½*
262 A34 1sh6p orange, blk & red .45 .45

Alfred Beit (1853-1906), philanthropist and friend of Cecil Rhodes.

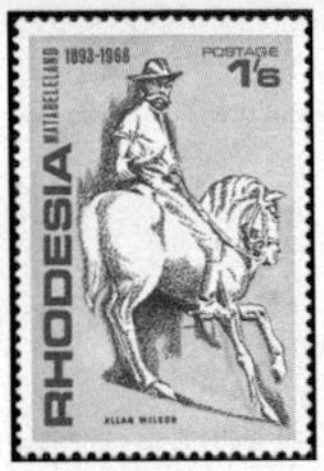

Allan Wilson, Matopos Hills — A38

Matabeleland, 75th Anniversary: 3p, Flag raising, Bulawayo, 1893. 9p, Bulawayo arms, view of Bulawayo.

**1968, Nov. 4** **Litho.** *Perf. 14½*
263 A38 3p multicolored .20 .20
264 A38 9p multicolored .25 .25
265 A38 1sh6p multicolored .35 .35
*Nos. 263-265 (3)* .80 .80

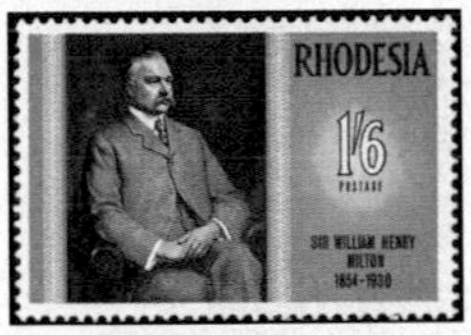

William Henry Milton (1854-1930), Adminstrator — A39

**1969, Jan. 15**
266 A39 1sh6p multicolored .50 .50

See Nos. 298-303.

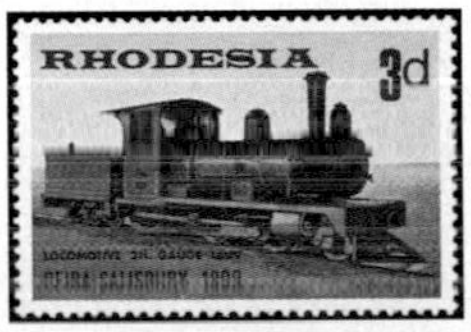

Locomotive, 1890's — A40

Beira-Salisbury Railroad, 70th Anniversary: 9p, Steam locomotive, 1901. 1sh6p, Garratt articulated locomotive, 1950. 2sh6p, Diesel, 1955.

**1969, May 22**
267 A40 3p multicolored 1.00 .20
268 A40 9p multicolored 1.75 .55
269 A40 1sh6p multicolored 5.00 3.00
270 A40 2sh6p multicolored 6.25 6.25
*Nos. 267-270 (4)* 14.00 10.00

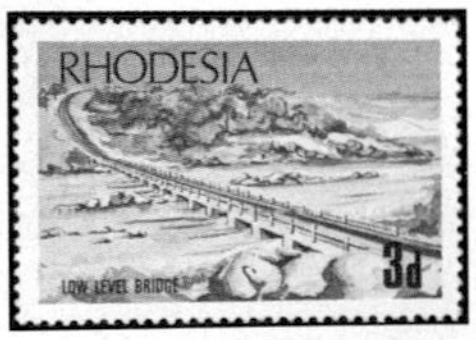

Low Level Bridge A41

Bridges: 9p, Mpudzi River. 1sh6p, Umniati River. 2sh6p, Birchenough over Sabi River.

**1969, Sept. 18**
271 A41 3p multicolored .25 .20
272 A41 9p multicolored .90 .50
273 A41 1sh6p multicolored 3.25 2.25
274 A41 2sh6p multicolored 4.25 2.75
*Nos. 272-274 (3)* 8.40 5.50

Blast Furnace — A42

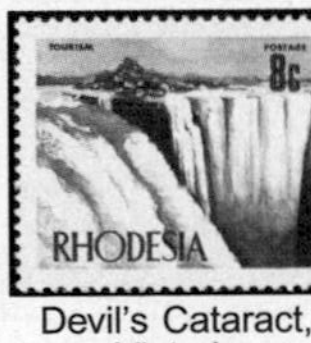

Devil's Cataract, Victoria Falls — A43

1c, Wheat harvest. 2½c, Ruins, Zimbabwe. 3c, Trailer truck. 3½c, 4c, Cecil Rhodes statue. 5c, Mining. 6c, Hydrofoil, "Seaflight." 7½c, like 8c. 10c, Yachting, Lake McIlwaine. 12½c, Hippopotamus. 14c, 15c, Kariba Dam. 20c, Irrigation canal. 25c, Bateleur eagles. 50c, Radar antenna and Viscount plane. $1, "Air Rescue." $2, Rhodesian flag.

**1970-73** **Litho.** *Perf. 14½*
**Size: 22x18mm**

275 A42 1c multicolored .20 .20
*a.* Booklet pane of 4 .25
*b.* Min. sheet of 4, Rhophil 2.50
276 A42 2c multicolored .20 .20
277 A42 2½c multicolored .20 .20
*a.* Booklet pane of 4 .20
*b.* Min. sheet of 4, Rhophil 2.50
278 A42 3c multi ('73) .75 .20
*a.* Booklet pane of 4 3.75
279 A42 3½c multicolored .20 .20
*a.* Booklet pane of 4 .70
*b.* Min. sheet of 4, Rhophil 2.50
280 A42 4c multi ('73) .85 .20
*a.* Booklet pane of 4 4.00
281 A42 5c multicolored .20 .20

**Size: 27x23mm**

282 A43 6c multi ('73) 2.75 1.40
283 A43 7½c multi ('73) 5.25 1.00
284 A43 8c multicolored 1.25 .80
285 A43 10c multicolored .40 .20
286 A43 12½c multicolored .75 .20
287 A43 14c multi ('73) 8.50 1.50
288 A43 15c multi 2.00 .20
289 A43 20c multicolored 1.50 .20

**Size: 30x25mm**

290 A43 25c multicolored 2.00 .40
291 A43 50c multicolored 2.00 .45
292 A43 $1 multicolored 6.25 5.00
293 A43 $2 multicolored 17.50 18.00
*Nos. 275-293 (19)* 52.75 30.75

Booklet panes and miniature sheets were made by altering the plates used to print the stamps, eliminating every third horizontal and vertical row of stamps. The perforations extend through the margins in four different versions. In 1972 sheets of 4 overprinted in the margins were issued for Rhophil '72 Philatelic Exhibition.

Issue dates: Feb. 17, 1970, Jan. 1, 1973.

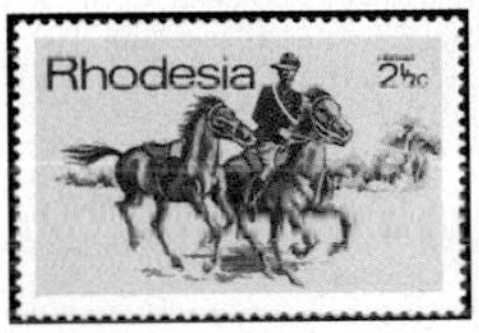

Despatch Rider, c. 1890 A44

Posts and Telecommunications Corporation, Inauguration: 3½c, Loading mail, Salisbury Airport. 15c, Telegraph line construction, c.1890. 25c, Telephone and telecommunications equipment.

**1970, July 1**
294 A44 2½c multicolored .25 .20
295 A44 3½c multicolored .60 .55
296 A44 15c multicolored 1.40 1.75
297 A44 25c multicolored 2.25 3.00
*Nos. 294-297 (4)* 4.50 5.50

Famous Rhodesians Type of 1969

13c Dr. Robert Moffat (1795-1883), missionary. #299, Dr. David Livingstone (1813-73), explorer. #300, George Pauling (1854-1919), engineer. #301, Thomas Baines (1820-75), self-portrait. #302, Mother Patrick (1863-1900), Dominican nurse and teacher. #303, Frederick Courteney Selous (1851-1917), explorer, big game hunter.

**1970-75** **Litho.** *Perf. 14½*
298 A39 13c multi ('72) 1.25 1.25
299 A39 14c multi ('73) 1.00 1.00
300 A39 14c multi ('74) 1.25 1.25
301 A39 14c multi ('75) 1.25 1.25
302 A39 15c multi .85 .85
303 A39 15c multi ('71) .70 .70
*Nos. 298-303 (6)* 6.30 6.30

Issued: 2/14/72; 4/2/73; 5/15/74; 2/12/75; 11/16/70; 3/1/71.

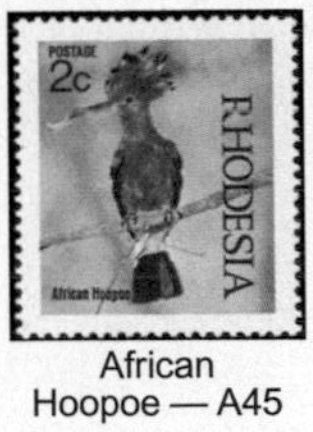

African Hoopoe — A45

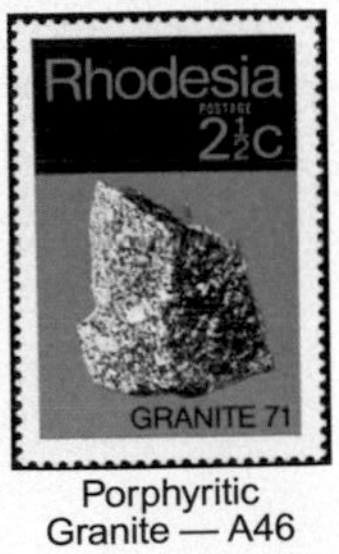

Porphyritic Granite — A46

Birds: 2½c, Half-collared kingfisher, horiz. 5c, Golden-breasted bunting. 7½c, Carmine bee-eater. 8c, Red-eyed bulbul. 25c, Wattled plover, horiz.

**1971, June 1**

| | | | | | |
|---|---|---|---|---|---|
| **304** | A45 | 2c | multicolored | 1.00 | .20 |
| **305** | A45 | 2½c | multicolored | 1.00 | .20 |
| **306** | A45 | 5c | multicolored | 2.50 | .85 |
| **307** | A45 | 7½c | multicolored | 3.25 | 1.00 |
| **308** | A45 | 8c | multicolored | 3.25 | 1.25 |
| **309** | A45 | 25c | multicolored | 7.00 | 3.50 |
| | | | *Nos. 304-309 (6)* | 18.00 | 7.00 |

**1971, Aug. 30**

Granite '71, Geological Symposium, 8/30-9/19: 7½c, Muscovite mica, seen through microscope. 15c, Granite, seen through microscope. 25c, Geological map of Rhodesia.

| | | | | | |
|---|---|---|---|---|---|
| **310** | A46 | 2½c | multicolored | .50 | .50 |
| **311** | A46 | 7½c | multicolored | 1.75 | 1.75 |
| **312** | A46 | 15c | multicolored | 3.25 | 3.25 |
| **313** | A46 | 25c | multicolored | 4.00 | 4.00 |
| | | | *Nos. 310-313 (4)* | 9.50 | 9.50 |

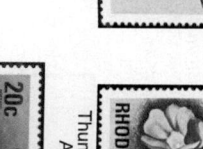

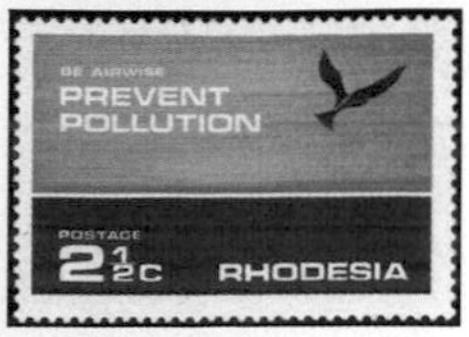
PREVENT POLLUTION
POSTAGE
2½c RHODESIA
"Be Airwise" A47

Prevent Pollution: 3½c, Antelope (Be Country-wise). 7c, Fish (Be Waterwise). 13c, City (Be Citywise).

**1972, July 17**

| | | | | | |
|---|---|---|---|---|---|
| **314** | A47 | 2½c | multicolored | .20 | .20 |
| **315** | A47 | 3½c | multicolored | .20 | .20 |
| **316** | A47 | 7c | multicolored | .30 | .30 |
| **317** | A47 | 13c | multicolored | .40 | .40 |
| | | | *Nos. 314-317 (4)* | 1.10 | 1.10 |

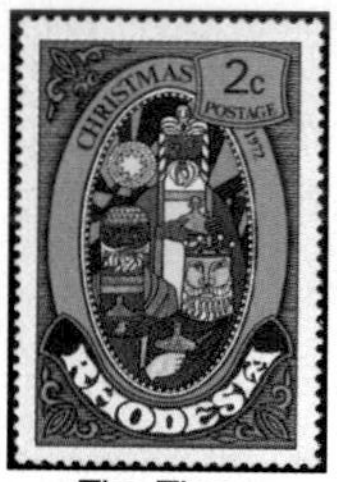
CHRISTMAS
2c
RHODESIA
The Three Kings — A48

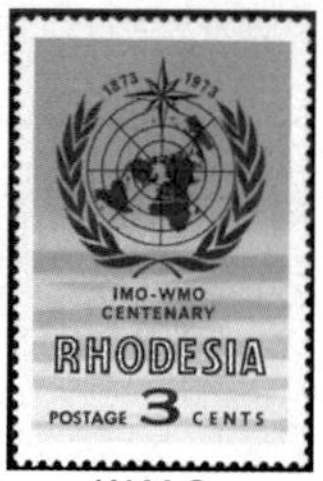
IMO-WMO CENTENARY
RHODESIA
POSTAGE 3 CENTS
W.M.O. Emblem — A49

**1972, Oct. 18**

| | | | | | |
|---|---|---|---|---|---|
| **318** | A48 | 2c | multicolored | .20 | .20 |
| **319** | A48 | 5c | multicolored | .20 | .20 |
| **320** | A48 | 13c | multicolored | .35 | .35 |
| | | | *Nos. 318-320 (3)* | .75 | .75 |

Christmas.

**1973, July 2**

| | | | | | |
|---|---|---|---|---|---|
| **321** | A49 | 3c | multicolored | .20 | .20 |
| **322** | A49 | 14c | multicolored | .60 | .45 |
| **323** | A49 | 25c | multicolored | .95 | *1.60* |
| | | | *Nos. 321-323 (3)* | 1.75 | 2.25 |

Intl. Meteorological Cooperation, cent.

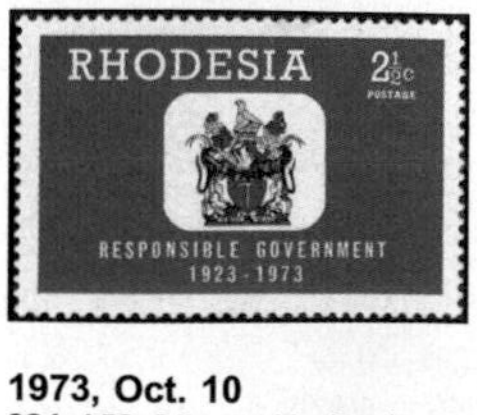
RHODESIA 2½c
RESPONSIBLE GOVERNMENT
1923-1973
Arms of Rhodesia A50

**1973, Oct. 10**

| | | | | | |
|---|---|---|---|---|---|
| **324** | A50 | 2½c | multicolored | .20 | .20 |
| **325** | A50 | 4c | multicolored | .20 | .20 |
| **326** | A50 | 7½c | multicolored | .50 | .50 |
| **327** | A50 | 14c | multicolored | .90 | *1.25* |
| | | | *Nos. 324-327 (4)* | 1.80 | 2.15 |

Responsible Government, 50th Anniversary.

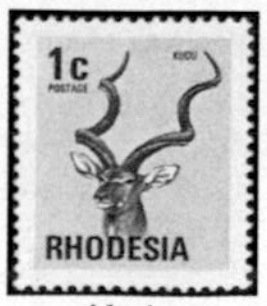
1c
RHODESIA
Kudu A51

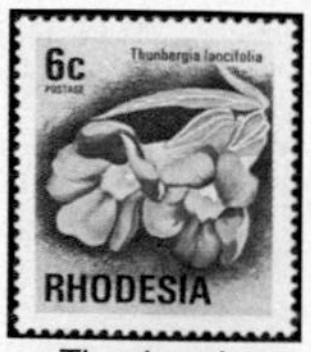
6c
RHODESIA
Thunbergia A52

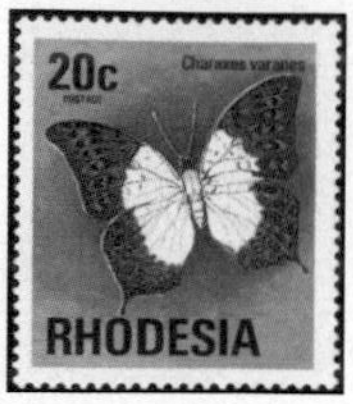
20c
RHODESIA
Pearl Charaxes — A53

**1974-76** **Litho.** ***Perf. 14½***

| | | | | | |
|---|---|---|---|---|---|
| **328** | A51 | 1c | shown | .20 | .20 |
| **329** | A51 | 2½c | Eland | .50 | .20 |
| **330** | A51 | 3c | Roan antelope | .20 | .20 |
| **331** | A51 | 4c | Reedbuck | .20 | .20 |
| **332** | A51 | 5c | Bushbuck | .20 | .20 |
| **333** | A52 | 6c | shown | .30 | .20 |
| **334** | A52 | 7½c | Flame lily | 3.25 | 1.75 |
| **335** | A52 | 8c | like 7½c ('76) | .25 | .20 |
| **336** | A52 | 10c | Devil thorn | .25 | .20 |
| **337** | A52 | 12c | Hibiscus ('76) | .40 | .20 |
| **338** | A52 | 12½c | Pink sabi star | 3.25 | 1.75 |
| **339** | A52 | 14c | Wild pimpernel | 4.75 | 2.50 |
| **340** | A52 | 15c | like 12½c ('76) | .50 | .25 |
| **341** | A52 | 16c | like 14c ('76) | .50 | .25 |
| **342** | A53 | 20c | shown | .50 | .25 |
| **343** | A53 | 24c | Yellow pansy ('76) | .95 | .50 |
| **344** | A53 | 25c | like 24c | 4.75 | 2.50 |
| **345** | A53 | 50c | Queen purple tip | 1.25 | .65 |
| **346** | A53 | $1 | Striped swordtail | 2.60 | 1.25 |
| **347** | A53 | $2 | Guinea fowl butterfly | 4.75 | 2.50 |
| | | | *Nos. 328-347 (20)* | 29.45 | 15.95 |

Issue dates: Aug. 14, 1974, July 1, 1976.
For surcharges see Nos. 364-366.

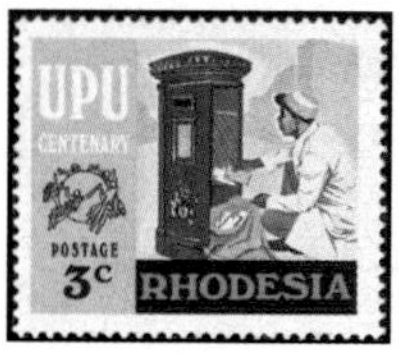
UPU CENTENARY
POSTAGE 3c RHODESIA
Mail Collection and UPU Emblem A54

**1974, Nov. 20** ***Perf. 14½***

| | | | | | |
|---|---|---|---|---|---|
| **348** | A54 | 3c | shown | .25 | .20 |
| **349** | A54 | 4c | Mail sorting | .25 | .20 |
| **350** | A54 | 7½c | Mail delivery | .50 | .45 |
| **351** | A54 | 14c | Parcel post | .75 | 1.40 |
| | | | *Nos. 348-351 (4)* | 1.75 | 2.25 |

Universal Postal Union Centenary.

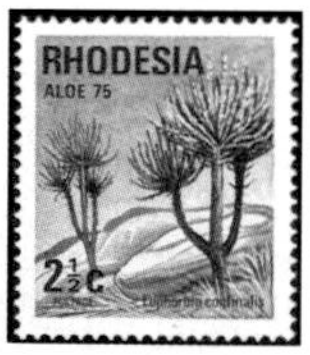
RHODESIA
ALOE 75
2½c
Euphorbia Confinalis — A55

**1975, July 16**

| | | | | | |
|---|---|---|---|---|---|
| **352** | A55 | 2½c | shown | .30 | .30 |
| **353** | A55 | 3c | Aloe excelsa | .30 | .30 |
| **354** | A55 | 4c | Hoodia lugardii | .30 | .30 |
| **355** | A55 | 7½c | Aloe ortholopha | .40 | .40 |
| **356** | A55 | 14c | Aloe musapana | .70 | .70 |
| **357** | A55 | 25c | Aloe saponaria | 1.25 | 1.25 |
| | | | *Nos. 352-357 (6)* | 3.25 | 3.25 |

Intl. Succulent Cong., Salisbury, July 1975.

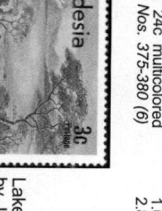

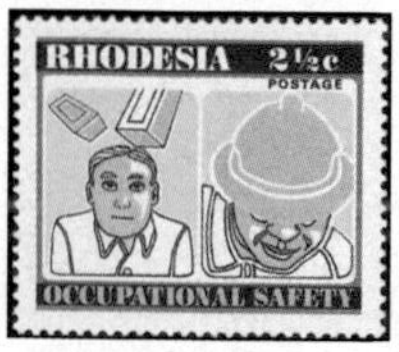
RHODESIA 2½c
POSTAGE
OCCUPATIONAL SAFETY
Head Injury and Safety Helmet — A56

Occupational Safety: 4c, Bandaged hand and safety glove. 7½c, Injured eye and safety eyeglass. 14c, Blind man and protective shield.

**1975, Oct. 15**

| | | | | | |
|---|---|---|---|---|---|
| **358** | A56 | 2½c | multicolored | .20 | .20 |
| **359** | A56 | 4c | multicolored | .20 | .20 |
| **360** | A56 | 7½c | multicolored | .30 | .30 |
| **361** | A56 | 14c | multicolored | .35 | .35 |
| | | | *Nos. 358-361 (4)* | 1.05 | 1.05 |

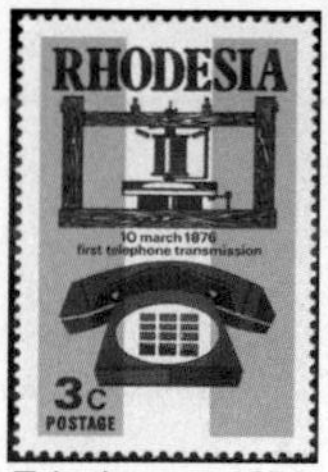
RHODESIA
3c
POSTAGE
Telephones, 1876 and 1976 — A57

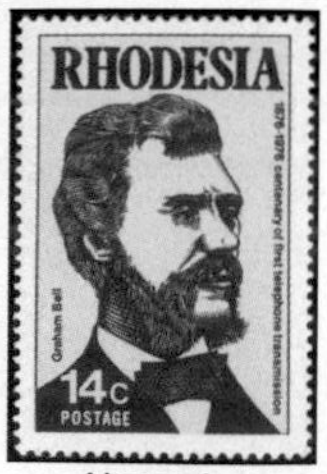
RHODESIA
14c
POSTAGE
Alexander Graham Bell — A58

**1976, Mar. 10**

| | | | | | |
|---|---|---|---|---|---|
| **362** | A57 | 3c | light blue & blk | .20 | .20 |
| **363** | A58 | 14c | buff & black | .20 | .20 |

Centenary of first telephone call, by Alexander Graham Bell, Mar. 10, 1876.

Nos. 334, 339 and 344 Surcharged with New Value and Two Bars

**1976, July 1**

| | | | | | |
|---|---|---|---|---|---|
| **364** | A52 | 8c | on 7½c multi | .20 | .20 |
| **365** | A52 | 16c | on 14c multi | .20 | .20 |
| **366** | A53 | 24c | on 25c multi | .35 | .35 |
| | | | *Nos. 364-366 (3)* | .75 | .75 |

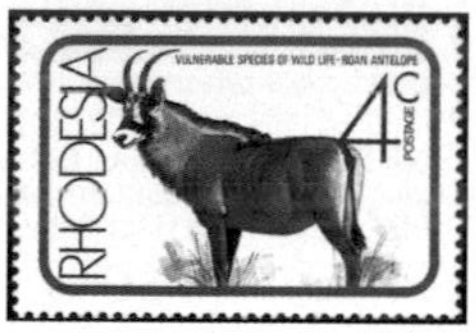
RHODESIA
4c
Wildlife Protection A59

**1976, July 21**

| | | | | | |
|---|---|---|---|---|---|
| **367** | A59 | 4c | Roan Antelope | .20 | .20 |
| **368** | A59 | 6c | Brown hyena | .20 | .20 |
| **369** | A59 | 8c | Wild dog | .30 | .30 |
| **370** | A59 | 16c | Cheetah | .40 | .40 |
| | | | *Nos. 367-370 (4)* | 1.10 | 1.10 |

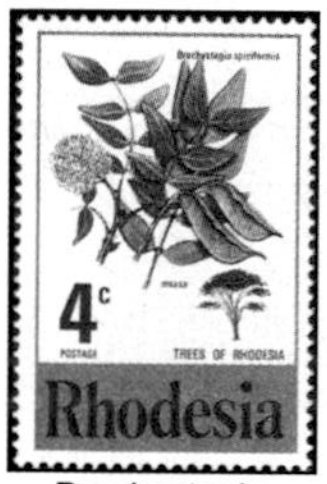
4c
Rhodesia
Brachystegia Spiciformis — A60

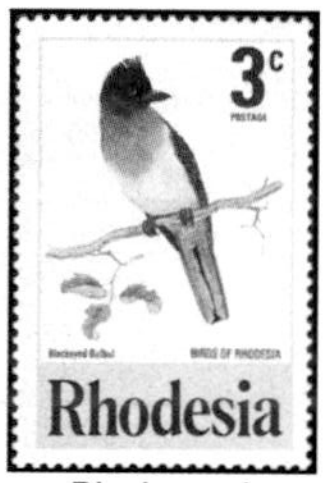
3c
Rhodesia
Black-eyed Bulbul — A61

**1976, Nov. 17**

| | | | | | |
|---|---|---|---|---|---|
| **371** | A60 | 4c | shown | .20 | .20 |
| **372** | A60 | 6c | Red mahogany | .20 | .20 |
| **373** | A60 | 8c | Pterocarpus angolensis | .20 | .20 |
| **374** | A60 | 16c | Rhodesian teak | .25 | .25 |
| | | | *Nos. 371-374 (4)* | .85 | .85 |

Flowering trees.

**1977, Mar. 16**

Birds: 4c, Yellow-mantled whydah. 6c, Orange-throated longclaw. 8c, Long-tailed shrike. 16c, Lesser blue-eared starling. 24c, Red-billed wood hoopoe.

| | | | | | |
|---|---|---|---|---|---|
| **375** | A61 | 3c | multicolored | .20 | .20 |
| **376** | A61 | 4c | multicolored | .20 | .20 |
| **377** | A61 | 6c | multicolored | .35 | .30 |
| **378** | A61 | 8c | multicolored | .45 | .35 |
| **379** | A61 | 16c | multicolored | .60 | .50 |
| **380** | A61 | 24c | multicolored | 1.00 | .70 |
| | | | *Nos. 375-380 (6)* | 2.80 | 2.25 |

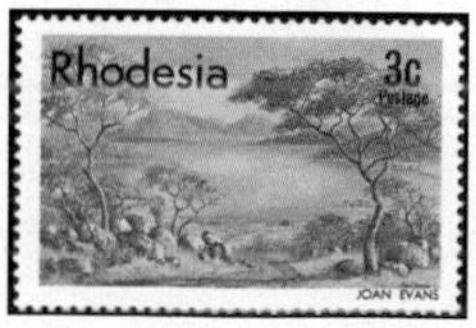
Rhodesia
3c
Lake Kyle, by Joan Evans A62

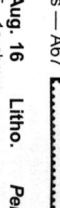

Landscape Paintings: 4c, Chimanimani Mountains, by Evans. 6c, Rocks near Bonsor Reef, by Alice Balfour. 8c, Dwala (rock) near Devil's Pass, by Balfour. 16c, Zimbabwe, by Balfour. 24c, Victoria Falls, by Thomas Baines.

**1977, July 20** **Litho.** ***Perf. 14½***

| | | | | | |
|---|---|---|---|---|---|
| **381** | A62 | 3c | multicolored | .20 | .20 |
| **382** | A62 | 4c | multicolored | .20 | .20 |
| **383** | A62 | 6c | multicolored | .20 | .20 |
| **384** | A62 | 8c | multicolored | .25 | .20 |
| **385** | A62 | 16c | multicolored | .35 | .25 |
| **386** | A62 | 24c | multicolored | .55 | .35 |
| | | | *Nos. 381-386 (6)* | 1.75 | 1.40 |

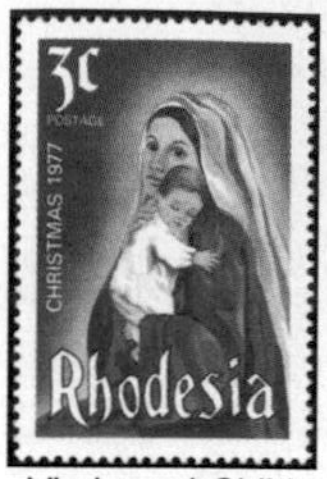
3c
CHRISTMAS 1977
Rhodesia
Virgin and Child A63

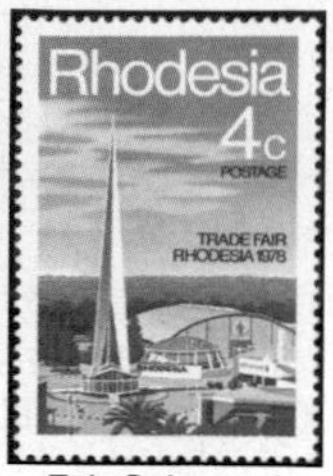
Rhodesia
4c
Fair Spire and Fairgrounds A64

**1977, Nov. 16**

| | | | | | |
|---|---|---|---|---|---|
| **387** | A63 | 3c | multicolored | .20 | .20 |
| **388** | A63 | 6c | multicolored | .20 | .20 |
| **389** | A63 | 8c | multicolored | .20 | .20 |
| **390** | A63 | 16c | multicolored | .40 | .40 |
| | | | *Nos. 387-390 (4)* | 1.00 | 1.00 |

Christmas.

**1978, Mar. 15**

19th Rhodesian Trade Fair, Bulawayo: 8c, Fair spire.

| | | | | | |
|---|---|---|---|---|---|
| **391** | A64 | 4c | multicolored | .20 | .20 |
| **392** | A64 | 8c | multicolored | .25 | .25 |

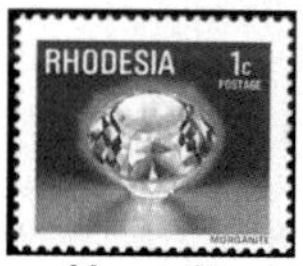
RHODESIA 1c
Morganite A65

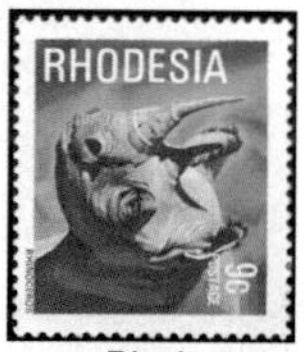
RHODESIA
Black Rhinoceros A66

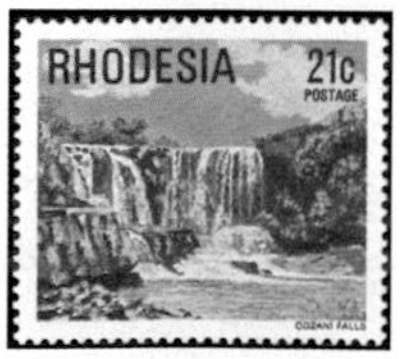
RHODESIA 21c
Odzani Falls — A67

**1978, Aug. 16** **Litho.** ***Perf. 14½***

| | | | | | |
|---|---|---|---|---|---|
| **393** | A65 | 1c | shown | .20 | .20 |
| **394** | A65 | 3c | Amethyst | .20 | .20 |
| **395** | A65 | 4c | Garnet | .20 | .20 |
| **396** | A65 | 5c | Citrine | .20 | .20 |
| **397** | A65 | 7c | Blue topaz | .20 | .20 |
| **398** | A66 | 9c | shown | .20 | .20 |
| **399** | A66 | 11c | Lion | .20 | .20 |
| **400** | A66 | 13c | Warthog | .20 | .20 |
| **401** | A66 | 15c | Giraffe | .20 | .20 |
| **402** | A66 | 17c | Zebra | .20 | .20 |
| **403** | A67 | 21c | shown | .25 | .20 |
| **404** | A67 | 25c | Goba Falls | .25 | .25 |
| **405** | A67 | 30c | Inyangombe Falls | .35 | .20 |
| **406** | A67 | $1 | Bridal Veil Falls | .55 | .75 |
| **407** | A67 | $2 | Victoria Falls | .90 | 1.00 |
| | | | *Nos. 393-407 (15)* | 4.30 | 4.40 |

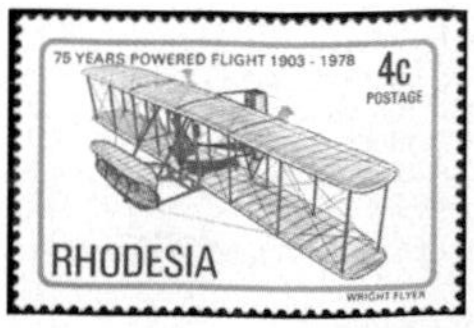
75 YEARS POWERED FLIGHT 1903 - 1978
4c
RHODESIA
Wright's Flyer A A68

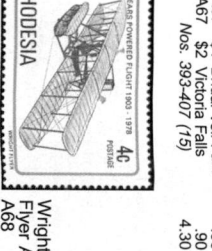

**1978, Oct. 18**

| | | | | | |
|---|---|---|---|---|---|
| **408** | A68 | 4c | shown | .20 | .20 |
| **409** | A68 | 5c | Bleriot XI | .20 | .20 |
| **410** | A68 | 7c | Vickers Vimy | .20 | .20 |
| **411** | A68 | 9c | A.W. 15 Atalanta | .20 | .20 |

**412** A68 17c Vickers Viking 1B .30 .25
**413** A68 25c Boeing 720 .45 .35
*Nos. 408-413 (6)* 1.55 1.40

75th anniversary of powered flight.

---

## POSTAGE DUE STAMPS

Type of Rhodesia and Nyasaland, 1961, Inscribed "RHODESIA"

***Hyphen Hole Perf. 5***

**1965, June 17 Typo. Unwmk.**
**J5** D1 1p vermilion .80 *13.50*
*a.* Rouletted 9½ 2.50 *13.50*

***Rouletted 9½***

**J6** D1 2p dark blue .60 *9.75*
**J7** D1 4p emerald .65 *9.75*
**J8** D1 6p purple .70 *7.00*
*Nos. J5-J8 (4)* 2.75 *40.00*

Soapstone Zimbabwe Bird — D2

**1966, Dec. 15 Litho. *Perf. 14½***
**J9** D2 1p crimson 1.60 *3.25*
**J10** D2 2p violet blue 2.25 *2.75*
**J11** D2 4p emerald 2.25 *4.75*
**J12** D2 6p lilac 2.25 *2.40*
**J13** D2 1sh dull red brown 2.25 *2.40*
**J14** D2 2sh black 2.75 *5.50*
*Nos. J9-J14 (6)* 13.35 *21.05*

**1970-73 Litho. *Perf. 14½***
**Size: 26x22½mm**
**J15** D2 1c bright green .95 *1.60*
**J16** D2 2c ultramarine .90 .80
**J17** D2 5c red violet 2.25 *3.00*
**J18** D2 6c lemon 3.75 *4.75*
**J19** D2 10c rose red 2.25 *4.00*
*Nos. J15-J19 (5)* 10.10 *14.15*

Issued: 6c, 5/7/73; others, 2/1/70.

---

# RIO DE ORO

ˌre-o de ˈör-ˌō

LOCATION — On the northwest coast of Africa, bordering on the Atlantic Ocean
GOVT. — Spanish Colony
AREA — 71,600 sq. mi.
POP. — 24,000
CAPITAL — Villa Cisneros

Rio de Oro became part of Spanish Sahara.

100 Centimos = 1 Peseta

King Alfonso XIII
A1 A2

Control Numbers on Back in Blue

**1905 Unwmk. Typo. *Perf. 14***
**1** A1 1c blue green 3.50 2.75
**2** A1 2c claret 4.25 2.75
**3** A1 3c bronze green 4.25 2.75
**4** A1 4c dark brown 4.25 2.75
**5** A1 5c orange red 4.25 2.75
**6** A1 10c dk gray brown 4.25 2.75
**7** A1 15c red brown 4.25 2.75
**8** A1 25c dark blue 75.00 30.00
**9** A1 50c dark green 37.50 12.00
**10** A1 75c dark violet 37.50 17.50
**11** A1 1p orange brown 26.00 7.25
**12** A1 2p buff 75.00 47.50
**13** A1 3p dull violet 55.00 16.00
**14** A1 4p blue green 55.00 16.00
**15** A1 5p dull blue 85.00 35.00
**16** A1 10p pale red 225.00 110.00
*Nos. 1-16 (16)* 700.00 310.50
Set, never hinged 1,000.

For surcharges see Nos. 17, 34-36, 60-66.

No. 8 Handstamp Surcharged in Rose

a

**1907**
**17** A1 15c on 25c dk blue 175.00 60.00
Never hinged 275.00

The surcharge exists inverted, double and in violet, normally positioned. Value for each, $450.

Control Numbers on Back in Blue

**1907 Typo.**
**18** A2 1c claret 2.25 2.00
**19** A2 2c black 2.75 2.00
**20** A2 3c dark brown 2.75 2.00
**21** A2 4c red 2.75 2.00
**22** A2 5c black brown 2.75 2.00
**23** A2 10c chocolate 2.75 2.00
**24** A2 15c dark blue 2.75 2.00
**25** A2 25c deep green 7.00 2.00
**26** A2 50c black violet 7.00 2.00
**27** A2 75c orange brown 7.00 2.00
**28** A2 1p orange 12.50 2.00
**29** A2 2p dull violet 4.00 2.00
**30** A2 3p blue green 4.00 2.00
*a.* Cliche of 4p in plate of 3p 300.00 200.00
**31** A2 4p dark blue 6.00 3.50
**32** A2 5p red 6.00 3.75
**33** A2 10p deep green 6.00 9.00
*Nos. 18-33 (16)* 78.25 42.25
Set, never hinged 140.00

For surcharges see Nos. 38-43, 67-70.

Nos. 9-10 Handstamp Surcharged in Red

**1907**
**34** A1 10c on 50c dk green 80.00 24.00
Never hinged 140.00
*a.* "10" omitted 140.00 75.00
Never hinged 190.00
**35** A1 10c on 75c dk violet 57.50 24.00
Never hinged 95.00

No. 12 Handstamp Surcharged in Violet

**1908**
**36** A1 2c on 2p buff 52.50 24.00
Never hinged 77.50

No. 36 is found with "1908" measuring 11mm and 12mm.

Same Surcharge in Red on No. 26
**38** A2 10c on 50c blk vio 22.50 3.75
Never hinged 35.00

A 5c on 10c (No. 23) was not officially issued.

Nos. 25, 27-28 Handstamp Surcharged Type "a" in Red, Violet or Green

**1908**
**39** A2 15c on 25c dp grn (R) 30.00 3.75
**40** A2 15c on 75c org brn (V) 45.00 17.50
*a.* Green surcharge 50.00 6.75
Never hinged 70.00
**41** A2 15c on 1p org (V) 40.00 15.00
**42** A2 15c on 1p org (R) 37.50 15.00
**43** A2 15c on 1p org (G) 26.00 6.75
*Nos. 39-43 (5)* 178.50 58.00
Set, never hinged 300.00

As this surcharge is handstamped, it exists in several varieties: double, inverted, in pairs with one surcharge omitted, etc.

A3

**Revenue stamps overprinted and surcharged**

**1908 *Imperf.***
**44** A3 5c on 50c green (C) 75.00 25.00
Never hinged 120.00
**45** A3 5c on 50c green (V) 110.00 42.50
Never hinged 175.00

The surcharge, which is handstamped, exists in many variations.

Nos. 44-45 are found with and without control numbers on back. Stamps with control numbers sell at about double the above values.

King Alfonso XIII — A4

Control Numbers on Back in Blue

**1909 Typo. *Perf. 14½***
**46** A4 1c red .70 .45
**47** A4 2c orange .70 .45
**48** A4 5c dark green .70 .45
**49** A4 10c orange red .70 .45
**50** A4 15c blue green .70 .45
**51** A4 20c dark violet 1.75 .65
**52** A4 25c deep blue 1.75 .65
**53** A4 30c claret 1.75 .65
**54** A4 40c chocolate 1.75 .65
**55** A4 50c red violet 3.25 .65
**56** A4 1p dark brown 4.50 3.00
**57** A4 4p carmine rose 5.50 4.25
**58** A4 10p claret 12.00 7.00
*Nos. 46-58 (13)* 35.75 19.75
Set, never hinged 60.00

Stamps of 1905 Handstamped in Black

**1910**
**10**
**Céntimos**

**1910**
**60** A1 10c on 5p dull bl 12.50 6.25
*a.* Red surcharge 67.50 40.00
Never hinged 110.00
**62** A1 10c on 10p pale red 12.50 6.25
*a.* Violet surcharge 110.00 47.50
Never hinged 100.00
*b.* Green surcharge 110.00 47.50
Never hinged 160.00
**65** A1 15c on 3p dull vio 12.50 6.25
*a.* Imperf. 82.50
Never hinged 140.00
**66** A1 15c on 4p blue grn 12.50 6.25
*a.* 10c on 4p bl grn 700.00 210.00
Never hinged 1,000.
*Nos. 60-66 (4)* 50.00 25.00
Set, never hinged 70.00

See note after No. 43.

Nos. 31 and 33 Surcharged in Red or Violet

**1911-13**
**67** A2 2c on 4p dk blue (R) 9.00 6.50
**68** A2 5c on 10p dp grn (V) 27.50 6.50

Nos. 29-30 Surcharged in Black

**10**
**Céntimos**

**69** A2 10c on 2p dull vio 15.00 6.50
**69A** A2 10c on 3p bl grn ('13) 175.00 40.00

**Nos. 30, 32 Handstamped Type "a"**
**69B** A2 15c on 3p bl grn ('13) 160.00 19.00
**70** A2 15c on 5p red 11.00 7.25
*Nos. 67-70 (6)* 397.50 85.75
Set, never hinged 525.00

King Alfonso XIII
A5 A6

Control Numbers on Back in Blue

**1912 Typo. *Perf. 13½***
**71** A5 1c carmine rose .30 .25
**72** A5 2c lilac .30 .25
**73** A5 5c deep green .30 .25
**74** A5 10c red .30 .25
**75** A5 15c brown orange .30 .25
**76** A5 20c brown .30 .25
**77** A5 25c dull blue .30 .25
**78** A5 30c dark violet .30 .25
**79** A5 40c blue green .30 .25
**80** A5 50c lake .30 .25
**81** A5 1p red 3.00 .65
**82** A5 4p claret 6.00 3.00
**83** A5 10p dark brown 8.50 4.75
*Nos. 71-83 (13)* 20.50 10.90
Set, never hinged 30.00

For overprints see Nos. 97-109.

Control Numbers on Back in Blue

**1914 *Perf. 13***
**84** A6 1c olive black .30 .25
**85** A6 2c maroon .30 .25
**86** A6 5c deep green .30 .25
**87** A6 10c orange red .30 .25
**88** A6 15c orange red .30 .25
**89** A6 20c deep claret .30 .25
**90** A6 25c dark blue .30 .25
**91** A6 30c blue green .30 .25
**92** A6 40c brown orange .30 .25
**93** A6 50c dark brown .30 .25
**94** A6 1p dull lilac 2.50 1.90
**95** A6 4p carmine rose 6.00 5.25
**96** A6 10p dull violet 8.00 5.25
*Nos. 84-96 (13)* 19.50 14.90
Set, never hinged 30.00

Nos. 71-83 Overprinted in Black

**1917 *Perf. 13½***
**97** A5 1c carmine rose 8.25 1.10
**98** A5 2c lilac 8.25 1.10
**99** A5 5c deep green 2.40 1.10
**100** A5 10c red 2.40 1.10
**101** A5 15c orange brn 2.40 1.10
**102** A5 20c brown 2.40 1.10
**103** A5 25c dull blue 2.40 1.10
**104** A5 30c dark violet 2.40 1.10
**105** A5 40c blue green 2.40 1.10
**106** A5 50c lake 2.40 1.10
**107** A5 1p red 11.50 3.75
**108** A5 4p claret 20.00 5.25
**109** A5 10p dark brown 32.50 7.75
*Nos. 97-109 (13)* 99.70 27.75
Set, never hinged 150.00

Nos. 97-109 exist with overprint inverted or double (value 50 percent over normal) and in dark blue (value twice normal).

King Alfonso XIII — A7

Control Numbers on Back in Blue

**1919 Typo. *Perf. 13***
**114** A7 1c brown .75 .40
**115** A7 2c claret .75 .40
**116** A7 5c light green .75 .40
**117** A7 10c carmine .75 .40
**118** A7 15c orange .75 .40
**119** A7 20c orange .75 .40
**120** A7 25c blue .75 .45
**121** A7 30c green .75 .45
**122** A7 40c vermilion .75 .45
**123** A7 50c brown .75 .45
**124** A7 1p lilac 6.00 3.00
**125** A7 4p rose 10.50 5.25
**126** A7 10p violet 18.00 7.50
*Nos. 114-126 (13)* 42.00 19.95
Set, never hinged 62.50

A8

A9

## Control Numbers on Back in Blue

**1920**    **Perf. 13**

| | | | | |
|---|---|---|---|---|
| 127 | A8 | 1c gray lilac | .70 | .40 |
| 128 | A8 | 2c rose | .70 | .40 |
| 129 | A8 | 5c light red | .70 | .40 |
| 130 | A8 | 5c lilac | .70 | .40 |
| 131 | A8 | 15c light brown | .70 | .40 |
| 132 | A8 | 20c greenish blue | .70 | .40 |
| 133 | A8 | 25c yellow | .70 | .45 |
| 134 | A8 | 30c dull rose | .70 | .45 |
| 135 | A8 | 40c orange | 4.25 | 3.50 |
| 136 | A8 | 50c dull blue | 2.50 | 1.50 |
| 137 | A8 | gray green | 2.50 | 1.50 |
| 138 | A8 | 4p lilac rose | 11.00 | 7.50 |
| 139 | A8 | 10p brown | 60.00 | |

Nos. 127-139 (13)

**1922**

### Control Numbers on Back in Blue

| | | | | |
|---|---|---|---|---|
| 140 | A9 | 1c yellow | .70 | .55 |
| 141 | A9 | 2c red brown | .70 | .55 |
| 142 | A9 | 5c blue green | .70 | .55 |
| 143 | A9 | 10c pale red | .70 | .55 |
| 144 | A9 | 15c myrtle green | .70 | .55 |
| 145 | A9 | 20c turq blue | .70 | .60 |
| 146 | A9 | 25c deep blue | 1.50 | .70 |
| 147 | A9 | 30c deep rose | 1.50 | 1.10 |
| 148 | A9 | 40c violet | 1.50 | 1.10 |
| 149 | A9 | 50c orange | 1.50 | 1.10 |
| 150 | A9 | 1p lilac | 4.00 | 1.50 |
| 151 | A9 | 4p claret | 6.50 | 3.50 |
| 152 | A9 | 10p dark brown | 9.50 | 7.50 |

Nos. 140-152 (13)    29.40   21.60

Set, never hinged    32.15   19.85    65.00

For subsequent issues see Spanish Sahara.

---

# RIO MUNI

rē-ō 'mü-nē

LOCATION — West Africa, bordering on Cameroun and Gabon Republics
GOVT. — Province of Spain
AREA — 9,500 sq. mi.
POP. — 183,377 (1960)
CAPITAL — Bata

100 Centimos = 1 Peseta

Rio Muni and the island of Fernando Po are the two provinces that constitute Spanish Guinea. Separate stamp issues for the two provinces were decreed in 1960.

Spanish Guinea Nos. 1-84 were used only in the territory now called Rio Muni. Rio Muni united with Fernando Po on Oct. 12, 1968, to form the Republic of Equatorial Guinea.

**Catalogue values for all unused stamps in this country are for Never Hinged items.**

Boy Reading and Missionary
A1

**1960**   **Unwmk.**   **Photo.**   **Perf. 13x12½**

| | | | | |
|---|---|---|---|---|
| 1 | A1 | 25c dull vio bl | .20 | .20 |
| 2 | A1 | 50c olive grn bl | .20 | .20 |
| 3 | A1 | 75c dull grysh pur | .20 | .20 |
| 4 | A1 | 1p orange ver | .20 | .20 |
| 5 | A1 | 1.50p brt blue grn | .20 | .20 |
| 6 | A1 | 2p red lilac | .25 | .20 |
| 7 | A1 | 3p sapphire | .25 | .20 |

Quina Plant
A2

**1960**

| | | | | |
|---|---|---|---|---|
| 8 | A1 | 5p red brown | 1.10 | .60 |
| 9 | A1 | 10p lt olive grn | 3.15 | 1.25 |

Nos. 1-9 (9)    1.85

See Nos. B1-B2.

**1960**

| | | | | |
|---|---|---|---|---|
| 10 | A2 | 35c shown | .20 | .20 |
| 11 | A2 | 80c Croton plant | .20 | .20 |

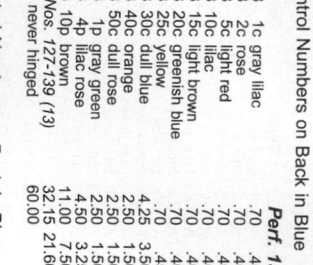
Map of Rio Muni — A3

**1961, Oct. 1**   **Perf. 12½x13**

| | | | | |
|---|---|---|---|---|
| 12 | A3 | 25c gray violet | .20 | .20 |
| 13 | A3 | 50c olive brown | .20 | .20 |
| 14 | A3 | 70c brt green | .20 | .20 |
| 15 | A3 | 1p red orange | .80 | .80 |

Nos. 12-15 (4)

Designs: 50c, 1p, Gen. Franco. 70c, Government Palace.

25th anniversary of the nomination of Gen. Francisco Franco as Chief of State.

Rio Muni Headdress — A4

**1962, July 10**   **Perf. 13**

| | | | | |
|---|---|---|---|---|
| 16 | A4 | 25c violet | .20 | .20 |
| 17 | A4 | 50c green | .20 | .20 |
| 18 | A4 | 1p brown | .60 | .60 |

Nos. 16-18 (3)

Issued for child welfare.

Cape Buffalo
A5

Design: 35c, Gorilla, vert.

**1962, Nov. 23**   **Perf. 13x12½, 12½x13**   **Photo.**   **Unwmk.**

| | | | | |
|---|---|---|---|---|
| 19 | A5 | 15c dark olive grn | .20 | .20 |
| 20 | A5 | 35c magenta | .20 | .20 |
| 21 | A5 | 1p brown orange | .60 | .60 |

Nos. 19-21 (3)

Mother and Child — A6

**1963, Jan. 29**

| | | | | |
|---|---|---|---|---|
| 22 | A6 | 50c green | .20 | .20 |
| 23 | A6 | 1p brown orange | .20 | .20 |

Issued to help the victims of the Seville flood.

Father Joaquin Juanola — A7

**1963, July 6**   **Perf. 13x12½**

| | | | | |
|---|---|---|---|---|
| 24 | A7 | 25c dull violet | .20 | .20 |
| 25 | A7 | 50c brown olive | .20 | .20 |
| 26 | A7 | 1p orange red | .60 | .60 |

Nos. 24-26 (3)

50c, Blessing hand, cross and palms.

Issued for child welfare.

Design: 50c, Rio Muni idol.

Praying Child and Arms — A8

**1963, July 12**   **Perf. 13x12½, 12½x13**   **Photo.**

| | | | | |
|---|---|---|---|---|
| 27 | A8 | 50c dull green | .20 | .20 |
| 28 | A8 | 1p redish brown | .20 | .20 |

Issued for Barcelona flood relief.

Branch of Copal Tree — A9

**1964, Mar. 6**   **Perf. 13x12½, 12½x13**   **Photo.**

| | | | | |
|---|---|---|---|---|
| 29 | A9 | 25c brt violet | .20 | .20 |
| 30 | A9 | 50c blue green | .20 | .20 |
| 31 | A9 | 1p dk carmine rose | .60 | .60 |

Nos. 29-31 (3)

Design: 50c, Flowering quina, horiz.

Issued for Stamp Day 1963.

Tree Pangolin A10

**1964, June 1**   **Perf. 13x12½**

| | | | | |
|---|---|---|---|---|
| 32 | A10 | 25c violet blk | .20 | .20 |
| 33 | A10 | 50c olive gray | .20 | .20 |
| 34 | A10 | 1p fawn | .60 | .60 |

Nos. 32-34 (3)

Design: 50c, Chameleon.

Issued for child welfare.

Dwarf Crocodile A11

**1964, July 1**

| | | | | |
|---|---|---|---|---|
| 35 | A11 | 15c lt brown | .20 | .20 |
| 36 | A11 | 15c violet | .20 | .20 |
| 37 | A11 | 25c violet | .20 | .20 |
| 38 | A11 | 50c olive | .20 | .20 |
| 39 | A11 | 70c green | .20 | .20 |
| 40 | A11 | 1p brown car | .55 | .55 |
| 41 | A11 | 1.50p blue green | .20 | .20 |
| 42 | A11 | 5p dark blue | 3.25 | .40 |
| 43 | A11 | 10p brown | 6.50 | .80 |

Nos. 35-43 (9)    13.00   2.60

15c, 70c, 3p, Dwarf crocodile. 25c, 1p, 5p, Leopard. 50c, 1.50p, 10p, Black rhinoceros.

Greshoff's Tree Frog A12

**1964, Nov. 23**   **Perf. 13x12½, 12½x13**   **Photo.**   **Unwmk.**

| | | | | |
|---|---|---|---|---|
| 44 | A12 | 50c green | .20 | .20 |
| 45 | A12 | 1p deep claret | .20 | .20 |
| 46 | A12 | 1.50p blue green | .60 | .60 |

Nos. 44-46 (3)

Stamp Day: 1p, Helmet guinea fowl, vert.

Issued for Stamp Day, 1964.

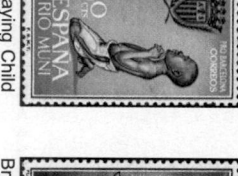
Woman's Head — A13

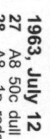
Woman Chemist — A14

**1964**   **Photo.**   **Perf. 13x12½**

| | | | | |
|---|---|---|---|---|
| 47 | A13 | 50c shown | .20 | .20 |
| 48 | A14 | 1p shown | .20 | .20 |
| 49 | A14 | 1.50p Logger | .60 | .60 |

Nos. 47-49 (3)

Issued to commemorate 25 years of peace.

Goliath Beetle A15

**1965, June 1**   **Photo.**   **Perf. 12½x13**

| | | | | |
|---|---|---|---|---|
| 50 | A15 | 50c shown | .20 | .20 |
| 51 | A15 | 1p sepia | .20 | .20 |
| 52 | A15 | 1.50p black | .60 | .60 |

Nos. 50-52 (3)

Beetle: 1p, Acridoxena hewaniana.

Issued for child welfare.

Ring-necked Pheasant — A16

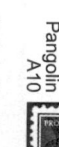
Leopard and Arms of Rio Muni A17

**1965, Nov. 23**   **Perf. 13x12½, 12½x13**   **Photo.**

| | | | | |
|---|---|---|---|---|
| 53 | A16 | 50c grnsh gray | .20 | .20 |
| 54 | A17 | 1p sepia | .25 | .20 |
| 55 | A16 | 2.50p brt Prus blue | 1.10 | .80 |

Nos. 53-55 (3)    1.55   .80

Issued for Stamp Day, 1965.

Elephant and Parrot A18

**1966, June 1**   **Perf. 12½x13**   **Photo.**   **Unwmk.**

| | | | | |
|---|---|---|---|---|
| 56 | A18 | 50c olive | .20 | .20 |
| 57 | A18 | 1p dk purple | .20 | .20 |
| 58 | A18 | 1.50p brt Prus blue | .60 | .60 |

Nos. 56-58 (3)

Design: 1.50p, Lion and boy.

Issued for child welfare.

Water Chevrotain A19

Designs: 40c, 4p, Tree pangolin, vert.

# SCHAUFIX MOUNTS

Made from archival quality materials, Schaufix mounts feature a rubberized base film and a crystal clear covering film for optimum protection and flexibility.

## PRE-CUT SIZES

| Item | WxH MM | | Mounts | Retail | *AA |
|---|---|---|---|---|---|
| HM701B | 40 x 25 | U.S. Standard Water-Activated Horizontal Commemoratives | 20 | 99¢ | 75¢ |
| HM702B | 25 x 40 | U.S. Standard Water-Activated Vertical Commemoratives | 20 | 99¢ | 75¢ |
| HM703B | 22 x 25 | U.S. Standard Water-Activated Horizontal Definitives | 20 | 99¢ | 75¢ |
| HM704B | 25 x 22 | U.S. Standard Water-Activated Vertical Definitives | 20 | 99¢ | 75¢ |
| HM705B | 41 x 31 | U.S. Horizontal Semi-Jumbo Commemoratives | 20 | 99¢ | 75¢ |
| HM706B | 40 x 26 | U.S. Standard SELF-ADHESIVE Horizontal Commemoratives | 20 | 99¢ | 75¢ |
| HM707B | 25 x 41 | U.S. Standard SELF-ADHESIVE Vertical Commemoratives | 20 | 99¢ | 75¢ |
| HM708B | 22 x 26 | U.S. Standard SELF-ADHESIVE Vertical Definitives | 20 | 99¢ | 75¢ |

## STRIPS 210 MM LONG

| Item | WxH MM | | Mounts | Retail | *AA |
|---|---|---|---|---|---|
| HM721B | 24 | U.S., Canada, Great Britain; | 5 | $1.49 | 99¢ |
| HM722B | 25 | U.S. Water-Activated Horizontal Commemorative & Definitives | 5 | $1.49 | 99¢ |
| HM723B | 26 | U.S. Standard SELF-ADHESIVE Horizontal Commemoratives & Definitives, Germany | 5 | $1.49 | 99¢ |
| HM724B | 27 | U.S. Famous Americans | 5 | $1.49 | 99¢ |
| HM725B | 28 | U.S. 19th Century, Liechtenstein | 5 | $1.49 | 99¢ |
| HM726B | 29 | Various Foreign Stamps | 5 | $1.49 | 99¢ |
| HM727B | 30 | U.S. Hunting Permit (Ducks), Canada | 5 | $1.49 | 99¢ |
| HM728B | 30 | U.S. Horizontal Jumbo & Semi-Jumbo | 5 | $1.49 | 99¢ |
| HM729B | 33 | U.S. Stampin' the Future | 5 | $1.49 | 99¢ |
| HM730B | 36 | U.S. Hunting Permit (Ducks), Canada | 5 | $1.49 | 99¢ |
| HM731B | 39 | U.S. Early 20th Century | 5 | $1.49 | 99¢ |
| HM732B | 40 | U.S. Standard Water-Activated Vertical Commemoratives | 5 | $1.49 | 99¢ |
| HM733B | 41 | U.S. Semi-Jumbo Vertical Commemoratives (Lafayette, Pottery, etc.) Self-Adhesive Vertical Commemoratives | 5 | $1.49 | 99¢ |
| HM734B | 44 | U.S. Vertical Coil Pairs, Booklet Panes (Garden Flowers); | 5 | $1.49 | 99¢ |
| HM735B | 63 | U.S. Jumbo Commemoratives, Horizontal Blocks of 4 | 5 | $1.49 | 99¢ |

---

**1966, Nov. 23   Photo.   Perf. 13**

| 59 | A19 | 10c brown & yel brn | .20 | .20 |
|---|---|---|---|---|
| 60 | A19 | 40c brown & yellow | .20 | .20 |
| 61 | A19 | 1.50p blue & rose lilac | .80 | .80 |
| 62 | A19 | 4p dk bl & emerald | .80 | .80 |

*Nos. 59-62 (4)*

Issued for Stamp Day, 1966.

Potto — A21

**1967, June 1   Photo.   Perf. 13**

| 63 | A20 | 10c green & yellow | .20 | .20 |
|---|---|---|---|---|
| 64 | A20 | 40c blk, rose car & grn | .20 | .20 |
| 65 | A20 | 1.50p blue & orange | .80 | .80 |
| 66 | A20 | 4p black & green | .80 | .80 |

*Nos. 63-66 (4)*

Issued for child welfare.

**1967, Nov. 23   Photo.   Perf. 13**

Designs: 1p, River hog, horiz. 3.50p, African golden cat, horiz.

| 67 | A21 | 1p black & red brn | .20 | .20 |
|---|---|---|---|---|
| 68 | A21 | 1.50p brown & grn | .20 | .20 |
| 69 | A21 | 3.50p org brn & grn | .25 | .20 |

*Nos. 67-69 (3)*

Issued for Stamp Day 1967.

## Zodiac Issue

Cancer — A22

1.50p, Taurus. 2.50p, Gemini.

**1968, Apr. 25   Photo.   Perf. 13**

| 70 | A22 | 1p brt mag, lt yel | .20 | .20 |
|---|---|---|---|---|
| 71 | A22 | 1.50p brown, pink | .20 | .20 |
| 72 | A22 | 2.50p dk vio, yel | .60 | .60 |

*Nos. 70-72 (3)*

Issued for child welfare.

## SEMI-POSTAL STAMPS

Type of Regular Issue, 1960

Designs: 10c+5c, Croton plant. 15c+5c, Flower and leaves of croton.

**1960 Unwmk.   Photo.   Perf. 13x12½**

| B1 | A22 | 10c + 5c maroon | .20 | .20 |
|---|---|---|---|---|
| B2 | A22 | 15c + 5c bister brown | .20 | .20 |

The surtax was for child welfare.

---

Mandrill SP2

Design: 25c+10c, Elephant, vert.

**Perf. 12½x13, 13x12½   Unwmk.**

**1961, June 21**

| B7 | SP2 | 10c + 5c rose brown | .20 | .20 |
|---|---|---|---|---|
| B8 | SP2 | 25c + 10c gray violet | .20 | .20 |
| B9 | SP2 | 80c + 20c dark green | .60 | .60 |

*Nos. B7-B9 (3)*

The surtax was for child welfare.

Statuette — SP3

Design: 25c+10c, 1p+10c, Male figure.

**Perf. 13x12½**

**1961, Nov. 23**

| B10 | SP3 | 10c + 5c rose brown | .20 | .20 |
|---|---|---|---|---|
| B11 | SP3 | 25c + 10c dark purple | .20 | .20 |
| B12 | SP3 | 30c + 10c olive black | .20 | .20 |
| B13 | SP3 | 1p + 10c red orange | .80 | .80 |

*Nos. B10-B13 (4)*

Issued for Stamp Day 1961.

---

**1961   Perf. 13x12½**

| B3 | SP1 | 10c + 5c rose brown | .20 | .20 |
|---|---|---|---|---|
| B4 | SP1 | 20c + 5c yellow | .20 | .20 |
| B5 | SP1 | 30c + 10c olive brown | .20 | .20 |
| B6 | SP1 | 50c + 20c brown | .80 | .80 |

*Nos. B3-B6 (4)*

Issued for Stamp Day, 1960.

Bishop Juan de Ribera — SP1

20c+5c, The clown Pablo de Valladolid by Velazquez. 30c+10c, Juan de Ribera statue.

# ROMANIA
### rō-mā-nēa
(Rumania, Roumania)

**LOCATION** — Southeastern Europe, bordering on the Black Sea
**GOVT.** — Republic
**AREA** — 91,699 sq. mi.
**POP.** — 22,600,000 (est. 1984)
**CAPITAL** — Bucharest

Romania was formed in 1861 from the union of the principalities of Moldavia and Walachia in 1859. It became a kingdom in 1881. Following World War I, the original territory was considerably enlarged by the addition of Bessarabia, Bukovina, Transylvania, Crisana, Maramures and Banat. The republic was established in 1948.

100 Bani = 1 Leu (plural "Lei")

40 Parale = 1 Piaster (1868)

**Catalogue values** for unused stamps in this country are for **Never Hinged** items, beginning with Scott 475 in the regular postage section, Scott C24 in the semi-postal section, Scott B82 in the semi-postal section, Scott CB1 in the airpost semi-postal section, Scott J82 in the postage due section, Scott O1 in the official section, Scott RA16 in the postal tax section, and Scott RAJ1 in the postal tax postage due section.

Wmk. 167 — Coat of Arms Covering 25 Stamps
Reduced illustration.

No. 163 is not a true watermark, having been impressed after the paper was manufactured.

Wmk. 95 — Wavy Lines

Wmk. 164 — PR

Watermarks

Wmk. 163 — Coat of Arms

Wmk. 165 — PR Interlaced

---

Wmk. 398 — Fr Multiple

Wmk. 358 — RPR Multiple in Endless Rows

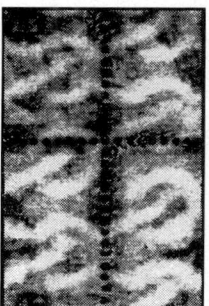

Wmk. 289 — RPR Multiple

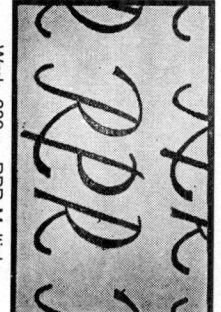

Wmk. 276 — Cross and Crown Multiple

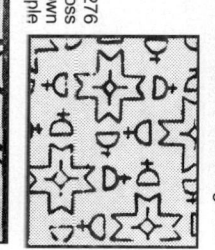

Wmk. 230 — Crowns and Monograms

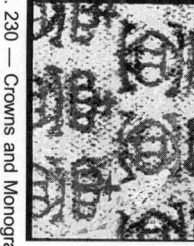

Wmk. 225 — Crown over PTT, Multiple

Wmk. 200 — PR

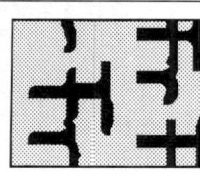

**Moldavia**

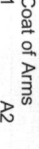
Coat of Arms
A1

Coat of Arms
A2

Values for unused stamps are for examples with original gum as defined in the catalogue introduction except for Nos. 1-4 which are valued without gum.

---

# ROMANIA

## Coat of Arms — A3

### Handstamped
**1858, July. Unwmk. Imperf.**

**Laid Paper**

| | | | | |
|---|---|---|---|---|
| 1 | A1 | 27pa blk, rose | 19,000 | — |
| 2 | a. | Tête bêche pair | 19,000 | — |
| 3 | A1 | 54pa blue, grn | 4,250 | 5,500. |
| | a. | A1 54pa blue | 4,250 | 2,250. |
| | A1 | 108pa blue, rose | 14,000 | 5,250. |

**Wove Paper**

| | | | | |
|---|---|---|---|---|
| 4 | A1 | 81pa blue, bl | 21,000. | 22,500. |

Cut to shape or octagonally, Nos. 1-4 sell for one-fourth of these prices.

**1858**

### Bluish Wove Paper

| | | | | |
|---|---|---|---|---|
| 5 | A2 | 5pa black | 12,000. | 4,750. |
| | a. | Tête bêche pair | | |
| | b. | Frame broken at bottom | | |
| 6 | A2 | 40pa blue | 175. | 125. |
| | a. | As "b," tête bêche pair | 750. | 2,000. |
| 7 | A2 | 80pa red | 6,750. | 400. |
| | a. | Tête bêche pair | | |

**1859**

### White Wove Paper

| | | | | |
|---|---|---|---|---|
| 8 | A2 | 5pa black | 9,000. | 5,000. |
| | a. | Tête bêche pair | | |
| | b. | Frame broken at bottom | 100. | |
| 9 | A2 | 40pa blue | 325. | 110. |
| | a. | A2 40pa blue | 375. | 100. |
| 10 | A2 | 80pa red | 300. | 150. |
| | b. | Tête bêche pair | 1,050. | 3,100. |

No. 8b has a break in the frame at bottom below "A." It was never placed in use.

### Moldavia-Walachia

## Printed by Hand from Single Dies
**1862**

### White Laid Paper

| | | | | |
|---|---|---|---|---|
| 11 | A3 | 3pa orange | 200.00 | 2,250. |
| | a. | A3 3pa yellow | 210.00 | 2,250. |
| 12 | A3 | 6pa carmine | 190.00 | 250.00 |
| 13 | A3 | 6pa red | 190.00 | 250.00 |
| 14 | A3 | 30pa blue | 55.00 | 75.00 |
| | | Nos. 11-14 (4) | 635.00 | |

### White Wove Paper

| | | | | |
|---|---|---|---|---|
| 15 | A3 | 3pa orange yel | 55.00 | 160.00 |
| | a. | 3pa lemon | 60.00 | 160.00 |
| 16 | A3 | 6pa carmine | 55.00 | 110.00 |
| 17 | A3 | 6pa vermilion | 35.00 | 90.00 |
| 18 | A3 | 30pa blue | 50.00 | 30.00 |
| | | Nos. 15-18 (4) | 195.00 | |

Nos. 11-18 were printed with a hand press, one at a time, from single dies. The impressions were very irregularly placed and occasionally overlapped. Sheets of 32 (4x8). The 3rd and 4th rows were printed inverted, making the second and third rows tête bêche. All values come in distinct shades, frequently even on the same sheet. The paper of No. 52 often shows a bluish, grayish or yellowish tint.

### Tête bêche pairs

| | | |
|---|---|---|
| 11b | 3pa orange | 1,000. |
| 12a | 3pa carmine | 1,000. |
| 14a | 3pa blue | 1,250. |
| 15a | 6pa blue | 1,000. |
| 15b | 3pa orange yellow | 140.00 |
| 16a | 6pa carmine | 150.00 |
| 17a | 6pa vermilion | 150.00 |
| 18a | 30pa blue | 140.00 |

**1864**

## Typographed from Plates
### White Wove Paper

| | | | | |
|---|---|---|---|---|
| 19 | A3 | 3pa yellow | 32.50 | 1,250. |
| | a. | Tête bêche pair | 200.00 | |
| | b. | Pair, one sideways | | |
| | c. | Bluish wove paper | | |
| 20 | A3 | 6pa deep rose | 4.50 | |
| | a. | Tête bêche pair | 27.50 | |
| | b. | Pair, one sideways | | |
| 21 | A3 | 30pa deep blue | 5.25 | 60.00 |
| | a. | Tête bêche pair | 32.50 | |
| | b. | Pair, one sideways | 12.00 | |
| | c. | Bluish wove paper | 125.00 | |
| | | Nos. 19-21 (3) | 42.25 | 1,310. |

Stamps of 1862 issue range from very clear to blurred impressions but rarely have broken or deformed characteristics. The 1864 issue, though rarely blurred, usually have various imperfections in the letters and numbers. These include breaks, malformations, occasional dots at left of the crown or above the "P" of "PAR," a dot on the middle stroke of the "F," and many other bulges, breaks and spots of color.

The 1864 issue were printed in sheets of 40 (5x8). The first and second rows were inverted. Cliches in the third row were placed sideways, 4 with head to right and 4 with head to left, making one tête bêche pair. The fourth and fifth rows were normally placed. No. 20 was never placed in use.

---

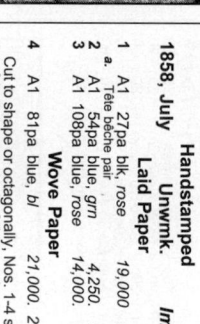

**Romania**

Prince Alexandru Ioan Cuza — A4

### 1865, Jan. Unwmk. Litho. Imperf.
**White Laid Paper**

| | | | | |
|---|---|---|---|---|
| 22 | A4 | 2pa orange | 30.00 | 125.00 |
| | a. | 2pa yellow | 42.50 | 150.00 |
| 23 | A4 | 2pa ocher | 90.00 | 175.00 |
| 24 | A4 | 5pa blue | 20.00 | 10.00 |
| | a. | 20pa rod, typo I | 7.50 | 7.60 |
| 25 | A4 | 20pa red, type II | 175.00 | 10.00 |
| | a. | Bluish paper, type I | 175.00 | |
| | | Nos. 22-25 (4) | 65.00 | |

The 20pa types are found se-tenant.

| | | | | |
|---|---|---|---|---|
| 26 | A4 | 2pa orange | 37.50 | 125.00 |
| 27 | A4 | 5pa blue | 60.00 | 275.00 |

TWENTY PARALES:
Type I — The central oval does not touch the inner frame. The "1" of "DECI" extends above and below the other letters.
Type II — The central oval touches the frame at the bottom. The "I" of "DECI" is the same height as the other letters.

Prince Carol — A5

Type II — A7

Type I — A6

TWENTY PARALES:
Type I — A6. The Greek border at the upper right goes from right to left.
Type II — A7. The Greek border at the upper right goes from left to right.

**1866-67**

### Thin Wove Paper

| | | | | |
|---|---|---|---|---|
| 29 | A5 | 2pa blk, yellow | 8.00 | 45.00 |
| | a. | Thick paper | 35.00 | 200.00 |
| 30 | A5 | 5pa blk, dk bl | 35.00 | 275.00 |
| | a. | Thick paper | 75.00 | |
| 31 | A6 | 20pa blk, indigo | 45.00 | 275.00 |
| | a. | Dot in Greek border, (I) | 45.00 | |
| | | paper | 9.00 | |
| | b. | Dot in Greek border, thin | 350.00 | |
| | | paper | 95.00 | 125.00 |
| | c. | Thick paper | | 45.00 |
| 32 | A7 | 20pa blk, rose, (II) | 125.00 | 72.50 |
| | a. | Thick paper | 9.00 | 9.00 |
| | | Nos. 29-32 (4) | 100.00 | 50.00 |
| | | | 61.00 | 338.00 |

The 20pa types are found se-tenant. Faked cancellations are known on No. 22-27, 29-32.
The white dot of Nos. 31a and 31c occurs in extreme upper right border. Thick paper was used in 1866, thin in 1867.

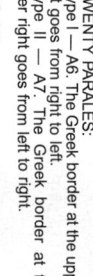

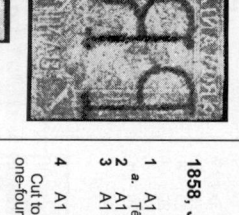

Three stamps in this design– 2pa, 5pa, 20pa– were printed on white wove paper in 1864, but never placed in use. Value, set $9.00.

All values exist in shades, light to dark. Counterfeit cancellations exist on #11-21.

## Prince Carol — A8, A9

**1868-70**

| No. | Type | Description | Unused | Used |
|---|---|---|---|---|
| 33 | A8 | 2b orange | 22.50 | 12.50 |
| a. | | 2b yellow | 30.00 | 27.50 |
| 34 | A8 | 3b violet ('70) | 22.50 | 20.00 |
| 35 | A8 | 4b dk blue | 45.00 | 25.00 |
| 36 | A8 | 18b scarlet | 175.00 | 9.00 |
| a. | | 18b rose | 265.00 | 66.50 |
| | | Nos. 33-36 (4) | | |

**1869**

| No. | Type | Description | Unused | Used |
|---|---|---|---|---|
| 37 | A9 | 5b orange yel | 52.50 | 20.00 |
| 38 | A9 | 5b deep orange | 55.00 | 50.00 |
| a. | | 10b blue | 25.00 | 12.50 |
| 39 | A9 | 10b blue | 55.00 | 17.50 |
| b. | | 10b ultramarine | 65.00 | 12.50 |
| 40 | A9 | 15b vermilion | 25.00 | 12.50 |
| 41 | A9 | 25b orange & blue | 25.00 | 17.50 |
| 42 | A9 | 50b blue & red | 140.00 | 20.00 |
| a. | | 50b indigo & red | 150.00 | 75.00 |
| | | Nos. 37-42 (5) | | |

No. 40 on vertically laid paper was not issued. Value $1,250.

## Prince Carol — A10, A11

**1871-72 — Imperf.**

| No. | Type | Description | Unused | Used |
|---|---|---|---|---|
| 43 | A10 | 5b rose | 32.50 | 11.00 |
| a. | | 5b vermilion | 35.00 | 12.50 |
| 44 | A10 | 10b orange yel | 47.50 | 17.50 |
| a. | | Vertically laid paper | 450.00 | 450.00 |
| 45 | A10 | 10b blue | 55.00 | 25.00 |
| 46 | A10 | 15b red | 125.00 | 65.00 |
| 47 | A10 | 25b olive brown | 30.00 | 21.00 |
| | | Nos. 43-47 (5) | 360.00 | 144.50 |

**1872**

| No. | Type | Description | Unused | Used |
|---|---|---|---|---|
| 48 | A10 | 10b ultra | 26.00 | |
| a. | | Vertically laid paper | 100.00 | |
| b. | | 10b greenish blue | 100.00 | |
| 49 | A10 | 50b blue & red | 150.00 | 165.00 |
| | | Nos. 50-52 (3) | | |

No. 48 is a provisional issue printed from a new plate in which the head is placed further right. Faked cancellations are found on No. 49.

No. 43a with faked perforation is frequently offered as No. 50a.

**1872 — Typo. — Perf. 14x13½**
**Paris Print, Fine Impression**
**Wove Paper**

| No. | Type | Description | Unused | Used |
|---|---|---|---|---|
| 50 | A11 | 5b rose | 40.00 | 20.00 |
| a. | | 5b vermilion | 1,000. | 500.00 |
| 51 | A11 | 10b blue | 47.50 | 50.00 |
| 52 | A11 | 10b ultramarine | 50.00 | 25.00 |
| a. | | 25b dark brown | 22.50 | 62.50 |
| | | | 110.00 | |

**1872 — Typo. — Tinted Paper**
**Perf. 12½**

| No. | Type | Description | Unused | Used |
|---|---|---|---|---|
| 53 | A11 | 1½b brnz grn, grn-ish | 7.50 | .75 |
| 54 | A11 | 3b green, bluish | 12.50 | 1.25 |
| 55 | A11 | 5b bis, pale buff | 9.00 | 1.00 |
| 57 | A11 | 15b red brn, pale buff | 8.50 | 1.10 |
| 58 | A11 | 25b org, pale buff | 75.00 | 7.50 |
| 59 | A11 | 50b rose, pale | 77.50 | 8.00 |
| | | Nos. 53-59 (7) | | |

Nos. 53-59 exist imperf.

**Bucharest Print, Rough Impression**
**1876-79 — Perf. 11, 11½, 13½, and Compound**

| No. | Type | Description | Unused | Used |
|---|---|---|---|---|
| 60 | A11 | 1½b brnz grn, grn-ish | 5.00 | .50 |
| a. | | 1½b brnz grn, yelsh | 13.00 | .55 |
| 61 | A11 | 5b bis, yelsh | | 75.00 |
| 62 | b. | 10b bl, yelsh ('77) | 14.00 | .75 |
| c. | | 10b dk bl, yelsh | 12.00 | 1.25 |
| d. | | Cliché of 5b in plate of 10b ('79) | | |
| 63 | A11 | 10b ultra, yelsh ('77) | 190.00 | |
| 64 | A11 | 15b red brn, yelsh | 25.00 | 1.25 |
| a. | | Printed on both sides | 27.50 | 100.00 |

| No. | Type | Description | Unused | Used |
|---|---|---|---|---|
| 65 | A11 | 30b org red, yelsh ('78) | 125.00 | 10.00 |
| | | Printed on both sides | 210.00 | |
| a. | | | 209.50 | 14.30 |

#60-65 are valued in the grade of fine. The originals are in dull blue. Value of reprint, $35.

#62d has been reprinted in dark blue. The originals are in dull blue. Value of reprint, $35.

**1879 — Perf. 11, 11½, 13½ and Compound**

| No. | Type | Description | Unused | Used |
|---|---|---|---|---|
| 66 | A11 | 1½b blk, yelsh | 2.50 | .35 |
| a. | | Imperf. | 7.00 | 12.00 |
| 67 | A11 | 3b ol grn, bluish | | 1.00 |
| | | Diagonal half used as 1½b on cover | | |
| 68 | A11 | 5b green, bluish | 2.50 | .35 |
| 69 | A11 | 10b rose, yelsh | 9.00 | .40 |
| b. | | Cliché of 5b in plate of 10b | 100.00 | 475.00 |
| 70 | A11 | 15b rose red, yelsh | | 5.00 |
| 71 | A11 | 25b blue, yelsh | 35.00 | 4.50 |
| 72 | A11 | 50b bister, yelsh | 186.00 | 6.50 |
| | | | | 18.10 |
| | | Nos. 66-72 (7) | | |

#66-72 are valued in the grade of fine. There are two varieties of the numerals on the 15b and 50b. No. 69b has been reprinted in dark rose. Originals are in pale rose. Value of reprint, $40.

## King Carol I — A12, A13

**1880 — White Paper**

| No. | Type | Description | Unused | Used |
|---|---|---|---|---|
| 73 | A12 | 15b brown | 7.50 | .40 |
| 74 | A12 | 25b blue | 14.00 | .60 |

Nos. 73-74 are valued in the grade of fine. No. 74 exists imperf.

**1885-89 — Perf. 13½, 11½ & Compound**

| No. | Type | Description | Unused | Used |
|---|---|---|---|---|
| 75 | A13 | 1½b black | 2.00 | .50 |
| | | Printed on both sides | | |
| 76 | A13 | 3b violet | 5.00 | .60 |
| | | Half used as 1½b on cover | | |
| 77 | A13 | 5b green | 52.50 | 6.00 |
| 78 | A13 | 15b red brown | 10.00 | .85 |
| 79 | A13 | 25b blue | 11.00 | 1.00 |
| | | Nos. 75-79 (5) | 80.50 | 8.95 |

**Tinted Paper**

| No. | Type | Description | Unused | Used |
|---|---|---|---|---|
| 80 | A13 | 1½b blk, yelsh | 3.50 | .65 |
| 81 | A13 | 3b vio, bluish | 3.50 | .75 |
| 82 | A13 | 5b grn, bluish | 4.25 | .60 |
| 83 | A13 | 5b grn, bluish | 4.25 | .60 |
| 84 | A13 | 15b red brn, bluish | 4.25 | .65 |
| 85 | A13 | 15b red brn, pale buff | | .75 |
| 86 | A13 | 25b bl, pale buff | 15.00 | 1.00 |
| 87 | A13 | 50b bis, pale buff | 55.00 | 6.00 |
| | | Nos. 80-87 (8) | 104.75 | 11.05 |

**1889 — Thin Pale Yellowish Paper — Wmk. 163**

| No. | Type | Description | Unused | Used |
|---|---|---|---|---|
| 88 | A13 | 1½b black | 22.50 | 3.00 |
| 89 | A13 | 3b violet | 17.50 | 3.00 |
| 90 | A13 | 5b green | 17.50 | 3.00 |
| 91 | A13 | 10b red brown | 50.00 | 3.25 |
| 92 | A13 | 15b red brown | 40.00 | 5.50 |
| 93 | A13 | 25b dark blue | 165.00 | 22.75 |
| | | Nos. 88-93 (6) | | |

## King Carol I — A14, A15

**1890 — Perf. 13½, 11½ & Compound**

| No. | Type | Description | Unused | Used |
|---|---|---|---|---|
| 94 | A14 | 1½b maroon | 4.25 | .80 |
| 95 | A14 | 3b violet | 22.50 | 1.10 |
| 96 | A14 | 5b emerald | 9.50 | 1.10 |
| 97 | A14 | 10b red | 15.00 | 3.50 |
| a. | | | 15.00 | 3.50 |
| 98 | A14 | 15b dk green | 13.00 | 1.60 |
| 99 | A14 | 25b gray blue | 65.00 | 13.50 |
| 100 | A14 | 50b orange | 142.75 | 22.10 |
| | | Nos. 94-100 (7) | | |

**1891 — Unwmk.**

| No. | Type | Description | Unused | Used |
|---|---|---|---|---|
| 101 | A14 | 1½b lilac rose | 1.40 | .30 |
| a. | | Printed on both sides | | 65.00 |
| 102 | A14 | 3b lilac | 1.10 | .50 |
| b. | | 3b violet | 2.00 | |
| c. | | Impressions of 5b on back | 100.00 | 75.00 |
| 103 | A14 | 5b emerald | 2.10 | .50 |
| 104 | A14 | 10b pale red | 7.75 | .60 |
| 105 | A14 | 15b gray brown | 9.50 | .40 |
| 106 | A14 | 15b gray blue | 5.50 | 6.00 |
| 107 | A14 | 50b orange | 57.50 | 8.90 |
| | | Nos. 101-107 (7) | 84.85 | |

Nos. 101-107 exist imperf.

**1891 — Wmk. 164**

| No. | Type | Description | Unused | Used |
|---|---|---|---|---|
| 108 | A15 | 1½b claret | 2.00 | 1.25 |
| 109 | A15 | 3b lilac | 2.00 | 1.25 |
| 110 | A15 | 5b red | 2.50 | 2.25 |
| 111 | A15 | 10b red | 2.75 | 2.25 |
| 112 | A15 | 15b gray brown | 2.25 | 2.00 |
| | | Nos. 108-112 (5) | 11.50 | 9.00 |

25th year of the reign of King Carol I.

**1894 — Wmk. 164**

| No. | Type | Description | Unused | Used |
|---|---|---|---|---|
| 113 | A14 | 3b lilac | 6.50 | 2.50 |
| 114 | A14 | 15b red brown | 6.50 | 2.50 |
| 115 | A14 | 25b gray blue | 10.00 | 4.50 |
| 116 | A14 | 50b orange | 20.00 | 10.00 |
| | | Nos. 113-116 (4) | 43.00 | 19.50 |

## King Carol I — A17, A18, A19, A20, A21, A23

**1893-98 — Wmk. 164 & 200**

| No. | Type | Description | Unused | Used |
|---|---|---|---|---|
| 117 | A17 | 1b pale brown | .80 | .20 |
| 118 | A17 | 1½b blue brown | .80 | .20 |
| 119 | A18 | 3b chocolate | .80 | .20 |
| 120 | A19 | 5b rose | 1.10 | .20 |
| a. | | Cliché of the 25b in the plate of 5b | | |
| 121 | A19 | 5b yel grn ('98) | 47.50 | 60.00 |
| 122 | A20 | 10b emerald | 3.25 | .35 |
| 123 | A20 | 10b rose ('98) | 4.00 | .35 |
| 124 | A21 | 15b black ('98) | 1.60 | .20 |
| 125 | A21 | 15b rose | 3.25 | .30 |
| 126 | A19 | 25b violet | 3.25 | .30 |
| 127 | A19 | 25b indigo ('98) | 2.50 | .45 |
| 128 | A19 | 40b gray grn | 5.75 | .50 |
| 129 | A19 | 50b orange | 13.50 | .25 |
| 130 | A23 | 1l bis & rose | 6.50 | .25 |
| 131 | A23 | 2l orange & brn | 13.50 | .35 |
| a. | | | 17.00 | |
| | | Nos. 117-131 (15) | 75.00 | 4.45 |

This watermark may be found in four versions (Wmks. 164, 200 and variations). The paper also varies in thickness.

A 3b rose, type A18; 10b brown, type A20; 15b rose, type A21, and 25b bright green with similar but different border, all watermarked "P R," were prepared but never issued. Value, each $15.

See Nos. 132-157, 224-229. For overprints and surcharges see Romanian Post Offices in the Turkish Empire Nos. 1-6, 10-11.

## King Carol I — A24

**1900-03 — Unwmk.**
**Perf. 11½, 13½ and Compound**
**Thin Paper, Tinted Rose on Back**

| No. | Type | Description | Unused | Used |
|---|---|---|---|---|
| 132 | A17 | 1b pale brown | .75 | .25 |
| 133 | A24 | 1b brown ('01) | .75 | .25 |
| 134 | A24 | 1b black ('03) | 1.00 | .20 |
| 135 | A18 | 3b red brown | | .20 |

| No. | Type | Description | Unused | Used |
|---|---|---|---|---|
| 136 | A19 | 5b emerald | 1.40 | .20 |
| 137 | A20 | 10b pale red | 1.75 | .20 |
| 138 | A21 | 15b black | 1.40 | .40 |
| 139 | A21 | 15b lil gray ('01) | 1.40 | .25 |
| 140 | A21 | 15b dk gray ('03) | | .70 |
| 141 | A19 | 25b blue | 2.50 | .30 |
| 142 | A19 | 40b gray grn | 5.00 | .40 |
| 143 | A19 | 50b orange | 9.50 | .65 |
| 144 | A23 | 1l bis & rose ('01) | 20.00 | .90 |
| 145 | A23 | 1l grn & blk ('03) | 14.00 | .90 |
| 146 | A23 | 2l org & brn ('01) | 14.00 | .90 |
| 147 | A23 | 2l red brn & blk | 1.00 | 6.40 |

#132 inscribed BANI; #133-134 BAN.

**1900, July — Wmk. 167**

| No. | Type | Description | Unused | Used |
|---|---|---|---|---|
| 148 | A17 | 1b pale brown | 5.50 | 2.00 |
| 149 | A18 | 3b red brown | 4.75 | 2.00 |
| 150 | A19 | 5b emerald | 5.50 | 2.00 |
| 151 | A20 | 10b rose | 5.50 | 2.00 |
| 152 | A21 | 15b black | 7.00 | 3.25 |
| 153 | A19 | 25b blue | 8.00 | 3.75 |
| 154 | A19 | 40b gray grn | 14.00 | 4.25 |
| 155 | A19 | 50b orange | 14.00 | 4.25 |
| 156 | A23 | 1l bis & rose | 16.00 | 5.25 |
| 157 | A23 | 2l orange & brn | 21.00 | 6.50 |
| | | Nos. 148-157 (10) | 101.25 | 35.25 |

## Mail Coach Leaving P.O. — A25
## King Carol I and Façade of New Post Office — A26

**1903 — Unwmk. — Perf. 14x13½**
**Thin Paper, Tinted Rose on Face**

| No. | Type | Description | Unused | Used |
|---|---|---|---|---|
| 158 | A26 | 1b gray brown | 1.00 | .40 |
| 159 | A26 | 3b brown violet | 1.75 | .75 |
| 160 | A25 | 5b pale green | 4.00 | 1.60 |
| 161 | A25 | 10b rose | 3.50 | 1.60 |
| 162 | A25 | 25b blue | 3.50 | 1.60 |
| 163 | A26 | 25b blue | 15.00 | 6.50 |
| 164 | A26 | 50b dull green | 20.00 | 8.50 |
| 165 | A26 | 50b dull green | 27.50 | 11.00 |
| | | Nos. 158-165 (8) | 76.25 | 31.95 |

Counterfeits are plentiful. See note after No. 172. See No. 428.

**1903 — Engr. — Perf. 13½x14**
**Thick Toned Paper**

| No. | Type | Description | Unused | Used |
|---|---|---|---|---|
| 166 | A26 | 1b gray brown | 2.00 | .80 |
| 167 | A26 | 25b blue | 6.00 | 2.00 |
| 168 | A26 | 25b blue | 8.00 | 3.25 |
| 169 | A26 | 40b gray grn | 8.00 | 3.50 |
| 170 | A26 | 1l dk brown | 75.00 | 30.00 |
| 171 | A26 | 2l dull red | 87.50 | 75.00 |
| a. | | 2l orange (error) | | |
| 172 | A26 | 5l red violet | 182.00 | 73.05 |
| | | Nos. 166-172a (7) | | |

Opening of the new PO in Bucharest (Nos. 158-172). Counterfeits exist.

## Prince Carol Taking Oath of Allegiance, 1866 — A27

## Prince in Royal Carriage — A28
## Prince Carol at Calafat in 1877 — A29

Prince Carol Shaking Hands with His Captive, Osman Pasha — A30

Carol I as Prince in 1866 and King in 1906 — A31

Romanian Army Crossing Danube A32

Romanian Troops Return to Bucharest in 1878 — A33

Prince Carol at Head of His Command in 1877 — A34

King Carol I at Cathedral in 1896 — A35

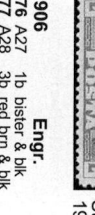

King Carol I at Shrine of St. Nicholas, 1904 — A36

King Carol I — A37

**Engr. Perf. 12**

**1906**

| | | | | |
|---|---|---|---|---|
| 176 | A27 | 1b bister & blk | .50 | .25 |
| 177 | A28 | 3b red brn & blk | 1.25 | .25 |
| 178 | A29 | 5b dp grn & blk | 1.50 | .75 |
| 179 | A30 | 10b carmine & blk | 1.50 | .25 |
| 180 | A31 | 15b dull vio & blk | .75 | .25 |
| 181 | A32 | 25b ultra & blk | 1.50 | .75 |
| 182 | A33 | 25b olive green & black | 5.50 | 4.50 |
| 183 | A34 | 40b dk brn & blk | 8.75 | 5.00 |
| 184 | A35 | 50b bis brn & blk | 1.60 | 1.50 |
| 185 | A36 | 1l vermilion & blk | 1.75 | 1.50 |
| a. | | 2l orange & blk | 2.00 | 1.90 |
| | | Nos. 176-185 (10) | 17.10 | 12.40 |

40 years' rule of Carol I as Prince & King. No. 181a was never placed in use. Cancellations were by favor.

**1906**

| | | | | |
|---|---|---|---|---|
| 186 | A37 | 1b bister & blk | 1.00 | |
| 187 | A37 | 3b red brn & blk | .45 | |
| 188 | A37 | 5b dp grn & blk | .25 | |
| 189 | A37 | 10b carmine & blk | .85 | |
| 190 | A37 | 15b dl vio & blk | .75 | |
| 191 | A37 | 25b ultra & blk | .75 | |
| 192 | A37 | 40b dk brn & blk | 12.00 | 6.75 |
| 193 | A37 | 50b bis brn & blk | 3.50 | 1.50 |
| 194 | A37 | 1l red & blk | 3.50 | 1.50 |
| 195 | A37 | 2l orange & blk | 3.50 | 1.50 |
| | | Nos. 186-195 (10) | 33.25 | 16.30 |

25th anniversary of the Kingdom.

Plowman and Angel — A38

Exposition Building — A39

Exposition Buildings A40

Exposition Building A41

King Carol I — A42

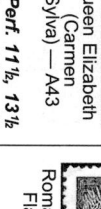

Queen Elizabeth (Carmen Sylva) — A43

**Typo. Perf. 11½, 13½**

**1906**

| | | | | |
|---|---|---|---|---|
| 196 | A38 | 5b yel grn & blk | 1.10 | .55 |
| 197 | A38 | 10b carmine & blk | .75 | .80 |
| 198 | A39 | 15b violet & blk | 1.75 | .80 |
| 199 | A40 | 25b blue & blk | 4.75 | 1.10 |
| 200 | A40 | 30b red & blk | 4.75 | 1.40 |
| 201 | A41 | 40b green & blk | 5.75 | 1.40 |

| | | | | |
|---|---|---|---|---|
| 202 | A42 | 50b orange & blk | 7.00 | 1.60 |
| 203 | A41 | 75b lt brn & dk brn | 5.75 | 2.00 |
| 204 | A42 | 1.50 l red lil & blk | 5.75 | 2.00 |
| a. | | Center inverted | | |
| 205 | A42 | 2.50 l yellow & brn | 65.00 | 35.00 |
| a. | | Center inverted | | |
| 206 | A43 | 3 l brn org & brn | 18.00 | 17.00 |
| a. | | 3 l brn org & brn | 24.00 | 18.00 |
| | | Nos. 196-206 (11) | 143.35 | 80.85 |

General Exposition. They were sold at post offices July 29-31, 1906, and were valid only for those three days. Those sold at the exposition are overprinted "S E" in black. Remainders were sold privately, both unused and canceled to order, by the Exposition promoters. Value, unused or used, $275.

King Carol I — A44

A45

King Carol I — A46

**No. 217 Handstamped in Red**

**1909-18 Perf. 13½x14, 11½, 13½ & Compound**

**Engr.**

| | | | | |
|---|---|---|---|---|
| 207 | A44 | 5b pale yel grn | 2.00 | .20 |
| 208 | A44 | 10b carmine | .70 | .20 |
| 209 | A45 | 5b purple | 11.50 | 2.25 |
| 210 | A44 | 25b deep blue | 1.25 | .20 |
| 211 | A44 | 40b brt green | .85 | .20 |
| 212 | A44 | 50b dk brn | 5.25 | 2.25 |
| 213 | A44 | 50b orange | .65 | .20 |
| 214 | A44 | 50b lt red ('18) | 2.00 | .70 |
| 215 | A44 | 1 l brown | 1.75 | .35 |
| 216 | A44 | 2 l red | 10.00 | 2.00 |
| | | Nos. 207-216 (10) | 35.95 | 8.80 |

**Typo.**

**1909-18**

| | | | | |
|---|---|---|---|---|
| 217 | A46 | 1b black | .60 | .20 |
| 218 | A46 | 3b red brown | 1.25 | .20 |
| 219 | A46 | 5b yellow grn | 1.25 | .20 |
| 220 | A46 | 10b green | 1.25 | .20 |
| 221 | A46 | 15b brt green | 17.50 | 11.00 |
| 222 | A46 | 15b dull violet | 1.25 | .20 |
| 223 | A46 | 15b red brn ('18) | 1.10 | .20 |
| | | Nos. 217-223 (7) | 23.55 | 12.65 |

No. 219 in black is a chemical changeling. For surcharge and overprints see Nos. 240-242, 245-247, J50-J51, RA1-RA2, RA11-RA12, Romanian Post Offices in the Turkish Empire 7-9.

Romania Holding Flag — A47

Romanian Crown and Old Fort on Danube — A48

Troops Crossing Danube — A49

**Types of 1893-99**

**1911-19 White Paper Unwmk.**

| | | | | |
|---|---|---|---|---|
| 224 | A17 | 1½b straw | 1.75 | .45 |
| 225 | A19 | 25b deep blue ('18) | .55 | .20 |
| 226 | A19 | 40b gray brn ('19) | 1.00 | .20 |
| 227 | A19 | 50b dull red ('19) | 1.00 | .20 |
| 228 | A23 | 1 l gray grn ('19) | 1.75 | .20 |
| 229 | A23 | 2 l orange ('18) | 2.00 | .20 |
| | | Nos. 224-229 (6) | 8.05 | 1.45 |

For overprints see Romanian Post Offices in the Turkish Empire Nos. 10-11.

View of Turtucaia — A50

View of Silistra — A52

Mircea the Great and Carol I — A51

**1913, Dec. 25 Perf. 11½x13½, 13½x11½**

| | | | | |
|---|---|---|---|---|
| 230 | A47 | 1b black | .55 | .20 |
| 231 | A48 | 3b red brn & choc | 1.75 | .40 |
| 232 | A49 | 5b yel grn & blk brn | 1.75 | .40 |
| 233 | A50 | 10b gray | 1.10 | .20 |
| 234 | A51 | 15b org & gray | 1.75 | .40 |
| 235 | A52 | 25b bister & blk & vio | 2.25 | .65 |

**1918 Perf. 13½x14, 11½, 13½ & Compound**

| | | | | |
|---|---|---|---|---|
| 236 | A49 | 40b bis & red vio | 3.50 | 1.40 |
| 237 | A48 | 50b yellow & bl | 4.25 | 3.25 |
| 238 | A48 | 1 l bl & ol bis | 11.50 | 7.50 |
| 239 | A48 | 2 l org red & rose | 43.70 | 22.95 |
| | | Nos. 230-239 (10) | | |

Romania's annexation of Silistra.

**No. 217 Handstamped in Red**

**1918, May 1**

| | | | | |
|---|---|---|---|---|
| 240 | A46 | 25b in black | 2.25 | 2.25 |

This handstamp is found inverted.

**No. 219 and 220 Overprinted in Black**

**1918**

| | | | | |
|---|---|---|---|---|
| 241 | A46 | 5b yellow green | .45 | .40 |
| 242 | A46 | 10b green | .40 | .40 |
| a. | | Inverted overprint | 3.25 | 3.25 |
| b. | | Double overprint | 3.50 | 3.50 |

**Nos. 217, 219 and 220 Overprinted in Red or Black**

**1919, Nov. 8**

| | | | | |
|---|---|---|---|---|
| 245 | A46 | 1b black (R) | .40 | .20 |
| a. | | Inverted overprint | 6.75 | 6.75 |
| 246 | A46 | 5b yel grn (Bk) | .40 | .20 |
| a. | | Inverted overprint | 10.00 | 10.00 |
| b. | | Double overprint | 2.25 | 2.25 |
| 247 | A46 | 10b rose (Bk) | 1.50 | .40 |
| a. | | Inverted overprint | .40 | .20 |
| b. | | Double overprint | 6.75 | 6.75 |
| | | Nos. 245-247 (3) | | |

Recovery of Transylvania and the return of the King to Bucharest.

King Ferdinand A53

A54

**1920-22 Typo.**

| | | | | |
|---|---|---|---|---|
| 248 | A53 | 1b black | .20 | .20 |
| 249 | A53 | 5b yellow grn | .20 | .20 |
| 250 | A53 | 10b rose | .40 | .20 |
| 251 | A53 | 15b red brown | 1.00 | .20 |
| 252 | A53 | 25b deep blue | .75 | .20 |
| 253 | A53 | 25b brown | .75 | .35 |
| 254 | A53 | 40b gray brown | .35 | .20 |
| 255 | A53 | 50b salmon | .35 | .20 |
| 256 | A53 | 1 l gray grn | .75 | .20 |
| 257 | A53 | 1 l rose | 1.25 | .20 |
| 258 | A53 | 2 l orange | 1.25 | .25 |
| 259 | A53 | 2 l dp blue | 1.25 | .25 |
| 260 | A53 | 2 l rose ('22) | 3.00 | 1.75 |
| | | Nos. 248-260 (13) | 12.70 | 4.75 |

Nos. 248-260 are printed on two papers: coarse, grayish paper with bits of colored fiber, and thinner white paper of better quality. Nos. 248-251, 253 exist imperf.

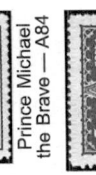

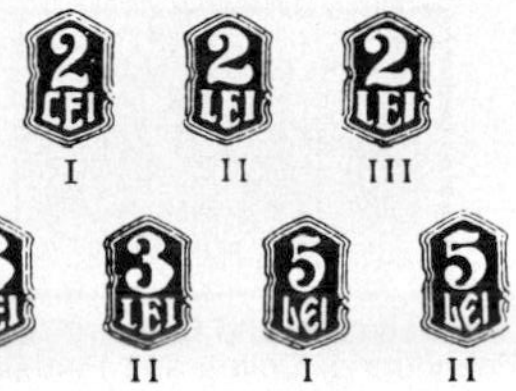
I
II
III
I
II
I
II

TWO LEI:
Type I — The "2" is thin, with tail 2½mm wide. Top of "2" forms a hook.
Type II — The "2" is thick, with tail 3mm wide. Top of "2" forms a ball.
Type III — The "2" is similar to type II. The "E" of "LEI" is larger and about 2mm wide.

THREE LEI:
Type I — Top of "3" begins in a point. Top and middle bars of "E" of "LEI" are without serifs.
Type II — Top of "3" begins in a ball. Top and middle bars of "E" of "LEI" have serifs.

FIVE LEI:
Type I — The "5" is 2½mm wide. The end of the final stroke of the "L" of "LEI" almost touches the vertical stroke.
Type II — The "5" is 3mm wide and the lines are broader than in type I. The end of the final stroke of the "L" of "LEI" is separated from the vertical by a narrow space.

***Perf. 13½x14, 11½, 13½ & Compound***

**1920-26**

| | | | | |
|---|---|---|---|---|
| **261** | A54 | 3b black | .20 | .20 |
| **262** | A54 | 5b black | .20 | .20 |
| **263** | A54 | 10b yel grn ('25) | .20 | .20 |
| a. | | 10b olive green ('25) | .40 | |
| **264** | A54 | 25b bister brn | .20 | .20 |
| **265** | A54 | 25b salmon | .20 | .20 |
| **266** | A54 | 30b violet | .20 | .20 |
| **267** | A54 | 50b orange | .20 | .20 |
| **268** | A54 | 60b gray grn | 1.00 | .45 |
| **269** | A54 | 1 l violet | .20 | .20 |
| **270** | A54 | 2 l rose (I) | 1.25 | .25 |
| a. | | 2 l claret (I) | 25.00 | |
| **271** | A54 | 2 l lt green (II) | .70 | .20 |
| a. | | 2 l light green (I) | .95 | .20 |
| b. | | 2 l light green (III) | .80 | .20 |
| **272** | A54 | 3 l blue (I) | 2.60 | .35 |
| **273** | A54 | 3 l buff (II) | 2.60 | .25 |
| a. | | 3 l buff (I) | 11.00 | .65 |
| **274** | A54 | 3 l salmon (II) | .20 | .20 |
| a. | | 3 l salmon (I) | 1.60 | 1.00 |
| **275** | A54 | 3 l car rose (II) | .65 | .20 |
| **276** | A54 | 5 l emer (I) | 2.10 | .25 |
| **277** | A54 | 5 l lt brn (II) | .45 | .20 |
| a. | | 5 l light brown (I) | 1.60 | .55 |
| **278** | A54 | 6 l blue | 2.60 | .85 |
| **279** | A54 | 6 l carmine | 5.75 | 1.40 |
| **280** | A54 | 6 l ol grn ('26) | 2.50 | .45 |
| **281** | A54 | 7½ l pale bl | 2.10 | .25 |
| **282** | A54 | 10 l deep blue | 2.10 | .25 |
| | | *Nos. 261-282 (22)* | 28.20 | 7.15 |

#273 and 273a, 274 and 274a, exist se-tenant. The 5b exists in three types.
For surcharge see No. Q7.

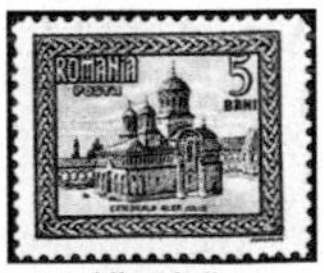
Alba Iulia Cathedral A55

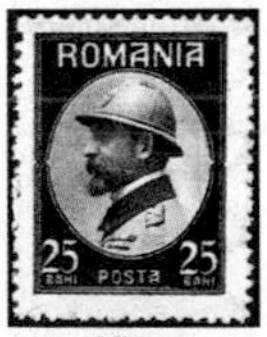
King Ferdinand A56

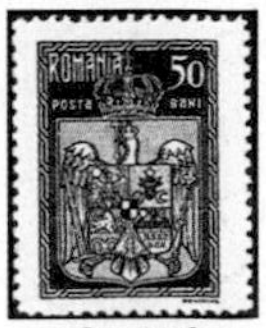
Coat of Arms — A57

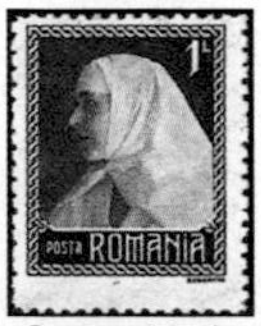
Queen Marie as Nurse — A58

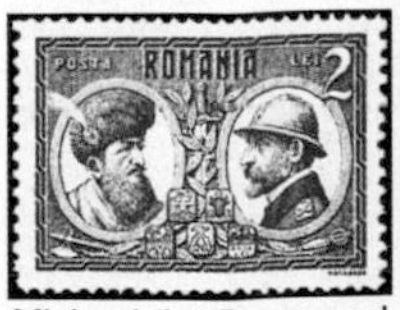
Michael the Brave and King Ferdinand A59

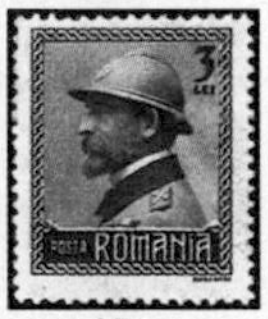
King Ferdinand A60

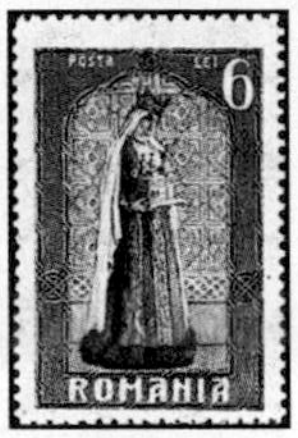
Queen Marie — A61

***Perf. 13½x14, 13½, 11½ & Compound***

**1922, Oct. 15 Photo. Wmk. 95**

| | | | | |
|---|---|---|---|---|
| **283** | A55 | 5b black | .20 | .25 |
| **284** | A56 | 25b chocolate | .65 | .25 |
| **285** | A57 | 50b dp green | .75 | .30 |
| **286** | A58 | 1 l olive grn | 1.00 | .60 |
| **287** | A59 | 2 l carmine | 1.10 | .60 |
| **288** | A60 | 3 l blue | 2.10 | 1.00 |
| **289** | A61 | 6 l violet | 8.50 | 6.00 |
| | | *Nos. 283-289 (7)* | 14.30 | 9.00 |

Coronation of King Ferdinand I and Queen Marie on Oct. 15, 1922, at Alba Iulia. All values exist imperforate. Value $90, unused or used.

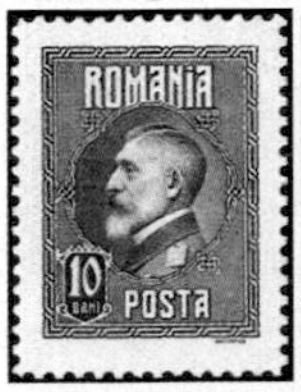
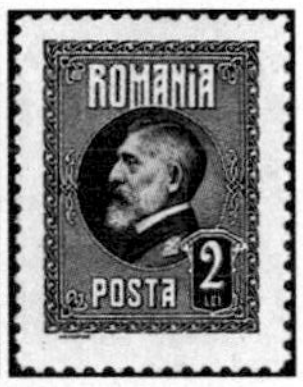
King Ferdinand
A62 A63

**1926, July 1 Unwmk. *Perf. 11***

| | | | | |
|---|---|---|---|---|
| **291** | A62 | 10b yellow grn | .40 | .30 |
| **292** | A62 | 25b orange | .40 | .30 |
| **293** | A62 | 50b orange brn | .40 | .30 |
| **294** | A63 | 1 l dk violet | .40 | .30 |
| **295** | A63 | 2 l dk green | .40 | .30 |
| **296** | A63 | 3 l brown car | .40 | .30 |
| **297** | A63 | 5 l black brn | .40 | .30 |
| **298** | A63 | 6 l dk olive | .40 | .30 |
| a. | | 6 l bright blue (error) | 65.00 | 65.00 |
| **300** | A63 | 9 l slate | .40 | .30 |
| **301** | A63 | 10 l brt blue | .40 | .30 |
| a. | | 10 l brown carmine (error) | 65.00 | 65.00 |
| | | *Nos. 291-301 (10)* | 4.00 | 3.00 |

60th birthday of King Ferdinand.
Exist imperf. Value $35, unused or used. Imperf. examples with watermark 95 are proofs.

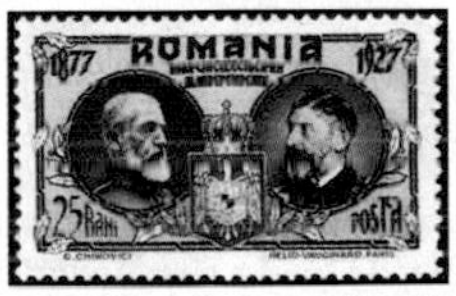
King Carol I and King Ferdinand A69

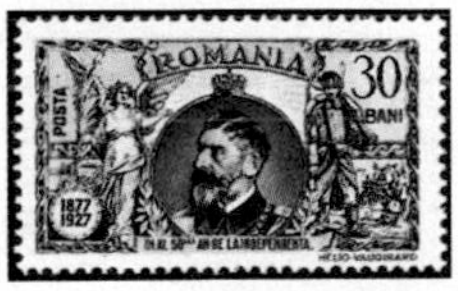
King Ferdinand A70

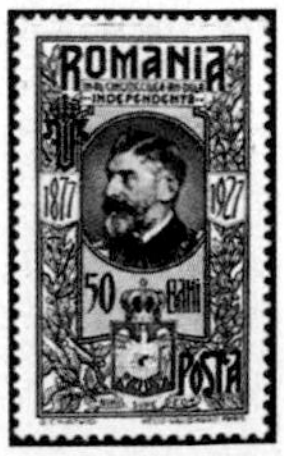
A71

**1927, Aug. 1 *Perf. 13½***

| | | | | |
|---|---|---|---|---|
| **308** | A69 | 25b brown vio | .25 | .20 |
| **309** | A70 | 30b gray blk | .20 | .20 |
| **310** | A71 | 50b dk green | .25 | .20 |
| **311** | A69 | 1 l bluish slate | .25 | .20 |
| **312** | A70 | 2 l dp green | .25 | .25 |
| **313** | A70 | 3 l violet | .35 | .35 |
| **314** | A71 | 4 l dk brown | .50 | .40 |
| **315** | A71 | 4.50 l henna brn | 1.50 | 1.00 |
| **316** | A70 | 5 l red brown | .35 | .35 |
| **317** | A71 | 6 l carmine | .85 | .45 |
| **318** | A69 | 7.50 l grnsh bl | .45 | .35 |
| **319** | A69 | 10 l brt blue | 1.50 | .45 |
| | | *Nos. 308-319 (12)* | 6.70 | 4.40 |

50th anniversary of Romania's independence from Turkish suzerainty.

Some values exist imperf. All exist imperf. and with value numerals omitted.

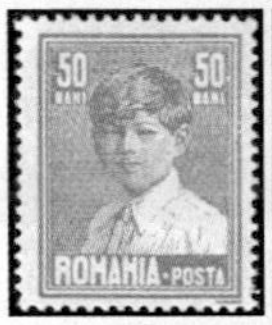
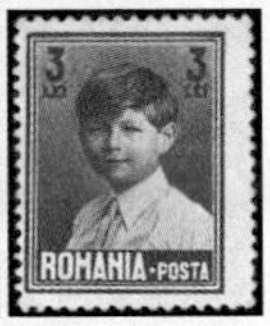
King Michael
A72 A73

***Perf. 13½x14 (25b, 50b); 13½***

**1928-29 Typo. Unwmk.**

**Size: 19x25mm**

| | | | | |
|---|---|---|---|---|
| **320** | A72 | 25b black | .25 | .20 |
| **321** | A72 | 30b fawn ('29) | .40 | .20 |
| **322** | A72 | 50b olive grn | .25 | .20 |

**Photo.**

**Size: 18½x24½mm**

| | | | | |
|---|---|---|---|---|
| **323** | A73 | 1 l violet | .45 | .20 |
| **324** | A73 | 2 l dp green | .45 | .20 |
| **325** | A73 | 3 l brt rose | .90 | .20 |
| **326** | A73 | 5 l red brown | 1.40 | .20 |
| **327** | A73 | 7.50 l ultra | 6.25 | .45 |
| **328** | A73 | 10 l blue | 5.25 | .20 |
| | | *Nos. 320-328 (9)* | 15.60 | 2.05 |

See Nos. 343-345, 353-357. For overprints see Nos. 359-368A.

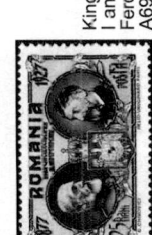

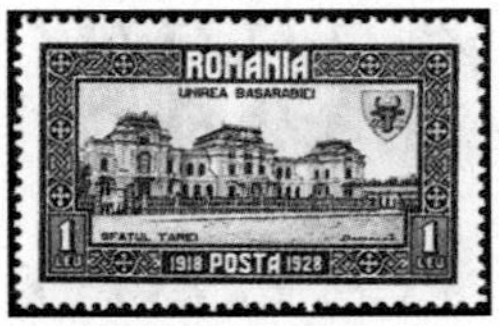
Parliament House, Bessarabia — A74

Designs: 1 l, 2 l, Parliament House, Bessarabia. 3 l, 5 l, 20 l, Hotin Fortress. 7.50 l, 10 l, Fortress Cetatea Alba.

**1928, Apr. 29 Wmk. 95 *Perf. 13½***

| | | | | |
|---|---|---|---|---|
| **329** | A74 | 1 l deep green | 1.10 | .65 |
| **330** | A74 | 2 l deep brown | 1.10 | .65 |
| **331** | A74 | 3 l black brown | 1.25 | .65 |
| **332** | A74 | 5 l carmine lake | 1.60 | .85 |
| **333** | A74 | 7.50 l ultra | 1.60 | .85 |
| **334** | A74 | 10 l Prus blue | 4.25 | 2.10 |
| **335** | A74 | 20 l black vio | 5.50 | 2.75 |
| | | *Nos. 329-335 (7)* | 16.40 | 8.50 |

Reunion of Bessarabia with Romania, 10th anniv.

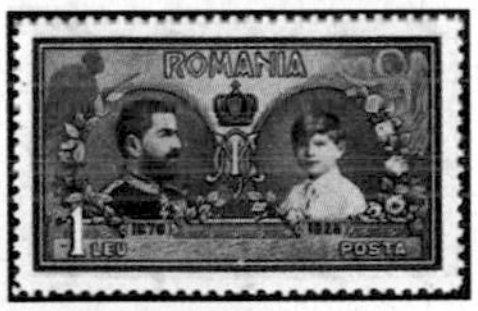
King Carol I and King Michael A77

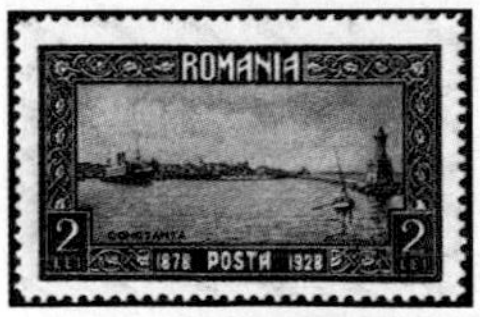
View of Constanta Harbor A78

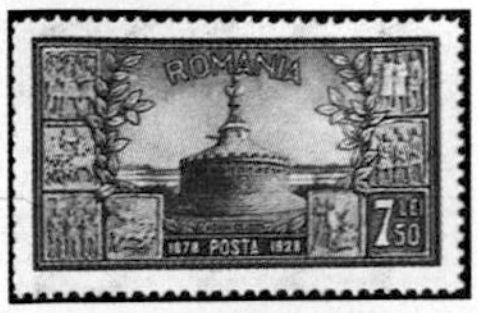
Trajan's Monument at Adam Clisi A79

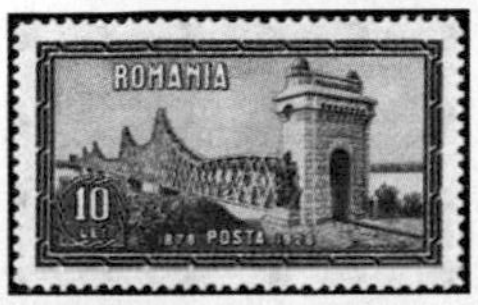
Cernavoda Bridge — A80

**1928, Oct. 25**

| | | | | |
|---|---|---|---|---|
| **336** | A77 | 1 l blue green | 1.10 | .40 |
| **337** | A78 | 2 l red brown | 1.10 | .45 |
| **338** | A77 | 3 l gray black | 1.40 | .50 |
| **339** | A79 | 5 l dull lilac | 1.75 | .60 |
| **340** | A79 | 7.50 l ultra | 2.10 | .80 |
| **341** | A80 | 10 l blue | 3.25 | 1.90 |
| **342** | A80 | 20 l carmine rose | 5.50 | 3.25 |
| | | *Nos. 336-342 (7)* | 16.20 | 7.90 |

Union of Dobruja with Romania, 50th anniv.

Michael Types of 1928-29

***Perf. 13½x14***

**1928, Sept. 1 Typo. Wmk. 95**

| | | | | |
|---|---|---|---|---|
| **343** | A72 | 25b black | .55 | .20 |

**Photo.**

| | | | | |
|---|---|---|---|---|
| **344** | A73 | 7.50 l ultra | 1.75 | .60 |
| **345** | A73 | 10 l blue | 3.75 | .35 |
| | | *Nos. 343-345 (3)* | 6.05 | 1.15 |

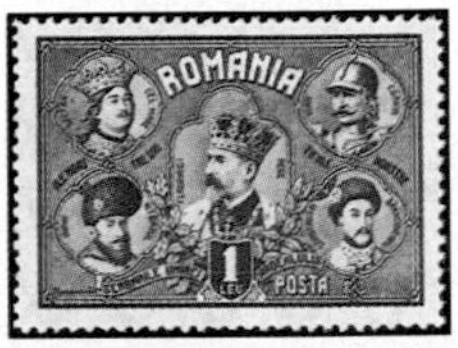
Ferdinand I; Stephen the Great; Michael the Brave; Corvin and Constantine Brancoveanu — A81

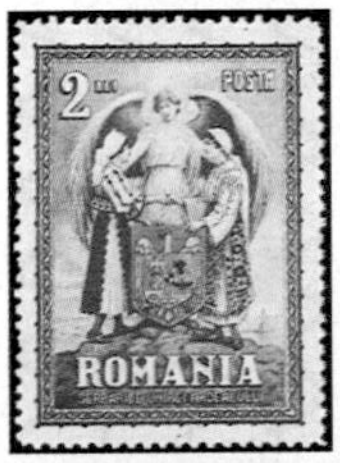
Union with Transylvania A82

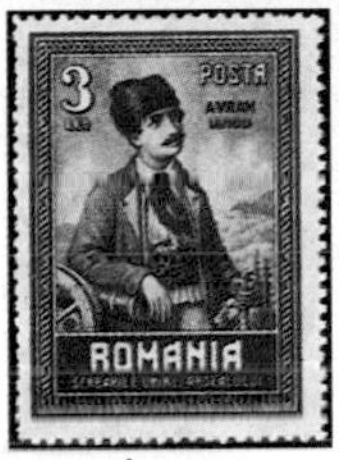
Avram Jancu — A83

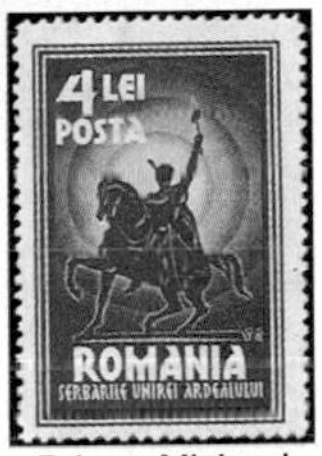
Prince Michael the Brave — A84

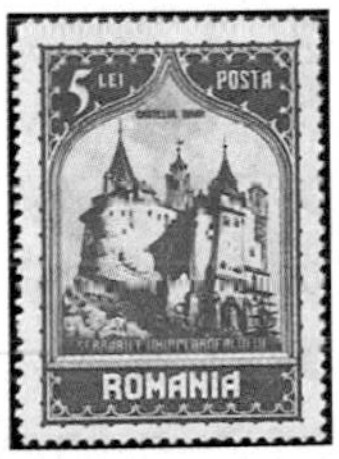
Castle Bran — A85

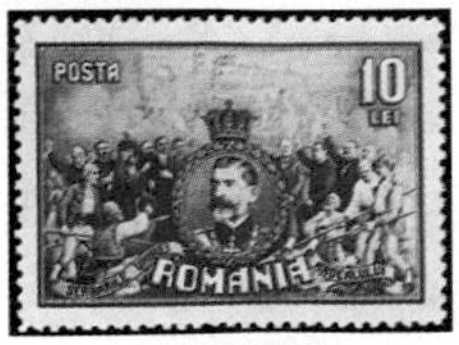
King Ferdinand I — A86

**1929, May 10 Photo. Wmk. 95**

| | | | | |
|---|---|---|---|---|
| **347** | A81 | 1 l dark violet | 1.75 | .75 |
| **348** | A82 | 2 l olive green | 1.75 | .85 |
| **349** | A83 | 3 l violet brown | 2.10 | .85 |
| **350** | A84 | 4 l cerise | 2.25 | 1.25 |
| **351** | A85 | 5 l orange | 3.75 | 1.25 |
| **352** | A86 | 10 l brt blue | 6.50 | 3.75 |
| | | *Nos. 347-352 (6)* | 18.10 | 8.70 |

Union of Transylvania and Romania.

Michael Type of 1928

**1930 Unwmk. *Perf. 14½x14***

**Size: 18x23mm**

| | | | | |
|---|---|---|---|---|
| **353** | A73 | 1 l deep violet | .70 | .20 |
| **354** | A73 | 2 l deep green | 1.00 | .20 |
| **355** | A73 | 3 l carmine rose | 1.90 | .20 |
| **356** | A73 | 7.50 l ultra | 4.25 | .20 |
| **357** | A73 | 10 l deep blue | 12.50 | 4.25 |
| | | *Nos. 353-357 (5)* | 20.35 | 5.05 |

## Stamps of 1928-30 Overprinted

### 1930, June 8
**On Nos. 320-322, 326, 328**
**Perf. 13½x14, 13½**
**Typo.**

| | | | | |
|---|---|---|---|---|
| 359 | A72 | 25b black | .20 | .20 |
| 360 | A72 | 30b fawn | .65 | .20 |
| 361 | A72 | 50b olive green | .65 | .20 |

**Photo.**
**Size: 18½x24½mm**

| | | | | |
|---|---|---|---|---|
| 362 | A73 | 5 l red brown | 1.10 | .20 |
| 362A | A73 | 10 l brt blue | 4.75 | .85 |

**On Nos. 343-344**
**Size: 18x23mm**

| | | | | |
|---|---|---|---|---|
| 363 | A73 | 1 l deep violet | .40 | .20 |
| 364 | A73 | 2 l deep green | .85 | .20 |
| 365 | A73 | 3 l carmine rose | 2.25 | .30 |
| 366 | A73 | 7.50 l ultra | 2.25 | .30 |
| 367 | A73 | 10 l deep blue | 2.10 | .45 |

**On Nos. 353-357**
**Perf. 14½x14**
**Photo.**

| | | | | |
|---|---|---|---|---|
| 368 | A72 | 25b black | .65 | .20 |

**Size: 18½x24½mm**

| | | | | |
|---|---|---|---|---|
| 368A | A73 | 7.50 l ultra | 3.25 | .85 |
| | | | 17.30 | 4.05 |

A72  A73

Accession to the throne by King Carol II.
This overprint exists on Nos. 323, 345.

*Nos. 359-368A (12)*

### King Carol II — A89

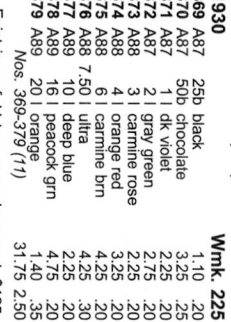

A87 A88

### 1930
**Perf. 13½, 14, 14x13½    Wmk. 225**

| | | | | |
|---|---|---|---|---|
| 369 | A87 | 25b black | 1.10 | .20 |
| 370 | A87 | 50b chocolate | 3.25 | .25 |
| 371 | A87 | 1 l dk violet | 3.25 | .20 |
| 372 | A87 | 2 l gray green | 2.75 | .20 |
| 373 | A88 | 3 l orange brn | 2.25 | .20 |
| 374 | A88 | 4 l carmine rose | 3.25 | .20 |
| 375 | A88 | 6 l orange red | 4.25 | .30 |
| 376 | A88 | 7.50 l ultra | 4.25 | .25 |
| 377 | A89 | 10 l deep blue | 2.25 | .20 |
| 378 | A89 | 16 l peacock grn | 4.75 | .20 |
| 379 | A89 | 20 l orange | 1.40 | .35 |
| | | *Nos. 369-379 (11)* | 31.75 | 2.50 |

Exist imperf. Value, unused or used, $125.
See Nos. 405-414.

A90    A91

### 1930, Dec. 24    Unwmk.    Perf. 13½

| | | | | |
|---|---|---|---|---|
| 380 | A90 | 1 l dull violet | 1.25 | .20 |
| 381 | A91 | 2 l green | 2.25 | .20 |
| 382 | A91 | 4 l vermilion | 2.50 | .20 |
| 383 | A91 | 6 l brown carmine | 12.50 | 1.00 |
| | | *Nos. 380-383 (4)* | | |

First census in Romania.

---

Using Bayonet — A97

Romanian Infantry 1830 — A99

Romanian Infantryman 1870 — A98

King Carol I — A93

King Carol II, King Ferdinand and King Carol I — A95

King Ferdinand — A96

King Carol II — A94

### 1931, May 10    Photo.    Wmk. 225

| | | | | |
|---|---|---|---|---|
| 384 | A92 | 1 l gray violet | 2.00 | .95 |
| 385 | A93 | 2 l green | 4.00 | 1.00 |
| 386 | A94 | 3 l red brown | 9.75 | 1.75 |
| 387 | A95 | 10 l blue | 14.00 | 2.50 |
| 388 | A96 | 20 l orange | 20.00 | 4.00 |
| | | *Nos. 384-388 (5)* | 49.75 | 10.20 |

50th anniversary of Romanian Kingdom.

### King Carol II — A92

King Carol I — A93

King Ferdinand — A96

### 1931, May 10

| | | | | |
|---|---|---|---|---|
| 389 | A97 | 25b gray black | 1.40 | .50 |
| 390 | A98 | 50b dk red brn | 2.10 | .80 |
| 391 | A99 | 1 l gray violet | 4.25 | .80 |
| 392 | A100 | 2 l deep green | 2.75 | 1.10 |
| 393 | A101 | 3 l carmine rose | 10.00 | 2.75 |
| 394 | A102 | 7.50 l ultra | 13.00 | 3.25 |
| 395 | A103 | 16 l blue green | 16.00 | 3.25 |
| | | *Nos. 389-395 (7)* | 49.50 | 16.20 |

Centenary of the Romanian Army.

Naval Cadet Ship "Mircea" A104

### 1931, May 10    Unwmk.    Engr.    Perf. 12

| | | | | |
|---|---|---|---|---|
| 396 | A104 | 6 l red brown | 4.50 | 2.25 |
| 397 | A104 | 10 l blue | 7.50 | 2.25 |
| 398 | A104 | 16 l blue green | 5.00 | 2.25 |
| 399 | A104 | 20 l orange | 8.00 | 1.75 |
| | | *Nos. 396-399 (4)* | 51.00 | 11.25 |

50th anniversary of the Romanian Navy.

King Carol II — A108

10 l, Ironclad. 16 l, Light cruiser. 20 l, Destroyer.

### 1931    Unwmk.    Perf. 12

| | | | | |
|---|---|---|---|---|
| 400 | A108 | 30 l ol bis & dk bl | 1.00 | .50 |
| 401 | A108 | 10 l red & dk bl | 2.00 | .45 |
| 402 | A108 | 100 l dk grn & dk bl | 8.00 | 1.75 |
| | | *Nos. 400-402 (3)* | | |

Exist imperf. Value, unused or used, $150.

---

King Ferdinand A102

King Carol I A100

Infantry Advance A101

King Carol II A103

Carol II, Ferdinand, Carol I — A109

### 1931, Nov. 1    Wmk. 230    Photo.    Perf. 13½

| | | | | |
|---|---|---|---|---|
| 403 | A109 | 16 l Prus green | 11.00 | .40 |

Exists imperf. Value, unused or used, $200.

### 1932    Perf. 13½, 14, 14½ and Compound
**Carol II Types of 1930-31    Wmk. 230**

| | | | | |
|---|---|---|---|---|
| 405 | A87 | 25b black | .50 | .20 |
| 406 | A87 | 50b dark brown | 1.00 | .20 |
| 407 | A87 | 1 l dark violet | 1.40 | .20 |
| 408 | A87 | 2 l gray green | 1.75 | .20 |
| 409 | A88 | 3 l carmine rose | 2.25 | .20 |
| 410 | A88 | 4 l orange red | 5.25 | .20 |
| 411 | A88 | 6 l carmine brn | 12.50 | .20 |
| 412 | A89 | 7.50 l ultra | 21.50 | .25 |
| 413 | A89 | 10 l deep blue | 125.00 | .25 |
| 414 | A89 | 20 l orange | 110.00 | .25 |
| | | *Nos. 405-414 (10)* | 281.15 | 6.40 |

Alexander the Good — A110

### 1932, May

| | | | | |
|---|---|---|---|---|
| 415 | A110 | 6 l carmine brown | 12.00 | 5.00 |

500th death anniv. of Alexander the Good, Prince of Moldavia, 1400-1432.

King Carol II — A111

### 1932, June

| | | | | |
|---|---|---|---|---|
| 416 | A111 | 10 l brt blue | 12.00 | .35 |

Exists imperf. Value, unused or used, $150.

---

Cantacuzino and Gregory Ghika, Founders of Coltea and Pantelimon Hospitals — A112

Aesculapius and Hygeia — A114

Session of the Congress A113

### 1932, Sept.    Perf. 13½

| | | | | |
|---|---|---|---|---|
| 417 | A112 | 1 l carmine rose | 7.25 | 3.75 |
| 418 | A113 | 6 l deep orange | 19.00 | 10.50 |
| 419 | A114 | 10 l brt blue | 32.50 | 19.75 |
| | | *Nos. 417-419 (3)* | 58.75 | 19.75 |

9th Intl. History of Medicine Congress, Bucharest.

---

Coat of Arms — A113

Dolphins A118

Bull's Head and Post Horn A116

Eagle and Castles A119

Lion Rampant and Bridge A117

Eagle and Post Horn A121

Bull's Head and Post Horn — A122

### 1932, Nov. 20    Typo.    Perf. 13½

| | | | | |
|---|---|---|---|---|
| 421 | A116 | 25b black | .85 | .30 |
| 422 | A117 | 1 l violet | .25 | .20 |
| 423 | A118 | 2 l green | .70 | .20 |
| 424 | A119 | 3 l car rose | 2.80 | .20 |
| 425 | A120 | 6 l red brown | 3.50 | 1.00 |
| 426 | A121 | 7.50 l lt blue | 4.25 | 1.00 |
| 427 | A122 | 10 l dk blue | 8.00 | 2.25 |
| | | *Nos. 421-427 (7)* | 23.90 | 6.75 |

**Imperf.**

| | | | | |
|---|---|---|---|---|
| | | | 2.00 | .30 |
| | | | .80 | |
| | | | 2.80 | |
| | | | 3.50 | |
| | | | 4.25 | |
| | | | 8.00 | |

75th anniv. of the first Moldavian stamps.

### Mail Coach Type of 1903    Perf. 13½

### 1932, Nov. 20

| | | | | |
|---|---|---|---|---|
| 428 | A25 | 16 l blue green | 11.00 | 3.25 |

30th anniv. of the opening of the new post office, Bucharest, in 1903.

## Souvenir Sheet

25 OCTOMVRIE 1937
Înălțarea în gradul de sublocotenent a MĂRIEI SALE MARELUI VOEVOD MIHAI

A146a

**Surcharged in Black with New Values**

**1937, Oct. 25    Unwmk.    Perf. 13½**

| | | | | |
|---|---|---|---|---|
| 469 | A146a | Sheet of 4 | 9.00 | 9.00 |
| a. | | 2 on 20 l orange | .35 | .35 |
| b. | | 6 on 10 l bright blue | .35 | .35 |
| c. | | 10 l on 6 l maroon | .46 | .45 |
| d. | | 20 l on 2 l green | 1.00 | 1.00 |

Promotion of the Crown Prince Michael to the rank of Lieutenant on his 17th birthday.

Arms of Romania, Greece, Turkey and Yugoslavia
A147

**1938, Feb. 10    Wmk. 230**

| | | | | |
|---|---|---|---|---|
| 470 | A147 | 7.50 l ultra | 1.50 | .60 |
| 471 | A147 | 10 l blue | 2.00 | .50 |

The Balkan Entente. Exist imperf. Value, unused or used, $100.

A148    A149

King Carol II
A150

**1938, May 10    Perf. 13½**

| | | | | |
|---|---|---|---|---|
| 472 | A148 | 3 l dk carmine | .75 | .25 |
| 473 | A149 | 6 l violet brn | 1.25 | .25 |
| 474 | A150 | 10 l blue | 2.00 | .40 |
| | | | 4.00 | .90 |

Nos. 472-474 (3)

New Constitution of Feb. 27, 1938. Exist imperf. Value, unused or used, $125.

**Catalogue values for unused stamps in this section, from this point to the end of the section, are for Never Hinged items.**

Prince Carol at Calatorie, 1866
A151

---

| | | | | |
|---|---|---|---|---|
| 450 | A142 | 3 l deep rose | .70 | .20 |
| 450A | A142 | 3 l grnsh bl ('40) | .85 | .30 |
| 451 | A141 | 4 l vermilion | 1.25 | .20 |
| 452 | A140 | 5 l rose car ('40) | 1.25 | .80 |
| 453 | A143 | 6 l maroon | 1.60 | .20 |
| 454 | A140 | 7.50 l ultra | 1.90 | .30 |
| 454A | A142 | 8 l magenta ('40) | 1.90 | .70 |
| 455 | A142 | 10 l brt ultra ('40) | 2.50 | .80 |
| 456 | A142 | 10 l brt blue | 1.00 | .20 |
| 456A | A143 | 12 l slate bl ('40) | 1.60 | 1.25 |
| 457 | A139 | 15 l dk brn ('40) | 1.60 | .95 |
| 458 | A143 | 16 l Prus blue | 2.10 | .25 |
| 459 | A143 | 20 l orange | 1.25 | .35 |
| 460 | A143 | 24 l dk car ('40) | 2.10 | .95 |
| | | | 23.35 | 8.50 |

Nos. 446-460 (79)

Exist imperf. Value, unused or used, $240.

**Nos. 454, 456 Overprinted in Red**

| | | | |
|---|---|---|---|
| 454 | | 3.75 | 2.25 |
| 456 | | 3.75 | 2.25 |

16th anniversary of the Little Entente. Overprints in silver or gold are fraudulent.

Birthplace of Ion Creanga
A144

**1936, Dec. 5**

| | | | | |
|---|---|---|---|---|
| 461 | A140 | 7.50 l ultra | 5.00 | 1.60 |
| 462 | A142 | 10 l brt blue | 5.00 | 1.60 |

Exist imperf.

Ion Creanga
A145

**1937, May 15**

| | | | | |
|---|---|---|---|---|
| 463 | A144 | 2 l green | 1.10 | .25 |
| 464 | A145 | 3 l carmine rose | 1.60 | .40 |
| 465 | A144 | 4 l dp violet | 1.75 | .45 |
| 466 | A145 | 6 l red brown | 4.50 | 1.10 |
| | | | 8.95 | 2.20 |

Nos. 463-466 (4)

Creanga (1837-89), writer. Exist imperf. Value, unused or used, $125.

Cathedral at Curtea de Arges — A146

**1937, July 1**

| | | | | |
|---|---|---|---|---|
| 467 | A146 | 7.50 l ultra | 1.25 | .50 |
| 468 | A146 | 10 l blue | 2.25 | .40 |

The Little Entente (Romania, Czechoslovakia, Yugoslavia). Exist imperf. Value, unused or used, $125.

---

King Carol II — A132

**Perf. 13½**

**1934, Aug.**

| | | | | |
|---|---|---|---|---|
| 436 | A130 | 50b brown | 1.00 | .20 |
| 437 | A131 | 2 l gray green | 2.00 | .20 |
| 438 | A131 | 4 l red | 3.50 | .25 |
| 439 | A132 | 6 l deep claret | 14.50 | .85 |

Nos. 436-439 (4)

See Nos. 446-460 for stamps inscribed "Posta." Nos. 436, 439 exist imperf. Value for both, unused or used, $100.

Woman and Fruit — A134

Child and Grapes — A133

**1934, Sept. 14**

| | | | | |
|---|---|---|---|---|
| 440 | A133 | 1 l dull green | 5.00 | 1.60 |
| 441 | A134 | 2 l violet brown | 5.00 | 1.60 |

Natl. Fruit Week, Sept. 14-21. Exist imperf. Value, unused or used, $125.

Crisan, Horia and Closca
A135

**1935, Feb. 28**

| | | | | |
|---|---|---|---|---|
| 442 | A135 | 1 l shown | .65 | .25 |
| 443 | A135 | 6 l Crisan | .90 | .30 |
| 444 | A135 | 6 l Closca | 2.25 | .35 |
| 445 | A135 | 10 l Horia | 5.00 | 1.25 |
| | | | 8.80 | 2.35 |

Nos. 442-445 (4)

150th anniversary of the death of three Romanian martyrs. Exist imperf. Value, unused or used, $110.

A140    A142

A139    A141

King Carol II — A143

**Wmk. 230    Photo.    Perf. 13½**

**1935-40**

| | | | | |
|---|---|---|---|---|
| 446 | A139 | 25b black brn | .20 | .20 |
| 447 | A142 | 50b brown | .20 | .20 |
| 448 | A140 | 1 l purple | .25 | .20 |
| 449 | A141 | 2 l green | .45 | .20 |
| 449A | A141 | 2 l dk bl grn ('40) | .65 | .25 |

---

Arms of City of Turnu-Severin, Ruins of Tower of Emperor Severus — A123

Inauguration of Trajan's Bridge — A124

Prince Carol Landing at Turnu-Severin — A125

Bridge over the Danube
A126

**Perf. 14½x14    Photo.**

**1933, June 2**

| | | | | |
|---|---|---|---|---|
| 429 | A123 | 25b gray green | .75 | .25 |
| 430 | A124 | 50b dull blue | 1.10 | .25 |
| 431 | A125 | 1 l black brn | 1.75 | .65 |
| 432 | A126 | 2 l olive blk | 3.25 | .90 |
| | | | 6.85 | 2.00 |

Nos. 429-432 (4)

Centenary of the incorporation in Walachia of the old Roman City of Turnu-Severin. Exist imperf. Value, unused or used, $150.

Queen Elizabeth and King Carol I — A127

Profiles of Kings Carol I, Ferdinand and Carol II — A128

Castle Peles, Sinaia
A129

**1933, Aug.**

| | | | | |
|---|---|---|---|---|
| 433 | A127 | 1 l dark violet | 2.00 | .80 |
| 434 | A128 | 3 l olive brown | 2.25 | .80 |
| 435 | A129 | 6 l vermilion | 3.75 | 1.50 |
| | | | 8.00 | 3.10 |

Nos. 433-435 (3)

50th anniversary of the erection of Castle Peles, the royal summer residence at Sinaia. Exist imperf. Value, unused or used, $125.

A131

A130

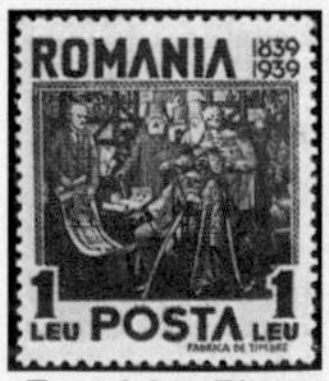

Examining Plans for a Monastery A153

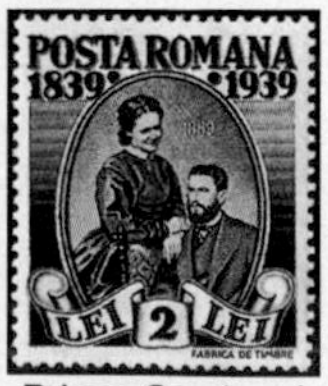

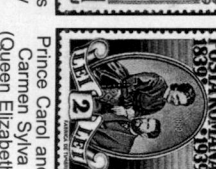

Prince Carol and Carmen Sylva (Queen Elizabeth) A155

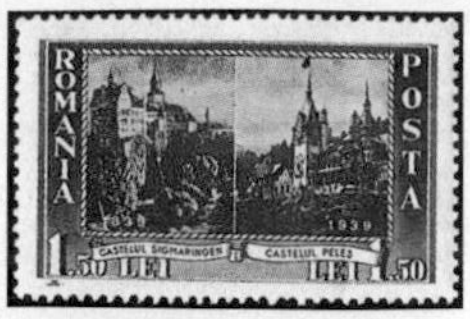

Sigmaringen and Peles Castles — A154

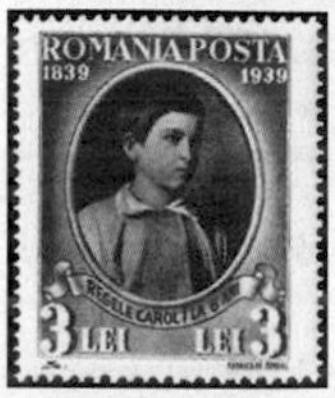

Prince Carol, Age 6 — A156

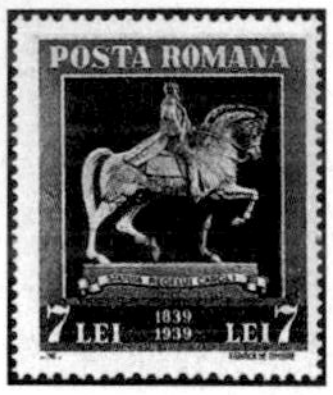

Equestrian Statue — A159

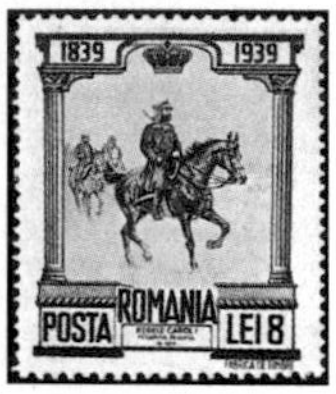

Battle of Plevna — A160

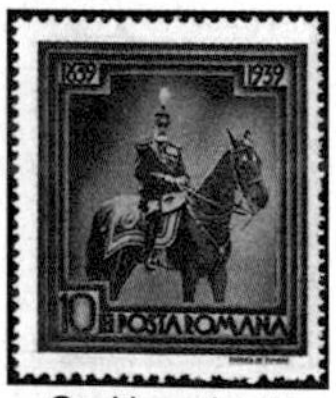

On Horseback A161

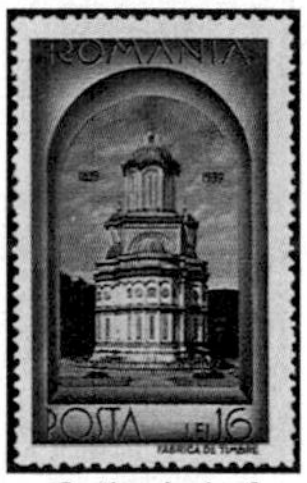

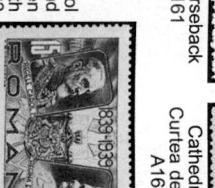

Cathedral of Curtea de Arges A164

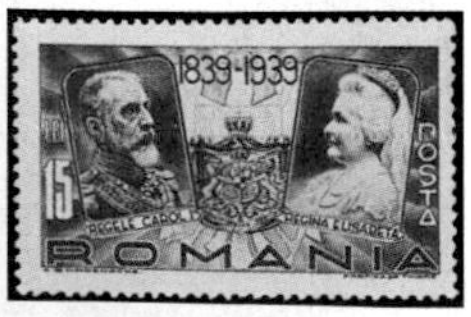

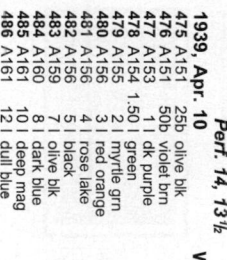

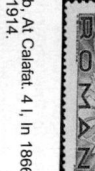

King Carol I and Queen Elizabeth A163

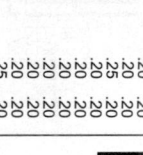

Designs: 50b, At Calafat. 4 l, In 1866. 5 l, In 1877. 12 l, in 1914.

*Perf. 14, 13½*

**1939, Apr. 10** **Wmk. 230**

**475** A151 25b olive blk .20 .20
**476** A151 50b violet brn .20 .20
**477** A153 1 l dk purple .25 .20
**478** A154 1.50 l green .20 .20
**479** A155 2 l myrtle grn .20 .20
**480** A156 3 l red orange .20 .20
**481** A156 4 l rose lake .20 .20
**482** A156 5 l black .20 .20
**483** A159 7 l olive blk .20 .20
**484** A160 8 l dark blue .25 .20
**485** A161 10 l deep mag .25 .20
**486** A161 12 l dull blue .30 .20
**487** A163 15 l ultra .35 .20
**488** A164 16 l Prus green .75 .40
*Nos. 475-488 (14)* 3.75 3.00

Centenary of the birth of King Carol I.

Nos 475-488 exist imperf. Value, unused or used, $150.

### Souvenir Sheets

**1939** *Perf. 14x13½*

**488A** Sheet of 3, #475-476, 478 1.50 1.50
*d.* Imperf. ('40) 3.50 3.50

*Perf. 14x15½*

**488B** Sheet of 4, #480-482, 486 1.50 1.50
*e.* Imperf. ('40) 3.50 3.50
**488C** Sheet of 4, #479, 483-485 1.50 1.50
*f.* Imperf. ('40) 3.50 3.50

No. 488A sold for 20 l, Nos. 488B-488C for 50 l, the surtax for national defense.

Nos. 488A-488C and 488Ad-488Cf were overprinted "PRO-PATRIA 1940" to aid the armament fund. Value, set of 6, $100.

Nos. 488A-488C exist with overprint of "ROMA BERLIN 1940" and bars, but these are not recognized as having been officially issued.

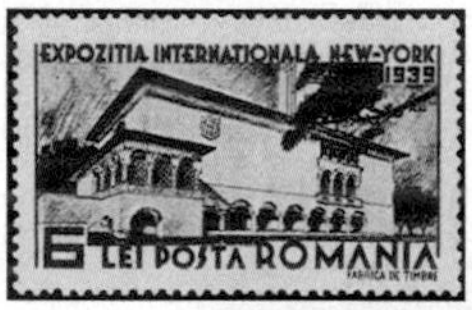

Romanian Pavilion A165

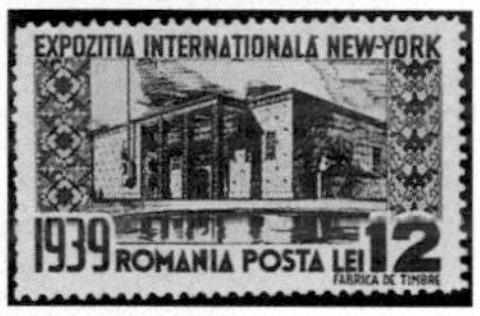

Romanian Pavilion A166

**1939, May 8** *Perf. 14x13½, 13½*

**489** A165 6 l brown carmine .55 .40
**490** A166 12 l brt blue .55 .40

New York World's Fair.

Nos 489-490 exist imperf. Value, unused or used, $250.

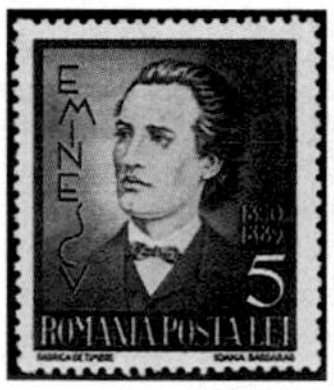

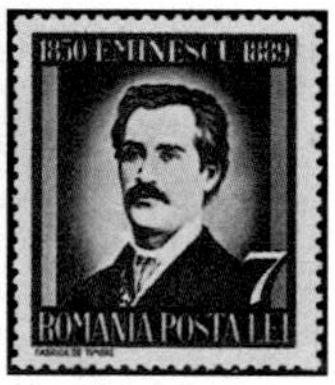

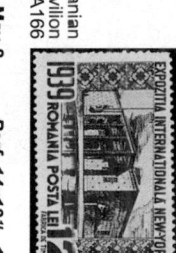

Mihail Eminescu
A167 A168

**1939, May 22** *Perf. 13½*

**491** A167 5 l olive gray .55 .40
**492** A168 7 l brown carmine .55 .40

Mihail Eminescu, poet, 50th death anniv.

Nos 491-492 exist imperf. Value, unused or used, $250.

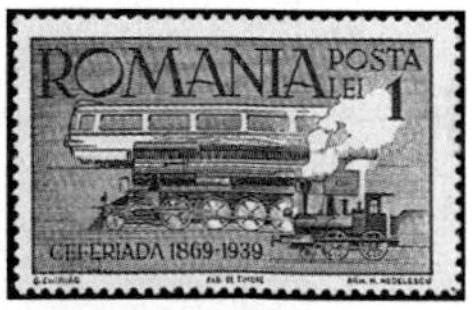

Three Types of Locomotives — A169

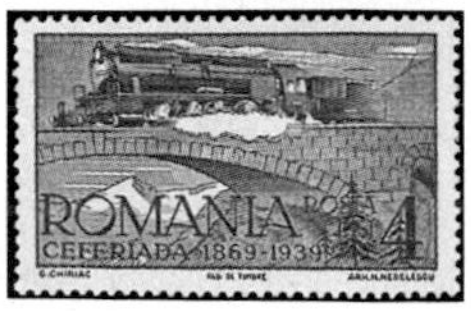

Modern Train A170

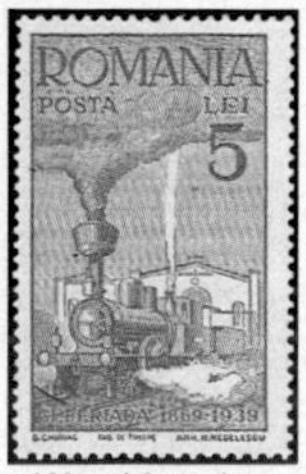

Wood-burning Locomotive A171

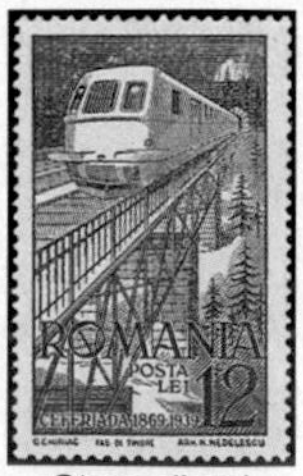

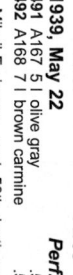

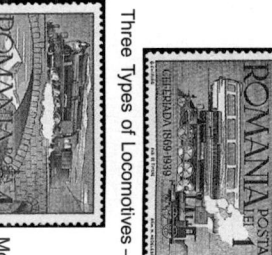

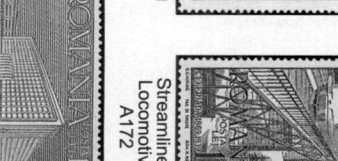

Streamlined Locomotive A172

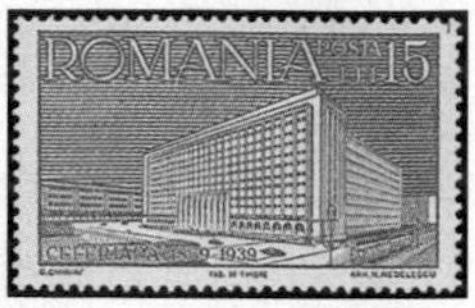

Railroad Terminal A173

**1939, June 10** **Typo.** *Perf. 14*

**493** A169 1 l red violet .95 .30
**494** A170 4 l deep rose .95 .30
**495** A171 5 l gray lilac .95 .30
**496** A171 7 l claret .95 .40
**497** A172 12 l blue 2.00 1.10
**498** A173 15 l green 2.00 1.50
*Nos. 493-498 (6)* 7.80 3.90

Romanian Railways, 70th anniversary.

Nos 493-498 exist imperf. Value, unused or used, $150.

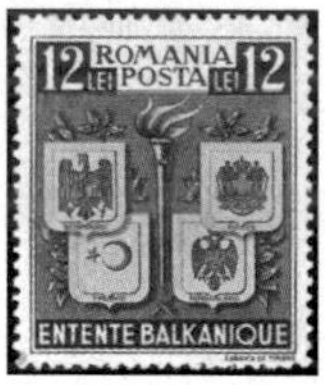

Arms of Romania, Greece, Turkey and Yugoslavia — A174

**Wmk. 230**

**1940, May 27** **Photo.** *Perf. 13½*

**504** A174 12 l lt ultra .75 .60
**505** A174 16 l dull blue .75 .60

The Balkan Entente.

Nos 504-505 exist imperf. Value, unused or used, $125.

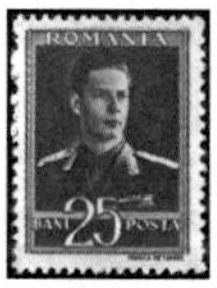

King Michael — A175

**1940-42** **Wmk. 230** *Perf. 14*

**506** A175 25b Prus green .20 .20
**506A** A175 50b dk grn ('42) .20 .20
**507** A175 1 l purple .20 .20
**508** A175 2 l red orange .20 .20
**508A** A175 4 l slate ('42) .20 .20
**509** A175 5 l rose pink .20 .20
**509A** A175 7 l dp blue ('42) .20 .20
**510** A175 10 l dp magenta .25 .20
**511** A175 12 l dull blue .20 .20
**511A** A175 13 l dk vio ('42) .20 .20
**512** A175 16 l Prus blue .30 .20
**513** A175 20 l brown 1.10 .20
**514** A175 30 l yellow grn .20 .20
**515** A175 50 l olive brn .20 .20
**516** A175 100 l rose brown .35 .20
*Nos. 506-516 (15)* 4.20 3.00

See Nos. 535A-553.

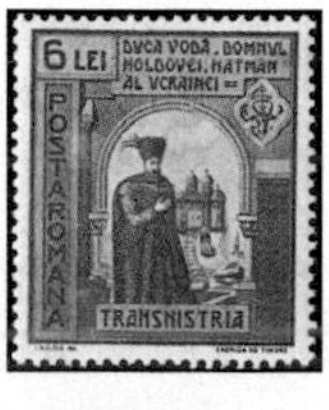

Prince Duca — A176

**1941, Oct. 6** *Perf. 13½*

**517** A176 6 l lt brown .20 .20
**518** A176 12 l dk violet .40 .20
**519** A176 24 l brt blue .50 .30
*Nos. 517-519 (3)* 1.10 .70

Crossing of the Dniester River by Romanian forces invading Russia.

Nos. 517-519 each exist in an imperf., ungummed souvenir sheet of 4. These were prepared by the civil government of Trans-Dniestria to be sold for 300 lei apiece to aid the Red Cross, but were not recognized by the national government at Bucharest. The sheets reached philatelic channels in 1946.

See Nos. 554-557.

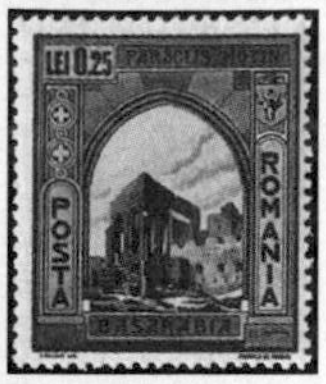

Hotin Chapel, Bessarabia A177

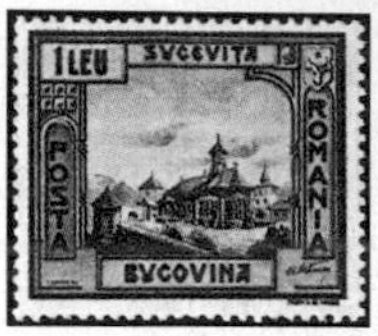

Sucevita Monastery, Bucovina A179

Inscribed "Basarabia" or "Bucovina" at bottom

Designs: 50b, 9.50 l, Hotin Fortress, Bessarabia. 1.50 l, Soroca Fortress, Bessarabia. 2 l, 5.50 l, Tighina Fortress, Bessarabia. 3 l, Dragomirna Monastery, Bucovina. 6.50 l, Cetatea Alba Fortress, Bessarabia. 10 l, 130 l, Putna Monastery, Bucovina. 13 l, Milisauti Monastery, Bucovina. 26 l, St. Nicholas Monastery, Suceava, Bucovina. 39 l, Rughi Monastery, Bessarabia.

**1941, Dec. 1** *Perf. 13½*

**520** A177 25b rose car .20 .20
**521** A179 50b red brn .20 .20
**522** A179 1 l dp vio .20 .20
**523** A179 1.50 l green .20 .20
**524** A179 2 l brn org .20 .20
**525** A177 3 l dk ol grn .20 .20
**526** A177 5 l olive blk .20 .20
**527** A179 5.50 l brown .20 .20
**528** A179 6.50 l magenta .30 .20
**529** A179 9.50 l gray blk .30 .20
**530** A179 10 l dk vio brn .20 .20
**531** A177 13 l slate blue .30 .20
**532** A179 17 l brn car .35 .20
**533** A179 26 l gray grn .40 .25
**534** A179 39 l bl grn .55 .45
**535** A179 130 l yel org 2.25 1.75
*Nos. 520-535,B179-B187 (25)* 10.75 8.50

Type of 1940-42

**1943-45** **Wmk. 276** *Perf. 14*

**535A** A175 25b Prus grn ('44) .20 .20
**536** A175 50b dk grn ('44) .20 .20
**537** A175 1 l dk vio ('43) .20 .20
**538** A175 2 l red org ('43) .20 .20
**539** A175 3 l red brn ('44) .20 .20
**540** A175 3.50 l brn ('43) .20 .20
**541** A175 4 l slate .20 .20
**542** A175 4.50 l dk brn ('43) .20 .20
**543** A175 5 l rose car .20 .20
**544** A175 6.50 l dl vio .20 .20
**545** A175 7 l dp bl .20 .20
**546** A175 10 l dp mag .20 .20
**547** A175 11 l brt ultra .20 .20
**548** A175 12 l dark blue .20 .20
**549** A175 15 l royal blue .20 .20
**550** A175 16 l dp blue .20 .20
**551** A175 20 l brn ('43) .20 .20
**551A** A175 29 l ultra ('45) .55 .35
**552** A175 30 l yel grn .20 .20
**553** A175 50 l olive blk .20 .20
*Nos. 535A-553 (20)* 4.35 4.15

Prince Duca Type of 1941

**1943** *Perf. 13½*

**554** A176 3 l red org .20 .40
**555** A176 6 l dl brn .20 .40
**556** A176 12 l dl vio .30 .55
**557** A176 24 l brt bl .40 .80
*Nos. 554-557 (4)* 1.10 2.15

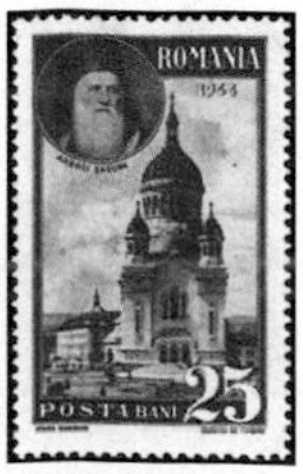

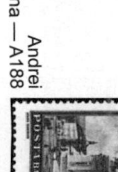

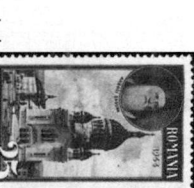

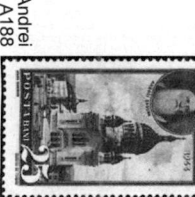

Andrei Saguna — A188

ROMANIA

## Andrei Muresanu — A189

Transylvanians: 4.50 l, Samuel Micu. 11 l, Gheorghe Sincai. 15 l, Michael the Brave. 31 l, Gheorghe Lazar. 35 l, Avram Iancu. 41 l, Simeon Barnutiu. 55 l, Three Heroes. 61 l, Petru Maior.

**1945    Inscribed "1944"    Perf. 14**

| | | | | |
|---|---|---|---|---|
| 558 | A188 | 25b rose red | .35 | .40 |
| 559 | A189 | 50b orange | .20 | .30 |
| 560 | A189 | 4.50 l brown | .20 | .30 |
| 561 | A188 | 11 l lt ultra | .20 | .30 |
| 562 | A189 | 15 l Prus grn | .20 | .30 |
| 563 | A189 | 31 l dl vio | .20 | .30 |
| 564 | A188 | 35 l bl blk | .20 | .30 |
| 565 | A189 | 41 l olive gray | .75 | .40 |
| 566 | A189 | 55 l red brown | .20 | .40 |
| 567 | A189 | 61 l deep magenta | 3.20 | 4.00 |

Nos. 558-567,B251 (11)

Romania's liberation.

---

A198 · A199 · A200 · A201 — **King Michael**

**Photo.**

**1945**

| | | | | |
|---|---|---|---|---|
| 568 | A198 | 50b gray blue | .20 | .20 |
| 569 | A199 | 1 l dl brn | .20 | .20 |
| 570 | A199 | 2 l violet | .20 | .20 |
| 571 | A190 | 4 l yel grn | .20 | .20 |
| 572 | A199 | 4 l sepia | .20 | .20 |
| 573 | A200 | 5 l dl vio | .20 | .20 |
| 574 | A198 | 5 l blue | .20 | .20 |
| 575 | A199 | 15 l magenta | .20 | .20 |
| 576 | A198 | 20 l dl blue | .20 | .20 |
| 577 | A200 | 25 l red org | .20 | .20 |
| 578 | A200 | 35 l brown | .20 | .20 |
| 579 | A200 | 40 l car rose | .20 | .20 |
| 580 | A199 | 50 l pale ultra | .20 | .20 |
| 581 | A199 | 55 l red | .20 | .20 |
| 582 | A200 | 75 l Prus grn | .20 | .20 |
| 583 | A201 | 80 l orange | .20 | .20 |
| 584 | A201 | 100 l dp red brn | .20 | .20 |
| 585 | A200 | 160 l yel grn | .20 | .20 |
| 586 | A201 | 200 l dk ol grn | .20 | .20 |
| 587 | A201 | 400 l dl vio | 4.00 | 4.00 |

Nos. 568-587 (20)

Nos. 571, 573, 580, 581, 585 and 587 are printed on toned paper. Nos. 576, 577, 583, 584 and 586 on both toned and white papers, others on white paper only.
See Nos. 610-624, 651-660.

**Mail Carrier A202**

**Telegraph Operator A203**

**Lineman A204**

---

## Post Office, Bucharest — A205

**1945, July 20    Wmk. 276    Perf. 13**

| | | | | |
|---|---|---|---|---|
| 588 | A202 | 100 l dk brn | .90 | .90 |
| 589 | A203 | 100 l gray olive | .90 | .90 |
| 590 | A203 | 150 l brown | 1.50 | 1.50 |
| 591 | A203 | 150 l brt rose | 1.50 | 1.50 |
| 592 | A204 | 250 l lt gray el | 1.75 | 1.75 |
| 593 | A204 | 250 l blue | 1.75 | 1.75 |
| 594 | A205 | 500 l dp mag | 12.50 | 12.50 |
| | | | 20.80 | 20.80 |

Nos. 588-594 (7)

Issued in sheets of 4.

## I. Ionescu, G. Titeica, A. O. Idachimescu and V. Cristescu — A207

## Allegory of Learning — A208

**1945, Sept. 5    Perf. 13½**

| | | | | |
|---|---|---|---|---|
| 596 | A207 | 2 l sepia | .20 | .20 |
| 597 | A208 | 80 l bl blk | .20 | .20 |

50th anniversary of "Gazeta Matematica," mathematics journal.

## Cernavoda Bridge, 50th Anniv. — A209

**1945, Sept. 26    Perf. 14**

| | | | | |
|---|---|---|---|---|
| 598 | A209 | 80 l bl blk | .25 | .20 |

## Blacksmith and Plowman — A210

**1946, Mar. 6**

| | | | | |
|---|---|---|---|---|
| 599 | A210 | 80 l blue | .25 | .20 |

Agrarian reform law of Mar. 23, 1945.

## Atheneum, Bucharest — A211

## Numeral in Wreath — A212

---

## Georges Enescu — A213

## Mechanic — A214

**1946, Apr. 26    Wmk. 276    Photo.    Perf. 13½**

| | | | | |
|---|---|---|---|---|
| 600 | A211 | 100 l dk brn | .20 | .20 |
| 601 | A212 | 20 l red brn | .20 | .20 |
| 602 | A212 | 55 l peacock bl | .20 | .20 |
| 603 | A213 | 80 l purple | .60 | .60 |
| a. | | Tête bêche pair | 2.50 | 2.50 |
| 604 | A212 | 160 l red org | .20 | .20 |

Nos. 600-604,B330-B331 (7)

Philharmonic Society, 25th anniv.

**1946, May 1    Perf. 13½x13**

Labor Day: No. 606, Laborer. No. 607, Sower. No. 608, Reaper. 200 l, Students.

| | | | | |
|---|---|---|---|---|
| 605 | A214 | 100 l Prus grn | .40 | .40 |
| 606 | A214 | 100 l dk car rose | .40 | .40 |
| 607 | A214 | 200 l dl bl | .20 | .20 |
| 608 | A214 | 200 l dk red brn | .20 | .20 |
| 609 | A214 | 200 l brt red | 1.40 | 1.40 |

Nos. 605-609 (5)

**Michael Types of 1945**

**1946    Wmk. 276    Photo.    Perf. 14**

**Toned Paper**

| | | | | |
|---|---|---|---|---|
| 610 | A198 | 10 l brt red brn | .20 | .20 |
| 611 | A198 | 10 l vio brn | .20 | .20 |
| 612 | A201 | 80 l blue | .20 | .20 |
| 613 | A198 | 137 l yel grn | .20 | .20 |
| 614 | A201 | 160 l chalky bl | .20 | .20 |
| 615 | A201 | 200 l red org | .20 | .20 |
| 616 | A201 | 300 l sapphire | .20 | .20 |
| 617 | A201 | 360 l sepia | .20 | .20 |
| 618 | A199 | 480 l brn red | .20 | .20 |
| 619 | A201 | 480 l red org | .20 | .20 |
| 620 | A201 | 600 l dk ol grn | .20 | .20 |
| 621 | A201 | 1000 l Prus grn | .20 | .20 |
| 622 | A198 | 1500 l Prus grn | .20 | .20 |
| 623 | A201 | 2400 l magenta | .20 | .20 |
| 624 | A201 | 3700 l dull bl | 3.00 | 3.00 |

Nos. 610-624 (15)

## Demetrius Cantemir — A219

## Soccer — A222

Designs: 100 l, "Cultural Ties." 300 l, "Economic Ties."

**1946, Oct. 20    Perf. 13½**

| | | | | |
|---|---|---|---|---|
| 625 | A219 | 80 l dk brn | .20 | .20 |
| 626 | A219 | 100 l dp bl | .20 | .20 |
| 627 | A219 | 300 l bl blk | 1.10 | .85 |

Nos. 625-627,B338 (4)

Romania-Soviet friendship. See No. B339.

**1946, Sept. 1    Perf. 11½, Imperf.**

Designs: 20 l, Diving. 50 l, Running. 80 l, Mountain climbing.

| | | | | |
|---|---|---|---|---|
| 628 | A222 | 100 l dp blue | .35 | .35 |
| 629 | A222 | 20 l brt red | .35 | .35 |
| 630 | A222 | 50 l dp violet | .35 | .35 |
| 631 | A222 | 80 l chocolate | 3.40 | 3.65 |

Nos. 628-631,B340,C26,CB6 (7)

Issued in sheets of 16.

## Weaving — A226

## Child Receiving Bread — A227

---

## Transporting Relief Supplies — A228

## CGM Congress Emblem — A229

**1946, Nov. 20    Wmk. 276    Photo.    Perf. 14**

| | | | | |
|---|---|---|---|---|
| 636 | A226 | 80 l dk ol brn | .20 | .20 |
| | | Nos. 636,B342-B345 (5) | 1.00 | 1.00 |

Democratic Women's Org. of Romania. See No. CB7.

**1947, Jan. 15    Perf. 13½x14, 14x13½**

| | | | | |
|---|---|---|---|---|
| 637 | A227 | 300 l dk ol brn | .20 | .20 |
| 638 | A228 | 600 l magenta | .20 | .20 |
| | | Nos. 637-638,B346-B347 (4) | .80 | .80 |

Social relief fund. See #B348.

## Peace in Chariot — A230

## Peace — A231

**1947, Feb. 10    Perf. 13½**

| | | | | |
|---|---|---|---|---|
| 639 | A229 | 200 l blue | .25 | .25 |
| 640 | A229 | 300 l orange | .30 | .30 |
| a. | | Pair, #639-640 | .75 | .75 |
| b. | | Pair, #640-641 | 1.00 | 1.00 |
| 641 | A229 | 600 l crimson | 1.05 | 1.05 |

Nos. 639-641 (3)

Congress of the United Labor Unions ("CGM").
Printed in sheets of 18 comprising 3 pairs of each denomination. Sheet yields 3 each of Nos. 640a and 640b.

## Flags of US, Russia, GB & Romania — A232

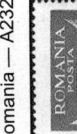

## Dove of Peace — A233

**1947, Feb. 25    Perf. 14x13½, 13½x14**

| | | | | |
|---|---|---|---|---|
| 642 | A230 | 1 l dl vio | .20 | .30 |
| 643 | A231 | 600 l dk org brn | .20 | .30 |
| 644 | A232 | 3000 l blue | .20 | .30 |
| 645 | A233 | 7200 l sage grn | .80 | 1.20 |

Nos. 642-645 (4)

Signing of the peace treaty of Feb. 10, 1947.

## King Michael — A234

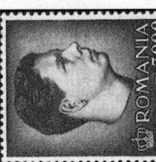

**1947**

**Perf. 13½**

| 646 | A234 | 3000 l blue | .20 | .20 |
| 647 | A234 | 7200 l di vio | .20 | .20 |
| 648 | A234 | 15,000 l brt bl | .20 | .20 |
| 649 | A234 | 21,000 l magenta | .20 | .20 |
| 650 | A234 | 36,000 l violet | 1.05 | 1.00 |

Nos. 646-650 (5)

See Nos. 661-664.

**Michael Types of 1945**

**1947, Wmk. 276 Photo. Perf. 14**

| 651 | A199 | 10 l red brn | .20 | .20 |
| 652 | A199 | 20 l magenta | .20 | .20 |
| 653 | A199 | 80 l blue | .20 | .20 |
| 654 | A199 | 200 l brt red | .20 | .20 |
| 655 | A199 | 500 l magenta | .20 | .20 |
| 656 | A200 | 860 l vio brn | .20 | .20 |
| 657 | A199 | 2500 l ultra | .20 | .20 |
| 658 | A199 | 5000 l sl gray | .20 | .20 |
| 659 | A198 | 5000 l Prus grn | .35 | .20 |
| 660 | A201 | 10,000 l red org | .25 | .20 |

Nos. 651-664 (14)

**Type of 1947**

**Size: 18x21½mm**

| 661 | A234 | 1000 l gray bl | .20 | .20 |
| 662 | A234 | 5000 l yel grn | .20 | .20 |
| 663 | A234 | 20,000 l ol brn | .20 | .20 |
| 664 | A234 | 50,000 l red org | 3.15 | 2.80 |

For surcharge see No. B368.

**Harvesting Wheat — A235**

**1947, Aug. 15 Perf. 14½x14**

| 666 | A235 | 50b red org | .20 | .20 |
| 667 | A235 | 1 l red brn | .20 | .20 |
| 668 | A235 | 3 l bl gray | .20 | .20 |
| 669 | A235 | 5 l rose crim | .20 | .20 |
| 670 | A235 | 6 l brt ultra | .25 | .20 |
| 671 | A235 | 10 l brt blue | .25 | .20 |
| 672 | A235 | 12 l violet | .55 | .20 |
| 673 | A235 | 15 l dp ultra | 1.00 | .20 |
| 674 | A235 | 20 l dk brown | 1.00 | .50 |
| 675 | A235 | 32 l violet brn | 2.00 | .25 |
| 676 | A235 | 36 l dk car rose | 7.15 | 2.60 |

For overprints & surcharge see #684-694, B369.

Designs: 1 l, Log raft. 2 l, River steamer. 3 l, Resita. 5 l, Cathedral of Curtea de Arges. 10 l, View of Bucharest. 12 l, 36 l, Cernavoda Bridge. 15 l, 32 l, Port of Constantsa. 20 l, Petroleum field.

**Beehive, Savings Emblem — A236**

**1947, Oct. 31 Perf. 13½**

| 677 | A236 | 12 l dk car rose | .30 | .20 |

World Savings Day, Oct. 31, 1947.

**People's Republic**

**1948, Jan. 25 Perf. 14½x14**

| 678 | A237 | 12 l brt ultra | .35 | .20 |

1948 census. For surcharge see #819A.

**Map, Workers and Children — A237**

---

**1948**

**Government Printing Plant and Press — A238**

75th anniversary of Stamp Division of Romanian State Printing Works.

Issued: No. 680, Feb. 12; No. 679, May 20.

**1948 Perf. 14½x14**

| 679 | A238 | 6 l magenta | .90 | .50 |
| 680 | A238 | 7.50 l dk Prus grn | .60 | .20 |
| b. | | Tête bêche pair | 1.50 | .90 |
| 680A | A239 | 32 l red brown | .50 | .20 |

**1948, Mar. 25 Wmk. 276**

Romanian-Bulgarian friendship.

For surcharge see No. 696.

**Romanian and Bulgarian Peasants Shaking Hands — A239**

**Allegory of the People's Republic — A240**

**1948, Apr. 8 Photo. Perf. 14x14½**

| 681 | A240 | 2 l car rose | .30 | .20 |
| 682 | A240 | 3 l dl org | .40 | .30 |
| 683 | A240 | 12 l deep blue | 1.25 | .45 |

Nos. 681-683 (3)

New constitution.

For surcharge see No. 820.

**R·P·R·**

Nos. 666 to 676 Overprinted in Black

**1948, Mar. Perf. 14½x14**

| 684 | A235 | 50b red org | .30 | .20 |
| 685 | A235 | 1 l red brn | .30 | .20 |
| 686 | A235 | 3 l bl gray | .30 | .20 |
| 687 | A235 | 5 l rose crim | .55 | .20 |
| 688 | A235 | 6 l brt ultra | .90 | .20 |
| 689 | A235 | 10 l brt bl | 1.25 | .20 |
| 690 | A235 | 12 l violet | 1.40 | .20 |
| 691 | A235 | 15 l dp ultra | 1.40 | .30 |
| 692 | A235 | 20 l dk brn | 1.75 | .50 |
| 693 | A235 | 32 l vio brn | 4.50 | 1.50 |
| 694 | A235 | 36 l dk car rose | 17.40 | 5.25 |

Nos. 684-694 (11)

**Romanian Newspapers — A241**

**1948, Sept. 12 Perf. 14½x14**

| 695 | A241 | 10 l red brn | .30 | .20 |

Nos. 696,B396-B398 (4)

Week of the Democratic Press, Sept. 12-19.

**No. 680A Surcharged with New Value in Black**

**1948, Aug. 17**

| 696 | A239 | 31 l on 32 l red brn | .55 | .20 |

**Lenin, 25th Death Anniv. — A246**

**Release from Bondage — A245**

**1948, Dec. 30 Perf. 13½**

| 700 | A245 | 5 l brt rose | .40 | .20 |

First anniversary of the Republic.

---

**ROMANIA**

**Monument to Soviet Soldier — A242**

**1948, Oct. 29 Photo. Perf. 14x14½**

| 697 | A242 | 10 l dk red | .45 | .35 |

Nos. 697,B399-B400,CB16 (4) 10.70 10.60

Sheets of 50 stamps and 50 labels.

**Proclamation of Islaz — A243**

**1948, June 1 Perf. 14½x14**

| 698 | A243 | 11 l car rose | .35 | .20 |

Nos. 698,B409-B412 (5) 2.60 2.45

Centenary of Revolution of 1848.

For surcharge see No. 820A.

**Arms of Romanian People's Republic — A243a**

**1948, July 8 Wmk. 276**

| 698A | A243a | 50b red ("Lei 0.50") | .40 | .30 |
| 698B | A243a | 1 l red brn | .25 | .20 |
| 698C | A243a | 2 l dk grn | .25 | .20 |
| 698D | A243a | 3 l grnsh blk | .35 | .20 |
| 698E | A243a | 4 l chocolate | .35 | .20 |
| 698F | A243a | 5 l ultra | .35 | .20 |
| 698G | A243a | 10 l dp bl | 1.10 | .20 |
| 698H | A243a | 50b red ("Bani 0.50") | .50 | .20 |

Nos. 698A-698H (8) 3.55 1.70

**"Bani" instead of "Lei"**

See Nos. 712-717.

**Nicolae Balcescu (1819-1852), Writer — A244**

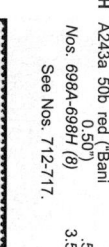

**1948, Dec. 20 Wmk. 289**

| 699 | A244 | 20 l scarlet | .35 | .20 |

---

**1949, Mar. 22 Perf. 14½x14**

| 703 | A248 | 20 l red | .35 | .20 |

Exists imperf. Values, unused 70c, used 35c.

**Ion C. Frimu and Revolutionary Scene — A248**

**Folk Dance — A247**

**1949, Jan. 21 Perf. 13½**

| 701 | A246 | 20 l black | .35 | .20 |

Exists imperf. Value, unused 70c, used 20c.

**1949, Jan. 24 Perf. 13½**

| 702 | A247 | 10 l dp bl | .35 | .20 |

90th anniv. of the union of the Danubian Principalities.

**Aleksander S. Pushkin, 150th Birth Anniv. — A249**

**1949, May 20 Perf. 14x14½**

| 704 | A249 | 11 l car rose | .50 | .20 |
| 705 | A249 | 30 l Prus grn | .70 | .30 |

For surcharges see Nos. 821-822.

**Evolution of Mail Transportation — A251**

**1949, June 30 Photo. Wmk. 289 Perf. 13½, 14½x14**

| 706 | A250 | 20 l dk brn | 1.50 | .90 |
| 707 | A251 | 30 l brt bl | 1.10 | .60 |

UPU, 75th anniv.

For surcharges see Nos. C43-C44.

**Globe and Post Horn — A250**

**Russian Army Entering Bucharest, August, 1944 — A252**

**1949, Aug. 23 Perf. 14½x14**

| 708 | A252 | 50 l choc, bl grn | .65 | .30 |

5th anniv. of the liberation of Romania by the Soviet army, Aug. 1944.

Exists imperf. Values, unused $1.30, used 40c.

ROMANIA

"Long Live Romanian-Soviet Amity" — A253

**Perf. 13½x14½**
709 A253 20 l dp red .35 .20
Natl. week of Romanian-Soviet friendship celebration, 11/1-7/49. Exists imperf. Values, unused 70c., used 20c.

Symbols of Transportation A254

Joseph V. Stalin — A256

**1949, Dec. 10  Wmk. 289  Perf. 13½**
710 A254 11 l blue .75 .65
711 A254 20 l crimson .75 .65
Intl. Conference of Transportation Unions, Dec. 10, 1949.
Alternate vertical rows of stamps and labels in sheet. Exist imperf. Value for set, unused $2.50, used $1.80.

**1949-50  Wmk. 289  Perf. 14x13½**
712 A243a sub red ("Lei 0.50") .35 .20
713 A243a 1 l red brn .35 .20
714 A243a 2 l dk grn .35 .20
714A A243a 3 l grnsh blk .65 .20
716 A243a 5 l ultra .50 .20
716 A243a 6 l rose vio (′50) .70 .20
717 A243a 10 l dp blue .90 .20
3.80 1.40
Nos. 712-717 (7)

**1949, Dec. 21  Perf. 13½**
718 A256 31 l olive black .50 .20
Stalin's 70th birthday. Exists imperf. Values, unused $1.50, used 20c.

Mihail Eminescu — A257

Poem: "Life" — A258

"Third Letter." #722, "Angel and Demon." #723, "Emperor and Proletariat."

**1950, Jan. 15  Photo.  Wmk. 289**
719 A257 11 l blue .50 .25
720 A258 11 l purple 1.00 .45
721 A258 11 l dk grn .50 .25
722 A258 11 l red brn .90 .25
723 A258 41 l rose pink 3.00 1.45
Birth cent. of Mihail Eminescu, poet.
For surcharges see Nos. 823-827.

---

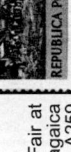 

Fair at Dragaica A259

Ion Andreescu (Self-portrait) A260

Village Well A261

**1950, Mar. 25  Perf. 14½x14, 14x14½**
724 A259 5 l dk gray grn .40 .30
725 A260 11 l ultra .75 .30
726 A261 20 l brown .85 .50
2.00 1.10
Nos. 724-726 (3)
Birth cent. of Ion Andreescu, painter. No. 725 also exists imperf. Values, unused $1.50, used 60c.
For surcharges see Nos. 827A-827B.

Graph and Factories A262

Design: 31 l, Tractor and Oil Derricks.
Inscribed: "Planul de Stat 1950."

**Perf. 14½x14**
**1950, Apr. 23  Wmk. 289**
727 A262 11 l red .85 .20
728 A262 31 l violet .90 .25
1950 plan for increased industrial production. No. 727 exists imperf. Values, unused 80c., used 20c.
For surcharges see Nos. 827C-827D.

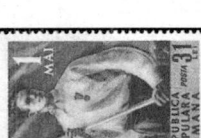

Young Man Holding Flag A263

**1950, May 1  Perf. 14x14½**
729 A263 31 l orange red .60 .20
Labor Day, May 1.
Exists imperf. Value, unused 70c., used 20c.
For surcharge see No. 827E.

Arms of Republic A264

**Canceled to Order**
Canceled sets of new issues have long been sold by the government. Values in the second ("used") column are for these canceled-to-order stamps. Postally used copies are worth more.

**1950  Photo.  Perf. 12½**
730 A264 50b black .20 .20
731 A264 1 l red .20 .20
732 A264 3 l violet .20 .20
733 A264 4 l rose lilac .20 .20
734 A264 5 l red brn .20 .20
735 A264 6 l dp grn .20 .20
736 A264 7 l vio brn .20 .20

---

737 A264 7 l vio brn .20 .20
738 A264 7.50 l blue .25 .20
739 A264 10 l dk brn .40 .20
740 A264 11 l rose car .40 .20
741 A264 15 l dp bl .25 .20
742 A264 20 l Prus grn .40 .20
743 A264 31 l dl grn .40 .30
744 A264 36 l dk org brn .60 .30
4.15 3.10
Nos. 730-744 (15)
See Nos. 947-961 which have similar design with white denomination figures. For overprint & surcharges see #758, 828-841.

Bugler and Drummer A265

Designs: 11 l, Three school children. 31 l, Drummer, flag-bearer and bugler.

**1950, May 25  Perf. 14½x14**
745 A265 8 l blue .65 .30
746 A265 11 l rose vio .85 .50
747 A265 31 l org ver 1.50 1.10
3.00 1.90
Nos. 745-747 (3)
Young Pioneers, 1st anniv.
For surcharges see Nos. 841A-841C.

Aurel Vlaicu and his First Plane — A267

Factory Worker — A266

**1950, July 20  Photo.  Perf. 14x14½**
748 A266 11 l red brn .40 .20
749 A266 11 l red .45 .20
750 A266 11 l bl .30 .20
751 A266 11 l blk brn .45 .30
1.50 .90
Nos. 748-751 (4)
Nationalization of industry, 2nd anniv.

**1950, July 22  Wmk. 289  Perf. 12½**
752 A267 3 l dk grn .35 .20
753 A267 6 l dk bl .40 .20
754 A267 8 l ultra .50 .25
1.25 .65
Nos. 752-754 (3)
Aurel Vlaicu (1882-1913), pioneer of Romanian aviation.
For surcharges see Nos. 842-844.

Lathe and Operator — A269

Mother and Child — A268

**1950, Sept. 9  Perf. 13½**
755 A268 11 l rose red .30 .20
756 A269 20 l dk ol brn .35 .20
Congress of the Committees for the Struggle for Peace.
For surcharge see No. 844A.

---

Statue of Soviet Soldier — A270

**1950, Oct. 6  Perf. 14x14½**
757 A270 30 l red brn .50 .25
Celebration of Romanian-Soviet friendship, Oct. 7-Nov. 7, 1950.

No. 741 Overprinted in Carmine

**1950, Oct. 6  Perf. 12½x14**
758 A264 15 l deep blue .40 .20
Romanian-Hungarian friendship.

"Agriculture," "Manufacturing" and Sports Badge — A271

5 l, Student workers & badge. 11 l, Track team & badge. 31 l, Calisthenics & badge.

**1950, Oct. 30  Perf. 14½x14**
759 A271 3 l rose car .65 .50
760 A271 5 l rose brn .35 .35
761 A271 5 l brt bl .60 .30
762 A271 11 l green 1.25 1.00
763 A271 31 l brn ol 3.40 2.55
Nos. 759-763 (5)
For surcharge see No. 845.

A272

"Industry" — A273

"Agriculture" — A274

**1950, Nov. 2  Perf. 13½**
764 A272 11 l blue .30 .20
765 A272 11 l red org .30 .20
3rd Soviet-Romanian Friendship Congress.

## 1951, Feb. 9 Photo. Wmk. 289
**Perf. 14x14½, 14½x14**

| | | | | |
|---|---|---|---|---|
| 766 | A273 | 11 l red brn | .20 | .20 |
| 767 | A274 | 31 l deep bl | .40 | .20 |

Industry and Agriculture Exposition. Exist imperf. Value for set, unused $1.50, used 40c.
For surcharge see No. 846.

Ski Jump — A275

Ski Descent A276

## 1951, Jan. 28 Perf. 13½

| | | | | |
|---|---|---|---|---|
| 768 | A275 | 4 l blk brn | 1.00 | .60 |
| 769 | A275 | 5 l vermilion | .75 | .45 |
| 770 | A276 | 11 l dp bl | .75 | .45 |
| 771 | A276 | 20 l org brn | .75 | .45 |
| 772 | A275 | 31 l dk gray grn | 5.00 | 3.05 |
| | | Nos. 768-772 (5) | | |

9th World University Winter Games. For surcharges see Nos. 847-848.
5 l, Skating, 20 l, Hockey, 31 l, Bobsledding.

Medal for Work — A277

## 1951, May 1 Perf. 13½

| | | | | |
|---|---|---|---|---|
| 773 | A277 | 2 l ol gray | .25 | .20 |
| 774 | A277 | 4 l blue | .30 | .20 |
| 775 | A277 | 11 l crimson | .40 | .25 |
| 776 | A277 | 35 l org brn | .50 | .30 |
| | | Nos. 773-776 (4) | 1.45 | .95 |

Orders: 4 l, Star of the Republic, Classes III, IV & V. 11 l, Work. 35 l, As 4 l, Classes I & II.
Labor Day. Exist imperf. Value for set, unused $1.65, used 95c.
For surcharges see Nos. 849-852.

Pioneers Greeting Stalin — A279

Camp of Young Pioneers A278

Stalin — A279

Admitting New Pioneers A280

## 1951, May 8 Perf. 14x14½, 14½x14

| | | | | |
|---|---|---|---|---|
| 777 | A278 | 2 l gray grn | .90 | .45 |
| 778 | A279 | 11 l blue | .90 | .45 |
| 779 | A280 | 35 l red | 1.25 | .70 |
| | | Nos. 777-779 (3) | 3.05 | 1.60 |

Romanian Young Pioneers Organization. For surcharge see No. 853.

---

Woman Orator and Flags — A281

Ion Negulici — A282

## 1951, Mar. 8 Perf. 14x14½

| | | | | |
|---|---|---|---|---|
| 780 | A281 | 11 l org brn | .40 | .20 |
| 781 | A282 | 11 l dk brn | .40 | .20 |

Woman's Day, March 8. Exists imperf. Values, unused 50c, used 20c.

## 1951, June 20 Perf. 14x14½

| | | | | |
|---|---|---|---|---|
| 782 | A283 | 11 l rose red | 2.00 | 1.25 |
| a. | | Tête bêche pair | | |

Death cent. of Ion Negulici, painter.

Bicyclists A283

## 1951, July 9

| | | | | |
|---|---|---|---|---|
| 782 | A283 | 11 l chnt brn | 1.50 | .50 |

The 1951 Bicycle Tour of Romania.

Festival Badge — A284

Youths Encircling Globe — A286

Boy and Girl with Flag — A285

## 1951, Aug. 1 Perf. 13½

| | | | | |
|---|---|---|---|---|
| 783 | A284 | 1 l scarlet | .40 | .25 |
| 784 | A285 | 5 l deep blue | .75 | .25 |
| 785 | A286 | 11 l deep plum | 2.25 | 1.00 |
| | | Nos. 783-785 (3) | | |

3rd World Youth Festival, Berlin.

Filimon Sarbu — A287

"Romania Raising the Masses" — A288

## 1951, July 23 Perf. 14x14½, 14½x14

| | | | | |
|---|---|---|---|---|
| 786 | A287 | 11 l dk brn | .35 | .20 |

10th death anniv. of Filimon Sarbu, patriot.

"Revolutionary Romania" — A289

## 1951, July 23 Perf. 14x14½, 14½x14

| | | | | |
|---|---|---|---|---|
| 787 | A288 | 11 l yel brn | 1.50 | .60 |
| 788 | A288 | 11 l rose vio | 1.50 | .60 |
| 789 | A289 | 11 l dk grn | 1.50 | .60 |
| 790 | A289 | 11 l org red | 1.50 | .60 |
| | | Nos. 787-790 (4) | 6.00 | 2.40 |

Death cent. of C. D. Rosenthal, painter.

Scanteia Building A290

## 1951, Aug. 16 Perf. 14x14½

| | | | | |
|---|---|---|---|---|
| 791 | A290 | 11 l blue | .40 | .25 |

20th anniv. of the newspaper Scanteia.

Miner in Dress Uniform — A291

Order for National Defense — A293

Design: 11 l, Miner in work clothes.

## 1951, Aug. 12 Perf. 14x14½

| | | | | |
|---|---|---|---|---|
| 792 | A291 | 5 l blue | .35 | .25 |
| 793 | A291 | 11 l plum | .45 | .20 |

Miner's Day. For surcharge see #854.

## 1951, Aug. 12

| | | | | |
|---|---|---|---|---|
| 794 | A293 | 10 l crimson | .45 | .20 |

For surcharge see No. 855.

Music Week Emblem — A295

Choir — A294

## 1951, Sept. 22 Wmk. 358 Photo. Perf. 13½

| | | | | |
|---|---|---|---|---|
| 795 | A294 | 11 l blue | .35 | .35 |
| 796 | A294 | 11 l red brown | .50 | .30 |
| 797 | A295 | 11 l purple | 1.20 | .80 |
| | | Nos. 795-797 (3) | | |

Music Week, Sept. 22-30, 1951.
Design: No. 796, Orchestra and dancers.

---

Soldier — A296

Oil Field — A297

## 1951, Oct. 2

| | | | | |
|---|---|---|---|---|
| 798 | A296 | 11 l blue | .35 | .20 |

Army Day, Oct. 2, 1951.

## 1951-52

Designs: 2 l, Coal mining. 3 l, Romanian soldier. 4 l, Smelting ore. 5 l, Agricultural machinery. 6 l, Canal construction. 7 l, Agriculture. 8 l, Self-education. 11 l, Hydroelectric production. 35 l, Manufacturing.

| | | | | |
|---|---|---|---|---|
| 799 | A297 | 1 l black brn | .30 | .20 |
| 800 | A297 | 2 l chocolate | .20 | .20 |
| 801 | A297 | 3 l scarlet | .35 | .25 |
| 802 | A297 | 4 l yel brn ('52) | .25 | .20 |
| 803 | A297 | 5 l green | .25 | .20 |
| 804 | A297 | 6 l brt bl ('52) | 1.00 | .40 |
| 805 | A297 | 7 l emerald | .60 | .40 |
| 806 | A297 | 8 l brown ('52) | .50 | .40 |
| 807 | A297 | 11 l brown | .35 | .20 |
| 808 | A297 | 35 l purple | 8.00 | 5.95 |
| | | Nos. 799-808, C35-C36 (12) | | |

1951-55 Five Year Plan.
2 l and 11 l exist with wmk. 289. Values same. For surcharges see Nos. 860-869.

Arms of Soviet Union and Romania A298

## 1951, Oct. 7 Wmk. 358

| | | | | |
|---|---|---|---|---|
| 809 | A298 | 4 l chestnut brn, cr | .80 | .30 |
| 810 | A298 | 35 l orange red | .85 | .45 |

Month of Romanian-Soviet friendship, Oct. 7-Nov. 7. For surcharges see Nos. 870-871.

Pavel Tcacenco A299

## 1951, Dec. 15 Perf. 14x14½

| | | | | |
|---|---|---|---|---|
| 811 | A299 | 10 l ol brn & dk brn | .40 | .25 |

Revolutionary, 26th death anniv. For surcharge see No. 872.

Railroad Conductor A300

## 1952, Mar. 24 Perf. 13½

| | | | | |
|---|---|---|---|---|
| 812 | A300 | 55b dark brown | 1.60 | .40 |

Railroad Workers' Day, Feb. 16.

Ion L. Caragiale — A301

Announcing Caragiale Celebration — A302

Designs: No. 814, Book and painting "1907." No. 815, Bust and wreath.

**1952, Apr. 1** *Perf. 13½, 14½x14*

**Inscribed: ". . . . I. L. Caragiale."**

**813** A301 55b chalky blue .90 .25
**814** A302 55b scarlet .90 .25
**815** A302 55b deep green .90 .25
**816** A302 1 l brown 2.50 .40
*Nos. 813-816 (4)* 5.20 1.15

Birth cent. of Ion L. Caragiale, dramatist.
For surcharges see Nos. 817-819.

Types of 1952 Surcharged with New Value in Black or Carmine

**1952-53**
**817** A302 20b on 11 l scar (as #814) 1.00 .60
**818** A302 55b on 11 l dp grn (as #815) (C) 1.40 .75
**819** A301 75b on 11 l chlky bl (C) 2.40 1.00

**Various Issues Surcharged with New Values in Carmine or Black**

**On No. 678, Census**

*Perf. 14x13½*

**819A** A237 50b on 12 l ultra 6.75 3.75

**On No. 683, New Constitution**

*Perf. 14*

**820** A240 50b on 12 l dp bl 2.75 1.25

**On No. 698, Revolution**

**820A** A243 1.75 l on 11 l car rose (Bk) 25.00 12.00

**On Nos. 704-705, Pushkin**

**1952** **Wmk. 358**
**821** A249 10b on 11 l (Bk) 2.50 1.75
**822** A249 10b on 30 l 2.50 1.75

**On Nos. 719-723, Eminescu**

*Perf. 13½x13, 13x13½*

**823** A257 10b on 11 l blue 2.25 1.75
**824** A258 10b on 11 l pur 2.25 1.75
**825** A258 10b on 11 l dk grn 2.25 1.75
**826** A258 10b on 11 l red brn (Bk) 2.25 1.75
**827** A258 10b on 11 l rose pink (Bk) 3.50 1.75

**On Nos. 724-725, Andreescu**

*Perf. 14*

**827A** A259 55b on 5 l dk gray grn 7.50 2.75
**827B** A260 55b on 11 l ultra 5.00 2.75

**On Nos. 727-728, Production Plan**

*Perf. 14½x14*

**827C** A262 20b on 11 l red (Bk) 2.00 .75
**827D** A262 20b on 31 l vio 3.75 .75

**On No. 729, Labor Day**

*Perf. 14*

**827E** A263 55b on 31 l (Bk) 3.75 2.75

**On Nos. 730-739 and 741-744, National Arms**

*Perf. 12½*

**828** A264 3b on 1 l red (Bk) .70 .45
**829** A264 3b on 2 l ol gray (Bk) 1.10 .55
**830** A264 3b on 4 l rose lil (Bk) .70 .30
**831** A264 3b on 5 l red brn (Bk) 1.10 .55
**832** A264 3b on 7.50 l bl (Bk) 3.25 1.40
**833** A264 3b on 10 l dk brn (Bk) 1.10 .55
**834** A264 55b on 50b blk brn 3.25 .45
**835** A264 55b on 3 l vio 3.25 .45
**836** A264 55b on 6 l dp grn 3.25 .45
**837** A264 55b on 7 l vio brn 3.25 .45
**838** A264 55b on 15 l dp bl 5.00 .45
**839** A264 55b on 20 l Prus grn 3.25 .45
**840** A264 55b on 31 l dl grn 3.25 .45
**841** A264 55b on 36 l dk org brn 5.00 .45

**On Nos. 745-747, Young Pioneers**

*Perf. 14*

**841A** A265 55b on 8 l 10.00 5.75
**841B** A265 55b on 11 l 10.00 5.75
**841C** A265 55b on 31 l (Bk) 10.00 5.75

**On Nos. 752-754, Vlaicu**

*Perf. 12½*

**842** A267 10b on 3 l dk grn 1.50 .75
**843** A267 10b on 6 l dk bl 1.50 .75
**844** A267 10b on 8 l ultra 1.50 .75

Original denomination canceled with an "X."

**On No. 756, Peace Congress**

*Perf. 13½*

**844A** A269 20b on 20 l 2.25 1.25

**On No. 759, Sports**

*Perf. 14½x14*

**845** A271 55b on 3 l (Bk) 15.00 11.50

**On No. 767, Exposition**

**846** A274 55b on 31 l dp bl 9.00 5.75

**On Nos. 771-772, Winter Games**

*Perf. 13½*

**847** A275 55b on 20 l (Bk) 25.00 8.00
**848** A275 55b on 31 l 25.00 8.00

**On Nos. 773-776, Labor Medals**

**849** A277 20b on 2 l 3.75 2.25
**850** A277 20b on 4 l 3.75 2.25
**851** A277 20b on 11 l (Bk) 3.75 2.25
**852** A277 20b on 35 l (Bk) 3.75 2.25

**On Nov. 779, Young Pioneers**

*Perf. 14x14½*

**853** A280 55b on 35 l (Bk) 15.00 9.50

**On No. 792, Miners' Day**

**854** A291 55b on 5 l bl 11.00 7.50

**On No. 794, Defense Order**

**855** A293 55b on 10 l (Bk) 6.00 3.75

**On Nos. B409-B412, 1848 Revolution**

**1952** **Wmk. 276** *Perf. 13x13½*
**856** SP280 1.75 l on 2 l + 2 l (Bk) 11.50 3.75
**857** SP281 1.75 l on 5 l + 5 l 11.50 3.75
**858** SP282 1.75 l on 10 l + 10 l 11.50 3.75
**859** SP280 1.75 l on 36 l + 18 l 11.50 3.75

**On Nos. 799-808, 5-Year Plan**

**Wmk. 358** *Perf. 13½*
**860** A297 35b on 1 l blk brn 1.90 .65
**861** A297 35b on 2 l choc 6.00 .75
**862** A297 35b on 3 l scar (Bk) 3.00 1.25
**863** A297 35b on 4 l yel brn (Bk) 3.50 1.50
a. Red surcharge 25.00 6.00
**864** A297 35b on 5 l grn 3.00 2.00
**865** A297 1 l on 6 l brt bl 4.75 3.00
**866** A297 1 l on 7 l emer 3.50 1.50
**867** A297 1 l on 8 l brn 3.50 2.25
**868** A297 1 l on 11 l bl 4.75 1.75
**869** A297 1 l on 35 l pur 4.75 1.50

Nos. 861, 868 exist with wmk. 289.

**On Nos. 809-810, Romanian-Soviet Friendship**

**870** A298 10b on 4 l (Bk) 1.50 .65
**871** A298 10b on 35 l (Bk) 1.50 .65

**On No. 811, Tcacenco**

*Perf. 13½x14*

**872** A299 10b on 10 l 1.90 .90

A302a

A303

*Perf. 13½x13*

**1952, Apr. 14** **Photo.** **Wmk. 358**
**873** A302a 1 l Ivan P. Pavlov 1.75 .40

Meeting of Romanian-Soviet doctors in Bucharest.

**1952, May 1**
**874** A303 55b Hammer & sickle medal .75 .20

Labor Day.

Medal for Motherhood A304

Leonardo da Vinci A305

Medals: 55b, Maternal glory. 1.75 l, Mother-Heroine.

**1952, Apr. 7** *Perf. 13x13½*
**875** A304 20b plum & sl gray .30 .20
**876** A304 55b henna brn .70 .20
**877** A304 1.75 l rose red & brn buff 1.75 .40
*Nos. 875-877 (3)* 2.75 .80

International Women's Day.

**1952, July 3**
**878** A305 55b purple 2.10 .50

500th birth anniv. of Leonardo da Vinci.

Gogol and Scene from Taras Bulba A306

Nikolai V. Gogol — A307

**1952, Apr. 1** *Perf. 13½x14, 14x13½*
**879** A306 55b deep blue 1.25 .20
**880** A307 1.75 l olive gray 2.00 .40

Gogol, Russian writer, death cent.

Pioneers Saluting — A308

Labor Day Paraders Returning A309

Design: 55b, Pioneers studying nature.

**1952, May 21** *Perf. 14*
**881** A308 20b brown .45 .20
**882** A308 55b dp green 1.25 .20
**883** A309 1.75 l blue 2.10 .40
*Nos. 881-883 (3)* 3.80 .80

Third anniversary of Romanian Pioneers.

Infantry Attack, Painting by Grigorescu A310

Miner — A311

1.10 l, Romanian and Russian soldiers.

**1952, June 7** *Perf. 13x13½*
**884** A310 50b rose brown .50 .20
**885** A310 1.10 l blue .80 .25

Independence Proclamation of 1877, 75th anniv.

**1952, Aug. 11** **Wmk. 358**
**902** A311 20b rose red 1.40 .25
**903** A311 55b purple 1.40 .20

Day of the Miner.

Book and Globe — A312

Students in Native Dress — A314

Chemistry Student A313

Design: 55b, Students playing soccer.

*Perf. 13½x13, 13½x14, 13x13½*

**1952, Sept. 5**
**904** A312 10b deep blue .30 .20
**905** A313 20b orange 1.75 .25
**906** A312 55b deep green 1.75 .35
**907** A314 1.75 l rose red 3.00 .55
*Nos. 904-907 (4)* 6.80 1.35

Intl. Student Union Congr., Bucharest, Sept.

Soldier, Sailor and Aviator — A316

**1952, Oct. 2** *Perf. 14*
**909** A316 55b blue .50 .20

Armed Forces Day, Oct. 2, 1952.

"Russia" Leading Peace Crusade — A317

Allegory: Romanian-Soviet
Friendship — A318

**1952, Oct. 7**    *Perf. 13½x13, 13x13½*
910 A317 55b vermilion .80 .20
911 A318 1.75 l black brown 2.10 .60

Month of Romanian-Soviet friendship, Oct.

Rowing on
Lake
Snagov — A319

Nicolae
Balcescu — A320

**1952, Oct. 20**
912 A319 20b deep blue 3.00 .50
913 A319 1.75 l rose red 5.50 1.10

Values are for copies with poor perforations.

1.75 l, Athletes marching with flags.

**1952, Nov. 29**
914 A320 55b gray 2.00 .50
915 A320 1.75 l lemon bister 4.00 1.25

Death cent. of Nicolae Balcescu, poet.

**1952, Dec. 6**    *Wmk. 358*
916 A321 55b dull green .75 .25

Arms of
Republic — A321

5th anniversary of socialist constitution.

**1953, Jan. 8**    *Perf. 12½x13½*
917 A322 55b blue, yellow & red .90 .35

5th anniv. of the proclamation of the People's Republic.

Arms and
Industrial
Symbols
A322

Matei Millo,
Costache
Caragiale and
Aristita
Romanescu
A323

**1953, Feb.**    *Photo.*    *Perf. 13x13½*
918 A323 55b brt ultra 1.50 .35

National Theater of I. L. Caragiale, cent.

---

Worker — A325

Iron Foundry
Worker — A324

**1953, Feb.**    *Perf. 13½x13, 13x13½*
919 A324 55b slate green .30 .20
920 A325 55b black brown .30 .20
929A A325 55b purple .25 .25
921 A325 55b orange 1.25 .65

Design: No. 921, Driving Tractor.

3rd Congress of the Syndicate of the
Romanian People's Republic.

"Strike at Grivita,"
Painted by G.
Miclossy
A326

**1953, Feb. 16**    *Perf. 13x13½*
922 A326 55b chestnut 1.25 .25

Oil industry strike, Feb. 16, 1933, 20th anniv.

**1953**
923 A327 5b crimson .25 .20
924 A327 55b purple 1.00 .20

Arms of
Romanian
People's
Republic
A327

**1953, Mar. 24**    *Perf. 12½*
925 A328 55b dk brn, *bl* 1.10 .25

5th anniv. of the signing of a treaty of friendship and mutual assistance between Russia
and Romania.

Flags of
Romania,
Russia,
Farm
Machinery
A328

Map and
Medal — A329

**1953, Mar. 24**
926 A329 55b dk gray green 4.00 .75
927 A329 55b chestnut 4.00 .75

20th World Championship Table Tennis
Matches, Budapest, 1953.

Folk Dance
— A330a

Rug — A330

**1953, May 24**
933 A332 35b deep green 1.10 .20
934 A332 55b dull blue 3.25 .45
935 A332 1.75 l brown 5.85 .85

Design: 55b, Flying model planes.

Nos. 933-935 (3)

Women and
Flags — A334

Students
Offering
Teacher
Flowers
A336

**1953, June 18**    *Perf. 13½x13*
936 A334 55b red brown 1.40 .25

3rd World Congress of Women, Copenhagen, 1953.

**1953, Aug. 2**    *Wmk. 358*    *Perf. 14*
937 A335 20b orange .60 .25
938 A335 55b deep blue 1.00 .35
939 A336 65b scarlet 1.00 .65
940 A336 1.75 l red violet 4.00 1.25

Designs: 55b, Students reaching toward
dove. 1.75 l, Dance in local costumes.

4th World Youth Festival, Bucharest, 8/2-16.

Nos. 937-940 (4)

Discus
Thrower — A335

---

**1953**
928 A330 10b deep green .75 .20
929 A330 20b red brown 1.25 .20
930 A330 35b purple 2.00 .20
930 A330 55b violet blue 3.00 .20
931 A330 1 l brt red violet 12.00 1.05

Designs: 10b, Ceramics. 20b, Costume of
Campulung (Muscel). 55b, Apuseni Mts.
costume.

Inscribed: "Arta Populara
Romaneasca"

Romanian Folk Arts.

Nos. 928-931 (5)

Karl Marx — A331

Physics
Class
A333

Children Planting
Tree — A332

**1953, May 21**    *Perf. 13½x13*
932 A331 1.55 l olive brown 1.90 .45

70th death anniv. of Karl Marx.

**1953, May 21**    *Perf. 14*

Vladimir V.
Mayakovsky, 60th
Birth
Anniv. — A339

Wheat
Field — A338

**1953, July 29**    *Photo.*
941 A338 20b violet blue .55 .20
942 A338 38b dull green 1.40 .30
943 A337 55b lt brown 1.50 .30
    3.45 1.00

Design: 55b, Forester holding seedling.

Month of the Forest.

Nos. 941-943 (3)

Waterfall — A337

Month of the Forest.

**1953, Aug. 22**
944 A339 55b brown .75 .25

Miner
Using Drill
A340

**1953, Sept. 19**
945 A340 1.55 l slate black 1.50 .40

Miners' Day.

Arms of
Republic — A342

**1952-53**     *Perf. 12½*

     *Size: 20x24mm*
947 A342 3b deep orange .60 .30
948 A342 5b crimson .80 .40
949 A342 7b dk blue grn .80 .20
950 A342 10b chocolate 1.00 .20
951 A342 20b deep blue 1.25 .20
952 A342 35b black brn 2.75 .20
953 A342 50b dk gray grn 3.25 .20
954 A342 55b purple 7.25 .20

     *Size: 24x29mm*
955 A342 1 l dk brown 6.50 .30
956 A342 1.75 l violet 24.00 .40
957 A342 2 l olive black 6.50 .20
958 A342 2.35 l orange brn 8.00 .35
959 A342 3 l dp orange 10.00 .40
960 A342 3 l dk gray grn 10.00 .35
961 A342 5 l deep crimson 94.70 4.50
    14.00 .70

Stamps of similar design with value figures
in color are Nos. 730-744.

Postal
Administration Building and
Telephone Employees — A343

Designs: 55b, Postal Adm. Bldg. and Letter carrier. 1 l, Map and communications symbols. 1.55 l, Postal Adm. Bldg. and Telegraph employees.

**1953, Oct. 20    Perf. 14    Wmk. 358**

| | | | |
|---|---|---|---|
| 964 | A343 | 20b dk red brn | .20 .20 |
| 965 | A343 | 55b olive green | .35 .20 |
| 966 | A343 | 1 l brt blue | .85 .20 |
| 967 | A343 | 1.55 l rose brown | 1.10 .40 |
| | | | 2.50 1.00 |

Nos. 964-967 (4)

50th anniv. of the construction of the Postal Administration Building.

Liberation Medal — A344

**1953, Oct. 20    Perf. 14x13½**

968  A344  55b dark brown    .80 .20

9th anniv. of the liberation of Romania.

Soldier and Flag — A345

**1953, Oct. 2    Perf. 13½**

969  A345  55b olive green    .80 .25

Army Day, Oct. 2.

Girl with Model Plane A346

Civil Aviation: 20b, Parachute landing. 55b, Glider and pilot. 1.75 l, Plane in flight.

**1953, Oct. 20    Perf. 14**

| | | | |
|---|---|---|---|
| 970 | A346 | 10b org & dk grav grn | 2.25 .30 |
| 971 | A346 | 20b org brn & dk ol grn | 4.50 .20 |
| 972 | A346 | 55b dk scar & rose lil | 7.25 .50 |
| 973 | A346 | 1.75 l dk rose vio & brn | 9.50 .75 |
| | | | 23.50 1.75 |

Nos. 970-973 (4)

Workers and Flags — A347

**1953, Nov. 25    Perf. 13½x13**

974  A347  55b brown    .50 .25
975  A347  1.55 l rose brown    .75 .25

Month of Romanian-Soviet friendship, Oct. 7-Nov. 7.

Hemispheres and Clasped Hands — A348

Workers, Flags and Globe — A349

**1953, Nov. 25    Perf. 14**

976  A348  55b dark olive    .40 .20
977  A349  1.25 l crimson    .90 .30

World Congress of Trade Unions.

Ciprian Porumbescu A350

**1953, Dec. 16    Perf. 13½**

978  A350  55b purple    .45

Ciprian Porumbescu (1853-1883), composer.

Harvesting Machine — A351

**1953, Dec. 16    Wmk. 358**

Designs: 35b, Tractor in field. 2.55 l, Cattle.

| | | | |
|---|---|---|---|
| 979 | A351 | 10b sepia | .30 .20 |
| 980 | A351 | 35b dark green | .40 .20 |
| 981 | A351 | 2.55 l orange brown | 3.50 .75 |
| | | | 4.20 1.15 |

Nos. 979-981 (3)

Aurel Vlaicu — A352

**1953, Dec. 26    Perf. 14**

982  A352  50b violet blue    .75 .20

Vlaicu, aviation pioneer, 40th death anniv.

Lenin — A353

**1954, Jan. 21    Perf. 13½**

983  A353  55b dk red brn, buff    .75 .20

30th death anniv. of Lenin.

Red Deer — A354

**1954, Apr. 1    Yellow Surface-colored Paper**

| | | | |
|---|---|---|---|
| 984 | A354 | 20b dark brown | 2.25 .25 |
| 985 | A354 | 55b violet | 1.75 .50 |
| 986 | A354 | 1.75 l dark blue | 2.75 .50 |
| | | | 6.75 1.00 |

Nos. 984-986 (3)

Month of the Forest.


Calimanesti Rest Home — A355

Workers' Rest Homes: 1.55 l, Sinaia. 2 l, Predeal. 2.35 l, Tusnad. 2.55 l, Govora.

**1954, Apr. 15    Perf. 14**

| | | | |
|---|---|---|---|
| 987 | A355 | 5b blk brn, cream | .25 .20 |
| 988 | A355 | 1.55 l dk vio brn, bl | 1.00 .20 |
| 989 | A355 | 2 l dk grn, pink | 1.75 .20 |
| 990 | A355 | 2.35 l ol blk, grnsh | 1.60 .45 |
| 991 | A355 | 2.55 l dk red brn, cit | 2.25 .65 |
| | | | 6.85 1.70 |

Nos. 987-991 (5)

Octav Bancila — A356

Globe, Child, Dove and Flowers A357

**1954, May 26    Perf. 13½**

992  A356  55b red brn & dk grn    2.75 1.25

10th death anniv. of Octav Bancila, painter.

**1954, June 1    Perf. 13½x13**

993  A357  55b brown    1.25 .25

Children's Day, June 1.

Girl Fondling Calf A358

Designs: 55b, Girl holding sheaf of grain. 1.75 l, Young students.

**1954, July 5    Perf. 14**

| | | | |
|---|---|---|---|
| 994 | A358 | 20b grnsh blk | .35 .20 |
| 995 | A358 | 55b blue | .60 .25 |
| 996 | A358 | 1.75 l car rose | 1.75 .35 |
| | | | 2.70 .80 |

Nos. 994-996 (3)

Stephen the Great — A359

**1954, July 10    Perf. 13½**

997  A359  55b violet brown    1.75 .40

Stephen of Moldavia (1433?-1504).

Loading Coal on Conveyor Belt — A360

**1954, Aug. 8    Perf. 13½x13**

998  A360  1.75 l black    1.75 .40

Miners' Day.


Victor Babes — A361

Applicant Requesting Loan — A362

**1954, Aug. 15    Perf. 14**

999  A361  55b rose red    1.75 .40

Birth cent. of Victor Babes, serologist.

**1954, Aug. 20**

Design: 55b, Mutual aid declaration.

1000  A362  20b deep violet    .30 .20
1001  A362  55b dk redsh brn    .50 .20

5th anniv. of the Mutual Aid Organization.

Sailor and Naval Scene — A363

**1954, Aug. 19    Perf. 13x13½**

1002  A363  55b deep blue    1.00 .25

Navy Day.

Monument to Soviet Soldier — A364

**1954, Aug. 23    Perf. 13½x13**

1003  A364  55b scarlet & purple    1.00 .25

10th anniv. of Romania's liberation.

House of Culture A365

Aviator — A367

Academy of Music, Bucharest — A366

55b, Scanteia building. 1.55 l, Radio station.

**1954, Sept. 6    Perf. 14, 13½x13**

| | | | |
|---|---|---|---|
| 1004 | A365 | 20b violet blue | .20 .20 |
| 1005 | A366 | 38b violet | .40 .20 |
| 1006 | A366 | 55b violet brown | .40 .20 |
| 1007 | A366 | 1.55 l red brown | .75 .80 |
| | | | 1.75 1.40 |

Nos. 1004-1007 (4)

Publicizing Romania's cultural progress during the decade following liberation.

**1954, Sept. 13    Wmk. 358**

1008  A367  55b blue    .90 .40

Aviation Day.

Chemical Plant and Oil Derricks — A368

**1954, Sept. 21** Perf. 13x13½
1009 A368 55b gray .25 .25
Intl. Conference of chemical and petroleum workers, Bucharest, Sept. 1954.

Dragon Pillar, Peking — A369

**1954, Oct. 7** Perf. 14
1010 A369 55b dk ol grn, cream 1.25 .25
Week of Chinese Culture.

Wild Boar — A374
1014 A373 1.75 l red brown
1015 A373 1.75 l red brown
Death cent. of Barbu Iscovescu, painter.

Glube and Clasped Hands — A375

**1954, Nov. 3**

**1954, Oct. 24**
Gheorghe Tattarescu A372
1014 A372 55b cerise

Barbu Iscovescu A373

**Perf. 13½x13**
1.50 .40

**Perf. 14**
2.50 .50

**1954, Oct. 17**
Dumitri T. Neculuta — A370
1011 A370 55b purple
Neculuta, poet, 50th death anniv.

**Perf. 13½x13**
1.10 .25

ARLUS Emblem — A371

**1954, Oct. 22**
65b, Romanian & Russian women
1012 A371 55b rose carmine .45 .20
1013 A371 65b dark purple .65 .20
Month of Romanian-Soviet Friendship.

**Perf. 14**

---

Month of the Forest; 65b, Couple planting tree, 1.20 l, Logging.

**1954, Apr. 5** Wmk. 358
1016 A374 35b brown 1.10 .20
1017 A374 65b turq blue 1.25 .25
1018 A374 1.20 l dark red 2.75 .55
Nos. 1016-1018 (3) 5.10 1.00

**Perf. 13½x13** Photo.
1019 A375 25b carmine rose .35 .20
Intl. Conference of Universal Trade Unions (Federation Syndicale Mondiale), Vienna, Apr. 1955.

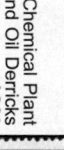

**1955, Mar. 15** Perf. 13½x13

**1955, Apr. 22** Perf. 13½x14
Various Portraits of Lenin.
1021 A377 20b ol bis & brn .45 .25
1022 A377 55b copper brown 1.40 .30
1023 A377 1 l vermilion 2.75 .75
Nos. 1021-1023 (3)
85th anniversary of the birth of Lenin.

Teletype — A376
1020 A376 50b lilac
Romanian telegraph system, cent.

**1955, Dec. 20** Perf. 13½x13
.45 .20

Globe, Flag and Dove — A379a
Girls with Dove and Flag — A380

**1955, May 7** Photo.
1035A A379a 55b ultra .75 .20
Peace Congress, Helsinki.

**1955, June 1** Perf. 13½x14
1036 A380 55b dark red brown .75 .20
International Children's Day, June 1.

---

Lenin — A377

**1955-56** Wmk. 358
1024 A378 3b blue .25 .20
1025 A378 5b violet .20 .20
1026 A378 10b chocolate .25 .20
1027 A378 20b lilac rose .30 .20
1027A A378 30b vio bl ('56) .60 .20
1028 A378 35b grnsh blue .45 .20
1028A A378 40b slate 1.00 .20
1029 A378 55b ol gray .90 .20
1030 A378 1 l purple 1.10 .20
1031 A378 1.55 l brown lake 1.75 .20
1032 A378 2.35 l bister brn 2.25 .35
1033 A378 2.55 l slate 3.25 .25
Nos. 1024-1033 (12) 12.30 2.60

Designs: 5b, Steelworker, 10b, Aviator, 20b, Miner, 30b, Tractor driver, 35b, Pioneer, 40b, Girl student, 55b, Mason, 1 l, Sailor, 1.55 l, Spinner, 2.35 l, Soldier, 2.55 l, Electrician.

Chemist A378

Volleyball A379

**1955, June 17**
European Volleyball Championships, Bucharest.

Design: 1.75 l, Woman volleyball player.
1034 A379 55b red vio, pink 3.00 .65
1035 A379 1.75 l lil rose, cr .65 .65

---

Bishop Dosoftei A385

Mother and Child — A386

**1955, Sept. 9** Photo.
Romanian writers: Constantin Cantacuzino, #1046, Stoilnicul Constantin Cantemir, #1047, Dimitrie Cantemir, #1048, Enachita Vacarescu, #1049, Anton Pann.
1045 A385 55b bluish gray 1.00 .30
1046 A385 55b dp vio 1.00 .30
1047 A385 55b ultra 1.00 .30
1048 A385 55b rose vio 1.00 .30
1049 A385 55b ol gray 1.00 .30
Nos. 1045-1049 (5) 5.00 1.50

**1955, July 7** Perf. 13½x14
1050 A386 55b ultra 1.10 .25
World Congress of Mothers, Lausanne.

Russian War Memorial, Berlin — A381
Theodor Aman Museum A382

**1955, May 9**
1037 A381 55b deep blue .60 .20
Victory over Germany, 10th anniversary.

**1955, June 28** Perf. 13½, 14
Bucharest Museums: 55b, Lenin and Stalin Arts Museum, 1.20 l, Popular Arts Museum, 2.55 l, Simu Museum.
1038 A382 20b rose lilac .25 .20
1039 A382 55b brown .90 .20
1040 A382 1.20 l gray black .95 .35
1041 A382 1.75 l slate green 1.50 .35
1042 A382 2.55 l rose violet 2.75 .45
Nos. 1038-1042 (5) 5.85 1.55
#1038, 1040, 1042 measure 29x24½mm, #1039, 1041 32½x23mm.

Sharpshooter A383

**1955, Sept. 11** Perf. 13½
1043 A383 1 l pale brn & sepia 4.00 .45
European Sharpshooting Championship meeting, Bucharest, Sept. 11-18.

---

I. V. Michurin — A390

Insect Pest Control A389

Designs: 20b, Pioneers studying nature, 55b, Home of the Pioneers.

**1955**
1051 A387 10b brt ultra .40 .20
1052 A387 20b grnsh bl .80 .20
1053 A387 55b dp plum 1.75 .25
Nos. 1051-1053 (3) 2.95 .65
Fifth anniversary of the Pioneer headquarters, Bucharest.

Pioneers and Train Set — A387
Rowing — A388

**1955, Aug. 22** Perf. 13x13½
1054 A388 55b shown 4.75 .50
1055 A388 1 l Sculling 8.25 .75
European Women's Rowing Championship on Lake Snagov, Aug. 4-7.

20b, Orchard, 55b, Vineyard, 1 l, Truck garden.

Fire Truck, Farm and Factory — A384

**1955, Sept. 13** Wmk. 358
1044 A384 55b carmine .75 .25
Firemen's Day, Sept. 13.

**ROMANIA**

---

### 1955, Oct. 15 — Perf. 14x13½
| | | | |
|---|---|---|---|
| 1056 | A389 | 10b brt grn | .60 .20 |
| 1057 | A389 | 20b lil rose | .60 .20 |
| 1058 | A389 | 55b vio bl | 1.60 .25 |
| 1059 | A389 | 1 l dp claret | 2.40 .90 |
| | | | 5.20 .90 |

*Nos. 1056-1059 (4)*

Quality products of Romanian agriculture. See Nos. 1068-1071.

### 1955, Oct. 25 — Perf. 13½x14
1060 A390 55b Prus bl .75 .20

Birth cent. of I. V. Michurin, Russian agricultural scientist.

Congress Emblem A391

### 1955, Oct. 20 — Perf. 13x13½
1061 A391 20b cream & ultra .30 .20

4th Soviet-Romanian Cong., Bucharest, Oct.

Globes and Olive Branches — A392

### 1955, Oct. 1 — Perf. 13½x13
1 l, Three workers holding FSM banner.
1062 A392 55b dk ol grn .30 .20
1063 A392 1 l ultra .45 .20

Intl. Trade Union Org. (Federation Syndicale Mondiale), 10th anniv.

Sugar Beets — A393

Sheep and Shepherd A394

20b, Cotton. 55b, Flax. 1.55l, Sunflower.

### 1955, Nov. 10 — Perf. 13½
| | | | |
|---|---|---|---|
| 1064 | A393 | 10b plum | .40 .20 |
| 1065 | A393 | 20b sl ultra | .75 .25 |
| 1066 | A393 | 55b brt ultra | 1.75 .40 |
| 1067 | A393 | 1.55 l dk red brn | 3.75 .60 |
| | | | 6.65 1.45 |

*Nos. 1064-1067 (4)*

### 1955, Dec. 10 — Perf. 14x13½
Stock Farming: 10b, Pigs. 35b, Cattle. 55b, Horses.
| | | | |
|---|---|---|---|
| 1068 | A394 | 5b yel grn & brn | .60 .20 |
| 1069 | A394 | 10b ol bis & dk vio | .60 .20 |
| 1070 | A394 | 35b brick red & brn | 1.60 .20 |
| 1071 | A394 | 55b dk ol bis & brn | 2.00 .40 |
| | | | 4.80 1.00 |

*Nos. 1068-1071 (4)*

Animal husbandry.

Hans Christian Andersen — A395

---

Bank Book and Savings Bank A396

### Perf. 13½x14 — Engr.
### 1955, Dec. 17
| | | | |
|---|---|---|---|
| 1072 | A395 | 20b sl bl | .30 .20 |
| 1073 | A395 | 20b dp ultra | .70 .20 |
| 1074 | A395 | 55b grnsh blk | 1.25 .20 |
| 1075 | A395 | 1 l vio brn | 2.25 .40 |
| 1076 | A395 | 1.75 l dl vio | 2.50 .75 |
| 1077 | A395 | 2 l rose lake | 3.00 .75 |
| | | | 10.00 2.50 |

*Nos. 1072-1077 (6)*

Anniversaries of famous writers.

Portraits: 55b, Adam Mickiewicz. 1 l, Friedrich von Schiller. 1.55 l, Baron de Montesquieu. 1.75 l, Walt Whitman. 2 l, Miguel de Cervantes.

**Unwmk.**

### Perf. 14x13½ — Photo.
### 1955, Dec. 29
1078 A396 55b dp vio 1.25 .25
1079 A396 55b blue 4.00 2.25

Advantages of systematic saving in a bank.

Census Date — A397

Design: 1.75 l, Family group.
Inscribed: "Recensamintul Populatiei"

### 1956, Feb. 3 — Perf. 13½
1080 A397 55b dp org .30 .20
1081 A397 1.75 l omar & red brn 1.25 .25
a. Center inverted 350.00 300.00

National Census, Feb. 21, 1956.

Ring-necked Pheasant A398

Great Bustard — A399

Street Fighting, Paris, 1871 — A400

Animals. No. 1082, Hare. No. 1083, Bustard. 35b, Trout. 50b, Boar. No. 1087, Brown bear. 1 l, Lynx. 1.55 l, Red squirrel. 2 l, Chamois. 3.25 l, Pintail (duck). 4.25 l, Fallow deer.

### 1956 — Wmk. 358 — Perf. 14
| | | | |
|---|---|---|---|
| 1082 | A398 | 20b grn & blk | 1.75 .30 |
| 1083 | A398 | 20b cit & gray blk | 1.75 .30 |
| 1084 | A399 | 35b brt bl & blk | 1.75 .30 |
| 1085 | A398 | 50b dp ultra & brn blk | 1.75 .30 |
| 1086 | A398 | 55b ol bis & ind | 1.75 .30 |
| 1087 | A398 | 55b dk bis & dk red brn | 1.75 .30 |
| 1088 | A398 | 1 l dk grn & red brn | 3.75 .60 |
| 1089 | A399 | 1.55 l lt ultra & red brn | 3.75 .60 |
| 1090 | A399 | 1.75 l sl grn & dk brn | 3.75 .60 |
| 1091 | A398 | 2 l ultra & brn blk | 14.50 7.25 |
| 1092 | A398 | 3.25 l lt grn & blk brn | 14.50 7.25 |

---

1093 A399 4.25 l brn org & dk brn 14.50 7.25
Nos. 1082-1093 (12) 65.25 25.35

Exist imperf. in changed colors. Value, set $25.

### 1956, May 29 — Perf. 13½
1094 A400 55b vermilion .75 .25

85th anniversary of Commune of Paris.

Oak Tree — A401

Globe and Child — A400a

### 1956, June 1 — Photo. — Perf. 13½x14
1095 A400a 55b dp vio 1.00 .25

Intl. Children's Day. The sheet of 100 contains 10 labels, each with "Peace" printed on it in one of 10 languages. Value for stamp with label, unused or used, $20.

### 1956, June 11 — Litho. — Wmk. 358
Design: 55b, Logging train in timberland.
1096 A401 20b dk bl grn, pale grn .65 .20
1097 A401 55b brn blk, pale grn 2.00 .50

Month of the Forest.

Romanian Academy A402

### 1956, June 19 — Photo. — Perf. 14
1098 A402 55b dk grn & dl yol .75 .20

90th anniversary of Romanian Academy.

Woman Speaker and Globe — A404

Red Cross Worker — A403

### 1956, June 7
1099 A403 55b olive & red 1.25 .40

Romanian Red Cross Congress, June 7-9.

### 1956, June 14
1100 A404 55b dk bl grn 1.00 .25

Intl. Conference of Working Women, Budapest, June 14-17.

Traian Vuia and Planes — A405

### 1956, June 21 — Perf. 13x13½
1101 A405 55b grnsh blk & brn 1.25 .25

1st flight by Vuia, near Paris, 50th anniv.

---

Ion Georgescu A406

### 1956, June 25 — Perf. 14x13½
1102 A406 55b dk red brn & dk 1.25 .25

Ion Georgescu (1856-1898), sculptor.

White Cabbage Butterfly A407

June Bug — A408

Design: 55b, Colorado potato beetle.

### 1956, July 30 — Perf. 14x13½, 13½x14
| | | | |
|---|---|---|---|
| 1103 | A407 | 10b dk vio, pale yel & blk | 2.50 .25 |
| 1104 | A407 | 55b ol blk & yel | 3.75 .30 |
| 1105 | A408 | 1.75 l lt ol & dp plum | 10.00 6.25 |
| 1106 | A408 | 1.75 l gray ol & dk vio brn | 8.00 .70 |
| | | | 24.25 7.50 |

*Nos. 1103-1106 (4)*

Campaign against Insect pests.

Dock Workers on Strike — A410

Girl Holding Sheaf of Wheat — A409

### 1956 — Perf. 13½x14
1107 A409 55b "1949-1956" 1.50 .25
a. "1951-1956" (error) 5.00 4.00

7th anniversary of collective farming.

### 1956, Aug. 6
1108 A410 55b dk red brn .75 .20

Dock workers' strike at Galati, 50th anniv.

Maxim Gorki — A412

Title Page and Printer — A411

### 1956, Aug. 13 — Perf. 13½
1109 A411 55b ultra .75 .20

25th anniv. of the publication of "Scanteia" (The Spark).

### 1956, Aug. 29 — Perf. 13½x14
1110 A412 55b brown .75 .20

Maxim Gorki (1868-1936), Russian writer.

ROMANIA

**1956, Sept. 24**
1111 A413 55b gray blk    1.25 .25

Theodor Aman
A413

Aman, painter, 125th birth anniv.

Primrose and
Snowdrops
A414

**1956, Sept. 26 Photo. Perf. 14x14½**

| | | | | |
|---|---|---|---|---|
| 1112 A414 | 5b bl, yel & red | | .50 | .25 |
| 1113 A414 | 5b blk, yel & red | | 1.75 | .35 |
| 1114 A414 | 1.75 l ind, pink & yel | | 4.00 | .50 |
| 1115 A414 | 3 l bl grn, dk bl grn & yel | | | |

Nos. 1112-1115 (4)   6.00   .65   12.25   1.75

Flowers in Natural Colors

55b, Daffodil and violets. 1.75 l, Snapdragon and bellflowers. 3 l, Poppies and lilies of the valley.

A XVI-a OLIMPIADA
MELBOURNE

Olympic Rings
and
Torch — A415

**1956, Oct. 25**
1121 A416 55b dp vio

16th Olympic Games, Melbourne, 11/22-12/8.

Designs: 55b, Water polo. 1 l, Gymnastics. 1.55 l, Canoeing. 1.75 l, High jump.

**1956, Oct.**    **Perf. 13½x14**

| | | | | |
|---|---|---|---|---|
| 1116 A415 | 20b vermilion | | .35 | .20 |
| 1117 A415 | 55b ultra | | .50 | .20 |
| 1118 A415 | 1 l lil rose | | 1.00 | .20 |
| 1119 A415 | 1.55 l lt bl grn | | 1.40 | .20 |
| 1120 A415 | 1.75 l dp pur | | 1.75 | .30 |

Nos. 1116-1120 (5)   5.00   1.10

Janos
Hunyadi — A416

**1956, Sept.**    **Wmk. 358**
1121 A416 55b dp vio    1.25 .45

Janos Hunyadi (1387-1456), national hero of Hungary. No. 1121 is found se-tenant with label showing Hunyadi Castle. Value for stamp with label, unused or used. $6.

B. FRANKLIN

Benjamin
Franklin — A417

Portraits: 35b, Sesshu (Toyo Oda). 40b, G. B. Shaw. 50b, Ivan Franco. 55b, Pierre Curie. 1 l, Henrik Ibsen. 1.55 l, Fedor Dostoevski. 1.75 l, Heinrich Heine. 2.55 l, Mozart. 3.25 l, Rembrandt.

**1956**    **Unwmk.**

| | | | | |
|---|---|---|---|---|
| 1122 A417 | 20b vio bl | | .25 | .20 |
| 1123 A417 | 35b rose lake | | .30 | .20 |
| 1124 A417 | 40b chocolate | | .35 | .20 |
| 1125 A417 | 50b brn blk | | .45 | .20 |
| 1126 A417 | 55b dk yel | | .45 | .20 |
| 1127 A417 | 1 l dk bl grn | | .85 | .20 |
| 1128 A417 | 1.55 l dp pur | | 1.25 | .20 |
| 1129 A417 | 1.75 l brt red | | 1.50 | .20 |
| 1130 A417 | 2.55 l rose vio | | 2.10 | .20 |
| 1131 A417 | 3.25 l dk ol | | 2.40 | .60 |

Nos. 1122-1131 (10)   10.00   2.55

Great personalities of the world.

George Enescu
as a Boy — A418

**1956, Dec. 29**    **Engr.**

| | | | | |
|---|---|---|---|---|
| 1132 A418 | 55b ultramarine | | .75 | .25 |
| 1133 A418 | 1.75 l deep claret | | 1.50 | .30 |

Portrait: 1.75 l, George Enescu as an adult.

75th birth anniv. of George Enescu, musician and composer.

A419

A420

**1957, Feb. 28 Photo. Wmk. 358**
1134 A419 55b dk bl gray    1.00 .25

50th anniversary of Peasant Uprising.

Fighting Peasants, by Octav Bancila.

**1957, Apr. 24**    **Perf. 13½x14**

| | | | | |
|---|---|---|---|---|
| 1147 A420 | 55b brown | | .85 | .20 |
| 1148 A420 | 55b olive black | | .50 | .30 |

Enthronement of Stephen the Great, Prince of Moldavia, 500th anniv.

Dr. George Marinescu, Marinescu
Institute and Congress
Emblem — A421

Dr. N. Kretzulescu, Medical School,
Dr. C. Davila — A422

**1957, May 5**    **Perf. 14x13½**

| | | | | |
|---|---|---|---|---|
| 1149 A421 | 20b dp grn | | .25 | .20 |
| 1150 A421 | 35b dp red brn | | .35 | .20 |
| 1151 A421 | 55b red lil | | .50 | .20 |
| 1152 A422 | 1.75 l brt ultra & dk red | | 1.90 | .50 |

Nos. 1149-1152 (4)   3.00   1.10

35b, Dr. I. Cantacuzino & Cantacuzino Hospital. 55b, Dr. V. Babes & Babes Institute.

RP.ROMINA

Dove and
Handle
Bars — A423

**1957, May 29**    **Perf. 13½x14**

| | | | | |
|---|---|---|---|---|
| 1153 A423 | 20b shown | | .25 | .20 |
| 1154 A423 | 55b Cyclist | | .60 | .20 |

10th International Bicycle Peace Race.

Woman Watching
Gymnast — A424

**1957, May 29**
1155 A424 55b shown

European Women's Gymnastic meet, Bucharest.

Designs: 55b, Girl with flags on hoop.

Slide Rule,
Caliper & Atomic
Symbol — A426

**1957, May 29**    **Wmk. 358**
1159 A426 55b blue    .85 .20
1160 A426 55b brn red    1.00 .20

2nd Congress of the Society of Engineers and Technicians, Bucharest, May 29-31.

Carpathian Mountain Flowers: 10b, Daphne Blagayana. 20b, Lilium Bulbiferum. L. 35b, Leontopodium Alpinum. 55b, Gentiana Acaulis L. 1 l, Dianthus Callizonus. 1.55 l, Primula Carpatica Griseb. 1.75 l, Anemone Montana Hoppe.

**1957, June 22 Litho. Unwmk.**

Light Gray Background

| | | | | |
|---|---|---|---|---|
| 1161 A427 | 5b brt rose | | .25 | .20 |
| 1162 A427 | 10b dk grn | | .35 | .20 |
| 1163 A427 | 20b red org | | .75 | .20 |
| 1164 A427 | 35b olive | | 1.00 | .20 |
| 1165 A427 | 55b ultra | | 1.00 | .20 |
| 1166 A427 | 1 l red | | 2.00 | .20 |
| 1167 A427 | 1.55 l yellow | | 2.00 | .25 |
| 1168 A427 | 1.75 l dk pur | | 10.00 | 1.85 |

Nos. 1161-1168 (8)   3.25   .40

Nos. 1161-1168 also come se-tenant with a decorative label. Value, set $30.

Rhododendron
Hirsutum — A427

**1957, May 21**    **Perf. 13½**

| | | | | |
|---|---|---|---|---|
| 1155 A424 | 20b shown | | .30 | .20 |
| 1156 A425 | 35b shown | | .45 | .20 |
| 1157 A425 | 55b Vaulting horse | | .85 | .25 |
| 1158 A424 | 1.75 l Acrobat | | 2.40 | .40 |

Nos. 1155-1158 (4)   4.00   1.00

Woman
Gymnast on
Bar — A425

Nicolae
Grigorescu — A429

**1957, June 29 Photo. Wmk. 358**

| | | | | |
|---|---|---|---|---|
| 1169 A428 | 20b dk bl grn | | .35 | .20 |
| 1170 A429 | 55b deep brown | | .90 | .20 |
| 1171 A428 | 1.75 l chalky blue | | 4.50 | 1.00 |

Nos. 1169-1171 (3)   3.25   .60

Grigorescu, painter, 50th death anniv.

Painting: 1.75 l, Battle scene.

"Oxcart" by
Grigorescu
A428

Festival Emblem — A432

Young
Couple — A431

Folk Dance — A433

**1957, July 28**
**Perf. 14x14½, 14x14x12½ (A432),**
**13½x12½x12½ (A433)**

| | | | | |
|---|---|---|---|---|
| 1173 A431 | 20b red lilac | | .20 | .20 |
| 1174 A431 | 55b emerald | | .30 | .20 |
| 1175 A432 | 1 l red orange | | .75 | .25 |
| 1176 A432 | 1.75 l ultra | | 2.50 | .85 |

Nos. 1173-1176 (4)   1.25   .20

Moscow 1957 Youth Festival. No. 1173 measures 23x34mm, No. 1174 22x38mm, No. 1175 24x36mm. No. 1176 36x24mm. No. 1175 was printed in sheets of 50, alternating with 40 labels inscribed "Peace and Friendship" in 20 languages. Value for stamp with label, unused or used. $10.

Warship
A430

**1957, Aug. 3**    **Perf. 13x13½**
1172 A430 1.75 l Prus bl    1.10 .25

Navy Day.

Bugler — A434

**1957, Aug. 30 Wmk. 358 Perf. 14**
1177 A434 20b brt pur    .75 .20

80th anniv. of the Russo-Turkish war.

Girl Holding
Dove — A435

**1957, Sept. 3 Photo. Perf. 13½**
1178 A435 55b Prus grn & red    .75 .20

Honoring the Red Cross.

Battle Scene
A436

**1957, Aug. 31**
1179 A436 1.75 l brown    .75 .25

Battle of Marasesti, 40th anniv.

Jumper and Dove — A437

**1957, Sept. 14    Photo.    Perf. 13½**
1180 A437 20b brt bl & blk    .30  .20
1181 A437 55b yel & blk    .85  .20
1182 A437 1.75 l brick red & blk    2.40  .50
  Nos. 1180-1182 (3)    3.55  .90

International Athletic Meet, Bucharest.
55b, Javelin thrower, bison. 1.75 l, Runner, stag.

Statue of Ovid, Constanta A438

**1957, Sept. 20    Photo.    Wmk. 358**
1183 A438 1.75 l vio bl    1.60  .45

2000th anniv. of the birth of the Roman poet Publius Ovidius Naso.

Oil Field — A439

**1957, Oct. 5**
1184 A439 20b dl red brn    .25  .20
1185 A439 20b indigo    .25  .20
1186 A439 55b vio blk    .60  .65
  Nos. 1184-1186 (3)    1.10

Design: 55b, Horse pulling drill, 1857.
Centenary of Romanian oil industry.

Congress Emblem A440

**1957, Sept. 28**
1187 A440 55b ultra    .50  .20

4th Intl. Trade Union Cong., Leipzig, 10/4-15.

Young Couple, Lenin Banner — A441

35b, Lenin & Flags. 55b, Lenin statue.

Endre Ady — A442

**1957, Nov. 6    Perf. 14x14½, 14½x14**
1188 A441 10b crimson    .20  .20
1189 A441 35b plum, horiz.    .25  .20
1190 A441 55b brown    .35  .60
  Nos. 1188-1190 (3)    .80

Russian Revolution, 40th anniversary.

**1957, Dec. 5    Perf. 14**
1191 A442 55b ol brn    .75  .20

Ady, Hungarian poet, 80th birth anniv.

Oath of Bobilna A443

Bobilna Monument — A444

**1957, Nov. 30**
1192 A443 50b deep plum    .35  .20
1193 A444 55b slate blue    .45  .20

520th anniversary of the insurrection of the peasants of Bobilna in 1437.

Black-winged Stilt — A445

Animals:  10b, Great white egret.  20b, White spoonbill.  50b, Sturgeon.  55b, Ermine, horiz. 1.30 l, White pelican, horiz.

**1957, Dec. 27    Photo.    Perf. 13½x14, 14x13½    Wmk. 358**
1194 A445 5b red brn & gray    .20  .20
1195 A445 10b emer & ocher    .20  .20
1196 A445 20b brt red & ocher    .2b  .50
1197 A445 50b bl grn & ocher    .50  .75
1198 A445 55b dp cl & gray    1.25  .30
1199 A445 1.30 l pur & org    9.40  2.55
  Nos. 1194-1199 (8)

Sputnik 2 and Laika A446

**1957, Dec. 20    Perf. 14x13½**
1200 A446 1.20 l bl & dk brn    1.40  .35
1201 A446 1.20 l grnsh bl & choc    1.40  .35

Dog Laika, "first space traveler."

Romanian Arms, Flags — A447

Designs: 55b, Arms, "Industry and Agriculture." 1.20 l, Arms, "Art, Science and Sport (soccer)."

**1957, Dec. 30    Perf. 13½**
1202 A447 25b ultra, red & ocher    .20  .20
1203 A447 55b dull yellow    .35  .25
1204 A447 1.20 l crimson rose    .75  .65
  Nos. 1202-1204 (3)    1.30

Proclamation of the Peoples' Republic, 10th anniv.

Flag and Wreath — A448

**1958, Feb. 15    Unwmk.    Perf. 13½**
1205 A448 1 l dk bl & red, buff    .65  .20
1206 A448 1 l brn & red, buff    .65  .20

Grivita Strike, 25th anniversary.

Television, Radio Antennas A449

Design: 1.75 l, Telegraph pole and wires.

**1958, Mar. 21    Perf. 14x13½**
1207 A449 55b brt vio    .45  .20
1208 A449 1.75 l dp mag    .85  .25

Telecommunications Conference, Moscow, Dec. 3-17, 1957.

Nicolae Balcescu — A450

Romanian Writers: 10b, Ion Creanga. 35b, Alexandru Vlahuta 55b, Mihail Eminescu. 1.75 l, Vasile Alecsandri. 2 l, Barbu S. Delavrancea.

**1958    Wmk. 358    Perf. 14x14½**
1209 A450 5b bluish blk    .20  .20
1210 A450 10b int blk    .20  .20
1211 A450 35b dk bl    .20  .20
1212 A450 55b dk red brn    .35  .20
1213 A450 1.75 l blk brn    .70  .20
1214 A450 2 l dk sl grn    1.25  1.20
  Nos. 1209-1214 (6)    2.90  1.20

See Nos. 1309-1314.

Fencer in Global Mask A451

**1958, Apr. 5    Perf. 14½x14**
1215 A451 1.75 l brt pink    1.10  .25

Youth Fencing World Championships, Bucharest.

Stadium and Health Symbol — A452

**1958, Apr. 16**
1216 A452 1.20 l lt grn & red    1.00  .20

25 years of sports medicine.

Globe and Dove — A453

**Photo.**
1217 A453 55b brt bl    .50  .20

4th Congress of the Intl. Democratic Women's Federation, June 1958.

Clavaria Aurea — A456

Carl von Linné — A454

Portraits:  20b, Auguste Comte.  40b, William Blake.  55b, Mikhail I. Glinka.  1 l, Henry W. Longfellow. 1.75 l, Carlo Goldoni. 2 l, Jan A. Komensky.

**1958, May 31    Perf. 14x14½    Unwmk.**
1218 A454 10b Prus grn    .20  .20
1219 A454 20b brown    .25  .20
1220 A454 40b dp lil    .40  .20
1221 A454 55b dp lil    .00  .20
1222 A454 1 l dp mag    .80  .20
1223 A454 1.75 l dp vio bl    1.00  .20
1224 A454 2 l olive    1.90  .30
  Nos. 1218-1224 (7)    5.15  1.50

Great personalities of the world.

**1958, July    Litho.    Unwmk.**

Mushrooms:  5b, Lepiota Procera.  20b, Amanita caesarea 30b, Lactarius deliciosus. 35b, Armillaria mellea.  55b, Coprinus comatus. 1 l, Morchella conica. 1.55 l, Psalliota campestris. 1.75 l, Boletus edulis. 2 l, Cantharellus cibarius.

1225 A456 6b gray bl & brn    .20  .20
1226 A456 10b ol, ocher & brn    .20  .20
1227 A456 20b gray, red & yel    .20  .20
1228 A456 30b grn & dp org    .20  .20
1229 A456 35b lt bl & yel brn    .20  .20
1230 A456 55b pale grn, fawn & brn    .35  .20
1231 A456 1 l bl grn, ocher & brn    .50
1232 A456 1.55 l gray, lt gray & pink    .85
1233 A456 1.75 l emer, brn & buff    1.00  .25
1234 A456 2 l dl bl & org yel    1.90  .25
  Nos. 1225-1234 (10)    5.60  2.05

Antarctic Map and Emil Racovita A457

Design: 1.20 l, Cave and Racovita.

**1958, July 30    Photo.    Perf. 14½x14**
1235 A457 55b indigo & lt bl    .50  .20
1236 A457 1.20 l ol bis & brt vio    1.25  .20

90th birth anniv. of Emil Racovita, explorer and naturalist.

## Armed Forces Monument — A458

**1958, Oct. 2**    **Perf. 13½x13**

Designs: 75b, Soldier guarding industry. 1.75 l, Sailor raising flag and ship.

| | | | | |
|---|---|---|---|---|
| 1237 | A458 | 75b orange brown | .20 | .20 |
| 1238 | A458 | 75b deep magenta | .25 | .25 |
| 1239 | A458 | 1.75 l bright blue | .65 | .25 |

Nos. 1237-1239,C55 (4)    2.35 1.05

Armed Forces Day.

---

## Woman & Man from Oltenia — A459

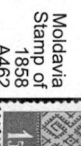

**1958, Unwmk. Litho. Perf. 13½x14**

| | | | | |
|---|---|---|---|---|
| 1240 | A459 | 35b | .40 | .20 |
| 1241 | A459 | 40b label | .40 | .20 |
| 1242 | A459 | 50b label | .50 | .20 |
| 1243 | A459 | 55b label | .80 | .20 |
| 1244 | A459 | 1 l label | 1.75 | .40 |
| 1245 | A459 | 1.75 l label | 2.00 | .50 |

Nos. 1240-1245 exist imperf. Value, set $20, unused or used.

Regional Costumes: 40b, Tara Oasului. 50b, Transylvania. 55b, Muntenia. 1 l, Banat. 1.75 l, Moldavia. Pairs: 'a' woman, 'b' man.

|  | Pair, #a.-b. + | | |
|---|---|---|---|
| 1240 | 35b | Pair, #a.-b. + | .20 .20 |
| 1241 | 40b | Pair, #a.-b. + | |
| 1242 | 50b | Pair, #a.-b. + | |
| 1243 | 55b | Pair, #a.-b. + | |
| 1244 | 1 l | Pair, #a.-b. + | 1.75 .40 |
| 1245 | 1.75 l | Pair, #a.-b. + | 5.85 1.70 |

---

## Printer and Hand Press A461

### Moldavia Stamp of 1858 A462

55b, Scissors cutting strips of 1858 stamps. 1.20 l, Postilion, mail coach. 1.30 l, Postilion blowing horn, courier on horseback. 1.75 l, 2 l, 3.30 l, Various denominations of 1858 issue.

**1958, Nov. 15 Engr. Perf. 14½x14**

| | | | | |
|---|---|---|---|---|
| 1252 | A461 | 35b vio bl | .20 | .20 |
| 1253 | A461 | 55b red brn | .35 | .20 |
| 1254 | A461 | 1.20 l dull bl | .70 | .20 |
| 1255 | A461 | 1.30 l brown vio | 1.00 | .20 |
| 1256 | A462 | 1.55 l gray brn | 1.10 | .20 |
| 1257 | A462 | 1.75 l rose claret | 1.25 | .25 |
| 1258 | A462 | 2 l dull vio | 1.60 | .45 |
| 1259 | A462 | 3.30 l dull red brn | 2.10 | .65 |

Nos. 1252-1259 (8)    8.30 2.25

Cent. of Romanian stamps. See No. C57. Exist imperf. Value, set $15.

---

## Bugler — A463    Runner — A464

**1958, Dec. 10 Photo. Perf. 13½x13**

| | | | | |
|---|---|---|---|---|
| 1260 | A463 | 55b crimson rose | .50 | .20 |

Decade of teaching reforms.

**1958, Dec. 9 Perf. 13½x14**

| | | | | |
|---|---|---|---|---|
| 1261 | A464 | 1 l deep brown | .90 | .25 |

Third Youth Spartacist Sports Meet. For overprint, see No. 1287.

---

## Building and Flag — A465

**1958, Dec. 16**

| | | | | |
|---|---|---|---|---|
| 1262 | A465 | 55b dk car rose | .30 | .20 |

Workers' Revolution, 40th anniversary.

---

## Prince Alexandru Ioan Cuza A466

**1959, Jan. 27 Perf. 14x13½**

| | | | | |
|---|---|---|---|---|
| 1263 | A466 | 1.75 l dk blue | .60 | .25 |

Centenary of the Romanian Union.

---

## Friedrich Handel — A467

## Sheep A469    Corn — A468

**1959, Apr. 25 Photo. Perf. 13½x14**

| | | | | |
|---|---|---|---|---|
| 1264 | A467 | 55b brown | .40 | .20 |
| 1265 | A467 | 55b indigo | .40 | .20 |
| 1266 | A467 | 55b slate | .40 | .20 |
| 1267 | A467 | 55b carmine | .40 | .20 |
| 1268 | A467 | 55b purple | .40 | .20 |

Nos. 1264-1268,C59 (6)    4.50 1.50

Portraits: No. 1265, Robert Burns. No. 1266, Charles Darwin. No. 1267, Alexander Popov. No. 1268, Shalom Aleichem.

Various cultural anniversaries in 1959.

---

**1959, June 1 Photo. Wmk. 358**

**Perf. 13½x14, 14x13½**

| | | | | |
|---|---|---|---|---|
| 1269 | A468 | 55b brt green | .30 | .20 |
| 1270 | A468 | 35b red org | .30 | .20 |
| 1271 | A468 | 40b red lilac | .30 | .20 |
| 1272 | A469 | 55b olive grn | .30 | .20 |
| 1273 | A469 | 55b red brown | .30 | .20 |
| 1274 | A469 | 55b blue | .30 | .20 |
| 1275 | A469 | 55b yellow brn | .30 | .20 |
| 1276 | A469 | 55b brown | .30 | .20 |

and grain. No. 1276, Loaded farm wagon. No. 1277, Farm couple and "10."

**1959 Unwmk.**

| | | | | |
|---|---|---|---|---|
| 1277 | A469 | 5 l dp red lilac | 2.75 | .50 |

Nos. 1269-1277 (9)    5.15 2.10

10th anniv. of collective farming. Sizes: #1272-1276 33x23mm; #1277 38x27mm.

Designs: No. 1270, Sunflower and bee. No. 1271, Sugar beet and refinery. No. 1273, Cattle. No. 1274, Rooster and hens. No. 1275, Tractor

---

## Young Couple — A470

Design: 1.60 l, Dancer in folk costume.

**1959, July 15 Perf. 13½x14**

**Unwmk.**

| | | | | |
|---|---|---|---|---|
| 1278 | A470 | 1 l brt blue | .35 | .20 |
| 1279 | A470 | 1.60 l car rose | .70 | .20 |

7th World Youth Festival, Vienna, 7/26-8/14.

---

## Steel Worker and Farm Woman — A471

**1959, Aug. 23 Litho. Perf. 13½x14**

| | | | | |
|---|---|---|---|---|
| 1280 | A471 | 55b multicolored | .50 | .20 |
| a. | Souvenir sheet of 1 | .40 | .40 |

15th anniv. of Romania's liberation from the Germans.

No. 1280a is ungummed and imperf. The blue, yellow and red vignette shows large "XV" and Romanian flag. Brown 1.20 l denomination and inscription in margin.

---

## Prince Vlad Tepes and Document — A472

Designs: 40b, Nicolae Balcescu Street. No. 1283, Atheneum. No. 1284, Printing Combine. 1.55 l, Opera House. 1.75 l, Stadium.

**1959, Sept. 20 Photo.**

| | | | | |
|---|---|---|---|---|
| 1281 | A472 | 20b blue | .60 | .20 |
| 1282 | A472 | 40b brown | .90 | .20 |
| 1283 | A472 | 55b bister brn | 1.00 | .20 |
| 1284 | A472 | 55b rose brn | 1.25 | .20 |
| 1285 | A472 | 1.55 l rose lilac | 2.75 | .50 |
| 1286 | A472 | 1.75 l pale violet | 3.00 | .75 |

Nos. 1281-1286 (6)    9.50 2.10

500th anniversary of the founding of Bucharest. See No. C71.

---

## Soccer — A473    Motorcycle Race — A474

**1959 Unwmk. Litho. Perf. 13½**

| | | | | |
|---|---|---|---|---|
| 1288 | A473 | 20b shown | .20 | .20 |
| 1289 | A473 | 35b shown | .25 | .20 |
| 1290 | A474 | 40b ice hockey | .30 | .20 |
| 1291 | A474 | 55b Field ball | .35 | .20 |
| 1292 | A474 | 1 l Horse race | .60 | .20 |
| 1293 | A473 | 1.50 l Boxing | 1.10 | .20 |
| 1294 | A473 | 1.50 l Rugby | 1.25 | .20 |
| 1295 | A474 | 1.60 l Tennis | 1.50 | .25 |

Nos. 1288-1295,C72 (9)    7.55 2.05

---

## Russian Icebreaker "Lenin" A475

**1959, Oct. 25 Perf. 14½x13½**

| | | | | |
|---|---|---|---|---|
| 1296 | A475 | 1.75 l blue vio | 1.25 | .25 |

First atomic ice-breaker.

---

## Stamp Album and Magnifying Glass — A476

**1959, Nov. 15 Wmk. 358 Perf. 14**

| | | | | |
|---|---|---|---|---|
| 1297 | A476 | 1.60 l + 40b label | 1.25 | .40 |

Issued for Stamp Day. Stamp and label were printed alternately in sheet. The 40b label went to the Romanian Association of Philatelists.

---

## Purple Foxglove — A477

**1959, Dec. 15 Typo. Unwmk.**

### Medicinal Flowers in Natural Colors

| | | | | |
|---|---|---|---|---|
| 1298 | A477 | 20b shown | .20 | .20 |
| 1299 | A477 | 40b Peppermint | .25 | .20 |
| 1300 | A477 | 55b Cornflower | .35 | .20 |
| 1301 | A477 | 55b Daisies | .50 | .20 |
| 1302 | A477 | 1 l Autumn crocus | .65 | .20 |
| 1303 | A477 | 1.20 l Monkshood | .75 | .20 |
| 1304 | A477 | 1.55 l Poppies | 1.00 | .20 |
| 1305 | A477 | 1.55 l Linden | 1.00 | .25 |
| 1306 | A477 | 1.75 l Dog rose | 1.10 | .20 |
| 1307 | A477 | 3.20 l Buttercup | 1.75 | .40 |

Nos. 1298-1307 (10)    7.55 2.30

---

**1959, Sept. 12 Wmk. 358**

| | | | | |
|---|---|---|---|---|
| 1287 | A464 | 1 l deep brown | 6.00 | 6.00 |

Balkan Games.

No. 1261 Overprinted with Shield in Silver, inscribed: "Jocurile Bucuresti Balcanice 1959"

**ROMANIA**

Petrushka, Russian Puppet — A493

Emblem — A492

Designs: Various Puppets.

**1960, Aug. 20    Typo.**

| | | | | |
|---|---|---|---|---|
| 1375 | A492 | 20b multi | .20 | .20 |
| 1376 | A492 | 40b multi | .20 | .20 |
| 1377 | A493 | 55b multi | .20 | .20 |
| 1378 | A493 | 1 l multi | .40 | .20 |
| 1379 | A493 | 1.20 l multi | .40 | .20 |
| 1380 | A493 | 1.75 l multi | .60 | .20 |
| | | Nos. 1375-1380 (6) | 2.00 | 1.20 |

International Puppet Theater Festival.

Globe and Peace — A495

Children on Sled — A494

Children's Sports: 35b, Ice skating, horiz. 1 l, Running, horiz. 55b, Boys playing ball, horiz. 1.75 l, Swimming, horiz.

**1960, Oct. 1    Unwmk.    Litho.**

**Perf. 14**

| | | | | |
|---|---|---|---|---|
| 1381 | A494 | 20b multi | .20 | .20 |
| 1382 | A494 | 35b multi | .20 | .20 |
| 1383 | A494 | 55b multi | .25 | .20 |
| 1384 | A494 | 1 l multi | .35 | .20 |
| 1385 | A494 | 1.75 l multi | .75 | 1.00 |
| | | Nos. 1381-1385 (5) | 1.75 | 1.00 |

Worker and Flags A496

**Perf. 13½x14    Wmk. 358**

**1960, Nov. 26    Photo.**

| | | | | |
|---|---|---|---|---|
| 1386 | A495 | 55b brt bl & yel | .25 | .20 |

Intl. Youth Federation, 15th anniv.

**Perf. 14x13    Litho.    Unwmk.**

**1960, Nov. 26**

| | | | | |
|---|---|---|---|---|
| 1387 | A496 | 55b dk car & red org | .30 | .20 |

40th anniversary of the general strike.

Carp A497

Fish: 20b, Pikeperch. 40b, Black Sea turbot. 55b, Allis shad. 1 l, Wels (catfish). 1.20 l, Sterlet. 1.60 l, Huchen (salmon).

**1960, Dec. 5    Typo.**

| | | | | |
|---|---|---|---|---|
| 1388 | A497 | 10b multi | .20 | .20 |
| 1389 | A497 | 20b multi | .20 | .20 |
| 1390 | A497 | 40b multi | .25 | .20 |
| 1391 | A497 | 55b multi | .30 | .20 |
| 1392 | A497 | 1 l multi | .45 | .20 |
| 1393 | A497 | 1.20 l multi | .70 | .25 |
| 1394 | A497 | 1.60 l multi | 1.00 | 1.45 |
| | | Nos. 1388-1394 (7) | 3.35 | 1.45 |

---

A488

**Perf. 13½    Unwmk.    Litho.**

**1960, June 20**

| | | | | |
|---|---|---|---|---|
| 1339 | A487 | 55b red org & dk car | .40 | .20 |

Romanian Workers' Party, 3rd congress.

**1960    Wmk. 358    Photo.    Perf. 14**

Portraits: 10b, Leo Tolstoy. 20b, Mark Twain. 35b, Hokusai. 40b, Alfred de Musset. 55b, Daniel Defoe. 1 l, Janos Bolyai. 1 l, Anton Chekov. 1.55 l, Robert Koch. 1.75 l, Frederick Chopin.

| | | | | |
|---|---|---|---|---|
| 1340 | A488 | 10b dull pur | .20 | .20 |
| 1341 | A488 | 20b olive | .20 | .20 |
| 1342 | A488 | 35b blue | .20 | .20 |
| 1343 | A488 | 40b slate green | .30 | .20 |
| 1344 | A488 | 55b dull brn vio | .40 | .20 |
| 1345 | A488 | 1 l Prus grn | .70 | .20 |
| 1346 | A488 | 1.20 l dk car rose | .90 | .20 |
| 1347 | A488 | 1.55 l gray blue | 1.25 | .20 |
| 1348 | A488 | 1.75 l brown | 1.40 | .25 |
| | | Nos. 1340-1348 (9) | 5.45 | 1.85 |

Various cultural anniversaries.

Piano and Books A490

Students A489

Designs: 5b, Diesel locomotive. 10b, Dam. 20b, Miner with drill. 30b, Ambulance and doctor. 35b, Textile worker. 50b, Nursery. 55b, Timber industry. 60b, Harvester. 75b, Feeding cattle. 1 l, Atomic reactor. 1.20 l, Oil derricks. 1.50 l, Coal mine. 1.55 l, Loading ship. 1.60 l, Tractor. 1.75 l, Chemist. 3 l, Radio and television.

**1960    Wmk. 358    Photo.    Perf. 14**

| | | | | |
|---|---|---|---|---|
| 1349 | A489 | 5b brt lil rose | .20 | .20 |
| 1350 | A489 | 10b olive bis | .20 | .20 |
| 1351 | A489 | 20b violet gray | .20 | .20 |
| 1352 | A489 | 30b blue vio | .20 | .20 |
| 1353 | A489 | 35b vermilion | .20 | .20 |
| 1354 | A490 | 40b ocher | .20 | .20 |
| 1355 | A490 | 50b crimson | .30 | .20 |
| 1356 | A490 | 55b blue | .30 | .20 |
| 1357 | A489 | 60b green | .35 | .20 |
| 1358 | A490 | 75b gray ol | .40 | .20 |
| 1359 | A490 | 1 l car rose | .50 | .20 |
| 1360 | A489 | 1.20 l black | .50 | .20 |
| 1361 | A489 | 1.50 l plum | .50 | .20 |
| 1362 | A490 | 1.55 l dp blue | .55 | .20 |
| 1363 | A490 | 1.60 l dp blue | .65 | .20 |
| 1364 | A490 | 1.75 l red brown | .80 | .20 |
| 1365 | A489 | 2 l red gray | 1.00 | .20 |
| 1367 | A489 | 2.40 l brt lilac | 1.50 | 1.00 |
| 1368 | A489 | 3 l grysh blue | 9.95 | 4.20 |
| | | Nos. 1349-1368,C86 (21) | | |

Ovid Statue at Constanta A491

Black Sea Resorts: 35b, Constanta harbor. 40b, Vasile Rosita beach and vase. 55b, Ionian column and Mangalia beach. 1 l, Eforie at night. 1.60 l, Eforie and sailboat.

**1960, Aug. 2    Unwmk.    Litho.**

| | | | | |
|---|---|---|---|---|
| 1369 | A491 | 20b multicolored | .20 | .20 |
| 1370 | A491 | 35b multicolored | .20 | .20 |
| 1371 | A491 | 40b multicolored | .20 | .20 |
| 1372 | A491 | 55b multicolored | .25 | .20 |
| 1373 | A491 | 1 l multicolored | .60 | .20 |
| 1374 | A491 | 1.60 l multicolored | .90 | 1.60 |
| | | Nos. 1369-1374,C87 (7) | 3.60 | 1.60 |

---

Swimming A484

Sports: 55b, Women's gymnastics. 1.20 l, High jump. 1.60 l, Boxing. 2.45 l, Canoeing.

**1960, June   Unwmk.   Typo.   Perf. 14**

**Gray Background**

| | | | | |
|---|---|---|---|---|
| 1326 | A484 | 40b blue & yel | .35 | .25 |
| 1327 | A484 | 55b blk, yel & emer | .40 | .30 |
| 1328 | A484 | 1.20 l emer & brick red | .95 | .70 |
| a. | | Strip of 3, #1326-1328 | 1.75 | |
| 1329 | A484 | 1.60 l blue, yel & blk | 1.75 | 1.25 |
| 1330 | A484 | 2.45 l blk, emer & brick red | 3.50 | |
| a. | | Pair, #1329-1330 + 2 labels | 5.20 | 3.75 |
| | | Nos. 1326-1330 (5) | | |

17th Olympic Games, Rome, 8/25-9/11. Nos. 1326-1330 were printed in one sheet, the top half containing No. 1328a, the bottom half No. 1330a, with gutter between. When the two strips are placed together, the Olympic rings join in a continuous design. Exist imperf. (3.70 l replaced 2.45 l). Value, set $7.75.

Swimming — A485

Olympic Flame, Stadium — A486

40b, Women's gymnastics. 55h, High jump. 1 l, Boxing. 1.60 l, Canoeing. 2 l, Soccer.

**1960    Photo.    Wmk. 358**

| | | | | |
|---|---|---|---|---|
| 1331 | A485 | 20b chalky blue | .20 | .20 |
| 1332 | A485 | 40b dk brn red | .30 | .20 |
| 1333 | A485 | 55b blue | .45 | .20 |
| 1334 | A485 | 1 l rose red | .60 | .20 |
| 1335 | A485 | 1.60 l rose lilac | .75 | .20 |
| 1336 | A485 | 2 l dull violet | 1.40 | .30 |
| | | Nos. 1331-1336 (6) | 3.70 | 1.30 |

**Souvenir Sheets**

**Perf. 11½**

| | | | | |
|---|---|---|---|---|
| 1337 | A486 | 5 l ultra | 4.50 | 2.25 |

**Imperf**

| | | | | |
|---|---|---|---|---|
| 1338 | A486 | 6 l dull red | 7.25 | 3.75 |

17th Olympic Games.

A487

---

Cuza University, Jassy, Centenary A478

**1959, Nov. 26   Photo.   Wmk. 358**

| | | | | |
|---|---|---|---|---|
| 1308 | A478 | 55b brown | .40 | .20 |

**Romanian Writers Type of 1958**

20b, Gheorghe Cosbuc. 40b, Ion Luca Caragiale. 50b, Grigore Alexandrescu. 55b, Alexandru Donici. 1 l, Costache Negruzzi. 1.55 l, Dimitrie Bolintineanu.

**1960, Jan. 20    Perf. 14**

| | | | | |
|---|---|---|---|---|
| 1309 | A450 | 20b bluish blk | .20 | .20 |
| 1310 | A450 | 40b dp lilac | .30 | .20 |
| 1311 | A450 | 50b brown | .40 | .20 |
| 1312 | A450 | 55b violet brn | .40 | .20 |
| 1313 | A450 | 1 l violet | .70 | .20 |
| 1314 | A450 | 1.55 l dk blue | 1.25 | .30 |
| | | Nos. 1309-1314 (6) | 3.25 | 1.30 |

Woman, Dove and Globe — A481

Huchen (Salmon) — A480

55b, Greek tortoise. 1.20 l, Shelduck.

**1960, Feb. 1    Engr.    Unwmk.**

| | | | | |
|---|---|---|---|---|
| 1315 | A480 | 20b blue | .20 | .20 |
| 1316 | A480 | 55b brown | .30 | .20 |
| 1317 | A480 | 1.20 l dk purple | .75 | .20 |
| | | Nos. 1315-1317,C76-C78 (6) | 4.85 | 1.60 |

**1960, Mar. 1    Photo.    Perf. 14**

| | | | | |
|---|---|---|---|---|
| 1318 | A481 | 55b violet blue | .50 | .20 |

50 years of Intl. Women's Day, Mar. 8.

A482

A483

40b, Lenin. 55b, Lenin statue, Bucharest. 1.55 l, Head of Lenin.

**1960, Apr. 22    Wmk. 358    Perf. 13½**

| | | | | |
|---|---|---|---|---|
| 1319 | A482 | 40b magenta | .30 | .20 |
| 1320 | A482 | 55b violet blue | .50 | .20 |

**Souvenir Sheet**

| | | | | |
|---|---|---|---|---|
| 1321 | A482 | 1.55 l carmine | 2.50 | 2.00 |

90th birth anniv. of Lenin.

**1960, May 9    Wmk. 358    Perf. 14**

| | | | | |
|---|---|---|---|---|
| 1322 | A483 | 40b Heroes Monument | .35 | .20 |
| 1323 | A483 | 55b Soviet war memorial | .45 | .75 |
| a. | | Strip of 2, #1322-1323 + label | 1.75 | .75 |

15th anniversary of the liberation. Nos. 1322-1323 exist imperf, printed in deep magenta. Value, set $3.25; label strip, $4.50.

## 1960, Dec. 20 — Litho. — Perf. 14

Kneeling Woman and Grapes — A498

1395 A498 20b brn & gray .20 .20
1396 A498 30b red org & pale grn .20 .20
1397 A498 40b dp ultra & buff ol .25 .20
1398 A498 55b emer & buff .35 .20
1399 A498 75b dk car rose & pale grn .35 .20
1400 A498 1 l Prus grn & gray .45 .20
1401 A498 1.20 l org brn & pale bl .75 .25
Nos. 1395-1401 (7) 2.55 1.45

**Souvenir Sheet**
**Imperf**
1402 A498 5 l dk car rose & bis 3.25 1.50

Each stamp represents a different wine-growing region: Dragasani, Dealul Mare, Odubesti, Cotnari, Tirnave, Minis, Murfatlar and Pietroasa.

Designs: 30b, Farmers drinking, horiz, 40b, Loading grapes into basket, 75b, Vintner with basket, 1 l, Woman filling basket with grapes, 1.20 l, Vintner with jug, 5 l, Antique wine jug.

## 1961, Feb. 16 — Photo. — Unwmk.
### Perf. 13½x14, 14x13½

Steelworker by I. Irimescu — A499

1403 A499 5b car rose .20 .20
1404 A499 10b violet .20 .20
1405 A499 20b ol blk .20 .20
1406 A499 40b ol bis .20 .20
1407 A499 50b org ver .20 .20
1408 A499 50b blk brn .20 .20
1409 A499 1 l dp plum .40 .20
1410 A499 1.55 l brt ultra .55 .20
1411 A499 1.75 l green .85 .25
Nos. 1403-1411 (9) 3.00 1.85

Modern Sculptures: 10b, G. Doja, I. Vlad. 20b, Meeting, B. Caragea. 40b, George Enescu, A. Angnel. 50b, Mihail Eminescu, C. Baraschi. 55b, Peasant Revolt, 1907, M. Constantinescu, horiz. 1 l, "Peace," I. Jalea. 1.55 l, Building Socialism, C. Medrea. 1.75 l, Birth of an Idea, A. Szobotka.

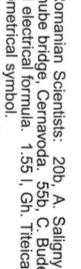

## 1961, Apr. 11 — Litho. — Perf. 13½x13

Peter Poni, and Chemical Apparatus — A500

1412 A500 10b pink & vio bl .20 .20
1413 A500 20b citron & mar .20 .20
1414 A500 55b blue & red .20 .20
1415 A500 1.55 l ocher & lilac .75 .20
Nos. 1412-1415 (4) 1.35 .80

Romanian Scientists: 20b, A. Saligny and Danube bridge, Cernavoda, 55b, C. Budeanu and electrical formula, 1.55 l, Gh. Titeica and geometrical symbol.

Freighter "Galati" A501

## 1961, Apr. 25 — Typo. — Perf. 14x13

1416 A501 20b multi .20 .20
1417 A501 40b multi .30 .30
1418 A501 55b multi .20 .20

Ships: 40b, Passenger ship "Oltenita," 55b, Motorboat "Tomis," 1 l, Freighter "Arad," 1.55 l, Tugboat 1.75 l, Freighter "Dobrogea."

## 1961 — Perf. 13x14, 14x13 — Typo.
### Unwmk. — Tinted Paper — Wmk. 358

1419 A501 1 l multi .40 .20
1420 A501 1.55 l multi .55 .35
1421 A501 1.75 l multi 2.50 1.25
Nos. 1416-1421 (6) 1.85 1.20

Marx, Lenin and Engels on Red Flag — A502

## 1961, Apr. 29 — Litho.

1422 A502 35b red, bl & ocher .20 .20
1423 A502 55b mar, red & gray .25 .20

**Souvenir Sheet**
**Imperf**
1424 A502 1 l multi 1.25 .50

Designs: 55b, Workers, 1 l, "Industry and Agriculture" and Workers Party Emblem.

40th anniv. of the Romanian Communist Party. #1424 contains one 55x33mm stamp.

Roe Deer and Bronze Age Hunting Scene — A503

Lynx and Prehistoric Hunter — A504

## 1961, July — Perf. 13x14, 14x13

1425 A503 10b multi .20 .20
1426 A503 20b multi .20 .20
1427 A503 35b multi .25 .20
1428 A503 40b multi .30 .20
1429 A503 55b multi .40 .20
1430 A503 75b multi .60 .20
1431 A503 1 l multi .60 .20
1432 A503 1.55 l multi .75 .20
1433 A503 1.55 l multi .90 .20
1434 A503 2 l multi 1.40 .35
Nos. 1425-1434 (10) 6.60 2.20

35b, Boar, Roman hunter. 40b, Brown bear, Roman tombstone. 55b, Red deer, 16th cent. hunter. 75b, Red fox, feudal hunter. 1 l, Black goat, modern hunter. 1.55 l, Rabbit, hunter with dog. 1.75 l, Badger, hunter. 2 l, Roebuck, hunter.

Georges Enescu A505

Peasant Playing Panpipe — A506

Heraclitus — A507

## 1961, Sept. 7 — Litho. — Perf. 14x13

1435 A505 3 l pale vio & dk brn 1.40 .25

2nd Intl. George Enescu Festival, Bucharest.

Peasants playing musical instruments: 20b, Alpenhorn, horiz, 40b, Flute, 55b, Guitar, 60b, Bagpipe, 1 l, Zither.

## 1961, Oct. 25 — Photo. — Wmk. 358

1436 A506 10b multi .20 .20
1437 A506 20b multi .20 .20
1438 A506 40b multi .20 .20
1439 A506 55b multi .20 .20
1440 A506 60b multi .20 .20
1441 A506 1 l multi .55 .20
Nos. 1436-1441 (6) 1.85 1.20

## 1961

1442 A507 10b maroon .20 .20
1443 A507 20b brown .20 .20
1444 A507 40b Prus grn .20 .20
1445 A507 55b cerise .20 .20
1446 A507 1.35 l brt bl .50 .20
1447 A507 1.75 l purple .70 .20
Nos. 1442-1447 (6) 2.00 1.20

Portraits: 20b, Francis Bacon, 40b, Rabindranath Tagore, 55b, Domingo F. Sarmiento, 1.35 l, Heinrich von Kleist, 1.75 l, Mikhail V. Lomonosov.

Swimming — A508

Gold Medal, Boxing A509

## 1961, Oct. 30 — Photo. — Unwmk.
### Perf. 14x14½

1448 A508 20b gray .20 .20
1449 A508 20b bl gray .20 .20
1450 A508 55b vermilion .50 .20
1451 A508 55b ultra .50 .20
Nos. 1448-1451 (4) 1.40 .80

#1449, Olympic torch. #1450, Water polo. #1451, Women's high jump.

**Medals in Ocher**

**Size: 33x33mm**
1452 A509 10b Prus grn .20 .20
1453 A509 35b brown .35 .20
1454 A509 40b plum .40 .20
1455 A509 55b org red .50 .20
1456 A509 1.35 l dp ultra .80 .20

**Size: 46x32mm**
1457 A509 1.75 l dk car rose 1.50 .35
Nos. 1452-1457 (6) 3.75 1.35
5.15 2.15

Gold Medals: 35b, Pistol shooting, Melbourne. 40b, Sharpshooting, Rome. 55b, Wrestling. 1.35 l, Woman's high jump. 1.75 l, Three medals for canoeing.

Romania's gold medals in 1956, 1960 Olympics. #1452-1457 exist imperf. Value, set $3.75. A souvenir sheet of one 4 l dark red & ocher was issued. Value unused $4.25, canceled $3.25.

Primrose A511

## 1961, Sept. 15

### Perf. 14x13½, 13½x14

1459 A511 10b multi .20 .20
1460 A511 20b multi .20 .20
1461 A511 25b multi .20 .20
1462 A511 35b multi .20 .20
1463 A511 40b multi .20 .20
1464 A511 55b multi .35 .20
1465 A511 1 l multi .90 .25
1466 A511 1.20 l multi .35 .20
1467 A511 1.55 l multi 3.00 1.85
Nos. 1459-1467 (9) 3.00 1.85

**Souvenir Sheet**
**Imperf**
1468 A511 1.75 l car, blk & grn 3.00 2.00

Designs: 20b, Sweet William. 25b, Peony. 35b, Prickly pear. 40b, Iris. 55b, Buttercup. 1 l, Hepatica. 1.20 l, Poppy. 1.55 l, Gentian. 1.75 l, Carol Davilla and Dimitrie Brandza. 20b, 25b, 40b, 55b, 1.20 l, 1.55 l, are vertical.

Bucharest Botanical Garden, cent. No. 1459-1467 exist imperf. Value, set $3.

Congress Emblem — A510

## 1961, Dec. — Litho. — Perf. 13½x14

1458 A510 55b dk car rose .50 .25

5th World Congress of Trade Unions, Moscow. Dec. 4-16.

United Nations Emblem — A512

Cock and Savings Book — A513

## 1961, Nov. 27 — Perf. 13½x14

1469 A512 20b bl, yel & pink .25 .20
1470 A512 40b multi .50 .20
1471 A512 55b org, lil & yel .65 .20
Nos. 1469-1471 (3) 1.40 .60

Designs: 20b, Map of Balkan peninsula and dove. 40b, Men of three races.

UN, 15th anniv. Nos. 1469-1470 are each printed with alternating yellow labels. Exist imperf. Value, set $2.75.

## 1962, Feb. 15 — Typo. — Perf. 13½

1472 A513 40b multi .20 .20
1473 A513 55b multi .25 .20

Savings Day: 55b, Honeycomb, bee and savings book.

Soccer Player and Map of Europe — A514

## 1962, Apr. 20 — Litho. — Perf. 13x14

1474 A514 55b emer & red brn .50 .20

European Junior Soccer Championships, Bucharest. For surcharge see No. 1510.

Wheat, Map and Tractor — A515

## 1962, Apr. 27 — Litho. — Perf. 13½x14

1475 A515 40b org & dk car .20 .20
1476 A515 55b yel, car & brn .25 .20
1477 A515 1.55 l multi .60 .60
Nos. 1475-1477 (3) 1.15 .60

Designs: 55b, Medal honoring agriculture. 1.55 l, Sheaf of wheat, hammer & sickle.

Collectivization of agriculture.

## Canoe Race A516

20b, Kayak. 40b, 8-man shell. 55b, 2-man skiff. 1 l, Yachts. 1.20 l, Motorboats. 1.55 l, Sailboat. 3 l, Water slalom.

**1962, May 15  Photo.  Perf. 14x13**
**Vignette in Bright Blue**

| | | | | |
|---|---|---|---|---|
| 1478 | A516 | 10b lil rose | .20 | .20 |
| 1479 | A516 | 20b ol gray | .20 | .20 |
| 1480 | A516 | 40b red brn | .20 | .20 |
| 1481 | A516 | 55b ultra | .20 | .20 |
| 1482 | A516 | 1 l red | .25 | .20 |
| 1483 | A516 | 1.20 l dp plum | .55 | .20 |
| 1484 | A516 | 1.55 l orange | .75 | .20 |
| 1485 | A516 | 3 l violet | 1.40 | 1.60 |
| | | Nos. 1478-1485 (8) | 3.75 | 1.60 |

## Ion Luca Caragiale — A517

40b, Jean Jacques Rousseau. 1.75 l, Alexander I. Herzen. 3.30 l, Ion Luca Caragiale (as a young man).

**1962, June 9  Perf. 13½x14**

| | | | | |
|---|---|---|---|---|
| 1486 | A517 | 40b dk sl grn | .20 | .20 |
| 1487 | A517 | 55b magenta | .20 | .20 |
| 1488 | A517 | 1.75 l dp bl | .75 | .25 |
| | | Nos. 1486-1488 (3) | 1.15 | .65 |

**Souvenir Sheet  Perf. 11½**

| | | | | |
|---|---|---|---|---|
| 1489 | A517 | 3.30 l brown | 3.00 | 1.75 |

Rousseau, French philosopher, 250th birth anniv., Caragiale, Romanian author, 50th death anniv., Herzen, Russian writer, 150th birth anniv. No. 1489 contains one 32x55mm stamp.

## Globes Surrounded with Flags — A518

**1962, July 6  Typo.  Perf. 11**

| | | | | |
|---|---|---|---|---|
| 1490 | A518 | 55b multi | .40 | .20 |

8th Youth Festival for Peace and Friendship, Helsinki, July 28-Aug. 6.

## Traian Vuia — A519
## Fieldball Player and Globe — A520

**1962, July 20  Perf. 13½x14  Photo.  Wmk. 358**

| | | | | |
|---|---|---|---|---|
| 1491 | A519 | 15b brown | .20 | .20 |
| 1492 | A519 | 20b red brn | .20 | .20 |
| 1493 | A519 | 35b brn mag | .20 | .20 |
| 1494 | A519 | 40b bl vio | .20 | .20 |
| 1495 | A519 | 55b brt bl | .20 | .20 |
| 1496 | A519 | 1 l dp ultra | .25 | .20 |
| 1497 | A519 | 1.20 l crimson | .35 | .20 |
| 1498 | A519 | 3 l Prus grn | .45 | .20 |
| 1499 | A519 | 1.55 l purple | .90 | .80 |
| | | Nos. 1491-1499 (9) | 2.90 | 1.80 |

**1962, May 12  Perf. 13x14  Litho.  Unwmk.**

| | | | | |
|---|---|---|---|---|
| 1500 | A520 | 55b yel & vio | .45 | .20 |

2nd Intl. Women's Fieldball Championships, Bucharest.

**Same Surcharged in Violet Blue:**
"Campionana Mondiala 5 lei"

**1962, July 31**

| | | | | |
|---|---|---|---|---|
| 1501 | A520 | 5 l on 55b yel & vio | 4.25 | 2.10 |

Romanian victory in the 2nd Intl. Women's Fieldball Championships.

## Rod Fishing A521

Various Fishing Scenes.

**1962, July 25  Perf. 14x13**

| | | | | |
|---|---|---|---|---|
| 1502 | A521 | 10b multi | .20 | .20 |
| 1503 | A521 | 25b multi | .20 | .20 |
| 1504 | A521 | 40b bl & brick red | .20 | .20 |
| 1505 | A521 | 55b multi | .20 | .20 |
| 1506 | A521 | 75b sl, gray & bl | .30 | .20 |
| 1507 | A521 | 1 l multi | .45 | .20 |
| 1508 | A521 | 1.75 l multi | .75 | .20 |
| 1509 | A521 | 3.25 l multi | 1.40 | 1.60 |
| | | Nos. 1502-1509 (8) | 3.70 | 1.60 |

**No. 1474 Surcharged in Dark Blue:**
"1962 Campioana Europeana 2 lei"

**1962, July 31**

| | | | | |
|---|---|---|---|---|
| 1510 | A514 | 2 l on 55b | 1.60 | 1.00 |

Romania's victory in the European Junior Soccer Championships, Bucharest.

## Child and Butterfly A522
## Handicraft A523

**1962, Aug. 25  Perf. 13x14, 14x13  Litho.**

Designs: 30b, Girl feeding bird. 40b, Boy and model sailboat. 55b, Children writing, horiz. 1.20 l, Girl at piano, and boy playing violin. 1.55 l, Pioneers camping, horiz.

| | | | | |
|---|---|---|---|---|
| 1511 | A522 | 20b lt bl, red & brn | .20 | .20 |
| 1512 | A522 | 30b org, bl & red brn | .20 | .20 |
| 1513 | A522 | 40b chalky bl, dp org & Prus bl | .20 | .20 |
| 1514 | A522 | 55b citron, bl & red | .35 | .20 |
| 1515 | A522 | 1.20 l car, brn & dk vio | .70 | .20 |
| 1516 | A522 | 1.55 l bis, red & vio | .90 | 1.20 |
| | | Nos. 1511-1516 (6) | 1.90 | 1.20 |

**1962, Oct. 12  Perf. 13x14**

Designs: 10b, Food and drink. 20b, Chemical industry. 40b, Chinaware. 55b, Leather industry. 75b, Textiles. 1 l, Furniture. 1.20 l, Electrical appliances. 1.55 l, Household goods (sewing machine and pots).

| | | | | |
|---|---|---|---|---|
| 1517 | A523 | 5b multi | .20 | .20 |
| 1518 | A523 | 10b multi | .20 | .20 |
| 1519 | A523 | 20b multi | .20 | .20 |
| 1520 | A523 | 40b multi | .20 | .20 |
| 1521 | A523 | 55b multi | .25 | .20 |
| 1522 | A523 | 75b multi | .30 | .20 |
| 1523 | A523 | 1 l multi | .30 | .20 |

These stamps were also issued imperf. with color of denomination and inscription changed. Value, set unused $4.50, canceled $2.

## Lenin — A524

| | | | | |
|---|---|---|---|---|
| 1524 | A523 | 1.20 l multi | .55 | .20 |
| 1525 | A523 | 1.55 l multi | .90 | .25 |
| | | Nos. 1517-1525,C126 (10) | 4.20 | 2.05 |

4th Sample Fair, Bucharest.

## Bull — A525

**1962, Nov. 7  Perf. 10½**

| | | | | |
|---|---|---|---|---|
| 1526 | A524 | 55b vio bl, red & bis | .35 | .20 |

Russian October Revolution, 45th anniv.

**1962, Nov. 20  Perf. 14x13, 13x14**

Designs: 20b, Sheep, horiz. 40b, Merino ram, horiz. 1 l, York pig. 1.35 l, Cow. 1.55 l, Heifer, horiz. 3 l, Pigs, horiz.

| | | | | |
|---|---|---|---|---|
| 1527 | A525 | 20b ultra & blk | .20 | .20 |
| 1528 | A525 | 40b bl, yel & sep | .20 | .20 |
| 1529 | A525 | 55b ocher, buff & sl grn | .25 | .20 |
| 1530 | A525 | 1 l gray, yel & brn | .35 | .20 |
| 1531 | A525 | 1.35 l dl grn, choc & gray | .35 | .20 |
| 1532 | A525 | 1.55 l org red, dk brn & blk | .60 | .20 |
| 1533 | A525 | 1.75 l dk vio bl, yel & org | .75 | .30 |
| | | Nos. 1527-1533 (7) | 2.55 | 1.50 |

## Arms, Factory and Harvester A526

**1962, Dec. 30  Litho.  Perf. 14½x13½**

| | | | | |
|---|---|---|---|---|
| 1534 | A526 | 1.55 l multi | .90 | .20 |

Romanian People's Republic, 15th anniv.

## Strikers at Grivita, 1933 A527

**1963, Feb. 16  Perf. 14x13½**

| | | | | |
|---|---|---|---|---|
| 1535 | A527 | 1 l red, vio & yel | .70 | .20 |

30th anniv. of the strike of railroad and oil industry workers at Grivita.

## Tractor Driver and "FAO" Emblem A528

## Tomatoes — A529

**1963, Mar. 21  Photo.  Perf. 14½x13**

| | | | | |
|---|---|---|---|---|
| 1536 | A528 | 40b vio bl | .20 | .20 |
| 1537 | A528 | 55b bis brn | .20 | .20 |
| 1538 | A528 | 1.55 l rose red | .45 | .25 |
| 1539 | A528 | 1.75 l green | .75 | .25 |
| | | Nos. 1536-1539 (4) | 1.60 | .85 |

FAO "Freedom from Hunger" campaign.

Designs: 55b, Farm woman, cornfield & combine. 1.55 l, Child drinking milk & milking machine. 1.75 l, Woman with basket of grapes & vineyard.

**Perf. 13½x14, 14x13½**
**1963, Apr. 25  Litho.  Unwmk.**

40b, Hot peppers. 55b, Radishes. 75b, Egg-plant. 1.20 l, Mild peppers. 3.25 l, Cucumbers. horiz.

| | | | | |
|---|---|---|---|---|
| 1540 | A529 | 35b multi | .20 | .20 |
| 1541 | A529 | 40b multi | .20 | .20 |
| 1542 | A529 | 55b multi | .20 | .20 |
| 1543 | A529 | 75b multi | .20 | .20 |
| 1544 | A529 | 1.20 l multi | .60 | .30 |
| 1545 | A529 | 3.25 l multi | 1.40 | 1.30 |
| | | Nos. 1540-1545 (6) | 2.80 | 1.30 |

## Woman Swimmer at Start — A530

## Chicks — A531

Designs: 30b, Crawl, horiz. 55b, Butterfly stroke, horiz. 1 l, Backstroke, horiz. 1.35 l, Breaststroke, horiz. 1.55 l, Woman diver. 2 l, Water polo.

**1963, June 15  Perf. 13x14, 14x13**

| | | | | |
|---|---|---|---|---|
| 1546 | A530 | 25b yel brn, emer & gray | .20 | .20 |
| 1547 | A530 | 30b ol grn, gray & yel | .20 | .20 |
| 1548 | A530 | 55b bl, gray & red | .20 | .20 |
| 1549 | A530 | 1 l grn, gray & red | .25 | .20 |
| 1550 | A530 | 1.35 l ultra, car & gray | .35 | .20 |
| 1551 | A530 | 1.55 l pur, gray & org | .70 | .20 |
| 1552 | A530 | 2 l car rose, gray & org | .75 | .35 |
| | | Nos. 1546-1552 (7) | 2.65 | 1.55 |

**1963, May 23  Perf. 10½**
**Fowl in Natural Colors; Inscription in Dark Blue**

Domestic poultry: 30b, Hen. 40b, Goose. 55b, White cock. 70b, Duck. 1 l, Hen. 1.35 l, Tom turkey. 3.20 l, Hen. horiz.

| | | | | |
|---|---|---|---|---|
| 1553 | A531 | 30b ultra | .20 | .20 |
| 1554 | A531 | 30b tan | .20 | .20 |
| 1555 | A531 | 40b org brn | .20 | .20 |
| 1556 | A531 | 55b brt grn | .25 | .20 |
| 1557 | A531 | 70b lilac | .35 | .20 |
| 1558 | A531 | 1 l blue | .35 | .20 |
| 1559 | A531 | 1.35 l ocher | .50 | .20 |
| 1560 | A531 | 3.20 l yel & brn | 1.10 | .35 |
| | | Nos. 1553-1560 (8) | 3.00 | 1.75 |

Portraits: 20b, Al. Davila. 35b, Vasile Pirvan. 40b, Ion Negulici. 55b, Grigore Cobilcescu. 1 l, Dr. Gheorghe Marinescu. 1.20 l, Ion Cantacuzino. 1.35 l, Victor Babes. 1.55 l, C. Levaditi.

**1963, June 15**   **Photo.**   **Perf. 14x13**
1561   A532   55b dark blue   .30   .20
Intl. Women's Cong., Moscow, June 24-29.

Women and
Globe
A532

William M.
Thackeray,
Writer
A533

**1963, July**   **Unwmk.**   **Perf. 14x13**
Portrait in Black
1562   A533   40b pale vio   .20   .20
1563   A533   50b bister brn   .25   .20
1564   A533   55b olive   .25   .20
1565   A533   1.55 l rose brn   .45   .20
1566   A533   3.25 l rose vio bl   .75   .20
  Nos. 1562-1566 (5)   1.85   1.00

Portraits: 50b, Eugene Delacroix, painter. 55b, Gheorghe Marinescu, physician. 1.55 l, Giuseppe Verdi, composer. 1.75 l, Stanislavski, actor and producer.

Walnuts
A534

**1963, Sept. 15**   **Litho.**   **Perf. 14x13½**
Fruits in Natural Colors
1567   A534   10b pale yel & brn   .20   .20
1568   A534   20b pale pink & red   .20   .20
1569   A534   40b lt bl & bl   .20   .20
1570   A534   55b dl yel & rose   .25   .20
1571   A534   1 l pale vio & vio   .25   .20
1572   A534   1.55 l yel grn & ultra   .45   .20
1573   A534   1.60 l yel & bis   .45   .20
1574   A534   1.75 l lt bl & grn   .75   .20
  Nos. 1567-1574 (8)   3.00   1.60

Designs: 20b, Plums. 40b, Peaches. 55b, Strawberries. 1 l, Grapes. 1.55 l, Apples. 1.60 l, Cherries. 1.75 l, Pears.

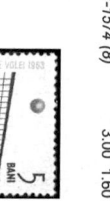

Women Playing
Volleyball and Map
of Europe — A535

**1963, Oct. 22**   **Perf. 13½x14**
1575   A535   5b gray & lil rose   .20   .20
1576   A535   40b gray & vio bl   .20   .20
1577   A535   55b gray & grnsh bl   .20   .20
1578   A535   1.75 l gray & org brn   .55   .20
1579   A535   3.20 l gray & vio   1.10   .30
  Nos. 1575-1579 (5)   2.35   1.15

Designs: 40b, 3 men players. 55b, 3 women players. 1.75 l, 2 men players. 3.20 l, Europa Cup.

European Volleyball Championships, Oct. 22-Nov. 4.

Design: 1.75 l, Beech forest and branch.

Pine Tree,
Branch and
Cone
A536

Design: 1.75 l, Pine forest and branch.

---

**1963, Dec. 5**   **Unwmk.**
        **Perf. 13½**
1580   A536   55b dk grn   .20   .20
        **Photo.**
1581   A536   1.75 l dk bl   .50   .20
Reforestation program.

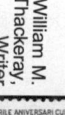

Silkworm
Moth — A537

**1963, Dec. 12**   **Litho.**   **Perf. 13x14**
1582   A537   10b multi   .20   .20
1583   A537   20b multi   .20   .20
1584   A537   40b multi   .20   .20
1585   A537   55b multi   .25   .20
1586   A537   60b multi   .35   .20
1587   A537   1.20 l multi   .60   .20
1588   A537   1.35 l multi   .75   .20
1589   A537   1.60 l multi   1.10   .25
  Nos. 1582-1589 (8)   3.65   1.65

Designs: 20b, Chrysalis, moth and worm. 40b, Silkworm on leaf. 60b, Bee over mountains, horiz. 55b, Bee over mountains, horiz. 1 l, 1.35 l, 1.60 l, Bees pollinating various flowers, horiz.

Ski
Jump
A539

**1963, Nov. 25**   **Litho.**   **Perf. 14**
1596   A539   5b red & dk bl   .20   .20
1597   A539   10b red & dk bl   .20   .20
1598   A539   20b ultra & red brn   .20   .20
1599   A539   40b emer & red brn   .20   .20
1600   A539   55b vio & red brn   .30   .20
1601   A539   60b org & vio bl   .40   .20
1602   A539   75b lil rose & dk bl   .50   .20
1603   A539   1 l bis & vio bl   .85   .25
1604   A539   1.20 l grnsh bl & vio   .90   .35
  Nos. 1597-1604 (8)   3.55   1.00

9th Winter Olympic Games, Innsbruck, Jan. 29-Feb. 9, 1964.

20b, Speed skating. 40b, Ice hockey. 55b, Women's figure skating. 60b, Slalom. 75b, Biathlon. 1 l, Bobsledding. 1.20 l, Cross-country skiing.

Exist imperf. in changed colors. Value, set $5.50.

A souvenir sheet contains one imperf. 1.50 l ultramarine and red stamp showing the ultramarine and red Olympic Ice Stadium at Innsbruck and the Winter Games emblem. Value $5.50.

18th Century
House,
Ploesti — A538

**1963, Dec. 25**   **Engr.**   **Perf. 13**
1590   A538   20b claret   .20   .20
1591   A538   40b blue   .20   .20
1592   A538   55b dl vio   .20   .20
1593   A538   75b green   .20   .20
1594   A538   1 l brn & mar   .35   .20
1595   A538   1.20 l gray ol   .45   .20
1596   A538   1.75 l dk brn & ultra   2.45   1.40
  Nos. 1590-1596 (7)

Peasant Houses from Village Museum, Bucharest: 40b, Oltenia, 1875, horiz. 55b, Hunedoara, 19th Cent., horiz. 75b, Oltenia, 19th Cent. 1 l, Brasov, 1847. 1.20 l, Bacau, 19th Cent. 1.75 l, Arges, 19th Cent.

---

**1964, Jan. 20**   **Photo.**   **Perf. 13**
Portrait in Dark Brown
1605   A540   10b olive   .20   .20
1606   A540   20b ultra   .20   .20
1607   A540   35b green   .20   .20
1608   A540   40b grnsh bl   .20   .20
1609   A540   55b car rose   .20   .20
1610   A540   75b lilac   .20   .20
1611   A540   1 l blue   .55   .20
1612   A540   1.35 l brt vio   .75   .20
1613   A540   1.55 l red org   1.10   .20
  Nos. 1605-1613 (9)   3.60   1.80

Designs: 10b, George Stephanescu, founder of Romanian opera, 35b, Ion Bajenaru as Petru Rares. 35b, D. Popovici as Alberich. 55b, Hariclea Darclée as Tosca. 75b, George Folescu as Boris Godunov. 1 l, Jean Athanasiu as Rigoletto. 1.35 l, Traian Grosavescu as Duke in Rigoletto. 1.55 l, N. Leonard as Hoffmann.

Elena Teodorini
as
Carmen — A540

Munteanu
Murgoci and
Congress
Emblem — A541

**1964, Feb. 5**   **Unwmk.**   **Perf. 13**
1614   A541   1.60 l brt bl, ind & bis   3.35   1.80
8th Intl. Soil Congress, Bucharest.

Asculaphid
A542

**1964, Feb. 20**   **Litho.**   **Perf. 14x13**
Insects in Natural Colors
1615   A542   5b pale lilac   .20   .20
1616   A542   10b lt bl & brn   .20   .20
1617   A542   35b pale grn   .20   .20
1618   A542   40b olive green   .20   .20
1619   A542   55b ultra   .40   .20
1620   A542   1 l pale grn & red   .60   .20
1621   A542   1.55 l yel & brn   .65   .20
1622   A542   1.75 l orange & red   2.65   1.60
  Nos. 1615-1622 (8)

Insects: 10b, Thread-waisted wasp. 35b, Wasp. 40b, Rhyparioides metelkana moth. 55b, Tussock moth. 1.20 l, Kanetisa circe butterfly. 1.55 l, Beetle. 1.75 l, Horned beetle.

Tobacco
Plant — A543

**1964, Mar. 25**   **Perf. 13x14**
1623   A543   10b dk bl, grn & bis   .20   .20
1624   A543   20b gray, grn & red   .20   .20
1625   A543   40b pale grn & red   .20   .20
1626   A543   55b grn, lt grn & lil   .25   .20
1627   A543   75b cit, red & grn   .25   .20
1628   A543   1 l dp cl, rose cl, grn & org   .40   .20
1629   A543   1.25 l sal, vio bl & grn   .45   .20
1630   A543   1.55 l red brn, yel & grn   2.45   1.60
  Nos. 1623-1630 (8)

Garden flowers: 20b, Geranium. 40b, Fuchsia. 55b, Chrysanthemum. 75b, Dahlia. 1 l, Lily. 1.25 l, Day lily. 1.55 l, Marigold.

Tourist Publicity: 55b, Lake Bilea and cottage. 1 l, Ski lift. 1.20 l, Polana Brasov. 1.35 l, Ceahlaul peak and Lake Bicaz, horiz. 1.75 l, Hotel Alpin.

Road through
Gorge — A547

**1964, June 29**   **Engr.**
1649   A547   40b rose brn   .20   .20
1650   A547   55b dk bl   .20   .20
1651   A547   1 l dl pur   .30   .20
1652   A547   1.35 l pale brn   .45   .20
1653   A547   1.55 l green   1.70   1.00
  Nos. 1649-1653 (5)

---

**1964, Apr. 25**   **Photo.**   **Perf. 13**
Horse Show Events: 40b, Dressage, horiz. 1.35 l, Jumping. 1.55 l, Galloping, horiz.
1631   A544   40b lt bl, rose brn & brn   .20   .20
1632   A544   55b lil, red & brn   .20   .20
1633   A544   1.35 l brt grn, red & dk claret   .55   .20
1634   A544   1.55 l pale yel, bl & dp   .80   .20
  Nos. 1631-1634 (4)   1.75   .80

Hogfish
A545

**1964, May 10**   **Litho.**   **Perf. 14**
1635   A545   5h multi   .20   .20
1636   A545   10b multi   .20   .20
1637   A545   20b multi   .20   .20
1638   A545   35b multi   .20   .20
1639   A545   40b multi   .25   .20
1640   A545   55b multi   .50   .20
1641   A545   1 l multi   .90   .25
1642   A545   1.35 l multi   2.75   1.60
  Nos. 1635-1642 (8)

Fish (Constanta Aquarium): 10b, Peacock blenny. 20b, Mediterranean scad. 40b, Sturgeon. 50b, Sea horses. 55b, Yellow gurnard. 1 l, Beluga. 3.20 l, Stingray.

High
Jump — A548

**1964, July 28**   **Photo.**
55b, Balkan Games: 40b, Javelin throw. 55b, Running. 1 l, Discus throw. 1.20 l, Hurdling. 1.55 l, Map and flags of Balkan countries.

Mihail
Eminescu — A546

**1964, June 20**   **Photo.**   **Perf. 13**
Portraits in Dark Brown
1643   A546   5b green   .20   .20
1644   A546   20b magenta   .20   .20
1645   A546   35b vermilion   .25   .20
1646   A546   40b bister   .30   .20
1647   A546   55b multi   .90   .25
1648   A546   1.75 l violet   2.35   1.25
  Nos. 1643-1648 (6)

Portraits: 20b, Ion Creanga. 35b, Emil Girleanu. 55b, Michelangelo. 1.20 l, Emil Galilei. 1.75 l, William Shakespeare.

50th death anniv. of Emil Girleanu, writer, the 75th death anniversaries of Ion Creanga and Mihail Eminescu, writers, the 400th anniv. of the death of Michelangelo and the births of Galileo and Shakespeare.

**Size: 23x37½mm**

**1654** A548 30b ver, yel & yel grn .20 .20
**1655** A548 40b grn, yel, brn & vio .20 .20
**1656** A548 55b gldn brn, yel & bl grn .20 .20
**1657** A548 1 l brt bl, yel, brn & red .45 .20
**1658** A548 1.20 l pur, yel, brn & grn .55 .20

**Litho.**

**Size: 23x45mm**

**1659** A548 1.55 l multi .90 .20
*Nos. 1654-1659 (6)* 2.50 1.20

Factory — A549

55b, Flag, Coat of Arms, vert. 75b, Combine. 1.20 l, Apartment buildings. 2 l, Flag, coat of arms, industrial & agricultural scenes. 55b, 2 l, Inscribed "A XX A aniversare a eliberarii patriei!"

**1964, Aug. 23 Photo. *Perf. 13***

**1660** A549 55b multi .20 .20
**1661** A549 60b multi .25 .20
**1662** A549 75b multi .25 .20
**1663** A549 1.20 l multi .50 .20
*Nos. 1660-1663 (4)* 1.20 .80

**Souvenir Sheet**

***Imperf***

**1664** A549 2 l multi 1.25 .55

20th anniv. of Romania's liberation. No. 1664 contains one stamp 110x70mm.

High Jump — A550

Sport: 30b, Wrestling. 35b, Volleyball. 40b, Canoeing. 55b, Fencing. 1.20 l, Women's gymnastics. 1.35 l, Soccer. 1.55 l, Sharpshooting.

**1964, Sept. 1 Litho.**

**Olympic Rings in Blue, Yellow, Black, Green and Red**

**1665** A550 20b yel & blk .20 .20
**1666** A550 30b lilac & blk .20 .20
**1667** A550 35b grnsh bl & blk .20 .20
**1668** A550 40b pink & blk .20 .20
**1669** A550 55b lt yel grn & blk .35 .20
**1670** A550 1.20 l org & blk .65 .20
**1671** A550 1.35 l ocher & blk .80 .20
**1672** A550 1.55 l bl & blk .90 .35
*Nos. 1665-1672 (8)* 3.50 1.75

18th Olympic Games, Tokyo, Oct. 10-25.
Nos. 1665-1669 exist imperf., in changed colors. Three other denominations exist, 1.60 l, 2 l and 2.40 l, imperf. Value, set of 8, unused $5.50, canceled $4.
An imperf. souvenir sheet contains a 3.25 l stamp showing a runner. Value unused $5.50 canceled $5.

George Enescu, Piano Keys and Neck of Violin — A551

Designs: 55b, Enescu at piano. 1.60 l, Enescu Festival medal. 1.75 l, Enescu bust by G. Anghel.

**1964, Sept. 5 Engr.**

**1673** A551 10b bl grn .20 .20
**1674** A551 55b vio blk .20 .20
**1675** A551 1.60 l dk red brn .50 .20
**1676** A551 1.75 l dk bl .85 .20
*Nos. 1673-1676 (4)* 1.75 .80

3rd Intl. George Enescu Festival, Bucharest, Sept., 1964.

Black Swans A552

5b, Indian python. 35b, Ostriches. 40b, Crowned cranes. 55b, Tigers. 1 l, Lions. 1.55 l, Grevy's zebras. 2 l, Bactrian camels.

***Perf. 14x13***

**1964, Sept. 28 Litho. Unwmk.**

**1677** A552 5b multi .20 .20
**1678** A552 10b multi .20 .20
**1679** A552 35b multi .20 .20
**1680** A552 40b multi .20 .20
**1681** A552 55b multi .20 .20
**1682** A552 1 l multi .35 .20
**1683** A552 1.55 l multi .75 .20
**1684** A552 2 l multi 1.00 .20
*Nos. 1677-1684 (8)* 3.10 1.60

Issued to publicize the Bucharest Zoo. No. 1683 inscribed "BANI."

C. Brincoveanu, Stolnicul Cantacuzino, Gheorghe Lazar and Academy — A553

Designs: 40b, Alexandru Ioan Cuza, medal and University. 55b, Masks, curtain, harp, keyboard and palette, vert. 75b, Women students in laboratory and auditorium. 1 l, Savings Bank building.

***Perf. 13x13½, 13½x13***

**1964, Oct. 14 Photo.**

**1685** A553 20b multi .20 .20
**1686** A553 40b multi .20 .20
**1687** A553 55b multi .20 .20
**1688** A553 75b multi .25 .20
**1689** A553 1 l dk brn, yel & org .40 .20
*Nos. 1685-1689 (5)* 1.25 1.00

No. 1685 for 250th anniv. of the Royal Academy; Nos. 1686, 1688 cent. of the University of Bucharest; No. 1687 cent. of the Academy of Art and No. 1689 cent. of the Savings Bank.

Soldier's Head and Laurel — A554

**1964, Oct. 25 Litho. *Perf. 12x12½***

**1690** A554 55b ultra & lt bl .30 .20

Army Day.

Canadian Kayak Singles Gold Medal, Melbourne, 1956 A555

Romanian Olympic Gold Medals: 30b, Boxing, Melbourne, 1956. 35b, Rapid Silhouette Pistol, Melbourne, 1956. 40b, Women's High Jump, Rome, 1960. 55b, Wrestling, Rome, 1960. 1.20 l, Clay Pigeon Shooting, Rome, 1960. 1.35 l, Women's High Jump, Tokyo, 1964. 1.55 l, Javelin, Tokyo, 1964.

**1964, Nov. 30 Photo. *Perf. 13½***

**Medals in Gold and Brown**

**1691** A555 20b pink & ultra .20 .20
**1692** A555 30b yel grn & ultra .20 .20
**1693** A555 35b bluish grn & ultra .25 .20
**1694** A555 40b lil & ultra .40 .20
**1695** A555 55b org & ultra .50 .20
**1696** A555 1.20 l ol grn & ultra .70 .20
**1697** A555 1.35 l gldn brn & ultra .90 .25
**1698** A555 1.55 l rose lil & ultra 1.25 .35
*Nos. 1691-1698 (8)* 4.40 1.80

Romanian athletes who won gold medals in three Olympic Games.
Nos. 1691-1695 exist imperf., in changed colors. Three other denominations exist, 1.60 l, 2 l and 2.40 l, imperf. Value, set of 8, unused $5.75, canceled $4.
A 10 l souvenir sheet shows the 1964 Olympic gold medal and world map. Value unused $5.50, canceled $4.

Strawberries A556

Designs: 35b, Blackberries. 40b, Raspberries. 55b, Rose hips. 1.20 l, Blueberries. 1.35 l, Cornelian cherries. 1.55 l, Hazelnuts. 2.55 l, Cherries.

**1964, Dec. 20 Litho. *Perf. 13½x14***

**1703** A556 5b gray, red & grn .20 .20
**1704** A556 35b ocher, grn & dk vio bl .20 .20
**1705** A556 40b pale vio, car & grn .20 .20
**1706** A556 55b yel grn, grn & red .20 .20
**1707** A556 1.20 l sal pink, grn, brn & ind .35 .20
**1708** A556 1.35 l lt bl, grn & red .40 .20
**1709** A556 1.55 l gldn brn, grn & ocher .75 .20
**1710** A556 2.55 l ultra, grn & red 1.50 .25
*Nos. 1703-1710 (8)* 3.80 1.65

Syncom 3 — A557

UN Headquarters, NY — A558

Space Satellites: 40b, Syncom 3 over TV antennas. 55b, Ranger 7 reaching moon, horiz. 1 l, Ranger 7 and moon close-up, horiz. 1.20 l, Voskhod. 5 l, Konstantin Feoktistov, Vladimir M. Komarov, Boris B. Yegorov and Voskhod.

***Perf. 13x14, 14x13***

**1965, Jan. 5 Litho. Unwmk.**

**Size: 22x38mm, 38x22mm**

**1711** A557 30b multi .20 .20
**1712** A557 40b multi .35 .20
**1713** A557 55b multi .45 .20
**1714** A557 1 l multi .50 .20
**1715** A557 1.20 l multi, horiz. .85 .20

***Perf. 13½x13***

**Size: 52x30mm**

**1716** A557 5 l multi 2.00 .50
*Nos. 1711-1716 (6)* 4.35 1.50

For surcharge see No. 1737.

**1965, Jan. 25 *Perf. 12x12½***

1.60 l, Arms, flag of Romania, UN emblem.

**1717** A558 55b ultra, red & gold .40 .20
**1718** A558 1.60 l ultra, red, gold & yel .75 .20

20th anniv. of the UN and 10th anniv. of Romania's membership in the UN.

Greek Tortoise — A559

Reptiles: 10b, Bull lizard. 20b, Three-lined lizard. 40b, Sand lizard. 55b, Slow worm. 60b, Sand viper. 1 l, Desert lizard. 1.20 l, Orsini's viper. 1.35 l, Caspian whipsnake. 3.25 l, Four-lined snake.

**1965, Feb. 25 Photo. *Perf. 13½***

**1719** A559 5b multi .20 .20
**1720** A559 10b multi .20 .20
**1721** A559 20b multi .20 .20
**1722** A559 40b multi .20 .20
**1723** A559 55b multi .20 .20
**1724** A559 60b multi .25 .20
**1725** A559 1 l multi .35 .20
**1726** A559 1.20 l multi .45 .20
**1727** A559 1.35 l multi .60 .20
**1728** A559 3.25 l multi 1.10 .25
*Nos. 1719-1728 (10)* 3.75 2.05

White Persian Cats — A560

Designs: 1.35 l, Siamese cat. Others; Various European cats. (5b, 10b, 3.25 l, horiz.)

**1965, Mar. 20 Litho.**

**Size: 41x29mm, 29x41mm**

**Cats in Natural Colors**

**1729** A560 5b brn org & blk .20 .20
**1730** A560 10b brt bl & blk .20 .20
**1731** A560 40b yel grn, yel & blk .20 .20
**1732** A560 55b rose red & blk .25 .20
**1733** A560 60b yel & blk .40 .20
**1734** A560 75b lt vio & blk .45 .20
**1735** A560 1.35 l red org & blk .85 .20

***Perf. 13x13½***

**Size: 62x29mm**

**1736** A560 3.25 l blue 1.60 .35
*Nos. 1729-1736 (8)* 4.15 1.75

No. 1714 Surcharged in Violet

**1965, Apr. 25 *Perf. 14x13***

**1737** A557 5 l on 1 l multi 12.50 12.50

Flight of the US rocket Ranger 9 to the moon, Mar. 24, 1965.

## Dante Alighieri — A561

**1965, May 10. Photo. Perf. 13½**
Portrait in Black

| | | | | |
|---|---|---|---|---|
| 1738 | A561 | 40b chalky blue | .20 | .20 |
| 1739 | A561 | 55b bister | .20 | .20 |
| 1740 | A561 | 60b light lilac | .20 | .20 |
| 1741 | A561 | 1 l dl red brn | .45 | .20 |
| 1742 | A561 | 1.35 l olive | 1.10 | .60 |
| 1743 | A561 | 1.75 l orange red | 2.75 | 1.25 |
| | | Nos. 1738-1743 (6) | | |

40b, Ion Bianu, philologist and historian. 55b, Anton Bacalbasa, writer. 60b, Vasile Conta, philosopher. 1.35 l, Jean Sibelius, Finnish composer. 1.35 l, Horace, Roman poet.

## ITU Emblem, Old and New Communication Equipment — A562

**1965, May 15. Engr.**

| | | | | |
|---|---|---|---|---|
| 1744 | A562 | 1.75 l ultra | .90 | .40 |

ITU, centenary.

## Iron Gate, Danube — A562a

**1965, Apr. 30. Litho. Perf. 12½x12**

| | | | | |
|---|---|---|---|---|
| 1745 | A562a | 30b (25d) lt bl & grn | .20 | .20 |
| 1746 | A562a | 55b (50d) lt bl & dk red | .25 | .20 |

## Arms of Yugoslavia and Romania and Djerdap Dam — A562b

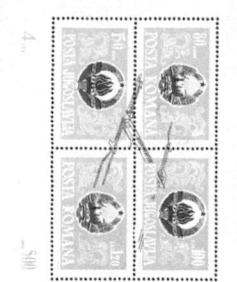

**Miniature Sheet**
**Perf. 13½x13**

| | | | | |
|---|---|---|---|---|
| 1747 | A562b | Sheet of 4 | 2.50 | 2.50 |
| a. | | 80b multi | .40 | .20 |
| b. | | 1.20 l multi | .20 | .20 |

55b (50d), Iron Gate hydroelectric plant & dam.

Issued simultaneously by Romania and Yugoslavia for the start of construction of the Iron Gate hydroelectric plant and dam. Valid for postage in both countries.

No. 1747 contains one each of Nos. 1747a, 1747b and Yugoslavia Nos. 771a and 771b. Only Nos. 1747a and 1747b were valid in Romania. Sold for 4 l. See Yugoslavia Nos. 769-771.

## Small-bore Rifle Shooting, Kneeling — A563

**1965, May 15. Litho. Unwmk.**
**Size: 23x43mm, 43x23mm**
**Perf. 12x12½, 12½x12**

| | | | | |
|---|---|---|---|---|
| 1748 | A563 | 20b multi | .20 | .20 |
| 1749 | A563 | 40b dl grn, pink & blk | .20 | .20 |
| 1750 | A563 | 55b multi | .20 | .20 |
| 1751 | A563 | 1 l pale grn, blk & ocher | .35 | .20 |
| 1752 | A563 | 1.60 l multi | .60 | .20 |
| 1753 | A563 | 2 l multi | .75 | .20 |
| | | Nos. 1748-1753 (6) | 2.30 | 1.20 |

Designs: 40b, Rifle shooting, prone. 55b, Rapid-fire pistol and map of Europe. 1 l, Free pistol and map of Europe. 1.60 l, Small-bore rifle, standing, and map of Europe. Marksmen in various shooting positions (all horizontal).

European Shooting Championships, Bucharest.

Nos. 1749-1752 were issued imperf. in changed colors. Two other denominations also exist, 3.25 l and 5 l, imperf. Value, set of 6, unused $4.25, canceled $1.75.

## Fat-Frumos and the Giant A564

**1965, June 25. Photo. Perf. 13**

| | | | | |
|---|---|---|---|---|
| 1756 | A564 | 20b multi | .20 | .20 |
| 1757 | A564 | 40b multi | .20 | .20 |
| 1758 | A564 | 55b multi | .20 | .20 |
| 1759 | A564 | 1 l multi | .25 | .20 |
| 1760 | A564 | 1.35 l multi | .40 | .20 |
| 1761 | A564 | 2 l multi | .85 | .20 |
| | | Nos. 1756-1761 (6) | 2.50 | 1.20 |

Fairy Tales: 40b, Fat-Frumos on horseback and Ileana Cosinzeana. 55b, Harap Alb and the Ox and the Bear. 1 l, "The Moralist Wolf." 1.35 l, "The Calif." 2 l, Wolf and bear pulling sled.

## Bee and Blossoms A565

**1965, July 28. Litho. Unwmk.**
**Perf. 12x12½, 12½x12**

| | | | | |
|---|---|---|---|---|
| 1762 | A565 | 55b org, bl & pink | .25 | .20 |
| 1763 | A565 | 1.60 l multi | .50 | .20 |

20th Congress of the Intl Federation of Bee-keeping Assocs. (Apimondia), Bucharest, Aug. 26-31.

## Space Achievements A566

**1965, Aug. 25. Litho. Perf. 12x12½**

| | | | | |
|---|---|---|---|---|
| 1764 | A566 | 1.75 l dk bl, bl & ver | .80 | .20 |
| 1765 | A566 | 2.40 l multi | 1.10 | .20 |
| 1766 | A566 | 3.20 l lt bl & ver | 2.25 | .35 |
| | | Nos. 1764-1766 (3) | 4.15 | .75 |

Designs: 1.75 l, Col. Pavel Belyayev, Lt. Col. Alexei Leonov and Voskhod 2. 2.40 l, Early Bird over globe. 3.20 l, Lt. Col. Gordon Cooper and Lt. Com. Charles Conrad, Gemini 3 and globe.

## European Quail — A567

**Birds in Natural Colors**

**1965, Sept. 10. Photo. Perf. 13½**
**Size: 34x34mm**

| | | | | |
|---|---|---|---|---|
| 1767 | A567 | 5b red brn & rose lil | .20 | .20 |
| 1768 | A567 | 10b brn & yel | .20 | .20 |
| 1769 | A567 | 20b brn & bl grn | .20 | .20 |
| 1770 | A567 | 40b lil & org brn | .25 | .20 |
| 1771 | A567 | 55b brt grn & lt brn | .25 | .20 |
| 1772 | A567 | 60b dl org & bl | .30 | .20 |
| 1773 | A567 | 1 l red & lil | .40 | .20 |
| 1774 | A567 | 1.20 l dk brn & grn | .60 | .20 |
| 1775 | A567 | 1.35 l org & ultra | .80 | .20 |

**Size: 32x73mm**

| | | | | |
|---|---|---|---|---|
| 1776 | A567 | 3.25 l ultra & sep | 2.10 | .30 |
| | | Nos. 1767-1776 (10) | 5.25 | 2.10 |

Birds: 10b, Eurasian woodcock. 20b, Eurasian snipe. 40b, Turtle dove. 55b, Mallard. 60b, White-fronted goose. 1 l, Eurasian crane. 1.20 l, Glossy ibis. 1.35 l, Mute swan. 3.25 l, White pelican.

## Marx and Lenin A568

**1965, Sept. 6. Photo.**

| | | | | |
|---|---|---|---|---|
| 1777 | A568 | 55b red, blk & yel | .40 | .20 |

6th Conference of Postal Ministers of Communist Countries, Peking, June 21-July 15.

## Vasile Alecsandri A569

**1965, Oct. 9. Unwmk. Perf. 13½**

| | | | | |
|---|---|---|---|---|
| 1778 | A569 | 55b red brn, dk brn & gold | .40 | .20 |

Alecsandri (1821-1890), statesman and poet.

## Bird-of-Paradise Flower — A570

**1965, Oct. 25. Litho. Perf. 12x12½, 12½x12**
**Flowers in Natural Colors**
**Size: 23x43mm, 43x23mm**

| | | | | |
|---|---|---|---|---|
| 1779 | A570 | 5b brown | .20 | .20 |
| 1780 | A570 | 10b green | .20 | .20 |
| 1781 | A570 | 20b dk bl | .20 | .20 |
| 1782 | A570 | 30b vio bl | .20 | .20 |
| 1783 | A570 | 40b red brn | .20 | .20 |
| 1784 | A570 | 55b dk red | .20 | .20 |
| 1785 | A570 | 60b lt grn | .20 | .20 |
| 1786 | A570 | 1 l grn | .30 | .20 |
| 1787 | A570 | 1.35 l violet | .45 | .20 |
| 1788 | A570 | 1.75 l dk grn | .80 | .20 |
| | | Nos. 1779-1788 (10) | 3.85 | 2.15 |

The orchid on No. 1780 is attached to the limb.

Flowers from Cluj Botanical Gardens: 10b, Stanhope orchid. 20b, Paphiopedilum insigne. 30b, Zanzibar water lily, horiz. 40b, Ferocactus, horiz. 55b, Cotton blossom, horiz. 1 l, Hibiscus, horiz. 1.35 l, Gloxinia, horiz. 1.75 l, Victoria water lily, horiz. 2.30 l, Hibiscus, bird-of-paradise flower and greenhouse.

## Running — A571

**1965, Nov. 10. Photo. Perf. 13½**

| | | | | |
|---|---|---|---|---|
| 1789 | A571 | 55b shown | .20 | .20 |
| 1790 | A571 | 1.55 l Soccer | .45 | .20 |
| 1791 | A571 | 1.75 l Woman diver | .55 | .20 |
| 1792 | A571 | Mountaineering | .60 | .20 |
| 1793 | A571 | 5 l Canoeing | 3.20 | 1.10 |
| | | Nos. 1789-1793 (5) | 1.40 | .30 |

Spartakist Games. No. 1793 commemorates the Romanian victory in the European Kayak Championships.

## Pigeon and Post Horn — A572

**1965, Nov. 15:**

Designs: 1 l, Pigeon on television antenna and post horn, horiz. 1.75 l, Flying pigeon and post horn, horiz.

| | | | | |
|---|---|---|---|---|
| 1794 | A572 | 55b + 45b label | .85 | .20 |
| 1795 | A572 | 1 l green & brown | .40 | .20 |
| 1796 | A572 | 1.75 l green & se- | 1.65 | .60 |
| | | Nos. 1794-1796 (3) | | |

Issued for Stamp Day. No. 1794 is printed with alternating label showing post rider and emblem of Romanian Philatelists' Association and 45b additional charge. Stamp and label are imperf. between.

## Chamois and Hunting Trophy A573

**1965, Dec. 10. Photo. Perf. 13½**
**Size: 37x22mm**

| | | | | |
|---|---|---|---|---|
| 1797 | A573 | 55b rose lil, yel & brn | .20 | .20 |
| 1798 | A573 | 1 l brt grn, red & brn | .20 | .20 |
| 1799 | A573 | 1.60 l lt vio bl, org & brn | .25 | .20 |
| 1800 | A573 | 1.75 l rose, grn & blk | .70 | .20 |

**Size: 48x36½mm**

| | | | | |
|---|---|---|---|---|
| 1801 | A573 | 3.20 l gray, gold, blk & org | .90 | .20 |
| | | Nos. 1797-1801 (5) | 3.45 | 1.10 |

Designs and sizes: Hunting Trophy and: 1 l, Brown bear. 1.60 l, Wild boar. 3.20 l, Antlers of red deer.

## Probe III Photographing Moon — A574

## Achievements in space research — A574

Designs: 5b, Proton 1 space station, vert. 15b, Molniya I telecommunication satellite, vert. 3.25 l, Mariner IV and Mars picture, vert. 5 l, Gemini 5.

**Perf. 12x12½, 12½x12**

**1965, Dec. 25    Litho.**

| No. | Type | Denom. | Description | Mint | Used |
|---|---|---|---|---|---|
| 1802 | A574 | 5b | multi | .20 | .20 |
| 1803 | A574 | 10b | vio bl, red & gray | .20 | .20 |
| 1804 | A574 | 15b | pur, gray & org | .20 | .20 |
| 1805 | A574 | 3.25 l | vio bl, blk & red | 2.25 | .20 |
| 1806 | A574 | 5 l | dk bl, gray & red org | 3.50 | .45 |
| | | | | 6.35 | 1.25 |

Nos. 1802-1806 (5)

Achievements in space research.

## Cocker Spaniel — A575

Hunting Dogs: 5b, Dachshund (triangle). 40b, Retriever. 55b, Terrier. 60b, Red setter. 75b, White setter. 1.55 l, Pointers (rectangle). 3.25 l, Duck hunter with retriever (rectangle).

**1965, Dec. 28    Photo.    Perf. 13½**

Size: 30x42mm

| No. | Type | Denom. | Description | Mint | Used |
|---|---|---|---|---|---|
| 1807 | A575 | 5b | multi | .20 | .20 |

Size: 33½x33½mm

| No. | Type | Denom. | Description | Mint | Used |
|---|---|---|---|---|---|
| 1808 | A575 | 10b | multi | .20 | .20 |
| 1809 | A575 | 40b | multi | .25 | .20 |
| 1810 | A575 | 55b | multi | .35 | .25 |
| 1811 | A575 | 60b | multi | .60 | .50 |
| 1812 | A575 | 75b | multi | .70 | .70 |

Size: 43x28mm

| No. | Type | Denom. | Description | Mint | Used |
|---|---|---|---|---|---|
| 1813 | A575 | 1.55 l | multi | 1.55 | .75 |
| 1814 | A575 | 3.25 l | multi | 2.75 | .75 |
| | | | | 6.35 | 2.15 |

Nos. 1807-1814 (8)

## Chessboard, Queen and Jester — A576

Chessboard and: 20b, 1.60 l, Pawn and emblem. 55b, 1 l, Rook and knight on horseback.

**1966, Feb. 25    Litho.    Perf. 13**

| No. | Type | Denom. | Description | Mint | Used |
|---|---|---|---|---|---|
| 1815 | A576 | 20b | multi | .20 | .20 |
| 1816 | A576 | 40b | multi | .20 | .20 |
| 1817 | A576 | 55b | multi | .25 | .20 |
| 1818 | A576 | 1 l | multi | .55 | .20 |
| 1819 | A576 | 1.60 l | multi | 1.00 | .65 |
| 1820 | A576 | 3.25 l | multi | 2.50 | .20 |
| | | | | 4.70 | 1.65 |

Nos. 1815-1820 (6)

Chess Olympics in Cuba.

## Tractor, Grain and Sun — A577

**1966, Mar. 5**

| No. | Type | Denom. | Description | Mint | Used |
|---|---|---|---|---|---|
| 1821 | A577 | 55b | lt grn & ocher | .25 | .20 |

Founding congress of the National Union of Cooperative Farms.

## Gheorghe Gheorghiu-Dej — A578

**1966, Mar.    Photo.**

| No. | Type | Denom. | Description | Mint | Used |
|---|---|---|---|---|---|
| 1822 | A578 | 55b | gold & blk | .30 | .20 |
| a. | | 5 l | souvenir sheet | 3.75 | 3.75 |

1st death anniv. of Pres. Gheorghe Gheorghiu-Dej (1901-65). No. 1822a contains design similar to No. 1822 with signature of Gheorghiu-Dej.

## Congress Emblem — A579

**1966, Mar. 21    Photo.    Perf. 13x14½**

| No. | Type | Denom. | Description | Mint | Used |
|---|---|---|---|---|---|
| 1823 | A579 | 55b | yel & red | .30 | .20 |

1966 Congress of Communist Youth.

## Folk Dancers of Moldavia — A580

Folk Dances: 40b, Oltenia. 55b, Maramaros. 1 l, Muntenia. 1.60 l, Banat. 2 l, Transylvania.

**Engr.    Perf. 13½**

Center In Black

**1966, Apr. 4**

| No. | Type | Denom. | Description | Mint | Used |
|---|---|---|---|---|---|
| 1824 | A580 | 30b | lilac | .20 | .20 |
| 1825 | A580 | 40b | brick red | .20 | .20 |
| 1826 | A580 | 55b | brt grn | .20 | .20 |
| 1827 | A580 | 1 l | maroon | .40 | .20 |
| 1828 | A580 | 1.60 l | dk bl | .75 | .75 |
| 1829 | A580 | 2 l | yel grn | 1.00 | 1.00 |
| | | | | 2.75 | 2.55 |

Nos. 1824-1829 (6)

## Soccer Game — A581

Designs: 10b, 15b, 55b, 1.75 l, Scenes of soccer play. 4 l, Jules Rimet Cup.

**1966, Apr. 25    Litho.    Unwmk.**

| No. | Type | Denom. | Description | Mint | Used |
|---|---|---|---|---|---|
| 1830 | A581 | 5b | multi | .20 | .20 |
| 1831 | A581 | 10b | multi | .20 | .20 |
| 1832 | A581 | 15b | multi | .20 | .20 |
| 1833 | A581 | 55b | multi | .45 | .20 |
| 1834 | A581 | 1.75 l | multi | 1.10 | .60 |
| 1835 | A581 | 4 l | gold & multi | 2.50 | .60 |
| | | | | 4.65 | 1.60 |
| 1835a | A581 | 10 l | souv sheet | 3.75 | 3.75 |

Nos. 1830-1835 (6)

World Cup Soccer Championship, Wembley, England, July 11-30. No. 1835a contains one imperf. 10 l multicolored stamp in design of 4 l, but larger (32x46mm). No gum. Issued June 20.

Red-breasted Flycatcher
A583

**Photo.**

.25 .20

**1966, May 14    Photo.**

| No. | Type | Denom. | Description | Mint | Used |
|---|---|---|---|---|---|
| 1836 | A582 | 55b | multi | .25 | .20 |

Romanian Trade Union Congress.

**1966, May 25    Photo.    Perf. 13½**

Song Birds: 10b, Red crossbill. 15b, Great reed warbler. 20b, European redstart. 55b, White-spotted bluethroat. 1.20 l, Yellow wagtail. 3.20 l, Common penduline tit.

| No. | Type | Denom. | Description | Mint | Used |
|---|---|---|---|---|---|
| 1837 | A583 | 5b | gold & multi | .20 | .20 |
| 1838 | A583 | 10b | gold & multi | .20 | .20 |
| 1839 | A583 | 15b | gold & multi | .20 | .20 |
| 1840 | A583 | 20b | sil & multi | .20 | .20 |
| 1841 | A583 | 55b | sil & multi | .25 | .20 |
| 1842 | A583 | 1.20 l | gold & multi | .35 | .30 |
| 1843 | A583 | 1.55 l | sil & multi | 1.00 | .50 |
| 1844 | A583 | 3.20 l | gold & multi | 1.60 | .50 |
| | | | | 4.00 | 2.10 |

Nos. 1837-1844 (8)

## Venus 3 (USSR) — A584

Designs: 20b, FR-1 (France) 1.60 l, Luna 9 (USSR). 5 l, Gemini 6 and 7 (US).

**1966, June 25**

| No. | Type | Denom. | Description | Mint | Used |
|---|---|---|---|---|---|
| 1845 | A584 | 10b | dp vio, gray & red | .20 | .20 |
| 1846 | A584 | 20b | ultra, blk & red | .20 | .20 |
| 1847 | A584 | 1.60 l | dk bl, blk & red | .55 | .20 |
| 1848 | A584 | 5 l | bl, blk, brn & red | 1.50 | .40 |
| | | | | 2.45 | 1.00 |

Nos. 1845-1848 (4)

International achievements in space.

## Urechia Nestor — A585

Portraits: 5b, George Cosbuc. 10b, Gheorghe Sincai. 40b, Aron Pumnul. 55b, Stefan Luchian. 1 l, Sun Yat-sen. 1.35 l, Romain Rolland. 1.60 l, Gottfried Wilhelm Leibniz. 1.75 l, Ion Ghica. 3.25 l, Constantin Cantacuzino.

**1966, June 28**

| No. | Type | Denom. | Description | Mint | Used |
|---|---|---|---|---|---|
| 1849 | A585 | 5b | grn, blk & dk bl | .20 | .20 |
| 1850 | A585 | 10b | rose car, grn & blk | .20 | .20 |
| 1851 | A585 | 20b | grn, plum & blk | .20 | .20 |
| 1852 | A585 | 40b | vio bl, brn & blk | .20 | .20 |
| 1853 | A585 | 55b | brn org, bl grn & blk | .25 | .35 |
| 1854 | A585 | 1 l | ocher, vio & blk | .25 | .35 |
| 1855 | A585 | 1.35 l | lt brn & blk | .35 | .25 |
| 1856 | A585 | 1.60 l | brt grn, dl vio & blk | .55 | .55 |
| 1857 | A585 | 1.75 l | org, dl vio & blk | .55 | .55 |
| 1858 | A585 | 3.25 l | red, dl car & blk | 1.75 | .25 |
| | | | | 3.70 | 2.05 |

Nos. 1849-1858 (10)

Cultural anniversaries.

Symbols of Industry
A582

Hottonia
Palustris
A587

Marine Flora: 10b, Ceratophyllum submersum. 20b, Aldrovanda vesiculosa. 40b, Callitriche verna 55b, Vallisneria spiralis. 1 l, Elodea Canadensis rich. 1.55 l, Hippuris vulgaris. 3.25 l Myriophyllum spicatum.

**1966, Aug. 25    Litho.    Perf. 13½**

Size: 28x40mm

| No. | Type | Denom. | Description | Mint | Used |
|---|---|---|---|---|---|
| 1865 | A587 | 5b | multi | .20 | .20 |
| 1866 | A587 | 10b | multi | .20 | .20 |
| 1867 | A587 | 20b | multi | .20 | .20 |
| 1868 | A587 | 40b | multi | .20 | .20 |
| 1869 | A587 | 55b | multi | .20 | .20 |
| 1870 | A587 | 1 l | multi | .45 | .20 |
| 1871 | A587 | 1.55 l | multi | .70 | .25 |

Size: 28x50mm

| No. | Type | Denom. | Description | Mint | Used |
|---|---|---|---|---|---|
| 1872 | A587 | 3.25 l | multi | 1.40 | .35 |
| | | | | 3.55 | 1.80 |

Nos. 1865-1872 (8)

Country House, by Gheorghe Petrascu — A586

Paintings: 10b, Peasant Woman, by Nicolae Grigorescu, vert. 20b, Reapers at Rest, by Camil Ressu. 55b, Man with the Blue Cap, by Van Eyck, vert. 1.55 l, Train Compartment, by Daumier. 3.25 l, Betrothal of the Virgin, by El Greco, vert.

**1966, July 25    Unwmk.**

Gold Frame

| No. | Type | Denom. | Description | Mint | Used |
|---|---|---|---|---|---|
| 1859 | A586 | 5b | Prus grn & brn org | .20 | .20 |
| 1860 | A586 | 10b | red brn & crim | .20 | .20 |
| 1861 | A586 | 20b | brn & brt grn | .20 | .20 |
| 1862 | A586 | 55b | vio bl & lil | .25 | .20 |
| 1863 | A586 | 1.55 l | dk sl grn & org | 1.25 | 1.00 |
| 1864 | A586 | 3.25 l | vio & ultra | 2.75 | 1.00 |
| | | | | 4.85 | 2.15 |

Nos. 1859-1864 (6)

See Nos. 1907-1912.

Derivation
of the
Meter — A588

Design: 1 l, Metric system symbols.

**1966, Sept. 10    Photo.    Perf. 13½**

| No. | Type | Denom. | Description | Mint | Used |
|---|---|---|---|---|---|
| 1873 | A588 | 55b | salmon & ultra | .25 | .20 |
| 1874 | A588 | 1 l | lt grn & vio | .35 | .20 |

Introduction of metric system in Romania, centenary.

Line Integral
Denoting
Work — A590

Statue of Ovid
and Medical
School
Emblem — A589

Design: 1 l, Academy centenary medal.

I. H. Radulescu, M. Kogalniceanu and T. Savulescu — A591

**1966, Sept. 30**
Size: 22x27mm
1875 A589 40b lil gray, ultra, sep & gold — .20 .20
1876 A590 55b gray, brn, red & gold — .20 .20
Size: 22x34mm
1877 A589 1 l ultra, brn & gold — .35 .20
Size: 66x28mm
1878 A591 3 l org, dk brn & gold — 1.70 .90
Nos. 1875-1878 (4) — .95 .30
Centenary of the Romanian Academy.

Stone Crab A592

 (Stone Crab — POSTA ROMANA 20 BANI)

**1966, Oct. 15**
**Animals in Natural Colors**
1879 A592 5b dp org — .20 .20
1880 A592 10b lt bl — .20 .20
1881 A592 20b pale lil — .20 .20
1882 A592 40b grn — .20 .20
1883 A592 55b car rose — .20 .20
1884 A592 1.35 l brt grn — .45 .20
1885 A592 1.75 l ultra — .55 .20
1886 A592 3.25 l brn — 1.40 .35
Nos. 1879-1886 (8) — 3.40 1.75

Molluscs and Crustaceans: 5b, Crawfish. 10b, Nassa reticulata, vert. 40b, Campylaea trizona. 55b, Helix lucorum. 1.35 l, Mytilus galloprovincialis. 1.75 l, Lymnaea stagnalis. 3.25 l, Anodonta cygnaea. (10j, 40b, 55b, 1.75 l, are snails; 1.35, 3.25 l, are bivalves).

Cave Bear A593

**1966, Nov. 25**
Size: 36x22mm
1887 A593 5b ultra, red brn — .20 .20
1888 A593 10b vio, emer & red brn — .20 .20
1889 A593 15b ol, grn & dk brn — .20 .20
1890 A593 55b car rose — .20 .20
1891 A593 1.55 l ultra, emer & brn — .30 .20
Size: 43x27mm
1892 A593 4 l rose car, grn & brn — 1.50 .50
Nos. 1887-1892 (6) — 1.50

Prehistoric Animals: 10b, Mammoth. 15b, Bison. 55b, Cave elephant. 1.55 l, Stags. 4 l, Dinotherium.

**1966**
1893 A594 2 l multi — .65 .20

Putna Monastery, 500th Anniv. A594

Photo. Perf. 13½

---

**1967, Feb. 15** Photo. Perf. 13½
1894 A595 10b silver & multi — .20 .20
1895 A595 20b silver & multi — .20 .20
1896 A595 25b silver & multi — .20 .20
1897 A595 40b silver & multi — .30 .20
1898 A595 55b silver & multi — 4.35 2.50
Nos. 1894-1898, C163-C166 (9)

Russian Achievements in Space: 10b, Trajectory of Sputnik 1 around globe, horiz. 25b, Valentina Tereshkova and globe with trajectory of Vostok 6. 40b, Andrian G. Nikolayev, Pavel R. Popovich and globe with trajectory of Vostok 8. 55b, Alexei Leonov walking in space.

Yuri A. Gagarin and Vostok 1 — A595

Ten years of space exploration.

Barn Owl A596

 (STRIGA · TYTO ALBA — POSTA ROMANA 10 BANI)

**1967, Mar. 20** Photo. Unwmk.
**Birds in Natural Colors**
1899 A596 10b vio & olive — .20 .20
1900 A596 20b bl & org — .25 .20
1901 A596 25b brt & org — .20 .20
1902 A596 40b emer & org — .20 .20
1903 A596 55b yel grn & ocher — .25 .20
1904 A596 75b rose lil & grn — .50 .20
1905 A596 1 l yel org & blk — .80 .20
1906 A596 1.75 l sal pink & gray — 3.75 1.90
Nos. 1899-1906 (8)

Birds of Prey: 20b, Eagle owl. 40b, Osprey. 1 l, Saker falcon. 25b, Egyptian vulture. 75b, Griffon vulture. 1.20 l, Lammergeier. 1.75 l, Cinereous vulture.

**1967, Mar. 30**
**Gold Frame**
1907 A586 10b dp bl & rose red — .20 .20
1908 A586 20b dp grn & bis — .20 .20
1909 A586 55b dp carmine & bl — .20 .20
1910 A586 1.55 l dp plum & lt ultra — .50 .20
1911 A586 3.20 l brown & grn — 2.00 .45
1912 A586 5 l org & org — 4.00 1.45
Nos. 1907-1912 (6)

Painting Type of 1966
10b, Woman in Fancy Dress, by Ion Andreescu. 20b, Washwomen, by Al. Steriadi. 40b, Women weavers, by St. Dimitrescu, vert. 1.55 l, Venus and Amor, by Lucas Cranach, vert. 3.20 l, Hercules & the Lion of Numea, by Rubens. 5 l, Haman Asking Esther's Forgiveness, by Rembrandt, vert.

 (Donnizara Pogany — POSTA ROMANA)

**1967, Apr. 27** Photo. Perf. 13½
1913 A597 5b dl yel, blk brn & ver — .20 .20
1914 A597 10b bl grn, blk & lil — .20 .20

Mlle. Pogany, by Brancusi A597

 (C. BRANCUSI 1876 1957 — POSTA ROMANA)

Sculptures: 5b, Girl's head. 10b, The Sleeping Muse, horiz. 20b, The Kiss, horiz. 40b, The Infinite Column. 55b, Earth Wisdom (seated woman). 3.25 l, Gate of the Kiss.

---

1915 A597 20b lt bl, blk & rose red — .20 .20
1916 A597 40b pink, sep & brt — .20 .20
1917 A597 55b yel grn, blk & ultra — .20 .20
1918 A597 1.20 l bluish lil, ol blk & org — .40 .20
1919 A597 3.25 l emer, blk & car — 1.10 .50
Nos. 1913-1919 (7) — 2.55 1.70
Constantin Brancusi (1876-1957), sculptor.

**1967, May 4**
1920 A598 55b multicolored — .25 .20
1921 A598 1.20 l multicolored — 1.10 .25
Centenary of Romanian monetary system.

Coins of 1867 A598

 (MONEDEI NATIONALE 1867-1967 — POSTA ROMANA 55 BANI)

Design: 1.20 l, Coins of 1966.

**1967, May 9** Unwmk. Perf. 13½
1922 A599 55b multicolored — .55 .20
90th anniv. of Romanian independence.

Infantry Soldier, by Nicolae Grigorescu A599

 (INDEPENDENTA ROMANIEI — POSTA ROMANA 55)

**1967, May 20** Unwmk. Perf. 13½
1923 A600 40b multicolored — .25 .20
1924 A600 1.55 l multicolored — 1.10 .70
60th anniversary of Peasant Uprising.

Painting: 40b, Fighting Peasants, by Octav Bancila, vert.

Peasants Marching, by Stefan Luchian — A600

 (ST. LUCHIAN - LA IMPARTIT PORUMBULUI — POSTA ROMANA 1.55)

**1967, June 10** Photo.
**Flowers in Natural Colors**
1925 A601 20b ocher — .20 .20
1926 A601 40b violet — .20 .20
1927 A601 55b bis & brn red — .20 .20
1928 A601 1.20 l yel & red brn — .30 .20
1929 A601 1.75 l bluish grn & car — 1.45 .20
1930 A601 2 l lt ultra — 2.60 1.20
Nos. 1925-1930 (6)

Carpathian Flora: 40b, Hedge mustard. 55b, Columbine. 1.20 l, Alpine violet. 1.75 l, Dryas, horiz. 2 l, Edelweiss.

Centaury — A601

 (POSTA ROMANA 20)

---

Fortifications, Sibiu — A602

 (TURNURILE BRESLELOR-SIBIU — POSTA ROMANA 20)

Map of Romania and ITY Emblem — A603

 (ANNEE INTERNATIONALE DU TOURISME — POSTA 5)

Designs: 40b, Cris Castle. 55b, Wooden Church, Plopis. 1.60 l, Ruins of Nuamtula Fortress. 1.75 l, Mogosoaia Palace. 2.25 l, Voronet Church.

**1967, June 29** Photo. Perf. 13½
Size: 33x33mm
1931 A602 20b blk & multi — .20 .20
1932 A602 40b vio & multi — .20 .20
1933 A602 55b red & multi — .20 .20
1934 A602 1.60 l multi — .35 .20
1935 A602 1.75 l multi — .45 .20
Size: 48x36mm
1936 A602 2.25 l bl & multi — .75 .20
**Souvenir Sheet**
**Imperf**
1937 A603 5 l lt bl, ultra & blk — 2.50 1.40
International Tourist Year.

**1967, July 24** Unwmk. Perf. 13½
1938 A604 55b gray, Prus bl & brn — .35 .20
Battle of Marasesti & Oituz, 50th anniv.

The Attack at Marasesti, by E. Stoica — A604

 (MARASTI-MARASESTI-OITUZ — POSTA ROMANA 55 / 1917 1967)

**1967, July 29** Photo. Perf. 13½
1939 A605 10b ultra, blk & pur — .20 .20
1940 A605 20b org brn, blk & ultra — .20 .20
1941 A605 40b bl grn, blk & org brn — .20 .20
1942 A605 55b dp rose, blk & ol grn — .20 .20
1943 A605 1.20 l ol, blk & brn — .70 .20
1944 A605 1.75 l dl bl, blk & bl — .35 .20
Nos. 1939-1944 (6) — 1.85 1.20

Designs: 20b, Al. Orascu, architect. 40b, Gr. Antipa, zoologist. 55b, M. Kogalniceanu, statesman. 1.20 l, Jonathan Swift, writer. 1.75 l, Marie Curie, scientist.

Cultural anniversaries.

Dinu Lipatti, Pianist — A605

 (POSTA ROMANA 10 BANI)

## Souvenir Sheet

Anemones, by Stefan Luchian — A619    **Imperf.**

**1968, Mar. 30    Litho.**
1993 A619  10 l  multi                  4.75  4.75

1993  Stefan Luchian, Romanian painter, birth cent.

Portrait of a Lady, by Misu Popp — A620

**Perf. 13½**

Paintings: 10b, The Reveille of Romania, by Gheorghe Tattarescu. 20b, Companilul, by Teodorescu Sionion, horiz. 35b, The Judgment of Paris, by Hendrick van Balen, horiz. 55b, Little Girl with Red Kerchief, by Nicolae Grigorescu. 60b, The Mystical Betrothal of St. Catherine, by Lamberto Sustris, horiz. 1 l, Old Nicolae, the "Zither Player", by Stefan Luchian. 1.60 l, Man with a Skull, by Dietrick Bouts (?). 1.75 l, Madonna and Child with Fruit Basket, by Jan van Bylert. 2.40 l, Medor and Angelica, by Sebastiano Ricci, horiz. 3 l, Summer, by Jacob Jordaens, horiz. 3.20 l, 5 l, Ecce Homo, by Titian.

**1968    Photo.    Gold Frame    Size: 28x49mm**

1994  A620  10b  multi              .20   .20

**Size: 48½x36½mm, 36x48½mm**

| | | | | |
|---|---|---|---|---|
| 1995 | A620 | 20b multi | .20 | .20 |
| 1996 | A620 | 35b multi | .20 | .20 |
| 1997 | A620 | 40b multi | .20 | .20 |
| 1998 | A620 | 55b multi | .20 | .20 |
| 1999 | A620 | 60b multi | .25 | .20 |
| 2000 | A620 | 1 l multi | .40 | .20 |
| 2001 | A620 | 1.60 l multi | .40 | .20 |
| 2002 | A620 | 1.75 l multi | .80 | .30 |
| 2003 | A620 | 2.40 l multi | .90 | .50 |
| 2004 | A620 | 3 l multi | 1.40 | .70 |
| 2005 | A620 | 3.20 l multi | 5.35 | 3.30 |

Nos. 1994-2005 (12)

**Miniature Sheet**

**Imperf**

2006  A620  5 l  multi              4.50  4.50

Issued: 40, 55b, 1, 1.60, 2.40, 3.20, 5 l, 3/28; others, 9/9.
See Nos. 2088-2094, 2124-2130.

---

Diesel Locomotive — A616

Map Showing Telephone Network — A617

Designs: 10b, Communications emblem, vert. 20b, Train. 35b, Plane. 50b, Telephone, vert. 60b, Small loading truck. 1.20 l, Autobus. 1.35 l, Helicopter. 1.50 l, Trolley bus. 1.55 l, Radio station and tower. 1.75 l, Highway. 2 l, Mail truck. 2.40 l, Television tower. 3.20 l, Jet plane. 3.25 l, Steamship. 4 l, Electric train. 5 l, World map and teletype.

**Photo.; Engr. (type A615)    Perf. 13½**

| 1967-68 | | | | |
|---|---|---|---|---|
| 1967 | A614 | 5b lt ol grn ('68) | .20 | .20 |
| 1968 | A614 | 10b henna brn ('68) | .20 | .20 |
| 1969 | A614 | 20b gray ('68) | .20 | .20 |
| 1970 | A614 | 35b bl blk ('68) | .20 | .20 |
| 1971 | A615 | 40b violet blue | .20 | .20 |
| 1972 | A614 | 50b orange ('68) | .20 | .20 |
| 1973 | A615 | 55b dull orange | .20 | .20 |
| 1974 | A614 | 60b orange brn ('68) | .20 | .20 |

**Size: 22½x28mm, 28x22½mm**

| 1975 | A616 | 1 l emerald ('68) | .20 | .20 |
|---|---|---|---|---|
| 1976 | A617 | 1.20 l red lil ('68) | .25 | .20 |
| 1977 | A617 | 1.35 l brt blue ('68) | .30 | .25 |
| 1978 | A617 | 1.50 l rose red ('68) | .35 | .35 |
| 1979 | A616 | 1.55 l dk brown ('68) | .40 | .35 |
| 1980 | A615 | 1.60 l rose red | .40 | .40 |
| 1981 | A617 | 1.75 l dp green ('68) | .60 | .60 |
| 1982 | A617 | 2 l dk blue ('68) | .75 | .75 |
| 1983 | A616 | 2.40 l dk blue ('68) | .75 | .75 |
| 1984 | A617 | 3 l grnsh blue | 1.00 | 1.00 |
| 1985 | A617 | 3.20 l ocher ('68) | 1.00 | 1.00 |
| 1986 | A616 | 3.25 l ultra ('68) | 1.25 | 1.20 |
| 1987 | A617 | 4 l lil rose ('68) | 1.00 | .85 |
| 1988 | A617 | 5 l violet ('68) | 10.80 | 1.40 |

Nos. 1067-1088 (22)

40th anniv. of the first automatic telephone exchange; introduction of automatic telephone service (No. 1984).

See Nos. 2078-2079, 2269-2284 and design A702.

Coat of Arms, Symbols of Agriculture and Industry A618

55b, Coat of arms. 1.60 l, Romanian flag. 1.75 l, Coat of arms, symbols of arts and education.

**1967, Dec. 26    Photo.    Perf. 13½**

**Size: 27x48mm**
| 1989 | A618 | 40b multicolored | .20 | .20 |
|---|---|---|---|---|
| 1990 | A618 | 55b multicolored | .20 | .20 |

**Size: 33½x48mm**
| 1991 | A618 | 1.60 l multicolored | .30 | .20 |

**Size: 27x48mm**
| 1992 | A618 | 1.75 l multicolored | .50 | .25 |
| | | | 1.20 | .85 |

Nos. 1989-1992 (4)

20th anniversary of the republic.

---

Romanian Academy Library, Bucharest, Cent. — A610

**1967, Sept. 25    Litho.**
1960  A610  55b  ocher, gray & dk bl  .30  .20

Karl Marx and Title Page — A611

**Photo.**
Lenin — A612

**1967, Nov. 4**
1961  A611  40b  rose claret, blk & yel  .25  .20

Centenary of the publication of "Das Kapital" by Karl Marx.

**1967, Nov. 3**
1962  A612  1.20 l  red, blk & gold  .35  .20

Russian October Revolution, 50th anniv.

Monorail Leaving US EXPO Pavilion A613

Designs: 1 l, EXPO emblem and atom symbol. 1.60 l, Cup, world map and EXPO emblem. 2 l, EXPO emblem.

**1967, Nov. 28    Photo.**
| 1963 | A613 | 55b grnsh bl, vio & blk | .20 | .20 |
|---|---|---|---|---|
| 1964 | A613 | 1 l red, blk & gray | .25 | .20 |
| 1965 | A613 | 1.60 l multicolored | .60 | .20 |
| 1966 | A613 | 2 l multicolored | 1.45 | .80 |

Nos. 1963-1966 (4)

EXPO '67 Intl. Exhib., Montreal, Apr. 28-Oct. 27.

Arms of the Republic — A615

Arms — A609

---

Wrestlers A606

Congress Emblem — A607

Designs: 20b, 55b, 1.20 l, 2 l, Various fight scenes and world map (20b, 2 l horizontal); on 2 l maps are large and wrestlers small.

**1967, Aug. 28**
| 1945 | A606 | 10b olive & multi | .20 | .20 |
|---|---|---|---|---|
| 1946 | A606 | 20b citron & multi | .20 | .20 |
| 1947 | A606 | 55b bister & multi | .25 | .20 |
| 1948 | A606 | 1.20 l multi | .20 | .20 |
| 1949 | A606 | 2 l ultra, gold & dp car | 1.00 | .30 |
| | | | 1.85 | 1.10 |

Nos. 1945-1949 (5)

World Greco-Roman Wrestling Championships, Bucharest.

**1967, Aug. 28**
1950  A607  1.60 l  lt bl, ultra & dp car  .50  .20

Intl. Linguists' Cong., Bucharest, 8/28-9/2.

Ice Skating — A608

Designs: 40b, Biathlon. 55b, 5 l, Bobsledding. 1 l, Skiing. 1.55 l, Ice Hockey. 2 l, Emblem of 10th Winter Olympic Games. 2.30 l, Ski jump.

**1967, Sept. 28    Photo.    Perf. 13½x13**
| 1951 | A608 | 20b lt bl & multi | .20 | .20 |
|---|---|---|---|---|
| 1952 | A608 | 40b multi | .20 | .20 |
| 1953 | A608 | 55b bl & multi | .20 | .20 |
| 1954 | A608 | 1 l lil & multi | .20 | .20 |
| 1955 | A608 | 1.55 l multi | .30 | .20 |
| 1956 | A608 | 2 l gray & multi | .50 | .50 |
| 1957 | A608 | 2.30 l multi | .85 | .35 |
| | | | 2.45 | 1.55 |

Nos. 1951-1957 (7)

**Souvenir Sheet**
**Imperf**
1958  A608  5 l  lt bl & multi  3.25  2.75

10th Winter Olympic Games, Grenoble, France, Feb. 6-18, 1968.
Nos. 1951-1957 issued in sheets of 10 (5x2) and 5 labels.

Truck — A614

Curtea de Arges Monastery, 450th Anniv. — A609

**1967, Nov. 1    Unwmk.    Perf. 13½**
1959  A609  55b  multicolored  .30  .20

**1968, May 9**  Human Rights Flame — A621  **Perf. 13½**
2007  A621  1 l multicolored  .45  .20
Int'l Human Rights Year.

**1968, May 14**  WHO Emblem — A622  **Photo.**
2008  A622  1.60 l multi  .50  .20
WHO, 20th anniversary.

**1968, May 17**  "Prince Dragos Hunting Bison," by Nicolae Grigorescu — A623
2009  A623  1.60 l multi  .60  .20
15th Hunting Cong., Mamaia, May 23-29.

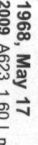

**1968, June 9**  Pioneers and Liberation Monument — A624  **Photo.**  **Perf. 13½**
2010  A624  5b multi  .20  .20
2011  A624  40b multi  .20  .20
2012  A624  55b multi  .20  .20
2013  A624  1 l multi  .30  .20
2014  A624  1.60 l multi  .50  .20
2015  A624  2.40 l multi  .70  .20
Nos. 2010-2015 (6)  2.10  1.20

Pioneers: 40b, receiving scarfs, 55b, building model planes and boat. 1 l, as radio amateurs. 1.60 l, folk dancing. 2.40 l, Girl Pioneers in camp.

IO N IONESCU DE LA BRAD 1818-1891

**1968**
2016  A625  40b multicolored  .45  .20
2017  A626  55b green & multi  .20  .20

**Size: 28x43mm**
2018  A625  1.60 l gold & multi  .85  .60
Nos. 2016-2018 (3)

Designs: 55b, Emil Racovita. 1.60 l, Prince Mircea of Walachia.

**Size: 28x48mm**
Ion Ionescu de la Brad — A625

Ion Ionescu de la Brad (1818-91); Emil Racovita (1868-1947), explorer and naturalist; Prince Mircea (1386-1418). Issue dates: 40b, 55b, June 24; 1.60 l, June 22.

---

**1968, July 20**  Geranium A626  **Photo.**  **Perf. 13½**
2019  A626  10b multicolored  .20  .20
2020  A626  20b multicolored  .20  .20
2021  A626  40b multicolored  .20  .20
2022  A626  55b multicolored  .20  .20
2023  A626  60b multicolored  .20  .20
2024  A626  1.20 l multicolored  .25  .20
2025  A626  1.35 l multicolored  .35  .20
2026  A626  1.60 l multicolored  .75  .20
Nos. 2019-2026 (8)  2.35  1.60

Designs: Various geraniums.

**1968, July 25**  Avram Iancu, by B. Iscovescu and Demonstrating Students — A627
2027  A627  55b gold & multi  .20  .20
2028  A627  1.20 l gold & multi  .45  .20
2029  A627  1.60 l gold & multi  .70  .20
Nos. 2027-2029 (3)  1.35  .60

Demonstrating Students and: 55b, Nicolae Balcescu, by Gheorghe Tattarescu. 1.20 l, Vasile Alecsandri, by N. Livaditti.

120th anniversary of 1848 revolution.

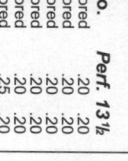
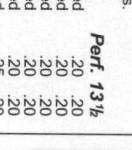
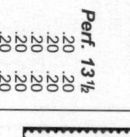

Boxing — A628

**1968, Aug. 28**
2030  A628  10b multi  .20  .20
2031  A628  20b multicolored  .20  .20
2032  A628  40b multi  .20  .20
2033  A628  55b multi  .20  .20
2034  A628  1 l multi  .20  .20
2035  A628  1.20 l multi  .35  .20
2036  A628  1.35 l multi  .40  .25
2037  A628  1.60 l multi  .65  .25
Nos. 2030-2037 (8)  2.40  1.70

Aztec Calendar Stone and: 10b, Javelin, Women's. 20b, Woman diver. 40b, Volleyball. 60b, Wrestling. 1.20 l, Fencing. 1.35 l, Canoeing. 1.60 l, Soccer. 5 l, Running

Atheneum and Harp — A629

---

**1968, Oct. 4**  Globe and Emblem — A630  **Litho.**  **Perf. 13½**
2040  A630  1.60 l ultra & gold  .50  .20
Int'l. Fed. of Photographic Art, 20th anniv.

**Souvenir Sheet**
*Imperf*
2038  A628  5 l multi  2.25  1.75
19th Olympic Games, Mexico City, 10/12-17.

**1968, Aug. 20**  **Litho.**  **Perf. 12x12½**
2039  A629  55b multicolored  .25  .20
Centenary of the Philharmonic Orchestra.

Moldovita Monastery Church — A631

**1968, Nov. 25**  **Engr.**  **Perf. 13½**
2041  A631  10b dk bl, ol & brn  .20  .20
2042  A631  40b rose car, bl &  .20  .20
2043  A631  55b ol, brn & vio  .20  .20
2044  A631  1.20 l yel, mar & gray  .30  .20
2045  A631  1.55 l vio brn, dk bl &  
2046  A631  1.75 l org, blk & ol  1.00  .20
Nos. 2041-2046 (6)  2.40  1.20

Historic Monuments: 10b, "The Triumph of Trajan," Roman metope, vert. 55b, Cozia monastery church. 1.20 l, Court of Tirgoviste Palace. 1.55 l, Palace of Culture, Jassy. 1.75 l, Corvinus Castle, Hunedoara.

Mute Swan — A632

**1968, Dec. 20**  **Photo.**  **Perf. 13½**
2047  A632  10b pink & multi  .20  .20
2048  A632  20b multicolored  .20  .20
2049  A632  40b multi  .20  .20
2050  A632  olive & multi  .20  .20
2051  A632  60b multicolored  .20  .20
2052  A632  1.20 l multicolored  .45  .20
2053  A632  1.35 l blue & multi  .60  .20
2054  A632  1.60 l multicolored  .60  .20
Nos. 2047-2054 (8)  2.55  1.60

Protected Birds and Animals: 20b, European stilts. 40b, Sheldrakes. 55b, Euro-bustards. 1.35 l, Chamois. 1.60 l, Bison.
bustards. 1.20 l, Great feeding young. 60b, Golden eagle. 1.20 l, Egret feeding.

---

**1968, Dec. 1**  **Litho.**  **Perf. 13½**
2055  A633  55b gold & multi  .30  .20
2056  A633  1 l gold & multi  .30  .20
2057  A633  1.75 l gold & multi  .40  .35
a.  Souv. sheet of 3, #2055-2057,  1.50  1.50
imperf.
Nos. 2055-2057 (3)  .90  .75

50th anniv. of the union of Transylvania and Romania. No. 2057a sold for 4 l.

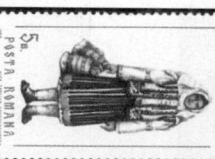

Woman from Neamt — A634

Regional Costumes: 40b, Man from Neamt. 55b, Woman from Hunedoara. 1 l, Man from Hunedoara. 1.60 l, Woman from Brasov. 2.40 l, Man from Brasov.

**1968, Dec. 28**  **Perf. 12x12½**
2058  A634  5b orange & multi  .20  .20
2059  A634  40b blue & multi  .20  .20
2060  A634  55b multi  .20  .20
2061  A634  1 l rose & multi  .55  .20
2062  A634  1.60 l brown & multi  .50  .20
2063  A634  2.40 l multi  .95  .35
Nos. 2058-2063 (6)  2.30  1.35

Michael the Brave's Entry into Alba Iulia — A633

Designs: 1 l, "The Round Dance of Union," by Theodor Aman. 1.75 l, Assembly of Alba Iulia.

**1969, Mar. 27**  **Photo.**  **Perf. 13½**
**Size: 37x49mm, 49x37mm**
**Gold Frame**
2088  A620  10b multi  .20  .20
2089  A620  20b multi  .20  .20
2090  A620  355b multi  .20  .20
2091  A620  60b multi  .30  .20
2092  A620  1.75 l multi  .70  .25

Painting Type of 1968
Paintings (Nudes): 10b, Woman Carrying Jug, by Gheorghe Tattarescu. 20b, Reclining Woman, by Theodor Pallady, horiz. 35b, Seated Woman, by Nicolae Tonitza. 60b, Venus and Amor, 17th century Flemish School. 1.75 l, Diana and Endimion, by Marco Liberi. 3 l, The Three Graces, by Alessandro Varotari.

**1969, Jan. 10**  **Photo.**  **Perf. 13½**
**Type of Regular Issue**
2078  A614  40b Power lines, vert.  .20  .20
2079  A614  55b Dam, vert.  .20  .20

Type of Regular Issue

**1969, Feb. 15**
2064  A634  5b multi  .20  .20
2065  A634  40b multi  .20  .20
2066  A634  55b lil & multi  .20  .20
2067  A634  1 l brn & multi  .25  .20
2068  A634  1.60 l brn & multi  1.00  .20
2069  A634  2.40 l multi  1.00  .25
Nos. 2064-2069 (6)  2.40  1.25

Regional Costumes: 5b, Woman from Dolj. 40b, Man from Hunedoara. 1 l, Man from Arges. 55b, Woman from Arges. 1.60 l, Man from Timisoara. 2.40 l, Man from Timisoara.

Fencing — A635

**1969, Mar. 10**  **Photo.**  **Perf. 13½**
**Denominations Black, Athletes in Gray**
2070  A635  10b pale brown  .20  .20
2071  A635  20b violet  .20  .20
2072  A635  40b blue  .20  .20
2073  A635  55b red  .20  .20
2074  A635  1 l green  .20  .20
2075  A635  1.20 l brt blue  .40  .20
2076  A635  1.35 l cerise  .45  .20
2077  A635  2.40 l dp green  .85  .20
Nos. 2070-2077 (8)  2.60  1.60

Sports: 20b, Women's javelin. 40b, Canoeing. 55b, Boxing. 1 l, Volleyball. 1.20 l, Swimming. 1.60 l, Wrestling. 2.40 l, Soccer.

The Last Judgment (detail), Voronet Monastery — A650

North Moldavian Monastery Frescoes: 10b, Stephen the Great and family, Voronet. 20b, Three prophets, Sucevita. 60b, St. Nicholas (scene from his life), Sucevita. vert. 1.75 l, Siege of Constantinople, 7th century, Moldovita. 3 l, Plowman, Voronet, vert.

**1969, Dec. 15** **Perf. 13½**

| | | | | |
|---|---|---|---|---|
| 2142 | A650 | 10b | gold & multi | .20 .20 |
| 2143 | A650 | 20b | gold & multi | .20 .20 |
| 2144 | A650 | 35b | gold & multi | .20 .20 |
| 2145 | A650 | 60b | gold & multi | .20 .20 |
| 2146 | A650 | 1.75 l | gold & multi | .30 .20 |
| 2147 | A650 | 3 l | gold & multi | 1.00 1.20 |
| | | Nos. 2142-2147 (6) | | 2.10 1.20 |

Ice Hockey A651

Designs: 55b, Goalkeeper. 1.20 l, Two players with puck. 2.40 l, Player and goalkeeper.

**1970, Jan. 20** **Perf. 13½**

| | | | | |
|---|---|---|---|---|
| 2148 | A651 | 20b | yellow & multi | .20 .20 |
| 2149 | A651 | 55b | multicolored | .35 .20 |
| 2150 | A651 | 1.20 l | pink & multi | 1.00 .30 |
| 2151 | A651 | 2.40 l | lt blue & multi | 1.75 .90 |
| | | Nos. 2148-2151 (4) | | |

World Ice Hockey Championships, Bucharest and Galati, Feb. 24–Mar. 5.

Pasqueflower A652

Flowers: 10b, Adonis vernalis. 20b, Thistle. 40b, Almond tree blossoms. 55b, Iris. 1 l, Flax. 1.20 l, Sage. 2.40 l, Peony.

**1970, Feb. 25** **Photo.** **Perf. 13½**

| | | | | |
|---|---|---|---|---|
| 2152 | A652 | 5b | yellow & multi | .20 .20 |
| 2153 | A652 | 10b | green & multi | .20 .20 |
| 2154 | A652 | 20b | violet & multi | .20 .20 |
| 2155 | A652 | 40b | lt blue & multi | .20 .20 |
| 2156 | A652 | 1 l | multicolored | .35 .20 |
| 2157 | A652 | 1.20 l | red & multi | .70 .20 |
| 2159 | A652 | 2.40 l | multicolored | 2.25 1.60 |
| | | Nos. 2152-2159 (8) | | |

Japanese Print and EXPO '70 Emblem A653

Design: 1 l, Pagoda, EXPO '70 emblem.

---

| | | | | |
|---|---|---|---|---|
| 2128 | A620 | 1.75 l | multi | .70 .20 |
| 2129 | A620 | 3 l | multi | 1.25 .35 |
| | | Nos. 2124-2129 (6) | | 2.90 1.35 |

**Miniature Sheet**

*Imperf*

| | | | | |
|---|---|---|---|---|
| 2130 | A620 | 5 l | gold & multi | 2.00 1.50 |

No. 2130 contains one stamp with simulated perforations.

Issue dates: 5 l, July 31. Others, Oct. 1.

**1969, Nov. 24** **Photo.** **Perf. 13½**

| | | | | |
|---|---|---|---|---|
| 2131 | A645 | 40b | Branesti | .20 .20 |
| 2132 | A645 | 55b | Tudora | .20 .20 |
| 2133 | A645 | 1.55 l | Birsesti | .50 .50 |
| 2134 | A645 | 1.75 l | Rudaria | .60 .20 |
| | | Nos. 2131-2134 (4) | | 1.50 .80 |

Armed Forces Memorial A646

**1969, Oct. 25**

| | | | | |
|---|---|---|---|---|
| 2135 | A646 | 55b | red, blk & gold | .20 .20 |

25th anniversary of the People's Army.

Locomotives of 1869 and 1969 — A647

**1969, Oct. 31**

| | | | | |
|---|---|---|---|---|
| 2136 | A647 | 55b | silver & multi | .25 .20 |

Bucharest-Filaret-Giurgevo railroad, cent.

A649

A648

Apollo 12 landing module

**1969, Nov. 24**

| | | | | |
|---|---|---|---|---|
| 2137 | A648 | 1.50 l | multi | .55 .50 |

2nd landing on the moon, Nov. 19, 1969, astronauts Captains Alan Bean, Charles Conrad, Jr. and Richard Gordon.

Printed in sheets of 4 with 4 labels (one label with names of astronauts, one with Apollo 12 emblem and 2 silver labels with picture of landing module, Intrepid).

**1969, Dec. 25** **Photo.** **Perf. 13½**

| | | | | |
|---|---|---|---|---|
| 2138 | A649 | 40b | bister & multi | .20 .20 |
| 2139 | A649 | 55b | lilac & multi | .20 .20 |
| 2140 | A649 | 1.50 l | blue & multi | .50 .25 |
| 2141 | A649 | 2.40 l | multicolored | 1.00 .25 |
| | | Nos. 2138-2141 (4) | | 1.90 .85 |

---

Communist Party Flag — A641

**1969, Aug. 6** **Photo.** **Perf. 13½**

| | | | | |
|---|---|---|---|---|
| 2111 | A641 | 55b | multicolored | .30 .20 |

10th Romanian Communist Party Congress.

Broken Chain — A643

Torch, Atom Diagram and Book — A642

Designs: 40b, Symbols of agriculture, science and industry. 1.75 l, Pylon, smokestack and cogwheel.

**1969, Aug. 10**

| | | | | |
|---|---|---|---|---|
| 2112 | A642 | 35b | multicolored | .20 .20 |
| 2113 | A642 | 40b | green & multi | .20 .20 |
| 2114 | A642 | 1.75 l | multicolored | .60 .60 |
| | | Nos. 2112-2114 (3) | | |

Exhibition showing the achievements of Romanian economy during the last 25 years.

**1969, Aug. 23**

| | | | | |
|---|---|---|---|---|
| 2115 | A643 | 10b | multicolored | .20 .20 |
| 2116 | A643 | 55b | yellow & multi | .20 .20 |
| 2117 | A643 | 60b | multicolored | .25 .20 |
| | | Nos. 2115-2117 (3) | | .65 .60 |

55b, Construction work. 60b, Flags.

25th anniversary of Romania's liberation from fascist rule.

Masks — A645

Circus Performers: 20b, Clown. 35b, Trapeze artists. 60b, Dressage and woman trainer. 1.75 l, Woman in high wire act. 3 l, Performing tiger and trainer.

**1969, Sept. 29** **Photo.** **Perf. 13½**

| | | | | |
|---|---|---|---|---|
| 2118 | A644 | 10b | lt blue & multi | .20 .20 |
| 2119 | A644 | 20b | lemon & multi | .20 .20 |
| 2120 | A644 | 35b | lilac & multi | .20 .20 |
| 2121 | A644 | 60b | multicolored | .55 .20 |
| 2122 | A644 | 1.75 l | multicolored | .90 .35 |
| 2123 | A644 | 3 l | ultra & multi | 2.25 1.35 |
| | | Nos. 2118-2123 (6) | | |

Juggler on Unicycle — A644

Painting Type of 1968

10b, Venetian Senator, Tintoretto School. 20b, Sofia Kretzulescu, by Gheorghe Tattarescu. 35b, Phillip IV, by Velazquez. 60b, Man Reading and Child, by Hans Memling. 1.75 l, Doamnei d'Aguesseau, by Madame Vigée-Lebrun. 3 l, Portrait of a Woman, by Rembrandt. 5 l, The Return of the Prodigal Son, by Bernardino Licinio, horiz.

**1969**

**Gold Frame**

**Size: 36½x49mm**

| | | | | |
|---|---|---|---|---|
| 2124 | A620 | 10b | multi | .20 .20 |
| 2125 | A620 | 20b | multi | .20 .20 |
| 2126 | A620 | 35b | multi | .20 .20 |
| 2127 | A620 | 60b | multi | .35 .20 |

---

**Size: 27½x48½mm**

**Miniature Sheet**

*Imperf*

| | | | | |
|---|---|---|---|---|
| 2093 | A620 | 3 l | multi | 1.50 .45 |
| | | Nos. 2088-2093 (6) | | 3.10 1.50 |
| 2094 | A620 | 5 l | multi | 3.00 3.00 |

No. 2094 contains one stamp 36½x48½mm. with simulated perforations. No. 2093 is incorrectly inscribed Hans von Aachen.

Symbolic Head — A637

ILO, 50th Anniv. — A636

**1969, Apr. 9** **Photo.**

| | | | | |
|---|---|---|---|---|
| 2095 | A636 | 55b | multicolored | |

**1969, Apr. 28** **Perf. 13½**

| | | | | |
|---|---|---|---|---|
| 2096 | A637 | 55b | ultra & multi | .35 .20 |
| 2097 | A637 | 1.50 l | red & multi | .90 .35 |

Romania's cultural and economic cooperation with European countries.

Communications Symbol — A638

**1969, May 12** **Photo.** **Perf. 13½**

| | | | | |
|---|---|---|---|---|
| 2098 | A638 | 55b | vio bl & bluish gray | .35 .20 |

7th Session of the Conference of Postal and Telecommunications Ministers, Bucharest.

Boxers, Referee and Map of Europe A639

Map of Europe and: 40h, Two boxers. 55b, Sparring. 1.75 l, Referee declaring winner.

**1969, May 24**

| | | | | |
|---|---|---|---|---|
| 2099 | A639 | 35b | multicolored | .20 .20 |
| 2100 | A639 | 40b | multicolored | .20 .20 |
| 2101 | A639 | 55b | multicolored | .25 .20 |
| 2102 | A639 | 1.75 l | blue & multi | .60 .20 |
| | | Nos. 2099-2102 (4) | | 1.25 .80 |

European Boxing Championships, Bucharest, May 31–June 8.

Apatura Ilia — A640

**1969, June 25** **Photo.** **Perf. 13½**

**Insects in Natural Colors**

| | | | | |
|---|---|---|---|---|
| 2103 | A640 | 5b | yellow grn | .20 .20 |
| 2104 | A640 | 10b | yellow mag | .20 .20 |
| 2105 | A640 | 20b | violet | .20 .20 |
| 2106 | A640 | 40b | blue grn | .20 .20 |
| 2107 | A640 | 55b | brt blue | .20 .20 |
| 2108 | A640 | 60b | brt blue | .30 .20 |
| 2109 | A640 | 1.20 l | violet bl | .40 .20 |
| 2110 | A640 | 2.40 l | yellow bis | .80 .20 |
| | | Nos. 2103-2110 (8) | | 2.50 1.60 |

Designs: Various butterflies and moths.

**1970, Mar. 23**

2160 A653 20b gold & multi .20 .20

**Size: 29x92mm**

2161 A653 1 l gold & multi .30 .20

EXPO '70 Intl. Exhib., Osaka, Japan, Mar. 15-Sept. 13.

A souvenir sheet exists with perforated label in pagoda design of 1 l. Issued Nov. 28, 1970. Value $1.65.

**1970, Apr. 19   Photo.   Perf. 13½**

2162 A654 1.50 l gold & multi .45 .20

Franco-Romanian Maximafil Phil. Exhib.

Camille, by Claude Monet (Maximum Card) — A654

Cuza, by C. Popp de Szathmary — A655

Lenin (1870-1924) A656

V. I. LENIN

**1970, Apr. 20**

2163 A655 55b gold & multi .20 .20

Alexandru Ioan Cuza (1820-1866), prince of Romania.

**1970, Apr. 21   Photo.   Perf. 13½**

2164 A656 40b dk red & multi .20 .20

**1970, Apr. 28**

2165 A657 40b grn, brn org & blk .50 .35
2166 A657 1.50 l ultra, yel brn & blk 1.00 .70

Map of Europe with Capital Cities A657

Inter-European cultural and economic cooperation.

---

**1970, May 9**

2167 A658 55b red & multi .20 .20

25th anniv. of victory over the Germans.

Victory Monument, Romanian and Russian Flags — A658

Greek Silver Drachm, 5th Century B.C. — A659

**1970, May 15**

2168 A659 10b ultra, blk & sil .20 .20
2169 A659 20b hn brn, blk & sil .20 .20
2170 A659 35b grn, dk brn & gold .20 .20
2171 A659 60b brn, blk & sil .20 .20
2172 A659 1 l brt bl, blk & sil .50 .20
2173 A659 3 l dk car, blk & sil 1.00 .20
Nos. 2168-2173 (6) 2.30 1.25

Coins: 20b, Getic-Dacian silver didrachm, 2nd-1st centuries B.C. 35b, Emperor Trajan's copper sestertius, 106 A.D. 60b, Mircea ducat, 1400. 1.75 l, Stephen the Great's silver groschen, 1460. 3 l, Brasov klippe-taler, 1601, vert.

Soccer Players and Ball — A660

**1970, May 26**

2174 A660 40b multi .20 .20
2175 A660 55b multi .20 .20
2176 A660 1.75 l blue & multi .45 .20
2177 A660 3.30 l multi 1.70 .90
Nos. 2174-2177 (4)

**Souvenir Sheet**

2178 Sheet of 4 2.00 1.50
   a. A660 1.20 l multi .20 .25
   b. A660 1.50 l multi .35 .20
   c. A660 1.55 l multi .40 .20
   d. A660 1.75 l multi .40 .20

9th World Soccer Championships for the Jules Rimet Cup, Mexico City, May 30-June 21. No. 2178 contains 4 stamps similar to Nos. 2174-2177, but with only one quarter of the soccer ball on each stamp, forming one large ball in the center of the block.

Soccer ball & various scenes from soccer game.

Moldovita Monastery — A661

Frescoes from North Moldavian Monasteries.

---

**1970, June 29   Perf. 13½**

2179 A661 10b gold & multi .20 .20

**Size: 36½x49mm**

2180 A661 20b gold & multi .20 .20

**Size: 27½x49mm**

2181 A661 40b gold & multi .20 .20
2182 A661 55b gold & multi .20 .20
2183 A661 1.75 l gold & multi .35 .20
2184 A661 3 l gold & multi 1.00 .35
Nos. 2179-2184 (6) 2.15 1.35

**Size: 36½x49mm, 48x37mm**

**Miniature Sheet**

2185 A661 5 l gold & multi 1.75 1.75

Friedrich Engels (1820-1895), German Socialist — A662

**1970, July 10   Photo.   Perf. 13½**

2186 A662 1.50 l multi .45 .20

Friedrich Engels (1820-1895), German Socialist.

Aerial View of Iron Gate Power Station A663

**1970, July 13**

2187 A663 35b blue & multi .20 .20

Hydroelectric plant at the Iron Gate of the Danube.

Cargo Ship A664

**1970, July 17**

2188 A664 55b blue & multi .20 .20

Romanian merchant marine, 75th anniv.

Exhibition Hall and Oil Derrick A665

**1970, July 20**

2189 A665 1.50 l multi .45 .20

International Bucharest Fair, Oct. 13-24.

**1970, Aug. 17   Photo.   Perf. 13½**

2190 A666 1.50 l ultra & slate green .45 .20

Opening of UPU Headquarters, Bern — A666

---

**1970, Aug. 21**

Roses: 35b, Wiener charme. 55b, Pink luster. 1 l, Piccadilly. 1.50 l, Orange Delbard. 2.40 l, Sibelius.

2192 A668 20b dk red, grn & blk .20 .20
2193 A668 35b vio, yel & grn .20 .20
2194 A668 55b blue, rose & grn .20 .20
2195 A668 1 l grn, car rose & yel .30 .20
2196 A668 1.50 l dk bl, red & grn .45 .20
2197 A668 2.40 l brt bl, dp red & grn .85 .20
Nos. 2192-2197 (6) 2.20 1.20

Education Year Emblem — A667

**1970, Aug. 17**

2191 A667 55b black, pur & red .20 .20

International Education Year.

Iceberg Rose — A668

---

Spaniel and Pheasant, by Jean B. Oudry A669

Paintings: 10b, The Hunt, by Domenico Brandi. 35b, The Hunt, by Jan Fyt. 60b, After the Chase, by Jacob Jordaens. 1.75 l, 5 l, Game Merchant, by Frans Snyders (horiz.). 3 l, The Hunt, by Adriaen de Gryert. Sizes: 37x49mm (10b, 35b); 35x33mm (20b, 60b; 3 l); 49x37mm (1.75 l, 3 l).

**1970, Sept. 20   Photo.   Perf. 13½**

2198 A669 10b gold & multi .20 .20
2199 A669 20b gold & multi .20 .20
2200 A669 35b gold & multi .20 .20
2201 A669 60b gold & multi .20 .20
2202 A669 1.75 l gold & multi .60 .20
2203 A669 3 l gold & multi 1.25 .45
Nos. 2198-2203 (6) 2.65 1.55

**Miniature Sheet**

2204 A669 5 l gold & multi 2.00 2.00

UN Emblem — A670

**1970, Sept. 29**

2205 A670 1.50 l lt bl, ultra & blk .45 .20

25th anniversary of the United Nations.

Mother and Child — A671

**1970, Sept. 25**

Designs: 1.50 l, Red Cross relief trucks and tents. 1.75 l, Rebuilding houses.

2206 A671 55b bl gray, blk & ol .20 .20
2207 A671 1.50 l ol, blk & car .45 .20
   a. Strip of 3, #2206-2207, C179 1.40 .55
2208 A671 1.75 l blue & multi .70 .20
Nos. 2206-2208 (3) 1.35 .60

Plight of the Danube flood victims.

ROMANIA

POSTA ROMANA
b20

**Arabian Thoroughbred — A672**
*pur sînge arab*

Horses: 35b, American trotter. 55b, Ghidran (Anglo-American). 1 l, Northern Moravian. 1.50 l, Trotter thoroughbred. 2.40 l, Lippizaner.

**1970, Oct. 10    Photo.    Perf. 13½**
| | | | | |
|---|---|---|---|---|
| 2209 | A672 | 20b | blk & multi | .20 .20 |
| 2210 | A672 | 35b | blk & multi | .20 .20 |
| 2211 | A672 | 55b | blk & multi | .25 .20 |
| 2212 | A672 | 1 l | blk & multi | .40 .20 |
| 2213 | A672 | 1.50 l | blk & multi | .95 .20 |
| 2214 | A672 | 2.40 l | blk & multi | 2.20 1.20 |
| | | | *Nos. 2209-2214 (6)* | |

JOAN MIRÓ
POSTA ROMANA
55b

**Ludwig van Beethoven (1770-1827), Composer — A673**

**1970, Nov. 2**
2215  A673  55b  multicolored     .25  .20

POSTA ROMANA
3 l
JOAN MIRÓ

**Abstract, by Joan Miró — A674**

**1970, Dec. 10    Photo.    Perf. 13½**
2216  A674  3 l  ultra & multi     .85  .70

**Souvenir Sheet**

**Imperf**
2217  A674  5 l  ultra & multi     1.90  1.90

Plight of the Danube flood victims. No. 2216 issued in sheets of 5 stamps and label with signature of Miró and date of flood. No 2217 contains one stamp with simulated perforation.

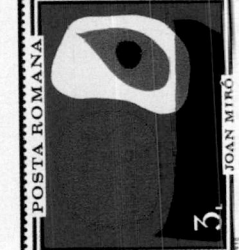
POSTA ROMANA
10b

**"The Senses," paintings by Gonzales Coques (1614-1684): 20b, Hearing. 35b, Smell. 60b, Taste. 1.75 l, Touch. 3 l, Bruckenthal Museum, Sibiu. 5 l, View of Sibiu, 1808, horiz.**

**The Sense of Sight, by Gonzales Coques A675**

**1970, Dec. 15    Photo.    Perf. 13½**
| | | | | |
|---|---|---|---|---|
| 2218 | A675 | 10b | gold & multi | .20 .20 |
| 2219 | A675 | 20b | gold & multi | .20 .20 |
| 2220 | A675 | 35b | gold & multi | .20 .20 |
| 2221 | A675 | 60b | gold & multi | .25 .20 |
| 2222 | A675 | 1.75 l | gold & multi | .60 .25 |
| 2223 | A675 | 3 l | gold & multi | 1.40 .45 |
| | | | *Nos. 2218-2223 (6)* | 2.40 1.50 |

**Miniature Sheet**

**Imperf**
2224  A675  5 l  gold & multi     2.00  2.00

---

POSTA ROMANA
1.50

**Men of Three Races A676**

**1971, Feb. 23    Photo.    Perf. 13½**
2225  A676  1.50 l  multi     .45  .20

Intl. year against racial discrimination.

150 POSTA ROMANA
1821 1971

**Tudor Vladimirescu, by Theodor Aman — A677**

**1971, Feb. 20**
2226  A677  1.50 l  gold & multi     .45  .20

Vladimirescu, patriot, 150th death anniv.

ROMANA
lup alsacian
POSTA
20 b

Dogs: 35b, Bulldog. 55b, Fox terrier. 1 l, Setter. 1.50 l, Cocker spaniel. 2.40 l, Poodle.

**German Shepherd A677a**

**1971, Feb. 22**
| | | | | |
|---|---|---|---|---|
| 2227 | A677a | 20b | blk & multi | .20 .20 |
| 2228 | A677a | 35b | blk & multi | .20 .20 |
| 2229 | A677a | 55b | blk & multi | .20 .20 |
| 2230 | A677a | 1 l | blk & multi | .25 .20 |
| 2231 | A677a | 1.50 l | blk & multi | .85 .40 |
| 2232 | A677a | 2.40 l | blk & multi | 2.10 1.40 |
| | | | *Nos. 2227-2232 (6)* | |

POSTA ROMANA
40

**Rock Formation A680**

Designs: 10b, Bicazului Gorge, vert. 55b, Winter resort. 1 l, Danube Delta view. 1.50 l, Lakeside resort. 2.40 l, Venus, Jupiter, Neptune Hotels on Black Sea.

**A SINDICATELOR DIN ROMANIA**
CONGRESUL
UNIUNII GENERALE
55 B
POSTA ROMANA

**Congress Emblem A679**

**1971, Mar. 15    Photo.    Perf. 13½**
2233  A678  40b  multicolored     .20  .20

Centenary of the Paris Commune.

1871-Commune de Paris 1971
POSTA ROMANA
40 b

**Paris Commune A678**

**1971, Mar. 23**
2234  A679  55b  multicolored     .20  .20

Romanian Trade Unions Congress.

---

**1971, Apr. 15**
**Size: 23x38mm, 38x23mm**
| | | | | |
|---|---|---|---|---|
| 2235 | A680 | 10b | multi | .20 .20 |
| 2236 | A680 | 40b | multi | .20 .20 |
| 2237 | A680 | 55b | multi | .20 .20 |
| 2238 | A680 | 1 l | multi | .30 .20 |
| 2239 | A680 | 1.50 l | multi | .50 .35 |

**Size: 76½x28mm**
2240  A680  2.40 l  multi     1.00 1.00
                                2.40 1.35
*Nos. 2235-2240 (6)*

POSTA ROMANA
55
BANI
COLABORAREA CULTURAL-ECONOMICA INTEREUROPEANA

**Arrow Pattern A681**

Design: 1.75 l, Wave pattern.

**1971, Apr. 28    Photo.    Perf. 13½**
2241  A681  55b  multi     .75  .60
2242  A681  1.75 l  multi     1.50 1.00

Inter-European Cultural and Economic Collaboration. Sheets of 10.

POSTA ROMANA
55 b
A. ANASTASIU

**Demonstration, by A. Anastasiu A684**

MUZEUL DE ISTORIE AL REPUBLICII SOCIALISTE ROMANIA
1971
posta romana
55 b

**Historical Museum A682**

**1971, May 7    Photo.    Perf. 13½**
2243  A682  55b  blue & multi     .20  .20

For Romania's Historical Museum.

POSTA ROMANA
50 ANI

**Communist Party Emblem — A683**

**1971, May 8**
35b, Reading Proclamation, by Stefan Szonyi
| | | | | |
|---|---|---|---|---|
| 2244 | A684 | 35b | multicolored | .20 .20 |
| 2245 | A683 | 40b | multicolored | .60 .60 |
| 2246 | A684 | 55b | multicolored | .60 .60 |
| | | | *Nos. 2244-2246 (3)* | |

Romanian Communist Party, 50th anniv.

**Souvenir Sheets**

120 l  POSTA ROMANA
KOLE IDROMENO
Motra Tone

**Motra Tone, by Kole Idromeno A685**

---

5 l  POSTA ROMANA
BALKANFILA III 1971

**Dancing the Hora, by Theodor Aman — A686**

Designs: b, Maid by V. Dimitrov-Maystora. c, Rosa Botzaris, by Joseph Stieler. d, Woman in Costume, by Katarina Ivanovic. e, Argeseanca, by Carol Popp de Szathmary. f, Woman in Modern Dress, by Calli Ibrahim.

**1971, May 25    Photo.    Perf. 13½**
2247  a.-f.  **Sheet of 6**     3.50 3.00
      A685  1.20 l  any single     .50  .35
2248  A686  5 l  multicolored     2.25 2.25

Balkanphila III Stamp Exhibition, Bucharest, June 27-July 2.
No. 2247 contains 6 stamps in 3 rows and 6 labels showing exhibition emblem and "60b."

POSTA ROMANA
l.20
Punica Granatum l.

**Pomegranate Flower — A687**

Flowers: 35b, Slipperwort. 55b, Lily. 1 l, Mimulus. 1.50 l, Morning-glory. 2.40 l, Leaf cactus, horiz.

**1971, June 20**
| | | | | |
|---|---|---|---|---|
| 2249 | A687 | 20b | ultra & multi | .20 .20 |
| 2250 | A687 | 35b | red & multi | .20 .20 |
| 2251 | A687 | 55b | ultra & multi | .20 .20 |
| 2252 | A687 | 1 l | car & multi | .35 .20 |
| 2253 | A687 | 1.60 l | car & multi | .60 .20 |
| 2254 | A687 | 2.40 l | ultra & multi | .95 .25 |
| | | | *Nos. 2249-2254 (6)* | 2.50 1.25 |

POSTA ROMANA
10

**Nude, by Iosif Iser A688**

Paintings of Nudes: 20b, by Camil Ressu. 35b, by Nicolae Grigorescu. 60b, by Eugene Delacroix (odalisque). 1.75 l, by Auguste Renoir. 3 l, by Palma il Vecchio (Venus and Amor). 5 l, by Il Bronzino (Venus and Amor). 60b, 3 l, 5 l, horiz.

**1971, July 25    Photo.    Perf. 13½**
**Size: 38x50mm, 49x39mm, 29x50mm (20b)**
| | | | | |
|---|---|---|---|---|
| 2255 | A688 | 10b | gold & multi | .20 .20 |
| 2256 | A688 | 20b | gold & multi | .20 .20 |
| 2257 | A688 | 35b | gold & multi | .20 .20 |
| 2258 | A688 | 60b | gold & multi | .20 .20 |
| 2259 | A688 | 1.75 l | gold & multi | .35 .20 |
| 2260 | A688 | 3 l | gold & multi | 1.40 .35 |
| | | | *Nos. 2255-2260 (6)* | 2.55 1.35 |

**Miniature Sheet**

**Imperf**
2261  A688  5 l  gold & multi     2.00  2.00

Paintings of Ships by: 20b, Ludolf Backhuysen; 35b, Andries van Eertvelt; 60b, M. W. Arnold; 1.75 l, Ivan Konstantinovich Aivazovski; 3 l, Jean Steriadi; 5 l, N. Darascu; vert.

Ships in Storm, by B. Peters — A689

**1971, Sept. 15    Photo.    Perf. 13½**

| | | | | |
|---|---|---|---|---|
| 2262 | A689 | 20b gold & multi | .20 | .20 |
| 2263 | A689 | 35b gold & multi | .20 | .20 |
| 2264 | A689 | 60b gold & multi | .20 | .20 |
| 2265 | A689 | 1.75 l gold & multi | .45 | .20 |
| 2266 | A689 | 3 l gold & multi | .50 | .30 |
| 2267 | A689 | 5 l gold & multi | 1.00 | .35 |

*Miniature Sheet*

| | | | | |
|---|---|---|---|---|
| 2268 | A689 | 5 l gold & multi | 2.25 | 1.35 |

Nos. 2262-2267 (6)

**Types of Regular Issue**

**1971**

Size: 16½x23mm, 23x16½mm

**Photo.    Perf. 13½**

| | | | | |
|---|---|---|---|---|
| 2269 | A616 | 1 l emerald | .20 | .20 |
| 2270 | A616 | 1.20 l red lilac | .25 | .20 |
| 2271 | A617 | 1.35 l brt blue | .30 | .20 |
| 2272 | A617 | 1.50 l orange red | .30 | .20 |
| 2273 | A616 | 1.55 l deep green | .35 | .20 |
| 2274 | A617 | 1.75 l sepia | .40 | .20 |
| 2275 | A617 | 2 l citron | .45 | .20 |
| 2276 | A616 | 2.40 l dark blue | .55 | .20 |
| 2277 | A617 | 3 l greenish bl | .70 | .20 |
| 2278 | A617 | 3.20 l ultra | .70 | .20 |
| 2280 | A616 | 3.25 l ocher | .85 | .20 |
| 2281 | A616 | 4 l grnsh blue | 1.00 | .20 |
| 2282 | A617 | 4.80 l blue | 1.25 | .20 |
| 2283 | A617 | 5 l violet | 1.40 | .20 |
| 2284 | A616 | 6 l dp magenta | 11.65 | 3.20 |

Designs as Before and: 3.60 l, Mail collector. 4.80 l, Maliman. 6 l, Ministry of Posts.

Nos. 2269-2284 (16)

Prince Neagoe Basarab A690

Theodor Pallady (Painter) — A691

**1971, Sept. 20    Photo.    Perf. 13½**

| | | | | |
|---|---|---|---|---|
| 2288 | A690 | 60b gold & multi | .20 | .20 |

450th anniversary of the death of Prince Neagoe Basarab of Walachia.

**1971, Oct. 12    Photo.    Perf. 13½**

Portraits of: 55b, Benvenuto Cellini (1500-1571), sculptor. 1.50 l, Antoine Watteau (1684-1721), painter. 2.40 l, Albrecht Dürer (1471-1528), painter.

| | | | | |
|---|---|---|---|---|
| 2289 | A691 | 40b gold & multi | .20 | .20 |
| 2290 | A691 | 55b gold & multi | .50 | .25 |
| 2291 | A691 | 1.50 l gold & multi | 1.00 | .50 |
| 2292 | A691 | 2.40 l gold & multi | 1.90 | .85 |

Anniversaries of famous artists.

Nos. 2289-2292 (4)

---

Proclamation of Cyrus the Great — A692

**1971, Oct. 12    Perf. 13½**

| | | | | |
|---|---|---|---|---|
| 2293 | A692 | 55b multicolored | .20 | .20 |

2500th anniversary of the founding of the Persian empire by Cyrus the Great.

Figure Skating — A693

**1971, Oct. 25    Imperf**

Designs: 20b, Ice hockey. 40b, Biathlon (skier). 55b, Bobsledding. 1.75 l, Skiing. 3 l, Sapporo '72 emblem. 5 l, Olympic flame and emblem.

| | | | | |
|---|---|---|---|---|
| 2294 | A693 | 10b lt bl & red | .20 | .20 |
| 2295 | A693 | 20b multicolored | .20 | .20 |
| 2296 | A693 | 40b multicolored | .20 | .20 |
| 2297 | A693 | 55b lt bl, blk & red | .20 | .20 |
| 2298 | A693 | 1.75 l lt bl, blk & red | .50 | .20 |
| 2299 | A693 | 3 l lt bl, blk & red | .80 | .25 |

*Miniature Sheet*

*Imperf*

| | | | | |
|---|---|---|---|---|
| 2300 | A693 | 5 l multicolored | 2.00 | 2.00 |

11th Winter Olympic Games, Sapporo, Japan, Feb. 3-13, 1972. Nos. 2294-2296 printed se-tenant in sheets of 15 (5x3); Nos. 2297-2298 printed se-tenant in sheets of 10 (5x2). No. 2300 contains one stamp 37x50mm.

Nos. 2294-2299 (6)

St. George and the Dragon A694

**1971, Nov. 30    Photo.    Perf. 13½**

| | | | | |
|---|---|---|---|---|
| 2301 | A694 | 10b gold & multi | .20 | .20 |
| 2302 | A694 | 20b gold & multi | .20 | .20 |
| 2303 | A694 | 40b gold & multi | .20 | .20 |
| 2304 | A694 | 55b gold & multi | .20 | .20 |
| 2305 | A694 | 1.75 l gold & multi | .60 | .20 |
| 2306 | A694 | 3 l gold & multi | .90 | .40 |

Frescoes from North Moldavian Monasteries: 10b, 20b, 40b, Moldovita. 55b, 1.75 l, 5 l, Voronet. 3 l, Arborea, horiz.

*Miniature Sheet*

*Imperf*

| | | | | |
|---|---|---|---|---|
| 2307 | A694 | 5 l gold & multi | 2.30 | 1.40 |

No. 2307 contains one stamp 44x56mm.

Ferdinand Magellan A695

**1971, Dec. 20    Photo.    Perf. 13½**

| | | | | |
|---|---|---|---|---|
| 2308 | A695 | 40b grn, brt rose & dk bl | .20 | .20 |
| 2309 | A695 | 55b lil, bl & gray grn | .30 | .20 |
| 2310 | A695 | 1 l violet & multi | .30 | .20 |
| 2311 | A695 | 1.50 l red brn, grn & bl | 1.20 | .80 |

Designs: 55b, Johannes Kepler and observation tower. 1 l, Yuri Gagarin and rocket orbiting earth. 1.50 l, Baron Ernest R. Rutherford, atom, nucleus and chemical apparatus.

Magellan (1480?-1521), navigator; Kepler (1571-1630), astronomer; Gagarin, 1st man in space, 10th anniv.; Ernest R. Rutherford (1871-1937), British physicist.

Nos. 2308-2311 (4)

---

Matei Millo — A696

Young Communists Union Emblem — A697

**1971, Dec.**

Design: 1 l, Nicolae Iorga.

| | | | | |
|---|---|---|---|---|
| 2312 | A696 | 55b blue & multi | .20 | .20 |
| 2313 | A696 | 1 l purple & multi | .25 | .20 |

Millo (1814-1896), playwright; Iorga (1871-1940), historian and politician.

**1972, Feb.**

| | | | | |
|---|---|---|---|---|
| 2314 | A697 | 55b dk bl, red & gold | .20 | .20 |

Young Communists Union, 50th anniv.

Young Animals — A698

**1972, Mar. 10    Photo.    Perf. 13½**

| | | | | |
|---|---|---|---|---|
| 2315 | A698 | 20b Lynx | .20 | .20 |
| 2316 | A698 | 35b Foxes | .20 | .20 |
| 2317 | A698 | 55b Roe fawns | .20 | .20 |
| 2318 | A698 | 1 l Wild pigs | .25 | .20 |
| 2319 | A698 | 1.50 l Wolves | .40 | .25 |
| 2320 | A698 | 2.40 l Bears | .85 | .25 |

Nos. 2315-2320 (6)

Wrestling — A699

**1972, Apr. 25    Photo.    Perf. 13½**

| | | | | |
|---|---|---|---|---|
| 2321 | A699 | 10b yel & multi | .20 | .20 |
| 2322 | A699 | 20b multicolored | .20 | .20 |
| 2323 | A699 | 55b gray & multi | .20 | .20 |
| 2324 | A699 | 1.55 l grn & multi | .35 | .20 |
| 2325 | A699 | 2.90 l multicolored | .80 | .50 |
| 2326 | A699 | 2.40 l multi | 1.25 | .50 |

Olympic Rings and: 20b, Canoeing. 55b, Boxing. 6.70 l, Field ball.

Soccer, 1.55 l. Women's high jump, 2.90 l.

Nos. 2321-2326 (6)

20th Olympic Games, Munich, Aug. 26-Sept. 10. See Nos. C186-C187.

---

UIC Emblem and Trains A701

Design: 1 l, Nicolae Iorga.

**1972, May 20    Photo.    Perf. 13½**

| | | | | |
|---|---|---|---|---|
| 2329 | A701 | 55b dp car rose, blk & gold | .20 | .20 |

50th anniv., Intl. Railroad Union (UIC).

"Summer," by Peter Brueghel, the Younger — A702

*Souvenir Sheet*

**1972, May 20**

| | | | | |
|---|---|---|---|---|
| 2330 | A702 | 6 l gold & multi | 2.00 | 2.00 |

Belgica '72, Intl. Phil. Exhib., Brussels, June 24-July 9.

Peony — A703

**1972, June 5    Photo.    Perf. 13**

Protected Flowers: 40b, Pink. 55b, Edelweiss. 60b, Nigritella rubra.

| | | | | |
|---|---|---|---|---|
| 2331 | A703 | 20b dk vio bl | .20 | .20 |
| 2332 | A703 | 40b chocolate | .20 | .20 |
| 2333 | A703 | 55b dp blue | .20 | .20 |
| 2334 | A703 | 60b dk green | .20 | .20 |
| 2335 | A703 | 1.35 l violet | .90 | .40 |
| 2336 | A703 | 2.90 l dk Prus bl | 2.20 | 1.40 |

2.90 l, Lady's slipper. 1.35 l, Narcissus.

Flowers in Natural Colors

Nos. 2331-2336 (6)

---

Stylized Map of Europe and Links A700

**1972, Apr. 28**

Design: 2.90 l, Entwined arrows and links.

| | | | | |
|---|---|---|---|---|
| 2327 | A700 | 1.75 l dp car, gold & blk | 1.10 | .75 |
| 2328 | A700 | 2.90 l grn, gold & blk | 2.60 | 2.00 |
| a. | Pair, #2327-2328 | | 1.50 | 1.00 |

Inter-European Cultural and Economic Collaboration.

Danube Bridges — A704

Danube Bridges: 1.75 l, Giurgeni Bridge, Vadul. 2.75 l, Friendship Bridge, Giurgiu-Ruse. 5 l, Saligny Bridge, Cernavoda — A704

ROMANIA

Venice, by Gheorge Petrascu — A713

Paintings of Venice by: 20b, N. Darascu. 55b, Petrascu. 1.55 l, Marius Bunescu. 2.75 l, N. Darascu, vert. 6 l, Petrascu. 6.40 l, Marius Bunescu.

**1972, Oct. 20**
| | | | |
|---|---|---|---|
| 2374 | A713 | 20b gray & multi | .20 .20 |
| 2375 | A713 | 20b gray & multi | .20 .20 |
| 2376 | A713 | 55b gray & multi | .20 .20 |
| 2377 | A713 | 1.55 l gray & multi | .25 .25 |
| 2378 | A713 | 2.75 l gray & multi | .35 .35 |
| 2379 | A713 | 6.40 l gray & multi | 1.40 1.35 |

**Souvenir Sheet**
| | | | |
|---|---|---|---|
| 2380 | A713 | 6 l gray & multi | 2.00 2.00 |

Nos. 2374-2379 (6)  2.80 1.35

Fencing, Bronze Medal — A714

20b, Team handball, bronze medal. 35b, Boxing, silver medal. 1.45 l, Hurdles, women's, silver medal. 2.75 l, Pistol shoot, silver medal. 6.20 l, Wrestling, gold medal.

**1972, Oct. 28**
| | | | |
|---|---|---|---|
| 2381 | A714 | 10b red org & multi | .20 .20 |
| 2382 | A714 | 20b l grn & multi | .20 .20 |
| 2383 | A714 | 35b multicolored | .20 .20 |
| 2384 | A714 | 1.45 l multi | .25 .20 |
| 2385 | A714 | 2.75 l ocher & multi | .55 .25 |
| 2386 | A714 | 6.20 l bl & multi | 1.40 .45 |

Nos. 2381-2386 (6)  2.80 1.50

Romanian medalists at 20th Olympic Games. See No. C191. For surcharge see No. 2493.

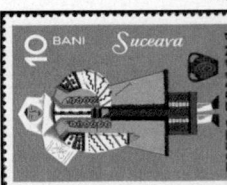

Nicolaus Copernicus — A719

Nicolaus Copernicus (1473-1543). Polish astronomer. Printed with alternating label publicizing Intl. Exhib., Philatelic Exhib., Poznan, 8/19-9/2.

**1973, Feb. 19.  Photo.  Perf. 13½13½.**
| | | | |
|---|---|---|---|
| 2405 | A719 | 2.75 l multi | .70 .25 |

---

Runner with Torch, Olympic Rings — A709

**1972, Aug. 13**
| | | | |
|---|---|---|---|
| 2352 | A709 | 55b sil, bl & claret | .20 .20 |

Olympic torch relay from Olympia, Greece, to Munich, Germany, passing through Romania.

City Hall Tower, Sibiu — A710

**1972**  **Photo.**  **Perf. 13**

Designs: 1.85 l, St. Michael's Cathedral, Cluj. 2.75 l, Sphinx Rock, Mt. Bucegi, horiz. 3.35 l, Heroes Monument, Bucharest. 3.45 l, Sinaia Castle, horiz. 5.15 l, Hydroelectric Works, Arges, horiz. 5.60 l, Church of the Epiphany, Iasi. 6.20 l, Bran Castle. 6.40 l, Hunedoara Castle, horiz. 6.80 l, Polytechnic Institute, Bucharest, horiz. 7.05 l, Black Church, Brasov. 8.45 l, Atheneum, Bucharest, horiz. 9.05 l, Excavated Coliseum, Sarmizegetusa, horiz. 9.10 l, Hydroelectric Station, Iron Gate. 9.85 l, Monument, Cetatea. 11.90 l, Republic Palace, horiz. 12.75 l, Television Station. 13.30 l, Arch, Alba Iulia, horiz. 16.20 l, Clock Tower, Sighisoara.

**Size: 23x18mm, 17x24mm**
| | | | |
|---|---|---|---|
| 2353 | A710 | 1.85 l brt purple | .35 .20 |
| 2354 | A710 | 2.75 l gray | .50 .20 |
| 2355 | A710 | 3.35 l magenta | .60 .20 |
| 2356 | A710 | 3.45 l green | .55 .20 |
| 2357 | A710 | 5.15 l brt blue | .95 .20 |
| 2358 | A710 | 5.60 l blue | 1.00 .20 |
| 2359 | A710 | 6.20 l cerise | 1.10 .20 |
| 2360 | A710 | 6.40 l sepia | 1.25 .20 |
| 2361 | A710 | 6.80 l rose red | 1.25 .20 |
| 2362 | A710 | 7.05 l black | 1.40 .20 |
| 2363 | A710 | 8.45 l rose red | 1.50 .20 |
| 2364 | A710 | 9.05 l dull green | 1.60 .20 |
| 2365 | A710 | 9.10 l ultra | 1.60 .20 |
| 2366 | A710 | 9.85 l green | 1.60 .20 |

**Size: 19½x29mm, 29x21mm**
| | | | |
|---|---|---|---|
| 2367 | A710 | 10 l dp brown | 1.90 .20 |
| 2368 | A710 | 11.90 l bluish blk | 2.25 .20 |
| 2369 | A710 | 12.75 l dk violet | 2.50 .20 |
| 2370 | A710 | 13.30 l dull red | 2.50 .20 |
| 2371 | A710 | 16.20 l olive grn | 3.00 .25 |

Nos. 2353-2371, C193 (20)  28.65 4.15

View of Satu-Mare — A711

**1972, Oct. 5**
| | | | |
|---|---|---|---|
| 2372 | A711 | 55b multicolored | .20 .20 |

Millennium of Satu-Mare.

Tennis Racket and Davis Cup — A712

**1972, Oct. 10**  **Perf. 13½**
| | | | |
|---|---|---|---|
| 2373 | A712 | 2.75 l multi | .75 .25 |

Davis Cup finals between Romania and US, Bucharest, Oct. 13-15.

---

North Railroad Station, Bucharest, Cent. A705

**1972, June 25  Photo.  Perf. 13½**
| | | | |
|---|---|---|---|
| 2337 | A704 | 1.35 l multi | .35 .20 |
| 2338 | A704 | 1.75 l multi | .50 .20 |
| 2339 | A704 | 2.75 l multi | .85 .60 |

Nos. 2337-2339 (3)  1.70

**1972, July 4**
| | | | |
|---|---|---|---|
| 2340 | A705 | 55b ultra & multi | .25 .20 |

Water Polo and Olympic Rings A706

Olympic Rings and: 20b, Pistol shoot. 55b, Discus. 1.55 l, Gymnastics, women's. 2.75 l, Canoeing. 6.40 l, Fencing.

**1972, July 5  Photo.  Perf. 13½**
| | | | |
|---|---|---|---|
| 2341 | A706 | 10b ol, gold & lil | .20 .20 |
| 2342 | A706 | 20b red, gold & grn | .20 .20 |
| 2343 | A706 | 55b grn, gold & brn | .20 .20 |
| 2344 | A706 | 1.55 l vio, gold & ol | .25 .20 |
| 2345 | A706 | 2.75 l bl, gold & gray | .45 .20 |
| 2346 | A706 | 6.40 l pur, gold & gray | 1.10 .35 |
| | | | 2.40 1.35 |

Nos. 2341-2346 (6)

20th Olympic Games, Munich, Aug. 26-Sept. 11. See No. C187.

Stamp Printing Press — A707

**1972, July 25**
| | | | |
|---|---|---|---|
| 2347 | A707 | 55b multicolored | .20 .20 |

Centenary of the stamp printing office.

Stefan Popescu, Self-portrait — A708

**1972, Aug. 10**
| | | | |
|---|---|---|---|
| 2348 | A708 | 55b shown | .20 .20 |
| 2349 | A708 | 1 l Octav Bancila | .25 .20 |
| 2350 | A708 | 2.90 l Gheorghe Petrascu | .50 .20 |
| 2351 | A708 | 6.50 l Ion Andreescu | 1.25 .30 |
| | | | 2.20 .90 |

Nos. 2348-2351 (4)

Self-portraits by Romanian painters.

---

**1972**
| | | | |
|---|---|---|---|
| 2393 | A715 | 1.85 l Apollo 13, 14 | .35 .20 |
| 2394 | A715 | 2.75 l Apollo 15, 16 | .60 .20 |
| 2395 | A715 | 3.60 l Apollo 17 | 1.10 .30 |

Nos. 2387-2395 (9)  3.30 1.90

Highlights of US Apollo space program. See No. C192.

"25" and Flags — A716

Designs: 1.20 l, "25" and national emblem. 1.75 l, "25" and factory.

**1972, Dec. 25**
| | | | |
|---|---|---|---|
| 2396 | A716 | 55b blue & multi | .20 .20 |
| 2397 | A716 | 1.20 l yel & multi | .35 .35 |
| 2398 | A716 | 1.75 l ver & multi | .60 .60 |

Nos. 2396-2398 (3)  1.15 .60

25th anniversary of the Republic.

Globeflowers A718

European Bee-eater A717

Nature Protection: No. 2400. Red-breasted goose. No. 2401. Penduline tit. No. 2403, Garden Turk's-cap. No. 2404, Gentian.

**1973, Feb. 5  Photo.  Perf. 13**
| | | | |
|---|---|---|---|
| 2399 | A717 | 1.40 l gray & multi | .20 .20 |
| 2400 | A717 | 1.85 l multi | .35 .20 |
| 2401 | A717 | 2.75 l blue & multi | .70 .20 |
| | | | 1.40 .60 |
| 2402 | A718 | 1.40 l multi | .25 .20 |
| 2403 | A718 | 1.85 l yellow & multi | .35 .20 |
| 2404 | A718 | 2.75 l multi | .70 .60 |
| | | Strip of 3, #2399-2401 | 1.40 .60 |
| | | Strip of 3, #2402-2404 | 1.40 .60 |

Nos. 2402-2404

POLSKA'73 — A719

Suceava Woman A720

---

Charity Labels

Stamp day issues frequently have an attached, fully perforated label with a face value. These are Romanian Philatelic Association charity labels. They are inscribed "AFR." The stamps are valued with label attached. When the "label" is part of the stamp, the stamp is listed in the semi-postal section. See Nos. B426-B430.

Stamp Day Semi-Postal Type of 1968

Design: Traveling Gypsies, by Emil Volkers.

**1972, Nov. 15  Photo.  Perf. 13½**
| | | | |
|---|---|---|---|
| 2386A | SP288 | 1.10 l + 90b label | .55 .35 |

Stamp Day.

**1972, Dec. 27  Photo.  Perf. 13½**
| | | | |
|---|---|---|---|
| 2387 | A715 | 10b shown | .20 .20 |
| 2388 | A715 | 35b Grissom, Chaffee and White, 1967 | .20 .20 |
| 2389 | A715 | 40b Apollo 4, 5, 6 | .20 .20 |
| 2390 | A715 | 55b Apollo 7, 8 | .20 .20 |
| 2391 | A715 | 1 l Apollo 9, 10 | .25 .20 |
| 2392 | A715 | 1.20 l Apollo 11, 12 | .25 .20 |

**1973, Mar. 15**

| 2406 | A720 | 10b lt bl & multi | .20 | .20 |
|---|---|---|---|---|
| 2407 | A720 | 40b multicolored | .20 | .20 |
| 2408 | A720 | 55b bis & multi | .20 | .20 |
| 2409 | A720 | 1.75 l lil & multi | .30 | .20 |
| 2410 | A720 | 2.75 l multi | .45 | .20 |
| 2411 | A720 | 6.40 l multi | 1.25 | .35 |
| | | Nos. 2406-2411 (6) | 2.60 | 1.35 |

**1973, Mar. 26**

| 2412 | A721 | 10b multi | .20 | .20 |
|---|---|---|---|---|
| 2413 | A721 | 40b multi | .20 | .20 |
| 2414 | A721 | 55b multi | .35 | .20 |
| 2415 | A721 | 6.40 l multi | 1.70 | .95 |
| | | Nos. 2412-2415 (4) | 1.10 | .35 |

Anniversaries of famous artists.
Portraits: 40b, I. Slavici (1848-1925), writer. 55b, G. Lazar (1779-1823), writer. 6.40 l, A. Flechtenmacher (1823-1898), composer.

D. Paciurea (Sculptor) — A721

Map of Europe A722

**1973, Apr. 28    Photo.    Perf. 13½**

| 2416 | A722 | 3.35 l dp bl & gold | 1.10 | .70 |
|---|---|---|---|---|
| 2417 | A722 | 3.60 l brt mag & gold | 1.25 | 1.00 |
| a. | | Pair, #2416-2417 | 2.40 | 2.00 |

Design: 3.60 l, Symbol of collaboration.

**Souvenir Sheet**

Inter-European cultural and economic cooperation. Printed in sheets of 10 with blue marginal inscription.

The Rape of Proserpina, by Hans von Aachen — A723

**1973, May 5**

| 2418 | A723 | 12 l gold & multi | 2.75 | 2.50 |
|---|---|---|---|---|

IBRA Munchen 1973, Intl. Stamp Exhib., Munich, May 11-20.

---

Prince Alexander I. Cuza — A724

Hand with Hammer and Sickle — A725

**1973, May 5    Photo.    Perf. 13½**

| 2419 | A724 | 1.75 l multi | .50 | .20 |
|---|---|---|---|---|

Alexander Ioan Cuza (1820-1873), prince of Romania, Moldavia and Walachia.

**1973, May 5**

| 2420 | A725 | 40b gold & multi | .20 | .20 |
|---|---|---|---|---|

Workers and Peasants Party, 25th anniv.

Romanian Flag, Bayonets Stabbing Swastika — A726

**1973, May 5**

| 2421 | A726 | 55b multicolored | .20 | .20 |
|---|---|---|---|---|

Anti-fascist Front, 40th anniversary.

**1973, June 15**

| 2422 | A727 | 2 l ultra & multi | .50 | .20 |
|---|---|---|---|---|

Intl. meteorological cooperation, cent.

WMO Emblem, Weather Satellite — A727

Dimitrie Ralet Holding Letter — A728

Dimitrie Cantemir — A729

**1973, June 20**

| 2423 | A728 | 40b multi | .20 | .20 |
|---|---|---|---|---|
| 2424 | A728 | 60b multi | .20 | .20 |
| 2425 | A728 | 1.55 l multi | .20 | .20 |
| | | Nos. 2423-2425,B432 (4) | 2.15 | 1.15 |

"The Letter on Romanian Portraits." Socfilex III Philatelic Exhibition, Bucharest, July 20-29. See No. B433.

Portraits with letters. 60b, Enachita Vacarescu, by A. Chladek. 1.55 l, Serdarul Dimitrie Aman, by C. Lecca.

**1973, June 25**

| 2426 | A729 | 1.75 l multi | .50 | .20 |
|---|---|---|---|---|

Portrait of Cantemir in oval frame.

**Souvenir Sheet**

| 2427 | A729 | 6 l multi | 2.00 | 1.40 |
|---|---|---|---|---|

Dimitrie Cantemir (1673-1723), Prince of Moldavia, writer. No. 2427 contains one 38x50mm stamp.

---

Plate — A730

**1973, July 25    Photo.    Perf. 13½**

| 2428 | A730 | 10b vio bl & multi | .20 | .20 |
|---|---|---|---|---|
| 2429 | A730 | 20b green & multi | .20 | .20 |
| 2430 | A730 | 55b red & multi | .20 | .20 |
| 2431 | A730 | 1.55 l multi | .35 | .20 |
| 2432 | A730 | 2.75 l plum & multi | .55 | .20 |
| 2433 | A730 | 6.80 l gold & multi | 1.50 | .35 |
| | | Nos. 2428-2433 (6) | 3.00 | 1.35 |

Designs: 10b, Fibulae, vert. 55b, Jug, vert. 1.55 l, Necklaces and fibula. 2.75 l, Plate, vert. 6.80 l, Octagonal bowl with animal handles. 12 l, Breastplate, vert.

**Souvenir Sheet**

| 2434 | A730 | 12 l multi | 2.75 | 2.50 |
|---|---|---|---|---|

Roman gold treasure of Pietroasa, 4th century.

Symbolic Flower, Map of Europe A731

**1973, Oct. 2    Photo.    Perf. 13½**

| 2435 | A731 | 2.75 l multi | 1.10 | .70 |
|---|---|---|---|---|
| 2436 | A731 | 5 l multi | 1.75 | 1.00 |
| a. | | Sheet, 2 each + 2 labels | 5.50 | 5.50 |

Conference for European Security and Cooperation, Helsinki, Finland, July 1973.

Design: 5 l, Map of Europe, symbolic tree.

Jug and Cloth, Oboga — A732

**1973, Oct. 15    Photo.    Perf. 13**

| 2437 | A732 | 10b multi | .20 | .20 |
|---|---|---|---|---|
| 2438 | A732 | 20b multi | .20 | .20 |
| 2439 | A732 | 55b multi | .20 | .20 |
| 2440 | A732 | 1.55 l multi | .35 | .20 |
| 2441 | A732 | 2.75 l multi | .55 | .20 |
| 2442 | A732 | 6.80 l multi | 1.50 | .35 |
| | | Nos. 2437-2442 (6) | 3.00 | 1.35 |

Designs: 20b, Plate and Pitcher, Vama. 55b, Bowl, Marginea. 1.55 l, Pitcher and plate, Sibiu-Saschiz. 2.75 l, Bowl and jug, Pisc. 6.80 l, Figurine (fowl), Oboga.

Pottery and cloths from various regions of Romania.

---

Women Workers, by G. Saru A733

**1973, Nov. 26    Photo.    Perf. 13½**

| 2443 | A733 | 10b gold & multi | .20 | .20 |
|---|---|---|---|---|
| 2444 | A733 | 40b gold & multi | .20 | .20 |
| 2445 | A733 | 55b gold & multi | .20 | .20 |
| 2446 | A733 | 1.55 l gold & multi | .35 | .20 |
| 2447 | A733 | 2.75 l gold & multi | .55 | .20 |
| 2448 | A733 | 6.80 l gold & multi | 1.50 | .35 |
| | | Nos. 2443-2448 (6) | 3.00 | 1.35 |

Paintings of Workers: 20b, Construction Site, by M. Bunescu. 55b, Shipyard Workers, by H. Catargi, horiz. 1.55 l, Worker, by Catargi. 2.75 l, Miners, by A. Phoebus. 6.80 l, Spinner, by Nicolae Grigorescu. 12 l, Farmers at Rest, by Stefan Popescu, horiz.

**Miniature Sheet**

| 2449 | A733 | 12 l gold & multi | 2.50 | 2.25 |
|---|---|---|---|---|

City Hall, Craiova — A734

Tugboat under Bridge — A735

**1973-74    Photo.    Perf. 13**

| 2450 | A734 | 5b lake | .20 | .20 |
|---|---|---|---|---|
| 2451 | A734 | 10b brt blue | .20 | .20 |
| 2452 | A734 | 20b orange | .20 | .20 |
| 2453 | A734 | 35b green | .20 | .20 |
| 2454 | A734 | 40b dk violet | .20 | .20 |
| 2455 | A734 | 50b ultra | .20 | .20 |
| 2456 | A734 | 55b orange brn | .25 | .20 |
| 2457 | A734 | 60b carmine | .30 | .20 |
| 2458 | A734 | 1 l olive grn | .30 | .20 |
| 2459 | A734 | 1.20 l gray | .35 | .20 |
| 2460 | A734 | 1.35 l blue | .35 | .20 |
| 2461 | A734 | 1.45 l dull blue | .35 | .20 |
| 2462 | A734 | 1.50 l car rose | .35 | .20 |
| 2463 | A735 | 1.55 l violet bl | .45 | .20 |
| 2464 | A735 | 1.75 l slate grn | .45 | .20 |
| 2465 | A735 | 2.20 l brt blue | .60 | .20 |
| 2466 | A735 | 3.65 l dull lilac | 1.00 | .20 |
| 2467 | A735 | 4.70 l violet brn | 1.40 | 1.00 |
| a. | A735 | 6 l violet brn | 7.00 | 3.60 |
| | | Nos. 2450-2467 (18) | | |

Designs: 10b, Infinite Column, by Constantin Brancusi, vert. 20b, Heroes' Mausoleum, Marasesti. 35b, Risnov Citadel. 40b, Densus Church, vert. 50b, B j Church, vert. 55b, Maidanesti Fortress. 60b, National Theater, Iasi. 1 l, Curtea-de-Arges Monastery, vert. 1.20 l, Tirgu-Mures Citadel. 1.45 l, Cargoship Dimbovita. 1.50 l, Muntenia passenger ship. 1.55 l, Three-master Mircea. 1.75 l, Motorship Transilvania. 2.20 l, Ore carrier Oltul. 3.65 l, Trawler Mures. 4.70 l, Tanker Arges.

Issued: #2450-2459, 12/15/73; #2460-2467, 1/28/74.

---

Postillion, by A. Verona A732a

**1973, Nov. 15    Photo.    Perf. 13½**

| 2442A | A732a | 1.10 + 90b label | .40 | .20 |
|---|---|---|---|---|

Stamp Day.

Boats at Montfleur, by Claude Monet — A736

**1974, Mar. 15    Photo.    Perf. 13½**

| 2468 | A736 | 20b blue & multi | .20 | .20 |
|---|---|---|---|---|
| 2469 | A736 | 40b blue & multi | .20 | .20 |
| 2470 | A736 | 55b blue & multi | .20 | .20 |

Impressionistic paintings: 40b, Church of Moret, by Alfred Sisley, vert. 55b, Orchard in Bloom, by Camille Pissarro. 1.75 l, Portrait of Jeanne, by Auguste Renoir, vert. 2.75 l, Landscape, vert. 3.60 l, Portrait of a Girl, by Paul Cezanne, vert. 10 l, Women Taking Bath, by Renoir, vert.

ROMANIA

## Romanians and Flags — A750

Design: 40b, Romanian and Communist flags forming "XXX", vert.

**1974, Aug. 20**
2510 A750 40b gold, ultra & car .20 .20
2511 A750 55b yellow & multi .20 .20

Romania's liberation from Fascist rule, 30th anniv.

## Souvenir Sheet

View, Stockholm — A751

**1974, Sept. 10  Photo.  Perf. 13**
2512 A751 10 l multicolored 2.00 2.00

Stockholmia 74 International Philatelic Exhibition, Stockholm, Sept. 21-29.

Thistle — A752

Nature Protection: 40b, Checkered lily. 55b, Yew. 1.75 l, Azalea. 2.75 l, Forget-me-not. 3.60 l, Pinks.

**1974, Sept. 15**
2513 A752 20b plum & multi .20 .20
2514 A752 40b multi .20 .20
2515 A752 55b multi .20 .20
2516 A752 1.75 l multi .40 .20
2517 A752 2.75 l brm & multi .60 .30
2518 A752 3.60 l multi .85 .30
    Nos. 2513-2518 (6) 2.45 1.30

Isis, First Century A.D. A753

Archaeological art works excavated in Romania: 40b, Serpent, by Glycon. 55b, Emperor Trajan, bronze bust. 1.75 l, Mithraic woman, statue, 3rd century. 2.75 l, Roman man, statue, 3rd century.

**1974, Oct. 20  Photo.  Perf. 13**
2519 A753 20b multi .20 .20
2520 A753 40b ultra & multi .20 .20
2521 A753 55b multi .20 .20
2522 A753 1.75 l multi .40 .20

---

2498 A743 2.75 l multi .60 .20
2499 A743 3.60 l vio & multi .85 .30
    Nos. 2494-2499 (6) 2.45 1.30

## Souvenir Sheet

2500 A743 10 l multi 2.50 2.00

World Cup Soccer Championship, Munich, June 13-July 7. No. 2500 contains one horizontal stamp 50x38mm.

An imperf. 10 l airmail souvenir sheet exists showing a globe as soccer ball and satellite. Gray blue margin showing World Cup, radio tower and control number. Value, unused $30, used $27.50.

**1974, June 10**
2501 A744 55b blue & multi .20 .20

25th anniv. of the Council for Mutual Economic Assistance (COMECON).

Hand Drawing Peace Dove — A746

**1974, June 25  Photo.  Perf. 13½**
2502 A745 2 l multicolored .50 .20

World Population Year.

UN Emblem and People — A745

**1974, June 28**
2503 A745 2 l ultra & multi .50 .20

25 years of the National and Intl. Movement to Uphold the Cause of Peace.

Ioan, Prince of Wallachia — A747

Soldier, Industry and Agriculture A748

Hunedoara Iron and Steel Works — A749

Designs: 1.10 l, Avram Iancu (1824-1872). 1.30 l, Dr. C. I. Parhon (1874-1969). 1.40 l, Bishop Dosoftei (1624-1693).

**1974  Photo.  Perf. 13**
2504 A747 20b blue .20 .20
2505 A748 55b carmine rose .25 .25
2506 A749 1 l slate green .25 .25
2507 A747 1.10 l dk gray olive .30 .25
2508 A747 1.30 l deep magenta .35 .20
2509 A747 1.40 l dark violet 1.55 1.20
    Nos. 2504-2509 (6) 3.25 2.50

No. 2505 for Army Day. No. 2506 for 220th anniv. of Hunedoara Iron and Steel works; others for anniversaries of famous Romanians.

Issue dates: 1l, June 17; others June 25.

---

Young Pioneers with Banners, by Pepene Cornelia — A741

**1974, Apr. 25  Photo.  Perf. 13½**
2485 A741 55b multicolored .20 .20

25th anniv. of the Romanian Pioneers Org.

Mail Motorboat, UPU Emblem A742

UPU Emblem and: 40b, Mail train. 55b, Mailplane and truck. 1.75 l, Mail delivery by motorcycle. 2.75 l, Mailman delivering letter to little girl. 3.60 l, Young stamp collectors. 4 l, Mail collection. 6 l, Modern post office.

**1974, May 15**
2486 A742 20b gray & multi .20 .20
2487 A742 40b multicolored .20 .20
2488 A742 55b ultra & multi .20 .20
2489 A742 1.75 l multi .40 .20
2490 A742 2.75 l brm & multi .60 .20
2491 A742 3.60 l org & multi .85 .30
    Nos. 2486-2491 (6) 2.45 1.30

## Souvenir Sheet

2492 Sheet of 2 3.25 2.50
a. A742 4 l multi 1.00
b. A742 6 l multi 1.40

Centenary of Universal Postal Union. Size of stamps of No. 2492, 28x24mm.

An imperf airmail UPU souvenir sheet of one (10 l) exists. The multicolored stamp is 49x38mm. This sheet is not known to have been sold to the public at post offices. Value, unused $30, used $27.50.

No. 2382 Surcharged with New Value and Overprinted: "ROMANIA / CAMPIOANA / MONDIALA / 1974"

**1974, May 13**
2493 A714 1.75 l on 20b multi 2.50 1.75

Romania's victory in World Handball Championship, 1974.

Soccer and Games Emblem A743

"25" — A744

Designs: Games emblem and various scenes from soccer game.

**1974, June 25  Perf. 13½**
2494 A743 20b purple & multi .20 .20
2495 A743 40b multi .20 .20
2496 A743 55b ultra & multi .20 .20
2497 A743 1.75 l brm & multi .40 .20

---

2471 A736 1.75 l blue & multi .40 .20
2472 A736 2.75 l blue & multi .60 .20
2473 A736 3.60 l multi .80 .25
    Nos. 2468-2473 (6) 2.40 1.25

## Souvenir Sheet

2474 A736 10 l blue & multi 2.25 2.00

Designs: Various horse races.

Harness Racing A737

**1974, Apr. 5  Photo.  Perf. 13½**
2475 A737 40b ver & multi .20 .20
2476 A737 55b blue & multi .20 .20
2477 A737 60b multi .20 .20
2478 A737 1.55 l multi .35 .20
2479 A737 2.45 l multi .60 .20
2480 A737 3.45 l multi .80 .30
    Nos. 2475-2480 (6) 2.35 1.30

Centenary of horse racing in Romania.

Nicolae Titulescu (1883-1941) A738

**1974, Apr. 16**
2481 A738 1.75 l multi .50 .20

Interparliamentary Session, Bucharest, Apr. 19/74. Titulescu was the first Romanian delegate to the League of Nations.

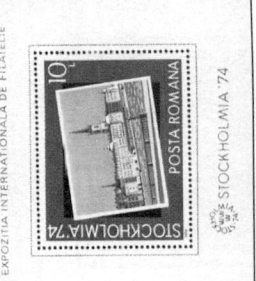

## Souvenir Sheet

Roman Memorial with First Reference to Napoca (Cluj) — A739

**1974, Apr. 18  Photo.  Perf. 13**
2482 A739 10 l multi 2.00 2.00

1850th anniv. of the elevation of the Roman settlement of Napoca (Cluj) to a municipality.

Stylized Map of Europe A740

**1974, Apr. 25  Photo.  Perf. 13½x13**
2483 A740 2.20 l multi 1.25 .70
2484 A740 3.45 l multi 1.50 1.00
a. Pair, #2483-2484 2.75 2.00

Inter-European Cultural Economic Cooperation.

Design: 3.45 l, Satellite over earth.

| | | | |
|---|---|---|---|
| 2523 | A753 | 2.75 l brn & multi | .60 .20 |
| 2524 | A753 | 3.60 l multi | .85 .30 |
| | | Nos. 2519-2524 (6) | 2.45 1.30 |

**Romanian Communist Party Emblem — A754**

**1974, Nov. 20**

| | | | |
|---|---|---|---|
| 2525 | A754 | 55b blk, red & gold | .20 .20 |
| 2526 | A754 | 1 l blk, red & gold | .30 .20 |

Design: 1 l, similar to 55b.

9th Romanian Communist Party Congress.

**Discobolus and Olympic Rings — A755**

**1974, Nov. 11**

| | | | |
|---|---|---|---|
| 2527 | A755 | 2 l ultra & multi | .45 .20 |

Romanian Olympic Committee, 60th anniv.

**Skylab A756**

**1974, Dec. 14    Photo.    Perf. 13**

| | | | |
|---|---|---|---|
| 2528 | A756 | 2.50 l multi | .60 .35 |

Skylab, manned US space laboratory. No. 2528 printed in sheets of 4 stamps and 4 labels. A 10 l imperf. souvenir sheet exists showing Skylab. Value, unused sheet $30, used $27.50.

**Field Ball and Games Emblem A757**

**1975, Jan. 3**

| | | | |
|---|---|---|---|
| 2529 | A757 | 55b ultra & multi | .20 .20 |
| 2530 | A757 | 1.75 l yellow & multi | .40 .20 |
| 2531 | A757 | 2.20 l multi | .50 .20 |
| | | Nos. 2529-2531 (3) | 1.10 .60 |

World University Field Ball Championship.

---

**Rocks and Birches, by Andreescu A758**

Paintings by Ion Andreescu (1850-1882): 40b, Farm Woman with Green Kerchief, 55b, Winter in the Woods, 1.75 l, Winter in Barbizon, horiz. 2.75 l, Self-portrait. 3.60 l, Main Road, horiz.

**1975, Jan. 24**

| | | | |
|---|---|---|---|
| 2532 | A758 | 20b multi | .20 .20 |
| 2533 | A758 | 40b multi | .20 .20 |
| 2534 | A758 | 55b multi | .20 .20 |
| 2535 | A758 | 1.75 l multi | .40 .20 |
| 2536 | A758 | 2.75 l multi | .60 .30 |
| 2537 | A758 | 3.60 l multi | .85 .35 |
| | | Nos. 2532-2537 (6) | 2.45 1.30 |

**Torch with Flame in Flag Colors and Coat of Arms — A759**

**1975, Feb. 1**

| | | | |
|---|---|---|---|
| 2538 | A759 | 40b multicolored | .20 .20 |

Romanian Socialist Republic, 10th anniv.

**Vaslui Battle, by O. Obedeanu A760**

**1975, Feb. 8    Photo.    Perf. 13½**

| | | | |
|---|---|---|---|
| 2539 | A760 | 55b gold & multi | .20 .20 |

Battle at the High Bridge, Stephan the Great's victory over the Turks, 500th anniv.

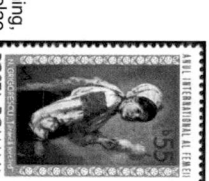

**Woman Spinning, by Nicolae Grigorescu — A761**

---

**Michelangelo, Self-portrait A762**

**1975, Mar. 1**

| | | | |
|---|---|---|---|
| 2540 | A761 | 55b gold & multi | .20 .20 |

International Women's Year.

**1975, Mar. 10**

| | | | |
|---|---|---|---|
| 2541 | A762 | 5 l multicolored | .85 .30 |

Michelangelo Buonarroti (1475-1564), Italian sculptor, painter and architect. For overprint see No. 2581.

**Souvenir Sheet**

**Escorial Palace and España 75 Emblem — A763**

**1975, Mar. 15    Photo.    Perf. 13**

| | | | |
|---|---|---|---|
| 2542 | A763 | 10 l multi | 2.00 1.75 |

Espana 75 Intl. Phil. Exhib., Madrid, 4/4-13.

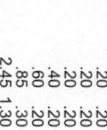

**Letter with Postal Code, Pigeon A764**

**1975, Mar. 26    Photo.    Perf. 13½**

| | | | |
|---|---|---|---|
| 2543 | A764 | 55b blue & multi | .20 .20 |

Introduction of postal code system.

**Children's Science Pavilion — A765**

**1975, Apr. 10    Photo.    Perf. 13**

| | | | |
|---|---|---|---|
| 2544 | A765 | 4 l multicolored | .75 .20 |

Oceanexpo 75, International Exhibition, Okinawa, July 20, 1975-Jan. 1976.

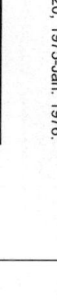

**Peonies, by N. Tonitza A766**

3.45 l, Chrysanthemums, by St. Luchian.

---

**1875 Meter Convention Emblem — A767**

**1975, Apr. 28**

| | | | |
|---|---|---|---|
| 2545 | A766 | 2.20 l gold & multi | .85 .50 |
| 2546 | A766 | 3.45 l gold & multi | .95 .95 |
| a. | | Pair, #2545-2546 | 2.10 1.75 |

Inter-European Cultural and Economic Cooperation. Printed checkerwise in sheets of 10 (2x5).

**1975, May 10    Photo.    Perf. 13**

| | | | |
|---|---|---|---|
| 2547 | A767 | 1.85 l blk & gold | .50 .20 |

Cent. of Intl. Meter Convention, Paris, 1875.

**Mihail Eminescu and his Home — A768**

**1975, June 5**

| | | | |
|---|---|---|---|
| 2548 | A768 | 55b multicolored | .20 .20 |

Mihail Eminescu (1850-1889), poet.

**Marble Plaque and Dacian Coins 1st-2nd Centuries — A769**

**1975, May 26**

| | | | |
|---|---|---|---|
| 2549 | A769 | 55b multicolored | .20 .20 |

2000th anniv. of the founding of Alba Iulia (Apulum).

**Souvenir Sheet**

**"On the Bank of the Seine," by Th. Pallady — A770**

**1975, May 26**

| | | | |
|---|---|---|---|
| 2550 | A770 | 10 l multicolored | 2.25 1.75 |

ARPHILA 75, Paris, June 6-16.

ROMANIA

Dr. Albert Schweitzer (1875-1965), Medical Missionary — A771

**1974, Dec. 20    Photo.    Perf. 13½**
2551  A771  40b  black brown                    .20  .20

Ana Ipatescu A772

**1975, June 2    Photo.    Perf. 13½**
2552  A772  55b  lilac rose                     .20  .20

Ana Ipatescu, fighter in 1848 revolution.

Policeman with Walkie-talkie A773

**1975, Sept. 1**
2553  A773  55b  brt blue                       .20  .20

Publicity for traffic rules.

Monument and Projected Reconstruction, Adam Clissi — A777

Roman Monuments: 55b, Emperor Trajan, bas-relief, vert. 1.20 l, Trajan's column, Rome, vert. 1.55 l, Governor Decibalus, bas-relief, vert. 2 l, Excavated Roman city, Turnu-Severin. 2.25 l, Trajan's Bridge, ruin and projected reconstruction. No. 2569, Roman fortifications, vert.

**1975, June 26    Photo.    Perf. 13½**
2563  A777  55b  red brn & blk                  .20  .20
2564  A777  1.20 l  vio bl & blk                .25  .20
2565  A777  1.55 l  green & blk                 .20  .20
2566  A777  1.75 l  dl rose & multi             .35  .20
2567  A777  2 l  dl yel & blk                   .40  .25
2568  A777  2.25 l  brt bl & blk                .55  .20
        Nos. 2563-2568 (6)                      2.00  1.20

**Souvenir Sheet**

2569  A777  multicolored                        2.75  2.00

European Architectural Heritage Year. An imperf. 10 l gold and dark brown souvenir sheet exists showing the Roman wolf suckling Romulus and Remus. Value $100, unused or used.

Michael the Brave, by Sadeler A778

01068

375 ANI DE LA PRIMA UNIRE A TARILOR ROMANE SUB MIHAI VITEAZUL

Michael the Brave Statue — A779

Designs: 1.20 l, Ottoman Messengers Offering Gifts to Michael the Brave, by Theodor Aman, horiz. 2.75 l, Michael the Brave in Battle of Calugareni, by Aman.

**1975, July 7**
2571  A778  55b  gold & blk                     .20  .20
2572  A778  1.20 l  gold & multi                .25  .20
2573  A778  2.75 l  gold & multi                .55  .60
        Nos. 2571-2573 (3)                      1.00  1.00

**Souvenir Sheet**
**Imperf**

2574  A779  10 l  gold & multi                  18.00  16.00

First political union of Romanian states under Michael the Brave, 375th anniv. No. 2574 issued Sept. 20.

Larkspur — A780

**1975, Aug. 15    Photo.    Perf. 13½**
2575  A780  20b  shown                          .20  .20
2576  A780  40b  Field poppies                  .20  .20
2577  A780  55b  Xeranthemum                    .20  .20
                annuum
2578  A780  1.75 l  Rockrose                    .40  .20
2579  A780  2.75 l  Meadow sage                 .60  .20
2580  A780  3.60 l  Wild chicory                .85  .25
        Nos. 2575-2580 (6)                      2.45  1.25

Tirg International de marci postale

Riccione — Italia
23-25 august 1975

No. 2541 Overprinted in Red:

**1975, Aug. 23**
2581  A762  5 l  multicolored                   1.75  .85

Intl. Phil. Exhib., Riccione, Italy, Aug. 23-25.

Map Showing Location of Craiova, 1750 — A781

Illustration reduced.

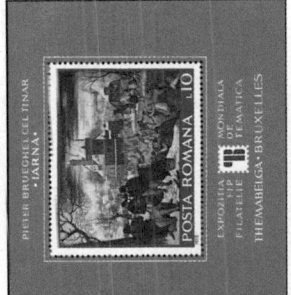

Muntenian Rug — A782

Romanian Peasant Rugs: 40b, Banat. 55b, Oltenia. 1.75 l, Moldavia. 2.75 l, Oltenia. 3.60 l, Maramures.

**1975, Oct. 5    Photo.    Perf. 13½**
2583  A782  20b  dk bl & multi                  .20  .20
2584  A782  40b  black & multi                  .20  .20
2585  A782  55b  multicolored                   .20  .20
2586  A782  1.75 l  black & multi               .40  .20
2587  A782  2.75 l  multicolored                .60  .20
2588  A782  3.60 l  black & multi               .80  .25
        Nos. 2583-2588 (6)                      2.40  1.20

Minibus A783

**1975, Nov. 5    Photo.    Perf. 13½**
2589  A783  20b  shown                          .20  .20
2590  A783  40b  Gasoline truck                 .20  .20
2591  A783  55b  Jeep                           .20  .20
2592  A783  1.75 l  Flat-bed truck              .40  .20
2593  A783  2.75 l  Furgo automo-               .60  .20
                bile
2594  A783  3.60 l  Dump truck                  .85  .25
        Nos. 2589-2594 (6)                      2.45  1.20

**Souvenir Sheet**

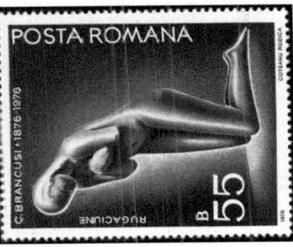

EXPOZITIA MONDIALA FILATELICA TEMATICA
PIETER BRUEGHEL CEL TINAR : IARNA
THEMABELGA-BRUXELLES

Winter, by Peter Brueghel, the Younger — A784

**1975, Nov. 25    Photo.**
2595  A784  10 l  multicolored                  2.50  2.00

THEMABELGA Intl. Topical Phil. Exhib., Brussels, Dec. 13-21.

*Muntenia B.20* POSTA ROMANA

*POSTA ROMANA 1776 - 1976*

**Souvenir Sheet**

Washington at Valley Forge, by W. T. Trego — A786

Paintings: 40b, Washington at Trenton, by John Trumbull. 55b, Washington Crossing the Delaware, by Emanuel Leutze. 1.75 l, The Capture of the Hessians, by Trumbull. 2.75 l, Jefferson, by Thomas Sully, vert. 3.60 l, Surrender of Cornwallis at Yorktown, by Trumbull. 10 l, Signing of the Declaration of Independence, by Trumbull.

**1976, Jan. 12    Photo.    Perf. 13½**
2596  A785  20b  blue & multi                   .20  .20
2597  A785  40b  multicolored                   .20  .20
2598  A785  55b  multicolored                   .20  .20
2599  A785  1.75 l  ol & multi                  .40  .20
2600  A785  2.75 l  multi                       .60  .35
2601  A785  3.60 l  multi                       2.40  1.35
        Nos. 2596-2601 (6)

**Souvenir Sheet**

2602  A785  10 l  multi                         2.50  2.00

12th Winter Olympic Games, Innsbruck, Austria, Feb. 4-15. An imperf. 10 l souvenir sheet exists showing slalom; Romanian flag, Games' emblem. Value, unused $30, used $27.50.

**1976, Jan. 25    Photo.    Perf. 13½**
2603  A786  20b  gold & multi                   .20  .20
2604  A786  40b  gold & multi                   .20  .20
2605  A786  55b  gold & multi                   .20  .20
2606  A786  1.75 l  gold & multi                .40  .20
2607  A786  2.75 l  gold & multi                .60  .25
2608  A786  3.60 l  gold & multi                .75  .35
        Nos. 2603-2608 (6)                      2.35  1.40

**Souvenir Sheet**

2609  A786  10 l  gold & multi                  2.50  2.00

American Bicentennial. No. 2609 also for Interphil 76 Intl. Phil. Exhib., Philadelphia, Pa., May 29-June 6. Printed in horizontal rows of 4; stamps with centered label showing Bicentennial emblem.

POSTA ROMANA

C. Brancusi 1876-1976

RUGACIUNE   B 55

Prayer, by Brancusi A787

Designs: 1.75 l, Architectural Assembly, by Brancusi. 3.60 l, Constantin Brancusi.

**1976, Feb. 15    Photo.    Perf. 13½**
2610  A787  55b  purple & multi                 .20  .20
2611  A787  1.75 l  blue & multi                .40  .20
2612  A787  3.60 l  multicolored                1.45  .75
        Nos. 2610-2612 (3)

Constantin Brancusi (1576-1957), sculptor. For surcharge see No. B440.

Archives Museum A789

55b, Vlad Tepes. 1.20 l, Costache Negri.

POSTA ROMANA 1926-1976   175 L

Anton Davidoglu 1876-1958   40

Anton Davidoglu A788

INNSBRUCK '76   B 20   POSTA ROMANA

Luge and Olympic Games' Emblem — A785

Innsbruck Olympic Games' Emblem and: 40b, Biathlon, vert. 55b, Woman skier. 1.75 l, Ski jump. 2.75 l, Woman figure skater. 3.60 l, Ice hockey. 10 l, Two-man bobsled.

**1976, Feb. 25**

Anniversaries: Anton Davidoglu (1876-1958), mathematician; Prince Vlad Tepes, commander in war against the Turks (d. 1476); Costache Negri (1812-1876), Moldavian freedom fighter; Romanian National Archives Museum, founded 1926.

| 2613 | A788 | 40b green & multi | .20 | .20 |
|---|---|---|---|---|
| 2614 | A788 | 55b green & multi | .20 | .20 |
| 2615 | A788 | 1.20 l green & multi | .30 | .20 |
| 2616 | A789 | 1.75 l green & multi | .40 | .20 |
| | | Nos. 2613-2616 (4) | 1.10 | .80 |

Dr. Carol Davila — A790

**1976, Apr. 20**

| 2617 | A790 | 55b multi | .20 | .20 |
|---|---|---|---|---|
| 2618 | A790 | 1.75 l multi | .40 | .20 |
| 2619 | A790 | 2.20 l yellow & multi | .50 | .20 |
| | | Nos. 2617-2619,C199 (4) | 1.70 | .85 |

Romanian Red Cross cent.

Vase with King Decebalus Portrait — A791

1.75 l, Nurse with patient. 2.20 l, First aid.

**1976, May 13**

Design: 3.45 l, Vase with portrait of King Michael the Bold.

| 2620 | A791 | 2.20 l bl & multi | 1.00 | .50 |
|---|---|---|---|---|
| 2621 | A791 | 3.45 l multi | 2.50 | 1.25 |

Inter-European Cultural Economic Cooperation. Nos. 2620-2621 each printed in sheets of 4 with marginal inscriptions.

Coat of Arms — A792

Spiru Haret — A793

**1976, June 12**

| 2622 | A792 | 1.75 l multi | .40 | .20 |
|---|---|---|---|---|

See design A615.

**1976, June 25**

| 2628 | A793 | 20b multicolored | .20 | .20 |
|---|---|---|---|---|

Spiru Haret (1851-1912), mathematician.

Woman Athlete — A794

**1976, June 25 Photo. Perf. 13½**

| 2629 | A794 | 20b org & multi | .20 | .20 |
|---|---|---|---|---|
| 2630 | A794 | 40b multi | .20 | .20 |
| 2631 | A794 | 55b multi | .20 | .20 |
| 2632 | A794 | 1.75 l multi | .40 | .20 |
| 2633 | A794 | 2.75 l vio & multi | .60 | .20 |
| 2634 | A794 | 3.60 l bl & multi | .85 | .45 |
| | | Nos. 2629-2634 (6) | 2.45 | 1.50 |

21st Olympic Games, Montreal, Canada, July 17-Aug. 1. No. 2635 contains one stamp 49x37mm.

**Souvenir Sheet**

| 2635 | A794 | 10 l rose & multi | 2.50 | 2.00 |
|---|---|---|---|---|

An imperf. airmail 10 l souvenir sheet exists showing Olympic Stadium, Montreal. Value, unused $25, used $22.50.

Romanian Olympic Emblem and: 40b, Boxing. 55b, Team handball. 1.75 l, 2-man scull, horiz. 2.75 l, 2-man canoe, horiz. 3.60 l, Gymnast on rings, horiz. 10 l, Woman gymnast, horiz.

Inscribed Stone Tablets, Banat — A795

Designs: 40b, Hekate, Bacchus, bas-relief. 55b, Ceramic fragment, bowl, coins. 1.75 l, Bowl, urn and cup. 2.75 l, Sword, lance and tombstone. 3.60 l, Lances, urn. 10 l, Clay vessel and silver coins.

**1976, July 25**

| 2636 | A795 | 20b multi | .20 | .20 |
|---|---|---|---|---|
| 2637 | A795 | 40b multi | .20 | .20 |
| 2638 | A795 | 55b org & multi | .20 | .20 |
| 2639 | A795 | 1.75 l multi | .40 | .20 |
| 2640 | A795 | 2.75 l fawn & multi | .60 | .25 |
| 2641 | A795 | 3.60 l multi | .85 | .35 |
| | | Nos. 2636-2641 (6) | 2.45 | 1.40 |

**Souvenir Sheet**

| 2642 | A795 | 10 l yel & multi | 2.50 | 2.00 |
|---|---|---|---|---|

Daco-Roman archaeological treasures. No. 2642 issued Mar. 25. An imperf. 10 l souvenir sheet exists showing a silver and gold vase and silver coins. Value, unused or used, $10.

Wolf Statue, 4th Century Map A796

**1976, Aug. 25**

| 2643 | A796 | 55b multi | .20 | .20 |
|---|---|---|---|---|

Founding of Buzau, 1600th anniv.

Dan Grecu, Bronze Medal — A798

Game — A797

**1976, Sept. 20**

| 2644 | A797 | 20b Red deer | .20 | .20 |
|---|---|---|---|---|
| 2645 | A797 | 40b Brown bear | .20 | .20 |
| 2646 | A797 | 55b Chamois | .20 | .20 |
| 2647 | A797 | 1.75 l Boar | .40 | .20 |
| 2648 | A797 | 2.75 l Red fox | .60 | .20 |
| 2649 | A797 | 3.60 l Lynx | .85 | .20 |
| | | Nos. 2644-2649 (6) | 2.45 | 1.20 |

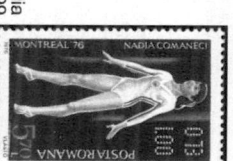

Nadia Comaneci — A799

40b, Fencing, bronze medal. 55b Gheorghe Megelea (Javelin), bronze medal. 1.75 l, Handball, silver medal. 2.75 l, Boxing, 1 bronze, 2 silver medals. 10 l, Wrestling, silver and bronze medals. 10 l, Vasile Daba (kayak), gold and silver medals, vert.

**1976, Oct. 20 Photo. Perf. 13½**

| 2650 | A798 | 20b multi | .20 | .20 |
|---|---|---|---|---|
| 2651 | A798 | 40b car & multi | .20 | .20 |
| 2652 | A798 | 55b grn & multi | .20 | .20 |
| 2653 | A798 | 1.75 l red & multi | .40 | .20 |
| 2654 | A798 | 2.75 l bl & multi | .60 | .25 |
| 2655 | A798 | 3.60 l multi | .80 | .40 |
| 2656 | A799 | 5.70 l multi | 1.40 | .45 |
| | | Nos. 2650-2656 (7) | 3.80 | 1.90 |

Romanian Olympic medalists. No. 2657 contains one 37x50mm stamp.

**Souvenir Sheet**

| 2657 | A798 | 10 l multi | 2.50 | 2.00 |
|---|---|---|---|---|

An imperf airmail 10 l souvenir sheet exists picturing gymnast, Nadia Comaneci. Value, unused $30, used $27.50.

Milan Cathedral — A800

**1976, Oct. 20 Photo. Perf. 13½**

| 2658 | A800 | 4.75 l multi | 1.10 | .40 |
|---|---|---|---|---|

ITALIA 76 Intl. Phil. Exhib., Milan, 10/14-24.

Oranges and Carnations, by Luchian — A801

**1976, Nov. 5**

| 2659 | A801 | 20b multi | .20 | .20 |
|---|---|---|---|---|
| 2660 | A801 | 40b multi | .20 | .20 |
| 2661 | A801 | 55b multi | .20 | .20 |
| 2662 | A801 | 1.75 l multi | .40 | .20 |
| 2663 | A801 | 2.75 l multi | .60 | .20 |
| 2664 | A801 | 3.60 l multi | .85 | .35 |
| | | Nos. 2659-2664 (6) | 2.45 | 1.40 |

Paintings by Stefan Luchian (1868-1916): 40b, Flower arrangement. 55b, Vase with flowers. 1.75 l, Roses. 2.75 l, Cornflowers. 3.60 l, Carnations in vase.

Arms of Alba — A802

Designs: Arms of Romanian counties.

**1976-77 Photo. Perf. 13½**

| 2665 | A802 | 55b shown | .25 | .20 |
|---|---|---|---|---|
| 2666 | A802 | 55b Arad | .25 | .20 |
| 2667 | A802 | 55b Arges | .25 | .20 |
| 2668 | A802 | 55b Bacau | .25 | .20 |
| 2669 | A802 | 55b Bihor | .25 | .20 |
| 2670 | A802 | 55b Bistrita-Nasaud | .25 | .20 |
| 2671 | A802 | 55b Botosani | .25 | .20 |
| 2672 | A802 | 55b Brasov | .25 | .20 |
| 2673 | A802 | 55b Braila | .25 | .20 |
| 2674 | A802 | 55b Buzau | .25 | .20 |
| 2675 | A802 | 55b Caras-Severin | .25 | .20 |
| 2676 | A802 | 55b Cluj | .25 | .20 |
| 2677 | A802 | 55b Constanta | .25 | .20 |
| 2678 | A802 | 55b Covasna | .25 | .20 |
| 2679 | A802 | 55b Dimbovita | .25 | .20 |
| 2680 | A802 | 55b Dolj | .25 | .20 |
| 2681 | A802 | 55b Galati | .25 | .20 |
| 2682 | A802 | 55b Gorj | .25 | .20 |
| 2683 | A802 | 55b Harghita | .25 | .20 |
| 2684 | A802 | 55b Hunedoara | .25 | .20 |
| 2685 | A802 | 55b Ialomita | .25 | .20 |
| 2686 | A802 | 55b Iasi | .25 | .20 |
| 2687 | A802 | 55b Ilfov | .25 | .20 |
| 2688 | A802 | 55b Maramures | .25 | .20 |
| 2689 | A802 | 55b Mehedinti | .25 | .20 |
| 2690 | A802 | 55b Mures | .25 | .20 |
| 2691 | A802 | 55b Neamt | .25 | .20 |
| 2692 | A802 | 55b Olt | .25 | .20 |
| 2693 | A802 | 55b Prahova | .25 | .20 |
| 2694 | A802 | 55b Salaj | .25 | .20 |
| 2695 | A802 | 55b Satu-Mare | .25 | .20 |
| 2696 | A802 | 55b Sibiu | .25 | .20 |
| 2697 | A802 | 55b Suceava | .25 | .20 |
| 2698 | A802 | 55b Teleorman | .25 | .20 |
| 2699 | A802 | 55b Timis | .25 | .20 |
| 2700 | A802 | 55b Tulcea | .25 | .20 |
| 2701 | A802 | 55b Vaslui | .25 | .20 |
| 2702 | A802 | 55b Vilcea | .25 | .20 |
| 2703 | A802 | 55b Vrancea | .25 | .20 |
| 2704 | A802 | 5b Postal emblem | .10 | .10 |
| | | Nos. 2665-2704 (40) | 10.00 | 8.00 |

Sheets of 50 (10x5) contain 5 designs: Nos. 2665-2669; 2670-2674; 2675-2679; 2680-2684; 2685-2689; 2690-2694; 2695-2699; 2700-2704. Each row of 10 contains 5 pairs of each design. Issued: #2665-2679, 12/20; #2680-2704, 9/5/77.

Oxcart, by Grigorescu — A803

ROMANIA

---

Paintings by Nicolae Grigorescu (1838-1907): 1 l, Self-portrait, vert. 1.50 l, Shepherdess. 2.15 l, Woman Spinning with Distaff. 3.40 l, Shepherd, vert. 4.80 l, Rest at Well.

**1977, Jan. 20 — Photo. — Perf. 13½**

| 2705 | A803 | 55b | gray & multi | .20 | .20 |
|---|---|---|---|---|---|
| 2706 | A803 | 1.50 l | gray & multi | .20 | .20 |
| 2707 | A803 | 2.15 l | gray & multi | .25 | .20 |
| 2708 | A803 | 3.40 l | gray & multi | .40 | .20 |
| 2709 | A803 | 4.80 l | gray & multi | .55 | .30 |
| 2710 | A803 | | gray & multi | .85 | .35 |
| Nos. 2705-2710 (6) | | | | 2.45 | 1.45 |

Cheia Telecommunications Station — A804

**1977, Feb. 1**

| 2711 | A804 | 55b | multi | .20 | .20 |
|---|---|---|---|---|---|

Red Deer A805

Protected Birds and Animals: 1 l, Mute swan. 1.50 l, Egyptian vulture. 2.15 l, Bison. 3.40 l, White-headed ruddy duck. 4.80 l, Kingfisher.

**1977, Mar. 20 — Photo. — Perf. 13½**

| 2712 | A805 | 55b | multi | .20 | .20 |
|---|---|---|---|---|---|
| 2713 | A805 | 1 l | multi | .20 | .20 |
| 2714 | A805 | 1.50 l | multi | .25 | .20 |
| 2715 | A805 | 2.15 l | multi | .35 | .20 |
| 2716 | A805 | 3.40 l | multi | .60 | .50 |
| 2717 | A805 | 4.80 l | multi | .75 | .20 |
| Nos. 2712-2717 (6) | | | | 2.40 | 1.20 |

Calafat Artillery Unit, by Sava Hentia — A806

Paintings: 55b, Attacking Infantryman, by Oscar Obedeanu, vert. 1.50 l, Infantry Attack in Winter, by Stefan Luchian, vert. 2.15 l, Battle of Plevna (after etching). 3.40 l, Artillery, by Nicolae Ion Grigorescu. 10 l, Battle of Grivita, 1877.

**1977**

| 2718 | A806 | 55b | gold & multi | .20 | .20 |
|---|---|---|---|---|---|
| 2719 | A806 | 1 l | gold & multi | .20 | .20 |
| 2720 | A806 | 1.50 l | gold & multi | .25 | .20 |
| 2721 | A806 | 2.15 l | gold & multi | .60 | .20 |
| 2722 | A806 | 3.40 l | gold & multi | .75 | .20 |
| Nos. 2718-2722,B442 (6) | | | | 3.25 | 1.35 |

**Souvenir Sheet**

| 2723 | A806 | 10 l | gold & multi | 2.75 | 2.00 |
|---|---|---|---|---|---|

Centenary of Romania's independence. A 10 l imperf. souvenir sheet exists showing victorious return of army, Dobruja, 1878. Value, unused or used, $10.
Issued: #2718-2722, May 9; #2723, Apr. 25.

---

Sinaia, Carpathian Mountains — A807

Design: 2.40 l, Hotels, Aurora, Black Sea.

**1977, May 17**

| 2724 | A807 | 2 l | gold & multi | 1.00 | .85 |
|---|---|---|---|---|---|
| 2725 | A807 | 2.40 l | gold & multi | 1.40 | 1.25 |

Inter-European Cultural and Economic Cooperation. Nos. 2724-2725 printed in sheets of 4 with marginal inscriptions.

Petru Rares — A808

Ion Luca Caragiale — A809

**1977, June 10 — Photo. — Perf. 13½**

| 2726 | A808 | 40b | multi | .20 | .20 |
|---|---|---|---|---|---|

450th anniversary of the elevation of Petru Rares to Duke of Moldavia.

**1977, June 10**

| 2727 | A809 | 55b | multi | .20 | .20 |
|---|---|---|---|---|---|

Ion Luca Caragiale (1852-1912), writer.

Red Cross Nurse, Children, Emblems A810

**1977, June 10**

| 2728 | A810 | 1.50 l | multi | .35 | .20 |
|---|---|---|---|---|---|

23rd Intl. Red Cross Conf. Bucharest.

Arch of Triumph, Bucharest A811

**1977, June 10**

| 2729 | A811 | 2.15 l | multi | .50 | .20 |
|---|---|---|---|---|---|

Battles of Marasesti and Oituz, 60th anniv.

---

Peaks of San Marino, Exhibition Emblem — A812

**1977, Aug. 28 — Photo. — Perf. 13½**

| 2730 | A812 | 4 l | brt bl & multi | 1.00 | .25 |
|---|---|---|---|---|---|

Centenary of San Marino stamps, and San Marino '77 Phil. Exhib., San Marino, 8/28-9/4.

Man on Pommel Horse — A813

Gymnasts: 40b, Woman dancer. 55b, Man on parallel bars. 1 l, Woman on balance beam. 2.15 l, Man on rings. 4.80 l, Woman on double bars.

**1977, Sept. 25 — Photo. — Perf. 13½**

| 2731 | A813 | 20b | multi | .20 | .20 |
|---|---|---|---|---|---|
| 2732 | A813 | 40b | multi | .20 | .20 |
| 2733 | A813 | 55b | multi | .20 | .20 |
| 2734 | A813 | 1 l | multi | .20 | .20 |
| 2735 | A813 | 2.15 l | multi | .35 | .20 |
| 2736 | A813 | 4.80 l | multi | 1.25 | .20 |
| Nos. 2731-2736 (6) | | | | 2.40 | 1.20 |

"Carpati" near Cazane, Iron Gate — A814

Designs: 1 l, "Mircesti" at Orsova. 1.50 l, "Oltenia" at Calafat. 2.15 l, Water bus at Giurgiu. 3 l, "Herculane" at Tulcea. 3.40 l, "Muntenia" in Nature preserve, Sulina. 4.80 l, Map of Danube Delta with Sulina Canal. 10 l, Danubius, god of Danube, from Trajan's Column, Rome, vert.

**1977, Dec. 28**

| 2737 | A814 | 55b | multi | .20 | .20 |
|---|---|---|---|---|---|
| 2738 | A814 | 1 l | multi | .20 | .20 |
| 2739 | A814 | 1.50 l | multi | .25 | .20 |
| 2740 | A814 | 2.15 l | multi | .40 | .20 |
| 2741 | A814 | 3 l | multi | .60 | .20 |
| 2742 | A814 | 3.40 l | multi | .65 | .30 |
| 2743 | A814 | 4.80 l | multi | 1.25 | .30 |
| Nos. 2737-2743 (7) | | | | 3.55 | 1.50 |

**Souvenir Sheet**

| 2744 | A814 | 10 l | multi | 2.75 | 2.00 |
|---|---|---|---|---|---|

European Danube Commission. A 10 l imperf. souvenir sheet exists showing map of Danube from Regensburg to the Black Sea. Value, unused $35, used $32.50.

---

Flag and Arms of Romania A815

Designs: 1.20 l, Computer production in Romania. 1.75 l, National Theater, Craiova.

Dancers A816

**1977, Dec. 30**

| 2745 | A815 | 55b | multi | .20 | .20 |
|---|---|---|---|---|---|
| 2746 | A815 | 1.20 l | multi | .20 | .20 |
| 2747 | A815 | 1.75 l | multi | .80 | .60 |
| Nos. 2745-2747 (3) | | | | | |

Proclamation of Republic, 30th anniversary.

Designs: Romanian male folk dancers.

**1977, Nov. 28 — Photo. — Perf. 13½**

| 2748 | A816 | 20b | multi | .20 | .20 |
|---|---|---|---|---|---|
| 2749 | A816 | 40b | multi | .20 | .20 |
| 2750 | A816 | 55b | multi | .20 | .20 |
| 2751 | A816 | 1 l | multi | .20 | .20 |
| 2752 | A816 | 2.15 l | multi | .35 | .20 |
| 2753 | A816 | 4.80 l | multi | 1.25 | 1.20 |
| Nos. 2748-2753 (6) | | | | 2.40 | 1.20 |

**Souvenir Sheet**

| 2754 | A816 | 10 l | multi | 2.00 | 2.00 |
|---|---|---|---|---|---|

Firiza Dam A817

Hydroelectric Stations and Dams: 40b, Negovanu. 55b, Piatra Neamt. 1 l, Izvorul Muntelui-Bicaz. 2.15 l, Vidraru. 4.80 l, Iron Gate.

**1978, Mar. 10 — Photo. — Perf. 13½**

| 2755 | A817 | 20b | multi | .20 | .20 |
|---|---|---|---|---|---|
| 2756 | A817 | 40b | multi | .20 | .20 |
| 2767 | A017 | 55b | multi | .20 | .20 |
| 2758 | A817 | 1 l | multi | .35 | .20 |
| 2759 | A817 | 2.15 l | multi | 1.00 | .20 |
| 2760 | A817 | 4.80 l | multi | 2.15 | 1.20 |
| Nos. 2755-2760 (6) | | | | | |

Soccer and Argentina '78 Emblem A818

Various soccer scenes & Argentina '78 emblem.

**1978, Apr. 15**

| 2761 | A818 | 20b | bl & multi | .20 | .20 |
|---|---|---|---|---|---|
| 2762 | A818 | 55b | org & multi | .20 | .20 |
| 2763 | A818 | 1 l | yel grn & multi | .30 | .20 |
| 2764 | A818 | 1.50 l | ver & multi | .30 | .20 |
| 2765 | A818 | 2.15 l | bl grn & multi | .50 | .20 |
| 2766 | A818 | 4.80 l | lil rose & multi | 1.00 | 1.20 |
| Nos. 2761-2766 (6) | | | | 2.40 | 1.20 |

11th World Cup Soccer Championship, Argentina '78, June 1-25. See No. C222.

King Decebalus of Dacia Statue, Deva A819

Design: 3.40 l, King Mircea the Elder of Walachia statue, Tulcea, and ship.

Worker, Factory,
Flag — A821

**1978, May 22      Photo.      Perf. 13½**
2767  A819  1.30 l, gold & multi ......... .90  .70
2768  A819  3.40 l, gold & multi ........ 1.60  1.25

Inter-European Cultural and Economic
Cooperation. Each printed in sheet of 4.

---

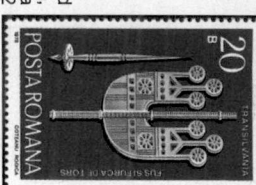

Spindle and
Handle,
Transylvania
A822

**1978, June 11      Photo.      Perf. 13½**
2770  A821  55b multi ...................... .20  .20

Nationalization of industry, 30th anniv.

---

Danube Delta — A823

**1978, June 20**
2771  A822  20b multi ...................... .20
2772  A822  40b multi ...................... .20
2773  A822  55b multi ...................... .20
2774  A822  1 l   multi ...................... .20
2775  A822  2.15 l multi .................. .20  .30
2776  A822  4.80 l multi .................. .20  1.20
            Nos. 2771-2776 (6)

Wood Carvings: 40b, Cheese molds,
Muntenia. 55b, Spoons, Oltenia. 1 l, Barrel,
Moldavia. 2.15 l, Ladle and mug, Transylvania.
4.80 l, Water bucket, Oltenia.

**1978, July 20      Photo.**
2777  A823  55b multi ...................... .20  .20
2778  A823      1 l  multi .................. .20  .20
2779  A823  1.50 l multi .................. .20  .20
2780  A823  2.15 l multi .................. .20  .30
2781  A823  3.40 l multi .................. .20  .50
2782  A823  4.80 l multi .................. .20  1.35
            Nos. 2777-2782 (6)         1.00

Tourist Publicity: 1 l, Bran Castle.
1.50 l, Monastery, Suceava. Moldavia. 2.15 l,
Caves, Oltenia. 3.40 l, Ski lift, Brasov. 4.80 l,
Mangalia, Black Sea. 10 l, Strehaia Fortress,
vert.

**Miniature Sheet**
2783  A823  10 l multi .................... 2.50  2.00

No. 2783 contains one 37x51mm stamp.
Issued July 30.

---

Electronic
Microscope
A824

Designs: 40b, Hydraulic excavator. 55b,
Computer center. 1.50 l, Oil derricks. 3 l, Harvester combine. 3.40 l, Petrochemical plant.

---

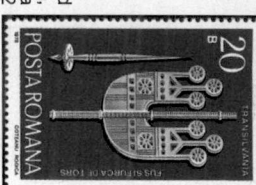

"Racial
Equality" — A826

**1978, Aug. 15      Photo.      Perf. 13½**
2784  A824  20b multi ...................... .20  .20
2785  A824  40b multi ...................... .20  .20
2786  A824  55b multi ...................... .20  .25
2787  A824  1.50 l multi, horiz. ....... .25  .25
2788  A824      3 l  multi, horiz. ....... .55  .55
2789  A824  3.40 l multi ................. .70  .70
            Nos. 2784-2789 (6)      2.10  1.20

Industrial development.

---

**1978, Aug. 25      Photo.      Perf. 13½**
2790  A825  55b multi ...................... .20  .20
2791  A825      1 l  multi .................. .20  .20
2792  A825  1.50 l multi .................. .20  .20
2793  A825  2.15 l multi .................. .20  .30
2794  A825  3.40 l multi .................. .20  .50
2795  A825  4.80 l multi .................. .20  1.20
            Nos. 2790-2795 (6)      1.00

Caves: 1 l, Topolnita. 1.50 l, Ponoare. 2.15 l,
Ratei. Mt. Bucegi. 3.40 l, Closani. Mt. Motrului.
4.80 l, Epuran. 1 l, 1.50 l, 4.80 l, Mt. Mehedinti.

---

Gold Bas-relief — A827

**1978, Sept. 25**
2797  A827  20b multi ...................... .20
2798  A827  40b multi ...................... .20
2799  A827  55b multi ...................... .20
2800  A827      1 l  multi .................. .20
2801  A827  2.15 l multi .................. .20  .30
2802  A827  4.80 l multi .................. .20  1.35
            Nos. 2797-2802 (6)      1.00

Designs: 40b, Gold armband. 55b, Gold
cameo ring. 1 l, Silver bowl. 2.15 l, Eagle from
Roman standard, vert. 4.80 l, Silver armband.

---

Woman
Gymnast,
Games
Emblem
A828

1 l, Running. 1.50 l, Skiing. 2.15 l, Equestrian. 3.40 l, Soccer. 4.80 l, Handball.

---

Polovraci Cave,
Carpathians
A825

**1978, Sept. 28**
2796  A826  3.40 l multi ............... .50  .20

Anti-Apartheid Year.

---

**1978, Sept. 15**
2803  A828  20b multi ...................... .20
2804  A828  40b multi ...................... .20
2805  A828  55b multi ...................... .20
2806  A828  1 l   multi .................. .20
2807  A828  3.40 l multi .................. .20  .50
2808  A828  4.80 l multi .................. .20  1.25
            Nos. 2803-2808 (6)      1.00

Designs: 55b, Meeting House of the
National Council, Arad. 1.75 l, Pottery vases,
8th-9th centuries, found near Arad.
2,000th anniversary of founding of Arad.

---

Ptolemaic
Map of
Dacia
A829

**1978, Oct. 21      Photo.      Perf. 13½**
2809  A829  40b multi ...................... .20
2810  A829  55b multi ...................... .20
2811  A829  1.75 l multi .................. .20  .50
 b.   Strip of 3, #2809-2811 ....... .30

---

Dacian Warrior, from Trajan's Column,
Rome — A829a

**1978, Nov. 5      Photo.      Perf. 13x13½**
2811A A829a  6 l + 3 l label ......... 1.60  .85

NATIONALA '78 Phil. Exhib., Bucharest.
Stamp Day.

---

Assembly at
Alba Iulia,
1919 — A830

**1978, Dec. 1**
2812  A830  55b gold & multi ....... .20  .20
2813  A830      1 l  gold & multi .... .20  .20

Design: 1 l, Open book and Romanian flag.
60th anniversary of national unity.

---

Warrior, Bas-
relief — A831

**1979**
2814  A831  1.50 l, Warrior on horseback, bas-relief.
2815  A831  1.50 l multi ................... .20  .20

2,050 years since establishment of first centralized and independent Dacian state.

---

Ice Hockey, Globe,
Emblem — A833

**1979, Mar. 1      Photo.      Perf. 13½**
2816  A832  55b multi ...................... .20
2817  A832      1 l  multi .................. .20
2818  A832  1.50 l multi .................. .20
2819  A832  2.15 l multi .................. .20  .30
2820  A832  3.40 l multi .................. .20  .50
2821  A832  4.80 l multi .................. .20  1.25
            Nos. 2816-2821 (6)      1.00

European Youth Ice Hockey Championship,
Miercurea-Ciuc (1.30 l) and World Ice Hockey
Championship, Galati (3.40 l).

---

**1979, Mar. 16      Photo.      Perf. 13½**
2822  A833  3.40 l, Ice hockey players, globe & emblem.
2823  A033  3.40 l multi ................. .30  .20
 a.   Pair, #2822-2823 .............. .55  .20
                                      .86  .50

European Youth Ice Hockey Championship,
Miercurea-Ciuc (1.30 l) and World Ice Hockey
Championship, Galati (3.40 l).

---

"Heroes of
Vaslui" — A832

Children's Drawings: 1 l, Building houses.
1.50 l, Folk music of Tica. 2.15 l, Industrial
landscape, horiz. 3.40 l, Winter customs, horiz.
4.80 l, Pioneer festival, horiz.
International Year of the Child.

---

Dog's-tooth
Violet — A834

**1979, Apr. 25      Photo.**
2824  A834  55b multi ...................... .20
2825  A834      1 l  multi .................. .20
2826  A834  1.50 l multi .................. .20
2827  A834  2.15 l multi .................. .20  .30
2828  A834  3.40 l multi .................. .20  .50
2829  A834  4.80 l multi .................. .20  1.25
            Nos. 2824-2829 (6)      1.00

Protected Flowers: 1 l, Alpine violet. 1.50 l,
Linum borzaeanum. 2.15 l, Persian bindweed.
3.40 l, Primula auricula. 4.80 l, Transylvanian
columbine.

---

Mail
Coach and
Post
Rider,
19th
Century
A835

**1979, May 3      Photo.      Perf. 13**
2830  A835  1.30 l multi ............... .40  .25

Inter-European Cultural and Economic
Cooperation. Printed in sheets of 4.
See No. C231.

---

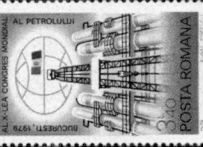
Oil Rig and Refinery — A836

**1979, May 24**    Photo.    *Perf. 13*
2832 A836 3.40 l multi   .50   .20
10th World Petroleum Congress, Bucharest.

Girl Pioneer — A837

**1979, June 20**
2833 A837 55b multi   .20   .20
30th anniversary of Romanian Pioneers.

Children with Flowers, IYC Emblem — A838

**1979, July 18**    Photo.    *Perf. 13½*
2834 A838 40b multi   .20   .20
2835 A838 1 l multi   .20   .20
2836 A838 2 l multi   .30   .20
2837 A838 4.60 l multi   .95   .80
Nos. 2834-2837 (4)   1.65

IYC Emblem and: 1 l, Kindergarten. 2 l, Pioneers with rabbit. 4.60 l, Drummer, trumpeters, flags.
International Year of the Child.

Lady in a Garden, by Tattarescu A839

Stefan Gheorghiu — A840

**1979, June 16**
2838 A839 20b multi   .20   .20
2839 A839 40b multi   .20   .20
2840 A839 55b multi   .30   .20
2841 A839 1 l multi   .30   .20
2842 A839 2.15 l multi   .50   .25
2843 A839 4.80 l multi   .90   1.20
Nos. 2838-2843 (6)   2.00

Paintings by Gheorghe Tattarescu: 40b, Mountain woman. 55b, Mountain man. 1 l, Portrait of Gh. Magheru. 2.15 l, The artist's daughter. 4.80 l, Self-portrait.

**1979, Aug.**
Designs: 55b, Gheorghe Lazar monument. 2.15 l, Lupeni monument. 4.60 l, Women in front of Memorial Arch.
2844 A840 40b multi   .20   .20
2845 A840 55b multi   .20   .20
2846 A840 2.15 l multi   .30   .20
2847 A840 4.60 l multi   .95   .80
Nos. 2844-2847 (4)   1.65

State Theater, Tirgu-Mures — A841

Modern Architecture: 40b, University, Brasov. 55b, Political Administration Buildings, Baia Mare. 1 l, Stefan Gheorghiu Academy, Bucharest. 2.15 l, Political Administration Building, Botosani. 4.80 l, House of Culture, Tirgoviste.

**1979, June 25**
2848 A841 20b multi   .20   .20
2849 A841 40b multi   .20   .20
2850 A841 55b multi   .20   .20
2851 A841 1 l multi   .20   .20
2852 A841 2.15 l multi   .25   .20
2853 A841 4.80 l multi   .85   1.20
Nos. 2848-2853 (6)   1.90

Flags of Russia and Romania — A842

1 l, Workers' Militia, by L. Suhar, horiz.

**1979, Aug. 20**    Photo.    *Perf. 13½*
2854 A842 55b multi   .20   .20
2855 A842 1 l multi   .20   .20
Liberation from Fascism, 35th anniversary.

Cargo Ship Galati A843

Romanian Ships: 1 l, Cargo ship Bucuresti. 1.50 l, Ure carrier Resita. 2.15 l, Ore carrier Tomis. 3.40 l, Tanker Dacia. 4.80 l, Tanker Independenta.

**1979, Aug. 27**    Photo.    *Perf. 13½*
2856 A843 55b multi   .20   .20
2857 A843 1 l multi   .20   .20
2858 A843 1.50 l multi   .20   .20
2859 A843 2.15 l multi   .25   .20
2860 A843 3.40 l multi   .45   .20
2861 A843 4.80 l multi   .90   .25
Nos. 2856-2861 (6)   2.20   1.25

Olympic Stadium, Melbourne, 1956, Moscow '80 Emblem — A844

Moscow '80 Emblem and Olympic Stadiums: 1 l, Rome, 1960. 1.50 l, Tokyo, 1964. 2.15 l, Mexico City, 1968. 3.40 l, Munich, 1972. 4.80 l, Montreal, 1976. 10 l, Moscow, 1980.

**1979, Oct. 23**    Photo.    *Perf. 13½*
2862 A844 55b multi   .20   .20
2863 A844 1 l multi   .20   .20
2864 A844 1.50 l multi   .20   .20
2865 A844 2.15 l multi   .30   .20
2866 A844 3.40 l multi   .50   .20
2867 A844 4.80 l multi   1.00   .25
Nos. 2862-2867 (6)   2.40   1.25

**Souvenir Sheet**
2868 A844 10 l multi   2.50   2.00
22nd Summer Olympic Games, Moscow, July 19-Aug. 3, 1980. No. 2868 contains one 50x38mm stamp. No. 2868 airmail.

Arms of Alba Iulia — A845

Designs: Arms of Romanian cities.

**1979, Oct. 25**
2869 A845 shown   .30   .20
2870 A845 1.20 l Arad   .30   .20
2871 A845 1.20 l Bacau   .30   .20
2872 A845 1.20 l Baia-Mare   .30   .20
2873 A845 1.20 l Birlad   .30   .20
2874 A845 1.20 l Botosani   .30   .20
2875 A845 1.20 l Braila   .30   .20
2876 A845 1.20 l Brasov   .30   .20
2877 A845 1.20 l Buzau   .30   .20
2878 A845 1.20 l Calarasi   .30   .20
2879 A845 1.20 l Cluj   .30   .20
2880 A845 1.20 l Constanta   .30   .20
2881 A845 1.20 l Craiova   .30   .20
2882 A845 1.20 l Dej   .30   .20
2883 A845 1.20 l Deva   .30   .20
2884 A845 1.20 l Turnu-Severin   .30   .20
2885 A845 1.20 l Focsani   .30   .20
2886 A845 1.20 l Galati   .30   .20
2887 A845 1.20 l Gheorghe Gheorghiu-Dej   .30   .20
2888 A845 1.20 l Giurgiu   .30   .20
2889 A845 1.20 l Hunedoara   .30   .20
2890 A845 1.20 l Iasi   .30   .20
2891 A845 1.20 l Lugoj   .30   .20
2892 A845 1.20 l Medias   .30   .20
2893 A845 1.20 l Odorheiu Seguiesc   .30   .20

**1980, Jan. 5**
2894 A845 1.20 l Oradea   .30   .20
2895 A845 1.20 l Petrosani   .30   .20
2896 A845 1.20 l Piatra-Neamt   .30   .20
2897 A845 1.20 l Pitesti   .30   .20
2898 A845 1.20 l Ploiesti   .30   .20
2899 A845 1.20 l Resita   .30   .20
2900 A845 1.20 l Rimnicu-Vilcea   .30   .20
2901 A845 1.20 l Roman   .30   .20
2902 A845 1.20 l Satu-Mare   .30   .20
2903 A845 1.20 l Sibiu   .30   .20
2904 A845 1.20 l Sighet-Marmatei   .30   .20
2905 A845 1.20 l Sighisoara   .30   .20
2906 A845 1.20 l Suceava   .30   .20
2907 A845 1.20 l Tecuci   .30   .20
2908 A845 1.20 l Timisoara   .30   .20
2909 A845 1.20 l Tirgoviste   .30   .20
2910 A845 1.20 l Tirgu-Jiu   .30   .20
2911 A845 1.20 l Tirgu-Mures   .30   .20
2912 A845 1.20 l Tulcea   .30   .20
2913 A845 1.20 l Turda   .30   .20
2914 A845 1.20 l Turnu Magurele   .30   .20
2915 A845 1.20 l Bucharest   .30
Nos. 2869-2915 (47)   14.10   9.40

A846

A847

Regional Costumes: 20b, Maramures Woman. 40b, Maramures man. 55b, Vrancea woman. 1.50 l, Vrancea man. 3 l, Padureni woman. 3.40 l, Padureni man.

**1979, Oct. 27**
2916 A846 20b multi   .20   .20
2917 A846 40b multi   .20   .20
2918 A846 55b multi   .20   .20
2919 A846 1.50 l multi   .25   .20
2920 A846 3 l multi   .45   .20
2921 A846 3.40 l multi   .55   .20
Nos. 2916-2921 (6)   1.85   1.20

**1979, July 27**
Flower Paintings by Stefan Luchian: 40b, Snapdragons. 60b, Triple chrysanthemums. 1.55 l, Potted flowers on stairs.
2922 A847 40b multi   .20   .20
2923 A847 60b multi   .20   .20
2924 A847 1.55 l multi   1.40   1.35
Nos. 2922-2924,B445 (4)   1.40   1.35

Socflex, International Philatelic Exhibition, Bucharest. See No. B446.

**Souvenir Sheet**

Romanian Communist Party, 12th Congress — A848

**1979, Oct.**
2925 A848 5 l multi   1.25   .50

Figure Skating, Lake Placid '80 Emblem, Olympic Rings — A849

**1979, Dec. 27**    Photo.    *Perf. 13½*
2926 A849 55b shown   .20   .20
2927 A849 1 l Downhill skiing   .20   .20
2928 A849 1.50 l Biathlon   .20   .20
2929 A849 2.15 l Two-man bobsledding   .25   .20
2930 A849 3.40 l Speed skating   .50   .20
2931 A849 4.80 l Ice hockey   1.00   1.20
Nos. 2926-2931 (6)   2.35

**Souvenir Sheet**
2932 A849 10 l Ice hockey, diff.   2.25   1.75
13th Winter Olympic Games, Lake Placid, NY, Feb. 12-24, 1980. No. 2932 contains one 38x50mm stamp. An imperf. 10 l air post souvenir sheet exists showing four-man bobsledding. Value, unused or used, $20.

"Calugareni", Expo Emblem — A850

**1979, Dec. 29**
2933 A850 55b shown   .20   .20
2934 A850 1 l "Orleans"   .20   .20
2935 A850 1.50 l #1059, type fawn   .20   .20
2936 A850 2.15 l #15021, type   .30   .20
2937 A850 3.40 l "Pacific"   .50   .20

Imperf 10 l souvenir sheets exist for the European Sports Conference and 1980 Olympics. Value for former, unused or used, $15. Value for latter, unused or used, $20.

ROMANIA

2938 A850 4.80 l Electric engine 1.00 .25
Nos. 2933-2938 (6) 2.40 1.25
060-EA

**Souvenir Sheet**

2939 A850 10 l Diesel electric 2.50 2.00

Intl. Transport Expo., Hamburg, June 8-July 1. #2939 contains one 50x40mm stamp.

Dacian Warrior,
Trajan's Column,
Rome — A851

Design: 1.50 l, Two warriors.

**1980, Feb. 9** Photo. *Perf. 13½*
2940 A851 55b multi .20 .20
2941 A851 1.50 l multi .30 .20

2,050 years since establishment of first centralized and independent Dacian state.

Vallota Purpurea
A854

Tudor
Vladimirescu
A855

George
Enescu
Playing
Violin
A853

Souvenir Sheets

Kingfisher — A852

**1980, Mar. 25** Photo. *Perf. 13½*
2942 A852 55b shown .20 .20
2943 A852 1 l Great white .20 .20
heron, vert.
2944 A852 1.50 l Red-breasted
goose .20 .20
2945 A852 2.15 l Red deer, vert. .25 .20
2946 A852 3.40 l Roe deer .25 .20
2947 A852 4.80 l European bison, vert. .45 .20
Nos. 2942-2947 (6)

European Nature Protection Year. A 10 l imperf. souvenir sheet exists showing bears; red control number. Value, unused or used. $30.

See No. C232.

**1980, May 6**
2948 Sheet of 4 1.50 1.50
a. A853 1.30 l shown .25 .20
b. A853 1.30 l Conducting .25 .20
c. A853 1.30 l Playing piano .25 .20
d. A853 1.30 l Composing .25 .20
2949 Sheet of 4 3.25 3.25
a. A853 3.40 l Beethoven in library .70 .25
b. A853 3.40 l Portrait .70 .25
c. A853 3.40 l At piano .70 .25
d. A853 3.40 l Composing .70 .25

Inter-European Cultural and Economic Cooperation.

---

A857

A856

**1980, Apr. 10** Photo. *Perf. 13½*
2950 A854 55b shown .20 .20
2951 A854 1 l Eichhornia
crasipes .20 .20
2952 A854 1.50 l Sprekelia
formosissima .20 .20
2953 A854 2.15 l Hypericum
calycinum .30 .20
2954 A854 3.40 l Camellia japonica .30 .20
2955 A854 4.80 l Nelumbo
nucifera .50 .20
Nos. 2950-2955 (6) 1.00 .25
2.40 .20

**1980, Apr. 24** Photo. *Perf. 13½*
2956 A855 40b multi .20 .20
2957 A855 55b multi .20 .20
2958 A855 1.50 l multi .20 .20
2959 A855 2.15 l multi .30 .20
2960 A855 3 l multi .40 .20
Nos. 2956-2960 (5) 1.30 1.00

Anniversaries: 40b, Tudor Vladimirescu (1780-1821), leader of 1821 revolution; 55b, Mihail Sadoveanu, 1.50 l, Battle against Hungarians, 2.15 l, Tudor Arghezi; 3 l, Horea.

Mihail Sadoveanu (1880-1961), author; 1.50 l, Victory of Posada; 2.15 l, Tudor Arghezi (1880-1967), poet; 3 l, Tudor, Horea (1730-1785), leader of 1784 uprising.

Dacian fruit bowl and cup.

**1980, May 8**
2961 A856 1 l multicolored .20 .20

Petrodava City, 2000th anniversary.

**1980, June 20** Photo. *Perf. 13½*
2962 A857 55b Javelin .20 .20
2963 A857 1 l Fencing .20 .20
2964 A857 1.50 l Shooting .20 .20
2965 A857 2.15 l Kayak .30 .20
2966 A857 3 l Wrestling .50 .20
2967 A857 3.40 l Rowing 1.00 .20
Nos. 2962-2967 (6) 2.40 1.25

**Souvenir Sheet**

2968 A857 10 l Handball 2.25 1.75

22nd Summer Olympic Games, Moscow, July 19-Aug. 3. No. 2968 contains one 38x50mm stamp. An imperf. 10 l air post souvenir sheet exists showing gymnast. Value, unused or used, $15.

---

Congress
Emblem — A858

Chinese and
Romanian
Young Pioneers
at Stamp
Show — A860

Fireman
Rescuing
Child — A859

**1980, Aug. 10** Photo. *Perf. 13½*
2969 A858 55b multicolored .20 .20

15th Intl. Historical Sciences Congress, Bucharest.

**1980, Aug. 25**
2970 A859 55b multicolored .20 .20

Firemen's Day, Sept. 13.

**Souvenir Sheet**

**1980, Sept. 18**
2971 A860 1 l multicolored .20 .20

Romanian-Chinese Phil. Exhib., Bucharest.

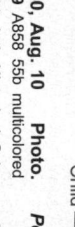

Parliament Building,
Bucharest — A861

**1980, Sept. 30**
2972 A861 10 l multicolored 2.00 1.65

European Security Conference, Madrid. An imperf. 10 l air post souvenir sheet exists showing Plaza Mayor, Madrid. Value, unused or used, $15.

Knights and Chessboard — A862

**1980, Oct. 1** Photo. *Perf. 13½*
2973 A862 55b shown .20 .20
2974 A862 1 l Rooks .20 .20
2975 A862 2.15 l Man .30 .20
2976 A862 4.80 l Woman 1.00 .20
Nos. 2973-2976 (4) 1.70 .85

Chess Olympiad, Valletta, Malta, Nov. 20-Dec. 8.

---

Dacian
Warrior — A863

**1980, Oct. 15** Photo. *Perf. 13½*
2977 A863 20b shown .20 .20
2978 A863 40b Moldavian soldier, 15th
cent. .20 .20
2979 A863 55b Walachian
horseman,
17th cent. .20 .20
2980 A863 1 l Flag bearer,
19th cent. .20 .20
2981 A863 1.50 l Infantryman,
19th cent. .20 .20
2982 A863 2.15 l Lancer, 19th
cent. .30 .20
2983 A863 4.80 l Mounted Elite
Corps Guard,
19th cent. 1.00 .35
Nos. 2977-2983 (7) 2.30 1.55

Burebista
Sculpture — A864

**1980, Nov. 5** Photo. *Perf. 13½*
2984 A864 2 l multicolored .35 .20

2050 years since establishment of first centralized and independent Dacian state.

George
Opresçu
(1881-1969),
Art
Critic — A865

National Dog
Show — A866

**1981, Feb. 20** Photo. *Perf. 13½*
2985 A865 1.50 l multi .20 .20
2986 A865 2.15 l multi .30 .20
2987 A865 3.40 l multi .50 .25
Nos. 2985-2987 (3) 1.00 .65

Famous Men: 2.15 l, Marius Bunescu (1881-1971), painter; 3.40 l, Ion Georgescu (1856-1898), sculptor.

**1981, Mar. 15**
Designs: Dogs. 40b, 1 l, 1.50 l, 3.40 l horiz.
2988 A866 40b Mountain
sheepdog .20 .20
2989 A866 55b Saint Bernard .20 .20
2990 A866 1 l Fox terrier .30 .20
2991 A866 1.50 l German shepherd .30 .20
2992 A866 2.15 l Boxer .30 .20
2993 A866 3.40 l Dalmatian .50 .20
2994 A866 4.80 l Poodle 1.00 .20
Nos. 2988-2994 (7) 2.60 1.40

River Steamer Stefan cel
Mare — A867

**1981, Mar. 25**
2995 A867 55b shown .20 .20
2996 A867 1 l Tudor
Vladimirescu .20 .20
2997 A867 1.50 l Vas de
Supraveghere .20 .20
2998 A867 2.15 l Dredger Sulina .30 .20

**Bucharest Central Military Hospital Sesquicentennial — A876**

**1981, Aug. 15   Photo.   Perf. 13½**
3025 A875 55b multicolored ... .20 .20

**1981, Sept. 1**
3026 A876 55b multicolored ... .20 .20

**1981, Sept. 20**
Designs: 40b, George Enescu (1881-1955). 55b, Paul Constantinescu (1909-1963). 1 l, Dinu Lipatti (1917-1950). 1.50 l, Ionel Perlea (1900-1970). 2.15 l, Ciprian Porumbescu (1853-1883). 3.40 l, Mihail Jora (1891-1971).
3027 A877 40b multi ... .20 .20
3028 A877 55b multi ... .20 .20
3029 A877 1 l multi ... .20 .20
3030 A877 1.50 l multi ... .25 .20
3031 A877 2.15 l multi ... .35 .25
3032 A877 3.40 l multi ... .50 .25
Nos. 3027-3032 (6) ... 1.70 1.25

**Stamp Day A879**

**1981, Nov. 5   Photo.   Perf. 13½**
3034 A879 2 l multicolored ... .35 .20

**Children's Games — A880**
Illustrations by Eugen Palade (40b, 55b, 1 l) and Norman Rockwell.
**1981, Nov. 25**
3035 A880 40b Hopscotch ... .20 .20
3036 A880 55b Soccer ... .20 .20
3037 A880 1 l Riding stick horse ... .20 .20
3038 A880 1.50 l Snagging the Big One ... .25 .20
3039 A880 2.15 l A Patient Friend ... .30 .20
3040 A880 3 l Doggone It ... .40 .20
3041 A880 4 l Puppy Love ... .45 .35
Nos. 3035-3041,C243 (8) ... 2.50 2.05

A882

**1981, Dec. 28**
3042 A881 55b multi ... .20 .20
3043 A881 1 l multi ... .20 .20
3044 A881 1.50 l multi ... .35 .25
3045 A881 2.15 l multi ... .50 .35
3046 A881 3.40 l multi ... 1.00 .35
3047 A881 4.80 l multi ... 2.50 1.40
**Souvenir Sheet**
3048 A881 10 l multi ... 2.00 2.00
Espana 82 World Cup Soccer. No. 3048 contains one 38x50mm stamp. An imperf. 10 l air post souvenir sheet exists showing game. Value, unused or used, $15.

**1982, Jan. 30   Photo.   Perf. 13½**
Designs: 1 l, Prince Alexander the Good of Moldavia (ruled 1400-1432), 1.50 l, Bogdan Petriceicu Hasdeu (1838-1907), scholar. 2.15 l, Nicolae Titulescu (1882-1941), diplomat.
3049 A882 1 l multi ... .20 .20
3050 A882 1.50 l multi ... .20 .20
3051 A882 2.15 l multi ... .40 .20
Nos. 3049-3051 (3) ... .85 .60

**Bucharest Subway System A883**

**1982, Feb. 25**
3052 A883 60b Union Square station entrance ... .20 .20
3053 A883 2.40 l Heroes' Station platform ... .40 .25

**60th Anniv. of Communist Youth Union — A884**
**1982**
3054 A884 1 l shown ... .20 .20
3055 A884 1.20 l Construction worker ... .20 .20
3056 A884 1.50 l Farm workers ... .25 .20
3057 A884 2 l Research ... .35 .20
3058 A884 2.50 l Workers ... .50 .25
3059 A884 4.80 l Musicians, dancers ... .60 .25
Nos. 3054-3059 (6) ... 2.10 1.30

**Dog Sled A885**
**1982, Mar. 28   Photo.   Perf. 13½**
3060 A885 55b Dog rescuing child ... .20 .20
3061 A885 1 l Shepherd, dog ... .20 .35
3062 A885 3 l Hunting dog ... .55 .35
3063 A885 3.40 l shown ... .60 .40
3064 A885 4 l Spitz, woman ... .70 .40
3065 A885 4.80 l Guide dog, woman ... .80 .45
3066 A885 5 l Dalmatian, girl ... .95 .50
3067 A885 6 l Saint Bernard ... 1.00 .40
Nos. 3060-3067 (8) ... 5.00 2.85
1 l, 3 l, 4 l, 4.80 l, 5 l, vertical.

**University '81 Games, Bucharest — A872**

**Theodor Aman, Artist, Birth Sesquicentennial — A873**

**1981, July 17**
3015 A872 1 l Book, flag ... .20 .20
3016 A872 2.15 l Emblem ... .35 .20
3017 A872 4.80 l Stadium, horiz. ... 1.00 .35
Nos. 3015-3017 (3) ... 1.55 .75

**1981, July 28**
Aman Paintings: 40b, Self-portrait. 55b, Battle of Giurgiu. 1 l, The Family Picnic. 1.50 l, The Painter's Studio. 2.15 l, Woman in Interior. 3.40 l, Aman Museum, Bucharest. 55b, 1 l, 1.50 l, 3.40 l horiz.
3018 A873 40b multi ... .20 .20
3019 A873 55b multi ... .20 .20
3020 A873 1 l multi ... .20 .20
3021 A873 1.50 l multi ... .25 .20
3022 A873 2.15 l multi ... .35 .25
3023 A873 3.40 l multi ... .60 .25
Nos. 3018-3023 (6) ... 1.80 1.25

**Thinker of Cernavoda, 3rd Cent. BC — A874**
**1981, July 30**
3024 A874 3.40 l multi ... .50 .25
16th Science History Congress.

**Romanian Musicians A877**

**Blood Donation Campaign A875**

---

2999 A867 3.40 l Republica Populara Romana ... .50 .25
3000 A867 4.80 l Sulina Canal ... 1.00 .35
Nos. 2995-3000 (6) ... 2.45 1.40
**Souvenir Sheet**
3001 A867 10 l Galati ... 2.50 2.00
European Danube Commission, 125th anniv. An imperf. 10 l souvenir sheet exists showing map of Danube. Value, unused or used, $15.

**Carrier Pigeon A868**
Various carrier pigeons and doves.
**1981, Apr. 15   Photo.   Perf. 13½**
3002 A868 40b multi ... .20 .20
3003 A868 55b multi ... .20 .20
3004 A868 1 l multi ... .20 .20
3005 A868 1.50 l multi ... .30 .20
3006 A868 2.15 l multi ... .50 .25
3007 A868 3.40 l multi ... 1.60 1.25
Nos. 3002-3007 (6)

**Romanian Communist Party, 60th Anniv. — A869**
**1981, Apr. 15**
3008 A869 1 l multicolored ... .20 .20

**Singing Romania Festival — A871**

**Folkdance, Moldavia — A870**

**1981, Apr. 22   Photo.   Perf. 13½**

**1981, May 4   Photo.   Perf. 13½**
Designs: Regional folkdances.
3009 Sheet of 4 ... 2.50 2.50
a. A870 2.50 l shown ... .45 .45
b. A870 2.50 l Transylvania ... .45 .45
c. A870 2.50 l Banat ... .45 .45
d. A870 2.50 l Muntenia ... .45 .45
3010 Sheet of 4 ... 2.50 2.50
a. A870 2.50 l Maramures ... .45 .45
b. A870 2.50 l Dobruja ... .45 .45
c. A870 2.50 l Oltenia ... .45 .45
d. A870 2.50 l Crisana ... .45 .45

Inter-European Cultural and Economic Cooperation.
**1981, July 15**
3011 A871 55b Industry ... .20 .20
3012 A871 1.50 l Electronics ... .25 .20
3013 A871 2.15 l Agriculture ... .35 .30
3014 A871 3.40 l Culture ... .50 .30
Nos. 3011-3014 (4) ... 1.30 .90

ROMANIA

## Bran Castle, Brasov, 1377 — A886

Inter-European Cultural and Economic Cooperation.

### Souvenir Sheet

**1982, May 6**
| | | | |
|---|---|---|---|
| 3068 | A886 | 2,50 shown | 2.50 .55 |
| 3069 | | Sheet of 4 | 2.50 |
| a. | A886 | 2,50 l Sinaia, 1873 | .55 |
| b. | A886 | 2,50 l Hunedoara, Corvinilor, 1409 | .55 |
| c. | A886 | 2,50 l Iasi, 1905 | .55 |
| | | Sheet of 4 | 2.50 |
| a. | A886 | 2,50 l Neuschwanstein | .55 |
| b. | A886 | 2,50 l Stolzenfels | .55 |
| c. | A886 | 2,50 l Katz-Loreley | .55 |
| d. | A886 | 2,50 l Lindenhof | .55 |

### Souvenir Sheet

EXPOZITIA INTERNATIONALA FILATELICA PHILEXFRANCE '82

## Constantin Brancusi in Paris Studio — A887

**1982, June 5**
| | | | |
|---|---|---|---|
| 3070 | A887 | 10 l multicolored | 2.00 1.60 |

PHILEXFRANCE '82 Intl. Stamp Exhibition, Paris, June 11-21.

## Gloria C-16 Combine Harvester — A888

**1982, June 29**
| | | | |
|---|---|---|---|
| 3071 | A888 | 50b shown | .20 .20 |
| 3072 | A888 | 1 l Dairy farm | .20 .20 |
| 3073 | A888 | 1,50 l Apple orchard | .25 .20 |
| 3074 | A888 | 2,50 l Vineyard | .40 .20 |
| 3075 | A888 | 3 l Irrigation | .50 .25 |

### Souvenir Sheet
| | | | |
|---|---|---|---|
| 3076 | A888 | 10 l Village | 2.00 1.60 |

Agricultural modernization. No. 3076 contains one 50x38mm stamp.
Nos. 3071-3075,C250 (6)   2.05 1.25

## A891

GENEZA POPORULUI ROMAN — A890

**1982, Aug. 30   Photo.   Perf. 13½**
| | | | |
|---|---|---|---|
| 3078 | A890 | 50b Baile Felix | .20 .20 |
| 3079 | A890 | 1 l Predeal | .20 .20 |
| 3080 | A890 | 1,50 l Baile Herculane | .25 .20 |
| 3081 | A890 | 2,50 l Eforie Nord | .40 .20 |
| 3082 | A890 | 3 l Olimp | .50 .20 |
| 3083 | A890 | 5 l Neptun | .95 .30 |
| | | Nos. 3078-3083 (6) | 2.60 1.30 |

Resort Hotels and Beaches. 1 l, 2.50 l, 3 l, 5 l horiz.

**1982, Sept. 6**

### Souvenir Sheet
| | | | |
|---|---|---|---|
| 3084 | A891 | 1 l multicolored | .20 .20 |
| 3085 | A891 | 1,50 l multicolored | .25 .20 |
| 3086 | A891 | 3,50 l multicolored | .60 .25 |
| 3087 | A891 | 4 l multicolored | .75 .35 |
| | | Nos. 3084-3087 (4) | 1.80 1.00 |

Designs: 1 l, Legend, horiz. 1,50 l, Contrasts, horiz. 3,50 l, Relay Runner, horiz. 4 l, Genesis of Romanian People, by Sabin Balasa.

### Souvenir Sheet

## Merry Peasant Girl, by Nicolae Grigorescu (d. 1907) — A892

**1982, Sept. 30   Photo.   Perf. 13½**
| | | | |
|---|---|---|---|
| 3088 | A892 | 10 l multicolored | 1.75 1.75 |

## Bucharest Intl. Fair — A893

**1982, Oct. 2**
| | | | |
|---|---|---|---|
| 3089 | A893 | 2 l Exhibition Hall, flag | .35 .20 |

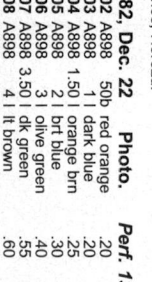

## Savings Week, Oct. 31 — A894

**1982, Oct. 25**
| | | | |
|---|---|---|---|
| 3090 | A894 | 1 l Girl holding bank book | .20 .20 |

## Stamp Day — A895

**1982, Oct. 25**
| | | | |
|---|---|---|---|
| 3091 | A894 | 2 l Poster | .35 .20 |

**1982, Nov. 10**
| | | | |
|---|---|---|---|
| 3092 | A895b | 1 l Woman letter carrier | .20 .20 |
| 3093 | A895 | 2 l Mailman | .35 .20 |

## Scene from Ileana Sinziana, by Petre Ispirescu A896

## Arms, Colors, Book — A897

**1982, Nov. 30**
| | | | |
|---|---|---|---|
| 3094 | A896 | 50b multicolored | .20 .20 |
| 3095 | A896 | 1 l multicolored | .20 .20 |
| 3096 | A896 | 1,50 l multicolored | .25 .20 |
| 3097 | A896 | 2,50 l multicolored | .40 .20 |
| 3098 | A896 | 3 l multicolored | .50 .20 |
| 3099 | A896 | 5 l multicolored | .95 .30 |
| | | Nos. 3094-3099 (6) | 2.50 1.30 |

Fairytales: 50b, The Youngest Child and the Golden Apples, by Petre Ispirescu. 1 l, The Bear Hoaxed by the Fox, by Ion Creanga. 1,50 l, The Prince of Tear, by Mihai Eminescu. 2,50 l, The Little Bag with Two Coins Inside, by Ion Creanga. 5 l, Danila Prepeleac, by Ion Creanga.

**1982, Dec. 16**
| | | | |
|---|---|---|---|
| 3100 | A897 | 1 l Closed book | .20 .20 |
| 3101 | A897 | 2 l Open book | .35 .20 |

Natl. Communist Party Conference, Bucharest, Dec. 16-18.

## A898

**1982, Dec. 22   Photo.   Perf. 13½**

Size: 23x29mm, 29x23mm
| | | | |
|---|---|---|---|
| 3102 | A898 | 50b red orange | .90 .20 |
| 3103 | A898 | 1 l dark blue | .20 .20 |
| 3104 | A898 | 1,50 l orange brn | .25 .20 |
| 3105 | A898 | 2 l brt blue | .30 .20 |
| 3106 | A898 | 3 l olive green | .40 .20 |
| 3107 | A898 | 3,50 l olive green | .55 .20 |
| 3108 | A898 | 4 l lt brown | .60 .20 |
| 3109 | A898 | 5 l gray blue | .75 .20 |
| 3110 | A898 | 6 l blue | .90 .20 |
| 3111 | A898 | 7 l lake | 1.10 .20 |
| 3112 | A898 | 7,50 l red violet | 1.25 .20 |
| 3113 | A898 | 8 l red | 1.50 .20 |
| 3114 | A898 | 10 l brt green | 1.50 .20 |
| 3115 | A898 | 20 l purple | 3.25 .25 |
| 3116 | A898 | 30 l Prus blue | 4.50 .25 |
| 3117 | A898 | 50 l dark brown | 8.00 .65 |
| | | Nos. 3102-3117 (16) | 25.00 3.85 |

50b, Wooden flask, Suceava. 1 l, Ceramic plate, Radauti. 1,50 l, Wooden scoop, Valea Mare, horiz. 2 l, Plate, jug, Vama. 3 l, Butter churn, wooden bucket, Moldavia. 3,50 l, Ceramic plates, Lehceni, horiz. 4 l, Wooden spoon, platter, Cluj. 5 l, Bowl, pitcher, Marginea. 6 l, Jug, flask, Bihor. 7 l, Spindle, shuttle, Transylvania. 7,50 l, Water buckets, Suceava. 8 l, Jug, Oboga; plate, Horezu. 10 l, Water buckets, Hunedoara, Suceava, horiz. 20 l, Wooden flask, beakers, Horezu. 30 l, Wooden spoons, Alba, horiz. 50 l, Ceramic dishes, Horezu.

## 35th Anniv. of Republic — A899

**1982, Dec. 27**
| | | | |
|---|---|---|---|
| 3118 | A899 | 1 l Symbols of development | .20 .20 |
| 3119 | A899 | 2 l Flag | .35 .20 |

## Grigore Manolescu (1857-92) as Hamlet — A900

**1983, Feb. 28**
| | | | |
|---|---|---|---|
| 3120 | A900 | 50b multi | .20 .20 |
| 3121 | A900 | 1 l multi | .20 .20 |
| 3122 | A900 | 1,50 l multi | .25 .20 |
| 3123 | A900 | 2 l multi | .35 .20 |
| 3124 | A900 | 2,50 l multi | .40 .20 |
| 3125 | A900 | 3 l multi | .50 .25 |
| 3126 | A900 | 4 l multi | .70 .30 |
| 3127 | A900 | 5 l multi | .85 .30 |
| | | Nos. 3120-3127 (8) | 3.45 1.75 |

Actors or Actresses in Famous Roles: 50b, Matei Millo (1814-1896) in The Discontented. 1 l, Mihail Pascaly (1829-1882) in Director. 1,50 l, Aristizza Romanescu (1854-1918) in The Dogs. 2 l, C. I. Nottara (1859-1935) in Snowstorm. 3 l, Agatha Birsescu (1857-1939) in Medea. 4 l, Ion Brezeanu (1869-1940) in The Lost Letter. 5 l, Aristide Demetriad (1872-1930) in The Despotic Prince.

## Hugo Grotius (1583-1645), Dutch Jurist — A901

**1983, Apr. 30**
| | | | |
|---|---|---|---|
| 3128 | A901 | 2 l brown | .35 .20 |

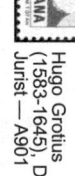

## Romanian-Made Vehicles — A902

**1983, May 3**
| | | | |
|---|---|---|---|
| 3129 | A902 | 50b ARO-10 | .20 .20 |
| 3130 | A902 | 1 l Dacia, 1300 station wagon | .20 .20 |
| 3131 | A902 | 1,50 l ARO-242 Jeep | .25 .20 |
| 3132 | A902 | 2,50 l ARO-244 | .40 .25 |
| 3133 | A902 | 4 l Dacia 1310 | .70 .35 |
| 3134 | A902 | 5 l OLTCIT club passenger car | .85 .40 |
| | | Nos. 3129-3134 (6) | 2.60 1.55 |

## Johannes Kepler (1571-1630) — A903

Famous Men: No. 3135: b, Alexander von Humboldt (1769-1859), explorer. c, Goethe (1749-1832). d, Richard Wagner (1813-1883), composer.

No. 3136: a, Ioan Andreescu (1850-1882), painter. b, George Constantinescu (1881-1965), engineer. c, Tudor Arghezi (1880-1967), poet. d, C.I. Parhon (1874-1969), endocrinologist.

**1983, May 16**
| | | | |
|---|---|---|---|
| 3135 | A903 | 3 l multicolored | 2.50 | 2.50 |
| *a.-d.* | A903 | 3 l multicolored | .55 | .55 |
| 3136 | Sheet of 4 | | 2.50 | 2.50 |
| *a.-d.* | A903 | 3 l multicolored | .55 | .55 |

Inter-European Cultural and Economic Cooperation.

---

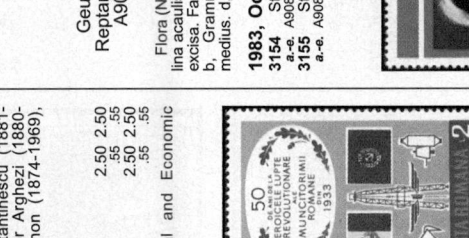

Souvenir Sheet

Orient Express Centenary (Paris-Istanbul) — A912

**1983, Dec. 30**
3165 A912 10 l Leaving Gara de Nord, Bucharest, 1883 2.50 2.50

1984 Winter Olympics A913

**1984, Jan. 14**
3166 A913 50b Cross-country skiing .20 .20

| | | | |
|---|---|---|---|
| 3167 | A913 | 1 l Biathlon | .20 | .20 |
| 3168 | A913 | 1.50 l Figure skating | .20 | .20 |
| 3169 | A913 | 3 l Speed skating | .30 | .20 |
| 3170 | A913 | 3 l Hockey | .50 | .40 |
| 3171 | A913 | 3.50 l Bobsledding | .60 | .25 |
| 3172 | A913 | 4 l Luge | .75 | .30 |
| 3173 | A913 | 5 l Skiing | 3.15 | 1.75 |
| | | *Nos. 3166-3173 (8)* | | |

A 10 l imperf souvenir sheet exists showing ski jumping. Value, unused or used, $15.

---

Geum Reptans A908

Flora (No. 3154): b, Papaver dubium. c, Carlina acaulis. d, Paeonia peregrina. e, Gentiana excisa. Fauna (No. 3155): a, Sciurus vulgaris. b, Grammia quenselii. c, Dendrocopos medius. d, Lynx. e, Tichodroma muraria.

**1983, Oct. 28  Photo.  Perf. 13½**
| | | | |
|---|---|---|---|
| 3154 | Strip of 5 | | 1.40 | 1.40 |
| *a.-e.* | A908 | 1 l multicolored | .25 | .25 |
| 3155 | Strip of 5 | | 1.40 | 1.40 |
| *a.-e.* | A908 | 1 l multicolored | .25 | .25 |

Issued in sheets of 15.

Lady with Feather, by Cornelius Baba — A909

**1983, Nov. 3**
| | | | |
|---|---|---|---|
| 3156 | A909 | 1 l shown | .20 | .20 |
| 3157 | A909 | 2 l Citizens | .35 | .20 |
| 3158 | A909 | 3 l Farmers, horiz. | .50 | .25 |
| 3159 | A909 | 4 l Resting in the Field, horiz. | .70 | .25 |
| | | *Nos. 3156-3159 (4)* | 1.75 | .85 |

---

Workers' Struggle, 50th Anniv. — A904

**1983, July 22  Photo.  Perf. 13½**
3137 A904 2 l silver & multi .35 .20

Birds — A905

**1983, Oct. 28  Photo.  Perf. 13½**
| | | | |
|---|---|---|---|
| 3138 | A905 | 50b Luscinia svecica | .20 | .20 |
| 3139 | A905 | 1 l Sturnus roseus | .20 | .20 |
| 3140 | A905 | 1.50 l Coracias garrulus | .20 | .20 |
| 3141 | A905 | 2.50 l Merops apiaster | .35 | .20 |
| 3142 | A905 | 4 l Emberiza schoeniclus | .65 | .35 |
| 3143 | A905 | 5 l Lanius minor | .75 | .40 |
| | | *Nos. 3138-3143 (6)* | 2.35 | 1.55 |

Luscinia svecica

Water Sports A906

**1983, Sept. 16  Photo.  Perf. 13½**
| | | | |
|---|---|---|---|
| 3144 | A906 | 50b Kayak | .20 | .20 |
| 3145 | A906 | 1 l Water polo | .20 | .20 |
| 3146 | A906 | 1.50 l Canadian one-man canoes | .20 | .20 |
| 3147 | A906 | 2.50 l Diving | .35 | .20 |
| 3148 | A906 | 4 l Singles rowing | .60 | .20 |
| 3149 | A906 | 5 l Swimming | .70 | .25 |
| | | *Nos. 3144-3149 (6)* | 2.25 | 1.25 |

A910

A911

**1983, Nov. 30**
| | | | |
|---|---|---|---|
| 3160 | A910 | 1 l Banner, emblem | .20 | .20 |
| 3161 | A910 | 2 l Congress building, flags | .30 | .20 |

Pact with Romania, 65th anniv.

**1983, Dec. 17**
| | | | |
|---|---|---|---|
| 3162 | A911 | 1 l multicolored | .20 | .20 |
| 3163 | A911 | 2 l multicolored | .30 | .20 |
| | | **Souvenir Sheet** | | |
| 3164 | A911 | 10 l multicolored | 1.60 | 1.60 |

BALKANFILA '83 Stamp Exhibition, Bucharest. #3164 contains one 38x50mm stamp.

Stamp Day A907

**1983, Oct. 24**
| | | | |
|---|---|---|---|
| 3150 | A907 | 1 l Mailman on bicycle | .20 | .20 |
| 3151 | A907 | 3.50 l with 3 l label, flag | 1.10 | .55 |
| | | **Souvenir Sheet** | | |
| 3152 | A907 | 10 l Unloading mail plane | 1.75 | 1.75 |

#3152 is airmail, contains one 38x51mm stamp.

---

15th Balkan Chess Match, Herculane A917

**1984, Feb. 8  multi**
| | | | |
|---|---|---|---|
| 3175 | A915 | 50b multi | .20 | .20 |
| 3176 | A916 | 1 l multi | .20 | .20 |
| 3177 | A916 | 1.50 l multi | .20 | .20 |
| 3178 | A916 | 2 l multi | .30 | .20 |
| 3179 | A916 | 3.50 l multi | .40 | .20 |
| 3180 | A916 | 4 l multi | .45 | .20 |
| | | *Nos. 3175-3180 (6)* | 1.65 | 1.20 |

See Nos. 3210-3213.

**Souvenir Sheet**

4 successive moves culminating in checkmate.

**1984, Feb. 20  Photo.  Perf. 13½**
| | | | |
|---|---|---|---|
| 3181 | Sheet of 4 | | 2.25 | 2.25 |
| *a.-d.* | A917 | 3 l, any single | .55 | .55 |

---

Orsova Bridge A918

Bridges: No. 3182b, Arges. c, Basarabi. d, Ohaba. No. 3183: a, Kohlbrand-Germany. b, Bosfor-Turcia. c, Europa-Austria. d, Turnului-Anglia.

**1984, Apr. 24**
| | | | |
|---|---|---|---|
| 3182 | Sheet of 4 | | 2.50 | 2.50 |
| *a.-d.* | A918 | 3 l multi | .55 | .65 |
| 3183 | Sheet of 4 | | 2.50 | 2.50 |
| *a.-d.* | A918 | 3 l multi | .55 | .55 |

Inter-European Cultural and Economic Cooperation.

Prince Alexandru Ioan Cuza, Arms — A914

**1984, Jan. 24  Photo.  Perf. 13½**
3174 A914 10 l multi 1.75 1.75

Union of Moldavia and Walachia Provinces, 125th anniv.

---

Summer Olympics — A919

**1984, May 25  Photo.  Perf. 13½**
| | | | |
|---|---|---|---|
| 3184 | A919 | 50b High jump | .20 | .20 |
| 3185 | A919 | 1 l Swimming | .20 | .20 |
| 3186 | A919 | 1.50 l Running | .25 | .20 |
| 3187 | A919 | 3 l Handball | .50 | .30 |
| 3188 | A919 | 4 l Rowing | .70 | .40 |
| 3189 | A919 | 5 l 2-man canoe | .85 | .50 |
| | | *Nos. 3184-3189 (6)* | 2.70 | 1.80 |

A 10 l imperf. airmail souvenir sheet containing a vert. stamp picturing a gymnast exists.

Miron Costin (1633-91), Poet — A916

Miron Costin

**Famous Men:** 1.50 l, Crisan (Marcu Giurgiu), (1733-85), peasant revolt leader. 2 l, Simion Barnutiu (1808-64), scientist. 3.50 l, Duiliu Zamfirescu (1858-1922), poet. 4 l, Nicolaus Milescu (1636-1708), Court official.

Palace of Udriste Natreul (1596-1658), Chancery Official — A915

---

Environmental Protection — A920

**1984, Apr. 26  Photo.  Perf. 13½**
| | | | |
|---|---|---|---|
| 3190 | A920 | 1 l Sunflower | .20 | .20 |
| 3191 | A920 | 2 l Stag | .45 | .20 |
| 3192 | A920 | 3 l Fish | .70 | .30 |
| 3193 | A920 | 4 l Bird | .90 | .30 |
| | | *Nos. 3190-3193 (4)* | 2.25 | .90 |

**Danube Flowers — A921**

**1984, Apr. 30**    **Photo.**    **Perf. 13½**
3194 A921 50b Sagittaria sagit-tifolia .20 .20
3195 A921 1 l Iris pseudacorus .20 .20
3196 A921 1.50 l Butomus umbellatus .25 .20
3197 A921 3 l Nymphaea al-ba, horiz. .50 .25
3198 A921 4 l Nymphoides peltata, horiz. .70 .30
3199 A921 5 l Nuphar luteum, horiz. .85 .45
Nos. 3194-3199 (6) 2.70 1.60

**1984, Apr. 30**    **Photo.**    **Perf. 13½**
45th Anniv., Youth Anti-Fascist Committee A922
3200 A922 2 l multicolored .40 .20

**1984, May 30**    **Photo.**    **Perf. 13½**
25th Congress, Ear, Nose and Throat Medicine — A923
3201 A923 2 l Congress seal .40 .20

Souvenir Sheets

**1984, June 7**    **Photo.**    **Perf. 13½**
European Soccer Cup Championships — A923a
3201A A923a 3 l Sheet of 4 2.50 2.50
  c.-f. A923a 3 l, any single .60 .60
3201B Sheet of 4 2.50 2.50
  g.-j. A923a 3 l, any single .60 .60

Soccer players and flags of: c. Romania. d. West Germany. e. Portugal. f. Spain. g. France. h. Belgium. i. Yugoslavia. j. Denmark.

**1984, July 2**    **Photo.**    **Perf. 13½**
Summer Olympics — A924
3202 A924 50b Boxing .20 .20
3203 A924 1 l Rowing .20 .20
3204 A924 1.50 l Team handball .20 .20
3205 A924 2 l Judo .25 .20
3206 A924 3 l Wrestling .40 .20
3207 A924 3.50 l Fencing .50 .20
3208 A924 4 l Kayak .55 .25
3209 A924 5 l Swimming .60 .30
Nos. 3202-3209 (8) 2.90 1.75

Two imperf. 10 l airmail souvenir sheets, showing long jumping and gymnastics exist. Value for each sheet, unused or used, $6.

**1984, July 28**    **Photo.**    **Perf. 13½**
Famous Romanians Type
3210 A916 2 l Mihai Ciuca .20 .20
3211 A916 2 l Petre Aurelian .35 .20
3212 A916 4 l Alexandru Vlahuta .70 .30
3213 A916 4 l Dimitrie Leonida .70 .30
Nos. 3210-3213 (4) 1.75 .90

**1984, Aug. 17**    **Photo.**    **Perf. 13½**
40th Anniv. Romanian Revolution A925
3214 A925 2 l multicolored .35 .20

**1984, Aug. 30**    **Photo.**    **Perf. 13½**
Romanian Horses — A926
3215 A926 50b Lippizaner .20 .20
3216 A926 1 l Hutul .20 .20
3217 A926 1.50 l Bucovina .25 .20
3218 A926 2.50 l Nonius .40 .20
3219 A926 4 l Arabian .65 .30
3220 A926 5 l Romanian Mix-ed-breed .80 .40
Nos. 3215-3220 (6) 2.50 1.50

**1984, Nov. 1**    **Photo.**    **Perf. 13½**
1784 Uprisings, 200th Anniv. — A927
3221 A927 2 l Monument .30 .20

**Children A928**

**1984, Nov. 10**    **Photo.**    **Perf. 13½**
3222 A928 50b multicolored .20 .20
3223 A928 1 l multicolored .20 .20
3224 A928 2 l multicolored .35 .20
3225 A928 3 l multicolored .50 .20
3226 A928 4 l multicolored .70 .30
3227 A928 5 l multicolored .85 .35
Nos. 3222-3227 (6) 2.80 1.45

Paintings: 50b, Portrait of Child, by T. Aman. 1 l, Shepherd, by N. Grigorescu. 2 l, Girl with Orange, by S. Luchian. 3 l, Portrait of Child, by N. Tonitza. 4 l, Portrait of Boy, by S. Popp. 5 l, Portrait of Girl, by I. Tuculescu.

**Stamp Day A929**

**1984, Nov. 15**    **Photo.**    **Perf. 13½**
3228 A929 2 l + 1 l label .50 .30

Souvenir Sheet

**13th Party Congress — A930**

**1984, Nov. 17**    **Photo.**    **Perf. 13½**
3229 A930 10 l Party symbols 1.75 1.75

Souvenir Sheets

**Romanian Medalists, 1984 Summer Olympic Games — A931**

**1984, Oct. 29**    **Photo.**    **Perf. 13½**
3230 A931 Sheet of 6 3.25 3.25
  a.-f. A931 3 l, any single .50 .50
3231 Sheet of 6 3.25 3.25
  a.-f. A931 3 l, any single .50 .50

No. 3230: a. Ecaterina Szabo, gymnastic floor exercise. b. 500-meter four-women kayak. c. Anisoara Stanciu, long jump. d. Greco-Roman wrestling. e. Mircea Fratica, half-middleweight judo. f. Corneliu Ion, rapid fire pistol.
No. 3231: a. 1000-meter two-man scull. b. Weight lifting. c. Women's relays. d. Canoeing, pair oars without coxswain. e. Fencing, team foil. f. Ecaterina Szabo, all-around gymnastics.

Pelicans of the Danube Delta.

**1984, Dec. 15**    **Photo.**    **Perf. 13½**
Pelicans of the Danube Delta. A932
3232 A932 50b Flying .40 .20
3233 A932 1 l On ground .75 .20
3234 A932 1 l In water .85 .20
3235 A932 2 l Nesting 1.60 .80
Nos. 3232-3235 (4) 3.50 .80

A933

**1984, Dec. 26**   
Famous Men — A933
3236 A933 50b multi .20 .20
3237 A933 1 l multi .35 .20
3238 A933 2 l multi .50 .20
3239 A933 3 l multi .70 .30
3240 A933 4 l multi .85 .35
3241 A933 5 l multi 2.80 1.45
Nos. 3236-3241 (6)

Famous Men: 50b, Dr. Petru Groza (1884-1968). 1 l, Alexandru Odobescu (1834-1895). 2 l, Dr. Carol Davila (1828-1884). 3 l, Dr. Nicolae G. Lupu (1884-1966). 4 l, Dr. Daniel Danielopolu (1884-1955). 5 l, Panait Istrati (1884-1935).

**Timisoara Power Station, Electric Street Lights, Cent. A934**

**1984, Dec. 29**   
3242 A934 1 l Generator, 1884 .20 .20
3243 A934 2 l Street arc lamp, Ti-misoara, 1884, vert. .35 .20

Souvenir Sheets

**European Music Year A935**

**1985, Mar. 28**
3244 A935 Sheet of 4 2.50 2.50
  a.-d. A935 3 l, any single .60 .60
3245 Sheet of 4 2.50 2.50
  a.-d. A935 3 l, any single .60 .60

Composers and opera houses: No. 3244a, Moscow Theater, Tchaikovsky (1840-1893). b, Bucharest Theater, George Enescu (1881-1955). c, Dresden Opera, Wagner (1813-1883). d, Warsaw Opera, Stanislaw Moniuszko (1819-1872). No. 3245a, Paris Opera, Gounod (1818-1893). b, Munich Opera, Strauss (1864-1949). c, Vienna Opera, Mozart (1756-1791). d, La Scala, Milan, Verdi (1813-1901).

**August T. Laurian (1810-1881), Linguist and Historian — A936**

## Danube-Black Sea Canal Opening, May 26, 1984 — A942

**Perf. 13½**
**1985, June 7**

| | | | | |
|---|---|---|---|---|
| 3266 | A942 | 1 l | Canal, map | .20 .20 |
| 3267 | A942 | 2 l | Bridge over lock, Cernavoda | .35 .20 |
| 3268 | A942 | 3 l | Bridge over canal, Medgidea | .50 .25 |
| 3269 | A942 | 4 l | Agigea lock, bridge | .70 .35 |
| | | | Nos. 3266-3269 (4) | 1.75 1.00 |

**Souvenir Sheet**

| 3270 | A942 | 10 l | Opening ceremony, Cernavoda, Ceaucescu | 1.75 1.75 |
|---|---|---|---|---|

No. 3270 contains one 54x42mm stamp.

## Audubon Birth Bicentenary — A943

No. American bird species. #3272-3275 vert.

**1985, June 26**

| | | | | |
|---|---|---|---|---|
| 3271 | A943 | 50b | Turdus migratorius | .20 .20 |
| 3272 | A943 | | Pelecanus occidentalis | .20 .20 |
| 3273 | A943 | 1.50 l | Nyctanassa violarea | .30 .20 |
| 3274 | A943 | 2 l | Ictorus galbula | .35 .20 |
| 3275 | A943 | 3 l | Podiceps grisegena | .55 .25 |
| 3276 | A943 | 5 l | Anas platyrhynchos | .70 .35 |
| | | | Nos. 3271-3276 (6) | 2.30 1.40 |

## 20th Century Paintings by Ion Tuculescu — A944

**1985, July 13**

| | | | | |
|---|---|---|---|---|
| 3277 | A944 | 1 l | Fire, vert. | .20 .20 |
| 3278 | A944 | 2 l | Circuit, vert. | .35 .25 |
| 3279 | A944 | 3 l | Interior | .55 .25 |
| 3280 | A944 | 4 l | Sunset | .70 .35 |
| | | | Nos. 3277-3280 (4) | 1.80 1.00 |

## Butterflies A945

**1985, July 15**

| | | | | |
|---|---|---|---|---|
| 3281 | A945 | 50b | Inachis io | .20 .20 |
| 3282 | A945 | 1 l | Papilio machaon | .20 .20 |
| 3283 | A945 | 2 l | Vanessa atalanta | .40 .20 |
| 3284 | A945 | 3 l | Saturnia pavonia | .60 .30 |
| 3285 | A945 | 4 l | Ammobiota festiva | .80 .40 |
| 3286 | A945 | 5 l | Smerinthus ocellatus | 1.00 .50 |
| | | | Nos. 3281-3286 (6) | 3.20 1.80 |

## Intl. Youth Year — A937

Famous men: 1 l, Grigore Alexandrescu (1810-1885), author. 1.50 l, Gheorghe Pop de Basesti (1835-1919), politician. 2 l, Mateiu Caragiale (1885-1936), author. 3 l, Gheorghe Ionescu-Sisesti (1885-1967), scientist. 4 l, Liviu Rebreanu (1885-1944), author.

**1985, Mar. 29**

| | | | | |
|---|---|---|---|---|
| 3246 | A936 | 50b | multi | .20 .20 |
| 3247 | A936 | 1 l | multi | .20 .20 |
| 3248 | A936 | 1.50 l | multi | .30 .20 |
| 3249 | A936 | 2 l | multi | .40 .20 |
| 3250 | A936 | 3 l | multi | .60 .30 |
| 3251 | A936 | 4 l | multi | .80 .40 |
| | | | Nos. 3246-3251 (6) | 2.50 1.50 |

**1985, Apr. 15**

| | | | | |
|---|---|---|---|---|
| 3252 | A937 | 1 l | Scientific research | .20 .20 |
| 3253 | A937 | 2 l | Construction | .35 .20 |

**Souvenir Sheet**

| 3254 | A937 | 10 l | Intl. solidarity | 1.75 1.75 |
|---|---|---|---|---|

No. 3254 contains one 54x42mm stamp.

## Wildlife Conservation A938

**1985, May 6**

| | | | | |
|---|---|---|---|---|
| 3255 | A938 | 50b | Nyctereutes procyonoides | .20 .20 |
| 3256 | A938 | 1 l | Perdix perdix | .20 .20 |
| 3257 | A938 | 1.50 l | Nyctea scandiaca | .25 .20 |
| 3258 | A938 | 2 l | Martes martes | .35 .25 |
| 3259 | A938 | 3 l | Meles meles | .55 .30 |
| 3260 | A938 | 3.50 l | Lutra lutra | .70 .35 |
| 3261 | A938 | 4 l | Tetrao urogallus | .75 .90 |
| 3262 | A938 | 5 l | Otis tarda | .90 1.90 |
| | | | Nos. 3255-3262 (8) | 3.90 3.90 |

## End of World War II, 40th Anniv. — A939

**1985, May 9**

| 3263 | A939 | 2 l | War monument, natl. and party flags | .35 .20 |
|---|---|---|---|---|

## Union of Communist Youth, 12th Congress A940

**1985, May 14**

| 3264 | A940 | 2 l | Emblem | .35 .20 |
|---|---|---|---|---|

## Natl. Communist Party Achievements — A946

Natl. and party flags, and: 1 l, Transfagarasan Mountain Road. 2 l, Danube-Black Sea Canal. 3 l, Bucharest Underground Railway. 4 l, Irrigation.

**1985, July 29**

| | | | | |
|---|---|---|---|---|
| 3287 | A946 | 1 l | multicolored | .20 .20 |
| 3288 | A946 | 2 l | multicolored | .35 .20 |
| 3289 | A946 | 3 l | multicolored | .55 .25 |
| 3290 | A946 | 4 l | multicolored | .70 .35 |
| | | | Nos. 3287-3290 (4) | 1.80 1.00 |

## Romanian Socialist Constitution, 20th Anniv. — A947

20th anniv. Election of Gen.-Sec. Nicolae Ceausescu; Natl. Communist Congress.

**1985, Aug. 5**

| | | | | |
|---|---|---|---|---|
| 3291 | A947 | 1 l | Arms, wheat, dove | .20 .20 |
| 3292 | A947 | 2 l | Arms, eternal flame | .35 .20 |

## 1986 World Cup Soccer Preliminaries — A948

Flags of participants; Great Britain, Northern Ireland, Romania, Finland, Turkey and: 50b, Sliding tackle. 1 l, Trapping the ball. 1.50 l, Heading the ball. 2 l, Dribble. 3 l, Tackle. 4 l, Scissor kick. 1 U, Dribble, diff.

**1985, Oct. 15**

| | | | | |
|---|---|---|---|---|
| 3293 | A948 | 50b | multi | .20 .20 |
| 3294 | A948 | 1 l | multi | .20 .20 |
| 3295 | A948 | 1.50 l | multi | .30 .20 |
| 3296 | A948 | 2 l | multi | .35 .20 |
| 3297 | A948 | 3 l | multi | .55 .30 |
| 3298 | A948 | 4 l | multi | .70 .35 |
| | | | Nos. 3293-3298 (6) | 2.30 1.45 |

## Motorcycle Centenary — A949

**Souvenir Sheet**

An imperf airmail 10 l souvenir sheet exists, showing flags, stadium and soccer players. Value, unused or used, $7.

**1985, Aug. 22 Photo.** *Perf. 13½*

| 3300 | A949 | 10 l | 1885 Daimler Einspur | 1.90 .90 |
|---|---|---|---|---|

## Retezat Natl. Park, 50th Anniv. — A950

**1985, Aug. 29**

| | | | | |
|---|---|---|---|---|
| 3301 | A950 | 50b | Senecio glaberrimus | .20 .20 |
| 3302 | A950 | 1 l | Rupicapra rupicapra | .20 .20 |
| 3303 | A950 | 2 l | Centaurea retezatensis | .35 .20 |
| 3304 | A950 | 3 l | Viola dacica | .55 .25 |
| 3305 | A950 | 4 l | Marmota marmota | .70 .35 |
| 3306 | A950 | 5 l | Aquila chrysaetos | .90 .45 |
| | | | Nos. 3301-3306 (6) | 2.90 1.65 |

**Souvenir Sheet**

| 3307 | A950 | 10 l | Lynx lynx | 1.90 .90 |
|---|---|---|---|---|

No. 3307 contains one 42x54mm stamp.

## Tractors Manufactured by Universal — A951

**1985, Sept. 10**

| | | | | |
|---|---|---|---|---|
| 3308 | A951 | 50b | 530 DTC | .20 .20 |
| 3309 | A951 | 1 l | 550 M HC | .20 .20 |
| 3310 | A951 | 1.50 l | 650 Super | .30 .20 |
| 3311 | A951 | | S 1801 IF | .50 .20 |
| 3312 | A951 | 3 l | S 1801 IF | .65 .30 |
| 3313 | A951 | 4 l | A 3602 IF | 2.10 1.35 |
| | | | Nos. 3308-3313 (6) | |

## Folk Costumes — A952

Women's and men's costumes from same region printed in continuous design.

**1985, Sept. 28**

| | | | | |
|---|---|---|---|---|
| 3314 | A952 | 50b | Muscel woman | .20 .20 |
| 3315 | A952 | 50b | Muscel man | .20 .20 |
| 3316 | A952 | 1.50 l | Bistrita-Nasaud woman | .20 .20 |
| | a. | | Pair, #3314-3315 | |
| 3317 | A952 | 1.50 l | Bistrita-Nasaud man | .25 .20 |
| | a. | | Pair, #3316-3317 | |
| 3318 | A952 | 3 l | Vrancea woman | .50 .30 |
| 3319 | A952 | 3 l | Vrancea man | .35 .20 |
| | a. | | Pair, #3318-3319 | |
| 3320 | A952 | 3 l | Vilcea woman | .70 .35 |
| 3321 | A952 | 3 l | Vilcea man | .50 .25 |
| | a. | | Pair, #3320-3321 | |
| | | | Nos. 3314-3321 (8) | 2.60 1.70 |

## Admission to UN, 30th Anniv. — A953

**1985, Oct. 21**

| 3322 | A953 | 2 l | multicolored | .35 .20 |
|---|---|---|---|---|

ROMANIA

**UN, 40th Anniv. — A954**

3323 A954 2 l multicolored

**1985, Oct. 21**

POSTA ROMANA

Mineral Flowers — A955

**1985, Oct. 21**
3324 A955 50b Quartz and cal-
cite, Herja         .35   .20
3325 A955   1 l Copper, Altin
Tepe                .20   .20
3326 A955   2 l Gypsum, Cavnic  .30   .20
3327 A955   3 l Quartz, Ocna de
Fier                .60   .30
3328 A955   4 l Stibium, Baiut   .80   .40
3329 A955   5 l Tetrahedrite,
Cavnic             1.00   .50
Nos. 3324-3329 (6)  3.10  1.80

Stamp Day — A956

**1985, Oct. 29**
3330 A956 2 l + 1 l label  .35   .20

A Connecticut Yankee in King Arthur's
Court, by Mark Twain — A957

**1985, Oct. 28**
3331 A957 50b Hank Morgan
awakes in
Camelot          .30   .20

© 1985 Walt Disney Productions

The Three Brothers, by Jacob and
Wilhelm Grimm — A958

**1985, Nov. 28**
3332 A958 50b Predicts
eclipse of sun     .30   .20
3333 A958 50b Mouating
horse              .30   .20
3334 A957 50b Sir Sagramor
horse              .30   .20
3335 A958   1 l Fencing with
shadow            4.00  4.00

Disney characters in classic fairy tales.

---

Fauna & flora: #3343: a, Felis silvestris. b,
Mustela erminea. c, Tetrao urogallus. d, Urso
arctos.
#3344: a, Dianthus callizonus. b, Pinus
cembra. c, Salix sp. d, Rose pendulina.

**1986, Mar. 25      Photo.      Perf. 13½**
3343      Sheet of 4         2.50  2.50
a.-d.  A959 3 l, any single   .60   .60
3344      Sheet of 4         2.50  2.50
a.-d.  A959 3 l, any single   .60   .60

3336 A958   1 l Fencing, father  4.00  4.00
3337 A958   1 l Shoeing a
horse             4.00  4.00
3338 A958   1 l Barber, rabbit  4.00  4.00
3339 A958   1 l Father, three
sons              4.00  4.00
Nos. 3331-3339 (9)  21.20 20.80

Souvenir Sheets

3340 A957  5 l Tournament of
knights          10.00 10.00
3341 A958  5 l Cottage      10.00 10.00

Intereuropa 1986 — A959

Miniature Sheets

---

Inventors and Adventurers — A960

Designs: 1 l, Orville and Wilbur Wright,
Wright Flyer. 1.50 l, Jacques Cousteau,
research vessel Calypso. 2 l, Amelia Earhart,
Lockheed Electra. 3.50 l, Charles Lindbergh,
Spirit of St. Louis. 3.50 l, Sir Edmund Hillary
(1919- ), first man to reach Mt. Everest summit. 4 l, Robert Edwin Peary, Arctic explorer. 5
l, Adm. Richard Byrd, explorer. 6 l, Neil Armstrong, first man on moon.

**1985, Dec. 25      Photo.      Perf. 13½**
3345 A960   1 l multi         .20   .20
3346 A960 1.50 l multi        .30   .20
3347 A960   2 l multi         .40   .20
3348 A960   3 l multi         .60   .40
3349 A960 3.50 l multi        .60   .60
3350 A960   4 l multi         .75   .60
3351 A960   5 l multi        1.00   .70
3352 A960   6 l multi        1.25   .85
Nos. 3345-3352 (8)  5.15  3.75

Paintings by Nicolae Tonitza — A961

**1986, Mar. 12      Photo.      Perf. 13½**
3353 A961   1 l Nina in Green  .25   .25
3354 A961   2 l Irina          .60   .30
3355 A961   3 l Woodman's
Daughter         .90   .45
3356 A961   4 l Woman on the Ve-
randah          1.25   .60
Nos. 3353-3356 (4)  3.00  1.55

---

Wait, Disney animated characters in the Band Concert,
1935.

**1986, Apr. 10      Photo.      Perf. 13½**
3357 A962 50b Clarabelle        .25   .20
3358 A962 50b Mickey Mouse      .25   .20
3359 A962 50b Paddy and Pe-
ter              .25   .20
3360 A962 50b Goofy             .25   .20
3361 A962 50b Donald Duck       .25   .20
3362 A962 50b Mickey Mouse,
diff.            .25   .20
3363 A962   1 l Mickey and
Donald          4.00  4.00
3364 A962   1 l Horace and
Donald          4.00  4.00
3365 A962   1 l trombonist      4.00  4.00
Nos. 3357-3365 (9)  21.00 20.80

Souvenir Sheet

3366 A962  5 l Finale        10.00 10.00

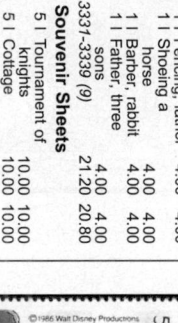

© 1986 Walt Disney Productions

Color Animated Films, 50th
Anniv. — A962

---

**1986, May 9**
3367 A963   1 l multi          .20   .20
3368 A963   1 l multi          .30   .20
3369 A963   1 l multi          .30   .20
3370 A963   3 l multi          .75   .35
3371 A963   4 l multi         1.00   .50
3372 A963   5 l multi         1.25   .70
Nos. 3367-3372 (6)  4.00  2.20

An imperf. 10 l airmail souvenir sheet exists
picturing stadium, flags of previous winners,
satellite and map. Value, unused or used,
$12.50.

Various soccer plays and flags: 50b, Italy vs.
Bulgaria. 1 l, Mexico vs. Belgium. 2 l, Canada
vs. France. 3 l, Brazil vs. Spain. 4 l, Uruguay
vs. Germany. 5 l, Morocco vs. Poland.

1986 World Cup Soccer
Championships, Mexico — A963

---

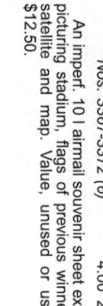

STATIUNEA BAILE HERCULANE

Hotels — A964

**1986, Apr. 23      Photo.      Perf. 13½**
3373 A964   1 l Diana, Herculane  .20   .20
3374 A964   1 l Termal, Felix    .20   .20
3375 A964   2 l Delfin, Meduza,
Mare, Eforie     .25   .20
Nord
3376 A964   3 l Caciulata,
Caciulata        .45   .20
3377 A964   4 l Palas, Slanic
Moldova          .65   .30
3378 A964   5 l Bradet, Sovata   .90   .45
Nos. 3373-3378 (6)  3.55  1.90

---

Flowers — A966

**1986, June 25      Photo.      Perf. 13½**
3380 A966 50b Tulipa gesneriana  .25   .20
3381 A966   1 l Iris hispanica   .25   .20
3382 A966   1 l Rosa hybrida     .50   .25
3383 A966   3 l Anemone
coronaria       .70   .35
3384 A966   4 l Freesia refracta 1.00   .50
3385 A966   5 l Chrysanthemum
indicum         3.90  2.10
Nos. 3380-3385 (6)

POSTA ROMANA

---

Nicolae Ceausescu, Party
Flag — A965

**1986, May 8      Photo.      Perf. 13½**
3379 A965 2 l multicolored       .60   .30
Natl. Communist Party, 65th anniv.

---

Mircea the Great, Ruler of Wallachia,
1386-1418 — A967

**1986, July 17      Photo.      Perf. 13½**
3386 A967 2 l multicolored       .60   .30
Ascent to the throne, 600th anniv.

Open Air Museum of Historic
Dwellings, Bucharest, 50th
Anniv. — A968

**1986, July 21      Photo.      Perf. 13½**
3387 A968 50b Alba              .20   .20
3388 A968   1 l Arges           .25   .20
3389 A968   1 l Constantia      .25   .20
3390 A968   1 l Timis           .45   .30
3391 A968   3 l Neamt           .90   .45
3392 A968   5 l Gorj           3.55  1.90
Nos. 3387-3392 (6)

Polar Research — A969

Exploration: 50b, Julius Popper, exploration
of Tierra del Fuego (1886-93). 1 l, Bazil G.

**Peasant Uprising of 1907, 80th Anniv. — A983**

1987, May 30
3443 A983 2 l multicolored .50 .25

**Men's World Handball Championships — A984**

Various plays.

1987, July 15
3444 A984 50b multi, vert. .20 .20
3445 A984 1 l multi. .20 .20
3446 A984 2 l multi. .35 .25
3447 A984 3 l multi. .50 .35
3448 A984 4 l multi, vert. .75 .50
3449 A984 5 l multi 1.00 .70
Nos. 3444-3449 (6) 3.00 1.70

A905

**Natl. Currency — A986**

A986 illustration reduced.

1987, July 15
3450 A985 1 l multicolored .20 .20

**Souvenir Sheet**

3451 A986 10 l multicolored 2.00 2.00

**Landscapes — A987**

---

65 DE ANI DE LA CREAREA UTC

1986, Dec. 30
3429 A978 1 l Metal .25 .20
3430 A978 2 l Trees .50 .25

**Young Communists' League, 65th Anniv. — A979** Photo. Perf. 13½

1987, Mar. 18
3431 A979 1 l Flags, youth .25 .20
3432 A979 2 l Emblem .50 .25
3433 A979 3 l Flags, youth, diff. .75 .40
Nos. 3431-3433 (3) 1.50 .85

**Miniature Sheets**

**Intereuropa — A980**

Modern architecture: No. 3434a, Exposition Pavilion, Bucharest. b, Intercontinental Hotel, Bucharest. c, Europa Hotel, Black Sea coast. d, Polytechnic Institute, Bucharest. Satu Mare. b, House of Young Pioneers, Bucharest; c, Valahia Hotel, Tirgoviste. d, Caciulata Hotel, Caciulata.

No. 3435a, Administration Building, Satu Mare.

Perf. 13½ Photo.
1987, May 18
3434 2.50 2.50
a.-d. A980 3 l, any single .60 .60
3435 Sheet of 4 2.50 2.50
a.-d. A980 3 l, any single .60 .50

**Collective Farming, 25th Anniv. — A981** Photo. Perf. 13½

1987, Apr. 25
3436 A981 2 l multicolored .50 .25

**Birch Trees by the Lakeside, by I. Andreescu — A982**

Paintings in Romanian museums: 1 l, Young Peasant Girls Spinning, by N. Grigorescu. 2 l, Washerwoman, by S. Luchian. 3 l, Inside the Peasant's Cottage, by S. Dimitrescu. 4 l, Winter Landscape, by A. Ciucurencu. 5 l, Winter in Bucharest, by N. Tonitza, vert.

1987, Apr. 28
3437 A982 50b multicolored .20 .20
3438 A982 1 l multicolored .20 .20
3439 A982 2 l multicolored .35 .25
3440 A982 3 l multicolored .45 .25
3441 A982 4 l multicolored 1.00 .50
3442 A982 5 l multicolored .... 3.00 1.70
Nos. 3437-3442 (6)

---

3410 A972 5 l Tremiscus helvelloides 1.25 .60
Nos. 3405-3410 (6) 3.90 2.10

**1986, Nov. 10** Photo. Perf. 13½

Famous Men: 50b, Petru Maior (b. 1761-1821), historian. 1 l, George Topirceanu (1886-1937), doctor. 2 l, Henri Coanda (1886-1972), engineer. 3 l, Constantin Budeanu (1886-1959), engineer.

3411 A973 50b dl cl, gold & dk bl grn .20 .20
3412 A973 1 l sl grn, gold & dk lil rose .25 .20
3413 A973 2 l rose cl, gold & brt bl .50 .25
3414 A973 3 l chky bl, gold & choc .70 .35
Nos. 3411-3414 (4) 1.65 1.00

ROMÂNIA XXX UNESCO

**UNESCO, 40th Anniv. A974**

1986, Nov. 10
3415 A974 4 l multicolored 1.00 .50

**Stamp Day — A975**

1986, Nov. 15
3416 A975 2 l + 1 label .75 .35

**Industry A976**

1986, Nov. 28
3417 A976 50b F-300 oil rigs, vert. .20 .20
3418 A976 1 l Promex excavator .25 .20
3419 A976 2 l Pitesti refinery, vert. .45 .20
3420 A976 3 l 110-ton dump truck .65 .30
3421 A976 4 l Coral computer, vert. .90 .45
3422 A976 5 l 350-megawatt turbine 1.10 .55
Nos. 3417-3422 (6) 3.55 1.90

**Folk Costumes — A977**

1986, Dec. 26
3423 A977 50b Capra .20 .20
3424 A977 1 l Sorcova .25 .20
3425 A977 2 l Plugusorul .45 .20
3426 A977 3 l Buhaiul .65 .30
3427 A977 4 l Caiutii .90 .45
3428 A977 5 l Uratorii 1.10 .55
Nos. 3423-3428 (6) 3.55 1.90

**Recycling Campaign — A978**

---

Assan, exploration of Spitzbergen (1896). 2 l, Emil Racovita, Antarctic expedition (1897-99). 3 l, Constantin Dumbrava, exploration of Greenland (1927-8). 4 l, Romanians with the 17th Soviet Antarctic expedition (1971-72). 5 l, Research on krill fishing (1977-80).

**1986, July 23** Photo. Perf. 13½
3393 A969 50b multi .20 .20
3394 A969 1 l multi .25 .20
3395 A969 2 l multi .45 .20
3396 A969 3 l multi .65 .30
3397 A969 4 l multi .90 .45
3398 A969 5 l multi 1.10 .55
Nos. 3393-3398 (6) 3.55 1.90

**Natl. Cycling Championships A970**

TURUL CICLIST AL ROMÂNIEI 1986

Various athletes.

1986, Aug. 29
3399 A970 1 l multicolored .25 .20
3400 A970 2 l multicolored .50 .25
3401 A970 3 l multicolored .70 .35
3402 A970 4 l multicolored 1.00 .50
Nos. 3399-3402 (4) 2.45 1.30

**Souvenir Sheet**

3403 A970 10 l multicolored 2.50 1.25

No. 3403 contains one 42x54mm stamp.

**Souvenir Sheet**

1986 anul international al păcii

**Intl. Peace Year — A971**

1986, July 25
3404 A971 5 l multicolored 1.25 .60

**Fungi — A972**

1986, Aug. 15
3405 A972 50b Amanita rubescens .20 .20
3406 A972 1 l Boletus luridus .50 .25
3407 A972 2 l Lactarius piperatus .70 .35
3408 A972 3 l Lepiota clypeolaria
3409 A972 4 l Russula cyanoxantha 1.00 .50

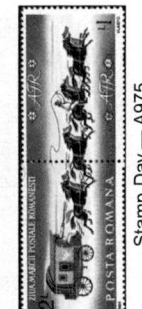

ROMANIA

A988

A988a illustration reduced.

Scenes from Fairy Tale by Peter Ispirescu (b. 1887) — A988a

**1987, July 31**    **Photo.**    **Perf. 13½**
| | | | | |
|---|---|---|---|---|
| 3452 | A987 | 50b Pelicans over the Danube Delta | | .20 .20 |
| 3453 | A987 | 1 l Transfagarasan Highway | | .20 .20 |
| 3454 | A987 | 2 l Hairpin curve, Bicazului | | .35 .20 |
| 3455 | A987 | 3 l Limestone peaks, Mt. Ceahlau | | .50 .25 |
| 3456 | A987 | 4 l Lake Capra, Mt. Fagaras | | .70 .35 |
| 3457 | A987 | 5 l Orchard, Borsa | | .90 .50 |

Nos. 3452-3457 (6)    2.85 1.70

**1987, Sept. 25**    **Photo.**    **Perf. 13½**
| | | | | |
|---|---|---|---|---|
| 3458 | A988 | 50b shown | | .20 .20 |
| 3459 | A988 | 1 l multi, diff. | | .20 .20 |
| 3460 | A988 | 2 l multi, diff. | | .35 .20 |
| 3461 | A988 | 3 l multi, diff. | | .50 .25 |
| 3462 | A988 | 4 l multi, diff. | | .70 .35 |
| 3463 | A988 | 5 l multi, diff. | | .85 .60 |

Nos. 3458-3463 (6)    2.80 1.60

**Souvenir Sheet**

3464   A988a   10 l shown    2.00 2.00

**1987, Oct. 16**

**Miniature Sheets**

Flora and Fauna — A989

Flora No. 3446a, Aquilegia alpina. b, Pulsatilla vernalis. c, Aster alpinus. d, Soldanella pusilla baumg. e, Lilium bulbiferum. f, Arctostaphylos uva-ursi. g, Crocus vernus. h, Crepis aurea. i, Cypripedium calceolus. j, Centaurea nervosa. k, Dryas octopetala. l, Gentiana excisa.

Fauna: No. 3466a. Martes martes. b, Felis lynx. c, Ursus marltinus. d, Lutra lutra. e, Bison bonasus. f, Branta ruficollis. g, Phoenicopterus ruber. h, Otis tarda. i, Lyrurus tetrix. j, Gypaetus barbatus. k, Vormela peregusna. l, Oxyura leucocephala.

**Sheets of 12**
| | | | |
|---|---|---|---|
| 3465 | A989 | 1 l #a.-l. | 3.25 1.50 |
| 3466 | A989 | 1 l #a.-l. | 3.25 1.50 |

PHILATELIA '87, Cologne — A990

**1987, Oct. 19**

3467    Sheet of 2 + 2 labels    3.75 3.75
   a.   A990 3 l Bucharest city seal    1.90 1.90
   b.   A990 3 l Cologne city arms    1.90 1.90

---

Locomotives — A991

**1987, Oct. 15**
| | | | | |
|---|---|---|---|---|
| 3468 | A991 | 50b L 45 H | | .20 .20 |
| 3469 | A991 | 1 l LDE 125 | | .20 .20 |
| 3470 | A991 | 1 l LDH 70 | | .20 .20 |
| 3471 | A991 | 2 l LDE 2100 | | .65 .30 |
| 3472 | A991 | 4 l LDE 3000 | | .90 .40 |
| 3473 | A991 | 5 l LE 5100 | | 1.00 .50 |

Nos. 3468-3473 (6)    3.35 1.80

Folk Costumes — A992

**1987, Nov. 7**
| | | | | |
|---|---|---|---|---|
| 3474 | 1 l Tirnave (woman) | | | .20 .20 |
| 3475 | 1 l Tirnave (man) | | | .20 .20 |

Nos. 3474-3475   A992 Pair, #3474-3475
| | | | | |
|---|---|---|---|---|
| 3476 | 2 l Buzau (woman) | | | .40 .20 |
| 3477 | 2 l Buzau (man) | | | .40 .20 |

A992 Pair, #3476-3477
| | | | | |
|---|---|---|---|---|
| 3478 | 3 l Dobrogea (woman) | | | .60 .30 |
| 3479 | 3 l Dobrogea (man) | | | .60 .30 |

A992 Pair, #3478-3479
| | | | | |
|---|---|---|---|---|
| 3480 | 4 l Ilfov (woman) | | | .80 .40 |
| 3481 | 4 l Ilfov (man) | | | .80 .40 |

A992 Pair, #3480-3481
| | | | | |
|---|---|---|---|---|
| 3482 | 4 l Illicu (man) | | | 1.25 .50 |

Nos. 3474-3481 (8)    4.00 2.20

Postwoman Delivering Mail — A993

**1987, Nov. 15**    **Photo.**    **Perf. 13½**
Stamp Day.

3482   A993   2 l + 1 l label    .75 .35

Apiculture — A994

**1987, Nov. 16**    **Photo.**    **Perf. 13½**
| | | | | |
|---|---|---|---|---|
| 3483 | A994 | 1 l Apis mellifica carpatica | | .25 .20 |
| 3484 | A994 | 2 l Bee pollinating sunflower | | .50 .25 |
| 3485 | A994 | 3 l Hives, Danube Delta | | .75 .35 |
| 3486 | A994 | 4 l Apiculture complex, Bucharest | | 1.00 .50 |

Nos. 3483-3486 (4)    2.50 1.30

1988 Winter Olympics, Calgary A995

**1987, Dec. 28**    **Photo.**    **Perf. 13½**
| | | | | |
|---|---|---|---|---|
| 3487 | A995 | 50b Biathlon | | .20 .20 |
| 3488 | A995 | 1 l Slalom | | .20 .20 |
| 3489 | A995 | 1.50 | | .30 .20 |
| 3490 | A995 | 2 l Luge | | .40 .20 |

---

Traffic Safety A996

Designs: 50b, Be aware of children riding bicycles in the road. 1 l, Young Pioneer girl as crossing guard. 2 l, Do not open car doors in path of moving traffic. 3 l, Be aware of pedestrian crossings. 4 l, Observe the speed limit. 5 l, Protect small children.

**1987, Dec. 10**    **Photo.**    **Perf. 13½**
| | | | | |
|---|---|---|---|---|
| 3495 | A996 | 50b multicolored | | .20 .20 |
| 3496 | A996 | 1 l multicolored | | .20 .20 |
| 3497 | A996 | 2 l multicolored | | .40 .20 |
| 3498 | A996 | 3 l multicolored | | .65 .30 |
| 3499 | A996 | 4 l multicolored | | .85 .40 |
| 3500 | A996 | 4 l multicolored | | 1.00 .45 |

Nos. 3495-3500 (6)    3.30 1.75

October Revolution, Russia, 70th Anniv. — A997

**1987, Dec. 26**

3501   A997   2 l multicolored    .45 .20

40th Anniv. of the Romanian Republic — A998

**1987, Dec. 30**

3502   A998   2 l multicolored    .45 .20

70th Birthday of President Nicolae Ceausescu — A999

**1988, Jan. 26**

3503   A999   2 l multicolored    .45 .25

---

An imperf. 10 l souvenir sheet picturing ski jumping also exists. Value, unused or used, $12.

| | | | | |
|---|---|---|---|---|
| 3491 | A995 | 3 l Speed skating | | .60 .30 |
| 3492 | A995 | 3.50 l Women's figure skating | | .65 .35 |
| 3493 | A995 | 4 l Downhill skiing | | .80 .40 |
| 3494 | A995 | 5 l Two-man bobsled | | 1.00 .50 |

Nos. 3487-3494 (8)    4.15 2.35

Transportation and communication: No. 3510a, Mail coach. b, ECS telecommunications satellite. c, Oltcit automobile. d, Airbus-A320. No. 3511a, Santa Maria, 15th cent. b, Cheia Ground Station satellite dish receivers. c, Bucharest subway. d, ICE highspeed electric train.

Intereuropa — A1001

**1988, Apr. 27**    **Photo.**    **Perf. 13½**
| | | | | |
|---|---|---|---|---|
| 3510 | A1001 | 3 l any single | | 2.50 2.50 |
| a.-d. | | Sheet of 4 | | 2.50 2.50 |
| 3511 | A1001 | 3 l any single | | 2.50 2.50 |
| a.-d. | | Sheet of 4 | | 2.50 2.50 |

Pottery A1000

**1988, Feb. 26**    **Photo.**    **Perf. 13½**
| | | | | |
|---|---|---|---|---|
| 3504 | A1000 | 50b Marginea | | .20 .20 |
| 3505 | A1000 | 1 l Oboga | | .20 .20 |
| 3506 | A1000 | 2 l Horezu | | .40 .20 |
| 3507 | A1000 | 3 l Curtea De Ar-ges | | .65 .25 |
| 3508 | A1000 | 4 l Birsa | | .85 .35 |
| 3509 | A1000 | 5 l Vama | | 1.00 .60 |

Nos. 3504-3509 (6)    3.30 1.60

**Miniature Sheets**

1988 Summer Olympics, Seoul — A1002

**1988, Jun. 28**
| | | | | |
|---|---|---|---|---|
| 3512 | A1002 | 50b Gymnastics | | .20 .20 |
| 3513 | A1002 | 1 l Boxing | | .30 .20 |
| 3514 | A1002 | 1.50 l Tennis | | .40 .20 |
| 3515 | A1002 | 2 l Judo | | .60 .25 |
| 3516 | A1002 | 4 l Rowing | | .80 .35 |
| 3517 | A1002 | 5 l Running | | 1.00 .60 |

Nos. 3512-3517 (6)    3.30 1.60

An imperf. 10 l souvenir sheet exists. Value, unused or used, $12.

19th-20th Cent. Clocks in the Ceasului Museum, Ploesti A1003

**1988, May 20**    **Photo.**    **Perf. 13½**
| | | | | |
|---|---|---|---|---|
| 3518 | A1003 | 50b Arad Region porcelain | | .20 .20 |
| 3519 | A1003 | 1.50 l French porcelain | | .35 .20 |
| 3520 | A1003 | 2 l French bronze | | .40 .20 |
| 3521 | A1003 | 3 l Gothic bronze, diff. | | .65 .25 |
| 3522 | A1003 | 4 l Saxony porcelain | | .85 .35 |
| 3523 | A1003 | 5 l Bohemian porcelain | | 1.10 .45 |

Nos. 3518-3523 (6)    3.55 1.65

19th-20th cent. timepiece (50b); others 19th cent.

## Miniature Sheets

### European Soccer Championships, Germany — A1003a

Soccer players and flags of: c, Federal Republic of Germany. d, Spain. e, Italy. f, Denmark. g, England. h, Netherlands. i, Ireland. j, Soviet Union.

**1988, June 9      Litho.      Perf. 13½**

| | | | |
|---|---|---|---|
| 3523A | Sheet of 4 | 3.25 | 3.25 |
| c.-f. | A1003a 3 l any single | .80 | .80 |
| 3523B | Sheet of 4 | 3.25 | 3.25 |
| g.-j. | A1003a 3 l any single | .80 | .80 |

### Accession of Constanin Brincoveanu as Prince Regent of Wallachia, 1688-1714, 300th Anniv. — A1004

**1988, June 20** A1004 2 l multicolored   .50   .25

### 1988 Summer Olympics, Seoul — A1005

**1988, Sept. 1      Photo.      Perf. 13½**

| | | | |
|---|---|---|---|
| 3525 | A1005 50b Women's running | .20 | .20 |
| 3526 | A1005 1 l Canoeing | .25 | .20 |
| 3527 | A1005 1.50 l Women's gymnastics | .40 | .25 |
| 3528 | A1005 2 l Kayaking | .55 | .55 |
| 3529 | A1005 3 l Weight lifting | | |
| 3530 | A1005 3.50 l Women's swimming | .60 | .25 |
| 3531 | A1005 4 l Fencing | .70 | .30 |
| 3532 | A1005 5 l Women's rowing (double) | .95 | .40 |
| | | 3.85 | 2.00 |

Nos. 3525-3532 (8)

### Romania-China Philatelic Exhibition — A1006

**1988, Aug. 5      Photo.      Perf. 13½**
3533 A1006 2 l multicolored   .50   .25

## Souvenir Sheet

PRAGA '88 — A1007

**1988, Aug. 26**
3534 A1007 5 l Carnations, by Stefan Luchian   2.00   2.00

## Miniature Sheets

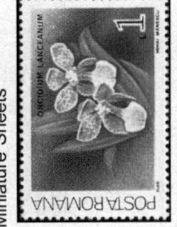

### Orchids A1008

#3535: a, Oncidium lanceanum. b, Cattleya trianae. c, Sophronitis cernua. d, Bulbophyllum lobbii. e, Lycaste cruenta. f, Mormolyce ringens. g, Phragmipedium schlimii. h, Angraecum sesquipedale. i, Laelia crispa. j, Encyclia atropurpurea. k, Dendrobium nobile. l, Oncidium splendidum.

#3536: a, Brassavola perrinii. b, Paphiopedilum maudiae. c, Sophronitis coccinea. d, Vandopsis lissochiloides. e, Phalaenopsis lueddemanniana. f, Chysis bractescens. g, Cochleanthes discolor. h, Phalaenopsis amabilis. i, Pleione precei. j, Sobralia macrantha. k, Aspasia lunata. l, Cattleya citrina.

**1988, Oct. 24**

| | | | |
|---|---|---|---|
| 3535 | Sheet of 12 | 3.25 | 3.25 |
| a.-l. | A1008 1 l any single | .25 | .25 |
| 3536 | Sheet of 12 | 3.25 | 3.25 |
| a.-l. | A1008 1 l any single | .25 | .25 |

## Miniature Sheets

### Events Won by Romanian Athletes at the 1988 Seoul Olympic Games A1009

Sporting event and medal: No. 3537a, Women's gymnastics. b, Free pistol shooting. c, Weight lifting (220 pounds). d, Featherweight boxing.

No. 3538a, Women's 1500 and 3000-meter relays. b, Women's 200 and 400-meter individual swimming medley. c, Wrestling (220 pounds). d, Rowing, coxless pairs and coxed fours.

**1988, Dec. 7      Photo.      Perf. 13½**

| | | | |
|---|---|---|---|
| 3537 | Sheet of 4 | 3.00 | 3.00 |
| a.-d. | A1009 3 l any single | .75 | .75 |
| 3538 | Sheet of 4 | 3.00 | 3.00 |
| a.-d. | A1009 3 l any single | .75 | .75 |

### Stamp Day — A1010

**1988, Nov. 13      Photo.      Perf. 13½**
3539 A1010 2 l + 1 l label   .75   .35

### Unitary Natl. Romanian State, 70th Anniv. A1011

**1988, Dec. 29**
3540 A1011 2 l multicolored   .50   .40

### Anniversaries — A1012

Designs: 50b, Athenaeum, Bucharest. 1.50 l, Trajan's Bridge, Drobeta, on a Roman bronze sestertius used in Romania from 103 to 105 A.D. 2 l, Ruins, Suceava. 3 l, Pitesti municipal coat of arms, scroll, architecture. 4 l, Trajan's Column (detail), 113 A.D. 5 l, Gold helmet discovered in Prahova County.

**1988, Dec. 30**

| | | | |
|---|---|---|---|
| 3541 | A1012 50b shown | .20 | .20 |
| 3542 | A1012 1.50 l multi | .30 | .20 |
| 3543 | A1012 2 l multi | .45 | .20 |
| 3544 | A1012 3 l multi | .65 | .35 |
| 3545 | A1012 4 l multi | .85 | .35 |
| 3546 | A1012 5 l multi | 1.10 | .45 |
| | | 3.55 | 1.65 |

Nos. 3541-3546 (6)

Athenaeum, Bucharest, cent. (50b). Suceava, capital of Moldavia from 1411-1565, 600th anniv. (2 l). & Pitesti municipal charter, 600th anniv. (3 l).

### Grand Slam Tennis Championships — A1013

No. 3547: a, Men's singles, stadium in Melbourne. b, Men's singles, scoreboard. c, Mixed doubles, spectators. d, Mixed doubles, Roland Garros stadium.

No. 3548: a, Women's singles, stadium in Wimbledon. b, Women's singles, spectators. c, Men's doubles, spectators. d, Men's doubles, stadium in Flushing Meadows.

**1988, Aug. 22      Photo.      Perf. 13½**

| | | | |
|---|---|---|---|
| 3547 | Sheet of 4 | 3.00 | 3.00 |
| a.-d. | A1013 3 l any single | .75 | .75 |
| 3548 | Sheet of 4 | 3.00 | 3.00 |
| a.-d. | A1013 3 l any single | .75 | .75 |

Australian Open (Nos. 3547a-3547b), French Open (Nos. 3547c-3547d), Wimbledon (Nos. 3548a-3548b) and US Open (Nos. 3548c-3548d).

### Architecture — A1014

Designs: 50b, Zapodeni, Vaslui, 17th cent. 1.50 l, Berbesti, Maramures, 18th cent. 2 l, Voitinel, Suceava, 18th cent. 3 l, Chiojdu mic, Buzau, 18th cent. 4 l, Cimpanii de sus, Bihor, 19th cent. 5 l, Naruja, Vrancea, 19th cent.

### Rescue and Relief Services — A1015

**1989, Feb. 8      Photo.      Perf. 13½**

| | | | |
|---|---|---|---|
| 3549 | A1014 50b multi | .20 | .20 |
| 3550 | A1014 1.50 l multi | .30 | .20 |
| 3551 | A1014 2 l multi | .45 | .25 |
| 3552 | A1014 3 l multi | .65 | .35 |
| 3553 | A1014 4 l multi | 1.10 | .45 |
| 3554 | A1014 5 l multi | 3.55 | 1.65 |

Nos. 3549-3554 (6)

**1989, Feb. 25**

| | | | |
|---|---|---|---|
| 3555 | A1015 50b Relief worker | .20 | .20 |
| 3556 | A1015 1 l shown | .20 | .20 |
| 3557 | A1015 1.50 l Fireman, child | .25 | .20 |
| 3558 | A1015 2 l Fireman's carry | .30 | .20 |
| 3559 | A1015 3 l Rescue team on skis | .50 | .20 |
| 3560 | A1015 3.50 l Mountain rescue | .60 | .25 |
| 3561 | A1015 4 l Water rescue | .70 | .30 |
| 3562 | A1015 5 l Water safety | .85 | .35 |
| | | 3.60 | 1.90 |

Nos. 3555, 3557-3558, 3560-3561 vert.
Nos. 3555-3562 (8)

### Industries — A1016

Designs: 50b, Fasca Bicaz cement factory. 1.50 l, Bridge on the Danube near Cernavoda. 2 l, Mangalia-Constanta ferry. 5 l, Gloria marine platform.

**1989, Apr. 10      Photo.**

| | | | |
|---|---|---|---|
| 3563 | A1016 50b multi | .20 | .20 |
| 3564 | A1016 1.50 l multi | .30 | .20 |
| 3565 | A1016 2 l multi | .40 | .25 |
| 3566 | A1016 4 l multi | .60 | .25 |
| 3567 | A1016 4 l multi | .80 | .35 |
| 3568 | A1016 5 l multi | 1.00 | .40 |
| | | 3.30 | 1.60 |

Nos. 3563-3568 (6)

### Anti-fascist March, 50th Anniv. — A1017

**1989, May 1      Photo.**
3569 A1017 2 l shown   .50   .25

### Souvenir Sheet

3570 A1017 10 l Patriots, flag   4.00   4.00

**1989, May 20**
3571 A1018 10 l Roses .50 .25

BULGARIA '89, Sofia, May 22-31 — A1018

Illustration reduced.

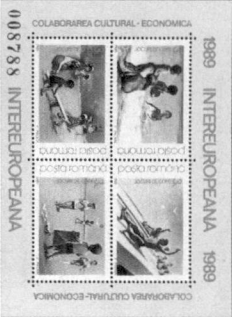

Miniature Sheets

**1989, May 20** Photo. *Perf. 13½*
3572 A1019 Sheet of 4 3.00 3.00
a.-d. 3 l any single .75 .75
3573 A1019 Sheet of 4 3.00 3.00
a.-d. 3 l any single .75 .75
3574 A1020 2 l multicolored .50 .25

Intereuropa 1989 — A1019

Children's activities and games: No. 3572a, Swimming. No. 3572b, Water slide. No. 3572c, Seesaw. No. 3572d, Flying kites. No. 3573a, Playing with dolls. No. 3573b, Playing ball. No. 3573c, Playing in the sand. No. 3573d, Playing with toy cars.

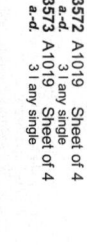 

**1989, Aug. 21** Photo. *Perf. 13½*
3575 A1020 2 l multicolored .50 .25

Socialist Revolution in Romania, 45th Anniv. A1020

**1989, Sept. 25**
Cartoons — A1021

3575 A1021 50b Pin-pin .20
3576 A1021 1 l Maria .25 .20
3577 A1021 1.50 l Gore and Grigore .30 .20
3578 A1021 2 l Pisoiul, Balanel, Ma-nole and Monk .30 .20
3579 A1021 3 l Gruia Lui Novac .45 .20
3580 A1021 3.50 l Mihaela .65 .25
3581 A1021 4 l Harap alb .80 .30
3582 A1021 5 l Homo sapiens 1.00 .40
Nos. 3575-3582 (8) 4.55 2.10

**1989, Aug. 18** Photo. *Perf. 13½*
3583 A1022 1 l multicolored .30 .20
3584 A1022 2 l multicolored .60 .25
3585 A1022 3 l multicolored .90 .35
Nos. 3583-3585 (3) 1.80 .80

Romanian Writers A1022

Portraits: 1 l, Ion Creanga (1837-1889), 2 l, Mihail Eminescu (1850-1889), poet. 3 l, Nico-lae Teclu (1839-1916).

**1989, Oct. 7**
3586 A1023 2 l + 1 l multicolored .75 .30

Stamp Day — A1023

No. 3586 has a second label picturing posthorn.

Storming of the Bastille, 1789 A1024

**1989, Oct. 14**
3587 A1024 50b shown .20 .20
3588 A1024 1 l multicolored .30 .20
3589 A1024 1.50 l multicolored .40 .20
3590 A1024 3 l multicolored .60 .25
3591 A1024 4 l multicolored .80 .30
3592 A1024 5 l multicolored 1.00 .40
Nos. 3587-3592 (6) 3.30 1.55

Souvenir Sheet

3593 A1025 10 l shown 3.00 3.00

Emblems of PHILEXFRANCE '89 and the Revolution — A1025

Designs: 1.50 l, Gavroche. 2 l, Robespierre, Diderot. 5 l, 1848 Uprising, Romania.

**1989, Nov. 20** Photo. *Perf. 13½*
3593A A1025a 2 l multicolored .50 .25

3593B A1025a 10 l multicolored 4.00 4.00

Souvenir Sheet

Revolution of Dec. 22, 1989 — A1026

**1990, Jan. 8** Photo. *Perf. 13½*
3594 A1026 2 l multicolored .40 .20

For surcharge, see No. 3633.

World Cup Soccer Preliminaries, Italy — A1027

**1990, Mar. 19** Photo. *Perf. 13½*
3595 A1027 50b multicolored .20 .20
3596 A1027 1 l multicolored .30 .20
3597 A1027 1.50 l multicolored .40 .20
3598 A1027 3 l multicolored .60 .25
3599 A1027 4 l multicolored .80 .30
3600 A1027 5 l multicolored 1.00 .40
Nos. 3595-3600 (6) 3.30 1.55

Various soccer players in action.

An imperf. 10 l airmail souvenir sheet exists. Value, $8.50.

Souvenir Sheet

First Postage Stamp, 150th Anniv. — A1028

**1990, May 2** Litho. *Perf. 13½*
3601 A1028 10 l multicolored 2.00 2.00

Stamp World London '90.

Illustration reduced.

World Cup Soccer Championships, Italy — A1029

**1990, May 7** Photo. *Perf. 13½*
3602 A1029 50b multicolored .20 .20
3603 A1029 1 l multicolored .20 .20
3604 A1029 1.50 l multicolored .20 .20
3605 A1029 3 l multicolored .25 .20
3606 A1029 4 l multicolored .25 .20
3607 A1029 3.50 l multicolored .30 .20

Various soccer players in action.

14th Romanian Communist Party Congress — A1025a

**1990, Aug. 24**
3618 A1031 2 l multicolored .50 .20

See No. 3856.

Riccione '90, Int. Philatelic Exhibition A1031

**1990, Sept. 8** Photo. *Perf. 13½*
3619 A1032 2 l multicolored .40 .20

For surcharge see No. 4186.

Romanian-Chinese Philatelic Exhibition, Bucharest — A1032

Paintings Damaged in 1989 Revolution — A1033

Designs: 50b, Old Nicolas, the Zither Player, by Stefan Luchian. 1.50 l, Woman in Blue by Ion Andreescu. 2 l, The Gardener by Luchian. 3 l, Vase of Flowers by Jan Brueghel, the Elder. 4 l, Springtime by Peter Brueghel, the Elder, horiz. 5 l, Madonna and Child by G. B. Paggi.

**1990, June 6**
Int'l. Dog Show, Brno, Czechoslovakia — A1030

3610 A1030 50b German shep-herd .20 .20
3611 A1030 1 l English setter .20 .20
3612 A1030 1.50 l Boxer .30 .20
3613 A1030 3 l Beagle .45 .20
3614 A1030 3 l Doberman pinscher .65 .25
3615 A1030 3.50 l Great Dane .75 .30
3616 A1030 4 l Afghan hound .90 .35
3617 A1030 5 l Yorkshire terri-er 1.10 .45
Nos. 3610-3617 (8) 4.55 2.15

An imperf. 10 l airmail souvenir sheet show-ing Olympic Stadium, Rome exists. Value, $7.50.

3608 A1029 4 l multicolored .35 .20
3609 A1029 5 l multicolored .45 .20
Nos. 3602-3609 (8) 2.15 1.60

## 1990, Oct. 25 — Photo. — Perf. 13½

| | | | | |
|---|---|---|---|---|
| 3620 | A1033 | 50b multicolored | .20 | .20 |
| 3621 | A1033 | 1.50 l multicolored | .20 | .20 |
| 3622 | A1033 | 2 l multicolored | .25 | .20 |
| 3623 | A1033 | 3 l multicolored | .40 | .20 |
| 3624 | A1033 | 4 l multicolored | .55 | .30 |
| 3625 | A1033 | 5 l multicolored | .70 | .35 |
| | | Nos. 3620-3625 (6) | 2.30 | 1.35 |

For surcharges see #4365-4369.

### Stamp Day — A1033a
1990, Nov. 10 — Photo. — Perf. 13½
3625A A1033a 2 l + 1 l label — .25 .20

### Famous Romanians — A1034

Designs: 50b, Prince Constantin Cantacuzino (1640-1716). 1.50 l, Ienachita Vacarescu (c. 1740-1797), historian. 2 l, Titu Maiorescu (1840-1917), writer. 3 l, Nicolae Iorga (1871-1940), historian. 4 l, Martha Bibescu (1890-1973). 5 l, Stefan Procopiu (1890-1972), scientist.

## 1990, Nov. 27 — Photo. — Perf. 13½

| | | | | |
|---|---|---|---|---|
| 3626 | A1034 | 50b sepia & dk bl | .20 | .20 |
| 3627 | A1034 | 1.50 l grn & brt pur | .20 | .20 |
| 3628 | A1034 | 2 l claret & dk bl | .20 | .20 |
| 3629 | A1034 | 3 l dk bl & brn | .25 | .20 |
| 3630 | A1034 | 4 l brn & dk bl | .30 | .20 |
| 3631 | A1034 | 5 l brt pur & grn | .40 | .20 |
| | | Nos. 3626-3631 (6) | 1.55 | 1.20 |

For surcharges see #4356-4360.

### National Day — A1035
1990, Dec. 1 — Photo. — Perf. 13½
3632 A1035 2 l multicolored — .25 .20

### No. 3594 Surcharged in Brown
1990, Dec. 22 — Photo. — Perf. 13½
3633 A1026 4 l on 2 l — .50 .20

---

### Vincent Van Gogh, Death Cent. — A1036
Paintings: 50b, Field of Irises. 2 l, Artist's Room. 3 l, Night on the Coffee Terrace, vert. 3.50 l, Blossoming Fruit Trees. 5 l, Vase with Fourteen Sunflowers, vert.

## 1991, Mar. 29 — Photo. — Perf. 13½

| | | | | |
|---|---|---|---|---|
| 3634 | A1036 | 50b multicolored | .20 | .20 |
| 3635 | A1036 | 2 l multicolored | .20 | .20 |
| 3636 | A1036 | 3 l multicolored | .35 | .20 |
| 3637 | A1036 | 3.50 l multicolored | .40 | .20 |
| 3638 | A1036 | 5 l multicolored | .60 | .25 |
| | | Nos. 3634-3638 (5) | 1.75 | 1.05 |

For surcharges see #4371-4372.

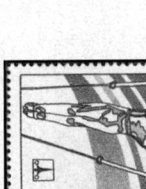

### A1037 / A1038

Birds: 50b, Larus marinus. 1 l, Sterna hirundo. 1.50 l, Recurvirostra avosetta. 2 l, Stercorarius pomarinus. 3 l, Vanellus vanellus. 3.50 l, Mergus serrator. 4 l, Egretta garzetta. 5 l, Calidris alpina. 6 l, Limosa limosa. 7 l, Childonias hybrida.

## 1991, Apr. 3 — Photo. — Perf. 13½

| | | | | |
|---|---|---|---|---|
| 3639 | A1037 | 50b ultra | .20 | .20 |
| 3640 | A1037 | 1 l blue green | .20 | .20 |
| 3641 | A1037 | 1.50 l bister | .20 | .20 |
| 3642 | A1037 | 2 l dark blue | .25 | .20 |
| 3643 | A1037 | 3 l light green | .30 | .20 |
| 3644 | A1037 | 3.50 l dark green | .30 | .20 |
| 3645 | A1037 | 4 l purple | .40 | .20 |
| 3646 | A1037 | 5 l brown | .50 | .20 |
| 3647 | A1037 | 6 l yel brown | .50 | .25 |
| 3648 | A1037 | 7 l light blue | .60 | .25 |
| | | Nos. 3639-3648 (10) | 3.45 | 2.05 |

Easter.
1991, Apr. 5 — Photo. — Perf. 13½
3649 A1038 4 l multicolored — .35 .20

### Europa — A1039

EUROPA '91
1991, May 10 — Photo. — Perf. 13½
3650 A1039 4.50 l Eutelsat I — .50 .20
For surcharge see No. 4185.

---

### Posthorn — A1040
Photo. — Perf. 13½
3651 A1040 4.50 l blue — .40 .20

### Gymnastics — A1041
1991, June 14

| | | | | |
|---|---|---|---|---|
| 3652 | A1041 | 1 l Rings | .20 | .20 |
| 3653 | A1041 | 1 l Parallel bars | .20 | .20 |
| 3654 | A1041 | 4.50 l Vault | .40 | .20 |
| 3655 | A1041 | 1.50 l Uneven parallel bars | .40 | .20 |
| 3656 | A1041 | 8 l Floor exercise | .70 | .30 |
| 3657 | A1041 | 9 l Balance beam | .80 | .35 |
| | | Nos. 3652-3657 (6) | 2.70 | 1.45 |

For other surcharges see Nos. 3944, 4237-4238.

### Monasteries — A1042
Photo. — Perf. 13½

| | | | | |
|---|---|---|---|---|
| 3658 | A1042 | 1 l Curtea de Arges, vert. | .20 | .20 |
| 3659 | A1042 | 1 l Putna, vert. | .20 | .20 |
| 3660 | A1042 | 4.50 l Varatoc, vert. | .40 | .20 |
| 3661 | A1042 | 4.50 l Agapia | .40 | .20 |
| 3662 | A1042 | 8 l Golia | .70 | .30 |
| 3663 | A1042 | 9 l Sucevita | .80 | .35 |
| | | Nos. 3658-3663 (6) | 2.70 | 1.45 |

For surcharges see #4354-4355.

### Hotels, Lodges, and Resorts — A1043 / A1044

Designs: 1 l, Hotel Continental, Timisoara, vert. 2 l, Valea Caprei Lodge, Fagaras. 4 l, Hotel Intercontinental, Bucharest, vert. 5 l, Lebada Lodge, Crisan. 6 l, Muntele Rosu Lodge, Ciucas. 8 l, Transylvania Hotel, Cluj-Napoca. 9 l, Hotel Orizont, Predeal. 10 l, Hotel Roman, Herculane, vert. 18 l, Rarau Lodge, Rarau, vert. 20 l, Alpine Hotel, Poiana Brasov. 25 l, Constanta Casino. 30 l, Miorija Lodge, Bucegi. 45 l, Sura Dacilor Lodge, Poiana Brasov. 60 l, Valea Draganului. Tourist Complex. 80 l, Hotel Florica, Venus Health Resort. 120 l, International Hotel, Baile Felix, vert. 160 l, Hotel Egreta, Tulcea. 250 l, Motel Valea de Pesti, Valea Jiului. 400 l, Tourist Complex, Baisoara. 500 l, Hotel Bradul, Covasna. 800 l, Hotel Gorj, Tirgu Jiu.

## 1991 — Photo. — Perf. 13½

| | | | | |
|---|---|---|---|---|
| 3664 | A1043 | 1 l blue | .20 | .20 |
| 3665 | A1043 | 2 l dark green | .20 | .20 |
| 3666 | A1043 | 4 l carmine | .20 | .25 |
| 3667 | A1043 | 5 l violet | .30 | .20 |
| 3668 | A1043 | 6 l olive brown | .30 | .20 |
| 3669 | A1043 | 8 l brown | .60 | .20 |
| 3670 | A1043 | 9 l red brown | .65 | .25 |
| 3671 | A1043 | 10 l olive green | .50 | .30 |
| 3672 | A1043 | 18 l bright red | .40 | .20 |
| 3673 | A1043 | 20 l brown org | .30 | .20 |
| 3674 | A1043 | 25 l bright blue | .35 | .20 |
| 3675 | A1043 | 30 l magenta | .40 | .20 |
| 3676 | A1043 | 45 l dark blue | .95 | .35 |
| 3677 | A1043 | 60 l brown olive | 1.25 | .40 |
| 3678 | A1044 | 80 l purple | 1.60 | .55 |

**Size: 27x41mm, 41x27mm**

| | | | | |
|---|---|---|---|---|
| 3679 | A1044 | 120 l gray bl & dk | .75 | |
| 3680 | A1044 | 160 l lt ver & dk bl vio | 1.80 | .60 |
| | | lt ver & dk ver | 2.25 | .75 |
| 3681 | A1044 | 250 l lt bl & dk bl | 2.90 | 1.00 |
| 3682 | A1044 | 400 l tan & dk brn | 3.75 | 1.25 |
| 3683 | A1044 | 500 l lt bl grn & dk bl grn | 4.25 | 1.50 |
| 3684 | A1044 | 800 l pink & dk lil rose | 5.25 | 1.75 |
| | | Nos. 3664-3684 (21) | 28.10 | 10.55 |

Issued: 1 l, 5 l, 9 l, 10 l, 8/27; 2 l, 4 l, 18 l, 25 l, 30 l, 10/8; 6 l, 8 l, 20 l, 45 l, 60 l, 80 l, 11/14; 120 l, 160 l, 250 l, 400 l, 500 l, 800 l, 12/5.
For surcharges see Nos. 4167-4174, 4204-4219.

### Riccione '91, Intl. Philatelic Exhibition — A1045
1991, Aug. 27
3685 A1045 4 l multicolored — .40 .20

### Romanian-Chinese Philatelic Exhibition. — A1046 / A1047
Vases: a, Decorated with birds. b, Decorated with flowers.
1991, Sept. 12
3686 A1046 5 l Pair, #a-b. — .70 .35

Romanian Academy, 125th anniv.
1991, Sept. 17
3687 A1047 1 l blue — .25 .20

### A1048 / A1049
1991, Sept. 20 — Cissa erythrorhyncha.
3688 A1048 4 l multicolored — .40 .20
3689 A1048 5 l multicolored — .45 .20

### Souvenir Sheet
3690 A1048 20 l multicolored — 1.75 1.75

Balkanfila '91 Philatelic Exhibition: 4 l, Flowers, by Nicu Enea. 5 l, Peasant Girl of Vlasca, by Georghe Tattarescu. 20 l, Sports Center, Bacau.

### Miniature Sheets
No. 3689 printed se-tenant with 2 l Romanian Philatelic Assoc. label. No. 3690 contains one 54x42mm stamp.

Birds: No. 3691a, Cissa erythrorhyncha. b, Malaconotus blanchoti. c, Sialia sialis. d, Sturnella neglecta. e, Harpactes fasciatus. f, Upupa epops. g, Malurus cyaneus. h, Brachypteracias squamigera. i, Leptopterus madagascariensis. j, Phoeniculus bollei. k, Melanerpes erythrocephalus. l, Pericrocotus flammeus.
No. 3692a, Melithreptus laetior. b, Rhynochetos jubatus. c, Turdus migratorius. d, Copsychus saularis. e, Monticola saxatilis. f,

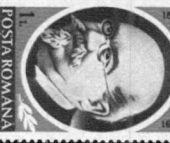

A1053

A1054

**1991, Oct. 7**
3691 A1049 2 l #a.-l.
3692 A1049 2 l #a.-l.

**Designs:** ... g, Scotope-
lia pelii. h, Ptilogonys caudatus. i, Todus mexi-
canus. j, Copsychus malabaricus. k,
Myzomela erythrocephala. l, Gymnostinops
montezuma.

Xanthocephalus xanthocephalus. g, Scotope-

**1991, Oct. 7**
3691 A1049 2 l #a.-l.  2.50 2.50
3692 A1049 2 l #a.-l.  2.50 2.50

**Sheets of 12**

**1991, Oct. 15**  Nat'l.
Census — A1050
3693 A1050 5 l multicolored  .30  .20

**1991, Nov. 13  Photo.  Perf. 13½**
Phila Nippon '91 — A1051
3694 A1051 10 l Sailing ship  .75  .25
3695 A1051 10 l Bridge building  .75  .25

**Miniature Sheets**

Butterflies and Moths A1052

**1991, Nov. 30  Photo.  Perf. 13½**
**Sheets of 12**
3696 A1052 3 l #a.-l.  3.00 3.00
3697 A1052 3 l #a.-l.  3.00 3.00
For surcharges see #4266-4267.

**Designs:** No. 3696a, Ornithoptera
paradisea. b, Bhutanitis lidderdalii. c, Ornithoptera
helena. d, Ornithoptera croesus. e, Phoebis
avellaneda. f, Ornithoptera victoriae. g, Teinopalpus imperialis. h, Hypolimnas dexithea. i,
Dabasa payeni. j, Morpho achilleana. k,
Heliconius melpomene. l, Agrias claudina
sardanapalus.
No. 3697a, Graellsia isabellae. b,
Antocharis cardamines. c, Anniobicta festiva.
d, Polygonia c-album. e, Catocala promissa. f,
Rhyparia purpurata. g, Arctia villica. h, Poly-
ommatus daphnis. i, Zerynthia polyxena. j,
Daphnis nerii. k, Licaena dispar rutila. l,
Pararge roxelana.

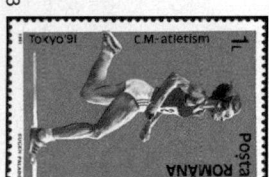

**1991, Nov. 21  Photo.  Perf. 13½**
3698 A1053 4 l Long jump  .20  .20
3699 A1053 4 l Running  .20  .20
3700 A1053 5 l High jump  .45  .30
3701 A1053 5 l Runner in
  blocks  .45  .30
3702 A1053 9 l Hurdles  .80  .35
3703 A1053 10 l Javelin  .90  .30
Nos. 3698-3703 (6)  3.15 1.35

World Track and Field Championships, Tokyo.

**1991, Dec. 10  Photo.  Perf. 13½**
Famous People: 1 l, Mihail Kogalniceanu
(1817-1891), politician. 4 l, Nicolae Titulescu
(1882-1941), politician. No. 3706, Andrei
Mureseanu (1816-1863), author. No. 3707,
Aron Pumnul (1818-1866), author. 9 l, George
Bacovia (1881-1957), author. 10 l, Perpes-
sicius (1891-1971), writer.
3704 A1054 1 l multi  .20  .20
3705 A1054 4 l multi  .20  .20
3706 A1054 5 l multi  .25  .20
3707 A1054 5 l multi  .25  .20
3708 A1054 9 l multi  .50  .20
3709 A1054 10 l multi  .50  .20
Nos. 3704-3709 (6)  2.00 1.20
See Nos. 3759-3761, 3776-3781.
For surcharges see Nos. 4238A-4248.

Stamp Day — A1055

**1991, Dec. 20  Photo.**
3710 A1055 8 l red brown  .50  .20

**1991, Dec. 23**
Central University Library, Bucharest. Cent. A1056
3711 A1056 8 l multicolored  .50  .20

**1991, Dec. 25  Photo.  Perf. 13½**
Christmas A1057
3712 A1057 8 l multicolored  .50  .20
See No. 3874.

**1992, Feb. 1  Photo.  Perf. 13½**
1992 Winter Olympics, Albertville A1058
3713 A1058 4 l Biathlon  .20  .20
3714 A1058 5 l Alpine skiing  .20  .20
3715 A1058 8 l Cross-country
  skiing  .20  .20
3716 A1058 10 l Two-man luge  .20  .20
3717 A1058 20 l Speed skating  .40  .20
3718 A1058 25 l Ski jumping  .50  .20
3719 A1058 30 l Ice hockey  .60  .25

3720 A1058 45 l Men's figure
  skating  .90  .30
Nos. 3713-3720 (8)  3.20 1.75

**Souvenir Sheets**
**Imperf**
3721 A1058 75 l Women's figure
  skating  2.25 2.25
3722 A1058 125 l 4-Man bobsled  6.00 6.00
No. 3721 is airmail and contains one
42x54mm stamp.

A1059

**1992, Feb. 20  Photo.  Perf. 13½**
Porcelain — A1059
3723 A1059 4 l multicolored  .20  .20
3724 A1059 4 l multicolored  .20  .20
3725 A1059 8 l multicolored  .20  .20
3726 A1059 8 l multicolored  .70  .25
3727 A1059 45 l multicolored  1.00  .35
Nos. 3723-3727 (5)  2.30 1.20
Designs: 4 l, Sugar and cream service. 5 l,
Tea service. 8 l, Goblet and pitcher, vert. 30 l,
Tea service, diff. 45 l, Vase, vert.

Fish A1060

**1992, Feb. 28  Photo.  Perf. 13½**
3728 A1060 4 l multicolored  .20  .20
3729 A1060 5 l multicolored  .20  .20
3730 A1060 8 l multicolored  .20  .20
3731 A1060 10 l multicolored  .30  .20
3732 A1060 30 l multicolored  .65  .20
3733 A1060 45 l multicolored  1.00  .20
Nos. 3728-3733 (6)  2.75 1.20
Designs: 4 l, Scomber scombrus. 5 l, Tinca
tinca. 8 l, Salvelinus fontinalis. 10 l,
Romanichthys valsanicola. 30 l, Chondros-
toma nasus. 45 l, Mullus barbatus ponticus.

A1060a

**Olympics Type of 1991 Surcharged**

**1992, Mar. 11  Photo.  Perf. 13½**
3735 A1041 90 l on 5 l like
  #3667  1.75  .60
No. 3735 not issued without surcharge.

**1992, Mar. 11  Photo.  Perf. 13½**
3734 A1060a 90 l on 5 l multi  1.75  .60
No. 3734 not issued without surcharge.

Horses A1061

**1992, Mar. 17  Photo.  Perf. 13½**
3736 A1061 6 l multi, vert.  .20  .20
3737 A1061 7 l multi, vert.  .20  .20
3738 A1061 11 l multi, vert.  .20  .20
3739 A1061 25 l multi, vert.  .50  .20
3740 A1061 30 l multi, vert.  .70  .20
3741 A1061 50 l multi, vert.  1.10  .20
Nos. 3736-3741 (6)  2.90 1.20
Various stylized drawings of horses walking,
running, or jumping.

**Miniature Sheet**

Discovery of America, 500th
Anniv. — A1062

**1992, Apr. 22  Photo.  Perf. 13½**
3742 A1062 35 l Sheet of 4,
  #a.-d.  12.50 12.50
Columbus and ships: a, Green background.
b, Violet background. c, Blue background. d,
Ship approaching island.
Europa.

**1992, Apr. 24  Photo.  Perf. 13½**
Granada '92, Philatelic
Exhibition — A1063
3743 A1063 Sheet of 3, #a.-c.  1.40 1.40
a, 25 l, Spain No. 1 and Romania No. 1. b,
10 l, Expo emblem. c, 30 l, Building and courtyard. Granada. Illustration reduced.

Icon of Christ's
Descent into
Hell. — A1064

**1992, Apr. 24  Photo.  Perf. 13½**
3744 A1064 10 l multicolored  .30  .20
Easter.

**1992, May 2  Photo.  Perf. 13½**
Fire Station, Bucharest.
Cent. — A1065
3745 A1065 10 l multicolored  .30  .20

## Chess Olympiad, Manila — A1066

1992, June 7    **Perf. 13½**

| | | | | |
|---|---|---|---|---|
| 3746 | A1066 | 10 l | shown | .30 | .20 |
| 3747 | A1066 | 10 l | Building, chess board | .30 | .20 |

**Souvenir Sheet**

| | | | | |
|---|---|---|---|---|
| 3748 | A1066 | 75 l | Shore, chess board | 2.25 | 2.25 |

No. 3748 contains one 42x54mm stamp.

## 1992 Summer Olympics, Barcelona — A1067

1992, July 17    **Photo.**    **Perf. 13½**

| | | | | | |
|---|---|---|---|---|---|
| 3749 | A1067 | 6 l | Shooting, vert. | .20 | .20 |
| 3750 | A1067 | 7 l | Weight lifting, vert. | .20 | .20 |
| 3751 | A1067 | 9 l | Two-man canoeing | .20 | .20 |
| 3752 | A1067 | 10 l | Handball, vert. | .30 | .20 |
| 3753 | A1067 | 25 l | Wrestling | .35 | .25 |
| 3754 | A1067 | 30 l | Fencing | .35 | .25 |
| 3755 | A1067 | 50 l | Running, vert. | .65 | .50 |
| 3756 | A1067 | 55 l | Boxing | .75 | .75 |
| | | | Nos. 3749-3756 (8) | 2.85 | 1.70 |

**Souvenir Sheets**

| | | | | | |
|---|---|---|---|---|---|
| 3757 | A1067 | 100 l | Rowing | 1.25 | 1.25 |

**Imperf**

| | | | | | |
|---|---|---|---|---|---|
| 3758 | A1067 | 200 l | Gymnastics | 5.00 | 5.00 |

Nos. 3757-3758 are airmail. No. 3757 contains one 54x42mm stamp. No. 3758 one 40x53mm stamp.

## Famous People Type of 1991

Designs: 10 l, Iuri I. C. Brătianu (1864-1927), prime minister. 25 l, Ion Gh. Duca (1879-1933), prime minister. 30 l, Grigore Gafencu (1892-1957), journalist and politician.

1992, July 27    **Photo.**    **Perf. 13½**

| | | | | | |
|---|---|---|---|---|---|
| 3759 | A1054 | 10 l | green & violet | .20 | .20 |
| 3760 | A1054 | 25 l | blue & lake | .30 | .20 |
| 3761 | A1054 | 30 l | lake & blue | .70 | .60 |
| | | | Nos. 3759-3761 (3) | | |

## Expo '92, Seville — A1068

Designs: 6 l, The Thinker, Cernavoda. 7 l, Trajan's bridge, Drobeta. 10 l, Mill. 25 l, Railroad bridge, Cernavoda. 30 l, Trajan Vuia's flying machine. 55 l, Herman Oberth's rocket. 100 l, Prayer sculpture, by C. Brancusi.

1992, Sept. 1

| | | | | | |
|---|---|---|---|---|---|
| 3762 | A1068 | 6 l | multicolored | .20 | .20 |
| 3763 | A1068 | 7 l | multicolored | .20 | .20 |
| 3764 | A1068 | 10 l | multicolored | .20 | .20 |
| 3765 | A1068 | 25 l | multicolored | .30 | .20 |
| 3766 | A1068 | 30 l | multicolored | .50 | .20 |
| 3767 | A1068 | 55 l | multicolored | 1.65 | 1.20 |
| | | | Nos. 3762-3767 (6) | | |

**Souvenir Sheet**

| | | | | | |
|---|---|---|---|---|---|
| 3768 | A1068 | 100 l | multicolored | .75 | .75 |

No. 3768 contains one 42x54mm stamp.

## World Post Day — A1069

1992, Oct. 9

| | | | | | |
|---|---|---|---|---|---|
| 3769 | A1069 | 10 l | multicolored | .20 | .20 |

For surcharge see No. 3945.

## Discovery of America, 500th Anniv. — A1070

Columbus and: 6 l, Santa Maria. 10 l, Nina. 25 l, Pinta. 55 l, Arrival in New World. 100 l, Sailing ship, vert.

1992, Oct. 30    **Photo.**    **Perf. 13½**

| | | | | | |
|---|---|---|---|---|---|
| 3770 | A1070 | 6 l | multicolored | .20 | .20 |
| 3771 | A1070 | 10 l | multicolored | .20 | .20 |
| 3772 | A1070 | 25 l | multicolored | .25 | .20 |
| 3773 | A1070 | 55 l | multicolored | .50 | .20 |
| | | | Nos. 3770-3773 (4) | 1.15 | .80 |

**Souvenir Sheet**

| | | | | | |
|---|---|---|---|---|---|
| 3774 | A1070 | 100 l | multicolored | .90 | .90 |

No. 3774 contains one 42x54mm stamp.

## Romanian Postal Reorganization, 1st Anniv. — A1071

1992, Nov. 5    **Photo.**    **Perf. 13½**

| | | | | | |
|---|---|---|---|---|---|
| 3775 | A1071 | 10 l | multicolored | .20 | .20 |

For surcharge see No. 4113.

## Famous People Type of 1991

Designs: 6 l, Iacob Negruzzi (1842-1932), author. 7 l, Grigore Antipa (1867-1944), naturalist. 9 l, Alexe Mateevici (1888-1917), poet. 10 l, Cezar Petrescu (1892-1961), author. 25 l, Octav Onicescu (1892-1983), mathematician. 30 l, Ecaterina Teodoroiu (1894-1917), World War I soldier.

1992, Nov. 9    **Photo.**    **Perf. 13½**

| | | | | | |
|---|---|---|---|---|---|
| 3776 | A1054 | 6 l | green & violet | .20 | .20 |
| 3777 | A1054 | 7 l | lilac & green | .20 | .20 |
| 3778 | A1054 | 9 l | gray blue & purple | .20 | .20 |
| 3779 | A1054 | 10 l | brown & blue | .20 | .20 |
| 3780 | A1054 | 25 l | blue & brown | .30 | .20 |
| 3781 | A1054 | 30 l | slate & blue | 1.30 | 1.20 |
| | | | Nos. 3776-3781 (6) | | |

## Wild Animals — A1072

Designs: 6 l, Haliaeetus leucocephalus, vert. 7 l, Strix occidentalis, vert. 9 l, Ursus arctos, vert. 10 l, Haematopus bachmani. 25 l, Canis lupus. 30 l, Odocoileus virginianus. 55 l, Alces alces.

## Romanian Anniversaries and Events — A1073

7 l, Building, Galea Victoria St., 300th anniv. 9 l, Statue, School of Commerce, 600th anniv. 10 l, Curtea de Arges Monastery, 475th anniv. 25 l, School of Architecture, Bucharest, 80th anniv.

1992, Nov. 16    **Litho.**    **Perf. 13½**

| | | | | | |
|---|---|---|---|---|---|
| 3782 | A1072 | 6 l | multicolored | .20 | .20 |
| 3783 | A1072 | 7 l | multicolored | .20 | .20 |
| 3784 | A1072 | 9 l | multicolored | .20 | .20 |
| 3785 | A1072 | 10 l | multicolored | .20 | .20 |
| 3786 | A1072 | 25 l | multicolored | .25 | .20 |
| 3787 | A1072 | 30 l | multicolored | .30 | .20 |
| 3788 | A1072 | 55 l | multicolored | .60 | 1.40 |
| | | | Nos. 3782-3788 (7) | 1.95 | 1.40 |

**Souvenir Sheet**

| | | | | | |
|---|---|---|---|---|---|
| 3789 | A1072 | 100 l | Orcinus orca | .90 | .90 |

1992, Dec. 3    **Photo.**    **Perf. 13½**

| | | | | | |
|---|---|---|---|---|---|
| 3790 | A1073 | 7 l | multicolored | .20 | .20 |
| 3791 | A1073 | 9 l | multicolored | .20 | .20 |
| 3792 | A1073 | 10 l | multicolored | .25 | .20 |
| 3793 | A1073 | 25 l | multicolored | .85 | .80 |
| | | | Nos. 3790-3793 (4) | | |

## Natl. Arms — A1074

1992, Dec. 7

| | | | | | |
|---|---|---|---|---|---|
| 3794 | A1074 | 15 l | multicolored | .20 | .20 |

## Christmas A1075

1992, Dec. 15

| | | | | | |
|---|---|---|---|---|---|
| 3795 | A1075 | 15 l | multicolored | .20 | .20 |

For surcharge see No. 4249.

## New Telephone Numbering System A1076

1992, Dec. 28    **Photo.**    **Perf. 13½**

| | | | | | |
|---|---|---|---|---|---|
| 3796 | A1076 | 15 l | blue, black & red | .20 | .20 |

For surcharges see #4268-4272.

**Souvenir Sheets**

1992 Summer Olympics, Barcelona A1077

No. 3797: a, Shooting. b, Wrestling. c, Weight lifting. d, Boxing.
No. 3798: a, Women's gymnastics. b, Four-man sculls. c, Fencing. d, High jump.

1992, Dec. 30    **Photo.**    **Perf. 13½**

| | | | | | |
|---|---|---|---|---|---|
| 3797 | A1077 | 35 l | Sheet of 4, #a-. | | |
| | | | d. | 1.10 | 1.10 |
| 3798 | A1077 | 35 l | Sheet of 4, #a-. | | |
| | | | d. | 1.10 | 1.10 |

## Historic Sites, Bucharest — A1078

Designs: 10 l, Mihai Voda Monastery. 15 l, Vacaresti Monastery. 25 l, Multi-purpose hall. 30 l, Mina Minovici Medical Institute.

1993, Feb. 11    **Photo.**    **Perf. 13½**

| | | | | | |
|---|---|---|---|---|---|
| 3799 | A1078 | 10 l | multicolored | .20 | .20 |
| 3800 | A1078 | 15 l | multicolored | .20 | .20 |
| 3801 | A1078 | 25 l | multicolored | .20 | .20 |
| 3802 | A1078 | 30 l | multicolored | .25 | .20 |
| | | | Nos. 3799-3802 (4) | .85 | .80 |

## Easter — A1079

1993, Mar. 25

| | | | | | |
|---|---|---|---|---|---|
| 3803 | A1079 | 15 l | multicolored | .20 | .20 |

## Medicinal Plants — A1080

1993, Mar. 30

| | | | | | |
|---|---|---|---|---|---|
| 3804 | A1080 | 10 l | Crataegus monogyna | .20 | .20 |
| 3805 | A1080 | 15 l | Gentiana phlogifolia | .20 | .20 |
| 3806 | A1080 | 25 l | Hippophae rhamnoides | .20 | .20 |
| 3807 | A1080 | 30 l | Vaccinium myrtillus | .25 | .20 |
| 3808 | A1080 | 50 l | Arnica montana | .35 | .25 |
| 3809 | A1080 | 90 l | Rosa canina | .65 | 1.25 |
| | | | Nos. 3804-3809 (6) | 1.85 | 1.25 |

## Nichita Stanescu (1933-1983), Poet — A1081

1993, Mar. 31

| | | | | | |
|---|---|---|---|---|---|
| 3810 | A1081 | 15 l | brown and blue | .25 | .20 |

Souvenir Sheet

Polska '93 — A1082

EXPOZITIA MONDIALA DE FILATELIE POLSKA '93
POZNAN 7-16V 1993

**1993, Apr. 28** **Photo.** **Perf. 13½**
3811 A1082 200 l multicolored 1.25 1.25

Birds A1083

**1993, Apr. 30**
| | | | | | |
|---|---|---|---|---|---|
| 3812 | A1083 | 5 l | Pica pica | .20 | .20 |
| 3813 | A1083 | 10 l | Aquila chrysaetos | .20 | .20 |
| 3814 | A1083 | 15 l | Pyrrhula pyrrhula | .20 | .20 |
| 3815 | A1083 | 20 l | Upupa epops | .20 | .20 |
| 3816 | A1083 | 25 l | Dendrocopos major | .20 | .20 |
| 3817 | A1083 | 50 l | Oriolus oriolus | .20 | .20 |
| 3818 | A1083 | 65 l | Loxia leucoptera | .35 | .25 |
| 3819 | A1083 | 90 l | Parus cyanus | .55 | .20 |
| 3820 | A1083 | 160 l | Hirundo rustica | .90 | .20 |
| 3821 | A1083 | 250 l | Sturnus roseus | 1.25 | .20 |
| | | | Nos. 3812-3821 (10) | 4.30 | 2.00 |

Cats — A1084

**1993, May 24** **Photo.** **Perf. 13½**
Various cats.
| | | | | | |
|---|---|---|---|---|---|
| 3822 | A1084 | 10 l | multicolored | .20 | .20 |
| 3823 | A1084 | 15 l | multicolored | .20 | .20 |
| 3824 | A1084 | 30 l | multicolored | .55 | .20 |
| 3825 | A1084 | 60 l | multicolored | .55 | .20 |
| 3826 | A1084 | 135 l | multicolored | .70 | .20 |
| 3827 | A1084 | 160 l | multicolored | .20 | .20 |
| | | | Nos. 3822-3827 (6) | 2.80 | 1.20 |

Europa — A1085

**1993, May 31** **Photo.** **Perf. 13½**
Paintings and sculpture by: a, Pablo Picasso. b, Constantin Brancusi. c, Ion Irimescu. d, Alexandru Ciucurencu.
3828 A1085 280 l Sheet of 4, #a-d. 2.75 2.75

---

A1086

A1087

**1993, June 30** **Photo.** **Perf. 13½**
| | | | | | |
|---|---|---|---|---|---|
| 3829 | A1086 | 10 l | Vipera berus | .20 | .20 |
| 3830 | A1086 | 15 l | Lynx lynx | .20 | .20 |
| 3831 | A1086 | 25 l | Tadorna tadorna | .40 | .20 |
| 3832 | A1086 | 75 l | Hucho hucho | .50 | .20 |
| 3833 | A1086 | 105 l | Limenitis populi | .75 | .20 |
| 3834 | A1086 | 280 l | Rosalia alpina | 2.25 | 1.20 |
| | | | Nos. 3829-3834 (6) | | |

Nos. 3829, 3831-3834 are horiz.

**1993, June 30**
| | | | | | |
|---|---|---|---|---|---|
| 3835 | A1087 | 10 l | Martes martes | .20 | .20 |
| 3836 | A1087 | 15 l | Uryctolagus cuniculus | .20 | .20 |
| 3837 | A1087 | 20 l | Sciurus vulgaris | .20 | .20 |
| 3838 | A1087 | 25 l | Rupicapra rupicapra | .20 | .20 |
| 3839 | A1087 | 30 l | Vulpes vulpes | .20 | .20 |
| 3840 | A1087 | 40 l | Ovis ammon | .20 | .20 |
| 3841 | A1087 | 75 l | Genetta genetta | .30 | .30 |
| 3842 | A1087 | 105 l | Eliomys quercinus | .45 | .20 |
| 3843 | A1087 | 150 l | Mustela erminea | .50 | .20 |
| 3844 | A1087 | 280 l | Herpestes ichneumon | 1.25 | .20 |
| | | | Nos. 3835-3844 (10) | 3.70 | 2.00 |

Nos. 3836, 3839, 3843-3844 are horiz.

Dinosaurs — A1088

Brontosaurus

**1993, July 30** **Photo.** **Perf. 13½**
| | | | | | |
|---|---|---|---|---|---|
| 3845 | A1088 | 29 l | Brontosaurus | .20 | .20 |
| 3846 | A1088 | 46 l | Plesiosaurus | .25 | .20 |
| 3847 | A1088 | 85 l | Triceratops | .35 | .20 |
| 3848 | A1088 | 171 l | Stegosaurus | .80 | .20 |
| 3849 | A1088 | 216 l | Tyrannosaurus | 1.00 | .20 |
| 3850 | A1088 | 319 l | Archaeopteryx | 1.40 | .20 |
| | | | Nos. 3845-3850 (6) | 4.00 | 1.20 |

Souvenir Sheet

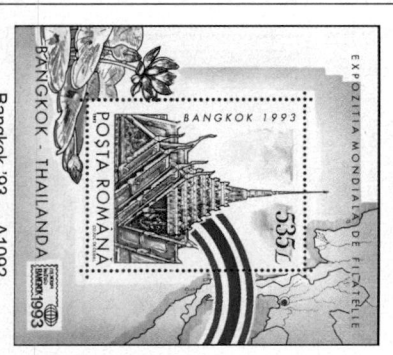

Telafila '93, Israel-Romanian Philatelic Exhibition — A1089

EXPOZITIA FILATELICA BINATIONALA ISRAFI - ROMANIA

Bangkok '93 — A1092

Souvenir Sheet

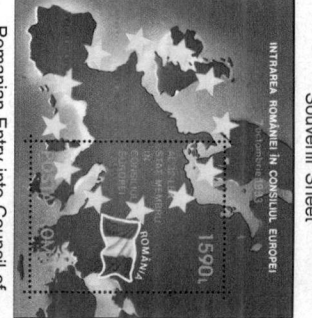

EXPOZITIA MONDIALA DE FILATELIE
BANGKOK - THAILANDA

**1993, Sept. 20**
3857 A1092 535 l multicolored 2.25 2.25
Illustration reduced.

No. 3618 Surcharged in Red

Riccione '93, 3-5 septembrie

**1993, Sept. 3**
3856 A1031 171 l on 2 l .65 .25

Rural Mounted Police, Cent. — A1091
**1993, Sept. 1**
3855 A1091 29 l multicolored .20 .20

---

Woman with Eggs, by Marcel Iancu. Illustration reduced.
**1993, Aug. 21**
3851 A1089 535 l multicolored 2.25 2.25

Icons — A1090
**1993, Aug. 31**
Designs: 75 l, St. Stephen. 171 l, Martyrs from Brancoveanu and Vacarescu families. 216 l, St. Anthony.
| | | | | | |
|---|---|---|---|---|---|
| 3852 | A1090 | 75 l | multicolored | .20 | .20 |
| 3853 | A1090 | 171 l | multicolored | .50 | .20 |
| 3854 | A1090 | 216 l | multicolored | 1.10 | .35 |
| | | | Nos. 3852-3854 (3) | 1.80 | .75 |

Famous Men — A1093

GEORGE BARITIU 1812-1893

**1993, Oct. 8**
Designs: 29 l, George Baritiu (1812-93), politician. 46 l, Horia Creanga (1892-1943), architect. 85 l, Armand Calinescu (1893-1939), politician. 171 l, Dumitru Bagdasar (1893-1946), physician. 216 l, Constantin Brailoiu (1893-1958), musician. 319 l, Iuliu Maniu (1873-1953), politician.
| | | | | | |
|---|---|---|---|---|---|
| 3858 | A1093 | 29 l | multicolored | .20 | .20 |
| 3859 | A1093 | 46 l | multicolored | .20 | .20 |
| 3860 | A1093 | 85 l | multicolored | .25 | .20 |
| 3861 | A1093 | 171 l | multicolored | .55 | .20 |
| 3862 | A1093 | 216 l | multicolored | .65 | .25 |
| 3863 | A1093 | 319 l | multicolored | 1.10 | .35 |
| | | | Nos. 3858-3863 (6) | 2.95 | 1.40 |

Romanian Entry into Council of Europe — A1094

INTRAREA ROMANIEI IN CONSILIUL EUROPEI

Souvenir Sheet

**1993, Nov. 26** **Photo.** **Perf. 13½**
3864 A1094 1590 l multi 4.75 4.75

Expansion of Natl. Borders, 75th Anniv. — A1095

75 ANI DE LA MAREA UNIRE
IANCU FLONDOR

**1993-94**
Government leaders: 115 l, Iancu Flondor (1865-1924). 245 l, Ion I. C. Bratianu (1864-1927). 255 l, Iuliu Maniu (1873-1953). 325 l, Pantelimon Halippa (1883-1979). 1060 l, King Ferdinand I (1865-1927).
| | | | | | |
|---|---|---|---|---|---|
| 3865 | A1095 | 115 l | multi | .35 | .20 |
| 3866 | A1095 | 245 l | multi | .70 | .25 |
| 3867 | A1095 | 255 l | multi | .80 | .25 |
| 3868 | A1095 | 325 l | multi | 1.00 | .35 |
| 3869 | A1095 | 1060 l | Romania in one color | 2.85 | 1.05 |
| | | | Nos. 3865-3868 (4) | | |

Souvenir Sheet
3869 A1095 1060 l Romania in one color 3.25 3.25
a. Romania in four colors 10.00 10.00

No. 3869a was redrawn because of an error in the map. Issued: No. 3869, Feb. 1994; Nos. 3865-3868, 3869a, Dec. 1, 1993.

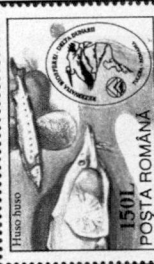

## Anniversaries and Events — A1096

Designs: 115 l, Emblem of the Diplomatic Alliance. 245 l, Statue of Johannes Honterus, founder of first Humanitarian School. 255 l, Arms, seal of Slatina, Olt River Bridge. 325 l, Map, arms of Braila.

**1993, Dec. 15**

| | | | | | |
|---|---|---|---|---|---|
| 3870 | A1096 | 115 l | multicolored | .30 | .20 |
| 3871 | A1096 | 245 l | multicolored | .60 | .20 |
| 3872 | A1096 | 255 l | multicolored | .65 | .25 |
| 3873 | A1096 | 325 l | multicolored | .85 | .95 |
| | Nos. 3870-3873 (4) | | | | |

Diplomatic Alliance, 75th anniv. (#3870). Birth of Johannes Honterus, 450th anniv. (#3871). City of Slatina, 625th anniv. (#3872). County of Braila, 625th anniv. (#3873).

### Christmas Type of 1991

**1993, Dec. 20**

| | | | | | |
|---|---|---|---|---|---|
| 3874 | A1057 | 45 l | like #3712 | .20 | .20 |

## Insects, Wildlife from Movile Cavern — A1097

Designs: 29 l, Clivina subterranea. 40 l, Nepa anophthalma. 85 l, Haemopis caeca. 171 l, Lascona cristiani. 216 l, Semisalsa dobrogica. 319 l, Armadilidium tabacarul. 535 l, Exploring cavern, vert.

**1993, Dec. 27**

| | | | | | |
|---|---|---|---|---|---|
| 3875 | A1097 | 29 l | multicolored | .20 | .20 |
| 3876 | A1097 | 40 l | multicolored | .20 | .20 |
| 3877 | A1097 | 85 l | multicolored | .30 | .20 |
| 3878 | A1097 | 171 l | multicolored | .55 | .20 |
| 3879 | A1097 | 216 l | multicolored | .70 | .25 |
| 3880 | A1097 | 319 l | multicolored | 1.00 | .35 |
| | Nos. 3875-3880 (6) | | | 2.95 | 1.40 |

**Souvenir Sheet**

| | | | | | |
|---|---|---|---|---|---|
| 3881 | A1097 | 535 l | multicolored | 1.75 | 1.75 |

## Alexandru Ioan Cuza — A1098

**1994, Jan. 24** Photo. Perf. 13

| | | | | | |
|---|---|---|---|---|---|
| 3882 | A1098 | 45 l | multicolored | .20 | .20 |

## Historic Buildings, Bucharest — A1099

115 l, Opera House. 245 l, Vacaresti Monastery. 255 l, Church of St. Vineri. 325 l, Dominican House, Vacaresti Monastery.

---

**1994, Feb. 7**

| | | | | | |
|---|---|---|---|---|---|
| 3883 | A1099 | 115 l | multicolored | .25 | .20 |
| 3884 | A1099 | 245 l | multicolored | .55 | .25 |
| 3885 | A1099 | 255 l | multicolored | .65 | .25 |
| 3886 | A1099 | 325 l | multicolored | .80 | .90 |
| | Nos. 3883-3886 (4) | | | 2.25 | |

## 1994 Winter Olympics, Lillehammer A1100

**1994, Feb. 12** Perf. 13½

| | | | | | |
|---|---|---|---|---|---|
| 3887 | A1100 | 70 l | Speed skating | .20 | .20 |
| 3888 | A1100 | 115 l | Slalom skiing | .25 | .20 |
| 3889 | A1100 | 125 l | Bobsled | .30 | .20 |
| 3890 | A1100 | 245 l | Biathlon | .55 | .20 |
| 3891 | A1100 | 255 l | Ski jumping | .60 | .25 |
| 3892 | A1100 | 325 l | Figure skating | .85 | .30 |
| | Nos. 3887-3892 (6) | | | 2.75 | 1.35 |

**Souvenir Sheet**

| | | | | | |
|---|---|---|---|---|---|
| 3893 | A1100 | 1590 l | Luge | 4.00 | 4.00 |

No. 3893 contains one 43x54mm stamp.

## Mills — A1101

**1994, Mar. 31** Perf. 13

| | | | | | |
|---|---|---|---|---|---|
| 3894 | A1101 | 70 l | Sarichioi | .20 | .20 |
| 3895 | A1101 | 115 l | Valea Nucarilor | .25 | .25 |
| 3896 | A1101 | 125 l | Caraorman | .30 | .20 |
| 3897 | A1101 | 245 l | Romanii de Jos | .60 | .25 |
| 3898 | A1101 | 255 l | Enisala, horiz. | .65 | .30 |
| 3899 | A1101 | 325 l | Nistoresti | .95 | 1.40 |
| | Nos. 3894-3899 (6) | | | 2.90 | 1.40 |

## Dinosaurs — A1102

**1994, Apr. 30** Photo. Perf. 13½

| | | | | | |
|---|---|---|---|---|---|
| 3900 | A1102 | 70 l | Struthiosaurs | .20 | .20 |
| 3901 | A1102 | 90 l | Megalosaurs | .25 | .20 |
| 3902 | A1102 | 150 l | Parasaurolophus | .25 | .25 |
| 3903 | A1102 | 280 l | Stenonychosaurus | .25 | .20 |
| 3904 | A1102 | 500 l | Camarasaurus | .55 | .25 |
| 3905 | A1102 | 635 l | Gallimimus | .95 | .30 |
| | Nos. 3900-3905 (6) | | | 2.95 | 1.35 |

## Romanian Legends A1103

Designs: 70 l, Calin the Madman. 115 l, Ileana Cosanzeana. 125 l, Ileana Cosanzeana, diff. 245 l, Ileana Cosanzeana, diff. 255 l, Ileana Cosanzeana, diff. 325 l, Agheran the Brave. 325 l, Wolf as Prince Charming, Ileana Cosanzeana.

**1994, Apr. 8** Photo. Perf. 13½

| | | | | | |
|---|---|---|---|---|---|
| 3906 | A1103 | 70 l | multicolored | .20 | .20 |
| 3907 | A1103 | 115 l | multicolored | .25 | .20 |
| 3908 | A1103 | 125 l | multicolored | .25 | .20 |
| 3909 | A1103 | 245 l | multicolored | .30 | .30 |
| 3910 | A1103 | 255 l | multicolored | .60 | .25 |
| 3911 | A1103 | 325 l | multicolored | .65 | .25 |
| | Nos. 3906-3911 (6) | | | 2.95 | 1.35 |

## Easter A1104

## Trees — A1105

**1994, Apr. 21**

| | | | | | |
|---|---|---|---|---|---|
| 3912 | A1104 | 60 l | multicolored | .20 | .20 |

**Wmk. 398**

**1994, May 27** Photo. Perf. 13¼

| | | | | | |
|---|---|---|---|---|---|
| 3913 | A1105 | 35 l | Abies alba | .20 | .20 |
| 3914 | A1105 | 35 l | Pinus sylvestris | .20 | .20 |
| 3915 | A1105 | 45 l | Populus alba | .20 | .20 |
| 3916 | A1105 | 60 l | Quercus robur | .20 | .20 |
| 3917 | A1105 | 70 l | Larix decidua | .20 | .20 |
| 3918 | A1105 | 125 l | Fagus sylvatica | .20 | .20 |
| 3919 | A1105 | 350 l | Acer pseudoplatanus | .40 | .40 |
| 3920 | A1105 | 940 l | Fraxinus excelsior | 1.00 | 1.00 |
| 3921 | A1105 | 1440 l | Picea abies | 1.60 | 1.60 |
| 3922 | A1105 | 3095 l | Tilia platyphyllos | 3.50 | 3.50 |
| | Nos. 3913-3922 (10) | | | 7.70 | 2.20 |

For surcharges see Nos. 4221-4224.

## 1994 World Cup Soccer Championships, US — A1106

**1994, June 17** Unwmk.

| | | | | | |
|---|---|---|---|---|---|
| 3923 | A1106 | 90 l | Group A | .20 | .20 |
| 3924 | A1106 | 130 l | Group B | .25 | .25 |
| 3925 | A1106 | 150 l | Group C | .25 | .25 |
| 3926 | A1106 | 280 l | Group D | .55 | .25 |
| 3927 | A1106 | 500 l | Group E | .75 | .25 |
| 3928 | A1106 | 635 l | Group F | .95 | .30 |
| | Nos. 3923-3928 (6) | | | 2.95 | 1.35 |

**Souvenir Sheet**

| | | | | | |
|---|---|---|---|---|---|
| 3929 | A1106 | 2075 l | Action scene | 3.50 | 3.50 |

No. 3929 is airmail and contains one 54x42mm stamp.

---

## Intl. Olympic Committee, Cent. — A1107

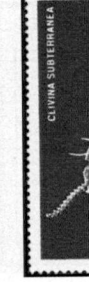

Ancient Olympians: 150 l, Torchbearer. 280 l, Discus thrower. 500 l, Wrestlers. 635 l, Arbitrator. 2075 l, Runners, emblem of Romanian Olympic Committee.

**1994, June 23**

| | | | | | |
|---|---|---|---|---|---|
| 3930 | A1107 | 150 l | multicolored | .25 | .20 |
| 3931 | A1107 | 280 l | multicolored | .50 | .30 |
| 3932 | A1107 | 500 l | multicolored | .85 | .35 |
| 3933 | A1107 | 635 l | multicolored | 1.10 | 1.05 |
| | Nos. 3930-3933 (4) | | | 2.70 | |

**Souvenir Sheet**

| | | | | | |
|---|---|---|---|---|---|
| 3934 | A1107 | 2075 l | multicolored | 3.50 | 3.50 |

No. 3934 contains one 54x42mm stamp. Romanian Olympic Committee, 80th anniv. (#3934).

## Miniature Sheets

### Mushrooms A1108

Edible: No. 3935a, 30 l, Craterellus cornucopioides. b, 60 l, Lepista nuda. c, 150 l, Boletus edulis. d, 940 l, Lycopordon perlatum. Poisonous: No. 3936a, 90 l, Boletus satanas. b, 280 l, Amanita phalloides. c, 350 l, Inocybe patonillardi. d, 500 l, Amanita muscaria.

**1994, Aug. 8** Photo.

| | | | | | |
|---|---|---|---|---|---|
| 3935 | A1108 | | Sheet of 4, #a-d. | 2.25 | 2.00 |
| 3936 | A1108 | | Sheet of 4, #a-d. | 2.25 | 2.00 |
| | Complete booklet, #3935-3936 | | | 4.75 | |

## PHILAKOREA '94 — A1109

Perf. 13½

60 l Tuning fork

**1994, Aug. 16**

| | | | | | |
|---|---|---|---|---|---|
| 3937 | A1109 | 60 l | Korean drummer | .20 | .20 |

**Souvenir Sheet**

| | | | | | |
|---|---|---|---|---|---|
| 3938 | A1109 | 2075 l | multicolored | 3.25 | 3.25 |

No. 3938 contains one 42x54mm stamp.

## Environmental Protection in Danube River Delta — A1110

Designs: 150 l, Huso huso. 280 l, Vipera ursini. 500 l, Haliaeetus albicilla. 635 l, Mustela lutreola. 2075 l, Periploca graeca.

**1994, Aug. 31**

| | | | | |
|---|---|---|---|---|
| 3939 | A1110 | 150 l | multicolored | .25 | .20 |
| 3940 | A1110 | 280 l | multicolored | .50 | .20 |
| 3941 | A1110 | 500 l | multicolored | .95 | .30 |
| 3942 | A1110 | 635 l | multicolored | 1.10 | .35 |

Nos. 3939-3942 (4)  2.80  1.05

**Souvenir Sheet**

3943 A1110 2075 l multicolored  3.50  3.50

No. 3943 contains one 54x42mm stamp.

Nos. 3654-3655 Surcharged

No. 3769 Surcharged

**1994**

| | | | | |
|---|---|---|---|---|
| 3944 | A1041 | 150 l | on 4.50 l | .25 | .20 |
| | | | #3654 | | |
| 3945 | A1069 | 150 l | on 10 l #3769 | .30 | .20 |
| 3946 | A1041 | 525 l | on 4.50 l | .90 | .30 |
| | | | #3655 | | |

Nos. 3944-3946 (3)  1.45  .70

Issued: #3944, 3946 9/9/94; #3945, 10/7/94.

**Perfs, Etc. as Before**

**1994, Sept. 15**    Photo.    Perf. 13

Circus Animal Acts — A1111

| | | | | |
|---|---|---|---|---|
| 3947 | A1111 | 90 l | Elephant | .20 | .20 |
| 3948 | A1111 | 130 l | Bear, vert. | .25 | .20 |
| 3949 | A1111 | 150 l | Monkeys | .25 | .20 |
| 3950 | A1111 | 280 l | Tiger | .50 | .20 |
| 3951 | A1111 | 500 l | Lion | .95 | .30 |
| 3952 | A1111 | 635 l | Horse | 1.10 | .35 |

Nos. 3947-3952 (6)  3.25  1.45

**1994, Oct. 10**

20th Intl. Fair, Bucharest — A1112

3953 A1112 525 l multicolored  .90  .30

**Fish**
A1113

World Wildlife Fund: 150 l, Acipenser ruthenus. 280 l, Acipenser guldenstaedti. 500 l, Acipenser stellatus. 635 l, Acipenser sturio.

**1994, Oct. 29**    Photo.    Perf. 13½

| | | | | |
|---|---|---|---|---|
| 3954 | A1113 | 150 l | multicolored | .30 | .20 |
| 3955 | A1113 | 280 l | multicolored | .60 | .20 |
| 3956 | A1113 | 500 l | multicolored | 1.00 | .35 |
| 3957 | A1113 | 635 l | multicolored | 1.25 | .40 |

Nos. 3954-3957 (4)  3.15  1.15

Issued in sheets of 10.

Chinese-Romanian Philatelic Exhibition — A1114

**1994, Oct. 29**    Photo.    Perf. 13½

| | | | | |
|---|---|---|---|---|
| 3958 | A1114 | 150 l | Serpent | .25 | .20 |
| 3959 | A1114 | 1135 l | Dragon | .60 | .20 |
| a. | | | Pair, #3958-3959 + label | 1.90 | |

  2.75  1.25

**1994, Oct. 31**

Romanian State Railway, 125th Anniv. A1115

3960 A1115 90 l multicolored  .20  .20

Famous People A1116

Designs: 30 l, Alex Drascu (1817-94). 60 l, Gh. Polizu (1819-86). 90 l, Gheorghe Tattarescu (1820-94), politician, prime minister. 150 l, Iulia Hasdeu (1869-88). 280 l, S. Mehedinti (1869-1962). 350 l, Camil Petrescu (1894-1957). 500 l, N. Paulescu (1869-1931). 940 l, L. Grigorescu (1894-1965).

**1994**    Photo.    Perf. 13½

| | | | | |
|---|---|---|---|---|
| 3961 | A1116 | 30 l | multicolored | .20 | .20 |
| 3962 | A1116 | 60 l | multicolored | .20 | .20 |
| 3962A | A1116 | 90 l | multicolored | .20 | .20 |
| 3963 | A1116 | 150 l | multicolored | .25 | .20 |
| 3964 | A1116 | 280 l | multicolored | .35 | .20 |
| 3965 | A1116 | 350 l | multicolored | .55 | .20 |
| 3966 | A1116 | 500 l | multicolored | .65 | .25 |
| 3967 | A1116 | 940 l | multicolored | 1.40 | .45 |

Nos. 3961-3967 (8)  3.80  1.90

Issued: 90 l, 12/28/94; others, 11/30/94.

**1994, Dec. 14**    Perf. 13½

Christmas — A1117

3968 A1117 60 l multicolored  .20  .20

For surcharge see No. 4250.

St. Mary's Romanian Orthodox Church, Cleveland, Ohio, 90th Anniv. — A1118

**1994, Dec. 21**    Photo.    Perf. 13½

3969 A1118 610 l multicolored  .90  .30

World Tourism Organization, 20th Anniv. — A1119

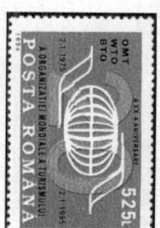

**1994, Dec. 22**

3970 A1119 525 l multicolored  .90  .30

Miniature Sheet

Romanian Military Decorations A1120

Year of medal - #3971: a, 30 l, Distinguished Flying Cross, 1938. b, 60 l, Military Cross, 3rd class, 1916. c, 150 l, Distinguished Service Medal, 1st Class, 1880. d, 940 l, Order of the Medal, Star, 1877.

**1994, Dec. 23**

3971 A1120  Sheet of 4, #a.-d.  2.00  2.00

Baby Animals A1121

**1994, Dec. 27**    Photo.    Perf. 13x½

| | | | | |
|---|---|---|---|---|
| 3972 | A1121 | 90 l | Kittens | .20 | .20 |
| 3973 | A1121 | 130 l | Puppies | .20 | .20 |
| 3974 | A1121 | 150 l | Kid goat | .20 | .20 |
| 3975 | A1121 | 280 l | Foal | .35 | .20 |
| 3976 | A1121 | 500 l | Bunnies | .80 | .25 |
| 3977 | A1121 | 635 l | Lambs | 1.00 | .35 |

Nos. 3972-3977 (6)  2.75  1.40

A1122

The Young Men of Brasov (Riders representing municipal districts of Brasov): 40 l, Tanar. 60 l, Batran. 150 l, Curcan. 280 l, Doro-bant. 350 l, Brasovechean. 500 l, Rosior. 635 l, Albior.

A1123

**1995, Jan. 31**    Photo.    Perf. 13½

3978 A1122 60 l dark blue  .20  .20

Save the Children organization.

**1995, Feb. 25**    Photo.    Perf. 13½

| | | | | |
|---|---|---|---|---|
| 3979 | A1123 | 40 l | multicolored | .20 | .20 |
| 3980 | A1123 | 60 l | multicolored | .20 | .20 |
| 3981 | A1123 | 150 l | multicolored | .20 | .20 |
| 3982 | A1123 | 280 l | multicolored | .35 | .20 |
| 3983 | A1123 | 350 l | multicolored | .55 | .20 |
| 3984 | A1123 | 500 l | multicolored | .65 | .25 |
| 3985 | A1123 | 635 l | multicolored | .90 | .30 |

Nos. 3979-3985 (7)  3.05  1.55

Liberation of Concentration Camps, 50th Anniv. — A1124

**1995, Mar. 24**    Perf. 13½

3986 A1124 960 l black & red  .90  .30

"50" UN emblem. 1615 l, Hand holding pen with flags of UN Charter countries.

Designs: 675 l, FAO emblem, grain. 960 l, "50" UN emblem.

**1995, Apr. 12**    Perf. 13½

| | | | | |
|---|---|---|---|---|
| 3987 | A1125 | 675 l | multicolored | .70 | .25 |
| 3988 | A1125 | 960 l | multicolored | .95 | .30 |
| 3989 | A1125 | 1615 l | multicolored | 1.60 | .55 |

Nos. 3987-3989 (3)  3.25  1.10

FAO & UN, 50th Anniv. A1125

Easter A1126

**1995, Apr. 14**

3990 A1126 60 l multicolored  .20  .20

Romanian Fairy Tales — A1127

Designs: 90 l, King riding horse across town. 130 l, Woman feeding animals, vert. 150 l, Man riding on winged horse. 280 l, Old man, young man. 500 l, Archer aiming at apple tree, vert. 635 l, Two people riding log pulled by galloping horses.

**1995, Apr. 20**    **Perf. 13½**
| | | | |
|---|---|---|---|
| 3991 A1127 | 90 l | multicolored | .20 .20 |
| 3992 A1127 | 130 l | multicolored | .20 .20 |
| 3993 A1127 | 150 l | multicolored | .20 .20 |
| 3994 A1127 | 280 l | multicolored | .25 .20 |
| 3995 A1127 | 500 l | multicolored | .50 .20 |
| 3996 A1127 | 635 l | multicolored | .65 .25 |
| Nos. 3991-3996 (6) | | | 2.00 1.25 |

Georges Enescu (1881-1955), Composer — A1128

**1995, May 5**    **Perf. 13½**
3997 A1128 960 l black & dp yellow    .95 .30

Peace & Freedom A1129

Europa: 150 l, Dove carrying piece of rainbow. 4370 l, Dove under rainbow with wings forming "Europa."

**1995, May 9**
3998 A1129 150 l multicolored    .20 .20
3999 A1129 4370 l multicolored    9.00 9.00

Lucian Blaga (1895-1961), Poet — A1130

**1995, May 9**
4000 A1130 150 l multicolored    .25 .20
See Nos. 4017-4021.

Methods of Transportation — A1131

Designs: 470 l, Bucharest Metro subway train, 1979. 675 l, Brasov aerial cable car, vert. 965 l, Sud Aviation SA 330 Puma helicopter, 1904 Trolleybus. 2550 l, Steam locomotive, 1869. 3410 l, Boeing 737-300.

**1995, May 30**    **Photo.**    **Perf. 13½**
| | | | |
|---|---|---|---|
| 4001 A1131 | 470 l | blk, gray & yel | .60 .30 |
| 4002 A1131 | 675 l | blk, gray & red | .90 .45 |
| 4003 A1131 | 965 l | blk, blk & gray | 1.25 .65 |
| 4004 A1131 | 2300 l | blk, gray & grn | 3.00 1.50 |
| 4005 A1131 | 2550 l | blk, gray & red | 3.25 1.60 |
| 4006 A1131 | 3410 l | bl, blk & gray | 4.50 2.25 |
| | | | 13.50 6.75 |

Nos. 4003, 4006 are airmail. No. 4006, 75th anniversary of Romanian air transportation. See Nos. 4055-4060.

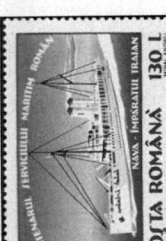
Romanian Maritime Service, Cent. — A1132

Ships: 90 l, Dacia, liner, vert. 130 l, Imparatul Traian, steamer. 150 l, Romania, steamer. 280 l, Costinesti, tanker. 960 l, Caransebes, container ship. 3410 l, Tutova, car ferry.

**1995, May 31**    **Photo.**    **Perf. 13½**
| | | | |
|---|---|---|---|
| 4007 A1132 | 90 l | multicolored | .20 .20 |
| 4008 A1132 | 130 l | multicolored | .20 .20 |
| 4009 A1132 | 150 l | multicolored | .20 .20 |
| 4010 A1132 | 280 l | multicolored | .30 .20 |
| 4011 A1132 | 960 l | multicolored | 1.00 .50 |
| 4012 A1132 | 3410 l | multicolored | 3.75 1.90 |
| Nos. 4007-4012 (6) | | | 5.65 3.20 |

A1133

European Nature Conservation Year: 150 l, Dama dama. 280 l, Otis tarda. 960 l, Cypripedium calceolus. 1615 l, Ghetarul scarisoara (stalagmites).

**1995, June 5**
| | | | |
|---|---|---|---|
| 4013 A1133 | 150 l | multicolored | .20 .20 |
| 4014 A1133 | 280 l | multicolored | .30 .20 |
| 4015 A1133 | 960 l | multicolored | 1.00 .50 |
| 4016 A1133 | 1615 l | multicolored | 1.75 .90 |
| Nos. 4013-4016 (4) | | | 3.25 1.80 |

A1134

Famous Romanians Type of 1995

Designs: 90 l, D.D. Rosca (1895-1980). 130 l, Vasile Conta (1845-1882). 280 l, Ion Barbu (1895-1961). 960 l, Iuliu Hatieganu (1885-1959). 1650 l, Dimitrie Brandza (1846-95).

**1995, June 26**    **Photo.**    **Perf. 13½**
| | | | |
|---|---|---|---|
| 4017 A1130 | 90 l | multicolored | .20 .20 |
| 4018 A1130 | 130 l | multicolored | .30 .20 |
| 4019 A1130 | 280 l | multicolored | .30 .20 |
| 4020 A1130 | 960 l | multicolored | 1.00 .50 |
| 4021 A1130 | 1650 l | multicolored | 1.75 .90 |
| Nos. 4017-4021 (5) | | | 3.45 2.00 |

**1995, July 10**    **Photo.**    **Perf. 13½**
4022 A1134 1650 l multicolored    1.75 .90
European Youth Olympic days.

Stamp Day — A1135

Illustration reduced.

**1995, July 15**
4023 A1135 960 l +715 l label    1.75 .90

Cernavoda Bridge, Cent. — A1136

**1995, July 27**    **Photo.**    **Perf. 13½**
4024 A1136 675 l multicolored    .75 .40

A1137

Fowl: 90 l, Anas platyrhynchos. 130 l, Gallus gallus (hen). 150 l, Numida meleagris. 280 l, Meleagris gallopavo. 960 l, Anser anser. 1650 l, Gallus gallus (rooster).

**1995, July 31**    **Photo.**    **Perf. 13½**
| | | | |
|---|---|---|---|
| 4025 A1137 | 90 l | multicolored | .20 .20 |
| 4026 A1137 | 130 l | multicolored | .20 .20 |
| 4027 A1137 | 150 l | multicolored | .20 .20 |
| 4028 A1137 | 280 l | multicolored | .30 .30 |
| 4029 A1137 | 960 l | multicolored | 1.00 1.00 |
| 4030 A1137 | 1650 l | multicolored | 1.75 1.75 |
| Nos. 4025-4030 (6) | | | 3.66 3.66 |

A1138

Institute of Air Medicine, 75th Anniv.; Gen. Dr. Victor Anastasiu (1886-1972).

**1995, Aug. 5**    **Perf. 13½**
4031 A1138 960 l multicolored    1.10 .55

Battle of Calugareni, 400th Anniv. — A1139

**1995, Aug. 13**
4032 A1139 100 l multicolored    .20 .20

Structure, year completed: 250 l, Giurgiu Castle, 1395. 500 l, Neamtului Castle, 1395, vert. 675 l, Sebes-Alba Mill, 1245. 1615 l, Dorohoi Church, 1495, vert. 1650 l, Military Observatory, Bucharest, 1895, vert.

Romanian Buildings — A1140

**1995, Aug. 28**
| | | | |
|---|---|---|---|
| 4033 A1140 | 250 l | multicolored | .25 .20 |
| 4034 A1140 | 500 l | multicolored | .55 .25 |
| 4035 A1140 | 675 l | multicolored | 1.10 .55 |
| 4036 A1140 | 1615 l | multicolored | 1.75 .90 |
| 4037 A1140 | 1650 l | multicolored | 1.75 .90 |
| Nos. 4033-4037 (5) | | | 5.40 2.80 |

A1141

Buildings: 675 l, Moldovita Monastery. 960 l, Hurez Monastery. 1615 l, Biertan Castle, horiz.

**1995, Aug. 31**
| | | | |
|---|---|---|---|
| 4038 A1141 | 675 l | multicolored | .75 .35 |
| 4039 A1141 | 960 l | multicolored | 1.00 .50 |
| 4040 A1141 | 1615 l | multicolored | 1.75 .75 |
| Nos. 4038-4040 (3) | | | 3.50 1.75 |

A1142

**1995, Sept. 8**
4041 A1142 1020 l multicolored    1.10 .55
Romania Open Tennis Tournament, Bucharest.

Magazine "Mathematics," Cent. — A1143

**1995, Sept. 15**
4042 A1143 100 l multicolored    .20 .20
Design: Ion N. Ionescu, founder.

Designs: 50 l, Albizia julibrissin. 100 l, Taxus baccata. 150 l, Paulownia tomentosa. 500 l, Strelitzia reginae. 960 l, Victoria amazonica. 2300 l, Rhododendron indicum.

Plants from Bucharest Botanical Garden — A1144

**1995, Sept. 29**    **Photo.**    **Perf. 13½**
| | | | |
|---|---|---|---|
| 4043 A1144 | 50 l | multicolored | .20 .20 |
| 4044 A1144 | 100 l | multicolored | .20 .20 |
| 4045 A1144 | 150 l | multicolored | .20 .20 |
| 4046 A1144 | 500 l | multicolored | .55 .30 |
| 4047 A1144 | 960 l | multicolored | 1.00 .50 |
| 4048 A1144 | 2300 l | multicolored | 2.50 1.25 |
| Nos. 4043-4048 (6) | | | 4.65 2.65 |

A1145

A1146

**1995, Oct. 1**    **Photo.**    **Perf. 13½**
4049 A1145 250 l Church of St. John .30 .20

City of Piatra Neamt, 600th anniv.

**1995, Nov. 9**

Emigres: 150 l, George Apostu (1934-86), sculptor. 250 l, Emil Cioran (1911-95), philosopher. 500 l, Eugen Ionescu (1909-94), writer. 960 l, Elena Vacarescu (1866-1947), writer. 1650 l, Mircea Eliade (1907-86), philosopher.
4050 A1146 150 l grn, gray & blk .20 .20
4051 A1146 250 l bl, gray & blk .30 .20
4052 A1146 500 l tan, brn & blk .55 .30
4053 A1146 960 l lake, mag & blk .55 .30
4054 A1146 1650 l tan, brn & blk 1.80 .90
Nos. 4050-4054 (5) 3.85 2.10

**1995, Nov. 16**
4055 A1131 285 l blk, gray & gray .30 .20

Transportation Type of 1995

285 l, IAR 80 fighter planes. 630 l, Training ship, Mesagerul. 715 l, IAR-316 Red Cross helicopter. 755 l, Cargo ship, Razboieni. 1575 l, IAR-818H seaplane. 1615 l, First electric tram, Bucharest, 1896, vert.

4056 A1131 630 l bl & red .70 .35
4057 A1131 715 l gray bl & red .80 .40
4058 A1131 755 l blk, bl & gray .85 .40
4059 A1131 1575 l blk, grn & gray 1.75 .85
4060 A1131 1615 l blk, grn & gray 1.75 .90
Nos. 4055, 4057, 4059 are air mail.
6.15 3.10

POSTA ROMÂNĂ
50 L
ATLETISM
CONCURSURILE PREOLIMPICE ATLANTA '95
A1147

1996 Summer Olympics, Atlanta — A1147

**1995, Dec. 8**
4061 A1147 50 l Track .20 .20
4062 A1147 100 l Gymnastics .20 .20
4063 A1147 150 l Two-man canoe .20 .20
4064 A1147 500 l Fencing .55 .25
4065 A1147 960 l Rowing-eights 1.10 .55
4066 A1147 2300 l Boxing 2.50 1.25
Nos. 4061-4066 (6) 4.75 2.65

**Souvenir Sheet**
4067 A1147 2610 l Gymnastics 2.75 1.40
No. 4067 contains one 42x54mm stamp.

---

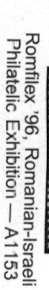

POSTA ROMÂNĂ
150 L
Tristan Tzara (1896-1963)
A1151

Tristan Tzara (1896-1963), Writer — A1151

**1995, Dec. 15**    **Photo.**    **Perf. 13½**
4068 A1148 100 l The Holy Family .20 .20

Christmas A1148

Insects A1154

POSTA ROMÂNĂ
250
MĂŞTI POPULARE - MARAMUREŞ
BULGAR, E
A1149

Folk Masks & Costumes — A1149

**1996, Jan. 31**
4069 A1149 250 l Maramures .25 .20
4070 A1149 500 l Moldova .55 .30
4071 A1149 960 l Moldova .90 .50
4072 A1149 1650 l Moldova, diff. 1.75 .90
Nos. 4069-4072 (4) vert. 3.55 1.90

ROMÂNIA 150 L
MĂRŢIŞOR
A1150

**1996, Mar. 27**    **Photo.**    **Perf. 13½**
4078 A1151 150 l multicolored .25 .20
4079 A1151 1500 l multicolored 1.60 .80

1500 l, Anton Pann (1796-1854), writer.

Illustration reduced.

ROMÂNIA 370 L
A1152

Easter A1152

**1996, Mar. 29**
4080 A1152 150 l multicolored .25 .20

---

posta română 70 L
Chrysomela vigintipunctata
A1154

**1996**

Designs: 70 l, Chrysomela vigintipunctata. 220 l, Cerambyx cerdo. 370 l, Entomoscelis adonidis. 650 l, Coccinella bipunctata. 700 l, Calosoma sycophanta. 740 l, Hedobia imperialis. 960 l, Oryctes nasicornis. 1000 l, Trichius fasciatus. 1500 l, Purpuricenus kaehleri. 2500 l, Anthaxia salicis.

4082 A1154 70 l multicolored .20 .20
4083 A1154 220 l multicolored .25 .20
4084 A1154 370 l multicolored .40 .20
4085 A1154 650 l multicolored .70 .35
4086 A1154 700 l multicolored .75 .40
4087 A1154 740 l multicolored .80 .40
4088 A1154 960 l multicolored .55 .20
4089 A1154 1000 l multicolored .55 .20
4090 A1154 1500 l multicolored .90 .20
4091 A1154 2500 l multicolored 1.40 .45
Nos. 4082-4091 (10) 5.25 2.25

Issued: 220, 740, 960, 1000, 1500, 4/16/96; 70, 370, 650, 700, 2500 l, 6/10/96. For surcharges see Nos. 4283-4289.

**Souvenir Sheet**

SPAMER
EXPOZITIA MONDIALA DE FILATELIE
2720
ROMÂNIA
A1155

Dumitru Prunariu, First Romanian Cosmonaut — A1155

**1996, Apr. 22**
4092 A1155 2720 l multicolored 3.00 1.50

ESPAMER '96, Aviation and Space Philatelic Exhibition, Seville, Spain.

ROMÂNIA 150 L
PE TERASĂ LA SINAIA
SPRELE PAŞTI
A1153

Romfilex '96, Romanian-Israeli Philatelic Exhibition — A1153

Paintings from National History Museum: a, 370 l, On the Terrace at Sinaia, by Theodor Aman. b, 150 l, The Palace, by M. Stoican. c, 1500 l, Old Jerusalem, by Reuven Rubin.

**1996, Apr. 5**
4081 A1153 Sheet of 3, #a-c. 2.25 1.10
For surcharges see No. 4202.

---

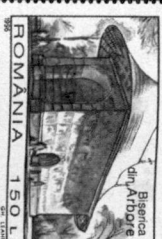

ROMÂNIA 150 L
Biserica din Arbore
A1159

UNESCO World Heritage Sites — A1159

Designs: 150 l, Arbore Church. 1500 l, Voronet Monastery. 2550 l, Humor Monastery.

**1996, Apr. 24**    **Photo.**    **Perf. 13½**
4099 A1159 150 l multicolored .20 .20
4100 A1159 1500 l multicolored 1.60 .80
4101 A1159 2550 l multicolored 2.75 1.25
Nos. 4099-4101 (3) 4.55 2.25

POSTA ROMÂNA 370 L
ANA ASLAN (1897-1988)
EUROPA '95
A1160

Famous Women — A1160

**1996, May 6**
4102 A1160 370 l multicolored .40 .20
4103 A1160 4140 l multicolored 4.25 2.25
a. Pair, #4102-4103 + 2 labels 4.75 2.50

Europa: 370 l, Ana Aslan (1897-1988), physician. 4140 l, Lucia Bulandra (1873-1961), actress.

ROMÂNIA 370 L
UNICEF
A1161

UNICEF, 50th Anniv. — A1161

Children's paintings: 370 l, Mother and children. 740 l, Winter Scene. 1500 l, Children and Sun over House. 2550 l, House on Stilts.

**1996, May 25**
4104 A1161 370 l multi .40 .20
4105 A1161 740 l multi .80 .40
4106 A1161 1500 l multi 1.60 .80
4107 A1161 2550 l multi, vert. 2.75 1.25
Nos. 4104-4107 (4) 5.55 2.65

Habitat II (#4107).

ROMÂNIA 220 L
TURNEUL FINAL AL CAMPIONATULUI EUROPEAN DE FOTBAL
ANGLIA 96
A1162

Euro '96, European Soccer Championships, Great Britain — A1162

Designs: a, 220 l, Goal keeper, ball. b, 370 l, Player with ball. c, Two players, ball. d, 1500 l, Three players, ball. e, 2550 l, Player dribbling ball.

**1996, May 27**
4108 A1162 Strip of 5, #a-e. 5.50 2.75

**Souvenir Sheet**
4109 A1162 4050 l multicolored 4.25 2.10
No. 4109 contains one 42x54mm stamp.

ROMÂNIA 220 L
ATLANTA '96
CENTENARUL JOCURILOR OLIMPICE
Box
A1158

1996 Summer Olympic Games, Atlanta — A1158

**1996, July 12**    **Photo.**    **Perf. 13½**
4093 A1158 220 l Boxing .20 .20
4094 A1158 370 l Athletics .40 .30
4095 A1158 740 l Rowing .50 .30
4096 A1158 1500 l Judo 1.10 .55
4097 A1158 2550 l Gymnastics 1.90 .95
Nos. 4093-4097 (5) 4.00 2.20

**Souvenir Sheet**
4098 A1158 4050 l Gymnastics, diff. 3.00 1.50
No. 4098 is airmail and contains one 54x42mm stamp. Olymphilex '96 (#4098).

**CAPEX '96 — A1163**

Designs: 150 l, Toronto Convention Center. 4050 l, CN Tower, Skydome, Toronto skyline.

**1996, May 29**
4110 A1163 150 l multicolored .20 .20

**Souvenir Sheet**
4111 A1163 4050 l multicolored 4.25 2.10
No. 4111 contains one 42x54mm stamp.

Resita Factory, 225th Anniv. A1164

**1996, June 20   Photo.   Perf. 13½**
4112 A1164 150 l dark red brown .20 .20
No. 3775 Surcharged

**1996, June 22**
4113 A1071 150 l on 10 l multi .20 .20

**Stamp Day — A1165**

Illustration reduced.

**1996, July 15**
4114 A1165 1500 l + 650 l label 1.60 .80

**Conifers — A1166**

**1996, Aug. 1**
4115 A1166 70 l Picea glauca .20 .20
4116 A1166 150 l Picea omori-ca .20 .20
4117 A1166 220 l Picea pungeus .20 .20
4118 A1166 740 l Picea stichen-sis .30 .20
4119 A1166 1500 l Pinus sylves-tris .65 .25
4120 A1166 3500 l Pinus pinas-ter 1.60 .40
Nos. 4115-4120 (6) 3.15 1.45

**Wildlife — A1167**

Designs: 70 l, Natrix natrix, vert. 150 l, Testudo hermanni, vert. 220 l, Alauda arvensis. 740 l, Vulpes vulpes. 1500 l, Phocaena phocaena, vert. 3500 l, Aquila chrysaetos, vert.

**1996, Sept. 12   Photo.   Perf. 13½**
4121 A1167 70 l multicolored .20 .20
4122 A1167 150 l multicolored .20 .20
4123 A1167 220 l multicolored .20 .20
4124 A1167 740 l multicolored .30 .20
4125 A1167 1500 l multicolored .65 .25
4126 A1167 3500 l multicolored 1.60 1.45
Nos. 4121-4126 (6) 3.15 1.45
For surcharge see No. 4348.

**Famous Men — A1168**

100 l, Stan Golestan (1875-1956). 150 l, Corneliu Coposu (1914-95). 370 l, Horia Vintila (1915-92). 1500 l, Alexandru Papana (1906-46).

**1996, Nov. 29**
4127 A1168 100 l black & rose red .20 .20
4128 A1168 150 l black & lake .20 .20
4129 A1168 370 l blk & yel brn .25 .20
4130 A1168 1500 l black & ver .95 .40
Nos. 4127-4130 (4) 1.60 1.00

**Madonna and Child — A1169**

**1996, Nov. 27**
4131 A1169 150 l multicolored .20 .20

**Antique Autombiles — A1170**

No. 4132: a, 280 l, 1933 Mercedes Benz. b, 70 l, 1930 Ford Spider. c, 150 l, 1932 Citroen. d, 220 l, 1936 Rolls Royce.
No. 4133: a, 2550 l, 1936 Mercedes Benz 500k Roadster. b, 2500 l, 1934 Bugatti "Type 59." c, 2550 l, 1931 Alfa Romeo 8C. d, 120 l, 1937 Jaguar SS 100.

**1996, Dec. 19   Photo.   Perf. 13½**
4132 A1170 Sheet of 4, #a.-d. .60 .30
4133 A1170 Sheet of 4, #a.-d. 6.25 3.00

Deng Xiaoping, China, and Margaret Thatcher, Great Britain — A1171

**1997, Jan. 20   Photo.   Perf. 13½**
4134 A1171 1500 l multicolored 1.10 .55
Hong Kong '97.

**Souvenir Sheet**

**1996, May 29**
4110 A1163 150 l multicolored .20 .20

**Fur-Bearing Animals — A1172**

Designs: 70 l, Mustela erminea. 150 l, Alopex lagopus. 220 l, Nyctereutes procyonoides. 740 l, Lutra lutra. 1500 l, Ondatra zibethica. 3500 l, Martes martes.

**1997, Feb. 14**
4135 A1172 70 l multicolored .20 .20
4136 A1172 150 l multicolored .20 .20
4137 A1172 220 l multicolored .20 .20
4138 A1172 740 l multicolored .30 .25
4139 A1172 1500 l multicolored .50 .55
4140 A1172 3500 l multicolored 1.10 1.60
Nos. 4135-4140 (6) 2.45
For surcharge see No. 4349.

Greenpeace, 25th Anniv. — A1173

Various views of MV Greenpeace.

**1997, Mar. 6**
4141 A1173 150 l multicolored .20 .20
4142 A1173 370 l multicolored .20 .20
4143 A1173 1940 l multicolored .55 .25
4144 A1173 2500 l multicolored .75 .35
Nos. 4141-4144 (4) 1.70 1.00

**Souvenir Sheet**
4145 A1173 4050 l multicolored 1.50 .75
No. 4145 contains one 49x38mm stamp.

**Famous People — A1174**

Designs: 200 l, Thomas A. Edison. 400 l, Franz Schubert. 3600 l, Miguel de Cervantes Saavedra (1547-1616), Spanish writer.

**1997, Mar. 27   Photo.   Perf. 13½**
4146 A1174 200 l multicolored .20 .20
4147 A1174 400 l multicolored .20 .20
4148 A1174 3600 l multicolored 1.00 .90
Nos. 4146-4148 (3) 1.40

Inauguration of Mobile Telephone Network in Romania — A1175

**1997, Apr. 7   Photo.   Perf. 13½**
4149 A1175 400 l multicolored .25 .20

Churches — A1176

**1997, Apr. 21   Photo.   Perf. 13½**
4150 A1176 200 l Surdesti .20 .20
4151 A1176 400 l Plopis .20 .20
4152 A1176 450 l Bogdan Voda .20 .20
4153 A1176 850 l Rogoz .25 .20
4154 A1176 3600 l Calinesti 1.00 .50
4155 A1176 6000 l Birsana 1.75 .90
Nos. 4150 4155 (6) 3.60 2.20

Shakespeare Festival, Craiova: a, 400 l, Constantin Serghe (1819-87) as Othello, 1855. b, 200 l, Al. Demetrescu Dan (1870-1948) as Hamlet, 1916. c, 3600 l, Ion Manolescu (1881-1959) as Hamlet, 1924. d, 2400 l, Gheorghe Cozorici (1933-93) as Hamlet, 1957.

**1997, Apr. 23   Photo.**
4156 A1177 Sheet of 4, #a.-d. + 4 labels 2.50 1.25

**1997, May 5**

Europa (Stories and Legends): 400 l, Vlad Tepes (Vlad the Impaler), prince upon which legend of Dracula said to be based. 4250 l, Dracula.

4157 A1178 400 l multicolored .20 .20
4158 A1178 4250 l multicolored 1.75 1.75
a. Pair, #4157-4158 + label 2.00 2.00

**1997, June 27    Photo.    Perf. 13½**

4159  A1179  450 l  multicolored    .20  .20

Natl. Theater, Cathedral, Statue of Mihai Viteazul.

Balcannax '97, Maximum Cards Exhibition, Cluj-Napoca.

Dolichothele uberiformis

Cacti
A1180

**1997, June 27**

Designs: 100 l, Dolichothele uberiformis; 250 l, Rebutia; 500 l, Ferocactus lamellosus; 450 l, Echinofossulocactus; 650 l, Thelocactus; 6150 l, Echinofossulocactus albatus.

4160  A1180  100 l  multicolored    .20  .20
4161  A1180  100 l  multicolored    .20  .20
4162  A1180  450 l  multicolored    .20  .20
4163  A1180  450 l  multicolored    .20  .20
4164  A1180  500 l  multicolored    .25  .20
4165  A1180  6150 l  multicolored    .25  .20
Nos. 4160-4165 (6)    2.40  1.25
                       3.45  2.25

Tourism Monument, Banat.

A1181b    A1181c

**1997, Aug. 3**

4175C  A1181b  950 l  multi    .60  .30

**1997, Aug. 13**

4175D  A1181c  450 l  multi    .30  .20

Stamp Printing Works, 125th anniv.

Belgian Antarctic Expedition, Cent. — A1181d

"Belgica" sailing ship and: 450 l, Emil Racovita, biologist; 650 l, Frederick A. Cook, anthropologist; 1600 l, photographer; 1600 l, Roald Amundsen; 3700 l, Adrien de Gerlache, expedition commander.

**1997, Aug. 18**

4175E  A1181d  450 l  multi    .30  .20
4175F  A1181d  650 l  multi    .45  .20
4175G  A1181d  1600 l  multi    1.00  .50
4175H  A1181d  3700 l  multi    2.25  1.10
Nos. 4175E-4175H (4)    4.00  2.00

**1997, Sept. 27**

4185  A1039  1050 l  on 4.50 l    .45  .25

No. 3619 Surcharged in Red

**1997, Oct. 28    Photo.    Perf. 13½**

4186  A1032  500 l  multi    .25  .20

Stamp Day — A1181

**1997, July 15    Photo.    Perf. 13½**

4166  A1181  3600 l + 1500 l label  3.00  1.50

Illustration reduced.

Ten different labels exist.

Nos. 3664-3670, 3672 Surcharged in Brownish Purple (#4167-4171, 4174) or Black (#4172-4173)

4167  A1043  250 l  on 2  #3664    .20  .20
4168  A1043  250 l  on 4  #3665    .20  .20
4169  A1043  250 l  on 4  #3666    .20  .20
4170  A1043  450 l  on 5 l  #3667    .30  .20
4171  A1043  450 l  on 6 l  #3668    .30  .20
4172  A1043  450 l  on 18 l  #3672    .30  .20
4173  A1043  950 l  on 9 l  #3670    .60  .30
4174  A1043  3600 l  on 8 l  #3669    2.25  1.10
Nos. 4167-4174 (8)    4.35  2.60

Sports
A1182

**1997, Nov. 21    Photo.    Perf. 13½**

4176  A1182  500 l  Rugby    .20  .20
4177  A1182  700 l  American football    .25  .20
4178  A1182  1750 l  Baseball    .65  .35
4179  A1182  3700 l  Mountain climbing, vert.    1.40  .70
Nos. 4176-4179 (4)    2.50  1.45

Design: 1050 l, King Carol I (1866-1914).

**1997, Nov. 8**

4187  A1184  500 l  multicolored    .20  .20
4188  A1184  1050 l  multicolored    .65  .30

Ion Mihalache, Politician (1882-1963). — A1184

Chamber of Commerce and Industry, Bucharest, 130th Anniv. — A1185

**1998, Jan. 29    Photo.    Perf. 13½**

4189  A1185  700 l  multicolored    .25  .20

No. 4189 is printed se-tenant with label.

**1997, July 31**

Designs: 650 l, Clocktower on Town Hall; 3700 l, Steps leading to castle and clocktower.

4175  A1181a  250 l  shown    .20  .20
4175A  A1181a  650 l    .40  .20
4175B  A1181a  3700 l  multi    2.25  1.10
Nos. 4175-4175B (3)    2.85  1.50

Castle Dracula, Sighisoara — A1181a

300 l, Tents at campsite; 700 l, Scouting emblem; 1050 l, Hands reaching toward each other; 1750 l, Carvings; 3700 l, Scouts seated around campfire.

**1997, Oct. 25    Photo.    Perf. 13½**

4180  A1183  300 l  multicolored    .20  .20
4181  A1183  700 l  multicolored    .25  .20
4182  A1183  1050 l  multicolored    .60  .30
4183  A1183  1750 l  multicolored    1.00  .50
4184  A1183  3700 l  multicolored    2.25  1.10
a.  A1183  Strip of 5, #4180-4184    4.50  2.25

Romanian Scouts
A1183

**1998, Feb. 5**

4190  A1186  900 l  Skiing    .30  .20
4191  A1186  3900 l  Figure skating    1.25  .65

1998 Winter Olympic Games, Nagano
A1186

EUROPA '91

**1998, Feb. 24    Photo.    Perf. 13½**

4192  A1187  900 l  multicolored    .30  .20

Illustration reduced.

Flag Day — A1187

Souvenir Sheet

**1998, Feb. 26    Photo.    Perf. 13x13½**

4193  A1188  900 l  4-Leaf clover    .50  .50
4194  A1188  3900 l  Heart    3.50  3.50

National Festivals and Holidays — A1188

Europa.

Famous People and Events of the 20th Century A1189

Designs: 700 l, Alfred Nobel, creation of Nobel Foundation, 1901; 900 l, Guglielmo Marconi, first radio transmission across Atlantic, 1901; 1500 l, Albert Einstein, theory of relativity, 1905; 3900 l, Trajan Vuia, flying machine, 1906.

**1998, Mar. 31    Photo.    Perf. 13½**

4195  A1189  700 l  multicolored    .25  .20
4196  A1189  900 l  multicolored    .30  .20
4197  A1189  1500 l  multicolored    .70  .40
4198  A1189  3900 l  multicolored    1.35  1.00
Nos. 4195-4198 (4)

See Nos. 4261-4265, 4312-4319, 4380-4383.

Roadside Shrines — A1190

**1998, Apr. 17**

4199  A1190  700 l  Cluj    .25  .20
4200  A1190  900 l  Prahova    .20  .20
4201  A1190  1500 l  Arges    .65  .60
Nos. 4199-4201 (3)

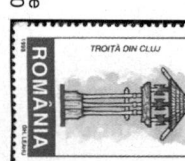

TROITA DIN CLUJ

ISRAEL '98

No. 4081 Surcharged in Red

**ROMANIA**

Designs: a, 900 l on 370 l. b, 700 l on 150 l. c, 3900 l on 1500 l.

**1998, May 12**

4202 A1153 Sheet of 3, #a.-c.   1.00   .50

Surcharge on #4202a, 4202c does not include '98 show emblem. This appears in the selvage to the right and left of the stamps.

**Romanian Surgical Society, Cent. — A1191**

Thoma Ionescu (1860-1926), founder.

**1998, May 18**

4203 A1191 1050 l multicolored   .20   .20

Nos. 3665-3669, 3672, 3676 Surcharged in Black, Red, Bright Green, Violet, Red Violet, Orange Brown, Dark Green, Violet Brown or Deep Blue

| | | | | |
|---|---|---|---|---|
| **1998** | **Photo.** | | **Perf. 13½** | |
| 4204 | A1043 | 50 l on 2 l #3665 (R) | .20 | .20 |
| 4205 | A1043 | 100 l on 8 l #3669 (BG) | .20 | .20 |
| 4206 | A1043 | 200 l on 4 l #3666 | .20 | .20 |
| 4207 | A1043 | 250 l on 45 l #3676 (Bl) | .20 | .20 |
| 4208 | A1043 | 350 l on 45 l #3676 (BG) | .40 | .25 |
| 4209 | A1043 | 400 l on 6 l #3670 | .20 | .25 |
| 4210 | A1043 | 400 l on 45 l #3676 (V) | .25 | .25 |
| 4211 | A1043 | 450 l on 45 l #3676 (BG) | .45 | .25 |
| 4212 | A1043 | 500 l on 18 l #3072 (Bl) | .50 | .25 |
| 4213 | A1043 | 850 l on 45 l #3676 (RV) | .55 | .25 |
| 4214 | A1043 | 900 l on 45 l #3676 (OB) | .90 | .45 |
| 4215 | A1043 | 1000 l on 45 l #3676 (V) | 1.00 | .50 |
| 4216 | A1043 | 1000 l on 45 l #3678 (DkG) | 1.10 | .55 |
| 4217 | A1043 | 1500 l on 45 l #3670 | 1.10 | .55 |
| 4218 | A1043 | 1600 l on 45 l #3667 (R) | 1.60 | .75 |
| 4219 | A1043 | 2500 l on 45 l #3676 (VB) | 1.60 | .80 |
| | | #3676 (R) | 2.75 | 1.40 |
| | | | 13.20 | 7.00 |

Nos. 4204-4219 (16)

Obliterator varies on Nos. 4204-4219.
Issued: Nos. 4204-4206, 4209, 4212, 5/21; 4216-4217, 7/6; others, 1998.

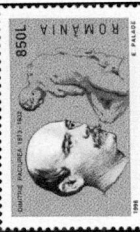

**1998 World Cup Soccer Championships, France — A1192**

Various soccer plays, stadium: a, 800 l. b, 1050 l. c, 1850 l. d, 4150 l.

**1998, June 10   Photo.   Perf. 13½**

4220 A1192 Sheet of 4, #a.-d.   .90   .45

Nos. 3913-3915, 3918 Surcharged in Red Violet, Blue, Black, or Red

**Wmk. 398   Photo.**
**Design A1105   Perf. 13**

Night Birds A1193

**1998, June 30**

| | | | | |
|---|---|---|---|---|
| 4221 | A1193 | 700 l on 125 l #3918 (RV) | .25 | .20 |
| 4222 | A1193 | 800 l on 35 l #3914 (Bl) | .25 | .20 |
| 4223 | A1193 | 1050 l on 45 l #3915 (Bk) | .35 | .20 |
| 4224 | A1193 | 4150 l on 15 l #3913 (R) | 1.25 | .65 |
| | | Nos. 4221-4224 (4) | 2.10 | 1.25 |

Designs: 700 l, Apteryx australis, vert. 1500 l, Tyto alba, vert. 1850 l, Rallus aquaticus. 2450 l, Caprimulgus europaeus.

**1998, Aug. 12   Unwmk.**

| | | | | |
|---|---|---|---|---|
| 4225 | A1193 | 700 l multicolored | .25 | .20 |
| 4226 | A1193 | 1500 l multicolored | .50 | .25 |
| a. | | Complete booklet, 4 each, | 3.00 | |
| 4227 | A1193 | 1850 l multicolored | .60 | .30 |
| 4228 | A1193 | 2450 l multicolored | .80 | .40 |
| a. | | Complete booklet, 4 each, | 5.75 | |
| | | Nos. 4225-4228 (4) | 2.15 | 1.15 |

Stamp Day A1194

**1998, July   Litho.   Perf. 13½**

| | | | | |
|---|---|---|---|---|
| 4229 | A1194 | 700 l + 850 l Romania #4 | .25 | .20 |
| 4230 | A1194 | 1050 l Romania #1 | .35 | .20 |
| a. | | Complete booklet, #4225,4226 | 1.75 | |

**Souvenir Sheet**

4231 A1194 4150 l +850 l Romania #2-3   1.60   1.60

No. 4231 contains one 54x42mm stamp.

**Natl. Uprising, 150th Anniv. — A1195**

**1998, Sept. 28   Photo.   Perf. 13½**

4232 A1195 1050 l multicolored   .20   .20

A1197

German Personalities in Banat: 800 l, Nikolaus Lenau (1802-50). 1850 l, Stefan Jäger (1877-1962). 4150 l, Adam Müller-Guttenbrunn (1852-1923).

**1998, Oct. 16   Photo.   Perf. 13½**

| | | | | |
|---|---|---|---|---|
| 4233 | A1196 | 800 l multicolored | .20 | .20 |
| 4234 | A1196 | 1850 l multicolored | .35 | .40 |
| 4235 | A1196 | 4150 l multicolored | .75 | .80 |
| | | Nos. 4233-4235 (3) | 1.30 | .80 |

**1998, Nov. 4**

4236 A1197 1100 l multicolored   .40   .20

Intl. Year of the Ocean.

Nos. 3652-3653, 3704-3709, 3776-3779, 3781, 3795, 3968 Surcharged in Green, Black, Red, Red Violet or Deep Blue

| | | | | |
|---|---|---|---|---|
| **1998** | | **Photo.** | **Perf. 13½** | |
| 4237 | A1041 | 50 l on #3652 (G) | .20 | .20 |
| 4238 | A1041 | 50 l on #3653 (Bk) | .20 | .20 |
| 4238A | A1054 | 50 l on #3704 (Bk) | .20 | .20 |
| 4239 | A1054 | 50 l on #3705 (R) | .20 | .20 |
| 4240 | A1054 | 50 l on #3706 (R) | .20 | .20 |
| 4241 | A1054 | 50 l on #3707 (R) | .20 | .20 |
| 4242 | A1054 | 50 l on #3708 (Bk) | .20 | .20 |
| 4243 | A1054 | 50 l on #3709 (R) | .20 | .20 |
| 4244 | A1054 | 50 l on #3776 (RV) | .20 | .20 |
| 4245 | A1054 | 50 l on #3777 (DB) | .20 | .20 |
| 4246 | A1054 | 50 l on #3778 (Bk) | .20 | .20 |
| 4247 | A1054 | 50 l on #3779 (G) | .20 | .20 |
| 4248 | A1054 | 50 l on #3781 (R) | .20 | .20 |
| 4249 | A1075 | 2000 l on #3795 (G) | .60 | .30 |
| 4250 | A1117 | 2600 l on #3968 (R) | .80 | .40 |
| | | Nos. 4237-4250 (15) | 4.00 | 3.30 |

Obliterator varies on Nos. 4237-4250.
Issued: 4237-4238, 11/10; 4238A, 11/27; 4249-4250, 12/22.

A1199

A1198

Lighthouses.

**1998, Dec. 28**

| | | | | |
|---|---|---|---|---|
| 4251 | A1198 | 900 l Genovez | .25 | .20 |
| 4252 | A1198 | 1000 l Constanta | .30 | .20 |
| 4253 | A1198 | 1100 l Sfantu Gheorghe | .35 | .40 |
| 4254 | A1198 | 2600 l Sulina | .75 | 1.00 |
| | | Nos. 4251-4254 (4) | 1.65 | 1.00 |

Flowers: 350 l, Tulipa gesneriana. 850 l, Dahlia variabilis. 1100 l, Lilium martagon. 4450 l, Rosa centifolia.

**1998, Nov. 25**

| | | | | |
|---|---|---|---|---|
| 4255 | A1199 | 350 l multicolored | .20 | .20 |
| 4256 | A1199 | 850 l multicolored | .25 | .20 |
| 4257 | A1199 | 1100 l multicolored | .30 | .20 |
| 4258 | A1199 | 4450 l multicolored | 1.25 | .65 |
| | | Nos. 4255-4258 (4) | 2.00 | 1.25 |

**Universal Declaration of Human Rights, 50th Anniv. — A1200**

**1998, Dec. 10**

4259 A1200 700 l multicolored   .25   .20

**Dimitrie Paciurea (1873-1932), Sculptor — A1200a**

**1998, Dec. 11   Photo.   Perf. 13¼**

4259A A1200a 850 l ocher & blk   .20   .20

**Total Eclipse of the Sun, Aug. 11, 1999 — A1201**

**1998, Dec. 28**

4260 A1201 1100 l multi + label   .35   .20

**Events of the 20th Cent. Type**

Designs: 350 l, Sinking of the Titanic, 1912. 1100 l, "Coanda 1910" aircraft with air-reactive (jet) engine, 1919, by Henri Coanda (1886-1972). 1600 l, Louis Blériot's (1872-1936) Calais-Dover flight, 1000. 2000 l, Opening of the Panama Canal, 1914. 2600 l, Russian Revolution, 1917.

**1998, Dec. 22   Photo.   Perf. 13½**

| | | | | |
|---|---|---|---|---|
| 4261 | A1189 | 350 l multicolored | .20 | .20 |
| 4262 | A1189 | 1100 l multicolored | .30 | .20 |
| 4263 | A1189 | 1600 l multicolored | .45 | .25 |
| 4264 | A1189 | 2000 l multicolored | .60 | .30 |
| 4265 | A1189 | 2600 l multicolored | .75 | .40 |
| | | Nos. 4261-4265 (5) | 2.30 | 1.35 |

No. 3687 Surcharged in Red or Black

**1999, Feb. 10   Photo.   Perf. 13½**

| | | | | |
|---|---|---|---|---|
| 4266 | A1047 | 100 l on 1 l (R) | .20 | .20 |
| 4267 | A1047 | 250 l on 1 l (Bk) | .20 | .20 |

Obliterator is a guitar on #4266 and a saxophone on #4267.

No. 3796 Surcharged in Black, Red, Green, or Brown

**1999, Jan. 22**

| | | | | |
|---|---|---|---|---|
| 4268 | A1076 | 50 l on 15 l (Blk) | .20 | .20 |
| 4269 | A1076 | 50 l on 15 l (R) | .20 | .20 |
| 4270 | A1076 | 400 l on 15 l (Grn) | .20 | .20 |

**1999, Jan. 17**

Monasteries — A1203

| 4271 | A1076 | 2300 l | on 15 l (Brn) | .70 | .35 |
| 4272 | A1076 | 3200 l | on 15 l (Blk) | 1.00 | .50 |

Nos. 4268-4272 (5)     2.30 1.45

Obliterator varies on Nos. 4268-4272.

| 4273 | A1203 | 500 l | Arnota | .20 | .20 |
| 4274 | A1203 | 700 l | Bistrita | .20 | .20 |
| 4275 | A1203 | 1100 l | Dintr'un Lemn | .30 | .20 |
| 4276 | A1203 | 2100 l | Govora | .60 | .30 |
| 4277 | A1203 | 4850 l | Tismana | 1.40 | .70 |

Nos. 4273-4277 (5)     2.70 1.60

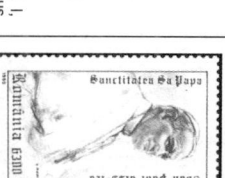

Shrub
Flowers
A1204

**1999, Feb. 15**

| 4278 | A1204 | 350 l | multicolored | .20 | .20 |
| 4279 | A1204 | 1000 l | multicolored | .30 | .20 |
| 4280 | A1204 | 1100 l | multicolored | .30 | .20 |
| 4281 | A1204 | 5350 l | multicolored | 1.50 | .75 |

Nos. 4278-4281 (4)     2.30 1.35

350 l, Magnolia x soulangiana. 1000 l, Stewartia malacodendron. 1100 l, Hibiscus rosa-sinensis. 5350 l, Clematis patens.

Easter
A1205

**1999, Mar. 15**     Photo.

4282 A1205 1100 l multi     .25 .20

posta româná
Chrysomela vigintipunctata

**1999, Mar. 22**     Litho.

| 4283 | A1154 | 100 l | on 70 l (BP) | .20 | .20 |
| 4284 | A1154 | 200 l | on 70 l (R) | .20 | .20 |
| 4285 | A1154 | 200 l | on 70 l (V) | .20 | .20 |
| 4286 | A1154 | 1500 l | on 70 l | .45 | .20 |
| 4287 | A1154 | 1600 l | on 70 l (G) | .45 | .20 |
| 4288 | A1154 | 3200 l | on 70 l (Bl) | .95 | .45 |
| 4289 | A1154 | 6000 l | on 70 l (G) | 1.75 | .90 |

Nos. 4283-4289 (7)     4.20 2.35

Obliterators on Nos. 4283-4289 are various dinosaurs.

No. 4082 Surcharged in Bright Pink, Red, Violet, Black, Green or Blue

Designs: 1200 l, Keys on chain. 2100 l, Necklace. 3200 l, Necklace, holder. 2600 l, Necklace. 3200 l, Key holder.

Jewelry — A1206

**1999, Mar. 29**     Photo.

4290-4293 A1206 Set of 4     1.75 .90

"Arakanga - Ara macao"

Birds — A1207

Perf. 13½     1.75 .90

---

**1999, Apr. 26**     Perf. 13½x13¼

| 4294 | A1207 | 1100 l | Ara macao | .30 | .25 |
| 4295 | A1207 | 2700 l | Pavo albus | .60 | .30 |
| 4296 | A1207 | 3700 l | Pavo cristatus | .80 | .45 |
| 4297 | A1207 | 5700 l | Cacatua galerita | 1.25 | .65 |

Nos. 4294-4297 (4)     2.95 1.70

Council of Europe, 50th
Anniv. — A1208

**1999, May 5**     Photo.

4298 A1208 2300 l multi + label     .30 .20

A1209

**1999, May 7**

4299 A1209 Sheet of 6     3.75 1.90

Issued in sheets containing one strip of #4299a-4299d, 1 ea #4299a, 4299d + 2 labels.

Visit of Pope John Paul II to Romania: a, 63300 l, Pope John Paul II. b, 1300 l, St. Peter's Basilica. c, 1600 l, Patriarchal Cathedral, Bucharest. d, 2300 l, Patriarch Teoctist.

A1210

**1999, May 17**

| 4300 | A1210 | 1100 l | multicolored | .20 | .20 |
| 4301 | A1210 | 5700 l | multicolored | .40 | .40 |

Nos. 4300-4301 printed with se-tenant label.

Europa: 1100 l, Anas clypeata. 5700 l, Ciconia nigra.

Famous Personalities — A1211

**1999, May 31**

| 4302 | A1211 | 600 l | multicolored | .20 | .20 |
| 4303 | A1211 | 1100 l | multicolored | .25 | .20 |
| 4304 | A1211 | 2600 l | multicolored | .55 | .25 |
| 4305 | A1211 | 7300 l | multicolored | 1.75 | .75 |

Nos. 4302-4305 (4)     2.50 1.40

Designs: 600 l, Gheorghe Cartan (1849-1911). 1100 l, George Calinescu (1899-1965), writer. 2600 l, Johann Wolfgang von Goethe (1749-1832), poet. 7300 l, Honoré de Balzac (1799-1850), novelist.

Total Solar Eclipse, Aug. 11 — A1212

**1999, June 21**     Photo.

4306 A1212 1100 l multicolored     .25 .20

No. 4306 printed se-tenant with label.

---

**1999, July 29**     Photo.

| 4307 | A1213 | 400 l | Smoking | .20 | .20 |
| 4308 | A1213 | 800 l | Alcohol | .20 | .20 |
| 4309 | A1213 | 1500 l | Drugs | .50 | .25 |
| 4310 | A1213 | 2300 l | AIDS | 1.15 | .85 |

Nos. 4307-4310 (4)

Health
Dangers
A1213

Luciano Pavarotti Concert in Bucharest on Day of Solar Eclipse — A1214

**1999, Aug. 9**

4311 A1214 8100 l multi     1.60 .80

Events of the 20th Century Type

**1999, Aug. 30**

| 4312 | A1189 | 800 l | multi | .20 | .20 |
| 4313 | A1189 | 3000 l | multi | .60 | .30 |
| 4314 | A1189 | 7300 l | multi | 1.40 | .75 |
| 4315 | A1189 | 17,000 l | multi | 5.70 | 3.00 |

Nos. 4312-4315 (4)

Designs: 800 l, Alexander Fleming discoverers penicillin, 1928. 3000 l, League of Nations, 1920. 7300 l, Harold C. Urey discovers heavy water, 1931. 17,000 l, First marine oil drilling platform, off Beaumont, Texas, 1934.

**1999, Sept. 24**     Photo.     Perf. 13¼

| 4316 | A1189 | 1500 l | multi | .30 | .30 |
| 4317 | A1189 | 3000 l | multi | .55 | .30 |
| 4318 | A1189 | 7300 l | multi | 1.40 | .70 |
| 4319 | A1189 | 17,000 l | multi | 3.25 | 1.60 |

Nos. 4316-4319 (4)     5.50 2.80

Designs: 1500 l, Karl Landsteiner (1868-1943), discoverer of blood groups. 3000 l, Nicolae C. Paulescu (1869-1931), diabetes researcher. 7300 l, Otto Hahn (1879-1968), discoverer of nuclear fission. 17,000 l, Ernst Ruska (1906-88), inventor of electron microscope.

UPU, 125th
Anniv. — A1215

**1999, Oct. 9**

4320 A1215 3100 l multi     .60 .30

Comic
Actors — A1216

**1999, Oct. 21**

| 4321 | A1216 | 900 l | blk & brn | .20 | .20 |
| 4322 | A1216 | 1500 l | blk & brn red | .25 | .20 |
| 4323 | A1216 | 3100 l | blk & brn red | .55 | .25 |
| 4324 | A1216 | 7950 l | blk & brn red | 1.40 | .70 |
| 4325 | A1216 | 8850 l | blk & brn red | 1.50 | .75 |

Nos. 4321-4325 (5)     3.90 2.10

Designs: 900 l, Grigore Vasiliu Birlic. 1500 l, Toma Caragiu. 3100 l, Constantin Tanase. 7950 l, Charlie Chaplin. 8850 l, Oliver Hardy and Stan Laurel, horiz.

---

New
Olympic
Sports
A1218

**1999, Nov. 10**     Perf. 13¼

| 4327 | A1218 | 1600 l | Snowboarding | .25 | .20 |
| 4328 | A1218 | 1700 l | Softball | .35 | .20 |
| 4329 | A1218 | 7950 l | Taekwondo | 1.40 | .70 |

Nos. 4327-4329 (3)

Stavropoleos Church, 275th
Anniv. — A1217

**1999, Oct. 29**

4326 A1217 2100 l multi     .40 .20

Christmas — A1219

**1999, Nov. 29**     Photo.     Perf. 13¼

4330-4331 A1219 Set of 2     .80 .40

Designs: 1500 l, Christmas tree, bell. 3100 l, Santa Claus.

UN Rights of the Child Convention, 10th Anniv. — A1220

**1999, Nov. 30**     Photo.     Perf. 13¼

| 4332 | A1220 | 900 l | multi | .20 | .20 |
| 4333 | A1220 | 3400 l | multi | .60 | .30 |
| 4334 | A1220 | 8850 l | multi | 2.30 | 1.25 |

Nos. 4332-4334 (3)

Children's art by: 900 l, A. Vieru. 3400 l, A. M. Bulete, vert. 8850 l, M. L. Rogojeanu.

Princess
Diana — A1221

**1999, Dec. 2**

4335 A1221 6000 l multi     1.00 .45

Issued in sheets of 4.

Ferrari Automobiles — A1222

**ROMÂNIA 9050L**

Printing of Bible in Latin by Johann Gutenberg, 550th Anniv. — A1231

**2000, May 19**

4374 A1231 9050 l multi    1.25   .60

No. 4084 Surcharged in Red

*Entomoscelis adonidis* — **10000 L** posta română

**2000, May 31   Photo.   Perf. 13¼**

| 4375 | A1154 | 10,000 l on 370 l | 1.40 | .70 |
| 4376 | A1154 | 19,000 l on 370 l | 2.50 | 1.25 |
| 4377 | A1154 | 34,000 l on 370 l | 4.75 | 2.40 |
|  |  |  | 8.65 | 4.35 |

Nos. 4375-4377 (3)

**Souvenir Sheet**

CAMPIONATUL EUROPEAN DE FOTBAL 2000

2000 European Soccer Championships — A1232

No. 4378: a, 3800 l, Romania vs. Portugal (red and green flag); b, 3800 l, England (red and white flag) vs. Romania. c, 10,150 l, Romania vs. Germany. d, 10,150 l, Goalie.

**2000, June 20**

4378 A1232   Sheet of 4, #a-d   3.75   1.90

First Zeppelin Flight, Cent. A1233

**2000, July 12**

4379 A1233 2100 l multi   .25   .20

Stamp Day.

**20th Century Type of 1998**

2100 l, Enrico Fermi, formula, 1st nuclear reactor, 1942. 2200 l, Signing of UN Charter, 1945. 2400 l, Edith Piaf sings "La Vie en Rose," 1947. 6000 l, 1st ascent of Mt. Everest, by Sir Edmund Hillary and Tenzing Norgay, 1953.

**2000, July 12**

4380-4383 A1189   Set of 4   1.60   .80

---

Flowers — A1229

 **1700 L POSTA ROMANA**

Designs: 1700 l, Senecio cruentus. 3100 l, Clivia miniata. 5800 l, Plumeria rubra. 10,050 l, Fuchsia hybrida.

**2000, Apr. 20   Photo.   Perf. 13¼**

| 4361 | A1229 | 1700 l multi | .25 | .20 |
| 4362 | A1229 | 3100 l multi | .40 | .40 |
| 4363 | A1229 | 5800 l multi | .80 | .40 |
| 4364 | A1229 | 10,050 l multi | 1.40 | .70 |
|  |  |  | 2.85 | 1.50 |

Nos. 3620-3624 Surcharged

 **1700 L POSTA ROMANA**

**Methods & Perfs. as Before**

**2000, Apr. 24**

| 4365 | A1033 | 1700 l on 50b | .25 | .20 |
| 4366 | A1033 | 1700 l on 1.50 l | .25 | .20 |
| 4367 | A1033 | 1700 l on 2 l | .25 | .20 |
| 4368 | A1033 | 1700 l on 3 l | .25 | .20 |
| 4369 | A1033 | 1700 l on 4 l | .25 | .20 |
|  |  |  | 1.25 | 1.00 |

Nos. 4365-4369 (5)

**Europa, 2000**   Common Design Type

**2000, May 9   Photo.   Perf. 13¼**

4370 CD17 10,150 l multi   1.40   .70

Nos. 3634, 3637 Surcharged in Red

 **1700 L POSTA ROMANĂ**

**Methods and Perfs as Before**

**2000, May 17**

| 4371 | A1036 | 1700 l on 50b | .40 | .20 |
| 4372 | A1036 | 1700 l on 3.50 l | .40 | .20 |

 **ROMÂNIA 3800L**

Unification of Walachia, Transylvania and Moldavia by Michael the Brave, 400th Anniv. — A1230

**2000, May 19   Photo.   Perf. 13¼**

4373 A1230 3800 l multi   .50   .25

---

 **1700 L ROMANIA**

Nos. 4121, 4135 Surcharged in Red

**Methods and Perfs. as Before**

**2000**

| 4348 | A1167 | 1700 l on 70 l multi | .30 | .20 |
| 4349 | A1172 | 1700 l on 70 l multi | .30 | .20 |

Issued: No. 4348, 3/14; No. 4349, 3/13. Obliterator on No. 4349 is a crown.

Birds A1228

 **1700 L ROMÂNIA** *Paradisaea apoda*

Designs: 1700 l, Paradisaea apoda. 2400 l, Diphyllodes magnificus. 9050 l, Lophorina superba. 10,050 l, Cicinnurus regius.

**2000, Mar. 20   Photo.   Perf. 13¼**

| 4350 | A1228 | 1700 l multi | .25 | .20 |
| 4351 | A1228 | 2400 l multi | .35 | .20 |
| 4352 | A1228 | 9050 l multi | 1.40 | .70 |
| 4353 | A1228 | 10,050 l multi | 1.50 | .75 |
|  |  |  | 3.50 | 1.85 |

Nos. 4350-4353 (4)

 **1900 L** MĂNĂSTIREA CURTEA DE ARGES

Nos. 3658-3659 Surcharged in Red

**Methods & Perfs. as Before**

**2000, Mar. 31**

| 4354 | A1042 | 1900 l on 1 l | (#3658) | .25 | .20 |
| 4355 | A1042 | 2000 l on 1 l | (#3659) | .30 | .20 |

 **STOLNIC CONSTANTIN CANTACUZINO 1640-1716   1700 L POSTA ROMANA**

Nos. 3626-3630 Surcharged

**Methods & Perfs. as Before**

**2000, Apr. 12**

| 4356 | A1034 | 1700 l on 50b | .25 | .20 |
| 4357 | A1034 | 1700 l on 1.50 l | .25 | .20 |
| 4358 | A1034 | 1700 l on 2 l | .25 | .20 |
| 4359 | A1034 | 1700 l on 3 l | .25 | .20 |
| 4360 | A1034 | 1700 l on 4 l | .25 | .20 |
|  |  |  | 1.25 | 1.00 |

Nos. 4356-4360 (5)

Appearance of obliterator varies.

---

Designs: 1500 l, 1968 365 GTB/4. 1600 l, 1970 Dino 246 GT. 1700 l, 1973 365 GT/4 BB. 7950 l, Mondial 3.2. 8850 l, 1994 F 355. 14,500 l, 1998 456M GT.

**1999, Dec. 17**

| 4336 | A1222 | 1500 l multi | .25 | .20 |
| 4337 | A1222 | 1600 l multi | .30 | .20 |
| 4338 | A1222 | 1700 l multi | .30 | .20 |
| 4339 | A1222 | 7950 l multi | 1.40 | .70 |
| 4340 | A1222 | 8850 l multi | 1.50 | .75 |
| 4341 | A1222 | 14,500 l multi | 2.50 | 1.25 |
|  |  |  | 6.25 | 3.30 |

Nos. 4336-4341 (6)

 **REVOLUȚIA ROMÂNĂ 2100 L**

Romanian Revolution, 10th Anniv. — A1223

**1999, Dec. 21   Perf. 13¼**

4342 A1223 2100 l multi   .35   .20

**ROMÂNIA 6100L**

Start of Accession Negotiations With European Union — A1224

**2000, Jan. 13   Photo.   Perf. 13¼**

4343 A1224 6100 l multi   1.00   .50

**Souvenir Sheet**

**3400 L** Mihail Eminescu (1850-89), Poet A1225

Scenes from poems and Eminescu: a, At R, clean-shaven. b, At R, with mustache. c, At L, with trimmed mustache. d, At L, with handle-bar mustache.

**2000, Jan. 15**

4344 A1225 3400 l   Sheet of 4   2.25   1.10

a.-d.   Any single   .55   .25

 **1500 ROMÂNIA**

Valentine's Day — A1226

**2000, Feb. 1   Photo.   Perf. 13¼**

| 4345 | A1226 | 1500 l Cupid | .25 | .20 |
| 4346 | A1226 | 7950 l Couple kissing | 1.25 | .65 |

**ROMÂNIA 1700 L**

Easter — A1227

**2000, Feb. 29**

4347 A1227 1700 l multi   .30   .20

No. 3680
Surcharged in
Green

**Methods and Perfs as Before**

**2000, July 31**
4384 A1044 1700 l on 160 l    .30   .20

**20th Century Type of 1998**
4385-4388 A1189    Set of 4

**2000, Aug. 28**    **Photo.**    **Perf. 13½**
   Set of 4    2.75 1.40

2000
Summer
Olympics,
Sydney
A1234

Designs: 1700 l, First artificial satellite, 1957, 3900 l, Yuri Gagarin, first man in space, 1961, 6400 l, First heart transplant performed by Christiaan Barnard, 1967. 11,300 l, Neil Armstrong, first man on the moon, 1969.

**2000, Sept. 7**
4389-4392 A1234    Set of 4

**Souvenir Sheet**
4393 A1234 11,300 l Runner    1.40   .70

No. 4393 contains one 42x54mm stamp.

Designs: 1700 l, Boxing, 2200 l, High jump, 3900 l, Weight lifting. 6200 l, Gymnastics.

**2000, Sept. 7**    **Photo.**    **Perf. 13½**
4389-4392    1.75   .85

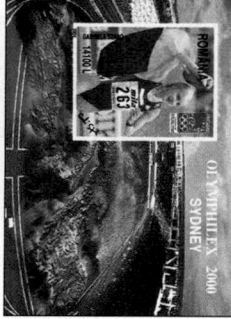

Souvenir Sheet

2000
Olymphilex 2000, Sydney — A1235

**2000, Sept. 7**    **Imperf.**
4394 A1235 14,100 l Gabriela Szabo    1.75   .85
   1.25   .60

Bucharest
Palaces
A1236

Designs: 1700 l, Agricultural Ministry Palace, vert. 2200 l, Cantacuzino Palace, 2400 l, Grigore Ghica Palace. 3900 l, Stirbei Palace.

**2000, Sept. 29**    **Photo.**    **Perf. 13½**
4395-4398 A1236    Set of 4

No. 4115 Surcharged in Brown

**2000, Oct. 11**    **Photo.**    **Perf. 13½**
4403 A1166 300 l on 70 l multi    .20   .20

---

No. 3664 Surcharged in
Blue

**2000, Oct. 26**    **Perf. 13½**
4404 A1043 300 l on 11 blue    .20   .20

No. 3991 Surcharged in Red Violet

**2000, Nov. 3**
4405 A1127 2000 l on 90 l multi    .90   .45

**2000, Nov. 3**
4406 A1237 11,300 l multi

European Human
Rights Convention,
50th
Anniv. — A1237

**2000, Nov. 3**    **Perf. 13½**
   .90   .45

No. 3858
Surcharged

**2000, Nov. 28**
4407 A1093 2000 l on 29 l multi    .20   .20

Endangered Wild Cats — A1238

Designs: 1200 l, Panthera pardus. 2000 l, Panthera uncia. 2200 l, Panthera leo. Lynx rufus. 4200 l, Puma concolor. 6500 l, Panthera tigris. 14,100 l, Panthera leo.

**2000, Nov. 29**    **Photo.**    **Perf. 13½**
4408 A1238    1200 l    .20   .20
4409 A1238    2000 l    .20   .20
4410 A1238    2200 l    .20   .20
4411 A1238    2300 l    .20   .20
4412 A1238    4200 l    .30   .20
4413 A1238    6500 l multi    .50   .25
   Nos. 4408-4413 (6)    1.60 1.25

**Souvenir Sheet**
4414 A1238 14,100 l multi    1.10   .55

No. 4414 contains one 54x42mm stamp.

---

2000
A1239

Designs: 2000 l, Camil Ressu (1880-1962), 2400 l, Jean A. Steriadi (1880-1956), 4400 l, Nicolae Tonitza (1886-1940). 15,000 l, Nicolae Grigorescu (1838-1907).

Self-portraits
A1239

**2000**    **Photo.**    **Perf. 13½**
4415 A1239    2000 l multi    .20   .20
4416 A1239    2400 l multi    .20   .20
4417 A1239    4400 l multi    .35   .20
4418 A1239    15,000 l multi    1.10   .55
   Nos. 4415-4418 (4)    1.85 1.15

Issued: 2000, 12/8; others, 12/13.

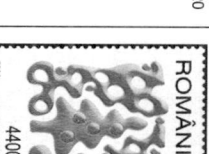

**2000, Dec. 15**    **Photo.**    **Perf. 13½**
4419 A1240 4400 l multi    .35   .20

Christmas — A1240

Stained glass windows: 2000 l, Resurrection of Jesus. 7000 l, Holy Trinity (22x38mm).

**2000, Dec. 22**    **Photo.**    **Perf. 13½**
4420-4421 A1241    Set of 2    .75   .40

Christianity,
2000th
Anniv. — A1241

No. 3922
Surcharged in
Brown

**2000, Dec. 28**    **Photo.**    **Perf. 13½**
4422 A1105 7000 l on 3095 l multi    .55   .25

**Wmk. 398**
4423 A1105 10,000 l on 3095 l multi    .75   .40
4424 A1105 11,500 l on 3095 l multi    .90   .45
   Nos. 4422-4424 (3)    2.20 1.10

Obliterator on No. 4423 is a bear and on No. 4424 a bison.

Advent of the Third
Millennium — A1242

---

No. 3844 Surcharged in Black or Red

**2001, Feb. 2**
4426 A1243    Horiz. pair, #a-b

Sculptures by Constantin Brancusi
(1876-1957) — A1243

**2001, Jan. 19**    **Photo.**    **Unwmk.**
4425 A1242 11,500 l multi    .90   .45

No. 4426: a, 4600 l, b, 7200 l.

   **Perf. 13½**
   .90   .45

**Methods and Perfs as Before**

**2001, Feb. 9**
4427 A1087 7400 l on 280 l    .55   .25
4428 A1087 13,000 l on 280 l multi (R)    .95   .45

Obliterator on No. 4428 is snake on branch.

Valentine's Day — A1244

Designs: 2200 l, Heart of rope. 11,500 l, Rope running through heart.

**2001, Feb. 15**    **Photo.**    **Perf. 13½**
4429-4430 A1244    Set of 2    1.00   .50

Nos. 3894,
3895, 3897
Surcharged in
Brown or Green

**Methods and Perfs as Before**

**2001, Feb. 21**    **Photo.**    **Perf. 13½**
4431 A1101 1300 l on 245 l    .20   .20
4432 A1101 2200 l on 115 l multi    .20   .20
4433 A1101 5000 l on 115 l multi    .35   .20
4434 A1101 16,500 l on 70 l multi (G)    1.25   .60
   Nos. 4431-4434 (4)    2.00 1.20

Appearance of obliterators differ. Obliterators on Nos 4432-4433 are ears of corn.

Famous
People
A1245

Designs: 1300 l, Hortensia Papadat-Bengescu (1876-1955), writer. 2200 l, Eugen Lovinescu (1881-1943), writer. 2400 l, Ion Minulescu (1881-1944), writer. 4600 l, André Malraux (1901-76), writer. 7200 l, George H.

ROMANIA

Gallup (1901-84), poster. 35,000 l, Walt Disney (1901-66), film producer.

**2001**    **Photo.**    **Perf. 13¼**
4435-4440   A1245   Set of 6    4.00   2.00

Issued: 2200 l, 4600 l, 7200 l, 3/9; others 3/15.

Easter — A1246

**2001, Mar. 23**
4441   A1246   2200 l multi    .20   .20

Fruit — A1247

**2001, Apr. 12**
Designs: 2200 l, Prunus spinosa. 4600 l, Ribes rubrum. 7400 l, Ribes uva-crispa. 11,500 l, Vaccinium vitis-idaea.
4442-4445   A1247   Set of 4    1.90   .95

Gheorghe Hagi, Soccer Player — A1248

**2001, Apr. 23**    **Perf. 13¼**
4446   A1248   2200 l multi    .20   .20

**Souvenir Sheet**
**Imperf**
**Without Gum**
4447   A1248   35,000 l multi    2.75   1.40

Designs: 2200 l, Wearing uniform. 35,000 l, Wearing team jacket.

No. 4447 is airmail and contains one 43x28mm stamp.

Europa — A1249

**2001, May 4**    **Perf. 13¼**
4448   A1249   13,000 l multi    1.00   .50

Dogs
A1250

**2001, June 16**
4449-4452   A1250   Set of 4    2.25   1.10

Designs: 1300 l, Collie. 5000 l, Basset hound. 8000 l, Siberian husky. 13,500 l, Sheepdog.

---

Romanian Presidency of Organization for Security and Cooperation in Europe — A1251

4453   A1251   11,500 l multi    .90   .45

Millennium — A1252

Events of the 20th Century: 1300 l, Mariner 9, 1971. 1500 l, Telephone pioneer Augustin Maior and circuit diagram, 1906. 2400 l, Discovery of cave drawings in Ardeche, France, 1994. 5000 l, First Olympic perfect score of gymnast Nadia Comaneci, 1976. 5300 l, Pioneer 10, 1972. 8000 l, Fall of the Iron Curtain, 1989. 13,500 l, First microprocessor, 1971. 15,500 l, Hubble Space Telescope, 1990.

**2001**
4454-4461   A1252   Set of 8    3.50   1.75

Issued: 1300 l, 2400 l, 5000 l, 8000 l, 7/13; others, 9/25.

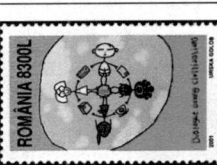

UN High Commissioner for Refugees, 50th Anniv. — A1253

**2001, July 26**
4462   A1253   13,500 l multi    1.00   .50

Nos. 3688, 3713, 3790, 3791, 3865, 3870, 3900, 3907, 3972, 4007, 4017, 4025, 4057, 4058, and 4060 Surcharged in Black, Red, Green or Blue

**2001**    **Photo.**    **Perf. 13½**
| | | | | | |
|---|---|---|---|---|---|
| 4463 | A1048 | 300 l on 4 l #3688 | | .20 | .20 |
| 4464 | A1058 | 300 l on 4 l #3713 | | .20 | .20 |
| | | (R) | | | |
| 4465 | A1073 | 300 l on 7 l #3790 | | .20 | .20 |
| | | (R) | | | |
| 4466 | A1073 | 300 l on 9 l #3791 | | .20 | .20 |
| | | (R) | | | |
| 4467 | A1102 | 300 l on 90 l #3900 | | .20 | .20 |
| 4468 | A1121 | 300 l on 90 l #3972 | | .20 | .20 |
| | | (G) | | | |
| 4469 | A1132 | 300 l on 90 l #4007 | | .20 | .20 |
| 4470 | A1130 | 300 l on 90 l #4017 | | .20 | .20 |
| 4471 | A1137 | 300 l on 90 l #4025 | | .20 | .20 |
| | | (G) | | | |
| 4472 | A1095 | 300 l on 115 l #3865 | | .20 | .20 |
| | | (R) | | | |
| 4473 | A1096 | 300 l on 115 l #3870 | | .20 | .20 |
| 4474 | A1103 | 300 l on 115 l #3907 | | .20 | .20 |
| | | (R) | | | |
| 4475 | A1131 | 2500 l on 715 l #4057 | | .20 | .20 |
| 4476 | A1131 | 2500 l on 755 l #4058 | | .20 | .20 |
| | | (B) | | | |
| 4477 | A1131 | 2500 l on 1615 l #4060 | | .20 | .20 |
| a.-e. | | Horiz. strip of 5 | | 3.00 | 3.00 |

Nos. 4463-4477 (15)    4.50   2.25

Numbers have been reserved for additional surcharges. Design and location of obliterators and new value varies.

---

Issued: No. 4472, 8/20; No. 4473, 8/24; Nos. 4467, 4469, 8/28; No. 4470, 8/29; Nos. 4463, 4464, 4465, 4466, Nos. 4468, 4471, 4474-4477, 8/31.

Equestrian Sports A1254

**2001, Aug. 21**    **Photo.**    **Perf. 13¼**
4478-4481   A1254   Set of 4    1.25   .60

Designs: 1500 l, Harness racing. 2500 l, Dressage. 5300 l, Steeplechase. 8300 l, Racing.

No. 3883 Surcharged

4482   A1099   300 l on 115 l multi    .20   .20

**Souvenir Sheets**

Corals and Anemones — A1256

**2001, Aug. 29**    **Photo.**    **Perf. 13½**
    **Sheets of 4, #a-d**
4483-4484   A1255   Set of 2    7.25   3.75

Designs: No. 4483: a, 2500 l. b, 3300 l. c, 13,500 l. d, 8300 l, Porites porites. b, Condylactis gigantea. c, Gorgonia ventalina. Anemonia tolla. 37,500 l, Corallium rubrum. No. 4484: a, 9000 l, Corallium rubrum. b, 16,500 l, Actinia equina. c, Anemonia palmata. d, 16,500 l, Metridium senile.

Issued: No. 4483, 9/27/01; No. 4484, 1/30/02.

Year of Dialogue Among Civilizations A1256

**2001, Oct. 9**
4485   A1256   8300 l multi    .55   .25

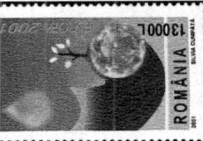

Comic Strip A1257

**2001, Oct. 31**
4486    Horiz. strip of 5    4.50   2.25
a.-e.   A1257   13,500 l Any single    .90   .45

Designs: No. 4486: a, Cat, bear, king. b, Fox with drum, cat. c, Fox plays drum for king. d, Cat gives drum to fox. e, Fox, exploding drum.

---

Christmas
A1258

**2001, Nov. 5**
4487   A1258   2500 l Pair, #a-b    .35   .20
    Booklet, 5 #4487    1.75

No. 4487: a, Ribbon extending from wreath. b, No ribbon extending from wreath.

Zodiac Signs A1259

Designs: No. 4488, 1500 l. 1500 l, Scorpio. No. 4489, 1500 l, Aries. No. 4490, 2500 l, Libra. No. 4491, 2500 l, Taurus. No. 4492, 5500 l, Capricorn. No. 4493, 5500 l, Gemini. 8700 l, Cancer. No. 4495, 9000 l, Pisces. No. 4496, 9000 l, Leo. 13,500 l, Aquarius. 16,500 l, Sagittarius. 23,500 l, Virgo.

**2001-02**
4488-4499   A1259   Set of 12    6.50   3.25

Issued: Nos. 4488, 4490, 4492, 4495, 4497, 4498, 11/23/01; others 1/4/02.

Bucharest Post Office, Cent. — A1260

No. 4500: a, Building. b, Medal. Illustration reduced.

**2001, Dec. 18**    **Photo.**    **Perf. 13¼**
4500   A1260   5500 l Horiz. pair, #a-b    .80   .40

Emanuil Gojdu (1802-70), Promoter of Romanian Orthodox Church in Hungary A1261

**2002, Feb. 6**
4501   A1261   2500 l multi    .20   .20

Valentine's Day A1262

**2002, Feb. 8**
4502-4503   A1262   Set of 2    3.25   1.60

Designs: 5500 l, Mice. 43,500 l, Elephants.

Famous Men A1263

Designs: 1500 l, Ion Mincu (1852-1912), architect. 2500 l, Costin D. Nenitescu (1902-70), chemist. 5500 l, Alexandre Dumas père (1802-70), writer. 9000 l, Şerban Cioculescu (1902-88), writer. 16,500 l, Leonardo da Vinci

(1452-1519), artist. 34,000 l, Victor Hugo (1802-85), writer.

**2002, Mar. 1**
4504-4509 A1263 Set of 6   4.50 2.25

United We Stand — A1264

**2002, Mar. 22**
4510 A1264 25,500 l Horiz. pair, #a-b   5.00 3.25
No. 4510: a, Statue of Liberty, US flag. b, Romanian flag.

Europa — A1268

**2002, May 9**
4520-4521 A1268 Set of 2   3.00 1.50
Clown with: 17,500 l, Yellow hair. 25,500 l, Brown hair.

Intl. Federation of Stamp Dealers' Associations, 50th Anniv. — A1269

**2002, June 10**
4522 A1269 Sheet of 4, #a-d   5.50 2.75
No. 4522: a, 10,000 l, Romanian flags #1, 2 and 4. b, 10,000 l, IFSDA emblem. c, 27,500 l, World Trade Center, Bucharest. d, 27,500 l, Romanian philatelic store.

Souvenir Sheet

German Fortresses in Romania — A1265

**2002, Apr. 2**
4511-4516 A1265 Set of 6   3.25 1.60
Designs: 1500 l, Saschiz, vert. 2500 l, Darjiu, vert. 6500 l, Viscri. 10,500 l, Vorumloc. 13,500 l, Calnic, vert. 17,500 l, Prejmer, vert.

Easter — A1266

**2002, Apr. 12**
4517-4518 A1266 Set of 2
Photo. Perf. 13¼
Designs: 2500 l, Crucifixion. 10,500 l, Resurrection.   1.00 .50

Souvenir Sheet

**2002, May 9**
4519 A1267 25,500 l multi   1.90 .95
Proclamation of Independence, 125th Anniv. — A1267

Intl. Year of Mountains A1270

**2002, June 14**
4523 A1270 2000 l multi   .20 .20

Intl. Year of Ecotourism A1271

**2002, June 14**
4524 A1271 3000 l multi   .25 .20

Sports A1272

**2002, July 11**
4525-4528 A1272 Set of 4   4.00 2.00
Designs: 7000 l, Cricket. 11,000 l, Polo. 15,500 l, Golf. 19,500 l, Baseball.

Stamp Day — A1273

**2002, July 15**
4529 A1273 10,000 l Horiz. pair, #a-b   1.60 .80
No. 4529: a, Ion Luca Caragiale (1852-1912), writer. b, National Theater, Bucharest, 150th anniv. Illustration reduced.

Postal Services A1278

**2002, Aug. 9**
4530 A1274 2000 l multi   .20 .20
4531 A1275 3000 l multi   .25 .20
4532 A1276 10,000 l multi   .75 .40
4533 A1277 15,500 l multi   1.25 .60
4534 A1278 27,500 l multi   1.00 1.00
Nos. 4530-4534 (5)   4.45 2.40

A1274

A1276

A1277

A1275

Butterflies — A1279

**2002, Sept. 2**
4535 A1279 44,500 l Sheet of 4, #a-d   13.50 13.50
No. 4535: a, Boloria pales carpathomeridionalis. b, Erebia pharte romaniae. c, Peridea korbi herculiana. d, Tomares nogelli dobrogensis.

Locomotives — A1280

**2002, Sept. 22**
4536-4541 A1280 Set of 6   5.75 2.75
Souvenir Sheet
4542 A1280 72,500 l multi   4.50 2.25
Photo. Perf. 13¼
Designs: 4500 l, Series 50025. 5000 l, Series 50115, 1930. 6500 l, Series 1921. 7000 l, Series 230128, 1933. 11,000 l, Series 764493, 1956. 19,500 l, Series 142072, 1939. 44,500 l, Series 704209, 1909.
No. 4542: 72,500 l, Locomotive #1, 1872, vert.
No. 4542 contains one 54x41mm stamp.

Postal Services A1283

**2002, Oct. 1**
4543 A1281 8000 l multi   .50 .25
4544 A1282 13,000 l multi   .80 .40
4545 A1283 20,500 l multi   1.25 .60
Nos. 4543-4545 (3)   2.55 1.25

A1283

A1281

A1282

35th Chess Olympiad, Bled, Slovenia — A1284

Souvenir Sheet

**2002, Oct. 23**
4546 A1284 20,500 l Sheet of 3, #a-c   3.75 1.90
No. 4546: a, Knight and bishop. b, Queen and knight. c, King and rook.

Fruit — A1285

**2002, Nov. 11**
4547-4550 A1285 Set of 4   9.25 4.75
Designs: 15,500 l, Cydonia oblonga. 20,500 l, Armeniaca vulgaris. 44,500 l, Cerasus vulgaris. 73,500 l, Morus nigra.

Christmas A1286

**2002, Nov. 19**
4551-4552 A1286 Set of 2   1.10 .55
Santa Claus and helper: 3000 l, With gifts. 15,500 l, At computers.

Invitation to Join NATO A1287

Souvenir Sheets

*Ciuperci otrăvitoare*    *Ciuperci otrăvitoare*

Mushrooms — A1301

No. 4594, 15,500 l: a, Agaricus xanthodermus. b, Clathrus ruber. c, Amanita pantherina.
No. 4595, 20,500 l: a, Leccinum aurantiacum. b, Laetiporus sulphureus. c, Russula xerampelina.

**2003, Sept. 19**    **Sheets of 3, #a-c**
4594-4595 A1301   Set of 2   6.50 3.25

Extreme
Sports
A1302

No. 4596, 5000 l, Skydiving, vert. 8000 l, Windsurfing. 10,000 l, Motorcycle racing. 30,500 l, Skiing, vert.

**2003, Sept. 30**
4596-4599 A1302   Set of 4   3.25 1.60

Reptiles and Amphibians — A1303

No. 4600: a, Lacerta viridis. b, Hyla arborea. c, Ablepharus kitaibelii ctopanekii d, Rana temporaria.

**2003, Oct. 28**
4600 A1303 18,000 l Sheet of 4,   4.25 2.10
  #a-d

COBZĂ    ROMÂNIA 1000l

Musical Instruments — A1304

Designs: 1000 l, Lute (cobza). 4000 l, Horn (bucium). 6000 l, Fiddle with horn (vioara cu goarna).

**2003, Oct. 31**
4601-4603 A1304   Set of 3   .65 .30

ROMÂNIA   16000L

Granting of Dobruja Region to
Romania, 125th Anniv. — A1305

**2003, Nov. 11**
4604 A1305 16,000 l multi   .95 .50

---

ROMÂNIA 20500 l   EUROPA

Europa
A1297

Poster art: 20,500 l, Butterfly emerging from chrysalis. 73,500 l, Man holding framed picture.

**2003, May 9**
4585-4586 A1297   Set of 2   5.75 5.75

**Famous Men Type of 2003**

Designs: 4500 l, Dumitru Staniloae (1903-93), theologian. 8000 l, Alexandru Ciucurecu (1903-77), painter. 30,500 l, Ilarie Voronca (1903-46), writer. 46,500 l, Victor Brauner (1903-66), painter.

**2003, June 6**    **Photo.**    ***Perf. 13¼***
4587-4590 A1292   Set of 4   5.50 2.75

CENTENARUL 1903-2003 VICTOR BRAUNER   PIATRA — NEAMT

Paintings by Victor Brauner — A1298

No. 4591 — Unidentified paintings: a, Two dragons in foreground. b, White and black arcs (20x30mm). c, Spheres at left. d, Landscape with house with red roof in center. e, Abstract with fish head (20x30mm). f, Landscape with white clouds at left and right. g, Mountain with rings. h, Line drawing of man (20x30mm). i, Fire-breathing dragon. j, Man standing (20x30mm).

**2003, June 24**
4591 A1298 10,000 l Sheet, #a-i,   7.50 3.75
  3 #j

FOMÂNIA 500   73500l ROMÂNIA

Nostradamus (1503-66),
Astrologer — A1299

No. 4592: a, Nostradamus, denomination at left. b, Astrological chart, denomination at bottom. Illustration reduced.

**2003, July 2**
4592 A1299 73,500 l Horiz. pair,   9.00 4.50
  #a-b

100   5000 L   ROMÂNIA

Stamp
Day
A1300

**2003, July 15**
4593 A1300 5000 l multi   .30 .20

---

ROMÂNIA 4500 L   PALATUL POŞTELOR

Buildings in
Bucharest — A1293

Designs: 4500 l, Postal Palace. 5500 l, Economics House. 10,000 l, National Bank of Romania, horiz. 15,500 l, Stock Exchange. 46,500 l, Carol I University. 46,500 l, Atheneum. 73,500 l, Palace of Justice.

**2003, Mar. 27**    **Photo.**    ***Perf. 13¼***
4569-4574 A1293   Set of 6   6.00 3.00

**Souvenir Sheet**
4575 A1293 73,500 l multi   4.50 2.25
No. 4575 contains one 42x53mm stamp.

ROMÂNIA

Natl. Map and Book Museum,
Bucharest — A1294

No. 4576 — Map of Dacia by Petrus Kaerius: a, Northwestern Dacia. b, Northeastern Dacia. c, Southwestern Dacia. d, Southeastern Dacia.
46,500 l, Museum, vert.

**2003, Apr. 4**    **Photo.**    ***Perf. 13¼***
4576 A1294   30,500 l Sheet of 4,   7.25 3.75
  #a-d

**Souvenir Sheet**
4577 A1294 46,500 l multi   2.75 1.40
No. 4577 contains one 42x54mm stamp.

ROMÂNIA 3000 L   SEMÎE PAŞTI

Easter — A1295

**2003, Apr. 10**
4578 A1295 3000 l multi   .20 .20

Owls — A1296

Designs: 5000 l, Otus scops. 8000 l, Strix uralensis. 10,000 l, Glaucidium passerinum. 13,000 l, Asio flammeus. 15,500 l, Asio otus. 20,500 l, Aegolius funereus.

**2003, Apr. 25**
4579-4584 A1296   Set of 6   4.50 2.25

---

**Litho. With Hologram Applied**
    ***Perf. 12¾***
2002, Nov. 22   131,000 l multi   8.00 4.00
4553 A1287
Printed in sheets of 2 + central label.

ROMÂNIA 4500L   J. AL. STERIADI – PORTUL BRĂILA

Paintings — A1288

Designs: 4500 l, Portul Braila, by J.A. Steriadi. 6500 l, Balcic, by N. Darascu. 30,500 l, Conversatie, by N. Vermont. 34,000 l, Dalmatia, by N. Danascu. 46,500 l, Barci Pescaresti, by Steriadi. 53,000 l, Nude, by B. Pietris. 83,500 l, Femeie pe Malul Marii, by N. Grigorescu, vert.

**2003, Jan. 22**    **Photo.**    ***Perf. 13¼***
4554-4559 A1288   Set of 6   11.00 5.50

**Souvenir Sheet**
4560 A1288 83,500 l multi   5.25 2.60
No. 4560 contains one 41x54mm stamp.

Natl.
Military
Palace,
80th Anniv.
A1289

PALATUL CERCULUI MILITAR NATIONAL – 80 DE ANI
ROMÂNIA 5000 L

**2003, Jan. 28**     .35 .20
4561 A1289 5000 l multi

3000 L   ROMÂNIA

St.
Valentine's
Day
A1290

Designs: 3000 l, Ladybug with heart-shaped spots. 5000 l, Man with ladder, vert.

**2003, Feb. 14**    Set of 2   .50 .25
4562-4563 A1290

ROMÂNIA 142000L

Admission
to
European
Union,
10th Anniv.
A1291

**2003, Feb. 20**
4564 A1291 142,000 l multi   8.75 4.50

6000L   Ion Irimescu (n. 1903)   ROMÂNIA

Famous
Men — A1292

Designs: 6000 l, Ion Irimescu, sculptor, cent. of birth. 18,000 l, Hector Berlioz (1803-69), composer. 20,000 l, Vincent Van Gogh (1853-90), painter. 36,000 l, Dr. Georges de Bellio (1828-94), art collector.

**2003, Feb. 27**    Set of 4   5.00 2.50
4565-4568 A1292

## Pope John Paul II and Patriarch Teoctist — A1306

No. 4605: a, Holding crosses. b, Embracing.

**2003, Nov. 29**
**4605** Horiz. pair with 2 central labels
a.-b. A1306 16,000 l Either single 1.00 .50
Pontificate of Pope John Paul II, 25th anniv.

## Christmas — A1307

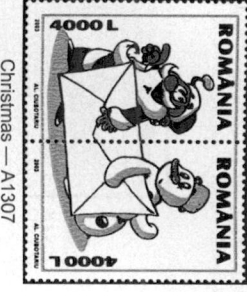

**2003, Dec. 5**
**4606** A1307 4000 l Horiz. pair, #a-b .50 .25

No. 4606: a, Santa Claus. b, Snowman.

## Women's Fashions in the 20th Century — A1308

No. 4607, 4000 l: a, 1921-30. b, 1931-40.
No. 4608, 21,000 l: a, 1901-10. b, 1911-20.

**2003, Dec. 13** Horiz. Pairs, #a-b + Label
4607-4608 A1308 Set of 2 3.25 1.60

## FIFA (Fédération Internationale de Football Association), Cent. (in 2004) — A1309

Designs: 3000 l, Women soccer players. 4000 l, Soccer players, television camera. 6000 l, Men, FIFA charter. 10,000 l, Players, equipment. 34,000 l, Rule book, field diagram.

**2003, Dec. 22** **Photo.**
4609-4613 A1309 Set of 5 3.50 1.75

---

## Birds — A1310

No. 4614 — UPU emblem and: a, Ardea cinerea. b, Anas platyrhynchos. c, Podiceps cristatus. d, Pelecanus onocrotalus.

**2004, Jan. 23** **Photo. Perf. 13¼**
**4614** A1310 16,000 l Sheet of 4, #a-d 4.00 2.00
Miniature Sheet

## Information Technology — A1311

No. 4615 — UPU emblem and: a, Earth, satellite, compact disc. b, Computer screen showing computer user. c, Earth, satellite dish. d, Computer keyboard, diskette.

**2004, Jan. 26**
**4615** A1311 20,000 l Sheet of 4, #a-d 5.00 2.50

## Amerigo Vespucci (1454-1512), Explorer — A1312

**2004, Jan. 31**
4616-4617 A1312 Set of 2 3.00 1.50
Designs: 16,000 l, Vespucci. 31,000 l, Ship.

## St. Valentine's Day — A1313

**2004, Feb. 10**
**4618** A1313 21,000 l multi 1.40 .70

## 23rd UPU Congress, Bucharest — A1314

No. 4619: a, UPU emblem. b, Congress emblem.
Illustration reduced.

---

## Miniature Sheet

## Easter — A1315

**2004, Mar. 5**
**4620** A1315 4000 l multi .25 .20

## High Speed Trains A1316

UPU Congress emblem and: 4000 l, Bullet Train, Japan. 6000 l, TGV, France. 10,000 l, KTX, South Korea. 16,000 l, AVE, Spain. 47,000 l, ICE, Germany. 56,000 l, Eurostar, Europe. 77,000 l, Sageata Albastra, Romania.

**2004, Mar. 11**
4621-4626 A1316 Set of 6 8.50 4.25
**Souvenir Sheet**
**4627** A1316 77,000 l multi 4.75 2.40
No. 4627 contains one 54x42mm stamp.

## Admission to NATO — A1317

**2004, Mar. 24**
**4628** A1317 4000 l multi .25 .20

## Women's Fashions Type of 2003

No. 4629, 5000 l: a, 1941-50. b, 1951-60. No. 4630, 21,000 l: a, 1981-90. b, 1991-2000. No. 4631, 31,000 l: a, 1961-70. b, 1971-80.

**2004, Mar. 31** Horiz. Pairs, #a-b + Label
4629-4631 A1308 Set of 3 6.75 3.50

## Intl. Council for Game and Wildlife Conservation, 51st General Assembly A1318

No. 4632 — Emblem and: a, Hunter. b, Dog and pheasant. c, Buck. d, Mountain goat. e, Bear.

**2004, Apr. 24** Horiz. strip of 5
**4632** A1318 16,000 l Any single 4.75 2.40
.95 .45
**Souvenir Sheet**
**4633** A1318 16,000 l multi .95 .45
No. 4633 contains one 54x42mm stamp.

---

## Europa A1319

**2004, May 7** **Photo. Perf. 13¼**
4634-4635 A1319 Set of 2 5.75 3.00
Stylized sun and: 21,000 l, Beach. 77,000 l, Mountains.

## Michael the Brave (1558-1601), Prince of Walachia — A1320

**2004, May 14**
**4636** A1320 3000 l multi .20 .20

## Naţional Philatelic and Romanian History Museum — A1321

**2004, May 21**
**4637** A1321 4000 l multi .25 .20
Souvenir Sheet

## Dracula — A1322

No. 4638: a, Bram Stoker, author of Dracula. b, Dracula and cross. c, Dracula and woman. d, Dracula in coffin.

**2004, May 21**
**4638** A1322 31,000 l Sheet of 4, #a-d 7.25 3.75
23rd UPU Congress, Bucharest. Exists imperf.

## Famous People A1323

Designs: 4000 l, Anghel Saligny (1854-1925), civil engineer. 16,000 l, Gheorge D. Anghel (1904-66), sculptor. 21,000 l, George D. Sand (1804-76), author. 31,000 l, Oscar Wilde (1854-1900), writer.

**2004, May 27**
4639-4642 A1323 Set of 4 4.25 2.10

Designs: 8000 l, Simfonia. 15,000 l, Foc de Tabara. 25,000 l, Golden Elegance. 36,000 l, Doamna in Mov.

**2004, Oct. 25**
4677-4680 A1339 Set of 4 5.50 2.75
4680a Souvenir sheet of #4677-4680 5.50 2.75

Ilie Nastase, Tennis Player — A1340

**2004, Nov. 16**    *Perf. 13¼*
4681 A1340 10,000 l multi .75 .35

**Souvenir Sheets**
*Perf. 13¼x13¾*
4682 A1340 72,000 l Nastase, diff. 5.25 2.60

***Imperf***
4683 A1340 72,000 l Like No. 4682 5.25 2.60

No. 4682 contains one 42x51mm stamp.
No. 4683 contains one 37x48mm stamp.

Christmas — A1341

**2004, Nov. 27**    *Perf. 13¼*
4684 A1341 5000 l multi .40 .20

Organizations A1342

Prince Dimitrie Cantemir (1673-1723), Writer — A1343

Designs: 12,000 l, Romanian Boy Scouts. 16,000 l, Lions International. 19,000 l, Red Cross and Red Crescent.

**2004, Dec. 8**    *Perf. 13¼*
4685-4687 A1342 Set of 3 3.25 1.60

**Souvenir Sheet**
*Perf. 13¼x13¾*
4688 A1343 87,000 l multi 6.00 3.00

Olympic Gold Medalists A1344

Sculptures by Idel Ianchelevici (1909-94) A1335

Designs: 21,000 l, L'appel. 31,000 l, Perennis Perdurat Poeta.

**2004, Sept. 20**    Set of 2
4666-4667 A1335 1.60 .80

Chinese and Romanian Handicrafts — A1336

No. 4668: a, Drum with tigers and birds, China. b, Cucuteni pottery jar, Romania. Illustration reduced.

**2004, Sept. 24**
4668 A1336 5000 l Pair, #a-b .60 .30

See People's Republic of China Nos. 3390-3391.

Souvenir Sheet

23rd UPU Congress, Bucharest — A1337

No. 4669: a, Gerardus Mercator and Jodocus Hondius, cartographers. b, UPU emblem. c, Amerigo Vespucci (1454-1512) explorer.

**2004, Oct. 5**    *Perf. 13½*
4669 A1337 118,000 l Sheet of 3, #a-c 21.50 10.50

Details From Trajan's Column, Rome A1338

Various details: 7000 l, 12,000 l, 19,000 l, 21,000 l, 31,000 l, 56,000 l, 145,000 l.

**2004**    *Perf. 13¼*
4670-4676 A1338 Set of 7 20.00 10.00

Issued: 7000 l, 12,000 l, 19,000 l, 56,000 l, 10/15; others, 12/4.

Roses — A1339

Flight of Zeppelin LZ-127 Over Brasov, 75th Anniv. A1330

**2004, July 29**
4653 A1330 31,000 l multi 1.90 .95

Savings Banks, 140th Anniv. A1331

**2004, July 30**
4654 A1331 5000 l multi .30 .20

Fire Fighters — A1332

No. 4655: a, Fire fighters leaving truck. b, Fire fighters in protective suits. Illustration reduced.

**2004, Aug. 12**
4655 A1332 12,000 l Horiz. pair, #a-b, + flanking label 1.50 .75

2004 Summer Olympics, Athens — A1333

Designs: 7000 l, Rowing. 12,000 l, Fencing. 21,000 l, Swimming. 31,000 l +9000 l, Gymnastics.

**2004, Aug. 20**    *Litho.*    *Perf. 13¼*
4656-4659 A1333 Set of 4 4.75 2.40

Olymphilex Philatelic Exhibition (#4659).

23rd UPU Congress, Bucharest A1334

Stamps commemorating UPU Congresses: 8000 l, Romania #4619b. 10,000 l, Switzerland #590. 19,000 l, South Korea #1794, horiz. 31,000 l, People's Republic of China #2868. 47,000 l, United States #2434, horiz. 77,000 l, Brazil #1629.

**2004, Sept. 10**
4660-4665 A1334 Set of 6 11.50 5.75

Romanian Athenaeum — A1324

**2004, May 28**
4643 A1324 10,000 l multi .60 .30

Johnny Weissmuller (1904-84), Olympic Swimming Gold Medalist, Actor — A1325

**2004, June 2**    *Photo.*
4644 A1325 21,000 l multi 1.25 .60

TAROM Airlines, 50th Anniv. A1326

**2004, June 7**    *Perf. 13¼*
4645 A1326 16,000 l multi .95 .45

FIFA (Fédération Internationale de Football Association), Cent. — A1327

**2004, June 15**
4646 A1327 31,000 l multi 1.90 .95

Miniature Sheets

Stephen the Great (1437-1504), Prince of Moldavia — A1328

No. 4647: 10,000 l: a, Portrait of Stephen the Great, Dobrovat-Iasi Monastery Church. b, Sucevei Fortress. c, Portrait of Stephen the Great, Putna Monastery. No. 4648, 16,000 l: a, Putna Monastery. b, Stephen the Great. c, Neamtului Fortress.

**2004, June 16**    Sheets of 3, #a-c
4647-4648 A1328 Set of 2 4.75 2.40

Famous Men A1329

Designs: 2000 l, Alexandru Macedonski (1854-1920), writer. 3000 l, Victor Babes (1854-1926), bacteriologist. 6000 l, Arthur Rimbaud (1854-91), writer. 56,000 l, Salvador Dali (1904-89), painter.

**2004, June 30**
4649-4652 A1329 Set of 4 4.25 2.10

Designs: 5000 l, Iolanda Balas, high jump, 33,000 l, Elisabeta Lipa, rowing. 77,000 l, Ivan Pazaichin, canoeing.

**2004, Dec. 15**    **Perf. 13¼**
4689-4691 A1344   Set of 3   8.00 4.00
Values are for stamps with surrounding selvage.

## Souvenir Sheets

No. 4692, 7000 l, a. Tristan Tzara, by M. H. Maxy. b. Baroness, by Merica Ramniceanu. c. No. 4693, 12,000 l, a. Composition, by Marcel Iancu. b. Female Care Viseaza, by Victor Brauner. c, Composition, by Hans Mattis-Teutsch.

**2004, Dec. 16**    **Litho.**
### Modern Paintings — A1345
4692-4693 A1345   Set of 2
   #a-c   4.00 2.00

Rotary International, Cent. A1347

**2005, Feb. 23**
4699 A1347 21,000 l multi   1.60 .80
Printed in sheets of 4.

Designs from: 3000 l, Oboga, Olt. 5000 l, Sacel, Maramures. 7000 l, Romania, Olt. 8000 l, Vadul Crisului, Bihor. 10,000 l, Tara Barsei, Brasov. 12,000 l, Horezu, Valcea. 16,000 l, Corund, Harghita.

### Pottery — A1348
**2005**    **Litho.**
**Background Color**    **Perf. 13¼**
4700 A1348 3000 l lilac   .20 .20
4701 A1348 5000 l lt blue   .40 .20
4702 A1348 7000 l rose brn   .50 .25
4703 A1348 8000 l lt green   .60 .30
4704 A1348 10,000 l orange   .70 .35

Gheorghe Magheru 1804-1880 ROMANIA 15 000 L

**2004, Jan. 20**    **Litho.**
### Famous People — A1346
4694-4698 A1346   Set of 5   15.50 7.75
See Nos. 4722-4726.

---

4705 A1348 12,000 l green   .90 .45
4706 A1348 16,000 l lt brown   1.25 .60
Nos. 4700-4706 (7)   4.55 2.35

Issued: 3000 l, 5000 l, 12,000 l, 16,000 l, 2/24. 7000 l, 8000 l, 10,000 l, 3/24. This is an expanding set.

Designs: 31,000 l, Elopteryx nopcsai. 35,000 l, Telmatosaurus transsylvanicus. 47,000 l, Struthiosaurus transsilvanicus. Hatzegopteryx thambema.

### Dinosaurs — A1349
**2005, Feb. 25**    **Litho.**    **Perf. 13¼**
4707-4710 A1349   Set of 4   9.75 5.00
4710a   Souvenir sheet, #4707-4710, + 2 labels   9.75 5.00

Carassius auratus

Designs: 21,000 l, Carassius auratus. 31,000 l, Symphysodon discus. 36,000 l, Labidochromis. 47,000 l, Betta splendens.

### Fish — A1350
**2005, Mar. 1**
**Stamp + Label**
4711-4714 A1350   Set of 4   9.75 5.00
4714a   Souvenir sheet, #4711-4714, + 4 labels   9.75 5.00

"Castelul din Carpati" Centenar Jules Verne 1905-2005 100061

Scenes from stories: 19,000 l, The Carpathians. 21,000 l, The Danube Pilot. 47,000 l, Claudius Bombarnac. 56,000 l, Keraban, the Inflexible.

### Jules Verne (1828-1905), Writer — A1351
**2005, Mar. 29**    **Litho.**    **Perf. 13¼**
4715-4718 A1351   Set of 4   10.50 5.25
4718a   Souvenir sheet, #4715-4718, + 2 labels   10.50 5.25

No. 4719: a, Last Supper. b, Crucifixion. c, Resurrection.

### Easter A1352
**2005, Apr. 1**
4719 A1352 5000 l Any single   .55 .20
a.-c.   Horiz. strip of 3   1.10 .35

---

### Pope John Paul II (1920-2005) — A1353
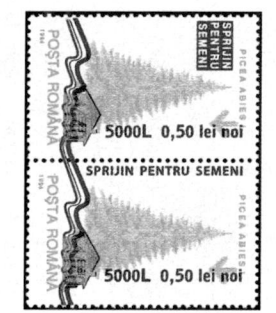

**2005, Apr. 8**    **Litho.**    **Perf. 13¼**
4720-4721 A1353   Set of 2   4.00 2.00
4721a   Souvenir sheet, 2 each #4720-4721   1.90 .95

### Famous People Type of 2005
Designs: 3000 l, Hans Christian Andersen (1805-75), author. 5000 l, Jules Verne (1828-1905), writer. 12,000 l, Albert Einstein (1879-1955), physicist. 21,000 l, Dimitrie Gusti (1880-1955), sociologist. 22,000 l, George Enescu (1881-1955), composer.

**2005, Apr. 18**
4722-4726 A1346   Set of 5   4.50 2.25

Pope John Paul II and: 5000 l, Dove, map of Romania. 21,000 l, St. Peter's Basilica.

### Romanian Accession to European Union — A1354
**2005, Apr. 25**
4727 A1354 5000 l Either single   .75 .35
a.-b.   Pair, #4727a-4727b   1.50 .20
4727b   Souvenir sheet, 2 each   .75
No. 4727: a, Map in gold. b, Map in silver.

SPRIJIN PENTRU SEMENI / POSTA ROMANA / PICEA ABIES / 5000L 0,50 lei noi

No. 4728 — "Sprijin Pentru Semeni": a, In box. b, Reading up at left.

**2005, May 9**    **Wmk. 398**    **Photo.**    **Perf. 13¼**
4728   Horiz. pair   .70 .35
a.-b.   single   .35 .20

---

No. 4731: a, Feteasca alba. b, Grasa de Cotnari. c, Feteasca neagra. d, Victoria.

### Viticulture — A1356
**2005, May 27**
4731 A1356 21,000 l Sheet of 4, #a-d, + 2 labels   5.75 3.00
Nos. 4731a-4731d also have face values expressed in revalued leu currency that was used as of July 1.

### Scouting A1357

CERCETASI ROMANIEI ROMANIA 22000L

Designs: No. 4732, 22,000 l, Scout climbing rocks. No. 4733, 22,000 l, Scout following marked trail. No. 4734, 22,000 l, Scouts building campfire. No. 4735, 22,000 l, Scouts reading map.

**2005, June 15**
4732-4735 A1357   Set of 4   6.00 3.00
4735a   Horiz. strip of 4, #4732-   6.00 3.00
4735b   Souvenir sheet of 4, #4732-4735   6.00 3.00
Nos. 4732-4735 also have face values expressed in revalued leu currency that was used as of July 1.

ROMANIA 21000L EUROPA

Designs: 21,000 l, Map of Dacia, archer on horseback, duck and stew pot. 77,000 l, Map, hunting dog, roasted game bird, vegetables, glass of wine.

### Europa — A1355
**2005, May 9**    **Litho.**    **Perf. 13¼**
4729-4730 A1355   Set of 2   13.50 6.75
4729a-4730a   Souvenir sheet, #4729-4730, 2 each at UL   6.75
4730b   As "a," #4730 at UL   13.50 6.75

---

ROMANIA 1 Ban nou / LEUL NOU: totul se simplifica — ROMANIA 30 Bani

National Bank of Romania, new and old coins or banknotes depicting revaluation of: 30b, 100 old lei to 1 new leu. 50b, 10,000 old lei to 1 new leu. 70b, 500 old lei to 5 new bani. 80b, 50,000 old lei to 5 new lei. 1 l, 100,000 old lei to 10 new lei. 1.20 l, 500,000 old lei to 50 new lei. 1.60 l, 1,000,000 old lei to 100 new lei. 2.10 l, 1000 old lei to 10 new bani. 2.20 l, 5,000,000 old lei to 500 new lei. 3.10 l, 5000 old lei to 50 new bani.

In the pairs, the "a" stamp has the colored denomination panel on the left and shows the obverse of coins at left and reverse of coins at right, or the obverse side of banknotes. The "b" stamp has the colored denomination panel on the right, shows the reverse of coins at left and obverse of coins at right, or the reverse side of banknotes.

### July 1 Currency Devaluation — A1358
**2005, July 1**    **Litho.**
**Horiz. or Vert. Pairs, #a-b**
**Panel Color**
4736 A1358 30b gray   .40 .20
4737 A1358 30b dk gray   .70 .35
4738 A1358 50b emerald   .95 .45
4739 A1358 80b red brown   1.10 .55
4740 A1358 1 l red violet   1.40 .70
4741 A1358 1.20 l dull brown   1.60 .80
4742 A1358 1.60 l olive green   2.25 1.10
4743 A1358 2.10 l blue green   2.75 1.40
4744 A1358 2.20 l bister   3.00 1.50
4745 A1358 3.10 l purple   4.25 2.10
c.   Miniature sheet of 10 horiz. pairs, #4736-4745   18.50 9.25

# ROMANIA

## Souvenir Sheet

**Pigeon Breeds — A1371**

No. 4765: a, English Pouter (green frame). b, Parlor rollers (lilac frame). c, Standard carrier (green frame). d, Andalusian (yellow orange frame).

**2005, Nov. 18**   *Litho.*
4765  A1371  2.50 l  Sheet of 4,   6.50 3.25
#a-d

**UNESCO, 60th Anniv. — A1372**

**2005, Nov. 21**   *Perf. 13¼*
4766  A1372  60b multi + label   .40  .20

Illustration reduced.

**Pottery Type of 2005**

Pottery from: 30b, Leheceni, Bihor. 50b, Vladesti, Valcea. 1 l, Curtea de Arges, Arges. 1.20 l, Vamu. Satu Mare. 2.20 l, Barsa, Arad. 2.50 l, Corund, Ilarghita. 4.70 l, Targu Neamt, Neamt. 5.60 l, Polaina Deleni, Iasi. 14.50 l, Valea Izei, Maramures.

**2005**

### Background Color

| No. | Type | Denom. | Color | | |
|---|---|---|---|---|---|
| 4767 | A1340 | 30b | greenish yel | .20 | .20 |
| 4768 | A1348 | 50b | blue green | .35 | .20 |
| 4769 | A1348 | 1 l | red orange | .65 | .30 |
| 4770 | A1348 | 1.20 l | pale salmon on | .80 | .40 |
| 4771 | A1348 | | | .80 | .40 |
| 4772 | A1348 | 2.20 l | gray | 1.40 | .70 |
| 4773 | A1340 | 2.50 l | blue | 1.60 | .80 |
| 4774 | A1348 | 4.70 l | blue violet | 3.00 | 1.50 |
| 4775 | A1348 | 14.50 l | bl grn | 3.75 | 1.90 |
| | | | redn | 9.25 | 4.75 |

Nos. 4767-4775 (9)   21.00 10.75

**Christmas — A1373**

No. 4776: a, The Annunciation (23x32mm). b, Nativity (47x32mm). c, Madonna and Child with Angels (23x32mm). Illustration reduced.

**2005, Dec. 2**
4776  A1373  50b  Horiz. strip of 3,   1.00  .50
#a-c

**Modern Art — A1374**

---

**World Summit on the Information Society, Tunis — A1366**

**2005, Oct. 10**
4758  A1366  5.60 l multi   3.75 1.90

**United Nations — A1367**

**2005, Oct. 24**   *Perf. 13¼*
4759-4761  A1367  Set of 3   2.75 1.40
4761a  Souvenir sheet, #4750-4761   2.75 1.40

Dove, UN emblem, Romanian flag and: 40b, Flags. 1.50 l, Security Council. 2.20 l, General Assembly building.

Romania's admission to UN, 50th anniv. (#4759); Romania's presidency of Security Council, 2004-05 (#4760); UN, 60th anniv. (#4761).

**Birthplace of Dimitrie Butculescu, Romanian Philatelic Federation Emblem — A1368**

**2005, Nov. 4**   *Perf. 13¼*
4762  Horiz. pair with flanking labels   .65 .30
a.-b.  A1368  50b  Either single + label   .30 .20

**Souvenir Sheet**   *Imperf*
4763  A1369  9 l multi   6.00 3.00

**Dimitrie Butculescu, Founder of Romanian Philatelic Society — A1369**

Design: No. 4762b, Butculescu, September 1892 edition of Romanian Philatelic Society Monitor.
Illustrations reduced.

**Central University Library, 110th Anniv. — A1370**

**2005, Nov. 10**   *Perf. 13¼*
4764  A1370  60b  Horiz. pair, #a-b   .80 .40
c.  Souvenir sheet, #4764a-4764b   .80 .40

No. 4764: a, Library building (47x32mm). b, Statue (23x32mm).
Illustration reduced.

---

**Children's Art — A1363**

Designs: 30b, Forest Mailman, by Bianca Paul. 40b, The Road to You, by Daniel Ciornei. 60b, A Messenger of Peace, by Stefan Ghiliman, horiz. 1 l, Good News for Everybody, by Adina Elena Mocanu, horiz.

**2005, Aug. 31**   *Litho.*   *Perf. 13¼*
4751-4754  A1363  Set of 4   1.75  .85

**No. 4669 Surcharged in Black and Blue**

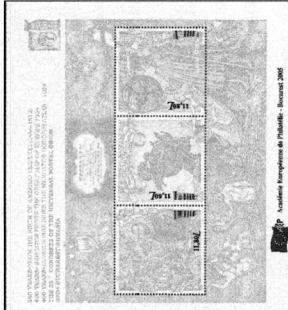

No. 4755: a, Gerardus Mercator and Jodocus Hondius, cartographers. b, UPU emblem. c, Amerigo Vespucci, explorer.

**2005, Sept. 26**   *Perf. 13½*
4755  A1337  11.80 l on 118,000 l   24.00 12.00
Sheet of 3, #a-o

Visit of members of European Philatelic Academy to Bucharest.

**Dogs — A1364**

No. 4756: a, Jagd terrier. b, Rhodesian ridgeback. c, Munsterlander. d, Bloodhound. e, Transylvanian hound (Copoi ardelenesc). f, Pointer.

**2005, Sept. 28**   *Perf. 13¼*
4756  Block of 6   9.00 4.50
a.-f.  A1364  2.20 l  Any single   1.50 .75
g.  Sheet, #4756a-4756f   9.00 4.50

**Natl. Philatelic Museum, 1st Anniv. — A1365**

**2005, Sept. 30**
4757  A1365  40b multi   .30  .20

---

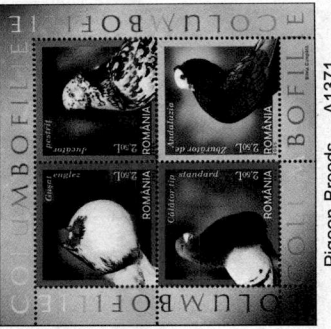

**Military Ships — A1359**

No. 4746: a, Training ship Constanta. b, Corvette Contraadmiral Horia Macellariu. c, Monitor ship Mihail Kogalniceanu. d, Frigate Marasesti.

**2005, July 15**   *Perf. 13¼*
4746  Vert. strip of 4   6.00 3.00
a.-d.  A1359  2.20 l  Any single   1.50 .75
e.  Souvenir sheet of 4, #4746a-4746d   6.00 3.00

Stamp Day.

**Rainbow and Genesis 1:9 — A1360**

**2005, Aug. 2**
4747  A1360  50b multi + label   .35  .20

July 2005 floods in Romania.
Illustration reduced.

**Election of Joseph Cardinal Ratzinger as Pope Benedict XVI — A1361**

Ratzinger in vestments of: 1.20 l, Cardinal. 2.10 l, Pope.

**2005, Aug. 18**
4748-4749  A1361  Set of 2   2.40 1.25
4740a  Souvenir sheet, #1748-4749   2.10 1.25

**European Philatelic Cooperation, 50th Anniv. (in 2006) — A1362**

No. 4750 — Christopher Columbus and: a, Denomination to right of face. b, Ship, denomination at lower right. c, Ship, denomination at lower left. d, Denomination to left of face.

**2005, Aug. 22**   *Perf. 13¼*
4750  Horiz. strip of 4   13.50 6.75
a.-d.  A1362  4.70 l  Any single   3.25 1.60
e.  Souvenir sheet, #4750a-4750d +2 labels   13.50 6.75

Europa stamps, 50th anniv. (in 2006). The vignettes of Nos. 4750a and 4750d are inside a 31x27mm perf. 13 hexagon. Values for singles of these stamps are for examples with surrounding selvage. No. 4750 exists imperf.

No. 4777: a, Inscriptions, by Virgil Preda. b, The Suspended Garden, by Alin Gheorghiu. c, Still Life with Bottle, by Constantin Ceraceanu. d, Monster 1, by Cristian Paleologu.
Illustration reduced.

**2005, Dec. 12**
**4777** A1374 1.50 l Block of 4, #a-d 4.00 2.00

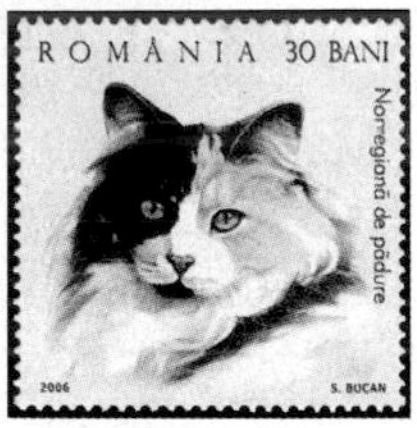
Cats A1375

Designs: 30b, Norwegian Forest. 50b, Turkish Van. 70b, Siamese. 80b, Ragdoll. 1.20 l, Persian. 1.60 l, Birman.

**2006, Jan. 20** ***Perf. 13¼***
**4778-4783** A1375 Set of 6 3.50 1.75
*4783a* Souvenir sheet, #4778-4783, imperf. 3.50 1.75

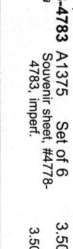

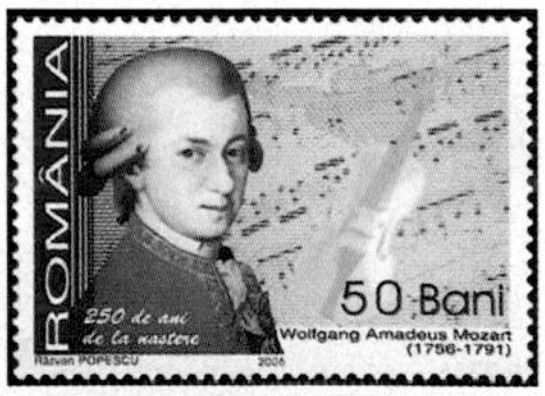
Famous People — A1376

Designs: 50b, Wolfgang Amadeus Mozart (1756-91), composer. 1.20 l, Ion C. Bratianu (1821-91), Prime Minister. 2.10 l, Grigore Moisil (1906-73), mathematician.

**2006, Jan. 27** ***Perf. 13¼***
**4784-4786** A1376 Set of 3 2.60 1.25

Souvenir Sheet

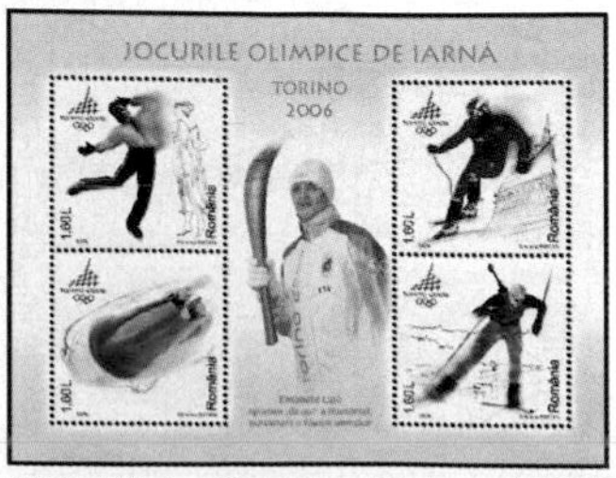
2006 Winter Olympics, Turin — A1377

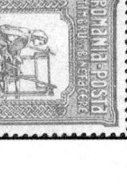

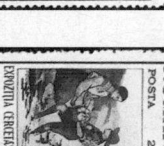

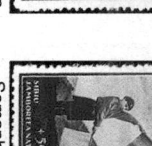

No. 4787: a, Figure skating. b, Downhill skiing. c, Bobsled. d, Biathlon.

**2006, Feb. 1**
**4787** A1377 1.60 l Sheet of 4, #a-d 4.25 2.10

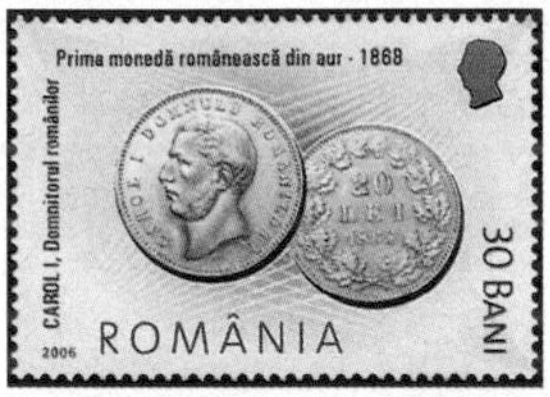
Gold Coins — A1378

Coin obverse and reverse: 30b, 1868 20 lei. 50b, 1906 50 lei. 70b, 1906 100 lei. 1 l, 1922 50 lei. 1.20 l, 1939 100 lei. 2.20 l, 1940 100 lei.

**2006, Feb. 22**
**4788-4793** A1378 Set of 6 4.00 2.00

## SEMI-POSTAL STAMPS

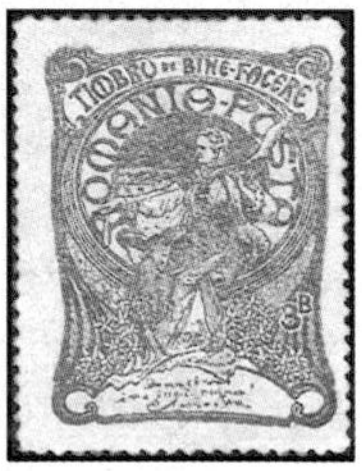
Queen Elizabeth Spinning — SP1

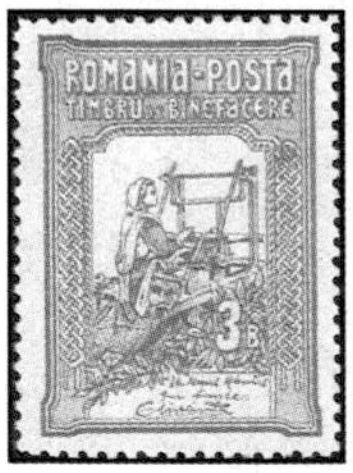
The Queen Weaving — SP2

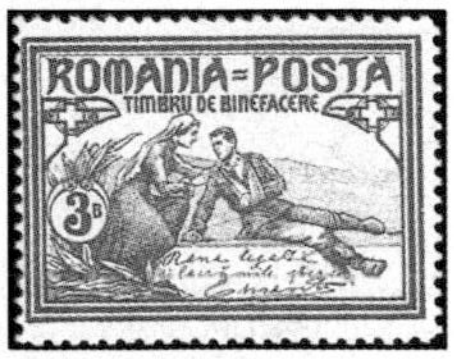
Queen as War Nurse SP3

***Perf. 11½, 11½x13½***
**1906, Jan. 14** **Typo.** **Unwmk.**
**B1** SP1 3b (+ 7b) brown 3.00 2.00
**B2** SP1 5b (+ 10b) lt grn 3.00 2.00
**B3** SP1 10b (+ 10b) rose red 14.00 6.50
**B4** SP1 15b (+ 10b) violet 10.00 4.50
*Nos. B1-B4 (4)* 30.00 15.00

**1906, Mar. 18**
**B5** SP2 3b (+ 7b) org brn 3.00 2.00
**B6** SP2 5b (+ 10b) bl grn 3.00 2.00
**B7** SP2 10b (+ 10b) car 16.50 6.50
**B8** SP2 15b (+ 10b) red vio 10.00 4.55
*Nos. B5-B8 (4)* 32.50 15.05

**1906, Mar. 23** ***Perf. 11½, 13½x11½***
**B9** SP3 3b (+ 7b) org brn 3.00 2.00
**B10** SP3 5b (+ 10b) bl grn 3.00 2.00
**B11** SP3 10b (+ 10b) car 16.50 6.50
**B12** SP3 15b (+ 10b) red vio 10.00 4.55
*Nos. B9-B12 (4)* 32.50 15.05
*Nos. B1-B12 (12)* 95.00 45.10

Booklet panes of 4 exist of Nos. B1-B3, B5-B7, B9-B12.
Counterfeits of Nos. B1-B12 are plentiful. Copies of Nos. B1-B12 with smooth, even gum are counterfeits.

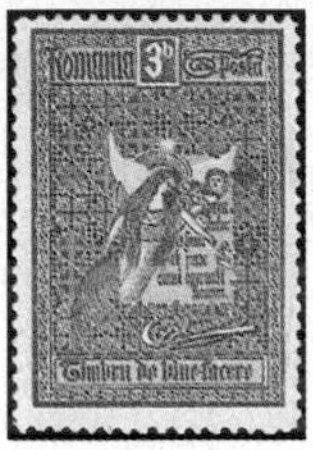
SP4

**1906, Aug. 4** ***Perf. 12***
**B13** SP4 3b (+ 7b) ol brn, buff & bl 1.50 1.00
**B14** SP4 5b (+ 10b) grn, rose & buff 1.50 1.00
**B15** SP4 10b (+ 10b) rose red, buff & bl 3.00 2.00
**B16** SP4 15b (+ 10b) vio, buff & bl 6.50 3.00
*Nos. B13-B16 (4)* 12.50 7.00

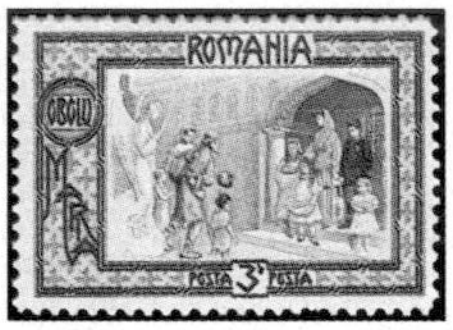
Guardian Angel Bringing Poor to Crown Princess Marie SP5

**1907, Feb.** **Engr.** ***Perf. 11***
**Center in Brown**
**B17** SP5 3b (+ 7b) org brn 3.25 1.90
**B18** SP5 5b (+ 10b) dk grn 2.25 1.00
**B19** SP5 10b (+ 10b) dk car 2.25 1.00
**B20** SP5 15b (+ 10b) dl vio 2.25 1.10
*Nos. B17-B20 (4)* 10.00 5.00

Nos. B1-B20 were sold for more than face value. The surtax, shown in parenthesis, was for charitable purposes.

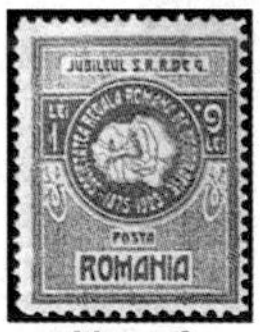
Map of Romania SP9

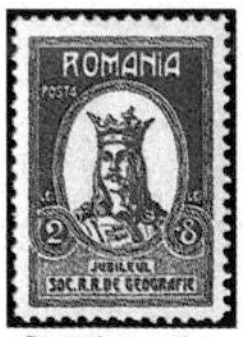
Stephen the Great SP10

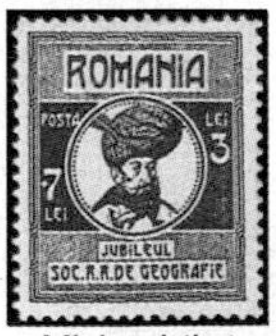
Michael the Brave SP11

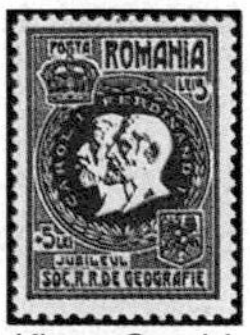
Kings Carol I and Ferdinand SP12

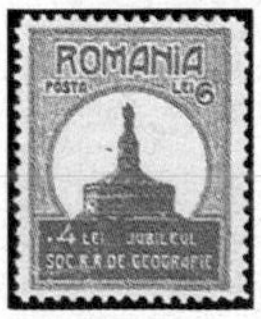
Adam Clisi Monument — SP13

**1927, Mar. 15** **Typo.** ***Perf. 13½***
**B21** SP9 1 l + 9 l lt vio .80 .45
**B22** SP10 2 l + 8 l Prus grn .80 .45
**B23** SP11 3 l + 7 l dp rose .80 .45
**B24** SP12 5 l + 5 l dp bl .80 .45
**B25** SP13 6 l + 4 l ol grn 2.25 .45
*Nos. B21-B25 (5)* 5.45 2.25

50th anniv. of the Royal Geographical Society. The surtax was for the benefit of that society. The stamps were valid for postage only from 3/15-4/14.

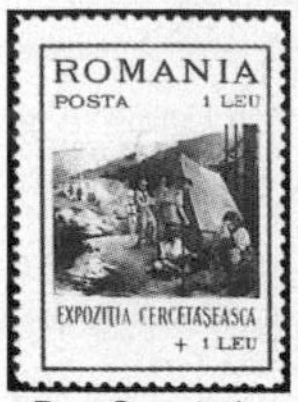
Boy Scouts in Camp — SP15

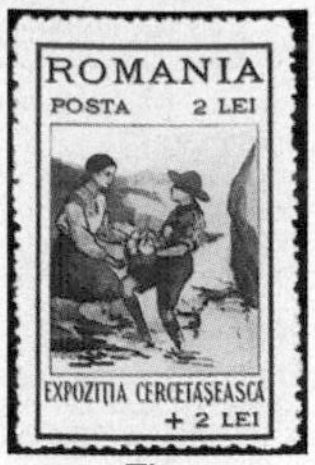
The Rescue — SP16

Designs: 3 l+3 l, Swearing in a Tenderfoot. 4 l+4 l, Prince Nicholas Chief Scout. 6 l+6 l, King Carol II in Scout's Uniform.

**1931, July 15** **Photo.** **Wmk. 225**
**B26** SP15 1 l + 1 l car rose 1.25 1.10
**B27** SP16 2 l + 2 l dp grn 1.60 1.25
**B28** SP15 3 l + 3 l ultra 2.00 1.50
**B29** SP16 4 l + 4 l ol gray 2.40 2.00
**B30** SP16 6 l + 6 l red brn 3.25 2.00
*Nos. B26-B30 (5)* 10.50 7.85

The surtax was for the benefit of the Boy Scout organization.

### Boy Scout Jamboree Issue

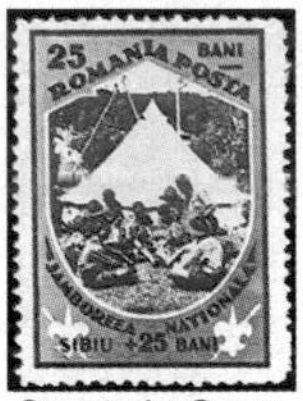
Scouts in Camp SP20

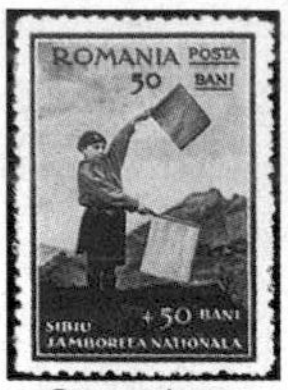
Semaphore Signaling SP21

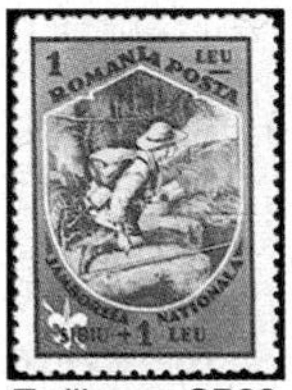
Trailing — SP22

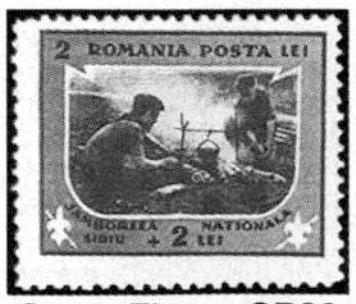
Camp Fire — SP23

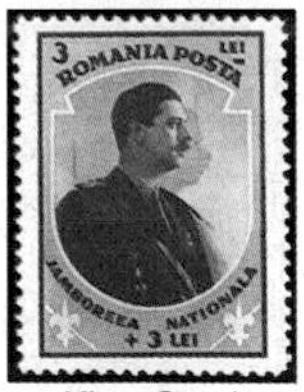
King Carol II — SP24

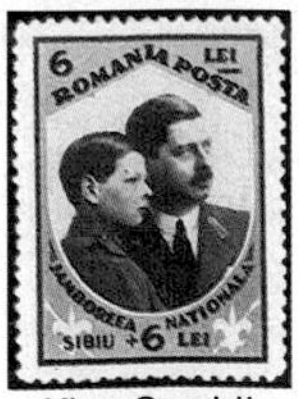
King Carol II and Prince Michael — SP25

**1932, June 8** **Wmk. 230**
**B31** SP20 25b + 25b pck grn 3.00 1.10
**B32** SP21 50b + 50b brt bl 4.00 2.25
**B33** SP22 1 l + 1 l ol grn 4.50 3.25
**B34** SP23 2 l + 2 l org red 7.50 4.50
**B35** SP24 3 l + 3 l Prus bl 14.00 9.00
**B36** SP25 6 l + 6 l blk brn 16.00 11.50
*Nos. B31-B36 (6)* 49.00 31.60

For overprints see Nos. B44-B49.

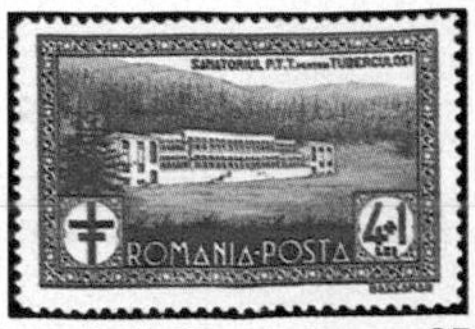
Tuberculosis Sanatorium — SP26

ROMANIA

Swimming SP54

Throwing the Javelin — SP55

Skiing — SP56

King Carol II Hunting — SP57

Horsemanship SP59

Rowing SP58

Founding of the U.F.S.R. SP60

**1937, June 8  Wmk. 230  Perf. 13½**

| | | | | | |
|---|---|---|---|---|---|
| B69 | SP53 | 25b + 25b ol blk | .20 | .20 |
| B70 | SP54 | 50b + 50b brown | .25 | .25 |
| B71 | SP55 | 1 l + 1 l violet | .30 | .30 |
| B72 | SP56 | 2 l + 1 l slate grn | .35 | .35 |
| B73 | SP57 | 3 l + 1 l rose lake | .50 | .45 |
| B74 | SP58 | 4 l + 1 l red org | .80 | .60 |
| B75 | SP59 | 6 l + 2 l dp claret | 1.00 | 1.00 |
| B76 | SP60 | 10 l + 4 l brt bluo | 1.25 | 1.25 |
| | | Nos. B69-B76 (8) | 4.70 | 4.40 |

25th anniversary of the Federation of Romanian Sports Clubs (U.F.S.R.); 7th anniversary of the accession of King Carol II. Exist imperf. Value $200, unused or uood.

Javelin Thrower — SP62

Start of Race — SP61

**1937, Sept. 1  Wmk. 230  Perf. 13½**

| | | | | | |
|---|---|---|---|---|---|
| B77 | SP61 | 1 l + 1 l purple | .40 | .40 |
| B78 | SP62 | 2 l + 1 l green | .50 | .50 |
| B79 | SP61 | 4 l + 1 l vermilion | .60 | .60 |
| B80 | SP62 | 6 l + 1 l maroon | 1.00 | 1.00 |
| B81 | SP61 | 10 l + 1 l brt bl | 2.50 | 2.50 |
| | | Nos. B77-B81 (5) | 5.00 | 5.00 |

8th Balkan Games, Bucharest. Exist imperf. Value $200, unused or used.

---

Catalogue values for unused stamps in this section, from this point to the end of the section, are for Never Hinged items.

---

Girl of Saliste — SP42

Youth from Gorj — SP44

Designs: 1 l+1 l, Girl of Banat. 3 l+1 l, Girl of Hateg. 6 l+3 l, Girl of Neamt. 10 l+5 l, Youth and girl of Bucovina.

**1936, June 8**

| | | | | | |
|---|---|---|---|---|---|
| B56 | SP40 | 50b + 50b brown | .45 | .30 |
| B57 | SP40 | 1 l + 1 l violet | .45 | .30 |
| B58 | SP42 | 2 l + 1 l Prus grn | .45 | .30 |
| B59 | SP42 | 3 l + 1 l car rose | .45 | .30 |
| B60 | SP44 | 4 l + 2 l red org | .80 | .65 |
| B61 | SP40 | 6 l + 3 l ol gray | .80 | .75 |
| B62 | SP42 | 10 l + 5 l brt brn | 1.60 | 1.40 |
| | | Nos. B56-B62 (7) | 5.00 | 4.00 |

6th anniv. of accession of King Carol II. The surtax was for child welfare. Exist imperf. Value $200, unused or used.

Insignia of Boy Scouts SP47

Jamboree Emblem — SP49

Submarine "Delfinul" SP50

**1936, Aug. 20**

| | | | | | |
|---|---|---|---|---|---|
| B63 | SP47 | 1 l + 1 l brt bl | 5.25 | 3.75 |
| B64 | SP48 | 3 l + 3 l ol gray | 8.75 | 4.25 |
| B65 | SP49 | 6 l + 6 l car rose | 11.50 | 4.75 |
| | | Nos. B63-B65 (3) | 25.50 | 12.75 |

Boy Scout Jamboree at Brasov (Kronstadt). Exist imperf. Value $225, unused or used.

**1936, Oct.**

Designs: 3 l+2 l, Training ship "Mircea." 6 l+3 l, Steamship "S.M.R."

| | | | | | |
|---|---|---|---|---|---|
| B66 | SP50 | 3 l + 2 l pur | 2.10 | 2.00 |
| B67 | SP50 | 3 l + 2 l ultra | 2.00 | 1.75 |
| B68 | SP50 | 6 l + 3 l car rose | 2.75 | 1.75 |
| | | Nos. B66-B68 (3) | 6.85 | 5.50 |

Marine Exhibition at Bucharest. Exist imperf. Value $250, unused or used.

Soccer SP53

---

## Boy Scout Mamaia Jamboree Issue

Semi-Postal Stamps of 1932 Overprinted in Black or Gold

**1934, July 8**

| | | | | | |
|---|---|---|---|---|---|
| B44 | SP20 | 25b + 25b pck grn | 2.00 | 2.00 |
| B45 | SP21 | 50b + 50b brt bl (G) | 3.25 | 2.50 |
| B46 | SP22 | 1 l + 1 l ol grn | 4.00 | 4.50 |
| B47 | SP23 | 2 l + 2 l org red | 4.50 | 4.50 |
| B48 | SP24 | 3 l + 3 l Prus bl | 8.75 | 8.00 |
| B49 | SP25 | 6 l + 6 l blk brn | 14.00 | 11.00 |
| | | Nos. B44-B49 (6) | 36.50 | 32.00 |

Scout Bugler SP35

Sea Scout Saluting SP34

Sea, Land and Girl Scouts — SP38

Sea and Land Scouts SP36

King Carol II — SP37

**1935, June 8**

| | | | | |
|---|---|---|---|---|
| B50 | SP34 | 25b ol blk | 1.00 | .75 |
| B51 | SP35 | 1 l violet | 2.25 | 2.00 |
| B52 | SP36 | 2 l green | 2.75 | 2.50 |
| B53 | SP37 | 6 l + 1 l red brn | 4.25 | 3.75 |
| B54 | SP38 | 10 l + 2 l dk ultra | 12.00 | 11.00 |
| | | Nos. B50-B54 (5) | 22.25 | 20.00 |

Fifth anniversary of accession of King Carol II, and a national sports meeting held June 8. Surtax aided the Boy Scouts. Nos. B50-B54 exist imperf. Value $200.

King Carol II — SP39

**1936, May**

| | | | | |
|---|---|---|---|---|
| B55 | SP39 | 6 l + 1 l rose car | .55 | .40 |

Bucharest Exhibition and 70th anniversary of the dynasty. Exists imperf. Value $125.

Girl of Oltenia — SP40

---

Memorial Tablet to Postal Employees Who Died in World War I — SP27

Carmen Sylva Convalescent Home — SP28

**1932, Nov. 1**

| | | | | |
|---|---|---|---|---|
| B37 | SP26 | 4 l + 1 l dk grn | 2.50 | 2.00 |
| B38 | SP27 | 6 l + 1 l chocolate | 2.50 | 2.25 |
| B39 | SP28 | 10 l + 1 l dp bl | 5.00 | 3.75 |
| | | Nos. B37-B39 (3) | 10.00 | 8.00 |

The surtax was given to a fund for the employees of the postal and telegraph services.

## Philatelic Exhibition Issue

Souvenir Sheet

*Expoziția Filatelică Romănă*  CITIRO

*Bucuresti 1932 Bucuresti*

King Carol II — SP29

**1932, Nov. 20  Unwmk.  Imperf.**

| | | | | |
|---|---|---|---|---|
| B40 | SP29 | 6 l + 5 l dk grn | 50.00 | 50.00 |

Intl. Phil. Exhib. at Bucharest, Nov. 20-24, 1932. Each holder of a ticket of admission to the exhibition could buy a copy of the stamp. The ticket cost 20 lei.

---

Woman Spinning — SP33

Woman Weaving SP32

Roadside Shrine — SP31

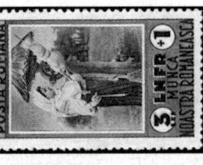

**1934, Apr. 16  Wmk. 230  Perf. 13½**

| | | | | |
|---|---|---|---|---|
| B41 | SP31 | 1 l + 1 l dk brn | .85 | .75 |
| B42 | SP32 | 2 l + 1 l blue | 1.10 | 1.00 |
| B43 | SP33 | 3 l + 1 l slate grn | 1.40 | 1.25 |
| | | Nos. B41-B43 (3) | 3.35 | 3.00 |

Weaving Exposition.

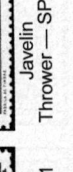

## 1938, May 24

B82 SP66 6 l + 11 l deep magenta .90 .20

King Carol II — SP66

Bucharest Exhibition (for local products), May 19-June 19, celebrating 20th anniversary of the union of Rumanian provinces.
Exists imperf. Value $150, unused or used.

Dimitrie Cantemir — SP67
Mircea the Great SP69
Constantine Brancoveanu SP70
Maria Doamna — SP68
Stephen the Great — SP71
Prince Cuza — SP72
Michael the Brave — SP75
King Carol I — SP77
King Ferdinand I — SP76
Queen Elizabeth I — SP74

## 1938, June 8

| | | | | |
|---|---|---|---|---|
| B83 | SP67 | 25b + 25b ol blk | .80 | .40 |
| B84 | SP68 | 50b + 50b brn | 1.00 | .40 |
| B85 | SP69 | 1 l + 1 l blk vio | 1.00 | .40 |
| B86 | SP70 | 2 l + 2 l dk brn grn | 1.25 | .40 |
| B87 | SP71 | 3 l + 3 l dp mag | 1.25 | .40 |
| B88 | SP72 | 4 l + 4 l scarlet | 1.25 | .40 |
| B89 | SP73 | 6 l + 2 l vio brn | 1.50 | .80 |

Perf 13½

| | | | | |
|---|---|---|---|---|
| B90 | SP74 | 7.50 l gray bl | 1.75 | .80 |
| B91 | SP75 | 10 l brt bl | 2.50 | 1.00 |
| B92 | SP76 | 16 l dk slate grn | 3.50 | 1.75 |
| B93 | SP77 | 20 l vermilion | 4.25 | 1.75 |
| | | | 19.80 | 9.25 |

Nos. B83-B93 (11)

8th anniv. of accession of King Carol II. Surtax was for Straja Tarii, a natl. org. for boys. Exist imperf. Value $175, unused or used.

"Rodica, the Water Carrier" SP81
Nicolae Grigorescu SP82
"Escorting Prisoners" SP79
"The Spring" — SP78

## 1938, June 23

Design: 4 l+1 l, "Returning from Market."

| | | | | |
|---|---|---|---|---|
| B94 | SP78 | 1 l + 1 l brt bl | 1.00 | .40 |
| B95 | SP79 | 2 l + 1 l yel grn | 1.00 | .65 |
| B96 | SP80 | 3 l + 1 l pale vio | 1.25 | .70 |
| B97 | SP81 | 4 l + 1 l lake | 1.75 | 1.00 |
| B98 | SP82 | 10 l + 1 l brt bl | 2.50 | 1.25 |
| | | | 7.75 | 4.00 |

Nos. B94-B98 (5)

Birth centenary of Nicolae Grigorescu, Romanian painter. Exist imperf. Value $175, unused or used.

Perf 13½

St. George and the Dragon — SP83

## 1939, June 8

| | | | | |
|---|---|---|---|---|
| B99 | SP83 | 25b + 25b ol gray | .45 | .30 |
| B100 | SP83 | 50b + 50b brn | .45 | .30 |
| B101 | SP83 | 1 l + 1 l pale vio | .45 | .30 |
| B102 | SP83 | 2 l + 2 l lt grn | .45 | .30 |
| B103 | SP83 | 3 l + 3 l red vio | .90 | .35 |
| B104 | SP83 | 6 l + 2 l car rose | 1.00 | .35 |
| B105 | SP83 | 6 l + 2 l gray vio | 1.00 | .35 |
| B106 | SP83 | 6 l + 2 l red org | 1.10 | .45 |
| B107 | SP83 | 10 l brt bl | 1.00 | .35 |
| B108 | SP83 | 12 l brt ultra | 1.40 | .55 |
| B109 | SP83 | 16 l bl grn | 2.00 | 1.10 |
| | | | 10.50 | 5.70 |

Nos. B99-B109 (11)

9th anniv. of accession of King Carol II. Exist imperf. Value $175, unused or used.

Photo.

King Carol II
SP87
SP88

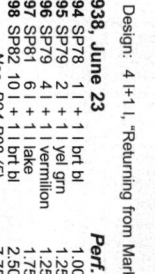 

## 1940, June 8    Wmk. 230

Photo.    Perf 13½

| | | | | |
|---|---|---|---|---|
| B113 | SP87 | 1 l + 50b dl pur | .65 | .20 |
| B114 | SP88 | 1 l fawn | .65 | .35 |
| B115 | SP89 | 6 l + 1 l dp | .45 | .25 |
| B116 | SP90 | 6 l rose brn | .90 | .55 |
| B117 | SP91 | 6 l dk vio brn | 1.10 | .20 |
| B118 | SP91 | 32 l dk vio brn | 1.60 | 1.10 |
| | | | 5.55 | 3.35 |

Nos. B113-B118 (6)

10th anniv. of accession of King Carol II. Exist imperf.

SP89
SP91

King Carol II
SP92
SP93

## 1940, June 1

| | | | | |
|---|---|---|---|---|
| B119 | SP92 | 1 l + 50b dk grn | .20 | .20 |
| B120 | SP93 | 2.50 l + 50b Prus grn | .25 | .20 |
| B121 | SP93 | 3 l + 1 l rose car | .35 | .25 |
| B122 | SP93 | 4 l + 50b choc | .35 | .35 |
| B123 | SP93 | 6 l + 1 l org brn | .50 | .35 |
| B124 | SP93 | 6 l + 1 l sapphire | .75 | .20 |
| B125 | SP93 | 9 l + 1 l brt bl | .85 | .70 |
| B126 | SP93 | 14 l + 1 l dk bl grn | 1.10 | .90 |
| | | | 4.35 | 3.15 |

Nos. B119-B126 (8)

Surtax was for Romania's air force. Exist imperf. Value $125, unused or used.

View of Danube SP94
Greco-Roman Ruins — SP95

## 1940, June 8    Perf 14½x14, 14x14½
Inscribed: "Straja Tarii 8 Junie 1940"

| | | | | |
|---|---|---|---|---|
| B127 | SP94 | 1 l + 1 l dp vio | .40 | .20 |
| B128 | SP94 | 2 l + 1 l red brn | .45 | .30 |
| B129 | SP94 | 3 l + 1 l yel grn | .50 | .35 |
| B130 | SP94 | 4 l + 1 l grnsh blk | .50 | .45 |
| B131 | SP94 | 5 l + 1 l org ver | .55 | .45 |
| B132 | SP94 | 6 l + 1 l brn car | .60 | .60 |
| B133 | SP95 | 10 l + 1 l ultra | .85 | .60 |
| B134 | SP95 | 16 l + 2 l dk bl gray | 1.00 | .90 |
| | | | 6.10 | 4.60 |

Designs: 3 l+1 l, Hotin Castle. 4 l+1 l, Hurez Monastery. 5 l+1 l, Church in Bucovina. 8 l+1 l, Tower. 16 l+2 l, Village church, Transylvania. 16 l+2 l, Arch in Bucharest.
Nos. B127-B134 (8)

Issued to honor Straja Tarii, a national organization for boys. Exist imperf. Value $140, unused or used.

Vasile Marin—SP104

Vasile Marin and Ion Mota, who died in the Spanish Civil War. No. B148 sold for 300 lei.

B148
a.
b.

## 1941, Jan. 13

Design: 15 l+15 l, Ion Mota.

| | | | | |
|---|---|---|---|---|
| B146 | SP104 | 7 l + 7 l rose | 2.50 | 2.50 |
| B147 | SP104 | 15 l + 15 l slate bl | 3.75 | 3.75 |

Souvenir Sheet
Imperf

| | | | | |
|---|---|---|---|---|
| B148 | | Sheet of 2 | 45.00 | 45.00 |
| a. | SP104 | 7 l + 7 l Prus grn | 9.00 | 9.00 |
| b. | SP104 | 15 l + 15 l Prus green | | 14.00 |

King Michael
SP102

## 1940-42    Photo.    Wmk. 230

| | | | | |
|---|---|---|---|---|
| B138 | SP102 | 1 l + 50b yel | .20 | .20 |
| B138A | SP102 | 2 l + 50b yel | .45 | .35 |
| B139 | SP102 | 2.50 l + 50b dk bl | .20 | .20 |
| B140 | SP102 | 3 l + 1 l grn | .20 | .20 |
| B141 | SP102 | 3.50 l + 50b rose | .20 | .20 |
| B141A | SP102 | 4 l + 50b org | .20 | .20 |
| B142 | SP102 | 4 l + 1 l brn | .20 | .20 |
| B142A | SP102 | 5 l + 1 l dp plum | .45 | .35 |
| B143 | SP102 | 6 l + 1 l lt ultra | .20 | .20 |
| B143A | SP102 | 6 l + 1 l sl grn | .20 | .20 |
| B143B | SP102 | 8 l + 1 l pur | .20 | .20 |
| B143C | SP102 | 12 l + 1 l dp | .20 | .20 |
| B144 | SP102 | 14 l + 1 l brt vio | .30 | .20 |
| B144A | SP102 | 19 l + 1 l lil rose | .30 | .35 |

Nos. B138-B144A (14)

Issue years: #B138A, B141A, B142A, B143A, B143B, B143C, B144A, 1942; others, 1940.

Crown, Leaves and Bible — SP107

## 1941, May 9    Wmk. 230    Photo.    Perf 13½
Inscribed: "1891 1941"

| | | | | |
|---|---|---|---|---|
| B149 | SP106 | 1.50 l + 43.50 l pur | 1.10 | 1.10 |
| B150 | SP107 | 2 l + 43 l rose | | |
| B151 | SP107 | 7 l + 38 l rose | 1.10 | 1.10 |
| B152 | SP107 | 10 l + 35 l ol blk | 1.10 | 1.10 |
| B153 | SP107 | 16 l + 29 l brown | 1.10 | 1.10 |
| | | | 5.50 | 5.50 |

Nos. B149-B153 (5)

50th anniv. of the Carol I Foundation, established to endow research and stimulate the arts.

Designs: 2 l+43 l, Library shelves. 7 l+38 l, Carol I Foundation, Bucharest. 10 l+35 l, King Carol I. 16 l+29 l, Kings Michael and Carol I.

Corneliu Codreanu
SP103

## 1940, Nov. 8    Unwmk.    Perf 13½

B145 SP103 7 l + 30 l dk grn 4.25 3.50

13th anniv. of the founding of the Iron Guard by Corneliu Codreanu.

ROMANIA

Avram Jancu,
National
Hero—SP138

**1943, Feb. 15**
B202 SP138 16 l + 4 l brown   .70 .70

Nurse
Aiding
Wounded
Soldier
SP139

**1943, Mar. 1**    *Perf. 14½x14*
B203 SP139 12 l + 88 l red brn &   .75 .75
     ultra
B204 SP139 16 l + 84 l brt ultra   .75 .75
     & red
B205 SP139 20 l + 80 l ol gray &   .75 .75
     red    2.25 2.25
     *Nos. B203-B205 (3)*

**Souvenir Sheet**
*Imperf*
B206    Sheet of 2    6.00 7.00
  *a.*    SP139 16 l + 84 l bright ultra &
     red    2.00 2.50
  *b.*    SP139 20 l + 80 l olive gray &
     red    2.00 2.50
Surtax on Nos. B203-B206 aided the
Romanian Red Cross.
No. B206 sold for 500 l.

Sword Severing
Chain—SP142

Sword
Hilt—SP141

Soldier and Family,
Guardian
Angel—SP143

**1943, June 22**    *Perf. 14x14½*
            *Wmk. 276*
B207 SP141 36 l + 164 l brn    1.75 1.75
B208 SP142 62 l + 138 l brt bl    1.75 1.75
B209 SP143 76 l + 124 l red org    5.25 5.25
     *Nos. B207-B209 (3)*

**Souvenir Sheet**
*Imperf*
B210    Sheet of 2    12.50 12.50
  *a.*    SP143 62 l + 138 l deep blue   3.25 3.25
  *b.*    SP143 76 l + 124 l red org   3.25 3.25
2nd anniv. of Romania's entrance into
WWII. No. B210 sold for 600 l.

Petru
Maior—SP145

Horia,
Closca
and Crisan
SP148

---

**Souvenir Sheet**
*Imperf*
**Without Gum**
B191 SP128    Sheet of 3    4.75 4.75
   The surtax aided war prisoners.
No. B191 contains one each of Nos. B188-
B190, imperf. Sold for 200 l.

**1942, Dec.**    *Perf. 13½*
B192 SP130   6 l + 44 l sepia   1.25 2.00
B193 SP130 12 l + 38 l violet   1.25 2.00
B194 SP130 24 l + 26 l blue   3.75 6.00
     *Nos. B192-B194 (3)*
Anniv. of the conquest of Transdniestria,
and for use only in this territory which includes
Odessa and land beyond the Duiester.

Michael,
Antonescu and
(inset) Stephen
of Moldavia
SP132

Romanian Troops Crossing Pruth
River to Retake Bessarabia — SP133

**1942, Wmk. 230   Photo.**   *Perf. 13½*
B195 SP131   9 l + 41 l red brn   2.00 2.25
B196 SP132 18 l + 32 l ul gray   2.00 2.25
B197 SP133 20 l + 30 l brt ultra   6.00 6.75
     *Nos. B195-B197 (3)*
First anniversary of liberation of Bessarabia.

Michael,
Antonescu,
Hitler, Mussolini
and Bessarabia
Map
SP131

Bucovina Coats of Arms
SP135

   Design: 20 l +30 l, Bucovina arms with
triple-barred cross.

**1942, Nov. 1**
B198 SP134   9 l + 41 l brt ver   2.00 2.25
B199 SP135 18 l + 32 l blue   2.00 2.25
B200 SP135 20 l + 30 l car rose   6.00 6.75
     *Nos. B198-B200 (3)*
First anniversary of liberation of Bucovina.

Andrei Muresanu
SP137

**1942, Dec. 30**
B201 SP137   5 l + 5 l violet    .60 .60
80th death anniv. of Andrei Muresanu, writer.

---

SP118

**Souvenir Sheet**
*Imperf*
**Without Gum**

**1941, Oct. 11**    *Perf. 14½x13½*
B170 SP113 10 l + 30 l ultra   2.25 2.75
B171 SP114 12 l + 28 l dl org   2.50 2.75
     red
B172 SP115 16 l + 24 l lt brn   2.50 2.75
B173 SP116 20 l + 20 l dk vio   9.50 11.00
     *Nos. B170-B173 (4)*

**Souvenir Sheet**
*Imperf*
**Without Gum**
B174 SP118    Sheet of 2   10.00 12.00
  *a.*    16 l blue gray   1.50 3.00
  *b.*    20 l brown carmine   1.50 3.00
No. B174 sold for 200 l. The surtax aided
the Anti-Bolshevism crusade.

**ODESA**
**16 Oct. 1941**

Nos. B170-B174 Overprinted

**1941, Oct.**    *Perf. 14½x13½*
B175 SP113 10 l + 30 l ultra   1.60 2.25
B176 SP114 12 l + 28 l dl   1.60
     org red    2.25
B177 SP115 16 l + 24 l lt brn   1.75 2.25
B178 SP116 20 l + 20 l dk   6.70 9.00
     vio
     *Nos. B175-B178 (4)*

**Souvenir Sheet**
*Imperf*
**Without Gum**
B178A SP118    Sheet of 2   10.00 10.00
   Occupation of Odessa, Russia.

**Types of Regular Issue, 1941**
Designs: 3 l+50b, Sucevita Monastery,
Bucovina. 5.50 l+50b, Rughi Monastery,
Soroca, Bessarabia. 5.50 l+1 l, Tighina For-
tresa, Bessarabia. 6.50 l+1 l, Soroca Fortresa,
Bessarabia. 8 l+1 l, St. Nicholas Monastery,
Suceava, Bucovina. 9.50 l+1 l, Milisauti
Monastery, Bucovina. 10.50 l+1 l, Putna
Monastery, Bucovina. 16 l+1 l, Cetatea Alba
Fortress, Bessarabia. 25 l+1 l, Hotin Fortress,
Bessarabia.

**1941, Dec. 1   Wmk. 230**   *Perf. 13½*
B179 A179   3 l + 50b rose    .25 .25
     brn
B180 A179   5 l + 50b red org   .30 .35
B181 A179   5.50 l + 1 l blk   .45 .35
B182 A179   6.50 l + 1 l dk brn   .45 .50
B183 A177   8 l + 1 l lt bl   .50 .50
B184 A177   9.50 l + 1 l gray bl   .50 .45
B185 A179 10.50 l + 1 l dk bl   .55 .25
B186 A179 16 l + 1 l vio   .60 .50
B187 A179 25 l + 1 l gray blk   .70 .55
     *Nos. B179-B187 (9)*   4.50 3.45

Statue of Miron
Costin at
Jassy—SP130

Titu
Maiorescu — SP128

**1942, Oct. 5**
B188 SP128   9 l + 11 l dl vio   .45 .45
B189 SP128 20 l + 20 l yel brn   1.25 1.25
B190 SP128 20 l + 30 l blue   3.10 3.10
     *Nos. B188-B190 (3)*

---

Same
Overprinted in
Red or Black

**1941, Aug.**
B154 SP107   1.50 l + 43.50 l (R)   1.60 2.00
B155 SP107   2 l + 43 l   1.60 2.00
B156 SP107   7 l + 38 l   1.60 2.00
B157 SP107 10 l + 35 l (R)   1.60 2.00
B158 SP107 16 l + 29 l   1.60 2.00
   Occupation of Cernauti, Bucovina.

Same
Overprinted in
Red or Black

**1941, Aug.**
B159 SP107   1.50 l + 43.50 l   1.60 2.00
     (R)
B160 SP107   2 l + 43 l   1.60 2.00
B161 SP107   7 l + 38 l   1.60 2.00
B162 SP107 10 l + 35 l (R)   1.60 2.00
B163 SP107 16 l + 29 l   16.00 20.00
     *Nos. B154-B163 (10)*
   Occupation of Chisinau, Bessarabia.

Romanian Red
Cross—SP111

     *Perf. 13½*

**1941, Aug.**
B164 SP111   1.50 l + 38.50 l   .85 .85
B165 SP111   2 l + 38 l   .85 .85
B166 SP111   7 l + 33 l   .85 .85
B167 SP111 10 l + 30 l   1.10 1.10
B168 SP111 16 l + 24 l   1.50 3.10
     *Nos. B164-B168 (5)*

**Souvenir Sheet**
*Imperf*
**Without Gum**
B169    Sheet of 2   11.00 11.00
  *a.*    SP111 7 l + 33 l brown & red   1.60 2.00
  *b.*    SP111 10 l + 30 l brt blue &   1.60 2.00
     red
The surtax on Nos. B164-B169 was for the
Romanian Red Cross.
No. B169 sold for 200 l.

King
Michael
and Stephen
the Great
SP113

Hotin and
Akkerman
Castles
SP114

Romanian
and German
Soldiers
SP115

Soldiers
SP116

32 l+118 l, Gheorghe Sincai. 36 l+114 l, Timotei Cipariu. 91 l+109 l, Gheorghe Cosbuc.

**1943, Aug. 15**   **Photo.**   **Wmk. 276**
**Perf. 13½; 14½x14 (No. B214)**

| | | | |
|---|---|---|---|
| B211 | SP145 16 l + 134 l red org | .45 | .45 |
| B212 | SP145 32 l + 118 l lt bl | .45 | .45 |
| B213 | SP145 36 l + 114 l vio | .45 | .45 |
| B214 | SP145 62 l + 138 l car rose | .45 | .45 |
| B215 | SP145 91 l + 109 l dk brn | .45 | .45 |
| | Nos. B211-B215 (5) | 2.25 | 2.25 |

King Michael and Ion Antonescu SP150

**1943, Sept. 6**
B216 SP150 16 l + 24 l blue   1.75  1.75

3rd anniv. of the government of King Michael and Marshal Ion Antonescu.
See Nos. B219-B223.

Roman Post Chariot SP168

Symbols of Sports — SP151

**1943, Sept. 26**   **Perf. 13½**
B217 SP151 16 l + 24 l ultra   .45  .35
B218 SP151 16 l + 24 l red brn   .45  .35

Surtax for the benefit of Romanian sports.

### Portrait Type of 1943

**1943, Oct. 1**

Designs: 16 l+134 l, Samuel Micu. 51 l+99 l, George Lazar. 56 l+144 l, Octavian Goga. 76 l+124 l, Simeon Barnutiu. 77 l+123 l, Andrei Saguna.

| | | | |
|---|---|---|---|
| B219 | SP145 16 l + 134 l red vio | .30 | .30 |
| B220 | SP145 51 l + 99 l orange | .30 | .30 |
| B221 | SP145 56 l + 144 l rose car | .30 | .30 |
| B222 | SP145 76 l + 124 l slate bl | .30 | .30 |
| B223 | SP145 77 l + 123 l brown | .30 | .30 |
| | Nos. B219-B223 (5) | 1.50 | 1.50 |

The surtax aided refugees.

Calafat, 1877 — SP157

**1943, Nov. 10**   **Photo.**   **Perf. 13½**

Designs: 2 l, +2 l, World War I scene. 3.50 l+3.50 l, Stalingrad, 1943. 4 l+4 l, Tisza, 1919. 5 l+5 l, Odessa, 1941. 6.50 l+6.50 l, Caucasus, 1942. 7 l+7 l, Sevastopol, 1942. 20 l+20 l, Prince Ribescu and King Michael.

| | | | |
|---|---|---|---|
| B224 | SP157 1 l + 1 l red brn | .20 | .20 |
| B225 | SP157 2 l + 2 l dl vio | .20 | .20 |
| B226 | SP157 3.50 l + 3.50 l lt ultra | | |
| B227 | SP157 4 l + 4 l mag | .20 | .20 |
| B228 | SP157 5 l + 5 l red org | .30 | .30 |
| B229 | SP157 6.50 l + 6.50 l bl | .30 | .30 |
| B230 | SP157 7 l + 7 l dp vio | .40 | .40 |
| B231 | SP157 20 l + 20 l crim | .50 | .50 |
| | Nos. B224-B231 (8) | 2.30 | 2.30 |

Centenary of Romanian Artillery.

Emblem of Romanian Engineers' Association — SP165

**1943, Dec. 19**   **Perf. 14**
B232 SP165 21 l + 29 l sepia   .80  .55

Society of Romanian Engineers, 25th anniv.

---

Motorcycle, Truck and Post Horn — SP166

Post Wagon SP167

Post Rider — SP169

**1944, Feb. 1**   **Wmk. 276**   **Perf. 14**

| | | | |
|---|---|---|---|
| B233 | SP166 1 l + 49 l org red | 1.40 | 1.40 |
| B234 | SP167 2 l + 48 l lili rose | 1.40 | 1.40 |
| B235 | SP168 4 l + 46 l ultra | 1.40 | 1.40 |
| B236 | SP169 10 l + 40 l dl vio | 1.40 | 1.40 |
| | Nos. B233-B236 (4) | 5.60 | 5.60 |

**Souvenir Sheets**   **Perf. 14**

| | | | |
|---|---|---|---|
| B237 | Sheet of 3 | 4.50 | 4.50 |
| a. | SP166 1 l + 49 l orange red | .80 | .80 |
| b. | SP167 2 l + 48 l orange red | .80 | .80 |
| c. | SP168 4 l + 46 l orange red | .80 | .80 |

**Imperf**

| | | | |
|---|---|---|---|
| B238 | Sheet of 3 | 4.50 | 4.50 |
| a. | SP166 1 l + 49 l dull violet | .80 | .80 |
| b. | SP167 2 l + 48 l dull violet | .80 | .80 |
| c. | SP168 4 l + 46 l dull violet | .80 | .80 |

The surtax aided communications employees. No. B238 is imperf, between the stamps. Nos. B237-B238 each sold for 200 l.

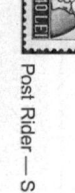

Nos. B233-B238 Overprinted

**1944, Feb. 28**

| | | | |
|---|---|---|---|
| B239 | SP166 1 l + 49 l org red | 3.25 | 3.25 |
| B240 | SP167 2 l + 48 l lil rose | 3.25 | 3.25 |
| B241 | SP168 4 l + 46 l ultra | 3.25 | 3.25 |
| B242 | SP169 10 l + 40 l dl vio | 3.25 | 3.25 |
| | Nos. B239-B242 (4) | 13.00 | 13.00 |

**Souvenir Sheets**   **Perf. 14**
B243 Sheet of 3   9.50  9.50

**Imperf**
B244 Sheet of 3   9.50  11.50

---

Rugby Player SP171

Dr. N. Cretzulescu SP172

**1944, Mar. 16**   **Perf. 15**
B245 SP171 16 l + 184 l crimson   3.75  3.75

30th anniv. of the Romanian Rugby Assoc. The surtax was used to encourage the sport.

Queen Mother Helen — SP173

**1944, Mar. 1**   **Photo.**   **Perf. 13½**
B246 SP172 35 l + 65 l brt ultra   .80  .80

Centenary of medical teaching in Romania.

Kings Ferdinand and Michael and Map SP174

**1945, Feb. 10**   **Perf. 15**

| | | | |
|---|---|---|---|
| B247 | SP173 4.50 l + 5.50 l multi | .25 | .25 |
| B248 | SP173 10 l + 40 l multi | .30 | .30 |
| B249 | SP173 15 l + 75 l multi | .35 | .35 |
| B250 | SP173 20 l + 80 l multi | .55 | .55 |
| | Nos. B247-B250 (4) | 1.45 | 1.45 |

The surtax aided the Romanian Red Cross.

**1945, Feb.**   **Perf. 14**
B251 SP174 75 l + 75 l dk ol brn   .50  .60

Romania's liberation.

Stefan Tomsa Church, Radaseni SP175

Municipal Home Radaseni SP176

Gathering Fruit — SP177

School SP178

---

King Michael and Carol I Foundation, Bucharest — SP179

**1944**   **Wmk. 276**   **Photo.**   **Perf. 14**

| | | | |
|---|---|---|---|
| B252 | SP175 5 l + 145 l brt bl | .55 | .55 |
| B253 | SP176 12 l + 138 l car rose | .55 | .55 |
| B254 | SP177 15 l + 135 l red org | .55 | .55 |
| B255 | SP178 32 l + 118 l dk brn | .55 | .55 |
| | Nos. B252-B255 (4) | 2.20 | 2.20 |

**1945, Feb. 10**   **Photo.**   **Perf. 13**

Design: 200 l, King Carol I and Foundation.

| | | | |
|---|---|---|---|
| B256 | SP179 20 l + 180 l dp org | .35 | .35 |
| B257 | SP179 25 l + 175 l slate | .35 | .35 |
| B258 | SP179 35 l + 165 l cl brn | .35 | .35 |
| B259 | SP179 75 l + 125 l pale vio | 1.40 | 1.40 |
| | Nos. B256-B259 (4) | | |

**Without Gum**   **Imperf**

**Souvenir Sheet**
B260 SP179 200 l blue   5.50  5.50

Surtax was to aid in rebuilding the Public Library, Bucharest. #B256-B259 were printed in sheets of 4. No. B260 sold for 1200 l.

Ion G. Duca SP181

**1945, Apr. 30**   **Perf. 13**

16 l+184 l, Virgil Madgearu. 20 l+180 l, Nikolai Jorga. 32 l+168 l, Ilie Pintilie. 35 l+165 l, Bernath Andrei. 36 l+164 l, Filimon Sarbu.

| | | | |
|---|---|---|---|
| B261 | SP181 12 l + 188 l dk bl | .40 | .40 |
| B262 | SP181 16 l + 184 l lt brn | .40 | .40 |
| B263 | SP181 20 l + 180 l blk | .40 | .40 |
| B264 | SP181 32 l + 168 l brn red | .40 | .40 |
| B265 | SP181 35 l + 165 l Prus bl | .40 | .40 |
| B266 | SP181 36 l + 164 l lt vio | 2.40 | 2.40 |
| | Nos. B261-B266 (6) | | |

**Souvenir Sheet**   **Imperf**

| | | | |
|---|---|---|---|
| B267 | | | |
| a. | SP181 32 l + 168 l mag | 14.00 | 14.00 |
| b. | SP181 35 l + 165 l mag | 2.75 | 3.00 |

Honoring six victims of Nazi terrorism. No. B267 sold for 1,000 l.

Books and Torch — SP188

**1945, May 20**

Designs: #B269, Flags of Russia and Romania. #B270, Kremlin, Moscow. #B271, Tudor Vladimirescu and Alexander Nevsky.

| | | | |
|---|---|---|---|
| B268 | SP188 20 l + 80 l grm | .25 | .25 |
| B269 | SP188 35 l + 165 l brt rose | .25 | .25 |
| B270 | SP188 75 l + 225 l blue | .25 | .25 |
| B271 | SP188 80 l + 420 l cl brn | 1.00 | 1.00 |
| | Nos. B268-B271 (4) | | |

**Souvenir Sheet**   **Imperf**

| | | | |
|---|---|---|---|
| B272 | Sheet of 2 | | |
| a. | SP189 35 l + 165 l bright red | 6.50 | 6.50 |
| b. | SP190 75 l + 225 l bright red | 1.60 | 1.60 |

**Without Gum**   **Perf. 14**

1st Soviet-Romanian Cong., May 20, 1945. No. B272 sold for 900 l.

## Karl Marx — SP193

Lenin. 120 l+380 l, Friedrich Engels. 155 l+445 l.

**1945, June 30**    **Perf. 13½**

| B273 | SP193 | 75 l + 425 l car rose | 2.00 | 2.00 |
|---|---|---|---|---|
| B274 | SP193 | 120 l + 380 l bl | 2.00 | 2.00 |
| B275 | SP193 | 155 l + 445 l dk vio brn | 2.00 | 2.00 |

**Imperf**

| B276 | SP193 | 75 l + 425 l rose | 5.25 | 5.25 |
|---|---|---|---|---|
| B277 | SP193 | 120 l + 380 l dk vio brn | 5.25 | 5.25 |
| B278 | SP193 | 155 l + 445 l car rose | 5.25 | 5.25 |
| | | Nos. B273-B278 (6) | 21.75 | 21.75 |

Nos. B276-B278 were printed in sheets of 4.

## Woman Throwing Discus — SP196

**Wmk. 278**

**1945, Aug. 5**    **Photo.**    **Perf. 13**

| B279 | SP196 | 12 l +188 l ol gray | 1.25 | 1.25 |
|---|---|---|---|---|

Designs: 16 l+184 l, Diving. 20 l+180 l, Skiing. 32 l+168 l, Volleyball. 35 l+165 l, Worker athlete.

| B280 | SP196 | 16 l +184 l lt ultra | 1.25 | 1.25 |
|---|---|---|---|---|
| B281 | SP196 | 20 l +180 l dp grn | 1.25 | 1.25 |
| B282 | 3P190 | 32 l +160 l mag | 1.25 | 1.25 |
| B283 | SP196 | 35 l +165 l brt bl | 1.25 | 1.25 |

**Imperf**

| B284 | SP196 | 12 l +188 l org red | 1.25 | 1.25 |
|---|---|---|---|---|
| B285 | SP196 | 16 l +184 l vio brn | 1.25 | 1.25 |
| B286 | SP196 | 20 l +180 l dp vio | 1.25 | 1.25 |
| B287 | SP196 | 32 l +168 l yel | 1.25 | 1.25 |
| B288 | SP196 | 35 l +165 l dk ol grn | 1.25 | 1.25 |
| | | Nos. B279-B288 (10) | 12.50 | 12.60 |

Printed in sheets of 9.

## Mail Plane and Bird Carrying Letter SP201

**1945, Aug. 5**    **Perf. 13½**

| B289 | SP201 | 200 l + 1000 l bl & dk bl | 5.00 | 5.00 |
|---|---|---|---|---|
| a. | | With label | 25.00 | 25.00 |

The surtax on Nos. B279-B289 was for the Office of Popular Sports.

Issued in sheets of 30 stamps and 10 labels, arranged 10x4 with second and fourth horizontal rows each having five alternating labels.

## Agriculture and Industry United — SP202

### King Michael SP203

**1945, Aug. 23**

| B290 | SP202 | 100 l + 400 l red | .45 | .45 |
|---|---|---|---|---|
| B291 | SP203 | 200 l + 800 l blue | .50 | .50 |

The surtax was for the Farmers' Front. For surcharges see Nos. B318-B325.

**Perf. 14**

## Political Amnesty SP204

## Military Amnesty SP205

## Agrarian Amnesty SP200

## Tudor Vladimirescu SP207

## Nicolae Horia SP208

## Reconstruction — SP209

**1945, Aug.**    **Perf. 13**

| B292 | SP204 | 20 l + 580 l grn | 9.00 | 9.00 |
|---|---|---|---|---|
| B293 | SP204 | 20 l + 580 l choc | 9.00 | 9.00 |
| B294 | SP205 | 40 l + 560 l mag | 9.00 | 9.00 |
| B295 | SP205 | 40 l + 560 l sl blue | 9.00 | 9.00 |
| B296 | SP206 | 55 l + 545 l grn | 9.00 | 9.00 |
| B297 | SP206 | 55 l + 545 l red | 9.00 | 9.00 |
| B298 | SP207 | 60 l + 540 l dk vio | 9.00 | 9.00 |
| B299 | SP207 | 60 l + 540 l ultra | 9.00 | 9.00 |
| B300 | SP208 | 80 l + 520 l choc | 9.00 | 9.00 |
| B301 | SP208 | 80 l + 520 l red | 9.00 | 9.00 |
| B302 | SP209 | 100 l + 500 l mag grn | 9.00 | 9.00 |
| B303 | SP209 | 100 l + 500 l red brn | 9.00 | 9.00 |
| | | Nos. B292-B303 (12) | 108.00 | 108.00 |

1st anniv. of Romania's armistice with Russia. Issued in panes of four.

Nos. B292-B303 also exist on coarse grayish paper, ungummed (same value).

### Electric Train SP210
### Coats of Arms SP211
### Truck on Mountain Road SP212
### Oil Field SP213
### "Agriculture" — SP214

**1945, Oct. 1**    **Perf. 14**

| B304 | SP210 | 10 l + 490 l ol grn | .35 | .35 |
|---|---|---|---|---|
| B305 | SP211 | 20 l + 480 l red brn | .35 | .35 |
| B306 | SP212 | 25 l + 475 l brn vio | .35 | .35 |
| B307 | SP213 | 55 l + 445 l ultra | .35 | .35 |
| B308 | SP214 | 100 l + 400 l brn | .35 | .35 |

**Imperf**

| B309 | SP210 | 10 l + 490 l blue | .35 | .35 |
|---|---|---|---|---|
| B310 | SP211 | 20 l + 480 l violet | .35 | .35 |
| B311 | SP212 | 25 l + 475 l bl grn | .35 | .35 |
| B312 | SP213 | 55 l + 445 l gray | .35 | .35 |
| B313 | SP214 | 100 l + 400 l dp mag | .35 | .35 |
| | | Nos. B304-B313 (10) | 3.50 | 3.50 |

16th Congress of the General Assoc. of Romanian Engineers.

## "Brotherhood" — SP215

**1945, Dec. 5**    **Perf. 14**

| B314 | SP215 | 80 l + 920 l mag | 11.00 | 11.00 |
|---|---|---|---|---|
| B315 | SP215 | 160 l + 1840 l org brn | 11.00 | 11.00 |
| B316 | SP215 | 320 l + 1680 l vio | 11.00 | 11.00 |
| B317 | SP215 | 440 l + 2560 l yel | 44.00 | 44.00 |
| | | Nos. B314-B317 (4) | | |

World Trade Union Congress at Paris, Sept. 25-Oct. 10, 1945.

160 l+1840 l, "Peace." 320 l+1680 l, Hammer crushing Nazism. 440 l+2560 l, "World Unity."

### Nos. B290 and B291 Surcharged in Various Colors

**1946, Jan. 20**

| B318 | SP202 | 10 l + 90 l (Bk) | .55 | .55 |
|---|---|---|---|---|
| B319 | SP203 | 10 l + 90 l (R) | .55 | .55 |
| B320 | SP202 | 20 l + 80 l (G) | .55 | .55 |
| B321 | SP203 | 20 l + 80 l (Bk) | .55 | .55 |
| B322 | SP202 | 80 l + 120 l (Bl) | .55 | .75 |
| B323 | SP203 | 80 l + 120 l (Bk) | .55 | .75 |
| B324 | SP202 | 100 l + 150 l (Bk) | .55 | .75 |
| B325 | SP203 | 100 l + 150 l (R) | .55 | .75 |
| | | Nos. B318-B325 (8) | 4.40 | 6.00 |

### Re-distribution of Land — SP219
### Sower SP220
### Ox Team Drawing Hay SP221
### Old and New Plowing Methods SP222

**1946, Mar. 6**

| B326 | SP219 | 50 l + 450 l rod | .30 | .30 |
|---|---|---|---|---|
| B327 | SP220 | 100 l + 900 l red vio | .30 | .30 |
| B328 | SP221 | 200 l + 800 l orange | .30 | .30 |
| B329 | SP222 | 400 l + 1600 l dk grn | .30 | .30 |
| | | Nos. B326-B329 (4) | 1.20 | 1.20 |

Agrarian reform law of Mar. 23, 1945.

### Philharmonic Typo of Regular Issue

**Perf. 13, 13½x13**    **Wmk. 276**

**1946, Apr. 26**    **Photo.**    **Perf. 13, 13½x13**

| B330 | A211 | 200 l + 800 l brt red | .70 | .70 |
|---|---|---|---|---|
| B331 | A213 | 350 l + 1650 l dk bl | 22.50 | 22.50 |
| a. | | A213 350 l + 1650 l dk bl | 20.00 | 20.00 |
| | | Sheet of 12 | 20.00 | 22.50 |

Issued in sheets containing 12 stamps and 4 labels, with bars of music in the margins.

### Dove SP228

### Agriculture SP223

**Wmk. 276**

**1946, July 28**    **Photo.**    **Perf. 11½**

| B332 | SP223 | 10 l + 200 l dk org | .30 | .30 |
|---|---|---|---|---|
| B333 | SP223 | 10 l + 200 l bl & brn & red brn | .30 | .30 |
| B334 | SP223 | 80 l + 200 l brn vio & brn | .30 | .30 |
| B335 | SP223 | 80 l + 300 l dk org brn & rose lil | .30 | .30 |
| B336 | SP223 | 200 l + 400 l Prus bl | .30 | .30 |
| | | Nos. B332-B336 (5) | 1.50 | 1.50 |

Issued in panes of 4 stamps with marginal inscription.

Designs: 10 l+200 l, Hurdling. 80 l+200 l, Research. 80 l+300 l, Industry. 200 l+400 l, Workers and flag.

**1946, Oct. 20**    **Perf. 13½x13, Imperf.**

| B338 | SP228 | 300 l + 1200 l scar | .50 | .25 |
|---|---|---|---|---|

### Souvenir Sheet

**Perf. 14x14½**

| B339 | SP228 | 1000 l scarlet | 2.00 | 2.25 |
|---|---|---|---|---|

Romanian-Soviet friendship. No. B339 sold for 6000 lei.

**Skiing — SP230**

B340 SP230 160 l + 1340 l dk grn .50 .50

**1946, Sept. 1    Perf. 11½, Imperf.**

Surtax for Office of Popular Sports.

Spinning SP231

Reaping SP232

**Riding — SP233**

Water Carrier — SP234

**1946, Nov. 20    Perf. 14**

B342 SP231 80 l + 320 l brt red .20 .20
B343 SP232 140 l + 360 l dp org .20 .20
B344 SP233 300 l + 450 l brn ol .20 .20
B345 SP234 600 l + 900 l ultra .80 .80
Nos. B342-B345 (4)

Democratic Women's Org. of Romania.

**Angel with Food and Clothing SP235**

Bread for Hungry Family SP236

**Care for Needy — SP237**

**1947, Jan. 15    Perf. 13½x14**

B346 SP235 1500 l + 3500 l red .20 .20
B347 SP236 3700 l + 5300 l dp .20 .20
          org

Miniature Sheet
**Without Gum    Imperf**

B348 SP237 5000 l + 5000 l ultra 1.10 1.25
          vio

Surtax helped the social relief fund. No. B348 is miniature sheet of one.

Victor Babes — SP244

#B356, Michael Eminescu. #B357, Nicolae Grigorescu. #B358, Peter Movila. #B359, Aleksander S. Pushkin. #B360, Mikhail V. Lomonosov. #B361, Peter I. Tchaikovsky. #B362, Ilya E. Repin.

**1947, Apr. 18    Perf. 14**

B355 SP244 1500 l + 1500 l red .20 .20
B356 SP244 1500 l + 1500 l org .20 .20
B357 SP244 1500 l + 1500 l dk .20 .20
          ol grn
B358 SP244 1500 l + 1500 l dk .20 .20
          bl
B359 SP244 1500 l + 1500 l plum .20 .20
B360 SP244 1500 l + 1500 l scar .20 .20
B361 SP244 1500 l + 1500 l rose .20 .20
          brn
B362 SP244 1500 l + 1500 l ultra .20 .20
          choc
Nos. B355-B362 (8) 1.60 1.60

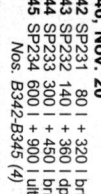

#B350, Weaving class. #B351, Young machinist. #B352, Romanian school.

**1947, Mar. 5    Photo.    Wmk. 276**

B349 SP238 200 l + 200 l vio bl .20 .20
B350 SP238 300 l + 300 l red .20 .20
          brn
B351 SP238 600 l + 600 l Prus .20 .20
          grn
B352 SP238 1200 l + 1200 l ultra .20 .20
B353 SP242 1500 l + 1500 l dp .20 .20
Nos. B349-B353 (5)

**Souvenir Sheet    Imperf**

B354 SP243 3700 l + 3700 l dl 1.25 1.50
          brn & dl bl

Romania's vocational schools, 50th anniv.

Allegory of Education — SP242

SP243

Student Reciting SP238

**1947, May 1**

B363 SP252 1000 l + 1000 l dk .20 .25
          ol brn
B364 SP252 1500 l + 1500 l red .20 .25
          brn
B365 SP252 2000 l + 2000 l blue .20 .25
B366 SP252 2500 l + 2500 l red .20 .25
          vio
B367 SP252 3000 l + 3000 l crim 1.00 1.25
          rose
Nos. B363-B367 (5)

Labor Day: No. B364, Farmer. No. B365, Farm woman. No. B366, Teacher and school. No. B367, Laborer and factory.

Transportation — SP252

**1947, Sept. 6    Perf. 13½**

B368 A234 2 l + 3 on 36,000 l vio .60 .60

Balkan Games of 1947, Bucharest.

**Type of 1947 Surcharged in Carmine**

Design: Cathedral of Curtea de Arges.

**1947, Oct. 30    Imperf.**

B369 A235 5 l + 5 l brt ultra .35 .35

Soviet-Romanian Congress, Nov. 1-7.

No. 650 Surcharged in Carmine

**Plowing — SP257**

**1947, Oct. 5    Photo.    Wmk. 276**

B370 SP257 1 l + 1 l shown .20 .20
B371 SP257 2 l + 2 l Sawmill .20 .20
B372 SP257 3 l + 3 l Refinery .20 .20
B373 SP257 4 l + 4 l Steel mill .20 .20
Nos. B370-B373,CB12 (5) 1.20 1.20

17th Congress of the General Assoc. of Romanian Engineers.

Allegory of Industry, Science and Agriculture — SP258

Winged Man Holding Hammer and Sickle SP259

**1947, Nov. 7    Perf. 14**

B376 SP260 1 l + 1 l dk gray bl .20 .20
B377 SP260 2 l + 2 l dk brn .20 .20
B378 SP260 3 l + 3 l rose lake .20 .20
B379 SP260 4 l + 4 l brt ultra .20 .20
B380 SP264 5 l + 5 l red 1.00 1.00
Nos. B376-B380 (5)

Designs: 1 l+1 l, Convoy of Food for Moldavia. 2 l+2 l, "Everything for the Front-Everything for Victory." 3 l+3 l, Woman, child and hospital. 4 l+4 l, "Help the Famine-stricken Regions." 5 l+5 l, "Three Years of Action."

Issued in sheets of eight.

**1947, Nov. 10    Perf. 14½x14**

B374 SP258 2 l + 10 l rose lake .20 .20
B375 SP259 7 l + 10 l bluish blk .20 .20

2nd Trade Union Conf., Nov. 10.

SP260

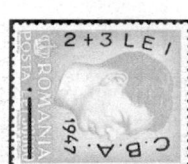

Discus Thrower — SP265

Labor — SP266

**1948, Feb.    Wmk. 276**
**Photo.    Perf. 13½**

B381 SP265 2 l + 2 l dk brn .30 .30
B382 SP265 3 l + 3 l car lake .40 .40
B383 SP265 5 l + 5 l blue .65 .65
Nos. B381-B383,CB13-CB14 (5) 3.75 2.85

Balkan Games of 1947: 2 l+2 l, Runner. 5 l+5 l, Boy and girl athletes.

Youths Following Filimon Sarbu Banner — SP269

**1948, Mar. 15    Imperf**

B384 SP266 2 l + 2 l dk sl bl .25 .20
B385 SP266 3 l + 3 l gray grn .30 .20
B386 SP266 5 l + 5 l red brn .40 .20

**1948, Mar. 15**

B387 SP269 8 l + 8 l dk car rose .60 .25
Nos. B384-B387,CB15 (5) 2.45 1.35

No. B387 issued in triangular sheets of 4.

SP264

SP266

## Gliders — SP270

## Sailboat Race SP271

Designs: No. B389, Early plane. No. B390, Plane over farm. No. B391, Transport plane. B393, Training ship. Mircea. B394, Danube ferry. B395, S.S. Transylvania.

**1948, July 26    Perf. 14x14½**

| | | | |
|---|---|---|---|
| B388 | SP270 10 l + 10 l choc | 1.50 | 1.50 |
| B389 | SP270 2 l + 2 l blue | 1.50 | 1.50 |
| B390 | SP270 8 l + 8 l dk car rose | 2.25 | 2.75 |
| B391 | SP270 10 l + 10 l choc | 2.25 | 2.75 |
| B392 | SP271 2 l + 2 l dk grn | 1.50 | 1.50 |
| B393 | SP271 5 l + 5 l slate | 1.50 | 1.50 |
| B394 | SP271 8 l + 8 l brt bl | 2.25 | 2.75 |
| B395 | SP271 10 l + 10 l ver | 2.75 | 2.75 |
| | Nos. B388-B395 (8) | 16.00 | 16.00 |

Air and Sea Communications Day.

## Type of Regular Issue and Torch, Pen, Ink and Flag SP272

## Alexandru Sahia SP273

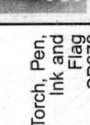

## Romanian-Soviet Association Emblem SP274

**Perf. 14x13½, 13½x14**

**1948, Sept. 12**

| | | | |
|---|---|---|---|
| B396 | A241 5 l + 5 l crimson | .65 | .65 |
| B397 | SP272 10 l + 10 l violet | 1.00 | 1.00 |
| B398 | SP273 15 l + 15 l blue | 1.40 | 1.40 |
| | Nos. B396-B398 (3) | 3.05 | 3.05 |

Week of the Democratic Press, Sept. 12-19. Nos. B396-B398 were also issued imperf. Value, unused $3.50, used $6. 1,500 sets of Nos. 695, B396-B398 perf and B396-B398 imperf were overprinted at "The Week of the Democratic Press" exposition. These stamps were not recognized by the Romanian PTT, although some examples were used on items mailed from the exposition post office.

**1948, Oct. 29    Perf. 14**

Design: 15 l+15 l, Spasski Tower, Kremlin.

| | | | |
|---|---|---|---|
| B399 | SP274 10 l + 10 l gray grn | 1.25 | 1.25 |
| B400 | SP274 15 l + 15 l dp ultra | 1.50 | 1.50 |

No. B399 was issued in sheets of 50 stamps and 50 labels.

## Symbols of United Labor SP275

## Agriculture SP276

## Industry SP277

## Automatic Riflemen SP278

## Soldiers Cutting Barbed Wire SP279

**1948, May 1    Perf. 14x13½, 13½x14**

| | | | |
|---|---|---|---|
| B401 | SP275 8 l + 8 l red | 1.10 | 1.75 |
| B402 | SP276 10 l + 10 l ol grm | 1.50 | 2.50 |
| B403 | SP277 12 l + 12 l red brn rose | 2.00 | 2.75 |
| | Nos. B401-B403 (3) | 4.60 | 7.00 |

Labor Day, May 1. See No. CB17.

**1948, May 9    Flags and Dates: 23 Aug 1944-9 Mai 1945**

| | | | |
|---|---|---|---|
| B404 | SP278 1.50 l + 1.50 l shown | .25 | .25 |
| B405 | SP279 2 l + 2 l shown | .25 | .25 |
| B406 | SP279 4 l + 4 l Field Artillery | .50 | .50 |
| B407 | SP279 7.50 l + 7.50 l tank | .85 | .85 |
| B408 | SP279 8 l + 8 l Warship | .90 | .90 |
| | Nos. B404-B408, CB18-CB19 (7) | 13.25 | 13.25 |

Honoring the Romanian Army.

## Nicolae Balcescu — SP280

## Balcescu and Revolutionists SP281

## Balcescu, Sandor Petöfi and Revolutionists — SP282

Revolution of 1848: #B412, Balcescu and revolutionists.

**1948, June 1    Perf. 13x13½**

| | | | |
|---|---|---|---|
| B409 | SP280 2 l + 2 l car lake | .25 | .25 |
| B410 | SP281 5 l + 5 l dk vio | .40 | .40 |
| B411 | SP282 10 l + 10 l dk brn | .50 | .50 |
| B412 | SP280 36 l + 18 l dp bl | 1.10 | 1.10 |
| | Nos. B409-B412 (4) | 2.25 | 2.25 |

For surcharges see Nos. 856-859.

## Loading Freighter SP283

Designs: 3 l+3 l, Lineman. 11 l+11 l, Transport plane. 15 l+15 l, Railroad train.

**1948, Dec. 10    Wmk. 289    Perf. 14    Photo. Center in Black**

| | | | |
|---|---|---|---|
| B413 | SP283 3 l + 3 l dk grn | .45 | .35 |
| B414 | SP283 3 l + 3 l redsh brn | .55 | .50 |
| B415 | SP283 11 l + 11 l dp bl | 2.25 | 1.75 |
| B416 | SP283 15 l + 15 l red | 2.75 | 2.40 |
| a. | Sheet of 4 | 15.00 | 15.00 |
| | Nos. B413-B416 (4) | 5.00 | 5.00 |

No. B416a contains four imperf. stamps similar to Nos. B413-B416 in changed colors, center in brown. No gum.

## Runners — SP284

## Parade of Athletes SP285

**1948, Dec. 31    Perf. 13x13½, 13½x13**

| | | | |
|---|---|---|---|
| B421 | SP284 5 l + 5 l grn | 2.00 | 2.00 |
| B422 | SP285 5 l + 5 l brn vio | 3.25 | 3.25 |

**Imperf**

| | | | |
|---|---|---|---|
| B423 | SP284 5 l + 5 l grn | 2.00 | 2.00 |
| B424 | SP285 5 l + 5 l red | 3.25 | 3.25 |
| | Nos. B421-B424, CB20-CB21 (6) | 32.50 | 32.50 |

Nos. B421-B424 were issued in sheets of 4.

## Souvenir Sheet

SP286

**1950, Jan. 27**

B425 SP286 10 l carmine    3.00  2.00

Philatelic exhib., Bucharest. Sold for 50 lei.

## Crossing the Buzau, by Denis Auguste Marie Raffet — SP287

**1967, Nov. 15    Engr.    Perf. 13½**

B426 SP287 55b + 45b ocher & indigo    .40  .30

Stamp Day.

## Old Bucharest, 18th Century Painting — SP288

**1968, Nov. 15    Photo.    Perf. 13½**

B427 SP288 55b + 45b label    .75  .40

Stamp Day. Label has printed perforations. See Nos. 2386A, B428-B429.

**1969, Nov. 15**

Design: Courtyard, by M. Bouquet.

B428 SP288 55b + 45b label    .65  .50

Stamp Day. Label at right of stamp has printed perforations.

**1970, Nov. 15**

Mail Coach in the Winter, by Emil Volkers.

B429 SP288 55b + 45b multi    .70  .55

Stamp Day.

## Lady with Letter, by Sava Henţia SP289

**1971, Nov. 15    Photo.    Perf. 13½**

B430 SP289 1.10 l + 90b multi    .80  .50

Stamp Day. Label portion below stamp has printed perforations and shows Romania No. 12.

## Portrait Type of Regular Issue

Designs: 4 l+2 l, Barbat at his Desk, by B. Iscovescu. 6 l+2 l, The Poet Alecsandri with his Family, by N. Livaditti.

**1973, June 20    Photo.    Perf. 13½**

B432 A728 4 l + 2 l multi    1.25  .50

**Souvenir Sheet**

B433 A728 6 l + 2 l multi    2.25  2.25

No. B433 contains one 38x50mm stamp.

## Map of Europe with Emblem Marking Bucharest SP291

**1974, June 25    Photo.    Perf. 13½**

B435 SP291 4 l + 3 l multi    1.25  .40

EUROMAX, European Exhibition of Maximaphily, Bucharest, Oct. 6-13.

## Marketplace, Sibiu — SP292

**1974, Nov. 15    Photo.    Perf. 13½**

B436 SP292 2.10 l + 1.90 l multi    .90  .30

Stamp Day.

No. B436 Overprinted in Red:
"EXPOZITIA FILATELICA 'NATIONALA
'74' / 15-24 noiembrie / Bucuresti"

**1974, Nov. 15**
B437 SP292 2.10 l +1.90 l multi   1.75 1.75
NATIONALA '74 Philatelic Exhibition,
Bucharest, Nov. 15-24.

Post
Office,
Bucharest
SP293

Stamp Day: 2.10 l +1.90 l, like No. B438,
side view.

**1975, Nov. 15**    **Photo.**    **Perf. 13½**
B438 SP293 1.50 l +1.50 l multi   .75 .40
B439 SP293 2.10 l +1.90 l multi   1.25 .60

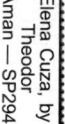

No. 2612 Surcharged and Overprinted:
"EXPOZITIA FILATELICA /
BUCURESTI / 12-19.IX.1976"

**1976, Sept. 12**    **Photo.**    **Perf. 13½**
B440 A787 3.60 l +1.80 l   3.00 2.50
Philatelic Exhibition, Bucharest, Sept. 12-19.

Elena Cuza, by
Theodor
Aman — SP294

**1976, Nov. 15**    **Photo.**    **Perf. 13½**
B441 SP294 2.10 l +1.90 l multi   .90 .60

Stamp Day.

Dispatch Rider
Handing Letter to
Officer — SP295

**1977, Nov.**    **Photo.**    **Perf. 13½**
B442 A806 4.80 l +2 l multi   1.25 .35
B443 SP295 2.10 l +1.90 l multi   .90 .75

Independence Type of 1977
Stamp Day: Battle of Rahova, after etching.

Socflex Type of 1979
Flower Paintings by Luchian: 4 l+2 l, Field
flowers, 10 l+5 l, Roses.

**1979, July 27**    **Photo.**    **Perf. 13½**
B444 SP296 2.10 l +1.90 l multi   .75 .75

Souvenir Sheet

B445 A847 4 l +2 l multi   2.50 2.50
B446 A847 10 l +5 l multi
Socflex Intl. Phil. Exhib., Bucharest, Oct.
26-Nov. 1. #B446 contains one 50x38mm
stamp.

**1979, Dec. 12**    **Photo.**    **Perf. 13½**
B447 SP297 2.10 l +1.90 l multi   .70 .25

Stamp
Day
SP297

---

Designs: 50b+50b, Palace on fire,
Bucharest, 1 l+1 l, Crowd, Timisoara,
1.50 l+1 l, Soldiers & crowd, Tirgu Mures,
2 l+1 l, Soldiers in Bucharest, vert, 3 l+1 l,
Funeral, Timisoara, 3.50 l+1 l, Crowd celebrat-
ing, Brasov, vert, 4 l+1 l, Crowd with flags,
Sibiu, 5 l+1 l, Cemetery, Bucharest. No.
B457, Foreign aid.

**1990, Oct. 1**    **Photo.**    **Perf. 13½**
B449 SP299 50b +50b multi   .20 .20
B450 SP299 1 l +1 l multi   .20 .20
B451 SP299 1.50 l +1 l multi   .25 .20
B452 SP299 2 l +1 l multi   .30 .20
B453 SP299 3 l +1 l multi   .35 .20
B454 SP299 3.50 l +1 l multi   .40 .20
B455 SP299 4 l +1 l multi   .45 .20
B456 SP299 5 l +1 l multi   .60 .25
Nos. B449-B456 (8)   2.75 1.65

Souvenir Sheet

B457 SP299 5 l +2 l multi   1.25 1.25
No. B457 contains one 54x42mm stamp.

December 1989 Revolution — SP299

Socflex Type of 1979

**1992, July 15**    **Photo.**    **Perf. 13½**
B458 SP300 10 l +4 l multi   .20 .20
For surcharge see No. B460.

Stamp Day — SP300

**1993, Apr. 26**    **Photo.**    **Perf. 13½**
B459 SP301 15 l +10 l multi   .20 .20

Stamp
Day —
SP301

---

Souvenir Sheet

**1980, July 1**
B448 SP298 5 l + 5 l multi   1.75 1.75

Stamp Day — SP298

**1993, Nov. 9**    **Photo.**    **Perf. 13½**
B460 SP300 70 l +45 l on 10 l+4 l   .40 .40

No. B458 Surcharged in Red

**1994, July 15**    **Photo.**    **Perf. 13½**
B461 SP302 90 l +60 l multi   .20 .20

National History
Museum,
Bucharest,
SP302

Souvenir Sheet

No. B462: a, Pierre de Coubertin, b, Greece
#125 (54x42mm), c, George V. Bibescu.

**2004, Mar. 25**    **Photo.**    **Perf. 13¼**
B462 SP303 16,000 l +5000 l   3.75 3.75
    Sheet of 3, #a-c
Romanian Olympic Committee, 90th
Anniv. — SP303

First Romanian Philatelic Exhibition,
80th Anniv. — SP304

**2004, July 15**    **Photo.**    **Perf. 13¼**
B463 SP304 21,000 l +10,000 l
   multi   1.90 1.90

**Litho.**
**Imperf.**
B464 SP304 21,000 l +10,000 l
   multi   1.90 1.90

---

**AIR POST STAMPS**

Capt. C.
G.
Craiu's
Airplane
AP1

**1928**    Wmk. 95 Vertical
     **Photo.**    **Perf. 13½**
C1 AP1 1 l red brown   2.00 2.00
C2 AP1 2 l brt blue   2.00 2.00
C3 AP1 5 l carmine rose   2.50 2.00
    Wmk. 95 Horizontal
C4 AP1 1 l red brown   2.75 2.75
C5 AP1 2 l brt blue   2.75 2.75
C6 AP1 5 l carmine rose   3.00 3.00
    Nos. C1-C6 (6)   14.25 14.25
Nos. C4-C6 also come with white gum.

**1930**    Nos. C4-C6 Overprinted
C7 AP1 1 l red brown   5.25 4.50
C8 AP1 2 l brt blue   5.25 4.50
    a. Vert. pair, imperf. btwn.
C9 AP1 5 l carmine rose   175.00
    Nos. C7-C9 (3)   13.50
   Same Overprint on Nos. C1-C3
    Wmk. 95 Vertical
C10 AP1 1 l red brown   37.50 37.50
C11 AP1 2 l brt blue   37.50 37.50
C12 AP1 5 l carmine rose   37.50 37.50
    Nos. C10-C12 (3)   128.25 126.00
#C7-C12 for the accession of King Carol II.
Excellent counterfeits are known of #C10-
C12.

King Carol II — AP2

**1930, Oct. 4**
    Bluish Paper    **Unwmk.**
C13 AP2 1 l dk violet   1.50 1.50
C14 AP2 2 l gray green   2.00 1.75
C15 AP2 5 l red brown   8.25 2.25
C16 AP2 10 l brt blue   5.00 5.00
    Nos. C13-C16 (4)   16.25 10.50
Never hinged   32.50

Junkers
Monoplane
AP3

Monoplanes
AP7

**1931, Nov. 4**    Wmk. 230
C17 AP3 2 l dull green   .50 .35
C18 AP3 3 l carmine   .60 .45
C19 AP3 5 l red brown   .90 .60
C20 AP3 10 l blue   2.00 1.25
C21 AP7 20 l dk violet   3.75 1.75
    Nos. C17-C21 (5)   7.75 4.40
Never hinged   17.50

3 l, Monoplane with biplane behind. 5 l,
Biplane. 10 l, Monoplane flying leftward.
Exist imperf. Value $200, unused or used.

## Souvenir Sheets

ASOCIATIA GENERALA A INGINERILOR DIN ROMANIA

AL XVI-LEA CONGRES

Plane over Resita — AP8

ASOCIATIA GENERALA A INGINERILOR DIN ROMANIA

AL XVI-LEA CONGRES

Plane over Sinaia — AP9

**1945, Oct. 1    Wmk. 276    Photo.    Perf. 13**
**Without Gum**
C22 AP8  80 l slate green    8.00  8.00
**Imperf**
C23 AP9  80 l magenta    5.50  5.50

16th Congress of the General Assoc. of Romanian Engineers.

Catalogue values for unused stamps in this section, from this point to the end of the section, are for Never Hinged items.

---

Plane AP10

Design: 500 l, Aviator and planes.

**1946, Sept. 5    Perf. 13½x13**
C24 AP10  200 l yel grn & bl    3.75  3.75
C25 AP10  500 l orq red & dl bl    3.75  3.75

Sheets of four with marginal inscription.

Lockheed 12 Electra — AP12

**1946, Oct.    Perf. 11½**
C26 AP12  300 l crimson    .50  .50
a.    Pair, #C26, C6b    1.75  1.75

Sheet contains 8 each of Nos. C26 and C6B, arranged so se-tenant or normal pairs are available.

CGM Congress Emblem — AP13

**1947, Mar.    Wmk. 276    Perf. 13x14**
C27 AP13  1100 l blue    .35  .35

Congress of the United Labor Unions ("CGM"). Printed in sheets of 15.

---

"May 1" Supported by Parachutes AP14

Plane and Conference Banner AP17

Designs: No. C29, Air Force monument. No. C30, Plane over rural road.

**1947, May 4    Perf. 11½**
C28 AP14  3000 l vermilion    .20  .20
C29 AP14  3000 l grnsh gray    .20  .20
C30 AP14  3000 l blk brown    .60  .60
Nos. C28-C30 (3)

Printed in sheets of four with marginal inscriptions.

**1947, Nov. 10    Perf. 14**
C31 AP17  11 l bl & dp car    .30  .30
2nd Trade Union Conference, Nov. 10.

Emblem of the Republic and Factories AP18

Industry and Agriculture — AP19

Transportation — AP20

---

**1948, Nov. 22    Wmk. 289    Perf. 14x13½**
C32 AP18  30 l cerise    .30  .30
a.    30 l carmine (50)    .40  .40
C33 AP19  50 l dk slate grn    .40  .40
C34 AP20  100 l ultra    1.80  1.00
Nos. C32-C34 (3)

No. C32a issued May 10. For surcharges see Nos. C37-C39.

Agriculture — AP21

**1951-52    Wmk. 358    Perf. 13½**
C35 AP21  30 l dk green (52)    1.50  1.25
C36 AP21  50 l red brown    2.00  1.75

1951-55 Five Year Plan.
For surcharges see Nos. C40-C41.

**Nos. C32-C36 Surcharged with New Values in Blue or Carmine**

**1952    Wmk. 289    Perf. 14x13½**
C37 AP18  3b on 30 l car (BI)    1.50  1.50
a.    3b on 30 l cerise (BI)    9.00  6.50
C38 AP19  3b on 50 l dk sl grm    .50  .40
C39 AP20  3b on 100 l ultra    .50  .40
**Perf. 13½**
**Wmk. 358**
C40 AP21  1 l on 30 l dk grm    6.75  1.25
C41 AP21  1 l on 50 l red brm    6.75  1.25
Nos. C37-C41 (5)    16.50  4.80

---

Nos. 706 and 707 Surcharged in Blue or Carmine

**1953    Wmk. 289    Perf. 13½, 14**
C43 A250  3 l on 20 l org brn    11.50  10.00
C44 A251  5 l on 30 l brt bl (C)    16.00  12.50

Plane facing right and surcharge arranged to fit design on No. C44.

Plane over City — AP22

Sputnik 1 and Earth — AP23

---

Designs: 55b, Plane over Mountains. 1.75 l, over Harvest fields.  2.25 l, over Seashore.

**Perf. 14½x14**
**1956, Dec. 15    Photo.    Wmk. 358**
C45 AP22  20b brt bl, org & grn    .35  .20
C46 AP22  55b brt bl, grn & ocher    .65  .20
C47 AP22  1.75 l brt bl & red org    1.75  .20
C48 AP22  2.55 l brt bl & red org    2.50  .40
a.    Pair, #C45-C48 (4)    5.25  1.00
Nos. C45-C48 (4)

**1957, Nov. 6    Perf. 14**
3.75 l, Sputniks 1 and 2 circling globe.
C49 AP23  25b brt ultra    .30  .20
C50 AP23  25b dk ultra    .30  .20
C51 AP23  3.75 l brt ultra    1.75  .60
a.    Pair, #C49, C51 + label    2.25  2.25
C52 AP23  3.75 l dk grm    1.90  .60
a.    Pair, #C50, C52 + label    4.25  1.00
Nos. C49-C52 (4)

Each sheet contains 27 triptychs with the center plane arranged tête-bêche. In 1958 Nos. C49-C52 were overprinted: 1.) "Expoziția Universală a Bruxelles 1958" and star. 2.) Large star. 3.) Small star.

---

**Animal Type of Regular Issue, 1957**
Birds: 3.30 l, Black-headed gull, horiz. 5 l, Sea eagle, horiz.

**Perf. 14x13½**
**1957, Dec. 27    Wmk. 358**
C53 A445  3.30 l ultra & gray    2.50  .50
C54 A445  5 l carmine & org    3.75  .75

**Armed Forces Type of Regular Issue**
Design:  Flier and planes.

**Perf. 13½x13**
**1958, Oct. 2    Unwmk.    Photo.**
C55 A458  3.30 l brt violet    1.25  .40
Day of the Armed Forces, Oct. 2.

Earth and Sputnik 3 Orbit AP24

**1958, Sept. 20    Perf. 14x13½**
C56 AP24  3.25 l indigo & ocher    2.75  .75
Launching of Sputnik 3, May 15, 1958.

**Type of Regular Issue, 1958 Souvenir Sheet**
Design: Tête bêche pair of 27pa of 1858.

---

**Perf. 11½    Unwmk.    Engr.**
**1958, Nov. 15**
C57 A462  10 l blue, bluish    25.00  25.00

A similar sheet, printed in dull red and imperf. exists. Value, unused $55, used $45. No. C57 on bluish and white papers was overprinted in 1959 in vermilion to commemorate the 10th anniv. of the State Philatelic Trade. Value $50, either unused or used.

Lunik I Leaving Earth AP25

Frederic Joliot-Curie — AP26

**1959, Feb. 4    Photo.    Perf. 14**
C58 AP25  3.25 l vio bl, pnksh    7.50  .90
Launching of the "first artificial planet of the solar system."
For surcharge see No. C70.

**1959, Apr. 25    Perf. 13½x14**
C59 AP26  3.25 l ultra    2.50  .50
Frederic Joliot-Curie; 10th anniv. of the World Peace Movement.

Rock Thrush AP27

---

**1959, June 25    Litho.    Perf. 14**
**Birds in Natural Colors**

Birds: 20b, European golden oriole. 35b, Lapwing. 40b, Barn swallow. No. C64, Gold-finch. No. C65, Great spotted woodpecker. No. C66, Great tit. 1 l, Bullfinch. 1.55 l, Long-tailed tit. 5 l, Wall creeper. Nos. C62-C67 vertical.

C60 AP27  10b gray, cr    .20  .20
C61 AP27  20b gray, grysh    .20  .20
C62 AP27  35b gray, grysh    .20  .20
C63 AP27  40b gray, & red, pnksh    .20  .20
C64 AP27  55b gray, buff    .25  .25
C65 AP27  55b gray, grnsh    .25  .25
C66 AP27  55b gray, & ol, grysh    .25  .20
C67 AP27  1 l gray and red, cr    .80  .20
C68 AP27  1.55 l gray & red, pnksh    .90  .20
C69 AP27  5 l gray, grnsh    3.75  .70
C60-C69 (10)    7.00  2.50

**No. C58 Surcharged in Red**

**1959, Sept. 14    Photo.    Unwmk.**
C70 AP25  5 l on 3.25 l    6.00  1.50
1st Russian rocket to reach the moon, 9/14/59.

## Prince Vlad Tepes and Document — AP28

**1959, Sept. 15   Engr.   Perf. 11½x11**

| | | | | |
|---|---|---|---|---|
| C71 | AP28 | 20 l violet brn | 65.00 | 65.00 |

500th anniv. of the founding of Bucharest.

**1959, Oct. 5   Litho.   Perf. 13½**

| | | | | |
|---|---|---|---|---|
| C72 | A474 | 2.80 l Boating | 2.00 | .40 |

Sport Type of Regular Issue, 1959

## Soviet Rocket, Globe, Dog and Rabbit — AP29

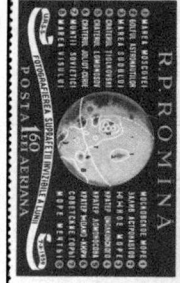

**1959, Dec.   Photo.   Wmk. 358**

| | | | | |
|---|---|---|---|---|
| C73 | AP29 | 1.55 l dk blue | 2.00 | .20 |
| C74 | AP30 | 1.60 l vio bl, buff | 2.50 | .40 |
| C75 | AP29 | 1.75 l dk blue | 7.00 | 1.00 |
| | | Nos. C73-C75 (3) | | |

## Photograph of Far Side of the Moon — AP30

Design: 1.75 l, Trajectory of Lunik 3, which hit the moon.

## Aurel Vlaicu and Plane of 1910 AP31

**1960, Mar. 3   Engr.   Perf. 14**

| | | | | |
|---|---|---|---|---|
| C76 | A480 | 1.30 l dk green | .85 | .30 |
| C77 | A480 | 1.75 l olive grn | 1.25 | .30 |
| C78 | A480 | 2 l dk carmine | 1.50 | .40 |
| | | Nos. C76-C78 (3) | 3.60 | 1.00 |

Animal Type of Regular Issue, 1960.
Designs: 1.30 l, Golden eagle. 1.75 l, Black grouse. 2 l, Lammergeier.

Soviet conquest of space.

---

## Bucharest Airport and Turbo-Jet — AP32

**1960, June 15   Litho.   Unwmk.**

| | | | | |
|---|---|---|---|---|
| C79 | AP31 | 10b yellow & brn | .20 | .20 |
| C80 | AP31 | 20b red org & brn | .20 | .20 |
| | | **Photo.   Wmk. 358** | | |
| C81 | AP31 | 35b crimson | .20 | .20 |
| C82 | AP31 | 40b violet | .30 | .20 |
| C83 | AP31 | 55b blue | .40 | .20 |

**1960   Litho.   Unwmk.**

| | | | | |
|---|---|---|---|---|
| C84 | AP32 | 1.60 l vio bl, yel & em-er | 1.25 | .35 |
| C85 | AP32 | 1.75 l bl, red, brn & pale grn | 3.50 | 1.55 |

Designs: 20b, Plane and Aurel Vlaicu. 35b, Amphibian ambulance plane. 40b, Plane spraying crops. 55b, Pilot and planes, vert. 1.75 l, Parachutes at aviation sports meet.

50th anniv. of the first Romanian airplane flight by Aurel Vlaicu. For surcharge see No. C145.

Nos. C79-C85 (7)

## Bucharest Airport — AP33

**1960   Wmk. 358   Photo.   Perf. 14**

| | | | | |
|---|---|---|---|---|
| C86 | AP33 | 3.20 l brt ultra | 1.25 | .20 |

Type of Regular Issue, 1960
Black Sea Resort: 2 l, Beach at Mamaia.

## Sputnik 4 Flying into Space AP34

**1960, June 8   Photo.   Wmk. 358**

| | | | | |
|---|---|---|---|---|
| C88 | AP34 | 55b deep blue | 1.25 | .25 |

**1960, Aug. 2   Litho.   Unwmk.**

| | | | | |
|---|---|---|---|---|
| C87 | A491 | 2 l grn, org & lt bl | 1.25 | .40 |

Launching of Sputnik 4, May 15, 1960.

## Saturnia Pyri AP35   Papilio Machaon AP36

## Limenitis Populi — AP37

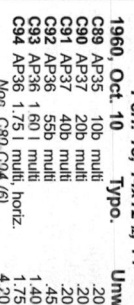

**1960, Oct. 10   Typo.   Unwmk.**

**Perf. 13, 14x12½, 14**

| | | | | |
|---|---|---|---|---|
| C89 | AP35 | 10b multi | .20 | .20 |
| C90 | AP37 | 20b multi | .20 | .20 |
| C91 | AP37 | 40b multi | .45 | .20 |
| C92 | AP36 | 55b multi | .40 | .20 |
| C93 | AP36 | 1.60 l multi | 1.40 | .20 |
| C94 | AP36 | 1.75 l multi, horiz. | 1.75 | .20 |
| | | Nos. C89-C94 (6) | 4.20 | 1.20 |

Designs: 40b, Chrisophanus virgaureae. 1.60 l, Acherontia atropos. 1.75 l, Apatura iris.

---

## Compass Rose and Jet — AP38

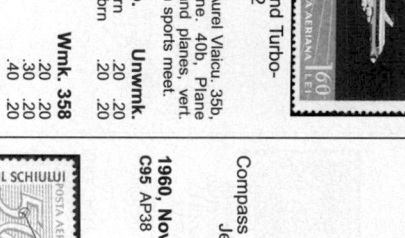

**1960, Nov. 1   Photo.   Wmk. 358   Perf. 13½x14**

| | | | | |
|---|---|---|---|---|
| C95 | AP38 | 55b brt bl + 45b label | .35 | .20 |

Stamp Day.

## Skier AP39   Slalom — AP40   Maj. Yuri A. Gagarin — AP41

**1961, Mar. 18   Litho.   Unwmk.**

**Perf. 14x13½, 13½x14**

| | | | | |
|---|---|---|---|---|
| C96 | AP39 | 10b olive & gray | .20 | .20 |
| C97 | AP40 | 20b gray & dk red | .20 | .20 |
| C98 | AP40 | 25b gray & bl grn | .25 | .20 |
| C99 | AP40 | 40b gray & pur | .30 | .20 |
| C100 | AP39 | 55b gray & ultra | .50 | .20 |
| C101 | AP40 | 1 l gray & brn lake | .80 | .20 |
| C102 | AP39 | 1.75 l gray & brn | 2.50 | 1.40 |
| | | Nos. C96-C102 (7) | | |

Designs: 25b, Skiers going up. 40b, Bobsled. 55b, Ski jump. 1 l, Mountain climber. 1.55 l, Long-distance skier.

**1961, Apr. 19   Photo.   Unwmk.**

| | | | | |
|---|---|---|---|---|
| C103 | AP41 | 1.35 l brt blue | .75 | .20 |
| C104 | AP41 | 3.20 l ultra | 1.75 | .40 |

Design: 3.20 l, Gagarin in space capsule and globe with orbit, horiz.

No. C104 exists imperf. in dark carmine rose. Value unused $4.50, canceled $2.

Exist imperf. with changed colors. Value, set $4.00.

## Eclipse over Republic Palace, Bucharest — AP42

**1961, June 13   Wmk. 358   Perf. 14x13½**

| | | | | |
|---|---|---|---|---|
| C106 | AP42 | 1.60 l ultra | .90 | .20 |
| C107 | AP42 | 1.75 l dk blue | 1.00 | .20 |

Total solar eclipse of Feb. 15, 1961.

1.75 l, Total Eclipse, Scinteia House, telescope.

## Maj. Gherman S. Titov — AP43   Globe and Stamps — AP44

**1961, Sept. 11   Perf. 13½x14   Unwmk.**

| | | | | |
|---|---|---|---|---|
| C108 | AP43 | 55b dp blue | .45 | .20 |
| C109 | AP43 | 1.35 l dp purple | .70 | .20 |
| C110 | AP43 | 1.75 l dk carmine | 2.25 | .60 |
| | | Nos. C108-C110 (3) | | |

Issued to honor the Russian space navigators Y. A. Gagarin and G. S. Titov.

55b, "Peace" and Vostok 2 rocket. 1.75 l, Yuri A. Gagarin and Gherman S. Titov, horiz.

---

## Railroad Station, Constanta AP45

**1961, Nov. 15   Litho.   Perf. 13½x14**

| | | | | |
|---|---|---|---|---|
| C111 | AP44 | 55b multi + 45b label | .60 | .20 |

Stamp Day.

**1961, Nov. 20   Perf. 13½x14, 14x13½**

| | | | | |
|---|---|---|---|---|
| C112 | AP45 | 20b multi | .20 | .20 |
| C113 | AP45 | 40b multi | .20 | .20 |
| C114 | AP45 | 55b multi | .20 | .20 |
| C115 | AP45 | 75b multi | .25 | .20 |
| C116 | AP45 | 1 l multi | .30 | .20 |
| C117 | AP45 | 1.20 l multi | .65 | .25 |
| C118 | AP45 | 1.75 l multi | .95 | .20 |
| | | Nos. C112-C118 (7) | 2.75 | 1.45 |

Buildings: 20b, Tower, RPR Palace place, vert. 55b, Congress hall, Bucharest. 75b, Mill, Hunedoara. 1 l, Apartment houses, Bucharest. 1.20 l, Circus, Bucharest. 1.75 l, Worker's Club, Mangalia.

## Space Exploration Stamps and Dove AP46

**1962, July 27   Perf. 14x13½**

| | | | | |
|---|---|---|---|---|
| C119 | AP46 | 35b yellow brn | .20 | .20 |
| C120 | AP46 | 40b violet | .20 | .20 |
| C121 | AP46 | 55b green | .45 | .20 |
| C122 | AP46 | 1.75 l rose red | .90 | .25 |
| a. | | Sheet of 4 | 1.75 | |
| | | Nos. C119-C122 (4) | | .85 |

Peaceful space exploration.

Design: Each stamp shows a different group of Romanian space exploration stamps.

No. C122a contains four imperf. stamps similar to Nos. C119-C122 in changed colors and with one dove covering all four stamps. Stamps are printed together without space between.

## Andrian G. Nikolayev — AP47

**1962, Aug. 20   Photo.   Perf. 13½x14**

| | | | | |
|---|---|---|---|---|
| C123 | AP47 | 55b purple | .35 | .20 |
| C124 | AP47 | 1.60 l dark blue | 1.00 | .30 |
| C125 | AP47 | 1.75 l rose claret | 2.60 | .75 |
| | | Nos. C123-C125 (3) | | |

Designs: 1.60 l, Globe and trajectories of Vostoks 3 and 4. 1.75 l, Pavel R. Popovich.

1st Russian group space flight of Vostoks 3 and 4, Aug. 11-15, 1962.

ROMANIA

Steam Locomotive
AP52

Designs: 55b, Diesel locomotive. 75b, Trolley bus. 1.35 l, Passenger ship. 1.75 l, Plane.

**1963, July 10    Litho.    Perf. 14½x13**
| | | | | |
|---|---|---|---|---|
| C137 | AP52 | 40b multi | .25 | .20 |
| C138 | AP52 | 55b multi | .30 | .20 |
| C139 | AP52 | 75b multi | .40 | .20 |
| C140 | AP52 | 1.35 l multi | .70 | .20 |
| C141 | AP52 | 1.75 l multi | 1.10 | 1.00 |

*Nos. C137-C141 (5)    2.75    1.00*

Valeri Bykovski
AP53

Designs: 1.20 l, Bykovski, vert. 1.60 l, Tereshkova, vert. 1.75 l, Valentina Tereshkova.

**1963    Photo.**
| | | | | |
|---|---|---|---|---|
| C142 | AP53 | 55b blue | .25 | .20 |
| C143 | AP53 | 1.75 l rose red | 1.00 | .20 |

**Souvenir Sheet**
**Perf. 13**
| | | | | |
|---|---|---|---|---|
| | | Sheet of 2 | 2.25 | .75 |
| C144 | | | | |
| a. | AP53 | 1.20 l ultra | .60 | .30 |
| b. | AP53 | 1.60 l ultra | .75 | .40 |

Space flights of Valeri Bykovski, June 14-19, and Valentina Tereshkova, first woman cosmonaut, June 16-19, 1963.

No. C79 Surcharged and Overprinted:
"1913-1963 50 ani de la moarte"

**1963, Sept. 15    Unwmk.    Perf. 14**
| | | | | |
|---|---|---|---|---|
| C145 | AP31 | 1.75 l on 10b | 2.00 | .75 |

50th death anniv. of Aurel Vlaicu, aviation pioneer.
Exists with "1" of "lei," missing.

Centenary Stamp of 1958
AP54

Stamps on Stamps: 40b, Sputnik 2 and Laika, #1200. 55b, Yuri A. Gagarin, #C104a. 1.20 l, Nikolayev and Popovich, #C123, C125. 1.55 l, Postal Administration Bldg. and letter carrier, #965.

**1963, Nov. 15    Photo.    Perf. 14x13½**
**Size: 38x26mm**
| | | | | |
|---|---|---|---|---|
| C146 | AP54 | 20b tl bl & dk brn | .20 | .20 |
| C147 | AP54 | 40b brt pink & dk bl | .20 | .20 |
| C148 | AP54 | 55b ll ultra & dk | .20 | .20 |
| | | car rose | | |
| C149 | AP54 | 1.20 l ocher & pur | .35 | .20 |
| C150 | AP54 | 1.55 l sal pink & ol | .50 | .20 |
| | | gray | | |

*Nos. C146-C150,CB22 (6)    2.45    1.50*

15th UPU Congress, Vienna.

Pavel R. Popovich
AP55

Astronauts and flag: 5b, Yuri A. Gagarin. 10b, Gherman S. Titov. 20b, John H. Glenn, Jr. 35b, M. Scott Carpenter. 40b, Andrian G. Nikolayev. 60b, Walter M. Schirra. 75b, Gordon L. Cooper. 1 l, Valeri Bykovski. 1.40 l, Valentina Tereshkova. (5b, 10b, 20b, 35b, 60b and 75b are diamond shaped.)

---

Exhibition Hall — AP48

**1962, Oct. 12    Litho.    Perf. 14x13**
| | | | | |
|---|---|---|---|---|
| C126 | AP48 | 1.60 l bl, vio bl & org | 1.25 | .20 |

4th Sample Fair, Bucharest.

The Coachmen by Szatmary — AP49

**1962, Nov. 15    Perf. 13½x14**
| | | | | |
|---|---|---|---|---|
| C127 | AP49 | 55b + 45b label | .75 | .25 |

Stamp Day. Alternating label shows No. 14 on cover.

No. C127 Overprinted in Violet

**1963, Mar. 30**
| | | | | |
|---|---|---|---|---|
| C128 | AP49 | 55b + 45b label | 2.25 | 1.25 |

Romanian Philatelists' Assoc. meeting at Bucharest, Mar. 30.

Sighisoara Glass and Crockery Factory
AP50

Industrial Plants: 40b, Govora soda works. 55b, Tirgul-Jiu wood chemical plant. 1 l, Savinesti chemical plant (synthetic fibers). 1.55 l, Hunedoara metal factory. 1.75 l, Brazi thermal power station.

**1963, Apr. 10    Unwmk.    Photo.**
**Perf. 14x13**
| | | | | |
|---|---|---|---|---|
| C129 | AP50 | 30b dk bl & red | .20 | .20 |
| C130 | AP50 | 40b sl grn & pur | .20 | .20 |
| C131 | AP50 | 55b brn red & dp bl | .20 | .20 |
| C132 | AP50 | 1 l vio & brn | .35 | .20 |
| C133 | AP50 | 1.55 l ver & dk bl | .50 | .20 |
| C134 | AP50 | 1.75 l dk bl & magen- | .70 | .20 |
| | | ta | | |

*Nos. C129-C134 (6)    2.00    1.20*

Industrial achievements.

Lunik 4 Approaching Moon — AP51

**1963, Apr. 29    Perf. 13½x14**
| | | | | |
|---|---|---|---|---|
| C135 | AP51 | 55b dk ultra & red | .45 | .20 |

**Imperf**
| | | | | |
|---|---|---|---|---|
| C136 | AP51 | 1.75 l vio & red | .75 | .20 |

Moon flight of Lunik 4, Apr. 2, 1963.

---

**1964, Jan. 15    Perf. 13½    Litho.    Unwmk.**
**Light Blue Background**
| | | | | |
|---|---|---|---|---|
| C151 | AP55 | 5b red, yel & vio | .20 | .20 |
| | | bl | | |
| C152 | AP55 | 10b red, yel & pur | .20 | .20 |
| C153 | AP55 | 20b red, ochr & ol | .20 | .20 |
| | | gray | | |
| C154 | AP55 | 35b red, ultra & sl | .20 | .20 |
| | | bl | | |
| C155 | AP55 | 40b red, yel & ultra | .20 | .20 |
| C156 | AP55 | 55b red, yel & ultra | .20 | .20 |
| C157 | AP55 | 60b red, ultra, red & | .40 | .20 |
| | | sep | | |
| C158 | AP55 | 75b red, ultra & dk | .40 | .20 |
| C159 | AP55 | 1 l red, yel & mar | .45 | .20 |
| C160 | AP55 | 1.40 l red, yel & mar | .75 | .20 |
| | | | .90 | .20 |

*Nos. C151-C160 (10)    3.90    2.00*

Nos. C151-C160 exist imperf. in changed colors. Value, set $6.50.
A miniature sheet contains one imperf. horizontal 2 l ultramarine and yellow stamp. Size of stamp: 59½x43mm. Value unused $7.50, canceled $3.75.

Modern and 19th Century Post Office Buildings
AP56

**1964, Nov. 15    Engr. & Typo.    Perf. 13½**
| | | | | |
|---|---|---|---|---|
| C161 | AP56 | 1.60 l ultra + 40b label | .75 | .25 |

Stamp Day. Stamp and label are imperf. between.

Plane Approaching Airport and Coach Leaving Gate — AP57

**1966, Oct. 20    Engr. & Typo.    Perf. 13½**
| | | | | |
|---|---|---|---|---|
| C162 | AP57 | 55b + 45b label | .60 | .20 |

Stamp Day.

Space Exploration Type of Regular Issue

US Achievements in Space: 1.20 l, Early Bird satellite and globe. 1.55 l, Mariner 4 transmitting pictures of the moon. 3.25 l, Gemini 6 & 7, rendezvous in space. 5 l, Gemini 8 meeting Agena rocket, and globe.

**1967, Feb. 15    Photo.    Perf. 13½**
| | | | | |
|---|---|---|---|---|
| C163 | A595 | 1.20 l silver & multi | .50 | .20 |
| C164 | A595 | 1.55 l silver & multi | .65 | .20 |
| C165 | A595 | 3.25 l silver & multi | .85 | .35 |
| C166 | A595 | 5 l silver & multi | 1.25 | .75 |
| | | | 3.25 | 1.50 |

*Nos. C163-C166 (4)*

10 years of space exploration.

---

Plane Spraying Crops — AP58

Moon, Earth and Path of Apollo 8 — AP59

Designs: 55b, Aerial ambulance over river, horiz. 1 l, Red Cross and plane. 2.40 l, Biplane and Mircea Zorileanu, aviation pioneer.

**1968, Feb. 28    Litho.    Unwmk.**
**Perf. 12x12½, 12½x12**
| | | | | |
|---|---|---|---|---|
| C167 | AP58 | 40b bl grn, blk & yel | .20 | .20 |
| | | brn | | |
| C168 | AP58 | 55b multicolored | .20 | .20 |
| C169 | AP58 | 1 l ultra, pale grn & | .20 | .20 |
| | | red org | | |
| C170 | AP58 | 2.40 l brt rose lil & | .50 | .30 |
| | | red org | 1.10 | .90 |

*Nos. C167-C170 (4)*

**1969    Photo.    Perf. 13½**

Design: No. C172, Soyuz 4 and 5 over globe with map of Russia.

| | | | | |
|---|---|---|---|---|
| C171 | AP59 | 3.30 l multi | 1.10 | 1.10 |
| C172 | AP59 | 3.30 l multi | 1.10 | 1.10 |

1st manned flight around the Moon, Dec. 21-27, 1968, and the first team flights of the Russian spacecrafts Soyuz 4 and 5, Jan. 16, 1969. See note after Hungary No. C284.
Issued in sheets of 4.
Issued: #C171, Jan. 17, #C172, Mar. 28.

Apollo 9 and Lunar Landing Module over Earth
AP60

Design: 2.40 l, Apollo 10 and lunar landing module over moon, vert.

**1969, June 15    Photo.    Perf. 13½**
| | | | | |
|---|---|---|---|---|
| C173 | AP60 | 60b multi | .20 | .20 |
| C174 | AP60 | 2.40 l multi | .70 | .25 |

US space explorations, Apollo 9 and 10.

First Man on Moon — AP61

**1969, July 24    Photo.    Perf. 13½**
| | | | | |
|---|---|---|---|---|
| C175 | AP61 | 3.30 l multi | 1.10 | .80 |

Man's first landing on the moon July 20, 1969. US astronauts Neil A. Armstrong and Col. Edwin E. Aldrin, Jr., with Lieut. Col. Michael Collins piloting Apollo 11. Printed in sheets of 4.

**1970, June 29**
| | | | | |
|---|---|---|---|---|
| C176 | AP61 | 1.50 l multi | .50 | .40 |

1.50 l, Apollo 13 capsule splashing down in Pacific.

Flight and safe landing of Apollo 13, Apr. 11-17, 1970. Printed in sheets of 4.

ROMANIA

---

## BAC 1-11 Jet AP62

**1970, Apr. 6**
C177  AP62  60b  multi    .20  .20
C178  AP62  21 l  multi    .55  .20
50th anniv. of Romanian civil aviation.
Design: 2 l, Fuselage BAC 1-11 and control tower, Bucharest airport.

### Flood Relief Type of Regular Issue
Design: 60b, Rescue by helicopter.

**1970, Sept. 25    Photo.    Perf. 13½**
C179  A671  60b b gray, blk & olive    .20  .20
Publicizing the plight of victims of the Danube flood. See No. 2207a.

## Henri Coanda's Model Plane AP63

**1970, Dec. 1**
C180  A663  60b  multicolored    .60  .20
Henri Coanda's first flight, 60th anniversary.

---

## Luna 16 on Moon AP64

**1971, Mar. 5    Photo.    Perf. 13½**
C181  AP64  3.30 l  silver & multi    1.00  1.00
C182  AP64  3.30 l  silver & multi    1.00  1.00
C182a.  Pair, #C181-C182 + 2 labels    2.00  2.00
C183  AP64  3.30 l  silver & multi    1.00  1.00
Nos. C181-C183 (3)    3.00  3.00

No. C181 commemorates Luna 16 Russian unmanned, automatic moon mission, Sept. 12-24, 1970. No. C182 commemorates Lunokhod 1 (Luna 17), Nov. 10-17, 1970. Nos. C181-C182 printed in sheets of 4 stamps, arranged checkerwise, and 4 labels. No. C183 commemorates Apollo 14 moon landing, Jan. 31-Feb. 9. Printed in sheets of 4 with 4 labels showing portraits of US astronauts Alan B. Shepard, Edgar D. Mitchell, Stuart A. Roosa, and Apollo 14 emblem.

#C182, Lunokhod 1, unmanned vehicle on moon. #C183, US astronaut & vehicle on moon.

---

## Cosmonauts Patsayev, Dobrovolsky and Volkov—AP65
### Souvenir Sheet

**1971, July 26    Litho.    Perf. 13½**
C184  AP65  6 l  black & ultra    4.50  4.50
In memory of Russian cosmonauts Viktor I. Patsayev, Georgi T. Dobrovolsky and Vladislav N. Volkov, who died during Soyuz 11 space mission, June 6-30, 1971.
No. C184 exists imperf. in black & blue green; size: 130x90mm. Value, unused $120, used $150.

---

## Lunar Rover on Moon AP66

**1971, Aug. 26    Photo.    Perf. 13½**
C185  AP66  1.50 l  blue & multi    1.10  1.10
US Apollo 15 moon mission, July 26-Aug. 7, 1971. No. C185 printed in sheets of 4 stamps, and 4 labels showing astronauts David Scott, James Irwin, Alfred Worden and Apollo 15 emblem with labels.
No. C185 exists imperf. in green & multicolored. The sheet has a control number. Value, unused $120, used $150.

### Olympic Souvenir Sheets
Designs: No. C186, Torchbearer and map of Romania. No. C187, Soccer.

**1972    Photo.    Perf. 13½**
C186  A699  6 l  pale grn & multi    5.00  5.00
C187  A699  6 l  blue & multi    5.00  5.00
20th Olympic Games, Munich, Aug. 26-Sept. 11. No. C186 contains one stamp 50x38mm. No. C187 contains one stamp 48½x37mm.
Issued: #C186, Apr. 25; #C187, Sept. 29. Two imperf. 6 l souvenir sheets exist, one showing equestrian, the other a satellite over globe. Value for either sheet, unused or used, $35.

---

## Lunar Rover on Moon — AP67

**1972, May 10    Photo.    Perf. 13½**
C188  AP67  3 l  vio bl, rose & gray grn    .90  .75
Apollo 16 US moon mission, Apr. 15-27, 1972. No. C188 printed in sheets of 4 stamps, Capt. John W. Young, Lt. Comdr. Thomas K. Mattingly 2nd, Col. Charles M. Duke, Jr., and Apollo 16 badge.

---

## Aurel Vlaicu and Monoplane — AP68

**1972, Aug. 15**
C189  AP68  60b  multicolored    .20  .20
C190  AP68  3 l  multicolored    .85  .30
Romanian Aviation Pioneers: 3 l, Traian Vuia and his flying machine.

### Olympic Medals Type of Regular Issue
#### Souvenir Sheet
Olympic silver and gold medals, horiz.

**1972, Sept. 29    Litho.    Perf. 13½**
C191  A714  6 l  multicolored    5.00  5.00
Romanian medalists at 20th Olympic Games. An imperf. 6 l souvenir sheet exists showing gold medal. Value, unused or used, $30.

### Apollo Type of Regular Issue
#### Souvenir Sheet

**1972, Dec. 27    Photo.    Perf. 13½**
C192  A715  6 l  vio bl, bis & dl grn    7.00  7.00
No. C192 contains one stamp 48½x36mm. An imperf. 6 l souvenir sheet exists showing surface of moon with landing sites of last 6 Apollo missions and landing capsule. Value, unused or used, $35.

---

### Type of Regular Issue, 1972
Design: Otopeni Airport, horiz.

**1972, Dec. 20    Photo.    Perf. 13**
Size: 29x21mm
C193  A710  14.60 l  brt blue    1.25  .30

## Apollo and Soyuz Spacecraft — AP69

**1975, July 14    Photo.    Perf. 13½**
C196  AP69  1.75 l  vio bl, red & ol    .75  .75
C197  AP69  3.25 l  vio bl, red & ol    1.25  1.25
Apollo Soyuz space test project (Russo-American cooperation), launching July 15; link-up, July 17. Nos. C196-C197 printed in sheets of 4 stamps, arranged checkerwise, and 4 rose lilac labels showing Apollo-Soyuz emblem.
3.25 l, Apollo and Soyuz after link-up.

---

## European Security and Cooperation Conference — AP70

**1975, July 30    Photo.    Perf. 13½**
C198  Sheet of 4    2.50  2.50
a.  2.75 l  Map of Europe    .35  .35
b.  2.75 l  Peace doves    .35  .35
c.  5 l  Open book    .75  .75
d.  5 l  Children playing    .75  .75
European Security and Cooperation Conference, Helsinki, July 30-Aug. 1. No. C198 inscribed "posta aeriana." An imperf. 10 l souvenir sheet exists showing Helsinki on map of Europe. Value, unused or used, $95.

### Red Cross Type of 1976
Design: Blood donors, Red Cross plane.

**1976, Apr. 20    Photo.    Perf. 13½**
C199  A790  3.35 l  multi    .60  .25

---

## De Havilland DH-9 — AP71

**1976, June 24    Photo.    Perf. 13½**
C200  AP71  20b  blue & multi    .20  .20
C201  AP71  40b  blue & multi    .20  .20
C202  AP71  1 l  multi    .40  .20
C203  AP71  1.75 l  blue & multi    .40  .20
C204  AP71  2.75 l  blue & multi    .55  .20
C205  AP71  3.60 l  multi    .85  .30
Nos. C200-C205 (6)    2.40  1.30
Romanian Airline, 50th anniversary.
Airplanes: 40b, I.C.A.R. Commercial, 60b, Douglas DC-3, 1.75 l, AN-24, 2.75 l, IL-62, 3.60 l, Boeing 707.

## Glider I.C.A.R.-1 — AP72

**1977, Feb. 20    Photo.    Perf. 13**
C206  AP72  20b  multi    .20  .20
C207  AP72  40b  multi    .20  .20
C208  AP72  55b  multi    .20  .20
C209  AP72  1.50 l  bl & multi    .30  .20
C210  AP72  3 l  multi    .90  .25
C211  AP72  3.40 l  multi    .95  .25
Nos. C206-C211 (6)    2.40  1.25
Gliders: 40b, I.S.-3d, 55b, R.G.-5, 1.50 l, I.S.-11, 3 l, I.S.-29D, 3.40 l, I.S.-28B.

## Boeing 707 over Bucharest Airport and Pioneers — AP73
### Souvenir Sheet

**1977, June 28    Photo.    Perf. 13½**
C212  AP73  10 l  multi    2.50  2.50
European Security and Cooperation Conference, Belgrade. An imperf. 10 l souvenir sheet exists showing Boeing 707, map of Europe and buildings. Value, unused or used, $35.

---

## Woman Letter Carrier, Mailbox AP74

**1977    Photo.    Perf. 13**
C213  AP74  2 l  multicolored    3.00  1.00
C214  AP74  3 l  multicolored    4.50  1.50
3 l, Plane, newspapers, letters, packages.
Issue dates: 2 l, July 25, 30; 3 l, Sept. 10.

## LZ-1 over Friedrichshafen, 1900 — AP75

**1978, Mar. 20    Photo.    Perf. 13½**
C215  AP75  60b  multi    .20  .20
C216  AP75  1 l  multi    .25  .20
C217  AP75  1.50 l  multi    .30  .20
C218  AP75  2.15 l  multi    .55  .20
C219  AP75  3.40 l  multi    .90  .25
C220  AP75  4.80 l  multi    1.25  .30
Nos. C215-C220 (6)    2.40  1.25
Airships: 1 l, Santos Dumont's dirigible over Paris, 1901, 1.50 l, British R-34 over New York and Statue of Liberty, 1919, 2.15 l, Italia over North Pole, 1928, 3.40 l, Zeppelin LZ-127 over Brasov, 1929, 4.80 l, "Zeppelin over Sibiu, 1929," 10 l, Zeppelin over Bucharest, 1929.

### Souvenir Sheet
C221  AP75  10 l  multicolored    2.25  2.25
History of airships. No. C221 contains one 50x37½mm stamp.

### Soccer Type of 1978
#### Souvenir Sheet
10 l, 2 soccer players, Argentina '78 emblem.

**1978, Apr. 15    Photo.    Perf. 13½**
C222  A818  10 l  blue & multi    2.25  2.25
11th World Cup Soccer Championship, Argentina, June 1-25. No. C222 contains one stamp 37x50mm. A 10 l imperf souvenir sheet exists showing goalkeeper. Value, unused or used, $25.

ROMANIA

**Wilbur and Orville Wright, Flyer A — AP76**

Aviation History: 1 l, Louis Blériot and his plane over English Channel, 1909. 1.50 l, Anthony Fokker and Fokker F-VII trimotor, 1926. 2.15 l, Andrei N. Tupolev and ANT-25 monoplane, 1937. 3.40 l, Otto Lilienthal and glider, 1891-96. 3.40 l, Traian Vuia and his plane, Montesson, France, 1906. 4.80 l, Aurel Vlaicu and 1st Romanian plane, 1910. 10 l, Henri Coanda and his "jet", 1910.

**1978, Dec. 18** — Photo. — Perf. 13½
| C223 | AP76 | 55b multi | .20 | .20 |
|---|---|---|---|---|
| C224 | AP76 | 1 l multi | .20 | .20 |
| C225 | AP76 | 1.50 l multi | .20 | .20 |
| C226 | AP76 | 2.15 l multi | .35 | .20 |
| C227 | AP76 | 3 l multi | .40 | .20 |
| C228 | AP76 | 3.40 l multi | .40 | .20 |
| C229 | AP76 | 4.80 l multi | .45 | .20 |
| Nos. C223-C229 (7) | | | 2.15 | 1.40 |

**Souvenir Sheet**
| C230 | AP76 | 10 l multi | 2.25 | 2.25 |
|---|---|---|---|---|

No. C230 contains one stamp 50x38mm.

**Inter-Europa Type of 1979**
3.40 l, Jet, mail truck and motorcycle.
**1979, May 3** — Photo. — Perf. 13
| C231 | A835 | 3.40 l multi | .40 | .40 |
|---|---|---|---|---|

**Animal Type of 1980**
**Souvenir Sheet**
**1980, Mar. 25** — Photo. — Perf. 13½
| C232 | A852 | 10 l Pelicans | .20 | .20 |
|---|---|---|---|---|

No. C232 contains one stamp 38x50mm.

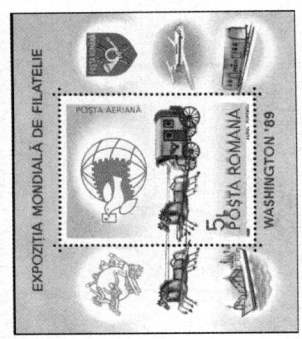

**Mercury — AP77**
**1981, June 30** — Photo. — Perf. 13½
| C233 | AP77 | 55b shown | .20 | .20 |
|---|---|---|---|---|
| C234 | AP77 | 1 l Venus, Earth, Mars | .20 | .20 |
| C235 | AP77 | 1.50 l Jupiter | .20 | .20 |
| C236 | AP77 | 2.15 l Saturn | .30 | .20 |
| C237 | AP77 | 3.40 l Uranus | .40 | .20 |
| C238 | AP77 | 4.80 l Neptune, Pluto | .55 | .30 |
| Nos. C233-C238 (6) | | | 1.75 | 1.30 |

**Souvenir Sheet**
| C239 | AP77 | 10 l Earth | 1.75 | 1.75 |
|---|---|---|---|---|

No. C239 contains one stamp 37x50mm. An imperf. 10 l souvenir sheet exists showing planets in orbit. Value, unused or used, $16.

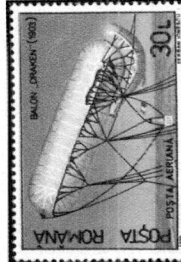

**Romanian-Russian Space Cooperation — AP78**
**1981** — Photo. — Perf. 13½
| C240 | AP78 | 55b Soyuz 40 | .20 | .20 |
|---|---|---|---|---|
| C241 | AP78 | 3.40 l Salyut 6, Soyuz 40 | .30 | .20 |

**Souvenir Sheet**
| C242 | AP78 | 10 l Cosmonauts, spacecraft | 1.50 | 1.50 |
|---|---|---|---|---|

No. C242 contains one stamp 50x39mm. Issued: 55b, 3.40 l, May 14; 10 l, June 30.

**Children's Games Type of 1981**
**1981, Nov. 25**
| C243 | A880 | 4.80 l Flying model planes | .50 | .50 |
|---|---|---|---|---|

**Standard Glider — AP79**
**1982, June 20** — Photo. — Perf. 13½
| C244 | AP79 | 50b shown | .20 | .20 |
|---|---|---|---|---|
| C245 | AP79 | 1 l Excelsior D | .20 | .20 |
| C246 | AP79 | 1 l Dedal I | .20 | .20 |
| C247 | AP79 | 1.50 l Enthusiast | .30 | .20 |
| C248 | AP79 | 2.50 l AK-22 | .40 | .25 |
| C249 | AP79 | 4 l Grifrom | .55 | .30 |
| Nos. C244-C249 (6) | | | 1.85 | 1.35 |

**Agriculture Type of 1982**
**1982, June 29**
| C250 | A888 | 4 l Helicopter spraying insecticide | .50 | .20 |
|---|---|---|---|---|

**Vlaicu's Glider, 1909 — AP80**
Aurel Vlaicu (1882-19), Aviator: 1 l, Memorial, Banesti-Prahova, vert. 2.50 l, Hero Aviators Memorial, by Kotzebue and Fekete, vert. 3 l, Vlaicu-1 glider, 1910.
**1982, Sept. 27** — Photo. — Perf. 13½
| C251 | AP80 | 50b multi | .20 | .20 |
|---|---|---|---|---|
| C252 | AP80 | 1 l multi | .20 | .20 |
| C253 | AP80 | 2.50 l multi | .40 | .20 |
| C254 | AP80 | 3 l multi | .45 | .25 |
| Nos. C251-C254 (4) | | | 1.25 | .80 |

**25th Anniv. of Space Flight — AP81**
Designs: 50b, H. Coanda, reaction motor, 1910. 1 l, H. Oberth, rocket, 1923. 1.50 l, Sputnik I, 1957. 2.50 l, Vostok I, 1961. 4 l, Apollo 11, 1969. 5 l, Columbia space shuttle, 1982. 10 l, Globe.
**1983, Jan. 24** — Photo. — Perf. 13½
| C255 | AP81 | 50b multi | .20 | .20 |
|---|---|---|---|---|
| C256 | AP81 | 1 l multi | .20 | .20 |
| C257 | AP81 | 1.50 l multi | .30 | .20 |
| C258 | AP81 | 2.50 l multi | .35 | .20 |
| C259 | AP81 | 4 l multi | .50 | .20 |
| C260 | AP81 | 5 l multi | .65 | .25 |
| Nos. C255-C260 (6) | | | 2.10 | 1.25 |

**Souvenir Sheet**
**1983, Jan. 25** — Photo. — Perf. 13½
| C261 | AP81 | 10 l Earth | 2.50 | 2.50 |
|---|---|---|---|---|

No. C261 contains one stamp 41x53mm.

**First Romanian-built Jet Airliner — AP82**
**1983, Jan. 25** — Photo. — Perf. 13½
| C262 | AP82 | 11 l Rombac 1-11 | 1.50 | .20 |
|---|---|---|---|---|

**World Communications Year — AP83**
**1983, July 25** — Photo. — Perf. 13½
| C263 | AP83 | 2 l Boeing 707, Postal van | .35 | .20 |
|---|---|---|---|---|

**40th Anniv., Intl. Civil Aviation Organization — AP84**
**1984, Aug. 15** — Photo. — Perf. 13½
| C265 | AP84 | 50b Lockheed L-14 | .20 | .20 |
|---|---|---|---|---|
| C266 | AP84 | 1.50 l BN-2 Islander | .25 | .20 |
| C267 | AP84 | 4 l Rombac | .45 | .20 |
| C268 | AP84 | 6 l Boeing 707 | .90 | .25 |
| Nos. C265-C268 (4) | | | 1.80 | .85 |

**Halley's Comet — AP86**
**1986, Jan. 27** — Photo. — Perf. 13½
| C269 | AP85 | 2 l shown | .30 | .20 |
|---|---|---|---|---|
| C270 | AP85 | 4 l Space probes | .60 | .30 |

An imperf. 10 l air post souvenir sheet exists showing comet and space probes, perf and control number. Value, unused or used, 30.

**Souvenir Sheet**
**Plane of Alexandru Papana, 1936 — AP86**
**1986, May 15** — Photo. — Perf. 13½
| C271 | AP86 | 10 l multi | 2.00 | 2.00 |
|---|---|---|---|---|

AMERIPEX '86.

**Aircraft — AP87**
**1987, Aug. 10**
| C272 | AP87 | 50b Henri Auguste glider, 1909 | .20 | .20 |
|---|---|---|---|---|
| C273 | AP87 | 1 l Sky diver, IS-28 B2 glider | .20 | .20 |
| C274 | AP87 | 2 l IS-29 D-2 glider | .25 | .20 |
| C275 | AP87 | 3 l IS-32 glider | .35 | .20 |
| C276 | AP87 | 4 l IAR-35 glider | .60 | .20 |
| C277 | AP87 | 5 l IS-28 M2, route | .75 | .30 |
| Nos. C272-C277 (6) | | | 2.35 | 1.30 |

**1st Moon Landing, 20th Anniv. — AP88**

Designs: 50b, C. Haas. 1.50 l, Konstantin Tsiolkovski (1857-1935), Soviet rocket science pioneer. 2 l, H. Oberth and equations. 3 l, Robert Goddard and diagram on blackboard. 4 l, Sergei Korolev (1906-66). Soviet aeronautical engineer. 5 l, Wernher von Braun (1912-77), lunar module.

**1989, Oct. 25** — Photo. — Perf. 13½
| C278 | AP88 | 50b multicolored | .20 | .20 |
|---|---|---|---|---|
| C279 | AP88 | 1.50 l multicolored | .30 | .20 |
| C280 | AP88 | 3 l multicolored | .40 | .20 |
| C281 | AP88 | 4 l multicolored | .55 | .20 |
| C282 | AP88 | 4 l multicolored | .75 | .20 |
| C283 | AP88 | 5 l multicolored | .95 | .25 |
| Nos. C278-C283 (6) | | | 3.15 | 1.25 |

**Souvenir Sheet**
A 10 l souvenir sheet picturing Armstrong and Eagle lunar module was also issued. Value, unused or used, $15.

**World Stamp Expo '89, Washington, DC, Nov. 17-Dec. 3 — AP89**
**1989, Nov. 17** — Photo. — Perf. 13½
| C284 | AP89 | 5 l Postal coach | 1.50 | 1.50 |
|---|---|---|---|---|

**Captured Balloons — AP90**
Balloons captured by Romanian army: 30 l, German balloon, Draken, 1903. 90 l, French balloon, Caquot, 1917.
**1993, Feb. 26** — Photo. — Perf. 13½
| C285 | AP90 | 30 l multicolored | .20 | .20 |
|---|---|---|---|---|
| C286 | AP90 | 90 l multicolored | .70 | .20 |

**European Inventions, Discoveries — AP91**
Europa: a, 240 l, Hermann Oberth (1894-1989), rocket scientist. b, 2100 l, Henri Doanda (1886-1972), aeronautical engineer. Illustration reduced.
**1994, May 25** — Photo. — Perf. 13
| C287 | AP91 | Sheet of 2, #a.-b. + 2 labels | 4.50 | 4.50 |
|---|---|---|---|---|

ICAO, 50th Anniv. AP92

Aircraft: 110 l, Traian Vuia, 1906. 350 l, Rombac 1-11. 500 l, Boeing 737-300. 635 l, Airbus A310.

**1994. Aug. 12** **Photo.** ***Perf. 13***

| | | | | |
|---|---|---|---|---|
| **C288** | AP92 | 110 l multicolored | .20 | .20 |
| **C289** | AP92 | 350 l multicolored | .55 | .20 |
| **C290** | AP92 | 500 l multicolored | .75 | .20 |
| **C291** | AP92 | 635 l multicolored | 1.00 | .20 |
| | | *Nos. C288-C291 (4)* | 2.50 | .80 |

For surcharges see #C294-C297.

French-Romanian Aeronautical Agreement, 75th Anniv. — AP93

**1995, Mar. 31** **Photo.** ***Perf. 13x13¼***

| | | | | |
|---|---|---|---|---|
| **C292** | AP93 | 60 l shown | .20 | .20 |
| **C293** | AP93 | 960 l Biplane Potez IX | 1.00 | .20 |

No. C291 Surcharged in Red

**Methods and Perfs as Before**

**2000, May 19**

| | | | | |
|---|---|---|---|---|
| **C294** | AP92 | 1700 l on 635 l multi | .20 | .20 |
| **C295** | AP92 | 2000 l on 635 l multi | .30 | .20 |
| **C296** | AP92 | 3900 l on 635 l multi | .55 | .25 |
| **C297** | AP92 | 9050 l on 635 l multi | 1.25 | .60 |
| | | *Nos. C294-C297 (4)* | 2.30 | 1.25 |

No. C293 Surcharged in Red

**2000, Oct. 27** **Photo.** ***Perf. 13¼***

| | | | | |
|---|---|---|---|---|
| **C298** | AP93 | 2000 l on 960 l multi | .20 | .20 |
| **C299** | AP93 | 4200 l on 960 l multi | .35 | .20 |
| **C300** | AP93 | 4600 l on 960 l multi | .35 | .20 |
| **C301** | AP93 | 6500 l on 960 l multi | .55 | .25 |
| | | *Nos. C298-C301 (4)* | 1.45 | .85 |

## AIR POST SEMI-POSTAL STAMPS

**Catalogue values for unused stamps in this section are for Never Hinged items.**

Corneliu Codreanu SPAP1

**Unwmk.**

**1940, Dec. 1** **Photo.** ***Perf. 14***

**CB1** SPAP1 20 l + 5 l Prus grn 2.00 1.10

Propaganda for the Rome-Berlin Axis.

No. CB1 exists with overprint "1 Mai 1941 Jamboreea Nationala." This was a private overprint, not authorized by the Romanian Postal Service.

Plane over Sinaia — SPAP2

200 l+800 l, Plane over Mountains.

**1945, Oct. 1** **Wmk. 276** ***Imperf.***

| | | | | |
|---|---|---|---|---|
| **CB2** | SPAP2 | 80 l + 420 l gray | 2.00 | 2.00 |
| **CB3** | SPAP2 | 200 l + 800 l ultra | 2.00 | 2.00 |

16th Congress of the General Assoc. of Romanian Engineers.

Souvenir Sheet

Re-distribution of Land — SPAP4

**1946, May 4** **Photo.** ***Perf. 14***

**CB4** SPAP4 80 l blue 10.00 *12.00*

Agrarian reform law of Mar. 23, 1945. The sheet sold for 100 lei.

Souvenir Sheet

Plane Skywriting — SPAP5

**1946, May 1** ***Perf. 13***

**CB5** SPAP5 200 l bl & brt red 16.50 *18.00*

Labor Day. The sheet sold for 10,000 lei.

Lockheed 12 Electra — SPAP6

**1946, Sept. 1** ***Perf. 11½***

**CB6** SPAP6 300 l + 1200 l dp bl 1.00 *1.25*

For se-tenant see No. C26a and note after No. C26.

The surtax was for the Office of Popular Sports.

Miniature Sheet

Women of Wallachia, Transylvania and Moldavia — SPAP7

**1946, Dec. 20** **Wmk. 276** ***Imperf.***

**CB7** SPAP7 500 l + 9500 l choc & red 1.90 2.25

Democratic Women's Org. of Romania.

SPAP8

**1946, Oct.** ***Imperf.***

**CB8** SPAP8 300 l deep plum 6.00 *7.00*

The surtax was for the Office of Popular Sports. Sheets of four. Stamp sold for 1300 l.

Laborer with Torch — SPAP9

**1947, Mar. 1**

**CB9** SPAP9 3000 l + 7000 l choc .50 .50

Sheets of four with marginal inscription.

Plane SPAP10

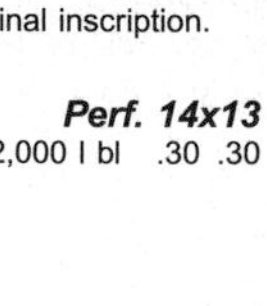

Plane above Shore Line SPAP11

**1947, June 27** ***Imperf.***

**CB10** SPAP10 15,000 l + 15,000 l .50 .50

Sheets of four with marginal inscription.

**1947, May 1** ***Perf. 14x13***

**CB11** SPAP11 3000 l + 12,000 l bl .30 .30

Planes over Mountains SPAP12

Plane over Athletic Field SPAP13

**1947, Oct. 5** ***Perf. 14x14½***

**CB12** SPAP12 5 l + 5 l blue .40 .40

17th Congress of the General Assoc. of Romanian Engineers.

**Wmk. 276**

**1948, Feb. 20** **Photo.** ***Perf. 13½***

**CB13** SPAP13 7 l + 7 l vio 1.00 .60

***Imperf***

**CB14** SPAP13 10 l + 10 l Prus grn 1.40 .90

Balkan Games. Sheets of four with marginal inscription.

Swallow and Plane SPAP14

**1948, Mar. 15** ***Perf. 14x13½***

**CB15** SPAP14 12 l + 12 l blue .90 .50

Bucharest-Moscow Passenger Plane, Douglas DC-3 Dakota — SPAP15

**1948, Oct. 29** ***Perf. 14***

**CB16** SPAP15 20 l + 20 l dp bl 7.50 7.50

Printed in sheets of 8 stamps and 16 small, red brown labels. Sheet yields 8 triptychs, each comprising 1 stamp flanked by label with Bucharest view and label with Moscow view.

Douglas DC-4 — SPAP16

**1948, May 1** ***Perf. 13½x14***

**CB17** SPAP16 20 l + 20 l blue 6.75 5.75

Issued to publicize Labor Day, May 1, 1948.

Pursuit Plane and Victim SPAP17

Launching Model Plane SPAP18

**1948, May 9** ***Perf. 13***

| | | | | |
|---|---|---|---|---|
| **CB18** | SPAP17 | 3 l + 3 l shown | 4.25 | 4.25 |
| **CB19** | SPAP17 | 5 l + 5 l Bomber | 6.25 | 6.25 |

Issued to honor the Romanian army.

## 1948, Dec. 31

| | | | | Perf. 13x13½ | |
|---|---|---|---|---|---|
| CB20 | SPAP18 | 20 l + 20 l dp ultra | | 11.00 | 11.00 |

**Imperf.**

| CB21 | SPAP18 | 20 l + 20 l Prus bl | | 11.00 | 11.00 |
|---|---|---|---|---|---|

Nos. CB20 and CB21 were issued in sheets of four stamps, with ornamental border and "1948" in contrasting color.

### UPU Type of Air Post Issue, 1963

Design: 1.60 l+50b, Globe, map of Romania, planes and UPU monument.

**1963, Nov. 15    Size: 75x27mm**
**Perf. 14x13½    Litho.    Unwmk.**

| CB22 | AP54 | 1.60 l + 50b multi | | 1.00 | .50 |
|---|---|---|---|---|---|

Surtax for the Romanian Philatelic Federation.

## POSTAGE DUE STAMPS

D1

**Perf. 11, 11½, 13½ and Compound**

### 1881    Typo.

| J1 | D1 | 2b brown | 4.00 | 1.25 |
|---|---|---|---|---|
| J2 | D1 | 5b brown | 22.50 | 2.00 |
| a. | | Tête bêche pair | 190.00 | 75.00 |
| J3 | D1 | 10b brown | 30.00 | 1.25 |
| J4 | D1 | 20b brown | 32.50 | 1.25 |
| J5 | D1 | 50b brown | 26.00 | 2.50 |
| J6 | D1 | 60b brown | 21.00 | 3.00 |
| | | Nos. J1-J6 (6) | 136.00 | 11.25 |

### 1885

| J7 | D1 | 10b pale red brown | 8.00 | .50 |
|---|---|---|---|---|
| J8 | D1 | 30b pale red brown | 8.00 | .50 |

### 1887-90

| J9 | D1 | 2b gray green | 4.00 | .75 |
|---|---|---|---|---|
| J10 | D1 | 5b gray green | 8.00 | 3.00 |
| J11 | D1 | 10b gray green | 8.00 | 3.00 |
| J12 | D1 | 30b gray green | 28.00 | 7.50 |
| | | Nos. J9-J12 (4) | | |

### 1888

| J14 | D1 | 2b green, yellowish | .90 | .75 |
|---|---|---|---|---|
| J15 | D1 | 5b green, yellowish | 2.25 | 2.25 |
| J16 | D1 | 10b green, yellowish | 32.50 | 2.75 |
| J17 | D1 | 30b green, yellowish | 17.50 | 3.15 |
| | | Nos. J14-J17 (4) | 53.15 | 7.00 |

### 1890-96    Wmk. 163

| J18 | D1 | 2b emerald | 1.60 | .45 |
|---|---|---|---|---|
| J19 | D1 | 5b emerald | .80 | .45 |
| J20 | D1 | 10b emerald | 1.25 | .45 |
| J21 | D1 | 30b emerald | 2.00 | .45 |
| J22 | D1 | 50b emerald | 6.50 | .95 |
| J23 | D1 | 60b emerald | 8.75 | 3.25 |
| | | Nos. J18-J23 (6) | 20.90 | 6.00 |

### 1898    Wmk. 200

| J24 | D1 | 2b blue green | .70 | .45 |
|---|---|---|---|---|
| J25 | D1 | 5b blue green | .90 | .30 |
| J26 | D1 | 10b blue green | 1.40 | .30 |
| J27 | D1 | 30b blue green | 1.90 | .90 |
| J28 | D1 | 50b blue green | 4.75 | 1.75 |
| J29 | D1 | 60b blue green | 5.50 | 4.00 |
| | | Nos. J24-J29 (6) | 15.15 | 4.00 |

### 1902-10    Unwmk.
**Thin Paper, Tinted Rose on Back**

| J30 | D1 | 2b green | .85 | .25 |
|---|---|---|---|---|
| J31 | D1 | 5b green | .50 | .50 |
| J32 | D1 | 10b green | .40 | .20 |
| J33 | D1 | 30b green | 2.50 | .90 |
| J34 | D1 | 50b green | 5.25 | 2.25 |
| J35 | D1 | 60b green | 10.00 | 4.00 |
| | | Nos. J30-J35 (6) | | |

### 1908-11    White Paper

| J36 | D1 | 2b green | .80 | .50 |
|---|---|---|---|---|
| J37 | D1 | 5b green | .60 | .60 |
| a. | | Tête bêche pair | 12.00 | 12.00 |
| J38 | D1 | 10b green | .40 | .30 |
| a. | | Tête bêche pair | 12.00 | 12.00 |
| J39 | D1 | 30b green | .50 | .30 |
| J40 | D1 | 50b green | 2.00 | 1.25 |
| a. | | Tête bêche pair | 4.30 | 2.85 |
| | | Nos. J36-J40 (5) | | |

### 1911    Wmk. 165

| J41 | D2 | 2b dark blue, green | .20 | .20 |
|---|---|---|---|---|
| J42 | D2 | 5b dark blue, green | .20 | .20 |
| J43 | D2 | 10b dark blue, green | .20 | .20 |
| J44 | D2 | 15b dark blue, green | .20 | .20 |
| J45 | D2 | 20b dark blue, green | .20 | .25 |
| J46 | D2 | 30b dark blue, green | .25 | .30 |
| J47 | D2 | 50b dark blue, green | .40 | .40 |
| J48 | D2 | 60b dark blue, green | .80 | .80 |
| J49 | D2 | 2 l dark blue, green | 2.75 | 2.75 |
| | | Nos. J41-J49 (9) | | |

D2

The letters "P.R." appear to be embossed instead of watermarked. They are often faint or entirely invisible.

The 20b, type D2 has two types, differing in the width of the head of the "2." This affects Nos. J45, J54, J58, and J63.

For overprints see Nos. J52-J77, J82, J87-J88, RAJ1-RAJ2, RAJ20-RAJ21, 3NJ1-3NJ7.

### Regular Issue of 1908 Overprinted

D3

### 1918    Unwmk.

| J50 | A46 | 5b yellow green | .75 | .25 |
|---|---|---|---|---|
| a. | | Inverted overprint | 5.00 | 5.00 |
| J51 | A46 | 10b rose | .75 | .25 |
| a. | | Inverted overprint | 3.75 | 3.75 |

### Postage Due Type of 1911    Wmk. 165
**1920**

| J52 | D2 | 5b black, green | .20 | .20 |
|---|---|---|---|---|
| J53 | D2 | 10b black, green | .20 | .20 |
| J54 | D2 | 20b black, green | .60 | .60 |
| J55 | D2 | 30b black, green | 4.00 | .40 |
| J55A | D2 | 50b black, green | 1.10 | .40 |
| | | Nos. J52-J55A (5) | | |

**Perf. 11½, 13½ and Compound**

### 1919    Unwmk.

| J56 | D2 | 5b black, green | .30 | .20 |
|---|---|---|---|---|
| J57 | D2 | 10b black, green | 1.00 | .20 |
| J58 | D2 | 20b black, green | .90 | .20 |
| J59 | D2 | 30b black, green | 2.25 | .40 |
| J60 | D2 | 50b black, green | 4.75 | 1.20 |
| | | Nos. J56-J60 (5) | | |

### 1920-26    White Paper

| J61 | D2 | 5b black | .20 | .20 |
|---|---|---|---|---|
| J62 | D2 | 10b black | .20 | .20 |
| J63 | D2 | 20b black | .20 | .40 |
| J64 | D2 | 30b black | .40 | .40 |
| J65 | D2 | 50b black | .30 | .30 |
| J66 | D2 | 60b black | .30 | .30 |
| J67 | D2 | 1 l black | .30 | .20 |
| J68 | D2 | 2 l black (26) | .20 | .20 |
| J69 | D2 | 3 l black (26) | | |
| J70 | D2 | 6 l black | .75 | .30 |
| | | Nos. J61-J70 (10) | | |

### 1923-24

| J74 | D2 | 1 l black, pale green | .25 | .20 |
|---|---|---|---|---|
| J75 | D2 | 2 l black, pale green | .45 | .25 |
| J76 | D2 | 3 l black, pale green ('24) | 1.10 | .55 |
| J77 | D2 | 6 l blk, pale green ('24) | 3.20 | 1.55 |
| | | Nos. J74-J77 (4) | | |

### Postage Due Stamps of 1920-26 Overprinted

[Stamp: ROMANA 2 LEI TAXA DE PLATA — 8 IUNIE 1930]

### 1930    Perf. 13½

| J78 | D2 | 1 l black | .20 | .20 |
|---|---|---|---|---|
| J79 | D2 | 2 l black | .20 | .20 |
| J80 | D2 | 3 l black | .30 | .20 |
| J81 | D2 | 6 l black | 1.15 | .85 |
| | | Nos. J78-J81 (4) | | |

Accession of King Carol II.

> Catalogue values for unused stamps in this section, from this point to the end of the section, are for Never Hinged items.

### 1931    Wmk. 225

| J82 | D2 | 2 l black | .70 | .35 |
|---|---|---|---|---|

**Type of 1911 Issue**

### 1932-37    Wmk. 230    Perf. 13½

| J83 | D3 | 1 l black | .20 | .20 |
|---|---|---|---|---|
| J84 | D3 | 2 l black | .20 | .20 |
| J85 | D3 | 3 l black ('37) | .20 | .20 |
| J86 | D3 | 6 l black ('37) | .80 | .80 |
| | | Nos. J83-J86 (4) | | |

See Nos. J89-J98.

### Type of 1911
**1942    Typo.**

| J87 | D2 | 50 l black | .25 | .20 |
|---|---|---|---|---|
| J88 | D2 | 100 l black | .40 | .25 |

### Type of 1932
**1946-47    Unwmk.**

| J89 | D3 | 20 l black | .60 | .55 |
|---|---|---|---|---|
| J90 | D3 | 100 l black | .45 | .25 |
| J91 | D3 | 200 l black ('47) | 1.10 | 1.35 |
| | | Nos. J89-J91 (3) | | |

**Perf. 14    Unwmk.**

### 1946-47    Wmk. 276

| J92 | D3 | 20 l black | .20 | .20 |
|---|---|---|---|---|
| J93 | D3 | 30 l black | .20 | .20 |
| J94 | D3 | 80 l bluish | .20 | .35 |
| J95 | D3 | 100 l black | .45 | .35 |
| J96 | D3 | 200 l black | .60 | .50 |
| J97 | D3 | 500 l black ('47) | 1.25 | 1.25 |
| J98 | D3 | 5000 l black ('47) | 1.10 | 2.90 |
| | | Nos. J92-J98 (7) | | |

### Crown and King Michael — D3a

**Perf. 14½x13½    Typo.**

### 1947

| J98A | D3a | 2 l carmine | .40 | .20 |
|---|---|---|---|---|
| J98B | D3a | 4 l gray blue | .75 | .30 |
| J98C | D3a | 5 l gray blue | 1.10 | .45 |
| J98D | D3a | 10 l violet brown | 4.25 | 1.70 |
| | | Nos. J98A-J98D (4) | | |

### Same Overprinted    **R.P.R.**

### 1948

| J98E | D3a | 2 l carmine | .30 | .20 |
|---|---|---|---|---|
| J98F | D3a | 4 l gray blue | .60 | .25 |
| J98G | D3a | 5 l gray blue | .75 | .30 |
| J98H | D3a | 10 l violet brown | 1.50 | .55 |
| | | Nos. J98E-J98H (4) | 3.15 | 1.30 |

In use, Nos. J98A-J106 and following issues were torn apart, one half being affixed to the postage due item and the other half being pasted into the postman's record book. Values are for unused and canceled-to-order pairs.

### General Post Office and Post Horn — D5

### 1950    Unwmk.    Photo.    Perf. 14½x14

| J99 | D4 | 2 l orange vermilion | .70 | .70 |
|---|---|---|---|---|
| J100 | D4 | 4 l deep blue | .70 | .70 |
| J101 | D4 | 5 l dark gray green | .90 | .90 |
| J102 | D4 | 10 l orange brown | 1.10 | 1.10 |

**Wmk. 358**

| J103 | D4 | 2 l orange vermilion | 1.00 | .70 |
|---|---|---|---|---|
| J104 | D4 | 4 l deep blue | 1.50 | .75 |
| J105 | D4 | 5 l dark gray green | 1.50 | .90 |
| J106 | D4 | 10 l orange brown | 2.00 | 1.25 |
| | | Nos. J99-J106 (8) | 8.90 | 7.00 |

### Postage Due Stamps of 1950 Surcharged with New Values in Black or Carmine

### 1952    Unwmk.

| J107 | D4 | 4b on 2 l | .25 | .25 |
|---|---|---|---|---|
| J108 | D4 | 10b on 4 l (C) | .25 | .25 |
| J109 | D4 | 20b on 5 l (C) | .45 | .45 |
| J110 | D4 | 50b on 10 l (C) | .75 | .75 |
| | | Nos. J107-J110 (4) | | |

**Wmk. 358**

| J111 | D4 | 4b on 2 l | | |
|---|---|---|---|---|
| J112 | D4 | 10b on 4 l (C) | | |
| J113 | D4 | 20b on 5 l (C) | 2.50 | 1.25 |
| J114 | D4 | 50b on 10 l (C) | 3.00 | 1.25 |
| | | Nos. J115-J120 (6) | | |

The existence of Nos. J111-J112 has been questioned.
See note after No. J98H.

### General Post Office and Post Horn — D6

### 1957    Wmk. 358    Perf. 14

| J115 | D5 | 3b black | .20 | .20 |
|---|---|---|---|---|
| J116 | D5 | 5b red orange | .20 | .20 |
| J117 | D5 | 5b red lilac | .20 | .20 |
| J118 | D5 | 20b brt red | .20 | .20 |
| J119 | D5 | 40b lt bl grn | .35 | .20 |
| J120 | D5 | 1 l brt ultra | 1.00 | .20 |
| | | Nos. J115-J120 (6) | 2.15 | 1.20 |

See note after No. J98H.

### 1967, Feb. 25    Photo.    Perf. 13

| J121 | D6 | 3b brt grn | .20 | .20 |
|---|---|---|---|---|
| J122 | D6 | 5b brt bl | .20 | .20 |
| J123 | D6 | 10b lilac rose | .20 | .20 |
| J124 | D6 | 20b brown | .20 | .20 |
| J125 | D6 | 40b brown | .20 | .20 |
| J126 | D6 | 1 l violet | 1.55 | 1.20 |
| | | Nos. J121-J126 (6) | | |

See note after No. J98H.

### 1970, Mar. 10    Unwmk.

| J127 | D6 | 3b brt grn | .20 | .20 |
|---|---|---|---|---|
| J128 | D6 | 5b brt bl | .20 | .20 |
| J129 | D6 | 10b lilac rose | .20 | .20 |
| J130 | D6 | 20b vermilion | .20 | .20 |
| J131 | D6 | 40b brown | .35 | .20 |
| J132 | D6 | 1 l violet | 1.35 | 1.20 |
| | | Nos. J127-J132 (6) | | |

See note after No. J98H.

### Symbols of Communications — D7

### 1974, Jan. 1    Photo.    Perf. 13

| J133 | D7 | 5b brt bl | .20 | .20 |
|---|---|---|---|---|
| J134 | D7 | 10b olive | .20 | .20 |
| J135 | D7 | 20b lilac rose | .20 | .20 |
| J136 | D7 | 40b purple | .20 | .20 |
| J137 | D7 | 50b brown | .20 | .20 |
| J138 | D7 | 1 l orange | .35 | .20 |
| | | Nos. J133-J138 (6) | | |

Designs: 10b, Like 5b. 20b, 40b, Pigeons, head of Mercury and post horn. 50b, 1 l, General Post Office, post horn and truck.

See #J139-J144. For surcharges see #J147-J151.

Communications Badge and Postwoman — D4

**1982, Dec. 23 Photo. *Perf. 13½***

| | | | |
|---|---|---|---|
| **J139** D7 25b like #J135 | .20 | .20 |
| **J140** D7 50b like #J133 | .20 | .20 |
| **J141** D7 1 l like #J135 | .20 | .20 |
| **J142** D7 2 l like #J137 | .35 | .20 |
| **J143** D7 3 l like #J133 | .50 | .20 |
| **J144** D7 4 l like #J137 | .70 | .20 |
| *Nos. J139-J144 (6)* | 2.15 | 1.20 |

See note after No. J98H.

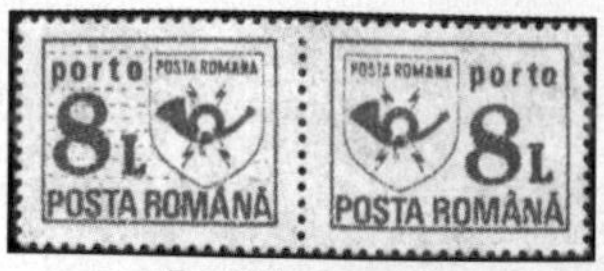


Post Horn — D8

**1992, Feb. 3 Photo. *Perf. 13½***

| | | |
|---|---|---|
| **J145** D8 4 l red | .25 | .20 |
| **J146** D8 8 l blue | .50 | .20 |

See note after No. J98H.

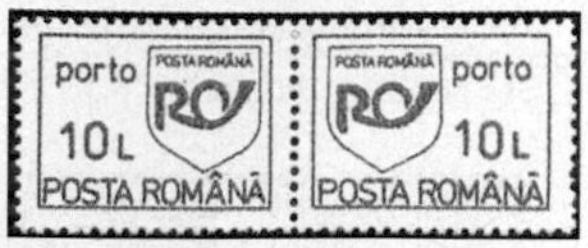


D9

**1994, Dec. 10 Photo. *Perf. 13¼***

| | | |
|---|---|---|
| **J146A** D9 10 l brown | .20 | .20 |
| **J146B** D9 45 l orange | .40 | .20 |

See note after No. J98H.

**L50**

Nos. J140-J142, J144 Surcharged in Green, Deep Blue, or Black

**1999, Mar. 12 Photo. *Perf. 13½***

| | | |
|---|---|---|
| **J147** D7 50 l on 50b #J140 (G) | .20 | .20 |
| **J148** D7 50 l on 1 l #J141 (Dbl) | .20 | .20 |
| **J149** D7 100 l on 2 l #J142 | .20 | .20 |
| **J150** D7 700 l on 1 l #J141 | .30 | .20 |
| **J151** D7 1100 l on 4 l #J144 | .45 | .25 |
| *Nos. J147-J151 (5)* | 1.35 | 1.05 |

Nos. J145, J146B Surcharged

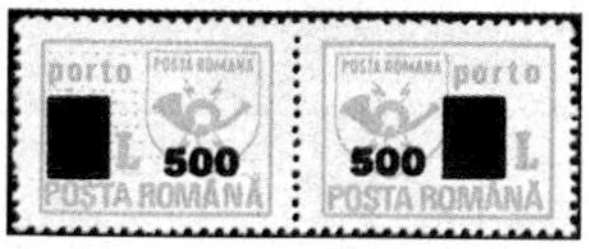


**2001, Jan. 17 Photo. *Perf. 13¼***

| | | |
|---|---|---|
| **J152** D8 500 l on 4 l red | .20 | .20 |
| **J153** D8 1000 l on 4 l red | .20 | .20 |
| **J154** D9 2000 l on 45 l org | .20 | .20 |
| *Nos. J152-J154 (3)* | .60 | .60 |

See note after No. J98H.

## OFFICIAL STAMPS

**Catalogue values for unused stamps in this section are for Never Hinged items.**

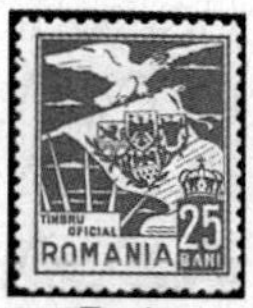

Eagle Carrying National Emblem O1

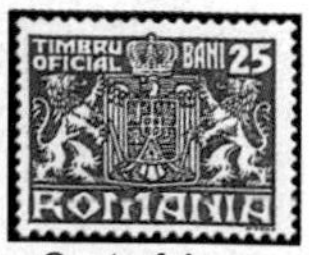

Coat of Arms O2

**1929 Photo. Wmk. 95 *Perf. 13½***

| | | |
|---|---|---|
| **O1** O1 25b red orange | .25 | .20 |
| **O2** O1 50b dk brown | .25 | .20 |
| **O3** O1 1 l dk violet | .30 | .20 |
| **O4** O1 2 l olive grn | .30 | .20 |
| **O5** O1 3 l rose car | .45 | .20 |
| **O6** O1 4 l dk olive | .45 | .20 |
| **O7** O1 6 l Prus blue | 2.50 | .20 |
| **O8** O1 10 l deep blue | .80 | .20 |
| **O9** O1 25 l carmine brn | 1.60 | 1.25 |
| **O10** O1 50 l purple | 4.75 | 3.50 |
| *Nos. O1-O10 (10)* | 11.65 | 6.35 |

Type of Official Stamps of 1929 Overprinted

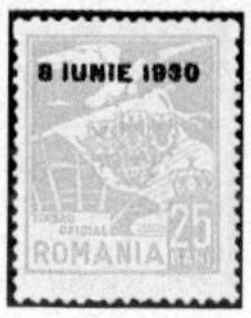


**1930 Unwmk.**

| | | |
|---|---|---|
| **O11** O1 25b red orange | .20 | .20 |
| **O12** O1 50b dk brown | .20 | .20 |
| **O13** O1 1 l dk violet | .35 | .20 |
| **O14** O1 3 l rose carmine | .50 | .20 |
| *Nos. O11-O14 (4)* | 1.25 | .80 |

Nos. O11-O14 were not placed in use without overprint.

**Same Overprint on Nos. O1-O10**

**Wmk. 95**

| | | |
|---|---|---|
| **O15** O1 25b red orange | .25 | .20 |
| **O16** O1 50b dk brown | .25 | .20 |
| **O17** O1 1 l dk violet | .25 | .20 |
| **O18** O1 2 l dp green | .25 | .20 |
| **O19** O1 3 l rose carmine | .60 | .20 |
| **O20** O1 4 l olive black | .75 | .20 |
| **O21** O1 6 l Prus blue | 2.00 | .20 |
| **O22** O1 10 l deep blue | .80 | .20 |
| **O23** O1 25 l carmine brown | 3.00 | 2.50 |
| **O24** O1 50 l purple | 4.00 | 3.50 |
| *Nos. O15-O24 (10)* | 12.15 | 7.60 |

Accession of King Carol II to the throne of Romania (Nos O11-O24).

***Perf. 13½, 13½x14½***

**1931-32 Typo. Wmk. 225**

| | | |
|---|---|---|
| **O25** O2 25b black | .30 | .20 |
| **O26** O2 1 l lilac | .30 | .20 |
| **O27** O2 2 l emerald | .60 | .40 |
| **O28** O2 3 l rose | 1.00 | .70 |
| *Nos. O25-O28 (4)* | 2.20 | 1.50 |

**1932 Wmk. 230 *Perf. 13½***

| | | |
|---|---|---|
| **O29** O2 25b black | .30 | .25 |
| **O30** O2 1 l violet | .40 | .35 |
| **O31** O2 2 l emerald | .65 | .55 |
| **O32** O2 3 l rose | .80 | .65 |
| **O33** O2 6 l red brown | 1.25 | 1.00 |
| *Nos. O29-O33 (5)* | 3.40 | 2.80 |

## PARCEL POST STAMPS

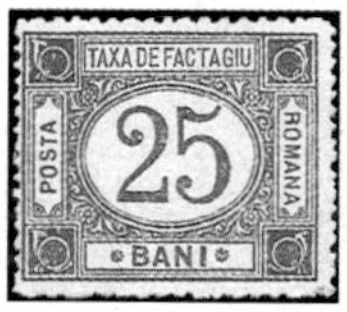


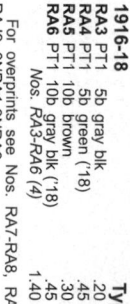

PP1

***Perf. 11½, 13½ and Compound***

**1895 Wmk. 163 Typo.**

| | | |
|---|---|---|
| **Q1** PP1 25b brown red | 12.50 | 2.25 |

**1896**

| | | |
|---|---|---|
| **Q2** PP1 25b vermilion | 10.00 | 1.25 |

***Perf. 13½ and 11½x13½***

**1898 Wmk. 200**

| | | |
|---|---|---|
| **Q3** PP1 25b brown red | 7.00 | 1.25 |
| *a.* Tete beche pair | | |
| **Q4** PP1 25b vermilion | 7.00 | .90 |

Thin Paper
Tinted Rose on Back

**1905 Unwmk. *Perf. 11½***

| | | |
|---|---|---|
| **Q5** PP1 25b vermilion | 6.00 | 1.25 |

**1911 White Paper**

| | | |
|---|---|---|
| **Q6** PP1 25b pale red | 6.00 | 1.25 |

No. 263 Surcharged in Carmine

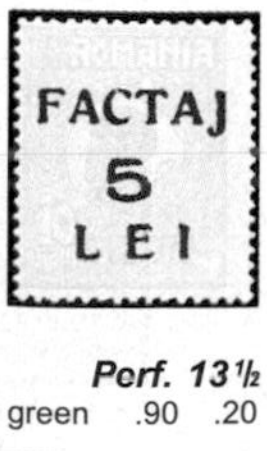


**1928 *Perf. 13½***

| | | |
|---|---|---|
| **Q7** A54 5 l on 10b yellow green | .90 | .20 |

## POSTAL TAX STAMPS

Regular Issue of 1908 Overprinted

***Perf. 11½, 13½, 11½x13½***

**1915 Unwmk.**

| | | |
|---|---|---|
| **RA1** A46 5b green | .20 | .20 |
| **RA2** A46 10b rose | .30 | .20 |

The "Timbru de Ajutor" stamps represent a tax on postal matter. The money obtained from their sale was turned into a fund for the assistance of soldiers' families.

Until 1923 the only "Timbru de Ajutor" stamps used for postal purposes were the 5b and 10b. Stamps of higher values with this inscription were used to pay the taxes on railway and theater tickets and other fiscal taxes. In 1923 the postal rate was advanced to 25b.

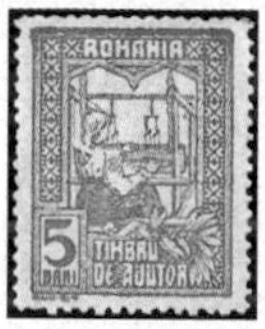

The Queen Weaving — PT1

**1916-18 Typo.**

| | | |
|---|---|---|
| **RA3** PT1 5b gray blk | .20 | .20 |
| **RA4** PT1 5b green ('18) | .45 | .20 |
| **RA5** PT1 10b brown | .30 | .20 |
| **RA6** PT1 10b gray blk ('18) | .45 | .20 |
| *Nos. RA3-RA6 (4)* | 1.40 | .80 |

For overprints see Nos. RA7-RA8, RAJ7-RAJ9, 3NRA1-3NRA8.

Stamps of 1916 Overprinted in Red or Black

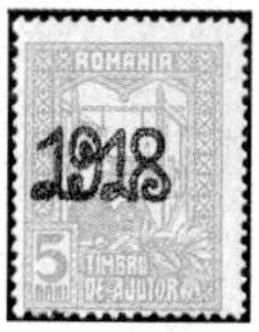


**1918 *Perf. 13½***

| | | |
|---|---|---|
| **RA7** PT1 5b gray blk (R) | .40 | .25 |
| *a.* Double overprint | 5.00 | |
| *c.* Black overprint | 5.00 | |
| **RA8** PT1 10b brn (Bk) | .45 | .25 |
| *a.* Double overprint | 5.00 | |
| *b.* Double overprint, one inverted | 5.00 | |
| *c.* Inverted overprint | 5.00 | |

Same Overprint on RA1 and RA2

**1919**

| | | |
|---|---|---|
| **RA11** A46 5b yel grn (R) | *19.00* | *12.50* |
| **RA12** A46 10b rose (Bk) | *19.00* | *12.50* |

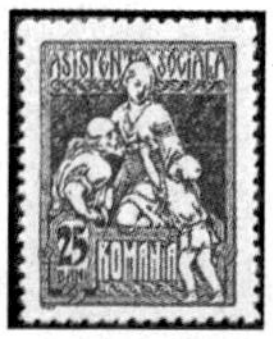

Charity — PT3

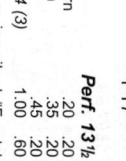

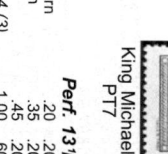

***Perf. 13½, 11½, 13½x11½***

**1921-24 Typo. Unwmk.**

| | | |
|---|---|---|
| **RA13** PT3 10b green | .20 | .20 |
| **RA14** PT3 25b blk ('24) | .20 | .20 |

Type of 1921-24 Issue

**1928 Wmk. 95**

| | | |
|---|---|---|
| **RA15** PT3 25b black | .75 | .25 |

Nos. RA13, RA14 and RA15 are the only stamps of type PT3 issued for postal purposes. Other denominations were used fiscally.

**Catalogue values for unused stamps in this section, from this point to the end of the section, are for Never Hinged items.**

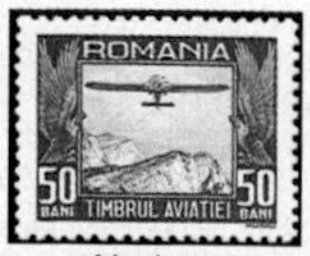

Airplane PT4

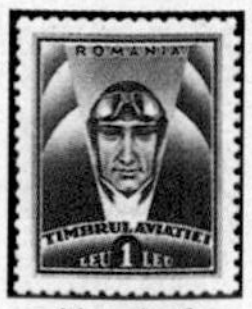

Head of Aviator PT5

**1931 Photo. Unwmk.**

| | | |
|---|---|---|
| **RA16** PT4 50b Prus bl | .30 | .20 |
| *a.* Double impression | 15.00 | |
| **RA17** PT4 1 l dk red brn | .30 | .20 |
| **RA18** PT4 2 l ultra | .60 | .20 |
| *Nos. RA16-RA18 (3)* | 1.20 | .60 |

The use of these stamps, in addition to the regular postage, was obligatory on all postal matter for the interior of the country. The money thus obtained was to augment the National Fund for Aviation. When the stamps were not used to prepay the special tax, it was collected by means of Postal Tax Due stamps Nos. RAJ20 and RAJ21.

Nos. RA17 and RA18 were also used for other than postal tax.

**1932 Wmk. 230 *Perf. 14 x 13½***

| | | |
|---|---|---|
| **RA19** PT5 50b Prus bl | .20 | .20 |
| **RA20** PT5 1 l red brn | .35 | .20 |
| **RA21** PT5 2 l ultra | .45 | .20 |
| *Nos. RA19-RA21 (3)* | 1.00 | .60 |

See notes after No. RA18.

After 1937 use of Nos. RA20-RA21 was limited to other than postal matter.

Nos. RA19-RA21 exist imperf.

Two stamps similar to type PT5, but inscribed "Fondul Aviatiei," were issued in 1936: 10b sepia and 20b violet.

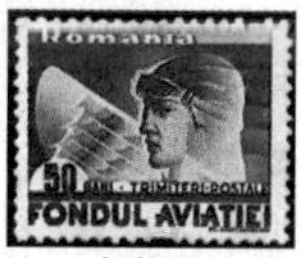


Aviator PT6

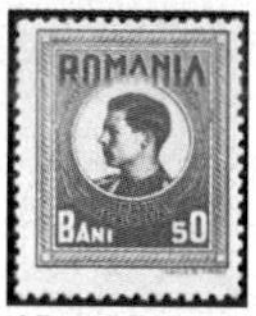

King Michael PT7

**1937 *Perf. 13½***

| | | |
|---|---|---|
| **RA22** PT6 50b Prus grn | .20 | .20 |
| **RA23** PT6 1 l red brn | .35 | .20 |
| **RA24** PT6 2 l ultra | .45 | .20 |
| *Nos. RA22-RA24 (3)* | 1.00 | .60 |

Stamps overprinted or inscribed "Fondul Aviatiei" other than Nos. RA22, RA23 or RA24 were used to pay taxes on other than postal matters.

**1943 Wmk. 276 Photo. *Perf. 14***

| | | |
|---|---|---|
| **RA25** PT7 50b org ver | .20 | .20 |
| **RA26** PT7 1 l lil rose | .20 | .20 |
| **RA27** PT7 2 l brown | .20 | .20 |
| **RA28** PT7 4 l lt ultra | .20 | .20 |
| **RA29** PT7 5 l dull lilac | .20 | .20 |
| **RA30** PT7 8 l yel grn | .20 | .20 |
| **RA31** PT7 10 l blk brn | .20 | .20 |
| *Nos. RA25-RA31 (7)* | 1.40 | 1.40 |

The tax was obligatory on domestic mail.

Examples of these stamps with an overprint consisting of a red cross and text are unissued franchise stamps.

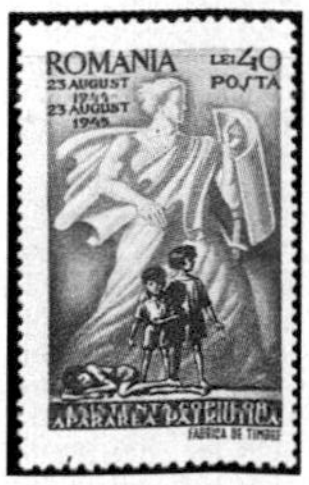

Protection of Homeless Children — PT8

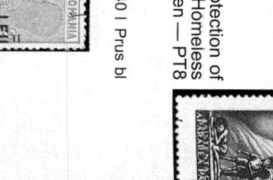

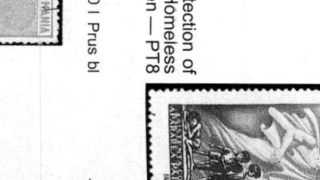

**1945**

| | | |
|---|---|---|
| **RA32** PT8 40 l Prus bl | .25 | .20 |

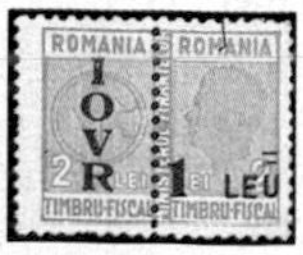

PT9

1918
3N13 A16 10pf carmine 7.50 10.00
3N14 A22 15pf dk vio 12.50 15.00
3N15 A16 20pf blue 1.25 1.50
3N16 A16 30pf org & blk, buff 10.00 12.50
Nos. 3N13-3N16 (4) 31.25 39.00

A set of 13 stamps similar to Austria Nos. M69-M81 was prepared for use in Romania in 1918, but not placed in use there. Denominations are in bani. It is reported that they were on sale after the armistice at the Vienna post office for a few days. Value $850.

## POSTAGE DUE STAMPS ISSUED UNDER GERMAN OCCUPATION

Postage Due Stamps and Type of Romania Overprinted in Red

**Perf. 11½, 13½ and Compound   Wmk. 165**

1918
3NJ1 D2 5b dk bl, grn 19.00 24.00
3NJ2 D2 10b dk bl, grn 26.00 30.00

The 20b, 30b and 50b with this overprint are fraudulent.

**Unwmk.**
3NJ3 D2 5b dk bl, grn 2.50 2.25
3NJ4 D2 10b dk bl, grn 2.50 2.25
3NJ5 D2 20b dk bl, grn 2.50 2.25
3NJ6 D2 30b dk bl, grn 2.50 2.25
3NJ7 D2 50b dk bl, grn 2.50 2.25
Nos. 3NJ1-3NJ7 (7) 57.50 65.25

## POSTAL TAX STAMPS ISSUED UNDER GERMAN OCCUPATION

Romanian Postal Tax Stamps and Type of 1916

Overprinted in Red or Black

**Perf. 11½, 13½ and Compound   Unwmk.**

1917
3NRA1 PT1 5b gray blk (R) .20 .20
3NRA2 PT1 10b brown (Bk) .20 .20

Same, Overprinted

1917-18
3NRA3 PT1 5b gray blk (R) .20
a. Black overprint .20
3NRA4 PT1 10b brown (Bk) 5.00
3NRA5 PT1 10b violet (Bk) .35 .60
Nos. 3NRA3-3NRA5 (3) 1.15

Same, Overprinted in Red or Black

1918
3NRA6 PT1 5b gray blk (R) 20.00
3NRA7 PT1 10b brown (Bk) 20.00

Same, Overprinted

1918
3NRA8 PT1 10b violet (Bk) .20 .20

## ISSUED UNDER BULGARIAN OCCUPATION

### Dobruja District

Bulgarian Stamps of 1915-16 Overprinted in Red or Blue

**Perf. 11½, 14   Unwmk.**

1916
2N1 A20 1s dk blue grn (R) .20 .20
2N2 A23 5s grn & brn (R) 1.75 .40
2N3 A24 10s brn & brnsh blk (Bl) .25 .20
2N4 A26 25s indigo & blk (Bl) 2.45 1.00
Nos. 2N1-2N4 (4)

Many varieties of overprint exist.

## ISSUED UNDER GERMAN OCCUPATION

German Stamps of 1905-17 Surcharged

**Wmk. 125   Perf. 14**

1917
3N1 A22 15b on 15pf dk vio (R) 1.00 1.00
3N2 A16 25b on 20pf ultra (Bk) 17.50 17.50
blk, buff (R) 19.50 19.50
Nos. 3N1-3N3 (3)

"M.V.iR." are the initials of "Militär Verwaltung in Rumänien" (Military Administration of Romania).

German Stamps of 1905-17 Surcharged

1917-18
3N4 A16 10b on 10pf car .85 .60
3N5 A22 15b on 15pf dk vio 4.50 4.50
3N6 A16 25b on 20pf ultra .75 1.50
3N7 A16 40b on 30pf org & blk, buff 1.00 1.00
a. "40" omitted 50.00 67.50
Nos. 3N4-3N7 (4) 7.10 7.60

German Stamps of 1905-17 Surcharged

1918
3N8 A16 5b on 5pf grn .20 .80
3N9 A16 10b on 5pf car .20 .75
3N10 A22 15b on 15pf dk vio .20 .75
3N11 A16 25b on 20pf bl vio 1.50 4.00
3N12 A16 40b on 30pf org & blk, buff .30 .30
Nos. 3N8-3N12 (5) 1.10 2.80

German Stamps of 1905-17 Overprinted

## OCCUPATION STAMPS

### ISSUED UNDER AUSTRIAN OCCUPATION

Emperor Karl of Austria   OS1 ... OS2

**Unwmk.   Engr.**

|  | | Perf. 11½ | 12½ |
|---|---|---|---|
1917
1N1 OS1 3b ol gray .75
1N2 OS1 5b ol grn .50
1N3 OS1 6b violet .50
1N4 OS1 10b org brn 1.00 .60
1N5 OS1 12b dp bl .80 .50
1N6 OS1 15b brt rose .20
1N7 OS1 20b red brn .20
1N8 OS1 25b ultra
1N9 OS1 30b slate
1N10 OS1 40b olive bis .30
a. Perf. 11½
1N11 OS1 50b dp grn 40.00 40.00
1N12 OS1 60b rose 45.00
1N13 OS1 80b dl bl .30
1N14 OS1 90b dk vio .25
1N15 OS2 2l rose, straw .45 .30
1N16 OS2 3l grn, bl .75 .40
1N17 OS2 4l rose, grn 8.75 6.00
Nos. 1N1-1N17 (17)

Nos. 1N1-1N14 have "BANI" surcharged in red.

Nos. 1N1-1N17 also exist imperforate. Value, set $20.

For overprints see Austria Nos. M51-M64 with "BANI" in red; Nos. M65-M67 for "LEI" in black.

---

"Hope" — PT10

1947   Unwmk.   Typo.   **Perf. 14x14½**
Black Surcharge
RA33 PT9 1l on 2l + 2l pink .30 .25
37.50
RA34 PT9 5l on 1l + 1l gray grm 4.50 3.75

**Perf. 14**
1948
RA35 PT10 1l rose 1.90 .20
RA36 PT10 1l rose violet 2.10 .20

A 2 lei blue and 5 lei ocher in type PT10 were issued primarily for revenue purposes.

## POSTAL TAX DUE STAMPS

Catalogue values for unused stamps in this section are for Never Hinged items.

Postage Due Stamps of 1911 Overprinted

PTD1

**Perf. 11½, 13½, 11½x13½   Unwmk.**

1915
RAJ1 D2 5b dk bl, grn .75 .20
RAJ2 D2 10b dk bl, grn .75 .20
a. Wmk. 165 10.00 1.00

1916   Typo.
RAJ3 PTD1 5b brn, grn .40 .20
RAJ4 PTD1 10b red, grn .40 .20

See Nos. RAJ5-RAJ6, RAJ10-RAJ11. For overprint see No. 3NRAJ1.

 PTD2

1918
RAJ5 PTD1 5b red, grn .25 .20
RAJ6 PTD1 10b brn, grn 1.00 .25
a. Wmk. 165

Type of 1916
RAJ7 PT1 5b gray blk (R) .40 .20
a. Inverted overprint 7.50
RAJ8 PT1 10b brn (Bk) .80 .20
a. Inverted overprint 7.50
RAJ9 PT1 10b brn (Bl) 5.00 5.00
Nos. RAJ7-RAJ9 (3) 6.20 5.40

1921
RAJ10 PTD1 5b red .50 .20
RAJ11 PTD1 10b brown .50 .20

1922-25   Typo.
Greenish Paper
RAJ12 PTD2 10b brown .20 .20
RAJ13 PTD2 20b brown .20 .20
RAJ14 PTD2 25b brown .30 .30
RAJ15 PTD2 50b brown .80 .80
Nos. RAJ12-RAJ15 (4) 3.85 3.85

1923-26
RAJ16 PTD2 10b lt brn .20 .20
RAJ17 PTD2 20b brown ('26) .20 .20
RAJ18 PTD2 25b brown ('26) .20 .20
RAJ19 PTD2 50b brown .80 .80
Nos. RAJ16-RAJ19 (4)

J82 and Type of 1911 Postage Due Stamps Overprinted in Red

1931   **Wmk. 225**
RAJ20 D2 1l black .20 .20
RAJ21 D2 2l black .20 .20

When the Postal Tax stamps for the Aviation Fund issue (Nos. RA16 to RA18) were not used to prepay the obligatory tax on letters, etc., it was collected by affixing Nos. RAJ20 and RAJ21.

OS3   OS4

## POSTAL TAX DUE STAMP ISSUED UNDER GERMAN OCCUPATION

Type of Romanian Postal Tax Due Stamp of 1916 Overprinted

**1918**

| | | | |
|---|---|---|---|
| 3NRA,1 | PTD1 | 10b red, green | 2.00 2.50 |

**Perf. 11½, 13½, and Compound Wmk. 165**

## ROMANIAN POST OFFICES IN THE TURKISH EMPIRE

King Carol I

A1     A2

40 Paras = 1 Piaster

**1896**

**Perf. 11½, 13½ and Compound Wmk. 200**

**Black Surcharge**

| 1 | A1 | 10pa on 5b blue | 32.50 | 30.00 |
| 2 | A1 | 20pa on 10b emer | 24.00 | 22.50 |
| 3 | A1 | 1pia on 25b violet | 80.50 | 75.00 |
| | | Nos. 1-3 (3) | | |

**Violet Surcharge**

| 4 | A1 | 10pa on 5b blue | 17.00 | 15.00 |
| 5 | A2 | 20pa on 10b emer | 17.00 | 15.00 |
| 6 | A1 | 1pia on 25b violet | 51.00 | 45.00 |
| | | Nos. 4-6 (3) | | |

All values exist with inverted overprint.

**1916, Jan. 12**     **Perf. 14x13½ Unwmk.**

| 1 | A2 | 5c green | 350.00 | 175.00 |
| 2 | A3 | 10c rose red | 350.00 | 175.00 |
| 3 | A5 | 1pi on 25c blue | 350.00 | 175.00 |

Dangerous counterfeits exist.

Stamps of French Offices in the Levant, 1902-06, Overprinted Horizontally

## ROUAD, ILE

êl-ru-ad

(Arwad)

LOCATION — An island in the Mediterranean, off the coast of Latakia, Syria

GOVT. — French Mandate

In 1916, while a French post office was maintained on Ile Rouad, stamps were issued by France.

Stamps of French Offices in the Levant, 1902-06, Overprinted

25 Centimes = 1 Piaster

**ILE ROUAD**

ILE ROUAD

**1916, Dec.**     **Unwmk.**

| 4 | A2 | 1c gray | .80 | .80 |
| 5 | A2 | 2c violet brown | .80 | .80 |
| 6 | A2 | 3c red orange | .80 | .80 |
| 7 | A2 | 5c green | 100.00 | |
| a. | | Double overprint | | |
| 8 | A3 | 10c rose | 1.10 | 1.10 |
| 9 | A3 | 15c pale red | 1.25 | 1.25 |
| 10 | A3 | 20c brown violet | 2.10 | 2.10 |
| 11 | A3 | 25c blue | 1.60 | 1.60 |
| 12 | A5 | 1pi on 25c blue | 1.60 | 1.60 |
| 13 | A4 | 30c violet | 3.00 | 3.00 |
| 14 | A6 | 40c red & pale bl | 1.25 | 1.25 |
| | | lavender | | |
| 15 | A6 | 50c bis brn & | | |
| 16 | A6 | 4pi on cf & ol grn | 5.00 | 5.00 |
| | | 20pi on 5fr dk bl & buff | 24.00 | 24.00 |
| | | Nos. 4-16 (13) | 52.55 | 52.55 |

There is a wide space between the two words of the overprint on Nos. 13 to 16 inclusive, Nos. 4, 5 and 6 are on white and coarse, grayish (G. C.) papers.

(Note on G. C. paper follows France No. 184.)

## RUANDA-URUNDI

rü-än-da ürün-dê

(Belgian East Africa)

LOCATION — In central Africa, bounded by Congo, Uganda and Tanganyika

GOVT. — Former United Nations trusteeship administered by Belgium

AREA — 20,540 sq. mi.

POP. — 4,700,000 (est. 1958)

CAPITAL — Usumbura

See German East Africa in Vol. 3 for stamps issued under Belgian occupation.

In 1962 the two parts of the trusteeship became independent states, the Republic of Rwanda and the Kingdom of Burundi.

100 Centimes = 1 Franc

Stamps of Belgian Congo, 1923-26, Overprinted

Belgian Congo Nos. 112-113 Overprinted in Red or Black

**1925-27**     **Perf. 12½**

| 24 | A44 | 45c dk vio (R) ('27) | .20 | .20 |
| 25 | A44 | 80c car rose (Bk) | .40 | .30 |

**1924-26**     **Perf. 12**

| 6 | A32 | 5c orange yel | .20 | .20 |
| 7 | A32 | 5c green | .20 | .20 |
| a. | | Double overprint | | |
| 8 | A32 | 15c olive brn | .20 | .20 |
| 9 | A32 | 20c green ('26) | .20 | .20 |
| 10 | A32 | 25c red brown | .20 | .20 |
| 11 | A44 | 25c rose red | .35 | .20 |
| 12 | A44 | 30c olive grn ('25) | .20 | .20 |
| 13 | A32 | 40c violet (R) ('25) | .20 | .20 |
| 14 | A44 | 40c red brown | — | .20 |
| 15 | A32 | 50c olive green | .20 | .20 |
| 16 | | Inverted overprint | | |
| 17 | A44 | 50c buff ('25) | .25 | .25 |
| 18 | A44 | 75c red org | .25 | .25 |
| 19 | A44 | 1fr gray blue ('25) | .35 | .25 |
| 20 | A44 | 1fr bister brown | .45 | .35 |
| 21 | A44 | 1fr dull blue | .45 | .35 |
| 22 | A44 | 5fr gray brown | 4.00 | 1.60 |
| 23 | A44 | 10fr gray black | 7.50 | 5.50 |
| | | Nos. 6-23 (18) | 14.50 | 12.00 |
| | | | 29.85 | 22.45 |

Stamps of Belgian Congo, 1923-1927, Overprinted

**1927-29**

| 26 | A32 | 10c green ('29) | .20 | .20 |
| 27 | A32 | 15c ol brn ('29) | .80 | .60 |
| 28 | A32 | 35c green | .20 | .20 |
| 29 | A44 | 75c salmon red | .25 | .25 |
| 30 | A44 | 1fr rose red ('29) | .40 | .30 |
| 31 | A44 | 1.25fr dull blue | .50 | .35 |
| 32 | A32 | 1.50fr dull blue | .45 | .35 |
| 33 | A32 | 1.75fr dull blue | 1.40 | .65 |

No. 32 Surcharged

| 34 | A32 | 1.75fr on 1.50fr dl bl | .45 | .40 |
| | | Nos. 26-34 (9) | 4.65 | 3.30 |

**1931**

| 35 | A44 | 1.25fr on 1fr rose red | 2.25 | 1.25 |
| 36 | A32 | 2fr on 1.75fr dl bl | 3.00 | 1.75 |

Nos. 30 and 33 Surcharged

**1931**

| 56 | A1 | 5c on 40c green | 3.25 | 3.25 |
| 57 | A2 | 60c on 50c gray lil | 1.90 | 1.90 |
| 58 | A2 | 2.50fr on 1.50fr brn vio | 2.00 | 2.00 |
| 59 | A2 | 3.25fr on 2fr dp dl bl | 8.50 | 8.50 |
| | | Set, never hinged | 15.65 | 15.65 |
| | | Nos. 56-59 (4) | 42.50 | |

**1941**

| 60 | A70 | 10c light gray | 6.50 | 6.50 |
| | | Never hinged | 14.00 | |

Inverts exist.

Stamps of Belgian Congo, 1923-1927, Overprinted

King Albert Memorial Issue

King Albert — A16

**1934**

| 55 | A16 | 1.50fr black | .35 | .35 |
| | | Never hinged | 1.25 | |

**Photo.**

Stamps of 1931-38 Surcharged in Black

Belgian Congo No. 173 Overprinted in Black

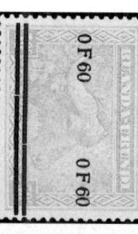

**1941**     **Perf. 11**

Mountain Scene — A2

Designs: 5c, 60c, Porter. 15c, Warrior. 25c, Kraal. 40c, Cattle herders. 50c, Cape buffalo. 75c, Bahutu greeting. 1fr, Barundi women. 1.25fr, Bahutu mother. 2.50fr, 3.25fr, Preparing wooden vessel. 2.50fr, Making hides. 4fr, Watuba potter. 5fr, Mututsi dancer. 20fr, Urundi prince.

**1931-38**     **Engr.**     **Perf. 11½**

| 37 | A1 | 5c dp lil rose ('38) | .20 | .20 |
| 38 | A2 | 10c gray | .20 | .20 |
| 39 | A2 | 15c pale red | .20 | .20 |
| 40 | A2 | 25c brown vio | .20 | .20 |
| 41 | A44 | 40c gray blue | .20 | .20 |
| 42 | A2 | 50c gray lilac | .20 | .20 |
| 43 | A2 | 60c lilac rose | .20 | .20 |
| 44 | A1 | 75c gray black | .25 | .25 |
| 45 | A2 | 1fr brown | .35 | .35 |
| 46 | A2 | 1fr rose red | .45 | .45 |
| 47 | A1 | 1.25fr brown ('37) | .45 | .45 |
| 48 | A2 | 1.50fr brown vio | .50 | .50 |
| 49 | A2 | 2.50fr brown vio | .20 | .20 |
| 50 | A2 | 3.25fr deep blue ('37) | .25 | .25 |
| 51 | A1 | 4fr gray | .30 | .30 |
| 52 | A1 | 5fr gray | .25 | .25 |
| 53 | A1 | 10fr brown violet | .40 | .40 |
| 54 | A1 | 20fr brown | 1.75 | 1.75 |
| | | Nos. 37-54 (18) | 5.80 | 5.70 |
| | | Set, never hinged | 13.00 | |

For surcharges see Nos. 56-59.

Watusi Warriors — A1

## ROMANIAN POST OFFICES IN THE TURKISH EMPIRE POSTAL TAX STAMP

Romanian Postal Tax Stamp of 1918 Overprinted

**1919**     **Perf. 11½, 11½x13½**

| RA1 | PT1 | 5b green | 1.25 | 1.25 |

Romanian Stamps of 1908-18 Overprinted in Black or Red

**1919**     **Typo.**     **Unwmk.**

| 7 | A46 | 5b yellow grn | .40 | .40 |
| 8 | A46 | 10b rose | .55 | .55 |
| 9 | A46 | 15b red brown | .55 | .55 |
| 10 | A19 | 25b dp blue | .70 | .70 |
| 11 | A19 | 40b gray brn (R) | 1.40 | 1.40 |
| | | Nos. 7-11 (5) | 3.60 | 3.60 |

All values exist with inverted overprint.

Catalogue values for unused stamps in this country are for Never Hinged items, beginning with Scott 151 in the regular postage section, Scott B26 in the semipostal section, and Scott J8 in the postage due section.

## Left section

**Belgian Congo Nos. 179, 181 Overprinted in Black**

**1941**

| | | | | |
|---|---|---|---|---|
| 61 | A70 | 1.75fr orange | 3.75 | 3.75 |
| 62 | A70 | 2.75fr vio bl | 3.75 | 3.75 |
| | | Set, never hinged | 21.00 | |

For surcharges see Nos. 64-65.

**Belgian Congo No. 168 Surcharged in Black**

**1941**    *Perf. 11½*

| | | | | |
|---|---|---|---|---|
| 63 | A66 | 5c on 1.50fr dp red brn & blk | .20 | .20 |
| | | Never hinged | | |

Inverts exist.

**Nos. 61-62 Surcharged with New Values and Bars in Black**

**1942**

| | | | | |
|---|---|---|---|---|
| 64 | A70 | 75c on 1.75fr org | 1.10 | 1.25 |
| 65 | A70 | 2.50fr on 2.75fr vio bl | 3.75 | 3.75 |
| | | Set, never hinged | 14.00 | |

Inverts exist.

**Belgian Congo Nos. 167, 183 Surcharged in Black:**

**1942**    *Perf. 11, 11½*

| | | | | |
|---|---|---|---|---|
| 66 | A65 | 75c on 90c car & brn | .70 | .65 |
| a. | | Inverted surcharge | 9.00 | |
| 67 | A70 | 2.50fr on 10fr rose red | 1.10 | .85 |
| a. | | Inverted surcharge | 8.00 | |
| | | Set, never hinged | 3.00 | |
| | | Nos. 66a-67a, never hinged | 35.00 | |

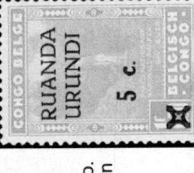

Oil Palms — A17    Oil Palms — A18    Watusi Chief — A19

Baluba Mask — A25

Carved Figures and Masks of Baluba Tribe: 10c, 50c, 2fr, 10fr, "Ndoha," figure of tribal king. 15c, 15c, 70c, 2.50fr, "Tshimanyi," an idol. 20c, 75c, 3.50fr, "Buangakokoma," statue of a kneeling beggar. 25c, 1fr, 5fr, "Mbuta," sacred double cup carved with two faces, Man and Woman. 40c, 1.25fr, 6fr, "Ngadimuashi," female mask. 50c, 1.50fr, 50fr, "Buadi-Muadi," mask with squared features (full face). 20fr, 100fr, "Mbowa," executioner's mask with buffalo horns.

Askari — A21    Leopard A20    Zebra — A22

Askari — A23

Design: 100fr, Watusi chief.

**Engr.**

**1942-43**

| | | | | |
|---|---|---|---|---|
| 68 | A17 | 5c red | .20 | .20 |
| 69 | A18 | 10c ol grn | .20 | .20 |
| 70 | A18 | 15c brn car | .20 | .20 |
| 71 | A18 | 20c dp ultra | .20 | .20 |
| 72 | A18 | 25c brn vio | .20 | .20 |
| 73 | A18 | 30c dull blue | .20 | .20 |
| 74 | A18 | 50c dp grn | .20 | .20 |
| 75 | A18 | 60c chestnut | .20 | .20 |
| 76 | A18 | 75c dl lil & blk | .20 | .20 |
| 77 | A19 | 1fr dk brn & blk | .25 | .20 |
| 78 | A19 | 1.25fr rose red & blk | .40 | .20 |
| 79 | A20 | 1.75fr dk gray brn | .80 | .80 |
| 80 | A20 | 2fr ocher | .80 | .80 |
| 81 | A20 | 2.50fr carmine | .55 | .55 |
| 82 | A21 | 3.50fr dk ol grn | .80 | .25 |
| 83 | A21 | 5fr orange | .80 | .30 |
| 84 | A21 | 6fr brn ultra | .80 | .30 |
| 85 | A21 | 7fr black | .95 | .35 |
| 86 | A21 | 10fr dp brn | .90 | |
| 87 | A22 | 20fr org brn & blk | 2.75 | 2.75 |
| 88 | A23 | 50fr red & blk ('43) | 3.25 | 1.10 |
| 89 | A23 | 100fr red & blk ('43) | 8.00 | 2.75 |
| | | | 22.75 | 9.15 |

Nos. 68-89 (22)

Nos. 68-89 exist imperforate, but have no franking value. Value, set never hinged $225, value set hinged $110.

Miniature sheets of Nos. 72, 76, 77 and 83 were printed in 1944 by the Belgian Government in London and given to the political review "Message," which distributed them to its subscribers, one a month. Value $20 each.

See note after Belgian Congo No. 225.

For surcharges see Nos. B17-B20.

Baluba Mask — A25


**1948-50**    *Unwmk.*    *Perf. 12x12½*

| | | | | |
|---|---|---|---|---|
| 90 | A25 | 10c dp org | .20 | .20 |
| 91 | A25 | 15c ultra | .20 | .20 |
| 92 | A25 | 20c brt bl | .30 | .30 |
| 93 | A25 | 25c rose car | .20 | .20 |
| 94 | A25 | 40c violet | .20 | .20 |
| 95 | A25 | 50c ol brn | .20 | .20 |
| 96 | A25 | 70c yel grn | .25 | .20 |
| 97 | A25 | 75c magenta | .30 | .20 |
| 98 | A25 | 1fr yel org & dk vio | .20 | .20 |
| 99 | A25 | 1.25fr lt bl grn & mag | .30 | .35 |
| 100 | A25 | 1.50fr ol & mag ('50) | .85 | .90 |
| 101 | A25 | 2fr org & mag | .40 | .20 |
| 102 | A25 | 2.50fr brn red & bl grn | .40 | .20 |
| 103 | A25 | 3.50fr lt bl & blk | .50 | .50 |
| 104 | A25 | 5fr bis & mag | .80 | .80 |
| 105 | A25 | 6fr brn org & ind | .80 | .20 |
| 106 | A25 | 10fr pale vio & red brn | 1.10 | .20 |
| 107 | A25 | 20fr red org & vio brn | 1.75 | .35 |
| 108 | A25 | 50fr dp org & blk | 3.25 | .90 |
| 109 | A25 | 100fr crim & blk brn | 6.00 | 2.25 |
| | | | 18.15 | 7.00 |

Nos. 90-109 (20)

**Nos. 102 and 105 Surcharged with New Value and Bars in Black**

**1949**

| | | | | |
|---|---|---|---|---|
| 110 | A25 | 3fr on 2.50fr | .35 | .20 |
| 111 | A25 | 4fr on 6fr | .45 | .25 |
| 112 | A25 | 6.50fr on 6fr | 1.15 | .65 |

Nos. 110-112 (3)

Dissotis — A27

St. Francis Xavier — A26

**1953**    *Unwmk.*    *Perf. 12½x13*

| | | | | |
|---|---|---|---|---|
| 113 | A26 | 1.50fr ultra & gray blk | .35 | .30 |

Death of St. Francis Xavier, 400th anniv.

**1953**    *Unwmk.*    *Photo.*    *Perf. 11½*

**Flowers in Natural Colors**

Flowers: 15c, Protea. 20c, Vellozia. 25c, Lintonia. 40c, Ipomoea. 50c, Angraecum. 60c, Haplolula. 75c, Oohna. 1fr, Nihhhals. 1.25fr, Protea. 1.50fr, Schizoglossum. 2fr, Ansellia. 3fr, Costus. 4fr, Nymphaea. 5fr, Thunbergia. 7fr, Gerbera. 8fr, Gloriosa 10fr, Silene. 20fr, Aristolochia.

| | | | | |
|---|---|---|---|---|
| 114 | A27 | 10c plum & ocher | .20 | .20 |
| 115 | A27 | 15c red & yel grn | .20 | .20 |
| 116 | A27 | 20c green & gray | .20 | .20 |
| 117 | A27 | 25c dk grn & dl org | .20 | .20 |
| 118 | A27 | 40c grn & sal | .20 | .20 |
| 119 | A27 | 50c dk car & aqua | .20 | .20 |
| 120 | A27 | 60c bl grn & pink | .20 | .20 |
| 121 | A27 | 75c dp plum & gray | .25 | .20 |
| 122 | A27 | 1fr car & yel | .25 | .20 |
| 123 | A27 | 1.25fr dk grn & bl | .50 | .40 |
| 124 | A27 | 1.50fr vio & ap grn | .50 | .40 |
| 125 | A27 | 2fr ol grn & buff | 1.90 | |
| 126 | A27 | 3fr ol grn & pink | .55 | .20 |
| 127 | A27 | 4fr choc & lil | .55 | .20 |
| 128 | A27 | 5fr dp plum & lt bl grn | .85 | .20 |
| 129 | A27 | 7fr dk grn & fawn | 1.00 | .30 |
| 130 | A27 | 8fr grn & lt yel | 1.40 | .30 |
| 131 | A27 | 10fr dp plum & pale grn | 2.50 | .25 |
| 132 | A27 | 20fr vio bl & dl sal | 4.00 | .80 |
| | | | 15.35 | 4.85 |

Nos. 114-132 (19)

King Baudouin and Tropical Scene A28

**1955**    *Engr. & Photo.*

**Portrait Photo. in Black**

Designs: Various African Views.

| | | | | |
|---|---|---|---|---|
| 133 | A28 | 1.50fr rose carmine | 2.25 | .35 |
| 134 | A28 | 3fr green | 2.25 | .35 |
| 135 | A28 | 4fr ultra | 2.25 | .50 |
| 136 | A28 | 6.50fr deep claret | 3.50 | .80 |
| | | | 10.00 | 2.00 |
| | | Set, never hinged | 25.00 | |

Nos. 133-136 (4)

## Right section

Mountain Gorilla — A29

Cape Buffaloes A30

Animals: 40c, 50c, 2fr, Black-and-white colobus (monkey). 50c, 6.50fr, Impalas. 3fr, 8fr, Elephants. 5fr, 10fr, Eland and Zebras. 20fr, Leopard. 50fr, Lions.

**1959-61**    *Unwmk.*    *Photo.*    *Perf. 11½*

**Granite Paper**

**Size: 23x33mm, 33x23mm**

| | | | | |
|---|---|---|---|---|
| 137 | A29 | 10c brn, crim, & blk | .20 | .20 |
| 138 | A30 | 20c blk, gray & ap grn brn | .20 | .20 |
| 139 | A29 | 40c mag, blk & gray grn | .20 | .20 |
| 140 | A30 | 50c grn, org yel & brn | .20 | .20 |
| 141 | A29 | 1fr brn, ultra & blk | .20 | .20 |
| 142 | A30 | 1.50fr blk, gray & org | .20 | .20 |
| 143 | A29 | 2fr grnsh bl, ind & blk | .20 | .20 |

**Size: 45x26½mm**

| | | | | |
|---|---|---|---|---|
| 144 | A30 | 3fr brn, dp car & blk | .30 | .30 |
| 145 | A29 | 5fr brn, dl yel, grn & blk | .45 | .45 |
| 146 | A30 | 6.50fr red, org yel & brn | .55 | .50 |
| 147 | A30 | 8fr bl, mag & blk | 1.25 | 1.00 |
| 148 | A30 | 10fr multi | 4.80 | 4.00 |
| 149 | A30 | 20fr multi ('61) | | |
| 150 | A30 | 50fr multi ('61) | | |

Nos. 137-150 (14)

For surcharge see No. 153.

> Catalogue values for unused stamps in this section, from this point to the end of the section, are for Never Hinged Items.

Map of Africa and Symbolic Honeycomb A31

**1960, Feb.19**    *Unwmk.*    *Perf. 11½*

**Inscription in French**

| | | | | |
|---|---|---|---|---|
| 151 | A31 | 3fr ultra & red | .20 | .20 |

**Inscription in Flemish**

| | | | | |
|---|---|---|---|---|
| 152 | A31 | 3fr ultra & red | .20 | .20 |

10th anniversary of the Commission for Technical Co-operation in Africa South of the Sahara (C. C. T. A.).

**No. 144 Surcharged with New Value and Bars**

**1960**

| | | | | |
|---|---|---|---|---|
| 153 | A30 | 3.50fr on 3fr | .30 | .20 |

## SEMI-POSTAL STAMPS

Belgian Congo Nos. B10-B11 Overprinted

**1925**    *Unwmk.*    *Perf. 12½*

| | | | | |
|---|---|---|---|---|
| B1 | SP1 | 25c + 25c car & blk | .20 | .20 |
| B2 | SP1 | 25c + 25c car & blk | .25 | .25 |
| | | Set, never hinged | 1.50 | |

No. B2 inscribed "BELGISCH CONGO."

Commemorative of the Colonial Campaigns in 1914-1918. Nos. B1 and B2 alternate in the sheet.

## 1930
### Belgian Congo Nos. B12-B20 Overprinted in Blue or Red

**Perf. 11½**

| | | | | |
|---|---|---|---|---|
| B3 | SP3 | 10c + 5c ver | .35 | .35 |
| B4 | SP3 | 20c + 10c dk brn | .70 | .70 |
| B5 | SP3 | 35c + 15c dp grn | 1.40 | 1.40 |
| B6 | SP3 | 60c + 30c dl vio | 1.60 | 1.60 |
| B7 | SP3 | 1fr + 50c dk car | 1.60 | 1.60 |
| B8 | SP5 | 1.75fr + 75c dp bl (R) | 2.75 | 2.75 |
| B9 | SP5 | 3.50fr + 1.50fr rose lake | 2.50 | 2.50 |
| B10 | SP5 | 5fr + 2.50fr red | 5.75 | 5.75 |
| B11 | SP5 | 10fr + 5fr gray blk | 4.50 | 4.50 |
| | | | 5.00 | 5.00 |
| | | Nos. B3-B11 (9) | 24.55 | 24.55 |
| | | Set, never hinged | 80.00 | |

On Nos. B3, B4 and B7 there is a space of 26mm between the two words of the overprint. The surtax was for native welfare.

## 1936
### Queen Astrid with Native Children — SP1

**Photo. Perf. 12½**

| | | | | |
|---|---|---|---|---|
| B12 | SP1 | 1.25fr + 5c dk brn | .45 | .45 |
| B13 | SP1 | 1.50fr + 10c dl rose | .45 | .45 |
| B14 | SP1 | 2.50fr + 25c dk bl | .55 | .55 |
| | | Nos. B12-B14 (3) | 1.45 | 1.45 |
| | | Set, never hinged | 4.00 | |

Issued in memory of Queen Astrid. The surtax was for the National League for Protection of Native Children.

### Lion of Belgium and Inscription "Belgium Shall Rise Again" — SP2

## 1942
**Engr.**

| | | | | |
|---|---|---|---|---|
| B15 | SP2 | 10fr + 40fr blue | 1.75 | 2.00 |
| B16 | SP2 | 10fr + 40fr dark red | 1.75 | 2.00 |
| | | Set, never hinged | 7.00 | |

Nos. 74, 78, 79 and 82 Surcharged in Red

a

b

---

## 1945

| | | | | |
|---|---|---|---|---|
| B17 | A18 (a) | 50c + 50fr | 1.75 | 1.75 |
| B18 | A19 (b) | 1.25fr + 100fr | 2.00 | 1.40 |
| B19 | A20 (c) | 1.75fr + 100fr | 1.75 | 1.60 |
| B20 | A21 (c) | 3.50fr + 100fr | 2.00 | 1.60 |
| | | Set, never hinged | 22.50 | 6.00 |
| | | Nos. B17-B20 (4) | 7.50 | |

**Unwmk. Perf. 12½**

### Mozart at Age 7 — SP3

## 1956

| | | | | |
|---|---|---|---|---|
| B21 | SP3 | 4.50fr + 1.50fr bluish vio | 1.00 | 1.75 |
| B22 | SP3 | 6.50fr + 2.50fr claret | 2.50 | 2.75 |
| | | Set, never hinged | 7.00 | |

**Engr. Perf. 11½**

200th anniv. of the birth of Wolfgang Amadeus Mozart. Surtax for the Pro-Mozart Committee.

### Queen Elizabeth and Mozart Sonata — SP4

## 1957
**Photo. Cross in Carmine Perf. 13x10½**

| | | | | |
|---|---|---|---|---|
| B23 | SP5 | 3fr + 50c dk blue | .50 | .45 |
| B24 | SP5 | 4.50fr + 50c dk grn | .65 | .60 |
| B25 | SP5 | 6.50fr + 50c red brn | .85 | .75 |
| | | Nos. B23-B25 (3) | 2.00 | 1.80 |
| | | Set, never hinged | 4.00 | |

Designs: 4.50fr+50c, Patient receiving injection. 6.50fr+50c, Patient being bandaged.

### Nurse and Children — SP5

> Catalogue values for unused stamps in this section, from this point to the end of the section, are for Never Hinged items.

---

## 1961, Dec. 18

| | | | | |
|---|---|---|---|---|
| B30 | SP6 | 6.50fr + 3.50fr ol grn & red | 1.25 | 1.25 |
| | | Nos. B26-B30 (5) | 3.10 | 3.10 |
| B31 | SP7 | 50c + 25c brn & buff | .20 | .20 |
| B32 | SP7 | 1fr + 50c grn & pale grn | .20 | .20 |
| B33 | SP7 | 1.50fr + 75c multi | .20 | .20 |
| B34 | SP7 | 3.50fr + 1.50fr lt bl & brt bl | .30 | .30 |
| B35 | SP7 | 5fr + 2fr car & sal | .40 | .40 |
| B36 | SP7 | 6.50fr + 3fr multi | 1.50 | 1.50 |
| | | Nos. B31-B36 (6) | | |

### Usumbura Cathedral — SP7

**Perf. 11½**

Designs: 5fr+2fr, Cathedral, sideview. 1.50fr+75c, Cathedral, stained glass window.

The surtax went for the construction and completion of the Cathedral at Usumbura.

---

# POSTAGE DUE STAMPS

### Belgian Congo Nos. J1-J7 Overprinted

## 1924-27  Unwmk.  Perf. 14

| | | | | |
|---|---|---|---|---|
| J1 | D1 | 10c black brn | .20 | .20 |
| J2 | D1 | 10c deep rose | .20 | .20 |
| J3 | D1 | 15c violet | .20 | .20 |
| J4 | D1 | 30c green | .25 | .25 |
| J5 | D1 | 50c ultra | .30 | .30 |
| J6 | D1 | 50c brt blue ('27) | .30 | .30 |
| J7 | D1 | 1fr gray | .40 | .40 |
| | | Nos. J1-J7 (7) | 1.85 | 1.85 |
| | | Set, never hinged | 3.50 | |

### Belgian Congo Nos. J8-J12 Overprinted in Carmine

## 1943  Perf. 14x14½, 12½

| | | | | |
|---|---|---|---|---|
| J8 | D2 | 10c olive green | .20 | .20 |
| J9 | D2 | 20c dk ultra | .20 | .20 |
| J10 | D2 | 50c green | .20 | .20 |
| J11 | D2 | 1fr dark brown | .20 | .20 |
| J12 | D2 | 2fr yellow orange | .20 | .20 |
| | | Nos. J8-J12 (5) | 1.00 | 1.00 |

Nos. J8-J12 values are for stamps perf. 14x14½. Those perf. 12½ sell for about three times as much.

## 1959  Engr.  Perf. 11½

| | | | | |
|---|---|---|---|---|
| J13 | D3 | 10c olive brown | .20 | .20 |
| J14 | D3 | 20c claret | .20 | .20 |
| J15 | D3 | 50c green | .20 | .20 |
| J16 | D3 | 1fr blue | .20 | .20 |
| J17 | D3 | 2fr vermilion | .30 | .30 |
| J18 | D3 | 4fr purple | .30 | .30 |
| J19 | D3 | 6fr violet blue | .40 | .40 |
| | | Nos. J13-J19 (7) | 1.70 | 1.70 |

### Belgian Congo Nos. J13-J19 Overprinted

Both capital and lower-case U's are found in this overprint.

---

Sports: #B26, High Jumper. #B27, Hurdlers. #B29, Javelin thrower. #B30, Discus thrower.

## 1960

| | | | | |
|---|---|---|---|---|
| B26 | SP6 | 50c + 25c int bd l & maroon | .20 | .20 |
| B27 | SP6 | 1.50fr + 50c dk car & blk | .20 | .20 |
| B28 | SP6 | 2fr + 1fr blk & dk car & grn | .20 | .20 |
| B29 | SP6 | 3fr + 1.25fr org ver & grn | 1.25 | 1.25 |

**Unwmk. Perf. 13½**

### Soccer SP6

> Catalogue values for unused stamps in this section, from this point to the end of the section, are for Never Hinged items.

17th Olympic Games, Rome, Aug. 25-Sept. 11. The surtax was for the youth of Ruanda-Urundi.

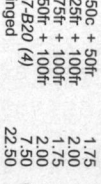

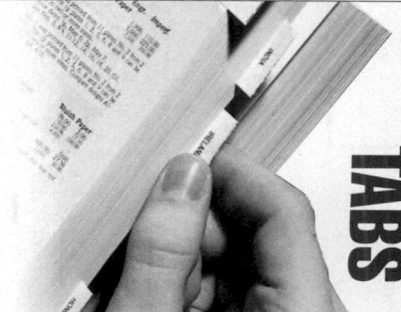

# RUSSIA
ˈrəsh-ə

(Union of Soviet Socialist Republics)

LOCATION — Eastern Europe and Northern Asia
GOVT. — Republic
AREA — 6,592,691 sq. mi.
POP. — 147,100,000 (1999 est.)
CAPITAL — Moscow

An empire until 1917, the government was overthrown in that year and a socialist union of republics was formed under the name of the Union of Soviet Socialist Republics. The USSR includes the following autonomous republics which have issued their own stamps: Armenia, Azerbaijan, Georgia and Ukraine.

With the breakup of the Soviet Union on Dec. 26, 1991, eleven former Soviet republics established the Commonwealth of Independent States. Stamps inscribed "Rossija" are issued by the Russian Republic.

100 Kopecks = 1 Ruble

Catalogue values for unused stamps in this country are for Never Hinged items, beginning with Scott 1021 in the regular postage section, Scott B58 in the semi-postal section, and Scott C82 in the airpost section.

## Watermarks

Wmk. 166 — Colorless Numerals ("1" for Nos. 1-2, "2" for No. 3, "3" for No. 4)

Wmk. 168 — Cyrillic EZGB & Wavy Lines

Initials are those of the State Printing Plant.

Wmk. 169 — Lozenges

Wmk. 170 — Greek Border and Rosettes

Wmk. 226 — Diamonds Enclosing Four Dots

Wmk. 171 — Diamonds

Wmk. 293 — Hammer and Sickle, Multiple

Wmk. 383 — Cyrillic Letters in Shield

### Empire

Coat of Arms
A1      A2      A3

**1857, Dec. 10    Typo.    Imperf.**

| | | | | |
|---|---|---|---|---|
| 1 | A1 | 10k brown & blue | 12,500. | 800. |
| | a. | Pen cancellation | | 675. |
| | | Penmark & postmark | | 700. |

Genuine unused copies of No. 1 are exceedingly rare. Most of those offered are used with pen cancellation removed. The unused value is for a specimen without gum. The very few known stamps with original gum sell for much more.

See Poland for similar stamp inscribed "ZALOT KOP. 10."

**1858, Jan. 10    Perf. 14½, 15**

| | | | | |
|---|---|---|---|---|
| 2 | A1 | 10k brown & blue | 1,750. | 125. |
| 3 | A1 | 20k blue & orange | 3,000. | 750. |
| 4 | A1 | 30k carmine & green | 4,500. | 1,250. |

**1858-64    Unwmk.    Wove Paper    Perf. 12½**

| | | | | |
|---|---|---|---|---|
| 5 | A2 | 1k black & yel (64) | 62.50 | 42.50 |
| | a. | 1k black & orange | 72.50 | 42.50 |
| 6 | A2 | 3k black & green (64) | 300.00 | 80.00 |
| 7 | A2 | 5k black & lilac (64) | 275.00 | 90.00 |
| 8 | A1 | 10k brown & blue | 175.00 | 10.00 |
| 9 | A1 | 20k blue & orange | 425.00 | 85.00 |
| | a. | Half used as 10k on cover | | |
| 10 | A1 | 30k carmine & green | 425.00 | 100.00 |
| | | Nos. 5-10 (6) | 1,662. | 407.50 |

**1863**

| | | | | |
|---|---|---|---|---|
| 11 | A3 | 5k black & blue | 25.00 | 150.00 |

No. 11 was issued to pay local postage in St. Petersburg and Moscow. It is known to have been used in other cities. Copies canceled after July, 1864, are worth considerably less.

**1865, June 2    Perf. 14½, 15**

| | | | | |
|---|---|---|---|---|
| 12 | A2 | 1k black & yellow | 75.00 | 15.00 |
| | a. | 1k black & orange | 80.00 | 20.00 |
| 13 | A2 | 3k black & green | 110.00 | 6.00 |
| 14 | A2 | 5k black & lilac | 120.00 | 8.50 |
| 15 | A1 | 10k brown & blue | 75.00 | 3.00 |
| | a. | Thick paper | 110.00 | 7.50 |
| 17 | A1 | 20k blue & orange | 250.00 | 18.50 |
| 18 | A1 | 30k carmine & green | 300.00 | 32.50 |
| | | Nos. 12-18 (6) | 930.00 | 83.50 |

**1866-70    Wmk. 168    Horizontally Laid Paper**

| | | | | |
|---|---|---|---|---|
| 19 | A2 | 1k black & yellow | 5.00 | .75 |
| | a. | 1k black & orange | 5.00 | .90 |
| | b. | Imperf. | | 1,000. |
| | c. | Vertically laid | 175.00 | 25.00 |
| | d. | Groundwork inverted | 3,000. | 25.00 |
| | e. | Thick paper | 1,750. | 30.00 |
| | f. | As "c," imperf. | | 2,250. |
| | g. | As "b," "c" & "d" | | 5,000. |
| 20 | A2 | 3k blk & org, vert. laid paper | 175.00 | 25.00 |
| | a. | 3k black & dp green | 5.00 | 1.00 |
| | b. | 3k black & yellow green | | 1.50 |
| | c. | V's in groundwork (error) (70) | | 1,500. |
| | d. | Vertically laid | 700.00 | 40.00 |
| 22 | A2 | 5k black & lilac | 4.50 | .50 |
| | a. | 5k black & gray | 6.50 | .85 |
| | b. | Imperf. | 85.00 | 10.00 |
| | c. | Vertically laid | 2,500. | 1,000. |
| | d. | As "c," imperf. | 1,050. | 1,000. |
| 23 | A1 | 10k brown & blue | 30.00 | 1.25 |
| | a. | Vertically laid | 250.00 | 11.00 |
| | b. | Center inverted | | 7,000. |
| | c. | Imperf. | | 4,000. |
| 24 | A1 | 20k blue & orange | 90.00 | 6.00 |
| | a. | Vertically laid | 1,100. | 65.00 |
| 25 | A1 | 30k carmine & green | 80.00 | 25.00 |
| | a. | Vertically laid | 80.00 | 40.00 |
| | | Nos. 19-25 (6) | 216.50 | 34.85 |

Arms — A4

**1875-79    Horizontally Laid Paper**

| | | | | |
|---|---|---|---|---|
| 26 | A2 | 2k black & red | 6.00 | .50 |
| | a. | Vertically laid | 6.00 | 75.00 |
| | b. | Groundwork inverted | | 7,500. |
| 27 | A4 | 7k gray & rose (79) | 6.00 | .25 |
| | a. | Imperf. | | 4,250. |
| | b. | Vertically laid | 450.00 | 60.00 |
| | c. | Wmkd. hexagons (79) | | 12,500. |
| | d. | Center inverted | | 25,000. |
| | e. | Center omitted | | 1,500. |
| | f. | 7k black & carmine (80) | | 1,500. |
| | g. | 7k pale gray & car (82) | 5.75 | .35 |
| 28 | A4 | 8k gray & rose | 6.25 | 2.50 |
| | a. | Vertically laid | 7.50 | .35 |
| | b. | Imperf. | 900.00 | .75 |
| | c. | "C" instead of "B" in "Bosem" | | 70.00 |
| | | | | 1,500. |
| 29 | A4 | 10k brown & blue | 200.00 | 4.50 |
| | a. | Center inverted | 25.00 | 9,000. |
| 30 | A4 | 20k blue & orange | 45.00 | 7.50 |
| | b. | Cross-shaped "T" in bottom word | 125.00 | 30.00 |
| | | Nos. 26-30 (5) | 89.50 | 13.50 |

The hexagon watermark of No. 27c is that of revenue stamps. No. 27c exists with Perm and Riga postmarks.

See Finland for stamps similar to designs A4-A15, which have "dot in circle" devices or are inscribed "Markka," "Markkaa," "Pen," or "Pennia."

## Imperial Eagle and Post Horns

A5   A6

### 1883-88

**Perf. 14 to 15 and Compound**
**Horizontally Laid Paper**
**Wmk. 168**

| | | | |
|---|---|---|---|
| 31 | A5 1k orange | 2.50 | .20 |
| a. | Imperf. | 600.00 | |
| b. | Groundwork inverted | 600.00 | |
| 32 | A5 2k dark green | 4.00 | .25 |
| a. | 1k yellow | 2.25 | |
| b. | 2k yellow green ('88) | 3.50 | .25 |
| c. | Imperf. | 500.00 | |
| d. | Wove paper | 500.00 | |
| 33 | A5 3k carmine | 5.00 | .20 |
| a. | Groundwork inverted | 450.00 | |
| b. | Imperf. | 450.00 | |
| c. | Wove paper | 4,000. | |
| 34 | A5 5k red violet | 6.50 | .20 |
| a. | Groundwork inverted | 500.00 | |
| 35 | A5 7k blue | 5.00 | .20 |
| a. | Groundwork inverted | 400.00 | |
| b. | Imperf. | 800.00 | |
| c. | Double impression of frame and center | 800.00 | |
| 36 | A6 14k blue & rose | 7.50 | .55 |
| a. | Center inverted | | 800.00 |
| b. | Imperf. | | 7,000. |
| 37 | A6 35k violet & green | 30.00 | 5.00 |
| 38 | A6 70k brown & orange | 30.00 | 5.00 |
| | Nos. 31-38 (8) | 90.50 | 11.60 |
| c. | Diagonal half surcharge "7" in red, on cover ('84) | 10,000. | |

Before 1882 the 1, 2, 3 and 5 kopecks had small numerals in the background; beginning with No. 31 these denominations have a background of network. the higher values, Nos. 31-38 (8) ... No. 36c is handstamped. It is known with cancellations of Tiflis and Kutais, both in Georgia. It is believed to be of philatelic origin.

---

## 1884

A7   A8

**Perf. 13½, 13½x11½**
**Vertically Laid Paper**

| | | | |
|---|---|---|---|
| 39 | A7 3.50r black & gray | 575. | 450. |
| a. | Horiz. laid | 45,000. | |
| 40 | A7 7r black & org | 6,500. | 550. |
| b. | 7r black & org | | 475. |

Forgeries exist, especially with forged postmarks.

A9

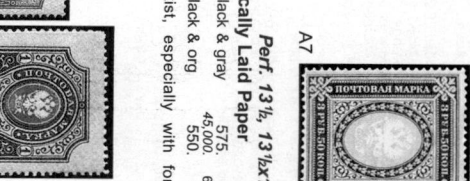

### 1889, May 14

**With Thunderbolts Across Post Horns**
**Perf. 14 to 15 and Compound**
**Horizontally Laid Paper**

| | | | |
|---|---|---|---|
| 41 | A8 4k rose | .75 | .30 |
| a. | Groundwork inverted | | 3.00 |
| 42 | A8 10k dark blue | .75 | .25 |
| 43 | A8 20k blue & carmine | 2.25 | .35 |
| 44 | A8 50k violet & green | 2.50 | .50 |
| a. | Nos. 41-45 (5) | 23.75 | 4.40 |

A10   A11

**Perf. 13½**

| | | | |
|---|---|---|---|
| 45 | A9 1r lt brn, brn & org | 17.50 | 3.00 |
| a. | Imperf., pair | 750.00 | |
| b. | Center omitted | | .50 |

See #57C, 60, 63, 66, 68, 82, 85, 87, 126, 129, 131. For surcharges see #216, 219, 223, 226.

---

## Imperial Eagle and Post Horns with Thunderbolts

A12   A13

### 1889-92

**With Thunderbolts Across Post Horns**
**Perf. 14½x15**
**Horizontally Laid Paper**

| | | | |
|---|---|---|---|
| 46 | A10 1k orange | 1.00 | .20 |
| a. | Imperf. | 500.00 | |
| 47 | A10 2k green | 1.00 | .20 |
| a. | Imperf. | 500.00 | |
| 48 | A10 3k carmine | 1.00 | .20 |
| a. | Imperf. | 350.00 | |
| 49 | A10 5k red violet | .70 | .20 |
| b. | Center inverted | 725.00 | |
| 50 | A10 7k dark blue | 1.00 | .20 |
| a. | Groundwork omitted | 500.00 | |
| b. | Center inverted | 6,000. | |
| 51 | A11 14k blue & rose | 4.00 | .20 |
| a. | Groundwork inverted | 200.00 | |
| b. | Center inverted | 6,000. | |
| 52 | A11 35k vio & car | 4.25 | .20 |
| a. | Center inverted | 4,500. | |
| | | 8.00 | .60 |

**Perf. 13½**

| | | | |
|---|---|---|---|
| 53 | A12 3.50r black & gray | 25.00 | 9.00 |
| 54 | A12 7r black & yel | 60.00 | 11.00 |
| a. | Dbl. impression of black | | 275.00 |
| | Nos. 46-54 (9) | 102.25 | 21.80 |

---

A14   A15

## Vertical Lozenges of Varnish on Face

### 1909-12

**Unwmk.   Perf. 14x14½**
**Wove Paper**

| | | | |
|---|---|---|---|
| 73 | A14 1k dull orange yellow | .20 | .20 |
| a. | 1k orange yellow ('09) | .20 | |
| b. | Double impression | 100.00 | |
| 74 | A14 2k dull green | .20 | .20 |
| a. | 2k green ('09) | .20 | |
| b. | Double impression | 100.00 | |
| 75 | A14 3k carmine | .20 | .20 |
| 76 | A14 4k carmine rose ('09) | .20 | .20 |
| 77 | A14 5k claret | .65 | .20 |
| a. | 5k lilac ('12) | .20 | |
| 78 | A14 7k blue | .65 | .20 |
| a. | 7k light blue ('09) | | |
| b. | Imperf. | 250.00 | |
| 79 | A15 10k dark blue | 1.00 | .20 |
| a. | 10k light blue ('09) | 6.00 | |
| b. | 10k pale blue | | .20 |
| 80 | A11 14k dk blue & rose ('09) | 85.00 | .20 |
| a. | 14k blue & rose ('09) | 1.00 | |

---

A1

### 1906

**Perf. 13½**

| | | | |
|---|---|---|---|
| 71 | A13 5r dk blue, grn & orange | 25.00 | 5.00 |
| 72 | A13 10r car rose, yel & gray | 225.00 | 275.00 |
| a. | Perf. 11½ | 100.00 | 11.50 |
| b. | Perf. 13½x11½, 11½x13½ | 204.25 | 33.85 |

The design of No. 72 differs in many details from the illustration. Nos. 71-72 were printed in sheets of 25. See Nos. 55-72 (19)

See Nos. 80-81, 83-84, 86, 108-109, 125, 127-128, 130, 132-135, 137-138. For surcharges see Nos. 217-218, 220-222, 224-225, 227-229.

---

### Perf. 14 to 15 and Compound
**1902-05   Vertically Laid Paper**

| | | | |
|---|---|---|---|
| 55 | A10 1k orange | 1.00 | .35 |
| a. | Imperf. | 600.00 | |
| b. | Groundwork inverted | 850.00 | |
| c. | Groundwork omitted | | |
| 56 | A10 2k yellow green | 1.00 | .35 |
| a. | 2k deep green | 7.50 | |
| d. | Groundwork omitted | 850.00 | |
| 57 | A10 3k rose red | 1.00 | .35 |
| a. | Groundwork omitted | 850.00 | |
| d. | Center inverted | 425.00 | |
| 57C | A8 4k rose red ('04) | .50 | .35 |
| f. | Double impression | | |
| 58 | A10 5k red violet | .70 | .35 |
| a. | Groundwork omitted | 600.00 | |
| 59 | A10 7k dark blue | .50 | .35 |
| a. | Center inverted | | |
| b. | Imperf. | 250.00 | |
| c. | Groundwork omitted | 250.00 | |
| 60 | A8 10k dk bl ('04) | .50 | .35 |
| a. | Center inverted | 4,000. | |
| b. | Groundwork inverted | 300.00 | |
| c. | Groundwork double | 375.00 | |
| d. | Imperf. | 800.00 | |
| 61 | A11 14k blue & rose | 1.25 | .35 |
| a. | Groundwork omitted | | |
| 62 | A11 15k brown vio & blue ('05) | 3.50 | 1.00 |
| 63 | A8 20k blue & car | 2.25 | .75 |
| 64 | A11 25k dull grn & lil ('04) | 3.50 | 1.00 |
| a. | Center inverted | 4,750. | |
| 65 | A11 35k dk vio & grn | 6.00 | 4,000. |
| a. | Center inverted | 1,100. | |
| 66 | A8 50k vio & grn ('05) | 11.00 | 11.00 |
| 67 | A11 70k brown & org | 11.00 | 1.25 |
| 68 | A9 1r lt brown, brn & orange | 12.50 | 1.00 |
| a. | Center inverted | 675.00 | 50.00 |

See Nos. 119-124. For surcharges see Nos. 117-118, B24-B29.

---

### Perf. 13½

| | | | |
|---|---|---|---|
| 81 | A11 15k red brown & dp blue | .20 | .25 |
| a. | Center omitted | 115.00 | |
| b. | Center double | 50.00 | |
| 82 | A8 20k dull bl & car | .85 | .55 |
| a. | Center omitted | 115.00 | |
| b. | 20k blue & carmine ('10) | .85 | 13.00 |
| c. | Groundwork omitted | 210.00 | |
| 83 | A11 25k dl grn & dk vio ('09) | .50 | .30 |
| a. | Center omitted | 85.00 | |
| d. | Center double | 25.00 | |
| 84 | A11 35k red brn & grn ('09) | 1.00 | .20 |
| a. | Center omitted | 115.00 | |
| b. | 35k red brn & yel grn ('09) | | |
| 85 | A8 50k red brn & grn ('09) | .50 | .40 |
| a. | 50k violet & green ('09) | | |
| b. | Center omitted | 32.50 | |
| 86 | A11 70k lt brown & orange ('09) | .30 | .25 |
| a. | Center omitted | 115.00 | |
| 87 | A9 1r pale brown, dk brn & orange | 3.00 | 3.05 |
| a. | Center omitted | | |
| b. | Pair, imperf. between | 22.50 | |
| f. | Center double | 22.50 | |
| | Nos. 73-87 (15) | | |

---

## SURCHARGES

Russian stamps of types A6-A15 with various surcharges may be found listed under Armenia, Batum, Far Eastern Republic, Georgia, Latvia, Siberia, South Russia, Transcaucasian Federated Republics, Ukraine, Russian Offices in China, Russian Offices in the Turkish Empire and Army of the Northwest.

Nos. 87g-87k are listed below No. 138a. Nearly all values of this issue are known without the lines of varnish.

I — The 7k has two types:

I — Inner lines of scroll at top left end in two first printing. Value of pair, type I with type II, unused $2,500.

---

A16   A17

Peter I — A16   Alexander II — A17

---

A18   A19

Alexander III — A18   Peter I — A19

---

A20   A21

Nicholas II

Catherine II — A22  
Nicholas I — A23  
Alexander I — A24  
Alexis Mikhailovich A25  
Paul I A26  
Elizabeth Petrovna A27  
Michael Feodorovich A28  
The Kremlin — A29  
Winter Palace — A30  
Romanov Castle — A31  
Nicholas II — A32

**Without Lozenges of Varnish**

**1913, Jan. 2     Typo.     Perf. 13½**

| | | | | |
|---|---|---|---|---|
| 88 | A16 | 1k brown orange | .30 | .20 |
| 89 | A17 | 2k yellow green | .30 | .20 |
| 90 | A18 | 3k rose red | .30 | .20 |
| b. | | Double impression | 700.00 | |
| 91 | A19 | 4k dull red | .25 | .20 |
| 92 | A20 | 7k brown | .25 | .20 |
| b. | | Double impression | 350.00 | 350.00 |
| 93 | A21 | 10k deep blue | .50 | .20 |
| 94 | A22 | 14k blue green | .45 | .20 |
| 95 | A23 | 15k yellow brown | .80 | .20 |
| 96 | A24 | 20k olive green | 1.00 | .20 |
| 97 | A25 | 25k red violet | 1.00 | .35 |
| 98 | A26 | 35k gray vio & dk grn | 1.00 | .35 |
| 99 | A27 | 50k brown & slate | 1.25 | .45 |
| 100 | A28 | 70k grn & brn | 2.50 | 1.25 |

**Engr.**

| | | | | |
|---|---|---|---|---|
| 101 | A29 | 1r deep green | 12.50 | 4.50 |
| 102 | A30 | 2r red brown | 27.50 | 8.00 |
| 103 | A31 | 3r dark violet | 27.50 | 13.50 |
| 104 | A32 | 5r black brown | 22.50 | 20.00 |
| | | Nos. 88-104 (17) | 92.40 | 50.20 |

**Imperf**

| | | | |
|---|---|---|---|
| 88a | A16 | 1k rose red | 775.00 |
| 90a | A18 | 3r brown | 775.00 |
| 92a | A20 | 7k brown | 775.00 |
| 93a | A21 | 10k deep blue | 775.00 |
| 102a | A30 | 2r red brown | 775.00 |
| 103b | A31 | 3r dark violet | 775.00 |

Tercentenary of the founding of the Romanov dynasty.
See #105-107, 112-116, 139-141. For surcharges see #105-107, 112-116, 139-141, Russian Offices in the Turkish Empire 213-227.

**Arms and 5-line Inscription on Back**

**1915, Oct.     Typo.     Perf. 13½**

**Thin Cardboard**

**Without Gum**

| | | | | |
|---|---|---|---|---|
| 105 | A21 | 10k blue | .75 | 3.75 |
| 106 | A23 | 15k brown | .75 | 3.75 |
| 107 | A24 | 20k olive green | .75 | 3.75 |
| | | Nos. 105-107 (3) | 2.25 | 11.25 |

**Imperf**

| | | | | |
|---|---|---|---|---|
| 105a | A21 | 10k | 75.00 | |
| 106a | A23 | 15k | 75.00 | 50.00 |
| 107a | A24 | 20k | 75.00 | |

Nos. 105-107, 112-116 and 139-141 were issued for use as paper money, but contrary to regulations were often used for postal purposes. Back inscription means: "Having circulation on par with silver subsidiary coins."

**Types of 1906 Issue**

**Vertical Lozenges of Varnish on Face**

**1915     Perf. 13½, 13½x13**

| | | | | |
|---|---|---|---|---|
| 108 | A13 | 5r ind, grn & lt blue | .25 | .20 |
| a. | | 5r dk bl, grn & pale bl (15) | .65 | |
| b. | | Perf. 12½ | 3.25 | 1.00 |
| c. | | Center double | 50.00 | |
| d. | | Pair, imperf. between | 200.00 | |
| 109 | A13 | 10r car lake yel & gray | .20 | .20 |
| a. | | 10r carmine, yel & light gray | .40 | .25 |
| b. | | 10r rose red, yel & gray (15) | .85 | .50 |
| c. | | 10r car, yel & gray blue (error) | 1,250. | |
| d. | | Groundwork inverted | 375.00 | |
| e. | | Center double | 50.00 | |

Nos. 108a and 109a were issued in sheets of 25. Nos. 108, 108a, 109 and 109a in sheets of 50. Chemical forgeries of No. 109c exist. Genuine copies usually are centered to upper right.

Nos. 92, 94 Surcharged

**1916**

| | | | | |
|---|---|---|---|---|
| 110 | A20 | 10k on 7k brown | .25 | .25 |
| a. | | Inverted surcharge | 70.00 | 70.00 |
| 111 | A22 | 20k on 14k bl grn | .25 | .25 |

**Types of 1913 Issue**

**Arms, Value & 4-line inscription on Back**

**Surcharged Large Numerals on Nos. 112-113**

**1916-17**

**Thin Cardboard**

**Without Gum**

| | | | | |
|---|---|---|---|---|
| 112 | A16 | 1 on 1k brn org ('17) | 2.50 | 5.00 |
| 113 | A17 | 2 on 2k yel green ('17) | 2.50 | 5.00 |

**Without Surcharge**

| | | | | |
|---|---|---|---|---|
| 114 | A16 | 1k brown orange | 25.00 | 32.50 |
| 115 | A17 | 2k yellow green | 35.00 | 55.00 |
| 116 | A18 | 3k rose red | .75 | 4.50 |

See note after No. 107.

Nos. 78a, 80a Surcharged:

a  
b

---

**1917     Perf. 14x14½**

| | | | | |
|---|---|---|---|---|
| 117 | A14 | 10k on 7k lt blue | .20 | .20 |
| a. | | Inverted surcharge | 50.00 | 60.00 |
| b. | | Double surcharge | 60.00 | |
| 118 | A11 | 20k on 14k bl & rose | 50.00 | 50.00 |
| a. | | Inverted surcharge | | |

**Provisional Government**

**Civil War**

**Type of 1889-1912 Issues**

**Vertical Lozenges of Varnish on Face**

Two types of 7r:
Type I — Single outer frame line.
Type II — Double outer frame line.

**1917     Typo.     Imperf.**

**Wove Paper**

| | | | | |
|---|---|---|---|---|
| 119 | A14 | 1k orange | .20 | .20 |
| 120 | A14 | 2k gray green | .20 | .20 |
| 121 | A14 | 3k red | .20 | .20 |
| 122 | A14 | 4k carmine | .20 | .20 |
| 123 | A14 | 5k claret | .20 | .20 |
| 124 | A15 | 10k dark blue | 18.00 | 18.00 |
| 125 | A11 | 15k red brn & dp blue | .20 | .20 |
| a. | | Center omitted | .35 | |
| 126 | A8 | 20k blue & car | 65.00 | |
| a. | | Groundwork double | | |
| 127 | A11 | 25k grn & gray vio | 25.00 | 25.00 |
| 128 | A11 | 35k red brn & grn | .75 | 1.00 |
| 129 | A8 | 50k brn vio & grn | .75 | .35 |
| a. | | Groundwork omitted | .25 | |
| 130 | A11 | 70k brn & orange | 25.00 | 25.00 |
| 131 | A9 | 1r pale brn, brn & red org | 115.00 | .40 |
| a. | | Center inverted | 20.00 | 20.00 |
| b. | | Center omitted | 20.00 | 20.00 |
| c. | | Center double | 20.00 | 20.00 |
| d. | | Groundwork double | 14.00 | 14.00 |
| e. | | Groundwork omitted | 22.50 | 22.50 |
| f. | | Groundwork omitted | 16.00 | 16.00 |
| g. | | Frame double | .20 | .25 |
| 132 | A12 | 3.50r mar & lt green | | .35 |
| 133 | A13 | 5r dk blue, grn & pale blue | | |
| a. | | 5r dk bl, grn & pale blue (error) | 1,000. | |
| b. | | Groundwork inverted | 400.00 | |
| 134 | A12 | 7r dk green & pink (I) | .75 | 5,000. |
| a. | | Center inverted | 1.00 | |

| | | | | |
|---|---|---|---|---|
| 135 | A13 | 10r scarlet, yel & gray | 40.00 | 35.00 |
| a. | | 10r scarlet, green & gray (error) | 1,250. | |
| | | Nos. 119-135 (17) | 62.20 | 58.35 |

Beware of trimmed copies of No. 109 offered as No. 135.

**Vertical Lozenges of Varnish on Face**

**Perf. 13½, 13½x13**

**1917**

| | | | | |
|---|---|---|---|---|
| 137 | A12 | 3.50r mar & lt grn | .20 | .20 |
| 138 | A12 | 7r dark green & pink (II) | 2.00 | 2.00 |

**Perf. 12½**

| | | | | |
|---|---|---|---|---|
| d. | | Type I | .20 | .20 |

**1917     Typo.     Imperf.**

| | | | | |
|---|---|---|---|---|
| 137a | A12 | 3.50r maroon & lt grn | .20 | .20 |
| 138a | A12 | 7r dk grn & pink (II) | 1.00 | 1.00 |

**Horizontal Lozenges of Varnish on Face**

**Perf. 13½x13**

| | | | | |
|---|---|---|---|---|
| 87g | A9 | 1r pale brown, brn & red orange | .20 | .20 |
| h. | | Imperf. | 12.50 | |
| i. | | As "h," center omitted | 25.00 | |
| j. | | As "h," center inverted | 25.00 | |
| k. | | As "h," center inverted | 25.00 | |
| 137b | A12 | 3.50r mar & lt green | .65 | .65 |
| d. | | Imperf. | 250.00 | |
| 138b | A12 | 7r dk grn & pink (II) | .65 | .65 |
| b. | | Imperf. | 250.00 | |

Nos. 87g, 137b and 138b often show the eagle with little or no embossing.

**Types of 1913 Issue**

**Surcharge & 4-line Inscription on Back**

**Surcharged Large Numerals**

**1917**

**Thin Cardboard, Without Gum**

| | | | | |
|---|---|---|---|---|
| 139 | A16 | 1 on 1k brown org | .85 | 6.00 |
| 140 | A17 | 2 on 2k yel green | .85 | 6.00 |
| a. | | Imperf. | 30.00 | 30.00 |
| b. | | Surch. omitted, imperf. | 45.00 | 45.00 |

# RUSSIAN TURKESTAN

Russian stamps of 1917-18 surcharged as above are frauds.

**Without Surcharge**

| | | |
|---|---|---|
| 141 A18 3k rose red | 1.25 | 6.00 |
| a. Imperf. | | |
| Nos. 139-141 (3) | 2.95 | 18.00 |

See note after No. 107.

Stamps overprinted with a Liberty Cap on Crossed Swords or with reduced facsimiles of pages of newspapers were a private speculation and without official sanction.

## Russian Soviet Federated Socialist Republic

### Severing Chain of Bondage — A33

**1918**    Typo.    Perf. 13½

| | | |
|---|---|---|
| 149 A33 35k blue | .25 | 5.00 |
| 150 A33 70k brown | 225.00 | 5.00 |
| a. A33, Imperf., pair | 750.00 | |

In 1918-1922 various revenue stamps were permitted to be used for postal duty, sometimes surcharged with new values, more often not.

For surcharges see Nos. B18-B23, J1-J9 and note following No. B17.

### Symbols of Agriculture — A40
### Symbols of Industry — A41
### Soviet Symbols of Agriculture and Industry — A42
### Science and Arts — A43

**1921**    Unwmk.    Litho.    Imperf.

| | | | |
|---|---|---|---|
| 177 A40 | 1r orange | 1.75 | 1.75 |
| 178 A40 | 2r lt brown | 1.75 | 1.75 |
| 179 A41 | 5r dull ultra | 1.50 | .45 |
| 180 A42 | 20r blue | 1.50 | 3.00 |
| a. Pelure paper | | 3.25 | 2.75 |
| 181 A40 | 100r orange | .20 | .20 |
| a. Pelure paper | | .20 | .20 |
| 182 A40 | 200r lt brown | .20 | .20 |
| a. Pelure paper | | .20 | .20 |
| 183 A43 | 250r dull violet | 15.00 | 15.00 |
| a. 200r olive brown | | | |
| b. Pelure paper | | 15.00 | 15.00 |
| 184 A42 | 300r green | .20 | .25 |
| a. Pelure paper | | .20 | .25 |
| 185 A41 | 500r blue | .20 | .35 |
| 186 A41 | 1000r carmine | .20 | .30 |
| a. Thick paper | | .20 | .30 |
| b. Pelure paper | | .20 | .30 |
| c. Chalk surfaced paper | | | |
| Nos. 177-186 (10) | | 7.20 | 8.00 |

See #203, 205. For surcharges see Nos. 191-194, 196-199, 201, 210, B40, B43-B47, J10.

### New Russia Triumphant A44

**1921, Aug. 10**    Wmk. 169    Engr.

| | | |
|---|---|---|
| 187 A44 40r slate, type II | .60 | 1.00 |
| a. Type I | 1.10 | 1.10 |

Type I — 37½mm by 23¾mm.
Type II — 38½mm by 23¾mm.

The types are caused by paper shrinkage, one type has the watermark sideways in relation to the other.

For surcharges see Nos. 195, 200.

### Initials Stand for Russian Soviet Federated Socialist Republic — A45

**1921**    Litho.    Unwmk.

| | | |
|---|---|---|
| 188 A45 100r orange | .20 | .55 |
| 189 A45 250r violet | .20 | .55 |
| 190 A45 1000r carmine rose | .75 | 1.40 |
| Nos. 188-190 (3) | 1.15 | 2.50 |

4th anniversary of Soviet Government. A 200r was not regularly issued. Value $45.

**1922**    Litho.    Unwmk.

| | | |
|---|---|---|
| 191 A40 5000r on 1r orange | 1.50 | .80 |
| a. Inverted surcharge | 100.00 | 22.50 |
| b. Double surch, red & blk | 125.00 | |
| c. Pair, one without surcharge | | |
| 192 A40 5000r on 2r lt brown | 1.25 | 1.25 |
| a. Double surcharge | 75.00 | 15.00 |
| 193 A41 5000r on 5r ultra | 2.00 | |
| a. Inverted surcharge | 75.00 | |
| b. Double surcharge | 75.00 | 30.00 |

No. 180 Surcharged

| | | |
|---|---|---|
| 194 A42 5000r on 20r blue | 1.75 | 2.50 |
| a. Pelure paper | 1.75 | 2.25 |
| b. Pair, one without surcharge | 100.00 | |

Nos. 177-180, 187-187a Surcharged in Black or Red

Nos. 177-179 Surcharged in Black

Beware of digitally created forgeries of the errors of Nos. 191-193 and 196-199.

**Wmk. Lozenges (169)**    Unwmk.

| | | |
|---|---|---|
| 195 A44 10,000r on 40r, type I | 2.50 | 3.25 |
| a. Type II | 2.75 | 2.50 |
| b. Inverted surcharge | | |
| c. "1000" instead of "10,000" | | |
| d. Double surcharge | | |

**Red Surcharge**

| | | |
|---|---|---|
| 196 A40 5000r on 1r org | 2.00 | 1.50 |
| 197 A40 5000r on 2r lt brn | 75.00 | 15.00 |
| 198 A41 5000r on 5r ultra | 2.25 | 2.00 |
| 199 A42 5000r on 20r blue | 2.25 | 2.25 |
| a. Inverted surcharge | 100.00 | 100.00 |
| b. Pelure paper | 100.00 | 5.00 |

**Wmk. Lozenges (169)**

| | | |
|---|---|---|
| 200 A44 10,000r on 40r, type I (R) | 1.50 | |
| a. Inverted surcharge | 75.00 | 15.00 |
| b. With letters | 100.00 | 18.00 |
| c. With periods after Russian | 100.00 | 18.00 |
| As "a", type II | 35.00 | |
| As "c", type II | 30.00 | |
| Type II | 30.00 | 45.00 |

### No. 183 Surcharged in Black or Blue

**1922, Mar.**    Unwmk.

| | | |
|---|---|---|
| 201 A43 7500r on 250r (Bk) | 2.00 | 1.50 |
| a. Pelure paper | .75 | .75 |
| b. Chalk surfaced paper | .20 | 2.00 |
| c. Blue black surcharge | .20 | .25 |
| Nos. 191-207 (11) | 20.45 | 19.75 |

Nos. 201, 201a and 201b exist with surcharge inverted (value about $25 each), and double (about $20 each). The horizontal surcharge was prepared but not issued.

### "Workers of the World Unite" A46

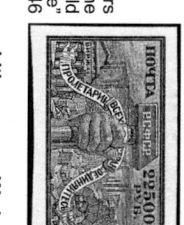

Type of 1921 and

**1922**    Litho.    Wmk. 171

| | | |
|---|---|---|
| 202 A46 5000r dark violet | .75 | 3.25 |
| 203 A43 5000r blue | .25 | .35 |
| 204 A46 10,000r blue | 25.00 | 18.00 |

**Unwmk.**

| | | |
|---|---|---|
| 205 A42 7500r blue, buff | 100.00 | |
| 206 A46 22,500r dk violet, buff | .50 | .60 |
| Nos. 202-206 (5) | 26.75 | 22.60 |

For surcharges see Nos. B41-B42.

Forgeries of No. 223-229 exist, including a dangerous digital forgery of No. 224.

No. 183 Surcharged Diagonally

Marking 5th Anniversary of October Revolution — A48

**1922**    Unwmk.

| | | |
|---|---|---|
| 210 A43 100,000r on 250r | .20 | .20 |
| a. Inverted surcharge | 60.00 | 60.00 |
| b. Pelure paper | .50 | .50 |
| c. Chalk surfaced paper | .20 | .20 |
| d. As "b," inverted surcharge | 100.00 | 100.00 |

### No. 183 Surcharged

**Worker A49**

**Soldier A50**

**1922-23**

**Pelure Paper**

| | | |
|---|---|---|
| 211 A48 5r ocher & black | .90 | .75 |
| 212 A48 10r brown & black | .20 | .25 |
| 213 A48 25r violet & black | .50 | .60 |
| 214 A48 27r rose & black | 1.25 | 1.00 |
| a. 27r violet & black | 60.00 | |
| 215 A48 45r blue & black | 3.05 | 2.85 |
| a. 45r rose & black | 65.00 | |
| Nos. 81, 82a, 85-86, 125-126, 129-130 Surcharged | | |

**Perf. 14½x15**

5th anniv. of the October Revolution. Sold in the currency of 1922 which was then valued at 10,000 times that of the preceding years. For surcharges see Nos. B38-B39.

**1922-23**

| | | |
|---|---|---|
| 216 A8 5r on 20k | .70 | 2.00 |
| 217 A11 20r on 70k | 1.10 | 2.00 |
| 218 A11 20r on 15k | .70 | .35 |
| 219 A8 30r on 50k | .50 | .50 |
| a. Groundwork omitted | | |
| 220 A11 40r on 15k | 1.10 | .35 |
| a. Inverted surcharge | | |
| b. Double surcharge | | |
| 221 A11 100r on 15k | .70 | .35 |
| a. Inverted surcharge | | |
| b. Double surcharge | | |
| 222 A11 100r on 15k | .70 | .35 |
| a. Inverted surcharge | | |
| b. Double surcharge | | |
| 223 A8 5r on 20k | 5.00 | 4.50 |
| 224 A11 20r on 15k | .30 | .30 |
| 225 A11 20r on 70k | .80 | 1.00 |
| 226 A8 30r on 50k brn vio | 17.50 | 17.50 |
| a. 30r & green | | |
| 227 A11 40r on 15k | .30 | 35.00 |
| a. Inverted surcharge | 27.50 | 35.00 |
| b. Double surcharge | 27.50 | 35.00 |
| 228 A11 100r on 15k | 2.25 | 1.10 |
| a. Inverted surcharge | 50.00 | 50.00 |
| 229 A11 200r on 15k | 2.25 | 1.00 |
| a. Inverted surcharge | 50.00 | 50.00 |
| b. Double surcharge | 35.00 | 35.00 |
| Nos. 216-223,225-229 (13) | 26.30 | 28.80 |

**Worker A49**

**1922-23**    Typo.    Imperf.

| | | |
|---|---|---|
| 230 A49 10r blue | .20 | .25 |
| 231 A49 50r blue | .20 | .25 |
| 232 A50 70r brown | .20 | .25 |
| 233 A50 100r red | .50 | .60 |

**Soldier A50**

**1923**    Perf. 14x14½

| | | |
|---|---|---|
| 234 A49 10r dp bl, perf. 13½ | .20 | .25 |
| 235 A50 50r brown | 15.00 | 16.00 |
| 236 A50 70r red | 1.00 | .85 |
| 237 A50 100r red | .20 | .25 |
| a. Corrected cliché | | |
| Nos. 234-237 (4) | | |

No. 237b has extra broken line at right.

**Soldier — Worker — Peasant A51, A52, A53**

A51 Soldier
A52 Worker
A53 Peasant

No. 180 Surcharged

**1923** *Perf. 14½x15*

| | | | | |
|---|---|---|---|---|
| **238** | A51 3r rose | .20 | .25 |
| **239** | A52 4r brown | .20 | .25 |
| **240** | A53 5r light blue | .20 | .25 |
| *a.* | Double impression | *50.00* | *50.00* |
| **241** | A51 10r gray | .20 | .25 |
| *e.* | Double impression | *75.00* | |
| **241A** | A51 20r brown violet | .20 | .75 |
| *b.* | Double impression | *75.00* | *75.00* |
| | *Nos. 238-241A (5)* | 1.00 | 1.75 |

***Imperf***

| | | | |
|---|---|---|---|
| *238a* | A51 3r rose | 10.00 | *20.00* |
| *239a* | A52 4r brown | 10.00 | *25.00* |
| *b.* | As "a," double impression | *75.00* | |
| *240b* | A53 5r light blue | 6.00 | *10.00* |
| *241d* | A51 10r gray | 7.50 | *10.00* |
| *f.* | As "d," double impression | *75.00* | |
| *241c* | A51 20r brown violet | 150.00 | 75.00 |

Stamps of 1r buff, type A52, and 2r green, type A53, perf. 12 and imperf. were prepared but not put in use. Value $1 each.

The imperfs of Nos. 238-241A were sold only by the philatelic bureau in Moscow.

Stamps of 20r, type A51, printed in gray black or dull violet are essays. Value, $75 each.

The stamps of this and the following issues were sold for the currency of 1923, one ruble of which was equal to 100 rubles of 1922 and 1,000,000 rubles of 1921.

## Union of Soviet Socialist Republics

Reaping — A54

Sowing — A55

Fordson Tractor A56

Symbolical of the Exhibition — A57

**1923, Aug. 19** **Litho.** ***Imperf.***

| | | | |
|---|---|---|---|
| **242** | A54 1r brown & orange | 1.50 | *3.00* |
| **243** | A55 2r dp grn & pale grn | 1.50 | *3.00* |
| **244** | A56 5r dp bl & pale blue | 1.50 | *4.00* |
| **245** | A57 7r rose & pink | 1.50 | *5.00* |

***Perf. 12½, 13½***

| | | | |
|---|---|---|---|
| **246** | A54 1r brown & orange | 3.00 | *3.50* |
| *a.* | Perf. 12½ | 20.00 | *35.00* |
| **247** | A55 2r dp grn & pale grn, perf. 12½ | 3.00 | 2.50 |
| **248** | A56 5r dp bl & pale bl | 3.00 | *4.25* |
| *a.* | Perf. 13½ | 16.00 | 16.00 |
| **249** | A57 7r rose & pink | 4.00 | *5.00* |
| *a.* | Perf. 12½ | 16.00 | *25.00* |
| | *Nos. 242-249 (8)* | 19.00 | 30.25 |

1st Agriculture and Craftsmanship Exhibition, Moscow.

Worker — Soldier — Peasant
A58 A59 A60

**1923** **Unwmk.** **Litho.** ***Imperf.***

| | | | |
|---|---|---|---|
| **250** | A58 1k orange | .60 | .25 |
| **251** | A60 2k green | .90 | .40 |
| **252** | A59 3k red brown | .80 | .40 |
| **253** | A58 4k deep rose | .80 | .65 |
| **254** | A58 5k lilac | 1.10 | .65 |
| **255** | A60 6k light blue | .60 | .30 |
| **256** | A59 10k dark blue | .60 | .30 |
| **257** | A58 20k yellow green | 2.50 | .55 |
| **258** | A60 50k dark brown | 4.00 | 1.90 |
| **259** | A59 1r red & brown | 7.50 | 5.00 |
| | *Nos. 250-259 (10)* | 19.40 | 10.40 |

**1924** ***Perf. 14½x15***

| | | | |
|---|---|---|---|
| **261** | A58 4k deep rose | 100.00 | 75.00 |
| **262** | A59 10k dark blue | 100.00 | 75.00 |
| **263** | A60 30k violet | 25.00 | 8.00 |
| **264** | A59 40k slate gray | 25.00 | 8.00 |
| | *Nos. 261-264 (4)* | 250.00 | 166.00 |

See Nos. 273-290, 304-321. For surcharges see Nos. 349-350.

Vladimir Ilyich Ulyanov (Lenin) A61

Worker A62

**1924** ***Imperf.***

| | | | |
|---|---|---|---|
| **265** | A61 3k red & black | 2.50 | 1.50 |
| **266** | A61 6k red & black | 2.50 | 1.50 |
| **267** | A61 12k red & black | 2.50 | 1.50 |
| **268** | A61 20k red & black | 2.50 | 1.50 |
| | *Nos. 265-268 (4)* | 10.00 | 6.00 |

Three printings of Nos. 265-268 differ in size of red frame.

***Perf. 13½***

| | | | |
|---|---|---|---|
| **269** | A61 3k red & black | 2.50 | 1.75 |
| **270** | A61 6k red & black | 2.50 | 1.75 |
| **271** | A61 12k red & black | 2.50 | 2.50 |
| **272** | A61 20k red & black | 3.75 | 3.00 |
| | *Nos. 269-272 (4)* | 11.25 | 9.00 |
| | *Nos. 265-272 (8)* | 21.25 | 15.00 |

Death of Lenin (1870-1924).

Forgeries of Nos. 265-272 exist.

### Types of 1923

There are small differences between the lithographed stamps of 1923 and the typographed of 1924-25. On a few values this may be seen in the numerals.

Type A58. Lithographed. The two white lines forming the outline of the ear are continued across the cheek. Typographed. The outer lines of the ear are broken where they touch the cheek.

Type A59: Lithographed. At the top of the right shoulder a white line touches the frame at the left. Counting from the edge of the visor of the cap, lines 5, 6 and sometimes 7 touch at their upper ends. Typographed. The top line of the shoulder does not reach the frame. On the cap lines 5, 6 and 7 run together and form a white spot.

Type A60: In the angle above the first letter "C" there is a fan-shaped ornament enclosing four white dashes. On the lithographed stamps these dashes reach nearly to the point of the angle. On the typographed stamps the dashes are shorter and often only three are visible.

On unused copies of the typographed stamps the raised outlines of the designs can be seen on the backs of the stamps.

**1924-25** **Typo.** ***Imperf.***

| | | | |
|---|---|---|---|
| **273** | A59 3k red brown | 1.40 | 1.00 |
| **274** | A58 4k deep rose | 1.40 | 1.00 |
| **275** | A59 10k dark blue | 2.50 | 1.00 |
| **275A** | A60 50k brown | 850.00 | 25.00 |

Other typographed and imperf. values include: 2k green, 5k lilac, 6k light blue, 20k green and 1r red and brown. Value, unused: $150, $100, $37.50, $150, and $1,000, respectively.

Nos. 273-275A were regularly issued. The 7k, 8k, 9k, 30k, 40k, 2r, 3r, and 5r also exist imperf. Value, set of 8, $75.

***Perf. 14½x15***
**Typo.**

| | | | |
|---|---|---|---|
| **276** | A58 1k orange | 65.00 | 5.50 |
| **277** | A60 2k green | 1.00 | .30 |
| **278** | A59 3k red brown | 1.25 | .40 |
| **279** | A58 4k deep rose | 1.00 | .40 |
| **280** | A58 5k lilac | 10.00 | 2.50 |
| **281** | A60 6k lt blue | 1.00 | .50 |
| **282** | A59 7k chocolate | 1.00 | .50 |
| **283** | A58 8k brown olive | 1.25 | .70 |
| **284** | A60 9k orange red | 1.25 | 1.10 |
| **285** | A59 10k dark blue | 1.60 | .55 |
| **286** | A58 14k slate blue | 35.00 | 4.00 |
| **287** | A60 15k yellow | *6,000.* | *150.00* |
| **288** | A58 20k gray green | 4.00 | .80 |
| **288A** | A60 30k violet | 200.00 | 7.50 |
| **288B** | A59 40k slate gray | 200.00 | 7.50 |
| **289** | A60 50k brown | 50.00 | 8.00 |
| **290** | A59 1r red & brown | 12.00 | 2.00 |
| **291** | A62 2r green & rose | 15.00 | 3.50 |
| | *Nos. 276-286,288-291 (17)* | 600.35 | 45.75 |

See No. 323. Forgeries of No. 287 exist.

**1925** ***Perf. 12***

| | | | |
|---|---|---|---|
| *276a* | A58 1k orange | .85 | .20 |
| *277a* | A60 2k green | 8.00 | .95 |
| *278a* | A59 3k red brown | 1.60 | .70 |
| *279a* | A58 4k deep rose | 55.00 | 3.25 |
| *280a* | A58 5k lilac | 4.00 | .80 |
| *282a* | A59 7k chocolate | 2.25 | .20 |
| *283a* | A58 8k brown olive | 80.00 | 12.50 |
| *284a* | A60 9k orange red | 13.00 | 7.50 |
| *285a* | A59 10k dark blue | 3.00 | .25 |
| *286a* | A58 14k slate blue | 3.50 | .40 |
| *287a* | A60 15k yellow | 4.50 | 1.00 |
| *288c* | A58 20k gray green | 18.00 | .45 |
| *288d* | A60 30k violet | 25.00 | 2.50 |
| *288e* | A59 40k slate gray | 20.00 | 2.75 |
| *289a* | A60 50k brown | 8.00 | 1.10 |
| *290a* | A59 1r red & brown | 750.00 | 150.00 |
| | *Nos. 276a-290a (16)* | 996.70 | 184.55 |

Soldier — A63

Worker — A64

**1924-25** ***Perf. 13½***

| | | | |
|---|---|---|---|
| **292** | A63 3r blk brn & grn | 15.00 | 4.75 |
| *a.* | Perf. 10 | 600.00 | 50.00 |
| *b.* | Perf. 13½x10 | 1,000. | 325.00 |
| **293** | A64 5r dk bl & gray brn | 35.00 | 9.25 |
| *a.* | Perf. 10½ | 50.00 | 65.00 |

See Nos. 324-325.

Lenin Mausoleum, Moscow — A65

**Wmk. 170**

**1925, Jan.** **Photo.** ***Imperf.***

| | | | |
|---|---|---|---|
| **294** | A65 7k deep blue | 3.75 | 3.00 |
| **295** | A65 14k dark green | 3.75 | 3.00 |
| **296** | A65 20k carmine rose | 3.75 | 3.00 |
| **297** | A65 40k red brown | 3.75 | 3.50 |
| | *Nos. 294-297 (4)* | 15.00 | 12.50 |

***Perf. 13½x14***

| | | | |
|---|---|---|---|
| **298** | A65 7k deep blue | 4.50 | 2.75 |
| **299** | A65 14k dark green | 5.00 | 2.75 |
| **300** | A65 20k carmine rose | 5.00 | 2.75 |
| **301** | A65 40k red brown | 5.50 | 4.00 |
| | *Nos. 298-301 (4)* | 20.00 | 12.25 |
| | *Nos. 294-301 (8)* | 35.00 | 24.75 |

First anniversary of Lenin's death.

Nos. 294-301 are found on both ordinary and thick paper. Those on thick paper sell for twice as much, except for No. 301, which is scarcer on ordinary paper.

Lenin — A66

**Wmk. 170**

**1925, July** **Engr.** ***Perf. 13½***

| | | | |
|---|---|---|---|
| **302** | A66 5r red brown | 27.50 | 6.00 |
| *a.* | Perf. 12½ | 35.00 | 11.00 |
| *b.* | Perf. 10½ ('26) | 30.00 | 8.00 |
| **303** | A66 10r indigo | 27.50 | 11.00 |
| *a.* | Perf. 12½ | 190.00 | 90.00 |
| *b.* | Perf. 10½ ('26) | 22.50 | 11.00 |

Imperfs. exist. Value, set $75.

See Nos. 407-408, 621-622

### Types of 1923 Issue

**1925-27** **Wmk. 170** **Typo.** ***Perf. 12***

| | | | |
|---|---|---|---|
| **304** | A58 1k orange | .50 | .35 |
| **305** | A60 2k green | .45 | .20 |
| **306** | A59 3k red brown | .50 | .35 |
| **307** | A58 4k deep rose | .30 | .25 |
| **308** | A58 5k lilac | .40 | .25 |
| **309** | A60 6k lt blue | .60 | .25 |
| **310** | A59 7k chocolate | .45 | .20 |
| **311** | A58 8k brown olive | .95 | .20 |
| *a.* | Perf. 14½x15 | 100.00 | 50.00 |
| **312** | A60 9k red | .70 | .40 |
| **313** | A59 10k dark blue | .70 | .30 |
| *a.* | 10k pale blue ('27) | 1.25 | 1.00 |
| **314** | A58 14k slate blue | 1.50 | .35 |
| **315** | A60 15k yellow | 2.25 | 1.00 |
| **316** | A59 18k violet | 1.50 | .25 |
| **317** | A58 20k gray green | 1.25 | .25 |
| **318** | A60 30k violet | 1.50 | .25 |
| **319** | A59 40k slate gray | 2.00 | .35 |
| **320** | A60 50k brown | 3.25 | .35 |
| **321** | A59 1r red & brown | 3.75 | .35 |
| *a.* | Perf. 14½x15 | 100.00 | 40.00 |
| **323** | A62 2r green & rose red | 22.50 | 5.50 |
| *a.* | Perf. 14½x15 | 11.00 | 2.75 |

***Perf. 13½***

| | | | |
|---|---|---|---|
| **324** | A63 3r blk brn & green | 7.50 | 4.75 |
| *a.* | Perf. 12½ | 40.00 | 14.00 |
| **325** | A64 5r dark blue & gray brown | 12.00 | 4.75 |
| | *Nos. 304-325 (21)* | 64.55 | 20.90 |

Nos. 304-315, 317-325 exist imperf. Value, set $60.

Mikhail V. Lomonosov and Academy of Sciences — A67

**1925, Sept.** **Photo.** ***Perf. 12½, 13½***

| | | | |
|---|---|---|---|
| **326** | A67 3k orange brown | 4.75 | 3.00 |
| *a.* | Perf. 12½x12 | 11.00 | 7.50 |
| *b.* | Perf. 13½x12½ | 45.00 | 27.50 |
| *c.* | Perf. 13½ | 20.00 | 10.00 |
| **327** | A67 15k dk olive green | 4.75 | 3.00 |
| *a.* | Perf. 12½ | 20.00 | 7.50 |

Russian Academy of Sciences, 200th anniv.

Exist unwatermarked, on thick paper with yellow gum, perf. 13½. These are essays, later perforated and gummed. Value, each $50.

Prof. Aleksandr S. Popov (1859-1905), Radio Pioneer — A68

**1925, Oct.** ***Perf. 13½***

| | | | |
|---|---|---|---|
| **328** | A68 7k deep blue | 2.00 | 1.50 |
| **329** | A68 14k green | 3.25 | 1.90 |

For surcharge see No. 353.

Decembrist Exiles — A69

Street Rioting in St. Petersburg — A70

Revolutionist Leaders — A71

**1925, Dec. 28** *Imperf.*

| | | |
|---|---|---|
| **330** A69 3k olive green | 2.25 | *3.00* |
| **331** A70 7k brown | 2.25 | *2.50* |
| **332** A71 14k carmine lake | 3.50 | *3.75* |

***Perf. 13½***

| | | |
|---|---|---|
| **333** A69 3k olive green | 2.50 | 2.25 |
| *a.* Perf. 12½ | 60.00 | 50.00 |
| **334** A70 7k brown | 2.00 | *2.25* |
| **335** A71 14k carmine lake | 3.00 | 2.50 |
| *Nos. 330-335 (6)* | 15.50 | 16.25 |

Centenary of Decembrist revolution.
For surcharges see Nos. 354, 357.

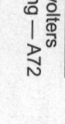

Revolters Parading — A72

Speaker Haranguing Mob — A73

Street Barricade, Moscow — A74

**1925, Dec. 20** *Imperf.*

| | | |
|---|---|---|
| **336** A72 3k olive green | 1.50 | 1.50 |
| **337** A73 7k brown | 1.75 | 1.60 |
| **338** A74 14k carmine lake | 2.25 | 2.00 |

***Perf. 12½, 12x12½***

| | | |
|---|---|---|
| **339** A72 3k olive green | 1.50 | 1.25 |
| *a.* Perf. 13½ | 4.50 | 4.25 |
| **340** A73 7k brown | 3.50 | 3.00 |
| *a.* Perf. 13½ | 15.00 | 10.50 |
| *b.* Horiz. pair, imperf. btwn. | 55.00 | 50.00 |
| **341** A74 14k carmine lake | 2.50 | 2.00 |
| *a.* Perf. 13½ | 22.50 | 12.00 |
| *Nos. 336-341 (6)* | 13.00 | 11.35 |

20th anniversary of Revolution of 1905.
For surcharges see Nos. 355, 358.

Lenin — A75

Liberty Monument, Moscow — A76

**1926 Wmk. 170 Engr.** *Perf. 10½*

| | | |
|---|---|---|
| **342** A75 1r dark brown | 5.00 | 2.50 |
| **343** A75 2r black violet | 10.00 | 4.50 |
| *a.* Perf. 12½ | 100.00 | 50.00 |
| **344** A75 3r dark green | 14.00 | 4.50 |
| *Nos. 342-344 (3)* | 29.00 | 11.50 |

Nos. 342-343 exist imperf.
See Nos. 406, 620.

**1926, July Litho.** *Perf. 12x12½*

| | | |
|---|---|---|
| **347** A76 7k blue green & red | 2.00 | 1.50 |
| **348** A76 14k blue green & violet | 2.50 | 1.50 |

6th International Esperanto Congress at Leningrad. Exist perf. 11½. Value, $500.
For surcharge see No. 356.

Nos. 282, 282a and 310 Surcharged in Black

**1927, June Unwmk.** *Perf. 14½x15*

| | | |
|---|---|---|
| **349** A59 8k on 7k chocolate | 4.00 | 1.25 |
| *a.* Perf. 12 | 8.50 | 7.50 |
| *b.* Inverted surcharge | 125.00 | 110.00 |

***Perf. 12***

**Wmk. 170**

| | | |
|---|---|---|
| **350** A59 8k on 7k chocolate | 2.50 | 1.25 |
| *a.* Inverted surcharge | 100.00 | 35.00 |

The surcharge on Nos. 349-350 comes in two types: With space of 2mm between lines, and with space of ¾mm. The latter is much scarcer.

**Same Surcharge on Stamps of 1925-26 in Black or Red**

***Perf. 13½, 12½, 12x12½***

| | | |
|---|---|---|
| **353** A68 8k on 7k dp bl (R) | 2.75 | *4.50* |
| *a.* Inverted "8" | 75.00 | *100.00* |
| **354** A70 8k on 7k brown | 8.00 | *9.25* |
| **355** A73 8k on 7k brown | 10.50 | *12.25* |
| **356** A76 8k on 7k blue green & red | 8.75 | *11.00* |

***Imperf***

| | | |
|---|---|---|
| **357** A70 8k on 7k brown | 3.50 | *5.25* |
| **358** A73 8k on 7k brown | 3.50 | *5.25* |
| *Nos. 349-350,353-358 (8)* | 43.50 | 50.00 |

Postage Due Stamps of 1925 Surcharged

Two settings: A's aligned (shown), bottom A to left.

**Lithographed or Typographed**

**1927, June Unwmk.** *Perf. 12*

| | | |
|---|---|---|
| **359** D1 8k on 1k red, typo. | 3.00 | 1.60 |
| *a.* Litho. | *750.00* | 100.00 |
| **360** D1 8k on 2k violet | 4.00 | 2.25 |

***Perf. 12, 14½x14***

| | | |
|---|---|---|
| **361** D1 8k on 3k lt blue | 4.25 | 2.25 |
| **362** D1 8k on 7k orange | 4.75 | 2.50 |
| **363** D1 8k on 8k green | 3.75 | 1.75 |
| **364** D1 8k on 10k dk blue | 4.50 | 2.50 |
| **365** D1 8k on 14k brown | 3.75 | 1.75 |
| *Nos. 359-365 (7)* | 28.00 | 14.60 |

Exist with inverted surcharge. Value each, $100.

**Wmk. 170**

**1927, June Typo.** *Perf. 12*

| | | |
|---|---|---|
| **366** D1 8k on 1k red | 1.50 | *1.90* |
| **367** D1 8k on 2k violet | 1.50 | *1.90* |
| **368** D1 8k on 3k lt blue | 3.00 | 2.25 |
| **369** D1 8k on 7k orange | 3.00 | 2.25 |
| **370** D1 8k on 8k green | 1.50 | *1.90* |
| **371** D1 8k on 10k dk blue | 1.50 | *1.90* |
| **372** D1 8k on 14k brown | 2.25 | *1.90* |
| *Nos. 366-372 (7)* | 14.25 | 14.00 |

Nos. 366, 368-372 exist with inverted surcharge. Value each, $100.

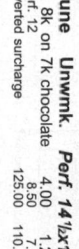

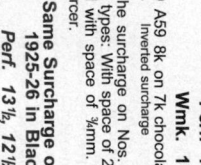

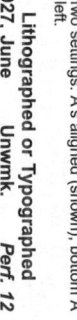

Dr. L. L. Zamenhof A77

**1927 Photo.** *Perf. 10½*

| | | |
|---|---|---|
| **373** A77 14k yel green & brown | 2.00 | 2.00 |

**Unwmk.**

| | | |
|---|---|---|
| **374** A77 14k yel green & brown | 2.00 | 2.00 |

40th anniversary of creation of Esperanto.
No. 374 exists perf. 10, 10x10½ and imperf. Value, imperf. pair $500.

Worker, Soldier, Peasant — A78

Worker and Sailor — A81

Lenin in Car Guarded by Soldiers A79

Smolny Institute, Leningrad A80

Map of the USSR A82

Men of Various Soviet Republics — A83

Workers of Different Races; Kremlin in Background — A84

**Typo. (3k, 8k, 18k), Engr. (7k), Litho. (14k), Photo. (5k, 28k)**

***Perf. 13½, 12½x12, 11***

**1927, Oct.** **Unwmk.**

| | | |
|---|---|---|
| **375** A78 3k bright rose | .95 | .80 |
| *a.* Imperf., pair | 500.00 | |
| **376** A79 5k deep brown | 2.50 | 2.25 |
| *a.* Imperf. | 500.00 | 175.00 |
| *b.* Perf. 12½ | 25.00 | 27.50 |
| *c.* Perf. 12½x10½ | 50.00 | 30.00 |
| **377** A80 7k myrtle green | 3.00 | 2.75 |
| *a.* Perf. 11½ | 50.00 | 30.00 |
| *b.* Imperf., pair | 500.00 | |
| **378** A81 8k brown & black | 1.60 | .95 |
| *a.* Perf. 10½x12½ | *32.50* | *27.50* |
| **379** A82 14k dull blue & red | 2.75 | 1.65 |
| **380** A83 18k blue | 2.00 | 1.65 |
| *a.* Imperf. | 1,000. | |
| **381** A84 28k olive brown | 10.00 | 5.75 |
| *a.* Perf. 10 | 40.00 | 35.00 |
| *Nos. 375-381 (7)* | 22.80 | 15.80 |

10th anniversary of October Revolution.
The paper of No. 375 has an overprint of pale yellow wavy lines.
No. 377b exists with watermark 170. Value, $1,000.

Worker — A85

Peasant — A86

Lenin — A87

**1927-28 Typo.** *Perf. 13½*

**Chalk Surfaced Paper**

| | | |
|---|---|---|
| **382** A85 1k orange | .30 | .20 |
| **383** A86 2k apple green | .30 | .20 |
| **385** A85 4k bright blue | .30 | .20 |
| **386** A86 5k brown | .30 | .20 |
| **388** A86 7k dark red ('28) | 1.75 | .75 |
| **389** A85 8k green | .90 | .20 |
| **391** A85 10k light brown | .90 | .20 |
| **392** A87 14k dark green ('28) | 1.25 | .30 |
| **393** A87 18k olive green | 1.25 | .30 |
| **394** A87 18k dark blue ('28) | 1.75 | .45 |
| **395** A86 20k dark gray green | 1.25 | .30 |
| **396** A85 40k rose red | 2.50 | .45 |
| **397** A86 50k bright blue | 3.00 | .85 |
| **399** A85 70k gray green | 3.50 | .85 |
| **400** A86 80k orange | 4.75 | 1.40 |
| *Nos. 382-400 (15)* | 24.00 | 6.85 |

The 1k, 2k and 10k exist imperf. Value, each $250.

Soldier and Kremlin — A88

Sailor and Flag — A89

Cavalryman A90

Aviator A91

**1928, Feb. 6**

**Chalk Surfaced Paper**

| | | |
|---|---|---|
| **402** A88 8k light brown | .85 | .35 |
| *a.* Imperf. | 250.00 | 200.00 |
| **403** A89 14k deep blue | 1.75 | .90 |
| **404** A90 18k carmine rose | 2.00 | 1.75 |
| *a.* Imperf. | 750.00 | |
| **405** A91 28k yellow green | 3.00 | 2.00 |
| *Nos. 402-405 (4)* | 7.60 | 5.00 |

10th anniversary of the Soviet Army.

**Lenin Types of 1925-26**

***Perf. 10, 10½***

**1928-29 Engr. Wmk. 169**

| | | |
|---|---|---|
| **406** A75 3r dark green ('29) | 7.00 | 2.00 |
| **407** A66 5r red brown | 8.00 | 2.50 |
| **408** A66 10r indigo | 15.00 | 4.50 |
| *Nos. 406-408 (3)* | 30.00 | 9.00 |

No. 406 exists imperf. Value, $500.

Bugler Sounding Assembly
A92 A93

***Perf. 12½x12***

**1929, Aug. 18 Photo. Wmk. 170**

| | | |
|---|---|---|
| **411** A92 10k olive brown | 10.00 | 5.00 |
| *a.* Perf. 10½ | 35.00 | 25.00 |
| *b.* Perf. 12½x12x10½x12 | 45.00 | 21.00 |
| **412** A93 14k slate | 6.50 | 2.00 |
| *a.* Perf. 12½x12x10½x12 | 75.00 | 45.00 |

First All-Soviet Assembly of Pioneers.

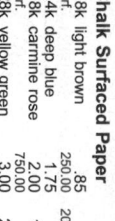

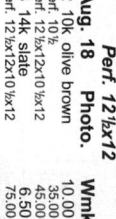

Factory Worker A95

Peasant A96

Farm Worker A97

Soldier A98

Worker, Soldier, Peasant A100

Worker A103

Lenin
A104

Peasant
A107

Factory
Worker
A109

Farm
Worker
A111

***Perf. 12x12½***

| | | | | |
|---|---|---|---|---|
| **1929-31** | **Typo.** | **Wmk. 170** | | |
| **413** A103 | 1k orange | | .20 | .20 |
| *a.* | Perf. 10½ | | 25.00 | 13.00 |
| *b.* | Perf. 14x14½ | | 50.00 | 35.00 |
| **414** A95 | 2k yellow green | | .20 | .20 |
| **415** A96 | 3k blue | | .20 | .20 |
| *a.* | Perf. 14x14½ | | 50.00 | 35.00 |
| **416** A97 | 4k claret | | .30 | .20 |
| **417** A98 | 5k orange brown | | .30 | .20 |
| *a.* | Perf. 10½ | | 75.00 | 75.00 |
| **418** A100 | 7k scarlet | | 1.10 | .90 |
| **419** A103 | 10k olive green | | .50 | .20 |
| *a.* | Perf. 10½ | | 27.50 | 22.50 |

**Unwmk.**

| | | | |
|---|---|---|---|
| **420** A104 | 14k indigo | 1.10 | 1.00 |
| *a.* | Perf. 10½ | 4.25 | 3.25 |

**Wmk. 170**

| | | | |
|---|---|---|---|
| **421** A100 | 15k dk ol grn ('30) | .85 | .25 |
| **422** A107 | 20k green | .85 | .25 |
| *a.* | Perf. 10½ | 50.00 | 27.50 |
| **423** A109 | 30k dk violet | 1.50 | .85 |
| **424** A111 | 50k dp brown | 2.00 | 1.75 |
| **425** A98 | 70k dk red ('30) | 2.10 | 1.90 |
| **426** A107 | 80k red brown ('31) | 2.00 | 1.90 |
| | *Nos. 413-426 (14)* | 13.20 | 10.00 |

Nos. 422, 423, 424 and 426 have a background of fine wavy lines in pale shades of the colors of the stamps.

See Nos. 456-466, 613A-619A. For surcharge see No. 743.

Symbolical of Industry
A112

Tractors Issuing from Assembly Line — A113

Iron Furnace (Inscription reads, "More Metal More Machines")
A114

Blast Furnace and Chart of Anticipated Iron Production
A115

| | | | |
|---|---|---|---|
| **1929-30** | | ***Perf. 12x12½*** | |
| **427** A112 | 5k orange brown | 1.75 | 1.50 |
| **428** A113 | 10k olive green | 1.75 | 2.00 |

***Perf. 12½x12***

| | | | |
|---|---|---|---|
| **429** A114 | 20k dull green | 4.00 | 3.50 |
| **430** A115 | 28k violet black | 2.50 | 2.25 |
| | *Nos. 427-430 (4)* | 10.00 | 9.25 |

Publicity for greater industrial production. No. 429 exists perf. 10½. Value, $800.

Red Cavalry in Polish Town after Battle
A116

Cavalry Charge
A117

Staff Officers of 1st Cavalry Army
A118

Plan of Action for 1st Cavalry Army — A119

| | | | |
|---|---|---|---|
| **1930, Feb.** | | ***Perf. 12x12½*** | |
| **431** A116 | 2k yellow green | 2.00 | 1.75 |
| **432** A117 | 5k light brown | 2.00 | 1.75 |
| **433** A118 | 10k olive gray | 3.75 | 2.75 |
| **434** A119 | 14k indigo & red | 1.60 | 1.75 |
| | *Nos. 431-434 (4)* | 9.35 | 8.00 |

1st Red Cavalry Army, 10th anniversary.

Students Preparing a Poster Newspaper
A120

| | | | |
|---|---|---|---|
| **1930, Aug. 15** | | | |
| **435** A120 | 10k olive green | 2.50 | 1.50 |

Educational Exhibition, Leningrad, 7/1-8/15/30.

Telegraph Office, Moscow
A121

Lenin Hydroelectric Power Station on Volkhov River
A122

| | | | |
|---|---|---|---|
| **1930** **Photo.** **Wmk. 169** | | ***Perf. 10½*** | |
| **436** A121 | 1r deep blue | 10.00 | 5.00 |

**Wmk. 170**

| | | | |
|---|---|---|---|
| **437** A122 | 3r yel green & blk brn | 11.50 | 6.00 |

See Nos. 467, 469.

Battleship Potemkin
A123

Inside Presnya Barricade
A124

Moscow Barricades in 1905 — A125

| | | | |
|---|---|---|---|
| **1930** **Typo.** | | ***Perf. 12x12½, 12½x12*** | |
| **438** A123 | 3k red | 1.40 | .55 |
| **439** A124 | 5k blue | 1.40 | .70 |
| **440** A125 | 10k dk green & red | 2.50 | 1.00 |
| | *Nos. 438-440 (3)* | 5.30 | 2.25 |
| **1931** | | ***Imperf.*** | |
| **452** A123 | 3k red | 5.00 | 1.75 |
| **453** A124 | 5k deep blue | 5.00 | 1.90 |
| **454** A125 | 10k dk green & red | 10.00 | 2.25 |
| | *Nos. 452-454 (3)* | 20.00 | 5.90 |
| | *Nos. 438-454 (6)* | 25.30 | 8.15 |

Revolution of 1905, 25th anniversary.

Types of 1929-31 Regular Issue

| | | | |
|---|---|---|---|
| **1931-32** | | ***Imperf.*** | |
| **456** A103 | 1k orange | 1.00 | 1.00 |
| **457** A95 | 2k yellow green | 1.00 | 1.25 |
| **458** A96 | 3k blue | 1.00 | 1.25 |
| **459** A97 | 4k claret | 22.50 | 12.50 |
| **460** A98 | 5k orange brown | 3.00 | 3.00 |
| **462** A103 | 10k olive green | 40.00 | 20.00 |
| **464** A100 | 15k dk olive green | 45.00 | 25.00 |
| **466** A109 | 30k dull violet | 70.00 | 35.00 |
| **467** A121 | 1r dark blue | 75.00 | 75.00 |
| | *Nos. 456-467 (9)* | 258.50 | 174.00 |

Nos. 459, 462-467 were sold only by the philatelic bureau.

**Type of 1930 Issue**

| | | | |
|---|---|---|---|
| **1931** **Wmk. 170** | | ***Perf. 12x12½*** | |
| **469** A121 | 1r dark blue | 2.00 | 1.00 |
| | Never hinged | 3.50 | |

Maxim Gorki — A133

| | | | |
|---|---|---|---|
| **1932-33** | | **Photo.** | |
| **470** A133 | 15k dark brown | 6.00 | 3.50 |
| *a.* | Imperf. | 125.00 | 125.00 |
| **471** A133 | 35k dp ultra ('33) | 15.00 | 11.00 |
| | Set, never hinged | 50.00 | |

40th anniversary of Gorki's literary activity.

Lenin Addressing the People
A134

Revolution in Petrograd (Leningrad)
A135

Dnieper Hydroelectric Power Station
A136

Asiatics Saluting the Soviet Flag — A139

Breaking Prison Bars — A140

Designs (dated 1917 1932): 15k, Collective farm. 20k, Magnitogorsk metallurgical plant in Urals. 30k, Radio tower and heads of 4 men.

| | | | |
|---|---|---|---|
| **1932-33** | | ***Perf. 12½x12; 12½ (30k)*** | |
| **472** A134 | 3k dark violet | 1.40 | .75 |
| **473** A135 | 5k dark brown | 1.40 | .75 |
| **474** A136 | 10k ultra | 3.25 | 1.40 |
| **475** A136 | 15k dark green | 2.00 | .85 |
| **476** A136 | 20k lake ('33) | 2.50 | 1.10 |
| **477** A136 | 30k dark gray ('33) | 50.00 | 15.00 |
| **478** A139 | 35k gray black | 75.00 | 57.50 |
| | *Nos. 472-478 (7)* | 135.55 | 77.35 |
| | Set, never hinged | 185.00 | |

October Revolution, 15th anniversary.

| | | | |
|---|---|---|---|
| **1932, Nov.** **Litho.** | | ***Perf. 12½x12*** | |
| **479** A140 | 50k dark red | 12.50 | 8.00 |
| | Never hinged | 25.00 | |

Intl. Revolutionaries' Aid Assoc., 10th anniv.

Trier, Birthplace of Marx — A141

Grave, Highgate Cemetery, London — A142

35k, Portrait & signature of Karl Marx (1818-83).

***Perf. 12x12½, 12½x12***

| | | | |
|---|---|---|---|
| **1933, Mar.** | | **Photo.** | |
| **480** A141 | 3k dull green | 3.50 | 1.25 |
| **481** A142 | 10k black brown | 5.50 | 2.50 |
| **482** A142 | 35k brown violet | 11.00 | 7.50 |
| | *Nos. 480-482 (3)* | 20.00 | 11.25 |
| | Set, never hinged | 50.00 | |

Fine Arts Museum, Moscow — A145

| | | | |
|---|---|---|---|
| **1932, Dec.** | | ***Perf. 12½*** | |
| **485** A145 | 15k black brown | 17.50 | 13.00 |
| **486** A145 | 35k ultra | 40.00 | 35.00 |
| *a.* | Perf. 10½ | 60.00 | 35.00 |
| | Set, never hinged | 150.00 | |

Moscow Philatelic Exhibition, 1932.

Nos. 485 and 486 were also issued in imperf. sheets of 4 containing 2 of each value, on thick paper for presentation purposes. They were not valid for postage. Replicas of the sheet were made for Moscow 97 by the Canadian Society of Russian Philately.

Nos. 485 and 486a Surcharged

## Peoples of the Soviet Union

**1933, Mar.**

| 487 | A145 | 30k on 15k black brn | 35.00 | 25.00 |
| 488 | A145 | 70k on 35k ultra | 65.00 | 35.00 |
| | | Set, never hinged | 200.00 | |

Leningrad Philatelic Exhibition, 1933.

**Perf. 10½**

**Perf. 12½**

Nientzians A155

Georgians A154

Abkhas A153

Chechens A152

Buryats — A151

Yakuts — A156

Crimean Tartars A148

Jews, Birobidzhan A149

Tungus A150

Lezghians A147

Kazaks A146

Bashkirs A165

Chuvashes A166

Koryaks A164

Byelorussians — A163

Uzbeks A162

Ukrainians — A161

Turkmen — A160

Transcaucasians — A159

Tadzhiks — A158

Great Russians — A157

# RUSSIA

**Perf. 12, 12x12½, 12½x12, 11x12, 12x11**

**1933, Apr. Photo.**

| 489 | A146 | 1k black brown | 2.00 | 1.00 |
| 490 | A147 | 2k ultra | 2.00 | 1.00 |
| 491 | A148 | 3k gray green | 2.00 | 1.00 |
| 492 | A149 | 4k gray black | 2.00 | 1.00 |
| 493 | A150 | 5k brown violet | 2.00 | 1.00 |
| 494 | A151 | 6k indigo | 1.00 | 1.00 |
| 495 | A152 | 7k black brown | 5.00 | 1.00 |
| 496 | A153 | 8k rose red | 5.00 | 1.00 |
| 497 | A154 | 9k ultra | 4.00 | 1.00 |
| 498 | A155 | 10k black brown | 4.00 | 3.00 |
| 499 | A156 | 14k olive green | 4.00 | 1.00 |
| 500 | A157 | 15k orange | 4.00 | 1.00 |
| 501 | A158 | 15k ultra | 5.00 | 1.00 |
| 502 | A159 | 15k dark brown | 5.00 | 1.00 |
| 503 | A160 | 15k black brown | 5.00 | 1.00 |
| 504 | A161 | 15k rose red | 5.25 | 1.00 |
| 505 | A162 | 15k violet brown | 4.75 | 1.00 |
| 506 | A163 | 15k gray black | 5.00 | 1.25 |
| 507 | A164 | 20k dull green | 13.00 | 3.00 |
| 508 | A165 | 30k brown violet | 27.50 | 5.00 |
| 509 | A166 | 35k black | 125.50 | 5.00 |
| | | Nos. 489-509 (21) | 250.00 | 35.00 |
| | | Set, never hinged | | |

3k, V. M. Volodarsky. 5k, M. S. Uritzky.

**1933, Oct.**    **Perf. 12x12½**

| 514 | A169 | 1k dull green | .90 | .55 |
| 515 | A169 | 3k blue black | 1.50 | .75 |
| 516 | A169 | 5k olive brown | 3.25 | .90 |
| | | Nos. 514-516 (3) | 5.65 | 2.20 |
| | | Set, never hinged | 30.00 | |

10th anniv. of the murder of Soviet Representative Vorovsky; 15th anniv. of the murder of the Revolutionists Volodarsky and Uritzky. See Nos. 531-532, 580-582.

V. V. Vorovsky A169

**1933, Nov. 17**    **Unwmk.**    **Perf. 14**

| 518 | A173 | 20k black, red & yellow | 1.75 | 1.50 |
| | | Never hinged | 30.00 | |

No. 518, perf. 9½, is a proof. Value $950.

Order of the Red Banner, 15th Anniv. — A173

**1933, Dec. 1**

| 519 | A174 | 4k brown | 12.00 | 2.00 |
| 520 | A175 | 5k dark gray | 12.00 | 2.00 |
| 521 | A176 | 20k purple | 8.00 | 2.00 |

Commissar Schaumyan A174

Commissar Prokofii A. Dzhaparidze A175

Commissars Awaiting Execution — A176

Designs: 35k, Monument to the 26 Commissars. 40k, Worker, peasant and soldier dipping flags in salute.

| 522 | A176 | 35k ultra | 35.00 | 7.75 |
| 523 | A176 | 40k carmine | 89.50 | 23.25 |
| | | Nos. 519-523 (5) | 22.50 | 9.50 |
| | | Set, never hinged | 185.00 | |

15th anniv. of the execution of 26 commissars at Baku. No. 521 exists imperf.

Lenin's Mausoleum A179

**1934, Feb. 7**    **Engr.**    **Perf. 14**

| 524 | A179 | 5k brown | 6.00 | .75 |
| a. | | Imperf. | 250.00 | 160.00 |
| 525 | A179 | 10k slate blue | 9.00 | 2.25 |
| a. | A179 | Imperf. | 160.00 | 140.00 |
| 526 | A179 | 15k dk carmine | 9.00 | 1.75 |
| 527 | A179 | 20k green | 13.50 | 1.75 |
| 528 | A179 | 35k dark brown | 46.50 | 2.75 |
| | | Nos. 524-528 (5) | 125.00 | 9.25 |
| | | Set, never hinged | 125.00 | |

10th anniversary of Lenin's death.

Ivan Fedorov A180

**1934, Mar. 5**

| 529 | A180 | 20k carmine rose | 12.50 | 3.50 |
| 530 | A180 | 40k indigo | 100.00 | 100.00 |
| | | Set, never hinged | 250.00 | |

350th anniv. of the death of Ivan Fedorov, founder of printing in Russia.

## Portrait Type of 1933

Designs: 10k, Yakov M. Sverdlov. 15k, Victor Pavlovich Nogin.

**1934, Mar.**    **Photo.**    **Wmk. 170**

| 531 | A169 | 10k ultra | 35.00 | 7.50 |
| 532 | A169 | 15k red | 40.00 | 12.50 |
| | | Imperf. | 150.00 | |
| | | Set, never hinged | | |

Deaths of Yakov M. Sverdlov, chairman of the All-Russian Central Executive Committee of the Soviets, 15th anniv.; Victor Pavlovich Nogin, chairman Russian State Textile Syndicate, 10th anniv.

Dmitri Ivanovich Mendeleev A185

A184

**1934, Sept. 15**    **Wmk. 170**    **Perf. 14**

| 536 | A184 | 5k emerald | 9.00 | 2.00 |
| 537 | A185 | 10k black brown | 21.00 | 3.75 |
| 538 | A185 | 15k vermilion | 18.00 | 3.50 |
| 539 | A184 | 20k ultra | 14.00 | 3.50 |
| | | Nos. 536-539 (4) | 62.00 | 12.75 |
| | | Set, never hinged | 150.00 | |

Prof. D. I. Mendeleev (1834-1907), chemist who discovered the Periodic Law of Classification of the Elements.

Imperfs. exist of 5k (value $400) and 15k (value $400).

## Lenin as Child and Youth A186

## Demonstration before Lenin Mausoleum — A190

Designs: 5k, Lenin in middle age. 10k, Lenin the orator. 30k, Lenin and Stalin.

**1934, Nov. 23    Unwmk.    Perf. 14**

| | | | | |
|---|---|---|---|---|
| 540 | A186 | 1k indigo & black | 5.00 | 1.50 |
| 541 | A187 | 3k indigo & black | 5.00 | 1.75 |
| 542 | A187 | 5k indigo & black | 9.50 | 2.50 |
| 543 | A187 | 10k indigo & black | 7.50 | 2.50 |
| 544 | A190 | 20k brn org & ultra | 17.50 | 5.00 |
| 545 | A190 | 30k brn org & car | 55.00 | 10.00 |
| | | Nos. 540-545 (6) | 99.50 | 23.25 |
| | | Set, never hinged | 200.00 | |

First decade without Lenin. See Nos. 931-935, 937.

## "Before War and Afterwards" A194

## Bombs Falling on City A192

Designs: 10k, Refugees from burning town. 20k, "Plowing with the sword." "Comradeship."

**1935, Jan. 1    Wmk. 170    Perf. 14**

| | | | | |
|---|---|---|---|---|
| 546 | A192 | 5k violet black | 7.50 | 5.00 |
| 547 | A192 | 10k ultra | 15.00 | 7.50 |
| 548 | A194 | 15k ultra | 17.50 | 7.50 |
| 549 | A194 | 20k dark brown | 15.00 | 7.50 |
| 550 | A194 | 35k dark brown | 60.00 | 15.00 |
| | | Nos. 546-550 (5) | 115.00 | 42.50 |
| | | Set, never hinged | 225.00 | |

Anti-war propaganda, the designs symbolize the horrors of modern warfare.

## Subway Tunnel A197

## Subway Station Cross Section A198

## Subway Station A199

## Train in Station — A200

**1935, Feb. 25    Wmk. 170    Perf. 14**

| | | | | |
|---|---|---|---|---|
| 551 | A197 | 5k orange | 11.00 | 2.00 |
| 552 | A198 | 10k dark ultra | 14.00 | 3.25 |
| 553 | A199 | 15k rose carmine | 52.50 | 12.00 |
| 554 | A200 | 20k emerald | 100.00 | 32.25 |
| | | Nos. 551-554 (4) | 250.00 | |
| | | Set, never hinged | | |

Completion of Moscow subway.

## Friedrich Engels (1820-1895), German Socialist and Collaborator of Marx — A201

**1935, May    Wmk. 170    Perf. 14**

| | | | | |
|---|---|---|---|---|
| 555 | A201 | 5k carmine | 15.00 | 1.25 |
| 556 | A201 | 10k dark green | 8.00 | 1.75 |
| 557 | A201 | 15k dark blue | 15.00 | 2.25 |
| 558 | A201 | 20k brown black | 12.00 | 3.50 |
| | | Nos. 555-558 (4) | 50.00 | 8.75 |
| | | Set, never hinged | 125.00 | |

## Running — A202

Designs: 2k, Diving. 3k, Rowing. 4k, Soccer. 5k, Skiing. 10k, Bicycling. 15k, Tennis. 20k, Skating. 35k, Hurdling. 40k, Parade of athletes.

**1935, Apr. 22    Unwmk.    Perf. 14**

| | | | | |
|---|---|---|---|---|
| 559 | A202 | 1k orange & ultra | 1.75 | .55 |
| 560 | A202 | 2k black & ultra | 2.25 | .55 |
| 561 | A202 | 3k grn & blk brn | 4.50 | 1.25 |
| 562 | A202 | 4k rose red & ultra | | |
| 563 | A202 | 5k pur & blk brn | 3.00 | .85 |
| 564 | A202 | 10k rose red & vio | 3.00 | .85 |
| 565 | A202 | 15k blk brn & blk brn | 11.50 | 3.00 |
| 566 | A202 | 20k blk brn & ultra | 22.50 | 5.00 |
| 567 | A202 | 35k ultra & blk brn | 19.00 | 5.00 |
| 568 | A202 | 40k brn blk & car | 27.50 | 9.00 |
| | | Nos. 559-568 (10) | 120.00 | 33.55 |
| | | Set, never hinged | | |

International Spartacist Games, Moscow. The games never took place.

## Silver Plate of Sassanian Dynasty A212

**1935, Sept. 10    Wmk. 170**

| | | | | |
|---|---|---|---|---|
| 569 | A212 | 5k orange red | 10.00 | 1.50 |
| 570 | A212 | 10k dk yellow green | 10.00 | 1.50 |

| | | | | |
|---|---|---|---|---|
| 571 | A212 | 15k dark violet | 11.00 | 2.50 |
| 572 | A212 | 35k black brown | 19.00 | 3.00 |
| | | Nos. 569-572 (4) | 50.00 | 8.50 |
| | | Set, never hinged | 150.00 | |

3rd International Exposition of Persian Art, Leningrad, Sept. 12-18, 1935.

## Mikhail Kalinin — A216

## Kalinin, the Worker — A213

Kalinin as: 5k, farmer. 10k, orator.

**1935, Nov. 20    Unwmk.    Perf. 14**

| | | | | |
|---|---|---|---|---|
| 573 | A213 | 3k rose lilac | 1.25 | .55 |
| 574 | A213 | 5k green | 1.25 | .55 |
| 575 | A213 | 10k blue slate | 1.40 | .80 |
| 576 | A216 | 20k brown black | 2.40 | 1.10 |
| | | Nos. 573-576 (4) | 6.30 | 3.00 |
| | | Set, never hinged | 25.00 | |

60th birthday of Mikhail Kalinin, chairman of the Central Executive Committee of the USSR. The 20k exists imperf. Value $110.

## Leo Tolstoy — A218

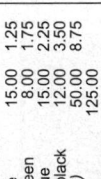

A217

Design: 20k, Statue of Tolstoy.

**1935, Dec. 4    Perf. 14**

| | | | | |
|---|---|---|---|---|
| 577 | A218 | 3k ol blk & vio | 1.00 | .75 |
| 578 | A218 | 10k vio blk & blk brn | 1.40 | .95 |
| 579 | A217 | 20k dk grn & blk brn | 5.50 | 3.00 |
| | | Nos. 577-579 (3) | 25.00 | 4.70 |

**Perf. 11**

| | | | | |
|---|---|---|---|---|
| 577a | A217 | 3k | 2.50 | .75 |
| 578a | A218 | 10k | 4.50 | 1.75 |
| 579a | A217 | 20k | 17.00 | 5.00 |
| | | Nos. 577a-579a (3) | | |

25th anniv. of the death of Count Leo N. Tolstoy (1828-1910).

## Portrait Type of 1933

Designs: 2k, Mikhail V. Frunze. 4k, N. E. Bauman. 40k, Sergei M. Kirov.

**1935, Nov.    Wmk. 170    Perf. 11**

| | | | | |
|---|---|---|---|---|
| 580 | A169 | 2k purple | 3.00 | 2.75 |
| 581 | A169 | 4k brown violet | 4.00 | 4.50 |
| 582 | A169 | 40k black brown | 8.00 | 6.50 |
| | | Nos. 580-582 (3) | 15.00 | 13.75 |
| | | Set, never hinged | | |

**Perf. 14**

| | | | | |
|---|---|---|---|---|
| 580a | A169 | 2k | 8.50 | .55 |
| 581a | A169 | 4k | 12.50 | .55 |
| 582a | A169 | 40k | 29.00 | 1.60 |
| | | Nos. 580a-582a (3) | 75.00 | 2.70 |

Death of three revolutionary heroes. Nos. 580-582 exist imperf, but were not regularly issued. Value, set $1,000.

## Pioneers Preventing Theft from Mailbox A223

Designs: 3k, 5k, Pioneers preventing destruction of property. 10k, Helping recover kite. 15k, Girl Pioneer saluting.

**1936, Apr.    Unwmk.    Perf. 14**

| | | | | |
|---|---|---|---|---|
| 583 | A223 | 1k yellow green | .65 | .35 |
| 584 | A223 | 2k copper red | 2.00 | .35 |
| 585 | A223 | 3k slate blue | 1.00 | .90 |
| 586 | A223 | 5k rose lake | .85 | .35 |
| 587 | A223 | 10k gray blue | 2.00 | 1.75 |
| 588 | A223 | 15k brown olive | 10.00 | 6.00 |
| | | Nos. 583-588 (6) | 16.50 | 9.70 |
| | | Set, never hinged | 50.00 | |

**Perf. 11**

| | | | |
|---|---|---|---|
| 583a | A223 | 1k | 1.25 | .55 |
| 584a | A223 | 2k | 1.25 | .55 |
| 585a | A223 | 3k | 3.50 | .75 |
| 586a | A223 | 5k | 1.50 | .75 |
| 587a | A223 | 10k | 15.00 | 1.75 |
| 588a | A223 | 15k | 29.40 | 2.00 |
| | | Nos. 583a-588a (6) | 60.00 | 7.10 |

## Nikolai A. Dobrolyubov, Writer and Critic, Birth Cent. — A227

**1936, Aug. 13    Typo.    Perf. 11½**

| | | | | |
|---|---|---|---|---|
| 589 | A227 | 10k rose lake | 3.00 | 1.75 |
| | | Never hinged | 6.00 | |
| a. | | Perf. 14 | 4.00 | 2.50 |
| | | Never hinged | 6.00 | |

## Aleksander Sergeyevich Pushkin — A228

## Statue of Pushkin, Moscow — A229

**1937, Feb. 1    Perf. 11 to 14 and Compound    Chalky or Ordinary Paper**

| | | | | |
|---|---|---|---|---|
| 590 | A228 | 10k yellow brown | .35 | .35 |
| 591 | A228 | 20k Prus green | .50 | .40 |
| 592 | A228 | 40k rose lake | .65 | .45 |
| 593 | A229 | 50k blue | 1.25 | .55 |
| 594 | A229 | 80k carmine rose | 1.90 | .75 |
| 595 | A229 | 1r green | 3.25 | 1.50 |
| | | Nos. 590-595 (6) | 7.90 | 4.00 |
| | | Set, never hinged | | |

**Souvenir Sheet    Imperf**

| | | | | |
|---|---|---|---|---|
| 596 | | Sheet of 2 | 9.00 | 125.00 |
| | | Never hinged | 15.00 | |
| a. | A228 | 10k brown | 2.50 | 12.50 |
| b. | A229 | 50k brown | 2.50 | 16.00 |

Pushkin (1799-1837), writer and poet.

## Tchaikovsky Concert Hall — A230

Designs: 5k, 15k, Telegraph Agency House. 10k, Tchaikovsky Concert Hall. 20k, 50k, Red Army Theater. 30k, Hotel Moscow. 40k, Palace of the Soviets.

## 1937, June — Unwmk. Photo. Perf. 12

| | | | | |
|---|---|---|---|---|
| 597 | A230 | 3k brown violet | 1.50 | .40 |
| 598 | A230 | 5k henna brown | 1.75 | .40 |
| 599 | A230 | 5k dark brown | 2.75 | .40 |
| 600 | A230 | 10k black | 3.50 | .40 |
| 601 | A230 | 15k dark brown | 1.50 | .90 |
| 601 | A230 | 20k olive green | 2.50 | .90 |
| 602 | A230 | 30k gray black | 21.50 | .90 |
| a. | | Perf. 11 | | |
| 603 | A230 | 40k dark violet | 3.00 | 1.25 |
| a. | | Souv. sheet of 4, imperf. | 12.50 | 37.50 |
| 604 | A230 | 50k gray black | 5.00 | 1.25 |
| | | Set, never hinged | 55.00 | 5.90 |

Nos. 597-601, 603-604 exist imperf. each $300.

First Congress of Soviet Architects. The 30k is watermarked Greek Border and Rosettes (170).

Feliks E. Dzerzhinski A235

## 1937, July 27 Typo. Perf. 12

| | | | | |
|---|---|---|---|---|
| 606 | A235 | 10k yellow brown | .75 | .25 |
| 607 | A235 | 20k Prus green | 1.50 | .50 |
| 608 | A235 | 40k rose lake | 2.25 | 1.00 |
| 609 | A235 | 80k carmine | 3.25 | 1.25 |
| | | Set, never hinged | 7.50 | 3.00 |

Nos. 606-609 (4)

Dzerzhinski, organizer of Soviet secret police, 10th death anniv. Exist imperf. Value, each $500.

Shota Rustaveli A236

## 1938, Feb. Unwmk. Photo.

| | | | | |
|---|---|---|---|---|
| 610 | A236 | 20k deep green | 1.00 | .50 |
| | | Never hinged | 3.00 | |

750th anniversary of the publication of the poem "Knight in the Tiger Skin," by Shota Rustaveli, Georgian poet. Exists imperf. Value, $500.

Statue Surmounting Pavilion A237

Soviet Pavilion at Paris Exposition A238

## 1938 Typo.

| | | | | |
|---|---|---|---|---|
| 611 | A237 | 5k red | .45 | .20 |
| | | Imperf. | | |
| 612 | A238 | 20k rose | .80 | .25 |
| 613 | A237 | 20k dark blue | 1.75 | .55 |
| | | Nos. 611-613 (3) | 3.00 | 1.00 |
| | | Set, never hinged | 10.00 | |

USSR participation in the 1937 International Exposition at Paris.

## Types of 1929-32 and Lenin Types of 1925-26

### 1937-52 Unwmk. Perf. 11½x12, 12

| | | | | |
|---|---|---|---|---|
| 613A | A103 | 1k dull org ('40) | 15.00 | 5.00 |
| 614 | A95 | 2k yel grn ('39) | 15.00 | 1.25 |
| 615 | A97 | 4k claret ('40) | 15.00 | 2.00 |
| 615A | A98 | 5k org brn ('46) | 100.00 | 15.00 |
| 616 | A109 | 10k blue ('39) | .50 | .30 |
| 616A | A103 | 10k olive ('40) | 100.00 | 20.00 |
| 616B | A109 | 10k black ('52) | .50 | .50 |
| 617 | A107 | 20k dull green | .50 | .35 |
| 617A | A107 | 20k dull green ('39) | 100.00 | 12.50 |
| 618 | A104 | 30k green ('39) | 15.00 | 4.50 |
| 619 | A109 | 40k indigo ('38) | 2.00 | .50 |
| 619A | A111 | 50k dp brn ('40) | | .50 |

### Engr.

| | | | | |
|---|---|---|---|---|
| 620 | A75 | 3r dk grn ('39) | 1.50 | .90 |
| 621 | A66 | 5r red brn ('39) | 2.00 | 1.25 |
| 622 | A66 | 10r indigo ('39) | 2.75 | 1.25 |
| | | Nos. 613A-622 (15) | 362.35 | 68.30 |
| | | Set, never hinged | 560.00 | |

#615-619 exist imperf but were not regularly issued.

Aviators Chkalov, Baidukov, Beliakov and Flight Route — A248

Infantryman A241

Soldier A242

Stalin Reviewing Cavalry A246

## 1938, Feb. 25 Litho. Perf. 12

| | | | | |
|---|---|---|---|---|
| 625 | A239 | 10k drab & black | 1.50 | .45 |
| 626 | A239 | 20k blue gray & blk | 1.60 | .65 |
| | | Set, never hinged | 5.35 | |

### Typo.

| | | | | |
|---|---|---|---|---|
| 627 | A240 | 40k dull green & blk | 5.00 | 2.50 |
| | | Imperf. | | |
| 628 | A240 | 80k rose car & car | 200.00 | |
| a. | | Imperf. | 90.00 | |
| | | Nos. 625-628 (4) | 10.00 | 5.35 |

Soviet flight to the North Pole.

Airplane Route from Moscow to North Pole — A239

Soviet Flag and Airplanes at North Pole — A240

## 1938, Apr. 10 Photo.

| | | | | |
|---|---|---|---|---|
| 636 | A248 | 10k black & red | | .60 |
| 637 | A248 | 20k brn blk & red | 1.75 | .90 |
| 638 | A248 | 40k dull violet & red | 2.50 | 2.00 |
| 639 | A248 | 50k brown vio & red | 4.50 | 2.00 |
| | | Set, never hinged | 10.00 | 5.50 |
| | | Nos. 636-639 (4) | 35.00 | |

639 exist imperf. Value $250 each.

First Trans-Polar flight, June 18-20, 1937, from Moscow to Vancouver, Wash. Nos. 636-639 exist imperf. Value, each $250.

## 1938, Apr. 13

| | | | | |
|---|---|---|---|---|
| 640 | A249 | 10k claret | 1.75 | .60 |
| 641 | A249 | 20k brown black | 2.00 | 1.25 |
| 642 | A249 | 50k dull violet | 2.25 | 1.50 |
| | | Set, never hinged | 6.00 | 3.35 |
| | | Nos. 640-642 (3) | 25.00 | |

First Trans-Polar flight, July 12-14, 1937, from Moscow to San Jacinto, Calif. Nos. 640-642 exist imperf. Value, each $500.

Aviators Gromov, Danilin, Yumashev, and Flight Route — A249

No. 616B was re-issued in 1954-56 in slightly smaller format, 14½x21mm, and in gray black. See note after No. 738.

Ivan Papanin and His Men Aboard Ice-breaker Yermak — A251

Arrival of the Rescuing Ice-breakers Taimyr and Murmansk A250

## 1938, June 21 Typo. Perf. 12, 12½

| | | | | |
|---|---|---|---|---|
| 643 | A250 | 10k violet brown | 1.25 | 1.00 |
| 644 | A250 | 20k dark blue | 2.25 | 1.25 |

### Photo.

| | | | | |
|---|---|---|---|---|
| 645 | A251 | 30k olive brown | 6.00 | 1.60 |
| 646 | A251 | 50k ultra | 16.50 | 6.10 |
| a. | | Imperf. | 300.00 | |
| | | Nos. 643-646 (4) | 50.00 | 2.25 |
| | | Set, never hinged | | |

Rescue of Papanin's North Pole Expedition.

## 1938, Mar. Unwmk. Photo. Perf. 12

| | | | | |
|---|---|---|---|---|
| 629 | A241 | 10k gray blk & dk red | .90 | .25 |
| 630 | A242 | 20k gray blk & dk red | 1.25 | .40 |
| 631 | A242 | 30k gray blk & dk red | 2.40 | .60 |
| 632 | A242 | 40k gray blk & dk red | 3.75 | 1.50 |
| 633 | A242 | 50k gray blk & dk red | 4.50 | 1.50 |
| 634 | A246 | 80k gray blk & dk red | 7.00 | 1.50 |

### Typo. Perf. 12x12½

| | | | | |
|---|---|---|---|---|
| 635 | A247 | 1r black & carmine | 2.00 | 1.50 |
| | | Nos. 629-635 (7) | 21.80 | 7.25 |
| | | Set, never hinged | 40.00 | |

No. 635 exists imperf. Value $500.

Designs: 30k, Sailor, 40k, Aviator, 50k, Antiaircraft soldier.

Chapayev and Boy — A247

Arms of USSR A253

Arms of Uzbek — A252

#650  #651

#654  #655  #656

Designs: Different arms on each stamp.

## 1937-38 Perf. 12, 12½ Unwmk. Typo.

| | | | | |
|---|---|---|---|---|
| 647 | A252 | 20k dp bl (Armenia) | 1.10 | .70 |
| 648 | A252 | 20k dull violet (Azerbaijan) | 1.10 | .70 |
| 649 | A252 | 20k brown orange (Byelorussia) | 7.00 | 5.00 |
| 650 | A252 | 20k carmine rose (Georgia) | | .95 |
| 651 | A252 | 20k bl grn (Kazakh) | 1.25 | .95 |
| 652 | A252 | 20k emer (Kirghiz) | 1.25 | .95 |
| 653 | A252 | 20k yel org (Uzbek) | 1.25 | .95 |
| 654 | A252 | 20k bl (R.S.F.S.R.) | 1.25 | .95 |
| 655 | A252 | 20k claret (Tadzhik) | 1.25 | .95 |
| 656 | A252 | 20k car (Turkmen) | 1.25 | .95 |
| 657 | A252 | 20k claret (Ukraine) | 1.25 | .95 |
| | | Set, never hinged | 22.20 | 17.00 |
| | | Nos. 647-658 (12) | 75.00 | |
| 658 | A253 | 40k brown red | 3.00 | 3.00 |

### Engr.

Constitution of USSR. No. 649 has inscriptions in Yiddish, Polish, Byelorussian and Russian. Issue dates: 40k, 1937. Others, 1938. See Nos. R41-R42.

Health Camp A267

Young Model Builders A268

Biology Lesson A266

Nurse Weighing Child — A264

Children at Lenin's Statue — A265

## 1938, Sept. 15 Unwmk. Perf. 12

| | | | | |
|---|---|---|---|---|
| 659 | A264 | 10k dk olive green | 2.50 | .65 |
| 660 | A265 | 15k dk olive green | 2.50 | 1.00 |
| 661 | A266 | 20k violet brown | 4.00 | 1.75 |
| 662 | A266 | 30k claret | 7.50 | 2.25 |
| 663 | A266 | 40k light brown | 7.50 | 3.00 |
| 664 | A268 | 50k deep blue | 12.00 | 3.00 |
| 665 | A268 | 80k deep blue | 50.00 | 12.65 |
| | | Nos. 659-665 (7) | 37.00 | |
| | | Set, never hinged | 50.00 | |

Child welfare.

View of Yalta A269

Crimean Shoreline — A272

Designs: No. 667, View along Crimean shore. No. 668, Georgian military highway. No, 670, View near Yalta. No. 671, "Swallows' Nest" Castle. 20k, Dzerzhinski Rest House for workers. 30k, Sunset in Crimea. 40k, Alupka. 50k, Gursuf. 80k, Crimean Gardens. 1r, "Swallows' Nest" Castle, horiz.

**Unwmk.**

| **1938, Sept. 21** | **Photo.** | ***Perf. 12*** | |
|---|---|---|---|
| **666** A269 | 5k brown | 1.50 | 1.25 |
| **667** A269 | 5k black brown | 1.50 | 1.25 |
| **668** A269 | 10k slate green | 2.25 | 1.25 |
| **669** A272 | 10k brown | 2.25 | 1.25 |
| **670** A269 | 15k black brown | 2.25 | 1.25 |
| **671** A272 | 15k black brown | 3.50 | 1.25 |
| **672** A269 | 20k dark brown | 4.00 | 1.25 |
| **673** A272 | 30k black brown | 4.00 | 1.75 |
| **674** A269 | 40k brown | 6.00 | 1.75 |
| **675** A272 | 50k slate green | 6.50 | 3.50 |
| **676** A269 | 80k brown | 9.00 | 3.50 |
| **677** A269 | 1r slate green | 15.00 | 5.50 |
| | *Nos. 666-677 (12)* | 57.75 | 24.75 |
| Set, never hinged | | 120.00 | |

Children Flying Model Plane A281

Glider A282

Captive Balloon — A283

Dirigible over Kremlin — A284

Parachute Jumpers — A285

Hydroplane A286

Balloon in Flight — A287

Balloon Ascent — A288

Four-motor Plane A289

**Unwmk.**

| **1938, Oct. 7** | **Typo.** | ***Perf. 12*** | |
|---|---|---|---|
| **678** A281 | 5k violet brown | 1.00 | .55 |
| **679** A282 | 10k olive gray | 1.00 | .55 |
| **680** A283 | 15k pink | 1.75 | .55 |
| **681** A284 | 20k deep blue | 1.75 | .55 |
| **682** A285 | 30k claret | 2.50 | .95 |
| **683** A286 | 40k deep blue | 3.00 | .95 |
| **684** A287 | 50k blue green | 6.25 | 1.40 |
| **685** A288 | 80k brown | 5.50 | 2.50 |
| **686** A289 | 1r blue green | 7.25 | 2.00 |
| | *Nos. 678-686 (9)* | 30.00 | 10.00 |
| Set, never hinged | | 75.00 | |

For overprints see Nos. C76-C76D.

Mayakovsky Station, Moscow Subway — A290

Sokol Terminal — A291

Kiev Station — A292

Dynamo Station A293

Train in Tunnel A294

Revolution Square Station A295

**Unwmk.**

| **1938, Nov. 7** | **Photo.** | ***Perf. 12*** | |
|---|---|---|---|
| **687** A290 | 10k deep red violet | 4.25 | .90 |
| **688** A291 | 15k dark brown | 4.25 | .90 |
| **689** A292 | 20k black brown | 4.25 | .90 |
| **690** A293 | 30k dark red violet | 4.25 | .90 |
| **691** A294 | 40k black brown | 4.25 | 1.40 |
| **692** A295 | 50k dark brown | 4.25 | 1.90 |
| | *Nos. 687-692 (6)* | 25.50 | 6.90 |
| Set, never hinged | | 50.00 | |

Second line of the Moscow subway opening.

Girl with Parachute A296

Young Miner A297

Harvesting A298

Designs: 50k, Students returning from school. 80k, Aviator and sailor.

| **1938, Dec. 7** | **Typo.** | ***Perf. 12*** | |
|---|---|---|---|
| **693** A296 | 20k deep blue | 2.00 | .60 |
| **694** A297 | 30k deep claret | 2.00 | .60 |
| **695** A298 | 40k violet brown | 2.50 | .60 |
| **696** A296 | 50k deep rose | 3.50 | 1.25 |
| **697** A298 | 80k deep blue | 10.00 | 2.10 |
| | *Nos. 693-697 (5)* | 20.00 | 5.15 |
| Set, never hinged | | 25.00 | |

20th anniv. of the Young Communist League (Komsomol).

Diving — A301

Discus Thrower — A302

Designs: 15k, Tennis. 20k, Acrobatic motorcyclists. 30k, Skier. 40k, Runners. 50k, Soccer. 80k, Physical culture.

**Unwmk.**

| **1938, Dec. 28** | **Photo.** | ***Perf. 12*** | |
|---|---|---|---|
| **698** A301 | 5k scarlet | 1.75 | .55 |
| **699** A302 | 10k black | 1.75 | .55 |
| **700** A302 | 15k brown | 2.00 | .55 |
| **701** A302 | 20k green | 2.00 | .90 |
| **702** A302 | 30k dull violet | 5.25 | 1.10 |
| **703** A302 | 40k deep green | 6.25 | 1.50 |
| **704** A302 | 50k blue | 5.25 | 1.50 |
| **705** A302 | 80k deep blue | 5.25 | 1.75 |
| | *Nos. 698-705 (8)* | 29.50 | 8.40 |
| Set, never hinged | | 90.00 | |

Gorki Street, Moscow — A309

Dynamo Subway Station A315

Foundryman A316

Moscow scenes: 20k, Council House & Hotel Moscow. 30k, Lenin Library. 40k, Crimea Bridge. 50k, Bridge over Moscow River. 80k, Khimki Station.

Paper with network as in parenthesis

| **1939, Mar.** | **Typo.** | ***Perf. 12*** | |
|---|---|---|---|
| **706** A309 | 10k brn *(red brown)* | .95 | .45 |
| **707** A309 | 20k dk sl grn *(lt blue)* | 1.10 | .45 |
| **708** A309 | 30k brn vio *(red brn)* | 1.10 | 1.00 |
| **709** A309 | 40k blue *(lt blue)* | 2.00 | 1.00 |
| **710** A309 | 50k rose lake *(red brn)* | 3.75 | 1.75 |
| **711** A309 | 80k gray ol *(lt blue)* | 4.00 | 1.75 |
| **712** A315 | 1r dk blue *(lt blue)* | 7.00 | 3.00 |
| | *Nos. 706-712 (7)* | 19.90 | 9.40 |
| Set, never hinged | | 75.00 | |

"New Moscow." On 30k, denomination is at upper right.

| **1939, Mar.** | | | |
|---|---|---|---|
| **713** A316 | 15k dark blue | 1.50 | .50 |
| | Never hinged | 2.00 | |
| ***a.*** | Imperf. | 300.00 | |
| | Never hinged | 500.00 | |

Statue on USSR Pavilion — A317

USSR Pavilion A318

| **1939, May** | | **Photo.** | |
|---|---|---|---|
| **714** A317 | 30k indigo & red | 1.75 | .35 |
| ***a.*** | Imperf. ('40) | 2.75 | .80 |
| **715** A318 | 50k blue & bister brn | 1.75 | .00 |
| ***a.*** | Imperf. ('40) | 2.75 | .90 |
| Set, never hinged | | 5.00 | |
| Set, imperf., never hinged | | 9.00 | |

Russia's participation in the NY World's Fair.

Paulina Osipenko A318a

Marina Raskova A318b

Design: 60k, Valentina Grizodubova.

| **1939, Mar.** | | | |
|---|---|---|---|
| **718** A318a | 15k green | 1.25 | .75 |
| **719** A318b | 30k brown violet | 1.25 | .75 |
| **720** A318b | 60k red | 2.75 | 1.50 |
| | *Nos. 718-720 (3)* | 5.25 | 3.00 |
| Set, never hinged | | 25.00 | |

Non-stop record flight from Moscow to the Far East.

Exist imperf. Value, each $350.

Shevchenko, Early Portrait — A319

Monument at Kharkov — A321

30k, Shevchenko portrait in later years.

**1939, Mar. 9**

| | | | | |
|---|---|---|---|---|
| 721 | A319 | 15k black brn & blk | 1.75 | .55 |
| 722 | A319 | 30k dark red & blk | 4.50 | 1.90 |
| 723 | A321 | 60k green & dk brn | 8.00 | 3.00 |
| | | Nos. 721-723 (3) | 22.50 | |
| | | Set, never hinged | | |

Taras G. Shevchenko (1814-1861), Ukrainian poet and painter.

**No. 416 Surcharged with New Value in Black**

**1939**  Wmk. 170

| | | | | |
|---|---|---|---|---|
| 743 | A97 | 30k on 4k claret | 10.00 | 8.00 |
| a. | | Unwmkd. | 100.00 | 30.00 |

**1939-43**  Unwmk.  Typo.  Perf. 12

| | | | | |
|---|---|---|---|---|
| 734 | A331 | 5k red | .20 | .20 |
| 735 | A332 | 15k dark green | .25 | .25 |
| 736 | A333 | 30k deep blue | .25 | .25 |
| 737 | A334 | 60k fawn ('43) | .60 | .25 |

**Photo.**

| | | | | |
|---|---|---|---|---|
| 738 | A335 | 60k rose carmine | .50 | .35 |
| | | Nos. 734-738 (5) | 1.80 | 1.30 |
| | | Set, never hinged | 3.00 | |

No. 734 was re-issued in 1954-56 in slightly smaller format: 14x21½mm, instead of 14¾x22½mm. Other values reissued in smaller format: 10k, 15k, 20k, 25k, 30k, 40k and 1r. (See notes following Nos. 622, 1260, 1347 and 1689.)

Arms of USSR A334
Worker-Soldier-Aviator A333

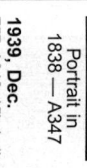

A331, A332, A335

**1939, Aug.**

| | | | | |
|---|---|---|---|---|
| 724 | A322 | 10k rose pink | .20 | |
| 725 | A323 | 15k red brown | .50 | .20 |
| 726 | A323 | 20k slate black | .50 | .20 |
| 727 | A323 | 30k purple | .50 | .20 |
| 728 | A323 | 30k red orange | .50 | .20 |
| 729 | A322 | 45k dark green | .75 | |
| 730 | A322 | 50k copper red | .75 | .80 |
| 731 | A322 | 60k bright purple | 1.40 | 1.10 |
| 732 | A322 | 80k dark violet | 1.40 | 1.10 |
| 733 | A322 | 1r dark blue | 3.00 | 1.40 |
| | | Nos. 724-733 (10) | 9.80 | 6.20 |
| | | Set, never hinged | 30.00 | |

Designs: 20k, Shepherd tending sheep. No. 727, Fair pavilion. No. 728, Fair emblem. 45k, Turkmen picking cotton. 50k, Drove of horses. 60k, Symbolizing agricultural wealth. 80k, Kolkhoz girl with sugar beets. 1r, Hunter with Polar foxes.

Soviet Agricultural Fair. A332

Milkmaid with Prize Cow — A322

Tractor-plow at Work on Abundant Harvest A323

**1939, Sept.**  Typo.  Unwmk.

| | | | | |
|---|---|---|---|---|
| 745 | A336 | 15k claret | .50 | .25 |
| 746 | A337 | 30k dark green | .75 | .50 |
| 747 | A336 | 45k olive gray | 1.25 | .50 |
| 748 | A337 | 60k dark blue | 1.75 | .75 |
| | | Nos. 745-748 (4) | 4.25 | 2.00 |
| | | Set, never hinged | 10.00 | |

Mikhail E. Saltykov (1826-89), writer & satirist who used pen name of N. Shchedrin.

M.E. Saltykov (N. Shchedrin) A336, A337

**1939, Nov.**  Photo.  Perf. 12

| | | | | |
|---|---|---|---|---|
| 749 | A338 | 5k dull brown | 1.10 | .20 |
| 750 | A338 | 10k carmine | 1.10 | .20 |
| 751 | A338 | 15k yellow green | 1.10 | .20 |
| 752 | A338 | 20k dk slate green | 1.10 | .25 |
| 753 | A338 | 30k bluish black | 2.50 | .40 |
| 754 | A338 | 50k gray black | 3.00 | .60 |
| 755 | A338 | 60k brown violet | 4.00 | .75 |
| 756 | A338 | 80k orange red | 15.00 | 2.80 |
| | | Nos. 749-756 (8) | 30.00 | |
| | | Set, never hinged | | |

Designs: 10k, 15k, Soviet Army sanatorium. 20k, Rest home, New Afyon. 30k, Clinical Institute. 50k, 80k, Sanatorium for workers in heavy industry. 60k, Rest home, Sukhumi.

Sanatorium of the State Bank — A338

Mikhail Y. Lermontov (1814-1841), Poet and Novelist, in 1837 — A346

Portrait in 1838 — A347
Portrait in 1841 — A348

**1939, Dec.**

| | | | | |
|---|---|---|---|---|
| 757 | A346 | 15k indigo & sepia | 1.50 | .35 |
| 758 | A347 | 30k dk grn & dull blk | 3.50 | .55 |
| 759 | A348 | 45k brick red & indigo | 10.00 | 2.10 |
| | | Nos. 757-759 (3) | 25.00 | 3.00 |
| | | Set, never hinged | | |

Nikolai Chernyshevski A349
Anton Chekhov A350

50th anniversary of the death of Nikolai Chernyshevski, scientist and critic.

**1939, Dec.**

| | | | | |
|---|---|---|---|---|
| 760 | A349 | 15k dark green | .60 | .25 |
| 761 | A349 | 30k dull violet | 1.25 | .45 |
| 762 | A349 | 60k Prus green | 5.00 | 1.15 |
| | | Nos. 760-762 (3) | 10.00 | |
| | | Set, never hinged | | |

**1940, Feb.**  Photo.  Unwmk.  Perf. 12

| | | | | |
|---|---|---|---|---|
| 763 | A350 | 10k dark yellow green | .60 | .25 |
| 764 | A350 | 15k ultra | 1.25 | .45 |
| 765 | A350 | 20k violet | 2.50 | .45 |
| 766 | A350 | 30k copper brown | 4.95 | 1.50 |
| | | Nos. 763-766 (4) | 10.00 | |
| | | Set, never hinged | | |

Chekhov (1860-1904), playwright.

**1940, Apr.**

| | | | | |
|---|---|---|---|---|
| 767 | A352 | 10k deep rose | 1.25 | .75 |
| 768 | A352 | 30k myrtle green | 1.25 | .75 |
| 769 | A352 | 50k gray black | 2.25 | 1.75 |
| 770 | A352 | 60k indigo | 3.00 | 3.00 |
| 771 | A352 | 1r red | 10.00 | 8.00 |
| | | Nos. 767-771 (5) | 20.00 | |
| | | Set, never hinged | | |

Designs: 30k, Villagers welcoming tank crew. 50k, 60k, Soldier giving newspapers to crowd. 1r, Crowd waving to tank column.

Welcome to Red Army by Western Ukraine and Western Byelorussia A352

Liberation of the people of Western Ukraine and Western Byelorussia.

Ice-breaker "Josef Stalin," Captain Beloussov and Chief Ivan Papanin A356

Vadygin and Papanin A358

Map of the Drift of the Sedov and Crew Members — A359

**1940, Apr.**

| | | | | |
|---|---|---|---|---|
| 772 | A356 | 15k dull yel green | 1.40 | .55 |
| 773 | A356 | 30k dull purple | 2.75 | .55 |
| 774 | A358 | 50k copper brown | 4.50 | 1.65 |
| 775 | A359 | 1r dark ultra | 10.90 | 3.30 |
| | | Nos. 772-775 (4) | 25.00 | |
| | | Set, never hinged | | |

Heroism of the Sedov crew which drifted in the Polar Basin for 812 days.

Design: 30k, Icebreaker Georgi Sedov, Captain Vadygin and First Mate Trofimov.

Vladimir V. Mayakovsky — A361

K.A. Timiryazev and Academy of Agricultural Sciences A362

In the Laboratory of Moscow University A363

Last Portrait A364

**1940, June**

| | | | | |
|---|---|---|---|---|
| 776 | A360 | 15k deep red | .30 | .20 |
| 777 | A360 | 30k copper brown | .55 | .25 |
| 778 | A361 | 60k dark gray blue | .60 | .35 |
| 779 | A361 | 80k bright ultra | 2.00 | .55 |
| | | Nos. 776-779 (4) | 5.00 | 1.15 |
| | | Set, never hinged | | |

Mayakovsky, poet (1893-1930).

**1940, June**

| | | | | |
|---|---|---|---|---|
| 780 | A362 | 10k indigo | .50 | .25 |
| 781 | A363 | 15k purple | .50 | .50 |
| 782 | A364 | 30k dk violet brown | 1.50 | .75 |
| 783 | A365 | 60k dark green | 3.00 | 2.00 |
| | | Nos. 780-783 (4) | 10.00 | 2.00 |
| | | Set, never hinged | | |

20th anniversary of the death of K. A. Timiryasev, scientist and professor of agricultural and biological sciences.

Monument in Moscow — A365

Relay Race — A366

Sportswomen Marching A367

Children's Sport Badge — A368

## 1940, July 21

Throwing the Grenade A370

Skier A369

| | | | | |
|---|---|---|---|---|
| 784 | A366 | 15k carmine rose | .75 | .30 |
| 785 | A367 | 30k sepia | 1.50 | .60 |
| 786 | A368 | 50k dk violet blue | 1.75 | .60 |
| 787 | A369 | 60k dk violet blue | 2.25 | .60 |
| 788 | A370 | 1r grayish green | 3.75 | 2.00 |

Nos. 784-788 (5) 10.00 3.80
Set, never hinged 30.00
2nd All-Union Physical Culture Day.

Tchaikovsky Museum at Klin A371

Tchaikovsky & Passage from his Fourth Symphony A372

Peter Ilich Tchaikovsky and Excerpt from Eugene Onegin — A373

## 1940, Aug.   Unwmk.   Typo.   Perf. 12

| | | | | |
|---|---|---|---|---|
| 789 | A371 | 15k Prus green | 1.90 | .75 |
| 790 | A372 | 20k brown | 1.90 | .75 |
| 791 | A372 | 30k dark blue | 1.90 | .75 |
| 792 | A371 | 50k rose lake | 2.40 | 1.75 |
| 793 | A373 | 60k red | 10.00 | 5.00 |

Nos. 789-793 (5) 25.00
Set, never hinged
Tchaikovsky (1840-1893), composer.

павильон грузинской ССР #801

павильон армянской ССР #802

у входа в павильон узбекской ССР #803

павильон туркменской ССР #804

павильон таджикской ССР #805

павильон киргизской ССР #806

павильон казахской ССР #807

павильон карело-финской ССР #808

## 1940, Oct.   Photo.

| | | | | |
|---|---|---|---|---|
| 794 | A374 | 10k shown | 1.25 | .50 |
| 795 | A374 | 15k Far East Provinces | | .50 |
| 796 | A376 | 30k Central Regions shown | 1.25 | .70 |
| 797 | A376 | 30k Ukrainian | 1.25 | .70 |
| 798 | A376 | 30k Byelorussian | 1.25 | .70 |
| 799 | A376 | 30k Azerbaijan | 1.25 | .70 |
| 800 | A374 | 30k Georgian | 1.25 | .70 |
| 801 | A376 | 30k Armenian | 1.25 | .70 |
| 802 | A376 | 30k Uzbek | 1.25 | .70 |
| 803 | A376 | 30k Turkmen | 1.25 | .70 |
| 804 | A374 | 30k Tadzhik | 1.25 | .70 |
| 805 | A376 | 30k Kirghiz | 1.25 | .70 |
| 806 | A376 | 30k Kazakh | 1.75 | 1.40 |
| 807 | A376 | 30k Karelian Finnish | 1.75 | 1.40 |
| 808 | A376 | 50k Main building | 1.75 | 1.40 |
| 809 | A376 | 50k Mechanization | 2.40 | 1.40 |
| 810 | A376 | 60k Pavilion, Stalin statue | 2.75 | 1.40 |

Nos. 794-810 (17) 25.40 15.00
Set, never hinged 75.00
All-Union Agricultural Fair.
Nos. 796-808 printed in three sheet formats with various vertical and horizontal se-tenant combinations.

Blast Furnace — A398

Coal Miners — A397

Bridge over Moscow-Volga Canal — A399

Three New Type Locomotives A400

Workers on a Collective Farm — A401

Automobiles and Planes A402

Oil Derricks — A403

## 1941, Jan.   Perf. 12

| | | | | |
|---|---|---|---|---|
| 817 | A397 | 10k deep blue | 65 | 20 |
| 818 | A398 | 15k dark violet | 65 | 20 |
| 819 | A399 | 20k deep blue | 65 | 20 |
| 820 | A400 | 30k dark brown | 85 | 20 |
| 821 | A401 | 50k olive brown | 85 | 40 |
| 822 | A402 | 60k olive brown | 1.10 | 55 |
| 823 | A403 | 1r dark blue green | 2.25 | 80 |

Nos. 817-823 (7) 7.00 2.55
Set, never hinged 17.50
Soviet industries.

Sailor — A405

Troops on Skis — A404

Soldiers with Cannon A406

20k, Cavalry. 30k, Machine gunners. 45k, Army horseman. 50k, Aviator. 1r, 3r, Marshal's Star.

Battle of Ismail — A412

Field Marshal Aleksandr Suvorov — A413

## 1941-43

| | | | | |
|---|---|---|---|---|
| 824 | A404 | 5k dark violet | .50 | .20 |
| 825 | A405 | 10k deep blue | .50 | .20 |
| 826 | A406 | 15k brt yellow green | .50 | .20 |
| 827 | A404 | 20k vermilion | .20 | .20 |
| 828 | A404 | 30k dull brown | .20 | .20 |
| 829 | A406 | 45k gray green | .60 | .50 |
| 830 | A404 | 50k dull blue | .40 | .20 |
| 831 | A404 | 1r dull blue green | .50 | .75 |
| 831A | A404 | 3r myrtle grn ('43) | 1.90 | 1.75 |

Nos. 824-831A (9) 5.00 4.70
Set, never hinged 17.50
Army & Navy of the USSR, 23rd anniv.

## 1941   Unwmk.

| | | | | |
|---|---|---|---|---|
| 832 | A412 | 10k dark green | .40 | .35 |
| 833 | A412 | 15k carmine rose | .55 | .55 |
| 834 | A413 | 30k blue black | .80 | .60 |
| 835 | A413 | 1r olive brown | 2.25 | 1.50 |

Nos. 832-835 (4) 4.00 3.00
Set, never hinged 10.00
150th anniversary of the capture of the Turkish fortress, Ismail.

Kirghiz Horse Breeder A414

Kirghiz Miner — A415

## 1941, Mar.   Perf. 12

| | | | | |
|---|---|---|---|---|
| 836 | A414 | 15k dull brown | 1.50 | .45 |
| 837 | A415 | 30k dull purple | 2.00 | .60 |

Set, never hinged 5.25
15th anniversary of the Kirghizian Soviet Socialist Republic.

Prof. N. E. Zhukovski A416

Zhukovski Lecturing A418

Military Air Academy A417

## 1941, Mar.

| | | | | |
|---|---|---|---|---|
| 838 | A416 | 15k deep blue | .75 | .35 |
| 839 | A417 | 30k carmine rose | .75 | .65 |
| 840 | A418 | 50k brown violet | 1.50 | 1.00 |

Nos. 838-840 (3) 3.00 2.00
Set, never hinged 7.50
Prof. Zhukovski, scientist (1847-1921).

**Arms Type of 1938**

Karelian-Finnish Soviet Socialist Republic.

Map of War Operations and M. V. Frunze — A393

Monument to Red Army Heroes — A391

Heroic Crossing of the Sivash A394

## 1940

| | | | | |
|---|---|---|---|---|
| 811 | A391 | 10k dark green | .75 | .30 |
| 812 | A391 | 15k orange ver | .75 | .30 |
| 813 | A393 | 30k dull brown & car | .75 | .50 |
| 814 | A394 | 50k violet brm | .75 | .50 |
| 815 | A394 | 60k indigo | .75 | .75 |
| 816 | A391 | 1r gray black | 1.25 | .75 |

Nos. 811-816 (6) 5.00 2.90
Set, never hinged 10.00
20th anniversary of battle of Perekop. Also issued perf. 12. Set price about 25% more.

*Imperf.*

Designs: 15k, Grenade thrower. 60k, Frunze's headquarters, Stroganovka. 1r, Victorious soldier.

Northeast Provinces Pavilion — A376

Volga Provinces Pavilion A374

павильон московской, рязанской и тульской обл. #797

павильон украинской ССР #798

павильон белорусской ССР #799

павильон азербайджанской ССР #800

**1941, Mar.**
| | | | |
|---|---|---|---|
| 841 | A252 | 30k rose | .60 | .40 |
| 842 | A252 | 45k dark blue green | .90 | .65 |

Set, never hinged 2.50

1st anniversary of the Karelian-Finnish Soviet Socialist Republic.

Kremlin and Moscow River — A421

Spasski Tower, Kremlin — A420

**1941, May** **Typo.** **Unwmk.**
| | | | |
|---|---|---|---|
| 843 | A420 | 1r dull red | .75 | .50 |
| 844 | A421 | 2r brown orange | 1.25 | 1.00 |

Set, never hinged 2.75

"Suvorov's March through the Alps, 1799" A422

Vasili Ivanovich Surikov, Self-portrait A424

"Stepan Rasin on the Volga" A423

**1941, June** **Photo.** **Perf. 12**
| | | | |
|---|---|---|---|
| 845 | A422 | 20k black | 1.25 | .60 |
| 846 | A423 | 30k scarlet | 2.25 | 1.10 |
| 847 | A422 | 50k dk violet brown | 7.50 | 4.00 |
| 848 | A424 | 1r gray green | 16.00 | 5.00 |
| 849 | A424 | 2r brown | 36.00 | 16.20 |

Set, never hinged 65.00

Nos. 845-849 (5)

Surikov (1848-1916), painter.

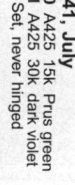

Mikhail Y. Lermontov, Poet, Death Centenary — A425

**1941, July**
| | | | |
|---|---|---|---|
| 850 | A425 | 15k Prus green | 9.00 | 4.00 |
| 851 | A425 | 30k dark violet | 11.00 | 6.00 |

Set, never hinged 40.00

Visitors in Lenin Museum A426

Lenin Museum A427

---

**1941-42**
| | | | |
|---|---|---|---|
| 852 | A426 | 30k dark violet ('42) | 2.00 | 4.00 |
| 853 | A427 | 45k dark violet ('42) | 8.25 | 8.00 |
| 854 | A426 | 1r Prus green | 3.75 | 4.50 |
| 855 | A427 | 1r orange brn ('42) | 11.00 | 8.00 |

Set, never hinged 65.00

Nos. 852-855 (4) 25.00 24.50

Fifth anniversary of Lenin Museum.

Mother's Farewell to a Soldier Son ("Be a Hero!") — A428

**1941, Aug.**
| | | | |
|---|---|---|---|
| 856 | A428 | 30k carmine | 12.50 | 12.50 |

Never hinged 25.00

Alisher Navoi — A429

People's Militia — A430

**1942, Jan.**
| | | | |
|---|---|---|---|
| 857 | A429 | 30k brown | 20.00 | 6.00 |
| 85B | A429 | 1r dark violet | 10.00 | 9.00 |

Set, never hinged 55.00

Alisher Navoi, Uzbekian poet, 500th birth anniv.

Junior Lieutenant Talalikhin Ramming German Plane in Midair A431

Captain Gastello and Burning Plane Diving into Enemy Gasoline Tanks A432

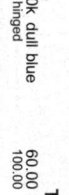

**1941, Dec.** **Typo.**
| | | | |
|---|---|---|---|
| 859 | A430 | 30k dull blue | 60.00 | 40.00 |

Never hinged 100.00

Major General Dovator and Cossack Cavalry in Action A433

Shura Chekalin Fighting Nazi Soldiers A434

---

Nazi Soldiers Leading Zoya Kosmodemjanskaja to her Death — A435

**1942-44** **Unwmk.** **Photo.** **Perf. 12**
| | | | |
|---|---|---|---|
| 860 | A431 | 20k bluish black | 1.25 | .45 |
| 860A | A431 | 30k Prus grn ('44) | 1.25 | .45 |
| 861 | A432 | 30k bluish black | 1.25 | .45 |
| 861A | A431 | 30k dp ultra ('44) | 1.25 | .45 |
| 862 | A433 | 30k black | 1.25 | .45 |
| 863 | A434 | 30k black | 1.25 | .45 |
| 863A | A434 | 30k brt yel green ('44) | 1.25 | .45 |
| 864 | A435 | 30k black | 1.25 | .45 |
| 864A | A435 | 30k rose vio ('44) | 1.25 | .45 |
| 865 | A434 | 1r slate green | 5.50 | 3.00 |
| 865A | A435 | 2r slate green | 9.00 | 4.50 |
| 866 | A435 | 2r slate green | 25.75 | 11.55 |

Set, never hinged 40.00

Nos. 860-866 (11)

Issued to honor Soviet heroes.

For surcharges see Nos. C80-C81.

Anti-tank Artillery A436

Signal Corps in Action A437

Guerrilla Fighters A438

Defense of Leningrad A440

War Worker A439

**1942-43**
| | | | |
|---|---|---|---|
| 867 | A436 | 20k black | .40 | .60 |
| 868 | A437 | 30k black | .40 | .80 |
| 869 | A438 | 30k sapphire | .70 | .80 |
| 870 | A439 | 30k Prus green ('43) | .70 | .80 |
| 871 | A440 | 60k blue black | 1.90 | 2.75 |
| 872 | A441 | 1r black brown | 3.25 | 4.25 |

Set, never hinged 15.00

Nos. 867-872 (6) 7.65 10.00

Red Army Scouts A441

Women Workers and Soldiers A442

---

Flaming Tank A443

Sewing Equipment for Red Army — A445

**1942-43** **Typo. Unwmk.**
| | | | |
|---|---|---|---|
| 873 | A442 | 20k dark blue | 1.75 | 1.00 |
| 874 | A443 | 20k dull rose violet | .75 | .50 |
| 875 | A444 | 20k brown violet ('43) | 1.00 | .60 |
| 876 | A445 | 45k dull rose red | 1.75 | 1.00 |
| 877 | A446 | 45k deep dull blue | 6.00 | 3.60 |

Set, never hinged 13.50

Nos. 873-877 (5) ('43)

Anti-Aircraft Battery in Action — A446

Women Preparing Food Shipments A444

Manufacturing Explosives — A447

**1943, Jan.** **Photo.** **Perf. 12**
Inscribed: "1917 XXV 1942"
| | | | |
|---|---|---|---|
| 878 | A447 | 5k black | .40 | .40 |
| 879 | A447 | 10k black brown | .40 | .40 |
| 880 | A447 | 15k black brown | .40 | .40 |
| 881 | A447 | 15k blue black | .55 | .40 |
| 882 | A447 | 20k black brown | .55 | .40 |
| 883 | A447 | 30k black brown | 1.25 | .50 |
| 884 | A447 | 60k black brown | 1.50 | .50 |
| 885 | A447 | 1r dull red brown | 4.50 | 1.75 |

Nos. 878-885 (8) 10.00 2.75

25th anniversary of October Revolution.

Designs: 10k, Agriculture. 15k, Group of Fighters. 20k, Storming the Palace. 30k, Lenin and Stalin. 60k, Tanks. 1r, Lenin. 2r, Revolution scene.

Mount St. Elias, Alaska A455

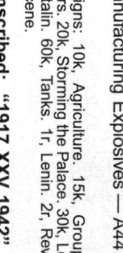

Bering Sea and Bering's Ship — A456

**1943, Apr.**
| | | | |
|---|---|---|---|
| 886 | A455 | 30k chalky blue | .60 | .30 |
| 887 | A455 | 60k Prus green | 1.00 | .30 |
| 888 | A455 | 1r yellow green | 1.90 | .30 |
| 889 | A456 | 2r bister brown | 3.50 | .75 |

Set, never hinged 7.00 1.00

Nos. 886-889 (4) 15.00 1.65

200th anniv. of the death of Vitus Bering, explorer (1681-1741).

## Bottom tier (1943, July etc.)

Medical Corpsmen and Wounded Soldier A457

Trench Mortar A458

Army Scouts A459

Repulsing Enemy Tanks A460

Snipers A461

**1943**
| | | | | | |
|---|---|---|---|---|---|
| 890 | A457 | 30k | myrtle green | .65 | .55 |
| 891 | A458 | 30k | brown bister | .65 | .55 |
| 892 | A459 | 30k | myrtle green | .70 | .55 |
| 893 | A460 | 60k | myrtle green | 2.00 | 1.90 |
| 894 | A461 | 60k | chalky blue | 2.00 | 1.90 |
| | | Nos. 890-894 (4) | | 12.50 | 5.45 |

Set, never hinged

Maxim Gorki (1868-1936), Writer A462

**1943, June**
| | | | | | |
|---|---|---|---|---|---|
| 895 | A462 | 30k | green | .35 | .20 |
| 896 | A462 | 60k | slate black | .45 | .30 |
| | | | | | 2.00 |

Set, never hinged

Order of Field Marshal Suvorov A464

Patriotic War Medal A463

**Engr.**
**1943, July**
| | | | | | |
|---|---|---|---|---|---|
| 897 | A463 | 1r | black | 1.00 | 1.00 |
| 898 | A464 | 10r | dk olive green | 4.00 | 4.00 |
| | | | | | 7.50 |

Set, never hinged

Sailors A465

Designs: 30k, Navy gunner and warship. 60k, Soldiers and tank.

## Middle-lower tier (1943, Oct. etc.)

**Photo.**
| | | | | | |
|---|---|---|---|---|---|
| | | | | .20 | .20 |
| | | | | .20 | .20 |
| | | | | .40 | .20 |
| | | | | 1.20 | .50 |
| | | | | 2.00 | 1.10 |
| | | | | | 4.00 |

**1943, Oct.**
| | | | |
|---|---|---|---|
| 899 | A465 | 20k | golden brown |
| 900 | A465 | 30k | dark myrtle green |
| 901 | A465 | 60k | brt yellow green |
| 902 | A465 | 3r | chalky blue |
| | | Nos. 899-902 (4) | |

Set, never hinged
25th anniv. of the Red Army and Navy.

Vladimir V. Mayakovsky A469

Karl Marx A468

**1943, Sept.**
| | | | | | |
|---|---|---|---|---|---|
| 903 | A468 | 30k | blue black | .40 | .25 |
| 904 | A468 | 60k | dk slate green | .60 | .25 |
| | | | | | 2.25 |

Set, never hinged
125th anniv. of the birth of Karl Marx.

**1943, Oct.**
| | | | | | |
|---|---|---|---|---|---|
| 905 | A469 | 30k | red orange | .40 | .25 |
| 906 | A469 | 60k | deep blue | .60 | .25 |
| | | | | | 2.00 |

Set, never hinged
Mayakovsky, poet, 50th birth anniv.

Flags of US, Britain, and USSR A470

Ivan Turgenev (1818-83), Poet — A471

**1943, Nov.**
| | | | | | |
|---|---|---|---|---|---|
| 907 | A470 | 30k | blk, dp red & dk bl | .40 | .30 |
| 908 | A470 | 3r | sl blue, red & lt blue | 2.60 | .05 |
| | | | | | 6.00 |

Set, never hinged
The Tehran conference.

Map of Stalingrad A472

Harbor of Sevastopol and Statue of Lenin A473

Leningrad A474

**1943, Oct.**
| | | | | | |
|---|---|---|---|---|---|
| 909 | A471 | 30k | myrtle green | 8.00 | 4.50 |
| 910 | A471 | 60k | dull purple | 12.00 | 5.50 |
| | | | | | 50.00 |

Set, never hinged

## Middle-upper tier (1944)

Odessa A475

**Perf. 12**
| | | |
|---|---|---|
| | .20 | .20 |

**1944, Mar.**
| | | | | | |
|---|---|---|---|---|---|
| 911 | A472 | 30k | dull brown & car | .35 | .20 |
| 912 | A473 | 30k | dark blue | .35 | .20 |
| 913 | A474 | 30k | dk slate green | .35 | .20 |
| 914 | A475 | 30k | yel green | .35 | .20 |
| | | Nos. 911-914 (4) | | 1.40 | .80 |
| | | | | | 3.00 |

Set, never hinged

Honoring the defenders of Stalingrad, Leningrad, Sevastopol and Odessa. See No. 959.
No. 911 measures 33x22mm and also exists in smaller size: 32x21½mm.

USSR War Heroes A476

**1944, Apr.**
915 A476 30k deep ultra .35 .25 / 1.00
Never hinged

Tanks — A478

Sailor Loading Gun — A477

Infantryman A480

Soldier Bayoneting a Nazi A479

Soldier Throwing Hand Grenade — A481

**Photo.**
**1943-44**
| | | | | | |
|---|---|---|---|---|---|
| 916 | A477 | 15k | deep ultra | .20 | .20 |
| 917 | A478 | 20k | red orange ('44) | .20 | .20 |
| 918 | A479 | 30k | dull brm & dk red ('44) | .25 | .20 |
| 919 | A480 | 1r | brt yel green ('44) | .85 | 1.00 |
| 920 | A481 | 2r | Prus green ('44) | 1.60 | 2.00 |
| | | Nos. 916-920 (5) | | 3.10 | 7.00 |

Set, never hinged
25th anniversary of the Young Communist League (Komsomol).

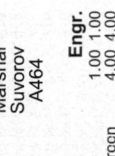
Flags of US, USSR, Great Britain — A482

## Top tier (1944, May 30 / June)

**Perf. 12 Unwmk.**
| | |
|---|---|
| .50 | .30 |
| 2.75 | 1.10 |
| | 5.00 |

**1944, May 30 Unwmk.**
| | | | | | |
|---|---|---|---|---|---|
| 921 | A482 | 60k | black, red & blue | | |
| 922 | A482 | 3r | dk bl, red & lt bl | | |

Set, never hinged
Day of the Nations United Against Germany, June 14, 1944.

Order of Prince Alexander Nevsky — A484

Order of Field Marshal Kutuzov — A486

Patriotic War Order — A483

Order of Field Marshal Suvorov — A485

**Paper with network as in parenthesis**

**Typo. Perf. 12, Imperf.**
**1944**
| | | | | | |
|---|---|---|---|---|---|
| 923 | A483 | 15k | dull red (rose) | .20 | .20 |
| 924 | A484 | 20k | blue (lt blue) | .20 | .20 |
| 925 | A485 | 30k | green (green) | .45 | .40 |
| 926 | A486 | 60k | dull red (rose) | .65 | 1.00 |
| | | Nos. 923-926 (4) | | 1.50 | 3.00 |

Set, never hinged
Beware of bogus perforation "errors" created from imperfs.

Order of Prince Alexander Nevski — A488

Order of Patriotic War — A487

Order of Field Marshal Suvorov A490

Order of Field Marshal Kutuzov A489

**Perf. 12 Engr. Unwmk.**
**1944, June**
| | | | | | |
|---|---|---|---|---|---|
| 927 | A487 | 1r | black | .25 | .25 |
| 928 | A488 | 3r | blue black | .55 | .45 |
| 929 | A489 | 5r | dark olive green | .95 | .60 |
| 930 | A490 | 10r | dark red | 1.60 | .75 |
| | | Nos. 927-930 (4) | | 3.35 | 2.00 |
| | | | | | 8.00 |

Set, never hinged

**Types of 1934, Inscribed 1924-1944 and**

Lenin's Mausoleum — A491

middle age. 60k, Lenin, the orator.

30k (#931); 3r, Lenin & Stalin. 50k, Lenin in

**Photo.**

| 931 | A190 | 30k orange & car | .20 | .20 |
| 932 | A186 | 30k slate & black | .20 | .20 |
| 933 | A187 | 45k slate & black | .25 | .25 |
| 934 | A187 | 50k slate & black | .35 | .25 |
| 935 | A491 | 60k slate & black | .90 | .35 |
| 936 | A491 | 1r indigo & brn blk | 2.00 | .75 |
| 937 | A190 | 3r bl blk & dull org | 4.35 | 2.25 |

Set, never hinged 7.50

Nos. 931-937 (7)

20 years without Lenin.

Nikolai Rimski-Korsakov
A492

**1944, June** Perf. 12, Imperf.

| 938 | A492 | 30k gray black | .20 | .20 |
| 939 | A493 | 60k slate green | .25 | .25 |
| 940 | A492 | 1r brt blue green | .55 | .30 |
| 941 | A493 | 3r purple | 1.25 | .40 |

Set, never hinged 3.50 1.15

Nos. 938-941 (4)

Rimski-Korsakov (1844-1909)), composer.

N.A. Schors
A494

Sergei A.
Chaplygin
A497

**1944, Sept.** Perf. 12

| 942 | A494 | 30k gray black | .35 | .35 |
| 943 | A494 | 30k dark slate green | .35 | .20 |
| 944 | A494 | 30k brt yellow green | 1.05 | .60 |

Set, never hinged 2.10

See Nos. 1209-1211, 1403.

Nos. 942-944 (3)

Heroes of the 1918 Civil War: No. 943, V.I. Chapayev. No. 944, S.G. Lazho.

Khanpasha
Nuradilov
A498

**1944, Sept.**

| 945 | A497 | 30k gray | .25 | .25 |
| 946 | A497 | 1r lt brown | .85 | .50 |

Set, never hinged 2.50

75th anniversary of the birth of Sergei A. Chaplygin, scientist and mathematician.

A. Matrosov
A499

---

Ilya E.
Repin — A503

Ivan A.
Krylov — A505

**1944, July**

| 947 | A498 | 30k slate green | .20 | .20 |
| 948 | A499 | 60k dull purple | .40 | .25 |
| 949 | A500 | 60k dull blue | .40 | .25 |
| 950 | A501 | 60k bright green | .60 | .25 |
| 951 | A502 | 60k slate black | 1.20 | .30 |

Set, never hinged 2.00 1.20

Nos. 947-951 (5)

Soviet war heroes.

"Cossacks'
Reply to
Sultan
Mohammed
IV" — A504

**1944, Nov.** Perf. 12½, Imperf.

| 952 | A503 | 30k slate green | .25 | .20 |
| 953 | A504 | 50k dk blue green | .45 | .20 |
| 954 | A504 | 60k chalky blue | .45 | .20 |
| 955 | A503 | 1r dk orange brown | .60 | .20 |
| 956 | A504 | 2r dark purple | 1.25 | .30 |

Set, never hinged 5.00 1.10

Nos. 952-956 (5)

I. E. Repin (1844-1930), painter.

**1944, Nov.** Perf. 12

| 957 | A505 | 30k yellow brown | .20 | .20 |
| 958 | A505 | 1r dk violet blue | .85 | .20 |

Set, never hinged

Krylov, fable writer, death centenary.

**1944, Dec. 6**

959 Sheet of 4 6.00 4.75

a. A474 30k dark slate green .40 .40

Liberation of Leningrad, Jan. 27, 1944.

Partisan
Medal — A507

Order for
Bravery — A508

**Leningrad Type**
**Souvenir Sheet**

**Imperf.**

970 Sheet of 4 27.50 27.50

a. Never hinged 25.00
Never hinged 7.50
Never hinged 15.00 10.00

Second anniv. of victory at Stalingrad.

---

M. S.
Polivanova
and N. V.
Kovshova
A501

Pilot B.
Safonov — A502

F. Louzan
A500

Aleksandr S.
Griboedov
A513

**1945, Jan.** Photo.

| 966 | A513 | 30k dk slate green | .30 | .20 |
| 967 | A513 | 60k gray brown | .55 | .30 |

Set, never hinged 1.25

Griboedov (1795-1829), poet & statesman.

**1945, Mar.** Perf. 12½

| 968 | A514 | 60k gray blk & henna | .50 | .55 |
| 969 | A514 | 3r gray blk & henna | 1.50 | 1.10 |

Set, never hinged 4.00

**Souvenir Sheet**
**Imperf**

Red Army
Soldier
A514

---

Order of
Ushakov
A511

Order of
Nakhimov
A512

**Paper with network as in
parenthesis**

**1945, Jan.** Typo. Unwmk.
Perf. 12½, Imperf.

| 960 | A507 | 15k black (green) | .20 | .20 |
| 961 | A508 | 30k dp blue (lt blue) | .20 | .20 |
| 962 | A509 | 45k dk blue | .20 | .20 |
| 963 | A510 | 60k dll rose (pale rose) | .30 | .20 |
| 964 | A511 | 1r dull blue (green) | .40 | .20 |
| 965 | A512 | 1r yel green (blue) | 1.70 | 1.20 |

Set, never hinged 5.00

Nos. 960-965 (6)

Beware of bogus perforation "errors" created from imperfs.

Order of Bogdan
Chmielnicki
A509

Order of
Victory
A510

**1945** Perf. 12

| 971 | A516 | 1r indigo | .50 | .35 |
| 972 | A517 | 2r black | 1.75 | .90 |
| 973 | A518 | 3r henna | 1.60 | .75 |

Set, never hinged 7.50

Nos. 971-973 (3)

See Nos. 1341-1342. For overprints see Nos. 992, 1709.

---

Order of
Bravery
A516

Order of
Bogdan
Chmielnicki
A517

**1945, Apr.** Photo. Perf. 12½

| 974 | A519 | 20k sl grn, org red & black | 1.00 | .60 |
| 975 | A520 | 30k bl blk & dull org | 1.00 | .60 |
| 976 | A521 | 30k blue black | 1.75 | 1.00 |
| 977 | A522 | 60k orange red | 1.75 | 1.00 |
| 978 | A523 | 1r sl grn & org red | 2.50 | 1.50 |
| 979 | A524 | 1r slate green | 9.75 | 5.80 |

Set, never hinged 15.00

Nos. 974-979 (6)

Red Army successes against Germany.

A523

A522

A519

Battle
Scenes
A524

A521

A520

Order of
Victory — A518

**1945**
Engr.

Parade in
Red Square,
Nov. 7,
1941 — A525

Designs: 60k, Soldiers and Moscow barricade, Dec. 1941. 1r, Air battle, 1941.

## 1945, June

| | | | |
|---|---|---|---|
| 980 | A525 | 30k dk blue violet | .25 .25 |
| 981 | A525 | 60k olive green | .35 .35 |
| 982 | A525 | 1r black brown | 1.40 1.40 |

Nos. 980-982 (3)    2.00 2.00
Set, never hinged    5.00

3rd anniversary of the victory over the Germans before Moscow.

Elite Guard Badge and Cannons A528

Motherhood Medal A529

Motherhood Glory — A530

Mother-Heroine Order — A531

**1945, Apr.**    **Typo.**
983 A528 60k red    .75 .25
Never hinged    1.10

## 1945

Paper with network as in parenthesis

**Perf. 12½, Imperf.**
**Size: 22x33¼mm**

| | | | |
|---|---|---|---|
| 984 | A529 | 20k brown (lt blue) | .20 .20 |
| 985 | A530 | 30k yel brown (green) | .25 .20 |
| 986 | A531 | 60k dull rose (pale rose) | .40 .20 |

**Perf. 12½**
**Engr.**
**Size: 20x30mm**

| | | | |
|---|---|---|---|
| 986A | A529 | 1r blk brn (green) | .40 .20 |
| 986B | A530 | 2r dp bl (lt blue) | .90 .35 |
| 986C | A531 | 3r brn red (lt blue) | 1.00 .60 |

Nos. 984-986C (6)    3.15 1.75
Set, never hinged    4.60

Academy Building, Moscow — A532

Academy at Leningrad and M. V. Lomonosov A533

**1945, June**    **Photo.**    **Perf. 12½**
987 A532 30k blue violet    .35 .20
   a. Horiz. pair, imperf. between    90.00
988 A533 2r grnsh black    1.25 .55
Set, never hinged    2.50

Academy of Sciences, 220th anniv.

---

Aleksandr S. Popov A535

Popov and his Invention A534

**1945, July**    **Unwmk.**
989 A534 30k dp blue violet    .40 .25
990 A534 60k dark red    .85 .35
991 A535 1r yellow brown    1.50 1.10
Nos. 989-991 (3)    2.75 4.50
Set, never hinged

"Invention of radio" by A. S. Popov, 50th anniv.

No. 973 Overprinted in Blue

**1945, Aug.**    **Perf. 12**
992 A518 3r henna    1.00 .50
Never hinged    1.60

Victory of the Allied Nations in Europe.

Iakovlev Fighter — A536

Petliakov-2 Dive Bombers — A537

Ilyushin-2 Bombers A538

#992A, 995, Iakovlev Fighter. #992B, 1000, Petliakov-2 dive bombers. #992C, 996, Ilyushin-2 bombers. #992D, 993, Petliakov-8 heavy bomber. #992E, 1001, Tupolev-2 bombers. #992F, 997, Ilyushin-4 bombers. #992G, 999, Polikarpov-2 biplane. #992H, 998, Lavochkin-7 fighters. #992I, 994, Iakovlev fighter in action.

**1945-46**   **Unwmk.**   **Photo.**   **Perf. 12**

| | | | |
|---|---|---|---|
| 992A | A536 | 5k dk violet (46) | .30 .20 |
| 992B | A537 | 10k henna brn (46) | .30 .20 |
| 992C | A538 | 15k henna brn (46) | |
| 992D | A536 | 15k Prus grm (46) | .40 .25 |
| 992E | A538 | 20k gray brn (46) | .45 .25 |
| 992F | A538 | 30k violet (46) | .45 .30 |
| 992G | A538 | 30k brown (46) | .45 .30 |
| 992H | A538 | 50k blue vio (46) | .95 .30 |
| 992I | A536 | 60k dl bl vio (46) | 1.40 .75 |
| 993 | A536 | 1r gray black | 1.90 |
| 994 | A536 | 1r henna brown | 2.50 1.90 |
| 995 | A538 | 1r brown | 2.50 1.90 |
| 996 | A538 | 1r deep brown | 2.50 1.90 |
| 997 | A538 | 1r intense black | 2.50 1.90 |
| 998 | A538 | 1r orange ver | 2.50 1.90 |
| 999 | A538 | 1r bright green | 2.50 1.90 |

---

| | | | |
|---|---|---|---|
| 1000 | A537 | 1r deep brown | 2.50 1.90 |
| 1001 | A538 | 1r violet blue | 2.50 1.90 |

Nos. 992A-1001 (18)    27.60 20.40
Set, never hinged    60.00
Issued: #992A-992I, 3/26; #993-1001, 8/19.

A545

Lenin, 75th Birth Anniv. — A546

Various Lenin portraits.

Dated "1870-1945"

**1945, Sept.**    **Perf. 12½**

| | | | |
|---|---|---|---|
| 1002 | A545 | 30k bluish black | .35 .25 |
| 1003 | A546 | 50k gray brown | .45 .25 |
| 1004 | A546 | 60k orange brown | .55 .25 |
| 1005 | A546 | 1r greenish black | .90 .35 |
| 1006 | A546 | 3r sepia | 2.75 .80 |

Nos. 1002-1006 (5)    5.00 1.90
Set, never hinged    9.00

Prince M. I. Kutuzov — A550

**1945, Sept. 16**
1007 A550 30k blue violet    .50 .40
1008 A550 60k brown    1.00 .60
Set, never hinged    3.00

Field Marshal Prince Mikhail Illarionovich Kutuzov (1745-1813).

Aleksandr Ivanovich Herzen A551

**1945, Oct. 26**
1009 A551 30k dark brown    .35 .40
1010 A551 2r greenish black    1.10 .60
Set, never hinged    3.25

Herzen, author, revolutionist, 75th death anniv.

Friedrich Engels A553

Ilya Mechnikov A552

**1945, Nov. 27**
1011 A552 30k greenish black    .65 .40
1012 A552 30k greenish black    1.25 .60
Set, never hinged    4.00

Ilya I. Mechnikov, zoologist and bacteriologist (1845-1916).

---

**1945, Nov.**    **Unwmk.**    **Perf. 12½**
1013 A553 30k dark brown    45 .20
1014 A553 60k Prussian green    60 .30
Set, never hinged    2.00

125th anniversary of the birth of Friedrich Engels, collaborator of Karl Marx.

Tank Leaving Assembly Line — A554

Designs: 30k, Harvesting wheat. 60k, Airplane designing. 1r, Moscow fireworks.

**1945, Dec. 25**    **Photo.**
1015 A554 20k indigo & brown    .50 .25
1016 A554 30k blk & org brn    .50 .40
1017 A554 60k brown & green    .90 .60
1018 A554 1r dk blue & orange    1.40 .90
Nos. 1015-1018 (4)    3.30 2.15
Set, never hinged    6.50

Artillery Observer and Guns A558

Heavy Field Pieces A559

**1945, Dec.**
1019 A558 30k brown    .65 .50
1020 A559 60k sepia    1.10 .75
Set, never hinged    3.50

Artillery Day, Nov. 19, 1945.

**Catalogue values for unused stamps in this section, from this point to the end of the section, are for Never Hinged items.**

Soldier with Victory Flag — A561

Victory Medal — A560

**1946, Jan. 23**
1021 A560 30k dk violet    .30 .20
1022 A560 30k brown    .30 .20
1023 A560 60k greenish black    .45 .20
1024 A560 60k henna    .45 .20
1025 A561 60k black & dull red    1.50 .70
Nos. 1021-1025 (5)    3.00 1.50

Red Square — A563

Arms of USSR — A562

**1946, Feb. 10**
1026 A562 30k henna    .25 .20
1027 A562 45k henna    .60 .45
1028 A562 60k greenish black    2.40 .85
Nos. 1026-1028 (3)    3.25 1.50

Elections to the Supreme Soviet of the USSR, Feb. 10, 1946.

## Artillery in Victory Parade — A564

## Victory Parade A565

**1946, Feb. 23**
| | | | | |
|---|---|---|---|---|
| 1029 | A564 | 60k dark brown | .75 | .30 |
| 1030 | A564 | 2r dull violet | 1.50 | .60 |
| 1031 | A565 | 3r black & red | 3.75 | .85 |
| | | Nos. 1029-1031 (3) | 6.00 | 1.75 |

Victory Parade, Moscow, June 24, 1945.

Order of Lenin — A566
Medal of Hammer and Sickle A568
Gold Star Medal — A570
Order of Token of Veneration A569
Order of Red Star — A567
Order of Red Banner — A571
Order of the Red Workers' Banner — A572

**1946  Unwmk.  Typo.  Perf. 12½x12**

**Paper with network as in parenthesis**

| | | | | |
|---|---|---|---|---|
| 1032 | A566 | 60k myrtle grn (green) | 1.40 | 1.10 |
| 1033 | A567 | 60k dk vio brn (brown) | 1.40 | 1.10 |
| 1034 | A568 | 60k plum (pink) | 1.40 | 1.10 |
| 1035 | A569 | 60k dp blue (green) | 1.40 | 1.10 |
| 1036 | A570 | 60k dk car (salmon) | 1.40 | 1.10 |
| 1037 | A571 | 60k red (salmon) | 1.40 | 1.10 |
| 1038 | A572 | 60k dk brn vio (buff) | 1.40 | 1.10 |
| | | Nos. 1032-1038 (7) | 9.80 | 7.70 |

See Nos. 1650-1654.

Workers' Achievement of Distinction A573
Workers' Gallantry A574
Marshal's Star — A575
Defense of Soviet Trans-Arctic Regions — A576
Meritorious Service in Battle A577
Defense of Caucasus A578
Defense of Moscow — A579
Bravery — A580

**1946**

**Paper with network as in parenthesis**

| | | | | |
|---|---|---|---|---|
| 1039 | A573 | 60k choc (salmon) | 1.40 | 1.10 |
| 1040 | A574 | 60k brown (salmon) | 1.40 | 1.10 |
| 1041 | A575 | 60k blue (pale blue) | 1.40 | 1.10 |
| 1042 | A576 | 60k dk grn (green) | 1.40 | 1.10 |
| 1043 | A577 | 60k dk blue (green) | 1.40 | 1.10 |
| 1044 | A578 | 60k dk yel grn (grn) | 1.40 | 1.10 |
| 1045 | A579 | 60k carmine (pink) | 1.40 | 1.10 |
| 1046 | A580 | 60k dk violet (blue) | 1.40 | 1.10 |
| | | Nos. 1039-1046 (8) | 11.20 | 8.80 |

## A581 / Maxim Gorki A582

**1946, June 18**
| | | | | |
|---|---|---|---|---|
| 1047 | A581 | 30k brown | .60 | .25 |
| 1048 | A582 | 60k dark green | 1.00 | .25 |

10th anniversary of the death of Maxim Gorki (Alexei M. Peshkov).

## Kalinin A583 / Chebyshev A584

**1946, June**
| | | | | |
|---|---|---|---|---|
| 1049 | A583 | 20k sepia | 2.00 | .60 |

**1946, May 25**
| | | | | |
|---|---|---|---|---|
| 1050 | A584 | 30k brown | .65 | .35 |
| 1051 | A584 | 60k gray brown | .95 | .65 |

Mikhail Ivanovich Kalinin (1875-1946). Pafnuti Lvovich Chebyshev (1821-94), mathematician.

## View of Sukhumi A585 / Sanatorium at Sochi — A587

Designs: #1053, Promenade at Gagri, 45k, New Afyon Sanatorium.

**1946, June 18**
| | | | | |
|---|---|---|---|---|
| 1052 | A585 | 15k dark brown | .40 | .20 |
| 1053 | A585 | 30k dk slate green | .50 | .20 |
| 1054 | A587 | 30k dark green | .50 | .20 |
| 1055 | A585 | 45k chestnut brown | 2.20 | .80 |
| | | Nos. 1052-1055 (4) | | .80 |

## All-Union Parade of Physical Culturists — A589

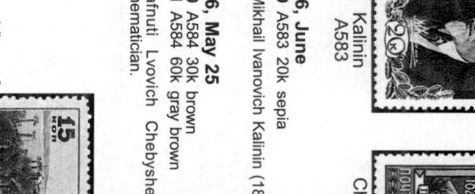

**1946, July 21**
| | | | | |
|---|---|---|---|---|
| 1056 | A589 | 30k dark green | 6.50 | 3.50 |

## Tank Divisions in Red Square A590

**1946, Sept. 8**
| | | | | |
|---|---|---|---|---|
| 1057 | A590 | 30k dark green | .75 | .40 |
| 1058 | A590 | 60k brown | 1.25 | .60 |

Honoring Soviet tankmen.

## Belfry of Ivan the Great, Kremlin — A591 / Bolshoi Theater, Moscow — A592

## Hotel Moscow A593 / Red Square — A597 / Spasski Tower and Statues of Minin and Pozharski — A598

**1946, Sept. 5**
| | | | | |
|---|---|---|---|---|
| 1059 | A591 | 5k brown | .35 | .20 |
| 1060 | A592 | 10k sepia | .35 | .20 |
| 1061 | A593 | 15k chestnut | .35 | .20 |
| 1062 | A593 | 20k light brown | .70 | .20 |
| 1063 | A593 | 45k dark green | 1.00 | .25 |
| 1064 | A593 | 50k brown | 1.50 | .40 |
| 1065 | A597 | 60k blue violet | 1.75 | .55 |
| 1066 | A598 | 1r chestnut brown | 8.50 | 2.50 |
| | | Nos. 1059-1066 (8) | | 2.50 |

Moscow scenes: 15k, Hotel Moscow; 20k, Bolshoi Theater, Sverdlov Square, 45k, View of Kremlin.

Meritorious Service in Battle A603
Workers' Achievement of Distinction A599
Partisan of the Patriotic War — A601
Workers' Gallantry A600
Defense of Soviet Trans-Arctic Regions — A602
Defense of Caucasus A604

## Perf. 12x12½, 12½x12, Imperf.

**1947, Feb. 23**    **Unwmk.**
| 1101 | A625 | 20k sepia | .20 | .20 |
| 1102 | A626 | 30k slate blue | .45 | .20 |
| 1103 | A627 | 30k brown | .45 | .20 |
| | | | 1.35 | .60 |

Nos. 1101-1103 (3)

29th anniversary of the Soviet Army. Exist imperf. Value, set $6.

### Reprints

From here through 1953 many sets exist in two distinct printings from different plates.

**Arms of:**

 Russian Socialist Federated Soviet Republic — A628

 Armenian SSR — A629

 Azerbaijan SSR — A630

 Byelorussian SSR — A631

Estonian SSR — A632

Georgian SSR — A633

Karelo Finnish SSR — A634

Kazakh SSR — A635

Kirghiz SSR — A636

Latvian SSR — A637

Lithuanian SSR — A638

Moldavian SSR — A639

---

 Lenin — A620

**1947, Jan. 21**
| 1091 | A619 | 30k slate blue | .65 | .65 |
| 1092 | A619 | 30k dark green | .65 | .65 |
| 1093 | A620 | 50k dark brown | 2.50 | 1.25 |
| | | | 3.80 | 2.55 |

Nos. 1091-1093 (3)

23rd anniversary of the death of Lenin.
See Nos. 1197-1199.

 F. P. Litke and Sailing Vessel A621

N. M. Przewalski, Mare and Foal — A622

**1947, Jan. 27**
| 1094 | A621 | 20k blue violet | 1.40 | .45 |
| 1095 | A621 | 20k sepia | 1.40 | .45 |
| 1096 | A622 | 60k olive brown | 1.60 | .55 |
| 1097 | A622 | 60k sepia | 6.00 | 2.00 |

Nos. 1094-1097 (4)

Soviet Union Geographical Society, cent.

 Nikolai Zhukovski (1847-1921), Scientist A623

**1947, Jan. 17**
| 1098 | A623 | 30k sepia | 1.50 | .40 |
| 1099 | A623 | 60k blue violet | 2.25 | .60 |

Stalin Prize Medal — A624    **Photo.**

**1946, Dec. 21**
| 1100 | A624 | 30k black brown | 2.25 | .75 |

 Russian Soldier A625

Military Instruction A626

 Aviator, Sailor and Soldier A627

---

 Stamps of Soviet Russia — A614

**1946, Nov. 6**    **Perf. 12½**
| 1080 | A612 | 15k black & dk red | .90 | .55 |
|   a. | | Sheet of 4, imperf. | 50.00 | 45.00 |
| 1081 | A613 | 30k dk green & brn | 1.40 | .60 |
|   a. | | Sheet of 4, imperf. | 50.00 | 45.00 |
| 1082 | A614 | 60k dk green & blk | 1.90 | .85 |
|   a. | | Sheet of 4, imperf. | 50.00 | 45.00 |
| | | | 4.20 | 2.00 |

Nos. 1080-1082 (3)

1st Soviet postage stamp, 25th anniv.

 Lenin and Stalin — A615

**Photo.**    **Perf. 12½**

**1946**
| 1083 | A615 | 30k dp brown org | 1.50 | 1.25 |
|   a. | | Sheet of 4, imperf. | 75.00 | 35.00 |
|   b. | | Single, imperf. | 3.00 | 3.00 |
| 1084 | A615 | 30k dk green | 1.50 | 1.25 |
|   a. | | Sheet of 4, imperf. | 50.00 | |
|   b. | | Single, imperf. | 3.00 | 2.00 |

October Revolution, 29th anniv.
Issued: #1083b-1084a, 11/6; #1083a-1084, 12/18; #1083a, 6/47.

 Dnieprostroy Dam and Power Station — A616

**Perf. 12½**

**1946, Dec. 23**
| 1085 | A616 | 30k sepia | 1.50 | .60 |
| 1086 | A616 | 60k chalky blue | 2.50 | .90 |

Nikolai A. Nekrasov A618

Aleksandr P. Karpinsky A617

**Unwmk.**

**1947, Jan. 17**
| 1087 | A617 | 30k dark green | .75 | .75 |
| 1088 | A617 | 50k | 1.75 | 1.00 |

Karpinsky (1847-1936), geologist.

**1946, Dec. 4**
| 1089 | A618 | 30k sepia | .50 | .25 |
| 1090 | A618 | 60k brown | 1.00 | .75 |

Nikolai A. Nekrasov (1821-1878), poet.

 Lenin's Mausoleum A619

### Canceled to Order

Canceled sets of new issues have long been sold by the government. Values in the second ("used") column are for these canceled-to-order stamps. Postally used copies are worth more.

---

 Defense of Moscow — A605

Bravery — A606

**1946, Sept. 5**    **Engr.**
| 1067 | A599 | 1r dark violet brown | 1.60 | .75 |
| 1068 | A600 | 1r dark carmine | 1.60 | .75 |
| 1069 | A601 | 1r carmine | 1.60 | .75 |
| 1070 | A602 | 1r blue black | 1.60 | .75 |
| 1071 | A603 | 1r black | 1.60 | .75 |
| 1072 | A604 | 1r black brown | 1.60 | .75 |
| 1073 | A605 | 1r olive black | 1.60 | .75 |
| 1074 | A606 | 1r deep claret | 12.80 | 6.00 |

Nos. 1067-1074 (8)

See Nos. 1650-1654.

 Give the Country Each Year: 127 Million Tons of Grain A607

60 Million Tons of Oil — A608

60 Million Tons of Steel — A610

 500 Million Tons of Coal — A609

 50 Million Tons of Cast Iron — A611

**1946, Oct. 6**    **Perf. 12½x12**    **Photo.**    **Unwmk.**
| 1075 | A607 | 5k olive brown | .20 | .20 |
| 1076 | A608 | 10k dk slate green | .20 | .20 |
| 1077 | A609 | 15k brown | .30 | .20 |
| 1078 | A610 | 20k dk blue violet | .50 | .20 |
| 1079 | A611 | 30k brown | .80 | 1.00 |
| | | | 2.00 | 1.00 |

Nos. 1075-1079 (5)

 Symbols of Transportation, Map and Stamps — A612

 Early Soviet Stamp A613

## RUSSIA

Tadzhikstan SSR — A640

Ukrainian SSR — A642

Turkmen SSR — A641

Uzbek SSR — A643

Soviet Union — A644

**1947 Unwmk. Photo. Perf. 12½**

| | | | | |
|---|---|---|---|---|
| 1104 | A628 | 30k henna brown | 1.40 | .35 |
| 1105 | A629 | 30k chestnut | 1.40 | .35 |
| 1106 | A630 | 30k olive brown | 1.40 | .35 |
| 1107 | A631 | 30k olive green | 1.40 | .35 |
| 1108 | A632 | 30k violet black | 1.40 | .35 |
| 1109 | A633 | 30k dark vio brown | 1.40 | .35 |
| 1110 | A634 | 30k dark violet | 1.40 | .35 |
| 1111 | A635 | 30k deep orange | 1.40 | .35 |
| 1112 | A636 | 30k dark violet | 1.40 | .35 |
| 1113 | A637 | 30k yellow brown | 1.40 | .35 |
| 1114 | A638 | 30k dark olive green | 1.40 | .35 |
| 1115 | A639 | 30k dark vio brown | 1.40 | .35 |
| 1116 | A640 | 30k dark green | 1.40 | .35 |
| 1117 | A641 | 30k gray black | 1.40 | .35 |
| 1118 | A642 | 30k blue violet | 1.40 | .35 |
| 1119 | A643 | 30k brown | 1.40 | .35 |
| 1120 | A644 | 1r dk brn, bl, gold & red | 4.00 | 1.00 |

Nos. 1104-1120 (17) 26.40 6.60

Aleksander S. Pushkin (1799-1837), Poet — A645

**1947, Feb. Photo. Perf. 12**

| | | | | |
|---|---|---|---|---|
| 1121 | A645 | 30k sepia | .75 | .35 |
| 1122 | A645 | 50k dk yellow green | 1.25 | .75 |

Classroom A646

Parade of Women — A647

---

Moscow Council Building A648

**1947, Mar. 11**

| | | | | |
|---|---|---|---|---|
| 1123 | A646 | 15k bright blue | 1.00 | .60 |
| 1124 | A647 | 30k red | 1.25 | .90 |

Int'l Day of Women, Mar. 8, 1947.

**1947**

| | | | | |
|---|---|---|---|---|
| 1125 | A648 | 30k sep, gray blue & brick red | 2.00 | 1.00 |

30th anniversary of the Moscow Soviet. Exists imperf. The imperf. exists also with gray blue omitted. Both perf. and imperf. stamps exist in two sizes: 40x27mm and 41x27mm.

**1947, June 10 Perf. 12½**

| | | | | |
|---|---|---|---|---|
| 1126 | A649 | 30k scarlet | .55 | .35 |
| 1127 | A649 | 1r dk olive green | 1.50 | .55 |

Labor Day, May 1, 1947.

May Day Parade in Red Square — A649

**1947, Sept. Perf. 12½x12**

| | | | | |
|---|---|---|---|---|
| 1128 | A593 | 20k lt brown | .75 | .20 |
| 1129 | A593 | 50k brown | 1.00 | .50 |
| 1130 | A597 | 60k blue violet | 1.25 | .60 |
| 1131 | A597 | 1r chestnut brown | 2.00 | .70 |

Overprint arranged in 4 lines on No. 1131. 5.00 2.00

Nos. 1128-1131 (4)

Nos. 1062, 1064-1066 Overprinted in Red

Crimea Bridge, Moscow — A650

Gorki Street, Moscow A651

View of Kremlin, Moscow — A652

**Litho.**

**1947, Sept.**

Designs: No. 1134, Central Telegraph Building. No. 1135, Kiev Railroad Station. No. 1136, Kazan Railroad Station. No. 1137, Kaluga St. No. 1138, Pushkin Square. No. 1139, View of Kremlin. No. 1140, "Old Moscow" by Vasnetsov. No. 1141, Grand Kremlin Palace. No. 1142, St. Basil Cathedral. 2r, View of Kremlin. 3r, View of Kremlin. 5r, Hotel Moscow and government building.

---

Karamyshevsky Dam — A653

**1947 Photo. Perf. 12½**

**Various Frames, Dated 1147-1947**

| | | | | |
|---|---|---|---|---|
| 1132 | A650 | 10k red brown & brn black | .35 | .25 |
| 1133 | A651 | 15k dk bl & dk brn | .35 | .25 |
| 1134 | A650 | 30k brown | .45 | .25 |
| 1135 | A650 | 30k dp yel green | .45 | .25 |
| 1136 | A650 | 30k dp Prus blue | .45 | .25 |
| 1137 | A650 | 30k ultra | .45 | .25 |
| 1138 | A651 | 30k yel green | .45 | .25 |
| 1139 | A650 | 30k dp yel green | .45 | .25 |
| 1140 | A652 | 60k red brown & | .65 | .40 |
| 1141 | A651 | 60k gray blue | .70 | .40 |
| 1142 | A651 | 1r dark violet | 1.50 | .95 |

**Colors: Blue, Yellow and Red. Typo.**

| | | | | |
|---|---|---|---|---|
| 1143 | A651 | 1r multicolored | 1.95 | |
| 1144 | A651 | 2r multicolored | 2.75 | 1.90 |
| 1145 | A650 | 3r multicolored | 5.25 | 1.90 |
| 1146 | A650 | 5r multicolored | 9.00 | 3.25 |
| a. | | Souv. sheet of 4, imperf. | 30.00 | 20.00 |
| b. | | | 25.00 | 11.90 |

Nos. 1128-1146 for founding of Moscow, 800th anniv.

Nos. 1143-1146 were printed in a single sheet containing a row of each denomination plus a row of labels.

Nos. 1132-1146 (15)

**1947, Sept. 7**

**Photo.**

| | | | | |
|---|---|---|---|---|
| 1147 | A653 | 30k sepia | .65 | .20 |
| 1148 | A653 | 30k red brown | .65 | .20 |
| 1149 | A653 | 45k henna brown | .65 | .20 |
| 1150 | A653 | 50k bright ultra | .65 | .20 |
| 1151 | A653 | 60k bright rose | .65 | .20 |
| 1152 | A663 | 1r violet | .90 | .20 |

Nos. 1147-1152 (6) 4.15 1.20

Designs: No. 1148, Direction towers, Yakromsky Lock. 45k, Yakromsky Pumping Station. 50k, Khimki Station. 1r, Lock #8.

Map Showing Moscow-Volga Canal — A654

Moscow-Volga Canal, 10th anniversary.

Mayakovsky Station — A656

Elektrozavodskaya Station — A655

Moscow Subway scenes: No. 1154, Ismailovsky Station. No. 1155, Stalinsky Station. No. 1156, Sokol Station. No. 1158, Kiev Station.

Planes and Flag — A657

---

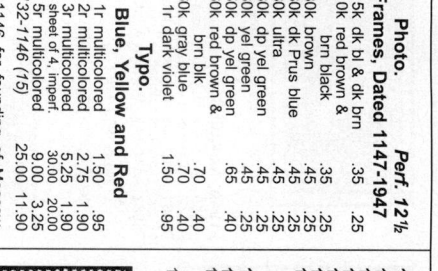

**1947, Sept.**

| | | | | |
|---|---|---|---|---|
| 1153 | A655 | 30k sepia | .65 | .55 |
| 1154 | A655 | 30k blue black | .90 | .55 |
| 1155 | A655 | 45k yellow brown | .90 | .55 |
| 1156 | A655 | 45k deep violet | .90 | .55 |
| 1157 | A666 | 60k henna brown | 1.50 | .65 |
| 1158 | A655 | 60k dp yel grn | 1.50 | .65 |

Nos. 1153-1158 (6) 6.10 3.60

**1947, Sept. 1**

| | | | | |
|---|---|---|---|---|
| 1159 | A657 | 30k deep violet | .35 | .20 |
| 1160 | A657 | 1r bright ultra | .85 | .30 |

Day of the Air Fleet. For overprints see Nos. 1246-1247.

**1947, Nov. Unwmk. Typo.**

| | | | | |
|---|---|---|---|---|
| 1161 | A658 | 60k dark red | 15.00 | 4.50 |

See No. 1260.

Spasski Tower, Kremlin — A658

Agave Plant at Sukhumi — A659

Gulripsh Sanatorium, Sukhumi A660

Peasants' Livadia A661

New Riviera A662

**1947, Nov. Perf. 12½ Unwmk. Typo.**

**1947, Nov. Photo.**

| | | | | |
|---|---|---|---|---|
| 1162 | A659 | 30k dark green | 1.50 | .50 |
| 1163 | A660 | 30k violet | 1.50 | .50 |
| 1164 | A661 | 30k olive | 1.50 | .50 |
| 1165 | A660 | 30k red brown | 1.50 | .50 |
| 1166 | A662 | 30k black violet | 1.50 | .50 |
| 1167 | A660 | 30k black | 1.50 | .50 |
| 1168 | A660 | 30k bright ultra | 1.50 | .50 |
| 1169 | A660 | 30k dk brown violet | 1.50 | .50 |
| 1170 | A659 | 30k dk brown violet | 1.50 | .50 |
| 1171 | A660 | 30k sepia | 1.50 | .50 |

Nos. 1162-1171 (10) 15.00 5.00

Russian sanatoria: No. 1166, Abkhasia, New Afyon. No. 1167, Kemeri, near Riga. No. 1168, Kirov Memorial, Kislovodsk. No. 1169, Voroshilov Memorial, Sochi. No. 1170, Riza, Gagri. No. 1171, Zapadugol, Sochi.

Blast Furnaces, Constantine A663

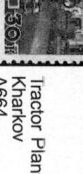
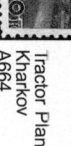
Tractor Plant, Kharkov A664

RUSSIA

Tractor Plant,
Stalingrad
A665

Maxim Gorki
Theater,
Stalingrad
A666

Government
Building,
Kiev — A670

50k, Dnieprostroy Dam. 60k, Wheat field,
granary. 1r, Steel mill, coal mine.

**1948, Jan. 25**    *Perf. 12½*
1193 A670 30k indigo .20 .40
1194 A670 50k violet 1.10 1.60
1195 A670 60k golden brown 2.25 .85
1196 A670 1r sepia 3.50 2.25
   *Nos. 1193-1196 (4)* 8.45 4.00

Ukrainian SSR, 30th anniv.

**Lenin Types of 1947**
Inscribed "1924-1948"    **Unwmk.**
1.00 .60
2.00 .70

**1948, Jan. 21**
1197 A619 30k brown violet 1.00 .60
1198 A619 60k dark gray blue 2.00 .70
1199 A620 60k deep yellow
    green 2.00 .70
   *Nos. 1197-1199 (3)* 5.00 2.00

24th anniversary of the death of Lenin.

Soviet Soldier
and
Artillery — A675

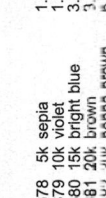

Vasili I.
Surikov — A672

Fliers and
Planes
A676

**1948, Feb. 15**    *Perf. 12*
1201 A672 30k red brown 1.40 .75
1202 A672 60k dark green 2.75 1.25

Vasili Ivanovich Surikov, artist, birth cent.

**1948, Feb. 23**    **Photo.**
No. 1206, Soviet sailor. 60k, Military class.
1205 A675 30k brown 1.10 .55
1206 A675 30k gray 1.10 .55
1207 A676 30k violet blue 1.10 .55
1208 A676 60k red brown 1.75 .85
   *Nos. 1205-1208 (4)* 5.05 2.50

**Hero Types of 1944**

Designs: No. 1209, N.A. Schors. No. 1210,
V.I. Chapayev. No. 1211, S.G. Lazho.

**1948, Feb. 23**
1209 A494 60k deep green 1.60 1.00
1210 A494 60k yellow brown 1.60 1.00
1211 A494 60k violet blue 4.80 3.00
   *Nos. 1209-1211 (3)* 

Nos. 1205-1211 for Soviet army, 30th anniv.

Karl Marx,
Friedrich Engels
and Communist
Manifesto
A677

**1948, Apr.**
1212 A677 30k black .60 .20
1213 A677 50k henna brown 1.40 .30

Centenary of the Communist Manifesto.

---

Miner
A678

Marine
A679

Aviator
A680

Woman
Farmer
A681

Arms of
USSR
A682

Scientist
A683

Spasski
Tower,
Kremlin
A684

Soldier
A685

**1948**    **Photo.**
1214 A678 5k sepia 1.50 .45
1215 A679 10k violet 1.50 .45
1216 A680 15k bright blue 3.50 1.25
1217 A681 20k brown 3.75 1.10
1218 A682 30k dk grn & vio brn 6.00 .75
1219 A683 45k brown violet 6.75 2.75
1220 A684 50k bright blue 8.25 4.25
1221 A685 60k bright green 14.00 6.00
   *Nos. 1214-1221 (8)* 16.25 18.00

See Nos. 1306, 1343-1347, 1689.

May Day Parade in Red
Square — A686

**1948, June 5**    *Perf. 12*
1222 A686 30k deep car rose 1.00 .80
1223 A686 30k bright blue 2.00 1.25

Labor Day, May 1, 1948.

Vissarion G. Belinski
(1811-48), Literary
Critic — A687

**1948, June 7**    **Unwmk.**    *Perf. 12*
1224 A687 30k brown .85 .85
1225 A687 50k dark green 1.40 .85
1226 A687 60k purple 4.00 2.55
   *Nos. 1224-1226 (3)*

---

Aleksandr N. Ostrovski
A690

A691

**1948, June 10**    **Photo.**    *Perf. 12*
1227 A690 30k bright green .60 .85
1228 A691 60k brown 2.25 1.50
1229 A691 1r brown violet 3.75 2.50
   7.90 4.85

Ostrovski (1823-1886), playwright.
Exist imperf. Value, set $250.

Ivan I. Shishkin
(1832-1898),
Painter — A692

"Field of
Rye," by
Shishkin
A693

60k, "Bears in a Forest," by Shishkin.

**Photo. (30k, 1r), Typo. (50k, 60k)**
**1948, June 12**
1230 A692 30k dk grn & vio brn 4.50 .55
1231 A693 50k multicolored 7.00 1.00
1232 A693 60k multicolored 13.50 1.10
1233 A692 1r brn & bl blk 35.00 3.00
   *Nos. 1230-1233 (4)*

Industrial
Expansion
A694

Public Gathering at Leningrad — A695

**Photo., Frames Litho. in Carmine**
**1948, June 25**
1234 A694 15k red brown 2.00 1.00
1235 A695 30k slate 2.50 1.50
1236 A694 60k brown black 4.00 2.25
   8.50 4.75

Industrial five-year plan.

Planting
Crops
A696

#1238, 1r, Gathering vegetables. 45k,
#1241, Baling cotton. #1242, Harvesting grain.

**1948, July 12**    **Photo.**
1237 A696 30k carmine rose .40 .30
1238 A696 30k blue green .40 .30
1239 A696 45k red brown .80 .70
1240 A696 50k brown black 1.25 .70
1241 A696 60k dark green .95 .80

---

Peter I
Monument — A669

**1948, Jan. 10**    *Perf. 12½*
1189 A668 30k violet .90 .40
1190 A668 50k dk slate green 1.60 .45
1191 A668 60k sepia 1.60 .75
1192 A669 1r dk brown violet 2.75 1.10
   *Nos. 1189-1192 (4)* 6.85 2.70

5th anniversary of the liberation of Leningrad from the German blockade.

Palace of the
Arts (Winter
Palace)
A668

Designs (Leningrad in 1947): 60k, Sts. Peter
and Paul Fortress. 1r, Smolny Institute.

---

20k, #1180, Kirov foundry, Makeevka.
#1175, 1179, Agricultural machine plant,
Rostov.

**1947, Nov.**    *Perf. 12½, Imperf.*
1172 A663 15k yellow brown .20 .20
1173 A663 20k sepia .35 .25
1174 A663 30k violet brown .55 .25
1175 A663 30k dark green .55 .25
1176 A664 30k brown .55 .25
1177 A665 30k black brown .55 .25
1178 A666 60k violet brown 1.25 .70
1179 A663 60k yellow brown 1.25 .70
1180 A663 1r black 2.00 .95
1181 A663 1r orange red 2.25 1.40
1182 A665 1r violet 2.25 1.40
   *Nos. 1172-1182 (11)* 12.00 7.00

Reconstruction of war-damaged cities and
factories, and as Five-Year-Plan publicity.

Revolutionists — A667

Designs: 30k. No. 1185, Revolutionists. 50k,
1r, Industry. No. 1186, 2r, Agriculture.

**1947, Nov.**    *Perf. 12½, Imperf.*
**Flame in Dark Red**
1183 A667 30k greenish black .50 .30
1184 A667 50k blue black .75 .40
1185 A667 50k brown black 1.25 .55
1186 A665 60k brown 1.25 .33
1187 A667 1r black 2.00 .95
1188 A667 2r greenish black 3.25 1.50
   *Nos. 1183-1188 (6)* 9.00 4.25

30th anniversary of October Revolution.

**1242** A696 60k dk blue green .80
**1243** A696 1r purple 3.25 1.40
8.00 5.00
Nos. 1237-1243 (7)

Agricultural five-year plan.

**Photo., Frames Litho. in Carmine**

**1948, July 25**
**1244** A697 30k slate 1.90 .90
**1245** A697 60k greenish black 2.25 1.10

25th anniv. of the USSR.

Arms and
Citizens of
USSR — A697

Soviet
Miners — A698

Nos. 1159 and 1160 Overprinted in
Red

**1948, Aug. 24** **Perf. 12½**
**1246** A657 30k deep violet 2.50 1.50
**1247** A657 1r bright ultra 2.50 1.50

Air Fleet Day, 1948. On sale one day.

**1948, Aug.** **Photo.** **Perf. 12½x12**
Miner's Day, Aug. 29: 60k. Scene in mine.
1r, Miner's badge.
**1248** A698 30k blue .75 .20
**1249** A698 60k purple 1.50 .45
**1250** A698 1r blue green 2.75 .85
Nos. 1248-1250 (3) 5.00 1.50

A. A.
Zhdanov — A699

Soviet
Sailor — A700

**1948, Sept. 3**
**1251** A699 40k slate 2.25 1.00

Andrei A. Zhdanov, statesman, 1896-1948.

**1948, Sept. 12** **Perf. 12**
**1252** A700 30k blue green 1.60 1.25
**1253** A700 60k bright blue 4.75 2.00

Navy Day, Sept. 12.

Slalom
A701

Motorcyclist — A702

**1948, Sept. 15** **Perf. 12½x12**
Designs: No. 1254, Foot race, 30k, Soccer
game, 45k, Motorboat race, 50k, Diving.
**1253** A701 15k dark blue 1.00 .25
**1253A** A701 15k violet 1.00 .25
**1254** A702 15k slate blue 1.25 .25
**1254A** A701 20k brown 1.40 .25
**1255** A701 30k brown 1.25 .25
**1256** A702 45k sepia 1.60 .25
**1257** A702 50k blue 2.50 .35
Nos. 1253A-1257 (6) 8.75 1.60

Tankmen
Group
A703

**1948, Sept. 25**
Design: 1r, Tank parade.
**1258** A703 30k sepia 2.75 1.50
**1259** A703 1r rose 6.75 3.50

Day of the Tankmen, Sept. 25.

**Spasski Tower Type of 1947**

**1940** **Litho.** **Perf. 12½x12½**
**1260** A658 1r brown red .90 .25

No. 1260 was re-issued in 1954-56 in
slightly smaller format: 14¾x21½mm, instead
of 14¾x22mm and in a paler shade. See note
after No. 738.

Train — A704

**1948, Sept. 30** **Perf. 12½x12**
Transportation 5-year plan: 60k, Auto and
bus at intersection, 1r, Steamships at anchor.
**1261** A704 30k brown 7.00 1.75
**1262** A704 50k dark green 10.00 2.00
**1263** A704 60k dark green 16.00 2.00
**1264** A704 1r blue violet 21.00 3.50
Nos. 1261-1264 (4) 54.00 9.25

Horses
A705

**1948, Sept. 30** **Perf. 12**
Livestock 5-year plan: 60k, Dairy farm.
**1265** A705 30k slate gray 3.00 1.10
**1266** A705 50k bright green 5.00 1.75
**1267** A705 1r brown 7.00 2.25
Nos. 1265-1267 (3) 15.00 5.10

Pouring
Molten Metal
A706

**1948, Oct. 14** **Perf. 12½**
Designs: 60k, 1r, Iron pipe manufacture.
**1268** A706 30k purple 1.25 .60
**1269** A706 50k brown 1.50 .80
**1270** A706 60k carmine 1.75 1.25
**1271** A706 1r dull blue 3.50 2.00
Nos. 1268-1271 (4) 8.00 4.65

Pioneers
Saluting — A714

Heavy
Machinery
Plant
A707

**1948, Oct. 14**
Design: 60k, Pump station interior.
**1272** A707 30k purple 1.90 .50
**1273** A707 50k sepia 1.75 1.40
**1274** A707 60k brown 2.50 1.25
Nos. 1272-1274 (3) 5.15 3.15

Nos. 1268-1274 publicize the 5-year plan for
steel, iron and machinery industries.

Khachatur Abovian
(1809-1848),
Armenian Writer
and Poet — A708

**1948, Oct. 16** **Perf. 12x12½**
**1275** A708 40k purple 3.00 2.50
**1276** A708 50k deep green 4.00 2.50

Farkhatz
Hydroelectric
Station
A709

**1948, Oct. 24** **Perf. 12½**
Design: 60k, Zouiev Hydroelectric Station.
**1277** A709 30k green 2.50 1.50
**1278** A709 60k red 5.25 2.75
**1279** A709 1r carmine rose 4.75 2.75
Nos. 1277-1279 (3) 12.50 7.00

Electrification five-year plan.

Coal
Mine — A710

**1948, Oct. 24** **Perf. 12½**
Designs: #1282, 1r, Oil field and tank cars.
**1280** A710 30k sepia 1.90 .75
**1281** A710 60k brown 2.00 1.10
**1282** A710 60k red brown 2.00 1.10
**1283** A710 1r blue green 4.00 2.50
Nos. 1280-1283 (4) 9.90 5.45

Coal mining and oil production 5-year plan.

Flying Model
Planes — A712

**1948, Oct. 24**
**1295** A719 40k gray blue 4.50 1.75
**1296** A720 1r violet brown 5.50 3.25

Moscow Art Theater, 50th anniv.

Marching
Pioneers
A713

**1948, Oct. 26** **Perf. 12½**
60k, Pioneer bugler, 1r, Pioneers at
campfire.
**1284** A712 30k dark bl grn 7.25 2.25
**1285** A713 45k dark violet 8.50 3.25
**1286** A714 45k deep carmine 7.25 3.00
**1287** A713 60k deep ultra 11.00 3.75
**1288** A713 1r deep blue 22.50 7.00
Nos. 1284-1288 (5) 56.50 19.25

Young Pioneers, a Soviet youth organization, and governmental supervision of children's summer vacations.

Marching
Youths
A715

Farm
Girl — A716

League Members
and Flag — A717

**1948, Oct. 29** **Perf. 12½**
Inscribed: "1918 1948 XXX"
Designs: 50k, Communist students, 1r, Flag
and badges, 2r, Young worker.
**1289** A716 20k violet brown 3.25 .80
**1290** A716 25k rose red 3.00 1.00
**1291** A717 40k olive green 4.25 1.25
**1292** A715 50k blue green 6.75 2.00
**1293** A717 1r multicolored 25.00 9.00
**1294** A716 2r purple 13.50 7.00
Nos. 1289-1294 (6) 55.75 21.05

30th anniversary of the Young Communist
League (Komsomol).

Stage of
Moscow Art
Theater
A719

K. S.
Stanislavski,
V. I. Nemirovich
Danchenko
A720

**Perf. 12½**

Flag and Moscow
Buildings — A721

## 1948, Nov. 7

Perf. 12½
| | | | |
|---|---|---|---|
| 1297 | A721 | 40k red | 1.50 1.25 |
| 1298 | A721 | 1r green | 2.25 1.75 |

31st anniversary of October Revolution.

### House of Unions, Moscow A722
### Player's Badge (Rook and Chessboard) A723

Perf. 12½

## 1948, Nov. 20
| | | | |
|---|---|---|---|
| 1299 | A722 | 30k greenish blue | 2.00 .35 |
| 1300 | A723 | 40k violet | 5.00 .90 |
| 1301 | A722 | 50k orange brown | 12.00 1.75 |
| | | Nos. 1299-1301 (3) | |

16th Chess Championship.

### Artillery Salute A724

Porf. 12½
| | | | |
|---|---|---|---|
| 1302 | A724 | 30k blue | 10.00 4.00 |
| 1303 | A724 | 1r rose carmine | 20.00 6.00 |

## 1948, Nov. 19

Artillery Day, Nov. 19, 1948.

### Vasili Petrovich Stasov — A725
### Stasov and Barracks of Paul's Regiment, Petrograd A726

Unwmk.

## 1948, Nov. 27
| | | | |
|---|---|---|---|
| 1304 | A725 | 40k brown | 1.40 .70 |
| 1305 | A726 | 1r sepia | 2.50 1.00 |

Stasov (1769-1848), architect.

### Arms Type of 1948

## 1948
Litho. Perf. 12x12½
| | | | |
|---|---|---|---|
| 1306 | A682 | 40k brown red | 5.50 .20 |

### Y. M. Sverdlov Monument A727

Design: 40k, Lenin Street, Sverdlovsk.

## 1948
Photo. Perf. 12½
| | | | |
|---|---|---|---|
| 1307 | A727 | 30k blue | .40 .20 |
| 1308 | A727 | 40k purple | .55 .20 |
| 1309 | A727 | 1r bright green | .90 .20 |
| | | 1r dark green | 1.85 .60 |
| | | Nos. 1307-1309 (3) | |

225th anniv. of the city of Sverdlovsk (before 1924, Ekaterinburg). Exist imperf. Value, set $7.50.

---

### Hot Spring, Piatigorsk A730
### "Swallow's Nest," Crimea A729
### Tree-lined Walk, Sochi A732
### Formal Gardens, Sochi A733
### Shoreline, Sukhumi A731
### Stalin Highway, Sochi — A734
### Colonnade, Kislovodsk A735
### Seascape, Gagri — A736

Perf. 12½

## 1948, Dec. 30
| | | | |
|---|---|---|---|
| 1310 | A729 | 40k brown | .65 .20 |
| 1311 | A730 | 40k bright red violet | .65 .20 |
| 1312 | A731 | 40k dark green | .65 .20 |
| 1313 | A732 | 40k violet | .65 .20 |
| 1314 | A733 | 40k dark purple | .65 .20 |
| 1315 | A734 | 40k dark blue green | .65 .20 |
| 1316 | A735 | 40k bright blue | .65 .20 |
| 1317 | A736 | 40k dark blue green | 5.20 1.60 |
| | | Nos. 1310-1317 (8) | |

### Byelorussian S.S.R. Arms — A737

## 1949, Jan. 4
| | | | |
|---|---|---|---|
| 1318 | A737 | 40k henna brown | 2.50 1.50 |
| 1319 | A737 | 1r blue green | 3.50 2.00 |

Byelorussian SSR, 30th anniv.

---

### Mikhail V. Lomonosov — A738
### Lomonosov Museum, Leningrad A739

## 1949, Jan. 10
| | | | |
|---|---|---|---|
| 1320 | A738 | 40k red brown | 2.25 1.75 |
| 1321 | A738 | 50k green | 2.50 1.75 |
| 1322 | A739 | 1r deep blue | 5.25 4.00 |
| | | Nos. 1320-1322 (3) | 10.00 7.50 |

### Cape Dezhnev (East Cape) A740

Design: 1r, Map and Dezhnev's ship.

## 1949, Jan. 30
| | | | |
|---|---|---|---|
| 1323 | A740 | 40k olive green | 5.50 3.25 |
| 1324 | A740 | 1r gray | 9.50 6.50 |

300th anniv. of the discovery of the strait between Asia and America by S. I. Dezhnev.

### Souvenir Sheet

A741

## 1949, Dec.
Imperf.
| | | | |
|---|---|---|---|
| 1325 | A741 | Sheet of 4 | 150.00 150.00 |
| | | Hinged | 100.00 |
| a. | | 40k Stalin's birthplace, Gorki | 12.00 17.00 |
| b. | | 40k Lenin & Stalin, Leningrad, 1917 | 12.00 17.00 |
| c. | | 40k Lenin & Stalin, Gorki | 12.00 17.00 |
| d. | | 40k Marshal Stalin | 12.00 17.00 |

70th birthday of Joseph V. Stalin.

### Lenin Mausoleum — A742

Perf. 12½

## 1949, Jan. 21
| | | | |
|---|---|---|---|
| 1326 | A742 | 40k ol green & org brown | 7.50 3.50 |
| 1327 | A742 | 1r gray black & org brown | 12.50 5.50 |
| a. | | Sheet of 4 | 250.00 250.00 |

25th anniversary of the death of Lenin. No. 1327a exists imperf. Value $700 mint, $850 used.

---

### Admiral S. O. Makarov — A743

## 1949, Mar. 15
| | | | |
|---|---|---|---|
| 1328 | A743 | 40k blue | 1.75 1.10 |
| 1329 | A743 | 1r red brown | 2.40 1.75 |

Centenary of the birth of Admiral Stepan Osipovich Makarov, shipbuilder.

### Kirov Military Medical Academy A744
### Professors Botkin, Pirogov and Sechenov A745

## 1949, Mar. 24
| | | | |
|---|---|---|---|
| 1330 | A744 | 40k red brown | 1.75 1.00 |
| 1331 | A745 | 50k blue | 2.75 1.50 |
| 1332 | A744 | 1r blue green | 5.50 2.25 |
| | | Nos. 1330-1332 (3) | 10.00 4.75 |

150th anniversary of the foundation of Kirov Military Medical Academy, Leningrad.

### Soviet Soldier A746

Photo.

## 1949, Mar. 16
| | | | |
|---|---|---|---|
| 1333 | A746 | 40k rose red | 12.00 6.00 |

31st anniversary of the Soviet army.

### Textile Weaving A747
### Political Leadership — A748

Designs: 25k, Preschool teaching. No. 1337. School teaching. No. 1338. Farm women. 1r, Women athletes.

## 1949, Mar. 8
Inscribed: "8 MAPTA 1949"
Perf. 12½
| | | | | |
|---|---|---|---|---|
| 1334 | A747 | 20k dark violet | .30 | .20 |
| 1335 | A747 | 25k blue | .40 | .20 |
| 1336 | A748 | 40k henna brown | .55 | .20 |
| 1337 | A747 | 40k slate gray | 1.00 | .35 |
| 1338 | A747 | 50k brown | 1.00 | .30 |
| 1339 | A747 | 1r green | 2.75 | .50 |
| 1340 | A748 | 2r copper red | 4.00 | 1.50 |
| | | Nos. 1334-1340 (7) | 10.00 | 3.30 |

International Women's Day, Mar. 8.

### Medal Types of 1945

1948-49
Engr.
| | | | | |
|---|---|---|---|---|
| 1341 | A517 | 2r green (49) | 2.25 | 1.00 |
| 1341A | A517 | 2r violet brown (49) | 11.00 | 5.25 |
| 1342 | A518 | 3r brown car (49) | 1.75 | .75 |
| | | Nos. 1341-1342 (3) | 15.00 | 7.00 |

For overprint see No. 1709.

## 1949 Types of 1948
Litho. Perf. 12x12½

| | | | | |
|---|---|---|---|---|
| 1343 | A678 | 15k black | 1.60 | .30 |
| 1344 | A681 | 20k green | 2.50 | .30 |
| 1345 | A680 | 25k dark blue | 3.75 | .30 |
| 1346 | A683 | 30k brown | 3.00 | .30 |
| 1347 | A684 | 50k deep blue | 58.35 | 9.70 |
| Nos. 1343-1347 (5) | | | | |

The 20k, 25k and 30k were re-issued in 1954-56 in slightly smaller format. The 20k measures 14x21mm, instead of 15x22mm. The 25k, 14½x21mm, instead of 15x22mm, and 30k, 14½x21mm, instead of 14½x22mm. The smaller-format 20k is olive green, instead of 25k, slate blue. The 15k was reissued in 1959 (?) in smaller format: 14x21mm, instead of 14½x22mm. See note after No. 738.
See No. 1709.

Vasili R. Williams (1863-1939), Agricultural Scientist A749

**1949, Apr. 18** Photo. Perf. 12½

| | | | | |
|---|---|---|---|---|
| 1348 | A749 | 25k blue green | 3.75 | 1.75 |
| 1349 | A749 | 50k brown | 5.25 | 2.50 |

Russian Citizens and Flag — A750

A. S. Popov and Radio — A751

Popov Demonstrating Radio to Admiral Makarov — A752

**1949, Apr. 30**

| | | | | |
|---|---|---|---|---|
| 1350 | A750 | 40k scarlet | 1.50 | .65 |
| 1351 | A750 | 1r blue green | 2.50 | 1.25 |

Labor Day, May 1, 1949.

**1949, May** Unwmk.

| | | | | |
|---|---|---|---|---|
| 1352 | A751 | 40k purple | 2.00 | .75 |
| 1353 | A752 | 50k brown | 3.25 | 1.50 |
| 1354 | A751 | 1r blue green | 6.75 | 2.75 |
| Nos. 1352-1354 (3) | | | 12.00 | 5.00 |

54th anniversary of Popov's discovery of the principles of radio.

Soviet Publications A753

Reading Pravda A754

**1949, May 4**

| | | | | |
|---|---|---|---|---|
| 1355 | A753 | 40k crimson | 3.50 | 2.25 |
| 1356 | A754 | 1r dark violet | 7.50 | 3.75 |

Soviet Press Day.

---

Ivan V. Michurin — A755

Pushkin Reading Poem A757

**1949, July 28**

| | | | | |
|---|---|---|---|---|
| 1357 | A755 | 40k blue gray | 1.75 | 1.00 |
| 1358 | A755 | 1r bright green | 3.50 | 2.25 |

Michurin (1855-1935), agricultural scientist.

A. S. Pushkin, 1822 — A756

**1949, June** Unwmk.

No. 1360, Pushkin portrait by Kiprensky, 1827. 1r, Pushkin Museum, Boldino.

| | | | | |
|---|---|---|---|---|
| 1359 | A756 | 25k indigo & sepia | 1.50 | .75 |
| 1360 | A756 | 40k org brn red & sep | 3.50 | 1.75 |
| a. | | Souv. sheet of 4, 2 each #1361, 1363, imperf. | 75.00 | 30.00 |
| 1361 | A757 | 40k brn red & dk violet | 3.50 | 2.00 |
| 1362 | A757 | 1r choc & slate | 8.50 | 4.00 |
| 1363 | A757 | 2r brown & vio bl | 13.00 | 6.50 |
| Nos. 1359-1363 (5) | | | 30.00 | 15.00 |

150th anniversary of the birth of Aleksander S. Pushkin.
Horizontal rows of Nos. 1361 and 1363 contain alternate stamps and labels.
No. 1360a issued July 20.

River Tugboat A758

**1949, July 13**

| | | | | |
|---|---|---|---|---|
| 1364 | A758 | 40k slate blue | 5.00 | 2.75 |
| 1365 | A758 | 1r red brown | 10.00 | 4.00 |

Centenary of the establishment of the Sormovo Machine and Boat Works.

1r, Freighter, motorship "Bolshaya Volga."

VCSPS No. 3, Kislovodsk A759

**1949, Sept. 10** Photo. Perf. 12½

| | | | | |
|---|---|---|---|---|
| 1366 | A759 | 40k violet | .60 | .20 |
| 1367 | A759 | 40k black | .60 | .20 |
| 1368 | A759 | 40k violet | .60 | .20 |
| 1369 | A759 | 40k carmine | .60 | .20 |
| 1370 | A759 | 40k blue | .60 | .20 |
| 1371 | A759 | 40k violet brown | .60 | .20 |
| 1372 | A759 | 40k red orange | .60 | .20 |
| 1373 | A759 | 40k dark brown | .60 | .20 |
| 1374 | A759 | 40k green | .60 | .20 |
| 1375 | A759 | 40k blue green | .60 | .20 |
| Nos. 1366-1375 (10) | | | 6.00 | 2.00 |

State Sanatoria for Workers: No. 1367, Communications, Khosta. No. 1368, Sanatorium No. 3, Khosta. No. 1369, Electric power, Kislovodsk. No. 1370, Sanatorium No. 1, Kislovodsk. No. 1371, State Theater, Sochi. No. 1372, Frunze Sanatorium, Sochi. No. 1373, Clinical, Chaltubo. No. 1375, Sanatorium No. 41, Zheleznovodsk.

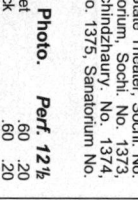

Regatta A760

---

**1949, Aug. 7**

Sports: "1949": 25k, Kayak race. 30k, Swimming. 40k, Bicycling. 1r, Soccer. 50k, Mountain climbing. 1r, Parachuting. 2r, High jump.

| | | | | |
|---|---|---|---|---|
| 1376 | A760 | 20k bright blue | .65 | .20 |
| 1377 | A760 | 25k blue green | .65 | .20 |
| 1378 | A760 | 30k violet | 1.10 | .20 |
| 1379 | A760 | 40k red brown | 1.10 | .20 |
| 1380 | A760 | 50k green | 1.40 | .20 |
| 1381 | A760 | 40k dk blue gray | 1.10 | .20 |
| 1382 | A760 | 1r carmine rose | 4.00 | .40 |
| 1383 | A760 | 2r gray black | 8.00 | .80 |
| Nos. 1376-1383 (8) | | | 18.00 | 2.40 |

V. V. Dokuchayev and Fields A761

**1949, Aug. 8**

| | | | | |
|---|---|---|---|---|
| 1384 | A761 | 40k brown | 1.00 | .30 |
| 1385 | A761 | 1r green | 1.50 | .45 |

Vasili V. Dokuchayev (1846-1903), pioneer soil scientist.

Vasili Bazhenov and Lenin Library, Moscow A762

**1949, Aug. 14** Photo. Perf. 12½

| | | | | |
|---|---|---|---|---|
| 1386 | A762 | 40k violet | 1.50 | .35 |
| 1387 | A762 | 1r red brown | 2.25 | .45 |

Bazhenov, architect, 150th death anniv.

Radishchev — A763

**1949, Aug. 31**

| | | | | |
|---|---|---|---|---|
| 1388 | A763 | 40k blue green | 3.00 | 1.00 |
| 1389 | A763 | 1r gray | 7.00 | 2.00 |

200th anniversary of the birth of Aleksandr N. Radishchev, writer.

Ivan P. Pavlov A764

**1949, Sept. 30** Unwmk.

| | | | | |
|---|---|---|---|---|
| 1390 | A764 | 40k deep brown | 1.00 | .25 |
| 1391 | A764 | 1r gray black | 3.00 | .35 |

Pavlov (1849-1936), Russian physiologist.

Globe Encircled by Letters A765

**1949, Oct.** Perf. 12½

| | | | | |
|---|---|---|---|---|
| 1392 | A765 | 40k org brn & indigo | .90 | .30 |
| a. | | Imperf. | 7.50 | 2.50 |
| 1393 | A765 | 50k indigo & gray vio | .90 | .30 |
| a. | | Imperf. | 7.50 | .30 |

75th anniv. of the UPU.

---

Map of European Russia — A767

**1949, Oct. 18** Perf. 12½

Designs: No. 1395, Peasants in grain field. 50k, Rural scene. 2r, Old man and children.

| | | | | |
|---|---|---|---|---|
| 1394 | A766 | 25k green | 11.50 | 4.25 |
| 1395 | A766 | 25k violet | 2.75 | 1.00 |
| 1396 | A767 | 40k gray grn & blk | 2.75 | 1.00 |
| 1397 | A766 | 50k deep blue | 1.50 | 1.50 |
| 1398 | A766 | 1r gray black | 7.50 | 3.00 |
| 1399 | A766 | 2r dark brown | 12.75 | 4.25 |
| Nos. 1394-1399 (6) | | | 38.75 | 15.00 |

Encouraging agricultural development. Nos. 1394, 1398, 1399 measure 33x19mm. Nos. 1395, 1397 measure 33x22mm.

Cultivators A766

**1949, Oct. 22** Photo.
Chapayev Type of 1944

| | | | | |
|---|---|---|---|---|
| 1403 | A494 | 40k brown orange | 5.00 | 3.00 |

30th anniversary of the death of V. I. Chapayev, a hero of the 1918 civil war. Portrait and outer frame same as type A494. Dates "1919 1949" are in upper corners. Other details differ.

Maly (Little) Theater, Moscow A768

M. N. Ermolova, I. S. Mochalov, A. N. Ostrovski, M. S. Shchepkin and P. M. Sadovsky A769

**1949, Oct. 27**

| | | | | |
|---|---|---|---|---|
| 1400 | A768 | 40k green | 1.00 | .25 |
| 1401 | A768 | 50k red orange | 1.50 | .40 |
| 1402 | A769 | 1r deep brown | 3.50 | .85 |
| Nos. 1400-1402 (3) | | | 6.00 | 1.50 |

125th anniversary of the Maly Theater (State Academic Little Theater)

125th Anniv. of the Birth of Ivan Savich Nikitin, Russian Poet (1824-1861) — A770

**1949, Oct. 24** Unwmk.

| | | | | |
|---|---|---|---|---|
| 1404 | A770 | 40k brown | 1.10 | .25 |
| 1405 | A770 | 1r slate blue | 1.90 | .35 |

Spasski lower and Russian Citizens A771

State University Museum — A790

Pushkin Museum A791

Museums: No. 1451, Tretiakov Gallery. No. 1452, Timiryazev Biology Museum. No. 1453, Lenin Museum. No. 1454, Museum of the Revolution. No. 1456, State History Museum.

Inscribed: "MOCKBA 1949" in Top Frame

**1950, Mar. 28    Litho.    Perf. 12½**
Multicolored Centers

| | | | |
|---|---|---|---|---|
| 1449 | A788 | 40k dark blue | 1.10 | .25 |
| 1450 | A788 | 40k dark blue | 1.10 | .25 |
| 1451 | A789 | 40k green | 1.10 | .25 |
| 1452 | A789 | 40k dark brown | 1.10 | .25 |
| 1453 | A789 | 40k olive brown | 1.10 | .25 |
| 1454 | A789 | 40k claret | 1.10 | .25 |
| 1455 | A790 | 40k red | 1.10 | .25 |
| 1456 | A790 | 40k chocolate | 1.10 | .25 |
| 1457 | A791 | 40k brown violet | 1.10 | .25 |
| | | Nos. 1449-1457 (9) | 9.90 | 2.25 |

A. S. Shcherbakov A793

**1950, May 1    Photo.    Perf. 12½**
1458 A792 40k org red & gray    2.50 1.75
1459 A792 1r red & gray black    5.00 3.00
Labor Day, May 1, 1950.

1r, 4 Russians and communist banner, horiz.

Soviets of Three Races A792

**1950, May    Unwmk.**
1460 A793 40k black, *pale blue*    2.25 1.00
1461 A793 1r dk green, *buff*    2.75 2.00
Shcherbakov, political leader (1901-1945).

Victory Medal A795

Monument A794

**1950    Wmk. 293**
1462 A794 40k dk brown & red    7.50 3.00

**Perf. 12x12½**
**Photo.**
**Unwmk.**
**1950    Photo.**
1463 A795 1r carmine rose    12.50 4.50
5th Intl. Victory Day, May 9, 1950.

---

**1950, Jan. 7    Photo.**
1438 A782 25k gray black    1.00 1.00
1439 A782 40k brown    1.40 .75
1440 A782 50k green    2.10 1.25
1441 A782 1r purple    4.50 2.50
Nos. 1438-1441 (4)    9.00 5.50
Turkmen Republic, 25th anniversary.

Motion Picture Projection A783

**1950, Feb.**
1442 A783 25k brown    10.00 5.00
Soviet motion picture industry, 30th anniv.

Kremlin — A785

Voter — A784

**1950, Mar. 8**
1443 A784 40k green, *yellow*    3.00 1.75
1444 A785 1r rose carmine    4.00 3.00
Supreme Soviet elections, Mar. 12, 1950.

Morozov Monument, Moscow — A786

**1950, Mar. 16    Perf. 12½**
1445 A786 40k black brn & red    3.25 1.75
1446 A786 1r dk green & red    6.75 3.00
Unveiling of a monument to Pavlik Morozov, Pioneer.

Globes and Communication Symbols — A787

**1950, Apr. 1**
1447 A787 40k deep green    3.00 2.00
1448 A787 50k deep blue    3.50 2.00
Meeting of the Post, Telegraph, Telephone and Radio Trade Unions.

State Polytechnic Museum A788

State Museum of Oriental Cultures A789

---

"Russia" versus "War" — A777

Byelorussians and Flag — A778

**1949, Dec. 25**
1425 A777 40k rose carmine    .75 .20
1426 A777 50k blue    1.25 .30
Issued to portray Russia as the defender of world peace.

**1949, Dec. 23    Unwmk.**
Design: No. 1428, Ukrainians and flag.
Inscribed: "1939 1949"
1427 A778 40k orange red    9.00 3.75
1428 A778 40k deep orange    9.00 3.75
Return of western territories to the Byelorussian and Ukrainian Republics, 10th anniv.

Teachers College A779

25k, State Theater. #1431, Government House. #1432, Navoi Street, Tashkent. 1r, Fergana Canal. 2r, Kuigonyarsk Dam.

**1950, Jan. 3**
1429 A779 20k blue    .30 .20
1430 A779 25k gray black    .30 .25
1431 A779 40k red orange    .65 .25
1432 A779 40k violet    .65 .25
1433 A779 1r green    1.40 .40
1434 A779 2r brown    3.00 .50
Nos. 1429-1434 (6)    6.30 1.80
Uzbek Republic, 25th anniversary.

Lenin at Razliv — A780

Lenin's Office, Kremlin — A781

Design: 1r, Lenin Museum.

**1950, Jan.    Unwmk.    Litho.    Perf. 12**
1435 A780 40k dk green & dk brn    .55 .20
1436 A780 50k dk brn, red brn & green    .90 .20
1437 A781 1r dk brn, dk grn & cream    1.65 .30
Nos. 1435-1437 (3)    3.10 .70
26th anniversary of the death of Lenin.

Textile Factory, Ashkhabad A782

Designs: 40k, 1r, Power dam and Turkmenian arms. 50k, Rug making.

---

**1949, Oct. 29    Perf. 12½**
1406 A771 40k brown orange    2.75 1.50
1407 A771 1r deep green    4.75 2.50
October Revolution, 32nd anniversary.

Sheep, Cattle and Farm Woman — A772

**1949, Nov. 2**
1408 A772 40k chocolate    1.00 .25
1409 A772 1r violet    1.50 .35
Encouraging better cattle breeding in Russia.

Arms and Flag of USSR — A773

**1949, Nov. 30    Engr.    Perf. 12**
1410 A773 40k carmine    10.00 6.00
Constitution Day.

Electric Trolley Car — A774

**1949, Nov. 19    Photo.    Perf. 12½**
1411 A774 25k red    1.00 .20
1412 A774 40k violet    1.25 .40
1413 A774 50k deep blue    2.25 .40
1414 A774 1r Prus green    4.50 1.00
Nos. 1411-1414 (4)    9.00 2.00
40k, 1r, Diesel train. 50k, Steam train

Ski Jump — A775

Designs: 40k, Girl on rings. 50k, Ice hockey. 1r, Weight lifter. 2r, Wolf hunt.

**1949, Nov. 12    Unwmk.**
1415 A775 20k dark green    .50 .20
1416 A775 40k orange red    1.25 .25
1417 A775 50k deep blue    1.50 .20
1418 A775 1r red    4.50 .25
1419 A775 2r violet    7.25 .80
Nos. 1415-1419 (5)    15.00 1.65

Textile Mills — A776

**1949, Dec. 7    Photo.    Perf. 12**
1420 A776 20k blue    .50 .20
1421 A776 40k green    .50 .25
1422 A776 40k red orange    .75 .25
1423 A776 50k violet    1.25 .25
1424 A776 1r gray black    2.00 .85
Nos. 1420-1424 (5)    5.00 1.75
Designs: 25k, Irrigation system. 40k, 1r, Government buildings, Stalinabad. 50k, University of Medicine.
Tadzhik Republic, 20th anniv.

## A. V. Suvorov — A796

### Various Designs and Sizes Dated "1800 1950"

**1950**

50k, Suvorov crossing Alps, 32½x47mm.
60k, Badge, flag and marchers, 24x39½mm.
2r, Suvorov facing left, 19x33½mm.

| | | | | |
|---|---|---|---|---|
| 1464 | A796 | 40k blue,pink | 7.75 | 3.25 |
| 1465 | A796 | 50k brown, pink | 7.75 | 3.75 |
| 1466 | A796 | 60k gray black, pale gray | 9.25 | 5.25 |
| 1467 | A796 | 1r dk brn, lemon | 19.00 | 9.00 |
| 1468 | A796 | 2r greenish blue | 50.00 | 25.00 |
| | | Nos. 1464-1468 (5) | | |

Field Marshal Count Aleksandr V. Suvorov (1730-1800).

## Farmers Studying Agronomic Techniques A797

No. 1470, 1r, Sowing on collective farm.

**1950, June**   **Perf. 12, 12½x12**

| | | | | |
|---|---|---|---|---|
| 1469 | A797 | 40k dk grn, pale grn | 3.00 | 1.50 |
| 1470 | A797 | 40k gray black, buff | 2.00 | 1.10 |
| 1471 | A797 | 1r blue, lemon | 4.00 | 2.25 |
| | | Nos. 1469-1471 (3) | 8.00 | 4.45 |

## George M. Dimitrov — A798

**1950, July 2**

| | | | | |
|---|---|---|---|---|
| 1472 | A798 | 40k gray black, citron | 2.00 | 1.10 |
| 1473 | A798 | 1r gray blk, salmon | 7.00 | 3.50 |

Dimitrov (1882-1949), Bulgarian-born revolutionary leader and Comintern official.

## Opera and Ballet Theater, Baku — A799

Designs: 40k, Azerbaijan Academy of Science. 1r, Stalin Avenue, Baku.

**1950, July**   **Photo.**   **Perf. 12½**

| | | | | |
|---|---|---|---|---|
| 1474 | A799 | 25k dp green, cit-ron | 4.25 | 1.25 |
| 1475 | A799 | 40k brown, buff | 6.75 | 5.50 |
| 1476 | A799 | 1r gray black, pink | 20.00 | 10.00 |
| | | Nos. 1474-1476 (3) | | |

Azerbaijan SSR, 30th anniversary.

## Victory Theater — A800

---

**1950, June**

| | | | | |
|---|---|---|---|---|
| 1477 | A800 | 20k dark blue | 1.75 | .80 |
| 1478 | A801 | 40k green | 2.40 | 1.25 |
| 1479 | A801 | 50k red orange | 5.00 | 2.00 |
| 1480 | A801 | 1r gray | 10.05 | 4.95 |
| | | Nos. 1477-1480 (4) | | |

Restoration of Stalingrad.

Designs: 50k, Gorky Theater. 1r, Monument marking Stalingrad defense line.

## Lenin Street A801

## Moscow Subway Stations: "Park of Culture" A802

**1950, July 30**   **Size: 33½x23mm**

| | | | | |
|---|---|---|---|---|
| 1481 | A802 | 40k deep carmine | .85 | .30 |
| 1482 | A802 | 40k dark green, buff | .85 | .30 |
| 1483 | A802 | 40k deep blue, buff | .85 | .30 |
| 1484 | A802 | 1r dark brn, citron | 1.90 | 1.00 |
| 1485 | A802 | 1r purple | 1.90 | 1.00 |
| 1486 | A802 | 1r dark grn, citron | 1.90 | 1.00 |

**Size: 33x18½mm**

| | | | | |
|---|---|---|---|---|
| 1487 | A802 | 1r black, pink | 1.75 | .75 |
| | | Nos. 1481-1487 (7) | 10.00 | 4.65 |

Designs: 40k, Kaluzskaya station. #1482, Taganskaya. #1483, Kurskaya. #1484, Pavelet-skaya. #1485, Kurskaya. #1486, Park of Culture. #1487, Taganskaya.

## Socialist Peoples and Flags A803

**1950, Aug. 4**   **Unwmk.**   **Perf. 12½**

| | | | | |
|---|---|---|---|---|
| 1488 | A803 | 40k multicolored | 1.25 | .20 |
| 1489 | A803 | 50k multicolored | 2.25 | .20 |
| 1490 | A803 | 1r multicolored | 3.00 | .30 |
| | | Nos. 1488-1490 (3) | 6.50 | .70 |

## Trade Union Building, Riga — A804

**1950**

| | | | | |
|---|---|---|---|---|
| 1491 | A804 | 25k dark brown | 1.50 | .50 |
| 1492 | A804 | 40k scarlet | 2.50 | .80 |
| 1493 | A804 | 50k dark green | 4.50 | 1.25 |
| 1494 | A804 | 60k deep blue | 5.50 | 1.60 |
| 1495 | A805 | 1r lilac | 7.50 | 2.10 |
| 1496 | A804 | 2r sepia | 13.50 | 4.75 |
| | | Nos. 1491-1496 (6) | 35.00 | 11.00 |

Designs: 40k, Latvian Cabinet building. 50k, Monument to Jan Rainis. 1r, Riga State Univ. 2r, Latvian Academy of Sciences.

Latvian SSR, 10th anniv.

## Opera and Ballet Theater, Riga — A805

---

## Marite Melnik — A807

**1950**

| | | | | |
|---|---|---|---|---|
| 1497 | A806 | 25k deep bl, bluish | 2.00 | 1.00 |
| 1498 | A807 | 40k brown | 3.00 | 1.00 |
| 1499 | A806 | 1r scarlet | 14.00 | 10.00 |
| | | Nos. 1497-1499 (3) | 20.00 | 10.00 |

Design: 1r, Cabinet building.

Lithuanian SSR, 10th anniv.

## Stalingrad Square, Tallinn A808

## Victor Kingisepp — A809

**1950**

| | | | | |
|---|---|---|---|---|
| 1500 | A808 | 25k dark green | 2.00 | .35 |
| 1501 | A808 | 40k scarlet | 2.40 | .65 |
| 1502 | A808 | 50k yellow | 4.00 | 1.25 |
| 1503 | A809 | 1r brown, blue | 12.00 | 4.75 |
| | | Nos. 1500-1503 (4) | 20.40 | 7.00 |

Designs: 40k, Government building, Tallinn. 50k, Estonia Theater, Tallinn.

Estonian SSR, 10th anniv.

## Citizens Signing Appeal for Peace A810

## Children and Governess — A811

**1950, Oct. 16**

| | | | | |
|---|---|---|---|---|
| 1504 | A810 | 40k red, salmon | 1.50 | .50 |
| 1505 | A811 | 40k black | 4.00 | 1.00 |
| 1506 | A811 | 50k dark red | 8.50 | 2.00 |
| 1507 | A810 | 1r brown, salmon | 24.00 | 7.00 |
| | | Nos. 1504-1507 (4) | 40.50 | 11.00 |

Design: 50k, Peace Demonstration.

## F. G. Bellingshausen, M. P. Lazarev and Globe — A812

---

## Lithuanian Academy of Sciences A806

**1950, Oct. 25**   **Blue Paper**
**Unwmk.**   **Perf. 12½**

| | | | | |
|---|---|---|---|---|
| 1508 | A812 | 40k dark carmine | 15.00 | 12.00 |
| 1509 | A813 | 1r purple | 30.00 | 15.00 |

## Route of Antarctic Expedition — A813

130th anniversary of the Bellingshausen-Lazarev expedition to the Antarctic.

## M. V. Frunze — A814

**1950, Oct. 31**

| | | | | |
|---|---|---|---|---|
| 1510 | A814 | 40k blue, buff | 4.00 | 4.00 |
| 1511 | A814 | 1r brown, blue | 16.00 | 8.50 |

Frunze, military strategist, 25th death anniv.

## M. I. Kalinin — A815

**1950, Nov. 20**   **Engr.**

| | | | | |
|---|---|---|---|---|
| 1512 | A815 | 40k deep green | 1.25 | .75 |
| 1513 | A815 | 1r reddish brown | 2.75 | 1.25 |
| 1514 | A815 | 5r violet | 6.00 | 2.25 |
| | | Nos. 1512-1514 (3) | 10.00 | 4.25 |

75th anniversary of the birth of M. I. Kalinin, Soviet Russia's first president.

## Gathering Grapes A816

## Armenian Government Building A817

## G. M. Sundukian — A818

**1950, Nov. 29**   **Photo.**   **Perf. 12½**

| | | | | |
|---|---|---|---|---|
| 1515 | A816 | 20k dp blue, buff | 1.75 | 1.00 |
| 1516 | A817 | 40k dp blue, buff | 3.00 | 1.50 |
| 1517 | A818 | 1r ol gray, yellow | 7.25 | 3.50 |
| | | Nos. 1515-1517 (3) | 12.00 | 6.00 |

Armenian Republic, 30th anniv. 1r also for birth of Sundukian, playwright.

## Apartment Building, Kotelnicheskaya Quay — A819

# Top row

**Furmanov at Work — A839**

**1951, Mar. 17**    *Perf. 12½*
- 1548 A838 40k brown   5.00 1.25
- 1549 A839 1r gray black, *buff*   6.00 2.00

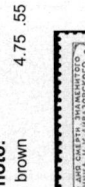

**Russian War Memorial, Berlin — A840**

**1951, Mar. 21**    *Perf. 12*
- 1550 A840 40k dk gray grn & dk red   10.00 3.00
- 1551 A840 1r brown blk & red   15.00 7.00

Stockholm Peace Conference.

**Kirov Machine Works — A841**

**1951, May 19**    *Photo.*
- 1552 A841 40k brown, *cream*   4.00 2.50

Kirov Machine Works, 150th anniv.

**Bolshoi Theater, Moscow — A842**

**Russian Composers — A843**

**1951, May**    *Unwmk.*
- 1553 A842 40k multicolored   5.00 .55
- 1554 A843 1r multicolored   7.00 1.25

Bolshoi Theater, Moscow, 175th anniv.

**Liberty Bridge, Budapest — A844**

# Second row

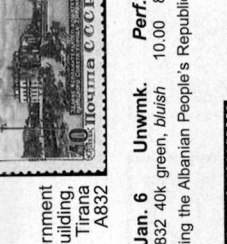

**1951, Feb. 2**    *Photo.*    *Perf. 12½*
- 1539 A830 25k dk brown, *blue*   3.50 1.90
- 1540 A831 40k dp green, *blue*   4.00 3.00

Kirghiz Republic, 25th anniv.

**Government Building, Tirana — A832**

**1951, Jan. 6**    *Unwmk.*    *Perf. 12*
- 1541 A832 40k green, *bluish*   10.00 8.00

Honoring the Albanian People's Republic.

**Bulgarians Greeting Russian Troops — A833**

**Lenin Square — A834**

Design: 60k, Monument to Soviet soldiers.

**1951, Jan. 13**
- 1542 A833 25k gray black, *bluish*   1.75 1.25
- 1543 A834 40k org red, *salmon*   3.25 2.50
- 1544 A834 60k blk brn, *salmon*   5.00 3.75
- Nos. 1542-1544 (3)   10.00 7.50

Honoring the Bulgarian People's Republic.

**Choibalsan State University — A835**

**State Theater, Ulan Bator — A836**

**Mongolian Republic Emblem and Flag — A837**

**1951, Mar. 12**
- 1545 A835 25k purple, *salmon*   .55 .45
- 1546 A836 40k dp orange, *yellow*   1.10 .45
- 1547 A837 1r multicolored   2.75 1.50
- Nos. 1545-1547 (3)   4.40 2.40

Honoring the Mongolian People's Republic.

**D. A. Furmanov (1891-1926) Writer — A838**

# Third row

**Hotel, Kalanchevkaya Square — A820**

**Various Buildings**
Inscribed: "Mockba, 1950"

**1950, Dec. 2**    *Unwmk.*
- 1518 A819 1r red brn, *buff*   25.00 19.00
- 1519 A819 1r gray black   25.00 19.00
- 1520 A819 1r brown, *blue*   25.00 19.00
- 1521 A819 1r dk green, *buff*   25.00 19.00
- 1522 A820 1r dp blue, *buff*   25.00 19.00
- 1523 A820 1r black, *buff*   25.00 19.00
- 1524 A820 1r red orange   25.00 19.00
- 1525 A819 1r dk grn, *yellow*   200.00 152.00
- Nos. 1518-1525 (8)   120.00
- Set, hinged

Skyscrapers planned for Moscow.

**Multicolored Centers**    *Litho.*
- 1529 A824 40k chocolate   1.75 .20
- 1530 A824 50k chocolate   1.75 .40
- 1531 A825 1r indigo   2.50 .90
- Nos. 1529-1531 (3)   6.00 1.50

**Flags and Newspapers Iskra and Pravda — A826**

1r, Flag and profiles of Lenin and Stalin.

**1950, Dec. 23**    *Photo.*
- 1532 A826 40k gray blk & red   25.00 6.25
- 1533 A826 1r dk brn & red   35.00 8.75

1st issue of the newspaper Iskra, 50th anniv.

**Presidium of Supreme Soviet, Alma-Ata — A827**

**1950, Dec. 27**    Inscribed: "ALMA-ATA" in Cyrillic
- 1534 A827 40k gray black, *blue*   7.25 3.00
- 1535 A827 1r red brn, *yellow*   7.50 4.00

Kazakh Republic, 30th anniversary. Cyrillic characters for "ALMA-ATA" are above building in vignette on 40k, immediately below building on right on 1r.

Design: 1r, Opera and Ballet Theater.

**Decembrists and Senatskaya Square, Leningrad — A828**

**1950, Dec. 30**    *Unwmk.*
- 1536 A828 1r black brn, *yellow*   7.00 4.00

Decembrist revolution of 1825.

**Lenin at Razliv — A829**

Design: 1r, Lenin and young communists.

**1951, Jan. 21**    *Litho.*    *Perf. 12½*
**Multicolored Centers**
- 1537 A829 40k olive green   2.50 .30
- 1538 A829 1r multicolored   4.50 .70

27th anniversary of the death of Lenin.

**Mountain Pasture — A830**

**Government Building, Frunze — A831**

# Bottom row

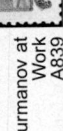

**Spasski Tower, Kremlin — A821**

**1950, Dec. 4**
- 1526 A821 1r dk grn, red brn & yel brown   15.00 5.50

October Revolution, 33rd anniversary.

**Golden Autumn by Levitan — A822**

**I. I. Levitan (1861-90), Painter — A823**

**1950, Dec. 6**    *Perf. 12½*
- 1527 A822 40k multicolored   3.25 .55

*Perf. 12*    *Photo.*
- 1528 A823 50k red brown   4.75 .55

**Black Sea by Aivazovsky — A824**

**Ivan K. Aivazovsky (1817-1900) Painter — A825**

Design: 50k, "Ninth Surge."

**1951, June 9**

Monument to Liberators — A845

Honoring the Hungarian People's Republic.

| | | | Perf. 12 | |
|---|---|---|---|---|
| 1555 | A844 | 25k emerald | .65 | .50 |
| 1556 | A844 | 40k bright blue | 1.10 | .75 |
| 1557 | A845 | 60k sepia | 1.50 | 1.00 |
| 1558 | A845 | 1r sepia, salmon | 2.75 | 2.25 |
| | | Nos. 1555-1558 (4) | 6.00 | 4.50 |

Budapest Buildings: 40k, Parliament. 60k, National Museum.

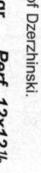

Harvesting Wheat A846

Designs: 40k, Apiary. 1r, Gathering citrus fruits. 2r, Cotton picking.

| 1559 | A846 | 25k dark green | .50 | .30 |
|---|---|---|---|---|
| 1560 | A846 | 40k green, bluish | .95 | .45 |
| 1561 | A846 | 1r brown, yellow | 1.75 | 1.25 |
| 1562 | A846 | 2r dk green, salmon | 3.00 | 2.50 |
| | | Nos. 1559-1562 (4) | 6.20 | 4.50 |

Kalinin Museum, Moscow — A847

Mikhail I. Kalinin — A848

Design: 1r, Kalinin statue.

**1951, June 25**    Perf. 12x12½, 12½x12

| 1563 | A847 | 20k org brn & black | .40 | .20 |
|---|---|---|---|---|
| 1564 | A848 | 40k dp green & choc | .75 | .25 |
| 1565 | A848 | 1r vio blue & gray | 1.50 | .55 |
| | | Nos. 1563-1565 (3) | 2.65 | 1.00 |

5th anniv. of the death of Kalinin.

F. E. Dzerzhinski, A849

Design: 1r, Profile of Dzerzhinski.

**1951, Aug. 4**    Engr.    Perf. 12x12½

| 1566 | A849 | 40k brown red | 3.75 | 1.75 |
|---|---|---|---|---|
| 1567 | A849 | 1r gray black | 5.25 | 3.25 |

1951, Aug. 4, 25th Death Anniv. — A849

---

**1951**    Unwmk.    Perf. 12½

Aleksandr M. Butlerov A850

P. K. Kozlov A850b

A. Kovalevski A850a

P. N. Lebedev A850d

N. S. Kurnakov A850c

A. N. Lodygin A850f

N. I. Lobachevski A850e

K. E. Tsiolkovsky A850h

A. N. Svertzov A850g

A. A. Aliabiev A851

Russian Scientists: No. 1570 Sonya Kovalevskaya. No. 1572, S. P. Krashenin-nikov. No. 1577, D. I. Mendeleev. No. 1578, N. N. Miklukho-Maklai. No. 1580, A. G. Stoletov. No. 1581, K. A. Timiryasev. No. 1583, P. N. Yablochkov.

**1951, Aug. 15**    Photo.    Perf. 12½

| 1568 | A850 | 40k org red, bluish | 1.75 | .80 |
|---|---|---|---|---|
| 1569 | A850a | 40k dk blue, sal | 1.10 | .30 |
| 1570 | A850 | 40k pur, salmon | 1.10 | .30 |
| 1571 | A850b | 40k orange red | 1.10 | .30 |
| 1572 | A850 | 40k purple | 1.10 | .30 |
| 1573 | A850c | 40k brown, salmon | 1.10 | .30 |
| 1574 | A850d | 40k blue | 1.10 | .30 |
| 1575 | A850e | 40k brown | 1.10 | .30 |
| 1576 | A850 | 40k green | 1.10 | .30 |
| 1577 | A850f | 40k deep blue | 1.10 | .30 |
| 1578 | A850 | 40k org red, sal | 1.10 | .30 |
| 1579 | A850g | 40k sepia, salmon | 1.10 | .30 |
| 1580 | A850 | 40k green, salmon | 1.10 | .30 |
| 1581 | A850 | 40k brown, salmon | 1.10 | .30 |
| 1582 | A850h | 40k gray blk, blue | 1.75 | .80 |
| 1583 | A850 | 40k sepia | 1.30 | .30 |
| | | Nos. 1568-1583 (16) | 18.90 | 5.80 |

**1951, Aug. 28**

| 1584 | A851 | 40k brown, salmon | 12.00 | 6.00 |
|---|---|---|---|---|
| 1585 | A851 | 40k gray, salmon | 12.00 | 7.50 |

Design: No. 1585, V. S. Kalinnikov.

Russian composers.

Two printings exist in differing stamp sizes of most of this issue.

---

Gathering Citrus Fruit — A853

Opera and Ballet Theater, Tbilisi — A852

**1951**    Unwmk.    Perf. 12½

40k, Principal street, Tbilisi. 1r, Picking tea.

| 1586 | A852 | 20k dp green, yel-low | 1.40 | .70 |
|---|---|---|---|---|
| 1587 | A853 | 25k pur, org & brn | 2.10 | .70 |
| 1588 | A853 | 40k dk brn, blue | 3.25 | 1.50 |
| 1589 | A853 | 1r red brn & dk grn | 8.25 | 3.50 |
| | | Nos. 1586-1589 (4) | 15.00 | 6.40 |

Georgian Republic, 30th anniversary.

Emblem of Aviation Society — A854

Planes and Emblem — A855

60k, Flying model planes. 1r, Parachutists.

**1951, Sept. 19**    Litho.
Dated: "1951"    Perf. 12½

| 1590 | A854 | 40k multicolored | .75 | .20 |
|---|---|---|---|---|
| 1591 | A854 | 60k emer, lt bl & brn | 1.40 | .30 |
| 1592 | A854 | 1r blue, sal & lilac | 2.00 | .45 |
| 1593 | A855 | 2r multicolored | 4.50 | .80 |
| | | Nos. 1590-1593 (4) | 8.65 | 1.75 |

Promoting interest in aviation.

---

Hydroelectric Station, Lenin and Stalin — A858

**1951, Nov. 6**    Photo.
Dated: "1917-1951"    Perf. 12½

| 1596 | A858 | 40k blue vio & red | 6.00 | 1.90 |
|---|---|---|---|---|
| 1597 | A858 | 1r dk brown & red | 9.00 | 3.25 |

Design: 1r, Spasski Tower, Kremlin.

34th anniversary of October Revolution.

Map, Dredge and Khakhovsky Hydroelectric Station — A859

Map, Volga Dam and Tugboat — A860

**1951, Nov. 28**    Perf. 12½

| 1598 | A859 | 20k multicolored | 5.75 | 1.75 |
|---|---|---|---|---|
| 1599 | A860 | 30k multicolored | 5.75 | 2.25 |
| 1600 | A860 | 40k multicolored | 7.50 | 3.75 |
| 1601 | A860 | 60k multicolored | 12.00 | 4.25 |
| 1602 | A860 | 1r multicolored | 18.00 | 8.50 |
| | | Nos. 1598-1602 (5) | 50.00 | 20.50 |

Designs (each showing map): 40k, Stalingrad Dam. 60k, Excavating Turkmenian canal. 1r, Kuibyshev dam.

Flag and Citizens Signing Peace Appeal — A861

**1951, Nov. 30**    Perf. 12½

| 1603 | A861 | 40k gray & red | 10.00 | 7.00 |
|---|---|---|---|---|

Third All-Union Peace Conference.

Three Heroes, by Vasnetsov — A857

Victor M. Vasnetsov (1848-1926), Painter — A856

**1951, Oct. 15**

| 1594 | A856 | 40k dk bl, brn & buff | 3.00 | .25 |
|---|---|---|---|---|
| 1595 | A857 | 1r multicolored | 4.50 | 1.00 |

Mikhail V. Ostrogradski, Mathematician, 150th Birth Anniv. — A862

**1951, Dec. 10**    Unwmk.

| 1604 | A862 | 40k black brn, pink | 8.00 | 3.50 |
|---|---|---|---|---|

Ogarev
A881

Zhukovski
A880

Design: No. 1636, K. P. Bryulov.

**Pale Blue Paper**

**1952, July 26**
1635 A880 40k gray black .75 .30
1636 A880 40k brt blue green .75 .30
V. A. Zhukovski, poet, and Bryulov, painter (1799-1852).

**1952, Aug. 29**
1637 A881 40k deep green .50 .25
75th anniversary of the death of N. P. Ogarev, poet and revolutionary.

Nakhimov — A883

Uspenski — A882

**1952, Sept. 4**
1638 A882 40k indigo & dk brown 1.00 .50
Gleb Ivanovich Uspenski (1843-1902), writer.

**1952, Sept. 9**
1639 A883 40k multicolored 2.00 .75
Adm. Paul S. Nakhimov (1802-1855).

**1952, Oct. 2**
1640 A884 40k black brn, *salmon* 3.00 1.25
150th anniversary of the enlargement of the University of Tartu, Estonia.

University Building, Tartu — A884

A. N. Radishchev
A886

Kajum Nasyri
A885

**1952, Nov. 5**
1641 A885 40k brown, *yellow* 1.25
Nasyri (1825-1902), Tartar educator.

**1952, Oct. 23**
1642 A886 40k blk, brn & dk red 2.00 1.00
Radishchev, writer, 150th death anniv.

---

**1952, May 15** **Unwmk.**
#1626, Aged citizens. #1627, Schoolgirl.
1624 A872 40k red & blk, *cream* 4.50 3.75
1625 A873 40k red & dk grn, *pale gray* 4.50 3.75
1626 A873 40k red & brown, *pale gray* 4.50 3.75
1627 A872 40k red & black, *pale gray* 4.50 3.75
*Nos. 1624-1627 (4)* 18.00 15.00
Adoption of Stalin constitution., 15th anniv

A. S. Novikov-Priboy and Ship — A874

**1952, June 5**
1628 A874 40k blk, pale cit & bl grn .50 .30
Novikov-Priboy, writer, 75th birthanniv.

150th anniv. of Birth of Victor Hugo (1802-1855), French Writer — A875

**1952, June 5** **Unwmk.**
1629 A875 40k brn org, gray & black .50 .25

*Perf. 12½*

Sedov — A877

**1952, June 28**
1630 A876 40k rose red, *pink* .60 .20
200th anniversary of the birth of Salavat Julaev, Bashkir hero who took part in the insurrection of 1773-1775.

Julaev — A876

**1952, July 4**
1631 A877 40k dk bl, dk brn & blue green 12.00 5.00
Georgi J. Sedov, Arctic explorer (1877-1914).

Arms and Flag of Romania — A878

University Square, Bucharest — A879

Design: 60k, Monument to Soviet soldiers.

**1952, July 26**
1632 A878 40k multicolored 2.75 .55
1633 A878 60k dk green, *pink* 4.50 1.25
1634 A879 1r bright ultra 5.75 2.50
*Nos. 1632-1634 (3)* 13.00 4.30

---

Kovalevski
A868

Semenov
A867

**1952, Feb. 1** **Unwmk.**
1615 A867 1r sepia, *blue* 7.00 5.00
Petr Petrovich Semenov-Tianshanski (1827-1914); traveler and geographer who explored the Tian Shan mountains.

**1952, Mar. 3**
1616 A868 40k sepia, *yellow* 12.50 10.00
V. O. Kovalevski (1843-1883), biologist and palaeontologist.

Skaters
A869

**1952, Mar. 3**
1617 A869 40k shown 1.25 .25
1618 A869 60k Skiers 2.25 .35

N. V. Gogol and Characters from "Taras Bulba" — A870

**1952, Mar. 4** **Dated: "1852-1952"**
1619 A870 40k sepia, *blue* .76 .20
1620 A870 60k multicolored 1.25 .20
1621 A870 1r multicolored 1.50 .25
*Nos. 1619-1621 (3)* 3.50 .65

Designs: 60k, Gogol und V. G. Belinski. 1r, Gogol and Ukrainian peasants.

Death centenary of N. V. Gogol, writter.

Workers and Soviet Flag
A872

Workers' Rest Home
A873

**1952, Apr. 23** **Photo.** *Perf. 12½*
1622 A871 40k dp green, *pink* 3.75 3.50
1623 A871 1r sepia, *blue* 3.75 3.50
15th anniv. of the death of Grigori K. Ordzhonikidze, Georgian party worker.

G. K. Ordzhonikidze
A871

---

Monument to Jan Zizka, Prague — A863

Monument to Soviet Liberators A864

25k, Monument to Soviet Soldiers, Ostrava. 40k, Julius Fucik. 60k, Smetana Museum, Prague.

**1951, Dec. 10** *Perf. 12½*
1605 A863 20k vio blue, *sal* 7.00 2.25
1606 A863 25k copper red, *yel* 14.00 4.75
1607 A863 40k red orange, *sal* 25.00 2.25
1608 A863 60k brnsh gray, *buff* 14.00 4.75
1609 A864 1r brnsh gray, *buff* 7.00 6.00
*Nos. 1605-1609 (5)* 67.00 20.00
Soviet-Czechoslovakian friendship.

Volkhovski Hydroelectric Station and Lenin Statue — A865

**1951, Dec. 19**
1610 A865 40k dk bl, gray & yel 2.50 .20
1611 A865 1r pur, gray & yel 5.50 .55
25th anniv. of the opening of the Lenin Volkhovski hydroelectric station.

Lenin as a Schoolboy
A866

**1952, Jan. 24** **Photo.** *Perf. 12½*
**Multicolored Centers**
1612 A866 40k dk blue green 1.75 .55
1613 A866 60k violet blue 2.25 .55
1614 A866 1r orange brown 3.50 .65
*Nos. 1612-1614 (3)* 7.50 1.75

Horizontal Designs: 60k, Lenin among children. 1r, Lenin and peasants.

28th anniversary of the death of Lenin.

## Composite Medal Types of 1946
### Frames as A599-A606
### Centers as Indicated

Medals: 1r, Token of Veneration. 2r, Red Star. 3r, Red Workers' Banner. 5r, Red Banner. 10r, Lenin.

M.S. Joseph Stalin at Entrance to Volga-Don Canal — A887

Design: 1r, Lenin, Stalin and red banners.

**1952, Nov. 6**    *Perf. 12½*
1643 A887 40k multicolored   3.00 1.50
1644 A887 1r brown, red & yel   5.00 3.00
35th anniversary of October Revolution.

Pavel Andreievitch Fedotov (1815-52), Artist — A888

**1952, Nov. 26**
1645 A888 40k red brn & black   1.00 .50

V. D. Polenov, Artist, 25th Death Anniv. — A889

"Moscow Courtyard" — A890

**1952, Dec. 6**
1646 A889 40k red brown & buff   1.25 .35
1647 A890 1r multicolored   2.25 .65

A. I. Odoyevski (1802-39) Poet — A891

**1952, Dec. 8**
1648 A891 40k gray blk & red org   .80 .25

D. N. Mamin-Sibiryak — A892

**1952, Dec. 15**
1649 A892 40k dp green, cream   1.00 .25
Centenary of the birth of Dimitri N. Mamin-Sibiryak (1852-1912), writer.

---

**1952-59**    **Engr.**    *Perf. 12½*
1650 A669 1r dark brown   7.00 7.00
1651 A567 2r red brown   1.10 .55
1652 A572 3r dp blue violet   1.50 .95
1653 A571 5r dk car ('53)   3.00 1.90
1654 A566 10r bright rose   3.50 1.90
   a.   10r dull rose ('54)   15.00 11.35
Nos. 1650-1654 (5)   15.00 11.35

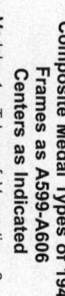

Vladimir M. Bekhterev (1857-1927), Neuropathologist — A893

**1952, Dec. 24**    **Photo.**
1655 A893 40k vio bl, slate & blk   .90 .30

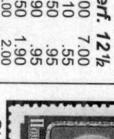

Byelorusskaya Station — A894

Designs (Moscow Subway stations): 40k, Botanical Garden Station. 40k, Novoslobodskaya Station. 40k, Komsomolskaya Station.

**1952, Dec. 30**
### Multicolored Centers
1656 A894 40k dull violet   .60 .30
1657 A894 40k light ultra   .60 .30
1658 A894 40k blue gray   .60 .30
1659 A894 40k dull green   .60 .30
   a.   Horiz. strip of 4, #1656-1659   2.50 2.00

USSR Emblem and Flags of 16 Union Republics — A895

**1952, Dec. 30**
1660 A895 1r grn, dk red & brn   2.50 1.75
30th anniversary of the USSR.

Lenin — A896

**1953, Jan. 26**
1661 A896 40k multicolored   5.00 4.00
29 years without Lenin.

---

Stalin Peace Medal — A897

Valerian V. Kuibyshev — A898

**1953, Apr. 30**    *Perf. 12½*
1662 A897 40k red brn, bl & dull yel   12.00 6.00

**1953, June 6**
1663 A898 40k red brn & black   1.00 .55
Kuibyshev (1888-1935), Bolshevik leader.

Count Leo N. Tolstoy (1828-1910), Writer — A903

**1953, Sept.**    *Perf. 12*
1673 A903 1r dark brown   6.00 4.00

Moscow University and Two Youths — A904

**1953, Oct. 29**    *Perf. 12½x12*
1674 A904 40k multicolored   2.50 1.40
1675 A904 1r multicolored   4.50 1.90

1r, Komsomol badge and four orders.

35th anniversary of the Young Communist League (Komsomol).

---

A899

A900

**1953, July 21**
1664 A899 40k buff & dk brown   2.00 1.25
Nikolai G. Chernyshevski (1828-1889), writer and radical leader, exiled to Siberia for 24 years.

**1953, July 19**
1665 A900 40k ver & gray brown   2.50 1.25
60th anniv. of the birth of Vladimir V. Mayakovsky, poet.

Tsymljanskaja Dam — A901

Volga-Don Canal: No. 1666, Lock No. 9, Volga-Don Canal; No. 1667, Lock 13, house; No. 1668, Lock 15; No. 1669, Volga River light-canal. No. 1671, M. S. "Joseph Stalin" in

**1953, Aug. 29**    **Litho.**
1666 A901 40k multicolored   1.00 .20
1667 A901 40k multicolored   1.00 .20
1668 A901 40k multicolored   1.00 .20
1669 A901 40k multicolored   1.00 .20
1670 A901 40k multicolored   1.00 .20
1671 A901 1r multicolored   2.25 .75
Nos. 1666-1671 (6)   7.25 1.75

V. G. Korolenko (1853-1921), Writer — A902

**1953, Aug. 29**    **Photo.**    *Perf. 12x12½*
1672 A902 40k brown   1.00 .25

---

Nationalities of the Soviet Union — A905

60k, Lenin and Stalin at Smolny monastery.

**1953, Nov. 6**
1676 A905 40k multicolored   4.50 3.25
1677 A905 60k multicolored   10.00 6.75
36th anniversary of October Revolution. No. 1676 measures 25½x38mm; No. 1677, 25⅛x42mm.

Lenin and His Writings — A906

1r, Lenin facing left and pages of "What to Do."

**1953**
1678 A906 40k multicolored   3.00 3.75
1679 A906 1r dk brn, org brn & red   6.50 4.75
Communist Party formation, 50th anniv. 2nd cong. of the Russian Socialist Party, 50th anniv. (1r) Issued: 40k, 11/12; 1r, 12/14.

Lenin Statue — A907

Peter I Statue, Decembrists'
Square — A908

Leningrad Views: Nos. 1681 & 1683, Admiralty building. Nos. 1685 & 1687, Smolny monastery.

**1953, Nov. 23**
| | | | | |
|---|---|---|---|---|
| 1680 | A907 | 40k brn blk, *yellow* | 2.25 | 1.25 |
| 1681 | A907 | 40k vio brn, *yellow* | 2.25 | 1.25 |
| 1682 | A907 | 40k dk brn, *pink* | 2.25 | 1.25 |
| 1683 | A907 | 40k blk, *cream* | 2.25 | 1.25 |
| 1684 | A908 | 1r dk brn, *blue* | 5.00 | 3.00 |
| 1685 | A908 | 1r dk green, *yellow* | 5.00 | 3.00 |
| 1686 | A908 | 1r violet, *yellow* | 5.00 | 3.00 |
| 1687 | A908 | 1r blk brn, *blue* | 5.00 | 3.00 |
| | | Nos. 1680-1687 (8) | 29.00 | 17.00 |

See Nos. 1944-1945, 1943a.

"Pioneers" and Model of Lomonosov Moscow University A909

Aleksandr S. Griboedov, Writer (1795-1829) A910

**1953, Dec. 22   Litho.   Perf. 12**
1688   A909   40k dk sl grn, dk brn & red   3.50   1.75

**1954-57**
1689   A682   40k scarlet   1.00   .50
  B ribbon turns on wreath at left   4.25   1.65
    (54)

No. 1689 was re-issued in 1954-56 typographed in slightly smaller format: 14½x21¾mm, instead of 14¾x21¾mm, and in a lighter shade. See note after No. 738. No. 1689 has 7 ribbon turns on left side of wreath.

**1954, Mar. 4   Photo.**
1690   A910   40k dp claret, *cream*   1.40   .75
1691   A910   1r black, *green*   1.60   1.50

Kremlin View — A911

V. P. Chkalov — A912

**1954, Mar. 7   Litho.   Perf. 12½x12**
1692   A911   40k red & gray   6.00   3.00

1954 elections to the Supreme Soviet.

**1954, Mar. 16   Perf. 12**
1693   A912   1r gray, vio bl & dk brown   6.00   1.25

50th anniversary of the birth of Valeri P. Chkalov (1904-1938), airplane pilot.

Lenin — A913

Lenin at Smolny A914

Designs: No. 1696, Lenin's home (later museum), Ulyanovsk. No. 1697, Lenin addressing workers. No. 1698, Lenin among students, University of Kazan.

**Photo.**
**1954, Apr. 16**
1694   A913   40k multicolored   4.00   2.00

**Size: 38x27½mm**
1695   A914   40k multicolored   4.00   2.00
1696   A914   40k multicolored   4.00   2.00

**Size: 48x35mm**
1697   A914   40k multicolored   4.00   2.00
1698   A914   40k multicolored   20.00   10.00
  Nos. 1694-1698 (5)

30th anniversary of the death of Lenin. For overprint see No. 2060.

Joseph V. Stalin — A915

**1954, Apr. 30   Unwmk.   Perf. 12**
1699   A915   40k dark brown   4.25   1.50

First anniversary of the death of Stalin.

Supreme Soviet Buildings in Kiev and Moscow A916

T. G. Shevchenko Statue, Kharkov — A917

Designs: No. 1701, University building, Kiev. No. 1702, Opera, Kiev. No. 1703, Ukrainian Academy of Science. No. 1705, Bogdan Chmielnicki statue. Kiev. No. 1706 Flags of Soviet Russia and Ukraine. No. 1707, T. G. Shevchenko statue, Kanev. No. 1708, Chmielnicki proclaiming reunion of Ukraine and Russia, 1654.

**1954, May 10   Litho.**
**Size: 37½x26mm, 26x37½mm**
| | | | | |
|---|---|---|---|---|
| 1700 | A916 | 40k red brn, sal, *cream* & black | .95 | .20 |
| 1701 | A916 | 40k ultra, vio bl & brn | .95 | .20 |
| 1702 | A916 | 40k red brn, buff, *blue* | .95 | .20 |
| 1703 | A916 | 40k org brn, *cream* & grn | .95 | .20 |
| 1704 | A917 | 40k rose red, blk, yel & brown | 1.25 | .20 |
| 1705 | A917 | 60k multicolored | 1.25 | .30 |
| 1706 | A917 | 1r multicolored | 2.75 | .50 |

**Size: 42x28mm**
1707   A916   1r multicolored   1.90   .50
**Size: 45x29½mm**
1708   A916   1r multicolored, *pink*   2.75   .50

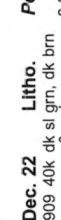

No. 1341 Overprinted in Carmine

1709   A517   2r green   6.25   1.60
  *Nos. 1700-1709 (10)*   19.95   4.40

300th anniversary of the union between the Ukraine and Russia.

Sailboat Race A918

Basketball A919

#1711, Hurdle race. #1712, Swimmers. #1713, Javelin. #1714, Track. #1715, Pole. #1716, Mountain climbing.

**1954, May 29**
**Frames in Orange Brown**
| | | | | |
|---|---|---|---|---|
| 1710 | A918 | 40k blue & black | 1.25 | .20 |
| 1711 | A918 | 40k vio gray & blk | 1.25 | .20 |
| 1712 | A918 | 40k dk blue & black | 1.25 | .20 |
| 1713 | A918 | 40k brn & buff | 1.25 | .20 |
| 1714 | A918 | 40k black brn & buff | 1.25 | .20 |
| 1715 | A918 | 1r blue & black | 2.75 | .25 |
| 1716 | A918 | 1r blue & black | 2.75 | .25 |
| 1717 | A919 | 1r dk brn & brn | 2.75 | .25 |
| | | *Nos. 1710-1717 (8)* | 14.50 | 1.75 |

For overprint see No. 2170.

Cattle A920

#1719, Potato planting and cultivation. #1720, Kolkhoz hydroelectric station.

**1954, June 8**
1718   A920   40k brn, *cream*, ind & black   1.90   .85
1719   A920   40k gray grn, buff & blue gray   1.90   .85
1720   A920   40k blk, bl grn & vio bl   1.90   .85
  *Nos. 1718-1720 (3)*   5.70   2.55

Anton P. Chekhov, Writer, 50th Death Anniv. — A921

**1954, July 15**
1721   A921   40k green & black brn   .75   .25

F. A. Bredichin, V. J. Struve, A. A. Belopolski and Observatory — A922

**1954, July 26**
1722   A922   40k vio bl, blk & blue   6.00   1.00

Restoration of Pulkov Observatory.

Mikhail I. Glinka, Composer, 150th Birth Anniv. — A923

Pushkin and Zhukovsky Visiting Glinka A924

**1954, July 26**
1723   A923   40k dp cl, *pink* & blk   4.50   .75
1724   A924   60k brown   5.50   1.00

Nikolai A. Ostrovsky (1904-36), Blind Writer — A925

**1954, Sept. 29   Photo.   Perf. 12½x12**
1725   A925   40k brn, dark red & yel   1.00   .40

Monument to Sunken Ships — A926

Defenders of Sevastopol — A927

Design: 1r, Admiral P. S. Nakhimov.

**1954, Oct. 17**     **Perf. 12½**
1726 A926 40k blue grn, blk & ol    .60 .20
1727 A927 60k org brn, blk & brn    .80 .25
1728 A926   1r brn, blk & ol
    green    1.60 .55
    3.00 1.00
Nos. 1726-1728 (3)
Centenary of the defense of Sevastopol during the Crimean War.

Sculpture at Exhibition Entrance — A928
Agriculture Pavilion — A929

Cattle Pavilion A929a

**1954, Nov. 5**     **Litho.**
1729 A928 40k multicolored    1.00 .50
   **Size: 26x37mm**
1730 A929 40k multicolored    1.00 .50
1731 A929a 40k multicolored    1.00 .50
1732 A929 40k multicolored    1.00 .50
   **Size: 40x29mm**
1733 A929   1r multicolored    3.50 2.00
   **Size: 40½x33mm**
1734 A928   1r multicolored    11.00 6.00
   **Size: 28½x40½mm**
Nos. 1729-1734 (6)    3.50 2.00
    11.00 6.00
Designs: No. 1732, Machinery pavilion. No. 1733, Main entrance. No. 1734, Main pavilion.
1954 Agricultural Exhibition.

**Perf. 12½, 12½x12, 12x12½**

Kazan University Building A931

Marx, Engels, Lenin and Stalin — A930

**1954, Nov. 6**   **Photo.**   **Perf. 12½x12**
1735 A930 1r dk brn, pale org &
   red    6.00 2.50
37th anniversary of October Revolution.

**1954, Nov. 11**    **Perf. 12x12½**
1736 A931 40k deep blue    1.00 .50
1737 A931 60k claret    1.25 1.00
Founding of Kazan University, 150th anniv.

---

Salome Neris A932

**1954, Nov. 17**    **Perf. 12½x12**
1738 A932 40k red org & ol gray    2.00 .50
50th anniversary of the birth of Salome Neris (1904-1945), Lithuanian poet.

Vegetables and Garden A933

Cultivating Flax — A934

**1954, Dec. 12**   **Litho.**   **Perf. 12½x12½**
1739 A933 40k multicolored    1.00 .25
1740 A934 40k multicolored    1.00 .25
1741 A933 40k multicolored    1.50 .35
1742 A934 60k multicolored    4.50 1.10
Nos. 1739-1742 (4)
Designs: No. 1741, Tractor plowing field. No. 1742, Loading ensilage.

Joseph Stalin, 75th Birth Anniv. — A935

**1954, Dec. 21**   **Engr.**   **Perf. 12½x12**
1743 A935 40k rose brown    .80 .50
1744 A935   1r dark blue    1.75 .60

Anton G. Rubinstein (1829-94), Composer A936

**1954, Dec. 30**   **Photo.**
1745 A936 40k claret, gray & blk    4.00 .50

Vsevolod M. Garshin (1855-1888), Writer — A937

**1955, Mar. 2**   **Unwmk.**
**Lithographed and Photogravure**    **Perf. 12**
1746 A937 40k buff, blk brn &
   green    .60 .25

---

K. A. Savitsky and Painting A938

**1955, Mar. 21**    **Photo.**
1747 A938 40k multicolored    1.00 .30
   a. Sheet of 4, black inscription    25.00 35.00
   b. As "a", red brown inscription    35.00 25.00
Design: K. A. Savitsky (1844-1905), painter.
Size: Nos. 1747a, 1747b, 152x108mm.

Globe and Clasped Hands — A939

**1955, Apr. 9**    **Litho.**
1748 A939 40k multicolored    .50 .25
International Conference of Public Service Unions, Vienna, April 1955.

Poets Pushkin and Mickiewicz — A940

Brothers in Arms Monument, Warsaw — A941

Palace of Culture and Science, Warsaw A942

Copernicus, Painting by Jan Matejko (in Medallion) — A943

**1955, Apr. 22**    **Unwmk.**   **Photo.**   **Perf. 12**
1749 A940 40k chalky blue, vio &
   black    1.25 .25
1750 A941 40k violet black    1.25 .25
1751 A942   1r brt red & gray
   black    2.75 .65
1752 A943   1r multicolored    2.75 .65
Nos. 1749-1752 (4)    8.00 1.80
Polish-USSR treaty of friendship, 10th anniv.

---

Lenin at Secret Printing House — A945
Friedrich von Schiller — A946
Lenin at Shushinskoe — A944

**1955, Apr. 22**
**Frame and Inscription in Dark Red**
1753 A944 60k multicolored    1.00 .35
1754 A944   1r multicolored    2.50 .45
1755 A945   1r multicolored    6.00 1.25
Nos. 1753-1755 (3)
85th anniversary of the birth of Lenin.
Design: 1r, Lenin and Krupskaya with peasants at Gorki, 1921.

**1955, May 10**
1756 A946 40k chocolate    1.00 .50
150th anniversary of the death of Friedrich von Schiller, German poet.

A. G. Venezianov and "Spring on the Land" — A947

**1955, June 21**    **Photo.**
1757 A947   1r multicolored    1.50 .50
   a. Souvenir sheet of 4    22.50 15.00
Venezianov, painter, 175th birth anniv.

Anatoli K. Liadov (1855-1914), Composer — A948

**1955, July 5**    **Litho.**
1758 A948 40k red brn, blk & lt
   brn    1.50 .50

Aleksandr Popov — A949

**1955, Nov. 5**
**Portraits Multicolored**
1759 A949 40k light ultra    1.10 .20
1760 A949   1r gray brown    2.25 .35
60th anniv. of the construction of a coherer for detecting Hertzian electromagnetic waves by A. S. Popov, radio pioneer.

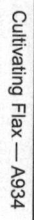

**Atomic Power Station A962**

Design: 60k, Atomic Reactor.

**1956, Jan. 31**
| | | | | |
|---|---|---|---|---|
| 1794 | A962 | 25k multicolored | .70 | .20 |
| 1795 | A962 | 60k multicolored | 1.10 | .25 |
| 1796 | A962 | 1r multicolored | 1.60 | .40 |
| | | | 3.40 | .85 |
| | | *Nos. 1794-1796 (3)* | | |

Establishment of the first Atomic Power Station of the USSR Academy of Science. Inscribed in Russian: "Atomic Energy in the service of the people."

**Statue of Lenin, Kremlin and Flags A963**

**1956, Feb.**
| | | | | |
|---|---|---|---|---|
| 1797 | A963 | 40k multicolored | .90 | .20 |
| 1798 | A963 | 1r ol, buff & red org | 1.10 | .30 |

20th Congress of the Communist Party of the Soviet Union.

**Khachatur Abovian, Armenian Writer, 150th Birth Anniv. — A964**

**1956, Feb. 25**    **Unwmk.**    **Perf. 12**
| | | | | |
|---|---|---|---|---|
| 1799 | A964 | 40k black brn, *bluish* | 5.00 | .40 |

**Workers with Red Flag — A965**

**1956, Mar. 14**
| | | | | |
|---|---|---|---|---|
| 1800 | A965 | 40k multicolored | 2.00 | .75 |

Revolution of 1905, 50th anniversary.

**Nikolai A. Kasatkin — A966**

**1956, Apr. 30**
| | | | | |
|---|---|---|---|---|
| 1801 | A966 | 40k carmine lake | .50 | .25 |

Kasatkin (1859-1930), painter.

**"On the Oka River" A967**

---

**Lomonosov Moscow State University, 200th Anniv. — A956**

Design: 1r, New University buildings.

**1955, June 9**    **Perf. 12**
| | | | | |
|---|---|---|---|---|
| 1786 | A956 | 40k multicolored | .65 | .25 |
| a. | | Sheet of 4 ('56) | 6.00 | 5.00 |
| 1787 | A956 | 1r multicolored | 1.40 | .30 |
| a. | | Sheet of 4 ('56) | 12.00 | 10.00 |

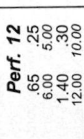

**Vladimir V. Mayakovsky — A957**

**1955, May 31**
| | | | | |
|---|---|---|---|---|
| 1788 | A957 | 40k multicolored | 1.00 | .25 |

Mayakovsky, poet, 25th death anniv.

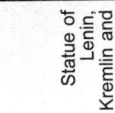

**Race Horse — A958**

**Trotter A959**

**1956, Jan. 9**
| | | | | |
|---|---|---|---|---|
| 1789 | A958 | 40k dark brown | .50 | .20 |
| 1790 | A959 | 60k Prus grn & blue | .90 | .25 |
| 1791 | A959 | 1r dull pur & blue vio green | 1.60 | .40 |
| | | | 3.00 | .85 |
| | | *Nos. 1789-1791 (3)* | | |

International Horse Races, Moscow, Aug. 14-Sept. 4, 1955.

**Alexei N. Krylov (1863-1945), Mathematician, Naval Architect — A960**

**1956, Jan. 9**
| | | | | |
|---|---|---|---|---|
| 1792 | A960 | 40k gray, brown & black | .50 | .20 |

**Symbol of Spartacist Games, Stadium and Factories — A961**

**1956, Jan. 18**
| | | | | |
|---|---|---|---|---|
| 1793 | A961 | 1r red vio & lt grn | .75 | .25 |

5th All-Union Spartacist Games of Soviet Trade Union sport clubs, Moscow, Aug. 12-18, 1955.

---

**Federal Socialist Republic Pavilion (R.S.F.S.R.) — A955**

| | |
|---|---|
| ПАВИЛЬОН ТАДЖИКСКОЙ ССР | #1771 |
| ПАВИЛЬОН БЕЛОРУССКОЙ ССР | #1772 |
| ПАВИЛЬОН АЗЕРБАЙДЖАНСКОЙ ССР | #1773 |
| ПАВИЛЬОН ГРУЗИНСКОЙ ССР | #1774 |
| ПАВИЛЬОН АРМЯНСКОЙ ССР | #1775 |
| ПАВИЛЬОН ТУРКМЕНСКОЙ ССР | #1776 |
| ПАВИЛЬОН УЗБЕКСКОЙ ССР | #1777 |
| ПАВИЛЬОН УКРАИНСКОЙ ССР | #1778 |
| ПАВИЛЬОН КАЗАХСКОЙ ССР | #1779 |
| ПАВИЛЬОН КИРГИЗСКОЙ ССР | #1780 |
| ПАВИЛЬОН КАРЕЛО-ФИНСКОЙ ССР | #1781 |
| ПАВИЛЬОН МОЛДАВСКОЙ ССР | #1782 |
| ПАВИЛЬОН ЭСТОНСКОЙ ССР | #1783 |
| ПАВИЛЬОН ЛАТВИЙСКОЙ ССР | #1784 |
| ПАВИЛЬОН ЛИТОВСКОЙ ССР | #1785 |

Designs: Pavilions.

**1955**    **Litho.**    **Unwmk.**
**Centers in Natural Colors; Frames in Blue Green and Olive**

| | | | | |
|---|---|---|---|---|
| 1770 | A955 | 40k shown | .70 | .30 |
| a. | | Sheet of 4 | 15.00 | 9.50 |
| 1771 | A955 | 40k Tadzhik | .70 | .30 |
| 1772 | A955 | 40k Byelorussian | .70 | .30 |
| a. | | Sheet of 4 | 15.00 | 9.50 |
| 1773 | A955 | 40k Azerbaijan | .70 | .30 |
| 1774 | A955 | 40k Georgian | .70 | .30 |
| 1775 | A955 | 40k Armenian | .70 | .30 |
| 1776 | A955 | 40k Turkmen | .70 | .30 |
| 1777 | A955 | 40k Uzbek | .70 | .30 |
| 1778 | A955 | 40k Ukrainian | .70 | .30 |
| a. | | Sheet of 4 | 15.00 | 9.50 |
| 1779 | A955 | 40k Kazakh | .70 | .30 |
| 1780 | A955 | 40k Kirghiz | .70 | .30 |
| 1781 | A955 | 40k Karelo-Finnish | .70 | .30 |
| 1782 | A955 | 40k Moldavian | .70 | .30 |
| 1783 | A955 | 40k Estonian | .70 | .30 |
| 1784 | A955 | 40k Latvian | .70 | .30 |
| 1785 | A955 | 40k Lithuanian | .70 | .30 |
| | | *Nos. 1770-1785 (16)* | 11.20 | 4.80 |

All-Union Agricultural Fair.

Nos. 1773-1785 were printed in sheets containing various stamps, providing a variety of horizontal se-tenant pairs and strips. Value, $50 per sheet.

---

**Lenin — A950**

**Storming the Winter Palace — A951**

Design: 1r, Lenin addressing the people.

**1955, Nov. 6**
| | | | | |
|---|---|---|---|---|
| 1761 | A950 | 40k multicolored | 1.25 | .75 |
| 1762 | A951 | 40k multicolored | 1.25 | .75 |
| 1763 | A951 | 1r multicolored | 3.00 | 1.00 |
| | | | 5.50 | 2.50 |
| | | *Nos. 1761-1763 (3)* | | |

38th anniversary of October Revolution.

**Apartment Houses, Magnitogorsk — A952**

**1955, Nov. 29**
| | | | | |
|---|---|---|---|---|
| 1764 | A952 | 40k multicolored | 3.00 | .25 |

25th anniversary of the founding of the industrial center, Magnitogorsk.

**Arctic Observation Post — A953**

Design: 1r, Scientist at observation post.

**1955, Nov. 29**    **Perf. 12½x12**
| | | | | |
|---|---|---|---|---|
| 1765 | A953 | 40k multicolored | 1.60 | .20 |
| 1766 | A953 | 60k multicolored | 1.90 | .30 |
| 1767 | A953 | 1r multicolored | 2.75 | .45 |
| a. | | Souvenir sheet of 4 ('58) | 35.00 | 25.00 |
| | | | 6.25 | .95 |
| | | *Nos. 1765-1767 (3)* | | |

Publicizing the Soviet scientific drifting stations at the North Pole.

In 1962, No. 1767a was overprinted in red "1962" on each stamp and, in the lower sheet margin, a three-line Russian inscription meaning "25 years from the beginning of the work of "NP-1" station."

Sheet value, $40 unused, $35 canceled.

**Fedor Ivanovich Shubin (1740-1805), Sculptor — A954**

**1955, Dec. 22**    **Perf. 12**
| | | | | |
|---|---|---|---|---|
| 1768 | A954 | 40k green & multi | .35 | .20 |
| 1769 | A954 | 1r brown & multi | .65 | .25 |

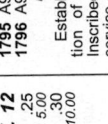
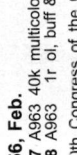

**1956, Apr. 30**
**Center Multicolored**

| | | | |
|---|---|---|---|
| 1802 | A967 | 40k bister & black | 1.50 .20 |
| 1803 | A967 | 1r ultra & black | 3.00 .30 |

A. E. Arkhipov, painter.

**1956, May 12**

| | | | |
|---|---|---|---|
| 1804 | A968 | 40k multicolored | 1.00 .25 |

I. P. Kulibin, Inventor, 220th Birth Anniv. — A968

Vassili Perov (1833-82), Painter — A969

"Birdcatchers" — A970

**1956, May 12**

| | | | |
|---|---|---|---|
| 1805 | A969 | 40k green | 1.10 .20 |
| 1806 | A970 | 1r brown | 2.10 .35 |
| 1807 | A970 | 1r orange brown | 2.10 .45 |
| | | Nos. 1805-1807 (3) | 5.30 1.00 |

Painting: No. 1807, "Hunters at Rest."

Ural Pavilion A971

**1956, May 12**
**Multicolored Centers**

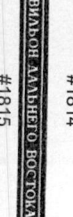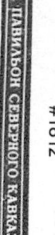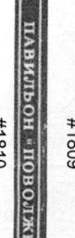

**1956, Apr. 25**
**Multicolored Centers**

| | | | |
|---|---|---|---|
| 1808 | A971 | 1r yel green & yel | 1.10 .40 |
| 1809 | A971 | 1r yel green & pale yel | 1.10 .40 |
| 1810 | A971 | 1r dk blue grn & pale yel | 1.10 .40 |
| 1811 | A971 | 1r dk bl grn & yel grn | 1.10 .40 |
| 1812 | A971 | 1r dk blue grn & buff | 1.10 .40 |
| 1813 | A971 | 1r ol gray & pale yel | 1.10 .40 |
| 1814 | A971 | 1r olive & yellow | 1.10 .40 |
| 1815 | A971 | 1r olive grn & yellow | 1.10 .40 |
| 1816 | A971 | 1r olive grn & lemon | 1.10 .40 |
| 1817 | A971 | 1r olive & lemon | 1.10 .40 |
| 1818 | A971 | 1r brown & yellow | 1.10 .40 |
| 1819 | A971 | 1r redsh brown & yel | 1.10 .40 |
| 1820 | A971 | 1r dk red brn & yel | 1.10 .40 |
| | | Nos. 1808-1820 (13) | 14.30 5.20 |

Pavilions: No. 1809, Tatar Republic. No. 1810, Volga District. No. 1811, Central Black Earth Area. No. 1812, Northeastern District. No. 1813, Northern Caucasus. No. 1814, Bashkir Republic. No. 1815, Far East. No. 1816, Central Asia. No. 1817, Young Naturalists. No. 1818, Siberia. No. 1819, Leningrad and Northwestern District. No. 1820, Moscow, Tula, Kaluga, Ryazan and Bryansk Districts.

All-Union Agricultural Fair, Moscow. Six of the Pavilion set were printed se-tenant in one sheet of 30 (6x5), the strip containing Nos. 1809, 1816, 1817, 1813, 1818 and 1810 in that order. Two others, Nos. 1819-1820, were printed se-tenant in one sheet of 35. Value, $50 per sheet.

Lenin A972

**1956, May 25**

| | | | |
|---|---|---|---|
| 1821 | A972 | 40k lilac & multi | 6.00 3.50 |

86th anniversary of the birth of Lenin.

Lobachevski A973

**1956, June 4**

| | | | |
|---|---|---|---|
| 1822 | A973 | 40k black brown | .50 .20 |

Nikolai Ivanovich Lobachevski (1793-1856), mathematician.

Nurse and Textile Factory A974

**1956, June 4**

| | | | |
|---|---|---|---|
| 1823 | A974 | 40k lt ol grn, grnsh bl & red | .50 .20 |
| 1824 | A974 | 40k red brn, lt bl & red | .50 .20 |

Design: 40k, First aid instruction.

Red Cross and Red Crescent. No. 1823 measures 37x25mm; No. 1824, 40x28mm.

V. K. Arseniev (1872-1930), Explorer and Writer — A975

**1956, June 15** **Litho.** **Perf. 12**

| | | | |
|---|---|---|---|
| 1825 | A975 | 40k violet, black & rose | 1.00 .25 |

I. M. Sechenov (1829-1905), Physiologist — A976

**1956, June 15**

| | | | |
|---|---|---|---|
| 1826 | A976 | 40k multicolored | 1.00 .25 |

A. K. Savrasov, Painter — A977

**1956, June 22**

| | | | |
|---|---|---|---|
| 1827 | A977 | 1r dull yel & brown | 1.00 .20 |

I. V. Michurin, Scientist, Birth Centenary A978

**1956, June 22**
**Center Multicolored**

| | | | |
|---|---|---|---|
| 1828 | A978 | 25k dark brown | .55 .20 |
| 1829 | A978 | 60k green & lt blue | 1.10 .40 |
| 1830 | A978 | 1r light blue | 2.25 .55 |
| | | Nos. 1828-1830 (3) | 3.90 1.15 |

Design: 60k, I. V. Michurin with Pioneers.

Nos. 1828 and 1830 measure 32x25mm. No. 1829 measures 47x26mm.

Nadezhda K. Krupskaya A979

**1956, June 28**

| | | | |
|---|---|---|---|
| 1831 | A979 | 40k brn, lt blue & pale brown | 2.50 .75 |

Krupskaya (1869-1939), teacher and wife of Lenin. See Nos. 1862, 1886, 1983, 2028.

S. M. Kirov (1886-1934), Revolutionary A980

**1956, June 28**

| | | | |
|---|---|---|---|
| 1832 | A980 | 40k red, buff & brown | .50 .25 |

Nikolai S. Leskov (1831-1895), Novelist — A981

**1956, July 10**

| | | | |
|---|---|---|---|
| 1833 | A981 | 40k olive bister & brn | .40 .20 |
| 1834 | A981 | 1r green & dk brown | .70 .40 |

Aleksandr A. Blok (1880-1921), Poet — A982

**1956, July 10**

| | | | |
|---|---|---|---|
| 1835 | A982 | 40k olive & brn, cream | .50 .40 |

Farm Machinery Factory A983

**1956, July 23** **Perf. 12½x12**

| | | | |
|---|---|---|---|
| 1836 | A983 | 40k multicolored | .50 .25 |

Rostov Farm Machinery Works, 25th anniv.

G. N. Fedotova (1846-1925), actress — A984

**1956, July 23** **Unwmk.**

| | | | |
|---|---|---|---|
| 1837 | A984 | 40k brown & rose vio | 1.00 .25 |

See No. 2026.

P. M. Tretiakov and Art Gallery A985

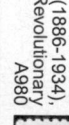

G. B. Shaw
A1000a

Dostoevski
A1000b

Portraits: #1876, Sesshu (Toyo Oda). #1877, Rembrandt. #1879, Mozart. #1880, Heinrich Heine. #1882, Ibsen. #1883, Pierre Curie.

**Photo.**
**1956, Oct. 17**

**Size: 25x37mm**
| 1875 | A1000 | 40k copper brown | 1.90 | .90 |
| 1876 | A1000 | 40k brt orange | 1.90 | .90 |
| 1877 | A1000 | 40k black | 1.90 | .90 |
| 1878 | A1000a | 40k black | 1.90 | .90 |

**Size: 21x32mm**
| 1879 | A1000 | 40k grnsh blue | 1.90 | .90 |
| 1880 | A1000 | 40k violet | 1.90 | .90 |
| 1881 | A1000b | 40k green | 1.90 | .90 |
| 1882 | A1000 | 40k black | 1.90 | .90 |
| 1883 | A1000 | 40k brt green | 17.10 | 8.10 |

Nos. 1875-1883 (9)

Great personalities of the world.

Antarctic Bases — A1001

**1956, Oct. 22   Litho.   Perf. 12x12½**
| 1884 | A1001 | 40k slate, grnsh bl & red | 1.00 | .50 |

Soviet Scientific Antarctic Expedition

G. I. Kotovsky (1881-1925), Military Commander A1002

**1956, Oct. 30**
| 1885 | A1002 | 40k magenta | 1.00 | .20 |

**Portrait Type of 1956**

Portrait: Julia A. Zemaite (1845-1921), Lithaunian novelist.

**1956, Oct. 30   Perf. 12**
| 1886 | A979 | 40k lt of green & brn | .50 | .25 |

Fedor A. Bredichin (1831-1904), Astronomer — A1004

**1956, Oct. 30**
| 1887 | A1004 | 40k sepia & ultra | 2.75 | .75 |

---

Aleksandr Andreevich Ivanov (1806-58), Painter — A996

**Unwmk.**
**1956, Sept. 22**
| 1865 | A996 | 40k gray & brown | .50 | .25 |

I. E. Repin and "Volga River Boatmen" — A997

"Cossacks Writing a Letter to the Turkish Sultan" — A998

**1956, Aug. 21**
**Multicolored Centers**
| 1866 | A997 | 40k org brn & black | 6.00 | .90 |
| 1867 | A998 | 1r chalky blue & blk | 12.00 | 1.10 |

Ilya E. Repin (1844-1930), painter.

Chicken Farm A999

Designs: No. 1869, Harvest. 25k, Harvesting corn. No. 1871, Women in corn field. No. 1872, Farm buildings. No. 1873, Cattle. No. 1874, Farm workers, inscriptions and silos.

**1956, Oct. 7**
| 1868 | A999 | 10k multicolored | .25 | .25 |
| 1869 | A999 | 10k multicolored | .25 | .25 |
| 1870 | A999 | 25k multicolored | .50 | .25 |
| 1871 | A999 | 40k multicolored | 1.00 | .25 |
| 1872 | A999 | 40k multicolored | 1.00 | .25 |
| 1873 | A999 | 40k multicolored | 1.00 | .25 |
| 1874 | A999 | 40k multicolored | 5.00 | 1.75 |

Nos. 1868-1874 (7)

#1868, 1872, 1873 measure 37x25½mm; #1869-1871 37x27½mm; #1874 37x21mm.

Benjamin Franklin — A1000

---

Builders' Day: 60k, Building a factory. 1r, Building a dam.

**1956   Photo.**
| 1855 | A990 | 40k deep orange | .35 | .20 |
| 1856 | A990 | 60k brown carmine | .65 | .20 |
| 1857 | A990 | 1r intense blue | 1.00 | .20 |

Nos. 1855-1857 (3)   2.00   .60

Makhmud Aivazov — A992

**1956, Aug. 27**
| 1858 | A991 | 40k deep claret | .75 | .25 |
| 1859 | A991 | 1r bright blue | 1.25 | .30 |

Franko, writer (1856-1916).

Ivan Franko — A991

**1956, Aug. 27**

Two types:
I — Three lines in panel with "148."
II — Two lines in panel with "148."

| 1860 | A992 | 40k emerald (II) | 7.50 | 4.00 |
| a. | | Type I | 21.00 | 18.00 |

148th birthday of Russia's oldest man, an Azerbaijan collective farmer.

Robert Burns, Scottish poet, 160th Death Anniv. — A993

**Photo.**
| 1861 | A993 | 40k yellow brown | 5.00 | 2.00 |

**Engr.**
| 1861A | A993 | 40k lt ultra & brn (57) | 3.60 | .85 |

For overprint see No. 2174.

**Portrait Type of 1956**

Lesya Ukrainka (1871-1913), Ukrainian writer.

**1956, Aug. 27   Litho.**
| 1862 | A979 | 40k olive, blk & brown | 2.00 | .50 |

Statue of Nestor — A995

**1956, Sept. 22   Perf. 12x12½**
| 1863 | A995 | 40k multicolored | 1.25 | .30 |
| 1864 | A995 | 1r multicolored | 1.75 | .30 |

900th anniversary of the birth of Nestor, first Russian historian.

---

"The Rooks Have Arrived" by A. K. Savrasov A986

**1956, July 31   Perf. 12**
| 1838 | A985 | 40k multicolored | 4.00 | .40 |
| 1839 | A986 | 40k multicolored | 4.00 | .40 |

Tretiakov Art Gallery, Moscow, cent.

Relay Race A987

Volleyball — A988

#1842, Rowing. #1843, Swimming. #1844, Medal with heads of man and woman. #1845, Tennis. #1846, Soccer. #1847, Fencing. #1848, Bicycle race. #1849, Stadium and flag. #1850, Diving. #1851, Boxing. #1852, Gymnast. #1853, Basketball.

**1956, Aug. 5**
| 1840 | A987 | 10k carmine rose | .20 | .20 |
| 1841 | A988 | 25k dk orange brn | .35 | .20 |
| 1842 | A988 | 25k brt grnsh blue | .35 | .20 |
| 1843 | A988 | 25k grn, blue & lt brn | .35 | .20 |
| 1844 | A988 | 40k org, pink, bis & yellow | .20 | .20 |
| 1845 | A988 | 40k orange brown | .50 | .50 |
| 1846 | A987 | 40k brt yel grn & dk brown | .50 | .20 |
| 1847 | A987 | 40k grn, brt grn & dk brn, grnsh | .50 | .20 |
| 1848 | A988 | 40k blue green | .50 | .70 |
| 1849 | A988 | 40k brt yel grn & red | .50 | .20 |
| 1850 | A988 | 40k greenish blue | .50 | .20 |
| 1851 | A988 | 60k violet | .80 | .20 |
| 1852 | A987 | 60k brt violet | .80 | .20 |
| 1853 | A987 | 1r red brown | 1.25 | .40 |

Nos. 1840-1853 (14)   7.60   3.00

All-Union Spartacist Games, Moscow, Aug. 5-16.

Parachute Landing — A989

**1956, Aug. 5   Perf. 12x12½**
| 1854 | A989 | 40k multicolored | .50 | .25 |

Third World Parachute Championships, Moscow, July 1956.

Building under Construction A990

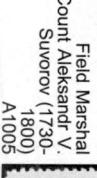

**1956, Nov. 17**
Field Marshal
Count Aleksandr V.
Suvorov (1730-
1800)
A1005

**Engr.**

| | | | |
|---|---|---|---|
| 1888 | A1005 | 40k org & maroon | .30 | .20 |
| 1889 | A1005 | 1r ol & dk red brn | .85 | .30 |
| 1890 | A1005 | 3r lt red brn & black | 2.10 | .75 |

Nos. 1888-1890 (3) 3.25 1.25

**1956**
1891 A1006 40k multicolored 1.00 .40
30th anniv. of the Shatura power station.

Shatura
Power
Station
A1006

**Litho.** **Perf. 12½x12**

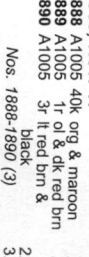

**1956, Nov. 17**
1892 A1007 40k lt brn, sepia & yel 1.00 .40
225th anniv. of the 1st balloon ascension of the Russian inventor, Kryakutni.

Kryakutni's Balloon, 1731 — A1007

**1956, Dec. 3**
1893 A1008 40k ultra & brown .75 .40
Yuli M. Shokalski (1856-1940), oceanographer and geodesist.

A1008 **Unwmk.** **Perf. 12**

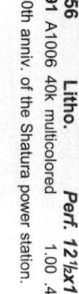

Apollinari
M.
Vasnetsov
"Winter
Scene"
A1009

**1956, Dec. 30**
1894 A1009 40k multicolored 1.50 .35
Vasnetsov (1856-1933), painter.

**1956, Dec. 26**
1895 A1010 40k deep carmine .40 .25
Kalidasa, 5th century deep carmine Indian poet.

Indian Building
and
Books — A1010

**1956, Dec. 26**
1896 A1011 40k slate green .50 .30
See Nos. 1858-1859.

Ivan Franko,
Ukrainian
Writer — A1011

**Engr.**

Leo N.
Tolstoy
A1012

**1956-57** **Litho.** **Perf. 12½x12**

Portraits of Writers: No. 1898, Mikhail V. Lomonosov. No. 1899, Aleksander S. Pushkin. No. 1900, Maxim Gorki. No. 1901, Shota Rustaveli. No. 1902, Vissarion G. Belinski. No. 1903, Mikhail Y. Lermontov, poet, and Darial Ravine in Caucasus.

**Size: 37½x27½mm**

| | | | |
|---|---|---|---|
| 1897 | A1012 | 40k brt grnish blue & brown | .60 | .20 |
| 1898 | A1012 | 40k dk red, ol & brn olive | .60 | .20 |

**Size: 35½x25½mm**

| | | | |
|---|---|---|---|
| 1899 | A1012 | 40k dk gray blue & brown | .60 | .20 |
| 1900 | A1012 | 40k black & brn car | .60 | .20 |
| 1901 | A1012 | 40k ol, brn & ol gray | .60 | .20 |
| 1902 | A1012 | 40k bis, ol & brn ('57) | .60 | .20 |
| 1903 | A1012 | 40k indigo & ol ('57) | .60 | .20 |

Nos. 1897-1903 (7) 4.20 1.40
Famous Russian writers.
See Nos. 1960-1962, 2031, 2112.

Fedor G.
Volkov
and
Theater
A1013

**1956, Dec. 31** **Unwmk.**
1904 A1013 40k mag, gray & yel .60 .30
200th anniversary of the founding of the St. Petersburg State Theater.

Vitus
Bering and
Map of
Bering
Strait
A1016

**1957, Feb. 6**
1905 A1016 40k brown & blue 1.10 .50
275th anniversary of the birth of Vitus Bering, Danish navigator and explorer.

Mikhail I.
Glinka — A1018

**1957, Feb. 23** **Perf. 12**
1907 A1018 40k dk red, buff & sep .50 .30
1908 A1018 1r multicolored 1.00 .30
Mikhail I. Glinka (1804-1857), composer.

Dmitri I.
Mendeleev
A1017

**1957, Feb. 6** **Perf. 12x12½**
1906 A1017 40k gray & gray & org 1.25 .60
D. I. Mendeleev (1834-1907), chemist.

All-Union Festival
of Soviet Youth,
Moscow — A1019

**1957, Feb. 23**
1909 A1019 40k dk blue, red & ocher .50 .25

23rd Ice Hockey
World
Championship,
Moscow — A1020

Designs: 25k, Emblem. 40k, Player. 60k, Goalkeeper.

**1957, Feb. 24** **Photo.**
1910 A1020 25k deep violet .70 .20
1911 A1020 40k bright blue .70 .20
1912 A1020 60k emerald .70 .60
Nos. 1910-1912 (3) 2.10 .60

Dove and Festival
Emblem — A1021

**1957** **Litho.** **Perf. 12**
1913 A1021 40k multicolored .60 .20
1914 A1021 60k multicolored .60 .20
6th World Youth Festival, Moscow. Exist imperf. Value, each $30.

Wooden
Products,
Hohloma
A1025

National Handicrafts: No. 1925, Lace maker, Vologda. No. 1926, Bone carver, North Russia. No. 1927, Woodcarver, Moscow area. No. 1928, Rug weaver, Turkmenistan. No. 1929, Painting.

**1957-58** **Unwmk.**
| | | | |
|---|---|---|---|
| 1924 | A1025 | 40k red org, yel & black | 1.50 | .40 |
| 1925 | A1025 | 40k brt car, yel & brown | 1.50 | .40 |
| 1926 | A1025 | 40k ultra, buff & gray | 1.50 | .40 |
| 1927 | A1025 | 40k brn, pale yel & tn brown | 1.50 | .40 |
| 1928 | A1025 | 40k buff, brn, bl & org ('58) | 1.00 | .50 |
| 1929 | A1025 | 40k multicolored ('58) | 1.00 | .50 |

Nos. 1924-1929 (6) 8.00 2.60

Assembly
Line — A1022

**1957, Mar. 15**
1915 A1022 40k Prus grn & dp org .50 .40
Moscow Machine Works centenary.

Black
Grouse
A1023

Axis
Deer — A1024

**1957, Mar. 28**
**Center in Natural Colors**

10k, Gray partridge. #1918, Polar bear. #1920, Bison. #1921, Mallard. #1922, European elk. #1923, Sable.

| | | | |
|---|---|---|---|
| 1916 | A1024 | 10k yel brown | .65 | .20 |
| 1917 | A1023 | 15k yel brown | .65 | .20 |
| 1918 | A1023 | 15k slate blue | .70 | .20 |
| 1919 | A1024 | 20k red orange | .70 | .20 |
| 1920 | A1023 | 30k ultra | .70 | .20 |
| 1921 | A1023 | 30k dk olive grn | .70 | .30 |
| 1922 | A1023 | 40k dk olive grn | 1.75 | .30 |
| 1923 | A1024 | 40k dk violet blue | 1.75 | .30 |
| | A1024 | 40k violet blue | 7.60 | 1.80 |

See Nos. 2213-2219, 2429-2431.

**Taras G. Shevchenko, Ukrainian Poet — A1041**

Design: #1962, Nikolai G. Chernyshevski, writer and politician.

1957, July 20
1961 A1041 40k grn & dk red brn .40 .20
1962 A1041 40k orange brn & grn .40 .20

**Woman Gymnast — A1043**

25k, Wrestling. No. 1965, Stadium. No. 1966, Youths of three races. 60k, Javelin thrower.

1957, July 15    Litho.    Perf. 12
1963 A1043 20k bluish vio & org brn .20 .20
1964 A1043 25k brt grn & claret .20 .20
1965 A1043 40k Prus bl, ol & red .35 .20
1966 A1043 40k crimson & violet .35 .20
1967 A1043 60k ultra & brown .40 .20
Nos. 1963-1967 (5) 1.50 1.00

Third International Youth Games, Moscow.

**Javelin Thrower — A1044**

Unwmk.

1957, July 20
1968 A1044 20k lt ultra & ol blk .35 .20
1969 A1044 20k brt grn, red vio & black .35 .20
1970 A1044 25k orange, ultra & blk .35 .20
1971 A1044 40k rose vio & blk .55 .20
1972 A1044 40k dp pink, bl, buff & black .55 .20
1973 A1044 60k lt violet & brn .85 .20
Nos. 1968-1973 (6) 3.00 1.20

Success of Soviet athletes at the 16th Olympic Games, Melbourne.

**Kremlin A1046**

**Kupala A1045**

1957, July 27
1974 A1045 40k dark gray 2.00 1.50

Yanka Kupala (1882-1942), poet.

**Photo.**

1957, July 27    Litho.

Moscow Views: No. 1976, Stadium. No. 1977, University. No. 1978, Bolshoi Theater.

---

**Kazakhstan Workers' Medal — A1036**

1957, May 20
1950 A1036 40k lt blue, blk & yel .50 .25

**A1037    A1037a    A1037b    Photo.**

1957    Various Frames
1951 A1037 40k dull red brown 6.50 4.50
1952 A1037a 40k sepia 3.50 3.50
1953 A1037 40k sepia 3.50 3.50
1954 A1037b 40k gray 3.50 3.50
1955 A1037 40k brown black 4.50 4.50
See Nos. 2036-2038, 2059. 21.50 19.50

Portraits: No. 1951, A. M. Liapunov. No. 1952, V. Mickevicius Kapsukas, writer. No. 1953, G. Bashindzhagian, Armenian painter. No. 1954, Yakub Kolas, Byelorussian poet. No. 1955, Carl von Linné, Swedish botanist.

**Bicyclist A1030**

1957, June 20    Litho.
1956 A1038 40k claret & vio blue .50 .25

10th Peace Bicycle Race.

**Telescope A1039**

Designs: No. 1958, Comet and observatory. No. 1959, Rocket leaving earth.

1957, July 4    **Size: 25½x37mm**
1957 A1039 40k brn, ocher & blue .50 .35
1958 A1039 40k indigo, lt bl & yel 1.40 .35

**Size: 14½x21mm**
1959 A1039 40k blue violet 1.10 .55
Nos. 1957-1959 (3) 3.00 1.25

International Geophysical Year, 1957-58. See Nos. 2089-2091.

**Folksinger A1040**

1957, May 20
1960 A1040 40k multicolored .50 .25

"The Song of Igor's Army," Russia's oldest literary work.

---

**Marine Museum Place and Neva — A1031**

Designs: No. 1942, Lenin monument. No. 1943, Nevski Prospect and Admiralty.

1957, May 27    **Photo.**
1941 A1031 40k blue green .50 .20
1942 A1031 40k reddish brown .50 .20
1943 A1031 40k bluish violet .50 .20
a. Souv. sheet of 3, red border 7.50 6.00
Nos. 1941-1943 (3) 1.50 .60

250th anniversary of Leningrad. No. 1943a contains imperf. stamps similar to #1941, 1680 (in reddish brown), 1943, and is for 40th anniv. of the October Revolution. Issued Nov. 7, 1957. A similar sheet is listed as No. 2002a.

**Henry Fielding — A1032**

**Perf. 12**

250 лет Ленинграда

**Type of 1953 Overprinted in Red**

Designs: No. 1944, Peter I Statue, Decembrists' Square. No. 1945, Smolny Institute.

1957, May 27    **Perf. 12½x12**
1944 A908 1r black brn, greenish .50 .20
1945 A908 1r green, pink .50 .20

250th anniversary of Leningrad. The overprint is in one line on No. 1945.

1957, June 20    Litho.
1946 A1032 40k multicolored .50 .25

Fielding (1707-54), English playwright, novelist.

**William Harvey — A1033**

**Photo.**

1957, May 20
1947 A1033 40k brown .50 .25

300th anniversary of the death of the English physician William Harvey, discoverer of blood circulation.

**M. A. Balakirev (1836-1910), Composer A1034**

1957, May 20
1948 A1034 40k bluish black .50 .25

**A. I. Herzen and N. P. Ogarev A1035**

**Engr.**

1957, May 20    Litho.
1949 A1035 40k blk vio & dk ol gray .50 .25

Centenary of newspaper Kolokol (Bell).

---

**Aleksei Nikolaievitch Bach (1857-1946), Biochemist A1026**

1957, Apr. 6    Litho.    **Perf. 12**
1930 A1026 40k ultra, brn & buff .60 .30

**Georgi Valentinovich Plekhanov (1856-1918), Political Philosopher A1027**

1957, Apr. 6    **Engr.**
1931 A1027 40k dull purple .40 .25

**Leonhard Euler A1028**

1957, Apr. 17    Litho.
1932 A1028 40k lilac & gray .60 .25

Leonhard Euler (1707-1783), Swiss mathematician and physicist.

**Lenin, 87th Birth Anniv. — A1029**

Designs: No. 1934, Lenin talking to soldier and sailor. No. 1935, Lenin building barricades.

1957, Apr. 22    **Multicolored Centers**
1933 A1029 40k magenta & bis 1.75 .40
1934 A1029 40k magenta & bis 1.75 .40
1935 A1029 40k magenta & bis 1.75 .40
Nos. 1933-1935 (3) 5.25 1.20

**Youths of All Races Carrying Festival Banner — A1030**

Design: 20k, Sculptor with motherhood statue. 40k, Young couples dancing. 1r, Festival banner and fireworks over Moscow University.

1957, May 27    **Perf. 12x12½**
1936 A1030 10k emer, pur & yel .20 .20
1937 A1030 20k multicolored .20 .20
1938 A1030 25k emer, pur & yel .45 .20
1939 A1030 40k rose, bl grn & bis brn .45 .20
1940 A1030 1r multicolored .50 1.00
Nos. 1936-1940 (5) 2.00 1.00

6th World Youth Festival in Moscow. The 10k, 20k, and 1r exist imperf. Value each about $25.

## Center in Black

| 1975 | A1046 | 40k dull red brown | .25 | .20 |
|------|-------|--------------------|-----|-----|
| 1976 | A1046 | 40k brown violet | .50 | .20 |
| 1977 | A1046 | 1r red | .50 | .20 |
| 1978 | A1046 | 1r brt violet blue | 1.50 | .80 |

Nos. 1975-1978 (4)

Sixth World Youth Festival, Moscow.

**1957, July 27**

| 1979 | A1047 | 40k brt grnsh blue | .50 | .25 |
|------|-------|--------------------|-----|-----|
| a. | | Souvenir sheet of 2, light imperf. | 10.00 | 10.00 |

Intl. Phil. Exhib., Moscow, July 29-Aug. 11. No. 1979 exists imperf. Value $10.

Lenin Library A1047

**Photo.**

**1957, Aug. 27**

| 1980 | A1048 | 40k brt blue green | .50 | .20 |

Pierre Jean de Beranger(1780-1857), French Song Writer — A1048

### Portrait Type of 1956

Portrait: 40k, Clara Zetkin (1857-1933), German communist.

**1957, Aug. 8**

| 1981 | A1049 | 40k bl, grn & bis brn | 1.50 | .60 |
|------|-------|------------------------|------|-----|
| 1982 | A1049 | 1r violet, grn & brn | 3.50 | 1.25 |

**Litho.**

**1957, Aug. 9**

| 1983 | A979 | 40k gray blue, brn & blk | 1.00 | .20 |

Publicity for world peace.

Globe, Dove and Olive Branch — A1049

**1957, Sept. 8**

| 1984 | A1050 | 40k black brown | .50 | .20 |

Centenary of Krenholm textile factory, Narva, Estonia.

Krenholm Factory, Narva A1050

Carrier Pigeon and Globes A1051

**1957, Sept. 26 Unwmk. Perf. 12**

| 1985 | A1051 | 40k blue | .30 | .20 |
|------|-------|----------|-----|-----|
| 1986 | A1051 | 60k lilac | .45 | .20 |

Intl. Letter Writing Week, Oct. 6-12

---

Konstantin E. Tsiolkovsky and Rockets A1055

**1957, Oct. 7**

| 1991 | A1055 | 40k dk blue & pale brown | 1.75 | .75 |

Tsiolkovsky (1857-1935), rocket and astronautics pioneer. For overprint see No. 2021.

Sputnik 1 Circling Globe — A1056

**1957**

| 1992 | A1056 | 40k indigo, bluish | 1.40 | .50 |
|------|-------|--------------------|------|-----|
| 1993 | A1056 | 40k bright blue | 1.40 | .50 |

Launching of first artificial earth satellite, Oct. 4. Issue dates: No. 1992, Nov. 5; No. 1993, Dec. 28.

**Photo.**

**1957, Nov. 20**

| 1994 | A1057 | 40k red brown | .50 | .20 |

All-Union Industrial Exhib See #2030.

Turbine Wheel, Kuibyshev Hydroelectric Station — A1057

---

**1957, Sept. 23**

| 1988 | A1053 | 40k brown | .35 | .20 |
|------|-------|-----------|-----|-----|
| 1989 | A1053 | 1r bluish black | .65 | .20 |

Vladimir Vasilievich Stasov (1824-1906), Art and Music Critic — A1053

**Engr.**

Congress Emblem A1054

**1957, Oct. 7 Litho. Perf. 12**

| 1990 | A1054 | 40k gray blue & blk, bluish | .50 | .25 |

4th International Trade Union Congress, Leipzig, Oct. 4-15.

Worker and Railroad A1061

#1999, Red flag, Lenin. #2000, Lenin addressing workers and peasants. 60k, Harvester.

**1957, Oct. 15 Perf. 12½x12, 12x12½, 12½ Litho.**

| 1998 | A1060 | 10k buff, sepia & red | .20 | .20 |
|------|-------|------------------------|-----|-----|
| 1999 | A1060 | 40k buff, red, sep & yel | .25 | .20 |
| 2000 | A1060 | 40k red, black & yel | .25 | .20 |
| 2001 | A1061 | 40k red, yel & green | .25 | .20 |
| 2002 | A1061 | 60k red, ocher & vio brn | .35 | .20 |
| a. | | Souvenir sheet of 3, #2000-2002, imperf. | 7.50 | 7.50 |

Nos. 1998-2002 (5) 1.30 1.00

40th anniv. of the October Revolution. A similar sheet is listed as No. 1943a. Nos. 1998-2002 exist imperf. Value, set $12.50.

---

Vyborzhets Factory, Lenin Statue A1052

**1957, Sept. 23 Litho.**

| 1987 | A1052 | 40k dark blue | .80 | .25 |

Krasny Vyborzhets factory, Leningrad, cent.

Meteor — A1058  Lenin — A1059

**1957, Oct. 30 Engr.**

| 1995 | A1058 | 40k multicolored | 2.25 | .50 |

Falling of Sihote Alin] meteor, 10th anniv.

**1957, Nov. 20**

| 1996 | A1059 | 40k blue | .75 | .25 |
|------|-------|----------|-----|-----|
| 1997 | A1059 | 60k rose red | .75 | .25 |

40th anniversary of October Revolution.

**1957, Oct. 30**

Design: 60k, Lenin reading Pravda, horiz.

Students and Moscow University — A1060

---

**No. 1991 Overprinted in Black**

**1957, Nov. 28**

| 2021 | A1055 | 40k | 12.50 | 5.00 |

Launching of Sputnik 1.

Artists and Academy of Art — A1064

**1957, Dec. 16**

| 2018 | A1064 | 40k black, pale salmon | .45 | .20 |
|------|-------|-------------------------|-----|-----|
| 2019 | A1065 | 60k black, pink | .85 | .20 |

Nos. 2018-2020 (3) 1.50 .60

200th anniversary of the Academy of Arts, Leningrad. Artists on 40k are K. P. Bryullov, Ilya Repin and V. I. Surikov. 1r, Worker and Peasant monument, Moscow.

Red Army Monument, Berlin — A1065

| 2006 | A1062 | 40k multicolored | .60 | .30 |
|------|-------|-------------------|-----|-----|
| 2007 | A1062 | 40k multicolored | .60 | .30 |
| 2008 | A1062 | 40k multicolored | .60 | .30 |
| 2009 | A1062 | 40k multicolored | .60 | .30 |
| 2010 | A1062 | 40k multicolored | .60 | .30 |
| 2011 | A1063 | 40k multicolored | .60 | .30 |
| 2012 | A1062 | 40k multicolored | .60 | .30 |
| 2013 | A1062 | 40k multicolored | .60 | .30 |
| 2015 | A1062 | 40k multicolored | .60 | .30 |
| 2016 | A1062 | 40k multicolored | .60 | .30 |
| 2017 | A1062 | 40k multicolored | .60 | .30 |

Nos. 2003-2017 (15) 9.00 4.50

40th anniversary of the October Revolution.

---

Federal Socialist Republic A1062

Uzbek Republic — A1063

**1957, Oct. 25**

| 2003 | A1062 | 40k multicolored | .60 | .30 |
|------|-------|-------------------|-----|-----|
| 2004 | A1062 | 40k multicolored | .60 | .30 |
| 2005 | A1062 | 40k multicolored | .60 | .30 |

Republic: #2005, Tadzhik (building, peasant girl). #2006, Byelorussia (truck). #2007, Azerbaijan (buildings). #2008, Georgia (valley, palm, couple). #2009, Armenia, (fruit, power line, mountains). #2010, Turkmen (couple, lambs). #2011, Ukraine (farmers). #2012, Kazakh (harvester, combine). #2013, Kirghiz (horseback rider, building). #2014, Moldavia (automatic sorting machine). #2015, Estonia (girl in national costume). #2016, Latvia (couple, sea, field). #2017, Lithuania (farmer couple).

Ukrainian Arms, Symbolic Figures A1066

**1957, Dec. 24**

| 2022 | A1066 | 40k yellow, red & blue | .50 | .25 |

Ukrainian Soviet Republic, 40th anniv.

Edvard Grieg A1067

**1957, Dec. 24 Photo.**

| 2023 | A1067 | 40k black, buff | .50 | .25 |

Grieg, Norwegian composer, 50th death anniv.

Giuseppe Garibaldi A1068

**1957, Dec. 24 Litho.**

| 2024 | A1068 | 40k plum, lt grn & blk | .45 | .20 |

Garibaldi, (1807-1882) Italian patriot.

Vladimir Lukich Borovikovsky (1757-1825), Painter — A1069

**1957, Dec. 24 — Photo.**
2025 A1069 40k brown .50 .25

### Portrait Type of 1956
Portrait: 40k, Mariya Nikolayevna Ermolova (1853-1928), actress.

**1957, Dec. 28 — Litho.**
2026 A984 40k red brn & brt violet .75 .20

Kuibyshev Hydroelectric Station and Dam A1070

**1957, Dec. 28**
2027 A1070 40k dark blue, *buff* .70 .20

### Type of 1956
Portrait: 40k, Rosa Luxemburg (1870-1919), German socialist.

**1958, Jan. 8**
2028 A979 40k blue & brown 1.00 .60

Flag and Symbols of Industry A1070b

**1958, Jan. 8 — Photo.**
2029 A1070a 40k deep violet 1.00 .25

Chi Pai-shih (1860-1957), Chinese painter.

**1958, Jan. 8 — Litho.**
2030 A1070b 60k gray vio, red & .50 .25

All-Union Industrial Exhib. Exists imperf. Value, $250.

Aleksei N. Tolstoi, Novelist & Dramatist (1883-1945) A1071

**1958, Jan. 28 — Photo. Perf. 12**
2031 A1071 40k brown olive .50 .30

See Nos. 2112, 2175-2178C.

Symbolic Figure Greeting Sputnik 2 — A1072

**Litho.**

### 1957-58 — Figure in Buff
2032 A1072 20k black & rose .45 .20
2033 A1072 40k black & grn ('58) .60 .25
2034 A1072 60k blk & lt brn ('58) .85 .25
2035 A1072 1r black & blue 1.10 .30
Nos. 2032-2035 (4) 3.00 1.00

Launching of Sputnik 2, Nov. 3, 1957.

### Small Portrait Type of 1957
#2036, Henry W. Longfellow, American poet. #2037, William Blake, English artist, poet, mystic. #2038, E. Sharents, Armenian poet.

**1958, Mar. — Unwmk.**
**Various Frames — Perf. 12**
2036 A1037 40k gray black 2.00 1.50
2037 A1037 40k gray black 2.00 1.50
2038 A1037 40k sepia 2.00 4.50
Nos. 2036-2038 (3) 6.00

Victory at Pskov A1073

Soldier and Civilian — A1074

Designs: No. 2040, Airman, sailor and soldier. No. 2042, Sailor and soldier. 60k, Storming of Berlin Reichstag building.

**1958, Feb. 21**
2039 A1073 25k multicolored .25 .20
2040 A1073 40k multicolored .50 .20
2041 A1074 40k multicolored .50 .20
2042 A1074 40k multicolored .50 .20
2043 A1073 60k multicolored .85 .20
Nos. 2039-2043 (5) 2.60 1.00

40th anniversary of Red Armed Forces.

Peter Ilich Tchaikovsky A1075

Swan Lake Ballet A1076

Design: 1r, Tchaikovsky, pianist and violinist.

**1958, Mar. 18**
2044 A1075 40k grn, bl, brn & red .45 .20
2045 A1076 40k grn, ultra, red & .45 .20
2046 A1075 1r lake & emerald yel 1.60 .35
Nos. 2044-2046 (3) 2.50 .75

Honoring Tchaikovsky and for the Tchaikovsky competitions for pianists and violinists. Exist imperf. Value, set $10. Nos. 2044-2045 were printed in sheets of 30, including 15 stamps of each value and 5 se-tenant pairs.

V. F. Rudnev — A1077

**1958, Mar. 25**
2047 A1077 40k green, blk & ocher 1.00 .25

Rudnev, naval commander.

Maxim Gorki — A1078 **Unwmk.**

**1958, Apr. 3 — Litho.**
2048 A1078 40k multicolored .75 .25

Gorki, writer, 90th birth anniv.

Spasski Tower — A1079

**1958, Apr. 9**
2049 A1079 40k dp violet, *pinkish* .25 .20
2050 A1079 60k rose red .35 .20

13th Congress of the Young Communist League (Komsomol).

Russian Pavilion, Brussels A1080

2051 A1080 10k multicolored .25 .20
2052 A1080 40k multicolored .35 .20

**1958, Apr.** Universal and International Exhibition at Brussels. Exist imperf. Value $2.

Lenin A1081

**Engr.**
.40 .20
.50 .20
.85 .20
1.75 .60

**1958, Apr. 22**
2053 A1081 40k dk blue gray
2054 A1081 40k rose brown
2055 A1081 1r brown
Nos. 2053-2055 (3)

88th anniversary of the birth of Lenin.

Jan A. Komensky (Comenius) A1082

Portrait: Nos. 2056-2058, Karl Marx.

**1958, May 5**
2056 A1081 40k brown .40 .20
2057 A1081 60k dark blue .50 .20
2058 A1081 1r dark red 1.10 .60
Nos. 2056-2058 (3) 2.00 .60

140th anniversary of the birth of Marx.

**1958, Apr. 17 — Photo.**
2059 A1082 40k green 1.90 1.25

### No. 1695 Overprinted in Blue
4.50 1.00
2060 A914 40k multicolored 4.50 1.00

**1958, Apr. 22**
Academy of Arts, Moscow, 200th anniv.

Carlo Goldoni — A1084

Lenin Order — A1083 **Litho.**
.50 .30
**Photo.**
.50 .30

**1958, Apr. 30**
2061 A1083 40k brown, yel & red

**1958, Apr. 28**
2062 A1084 40k blue & dk gray

Carlo Goldoni, Italian dramatist.

Radio Tower, Ship and Planes A1085

**1958, May 7**
2063 A1085 40k blue green & red 3.00 .35

Issued for Radio Day, May 7

Globe and Dove A1086

**1958, May 6**
2064 A1086 40k blue & black .20 .20
2065 A1086 60k blue & black .45 .20

4th Congress of the Intl. Democratic Women's Federation, June, 1958, at Vienna.

Ilya Chavchavadze A1087 **Litho.**
.30 .20
.45 .20
**Photo.**
.50 .20

**1958, May 12**
2066 A1087 40k black & blue .50 .20

50th anniversary of the death of Ilya Chavchavadze, Georgian writer.

Flags and Communication Symbols — A1088 **Litho.**
6.00 3.00
7.50 3.00

**1958-59**
2067 A1088 40k blue, red, yel & blk 6.00 3.00
a. Red half of Czech flag at bottom 7.50 3.00

Communist ministers' meeting on social problems in Moscow, Dec. 1957. On No. 2067, the Czech flag (center flag in vertical row of five) is incorrectly pictured with red stripe on top. This error is corrected on No. 2067a.

**Bugler — A1089**

**1958, May 29    Unwmk.    Perf. 12**
2068 A1089 10k ultra, red & red brn  .25  .20
2069 A1089 25k ultra, yel & red brn  .25  .20

Pioneers: 25k, Boy with model plane.

**Children of Three Races — A1090**

**1958, May 29**
2070 A1090 40k car, ultra & brn  .35  .20
2071 A1090 40k carmine & brown  .35  .20

Int'l Day for the Protection of Children.

Design: No. 2071, Child and bomb.

**Rimski-Korsakov A1092**

**Soccer Players and Globe A1091**

**1958, June 5**
2072 A1091 40k blue, red & buff  .30  .20
2073 A1091 60k blue, red & buff  .70  .30

6th World Soccer Championships, Stockholm, June 8-29. Exist imperf. Value $4.

**1958, June 5    Photo.**
2074 A1092 40k blue & brown  1.25  .20

Nikolai Andreevich Rimski-Korsakov (1844-1908), composer.

**Girl Gymnast — A1093**

**1958, June 24**
2075 A1093 40k ultra, red & buff  .50  .20
2076 A1093 40k blue, red buff & grn  .50  .20

14th World Gymnastic Championships, Moscow, July 6-10.

No. 2076, Gymnast on rings and view.

**Bomb, Globe, Atom, Sputniks, Ship A1094**

**1958, July 1**
2077 A1094 60k dk blue, blk & org  1.75  .50

Conference for peaceful uses of atomic energy, held at Stockholm.

---

**Street Fighters A1095**

**Moscow State University A1096**

**Congress Emblem A1097**

**1958, July 5**
2078 A1095 40k red & violet blk  .50  .25

Communist Party in the Ukraine, 40th anniv.

**1958, July 8    Perf. 12**
2079 A1096 40k red & blue  .25  .20
2080 A1097 60k lt grn, blue & red
a.  Souvenir sheet of 2  10.00  5.50

5th Congress of the International Architects' Organization, Moscow. No. 2080a contains Nos. 2079-2080, imperf., with background design in yellow, brown, blue and red. Issued Sept. 8, 1958.

**Young Couple A1098**

**1958, June 25**
2081 A1098 40k blue & ocher  .20  .20
2082 A1098 60k yel green & ocher  .35  .20

Day of Soviet Youth.

**Sputnik 3 Leaving Earth A1099**

**1958, June 16**
2083 A1099 40k vio blue, grn & rose  1.00  .25

Launching of Sputnik 3, May 15. Printed in sheets with alternating labels, giving details of launching.

**Sadriddin Aini — A1100**

**1958, July 15**
2084 A1100 40k rose, black & buff  .40  .20

80th birthday of Aini, Tadzhik writer.

Design: 1r, Telescope.

**Crimea Observatory A1104**

**Moscow University A1105**

**1958, Aug.    Photo.**
2092 A1104 40k brn & brt grnsh bl  .55  .20
2093 A1105 60k lt blue, vio & yel  .70  .20
2094 A1104 1r dp blue & org brn  1.00  .20
Nos. 2092-2094 (3)  2.25  .60

10th Congress of the International Astronomical Union, Moscow.

---

**1958, July 21    Typo.**
2085 A1101 40k lilac & blk  .50  .25

1st World Trade Union Conference of Working Youths, Prague, July 14-20.

**Emblem A1101**

**Type of 1958-59 and**

**TU-104 and Globe A1102**

**1958, Aug.    Litho.**
2086 A1102 60k blue, red & bis  .35  .20
2087 A1123 1r yel, red & black  .75  .20

Soviet civil aviation. Exist imperf. Value, set $5.50. See Nos. 2147-2151.

Design: 1r, Turbo-propeller liner AN-10.

**L. A. Kulik A1103**

**1958, Aug. 12**
2088 A1103 40k sep, bl, yel & claret  1.00  .25

50th anniv. of the falling of the Tungus meteor and the 75th anniv. of the birth of L. A. Kulik, meteorist.

**IGY Type of 1957**

**1958, July 29    Size: 25½x37mm**
2089 A1039 40k blue & brt yel  .90  .25
2090 A1039 40k blue green  .90  .25
2091 A1039 40k bright ultra  2.70  .75

International Geophysical Year, 1957-58.

Designs: No. 2089, Aurora borealis and camera. No. 2090, Schooner "Zarja" exploring's earth magnetism. No. 2091, Weather balloon and radar.

---

**Postillion, 16th Century A1106**

**1958, Aug.    Unwmk.    Litho.    Perf. 12**
2095 A1106 40k red, blk, yel & lil  .30  .20
2096 A1106 10k multicolored  .25  .20
2097 A1106 40k ultra & slate  .25  .20
2098 A1106 25k black & ultra  .25  .20
2099 A1106 25k car lake & brn  .25  .20
2100 A1106 60k grnsh bl & blk  .30  .20
2101 A1106 40k red, org & gray  .30  .20
2102 A1106 40k salmon & brown  .30  .20
2103 A1106 60k grnsh blue & red  .30  .20
2104 A1106 60k grnsh bl & lilac  .45  .20
2105 A1106 1r multicolored  .65  .25
2106 A1106 1r multicolored  .65  .25
Nos. 2095-2106 (12)  4.30  2.50

Designs: #2095, 15th cent. letter writer. #2097, A. L. Ordyn-Naishokin and sleigh mail coach, 17th cent. No. 2098, Mail coach and post office, 18th cent. #2099, Troika, 19th cent. #2100, Lenin stamp ship and Moscow University. #2102, Jet plane and postillion. vert. #2103, V. N. Podbielski and letter carriers. #2104, Mail train. #2105, Loading mail on plane. #2106, Ship, plane, train and globe.

Centenary of Russian postage stamps. Two imperf. souvenir sheets exist, measuring 155x106mm. Nos. 2095-2099, with background design in red, ultramarine, yellow and brown. The other contains one each of Nos. 2100, 2103-2106, with background design in blue, gray, ocher, pink and brown. Value for both, $15 unused, $10 canceled. Nos. 2096, 2100-2101 exist imperf. Value for both, $20 unused, $10 canceled.

**1958, Aug. 30**
2107 A1107 40k black & emerald  .50  .30

M. I. Chigorin, Chess Player, 50th Death Anniv. — A1107

**Golden Gate, Vladimir A1108**

**1958, Aug. 23    Litho.**
2108 A1108 40k multicolored  .30  .20
2109 A1108 60k lt violet, yel & blk  .45  .30

850th anniv. of the city of Vladimir.

**Nurse Bandaging Man's Leg — A1109**

**1958, Sept. 15    Photo.**
2110 A1109 40k multicolored  .30  .20
2111 A1109 40k olive, lemon & red  .30  .20

40 years of Red Cross-Red Crescent work.

2111, Hospital, & people of various races.

**Portrait Type of 1958**

**1958, Sept. 15**
2112 A1071 40k brn black & mar  .75  .20

Mikhail E. Saltykov (Shchedrin), writer.

RUSSIA

Fuzuli — A1127

K. F. Rulye — A1126

**1958, Dec. 26**
2154 A1126 40k ultra & black .50 .25
Rulye, educator, death cent.

**1958, Dec. 23** Photo.
2155 A1127 40k grnsh bl & brn .50 .25
400th anniv. of the death of Fuzuli (Mehmet Suleiman Ogiou), Turkish poet.

Census Emblem and Family — A1128

Lunik and Sputniks over Kremlin — A1129

**1958, Dec.**
2156 A1128 40k multicolored .25 .20
2157 A1128 40k yel, gray, bl & red .25 .20
1969 Soviet census.
Design: No. 2157, Census emblem.

**1959, Jan.** Unwmk. *Perf. 12*
Designs: 40k, Lenin and view of Kremlin. 60k, Workers and Lenin power plant on Volga.
2158 A1129 40k multicolored .30 .20
2159 A1129 60k multicolored .45 .30
2160 A1129 1r red, yel & vio bl 1.25 .75
Nos. 2158-2160 (3) 2.00 1.25
21st Cong. of the Communist Party and "the conquest of the cosmos by the Soviet people."

Lenin Statue, Minsk Buildings — A1130

**1958, Dec. 20**
2161 A1130 40k red, buff & brown .50 .20
Byelorussian Republic, 40th anniv.

Atomic Icebreaker "Lenin" A1131

Design: 60k, Diesel Locomotive "TE-3."

**1958, Dec. 31**
2162 A1131 40k multicolored .85 .50
2163 A1131 60k multicolored 1.40 .75

---

Sergei Esenin (1895-1925), Poet — A1120

2144 A1120 40k multicolored .50 .20
**1958, Nov. 29**

Kuan Han-ching A1122
*Perf. 12*

G. K. Ordzhonikidze A1121

**1958, Dec. 12**
2145 A1121 40k multicolored .50 .20
G. K. Ordzhonikidze (1886-1937), Georgian party worker.

**1958, Dec. 5**
2146 A1122 40k dk blue & gray .50 .20
700th anniversary of the theater of Kuan Han-ching, Chinese dramatist.

Airliner IL-14 and Globe A1123

Soviet civil aviation: No. 2148, Jet liner TU-104. No. 2149, Turbo-propeller liner TU-114. 60k, Jet liner TU-110. 2r, Turbo-propeller liner IL-18.

**1958-59**
2147 A1123 20k ultra, blk & red .20 .20
2148 A1123 20k grn, blk & red .20 .20
2149 A1123 40k brt bl, blk & red .30 .20
2150 A1123 60k rose car & black .30 .20
2151 A1123 2r plum, red & black (59) .90 .20
Nos. 2147-2151 (5) 2.00 1.00
Exist imperf., value $10.
See Nos. 2086-2007.

John Milton — A1125

Eleonora Duse — A1124

**1958, Dec. 26**
2152 A1124 40k blue green & gray .50 .20
Duse, Italian actress, birth cent.

**1958, Dec. 17**
2153 A1125 40k brown .50 .20
John Milton (1608-1674), English poet.

---

Capitals of Soviet Republics: #2121, Lenin Square, Alma Ata. #2122, Lenin statue, Ashkhabad. #2123, Lenin statue, Tashkent. #2124, Lenin Square, Stalinabad. #2125, Rustaveli Ave., Tbilisi. #2126, View from Dvina River, Riga. #2127, University Square, Frunze. #2128, View, Yerevan. #2129, Communist Street, Baku. #2130, Lenin Prospect, Kishinev. #2131, Round Square, Minsk. #2132, Viru Gate, Tallinn. #2133, Main Street, Kiev. #2134, View, Vilnius.

**1958** Engr.
2120 A1115 40k violet .60 .30
2121 A1115 40k brt blue green .60 .30
2122 A1115 40k greenish gray .60 .30
2123 A1115 40k dark gray .60 .30
2124 A1115 40k blue .60 .30
2125 A1115 40k violet blue .60 .30
2126 A1115 40k brown red .60 .30
2127 A1115 40k dk blue gray .60 .30
2128 A1115 40k brown .60 .30
2129 A1115 40k purple .60 .30
2130 A1115 40k olive .60 .30
2131 A1115 40k gray brown .60 .30
2132 A1115 40k emerald .60 .30
2133 A1115 40k lilac rose .60 .30
2134 A1115 40k orange ver 9.00 4.50
Nos. 2120-2134 (15)
See No. 2836.

Young Civil War Soldier 1919 — A1116

20k, Industrial brigade. 25k, Youth in World War II. 40k, Girl farm worker. 60k, Youth building new towns. 1r, Students, fighters for culture.

**1958, Oct. 25** Litho.
2135 A1116 10k multicolored .20 .20
2136 A1116 20k multicolored .35 .20
2137 A1116 25k multicolored .45 .20
2138 A1116 40k multicolored .70 .20
2139 A1116 60k multicolored 1.10 .20
2140 A1116 1r multicolored 2.25 1.80
Nos. 2135-2140 (6) 5.05 1.80
40th anniversary of the Young Communist League (Komsomol).

Marx and Lenin — A1117

Lenin, Intellectual, Peasant and Miner A1118

**1958, Oct. 31**
2141 A1117 40k multicolored .40 .20
2142 A1118 1r multicolored .60 .30
41st anniversary of Russian Revolution.

Torch, Wreath and Family A1119

**1958, Nov. 5**
2143 A1119 60k blk, beige & dull bl .50 .25
10th anniversary of the Universal Declaration of Human Rights.

---

V. V. Kapnist — A1111
*Perf. 12*

2113 A1110 40k multicolored .50 .20
1100th anniversary of the birth of Rudagi, Persian poet.

Rudagi — A1110

**1958, Oct. 10** Litho.

**1958, Sept. 30**
2114 A1111 40k blue & gray .55 .25
200th anniversary of the birth of V. V. Kapnist, poet and dramatist.

Book, Torch, Lyre, Flower A1112

**1958, Oct. 4**
2115 A1112 40k red org, ol & blk .50 .25
Conf. of Asian & African Writers, Tashkent.

Chelyabinsk Tractor Factory A1113

Designs: No. 2117, Zaporozhstal foundry. No. 2118, Ural machine building plant.

**1958, Oct. 20** Photo.
2116 A1113 40k green & yellow .40 .20
2117 A1113 40k brown red & yel .40 .20
2118 A1113 40k blue 1.20 .60
Nos. 2116-2118 (3)
Pioneers of Russian Industry.

Ancient Georgian on Horseback A1114

**1958, Oct. 18** Litho.
2119 A1114 40k ocher, ultra & red 1.25 .20
1500th anniv. of Tbilisi, capital of Georgia

Red Square, Moscow — A1115

АЛМА-АТА · ПЛОЩАДЬ им. В. И. ЛЕНИНА #2121

ТБИЛИСИ · ПРОСПЕКТ РУСТАВЕЛИ #2125

ФРУНЗЕ · УНИВЕРСИТЕТСКАЯ ПЛОЩАДЬ #2127

ОБЩИЙ ВИД ГОРОДА ЕРЕВАН #2128

МИНСК · КРУГЛАЯ ПЛОЩАДЬ #2131

## Shalom Aleichem A1132

**1959, Feb. 10**
2164 A1132 40k chocolate .40 .20
Aleichem, Yiddish writer, birth cent.

**1959, Feb.**
Scientists: #2166, Charles Darwin, English biologist; #2167, N. N. F. Gamaleya, microbiologist.

**Various Frames**
2165 A1133 40k blue green & blk .45 .20
2166 A1133 40k chalky blue & brn .55 .20
2167 A1133 40k dk red & black .50 .20
Nos. 2165-2167 (3) 1.50 .60

## Woman Skater A1134

**1959, Feb. 5**
2168 A1134 25k ultra, black & ver .30 .20
2169 A1134 40k ultra & black .45 .20
Women's International Ice Skating Championships, Sverdlovsk.

## Frederic Joliot-Curie A1135

**No. 1717 Overprinted in Orange Brown**

**1959, Mar. 3**
**Litho.** **Perf. 12**
2171 A1135 40k turq bl & gray brn. .50 .25
Joliot-Curie (1900-58), French scientist.

**1959, Feb. 12**
2170 A919 1r 7.50 5.00
"Victory of the USSR Basketball Team — Chile 1959." However, the 3rd World Basketball Championship honors went to Brazil when the Soviet team was disqualified for refusing to play Nationalist China.

## Evangelista Torricelli A1133

---

## Selma Lagerlöf A1136

**1959, Feb. 26**
2172 A1136 40k red brown & black .50 .25
Lagerlöf (1858-1940), Swedish writer.

## Peter Zwirka A1137

**1959, Mar. 3**
2173 A1137 40k hn brn & blk, yel .50 .25
Zwirka (1909-1947), Lithuanian writer.

**No. 1861A Overprinted in Red: "1759 1959"**

**1959, Feb. 26**
**Engr.**
2174 A993 40k lt ultra & brown 10.00 10.00
200th anniversary of the birth of Robert Burns, Scottish poet.

## Type of 1958

**1959**
Russian Writers: No. 2175, A. S. Griboedov, No. 2176; A. N. Ostrovski; No. 2177, Anton Chekhov; No. 2178, I. A. Krylov; No. 2178A, Nikolai V. Gogol; No. 2178B, S. T. Aksakov; No. 2178C, A. V. Koltzov, poet, and reaper.

**Litho.**
2175 A1071 40k buff, cl, blk & vio .40 .40
2176 A1071 40k vin & brown .40 .40
2177 A1071 40k slate & lnn brn .40 .40
2178 A1071 40k ol bister & brn .40 .40
2178A A1071 40k ol, gray & bis .40 .40
2178B A1071 40k brn, vio & bis .40 .40
2178C A1071 40k violet & black .40 .40
Nos. 2175-2178C (7) 2.80 2.80
No. 2178A for the 150th birth anniv. of Nikolai V. Gogol, writer, No. 2178B the centenary of the death of S. T. Aksakov, writer.

## A. S. Popov and Rescue from Ice Float A1138

**1959, Mar. 13**
2179 A1138 40k brn, blk & dk blue .40 .25
2180 A1138 60k multicolored .60 .25
Centenary of the birth of A. S. Popov, pioneer in radio research.

60k. Radio broadcasting "Peace" in 5 languages.

## M.S. Rossija at Odessa A1139

**1959**
**Litho.** **Unwmk.**
2181 A1139 10k multicolored .25 .20
2182 A1139 20k red, lt grn & dk bl .35 .20
2183 A1139 40k multicolored .65 .20
2184 A1139 40k blue, buff & red 1.00 .20
2185 A1139 60k ln grn, red & buff 1.25 .30
2186 A1139 1r ultra, red & yel 5.00 1.85
Nos. 2181-2186 (6)

Ships: 10k, Steamer, Vladivostok-Petropaviovsk-Kamchatka line, 20k, M.S. Feliks Dzerzhinski, Odessa-Latakia line. No. Ship, Murmansk-Tyksi line. 60k, M.S. Mikhail Kalinin at Leningrad, 1r, M.S. Baltika, Leningrad-London line.

Honoring the Russian fleet.

---

## Globe and Luna 1 A1140

Luna 1, launched Jan. 2, 1959: No. 2188, Globe and route of Luna 1.

**1959, Apr. 13**
2187 A1140 40k red brown & rose .55 .20
2188 A1140 40k ultra & blue .55 .20

## Saadi and "Gulistan" A1141

**1959, Mar. 20**
**Photo.**
2189 A1141 40k dk blue & black .40 .25
Persian poet Saadi (Muslih-ud-Din) and 700th anniv. of his book, "Gulistan" (1258).

## Suahan S. Orbeliani A1142

**1959, Apr. 2**
2190 A1142 40k dull rose & black .40 .20
Orbeliani (1658-1725), Georgian writer.

## Drawing by Korin A1143

**1959, Apr. 10**
**Litho.**
2191 A1143 40k multicolored 1.00 .50
Ogata Korin (1653?-1716), Japanese artist.

## Lenin — A1144

**1959, Apr. 17**
2192 A1144 40k sepia .50 .25
89th anniversary of the birth of Lenin.

## Cachin — A1146

**1959, Apr. 27**
**Engr.**
2194 A1146 60k dark brown .40 .20
Marcel Cachin (1869-1958), French Communist Party leader.

## Joseph Haydn A1147

## Alexander von Humboldt A1148

---

**1959, May 8**
2195 A1147 40k dk bl, gray & brn black .75 .20
Sesquicentennial of the death of Joseph Haydn, Austrian composer.

**1959, May 6**
2196 A1148 40k violet & brown .50 .25
Alexander von Humboldt, German naturalist and geographer; death centenary.

## Three Races Carrying Flag of Peace — A1149

## Mountain Climber — A1150

**1959, Apr. 30**
**Litho.**
2199 A1149 40k multicolored 1.00 .25
10th anniv. of World Peace Movement.

**1959, May 15**
Sports and Travel: No. 2201, Tourists reading map; No. 2202, Canoeing; No. 2203, Skiers.
2200 A1150 40k multicolored .30 .20
2201 A1150 40k multicolored .30 .20
2202 A1150 40k multicolored .30 .20
2203 A1150 40k multicolored .30 .20
Nos. 2200-2203 (4) 1.20 .80

## I. E. Repin Statue, Moscow A1151

## N. Y. Coliseum and Spasski Tower A1152

**1959**
Statues: No. 2205, Lenin, Ulyanovsk, 20k, V. V. Mayakovski, Moscow, 20k, Pushkin, Leningrad, 60k, Maxim Gorki, Moscow. 1r, Tchaikovsky, Moscow.

**Photo.** **Unwmk.**
2204 A1151 10k ocher & sepia .20 .20
2205 A1151 10k red & black .20 .20
2206 A1151 20k violet & sepia .20 .20
2207 A1151 25k grnsh blue & blk .20 .20
2208 A1151 60k lt green & slate .35 .20
2209 A1151 1r ultra & gray 1.35 1.20
Nos. 2204-2209 (6)

**1959, June 25**
**Litho.** **Perf. 12**
2210 A1152 20k multicolored .20 .20
2211 A1152 40k multicolored .30 .20
a. Souv. sheet of 1, imperf. 2.50 1.25
Soviet Exhibition of Science, Technology and Culture, New York, June 20-Aug. 10. No. 2211a issued July 20.

## Animal Types of 1957

**1959-60**
**Center in Natural Colors**
**Litho.** **Perf. 12**
20k. Hare, #2214, Siberian horse, #2215, Tiger, #2216, Red squirrel, #2217, Pine marten, #2218, Hazel hen, #2219, Mute swan.
2213 A1023 20k vio blue ('60) .30 .20
2214 A1023 25k blue black .30 .20
2215 A1023 25k brown .30 .20
2216 A1023 40k deep green .40 .20
2217 A1023 40k dark green .40 .20
2218 A1023 40k dark green .60 .40
2219 A1023 1r bright blue .95 .85
Nos. 2213-2219 (7) 3.25 2.25

RUSSIA

## Louis Braille — A1153 / Musa Djalil — A1154

**1959, July 16**
2220 A1153 60k blue grn, bis & brn .50 .25
150th anniversary of the birth of Louis Braille, French educator of the blind.

**Photo.**
**1959, July 16**
2221 A1154 40k violet & black .50 .25
Musa Djalil, Tatar poet.

## Sturgeon A1155

**1959, July 16**
2222 A1155 40k shown .40 .20
2223 A1155 60k Chum salmon .60 .20
See Nos. 2375-2377.

## Schoolboys in Workshop — A1160

**Photo.**
**1959, Aug. 27**
2230 A1160 40k dark purple .20 .20
2231 A1160 1r dark blue .50 .20
Design: 1r, Workers in night school.
Strengthening the connection between school and life.

## Letter Carrier A1165

**1959, Sept.**
2239 A1165 40k dk car rose & black .30 .20
2240 A1165 60k blue & black .60 .20
Intl. Letter Writing Week, Oct. 4-10.

## Makhtumkuli A1166

**Photo.**
**1959, Sept. 30**
2241 A1166 40k brown .50 .20
225th anniversary of the birth of Makhtumkuli, Turkmen writer.

## Arms of Tadzhikistan A1170

**1959, Oct. 13**
2258 A1170 40k red, emer, ocher & black .50 .20
Tadzhikistan statehood, 30th anniversary.

## Path of Luna 3 and Electronics Laboratory A1171

**1959, Oct. 12**
2259 A1171 40k violet .75 .25
Flight of Luna 3 around the moon, Oct. 4, 1959.

## Red Square, Moscow A1172

**Engr.**
**1959, Oct. 26**
2260 A1172 40k dark red .40 .20
42nd anniversary of October Revolution.

## US Capitol, Globe and Kremlin — A1173

**Photo.**
**1959, Oct. 27**
2261 A1173 60k blue & yellow .50 .20
Visit of Premier Nikita Khrushchev to the US, Sept. 1959.

## Helicopter — A1174

25k, Diver. 40k, Motorcyclist. 60k, Parachutist.
**Photo.**
**1959, Oct. 28**
2262 A1174 10k vio blue & mar .20 .20
2263 A1174 25k blue & brown .20 .20
2264 A1174 40k red brn & indigo .30 .20
2265 A1174 60k blue & ol bister .90 .80
Nos. 2262-2265 (4)
Honoring voluntary aides of the army.

## Glacier Survey — A1161 / Rocket and Observatory A1162

**1959**
2232 A1161 10k blue green .20 .20
2233 A1161 25k brt blue & red .30 .20
2234 A1161 40k ultra & red .50 .30
2235 A1162 1r ultra & buff 1.50 .90
Nos. 2232-2235 (4) 2.50 .90
Designs: 25k, Oceanographic ship "Vityaz" and map. 40k, Plane over Antarctica, camp and emperor penguin.
Intl. Geophysical Year. 1st Russian rocket to reach the moon, Sept. 14, 1959 (#2235).

## East German Emblem and Workers A1167

**1959, Oct. 6**
2242 A1167 40k multicolored .20 .20

## City Hall, East Berlin — A1168

**Photo.**
**Litho.**
2243 A1168 60k dp claret & buff .35 .20
German Democratic Republic, 10th anniv.

## Steel Production — A1169

7-Year Production Plan (Industries): #2244, Chemicals. #2245, Spasski Tower, hammer and sickle. #2246, Home building. #2247, Meat production, woman with farm animals. #2248, Machinery. #2249, Grain production, woman tractor driver. #2250, Oil. #2251, Textiles. #2252, Steel. #2253, Coal. #2254, Iron. #2255, Electric power.

**Litho.**
**1959-60**
2244 A1169 10k vio, grnsh blue .20 .20
2245 A1169 10k orange & dk car & maroon .20 .20
2246 A1169 15k brn, grn & mar .20 .20
2247 A1169 15k bl grn, yel & red .20 .20
2248 A1169 20k green, yel & red .20 .20
2249 A1169 20k lilac, sal & red .20 .20
2250 A1169 30k gldn brm, lil, red .20 .20
2251 A1169 30k vio bl, yel & org & green (60) .20 .20
2252 A1169 40k vio bl, yel & org & green .20 .20
2253 A1169 40k dk blue, pink & dp rose .20 .20
2254 A1169 60k org red, yel, bl & maroon .30 .20
2255 A1169 60k ultra, buff & red .60 .20
Nos. 2244-2255 (12) 2.60 2.40

## Gymnast A1156

Designs: 25k, Runner. 60k, Water polo.
**1959, Aug. 7**
2224 A1156 15k lilac rose & gray .20 .20
2225 A1156 25k yel green & red .20 .20
2226 A1156 30k brt red & gray .35 .20
2227 A1156 60k blue & org yel 1.00 .80
Nos. 2224-2227 (4)
2nd National Spartacist Games.

## Athletes Holding Trophy — A1157 / Globe and Hands — A1158

**Litho.**
**1959, Aug. 12**
2228 A1158 40k yel, blue & red .40 .20
2nd Intl. Conf. of Public Employees Unions.

## Workers and Farmers Holding Atom Symbol — A1163

**Litho.**
**1959, Sept. 23**
2236 A1163 40k red org & bister .40 .20
All-Union Economic Exhibition, Moscow.

## Russian and Chinese Students A1164

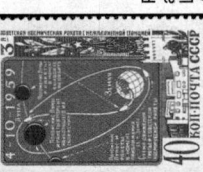

40k, Russian miner and Chinese steel worker.
**Litho.**
**1959, Sept. 25**
2237 A1164 20k multicolored .40 .25
2238 A1164 40k multicolored .60 .25
People's Republic of China, 10th anniv.

## Cathedral and Modern Building A1159

**Unwmk.**
**Perf. 12**
**1959, Aug. 21**
2229 A1159 40k blue, ol, yel & red .40 .20
1100th anniv. of the city of Novgorod.

---

**1959, Nov. 9**    *Perf. 12x12½, 12½x12*
2268 A1176 20k gray & ol bister .20 .20
2269 A1177 40k multicolored .30 .20

Soviet-Hungarian friendship.
For overprint see No. 2308.

Sandor Petőfi
A1176

Victory Statue and View of Budapest — A1177

---

No. 2267. Kremlin and diagram showing rocket and positions of moon and earth.

**1959, Nov. 1**
2266 A1175 40k bl, dk bl, red & bis .50 .20
2267 A1175 40k gray, pink & red .50 .20

Landing of the Soviet rocket on the moon, Sept. 14, 1959.

Moon, Earth and Path of Rocket A1175

---

**1959, Dec. 7**
2271 A1179 40k ultra & brown .40 .20

Chusovaya River, Ural — A1180

---

**1959, Dec.**    *Engr.*    *Perf. 12½*
2272 A1180 10k purple .20 .20
2273 A1180 10k rose carmine .20 .20
2274 A1180 25k dark blue .20 .20
2275 A1180 25k olive .30 .20
2276 A1180 25k dark red .30 .20
2277 A1180 40k claret .55 .25
2278 A1180 60k Prus blue .65 .30
2279 A1180 1r olive green 1.40 .60
2280 A1180 1r deep orange 5.30 2.75

Nos. 2272-2280 (9)

#2273, Lake Ritza, Caucasus. #2274, Lena River, Siberia. #2275, Seashore, Far East. #2276, Lake Iskander, Central Asia. #2277, Lake Baikal, Siberia. #2278, Belukha Mountain, Altai range. #2279, Crimea. #2280, Gur-suf region, Crimea.

---

**1959, Dec. 30**    *Litho.*    *Perf. 12½x12*
2283 A1181 40k multicolored .50 .35

40th anniversary of the 1st Cavalry.

"Trumpeters of 1st Cavalry" by M. Grekov — A1181

---

**1958-60**    *Engr.*    *Perf. 12½*
2286 A1182 20k slate grn ('59) 7.00 3.75
2287 A1182 25k sepia ('59) 3.25 1.60
2288 A1182 60k carmine 9.25 4.25

*Perf. 12x12½*
2290 A1182 20k green ('60) .20 .20
2291 A1182 25k sepia ('60) .35 .20
2292 A1182 60k vermilion ('59) .25 .20
2293 A1182 60k blue ('60) .70 .20

Nos. 2286-2293 (7) 21.00 10.40

Designs: 25k, Architect. 60k, Steel worker.

Farm Woman — A1182

---

**1959, Dec. 12**    *Photo.*    *Perf. 12x12½*
2270 A1178 40k ultra & brown 9.00 5.00

Manolis Glezos, Greek communist.

Manolis Glezos and Acropolis A1178

---

**1959, Dec. 7**    *Perf. 12½x12*
2271 A1179 40k ultra & brown .40 .20

A. A. Voskresensky, Chemist, 150th Birth Anniv. — A1179

---

**1960, Jan. 20**    *Litho.*    *Perf. 12½x12*
2297 A1185 20k red, gray & vio bl .50 .20
2298 A1185 40k dk blue, buff & brn .30 .20

40k, Chekhov in later years, Yalta home.
Anton P. Chekhov (1860-1904), playwright.

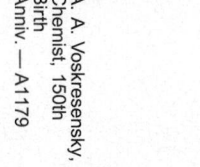

Anton Chekhov and Moscow Home A1185

---

**1960, Feb. 5**    *Photo.*    *Perf. 12½x12*
2299 A1186 40k chocolate .40 .20

Vera Komissar-zhevskaya (1864-1910), Actress — A1186

---

**1960, Jan. 25**    *Photo.*    *Perf. 12½*
2295 A1183 40k dark red brown .40 .20

Mikhail V. Frunze (1885-1925), Revolutionary A1183

---

**1960, Jan. 30**    *Unwmk.*
2296 A1184 40k brt violet & brown .50 .20

G.N. Gabrichevski, Microbiologist, Birth Cent. — A1184

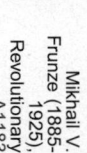

---

**1960, Feb. 18**    *Litho.*    *Perf. 11½*
2300 A1187 10k ocher & vio blue .25 .20
2301 A1187 25k multicolored .30 .20
2302 A1187 40k org, rose & vio blue .20 .20
2303 A1187 60k vio, grn & buff .35 .20
2304 A1187 1r bl, grn & brn .60 .20

Nos. 2300-2304 (5) 2.50 1.00

Sports: 10k, Ice hockey. 25k, Speed skating. 40k, Skier. 60k, Woman figure skater. 1r, Ski jumper.

8th Olympic Winter Games, Squaw Valley, Calif., Feb. 18-29. A1187

---

**1959, Nov. 1**
2283 ...

Sword into Plowshare Statue, UN, NY — A1188

---

**1960, Mar. 8**
2306 A1189 40k multicolored .50 .20

50 years of Int'l Woman's Day, Mar. 8.

Women of Various Races A1189

---

**1960, Feb. 23**    *Perf. 12½x12*
2307 A1190 40k multicolored 1.75 1.00

Lieut. Timur Frunze, World War II hero.

Planes in Combat and Timur Frunze A1190

---

**1960**
2305 A1188 40k grnsh bl, yel & brown .40 .20
   a.    Souvenir sheet 1.50 .75

No. 2305a for Premier Nikita Khrushchev's visit to the 15th General Assembly of the UN in NYC.

---

**1960, Apr. 4**
2308 A1177 40k multicolored 4.00 2.00

15th anniversary of Hungary's liberation from the Nazis.

---

**1960**
2309 A1191 40k pale bl, dk bl & yel .60 .25

No. 2269 Overprinted in Red

---

**1960**    *Photo.*    *Perf. 12x12½*
2309 A1191 40k pale bl, dk bl & citron .60 .25

Photographing of the far side of the moon, Oct. 7, 1959.

Lunik 3 Photographing Far Side of Moon — A1191

Design: 60k, Far side of the moon.

**1960, Photo.**
2310 A1191 60k lt bl, dk bl & citron .60 .25

---

**1960, Apr. 10**    *Litho.*    *Perf. 12½x12*
2311 A1192 10k multicolored .20 .20
2312 A1192 20k red, green & blk .20 .20
2313 A1192 30k multicolored .20 .20
2314 A1192 40k multicolored .25 .20

Various Lenin Portraits and: 20k, Lenin with children and Christmas tree: 30k, Flag, workers and ship. 40k, Kremlin, banners and marchers. 60k, Map of Russia, buildings and ship. 1r, Peace proclamation and globe.

Lenin as Child A1192

**Children's Friendship A1202**

Drawings by Children: 20k, Collective farm, vert. 25k, Winter joys. 40k, "In the Zoo."

**1960, June 1**    **Perf. 12x12½, 12½x12**    **Litho.**

| | | | | |
|---|---|---|---|---|
| 2345 | A1202 | 10k multicolored | .20 | .20 |
| 2346 | A1202 | 20k multicolored | .20 | .20 |
| 2347 | A1202 | 25k multicolored | .20 | .20 |
| 2348 | A1202 | 40k multicolored | .80 | .80 |
| | | Nos. 2345-2348 (4) | | |

**Lomonosov University and Congress Emblem — A1203**

**1960, June 17**    **Photo.**    **Perf. 12½x12**
2349 A1203 60k yellow & dk brown .70 .25

1st congress of the International Federation for Automation Control, Moscow.

**Sputnik 4 and Globe — A1204**

**1960, June 17**
2350 A1204 40k vio blue & dp org 1.00 .50

Launching on May 15, 1900, of Sputnik 4, which orbited the earth with a dummy cosmonaut.

**Kosta Hetagurov (1859-1906), Ossetian Poet — A1205**

**1960, June 20**    **Litho.**    **Perf. 12½**
2351 A1205 40k gray blue & brown .40 .20

**Flag and Tallinn, Estonia A1206**

Soviet Republics, 20th Annivs.: No. 2353, Flag and Riga, Latvia. No. 2354, Flag and Vilnius, Lithuania.

**1960**    **Perf. 12½x12½, 12½ (#2353)**    **Photo.**
2352 A1206 40k red & ultra .45 .20
**Typo.**
2353 A1206 40k blue, gray & red .45 .20
**Litho.**
2354 A1206 40k blue, red & grn 1.35 .60
Nos. 2352-2354 (3)

---

КОМИ АССР    1961    г.СЫКТЫВКАР. СО   #2341

НАХИЧЕВАНСКАЯ АССР   НАХЧЫВАН МССР   1961   г.НАХИЧЕВАНЬ. У   #2342

Capitals, Soviet Autonomous Republics: No. 2327, Lenin street, Batum. No. 2328, Cultural Palace, Izhevsk. Udmurt. No. 2329, August street, Grozny, Chechen-Ingush. No. 2330, Soviet House, Cheboksary, Chuvash. No. 2331, Buinak Street, Makhachkala, Dagestan. No. 2332, Soviet street, Ioshkar Ola, Mari. No. 2333, Chkalov street, Dzaudzhikau, North Ossetia. No. 2334, October street, Yakutsk, Yakut. No. 2335, House of Ministers, Nukus, Kara-Kalpak.

**1960**    **Engr.**    **Perf. 12½**

| | | | | |
|---|---|---|---|---|
| 2326 | A1201 | 40k Prus green | .55 | .35 |
| 2327 | A1201 | 40k violet blue | .55 | .35 |
| 2328 | A1201 | 40k green | .55 | .35 |
| 2329 | A1201 | 40k maroon | .55 | .35 |
| 2330 | A1201 | 40k dull red | .45 | .25 |
| 2331 | A1201 | 40k carmine | .45 | .25 |
| 2332 | A1201 | 40k dark brown | .45 | .25 |
| 2333 | A1201 | 40k orange brown | .45 | .25 |
| 2334 | A1201 | 40k dark blue | .45 | .25 |
| 2335 | A1201 | 40k brown | 5.00 | 3.00 |
| | | Nos. 2326-2335 (10) | | |

See Nos. 2338-2344C. For overprints see Nos. 2336-2337.

No. 2326 Overprinted in Red

**1960, June 9**
2336 A1201 40k Prus green 5.00 2.00

Karelian Autonomous Rep., 40th anniv.

No. 2328 Overprinted in Red

**1960, Nov. 4**
2337 A1201 40k green 2.50 1.25

Udmurt Autonomous Rep., 40th anniv.

**1961-62**    **Perf. 12½, 12½x12**

Capitals, Soviet Autonomous Republics: #2338, Rustaveli Street, Sukhumi, Abkhazia. #2339, House of Soviets, Nalchik, Kabardino-Balkar. #2340, Lenin Street, Ulan-Ude, Buriat. #2341, Soviet Street, Syktyvkar, Komi. #2342, Lenin Street, Nakhichevan, Nakhichevan. #2343, Elista, Kalmyk. #2344, Ufa, Bashkir. #2344A, Lobachevsky Square, Kazan, Tartar. #2344B, Kizil, Tuvinia. #2344C, Saransk, Mordovia.

| | | | | |
|---|---|---|---|---|
| 2338 | A1201 | 4k orange ver | .25 | .20 |
| 2339 | A1201 | 4k dark violet | .25 | .20 |
| 2340 | A1201 | 4k dark blue | .25 | .20 |
| 2341 | A1201 | 4k gray | .25 | .20 |
| 2342 | A1201 | 4k dk car rose | .25 | .20 |
| 2343 | A1201 | 4k olive green | .25 | .20 |
| 2344 | A1201 | 4k dull purple | .25 | .20 |
| 2344A | A1201 | 4k grnsh blk ('62) | .25 | .20 |
| 2344B | A1201 | 4k claret ('62) | .25 | .20 |
| 2344C | A1201 | 4k deep grn ('62) | 2.50 | 2.00 |
| | | Nos. 2338-2344C (10) | | |

Denominations of Nos. 2338-2344C are in the revalued currency.

---

**Robert Schumann (1810-56), German Composer A1198**

**1960, May 20**    **Photo.**    **Perf. 12x12½**
2323 A1198 40k ultra & black .50 .25

**Yakov M. Sverdlov (1885-1919), 1st USSR Pres. — A1199**

**1960, May 24**    **Perf. 12½x12**
2324 A1199 40k dk brn & org brn .75 .35

**Stamp of 1957 Under Magnifying Glass A1200**

**1960, May 28**    **Litho.**    **Perf. 11½**
2325 A1200 60k multicolored .75 .35

Stamp Day.

**Karl Marx Avenue, Petrozavodsk, Karelian Autonomous Republic — A1201**

АДЖАРСКАЯ АССР   г.БАТУМИ. УЛИ   #2327

ЧЕЧЕНО-ИНГУШСКАЯ АССР   НОХЧ-ГАЛГАЙН АССР   г.ГРОЗНЫЙ. АВГУС   #2329

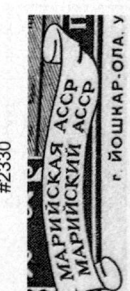

ЧУВАШСКАЯ АССР   ЧӐВАШ АССР-ĕ   г.ЧЕБОКСАРЫ. Ч   #2330

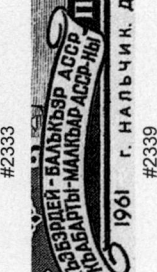

МАРИЙСКАЯ АССР   МАРИЙСКИЙ АССР   г.ЙОШКАР-ОЛА. У   #2332

СЕВЕРО-ОСЕТИНСКАЯ АССР   ЦӔГАТ-ИРЫСТОНЫ АССР   г.ОРДЖОНИКИДЗЕ.   #2333

КЪАБАРДЕЙ-БАЛЪКЪАР АССР   КАБАРДИНО-БАЛКАР АССР-НЫ   1961   г.НАЛЬЧИК. Д   #2339

---

2315 A1192 60k multicolored .75 .20
2316 A1192 1r red, vio bl & brn 2.35 1.20
Nos. 2311-2316 (6)

90th anniversary of the birth of Lenin.

**Steelworker A1193**

**1960, Apr. 30**    **Photo.**
2317 A1193 40k brown & red .40 .20

Industrial overproduction by 50,000,000r during the 1st year of the 7-year plan.

**Government House, Baku A1194**

**1960, Apr.**    **Litho.**    **Perf. 12½x12**
2318 A1194 40k bister & brown .20 .20

Azerbaijan, 40th anniv.
For surcharge see #2898.

**Brotherhood Monument, Prague — A1195**

Design: 60k, Charles Bridge, Prague.

**1960, Apr. 29**    **Photo.**    **Perf. 12½x12**
2319 A1195 40k brt blue & black .20 .20
2320 A1195 60k black brn & yellow .35 .20

Czechoslovak Republic, 15th anniv.

**Radio Tower and Popov Central Museum of Communications, Leningrad — A1196**

**1960, May 6**    **Litho.**
2321 A1196 40k blue, ocher & brn .50 .25

Radio Day.

**Gen. I. D. Tcherniakovski and Soldiers — A1197**

**1960, May 4**
2322 A1197 1r multicolored .60 .35

Gen. I. D. Tcherniakovski, World War II hero and his military school.

### Cement Factory, Belgorod A1207

Design: 40k, Factory, Novy Krivoi.

**1960, June 28**    *Perf. 12½x12*
| | | | |
|---|---|---|---|
| 2355 | A1207 | 25k ultra & black | .25 .20 |
| 2356 | A1207 | 40k rose brown & blk | .25 .20 |

"New buildings of the 1st year of the 7-year plan."

### Automatic Production Line and Roller Bearing A1208

**1960, June 13**    *Perf. 11½*
| | | | |
|---|---|---|---|
| 2357 | A1208 | 40k rose violet | .35 .20 |
| 2358 | A1208 | 40k Prus green | .35 .20 |

#2358, Automatic production line and gear.

Publicizing mechanization and automation of factories.

### Running A1209

 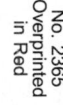

**1960, Aug. 1**    *Litho.*    *Perf. 11½*
| | | | |
|---|---|---|---|
| 2359 | A1209 | 5k multicolored | .20 .20 |
| 2360 | A1209 | 10k brn, blue & yel | .20 .20 |
| 2361 | A1209 | 15k multicolored | .20 .20 |
| 2362 | A1209 | 20k blk, crim & sal | .20 .20 |
| 2363 | A1209 | 25k lake, sl & rose | .20 .20 |
| 2364 | A1209 | 40k vio bl, bl & bis | .20 .20 |
| 2365 | A1209 | 40k vio, gray & pink | .20 .20 |
| 2366 | A1209 | 60k multicolored | .30 .20 |
| 2367 | A1209 | 1r brown, lilac & pale green | .60 .40 |
| 2368 | A1209 | 1r brown, lilac & pale green | 2.50 2.20 |
| | | Nos. 2359-2368 (10) | 2.50 2.20 |

Sports: 10k, Wrestling. 15k, Basketball. 20k, Weight lifting. 25k, Boxing. No. 2364, Fencing. No. 2365, Diving. No. 2366, Women's gymnastics. 60k, Canoeing. 1r, Steeplechase.

17th Olympic Games, Rome, 8/25-9/11.

### No. 2365 Overprinted in Red

**1960, Aug. 23**
| | | | |
|---|---|---|---|
| 2369 | A1209 | 40k | 7.50 5.00 |

12th San Marino-Riccione Stamp Fair.

### Kishinev, Moldavian Republic A1210

**1960, Aug. 2**
| | | | |
|---|---|---|---|
| 2370 | A1210 | 40k multicolored | .50 .20 |

20th anniversary of Moldavian Republic.

### Tractor and Factory A1211 — Book Museum, Hanoi A1212

**1960, Aug. 25**    *Perf. 12x12½, 12½x12*
| | | | |
|---|---|---|---|
| 2371 | A1211 | 40k green, ocher & blk | .35 .20 |
| 2372 | A1212 | 60k blue, lilac & brn | .40 .20 |

15th anniversary of North Viet Nam.

### Gregory N. Minkh, Microbiologist, 125th Birth Anniv. — A1213

**1960, Aug. 25**    *Photo.*    *Perf. 12½x12*
| | | | |
|---|---|---|---|
| 2373 | A1213 | 40k bister brn & dk brn | .50 .25 |

### "March," by I. I. Levitan A1214

**1960, Aug. 29**
| | | | |
|---|---|---|---|
| 2374 | A1214 | 40k ol bister & black | .50 .30 |

I. I. Levitan, painter, birth cent.

### Fish Type of 1959

**1960, Sept. 3**    *Perf. 12½*
| | | | |
|---|---|---|---|
| 2375 | A1155 | 20k blue & black | .20 .20 |
| 2376 | A1155 | 25k vio gray & red brn | .20 .20 |
| 2377 | A1155 | 40k rose lilac & purple | .60 .60 |
| | | Nos. 2375-2377 (3) | .60 .60 |

Designs: 20k, Pikeperch. 25k, Fur seals. 40k, Ludogan whitefish.

### Forest by I. I. Shishkin — A1215

**1960, Aug. 29**    *Engr.*
| | | | |
|---|---|---|---|
| 2378 | A1215 | 1r red brown | 1.50 .30 |

5th World Forestry Congress, Seattle, Wash., Aug. 29-Sept. 10.

### Globe with USSR and Letter A1216

**1960, Sept. 10**    *Litho.*    *Perf. 12x12½*
| | | | |
|---|---|---|---|
| 2379 | A1216 | 40k multicolored | .25 .20 |
| 2380 | A1216 | 60k multicolored | .35 .20 |

Intl. Letter Writing Week, Oct. 3-9.

### Farmer, Worker, Scientist A1217

**1960, Oct. 4**    *Typo.*    *Perf. 12½*
| | | | |
|---|---|---|---|
| 2381 | A1217 | 40k multicolored | .50 .20 |

Kazakh SSR, 40th anniv.

### Globes and Olive Branch — A1218

**1960, Sept. 29**    *Litho.*    *Perf. 12½x12*
| | | | |
|---|---|---|---|
| 2382 | A1218 | 60k pale vio, bl & gray | .50 .20 |

World Federation of Trade Unions, 15th anniv.

### Kremlin, Sputnik 5 and Dogs Belka and Strelka A1219

**1960, Sept. 29**    *Photo.*
| | | | |
|---|---|---|---|
| 2383 | A1219 | 40k brt pur & yellow | .55 .20 |
| 2384 | A1219 | 1r blue & salmon | .85 .25 |

Flight of Sputnik 5, Aug. 19-20, 1960.

### Passenger Ship "Karl Marx" A1220

Ships: 40k, Turbo-electric ship "Lenin." 60k, Speedboat "Raketa" (Rocket).

**1960, Oct. 24**    *Litho.*    *Perf. 12½x12½*
| | | | |
|---|---|---|---|
| 2385 | A1220 | 25k bl, blk, red & yel | .20 .20 |
| 2386 | A1220 | 40k blue, black & red | .35 .20 |
| 2387 | A1220 | 60k blue, blk & rose | 1.00 .60 |
| | | Nos. 2385-2387 (3) | 1.00 .60 |

### A. N. Voronikhin and Kasansky Cathedral, Leningrad A1221

**1960, Oct. 24**    *Photo.*
| | | | |
|---|---|---|---|
| 2388 | A1221 | 40k gray & brn black | .50 .25 |

Voronikhin, architect, 200th birth anniv.

### J. S. Gogebashvili A1222

**1960, Oct. 29**
| | | | |
|---|---|---|---|
| 2389 | A1222 | 40k dk gray & mag | .50 .25 |

120th anniversary of the birth of J. S. Gogebashvili, Georgian teacher and publicist.

### Red Flag, Electric Power Station and Factory — A1223

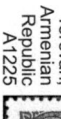

**1960, Oct. 29**    *Litho.*
| | | | |
|---|---|---|---|
| 2390 | A1223 | 40k red, yel & brown | .50 .20 |

43rd anniversary of October Revolution.

### Leo Tolstoy A1224

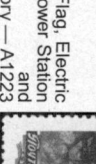

**1960, Nov. 14**    *Perf. 12x12½, 12½x12*
| | | | |
|---|---|---|---|
| 2391 | A1224 | 20k violet & brown | .25 .20 |
| 2392 | A1224 | 40k blue & lt brown | .35 .20 |
| 2393 | A1224 | 60k dp claret & se-pia | .50 .20 |
| | | Nos. 2391-2393 (3) | 1.10 .60 |

Designs: 40k, Tolstoy in Yasnaya Polyana. 60k, Portrait, vert.

50th anniversary of the death of Count Leo Tolstoy, writer.

### Yerevan, Armenian Republic A1225

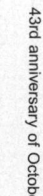

**1960, Nov. 14**
| | | | |
|---|---|---|---|
| 2394 | A1225 | 40k bl, red, buff & brn | .40 .20 |

Armenian Soviet Rep., 40th anniv.

### Friedrich Engels, 140th Birth Anniv. — A1226

**1960, Nov. 25**    *Engr.*    *Perf. 12½*
| | | | |
|---|---|---|---|
| 2395 | A1226 | 60k slate | .60 .25 |

### Badge of Youth Federation A1227

**1960, Nov. 2**    *Litho.*    *Perf. 12½*
| | | | |
|---|---|---|---|
| 2396 | A1227 | 40k brt pink, blk & yel | .75 .25 |

Intl. Youth Federation, 15th anniv.

### 40-ton Truck MAL-530 A1228

Automotive Industry: 40k, "Volga" car. 60k, "Moskvitch 407" car. 1r, "Tourist" Bus.

**1960, Oct. 29**    *Photo.*    *Perf. 12½x12½*
| | | | |
|---|---|---|---|
| 2397 | A1228 | 25k ultra & gray | .20 .20 |
| 2398 | A1228 | 40k ol bister & ultra | .25 .20 |

2399 A1228 60k Prus green & dp car .40 .20
2400 A1228 1r multicolored .90 .20
1.75 .80
**Litho.**
Nos. 2397-2400 (4)

N. I. Pirogov — A1229

**1960, Dec. 13 Photo. Perf. 12x12½**
2401 A1229 40k green & brn black .40 .20
Pirogov, surgeon, 125th birth anniv.

Friendship University and Students — A1230

**1960, Nov. Perf. 12x12½**
2402 A1230 40k brown carmine .50 .20
Completion of Friendship of Nations University in Moscow.
For surcharge see No. 2462.

Mark Twain A1231

**1960, Nov. 30 Perf. 12½x12**
2403 A1231 40k dp org & brown .75 .40
Mark Twain, 125th birth anniv.

Dove and Globe A1232

**1960, Oct. 29 Photo.**
2404 A1232 60k maroon & gray .50 .25
Intl. Democratic Women's Fed., 15th anniv.

Akaki Zeretely A1233

**1960, Dec. 27 Perf. 12½x12**
2405 A1233 40k violet & black brn .60 .20
Zeretely, Georgian poet, 120th birth anniv.

Frederic Chopin, after Delacroix A1234

**1960, Dec. 24 Perf. 12x11½**
2406 A1234 40k bister & brown .50 .20
Chopin, Polish composer, 150th birth anniv.


Crocus — A1236

North Korean Flag and Flying Horse — A1235

**1960. Dec. 24 Litho. Perf. 12½x12**
2407 A1235 40k multicolored .50 .20
15th anniversary of "the liberation of the Korean people by the Soviet army."

**1960 Perf. 12x12½**

**Flowers in Natural Colors**
Asiatic Flowers: No. 2409, Tulip. No. 2410, Trollius. No. 2411, Tulip. No. 2412, Ginseng. No. 2413, Iris. No. 2414, Hypericum. 1r, Dog rose.

2408 A1236 20k green & violet .25 .20
2409 A1236 20k vio blue & black .25 .20
2410 A1236 25k gray .30 .20
2411 A1236 40k ol bister & black .35 .20
2412 A1236 40k grn & blk, wmkd. .20 .20
2413 A1236 60k yel, green & red .35 .20
2414 A1236 60k bluish grn & blk .70 .20
2415 A1236 1r slate grn & blk 1.10 .20
Nos. 2408-2415 (8) 4.00 1.60
The watermark on No. 2412 consists of vertical rows of chevrons.

Lithuanian Costumes A1237

Regional Costumes: 60k, Uzbek.

**Perf. 12½ (10k), 11½ (60k)**
**1960, Dec. 24 Typo. Unwmk.**
2416 A1237 10k multicolored .26 .20
2417 A1237 60k multicolored .75 .20

**Currency Revalued**
**1961-62 Litho. Perf. 11½**
Regional Costumes: No. 2418, Moldavia. No. 2419, Georgia. No. 2420, Ukrainia. No. 2421, White Russia. No. 2422, Kazakhstan. No. 2422A, Latvia. 4k, Koryak. 6k, Russia. 10k, Armenia. 12k, Estonia.

2418 A1237 2k buff, brn & ver .20 .20
2419 A1237 2k red, brn, ocher & black .20 .20
2420 A1237 3k ultra, buff, red & brown .25 .20
2421 A1237 3k red org, ocher & black .25 .20
2422 A1237 3k buff, brn, grn & red .25 .20
2422A A1237 3k org red, gray ol & blk (62) .25 .20
2423 A1237 4k multicolored .25 .20
2424 A1237 6k multicolored .45 .25
2425 A1237 10k brn, ol bis & vermilion .55 .30
2426 A1237 12k red, ultra & black .80 .30
1.10 .40
Nos. 2418-2426 (10) 4.30 2.35

Lenin and Map Showing Electrification — A1238


**1961 Perf. 12½x12 Perf. 12½**
2427 A1238 4k blue, buff & brown .20 .20
2428 A1238 10k red org & blue blk .40 .25
State Electrification Plan, 40th anniv. (in 1960).

**Animal Types of 1957**
**1961, Jan. 7 Perf. 12½**
2429 A1024 1k Brown bear .20 .20
2430 A1023 6k Beaver .70 .35
2431 A1023 10k Roe deer .90 .55
Nos. 2429-2431 (3) 1.80 1.10

Georgian Flag and Views A1239

**1961, Feb. 15 Perf. 12½x12**
2432 A1239 4k multicolored .30 .20
40th anniv. of Georgian SSR.

Nikolai D. Zelinski, Chemist, Birth Cent. A1240

**1961, Feb. 6 Photo. Perf. 12x12½**
2433 A1240 4k rose violet .30 .20

Nikolai A. Dobrolyubov (1836-61), Journalist and Critic — A1241

**1961, Feb. 5 Perf. 11½x12**
2434 A1241 4k brt blue & brown .50 .20

A1242

Designs: 3k, Cattle. 4k, Tractor in cornfield. 6k, Mechanization of Grain Harvest. 10k, Women picking apples.

**Perf. 12x12½, 12x11½**
**1961**
2435 A1242 3k blue & magenta .25 .20
2436 A1242 4k green & dk gray .25 .20
2437 A1242 6k vio blue & brn .60 .20
2438 A1242 10k maroon & ol grn .90 .80
Nos. 2435-2438 (4) 1.90
Agricultural development.

A1243

**Perf. 12x12½; 12x11½ (Nos. 2439A, 2442 & 12k) Unwmk.**
**1961-65**
Designs: 1k, "Labor" Holding Peace Flag. 2k, Harvester and silo. 3k, Space rockets. 4k, Arms and flag of USSR. 6k, Spasski tower. 10k, Workers' monument. 12k, Minin and Pozharsky Monument and Spasski tower. 16k, Plane over power station and dam.

**Engr.**
2439 A1243 1k olive bister 1.90
**Litho.**
2439A A1243 1k olive bister .75 .20
2440 A1243 2k green 2.50
2441 A1243 3k dk violet .20 .20
**Engr.**
2442 A1243 4k red 4.25 .95
**Litho.**
2443 A1243 4k red .75 .20
2443A A1243 4k org brn ('65) 10.00 .65
2444 A1243 6k vermilion 3.00 .35
2445 A1243 6k dk car rose 1.90 .20


**Perf. 12½x12**
2446 A1243 10k orange .20
**Photo.**
2447 A1243 12k brt magenta .30
**Litho.**
2448 A1243 16k ultra 5.25 1.10
Nos. 2439-2448 (12) 37.50 4.75

V. P. Miroshnitchenko — A1244

**1961, Feb. 23 Photo. Perf. 12½x12**
2449 A1244 4k violet brn & slate .30 .20
Soldier hero of World War II.
See Nos. 2570-2571.

Taras G. Shevchenko and Birthplace — A1245

Shevchenko Statue, Kharkov A1246

Andrei Rubljov A1247

6k, Book, torch and Shevchenko with beard.

**Perf. 12½, 11½x12 Litho.; Photo. (4k)**
**1961, Mar.**
2450 A1245 3k brown & violet .30 .20
2451 A1246 4k red orange & gray .60 .20
2452 A1245 6k black, grn & red brn .85 .25
Nos. 2450-2452 (3) 1.75 .65
Shevchenko, Ukrainian poet, death cent. No. 2452 was printed with alternating green and black label, containing a quotation. See No. 2852.

**1961, Mar. 13 Litho. Perf. 12½x12**
2453 A1247 4k ultra, bister & brn .30 .20
Rubljov, painter, 600th birth anniv.

N. V. Sklifosovsky A1248

Robert Koch A1249

**1961, Mar. 26 Photo. Perf. 11½x12**
2454 A1248 4k ultra & black .30 .20
Sklifosovsky, surgeon, 125th birth anniv.

**1961, Mar. 26**
2455 A1249 6k dark brown .30 .20
Koch, German microbiologist, 59th death anniv.

## Globe and Sputnik 8 — A1250

Maj. Yuri A. Gagarin — A1254

Open Book and Globe — A1251

**1961, Apr.**
**Litho.**
2456 A1250 6k dk & lt blue & org .60 .20
**Photo.**
2457 A1250 10k vio blue & yel .85 .30

10k, Space probe and its path to Venus.
Launching of the Venus space probe, 2/12/61.

**1961, Apr. 7 Litho. Perf. 11½**
2458 A1251 6k ultra & sepia .70 .20

Centenary of the children's magazine "Around the World."

## Musician, Dancers and Singers — A1252

**1961, Apr. 7 Perf. 12½x12 Unwmk.**
2459 A1252 4k yel, red & black .40 .20

Russian National Choir, 50th anniv.

## African Breaking Chains and Map — A1253

**1961, Apr. 15 Perf. 12½**
2460 A1253 4k multicolored .35 .20
2461 A1253 6k blue, purple & org .35 .20

6k, Globe, torch & black & white handshake.
Africa Day and 3rd Conference of Independent African States, Cairo, Mar. 25-31.

## No. 2402 Surcharged in Red

**1961, Apr. 15 Photo. Perf. 12x12½**
2462 A1230 4k on 40k brown car .90 .20

Naming of Friendship University, Moscow, in memory of Patrice Lumumba, Premier of Congo.

---

6k, Kremlin, rockets and radar equipment. 10k, Rocket, Gagarin with helmet and Kremlin.

**1961, Apr. Litho. Perf. 11½ (3k), 12½x12**
2463 A1254 3k Prus blue .25 .20
2464 A1254 6k blue, violet & red .65 .20
**Photo.**
2465 A1254 10k red, blue grn & brn 1.10 .35
Nos. 2463-2465 (3) 2.00 .75

1st man in space, Yuri A. Gagarin, Apr. 12, 1961. No. 2464. First issued with alternating light blue and red label. Nos. 2463-2465 exist imperf. Value $1.75.

## Lenin — A1255

**1961, Apr. 22 Litho. Perf. 12½x12**
2466 A1255 4k dp car, sal & blk .75 .20

91st anniversary of Lenin's birth.

## Rabindranath Tagore — A1256

**1961, May 8 Engr. Perf. 11½x12**
2467 A1256 6k bis, maroon & blk .60 .20

Tagore, Indian poet, birth cent.

## The Hunchbacked Horse — A1257

Fairy Tales: 1k, The Geese and the Swans. 3k, Fox, Hare and Cock. 6k, The Peasant and the Bear. 10k, Ruslan and Ludmilla.

**1961 Litho. Perf. 12½**
2468 A1257 1k multicolored .20 .20
2469 A1257 3k multicolored .50 .30
2470 A1257 4k multicolored .50 .30
2471 A1257 6k multicolored .55 .35
2472 A1257 10k multicolored .55 .40
Nos. 2468-2472 (5) 2.10 1.45

## "Man Conquering Space" — A1258

Design: 6k, Giuseppe Garibaldi.

**1961, May 24**
2481 A1258 4k orange brown .25 .20
2482 A1258 6k lilac & salmon .45 .20

International Labor Exposition, Turin.

---

Lenin A1259

Patrice Lumumba A1260

Various portraits of Lenin.

**Photo. Olive Bister Frame — A1259**
**1961 Perf. 12½x12**
2483 A1259 20k dark green 1.50 .85
2484 A1259 30k dark blue 2.50 1.90
2485 A1259 50k rose red 4.50 2.75
Nos. 2483-2485 (3) 8.50 5.50

**1961, May 29 Litho.**
2486 A1260 2k yellow & brown .35 .20

Lumumba (1925-61), premier of Congo.

## Kindergarten — A1261

Children's Day: 3k, Young Pioneers in camp. 4k, Young Pioneers.

**1961, May 31 Perf. 12½x12, 12½x12½**
2487 A1261 2k orange & ultra .20 .20
2488 A1261 3k ol bister & purple .20 .20
2489 A1261 4k red & gray .60 .60
Nos. 2487-2489 (3)

## Dog Zvezdochka and Sputnik 10 — A1263

Sputniks 9 and 10: 4k Dog Chernushka and Sputnik 9, vert.

**1961, June 8 Litho. Perf. 12½, 11½**
2491 A1263 2k vio, Prus blue & blk 1.50 .20
**Photo.**
2492 A1263 4k Prus blue & brt grn 1.50 .20

## Vissarion G. Belinski, Author, 150th Birth Anniv. — A1265

**1961, June 13**
2493 A1265 4k carmine & black .30 .20

Engraved and Photogravure Perf. 11½x12

---

Lt. Gen. D.M. Karbishev A1266

**1961, June 22 Litho. Perf. 12½**
2494 A1266 4k black, red & yel .30 .20

Karbishev was tortured to death in the Nazi prison camp at Mauthausen, Austria.

## Hydro-meteorological Map and Instruments — A1267

**1961, June 21 Perf. 12½x12½**
2495 A1267 6k ultra & green .50 .20

40th anniversary of hydro-meteorological service in Russia.

## Gliders — A1268

6k, Motorboat race. 10k, Motorcycle race.

**1961, July 5 Photo. Perf. 12½**
2497 A1268 4k dk slate grn & crim .30 .20
**Litho.**
2498 A1268 6k slate & vermilion .40 .20
2499 A1268 10k slate & vermilion 1.25 .20
Nos. 2497-2499 (3) 1.95 .60

USSR Technical Sports Spartakiad.

## Javelin Thrower — A1269

**1961, Aug. 8 Photo. Perf. 12½x12½**
2500 A1209 6k dp carmine & pink .30 .20

7th Trade Union Spartacist Games.

## S. I. Vavilov A1270

**1961, July 25 Photo. Perf. 11½x12**
2501 A1270 4k lt green & sepia .30 .20

Vavilov, president of Academy of Science.

## Vazha Pshavela A1271

**1961 Photo. Perf. 11½x12**
2502 A1271 4k dk brown & cream .35 .20

Pshavela, Georgian poet, birth cent.

RUSSIA

**1961, Sept. 28   Litho.   *Perf. 12½x12***
| 2530 | A1287 | 2k plum & red, cream | .20 | .20 |
| 2531 | A1287 | 3k brn & red, yellow | .20 | .20 |
| 2532 | A1287 | 4k vio blue & red, cr | .65 | .60 |

*Nos. 2530-2532 (3)*

Publicizing Communist labor teams in their efforts for labor, education and relaxation.

Rocket and Stars — A1288

**Engraved on Aluminum Foil**
**1961, Oct. 17          *Perf. 12½***
2533  A1288  1r black & red          20.00  20.00

Soviet scientific and technical achievements in exploring outer space.

**Overprinted in Red**
**XXII съезд КПСС**
**1961, Oct. 23**
2534  A1288  1r black & red          25.00  25.00

22nd cong. Communist Party of the USSR.

Amangaldi Imanov — A1289

**1961, Oct. 25   Photo.   *Perf. 11½x12***
2535  A1289  4k green, buff & brn     .20  .20

Amangaldi Imanov (1873-1919), champion of Soviet power in Kazakhstan.

Franz Liszt (1811-86), Composer A1290

**1961, Oct. 31          *Perf. 12x11½***
2536  A1290  4k mar, dk brn & ocher   .60  .20

Flags and Slogans A1291

**1961, Nov. 4          *Perf. 11½***
2537  A1291  4k red, yel & dark red   .50  .20

44th anniversary of October Revolution.

Hand Holding Hammer — A1292

---

**1961          Photo.          *Perf. 11½x12***
| 2520 | A1282 | 2k lt ultra & sepia | .30 | .20 |
| 2521 | A1282 | 4k rose vio & sepia | .30 | .20 |

Letters and Means of Transportation — A1283

**1961, Sept. 15          *Perf. 11½***
2522  A1283  4k dk car & black       .30  .20

International Letter Writing Week.

Angara River Bridge, Irkutsk A1284

**1961, Sept. 15   Litho.   *Perf. 12½x12***
2523  A1284  4k ol bis, lilac & black  .30  .20

300th anniversary of Irkutsk.

Lenin, Marx, Engels and Marchers — A1285

**1961          Litho.**
| 2524 | A1285 | 2k ver, yel & brown | .55 | .25 |
| 2525 | A1285 | 3k org & deep blue | .85 | .25 |
| 2526 | A1285 | 4k mar, bis & red | .55 | .25 |
| 2527 | A1285 | 4k car rose, brn, org & blue | .55 | .25 |
| 2528 | A1285 | 4k red & dk brown | 3.05 | 1.25 |

*Nos. 2524-2528 (5)*

22nd Congress of the Communist Party of the USSR, Oct. 17-31.

3k, Obelisk commemorating conquest of space and Moscow University. #2526, Harvester combine. #2527, Industrial control center. #2528, Worker pointing to globe.

Soviet Soldier Monument, Berlin — A1286

**1961, Sept. 28   Photo.   *Perf. 12x12½***
2529  A1286  4k red & gray violet    .40  .20

10th anniversary of the International Federation of Resistance, FIR.

Workers Studying Mathematics — A1287

Designs: 2k, Communist labor team. 4k, Workers around piano.

---

A. D. Zacharov and Admiralty Building, Leningrad A1278

**1961, Aug. 8          *Perf. 12x11½***
2511  A1278  4k blue, dk brn & buff   .30  .20

Zacharov (1761-1811), architect.

Defense of Brest, 1941 A1279

Designs: No. 2512, Defense of Moscow. No. 2514, Defense of Odessa. No. 2514A, Defense of Sevastopol. No. 2514B, Defense of Leningrad. No. 2514C, Defense of Kiev. No. 2514D, Battle of the Volga (Stalingrad).

**1961-63          Photo.          *Perf. 12½x12***
2512  A1279  4k blk & red brn (Moscow)   .35  .20

**Litho.**
| 2513 | A1279 | 4k (Brest) | .35 | .20 |
| 2514 | A1279 | 4k (Odessa) | .35 | .20 |
| 2514A | A1279 | 4k (Sevastopol; '62) | .35 | .20 |
| 2514B | A1279 | 4k brn, dl bl & bis (Leningrad; '63) | .35 | .20 |
| 2514C | A1279 | 4k blk & multi (Kiev; '63) | .35 | .20 |
| 2514D | A1279 | dl org & multi (Volga; '63) | .35 | .20 |

*Nos. 2512-2514D (7)*          2.45  1.40

"War of Liberation", 1941-1945. See Nos. 2757-2758.

Students' Union Emblem A1280

**1961, Aug. 8   Litho.   *Perf. 12½***
2515  A1280  6k ultra & red          .40  .20

15th anniversary of the founding of the International Students' Union.

Soviet Stamps A1281

Stamps and background different on each denomination.

**1961, Aug.          *Perf. 12½x12***
| 2516 | A1281 | 2k multicolored | .25 | .20 |
| 2517 | A1281 | 4k multicolored | .45 | .25 |
| 2518 | A1281 | 6k multicolored | .60 | .30 |
| 2519 | A1281 | 10k multicolored | .85 | .40 |

*Nos. 2516-2519 (4)*          2.15  1.15

40 years of Soviet postage stamps.

Nikolai A. Schors Statue, Kiev — A1282

Statue: 4k, Gregori I. Kotovski, Kishinev.

---

Scientists at Control Panel for Rocket — A1272

**1961          Unwmk.          *Perf. 11½***
| 2503 | A1273 | 2k orange & sepia | .20 | .20 |
| 2504 | A1272 | 4k lilac & dk green | .35 | .20 |
| 2505 | A1273 | 6k ultra & citron | .45 | .20 |

*Nos. 2503-2505 (3)*          1.00  .60

International Youth Forum, Moscow.

Globe and Youth Activities A1273

Design: 2k, Men pushing tank into river.

Arms of Mongolian Republic and Sukhe Bator Statue A1274

**1961, July 25   Litho.   *Perf. 12½x12***
2506  A1274  4k multicolored          .40  .20

Mongol national revolution, 40th anniv.

Knight Kalevipoog A1275

**1961, July 31**
2507  A1275  4k black, blue & yel     .30  .20

1st publication of "Kalevipoog," Estonian national saga, recorded by R. K. Kreutzwald, Estonian writer, cent.

Symbols of Biochemistry A1276

**1961, July 31**
2508  A1276  6k multicolored          .35  .20

5th Intl. Biochemistry Congress, Moscow.

Major Titov and Vostok 2 — A1277

**1961, Aug.          Photo.          *Perf. 11½***
| 2509 | A1277 | 4k vio blue & dp plum | .25 | .20 |
| 2510 | A1277 | 6k brown, grn & org | .35 | .20 |

1st manned space flight around the world, Maj. Gherman S. Titov, Aug. 6-7, 1961. Nos. 2509-2510 exist imperf. Value, set $2.50.

Congress Emblem A1293

**1961, Nov.**    **Perf. 12, 12½, 11½**
2538 A1293 2k scarlet & bister .20 .20
2539 A1293 2k dk purple & gray .20 .20
2540 A1293 4k plum, org & blue .35 .20
2541 A1293 4k blk, lt blue & pink .20 .20
2542 A1293 6k grn, bister & red .70 .20
2543 A1293 6k ind, dull yel & red 1.20
   Nos. 2538-2543 (6) 2.35 1.20

Fifth World Congress of Trade Unions, Moscow. Dec. 4-16.

Designs: Nos. 2538, 2542, Congress emblem. Nos. 2539, 2543, African breaking chains. No. 2541, Three hands holding globe.

Lomonosov Statue — A1294

Hands Holding Hammer and Sickle — A1295

**1961, Nov. 19**    **Perf. 11½x12, 12x11½**
2544 A1294 4k Prus blue, yel grn & brown .25 .20
2545 A1294 6k green, yel & black .40 .20
2546 A1294 10k maroon, slate & brn .95 .25
   Nos. 2544-2546 (3) 1.60 .65

250th anniversary of the birth of M. V. Lomonosov, scientist and poet.

**1961, Nov. 27**    **Litho.**    **Perf. 12x12½**
2547 A1295 4k red & yellow .30 .20

USSR constitution, 25th anniv.

Designs: 6k, Lomonosov at desk. 10k, Lomonosov, his birthplace and Leningrad Academy of Science, horiz.

Romeo and Juliet Ballet — A1296

**1961-62**    **Perf. 12x12½**
2548 A1296 2k brn, car & lt green ('62) .20 .20
2549 A1296 3k multicolored ('62) .20 .20
2550 A1296 6k dk brn, bis & vio .40 .20
2551 A1296 10k blue, pink & dk brn .60 .20
   Nos. 2548-2551 (4) 1.40 .80

Ballets: 2k, Red Flower. 3k, Paris Flame. 10k, Swan Lake.

Honoring the Russian Ballet.

Linemen A1297

**1961**    **Perf. 12½**
2552 A1297 3k shown .20 .20
2553 A1297 4k Welders .25 .20
2554 A1297 6k Surveyor .35 .20
   Nos. 2552-2554 (3) .80 .60

Honoring self-sacrificing work of youth in the 7-year plan.

Andrejs Pumpurs (1841-1902), Latvian Poet and Satirist A1298

**1961, Dec. 20**    **Perf. 12x11½**
2555 A1298 4k gray & claret .30 .20

Bulgarian Couple, Flag, Emblem and Building A1299

**1961, Dec. 28**    **Perf. 12½x12**
2556 A1299 4k multicolored .30 .20

Bulgarian People's Republic, 15th anniv.

Fridtjof Nansen A1300

**1961, Dec. 30**    **Photo.**    **Perf. 11½**
2557 A1300 6k dk blue & brown 1.50 .55

Centenary of the birth of Fridtjof Nansen, Norwegian Polar explorer.

Mihael Ocipovich Dolivo-Dobrovolsky — A1301

**1962, Jan. 25**    **Perf. 12x11½**
2558 A1301 4k bister & dark blue .30 .20

Dolivo-Dobrovolsky, scientist and electrical engineer, birth cent.

Woman and Various Activities A1302

**1962, Jan. 26**    **Perf. 11½**
2559 A1302 4k bister, blk & dp org .30 .20

Honoring Soviet Women.

Aleksander S. Pushkin, 125th Death Anniv. — A1303

**1962, Jan. 26**    **Litho.**    **Perf. 12½x12**
2560 A1303 4k buff, dk brown & ver .30 .20

Dancers A1304

**1962, Feb. 6**    **Perf. 12½x12**
2561 A1304 4k bister & ver .30 .20

State ensemble of folk dancers, 25th anniv.

Speed Skating, Luzhniki Stadium — A1305

**1962, Feb. 17**    **Unwmk.**    **Photo.**
2562 A1305 4k orange & ultra .45 .20

Intl. Winter Sports Championships, Moscow.

No. 2562 Overprinted

**1962, Mar. 3**    **Perf. 11½**
2563 A1305 4k orange & ultra 1.50 .75

Victories of I. Voronina and V. Kosichkin, world speed skating champions, 1962.

Ski Jump A1305a

**1962, May 31**    **Perf. 11½**
2564 A1305a 2k ultra, brn & red .25 .20
2565 A1305a 10k org, ultra & black .45 .20

Intl. Winter Sports Championships, Zakopane.

10k, Woman long distance skier, vert.

Hero Type of 1961

**1962, Feb. 22**    **Perf. 12½x12**
2570 A1244 4k dk blue & brown 1.50 .75
2571 A1244 6k brn & slate grm 1.50 .75

4k, V. S. Shalandin. 6k, Magomet Gadgiev.

Soldier heroes of World War II.

Skier A1306

**1962, Mar. 3**    **Perf. 11½**
2572 A1306 4k shown .30 .20
2573 A1306 6k Ice hockey .35 .20
2574 A1306 10k Ice skating .80 .20
   Nos. 2572-2574 (3) 1.45 .60

First People's Winter Games, Sverdlovsk.

For overprints see Nos. 2717, 3612.

Aleksandr Ivanovich Herzen (1812-70), Political Writer A1307

**1962, Mar. 28**    **Litho.**    **Perf. 12½x12½**
2575 A1307 4k ultra, black & buff .20 .20

Ulyanov (Lenin) Family Portrait A1312

Lenin — A1308

Design: 6k, Lenin, horiz.

**1962, Mar. 28**    **Perf. 12x12½, 12½x12**
2576 A1308 4k brown, red & yel .30 .20
2577 A1308 6k blue, org & brn .30 .20

14th congress of the Young Communist League (Komsomol).

Vostok 1 — A1309

**1962, Apr.**    **Unwmk.**    **Perf. 11x11½**
2578 A1309 10k multicolored 1.00 .50

1st anniv. of Yuri A. Gagarin's flight into space. No. 2578 was printed in sheets of 20 stamps alternating with 20 labels. No. 2578 was also issued imperf. Value $3.

Bust of Tchaikovsky A1310

**1962, Apr. 19**    **Photo.**    **Perf. 11½x12**
2579 A1310 4k blue, black & bister .45 .25

Second International Tchaikovsky Competition in Moscow.

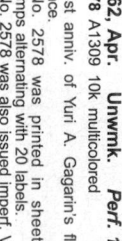

Youths of 3 Races, Broken Chain, Globe A1311

**1962, Apr. 19**    **Perf. 11½**
2580 A1311 6k black, brn & yel .30 .20

International Day of Solidarity of Youth against Colonialism.

**1962, June 30**    *Perf. 12x12½*
2612 A1327 2k multicolored .30 .20
2613 A1328 4k multicolored .30 .20
Program of the Communist Party of the Soviet Union for Peace and Friendship among all people.

Hands Breaking Bomb A1329

**1962, July 7**    *Perf. 11½*
2614 A1329 6k blue, blk & olive .30 .20
World Congress for Peace and Disarmament, Moscow, July 9-14.

Yakub Kolas and Yanka Kupala A1330

**1962, July 7**   Photo.   *Perf. 12½x12*
2615 A1330 4k henna brn & buff .30 .20
Byelorussian poets: Kolas (1882-1956), and Kupala (1882-1942).

Alepker Sabir (1802-1911), Azerbaijani Poet, Satirist — A1331

**1962, July 16**   *Perf. 11½*
2616 A1331 4k buff, dk brn & blue .30 .20
Copies inscribed "Azerbaijanyn" were withdrawn before release. Value, $250.

Cancer Congress Emblem A1332

**1962, July 16**   Litho.   *Perf. 12½*
2617 A1332 6k grnsh blue, blk & red .35 .20
8th Anti-Cancer Cong., Moscow. July 1962.

N. N. Zinin, Chemist, 150th Birth Anniv. A1333

**1962, July 16**   Photo.   *Perf. 12x11½*
2618 A1333 4k violet & dk brown .35 .20

I. M. Kramskoy, Painter — A1334

---

Louis Pasteur A1324

Volleyball A1323

2k, Bicyclists, horiz. 10k, Eight-man shell. 12k, Goalkeeper, soccer, horiz. 16k, Steeplechase.

**1962, June 27**   *Perf. 11½*
2603 A1323 2k lt brn, blk & ver .20 .20
2604 A1323 4k brn org, black & buff .30 .20
2605 A1323 10k ultra, black & yel .30 .20
2606 A1323 12k lt blue, brn & yel .70 .20
2607 A1323 16k lt green, blk & red .90 .20
Nos. 2603-2607 (5)   1.10 1.00
  3.20 1.00
Intl. Summer Sports Championships, 1962.

**1962, June 30**   *Perf. 12½x12*
2608 A1324 6k black & brown org .30 .20
Invention of the sterilization process by Louis Pasteur, French chemist, cent.

Library, 1862 A1325

Photo.
2609 A1325 4k slate & black .20 .20
2610 A1325 4k slate & black .20 .20
a.   Pair, #2609-2610 .... 1.00
**1962, June 30**
Design: No. 2610, New Lenin Library.
Centenary of the Lenin Library, Moscow.

Auction Building and Ermine — A1326

**1962, June 30**   Litho.
2611 A1326 6k multicolored .50 .20
International Fur Auction, Leningrad.

Young Couple, Lenin, Kremlin — A1327

Workers of Three Races and Dove — A1328

---

Lenin Reading Pravda — A1318

No. 2592, Pravda, Lenin and rocket.

**1962, May 4**   Litho.
2591 A1317 4k black, bister & red .30 .20
2592 A1317 4k red, black & ocher .30 .20
*Perf. 11½*   Photo.
2593 A1318 4k ocher, dp claret & red .30 .20
Nos. 2591-2593 (3)   .90 .60
50th anniversary of Pravda, Russian newspaper founded by Lenin.

Malaria Eradication Emblem and Mosquito A1319

**1962**
2594 A1319 4k Prus blue, red & blk .45 .20
2595 A1319 6k ol green, red & blk .45 .20
WHO drive to eradicate malaria. Issue dates: 4k, May 6; 6k, June 23. No. 2595 exists imperf. Value $1.

Pioneers Taking Oath before Lenin and Emblem A1320

Designs (Emblem and): 3k, Lenja Golikov and Valja Kotlik. No. 2598, Pioneers building rocket model. No. 2599, Red Cross, Red Crescent and nurse giving health instruction. 6k, Pioneers of many races and globe.

**1962, May 19**   Litho.   *Perf. 12½x12*
2596 A1320 2k green, red & brn .20 .20
2597 A1320 3k multicolored .20 .20
2598 A1320 4k multicolored .25 .20
2599 A1320 4k multicolored .25 .20
2600 A1320 6k multicolored .45 .20
Nos. 2596-2600 (5)   1.35 1.00
All-Union Lenin Pioneers, 40th anniv.

Ivan A. Goncharov A1322

Mesrob A1321

**1962, May 27**   Photo.   *Perf. 12½x12*
2601 A1321 4k yellow & dk brown .75 .20
"1600th" anniversary of the birth of Bishop Mesrob (350?-439), credited as author of the Armenian and Georgian alphabets.

**1962, June 18**
2602 A1322 4k gray & brown .40 .20
Ivan Aleksandrovich Goncharov (1812-91), novelist, 150th birth anniv.

---

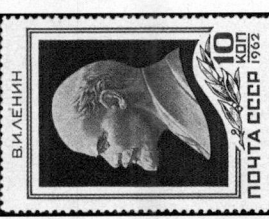

Lenin A1313

**1962, Apr. 21**   *Perf. 12x11½*
2581 A1312 4k gray, red & dk brn .35 .20
Typographed and Emboss
*Perf. 12½*
2582 A1313 10k dk red, gray & blk .65 .20
a.   Souv. sheet of 2, perf. 12   5.00 3.00
92nd anniversary of the birth of Lenin. No. 2582a for 94th anniv. of the birth of Lenin. Issued Nov. 6, 1964.

Cosmos 3 Satellite — A1314

**1962, Apr. 26**   Litho.   *Perf. 12½x12*
2586 A1314 6k blk, lt blue & vio .35 .20
Cosmos 3 earth satellite launching, Apr. 24.

Charles Dickens A1315

**1962, Apr. 29**   *Perf. 11½x12*
2588 A1315 6k blue, brn & pur .35 .20
*Perf. 11½*   Photo.
2589 A1315 6k gray, lilac & brn .35 .20
Charles Dickens, English writer, 150th birth anniv., and Jean Jacques Rousseau, French writer, 250th birth anniv.

No. 2589, Jean Jacques Rousseau.

Karl Marx Monument, Moscow A1316

**1962, Apr. 29**   *Perf. 12x12½*
2590 A1316 4k deep ultra & gray .30 .20

Pravda, Lenin, Revolutionists A1317

I. D. Shadr, Sculptor, A1335

M. V. Nesterov, Painter, A1336

**1962, July 28**    **Perf. 11½x12, 12x12½**
2619 A1334 4k gray, mar & dk brn .35 .20
2620 A1335 4k black & red brown .35 .20
2621 A1336 4k multicolored .35 .20
   Nos. 2619-2621 (3) 1.05 .60

Vostok 2 Going into Space — A1337

**1962, Aug. 7**    **Unwmk.**    **Perf. 11½**
2622 A1337 10k blk, lilac & blue .60 .20
2623 A1337 10k blk, orange & blue .60 .20
   1st anniv. of Gherman Titov's space flight. Issued imperf. on Aug 6. Value, set $4.50.

Friendship House, Moscow A1338

**1962, Aug. 15**    **Photo.**    **Perf. 12½x12½**
2624 A1338 6k ultra & gray .30 .20

Kremlin and Atom Symbol — A1339

Design: 6k, Map of Russia, atom symbol and "Peace" in 10 languages.

**1962, Aug. 15**    **Litho.**    **Perf. 12½x12**
2625 A1339 4k multicolored .35 .20
2626 A1339 6k multicolored .35 .20
   Use of atomic energy for peace.

Andrian G. Nikolayev A1340

Cosmonauts in Space Helmets — A1341

---

"To Space" Monument by G. Postnikov — A1342

Design: No. 2628, Pavel R. Popovich, with inscription at left and dated "12-15-VIII, 1962."

**1962**    **Photo.**    **Perf. 11½**
2627 A1340 4k blue, brn & red .35 .20
2628 A1340 4k blue, brn & red .35 .20

**Litho.**    **Perf. 12½x12**
2629 A1341 6k dk bl, bl bl, org & yellow .95 .20

**Photo.**
2630 A1342 6k brt blue & multi .90 .20
2631 A1342 10k violet & multi .95 .20
   Nos. 2627-2631 (5) 3.50 1.00

**1962, Nov. 27**    **Litho.**    **Perf. 12½**
2631A A1342 1r brt bl, blk & sil 7.50 3.50
   Nos. 2627-2631A honor the four Russian "conquerors of space," with Nos. 2627-2629 for the 1st group space flight, by Vostoks 3 and 4, Aug. 11-15, 1962. Also issued imperf. Value, set $10, souvenir sheet $17.50. For overprint see No. 2662.

Souvenir Sheet

**1962, Nov. 27**
Design: 1r, Monument and portraits of Gagarin, Titov, Nikolayev and Popovich.

Carp and Bream — A1343

Design: 6k, Freshwater salmon.

**1962, Aug. 28**    **Photo.**    **Perf. 11½x12**
2632 A1343 4k blue & orange .25 .20
2633 A1343 6k blue & orange .55 .20
   Fish preservation in USSR.

Feliks E. Dzerzhinski — A1344

**1962, Sept. 6**    **Litho.**    **Perf. 12½x12**
2634 A1344 4k ol green & dk blue .30 .20
   Dzerzhinski (1877-1926), organizer of Soviet secret police, 85th birth anniv.

O. Henry and New York Skyline A1345

**1962, Sept. 10**    **Photo.**    **Perf. 12x11½**
2635 A1345 6k yel, red brn & black .30 .20
   O. Henry (William Sidney Porter, 1862-1910), American writer.

---

Barclay de Tolly, Mikhail I., Kutuzov, Petr I. Bagration A1346

**1962, Sept. 25**    **Perf. 12½x12**
2636 A1346 3k orange brown .25 .20
2637 A1346 4k ultra .25 .20
2638 A1346 6k blue gray .60 .20
2639 A1346 10k violet .70 .20
   Nos. 2636-2639 (4) 1.80 .80
   War of 1812 against the French, 150th anniv.

Design: 4k, Denis Davidov leading partisans, 6k, Battle of Borodino. 10k, Wasilisa Kozhina and partisans.

Street in Vinnitsa A1347

**1962, Sept. 25**    **Photo.**
2640 A1347 4k yel bister & black .30 .20
   Town of Vinnitsa, Ukraine, 600th anniv.

"Mail and Transportation" — A1348

**1962, Sept. 25**    **Perf. 11½**
2641 A1348 4k blue grn, blk & lilac .30 .20
   Intl. Letter Writing Week, Oct. 7-13.

Cedar — A1349

Designs: No. 2642, Cedar. 4k, Canna. 6k, Arbutus. 10k, Chrysanthemum.

**1962, Sept. 27**    **Engr. & Photo.**
2642 A1349 3k ver, black & grn .25 .20
2643 A1349 4k multicolored .25 .20
2644 A1349 6k multicolored .65 .20
2645 A1349 10k multicolored 1.40 .80
   Nos. 2642-2645 (4) 2.55 1.40
   Nikitsky Botanical Gardens, 150th anniv.

Construction Worker — A1350

**1962, Sept. 29**    **Litho.**    **Perf. 12x12½**
2646 A1350 4k org, gray & vio .20 .20
2647 A1350 4k yel, gray, grn & blue .20 .20
2648 A1350 4k grn, gray & lilac rose .20 .20
2649 A1350 4k ver, gray & lilac .20 .20
   Designs: No. 2647, Hiker. No. 2648, Surgeon. No. 2649, Worker and lathe. No. 2650, Farmer's wife. No. 2651, Textile worker. No. 2652, Teacher.

---

M. F. Ahundov, Azerbaijan Poet and Philosopher, 150th Birth Anniv. — A1351

**1962, Oct. 4**    **Perf. 12½x12**
2650 A1350 4k bl, gray & emer .20 .20
2651 A1350 4k brt pink, gray & vio .20 .20
2652 A1350 4k yel, gray, dp vio, red & brown .20 .20
2653 A1351 10k multicolored .90 .25
   Nos. 2646-2652 (7) 1.40 1.40
   5th anniversary, launching of Sputnik 1.

Sputnik and Stars A1351

**1962, Oct. 2**    **Photo.**
2654 A1352 4k lt green & dk brown .30 .20

Farm and Young Couple with Banner A1353

**1962, Oct. 18**    **Litho.**    **Perf. 12½x12**
2655 A1353 4k multicolored .70 .40
2656 A1353 4k multicolored .70 .40
2657 A1353 4k brown, yel & red .70 .40
   Nos. 2655-2657 (3) 2.10 1.20
   Honoring pioneer developers of virgin soil.

Designs: No. 2656, Tractors, map and surveyor. No. 2657, Farmer, harvester and map.

N. N. Burdenko A1354

V. P. Filatov A1355

**1962, Oct. 20**    **Perf. 12½x12**
2658 A1354 4k red brn, lt brn & blk .30 .20
2659 A1355 4k multicolored .30 .20
   Scientists and academicians.

Lenin Mausoleum, Red Square — A1356

**1962, Oct. 26**    **Litho.**
2660 A1356 4k multicolored .35 .20
   92nd anniversary of Lenin's birth.

## Map of Russia, Bank Book and Number of Savings Banks A1372

Design: 6k, as 4k, but with depositors.

**1962, Dec. 30    Litho.    Perf. 12½x12**
2690 A1372 4k multicolored .30 .20
2691 A1372 6k multicolored .30 .20
40th anniv. of Russian savings banks.

## Rustavsky Fertilizer Plant — A1373

Hydroelectric Power Stations: No. 2693, Bratskaya. No. 2964, Volzhskaya.

**1962, Dec. 30    Photo.    Perf. 12½**
2692 A1373 4k ultra, lt blue & black .30 .20
2693 A1373 4k yel grn, bl grn & blk .30 .20
2694 A1373 4k gray bl, brt bl & blk .90 .60
Nos. 2692-2694 (3)

## Stanislavski A1374

**Engr.**   .30 .20
**Perf. 12½    Unwmk.**
2695 A1374 4k slate green

Stanislavski (professional name of Konstantin Sergeevich Alekseev, 1863-1938), actor, producer and founder of the Moscow Art Theater.

## A. S. Serafimovich (1863-1949) Writer — A1375

**1963, Jan. 19    Photo.    Perf. 11½**
2696 A1375 4k mag. dk brn & gray .30 .20

## Children in Nursery A1376

Designs: No. 2698, Kindergarten. No. 2699, Pioneers marching and camping. No. 2700, Young people studying and working.

**1963, Jan. 31**
2697 A1376 4k brn org, org red & black .35 .20
2698 A1376 4k blue, mag & org .35 .20
2699 A1376 4k brt grn, red & blk .35 .20
2700 A1376 4k multicolored 1.40 .80
Nos. 2697-2700 (4)

---

## Makharenko A1366 / Gaidar A1367

A. S. Makharenko (1888-1939) and Arkadi Gaidar (1904-1941), writers.

**1962, Nov. 30    Perf. 11½x12**
2679 A1366 4k multicolored .25 .20
2680 A1367 4k multicolored .25 .20

## Dove and Globe — A1368

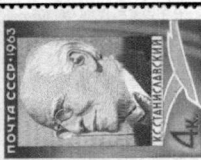

**1962, Dec. 22    Litho.    Perf. 12½x12**
2681 A1368 4k multicolored .30 .20
New Year 1963. Has alternating label inscribed "Happy New Year" issued imperf. on Dec. 20. Value $1.

## D. N. Prjanishnikov A1369

**1962, Dec. 22    Perf. 12x12½**
2682 A1369 4k multicolored .30 .20
Prjanishnikov, founder of Russian agricultural chemistry.

## Rose-colored Starlings — A1370

Designs: 4k, Red-breasted geese. 6k, Snow geese. 10k, White storks. 16k, Greater flamingos.

**1962, Dec. 26    Photo.    Perf. 11½**
2683 A1370 3k grn, blk & pink .20 .20
2684 A1370 4k brn, blk & dp org .20 .20
2685 A1370 6k gray, blk & red .25 .20
2686 A1370 10k blue, blk & red .65 .25
2687 A1370 16k lt bl, rose & blk 1.10 .25
  2.40 1.05
Nos. 2683-2687 (5)

## FIR Emblem A1371

**1962, Dec. 26    Perf. 12x12½**
2688 A1371 4k violet & red .30 .20
2689 A1371 6k grnsh blue & red .30 .20
4th Cong. of the Intl. Federation of Resistance.

---

## Electric Power Industry — A1362

Designs: No. 2668, Machines. No. 2669, Chemicals and oil. No. 2670, Factory construction. No. 2671, Transportation. No. 2672, Telecommunications and space. No. 2673, Metals. No. 2674, Grain farming. No. 2675, Dairy, poultry and meat.

**1962    Litho.    Perf. 12½x12**
2667 A1362 4k ultra, red, blk & gray .35 .20
2668 A1362 4k ultra, gray, yel & cl .35 .20
2669 A1362 4k yel, pink, blk, gray & brown .35 .20
2670 A1362 4k yel, blue, red brn & gray .35 .20
2671 A1362 4k mar, yel, red & blue .35 .20
2672 A1362 4k brt yel, blue & brn .35 .20
2673 A1362 4k lil, org, yel & dk brn .35 .20
2674 A1362 4k vio, bis, org red & dk brown .35 .20
2675 A1362 4k emer, dk brn, brn & gray 3.15 1.80
  3.15 1.80
Nos. 2667-2675 (9)
"Great decisions of the 22nd Communist Party Congress" and Russian people at work. Issued: #2667-2669, 11/19; others, 12/28.

## Queen, Rook and Knight — A1363

**1962, Nov. 24    Unwmk.    Photo.    Perf. 12½**
2676 A1363 1k orange yel & black .50 .25
30th Russian Chess Championships.

## Gen. Vasili Blucher A1364

**1962, Nov. 27    Perf. 11½**
2677 A1364 4k multicolored .30 .20
General Vasili Konstantinovich Blucher (1889-1938).

## V. N. Podbelski (1887-1920), Minister of Posts — A1365

**1962, Nov. 27    Perf. 12½x12**
2678 A1365 4k red brn, gray & blk .30 .20

---

## Worker, Flag and Factories A1357

**1962, Oct. 29    Perf. 12x12½**
2661 A1357 4k multicolored .35 .20
45th anniv. of the October Revolution.

## No. 2631 Overprinted in Dark Violet

**1962, Nov. 3    Photo.    Perf. 11½**
2662 A1342 10k violet & multi 2.50 1.00
Launching of a rocket to Mars.

## Togolok Moldo (1860-1942), Kirghiz Poet A1358 / Sajat Nova (1712-1795), Armenian Poet A1359

**1962, Nov. 17    Perf. 12½x12½**
2663 A1358 4k brn red & black .20 .20
2664 A1359 4k ultra & black .20 .20

## Arms, Hammer & Sickle and Map of USSR A1360

**1962, Nov. 17    Perf. 11½**
2665 A1360 4k red, org & dk red .30 .20
USSR founding, 40th anniv.

## Space Rocket, Earth and Mars — A1361

Size: 73x27mm

**1962, Nov. 17    Perf. 12½x12**
2666 A1361 10k purple & org red .90 .25
Launching of a space rocket to Mars, Nov. 1, 1962.

**1963, Jan. 31    Litho.    Perf. 12x12½**

| 2701 | A1377 | 4k multicolored | .20 | .20 |
| 2702 | A1377 | 6k multicolored | .20 | .20 |
| 2703 | A1377 | 10k multicolored | .50 | .20 |
| 2704 | A1377 | 12k multicolored | .20 | .20 |
| | | ultra, org & black | .65 | .20 |
| | | Nos. 2701-2704 (4) | 1.55 | .80 |

Wooden Dolls and Toys,
Russia — A1377

National Handicrafts: 6k, Pottery, Ukraine.
10k, Bookbinding, Estonia. 12k, Metalware,
Dagestan.

Designs: No. 2706, U. M. Avetisian. No.
2707, A. M. Matrosov. No. 2708, J. V. Panfilov.
No. 2709, V. F. Fabricius.

Gen. Mikhail N.
Tukhachevski — A1378

**1963, Feb.    Photo.    Unwmk.**

| 2705 | A1378 | 4k blue grn & slate | .30 | .20 |
| | | **Perf. 12½x12** | | |
| 2706 | A1378 | 4k org brown & blk | .30 | .20 |
| 2707 | A1378 | 4k ultra & dk brown | .30 | .20 |
| 2708 | A1378 | 4k dp rose & black | .30 | .20 |
| 2709 | A1378 | 4k rose lil & vio bl | 1.50 | 1.00 |
| | | Nos. 2705-2709 (5) | 1.50 | 1.00 |

45th anniv. of the Soviet Army and honoring
its heroes. No. 2705 for Gen. Mikhail Nikolaevich Tukhachevski (1893-1937).

E. O. Paton and
Dnieper Bridge,
Kiev — A1379a

M. A.
Pavlov — A1379

**1963**

| 2710 | A1379 | 4k gray, buff & dk bl | .30 | .20 |
| | | **Size: 21x32mm** | | |
| 2711 | A1379 | 4k slate & brown | .30 | .20 |
| | | **Perf. 12** | | |
| 2712 | A1379 | 4k lilac gray & lt brn | .30 | .20 |
| | | **Size: 23x34½mm** | | |
| | | **Perf. 11½** | | |
| 2713 | A1379 | 4k dk blue, sep & red | .30 | .20 |
| 2714 | A1379 | 4k brn ol, gray & red | .30 | .20 |
| 2715 | A1379a | 4k grnsh bl, blk & red | .30 | .20 |
| | | Nos. 2710-2715 (6) | 1.80 | 1.20 |

Portraits: #2711, I. V. Kurchatov. #2712, V.
I. Vernadski; #2713, Aleksei N. Krylov, #2714,
V. A. Obruchev, geologist.

Members of the Russian Academy of Science. No. 2715 for Eugene Oskarovich Paton
(1870-1963), bridge building engineer.

---

**1963, Feb. 28    Perf. 11½**

2716  A1380  4k brt blue, org & blk  .20  .20

5th Trade Union Spartacist Games. Printed
in sheets of 50 (5x10) with every other row
inverted.

No. 2573
Overprinted

2717  A1306  6k Prus blue & plum  1.25  .50

Victory of the Soviet ice hockey team in the
World Championships, Stockholm. For overprint see No. 3612.

**1963, Mar. 20**

Victor
Kingisepp
A1381

**1963, Mar. 24    Perf. 12x12½**

2718  A1381  4k blue gray & choc  .30  .20

75th anniversary of the birth of Victor
Kingisepp, communist party leader. Exists
imperf.

Rudolfs Blaumanis
(1863-1908),
Latvian
Writer — A1382

**1963, Mar. 24    Perf. 12½x12**

2719  A1382  4k ultra & dk red brn  .30  .20

---

**1963, Mar. 28    Perf. 11½**

Winter
Sports
A1380

**1963, Mar. 30    Engr.    Perf. 12**

2727  A1384  4k red & brown  1.25  .60

93rd anniversary of the birth of Lenin.

Luna 4
Approaching
Moon — A1385

**1963, Apr. 2    Photo.**

2728  A1385  6k black, lt blue & red  .50  .20

Soviet rocket to the moon, Apr. 2, 1963.
Exists imperforate. Value, $3.
For overprint see No. 3160.

Woman
and Beach
Scene
A1386

**1963, Apr. 7    Litho.    Perf. 12½x12**

| 2729 | A1386 | 2k multicolored | .30 | .25 |
| 2730 | A1386 | 4k multicolored | .30 | .25 |
| 2731 | A1386 | 10k multicolored | 1.05 | .75 |
| | | Nos. 2729-2731 (3) | | |

Designs: 4k, Young man's head and factory.
10k, Child's head and kindergarten.

15th anniversary of World Health Day.

---

**1963, Mar. 30    Engr.**

Lenin
A1384

Demian Bednii
(1883-1945),
Poet — A1388

**1963, Apr. 13    Photo.**

2735  A1388  4k brown & black  .30  .20

Soldiers on
Horseback and
Cuban
Flag — A1389

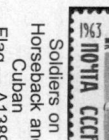

**1963, Apr. 25    Perf. 11½**

| 2736 | A1389 | 4k blk, red & ultra | .25 | .25 |
| 2737 | A1389 | 6k blk, red & ultra | .25 | .20 |
| 2738 | A1389 | 10k red, ultra & blk | .50 | .20 |
| | | Nos. 2736-2738 (3) | 1.00 | .60 |

Soviet-Cuban friendship: 6k, Cuban flag,
hands with gun and plant. 10k, Cuban and
USSR flags and crane lifting tractor.

Karl Marx — A1390

**1963, May 9    Perf. 12x12½**

2739  A1390  4k dk red brn & black  .30  .20

145th anniversary of the birth of Marx.

Hasek — A1391

**1963, Apr. 29    Perf. 11½x12**

2740  A1391  4k black  .30  .20

Jaroslav Hasek (1883-1923), Czech writer.

---

Costume Type of 1960-62

**1963, Mar. 31    Litho.    Perf. 11½**

| 2723 | A1237 | 3k blk, red, ocher & org | .40 | .20 |
| 2724 | A1237 | 4k brown, ver, ocher & ultra | .50 | .20 |
| 2725 | A1237 | 4k blk ocher, red & grn | .50 | .20 |
| 2726 | A1237 | 4k red, lil, ocher & blk | 1.90 | .80 |
| | | Nos. 2723-2726 (4) | | |

Regional Costumes: 3k, Tadzhik. No. 2724,
Kirghiz. No. 2725, Azerbaijan. No. 2726,
Turkmen.

Flower and
Globe — A1383

**1963, Mar. 26    Perf. 11½**

| 2720 | A1383 | 4k red, ultra & grn | .25 | .20 |
| 2721 | A1383 | 6k red, grn & lilac | .35 | .20 |
| 2722 | A1383 | 10k red, vio & lt blue | .80 | .20 |
| | | Nos. 2720-2722 (3) | 1.40 | .60 |

Designs: 6k, Atom diagram and power line.
10k, Rocket in space.

"World without Arms and Wars."
The 10k exists imperf. Value $2.50.
For overprint see No. 2754.

A1387

Block of 6

2732  A1387  10k "10k" blk, blue & lil  7.50  2.10

#2732: a, d, Sputnik & Earth. b, e, Vostok 1,
earth & moon. c, f, Rocket & Sun.

**1963, Apr. 12**

2732
a.  A1387  10k "10k" blk, blue & lil  1.25  .35
b.  A1389  10k "10k" lil rose, blue & blk  1.25  .35
c.  A1387  10k "10k" black, red & yel  1.25  .35
d.  A1387  10k "10k" blue  1.25  .35
e.  A1387  10k "10k" lilac rose  1.25  .35
f.  A1387  10k "10k" yellow  1.25  .35

Cosmonauts Day.

---

**1963, Apr. 30    Perf. 12**

Moscow
P.O. for
Foreign
Mail
A1392

**1963, May 9    Perf. 11½**

2741  A1392  6k brt violet & red brn  .30  .20

5th Conference of Communications Ministers of Socialist countries, Budapest.

King and
Pawn
A1393

**1963, May 22    Photo.**

| 2742 | A1393 | 4k multicolored | .25 | .20 |
| 2743 | A1393 | 6k ultra, brt pink & grnsh blue | .35 | .20 |
| 2744 | A1393 | 16k brt plum, brt pink & black | .90 | .20 |
| | | Nos. 2742-2744 (3) | 1.50 | .60 |

Designs: 6k, Queen, bishop. 16k, Rook, knight.

25th Championship Chess Match, Moscow.
Exists imperf, issued May 18. Value $5.

Richard
Wagner — A1394

Map of Antarctica, Penguins, Research Ship and Southern Lights — A1410

Designs: 4k, Map, southern lights and snocats (trucks). 6k, Globe, camp and various planes. 12k, Whaler and whales.

**1963, Sept. 16 Litho. *Perf. 12½x12***
| 2779 | A1410 | 3k multicolored | .20 | .20 |
|---|---|---|---|---|
| 2780 | A1410 | 4k multicolored | .30 | .20 |
| 2781 | A1410 | 6k vio, blue & red | .45 | .20 |
| 2782 | A1410 | 12k multicolored | 1.50 | .80 |

Nos. 2779-2782 (4) | 2.45 | .80

"The Antarctic - Continent of Peace."

Letters, Globe, Plane, Train and Ship A1411

**1963, Sept. 20 Photo. *Perf. 11½***
2783 A1411 4k violet, black & org .30 .20

International Letter Writing Week.

Gleb Uspenski A1414

Denis Diderot A1412

**1963, Oct. 10 Unwmk. *Perf. 11½***
2784 A1412 4k dk blue, brn & yel bister .30 .20

Denis Diderot (1713-84), French philosopher and encyclopedist.

**1963, Oct. 10**

Portraits: No. 2787, N. P. Ogarev. No. 2788, V. Brusov. No. 2789, F. Gladkov.

| 2786 | A1414 | 4k buff, red brn & dk brown | .40 | .20 |
|---|---|---|---|---|
| 2787 | A1414 | 4k black & pale green | .40 | .20 |
| 2788 | A1414 | 4k car, brown & gray | .40 | .20 |
| 2789 | A1414 | 4k car, ol brn & gray | .40 | .20 |

Nos. 2786-2789 (4) | 1.60 | .80

Gleb Ivanovich Uspenski (1843-1902), historian and writer; Ogarev, politician, 150th birth anniv.; Brusov, poet, 90th birth anniv.; Fyodor Gladkov (1883-1958), writer.

Kirghiz Academy and Spasski Tower — A1416

"Peace" Worker, Student, Astronaut and Lenin — A1415

Designs: No. 2794, "Labor," automatic controls. No. 2795, "Liberty," painter, lecturer; electations, regional costumes. No. 2797, "Brotherhood," Recognition of achievement. No. 2798, "Happiness," Family.

---

Freighter and Relief Shipment — A1404

Design: 12k, Centenary emblem.

**1963, Aug. 8 *Perf. 12½***
| 2766 | A1404 | 6k Prus green & red | .35 | .20 |
|---|---|---|---|---|
| 2767 | A1404 | 12k dark blue & red | .80 | .20 |

Centenary of International Red Cross.

Lapp Reindeer Race A1405

Designs: 4k, Pamir polo, vert. 6k, Burjat archery. 10k, Armenian wrestling, vert.

**1963, Aug. 8 *Perf. 11½***
| 2768 | A1405 | 3k lt vio bl, brn & red | .25 | .20 |
|---|---|---|---|---|
| 2769 | A1405 | 4k bis brn, red & blk | .30 | .20 |
| 2770 | A1405 | 6k yel, black & red | .30 | .20 |
| 2771 | A1405 | 10k sepia, blk & dk red | .45 | .20 |

Nos. 2768-2771 (4) | 1.30 | .80

A. F. Mozhaisky (1825-1890), Pioneer Airplane Builder — A1406

Aviation Pioneers: 10k, P. N. Nesterov (1887-1914), pioneer stunt flyer. 16k, N. E. Zhukovsky (1847-1921), aerodynamics pioneer, and pressurized air tunnel.

**1963, Aug. 18 Engr. & Photo.**
| 2772 | A1406 | 6k black & brt blue | .25 | .25 |
|---|---|---|---|---|
| 2773 | A1406 | 10k black & brt blue | .55 | .25 |
| 2774 | A1406 | 16k black & brt blue | .90 | .25 |

Nos. 2772-2774 (3) | 1.70 | .75

Alexander S. Dargomyzhski and Scene from "Rusalka" — A1408

S. S. Gulak-Artemovsky and Scene from "Cossacks on the Danube" — A1409

No. 2777, Georgi O. Eristavi and theater.

**1963, Sept. 10 *Perf. 11½x12, 12x12½* Photo.**
| 2776 | A1408 | 4k violet & black | .30 | .20 |
|---|---|---|---|---|
| 2777 | A1408 | 4k gray violet & brn | .30 | .20 |
| 2778 | A1409 | 4k red & black | .90 | .60 |

Nos. 2776-2778 (3)

Dargomyzhski, Ukrainian composer; Eristavi, Georgian writer, and Gulak-Artemovsky, Ukrainian composer, 150th birth annivs.

---

Vladimir V. Mayakovsky, Poet, 70th Birth Anniv. — A1399

**1963, July 19 Engr. *Perf. 12½***
2756 A1399 4k red brown .30 .20

Tanks and Map A1400

Design: 6k, Soldier, tanks and flag.

**1963, July Litho. *Perf. 12½x12***
| 2757 | A1400 | 4k sepia & orange | .40 | .25 |
|---|---|---|---|---|
| 2758 | A1400 | 6k org, slate green & blk | .40 | .25 |

20th anniversary of the Battle of Kursk in the "War of Liberation," 1941-1945.

Bicyclist — A1401

Sports: 4k, Long jump. 6k, Women divers, horiz. 12k, Basketball. 16k, Soccer.

**1963, July 27 *Perf. 12½x12, 12x12½***
| 2759 | A1401 | 3k multicolored | .20 | .20 |
|---|---|---|---|---|
| 2760 | A1401 | 4k multicolored | .20 | .20 |
| 2761 | A1401 | 6k multicolored | .35 | .20 |
| 2762 | A1401 | 12k multicolored | .60 | .70 |
| 2763 | A1401 | 16k multicolored | .75 | .20 |
| a. | | Souvenir sheet of 4, imperf. | 4.00 | 3.00 |

Nos. 2759-2763 (5) | 2.10 | 1.00

3rd Spartacist Games.

Exist imperf. Value $2.50.

No. 2763a contains stamps similar to the 3k, 4k, 12k and 16k, with colors changed. Issued Dec. 22.

Lenin — A1403

**Photo.**
2765 A1403 4k red & black .30 .20

60th anniversary of the 2nd Congress of the Social Democratic Labor Party.

Ice Hockey — A1402

**1963, July 27 Photo.**
2764 A1402 6k red & gray blue .50 .25

World Ice Hockey Championship, Stockholm. For overprint see No. 3012.

**1963, July 29**

---

Design: No. 2745A, Giuseppe Verdi.

**1963 Unwmk. *Perf. 11½x12***
| 2745 | A1394 | 4k black & red | .75 | .25 |
|---|---|---|---|---|
| 2745A | A1394 | 4k red & violet brn | .75 | .25 |

150th annivs. of the births of Wagner and Verdi, German and Italian composers.

15th European Boxing Championships, Moscow A1395

4k, Boxers. 6k, Referee proclaiming victor.

**1963, May 29 Litho. *Perf. 12½***
| 2746 | A1395 | 4k multicolored | .30 | .20 |
|---|---|---|---|---|
| 2747 | A1395 | 6k multicolored | .30 | .20 |

Valeri Bykovski — A1396

Valentina Tereshkova — A1397

Designs: No. 2749, Tereshkova. No. 2751, Bykovski. No. 2752, Tereshkova. No. 2753, Tereshkova, vert.

**Litho. (A1396); Photo. (A1397)**
**1963 *Perf. 12½x12, 12x12½***
| 2748 | A1396 | 4k multicolored | .25 | .20 |
|---|---|---|---|---|
| 2749 | A1396 | 4k multicolored | .25 | .20 |
| 2750 | | Pair #2748-2749 | .50 | |
| | A1397 | 6k grn & dk car rose | .25 | .20 |
| 2751 | A1397 | 6k purple & brown | .20 | .20 |
| 2752 | A1397 | 10k blue & red | .85 | .20 |
| 2753 | A1397 | 10k multicolored | 1.50 | .35 |

Nos. 2748-2753 (6) | 3.30 | 1.35

Space flights of Valeri Bykovski, June 14-19, and Valentina Tereshkova, 1st woman cosmonaut, June 16-19, 1963, in Vostoks 5 and 6.

No. 2749a has continuous design. Nos. 2750-2753 exist imperf. Value $5.

No. 2720 Overprinted in Red

Globe, Camera and Film A1398

**1963, June 24 Photo.**
2754 A1383 4k red, ultra & green .50 .25

Intl. Women's Cong., Moscow, June 24-29.

**1963, July 7 Photo. *Perf. 11½***
2755 A1398 4k gray & ultra .40 .30

3rd International Film Festival, Moscow.

**1963, Oct. 15   Litho.   Perf. 12½x12**

| 2793 | A1415 | 4k dk red, red & blk | .50 | .35 |
|---|---|---|---|---|
| 2794 | A1415 | 4k red, dk red & blk | .50 | .35 |
| 2795 | A1415 | 4k dk red, red & blk | .50 | .35 |
| 2796 | A1415 | 4k dk red, red & blk | .50 | .35 |
| 2797 | A1415 | 4k dk red, red & blk | .50 | .35 |
| 2798 | A1415 | 4k dk red, red & blk | .50 | .35 |
| a. | | Strip of 6, #2793-2798 | 2.75 | 2.25 |

Proclaiming Peace, Labor, Liberty, Equality, Brotherhood and Happiness.

**1963, Oct. 22**

| 2799 | A1416 | 4k red, yel & vio blue | .30 | .20 |
|---|---|---|---|---|

Russia's annexation of Kirghizia, cent.

Lenin and Young Workers A1417

Design: No. 2801, Lenin and Palace of Congresses, the Kremlin.

**1963, Oct. 24   Photo.   Perf. 11½**

| 2800 | A1417 | 4k crimson & black | .20 | .20 |
|---|---|---|---|---|
| 2801 | A1417 | 4k carmine & black | .20 | .20 |

13th Cong. of Soviet Trade Unions, Moscow.

Olga Kobylyanskaya, Ukrainian Novelist, Birth Cent. — A1418

**1963, Oct. 24   Photo.   Perf. 11½x12**

| 2802 | A1418 | 4k tan & dk car rose | .50 | .25 |
|---|---|---|---|---|

Ilya Mechnikov A1419

**1963, Oct. 28   Perf. 12**

| 2803 | A1419 | 4k green & bister | .20 | .25 |
|---|---|---|---|---|
| 2804 | A1419 | 6k purple & bister | .30 | .25 |
| 2805 | A1419 | 12k blue & bister | 1.00 | .25 |
| | | Nos. 2803-2805 (3) | 1.50 | .75 |

6k, Louis Pasteur. 12k, Albert Calmette.

Pasteur Institute, Paris, 75th anniv., 12k for Albert Calmette (1863-1933), bacteriologist.

Cruiser Aurora and Rockets A1420

**1963, Nov. 1**

| 2806 | A1420 | 4k mar, blk, gray & red orange | .40 | .20 |
|---|---|---|---|---|
| 2807 | A1420 | 4k mar, blk, gray & brt rose red | .40 | .20 |

Development of the Armed Forces, and 46th anniv. of the October Revolution. The bright rose red ink of No. 2807 is fluorescent.

Mausoleum Gur Emi, Samarkand A1421

**1963, Nov. 14   Litho.   Perf. 12**

Size: 27½x27½mm

| 2808 | A1421 | 4k bl, yel & red brn | .30 | .20 |
|---|---|---|---|---|
| 2809 | A1421 | 4k bl, yel & red brn | .30 | .20 |

Size: 55x27½mm

| 2810 | A1421 | 6k bl, yel & red brn | .70 | .60 |
|---|---|---|---|---|
| | | Nos. 2808-2810 (3) | 1.30 | .60 |

Architecture in Samarkand, Uzbekistan: #2809, Shahi-Zind Mosque. 6k, Registan Square.

Proclamation, Spasski Tower and Globe A1422

**1963, Nov. 15   Photo.   Perf. 12x11½**

| 2811 | A1422 | 6k purple & lt blue | .50 | .20 |
|---|---|---|---|---|

Signing of the Nuclear Test Ban Treaty between the US and the USSR.

Pushkin Monument, Kiev — A1423

M. S. Shchepkin A1424

**1963   Engr.   Perf. 12x12½**

| 2812 | A1423 | 4k dark brown | .20 | .20 |
|---|---|---|---|---|
| 2813 | A1424 | 4k brown | .20 | .20 |
| 2814 | A1424 | 4k brown black | .60 | .60 |
| | | Nos. 2812-2814 (3) | .60 | .60 |

Portrait No. 2814, V. L. Durov (1863-1934), circus clown.

No. 2813 for M. S. Shchepkin, actor, 75th birth anniv.

Yuri M. Steklov, 1st Editor of Izvestia, 90th Birth Anniv. A1425

**1963, Nov. 17   Photo.   Perf. 11½**

| 2815 | A1425 | 4k black & lilac rose | .30 | .20 |
|---|---|---|---|---|

Vladimir G. Shuhov and Moscow Radio Tower — A1426

**1963, Nov. 17   Perf. 12½x12½**

| 2816 | A1426 | 4k green & black | .30 | .20 |
|---|---|---|---|---|

Shuhov, scientist, 110th birth anniv.

USSR and Czech Flags, Kremlin and Hradcany A1427

**1963, Nov. 25   Litho.   Perf. 11½**

| 2817 | A1427 | 6k red, ultra & brown | .40 | .25 |
|---|---|---|---|---|

Russo-Czechoslovakian Treaty, 20th anniv.

Fyodor A. Poletaev — A1428

**1963, Nov. 25   Litho.   Perf. 12½x12**

| 2818 | A1428 | 4k multicolored | .40 | .30 |
|---|---|---|---|---|

F. A. Poletaev, Hero of the Soviet Union, National Hero of Italy, and holder of the Order of Garibaldi.

Julian Grimau and Worker Holding Flag — A1429

**1963, Nov. 29   Photo.   Perf. 11½**

| 2819 | A1429 | 6k vio black, red & buff | .30 | .20 |
|---|---|---|---|---|

Spanish anti-fascist fighter Julian Grimau.

Rockets, Sky and Tree — A1430

**1963, Dec. 12   Litho.   Perf. 12x12½**

| 2820 | A1430 | 6k multicolored | .30 | .20 |
|---|---|---|---|---|

"Happy New Year!" — A1431

**Photogravure and Embossed**

**1963, Dec. 20   Perf. 11½**

| 2821 | A1431 | 4k grn, dk blue & red | .30 | .20 |
|---|---|---|---|---|
| 2822 | A1431 | 6k grn, dk bl & fluor. rose red | .30 | .20 |

Nos. 2820-2822 issued for New Year 1964.

Mikas J. Petrauskas, Lithuanian Composer, 90th Birth Anniv. A1432

**1963, Dec. 20   Photo.   Perf. 11½x12**

| 2823 | A1432 | 4k brt green & brown | .75 | .35 |
|---|---|---|---|---|

Topaz — A1433

Precious stones of the Urals: 4k, Jasper. 6k, Amethyst. 10k, Emerald. 12k, Rhodonite. 16k, Malachite.

**1963, Dec. 26   Litho.   Perf. 12**

| 2824 | A1433 | 2k brn, yel & blue | .25 | .20 |
|---|---|---|---|---|
| 2825 | A1433 | 4k multicolored | .70 | .20 |
| 2826 | A1433 | 6k multicolored | .60 | .20 |
| 2827 | A1433 | 10k brn & purple | 1.00 | .20 |
| 2828 | A1433 | 12k multicolored | 1.25 | .20 |
| 2829 | A1433 | 16k multicolored | 1.40 | .20 |
| | | Nos. 2024-2829 (6) | 5.20 | 1.20 |

Coat of Arms and Sputnik A1434

**1963, Dec. 27   Litho. & Embossed**

| 2830 | A1434 | 10k red, gold & gray | .60 | .20 |
|---|---|---|---|---|
| 2831 | A1434 | 10k red, gold & gray | .60 | .20 |
| 2832 | A1434 | 10k red, gold & gray | .60 | .20 |
| 2833 | A1434 | 10k red, gold & gray | .60 | .20 |
| 2834 | A1434 | 10k red, gold & gray | .60 | .20 |
| 2835 | A1434 | 10k red, gold & gray | .60 | .20 |
| a. | | Vert. strip of 6, #2830-2835 | 3.60 | 1.25 |

Soviet achievements in space.

Rockets: No. 2831, Luna I. No. 2832, Rocket around the moon. No. 2833, Vostok I, first man in space. No. 2834, Vostok III & IV. No. 2835, Vostok VI, first woman astronaut.

Dyushambe, Tadzhikistan — A1435

**1963, Dec. 30   Engr.**

| 2836 | A1435 | 4k dull blue | .50 | .30 |
|---|---|---|---|---|

No. 2836 was issued after Stalinabad was renamed Dyushambe. For overprint see No. 2943.

**Flame, Broken Chain and Rainbow A1436**

**1963, Dec. 30**   **Litho.**
2837 A1436 6k multicolored   .50 .25
15th anniversary of the Universal Declaration of Human Rights.

**F. A. Sergeev A1437**

**1963, Dec. 30**   **Photo.**   **Perf. 12x12½**
2838 A1437 4k gray & red   .35 .45
80th anniversary of the birth of the revolutionist Artjem (F. A. Sergeev).

**Sun and Radar A1438**

**1964, Jan. 1**   **Photo.**   **Perf. 11½**
2839 A1438 4k brt mag, org & blk   .25 .25
2840 A1438 8k org yel, red & bl   .45 .25
2841 A1438 10k blue, vio & org   1.10 .75
Nos. 2839-2841 (3)
6k, Sun, Earth, vert. 10k, Earth, Sun.
International Quiet Sun Year, 1964-65.

**Christian Donalitius A1439**

**1964, Jan. 1**   **Unwmk.**   **Perf. 12**
2842 A1439 4k green & black   .30 .20
Lithuanian poet Christian Donalitius (Donelaitis), 250th birth anniv.

**Women's Speed Skating A1440**

**1964, Feb. 4**   **Perf. 11½, Imperf.**
2843 A1440 2k ultra, blk & lilac rose   .25 .20
2844 A1440 4k lilac rose, blk & ultra   .25 .20
2845 A1440 6k dk bl, red & blk   .30 .20
2846 A1440 10k grn, lil & blk   .55 .25
2847 A1440 12k blk, blk & grn   .75 .25
Nos. 2843-2847 (5)   2.10 1.10
Designs: 4k, Women's cross country skiing. 6k, 1964 Olympic emblem and torch. 10k, Biathlon. 12k, Figure skating pair.
9th Winter Olympic Games, Innsbruck Jan. 29-Feb. 9, 1964. See Nos. 2865, 2867-2870.

**Anna S. Golubkina (1864-1927), Sculptor — A1441**

**1964, Feb. 4**   **Photo.**   .30 .20
2848 A1441 4k gray, brown & buff
No. 2450 Overprinted

**Taras G. Shevchenko A1443**

Designs: 4k, Shevchenko statue, Kiev. 10k, Shevchenko by Ilya Repin. (Portrait on 6k by I. Kramskoi.)

**1964**   **Litho.**   **Perf. 12**
2852 A1245 3k brown & violet   .30 .20
**Engr.**
2853 A1443 4k magenta   .30 .20
2854 A1443 4k deep green   .45 .20
2855 A1443 6k red brown   .45 .20
2856 A1443 6k indigo   .45 .20
**Photo.**
2857 A1443 10k bister & brown   1.10 .20
2858 A1443 10k buff & dull violet   1.10 1.40
Nos. 2852-2858 (7)   4.15 1.40
Shevchenko, Ukrainian poet, 150th birth anniv. Issued: #2852, 2857-2858, 2/22; Others, 3/1.

**K. S. Zaslonov A1444**

**1964-65**   **Photo.**
2859 A1444 4k hn brn & brn blk   .30 .20
2860 A1444 4k Prus bl & vio blk   .30 .20
2861 A1444 4k brn red & ind   .30 .20
2862 A1444 4k bluish gray & dk brown   .30 .20
2862A A1444 4k lil & blk (65)   .30 .20
2862B A1444 4k blue & dk brm (65)   1.80 1.20
Nos. 2859-2862B (6)
Soviet Heroes: No. 2860, N. A. Vilkov. No. 2861, J. V. Smirnov. No. 2862, V. S. Khorujaia (heroine). No. 2862A, I. M. Sivko. No. 2862B, I. S. Polbin.

**Printer Inking Form, 16th Century A1445**

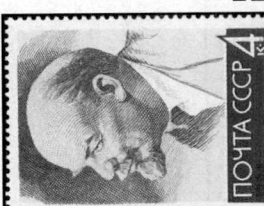

6k, Statue of Ivan Fedorov, 1st Russian printer.

**1964, Mar. 1**   **Litho.**   **Unwmk.**
2863 A1445 4k multicolored   .35 .20
2864 A1445 6k multicolored   .35 .20
400th anniv. of book printing in Russia.
Nos. 2843-2847 Overprinted

and

**Ice Hockey A1446**

Design: 3k, Ice hockey.

**1964, Mar. 9**   **Photo.**   **Perf. 11½**
2865 A1440 2k ultra, blk & lilac rose   .20 .20
2866 A1446 3k blk, bl grn & red   .25 .20
2867 A1440 4k lil rose, blk & ultra   .20 .20
2868 A1440 6k dk bl, red & blk   .70 .20
2869 A1440 10k grn, lil & blk   .80 .20
2870 A1440 12k lilac, blk & grn   .90 .20
**Perf. 12**
2871 A1447 16k org red & gldn brown   1.25 .25

**Olympic Gold Medal, "11 Gold, 8 Silver, 6 Bronze" A1447**

Nos. 2865-2871 (7)   4.40 1.45
Soviet victories at the 9th Winter Olympic Games.
On Nos. 2865, 2867-2870 the black overprints commemorate victories in various events and are variously arranged in 3 to 6 lines, with "Innsbruck" in Russian added below "1964" on 2k, 4k, 10k and 12k.

**Rubber Industry — A1448**

**1964**   **Litho.**   **Perf. 12x12½**
2872 A1448 4k org, lilac, ultra & blk   .30 .20
2873 A1448 4k org, blk, grn & ultra   .30 .20
2874 A1448 4k org, blk, ol, red & bl   .90 .60
Nos. 2872-2874 (3)
Designs: No. 2873, Textile industry. No. 2874, Cotton, wheat, corn and helicopter spraying land.
Importance of the chemical industry to the Soviet economy.
Issued: #2872, 2/10; #2873-2874, 3/27.

**Regular and Volunteer Militiamen A1449**

**1964, Mar. 27**   **Photo.**   **Perf. 12**
2875 A1449 4k red & deep ultra   .30 .30
Day of the Militia.

**Sailor and Odessa Lighthouse — A1450**

**Liberation Monument, Minsk — A1451**

**1964**   **Litho.**   **Perf. 12½x12**
2876 A1450 4k red, lt grn, ultra & black   .30 .20
2877 A1450 4k red, yel, grn, brn & black   .30 .20
2878 A1451 4k bl, gray, red & emer   .90 .60
Nos. 2876-2878 (3)
Liberation of Odessa (#2876), Leningrad (#2877), Byelorussia (#2878), 20th anniv. Issued: #2876, 4/10; #2877, 5/9; #2878, 6/30.

**First Soviet Sputniks A1452**

**F. A. Tsander — A1453**

Designs: 6k, Mars 1 spacecraft. No. 2886, Konstantin E. Tsiolkovsky. No. 2887, N. I. Kibalchitch. No. 2888, Statue honoring 3 balloonists killed in 1934 accident. 12k, Gagarin and Kosmos 3.

**1964, Apr.**   **Perf. 11½, Imperf.**
2883 A1452 4k red org, blk & blue green   .30 .20
2884 A1452 6k dk bl & org red   .60 .20
2885 A1453 10k grn, blk & fluor. pink   .75 .20
2886 A1453 10k dk bl grn, blk & lt grn fluor. pink   .75 .20
2887 A1453 10k lilac, blk & lt grn   .75 .20
2888 A1453 10k blue & black   .75 .20
2889 A1452 12k blue grn, org brn & black   .75 .25
Nos. 2883-2889 (7)   4.65 1.45
Leaders in rocket theory and technique.

**Lenin, 94th Birth Anniv. A1454**

## Engraved and Photogravure

**1964-65**   *Perf. 12x11½*

2890 A1454 4k blk, buff & lilac
  rose   4.50   3.50
  a. Re-engraved ('65)   3.50   2.00

On No. 2890a, the portrait shading is much heavier, rather than dotted. Lines on collar are straight and unbroken. For souvenir sheet see No. 2582a.

**William Shakespeare, 400th Birth Anniv. — A1455**

**1964, Apr. 23**   *Perf. 11½*

2891 A1455 10k gray & red brown   .60   .25
See Nos. 2985-2986.

**"Irrigation" — A1456**

**1964, May 12**   *Litho.*   *Perf. 12x12½*

2892 A1456 4k multicolored   .30   .20

A1457

**1964, May 12**   *Perf. 12x11½*

*Photo.*

2893 A1457 4k blue & gray brown   .30   .20

Y. B. Gamarnik, army commander, 70th birth anniv.

A1457

**D. I. Gulia**
**A1458**

## Engraved and Photogravure

**1964**   **Unwmk.**   *Perf. 12x11½*

2894 A1458 4k grn, buff & blk   .25   .20
2895 A1458 4k red, ocher, buff & blk   .25   .20
2896 A1458 4k brn lake, blk & buff   .25   .20
2896A A1458 4k blue, pale bl & buff   .25   .20
2896B A1458 4k brn & blk   .25   .20
2896C A1458 4k red brn & blk   .25   .20
Nos. 2894-2896C (6)   1.50   1.20

Portraits: No. 2895, Hamza Hakim-Zade Nijazi; No. 2896, Saken Seifullin. No. 2896A, M. M. Kotsyubinsky; No. 2896B, Stepanos Nazaryan. No. 2896C, Toktogil Satyiganov.

Abkhazian poet Gulia, 90th birth anniv.; Uzbekian writer and composer Nijazi, 75th birth anniv.; Kazakian poet Seifullin, 70th birth anniv.; Ukrainian writer Kotsyubinsky (1864-1913); Armenian writer Nazaryan (1814-1879); Kirghiz poet Satyiganov (1864-1933).

**Arkadi Gaidar (1904-41)**
**A1459**

---

**Writers:** No. 2897A, Nikolai Ostrovsky (1904-36) and battle scene (portrait at left). No. 2318 Surcharged:

**1964**   *Photo.*   *Perf. 12*

2897 A1459 4k red orange & gray   .30   .20
  **Engr.**
2897A A1459 4k brn lake & blk   .30   .20

**"Romania" — A1460**

**1964, May 27**   *Litho.*   *Perf. 12*

2898 A1194 4k on 40k bis & brn   3.00   .20

Azerbaijan's joining Russia, 150th anniv.

**1964-65**   *Litho.*   *Perf. 12*

2899 A1460 6k gray & multi   .25   .20
2900 A1460 6k ocher, red & brn   .25   .20
2901 A1460 6k tan, grn & red   .25   .20
2902 A1460 6k red, blk, dl bl, ol & red   .25   .20
2903 A1460 6k ultra, black & red ('65)   .25   .20
2903A A1460 6k brn, red & green ('65)   .25   .20
2903B A1460 6k dp org, gray bl & blk ('65)   .25   .20
2904 A1460 6k blue, red, yel & bister ('65)   .25   .20
Nos. 2899-2904 (8)   2.00   1.60

No. 2900, "Poland," (map, Polish eagle, industrial and agricultural symbols). No. 2901, "Bulgaria" (flag, rose, industrial and agricultural symbols). No. 2902, Soviet and Yugoslav soldiers and embattled Belgrade. No. 2903, "Czechoslovakia" (view of Prague, arms, Russian soldier and woman). No. 2903A, Map and flag of Hungary, Liberty statue. No. 2903B, Statue of Russian Soldier and Belvedere Palace, Vienna. No. 2904, Buildings under construction, Warsaw. Polish flag and medal.

20th anniversaries of liberation from German occupation of Romania, Poland, Bulgaria, Belgrade, Czechoslovakia, Hungary, Vienna and Warsaw.

---

**Corn — A1463**

**1964**   *Photo.*   *Perf. 11½, Imperf.*

2913 A1463 2k shown   .20   .20
2914 A1463 3k Wheat   .20   .20
2915 A1463 6k Potatoes   .20   .20
2916 A1463 6k Beans   .25   .20
2917 A1463 6k Beets   .30   .20
2918 A1463 12k Cotton   .60   .20
2919 A1463 16k Flax   .90   .20
Nos. 2913-2919 (7)   2.65   1.40

Issue dates: Perf., July 10. Imperf., June 25.

**Thorez — A1464**

**1964, July 31**

2920 A1464 4k black & red   .75   .25

Maurice Thorez, chairman of the French Communist party.

**Leningrad Post Office A1462**

**1964, June 30**   *Litho.*   *Perf. 12*

2912 A1462 4k citron, black & red   .30   .20

Leningrad postal service, 250th anniv.

**1964**   *Perf. 12½x12, 12x12½*
*Size: 36x25mm, 25x36mm*

2910 A1461 12k brn, ocher & blk   1.25   .40
2911 A1461 16k ultra, blk, bis & yellow   1.60   .60
Nos. 2905-2911 (7)   5.00   2.25

100th anniv. of the Moscow zoo.
Issue dates: Perf., June 18. Imperf., May.

---

**Elephant A1461**

Designs: 2k, Giant panda, horiz. 4k, Polar bear. 6k, European elk. 10k, Pelican. 12k, Tiger. 16k, Lammergeier.

**1964**   *Perf. 12½x12, 12x12½, Imperf.*   *Photo.*
*Size: 25x36mm, 36x25mm*

2905 A1461 1k red & black   .20   .20
2906 A1461 2k tan & black   .20   .20

*Perf. 12x12½*
*Size: 26x28mm*

2907 A1461 4k grnsh gray, black & tan   .25   .20

*Perf. 12*
*Size: 25x36mm*

2908 A1461 6k ol, brn & tan   .60   .25

*Perf. 12*
*Size: 26x28mm*

2909 A1461 10k ver, gray & blk   .90   .40

---

**Equestrian and Russian Olympic Emblem A1465**

**1964, July**   *Perf. 11½, Imperf.*

2921 A1465 3k lt yel grn, red, brn & black   .20   .20
2922 A1465 4k yel, black & red   .20   .20
2923 A1465 6k lt blue, blk & red   .25   .20
2924 A1465 6k bl grn, red & blk   .50   .20
2925 A1465 12k gray, blk & red   .60   .20
2926 A1465 16k lt ultra, blk & red   .75   .20
Nos. 2921-2926 (6)   2.50   1.20

Designs: 4k, Weight lifter. 6k, High jump. 10k, Canoeing. 12k, Girl gymnast. 16k, Fencing.

18th Olympic Games, Tokyo, 10/10-25/64. Two 1r imperf. souvenir sheets exist, showing emblem, woman gymnast and stadium. Size: 91x71mm.

Value, green sheet, $4.75 unused, $1.75 canceled; green sheet, $165 unused, $225 canceled.

---

**Marx and Engels A1468**

**1964, Aug. 27**   *Photo.*   *Perf. 11½x12*

2931 A1468 4k red brn & brown   .30   .20
2932 A1468 4k red, brn & slate   .30   .20
2933 A1468 4k blue, fluor. brt rose & black   .30   .20

**Litho.**

2934 A1468 4k ol blk, red & red   .30   .20
2935 A1468 4k bl, red & ol bis   .30   .20
Nos. 2931-2935 (5)   1.50   1.00

Designs: No. 2932, Lenin and title page of "CPSS Program." No. 2933, Worker breaking chains around the globe. No. 2934, Title pages of "Communist Manifesto" in German and Russian. No. 2935, Globe and banner inscribed "Workers of the World Unite."

Centenary of First Socialist International.

---

**Indian Prime Minister Nehru (1889-1964) A1467**

**1964, Aug. 20**   *Perf. 11½*

2930 A1467 4k brown & black   .40   .20

**Conquest of Space**
**Souvenir Sheet**

**1964, Aug. 20**   *Perf. 11½x12*

2930A sheet of 6   3.75   1.50
  b. On glossy paper   10.00   6.00

---

**Three Races — A1466**

**1964, Aug. 8**   *Photo.*   *Perf. 12*

2929 A1466 6k orange & black   .40   .35

International Congress of Anthropologists and Ethnographers, Moscow.

**A. V. Vishnevsky A1469**

**1964**   *Litho.*   *Perf. 12½x12*
*Size: 23½x35mm*

2936 A1469 4k gray & brown   .30   .20
2937 A1469 4k buff, sepia & red   .30   .20

**Litho.**   *Perf. 11½*
*Size: 22x32½mm*

**1964, Aug. 8**   *Photo.*   *Perf. 11½*

2938 A1469 4k tan, gray & brown   .30   .20
Nos. 2936-2938 (3)   .90   .60

Portraits: No. 2937, N. A. Semashko. No. 2938, D. Ivanovsky.

90th birth annivs, Vishnevsky, surgeon, and Semashko, founder of the Russian Public Health Service; Ivanovsky (1864-1920), physician.

"Happy New Year — A1486

V. J. Struve — A1487

## Photogravure and Engraved

**1964, Nov. 30**    *Perf. 11½*
2969 A1486 4k multicolored   .50 .30
New Year 1965. The bright rose ink is fluorescent.

**1964-65**   Photo.   *Perf. 12½x11½*
Portraits: No. 2971, N. P. Kravkov. No. 2971A, P. K. Sternberg. No. 2971B, Ch. Valikhanov. No. 2971C, V. A. Kistjakovski.
2970   A1487   4k sl bl & dk brn   .65 .20
*Litho.*
2971   A1487   4k brn, red & blk   .35 .20
*Photo.*   *Perf. 11½*
2971A   A1487   4k dk bl & dk brn   .35 .20
*Perf. 12*
2971B   A1487   4k rose vio & blk   .35 .20
*Litho.*
2971C   A1487   4k brn vio, blk & cit   .35 .20
  2.05 1.00
Nos. 2970-2971C (5)
Astronomer Struve (1793-1864), founder of Pulkov Observatory; Kravkov (1865-1924), pharmacologist; Sternberg (1865-1920), astronomer; Valikhanov (1835-1865), Kazakh scientist; Kistjakovski (1865-1952), chemist. Issued: #2970, 11/30; #2971A-2971B, 1/31/65; 9/21/65; #2971C, 12/24.

S. V. Ivanov and Skier's — A1488

**1964, Dec. 22**   Engr.   *Perf. 12½*
2972 A1488 1k black & brown   .50 .30
S. V. Ivanov (1864-1910), painter.

### Chemical Industry: Fertilizers and Pest Control — A1489
Importance of the chemical industry for the national economy: 6k, Synthetics factory.
**1964, Dec. 25**   *Photo.*   *Perf. 12*
2973 A1489 4k olive & lilac rose   .30 .20
2974 A1489 6k dp ultra & black   .30 .20

European Cranberries — A1490

**1964, Dec. 25**   *Perf. 11½x12*
2975 A1490 1k pale grn & car   .20 .20
2976 A1490 3k gray, vio bl & grn   .20 .20
2977 A1490 4k gray, org red & brown   .25 .20
Wild Berries: 3k, Huckleberries. 4k, Mountain ash. 10k, Blackberries. 16k, Cranberries.

---

*Imperf*   *Litho.*
**Size: 90x45½mm**
  5.00 1.40
  6.70 2.40
2957 A1480 50k vio, red & gray (6)
Nos. 2952-2957
3-men space flight of Komarov, Yegorov and Feoktistov, Oct. 12-13. Issued: #2952-2954, 10/19; #2955, 10/17; #2956, 10/13; #2957, 11/20.

A. I. Yelizarova-Ulyanova — A1482

Portrait: #2961, Nadezhda K. Krupskaya.
**1964, Nov. 6**   Photo.   *Perf. 11½*
2960 A1482 4k brn, org & indigo   .30 .20
2961 A1482 4k indigo, red & brn   .30 .20
Yelizarova-Ulyanova, Lenin's sister, birth cent. & Krupskaya, Lenin's wife, 95th birth anniv.

Farm Woman, Sheep, Flag of Mongolia — A1483
**1964, Nov. 20**   *Litho.*
2962 A1483 6k multicolored   .30 .20
Mongolian People's Republic, 40th anniv.

Mushrooms — A1484
Designs: Various mushrooms.
**1964, Nov. 25**   *Litho.*   *Perf. 12*
2963 A1484 2k ul grn, red brn & yellow   .20 .20
2964 A1484 4k green & yellow   .20 .20
2965 A1484 6k bluish grn, brn & yellow   .50 .20
2966 A1484 10k grn, org red & brn   .65 .20
2967 A1484 12k ultra, yel & grn   1.25 .20
Nos. 2963-2967 (5)   2.80 1.00
Nos. 2963-2967 exist varnished, printed in sheets of 25 with 10 labels in outside vertical rows. Issued Nov. 30. Value, set $5.

A. P. Dovzhenko — A1485
Design: 6k, Scene from "Tchapaev" (man and boy with guns).
**1964, Nov. 30**   *Photo.*   *Perf. 12*
2968 A1485 4k gray & dp ultra   .45 .25
2968A A1485 6k pale olive & blk   .45 .25
Dovzhenko (1894-1956), film producer, and 30th anniv. of the production of the film "Tchapaev."

---

**1964, Oct.**   *Litho.*
2944 A1473 4k red, green & brn   .40 .20
2945 A1474 4k red yel & claret   .40 .20
2946 A1475 4k red, black & red brn   .40 .20
  1.20 .60
40th anniv. of the Moldavian, Uzbek and Turkmen Socialist Republics. Issue dates: #2944, Oct. 7; others, Oct. 26. Nos. 2944-2946 (3)

Soldier and Flags — A1476

**1964, Oct. 14**
2947 A1476 4k red, bis, dk brn & bl   .30 .20
Liberation of the Ukraine, 20th anniv.

Mikhail Y. Lermontov (1814-41), Poet — A1477

**1964, Oct. 14**   Engr.; Litho. (10k)
2948 A1477 4k violet black   .20 .20
2949 A1477 6k black   .25 .20
2950 A1477 10k dk red brn & buff   .70 .20
  1.15 .60
Designs: 4k, Birthplace of Tarchany. 10k, Lermontov and Vissarion G. Belinski.
Nos. 2948-2950 (3)

Hammer and Sickle — A1478

**1964, Oct. 14**   *Litho.*
2951 A1478 4k dk blue, rod, ocher & yellow   .30 .20
47th anniversary of October Revolution

Col. Vladimir M. Komarov — A1479

Komarov, Feoktistov and Yegorov — A1480

Designs: No. 2953, Boris B. Yegorov, M.D. No. 2954, Konstantin Feoktistov, scientist. 10k, Spacecraft Voskhod I and cosmonauts. 50k, Red flag with portraits of Komarov, Feoktistov and Yegorov, and trajectory around earth.

**1964**   *Perf. 11½ (A1479), 12½x12*   Photo.
2952 A1479 4k bl grn, blk & org   .20 .20
2953 A1479 4k bl grn, blk & org   .20 .20
2954 A1479 4k bl grn, blk & org   .20 .20
**Size: 73x23mm**
2955 A1480 6k vio & dk brn   .25 .20
2956 A1480 10k dp ultra & pur   .85 .20

---

Palmiro Togliatti (1893-1964), General Secretary of the Italian Communist Party — A1470
**1964, Sept. 15**   *Perf. 12½x12*
2939 A1470 4k black & red   .30 .20

Letter, Aerogram and Globe — A1471
**1964, Sept. 20**   *Litho.*
2940 A1471 4k tan, lilac rose & ultra   .30 .20
Intl. Letter Writing Week, Oct. 5-11.

Arms of German Democratic Republic, Factories, Ship and Train — A1472
**1964, Oct. 7**   *Perf. 12*
2942 A1472 6k blk, yel, red & bister   .30 .20
German Democratic Republic, 15th anniv.

No. 2836 Overprinted in Red
**1964, Oct. 7**   Engr.
2943 A1435 4k dull blue   3.00 3.00
40th anniversary of Tadzhik Republic.

Woman Holding Bowl of Grain and Fruit — A1473

Uzbek Farm Couple and Arms — A1474

Turkmen Woman Holding Arms — A1475

**1964, Dec. 25**    **Typo.**    **Perf. 12x12½**
2978  A1490  10k lt grn, dk vio
              blue & claret                      .40  .20
2979  A1490  16k gray, brt green
              & car rose                         .50  .20
Nos. 2975-2979 (5)                              1.55  1.00

**1964, Dec. 25    Typo.**    **Perf. 12x12½**
2980  A1491  16k blk, pale grn & red     .30  .20

250th anniv. of the founding of the Academy
of Science Library, Leningrad.

Academy
of Science
Library
A1491

**1964, Dec. 25**    **Typo.**    **Perf. 12x12½**
2981  A1492  1r dark blue                4.50  1.00

Congress Palace,
Kremlin — A1492

**1964, Dec. 29**    **Photo.**    **Perf. 11½**
2982  A1493  4k grnsh bl, vio bl &
              buff                        .30  .20
2983  A1493  6k  yel, dk brn & ol        .30  .20
2984  A1493  12k lt yel, grn & pur        .40  .20
Nos. 2982-2984 (3)                       1.00  .60

Development of mountaineering in Russia.

Mountains: 6k, Kazbek, horiz. 12k, Twin
peaks of Ushba.

**1964, Dec. 29**    **Photo.**    **Perf. 11½**
2985  A1455  6k sep, red brn &
              org                         .20  .20
2986  A1455  12k dk brn & green          .80  .25

Michelangelo Buonarroti, artist, 400th death
anniv. and Galileo Galilei, astronomer and
physicist, 400th birth anniv.

**Portrait Type of 1964**

Design: 6k, Michelangelo. 12k, Galileo.

**Engraved and Photogravure**

**1964, Dec. 30**    **Perf. 11½**

Helmet
A1494

Khan
Tengri — A1493

Treasures from Kremlin Treasury: 6k, Saddle. 10k, Jeweled fur crown. 12k, Gold ladle.
16k, Bowl.

**1964, Dec. 30**    **Litho.**
2987  A1494  4k multicolored             .20  .20
2988  A1494  6k multicolored             .30  .20
2989  A1494  10k multicolored            .45  .20
2990  A1494  12k multicolored           1.10  .20
2991  A1494  16k multicolored           1.25  .20
Nos. 2987-2991 (5)                      3.30  1.00

Dante Alighieri
(1265-1321), Italian
Poet — A1495

**1965, Jan. 29**    **Photo.**    **Perf. 11½**
2995  A1495  4k dk red brn & ol bis     .35  .25

Communications Symbols — A1500

---

Blood
Donor — A1496

Honoring blood donors: No. 2997, Hand
holding blood carnation, and donors' emblem.

**1965, Jan. 31**    **Litho.**    **Perf. 12**
2996  A1496  4k car, red, vio bl &
              grn                         .30  .20
2997  A1496  4k brn, grn, red & dk       .30  .20

Bandy — A1497

**1965, Feb.**    **Photo.**    **Perf. 11½x12**
2998  A1497  4k blue, red & yellow       .30  .20
2999  A1497  6k green, blk & red         .30  .20

4k issued Feb. 21, for the victory of the
Soviet team in the World Bandy Championship, Moscow, Feb. 21-27. 6k issued Feb. 12,
for the European Figure Skating Championship. For overprint see No. 3017.

6k, Figure skaters and Moscow Sports
Palace.

Police
Dog — A1498

**1965, Feb.**    **Perf. 12x11½, 11½x12 (Photo.
stamps); 12x12½, 12½x12 (Litho.)**
**Photo., Litho. (1k, 10k, 12k, 16k)**
**1965, Feb. 26**

Dogs: 1k, Russian hound. 2k, Irish setter.
No. 3003, Pointer. No. 3004, Fox terrier. No.
3005, Sheepdog. No. 3006, Borzoi. 10k, Collie. 12k, Husky. 16k, Caucasian sheepdog.
(1k, 2k, 4k, 12k and No. 3006 horiz.)

3000  A1498  1k black, yel & mar         .20  .20
3001  A1498  2k ultra, blk & red         .20  .20
3002  A1498  3k blk, ocher &
              brown                       .25  .20
3003  A1498  4k org, yel grn &
              blk                         .25  .20
3004  A1498  4k brn, blk & lt grn        .40  .20
3005  A1498  6k chalky blue, sep         .40  .20
3006  A1498  6k chalky bl, org
              & red                       .50  .20
3007  A1498  10k yel green, ocher
              & red                       .50  .20
3008  A1498  12k gray, blk &
              ocher                       .90  .20
3009  A1498  16k multicolored           1.10  .20
Nos. 3000-3009 (10)                     5.75  2.05

First man walking in space, Lt. Col. Alexei
Leonov, Mar. 17, 1965 ("18 March" on stamp).
Exists Impert. Value $1.

Lt. Col. Alexei Leonov Taking Movies
in Space — A1501

**1965, Apr. 12**
3012  A1402  6k red & gray blue          1.00  .30

Soviet victory in the European and World
Ice Hockey Championships.

**1965, Mar. 20**    **Photo.**    **Perf. 12**

No. 2764
Overprinted

No. 2999
Overprinted

**1965, Mar. 26**
3017  A1497  6k green, black & red       .80  .25

Soviet victory in the World Figure Skating
Championships.

Souvenir Sheet

**1965, Apr. 12**    **Litho.**
3016  A1501  1r multicolored            5.50  2.00

Space flight of Voskhod 2. No. 3016 contains one 81x27mm stamp.

Richard Sorge
(1895-1944),
Soviet spy and
Hero of the
Soviet
Union — A1499

**1965, Mar. 6**    **Photo.**    **Perf. 12x12½**
3010  A1499  4k henna brn & black        .75  .30

Tsiolkovsky
Monument, Kaluga;
Globe and
Rockets — A1503

Flags of USSR
and Poland
A1502

20th anniversary of the signing of the Polish-
Soviet treaty of friendship, mutual assistance
and postwar cooperation.

**1965, Apr. 12**    **Photo.**    **Perf. 12**
3018  A1502  6k bister & red             .50  .20

---

**1965, Mar. 6**    **Perf. 12½x12**
3011  A1500  6k grnsh blue, vio & brt
              purple                      .50  .30

Intl. Telecommunication Union, cent.

**1965, Mar. 23**    **Photo.**    **Perf. 12**
**Size: 73x23mm**
3015  A1501  10k brt ultra, org &
              gray                        .80  .35

**1965, Apr. 16**    **Engr.**    **Perf. 12**
3024  A1505  10k tan & indigo           .50  .25

95th anniversary of the birth of Lenin.

Lenin — A1505

Rockets, Radio
Telescope, TV
Antenna
A1504

Designs: 12k, Space monument, Moscow.
16k, Cosmonauts' monument, Moscow. No.
3023, Globe with trajectories, satellite and
astronauts.

**1965, Apr. 12**    **Perf. 11½**
3019  A1503  4k pale grn, black
              & brt rose                  .20  .20
3020  A1503  12k vio, pur & brt
              rose                        .50  .20
3021  A1503  16k multicolored            .80  .20

**Lithographed on Aluminum Foil**
**Perf. 12½x12**
3022  A1504  20k black & red            5.00  3.00
3023  A1504  20k blk, blue & red        5.00  3.00
Nos. 3019-3023 (5)                     11.50  6.60

National Cosmonauts' Day. On Nos. 3019-
3021 the bright rose is fluorescent.

Poppies — A1506

Flowers: 3k, Daisies. 4k, Peony. 6k, Carnation. 10k, Tulips.

**1965, Apr. 23**    **Photo.**    **Perf. 11**
3025  A1506  1k mar, red & grn          .20  .20
3026  A1506  3k dk brn, yel & grn
              grn                         .20  .20
3027  A1506  4k dk red & grn            .45  .20
3028  A1506  6k dk si grn, grn &
              lilac                       .65  .20
3029  A1506  10k dk plum, yel &
              grn                        1.00  .20
Nos. 3025-3029 (5)                      2.50  1.00

Soviet Flag,
Broken
Swastikas,
Fighting in
Berlin
A1507

Designs: 2k, "Fatherland Calling!" (woman
with proclamation) by I. Toidze. 3k, "Attack on
Moscow" by V. Bogatkin. No. 3033, "Rest after
the Battle" by Y. Neprintsev. No. 3034,
"Mother of Partisan" by S. Gerasimov. 6k, "Our
Flag — Symbol of Victory" by V. Ivanov. 10k,
(mourners at bier) by F. Bogorodsky. 12k,
"Invincible Nation and Army" (worker and soldier holding shell) by L. Koretsky. 16k, Victory
celebration on Red Square by K. Yuan. 20k,
Soldier and symbols of war.

## 1965
Perf. 11½
| 3030 | A1507 | 1k red, blk & gold | .25 | .20 |
|---|---|---|---|---|
| 3031 | A1507 | 2k crim, blk & gold | .25 | .20 |
| 3032 | A1507 | 3k ultra & gold | .30 | .20 |
| 3033 | A1507 | 4k green & gold | .45 | .20 |
| 3034 | A1507 | 4k violet & gold | .45 | .20 |
| 3035 | A1507 | 10k plum & gold | .60 | .20 |
| 3036 | A1507 | 10k dp claret & gold | 1.25 | .20 |
| 3037 | A1507 | 12k blk, red & gold | 1.40 | .20 |
| 3038 | A1507 | 16k lilac rose & gold | 1.50 | .20 |
| 3039 | A1507 | 20k red, blk & gold | 2.50 | .30 |
| | | Nos. 3030-3039 (10) | 8.95 | 2.10 |

20th anniv. of the end of World War II. Issued Apr. 25-May 1.

**Souvenir Sheet**

Perf. 11½
3040 A1508 1r blue & multi 5.50 3.00

70th anniv. of Aleksandr S. Popov's radio pioneer work. No. 3040 contains 6 labels without denominations or country name.

From Popov's Radio to Space Telecommunications — A1508

1965, May 7  Litho.  Perf. 12x12½
3041 A1509 6k red & black .30 .20

6th conference of Postal Ministers of Communist Countries, Peking, June 21-July 15.

Marx, Lenin and Crowd with Flags — A1509

1965, May 9  Photo.
3042 A1510 6k grnsh blue, bis & blk .30 .20

International Theater Day.

Bolshoi Theater, Moscow — A1510

Col. Pavel Belyayev A1511

Design: No. 3044, Lt. Col. Alexei Leonov.

1965, May 23  Perf. 12x11½
3043 A1511 6k magenta & silver .30 .20
3044 A1511 6k purple & silver .30 .20

Space flight of Voskhod 2, Mar. 18-19, 1965, and the 1st man walking in space, Lt. Col. Alexei Leonov.

1965, May 20  Perf. 11x11½

Sverdlov A1512

Grothewohl A1513

**Photogravure and Engraved**

1965, May 30  Perf. 11x12
3045 A1512 4k orange brn & blk .60 .30
3046 A1512 4k lt violet & blk .60 .30

Yakov M. Sverdlov, 1885-1919, 1st pres. of USSR, and J. Akhunbabaev, 1885-1943, pres. of Uzbek Republic.

1965, June 12  Photo.  Perf. 12
3051 A1513 4k black & magenta .30 .20

Otto Grotewohl, prime minister of the German Democratic Republic (1894-1964).

Portrait: No. 3046, Juldash Akhunbabaev.

Maurice Thorez A1514

Communica-tion by Satellite A1515

1965, June 12
3052 A1514 6k brown & red .30 .20

Maurice Thorez (1900-1964), chairman of the French Communist party.

1965, June 15  Litho.
Designs. No. 3054, Pouring ladle, steel mill and map of India. No. 3055, Stars, satellites and names of international organizations.
3053 A1515 3k olive, blk & gold .25 .20
3054 A1515 6k emer, dk grn & gold .25 .20
3055 A1515 6k vio blue, gold & blk .75 .60
Nos. 3053-3055 (3)

Emphasizing international cooperation through communication, economic cooperation and international organizations.

Symbols of Chemistry A1516

1965, June 15  Photo.  Perf. 11½
3056 A1516 4k blk, brt rose & brt bl .30 .20

20th Cong. of the Intl. Union of Pure and Applied Chemistry (IUPAC), Moscow. The bright rose ink is fluorescent.

V. A. Serov A1517

Design: 6k. Full-length portrait of Feodor Chaliapin, the singer, by Serov.

1965, June 25  Typo.  Perf. 12½
3057 A1517 4k red brn, buff & blk .30 .25
3058 A1517 6k olive bister & black .30 .25

Serov (1865-1911), historical painter.

Abay Kunanbaev, Kazakh Poet — A1518

Designs (writers and poets): No. 3060, Vsevolod Ivanov (1895-1963). No. 3060A, Eduard Vilde, Estonian writer. No. 3061, Mark Kropivnitsky, Ukrainian playwright. No. 3062, Manuk Apeghyan, Armenian writer and critic. No. 3063, Musa Djalil, Tartar poet. No. 3064, Hagop Hagopian, Armenian poet. No. 3064A, Djalil Mamedkulizade, Azerbaijan writer.

1965-66  Photo.  Perf. 12½x12
3059 A1518 4k lt violet & blk .55 .30
3060 A1518 4k rose lilac & blk .55 .30
3060A A1518 4k gray & black .55 .30
3061 A1518 4k black & org brn .55 .30

Typo.  Perf. 12½
3062 A1518 4k crim, blue grn & blk .55 .30

**Photogravure and Engraved**  Perf. 11½
3063 A1518 4k black & org brn (66) .55 .30
3064 A1518 4k grn & blk (66) .55 .30

Photo.
3064A A1518 4k Prus green & blk (66) .55 .30
3064B A1518a 4k dull blue & black .35 .25

Nos. 3059-3064A (8) 4.40 2.40
Sizes: Nos. 3059-3062, 38x25mm. Nos. 3063-3064A, 35x23mm.

Jan Rainis A1518a

1965, Sept. 0  Photo.  Perf. 12½x12

Rainis (1865-1929), Latvian playwright. "Rainis" was pseudonym of Jan Plieksans.

Film, Screen, Globe and Star A1519

1965, July 5  Litho.  Perf. 12
3065 A1519 6k brt blue, gold & blk .35 .20

4th Intl. Film Festival, Moscow: "For Humanism in Cinema Art, for Peace and Friendship among Nations."

Concert Bowl, Tallinn A1520

"Lithuania" A1521

"Latvia" A1522

1965, July  Perf. 12x11½, 11½x12
3066 A1520 4k ultra, blk, red & ocher .30 .25
3067 A1521 4k red & brown .30 .20
3068 A1522 4k yel, red & blue .90 .60

25th anniversaries of Estonia, Lithuania and Latvia as Soviet Republics. Issued: #3066, 7/7; #3067, 7/14; #3068, 7/16.

"Keep Peace" — A1523

1965, July 10  Photo.  Perf. 11x11½
3069 A1523 6k yellow, black & blue .40 .20

Protesting Women and Czarist Eagle A1524

Designs: No. 3071, Soldier attacking distributor of handbills. No. 3072, Fighters on barricades with red flag. No. 3073, Monument for sailors of Battleship "Potemkin," Odessa.

1965, July 20  Litho.  Perf. 11½
3070 A1524 4k black, red & ol grn .25 .20
3071 A1524 4k red, ol green & blk .25 .20
3072 A1524 4k red, black & brn .25 .20
3073 A1524 4k red & violet blue 1.00 .80
Nos. 3070-3073 (4)

60th anniversary of the 1905 revolution.

Gheorghe Gheorghiu-Dej (1901-1965), President of Romanian State Council (1961-1965) A1525

1965, July 26  Photo.  Perf. 12
3074 A1525 4k black & red .30 .20

Relay Race A1526

Sport: No. 3076, Bicycle race. No. 3077, Gymnast on vaulting horse.

**1965, Aug. 5** **Litho.** *Perf. 12½x12*
| 3075 | A1526 | 4k vio blue, bis brn & red brown | .30 | .20 |
| 3076 | A1526 | 4k buff, red brn, gray & maroon | .30 | .20 |
| 3077 | A1526 | 4k bl, mar, buff & lt brn | .35 | .20 |

Nos. 3075-3077 (3) .95 .60

8th Trade Union Spartacist Games.

Electric Power — A1527

Designs: 2k, Metals in modern industry. 3k, Modern chemistry serving the people. 4k, Mechanization, automation and electronics. 6k, New materials for building industry. 10k, Mechanization and electrification of agriculture. 12k, Technological progress in transportation. 16k, Application of scientific discoveries to industry.

**1965, Aug. 5** **Photo.** *Perf. 12x11½*
| 3078 | A1527 | 1k olive, bl & blk | .20 | .20 |
| 3079 | A1527 | 2k org, blk & yel | .20 | .20 |
| 3080 | A1527 | 3k yel, vio & bister | .20 | .20 |
| 3081 | A1527 | 4k ultra, ind & red | .20 | .20 |
| 3082 | A1527 | 6k ultra & bister | .35 | .20 |
| 3083 | A1527 | 10k yel, org & red | .70 | .20 |
| 3084 | A1527 | 12k Prus blue & red | .80 | .20 |
| 3085 | A1527 | 16k rose lilac, blk & violet blue | 1.25 | .30 |

Nos. 3078-3085 (8) 3.95 1.70

Creation of the material and technical basis of communism.

---

Gymnast — A1528

Javelin and Running — A1529

**1965, Aug. 12**
Design: 6k, Bicycling. *Perf. 11½*
| 3086 | A1528 | 4k multi & red | .25 | .20 |
| 3087 | A1528 | 6k grnsh bl, red & brn | .25 | .20 |

9th Spartacist Games for school children.

**1965, Aug. 27**
Designs: 6k, High jump and shot put. 10k, Hammer throwing and hurdling.
| 3088 | A1529 | 4k brn, lilac & red | .25 | .20 |
| 3089 | A1529 | 6k brn, yel green & red | .25 | .20 |
| 3090 | A1529 | 10k brn, chlky bl & red | .60 | .20 |

Nos. 3088-3090 (3) 1.10 .60

US-Russian Track and Field Meet, Kiev.

---

Worker and Globe — A1530

**1965, Sept. 1**
Designs: No. 3092, Heads of three races and torch. No. 3093, Woman with dove.
| 3091 | A1530 | 6k dk purple & tan | .30 | .20 |
| 3092 | A1530 | 6k brt bl, brn & red | .30 | .20 |
| 3093 | A1530 | 6k Prus green & tan | .90 | .60 |

Nos. 3091-3003 (3)

Int'l. Fed. of Trade Unions (#3091), Fed. of Democratic Youth (#3092), Democratic Women's Fed. (#3093), 20th anniv.

---

Flag of North Viet Nam, Factory and Palm — A1531

**1965, Sept. 1** **Litho.** *Perf. 12*
3094 A1531 6k red, yel, brn & gray .50 .30
Republic of North Viet Nam, 20th anniv.

Film Scenes: 6k, "Young Guard." 12k, "Ballad of a Soldier."

Scene from Film "Potemkin" A1532

**1965, Sept. 29** **Litho.** *Perf. 12½x12*
| 3095 | A1532 | 4k blue, blk & red | .35 | .25 |
| 3096 | A1532 | 6k multicolored | .35 | .25 |
| 3097 | A1532 | 12k multicolored | .55 | .50 |

Nos. 3095-3097 (3) 1.25 .75

---

Post Rider, 16th Century — A1533

History of the Post: No. 3099, Mail coach, 17th-18th centuries. 2k, Train, 19th century. 4k, Mail truck. 1920. 6k, Train, ship and plane. 12k, New Moscow post office, helicopter, automatic sorting and canceling machines. 16k, Lenin, airport and map of USSR.

**1965 Photo. Unwmk.** *Perf. 11½x12*
| 3098 | A1533 | 1k org brn, dk gray & dk green | .35 | .30 |
| 3099 | A1533 | 1k gray, ocher & dk brown | .35 | .30 |
| 3100 | A1533 | 2k dl lil, brt bl & brn | .20 | .20 |
| 3101 | A1533 | 4k bis, rose lake & blk | .35 | .20 |
| 3102 | A1533 | 6k pale brn, Prus grn & black | .55 | .20 |
| 3103 | A1533 | 12k lt ultra, lt brn & black | 1.10 | .40 |
| 3104 | A1533 | 16k gray, rose red & vio black | 1.10 | .55 |

Nos. 3098-3104 (7) 4.00 2.15

For overprint see No. 3175.

---

Atomic Icebreaker "Lenin" A1534

**1965, Oct. 23** **Litho.** *Perf. 12*
| 3106 | A1534 | 4k blk, blk & org | .25 | .25 |
| 3107 | A1534 | 4k bl, blk & org | .25 | .25 |
| | a. | Pair #3106-3107 | .50 | .50 |
| 3108 | A1534 | 6k sepia & dk vio | .65 | .25 |
| | | **Size: 33x33mm** | | |
| 3109 | A1534 | 10k red, black & buff | .80 | .25 |
| | | **Size: 37x25mm** | | |
| 3110 | A1534 | 16k vio blk & red brn | 1.00 | .25 |

Nos. 3106-3110 (5) 2.95 1.25

#3106, Icebreakers "Taimir" and "Vaigtich." 6k, Dickson Settlement. 10k, Sailing ships "Vostok" and "Mirni." Bellingshausen-Lazarev expedition & icebergs. 16k, Vostok South Pole station.

Scientific conquests of the Arctic and Antarctic. No. 3107a has continuous design.

---

Timiryazev Agriculture Academy, Moscow — A1536

**1965, Oct. 30** **Photo.** *Perf. 11*
3112 A1536 4k brt car, gray & vio bl .30 .20
Agriculture Academy, Moscow, cent.

Souvenir Sheet

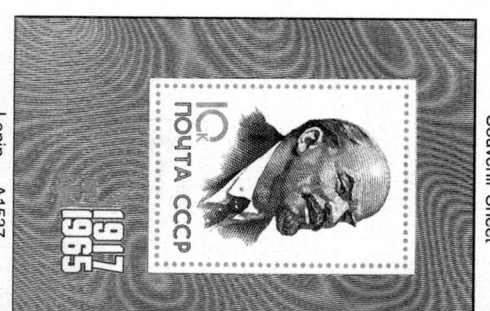

**1965, Oct. 30**
3113 A1537 10k sil, blk & dp org 5.00 1.00
48th anniv. of the October Revolution.

Lenin — A1537

Lithographed and Engraved *Imperf.*

---

Basketball, Map of Europe and Flags — A1535

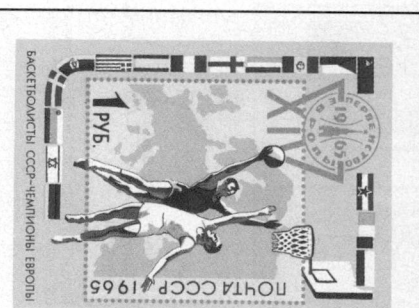

**1965, Oct. 29** **Litho.** *Imperf.*
3111 A1535 1r multicolored 4.00 1.00
14th European Basketball Championship, Moscow.

Souvenir Sheet

---

Mikhail Ivanovich Kalinin (1875-1946), USSR President (1923-1946) A1540

**1965, Nov. 19** *Perf. 12½*
3116 A1540 4k dp claret & red .30 .20

Klyuchevskaya Sopka — A1541

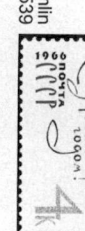

**1965, Nov. 30** **Litho.** *Perf. 12*
| 3117 | A1541 | 4k multicolored | .20 | .20 |
| 3118 | A1541 | 12k multicolored | .45 | .20 |
| 3119 | A1541 | 16k multicolored | .75 | .20 |

Nos. 3117-3119 (3) 1.40 .60

Kamchatka Volcanoes: 12k, Karumski erupting, vert. 16k, Konyakski snowcovered.

---

Kremlin A1539

**1965, Nov. 16** **Photo.** *Perf. 11½*
3114 A1538 4k gray blue, dk bl & dk brown
3115 A1539 4k black, ver & silver .30 .20
New Year 1966.

---

Nicolas Poussin (1594-1665) French Painter — A1538

**1965, Oct. 30** **Litho.** *Size: 37x25mm*
3113 A1537 10k sil, blk & dp org

Buzzard — A1543

Birds: 2k, Kestrel. 3k, Tawny eagle. 4k, Red kite. 10k, Peregrine falcon. 12k, Golden eagle, horiz. 14k, Lammergeier, horiz. 16k, Gyrfalcon.

---

October Subway Station, Moscow — A1542

**1965, Nov. 30**
Subway Stations: 12k, Lenin Avenue, Moscow No. 3121, Moscow Gate, Leningrad. No. 3123, Bolshevik Factory, Kiev.
| 3120 | A1542 | 6k indigo | .30 | .25 |
| 3121 | A1542 | 6k brown | .30 | .25 |
| 3122 | A1542 | 6k gray brown | .30 | .25 |
| 3123 | A1542 | 6k slate green | .30 | .25 |

Nos. 3120-3123 (4) 1.20 1.00

*Engr.*

Kremlin
Congress
Hall — A1556

**1966, Feb. 28**    **Typo.**    **Perf. 12**
3172 A1556 4k gold, red & lt ultra   .30   .20
23rd Communist Party Congress.

Hamlet
and
Queen
from Film
"Hamlet"
A1557

Film Scene: 4k, Two soldiers from "The Quick and the Dead."

**1966, Feb. 28**    **Litho.**
3173 A1557 4k red, black & olive   .35   .20
3174 A1557 10k ultra & black   .35   .20

**1966, Mar. 10**   **Photo.**   **Perf. 11½x12**
3175 A1533 16k multicolored   5.00   3.00

Constituent assembly of the All-Union Society of Philatelists, 1966.

No. 3104 Overprinted

Emblem and Skater — A1558

Designs: 6k, Emblem and ice hockey. 10k, Emblem and slalom skier.

**1966, Mar. 11**    **Perf. 11**
3176 A1558 4k ol, brt ultra & red   .35   .20
3177 A1558 6k bluish lilac, red   .50   .20
3178 A1558 10k lt bl, red & dk brown   .65   .20
    Nos. 3176-3178 (3)   1.50   .60

Second Winter Spartacist Games, Sverdlovsk. The label-like upper halves of Nos. 3176-3178 are separated from the lower halves by a row of perforations.

Electric Locomotive — A1559

Designs: 6k, Map of the Lenin Volga-Baltic Waterway, Admiralty, Leningrad, and Kremlin. 10k, Ship passing through lock in waterway,

Map of Antarctica With Soviet Stations — A1552

Diesel Ship "Ob" and Emperor Penguins — A1553

#3164, Snocat tractors and aurora australis.

**1966, Feb. 14**    **Photo.**    **Perf. 11**
3162 A1552 10k sky bl, sil & dk   .70   .25
3163 A1553 10k silver & dk car   .70   .25
3164 A1553 10k dk car, sil & sky bl   2.25   .75
   a.   Strip of 3, #3162-3164

10 years of Soviet explorations in Antarctica. No. 3162 has horizontal rows of perforation extending from either mid-side up to the map.

Lenin
A1554

**1966, Feb. 22**   **Photo.**   **Perf. 12x11½**
3165 A1554 10k grnsh black & gold   .65   .25
3166 A1554 10k dk red & silver   .65   .25

96th anniversary of the birth of Lenin.

N.Y. Iljin,
Guardsman
A1555

Soviet Heroes: #3168, Lt. Gen. G. P. Kravchenko. #3169, Pvt. Anatoli Uglovsky.

**1966**    **Perf. 11½x12**
3167 A1555 4k dp org & vio black   .30   .25
3168 A1555 4k grnsh bl & dk pur   .30   .25
3169 A1555 4k green & brown   .90   .75
    Nos. 3167-3169 (3)

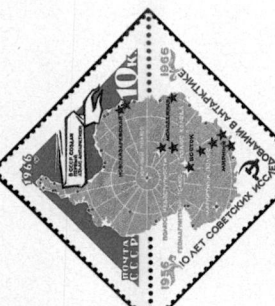

**1966**    **Photo.**    **Perf. 11½**
3147 A1548 6k dull bl, blk & red   .25   .20
3148 A1548 6k gray, pur & black   .25   .20
3149 A1548 6k ol bis, blk & bl   .25   .20
3150 A1548 6k grnsh blue & blk   .25   .20
3151 A1548 6k dull yel, red brn & blk   1.00   .35
    Nos. 3147-3151 (5)   1.25   1.00

Intl. congresses to be held in Moscow: 9th Cong. of Microbiology (#3147); 13th Cong. on Poultry Raising (#3148); 7th Cong. on Crystallography (#3149); 2nd Intl. Cong. of Oceanography (#3150); Intl. Cong. of Mathematicians (#3151).
    See Nos. 3309-3310.

Mailman and Milkmaid, 19th Century Figurines — A1549

**1966, Jan. 28**    **Litho.**
3152 A1549 6k shown   .25   .25
3153 A1549 10k Tea set   .35   .25

Bicentenary of Dimitrov Porcelain Works.

Romain Rolland (1866–1944), French Writer — A1550

Portrait: No. 3155, Eugène Pottier (1816–1887), French poet and author of the "International."

**1966**   **Photo. & Engr.**   **Perf. 11½**
3154 A1550 4k uk blue & brn org   .30   .20
3155 A1550 4k sl, red & dk red brn   .30   .20

Horseback
Rider, and
Flags of
Mongolia and
USSR — A1551

**1966, Jan. 31**   **Litho.**   **Perf. 12½x12**
3159 A1551 4k red, ultra & vio brn   .35   .25

20th anniversary of the signing of the Mongolian-Soviet treaty of friendship and mutual assistance.

No. 2728
Overprinted
in Silver

**1966, Feb. 5**    **Photo.**    **Perf. 12**
3160 A1385 6k blk, lt blue & red   5.00   2.00

1st soft landing on the moon by Luna 9, Feb. 3, 1966.

**1965**    **Photo.**    **Perf. 11½x12**
3124 A1543 1k gray grn & black   .20   .20
3125 A1543 2k pale brn & blk   .20   .20
3126 A1543 3k lt grn & black   .20   .20
3127 A1543 4k lt gray brn & blk   .35   .25
3128 A1543 10k lt vio brn & blk   .75   .35
3130 A1543 14k bluish gray & blk   1.10   .45
3131 A1543 16k dl red brn & blk   1.10   .50
    Nos. 3124-3131 (8)   5.00   2.35

Issued: 4k, 10k, Nov.; 1k, 2k, 12k, 14k, 12/24; 3k, 16k, 12/29.

Red Star
Medal, War
Scene and
View of
Kiev
A1544

Red Star Medal, War Scene and view of: No. 3133, Leningrad. No. 3134, Odessa. No. 3135, Moscow. No. 3136, Brest Litovsk. No. 3137, Volgograd (Stalingrad). No. 3138, Sevastopol.

**1965, Dec.**
3132 A1544 10k brown   .45   .20
3133 A1544 10k dark blue   .45   .20
3134 A1544 10k Prussian blue   .45   .20
3135 A1544 10k dark violet   .45   .20
3136 A1544 10k dark brown   .45   .20
3137 A1544 10k black   .45   .20
3138 A1544 10k gray   .45   .20
    Nos. 3132-3138 (7)   3.15   1.40

Honoring the heroism of various cities during World War II.
Issued: #3136-3138, 12/30; others, 12/20.

Map and Flag
of Yugoslavia,
and National
Assembly
Building
A1545

**1965, Dec. 30**   **Litho.**   **Perf. 12**
3139 A1545 6k vio blue, red & bis   .40   .20

Republic of Yugoslavia, 20th anniv.

Collective
Farm
Watchman
by S.V.
Gerasimov
A1547

Painting: 16k, "Major's Courtship" by Pavel Andreievitch Fedotov, horiz.

**1965, Dec. 31**    **Engr.**
3145 A1547 12k red & sepia   1.10   .25
3146 A1547 16k red & dark blue   1.40   .50

Painters: Gerasimov, 80th birth anniv; Pavel A. Fedotov (1815-52).

Turkeys,
Geese,
Chicken
and Globe
A1548

Congress Emblems: No. 3147, Microscope and Moscow University. No. 3149, Crystals. No. 3150, Oceanographic instruments and ship. No. 3151, Mathematical symbols.

vert, 12k, M.S. Aleksander Pushkin, 16k, Passenger liner and globe.

**1966** **Litho. Perf. 12½x12, 12x12½**
| 3179 | A1559 | 4k multicolored | .20 | .20 |
| 3180 | A1559 | 6k gray, ultra, red & black | .20 | .20 |
| 3181 | A1559 | 10k Prus bl, gray brn & black | .45 | .20 |
| 3182 | A1559 | 12k blue, ver & blk | .40 | .20 |
| 3183 | A1559 | 16k blue, red & multi | .55 | .20 |
| | | Nos. 3179-3183 (5) | 1.80 | 1.00 |

Modern transportation.
Issued: #3179-3181, 8/6; #3182-3183, 3/25.

Supreme Soviet Building, Frunze — A1560

**1966, Mar. 25** **Photo. Perf. 12**
| 3184 | A1560 | 4k deep red | .35 | .25 |

40th anniv. of the Kirghiz Republic.

**1966** **Engr. Perf. 12**
Portraits: No. 3186, Grigori Ordzhonikidze. No. 3187, Ion Yakir.
| 3185 | A1561 | 4k dk red brown | .50 | .25 |
| 3186 | A1561 | 4k slate green | .50 | .25 |
| 3187 | A1561 | 4k dark gray violet | 1.50 | .75 |
| | | Nos. 3185-3187 (3) | | |

Kirov (1886-1934), revolutionist and Secretary of the Communist Party Central Committee; Ordzhonikidze (1886-1937), a political leader of the Red Army and government official; Yakir, military leader in October Revolution, 70th birth anniv.
Issued: #3185, 3/27; #3186, 6/22; #3187, 7/30.

Souvenir Sheet

Lenin — A1563

**1966, Mar. 25** **Embossed and Typographed Imperf.**
| 3188 | A1563 | 50k red & silver | 3.00 | 1.00 |

23rd Communist Party Congress.

Aleksandr E. Fersman (1883-1945), Mineralogist A1564

**1966, Mar. 30** **Litho. Perf. 12½x12**
| 3188 | A1564 | 4k vio blue & multi | .50 | .50 |
| 3189 | A1564 | 4k red, brn & multi | .50 | .25 |
| 3190 | A1564 | 4k lilac & multi | .50 | .25 |
| 3191 | A1564 | 4k Prus bl & multi | .50 | .25 |
| 3191A | A1564 | 4k Prus bl & brn | 2.00 | 1.00 |
| | | Nos. 3189-3191A (4) | | |

Soviet Scientists: #3190, D. K. Zabolotny (1866-1929), microbiologist; #3191, M. A. Shatelen (1866-1957), physicist; #3191A, Otto Yulievich Schmidt (1891-1956), scientist and arctic explorer.

Luna 10 Automatic Moon Station — A1565

**1966, Apr. 3** **Typo. Imperf.**
| 3192 | A1565 | 10k gold, blk, brt bl & brt rose | 1.75 | .60 |

Launching of the 1st artificial moon satellite, Luna 10. The bright rose ink is fluorescent on Nos. 3192-3194.

**1966, Apr. 12** **Perf. 12**
Design: 12k, Station on moon.
| 3193 | A1565 | 10k multicolored | .40 | .30 |
| 3194 | A1565 | 12k multicolored | .60 | .30 |

Day of Space Research, Apr. 12, 1966.

Type A1565 Without Overprint

Moiniya 1 and Television Screens A1566

**1966, Apr. 12** **Litho. Perf. 12½**
| 3195 | A1566 | 10k gold, blk, brt bl & red | .50 | .25 |

Launching of the communications satellite "Lightning 1," Apr. 23, 1965.

Ernst Thälmann A1567

**1966-67** **Engr. Perf. 12½x12**
Portraits: No. 3197, Wilhelm Pieck. No. 3198, Sun Yat-sen. No. 3199, Sen Katayama.
| 3196 | A1567 | 6k rose claret | .50 | .25 |
| 3197 | A1567 | 6k blue violet | .50 | .25 |
| 3198 | A1567 | 6k reddish brown | .50 | .25 |
| 3199 | A1567 | 6k gray green ('67) | .50 | .25 |
| | | Nos. 3196-3199 (4) | 2.00 | 1.00 |

Thälmann (1886-1944), German Communist leader; Pieck (1876-1960), German Dem. Rep. Pres.; Sun Yat-sen (1866-1925), leader of the Chinese revolution; Katayama (1859-1933), founder of Social Democratic Party in Japan in 1901.
Issued: #3196, 4/16; #3197-3198, 6/22; #3199, 11/2/67.

Soldier, 1917, and Astronaut A1568

**1966, Apr. 30** **Litho. Perf. 11½**
| 3200 | A1568 | 4k brt rose & black | .30 | .20 |

15th Congress of the Young Communist League (Komsomol).

Ice Hockey Player — A1569

**1966, Apr. 30**
| 3201 | A1569 | 10k red, ultra, gold & brt rose | .40 | .25 |

Soviet victory in the World Ice Hockey Championships. For souvenir sheet see No. 3232. For overprint see No. 3315.

Nicolai Kuznetsov A1570

**1966, May 9** **Photo. Perf. 12x12½**
Heroes of Guerilla Warfare during WWII (Gold Star of Hero of the Soviet Union and): No. 3203, Imant Sudmalia. No. 3204, Anya Morozova. No. 3205, Filipp Strelets. No. 3206, Tikhon Rumazhikov.
| 3202 | A1570 | 4k green & black | .20 | .20 |
| 3203 | A1570 | 4k ocher & black | .20 | .20 |
| 3204 | A1570 | 4k blue & black | .20 | .20 |
| 3205 | A1570 | 4k brt rose & black | .20 | .20 |
| 3206 | A1570 | 4k violet & black | .20 | .20 |
| | | Nos. 3202-3206 (5) | 1.00 | 1.00 |

Peter I. Tchaikovsky A1571

**1966, May 26** **Typo. Perf. 12½**
| 3207 | A1571 | 4k red, yel & black | .25 | .25 |
| 3208 | A1571 | 6k yel, red & black | .40 | .30 |
| 3209 | A1571 | 16k red, bluish gray & black | .85 | .35 |
| | | Nos. 3207-3209 (3) | 1.50 | .90 |

Third International Tchaikovsky Contest, Moscow, May 30-June 29.

Runners — A1572

**1966, May 26** **Photo. Perf. 11x11½**
| 3210 | A1572 | 4k emer, olive & brn | .20 | .20 |
| 3211 | A1572 | 6k org, blk & lt brn | .30 | .20 |
| 3212 | A1572 | 12k grnsh bl, brn ol & black | .45 | .20 |
| | | Nos. 3210-3212 (3) | .95 | .60 |

Designs: 6k, Weight lifters. 12k, Wrestlers.
Competitions: No. 3210, Znamensky Brothers Intl. Track Competitions; No. 3211, Intl. Weightlifting Competitions; No. 3212, Intl. Wrestling Competitions for Ivan Poddubny Prize.

Jules Rimet World Soccer Cup, Ball and Laurel — A1573

**1966, May 31** **Litho. Perf. 11½**
| 3213 | A1573 | 4k rose red, gold & black | .20 | .20 |
| 3214 | A1573 | 6k emer, tan, blk & black | .30 | .20 |
| 3215 | A1573 | 6k brn, gold, blk & white | .30 | .20 |

Chessboard, Gold Medal, Pawn and King A1574

| 3216 | A1573 | 12k brt bl, ol & blk | .70 | .20 |
| 3217 | A1573 | 10k multicolored | 2.25 | 1.00 |
| | | Nos. 3213-3217 (5) | | |

Designs: No. 3214, Soccer. 12k, Fencers. 16k, Fencer, mask, foil and laurel branch.

Nos. 3213-3214 for World Cup Soccer Championship, Wembley, England, July 11-30; No. 3215, the World Chess Title Match between Tigran Petrosian and Boris Spassky; Nos. 3216-3217 the World Fencing Championships. For souvenir sheet see No. 3232.

Sable and Lake Baikal, Map of Barguzin Game Reserve — A1575

**1966, June 25** **Photo. Perf. 12**
| 3218 | A1575 | 4k steel blue & black | .35 | .25 |
| 3219 | A1575 | 6k rose bl & black | .35 | .25 |

Design: 6k, Map of Lake Baikal region and Game Reserve, brown bear on lake shore.

Barguzin Game Reserve, 50th anniv.

Pink Lotus — A1576

**1966, June 30** **Perf. 11½**
| 3220 | A1576 | 4k grn, pink & yel | .20 | .20 |
| 3221 | A1576 | 3k grnsh bl, ol brn | .30 | .20 |
| 3222 | A1576 | 12k multicolored | 1.00 | .60 |
| | | Nos. 3220-3222 (3) | | |

Sukhum Botanical Garden, 125th anniv.

6k, Palms and cypresses. 12k, Victoria cruziana.

Scene from Opera "Nargiz" by M. Magomayev—A1590

#3254. Scene from opera "Keroglu" by Y. Gadjubekov (knight on horseback and armed men).

1966, Oct. 12
3253 A1590 4k black & ocher .20 .20
3254 A1590 4k blk & blue green .30 .20
a. Pair, #3253-3254 .60 .20
Azerbaijan opera. Printed in checkerboard arrangement.

Fighters A1591
1966, Oct. 26
3255 A1591 6k red, blk & ol bister .40 .20
30th anniversary of Spanish Civil War.

National Militia—A1592
Protest Rally—A1592a

1966, Oct. 26 Litho. Perf. 12x12½
3256 A1592 4k red & dark brown .35 .20
25th anniv. of the National Militia.

1966, Oct. 26 Perf. 12
3256A A1592a 6k yel, black & red .40 .25
"Hands off Viet Nam!"

Soft Landing on Moon, Luna 9—A1593

Symbols of Agriculture and Chemistry A1594

Designs: 1k, Congress Palace, Moscow, and map of Russia. 3k, Boy, girl and Lenin banner. 4k, Flag. 6k, Plane and Ostankino Television Tower. 10k, Soldier and Soviet star. 12k, Steel worker. 16k, "Peace," woman with dove. 20k, Demonstrators in Red Square, flags, carnation and globe. 50k, Newspaper, plane, train and Communications Ministry. 1r, Lenin and industrial symbols.

---

1966, Sept. 25 Photo. & Engr.
3240 A1585 2k multicolored .20 .20
3241 A1585 4k multicolored .20 .20
3242 A1585 6k multicolored .30 .20
3243 A1585 10k multicolored .60 .20
3244 A1585 12k gray, dk grn & red brown .70 1.00
Nos. 3240-3244 (5) 2.00 1.00
Fish resources of Lake Baikal.

Map of USSR and Symbols of Transportation and Communication—A1586

Designs (map of USSR and): No. 3246, Technological education. No. 3247, Agriculture and mining. No. 3248, Increased productivity through five-year plan. No. 3249, Technology and inventions.

1966, Sept. 29 Photo. Perf. 11½x12
3245 A1586 4k ultra & silver .40 .20
3246 A1586 4k car & silver .40 .20
3247 A1586 4k red brn & silver .40 .20
3248 A1586 4k red & silver .40 .20
3249 A1586 4k dp green & silver .40 .20
Nos. 3245-3249 (5) 2.00 1.00
23rd Communist Party Congress decisions.

Government House, Kishinev, and Moldavian Flag—A1587
1966, Oct. 8 Litho. Perf. 12½x12
3250 A1587 4k multicolored .50 .30
500th anniversary of Kishinev.

Symbolic Water Cycle A1588
1966, Oct. 12 Perf. 11½
3251 A1588 6k multicolored .35 .20
Hydrological Decade (UNESCO), 1965-1974.

Nikitin Monument in Kalinin, Ship's Prow and Map—A1589
1966, Oct. 12 Photo.
3252 A1589 4k multicolored .40 .25
Afanasii Nikitin's trip to India, 500th anniv.

---

Congress Emblem, Congress Palace and Kremlin Tower—A1581
1966, Aug. 6 Photo. Perf. 11½x12
3233 A1581 4k brown & yellow .30 .20
Consumers' Cooperative Societies, 7th Cong.

Dove, Crane, Russian and Japanese Flags A1582
1966, Aug. 9 Perf. 12½x11½
3234 A1582 6k gray & red .40 .25
Soviet-Japanese friendship, and 2nd meeting of Russian and Japanese delegates at Khabarovsk.

"Knight Fighting with Tiger" by Rustaveli A1583

Designs: 4k, Shota Rustaveli, bas-relief. 6k, "Avtandil at a Mountain Spring." 50k, Shota Rustaveli Monument and design of 3k stamp.

1966, Aug. 31 Engr. Perf. 11½x12½
3235 A1583 3k blk, olive green .25 .20
3236 A1583 4k olivin, yellow .20 .20
3237 A1583 6k bluish black, lt ultra .35 .20
Nos. 3235-3237 (3) .85 .60

Souvenir Sheet
Imperf
Engraved and Photogravure
3238 A1583 50k slate grn & bis 3.50 1.25
800th anniv. of the birth of Shota Rustaveli, Georgian poet, author of "The Knight in the Tiger's Skin." No. 3238 contains one 32x49mm stamp; dark green margin with design of 6k stamp.

Coat of Arms and Fireworks over Moscow A1584
Lithographed (Lacquered) Perf. 11½
1966, Sept. 14 Litho. .30 .20
3239 A1584 4k multicolored
49th anniversary of October Revolution.

Grayling A1585

Designs (Fish and part of design of 6k stamp): 4k, Sturgeon. 6k, Trawler, net and map of Lake Baikal, vert. 10k, Two Baikal cisco. 12k, Two Baikal whitefish.

---

Dogs Ugolek and Veterok after Space Flight A1577

Designs: No. 3224, Diagram of Solar System, globe and medal of Venus 3 flight. No. 3225, Luna 10, earth and moon.

1966, July 15 Perf. 12x11½
3223 A1577 6k ocher, ind & org .30 .20
3224 A1577 6k crim, blk & silver .30 .20
Perf. 12x12½
3225 A1577 6k dk blue & bister brn .30 .20
Nos. 3223-3225 (3) .90 .60
Soviet achievements in space.

Itkol Hotel, Mount Cheget and Map of USSR A1578

Arch of General Headquarters, Winter Palace and Alexander Column A1579

Resort Areas: 4k, Ship on Volga River and Zhigul Mountain. 10k, Castle, Kislovodsk. 12k, Ismail Samani Mausoleum, Bukhara, Uzbek. 16k, Hotel Caucasus, Sochi.

1966, Litho. Perf. 12½x12, 12½ (6k)
3226 A1578 1k multicolored .20 .20
3227 A1578 4k multicolored .20 .20
3228 A1578 6k multicolored .20 .20
3229 A1578 10k multicolored .25 .20
3230 A1578 12k multicolored .40 .20
3231 A1578 16k multicolored .55 .20
Nos. 3226-3231 (6) 1.80 1.20
Issue dates: 10k, Sept. 14; others, July 20.

Souvenir Sheet
A1580
1966, July 26 Litho. Perf. 11½
3232 A1580 Sheet of 4 10.00 1.75
a. 10k Fencers 2.00 .40
b. 10k Chess 2.00 .40
c. 10k Soccer cup 2.00 .40
d. 10k Ice hockey 2.00 .40
World fencing, chess, soccer and ice hockey championships.
See Nos. 3201, 3213-3217.

**1966**

Litho.  *Perf. 12*

| | | | |
|---|---|---|---|
| 3257 | A1593 | 1k dk red brown | .20 .20 |
| 3258 | A1593 | 2k violet | .20 .20 |
| 3259 | A1593 | 3k red lilac | .20 .20 |
| 3260 | A1593 | 4k bright red | .20 .20 |
| 3261 | A1593 | 6k olive | .20 .20 |
| 3262 | A1593 | 10k olive | .35 .20 |
| 3263 | A1593 | 12k red brown | .65 .20 |
| 3264 | A1593 | 16k violet blue | .70 .20 |

No. 3260 was issued on fluorescent paper in 1969.
See Nos. 3470-3481.

**1966, Nov. 19**  *Perf. 11½*

Photo.

| | | | |
|---|---|---|---|
| 3265 | A1594 | 20k bis, red & dk bl | 1.10 .20 |
| 3266 | A1594 | 30k grn & green | 1.40 .30 |
| 3267 | A1594 | 50k blue & violet bl | 3.00 .55 |
| 3268 | A1594 | 1r black & red | 12.95 3.00 |

Ostankino Television Tower, Molniya 1 Satellite and Kremlin — A1595

**1966, Nov. 25**  *Perf. 12*

3273 A1595 4k multicolored  .35 .20

New Year, 1967, the 50th anniversary of the October Revolution.

Diagram of Luna 9 Flight — A1596

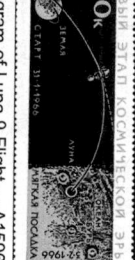

**1966, Nov. 25**  *Typo.  Perf. 12*

| | | | |
|---|---|---|---|
| 3274 | A1596 | 10k black & silver | .50 .25 |
| 3275 | A1597 | 10k red & silver | .50 .25 |
| 3276 | A1596 | 10k black & silver | 2.00 2.00 |
| a. | Strip of 3, #3274-3276 | | |

#3276, Luna 9 & photograph of moonscape.

Arms of Russia and Pennant Sent to Moon — A1597

Soft landing on the moon by Luna 9, Jan. 31, 1966, and the television program of moon pictures on Feb. 2.

Battle of Moscow, 1941 — A1598

Details from "Defense of Moscow" Medal and Golden Star Medal A1599

**1966, Dec. 1**  *Perf. 12, 11½ (A1599)*

| | | | |
|---|---|---|---|
| 3277 | A1598 | 4k red brown | .20 .20 |
| 3278 | A1599 | 6k bister & brown | .45 .20 |
| 3279 | A1598 | 10k dp bister & yel | .60 |

Nos. 3277-3279 (3)

25th anniv. of Battle of Moscow: 10k, Sun rising over Kremlin. Ostankino Tower, chemical plant and rockets.

Cervantes and Don Quixote A1600

**1966, Dec. 15**  *Photo.  Perf. 11½*

3280 A1600 6k gray & brown  .30 .20

Miguel Cervantes Saavedra (1547-1616), Spanish writer.

Bering's Ship and Map of Voyage to Commander Islands — A1601

Far Eastern Territories: 2k, Medny Island and map. 4k, Petropavlovsk-Kamchatski Harbor. 6k, Geyser, Kamchatka. 10k, Avachinskaya Bay, Kamchatka. vert. 10k, Bering Island. 16k, Guillemots in bird sanctuary, Kuril Islands.

**1966, Dec. 25**  *Litho.  Perf. 12*

| | | | |
|---|---|---|---|
| 3281 | A1601 | 1k bister & multi | .20 .20 |
| 3282 | A1601 | 2k bister & multi | .20 .20 |
| 3283 | A1601 | 4k dp blue & multi | .30 .20 |
| 3284 | A1601 | 6k multicolored | .40 .20 |
| 3285 | A1601 | 10k dp blue & multi | .60 .20 |
| 3286 | A1601 | 12k olive & multi | 1.00 .20 |
| 3287 | A1601 | 16k lt blue & multi | 1.75 .20 |

Nos. 3281-3287 (7)  4.45 1.40

Communications Satellite, Molniya 1 — A1602

**1966, Dec. 29**  *Photo.  Perf. 12x11½*

| | | | |
|---|---|---|---|
| 3288 | A1602 | 6k blk, vio bl & brt rose | .40 .20 |
| 3289 | A1602 | 6k black & brt rose | .40 .20 |

Space explorations. The bright rose is fluorescent.

Design: No. 3289, Luna 11 moon probe, moon, earth and Soviet emblem.

Golden Stag, Scythia, 6th Century B.C. — A1603

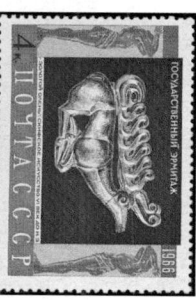

Treasures from the Hermitage, Leningrad: 6k, Silver jug, Persia, 5th Century A.D. 10k, Statue of Voltaire by Jean Antoine Houdon, 12k, Malachite vase, Ural, 1840. 16k, Lute Player, by Michelangelo de Caravaggio. (6k, 10k, 12k are vertical.)

**1966, Dec. 29**  *Typo.  Perf. 12*

3302 A1603 4k black & silver  .50 .25

Space exploration. The bright rose is fluorescent.

Sea Water Converter and Pavilion at EXPO '67 A1604

**1966, Dec. 29**  *Engr.  Perf. 12*

| | | | |
|---|---|---|---|
| 3290 | A1603 | 4k yellow & black | .20 .20 |
| 3291 | A1603 | 6k gray & black | .30 .20 |
| 3292 | A1603 | 10k dull vio & black | .50 .30 |
| 3293 | A1603 | 12k emer & black | .75 .35 |
| 3294 | A1603 | 16k other & black | .85 .35 |

Nos. 3290-3294 (5)  2.60 1.25

"Proton space station. 30k, Soviet pavilion.

Pavilion and: 6k, Splitting atom, vert. 10k, "Proton space station. 30k, Soviet pavilion.

**1967, Jan. 25**  *Litho.  Perf. 12*

| | | | |
|---|---|---|---|
| 3295 | A1604 | 4k multicolored | .25 .20 |
| 3296 | A1604 | 6k multicolored | .30 .20 |
| 3297 | A1604 | 10k multicolored | .30 .20 |

Nos. 3295-3297 (3)

Souvenir Sheet

3298 A1604 30k multicolored  3.00 1.25

EXPO '67, Intl. Exhib., Montreal, 4/28-10/27.

1st Lieut. B. I. Sizov A1605

**1967, Feb. 16**  *Photo.  Perf. 12x11½*

| | | | |
|---|---|---|---|
| 3299 | A1605 | 4k dull yel & ocher | .25 .25 |
| 3300 | A1605 | 4k gray & dk gray | .25 .25 |

Heroes of World War II.

Design: No. 3300, Sailor V. V. Khodyrev.

Congress Type of 1966

**1967, Mar. 10**  *Photo.  Perf. 11½*

| | | | |
|---|---|---|---|
| 3309 | A1548 | 6k ultra, brt blue & blk | .30 .20 |
| 3310 | A1548 | 6k blk, org red & blue | .30 .20 |

Intl. congresses to be held in Moscow: 7th General Assembly Session of the Intl. Standards Association (#3309); 5th Intl. Mining Cong. (#3310).

50th anniversary of newspaper Izvestia.

Newspaper Forming Hammer and Sickle, Red Flag — A1609

**1967, Mar. 13**  *Litho.  Perf. 11½*

3308 A1609 4k cl brn, red, yel & brn  .30 .20

Ships in Black and Red

**1967, Feb. 28**  *Litho.  Perf. 12x11½*

| | | | |
|---|---|---|---|
| 3303 | A1608 | 6k blue & black | .40 .25 |
| 3304 | A1608 | 6k blue & gray | .40 .25 |
| 3305 | A1608 | 6k blue & blk | .40 .25 |
| 3306 | A1608 | 6k blue & blue | .40 .25 |
| 3307 | A1608 | 6k blue & gray | .40 .25 |

a. Vert. strip of 5, #3303-3307  2.00 1.25

Designs: No. 3304, Refrigeration. No. 3305, Crab canning ship. No. 3306, Fishing trawler; No. 3307, Black Sea seiner.

Soviet fishing industry.

Woman's Head and Pavlov Shawl — A1606

**1967, Feb. 16**  *Perf. 11*

3301 A1606 4k violet, red & green  .30 .20

International Woman's Day, Mar. 8.

Movie Camera and Film — A1607

**1967, Feb. 16**  *Photo.  Perf. 11½*

3302 A1607 6k multicolored  .40 .25

5th Intl. Film Festival, Moscow, July 5-20.

Trawler Fish Factory and Fish — A1608

International Tourist Year Emblem and Travel Symbols — A1610

**1967, Mar. 10**  *Perf. 11*

3314 A1610 4k blk, sky bl & silver  .30 .20

International Tourist Year, 1967.

No. 3201 Overprinted

**1967, Mar. 29**  *Litho.  Perf. 11½*

3315 A1569 10k multicolored  1.50 .75

Victory of the Soviet team in the Ice Hockey Championships, Vienna, Mar. 18-29. Overprint reads: "Vienna-1967."

Space Walk — A1611

Designs: 10k, Rocket launching from satellite. 16k, Spaceship over moon, and earth.

Arms of USSR and Laurel — A1627

| | | |
|---|---|---|
| АРМЯНСКАЯ ССР ... | #3343 | |
| АЗЕРБАЙДЖАНСКАЯ ССР ... | #3344 | |
| БЕЛОРУССКАЯ ССР БЕЛАРУСКАЯ ССР | #3345 | |
| ГРУЗИНСКАЯ ССР ... | #3347 | |
| КИРГИЗСКАЯ ССР КЫРГЫЗ ССР | #3349 | |
| МОЛДАВСКАЯ ССР РСС МОЛДОВЕНЯСКЭ | #3352 | |
| ТАДЖИКСКАЯ ССР РСС ТОҶИКИСТОН | #3353 | |
| ТУРКМЕНСКАЯ ССР ТУРКМЕНИСТАН ССР | #3354 | |
| УКРАИНСКАЯ ССР УКРАЇНСЬКА РСР | #3355 | |
| УЗБЕКСКАЯ ССР ЎЗБЕКИСТОН ССР | #3356 | |

Flag, Crest and Capital of Republic.

**1967, Aug. 4    Litho.    Perf. 12½x12**

| | | | |
|---|---|---|---|
| 3342 | A1626 | 4k shown | .40 .20 |
| 3343 | A1626 | 4k Armenia | .40 .20 |
| 3344 | A1626 | 4k Azerbaijan | .40 .20 |
| 3345 | A1626 | 4k Byelorussia | .40 .20 |
| 3346 | A1626 | 4k Estonia | .40 .20 |
| 3347 | A1626 | 4k Georgia | .40 .20 |
| 3348 | A1626 | 4k Kazakhstan | .40 .20 |
| 3349 | A1626 | 4k Kirghizia | .40 .20 |
| 3350 | A1626 | 4k Latvia | .40 .20 |
| 3351 | A1626 | 4k Lithuania | .40 .20 |
| 3352 | A1626 | 4k Moldavia | .40 .20 |
| 3353 | A1626 | 4k Tadzhikistan | .40 .20 |
| 3354 | A1626 | 4k Turkmenistan | .40 .20 |
| 3355 | A1626 | 4k Ukraine | .40 .20 |
| 3356 | A1626 | 4k Uzbekistan | .40 .25 |
| 3357 | A1627 | 4k red, gold & black | 6.40 3.20 |

*Nos. 3342-3357 (16)*    6.00

50th anniversary of October Revolution.

---

Motorcyclist A1621

**Photogravure and Engraved**

**1967, June 24    Perf. 12x11½**
3334 A1621 10k multicolored    .40 .20

Intl. Motor Rally, Moscow, July 19.

G. D. Gai (1887-1937), Corps Commander of the First Cavalry, 1920 — A1622

**1967, June 30    Perf. 12**
3335 A1622 4k red & black    .30 .20

Children's Games Emblem and Trophy A1623

**1967, July 8    Perf. 11½**
3336 A1623 4k silver, red & black    .30 .20

10th National Athletic Games of School Children, Leningrad, July, 1967.

Games Emblem and Trophy A1624

**1967, July 20**

| | | | |
|---|---|---|---|
| 3337 | A1624 | 4k silver, red & black | .20 .20 |
| 3338 | A1624 | 4k silver, red & black | .20 .20 |
| a. | | Pair, #3337 3338 | .40 .20 |
| 3339 | A1624 | 4k silver, red & black | .20 .20 |
| 3340 | A1624 | 4k silver, red & black | .20 .20 |
| a. | | Pair, #3339-3340 | .40 .20 |

#3338, Cup and dancer. #3339, Cup and bicyclists. #3340, Cup and diver.

4th Natl. Spartacist Games, & USSR 50th anniv. Se-tenant in checkerboard arrangement.

V. G. Klochkov (1911-41), Hero of the Soviet Union — A1625

**1967, July 20    Perf. 12½x12**
3341 A1625 4k red & black    .40 .25

Alternating label shows citation.

Soviet Flag, Arms and Moscow Views A1626

---

Views of Old and New Minsk A1616

**1967, May 9**
3329 A1616 4k slate green & black    .35 .20

900th anniversary of Minsk.

Red Cross and Tulip — A1617

**1967, May 15    Perf. 12**
3330 A1617 4k yel brown & red    .30 .20

Centenary of the Russian Red Cross.

Stamps of 1918 and 1967 — A1618

**1967    Photo.    Perf. 11½**
3331 A1618 20k blue & black    .90 .30
a. Souv. sheet of 2, imperf.    4.00 1.25

All-Union Philatelic Exhibition "50 Years of the Great October," Moscow, Oct. 1-10. Se-tenant with label showing exhibition emblem. Issue dates: 20k, May 25. Sheet, Oct. 1. No. 3331 was re-issued Oct. 1 with "Oct. 1-10" printed in blue on the label. Value $2.

Komsomolsk-on-Amur and Map of Amur River — A1619

**1967, June 12    Perf. 12x12½**
3332 A1619 4k red & brown    .40 .20

35th anniv. of the Soviet youth town, Komsomolsk-on-Amur. Printed with label showing boy and girl of Young Communist League and tents.

Souvenir Sheet

Sputnik Orbiting Earth — A1620

**1967, June 24    Litho.    Perf. 13x12**
3333 A1620 30k black & multi    6.00 6.00

10th anniv. of the launching of Sputnik 1, the 1st artificial satellite, Oct. 4, 1957.

---

**1967, Mar. 30    Litho.    Perf. 12**

| | | | |
|---|---|---|---|
| 3316 | A1611 | 4k bister & multi | .25 .20 |
| 3317 | A1611 | 10k black & multi | .70 .20 |
| 3318 | A1611 | 16k lilac & multi | 1.00 .30 |

*Nos. 3316-3318 (3)*    1.95 .70

National Cosmonauts' Day.

Lenin as Student, by V. Tsigal A1612

**1967    Photo.    Perf. 12x11½, 11½x12**

| | | | |
|---|---|---|---|
| 3319 | A1612 | 2k grn, sepia & buff | .20 .20 |
| 3320 | A1612 | 3k maroon & brn | .20 .20 |
| 3321 | A1612 | 4k ol black & gold | .30 .20 |
| 3322 | A1612 | 6k dk bl, sil & blk | .40 .20 |
| 3323 | A1612 | 10k sil, gray bl & blk | .75 .20 |
| 3323A | A1612 | 10k gold, gray & black | .75 .20 |

*Nos. 3319-3323A (6)*    2.60 1.20

97th anniversary of the birth of Lenin. Issued: #3323A, Oct. 25; others, Apr. 22.

Lt. M. S. Kharchenko and Battle Scenes — A1613

**1967, Apr. 24    Perf. 12x11½**

| | | | |
|---|---|---|---|
| 3324 | A1613 | 4k brt purple & ol bis | .25 .20 |
| 3325 | A1613 | 4k ultra & ol bister | .25 .20 |
| 3326 | A1613 | 4k org brn & ol bister | .25 .20 |

*Nos. 3324-3326 (3)*    .75 .60

Designs: No. 3325, Maj. Gen. S. V. Rudnev. No. 3326, M. Shmyrev.

Partisan heroes of WWII.

Marshal S. S. Biryuzov, Hero of the Soviet Union — A1614

**1967, May 9    Photo.    Perf. 12**
3327 A1614 4k ocher & slate green    .40 .40

Driver Crossing Lake Ladoga A1615

**1967, May 9    Perf. 11½**
3328 A1615 4k plum & blue gray    .30 .20

25th anniversary of siege of Leningrad.

**Communication Symbols — A1628**

**1967, Aug. 16    Photo.    Perf. 12**
3358 A1628 4k crimson & silver    1.50 .30
Development of communications in USSR.

**Flying Crane, Dove and Anniversary Emblem — A1629**

**1967, Aug. 20**
3359 A1629 16k silver, red & blk    .50 .30
Russo-Japanese Friendship Meeting, held at Khabarovsk. Emblem is for 50th anniv. of October Revolution.

**Karl Marx and Title Page of "Das Kapital" — A1630**

**1967, Aug. 22    Engr.    Perf. 12½x12**
3360 A1630 4k sepia & dk red    .40 .30
Centenary of the publication of "Das Kapital."

**Russian Checkers Players A1631**

Design: 6k, Woman gymnast.

**Photogravure and Engraved**
**1967, Sept. 9    Perf. 12½x11½**
3361 A1631 1k lt brn, dp brn & sl    .30 .30
3362 A1631 6k ol bister & maroon    .30 .20
World Championship of Russian Checkers (Shashki) at Moscow, and World Championship of Rhythmic Gymnastics.

**Javelin A1632**

**1967, Sept. 9    Engr.    Perf. 12x12½**
3363 A1632 2k shown    .25 .20
3364 A1632 3k Running    .25 .20
3365 A1632 4k Jumping    .75 .60
Europa Cup Championships, Kiev, Sept. 15-17.

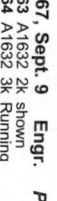

---

**Ice Skating and Olympic Emblem A1633**

**Photogravure and Engraved**
**1967, Sept. 20    Perf. 11½**
3366 A1633 2k gray, blk & bl    .20 .20
3367 A1633 3k bis, ocher, blk &
    green    .20 .20
3368 A1633 4k grn, red &
    blk    .20 .20
3369 A1633 10k bis, brn, bl & blk    .50 .20
3370 A1633 12k gray, blk, lilac &
    green    .65 .20
Nos. 3366-3370 (5)    1.75 1.00

Designs: 3k, Ski jump. 4k, Emblem of Winter Olympics, vert. 10k, Ice hockey. 12k, Long-distance skiing.

10th Winter Olympic Games, Grenoble, France, Feb. 6-18, 1968.

**Silver Fox A1634**

**1967, Sept. 20    Photo.**
3371 A1634 2k blue, blk & gray    .20 .20
3372 A1634 4k brn, blue    .20 .20
3373 A1634 6k tan, dk brn &
    gray grn    .30 .20
3374 A1634 10k yel grn, dk brn
    & black    .45 .20
3375 A1634 12k lilac, blk & bis    .75 .20
3376 A1634 16k org, brn & black    .80 .20
3377 A1634 20k gray blue, blk &
    dk brown    .90 .20
Nos. 3371-3377 (7)    3.60 1.40

Fur-bearing Animals: 2k, Arctic blue fox, horiz. 6k, Red fox, horiz. 10k, Muskrat, horiz. 12k, Ermine. 16k, Sable. 20k, Mink, horiz.

**Young Guards Memorial A1635**

**1967, Sept. 23**
3378 A1635 4k magenta, org & blk    .30 .20
25th anniv. of the fight of the Young Guards at Krasnodon against the Germans.

International Fur Auctions in Leningrad.

**Map of Cedar Valley Reservation and Snow Leopard — A1636**

**1967, Oct. 14    Photo.**
3379 A1636 10k ol bister & black    .40 .20
Far Eastern Cedar Valley Reservation.

**Planes and Emblem A1637**

**1967, Oct. 14    Perf. 11½**
3380 A1637 6k dp blue, red & gold    .30 .20
French Normandy-Neman aviators, who fought on the Russian Front, 25th anniv.

---

**Ice Skating and Olympic Emblem A1633**

**1967, Oct. 14    Perf. 12½x12**
3381 A1638 4k ver & ultra    .30 .20
50th anniversary of the Soviet Militia.

**Space Station Orbiting Moon — A1639**

**1967    Litho.    Perf. 12x12½, 12½x12**
3382 A1639 4k multicolored    .20 .20
3383 A1639 6k multicolored    .35 .20
3384 A1639 10k multicolored    .35 .20
3385 A1639 12k multicolored    .65 .20
3386 A1639 16k multicolored    .85 .20
Nos. 3382-3386 (5)    2.55 1.00

Science Fiction: 6k, Explorers on the moon, horiz. 10k, Rocket flying to the stars. 12k, Landscape on Red Planet, horiz. 16k, Satellites from outer space.

**Emblem of USSR and Red Star — A1640**

**Lenin Addressing 2nd Congress of Soviets, by V. A. Serov — A1641**

**1967, Oct. 25**
3387 A1640 4k gold, yel, red &
    dk brown    .20 .20

**Lithographed and Embossed    Perf. 11½**
3388 A1641 4k gold & multi    .20 .20
3389 A1641 4k gold & multi    .20 .20
3390 A1641 4k gold & multi    .20 .20
3391 A1641 4k gold & multi    .20 .20
3392 A1641 4k gold & multi    .20 .20
3393 A1641 4k gold & multi    .20 .20
3394 A1641 4k gold & multi    .20 .20
3395 A1641 4k gold & multi    .20 .20
3396 A1641 4k gold & multi    .20 .20
a.    A1641a 4k gold & multi    3.00 3.00
Souvenir sheet of 2
Nos. 3387-3396 (10)    2.00 1.00

50th anniversary of October Revolution.

Paintings: #3389, Lenin pointing to Map, by L. A. Schmeljko, 1957. #3390, The First Cavalry Army, by M. B. Grekov, 1924. #3391, Working Students on the March, by B. V. Yoganson, 1928. #3392, Russian Friendship for the World, by S. M. Karpov, 1924. #3393, Five-Year Plan Morning, by Y. D. Romas, 1934. #3394, Farmers' Holiday, by Y. I. Pimenov, 1937. #3395, Victory in the Great Patriotic War, by Y. K. Korolev, 1965.

Builders of Communism, by L. M. Merpert and Y. N. Skripkov — A1641a

---

**Militiaman and Soviet Emblem A1638**

**1967, Nov. 5    Engr.    Perf. 12½x12**
3397 A1642 1r lake    5.00 2.00
50th anniv. of the October Revolution. Margin contains "50" as a watermark.

**Hammer, Sickle and Sputnik — A1642**

**Souvenir Sheet**

No. 3396a contains two 40k imperf. stamps similar to Nos. 3388 and 3396. Issued Nov. 5.

**Ostankino Television Tower — A1643**

**1967, Nov. 5    Litho.    Perf. 11½**
3398 A1643 16k gray, org & black    .60 .25

**Jurmala Resort and Hepatica A1644**

Health Resorts of the Baltic Region: 6k, Narva-Joesuu and Labrador tea. 10k, Druskininkai and cranberry blossoms. 12k, Zelenogradsk and Scotch heather. 16k, Svetlogorsk and club moss, vert.

**1967, Nov. 30    Perf. 12½x12, 12x12½**
**Flowers in Natural Colors.    Litho.**
3399 A1644 4k blue & black    .20 .20
3400 A1644 6k ocher & black    .45 .20
3401 A1644 10k green & black    .45 .20
3402 A1644 12k gray olive & blk    .55 .20
3403 A1644 16k brown & blk    .75 .20
Nos. 3399-3403 (5)    2.45 1.00

---

**Hotel Russia and Kremlin A1646**

**Emergency Commission Emblem — A1645**

**1967, Dec. 11    Photo.    Perf. 11½**
3404 A1616 4k ultra & red    .40 .25
All-Russia Emergency Commission (later the State Security Commission), 50th anniv.

**1967, Dec. 14**
3405 A1646 4k silver, dk brn & brt pink    .30 .20

New Year 1968. The pink is fluorescent.

**Soldiers, Sailors, Congress Building, Kharkov, and Monument to the Men of Arsenal — A1647**

**1967, Dec. 20**    **Litho.**    **Perf. 12½**
3406 A1647 4k multicolored    .30 .20
3407 A1647 6k multicolored    .30 .20
3408 A1647 10k multicolored    .35 .60
   Nos. 3406-3408 (3)

50th anniv. of the Ukrainian SSR.

**Monument to the Unknown Soldier, Moscow — A1650**

**1967, Dec. 25**
3419 A1650 4k carmine    .35 .25

Dedication of the Monument of the Unknown Soldier of WWII in the Kremlin Wall.

**Three Kremlin Towers A1648**

**Engraved and Photogravure**

**1967, Dec. 25**    **Perf. 12x11½, 11½x12**
3409 A1648 4k dk brn & claret    .20 .20
3410 A1648 6k dk brn, yel & grn    .20 .20
3411 A1648 10k maroon & slate    .20 .20
3412 A1648 12k sl grn, yel & vio    .55 .20
3413 A1648 16k brn, pink & red    .80 .20
   Nos. 3409-3413 (5)    2.35 1.00

Kremlin: 6k, Cathedral of the Annunciation, horiz. 10k, Konstantin and Elena, Nabatnaya and Spasski towers. 12k, Ivan the Great bell tower. 16k, Kutafya and Troitskaya towers.

**Coat of Arms, Lenin's Tomb and Rockets A1649**

**1967, Dec. 25**    **Engr.**
3414 A1649 4k maroon    .20 .20
3415 A1649 4k green    .20 .20
3416 A1649 4k red brown    .20 .20
3417 A1649 4k violet blue    .20 .20
3418 A1649 4k dark blue    1.00 1.00
   Nos. 3414-3418 (5)    1.00 1.00

Designs: No. 3415, Agricultural Progress: Wheat, reapers and silo. No. 3416, Industrial Progress: Computer tape, atom symbol, cogwheel and factories. No. 3417, Scientific Progress: Radar, microscope, university buildings. No. 3418, Communications progress: Ostankino TV tower, railroad bridge, steamer and Aeroflot emblem, vert.

Material and technical basis of Russian Communism.

**Seascape by Ivan Aivazovsky — A1651**

**1967, Dec. 29**    **Litho.**
**Perf. 12½x12, 12x12½, 12, 11½**
**Size: 47x33mm, 33x47mm**
3420 A1651 3k multicolored    .20 .20
3421 A1651 4k multicolored    .20 .20
3422 A1651 4k multicolored    .20 .20
**Size: 60x35mm, 35x60mm**
3423 A1651 6k multicolored    .20 .20
3424 A1651 6k multicolored    .20 .20
3425 A1651 6k multicolored    .20 .20
**Size: 47x33mm, 33x47mm**
3426 A1651 10k multicolored    .35 .20
3427 A1651 10k multicolored    .35 .20
3428 A1651 16k multicolored    .45 .20
   Nos. 3420-3428 (9)    2.35 1.80

Tretiakov Art Gallery, Moscow.

Paintings: 3k, Interrogation of Communists by B. V. Yoganson, 1933. #3422, The Lacemaker, by V. A. Tropinin, 1823, vert. #3423, Bread-makers, by T. M. Yablonskaya, 1949. #3424, Alexander Nevsky, by P. D. Korin, 1942-43, vert. #3425, The Boyar Morozov Going into Exile by V. I. Surikov, 1887. #3426, The Swan Maiden, by M. A. Vrubel, 1900, vert. #3427, The Arrest of a Propagandist by Ilya E. Repin, 1878. 16k, Moscow Suburb in February by G. G. Nissky, 1957.

**Globe, Wheel and Workers of the World — A1652**

**1968, Jan. 18**    **Photo.**    **Perf. 12**
3429 A1652 6k ver & green    .35 .20

14th Trade Union Congress.

**Lt. S. Baikov and Velikaya River Bridge A1653**

**1968, Jan. 20**    **Perf. 12½x12**
3430 A1653 4k blue gray & black    .30 .20
3431 A1653 4k rose & black    .30 .20
3432 A1653 4k gray green & black    .90 .60
   Nos. 3430-3432 (3)

Heroes of WWII (War Memorial and): #3431. Lt. A. Pokalchuk. #3432, P. Gutchenko.

**Thoroughbred and Horse Race — A1654**

Horses: 6k, Arab mare and dressage, vert. 10k, Orlovski trotters. 12k, Altekin horse performing, vert. 16k, Donskay race horse.

**1968, Jan. 23**    **Perf. 11½**
3433 A1654 4k ultra, blk & red    .40 .20
3434 A1654 6k crim, blk & ultra    .65 .20
3435 A1654 10k grnsh blue, blk & orange    .95 .40
3436 A1654 12k org brn, black & apple green    1.25 .50
3437 A1654 16k ol grn, blk & red    1.75 .70
   Nos. 3433-3437 (5)    5.00 2.00

Horse breeding.

**Maria I. Ulyanova (1878-1937), Lenin's Sister — A1655**

**1968, Jan. 30**    **Perf. 12x12½**
3438 A1655 4k indigo & pale green    .30 .20

**Soviet Star and Flags of Army, Air Force and Navy A1656**

**Lenin Addressing Troops in 1919 — A1657**

#3441, Dneprostroi Dam & sculpture "On Guard." #3442, 1918 poster & marching volunteers. #3443, Red Army entering Vladivostok, 1922, & soldiers' monument in Primorie. #3444, Poster "Red Army as Liberator." Western Ukraine. #3445, Poster "Westward," defeat of German army. #3446, "Battle of Stalingrad" monument & German prisoners of war. #3447, Victory parade on Red Square, May 24, 1945, & Russian War Memorial, Berlin. Nos. 3448-3449, Modern weapons and Russian flag.

**1968, Feb. 20**    **Typo.**    **Perf. 12x12½**
3439 A1656 4k gold & multi    .20 .20
**Photo.**
**Perf. 11½x12**
3440 A1657 4k blk, red, pink & silver    .20 .20
3441 A1657 4k gold, black & red    .20 .20
**Litho.**
**Perf. 12½x12**
3442 A1657 4k yel grn, blk, red & buff    .20 .20
3443 A1657 4k grn, dk brn, red & bis    .20 .20
3444 A1657 4k green & multi    .20 .20
3445 A1657 4k yel green & multi    .20 .20

**Perf. 11½x12, 12x11½**    **Photo.**
3446 A1657 4k blk, silver & red    .20 .20
3447 A1657 4k gold, blk, pink & red    .20 .20
3448 A1657 4k blk, red & silver    2.00 2.00

**Souvenir Sheet**    **Imperf.**

**1968, Feb. 23**    **Litho.**
3449 A1656 1r blk, silver & red    3.50 1.50

50th anniv. of the Armed Forces of the USSR. No. 3449 contains one 25x37½mm stamp with simulated perforations.

**Maxim Gorki (1868-1936), Writer — A1658**

**1968, Feb. 29**    **Photo.**    **Perf. 12**
3450 A1658 4k gray ol & dk brown    .30 .20

**Fireman, Fire Truck and Boat — A1659**

**1968, Mar. 30**    **Photo.**    **Perf. 12x12½**
3451 A1659 4k red & black    .30 .20

50th anniversary of Soviet Fire Guards.

**Link-up of Cosmos 186 and 188 Satellites — A1660**

**1968, Mar. 30**    **Photo.**    **Perf. 11½**
3452 A1660 6k blk, dp lilac rose & gold    .30 .20

First link-up in space of two satellites, Cosmos 186 and Cosmos 188, Oct. 30, 1967.

**N. N. Popudrenko — A1661**

**1968, Mar. 30**    **Perf. 12½x12**
3453 A1661 4k gray green & black    .30 .20
3454 A1661 4k lt purple & black    .30 .20

Design: No. 3453, P. P. Vershigora.

Partisan heroes of World War II.

**1968, Apr. 11** Perf. 11½
3455 A1662 6k sil, mar, ver & black .50 .35

Globe and Hand Shielding from War A1662

Emergency session of the World Federation of Trade Unions and expressing solidarity with the people of Vietnam.

Space Walk A1663

**1968, Apr. 12** Litho.
3456 A1663 4k multicolored .20 .20
3457 A1663 6k multicolored .35 .20
3458 A1663 10k multicolored .75 .50
a. Block of 3, #3456-3458 + 3 labels

6k, Docking operation of Kosmos 186 & Kosmos 188. 10k, Exploration of Venus.

National Astronauts Day.

Lenin, 1919 A1664

Lenin Portraits: No. 3460, Addressing crowd on Red Square, Nov. 7, 1918. No. 3461, Full-face portrait, taken in Petrograd, Jan. 1918.

**1968, Apr. 16** Engraved and Photogravure Perf. 12x11½
3459 A1664 4k gold, brown & red .30 .20
3460 A1664 4k gold, red & black .30 .20
3461 A1664 4k gold, brn, buff & red .90 .60
Nos. 3459-3461 (3)

98th anniversary of the birth of Lenin.

Alisher Navoi, Uzbek Poet, 525th Birth Anniv. — A1665

**1968, Apr. 29** Photo. Perf. 12x12½
3462 A1665 4k deep brown .30 .20

---

Karl Marx (1818-83) A1666

**1968, May 5** Engr. Perf. 11½x12
3463 A1666 4k black & red .30 .20

Frontier Guard — A1667
Jubilee Badge — A1668

**1968, May 22** Photo. Perf. 11½
3464 A1667 4k sl green, ocher & red .30 .20
3465 A1668 6k sil, grn, blk & red brn .30 .20
Russian Frontier Guards, 50th anniv.

Crystal and Congress Emblem A1669

**1968, May 30** Engr. Perf. 12
3466 A1669 6k blue, dk blue & grn .25 .20
3467 A1669 6k org, gold & dk brn .25 .20
3468 A1669 6k red brn, gold & blk .25 .20
3469 A1669 6k lil rose, org & blk .25 .20
Nos. 3466-3469 (4) 1.00 .80

Intl. congresses: Leningrad: 7th World Power Conf.; 13th Entomological Cong.; 4th Cong. for the Study of Volatile Oils.

Congress Emblems and: No. 3467, Power lines and factories. No. 3468, Ground beetle. No. 3469, Roses and carbon rings.

Types of 1966
Designs as before.

**1968, June 20** Engr. Perf. 12
3470 A1593 1k dk red brown .20 .20
3471 A1593 2k deep violet .20 .20
3472 A1593 3k plum .20 .20
3473 A1593 4k bright red .20 .20
3474 A1593 6k blue .20 .20
3475 A1593 10k olive .40 .20
3476 A1593 12k red brown .60 .20
3477 A1593 16k violet blue .90 .20

Perf. 12½
3478 A1594 20k red 1.00 .20
3479 A1594 30k bright green 1.65 .20
3480 A1594 50k violet blue 2.75 .30

Perf. 12½x12
3481 A1594 1r gray, red brn & black 6.00 .50
Nos. 3470-3481 (12) 14.85 2.00

Sadriddin Aini A1670

**1968, June 30** Photo. Perf. 12½x12
3482 A1670 4k olive bister & mar .30 .20
Aini (1878-1954), Tadzhik poet.

---

Post Rider and C.C.E.P. Emblem A1671

**1968, June 30**
3483 A1671 6k gray & red brown .30 .20
3484 A1671 6k orange brn & bister .30 .20
#3484, Modern means of communications (train, ship, planes and C.C.E.P. emblem).

Annual session of the Council of the Consultative Commission on Postal Investigation of the UPU (C.C.E.P.), Moscow, 9/20-10/5.

Bolshevik Uprising, Kiev — A1672

**1968, July 5** Photo. Perf. 11½
3485 A1672 4k gold, red & plum .30 .20
Ukrainian Communist Party, 50th anniv.

Athletes A1673

**1968, July 9**
3486 A1673 4k yel, dp car & bister .30 .20
1st Youth Summer Sports Games for 50th anniv. of the Leninist Young Communists League.

Field Ball — A1674
Table Tennis A1675

**1968, July 18** Perf. 12x12½, 12½x12 Litho.
3487 A1674 2k red & multi .20 .20
3488 A1675 4k purple & multi .20 .20
3489 A1674 6k blue & multi .25 .20
3490 A1674 10k multicolored .35 .20
3491 A1675 12k green & multi .45 .20
Nos. 3487-3491 (5) 1.45 1.00

Designs: 6k, 20th Baltic Regatta. 10k, Soccer player and cup. 12k, Scuba divers.

European youth sports competitions.

Rhythmic Gymnast A1676

---

**1968, July 31** Photo. Perf. 11½
Gold Background
3492 A1676 4k blue & green .20 .20
3493 A1676 4k dp rose & pur .20 .20
3494 A1676 10k yel grn & pur .55 .20
3495 A1676 12k org & red grn .60 .20
3496 A1676 16k ultra & pink .70 .20
Nos. 3492-3496 (5) 2.35 1.00

6k, Weight lifting. 10k, Rowing. 12k, Women's hurdling. 16k, Fencing. 40k, Running.

19th Olympic Games, Mexico City, 10/12-27.

Souvenir Sheet Lithographed and Photogravure Perf. 12½x12
3497 A1676 40k gold, grn, org & gray 1.75 1.00

Gediminas Tower, Vilnius — A1677

**1968, Aug. 14** Photo. Perf. 11½
3498 A1677 4k magenta, tan & red .30 .20
Soviet power in Lithuania, 50th anniv.

Tbilisi State University A1678

**1968, Aug. 14** Perf. 12
3499 A1678 4k slate grn & lt brn .30 .20
Tbilisi State University, Georgia, 50th anniv.

Laocoon — A1679

**1968, Aug. 16** Perf. 11½
3500 A1679 6k sepia, blk & mar 2.75 2.00
"Promote solidarity with Greek democrats."

Red Army Man, Cavalry Charge and Order of the Red Banner of Battle — A1680

**1968, Aug. 25** Litho. Perf. 12½x12
3501 A1680 2k gray, red & ocher .20 .20
3502 A1680 3k multicolored .20 .20
3503 A1680 4k org, ocher & rose car .20 .20
3504 A1680 6k multicolored .20 .20
3505 A1680 10k olive & multi 1.00 1.00
Nos. 3501-3505 (5)

Designs: 3k, Young man and woman. Dneprostroi Dam and Order of the Red Banner of Labor. 4k, Soldier, storming of the Reichstag, Berlin, and Order of Lenin. 6k, "Restoration of National Economy" (workers), and Order of Lenin. 10k, Young man and woman cultivating virgin land and Order of Lenin, like 2k.

## Souvenir Sheet

Imperf

3506 A1680  50k ultra, red & bister  2.50 1.00

50th anniv. of the Lenin Young Communist League, Komsomol.

Chemistry Institute and Dimeric Molecule A1681

1968, Sept. 3    Photo.    Perf. 11½

3507 A1681  4k vio bl, dp lil rose & black  .30  .20

50th anniversary of Kurnakov Institute for General and Inorganic Chemistry.

Letter, Compass Rose, Ship and Plane A1682

1968, Sept. 16    Photo.    Perf. 11½

3508 A1682  4k dk car rose, brn & brt rod  .30  .20
3509 A1683  4k dk blue, lilac & blue       .30  .20

No. 3508 for Letter Writing Week, Oct. 7-13, and No. 3509 for Stamp Day and the Day of the Collector.

Compass Rose and Stamps of 1921 and 1965 A1683

The 26 Baku Commissars, Sculpture by Merkurov — A1684

1968, Sept. 20

3510 A1684  4k multicolored    .40  .20

50th anniversary of the shooting of the 26 Commissars, Baku, Sept. 20, 1918.

Toyvo Antikaynen (1898-1941), Finnish Workers' Organizer — A1685

1968, Sept. 30    Perf. 12

3511 A1685  6k gray & sepia    .60  .20

Russian Merchant Marine Emblem A1686

1968, Sept. 30    Perf. 12x11½

3512 A1686  6k blue, red & indigo  .40  .20

Russian Merchant Marine.

---

Order of the October Revolution — A1687

Typographed and Embossed

1968, Sept. 30    Perf. 12½x12

3513 A1687  4k gold & multi    .35  .25

51st anniv. of the October Revolution. Printed with alternating label.

Pavel P. Postyshev — A1688

1968-70    Engr.    Perf. 12½x12

Designs: No. 3515, Stepan G. Shaumian (1878-1918). No. 3516, Amkal Ikramov (1898-1938). No. 3516A, N. G. Markin (1893-1918). No. 3516B, P. E. Dybenko (1889-1938). No. 3516C, S. V. Kosior (1889-1939). No. 3516D, Vasili Kikvidze (1895-1919).

Size: 21½x32½mm

3514  A1688  4k bluish black      .55  .20
3515  A1688  4k bluish black      .55  .20
3516  A1688  4k gray black        .55  .20
3516A A1688  4k black             .55  .20
3516B A1688  4k dark car ('69)    .55  .20
3516C A1688  4k indigo ('69)      .55  .20
3516D A1688  4k dk brown ('70)    .66  .20
              Nos. 3514-3516D (7) 3.85 1.40

American Bison and Zebra A1689

Designs: No. 3518, Purple gallinule and lotus. No. 3519, Great white egrets, vert. No. 3520, Ostrich and golden pheasant, vert. No. 3521, Eland and guanaco. No. 3522, European spoonbill and glossy ibis.

1968, Oct. 16    Perf. 12½x12, 12x12½    Litho.

3517 A1689  4k ocher, brn & blk    .65  .30
3518 A1689  4k ocher & black       .65  .30
3519 A1689  6k olive & black       .75  .30
3520 A1689  6k gray & black        .75  .35
3521 A1689  10k dp grn & multi    1.10  .40
3522 A1689  10k emerald & multi   1.10  .40
              Nos. 3517-3522 (6)  5.00 2.00

Askania Nova and Astrakhan state reservations.

Ivan S. Turgenev (1818-83), Writer — A1690

1968, Oct. 10    Engr.    Perf. 12x12½

3523 A1690  4k green    4.50  .50

---

Warrior, 1880 B.C. and Mt. Ararat — A1691

Design: 12k, David Sasountsi monument, Yerevan, and Mt. Ararat.

Engraved and Photogravure

1968, Oct. 18    Perf. 11½

3524 A1691  4k blk & dk blue, gray   .25  .20
3525 A1691  12k dk brn & choc, bis   .35  .20

Yerevan, capital of Armenia, 2,750th anniv.

First Radio Tube Generator and Laboratory A1692

1968, Oct. 26    Photo.    Perf. 11½

3526 A1692  4k dk bl, dp bis & blk   .30  .20

50th anniversary of Russia's first radio laboratory at Gorki (Nizhni Novgorod).

Prospecting Geologist and Crystals A1693

1968, Oct. 31    Litho.    Perf. 11½

3527 A1693  4k blue & multi     .40  .20
3528 A1693  6k multicolored     .20  .20
3529 A1693  10k multicolored   1.15  .60
              Nos. 3527-3529 (3)

6k, Prospecting for metals: seismographic test apparatus with shock wave diagram, plane, truck. 10k, Oil derrick in the desert.

Geology Day. Printed with alternating label.

Borovoe, Kazakhstan — A1694

Landscapes: #3531, Djely-Oguz, Kirghizia, vert. #3532, Issyk-kul Lake, Kirghizia. #3533, Borovoe, Kazakhstan, vert.

1968, Nov. 20    Perf. 12½x12, 12x12½    Typo.

3530 A1694  4k dk red brn & multi  .20  .20
3531 A1694  4k gray & multi        .20  .20
3532 A1694  6k dk red brn & multi  .20  .20
3533 A1694  6k black & multi       .80  .80
              Nos. 3530-3533 (4)

Recreational areas in the Kazakh and Kirghiz Republics.

Medals and Cup, Riccione, 1952, 1961 and 1965 — A1695

4k, Medals, Eiffel Tower and Arc de Triomphe, Paris, 1964. 6k, Porcelain plaque, gold medal and Brandenburg Gate, Debria, Berlin, 1950, 1959. 12k, Medal and prize-winning stamp #2888, Buenos Aires. 16k, Cups and medals, Rome, 1952, 1954. 20k, Medals, awards and views, Vienna, 1961, 1965. 30k, Trophies, Prague, 1950, 1955, 1962.

1968, Nov. 27    Photo.    Perf. 11½x12

3534 A1695  4k dp cl, sil & blk     .20  .20
3535 A1695  6k dl bl, gold & blk    .25  .20
3536 A1695  10k light ultra, gold
                     & black         .40  .20
3537 A1695  12k blue, silver & blk  .50  .50
3538 A1695  16k red, gold & blk     .55  .55
3539 A1695  20k bright blue, gold
                     & black         .70  .20
3540 A1695  30k orange brown,
                 gold & black      1.00  .30
              Nos. 3534-3540 (7)   3.60 1.50

Awards to Soviet post office at foreign stamp exhibitions.

---

V. K. Lebedinsky and Radio Tower — A1697

Worker with Banner — A1696

1968, Nov. 29    Perf. 12x12½

3541 A1696  4k red & black    .50  .35

Estonian Workers' Commune, 50th anniv.

1968, Nov. 29    Perf. 11½x12

3542 A1697  4k gray grn, blk & gray  .50  .25

V. K. Lebedinsky (1868-1937), scientist.

Souvenir Sheet

Communication via Satellite — A1698

1968, Nov. 29    Litho.    Perf. 12

3543 A1698  Sheet of 3     3.00  .70
  a.  16k Molniya I                .70  .20
  b.  16k Map of Russia            .70  .20
  c.  16k Ground Station "Orbite"  .70  .20

Television transmission throughout USSR with the aid of the earth satellite Molniya I.

Sprig, Spasski Tower, Lenin Univ. and Library A1699

1968, Dec. 1    Perf. 11½

3544 A1699  4k ultra, sil, grn & red  .60  .30

New Year 1969.

Maj. Gen. Georgy T.
Beregovoi
A1700

**1968, Dec. 14    Photo.    Perf. 11½**
3545  A1700  10k  Prus blue, blk &
red ............................. .40 .25

Flight of Soyuz 3, Oct. 26-30.

Rail-laying
and
Casting
Machines
A1701

**1968, Dec. 14    Perf. 12½x12**
3546  A1701  4k  rose mag & org .25 .20
3547  A1701  10k  brown & emerald .25 .20

Soviet railroad transportation: 4k, Railroad
map of the Soviet Union and Train.

Newspaper Banner
and Monument
A1702

**1968, Dec. 23**
3548  A1702  4k tan, red & dk brn .40 .25
Byelorussian communist party, 50th anniv.

The
Reapers, by
A.
Venetzianov
A1703

Knight at the Crossroads, by Viktor M.
Vasnetsov — A1704

**1968, Dec. 25    Litho.**
Paintings: 2k, The Last Day of Pompeii, by
Karl P. Bryullov. 4k, Capture of a Town in Win-
ter, by Vasili I. Surikov. 6k, On the Lake, by I.I.
Levitan. 10k, Alarm, 1919 (family), by K.
Petrov-Vodkin. 16k, Defense of Sevastopol,
1942, by A. Deineka. 20k, Sculptor with a Bust
of Homer, by G. Korzhev. 30k, Celebration on
Uristsky Square, 1920, by G. Koustodiev. 50k,
Duel between Peresvet and Chelubey, by
Avilov.

**1968, Dec. 25    Perf. 12x12½, 12½**
3549  A1703  1k  multicolored .20 .20
3550  A1703  2k  multicolored .20 .20
3551  A1703  3k  multicolored .20 .20
3552  A1704  4k  multicolored .25 .20
3553  A1704  6k  multicolored .20 .20
3554  A1703  10k  multicolored .20 .20
3555  A1703  16k  multicolored .35 .20
3556  A1703  20k  multicolored .65 .20

---

3557  A1704  30k  multicolored .85 .30
3558  A1704  50k  multicolored 1.65 .40
Nos. 3549-3558 (10) 5.50 2.30

House, Zaoneje,
1876 — A1705

Russian State Museum, Leningrad.

**1968, Dec. 27    Engr.    Perf. 12½x12**
Russian Architecture: 4k, Carved doors,
Gorki Oblast, 1848. 6k, Castle, Kizhi, 1714.
10k, Fortress wall, Rostov-Yaroslav, 16th-17th
centuries. 12k, Gate, Tsaritsino, 1785. 16k,
Architect Rossi Street, Leningrad.
3559  A1705  4k  dp brown, ocher .25 .20
3560  A1705  6k  green, yellow .25 .20
3561  A1705  10k  vio, gray violet .35 .20
3562  A1705  10k  dl bl, grnsh gray .45 .20
3563  A1705  12k  car, gray .55 .20
3564  A1705  16k  blue, yellowish 2.55 1.20
Nos. 3559-3564 (6)

Banners of Young Communist League,
October Revolution Medal — A1707

**1968, Dec. 31    Litho.    Perf. 12**
3566  A1707  12k  red, yel & black .40 .30
Award of Order of October Revolution to the
Young Communist League on its 50th
anniversary.

Revolutionaries and
Monument — A1709

**1969, Jan.    Photo.    Perf. 11½**
3567  A1708  4k orange & claret .40 .20
Latvian Soviet Republic, 50th anniv.

Soldiers on
Guard — A1708

**1969, Jan. 1    Perf. 12x12½**
3567  A1708  4k orange & claret .40 .20

**1969, Jan.    Photo.    Perf. 11½**
3568  A1709  2k  ocher & rose claret ........................... .25 .20
3569  A1709  4k  ocher & red .25 .20
3570  A1709  6k  dk olive, mag &
red ........................... .75 .60
Nos. 3568-3570 (3)

Designs: 4k, Partisans and sword. 6k, Workers and Lenin Medals.

Byelorussian Soviet Republic, 50th anniv.

---

Russian State Museum, Leningrad.

Nikolai Filchenkov
A1713

**1969**
3574  A1713  4k  dull rose & black .20 .20
3575  A1713  4k  emerald & dk brn .20 .20
3575A A1713  4k  blue & black .60 .60
Nos. 3574-3575A (3)

Designs: No. 3575, Alexander Kosmodemi-
ansky; No. 3575A, Otakar Yarosh, member of
Czechoslovak Svoboda Battalion.

Heroes of World War II. Issued: #3575A,
May 9; others, Feb. 23.

Vladimir Shatalov, Boris Volynov,
Alexei S. Elisseyev, Evgeny
Khrunov — A1710

**1969, Jan. 22    Imperf.**
3571  A1710  50k dp bis & dk brn .40 .20
1st team flights of Soyuz 4 and 5, 1/16/69.

Souvenir Sheet

Leningrad
University
A1711

**1969, Jan. 23    Photo.    Perf. 12½x12**
3572  A1711  10k black & maroon .40 .20
University of Leningrad, 150th anniv.

Ivan A. Krylov
(1769?-1844),
Fable
Writer — A1712

**1969, Feb. 13    Litho.    Perf. 12x12½**
3573  A1712  4k black & multi .50 .30

---

Lenin
University,
Kazan, and
Kremlin
A1718

**1969**
3578  A1716  10k  black, vio & grn .25 .20
3579  A1716  10k  dk brn, yel &
brn red ........................ .25 .20
3580  A1717  10k  multicolored .75 .60
Nos. 3578-3580 (3)

Souvenir Sheet

Vostok on
Launching
Pad — A1717

**Perf. 12½x12, 12½x12½    Litho.**

Nat. Cosmonauts' Day; No. 3579, Zond 2
orbiting moon, and photograph of earth made
by Zond 5. 80k, Spaceship Soyuz 3.

**Perf. 12**
3581  A1716  80k vio, green & red 3.00 1.25
No. 3581 contains one 37x24mm stamp.

**1969, Mar. 21    Typo.    Perf. 11½**
3576  A1714  6k black, ver & lt grn .30 .20
Hungarian Soviet Republic, 50th anniv.

Design: "Shoulder to the Wheel" is a sculpture by Zigmond Kisfaludi-Strobl.

"Shoulder to
the Wheel,"
Parliament,
Budapest
A1714

Oil Refinery and Salavat Tualeyev
Monument — A1715

**1969, Mar. 22    Litho.    Perf. 12**
3577  A1715  4k multicolored .30 .20
50th anniv. of the Bashkir Autonomous
Socialist Republic.

Sergei P. Korolev, Sputnik 1, Space
Monument, Moscow — A1716

**1969, Apr. 12**

Lenin
House,
Pskov
A1718b

Lenin
House,
Kuibyshev
A1718a

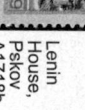

RUSSIA

No. 2717
Overprinted
in Vermilion

**1969, June 25** **Photo.** **Perf. 11½**
3612 A1306 6k Prus blue & plum 2.50 1.50
Soviet victory in the Ice Hockey World
Championships, Stockholm, 1969.

"Hill of Glory"
Monument
and Minsk
Battle Map
A1732

**1969, July 3** **Litho.** **Perf. 12x12½**
3613 A1732 4k red & olive .20 .20
25th anniv. of the liberation of Byelorussia
from the Germans.

Eagle, Flag and
Map of Poland
A1733

#3615, Hands holding torch, flags of Bulga-
ria, USSR, Bulgarian coat of arms.
**1969, July 10** **Photo.** **Perf. 12**
3614 A1733 6k red & bister .60 .20
**Litho.**
3615 A1733 6k bis, red, grn & blk .60 .20
25th anniv. of the Polish Republic; liberation
of Bulgaria from the Germans.

Monument to 68 Heroes — A1734

**1969, July 15** **Photo.** **Perf. 12**
3616 A1734 4k red & maroon .50 .30
25th anniversary of the liberation of Nikolayev from the Germans.

Old
Samarkand
A1735

Design: 6k, Intourist Hotel, Samarkand.

**1969, July 15** **Typo.**
3617 A1735 4k multicolored .30 .20
3618 A1735 6k multicolored .30 .20
2500th anniversary of Samarkand.

---

Estonian Singer
and Festival
Emblem — A1727

**1969, June 14** **Perf. 12x12½**
3606 A1727 4k ver & bister .50 .25
Centenary of the Estonian Song Festival.

Mendeleev and Formula with Author's
Corrections — A1728
**Engraved and Lithographed** **Perf. 12**
3607 A1728 6k brown & rose .50 .30
**Souvenir Sheet**
3608 A1728 30k carmine rose 3.00 1.25

30k, Dmitri Ivanovich Mendeleev, vert.

Cent. of the Periodic Law (classification of
elements), formulated by Dimitri I. Mendeleev
(1834-1907). No. 3608 contains one engraved
29x37mm stamp.

Hand
Holding
Peace
Banner
and World
Landmarks
A1729

**1969, June 20** **Photo.** **Perf. 11½**
3609 A1729 10k bl, dk brn & gold .40 .25
20th anniversary of the Peace Movement.

Laser Beam
Guiding Moon
Rocket — A1730

**1969, June 20** **Photo.**
3610 A1730 4k silver, black & red .50 .25
Soviet scientific inventions, 50th anniv.

Ivan Kotlyarevski (1769-1838),
Ukrainian Writer — A1731
**Typographed and Photogravure**
**1969, June 25** **Perf. 12½x12**
3611 A1731 4k blk, olive & lt brn .50 .25

---

Yasnaya
Polyana
Rose
A1722

4k, "Stroynaya" lily. 10k, Cattleya orchid.
12k, "Listopad" dahlia. 14k, "Ural Girl" gladioli.
**1969, May 15** **Litho.** **Perf. 11½**
3596 A1722 2k multicolored .20 .20
3597 A1722 4k multicolored .20 .20
3598 A1722 10k multicolored .25 .20
3599 A1722 12k multicolored .40 .20
3600 A1722 14k multicolored 1.45 1.00
*Nos. 3596-3600 (5)*
Work of the Botanical Gardens of the Academy of Sciences.

Ukrainian Academy
of
Sciences
A1723

**1969, May 22** **Photo.** **Perf. 12½x12**
3601 A1723 4k brown & yellow .30 .25
Ukrainian Academy of Sciences, 50th anniv.

Film, Camera
and Medal
A1724

Ballet
Dancers
A1725

**1969, June 3** **Litho.** **Perf. 12½x12**
3602 A1724 4k rose car, blk & gold .30 .25
3603 A1725 6k dk brown & multi .30 .20
Intl. Film Festival in Moscow, and 1st Intl.
Young Ballet Artists' Competitions.

Congress Emblem
and Cell
Division — A1726

**1969, June 10** **Photo.** **Perf. 11½**
3605 A1726 6k dp claret, lt bl & yal .50 .30
Protozoologists, 3rd Intl. Cong., Leningrad.

---

Lenin House, Shushensko — A1718c

Smolny
Institute,
Leningrad
A1718d

Places Connected with Lenin: #3586, Straw
Hut, Razliv. #3587, Lenin Museum, Gorki.
#3589, Lenin's room, Kremlin. #3590, Lenin
Museum, Ulyanovsk. #3591, Lenin House,
Ulyanovsk.

**1969** **Photo.** **Perf. 11½**
3582 A1718 4k pale rose & multi .20 .20
3583 A1718a 4k beige & multi .20 .20
3584 A1718b 4k bis brn & multi .20 .20
3585 A1718c 4k gray vio & multi .20 .20
3586 A1718 4k violet & multi .20 .20
3587 A1718 4k blue & multi .20 .20
3588 A1718d 4k brick red & multi .20 .20
3589 A1718 4k rose red & multi .20 .20
3590 A1718 4k lt red brn & multi .20 .20
3591 A1718 4k dull grn & multi .20 .20
*Nos. 3582-3591 (10)* 2.00 2.00
99th anniv. of the birth of Lenin.

Telephone, Transistor Radio and
Trademark — A1719

**1969, Apr. 25** **Perf. 12½x12**
3592 A1719 10k sepia & dp org .40 .20
50th anniversary of VEF Electrical Co.

ILO Emblem and Globe — A1720

**1969, May 9** **Perf. 11**
3593 A1720 6k car rose & gold .35 .20
50th anniversary of the ILO.

Suleiman
Stalsky
A1721

**1969, May 15** **Photo.** **Perf. 12½x12**
3595 A1721 4k tan & ol green .40 .25
Stalsky (1869-1937), Dagestan poet.

Volleyball
A1736

Munkacsy &
"Woman Churning
Butter"
A1737

Design: 6k, Kayak race.

**1969, July 20**     **Photogravure and Engraved**
3619 A1736 4k dp org & red brn   .35 .20
3620 A1736 6k multicolored   .35 .20

Championships; European Junior Volleyball;
European Rowing.

**1969, July 20**     **Photo.**
3621 A1737 6k dk brn, blk & org   .40 .25

Mihaly von Munkacsy (1844-1900), Hungarian painter.

Miners' Monument
A1738

**1969, July 30**
3622 A1738 4k silver & magenta   .40 .20

Centenary of the founding of the city of Donetsk, in the Donets coal basin.

Machine Gun Cart, by Mitrofan
Grekov — A1739

**1969, July 30**     **Engr.**   **Perf. 12½x12**
3623 A1739 4k red brn & brn red   .40 .25

First Mounted Army, 50th anniv.

Barge Pullers Along the Volga, by
Repin — A1740

Ilya E. Repin
(1844-1930),
Self-portrait
A1741

Design: 6k, "Not Expected." 12k,
Confession. 16k, Dnieper Cossacks.

**Perf. 12½x12, 12x12½**    **Litho.**
3624 A1740 4k multicolored   .25 .20
3625 A1740 6k multicolored   .25 .20
3626 A1740 10k bis, red brn &
    blk   .35 .20
3627 A1740 12k multicolored   .50 .20
3628 A1740 16k multicolored   .65 .20
Nos. 3624-3628 (5)   2.00 1.00

Repin Paintings: 6k, "Not Expected." 12k,
Confession. 16k, Dnieper Cossacks.

---

Runner
A1742

Komarov
A1743

Design: 10k, Athlete on rings.

**1969, Aug. 5**     **Perf. 12½x12½**
3629 A1742 4k red, green & blk   .25 .25
3630 A1742 10k grn, lt bl & blk   .25 .25

**Souvenir Sheet**

**Imperf**
3631 A1742 20k red, bister & blk   1.75 .60

9th Trade Union Spartakiad, Moscow.

**1969, Aug. 22**     **Photo.**   **Perf. 12x11½**
3632 A1743 4k olive & brown   .30 .20

V. L. Komarov (1869-1945), botanist.

Hovannes Tumanian, Armenian
Landscape — A1744

Turkmenian Wine
Horn, 2nd
Century — A1745

**1969, Sept. 1**     **Typo.**   **Perf. 12½x12**
3633 A1744 10k blk & peacock blue   .40 .25

Tumanian (1869-1923), Armenian poet.

Designs: 6k, Persian Simurg vessel (giant anthropomorphic bird), 13th century;
Head of goddess Kannon, Korea, 8th century, 12k, Bodhisattva, Tibet, 7th century, 20k,
Statue of Ebisu (tai), Japan, 17th century.

**1969, Sept. 3**    **Litho.**   **Perf. 12½x12½**
3634 A1745 4k blue & multi   .25 .20
3635 A1745 6k lilac & multi   .35 .20
3636 A1745 12k red & multi   .60 .20
3637 A1745 16k blue vio & multi   .70 .20
3638 A1745 20k pale grn & multi   .95 .30
Nos. 3634-3638 (5)   2.85 1.10

Treasures from the State Museum of Oriental Art.

---

Hovannes Tumanian, Armenian (repeated)

Black Stork
Feeding
Young
A1747

**1969, Sept. 10**     **Photo.**   **Perf. 12**
Size: 75x23mm, 10k, 35x23mm,
others

Belovezhskaya Forest reservation: 6k, Doe
and fawn (red deer). 10k, Fighting bison. 12k,
Lynx and cubs. 16k, Wild pig and piglets.

3640 A1747 4k blk, yel grn &
    red   .20 .20
3641 A1747 6k blue grn, dk brn
    & ocher   .25 .20
3642 A1747 10k dk brn, dull org
    & dp org   .55 .20
3643 A1747 12k dk & yel green,
    brn & gray   .65 .20
3644 A1747 16k gray, yel grn &
    dk brown   .65 .20
Nos. 3640-3644 (5)   2.20 1.00

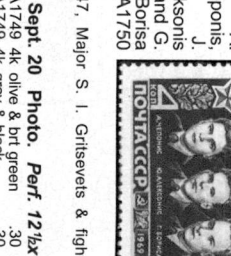

Komitas
A1748

Lisa
Chaikina
A1749

**1969, Sept. 18**    **Typo.**   **Perf. 12½x12**
3645 A1748 6k blk, gray & salmon   .50 .30

Komitas (S. N. Sogomonian, 1869-1935),
Armenian composer.

#3647, Major S. I. Gritsevets & fighter planes.

A.
Cheponis,
J.
Aleksonis
and G.
Borisa
A1750

**1969, Sept. 20**    **Photo.**   **Perf. 12½x12**
3646 A1749 4k olive & brt green   .30 .20
3647 A1749 4k gray & black   .30 .20

**Perf. 11½**
3648 A1750 4k hn brn, brn & buff   .30 .20
Nos. 3646-3648 (3)   .90 .60

Heroes of the Soviet Union.

---

Mahatma Gandhi
(1869-1948)
A1746

**1969, Sept. 10**     **Engr.**
3639 A1746 6k deep brown   .40 .35

East German
Arms, TV Tower
and
Brandenburg
Gate — A1752

**1969, Oct. 7**     **Litho.**
3650 A1752 6k red, black & yel   .35 .20

German Democratic Republic, 20th anniv.

Ivan Petrovich Pavlov (1849-1936),
Physiologist — A1751

**1969, Sept. 26**     **Engr.**
3649 A1751 4k multicolored   .40 .25

National
Emblem
A1754

**1969, Oct. 14**   **Photo.**   **Perf. 12x12½**
3653 A1754 4k gold & red   .40 .25

25th anniversary of the liberation of the
Ukraine from the Nazis.

Aleksei
Vasilievich
Koltsov (1809-
42),
Poet — A1753

**1969, Oct. 14**   **Photo.**   **Perf. 12x12½**
3652 A1753 4k lt blue & brown   .40 .25

---

Stars,
Hammer and
Sickle
A1755

**1969, Oct. 21**    **Typo.**   **Perf. 11½**
3654 A1755 4k vio blue, gold, yel &
    red   .50 .30

52nd anniversary of October Revolution.

Georgy
Shonin
and
Valery
Kubasov
A1756

Designs: No. 3656, Anatoly Filipchenko,
Vladislav Volkov and Viktor Gorbatko. No.
3657, Vladimir Shatalov and Alexey Elisyev.

**Souvenir Sheet**

*Imperf*

Litho.

| | | | |
|---|---|---|---|
| **3683** | | 4.00 | 2.00 |
| a. | A1768 50k indigo & multi | 1.65 | .90 |
| | A1768 50k dark brown & multi | 1.65 | .90 |

Space explorations of the automatic stations Zond 6, Nov. 10-17, 1968, and Zond 7, Aug. 8-14, 1969. No. 3683 contains 27x40mm stamps with simulated perforations.

Model Aircraft — A1769

Technical Sports: 4k, Motorboats. 6k, Parachute jumping.

**1969, Dec. 26** **Engr.** **Perf. 12½x12**

| **3684** | A1769 3k bright magenta | .30 | .20 |
| **3685** | A1769 4k dull blue green | .30 | .20 |
| **3686** | A1769 6k red orange | .30 | .20 |
| | Nos. 3684-3686 (3) | .90 | .60 |

Romanian Arms and Soviet War Memorial, Bucharest — A1770

**1969, Dec. 31** **Photo.** **Perf. 11½**

**3687** A1770 6k rose red & brown .60 .35

25th anniversary of Romania's liberation from fascist rule.

Ostankino Television Tower, Moscow — A1771

**1969, Dec. 31** **Perf. 12**

**3688** A1771 10k multicolored .60 .35

Conversation with Lenin, by A. Shirokov (in front of red table) — A1772

**Typo.**

Paintings: No. 3689, No. 3690, Lenin, by N. Andreyev. Lenin at Marxist Meeting, St. Petersburg, by A. Moravov (behind table). No. 3691, Lenin at Second Party Day, by Y. Vinogradov (leading crowd). No. 3692, First Day of Soviet Power, by F. Modorov (leading Lenin, by Modorov (seated at desk). No. 3695, With Lenin, by V. A. Serov (with cap, in background). No. 3696, Lenin on May 1, 1920, by I. Brodsky (with cap, in foreground). No. 3697, Builder of Communism, by a group of painters (in red). No. 3698, Mastery of Space, by A. Deyneka (rockets).

---

MiG Jet and First MiG Fighter Plane — A1765

**1969, Dec. 12** **Perf. 11½x12**

**3671** A1765 6k red, black & gray .40 .25

Soviet aircraft builders.

Lenin and Flag — A1766

**Typographed and Lithographed**

**1969, Dec. 25** **Perf. 11½**

**3672** A1766 4k gold, blue, red & blk. .40 .25

Happy New Year 1970, birth cent. of Lenin.

Antonov 2 — A1767

Aircraft: 3k, PO-2. 4k, AN1-9. 6k, TsAGI 1-EA, 10k, ANT-20 "Maxim Gorki". 12k, Tupolev-104. 10k, MI3-10 Helicopter. 20k, Ilyushin 62. 50k, Tupolev-144.

**Photogravure and Engraved**

**1969** **Perf. 11½x12**

| **3673** | A1767 2k bister & multi | .20 | .20 |
| **3674** | A1767 3k multicolored | .20 | .20 |
| **3675** | A1767 4k multicolored | .20 | .20 |
| **3676** | A1767 6k multicolored | .25 | .20 |
| **3677** | A1767 10t vio & multi | .40 | .20 |
| **3678** | A1767 12k multicolored | .55 | .20 |
| **3679** | A1767 16k multicolored | .65 | .20 |
| **3680** | A1767 20k multicolored | .70 | .20 |
| | Nos. 3673-3680 (8) | 3.15 | 1.60 |

**Souvenir Sheet**

*Imperf*

**3681** A1767 50k blue & multi 2.50 1.00

History of national aeronautics and aviation. No. 3681 margin contains signs of the zodiac, partly overlapping the stamp.

Designs: #3679, 3681, 12/31; others 12/25.

Photograph of Earth by Zond 7 — A1768

Designs: No. 3683a, same as 10k. No. 3683b, Photograph of moon.

**1969, Dec. 26** **Photo.** **Perf. 12x11½**

**3682** A1768 10k black & multi .40 .30

---

Vasilissa, the Beauty, by Ivan Y. Bilibin — A1761

Designs (Book Illustrations by Ivan Y. Bilibin): 10k, Marya Morevna. 16k, Finist, the Fine Fellow. horiz. 20k, The Golden Cock. 50k, The Sultan and the Czar. The inscriptions on the 16k and 20k are transposed. 4k, 10k, 16k are fairy tales; 20k and 50k are tales by Pushkin.

**1969, Nov. 20** **Litho.**

| **3662** | A1761 4k gray & multi | .25 | .20 |
| **3663** | A1761 10k gray & multi | .60 | .50 |
| **3664** | A1761 16k gray & multi | .75 | .75 |
| **3665** | A1761 20k gray & multi | .85 | .85 |
| **3666** | A1761 50k gray & multi | 3.00 | 1.40 |
| a. | Strip of 5, #3662-3666 | 5.50 | 4.50 |

Illustrator and artist Ivan Y. Bilibin.

USSR Emblems Dropped on Venus, Radar Installation and Orbits — A1762

6k, Interplanetary station, space capsule, orbits.

**1969, Nov. 25** **Photo.** **Perf. 12x11½**

**3667** A1762 4k bister, black & red .25 .20
**3668** A1762 6k gray, lilac rose & blk .25 .20

Completion of the fights of the space stations Venera 5 and Venera 6.

Flags of USSR and Afghanistan — A1763

**1969, Nov. 30** **Photo.** **Perf. 11½**

**3669** A1763 6k red, black & green .35 .25

50th anniversary of diplomatic relations between Russia and Afghanistan.

**Coil Stamp**

Russian State Emblem and Star — A1764

**1969, Nov. 13** **Perf. 11x11½**

**3670** A1764 4k red .60 .30

---

**1969, Oct. 22** **Photo.** **Perf. 12½x12**

| **3655** | A1756 10k black & gold | .30 | .20 |
| **3656** | A1756 10k black & gold | .30 | .20 |
| **3657** | A1756 10k black & gold | .30 | .20 |
| | a. Strip of 3, #3655-3657 | 1.25 | .30 |

Group flight of the space ships Soyuz 6, Soyuz 7 and Soyuz 8, Oct. 11-13.

Lenin as a Youth — A1757

**1969, Oct. 25** **Engr.** **Perf. 11½**

**3658** A1757 4k dark red, pink .40 .25

1st Soviet Youth Philatelic Exhibition, Kiev, dedicated to Lenin's 100th birthday.

Emblem of Communications Unit of Army — A1758

**Photo.**

**3659** A1758 4k red, red & bister .40 .25

50th anniversary of the Communications Troops of Soviet Army.

**1969, Oct. 30**

**Souvenir Sheet**

Lenin and Quotation — A1759

**Lithographed and Embossed**

**1969, Nov. 6** *Imperf.*

**3660** A1759 50k red, gold & pink 2.25 1.00

52nd anniv. of the October Revolution.

Cover of "Rules of the Kolkhoz" and Farm Woman's Monument — A1760

**1969, Nov. 18** **Photo.** **Perf. 12½x12**

**3661** A1760 4k brown & gold .40 .25

3rd All Union Collective Farmers' Congress, Moscow, Nov.-Dec.

**1970, Jan. 1    Litho.    Perf. 12**

| | | | |
|---|---|---|---|
| 3689 | A1772 | 4k multicolored | .20 .20 |
| 3690 | A1772 | 4k multicolored | .20 .20 |
| 3691 | A1772 | 4k multicolored | .20 .20 |
| 3692 | A1772 | 4k multicolored | .20 .20 |
| 3693 | A1772 | 4k multicolored | .20 .20 |
| 3694 | A1772 | 4k multicolored | .20 .20 |
| 3695 | A1772 | 4k multicolored | .20 .20 |
| 3696 | A1772 | 4k multicolored | .20 .20 |
| 3697 | A1772 | 4k multicolored | .20 .20 |
| 3698 | A1772 | 4k multicolored | .20 .20 |
| | | Nos. 3689-3698 (10) | 2.00 2.00 |

Centenary of birth of Lenin (1870-1924).

Map of Antarctic, "Mirny" and "Vostok" — A1773

150th anniversary of the Bellingshausen-Lazarev Antarctic expedition.

**1970, Jan. 27    Photo.    Perf. 11½**

| | | | |
|---|---|---|---|
| 3699 | A1773 | 4k multicolored | .25 .25 |
| 3700 | A1773 | 16k multicolored | .70 .25 |

Design: 16k, Camp and map of the Antarctic with Soviet Antarctic bases.

F. W. Sychkov and "Tobogganing" — A1774

**1970, Jan. 27    Perf. 12½x12**

| | | | |
|---|---|---|---|
| 3701 | A1774 | 4k sepia & vio blue | .40 .25 |

F. W. Sychkov (1870-1958), painter.

**1970, Feb. 10    Perf. 12x12½**

| | | | |
|---|---|---|---|
| 3702 | A1775 | 4k brown olive & brn | .30 .20 |
| 3703 | A1775 | 4k dark gray & plum | .30 .20 |

Heroes of the Soviet Union.

Design: No. 3703, Sgt. V. Peshekhonov.

Col. V. B. Borsoyev A1775

**1970, Feb. 26    Photo.    Perf. 11½**

| | | | |
|---|---|---|---|
| 3704 | A1776 | 6k bis, Prus bl & dk brn | .40 .30 |

Russian Geographical Society, 125th anniv.

Geographical Society Emblem and Globes — A1776

Torch of Peace — A1777

**1970, Mar. 3    Litho.    Perf. 12**

| | | | |
|---|---|---|---|
| 3705 | A1777 | 6k blue green & tan | .30 .20 |

Int'l. Women's Solidarity Day, Mar. 8.

Symbols of Russian Arts and Crafts — A1778

**1970, Mar. 10    Photo.    Perf. 11½**

| | | | |
|---|---|---|---|
| 3706 | A1778 | 4k dk blue grn, red & black | .20 .20 |
| 3707 | A1778 | 6k blk, silver & red | .25 .20 |
| 3708 | A1778 | 10k vio bl, sil & red | .25 .20 |
| | | Nos. 3706-3708 (3) | .75 .60 |

Designs: 6k, Russian EXPO '70 pavilion. 10k, Boy holding model ship.

Lenin — A1779

**1970, Mar. 14    Photo.    Perf. 11½**

| | | | |
|---|---|---|---|
| 3709 | A1779 | 50k dark red | 2.00 1.00 |

EXPO '70 Int'l. Exhibition, Osaka, Japan, 3/15-4/13.

**Souvenir Sheet**
**Engr. & Litho.**
**Perf. 12x12½**

| | | | |
|---|---|---|---|
| 3710 | A1780 | 4k red, blk & gold | .40 .30 |

**1970, Mar. 14    Imperf**

| | | | |
|---|---|---|---|
| 3711 | A1780 | 20k red, blk & gold | 2.00 1.00 |

**Photogravure and Embossed**
**Souvenir Sheet**

USSR Philatelic Exhibition dedicated to the centenary of the birth of Lenin.

Friendship Tree, Sochi — A1781

**1970, Mar. 18    Litho.    Perf. 11½**

| | | | |
|---|---|---|---|
| 3712 | A1781 | 10k multicolored | .50 .30 |

Friendship among people. Printed with alternating label.

National Emblem, Hammer and Sickle, Oil Derricks A1782

**1970, Mar. 18    Photo.    Perf. 11½**

| | | | |
|---|---|---|---|
| 3713 | A1782 | 4k car rose & gold | .35 .25 |

Azerbaijan Republic, 50th anniversary.

Ice Hockey Players A1783

**1970, Mar. 18**

| | | | |
|---|---|---|---|
| 3714 | A1783 | 6k blue & slate green | .35 .20 |

World Ice Hockey Championships, Sweden.

Overprinted Inscription

**1970, Apr. 1    Photo.    Perf. 11½**

| | | | |
|---|---|---|---|
| 3715 | A1783 | 6k blue & slate green | .40 .25 |

Soviet hockey players as the tenfold world champions.

D. N. Medvedev A1784

Portrait No. 3717, K. P. Orlovsky.

**1970, Mar. 26    Engr.    Perf. 12x12½**

| | | | |
|---|---|---|---|
| 3716 | A1784 | 4k chocolate | .25 .20 |
| 3717 | A1784 | 4k dk redsh brown | .25 .20 |

Heroes of the Soviet Union.

Worker, Books, Globes and UNESCO Symbol A1785

**1970, Mar. 26    Photo.    Perf. 12½x12**

| | | | |
|---|---|---|---|
| 3718 | A1785 | 6k car lake & ocher | .30 .20 |

UNESCO-sponsored Lenin Symposium, Tampere, Finland, Apr. 6-10.

Hungarian Arms, Budapest Landmarks A1786

**1970, Apr. 4    Typo.    Perf. 11½**

| | | | |
|---|---|---|---|
| 3719 | A1786 | 6k multicolored | .30 .20 |

Liberation of Hungary, 25th anniv.

Cosmonauts' Emblem A1787

**1970, Apr. 12    Litho.    Perf. 11½**

| | | | |
|---|---|---|---|
| 3720 | A1787 | 6k buff & multi | .30 .20 |

Cosmonauts' Day.

Lenin, 1891 — A1788

Designs: Various portraits of Lenin.

**1970, Apr. 15    Lithographed and Typographed    Perf. 12½x12**

| | | | |
|---|---|---|---|
| 3721 | A1788 | 2k green & gold | .20 .20 |
| 3722 | A1788 | 2k oil gray & gold | .20 .20 |
| 3723 | A1788 | 4k vio blue & gold | .20 .20 |
| 3724 | A1788 | 4k dark brn & gold | .20 .20 |
| 3725 | A1788 | 6k red brn & gold | .20 .20 |
| 3726 | A1788 | 6k lake & gold | .20 .20 |
| 3727 | A1788 | 6k dk brn & gold | .20 .20 |
| 3728 | A1788 | 10k dk brn & gold | .25 .20 |
| 3729 | A1788 | 10k dark rose brown & gold | .35 .20 |
| 3730 | A1788 | 12k blk, sil & gold | .45 .20 |
| | | Nos. 3721-3730 (10) | 2.70 2.00 |

**Souvenir Sheet**
**Photo.**
**1970, Apr. 22    Litho.    Typo.**

| | | | |
|---|---|---|---|
| 3731 | A1788 | 20k blk, silver & gold | 2.00 .70 |

Cent. of the birth of Lenin. Issued in sheets of 8 stamps surrounded by 16 labels showing Lenin-connected buildings, books, coats of arms and medals. No. 3731 contains one stamp in same design as No. 3729.

Order of Victory — A1789

**1970, May 8    Photo.    Perf. 11½**

| | | | |
|---|---|---|---|
| 3732 | A1789 | 1k red lilac, gold & gray | .20 .20 |
| 3733 | A1789 | 2k dark brn, gold & red | .20 .20 |
| 3734 | A1789 | 3k dark brn, gold & red | .20 .20 |
| 3735 | A1789 | 4k dark brn, gold & red | .20 .20 |

Designs: 2k, Monument to the Unknown Soldier, Moscow. 3k, Victory Monument, Berlin-Treptow. 4k, Order of the Great Patriotic War. 10k, Gold Star of Order of Hero of the Soviet Union. 30k, Like 1k.

Magnifying Glass over Stamp, and Covers — A1804

**1970, Aug. 31   Photo.   Perf. 12x12½**
3764   A1804   4k red & silver   .50   .25
2nd All-Union Philatelists' Cong., Moscow.

Pioneers' Badge — A1805

Soviet general education: 2k, Lenin and Children, monument, 4k, Star and scenes from play "Zarnitsa."

**1970, Sept. 24   Photo.   Perf. 11½**
3765   A1805   1k gray, red & gold   .25   .20
3766   A1805   2k brn red & slate grn   .25   .20
3767   A1805   4k lt ol, car & gold   .75   .60
Nos. 3765-3767 (3)

Yerevan University A1806

**1970, Sept. 24   Photo.   Perf. 12½x12**
3768   A1806   4k ultra & salmon pink   .30   .20
Yerevan State University, 50th anniv.

Library Bookplate, Vilnius University A1807

**1970, Oct.   Typo.   Perf. 12x12½**
3772   A1807   4k silver, gray & blk   .50   .25
Vilnius University Library, 400th anniv.

Woman Holding Flowers — A1808

**1970, Oct. 30   Photo.   .30   .20**
3773   A1808   6k blue & lt brown
25th anniversary of the International Democratic Federation of Women.

---

Armenian Woman and Symbols of Agriculture and Industry A1799

Design: No. 3751, Kazakh woman and symbols of agriculture and industry.

**1970, June 16   Photo.   Perf. 11½**
3750   A1799   4k red brn & silver   .30   .30
3751   A1799   4k brt rose lilac & gold   .30   .30
50th anniv. of the Armenian & Kazakh Soviet Socialist Republics.

Missile Cruiser "Grozny" — A1800

Soviet Warships: 3k, Cruiser "Aurora." 10k, Cruiser "October Revolution." 12k, Missile cruiser "Varyag." 20k, Atomic submarine "Leninsky Komsomol."

**1970, July 26   Photo.   Perf. 11½x12**
3752   A1800   3k lilac, pink & blk   .25   .20
3753   A1800   4k yellow & black   .25   .20
3754   A1800   10k rose & black   .45   .25
3755   A1800   12k buff & dk brown   .45   .20
3756   A1800   20k blue grn, dk brn & vio blue   .90   .20
   2.25   1.00
Nos. 3752-3756 (5)

Navy Day.

"History," Petroglyphs, Sputnik and Emblem — A1802

Soviet and Polish Workers and Flags — A1801

**1970, July 26   Perf. 12**
3757   A1801   6k red & slate   .30   .20
25th anniversary of the Treaty of Friendship, Collaboration and Mutual Assistance between USSR and Poland.

**1970, Aug. 16   Perf. 11½**
3758   A1802   4k red brn, buff & blue   .40   .25
13th International Congress of Historical Sciences in Moscow.

Mandarin Ducks A1803

Animals from the Sikhote-Alin Reserve: 6k, Pine marten. 10k, Asiatic black bear, vert. 16k, Red deer. 20k, Ussurian tiger.

**Perf. 12½x12, 12x12½   Litho.**
3759   A1803   4k multicolored   .20   .20
3760   A1803   6k multicolored   .25   .20
3761   A1803   10k multicolored   .45   .20
3762   A1803   16k ultra & multi   .45   .20
3763   A1803   20k gray & multi   1.80   1.00
Nos. 3759-3763 (5)

---

Petrozavodsk. No. 3744, Cheboksary. No. 3744A, Elista. No. 3744B, Izhevsk. No. 3744C, Yoshkar-Ola.

**1970   Engr.   Perf. 12x12½**
3742   A1794   4k violet blue   .50   .20
3743   A1794   4k green   .50   .20
3744   A1794   4k dark carmine   .50   .20
3744A   A1794   4k red   .50   .20
3744B   A1794   4k dark green   .50   .20
3744C   A1794   4k dark carmine   .50   1.20
   3.00   1.20
Nos. 3742-3744C (6)

50th annivs. of the Tatar (#3742), Karelian (#3743), Chuvash (#3744), Kalmyk (#3744A), Udmurt (#3744B) and Mari (#3744C) autonomous SSRs.
Issued: #3742, 5/27; #3743, 6/5; #3744, 6/24; #3744A-3744B, 10/22; #3744C, 11/4.
See Nos. 3814-3823, 4286, 4806.

9th World Soccer Championships for the Jules Rimet Cup, Mexico City, May 29-June 21 — A1795

10k, Woman athlete on balancing bar.

**1970, May 31   Photo.   Perf. 11½**
3745   A1795   10k lt gray & brt rose   .40   .20
3746   A1795   16k dk grn & org brn   .65   .20
17th World Gymnastics Championships, Ljubljana, Oct. 22-27 (#3745).

Sword into Plowshare Statue, UN, NY   A1706

**1970, June 1   Litho.   Perf. 12x12½**
3747   A1796   12k gray & lake   .50   .25
26th anniversary of the United Nations.

Soyuz 9, Andrian Nikolayev, Vitaly Sevastyanov A1797

**1970, June 7   Photo.   Perf. 12x11½**
3748   A1797   10k multicolored   .40   .20
424 hour space flight of Soyuz 9, June 1-19.

Friedrich Engels A1798

**1970, June 16   Engr.   Perf. 12x12½**
3749   A1798   4k chocolate & ver   .35   .20
Friedrich Engels (1820-1895). German socialist, collaborator with Karl Marx.

---

3736   A1789   10k red lil, gold & red   .35   .20
Nos. 3732-3736 (5)   1.15   1.00

**Souvenir Sheet**

*Imperf*
3737   A1789   30k dark red, gold & gray   1.75   .60
25th anniv. of victory in WWII. No. 3737 has simulated perforations.

**Arms-Landmark Type of 1970**

Czechoslovakia arms and view of Prague.

**1970, May 8   Typo.   Perf. 12½**
3738   A1786   6k dk brown & multi   .35   .20
25th anniversary of the liberation of Czechoslovakia from the Germans.

Young Fighters, and Youth Federation Emblem A1791

**1970, May 20   Litho.   Perf. 12**
3739   A1791   6k blue & black   .30   .20
25th anniversary of the World Federation of Democratic Youth.

Lenin A1792

**1970, May 20   Photo.   Perf. 11½**
3740   A1792   6k red   .30   .20
Intl. Youth Meeting dedicated to the cent. of the birth of Lenin, UN, NY, June 1970.

Komsomol Emblem with Lenin — A1793

**1970, May 20   Litho.   Perf. 12**
3741   A1793   4k red, yel & purple   .30   .20
16th Congress of the Young Communist League, May 26-30.

Hammer and Sickle Emblem and Building of Supreme Soviet in Kazan A1794

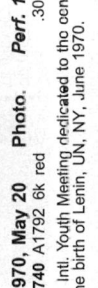

#3744

#3744B

#3744C

Designs (Hammer-Sickle Emblem and Supreme Soviet Building in): No. 3743,

## Farm Woman, Cattle Farm — A1809

**1970, Oct. 30**    **Perf. 11½x12**
3774 A1809 4k olive & red .20 .20
3775 A1809 4k ocher, yellow & red .20 .20
3776 A1809 4k lt vio, yellow & red .20 .20
   Nos. 3774-3776 (3) .60 .60

Designs: No. 3775, Farmer and mechanical farm equipment. No. 3776, Farmer, fertilization equipment and plane.

Aims of the new agricultural 5-year plan.

## Lenin — A1810

СЛАВА ОКТЯБРЮ!

**Lithographed and Embossed**

**1970, Nov. 3**    **Perf. 12½x12**
3777 A1810 4k red & gold .30 .20

**Souvenir Sheet**

**1970, Nov. 3**
3778 A1810 30k red & gold 1.75 .75

53rd anniv. of the October Revolution.

### No. 3389 Overprinted in Gold

**1970, Nov. 3**    **Perf. 11½**
3779 A1641 4k gold & multi .80 .75

50th anniversary of the GOELRO Plan for the electrification of Russia.

## Spasski Tower and Fir Branch — A1811

**1970, Nov. 23 Litho.**    **Perf. 12½x12**
3780 A1811 6k multicolored .30 .20

New Year, 1971.

## Baykov — A1812

**1970, Nov. 25 Photo.**    **Perf. 12x12½**
3781 A1812 4k sepia & golden brn .30 .20

Baykov (1870-1946), metallurgist and academician.

### Portrait Type of 1968

Portrait: No. 3782, A. D. Tsyurupa.

**1970, Nov. 25 Photo.**    **Perf. 12x12½**
3782 A1688 6k brown & salmon .35 .25

Tsyurupa (1870-1928), First Vice Chairman of the Soviet of People's Commissars.

---

## Vasily Blazhenny Church, Red Square A1813

Tourist publicity: 6k, Performance of Swan Lake. 10k, Two deer. 12k, Folk art. 14k, Sword into Plowshare statue, by E. Vouchetich, and museums. 16k, Automobiles and woman photographer.

### Photogravure and Engraved

**1970, Nov. 29**    **Perf. 12x11½**

**Frame in Brown Orange**
3783 A1813 4k multicolored .35 .20
3784 A1813 6k multicolored .45 .20
3785 A1813 10k brn org & sl .50 .20
3786 A1813 12k multicolored .35 .20
3787 A1813 14k multicolored .50 .20
3788 A1813 16k multicolored .65 .20
   Nos. 3783-3788 (6) 2.35 1.20

## Daisy — A1814

**1970, Nov. 29 Litho.**    **Perf. 11½**
3789 A1814 4k shown .20 .20
3790 A1814 6k Dahlia .20 .20
3791 A1814 10k Phlox .40 .20
3792 A1814 12k Aster .50 .20
3793 A1814 16k Clementis .85 .20
   Nos. 3789-3793 (5) 2.15 1.00

## UN Emblem, African Mother and Child, Broken Chain — A1815

**1970, Dec. 10 Photo.**    **Perf. 12x12½**
3794 A1815 10k blue & dk brown .50 .20

United Nations Declaration on Colonial Independence, 10th anniversary.

## Ludwig van Beethoven (1770-1827), Composer — A1816

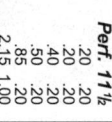 

**1970, Dec. 16 Engr.**    **Perf. 12½x12**
3795 A1816 10k deep claret, pink .50 .30

---

## Skating — A1817

Design: 10k, Skiing.

**1970, Dec. 18 Photo.**    **Perf. 11½**
3796 A1817 4k light gray, ultra & .20 .20
   dark red
3797 A1817 10k light gray, brt .30 .20
   green & brown

1971 Trade Union Winter Games.

## Luna 16 — A1818

**1970, Dec. Photo.**    **Perf. 11½**
3798 A1818 10k gray blue .35 .20
3799 A1818 10k dk purple .35 .20
3800 A1818 10k gray blue 1.05 .60
   Nos. 3798-3800 (3)

**Souvenir Sheet**
3801    Sheet of 3
  a. A1818 20k blue 2.10 1.00
  b. A1818 20k dark purple .70 .25
  c. A1818 20k blue .70 .25

Designs: No. 3799, 3801b, Luna 16 leaving moon. No. 3800, 3801c, Capsule landing on earth. No. 3801a, like Nos. 3798.

Luna 16 unmanned, automatic moon mission, Sept. 12-24, 1970.

Nos. 3801a-3801c have attached labels (no perf. between vignette and label). Issue dates: No. 3801, Dec. 18; Nos. 3798-3800, Dec. 28.

---

## The Constabile Madonna, by Raphael A1819

**1970, Dec. 23 Litho.**    **Perf. 12x12½, 12½x12**
3802 A1819 3k gray & multi .20 .20
3803 A1819 4k gray & multi .20 .20
3804 A1819 10k gray & multi .50 .20
3805 A1819 12k gray & multi .50 .20
3806 A1819 16k gray & multi .60 .20
3807 A1819 20k gray & multi .85 .20
3808 A1819 30k gray & multi 1.75 .25
   Nos. 3802-3808 (7) 4.60 1.45

**Souvenir Sheet**
**Imperf.**
3809 A1819 50k gold & multi 3.00 .90

Paintings: 4k, Apostles Peter and Paul, by El Greco. 10k, Perseus and Andromeda, by Rubens. 12k, The Prodigal Son, by Rembrandt. 16k, Family Portrait, by van Dyck. 20k, The Actress Jeanne Samary, by Renoir. 30k, Woman with Fruit, by Gauguin. 50k, The Litte Madonna, by da Vinci. All paintings from the Hermitage in Leningrad, except 20k from Pushkin Museum, Moscow.

## Harry Pollyt and Shipyard A1820

**1970, Dec. 31 Photo.**    **Perf. 12**
3810 A1820 10k maroon & brown .40 .30

Pollyt (1890-1960), British labor leader.

---

## International Cooperative Alliance A1821

**1970, Dec. 31**    **Perf. 11½x12**
3811 A1821 12k yel green & red .40 .30

Intl. Cooperative Alliance, 75th anniv.

## Lenin — A1822

**1971, Jan. 1**    **Perf. 12**
3812 A1822 4k red & gold .25 .20

Year of the 24th Congress of the Communist Party of the Soviet Union.

## Georgian Republic Flag A1823

**Republic Anniversaries Type of 1970**

**1971, Jan. 12 Litho.**    **Perf. 11½**
3813 A1823 4k ol bister & multi .25 .20

Georgian SSR, 50th anniversary.

#3816    #3818

**1971-74 Engr.**    **Perf. 12½x12**
3814 A1794 4k dk blue green .20 .20
3815 A1794 4k rose red .20 .20
3816 A1794 4k red .20 .20
3817 A1794 4k blue .20 .20
3818 A1794 4k brt bl (72) .20 .20
3819 A1794 4k car rose (72) .20 .20
3820 A1794 4k rose (73) .20 .20
3821 A1794 4k brt ultra (73) .20 .20
3822 A1794 4k golden brn (74) .20 .20

**Litho.**
3823 A1794 4k dark red (74) .20 .20
   Nos. 3814-3823 (10) 2.00 2.00

Designs (Hammer-Sickle Emblem and): No. 3814, Supreme Soviet Building, Makhachkala. No. 3815, Fruit, ship, mountain, conveyor. No. 3816, Grapes, refinery, ship. No. 3817, Supreme Soviet Building, Nalchik. No. 3818, Supreme Soviet Building, Syktyvkar, and lumber industry. No. 3819, Natural resources, dam, mining. No. 3820, Industrial installations and natural products. No. 3821, Ship, "industry." No. 3822, Grapes, pylons and mountains. No. 3823, Kazbek Mountain, industrial installations, produce.

50th anniversaries of Dagestan (#3814), Abkhazian (#3815), Adzhar (#3816), Kabardino-Balkarian (#3817), Komi (#3818), Yakut (#3819), Checheno-Ingush (#3820), Buryat (#3821), Nakhichevan (#3822), and North Ossetian (#3823) autonomous SSRs.

No. 3823 also for bicentenary of Ossetia's union with Russia.

Issued: #3814, 1/20; #3815, 3/3; 6/16; #3817-3818, 8/17; #3819, 4/20; #3816, 11/22; #3021, 5/24; #3822, 2/6; #3823, 7/7.

RUSSIA

Lt. Col. Nikolai I.
Vlasov — A1839

*Perf. 12x12½*

**1971, May 9   Photo.**
3846  A1839  4k gray olive & brn    .30  .20
Hero of the Soviet Union.

Khafiz Shirazi,
Tadzhik-Persian
Poet, 650th Birth
Anniv. — A1840

**1971, May 9      Litho.**    .25  .20
3847  A1840  4k olive, brn & black

GAZ-66 — A1841

Soviet Cars: 3k, BelAZ-540 truck. No. 3850,
Moskvich-412.  No.  3851,  7AZ-968.  10k,
Volga.

*Perf. 11x11½*

**1971, May 12   Photo.**
3848  A1841  2k yellow & multi    .20  .20
3849  A1841  3k lt blue & multi    .20  .20
3850  A1841  4k lt blue & multi    .20  .20
3851  A1841  4k lt gray & multi    .20  .20
3852  A1841  10k lt lilac & multi    1.00  1.00
Nos. 3848-3852 (5)

Satellite
A1843

Bogomolets
A1842

**1971, May 24     Photo.**
3853  A1842  4k orange & black    .25  .20
A. A. Bogomolets, physician, 90th birth
anniv.

*Perf. 11½*

**1971, June 9**      .25  .20
3854  A1843  6k blue & multi
15th General Assembly of the International
Union of Geodesics and Geophysics.

Symbols of
Science
and History
A1844

*Perf. 12*

**1971, June 9**      .25  .20
3855  A1844  6k green & gray
13th Congress of Science History.

---

Space
Research
A1834

**1971, Mar. 30**      .40  .20
3841  A1834  12k slate bl & vio brn
Cosmonauts' Day, Apr. 12.

E. Birznieks-
Upitis (1871-
1960), Latvian
Writer — A1835

*Perf. 12x12½*      .25  .20

**1971, Feb. 25**
3842  A1835  4k red brown & gray

Bee and
Blossom — A1836

*Perf. 11½*      .25  .20

**1971, Apr. 1**
3843  A1836  6k olive & multi
23rd International Beekeeping Congress,
Moscow, Aug. 22-Sept. 2.

Souvenir Sheet

Cosmonauts and Spacecraft — A1837

Designs:  10k,  Vostok.  No.  3844b,  Yuri
Gagarin.  No.  3844c,  First  man  walking  in
space. 16k, First orbital station.

*Perf. 12*

**1971, Apr. 12      Litho.**
3844  A1837   Sheet of 4    3.00  1.00
   a.    10k violet brown    .45  .20
  b.-c.   12k Prussian green    .45  .20
   d.    16k violet brown    .50  .20
10th anniv. of man's 1st flight into space.
Size of stamps: 26x19mm.

Lenin Memorial, Ulyanovsk — A1838

*Perf. 12*

**1971, Apr. 16      Photo.**      .25  .20
3845  A1838  4k cop red & ol bister
Lenin's birthday. Memorial was built for centenary celebration of his birth.

---

"Summer" Dance — A1829

Dancers of Russian Folk Dance Ensemble:
No. 3830, "On the Skating Rink." No. 3831,
Ukrainian  dance  "Hopak."  No.  3832,
Adzharian dance. No. 3833, Gypsy dance.

*Perf. 12½x12*

**1971, Feb. 25   Litho.**
3829  A1829  10k bister & multi    .40  .20
3830  A1829  10k olive & multi    .40  .20
3831  A1829  10k olive bis & multi    .40  .20
3832  A1829  10k gray & multi    .40  .20
3833  A1829  10k grnsh gray &
                        multi    .40  1.00
Nos. 3829-3833 (5)    2.00  1.00

Luna 17 on
Moon
A1830

Designs:  No.  3835,  Ground  control.  No.
3836, Separation of Lunokhod 1 and carrier.
16k, Lunokhod 1 in operation.

*Perf. 11½*

**1971, Mar. 16   Photo.**
3834  A1830  10k dp vio & sepia    .35  .20
3835  A1830  10k dk blue & sepia    .50  .20
3836  A1830  12k dk blue & sepia    .50  .20
3837  A1830  16k dp vio & sepia    .65  .20
   a.    Souv. sheet of 4    2.50  1.00
Nos. 3834-3837 (4)    2.00  .80

Luna 17 unmanned, automated moon mission, Nov. 10-17, 1970. No. 3837a contains
Nos. 3834-3037, size 32x21mm each.

Paris Commune,
Cent. — A1831

*Perf. 12*

**1971, Mar. 18   Litho.**    .30  .20
3838  A1831  6k red & black

Industry,
Science,
Culture
A1832

*Perf. 11½*

**1971, Mar. 29**      .25  .20
3839  A1832  6k bister, brn & red
24th Communist Party Cong., 3/30-4/3.

Yuri
Gagarin
Medal
A1833

*Perf. 11½*

**1971, Mar. 30   Photo.**      .40  .20
3840  A1833  10k brown & lemon
10th anniv. of man's first flight into space.

---

Tower of
Genoa,
Cranes,
Hammer and
Sickle
A1824

*Perf. 12*

**1971, Jan. 28   Typo.**      .30  .20
3824  A1824  10k dk red, gray & yel
Founding  of  Feodosiya,  Crimea,  2500th
anniv.

Palace of Culture,
Kiev — A1825

*Perf. 11½*

**1971, Feb. 16      Photo.**      .25  .20
3825  A1825  4k red, bister & blue
Ukrainian Communist Party, 24th cong.

N. Gubin, I.
Chernykh, S.
Kosinov
A1826

*Perf. 12½x12*

**1971, Feb. 16**      .25  .20
3826  A1826  4k slate grn & vio brn
Heroes of the Soviet Union.

"Industry and
Agriculture"
A1827

*Perf. 12x12½*

**1971, Feb. 16**      .25  .20
3827  A1827  6k olive bister & red
State Planning Organization, 50th anniv.

Lesya Ukrayinka
(1871-1913),
Ukrainian
Poet — A1828

**1971, Feb. 25**      .25  .20
3828  A1828  4k orange red & bister

Oil Derrick
& Symbols
A1845

**1971, June 9**
3856 A1845 6k multicolored

8th World Oil Congress.

**Perf. 11½**
.20 .20

**1971, June 16**
3857 A1846 6k red, gold & black

50th anniversary of Mongolian revolution.

Sukhe Bator Monument — A1846

**Typo.**
**Perf. 12**
.25 .20

Monument
of
Defenders
of Liepaja
A1847

**1971, June 21**
3858 A1847 4k gray, black & brn

30th anniversary of the defense of Liepaja
(Libau) against invading Germans.

**Photo.**
.30 .25

**1971, June 21**
3859 A1848 6k black, grn & ultra

Antarctic Treaty pledging peaceful uses of &
scientific co-operation in Antarctica, 10th
anniv.

Map of Antarctica
and
Station — A1848

**Perf. 12**
.25 .20

**1971, June 21**
3860 A1849 10k black, red & ultra

50th anniversary of Soviet Hydrometeoro-
logical service.

Weather Map,
Plane, Ship and
Satellite — A1849

**Engraved and Photogravure**
**Perf. 11½**
.50 .30

**1971, June 21**
3861 A1850 6k dk red & slate

International Federation of Resistance
Fighters (FIR), 20th anniversary.

FIR Emblem,
"Homeland," by E.
Vouchetich
A1850

**Perf. 12x12½**
.25 .20

---

Designs: 4k, Archery (women). 6k,
Dressage. 10k, Basketball. 12k, Wrestling.

Discus and
Running
A1851

**Lithographed and Engraved**
**1971, June 24**
**Perf. 11½**
3862 A1851 3k violet blue, rose .20 .20
3863 A1851 4k slate grn, pale pink .20 .20
3864 A1851 6k red brn, apple grn .30 .20
3865 A1851 10k dk pur, gray blue .40 .20
3866 A1851 12k red brn, yellow .50 .20
Nos. 3862-3866 (5) 1.60 1.00

5th Summer Spartakiad.

Benois
Madonna, by
da Vinci
A1852

Paintings: 4k, Mary Magdalene, by Titian.
10k, The Washerwoman, by Jean Simeon
Chardin, horiz. 12k, Portrait of a Young Man,
by Frans Hals. 14k, Tancred and Arminia, by
Nicolas Poussin, horiz. 16k, Girl with Fruit, by
Murillo. 20k, Girl with Ball, by Picasso.

**1971, July 7**
**Perf. 12x12½, 12½x12**
**Litho.**
3867 A1852 2k bister & multi .20 .20
3868 A1852 4k bister & multi .20 .20
3869 A1852 10k bister & multi .40 .20
3870 A1852 12k bister & multi .45 .20
3871 A1852 14k bister & multi .55 .20
3872 A1852 16k bister & multi .75 .20
3873 A1852 20k bister & multi 3.20 1.40
Nos. 3667-3873 (7)

Foreign master works in Russian museums.

Star
Emblem
and Letters
A1854

**1971, July 14**
3875 A1854 4k oliver, blue & black .25 .20

International Letter Writing Week.

Kazakhstan Flag, Lenin
Badge — A1853

**1971, July 7**
**Photo.**
**Perf. 11½**
3874 A1853 4k blue, red & brown .25 .20

50th anniversary of the Kazakh Communist
Youth League.

---

Nikolai A.
Nekrasov, by
Ivan N.
Kramskoi
A1855

**1971, July 14**
**Litho.**
**Perf. 12x12½**
3876 A1855 4k citron & multi .20 .20
3877 A1855 10k gray blue & multi .25 .20
3878 A1855 12k multicolored .30 .20
Nos. 3876-3878 (3) .75 .60

Nikolai Alekseevich Nekrasov (1821-1877),
poet, Fedor Mikhailovich Dostoevski (1821-
1881), novelist, Spendiarov
Armenian composer (1871-1928).
See Nos. 4056-4057.

Zachary
Paliashvili (1871-
1933), Georgian
Composer and
Score — A1856

**1971, Aug. 3**
**Photo.**
**Perf. 12x12½**
3879 A1856 4k brown .25 .20

Gorki
Kremlin, Stag
and Hydrofoil
A1857

**1971, Aug. 3**
**Litho.**
**Perf. 12**
3880 A1857 16k multicolored .60 .25

Gorki (formerly Nizhni Novgorod), 750th
anniv. See Nos. 3889, 3910-3914.

Federation
Emblem
and
Students
A1858

**1971, Aug. 3**
**Photo.**
**Perf. 11½**
3881 A1858 6k ultra & multi .25 .20

Intl. Students Federation, 25th anniv.

Common
Dolphins
A1859

**Photogravure and Engraved**
**1971, Aug. 12**
**Perf. 11½**
3882 A1859 4k silver & multi .20 .20
3883 A1859 6k silver & multi .20 .20
3884 A1859 10k silver & multi .30 .20

Sea Mammals: 6k, Sea otter. 10k, Nar-
whals. 12k, Walrus. 14k, Ribbon seals.

---

Miner's Star of
Valor — A1860

**1971, Aug. 17**
**Photo.**
**Perf. 11½**
3887 A1860 4k bister, black & red .25 .20

250th anniversary of the discovery of coal in
the Donets Basin.

**1971, Aug. 24**
**Photo.**
**Perf. 12**
3888 A1861 6k magenta & dk ol .25 .20

Ernest
Rutherford
and
Diagram of
Movement
of Atomic
Particles
A1861

Rutherford (1871-1937), British physicist.

Gorki and Gorki
Statue — A1862

**1971, Sept. 14**
**Perf. 11½**
3889 A1862 4k steel blue & multi .25 .20

Gorki (see #3880).

**1971, Sept. 14**
3890 A1863 10k black, red & gold .30 .20

New Year 1972.

Troika and
Spasski
Tower
A1863

Automatic Production Center — A1864

**1971, Sept. 29**
**Photo.**
**Perf. 12x11½**
3891 A1864 4k purple, red & blk .20 .20
3892 A1864 4k ocher, red & brn .20 .20
3893 A1864 4k yel, olive & red .20 .20
3894 A1864 4k bister, red & brn .20 .20
3895 A1864 4k ultra, red & slate 1.00 1.00
Nos. 3891-3895 (5)

#3892, Agricultural development. #3893,
Family in shopping center. #3894, Hydro-gen-
erators, thermoelectric station. #3895, Marchers, flags, books inscribed Marx and Lenin.

Resolutions of 24th Soviet Union Communist Party Congress.

**1971, Aug. 17**
3885 A1859 12k silver & multi .35 .20
3886 A1859 14k silver & multi .45 .20
Nos. 3882-3886 (5) 1.50 1.00

**Peter I Reviewing Fleet, 1723 — A1877**

History of Russian Fleet: 4k, Oriol, first ship built in Eddinovo, 1668, vert. 6k, Battleship Poltava, 1712, vert. 12k, Armed ship Ingermanland, 1715, vert. 16k, Frigate Vladimir, 1848.

**1971, Dec. 15    Engr. & Photo.    *Perf. 11½x12, 12x11½***
| | | | | |
|---|---|---|---|---|
| 3930 | A1877 | 1k multicolored | .30 | .25 |
| 3931 | A1877 | 4k brown & multi | .35 | .35 |
| 3932 | A1877 | 10k multicolored | .75 | .35 |
| 3933 | A1877 | 12k multicolored | .75 | .35 |
| 3934 | A1877 | 16k lt green & multi | 1.50 | .40 |
| | | Nos. 3930-3934 (5) | 3.65 | 1.60 |

**Ice Hockey A1878**

**1971, Dec. 15    Litho.    *Perf. 12½***
3935  A1878  6k multicolored    .30    .25
25th anniversary of Soviet ice hockey.

A1879

**A1880**

Oil rigs and causeway in Caspian Sea.

**1971, Dec. 30    *Perf. 11½***
3936  A1879  4k dp blue, org & blk    .25    .20
Baku oil industry.

**1972, Jan. 5    Engr.**
3937  A1880  4k yellow brown    .25    .20
G. M. Krzhizhanovsky (1872-1959), scientist and co-worker with Lenin.

**Alexander Scriabin (1872-1915), Composer A1881**

**1972, Jan. 6    Photo.    *Perf. 12x12½***
3938  A1881  4k indigo & olive    .30    .25

**Bering's Cormorant A1882**

---

**Aleksandr Fadeyev and Cavalrymen — A1873**

**1971, Nov. 25    Photo.    *Perf. 12½x12***
3916  A1873  4k slate & orange    .30    .25
Aleksandr Fadeyev (1901-1956), writer.

**Amethyst and Diamond Brooch A1874**

Precious Jewels: #3918, Engraved Shakh diamond, India, 16th cent. #3919, Diamond daffodils, 18th cent. #3920, Amethyst & diamond pendant. #3921, Diamond rose made for centenary of Lenin's birth. 30k, Diamond & pearl pendant.

**1971, Dec. 8    Litho.    *Perf. 11½***
| | | | | |
|---|---|---|---|---|
| 3917 | A1874 | 10k brt blue & multi | .20 | .20 |
| 3918 | A1874 | 10k dk red & multi | .20 | .20 |
| 3919 | A1874 | 10k grnsh black & multi | .20 | .20 |
| 3920 | A1874 | 20k grnsh black & multi | .40 | .25 |
| 3921 | A1874 | 20k rose red & multi | .40 | .40 |
| 3922 | A1874 | 30k black & multi | .60 | .40 |
| | | Nos. 3917-3922 (6) | 2.00 | 1.50 |

**Souvenir Sheet**

**Workers with Banners, Congress Hall and Spasski Tower — A1875**

**1971, Dec. 15    Photo.    *Perf. 11x11½***
3923  A1875  20k rod, pale green & brown    2.00    1.00

See note after No. 3895. No. 3923 contains one partially perforated stamp.

**Vanda Orchid — A1876**

Flowers: 1k, shown. 2k, Anthurium. 4k, #3929c, Flowering crab cactus. 12k, #3929a, Amaryllis. 14k, #3929d, Medinilla magnifica.

**1971, Dec. 15    Litho.    *Perf. 12x12½***
| | | | | |
|---|---|---|---|---|
| 3924 | A1876 | 1k olive & multi | .20 | .20 |
| 3925 | A1876 | 2k green & multi | .25 | .20 |
| 3926 | A1876 | 4k blue & multi | .40 | .20 |
| 3927 | A1876 | 12k multicolored | .50 | .20 |
| 3928 | A1876 | 14k multicolored | .65 | 1.00 |
| | | Nos. 3924-3928 (5) | 2.00 | .90 |

**Miniature Sheet    *Perf. 12***
Sheet of 4
3929    a.-d.    2.00    .90
a.-d.    A1876  10k any single    .25

Nos. 3929a-3929d have white background, black frame line and inscription. Size of stamps 19x57mm.
Issued: #3924-3928, 12/15; #3929, 12/30.

---

**Order of October Revolution — A1869**

**1971, Oct. 20    Litho.    *Perf. 12***
3905  A1869  4k red, yel & black    .25    .20
54th anniversary of October Revolution.

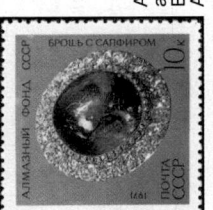

**E. Vakhtangov and "Princess Turandot" A1870**

Designs: No. 3907, Boris Shchukin and scene from "Man with Rifle (Lenin)," horiz. No. 3908, Ruben Simonov and scene from "Cyrano de Bergerac," horiz.

**1971, Oct. 26    *Perf. 12x12½, 12½x12    Photo.***
| | | | | |
|---|---|---|---|---|
| 3906 | A1870 | 10k mar & red brn | .35 | .20 |
| 3907 | A1870 | 10k brown & dull red | .35 | .20 |
| 3908 | A1870 | 10k red brn & ocher | 1.05 | .60 |
| | | Nos. 3906-3908 (3) | | |

Vakhtangov Theater, Moscow, 50th anniv.

**Dzhambul Dzhabayev(1846-1945), Kazakh Poet — A1871**

**1971, Nov. 16    *Perf. 12x12½***
3909  A1871  4k orange & brown    .30    .25

**Gorki Kremlin Type, 1971**

Designs: 3k, Pskov Kremlin and Velikaya River. 4k, Novgorod Kremlin and eternal flame memorial. 6k, Smolensk Fortress and liberation monument. 10k.Kolomna Kremlin and buses. 50k, Moscow Kremlin.

**1971, Nov. 16    Litho.    *Perf. 12***
| | | | | |
|---|---|---|---|---|
| 3910 | A1857 | 3k multicolored | .25 | .20 |
| 3911 | A1857 | 4k multicolored | .25 | .20 |
| 3912 | A1857 | 6k gray & multi | .25 | .20 |
| 3913 | A1857 | 10k olive & multi | .50 | .20 |
| | | Nos. 3910-3913 (4) | 1.00 | .80 |

**Souvenir Sheet
Engraved and Lithographed
*Perf. 11½***
3914  A1857  50k yellow & multi    1.75    1.00
Historic buildings. No. 3914 contains one 21½x32mm stamp.

**William Foster, View of New York A1872**

**1971    Litho.    *Perf. 12***
| | | | | |
|---|---|---|---|---|
| 3915 | A1872 | 10k brn & blk ("-1964") | .50 | .25 |
| a. | | "-1961" | 10.00 | 7.25 |

William Foster (1881-1961), chairman of Communist Party of US.
No. 3915a was issued Nov. 16 with incorrect death date (1964). No. 3915, with corrected date (1961), was issued Dec. 8.

---

**The Meeting, by Vladimir Y. Makovsky A1865**

**Ivan N. Kramskoi, Self-portrait — A1866**

Paintings: 4k, Woman Student, by Nikolai A. Yaroshenko. 6k, Woman Miner, by Nikolai A. Kasatkin. 10k, Harvest, by G. G. Myasoyedov, horiz. 16k, Country Road, by A. K. Savrasov. 20k, Pine Forest, by I. I. Shishkin, horiz.

**1971, Oct. 14    *Perf. 12x12½, 12½x12    Litho.***
| | | | | |
|---|---|---|---|---|
| 3896 | A1865 | 2k multicolored | .20 | .20 |
| 3897 | A1865 | 4k multicolored | .20 | .20 |
| 3898 | A1865 | 6k multicolored | .25 | .20 |
| 3899 | A1865 | 10k multicolored | .50 | .20 |
| 3900 | A1865 | 16k multicolored | .55 | .20 |
| 3901 | A1865 | 20k multicolored | 1.10 | 1.20 |
| | | Nos. 3896-3901 (6) | 2.80 | 1.20 |

**Souvenir Sheet
Lithographed and Gold Embossed**
3902  A1866  50k dk green & multi    2.00    .60
History of Russian painting.

**V. V. Vorovsky, Bolshevik Party Leader and Diplomat, Birth Cent. — A1867**

**1971, Oct. 14    Engr.    *Perf. 12***
3903  A1867  4k red brown    .25    .20

**Cosmonauts Dobrovolsky, Volkov and Patsayev — A1868**

**1971, Oct. 20    Photo.    *Perf. 11½x12***
3904  A1868  4k black, lilac & org    .25    .20

In memory of cosmonauts Lt. Col. Georgi T. Dobrovolsky, Vladislav N. Volkov and Viktor I. Patsayev, who died during the Soyuz 11 space mission, June 6-30, 1971.

Birds: 6k, Ross' gull, horiz. 10k, Barnacle geese. 12k, Spectacled eiders, horiz. 16k, Mediterranean gull.

**1972, Jan. 12** *Perf. 11½*

| | | | | |
|---|---|---|---|---|
| **3939** A1882 | 4k dk grn, blk & yel | .20 | .20 |
| **3940** A1882 | 6k ind, pink & blk | .30 | .20 |
| **3941** A1882 | 10k grnsh blue, blk & brown | .55 | .20 |
| **3942** A1882 | 12k multicolored | .60 | .20 |
| **3943** A1882 | 16k ultra, gray & red | .65 | .20 |
| | *Nos. 3939-3943 (5)* | 2.30 | 1.00 |

Waterfowl of the USSR.

11th Winter Olympic Games, Sapporo, Japan, Feb. 3-13 — A1883

Designs (Olympic Rings and): 4k, Speed skating. 6k, Women's figure skating. 10k, Ice hockey. 12k, Ski jump. 16k, Long-distance skiing. 50k, Sapporo '72 emblem.

**1972, Jan. 20** **Litho.** *Perf. 12x12½*

| | | | |
|---|---|---|---|
| **3944** A1883 | 4k bl grn, red & brn | .20 | .20 |
| **3945** A1883 | 6k yel grn, blue & dp orange | .20 | .20 |
| **3946** A1883 | 10k vio, bl & dp org | .35 | .20 |
| **3947** A1883 | 12k light blue, blue & brick red | .40 | .20 |
| **3948** A1883 | 16k gray, bl & brt rose | .70 | .20 |
| | *Nos. 3944-3948 (5)* | 1.85 | 1.00 |

**Souvenir Sheet**

| | | | |
|---|---|---|---|
| **3949** A1883 | 50k multicolored | 1.50 | .75 |

For overprint see No. 3961.

Heart, Globe and Exercising Family — A1884

**1972, Feb. 9** **Photo.**

| | | | |
|---|---|---|---|
| **3950** A1884 | 4k brt grn & rose red | .25 | .20 |

Heart Month sponsored by the WHO.

Leipzig Fair Emblem and Soviet Pavilion — A1885

**1972, Feb. 22** *Perf. 11½*

| | | | |
|---|---|---|---|
| **3951** A1885 | 16k red & gold | .60 | .25 |

50th anniversary of the participation of the USSR in the Leipzig Trade Fair.

Hammer, Sickle and Cogwheel Emblem — A1886

**1972, Feb. 29** *Perf. 12x12½*

| | | | |
|---|---|---|---|
| **3952** A1886 | 4k rose red & lt brown | .25 | .20 |

15th USSR Trade Union Congress, Moscow, March 1972.

Aloe A1887

Aleksandra Kollontai A1888

Medicinal Plants: 2k, Horn poppy. 4k, Groundsel. 6k, Orthosiphon stamineus. 10k, Nightshade.

**1972, Mar. 14** **Litho.** *Perf. 12x12½*

**Flowers in Natural Colors**

| | | | |
|---|---|---|---|
| **3953** A1887 | 1k olive bister | .20 | .20 |
| **3954** A1887 | 2k slate green | .20 | .20 |
| **3955** A1887 | 4k brt purple | .20 | .20 |
| **3956** A1887 | 6k violet blue | .20 | .20 |
| **3957** A1887 | 10k dk brown | .35 | .25 |
| | *Nos. 3953-3957 (5)* | 1.15 | 1.05 |

**1972, Mar. 20** **Engr.** *Perf. 12½x12*

#3959, Georgy Chicherin. #3960, Kamo (pseudonym of S.A. Ter-Petrosyan).

| | | | |
|---|---|---|---|
| **3958** A1888 | 4k red brown | .20 | .20 |
| **3959** A1888 | 4k claret | .20 | .20 |
| **3960** A1888 | 4k olive bister | .20 | .20 |
| | *Nos. 3958-3960 (3)* | .60 | .60 |

Outstanding workers of the Communist Party of the Soviet Union and for the State.

No. 3949 Overprinted in Margin Souvenir Sheet

**1972, Mar. 20** **Litho.** *Perf. 12x12½*

| | | | |
|---|---|---|---|
| **3961** A1883 | 50k multicolored | 4.00 | 2.00 |

Victories of Soviet athletes in the 11th Winter Olympic Games (8 gold, 5 silver, 3 bronze medals).

For similar overprints see Nos. 4028, 4416.

Orbital Station Salyut and Spaceship Soyuz Docking Above Earth — A1889

Designs: No. 3963, Mars 2 approaching Mars, and emblem dropped on Mars. 16k, Mars 3, which landed on Mars, Dec. 2, 1971.

**1972, Apr. 5** **Photo.** *Perf. 11½x12*

| | | | |
|---|---|---|---|
| **3962** A1889 | 6k vio, blue & silver | .20 | .20 |
| **3963** A1889 | 6k pur, ocher & sil | .20 | .20 |
| **3964** A1889 | 16k pur, blue & silver | 1.00 | .20 |
| | *Nos. 3962-3964 (3)* | 1.40 | .60 |

Cosmonauts' Day.

Shield and Products of Izhory Factory A1890

**1972, Apr. 20** *Perf. 12½x12*

| | | | |
|---|---|---|---|
| **3965** A1890 | 4k purple & silver | .25 | .20 |

250th anniversary of Izhory Factory, founded by Peter the Great.

Leonid Sobinov in "Eugene Onegin," by Tchaikovsky — A1891

**1972, Apr. 20**

| | | | |
|---|---|---|---|
| **3966** A1891 | 10k dp brown & buff | .30 | .20 |

Sobinov (1872-1934), opera singer.

Book, Torch, Children and Globe A1892

**1972, May 6** *Perf. 11½*

| | | | |
|---|---|---|---|
| **3967** A1892 | 6k brn, grnsh bl & buff | .25 | .20 |

International Book Year 1972.

Girl in Laboratory and Pioneers A1893

Designs: 1k, Pavlik Morosov (Pioneer hero), Pioneers saluting and banner. 3k, Pioneers with wheelbarrow, Chukchi boy, and Chukotka Pioneer House. 4k, Pioneer Honor Guard and Parade. 30k, Pioneer Honor Guard, vert.

**1972, May 10**

| | | | |
|---|---|---|---|
| **3968** A1893 | 1k red & multi | .20 | .20 |
| **3969** A1893 | 2k multicolored | .20 | .20 |
| **3970** A1893 | 3k multicolored | .20 | .20 |
| **3971** A1893 | 4k gray & multi | .20 | .20 |
| | *Nos. 3968-3971 (4)* | .80 | .80 |

**Souvenir Sheet**

*Perf. 12x12½*

| | | | |
|---|---|---|---|
| **3972** A1893 | 30k multicolored | 2.00 | .75 |

50th anniversary of the Lenin Pioneer Organization of the USSR.

Pioneer Bugler A1894

**1972, May 27** **Photo.** *Perf. 11½*

| | | | |
|---|---|---|---|
| **3973** A1094 | 4k red, ochr & plum | .25 | .20 |

2nd Youth Philatelic Exhibition, Minsk, and 50th anniv. of Lenin Pioneer Org.

M. S. Ordubady (1872-1950), Azerbaijan Writer and Social Worker — A1895

**1972, May 25** *Perf. 12x12½*

| | | | |
|---|---|---|---|
| **3974** A1895 | 4k orange & rose brn | .30 | .20 |

Globe A1896

**1972, May 25** *Perf. 11½*

| | | | |
|---|---|---|---|
| **3975** A1896 | 6k multicolored | .60 | .30 |

European Safety and Cooperation Conference, Brussels.

Cossack Leader, by Ivan Nikitin A1897

Paintings: 4k, Fedor G. Volkov (actor), by Anton Losenko. 6k, V. Majkov (poet), by Fedor Rokotov. 10k, Nikolai I. Novikov (writer), by Dimitri Levitsky. 12k, Gavriil R. Derzhavin (poet, civil servant), by Vladimir Borovikovsky. 16k, Peasants' Supper, by Mikhail Shibanov, horiz. 20k, View of Moscow, by Fedor Alexeyev, horiz.

*Perf. 12x12½, 12½x12*

**1972, June 7** **Litho.**

| | | | |
|---|---|---|---|
| **3976** A1897 | 2k gray & multi | .20 | .20 |
| **3977** A1897 | 4k gray & multi | .20 | .20 |
| **3978** A1897 | 6k gray & multi | .20 | .20 |
| **3979** A1897 | 10k gray & multi | .30 | .20 |
| **3980** A1897 | 12k gray & multi | .30 | .20 |
| **3981** A1897 | 16k gray & multi | .45 | .20 |
| **3982** A1897 | 20k gray & multi | .60 | .25 |
| | *Nos. 3976-3982 (7)* | 2.25 | 1.45 |

History of Russian painting. See Nos. 4036-4042, 4074-4080, 4103-4109.

George Dimitrov (1882-1949), Bulgarian Communist Party Leader — A1898

**1972, June 15** **Photo.** *Perf. 12½x12*

| | | | |
|---|---|---|---|
| **3983** A1898 | 6k brown & ol bister | .30 | .20 |

20th Olympic Games, Munich, 8/26-9/11 A1899

Olympic Rings and: 4k, Fencing. 6k, Women's gymnastics. 10k, Canoeing. 14k, Boxing. 16k, Running. 50k, Weight lifting.

**1972, July 1    Perf. 12x11½**
3984 A1899 4k brt mag & gold  .20 .20
3985 A1899 6k dp green & gold  .20 .20
3986 A1899 10k brt blue & gold  .55 .55
3987 A1899 14k Prus bl & gold  .60 .60
3988 A1899 16k red & gold  .85 1.00
Nos. 3984-3988 (5)  2.40 1.00

**Souvenir Sheet**
**Perf. 11½**
3989 A1899 50k gold & multi  2.00 .80
#3989 contains one 25x35mm stamp.
For overprint see No. 4028.

Congress Palace, Kiev A1900

**1972, July 1    Photo. & Engr.**
3990 A1900 6k Prus blue & bister  .25 .20
9th World Gerontology Cong., Kiev, 7/2-7.

Roald Amundsen, "Norway," Northern Lights A1901

**1972, July 13    Photo.    Perf. 11½**
3991 A1901 6k vio blue & dp bister  .40 .25
Roald Amundsen (1872-1928), Norwegian polar explorer.

17th Century House, Chernigov A1902

**1972, July 18    Litho.**
**Perf. 12x12½, 12½x12**
3992 A1902 4k citron & multi  .20 .20
3993 A1902 6k gray & multi  .25 .20
3994 A1902 10k ocher & multi  .40 .20
3995 A1902 16k salmon & multi  .60 .80
Nos. 3992-3995 (4)  1.40 .80
Designs: 4k, Market Square, Lvov, vert. 10k, Kuvnirov Building, Klev. 16k, Fortress, Kamenets-Podolski, vert.
Historic and architectural treasures of the Ukraine.

Asoka Pillar, Indian Flag, Red Fort, New Delhi A1903

**1972, July 27    Photo.    Perf. 11½**
3996 A1903 6k dk blue, emer & red  .25 .20
25th anniversary of India's independence.

Miners' Emblem A1904

**1972, Aug. 10**
3997 A1904 4k violet gray & red  .25 .20
25th Miners' Day.

Far East Fighters' Monument A1905

**1972, Aug. 10**
3998 A1905 3k red org, car & black  .20 .20
3999 A1905 4k yel, sepia & blk  .20 .20
4000 A1905 6k pink, dk car & black  .60 .60
Nos. 3998-4000 (3)
Designs: 4k, Monument for Far East Civil War heroes, industrial view. 6k, Vladivostok rostral column, Pacific fleet ships.
50th anniversary of the liberation of the Far Eastern provinces.

Boy with Dog, by Murillo A1906

Paintings from the Hermitage, Leningrad: 4k, Breakfast, Velazquez. 6k, Milkmaid's Family, Louis Le Nain. 16k, Sad Women, Watteau. 20k, Moroccan Saddling Steed, Delacroix. 50k, Self-portrait, Van Dyck. 4k, 6k horiz.

**1972, Aug. 15    Perf. 12½x12, 12½x12½**
4001 A1906 4k multicolored  .20 .20
4002 A1906 6k multicolored  .25 .20
4003 A1906 10k multicolored  .25 .20
4004 A1906 16k multicolored  .35 .20
4005 A1906 20k multicolored  .50 .20
Nos. 4001-4005 (5)  2.05 1.00

**Souvenir Sheet**
**Perf. 12**
4006 A1906 50k multicolored  2.50 1.00

Sputnik 1 — A1907

**1972, Sept. 14    Litho.    Perf. 12x11½**
4007 A1907 6k shown  .20 .20
4008 A1907 6k Launching of Vostok 2  .20 .20
4009 A1907 6k Lenov floating in space  .20 .20
4010 A1907 6k Lunokhod on moon  .20 .20
4011 A1907 6k Venera 7 descending to Venus  .20 .20
4012 A1907 6k Mars & descending to Mars  1.20 1.20
Nos. 4007-4012 (6)
15 years of space era. Sheets of 6.

Konstantin Aleksandrovich Mardzhanishvili (1872-1933), Theatrical Producer A1908

**1972, Sept. 20    Engr.    Perf. 12x12½**
4013 A1908 4k slate green  .30 .25

Museum Emblem, Communications Symbols — A1909

**1972, Sept. 20    Photo.    Perf. 11½**
4014 A1909 4k slate green & multi  .25 .20
Centenary of the A. S. Popov Central Museum of Communications.

"Stamp" and Topical Collecting Symbols A1910

**Engraved and Lithographed**
**1972, Oct. 4    Perf. 12**
4015 A1910 4k yel, black & red  .25 .20
Philatelic Exhibition in honor of 50th anniversary of the USSR.

Lenin A1911

**1972, Oct. 12    Photo.    Perf. 11½**
4016 A1911 4k gold & red  .25 .20
55th anniversary of October Revolution.

Militia Badge — A1912

**1972, Oct. 12**
4017 A1912 4k gold, red & dk brn  .25 .20
55th anniv. of the Militia of the USSR.

Arms of USSR A1913

USSR, 50th anniv.: #4019, Arms and industrial scene. #4020, Arms, Supreme Soviet, Kremlin. #4021, Lenin. #4022, Arms, worker, book (Constitution). 30k, Coat of arms and Spasski Tower, horiz.

**1972, Oct. 28    Perf. 12x11½**
4018 A1913 4k multicolored  .20 .20
4019 A1913 4k multicolored  .20 .20
4020 A1913 4k multicolored  .20 .20
4021 A1913 4k multicolored  .20 .20
4022 A1913 4k multicolored  .20 .20
Nos. 4018-4022 (5)  1.00 1.00

**Souvenir Sheet**
**Lithographed; Embossed**
**Perf. 12**
4023 A1913 30k red & gold  1.50 .40

Kremlin and Snowflake A1914

**Engraved and Photogravure**
**1972, Nov. 15    Perf. 11½**
4024 A1914 6k multicolored  .25 .20
New Year 1973.

Savings Bank Book — A1915

**1972, Nov. 15    Photo.    Perf. 12x12½**
4025 A1915 4k lilac & slate  .25 .20
50th anniv. of savings banks in the USSR.

Soviet Olympic Emblem and Laurel A1916

Design: 30k, Soviet Olympic emblem and obverse of gold, silver and bronze medals.

**1972, Nov. 15    Perf. 11½**
4026 A1916 20k brn ol, red & gold  .50 .40
4027 A1916 30k dp car, gold & brn  1.00 .60

No. 3989 Overprinted in Red

4028 A1899 50k gold & multi 2.00 1.25
Soviet medalists at 20th Olympic Games.

**Souvenir Sheet**

Battleship Peter the Great, 1872—A1917

History of Russian Fleet: 3k, Cruiser Varyag, 1899. 4k, Battleship Potemkin, 1900. 6k, Cruiser Ochakov, 1902. 10k, Mine layer Amur, 1907.

**Engraved and Photogravure**

**1972, Nov. 22**    **Perf. 11½x12**
4029 A1917 2k multicolored .35 .20
4030 A1917 3k multicolored .35 .20
4031 A1917 4k multicolored .45 .20
4032 A1917 6k multicolored .70 .20
4033 A1917 10k multicolored 1.10 .20
Nos. 4029-4033 (5) 2.95 1.00

Grigory S. Skovoroda (1722-1794), Ukrainian Philosopher and Humanist A1918

**Engr.**    **Perf. 12**
**1972, Dec. 7**    **Photo.**
4034 A1918 4k violet blue .30 .20
4035 A1919 4k Prus blue, blk & red .25 .20
Traffic safety campaign.

Child Reading Traffic Rules—A1919

**Russian Painting Type of 1972**
2k, Meeting of Village Party Members, by E. M. Cheptsov, horiz. 4k, Pioneer Girl, by Nicolai A. Kasatkin. 6k, Woman Delegate, by G. G. Ryazhsky. 10k, Winter's End, by K. F. Yuon, horiz. 16k, The Partisan A. G. Lunev, by N. I. Strunnikov. 20k, Igor E. Grabar, self-portrait. 50k, Blue Space (seascape with flying geese), by Arcadi A. Rylov, horiz.

**Perf. 12x12½, 12½x12    Litho.**
**1972, Dec. 7**
4036 A1897 2k olive & multi .20 .20
4037 A1897 4k olive & multi .20 .20
4038 A1897 10k olive & multi .40 .20
4039 A1897 16k olive & multi .55 .20
4040 A1897 20k olive & multi .80 .25
4041 A1897 olive & multi 2.35 1.25
Nos. 4036-4041 (6)

**Souvenir Sheet**
**Perf. 12**
4042 A1897 50k multicolored 1.75 1.25
History of Russian painting.

**Engraved and Photogravure**
**1972, Dec. 7**    **Perf. 11½**
4043 A1920 4k sl grn, yel & red brn .30 .20
Centenary of Polytechnic Museum, Moscow.

Symbolic of Theory and Practice—A1920

Venera 8 and Parachute A1921

**1972, Dec. 28**    **Photo.**    **Perf. 11½**
4044 A1921 6k dl claret, bl & blk .30 .20

**Souvenir Sheet**
**Imperf**
4045 Sheet of 2
a. A1921 50k Venera 8 9.00 3.00
b. A1921 50k Mars 3 2.50 .90
Soviet space research. No. 4045 contains 2 40x20mm stamps with simulated perforations.

**1973, Jan. 5**    **Perf. 11x11½**
4046 A1922 10k tan, vio blue & red .35 .30
15th anniversary of Afro-Asian Peoples' Solidarity Organization (AAPSO).

Globe, Torch and Palm—A1922

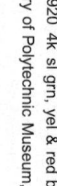

I. V. Babushkin A1923
**1973, Jan. 10**    **Engr.**    **Perf. 12**
4047 A1923 4k greenish black .25 .20
Babushkin (1873-1906), revolutionary.

**1973, Jan. 10**    **Photo.**    **Perf. 11½**
4048 A1924 4k pale brown, ocher & black .25 .20
30th anniversary of the breaking of the Nazi blockade of Leningrad.

"30." Map and Admiralty Tower, Leningrad A1924

**1973, Jan. 10**    **Litho.**    **Perf. 12**
4049 A1925 6k multicolored .40 .25
50th anniversary of Soviet Civil Aviation.

TU-154 Turbojet Passenger Plane—A1925

**1973, Jan. 10**    **Photo.**    **Perf. 11½**
4050 A1926 10k gray, red & green .40 .30
650th anniversary of Vilnius.

Gediminas Tower, Flag, Modern Vilnius A1926

**1973, Feb. 1**    **Litho.**    **Perf. 11½**
4051 A1927 3k dp org & blk .25 .20
4052 A1927 4k dp yel & blk .25 .20
4053 A1927 10k olive & multi .25 .20
4054 A1927 12k dp car & black .80 .80
Nos. 4051-4054 (4) 1.00

**Souvenir Sheet**
**Perf. 12x12½, 12½x12**
4055 Sheet of 2 1.50 .75
a.-b. A1927 20k any single .45 .20
30th anniv. of the victory over the Germans at Stalingrad. #4055 contains 2 40x18mm stamps.

Heroes' Memorial, Stalingrad—A1927

Designs (Details from Monument): 3k, Man with rifle and "Mother Russia," vert. 10k, Mourning mother and child. 12k, Arm with torch, vert. No. 4055a, Red star, hammer and sickle emblem and statuary like 3k. No. 4055b, "Mother Russia," vert.

**1973, Feb. 8**    **Engr. & Photo.**    **Perf. 11½**
4060 A1930 10k ultra & sepia .40 .25
500th anniversary of the birth of Nicolaus Copernicus (1473-1543), Polish astronomer.

Copernicus and Solar System A1930

Ice Hockey A1931
**1973, Mar. 14**    **Photo.**    **Perf. 11½**
4061 A1931 6k gold, blue & sep .40 .25

**Souvenir Sheet**
4062 A1931 50k bl grn, gold & sep 1.75 1.00
European and World ice Hockey Championships, Moscow. See No. 4082.

Design: 50k. Two players, vert.

**1973, Mar. 14**    **Perf. 11½**
4063 A1932 4k bright blue & multi .30 .20
Sports Society of Soviet Army, 50th anniv.

Athletes and Banners of Air, Land and Naval Forces—A1932

**1973, Mar. 14**
4064 A1933 4k gray, black & red .30 .20
30th anniversary of Soviet victory in the Battle of Kursk during World War II.

Tank, Red Star and Map of Battle of Kursk—A1933

**Large Portrait Type of 1971**
Designs: 4k, Mikhail Prishvin (1873-1954), author. 10k, Fedor Chaliapin (1873-1938), opera singer, by K. Korovin.

**1973**    **Litho.**    **Perf. 11½x12**
4056 A1855 4k pink & multi .20 .20
4057 A1855 10k lt blue & multi .20 .20
Issue dates: 4k, Feb. 1. 10k, Feb. 8.

**1973, Feb. 1**    **Photo.**    **Perf. 11½**
4058 A1928 10k red, grey & indigo .30 .20
4059 A1929 10k red, mag & gray .30 .20
50th anniversary of the Mayakovsky and Mossovet Theaters in Moscow.

"Mayakovsky Theater"—A1928

"Mossovet Theater"—A1929

Nikolai E. Bauman (1873-1905), Bolshevist Revolutionary A1934
**1973, Mar. 20**    **Engr.**    **Perf. 12½x12**
4065 A1934 4k brown .30 .20

**1973, Mar. 20**    **Photo.**    **Perf. 11**
4066 A1935 4k gray, grn & red .20 .20
4067 A1935 6k violet blue & red .25 .20
4068 A1935 16k multicolored .80 .20
Nos. 4066-4068 (3) 1.25 .60
Union of Red Cross and Red Crescent Societies of the USSR, 50th anniv.; 15th Cong. of

Red Cross and Red Crescent—A1935

6k, Theater curtain & mask. 16k, Youth Festival emblem & young people.

the Intl. Theater Institute; 10th World Festival of Youth and Students, Berlin.

**Aleksandr N. Ostrovsky, by V. Perov — A1936**

**1973, Apr. 5  Litho.  Perf. 12x12½**
4069 A1936 4k tan & multi  .30 .20
Ostrovsky (1823-1886), dramatist.

**Earth Satellite "Interkosmos" — A1937**

**1973, Apr. 12  Photo.  Perf. 12x12½**
4070 A1937 6k brn ol & dull cl  .25 .20
4071 A1938 6k vio blue & multi  .25 .20

**Lunokhod 2 on Moon and Lenin Moon Plaque A1938**

**Souvenir Sheets**
**Perf. 12x12½**
4072 Sheet of 3, purple & multi  2.50 1.00
a. A1938 20k Lenin plaque  .55 .30
b. A1938 20k Lunokhod 2  .55 .30
c. A1938 20k Telecommunications  .55 .35
4073 Sheet of 3, slate grn & multi  2.50 1.00
a. A1930 20k Lenin plaque  .55 .30
b. A1938 20k Lunokhod 2  .55 .30
c. A1938 20k Telecommunications  .55 .35

Cosmonauts' Day No. 4070 for cooperation in space research by European communist countries. Souvenir sheets contain 3 50x21mm stamps.

**Russian Painting Type of 1972**
Paintings: 2k, Guitarist, V. A. Tropinin. 4k, Young Widow, by P. A. Fedotov. 6k, Self-portrait, by O. A. Kiprensky. 10k, Woman with Grapes ("An Afternoon in Italy") by K. P. Bryullov. 12k, Boy with Dog ("That was my Father's Dinner"), by A. Venetsianov. 16k, "Lower Gallery of Albano," by A. A. Ivanov. 20k, Soldiers ("Conquest of Siberia"), by V. I. Surikov, horiz.

**Perf. 12x12½, 12½x12**
**1973, Apr. 18  Litho.**
4074 A1897 2k gray & multi  .20 .20
4075 A1897 4k gray & multi  .20 .20
4076 A1897 6k gray & multi  .25 .20
4077 A1897 10k gray & multi  .45 .25
4078 A1897 12k gray & multi  .60 .25
4079 A1897 16k gray & multi  .65 .25
4080 A1897 20k gray & multi  .80 .35
Nos. 4074-4080 (7)  3.15 1.70

**Athlete, Ribbon of Lenin Order — A1939**

**1973, Apr. 18  Photo.  Perf. 11½**
4081 A1939 4k blue, red & ocher  .25 .20
50th anniversary of Dynamo Sports Society.


**No. 4062 with Blue Green Inscription and Ornaments Added in Margin**
**Souvenir Sheet**
**1973, Apr. 26  Photo.  Perf. 11½**
4082 A1931 50k multicolored  4.00 2.00
Soviet victory in European and World Ice Hockey Championships, Moscow.

**"Mikhail Lermontov," Route Leningrad to New York — A1940**

**1973, May 20  Photo.  Perf. 11½**
4083 A1940 16k multicolored  .60 .25
Inauguration of transatlantic service Leningrad to New York.

**Ernest E. T. Krenkel, Polar Stations and Ship Chelyuskin A1941**

**1973, May 20  Litho. & Engr.  Perf. 12x12½**
4084 A1941 4k dull blue & olive  .40 .30
Krenkel (1903-1971), polar explorer.

**Emblem and Sports — A1942**

**1973, May 20  Litho.  Perf. 12x12½**
4085 A1942 4k multicolored  .25 .20
Sports Association for Labor and Defense.

**Latvian Song Festival, Cent. — A1943**  .35 .25

**1973, May 24**
4086 A1943 10k Singers

**Throwing the Hammer — A1944**

Designs: 3k, Athlete on rings. 4k, Woman diver. 16k, Fencing. 50k, Javelin.


**1973, June 14  Litho.  Perf. 11½**
4087 A1944 2k lemon & multi  .20 .20
4088 A1944 3k blue & multi  .20 .20
4089 A1944 4k citron & multi  .35 .25
4090 A1944 16k lilac & multi  .95 .80
**Souvenir Sheet**
4091 A1944 50k gold & multi  1.75 1.25
Universiad, Moscow, 1973.

**Souvenir Sheet**

**Valentina Nikolayeva-Tereshkova — A1945**

**1973, June 14  Photo.  Perf. 12x11½**
4092 A1945 Sheet of 3 + label  3.00 1.25
a. 20k as cosmonaut  .55 .25
b. 20k with Indian and African women  .55 .25
c. 20k with daughter  .55 .25
Flight of the 1st woman cosmonaut, 10th anniv.

**European Bison — A1946**

**1973, July 26  Photo.  Perf. 11x11½**
4093 A1946 1k shown  .20 .20
4094 A1946 3k Ibex  .20 .20
4095 A1946 4k Caucasian chamois  .20 .20
4096 A1946 6k Beaver  .35 .20
4097 A1946 10k Deer and fawns  .50 .20
Nos. 4093-4097 (5)  1.45 1.00
Caucasus and Voronezh wildlife reserves.

**Party Membership Card with Lenin Portrait — A1947**

**1973, July 26  Litho.  Perf. 11½**
4098 A1947 4k multicolored  .25 .20
70th anniversary of 2nd Congress of the Russian Social Democratic Workers' Party.

**Abu-al-Rayhan al-Biruni (973-1048), Arabian (Persian) Scholar and Writer — A1948**

**1973, Aug. 9  Engr.  Perf. 12x12½**
4099 A1948 6k red brown  .25 .20

**White House, Spasski Tower, Hemispheres — A1949**

**1973, Aug. 10  Photo.  Perf. 11½x12**
4100 A1949 10k magenta & multi  .50 .50
4101 A1949 10k brown & multi  .50 .50
4102 A1949 10k dp car & multi  .50 .50
a. Souv. sheet of 3 + 3 labels  2.50 2.50
Nos. 4100-4102 (3)  1.50 1.50

Visit of General Secretary Leonid I. Brezhnev to Washington, Paris and Bonn. Nos. 4100-4102 each printed with se-tenant label with different statements by Brezhnev in Russian and English, French and German, respectively.
No. 4102a contains 4k stamps similar to Nos. 4100-4102 in changed colors. Issued Nov. 26.
See Nos. 4161-4162.

**Russian Painting Type of 1972**
2k, S. T. Konenkov, sculptor, by P. D. Korin. 4k, Tractor Operators at Supper, by A. A. Plastov. 6k, Letter from the Front, by A. I. Laktionov. 10k, Mountains. by M. S. Saryan. 16k, Wedding on a Future Street, by Y. I. Pimenov. 20k, Ice Hockey, mosaic by A. A. Deineka. 50k, Lenin at 3rd Congress of Young Communist League, by B. V. Yoganson.

**1973, Aug. 22  Litho.  Perf. 12x12½**
**Frame in Light Gray**
4103 A1897 2k multicolored  .20 .20
4104 A1897 4k multicolored  .20 .20
4105 A1897 6k multicolored  .20 .20
4106 A1897 10k multicolored  .35 .20
4107 A1897 16k multicolored  .60 .20
4108 A1897 20k multicolored  .70 .20
Nos. 4103-4108 (6)  2.25 1.20
**Souvenir Sheet**
**Perf. 12**
4109 A1897 50k multicolored  2.00 1.25
History of Russian Painting.

**Museum, Tashkent — A1950**

**Y. M. Steklov — A1951**

**1973, Aug. 23  Photo.  Perf. 12x12½**
4110 A1950 4k multicolored  .25 .20
Lenin Central Museum, Tashkent branch.

**1973, Aug. 27  Photo.  Perf. 11½x12**
4111 A1951 4k multicolored  .25 .20
Steklov (1873-1941), party worker, historian, writer.

**Book, Pen and Torch — A1952**

**Echinopanax Elatum — A1953**

**1973, Aug. 31  Perf. 11½**
4112 A1952 6k multicolored  .25 .20
Conf. of Writers of Asia & Africa, Alma-Ata.

Medicinal Plants: 2k, Ginseng. 4k, Orchis maculatus. 10k, Arnica montana. 12k, Lily of the valley.

**1973, Sept. 5  Litho.  Perf. 12x12½**
4113 A1953  1k yellow & multi  .20 .20
4114 A1953  2k lt blue & multi  .20 .20
4115 A1953  4k gray & multi  .20 .20
4116 A1953  10k sepia & multi  .30 .20
4117 A1953  12k green & multi  .55 .20
Nos. 4113-4117 (5)  1.45 1.00

**1973, Sept. 12**
**Engraved and Photogravure  Perf. 11½x12**
4119 A1955  3k violet & multi  .20 .20
4120 A1955  4k green & multi  .20 .20
4121 A1955  6k multicolored  .20 .20
4122 A1955  10k blue grn & multi  .30 .20
4123 A1955  16k multicolored  .50 .20
Nos. 4119-4723 (5)  1.40 1.00

Soviet Warships: 4k, Battleship October Revolution. 6k, Submarine Krasnogvardeyets. 10k, Torpedo boat Soobrazitelny. 16k, Cruiser Red Caucasus.

Globe and Red Flag Emblem — A1956

**1973, Sept. 25  Photo.  Perf. 11½**
4124 A1956  6k gold, buff & red  .25 .20
15th anniversary of the international communist review "Problems of Peace and Socialism," published in Prague.

**Engraved and Photogravure**
Emelyan I. Pugachev and Peasant Army — A1957

**1973, Sept. 25  Perf. 11½x12**
4125 A1957  4k brn, bister & red  .25 .20
Bicentenary of peasant revolt of 1773-75 led by Emelyn Ivanovich Pugachev.

---

**1973, Sept. 5 — A1954**
4118 A1954  4k sepia  Engr.  .30 .20

Imadeddin Nasimi, Azerbaijani Poet, 600th Birth Anniv. — A1954

Cruiser Kirov — A1955

**1973, Oct. 5**
4126 A1958  4k black & multi
Leningrad Mining Institute, 150th anniv.
**Perf. 11½**
Crystal, Institute Emblem and Building — A1958

Palm, Globe, Flower A1959
**1973, Oct. 5**
4127 A1959  6k red, gray & dk blue  .25 .20
World Cong. of Peace-loving Forces, Moscow.

Elena Stasova A1960
**1973, Oct. 5  Photo.  Perf. 11½x12**
4128 A1960  4k deep claret  .25 .20
Elena Dmitriyevna Stasova (1873-1966), communist party worker. See Nos. 4228-4229.

Order of Friendship — A1961
**1973, Oct. 5  Litho.  Perf. 11½**
4129 A1961  4k red & multi  .25 .20
56th anniv. of the October Revolution. Printed se-tenant with coupon showing Arms of USSR and proclamation establishing Order of Friendship of People, in 1972, on the 50th anniv. of the USSR.

---

Marshal Malinovsky A1962
**1973, Oct. 17  Engr.  Perf. 12x12½**
4130 A1962  4k slate  .25 .20
See Nos. 4203-4205.
Rodion Y. Malinovsky (1898-1967).

Ural Man, Red Guard, Worker A1963
**1973, Oct. 5  Photo.  Perf. 11½**
4131 A1963  4k red, gold & black  .25 .20
250th anniversary of the city of Sverdlovsk.

Russo-Balt, 1909 — A1968
**1973, Nov. 30  Photo.  Perf. 12x11½**
4136 A1968  2k purple & multi  .20 .20
4137 A1968  3k olive & multi  .20 .20
4138 A1968  4k ocher & multi  .20 .20
4139 A1968  12k vio blue & multi  .45 .20
4140 A1968  16k red & multi  .75 .20
Nos. 4136-4140 (5)  1.80 1.00
Designs: 3k, AMO-F15 truck, 1924. 4k, Spartak, NAMI-1 car, 1927. 12k, GAZ-A car, 1932. 16k, Ya-6 autobus, 1929.
Development of Russian automotive industry. See Nos. 4216-4220, 4325-4329, 4440-4444.

---

Dimitri Cantemir (1673-1723), Prince of Moldavia, Writer — A1964
**1973, Oct. 17  Engr.  Perf. 12x12½**
4132 A1964  4k rose claret  .25 .20

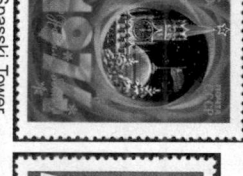
Salvador Allende (1908-73), Pres. of Chile A1965
**1973, Nov. 26  Photo.  Perf. 11½**
4133 A1965  6k rose brn & black  .25 .20

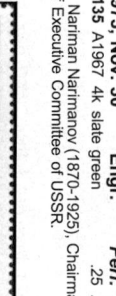 
Spasski Tower, Kremlin A1966
**1973, Nov. 30  Engr.  Perf. 12**
4134 A1966  6k brt blue & multi  .25 .20
New Year 1974.

Nariman Narimanov A1967
**1973, Nov. 30  Litho.  Perf. 12x12½**
4135 A1967  4k slate green  .25 .20
Nariman Narimanov (1870-1925), Chairman of Executive Committee of USSR.

---

Still Life, by Frans Snyders — A1969

Paintings: 6k, Woman Trying on Earrings, by Rembrandt, vert. 10k, Sick Woman and Physician, by Jan Steen, vert. 12k, Still Life with Lady in Garden, by Jean-Baptiste Chardin. 14k, Young Love, by Jules Bastien-Lepage, vert. 20k, Girl with Fan, by Auguste Renoir, vert. 50k, Flora, by Rembrandt, vert.

---

Pablo Picasso (1881-1973), Painter A1970
**1973, Dec. 12 — A1970**
4149 A1970  6k gold, slate grn & red  .25 .20

Organ Pipes and Dome, Riga — A1971
**1973, Dec. 20  Photo.  Perf. 12x11½**
4150 A1971  4k blk, red & slate grn  .20 .20
4151 A1971  4k gray, red & buff  .20 .20
4152 A1971  4k black, red & grn  .20 .20
4153 A1971  10k sep, grn, red & blk  .85 .80
Nos. 4150-4153 (4)
**1973, Dec. 20  Engr.  Perf. 12x12½**
Architecture of the Baltic area.
#4151, Small Trakai Castle, Lithuania. #4152, Great Sea Gate, Tallinn, Estonia. 10k, Town Hall and "Old Thomas" weather vane, Tallinn.

**1973, Dec. 12**
**Perf. 12x11½, 11½x12**
4141 A1969  4k bister & multi  .20 .20
4142 A1969  6k bister & multi  .20 .20
4143 A1969  10k bister & multi  .25 .20
4144 A1969  12k bister & multi  .40 .20
4145 A1969  14k bister & multi  .50 .20
4146 A1969  16k bister & multi  .55 .20
4147 A1969  20k bister & multi  .70 .20
Nos. 4141-4147 (7)  3.05 1.40
**Litho.**

**Souvenir Sheet**
**Perf. 12**
4148 A1969  50k multicolored  2.00 1.00
Foreign paintings in Russian museums.

---

I. G. Petrovsky A1972
4154 A1972  4k orange & multi  .20 .20
**1973-74  Photo.  Perf. 12x12½**
4155 A1973  4k blk brn & olive  .20 .20

L. A. Artsimovich A1973
4156 A1973  4k multicolored  **Engr.  Perf. 12x12½**  .25 .20
4157 A1973  4k multicolored  **Litho.  Perf. 12**  .25 .20

#4154, I. G. Petrovsky (1901-73), mathematician, rector of Moscow State University. #4155, L. A. Artsimovich (1909-73), physician, academician. #4156, K. D. Ushinsky (1824-71), teacher. #4157, M. D. Millionschikov (1913-73), vice president of Academy of Sciences.

Issued: #4154, 12/28/73; others, 2/6/74.

Rainbow, Swallow over Clouds — A1990

Congress Emblem and Clover — A1991

6k, Fish in water. 10k, Crystal. 16k, Rose. 20k, Fawn. 50k, Infant.

**1974, Apr. 24    Photo.    Perf. 11½**
4188 A1990 4k lilac & multi  .20 .20
4189 A1990 6k multicolored  .20 .20
4190 A1990 10k multicolored  .35 .20
4191 A1990 16k blue & multi  .50 .20
4192 A1990 20k citron & multi  .55 .20
Nos. 4188-4192 (5)  1.80 1.00

**Souvenir Sheet**
**Litho.**
**Perf. 12x12½**
4193 A1990 50k blue & multi  1.50 .80
EXPO '74 World's Fair, theme "Preserve the Environment," Spokane, WA, May 4-Nov. 4.

**1974, May 7    Photo.    Perf. 11½**
4194 A1991 4k green & multi  .25 .20
12th International Congress on Meadow Cultivation, Moscow, 1974.

"Cobblestones, Weapons of the Proletariat," by I. D. Shadra — A1992
**1974, May 7**
4195 A1992 4k gold, red & olive  .25 .20
50th anniversary of the Lenin Central Revolutionary Museum of the USSR.

Saiga — A1993

Fauna of USSR: 3k, Koulan (wild ass). 4k, Desman. 6k, Sea lion. 10k, Greenland whale.
**1974, May 22    Litho.    Perf. 11½**
4196 A1993 1k olive & multi  .40 .35
4197 A1993 3k green & multi  .80 .35
4198 A1993 4k multicolored  .80 .35
4199 A1993 6k multicolored  1.10 .50
4200 A1993 10k multicolored  1.00 .60
Nos. 4196-4200 (5)  5.00 2.00

Peter Ilich Tchaikovsky — A1994
**1974, May 22    Photo.    Perf. 11½**
4201 A1994 6k multicolored  .25 .20
5th International Tchaikovsky Competition, Moscow.

---

**Perf. 12x11½**
4176 A1985 10k grnsh blue & multi  .35 .20
4177 A1985 10k dull yel & multi  1.00 .60
Nos. 4175-4177 (3)
Cosmonauts' Day.

Odessa by Moonlight, by Aivazovski — A1986

Seascapes by Aivazovski: 4k, Battle of Chesma. 1848, vert. 6k, St. George's Monastery. 10k, Stormy Sea. 12k, Rainbow (shipwreck). 16k, Shipwreck. 50k, Portrait of Aivazovski, by Kramskoy, vert.

**Perf. 12x11½, 11½x12    Litho.**
**1974, Mar. 30**
4178 A1986 2k gray & multi  .20 .20
4179 A1986 4k gray & multi  .20 .20
4180 A1986 6k gray & multi  .35 .20
4181 A1986 10k gray & multi  .50 .20
4182 A1986 12k gray & multi  .85 .25
4183 A1986 16k gray & multi  2.65 1.25
Nos. 4178-4183 (6)

**Souvenir Sheet**
4184 A1986 50k gray & multi  1.25 .90
Ivan Konstantinovich Aivazovski (1817-1900), marine painter. Sheets of Nos. 4178-4183 each contain 2 labels with commemorative inscriptions.
See Nos. 4230-4234.

Young Man and Woman, Bunner A1987
**1974, Mar. 30    Litho.    Perf. 12½x12**
4185 A1987 4k red, yel & brown  .25 .20
17th Cong. of the Young Communist League.

Lenin, by V. E. Tsigal A1988
**1974, Mar. 30**
4186 A1988 4k yel, red & brown  .25 .20
50th anniversary of naming the Komsomol (Young Communist League) after Lenin.

Lenin at the Telegraph, by Igor E. Grabar — A1989

**Souvenir Sheet**
**1974, Apr. 16    Litho.    Perf. 12**
4187 A1989 50k multicolored  1.40 .90
104th anniv. of the birth of Lenin.

---

Skaters and Rink, Medeo A1979
**1974, Jan. 28**
4170 A1979 6k slate, brn red & bl  .25 .20
European Women's Skating Championships, Medeo, Alma-Ata.

Art Palace, Leningrad, Academy, Moscow A1980
**1974, Jan. 30    Photo. & Engr.**
4171 A1980 10k multicolored  .35 .25
25th anniversary of the Academy of Sciences of the USSR.

Young People and Emblem — A1982
**1974, Mar. 20    Photo.    Perf. 11½**
4172 A1981 10k gold & multi  .35 .25
Third Winter Spartakiad.

3rd Winter Spartiakad Emblem — A19R1
**1974, Mar. 20    Photo. & Engr.**
4173 A1982 4k multicolored  .25 .20
Youth scientific-technical work.

Azerbaijan Theater — A1983
**1974, Mar. 20    Photo.    Perf. 11½**
4174 A1983 6k org, red brn & brn  .30 .25
Centenary of Azerbaijan Theater.

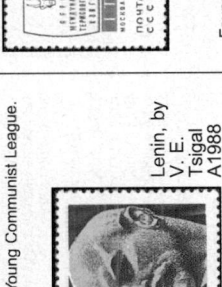

Meteorological Satellite "Meteor" — A1984

Cosmonauts V. G. Lazarev and O. G. Makarov and Soyuz 12 — A1985
Design: No. 4177, Cosmonauts P. I. Klimuk and V. V. Lebedev, and Soyuz 13.
**1974, Mar. 27    Perf. 11½**
4175 A1984 6k violet & multi  .30 .20

---

Flags of India and USSR, Red Fort, Taj Mahal and Kremlin — A1974

Design: No. 4162, Flags of Cuba and USSR, José Marti Monument, Moncada Barracks and Kremlin.
**1973-74    Litho.    Perf. 12**
4161 A1974 4k lt ultra & multi  .25 .20
4162 A1974 4k lt green & multi  .25 .20 ('74)
Visit of General Secretary Leonid I. Brezhnev to India and Cuba. Nos. 4161-4162 each printed with se-tenant label with different statements by Brezhnev in Russian and Hindi, and Russian and Spanish respectively.

Red Star, Soldier, Newspaper A1975
**1974, Jan. 1    Photo.    Perf. 11x11½**
4166 A1975 4k gold, red & black  .25 .20
50th anniversary of the Red Star newspaper.

Victory Monument, Peter-Paul Fortress, Statue of Peter I — A1976
**1974, Jan. 16    Litho.    Perf. 11½**
4167 A1976 4k multicolored  .25 .20
30th anniversary of the victory over the Germans near Leningrad.

Comecon Building — A1978
**1974, Jan. 16    Photo.    Perf. 11½**
4168 A1977 4k dull blue, red & blk  .25 .20
10th anniversary of the Tyumen oilfields.

Oil Workers, Refinery — A1977
**1974, Jan. 16    Photo.    Perf. 11½**
4169 A1978 16k red brn, ol & red  .35 .25
25th anniversary of the Council for Mutual Economic Assistance.

Souvenir Sheet

Aleksander S. Pushkin, by O. A.
Kiprensky — A1995

**1974, June 4    Litho.    Imperf.**
4202 A1995 50k multicolored    1.75 .80

Aleksander S. Pushkin (1799-1837).

Marshal Type of 1973

Designs: #4203, Marshal F. I. Tolbukhin
(1894-1949); #4204, Admiral I. S. Isakov
(1894-1967); #4205, Marshal S. M. Budenny
(1883-1973).

**1974    Engr.    Perf. 12**
4203 A1962 4k olive green    .20 .20
4204 A1962 4k indigo    .20 .20
4205 A1962 4k slate green    .20 .20
Nos. 4203-4205 (3)    .60 .60
Issued: #4203, 6/5; #4204, 7/18; #4205,
8/20.

Stanislavski and Nemirovich-
Danchenko — A1996

**1974, June 12    Litho.    Perf. 11½**
4211 A1996 10k yel, black & dk red    .35 .20

75th anniv. of the Moscow Arts Theater.

Runner,
Track,
Open Book
A1997

**1974, June 12    Photo.    Perf. 12**
4212 A1997 4k multicolored    .25 .20

13th Nat'l School Spartakiad, Alma-Ata.

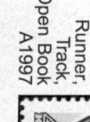

Railroad
Car
A1998

**1974, June 12**
4213 A1998 4k multicolored    .30 .25

Egorov Railroad Car Factory, cent.

Victory Monument,
Minsk — A1999

Liberation
Monument,
Poltava — A2000

#4215, Monument & Government House,
Kiev.

---

**1974, June 20    Perf. 12x11½**
4214 A1999 4k violet, black & yel    .25 .20
4215 A1999 4k blue, black & yel    .25 .20

30th anniversary of liberation of Byelorussia
(No. 4214), and of Ukraine (No. 4215).
Issued: #4214, June 20; #4215, July 18.

Automotive Type of 1973

Designs: 2k, GAZ AA truck, 1932. 3k, GAZ
03-30 bus, 1933. 4k, Zis 5 truck, 1933. 14k, GAZ
Zis 8 bus, 1934. 16k, Zis 101 car, 1936.

**1974, June 20    Perf. 12x11½**
4216 A1968 2k brown & multi    .20 .20
4217 A1968 3k multicolored    .20 .20
4218 A1968 4k orange & multi    .20 .20
4219 A1968 14k multicolored    .50 .20
4220 A1968 16k multicolored    .60 .20
Nos. 4216-4220 (5)    1.70 1.00

Soviet automotive industry.

**1974, July 7    Perf. 11½**
4221 A2000 4k dull red & sepia    .25 .20

800th anniversary of city of Poltava.

Nike Monument, Warsaw and Polish
Flag — A2001

**1974, July 7    Litho.    Perf. 12½x12**
4222 A2001 6k olive & red    .25 .20

Polish People's Republic, 30th anniversary.

Mine Layer — A2002

Soviet Warships: 4k, Landing craft. 6k, Anti-
submarine destroyer and helicopter. 16k, Anti-
submarine cruiser.

**1974, July 25    Engraved and Photogravure    Perf. 11½x12**
4223 A2002 3k multicolored    .20 .20
4224 A2002 4k multicolored    .20 .20
4225 A2002 6k multicolored    .40 .20
4226 A2002 16k multicolored    .75 .20
Nos. 4223-4226 (4)    1.55 .80

Pentathlon
A2003

**1974, Aug. 7    Photo.    Perf. 11½**
4227 A2003 16k gold, blue & brown    .50 .25

World Pentathlon Championships, Moscow.

Portrait Type of 1973

No. 4228, Dimitri Ulyanov (1874-1943),
Soviet official and Lenin's brother. No. 4229,
V. Menzhinsky (1874-1934), Soviet official.

**1974, Aug. 7    Engr.    Perf. 12½x12**
4228 A1960 4k slate green    .25 .20

**Litho.**
4229 A1960 4k rose lake    .25 .20

Painting Type of 1974

Russian paintings: 4k, Lilac, by W. Kontch-
alovski. 6k, "Towards the Wind" (sailboats), by
E. Kalnins. 10k, "Spring" (girl and landscape),
by O. Zardarian. 16k, Northern Harbor, G.
Nissky. 20k, Kirghiz Girl, by S. Chuikov, vert.

---

**Perf. 12x11½, 11½x12    Litho.**
4230 A1986 4k gray & multi    .20 .20
4231 A1986 6k gray & multi    .20 .20
4232 A1986 10k gray & multi    .35 .20
4233 A1986 16k gray & multi    .55 .20
4234 A1986 20k gray & multi    .75 .20
Nos. 4230-4234 (5)    2.05 1.00

Printed in sheets of 18 stamps and 2 labels.

Page of First
Russian
Primer — A2004

**1974, Aug. 20    Photo.    Perf. 11½**
4235 A2004 4k black, red & gold    .25 .20

1st printed Russian primer, 400th anniv.

**1974, Aug. 23**
4236 A2005 6k dk blue, red & yel    .25 .20

Romania's liberation from Fascist rule, 30th
anniversary.

Monument,
Russian and
Romanian
Flags — A2005

Vitebsk
A2006

**1974, Sept. 4    Litho.    Perf. 12**
4237 A2006 4k dk gray & olive    .25 .20

Millennium of city of Vitebsk.

Kirghiz
Republic
A2007

**1974, Sept. 4    Perf. 11½x11**
4238 A2007 4k vio blue & multi    .20 .20
4239 A2007 4k maroon & multi    .20 .20
4240 A2007 4k yellow & multi    .20 .20
4241 A2007 4k green & multi    .20 .20
4242 A2007 4k lt blue & multi    .20 .20
Nos. 4238-4242 (5)    1.00 1.00

50th Anniv. of Founding of Republics (Flags,
industrial and agricultural themes): No. 4238,
Uzbek. No. 4239, Moldavia. No. 4240,
Turkmen. No. 4241, Tadzhik. No. 4242,
Kirghiz.

Arms and Flag of
Bulgaria — A2008

**1974, Sept. 4    Photogravure and Engraved    Perf. 11½**
4243 A2008 6k gold & multi    .25 .20

30th anniv. of the Bulgarian revolution.

---

Arms of
DDR and
Soviet War
Memorial,
Treptow
A2009

**1974, Sept. 4    Photo.**
4244 A2009 6k multicolored    .25 .20

German Democratic Republic, 25th anniv.

Souvenir Sheet

Soviet Stamps and Exhibition
Poster — A2010

**1974, Sept. 4    Litho.    Perf. 12x12½**
4245 A2010 50k multicolored    7.50 3.00

3rd Cong. of the Phil. Soc. of the USSR.

Maly State
Theater — A2011

**1974, Oct. 3    Photo.    Perf. 11x11½**
4246 A2011 4k red, black & gold    .25 .20

150th anniversary of the Maly State Theater, Moscow.

"Guests from Overseas," by N. K.
Roerich — A2012

**1974, Oct. 3    Litho.    Perf. 12**
4247 A2012 6k multicolored    .25 .20

Nicholas Konstantin Roerich (1874-1947),
painter and sponsor of Roerich Pact and Banner of Peace.

UPU
Monument,
Bern, and
Arms of
USSR
A2013

RUSSIA

## Souvenir Sheet

**1974, Dec. 25**  **Photo.**  **Perf. 11½x12**
| | | | | |
|---|---|---|---|---|
| 4276 | A2027 | 6k olive & multi | .25 | .20 |
| 4277 | A2027 | 6k ultra & multi | .25 | .20 |
| 4278 | A2027 | 6k magenta & multi | .25 | .20 |
| 4279 | A2027 | 6k red & multi | .25 | .20 |
| 4280 | A2027 | 6k brown & multi | 1.25 | 1.00 |

Nos. 4276-4280 (5)
Russian aircraft history, 1882-1914.

### Sports and Sport Buildings, Moscow — A2028

**1974, Dec. 25**  **Perf. 11½**
| | | | |
|---|---|---|---|
| 4281 | A2028 Sheet of 4 | 1.60 | .50 |
| a. | 10k Woman gymnast | .30 | .20 |
| b. | 10k Running | .30 | .20 |
| c. | 10k Soccer | .30 | .20 |
| d. | 10k Canoeing | .30 | .20 |

Moscow preparing for Summer Olympic Games, 1980.

### Rotary Press, Masthead — A2029

**1975, Jan. 20**
4282  A2029  4k multicolored    .25  .20
Komsomolskaya Pravda newspaper, 50th anniv.

### Masthead and Pioneer Emblems — A2030

### Spartakiad Emblem and Skiers A2031

### Games' Emblem, Hockey Player and Skier A2032

**1975, Jan. 20**
4283  A2030  4k red, blk & silver    .25  .20
Pioneers' Pravda newspaper, 50th anniv.

**1975, Jan. 20**
4284  A2031  4k blue & multi    .25  .20
8th Winter Spartakiad of USSR Trade Unions.

**1975, Jan. 20**
4285  A2032  16k multicolored    .50  .25
5th Winter Spartakiad of Friendly Armies, Feb. 23-Mar. 1.

---

Chardin. 20k, The Spoiled Child, by Jean Greuze. 50k, Self-portrait, by Jacques Louis David.

**Perf. 12x12½, 12½x12**  **Litho.**
| | | | | |
|---|---|---|---|---|
| 4262 | A2023 | 4k bister & multi | .20 | .20 |
| 4263 | A2023 | 6k bister & multi | .25 | .20 |
| 4264 | A2023 | 10k bister & multi | .35 | .20 |
| 4265 | A2023 | 14k bister & multi | .50 | .20 |
| 4266 | A2023 | 16k bister & multi | .55 | .20 |
| 4267 | A2023 | 20k bister & multi | .75 | .30 |

Nos. 4262-4267 (6)    2.60  1.30

### Souvenir Sheet    Perf. 12

4268  A2023  50k multicolored    1.50  .75
Foreign paintings in Russian museums. Printed in sheets of 16 stamps and 4 labels.

### Morning Glory — A2024

Designs: Flora of the USSR.
**1974, Nov. 20**  **Perf. 12x12½**
| | | | | |
|---|---|---|---|---|
| 4269 | A2024 | 1k red brn & multi | .20 | .20 |
| 4270 | A2024 | 2k green & multi | .20 | .20 |
| 4271 | A2024 | 4k multicolored | .20 | .20 |
| 4272 | A2024 | 4k brown & multi | .50 | .20 |
| 4273 | A2024 | 12k dk blue & multi | .65 | 1.00 |

Nos. 4269-4273 (5)

### Ivan S. Nikitin (1824-1861), Poet — A2025

**Photo.**  **Perf. 11½**
4274  A2025  4k gray grn, grn & blk    .30  .25

### Leningrad Mint — A2026

**Photogravure and Engraved**  **Perf. 11**
**1974, Dec. 11**
4275  A2026  6k silver & multi    .25  .20
250th anniversary of the Leningrad Mint.

### Mozhajsky Plane, 1882 — A2027

Early Russian Aircraft: No. 4277, Grizidubov-N biplane, 1910. No. 4278, Russia-A, 1910. No. 4279, Russian Vityaz (Sikorsky), 1913. No. 4280, Grigorovich flying boat, 1914.

---

**1974, Oct. 28**  **Perf. 12x11½, 11½**  **Photo.**
| | | | | |
|---|---|---|---|---|
| 4255 | A2017 | 6k multicolored | .25 | .20 |
| 4256 | A2018 | 10k multicolored | .40 | .20 |
| 4257 | A2018 | 10k multicolored | .40 | .20 |
| | | | 1.05 | .60 |

Russian explorations of Mars (6k); flight of Soyuz 14 (No. 4256) and of Soyuz 15, Aug. 26-28 (No. 4257).

### Mongolian Flag and Arms A2019

**1974, Nov. 14**  **Photo.**  **Perf. 11½**
4258  A2019  6k gold & multi    .25  .20
Mongolian People's Republic, 50th anniv.

### Guards' Ribbon, Estonian Government Building, Tower — A2020

**1974, Nov. 14**
4259  A2020  4k multicolored    .25  .20
Liberation of Estonia, 30th anniversary.

### Tanker, Passenger and Cargo Ships — A2021

**1974, Nov. 14**  **Typo.**  **Perf. 12½x12**
4260  A2021  4k multicolored    .25  .20
USSR Merchant Marine, 50th anniversary.

### Spasski Tower Clock — A2022

**1974, Nov. 14**  **Litho.**  **Perf. 12**
4261  A2022  4k multicolored    .30  .20
New Year 1975.

### The Fishmonger, by Pieters A2023

Paintings: 4k. The Marketplace, by Beukelaer, 1564. 10k, A Drink of Lemonade, by Gerard Terborch. 14k, Girl at Work, by Gabriel Metsu. 16k, Saying Grace, by Jean

---

### Development of Postal Service — A2014

UPU Cent.: No. 4248, Ukrainian coat of arms, letters, UPU emblem and headquarters, Bern. No. 4249, Arms of Byelorussia, UPU emblem, letters, stagecoach and rocket.

**Photogravure and Engraved**  **Perf. 12x11½**
| | | | | |
|---|---|---|---|---|
| 4248 | A2013 | 10k red & multi | .35 | .20 |
| 4249 | A2013 | 10k red & multi | .35 | .20 |
| 4250 | A2013 | 10k red & multi | .35 | .20 |

Nos. 4248-4250 (3)    1.05  .60

### Souvenir Sheet    Typo.    Perf. 11½x12

| | | | |
|---|---|---|---|
| 4251 | A2014 Sheet of 3 | 7.50 | 3.00 |
| a. | 30k Jet and UPU emblem | 2.00 | .80 |
| b. | 30k Mail coach, UPU emblem | 2.00 | .80 |
| c. | 40k UPU emblem | 2.00 | .80 |

### Order of Labor, 1st, 2nd and 3rd Grade A2015

### KAMAZ Truuk Leaving Kama Plant — A2016

Design: #4254, Nurek Hydroelectric Plant.
**1974, Oct. 16**  **Litho.**  **Perf. 12½x12**
| | | | | |
|---|---|---|---|---|
| 4252 | A2015 | 4k multicolored | .25 | .20 |
| 4253 | A2016 | 4k multicolored | .25 | .20 |
| 4254 | A2016 | 4k multicolored | .75 | .60 |

Nos. 4252-4254 (3)

### Space Stations Mars 4-7 over Mars A2017

### P. R. Popovich, Y. P. Artyukhin and Soyuz 14 — A2018

Design: No. 4257, Cosmonauts G. V. Sarafanov and L. S. Demin, Soyuz 15. horiz.

## Republic Anniversaries Type of 1970

Design (Hammer-Sickle Emblem and): No. 4286, Landscape and produce.

**1975, Jan. 24    Engr.    Perf. 12x12½**
4286    A1794    4k green    .30    .20

50th anniversary of Karakalpak Autonomous Soviet Socialist Republic.

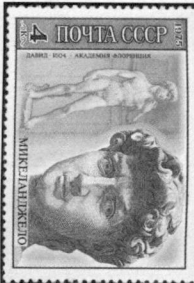

David, by Michelangelo — A2033

Works by Michelangelo: 6k, Squatting Boy. 10k, Rebellious Slave. 14k, The Creation of Adam. 20k, Staircase, Laurentian Library, Florence. 30k, The Last Judgment.

Michelangelo, Self-portrait — A2034

**1975, Feb. 27    Lithographed and Engraved**
**Perf. 12½x12**
4296    A2033    4k slate grn & grn    .20    .20
4297    A2033    6k red brn & bister    .20    .20
4298    A2033    10k slate grn & grn    .35    .20
4299    A2033    14k red brn & bister    .50    .50
a.    Min. sheet, 2 ea #4296-4298         5.00
4300    A2033    20k slate grn & grn    .70    .40
4301    A2033    30k red brn & bister    .85    .60
a.    Min. sheet 2 ea #4299-4301         2.00
Nos. 4296-4301(6)         2.80    1.80

4302    A2034    50k gold & multi    3.00    .80

Souvenir Sheet
**Perf. 12x11½**

Michelangelo Buonarroti (1475-1564), Italian sculptor, painter and architect. Issued only in the min. sheets of 6.

Mozhajski, Early Plane and Supersonic Jet TU-144 — A2035

**1975, Feb. 27    Photo.    Perf. 12½x11½**
4303    A2035    6k violet blue & ocher    .25    .20

A. F. Mozhajski (1825-1890), pioneer aircraft designer, birth sesquicentennial.

"Metric System" — A2036

**1975, Mar. 14    Perf. 11½**
4304    A2036    6k blk, vio blue & org    .25    .20

Int. Meter Convention, Paris, 1875, cent.

Spartakiad Emblem and Sports — A2037

**1975, Mar. 14**
4305    A2037    6k red, silver & black    .25    .20

6th Summer Spartakiad.

---

**1975, Mar. 14**
4306    A2038    6k gold & multi    .25    .20
4307    A2039    6k gold & multi    .25    .20

30th anniv. of liberation from fascism, Hungary (#4306) & Czechoslovakia (#4307).

Liberation Monument, Parliament, Arms — A2038

Charles Bridge Towers, Arms and Flags — A2039

Flags of France and USSR — A2040

**1975, Mar. 25    Litho.    Perf. 12**
4308    A2040    6k lilac & multi    .25    .20

50th anniv. of the establishment of diplomatic relations between France and USSR. 1st foreign recognition of Soviet State.

A. V. Filipchenko, N.N. Rukavishnikov, Russo-American Space Emblem, Soyuz 16 — A2042

Yuri A. Gagarin, by L. Kerbel — A2041

**1975, Mar. 28    Photo.**
**Perf. 11½x12, 12x11½**

Cosmonauts' Day: 10k A. A. Gubarev, G. M. Grechko aboard Soyuz 17 & orbital station Salyut 4.

4309    A2041    6k blue, sil & red    .20    .20
4310    A2042    10k blk, blue & red    .40    .20
4311    A2042    16k multicolored    .50    .20
Nos. 4309-4311(3)    1.10    .60

Warsaw Treaty Members' Flags — A2043

**1975, Apr. 16    Litho.    Perf. 12**
4312    A2043    6k multicolored    .30    .20

Signing of the Warsaw Treaty (Bulgaria, Czechoslovakia, German Democratic Rep., Hungary, Poland, Romania, USSR), 20th anniv.

---

Communications Emblem and Exhibition Pavilion — A2045

**1975, Apr. 22    Perf. 11½**
4314    A2045    6k ultra, red & silver    .25    .20

International Communications Exhibition, Sokolniki Park, Moscow, May 1975.

Lenin on Steps of Winter Palace, by V. G. Zyplakow — A2044

**1975, Apr. 22    Perf. 12x12½**
4313    A2044    4k multicolored    .30    .20

105th anniversary of the birth of Lenin.

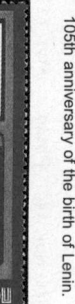

Lenin and Red Flag — A2046

War Memorial, Berlin-Treptow — A2048

Order of Victory — A2047

**1975, Apr. 22    Typo.    Perf. 12**
4315    A2046    4k shown    .25    .20
4316    A2046    4k Eternal Flame and guard    .25    .20
4317    A2046    4k Woman muni-tions worker    .25    .20
4318    A2046    4k Partisans    .25    .20
4319    A2046    4k Soldier destroying swastika    .25    .20
4320    A2046    4k Soldier with gun and banner    .25    .20
Nos. 4315-4320(6)    1.50    1.20

**Souvenir Sheet**
**Litho., Typo. & Photo.**
**Imperf**
4321    A2047    50k multicolored    5.00    3.00

World War II victory, 30th anniversary.

---

Soyuz-Apollo Docking Emblem and Painting by Cosmonaut A. A. Leonov — A2049

**1975, May 23    Photo.    Perf. 12x11½**
4324    A2049    20k multicolored    .60    .35

Russo-American space cooperation.

**Automobile Type of 1973**
4325    A1968    4k dp org & multi    .20    .20
4326    A1968    3k green & multi    .20    .20
4327    A1968    12k maroon & multi    .30    .20
4328    A1968    12k green & multi    .45    .20
4329    A1968    16k olive & multi    .20    .20
Nos. 4325-4329(5)    1.35    1.00

2k, GAZ-M-I car, 1936. 3k, 5-ton truck, YAG-6, 1936. 4k, ZIZ-16, autobus, 1938. 12k, KIM-10 car, 1940. 16k, GAZ-67B Jeep, 1943.

**1975, May 23    Photo.**
4330    A2050    6k multicolored    .25    .20

9th Int. Congress on Irrigation and Drainage, Moscow, and International Commission on Irrigation and Drainage, 25th anniv.

Canal, Emblem, Produce — A2050

Flags and Arms of Poland and USSR, Factories A2051

**1975, May 23**
4331    A2051    6k multicolored    .25    .20

Treaty of Friendship, Cooperation and Mutual Assistance between Poland & USSR, 30th anniv.

Man in Space and Earth A2052

**1975, May 23**
4332    A2052    6k multicolored    .25    .20

First man walking in space, Lt. Col. Alexei Leonov, 10th anniversary.

---

**1975, Apr. 25    Litho.    Perf. 12x12½**
4322    A2048    6k buff & multi    .25    .20

**Souvenir Sheet**
4323    A2048    50k dull blue & multi    3.00    .60

Socfilex 75 Int. Phil. Exhib. honoring 30th anniv. of WWII victory, Moscow, May 8-18.

**Avetik Isaakyan, by Martiros Saryan A2065**

**1975, Aug. 20 Litho. Perf. 12x12½**
4358 A2065 4k multicolored .20 .20
Isaakyan (1875-1957), Armenian poet.

**Jacques Duclos — A2066**

**1975, Aug. 20 Photo. Perf. 11½x12**
4359 A2066 6k maroon & silver .25 .20
Duclos (1896-1975), French labor leader.

**al-Farabi — A2067**

**1975, Aug. 20 Perf. 11½**
4360 A2067 6k grnsh blue, brn & bis .25 .20
Nasr al-Farabi (870?-950), Arab philosopher.

**Male Ruffs A2068**

**1975, Aug. 25 Litho. Perf. 12½x12**
4361 A2068 1k shown .20 .20
4363 A2068 4k Altai roebuck .20 .20
4364 A2068 6k Siberian marten .20 .20
4305 A2000 10k Old squaw (duck) .40 .20
10k Dajuj .55 1.00
Nos. 4361-4365 (5) 1.55 1.00

A2070
A2069

Designs: #4366, Flags of USSR, North Korea, arms of N. K., Liberation monument, Pyongyang; #4367, Flags of USSR, North Viet Nam, arms of N.V., industrial development.

**1975, Aug. 28 Perf. 12**
4366 A2069 6k multicolored .30 .20
4367 A2070 6k multicolored .30 .20
Liberation of North Korea from Japanese occupation (#4366); and establishment of Democratic Republic of Viet Nam (#4367), 30th anniv.

---

**Souvenir Sheet Perf. 12x11½**
Sheet of 2 2.00 .90
4349 a. A2061 30k Dolphin rising .80 .30
b. A2061 30k Dolphin diving .80 .30
Oceanexpo 75, 1st Intl. Oceanographic Exhib., Okinawa, July 20, 1975-Jan. 1976. No. 4349 contains 55x25mm stamps.

**Parade, Red Square, 1941, by K. F. Yuon — A2062**

Paintings: 2k, Morning of Industrial Moscow, by Yuon. 6k, Soldiers Inspecting Captured Artillery, by Lansere. 10k, Excavating Metro Tunnel, by Lansere. 16k, Pushkin and His Wife at Court Ball, by Ulyanov, vert. 20k, De Lauriston at Kutuzov's Headquarters, by Ulyanov.

**1975, July 22 Litho. Perf. 12½x11½**
4350 A2062 1k gray & multi .20 .20
4351 A2062 2k gray & multi .20 .20
4352 A2062 6k gray & multi .25 .20
4353 A2062 10k gray & multi .40 .20
4354 A2062 16k gray & multi .80 .25
4355 A2062 20k gray & multi .90 .30
Nos. 4350-4355 (6) 2.75 1.35
Konstantin F. Yuon (1875-1958), Yevgeni Y. Lansere (1875-1946), Nikolai Y. Ulyanov (1875-1949). Nos. 4350-4355 issued in sheets of 16 plus 4 labels.

**Finlandia Hall, Map of Europe, Laurel — A2063**

**1975, Aug. 18 Photo. Perf. 11½**
4356 A2063 6k brt blue, gold & blk .25 .20
European Security and Cooperation Conference, Helsinki, July 30-Aug. 1. Printed se-tenant with label with quotation by Leonid I. Brezhnev, first secretary of Communist party.

**Chuyrlenis, Waves and Lighthouse A2064**

**1975, Aug. 20 Photo. & Engr.**
4357 A2064 4k grm, indigo & gold .50 .20
M. K. Chuyrlenis, Lithuanian composer, birth centenary.

---

**Soviet and American Astronauts and Flags — A2058**

**Apollo and Soyuz After Link-up and Earth — A2059**

**Soyuz Launch A2060**

Designs: No. 4340, Spacecraft before linkup, earth and project emblem. 50k, Soviet Mission Control Center.

**1975, July 15 Litho. Perf. 11½**
4338 A2058 10k multicolored .55 .20
4339 A2059 12k multicolored .80 .20
4340 A2059 12k multicolored .80 .20
a. Vert. pair, #4339-4340 2.00 1.00
4341 A2060 16k multicolored .90 .40
Nos. 4338-4341 (4) 3.05 1.00

**Souvenir Sheet Photo. Perf. 12x11½**
4342 A2058 50k multicolored 2.00 1.25
Apollo-Soyuz space test project (Russo-American space cooperation), launching, July 1½; link-up, July 17. No. 4342 contains one 50x21mm stamp. See US Nos. 1569-1570.

**Sturgeon, Caspian Sea, Oceanexpo 75 Emblem — A2061**

Designs (Oceanexpo 75 Emblem and): 4k, Salt-water shell, Black Sea. 6k, Eel, Baltic Sea. 10k, Sea duck, Arctic Sea. 16k, Crab, Far Eastern waters. 20k, Chrisipher (fish), Pacific Ocean.

**1975, July 22 Photo. Perf. 11**
4343 A2061 3k multicolored .20 .20
4344 A2061 4k multicolored .20 .20
4345 A2061 6k green & multi .25 .20
4346 A2061 10k dk blue & multi .40 .30
4347 A2061 16k purple & multi .60 .30
4348 A2061 20k multicolored .70 .65
Nos. 4343-4340 (6) 2.35 1.05

---

**Yakov M. Sverdlov (1885-1919), Organizer and Early Member of Communist Party — A2053**

**1975, June 4**
4333 A2053 4k multicolored .30 .20

**Congress, Emblem, Forest and Field A2054**

**1975, June 4 Litho. Perf. 11½**
4334 A2054 6k multicolored .25 .20
8th International Congress for Conservation of Plants, Moscow.

**Symbolic Flower with Plants and Emblem A2055**

**1975, June 20 Litho. Perf. 11½**
4335 A2055 6k multicolored .25 .20
12th International Botanical Congress.

**Souvenir Sheet**

**UN Emblem — A2056**

**1975, June 20 Photo. Perf. 11½x12**
4336 A2056 50k gold & blue 2.50 1.00
30th anniversary of United Nations.

**Globe and Film A2057**

**1975, June 20 Photo. Perf. 11½**
4337 A2057 6k multicolored .25 .20
9th Intl. Film Festival, Moscow, 1975.

**1975, Sept. 12 Photo. Perf. 12x11½**
4368 A2071 10k ultra, blk & dp org .30 .20
Docking of space ship Soyuz 18 and space station Salyut 4.

P. Klimuk and V. Sevastyanov, Soyuz 18 and Salyut 4 Docking — A2071

S. A. Esenin and Birches A2072

**1975, Sept. 12 Photogravure and Engraved Perf. 11½**
4369 A2072 6k brown & ocher .25 .20
Sergei A. Esenin (1895-1925), poet.

Standardization Symbols — A2073

**1975, Sept. 12 Photo. Perf. 11½**
4370 A2073 4k red & multi .25 .20
USSR Committee for Standardization of Communications Ministry, 50th anniversary.

Karakul Lamb A2074

**1975, Sept. 22 Photo. Perf. 11½**
4371 A2074 6k black, yel & grn .25 .20
3rd International Symposium on astrakhan production, Samarkand, Sept. 22-27.

Dr. M. P. Konchalovsky A2075

Exhibition Emblem A2076

**1975, Sept. 30 Perf. 11½x12**
4372 A2075 4k brown & red .25 .20
Konchalovsky (1875-1942), physician.

**1975, Sept. 30 Perf. 11½**
4373 A2076 4k deep blue & red .25 .20
3rd All-Union Youth Phil. Exhib., Erevan.

---

IVY Emblem and Rose — A2077

**1975, Sept. 30 Litho. Perf. 12x11½**
4374 A2077 6k multicolored .25 .20
International Women's Year 1975.

Yugoslavian Flag and Parliament A2078

**1975, Sept. 30 Photo. Perf. 11½**
4375 A2078 6k gold, red & blue .25 .20
Republic of Yugoslavia, 30th anniv.

Illustration from 1938 Edition, by V. A. Favorsky — A2079

**1975, Oct. 20 Typo. Perf. 12**
4376 A2079 4k buff, red & black .30 .20
175th anniversary of the 1st edition of the old Russian saga "Slovo o polku igoreve."

Mikhail Ivanovich Kalinin — A2080

**1975, Oct. 20 Engr. Perf. 12**
4377 A2080 4k sepia .25 .20
4378 A2080 4k sepia .25 .20
#4378, Anatoli Vasilievich Lunacharski.
Kalinin (1875-1946), chairman of Central Executive Committee and Presidium of Supreme Soviet; Lunacharski, writer, commissar for education.

Hand Holding Torch and Lenin Quotation — A2081

**1975, Oct. 20 Engr.**
4379 A2081 4k red & olive .25 .20
First Russian Revolution (1905), 70th anniv.

Building Baikal-Amur Railroad — A2082

---

Novolipetsk Metallurgical Plant — A2083
Nevynomyssk Chemical Plant, Fertilizer Formula — A2084

**1975, Oct. 30 Photo. Perf. 11½**
4380 A2082 4k gold & multi .20 .20
4381 A2083 4k red, gray & sl green .20 .20
4382 A2084 4k red, blue & silver .20 .20
Nos. 4380-4382 (3) .60 .60
58th anniversary of October Revolution.

Bas-relief of Decembrists and "Decembrists at the Senate Square," by D. N. Kardovsky — A2085

**1975, Nov. 12 Litho. & Engr. Perf. 11½**
4383 A2085 4k gray & multi .25 .20
Sesquicentennial of Decembrist rising.

Star and "1976" — A2086

**1975, Nov. 12 Litho. Perf. 12x12½**
4384 A2086 4k green & multi .35 .20
New Year 1976.

Village Street, by A. Vasilev A2087

**1975, Nov. 25 Perf. 12x12½, 12½x12**
4385 A2087 2k gray & multi .20 .20
4386 A2087 4k gray & multi .20 .20
4387 A2087 6k gray & multi .20 .20
4388 A2087 10k gray & multi .30 .20
4389 A2087 12k gray & multi .45 .20
4390 A2087 16k gray & multi .55 .25
Nos. 4385-4390 (6) 2.40 1.25

**Souvenir Sheet Perf. 12**
4391 A2087 50k gray & multi 2.00 .90

Paintings by Vasilov: 4k, Road in Birch Forest. 6k, After the Thunderstorm. 10k, Swamp, Meadow, horiz. 12k, In the Crimean Mountains. 16k, Portrait, by Kramskoi.
Fedor Aleksandrovich Vasiliev (1850-1873), landscape painter. Nos. 4385-4390 printed in sheets of 7 stamps and one label.

---

Landing Capsule, Venus Surface, Lenin Banner A2088

**1975, Dec. 8 Photo. Perf. 11½**
4392 A2088 10k multicolored .35 .25
Flights of Soviet interplanetary stations Venera 9 and Venera 10.

Gabriel Sundoukian — A2089

**1975, Dec. 8 Litho. Perf. 12**
4393 A2089 4k multicolored .50 .30
Sundoukian (1825-1912), Armenian playwright.

Polar Poppies, Taiga A2090

**1975, Dec. 25 Photogravure and Engraved Perf. 12x11½**
4394 A2090 4k black & multi .20 .20
4395 A2090 6k black & multi .25 .20
4396 A2090 10k black & multi .35 .20
4397 A2090 12k black & multi .40 .20
4398 A2090 16k black & multi .50 .25
Nos. 4394-4398 (5) 1.70 1.05

Regional Flowers: 6k, Globeflowers, tundra. 10k, Buttercups, oak forest. 12k, Wood anemones, steppe. 16k, Erminum Lehmannii, desert.

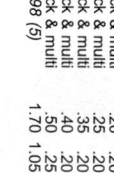

A. L. Mints (1895-1974), Academician A2091

**1975, Dec. 31 Photo. Perf. 11½x12**
4399 A2091 4k dp brown & gold .25 .20

Demon, by A. Kochupalov A2092

**1975, Dec. 31 Litho. Perf. 12**
4400 A2092 4k bister & multi .20 .20
4401 A2092 6k bister & multi .30 .20
4402 A2092 10k bister & multi .50 .20
Paintings: 6k, Vasilisa the Beautiful, by I. Vakurov. 10k, Snow Maiden, by T. Zubkova. 16k, Summer, by K. Kukulieva. 20k, The Fisherman and the Goldfish, by I. Vakurov, horiz.

Designs: 6k, Meteor and Molniya Satellites, Orbita Ground Communications Center. 10k, Cosmonauts on board Salyut space station and Mars planetary station. 12k, Interkosmos station and Apollo-Soyuz linking.

**Lithographed and Engraved**

**1976, Apr. 12** **Perf. 11½**

| | | | |
|---|---|---|---|
| 4427 | A2104 | 4k multicolored | .20 .20 |
| 4428 | A2104 | 6k multicolored | .25 .20 |
| 4429 | A2104 | 10k multicolored | .35 .20 |
| 4430 | A2104 | 12k multicolored | .55 .20 |
| | | Nos. 4427-4430 (4) | 1.35 .80 |

**Souvenir Sheet**

**Engr.** **Perf. 12**

4431 A2105 50k black    10.00 2.00

1st manned flight in space, 15th anniv.

Samed Vurgun and Derrick A2107

I. A. Dzhavakhishvili A2106

**1976, Apr. 20** **Photo.** **Perf. 11½x12**

4432 A2106 4k multicolored    .25 .20

Dzhavakhishvili (1876-1940), scientist.

**1976, Apr. 20** **Perf. 11½**

4433 A2107 4k multicolored    .25 .20

Vurgun (1906-56), natl. poet of Azerbaijan.

USSR Flag, Worker and Farmer Monument.

1st All-Union Festival of Amateur Artists — A2108

**1976, May 12** **Litho.** **Perf. 11½x12**

4434 A2108 4k multicolored    .25 .20

Intl. Federation of Philately, 50th Anniv. — A2109

**1976, May 12** **Photo.** **Perf. 11½**

4435 A2109 6k FIP Emblem    .25 .20

---

Atom Symbol and Dubna Institute — A2101

**1976, Mar. 10** **Photo.** **Perf. 11½**

4420 A2101 6k vio bl, red & silver    .25 .20

Joint Institute of Nuclear Research, Dubna, 20th anniversary.

Bolshoi Theater — A2102

**1976, Mar. 24** **Litho.** **Perf. 11x11½**

4421 A2102 10k yel, blue & dk brn    .30 .20

Bicentenary of Bolshoi Theater.

Back from the Fair, by Konchalovsky — A2103

Paintings by P. P. Konchalovsky. 2k, The Green Glass. 6k, Peaches. 16k, Meat, Game and Vegetables. 20k, Self-portrait, 1943, vert.

**1976, Apr. 6** **Perf. 12½x12, 12x12½**

| | | | |
|---|---|---|---|
| 4422 | A2103 | 1k yellow & multi | .20 .20 |
| 4423 | A2103 | 2k yellow & multi | .20 .20 |
| 4424 | A2103 | 6k yellow & multi | .20 .20 |
| 4425 | A2103 | 16k yellow & multi | .70 .20 |
| 4426 | A2103 | 20k yellow & multi | .85 .30 |
| | | Nos. 4422-4426 (5) | 2.25 1.10 |

Birth centenary of P. P. Konchalovsky.

Vostok, Salyut-Soyuz Link-up — A2104

Yuri A. Gagarin — A2105

---

| | | | |
|---|---|---|---|
| 4403 | A2092 | 16k bister & multi | .60 .20 |
| 4404 | A2092 | 20k bister & multi | .80 .25 |
| a. | | Strip of 5, #4400-4404 | 2.40 .60 |

Palekh Art State Museum, Ivanov Region.

Wilhelm Pieck (1876-1960), Pres. of German Democratic Republic — A2093

**1976, Jan. 3** **Engr.** **Perf. 12½x12**

4405 A2093 6k bluish black    .20 .20

M. E. Saltykov-Shchedrin, by I.N. Kramskoi — A2094

**1976, Jan. 14** **Litho.** **Perf. 12x12½**

4406 A2094 4k multicolored    .25 .20

Mikhail Evgrafovich Saltykov-Shchedrin (1826-1889), writer and revolutionist.

Congress Emblem — A2095

**1976, Feb. 2** **Photo.** **Perf. 11½**

4407 A2095 4k red, gold & mar    .25 .20

**Souvenir Sheet**

**Perf. 11½x12**

4408 A2095 50k red, gold & mar    1.75 .65

25th Congress of the Communist Party of the Soviet Union.

**1976, Feb. 2** **Perf. 11½**

4409 A2096 4k red, black & blue    .25 .20

Ukrainian Communist Party, 25th Congress.

Ice Hockey, Games' Emblem A2097

Designs (Winter Olympic Games' Emblem and): 4k, Cross-country skiing. 6k, Figure skating, pairs. 10k, Speed skating. 20k, Luge. 50k, Winter Olympic Games' emblem, vert.

**1976, Feb. 4** **Litho.** **Perf. 12½x12**

| | | | |
|---|---|---|---|
| 4410 | A2097 | 2k multicolored | .20 .20 |
| 4411 | A2097 | 4k multicolored | .20 .20 |
| 4412 | A2097 | 6k multicolored | .30 .20 |
| 4413 | A2097 | 10k multicolored | .45 .20 |
| 4414 | A2097 | 20k multicolored | .95 .30 |
| | | Nos. 4410-4414 (5) | 2.10 1.10 |

**Souvenir Sheet**

**Perf. 12x12½**

4415 A2097 50k vio bl, org & red    2.00 1.00

12th Winter Olympic Games, Innsbruck, Austria, Feb. 4-15. No. 4415 contains one stamp; silver and violet blue margin showing designs of Nos. 4410-4414. Size: 90x80mm.

No. 4415 Overprinted in Red

**Souvenir Sheet**

4416 A2097 50k multicolored    6.00 4.00

Success of Soviet athletes in 12th Winter Olympic Games. Translation of overprint: "Glory to Soviet Sport! The athletes of the USSR have won 13 gold, 6 silver and 8 bronze medals."

K.E. Voroshilov A2098

**1976, Feb. 4** **Engr.** **Perf. 12**

4417 A2098 4k slate green    .40 .20

Kliment Efremovich Voroshilov (1881-1969), pres. of revolutionary military council, commander of Leningrad front, USSR pres. 1953-60. See Nos. 4487-4488, 4545-4548.

Flag over Kremlin Palace of Congresses, Troitskaya Tower A2099

**Photogravure on Gold Foil**

**1976, Feb. 24** **Perf. 12x11½**

4418 A2099 20k gold, grn & red    4.00 2.00

25th Congress of the Communist Party of the Soviet Union (CPSU).

Lenin on Red Square, by P. Vasiliev — A2100

**1976, Mar. 10** **Litho.** **Perf. 12½x12**

4419 A2100 4k yellow & multi    .25 .20

106th anniversary of the birth of Lenin.

Souvenir Sheet

**1976, May 12 Litho. Perf. 12**
V. A. Tropinin, Self-portrait.—A2110
4436 A2110 50k multicolored 1.75 1.00
Vasily Andreevich Tropinin (1776-1857), painter.

Emblem, Dnieper Bridge
A2111

**1976, May 20 Perf. 12**
4437 A2111 4k Prus blue, gold & blk .25 .20
Bicentenary of Dnepropetrovsk.

Dr. N. N. Burdenko
A2112

**1976, May 20 Perf. 11½x12**
4438 A2112 4k deep brown & red .25 .20
Burdenko (1876-1946), neurosurgeon.

K. A. Trenev (1876-1945), Playwright
A2113

**1976, May 20 Photo. Perf. 12x11½**
4439 A2113 4k black & multi .25 .20

**Automobile Type of 1973**
2k, ZIS-110 passenger car. 3k, GAZ-51
Gorky truck. 4k, GAZ-M-20 Pobeda passenger
car. 12k, ZIS-150 Moscow Motor Works truck.
16k, ZIS-154 Moscow Motor Works bus.

**1976, June 15 Photo. Perf. 12x11½**
4440 A1968 2k grnsh bl & multi .20 .20
4441 A1968 3k bister & multi .20 .20
4442 A1968 4k dk blue & multi .20 .20
4443 A1968 12k brown & multi .20 .20
4444 A1968 16k deep car & multi .20 .20
Nos. 4440-4444 (5) 2.00 1.00

USSR National Olympic Committee
Emblem and: 6k, Basketball vert. 10k, Greco-
Roman wrestling. 14k, Women's discus, vert.
16k. Target shooting. 50k, Olympic medal, vert.
obverse and reverse.

Canoeing
A2114

---

**1976, June 23 Perf. 12½x12, 12x12½ Litho.**
4445 A2114 4k red & multi .20 .20
4446 A2114 6k red & multi .20 .20
4447 A2114 10k red & multi .45 .20
4448 A2114 14k red & multi .60 .20
4449 A2114 16k red & multi .65 .20
Nos. 4445-4449 (5) 2.10 1.05

Souvenir Sheet

4450 A2114 50k red & multi 3.00 .75
21st Olympic Games, Montreal, Canada,
July 17-Aug. 1.
For overprint see No. 4472.

Electric Trains, Overpass
A2115

**1976, June 23 Photo. Perf. 11½**
4451 A2115 4k multicolored 1.00 .20
Electrification of USSR railroads, 50th
anniversary.

L. Emilio Rekabarren—A2116

**1976, July 6 Perf. 11½**
4452 A2116 6k gold, red & blk .25 .20
Luis Emilio Rekabarren (1876-1924),
founder of Chilean Communist Party.

Ljudmila Pavlichenko (1916-1974), WWII Heroine—A2117

**1976, July 6 Perf. 11½**
4453 A2117 4k dp brn, silver & yel .25 .20

Pavel Andreevich Fedotov (1815-1852), Painter
A2118

Paintings: 2k, New Partner, by P. A.
Fedotov. 4k, The Fastidious Fiancée, horiz.
6k, Aristocrat's Breakfast. 10k, Gamblers,
horiz. 16k, The Outing. 50k, Self-portrait.

**1976, July 15 Perf. 12x12½, 12½x12**
4454 A2118 2k black & multi .20 .20
4455 A2118 4k black & multi .20 .20
4456 A2118 6k black & multi .20 .20
4457 A2118 10k black & multi .20 .20
4458 A2118 16k black & multi .25 .25
Nos. 4454-4458 (5) 1.70 1.05

Souvenir Sheet
Perf. 12
4459 A2118 50k multicolored 2.50 .75
Nos. 4454-4458 each printed in sheets of 20
stamps and center label with black commemorative inscription.

---

**1976, Aug. 18 Litho.**
S. S. Nametkin
A2119

**1976, Aug. 18 Litho. Perf. 12x12½**
4460 A2119 4k blue, black & buff .25 .20
Sergei Semenovich Nametkin (1876-1950),
organic chemist.

Squacco Heron
A2120

Waterfowl: 3k, Arctic loon. 4k, European
coot. 6k, Atlantic puffin. 10k, Slender-billed
gull.

**1976, Aug. 20 Photo. Perf. 11½x12½**
4465 A2120 1k green & multi .20 .20
4466 A2120 3k ol green & multi .50 .50
4467 A2120 4k orange & multi .80 .80
4468 A2120 6k purple & multi 1.10 1.10
4469 A2120 10k brt blue & multi 2.40 2.40
Nos. 4465-4469 (5) 5.00 5.00
Nature protection.

Peace Dove
A2121

**1976, Aug. 25 Photo. Perf. 11½**
4470 A2121 4k salmon, gold & blue .25 .20
2nd Stockholm appeal and movement to
stop arms race.

Resistance Movement Emblem
A2122

**1976, Aug. 25**
4471 A2122 6k dk bl, blk & gold .25 .20
Intl. Resistance Movement Fed., 25th anniv.

No. 4450 Overprinted in Gold in Margin
Souvenir Sheet

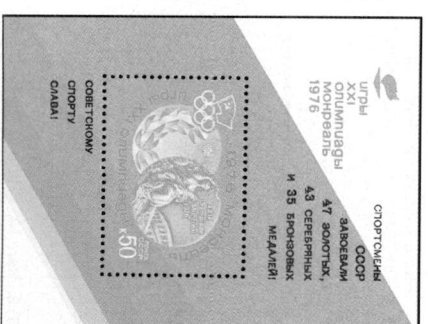

**1976, Aug. 25 Litho. Perf. 12½x12**
4472 A2114 50k red & multi 4.50 .75
Victories of Soviet athletes in 21st Olympic
Games (47 gold, 43 silver and 35 bronze
medals).

---

**1976, Sept. 8**
4473 A2123 4k multicolored .25 .20
Friendship and cooperation between USSR
and India.

Flags of India and USSR—A2123

**1976, Sept. 8 Engr. Perf. 12x12½**
UN, UNESCO Emblems, Open Book—A2124
4474 A2124 16k multicolored .40 .30
UNESCO, 30th anniv.

B. V. Volynov, V. M. Zholobov, Star Circling Globe—A2125

**1976, Sept. 8 Photo. Perf. 12x11½**
4475 A2125 10k brn, blue & black .50 .35
Exploits of Soyuz 21 and Salyut space
station.

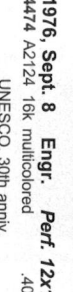 

"Industry"—A2126

**1976, Sept. 17**
4476 A2126 4k shown .25 .20
4477 A2126 4k Farm industry .25 .20
4478 A2126 4k Science .25 .20
4479 A2126 4k Transport & com- .25 .20
4480 A2126 4k Intl. cooperation .25 .20
Nos. 4476-4480 (5) 1.25 1.00
25th Congress of the Communist Party of
the Soviet Union.

Victory, by I. I. Vakurov
A2127

Paintings: 2k, Plower, by I. I. Golikov, horiz.
4k, Au (woman), by I. V. Markichev. 12k, Firebird, by A. V. Kotuhin, horiz. 14k, Festival, by
A. I. Vatagin. 20k.

**1976, Sept. 22 Perf. 12½x12, 12x12½ Litho.**
4481 A2127 2k black & multi .20 .20
4482 A2127 4k black & multi .25 .20
4483 A2127 12k black & multi 1.10 .20

| | | | | |
|---|---|---|---|---|
| 4520 | A2138 | 4k brick red | .20 | .20 |
| 4521 | A2139 | 6k Prus blue | .20 | .20 |
| 4522 | A2138 | 10k olive green | .20 | .20 |
| 4523 | A2139 | 12k violet blue | .45 | .20 |
| 4524 | A2139 | 16k deep green | .60 | .20 |
| 4525 | A2140 | 20k brown red | .80 | .20 |
| 4526 | A2141 | 30k brick red | 1.10 | .20 |
| 4527 | A2142 | 50k dark brown | 1.90 | .20 |
| 4528 | A2143 | 1r dark green | 4.00 | 2.40 |
| | | Nos. 4517-4528 (12) | 10.40 | 2.40 |

Issued: #4517-4524, 12/17; #4525-4528, 8/10. For overprint see #5720. See #4596-4607.

Luna 24 Emblem and Moon Landing A2144

**1976, Dec. 17 Photo. Perf. 11½**
4531 A2144 10k multicolored .30 .20
Moon exploration of automatic station Luna 24.

Icebreaker "Pilot" — A2145
**Perf. 12x11½, 11½x12**

Icebreakers: 6k, Ermak, vert. 10k, Fedor Litke. 16k, Vladimir Ilich, vert. 20k, Krassin.

**1976, Dec. 22 Litho. & Engr.**
| | | | | |
|---|---|---|---|---|
| 4532 | A2145 | 4k multicolored | .20 | .20 |
| 4533 | A2145 | 6k multicolored | .20 | .20 |
| 4534 | A2145 | 10k multicolored | .45 | .20 |
| 4535 | A2145 | 16k multicolored | .55 | .25 |
| 4536 | A2145 | 20k multicolored | .70 | .30 |
| | | Nos. 4532-4536 (5) | 2.10 | 1.15 |

See Nos. 4579-4585.

Soyuz 22 Emblem, Cosmonauts V. F. Bykofsky and V. V. Aksenov — A2146
**1976, Dec. 28 Photo. Perf. 12x11½**
4537 A2146 10k multicolored .30 .25
Soyuz 22 space flight, Sept. 15-23.

Society Emblem — A2147
**1977, Jan. 1 Perf. 11½**
4538 A2147 4k multicolored .25 .20
Red Banner Voluntary Soc., supporting Red Army, Navy & Air Force, 50th anniv.

---

Spasski Tower Clock, Greeting Card A2136

**1976, Nov. 25 Litho. Perf. 12½x12**
4510 A2136 4k multicolored .25 .20
New Year 1977.

Parable of the Workers in the Vineyard, by Rembrandt — A2137

Rembrandt Paintings in Hermitage: 6k, birth anniversary. 10k, 14k, Holy Family, vert. 20k, Rembrandt's brother Adrian. 1654, vert. 50k, Artakerxes, Esther and Haman.

**1976, Nov. 25 Perf. 12½x12, 12x12½ Photo.**
| | | | | |
|---|---|---|---|---|
| 4511 | A2137 | 4k multicolored | .20 | .20 |
| 4512 | A2137 | 6k multicolored | .20 | .20 |
| 4513 | A2137 | 10k multicolored | .50 | .20 |
| 4514 | A2137 | 14k multicolored | .65 | .20 |
| 4515 | A2137 | 20k multicolored | .90 | .30 |
| | | Nos. 4511-4515 (5) | 2.45 | 1.10 |

**Souvenir Sheet**
4516 A2137 50k multicolored 6.50 2.00
Rembrandt van Rijn (1606-69). Nos. 4511 and 4515 printed in sheets of 7 stamps and decorative label.

Worker and Farmer, by V. I. Muhina A2139

Armed Forces Order A2138

Council for Mutual Economic Aid Building A2141

Globe and Sputnik Orbits A2143

Marx and Lenin, by Fridman and Belostotsky A2140

Lenin, 1920 Photograph A2142

Designs: 2k, Golden Star and Hammer and Sickle medals. 4k, Coat of arms and "CCCP." 6k, TU-154 plane, globe and airmail envelope. 10k, Order of Labor. 12k, Space exploration medal with Gagarin portrait. 16k, Lenin Prize medal.

**1976 Engr. Perf. 12x12½**
4517 A2138 1k greenish black .20 .20
4518 A2138 2k brt magenta .20 .20
4519 A2139 3k red .20 .20

---

Petrov Tumor Research Institute A2132

M. A. Novinski — A2133

**1976, Oct. 28 Perf. 11½x12**
4498 A2132 4k vio blue & gold .50 .20
4499 A2133 4k dk brn, buff & blue .40 .20
Petrov Tumor Research Institute, 50th anniversary, and 135th birth anniversary of M. A. Novinski, cancer research pioneer.

Aviation Emblem, Gakkel VII, 1911 A2134

Russian Aircraft (Russian Aviation Emblem and): 6k, Gakkel IX, 1912. 12k, I. Steglau No. 2, 1912. 14k, Dybowski's Dolphin, 1913. 16k, Iliya Muromets, 1914.

**1976, Nov. 4 Lithographed and Engraved Perf. 12x12½**
| | | | | |
|---|---|---|---|---|
| 4500 | A2134 | 3k multicolored | .20 | .20 |
| 4501 | A2134 | 6k multicolored | .20 | .20 |
| 4502 | A2134 | 12k multicolored | .50 | .35 |
| 4503 | A2134 | 14k multicolored | .55 | .35 |
| 4504 | A2134 | 16k multicolored | .60 | .50 |
| | | Nos. 4500-4504 (5) | 2.05 | 1.60 |

See Nos. C109-C120.

Saffron A2135

Flowers of the Caucasus: 2k, Pasqueflowers. 3k, Gentian. 4k, Columbine. 6k, Checkered lily.

**1976, Nov. 17 Perf. 12x11½**
| | | | | |
|---|---|---|---|---|
| 4505 | A2135 | 1k multicolored | .40 | .40 |
| 4506 | A2135 | 2k multicolored | .40 | .40 |
| 4507 | A2135 | 3k multicolored | .40 | .40 |
| 4508 | A2135 | 4k multicolored | .40 | .40 |
| 4509 | A2135 | 6k multicolored | .40 | .40 |
| | | Nos. 4505-4509 (5) | 2.00 | 2.00 |

---

Shostakovich, Score from 7th Symphony, Leningrad — A2128

4484 A2127 14k black & multi 1.25 .20
4485 A2127 20k black & multi 1.65 .35
Nos. 4481-4485 (5) 4.45 1.15
Palekh Art State Museum, Ivanov Region.

**1976, Sept. 25 Engr. Perf. 12½x12**
4486 A2128 6k dk vio blue .25 .20
Dimitri Dimitrievich Shostakovich (1906-1975), composer.

**Voroshilov Type of 1976**
#4487, Zhukov. #4488, Rokossovsky.

**1976, Oct. 7 Engr. Perf. 12**
4487 A2098 4k slate green .20 .20
4488 A2098 4k brown .20 .20
Marshal Georgi Konstantinovich Zhukov (1896-1974), commander at Stalingrad and Leningrad and Deputy of Supreme Soviet; Marshal Konstantin K. Rokossovsky (1896-1968), commander at Stalingrad.

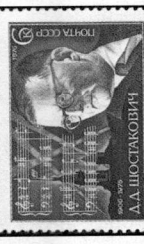

Intercosmos-14 A2129

10k, India's satellite Arryabata. 12k, Soyuz 19 and Apollo before docking. 16k, French satellite Aureole and Northern Lights. 20k, Dockings and Northern Lights. Interkosmos-14 and Aureole.

**1976, Oct. 15 Photo. Perf. 11½**
| | | | | |
|---|---|---|---|---|
| 4489 | A2129 | 6k black & multi | .20 | .20 |
| 4490 | A2129 | 10k black & multi | .20 | .20 |
| 4491 | A2129 | 12k black & multi | .45 | .20 |
| 4492 | A2129 | 16k black & multi | .50 | .20 |
| 4493 | A2129 | 20k black & multi | .65 | 1.00 |
| | | Nos. 4489-4493 (5) | 2.10 | 1.90 |

Interkosmos Program for Scientific and Experimental Research.

Vladimir I. Dahl A2130

**1976, Oct. 15 Photo. Perf. 11½**
4494 A2130 4k green & dk grm .25 .20
Vladimir I. Dahl (1801-1872), physician, writer, compiled Russian Dictionary.

Electric Power Industry A2131

**Photogravure and Engraved**

**1976, Oct. 20 Photo. Perf. 11½**
4495 A2131 4k dk blue & multi .20 .20
4496 A2131 4k rose brn & multi .20 .20
4497 A2131 4k slate grn & multi .60 .60
Nos. 4495-4497 (3)

#4496, Balashovo textile mill. #4497, Laying of drainage pipes and grain elevator.

59th anniversary of the October Revolution.

**S. P. Korolev, Vostok Rocket and Satellite A2148**

**1977, Jan. 12**
4539 A2148 4k multicolored .25 .20
Sergei Pavlovich Korolev (1907-1966), creator of first Soviet rocket space system.

**Globe and Palm A2149**

**1977, Jan. 12**
4540 A2149 4k multicolored .25 .20
World Congress of Peace Loving Forces, Moscow, Jan. 1977.

**Sedov and "St. Foka" A2150**

**1977, Jan. 25 Photo. Perf. 11½**
4541 A2150 4k multicolored .25 .20
G. Y. Sedov (1877-1914), polar explorer and hydrographer.

**Worker and Farmer Monument and Izvestia Front Page — A2151**

**1977, Jan. 25**
4542 A2151 4k silver, black & red .25 .20
60th anniversary of newspaper Izvestia.

**Ship Sailing Across the Oceans — A2152**

**1977, Jan. 25**
4543 A2152 6k deep blue & gold .30 .20
24th Int. Navigation Cong., Leningrad.

**Congress Hall and Troitskaya Tower, Kremlin — A2153**

**1977, Feb. 9 Photo. Perf. 11½**
4544 A2153 4k red, gold & black .25 .20
16th Congress of USSR Trade Unions.

**Voroshilov Type of 1976**

Marshals of the Soviet Union: #4545, Leonid A. Govorov (1897-1955). #4546, Ivan S. Koniev. #4547, K. A. Merezhkov. #4548, W. D. Sokolovsky.

**1977 Engr. Perf. 12**
4545 A2154 4k brown .20 .20
4546 A2154 4k slate green .20 .20
4547 A2154 4k brown .20 .20
4548 A2154 4k black .20 .20
Issue dates: #4545, Feb. 9; others, June 7.
Nos. 4545-4548 (4) .80 .80

**Academy, Crest, Anchor and Ribbons A2155**

**Photogravure and Engraved**

**1977, Feb. 9 Perf. 11½**
4549 A2155 6k multicolored .25 .20
A. A. Grechko Naval Academy, Leningrad, sesquicentennial.

**Jeanne Labourbe A2156**

**1977, Feb. 25 Photo. Perf. 11½**
4550 A2156 4k multicolored .25 .20
Jeanne Labourbe (1877-1919), leader of French communists in Moscow.

**Queen and Knights A2157**

**1977, Feb. 25 Perf. 12x11½**
4551 A2157 6k multicolored .30 .20
4th European Chess Championships.

**Cosmonauts V. D. Zudov and V. I. Rozhdestvensky — A2158**

**1977, Feb. 25**
4552 A2158 10k multicolored .25 .20
Soyuz 23 space flight, Oct. 14-16, 1976.

**A. S. Novikov-Priboy (1877-1944), Writer — A2159**

**1977, Mar. 16 Photo. Perf. 11½**
4553 A2159 4k multicolored .25 .20

**Welcome, by M. N. Soloninkin A2160**

Folk Tale Paintings from Fedoskino Artists' Colony: 6k, Along the Street, by V. D. Antonov, horiz. 10k, Northern Song, by J. V. Karapaev. 12k, Tale of Czar Saltan, by A. I. Kozlov. 14k, Summer Troika, by V. A. Nalimov, horiz. 16k, Red Flower, by V. D. Lipitsky.

**1977, Mar. 16 Perf. 12x12½, 12½x12**
4554 A2160 4k black & multi .20 .20
4555 A2160 6k black & multi .25 .20
4556 A2160 10k black & multi .30 .20
4557 A2160 12k black & multi .50 .20
4558 A2160 14k black & multi .60 .20
4559 A2160 16k black & multi .70 .75
Nos. 4554-4559 (6) 3.00 1.20

**Lenin on Red Square, by K. V. Filatov — A2161**

**1977, Apr. 12 Perf. 12½x11½**
4560 A2161 4k multicolored .25 .20
107th anniversary of the birth of Lenin.

**Electricity Congress Emblem A2162**

**1977, Apr. 12 Photo. Perf. 11½**
4561 A2162 6k blue, red & gray .25 .20
World Electricity Congress, Moscow 1977.

**Yuri Gagarin, Sputnik, Soyuz and Salyut — A2163**

**1977, Apr. 12 Perf. 12x11½**
4562 A2163 6k multicolored .25 .20
Cosmonauts' Day.

**N. I. Vavilov A2164**

**1977, Apr. 26 Photo. Perf. 11½**
4563 A2164 4k multicolored .25 .20
Vavilov (1887-1943), agricultural geneticist.

**Feliks E. Dzerzhinski A2165**

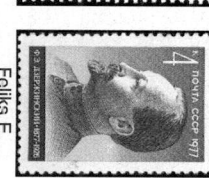

**1977, May 12 Engr. Perf. 12½x12**
4564 A2165 4k black .30 .20
Feliks E. Dzerzhinski (1877-1926), organizer and head of secret police (OGPU).

**V. V. Gorbatko, Y. N. Glazkov, Soyuz 24 Rocket A2167**

**1977, May 16 Photo. Perf. 12x11½**
4570 A2167 10k multicolored .40 .25
Space explorations of cosmonauts on Salyut 5 orbital station, launched with Soyuz 24 rocket.

**Saxifraga Sibirica — A2166**

Siberian Flowers: 3k, Dianthus repens. 4k, Novosieversia glacialis. 6k, Cerastium maxinicem. 16k, Golden rhododendron.

**1977, May 12 Litho. Perf. 12x12½**
4565 A2166 2k multicolored .20 .20
4566 A2166 3k multicolored .20 .20
4567 A2166 4k multicolored .20 .20
4568 A2166 6k multicolored .30 .20
4569 A2166 16k multicolored .80 .20
Nos. 4565-4569 (5) 1.70 1.00

**Film and Globe — A2168**

**1977, June 21 Photo. Perf. 11½**
4571 A2168 6k multicolored .25 .20
10th Int. Film Festival, Moscow 1977.

**Lion Hunt, by Rubens — A2169**

Rubens Paintings, Hermitage, Leningrad: 4k, Lady in Waiting. 10k, Workers in Quarry. 12k, Landscape with Rainbow. 20k, Alliance of Water and Earth, vert. 50k, Landscape with Rainbow. Self-portrait.
Peter Paul Rubens (1577-1640), painter.

**1977, June 24 Perf. 12x12½, 12½x12**
4572 A2169 4k yellow & multi .20 .20
4573 A2169 6k yellow & multi .20 .20
4574 A2169 10k yellow & multi .40 .20
4575 A2169 12k yellow & multi .50 .20
4576 A2169 20k yellow & multi .75 .30
Nos. 4572-4576 (5) 2.05 1.10

**Souvenir Sheet**

4577 A2169 50k yellow & multi 2.50 .80
Sheets of No. 4575 contain 2 labels with commemorative inscriptions and Atlas statue from Hermitage entrance.

## Souvenir Sheet

Leonid Brezhnev — A2180

**Lithographed and Embossed**

**1977, Nov. 2**   *Perf. 11½x12*
4618 A2180 50k gold & multi   1.75 1.00

Adoption of new constitution, General Secretary Brezhnev, chairman of Constitution Commission.

Postal Official and Postal Code — A2181

Mail Processing (Woman Postal Official and): No. 4620, Mail collection and Moskvich 430 car. No. 4621, Automatic letter sorting machine. No. 4622, Mail transport by truck, train, ship and planes. No. 4623, Mail delivery in city and country.

**Lithographed and Engraved**

**1977, Nov. 16**   *Perf. 12½x12*
| | | | |
|---|---|---|---|
| 4619 | A2181 | 4k multicolored | .20 .20 |
| 4620 | A2181 | 4k multicolored | .20 .20 |
| 4621 | A2181 | 4k multicolored | .20 .20 |
| 4622 | A2181 | 4k multicolored | .20 .20 |
| 4623 | A2181 | 4k multicolored | .20 .20 |
| | | | 1.00 1.00 |

Nos. 4619-4623 (5)

Capital, Asoka Pillar, Red Fort — A2182

**1977, Dec. 14**   Photo.   *Perf. 11½*
4624 A2182 6k maroon, gold & red   .25 .20

30th anniversary of India's independence.

Proclamation Monument, Charkov A2183

**1977, Dec. 14**   Litho.   *Perf. 12x12½*
4625 A2183 6k multicolored   .25 .20

60th anniv. of Soviet power in the Ukraine.

Lebetina Viper — A2184

Protected Fauna: 1k to 12k, Venomous snakes, useful for medicinal purposes. 16k,

---

Fir, Snowflake, Molniya Satellite — A2176

**1977, Oct. 12**   *Perf. 12x12½*
4609 A2176 4k multicolored   .30 .20

New Year 1978.

Cruiser Aurora and Torch A2177

60th Anniversary of Revolution Medal — A2178

60th Anniv. of October Revolution: #4611, Lenin speaking at Finland Station (monument), 1017. #4612, 1017 Роаоо Dooroo, Brozhnev's book about Lenin. #4613, Kremlin tower with star and fireworks.

**1977, Oct. 26**   Photo.   *Perf. 12x11½*
| | | | |
|---|---|---|---|
| 4610 | A2177 | 4k gold & black | .20 .20 |
| 4611 | A2177 | 4k gold, red & black | .20 .20 |
| 4612 | A2177 | 4k gold, red & black | .20 .20 |
| 4613 | A2177 | 4k gold, red & black | .80 .80 |

Nos. 4610-4613 (4)

**Souvenir Sheet**

*Perf. 11½*
4614 A2178 30k gold, red & black   1.50 .70

Flag of USSR, Constitution (Book) with Coat of Arms — A2179

Designs: No. 4616, Red banner, people and cover of constitution. 50k, Constitution, Kremlin and olive branch.

**1977, Oct. 31**   Litho.   *Perf. 12½x12*
4615 A2179 4k red, black & yel   .20 .20
4616 A2179 4k red, black & yel   .20 .20

**Souvenir Sheet**

*Perf. 11½x12½*

**Lithographed and Embossed**
4617 A2179 50k red, gold & yel   1.75 1.00

Adoption of new constitution. No. 4617 contains one 70x50mm stamp.

---

Yuri A. Gagarin and Spacecraft — A2174

No. 4590, Alexei Leonov floating in space. No. 4591, Orbiting space station, cosmonauts at control panel. No. 4592-4594. Various spacecraft: No. 4592, International cooperation for space research; No. 4593, Interplanetary flights; No. 4594, Exploring earth's atmosphere. 50k, "XX" laurel, symbolic Sputnik with Red Star.

**1977, Oct. 4**   Photo.   *Perf. 11½x12*
| | | | |
|---|---|---|---|
| 4589 | A2174 | 10k sepia & multi | .25 .20 |
| 4590 | A2174 | 10k gray & multi | .25 .20 |
| 4591 | A2174 | 10k gray green & multi | .20 .20 |
| 4592 | A2174 | 20k green & multi | .60 .35 |
| 4593 | A2174 | 10k vio & multi | .60 .35 |
| 4594 | A2174 | 20k bister & multi | .60 .35 |
| | | | 2.55 1.65 |

Nos. 4589-4594 (6)

**Souvenir Sheet**
4595 A2174 50k claret & gold   7.50 7.50

20th anniv. of space research. No. 4595 contains one stamp, size: 22x32mm.

### Types of 1976

Designs: 15k, Communications emblem and globes; others as before.

**1977-78**   Litho.   *Perf. 12x12½*
| | | | |
|---|---|---|---|
| 4596 | A2138 | 1k olive green | .20 .20 |
| 4597 | A2138 | 2k lilac rose | .20 .20 |
| 4598 | A2139 | 3k brick red | .20 .20 |
| 4599 | A2139 | 4k vermilion | .20 .20 |
| 4600 | A2139 | 6k Prus blue | .20 .20 |
| 4601 | A2139 | 10k gray green | .40 .20 |
| 4602 | A2139 | 12k vio blue | .45 .20 |
| 4602A | A2139 | 12k blue (78) | .55 .20 |
| 4603 | A2139 | 16k slate green | .60 .20 |

*Perf. 12½x12*
| | | | |
|---|---|---|---|
| 4604 | A2140 | 20k brown red | .75 .20 |
| 4605 | A2141 | 30k dull brick rod | 1.00 .20 |
| 4606 | A2142 | 50k brown | 2.00 .20 |
| 4607 | A2143 | 1r dark blue | 3.75 2.60 |
| | | | 10.50 2.60 |

Nos. 4596-4607 (13)

Nos. 4596-4602A, 4604-4607 were printed on dull and shiny paper.
For surcharges see #5720. For overprint see Uzbekistan #16-17, 23, 27-29, 61A.

Bas-relief, 12th Century, Cathedral of St. Dimitri, Vladimir — A2175

6k, Necklace, Ryazan excavations. 12th cent. 10k, Mask. Cathedral of the Nativity, Suzdal, 13th cent. 12k, Archangel Michael, 15th cent. icon. 16k, Chalice by Ivan Fomin, 1449. 20k, St. Basil's Cathedral, Moscow, 16th cent.

**1977, Oct. 12**   Litho.   *Perf. 12*
| | | | |
|---|---|---|---|
| 4608 | | Sheet of 6 | 2.50 1.25 |
| a. | A2175 | 6k gold & black | .20 .20 |
| b. | A2175 | 10k gold & multi | .35 |
| c. | A2175 | 12k gold & multi | .45 |
| d. | A2175 | 12k gold & multi | .45 |
| e. | A2175 | 16k gold & multi | .50 |
| f. | A2175 | 20k gold & multi | .60 |

Masterpieces of old Russian culture.

---

## Souvenir Sheet

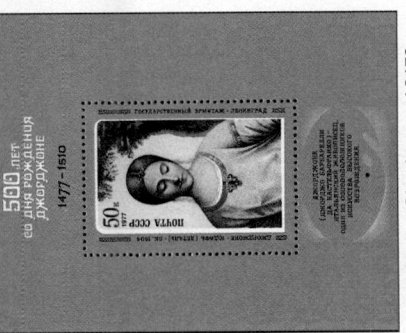

Judith, by Giorgione — A2170

**1977, July 15**   Litho.   *Perf. 12x12½*
4578 A2170 50k multicolored   2.00 1.00

Il Giorgione (1478-1511), Venetian painter.

### Icebreaker Type of 1976

Icebreakers: 4k, Aleksandr Sibiryukov. 6k, Georgi Sedov. 10k, Sadko. 12k, Dezhnev. 14k, Siberia. 16k, Lena. 20k, Amguyema.

**1977, July 27**   *Perf. 12½x12*

**Lithographed and Engraved**
| | | | |
|---|---|---|---|
| 4579 | A2145 | 4k multicolored | .20 .20 |
| 4580 | A2145 | 6k multicolored | .20 .20 |
| 4581 | A2145 | 10k multicolored | .35 .20 |
| 4582 | A2145 | 12k multicolored | .40 .25 |
| 4583 | A2145 | 14k multicolored | .45 .25 |
| 4584 | A2145 | 16k multicolored | .50 .35 |
| 4585 | A2145 | 20k multicolored | .65 .45 |
| | | | 2.75 1.85 |

Nos. 4579-4585 (7)

**Souvenir Sheet**

Icebreaker Arctica — A2171

**Lithographed and Engraved**

**1977, Sept. 15**   *Perf. 12½x12*
4586 A2171 50k multicolored   6.00 5.00

Arctica, first ship to travel from Murmansk to North Pole, Aug. 9-17.

View and Arms of Stavropol A2172

**1977, Aug. 16**   Photo.   *Perf. 11½*
4587 A2172 4k multicolored   .25 .20

200th anniversary of Stavropol.

Stamps and Exhibition Emblem A2173

**1977, Aug. 16**   Photo.   *Perf. 11½*
4588 A2173 4k multicolored   .25 .20

October Revolution Anniversary Philatelic Exhibition, Moscow.

Polar bear and cub, 20k, Walrus and calf, 30k, Tiger and cub.

**Photogravure and Engraved**
**Perf. 11½x12**
**1977, Dec. 16**

| | | | | |
|---|---|---|---|---|
| 4626 | A2184 | 1k | black & multi | .20 .20 |
| 4627 | A2184 | 4k | black & multi | .20 .20 |
| 4628 | A2184 | 4k | black & multi | .20 .20 |
| 4629 | A2184 | 6k | black & multi | .20 .20 |
| 4630 | A2184 | 10k | black & multi | .35 .20 |
| 4631 | A2184 | 12k | black & multi | .45 .20 |
| 4632 | A2184 | 16k | black & multi | .55 .25 |
| 4633 | A2184 | 30k | black & multi | .75 .25 |

Nos. 4626-4633 (8) 3.70 1.80

Wheat, Combine, Silos — A2185

**1978, Jan. 27 Photo. Perf. 11½**
4634 A2185 4k multicolored .25 .20
Gigant collective grain farm, Rostov Region, 50th anniversary.

Young Communist League, Lenin's Komsomol, 60th anniv. and its 25th Cong.

**1978, Jan. 27 Litho. Perf. 12x12½**
4635 A2186 4k multicolored .25 .20

Congress Palace, Spasski Tower — A2186

8th Congress of International Federation of Resistance Fighters, Minsk, Belorussia.

**1978, Jan. 27 Photo. Perf. 11½**
4636 A2187 6k multicolored .25 .20

Liberation Obelisk, Dove — A2187

Soldiers Leaving for the Front — A2188

**1978, Feb. 21 Litho. Perf. 12½x12**
4637 A2188 4k red & multi .20 .20
4638 A2188 4k red & multi .20 .20
4639 A2188 4k red & multi .20 .20
Nos. 4637-4639 (3) .60 .60

Designs: No. 4638, Defenders of Moscow Monument, Lenin banner. No. 4639, Soldier as defender of the people.
60th anniversary of USSR Military forces.

Celebration in Village — A2189

**1978, Mar. 3 Size: 70x33mm Perf. 11½**
4640 A2189 4k lilac & multi .20 .20
4641 A2189 6k lilac & multi .20 .20

**Size: 47x32mm**
**Perf. 12½x12**
4642 A2189 10k lilac & multi .40 .20
4643 A2189 12k lilac & multi .50 .20
4644 A2189 20k lilac & multi .70 .25
Nos. 4640-4644 (5) 2.00 1.05

**Souvenir Sheet**
**Size: 70x33mm**
**Perf. 11½**
4644A A2189 50k lilac & multi 1.75 .75

Kustodiev Paintings: 6k, Shrovetide (winter landscape). 10k, Morning, by Kustodiev. 12k, Merchant's Wife Drinking Tea. 20k, Bolshevik. 50k, Self-portrait, vert.

Boris Mikhailovich Kustodiev (1878-1927), painter. Nos. 4640-4643 have se-tenant label showing museum where painting is kept. No. 4644A has label giving short biography.

Docking in Space, Intercosmos Emblem A2190

Designs: 6k, Rocket, Soviet Cosmonaut Aleksei Gubarev and Czechoslovak Capt. Vladimir Remek on launching pad. 32k, Parachute, helicopter, Intercosmos emblem, USSR and Czechoslovakian flags.

**1978, Mar. 10 Litho. Perf. 12x12½**
4645 A2190 6k multicolored .20 .20
4646 A2190 15k multicolored .40 .20
4647 A2190 32k multicolored .85 .40
Nos. 4645-4647 (3) 1.45 .80

Intercosmos, Soviet-Czechoslovak cooperative space program.

Festival Emblem — A2191
11th Youth & Students' Cong., Havana.

**1978, Mar. 17 Litho. Perf. 12x12½**
4648 A2191 4k blue & multi .25 .20

Tulip, Bolshoi Theater A2192

Moscow Flowers: 2k, Rose "Moscow morning" and Lomonosov University. 4k, Gladiolus "Red Star" and Spasski Tower. 10k, Gladiolus "Moscovite" and VDNH Building. 12k, Ilich anniversary iris and Lenin Central Museum.

**1978, Mar. 17 Perf. 12½x12**
4649 A2192 1k multicolored .20 .20
4650 A2192 2k multicolored .20 .20
4651 A2192 4k multicolored .20 .20
4652 A2192 10k multicolored .25 .20
4653 A2192 12k multicolored 1.05 1.00
Nos. 4649-4653 (5)

IMCO Emblem and Waves — A2193

**1978, Mar. 17 Litho. Perf. 12x12½**
4654 A2193 6k multicolored .25 .20
Intergovernmental Maritime Consultative Org., 20th anniv., and World Maritime Day.

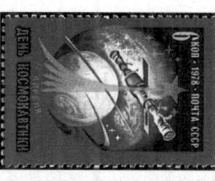

Spaceship, Orbits of Salyut 5, Soyuz 26 and Soyuz 27 — A2194

**1978, Apr. 12 Photo. Perf. 12**
4655 A2194 6k blue, dk blue & gold .25 .20
Cosmonauts' Day, Apr. 12.

World Federation of Trade Unions Emblem — A2195

**1978, Apr. 16 Perf. 12**
4656 A2195 6k multicolored .25 .20
9th World Trade Union Congress, Prague.

Locomotive, 1845, Petersburg and Moscow Stations — A2196

Locomotives: 1k, 1st Russian model by E. A. and M. W. Cherepanov, vert. 2k, 1-3-0 freight, 1845. 16k, Aleksandrov 0-3-0, 1863. 20k, 2-2-0 passenger and Sergievsk Pustyn platform, 1863.

**1978, Apr. 20 Litho. Perf. 11½**
4657 A2196 1k orange & multi .20 .20
4658 A2196 2k ultra & multi .20 .20
4659 A2196 3k yellow & multi .20 .20
4660 A2196 16k green & multi .60 .20
4661 A2196 20k rose & multi .70 .25
Nos. 4657-4661 (5) 1.90 1.05

Lenin, by V. A. Serov — A2197

**Souvenir Sheet**
**1978, Apr. 22 Perf. 12½x12**
4662 A2197 50k multicolored 1.50 .75
108th anniversary of the birth of Lenin.

A2198

**1978, June 15 Perf. 12**
4663 A2198 15k multicolored .40 .20
4664 A2198 15k multicolored .40 .20
a. Pair, #4663-4664 .40 .40

No. 4663, Soyuz and Salyut 6 docking in space. No. 4664, Y. V. Romanenko and G. M. Grechko.

Photographic survey and telescopic observations of stars by crews of Soyuz 26, Dec. 10, 1977-Mar. 16, 1978 Nos. 4663-4664, printed se-tenant with label showing schematic pictures of various experiments.

Space Meteorology, Rockets, Spaceship, Earth — A2200

No. 4665, Natural resources of earth and "Orbita" Station and Molniya satellite. No. 4667, Space communications, No. 4668, Man, earth and Vostok. 50k, Study of magnetosphere, Prognoz over earth.

**1978, June 23 Perf. 12x12½**
4665 A2200 10k green & multi .20 .20
4666 A2200 10k blue & multi .25 .20
4667 A2200 10k violet & multi .25 .20
4668 A2200 10k rose lil & multi .80 .20
Nos. 4665-4668 (4) 1.00 .80

**Souvenir Sheet**
**Perf. 11½x12½**
4669 A2200 50k multicolored 1.50 .75

Space explorations of the Intercosmos program. #4669 contains one 36x51mm stamp.

Soyuz 31 in Shop, Intercosmos Emblem, USSR and DDR Flags — A2210

**1978.** **Litho.** **Perf. 12x12½**
| | | | |
|---|---|---|---|
| 4690 | A2210 | 6k multicolored | .20 .20 |
| 4691 | A2210 | 6k multicolored | .85 .20 |
| 4692 | A2210 | 32k multicolored | 1.65 .45 |
| | | | 2.70 .85 |
| | | Nos. 4690-4692 (3) | |

Designs (Intercosmos Emblem, USSR and German Democratic Republic Flags and): 15k, Pamir Mountains photographed from space; 32k, Soyuz 29 and 31 complex and spectrum. 32k, Soyuz 31 docking, photographed from Salyut 6.

Intercosmos, Soviet-East German cooperative space program.
Issued: 6k, 8/27; 15k, 8/31; 32k, 9/3.

PRAGA '78 Emblem, Plane, Radar, Spaceship A2211

**Photogravure and Engraved**
**1978, Aug. 29** **Perf. 11½**
4693 A2211 6k multicolored .25 .20

PRAGA '78 International Philatelic Exhibition, Prague, Sept. 8-17.

Leo Tolstoi (1828-1910), Novelist and Philosopher — A2212

**1978, Sept. 7** **Engr.** **Perf. 12x12½**
4694 A2212 4k slate green 1.25 .90

Stag, Conference Emblem — A2213

**1978** **Photo.** **Perf. 11½**
4695 A2213 4k multicolored .25 .20

14th General Assembly of the Society for Wildlife Preservation, Ashkhabad.

Bronze Figure, Erebuni, 8th Century A2214

Armenian Architecture: 6k, Etchmiadzin Cathedral, 4th century. 10k, Stone crosses, Dzaghkazor, 13th century. 12k, Library, Erevan, horiz. 16k, Lenin statue, Lenin Square, Erevan, horiz.

**1978.** **Litho.** **Perf. 12x12½, 12½x12**
| | | | |
|---|---|---|---|
| 4696 | A2214 | 4k multicolored | .20 .20 |
| 4697 | A2214 | 6k multicolored | .20 .20 |
| 4698 | A2214 | 10k multicolored | .30 .20 |
| 4699 | A2214 | 12k multicolored | .40 .20 |
| 4700 | A2214 | 16k multicolored | .50 .20 |
| | | | 1.60 1.00 |
| | | Nos. 4696-4700 (5) | |

Issued: 4k, 10k, 16k, 9/12; others, 10/14.

Memorial, Messina, Russian Warships A2215

**1978, Sept. 12** **Photo.** **Perf. 11½**
4701 A2215 6k multicolored .25 .20

70th anniversary of aid given by Russian sailors during Messina earthquake.

Communications Emblem, Ostankino TV Tower — A2216

**1978, Sept. 20** **Photo.** **Perf. 11½**
4702 A2216 4k multicolored .25 .20

Organization for Communication Cooperation of Socialist Countries, 20th anniv.

No. 4673 Overprinted

**1978, Sept. 20** **Litho.** **Perf. 12x12½**
4703 A2202 4k multicolored 1.25 .70

Philatelic Exhibition for the Leninist Young Communist League.

Souvenir Sheet

Diana, by Paolo Veronese — A2217

**1978, Sept. 28** **Litho.** **Perf. 12x11½**
4704 A2217 50k multicolored 1.50 1.00

Veronese (1528-88), Italian painter.

---

Dr. William Harvey (1578-1657), Discoverer of Blood Circulation — A2206

**1978, July 25** **Perf. 12**
4677 A2206 6k blue, black & dp grn .25 .20

Nikolai Gavilovich Chernyshevsky (1828-1889), Revolutionary — A2207

**1978, July 30** **Engr.** **Perf. 12x12½**
4678 A2207 4k brown, yellow .25 .20

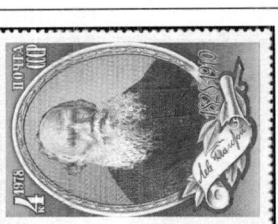

Whitewinged Petrel A2208

Antarctic Fauna: 1k, Crested penguin, horiz. 4k, Emperor penguin and chick. 6k, Whiteblooded pikes. 10k, Sea elephant, horiz.

**1978, July 30** **Perf. 12x11½, 11½x12**
| | | | |
|---|---|---|---|
| 4679 | A2208 | 1k multicolored | .25 .20 |
| 4680 | A2208 | 3k multicolored | .30 .20 |
| 4681 | A2208 | 4k multicolored | .60 .20 |
| 4682 | A2208 | 6k multicolored | .60 .20 |
| 4683 | A2208 | 10k multicolored | 1.25 1.00 |
| | | | 3.00 1.80 |
| | | Nos. 4679-4683 (5) | |

The Red Horse, by Petrov-Votkin — A2209

Paintings by Petrov-Votkin: 6k, Mother and Child, Petrograd, 1918. 10k, Death of the Commissar. 12k, Still-life with Fruit. 16k, Still-life with Teapot and Flowers. 50k, Self-portrait, 1918, vert.

**1978, Aug. 16** **Litho.** **Perf. 12½x12**
| | | | |
|---|---|---|---|
| 4684 | A2209 | 4k silver & multi | .20 .20 |
| 4685 | A2209 | 6k silver & multi | .20 .20 |
| 4686 | A2209 | 10k silver & multi | .45 .20 |
| 4687 | A2209 | 12k silver & multi | .55 .20 |
| 4688 | A2209 | 16k silver & multi | 1.00 1.00 |
| | | | 2.05 1.80 |
| | | Nos. 4684-4688 (5) | |

Souvenir Sheet

**Perf. 11½x12**
4689 A2209 50k silver & multi 1.50 1.00

Kozma Sergeevich Petrov-Votkin (1878-1939), painter. Nos. 4684-4688 have se-tenant labels. No. 4689 has label the size of stamp.

---

Soyuz Rocket on Carrier — A2201

Designs (Flags of USSR and Poland, Intercosmos Emblem): 15k, Crystal, spaceship (Sirena, experimental crystallogenesis in space). 32k, Research ship "Cosmonaut Vladimir Komarov," spaceship, world map and paths of Salyut 6, Soyuz 29-30.

**1978.** **Litho.** **Perf. 12½x12**
| | | | |
|---|---|---|---|
| 4670 | A2201 | 6k multicolored | .20 .20 |
| 4671 | A2201 | 15k multicolored | .40 .40 |
| 4672 | A2201 | 32k multicolored | .80 .80 |
| | | | 1.40 1.40 |
| | | Nos. 4670-4672 (3) | |

Intercosmos, Soviet-Polish cooperative space program. Issued: 6k, 6/28; 15k, 6/30; 32k, 7/5.

Lenin, Awards Received by Komsomol A2202

**1978, July 5**
| | | | |
|---|---|---|---|
| 4673 | A2202 | 4k multicolored | .20 .20 |
| 4674 | A2203 | 4k multicolored | .20 .20 |

Leninist Young Communist League (Komsomol), 60th anniv. (#4673); Komsomol's participation in 5-year plan (#4674). For overprint see No. 4703.

Калмаз Сат, Тали, Bildge, Hammer and Sickle — A2203

M. V. Zaharov (1898-1972), Marshal of the Soviet Union — A2204

**1978, July 5** **Engr.** **Perf. 12**
4675 A2204 4k sepia .25 .20

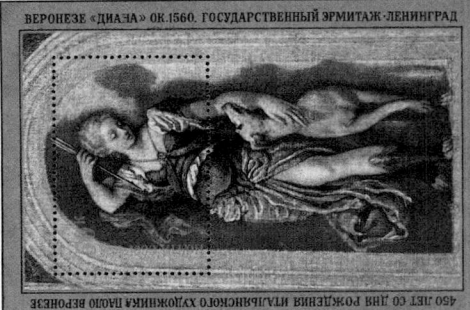

Torch, Flags of Participants A2205

**1978, July 25** **Litho.** **Perf. 12x12½**
4676 A2205 4k multicolored .25 .20

Construction of Soyuz gas-pipeline (Friendship Line), Orenburg. Flags of participating countries shown: Bulgaria, Hungary, German Democratic Republic, Poland, Romania, USSR, Czechoslovakia.

Kremlin,
Moscow
A2218

**Souvenir Sheet**

**1978, Oct. 7 Lithographed and Embossed**
4705 A2218 30k gold & multi
    *Perf. 11½x12*
Russian Constitution, 1st anniversary.     1.50 .65

Stepan Georgevich
Shaumyan (1878-
1918), Communist
Party Functionary
A2219

**1978, Oct. 11 Engr.**
4706 A2219 4k slate green
    *Perf. 12½x12*
61st anniversary of October Revolution.  .25 .20

Ferry, Russian
and Bulgarian
Colors — A2220

**1978, Oct. 14 Photo.**
4707 A2220 6k multicolored
    *Perf. 11½*
Opening of Ilychovsk-Varna Ferry.    .25 .20

Hammer and
Sickle,
Flags — A2221

**1978, Oct. 26 Photo.**
4708 A2221 4k gold & multi
    *Perf. 11½*     .25 .20

Silver Gilt Cup, Novgorod, 12th
Century — A2222

Old Russian Art: 10k, Pokrovna Nerli
Church, 12th century; vert. 12k, St. George
Slaying the Dragon, icon, Novgorod, 15th cen-
tury, vert. 16k, The Czar, cannon, 1586.

**1978, Nov. 28 Litho.**
4709 A2222 6k multicolored   .20 .20
4710 A2222 10k multicolored   .40 .20
4711 A2222 12k multicolored   .60 .20
4712 A2222 16k multicolored   .80 .20
    *Perf. 12½x12, 12x12½*
Nos. 4709-4712 (4)       1.70 .80

Oncology Institute,
Emblem — A2223

**1978, Dec. 1 Photo.**
4713 A2223 4k multicolored
    *Perf. 11½*
P.A. Herzen Tumor Institute, 75th anniv.  .25 .20

Savior Tower,
Kremlin — A2224

**1978, Dec. 20 Litho.**
4714 A2224 4k silver, blue & red
    *Perf. 12x12½*
New Year 1979.     .25 .20

Nestor Pechersky, Chronicler, c.
885 — A2225

History of Postal Service: 6k, Birch bark letter and stylus. 10k, Messenger with trumpet
and staff, from 14th century Psalm book. 12k,
Winter traffic, from 16th century book by
Sigizmund Gerberstein. 16k, Prikaz post-
office, from 17th century icon.

**1978, Dec. 20 Lithographed and Engraved**
    *Perf. 12½x12*
4715 A2225 4k multicolored   .20 .20
4716 A2225 6k multicolored   .20 .20
4717 A2225 10k multicolored   .50 .20
4718 A2225 12k multicolored   .55 .20
4719 A2225 16k multicolored   .65 .20
Nos. 4715-4719 (5)     2.10 1.00

Kovalenok and Ivanchenkov, Salyut 6-
Soyuz — A2226

**1978, Dec. 20 Photo.**
4720 A2226 10k multicolored
    *Perf. 11½x12*
Cosmonauts V. V. Kovalenok and A. S.
Ivanchenkov spent 140 days in space, June
15-Nov. 2, 1978.     .30 .20

Vasilii Pronchishchov — A2227

Icebreakers: 6k, Captain Belousov, 1954,
vert. 10k, Moscow. 12k, Admiral Makarov,

1974. 16k, Lenin, 1959, vert. 20k, Nuclear-
powered Arctica.

**1978, Dec. 20 Photo. & Engr.**
    *Perf. 11½x12, 12x11½*
4721 A2227 4k multicolored   .20 .20
4722 A2227 6k multicolored   .20 .20
4723 A2227 10k multicolored   .25 .20
4724 A2227 12k multicolored   .35 .20
4725 A2227 16k multicolored   .40 .25
4726 A2227 20k multicolored   .25 .20
Nos. 4721-4726 (6)    1.65 1.25

**Souvenir Sheet**

Mastheads and Globe with
Russia — A2228

**1978, Dec. 28 Litho.**
4727 A2228 30k multicolored
    *Perf. 12*     1.00 .35
Distribution of periodicals through the Post
and Telegraph Department, 60th anniversary.

Cuban Flags
Forming
Star — A2229

**1979, Jan. 1 Photo.**
4728 A2229 6k multicolored
    *Perf. 11½*
Cuban Revolution, 20th anniversary.  .25 .20

Russian and Byelorussian Flags,
Government Building, Minsk — A2230

**1979, Jan. 1**
4729 A2230 4k multicolored
Byelorussian SSR and Byelorussian Communist Party, 60th anniv.     .25 .20

Ukrainian and
Russian Flags,
Reunion
Monument
A2231

**1979, Jan. 16**
4730 A2231 4k multicolored
Reunion of Ukraine & Russia, 325th anniv.
    .30 .20

Old and
New Vilnius
University
Buildings
A2232

**1979, Jan. 16 Photo. & Engr.**
4731 A2232 4k black & salmon
    *Perf. 11½x12½*
400th anniversary of University of Vilnius.
    .25 .20

Bulgaria
No. 1 and
Exhibition
Hall
A2233

**1979, Jan. 25 Litho.**
4732 A2233 15k multicolored
    *Perf. 12½x12*
Filaserdica '79 Philatelic Exhibition, Sofia,
for centenary of Bulgarian postal service.
    .35 .20

Sputniks, Soviet
Radio Hams
Emblem — A2234

**1979, Feb. 23 Photo.**
4733 A2234 4k multicolored
    *Perf. 11½*
Sputnik satellites Radio 1 and Radio 2,
launched, Oct. 1978.     .25 .20

1-3-0 Locomotive, 1878 — A2235

Locomotives: 3k, 1-4-0, 1912. 4k, 2-3-1,
1915. 6k, 1-3-1, 1925. 15k, 1-5-0, 1947.

**1979, Feb. 23 Litho.**
    *Perf. 11½*
4734 A2235 2k multicolored   .20 .20
4735 A2235 3k multicolored   .20 .20
4736 A2235 4k multicolored   .20 .20
4737 A2235 6k multicolored   .20 .20
4738 A2235 15k multicolored   .65 1.00
Nos. 4734-4738 (5)    1.50 1.00

**Souvenir Sheet**

Medal for Land Development — A2236

**1979, Mar. 14**
4739 A2236 50k multicolored
    *Perf. 11½x12½*
25th anniv. of drive to develop virgin lands.
    1.50 .75

COMECON Building, Members, Flags — A2250

Scene from "Potemkin" and Festival Emblem — A2251

**Perf. 12**
1979, June 26
4759 A2250 16k multicolored .50 .20
Council for Mutual Economic Aid of Socialist Countries, 30th anniversary.

**Photogravure and Engraved**
**Perf. 11½**
1979, July
4760 A2251 15k multicolored .20 .20
11th International Film Festival, Moscow, and 60th anniversary of Soviet film industry.

Lenin Square Station, Tashkent A2252

**Perf. 12**
1979, July
4761 A2252 4k multicolored .25 .20
Tashkent subway.

**Souvenir Sheets**

Atom Symbol, Factories, Dam — A2253

**Perf. 11½x12**
1979, July 23
4762 A2253 30k multicolored 1.00 .45
50th anniversary of 1st Five-Year Plan.

USSR Philatelic Society Emblem — A2254

**Litho.** **Perf. 12x12½**
1979, July 25
4763 A2254 50k gray grn & red 1.50 .70
4th Cong. of USSR Phil. Soc. Moscow.

---

**Souvenir Sheet**

No. 4745 Overprinted in Margin in Red
**Perf. 12x11½**
1979, May 24
4751 A2242 50k multicolored 3.00 .80
Victory of Soviet team in World and European Ice Hockey Championships.

Infant, Flowers, IYC Emblem — A2247

**Perf. 12x12½**
1979, June 1  **Litho.**
4752 A2247 4k multicolored .25 .20
International Year of the Child.

Horn Player and Bears Playing Balalaika, Bogorodsk Wood Carvings — A2248

Folk Art: 3k, Decorated wooden bowls, Khokhloma. 4k, Tray decorated with flowers, Zhestovo. 6k, Carved bone boxes, Kholmogory. 15k, Lace, Vologda.
**Perf. 12½x12**
1979, June 14  **Litho.**
4753 A2248 2k multicolored .20 .20
4754 A2248 3k multicolored .20 .20
4755 A2248 4k multicolored .20 .20
4756 A2248 6k multicolored .20 .20
4757 A2248 15k multicolored .50 .25
Nos. 4753-4757 (5) 1.30 1.05
Nos. 4753-4757 printed in sheets of 7 stamps and decorative label.

V. A. Djanibekov, O. G. Makarov, Spacecraft A2249

**Perf. 12x11½**
1979, June
4758 A2249 4k multicolored .35 .20
Flights of Soyuz 26-27 and work on board of orbital complex Salyut 26-27.

---

**Souvenir Sheet**

Lenin — A2243

1979, Apr. 18
4746 A2243 50k red, gold & brn 1.50 .75
109th anniversary of the birth of Lenin.

Astronauts' Training Center A2244

Design: 32k, Astronauts, landing capsule, radar, helicopter and emblem.
**Perf. 11½**
1979, Apr. 12  **Litho.**
4747 A2244 6k multicolored .20 .20
4748 A2244 32k multicolored .90 .40
Joint Soviet-Bulgarian space flight.

Exhibition Emblem — A2245

**Photo.** **Perf. 11½**
1979, Apr. 18
4749 A2245 15k sil, red & vio blue .60 .20
National USSR Exhibition in the United Kingdom. Se-tenant label with commemorative inscription.

Blast Furnace, Pushkin Theater, "Tent" Sculpture — A2246

**Perf. 11½**
1979, May 24  **Photo.**
4750 A2246 4k multicolored .25 .20
50th anniversary of Magnitogorsk City.

---

Venera 11 and 12 over Venus — A2237

1979, Mar. 16  **Photo.** **Perf. 11½**
4740 A2237 10k multicolored .30 .20
Interplanetary flights of Venera 11 and Venera 12, December 1978.

Albert Einstein, Equation and Signature A2238

1979, Mar. 16
4741 A2238 6k multicolored .30 .20
Einstein (1879-1955), theoretical physicist.

Congress Emblem A2239

1979, Mar. 16
4742 A2239 6k multicolored .25 .20
21st World Veterinary Congress, Moscow.

"To Arms," by R. Berens A2240

1979, Mar. 21
4743 A2240 4k multicolored .26 .20
Soviet Republic of Hungary, 60th anniv.

Salyut 6, Soyuz, Research Ship, Letters — A2241

1979, Apr. 12  **Litho.** **Perf. 11½x12**
4744 A2241 15k multicolored .50 .20
Cosmonauts' Day.

**Souvenir Sheet**

Ice Hockey — A2242

1979, Apr. 14  **Photo.** **Perf. 12x11½**
4745 A2242 50k multicolored 1.50 .75
World and European Ice Hockey Championships, Moscow, Apr. 14-27.
For overprint see No. 4751.

Exhibition Hall, Scene from "Chapayev" — A2255

**1979, Aug. 8    Photo.    Perf. 11½**
4764  A2255  4k multicolored                .25  .20

60th anniversary of Soviet Film and Exhibition of History of Soviet Film.

Russian Flower Paintings: 1k, Flowers and Fruit, by I. F. Khrutsky, 1830. 2k, Phlox, by I. N. Kramskoi, 1884. 3k, Lilac, by K. A. Korovin, 1915. 15k, Bluebells, by S. V. Gerasimov, 1944. 2k. 3k. 15k. vert.

**1979, Aug. 16    Litho.    Perf. 12½x12, 12, 12x12½**
4765  A2256  1k multicolored                .20  .20
4766  A2256  2k multicolored                .20  .20
4767  A2256  3k multicolored                .40  .30
4768  A2256  15k multicolored               .75  .55
4769  A2256  32k multicolored              1.75  1.45
Nos. 4765-4769 (5)

Roses, by P. P. Konchalovsky, 1955 — A2256

John McClean — A2257

**1979, Aug. 29    Litho.    Perf. 11½**
4770  A2257  4k red & black                 .25  .20

John McClean (1879-1923), British Communist labor leader.

Soviet Circus Emblem — A2258

**1979, Sept.**
4771  A2258  4k multicolored                .25  .20

Soviet Circus, 60th anniversary.

Friendship — A2259

**1979, Sept. 10    Perf. 12½x12**
4772  A2259  2k multicolored                .20  .20
4773  A2259  3k multicolored                .20  .20
4774  A2259  4k multicolored                .30  .20
4775  A2259  15k multicolored               .90  .80
Nos. 4772-4775 (4)

Children's Drawings: 3k, Children and Horses. 4k, Dances. 15k, The Excursion.

International Year of the Child. Exist imperf. Value, $50 each.

---

Birds: 3k, Dendrocopus minor, 4k, Parus cristatus. 10k, Tyto alba. 15k, Caprimulgus europaeus.

Oriolus oriolus — A2260

**1979, Sept. 18    Litho.    Perf. 12x12½**
4776  A2260  2k multicolored                .20  .20
4777  A2260  3k multicolored                .20  .20
4778  A2260  4k multicolored                .20  .20
4779  A2260  10k multicolored               .35  .20
4780  A2260  15k multicolored               .50  .20
Nos. 4776-4780 (5)                         1.45 1.00

German Arms, Marx, Engels, Lenin, Berlin — A2261

**1979, Oct. 7    Photo.    Perf. 11½**
4781  A2261  6k multicolored                .25  .20

German Democratic Republic, 30th anniv.

Valery Ryumin, Vladimir Lyakhov, Salyut 6 — A2262

**1979, Oct. 10    Perf. 12x11½**
4782  A2262  15k multicolored               .40  .25
4783  A2262  15k multicolored               .40  .25
a.  Pair, #4782-4783                        .80  .50

Design: No. 4783, Spacecraft.

175 days in space, Feb. 25-Aug. 19. No. 4783a has continuous design.

Star — A2264

**1979, Oct. 18**
4784  A2264  4k multicolored                .25  .20

USSR Armed Forces, 60th anniversary.

Hammer and Sickle — A2265

**1979, Oct. 18    Perf. 11½**
4785  A2265  4k multicolored                .25  .20

October Revolution, 62nd anniversary.

---

Katherina, by T. G. Shevchenko — A2266

**1979, Nov. 18    Litho.    Perf. 12x12½**
4786  A2266  2k multicolored                .20  .20
4787  A2266  3k multicolored                .20  .20
4788  A2266  4k multicolored                .20  .20
4789  A2266  10k multicolored               .30  .20
4790  A2266  15k multicolored              1.10 1.00
Nos. 4786-4790 (5)

Ukrainian Paintings: 3k, Working Girl, by K.K. Kostandi. 4k, Lenin's Return to Petrograd, by A.M. Lopuhov. 10k, Soldier's Return, by N.V. Kostesky. 15k, Going to Work, by M.G. Belsky.

Shabolovka Radio Tower, Moscow — A2267

**1979, Nov. 28    Photo.    Perf. 12**
4791  A2267  32k multicolored              1.00  .50

Radio Moscow, 50th anniversary.

Mischa Holding Stamp — A2268

**1979, Nov. 28    Perf. 12x12½**
4792  A2268  4k multicolored                .50  .20

New Year 1980.

Hand Holding Peace Message — A2269

Peace Program in Action: No. 4794, Hands holding cultural symbols. No. 4795, Hammer and sickle, flag.

**1979, Dec. 5    Litho.    Perf. 12**
4793  A2269  4k multicolored                .20  .20
4794  A2269  4k multicolored                .20  .20
4795  A2269  4k multicolored                .20  .20
Nos. 4793-4795 (3)                          .60  .60

Policeman, Patrol Car, Helicopter — A2270

Traffic Safety: 4k, Car, girl and ball. 6k, Speeding cars.

**1979, Dec. 20    Perf. 12x12½**
4796  A2270  3k multicolored                .20  .20
4797  A2270  4k multicolored                .20  .20
4798  A2270  6k multicolored                .60  .60
Nos. 4796-4798 (3)

---

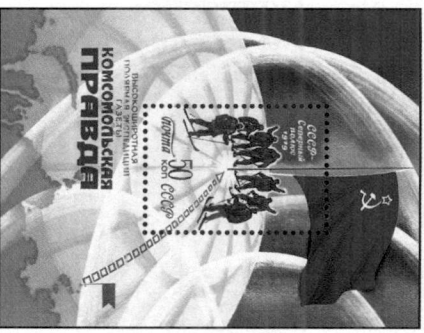

Explorers Raising Red Flag at North Pole — A2272

**1979, Dec. 25    Photo.    Perf. 11½x12**
4805  A2272  50k multicolored              1.50  .75

Komsomolskaya Pravda North Pole expedition.

**Type of 1970**

**1980, Jan. 10    Litho.    Perf. 12x12½**
4806  A1794  4k carmine                     .25  .20

Mordovian Autonomous SSR, 50th anniv.

Freestyle Skating — A2273

**1980, Jan. 22    Perf. 12x12½, 12½x12**
4807  A2273  4k Speed skating              .20  .20
4808  A2273  6k shown                       .20  .20
4809  A2273  10k Ice hockey                 .25  .20
4810  A2273  15k Downhill skiing            .35  .25
4811  A2273  20k Luge, vert.                .50  .35
Nos. 4807-4811 (5)                         1.50 1.20

**Souvenir Sheet**
4812  A2273  50k Cross-country skiing, vert.  1.50 1.00

13th Winter Olympic Games, Lake Placid, NY, Feb. 12-24. Nos. 4808, 4809 exist imperf. Value, $50 for both.

Vulkanolog — A2271

**Lithographed and Engraved**

Research Ships and Portraits: 2k, Professor Bogorov. 4k, Ernst Krenkel. 10k, Cosmonaut Yuri Gagarin. 15k, Academician E.B. Kurchatov.

**1979, Dec. 25    Perf. 12x11½**
4799  A2271  1k multicolored                .20  .20
4800  A2271  2k multicolored                .20  .20
4801  A2271  4k multicolored                .20  .20
4802  A2271  6k multicolored                .30  .20
4803  A2271  10k multicolored               .45  .20
4804  A2271  15k multicolored              1.55 1.20
Nos. 4799-4804 (6)

See Nos. 4881-4886.

**Souvenir Sheet**

RUSSIA

Ho Chi
Minh — A2291

College — A2290

**1980, July 1** **Photo.** **Perf. 11½**
4844 A2290 4k multicolored .25 .20
Bauman Technological College, Moscow,
150th anniversary.

**1980, July 7**
4845 A2291 6k multicolored .25 .20

Red Flag,
Lithuanian
Arms, Flag,
Red
Guards
Monument
A2292

**1980, July 12** **Perf. 12**
4846 A2292 4k multicolored .25 .20
Lithuanian SSR, 40th anniv.

Russian
Flag and
Arms,
Latvian
Flag,
Monument,
Buildings
A2293

Design: No. 4848, Russian flag and arms,
Estonian flag, monument, buildings.

**1980, July 21** **Litho.** **Perf. 12**
4847 A2293 4k multicolored .20 .20
4848 A2293 4k multicolored .20 .20
Restoration of Soviet power.

Cosmonauts
Boarding
Soyuz
A2294

**1980, July 24** **Perf. 12x12½**
4849 A2294 6k shown .20 .20
4850 A2294 15k Working aboard .45 .25
spacecraft
4851 A2294 32k Return flight .80 .55
Nos. 4849-4851 (3) 1.45 1.00
Center for Cosmonaut Training, 20th anniv.

Avicenna (980-
1037), Philosopher
and
Physician — A2295

**Photogravure and Engraved**
**1980, Aug. 16** **Perf. 11½**
4852 A2295 4k multicolored .25 .20

---

**1980, May 15** **Litho.** **Perf. 12½x12**
4828 A2285 1k shown .20 .20
4829 A2285 2k MI-8, 1962 .20 .20
4830 A2285 3k KA-26, 1965 .20 .20
4831 A2285 6k MI-6, 1957 .20 .20
4832 A2285 15k MI-10 .25 .40
4833 A2285 32k V-12 1.60 1.40
Nos. 4828-4833 (6)
Nos. 4832, 4833 exist imperf. Value, $50 for
both.

David Anacht,
Illuminated
Manuscript
A2286

**1980, May 16** **Perf. 12**
4834 A2286 4k multicolored .25 .20
David Anacht, Armenian philosopher,
1500th birth anniversary.

Emblem,
Training
Lab — A2287

**1980, June 4**
4835 A2287 6k shown .20 .20
4836 A2287 15k Cosmonauts .40 .25
meeting
4837 A2287 32k Press confer- .80 .55
ence 1.40 1.00
Nos. 4835-4837 (3)
Intercosmos cooperative space program
(USSR-Hungary).

Polar Fox
A2288

**1980, June 25** **Litho.** **Perf. 12x12½**
4838 A2288 2k Dark silver .20 .20
fox,vert.
4839 A2288 4k shown .20 .20
4840 A2288 6k Mink .20 .20
4841 A2288 15k Azerbaijan nu- .30 .20
tria, vert.
4842 A2288 15k Black sable 1.10 1.00
Nos. 4838-4842 (5)

Factory,
Buildings,
Arms of
Tatar
A.S.S.R.
A2289

**1980, June 25** **Perf. 12**
4843 A2289 4k multicolored .25 .20
Tatar Autonomous SSR, 60th anniv.

---

"Mother Russia,"
Fireworks over
Moscow — A2282

Flags and Arms of
Azerbaijan,
Government
House — A2280

**1980, Apr. 22** **Photo.**
4821 A2280 4k multicolored .25 .20
Azerbaijan Soviet Socialist Republic, Communist Party of Azerbaijan, 60th anniv.

**Souvenir Sheet**

Lenin, 110th Birth
Anniversary — A2281

**1980, Apr. 22** **Perf. 12x11½**
4822 A2281 30k multicolored 1.25 .75

**1980, Apr. 25** **Litho.**
#4824, Soviet War Memorial, Berlin, raising
of Red flag. #4825, Parade, Red Square,
Moscow.

4823 A2282 4k multicolored .20 .20
4824 A2282 4k multicolored .20 .20
4825 A2282 6k multicolored .60 .60
Nos. 4823-4825 (3)
35th anniv. of victory in World War II.
Nos. 4824, 4825 exist imperf.

"XXV"
A2284

**1980, May 12** **Litho.** **Perf. 12**
4826 A2283 4k multicolored .25 .20
Workers' Delegates in Ivanovo-Voznesensk,
75th anniversary.

Workers'
Monument
A2283

**1980, May 14** **Photo.** **Perf. 11½**
4827 A2284 32k multicolored 1.25 .75
Signing of Warsaw Pact (Bulgaria, Czechoslovakia, German Democratic Rep., Hungary,
Poland, Romania, USSR), 25th anniv.

YaK-24 Helicopter, 1953 — A2285

---

Nikolai Ilyitch
Podvoiski (1880-
1948), Revolutionary
A2274

**1980, Feb. 16** **Engr.** **Perf. 12½x12**
4813 A2274 4k claret brown .25 .20

Rainbow, by A.K. Savrasov — A2275

#4815, Summer Harvest, by A.G. Venetsia-
nov, vert. #4816, Old Erevan, by M.S. Saryan.

**1980, Mar. 4** **Litho.** **Perf. 11½**
4814 A2275 6k multicolored .25 .20
4815 A2275 6k multicolored .25 .20
4816 A2275 6k multicolored .75 .60
Nos. 4814-4816 (3)

**Souvenir Sheet**

Cosmonaut Alexei Leonov — A2276

**1980, Mar. 18** **Litho.** **Perf. 12½x12**
4817 A2276 50k multicolored 1.50 .75
Man's first walk in space (Voskhod 2, Mar.
18-19, 1965).

Lenin Order, 50th
Anniversary
A2278

**1980, Mar. 21** **Engr.**
4818 A2277 4k slate blue .25 .20

Georg Ots,
Estonian Artist
A2277

**1980, Apr. 6** **Photo.** **Perf. 11½**
4819 A2278 4k multicolored .25 .20

**Souvenir Sheet**

Cosmonauts, Salyut 6 and
Soyuz — A2279

**1980, Apr. 12** **Litho.** **Perf. 12**
4820 A2279 50k multicolored 1.50 1.00
Intercosmos cooperative space program.

Soviet Racing Car KHADI-7 — A2296

**1980, Aug. 25   Litho.   Perf. 12**

| 4853 | A2296 | 2k shown | .20 | .20 |
|---|---|---|---|---|
| 4854 | A2296 | 6k KHADI-10 | .20 | .20 |
| 4855 | A2296 | 15k KHADI-113 | .35 | .20 |
| 4856 | A2296 | 32k KHADI-133 | .65 | .45 |
| | | Nos. 4853-4856 (4) | 1.40 | 1.10 |

No. 4856 exists imperf. Value, $50.

**1980, Aug. 26   Perf. 12**

4857 A2297 4k multicolored   .50   .20

Kazakhstan Republic, 60th Anniversary A2297

**1980, Aug. 29**

4858 A2298 32k multicolored   1.00   .50

Ingres, Self-portrait, and Nymph A2298

Jean Auguste Dominique Ingres (1780-1867), French painter. Exists imperf.

**1980, Sept. 6   Litho.   Perf. 12½x12½**

4859 A2299 4k multicolored   .25   .20

Morning on the Field of Kulikovo, by A. Bubnov — A2299

Battle of Kulikovo, 600th anniversary.

**1980, Sept. 15   Photo.   Perf. 11½**

4860 A2300 4k multicolored   .25   .20

Town Hall, Tartu — A2300

Tartu, 950th anniversary.

---

**1980, Sept. 15   Litho.   Perf. 12x12½**

4861 A2301 10k multicolored   .30   .25

V.V. Malyshev, V.V. Aksenov A2301

Soyuz T-2 space flight.

**1980, Sept. 15   Photo.   Perf. 11½x12**

| 4862 | A2302 | 6k shown | .20 | .20 |
|---|---|---|---|---|
| 4863 | A2302 | 15k Space walk | .40 | .25 |
| 4864 | A2302 | 32k Endurance test | .80 | .45 |
| | | Nos. 4862-4864 (3) | 1.40 | .90 |

Flight Training, Yuri Gagarin — A2302

Gagarin Cosmonaut Training Center, 20th anniversary.

**1980, Sept. 15   Litho.   Perf. 12½x12½**

| 4865 | A2303 | 6k multicolored | .20 | .20 |
|---|---|---|---|---|
| 4866 | A2303 | 15k multicolored | .40 | .25 |
| 4867 | A2303 | 32k multicolored | .80 | .45 |
| | | Nos. 4865-4867 (3) | 1.40 | .90 |

Intercosmos A2303

6k, Intercosmos Emblem, Flags of USSR and Cuba, and Cosmonauts training. 15k, Inside weightless cabin. 32k, Landing.

Intercosmos cooperative space program (USSR-Cuba).

**1980, Sept. 20   Photo.   Perf. 11½**

4868 A2304 6k multicolored   .25   .20

October Revolution, 63rd Anniversary A2304

---

Design: No. 4869B, Countess Tarakanova, by K.D. Flavitsky (1830-1866), vert.

**1980, Sept. 25   Litho.   Perf. 11½**

| 4869 | A2305a | 6k multicolored | .25 | .25 |
|---|---|---|---|---|
| 4869A | A2305a | 6k multicolored | .25 | .25 |
| 4869B | A2305a | 6k multicolored | | |

Family with Serfs, by N.V. Nevrev (1830-1904) — A2305a

David Gurumishvily (1705-1792), Poet — A2305

**1980, Sept. 20**

4869 A2305 6k multicolored   .25   .20

A.F. Joffe (1880-1960), Physicist — A2306

**1980, Sept. 29**

4870 A2306 4k multicolored   .25   .20

Siberian Pine A2307

**1980, Sept. 29   Litho.   Perf. 12½x12**

| 4871 | A2307 | 2k shown | .20 | .20 |
|---|---|---|---|---|
| 4872 | A2307 | 4k Oak | .20 | .20 |
| 4873 | A2307 | 6k Lime tree, vert. | .20 | .20 |
| 4874 | A2307 | 10k Sea buckthorn | .20 | .20 |
| 4875 | A2307 | 15k European ash | .30 | .20 |
| | | Nos. 4871-4875 (5) | 1.10 | 1.00 |

**1980, Sept. 30   Engr.   Perf. 12**

4876 A2308 4k dark green   .25   .20

A.M. Vasilevsky (1895-1977), Soviet Marshal — A2308

---

Mischa Holding Olympic Torch — A2309

**1980, Nov. 24   Perf. 12x12½**

4877 A2309 1r multicolored   7.50   1.75

Completion of 22nd Summer Olympic Games, Moscow, July 19-Aug. 3.

Souvenir Sheet

**1980, Nov. 24**

4878 A2310 4k slate   .25   .20

A.V. Suvorov (1730-1800), General and Military Theorist A2310

A2311

**1980, Nov. 24   Litho.   Perf. 12**

4879 A2311 4k multicolored   .50   .20

Armenian SSR & Armenian Communist Party, 60th anniv.

**1980, Nov. 24**

4880 A2312 4k multicolored   .25   .20

Aleksandr Blok (1880-1921), Poet — A2312

**1980, Nov. 24**

Research Ship Type of 1979

**Lithographed and Engraved   Perf. 12x11½**

| 4881 | A2271 | 2k Aju Dag, Fleet arms | .20 | .20 |
|---|---|---|---|---|
| 4882 | A2271 | 3k Valerian Urywaev | .20 | .20 |
| 4883 | A2271 | 4k Mikhail Somov | .20 | .20 |
| 4884 | A2271 | 6k Sergei Korolev | .20 | .20 |
| 4885 | A2271 | 10k Otto Schmidt | .20 | .20 |
| 4886 | A2271 | 15k Mstislav Keldysh | .30 | .20 |
| | | Nos. 4881-4886 (6) | 1.30 | 1.20 |

For overprint see No. 5499.

Russian Flag — A2313

Georgian Soviet Socialist Republic, 60th Anniv. — A2331

**1981, Feb. 25**    *Perf. 12*
4914 A2331 4k multicolored    .25 .20

Abkhazian Autonomous Soviet Socialist Republic, 60th Anniv. — A2332

**1981, Mar. 4**
4915 A2332 4k multicolored    .25 .20
Exists imperf.

Communications Institute A2333

**1901, Mar. 12**    *Photo.*
4916 A2333 4k multicolored    .25 .20
Moscow Electrotechnical Institute of Communications, 60th anniv.

Satellite, Radio Operator A2334

**1981, Mar. 12**    *Perf. 11½*
4917 A2334 4k multicolored    .35 .25
30th All-Union Amateur Radio Designers Exhibition.

Cosmonauts L.I. Popov and V.V. Rumin A2335

**1981, Mar. 20**    *Litho.*
4918 A2335 15k shown    .40 .25
4919 A2335 15k Spacecraft complex    .60 .25
   a.   Pair, #4918-4919 + label    1.00 .50
185-day flight of Cosmos 35-Salyut 6-Cosmos 37 complex, Apr. 9-Oct. 11, 1980. No. 4919a has a continuous design.

Cosmonauts O. Makarov, L. Kizim and G. Strekalov — A2336

**1981, Mar. 20**    *Perf. 12½x12*
4920 A2336 10k multicolored    .25 .20
Soyuz T-3 flight, Nov. 27-Dec. 10, 1980.

Lenin and Congress Building — A2326

Banner and Kremlin — A2327

**1981**    *Photo.*    *Perf. 11½*
4903 A2325 4k multicolored    .25 .20

**Photogravure and Embossed**    *Perf. 11½x12*
**1982**
4904 A2326 20k multicolored    1.50 .75

**Souvenir Sheet**
*Litho.*    *Perf. 12x12½*
4905 A2327 50k multicolored    1.50 .75
26th Communist Party Congress. Issue dates: 4k, 20k, Jan. 22; 50k, Feb. 16.

Freighter, Flags of USSR and India A2329

**1981, Feb. 10**    *Photo.*    *Perf. 11½x12*
4906 A2328 4k multicolored    .25 .20
Mstislav Vsevolodovich Keldysh (1911-1978), mathematician.

Mstislav V. Keldysh A2328

**1981, Feb. 10**    *Litho.*    *Perf. 12*
4907 A2329 15k multicolored    .50 .30
Soviet-Indian Shipping Line, 25th anniv.

Baikal-Amur Railroad and Map — A2330

**1981, Feb. 18**    *Perf. 12½x12*
4908 A2330 4k multicolored    .25 .20
4909 A2330 4k multicolored    .25 .20
4910 A2330 4k multicolored    .25 .20
4911 A2330 4k multicolored    .25 .20
4912 A2330 4k multicolored    .25 .20
4913 A2330 4k multicolored    1.50 1.20
   Nos. 4908-4913 (6)
10th Five-Year Plan Projects (1976-1980): No. 4909, Gas plant, Urengoi (spherical tanks); No. 4910, Enisei River power station (dam); No. 4911, Atomic power plant. No. 4912, Paper mill. No. 4913, Coal mining. Ekibstuy.

Flags of India and USSR, Government House, New Delhi A2320

**1980, Dec. 30**    *Litho.*    *Perf. 12x12½*
4896 A2320 4k multicolored    .50 .35
Visit of Pres. Brezhnev to India. Printed se-tenant with inscribed label.

Mirny Base — A2321

**1981, Jan. 5**    *Perf. 12*
4897 A2321 4k shown    .20 .20
4898 A2321 6k Earth station, rocket    .20 .20 .30 .20
4899 A2321 15k Map, supply ship    .70 .60
   Nos. 4897-4899 (3)
Soviet Antarctic research, 25th anniv.

Dagestan Soviet Socialist Republic, 60th Anniversary A2322

**1981, Jan. 20**
4900 A2322 4k multicolored    .25 .20

Bandy World Championship, Cheborovsk — A2323

**1981, Jan. 20**
4901 A2323 6k multicolored    .25 .20

26th Congress of Ukrainian Communist Party. A2324

**1981, Jan. 23**    *Photo.*    *Perf. 11½*
4902 A2324 4k multicolored    .25 .20

Lenin, "XXVI" A2325

Soviet Medical College, 50th Anniversary A2314

**1980, Dec. 1**    *Engr.*    *Perf. 12x12½*
4887 A2313 3k orange red    .25 .20
**1980, Dec. 1**    *Photo.*    *Perf. 11½*
4888 A2314 4k multicolored    .25 .20

New Year 1981 A2315

**1980, Dec. 1**    *Litho.*
4889 A2315 4k multicolored    .25 .20

Lenin, Electrical Plant A2316

**1980, Dec. 18**
4890 A2316 4k multicolored    .25 .20
60th anniversary of GOELRO (Lenin's electro-economic plan).

A.N. Nesmeyanov (1899-1980), Chemist — A2317

**1980, Dec. 19**    *Perf. 12½x12*
4891 A2317 4k multicolored    .25 .20

Nagatinski Bridge, Moscow — A2318

**Photogravure and Engraved**
**1980, Dec. 23**    *Perf. 11½x12*
4892 A2318 4k shown    .20 .20
4893 A2318 6k Luzhniki Bridge    .20 .20
4894 A2318 15k Kalininski Bridge    .30 .20 .70 .60
   Nos. 4892-4894 (3)

S.K. Timoshenko (1895-1970), Marshal — A2319

**1980, Dec. 25**    *Engr.*    *Perf. 12*
4895 A2319 4k rose lake    .25 .20

## Lift-Off, Baikonur Base — A2337

**1981, Mar. 23**
| 4921 | A2337 | 6k shown | .20 | .20 |
| 4922 | A2337 | 15k Mongolians watching flight on TV | .40 | .25 |
| 4923 | A2337 | 32k Re-entry | .80 | .95 |
| | | Nos. 4921-4923 (3) | 1.40 | .95 |

Intercosmos cooperative space program (USSR-Mongolia).

### Vitus Bering A2338

**1981, Mar. 25    Engr.    Perf. 12x12½**
| 4924 | A2338 | 4k dark blue | .25 | .20 |

Bering (1680-1741), Danish navigator.

Yuri Gagarin and Earth — A2339

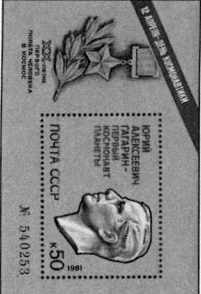

Yuri Gagarin — A2340

**1981, Apr. 12    Photo.    Perf. 11½x12**
| 4925 | A2339 | 6k shown | .20 | .20 |
| 4926 | A2339 | 15k S.P. Korolev (craft designer) | .40 | .25 |
| 4927 | A2339 | 32k Monument | .80 | .50 |

**Souvenir Sheet**
| 4928 | A2340 | 50k shown | 1.40 | .95 |

| 4928 | A2340 | 50k shown | 5.00 | 1.00 |

Soviet space flights, 20th anniv. Nos. 4925-4927 each se-tenant with label.

---

### Salyut Orbital Station, 10th Anniv. of Flight A2341

**1981, Apr. 19    Litho.    Perf. 12x12½**
| 4929 | A2341 | 32k multicolored | 1.00 | .50 |

### 111th Birth Anniv. of Lenin — A2342

**Souvenir Sheet**

**1981, Apr. 22    Perf. 11½x12½**
| 4930 | A2342 | 50k multicolored | 1.50 | .60 |

### Sergei Prokofiev (1891-1953), Composer A2343

**1981, Apr. 23    Engr.    Perf. 12**
| 4931 | A2343 | 4k dark purple | .40 | .25 |

### New Hofburg Palace, Vienna A2344

**1981, May 5    Litho.**
| 4932 | A2344 | 15k multicolored | .50 | .20 |

WIPA 1981 Phil. Exhib., Vienna, May 22-31.

### Adzhar Autonomous Soviet Socialist Republic, 60th Anniv. — A2345

**1981, May 7**
| 4933 | A2345 | 4k multicolored | .25 | .20 |

### Centenary of Welding (Invented by N.N. Benardos) A2346

**1981, May 12    Lithographed and Engraved    Perf. 11½**
| 4934 | A2346 | 6k multicolored | .25 | .20 |

---

### Int. Architects Union, 14th Congress, Warsaw — A2347

**1981, May 12    Photo.**
| 4935 | A2347 | 15k multicolored | .50 | .25 |

### Albanian Girl, by A.A. Ivanov A2348

**1981, May 15    Litho.    Perf. 12x12½**
| 4936 | A2348 | 10k multicolored | .25 | .20 |
| 4937 | A2348 | 10k multicolored | .25 | .20 |
| 4938 | A2348 | 10k multicolored | .25 | .20 |
| 4939 | A2348 | 10k multicolored | .25 | .20 |
| | | Nos. 4936-4939 (4) | 1.00 | .80 |

#4937, Horseman, by F.A. Roubeau. #4938, The Demon, by M.A. Wrubel, horiz. #4939, Sunset over the Sea, by N.N. Ge, horiz.

### Cosmonauts in Training A2349

**1981, May 15**
| 4940 | A2349 | 6k shown | .20 | .20 |
| 4941 | A2349 | 15k In space | .40 | .20 |
| 4942 | A2349 | 32k Return | .80 | .50 |
| | | Nos. 4940-4942 (3) | 1.40 | .95 |

Intercosmos cooperative space program (USSR-Romania).

### Dwarf Primrose — A2350

**1981, May 20    Perf. 12**
| 4943 | A2350 | 4k multicolored | .20 | .20 |
| 4944 | A2350 | 6k multicolored | .20 | .20 |
| 4945 | A2350 | 10k multicolored | .25 | .20 |
| 4946 | A2350 | 15k multicolored | .40 | .25 |
| 4947 | A2350 | 32k multicolored | 1.85 | 1.35 |
| | | Nos. 4943-4947 (5) | | |

Flowers of the Carpathian Mountains: 6k, Great carline thistle. 10k, Mountain parageum. 15k, Alpine bluebell. 32k, Rhododendron kotschyi.

---

### Luigi Longo, Italian Labor Leader, 1st Death Anniv. — A2351

**1981, May 24    Photo.    Perf. 11½**
| 4948 | A2351 | 6k multicolored | .25 | .20 |

### Nizami Gianshevi (1141-1209), Azerbaijan Poet — A2352

**1981, May 25    Photo. & Engr.**
| 4949 | A2352 | 4k multicolored | .25 | .20 |

A2353

**1981, June 18    Litho.    Perf. 12**
| 4950 | A2353 | 4k Running | .20 | .20 |
| 4951 | A2353 | 6k Soccer | .20 | .20 |
| 4952 | A2353 | 10k Discus throwing | .25 | .20 |
| 4953 | A2353 | 15k Boxing | .30 | .25 |
| 4954 | A2353 | 32k Diving | .60 | .35 |
| | | Nos. 4950-4954 (5) | 1.50 | 1.20 |

### Mongolian Revolution, 60th anniv. — A2354

**1981, July 6**
| 4955 | A2354 | 6k multicolored | .25 | .20 |

### 12th Int. Film Festival, Moscow — A2355

**1981, July 6    Photo.    Perf. 11½**
| 4956 | A2355 | 15k multicolored | .50 | .25 |

### River Tour Boat Lenin A2356

**1981, July 9    Litho.    Perf. 12½**
| 4957 | A2356 | 4k shown | .20 | .20 |
| 4958 | A2356 | 6k Cosmonaut Gagarin | .20 | .20 |
| 4959 | A2356 | 15k Valerian Kuibyshev | .35 | .20 |
| 4960 | A2356 | 32k Freestyle Baltiyski | .75 | .40 |
| | | Nos. 4957-4960 (4) | 1.50 | 1.00 |

RUSSIA

**Birth Centenary of Pablo Picasso — A2375**

Souvenir Sheet

*Perf. 12x12½*

**1981, Oct. 25**
4993 A2375 50k multicolored    2.75 .90

**Photogravure and Engraved**

*Perf. 11½*    .25 .20

**1981, Nov. 5**
4994 A2376 4k multicolored

Sergei Dmitrievich Merkurov (1881-1952), artist.

Paintings: 6k, Guriyka, by M.G. Kokodze, 1921. 10k, Fellow Travelers, by U.M. Dzhaparidze, 1936, horiz. 15k, Shota Rustaveli, by G.S. Kobuladze, 1038. 32k, Collecting Tea, by V.D. Gudiashvili, 1964, horiz.

Autumn, by Nino Pirosmanas, 1913 — A2377

*Perf. 12½x12½, 12½x12*

**1981, Nov. 5**    Litho.
4995 A2377 4k multicolored   .20 .20
4996 A2377 6k multicolored   .20 .20
4997 A2377 10k multicolored   .50 .25
4998 A2377 15k multicolored   .65 .25
4999 A2377 32k multicolored   1.40 .50
Nos. 4995-4999 (5)   2.95 1.35

**New Year 1982 — A2378**

Litho.    *Perf. 12*    .25 .20

**1981, Dec. 2**
5000 A2378 4k multicolored

**Public Transportation 19th-20th Cent. — A2379**

**Photogravure and Engraved**

*Perf. 11½x12*

**1981, Dec. 10**
5001 A2379 4k Sled   .20 .20
5002 A2379 6k Horse-drawn trolley   .20 .20
5003 A2379 10k Coach   .30 .20

---

Training ships. 4k, 6k, 15k, 20k, horiz.

*Perf. 12½x12, 12x12½*    Litho.

**1981, Sept. 18**
4981 A2368 4k 4-masted bark Tovarich I   .20 .20
4982 A2368 6k Barkentine Vega   .20 .20
4983 A2368 10k shown   .20 .20
4984 A2368 15k 3-masted bark Tovarich   .25 .20
4985 A2368 20k 4-masted bark Kruzenstern   .30 .25
4986 A2368 32k 4-masted bark Sedov   .50 .30
Nos. 4981-4986 (6)   1.65 1.35

A2370

A2369

*Perf. 12*    .25 .20

**1981, Oct. 10**
4987 A2369 4k multicolored   Kazakhstan's Union with Russia, 250th Anniv.

*Perf. 11½*    .75 .50

Photo.    .25 .20

**1981, Oct. 10**
4988 A2370 4k multicolored   Mikhail Alekseevich Lavrentiev (1900-80), mathematician. Exists imperf.

**64th Anniv. of October Revolution — A2371**

Litho.    .25 .20

**1981, Oct. 15**
4989 A2371 4k multicolored

**Ekran Satellite TV Broadcasting System — A2372**

*Perf. 12*    .25 .20

**1981, Oct. 15**
4990 A2372 4k multicolored

Salyut 6-Soyuz flight of V.V. Kovalionok and V.P. Savinykh — A2373

*Perf. 12*
4991 A2373 10k Text   .30 .20
4992 A2373 10k Cosmonauts   .60 .30
  a. A2373 Pair, #4991-4992

**1981, Oct. 15**

---

Siberian Tit — A2363

Designs: Song birds.

*Perf. 12½x12, 12x12½*    Litho.

**1981, Aug. 20**
4972 A2363 6k shown   .20 .20
4973 A2363 10k Tersiphone paradisi, vert.   .35 .20
4974 A2363 15k Emberiza jankowski   .45 .25
4975 A2363 20k Sutora webbiana, vert.   .55 .30
4976 A2363 32k Saxicola torquata, vert.   .90 .45
Nos. 4972-4976 (5)   2.45 1.40

**60th Anniv. of Komi Autonomous Soviet Socialist Republic — A2364**

*Perf. 12*    .35 .20

**1981, Aug. 22**
4977 A2364 4k multicolored

**Svyaz-'81 Intl. Communications Exhibition — A2365**

**Photogravure and Engraved**

*Perf. 11½*    .25 .20

**1981, Aug. 22**
4978 A2365 4k multicolored

**60th Anniv. of Kabardino-Balkar Autonomous Soviet Socialist Republic — A2366**

*Perf. 12*    .25 .20    Litho.

**1981, Sept. 1**
4979 A2366 4k multicolored

War Veterans' Committee, 25th Anniv. — A2367

Photo.    *Perf. 11½*    .25 .20

**1981, Sept. 1**
4980 A2367 4k multicolored

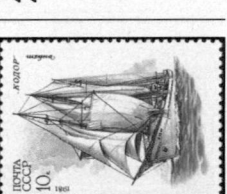

Schooner Kodor — A2368

---

Icebreaker Malgin — A2357

**Photogravure and Engraved**

*Perf. 11½x12*    .50 .25

**1981, July 9**
4961 A2357 15k multicolored

**26th Party Congress Resolutions (Intl. Cooperation) — A2358**

*Perf. 12x11½*
4962 A2358 4k shown   .20 .20
4963 A2358 4k Industry   .20 .20
4964 A2358 4k Energy   .20 .20
4965 A2358 4k Agriculture   .20 .20
4966 A2358 4k Communications   .20 .20
4967 A2358 4k Arts   1.20 1.20
Nos. 4962-4967 (6)

**1981, July 15**    Photo.

I.N. Ulyanov (Lenin's Father), 150th Anniv. of Birth — A2359

*Perf. 11½*    .25 .20

**1981, July 25**    Engr,
4968 A2359 4k multicolored

Leningrad Theater, 225th Anniv. — A2360

*Perf. 11½*    .25 .20    Photo.

**1981, Aug. 12**
4969 A2360 6k multicolored

A.M. Gerasimov, Artist, Birth Centenary A2361

*Perf. 12*    .25 .20

**1981, Aug. 12**
4970 A2361 4k multicolored

Physical Chemistry Institute, Moscow Academy of Science, 50th Anniv. A2362

Litho.    *Perf. 11½*    .25 .20

**1981, Aug. 12**
4971 A2362 4k multicolored

Souvenir Sheet

| | | | | |
|---|---|---|---|---|
| 5004 | A2379 | 15k Taxi, 1926 | .40 | .25 |
| 5005 | A2379 | 20k Bus, 1926 | .50 | .30 |
| 5006 | A2379 | 32k Trolley, 1912 | .80 | .50 |

Nos. 5001-5006 (6)  2.40 1.65

**1981, Dec. 17**
5007 A2380 50k multicolored  1.50 .75
Kremlin and New Delhi Parliament — A2380
1st direct telephone link with India.  **Photo.**

A2382

A2381

**1982, Jan. 11    Litho.    Perf. 12**
5008 A2381 4k multicolored  .20 .20
5009 A2382 4k multicolored  .20 .20
60th anniv. of Chechen-Ingush Autonomous SSR and of Yakutsk Autonomous SSR.

**1982, Jan. 12    Photo.    Perf. 11½x12**
5010 A2383 10k multicolored  .30 .25
1500th Anniv. of Kiev — A2383

S.P. Korolev (1907-66), Rocket Designer — A2384

**1982, Jan. 12    Perf. 11½**
5011 A2384 4k multicolored  .25 .20

Nazim Khikmet (1902-1963), Turkish Poet — A2385

**1982, Jan. 20    Litho.    Perf. 12**
5012 A2385 6k multicolored  .25 .20

---

**1982, Feb. 1    Photo.    Perf. 11½**
5013 A2386 15k multicolored  .50 .25
10th World Trade Union Congress, Havana — A2386

17th Soviet Trade Union Congress A2387

**1982, Feb. 10    Litho.**
5014 A2387 4k multicolored  .25 .20

Edouard Manet (1832-1883) A2388

**1982, Feb. 10    Perf. 12x12½**
5015 A2388 32k multicolored  1.00 .45

Equestrian Sports A2389

**1982, Feb. 16    Photo.    Perf. 11½**
5016 A2389 4k Hurdles  .20 .20
5017 A2389 6k Riding  .20 .20
5018 A2389 15k Racing  .70 .30
Nos. 5016-5018 (3)  .60
No. 5016 exists imperf.

2nd Death Anniv. of Marshal Tito of Yugoslavia A2390

**1982, Feb. 25    Litho.    Perf. 12**
5019 A2390 6k olive black  .25 .20

---

**1982, Mar. 4    Photo.    Perf. 11½**
5020 A2392 4k multicolored  .25 .20
350th Anniv. of State University of Tartu A2392

9th Int'l. Cardiologists Congress, Moscow — A2393

**1982, Mar. 4**
5021 A2393 15k multicolored  .50 .20

Souvenir Sheet

Biathlon, Speed Skating — A2391

**1982, Mar. 6    Litho.    Perf. 12½x12**
5022 A2394 50k multicolored  1.50 .70
5th Nat'l. Athletic Meet.

Blueberry Bush — A2395

**1982, Mar. 10    Litho.    Perf. 12x12½**
5023 A2395 4k Blackberries  .20 .20
5024 A2395 4k shown  .20 .20
5025 A2395 10k Cranberries  .25 .20
5026 A2395 15k Cherries  .70 .30
5027 A2395 32k Strawberries  1.65 1.10
Nos. 5023-5027 (5)

Venera 13 and Venera 14 Flights — A2396

**1982, Mar. 10    Photo.    Perf. 11½**
5028 A2396 10k multicolored  .30 .25

---

Paintings: No. 5030, M.I. Lopuchino, by Vladimir Borowikowsky (1757-1825). No. 5031, E.W. Davidov, by O.A. Kiprensky (1782-1836). No. 5032, Landscape.

**1982, Mar. 18    Perf. 12**
5029 A2397 6k multicolored  .20 .20
5030 A2397 6k multicolored  .20 .20
5031 A2397 6k multicolored  .20 .20
5032 A2397 6k multicolored  .80 .80
Nos. 5029-5032 (4)

Marriage Ceremony, by W.W. Pukirev (1832-1890) A2397

K.I. Tchukovsky (1882-1969), Writer — A2398

**1982, Mar. 31    Engr.**
5033 A2398 4k black  .25 .20

Cosmonauts' Day — A2399

**1982, Apr. 12    Photo.    Perf. 12x11½**
5034 A2399 6k multicolored  .25 .20

Souvenir Sheet

112th Birth Anniv. of Lenin — A2400

**1982, Apr. 22    Photo.    Perf. 11½x12**
5035 A2400 50k multicolored  1.50 .70

V.P. Soloviev-Sedoi (1907-79), Composer A2401

**1982, Apr. 25    Engr.    Perf. 12**
5036 A2401 4k brown  .25 .20

G. Dimitrov (1882-1949), 1st Bulgarian Prime Minister A2402

**1982, Apr. 25    Engr.    Perf. 12**
5037 A2402 6k green  .25 .20

Kremlin Tower, Moscow — A2403

**1982** **Litho.** **Perf. 12½x12**
5038 A2403 45k brown 1.10 .70
a. Engraved 1.10 .70
Issued: #5038, Apr. 25. #5038a, Oct. 12.

70th Anniv. of Pravda Newspaper A2404

**Photo.**
1982, May 5
5039 A2404 4k multicolored .25 .20

UN Conf. on Human Environment, 10th anniv. — A2405

1982, May 10
5040 A2405 6k multicolored .25 .20

Pioneers' Org., 60th anniv. — A2406
**Perf. 11½**
1982, May 19
5041 A2406 4k multicolored .25 .20

Communist Youth Org. 19th Cong. — A2407
1982, May 19
5042 A2407 4k multicolored .50 .25

ITU Delegates Conf. Nairobi — A2408

1982, May 19
5043 A2408 15k multicolored .50 .25

TUL-80 Electric Locomotive — A2409

**Perf. 12x11½**
1982, May 20
5044 A2409 4k shown .20 .20
5045 A2409 6k TEP-75 diesel .20 .20
5046 A2409 10k TEP-7 diesel .25 .20
5047 A2409 15k WL-82m electric .40 .20
5048 A2409 32k EP-200 electric .85 .35
Nos. 5044-5048 (5) 1.90 1.15

1982 World Cup — A2410

**Perf. 11½x12**
1982, June 4
5049 A2410 20k olive & purple .50 .30

Birds — A2411
Rare
18th Ornithological Cong., Moscow.

**Litho.** **Perf. 12x12½**
1982, June 10
5050 A2411 2k Grus Monacha .20 .20
5051 A2411 4k Haliaeetus pelagicus .20 .20
5052 A2411 6k Eurynorhynchus .20 .20
5053 A2411 10k Eulabeia indica .20 .20
5054 A2411 15k Chettusia gregaria .25 .20
5055 A2411 32k Ciconia boyciana .55 .35
Nos. 5050-5055 (6) 1.60 1.35

Komomolok on Amur City, 60th Anniv. — A2412

**Photogravure and Engraved**
**Perf. 11½**
1982, June 10
5056 A2412 4k multicolored .25 .20

Tatchanka, by M.B. Grekov (1882-1934) — A2413

**Litho.** **Perf. 12½x12**
1982, June 15
5057 A2413 6k multicolored .25 .20

2nd UN Conference on Peaceful Uses of Outer Space, Vienna, Aug. 9-21 — A2414

**Photo.** **Perf. 11½**
1982, June 15
5058 A2414 15k multicolored .50 .20

Intercosmos Cooperative Space Program (USSR-France) — A2415

**Litho.** **Perf. 12½x12**
1982
5059 A2415 6k Cosmonauts .20 .20
5060 A2415 20k Rocket, globe .35 .20
5061 A2415 45k Satellites .80 .40
Miniature sheet of 8 50.00
Nos. 5059-5061 (3) 1.35 .80

**Souvenir Sheet**
5062 A2415 50k Emblem, satellite 1.50 .75
#5062 contains one 41x29mm stamp. Issue dates: 6k, 50k, June 24. 20k, 45k, July 2.

The Legend of the Goldfish, by P. Sosin, 1968 — A2416

Lacquerware Paintings, Ustera: 10k, Minin's Appeal to Count Posharski, by J. Phomitchev, 1953. 15k, Two Peasants, by A. Kotjagin, 1933. 20k, The Fisherman, by N. Klykov, 1933. 32k, The Arrest of the Propagandists, by N. Shishakov, 1968.
**Litho.** **Perf. 12½x12**
1982, July 6
5063 A2416 6k multicolored .20 .20
5064 A2416 10k multicolored .25 .20
5065 A2416 15k multicolored .30 .20
5066 A2416 20k multicolored .45 .20
5007 A2416 32k multicolored .65 .30
Nos. 5063-5067 (5) 1.85 1.10

Telephone Centenary A2417

**Perf. 12**
1982, July 13
5068 A2417 4k Phone, 1882 .20 .20

P. Schilling's Electro-magnetic Telegraph Sesquicentennial — A2418

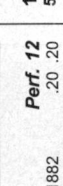

**Photogravure and Engraved**
**Perf. 11½**
1982, July 16
5069 A2418 6k Voltaic cells .25 .20

Intervision Gymnastics Contest A2419

**Photo.**
1982, Aug. 10
5070 A2419 15k multicolored .50 .30

Gliders A2420

**1982, Aug. 20** **Litho.** **Perf. 12½x12**
5071 A2420 4k Masljahart Glider, 1923 .20 .20
5072 A2420 6k Red Star, 1930 .20 .20
5073 A2420 10k ZAGI-1, 1934 .20 .20
**Size: 60x28mm**
**Perf. 11½x12**
5074 A2420 20k Stakhanovets, 1939 .35 .20
5075 A2420 32k Troop carrier GR-29, 1941 .55 .35
1.50 1.15
Nos. 5071-5075 (5)
See Nos. 5118-5122.

Garibaldi (1807-1882) A2421

**Perf. 11½**
1982, Aug. 25
5076 A2421 6k multicolored .25 .20

Intl. Atomic Energy Authority, 25th Anniv. A2422
**Photo.**
1982, Aug. 30
5077 A2422 20k multicolored .75 .30
Exists imperf.

World Chess Championship A2424

Marshal B.M. Shaposhnikov (1882-1945) A2423
**Engr.**
1982, Sept. 10
5078 A2423 4k red brown .25 .20

**Photo.**
1982, Sept. 10
5079 A2424 4k King .25 .20
5080 A2424 6k Queen .25 .20
See #5084.

African Natl. Congress, 70th Anniv. A2425
1982, Sept. 10
5081 A2425 6k multicolored .25 .20

S.P. Botkin (1832-89), Physician A2426

**Engr.** **Perf. 12½x12**
1982, Sept. 17
5082 A2426 4k green .25 .20

RUSSIA

## Souvenir Sheet

**1982, Sept. 17    Litho.    Perf. 12x12½**

25th Anniv. of Sputnik—A2427

5083  A2427  50k multicolored    5.00  .85

No. 5079 Overprinted in Gold for Karpov's Victory

**1982, Sept. 22    Photo.    Perf. 11½**

5084  A2424  6k multicolored    .60  .30

## World War II Warships — A2428

**Photogravure and Engraved**

**1982, Sept. 22    Perf. 11½x12**

5085  A2428  4k Submarine S-56    .20  .20
5086  A2428  6k Minelayer Gremjashtsky    .20  .20
5087  A2428  15k Mine sweeper T-205    .35  .20
5088  A2428  20k Cruiser Red Crimea    .40  .25
5089  A2428  45k Cruiser Sebastopol    .90  .45
Nos. 5085-5089 (5)    2.05  1.30

65th Anniv. of October Revolution A2429

**1982, Oct. 12    Litho.    Perf. 12**

5090  A2429  4k multicolored    .25  .20

## House of the Soviets, Moscow — A2430

**1982, Oct. 25    Photo.    Perf. 11x12**

5091  A2430  10k multicolored    .25  .20
5092  A2430  10k multicolored    .25  .20
5093  A2430  10k multicolored    .25  .20
5094  A2430  10k multicolored    .25  .20
5095  A2430  10k multicolored    .65  .20
5096  A2430  10k multicolored    1.90  1.20
Nos. 5091-5096 (6)

60th Anniv. of USSR. No. 5092, Dnieper Dam, Komosomol Monument, Statue of worker. No. 5093, Soviet War Memorial, resistance poster. No. 5094, Worker at podium, decree text. No. 5095, Workers Monument, Moscow, Rocket, jet. No. 5096, Arms, Kremlin.

No. 5095 Overprinted in Red for All-Union Philatelic Exhibition, 1984

**1982, Nov. 10**

5097  A2430  10k multicolored    .75  .20

## Portrait of an Actor, by Domenico Fetti A2431

Paintings from the Hermitage. 10k, St. Sebastian, by Perugino. 20k, Danae, by Titian, horiz. 45k, Portrait of a Woman, by Correggio. No. 5102, Portrait of a Young Man, by Capriola. No. 5103a, Portrait of a Young Woman, by Melzi.

**1982, Nov. 25    Litho.    Perf. 12x12½**

5098  A2431  4k multicolored    .20  .20
5099  A2431  10k multicolored    .25  .20
5100  A2431  20k multicolored    .40  .20
5101  A2431  45k multicolored    .75  .40
5102  A2431  50k multicolored    .75  .45
Nos. 5098-5102 (5)    2.35  1.45

## Souvenir Sheet

5103    Sheet of 2    4.00  1.65
a.  A2431  50k multicolored    1.00  .65

Printed in sheets of 24 stamps + label and 15 stamps + label.
See Nos. 5129-5134, 5199-5204, 5233-5238, 5310-5315, 5335-5340.

New Year 1983 — A2432

**1982, Dec. 1    Unwmk.**

5104  A2432  4k multicolored    .25  .20

Exists imperf. Value, $50.

## Souvenir Sheet

**1982, Dec. 3    Perf. 12½x12**

5105  A2433  50k multicolored    1.50  .90

60th Anniv. of USSR — A2433

## Mountain Climbers Scaling Mt. Everest—A2434

Souvenir Sheet

**1982, Dec. 20    Photo.    Perf. 11½x12**

5106  A2434  50k multicolored    2.00  .90

Lighthouses A2435

Mail Transport A2436

**1982, Dec. 29    Litho.    Perf. 12**

5107  A2435  6k green & multi    .20  .20
5108  A2435  6k lilac & multi    .20  .20
5109  A2435  6k salmon & multi    .20  .20
5110  A2435  6k gldn brn & multi    .20  .20
5111  A2435  6k lt brown & multi    .20  1.00
Nos. 5107-5111 (5)    1.00  1.00

No. 5111 exists imperf.
See Nos. 5179-5183, 5265-5269.

**1982, Dec. 22    Perf. 12**

5112  A2436  5k greenish blue    5.00  1.00

**1983, May 20    Litho.    Perf. 12**

5113  A2436  5k blue    2.00  .35

For surcharge see Uzbekistan #61E.

## Iskra Newspaper Masthead A2438

**1983, Jan. 5    Litho.    Perf. 12x12½**

5114  A2438  4k multicolored    .25  .20

80th anniv. of 2nd Social-Democratic Workers' Party.

Fedor P. Tolstoi (1783-1873), Painter—A2439

**1983, Jan. 5    Photo.    Perf. 11½**

5115  A2439  4k multicolored    .25  .20

## 65th Anniv. of Armed Forces — A2440

**1983, Jan. 25    Litho.    Perf. 12**

5116  A2440  4k multicolored    .25  .20

Exists imperf.

## Souvenir Sheet

60th Anniv. of Aeroflot Airlines — A2441

**1983, Feb. 9    Perf. 12½**

5117  A2441  50k multicolored    1.50  1.00

## Glider Type of 1982

**1983, Feb. 10    Perf. 12½x12**

5118  A2420  2k A-9, 1948    .20  .20
5119  A2420  4k KAI-12, 1957    .20  .20
5120  A2420  6k A-15, 1960    .20  .20
5121  A2420  20k SA-7, 1970    .55  .85
5122  A2420  45k LAI-12, 1979    1.85  1.40
Nos. 5118-5122 (5)

B.N. Petrov (1913-1980), Scientist—A2443

**1983, Feb. 17    Photo.    Perf. 11½**

5124  A2443  4k multicolored    .25  .20

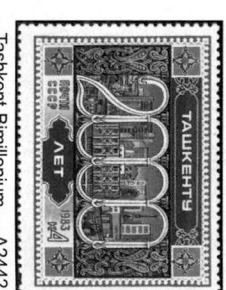

## Tashkent Bimillenium — A2442

**1983, Feb. 17    Perf. 12½x12**

5123  A2442  4k View    .25  .20

A.I. Khachaturian (1903-1978), Composer — A2458

**1983, May 25 Engr. Perf. 12½x12**
5144 A2458 4k violet brown .50 .30

Chelyabinsk Tractor Plant, 50th Anniv. — A2459

**1983, June 1 Photo. Perf. 11½**
5145 A2459 4k multicolored .25 .20

Simon Bolivar Bicentenary A2460

**Photogravure and Engraved Perf. 12**
**1983, June 10**
5146 A2460 6k brown & dk brown .25 .20

City of Sevastopol, 200th Anniv. — A2461

**1983, June 14 Photo. Perf. 11½x12**
5147 A2461 5k multicolored .25 .20

Spring Flowers — A2462

**1983, June 14 Litho. Perf. 12x12½**
5148 A2462 4k multicolored .20 .20
5149 A2462 6k multicolored .20 .20
5150 A2462 10k multicolored .25 .25
5151 A2462 15k multicolored .35 .30
5152 A2462 20k multicolored .45 .35
Nos. 5748-5752 (5) 1.45 1.25

Valentina Tereshkova's Spaceflight, 20th Anniv. — A2463

---

**1983, Apr. 25 Litho. Perf. 12½x12**
5137 A2451 10k multicolored .30 .25
5138 A2452 10k multicolored .30 .25
a. Pair, #5137-5138 .60 .50
Salyut 7-Soyuz 7 211-Day Flight. Exists se-tenant with label.

Karl Marx (1818-1883) A2453

**1983, May 5 Perf. 12x12½**
5139 A2453 4k multicolored .25 .20

View of Rostov-on-Don — A2454

**1983, May 5 Photo. Perf. 11½**
5140 A2454 4k multicolored .25 .20
Exists imperf. Value, $50.

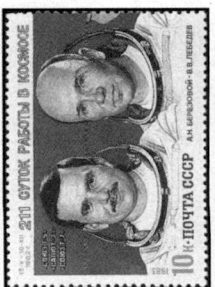

Buriat Autonomous Soviet Socialist Republic, 60th Anniv. — A2455

**1983, May 12 Litho. Perf. 12**
5141 A2455 4k multicolored .25 .20

Kirov Opera and Ballet Theater, Leningrad, 200th Anniv. — A2456

**Photogravure and Engraved Perf. 11½x12**
**1983, May 12**
5142 A2456 4k multicolored .20 .20

Emblem of Motorcycling, Auto Racing, Shooting, Motorboating, Parachuting Organization — A2457

**1983, May 20 Litho. Perf. 11½**
5143 A2457 6k multicolored .25 .20

---

5132 A2431 45k multicolored 1.40 .90
5133 A2431 50k multicolored 1.50 .95
Nos. 5129-5133 (5) 4.00 2.60

**Souvenir Sheet**
**Lithographed and Embossed**
5134 Sheet of 2 + label 4.00 3.00
a. A2431 50k multicolored 1.65 .70

Cosmonauts' Day — A2449

**Perf. 12½x12 Litho. Unwmk.**
**1983, Apr. 12 50k Soyuz T 5.00 3.50**
5135 A2449 50k Soyuz T
Souvenir Sheet

113th Birth Anniv. of Lenin — A2450

**Photogravure and Engraved Perf. 11½x12**
**1983, Apr. 22 50k multicolored 1.50 .80**
5136 A2450 50k multicolored

A. Berezovoy, V. Lebedev — A2451

Salyut 7-Soyuz 7 Spacecraft — A2452

---

Holy Family, by Raphael A2444

**1983, Feb. 17 Perf. 12x12½**
5125 A2444 50k multicolored 1.50 1.00

Soyuz T-7-Salyut 7-Soyuz T-5 Flight A2445

**1983, Mar. 10 Perf. 12x12½**
5126 A2445 10k L. Popov, A. Serebrav, S. Savitskaya .30 .20

World Communications Year — A2446

**1983, Mar. 10 Photo. Perf. 11½**
5127 A2446 50k multicolored 1.50 1.25
Souvenir Sheet
Exists imperf. Value, $50.

A.W. Aleksandrov, Natl. Anthem Composer — A2447

**1983, Mar. 22 Litho. Perf. 12**
5128 A2447 4k multicolored .50 .25

**Hermitage Type of 1982**
Rembrandt Paintings, Hermitage, Leningrad: 4k, Portrait of an Old Woman, 10k, Portrait of a Learned Man. 20k, Old Warrior. 45k, Portrait of Mrs. B. Martens Doomer. No. 5133, Portrait of Abraham. No. 5134a, Portrait of an Old Man in a Red Garment.

**1983, Mar. 25 Wmk. 383**
5129 A2431 4k multicolored .20 .20
5130 A2431 10k multicolored .30 .30
5131 A2431 20k multicolored .60 .35

**Perf. 12x12½**

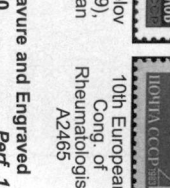

P.N. Pospelov (1898-1979), Academician A2464

Photogravure and Engraved
**1983, June 20** Perf. 11½
5154 A2464 4k multicolored .25 .20

**1983, June 21** Photo. Perf. 11½
5155 A2465 4k multicolored .20 .20

10th European Cong. of Rheumatologists A2465

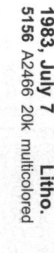

13th International Film Festival, Moscow — A2466
**1983, July 7** Litho. Perf. 12
5156 A2466 20k multicolored .50 .25

Ships of the Soviet Fishing Fleet — A2467

Photogravure and Engraved
**1983, July 20** Perf. 12x11½
5157 A2467 4k Two trawlers .20 .20
5158 A2467 6k Refrigerated trawler .20 .20
5159 A2467 10k Large trawler .20 .20
5160 A2467 15k Large refrigerated ship .35 .20
5161 A2467 20k Base ship .40 .25
Nos. 5157-5161 (5) 1.65 1.05

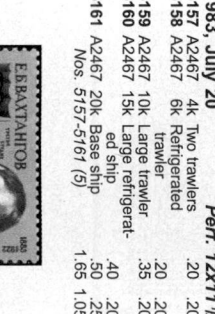

E.B. Vakhtangov (1883-1922), Actor and Producer — A2468
**1983, July 20** Photo. Perf. 11½
5162 A2468 5k multicolored .25 .20

"USSR-1" Stratospheric Flight, 50th Anniv. — A2469

**1983, July 25** Photo. Perf. 12
5163 A2469 20k multicolored .50 .40
a. Miniature sheet of 8 50.00

**1983, June 16** Litho. Perf. 12
5153 A2463 10k multicolored .35 .20
a. Miniature sheet of 8 50.00

---

Food Fish A2470

**1983, Aug. 5** Litho. Perf. 12½x12
5164 A2470 4k multicolored .20 .20
5165 A2470 6k multicolored .20 .20
5166 A2470 15k multicolored .35 .30
5167 A2470 20k multicolored .40 .30
5168 A2470 45k multicolored .90 .55
Nos. 5164-5168 (5) 2.05 1.50

4k, Oncorhynchus nerka. 6k, Perciformes. 15k, Anarhichas minor. 20k, Neogobius fluviatilis. 45k, Platichthys stellatus.

A2471

SOZPHILEX '83 Philatelic Exhibition — A2472
**1983, Aug. 18** Photo. Perf. 11½
5169 A2471 6k multicolored .25 .20
5170 A2472 50k Moscow Skyline 1.50 .80

Souvenir Sheet

Miniature Sheet

First Russian Postage Stamp, 125th Anniv. — A2473
**1983, Aug. 25** Photogravure and Engraved Perf. 11½x12
5171 A2473 50k pale yel & black 1.50 .70

No. 5171 Ovptd. on Margin in Red for the 5th Philatelic Society Congress
**1984, Oct. 1**
5171A A2473 50k pale yel & blk 5.00 4.50

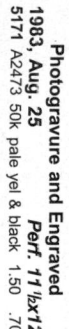

---

Namibia Day A2474
**1983, Aug. 26** Photo. Perf. 11½
5172 A2474 5k multicolored .25 .20

Palestinian Solidarity A2475
**1983, Aug. 29** Photo. Perf. 11½
5173 A2475 5k multicolored .25 .20

1st European Championship of Radio-Telegraphy, Moscow — A2476
**1983, Sept. 1** Photo. Perf. 11½
5174 A2476 6k multicolored .25 .20
Exists imperf. Value, $50.

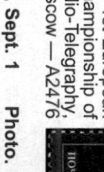

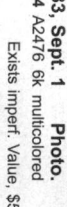

4th UNESCO Council on Communications Development — A2477
**1983, Sept. 2** Photo. Perf. 12x11½
5175 A2477 10k multicolored .30 .20

Muhammad Al-Khorezmi, Uzbek Mathematician, 1200th Birth Anniv. — A2478
**1983, Sept. 6** Photogravure and Engraved Perf. 11½
5176 A2478 4k multicolored .25 .20

---

Marshal A.I. Egorov (1883-1939) A2479
**1983, Sept. 8** Engr. Perf. 12
5177 A2479 4k brown violet .25 .20

Union of Georgia and Russia, 200th Anniv. — A2480
**1983, Sept. 8** Photo. Perf. 11½
5178 A2480 6k multicolored .25 .20

Lighthouse Type of 1982
Baltic Sea lighthouses.
**1983, Sept. 19** Litho. Perf. 12
5179 A2435 1k Kipu .20 .20
5180 A2435 5k Keri .20 .20
5181 A2435 10k Stirsudden .25 .20
5182 A2435 12k Tankun .30 .20
5183 A2435 20k Tallinn .50 .25
Nos. 5179-5183 (5) 1.45 1.05

Early Spring, by V.K. Bialynitzky-Birulia, 1912 — A2481

Paintings by White Russians: 4k, Portrait of the Artist's Wife with Fruit and Flowers, by J.F. Krutzky, 1838. 15k, Young Partisan, by E.A. Zaitsev, 1943. 20k, Partisan Madonna, by M.A. Savitsky, 1967. 45k, Harvest, by V.K. Tsvirko, 1972.
**1983, Sept. 28** Perf. 12½x12, 12x12½
5184 A2481 4k multicolored .20 .20
5185 A2481 6k multicolored .20 .20
5186 A2481 15k multicolored .25 .20
5187 A2481 20k multicolored .30 .20
5188 A2481 45k multicolored .70 .45
Nos. 5184-5188 (5) 1.65 1.25

Hammer and Sickle Steel Mill, Moscow, Centenary A2482
**1983, Oct. 1** Photo. Perf. 11½
5189 A2482 4k multicolored .25 .20

Natl. Food Program A2483
**1983, Oct. 10** Photo. Perf. 11½
5190 A2483 5k Wheat production .20 .20
5191 A2483 5k Cattle, dairy products .20 .20
5192 A2483 5k Produce .20 .20
Nos. 5190-5192 (3) .60 .60

## 1984 Winter Olympics — A2499

**1984, Feb. 8**   **Photo.**   *Perf. 11½x12*

| | | | | |
|---|---|---|---|---|
| 5222 | A2499 | 5k Biathlon | .20 | .20 |
| | a. | Miniature sheet of 8 | 20.00 | |
| 5223 | A2499 | 10k Speed skating | .25 | .20 |
| | a. | Miniature sheet of 8 | 20.00 | |
| 5224 | A2499 | 20k Hockey | .50 | .25 |
| | a. | Miniature sheet of 8 | 20.00 | |
| 5225 | A2499 | 45k Figure skating | .90 | .45 |
| | a. | Miniature sheet of 8 | 20.00 | |

Nos. 5222-5225 (4)   1.85   1.10
Exist imperf. Value, each $50.

## Moscow Zoo, 120th Anniv. — A2500

**1984, Feb. 16**   **Litho.**   *Perf. 12½x12*

| | | | | |
|---|---|---|---|---|
| 5226 | A2500 | 2k Mandrill | .20 | .20 |
| 5227 | A2500 | 3k Gazelle | .20 | .20 |
| 5228 | A2500 | 4k Snow leopard | .20 | .20 |
| 5229 | A2500 | 5k Crowned crane | .20 | .25 |
| 5230 | A2500 | 20k Macaw | .40 | .25 |
| | a. | Miniature sheet of 8 | 1.20 | 1.05 |

Nos. 5226-5230 (5)

## Yuri Gagarin (1934-68) — A2501

**1984, Mar. 9**   **Engr.**   *Perf. 12½x12*

| | | | | |
|---|---|---|---|---|
| 5231 | A2501 | 15k Portrait, Vostok | .35 | .25 |
| | a. | Miniature sheet of 8 | 50.00 | |

## Souvenir Sheet

Mass Development of Virgin and Unused Land, 30th Anniv. — A2502

**1984, Mar. 14**   **Photo.**   *Perf. 11½x12*

5232 A2502 50k multicolored   1.50   .75

### Hermitage Painting Type of 1982

Paintings by English Artists: 4k, E.K. Vorontsova, by George Hayter. 10k, Portrait of Mrs. Greer, by George Romney. 20k, Approaching Storm, by George Morland, horiz. 45k, Portrait of an Unknown Man, by Marcus Gheeraerts Jr. No. 5237, Cupid and Venus, by Joshua Reynolds. No. 5238a, Portrait of a Lady in Blue, by Thomas Gainsborough.

---

## Souvenir Sheet

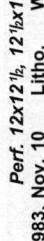

Environmental Protection Campaign — A2494

**1983, Dec. 20**   **Photo.**   *Perf. 11½*

5213 A2494 50k multicolored   5.00   5.00

№ 501708

## Moscow Local Broadcasting Network, 50th anniv. — A2495

**1984, Jan. 1**

5214 A2495 4k multicolored   .25   .20

## European Women's Skating Championships — A2496

**1984, Jan. 1**   *Perf. 12x11½*

5215 A2496 5k multicolored   .25   .20
Exists imperf. Value, $50.

## Cuban Revolution, 25th Anniv. A2497

**1984, Jan. 1**   *Perf. 11½*

5216 A2497 5k Flag, "25"   .25   .20
Exists imperf. Value, $50.

## World War II Tanks — A2498

**1984, Jan. 25**   **Litho.**   *Perf. 12½x12*

| | | | | |
|---|---|---|---|---|
| 5217 | A2498 | 10k KW | .25 | .20 |
| 5218 | A2498 | 10k IS-2 | .25 | .20 |
| 5219 | A2498 | 10k T-34 | .25 | .20 |
| 5220 | A2498 | 10k ISU-152 | .25 | .20 |
| 5221 | A2498 | 10k SU-100 | .25 | .20 |

Nos. 5217-5221 (5)   1.25   1.00
No. 5220 exists imperf. Value, $50.

---

*Perf. 12x12½, 12½x12*   **Litho.**   **Wmk. 383**

| | | | | |
|---|---|---|---|---|
| 5199 | A2431 | 4k multicolored | .20 | .20 |
| 5200 | A2431 | 10k multicolored | .40 | .35 |
| 5201 | A2431 | 20k multicolored | .60 | .70 |
| 5202 | A2431 | 45k multicolored | 1.25 | .75 |
| 5203 | A2431 | 50k multicolored | 1.50 | .75 |

Nos. 5199-5203 (5)   3.95   2.20

## Souvenir Sheet

| | | | | |
|---|---|---|---|---|
| | | Sheet of 2 | 4.00 | 2.50 |
| 5204 | a. | A2431 50k multicolored | 1.65 | .65 |

## Physicians Against Nuclear War Movement A2490

**1983, Nov. 17**   *Perf. 11½*   **Photo.**   **Unwmk.**

5205 A2490 5k Baby, dove, sun   .20   .20

## Sukhe Bator (1893-1923), Mongolian People's Rep. Founder — A2491

**1983, Nov. 17**

5206 A2491 5k Portrait   .25   .20

## New Year 1984 A2492

**1983, Dec. 1**

5207 A2492 5k Star, snowflakes   .25   .20
Exists imperf. Value, $50.

## Newly Completed Buildings, Moscow — A2493

**1983, Dec. 15**   *Perf. 12½x12, 12x12½*   **Engr.**

| | | | | |
|---|---|---|---|---|
| 5208 | A2493 | 3k Children's Musical Theater | .20 | .20 |
| 5209 | A2493 | 4k Tourist Hotel, vert. | .20 | .20 |
| 5210 | A2493 | 6k Council of Ministers | .20 | .20 |
| 5211 | A2493 | 20k Ismaelovo Hotel | .20 | .35 |
| 5212 | A2493 | 45k Novosti Press Agency | .70 | .70 |

Nos. 5208-5212 (5)   1.50   1.65
  2.80

---

## October Revolution, 66th anniv. — A2484

**1983, Oct. 12**   **Litho.**   *Perf. 12*

5193 A2484 4k multicolored   .25   .20

## Ivan Fedorov — A2485

**1983, Oct. 12**   **Engr.**   *Perf. 12½x12½*

5194 A2485 4k dark brown   .25   .20
Ivan Fedorov, first Russian printer (Book of the Apostles), 400th death anniv.

## Urengoy-Uzgorod Transcontinental Gas Pipeline Completion — A2486

**1983, Oct. 12**   **Photo.**   *Perf. 12x11½*

5195 A2486 5k multicolored   .25   .20

## A.W. Sidorenko (1917-82), Geologist A2487

**1983, Oct. 19**   **Litho.**   *Perf. 12*

5196 A2487 4k multicolored   .25   .20

## Campaign Against Nuclear Weapons A2488

**1983, Oct. 19**   **Photo.**   *Perf. 11½*

5197 A2488 5k Demonstration   .25   .20
Exists imperf. Value $50.

## Machtumkuli, Turkmenistan Poet, 250th Birth Anniv. — A2489

**1983, Oct. 27**

5198 A2489 5k multicolored   .25   .20

### Hermitage Painting Type of 1982

Paintings by Germans: 4k, Madonna and Child with Apple Tree, by Lucas Cranach the Elder. 10k, Self-portrait, by Anton R. Mengs. 20k, Self-portrait, by Jurgen Owen. 45k, Sailboat, by Caspar David Friedrich. No. 5203, Rape of the Sabines, by Johann Schoenfeld, horiz. No. 5204a, Portrait of a Young Man, by Ambrosius Holbein.

**Perf. 12x12½, 12½x12**

**Wmk. 383**

**1984, Mar. 20 Litho.**

| | | | |
|---|---|---|---|
| 5233 | A2431 | 4k multicolored | .20 .20 |
| 5234 | A2431 | 10k multicolored | .40 .20 |
| 5235 | A2431 | 20k multicolored | .60 .35 |
| 5236 | A2431 | 45k multicolored | 1.40 .70 |
| 5237 | A2431 | 50k multicolored | 1.65 .75 |

Nos. 5233-5237 (5) 4.25 2.20

**Souvenir Sheet**

| | | | |
|---|---|---|---|
| 5238 | A2432 50k multicolored | 5.00 1.70 | |
| a. | Sheet of 2 | 2.00 .65 | |

Nos. 5233-5237 each se-tenant with label showing text and embossed emblem.

S.V. Ilyushin
A2503

Andrei S. Bubnov
A2504

**1984, Mar. 23 Photo.**

5239 A2503 Aircraft designer, (1894-1977) .30 .20

**Perf. 11½x12 Unwmk.**

**1984, Apr. 3 Perf. 11½**

5240 A2504 5k Statesman, (1884-1940) .25 .20

**1984**

| | | | |
|---|---|---|---|
| 5241 | A2505 | 5k multicolored | .20 .20 |
| 5242 | A2505 | 20k multicolored | .45 .20 |
| 5243 | A2505 | 45k multicolored | 1.00 .45 |

Nos. 5241-5243 (3) 1.65 .85

**Souvenir Sheet**

**Perf. 12x11½**

5244 A2505 50k multicolored 1.50 .75

Designs: 5k. Weather Station M-100 launch. 20k. Geodesy (satellites, observatory). 45k. Rocket, satellites, dish antenna. 50k. Flags, cosmonauts.
Issue dates: 50k. Apr. 5; others, Apr. 3.

Intercosmos Cooperative Space Program (USSR-India) A2505

**1984, Apr. 12**

5245 A2506 10k Futuristic space-man .50 .30

Cosmonauts' Day — A2506

**Perf. 11½x12**

---

**Photogravure and Engraved**

Tchelyuskin Arctic Expedition, 50th Anniv. — A2507

**1984, Apr. 13 Perf. 11½x12**

| | | | |
|---|---|---|---|
| 5246 | A2507 | 6k Ship | .20 .20 |
| a. | Miniature sheet of 8 | .50 .25 | |
| 5247 | A2507 | 15k Shipwreck | 16.00 |
| a. | Miniature sheet of 8 | 16.00 | |
| 5248 | A2507 | 45k Rescue | .70 |
| a. | Miniature sheet of 8 | 2.20 1.15 | |

Nos. 5246-5248 (3)

**Souvenir Sheet**

**Photo.**

5249 A2507 50k Hero of Soviet Union medal 1.50 .70

First HSU medal awarded to rescue crew. No. 5249 contains one 27x39mm stamp.

**1984, Apr. 22 Litho. Perf. 11½x12½**

5250 A2508 50k Portrait 1.50 .70

114th Birth Anniv. of Lenin — A2508

**Souvenir Sheet**

Aquatic Plants — A2509

**1984, May 5 Perf. 12x12½, 12½x12**

| | | | |
|---|---|---|---|
| 5251 | A2509 | 1k Lotus | .20 .20 |
| 5252 | A2509 | 2k Euridia | .20 .20 |
| 5253 | A2509 | 3k Water lilies, horiz. | .20 .20 |
| 5254 | A2509 | 10k White nymphaea, horiz. | .20 .20 |
| a. | Miniature sheet of 8 | 15.00 | |
| 5255 | A2509 | 20k Marshflowers, horiz. | .40 .25 |

Nos. 5251-5255 (5) 1.20 1.05

Soviet Peace Policy — A2510

**1984, May 8 Photo. Perf. 11½**

| | | | |
|---|---|---|---|
| 5256 | A2510 | 5k Marchers, banners (at left) | .20 .20 |
| 5257 | A2510 | 5k Text | .20 .20 |
| 5258 | A2510 | 5k Marchers, banners (at right) | .20 .20 |
| a. | Strip of 3, #5256-5258 | .45 .30 | |

Nos. 5257-5255 (5)

---

**1984, May 15 Photo. Perf. 11½**

5259 A2511 10k multicolored .30 .25

E.O. Paton Institute of Electric Welding, 50th anniv.

**1984, May 21**

5260 A2512 10k multicolored .30 .30

25th Conf. for Electric and Postal Communications Cooperation.

A2511

A2512

**1984, May 29**

5261 A2513 5k violet brown .25 .20

Maurice Bishop, Grenada Prime Minister (1944-03).

**1984, May 31**

5262 A2514 5k multicolored .25 .20

V.I. Lenin Central Museum, 60th anniv.

A2513

A2514

**1984, June 1 Photo. & Engr.**

5263 A2515 5k multicolored .25 .20

City of Archangelsk, 400th Anniv. — A2515

**1984, June 1 Photo. Perf. 12x11½**

5264 A2516 15k multicolored .50 .30

European Youth Soccer Championship — A2516

**1984, June 14 Litho. Perf. 12**

**Lighthouse Type of 1982**

| | | | |
|---|---|---|---|
| 5265 | A2435 | 1k Petropavlovsk | .20 .20 |
| 5266 | A2435 | 2k Tokarev | .20 .20 |
| 5267 | A2435 | 4k Basargin | .20 .20 |
| 5268 | A2435 | 5k Kronitsky | .20 .20 |
| 5269 | A2435 | 10k Marekan | 1.00 1.00 |

Nos. 5265-5269 (5)

Far Eastern seas lighthouses.

---

**1984, June 27 Litho. Perf. 12**

5270 A2517 15k multicolored .35 .20

Salyut 7-Soyuz T-9 150-Day Flight — A2517

**Photogravure and Engraved**

**1984, July 1 Perf. 11½**

5271 A2518 10k multicolored .30 .25

Morflot, Merchant & Transport Fleet, 60th anniv.

A2518

**1984, July 1 Photo. Perf. 11½x12**

5272 A2519 5k multicolored .25 .20

60th Anniv. of Awarding V.I. Lenin Name to Youth Communist League — A2519

**1984, July 3 Photo. Perf. 12x11½**

5273 A2520 5k multicolored .25 .20

Liberation of Byelorussia, 40th Anniv. A2520

**1984, June 12 Photo. Perf. 11½**

5274 A2521 5k multicolored .25 .20

CMEA Conference, Moscow — A2521

CMEA Building & Kremlin

A2540

A2539

**1984, Oct. 23    Photo.    Perf. 11½**
5307  A2539  5k  Kremlin, 1917 flag    .25  .20
October Revolution, 67th anniv.

**1984, Nov. 6    Photo.    Perf. 11½**
5308  A2540  5k  Aircraft, spacecraft    .25  .20
M. Frunze Inst. of Aviation & Cosmonautics.

Baikal —
Amur
Railway
Completion
A2541

**1984, Nov. 7    Photo.    Perf. 11½**
5309  A2541  5k  Workers, map, engine    .30  .20

**Hermitage Type of 1982**
Paintings by French Artists: 4k, Girl in a Hat, by Jean Louis Voille. 10k, A Stolen Kiss, by Jean-Honore Fragonard. 20k, Woman Combing her Hair, by Edgar Degas. 45k, Pigmalion and Galatea, by Francois Boucher. 50k, Landscape with Polyphenus, by Nicholas Poussin. No. 5315a, Child with a Whip, by Pierre-Auguste Renoir.

**Perf. 12x12½, 12½x12**
**1984, Nov. 20    Litho.    Wmk. 383**
5310  A2431  4k  multicolored    .20  .20
5311  A2431  10k  multi. horiz.    .35  .20
5312  A2431  20k  multicolored    .55  .45
5313  A2431  45k  multi. horiz.    1.25  .75
5314  A2431  50k  multi. horiz.    1.40  .90
Nos. 5310-5314 (5)    3.75  2.50

**Souvenir Sheet**
5315  A2431  50k  multicolored    2.50  2.00
a.    A2431  50k multicolored    1.00  .60

Mongolian
Peoples' Republic,
60th
Anniv. — A2542

Unwmk.

**1984, Nov. 26    Photo.    Perf. 11½**
5316  A2542  5k  Mongolian flag, arms    .30  .20

New Year 1985 — A2543

**1984, Dec. 4    Litho.    Perf. 11½**
5317  A2543  5k  Kremlin, snowflakes    .25  .20
a.    Miniature sheet of 8    15.00

---

Nakhichevan ASSR, 60th
Anniv. — A2534

**1984, Sept. 20    Litho.    Perf. 12**
5295  A2534  5k  Arms    .25  .20

Television
from
Space,
25th Anniv.
A2535

**1984, Oct. 4    Photo.    Perf. 11½**
5296  A2535  5k  Luna 3    .20  .20
5297  A2535  20k  Venera 9    .35  .25
5298  A2535  45k  Meteor satellite    .80  .55
Nos. 5296-5298 (3)    1.35  1.00

**Souvenir Sheet**
**Perf. 11½x12**
5299  A2535  50k  Camera, space walker, vert.    1.50  .75
No. 5299 contains one 26x37mm stamp.

German
Democratic
Republic,
35th Anniv.
A2536

**1984, Oct. 7    Photo.    Perf. 11½**
5300  A2536  5k  Flag, arms    .25  .20

Ukrainian
Liberation,
40th Anniv.
A2537

**1984, Oct. 8    Photo.    Perf. 12x11½**
5301  A2537  5k  Motherland statue, Kiev    .25  .20

Soviet
Republics
and
Parties,
60th Anniv.
A2538

**1984    Litho.    Perf. 12**
5302  A2538  5k  multicolored    .20  .20
5303  A2538  5k  multicolored    .20  .20
5304  A2538  5k  multicolored    .20  .20
5305  A2538  5k  multicolored    .20  .20
5306  A2538  5k  multicolored    1.00  1.00
Nos. 5302-5306 (5)    1.00  1.00

SSR, Flags, & Arms: #5302, Moldavian. #5303, Kirgiz. #5304, Tadzhik. #5305, Uzbek. #5306, Turkmen.

Issued: #5302, 10/12; #5303-5304, 10/14; #5305-5306, 10/27.

---

A2529

A2528

**1984, Aug. 23    Litho.    Perf. 12**
5285  A2528  5k  Flag, monument    .25  .20
Liberation of Romania, 40th anniv.

**1984, Sept. 5    Litho.    Perf. 12½x12**
Subjects: 35k, 3r, Environmental protection. 2r, Arctic development. 5r, World peace.
5286  A2529  35k  Sable    .65  .35
5287  A2529  2r  Ship, arctic map    .80  .45

**Engr.**
5288  A2529  3r  Child and globe    5.75  1.10
5289  A2529  5r  Palm frond and globe    9.00  1.90
Nos. 5286-5289 (4)    16.20  3.80

Nos. 5286 and 5287 were issued in 1984 on chalky paper, which fluoresces under UV light. Reprints on ordinary paper were made in 1988 and 1991, respectively. Values above are for the later printings. The 1984 printings are valued, mint or used, at 80c for No. 5286, and $2.50 for No. 5287. See Nos. 6016B-6017A.

Bulgarian
Revolution, 40th
Anniv.
A2531

**1984, Sept. 7    Photo.    Perf. 11½**
5290  A2530  15k  Motherland statue, Volgograd    .50  .30
5291  A2530  15k  Spasski Tower, Moscow    .50  .30

World Chess
Championships
A2530

**1984, Sept. 9    Photo.    Perf. 11½**
5292  A2531  5k  Bulgarian arms    .25  .20

Ethiopian
Revolution,
10th Anniv.
A2532

**1984, Sept. 12    Litho.    Perf. 12**
5293  A2532  5k  Ethiopian flag, seal    .25  .20

Novokramatorsk Machinery Plant, 50th
Anniv. — A2533

**Photogravure and Engraved**
**1984, Sept. 20    Perf. 11½**
5294  A2533  5k  Excavator    .25  .20

---

A2523

**1984, July 20    Photo.    Perf. 11½**
5275  A2522  5k  Convention seal    .25  .20
27th Intl. Geological Cong., Moscow.

**1984, July 22    Photo.    Perf. 11½**
5276  A2523  5k  Arms, draped flag    .25  .20
People's Republic of Poland, 40th anniv.

A2522

B. V. Asafiev (1884-1949),
Composer — A2524

**1984, July 25    Engr.    Perf. 12½x12**
5277  A2524  5k  greenish black    .25  .20

Relations
with
Mexico,
60th Anniv.
A2525

**1984, Aug. 4    Litho.    Perf. 12**
5278  A2525  5k  USSR, Mexican flags    .25  .20

Russian Folk
Tales
A2526

Miniature Sheet

**1984, Aug. 10    Litho.    Perf. 12x12½**
5279    Sheet of 12    6.00  2.50
a.-l.    A2526  5k, any single    .30  .20

Designs: a, 3 archers. b, Prince and frog. c, Old man and prince. d, Crowd and swans. e, Wolf and men. f, Bird and youth. g, Youth on white horse. h, Couple with Tsar. i, Village scene. j, Man on black horse. k, Old man. l, Young woman.

Friendship
'84 Games
A2527

**1984, Aug. 15    Photo.    Perf. 11½**
5280  A2527  1k  Basketball    .20  .20
5281  A2527  5k  Gymnastics, vert.    .20  .20
5282  A2527  10k  Weightlifting    .25  .20
5283  A2527  15k  Wrestling    .40  .20
5284  A2527  20k  High jump    .50  .25
Nos. 5280-5284 (5)    1.55  1.05

Souvenir Sheet

**1984, Dec. 4    Litho.    Perf. 12½x12**
5318  A2544  50k  Leaf, pollution
sources    1.50    .75

Environmental Protection — A2544

Russian Fire Vehicles — A2545

**1984, Dec. 12    Photogravure and Engraved**

**1984, Dec. 15    Photo.    Perf. 12x11½**
5319  A2545  3k  Crew wagon,
19th cent.    .20    .20
5320  A2545  5k  Pumper, 19th
cent.    .20    .20
5321  A2545  10k  Ladder truck,
1904    .25    .20
5322  A2545  15k  Pumper, 1904    .35    .20
5323  A2545  20k  Ladder truck,
1913    .40    .20
Nos. 5319-5323 (5)    1.40  1.00

See Nos. 5410-5414.

Int. Venus-Halley's Comet
Project — A2546

**1984, Dec. 15    Photo.    Perf. 12x11½**
5324  A2546  15k  Satellite, flight
path    .50    .25
a.    Miniature sheet of 8    15.00

Photogravure and Engraved

**1984, Dec. 28    Litho.    Perf. 12**
5325  A2547  5k  Portrait    1.00    .75

Indira Gandhi
(1917-1984),
Indian Prime
Minister — A2547

**1985, Jan. 22    Photo.    Perf. 11½**
5326  A2548  5k  Flag, Moscow memorial    .25    .20

1905
Revolution
A2548

**1985, Jan. 24**
5327  A2549  5k  multicolored    .25    .20

Patrice Lumumba Peoples' Friendship University, 25th Anniv.

A2549

**1985, Feb. 2**
5328  A2550  5k  bluish, blk & ocher    .25    .20

Mikhail Vasilievich Frunze (1885-1925),
party leader.

A2550

**1985, Feb. 16    Perf. 12**
5329  A2551  5k  Republic arms    .25    .20

Karakalpak
ASSR, 60th
Anniv.
A2551

**1985, Feb. 23    Perf. 11½**
5330  A2552  5k  Hockey player, emblem    .25    .20

10th Winter
Spartakiad of
Friendly
Armies — A2552

Kalevala,
150th
Anniv.
A2553

**1985, Feb. 25    Litho.    Perf. 12**
5331  A2553  5k  Rune singer, frontis-
piece    .25    .20

Finnish Kalevala, collection of Karelian
poetry compiled by Elias Lonrot.

A2554

**1985, Mar. 3    Engr.    Perf. 12½x12**
5332  A2554  5k  rose lake    .25    .20

Yakov M. Sverdlov (1885-1919), party leader.

A2555

**1985, Mar. 6    Photo.    Perf. 11½**
5333  A2555  5k  Pioneer badge,
awards    .25    .20

Pionerskaya Pravda, All-Union children's
newspaper, 60th Anniv.

**1985, Mar. 6    Engr.    Perf. 12½x12**
5334  A2556  5k  black    .30    .20

Maria Alexandrovna
Ulyanova (1835-
1916), Lenin's
Mother — A2556

Hermitage Type of 1982

Paintings by Spanish artists: 4k, The Young
Virgin Praying, vert., by Francisco de Zurbaran
(1598-1664), 10k, Still-life, by Antonio Pereda
(c. 1608-1678), 20k, The Immaculate Conception, vert., by Murillo (1617-1682), 45k, The
Grinder, by Antonio Puga, No. 5339, Count
Olivares, vert., by Diego Velazques (1599-
1660). No. 5340a, Portrait of the actress Antonia Zarate, vert., by Goya (1746-1828).

**1985, Mar. 14    Litho.    Wmk. 383**
**Perf. 12½x12½, 12½x12**
5335  A2431  4k  multicolored    .20    .20
5336  A2431  10k  multicolored    .30    .20
5337  A2431  20k  multicolored    .50    .40
5338  A2431  45k  multicolored    1.25    .90
5339  A2431  50k  multicolored    1.40    .95
Nos. 5335-5339 (5)    3.65  2.65

Souvenir Sheet

Lithographed and Embossed
5340    Sheet of 2 + label    3.00  2.00
a.    A2431 50k multicolored    1.10    .75

EXPO '85,
Tsukuba,
Japan
A2557

Soviet exhibition, Expo '85 emblems and:
5k. Cosmonauts in space. 10k. Communications satellite. 20k. Alternative energy sources
development. 45k. Future housing systems.

**1985, Mar. 17    Photo.    Perf. 12x11½**
**Unwmk.**
5341  A2557  5k  multicolored    .20    .20
5342  A2557  10k  multicolored    .20    .20
5343  A2557  20k  multicolored    .40    .35
5344  A2557  45k  multicolored    .95    .70
Nos. 5341-5344 (4)    1.75  1.45

Souvenir Sheet
5345  A2557  50k  Soviet exhibition
emblem, globe    1.50    .90
Nos. 5341-5344 issued in sheets of 8.

**1985, Mar. 21    Photogravure and Engraved**
**Perf. 12x11½**
5346  A2558  50k  black    1.50  1.00

Souvenir Sheet

Johann Sebastian Bach (1685-1750),
Composer — A2558

**1985, Apr. 4    Litho.    Perf. 12**
5347  A2559  5k  Natl. crest, Budapest memorial    .25    .20

Hungary liberated from German occupation,
40th Anniv.

A2559

**1985, Apr. 5    Photo.    Perf. 11½**
5348  A2560  15k  Emblem    .40    .30

Society for Cultural Relations with Foreign
Countries, 60th anniv.

A2560

**1985, Apr. 20    Perf. 12x11½**
5349  A2561  5k  multicolored    .25    .20
5350  A2561  5k  multicolored    .25    .20
5351  A2561  5k  multicolored    .25    .20
5352  A2561  5k  multicolored    .25    .20
5353  A2561  5k  multicolored    1.25  1.00
Nos. 5349-5353 (5)

Souvenir Sheet
**Perf. 11½**
5354  A2561  50k  multicolored    1.50    .50

#5349, Battle of Moscow, soldier, Kremlin,
portrait of Lenin. #5350, Soldier, armed forces.
#5351, Armaments production, worker. #5352,
Partisan movement, cavalry. #5353, Berlin-
Treptow war memorial, German Democratic
Republic. Order of the Patriotic War,
second class.

No. 5354 contains one 28x40mm stamp.
issued in sheets of 8.

Victory over
Fascism,
40th Anniv.
A2561

No. 5353
Ovptd. in
Red for 40th
Year Since
World War II
Victory All-
Union
Philatelic
Exhibition

**1985, Apr. 29    Photo.    Perf. 12x11½**
5354A  A2561  5k  brn lake, gold &
vermilion    .50    .50

Yuri Gagarin Center for Training
Cosmonauts, 25th Anniv. — A2562

Cosmonauts day: Portrait, cosmonauts, Soyuz-T spaceship.

**1985, Apr. 12** *Photo.* *Perf. 11½x12*
5355 A2562 15k multicolored .50 .25
a. Miniature sheet of 8 20.00

12th World Youth Festival, Moscow A2563

**1985, Apr. 15** *Litho.* *Perf. 12x12½*
5356 A2563 1k Three youths .20 .20
5357 A2563 3k African girl .20 .20
5358 A2563 5k Girl, rainbow .20 .20
5359 A2563 20k Asian youth, camera .95 .35
5360 A2563 45k Emblem 2.25 .75
Nos. 5356-5360 (5) 3.80 1.70
No. 5358 issued in sheets of 8.

**Souvenir Sheet**

**1985, July 4**
5361 A2563 30k Emblem 1.50 1.00

115th Birth Anniv. of Lenin — A2564

Portrait and: No. 5362, Lenin Museum, Tampere, Finland. No. 5363, Memorial apartment, Paris, France.

**1985, Apr. 22** *Photo.* *Perf. 12x12½*
5362 A2564 5k multicolored .20 .20
5363 A2564 5k multicolored .20 .20

**Souvenir Sheet**
*Perf. 12x12½*
5364 A2564 30k Portrait 1.50 1.00
No. 5364 contains one 30x42mm stamp.

Order of Victory — A2565

**Photogravure and Engraved**
**1985, May 9** *Perf. 11½*
5365 A2565 20k sil, royal bl, dk red & gold .60 .35
Allied World War II victory over Germany and Japan, 40th anniv.

---

A2566 / A2567

**1985, May 9** *Litho.* *Perf. 12½x12*
5366 A2566 5k Arms .25 .20
Liberation of Czechoslovakia from German occupation, 40th Anniv.

**1985, May 14** *Photo.* *Perf. 11½*
5367 A2567 5k Flags of member nations .25 .20
Warsaw Treaty Org., 30th anniv.

Mikhail Alexandrovich Sholokhov (1905-1984), Novelist & Nobel Laureate — A2568

Portraits and book covers: No. 5368, Tales from the Don, Quiet Flows the Don, A Human Tragedy. No. 5369, The Quiet Don, Virgin Lands Under the Plow, Thus They Have Fought for Their Homeland. No. 5370, Portrait.

**1985, May 24** *Litho.* *Perf. 12½x12*
5368 A2568 5k Portrait at left .20 .20
5369 A2568 5k Portrait at right .20 .20

*Photo.*
*Perf. 12x11½*
**Size: 37x52mm**
5370 A2568 5k brn, gold & black .60 .60
Nos. 5368-5370 (3)

INTERCOSMOS Project Halley-Venus — A2570

**1985, June 11** *Litho.* *Perf. 12*
5372 A2570 15k Spacecraft, satellites, Venus .35 .20
a. Miniature sheet of 8 25.00

Artek Pioneer Camp, 60th Anniv. A2571

**1985, June 14** *Photo.* *Perf. 11½*
5373 A2571 4k Camp, badges, Lenin Pioneers emblem .50 .20

Mutiny on the Battleship Potemkin, 80th Anniv. — A2572

---

**Photogravure and Engraved**
**1985, June 16** *Perf. 11½x12*
5374 A2572 5k dk red, gold & black .30 .20

**Miniature Sheet**

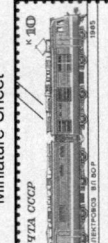

Soviet Railways Rolling Stock — A2573

Designs: a, Electric locomotive WL 80-R (grn). b, Tanker car (bl). c, Refrigerator car (bl). d, Sleeper car (brn). e, Tipper car (brn). f, Box car (brn). g, Shunting diesel locomotive (bl). h, Mail car (grn).

**1985, June 15** *Engr.* *Perf. 12½x12*
5375 A2573 Sheet of 8 2.50 1.65
a.-h. 10k any single .25 .20

Cosmonauts L. Kizim, V. Soloviov, O. Atkov and Salyut-7 Spacecraft — A2574

**1985, June 25** *Litho.*
5376 A2574 15k multicolored .50 .25
a. Miniature sheet of 8 15.00
Soyuz T-10, Salyut-7 and Soyuz T-11 flights, Feb. 8-Oct. 2, 1984.

Beating Sword into Plowshares, Sculpture Donated to UN Hdqtrs. by USSR — A2575

**Photogravure and Engraved**
**1985, June 26** *Perf. 11½*
5377 A2575 45k multicolored 1.50 .75
UN 40th anniv.

Intl. Youth Year A2576

*Perf. 12*
**1985, June 26** *Photo.*
5378 A2576 10k multicolored .30 .25

Medicinal Plants from Siberia — A2577

**1985, July 10** *Litho.* *Perf. 12½x12*
5379 A2577 2k dictocarpum .20 .20
5380 A2577 3k Thermopsis lanceolata .20 .20
5381 A2577 5k Rosa acicularis .20 .20
5382 A2577 20k Rhaponticum carthamoides .70 .35
a. Miniature sheet of 8 15.00
5383 A2577 45k Bergenia crassifolia fritsch 1.50 .70
Nos. 5379-5383 (5) 2.80 1.65

---

Cosmonauts V. A. Dzhanibekov, S. E. Savistskaya, and I. P. Volk, Soyuz T-12 Mission, July 17-29, 1984 — A2578

**1985, July 17**
5384 A2578 10k multicolored .40 .20
a. 15.00
1st woman's free flight in space.

A2579 / A2580

Caecilienhof Palace, Potsdam, Flags of UK, USSR, & US.

**1985, July 17**
5385 A2579 15k multicolored .50 .25
Potsdam Conference, 40th anniv.

**1985, July 25** *Photo.*
5386 A2580 20k Finlandia Hall, Helsinki .50 .30
a. Miniature sheet of 8 20.00
Helsinki Conference on European security and cooperation, 10th anniv.

Flags of USSR, North Korea, Liberation Monument in Pyongyang — A2581

**1985, Aug. 1**
5387 A2581 5k multicolored .25 .20
Socialist Rep. of North Korea, 40th anniv.

Endangered Wildlife — A2582

Designs: 2k, Sorex bucharensis, vert. 3k, Cardiocranius paradoxus. 5k, Selevinia betpakdalensis, vert. 20k, Felis caracal. 45k, Gazella subgutturosa, 50k, Panthera pardus.

**1985, Aug. 15** *Perf. 12x12½, 12½x12* *Litho.*
5388 A2582 2k multicolored .20 .20
5389 A2582 3k multicolored .20 .20
5390 A2582 5k multicolored .20 .20
**Size: 47x32mm**
5391 A2582 20k multicolored .60 .30
5392 A2582 45k multicolored 1.40 .60
a. Miniature sheet of 8 25.00
Nos. 5388-5392 (5) 2.60 1.50

**Souvenir Sheet**
5393 A2582 50k multicolored 2.50 .75

**1985, Aug. 24**
5394 A2583 5k multicolored .30 .25

Youth World Soccer Cup Championships, Moscow — A2583
**Perf. 12**

**1985, Aug. 30**    **Photo.**    **Perf. 11½**
5395 A2584 5k multicolored .25 .20

Alexander G. Stakhanov, Coal Miner & Labor Leader A2584

Stakhanovite Movement for high labor productivity, 50th anniv.

**1985, Sept. 1**
5396 A2585 5k multicolored .30 .25

Bryansk Victory Memorial, Buildings, Arms A2585

Millennium of Bryansk.

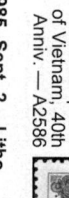

**1985, Sept. 2**    **Photo.**    **Perf. 11½x12**
5397 A2586 5k Arms .25 .20

Socialist Republic of Vietnam, 40th Anniv. — A2586

**1985, Sept. 2**    **Litho.**    **Perf. 11½**
5398 A2587 10k multicolored .50 .20

1985 World Chess Championship match. A. Karpov Vs. G. Kasparov, Moscow.
A2587

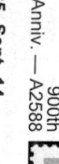

**1985, Sept. 14**
5399 A2588 5k Lutsk Castle .25 .20

Lutsk City, Ukrainian SSR., 900th Anniv. — A2588

Open Book, the Weeping Jaroslavna and Prince Igor's Army — A2589

**1985, Sept. 14**    **Photogravure and Engraved**    **Perf. 11½x12**
5400 A2589 10k multicolored .30 .20

The Song of Igor's Campaign, epic poem, 800th anniv.

**1985, Sept. 26**    **Perf. 12x11½**
5401 A2590 5k Portrait .25 .20

Sergei Vasilievich Gerasimov Painter (1885-1964), A2590

**1985, Oct. 10**    **Photo.**    **Perf. 11½**
5402 A2591 5k multicolored .25 .20

October Revolution, 68th Anniv. — A2591

**1985, Oct. 24**
5403 A2592 15k multicolored .50 .25

UN 40th Anniv. — A2592

**1985, Oct. 31**    **Lithographed and Engraved**
5404 A2593 5k beige & black .30 .20

Krushjanis Baron (1835-1923), Latvian Folklorist — A2593

**1985, Nov. 20**    **Photo.**
5405 A2594 5k multicolored .25 .20

Petersburg Union struggle for liberation of the working classes, founded by Lenin, 90th anniv.

Lenin, Laborer Breaking Chains A2594

**1985, Nov. 20**    **Engr.**    **Perf. 12x11½**
5406 A2595 10k dark blue .50 .25

Largest Soviet Telescope, 10th Anniv. — A2595

Soviet Observatory inauguration.

**1985, Nov. 25**    **Photo.**    **Perf. 11½**
5407 A2596 5k multicolored .25 .20
A2596

Angolan Independence, 10th anniv. — A2596

**1985, Nov. 29**    **Perf. 11½**
5408 A2597 5k multicolored .25 .20
A2597

Socialist Federal Republic of Yugoslavia, 40th anniv.

**1985, Dec. 3**    **Litho.**    **Perf. 12**
5409 A2598 5k multicolored .25 .20
a. Miniature sheet of 8   11.00

New Year — A2598

Samantha Smith — A2599

**1985, Dec. 25**
5415 A2599 5k vio blue, choc & ver .50 .20

American student invited to meet with Soviet leaders in 1984.

**1985, Dec. 18**    **Photo.**    **Perf. 12x11½**

Vehicle Type of 1984

| No. | Type | Denom. | Description | | |
|-----|------|--------|-------------|---|---|
| 5410 | A2545 | 3k | AMO-F15, 1926 | .20 | .20 |
| 5411 | A2545 | 5k | PMZ-1, 1933 | .20 | .20 |
| 5412 | A2545 | 10k | AC-40, 1977 | .35 | .20 |
| 5413 | A2545 | 20k | AL-30, 1970 | .35 | .20 |
| 5414 | A2545 | 45k | AA-60, 1978 | .70 | .35 |
| Nos. 5410-5414 (5) | | | | 2.60 | 1.65 |

**1985, Dec. 30**    **Perf. 12**
5416 A2600 5k multicolored .25 .20

N.M. Emanuel (1915-1984), chemist.
A2600

**1985, Dec. 30**    **Litho.**
5417 A2601 5k Sightseeing .20 .20
5418 A2601 5k Sports .20 .20

Family leisure activities.
A2601

**1986, Jan. 2**    **Photo.**    **Perf. 11½**
5419 A2602 20k brt blue, bluish grn & silver .50 .30

Intl. Peace Year — A2602

**1986, Jan. 3**
5420 A2603 5k multicolored .20 .20

Flags, Congress Palace, Carnation A2603

5421 A2604 20k multicolored .70 .30

Lenin, Troitskaya Tower, Congress Palace A2604

**1986, Jan. 3**    **Photogravure and Engraved**    **Souvenir Sheet**    **Photo.**    **Perf. 11½**
5422 A2605 50k multicolored 1.75 .70

27th Communist Party Congress.

Lenin — A2605

**1986, Jan. 15**    **Perf. 12½x12, 12x12½**    **Litho.**
5423 A2606 15k multicolored .50 .25

Flora of Russian Steppes, different.
A2606

Modern Olympic Games, 90th anniv.

**1986, Jan. 10**    **Perf. 12½x12, 12x12½**    **Litho.**

| No. | Type | Denom. | Description | | |
|-----|------|--------|-------------|---|---|
| 5424 | A2607 | 4k | multicolored | .20 | .20 |
| 5425 | A2607 | 5k | multi. horiz. | .20 | .20 |
| 5426 | A2607 | 10k | multicolored | .30 | .20 |
| 5427 | A2607 | 15k | multicolored | .40 | .30 |
| 5428 | A2607 | 20k | multicolored | .50 | .35 |
| a. Miniature sheet of 8 | | | | 15.00 | |
| Nos. 5424-5428 (5) | | | | 1.60 | 1.25 |

A2607

**Perf. 11½   Photo.**

1986, May 19
5459  A2624  10k multicolored   .35  .20
UNESCO Campaign, Man and Biosphere.

1986, May 20
5460  A2625  10k multicolored   .35  .20
9th Soviet Spartakiad.

Design: Lenin's House, Eternal Glory and V. I. Chapaiev monuments, Gorky State Academic Drama Theater.

1986, May 24
5461  A2626  5k multicolored   .25  .20
City of Kuibyshev, 400th anniv.

1986, May 25
5462  A2627  5k multicolored   .25  .20
"COMMUNICATION '86, Moscow."

**1986 World Cup Soccer Championships, Mexico — A2628**

5k, Various soccer plays. 15k, World Cup on FIFA commemorative gold medal.

1986, May 31   **Perf. 12x12½, 12½x12   Litho.**

5463  A2628  5k multicolored   .20  .20
5464  A2628  10k multicolored   10.00  10.00
  a.  Miniature sheet of 8   .40  .40
5465  A2628  15k multicolored   10.00  10.00
  a.  Miniature sheet of 8   .85  .65
Nos. 5463-5465 (3)

**Paintings in the Tretyakov Gallery, Moscow — A2629**

Designs: 4k, Lane in Albano, 1837, by M.I. Lebedev, vert. 5k, View of the Kremlin in Foul Weather, 1851, by A.K. Savrasov. 10k, Sunlit Pine Trees, 1896, by I.I. Shishkin, vert. 15k, Return, 1896, by A.E. Arkhipov. 45k, Wedding Procession in Moscow, the 17th Century, 1901, by A.P. Ryabushkin.

1986, June 11   **Perf. 12x12½, 12½x12   Litho.**

5466  A2629  4k multicolored   .20  .20
5467  A2629  5k multicolored   .20  .20
5468  A2629  10k multicolored   .35  .20

---

**Lenin, 116th Birth Anniv. — A2619**

Portraits and architecture: No. 5448, Socialist-Democratic People's House, Prague. No. 5449, Lenin Museum, Leipzig. No. 5450, Lenin Museum, Poronino, Poland.

1986, Apr. 22   **Photo.   Perf. 11½x12**

5448  A2619  5k multicolored   .20  .20
5449  A2619  5k multicolored   .20  .20
5450  A2619  5k multicolored   .20  .20
  a.  Nos. 5448-5450 (3)   .60  .60

Tambov City, 350th Anniv. A2620

1986, Apr. 27   **Perf. 11½**
5451  A2620  5k Buildings, city arms   .25  .20

Soviet Peace Fund, 25th Anniv. A2621

1986, Apr. 27
5452  A2621  10k chalky bl, gold & brt ultra   .40  .20

29th World Cycle Race, May 6-22 A2622

1986, May 6
5453  A2622  10k multicolored   .40  .20

Toadstools A2623

1986, May 15   **Litho.   Perf. 12**
5454  A2623  4k Amanita phalloides   .20  .20
5455  A2623  5k Amanita muscaria   .20  .20
5456  A2623  10k Amanita pantherina   .45  .30
5457  A2623  15k Tylopilus felleus   .50  .35
5458  A2623  20k Hypholoma fasciculare   .65  .55
Nos. 5454-5458 (5)   2.00  1.25

---

EXPO '86, Vancouver A2614

1986, Mar. 25   **Photo.   Perf. 12x11½**
5440  A2614  20k Globe, space station   .75  .30
  a.  Miniature sheet of 8   6.00

S.M. Kirov (1886-1934), Party Leader — A2615

1986, Mar. 27   **Engr.   Perf. 12½x12**
5441  A2615  5k black   .30  .20

**Cosmonauts' Day — A2616**

Designs: 5k, Konstantin E. Tsiolkovsky (1857-1935), aerodynamics innovator, and futuristic space rocket. 10k, Sergei P. Korolev (1906-1966), rocket scientist, and Vostok spaceship, vert. 15k, Yuri Gagarin, 1st cosmonaut, Sputnik I and Vega probe.

1986, Apr. 12   **Perf. 12½x12, 12x12½   Litho.**
5442  A2616  5k multicolored   .20  .20
5443  A2616  10k multicolored   .25  .20
  a.  Miniature sheet of 8   25.00  25.00
5444  A2616  15k multicolored   .35  .25
  a.  Miniature sheet of 7 + label   1.10  .85
Nos. 5441-5444 (4)

No. 5444 printed se-tenant with label picturing Vostok and inscribed for the 25th anniv. of first space flight.

**1986 World Ice Hockey Championships, Moscow — A2617**

1986, Apr. 12   **Photo.   Perf. 11½**
5445  A2617  15k multicolored   .50  .25

Ernst Thalmann (1886-1944), German Communist Leader — A2618

1986, Apr. 16   **Engr.   Perf. 12½x12**
5446  A2618  10k dark brown   .20  .20
5447  A2618  10k reddish brown   .30  .20

---

Vodovzvodnaya Tower, Grand Kremlin Palace.

1986, Jan. 20   **Perf. 12½x12**
5429  A2608  50k grayish green   1.50  .70

1986, Feb. 20   **Perf. 11½**
5430  A2609  5k multicolored   .30  .20
Voronezh City, 400th anniv.

1986, Feb. 20   **Engr.   Perf. 12**
5431  A2610  10k bluish black   .35  .20
Bela Kun (1886-1939), Hungarian party leader.

1986, Feb. 28   **Perf. 12½x12**
5432  A2611  5k grayish black   .25  .20
Karolis Pozhela (1896-1926), Lithuanian party founder.

Intercosmos Project Halley. Final Stage — A2612

1986, Mar. 6   **Litho.   Perf. 12**
5433  A2612  15k Vega probe, comet   .50  .25

**Souvenir Sheet   Perf. 12½x12**
5434  A2612  50k Vega I, comet   1.75  .75
No. 5434 contains one 42x30mm stamp.

Butterflies A2613

1986, Mar. 18   **Perf. 12x12½**
5435  A2613  4k Utetheisa pulchella   .20  .20
5436  A2613  5k Allancastria caucasica   .20  .20
5437  A2613  10k Zegris eupheme   .40  .40
5438  A2613  15k Catocala sponsa   .50  .50
5439  A2613  20k Satyrus bischoffi   .65  .55
  a.  Miniature sheet of 8   20.00
Nos. 5435-5439 (5)   1.95  1.65

RUSSIA

**Size: 74x37mm** **Perf. 11½**
5469 A2629 15k multicolored .40 .30
5470 A2629 45k multicolored .75
Nos. 5466-5470 (5) 2.25 1.65
Issued in sheets of 8.

1.10

Irkutsk City, 300th Anniv. — A2630

Goodwill Games, Moscow, July 5-20 — A2631

UNESCO Projects in Russia — A2632

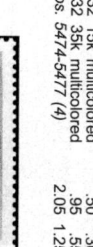

**1986, June 28 Photo. Perf. 11½**
5471 A2630 5k multicolored .25 .20

**1986, July 4 Photo. Perf. 11½**
5472 A2631 10k Prus bl, gold & blk .35 .20
5473 A2631 10k brt blue, gold & blk .35 .20

**1986, July 15**
Designs: 5k, Information sciences. 10k, Geological correlation. 15k, Inter-governmental oceanographic commission. 35k, Intl. hydrologic program.
5474 A2632 5k multicolored .20 .20
5475 A2632 10k multicolored .40 .20
5476 A2632 15k multicolored .50 .30
5477 A2632 35k multicolored .95 .55
Nos. 5474-5477 (4) 2.05 1.25

Tyumen, 400th Anniv. — A2633
**1986, July 27**
5478 A2633 5k multicolored .25 .20

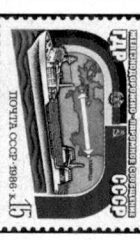

A2634

**1986, Aug. 1 Photo. Perf. 11½**
5479 A2634 10k multicolored .35 .20
Olof Palme (1927-86); Prime Minister of Sweden.

A2635

**1986, Aug. 8**
5480 A2635 15k multicolored .50 .25
10th World Women's Basketball Championships, Moscow, Aug. 15-17.

Natl. Sports Committee Intl. Alpinist Camps — A2636

---

**1986, Sept. 5 Litho. Perf. 12**
5481 A2636 4k Mt. Lenin .20 .20
5482 A2636 5k Mt. E. Korzhenevskaya .20 .20
5483 A2636 10k Mt. Belukha .30 .20
5484 A2636 15k Mt. Communism 10.00
5485 A2636 30k Mt. Elbrus .35 .20
a. Miniature sheet of 8 .65 .30
Nos. 5481-5485 (5) 1.70 1.10
See Nos. 5532-5535.

Red Book, Rainbow, Earth — A2637

Souvenir Sheet

**1986, Sept. 10**
5486 A2637 50k multicolored 1.75 .75
Nature preservation. **Perf. 11½**

A2638

A2640

A2639

**1986, Sept. 13 Photo.**
5487 A2638 5k multicolored .25 .20
Chelyabinsk, 250th anniv.

**1986, Sept. 23**
5488 A2639 15k multicolored .40 .25
Mukran, DDR to Klaipeda, Lithuania, train ferry, inauguration.

**1986, Sept. 26**
5489 A2640 5k multicolored .25 .20
Siauliai, Lithuanian SSR, 750th anniv.

Trucks — A2641

**1986, Oct. 15 Perf. 11½x12**
5490 A2641 4k Ural-375D, 1964 .20 .20
5491 A2641 5k GAZ-53A, 1965 .20 .20
5492 A2641 10k KrAZ-256B, 1966 .35 .20
5493 A2641 15k MAZ-515B, 1974 .50 .30
5494 A2641 20k ZIL-133GY, 1979 .60 .35
Nos. 5490-5494 (5) 1.85 1.25

---

October Revolution, 69th anniv. — A2642
Design: Lenin Monument in October Square, Kremlin, Moscow.
**1986, Oct. 1 Litho. Perf. 12**
5495 A2642 5k multicolored .25 .20

A2643

**1986, Oct. 10 Photo. Perf. 11½**
5496 A2643 5k Icebreaker, helicopters .20 .20
5497 A2643 10k Mikhail Somov port .20 .20
a. A2643 Pair, #5496-5497 .20
b. Miniature sheet of 8, 4 each side 15.00

Mikhail Somov — A2643
Souvenir Sheet
**1986, Oct. 10 Perf. 12½x11½**
5498 A2643 50k Trapped in ice 2.25 .65
Mikhail Somov trapped in the Antarctic. No. 5497a has a continuous design. No. 5498 contains one 51½x36½mm stamp.

No. 4883 Ovptd. in Black for Rescue of the Mikhail Somov

**1986, Oct. 10**
5499 A2271 4k multicolored .75 .20
Lithographed & Engraved **Perf. 12x11½**

Locomotives — A2644

**1986, Oct. 15 Litho. Perf. 12**
5500 A2644 4k EU 684-37, 1929 .20 .20
5501 A2644 5k FD 21-3000, 1941 .20 .20
5502 A2644 10k OV-5109, 1907 .20 .20
5503 A2644 20k CO17-1613, 1944 .55 .20
5504 A2644 30k FDP 20-578, 1941 .95 .40
a. Miniature sheet of 8 16.00
Nos. 5500-5504 (5) 1.25 .65
3.15 1.65

---

**1986, Oct. 18 Engr. Perf. 12½x12**
5505 A2645 5k dark blue green .25 .20
Grigori Konstantinovich Ordzhonikidze (1886-1937), Communist Party Leader — A2645

A.G. Novikov (1896-1984), Composer — A2646
**1986, Oct. 30**
5506 A2646 5k brown black .25 .20

A2647

**1986, Nov. 4 Photo. Perf. 11½**
5507 A2647 10k blue & silver .35 .20
UNESCO, 40th anniv.

A2648

**1986, Nov. 12**
5508 A2648 5k lt grnsh gray & blk .25 .20
Sun Yat-sen (1866-1925), Chinese statesman.

Mikhail Vasilyevich Lomonosov, Scientist — A2649
**1986, Nov. 19 Engr. Perf. 12x12½**
5509 A2649 5k dk violet brown .25 .20

Aircraft by A.S. Yakovlev — A2650
**1986, Nov. 25 Photo. Perf. 11½x12**
5510 A2650 4k 1927 .20 .20
5511 A2650 5k 1935 .20 .20
5512 A2650 10k 1946 .35 .20
5513 A2650 16k 1972 .65 .35
5514 A2650 30k 1981 .95 .50
a. Miniature sheet of 8 15.00
Nos. 5510-5514 (5) 2.40 1.45

Paintings: No. 5549, Lenin's Birthday, by N.A. Sysoyev. No. 5550, Lenin with Delegates at the 3rd Congress of the Soviet Young Communist League, by P.O. Belousov. No. 5551a, Lenin's Underground Activity (Lenin, lamp), by D.A. Nalbandyan. No. 5551b, Before the Assault (Lenin standing at table), by S.P. Viktorov. No. 5551c, We'll Show the Earth the New Way (Lenin, soldiers, flags), by A.G. Lysenko. No. 5551d, Lenin in Smolny, October 1917 (Lenin seated), by M.G. Sokolov. No. 5551e, Lenin, by N.A. Andreyev.

**1987, Apr. 22    Litho.    Perf. 12½x12**
5549 A2667 5k multicolored .20 .20
5550 A2667 5k multicolored .20 .20

**Souvenir Sheet**
**Perf. 12**
5551 Sheet of 5 1.75 .75
a.-e. A2667 10k any single .30 .20
Sizes: Nos. 5551a-5551d, 40x28mm; No. 5551e, 40x56mm.

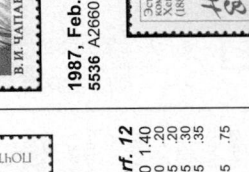

**1987, May 5    Photo.    Perf. 11½**
5552 A2668 10k multicolored .30 .20
European Gymnastics Championships, Moscow, May 18-26.

Bicycle Race — A2669

**1987, May 6**
5553 A2669 10k multicolored .30 .20
40th Peace Bicycle Race, Poland-Czechoslovakia-German Democratic Republic, May.

Fauna — A2670

**Perf. 12½x12 (#5554), 12x12½**
**1987, May 15    Litho.**
5554 A2670 5k Menzbira marmot .20 .20
       15.00
5555 A2670 10k Bald badger, horiz. .30 .20

**Size: 32x47mm**
5556 A2670 15k Snow leopard .40 .25
       .90 .65
Nos. 5554-5556 (3)

Passenger Ships — A2671

**1987, May 20    Photo.    Perf. 12x11½**
5557 A2671 5k Maxim Gorki .20 .20
5558 A2671 10k Alexander Pushkin .35 .20
       15.00
a. Miniature sheet of 8
5559 A2671 30k The Soviet Union 1.10 .45
       1.65 .85
Nos. 5557-5559 (3)

---

A2662    A2663

**1987, Mar. 8    Photo.    Perf. 11½x12**
5538 A2662 5k multicolored .25 .20

**Souvenir Sheet**
**Perf. 11½x12**
5539 A2663 50k "XX," and colored bands 1.75 .75
All-Union Leninist Young Communist League 20th Congress, Moscow. No. 5539 contains one 26x37mm stamp.

**Photogravure and Engraved**
**1987, Mar. 20    Perf. 11½**
5540 A2663 5k buff & sepia .25 .20
Iosif Agarovich Orbeli (1887-1961), first president of the Armenian Academy of Sciences.

World Wildlife Fund — A2664

Polar bears.

**1987, Mar. 25    Photo.    Perf. 11½x12**
5541 A2664 5k multicolored .20 .20
 Miniature sheet of 8 100.00
5642 A2664 10k multicolored .20 .10
 Miniature sheet of 8 100.00 .40
5543 A2664 20k multicolored .70 .75
 Miniature sheet of 8 100.00
5544 A2664 35k multicolored 1.00 1.00
 Miniature sheet of 8 100.00 1.55
d. Miniature sheet of 8 2.20
Nos. 5541-5544 (4)

UN Emblem, ESCAP Headquarters, Bangkok — A2666

**1987, Apr. 12    Perf. 11½**
5545 A2665 10k Sputnik, 1957 .35 .20
5546 A2665 10k Vostok 3 and 4, 1962 .35 .20
 Miniature sheet of 8 25.00
5547 A2665 10k Mars 1, 1962 .35 .20
a. Miniature sheet of 8 1.05 .60
Nos. 5545-5547 (3)

Cosmonauts' Day — A2665

**1987, Apr. 21**
5548 A2666 10k multicolored .30 .20
UN Economic and Social Commission for Asia and the Pacific, 40th anniv.

Lenin, 117th Birth Anniv. — A2667

---

18th Soviet Trade Unions Congress, Feb. 24- — A2656

**1987, Jan. 7    Photo.    Perf. 11½**
5524 A2656 5k multicolored .25 .20

Butterflies A2657

**1987, Jan. 15    Litho.    Perf. 12x12½**
5525 A2657 4k Atrophaneura alcinous .20 .20
5526 A2657 5k Papilio machaon .20 .20
5527 A2657 10k Papilio alexanor .30 .20
5528 A2657 15k Papilio maackii .35 .30
5529 A2657 30k Iphiclides podalirius .70 .50
       1.75 1.40
Nos. 5525-5529 (5)

A2658

**1987, Jan. 31    Perf. 12½x12½**
5530 A2658 5k multicolored .25 .20

**1987, Feb. 4    Perf. 12**
5531 A2659 5k buff & lulw .25 .20
Stasis Shimkus (1887-1943), composer.

**Alpinist Camps Type of 1986**
**1987, Jan. 31**
5532 A2636 4k Chimbulak Gorge .20 .20
5533 A2636 10k Shavla Gorge .30 .20
5534 A2636 20k Mts. Donguzorun, Nakra-tau .50 .35
5535 A2636 35k Mt. Kazbek .75 .55
       1.75 1.30
Nos. 5532-5535 (4)

Vasily Ivanovich Chapayev (1887-1919), Revolution Hero — A2660

**1987, Feb. 9**
5536 A2660 5k dark red brown .25 .20

Heino Eller (1887-1970), Estonian Composer — A2661

**1987, Mar. 7    Litho.    Perf. 12**
5537 A2661 5k buff & brown .25 .20

---

New Year 1987 A2651

**1986, Dec. 4    Litho.    Perf. 11½**
5515 A2651 5k Kremlin towers .25 .20
a. Miniature sheet of 8 15.00

27th Communist Party Cong., 2/25-3/6 — A2652

Red banner and: No. 5516, Engineer, computer, dish receivers. No. 5517, Engineer, computer, dish receivers. No. 5518, Aerial view of city. No. 5519, Council for Mutual Economic Assistance building, workers. No. 5520, Spasski Tower, Kremlin Palace.

**1986, Dec. 12    Photo.    Perf. 11½x12**
5516 A2652 5k multicolored .20 .20
5517 A2652 5k multicolored .20 .20
5518 A2652 5k multicolored .20 .20
5519 A2652 5k multicolored .20 .20
5520 A2652 5k multicolored .20 .20
       1.00 1.00
Nos. 5516-5520 (5)

A2653
A2654

**1986, Dec. 24    Engr.    Perf. 12½x12**
5521 A2653 5k black .25 .20
Alexander Yakovlevich Parkhomenko (1886-1921), revolution hero.

**1986, Dec. 25    Photo.    Perf. 11½**
5522 A2654 5k brown & buff .25 .20
Samora Moises Machel (1933-1986) Pres. of Mozambique.

Palace Museums in Leningrad — A2655

**Miniature Sheet**
**1986, Dec. 25    Engr.    Perf. 12**
5523 Sheet of 5 + label 3.00 1.40
a. A2655 5k State Museum, 1898 .20 .20
b. A2655 10k The Hermitage, 1764 .35 .30
c. A2655 15k Petrodvorets, 1728 .45 .35
d. A2655 20k Yekaterininsky, 1757 .55 .55
e. A2655 50k Pavlovsk, restored c. 1945 1.25 .75

Paintings by Foreign Artists in the Hermitage Museum A2672

**1987,** Perf. 12x12½, 12½x12
| | | | | |
|---|---|---|---|---|
| 5560 | A2672 | 4k multicolored | .20 | .20 |
| 5561 | A2672 | 5k multicolored | .20 | .20 |
| 5562 | A2672 | 10k multicolored | .30 | .20 |
| a. | | Miniature sheet of 8 | 20.00 | |
| 5563 | A2672 | 30k multicolored | .70 | .50 |
| 5564 | A2672 | 50k multicolored | 1.25 | .75 |
| | | Nos. 5560-5564 (5) | 2.65 | 1.85 |

4k, Portrait of a Woman, by Lucas Cranach Sr. (1472-1553). 5k, St. Sebastian, by Titian. 10k, Justice, by Durer. 30k, Adoration of the Magi, by Pieter Brueghel the Younger (c. 1564-1638). 50k, Ceres, by Rubens.

Lenin Hydroelectric plant.

**1987, June 6** Photo. Perf. 11½
| | | | | |
|---|---|---|---|---|
| 5565 | A2673 | 5k multicolored | .25 | .20 |

Aleksander Pushkin (1799-1837), Poet — A2674

**1987, June 6** Litho.
| | | | | |
|---|---|---|---|---|
| 5566 | A2674 | 5k buff, yel brn & deep brown | .25 | .20 |

Printed se-tenant with label.

Toljatti City, 250th Anniv. — A2673

Design: Zhiguli car, Volga Motors factory.

A2675

A2676

**1987, June 5** Engr. Perf. 12½x12
| | | | | |
|---|---|---|---|---|
| 5567 | A2675 | 5k black | .25 | .20 |

Maj.-Gen. Sidor A. Kovpak (1887-1967), Vice-Chairman of the Ukranian SSR.

**1987, June 7** Photo. Perf. 11½
| | | | | |
|---|---|---|---|---|
| 5568 | A2676 | 10k multicolored | .30 | .20 |

Women's World Congress on Nuclear Disarmament, Moscow, June 23-27.

**1987, June 23**

---

Tobolsk City, 400th Anniv. — A2677

**1987, June 25** Litho.
| | | | | |
|---|---|---|---|---|
| 5569 | A2677 | 5k multicolored | .25 | .20 |

Design: Tobolsk Kremlin, port, theater and Ermak Monument.

Mozambique-USSR Peace Treaty, 10th anniv. — A2678

**1987, June 25**
| | | | | |
|---|---|---|---|---|
| 5570 | A2678 | 5k Flag of Congo, man | .20 | .20 |
| 5571 | A2678 | 5k Flags of Frelimo, USSR | .20 | .20 |
| a. | | Pair, #5570-5571 | .30 | .30 |

Ferns — A2679

**1987, July 2** Litho. Perf. 12
| | | | | |
|---|---|---|---|---|
| 5572 | A2679 | 4k Scolopendrium vulgare | .20 | .20 |
| 5573 | A2679 | 5k Ceterach officinarum | .20 | .20 |
| 5574 | A2679 | 10k Salvinia natans, horiz. | .20 | .20 |
| 5575 | A2679 | 15k Matteuccia struthiopteris | .40 | .30 |
| 5576 | A2679 | 50k Adiantum pedatum | 1.10 | .75 |
| | | Nos. 5572-5576 (5) | 2.20 | 1.65 |

**1987, July 3**

Designs: #5577, Kremlin and 2000 Year-old Coin of India. #5578, Red Fort, Delhi, Soviet hammer & sickle.
| | | | | |
|---|---|---|---|---|
| 5577 | A2680 | 5k shown | .20 | .20 |
| 5578 | A2680 | 5k multicolored | .20 | .20 |
| a. | | Pair, #5577-5578 | .30 | .30 |

Festivals 1987-88: India in the USSR (No. 5577) and the USSR in India (No. 5578).

15th Intl. Film Festival, July 16-17, Moscow — A2681

**1987, July 6** Photo. Perf. 11½
| | | | | |
|---|---|---|---|---|
| 5579 | 2681 | 10k multicolored | .35 | .20 |

---

Mir Space Station — A2683

**1987**
| | | | | |
|---|---|---|---|---|
| 5580 | A2682 | 5k multicolored | .20 | .20 |
| 5581 | A2682 | 10k multicolored | .25 | .20 |
| 5582 | A2682 | 15k multicolored | .25 | .25 |
| | | Nos. 5580-5582 (3) | .65 | .65 |

**Souvenir Sheet**
| | | | | |
|---|---|---|---|---|
| 5583 | A2683 | 50k multicolored | 1.75 | .75 |

Issued: 5k, 1/22; 10k, 7/24; 15k, 50k 7/30.

Flags, Intercosmos emblem and; 5k, Cosmonaut training and launch. 10k, Mir space station, Syrian parliament and satellite. 15k, Gagarin Memorial, satellite dishes and cosmonauts wearing space suits.

Joint Soviet-Syrian Space Flight A2682

Intl. Atomic Energy Agency, 30th Anniv. — A2684

**1987, July 29** Photo. Perf. 11½
| | | | | |
|---|---|---|---|---|
| 5584 | A2684 | 20k multicolored | .60 | .30 |

14th-16th Century Postrider — A2685

**1987, Aug. 25** Photo. & Engr. Perf. 11½x12
| | | | | |
|---|---|---|---|---|
| 5585 | A2685 | 4k buff & black | .20 | .20 |
| 5586 | A2685 | 5k buff & black | .20 | .20 |
| 5587 | A2685 | 10k buff & black | .30 | .20 |
| 5588 | A2685 | 30k buff & black | .90 | .50 |
| 5589 | A2685 | 35k buff & black | 1.00 | .55 |
| | | Nos. 5585-5589 (5) | 2.60 | 1.65 |

**Souvenir Sheet**
| | | | | |
|---|---|---|---|---|
| 5590 | A2685 | 50k pale yel, dull gray grn & blk | 1.75 | .90 |

Designs: 5k, 17th cent. postman and 17th cent. kibitka (sled). 10k, 16th-17th cent. ship and 18th cent. packet. 30k, Railway station and 19th cent. mailcars. 35k, AMO-F-15 bus and car, 1905. 50k, Postal headquarters, Moscow, and modern postal delivery trucks.

---

October Revolution, 70th Anniv. — A2687

Paintings by Russian artists: No. 5591, Long Live the Socialist Revolution! by V.V. Kuznetsov. No. 5592, V.I. Lenin Proclaims the Soviet Power (Lenin pointing), by V.A. Serov. No. 5593, V.I. Lenin (with pencil), by P.V. Vasiliev. No. 5594, On the Eve of the Storm (Lenin, Trotsky, Dzerzhinski), by V.V. Pimenov. No. 5595, Taking the Winter Palace by Storm, by V.A. Serov.

**1987, Aug. 25** Litho. Perf. 12½x12
| | | | | |
|---|---|---|---|---|
| 5591 | A2686 | 5k shown | .20 | .20 |
| 5592 | A2686 | 5k multicolored | .20 | .20 |
| 5593 | A2686 | 5k multicolored | .20 | .20 |
| 5594 | A2686 | 5k multicolored | .20 | .20 |
| 5595 | A2686 | 5k multicolored | .20 | .20 |
| | | Nos. 5591-5595 (5) | 1.00 | 1.00 |

Size: 70x33mm

**Souvenir Sheet**
Photo. & Engr. Perf. 12x11½
| | | | | |
|---|---|---|---|---|
| 5596 | A2687 | 30k gold and black | 1.50 | .45 |

For overprint see No. 5604.

Battle of Borodino, 175th Anniv. — A2688

**1987, Sept. 7** Litho. Perf. 12½x12
| | | | | |
|---|---|---|---|---|
| 5597 | A2688 | 1r black, yel brn & blue gray | 3.00 | 1.50 |

A2689

**1987, Sept. 18** Engr.
| | | | | |
|---|---|---|---|---|
| 5598 | A2689 | 5k intense blue | .25 | .20 |

Pavel Petrovich Postyshev (1887-1939), party leader.

A2690

Design: 5k, Monument to founder Yuri Dolgoruki, by sculptor S. Orlov, A. Antropov, N. Stamm and architect V. Andreyev, in Sovetskaya Square, and buildings in Moscow.

**1987, Sept. 19** Photo. Perf. 11½
| | | | | |
|---|---|---|---|---|
| 5599 | A2690 | 5k dk red brn, or & dk org | .25 | .20 |

Moscow, 840th anniv.

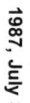

RUSSIA

A2709

A2708

Marshal Ivan Khristoforovich Bagramyan (1897-1982) — A2704

**1987, Dec. 2**    **Engr.**    **Perf. 12½x12**
5622 A2704 5k black    .25 .20

**Miniature Sheet**

18th-19th Cent. Naval Commanders and War Ships — A2705

Designs: 4k, Adm. Grigori Andreyevich Spiridov (1713-1790), Battle of Chesmen. 5k, Fedor Fedorovich Ushakov (1745-1817), Storming of Corfu. 10k, Adm. Dimitri Nikolayevich Senyavin (1763-1831) and flagship at the Battle of Afon off Mt. Athos. 25k, Mikhail Petrovich Lazarev (1788-1851), Battle of Navarin. 30k, Adm. Pavel Stepanovich Nakhimov (1802-1855), Battle of Sinop.

**1987, Dec. 22**
5623    Sheet of 5 + label    2.50 1.25
   a. A2705 4k dark blue & indigo    .20 .20
   b. A2705 5k maroon & indigo    .20 .20
   c. A2705 10k maroon & indigo    .20 .20
   d. A2705 25k dark blue & indigo    .80 .40
   e. A2705 30k dark blue & indigo    1.00 .50

No. 5623 contains corner label (LR) picturing national ensign of period Russian Navy vessels and anchor.
See No. 5850.

Asia-Africa Peoples Solidarity Organization, 30th Anniv. — A2706

**1987, Dec. 26**    **Photo.**
5624 A2706 10k multicolored    .35 .20

1st Soviet Postage Stamp, 70th Anniv. — A2707

**1988, Jan. 4**    **Photo.**    **Perf. 11½**
5625 A2707 10k #149, #150 UR    .50 .20
5626 A2707 10k #150, #149 UR    .50 .20
   a.    Pair, #5625-5626    1.00 .30

Lettering in brown on No. 5625, in blue on No. 5626.

---

A2698      A2699

**1987, Nov. 19**    **Photo.**    **Perf. 11½**
5614 A2698 5k black & brown    .25 .20
   Indira Gandhi (1917-1984).

**1987, Nov. 25**    **Perf. 12½x12**
5615 A2699 5k black    .25 .20
   Vadim Nikolaevich Podbelsky (1887-1920), revolution leader.

A2700      A2701

**1987, Nov. 25**
5616 A2700 5k dark blue gray    .25 .20
   Nikolai Ivanovich Vavilov (1887-1943), botanist.

**1987, Nov. 25**    **Photo. & Engr.**    **Perf. 11½**

Modern Science: 5k, TOKAMAK, a controlled thermonuclear reactor. 10k, Kola Project (Earth strata study). 20k, RATAN-600 radiotelescope.

5617 A2701    5k grnsh gray & brn    .20 .20
5618 A2701    10k dull grn, lt blue    .35 .20
5619 A2701    20k gray olive, blk & buff    .70 .30
   Nos. 5617-5619 (3)    1.25 .70

U.S. and Soviet Flags, Spasski Tower and US Capitol — A2702

**1987, Dec. 17**    **Photo.**
5620 A2702 10k multicolored    .50 .20

INF Treaty (eliminating intermediate-range nuclear missiles) signed by Gen.-Sec. Gorbachev and Pres. Reagan, Dec. 8.

New Year 1988 — A2703

**1987, Dec. 2**    **Litho.**    **Perf. 12x12½**
5621 A2703 5k Kremlin    .25 .20
   a.    Miniature sheet of 8

---

The Sun Above Red Square, by P.P. Ossovsky — A2694

Paintings by Soviet artists exhibited at the 7th Republican Art Exhibition, Moscow, 1985: 4k, There Will be Cities in the Taiga, by A.A. Yakovlev. 5k, Mother, by V.V. Shcherbakov. 30k, On Jakutian Soil, by A.N. Osipov. 35k, Ivan's Return, by V.I. Yerofeyev.

**1987, Oct. 20**    **Perf. 12x12½, 12½x12**
5605 A2693    4k multi, vert.    .20 .20
5606 A2693    5k multi, vert.    .20 .20
5607 A2693    10k multicolored    .35 .20
5608 A2693    30k multicolored    .75 .45
5609 A2693    35k multicolored    .85 .50
   Nos. 5605-5609 (5)    2.35 1.55

**Souvenir Sheet**

**Perf. 11½x12½**
5610 A2694 50k multicolored    2.50 1.00

John Reed (1887-1920), American Journalist — A2695

**Perf. 11½**
5611 A2695 10k buff & dark brown    .35 .20

Samuil Yakovlevich Marshak (1887-1964), Author — A2696

**1987, Nov. 3**    **Engr.**    **Perf. 12½x12**
5612 A2696 5k deep claret    .25 .20

A2697

**1987, Nov. 8**
5613 A2697 5k slate blue    .50 .20
   Ilja Grigorjevich Chavchavadze (1837-1907), Georgian author.

---

Scientists — A2691

Designs: No. 5600, Muhammed Taragai Ulugh Begh (1394-1449), Uzbek astronomer and mathematician. No. 5601, Sir Isaac Newton (1642-1727), English physicist and mathematician. No. 5602, Marie Curie (1867-1934), physicist, chemist, Nobel laureate.

**1987, Oct. 3**    **Photo. & Engr.**
5600 A2691    5k dk blk, org brn & blk    .20 .20
5601 A2691    5k dull grn, blk & dk ultra    .20 .20
5602 A2691    5k brown & deep blue    .60 .60
   Nos. 5600-5602 (3)

Nos. 5600-5602 each printed se-tenant with inscribed label.

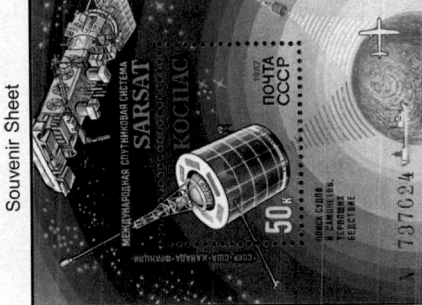

Souvenir Sheet

COSPAS-SARSAT Intl. Satellite System for Tracking Disabled Planes and Ships — A2692

   **Photo.**
**1987, Oct. 15**      2.25 .75
5603 A2692 50k multicolored

No. 5595 Overprinted in Gold

   **Litho.**
**1987, Oct. 17**      1.00 .20
5604 A2686 5k multicolored

All-Union Philatelic Exhibition and the 70th Anniv. of the October Revolution. Sheet of 8 No. 5595 has the overprint in the margin.

My Quiet Homeland, by V.M. Sidorov — A2693

**1988, Jan. 4**
5627 A2708 5k Biathlon .20 .20
a. Miniature sheet of 8 75.00
5628 A2708 10k Cross-country skiing 75.00
a. Miniature sheet of 8 75.00
5629 A2708 15k Slalom .30 .20
a. Miniature sheet of 8 75.00
5630 A2708 20k Pairs figure skating .50 .35
a. Miniature sheet of 8 75.00
5631 A2708 30k Ski jumping .70 .50
a. Miniature sheet of 8 75.00
Nos. 5627-5631 (5) 2.10 1.55

1988 Winter Olympics, Calgary, Canada.
For overprint see No. 5665.

**Souvenir Sheet**

**1988, Jan. 7**
5632 A2709 50k Ice hockey, horiz. 1.50 1.00
World Health Org., 40th anniv.

**1988, Jan. 7**
5633 A2709 35k blue & gold 1.00 .65

Lord Byron (1788-1824), English Poet

**1988, Jan. 22**
5634 A2710 15k Prus blue, blk & grn black .50 .30

**Photo. & Engr. Perf. 12x11½**

**1988, Jan. 27**
5635 A2711 20k multicolored .60 .40

Cultural, Technical and Educational Agreement with the US, 30th anniv.

**Photo. Perf. 11½**

**1988, Feb. 5**
5636 A2712 5k black & tan .25 .20

G.I. Lomov-Oppokov (1888-1938), party leader. See Nos. 5649, 5660, 5666, 5673, 5700, 5704, 5721, 5812.

**1988, Feb. 18 Litho. Perf. 12½x12**
5637 A2713 1k Little Humpback Horse, 1947 .20 .20
5638 A2713 3k Winnie-the-Pooh, 1969 .20 .20
5639 A2713 4k Gena, the Crocodile, 1969 .20 .20
5640 A2713 5k Just you Wait! 1969 .20 .20
5641 A2713 10k Hedgehog in the Mist, 1975 .30 .20
Nos. 5637-5641 (5) 1.10 1.00

**Souvenir Sheet**

5642 A2713 30k Post, 1929 1.00 .60

**Animated Soviet Cartoons — A2713**

---

Mikhail Alexandrovich Bonch-Bruevich (1888-1940), broadcast engineer.

**1988, Feb. 21 Photo. Perf. 11½**
5643 A2714 10k buff & black .30 .20

Intl. Red Cross and Red Crescent Organizations, 125th anniv.

**1988, Feb. 25**
5644 A2715 15k blk, brt bl & dk red .50 .30
a. Miniature sheet of 8 15.00

World Speed Skating Championships, Mar. 5-6, Alma-Ata — A2716

**1988, Mar. 13 Photo. Perf. 11½**
5645 A2716 15k blk, vio & brt blue .45 .30
No. 5645 printed se-tenant with label picturing Alma-Ata skating rink, Modoo.

Anton Semenovich Makarenko (1888-1939), teacher, youth development expert.

**1988, Mar. 13 Litho. Perf. 12½x12**
5646 A2717 10k dark olive green .30 .20

Franzisk Skorina (b. 1488), 1st Printer in Byelorussia

**1988, Mar. 17 Engr. Perf. 12x12½**
5647 A2718 5k gray black .25 .20

**1988, Mar. 22 Photo. Perf. 11½**
5648 A2719 5k multicolored .25 .20

Labor Day — A2719

**Party Leader Type of 1988**

**1988, Mar. 24 Engr. Perf. 12**
5649 A2712 5k dark green .25 .20

Victor Eduardovich Kinglisepp (1888-1922).

---

Marietta Sergeyevna Shaginyan (1888-1982), Author — A2722

**1988, Apr. 2 Litho. Perf. 12½x12**
5651 A2722 10k brown .30 .20

Soviet-Finnish Peace Treaty, 40th Anniv. — A2723

**1988, Apr. 6 Photo. Perf. 11½**
5652 A2723 15k multicolored .50 .30

MIR space station, Soyuz TM transport ship, automated cargo ship Progress & Quant module.

Cosmonaut's Day — A2724

**1988, Apr. 12**
5653 A2724 15k multicolored .50 .30
a. Miniature sheet of 8 15.00

Victory, 1948, Painted by P.A. Krivonogov A2725

**1988, Apr. 20 Litho. Perf. 12x12½**
5654 A2725 15k multicolored .25 .20

Victory Day (May 9).

Sochi City, 150th Anniv. A2726

**1988, Apr. 20 Photo. Perf. 11½**
5655 A2726 5k multicolored .25 .20

---

Organized Track and Field Events in Russia, Cent. A2721

**1988, Mar. 24 Photo. Perf. 11½**
5650 A2721 15k multicolored .50 .30

Branches of the Lenin Museum — A2727

**1988, Apr. 22 Litho. Perf. 12**
5656 A2727 5k vio brown & gold .20 .20
5657 A2727 5k brn vio, dk gold .20 .20
5658 A2727 5k vio brown & gold .20 .20
5659 A2727 5k dark green & gold .20 .20
a. Block of 4, Nos. 5656-5659 .80 .40

See Nos. 5765-5767, 5885-5887.

Portrait of Lenin and museum, Moscow, opened May 15, 1936. Central museum, Leningrad, opened in 1937. No. 5657, Branch, Kiev, opened in 1938. No. 5658, Branch, Krasnoyarsk, opened in 1987.

**Party Leader Type of 1988**

**1988, Apr. 24 Photo. Perf. 11½**
5660 A2712 5k blue black .25 .20

Ivan Alexeyevich Akulov (1888-1939).

---

No. 5632 Ovprtd. in Dark Red

**1988, May 5 Photo. Perf. 12½x11½**
5663 A2731 5k multicolored .20 .20
5664 A2731 5k multicolored .20 .20

Designs: No. 5663, Cruiser Aurora, revolutionary soldiers, workers and slogans Speeding Up, Democratization, and Glasnost against Kremlin Palace No. 5664, Worker, agriculture and industries.

Social and Economic Reforms — A2731

EXPO '88, Brisbane, Australia.

**1988, Apr. 30**
5661 A2729 20k multicolored .55 .35

**1988, May 5**
5662 A2730 5k chocolate .25 .20

**Engr. Perf. 12**

Karl Marx — A2730

## Souvenir Sheet    Photo.    Perf. 11½

**1988, May 12**
5665 A2708 50k multicolored    2.00  1.25

Victory of Soviet athletes at the 1988 Winter Olympics, Calgary. No. 5665 overprinted below stamp on souvenir sheet margin. Soviet sportsmen won 11 gold, 9 silver and 9 bronze medals.

### Party Leader Type of 1988

**1988, May 19    Engr.    Perf. 12**
5666 A2712 5k black    .25  .20

Nikolai Mikhailovich Shvernik (1888-1970).

## Hunting Dogs — A2733

Designs: 5k, Russian borzoi, fox hunt. 10k, Kirghiz greyhound, falconry. 15k, Russian retrievers. 20k, Russian spaniel, duck hunt. 35k, East Siberian husky, bear hunt.

**1988, May 20    Litho.**

| 5667 A2733 | 5k multicolored | .20 | .20 |
|---|---|---|---|
| 5668 A2733 | 10k multicolored | .35 | .35 |
| 5669 A2733 | 15k multicolored | .50 | .35 |
| 5670 A2733 | 20k multicolored | .75 | .50 |
| 5671 A2733 | 35k multicolored | 1.10 | .80 |
| | Nos. 5667-5671 (5) | 2.90 | 2.10 |

A2734

**1988, May 29    Photo.    Perf. 11½**
5672 A2734 5k multicolored    .30  .20

Soviet-US Summit Conf., May 29-June 2, Moscow.

### Party Leader Type of 1988

**1988, June 6    Engr.    Perf. 12**
5673 A2712 5k brown black    .25  .20

Valerian Vladimirovich Kuibyshev (1888-1935).

A27.34

**1988, June 7    Photo.    Perf. 11½**
5674 A2736 15k multicolored    .50  .35

Design: Flags, Mir space station and Soyuz TM spacecraft.

Shipka '88, USSR-Bulgarian joint space flight, June 7.

A2737

**1988, June 16**
5675 A2737 35k multicolored    1.00  .80

Soviet-Canada transarctic ski expedition, May-Aug.

Design: Natl. & Canadian flags, skis & obe.

A2738

**1988, June 16**
5676 A2738 5k multicolored    .25  .20

For a world without nuclear weapons.

---

A2739

A2740

## 19th All-union Communist Party Conference, Moscow — A2741

**1988, June 16    Litho.    Perf. 12**
5677 A2739 5k multicolored    .20  .20

**Photo.    Perf. 11½**
5678 A2740 5k multicolored    .20  .20

**Souvenir Sheet    Perf. 11½x12**
5679 A2741 50k multicolored    1.75  1.00

**1988 Summer Olympics, Seoul — A2742**

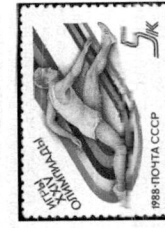

**1988, June 29    Litho.    Perf. 12**

| 5680 A2742 | 5k Hurdling | .20 | .20 |
|---|---|---|---|
| a. | Miniature sheet of 8 | 5.00 | |
| 5681 A2742 | 10k Long jump | .25 | .20 |
| a. | Miniature sheet of 8 | 5.00 | |
| 5682 A2742 | 15k Basketball | .40 | .30 |
| a. | Miniature sheet of 8 | 5.00 | |
| 5683 A2742 | 20k Rhythmic gymnastics | .50 | .35 |
| a. | Miniature sheet of 8 | 5.00 | |
| 5684 A2742 | 30k Swimming | .70 | .50 |
| a. | Miniature sheet of 8 | 2.05 | 1.55 |
| | Nos. 5680-5684 (5) | 1.75 | 1.10 |

**Souvenir Sheet**
5685 A2742 50k Soccer

For overprint see No. 5722.

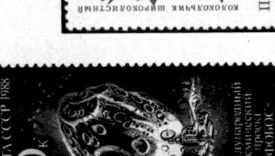

## Flowers Populating Deciduous Forests — A2744

## Phobos Intl. Space Project — A2743

**1988, July 7    Photo.    Perf. 11½x12**
5686 A2743 10k Satellite, space probe    .30  .20

For the study of Phobos, a satellite of Mars.

---

**1988, July 7    Litho.    Perf. 12**

| 5687 A2744 | 5k Campanula latifolia | .20 | .20 |
|---|---|---|---|
| 5688 A2744 | 10k Orobus vernus, horiz. | .35 | .25 |
| 5689 A2744 | 15k Pulmonaria obscura | .50 | .35 |
| 5690 A2744 | 20k Lilium martagon | .65 | .45 |
| 5691 A2744 | 35k Ficaria verna | 1.10 | .75 |
| | Nos. 5687-5691 (5) | 2.80 | 2.00 |

A2745    A2746

**1988, July 14    Photo.    Perf. 11½**
5692 A2745 5k multicolored    .25  .20

Leninist Young Communist League (Komsomol), 70th anniv. For overprint see No. 5699.

**1988, July 18**
5693 A2746 10k multicolored    .30  .20

Nelson Mandela (b. 1918), South African anti-apartheid leader.

## Paintings in the Timiriazev Equestrian Museum of the Moscow Agricultural Academy — A2747

Paintings: 5k, *Light Gray Arabian Stallion,* by N.E. Sverchkov, 1860. 10k, *Konvoets, a Kabardian,* by M.A. Vrubel, 1882. vert. 15k, *Horsewoman Riding an Orlov-Rastopchinsky,* by N.E. Sverchkov. 20k, *Letuchya, a Gray Orlov Trotter,* by V.A. Serov, 1886. vert. 30k, *Sardar, an Akhaltekinsky Stallion,* by A.B. Villevalde, 1882.

**1988, July 20    Litho.    Perf. 12½x12**

| 5694 A2747 | 5k multicolored | .20 | .20 |
|---|---|---|---|
| 5695 A2747 | 10k multicolored | .25 | .20 |
| 5696 A2747 | 15k multicolored | .40 | .25 |
| 5697 A2747 | 20k multicolored | .55 | .35 |
| 5698 A2747 | 30k multicolored | .90 | .65 |
| | Nos. 5694-5698 (5) | 2.30 | 1.65 |

No. 5692 Ovptd. for the All-Union Philatelic Exhibition, Moscow, Aug. 10-17

**1988, Aug. 10    Photo.    Perf. 11½**
5699 A2745 5k multicolored    .40  .30

### Party Leader Type of 1988

**1988, Aug. 13    Engr.    Perf. 12½x12**
5700 A2712 5k black    .25  .20

Petr Lazarevich Voykov (1888-1927), economic and trade union plenipotentiary.

## Intl. Letter-Writing Week — A2749

---

**1988, Aug. 25    Photo.    Perf. 11½**
5701 A2749 5k blue grn & dark blue green    .25  .20

A2750    A2751

**1988, Aug. 29**
5702 A2750 15k Earth, Mir space station and Soyuz-TM    .50  .30

Soviet-Afghan joint space flight.

**1988, Sept. 1    Photo.    Perf. 11½**
5703 A2751 10k multicolored    .30  .20

*Problems of Peace and Socialism* magazine, 30th anniv.

### Party Leader Type of 1988

**1988, Sept. 13    Engr.    Perf. 12**
5704 A2712 5k black    .25  .20

Emmanuil Ionovich Kviring (1888-1937).

A2753

A2753a

A2753b

A2753c

A2753d

Designs: No. 5705, *Ilya Muromets,* Russian lore. No. 5706, *Ballad of the Cossack Golota,* Ukrainian lore. No. 5707, *Musician-Magician,* a Byelorussian fairy tale. No. 5708, *Koblandybatyr,* a poem from Kazakh. No. 5709, *Alpamysh,* a fairy tale from Uzbek.

## 1988, Sept. 22    Perf. 12x12½, 12½x12    Litho.

| No. | Type | Description | | |
|---|---|---|---|---|
| 5705 | A2753 | 10k multicolored | .30 | .20 |
| 5706 | A2753a | 10k multicolored | .30 | .20 |
| 5707 | A2753b | 10k multicolored | .30 | .20 |
| 5708 | A2753c | 10k multicolored | .30 | .20 |
| 5709 | A2753d | 10k multicolored | .30 | .20 |
| | | Nos. 5705-5709 (5) | 1.50 | 1.00 |

Nos. 5705-5709 each printed se-tenant with inscribed labels. See design A2795.

**Appeal of the Leader, 1947, by I.M. Toidze — A2754**

## 1988, Oct. 5    Perf. 12x12½

| 5710 | A2754 | 5k multicolored | .25 | .20 |
|---|---|---|---|---|

October Revolution, 71st anniv.

A2755

## 1988, Oct. 18    Engr.

| 5711 | A2755 | 10k black | .25 | .20 |
|---|---|---|---|---|

Andrei Timofeyevich Bolotov (1738-1833), agricultural scientist, publisher.

A2756

## 1988, Oct. 18    Perf. 12

| 5712 | A2756 | 10k steel blue | .30 | .20 |
|---|---|---|---|---|

Andrei Nikolayevich Tupolev (1888-1972), aeronautical engineer.

A2757

## 1988, Oct. 25    Litho.

| 5713 | A2757 | 20k multicolored | .60 | .40 |
|---|---|---|---|---|

North Pole expedition (in 1987). Exists imperf.

20k. Map of expedition route, atomic icebreaker *Sibij* & expedition members.

A2758

## 1988, Oct. 30    Engr.

| 5714 | A2758 | 5k brown black | .25 | .20 |
|---|---|---|---|---|

Dmitry F. Ustinov (1908-84), minister of defense.

**Soviet-Vietnamese Treaty, 10th Anniv. — A2759**

## 1988, Nov. 3    Photo.    Perf. 11½

| 5715 | A2759 | 10k multicolored | .30 | .20 |
|---|---|---|---|---|

**State Broadcasting and Sound Recording Institute, 50th Anniv. — A2760**

## 1988, Nov. 3    Perf. 11½

| 5716 | A2760 | 10k multicolored | .30 | .20 |
|---|---|---|---|---|

**UN Declaration of Human Rights, 40th Anniv. A2761**

## 1988, Nov. 21

| 5717 | A2761 | 10k multicolored | .30 | .20 |
|---|---|---|---|---|

**New Year 1989 — A2762**

## 1988, Nov. 24    Litho.    Perf. 12x11½

| 5718 | A2762 | 5k multicolored | .25 | .20 |
|---|---|---|---|---|

Design: Preobrazhensky Regiment bodyguard riding to announce decree to celebrate new year's eve as of January 1, 1700.

**Soviet-French Joint Space Flight — A2763**

## 1988, Nov. 26    Photo.    Perf. 11½

| 5719 | A2763 | 15k Space walkers | .45 | .30 |
|---|---|---|---|---|

**No. 4607 Overprinted in Red**

## 1988, Dec. 16    Litho.    Perf. 12½x12

| 5720 | A2143 | 1r dark blue | 3.50 | 2.25 |
|---|---|---|---|---|

Space mail.

**Party Leader Type of 1988**

## 1988, Dec. 16    Engr.

| 5721 | A2712 | 5k slate green | .25 | .20 |
|---|---|---|---|---|

Martyn Ivanovich Latsis (1888-1938).

**19th Communist Party Congress — A2764**

Panes have photogravure margin. Panes are printed bilaterally and separated in the center by perforations so that stamps in the 2nd pane are arranged in reverse order from the 1st pane.

**Post Rider A2765**

## 1988, Dec. 22    Engr.    Perf. 12x11½

| 5723 | A2765 | 1k dark brown | .20 | .20 |
|---|---|---|---|---|
| 5724 | A2765 | 3k dark blue green | .20 | .20 |
| 5725 | A2765 | 4k indigo | .20 | .20 |
| 5726 | A2765 | 5k red | .20 | .20 |
| 5727 | A2765 | 10k claret | .30 | .20 |
| 5728 | A2765 | 15k deep blue | .45 | .30 |
| 5729 | A2765 | 20k olive gray | .60 | .40 |
| 5730 | A2765 | 25k dark gray | .75 | .50 |
| 5731 | A2765 | 30k dark blue | .90 | .60 |
| 5732 | A2765 | 35k dark red brown | 1.00 | .70 |
| 5733 | A2765 | 50k sapphire | 1.50 | 1.00 |

Designs: 3k, Cruiser *Aurora*. 4k, Spasski Tower, Lenin Mausoleum. 5k, Natl. flag, crest. 10k, *The Worker and the Collective Farmer*, 1935, sculpture by V.I. Mukhina. 15k, Satellite dish. 20k, Lyre, art tools, quill pen, parchment (arts and literature). 25k, *Discobolus*, 5th cent. sculpture by Myron (c. 480-440 B.C.). 30k, Map of the Antarctic, penguins. 35k, Mercury, sculpture by Giambologna (1529-1608). 50k, White cranes (nature conservation). 1r, UPU emblem.

## Perf. 12x12½

| 5734 | A2765 | 1r blue gray | 3.00 | 2.00 |
|---|---|---|---|---|
| | | Nos. 5723-5734 (12) | 9.30 | 6.50 |

See Nos. 5838-5849, 5984-5987. For surcharges see Uzbekistan #15, 22, 25-26, 61B, 61D, 61F.

**Fountains of Petrodvorets A2766**

## 1988, Dec. 25    Engr.    Perf. 11½x12

| 5735 | A2766 | 5k myrtle green | .20 | .20 |
|---|---|---|---|---|
| 5736 | A2766 | 10k myrtle green | .20 | .20 |
| 5737 | A2766 | 15k myrtle green | .30 | .20 |
| 5738 | A2766 | 30k myrtle green | .60 | .40 |
| 5739 | A2766 | 50k myrtle green | 1.00 | .70 |
| | a. | Pane of 5 #5735-5739 | 2.25 | 1.50 |

Designs: 5k, Samson Fountain, 1723, and Great Cascade. 10k, Adam Fountain, 1722, and sculptures, 1718, by D. Bonazza. 15k, Golden Mountain Cascade, by N. Miketti (1721-1723) and M.G. Zemtsov. 30k, Roman Fountains, 1763. 50k, Oak Tree Fountain, 1735.

Panes have photogravure margin. Panes are printed bilaterally and separated in the center by perforations so that stamps in the 2nd pane are arranged in reverse order from the 1st pane.

**No. 5685 Overprinted in Bright Blue**

## 1988, Dec. 20    Litho.    Perf. 12

| 5722 | A2742 | 50k multicolored | 1.75 | 1.00 |
|---|---|---|---|---|

Victory of Soviet athletes at the 1988 Summer Olympics, Seoul. Overprint on margin of No. 5722 specifies that Soviet athletes won 55 gold, 31 silver and 46 bronze medals.

**Souvenir Sheet**

## 1988, Dec. 30    Photo.    Perf. 12x11½

Multicolored and:

| 5740 | A2767 | 5k deep car (power) | .20 | .20 |
|---|---|---|---|---|
| 5741 | A2767 | 5k deep blue vio (industry) | .20 | .20 |
| 5742 | A2767 | 5k green (land) | .20 | .20 |
| | | Nos. 5740-5742 (3) | .60 | .60 |

**Inaugural Flight of the *Buran* Space Shuttle, Nov. 15 — A2768**

**Souvenir Sheet**

## 1988, Dec. 30    Perf. 11½x12

| 5743 | A2768 | 50k multicolored | 1.50 | 1.00 |
|---|---|---|---|---|

**Luna 1, 30th Anniv. — A2769**

## 1988, Dec. 30    Perf. 11½

| 5744 | A2769 | 15k multicolored | .50 | .30 |
|---|---|---|---|---|

**Jalmari Virtanen (1889-1939), Karelian Poet — A2770**

## 1989, Jan. 2    Photo.    Perf. 11½

| 5745 | A2770 | 5k olive brown | .25 | .20 |
|---|---|---|---|---|

**Council for Mutual Economic Assistance, 40th Anniv. A2771**

## 1989, Jan. 8

| 5746 | A2771 | 10k multicolored | .30 | .20 |
|---|---|---|---|---|

**Environmental Protection — A2772**

## 1989, Jan. 18    Litho.    Perf. 12½x12

| 5747 | A2772 | 5k Forest | .45 | .30 |
|---|---|---|---|---|
| 5748 | A2772 | 10k Arctic deer | .30 | .20 |
| 5749 | A2772 | 15k Stop desert encroachment | .95 | .70 |
| | | Nos. 5747-5749 (3) | | |

Nos. 5747-5749 printed se-tenant with inscribed labels picturing maps.

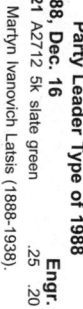

RUSSIA

## Jean Racine (1639-1699), French Dramatist A2789

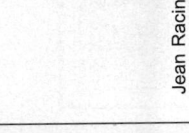

Photo. & Engr. Perf. 12x11½
1989, June 16 15k multicolored .35 .25
5777 A2789

## Europe, Our Common Home — A2790

Designs: 5k, Map of Europe, stylized bird. 10k, Crane, two men completing a bridge, globe. 15k, Stork's nest, globe.

1989, June 20 Photo. Perf. 11½
5778 A2790 5k multicolored .20 .20
5779 A2790 10k multicolored .35 .35
5780 A2790 15k multicolored .50 .35
Nos. 5778-5780 (3) 1.05 .75

## Mukhina, by Nesterov A2791

1989, June 25 Litho. Perf. 12x12½
5781 A2791 5k chalky blue .20 .20
Vera I. Mukhina (1889-1953), sculptor.

## 13th World Youth and Student Festival, Pyongyang A2792

1989, July 1 Litho. Perf. 12
5782 A2792 10k multicolored .35 .20

## Ducks A2793

1989, July 1
5783 A2793 5k *Tadorna tadorna* .20 .20
5784 A2793 15k *Anas crecca* .40 .25
5785 A2793 20k *Tadorna ferruginea* .50 .40
a. Min. sheet, 2 ea, 4 15k, 3 20k 4.25 3.00
Nos. 5783-5785 (3) 1.10 .85

## Souvenir Sheet

Launch of Interplanetary Probe Phobos — A2783
1989, Apr. 24 Perf. 11½x12
5768 A2783 50k multicolored 1.75 1.00

A2784 ... A2785
1989, May 5 Photo. Perf. 11½
5769 A2784 5k multicolored .25 .20
Hungarian Soviet Republic, 70th anniv.
1989, May 5 Photo. & Engr. Perf. 11½
5770 A2785 5k multicolored .25 .20
Volgograd, 400th anniv.

## Honeybees A2786

1989, May 18 Litho. Perf. 12
5771 A2786 6k Drone .20 .20
5772 A2786 10k Workers, flowers, man-made hive .20 .20
5773 A2786 20k Worker collecting pollen .45 .25
5774 A2786 35k Queen, drones, honeycomb .75 .50
Nos. 5771-5774 (4) 1.60 1.15
No. 5771 exists imperf.

## Photography, 150th Anniv. — A2787

1989, May 24 Photo. Perf. 11½
5775 A2787 5k multicolored .25 .20

## I.A. Kuratov (1839-1875), Author — A2788

1989, June 26 Litho. Perf. 12½x12
5776 A2788 5k dark golden brown .25 .20

## Souvenir Sheet

Labor Day, Cent. — A2778
1989, Mar. 25 Perf. 11½x12
5761 A2778 30k multicolored 1.00 .60

## Victory Banner, by P. Loginov and V. Pamfilov A2779

1989, Apr. 5 Litho. Perf. 12x12½
5762 A2779 5k multicolored .25 .20
World War II Victory Day.

## Cosmonauts' Day — A2780

Illustration reduced.
1989, Apr. 12 Photo. Perf. 11x11½
5763 A2780 15k Mir space station .45 .30

A2781
1989, Apr. 14 Perf. 11½
5764 A2781 10k multicolored .30 .20
Bering Bridge Soviet-American Expedition, Anadyr and Kotzebue.

## Type of 1988

Portraits and branches of the Lenin Central Museum: No. 5765, Kazan. No. 5766, Kuibyshev. No. 5767, Frunze.
1989, Apr. 14 Litho. Perf. 12
5765 A2727 5k rose brown & multi .20 .20
5766 A2727 5k olive gray & multi .20 .20
5767 A2727 5k deep brown & multi .20 .20
Nos. 5765-5767 (3) .60 .60
Lenin's 119th Birth Anniv.

## Samovars A2773

Samovars in the State Museum, Leningrad: 5k, Pear-shaped urn, late 18th cent. 10k, Barrel-shaped urn by Ivan Listisin, early 19th cent. 20k, "Kabachok" urn by the Sokolov Bros., Tula, c. 1830. 30k, Vase-shaped urn by the Nikolari Malikov Studio, Tula, c. 1840.

1989, Feb. 8 Photo. Perf. 11½
5750 A2773 5k multicolored .20 .20
5751 A2773 10k multicolored .25 .20
5752 A2773 20k multicolored .45 .30
5753 A2773 30k multicolored .65 .45
Nos. 5750-5753 (4) 1.55 1.15

## Modest Petrovich Mussorgsky (1839-1881), Composer — A2774

1989, Feb. 15 Litho. Perf. 12½x12
5754 A2774 10k dull vio & vio brn .30 .20

## P.E. Dybenko (1889-1938), Military Commander A2775

1989, Feb. 28 Engr. Perf. 12
5755 A2775 5k black .25 .20

## T.G. Shevchenko (1814-1861), Poet A2776

1989, Mar. 6 Litho. Perf. 11½
5756 A2776 5k pale grn, blk & brn .25 .20
Exists imperf. Value, $25.

## Cultivated Lilies — A2777

1989, Mar. 15 Perf. 12½x12
5757 A2777 5k Lilium speciosum .20 .20
5758 A2777 10k African queen .25 .20
5759 A2777 15k Eclat du soil .40 .55
5760 A2777 30k White tiger .80 .55
Nos. 5757-5760 (4) 1.65 1.20

## French Revolution, Bicent., A2794

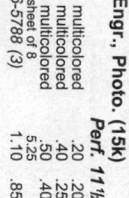

Designs: 5k, PHILEXFRANCE '89 emblem and Storming of the Bastille. 15k, Marat, Danton, Robespierre. 20k, "La Marseillaise," from the Arc de Triomphe carved by Francois Rude (1784-1855).

**1989, July 7    Photo. & Engr., Photo. (15k)    Perf. 11½**

| 5786 | A2794 | 5k multicolored | .20 | .20 |
|---|---|---|---|---|
| 5787 | A2794 | 15k multicolored | .40 | .25 |
| 5788 | A2794 | 20k multicolored | .50 | .40 |
| a. | | Miniature sheet of 8 | 5.25 | 1.10 |
| | | Nos. 5786-5788 (3) | | .85 |

A2795
A2795a
A2795b
A2795c
A2795d

### Folklore and Legends, A2795d

**1989, July 12    Litho.    Perf. 12x12½**

| 5789 | A2795 | 10k multicolored | .35 | .20 |
|---|---|---|---|---|
| 5790 | A2795a | 10k multicolored | .35 | .20 |
| 5791 | A2795b | 10k multicolored | .35 | .20 |
| 5792 | A2795c | 10k multicolored | .35 | .20 |
| 5793 | A2795d | 10k multicolored | .35 | .20 |
| | | Nos. 5789-5793 (5) | 1.75 | 1.00 |

Designs: No. 5789, Amiraniani, Georgian lore. No. 5790, Koroglu, Azerbaijan lore. No. 5791, Fir, Queen of the Grass-snakes, Lithuanian lore. No. 5792, Mioritsa, Moldavian lore. No. 5793, Lachplesis, Latvian lore.

Each printed with a se-tenant label. See types A2753-A2753d & #5890-5894.

### Tallinn Zoo, 50th Anniv. — A2796

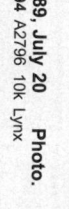

**1989, July 20    Photo.    Perf. 11½**

| 5794 | A2796 | 10k Lynx | .35 | .20 |
|---|---|---|---|---|

### Intl. Letter Writing Week — A2797

**1989, July 20    Litho.    Perf. 12**

| 5795 | A2797 | 5k multicolored | .25 | .20 |
|---|---|---|---|---|

Exists imperf.

### Pulkovskaya Observatory, 150th Anniv. — A2798

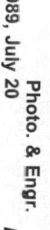

**1989, July 20    Photo. & Engr.    Perf. 11½**

| 5796 | A2798 | 10k multicolored | .35 | .20 |
|---|---|---|---|---|

### Souvenir Sheet

### Peter the Great and Battle Scene — A2799

**1989, July 27    Photo.    Perf. 11½x12**

| 5797 | A2799 | 50k dk bl & dk brn | 1.75 | 1.10 |
|---|---|---|---|---|

Battle of Hango, 275th anniv.

### City of Nikolaev, Bicent., A2800

**1989, Aug. 3    Photo.    Perf. 11½**

| 5798 | A2800 | 5k multicolored | .25 | .20 |
|---|---|---|---|---|

### 80th Birth Anniv. of Kwame Nkrumah, 1st Pres. of Ghana — A2801

**1989, Aug. 9**

| 5799 | A2801 | 10k multicolored | .35 | .20 |
|---|---|---|---|---|

### 6th Congress of the All-Union Philatelic Soc., Moscow, A2802

**1989, Aug. 9    Perf. 12**

| 5800 | A2802 | 10k bl, blk & pink | .35 | .20 |
|---|---|---|---|---|

Printed se-tenant with label picturing simulated stamps and congress emblem.

### James Fenimore Cooper (1789-1851), American Novelist, A2803

**1989, Aug. 19    Photo. & Engr.    Perf. 12x11½**

| 5801 | A2803 | 15k multicolored | .50 | .35 |
|---|---|---|---|---|

### Soviet Circus Performers — A2805

**1989, Aug. 22    Litho.    Perf. 12**

| 5802 | A2804 | 1k multicolored | .20 | .20 |
|---|---|---|---|---|
| 5803 | A2804 | 3k multicolored | .20 | .20 |
| 5804 | A2804 | 4k multicolored | .20 | .20 |
| 5805 | A2804 | 5k multicolored | .20 | .20 |
| 5806 | A2804 | 10k multicolored | .20 | .20 |
| | | Nos. 5802-5806 (5) | 1.00 | 1.00 |

### Souvenir Sheet

| 5807 | A2805 | 30k multicolored | 1.00 | .70 |
|---|---|---|---|---|

Nos. 5802-5806 exist imperf. Value, $25

Performers and scenes from their acts: 1k, V.L. Durov, clown and trainer. 3k, M.N. Rumyantsev, clown. 4k, V.I. Filatov, bear trainer. 5k, E.T. Kio, magician. 10k, V.E. Lazarenko, acrobat and clown. 30k, Moscow Circus, Tsvetnoi Boulevard.

### 5th World Boxing Championships, Moscow — A2806

**1989, Aug. 25    Photo.    Perf. 11½**

| 5808 | A2806 | 15k multicolored | .50 | .35 |
|---|---|---|---|---|

### Aleksandr Popov (1859-1905), Inventor of Radio in Russia — A2807

Design: Demonstration of the First Radio Receiver, 1895, by N. Sysoev.

**1989, Oct. 5    Litho.    Perf. 12x12½**

| 5809 | A2807 | 10k multicolored | .35 | .20 |
|---|---|---|---|---|

### Polish People's Republic, 45th Anniv., A2809

**1989, Oct. 7    Photo.    Perf. 11½**

| 5810 | A2808 | 5k multicolored | .20 | .20 |
|---|---|---|---|---|
| 5811 | A2809 | 5k multicolored | .20 | .20 |

German Democratic Republic, 40th anniv.

### Party Leader Type of 1988

**1989, Oct. 10    Engr.    Perf. 12**

| 5812 | A2712 | 5k black | .25 | .20 |
|---|---|---|---|---|

S.V. Kosior (1889-1939).

**1989, Oct. 10**

| 5813 | A2811 | 15k dark red brown | .25 | .25 |
|---|---|---|---|---|

Jawaharlal Nehru, 1st prime minister of independent India.

### Guardsmen of October, by M.M. Chepik — A2812

**1989, Oct. 14    Litho.    Perf. 12½x12**

| 5814 | A2812 | 5k multicolored | .25 | .20 |
|---|---|---|---|---|

October Revolution, 72nd anniv. Exists imperf. Value, $25.

### Kosta Khetagurov (1859-1906), Ossetic Poet — A2813

**1989, Oct. 14**

| 5815 | A2813 | 5k dark red brown | .25 | .20 |
|---|---|---|---|---|

Exists imperf.

A2814

A2815

**1989, Oct. 14 Photo. *Perf. 11½***

| | | | | |
|---|---|---|---|---|
| **5816** | A2814 5k buff, sepia & black | .25 | .20 |

Li Dazhao (1889-1927), communist party leader of China.

**1989, Oct. 20 Engr. *Perf. 12***

| | | | |
|---|---|---|---|
| **5817** | A2815 5k black | .25 | .20 |

Jan Karlovich Berzin (1889-1938), army intelligence leader.

Russian — A2816

Musical Instruments: No. 5819, Byelorussian. No. 5820, Ukrainian. No. 5821, Uzbek.

**Photo. & Engr.**

**1989, Oct. 20 *Perf. 12x11½***

**Denomination Color**

| | | | |
|---|---|---|---|
| **5818** | A2816 10k blue | .30 | .20 |
| **5819** | A2816 10k brown | .30 | .20 |
| **5820** | A2816 10k lemon | .30 | .20 |
| **5821** | A2816 10k blue green | .30 | .20 |
| | *Nos. 5818-5821 (4)* | 1.20 | .80 |

See Nos. 5929-5932, 6047-6049.

Scenes from Novels by James Fenimore Cooper A2817

Designs: No. 5822, *The Hunter,* (settlers, canoe). No. 5823, *Last of the Mohicans* (Indians, settlers). No. 5824, *The Pathfinder,* (couple near cliff). No. 5825, *The Pioneers* (women, wild animals). No. 5826, *The Prairie* (injured Indians, horse).

**1989, Nov. 17 Litho. *Perf. 12x12½***

| | | | |
|---|---|---|---|
| **5822** | A2817 20k multicolored | .60 | .40 |
| **5823** | A2817 20k multicolored | .60 | .40 |
| **5824** | A2817 20k multicolored | .60 | .40 |
| **5825** | A2817 20k multicolored | .60 | .40 |
| **5826** | A2817 20k multicolored | .60 | .40 |
| *a.* | Strip of 5, #5822-5826 | 3.00 | 2.00 |

Printed in a continuous design.

Monuments A2818

#5827, Pokrovsky Cathedral, St. Basil's, statue of K. Minin and D. Pozharsky, Moscow. #5828, Petropavlovsky Cathedral, statue of Peter the Great, Leningrad. #5829, Sofiisky Cathedral, Bogdan Chmielnicki monument, Kiev. #5830, Khodzha Akhmed Yasavi Mausoleum, Turkestan. #5831, Khazret-Khyzr Mosque, Samarkand.

**1989, Nov. 20 *Perf. 11½***

**Color of "Sky"**

| | | | |
|---|---|---|---|
| **5827** | A2818 15k tan | .50 | .30 |
| **5828** | A2818 15k gray green | .50 | .30 |
| **5829** | A2818 15k blue green | .50 | .30 |
| **5830** | A2818 15k violet blue | .50 | .30 |
| **5831** | A2818 15k bright blue | .50 | .30 |
| | *Nos. 5827-5831 (5)* | 2.50 | 1.50 |

New Year 1990 A2819

**1989, Nov. 22 *Perf. 12***

| | | | |
|---|---|---|---|
| **5832** | A2819 5k multicolored | .25 | .20 |

Space Achievements A2820

Designs: Nos. 5833, 5837a, Unmanned Soviet probe on the Moon. Nos. 5834, 5837b, American astronaut on Moon, 1969. Nos. 5835, 5837c, Soviet cosmonaut and American astronaut on Mars. Nos. 5836, 5837d, Mars, planetary body, diff.

**1989, Nov. 24**

| | | | |
|---|---|---|---|
| **5833** | A2820 25k multicolored | .75 | .55 |
| **5834** | A2820 25k multicolored | .75 | .55 |
| **5835** | A2820 25k multicolored | .75 | .55 |
| **5836** | A2820 25k multicolored | .75 | .55 |
| *a.* | Block of 4, #5833-5836 | 3.00 | 2.20 |

**Souvenir Sheet**

***Imperf***

| | | | |
|---|---|---|---|
| **5837** | Sheet of 4 | 3.00 | 2.20 |
| *a.-d.* | A2820 25k any single | .75 | .55 |

World Stamp Expo '89, Washington DC, Nov. 17-Dec. 3; 20th UPU Cong.

See US No. C126.

**Type of 1988**

**Dated 1988**

**1989, Dec. 25 Litho. *Perf. 12x12½***

| | | | |
|---|---|---|---|
| **5838** | A2765 1k dark brown | .20 | .20 |
| **5839** | A2765 3k dark blue green | .20 | .20 |
| **5840** | A2765 4k indigo | .20 | .20 |
| **5841** | A2765 5k red | .20 | .20 |
| **5842** | A2765 10k claret | .30 | .20 |
| **5843** | A2765 15k deep blue | .45 | .30 |
| **5844** | A2765 20k olive gray | .60 | .40 |
| **5845** | A2765 25k dark green | .75 | .50 |
| **5846** | A2765 30k dark blue | .90 | .60 |
| **5847** | A2765 35k dark red brown | 1.00 | .70 |
| **5848** | A2765 50k sapphire | 1.50 | 1.00 |
| **5849** | A2765 1r blue gray | 3.00 | 2.00 |
| | *Nos. 5838-5849 (12)* | 9.30 | 6.50 |

For surcharges see Uzbekistan #15, 22, 25-26, 61B, 61D, 61F.

**Admirals Type of 1987**

Miniature Sheet

Admirals & battle scenes: 5k, V.A. Kornilov (1806-54). 10k, V.I. Istomin (1809-55). 15k, G.I. Nevelskoi (1813-76). 20k, G.I. Butakov (1820-82). 30k, A.A. Popov (1821-98). 35k, Stepan O. Makarov (1849-1904).

**1989, Dec. 28 Engr. *Perf. 12½x12***

| | | | |
|---|---|---|---|
| **5850** | Sheet of 6 | 3.00 | 2.00 |
| *a.* | A2705 5k brown & Prus blue | .20 | .20 |
| *b.* | A2705 10k brown & Prus blue | .25 | .20 |
| *c.* | A2705 15k dark blue & Prus blue | .40 | .25 |
| *d.* | A2705 20k dark blue & Prus blue | .50 | .35 |
| *e.* | A2705 30k brown & Prus blue | .75 | .50 |
| *f.* | A2705 35k brown & Prus blue | .85 | .60 |

Global Ecology — A2821

10k, Flower dying, industrial waste entering the environment. 15k, Bird caught in industrial waste, Earth. 20k, Sea of chopped trees.

**1990, Jan. 5 Photo. *Perf. 11½***

| | | | |
|---|---|---|---|
| **5851** | A2821 10k multicolored | .35 | .20 |
| **5852** | A2821 15k multicolored | .50 | .35 |
| **5853** | A2821 20k multicolored | .65 | .45 |
| | *Nos. 5851-5853 (3)* | 1.50 | 1.00 |

Capitals of the Republics

A2822

A2822a

A2822b

A2822c

A2822d

A2822e

A2822f

A2822g

A2822h

A2822i

A2822j

A2822k

A2822l

A2822m

A2822n

**1990, Jan. 18 Litho. *Perf. 12x12½***

| | | | |
|---|---|---|---|
| **5854** | A2822 5k Moscow | .20 | .20 |
| **5855** | A2822a 5k Tallinn | .20 | .20 |
| **5856** | A2822b 5k Riga | .20 | .20 |
| **5857** | A2822c 5k Vilnius | .20 | .20 |
| **5858** | A2822d 5k Minsk | .20 | .20 |
| **5859** | A2822e 5k Kiev | .20 | .20 |
| **5860** | A2822f 5k Kishinev | .20 | .20 |
| **5861** | A2822g 5k Tbilisi | .20 | .20 |
| **5862** | A2822h 5k Yerevan | .20 | .20 |
| **5863** | A2822i 5k Baku | .20 | .20 |
| **5864** | A2822j 5k Alma-Ata | .20 | .20 |
| **5865** | A2822k 5k Tashkent | .20 | .20 |
| **5866** | A2822l 5k Frunze | .20 | .20 |
| **5867** | A2822m 5k Ashkhabad | .20 | .20 |
| **5868** | A2822n 5k Dushanbe | .20 | .20 |
| | *Nos. 5854-5868 (15)* | 3.00 | 3.00 |

A2823

A2824

**1990, Feb. 3 *Perf. 11½***

| | | | |
|---|---|---|---|
| **5869** | A2823 10k black & brown | .35 | .25 |

Ho Chi Minh (1890-1969).

**1990, Feb. 3 Photo.**

| | | | |
|---|---|---|---|
| **5870** | A2824 5k multicolored | .20 | .20 |

Vietnamese Communist Party, 60th anniv.

Owls A2825

***Perf. 12x12½, 12½x12***

**1990, Feb. 8 Litho.**

| | | | |
|---|---|---|---|
| **5871** | A2825 10k *Nyctea scandiaca* | .30 | .20 |
| **5872** | A2825 20k *Bubo bubo,* vert. | .60 | .40 |
| **5873** | A2825 55k *Asio otus* | 1.60 | 1.00 |
| | *Nos. 5871-5873 (3)* | 2.50 | 1.60 |

Penny Black, 150th Anniv. A2826

Emblems and various Penny Blacks: No. 5875, Position TP. No. 5876, Position TF. No. 5877, Position AH. No. 5878, Position VK. No. 5879, Position AE.

**1990, Feb. 15 Photo. *Perf. 11½***

| | | | |
|---|---|---|---|
| **5874** | A2826 10k shown | .35 | .20 |
| **5875** | A2826 20k gold & black | .65 | .45 |
| **5876** | A2826 20k gold & black | .65 | .45 |
| **5877** | A2826 35k multicolored | 1.10 | .75 |
| **5878** | A2826 35k multicolored | 1.10 | .75 |
| | *Nos. 5874-5878 (5)* | 3.85 | 2.60 |

**Souvenir Sheet**

***Perf. 12x11½***

| | | | |
|---|---|---|---|
| **5879** | A2826 1r dk green & blk | 3.25 | 2.25 |

Stamp World London '90 (35k).

No. 5879 contains one 37x26mm stamp.

ITU, 125th Anniv. A2827

**1990, Feb. 20 Photo. *Perf. 11½***

| | | | |
|---|---|---|---|
| **5880** | A2827 20k multicolored | .70 | .45 |

**1990, Mar. 28** Photo. Perf. 11½
5881 A2828 5k multicolored .20 .20

Labor Day
A2828

**1990, Mar. 28** Photo.
5882 A2829 5k multicolored .20 .20

Victory,
1945, by A.
Lysenko
A2829

End of World War II, 45th anniv.

**1990, Apr. 12** Litho. Perf. 12½x12½
5883 A2830 20k multicolored .60 .45

Mir Space
Station,
Cosmonaut
A2830

Cosmonauts' Day.

**1990, Apr. 14** Engr. Perf. 11½
5884 A2831 5k red brown .20 .20

Lenin, 120th Birth
Anniv. — A2831

LENINIANA '90 all-union philatelic exhibition.

**Lenin Birthday Type of 1988**

Portrait of Lenin and: No. 5885, Lenin
Memorial (birthplace), No. 5886, Lenin
Branch of the Central Lenin Museum, Baku.
No. 5887, Branch of the Central Lenin
Museum, Tashkent.

**1990, Apr. 14** Litho. Perf. 12
5885 A2727 5k dark car & multi .20 .20
5886 A2727 5k rose vio & multi .20 .20
5887 A2727 5k dark grn & multi .20 .20
  Nos. 5885-5887 (3) .60 .60

Lenin, 120th Birth Anniv.

**1990, Apr. 25** Engr. Perf. 12½x12
5888 A2832 15k black .45 .30

Tchaikovsky, Scene from
Iolanta — A2832

Tchaikovsky (1840-1893), composer.

---

**1990, May 22** Litho. Perf. 12½x12, 12½x12½
5889 A2833 10k blk & blk brn .30 .25

Kalmyk Legend
Dzhangar, 550th
Anniv. — A2833

**Folklore Type of 1989**

Designs: No. 5890, Manas, Kirghiz legend
(Warrior with saber leading battle). No. 5891,
Guragüli, Tadzhik legend (Armored warriors
and elephant). No. 5892, David Sasunsky,
Armenian legend (Men, arches), vert. No.
5893, Geroglu, Turkmen legend (Sleeping
woman, man with lute), vert. No. 5894, Kalevi-
poeg, Estonian legend (Man with boards),
vert. Nos. 5890-5894 printed se-tenant with
descriptive label.

**1990, May 22** Perf. 12½x12, 12½x12½
5890 A2795 10k multicolored .30 .20
5891 A2795 10k multicolored .30 .20
5892 A2795 10k multicolored .30 .20
5893 A2795 10k multicolored .30 .20
5894 A2795 10k multicolored .30 .20
  Nos. 5890-5894 (5) 1.50 1.00

**1990, May 25** Perf. 12½x12½
5895 A2834 5k multicolored .20 .20
5896 A2834 10k multicolored .35 .25
5897 A2834 15k multicolored .45 .30
5898 A2834 25k multicolored .80 .75
5899 A2834 35k multicolored 1.10 3.00
  a. Strip of 5, #5895-5899 1.00 2.00

World Cup Soccer Championships,
Italy 1990 — A2834

Various soccer players.

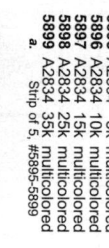

**1990, June 5** Litho. Perf. 11½
5900 A2835 15k multicolored .45 .30

Final agreement, European Conference on
Security and Cooperation, 15th anniv.

**1990, June 5**
5901 A2836 15k multicolored .20 .20

45th World
Championships,
Moscow — A2836

**1990, June 13** Litho. Perf. 12x12½
5902 A2837 5k Scientists on ice .20 .20
5903 A2837 60k Krill 1.50 1.00
  a. Souv. sheet of 2, #5902-5903 1.75

Cooperation
in Antarctic
Research
A2837

See Australia Nos. 1182-1183.

---

**1990, June 14** Litho. Perf. 11½
5904 A2838 10k multicolored .35 .25

Goodwill
Games
A2838

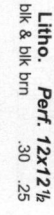

**1990, June 20** Litho. Perf. 12½x12
5905 A2839 50k multicolored 1.75 1.25

Battle of the Neva River, 750th
Anniv. — A2839

Souvenir Sheet

**1990, July 1** Litho. Perf. 12
5906 A2840 5k Anas
      platyrhynchos .20 .20
5907 A2840 15k Bucephala
      clangula .55 .35
5908 A2840 20k Netta rufina .75 .50
  Nos. 5906-5908 (3) 1.50 1.05

Duck Conservation — A2840

**1990, July 1** Perf. 12x12½
5909 A2841 5k Oboroshinsky
      geese .20 .20
5910 A2841 10k Adler rooster &
      hen .35 .25
5911 A2841 15k North Caucasian
      turkeys .55 .35
  Nos. 5909-5911 (3) 1.10 .80

Poultry
A2841

Spaso-Efrosinievsky Monastery,
Polotsk — A2842

Statue of Nicholas
Baratashvili and
Pantheon,
Mtasminda
A2843

Palace of
Shirvanshahs,
Baku
A2844

---

**1990, Aug. 1** Litho. Perf. 11½
5912 A2842 15k multicolored .40 .25
5913 A2843 15k multicolored .40 .25
5914 A2844 15k multicolored .40 .25
5915 A2845 15k multicolored .40 .25
5916 A2842 15k multicolored .40 .25
5917 A2842 15k multicolored .40 .25
5918 A2846 15k multicolored .40 .25
5919 A2842 15k multicolored .40 .25
  Nos. 5912-5919 (8) 3.20 2.00

Statue of Stefan
III the Great,
Kishinev — A2845

St. Nshan's
Church,
Akhpat — A2846

Historic Architecture: No. 5915, Cathedral,
Vilnius. No. 5917, St. Peter's Church, Riga.
No. 5919, Niguliste Church, Tallinn.

**1990, Aug. 15** Litho. Perf. 11½
5920 A2847 1k Sordes .20 .20
5921 A2847 3k Chalicotherium .20 .20
5922 A2847 5k Indricotherium .20 .20
5923 A2847 10k Saurolophus .30 .20
5924 A2847 10k Thyestes .60 .45
  Nos. 5920-5924 (5) 1.50 1.25

Prehistoric Animals — A2847

See Nos. 5968-5970.

**1990, Aug. 15**
5925 A2848 10k multicolored .35 .25
5926 A2848 10k multicolored .35 .25
  a. Pair, #5925-5926 .70 .50

Indian
Child's
Drawing of
the Kremlin
A2848

No. 5926, Russian child's drawing of India.

See India Nos. 1318-1319.

**1990, Sept. 12** Perf. 11½
5927 A2849 5k blue .20 .20

A2849

Letter Writing Week.

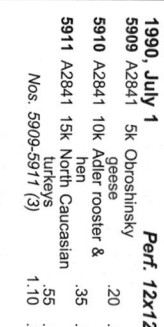

**1990, Sept. 12** Engr. Perf. 12x11½
5928 A2850 5k multicolored .20 .20

A2850

Traffic safety.

**Musical Instruments Type of 1989**

#5929, Kazakh. #5930, Georgian. #5931,
Azerbaijanian. #5932, Lithuanian.

RUSSIA

Designs: 10k, Bell tower near Kaliazin, Volga River region. 15k, Lake Baikal. 20k, Desert zone of former Aral Sea.

**1991, Feb. 5** **Litho.** **Perf. 11½**
5965 A2871 10k multicolored .30 .25
5966 A2871 15k multicolored .50 .35
5967 A2871 20k multicolored .65 .45
Nos. 5965-5967 (3) 1.45 1.05

Moslem Tower, Uzgen, Kirghizia A2872

Mukhammed Bashar Mausoleum, Tadzhikistan A2873

Talkhatan-baba Mosque, Turkmenistan A2874

**1991, Mar. 5**
5968 A2872 15k multicolored .20 .20
5969 A2873 15k multicolored .20 .20
5970 A2874 15k multicolored .60 .60
Nos. 5968-5970 (3)

Russian Settlements in America — A2875

Designs: 20k, G. I. Shelokhov (1747-1795), Alaska colonizer. 30k, A. A. Baranuv, (1746-1819), first governor of Russian America. 50k, I. A. Kuskov, founder of Fort Ross, California.

**1991, Mar. 14** **Perf. 12x11½**
5971 A2875 20k brt blue & black .45 .35
5972 A2875 30k olive brn & blk .75 .55
5973 A2875 50k red brn & black 1.25 .80
Nos. 5971-5973 (3) 2.45 1.70

Yuri A. Gagarin A2876

---

Marine Life A2866

**1991, Jan. 4** **Litho.** **Perf. 12**
5954 A2866 4k Rhizostoma pulmo .20 .20
5955 A2866 5k Anemonia sulcata .20 .20
5956 A2866 10k Squalus acanthias .30 .20
5957 A2866 15k Engraulis encrasicolus .50 .35
5958 A2866 20k Tursiops truncatus .65 .45
Nos. 5954-5958 (5) 1.85 1.40

Chernobyl Nuclear Disaster, 5th Anniv. A2867

**1991, Jan. 22** **Perf. 11½**
5959 A2867 15k multicolored .55 .40

Sorrento Coast with View of Capri, 1826, by S. F. Shchedrin (1791-1830) — A2000

Evening in the Ukraine, 1878, by A.I. Kuindzhi (1841-1910) — A2869

Paintings: No. 5961, New Rome, St. Angel's Castle, 1823, by Shchedrin. No. 5963, Birch Grove, 1879, by Kuindzhi.

**1991, Jan. 25** **Perf. 12½x12**
5960 A2868 10k multicolored .35 .25
5961 A2868 10k multicolored .35 .25
a. Pair, #5960-5961+label .70 .50
5962 A2869 10k multicolored .35 .25
5963 A2869 10k multicolored .35 .25
a. Pair, #5962-5963+label .70 .50
Nos. 5960-5963 (4) 1.40 1.00

Paul Keres (1916-1975), Chess Grandmaster — A2870

**1991, Jan. 7** **Litho.** **Perf. 11½**
5964 A2870 15k dark brown .55 .40

Environmental Protection — A2871

---

Submarines — A2861

**1990, Nov. 14** **Perf. 12**
5941 A2861 5k Sever-2 .20 .20
5942 A2861 10k Tinro-2 .30 .30
5943 A2861 15k Argus .50 .50
5944 A2861 25k Paisis .80 .55
5945 A2861 35k Mir 1.10 .75
Nos. 5941-5945 (5) 2.90 2.00

A2862

A2863

Armenia-Mother Monument by E. Kochar.

**1990, Nov. 27** **Litho.** **Perf. 11½**
5946 A2862 10k multicolored .35 .25

Armenia '90 Philatelic Exhibition.

**1990, Nov. 29** **Photo.** **Perf. 11½**

Soviet Agents: #5947, Rudolf I. Abel (1903-71). #5948, Kim Philby (1912-88). #5949, Konon T. Molody (1922-70). #5950, S.A. Vaupshasov (1899-1976). #5951, I.D. Kudrya (1912-42).

5947 A2863 5k black & brown .20 .20
5948 A2863 5k black & bluish blk .20 .20
5949 A2863 5k black & yel brown .20 .20
5950 A2863 5k black & yel green .20 .20
5951 A2863 5k black & brown .20 .20
Nos. 5947-5951 (5) 1.00 1.00

Joint Soviet-Japanese Space Flight — A2864

**1990, Dec. 2** **Litho.** **Perf. 12**
5952 A2864 20k multicolored .70 .50

Happy New Year — A2865

Illustration reduced.

**1990, Dec. 3** **Perf. 11½**
5953 A2865 5k multicolored .20 .20
b. Miniature sheet of 8

Charter for a New Europe — A2865a

**1990, Dec. 31** **Litho.** **Perf. 11½**
5953A A2865a 30k multicolored, Globe, Eiffel Tower 1.10 .80

---

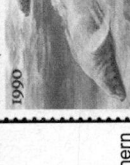

**1990, Sept. 20** **Photo. & Engr.**
**Denomination Color** **Perf. 12x11½**
5929 A2816 10k brown .35 .25
5930 A2816 10k green .35 .25
5931 A2816 10k orange .35 .25
5932 A2816 10k blue 1.40 1.00
Nos. 5929-5932 (4)

Killer Whales A2855

Northern Sea Lions A2856

Sea Otter A2857

Common Dolphin A2858

See US Nos. 2508-2511.

**1990, Oct. 3** **Litho.** **Perf. 12x11½**
5933 A2855 25k multicolored .80 .55
5934 A2856 25k multicolored .80 .55
5935 A2857 25k multicolored .80 .55
5936 A2858 25k multicolored .80 .55
a. Block of 4, #5933-5936 3.25 2.25

October Revolution, 73rd Anniv. — A2859

Design: Lenin Among the Delegates to the 2nd Congress of Soviets, by S.V. Gerasimov.

**1990, Oct. 10** **Litho.** **Perf. 12x12½**
5937 A2859 5k multicolored .20 .20

Nobel Laureates in Literature — A2860

**1990, Oct. 22** **Perf. 12**
#5938, Ivan A. Bunin (1870-1953). #5939, Boris Pasternak (1890-1960). #5940, Mikhail A. Sholokov (1905-1984).
5938 A2860 15k brown olive .40 .25
5939 A2860 15k bluish black .40 .25
5940 A2860 15k black 1.20 .75
Nos. 5938-5940 (3)

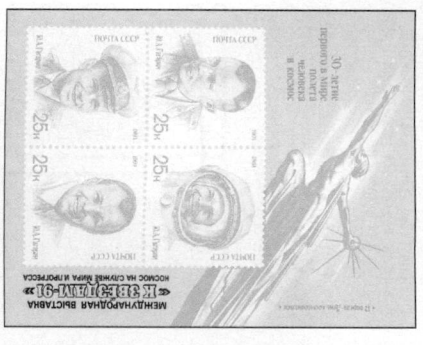

**No. 5977c Inscription**

**1991, Apr. 6** Perf. 11½x12
5974 A2876 25k Pilot .90 .70
5975 A2876 25k Cosmonaut .90 .70
5976 A2876 25k Pilot, wearing
hat .90 .70
5977 A2876 25k As civilian .90 .70
a. Block of 4, #5974-5977. 3.60 2.80
b. Sheet of 4, imperf. 3.60 2.80
c. As "b," inscribed
Sheet 2 each, #5974-5977,
Perf. 12x11½ 7.20 5.50
d. Perf. 12x11½ 3.60 2.80

#5977b-5977c have simulated perforations.

#5977b-5977c have simulated perforations.

**1991, Apr. 10** Perf. 12
5978 A2877 5k multicolored .25 .20

World War II Victory Day.

**May 1945**
by A. and
S. Tkachev
A2877

**1991, Apr. 15** Perf. 11½
5979 A2878 10k multicolored .25 .20

Asia and Pacific
Transport Network,
10th
Anniv. — A2878

**Type of 1988**
**Dated 1991**

Designs: 2k. Early ship, train, and carriage.
7k. Airplane, helicopter, ocean liner, cable car,
van. 12k. Space shuttle. 13k. Space station.

**1991, Apr. 15   Litho.** Perf. 12x12½
5984 A2765 2k orange brown .25 .20
a. Imperf .25 .20
5985 A2765 7k bright blue .25 .20
b. As "a," #5974-5977, im- .25 .20
5986 A2765 12k lilac rose .45 .35
5987 A2765 13k deep violet .50 .35
Nos. 5984-5987 (4) 1.40 1.05

For surcharges see Tadjikistan #10-11,
Uzbekistan #18, 61C.

Lenin,
121st Birth
Anniv.
A2879

**1991, Apr. 22   Litho.** Perf. 12
5992 A2879 5k multicolored .20 .20

Painting: Lenin working on "Materialism and
Empirical Criticism" by P.P. Belousov.

---

**1991, Apr. 23** Perf. 12½x12
5993 A2880 15k brown .50 .40

Sergei Prokofiev (1891-1953),
Composer — A2880

**1991, May 7** Perf. 12
5994 A2881 3k Cypripedium
calceolus .20 .20
5995 A2881 5k Orchis purpurea .20 .20
5996 A2881 10k Ophrys apifera .25 .20
5997 A2881 20k Calypso bulbosa .45 .35
5998 A2881 25k Epipactis palustris .60 .40
Nos. 5994-5998 (5) 1.70 1.35

Orchids — A2881

**1991, May 14**
Nobel Prize Winners: #5999, Ivan P. Pavlov
(1849-1936), 1904, Physiology; #6000, Ilya
Metchnikoff (1845-1916), 1908, Physiology,
Peace.

5999 A2882 15k black .40 .30
6000 A2882 15k black .40 .30
6001 A2882 15k blue black .40 .30
#6001, Andrei D. Sakharov, (1921-89), 1975,
Peace.
Nos. 5999-6001 (3) 1.20 .90

**1991, May 18** Perf. 12
6002 A2883 1r multicolored 3.00 2.25

William Saroyan (1908-1981),
American Writer — A2883

**1991, May 22** Perf. 11½
6003 A2884 20k multicolored .70 .50

See US No. 2538.

Russia-Great Britain Joint Space
Mission — A2884

Designs: 10k. Miniature from "Ostomirov
Gospel," by Sts. Cyril & Methodius, 1056-
1057. 15k. "Russian Truth," manuscript, 11th-
13th century by Jaroslav Mudrin, 20k. Sergei
Radonezhski by Troitse Sergeiev Lavra, 1424.

Cultural
Heritage
A2885

---

25k. Trinity, icon by Andrei Rublev, c. 1411.
30k. Oxyura leucocephala.
by Ivan Feodorov and Petr Mstislavetz, 1564.

**1991, June 20   Litho.** Perf. 12x12½
6004 A2885 15k multicolored .30 .30
6005 A2885 15k multicolored .45 .35
6006 A2885 20k multicolored .65 .50
6007 A2885 25k multicolored .80 .80
6008 A2885 30k multicolored 1.00 .80
a. Strip of #6004-6008 3.25 2.50

Designs: 5k. Anas acuta. 15k. Aythya
marila. 20k. Oxyura leucocephala.

**1991, July 1** Perf. 12
6009 A2886 5k multicolored .20 .20
6010 A2886 15k multicolored .45 .35
6011 A2886 20k multicolored .60 .45
a. Min. sheet of 9, 2 #6010, 4
#6011 3.25 3.25
Nos. 6009-6011 (3) 1.25 1.00

Ducks
A2886

**1991, July 1**
Designs: 1k. Albatross, 1910, vert. 3k. GA-
42, 1987, vert. 4k. Norge, 1923, 5k. Victory,
1944. 20k. Graf Zeppelin, 1928.

6012 A2887 1k multicolored .20 .20
6013 A2887 3k multicolored .20 .20
6014 A2887 4k multicolored .20 .20
6015 A2887 5k multicolored .20 .20
6016 A2887 20k multicolored .20 .20
a. Miniature sheet of 8 1.00 1.00
Nos. 6012-6076 (5)

Airships
A2887

**Types of 1984**

**1991-92   Litho.** Perf. 12½x12
6016B A2529 2r Ship, Arctic map 1.00 .45
c. Imperf .40 .30
6017 A2529 3r Child & globe .60 .60
6017A A2529 5r Palm frond and
globe 2.50 1.25
Issued: 3r, 6/25; 5r, 11/10; No. 6016B,
8/22/91; No. 6016Bc, 4/20/92. 9.00 4.20

Conf. on Security
and Cooperation in
Europe — A2888

**1991, July 1** Photo. Perf. 11½
6018 A2888 10k multicolored .25 .20

Bering & Chirikov's Voyage to Alaska,
250th Anniv. — A2889

Design: No. 6020. Sailing ship, map.

**1991, July 27** Perf. 12x11½
6019 A2889 30k multicolored .40 .25
6020 A2889 30k multicolored .40 .25

---

**1991, Aug. 1   Litho.** Perf. 12½x11½
6021 A2890 30k multicolored .40 .25

Ukrainian declaration of sovereignty.

A2890

**1991, Sept. 4   Litho.** Perf. 12x12½
6023 A2892 10k Canoeing .20 .20
a. Miniature sheet of 8
6024 A2892 20k Running .25 .20
a. Miniature sheet of 8
6025 A2892 30k Soccer .40 .25
a. Miniature sheet of 8
Nos. 6023-6025 (3) .85 .65

1992
Summer
Olympic
Games,
Barcelona
A2892

A2891

**1991, Aug. 1** Perf. 12
6022 A2891 7k brown .40 .25

Letter Writing Week.

Victims of Aug.
1991 Failed
Coup — A2893

**Citizens Protecting Russian "White
House" — A2893a**

**1991, Oct. 11   Litho.** Perf. 11½
6026 A2893 7k Vladimir Usov,
b. 1954 .20 .20
6027 A2893 7k Illya Krichev-
sky, b. 1963 .20 .20
6028 A2893 7k Dmitry Komar,
b. 1968 .20 .20
Nos. 6026-6028 (3) .60 .60
6029 A2893a 50k multicolored .75 .35

Souvenir Sheet

USSR-Austria Joint Space
Mission — A2894

**1991, Oct. 2   Litho.** Perf. 11½
6030 A2894 20k multicolored .25 .20

RUSSIA

## Souvenir Sheet

Battle on the Ice, 750th Anniv. — A2901

**1992, Feb. 20** **Litho.** **Perf. 12½x12**
6059 A2901 50k multicolored .75 .75

A2902

Designs: 10k, Golden Portal, Vladimir. 15k, Kremlin, Pskov. 20k, Georgy the Victor. 25k, 55k, Triumph Gate, Moscow. 30k, "Millennium of Russia," by M.O. Mikeshin, Novgorod. 50k, St. George Slaying the Dragon. 60k, Minin-Posharsky Monument, Moscow. 80k, "Millenium of Russia," by M.O. Mikeshin, Novgorod. 1r, Church, Kizki. 1.50r, Monument to Peter the Great, St. Petersburg. 2r, St. Basil's Cathedral, Moscow. 3r, Tretyakov Gallery, Moscow. 5r, Morosov House, Moscow. 10r, St. Isaac's Cathedral, St. Petersburg. 25r, Monument to Yuri Dolgoruky, Moscow. 100r, Kremlin, Moscow.

**Perf. 12½x12, 11½x12 (15k, 25k, 3r) Litho.**

**1992**
| | | | | |
|---|---|---|---|---|
| 6060 | A2902 | 10k salmon | .20 | .20 |
| 6060A | A2902 | 15k dark brn | .20 | .20 |
| 6061 | A2902 | 20k red | .20 | .20 |
| 6062 | A2902 | 25k red brown | .20 | .20 |
| 6063 | A2902 | 30k black | .20 | .20 |
| 6064 | A2902 | 50k dark blue | .20 | .20 |
| 6065 | A2902 | 55k dark bl grm | .20 | .20 |
| 6066 | A2902 | 60k blue green | .20 | .20 |
| 6066A | A2902 | 80k lake | .20 | .20 |
| 6067 | A2902 | 1r yel brown | .25 | .25 |
| 6067A | A2902 | 1.50r olive | .25 | .25 |
| 6068 | A2902 | 2r blue | .70 | .70 |
| 6068A | A2902 | 3r red | .20 | .20 |
| 6069 | A2902 | 5r dark brn | .30 | .25 |
| 6070 | A2902 | 10r bright blue | .35 | .35 |
| 6071 | A2902 | 25r dark red | 1.00 | .50 |
| 6071A | A2902 | 100r brt olive | 1.00 | 1.00 |
| | | Nos. 6060-6071A (17) | 6.30 | 4.60 |

Issued: 20k, 30k, 2/26; 10k, 60k, 2r, 4/20; 25r, 5/25; 10r, 100r, May; 1r, 1.50r, 5r, 6/25; 55k, 8/11; 50k, 80k, 8/18; 15k, 25k, 3r, 9/10.
See Nos. 6109-6124.

Victory by N. N. Baskakov
A2903

**1992, Mar. 5** **Perf. 12x12½**
6072 A2903 5k multicolored .20 .20
End of World War II, 47th anniv.

Prioksko-Terrasny Nature Reserve — A2904

**1992, Mar. 12** **Perf. 12**
6073 A2904 50k multicolored .20 .20

---

A2896

**1991, Oct. 29** **Litho.** **Perf. 11½**
6046 A2896 7k multicolored .25 .20
Election of Boris Yeltsin, 1st president of Russian Republic, June 12, 1991.

## Musical Instruments Type of 1989

Musical Instruments: No. 6048, Moldavia. No. 6049, Latvia. No. 6050, Kirgiz.

**1991, Nov. 19** **Photo. & Engr.**
**Denomination Color**
| | | | | |
|---|---|---|---|---|
| 6047 | A2816 | 10k red | .20 | .20 |
| 6048 | A2816 | 10k brt greenish bl | .20 | .20 |
| 6049 | A2816 | 10k red lilac | .60 | .60 |
| | | Nos. 6047-6049 (3) | | |

New Year 1992
A2897

**1991, Dec. 8** **Litho.** **Perf. 12x12½**
6050 A2897 7k multicolored .25 .20

A2900

В.Н.ТАТИЩЕВ
A2099

Russian Historians: #6052, V. N. Tatischev (1686-1750). #6053, N. M. Karamzin (1766-1826). #6054, S. M. Suluviev (1820-70). #6055, Vasili O. Klyuchevsky (1841-1911).

**1991, Dec. 12** **Photo. & Engr.**
| | | | | |
|---|---|---|---|---|
| 6052 | A2099 | 10k multicolored | .20 | .20 |
| 6053 | A2099 | 10k multicolored | .20 | .20 |
| 6054 | A2099 | 10k multicolored | .20 | .20 |
| 6055 | A2099 | 10k multicolored | .80 | .80 |
| | | Nos. 6052-6055 (4) | | |

With the breakup of the Soviet Union on Dec. 26, 1991, eleven former Soviet republics established the Commonwealth of Independent States. Stamps inscribed "Rossija" are issued by the Russian Republic.

**1992, Jan. 10** **Litho.** **Perf. 11½x12**
6056 A2900 14k Cross-country skiing, ski jumping .20 .20
**a.** 6057 A2900 1r Freestyle skiing .25 .25
Miniature sheet of 8
6058 A2900 2r Bobsleds .55 .25
**a.** Miniature sheet of 8 1.00 .65
Nos. 6056-6058 (3)
1992 Winter Olympics, Albertville.

---

## Folk Holidays

Ascension, Armenia
A2895

New Year, Azerbaijan
A2895a

Ivan Kupala Day, Byelorussia
A2895b

New Year, Estonia
A2895c

Biжkauia, Georgia
A2895d

Kazakhstan — A2895e

Kys Kumai, Kirgizia — A2895f

Ivan Kupala Day, Latvia — A2895g

Palm Sunday, Lithuania
A2895h

Plugushorul, Moldavia
A2895i

Shrovetide, Russia — A2895j

New Year, Tadzhikistan A2895k

Spring Tulips, Uzbekistan A2895n

Harvest, Turkmenistan — A2895l

Christmas, Ukraine — A2895m

**Perf. 12x12½, 12½x12** **Litho.**
**1991, Oct. 4**
| | | | | |
|---|---|---|---|---|
| 6031 | A2895 | 15k multicolored | .20 | .20 |
| 6032 | A2895a | 15k multicolored | .20 | .20 |
| 6033 | A2895b | 15k multicolored | .20 | .20 |
| 6034 | A2895c | 15k multicolored | .20 | .20 |
| 6035 | A2895d | 15k multicolored | .20 | .20 |
| 6036 | A2895e | 15k multicolored | .20 | .20 |
| 6037 | A2895f | 15k multicolored | .20 | .20 |
| 6038 | A2895g | 15k multicolored | .20 | .20 |
| 6039 | A2895h | 15k multicolored | .20 | .20 |
| 6040 | A2895i | 15k multicolored | .20 | .20 |
| 6041 | A2895j | 15k multicolored | .20 | .20 |
| 6042 | A2895k | 15k multicolored | .20 | .20 |
| 6043 | A2895l | 15k multicolored | .20 | .20 |
| 6044 | A2895m | 15k multicolored | .20 | .20 |
| 6045 | A2895n | 15k multicolored | .20 | .20 |
| | | Min. sheet, 2 each #6031-6045 | 11.25 | |
| **a.** | | | 3.00 | 3.00 |
| | | Nos. 6031-6045 (15) | | |

## 1992, Mar. 17
6074 A2905 5r multicolored .40 .30

**Russia-Germany Joint Space Mission — A2905**

**Souvenir Sheet**

## 1992, Mar. 18    Perf. 12x11½
6075 A2906 3r Ship, Columbus .90 .90

**Discovery of America, 500th Anniv. — A2906**

**Characters from Children's Books — A2907**

## 1992, Apr. 22   Litho.   Perf. 12
6076 A2907 25k Pinocchio .20 .20
6077 A2907 30k Cipollino .20 .20
6078 A2907 35k Dunno .20 .20
6079 A2907 50k Karlson .80 .80
   Nos. 6076-6079 (4)

Designs: No. 6081, Astronaut, Russian space station and space shuttle. No. 6082, Sputnik, Vostok, Apollo Command and Lunar modules. No. 6083, Soyuz, Mercury and Gemini spacecraft.

**Space Accomplishments — A2908**

## 1992, May 29   Litho.   Perf. 11½x12
6080 A2908 25r multicolored .50 .35
6081 A2908 25r multicolored .50 .35
6082 A2908 25r multicolored .50 .35
6083 A2908 25r multicolored .50 .35
   a. Block of 4, #6080-6083 2.00 1.50

See US Nos. 2631-2634.

**1992 Summer Olympics, Barcelona A2909**

## 1992, June 5   Perf. 11½x12, 12x11½   Photo.
6084 A2909 1r Team handball, vert. .20 .20
6085 A2909 2r Fencing .85 .65
   a. Miniature sheet of 8 .25 .25
6086 A2909 3r Judo 1.75 1.40
   a. Miniature sheet of 8 .40 .25
   Nos. 6084-6086 (3) .85 .65

---

Designs: 55r, L. A. Zagoskin, Alaska-Yukon. 70r, N. N. Miklucho-Maklai, New Guinea. 1r, G. I. Langsdorf, Brazil.

**Explorers — A2910**

## 1992, June 23   Litho.   Perf. 12x11½
6087 A2910 55k multicolored .20 .20
6088 A2910 70k multicolored .20 .20
6089 A2910 1r multicolored .60 .60
   Nos. 6087-6089 (3)

**Ducks A2911**

## 1992, July 1   Litho.   Perf. 12
6090 A2911 1r Anas querquedula .20 .20
6091 A2911 2r Aythya ferina .20 .20
6092 A2911 3r Anas falcata .20 .20
   a. Min. sheet of 9, 3 #6090, 4 #6091, 2 #6092
   Nos. 6090-6092 (3)

**The Saviour, by Andrei Rublev A2912**

## 1992, July 3   Perf. 12x12½
6093 A2912 1r multicolored .20 .20
   a. Miniature sheet of 8 1.40 1.25

**The Taj Mahal Mausoleum in Agra, by Vasili Vereshchagin (1842-1904) — A2913**

Design: No. 6095, Let Me Approach (detail), by Vereshchagin.

## 1992, July 3   Perf. 12½x12
6094 A2913 1.50r multicolored .25 .20
6095 A2913 1.50r multicolored .50 .25
   Pair #6094-6095 + label

**Cathedral of the Assumption, Moscow A2914**

**Cathedral of the Annunciation, Moscow A2915**

No. 6098, Archangel Cathedral, Moscow.

## 1992, Sept. 3   Litho.   Perf. 11½
6096 A2914 1r multicolored .20 .20
   a. Miniature sheet of 9 1.10
6097 A2915 1r multicolored .20 .20
   a. Miniature sheet of 9 1.10
6098 A2919 1r multicolored .20 .20
   a. Miniature sheet of 9 1.10
   Nos. 6096-6098 (3) .60 .60

---

**The Nutcracker, by Tchaikovsky, Cent. — A2916**

Designs: No. 6099, Nutcrackers, one holding rifle. No. 6100, Nutcrackers, diff. No. 6101, Pas de deux before Christmas tree. No. 6102, Ballet scene.

## 1992, Nov. 4   Litho.   Perf. 12½x12
6099 A2916 10r multicolored .35 .25
6100 A2916 10r multicolored .35 .25
6101 A2916 25r multicolored .70 .50
6102 A2916 25r multicolored .70 .50
   a. Block of 4, #6099-6102 2.10 1.75

**Icons**

A2917   A2919

A2920   A2918

Christmas: No. 6103, Joachim and Anna, 16th cent. No. 6104, Madonna and Child, 14th cent. No. 6105, Archangel Gabriel, 12th cent. No. 6106, St. Nicholas, 16th cent.

## 1992, Nov. 27   Perf. 11½
6103 A2917 10r multicolored .45 .35
6104 A2918 10r multicolored .45 .35
6105 A2919 10r multicolored .45 .35
6106 A2920 10r multicolored .45 .35
   a. Block of 4, #6103-6106 1.90 1.75

See Sweden Nos. 1979-1982.

**New Year 1993 A2921**

## 1992, Dec. 2   Litho.   Perf. 12x12½
6107 A2921 50k multicolored .20 .20
   a. Miniature sheet of 9 1.50

**Discovery of America, 500th Anniv. — A2922**

## 1992, Dec. 29   Perf. 11½x12
6108 A2922 15r Flags, sculpture .60 .40

---

**Monuments Type of 1992**

Designs: 4r, Church, Kizki. 6r, Monument to Peter the Great, St. Petersburg. 15r, 45r, The Horsebreaker, St. Petersburg. 50r, Kremlin, Rostov. 75r, Monument to Yuri Dolgoruky, Moscow. 150r, Golden Gate of Vladimir. 250r, Church, Bogolubova. 300r, Monument of Minin and Pozharsky, Moscow. 500r, Lomonosov University, Moscow. 750r, State Library, Moscow. 1000r, Fortress of St. Peter and St. Paul, St. Petersburg. 1500r, Pushkin Museum, Moscow. 2500r, Admiralty, St. Petersburg. 5000r, Bolshoi Theater, Moscow.

## 1992-95
**Litho., Photo. (50r, 250r, 500r)**
**Perf. 12½x12, 12x11½ (1000r)**

6109 A2902 4r red brown .20 .20
6110 A2902 6r gray blue .20 .20
6111 A2902 15r brown .25 .20
   a. Photo.
6112 A2902 45r slate .90 .45
6113 A2902 50r purple .25 .20
6114 A2902 75r red brown 1.75 .70
6115 A2902 150r blue .30 .25
6116 A2902 250r green .45 .30
6117 A2902 250r red brown .45 .45
6118 A2902 300r violet .60 .60
6119 A2902 500r violet .60 .45
6120 A2902 750r olive grn .35 .35
6121 A2902 1000r slate .70 .50
6122 A2902 1500r green .90 .60
6123 A2902 2500r olive brn 1.50 1.00
     A2902 5000r blue grn 3.00 2.00
   Nos. 6109-6123 (15) 12.35 8.00

Values reflect cost as of date of issue. Because of inflation during period of use, lower denominations were later sold for much higher prices.

Issued: 12/25/92; #6109-6110, 6/4/93; #6111a, 6113, 6116, 6114, 6112, 6115, 1/25/93: 150r, 300r. 12/30/93: 1000r, 1/27/95; 750r, 1500r, 2500r, 5000r, 2/21/95. For surcharge see #6529.

**Marius Petipa (1818-1910), Choreographer — A2923**

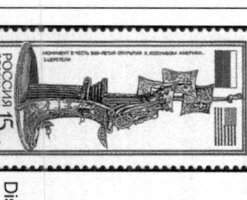

Ballets: No. 6126, Paquita (1847). No. 6127, Sleeping Beauty (1890). No. 6128, Swan Lake (1895). No. 6129, Raymonda (1898).

## 1993, Jan. 14   Litho.   Perf. 12½x12
6126 A2923 25r multicolored .35 .25
6127 A2923 25r multicolored .35 .25
6128 A2923 25r multicolored .35 .25
6129 A2923 25r multicolored .35 .25
   a. Block of 4, #6126-6129 1.75 1.50

A2924   A2925

Characters from Children's Books: a, 2r, Scrub and Rub. b, 3r, Big Cockroach. c, 10r, The Buzzer Fly. d, 15r, Doctor Doolittle. e, 25r, Barmalei.

## 1993, Feb. 25   Litho.   Perf. 12½x12
6130 A2924 Strip of 5, #a.-e. 1.25 1.00

## 1993, Mar. 18   Photo.   Perf. 11½x12
6131 A2925 10r Vyborg Castle .25 .20

City of Vyborg, 700th anniv.
No. 6130 printed in continuous design.

**Battle of Kursk, 50th Anniv. A2926**

## 1993, Mar. 25   Perf. 12x12½
6132 A2926 10r multicolored .25 .20

Victory Day.

## New Year 1994 — A2941

1993, Dec. 2    Photo.    Perf. 11½
6182 A2941 25r multicolored    .20   .20
a.   Sheet of 8    .90

Koala — A2942

A2942    Wildlife — A2943

1993, Nov. 25    Photo.    Perf. 11½x12
6183 A2942 90r gray, blk & red    .20   .20
Prevention of AIDS.

1993, Dec. 30    Litho.    Perf. 12½x12
6184 A2943 250r Phascolarctos cinereus    .35   .35
6185 A2943 250r Monachus schauinslandi    .35   .35
6186 A2943 250r Haliaeetus leucocephalus    .35   .35
6187 A2943 250r Elephas maximus    .35   .35
6188 A2943 250r Grus vipio    .35   .35
6189 A2943 250r Ailuropoda melanoleuca    .35   .35
6190 A2943 250r Phocoenoides dalli    .35   .35
6191 A2943 250r Lophiohlius robustus    .35   .35
a.   Min. sheet of 8, #6184-6191    3.50   3.50
Nos. 6184-6191 (8)    2.00   2.00

### Nikolai Rimsky-Korsakov (1844-1908)
### Scene from "Sariko" — A2944

Scenes from operas: No. 6193, "Golden Cockerel," 1907. No. 6194, "The Czar's Bride," 1898. No. 6195, "The Snow Maiden," 1881.

1994, Jan. 20    Litho.    Perf. 12½x12
6192 A2944 250r multicolored    .35   .35
6193 A2944 250r multicolored    .35   .35
6194 A2944 250r multicolored    .35   .35
6195 A2944 250r multicolored    .35   .35
a.   Block of 4, #6192-6195    1.40   1.25

### Flower Type of 1993

Designs: 50r, Epiphyllum peacockii. No. 6197, Mammillaria swinglei. No. 6198, Lophophora williamsii. No. 6199, Opuntia basilaris. No. 6200, Selenicereus grandiflorus.

1994, Feb. 25    Litho.    Perf. 12½x12
6196 A2927 50r multicolored    .20   .20
6197 A2927 50r multicolored    .25   .25
6198 A2927 100r multicolored    .25   .25
6199 A2927 250r multicolored    .25   .25
6200 A2927 250r multicolored    .25   .25
a.   Block of 4, #6196-6200 (5)    1.40   1.10

### Cathedral of St. Peter, York, Great Britain — A2945

---

### Goznak (Bank Note Printer and Mint), 175th Anniv. A2936

1993, Sept. 2    Litho.    Perf. 12
6168 A2936 100r multicolored    .35   .25

### Shipbuilders — A2937

#6169, Peter the Great (1672-1725), Goto Predestinatsia. #6170, K.A. Shilder (1786-1854), first all-metal submarine. #6171, I.A. Amosov (1800-78), screw steamship Archimedes. #6172, I.G. Bubnov (1872-1919), submarine Bars. #6173, B.M. Malinin (1889-1949), submarine Dekabrist. #6174, A.I. Maslov (1894-1968), cruiser Kirov.

1993, Sept. 7
6169 A2937 100r multicolored    .20   .20
6170 A2937 100r multicolored    .20   .20
6171 A2937 100r multicolored    .20   .20
6172 A2937 100r multicolored    .20   .20
6173 A2937 100r multicolored    .20   .20
6174 A2937 100r multicolored    .20   .20
a.   Block of 6, #6169-6174    1.25   1.00

A2938

### Moscow Kremlin A2939

#6175, Granovitaya Chamber (1487-91). #6176, Church of Rizpolozheniye (1484-88). #6177, Teremnoi Palace (1635-36).

1993, Oct. 28    Litho.    Perf. 12
6175 A2938 100r multicolored    .20   .20
6176 A2939 100r multicolored    .60   .60
6177 A2939 100r multicolored    .60   .60
Nos. 6175-6177 (3)

### Panthera Tigris A2940

Designs: 100r, Adult in woods. 250r, Two cubs. 500r, Adult in snow.

1993, Nov. 25    Litho.    Perf. 12½x12
6178 A2940 100r multicolored    .25   .25
6179 A2940 100r multicolored    .25   .25
6180 A2940 250r multicolored    .55   .55
6181 A2940 500r multicolored    .80   .80
a.   Block of 4, #6178-6181    1.90   1.45
b.   Miniature sheet, 2 #6181a    4.00
World Wildlife Fund.

---

1993, June 4    Litho.    Perf. 12
6150 A2930 25r multicolored    .20   .20
6151 A2931 25r multicolored    .20   .20
6152 A2931 25r multicolored    .20   .20
a.   Sheet, 3 each #6150-6152    .75   .60
Nos. 6150-6152 (3)    .60   .60
Souvenir Sheet    Perf. 12½x12
6153 A2930 250r multicolored    1.40   1.25
No. 6153 contains one 42x30mm stamp.

### Russian-Danish Relations, 500th Anniv. — A2932

1993, June 17    Litho.    Perf. 11½
6154 A2932 90r grn & light grn    .35   .25
See Denmark No. 985.

### Ducks A2933

90r, Somateria stelleri. 100r, Somateria mollissima. 250r, Somateria spectabilis.

1993, July 1    Litho.    Perf. 12
6155 A2933 90r multicolored    .20   .20
6156 A2933 100r multicolored    .20   .20
6157 A2933 250r multicolored    .45   .30
a.   Min. sheet, 4 each #6155-6157    3.00
Nos. 6155-6157 (3)    .85   .70

### Sea Life A2934

1993, July 6    Litho.    Perf. 12
6158 A2934 50r Pusa hispida    .20   .20
6159 A2934 60r Paralithodes brevipes    .20   .20
6160 A2934 90r Todarodes pacificus    .35   .25
6161 A2934 100r Oncorhynchus masu    .35   .25
6162 A2934 250r Fulmarus glacialis    1.00   .75
a.   Sheet, #6162, 2 each #6158-6161    2.50
Nos. 6158-6162 (5)    2.10   1.65

### Natl. Museum of Applied Arts and Folk Crafts, Moscow — A2935

Designs: No. 6163, Skopino earthenware candlestick. No. 6164, Painted tray, horiz. No. 6165, Painted box, distaff. No. 6166, Enamel icon of St. Dmitry of Solun. 250r, Fedoskino lacquer miniature Easter egg depicting the Resurrection.

1993, Aug. 11    Perf. 12x12½, 12½x12    Litho.
6163 A2935 50r multicolored    .35   .25
6164 A2935 50r multicolored    .35   .25
6165 A2935 100r multicolored    .35   .25
6166 A2935 250r multicolored    .80   .55
6167 A2935 250r multicolored    1.90   1.45
Nos. 6163-6167 (5)

---

### Flowers A2927

1993, Mar. 25    Perf. 12½x12
6133 A2927 10r Saintpaulia ionantha    .20   .20
6134 A2927 15r Hibiscus rosa-sinensis    .20   .20
6135 A2927 25r Cyclamen persicum    .25   .25
6136 A2927 50r Fuchsia hybrida    .45   .45
6137 A2927 100r Begonia semperflorens    .90   .60
Nos. 6133-6137 (5)    2.00   1.50

### Communications Satellites A2928

1993, Apr. 12    Photo.    Perf. 12x11½
6138 A2928 25r Molniya-3    .20   .20
6139 A2928 45r Ekran-M    .30   .30
6140 A2928 50r Gorizont    .35   .35
6141 A2928 75r Luch    .55   .40
6142 A2928 100r Express    .70   .55
Souvenir Sheet    Perf. 12x11½
6143 A2928 250r Ground station, horiz.    2.00   1.40
No. 6143 contains one 37x26mm stamp.

### Antique Silver A2929

15r, Snuff box, 1820, mug, 1849. 25r, Tea pot, 1896-1908. 45r, Vase, 1896-1908. 75r, Tray, candlestick holder, 1896-1908. 100r, Coffee pot, cream and sugar set, 1852. 250r, Sweet dish, 1896-1908, biscuit dish, 1844.

1993, May 5    Litho.    Perf. 11½
6144 A2929 15r multicolored    .20   .20
6145 A2929 25r multicolored    .30   .20
6146 A2929 45r multicolored    .30   .30
6147 A2929 75r multicolored    .50   .35
6148 A2929 100r multicolored    .70   .50
Nos. 6144-6148 (5)    1.90   1.45
Souvenir Sheet    Perf. 12½x12
6149 A2929 250r multicolored    1.75   1.25
No. 6149 contains one 52x37mm stamp.

### Nowgorod Kremlin A2931
### A2930

Designs: No. 6150, Kremlin towers, 14th-17th cent. No. 6151, St. Sofia's Temple, 11th cent. No. 6152, Belfry of St. Sophia's, 15th-18th cent. No. 6152, Icon, "Sign of the Virgin," 12th cent.

Metropolis Church, Athens — A2946

Space Research A2953

6208 A2951 150r multicolored .25 .20
6209 A2952 150r multicolored .25 .20
a. Min. sheet of 9, #6201-6209 2.75

Designs: 100r, TS-18 Centrifuge, Soyuz landing module during re-entry. 250r, Soyuz spacecraft docked at Mir space station. 500r, Training in hydrolaboratory, cosmonaut during space walk.

**1994, Apr. 12 Litho. Perf. 12x11½**
6210 A2953 100r multicolored .20 .20
6211 A2953 250r multicolored .35 .25
6212 A2953 500r multicolored .70 .45
Nos. 6210-6212 (3) 1.25 .90

Gothic Church, Roskilde, Denmark A2947

Liberation of Soviet Areas, 50th Anniv. A2954

Battle maps and: a. Katyusha rockets, liberation of Russia. b, Fighter planes, liberation of Ukraine. c, Combined offensive, liberation of Belarus.

**1994, Apr. 26 Perf. 12**
6213 A2954 100r Block of 3 + label .55 .46

See Belarus No. 78, Ukraine No. 195.

Notre Dame Cathedral, Paris — A2948

St. Peter's Basilica, Vatican City — A2949

Russian Architecture A2955

Structure, architect: 50r, Krasnye Vorota, Moscow, Prince D.V. Ukhtomsky (1719-74), 100r, Academy of Science, St. Petersburg, Giacomo Quarenghi (1744-1817). 150r, Trinity Cathedral, St. Petersburg, V.P. Stasov (1769-1848). 300r, Church of Christ the Saviour, Moscow, K.A. Ton (1794-1881).

**1994, May 25 Litho. Perf. 12½x12**
6214 A2955 50r lt brown & blk .20 .20
6215 A2955 100r red brn & blk .20 .20
6216 A2955 150r olive grn & blk .20 .20
6217 A2955 300r gray vio & blk .90 .85
Nos. 6214-6217 (4)

Cologne Cathedral, Germany A2950

Painting Type of 1992

Paintings by V. D. Polenov (1844-1927): No. 6218, Christ and the Adultress, 1886-87. No. 6219, Golden Autumn, 1893.

**1994, June 1 Litho. Perf. 12½x12**
6218 A2913 150r multicolored .20 .20
6219 A2913 150r multicolored .20 .20
a. Pair, #6218-6219 + label .35

St. Basil's Cathedral, Moscow — A2951

Ducks A2956

**1994, July 1**
6220 A2956 150r Anas penelope .20 .20
6221 A2956 250r Aythya fuligula .25 .20
6222 A2956 300r Anas formosa .35 .25
a. "a," overprinted 2.10 2.00
b. As "a," overprinted

Seville Cathedral, Spain — A2952

**1994, Mar. 24 Litho. Perf. 12x12½**
6201 A2945 150r multicolored .25 .20
6202 A2946 150r multicolored .25 .20
6203 A2947 150r multicolored .25 .20
6204 A2948 150r multicolored .25 .20
6205 A2949 150r multicolored .25 .20
6206 A2950 150r multicolored .25 .20
6207 A2951 150r multicolored .25 .20
#6207, St. Patrick's Cathedral, NYC, US.

No. 6222h is overprinted in sheet margin: "World Philatelic Exhibition Moscow-97" in Cyrillic and Latin with four exhibition emblems.
No. 6222b Nos. 6220-6222 (3)

A2957

A2958

**1994, July 5 Photo. Perf. 11½x12**
6223 A2957 100r multicolored .20 .20
1994 Goodwill Games, St. Petersburg.

Nobel Prize Winners in Physics: No. 6224, P.L. Kapitsa (1894-1984). No. 6225, P.A. Cherenkov (1904-90).

**1994, July 5 Litho. Perf. 12**
6224 A2958 150r sepia .20 .20
6225 A2958 150r sepia .20 .20

Intl. Olympic Committee, Cent. A2959

Russian Postal Day — A2960

**1994, July 5**
6226 A2959 250r multicolored .30 .20

**1994, July 8**
6227 A2960 125r multicolored .25 .20

Porcelain A2961

Designs: 50r, Snuff box, 1752. 100r, Candlestick, 1750-1760. 150r, Statue of watercarrier, 1818. 250r, Vase, 1910. 500r, Statue of lady with mask, 1910. 500r, Monogramed dinner service, 1848.

**1994, Aug. 10 Litho. Perf. 11½**
6228 A2961 50r multicolored .20 .20
6229 A2961 100r multicolored .20 .20
6230 A2961 150r multicolored .20 .20
6231 A2961 250r multicolored .25 .20
6232 A2961 300r multicolored .35 .25
6233 A2961 500r multicolored .65 .65
Nos. 6228-6232 (5)

Souvenir Sheet

6234 A2962 125r 1.25 1.05

No. 6228b is overprinted in sheet margin: "World Philatelic Exhibition Moscow 97" in Cyrillic and Latin with four exhibition logos.

Russia 1994

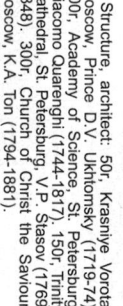

Painting Type of 1992

Alexander Griboedov (1795-1829), Poet, Diplomat A2965

**1994, Dec. 6 Photo. Perf. 12x11½**
6239 A2964 125r multicolored .20 .20
a. Min. sheet of 8
New Year 1995 — A2964

**1994, Nov. 22 Photo. & Engr. Perf. 12x11½**
6235 A2963 250r multicolored .20 .20
6236 A2963 250r multicolored .20 .20
a. Miniature sheet of 8 1.25 1.10
6237 A2963 250r multicolored .20 .20
6238 A2963 250r multicolored .80 .80
Nos. 6235-6238 (4)

Russian Fleet, 300th anniv. (#6236a).

**1995, Jan. 5 Litho. Perf. 11½**
6240 A2965 250r sepia & black .25 .20
No. 6240 printed se-tenant with label.

Russian Voyages of Exploration — A2963

Sailing ships and: No. 6235, V.M. Golovnin, Kurile Islands expedition, 1811. No. 6236, I.F. Kruzenstern, trans-global expedition, 1803-06. No. 6237, F.P. Wrangel, North American expedition, 1829-35. No. 6238, F.P. Litke, Novaya Zemlya expedition, 1821-24.

Ducks A2956

Russia 1994

A2966

Mikhail Fokine (1880-1942), Choreographer — A2967

Scenes from ballets: No. 6241, Scheherazade. No. 6242, The Fire Bird. No. 6243, Petrouchka.

**1995, Jan. 18 Litho. Perf. 12½x12**
6241 A2966 500r multicolored .30 .20
6242 A2967 500r multicolored .30 .20
6243 A2967 500r multicolored 1.05 .75
a. Block of 3 + label

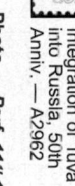

Integration of Tuva into Russia, 50th Anniv. — A2962

**1994, Oct. 13 Photo. Perf. 11½x12**
6234 A2962 125r multicolored .20 .20

Mikhail Kutuzov (1745-1813), Field Marshal — A2968

**1995, Jan. 20**
6244 A2968 300r multicolored .20 .20
a. Miniature sheet of 8 1.50 1.25

16th-17th Cent. Architecture, Moscow — A2969

Designs: 125r, English Yard, Varvarka St. 250r, Averki Kirillov's house, Bersenevskaya Embankment. 300r, Volkov's house, Kharitonievsky Lane.

**1995, Feb. 15  Litho.  Perf. 12x12½**
6245 A2969 125r multicolored .20 .20
6246 A2969 250r multicolored .20 .20
6247 A2969 300r multicolored .20 .20
a. Min. sheet, 2 #6245, 4 #6246. 1.10 1.10
b. Min. sheet, as "a," diff. margin 1.75 1.10
Nos. 6245-6247 (3) .60 .60

Sheet margin on No. 6247b has emblems and inscriptions in Cyrillic and Latin for "World Philatelic Exhibition Moscow '97."

UN Fight Against Drug Abuse — A2970

**1995, Mar. 1  Perf. 12x12½**
6248 A2970 150r multicolored .20 .20

Endangered Species — A2971
a, Lake. b, Pusa hispida. c, Lynx. d, River, trees.

**1995, Mar. 1  Perf. 12x12½**
6249 A2971 250r Block of 4, #a.-d. .75 .65

Nos. 6249a-6249b, 6249c-6249d are continuous designs. See Finland No. 960.

End of World War II, 50th Anniv. A2972

#6250, Churchill, Roosevelt, Stalin at Yalta. #6251, Ruins of Reichstag, Berlin. #6252, Monument to concentration camp victims. #6253, Tomb of the Unknown Soldier, Moscow, vert. #6254, Potsdam Conference, map of divided Germany, vert. #6255, Russian planes over Manchuria. #6256, Victory parade, Moscow, vert.

**1995, Apr. 7  Perf. 12x12½, 12½x12**
6251 A2972 250r multicolored .20 .20
6252 A2972 250r multicolored .20 .20
6253 A2972 250r multicolored .20 .20
6254 A2972 250r multicolored .20 .20
6255 A2972 250r multicolored .20 .20
Size: 37x52mm
6256 A2972 500r multicolored .25 .25
a. Souv. sheet of 1, perf 11½x12 .40 .40
Nos. 6250-6256 (7) 1.45 1.40

MIR-Space Shuttle Docking, Apollo-Soyuz Link-Up — A2973

a, Space shuttle Atlantis. b, MIR space station. c, Apollo command module. d, Soyuz spacecraft.

**1995, June 29  Litho.  Perf. 12x12½**
6257 A2973 1500r Block of 4, #a.-d. 3.00 2.50

No. 6257 is a continuous design.

Radio, Cent. A2974
Design: 250r, Alexander Popov (1859-1905), radio-telegraph.

**1995, May 3  Litho.  Perf. 11½**
6258 A2974 250r multicolored .20 .20

Songbirds A2976

Flowers A2975

#6259, Campanula patula. #6260, Leucanthemum vulgare. #6261, Trifolium pratense. #6262, Centaurea jacea. 500r, Geranium pratense.

**1995, May 18  Litho.  Perf. 12½x12**
6259 A2975 250r multicolored .20 .20
6260 A2975 250r multicolored .20 .20
6261 A2975 300r multicolored .20 .20
a. Min. sheet of 8 1.50
b. As "a," different margin 1.50
6262 A2975 300r multicolored .20 .20
6263 A2975 500r multicolored .30 .25
Nos. 6259-6263 (5) 1.10 1.00

**1995, June 15  Litho.  Perf. 12½x12**
6264 A2976 250r Alauda arvensis .20 .20
6265 A2976 250r Turdus philomelos .20 .20
6266 A2976 500r Carduelis carduelis .25 .25
6267 A2976 500r Cyanosylvia svecica .25 .25
6268 A2976 750r Luscinia luscinia .35 .25
a. Min. sheet, 2 #6264-6265, 1 #6268 + label 1.25 1.10
b. Min. sheet, 1 #6266-6267, 1 #6268 + label 1.75 1.50
Nos. 6264-6268 (5) 1.25 1.05

St. Trinity, Jerusalem A2977
Sts. Peter & Paul, Karlovy Vary — A2978
St. Nicholas, Vienna — A2979
St. Nicholas, New York — A2980

Russian Orthodox Churches abroad: 750r, St. Alexei, Leipzig.

**1995, July 5  Litho.  Perf. 12x12½**
6269 A2977 250r multicolored .20 .20
6270 A2978 300r multicolored .20 .20
6271 A2979 500r multicolored .20 .20
6272 A2980 500r multicolored .30 .25
6273 A2980 750r multicolored .35 .25
a. Min. sheet, 2 ea #6269-6273 (5) 2.50 2.25
Nos. 6269-6273 (5) 1.35 1.05

Principality of Ryazan, 900th Anniv. — A2981

**1995, July 20  Photo.  Perf. 11½**
6274 A2981 250r Kremlin Cathedral .20 .20

Fabergé Jewelry in Kremlin Museums — A2982

Designs: 150r, Easter egg, 1909, St. Petersburg. 250r, Goblet, 1899-1908, Moscow. 300r, Cross, 1899-1908, St. Petersburg. 600r, Ladle, 1890, Moscow. 750r, Easter egg, 1910, St. Petersburg. 1500r, Easter egg, 1904-06, St. Petersburg.

**1995, Aug. 15  Litho.  Perf. 11½**
6275 A2982 150r multicolored .20 .20
6276 A2982 250r multicolored .20 .20
6277 A2982 300r multicolored .25 .25
6278 A2982 500r multicolored .25 .25
6279 A2982 750r multicolored .35 .30
Nos. 6275-6279 (5) 1.20 1.10

**Souvenir Sheet**
6280 A2982 1500r multicolored .75 .65
No. 6280 contains one 37x51mm stamp.

**Souvenir Sheet**

Singapore '95 — A2983

Illustration reduced.

**1995, Sept. 1  Perf. 12½x12**
6281 A2983 2500r multicolored 1.10 1.00

Ducks A2984
Designs: 500r, Histrionicus histrionicus. 750r, Aythya baeri. 1000r, Mergus merganser.

**1995, Sept. 1  Perf. 12**
6284 A2984 500r multicolored .25 .20
6285 A2984 750r multicolored .35 .35
6286 A2984 1000r multicolored .50 .40
a. Miniature sheet, 2 #6284, 4 #6286 3.75 3.50
Nos. 6284-6286 (3) 1.10 .85

Russian Fleet, 300th Anniv. — A2985

Paintings: 250r, Battle of Grengam, 1720. 300r, Bay of Cesme, 1770. 500r, Battle of Revel Roadstead, 1790. 750r, Kronstadt Roadstead, 1840.

**1995, Sept. 14  Litho.  Perf. 12**
6287 A2985 250r multicolored .20 .20
6288 A2985 300r multicolored .20 .20
6289 A2985 500r multicolored .25 .25
6290 A2985 750r multicolored .35 .25
Nos. 6287-6290 (4) 1.00 .85

Arms & Flag of the Russian Federation — A2986

**1995, Oct. 4  Litho.  Perf. 12x12½**
6291 A2986 500r multicolored .30 .25
No. 6291 is printed with se-tenant label.

## 1995, Oct. 4
| | | | | |
|---|---|---|---|---|
| 6292 | A2987 | 500r multicolored | .30 | .25 |

UN, 50th Anniv. — A2987

### Peace and Freedom — A2988

Europa: No. 6293, Storks in nest, countryside. No. 6294, Stork in flight.

**1995, Nov. 15**   **Litho.**   **Perf. 12½**
| | | | |
|---|---|---|---|
| 6293 | 1500r multicolored | .75 | .70 |
| 6294 | 1500r multicolored | 1.50 | 1.40 |
| a. A2988 | Pair, Nos. 6293-6294 | | |

No. 6294a is a continuous design.

### Christmas A2989

**1995, Dec. 1**     **Perf. 12**
| | | | |
|---|---|---|---|
| 6295 | A2989 500r multicolored | .25 | .20 |

A2990c

A2990b

A2990a

A2990

### Early Russian Dukes — A2990c

Designs: No. 6296, Yuri Dolgorouki (1090-1157), Duke of Souzdal, Grand Duke of Kiev, founder of Moscow. No. 6297, Alexander Nevski (1220-63), Duke of Moscow. No. 6298, Duke of Vladimir. No. 6298, Michael Alexandrovitch (1333-39), Prince of Tver. No. 6299, Dimitri Donskoi (1350-89), Duke of Moscow, Vladimir. No. 6300, Ivan III (1440-1505), Grand Duke of Moscow.
Illustrations reduced.

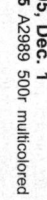

**1995, Dec. 21**   **Litho. & Engr.**   **Perf. 12**
| | | | | |
|---|---|---|---|---|
| 6296 | A2990 | 1000r multicolored | .50 | .35 |
| 6297 | A2990a | 1000r multicolored | .50 | .35 |
| 6298 | A2990b | 1000r multicolored | .50 | .35 |
| 6299 | A2990c | 1000r multicolored | .50 | .35 |
| 6300 | A2990c | 1000r multicolored | .50 | .35 |
| | Nos. 6296-6300 (5) | | 2.50 | 1.75 |

See #6359-6362.

A2991

**1996, Jan. 31**   **Litho.**   **Perf. 12**
| | | | |
|---|---|---|---|
| 6301 | A2991 750r dull olive black | .30 | .25 |

Nikolai N. Semenov (1896-1986), chemist.

A2992

**1996, Feb. 22**   **Litho.**   **Perf. 12**
| | | | | |
|---|---|---|---|---|
| 6302 | A2992 | 500r multicolored | .20 | .20 |
| 6303 | A2992 | 500r multicolored | .20 | .20 |
| 6304 | A2992 | 750r multicolored | .30 | .20 |
| 6305 | A2992 | 750r multicolored | .30 | .20 |
| 6306 | A2992 | 1000r multicolored | .40 | .30 |
| a. | A2992 | 1000r multicolored | .40 | .30 |
| | Min. sheet of 20, 4 each #6302-6306 + 4 labels | | 6.25 | 5.50 |
| | Nos. 6302-6306 (5) | | 1.60 | 1.20 |

Flowers: 500r, Viola wittrockiana. No. 6303, Dianthus barbatus. No. 6304, Lathyrus odoratus. No. 6305, Fritillaria imperialis. No. 6306, Antirrhinum majus.

### Domestic Cats A2993

**1996, Mar. 21**   **Color of Background**
| | | | | |
|---|---|---|---|---|
| 6307 | A2993 | 1000r orange | .40 | .30 |
| 6308 | A2993 | 1000r brown | .40 | .30 |
| 6309 | A2993 | 1000r red | .40 | .30 |
| 6310 | A2993 | 1000r blue violet | .40 | .30 |
| 6311 | A2993 | 1000r green | .40 | .30 |
| a. | | Sheet, 2 each #6307-6311 | 4.00 | |
| | Nos. 6307-6311 (5) | | 2.00 | 1.50 |

Designs: No. 6307, European tiger. No. 6308, Russian blue. No. 6309, Persian white. No. 6310, Siamese. No. 6311, Siberian.

### Souvenir Sheet

№ 051385

### Modern Olympic Games, Cent. — A2994

Illustration reduced.

**1996, Mar. 27**
| | | | |
|---|---|---|---|
| 6312 | A2994 5000r multicolored | 1.90 | 1.75 |

### Victory Day — A2995

A2995

Design: Painting "Plunged Down Banners," by A. S. Mikhailov. Illustration reduced.

**1996, Apr. 19**   **Litho.**   **Perf. 12**
| | | | | |
|---|---|---|---|---|
| 6313 | A2995 | 1000r multicolored | .40 | .30 |
| a. | A2995 | Sheet of 8 + label | 3.00 | |

### Tula, 850th Anniv. A2996

**1996, May 14**   **Litho.**   **Perf. 12½x12**
| | | | |
|---|---|---|---|
| 6314 | A2996 1500r Tula Kremlin | .60 | .40 |

### Russian Trams A2997

**1996, May 16**   **Photo.**   **Perf. 11½**
| | | | | |
|---|---|---|---|---|
| 6315 | A2997 | 500r multicolored | .20 | .20 |
| 6316 | A2997 | 750r multicolored | .30 | .20 |
| 6317 | A2997 | 750r multicolored | .30 | .20 |
| 6318 | A2997 | 1000r multicolored | .40 | .30 |
| 6319 | A2997 | 1000r multicolored | .40 | .30 |
| 6320 | A2997 | 2500r multicolored | .90 | .90 |
| a. | A2997 | Souvenir sheet | 1.25 | 1.10 |
| b. | | Sheet of 6, #6315-6320 | 2.85 | 2.10 |
| | Nos. 6315-6320 (6) | | | |

Designs: 500r, Putilovsky plant. No. 6316, Sormovo, 1912. No. 6317, "X" series, 1928. No. 6318, "KM" series, 1931. No. 6319, 1928-57, 1957. 2500r, Model 71-608 K, 1993.

A2998

A2999

Europa (Famous Women): No. 6321, E.R. Daschkova (1744-1810), scientist. No. 6322, S.V. Kovalevskaya (1850-91), mathematician.

**1996, May 20**   **Litho.**   **Perf. 12x12½**
| | | | | |
|---|---|---|---|---|
| 6321 | A2998 | 1500r green & black | .60 | .30 |
| 6322 | A2998 | 1500r lilac & black | .60 | .30 |

**1996, June 1**   **Litho.**   **Perf. 12½x12**
| | | | | |
|---|---|---|---|---|
| 6323 | A2999 | 2000r multicolored | .50 | .35 |

UNICEF, 50th anniv.

Summer, by P.P. Sokolov A3000

Post Troika, by P.N. Gruzinsky A3001

Design: No. 6326, Winter, by Sokolov.

**1996, June 14**   **Litho.**   **Perf. 12**
| | | | | |
|---|---|---|---|---|
| 6324 | A3000 | 1500r multicolored | .75 | .60 |
| 6325 | A3001 | 1500r multicolored | .75 | .60 |
| 6326 | A3002 | 1500r multicolored | .75 | .60 |
| | Nos. 6324-6326 (3) | | 2.25 | 1.80 |

### Moscow, 850th Anniv. — A3002

**1996, June 20**   **Litho.**   **Perf. 12**
| | | | | |
|---|---|---|---|---|
| 6327 | A3002 | 500r multicolored | .20 | .20 |
| 6328 | A3002 | 500r multicolored | .20 | .20 |
| 6329 | A3002 | 500r multicolored | .20 | .20 |
| 6330 | A3002 | 750r multicolored | .35 | .25 |
| 6331 | A3002 | 1000r multicolored | .40 | .25 |
| 6332 | A3002 | 1000r multicolored | .40 | .20 |
| a. | A3002 | Sheet, 2 ea #6327, 6330-6331 | 2.50 | |
| b. | A3002 | Sheet of 6, #6327-6332 | 2.50 | |
| | Nos. 6327-6332 (6) | | 1.90 | 1.30 |

Paintings of urban views: No. 6327, Yauza River, 1790's. No. 6328, Kremlin Palace, 1797. No. 6329, Kamenny Bridge, 1811. No. 6330, Volkhonka Steet, 1830's. No. 6331, Vorvarka St. 1830-40's. No. 6332, Petrovsky Park, troikas.

### Traffic Police, 60th Anniv. A3003

**1996, July 3**   **Litho.**   **Perf. 12x12½**
| | | | | |
|---|---|---|---|---|
| 6333 | A3003 | 1500r Sheet of 3, #a.-c. | 1.10 | .55 |

a. Pedestrian crossing guard. b. Children receiving traffic safety education. c. Officer writing citation.

### 1996 Summer Olympic Games, Atlanta — A3004

**1996, July 10**   **Litho.**   **Perf. 12**
| | | | | |
|---|---|---|---|---|
| 6334 | A3004 | 500r Basketball | .20 | .20 |
| 6335 | A3004 | 500r Boxing | .20 | .20 |
| 6336 | A3004 | 1000r Swimming | .40 | .20 |
| 6337 | A3004 | 1000r Women's gymnastics | .60 | .30 |
| 6338 | A3004 | 1500r Hurdles | .75 | .30 |
| a. | A3004 | Sheet of 8 | 4.75 | |
| | Nos. 6334-6338 (5) | | 2.20 | 1.20 |

### Russian Navy, 300th Anniv. A3006

A3005

A3006

Ships: 750r, Yevstafy, 1762. No. 6340, Petropavlovsk, 1894. No. 6341, Novik, 1913. Nos. 6342, 6343a, Galera, 1696. Nos. 6343, 6364d, Aircraft carrier Admiral Kuznetzov, 1985. No. 6344, Tashkent, 1937. No. 6345, Submarine C-13, 1939.

No. 6346: b, Atomic submarine, 1981. c, Sailing ship Azov, 1826.

**Litho. & Engr.**

**1996, July 26** *Perf. 12*

**6339** A3005 750r multicolored .25 .20
**6340** A3005 1000r multicolored .35 .20
**6341** A3005 1000r multicolored .35 .20
**6342** A3006 1000r multicolored .35 .20
**6343** A3006 1000r multicolored .35 .20
*a.* Sheet, 3 each #6342-6343 2.25 1.20
**6344** A3005 1500r multicolored .50 .25
**6345** A3005 1500r multicolored .50 .25
*Nos. 6339-6345 (7)* 2.65 1.50

**Souvenir Sheet**

**6346** A3006 1000r Sheet of 4, #a.-d. + label 1.75 .90

No. 6346 has blue background.

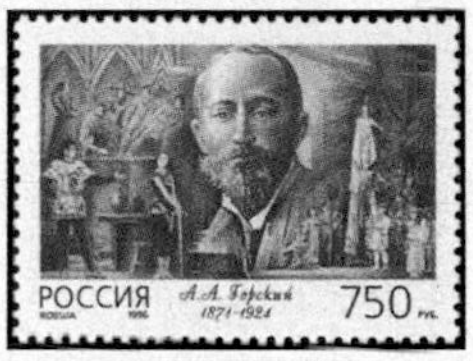


Aleksandr Gorsky (1871-1924), Choreographer — A3006a

a, 750r, Portrait, scenes from "The Daughter of Gudule," "Salambo." b, 1500r, Don Quixote. c, 1500r, Giselle. d, 750r, La Bayadere.

**1996, Aug. 7 Litho.** *Perf. 12½x12*

**6347** A3006a Block of 4, #a.-d. 1.90 .95
*e.* Sheet of 6, #6347b 3.50 1.75

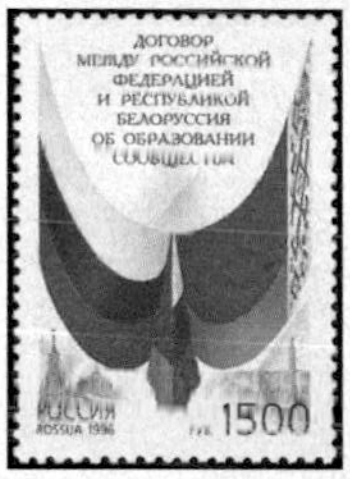


Treaty Between Russia and Belarus A3006b

**1996, Aug 27** *Perf. 12x12½*

**6348** A3006b 1500r Natl. flags .60 .30

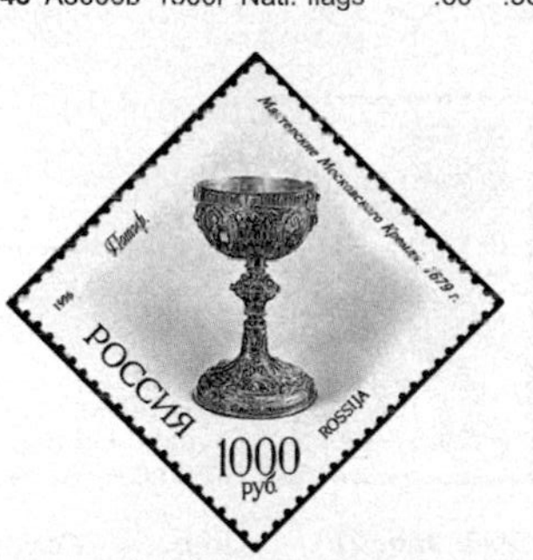


17th-20th Cent. Enamelwork — A3007

Designs: No. 6349, Chalice, 1679. No. 6350, Aromatic bottle, 17th cent. No. 6351, Ink pot, ink set, 17th-18th cent. No. 6352, Coffee pot, 1750-1760. No. 6353, Perfume bottle, 19th-20th cent.

5000r, Icon, Our Lady of Kazan, 1894.

**1996, Sept. 10** *Perf. 11½*

**6349** A3007 1000r multicolored .40 .20
**6350** A3007 1000r multicolored .40 .20
*a.* Sheet of 9 3.60
**6351** A3007 1000r multicolored .40 .20
**6352** A3007 1500r multicolored .60 .30
**6353** A3007 1500r multicolored .60 .30
*a.* Sheet of 9 5.50
*Nos. 6349-6353 (5)* 2.40 1.20

**Souvenir Sheet**

**6354** A3007 5000r multicolored 2.00 1.00

No. 6353a inscribed in sheet margin for Moscow '97.

No. 6354 contains one 35x50mm stamp.

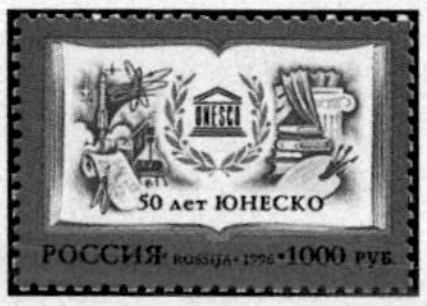


UNESCO, 50th Anniv. A3008

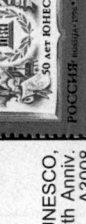

**1996, Oct. 15** *Perf. 12x12½*

**6355** A3008 1000r multicolored .40 .20

No. 6355 issued in sheets of 8.

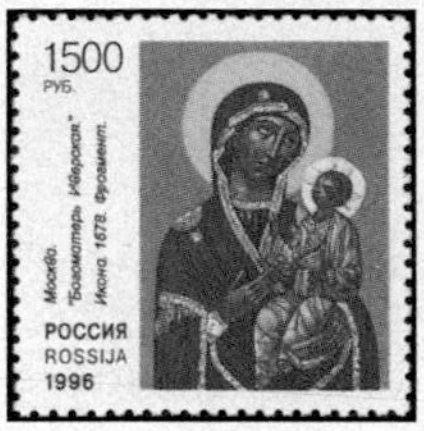


Icons, Religious Landmarks A3009

Designs: a, Icon of Our Lady of Iverone, Moscow. b, Holy Monastery of Stavrovouni, Cyprus. c, Icon of St. Nicholas, Cyprus. d, Resurrection (Iverone), Gate, Moscow.

**1996, Nov. 13** *Perf. 11½*

**6356** A3009 1500r Block of 4, #a.-d. 2.40 1.20

See Cyprus Nos. 893-896.

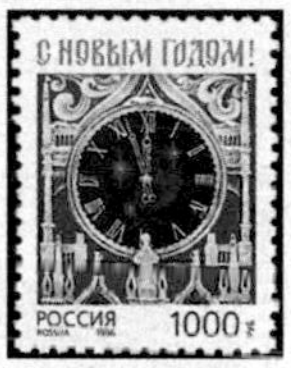


New Year 1997 — A3010

Design: Chiming Clock of Moscow, Kremlin.

**1996, Dec. 5**

**6357** A3010 1000r multicolored .40 .20
*a.* Sheet of 8 3.25 1.60

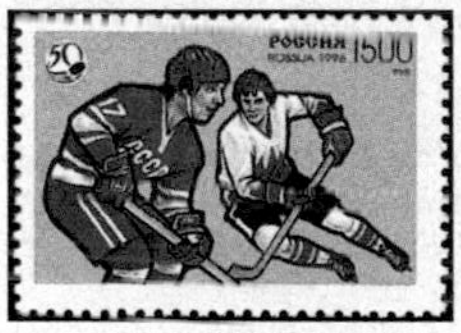


Natl. Ice Hockey Team, 50th Anniv. A3011

Action scenes: a, Two players. b, Three players. c, Three players, referee.

**1996, Dec. 5** *Perf. 12*

**6358** A3011 1500r Strip of 3, #a.-c. 1.75 .90

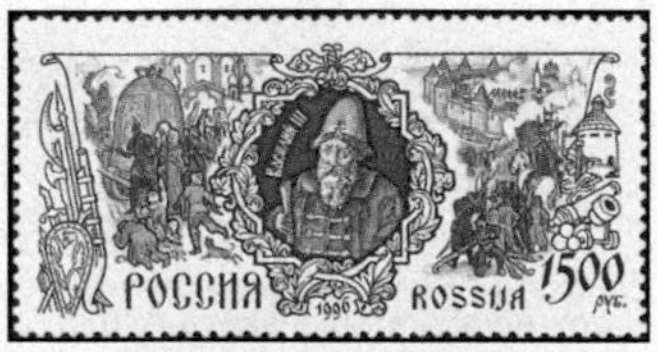


Basil III — A3012

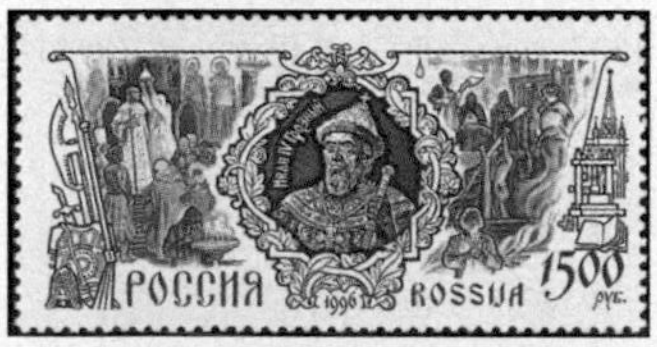


Ivan IV (the Terrible) — A3013

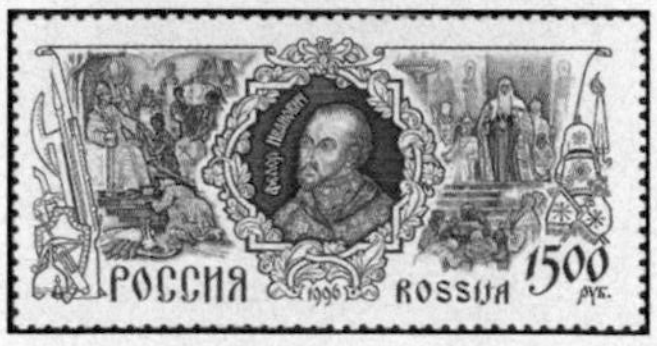


Feodor Ivanovich — A3014

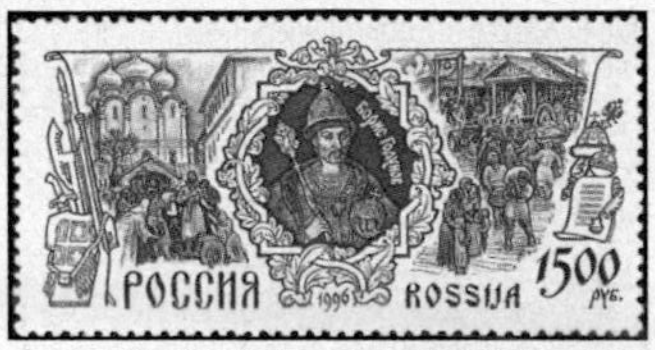


Boris Godunov — A3015

**Litho. & Engr.**

**1996, Dec. 20** *Perf. 12*

**6359** A3012 1500r multicolored .60 .30
**6360** A3013 1500r multicolored .60 .30
**6361** A3014 1500r multicolored .60 .30
**6362** A3015 1500r multicolored .60 .30
*Nos. 6359-6362 (4)* 2.40 1.20

See #6296-6300.

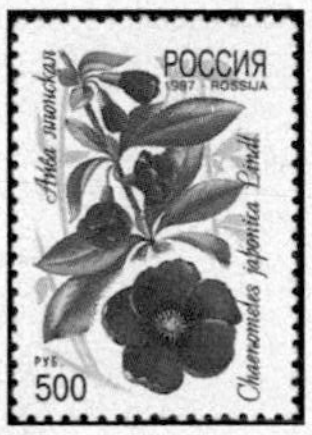


Flowers — A3016

Designs: No. 6363, Chaenomeles japonica. No. 6364, Amygdalus triloba. No. 6365, Cytisus scoparius. No. 6366, Rosa pimpinellifolia. No. 6367, Philadelphus coronarius.

**1997, Jan. 21 Litho.** *Perf. 12½x12*

**6363** A3016 500r multicolored .25 .20
**6364** A3016 500r multicolored .25 .20
**6365** A3016 1000r multicolored .45 .25
**6366** A3016 1000r multicolored .45 .25
**6367** A3016 1000r multicolored .45 .25
*Nos. 6363-6367 (5)* 1.85 1.15

**Souvenir Sheet**

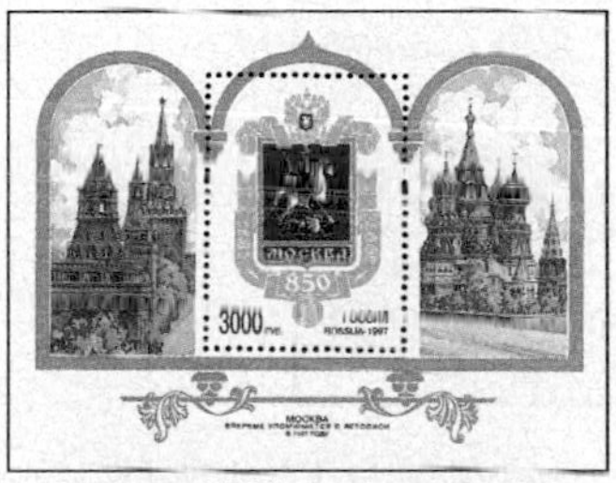

Moscow, 850th Anniv. — A3017

Illustration reduced.

**1997, Feb. 20** *Perf. 12x12½*

**6368** A3017 3000r Coat of arms 1.40 .70

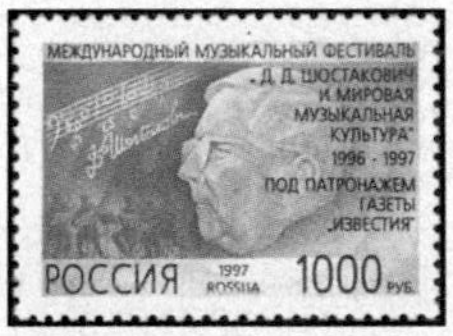


Shostakovich Intl. Music Festival — A3018

Dmitri D. Shostakovich (1906-75), composer.

**1997, Feb. 26** *Perf. 12*

**6369** A3018 1000r multicolored .45 .25

**Souvenir Sheet**

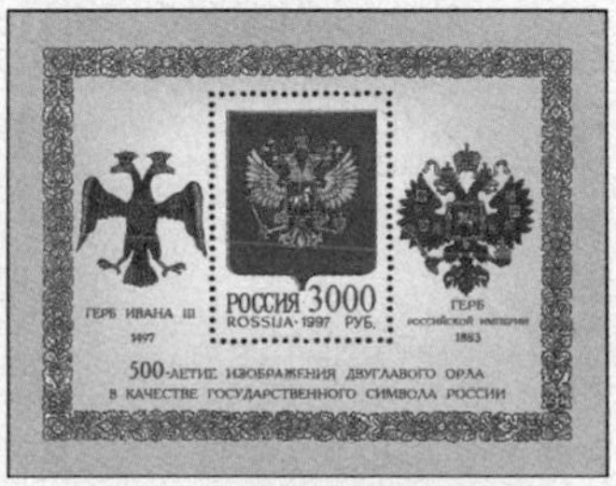


Coat of Arms of Russia, 500th Anniv. — A3019

Illustration reduced.

**1997, Mar. 20**

**6370** A3019 3000r multicolored 1.40 .70

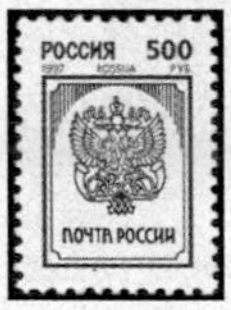


Post Emblem — A3020

Designs: 100r, Agriculture. 150r, Oil rig. 250r, Cranes (birds). 300r, Radio/TV tower. 500r, Russian Post emblem. 750r, St. George slaying dragon. 1000r, Natl. flag, arms. 1500r, Electric power. 2000r, Train. 2500r, Moscow Kremlin. 3000r, Satellite. 5000r, Fine arts.

**1997** *Perf. 12x12½*

**6371** A3020 100r blk & yel brn .20 .20
**6372** A3020 150r blk & red lilac .20 .20
**6373** A3020 250r blk & olive .20 .20
**6374** A3020 300r blk & dk grn .20 .20
**6375** A3020 500r blk & dk bl .20 .20
**6376** A3020 750r blk & brown .30 .20
**6377** A3020 1000r blue & red .40 .20
**6378** A3020 1500r blk & grn bl .60 .30
**6379** A3020 2000r blk & green .80 .40
**6380** A3020 2500r blk & red .90 .45
**6381** A3020 3000r blk & purple 1.25 .60
**6382** A3020 5000r blk & brown 2.00 1.00
*Nos. 6371-6382 (12)* 7.25 4.15

Issued: 500r, 750r, 1000r, 1500r, 2500r, 3/31; 100r, 150r, 250r, 300r, 2000r, 3000r, 5000r, 4/30.

See Nos. 6423-6433, 6550-6560.

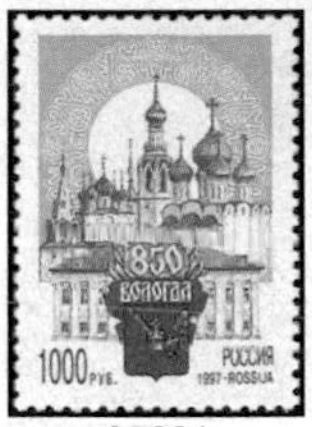


A3021

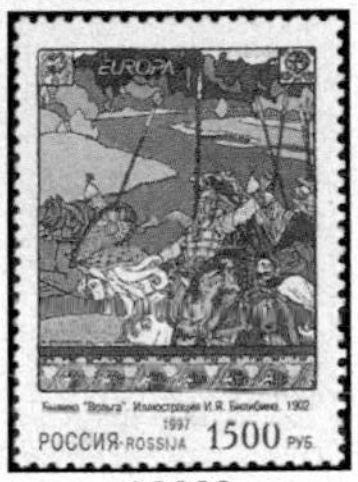


A3022

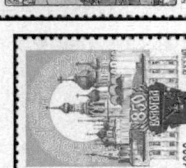

**1997, Mar. 31 Litho.** *Perf. 12*

**6383** A3021 1000r multicolored .40 .20

City of Vologda, 850th anniv.

**1997, May 5 Litho.** *Perf. 12x12½*

Europa (Stories and Legends): Legend of Volga.

**6384** A3022 1500r multicolored .60 .30

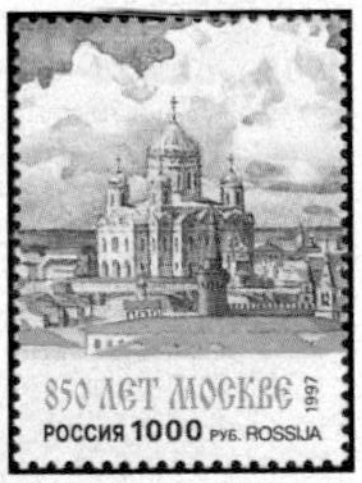


Moscow, 850th Anniv. — A3023

Historic buildings: a, Cathedral of Christ the Savior. b, Turrets and roofs of the Kremlin. c, Grand Palace of the Kremlin, cathedral plaza. d, St. Basil's Cathedral. e, Icon, St. George slaying the Dragon. f, Text of first chronicled record of Moscow, 1147. g, Prince Aleksandr Nevski, Danilov Monastery. h, 16th cent. miniature of Moscow Kremlin. i, Miniature of coronation of Czar Ivan IV. j, 16th cent. map of Moscow.

**1997, May 22**

**6385** A3023 1000r Sheet of 10, #a.-j. 3.75 1.90

Nos. 6385c, 6385h are 42x42mm.

## Helicopters — A3024

**1997, May 28    Litho.    Perf. 12½x12**

| | | | | |
|---|---|---|---|---|
| 6386 | A3024 | 500r. | .20 | .20 |
| 6387 | A3024 | 1000r. | .40 | .20 |
| 6388 | A3024 | 1500r. | .55 | .55 |
| 6389 | A3024 | 2000r. | .75 | .40 |
| 6390 | A3024 | 2500r. | .95 | .45 |
| | | Sheet of 6 | 2.85 | 1.80 |
| | | Nos. 6386-6390 (5) | 4.50 | 1.80 |

## Fairy Tales — A3025

**1997, June 6    Perf. 12½**

| | | | | |
|---|---|---|---|---|
| 6391 | A3025 | 500r. | .20 | .20 |
| 6392 | A3025 | 1000r. | .40 | .20 |
| 6393 | A3025 | 1500r. | .60 | .30 |
| 6394 | A3025 | 2000r. | .80 | .40 |
| 6395 | A3025 | 3000r. | 1.25 | .60 |
| a. | | Strip of 5 | 3.25 | 1.65 |
| b. | | Sheet of 2 | 6.40 | |
| | | Nos. 6391-6395 | | |

Designs: 500r, Man holding rope beside lake, devil running, from "Priest and Worker." 1000r, Two women, two men, from "Czar Saltan." 1500r, Man fishing in lake, fish, man, castle, from "Fisherman/Golden Fish." 2000r, Princess on steps, old woman holding apple, from "Dead Princess/Seven Knights." 3000r, Woman, King bowing with holding scepter, rooster up in air, from "Golden Cockerel."

## Diplomatic Relations Between Russia and Thailand — A3026

Design: St. Petersburg, Russian flag, Bangkok, Thailand flag.

**1997, June 20    Litho.    Perf. 12½x12**

| | | | | |
|---|---|---|---|---|
| 6396 | A3026 | 1500r. multicolored | .60 | .30 |

**Photo. & Engr.    Perf. 12½**

| | | | | |
|---|---|---|---|---|
| | | | .60 | .30 |

## Wildlife — A3027

**1997, July 10    Perf. 12½x12**

| | | | | |
|---|---|---|---|---|
| 6397 | A3027 | 1500r. multicolored | .60 | .30 |
| | | Block of 5 + label | 2.60 | 1.30 |

Designs: a, 500r, Pteromys volans. b, 750r, Felix lynx. c, 1000r, Tetrao urogallus. d, 2000r, Lutra lutra. e, 3000r, Numenius arguata.

## Russian Regions — A3028

**1997, July 15    Perf. 12½x12, 12x12½**

| | | | | |
|---|---|---|---|---|
| 6398 | A3028 | 500r. multicolored | .55 | .30 |
| 6399 | A3028 | 1500r. multicolored | .55 | .30 |
| 6400 | A3028 | 1500r. multicolored | .55 | .30 |

Designs: #6398, Winter scene, Archangel Oblast. #6399, Ocean, beach, Kaliningrad Oblast, vert. #6400, Ship, Krasnodarsky Krai, vert. #6401, Mountains, Yakutia, vert. #6402, Mountain, sailing ship monument, Kamchatka Oblast.

## Kljopa Puppets — A3029

**1997, July 25    Perf. 11½**

| | | | | |
|---|---|---|---|---|
| 6403 | A3029 | 500r. multicolored | .20 | .20 |
| 6404 | A3029 | 1000r. multicolored | .35 | .20 |

Designs: 500r, Rainbow, balloons. 1000r, Hang glider. 1500r, Troika.

| | | | | |
|---|---|---|---|---|
| 6405 | A3029 | 1500r. multicolored | .55 | .30 |

Size: 45x33mm

Nos. 6403-6405 (3)  1.10  .70

## World Philatelic Exhibition, Moscow, '97 — A3030

**1997, Aug. 5    Perf. 11½**

| | | | | |
|---|---|---|---|---|
| 6406 | A3030 | 1500r. Pair, #a.-b. | 1.10 | .55 |
| c. | | Sheet of 6 stamps | 4.25 | |

Designs: a, #1. b, #6061.

## A3031

History of Russia, Peter I: No. 6407, Planning new capital. No. 6408, Reforming the military. No. 6409, In Baltic Sea naval battle. No. 6410, Ordering administrative reform. No. 6411, Advocating cultural education. 5000r, Peter I (1672-1725).

**1997, Aug. 15    Perf. 12½x12½**

| | | | | |
|---|---|---|---|---|
| 6407 | A3031 | 2000r. multicolored | .75 | .35 |
| 6408 | A3031 | 2000r. multicolored | .75 | .35 |
| 6409 | A3031 | 2000r. multicolored | .75 | .35 |
| 6410 | A3031 | 2000r. multicolored | .75 | .35 |
| 6411 | A3031 | 2000r. multicolored | .75 | .35 |
| | | Nos. 6407-6411 (5) | 3.75 | 1.75 |

**Souvenir Sheet**

**Litho. & Engr.**

| | | | | |
|---|---|---|---|---|
| 6411A | A3031 | 5000r. multicolored | 3.25 | 1.60 |

## Indian Independence, 50th Anniv. — A3032

**1997, Aug. 15    Perf. 12**

| | | | | |
|---|---|---|---|---|
| 6412 | A3032 | 500r. multicolored | .20 | .20 |

## Russian Pentathlon, 50th Anniv. — A3033

**1997, Sept. 1    Perf. 12½x12**

| | | | | |
|---|---|---|---|---|
| 6413 | A3033 | 1000r. multicolored | .35 | .20 |

## Russian Soccer, Cent. — A3034

**1997, Sept. 4    Perf. 12½x12**

| | | | | |
|---|---|---|---|---|
| 6414 | A3034 | 2000r. multicolored | .75 | .35 |

## World Ozone Layer Day — A3035

**1997, Sept. 16    Perf. 12x12½**

| | | | | |
|---|---|---|---|---|
| 6415 | A3035 | 1000r. multicolored | .35 | .20 |

## A3036

**1997, Oct. 1    Perf. 12½x12½**

| | | | | |
|---|---|---|---|---|
| 6416 | A3036 | 1000r. multicolored | .35 | .20 |

Russia's admission to European Council. No. 6416 printed with se-tenant label.

## Souvenir Sheet

Pushkin's "Eugene Onegin," Translated by Abraham Shlonsky — A3038

**1997, Nov. 19    Litho.    Perf. 12**

| | | | | |
|---|---|---|---|---|
| 6418 | A3038 | 3000r. multicolored | 1.25 | .60 |

Illustration reduced.

See Israel No. 1319.

## Russian State Museum, St. Petersburg, Cent. — A3039

**1997, Nov. 12    Litho.    Perf. 12x12½**

| | | | | |
|---|---|---|---|---|
| 6419 | A3039 | 500r. multi, vert. | .20 | .20 |
| 6420 | A3039 | 1000r. multi, vert. | .40 | .20 |
| 6421 | A3039 | 1500r. multi, vert. | .60 | .30 |
| 6422 | A3039 | 2000r. multi, vert. | .80 | .40 |
| | | Nos. 6419-6422 (4) | 2.00 | 1.10 |

500r, Boris and Gleb, 14th cent. icon. 1000r, "The Volga Boatmen," by I. Repin. 1500r, "Promenade," by Marc Chagall. 2000r, "A Merchant's Wife Having Tea," by Kustodiyev.

Nos. 6419-6422 each issued in sheets of 8 + label. See Nos. 6446-6450.

## Post Emblem Type of 1997

**1998, Jan. 1    Litho.    Perf. 12x12½**

| | | | | |
|---|---|---|---|---|
| 6423 | A3020 | 10k like #6371 | .20 | .20 |
| 6424 | A3020 | 15k like #6372 | .20 | .20 |
| 6425 | A3020 | 25k like #6373 | .20 | .20 |
| 6426 | A3020 | 30k like #6374 | .20 | .20 |
| 6427 | A3020 | 50k like #6375 | .30 | .20 |
| 6428 | A3020 | 1.50r like #6377 | .60 | .45 |
| 6429 | A3020 | 2.50r like #6378 | .90 | .70 |
| 6430 | A3020 | 1.25r like #6379 | .90 | .45 |
| 6431 | A3020 | 1.40r like #6380 | 1.25 | .60 |
| 6432 | A3020 | 3r like #6381 | 1.40 | .70 |
| 6433 | A3020 | 9.90r like #6382 | 2.90 | 1.40 |
| | | Nos. 6423-6433 (11) | 9.90 | 5.35 |

## Vasily Surikov (1848-1916), V. Vasnetsov (1848-1926), Painters — A3040

**1998, Jan. 24    Perf. 12**

| | | | | |
|---|---|---|---|---|
| 6434 | A3040 | 1.50r multicolored | .90 | .45 |
| 6435 | A3040 | 1.50r multicolored | .90 | .45 |
| a. | | Pair, #6434-6435 + label | 1.80 | .90 |
| 6436 | A3040 | 1.50r multicolored | .90 | .45 |
| 6437 | A3040 | 1.50r multicolored | .90 | .45 |
| a. | | Pair, #6436-6437 + label | 1.80 | .90 |

Entire paintings or details by Surikov: No. 6434, Menchikov and Beresov, 1887. No. 6435, Russian Women of Morozov, 1887. By Vasnetsov, vert.: No. 6436, The Struggle of Slavs with the Nomads, 1881. No. 6437, Ivan Tsarevitch on a Wolf, 1889.

## 1998 Winter Olympic Games, Nagano — A3041

**1998, Jan. 27    Litho.    Perf. 12**

| | | | | |
|---|---|---|---|---|
| 6438 | A3041 | 50k Cross country skiing | .30 | .20 |
| 6439 | A3041 | 1r Pairs figure skating | .60 | .30 |
| 6440 | A3041 | 1.50r Biathlon | .90 | .45 |
| a. | | Sheet 2, each #6438-6440 | 3.60 | 1.80 |
| | | Nos. 6438-6440 (3) | 1.80 | .95 |

## Aquarium Fish — A3042

**1998, Feb. 25    Litho.    Perf. 12½x12**

| | | | | |
|---|---|---|---|---|
| 6441 | A3042 | 50k multicolored | .20 | .20 |
| 6442 | A3042 | 50k multicolored | .20 | .20 |
| 6443 | A3042 | 1r multicolored | .40 | .20 |
| 6444 | A3042 | 1.50r multicolored | .60 | .30 |
| a. | | Sheet of 6 | 2.40 | 1.20 |
| 6445 | A3042 | 1.50r multicolored | .60 | .30 |
| a. | | Sheet of 6 | 2.40 | 1.20 |
| | | Nos. 6441-6445 (5) | 2.00 | 1.20 |

Designs: No. 6441, Hyphessobrycon callistus. No. 6442, Epalzeorhynchus bicolor. 1r, Synodontis galinae. No. 6444, Botia kristinae. No. 6445, Cichlasoma labiatum.

## Russian State Museum, St. Petersburg, Cent., Type of 1997

#6446, The Last Day of Pompeii, by K.P. Bryulov, 1833. #6447, Our Lady of Malevolent Hearts Tenderness, by K.S. Petrov-Vodkin, 1914-15. #6448, Mast Pine Grove, by I.I. Shishkin, 1898. #6449, The Ninth Wave, by I.K. Aivazovsky, 1850.

3r, The Mihailovksy Palace (detail), by K.P. Beggrov, 1832.

**1998, Mar. 17    Perf. 12x12½**

| 6446 | A3039 | 1.50r multicolored | .60 | .30 |
|---|---|---|---|---|
| 6447 | A3039 | 1.50r multicolored | .60 | .30 |
| 6448 | A3039 | 1.50r multicolored | .60 | .30 |
| 6449 | A3039 | 1.50r multicolored | .60 | .30 |
| a. | | Sheet, 2 each #6446-6449 + label | 4.80 | 2.40 |
| | | Nos. 6446-6449 (4) | 2.40 | 1.20 |

**Souvenir Sheet**

| 6450 | A3039 | 3r multicolored | 1.20 | .60 |
|---|---|---|---|---|

**Souvenir Sheet**

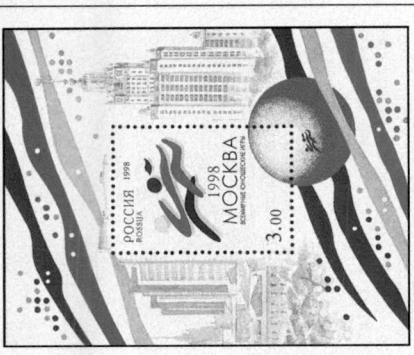

Expo '98, Lisbon — A3043

Illustration reduced.

**1998, Apr. 15    Perf. 12½x12**

| 6451 | A3043 | 3r Emblem, dolphins | 1.10 | .55 |
|---|---|---|---|---|

Theater of Arts, Moscow, Cent. — A3044

**1998, Apr. 24    Perf. 12**

| 6452 | A3044 | 1.50r multicolored | .55 | .30 |
|---|---|---|---|---|

No. 6452 was printed se-tenant with label.

Shrove-tide Natl. Festival — A3045

**1998, May 5    Litho.    Perf. 12½x12**

| 6453 | A3045 | 1.50r multicolored | .55 | .30 |
|---|---|---|---|---|

Europa.

A3046

A3046a

---

**Souvenir Sheet**

A3046b

Aleksander S. Pushkin (1799-1837), Poet — A3046c

Pushkin's drawings: No. 6454, Lyceum where Pushkin studied 1811-17. No. 6455, A. N. Wolf, contemporary of Pushkin's. No. 6456, Tatyana, heroine of novel "Eugene Onegin." No. 6457, Cover of 1830 manuscript. No. 6458, Self-portrait.

**1998, May 28    Litho. & Engr.    Perf. 12x12½**

| 6454 | A3046 | 1.50r multicolored | .55 | .30 |
|---|---|---|---|---|
| 6455 | A3046a | 1.50r multicolored | .55 | .30 |
| 6456 | A3046b | 1.50r multicolored | .55 | .30 |
| 6457 | A3046c | 1.50r multicolored | .55 | .30 |
| 6458 | A3046c | 1.50r multicolored | .55 | .30 |
| a. | | Sheet, 2 each #6454-6458 | 5.50 | 3.00 |
| | | Nos. 6454-6458 (5) | 2.75 | 1.50 |

City of Ulyanovsk (Simbirsk), 350th Anniv. — A3047

**1998, May 28    Litho.    Perf. 12½x12**

| 6459 | A3047 | 1r multicolored | .40 | .20 |
|---|---|---|---|---|

Czar Nicholas II (1868-1918) — A3048

**Perf. 11½**

**1998, June 30    Litho.**

| 6460 | A3048 | 3r multicolored | 1.10 | .55 |
|---|---|---|---|---|

Printed se-tenant with label.

City of Taganrog, 300th Anniv. — A3049

**1998, June 10    Litho.    Perf. 12½x12**

| 6461 | A3049 | 1r multicolored | .35 | .20 |
|---|---|---|---|---|

---

**Souvenir Sheet**

1998 World Youth Games, Moscow — A3049a

**1998, June 25    Litho.    Perf. 12½x12**

| 6461A | A3049a | 3r multicolored | 1.25 | .65 |
|---|---|---|---|---|

A3051

A3050

Wild Berries: 50k, Rubus idaeus. 75k, Vitis amurensis. 1r, Schisandra chinensis. 1.50r, Vaccinium vitis-idaea. 2r, Rubus arcticus.

**1998, July 10    Litho.**

| 6462 | A3050 | 50k multicolored | .20 | .20 |
|---|---|---|---|---|
| 6463 | A3050 | 75k multicolored | .30 | .20 |
| 6464 | A3050 | 1r multicolored | .35 | .20 |
| 6465 | A3050 | 1.50r multicolored | .55 | .30 |
| 6466 | A3050 | 2r multicolored | .75 | .35 |
| | | Nos. 6462-6466 (b) | 2.15 | 1.25 |

**1998, July 15**

| 6467 | A3051 | 1r multicolored | .35 | .20 |
|---|---|---|---|---|

Ekaterinburg, 275th anniv.

Heroes of the Russian Federation A3052

#6468, L. R. Kvasnikov (1905-93). #6469, Morris Cohen (1910-95). #6470, Leontina Cohen (1913-92). #6471, A.A. Yatskov (1913-93).

**1998, Aug. 10    Litho.    Perf. 12**

| 6468 | A3052 | 1r green & black | .35 | .20 |
|---|---|---|---|---|
| 6469 | A3052 | 1r brn, bister & blk | .35 | .20 |
| 6470 | A3052 | 1r slate & black | .35 | .20 |
| 6471 | A3052 | 1r claret & black | 1.40 | .80 |
| | | Nos. 6468-6471 (4) | | |

Orders of Russia — A3053

1r, St. Andrey Pervozvanny. 1.50r St. Catherine. 2r, St. Alexander Nevsky. 2.50r, St. George.

---

**Perf. 12x12½**

**1998, Aug. 20    Litho.**

| 6472 | A3053 | 1r multi | .35 | .20 |
|---|---|---|---|---|
| 6472A | A3053 | 1.50r multi | .55 | .25 |
| 6472B | A3053 | 2r multi | .70 | .45 |
| 6472C | A3053 | 2.50r multi | .90 | .45 |
| d. | | Block of 4, #6472-6472C | 2.50 | 1.25 |
| e. | | Souvenir sheet of 4, #6472-6472C + label | 2.50 | 1.25 |

See #6496-6500.

Murmansk Oblast A3054

Khabarovsk Krai — A3055

Karelia Republic — A3056
Buryat Republic — A3057

**1998, Sept. 15    Litho.**

| 6473 | A3054 | 1.50r multicolored | .55 | .25 |
|---|---|---|---|---|
| 6474 | A3055 | 1.50r multicolored | .55 | .25 |
| 6475 | A3056 | 1.50r multicolored | .55 | .25 |
| 6476 | A3057 | 1.50r multicolored | .55 | .25 |
| 6477 | A3054 | 1.50r Primorski Krai | .55 | .25 |
| | | Nos. 6473-6477 (5) | 2.75 | 1.25 |

World Stamp Day A3058

**Perf. 12**

**1998, Oct. 9    Litho.**

| 6478 | A3058 | 1r multicolored | .35 | .20 |
|---|---|---|---|---|

Universal Declaration of Human Rights, 50th Anniv. — A3059

**1998, Oct. 15**

| 6479 | A3059 | 1.50r multicolored | .55 | .25 |
|---|---|---|---|---|

No. 6479 released with se-tenant label.

Menatep Bank, 10th Anniv. — A3060

**1998, Oct. 29**

| 6480 | A3060 | 2r multicolored | .70 | .35 |
|---|---|---|---|---|

**20th Cent. Achievements — A3061**

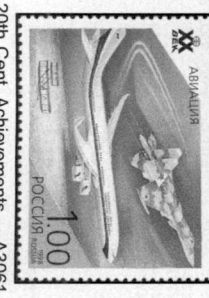

**1998, Nov. 12**
| | | | | |
|---|---|---|---|---|
| 6481 | A3061 | 1r Aviation | .20 | |
| 6482 | A3061 | 1r Space | .20 | |
| 6483 | A3061 | 1r Television | .20 | |
| 6484 | A3061 | 1r Genetics | .20 | |
| 6485 | A3061 | 1r Nuclear power | .20 | |
| 6486 | A3061 | 1r Computers | .20 | |
| | | Nos. 6481-6486 (6) | 1.20 | |

Illustration reduced.

**M.I. Koshkin (1898-1940), Tank Designer — A3062**

**1998, Nov. 20**
| 6487 | A3062 | 1r multicolored | .35 | .20 |
|---|---|---|---|---|

**New Year — A3063**

**1998, Dec. 1 Litho. Perf. 11½**
| 6488 | A3063 | 1r multicolored | .25 | .20 |
|---|---|---|---|---|
| a. | | Sheet of 9 | 2.25 | 1.10 |

**Moscow-St. Petersburg Telephone Line, Cent. — A3064**

**1999, Jan. 13**
| 6489 | A3064 | 1r multicolored | .25 | .20 |
|---|---|---|---|---|

**Hunting A3065**

**1999, Jan. 29 Litho. Perf. 11¼**
| 6490 | A3065 | 1r Wild turkey | .25 | .20 |
|---|---|---|---|---|
| 6491 | A3065 | 1.50r Ducks | .35 | .20 |
| 6492 | A3065 | 2r Releasing raptor | .45 | .20 |
| 6493 | A3065 | 2.50r Wolves | .60 | .30 |
| 6494 | A3065 | 3r Bear | .70 | .35 |
| | | Nos. 6490-6494 (5) | 2.35 | 1.25 |

**Souvenir Sheet**

**Mediterranean Cruise of Feodor F. Ushakov, Bicent. — A3066**

**1999, Feb. 19 Perf. 12½x12**
| 6495 | A3066 | 5r multicolored | 1.25 | .60 |
|---|---|---|---|---|

Illustration reduced.

**Order of Russia Type of 1998**

**1999, Feb. 25 Litho. Perf. 12x12½**
| 6496 | A3053 | 1r multicolored | .20 | .20 |
|---|---|---|---|---|
| 6497 | A3053 | 1.50r multicolored | .25 | .20 |
| 6498 | A3053 | 2r multicolored | .30 | .20 |
| 6499 | A3053 | 2.50r multicolored | .40 | .20 |
| 6500 | A3053 | 3r multicolored | .50 | .20 |
| a. | | Sheet of 5, #6496-6500 | 1.60 | .80 |

1r, St. Vladimir, 1782. 1.50r, St. Anne, 1797. 2r, St. John of Jerusalem, 1798. 2.50r, White Eagles, 1815. 3r, St. Stanislas, 1815.

**Children's Paintings — A3067**

**1999, Mar. 24 Litho. Perf. 12½x12**
| 6501 | A3067 | 1.20r multicolored | .20 | .20 |
|---|---|---|---|---|
| 6502 | A3067 | 1.20r multicolored | .20 | .20 |
| 6503 | A3067 | 1.20r multicolored | .20 | .20 |
| | | Nos. 6501-6503 (3) | .60 | .60 |

Designs: No. 6501, Family picnic. No. 6502, City, bridge, boats on water, helicopter. No. 6503, Stylized city, vert.

**Russian Navy's Use of Flag with St. Andrew's Cross, 300th Anniv. — A3068**

**Souvenir Sheet**

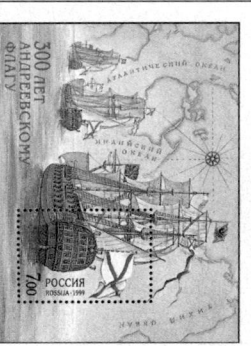

**1999, Mar. 24 Litho. Perf. 12½x12**
| 6504 | A3068 | 7r multicolored | 1.10 | .55 |
|---|---|---|---|---|

Illustration reduced.

**Intl. Space Station — A3069**

**1999, Apr. 12 Perf. 11½x12½**
| 6505 | A3069 | 7r multicolored | 1.00 | .50 |
|---|---|---|---|---|

Illustration reduced.

**Souvenir Sheet**

**IBRA '99 World Philatelic Exhibition, Nuremberg — A3070**

**1999, Apr. 27 Perf. 12½x12**
| 6506 | A3070 | 3r multicolored | .45 | .25 |
|---|---|---|---|---|

**Fishermen and Fishing Gear — A3071**

**1999, Apr. 30 Perf. 11¾**
| 6507 | A3071 | 1r Raft | .20 | .20 |
|---|---|---|---|---|
| 6508 | A3071 | 2r Three fishermen | .30 | .20 |
| 6509 | A3071 | 2r Fisherman, boat | .30 | .20 |
| 6510 | A3071 | 3r Spear fishing | .45 | .25 |
| 6511 | A3071 | 3r Ice fishermen | .45 | .25 |
| | | Nos. 6507-6511 (5) | 1.70 | 1.10 |

**Council of Europe, 50th Anniv. A3072**

**1999, May 5 Perf. 12x12½**
| 6512 | A3072 | 3r multicolored | .45 | .25 |
|---|---|---|---|---|

**Europa A3073**

**1999, May 5 Perf. 12½x12**
| 6513 | A3073 | 5r multicolored | .75 | .35 |
|---|---|---|---|---|

**Red Deer — A3074**

**1999, May 18 Perf. 12½x12**
| 6514 | A3074 | 2.50r Pair, #a.-b. | .75 | .35 |
|---|---|---|---|---|

Designs: a, Bucks. b, Does.
Complete booklet #6514.
See People's Republic of China #2958-2959.

**Aleksander Pushkin (1799-1837), Poet A3075**

**1999, May 27 Litho. & Engr. Perf. 12**
| 6515 | A3075 | 1r multicolored | .20 | .20 |
|---|---|---|---|---|
| 6516 | A3075 | 3r multicolored | .45 | .25 |
| 6517 | A3075 | 5r multicolored | .75 | .35 |
| a. | | Min. sheet, 2 ea #6515-6517 | 2.75 | 1.40 |
| | | Nos. 6515-6517 (3) | 1.40 | .80 |

Paintings of Pushkin by: 1r, S. G. Chirikov, 1815. 3r, J. E. Vivien, 1826. 5r, Karl P. Bryulov, 1836. 7r, Vasily A. Tropinin, 1827.

**Souvenir Sheet**
| 6518 | A3075 | 7r multicolored | 1.00 | .50 |
|---|---|---|---|---|

No. 6518 contains one 30x41mm stamp.

**North Ossetia Republic A3076**

**Stavropol Kray A3077**

**Evenki Autonomous Okrug — A3078**

**1999, June 2 Litho. Perf. 12**
| 6519 | A3078 | 2r multicolored | .30 | .20 |
|---|---|---|---|---|

**Bashkir Republic — A3079**
| 6520 | A3079 | 2r multicolored | .30 | .20 |
|---|---|---|---|---|
| 6521 | A3079 | 2r multicolored | .30 | .20 |
| 6522 | A3079 | 2r multicolored | .30 | .20 |
| 6523 | A3079 | 2r Kirov Oblast | .30 | .20 |
| | | Nos. 6519-6523 (5) | 1.50 | 1.00 |

**Roses — A3080**

  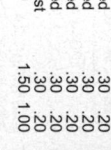

**1999, June 10 Perf. 12½x11¾**

*Color of Rose*
| 6524 | A3080 | 1.20r pink | .20 | .20 |
|---|---|---|---|---|
| 6525 | A3080 | 1.20r yellow | .20 | .20 |
| 6526 | A3080 | 1.20r red & yellow | .30 | .20 |
| 6527 | A3080 | 3r white | .45 | .25 |
| 6528 | A3080 | 4r red | .60 | .30 |
| a. | | Min. sheet of 5, #6524-6528 | 1.75 | 1.10 |
| b. | | Strip of 5, #6524-6528 | 1.75 | 1.10 |
| | | Nos. 6524-6528 (5) | 1.75 | 1.15 |

**No. 6125A Surcharged**

**1999, June 22 Litho. Perf. 12½x12**
| 6529 | A2902 | 1.20r on 500r | .20 | .20 |
|---|---|---|---|---|

**Rostov-on-Don, 250th Anniv. — A3081**

**1999, July 8 Litho. Perf. 11¾x12¼**
| 6530 | A3081 | 1.20r multi | .20 | .20 |
|---|---|---|---|---|

## UPU, 125th Anniv. — A3082

3.00 РОССИЯ ROSSIJA 1999 — 125 ЛЕТ ВСЕМИРНОМУ ПОЧТОВОМУ СОЮЗУ — UPU

**1999, Aug. 23**  **Perf. 11¾**
6531 A3082 3r multi  .45  .25

## Paintings of Karl P. Bryulov (1799-1852) — A3083

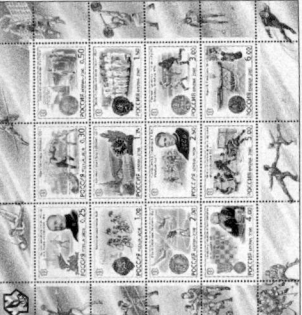

Paintings: a, Horsewoman, 1832. b, Portrait of Y. P. Samoilova and Amacillia Paccini. Illustration reduced.

**1999, Aug. 25**  **Litho.**  **Perf. 11¾x12**
6532 A3083 2.50r Pair, #a-b, + central label  .70  .35

## Motorcycles — A3084

Designs: a, 1r, IZ-1, 1929. b, 1.50r, L-300, 1930. c, 2r, M-72, 1941. d, 2.50r, M-1A, 1945. e, 5r, IZ Planet 5, 1987.

**1999, Sept. 9**  **Litho.**  **Perf. 11¾**
6533 A3084 Block of 5, #a-e,  1.75  4.25
Booklet No. #6533

The booklet also contains an unfranked cacheted envelope with First Day Cancel.

## Field Marshal Aleksandr Suvorov's Alpine Campaign, Bicent. — A3085

Designs: No. 6534, Suvorov and soldiers, monument at Schöllenen Gorge. No. 6535, Suvorov's vanguard at Lake Klöntal.

**1999, Sept. 24**  **Litho.**  **Perf. 12x11½**
6534 A3085 2.50r multi  .35  .20
6535 A3085 2.50r multi  .35  .20

See Switzerland Nos. 1056-1057.

## Native Sports — A3086

#6536, Kalmyk wrestling. #6537, Horse racing. #6538, Stick tossing. #6539, Reindeer racing. #6540, Weight lifting.

**1999, Sept. 30**
**Perf. 11¾x11½, 11½x11¾**
6536 A3086 2r multi  .30  .20
6537 A3086 2r multi  .30  .20
6538 A3086 2r multi  .30  .20
6539 A3086 2r multi  .30  .20
6540 A3086 2r multi, vert.  .30  .20
Nos. 6536-6540 (5)  1.50  1.00

## Popular Singers A3087

2.00 РОССИЯ 1999 — Леонид Утёсов 1895-1982

Designs: No. 6542, Leonid Utesov (1895-1982). No. 6543, Mark Bernes (1911-69). No. 6544, Claudia Shulzhenko (1906-84). No. 6545, Lidia Ruslanova (1900-73). No. 6546, Bulat Okudzhava (1924-97). No. 6547, Vladimir Visotsky (1938-80). No. 6548, Viktor Tsoi (1962-90). No. 6549, Igor Talkov (1956-91).

**1999, Oct. 6**  **Litho.**  **Perf. 12x12½**
6542 A3087 2r multi  .30  .20
6543 A3087 2r multi  .30  .20
6544 A3087 2r multi  .30  .20
6545 A3087 2r multi  .30  .20
6546 A3087 2r multi  .30  .20
6547 A3087 2r multi  .30  .20
6548 A3087 2r multi  .30  .20
6549 A3087 2r multi  .30  .20
a. Miniature sheet of #6542-6549 (8)  2.40  1.60
Nos. 6542-6549 (8)  2.40

## Types of 1997 Redrawn with Microprinting Replacing Vertical Lines

**1999, Oct. 26**  **Litho.**  **Perf. 12x12½**
Granite Paper
6550 A3020 10k Like #6371  .20  .20
6551 A3020 15k Like #6372  .20  .20
6552 A3020 25k Like #6373  .20  .20
6553 A3020 30k Like #6374  .20  .20
6554 A3020 50k Like #6375  .20  .20
6555 A3020 1r Like #6377  .20  .20
6556 A3020 1.50r Like #6378  .20  .20
6557 A3020 2r Like #6379  .30  .20
6558 A3020 2.50r Like #6380  .30  .20
6559 A3020 5r Like #6381  .40  .20
6560 A3020 5r Like #6382  .65  .30
Nos. 6550-6560 (11)  3.05  2.30

Dated 1998.

## Spartak, Russian Soccer Champions A3088

РОССИЯ 2.00 — СПАРТАК АЛАНИЯ

**1999, Nov. 27**  **Perf. 12x12½**
6561 A3088 2r multi  .30  .20

## New Year 2000 — A3089

Designs: a, Grandfather Frost, planets. b, Tree, earth in shell. Illustration reduced.

**1999, Dec. 1**  **Perf. 11½x11¾**
6562 A3089 1.20r Pair, #a-b  .35  .20
c. Sheet of 6 #6562a  .95
d. Sheet of 6 #6562b  .95

No. 6562 printed in sheets of 30 stamps.

## Christianity, 2000th Anniv. — A3090

РОССИЯ 3.00

Paintings: No. 6563, The Raising of the Daughter of Jairus, by Vassili D. Polenov, 1871. No. 6564, Christ in the Wilderness, by Ivan N. Kramskoy, 1872. No. 6565, Christ in the House of Mary and Martha, by G. I. Semiradsky, 1886. No. 6566, What is Truth?, by Nikolai N. Gay, 1890, vert. 7r, Appearance of the Risen Christ, by Alexander A. Ivanov, 1837-57.

**2000, Jan. 1**  **Litho.**  **Perf. 12**
6563 A3090 3r multi  .40  .20
6564 A3090 3r multi  .40  .20
6565 A3090 3r multi  .40  .20
6566 A3090 3r multi  .40  .20
Nos. 6563-6566 (4)  1.60  .80

Souvenir Sheet
**Perf. 12½x12**
6567 A3090 7r multi  .90  .45

No. 6567 contains one 52x37mm stamp.

## Christianity, 2000th Anniv. — A3091

Souvenir Sheet

2000-ЛЕТИЕ ХРИСТИАНСТВА

a, Mother of God mosaic, St. Sofia Cathedral, Kiev, 11th cent. b, Christ Pantocrator fresco, Church of the Savior's Transfiguration, Polotsk, Belarus, 12th cent. c, Volodymyr Madonna, Tretiakov Gallery, Moscow, 12th cent.
Illustration reduced.

**2000, Jan. 5**  **Perf. 12x12½**
6568 A3091 3r Sheet of 3, #a-c  .90  .45

See Belarus No. 330, Ukraine No. 370.

## Nikolai D. Psurtsev (1900-80), Communications Minister — A3092

Н.Д. ПСУРЦЕВ 1900-1980 — РОССИЯ 2000 — 2.50

**2000, Feb. 1**  **Litho. & Engr.**  **Perf. 12x12½**
6569 A3092 2.50r multi  .35  .20

## Christianity, 2000th Anniv. — A3093

Souvenir Sheet

Illustration reduced.

**2000, Feb. 10**  **Litho.**  **Perf. 12½**
6570 A3093 10r Kremlin Cathedrals  1.40  .70

No. 6570 contains two 37x52mm labels.

## Polar Explorers — A3094

РОССИЯ 2000 — 2.00 — Р. Л. Самойлович

Designs: No. 6571, R. L. Samoilovich (1881-1940). No. 6572, V. Y. Vize (1886-1954). No. 6573, Mikhail M. Somov (1908-73). No. 6574, P. A. Gordienko (1913-82). No. 6575, A. F. Treshnikov (1914-91).
Illustration reduced.

**2000, Feb. 24**  **Perf. 11¾**
6571 A3094 2r multi  .30  .20
6572 A3094 2r multi  .30  .20
6573 A3094 2r multi  .30  .20
6574 A3094 2r multi  .30  .20
6575 A3094 2r multi  .30  .20
a. Miniature sheet of 5, #6571-6575, + label  1.50  .75

## National Sporting Milestones of the 20th Century — A3095

a, 25k, N. A. Panin-Kolomenkin, 1st Olympic champion, 1908. b, 30k, Stockholm Olympics, 1912. c, 50k, All-Russian Olympiad, 1913-14. d, 1r, All-Union Spartacist Games, 1928. e, 1.35r, Sports Association for Labor & Defense, 1931. f, 1.50r, Honored Master of Sport award, 1934. g, 2r, Helsinki Olympics, 1952. h, 2.50r, Vladimir P. Kuts, gold medalist at Melbourne Olympics, 1956. i, 3r, Gold medalist soccer team at Melbourne, 1956. j, 4r, Mikhail M. Botvinnik, chess champion. k, 5r, Hockey series between Canada and Soviet Union, 1972. l, 6r, Moscow Olympics, 1980.

**2000, Mar. 15**  **Perf. 12½x12**
6576 A3095 Sheet of 12, #a-l  3.75  1.90

## World Meteorological Organization, 50th Anniv. — A3096

7.00 — 1951 2000 50

**2000, Mar. 20**  **Perf. 12½x12**
6577 A3096 7r multi  .90  .45

## End of World War II, 55th Anniv. — A3099

С ПОБЕДОЙ — КРАСНОЙ АРМИИ СЛАВА — 55 — РОССИЯ 2000 — 1.50

A3098  A3097

War effort posters: No. 6581, Soldier holding child. 5r, Soldier and medal.

**2000, Apr. 10**
6578 A3097 1.50r multi  .20  .20
6579 A3098 1.50r multi  .20  .20
6580 A3099 1.50r multi  .20  .20
6581 A3099 1.50r multi  .80  .80
Nos. 6578-6581 (4)  .65  .30

Souvenir Sheet
6582 A3099 5r multi  2.10  1.10
a. Miniature sheet, #6578-6581, #6582

RUSSIA

International Space Cooperation — A3100

**2000, Apr. 12**
6583 A3100 2r multi ........................ .20 .20
a. Miniature sheet of 6 ............... 1.50 .75
6584 A3100 3r multi ........................ .30 .25
6585 A3100 5r multi, vert. ............. .50 .25
Nos. 6583-6585 (3) ...................... 1.05 .65

2r, Apollo-Soyuz mission, 3r, Int'l. Space Station. 5r, Sea-based launching station.

Traffic Safety Week — A3101

**2000, Apr. 20    Litho.    Perf. 12**
6586 A3101 1.75r multi ........................ .25 .20

Holocaust — A3102

1933-1945

**2000, May 5    Litho.    Perf. 12½x12½**
6587 A3102 2r multi ........................ .25 .20

Election of Vladimir V. Putin as President — A3103

РОССИЯ 2000    1.75

**2000, May 7    Litho.    Perf. 12**
6588 A3103 1.75r multi ........................ .25 .20

Europa, 2000
Common Design Type

**2000, May 9    Litho.    Perf. 12½x12**
6589 CD17 7r multi ........................ .90 .90
Booklet #6589

Expo 2000, Hanover — A3104

**2000, May 17    Litho.    Perf. 12½x12**
6590 A3104 10r multi ........................ 1.25 .60
Souvenir Sheet

National Scientific Milestones in the 20th Century — A3109

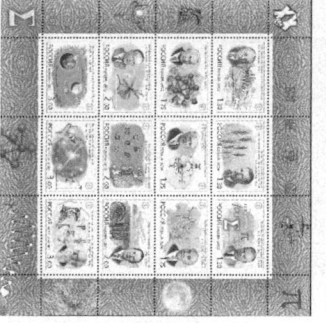

**2000, May 25    Perf. 12**
6591 A3105 3r shown ................. .35 .20
6592 A3105 3r Chuvash Republic ...... .35 .20
6593 A3106 3r shown ................. .35 .20
6594 A3107 3r shown ................. .35 .20
6595 A3108 3r shown ................. .35 .20
6596 A3108 3r Udmurtia Repub-
    lic ........................ 2.10 1.20
Nos. 6591-6596 (6)

No. 6597: a.1.30r, Observation of ferromagnetic resonance by V. K. Arkadiev, 1913. b. 1.30r, Botanical diversity studies by N. I. Vavilov, 1920. c. 1.30r, Moscow Mathematical School, N. N. Luzin, 1920-30. d. 1.75r, Theories on light wave emissions by I. Y. Tamm, 1929. e. 1.75r, Discovery of superfluidity of liquid helium, by P. L. Kapitsa, 1938. f. 1.75r, Research in chemical chain reactions by N. N. Semenov, 1934. g. 2r, Phase stability in particle accelerators, by V. I. Veksler, 1944-45. h. 2r, Translation of Mayan texts by Y. V. Knorozov, 1950s. i. 2r, Research into pogonophorans by A. V. Ivanov. j. 3r, Photographing of the dark side of the moon by Luna 3, 1959. k. 3r, Research in quantum electronics by N. G. Basov and A. M. Prokhorov, 1960s. l. 3r, Slavic ethnolinguistic dictionary by N. I. Tolstoi, 1995.

**2000, June 20    Perf. 12½x12**
6597 A3109 Sheet of 12, #a-l ......... 3.00 1.50

Dogs — A3110

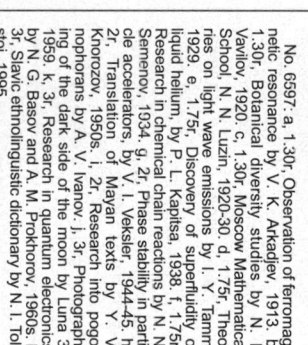 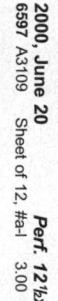

Чихуахуа    1.00

Dogs — A3110

Yamalo-Nenets Autonomous Okrug — A3105

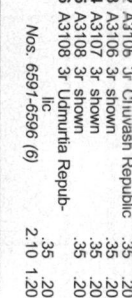

РОССИЯ 2000    3.00

Kalmykia Republic — A3106

РОССИЯ 2000    3.00

Mari El Republic — A3107

РОССИЯ 2000    3.00

Tatarstan Republic — A3108

РОССИЯ 2000    3.00

2000 Summer Olympics, Sydney — A3111

РОССИЯ 2000    2.00

Designs: 2r, Fencing. 3r, Synchronized swimming. 5r, Volleyball.

**2000, Aug. 15    Litho.    Perf. 12**
6599-6601 A3111    Set of 3 ...... 1.25 .65

Geological Service, 300th Anniv. — A3112

ЧАРОИТ    300

РОССИЯ 2000    1.00

Minerals: 1r, Charoite. 2r, Hematite. 3r, Rock crystals. 4r, Gold.

**2000, Aug. 22    Perf. 11¾**
6602-6605 A3112    Set of 4 ...... 1.25 .60

National Cultural Milestones in the 20th Century — A3113

No. 6606: a. 30k, Tours of Russian ballet and opera companies, 1908-14. b. 50k, Black Square on White, by Kazimir S. Malevich, 1913. c. 1r, Battleship Potemkin, movie by Sergein Eisenstein, 1925. d. 1.30r, Maxim Gorki, writer. e. 1.50r, Symbols of socialism. f. 1.75r, Vladimir V. Mayakovsky, poet, and propaganda posters. g. 2r, Vsevolod V. Meyerhold, Konstantin S. Stanislavsky, actors. h. 2.50r, Dmitry D. Shostakovich, composer. i. 3r, Galina S. Ulanova, ballet dancer. j. 4r, A. T. Tvardovsky, poet. k. 5r, Restoration of historical monuments and buildings. l. 6r, D. S. Likhachev, literary critic.

**2000, Sept. 20    Litho.    Perf. 12½x12**
6606 A3113 Sheet of 12, #a-l ........ 2.25 1.10

Fish in Lake Peipus — A3114

2.50

No. 6607: a. Stizostedion lucioperka. b. Coregonus lavaretus maraenoides. c. Osmerus eperlanus spirinchus. d. Coregonus albula.

**2000, Oct. 25    Perf. 12½x12½**
6607    Horiz. pair + central label ......... .40 .40
a.-b. Any single ...................... .20 .20
Booklet, #6607

See Estonia No. 403.

National Technological Milestones in the 20th Century — A3115

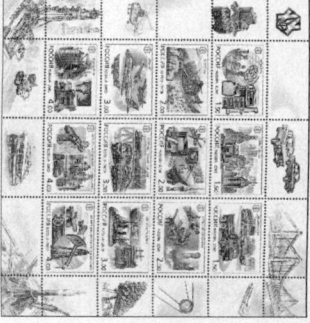

No. 6608: a. 1.50r, Medicine. b. 1.50r, Construction. c. 1.50r, Motor transport. d. 2r, Power generation. e. 2r, Communications. f. 2r, Space technology. g. 3r, Aviation. h. 3r, Rail transport. i. 3r, Sea transport. j. 4r, Metallurgy. k. 4r, Oil refining. l. 4r, Mineral extraction.

**2000, Nov. 28    Perf. 12½x12**
6608 A3115    Sheet of 12, #a-l ...... 2.50 1.25

Foreign Intelligence Service, 80th Anniv. — A3117

80 ЛЕТ    РОССИЯ    2.50

**2000, Dec. 14    Litho.    Perf. 12½x12½**
6610 A3117 2.50r multi ............... .25 .20

Happy New Millennium — A3116

РОССИЯ 2000    2.00

**2000, Dec. 1    Perf. 12**
6609 A3116 2r multi ......... .20 .20
a. Sheet of 6 ............... 1.00 .50

2000, July 20    Perf. 12x11¾
6598    Horiz. strip of 5 ...... 1.10 .55
a. A3110 1r Chihuahua .......... .20 .20
b. A3110 1.50r Toy terrier ...... .20 .20
c. A3110 2r Miniature poodle .... .20 .20
d. A3110 2.50r French bulldog ... .30 .20
e. A3110 3r Japanese chin ....... .30 .20
f. Souvenir sheet, #6598a, 2 each
    #6598a-6598e, perf. 11¾ ...... 2.00 1.00
Booklet, #6598
#6598a-6598d,
Souvenir sheet, #6598e ......... 1.10

Kabardino-Balkaria Republic — A3118

 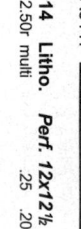

РОССИЯ 2001    3.00

Samara Oblast — A3120

РОССИЯ 2001    3.00

Dagestan Republic — A3119

РОССИЯ 2001    3.00

**2001, Jan. 10    Perf. 12**
6611 A3118 3r shown .......... .25 .20
6612 A3119 3r shown .......... .25 .20
6613 A3120 3r shown .......... .25 .20
6614 A3118 3r Chita Oblast .... .25 .20
6615 A3118 3r Komi Republic ... 1.25 1.00
Nos. 6611-6615 (5)

## Souvenir Sheet

### Naval Education in Russia, 300th Anniv. — A3121

No. 6616: a, 1.50r, Mathematics and Navigation School, Moscow. b, 2r, Geographical expeditions. c, 8r, St. Petersburg Naval Institute.

2001, Jan. 10    **Perf. 12x12¼**
6616 A3121 Sheet of 3, #a-c   .95   .50

### Type of 1997 With Lines of Microprinting for Vertical Lines

Design: 10r, Ballerina.

2001, Jan. 24   Litho.   **Perf. 11¾x12¼**
6617 A3020 10r multi   .65   .30

### Type of 1997 With Lines of Microprinting for Vertical Lines

Designs: 25r, Rhythmic gymnast. 50r, Earth and computer. 100r, UPU emblem.

2001, Jan. 24   Litho.   **Perf. 11¾x12¼**
6618 A3020 25r blk & yel brn   1.60   .80
6619 A3020 50r blk & blue   3.25   1.60
6620 A3020 100r blk & claret   6.50   3.25
Nos. 6618-6620 (3)   11.35   5.65

A number has been reserved for an additional stamp in this set.

---

### Paintings — A3126

No. 6626, 3r (brown background): a, Portrait of P. A. Bulakhov, by Vasily Andreevich Tropinin, 1823. b, Portrait of E. I. Karzinkina, by Tropinin, 1838.
No. 6627, 3r (tan and white background): a, Portrait of I. A. Galitsin, by A. M. Matveev, 1728. b, Portrait of A. P. Galitsina, by Matveev, 1728.
Illustration reduced.

2001, Feb. 15   Litho.   **Perf. 12**
**Pairs, #a-b, + Central Label**
6626-6627 A3126 Set of 2   1.00   .50

### St. Petersburg, 300th Anniv. — A3127

Paintings: 1r, Senate Square and Peter the Great Monument, by B. Patersen, 1799. 2r, English Embankment Near senate, by Patersen, 1801. 3r, View of Mikhailovsky Castle From Fontanka Embankment, by Patersen, 1801. 4r, View of the River Moika Near the Stable Department Building, by A. E. Martynov, 1809. 5r, View of the Neva River From the Peter and Paul Fortress, by K. P. Beggrov, 19th cent.

2001, Mar. 15   **Perf. 12x11¾**
6628-6632 A3127 Set of 5   1.25   .60
6632a Sheet, #6628-6632, + label   1.25   .60

### Dragonflies — A3128

No. 6633: a, 1r, Pyrrhosoma nymphula. b, 1.50r, Epitheca bimaculata. c, 2r, Aeschna grandis. d, 3r, Libellula depressa. e, 5r, Coenagrion hastulatum.
Illustration reduced.

2001, Apr. 5   **Perf. 12x12¼**
6633 A3128 Block of 5, #a-e, + label   1.00   .50

### First Manned Space Flight, 40th Anniv. — A3129

No. 6634: a, Cosmonaut Yuri Gagarin and rocket designer Sergei Korolev. b, Gagarin saluting.
Illustration reduced.

2001, Apr. 12   Litho.   **Perf. 12½x12**
6634 A3129 3r Horiz. pair, #a-b   .50   .25
c. Sheet, 3 #6634   1.50   .75

### Europa — A3130

2001, May 9   Litho.   **Perf. 11¾**
6635 A3130 8r multi   .65   .30
a. Sheet of 6   4.00   2.00

---

### Intl. Federation of Philately, 75th Anniv. — A3131

2.50

2001, May 17   **Perf. 11½**
6636 A3131 2.50r multi   .20   .20

### Declaration of State Sovereignty Day — A3132

5.00

**Perf. 13¼**
**Litho. & Embossed**
2001, June 5
6637 A3132 5r multi   .40   .20

### Russian Emblems A3133

2.50

Designs: No. 6638a, Flag. No. 6638b, Arms.
National anthem. Nos. 6638c, 6639a, Arms.

**Perf. 13¼**
**Litho. & Embossed**
2001, June 5
6638 Horiz. strip of 3   .80   .40
a. A3133 2.50r multi   .10   .20
b.    2.50r multi   .10
c.    .25   .25
d. Booklet pane of 1, #6638a
e. Booklet pane of 1, #6638b

### Souvenir Sheet

6639   Sheet of 3, #6638a-6638b, 6639a
a. A3133 100r multi   4.00
b. Booklet pane of 1, #6639a 4.25
   Booklet, #6638d, 6638e, 6639b 13.00

A3134

### Houses of Worship — A3135

Designs: No. 6640, Cathedral, Vladimir, 1189. No. 6641, Cathedral, Zvenigorod, 1405. No. 6642, Cathedral, Rostov-on-Don, 1792. No. 6643, Cathedral, Rostov-on-Don, 1792. No. 6644, Mosque, Ufa, 1830. No. 6645, Church,

---

St. Petersburg, 1838. No. 6646, Mosque, Kazan, 1849. No. 6647, Synagogue, Moscow, 1891. No. 6648, Synagogue, St. Petersburg, 1893. No. 6649, Cathedral, Moscow, 1911. No. 6650, Temple, Ulan-Ude, 1976. No. 6651, Church, Bryansk, 1996. No. 6652, Church, Ryazan, 1996. No. 6653, Church, Lesosibirsk, 1999.

**Perf. 11½**   Litho.
2001, July 12
6640 A3134 2.50r multi   .20   .20
6641 A3134 2.50r multi   .20   .20
6642 A3134 2.50r shown   .20   .20
6643 A3134 2.50r multi   .20   .20
6644 A3134 2.50r multi   .20   .20
6645 A3134 2.50r multi   .20   .20
6646 A3134 2.50r multi   .20   .20
6647 A3134 2.50r multi   .20   .20
6648 A3134 2.50r multi   .20   .20
6649 A3134 2.50r multi   .20   .20
6650 A3135 2.50r shown   .20   .20
6651 A3135 2.50r multi   .20   .20
6652 A3135 2.50r multi   .20   .20
6653 A3135 2.50r multi   .20   .20
Nos. 6640-6653 (14)   2.80   2.80

### Souvenir Sheet

12.00

### First Russian Railroad, 150th Anniv. — A3136

2001, July 25
6654 A3136 12r multi   .95   .50

### Flight of Gherman Titov on Vostok 2, 40th Anniv. A3137

**Perf. 12**
2001, Aug. 6   Litho.
6655 A3137 3r multi   .95   .95

### Film Stars A3138

3.00

**Perf. 12½x12**
Designs: No. 6656, 2.50r, Mikhail Zharov (1899-1981). No. 6657, 2.50r, Faina Ranevskaya (1896-1984). No. 6658, 2.50r, Nikolai Kryuchkov (1910-94). No. 6659, 2.50r, Nikolai Rybnikov (1930-90). No. 6660, 2.50r, Lubov Orlova (1902-75). No. 6661, 2.50r, Yuri Nikulin (1921-97). No. 6662, 2.50r, Evgeny Leonov (1926-94). No. 6663, 2.50r, Anatoly Papanov (1922-87). No. 6664, 2.50r, Andrei Mironov (1941-87).

2001, Sept. 20
6656-6664 A3138 Set of 9   1.90   .95
6664a Sheet, #6656-6664   1.90   .95

### Ivan Lazarev (1735-1801) and Institute of Eastern Languages — A3139

2.50

**Perf. 11¾**
2001, Sept. 26
6665 A3139 2.50r multi   .20   .20

---

### Tulips — A3125

2001, Feb. 2   Litho.   **Perf. 12½x12**
6625   Horiz. strip of 5   .80   .40
a. A3122 2r Happy Birthday   .20   .20
b. A3123 2r Be Happy   .20   .20
c. A3124 2r Congratulations   .20   .20
d. A3124a 2r Good luck   .20   .20
e. A3125 2r With Love   .20   .20
f. Sheet, #6625a-6625e + label   .80   .40

2.00   С днем рождения!   A3122
2.00   Желаем удачи!   A3123
2.00   поздравляем!   A3124
2.00   Будьте счастливы!   A3124a
2.00   С любовью!   A3125

**2001, Oct. 9**

Perf. 12

6666 A3140 2r gray & black ... 2.00 .20 .20

Arkady Raikin (1911-87), Comedian — A3140

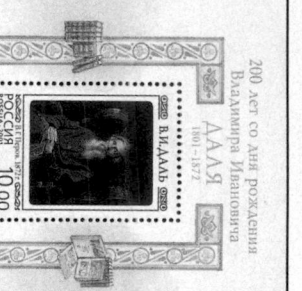

Year of Dialogue Among Civilizations — A3141

Souvenir Sheet

**2001, Oct. 9**

6667 A3141 5r multi ... .40 .20

200 лет со дня рождения Владимира Ивановича

**2001, Oct. 16**

6668 A3142 10r multi

Vladimir Dal (1801-72), Author — A3142

Perf. 12x12½ ... .80 .40

A3142

**2001, Nov. 1**

6669 A3143 3r multi

Constitutional Court, 10th Anniv. A3143

Perf. 11¾x12 ... .25 .20

3.00

A3143

**2001, Nov. 2**

6670 A3144 2.20r multi

Savings Bank of Russia, 160th Anniv. — A3144

Perf. 12x11¾ ... .20 .20

2.20

A3144

---

Defense of Moscow, 60th Anniv. — A3145

Souvenir Sheet

**2001, Nov. 15**

6671 A3145 10r multi ... .80 .40

Perf. 12x12½

Commonwealth of Independent States, 10th Anniv. — A3146

**2001, Nov. 28**

6672 A3146 2r multi ... .20 .20

Perf. 12

Happy New Year — A3147

**2001, Dec. 4**

6673 A3147 2.50r multi ... .20 .20
a. Sheet of 6 ... 1.25 .60

Perf. 12x12¼

Amur Oblast A3148

Khakassia Republic A3149

Karachay-Cherkessia Republic — A3150

Sakhalin Oblast A3151

Altai Republic — A3152

**2002, Jan. 2 Perf. 12x12¼, 12¼x12**

6674 A3148 3r multi ... .25 .20
6675 A3149 3r multi ... .25 .20
6676 A3150 3r multi ... .25 .20
6677 A3151 3r multi ... .25 .20
6678 A3152 3r multi ... .25 .20
Nos. 6674-6678 (5) ... 1.25 1.00

2002 Winter Olympics, Salt Lake City A3153

Designs: 3r, Skier. 4r, Figure skater. 5r, Ski jumper.

Souvenir Sheet

**2002, Jan. 24 Perf. 12x12¼**

6679-6681 A3153 Set of 3 ... .90 .45

World Unity Against Terrorism A3154

**2002, Jan. 30**

6682 A3154 5r multi ... .40 .20

Trans-Siberian Railway, Cent. — A3155

Souvenir Sheet

**2002, Jan. 30**

6683 A3155 12r multi ... .90 .45

Perf. 12¼x12

New Hermitage, 150th Anniv. A3156

Designs: No. 6684, Ecce Homo, by Peter Paul Rubens, before 1612. No. 6685, Courtesan, by Hendrick Goltzius, 1606. No. 6686, Helmet, by Philippo Negroli, 1530s. No. 6687, Gonzaga Cameo, 3rd Cent. B.C. No. 6688, New Hermitage, 1861, by Luigi Premazzi.

**2002, Feb. 15 Litho. & Embossed Perf. 13¼**

6684 A3156 2.50r multi ... .20 .20
6685 A3156 2.50r multi ... .20 .20
a. Booklet pane of 1 ... 1.25
6686 A3156 5r multi ... .40 .20
a. Booklet pane of 1 ... 1.25
6687 A3156 5r multi ... .40 .20
a. Booklet pane of 1 ... 2.25
6688 A3156 15r multi ... 1.20 .80
a. Booklet pane of 1 ... 2.25

Souvenir Sheet

Nos. 6684-6687 (4) ... 1.10 .55
a. Booklet, #6604a-6688a ... 14.00

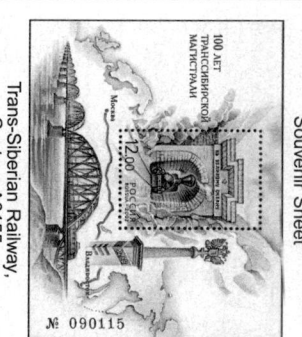

St. Petersburg, 300th Anniv. (in 2003) — A3160

Designs: No. 6695, Kazan Cathedral (semicircular colonnade); monument to Marshal Barclay de Tolly. No. 6696, St. Isaac's Cathedral and sculpture. No. 6697, Resurrection, bridge, griffin. No. 6698, Peter and Paul Cathedral, angel and cross steeple, vert. No. 6699, Admiralty and ship steeple, vert.

**2002, Apr. 25 Litho. & Embossed Perf. 13¼**

6695 A3160 5r multi ... .40 .20
a. Booklet pane of 1 ... 1.00
6696 A3160 5r multi ... .40 .20
a. Booklet pane of 1 ... 1.25 .20
6697 A3160 5r multi ... .40 .20
a. Booklet pane of 1 ... 1.25 .20
6698 A3160 25r multi ... 1.90 .95
a. Booklet pane of 1 ... 5.00
6699 A3160 25r multi ... 1.90 .95
a. Booklet pane of 1 ... 5.00
Nos. 6695-6699 (5) ... 6.50 3.25
17.00

Dogs — A3159

**2002, Mar. 15 Horiz. strip of 5 Perf. 11¼**

6694
a. A3159 1r Cane Corso ... 1.10 .55
b. A3159 2r Shar-pei ... .40 .20
c. A3159 3r Bull mastiff ... .20 .20
d. A3159 4r Fila Brasileiro ... .35 .20
e. A3159 5r Neapolitan mastiff ... .20 .20
f. Miniature sheet of 9, #6694d, 6694e, 2 # 6694a, 4 #6694b ... 1.75 .85

Lilies A3157 A3158

Flower color: No. 6690, White. No. 6692, White with red spots. No. 6693, Red and white with red spots.

**2002, Feb. 20 Perf. 12¼x11¾ Litho.**

6689 A3157 2.50r multi ... .20 .20
6690 A3157 2.50r multi ... .20 .20
6691 A3158 2.50r multi ... .20 .20
6692 A3157 2.50r multi ... .20 .20
6693 A3157 2.50r multi ... .20 .20
a. Miniature sheet, #6689-6693 + label ... 1.00 .50
Nos. 6689-6693 (5) ... 1.00 1.00

Security Services, 80th Anniv. — A3161

No. 6700: a. A. K. Artuzov (1891-1937), b. N. I. Demidenko (1896-1934), c. J. K. Olsky (1898-1937), d. S. V. Puzitsky (1895-1937), e.

Souvenir Sheet

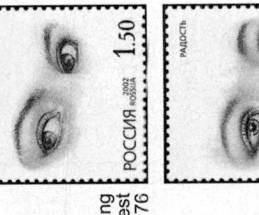

**Battle of Stalingrad, 60th Anniv. — A3175**

2002, Oct. 4
6721 A3175 10r multi .75 .40

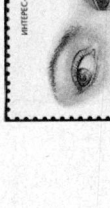 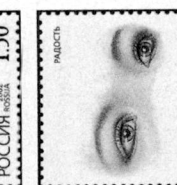

**Eyes Displaying Interest** — A3176

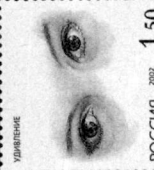

**Eyes Displaying Gladness** — A3177

**Eyes Displaying Astonishment** — A3178

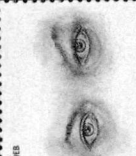

**Eyes Displaying Grief** — A3179

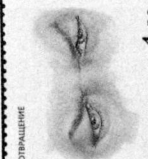

**Eyes Displaying Anger** — A3180

**Eyes Displaying Disgust** — A3181

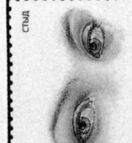

**Eyes Displaying Shame** — A3182

---

**Russian State, 1140th Anniv. — A3172**

*Perf. 11½x11¾*
2002, Sept. 17
6717 A3172 3r multi .25 .20

**2002 Census — A3173**

*Perf. 13½x13*
Litho. & Embossed
**Stamp + label**
2002, Sept. 17
6718 A3173 4r shown .30 .20
a. Booklet pane of 4, no labels 16.50
Complete booklet, #6718a 16.50

Litho.
**Self-Adhesive**
*Serpentine Die Cut 10⅞x11*
6719 A3173 3r Emblem, people .25 .20
a. Booklet pane of 8, no labels 2.00

**Customs Service — A3174**

No. 6720: a, 2r, Customs house, Arkhangelsk, 18th cent. b, 3r, Customs officers, St. Petersburg, 1830s. c, 5r, Kalanchovsky customs warehouse, Moscow, 19th cent.

2002, Sept. 25 Litho. *Perf. 12x12¼*
6720 A3174 Sheet of 3, #a-c .75 .40

---

Booklet, #6705-6705j 16.00
**Souvenir Sheet**
6706 A3166 25r Sheet of 3, #a-c 5.50 5.50

**Kamov Helicopters — A3167**

2002, Aug. 8 Litho. *Perf. 12½x12*
6707
a. A3167 1r KA-10 .90 .45
b. A3167 1.50r KA-22 .20 .20
c. A3167 2r KA-26 .20 .20
d. A3167 2.50r KA-27 .20 .20
e. A3167 5r KA-50 .35 .20
Block of 5 + label

**Anatoly A. Sobchak, Mayor of St. Petersburg (1937-2000) — A3168**

*Perf. 12x12½*
2002, Aug. 10
6708 A3168 3.25r multi .25 .20

**Birds — A3169**

No. 6709: a, Anthropoides virgo. b, Larus ichthyaetus.

2002, Aug. 29 *Perf. 12½x12*
6709 A3169 2.50r Horiz pair, #a-b .40 .20

See Kazakhstan No. 385.

**Kostroma, 850th Anniv. A3170**

2002, Sept. 2 Litho. *Perf. 12x12¼*
6710 A3170 2r multi .20 .20

**Government Ministries, 200th Anniv. — A3171**

Arms and/or Russian flag and ministry buildings or symbols: No. 6711, 3r, Defense (light green background, dark green frame). No. 6712, 3r, Foreign Affairs (light blue background, dark green frame). No. 6713, 3r, Internal Affairs (light blue background, dark blue frame). No. 6714, 3r, Education (pink background, red frame). No. 6715, 3r, Finance (lilac background, dark blue frame). No. 6716, 3r, Justice (light yellow background, gray blue frame).

2002, Sept. 2 *Perf. 12*
6711-6716 A3171 Set of 6 1.40 .70

---

V. A. Styrne (1897-1937), f, G. S. Syroezhkin (1900-37).

2002, Apr. 30 Litho. *Perf. 12x12½*
6700 A3161 2r Sheet of 6, #a-f .95 .50

**Europa A3162**

2002, May 9 *Perf. 12½x12*
6701 A3162 8r multi .65 .30
a. Miniature sheet of 6 4.00 2.00

**Admiral P. S. Nakhimov (1802-55) — A3163**

*Perf. 12x11¾*
2002, May 24 .20 .20
6702 A3163 2r multi 1.25 .60
a. Miniature sheet of 8

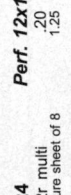

**European Organization of Supreme Audit Institutions, 5th Congress A3164**

*Perf. 12x12½*
2002, May 24 .20 .20
6703 A3164 2r multi

**Kamchatka Peninsula Volcanos — A3165**

No. 6704: a, 1r, Steaming geysers. b, 2r, Mud hole. c, 3r, Karymski Volcano. d, 5r, Crater lake.
Illustration reduced.

2002, June 20 Litho. *Perf. 12*
6704 A3165 Block of 4, #a-d .80 .40

**Carriages A3166**

Designs: No. 6705a, Russian carriage, 1640s. No. 6705b, Closed sleigh, 1732. Nos. 6705c, Coupe carriage, 1746. Nos. 6706a, 6706b, 25r, Berlin calash, 1770s. Nos. 6705e, 6706c, Berline carriage, 1769.

Litho. & Embossed
2002, July 25 *Perf. 13x13¼*
6705 Block of 5 + label 1.50 .75
a.-b. A3166 2.50r Any single .20 .20
c.-f. A3166 5r Any single .35 .35
f. Booklet pane, #6705a 2.00
g. Booklet pane, #6705b 2.00
h. Booklet pane, #6705c 4.00
i. Booklet pane, #6705d 4.00
j. Booklet pane, #6705e 4.00

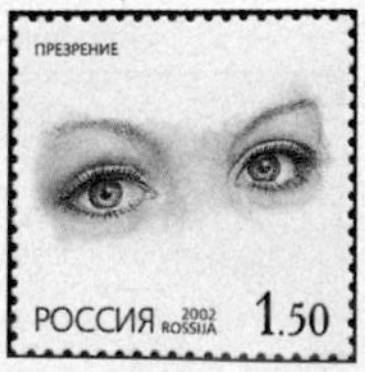

Eyes Displaying Contempt A3183

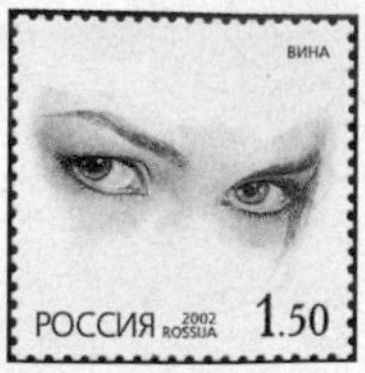

Eyes Displaying Guilt — A3184

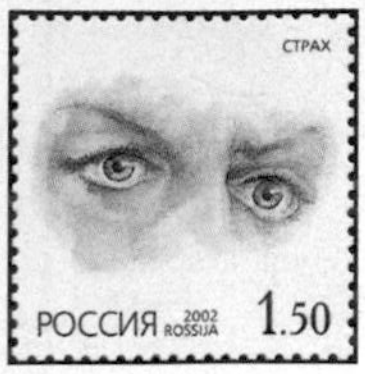

Eyes Displaying Fear — A3185

**2002, Oct. 17** ***Perf. 12x11¾***

| | | | |
|---|---|---|---|
| **6722** | Sheet of 10 | 1.10 | .55 |
| *a.* | A3176 1.50r multi | .20 | .20 |
| *b.* | A3177 1.50r multi | .20 | .20 |
| *c.* | A3178 1.50r multi | .20 | .20 |
| *d.* | A3179 1.50r multi | .20 | .20 |
| *e.* | A3180 1.50r multi | .20 | .20 |
| *f.* | A3181 1.50r multi | .20 | .20 |
| *g.* | A3182 1.50r multi | .20 | .20 |
| *h.* | A3183 1.50r multi | .20 | .20 |
| *i.* | A3184 1.50r multi | .20 | .20 |
| *j.* | A3185 1.50r multi | .20 | .20 |

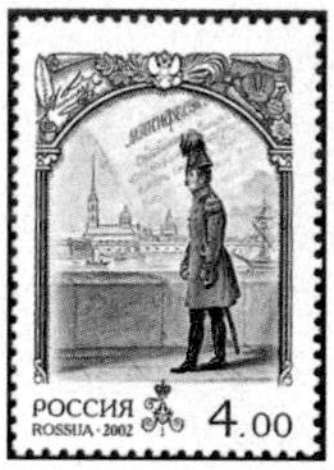

Emperor Alexander I (1777-1825) A3186

Alexander I: No. 6723, 4r, And Manifesto of March 12, 1801 (blue frame). No. 6724, 4r, Taking over codification of laws from his secretary Mikhail M. Speransky, Oct. 1809 (green frame). No. 6725, 7r, Receiving historian N. M. Karamzin ( red frame). No. 6726, 7r, Entering Paris with troops, Mar. 1814 (brown frame).

10r, Portrait of Alexander I, by Francois Gérard.

**Litho. & Engr.**

**2002, Nov. 12** ***Perf. 12x12½***

**6723-6726** A3186 Set of 4 1.60 .80

**Souvenir Sheet**

**6727** A3186 10r multi .75 .75

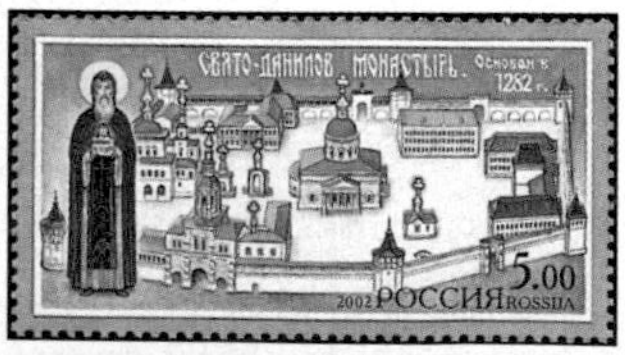

Russian Orthodox Monasteries — A3187

Designs: No. 6728, 5r, Monastery of St. Daniel, 1282. No. 6729, 5r, Sergii Lavra, 1337. No. 6730, 5r, Valaam Monastery, 14th cent. No. 6731, 5r, Monastery of Reverend Savva, 1398. No. 6732, 5r, Pskov Cave Monastery, 1470.

**Litho. & Embossed**

**2002, Nov. 26** ***Perf. 12½***

| | | | |
|---|---|---|---|
| **6728-6732** | A3187 Set of 5 | 1.90 | .95 |
| *6732a* | Souvenir sheet, #6728-6732 + label | 1.90 | .95 |

Nos. 6728-6732 each were issued in sheets of 9 stamps + label. The labels on these sheets differ from the label on No. 6732a.

See Nos. 6756-6761.

A limited edition booklet exists containing booklet panes of one of each of Nos. 6728-6732 and 6756-6761.

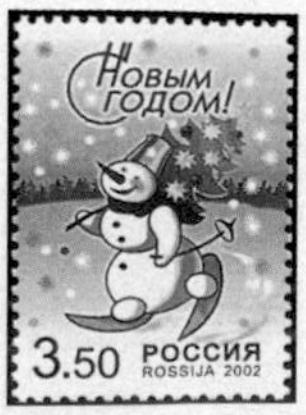

Happy New Year — A3188

**2002, Dec. 2 Litho.** ***Perf. 12¼x11¾***

| | | | |
|---|---|---|---|
| **6733** | A3188 3.50r multi | .25 | .20 |
| *a.* | Sheet of 6 | 1.50 | .75 |

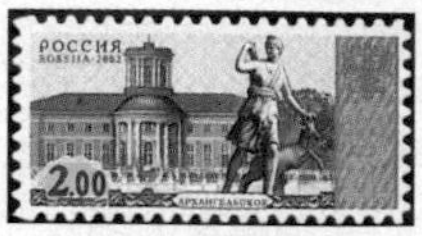

Sculpture and Buildings A3189

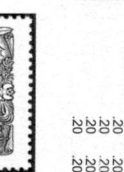

Designs: 2r, Sculpture "Artemis with Deer," Palace, Arkhangelsk. 2.50r, Sculpture "Omphala," Chinese Palace, Oranienbaum. 3r, Sculpture of griffin, mansion, Marfino. 4r, Sculpture "Erminia," Grand Palace, Pavlovsk. 5r, Allegorical sculpture of Scamander River, Palace, Kuskovo.

***Serpentine Die Cut 11***

**2002, Dec. 16**

**Self-Adhesive**

**Town name Panels with Colored Backgrounds**

**Denomination Color**

| | | | |
|---|---|---|---|
| **6734** | A3189 2r brown | .20 | .20 |
| **6735** | A3189 2.50r blue | .20 | .20 |
| **6736** | A3189 3r indigo | .20 | .20 |
| **6737** | A3189 4r violet | .30 | .20 |
| **6738** | A3189 5r purple | .35 | .20 |
| | *Nos. 6734-6738 (5)* | 1.25 | 1.00 |

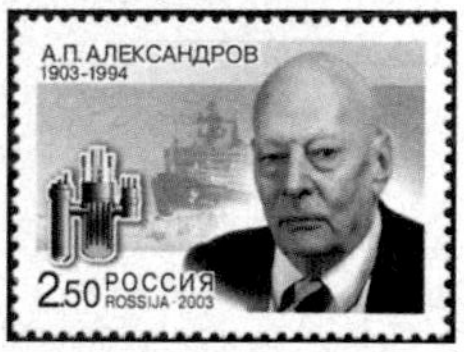

Nuclear Physicists A3190

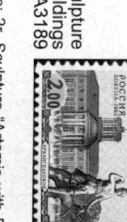

Reactor diagrams and: No. 6739, 2.50r, Anatoly P. Alexandrov (1903-94). No. 6740, 2.50r, Igor V. Kurchatov (1903-60).

**2003, Jan. 8** ***Perf. 12½x12***

**6739-6740** A3190 Set of 2 .40 .20

**Souvenir Sheet**

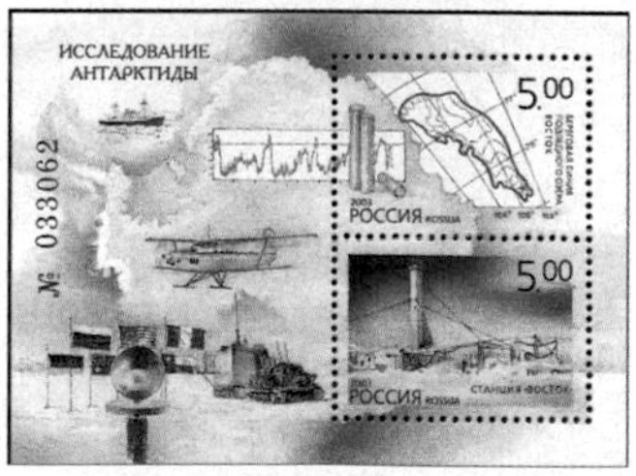

Antarctic Research — A3191

No. 6741: a, Ice borings, map. b, Vostok research station.

**2003, Jan. 8** ***Perf. 11½x12¼***

**6741** A3191 5r Sheet of 2, #a-b .75 .40

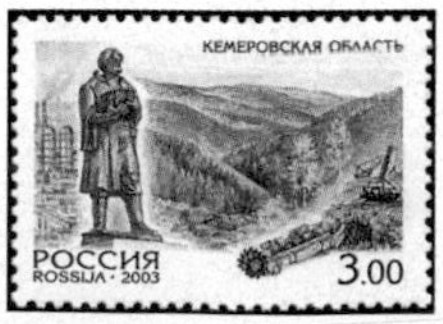

Kemerovo Oblast A3192

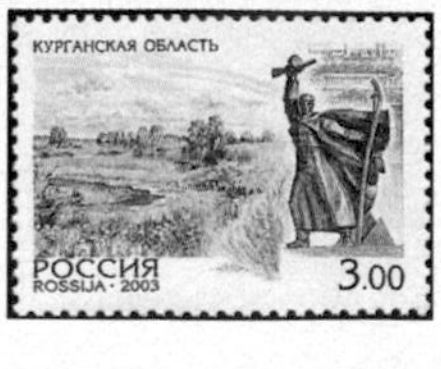

Kurgan Oblast A3193

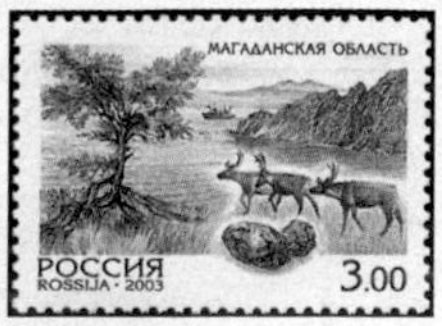

Magadan Oblast A3194

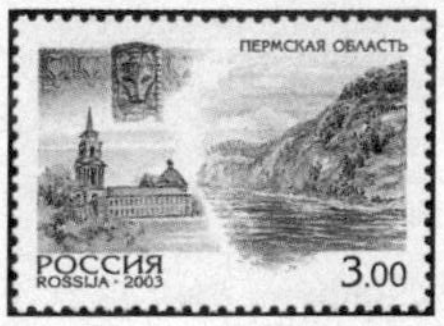

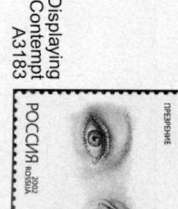

Perm Oblast A3195

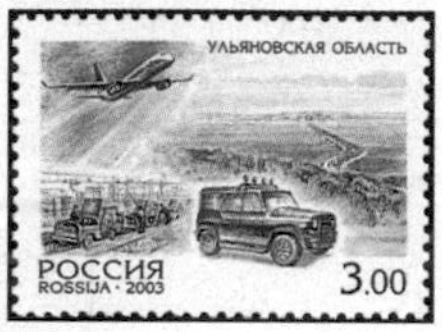

Ulyanovsk Oblast A3196

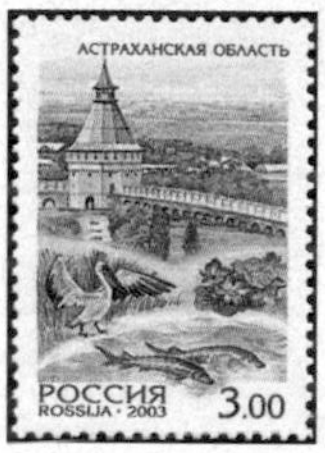

Astrakhan Oblast — A3197

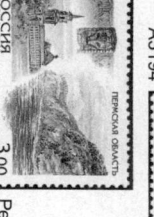

**2003, Jan. 10** ***Perf. 12x12¼, 12¼x12***

| | | | |
|---|---|---|---|
| **6742** | A3192 3r multi | .25 | .20 |
| **6743** | A3193 3r multi | .25 | .20 |
| **6744** | A3194 3r multi | .25 | .20 |
| **6745** | A3195 3r multi | .25 | .20 |
| **6746** | A3196 3r multi | .25 | .20 |
| **6747** | A3197 3r multi | .25 | .20 |
| | *Nos. 6742-6747 (6)* | 1.50 | 1.20 |

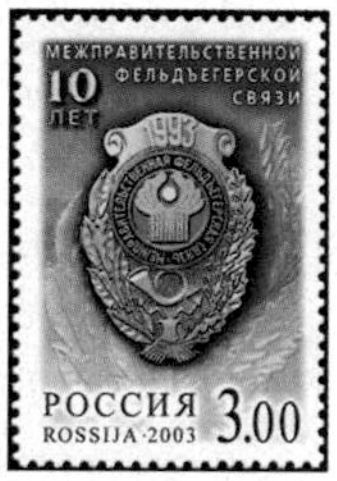

Commonwealth of Independent States Intergovernmental Communications by Courier, 10th Anniv. — A3198

**2003, Jan. 16** ***Perf. 12x12½***

**6748** A3198 3r multi .25 .20

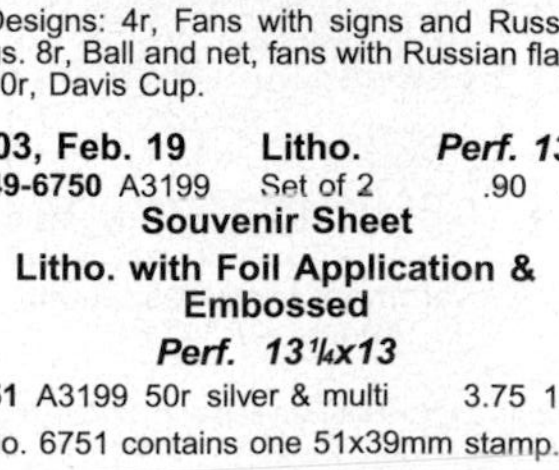

Victory at 2002 Davis Cup Tennis Championships — A3199

Designs: 4r, Fans with signs and Russian flags. 8r, Ball and net, fans with Russian flags. 50r, Davis Cup.

**2003, Feb. 19 Litho.** ***Perf. 13¼***

**6749-6750** A3199 Set of 2 .90 .45

**Souvenir Sheet**

**Litho. with Foil Application & Embossed**

***Perf. 13¼x13***

**6751** A3199 50r silver & multi 3.75 1.90

No. 6751 contains one 51x39mm stamp.

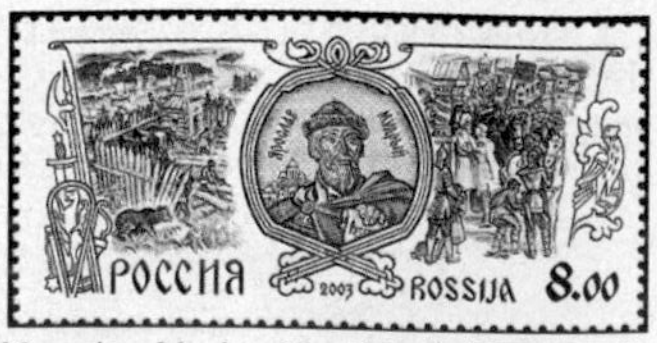

Yaroslav Mudry (the Wise) (978-1054), Grand Prince of Kiev — A3200

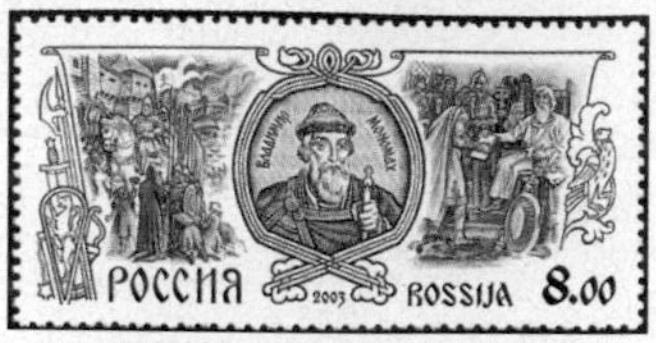

Vladimir II Monomakh (1053-1125), Grand Prince of Kiev — A3201

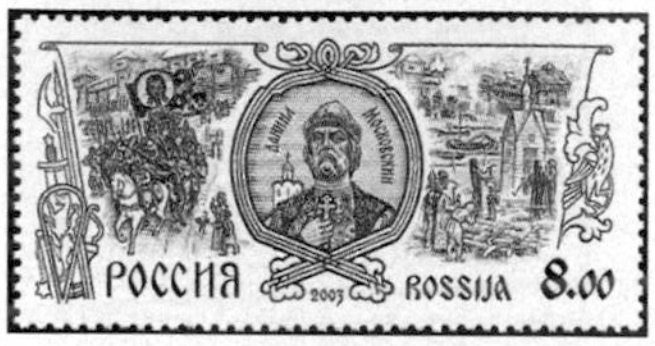

Daniel Aleksandrovich Moscowsky (1261-1303), Grand Prince of Moscow — A3202

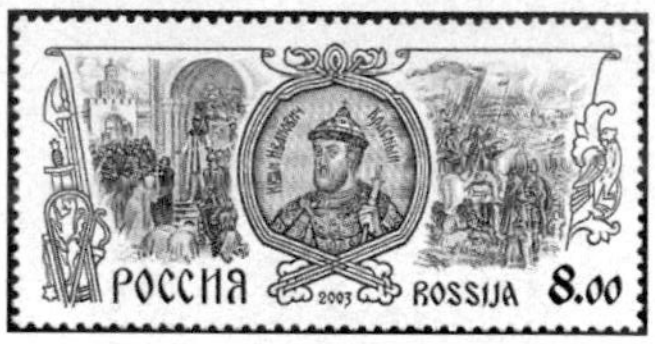

Ivan II Ivanovich Krasny (the Red) (1320-1359), Grand Prince of Moscow — A3203

Illustrations reduced.

**Litho. & Engr.**

**2003, Mar. 4** ***Perf. 11¾***

| | | | |
|---|---|---|---|
| **6752** | A3200 8r multi | .60 | .30 |
| **6753** | A3201 8r multi | .60 | .30 |
| **6754** | A3202 8r multi | .60 | .30 |
| **6755** | A3203 8r multi | .60 | .30 |
| | *Nos. 6752-6755 (4)* | 2.40 | 1.20 |

**Monasteries Type of 2002**

Designs: No. 6756, 5r, Yuriev Monastery, Novgorod, 1030. No. 6757, 5r, Tolgsky Nunnery, 1314. No. 6758, 5r, Kozelsk Optina Pustyn Monastery, 14th-15th cent. No. 6759, 5r, Solovetsky Zosima and Savvatii Monastery, 15th cent. No. 6760, 5r, Novodevichy Nunnery, 1524. No. 6761, 5r, Seraphim Nunnery, Diveyevo, 1780.

**Litho. & Embossed**

**2003, Mar. 26** ***Perf. 12½***

| | | | |
|---|---|---|---|
| **6756-6761** | A3187 Set of 6 | 2.25 | 1.10 |
| *6761a* | Souvenir sheet, #6756-6761 | 2.25 | 1.10 |

Nos. 6756-6761 each were issued in sheets of 9 stamps + label. A limited edtion booklet exists containing booklet panes of one of each of Nos. 6728-6732 and 6756-6761.

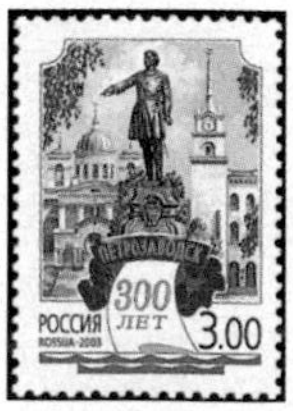

Petrozavodsk, 300th Anniv. — A3204

***Perf. 12¼x11¾***

**2003, Mar. 26** **Litho.**

**6762** A3204 3r multi .20 .20

## Souvenir Sheet

St. Petersburg Postal Service, 300th Anniv. — A3224

**Perf. 12½x12**

**2003, June 29**
6784  A3224  12r multi  .90  .45

### Beetles A3225

1.00

No. 6785: a, Lucanus cervus. b, Calosoma sycophanta. c, Carabus lopatini. d, Carabus constricticollis. e, Carabus caucasicus.

**Perf. 12**

**2003, July 22**   Horiz. strip of 5
6785  A3225  1r multi  1.10  .55
a.  A3225  1r multi  .20  .20
b.  A3225  2r multi  .20  .20
c.  A3225  3r multi  .20  .20
d.  A3225  4r multi  .35  .20
e.  A3225  5r multi  1.10  .55
f.  Sheet, #6785a-6785e, + label

Intl. Association of Academies of Science, 10th Anniv. A3226

2.50

**Perf. 12x12½**  .20  .20

**2003, July 30**
6786  A3226  2.50r multi

Chita, 350th Anniv. A3227

3.00

**Perf. 11¼**  .20  .20

**2003, Aug. 14**
6787  A3227  3r multi

World Conference on Climate Fluctuations, Moscow — A3228

4.00

**Perf. 12x12½**  .20  .20

**2003, Aug. 14**
6788  A3228  4r multi

### Mushrooms A3229

**Perf. 11¾**  .25  .20

Various mushrooms.

2.00

**Perf. 11¾**  1.25  .60

**2003, July 22**   Horiz. strip of 5
6789  A3229  2r multi
a.  A3229  2r multi  .20  .20
b.  A3229  2.50r multi  .20  .20

---

Second World Anti-Narcotics Congress A3218

3.00

**Perf. 12x12½**  .20  .20

**2003, May 25**   Litho.
6778  A3218  3r multi

Pskov, 1100th Anniv. A3219

3.00

**Perf. 11¾x12¼**  .20  .20

**2003, June 3**
6779  A3219  3r multi

Krasnoyarsk, 375th Anniv. A3220

4.00

**Perf. 11¾x12¼**  .25  .20

**2003, June 10**
6780  A3220  4r multi

Symbols of Industry, 5 Ruble Coin A3221

5.00

**Perf. 12½x12**  .35  .20

**2003, June 10**
6781  A3221  5r multi

Promotion of "Transparent Economy."

## Souvenir Sheet

10r

Battle of Kursk, 60th Anniv. — A3222

**Perf. 12x12½**  .75  .35

**2003, June 10**
6782  A3222  10r multi

Komi Republic Forests — A3223

2.00  5.00

No. 6783: a, 2r, Stone pillars, Man-Pupuner Mountain. b, 3r, Kozhim River. c, 5r, Upper Pechora River. Illustration reduced.

**Perf. 12x12½**  .75  .35

**2003, June 25**   Block of 3, #a-c, + label
6783  A3223

---

Anichkov Bridge — A3210   5.00
Neva River Drawbridge — A3211   5.00
Vasilievsky Island — A3212   5.00
Palace Square — A3213   5.00
Winter Palace — A3214   5.00
Summer Garden — A3215   5.00

Peter I Monument — A3216

Designs: 75r, 100r, Peter I Monument.

**Litho. & Embossed**

**Perf. 13x13½**

**2003, May 15**
6768  A3210  5r multi  .35  .20
6769  A3211  5r multi  .35  .20
6770  A3212  5r multi  .35  .20
6771  A3213  5r multi  .35  .20
6772  A3214  5r multi  .35  .20
6773  A3215  5r multi  .35  .20
Nos. 6768-6773 (6)  2.10  1.20

### Souvenir Sheet

**Perf. 13½**

**2003, May 15**
6774  A3216  50r multi  3.75  1.90
6775  A3216  75p multi  5.75  2.75
6776  A3216  100p multi  7.75  4.00

St. Petersburg, 300th anniv. Nos. 6775 and 6776 contain one 37x51mm stamp. A booklet exists containing one pane of Nos. 6768-6773 and one pane of No. 6774 with an extended margin.

Space Flight of Valentina Tereshkova, 40th Anniv. — A3217

3.00

**Perf. 12½x11¾**  .20  .20
1.25  .60

**2003, May 20**   Litho.
6777  A3217  3r multi
a.  Sheet of 6

---

Novosibirsk, Cent. A3205

3.00

**Perf. 11¾x12½**  .20  .20

**2003, Apr. 15**
6763  A3205  3r multi

## Souvenir Sheet

Baltic Fleet, 300th Anniv. — A3206

12r

**Perf. 12¼x11¾**  .90  .45

**2003, Apr. 15**
6764  A3206  12r multi

Aram Khatchaturian (1903-78), Composer — A3207

2.50

**2003, Apr. 23**
6765  A3207  2.50r multi

Europa — A3208

8.00

**Perf. 12½x11¾**  .60  .30
3.60  1.80

**2003, May 5**
6766  A3208  8r multi
a.  Sheet of 6

Carillons — A3209

5.00  5.00

No. 6767: a, St. Rombout's Cathedral, Mechelen, Belgium, and bells (denomination at left). b, Sts. Peter and Paul Cathedral, St. Petersburg, and bells (denomination at right). Illustration reduced.

**Litho. & Engr.**

**Perf. 12**

**2003, May 15**
6767  A3209  5r Horiz. pair, #a-b  .75  .40
c.  Sheet, 3 #6767  2.25  1.20

See Belgium No. 1956.

| | | | |
|---|---|---|---|
| *c.* | A3229 3r multi | .20 | .20 |
| *d.* | A3229 4r multi | .25 | .20 |
| *e.* | A3229 5r multi | .35 | .20 |
| *f.* | Sheet, #6789a-6789e, + label | 1.25 | .60 |

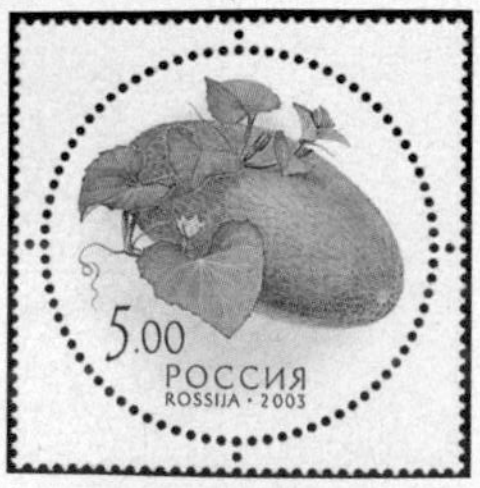

Fruit
A3230

Designs: No. 6790, 5r, Melon. No. 6791, 5r, Apples. No. 6792, 5r, Pear. No. 6793, 5r, Pineapple. No. 6794, 5r, Strawberries.

**2003, Aug. 27** ***Perf. 13½***

**6790-6794** A3230 Set of 5 1.75 .90

Nos. 6790-6794 are impregnated with fruit scents. Values are for stamps with surrounding selvage.

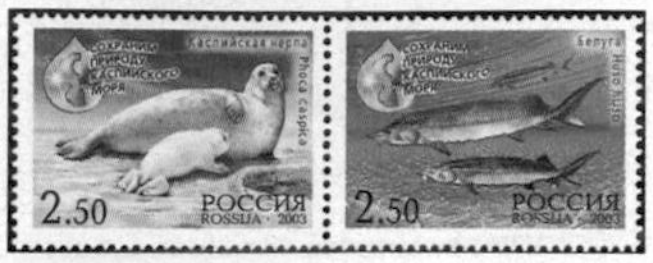

Caspian Sea Fauna — A3231

No. 6795: a, Phoca caspica. b, Huso huso. Illustration reduced.

**2003, Sept. 9** ***Perf. 12½x12***

**6795** A3231 2.50r Horiz. pair, #a-b .35 .20

*c.* Sheet, 3 each #6795a-6795b 1.10 .55

See Iran No. 2873.

Souvenir Sheet

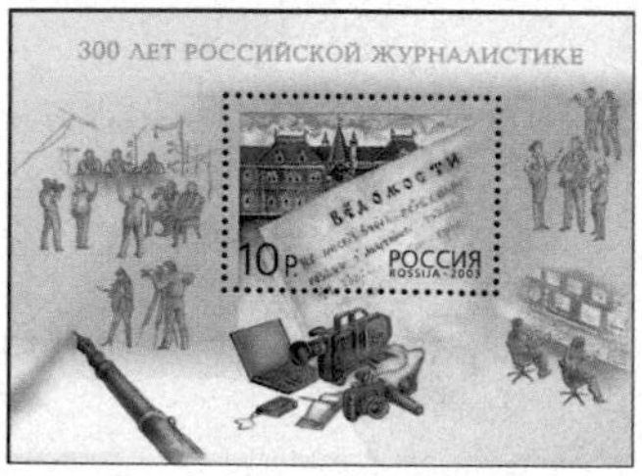

Russian Journalism, 300th Anniv. — A3232

**2003, Sept. 12** ***Perf. 12x12¼***

**6796** A3232 10r multi .75 .35

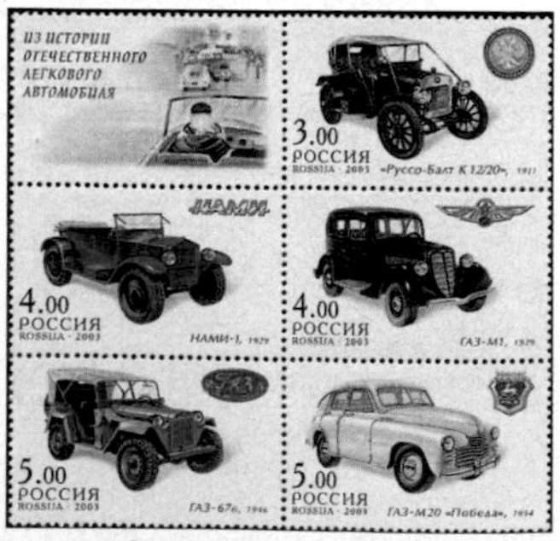

Automobiles — A3233

Designs: a, 3r, 1911 Russo-Balt K 12/20. b, 4r, 1929 NAMI-1. c, 4r, 1939 GAZ-M1. d, 5r, 1946 GAZ-67b. e, 5r, 1954 GAZ-M20 Pobeda. Illustration reduced.

**2003, Sept. 17** ***Perf. 11¾x11½***

**6797** A3233 Block of 5, #a-e, + label 1.50 .75

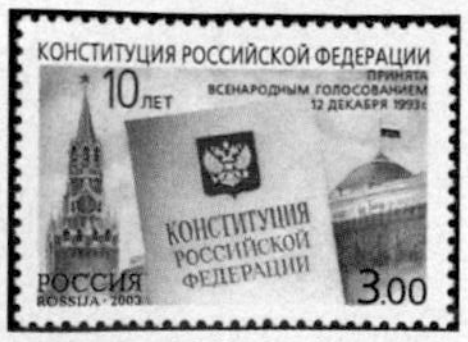

Constitution, 10th Anniv. — A3234

**2003, Oct. 15** ***Perf. 12½x12***

**6798** A3234 3r multi .20 .20

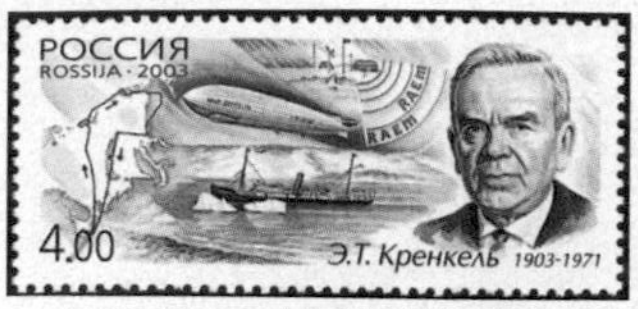

E. T. Krenkel (1903-71), Polar Explorer — A3235

**2003, Oct. 15** ***Perf. 12x12½***

**6799** A3235 4r multi .25 .20

Souvenir Sheet

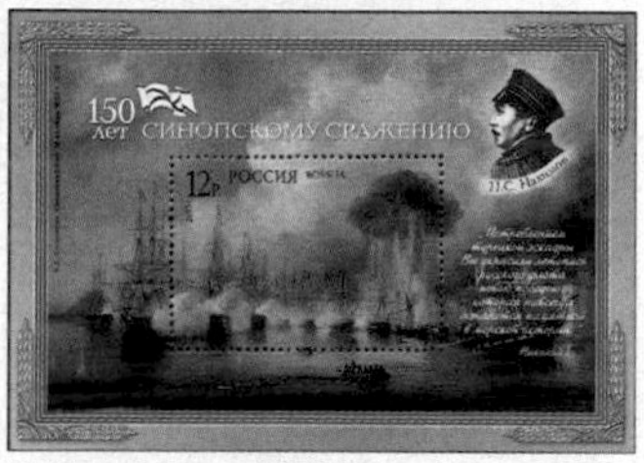

Battle of Sinop, 150th Anniv. — A3236

**2003, Nov. 5** ***Perf. 12¼x12***

**6800** A3236 12r multi .90 .45

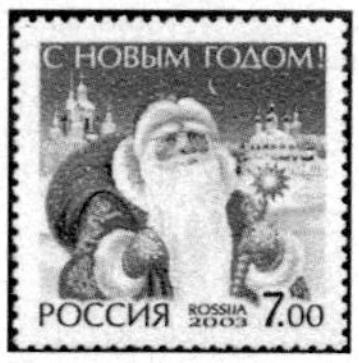

Happy New Year — A3237

**2003, Dec. 1** ***Perf. 12½***

**Flocked Paper**

**6801** A3237 7r multi .50 .25

**Sculpture and Buildings Type of 2002**

Designs: 1r, Ostankino Palace. 1.50r, Gatchinsky Palace. 6r, Grand Palace, Petrodvorets. 10r, Empress Catherine's Palace, Tsarskoye Selo.

**2003, Dec. 5** ***Serpentine Die Cut 11***

**Self-Adhesive**

| | | | | |
|---|---|---|---|---|
| **6802** | A3189 | 1r multi | .20 | .20 |
| **6803** | A3189 | 1.50r multi | .20 | .20 |
| **6804** | A3189 | 6r multi | .40 | .20 |
| **6805** | A3189 | 10r multi | .75 | .35 |
| | | *Nos. 6802-6805 (4)* | 1.55 | .95 |

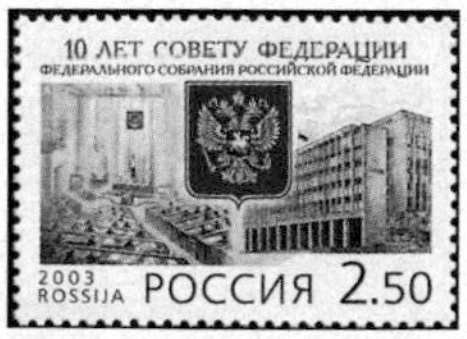

Legislative Bodies, 10th Anniv. A3238

No. 6806: a, Federation Council (denomination at right). b, State Duma (denomination at left).

**2003, Dec. 10** ***Perf. 12¼x12***

**6806** Horiz. pair + central label .35 .20

***a.-b.*** A3238 2.50r Either single .20 .20

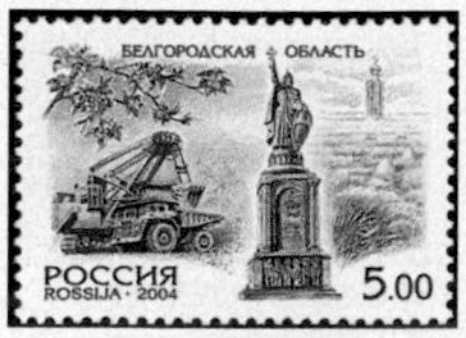

Belgorod Oblast A3239

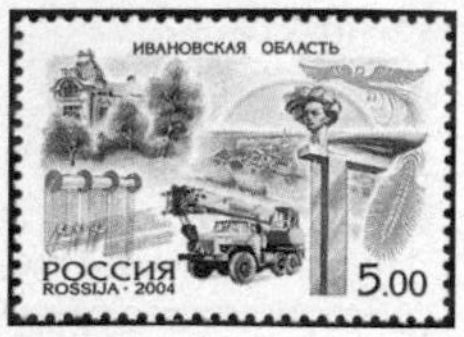

Ivanovo Oblast A3240

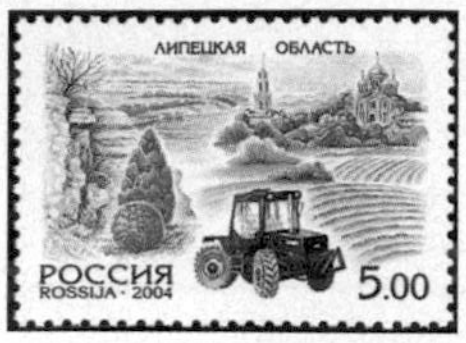

Lipetsk Oblast A3241

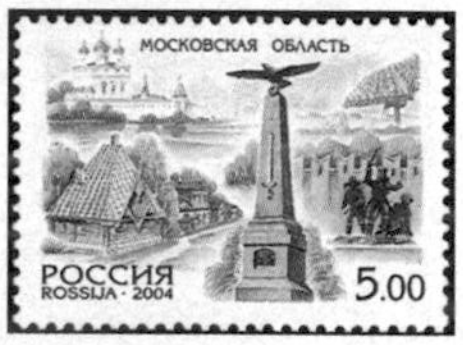

Moscow Oblast A3242

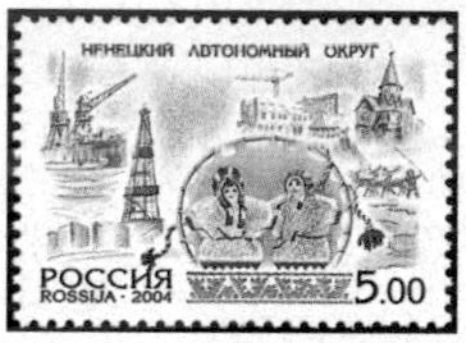

Nenetsky Okrug A3243

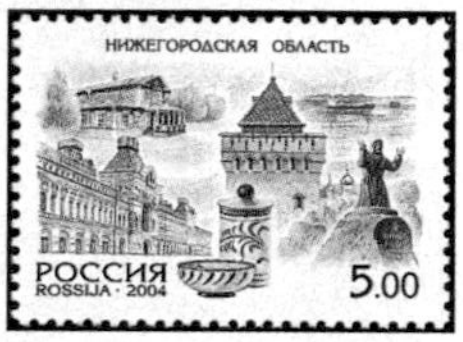

Nizhny Novgorod Oblast A3244

**2004, Jan. 6** ***Perf. 12x12¼***

| | | | | |
|---|---|---|---|---|
| **6807** | A3239 | 5r multi | .35 | .20 |
| **6808** | A3240 | 5r multi | .35 | .20 |
| **6809** | A3241 | 5r multi | .35 | .20 |
| **6810** | A3242 | 5r multi | .35 | .20 |
| **6811** | A3243 | 5r multi | .35 | .20 |
| **6812** | A3244 | 5r multi | .35 | .20 |
| | | *Nos. 6807-6812 (6)* | 2.10 | 1.20 |

Souvenir Sheet

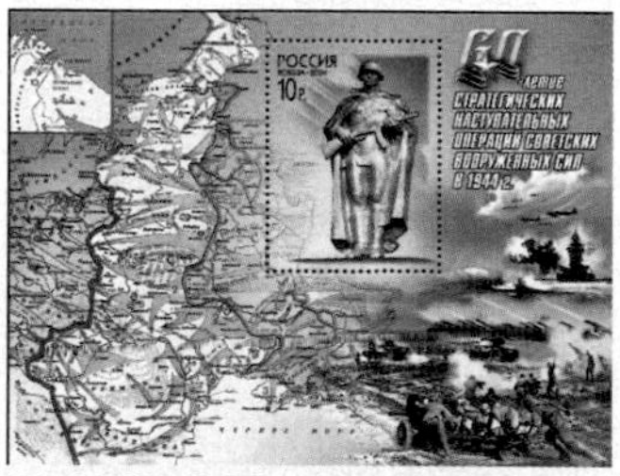

World War II Offensives of 1944, 60th Anniv. — A3245

**2004, Jan. 16 Litho.** ***Perf. 12x12¼***

**6813** A3245 10r multi .75 .35

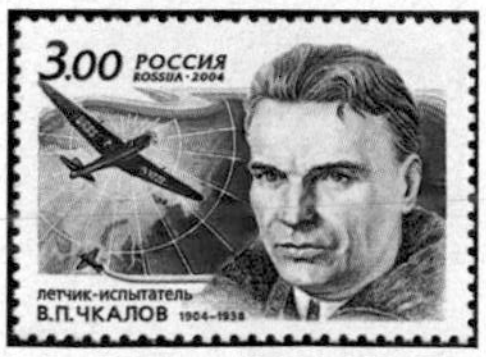

V. P. Chkalov (1904-38), Test Pilot — A3246

**2004, Jan. 23** ***Perf. 11¾x12***

**6814** A3246 3r multi .20 .20

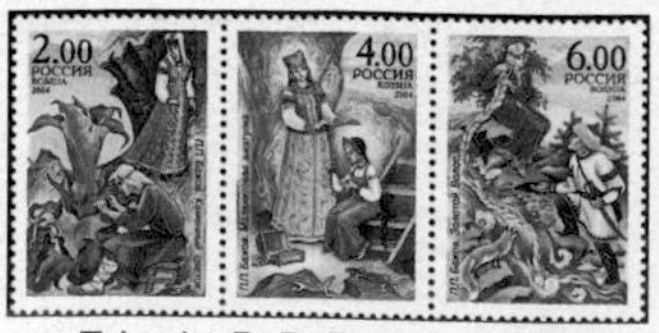

Tales by P. P. Bazhov (1879-1950) — A3247

No. 6815: a, 2r, The Stone Flower. b, 4r, The Malachite Box. c, 6r, The Golden Hair.

**2004, Jan. 27** ***Perf. 12x11¾***

**6815** A3247 Horiz. strip of 3, #a-c .90 .45

*d.* Miniature sheet, 2 #6815 1.80 .90

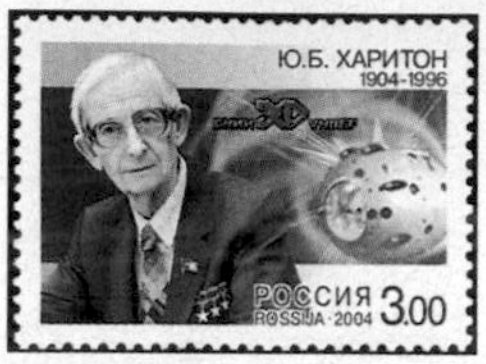

Yuly B. Khariton (1904-66), Physicist — A3248

**2004, Feb. 12 Litho.** ***Perf. 12¼x12***

**6816** A3248 3r multi .20 .20

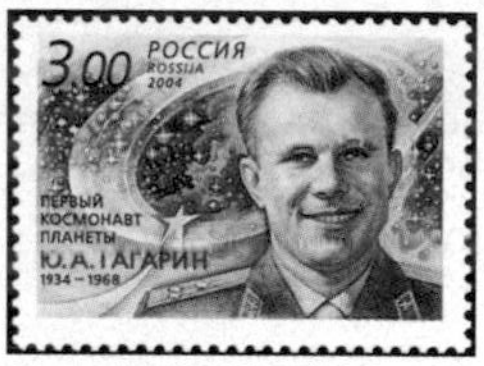

Yuri Gagarin (1934-68), First Man in Space — A3249

**2004, Feb. 20** ***Perf. 12***

**6817** A3249 3r multi .20 .20

**Monasteries Type of 2002**

Designs: No. 6818, 8r, St. Panteleimon Monastery, Mt. Athos, Greece, 11th cent. No. 6819, 8r, Holy Assumption Kiev-Pecherskaya Lavra, Ukraine, 1051. No. 6820, 8r, Convent of the Savior and Efrosinia, Polotsk, Belarus, 1128. No. 6821, 8r, Gorney Convent, Israel, 1886. No. 6822, 8r, Pyukhtitsky Convent of the Assumption, Estonia.

**Litho. & Embossed**

**2004, Mar. 16** ***Perf. 12½***

**6818-6822** A3187 Set of 5 3.00 1.50

*6822a* Miniature sheet, #6818-6822 + label 3.00 1.50

A limited edition booklet exists containing booklet panes of one of each of Nos. 6818-6822.

**Sculptures and Buildings Type of 2002 Redrawn**

Designs as before.

**2004 Litho.** ***Serpentine Die Cut 11***

**Self-Adhesive**

**Town Name Panels At Bottom With White Background**

**Denomination Color**

| | | | | |
|---|---|---|---|---|
| **6823** | A3189 | 2r brown | .20 | .20 |
| **6824** | A3189 | 2.50r blue | .20 | .20 |
| **6825** | A3189 | 3r indigo | .20 | .20 |
| **6826** | A3189 | 4r violet | .30 | .20 |
| **6827** | A3189 | 5r purple | .35 | .20 |
| | | *Nos. 6823-6827 (5)* | 1.25 | 1.00 |

Issued: 2r, 4r, 4/5; 2.50r, 5r, 4/12; 3r, 4/15.

Nos. 6823-6827 have a crest with stronger lines and vignettes in slightly different shades than Nos. 6734-6738. The background of the town name panels on Nos. 6734-6738 have dots of color, which on some stamps are faint, but are easily seen under magnification.

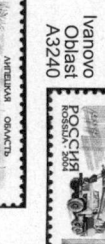

RUSSIA

## Souvenir Sheet

**2004, July 20**   *Perf. 12*
6854  Horiz. pair with central label  .75  .40
  *a.* A3267 3r Running  .20  .20
  *b.* A3267 8r Wrestling  .55  .25

Admiralty of the Wharves, 300th Anniv. — A3268

**2004, July 22**  *Perf. 12x12½*
6855 A3268 12r multi  .85  .40

## Miniature Sheet

Children and Road Safety — A3269

No. 6856: a, Ducks crossing street at pedestrian crossing. b, Boy and turtle crossing street with green light. c, Driver near fenced garden. d, Girl playing in street. e, Accident showing eggs flying out of car.

**2004, Aug. 5**  *Perf. 12*
6856 A3269 4r Sheet of 5, #a-e, + label  1.40  .70

Worldwide Fund for Nature (WWF) — A3270

Gulo gulo: a, With pine branches. b, With dead bird. c, On tree branch. d, With young.

**2004, Aug. 12**  *Perf. 11¼*
6857  Block of 4  2.25  1.10
  *a.-d.* A3270 8r Any single  .55  .25
  *e.* Miniature sheet, #6857a, 2 each #6857b-6857c, 3 #6857d + label  4.50  2.25

---

German - Russian Youth Meeting A3258

**2004, June 3**  Litho.  *Perf. 11¼*
6845 A3258 8r multi  .55  .30
See Germany No. 2287.

Vladimir K. Kokkinaki (1904-85), Test Pilot — A3259

**2004, June 8**  *Perf. 12*
6846 A3259 3r multi  .20  .20

Victory — A3260

Who Comes With the Sword Will Die by the Sword — A3201

Patriotic paintings by S. Prisekin: No. 6848, Marshal Zhukov. No. 6850, The Oath of Allogiance We Have Ilonorod, Smolensk, 1812.
Illustration A3261 reduced.

**2004, June 8**  *Perf. 11¼x11½*
6847 A3260 5r shown  .35  .20
6848 A3260 5r multi  .35  .20
   *Perf. 11¾*
6849 A3261 5r shown  .35  .20
6850 A3261 5r multi  1.40  .80
  Nos. 6847-6850 (4)

Women's Riding Habits — A3262

Designs: No. 6851, 4r, Three women, horse. No. 6852, 4r, Three women, horse, dog. No. 6853, 4r, Two women, horse, two dogs.

**2004, July 15**  *Perf. 12x11¾*
6851-6853 A3262  Set of 3  .85  .40
6853a  Miniature sheet, 2 each #6851-6853  1.75  .85

2004 Summer Olympics, Athens A3267

---

## Souvenir Sheet

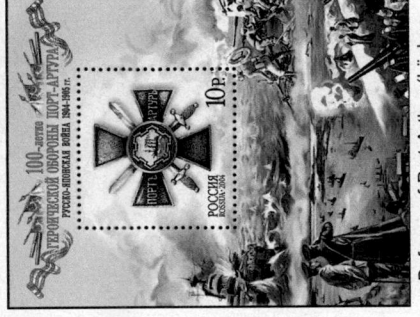

Defense of Port Arthur (Lüshun, China) in Russo-Japanese War, Cent. — A3254

**2004, May 12**  *Perf. 11¼*
6839 A3254 10r multi  .70  .35

Mikhail I. Glinka (1804-57), Composer — A3255

No. 6840: a, Portrait. b, Scene from opera "Life for the Tsar," 1836. c, Scene from opera "Ruslan and Ludmila," 1842.
Illustration reduced.

**2004, May 20**  *Perf. 12*
6840 A3255 4r Block of 3, #a-c, + label  .85  .40

Russian Crown — A3256

Carved Head — A3257

Treasures from the Amber Room, State Museum, St. Petersburg: No. 6842, Cameo depicting Moses and Pharaoh, vert. 25r; Touch and Smell, Florentine mosaic.

**2004, May 25**  Litho. & Embossed  *Perf. 13¼*
6841 A3256 5r multi  .35  .20
6842 A3256 5r multi  .35  .20
6843 A3257 5r multi  1.05  .60
  Nos. 6841-6843 (3)

## Souvenir Sheet
  *Perf. 13*
6844 A3257 25r multi  1.75  .85

A limited edition booklet exists containing booklet panes of one of each of Nos. 6841-6844.

---

Kronshtadt, 300th Anniv. — A3250

**2004, Apr. 15**  *Perf. 12½x12*
6828 A3250 4r multi  .30  .20

Zodiac Signs A3251

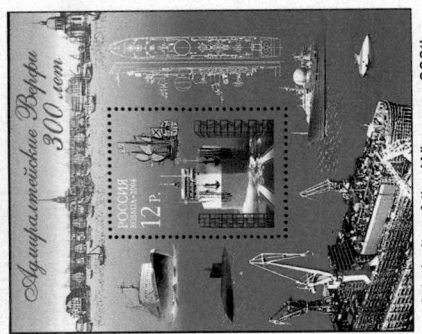

No. 6829: a, Aries. b, Leo. c, Sagittarius. No. 6830: a, Gemini. b, Aquarius. c, Libra. No. 6831: a, Capricorn. b, Taurus. c, Virgo. No. 6832: a, Pisces. b, Cancer. c, Scorpio.

**2004, Apr. 21**  Litho. & Embossed  *Perf. 13½x13*
6829  Horiz. strip of 3  1.10  .55
  *a.-c.* A3251 5r Any single  .35  .20
6830  Horiz. strip of 3  1.10  .55
  *a.-c.* A3251 5r Any single  .35  .20
6831  Horiz. strip of 3  1.10  .55
  *a.-c.* A3251 5r Any single  .35  .20
6832  Horiz. strip of 3  1.10  .55
  *a.-c.* A3251 5r Any single  .35  .20
  *a.-d.* Miniature sheet, #6829a-6829c, 6830a-6830c, 6831a-6831c, 6832a-6832c  4.50  2.25

Empress Cathorna II (1729-96) — A3252

Catherine the Great: 6r, Watching scientific presentation of Mikhail Lomonosov, 7r, Giving money to support education, vert. 8r, At legislative commission meeting, vert. 9r, Viewing ships at Inkerman Palace, Crimea.

**2004, Apr. 27**  Litho. & Engr.  *Perf. 12½x12, 12x12½*
6833-6836 A3252  Set of 4  2.10  1.10

## Souvenir Sheet
  *Perf. 11¾x12¼*
6837 A3252 15r multi  1.10  .55
No. 6837 contains one 33x47mm stamp.

Europa A3253

**2004, May 5**  Litho.  *Perf. 11¾x12¼*
6838 A3253 8r multi  .55  .30
  *a.* Miniature sheet of 8  4.50  2.40

**2004, Aug. 20**
Tomsk, 400th Anniv. — A3271
Perf. 12½x12
6858 A3271 4r multi | .30 .20

**2004, Aug. 20**
ITAR-TASS News Agency, Cent. — A3272
Perf. 12
6859 A3272 4r multi | .30 .20

Famous Men — A3273
Designs: No. 6860, 5r, B. G. Muzrukov (1904-79), organizer of defense industry. No. 6861, 5r, N. L. Dukhov (1904-64), rocket designer.

**2004, Sept. 8**
6860-6861 A3273 | Set of 2 | .70 .35

**2004, Sept. 10**
Tsar Paul I (1754-1801) A3274
Litho. & Engr. | Perf. 12
6862-6863 A3274 | Set of 2 | 1.40 .70
Souvenir Sheet
6864 A3274 20r multi | 1.40 .70

**2004, Sept. 16**
S. N. Rerikh (1904-93), Painter — A3275
Litho. | Perf. 11¾x11½
6865 A3275 4r multi | .30 .20

**2004, Oct. 7**
Vsevolod III (1154-1212), Grand Prince of Novgorod — A3276
Illustration reduced.
Litho. & Engr. | Perf. 11¾
6866 A3276 12r multi | .85 .40

**2004, Oct. 20**
Kazan State University, 200th Anniv. — A3277
Litho. | Perf. 12x11¾
6867 A3277 5r multi | .35 .20

Silver Containers — A3278
Designs: No. 6868, 4.70r, Bowl, c. 1880-1890. No. 6869, 4.70r, Vase, c. 1900-08, vert. No. 6870, 4.70r, Ladle, 1910. No. 6871, 4.70r, Milk container, 1900.

**2004, Oct. 26**
Litho. & Embossed | Perf. 13¼
6868-6871 A3278 | Set of 4 | 1.40 .70

Happy New Year — A3279
Serpentine Die Cut
Self-Adhesive

**2004, Nov. 12**
Litho.
6872 A3279 5r multi | .35 .35

Altai Republic Landscapes — A3280
Illustration reduced.
Designs: No. 6873: a, 2r, Belukha Mountain. b, 3r, Katun River. c, 5r, Teletskoye Lake.

**2004, Nov. 18**
Perf. 12
6873 A3280 | Block of 3, #a-c, + label | .75 .35

Baikonur Cosmodrome, 50th Anniv. — A3281

**2004, Dec. 1**
| | | | |
|---|---|---|---|
| 6874 | Horiz. strip of 4 | | 1.25 .60 |
| a. | A3281 2.50r R-7 missile | .20 .20 |
| b. | A3281 3.50r Proton rocket | .25 .20 |
| c. | A3281 4r Soyuz rocket | .30 .20 |
| d. | A3281 6r Zenit rocket | .45 .20 |
| e. | Miniature sheet, 2 #6874 | 2.50 1.25 |

**2005, Jan. 10**
Mordovian Republic A3282
Smolensk Oblast A3283
Tver Oblast A3284
Chukotsky Autonomous Okrug — A3285
Koryak Autonomous Okrug — A3286
Taimyr Autonomous Okrug — A3287
| | | |
|---|---|---|
| 6875 A3282 5r multi | .35 .20 |
| 6876 A3283 5r multi | .35 .20 |
| 6877 A3284 5r multi | .35 .20 |
| 6878 A3285 5r multi | .35 .20 |
| 6879 A3286 5r multi | .35 .20 |
| 6880 A3287 5r multi | .35 .20 |
| Nos. 6875-6880 (6) | 2.10 1.20 |

**2005, Jan. 12**
Moscow M. V. Lomonosov State University, 250th Anniv. — A3288
Souvenir Sheet
6881 A3288 5r multi | .35 .20

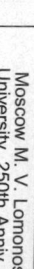

**2005, Feb. 21**
Expo 2005, Aichi, Japan — A3289
Souvenir Sheet
Litho. | Perf. 12½x12
6882 A3289 15r multi | 1.10 .55

Archaeological Treasures of Sarmatia — A3290
Designs: No. 6883, 5r, Silver bowl with bull design (shown). No. 6884, 5r, Gold and wood bowl with bear design. No. 6885, 7r, Gold ornament with camel design. No. 6886, 7r, Gold ornament with deer design, vert.

**2005, Feb. 25**
Litho. & Embossed | Perf. 13¾
6883-6886 A3290 | Set of 4 | 1.75 .85

Submarine Force, Cent. — A3291
Designs: 2r, Type M. VI-bis series, 3r, Type S, IX-bis series, 5r, Type Sch, X-bis series, 8r, Type K.

**2005, Mar. 3**
Litho. | Perf. 12x12½
6887-6890 A3291 | Set of 4 | 1.40 .70

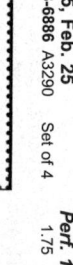

Kazan, 1000th Anniv. A3292
Designs: No. 6891, 5r, Suyumbike Tower (shown). No. 6892, 5r, Kul Sharif Mosque. 7r, Cathedral of the Annunciation.

**2005, Mar. 10**
Perf. 11¾x12
6891-6893 A3292 | Set of 3 | 1.25 .60
6893a | Souvenir sheet, #6891-6893 | .60

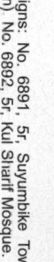

## Souvenir Sheet

Water — A3308

No. 6924: a, 3r, Hands in water. b, 3.50r, Ocean wave. c, 4r, Iceberg. d, 4.50r, Waterfall. e, 5r, Water droplets on leaf.

**2005, Aug. 16**      **Perf. 12**
6924 A3308   Sheet of 5, #a-e, +   1.50   .75
     label

Field Marshal Aleksandr V. Suvorov (1729–1800) — A3309

**2005, Sept. 15**   **Litho.**   **Perf. 12x11¾**
6925 A3309   4r multi     2.40   1.25
   a.   Miniature sheet of 8   .30   .20

**2005, June 15**      **Perf. 11¼**
6912   Horiz. strip of 5   1.75   .85
  a.   A3302 3r Bombus armeniacus   .20
  b.   A3302 4r Bombus fragrans   .25   .20
  c.   A3302 5r Bombus anachoreta   .25   .20
  d.   A3302 6r Bombus unicus   .45   .20
  e.   A3302 7r Bombus czerskii   .50   .25
  f.   Souvenir sheet, #6912a-6912e, +   1.75   .85
    label

Kaliningrad, 750th Anniv. — A3303

**2005, June 23**      **Perf. 12¼x12**
6913 A3303   5r multi     .35   .20

N. E. Bauman Moscow State Technical University, 175th Anniv. — A3304

**2005, July 1**      **Perf. 12**
6914 A3304   5r multi     .35   .20

Lighthouses — A3305

Map and: 5r, Mudyugsky Lighthouse. 6r, Solovetsky Lighthouse. 8r, Svyatonossky Lighthouse.

**2005, July 4**      **Litho.**
6915-6917 A3305   Set of 3   1.40   .70

MiG Fighters A3306

Designs: No. 6918, 5r, MiG-3. No. 6919, 5r, MiG-15. No. 6920, 5r, MiG-21. No. 6921, 5r, MiG-25. No. 6922, 5r, MiG-29.

**2005, July 6**
6918-6922 A3306   Set of 5, #6918-   1.75   .85
    6922, + label
  6922a   Souvenir sheet, #6918-   1.75   .85
    6922, + label

Battle of Kulikovo, 625th Anniv. — A3307

**2005, Aug. 2**      **Perf. 12½x12**
6923 A3307   15r multi     1.10   .55

## Souvenir Sheet

Opening of First Line of Moscow Metro, 70th Anniv. — A3297

No. 6907: a, 5r, Old train, stations, map of first line. b, 10r, Modern train, modern Metro map.

**2005, Apr. 25**      **Perf. 11½x12¼**
6907 A3297   Sheet of 2, #a-b   1.10   .55

Bid of Moscow to Host 2012 Summer Olympics A3298

**2005, May 5**      **Perf. 12**
6908 A3298   4r multi     .30   .20

Europa — A3299

**2005, May 5**      **Perf. 12¼x12**
6909 A3299   8r multi     .60   .30
   a.   Sheet of 6     3.75   1.90

Mikhail A. Sholokhov (1905–84), 1965 Nobel Laureate in Literature A3300

**2005, May 20**      **Perf. 11¾**
6910 A3300   5r multi     .35   .20

Fauna A3301

No. 6911: a, Martes zibellina. b, Panthera tigris altaica.

**2005, June 1**      **Perf. 12**
6911   Horiz. pair, #a-b, +   1.25   .60
    central label
  a.-b.   A3301 8r Either single   .60   .30

Bees A3302

Emperor Alexander II (1818-81) A3293

Alexander II and: No. 6894, 10r, Educator Vasily Zhukovsky, pillar (blue frame). No. 6895, 10r, Coronation (red frame). No. 6896, 10r, At desk (green frame). No. 6897, 10r, On horse (brown frame).

**2005, Mar. 28**   **Litho. & Engr.**
6894-6897 A3293   Set of 4   3.00   1.50

**Souvenir Sheet**      **Perf. 12x12½**
6898 A3293   25r multi     1.90   .95

Victory in World War II, 60th Anniv. — A3294

Designs: No. 6899, 2r, Soldier at column with grafitti. No. 6900, 2r, Soldiers and tank. No. 6901, 3r, Soldier watching pigeons eat. No. 6902, 3r, Jubilant soldiers return to Moscow. 5r, Soldiers and captured Nazi banners. 10r, Soldiers saluting Soviet flag over Reichstag building.

**2005, Apr. 5**      **Perf. 12**
6899-6903 A3294   Set of 5   1.10   .55
  0000a   Sheet of 0 + la-   1.40   .70
    bel
  6903a   Souvenir sheet, #6899-   1.10   .55
    6903, + label

Liberation of Vienna by Soviet Troops, 60th Anniv. — A3295

**Souvenir Sheet**      **Perf. 12x12¼**
6904 A3294   10r multi     .75   .35

**2005, Apr. 13**   **Litho.**
6905 A3295   6r multi     .45   .25

**Souvenir Sheet**

Fauna — A3296

No. 6906: a, Aquila danga (eagle). b, Catocala sponsa (butterflies). c, Castor fiber (beaver). d, Meles meles (badger).

**2005, Apr. 15**
6906 A3296   5r Sheet of 4, #a-d,   1.50   .75
    + label

See Belarus No. 554.

**Sea Infantry, 300th Anniv. — A3310**

No. 6926 — Sea infantrymen from: a, 2r, 18th cent. b, 3r, 19th cent. c, 4r, 20th cent. d, 5r, 21st cent. Illustration reduced.

**2005, Oct. 19** Litho. Perf. 11¾
6926 A3310 Block of 4, #a-d
a. 3r. 1.00 .50

**2005, Oct. 26**
6927 A3311 5r multi .35 .20

Printed in sheets of 8.

**UNESCO, 60th Anniv. A3312**

**2005, Nov. 1** Perf. 11¼
6928 A3312 5.60r multi .40 .20

Santa Claus (Ded Moroz) A3311

**2005, Dec. 1**
6929 A3313 5.60r multi
a. Sheet of 9 .40 .20
3.75 1.90

Christmas and New Year's Day A3313

---

**Designs:** No. 6930, 5.60r, An-3T. No. 6931, 5.60r, An-12. No. 6932, 5.60r, An-24. No. 6933, 5.60r, An 74. No. 6934, 5.60r, An-124.

**2006, Jan. 12** Litho. Perf. 12
6930-6934 A3314 Set of 5 2.00 1.00
6934a Sheet, #6930-6934, + label 2.00 1.00

Antonov Airplanes A3314

**Designs:** No. 6935, 4r, Luge. No. 6936, 4r, Speed skating. No. 6937, 4r, Snowboarding.

**2006, Jan. 18**
6935-6937 A3315 Set of 3 .85 .40

2006 Winter Olympics, Turin A3315

**2006, Jan. 22**
6938 A3316 10r multi .70 .35

Armenia Day in Russia — A3316

**Designs:** 3k, Underwater researcher, transport vehicle. 7k, Scientific ship, airplane. No. 6940, 7r, Icebreaker, penguins.

**2006, Jan. 26**
6939-6941 A3317 Set of 3 1.50 .75
6941a Sheet of 6 #6941 3.00 1.50

Antarctic Research, 50th Anniv. A3317

**Designs:** 3k, Don Cossack Bidding Farewell to His Sweetheart. 7k, Symbolical of Charity. 10k, St. George Slaying the Dragon.

Ilya Murometz Legendary Russian Hero — SP5

---

**SEMI-POSTAL STAMPS**

**2006, Feb. 16**
6942-6943 A3318 Set of 2 .80 .40

Peter I Interrogating Tsarevich Aleksei, by N. N. Ge (1851-94) — A3318

Design, by I. E. Repin, vert.

### Empire

Admiral Kornilov Monument, Sevastopol SP1

Pozharski and Minin Monument, Moscow SP2

Statue of Peter the Great, Leningrad SP3

Alexander II Memorial and Kremlin, Moscow SP4

**1905** Typo. Unwmk.
B1 SP1 3k red, brn & grn 3.00 2.25
a. Perf. 13½x 11½ 190.00 160.00
b. Perf. 13½x 13½ 27.50 27.50
B2 SP2 5k lilac, vio & straw 2.25 1.75
B3 SP3 7k lt bl, dk bl & pink 3.50 2.25
a. Perf. 13½ 45.00 45.00
B4 SP4 10k lt blue, dk bl & yel 6.00 3.25
Nos. B1-B4 (4) 14.75 9.50

**Perf. 11½ to 13½ and Compound**

These stamps were sold for 3 kopecks over face value. The surtax was donated to a fund for the orphans of soldiers killed in the Russo-Japanese war.

---

### Russian Soviet Federated Socialist Republic

**Volga Famine Relief Issue**

Relief Work on Volga River — SP9

Administering Aid to Famine Victim — SP10

**1921** Litho.
B14 SP9 2250r green 3.00
B15 SP9 2250r deep red 2.50
B16 SP9 2250r brown 6.00
B17 SP10 2250r dark blue 14.00
Nos. B14-B17 (4)

Imperf.
100.00 55.00
15.00 12.50
2.50 1.50
14.00
36.00

Forged cancels and counterfeits of Nos. B14-B17 are plentiful.

---

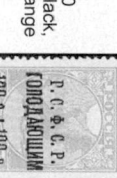

**P.C.P.C.P.**

Nos. 149-150 Surcharged in Black, Red, Blue or Orange

Stamps of type A33 with this overprint were not charity stamps nor did they pay postage in any form.

They represent taxes paid on stamps exported from or imported into Russia. In 1925 the semi-postal stamps of 1914-15 were surcharged for the same purpose. Stamps of the regular issues of 1918 and 1921 have also been surcharged with inscriptions and new values, to pay the importation and exportation taxes.

---

Peter I Interrogating Tsarevich Aleksei section, design by N. N. Ge, portrait of N. N.

**1914** Perf. 11½, 12½
B5 SP5 1k red & dk grn, straw .30 .45
B6 SP5 3k mar & gray grn, pink .35 .45
B7 SP5 7k dk brn & dk grn, buff .40 .45
B8 SP5 10k dk blue & brn, blue 1.90 2.25
Nos. B5-B8 (4) 3.10 3.60

**Perf. 13½**
**1915** White Paper
B9 SP5 1k orange brn & grn .25 .35
B10 SP5 3k car & gray black .35 .45
a. Horiz. pair, imperf btwn. 125.00
B12 SP5 7k dk brn & dk grn 6.00
B13 SP5 10k dk blue & brown .20 .35
Nos. B9-B13 (4) 6.80

B5a SP5 1k 35.00 32.50
B6a SP5 3k .25 .45
B7a SP5 7k 5.75 7.25
B8a SP5 10k 41.30 40.65
Nos. B5a-B8a (4)

## 1922, Feb. — Perf. 13½

| | | | | |
|---|---|---|---|---|
| B18 | A33 | 100r + 100r on 70k | .60 | 1.65 |
| a. | | 100 (r.) + 100r on 70k | 100.00 | 100.00 |
| B19 | A33 | 100r + 100r on 70k (R) | .60 | 1.65 |
| B20 | A33 | 100r + 100r on 70k (Bl) | .30 | .85 |
| B21 | A33 | 250r + 250r on 35k | .30 | .85 |
| B22 | A33 | 250r + 250r on 35k | .60 | 1.65 |
| B23 | A33 | 250r + 250r on 35k | 1.10 | 3.25 |
| | | | 3.50 | 9.90 |

Nos. B18-B23 (6)

Issued to raise funds for Volga famine relief. Values $20 to $40.

### Regular Issues of 1909-18 Overprinted

РСФСР
Филателия
—детям
19-8-22

## 1922, Aug. 19 — Perf. 14

| | | | | |
|---|---|---|---|---|
| B24 | A14 | 1k orange | 200.00 | 200.00 |
| B25 | A14 | 2k green | 15.00 | 15.00 |
| B26 | A14 | 3k red | 12.00 | 25.00 |
| B27 | A14 | 5k claret | 14.00 | 25.00 |
| B28 | A15 | 10k dark blue | 15.00 | 25.00 |

**Imperf**

| | | | | |
|---|---|---|---|---|
| B29 | A14 | 1k orange | 175.00 | 200.00 |
| | | | 432.00 | 50.00 |

Nos. B24-B29 (6)

The overprint means "Philately for the Children." The stamps were sold at five million times their face values and 80% of the amount was devoted to child welfare. The stamps were sold only at Moscow and for one day. Counterfeits exist including those with overprint reading up. Reprints exist.

Worker and Peasant (Industry and Agriculture) — SP11

Allegory: Agriculture Will Help End Distress SP12

Star of Hope, Wheat and Worker-Peasant Handclasp — SP13

---

Counterfeits of No. B42 exist.

### Leningrad Flood Issue

С.С.С.Р. пострадавшему от наводнения Ленинграду: 7 к. + 20 к.

Nos. 181-182, 184-186 Surcharged

## 1924 — Unwmk. — Imperf.

| | | | | |
|---|---|---|---|---|
| B43 | A40 | 3k + 10k on 100r | .80 | 1.25 |
| a. | | Pelure paper | 3.00 | 4.00 |
| b. | | Inverted surcharge | 250.00 | 250.00 |
| B44 | A40 | 7k + 20k on 200r | .80 | 1.25 |
| a. | | Pelure paper | 125.00 | 125.00 |
| B45 | A40 | 14k + 30k on 300r | .90 | 2.50 |
| a. | | Pelure paper | 250.00 | 210.00 |

**Similar Surcharge in Red or Black**

| | | | | |
|---|---|---|---|---|
| B46 | A41 | 12k + 40k on 500r | 1.65 | 2.50 |
| a. | | Double surcharge | | 250.00 |
| b. | | Inverted surcharge | 250.00 | 250.00 |
| B47 | A41 | 20k + 50k on 1000r | 1.10 | 2.50 |
| a. | | Thick paper | 11.50 | 18.00 |
| b. | | Pelure paper | 10.00 | 25.00 |
| c. | | Chalk surfaoo paper | | 12.50 |

Nos. B43-B47 (5) ... 5.25 10.00

The surcharge on Nos. B43 to B45 reads: "S.S.S.R. For the sufferers by the inundation at Leningrad." That on Nos. B46 and B47 reads: "S.S.S.R. For the Leningrad Proletariat, 23, IX, 1924." No. B46 is surcharged vertically, reading down, with the value as the top line.

Orphans SP19

Lenin as a Child SP20

## 1926 — Typo. — Perf. 13½

| | | | | |
|---|---|---|---|---|
| B48 | SP19 | 10k brown | 3.25 | 3.00 |
| R49 | SP20 | 20k deep blue | 4.00 | 4.25 |

**Wmk. 170**

| | | | | |
|---|---|---|---|---|
| B50 | SP19 | 10k brown | 1.00 | .90 |
| B51 | SP20 | 20k deep blue | 1.50 | 1.65 |

Nos. B48-B51 (4) ... 9.75 9.80

Two kopecks of the price of each of these stamps was donated to organizations for the care of indigent children.

### Types of 1926 Issue

## 1927

| | | | | |
|---|---|---|---|---|
| B52 | SP19 | 8k + 2k yel green | 1.25 | .35 |
| B53 | SP20 | 18k + 2k deep rose | 3.50 | 1.00 |

Surtax was for child welfare.

Industrial Training SP21

Agricultural Training SP22

## 1929-30 — Perf. 10, 10½, 12½ — Photo. — Unwmk.

| | | | | |
|---|---|---|---|---|
| B54 | SP21 | 10k +2k ol brn & org brn | 2.50 | 2.50 |
| | | | 75.00 | 75.00 |
| a. | | Perf. 10½ | | |

---

| | | | | |
|---|---|---|---|---|
| B55 | SP21 | 10k +2k ol grn ('30) | 1.50 | 1.25 |
| B56 | SP22 | 20k +2k blk brn & bl, perf. 10½ | 2.00 | 3.50 |
| | | | 35.00 | 35.00 |
| a. | | Perf. 12½ | | 10.00 |
| b. | | Perf. 10 | | |
| B57 | SP22 | 20k +2k bl grn ('30) | 8.00 | 10.75 |

Nos. B54-B57 (4)

Surtax was for child welfare.

> Catalogue values for unused stamps in this section, from this point to the end of the section, are for Never Hinged items.

"Montreal Passing Torch to Moscow" — SP23

Moscow '80 Olympic Games Emblem — SP24

22nd Olympic Games, Moscow, 1980: 16k+6k, like 10k+5k, 60k+30k, Aerial view of Kremlin and Moscow 80 emblem.

## 1976, Dec. 28 — Litho. — Perf. 12x12½

| | | | | |
|---|---|---|---|---|
| B58 | SP23 | 4k + 2k multi | .25 | .20 |
| B59 | SP24 | 4k + 5k multi | .45 | .35 |
| B60 | SP24 | 16k + 6k multi | .85 | .40 |

Nos. B58-B60 (3)

**Souvenir Sheet — Photo. — Perf. 11½**

| | | | | |
|---|---|---|---|---|
| B61 | SP23 | 60k + 30k multi | 2.25 | 1.65 |

Greco-Roman Wrestling — SP25

Moscow '80 Emblem and: 6k+3k, Free-style wrestling, 10k+5k, Judo, 16k+6k, Boxing, 20k+10k, Weight lifting.

## 1977, June 21 — Litho. — Perf. 12½x12

| | | | | |
|---|---|---|---|---|
| B62 | SP25 | 4k + 2k multi | .20 | .20 |
| B63 | SP25 | 6k + 3k multi | .30 | .20 |
| B64 | SP25 | 10k + 5k multi | .40 | .30 |
| B65 | SP25 | 16k + 6k multi | .60 | .35 |
| B66 | SP25 | 20k + 10k multi | .80 | .45 |

Nos. B62-B66 (5) ... 2.30 1.50

**Perf. 12½x12, 12x12½**

| | | | | |
|---|---|---|---|---|
| B67 | SP25 | 4k + 2k multi | .20 | .20 |
| B68 | SP25 | 6k + 3k multi | .30 | .20 |
| B69 | SP25 | 10k + 5k multi | .40 | .35 |
| B70 | SP25 | 16k + 6k multi | .55 | .35 |
| B71 | SP25 | 20k + 10k multi | .70 | .45 |

Nos. B67-B71 (5) ... 2.10 1.50

**Souvenir Sheet — Perf. 12½x12**

| | | | | |
|---|---|---|---|---|
| B72 | SP25 | 50k + 25k multi | 3.00 | 1.65 |

## 1977, Sept. 22

Designs: 4k+2k, Bicyclist, 6k+3k, Woman archer, vert. 10k+5k, Sharpshooting, 16k+6k, Equestrian, vert. 20k+10k, Fencer, 50k+25k, Equestrian and fencer.

## 1978, Mar. 24 — Perf. 12½x12

Designs: 4k+2k, Swimmer at start, 6k+3k, Woman diver, vert. 10k+5k, Water polo.

---

Sower — SP14

## 1922 — Litho. — Imperf.

**Without Gum**

| | | | | |
|---|---|---|---|---|
| B30 | SP11 | 2t (2000r) green | 8.50 | 20.00 |
| B31 | SP12 | 2t (2000r) rose | 14.00 | 35.00 |
| B32 | SP13 | 4t (4000r) rose | 14.00 | 35.00 |
| B33 | SP14 | 6t (6000r) green | 14.00 | 35.00 |

Nos. B30-B33 (4) ... 50.50 125.00

Nos. B30-B33 exist with double impression. Value, each $150. Counterfeits of Nos. B30-B33 exist; beware also of forged cancellations. Miniature copies of Nos. B30-B33 exist, taken from the 1933 Soviet catalogue.

Automobile SP15

Steamship SP16

Railroad Train SP17

Airplano SP18

## 1922 — Imperf.

| | | | | |
|---|---|---|---|---|
| B34 | SP15 | (20r+5r) light violet | .20 | .20 |
| B35 | SP16 | (20r+5r) violet | .20 | .20 |
| B36 | SP17 | (20r+5r) gray blue | .20 | 4.50 |
| B37 | SP18 | (20r+5r) blue gray | 3.10 | 5.10 |

Nos. B34-B37 (4)

Inscribed "For the Hungry." Counterfeits of Nos. B34-B37 exist.

1 мая 1923 г.

Филателия — трудящимся.

Nos. 212, 183, 202 Surcharged in Bronze, Gold or Silver

2 р. + 2 р.

## 1923 — Imperf.

| | | | | |
|---|---|---|---|---|
| B38 | A48 | 1r + 1r on 10r | 125.00 | 125.00 |
| a. | | Inverted surcharge | 250.00 | 300.00 |
| B39 | A48 | 1r + 1r on 10r (G) | 20.00 | 30.00 |
| a. | | Inverted surcharge | 250.00 | 300.00 |
| B40 | A43 | 2r + 2r on 250r | 16.00 | 22.50 |
| a. | | Pelure paper | 200.00 | 200.00 |

**Wmk. 171**

| | | | | |
|---|---|---|---|---|
| B41 | A46 | 4r + 4r on 5000r | 17.50 | 22.50 |
| a. | | Inverted surcharge | 160.00 | 160.00 |
| B42 | A46 | 4r + 4r on 5000r (S) | 450.00 | 400.00 |
| a. | | Inverted surcharge | 1,000. | 850.00 |
| b. | | Date spaced "1 923" | 1,000. | 850.00 |
| c. | | As "b," inverted surch. | 628.50 | 602.50 |

Nos. B38-B42 (5)

The inscriptions mean "Philately's Contribution to Labor." The stamps were on sale only at Moscow and for one day. The surtax was for charitable purposes.

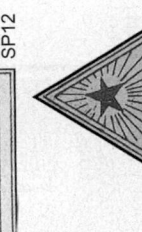

**16k+6k,** Canoeing. **20k+10k,** Canadian single. **50k+25k,** Start of double scull race.

| | | | | |
|---|---|---|---|---|
| B73 | SP25 | 4k + 2k multi | .20 | .20 |
| B74 | SP25 | 6k + 3k multi | .25 | .20 |
| B75 | SP25 | 10k + 5k multi | .40 | .25 |
| B76 | SP25 | 16k + 6k multi | .55 | .30 |
| B77 | SP25 | 20k + 10k multi | .70 | .45 |
| | | Nos. B73-B77 (5) | 2.10 | 1.40 |

| | | | | |
|---|---|---|---|---|
| B78 | SP25 | 50k + 25k grn & blk | 2.50 | 2.50 |

**Souvenir Sheet**

Star-class Yacht — SP26

Keel Yachts and Moscow '80 Emblem: **6k+3k,** Soling class. **10k+5k,** Centerboarder 470. **16k+6k,** Finn class. **20k+10k,** Flying Dutchman class. **50k+25k,** Catamaran Tornado, horiz.

**1978, Oct. 26    Litho.    Perf. 12½x12½**

| | | | | |
|---|---|---|---|---|
| B79 | SP26 | 4k + 2k multi | .20 | .20 |
| B80 | SP26 | 6k + 3k multi | .25 | .20 |
| B81 | SP26 | 10k + 5k multi | .40 | .20 |
| B82 | SP26 | 16k + 6k multi | .55 | .30 |
| B83 | SP26 | 20k + 10k multi | .70 | .40 |
| | | Nos. B79-B83 (5) | 2.10 | 1.30 |

| | | | | |
|---|---|---|---|---|
| B84 | SP26 | 50k + 25k multi | 2.50 | 1.40 |

**Souvenir Sheet**

**1978, Mar. 21    Litho.    Perf. 12½x12, 12x12½**

| | | | | |
|---|---|---|---|---|
| B85 | SP27 | 4k + 2k multi | .20 | .20 |
| B86 | SP27 | 6k + 3k multi | .25 | .20 |
| B87 | SP27 | 10k + 5k multi | .40 | .20 |
| B88 | SP27 | 16k + 6k multi | .55 | .30 |
| B89 | SP27 | 20k + 10k multi | .70 | .40 |
| | | Nos. B85-B89 (5) | 2.10 | 1.30 |

Designs: **6k+3k,** Man on parallel bars. **10k+5k,** Man on horizontal bar. **16k+6k,** Woman on balance beam. **20k+10k,** Woman on uneven bars. **50k+25k,** Man on rings.

| | | | | |
|---|---|---|---|---|
| B90 | SP26 | 50k + 25k multi | 2.00 | 1.40 |

**Souvenir Sheet**

Women's Gymnastics SP27

**1979, June    Perf. 12½x12, 12x12½**

Designs: **4k+2k,** Soccer. **6k+3k,** Basketball. **10k+5k,** Women's volleyball. **16k+6k,** Handball. **20k+10k,** Field hockey.

| | | | | |
|---|---|---|---|---|
| B91 | SP27 | 4k + 2k multi | .20 | .20 |
| B92 | SP27 | 6k + 3k multi | .25 | .20 |
| B93 | SP27 | 10k + 5k multi | .40 | .20 |
| B94 | SP27 | 16k + 6k multi | .55 | .30 |
| B95 | SP27 | 20k + 10k multi | .70 | .40 |
| | | Nos. B91-B95 (5) | 2.10 | 1.30 |

Running, Moscow '80 Emblem SP27a

**1980**

| | | | | |
|---|---|---|---|---|
| B96 | SP27a | 4k + 2k shown | .20 | .20 |
| B97 | SP27a | 6k + 3k Pole vault | .25 | .20 |
| B98 | SP27a | 6k + 3k Discus | .25 | .20 |
| B99 | SP27a | 6k + 3k Hurdles | .25 | .20 |
| B100 | SP27a | 10k + 5k Javelin | .40 | .20 |
| B101 | SP27a | 10k + 5k Walking, vert. | .40 | .20 |

**Litho.    Perf. 12½x12, 12x12½**

22nd Olympic Games, Moscow, July 19-Aug. 3, 1980.

Moscow '80 Emblem, Relief from St. Dimitri's Cathedral, Arms of Vladimir — SP28

Moscow '80 Emblem and: No. B108, Bridge over Klyazma River and Vladimir Hotel. No. B109, Relief from Nativity Cathedral and coat of arms (falcon), Suzdal. No. B110, Tourist complex and Poznarski Monument, Suzdal. No. B111, Frunze Monument, Ivanovo, torch and spindle. No. B112, Museum of First Soviets, Fighters of the Revolution Monument, Ivanovo.

| | | | | |
|---|---|---|---|---|
| B102 | SP27a | 16k + 6k Hammer throw | .70 | .30 |
| B103 | SP27a | 16k + 6k High jump | .70 | .30 |
| B104 | SP27a | 20k + 10k Shot put | .90 | .40 |
| B105 | SP27a | 20k + 10k Long jump | .90 | .40 |
| | | Nos. B96-B105 (10) | 4.90 | 2.60 |

| | | | | |
|---|---|---|---|---|
| B106 | SP27a | 50k + 25k Relay race | 2.00 | 1.00 |

**Souvenir Sheet**

22nd Olympic Games, Moscow, July 19-Aug. 3. Issued: Nos. B96, B99, B101, B103, B105, Feb. 6; others, Mar. 12.

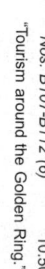

Fortifications and Arms of Zagorsk SP29

**1977, Dec. 30    Photogravure and Engraved    Perf. 11½x12**

| | | | | |
|---|---|---|---|---|
| B107 | SP28 | 1r + 50k multi | 1.75 | .90 |
| B108 | SP28 | 1r + 50k multi | 1.75 | .90 |
| B109 | SP28 | 1r + 50k multi | 1.75 | .90 |
| B110 | SP28 | 1r + 50k multi | 1.75 | .90 |
| B111 | SP28 | 1r + 50k multi | 1.75 | .90 |
| B112 | SP28 | 1r + 50k multi | 1.75 | .90 |
| | | Nos. B107-B112 (6) | 10.50 | 5.40 |

"Tourism around the Golden Ring."

Moscow '80 Emblem and (Coat of Arms design): No. B114, Gagarin Palace of Culture and new arms of Zagorsk (building & horse). No. B115, Rostov Kremlin with St. John the Divine Church and No. B116, View of Rostov from Nero Lake (deer). No. B117, Alexander Nevski and WWII soldiers' monuments, Pereyaslav and No. B118, Peter the Great monument, Pereyaslav (lion & fish). No. B119, Tower and wall of Monastery of the Transfiguration, Jaroslaw and No. B120, Dock and monument for Soviet heroes, Jaroslaw (bear).

**1978    Multicolored and:    Perf. 12½x11½**

| | | | | |
|---|---|---|---|---|
| B113 | SP29 | 1r + 50k gold | 2.00 | .80 |
| B114 | SP29 | 1r + 50k gold | 2.00 | .80 |
| B115 | SP29 | 1r + 50k gold | 2.00 | .80 |
| B116 | SP29 | 1r + 50k gold | 2.00 | .80 |
| B117 | SP29 | 1r + 50k gold | 2.00 | .80 |
| B118 | SP29 | 1r + 50k gold | 2.00 | .80 |
| B119 | SP29 | 1r + 50k silver | 2.00 | .80 |
| B120 | SP29 | 1r + 50k silver | 2.00 | .80 |
| | | Nos. B113-B120 (8) | 16.00 | 6.40 |

Issued: #B113-B116, 10/16; #B117-B120, 12/25.

**Multicolored and:**

| | | | | |
|---|---|---|---|---|
| B121 | SP29 | 1r+50k sil, bl circle | 2.25 | 1.40 |
| B122 | SP29 | 1r+50k gold, yel circle | 2.25 | 1.40 |
| B123 | SP29 | 1r+50k sil, bl 8-point star | 2.25 | 1.40 |
| B124 | SP29 | 1r+50k gold, red 8-point star | 2.25 | 1.40 |
| B125 | SP29b | 1r+50k sil, bl diamond | 2.25 | 1.40 |
| B126 | SP29b | 1r+50k gold, red diamond | 2.25 | 1.40 |

Issued: #B121-B124, 9/5; #B125-B126, Oct.

13.50 8.40

Kremlin Moscow SP29a

Kalinin Prospect, Moscow SP29b

Admiralteistvo, St. Isaak Cathedral, Leningrad — SP29c

World War II Defense Monument, Leningrad SP29d

Bogdan Khmelnitsky Monument, St. Sophia's Monastery, Kiev SP29e

Republican House of Cinematography, Minsk — SP29h

Palace of Sports, Obelisk, Minsk SP29g

Vyshgorodsky Castle, Town Hall, Tallinn SP29i

Metro Bridge, Dnieper River, Kiev — SP29f

Viru Hotel, Tallinn SP29j

**1979    Perf. 12½x11½**

Moscow '80 Emblem and: No. B121, Narikaly Fortress, Tbilisi. 4th century. No. B122, "Georgia Philharmonic Concert Hall, Tbilisi." No. B123, Chit-Dor Mosque, 17th century, Samarkand. No. B124, Peoples Friendship Museum, "Courage" monument, Tashkent. No. B125, Landscape, Erevan. B126, Armenian State Opera and Ballet Theater, Erevan.

**1980    Moscow '80 Emblem, Coat of Arms.    Perf. 12½x11½**

| | | | | |
|---|---|---|---|---|
| B127 | SP29g | 1r + 50k multi | 1.90 | .75 |
| B128 | SP29g | 1r + 50k multi | 2.25 | .90 |
| B129 | SP29c | 1r + 50k multi | 2.25 | .90 |
| B130 | SP29d | 1r + 50k multi | 2.25 | .90 |
| B131 | SP29e | 1r + 50k multi | 2.25 | .90 |
| B132 | SP29f | 1r + 50k multi | 2.25 | .90 |
| B133 | SP29g | 1r + 50k multi | 2.25 | .90 |
| B134 | SP29h | 1r + 50k multi | 2.25 | .90 |
| B135 | SP29i | 1r + 50k multi | 2.25 | .90 |
| B136 | SP29j | 1r + 50k multi | 2.25 | .90 |
| | | Nos. B127-B136 (10) | 21.80 | 8.70 |

Tourism. Issue dates: #B127-B128, Feb. 29. #B129-B130, Mar. 25; #B131-B136, Apr. 30.

## Soviet Culture Fund — SP30

Art treasures: No. B137, Z.E. Serebriakova, 1910, by O.K. Lansere, vert. No. B138, Boyar's Wife Examining an Embroidery Design, 1905, by K.V. Lebedev. No. B139, Talent, 1910, by N.P. Bogdanov-Belsky, vert. No. B140, Trinity, 15th-16th cent., Novgorod School, vert.

**Perf. 12x12½, 12½x12  Litho.**

**1988, Aug. 22**

| | | | | |
|---|---|---|---|---|
| B137 | SP30 | 10k +5k multi | .40 | .25 |
| B138 | SP30 | 15k +7k multi | .55 | .35 |
| B139 | SP30 | 30k +15k multi | 1.10 | .75 |
| a. | | Nos. #B137-B139 (3) | 2.05 | 1.35 |

**Souvenir Sheet**

| | | | | |
|---|---|---|---|---|
| B140 | SP30 | 1r +50k multi | 4.50 | 3.00 |

SP31

SP33

Lenin Children's Fund SP32

**1988, Oct. 20  Litho.  Perf. 12**

| | | | | |
|---|---|---|---|---|
| B141 | SP31 | 5k +2k multi | .25 | .20 |
| B142 | SP31 | 5k +2k Wolf | .25 | .20 |
| B143 | SP31 | 10k +5k Fox | .50 | .35 |
| B144 | SP31 | 20k +10k Boar | .50 | .35 |
| B145 | SP31 | 20k +10k Lynx | .75 | .45 |
| a. | | Block of 5+label, #B141-B145 | 2.00 | 1.40 |

Zoo Relief Fund. See #B152-B156, B166-B168.

**1988, Dec. 12  Litho.  Perf. 12**

| | | | | |
|---|---|---|---|---|
| B146 | SP32 | 5k +2k multi | .25 | .20 |
| B147 | SP32 | 5k +2k multi | .25 | .20 |
| B148 | SP32 | 5k +2k multi | .75 | .45 |
| a. | | Block of 3+label, #B146-B148 | | |

Children's drawings and fund emblem: No. B146, Skating Rink. No. B147, Rooster. No. B148, May (girl and flowers).

See Nos. B169-B171.

**1988, Dec. 27  Perf. 12½x12**

#B149, Tigranes I (c. 140-55 B.C.), king of Armenia, gold coin. #B150, St. Ripsime Temple, c. 618. #B151, Virgin and Child, fresco (detail) by Ovnat Ovnatanyan, 18th cent., Echmiadzin Cathedral.

| | | | |
|---|---|---|---|
| | | .60 | .40 |
| | | .90 | .60 |
| | | 1.50 | 1.00 |
| a. | Block of 3+label. | 2.00 | 2.00 |

Armenian earthquake relief. For surcharges see Nos. B173-B175.

**Zoo Relief Type of 1988**

**1989, Mar. 20  Litho.  Perf. 12**

| | | | | |
|---|---|---|---|---|
| B152 | SP31 | 10k+5k Marten | .45 | .30 |
| B153 | SP31 | 10k+5k Squirrel | .45 | .30 |
| B154 | SP31 | 20k+10k Hare | .90 | .60 |
| B155 | SP31 | 20k+10k Hedgehog | .90 | .60 |
| B156 | SP31 | 20k+10k Badger | 3.60 | 2.50 |
| a. | | Block of 5+label, #B152-B156 | | |

## Lenin Children's Fund Type of 1988

Fund emblem and children's drawings: No. B157, Rabbit. No. B158, Cat. No. B159, Doctor. Nos. B157-B159 vert.

---

**1989, June 14  Litho.  Perf. 12**

| | | | | |
|---|---|---|---|---|
| B157 | SP32 | 5k +2k multi | .25 | .20 |
| B158 | SP32 | 5k +2k multi | .25 | .20 |
| B159 | SP32 | 5k +2k multi | .75 | .45 |
| a. | | Block of 3+label, #B157-B159 | | |

Surtax for the fund.

Soviet Culture Fund SP34

Paintings and porcelain: No. B160, Village Market, by A. Makovsky. No. B161, Lady Wearing a Hat, by E. Zelenin. No. B162, Portrait of the Actress Bazhenova, by A. Sofronova. No. B163, Two Women, by H. Shaiber. No. B164, Popov porcelain coffee pot and plates, 19th cent.

**1989  Litho.  Perf. 12x12½**

| | | | | |
|---|---|---|---|---|
| B160 | SP34 | 4k +2k multi | .20 | .20 |
| B161 | SP34 | 5k +2k multi | .20 | .20 |
| B162 | SP34 | 10k +5k multi | .60 | .35 |
| B163 | SP34 | 20k +10k multi | 1.10 | .65 |
| B164 | SP34 | 30k +15k multi | 1.75 | .95 |
| a. | | Nos. #B160-B164 (5) | 3.90 | 2.35 |

**Souvenir Sheet**

## Nature Conservation — SP35

**1989, Dec. 14  Photo.  Perf. 11½**

| | | | | |
|---|---|---|---|---|
| B165 | SP35 | 20k +10k Swallow | 5.00 | 5.00 |

Surtax for the Soviet Union of Philatelists.

**Zoo Relief Type of 1988**

**1990, May 4  Litho.  Perf. 12**

| | | | | |
|---|---|---|---|---|
| B166 | SP31 | 10k +5k Aquila chrysaetos | .45 | .30 |
| B167 | SP31 | 20k +10k Falco cherrug | 1.00 | .65 |
| B168 | SP31 | 20k +10k Corvus corax | 1.00 | .65 |
| a. | | Block of 3 + label, #B166-B168 | 2.50 | 1.65 |

Nos. B166-B168 horiz.

## Lenin's Children Fund Type of 1988

#B169, Clown. #B170, Group of women. #B171, Group of children. #B169-B171, vert.

**1990, July 3  Litho.  Perf. 12**

| | | | | |
|---|---|---|---|---|
| B169 | SP32 | 5k +2k multi | .25 | .20 |
| B170 | SP32 | 5k +2k multi | .25 | .20 |
| B171 | SP32 | 5k +2k multi | .75 | .45 |
| a. | | Block of 3, #B169-B171 + label | | |

---

## Nature Conservation — SP36

**1990, Sept. 12  Litho.  Perf. 12**

| | | | | |
|---|---|---|---|---|
| B172 | SP36 | 20k +10k multi | 1.10 | 1.10 |

Surtax for Soviet Union of Philatelists.

Nos. B149-B151 Overprinted

#B173

#B174-B175

**1990, Nov. 24  Litho.  Perf. 12½x12½**

| | | | | |
|---|---|---|---|---|
| B173 | SP33 | 20k +10k multi | .75 | |
| B174 | SP33 | 30k +15k multi | 1.10 | |
| B175 | SP33 | 50k +25k multi | 1.80 | |
| a. | | Block of 3+label, #B173-B175 | 3.75 | |

Armenia '90 Philatelic Exhibition.

## Soviet Culture Fund — SP37

**1990, Dec. 20  Litho.  Perf. 12½x12**

| | | | | |
|---|---|---|---|---|
| B176 | SP37 | 10k +5k multi | .55 | .35 |
| B177 | SP37 | 20k +10k multi | 1.10 | .75 |

Paintings by N. K. Roerich: 10k+5k, Unkrada, 1909. 20k+10k, Pskovo-Pechorsky Monastery, 1907.

**Souvenir Sheet**

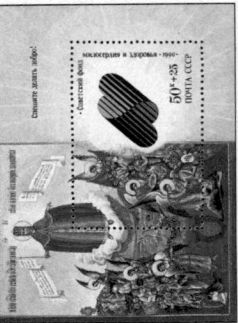

Joys of All Those Grieving, 18th Cent. — SP38

**1990, Dec. 23  Perf. 12½x12**

| | | | | |
|---|---|---|---|---|
| B178 | SP38 | 50k +25k multi | 2.75 | 2.75 |

Surtax for Charity and Health Fund.

---

Ciconia Ciconia SP39

**1991, Feb. 4  Litho.  Perf. 12**

| | | | | |
|---|---|---|---|---|
| B179 | SP39 | 10k +5k multi | .55 | .35 |

Surtax for the Zoo Relief Fund.

**Souvenir Sheet**

USSR Philatelic Society, 25th Anniv. — SP40

**1991, Feb. 15**

| | | | | |
|---|---|---|---|---|
| B180 | SP40 | 20k +10k multi | 1.10 | 1.10 |

The Universe by V. Lukianets SP41

No. B182, Another Planet by V. Luklianets.

**1991, June 1  Litho.  Perf. 12x12½**

| | | | | |
|---|---|---|---|---|
| B181 | SP41 | 10k +5k multi | .20 | .20 |
| B182 | SP41 | 10k +5k multi | .20 | .20 |

Lenin's Children's Fund.

SP42

**1991, July 10  Litho.  Perf. 12x12½**

| | | | | |
|---|---|---|---|---|
| B183 | SP42 | 20k +10k multi | .35 | .25 |

Surtax for Soviet Culture Fund.

SP43

**1991, July 10  Perf. 12**

| | | | | |
|---|---|---|---|---|
| B184 | SP43 | 20k +10k multi | .35 | .25 |

Surtax for Soviet Charity & Health Fund.

# RUSSIA

Souvenir Sheet

**1992, Jan. 22. Litho. Perf. 12½x12**
B185 SP44 3r +50k multi .70 .70
Surtax for Nature Preservation.

SP44

---

## AIR POST STAMPS

AP1

Fokker F-
111 — AP2

**1922**
C1 AP1 45r green & black .. 9.00 12.00
5th anniversary of October Revolution.
No. C1 was on sale only at the Moscow General Post Office. Counterfeits exist.

**1923 Photo. Imperf.**
C2 AP2 10r carmine 1.25 1.00
C3 AP2 3r deep blue 4.50
C4 AP2 5r green 4.00
C5 AP2 5k on 3r dp blue 3.25
Nos. C2-C5 Surcharged
C6 AP2 5k on 3r dp blue 1.00 1.00
C7 AP2 10k on 5r green 1.25 1.00
   a. Wide "5" 250.00 250.00
C8 AP2 15k on 1r red 900.00 450.00
   a. Wide "5" 5.00 4.00
C9 AP2 20k on 10r car 1,000. 500.00
   a. Inverted surcharge 1,000. 500.00
Nos. C2-C5 were not placed in use.

Nos. C2-C5
Surcharged

**1924 Plane Overprint in Red. Unwmk.**
Airplane over Map of World
AP3

C10 AP3 10k dk bl & yel brn 6.50 4.00
C11 AP3 15k dp red & ol grn 7.50 7.00
1st Intl. Air Post Cong. at The Hague, initiated by the USSR.

**1927, Sept. 1 Litho. Perf. 13x12**

**1930 Photo. Wmk. 226 Perf. 12½**
Graf Zeppelin and "Call to Complete 5-Year Plan in 4 Years" — AP4
C12 AP4 40k dk & dl blue 18.00 10.00
   a. Imperf. 10½ 1,000. 700.00
C13 AP4 80k dk car & rose 22.50 15.00
   a. Perf. 10½ 1,000. 700.00
   b. Imperf. 1,000. 700.00
Flight of the Graf Zeppelin from Friedrichshafen to Moscow and return.

Airship over Tundra to the Steppes — AP5

Symbolical of Airship Communication from Friedrich-

Airship over Dneprostroi Dam — AP6

**1931 Wmk. 170 Imperf.**
C26 AP10 30k dark violet 12.50
C27 AP10 35k dark green 12.50 12.50
C28 AP10 1r gray black 15.00 15.00
C29 AP10 2r deep ultra 60.00
Nos. C26-C29 (4)

**Perf. 12x12½**
C30 AP10 30k dark violet 32.50
C31 AP10 35k dark green 32.50
C32 AP10 1r gray black 32.50 32.50
C33 AP10 2r deep ultra 130.00 110.00
Nos. C30-C33 (4)

Graf Zeppelin and Icebreaker "Malygin" Transferring Mail — AP10

North Pole Issue

I. D. Usyskin
AP18

**Perf. 12½ Unwmk. Engr.**
C25 AP6 15k gray blk ('32) 1.00 .50
   a. Perf. 10½ 475.00 125.00
   b. Perf. 14 57.50 37.50
   c. Imperf. 325.00
Nos. C20-C25 (6) 31.50 12.75

The 11½ perforation on Nos. C20-C25 is of private origin; beware also of bogus perforation "errors."

**1931 Wmk. 170**
**Perf. 12x12½**
C34 AP11 50k carmine rose 24.00 15.00
   a. Perf. 10½ 2,750. 3,000.
C35 AP11 1r green 24.00 15.00
   a. Perf. 10½x12 125.00 40.00

Map of Polar Region, Airplane and Icebreaker "Sibiryakov" — AP11

2nd International Polar Year in connection with proposed flight from Franz-Josef Land to Archangel, which, being impossible, actually went from Archangel to Moscow to destinations.

Airship Exploring Arctic Regions — AP8

Airship over Lenin Mausoleum — AP7

Constructing an Airship AP9

**1931-32 Wmk. 170 Photo. Imperf.**
C15 AP5 10k dark violet
C16 AP6 15k gray blue 20.00 16.00
C17 AP7 20k dk carmine 20.00 22.50
**Typo.**
C18 AP8 50k black brown 20.00 22.50
C19 AP9 1r dark green 100.00 106.00
Nos. C15-C19 (5)

**Perf. 10½, 12, 12½ and Compound**
C20 AP5 10k dark violet 4.75 2.50
C21 AP6 15k gray blue
C22 AP7 20k dk carmine 9.00 3.75
**Typo.**
C23 AP8 50k black brown 6.50 7.50
C24 AP9 1r dark green 5.50 3.00
**Photo.**

Furnaces of Kuznetsk AP13

Designs: 10k, Oil wells. 20k, Collective farm. 50k, Map of Moscow-Volga Canal project. 80k, Arctic cargo ship.

**1933 Photo. Perf. 14**
C37 AP12 5k ultra 45.00 8.50
C38 AP12 10k carmine 45.00
   a. Vert. pair, imperf. btwn. 1,700.
C39 AP12 20k violet 116.00 25.50
   a. Horiz. pair, imperf. btwn. 26.00
Nos. C37-C39 (3)

Stratostat "U.S.S.R." — AP12

Ascent into the stratosphere by Soviet aeronauts, Sept. 30th, 1933.

**1933 Wmk. 170 Unwmk.**
C40 AP13 5k ultra 13.50 4.75
C41 AP13 10k green 13.50 4.75
C42 AP13 20k carmine 9.00
C43 AP13 50k dull blue 37.50 9.00
C44 AP13 80k dull blue 124.50 36.50
Nos. C40-C44 (5)

**Unwmk.**
C45 AP13 5k ultra 15.00 3.25
C46 AP13 10k green 15.00 350.00
   a. Horiz. pair, imperf. btwn.
C47 AP13 20k carmine 21.00 5.50
C48 AP13 50k dull blue 40.00 11.00
C49 AP13 80k purple 29.00 5.50
Nos. C45-C49 (5)

10th anniversary of Soviet civil aviation and airmail service. Counterfeits exist, perf 11½.

**1934 Wmk. 170 Perf. 11**
C50 AP18 5k vio brown 11.50 3.25
   a. Imperf. 185.00
C51 AP18 10k brown 32.50 3.25
C52 AP18 20k ultra 76.50 9.75
Nos. C50-C52 (3)

**Perf. 14**
C50a AP18 5k 110.00 95.00
C51a AP18 10k 185.00
C52a 520.00 505.00
Nos. C50a-C52a (3)

Honoring victims of the stratosphere disaster. See Nos. C77-C79.
Beware of copies of Nos. C50-C52 reperforated to resemble Nos. C50a-C52a.

Sideview of Airship — AP22

Airship "Lenin" — AP23

Airship "Voroshilov" — AP21

Airship Landing — AP20

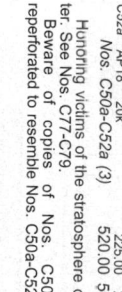

Airship "Pravda" — AP19

Design: 1r, Plane over river.

**1955    Litho.    Perf. 12½x12**

| | | | | |
|---|---|---|---|---|
| C91 | AP46 | 1r multicolored | 1.75 | .55 |
| C92 | AP46 | 2r black & yel grn | 3.50 | .75 |

For overprints see Nos. C95-C96.

**Photo.**

**1955, May 31**

| | | | | |
|---|---|---|---|---|
| C93 | AP47 | 2r chocolate | 1.40 | .50 |
| C94 | AP47 | 2r deep blue | 1.40 | .50 |

Nos. C91 and C92 Overprinted in Red

**1955, Nov. 22    Litho.    Perf. 12x12½    Unwmk.**

| | | | | |
|---|---|---|---|---|
| C95 | AP46 | 1r multicolored | 2.75 | 2.00 |
| C96 | AP46 | 2r black & yel grn | 4.75 | 3.00 |

Issued for use at the scientific drifting stations North Pole-4 and North Pole-5. The inscription reads "North Pole-Moscow, 1955." Counterfeits exist.

Arctic Camp AP48

**1956, June 8    Perf. 12½x12**

| | | | | |
|---|---|---|---|---|
| C97 | AP48 | 1r blue, grn, brn, yel & red | 1.50 | .65 |

Opening of scientific drifting station North Pole-6.

Air Force Emblem and Arms of Normandy AP50

Helicopter over Kremlin AP49

**1960, Mar. 5    Photo.    Perf. 12**

| | | | | |
|---|---|---|---|---|
| C98 | AP49 | 60k ultra | 1.00 | .30 |

**Surcharged with New Value, Bars and "1961"**

**1961, Dec. 20**

| | | | | |
|---|---|---|---|---|
| C99 | AP49 | 6k on 60k ultra | .80 | .30 |

**1962, Dec. 30    Unwmk.    Perf. 11½**

| | | | | |
|---|---|---|---|---|
| C100 | AP50 | 6k blue grn, ocher & car | .60 | .20 |

French Normandy-Neman Escadrille, which fought on the Russian front, 20th anniv.

Jet over Map Showing Airlines in USSR AP51

Designs: 12k, Aeroflot emblem and globe. 16k, Jet over map showing Russian international airlines.

---

Nos. 860A and 861A Surcharged in Red

**1944, May 25**

| | | | | |
|---|---|---|---|---|
| C80 | A431 | 1r on 30k Prus green | .50 | .20 |
| C81 | A432 | 1r on 30k deep ultra | .50 | .20 |
| | | Set, never hinged | 1.25 | |

> Catalogue values for unused stamps in this section, from this point to the end of the section, are for Never Hinged items.

Planes and Soviet Air Force Flag — AP42

**1948, Dec. 10    Litho.    Perf. 12½**

| | | | | |
|---|---|---|---|---|
| C82 | AP42 | 1r dark blue | 4.00 | 1.00 |

Air Force Day.

Plane over Zages, Caucasus — AP43

Plane over Farm Scene AP44

Map of Russian Air Routes and Transport Planes — AP45

#C85, Sochi, Crimea. #C86, Far East. #C87, Leningrad. 2r, Moscow. 3r, Arctic.

**1949, Nov. 9    Photo.    Perf. 12x12½    Unwmk.**

| | | | | |
|---|---|---|---|---|
| C83 | AP43 | 50k red brn, lemon | 2.50 | .65 |
| C84 | AP44 | 60k sepia, pale buff | 4.75 | .80 |
| C85 | AP44 | 1r org brn, yelsh | 4.75 | 1.10 |
| C86 | AP43 | 1r blue, bluish | 4.75 | 1.10 |
| C87 | AP43 | 1r red brn, pale fawn | 4.75 | 1.10 |
| C88 | AP45 | 1r blk, ultra & red, gray | 10.00 | 3.25 |
| C89 | AP43 | 2r org brn, bluish | 15.00 | 8.75 |
| C90 | AP43 | 3r dk green, bluish | 24.00 | 3.25 |
| | | Nos. C83-C90 (8) | 70.50 | 20.00 |

Globe and Plane AP47

Plane and Mountain Stream AP46

---

No. C61 Surcharged in Red

**1935, Aug.**

| | | | | |
|---|---|---|---|---|
| C68 | AP27 | 1r on 10k dk brn | 250.00 | 325.00 |
| a. | | Never hinged | 600.00 | |
| b. | | Inverted surcharge | 5,000. | 5,000. |
| c. | | Small Cyrillic "r" | 350.00 | 300.00 |
| | | As "b," inverted surcharge | 20,000. | |

Moscow-San Francisco flight. Counterfeits exist.

Single-Engined Monoplane — AP34

Five-Engined Transport — AP35

20k, Twin-engined cabin plane. 30k, 4-motored transport. 40k, Single engined amphibian. 50k, Twin-motored transport. 80k, 8-motored transport.

**1937    Unwmk.    Perf. 12**

| | | | | |
|---|---|---|---|---|
| C69 | AP34 | 10k yel brn & blk | 1.40 | .75 |
| a. | | Imperf. | 175.00 | |
| C70 | AP34 | 20k gray grn & blk | 1.40 | .75 |
| C71 | AP34 | 30k red brn & blk | 1.75 | .75 |
| C72 | AP34 | 40k vio brn & blk | 2.50 | .95 |
| C73 | AP34 | 50k blk vio & blk | 4.00 | 1.50 |
| C74 | AP35 | 80k bl vio & brn | 3.75 | 1.50 |
| C75 | AP35 | 1r black, brown & buff | 10.50 | 3.00 |
| a. | | Sheet of 4, imperf | 125.00 | 150.00 |
| | | Nos. C69-C75 (7) | 25.30 | 9.20 |
| | | Set, never hinged | 125.00 | |

Jubilee Aviation Exhib., Moscow, Nov. 15-20. Vertical pairs, imperf. between, exist for No. C71, value $500; No. C73, value $350.

Types of 1938 Regular Issue Overprinted in Various Colors

**1939    Typo.**

| | | | | |
|---|---|---|---|---|
| C76 | A282 | 10k red (C) | 1.40 | .40 |
| C76A | A285 | 30k blue (R) | 1.40 | .40 |
| C76B | A286 | 40k dull green (Br) | .40 | .40 |
| C76C | A287 | 50k dull violet (R) | 2.25 | .55 |
| C76D | A289 | 1r brown (Bl) | 3.00 | 1.75 |
| a. | | Double overprint | 1,000. | |
| | | Nos. C76-C76D (5) | 9.45 | 3.50 |
| | | Set, never hinged | 25.00 | |

Soviet Aviation Day, Aug. 18, 1939.

**Types of 1934 with "30.1.1944" Added at Lower Left**

Designs: No. C77, P. F. Fedoseinko. No. C78, I. D. Usyskin. No. C79, A. B. Vasenko.

**1944    Photo.    Perf. 12**

| | | | | |
|---|---|---|---|---|
| C77 | AP18 | 1r deep blue | 1.75 | .60 |
| C78 | AP18 | 1r slate green | 1.75 | .60 |
| C79 | AP18 | 1r brt yellow green | 1.75 | .75 |
| | | Nos. C77-C79 (3) | 5.25 | 1.95 |
| | | Set, never hinged | 6.50 | |

1934 stratosphere disaster, 10th anniv.

---

**1934    Perf. 14**

| | | | | |
|---|---|---|---|---|
| C53 | AP19 | 5k red orange | 18.00 | 2.75 |
| C54 | AP20 | 10k claret | 16.00 | 4.25 |
| C55 | AP21 | 15k brown | 16.00 | 5.75 |
| C56 | AP22 | 20k black | 35.00 | 8.75 |
| C57 | AP23 | 30k ultra | 65.00 | 8.75 |
| | | Nos. C53-C57 (5) | 150.00 | 30.25 |

Capt. V. Voronin and "Chelyuskin" — AP24

Prof. Otto Y. Schmidt — AP25

A. V. Lapidevsky AP26

S. A. Ievanevsky AP27

"Schmidt Camp" — AP28

**1935    Perf. 14**

| | | | | |
|---|---|---|---|---|
| C58 | AP24 | 1k red orange | 5.50 | 2.50 |
| C59 | AP25 | 3k rose carmine | 6.50 | 2.50 |
| C60 | AP26 | 5k emerald | 5.50 | 2.50 |
| C61 | AP27 | 10k dark brown | 6.50 | 2.50 |
| C62 | AP25 | 15k black | 6.50 | 4.75 |
| C63 | AP27 | 20k deep claret | 11.00 | 9.25 |
| C64 | AP27 | 25k indigo | 27.50 | 9.25 |
| C65 | AP27 | 30k dull green | 40.00 | 11.00 |
| C66 | AP27 | 40k purple | 27.50 | 7.00 |
| C67 | AP28 | 50k dark ultra | 27.50 | 9.25 |
| | | Nos. C58-C67 (10) | 165.50 | 53.75 |

Designs: 15k, M. G. Slepnev. 20k, I. V. Doronin. 25k, M. V. Vodopianov. 30k, V. S. Molokov. 40k, N. P. Kamanin.

Aerial rescue of ice-breaker Chelyuskin crew and scientific expedition.

## 1963, Feb.

Aeroflot, the civil air fleet, 40th anniv.

Nos. C101-C103 (3)

| | | | | |
|---|---|---|---|---|
| C101 | AP51 | 10k red, blk & tan | .60 | .20 |
| C102 | AP51 | 12k blue, red, tan & blk | .85 | .25 |
| C103 | AP51 | 16k blue, blk & red | 1.00 | .35 |
| | | | 2.45 | .80 |

Tupolev 134 at Sheremetyevo Airport, Moscow — AP52

## 1965, Dec. 31

Civil Aviation: 10k, An-24 (Antonov) and Vnukovo Airport, Moscow. 12k, Mi-10 (Mil helicopter) and Central Airport, Moscow. 16k, Be-10 (Beriev) and Chinki Riverport, Moscow. 20k, Antei airliner and Domodedovo Airport, Moscow.

Nos. C104-C108 (5)

| | | | | |
|---|---|---|---|---|
| C104 | AP52 | 6k org, red & vio | .30 | .20 |
| C105 | AP52 | 10k lt green, org red & gray | .45 | .20 |
| C106 | AP52 | 12k lilac, dk sep & lt grn | .45 | .20 |
| C107 | AP52 | 16k lilac, lt brn, red & grn | .70 | .20 |
| C108 | AP52 | 20k org red, pur & gray | .85 | .25 |
| | | | 2.75 | 1.05 |

### Aviation Type of 1976

Aviation 1917-1930 (Aviation Emblem and):
4k, P-4 BIS biplane, 1917. 6k, AK-1 monoplane, 1924. 10k, R-3 (ANT-3) biplane, 1925. 12k, TB-1 (ANT-4) monoplane, 1925. 16k, R-5 biplane, 1929. 20k, Shcha-2 amphibian, 1930.

## 1977, Aug. 16

### Lithographed and Engraved

Perf. 12x11½

| | | | | |
|---|---|---|---|---|
| C109 | A2134 | 4k multicolored | .20 | .20 |
| C110 | A2134 | 6k multicolored | .20 | .20 |
| C111 | A2134 | 10k multicolored | .20 | .20 |
| C112 | A2134 | 12k multicolored | .30 | .20 |
| C113 | A2134 | 16k multicolored | .45 | .30 |
| C114 | A2134 | 20k multicolored | .65 | .35 |

Nos. C109-C114 (6) 2.10 1.45

## 1978, Aug. 10

Aviation 1928-1930.
4k, PO-2 biplane, 1928. 6k, K-5 passenger plane, 1929. 10k, TB-3, cantilever monoplane, 1930. 12k, Stal-2, 1931. 16k, MBR-2 hydro-plane, 1932. 20k, I-16 fighter plane, 1934.

| | | | | |
|---|---|---|---|---|
| C115 | A2134 | 4k multicolored | .20 | .20 |
| C116 | A2134 | 6k multicolored | .20 | .20 |
| C117 | A2134 | 10k multicolored | .30 | .20 |
| C118 | A2134 | 12k multicolored | .35 | .20 |
| C119 | A2134 | 16k multicolored | .45 | .25 |
| C120 | A2134 | 20k multicolored | .60 | .25 |

Nos. C115-C120 (6) 2.10 1.25

Jet and Compass Rose — AP53

## 1978, Aug. 4    Litho.

| | | | | |
|---|---|---|---|---|
| C121 | AP53 | 32k dark blue | .80 | .30 |

Aeroflot Plane AH-28 — AP54

## 1979    Photogravure and Engraved    Perf. 11½x12

Designs: Various Aeroflot planes.

| | | | | |
|---|---|---|---|---|
| C122 | AP54 | 2k shown | .20 | .20 |
| C123 | AP54 | 3k YAK-42 | .20 | .20 |
| C124 | AP54 | 10k T4-154 | .30 | .20 |
| C125 | AP54 | 15k IL76 transport | .45 | .20 |
| C126 | AP54 | 32k IL86 jet liner | .45 | .45 |

Nos. C125-C126 (2) 2.00 1.25

## AIR POST OFFICIAL STAMPS

Used on mail from Russian embassy in Berlin to Moscow. Surcharged on Consular Fee stamps. Currency: the German mark.

### 1922, July    Surcharge in Carmine

### Litho.    Bicolored Burelage    Perf. 13½

OA1

| | | | |
|---|---|---|---|
| CO1 | OA1 | 12m on 2.25 | 67.50 |
| CO2 | OA1 | 24m on 3r | 67.50 |
| CO3 | OA1 | 120m on 2.25 | 77.50 |
| CO4 | OA1 | 600m on 3r | 97.50 |
| CO5 | OA1 | 1200m on 10k | 140.00 |
| CO6 | OA1 | 1200m on 50k | 15,000. |
| CO7 | OA1 | 1200m on 2.25 | 850.00 |
| CO8 | OA1 | 1200m on 3r | 1,000. |

Three types of each denomination, distinguished by shape of "C" in surcharge and length of second line of surcharge. Used copies have pen or crayon cancel. Forgeries exist.

## SPECIAL DELIVERY STAMPS

Motorcycle Courier — SD1

Express Truck — SD2

### 1932

Design: 80k, Locomotive.

Perf. 12½x12, 12x12½    Photo.

| | | | | |
|---|---|---|---|---|
| E1 | SD1 | 5k dull brown | 7.50 | 6.25 |
| E2 | SD1 | 10k violet brown | 9.75 | 6.25 |
| E3 | SD2 | 80k dull green | 40.00 | 12.50 |

Nos. E1-E3 (3) 57.25 25.00

Set, never hinged 100.00

Used values are for c-to.

## POSTAGE DUE STAMPS

### Regular Issue of 1918 Surcharged in Red or Carmine

### 1924-25    Unwmk.    Perf. 13½

| | | | | |
|---|---|---|---|---|
| J1 | A33 | 1k on 35k blue | | .90 |
| J2 | A33 | 3k on 35k blue | .25 | .90 |
| J3 | A33 | 5k on 35k blue | .25 | |
| J4 | A33 | 8k on 35k blue | | .90 |
|   a. | | Imperf. | | |
| J5 | A33 | 10k on 35k blue ('25) | | 1.10 |
|   a. | | Pair, one without surcharge | | |
| J6 | A33 | 14k on 35k blue | | .90 |
|   a. | | Imperf. | | |
| J7 | A33 | 14k on 70k brown ('25) | | .90 |
|   a. | | Imperf. | | |

### Regular Issue of 1921 Surcharged in Violet

| | | | | |
|---|---|---|---|---|
| J8 | A33 | 32k on 35k blue | .35 | 1.10 |
| J9 | A33 | 40k on 35k blue | | |
|   a. | | Imperf. | 60.00 | 12.50 |
| | | | 3.05 | 8.70 |

Nos. J1-J9 (9)

Surcharge is found inverted on Nos. J1-J2. J4, J6-J9, value $25-$50. Double on Nos. J2. J4-J6; value, $40-$50.

### 1924

| | | | | |
|---|---|---|---|---|
| J10 | A40 | 1k on 100r orange | .35 | |
|   a. | | 1k on 100r yellow | 5.00 | 6.00 |
|   b. | | Pelure paper | 6.00 | 12.50 |
|   c. | | Inverted surcharge | 100.00 | |

### 1925    Lithographed or Typographed

D1

Perf. 12

| | | | | |
|---|---|---|---|---|
| J11 | D1 | 1k red | 2.00 | 1.50 |
| J12 | D1 | 2k violet | 2.00 | 2.25 |
| J13 | D1 | 3k light blue | 1.00 | 2.25 |
| J14 | D1 | 7k orange | 1.00 | 3.00 |
| J15 | D1 | 8k green | 1.65 | 4.50 |
| J16 | D1 | 10k dark blue | 2.00 | 4.50 |
| J17 | D1 | 14k brown | 9.65 | 20.25 |

Perf. 14½x14

| | | | | |
|---|---|---|---|---|
| J13a | | 3k | 4.00 | 6.00 |
| J14a | | 7k | 8.25 | 12.50 |
| J16a | | 10k | 12.50 | 40.00 |
| J17a | | 14k | 2.25 | 3.50 |

Nos. J11-J17 (7) 14.50 62.00

### 1925    Wmk. 170    Typo.    Perf. 12

| | | | | |
|---|---|---|---|---|
| J18 | D1 | 1k red | .45 | .85 |
| J19 | D1 | 2k violet | .45 | .85 |
| J20 | D1 | 3k light blue | .60 | 1.10 |
| J21 | D1 | 7k orange | .60 | 1.10 |
| J22 | D1 | 8k green | .60 | 1.10 |
| J23 | D1 | 10k dark blue | .75 | 1.60 |
| J24 | D1 | 14k brown | 1.10 | 2.25 |

Nos. J18-J24 (7) 4.55 8.85

For surcharges see Nos. 359-372.

## WENDEN (LIVONIA)

A former district of Livonia, a province of the Russian Empire, which became part of Latvia, under the name of Vidzeme.

Used values for Nos. L2-L12 are for pen-canceled copies. Postmarked specimens sell for considerably more.

A1

### 1862    Unwmk.    Imperf.

| | | | | |
|---|---|---|---|---|
| L1 | A1 | (2k) blue | 30.00 | 350.00 |

No. L1 may have been used for a short period of time but withdrawn because of small size. Some consider it an essay.

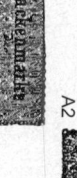

A2    A3

### 1863

| | | | | |
|---|---|---|---|---|
| L2 | A2 | (2k) rose & black | 175.00 | 160.00 |
|   a. | | Background inverted | 500.00 | 500.00 |
| L3 | A3 | (4k) blue grn & blk | 75.00 | 75.00 |
|   a. | | Yellow green & black | 150.00 | |
|   b. | | Half used as 2k on cover | 150.00 | |
|   c. | | As "a," background inverted | | |

The official imitations of Nos. L2 and L3 have a single hyphen instead of a double hyphen after "WENDEN."

### Coat of Arms

A4    A5    A6

### 1863-71

| | | | | |
|---|---|---|---|---|
| L4 | A4 | (2k) rose & green | 37.50 | |
|   a. | | Tête bêche pair | 1,800. | |
|   b. | | Yellowish paper | | |
|   c. | | Green frame around central oval | | |
| L5 | A5 | (4k) rose & grn ('64) | 35.00 | 30.00 |
| L6 | A6 | (2k) rose & green | 126.00 | 108.50 |

Nos. L4-L6 (3) 21.00

### Coat of Arms

A7    A8

### 1872-75    Perf. 12½

| | | | | |
|---|---|---|---|---|
| L7 | A7 | (2k) red & green | 75.00 | 50.00 |
| L8 | A8 | 2k yel grn & red ('75) | 8.00 | 10.00 |
|   a. | | Numeral in upper right corner resembles an inverted "3" | 27.50 | 27.50 |

Official imitations of Nos. L4b and L5 have a rose instead of a green line around the central oval. The first official imitation of No. L6 has the second oval 5½mm instead of 6½mm wide, than the original and the top of the "r" of "Briefmarke" is too much hooked.

A9

### 1878-80

| | | | | |
|---|---|---|---|---|
| L9 | A7 | (2k) green & red | 7.00 | 8.00 |
| L10 | A9 | 2k blk, grn & red ('80) | 9.00 | 30.00 |
|   a. | | Imperf, pair | | |

No. L9 has been reprinted in blue green and yellow green with perforation 11½ and in gray green with perforation 12½ or imperforate.

Wenden Castle — A10

### 1884

| | | | | |
|---|---|---|---|---|
| L11 | A9 | 2k black, green & red | 10.00 | 3.00 |
|   a. | | Arm omitted | 21.00 | |
| L12 | A10 | 2k dk green & brown | 12.00 | 7.50 |
|   a. | | Tête bêche pair | 21.00 | |
|   b. | | Imperf, pair | 27.00 | |

### 1901    Litho.    Perf. 11½

| | | | | |
|---|---|---|---|---|
| L12 | A10 | 2k dk green & brown | 12.00 | |
|   a. | | Arm double | 45.00 | |
|   b. | | Imperf, pair | 120.00 | |

Reprints of No. L8 have no horizontal lines in the background. Those of No. L6 have impression blurred and only traces of the horizontal lines.

A8

## OCCUPATION STAMPS

### Issued under Finnish Occupation

Finnish Stamps of 1917-18 Overprinted

# OFFICES IN CHINA

100 Kopecks = 1 Ruble
100 Cents = 1 Dollar (1917)

Russian Stamps Overprinted in Blue or Red

## On Issues of 1889-92
### Horizontally Laid Paper
1899-1904  Wmk. 168  Perf. 14½x15

| # | Type | Description | Unused | Used |
|---|------|-------------|--------|------|
| 1 | A10 | 1k orange (Bl) | .75 | 1.00 |
| 2 | A10 | 2k green (Bl) | .75 | 1.00 |
| 3 | A10 | 3k carmine (Bl) | .75 | 1.00 |
| 4 | A10 | 5k red violet (Bl) | .75 | 1.00 |
| 5 | A10 | 7k dk org | 1.50 | 2.50 |
| | | a. Inverted overprint | 500.00 | |
| 6 | A8 | 10k dk blue (R) | | 2.50 |
| 7 | A8 | 50k vio & grn (R) ('04) | 4.50 | 5.00 |

Perf. 13½

| 8 | A9 | 1r lt brn, brn & org ('04) | 50.00 | 50.00 |
|---|----|------|------|------|
| | | | 60.50 | 64.00 |

Nos. 1-8 (8)

## On Issues of 1902-05
### Vertically Laid Paper
Perf. 14½ to 15 and Compound
Overprinted in Black, Red or Blue
1904-08

| # | Type | Description | Unused | Used |
|---|------|-------------|--------|------|
| 9 | A10 | 4k rose red (R) | 2.00 | 2.50 |
| 10 | A10 | 7k dk blue (R) | 10.00 | 12.50 |
| 11 | A11 | 10k dk blue (R) | 1,200. | 1,200. |
| | | a. Groundwork inverted | 3,250. | |
| 12 | A11 | 14k bl & rose (R) | 5.00 | 3.50 |
| 13 | A11 | 35k brn vio & blue (Bl) ('08) | 4.50 | 5.00 |
| 14 | A8 | 20k dull grn & lil | 1.50 | 2.50 |
| 15 | A11 | 25k dull grn & lil (R) ('08) | 6.50 | |
| 16 | A11 | 35k dk vio & grn | 10.00 | |
| 17 | A8 | 50k vio & grn (Bl) | 2.50 | 3.25 |
| 18 | A11 | 70k brn & org (Bl) | 75.00 | 55.00 |

Perf. 13½

| 19 | A9 | 1r lt brn, brn & org (R) | 15.00 | 11.50 |
|----|----|------|------|------|
| 20 | A12 | 3.50r blk & gray (R) | 8.00 | 10.00 |
| 21 | A13 | 5r dk bl, grn & pale bl (R) ('07) | 375.00 | |
| 22 | A12 | 10r scar, yel & gray (Bl) ('07) | 40.00 | 50.00 |
| 23 | A13 | | 216.50 | 197.25 |
| | | a. Inverted overprint | | |

Nos. 9-10,12-23 (14)

## On Issues of 1909-12
### Wove Paper
Lozenges of Varnish on Face
1910-16  Unwmk.  Perf. 14x14½

| # | Type | Description | Unused | Used |
|---|------|-------------|--------|------|
| 24 | A14 | 1k orange yel (Bl) | .40 | .50 |
| 26 | A14 | 1k org yel (Bk) | 4.50 | 5.00 |
| 27 | A14 | 2k green (Bk) | .40 | .50 |
| 28 | A14 | 2k green (Bl) | 5.50 | 6.25 |
| | | a. Double ovpt. (Bk and Bl) | | |
| 28 | A14 | 3k rose red (Bl) | .30 | .50 |
| 29 | A14 | 3k rose red (Bk) | 10.00 | |
| 30 | A14 | 4k carmine (Bl) | .40 | .35 |
| 31 | A15 | 4k carmine (Bk) | 7.00 | 7.25 |
| 32 | A11 | 7k blue (Bk) | .40 | .40 |
| 33 | A15 | 10k blue (Bk) | .65 | .65 |
| 34 | A11 | 14k blue & rose (Bk) | .45 | 1.00 |
| 35 | A15 | 15k dl vio & bl (Bk) | .65 | .65 |
| 37 | A8 | 20k green & vio (Bk) | 3.00 | 1.60 |
| 38 | A11 | 25k grn & vio (Bk) | .60 | 5.00 |
| 39 | A11 | 35k brn vio & grn (Bk) | .50 | 1.60 |
| 40 | A11 | 35k brn, vio & grn (R) | .25 | .35 |
| 42 | A8 | 50k brn vio (Bk) | .40 | .40 |
| 43 | A8 | 50k brn vio & grn (Bk) | .40 | .35 |
| 44 | A11 | 70k lt brn & org (Bl) | 15.00 | .50 |

Perf. 13½

| 45 | A9 | 1r pale brn, brn & org, (Bl) | 1.00 | 1.75 |
|----|----|------|------|------|
| 47 | A13 | 5r dk bl, grn & pale bl | 25.00 | 15.00 |
| | | | 76.40 | 74.05 |

Nos. 24-34,36-47 (21)
The existence of #35 is questioned.

## On Stamps of 1909-12
1917  Perf. 11½, 13½, 14, 14½x15

| # | Type | Description | Unused | Used |
|---|------|-------------|--------|------|
| 50 | A14(a) | 1c on 1k dl org yel | .60 | 5.50 |
| 51 | A14(a) | 2c on 2k dull grn | .60 | 5.50 |
| | | a. Double surcharge | 65.00 | |
| | | b. Inverted surcharge | 150.00 | |
| 52 | A14(a) | 3c on 3k car | 1.25 | 4.25 |
| 53 | A15(a) | 4c on 4k car | 1.25 | 15.00 |
| 54 | A14(a) | 5c on 5k claret | 1.25 | 15.00 |
| 55 | A15(a) | 10c on 10k dk bl | 85.00 | 85.00 |
| | | a. Inverted surcharge | 115.00 | |
| | | b. Double surcharge | | |
| 56 | A11(b) | 14c on 14k dk bl & car | 1.25 | 10.00 |
| | | a. Imperf. | 6.00 | |
| | | b. Inverted surcharge | 1.25 | |
| 57 | A11(a) | 15c on 15k brn lil & dp bl | 1.25 | 15.00 |
| 58 | A8(b) | 20c on 20k bl & car | 1.25 | 15.00 |
| 59 | A11(a) | 25c on 25k grn & violet | 1.25 | 15.00 |
| 60 | A11(a) | 35c on 35k brn vio & green | 1.50 | 15.00 |
| | | a. Inverted surcharge | 27.50 | |
| 61 | A8(a) | 50c on 50k brn vio & green | 1.25 | 15.00 |
| 62 | A11(a) | 70c on 70k brn & red orange | 15.00 | 15.00 |
| 63 | A9(c) | $1 on 1r pale brn, brn & org | 15.80 | 165.75 |

Nos. 50-63 (14)

## On Stamps of 1902-05
### Vertically Laid Paper
Perf. 11½, 13, 13½, 13½x11½
Wmk. Wavy Lines (168)

| 64 | A12 | $3.50 on 3.50r blk & gray | 9.00 | 32.50 |
|----|----|------|------|------|
| 65 | A13 | $5 on 5r dk bl, grn & pale blue | 9.00 | 32.50 |
| 66 | A12 | $7 on 7r blk & yel | 8.50 | 32.50 |

## On Stamps of 1915
Unwmk.  Perf. 13½
### Wove Paper

| 68 | A13 | $5 on 5r ind, grn & lt blue | 13.00 | 42.50 |
|----|----|------|------|------|
| | | a. Inverted surcharge | 250.00 | |
| 70 | A13 | $10 on 10r car lake, yel & grn | 12.50 | 100.00 |
| | | | 52.00 | 240.00 |

Nos. 64-70 (5)
The surcharge on Nos. 64-70 is in larger type than on the $1.

Russian Stamps of 1909-18 Surcharged in Black or Red

## On Stamps of 1909-12
Perf. 14, 14½x15
1920

| # | Type | Description | Unused | Used |
|---|------|-------------|--------|------|
| 72 | A14 | 1c on 1k dull org yellow | 75.00 | 37.50 |
| 73 | A14 | 2c on 2k dull grn | 16.00 | 15.00 |
| 74 | A14 | 3c on 3k car | 16.00 | 15.00 |
| 75 | A15 | 5c on 5k claret (R) | 130.00 | 15.00 |
| 76 | A11 | 10c on 10k dk bl | 16.00 | 15.00 |
| 77 | A15 | 10c on 10k dk bl (R) | 100.00 | 57.50 |
| 78 | A14 | 10c on 10k on 7k blue (R) | 95.00 | 57.50 |

On Stamps of 1917-18
Imperf

| 79 | A14 | 1c on 1k orange (R) | 22.50 | 15.00 |
|----|----|------|------|------|
| | | a. Inverted surcharge | 45.00 | 75.00 |
| 80 | A14 | 5c on 5k claret | 140.00 | 30.00 |
| | | b. Double surcharge | 200.00 | |
| | | c. Surcharged "Ceil" only | | |

Nos. 72-80 (9) 386.50 257.50

---

# ARMY OF THE NORTH

A3, A5, A2, A1, A4

The letters OKCA are the initials of Russian words meaning "Special Corps, Army of the North." The stamps were in use from about the end of September to the end of December, 1919.
Used values are for c-t-o stamps.

1919, Sept.  Typo.  Imperf.

| # | Type | Description | | Used |
|---|------|-------------|---|------|
| 1 | A1 | 5k brown violet | .40 | .70 |
| 2 | A2 | 10k blue | .40 | .70 |
| 3 | A3 | 15k yellow | .40 | .70 |
| 4 | A4 | 20k rose | .40 | .70 |
| 5 | A5 | 50k green | 2.00 | 3.50 |

Nos. 1-5 (5)

---

# RUSSIAN OFFICES ABROAD

For various reasons the Russian Empire maintained Post Offices to handle its correspondence in several foreign countries. These were similar to the Post Offices in foreign countries maintained by other world powers.

(General Miller)

A set of seven stamps of this design was prepared in 1919, but not issued. Value, set $35. Counterfeits exist.

---

## On Stamps of 1917

| 6 | A11 | 25k grn & gray violet | 8.50 | 3.50 |
|---|----|------|------|------|
| 7 | A8 | 50k brn vio & grn | 5.00 | 27.50 |

Perf. 13½

| 8 | A9 | 1r pale brn, dk brn & org | 14.00 | 25.00 |
|---|----|------|------|------|

On Stamps of 1917
Imperf

| 10 | A14 | 3k red | 1.40 | 3.50 |
|----|----|------|------|------|
| 11 | A12 | 3.50r mar & lt grn | 17.50 | 27.50 |
| 12 | A13 | 5r dk blue, grn & pale bl | 14.00 | 25.00 |
| 13 | A12 | 7r dk green & pink | 77.50 | 125.00 |

No. 2 Surcharged
Perf. 14, 14½x15

| 9 | A13 | 10r scar, yel & gray | 1.75 | 3.75 |
|---|----|------|------|------|
| 14 | A14 | 10k on 5k claret | 181.65 | 295.50 |

Nos. 1-14 (14)

Nos. 1-14 exist with inverted overprint or surcharge. The 1, 3½, 5, 7 and 10 rubles with red overprint are trial printings (value $40 each). The 20k on 14k, perforated, and the 1, 2, 5, 15, 70k and 1r imperforate were overprinted but never placed in use. Value: $80; $30, $40, $40, $45, $40 and $60. These stamps were in use from Aug. 1 to Oct. 15, 1919.
Counterfeits of Nos. 1-14 abound.

---

## 1919

| # | Type | Description | Unused | Used |
|---|------|-------------|--------|------|
| N1 | A19 | 5p green | 12.50 | 12.00 |
| N2 | A19 | 10p rose | 12.50 | 6.25 |
| N3 | A19 | 20p buff | 12.50 | |
| N4 | A19 | 40p red violet | 100.00 | |
| N5 | A19 | 50p purple | 105.00 | 105.00 |
| N6 | A19 | 1m dl rose & blk | 325.00 | 325.00 |
| N7 | A19 | 5m violet & blk | 575.00 | 575.00 |
| N8 | A19 | 10m brown & blk | 1,155. | 1,155. |

Nos. N1-N8 (8)
"Aunus" is the Finnish name for Olonets, a town of Russia.
Counterfeits overprints exist.

---

# Issued under German Occupation

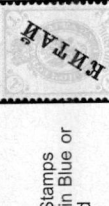

Germany Nos. 506 to 523 Overprinted in Black

1941-43  Unwmk.  Typo.  Perf. 14

| N9 | A115 | 1pf gray black | .20 | .20 |
|----|------|------|------|------|
| N10 | A115 | 3pf light brown | .20 | .20 |
| N11 | A115 | 4pf slate | .20 | .20 |
| N12 | A115 | 5pf dp yellow green | .20 | .20 |
| N13 | A115 | 6pf purple | .20 | .20 |
| N14 | A115 | 8pf red | .20 | .20 |

Engr.

| N15 | A115 | 10pf dk brown ('43) | .20 | 1.75 |
|-----|------|------|------|------|
| N16 | A115 | 12pf carmine ('43) | .20 | 1.75 |
| N17 | A115 | 10pf dark brown | .25 | .40 |
| N18 | A115 | 12pf brt carmine | .25 | .40 |
| N19 | A115 | 15pf brown lake | .25 | .25 |
| N20 | A115 | 16pf peacock grn | .25 | .25 |
| N21 | A115 | 20pf blue | .25 | .25 |
| N22 | A115 | 24pf orange brown | .25 | .25 |
| N23 | A115 | 25pf red ultra | .25 | .25 |
| N24 | A115 | 30pf olive green | .25 | .25 |
| N25 | A115 | 40pf brt red violet | .25 | .25 |
| N26 | A115 | 50pf myrtle green | .25 | .25 |
| N27 | A115 | 60pf dk red brown | .25 | .25 |
| N28 | A115 | 80pf indigo | 4.60 | 7.50 |

Nos. N9-N28 (20)
Issued for use in Estonia, Latvia and Lithuania.

Same Overprinted in Black

| N29 | A115 | 1pf gray black | .20 | .20 |
|-----|------|------|------|------|
| N30 | A115 | 3pf lt brown | .20 | .20 |
| N31 | A115 | 4pf slate | .20 | .20 |
| N33 | A115 | 6pf purple | .20 | .20 |
| N34 | A115 | 8pf red | .20 | .20 |

Engr.

| N35 | A115 | 10pf dk brown ('43) | .20 | 1.75 |
|-----|------|------|------|------|
| N36 | A115 | 12pf carmine ('43) | .20 | 1.75 |

1919, Sept.  Typo.

| N37 | A115 | 1pf gray black | .20 | .55 |
|-----|------|------|------|------|
| N38 | A115 | 3pf lt carmine | .60 | .55 |
| N39 | A115 | 4pf brown lake | .60 | .55 |
| N40 | A115 | 6pf purple | .25 | |
| N41 | A115 | 8pf green | .25 | |
| N42 | A115 | 24pf orange brown | .25 | |
| N43 | A115 | 25pf bright ultra | .25 | |
| N44 | A115 | 30pf olive green | .25 | |
| N45 | A115 | 40pf brt red violet | .25 | |
| N46 | A115 | 50pf myrtle green | .25 | |
| N47 | A115 | 60pf dk red brown | .25 | |
| N48 | A115 | 80pf indigo | 5.70 | 7.50 |

Nos. N29-N48 (20)

---

# ARMY OF THE NORTHWEST

(Gen. Nicolai N. Yudenich)

Russian Stamps of 1909-18 Overprinted in Black or Red

## On Stamps of 1909-12
Perf. 14 to 15 and Compound
1919, Aug. 1

| # | Type | Description | Unused | Used |
|---|------|-------------|--------|------|
| 1 | A14 | 2k green | 2.50 | 4.25 |
| 2 | A14 | 5k claret | 2.50 | 4.25 |
| 3 | A11 | 10k dk blue (R) | 2.75 | 5.00 |
| 4 | A15 | 15k red brn & bl | 2.50 | 5.00 |
| 5 | A8 | 20k blue & car | 5.00 | 7.50 |

---

c

a  1 CENT

b  10 CENTS

The existence of #35 is questioned.

Russian Stamps of 1902-12 Surcharged:

# OFFICES IN THE TURKISH EMPIRE

Various powers maintained post offices in the Turkish Empire before World War I by authority of treaties which ended with the signing of the Treaty of Lausanne in 1923. The foreign post offices were closed Oct. 27, 1923.

100 Kopecks = 1 Ruble
40 Paras = 1 Piaster (1900)

Coat of Arms
A1

A2

A3

A4  A5  A6

**1863  Unwmk.  Typo.  Imperf.**

| | | | |
|---|---|---|---|
| 1 | A1 | 6k blue | 275.00 1,000. |
| a. | | 6k light blue, thin paper | 350.00 1,350. |
| b. | | 6k light blue, medium paper | 325.00 1,350. |
| c. | | 6k dark blue, chalky paper | 200.00 |

Forgeries exist.

**1865**

| | | | |
|---|---|---|---|
| 2 | A2 | (2k) brown & blue | 700.00 625.00 |
| 3 | A3 | (20k) blue & red | 900.00 850.00 |

Twenty-eight varieties of each.

**Litho.**

**1866**  Horizontal Network

| | | | |
|---|---|---|---|
| 4 | A4 | (2k) rose & pale bl | 35.00 52.50 |
| 5 | A5 | (20k) dp blue & rose | 55.00 57.50 |

**1867**  Vertical Network

| | | | |
|---|---|---|---|
| 6 | A4 | (2k) rose & pale bl | 70.00 87.50 |
| 7 | A5 | (20k) dp rose & rose | 100.00 150.00 |

**1868  Typo.  Wmk. 168  Perf. 11½**

| | | | |
|---|---|---|---|
| 8 | A6 | 1k brown | 35.00 19.00 |
| 9 | A6 | 3k green | 35.00 19.00 |
| 10 | A6 | 5k blue | 35.00 19.00 |
| 11 | A6 | 10k car & green | 140.00 76.00 |

Nos. 8-11 dissolve in water.

**Horizontally Laid Paper**

**1872-90  Perf. 14½x15**

| | | | |
|---|---|---|---|
| 12 | A6 | 1k brown | 6.25 3.00 |
| 13 | A6 | 3k green | 2.00 1.00 |
| 14 | A6 | 5k blue | 3.75 1.00 |
| 15 | A6 | 10k pale red & grn | |
| b. | | 10k carmine & grn (90) | 31.00 |

Nos. 12-15 (4)

**Vertically Laid Paper**

| | | | |
|---|---|---|---|
| 12a | A6 | 1k brown | 1.00 .50 |
| 13a | A6 | 3k green | 3.75 |
| 14a | A6 | 5k blue | 1.00 .50 |
| 15a | A6 | 10k | 37.50 12.50 |

Nos. 12a-15a (4)

Colors of Nos. 8-11 exist imperf.
Nos. 12-15a exist imperf.

---

No. 15 Surcharged in Black or Blue:

A13  A14

**1876**

| | | | |
|---|---|---|---|
| 16 | A6(a) | 8k on 10k (Bk) | 75.00 45.00 |
| a. | | Vertically laid | |
| 17 | A6(a) | 8k on 10k (Bl) | 375.00 |
| a. | | Inverted surcharge | |
| b. | | Vertically laid | 85.00 |

**1879**

| | | | |
|---|---|---|---|
| 18 | A6(b) | 7k on 10k (Bk) | 85.00 65.00 |
| a. | | Vertically laid | 750.00 750.00 |
| 19 | A6(b) | 7k on 10k (Bl) | 65.00 |
| a. | | Inverted surcharge | |
| b. | | Vertically laid | |
| 19C | A6(c) | 7k on 10k (Bk) | 750.00 500.00 |
| 19D | A6(c) | 7k on 10k (Bl) | |

Nos. 16-19D have been counterfeited.

**1884  Perf. 14½x15**

| | | | |
|---|---|---|---|
| 20 | A6 | 1k black & yellow | 3.00 1.50 |
| a. | | Vertically laid | 9.00 7.50 |
| 21 | A6 | 2k black & rose | 4.50 4.25 |
| 22 | A6 | 7k carmine & rose | 6.50 6.00 |
| a. | | Vertically laid | 27.50 1.75 |

Nos. 20-22 (3)

**1879**

| | | | |
|---|---|---|---|
| 23 | A6 | 1k orange | .45 .30 |
| 24 | A6 | 2k green | .70 .40 |
| 25 | A6 | 5k pale red violet | 2.75 .40 |
| 26 | A6 | 7k blue | 5.30 2.00 |

Nos. 23-26 (4)

Nos. 23-26 imperforate are believed to be proofs. No. 23 surcharged "40 PARAS" is bogus, though some copies were postally used.

---

Russian Company of Navigation and Trade

**Р.О.П.и.Т.**

This overprint, in two sizes, was privately applied in various colors to Russian Offices in the Turkish Empire stamps of 1900-1910.

**Nos. 40-48 Overprinted with Names of Various Cities**

A7  A8  A9

A10  A11

A12

A13  A14

**1900**

**Surcharged in Blue, Black or Red**

| | | | |
|---|---|---|---|
| 27 | A7 | 4pa on 1k orange | .20 .20 |
| a. | | Inverted surcharge | 30.00 30.00 |
| 28 | A7 | 4pa on 1k orange (Bl) | 30.00 |
| | | (Bk) | 30.00 30.00 |
| 29 | A7 | 10pa on 2k green | .20 .20 |
| a. | | Inverted surcharge | 30.00 30.00 |
| 30 | A7 | 1pi on 10k dk blue | .50 .60 |
| a. | | Inverted surcharge | 1.15 1.25 |

Nos. 27-30 (4)

**1903-05**

**Vertically Laid Paper**

| | | | |
|---|---|---|---|
| 31 | A7 | 10pa on 2k yel green | .30 .50 |
| a. | | Inverted surcharge | 70.00 |
| 32 | A8 | 20pa on 4k rose red | .30 .50 |
| a. | | Inverted surcharge | 25.00 |

---

**1909**

**Lozenges of Varnish on Face**

**Wove Paper**

**1909  Unwmk.  Perf. 14½x15**

| | | | |
|---|---|---|---|
| 40 | A12 | 5pa on 1k orange | .30 .35 |
| 41 | A12 | 10pa on 2k green | .25 .35 |
| 42 | A12 | 20pa on 4k carmine | .65 .60 |
| 43 | A12 | 1pi on 10k | .65 .70 |
| 44 | A12 | 5pi on 50k vio & grn | 1.40 1.75 |
| 45 | A12 | 7pi on 70k brn & org | 2.00 2.75 |

**Perf. 13½**

| | | | |
|---|---|---|---|
| 46 | A13 | 10pi on 1r brn & org | 3.00 5.00 |
| 47 | A14 | 35pi on 3.50r mar & lt | |
| | | brn | 12.50 14.00 |
| 48 | A14 | 70pi on 7r dk grn & | |
| | | pink | 20.00 25.00 |

Nos. 40-48 (9)  40.70 51.30

50th anniv. of the establishing of the Russian Post Offices in the Levant.

---

Overprinted "Constantinople"
Black Overprint

**1909-10  Perf. 14½x15**

| | | | |
|---|---|---|---|
| 61 | A12 | 5pa on 1k | .20 .30 |
| 62 | A12 | 10pa on 2k | .20 .30 |
| 63 | A12 | 20pa on 4k | .35 .45 |
| 64 | A12 | 1pi on 10k | .35 .55 |
| 65 | A12 | 5pi on 50k | .65 .90 |
| 66 | A12 | 7pi on 70k | 1.50 2.00 |

**Perf. 13½**

| | | | |
|---|---|---|---|
| 67 | A13 | 10pi on 1r | 6.25 8.75 |
| 68 | A14 | 35pi on 3.50r | 15.00 |
| 69 | A14 | 70pi on 7r | 17.50 27.50 |

Nos. 61-69 (9)

**"Constantinople"**
**Blue Overprint**

| | | | |
|---|---|---|---|
| 70 | A12 | 5pa on 1k | 3.00 3.50 |

Nos. 61-70 (10)  62.50 86.75

**Overprinted "Constantinople"**
**Black Overprint**

| | | | |
|---|---|---|---|
| 71 | A12 | 5pa on 1k | 1.40 2.50 |
| 72 | A12 | 10pa on 2k | 1.50 2.75 |
| 73 | A12 | 20pa on 4k | 2.00 3.50 |
| 74 | A12 | 1pi on 10k | 2.50 3.50 |
| a. | | Double overprint | 32.50 |

Nos. 71-74 (4)

---

Overprinted "Jaffa"
Black Overprint

| | | | |
|---|---|---|---|
| 75 | A12 | 5pa on 50k | 6.00 7.00 |
| 76 | A12 | 7pi on 70k | 7.25 9.75 |

**Perf. 13½**

**Blue Overprint**

| | | | |
|---|---|---|---|
| 77 | A12 | 5pa on 50k | 30.00 37.50 |
| 78 | A14 | 35pi on 3.50r | 75.00 87.50 |
| 79 | A14 | 70pi on 7r | 100.00 125.00 |

**Overprinted "Ierusalem"**
**Black Overprint**

| | | | |
|---|---|---|---|
| 80 | A12 | 5pa on 1k | 10.00 10.00 |

Nos. 71-80 (10)  235.90 289.00

**Perf. 14½x15**

| | | | |
|---|---|---|---|
| 81 | A12 | 5pa on 1k | 1.50 2.00 |
| 82 | A12 | 10pa on 2k | 25.00 |
| a. | | Inverted overprint | 8.25 |
| 83 | A12 | 20pa on 4k | 13.00 |
| | | "Ierusalem" | 3.00 4.00 |
| 84 | A12 | 1pi on 10k | 13.00 |
| | | "Ierusalem" | 8.25 |
| 85 | A12 | 5pi on 50k | 3.00 |
| | | "Ierusalem" | 11.50 |
| 86 | A12 | 7pi on 70k | 8.00 |
| | | "Ierusalem" | 13.00 |

---

**Perf. 13½**

| | | | |
|---|---|---|---|
| 87 | A13 | 10pi on 1r | 50.00 |
| 88 | A14 | 35pi on 3.50r | 85.00 100.00 |
| 89 | A14 | 70pi on 7r | 100.00 150.00 |

**Overprinted "Kerassunde"**
**Black Overprint**

| | | | |
|---|---|---|---|
| 90 | A12 | 5pa on 1k | 6.50 |

Nos. 81-90 (10)  254.50 340.50

**Perf. 14½x15**

| | | | |
|---|---|---|---|
| 91 | A12 | 5pa on 1k | .30 .45 |
| 92 | A12 | 10pa on 2k | 20.00 |
| a. | | Inverted overprint | .30 |
| 93 | A12 | 20pa on 4k | 8.75 |
| 94 | A12 | 1pi on 10k | 10.50 |
| 95 | A12 | 5pi on 50k | 1.00 1.25 |
| 96 | A12 | 7pi on 70k | 1.50 2.00 |

**Perf. 13½**

| | | | |
|---|---|---|---|
| 97 | A13 | 10pi on 1r | 6.00 7.75 |
| 98 | A14 | 35pi on 3.50r | 19.00 21.00 |
| 99 | A14 | 70pi on 7r | 27.50 30.00 |

**Blue Overprint**

| | | | |
|---|---|---|---|
| 100 | A12 | 5pa on 1k | 4.00 5.50 |

Nos. 91-100 (10)  60.60 69.70

---

Overprinted "Mont Athos"
Black Overprint

**Perf. 14½x15**

| | | | |
|---|---|---|---|
| 101 | A12 | 5pa on 1k | .35 .70 |
| 102 | A12 | 10pa on 2k | 14.00 |
| 103 | A12 | 20pa on 4k | 14.00 |
| a. | | Inverted overprint | .40 |
| 104 | A12 | 1pi on 10k | 15.00 |
| a. | | Double overprint | 22.50 |
| 105 | A12 | 5pi on 50k | 2.25 |
| 106 | A12 | 7pi on 70k | 3.50 5.00 |
| b. | | Pair, one without "Mont Athos" | 16.00 |

**Perf. 13½**

| | | | |
|---|---|---|---|
| 107 | A13 | 10pi on 1r | 11.50 15.00 |
| 108 | A14 | 35pi on 3.50r | 25.00 32.50 |
| 109 | A14 | 70pi on 7r | 45.00 65.00 |

**"Mont Athos"**
**Blue Overprint**

| | | | |
|---|---|---|---|
| 110 | A12 | 5pa on 1k | 4.00 7.25 |

Nos. 101-110 (10)  93.05 131.00

---

Overprinted

| | | | |
|---|---|---|---|
| 111 | A12 | 5pa on 1k | .40 .60 |
| 112 | A12 | 10pa on 2k | .40 .60 |
| 113 | A12 | 20pa on 4k | .55 1.00 |
| 114 | A12 | 1pi on 10k | 1.10 3.00 |
| 115 | A12 | 5pi on 50k | 2.10 3.75 |
| 116 | A12 | 7pi on 70k | 11.50 |

**Perf. 13½**

| | | | |
|---|---|---|---|
| 117 | A13 | 10pi on 1r | 22.50 27.50 |
| a. | | | 30.80 40.45 |

The overprint is larger on No. 117.

Nos. 111-117 (7)

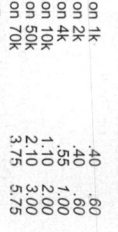

### Overprinted "Salonique"
#### Black Overprint
*Perf. 14½x15*

131 A12 5pa on 1k .30 .60
a. Inverted overprint 25.00
b. Pair, one without overprint
132 A12 10pa on 2k .45 .90
a. Inverted overprint 25.00
133 A12 20pa on 4k .60 .90
a. Inverted overprint 25.00
134 A12 1pi on 10k .60 .90
135 A12 5pi on 50k 1.25 1.75
136 A12 7pi on 70k 2.75 3.00

*Perf. 13½*

137 A13 10pi on 1r 16.00 15.00
138 A14 35pi on 3.50r 30.00 32.50
139 A14 70pi on 7r 52.50 50.00

#### Blue Overprint
*Perf. 14½x15*

140 A12 5pa on 1k 7.50 8.00
*Nos. 131-140 (10)* 111.95 113.55

### Overprinted "Smyrne"
#### Black Overprint

141 A12 5pa on 1k .50 1.00
a. Double overprint
b. Inverted overprint 5.00
142 A12 10pa on 2k .50 1.00
a. Inverted overprint 8.25
143 A12 20pa on 4k 1.00 1.30
a. Inverted overprint 10.00
144 A12 1pi on 10k 1.00 1.40
145 A12 5pi on 50k 2.25 2.50
146 A12 7pi on 70k 3.25 4.75

*Perf. 13½*

147 A13 10pi on 1r 13.50 17.50
148 A14 35pi on 3.50r 25.00 32.50
149 A14 70pi on 7r 37.50 50.00

#### Blue Overprint
*Perf. 14½x15*

150 A12 5pa on 1k 5.00 7.50
*Nos. 141-150 (10)* 89.50 119.45

#### "Smyrn"

141c A12 5pa on 1k 3.50 4.00
142b A12 10pa on 2k 3.25 4.00
143b A12 20pa on 4k 3.25 4.00
144a A12 1pi on 10k 4.50 5.75
145a A12 5pi on 50k 4.50 5.25
146a A12 7pi on 70k 6.50 6.50
*Nos. 141c-146a (6)* 25.50 29.50

### Overprinted "Trebizonde"
#### Black Overprint

151 A12 5pa on 1k .40 .60
a. Inverted overprint 20.00
152 A12 10pa on 2k .40 .60
a. Inverted overprint 6.50
b. Pair, one without "Trebizonde" 50.00
153 A12 20pa on 4k .50 .40
a. Inverted overprint 20.00
154 A12 1pi on 10k .50 .75
a. Pair, one without "Trebizonde" 27.50
155 A12 5pi on 50k 1.25 1.50
156 A12 7pi on 70k 2.25 3.00

*Perf. 13½*

157 A13 10pi on 1r 10.00 10.50
158 A14 35pi on 3.50r 20.00 21.00
159 A14 70pi on 7r 30.00 32.50

#### Blue Overprint
*Perf. 14½x15*

160 A12 5pa on 1k 4.00 4.75
*Nos. 151-160 (10)* 69.30 75.60

On Nos. 158 and 159 the overprint is spelled "Trebisonde."

### Overprinted "Beyrouth"
#### Black Overprint

**1910**

161 A12 5pa on 1k .25 .45
162 A12 10pa on 2k .25 .45
a. Inverted overprint 20.00
163 A12 20pa on 4k .40 .60
164 A12 1pi on 10k .40 .75
165 A12 5pi on 50k 1.00 1.50
166 A12 7pi on 70k 2.00 3.00

*Perf. 13½*

167 A13 10pi on 1r 10.00 10.50
168 A14 35pi on 3.50r 20.00 21.00
169 A14 70pi on 7r 30.00 32.50
*Nos. 161-169 (9)* 64.30 70.75

### Overprinted "Dardanelles"
*Perf. 14½x15*

171 A12 5pa on 1k .30 .60
172 A12 10pa on 2k .30 .60
a. Pair, one without overprint
173 A12 20pa on 4k .75 .75
a. Inverted overprint 10.00
174 A12 1pi on 10k .75 .90
175 A12 5pi on 50k 1.50 1.75
176 A12 7pi on 70k 3.25 3.00

*Perf. 13½*

177 A13 10pi on 1r 10.00 10.50
178 A14 35pi on 3.50r 20.00 21.00
a. Center and ovpt. inverted
179 A14 70pi on 7r 30.00 32.50
*Nos. 171-179 (9)* 66.85 71.60

### Overprinted "Metelin"
*Perf. 14½x15*

181 A12 5pa on 1k .50 .75
a. Inverted overprint 25.00
182 A12 10pa on 2k .50 .75
a. Inverted overprint 25.00
183 A12 20pa on 4k 1.10 1.25
a. Inverted overprint 13.00
184 A12 1pi on 10k 1.10 1.25
185 A12 5pi on 50k 2.75 2.50
186 A12 7pi on 70k 3.50 3.50

*Perf. 13½*

187 A13 10pi on 1r 17.50 15.00
188 A14 35pi on 3.50r 40.00 32.50
189 A14 70pi on 7r 55.00 45.00
*Nos. 181-189 (9)* 121.95 102.50

### Overprinted "Rizeh"
*Perf. 14½x15*

191 A12 5pa on 1k .40 .65
a. Inverted overprint 25.00
192 A12 10pa on 2k .40 .65
a. Inverted overprint 25.00
193 A12 20pa on 4k .65 .85
a. Inverted overprint 25.00
194 A12 1pi on 10k .65 .85
195 A12 5pi on 50k 1.10 2.25
196 A12 7pi on 70k 2.10 3.75

*Perf. 13½*

197 A13 10pi on 1r 11.00 12.50
198 A14 35pi on 3.50r 17.50 21.00
199 A14 70pi on 7r 27.50 32.50
*Nos. 191-199 (9)* 61.30 75.00

Nos. 61-199 for the establishing of Russian Post Offices in the Levant, 50th anniv.

A15 A16 A17

#### Vertically Laid Paper

**1910** **Wmk. 168** *Perf. 14½x15*

200 A15 20pa on 5k red violet (Bl) .60 .60

#### Wove Paper
#### Vertical Lozenges of Varnish on Face

**1910** **Unwmk.** *Perf. 14x14½*

201 A16 5pa on 1k org yel (Bl) .20 .25
202 A16 10pa on 2k green (R) .20 .25
203 A17 20pa on 4k car rose (Bl) .20 .25
204 A17 1pi on 10k blue (R) .20 .25
205 A8 5pi on 50k vio & grn (Bl) .40 .60
206 A9 7pi on 70k lt brn & org (Bl) .40 .65

*Perf. 13½*

207 A10 10pi on 1r pale brn, brn & org (Bl) .50 .75
*Nos. 201-207 (7)* 2.10 3.00

Russian Stamps of 1909-12 Surcharged in Black:

No. 208

Nos. 209-212

**1912** *Perf. 14x14½*

208 A14 20pa on 5k claret .20 .20
209 A11 1½pi on 15k dl vio & blue .20 .25
210 A8 2pi on 20k bl & car .20 .30
211 A11 2½pi on 25k grn & vio .25 .45
a. Double surcharge 50.00 50.00
212 A11 3½pi on 35k vio & grn .40 .55
*Nos. 208-212 (5)* 1.25 1.75

Russia Nos. 88-91, 93, 95-104 Surcharged:

c

d

e

f

g

**1913** *Perf. 13½*

213 A16(c) 5pa on 1k .20 .20
214 A17(d) 10pa on 2k .20 .20
215 A18(c) 15pa on 3k .20 .20
216 A19(c) 20pa on 4k .20 .20
217 A21(e) 1pi on 10k .20 .20
218 A23(f) 1½pi on 15k .45 .50
219 A24(f) 2pi on 20k .45 .50
220 A25(f) 2½pi on 25k .60 .70
221 A26(f) 3½pi on 35k 1.50 1.40
222 A27(e) 5pi on 50k 1.75 1.75
223 A28(f) 7pi on 70k 7.00 7.00
224 A29(e) 10pi on 1r 7.00 7.00
225 A30(e) 20pi on 2r 1.50 1.40
226 A31(g) 30pi on 3r 2.25 2.00
227 A32(e) 50pi on 5r 65.00 62.50
*Nos. 213-227 (15)* 88.50 85.75

Romanov dynasty tercentenary.
Forgeries exist of overprint on No. 227.

Russia Nos. 75, 71, 72 Surcharged:

h

i

#### *Perf. 14x14½*
#### Wove Paper

228 A14(h) 15pa on 3k .20 .20

*Perf. 13, 13½*

230 A13(i) 50pi on 5r 5.00 10.00

#### Vertically Laid Paper
#### Wmk. Wavy Lines (168)

231 A13(i) 100pi on 10r 10.00 20.00
a. Double surcharge 500.00 100.00
*Nos. 228-231 (3)* 15.20 30.20

No. 228 has lozenges of varnish on face but No. 230 has not.

### Wrangel Issues

For the Posts of Gen. Peter Wrangel's army and civilian refugees from South Russia, interned in Turkey, Serbia, etc.

Very few of the Wrangel overprints were actually sold to the public, and many of the covers were made up later with the original cancels. Reprints abound. Values probably are based on sales of reprints in most cases.

Russian Stamps of 1902-18 Surcharged in Blue, Red or Black

### On Russia Nos. 69-70
#### Vertically Laid Paper

**1921** **Wmk. 168** *Perf. 13½*

232 A12 10,000r on 3.50r 50.00 25.00
233 A12 10,000r on 7r 50.00 25.00
234 A12 20,000r on 3.50r 50.00 25.00
235 A12 20,000r on 7r 50.00 25.00
*Nos. 232-235 (4)* 200.00 100.00

### On Russia Nos. 71-86, 87a, 117-118, 137-138
#### Wove Paper
*Perf. 14x14½, 13½*
#### Unwmk.

236 A14 1000r on 1k .65 .65
237 A14 1000r on 2k (R) .65 .65
237A A14 1000r on 2k (Bk) 9.50 9.50
238 A14 1000r on 3k .20 .20
a. Inverted surcharge 10.00 10.00
239 A15 1000r on 4k .20 .20
a. Inverted surcharge 10.00 10.00
240 A14 1000r on 5k .20 .20
a. Inverted surcharge 10.00 10.00
241 A14 1000r on 7k .20 .20
a. Inverted surcharge 10.00 10.00
242 A15 1000r on 10k .20 .20
a. Inverted surcharge 10.00 10.00
243 A14 1000r on 10k on 7k .20 .20
244 A14 5000r on 3k .20 .20
245 A11 5000r on 14k 2.25 2.25
246 A11 5000r on 15k .20 .20
a. "PYCCKIN" 3.50 3.50
247 A8 5000r on 20k .70 .70
a. "PYCCKIN" 3.50 3.50
248 A11 5000r on 20k on 14k .70 .70
249 A11 5000r on 25k .20 .20
250 A11 5000r on 35k .20 .20
a. Inverted surcharge 10.00 10.00
b. New value omitted
251 A8 5000r on 50k .20 .20
a. Inverted surcharge 10.00 10.00
252 A11 5000r on 70k .20 .20
a. Inverted surcharge 10.00 10.00
253 A9 10,000r on 1r (Bl) .20 .20
254 A9 10,000r on 1r (Bk) 1.60 1.60
255 A12 10,000r on 3.50r .70 .70
256 A13 10,000r on 5r 9.50 9.50
257 A13 10,000r on 10r .85 .85
258 A9 20,000r on 1r .50 .50
259 A12 20,000r on 3.50r .50 .50
a. Inverted surcharge 10.00 10.00
b. New value omitted 55.00 55.00
260 A12 20,000r on 7r 19.00 19.00
261 A13 20,000r on 10r .50 .50
*Nos. 236-261 (27)* 50.20 50.20

### On Russia No. 104

261A A32 20,000r on 5r *250.00*

### On Russia Nos. 119-123, 125-135
*Imperf*

262 A14 1000r on 1k .20 .25
263 A14 1000r on 2k (R) .20 .25
263A A14 1000r on 2k (Bk) .25 .30
264 A14 1000r on 3k .20 .25
265 A15 1000r on 4k 6.50 6.50
266 A14 1000r on 5k .25 .30
267 A14 5000r on 3k .20 .25
268 A11 5000r on 15k .25 .30
268A A8 5000r on 20k 10.00
268B A11 5000r on 25k 10.00
269 A11 5000r on 35k .50 .50
270 A8 5000r on 50k .50 .50
271 A11 5000r on 70k .20 .20
272 A9 10,000r on 1r (Bl) .20 .20
a. Inverted surcharge 10.00 10.00
273 A9 10,000r on 1r (Bk) .20 .25
274 A12 10,000r on 3.50r .20 .25
275 A13 10,000r on 5r 1.75 1.75
276 A12 10,000r on 7r 10.00 10.00
276A A13 10,000r on 10r 32.50
277 A9 20,000r on 1r (Bl) .20 .20
a. Inverted surcharge 10.00 10.00
278 A9 20,000r on 1r (Bk) .20 .25
279 A12 20,000r on 3.50r 1.75 1.75
280 A13 20,000r on 5r .20 .20
281 A12 20,000r on 7r 8.00 8.00
281A A13 20,000r on 10r 60.00
*Nos. 262-268,269-276,277-281 (21)* 31.95 32.45

A18

A19

### On Postal Savings Stamps
*Perf. 14½x15*
#### Wmk. 171

282 A18 10,000r on 1k red, *buff* .35 .35
283 A19 10,000r on 5k grn, *buff* .35 .35
a. Inverted surcharge 10.00
284 A19 10,000r on 10k brn, *buff* .35 .35
a. Inverted surcharge 10.00
*Nos. 282-284 (3)* 1.05 1.05

### On Stamps of Russian Offices in Turkey
#### On No. 38-39
#### Vertically Laid Paper
#### Wmk. Wavy Lines (168)

284B A11 20,000r on 35pi on 3.50r *250.00*

**284C** A11 20,000r on 70pi on 7r .......... 250.00

## Vertically Laid Paper
### On Nos. 200-207
**284D** A15 1000r on 20pa on 5k .......... 3.00

## Wove Paper
### Unwmk.
| No. | Type | Description | | |
|---|---|---|---|---|
| 285 | A16 | 1000r on 1k | 1.00 | 1.00 |
| 286 | A16 | 1000r on 10pa on | 1.00 | 1.00 |
| 287 | A17 | 1000r on 20pa on | 1.00 | 1.00 |
| 288 | A17 | 1000r on 1pi on 10k | 1.00 | 1.00 |
| 289 | A8 | 5000r on 5pi on 50k | 4.75 | 4.75 |
| 290 | A9 | 5000r on 7pi on 70k | 4.75 | 4.75 |
| 291 | A10 | 10,000r on 10pi on 1r | 4.50 | 4.50 |
| a. | | Pair, one without surcharge | | |
| 292 | A10 | 20,000r on 10pi on 1r | 4.75 | 4.75 |
| b. | | Pair, one without surcharge | | |

Nos. 284D-292 (9) .......... 14.50 14.50

### On Nos. 208-212
| No. | Type | Description | | |
|---|---|---|---|---|
| 293 | A14 | 1000r on 20pa on 35k | 1.25 | 1.25 |
| 294 | A11 | 1000r on 1½pi on 5k | 1.00 | 1.00 |
| 295 | A8 | 5000r on 2pi on 20k | 1.00 | 1.00 |
| 296 | A11 | 5000r on 2½pi on | 1.00 | 1.00 |
| 297 | A11 | 5000r on 3½pi on | 1.00 | 1.00 |

Nos. 293-297 (5) .......... 5.25 5.25

### On Nos. 228, 230-231
| No. | Type | Description | | |
|---|---|---|---|---|
| 298 | A14 | 1000r on 15pa on 3k | .30 | .30 |
| 299 | A13 | 10,000r on 50pi on 5r | 17.50 | 17.50 |
| 300 | A13 | 10,000r on 100pi on 10r | 25.00 | 25.00 |
| 301 | A13 | 20,000r on 50pi on 5r | .30 | .30 |
| 302 | A13 | 20,000r on 100pi on 10r | 25.00 | 25.00 |

Nos. 298-302 (5) .......... 68.10 68.10

## On Stamps of South Russia
### Denikin Issue
*Imperf*
| No. | Type | Description | | |
|---|---|---|---|---|
| 303 | A5 | 5000r on 5k org | .20 | .20 |
| a. | | Inverted surcharge | | |
| 304 | A5 | 5000r on 10k red | .20 | .20 |
| 305 | A5 | 5000r on 15k red | .20 | .20 |
| 306 | A5 | 5000r on 35k lt bl | .20 | .20 |
| 307 | A5 | 5000r on 70k dk bl | .20 | .20 |
| 307A | A5 | 10,000r on 70k dk bl | 10.00 | 10.00 |
| 308 | A6 | 10,000r on 1r brn & | .20 | .20 |
| 309 | A6 | 10,000r on 10r red & | .20 | .20 |
| a. | | Inverted surcharge | | |
| 310 | A6 | 10,000r on 3r dull red | .25 | .30 |
| 311 | A6 | 10,000r on 5r slate & vio | .50 | .55 |
| 312 | A6 | 10,000r on 7r gray (Bl) | .20 | .20 |
| 313 | A6 | 20,000r on 2r gray (Bl) | 7.50 | 7.50 |
| 315B | A6 | 20,000r on 10r red & grn & rose | 10.00 | 10.00 |
| a. | | Inverted surcharge | | |
| 314 | A6 | 20,000r on 1r brn & vio & yel | .45 | .50 |
| 315 | A6 | 20,000r on 5r slate & vio & yel | .75 | .75 |
| 316 | A6 | 20,000r on 3r dull rose & grn | 10.00 | 10.00 |
| 316A | A6 | 20,000r on 3r dull rose & grn | 10.00 | 10.00 |
| 317 | A6 | 20,000r on 5r slate & rose | 6.00 | 6.00 |
| 318 | A6 | 20,000r on 7r gray | .20 | .25 |
| 319 | A6 | 20,000r on 10r red & grn gray | 12.50 | 12.50 |

Nos. 303-319 (20) .......... 69.95 70.25

## 1921
Trident Stamps of Ukraine Surcharged in Blue, Red, Black or Brown

*Perf. 14, 14½x15*
| No. | Type | Description | | |
|---|---|---|---|---|
| 320 | A14 | 10,000r on 1k org | .20 | .20 |
| 321 | A14 | 10,000r on 2k grn | 2.25 | 2.50 |
| 322 | A14 | 10,000r on 3k red | .20 | .20 |
| a. | | Inverted surcharge | | |
| 323 | A14 | 10,000r on 4k car | .20 | .20 |
| 324 | A14 | 10,000r on 5k cl | .20 | .20 |
| 325 | A14 | 10,000r on 7k lt bl | .20 | .20 |
| a. | | Inverted surcharge | | |
| 326 | A15 | 10,000r on 10k dk bl | .20 | .20 |
| a. | | Inverted surcharge | | |
| 327 | A14 | 10,000r on 10k on 7k lt bl | .20 | .20 |
| a. | | Inverted surcharge | | |
| 328 | A8 | 20,000r on 20k bl & car (Br) | .20 | .20 |
| 329 | A8 | 20,000r on 50k brn & grn | .20 | .20 |
| 330 | A11 | 20,000r on 20k bl & car (Bk) | .20 | .20 |
| a. | | Inverted surcharge | | |
| 331 | A8 | 20,000r on 35k red & grn | 35.00 | 35.00 |
| 332 | A8 | 20,000r on 50k brn vio & grn | .75 | .75 |

Nos. 320-332 (13) .......... 39.45 39.75

*Imperf*
| No. | Type | Description | | |
|---|---|---|---|---|
| 333 | A14 | 10,000r on 1k org | .20 | .20 |
| a. | | Inverted surcharge | | |
| 334 | A8 | 20,000r on 2k grn | 10.00 | 10.00 |
| 335 | A14 | 20,000r on 3k red | .75 | .75 |
| 336 | A8 | 20,000r on 20k bl & car | .20 | .20 |
| 337 | A11 | 20,000r on 35k red | .20 | .20 |
| 338 | A8 | 20,000r on 50k brn | 20.00 | 20.00 |

Nos. 333-338 (6) .......... 22.35 22.35

There are several varieties of the trident surcharge on Nos. 320 to 338.

## Same Surcharge on Russian Stamps
### On Stamps of 1909-18
*Perf. 14x14½*
| No. | Type | Description | | |
|---|---|---|---|---|
| 338A | A11 | 10,000r on 1k dl org yel | .50 | .50 |
| 339 | A14 | 10,000r on 2k dl org | .50 | .50 |
| 340 | A14 | 10,000r on 3k grn | 1.00 | 1.00 |
| 341 | A14 | 10,000r on 3k car | .20 | .20 |
| 343 | A14 | 10,000r on 5k dk cl | .20 | .20 |
| 344 | A14 | 10,000r on 7k blue | .20 | .20 |
| 344A | A14 | 10,000r on 10k dk | .50 | .50 |
| 345 | A11 | 20,000r on 14k dk bl & car | 1.50 | 1.00 |
| 346 | A8 | 20,000r on 20k dl bl brn & dp | 1.00 | .50 |
| 347 | A11 | 20,000r on 20k on 14k dk bl | .50 | .50 |
| 348 | A11 | 20,000r on 35k red brn & grn | 1.50 | 1.00 |
| 349 | A8 | 20,000r on 50k brn vio & grn | .80 | .40 |
| 349A | A11 | 20,000r on 70k brn org | 1.00 | .50 |

Nos. 338A-349A (15) .......... 24.20 13.30

### On Stamps of 1917-18
*Imperf*

## Same Surcharge on Stamps of Russian Offices in Turkey
### On Nos. 40-45
*Perf. 14½x15*
| No. | Type | Description | | |
|---|---|---|---|---|
| 350 | A14 | 10,000r on 1k org | .35 | .20 |
| 351 | A14 | 10,000r on 2k gray | .35 | .20 |
| 352 | A14 | 10,000r on 3k red | .35 | .20 |
| 353 | A14 | 10,000r on 5k red | 22.50 | 15.00 |
| 354 | A14 | 10,000r on 4k car | .35 | .20 |
| 355 | A11 | 20,000r on 15k red brn & | .35 | .20 |
| 356 | A8 | 20,000r on 50k brn vio & grn | 1.00 | .55 |
| 357 | A11 | 20,000r on 70k brn & org | .35 | .30 |

Nos. 350-357 (8) .......... 25.60 16.85

### On Nos. 201-206
| No. | Type | Description | | |
|---|---|---|---|---|
| 358 | A12 | 10,000r on 5pa on 1k | 2.50 | 1.60 |
| 359 | A12 | 10,000r on 10pa on | 2.50 | 1.60 |
| 360 | A12 | 10,000r on 20pa on 4k | 2.50 | 1.60 |
| 361 | A12 | 20,000r on 1pi on 10k | 2.50 | 1.60 |
| 363 | A12 | 20,000r on 5pi on 50k | 2.50 | 1.60 |

Nos. 358-363 (6) .......... 15.00 9.60

### On Nos. 228, 208-212, Stamps of 1912-13
*Perf. 14½x15*
| No. | Type | Description | | |
|---|---|---|---|---|
| 364 | A16 | 10,000r on 5pa on 1k | 3.00 | 3.00 |
| 365 | A16 | 10,000r on 10pa on 2k | 3.00 | 3.00 |
| 366 | A17 | 10,000r on 20pa on 4k | 3.00 | 3.00 |
| 367 | A17 | 10,000r on 1pi on 10k | 3.00 | 3.00 |
| 368 | A8 | 20,000r on 2pi on 20k | 3.00 | 3.00 |
| 369 | A9 | 20,000r on 7pi on 70k | 18.00 | 18.00 |

Nos. 364-369 (6)

| No. | Type | Description | | |
|---|---|---|---|---|
| 370 | A14 | 10,000r on 15pa on 3k | 3.00 | 3.00 |
| 371 | A14 | 10,000r on 20pa on 5k | 3.00 | 3.00 |

| No. | Type | Description | | |
|---|---|---|---|---|
| 372 | A11 | 20,000r on 1½pi on 15k | 3.00 | 3.00 |
| 373 | A8 | 20,000r on 2pi on 20k | 3.00 | 3.00 |
| 374 | A11 | 20,000r on 2½pi on 25k | 3.00 | 3.00 |
| 375 | A11 | 20,000r on 3½pi on 35k | 3.00 | 3.00 |

## Same Surcharge on Stamp of South Russia, Crimea Issue
| No. | Type | Description | | |
|---|---|---|---|---|
| 376 | A8 | 20,000r on 5r on 20k bl & car | 16.00 | 34.00 |

Nos. 370-376 (7)

# RWANDA

RWANDA

ru-än-da

(Rwandaise Republic)

LOCATION—Central Africa, adjoining the ex-Belgian Congo, Tanganyika, Uganda and Burundi.
GOVT.—Republic
AREA—10,169 sq. mi.
POP.—8,154,933(?) (1999 est.)
CAPITAL—Kigali

Rwanda was established as an independent republic on July 1, 1962. With Burundi, it had been a UN trusteeship territory administered by Belgium. See Ruanda-Urundi.

100 Centimes = 1 Franc

**Catalogue values for all unused stamps in this country are for Never Hinged items.**

Watermark

Wmk. 368 — JEZ Multiple

Gregoire Kayihanda and Map of Africa — A1

Design: 40c, 1.50fr, 6.50fr, 20fr, Rwanda map spotlighted, "R" omitted.

**1962, July 1    Perf. 11½    Unwmk.    Photo.**

| | | | | |
|---|---|---|---|---|
| 1 | A1 | 10c brown & gray grn | .20 | .20 |
| 2 | A1 | 40c grn & rose lil | .20 | .20 |
| 3 | A1 | 1fr brown & blue | .60 | .30 |
| 4 | A1 | 1.50fr brown & lt brn | .20 | .20 |
| 5 | A1 | 3.50fr brown & dp org | .20 | .20 |
| 6 | A1 | 6.50fr brown & lt vio bl | .20 | .20 |
| 7 | A1 | 10fr brown & citron | .20 | .20 |
| 8 | A1 | 20fr brown & rose | .40 | .20 |
| | | Nos. 1-8 (8) | 2.20 | 1.70 |

Rwanda's admission to UN, Sept. 18, 1962.

Map of Africa and Symbolic Honeycomb A2

**1963, Jan. 28    Unwmk.    Perf. 11½**

| | | | | |
|---|---|---|---|---|
| 9 | A2 | 3.50fr sil, blk, ultra & red | .20 | .20 |
| 10 | A2 | 6.50fr brnz, blk, ultra & red | .35 | .35 |
| 11 | A2 | 10fr stl bl, blk, ultra & red | .30 | .20 |
| 12 | A2 | 20fr sil, blk, ultra & red | .50 | .35 |
| | | Nos. 9-12 (4) | 1.95 | 1.35 |

Ruanda-Urundi Nos. 151-152 Overprinted with Metallic Frame Obliterating Previous Inscription and Denomination. Black Commemorative Inscription and "REPUBLIQUE RWANDAISE." Surcharged with New Value.

Littonia — A3

Designs as before.

**1963, Mar. 21    Unwmk.    Perf. 11½;**
**Flowers in Natural Colors; Metallic and Black Overprint**

| | | | | |
|---|---|---|---|---|
| 13 | A3 | 25c dk grn & dl org | .35 | .20 |
| 14 | A3 | 40c green & salmon | .35 | .20 |
| 15 | A3 | 60c bl grn & pink | .35 | .20 |
| 16 | A3 | 1.25fr dk green & blue | 1.50 | .65 |
| 17 | A3 | 1.50fr violet & apple grn | 1.10 | .50 |
| 18 | A3 | 2fr on 1.50fr vio & ap grn | 1.75 | .80 |
| 19 | A3 | 4fr on 1.50fr vio & ap grn | 1.75 | .80 |
| 20 | A3 | 5fr dp plum & lt bl | 1.75 | .80 |
| 21 | A3 | 7fr dk green & fawn | 1.75 | .80 |
| 22 | A3 | 10fr dp plum & pale ol | 12.40 | 5.75 |
| | | Nos. 13-22 (10) | | |

The overprint consists of silver panels with black lettering. The panels on No. 19 are bluish gray.

**Imperforates** exist of practically every issue, starting with Nos. 1-8, except Nos. 9-12, 13-22, 36 and 55-69.

Wheat Emblem, Bow, Arrow, Hoe and Billhook — A4

**1963, June 25    Photo.    Perf. 13½**

| | | | | |
|---|---|---|---|---|
| 23 | A4 | 2fr brown & green | .20 | .20 |
| 24 | A4 | 4fr magenta & ultra | .20 | .20 |
| 25 | A4 | 7fr red & gray | .25 | .40 |
| 26 | A4 | 10fr olive grn & yel | 1.15 | 1.00 |
| | | Nos. 23-26 (4) | | |

FAO "Freedom from Hunger" campaign.

The 20fr leopard and 50fr lion designs of Ruanda-Urundi, Nos. 149-150, overprinted "Republique Rwandaise" at top and "Contre la Faim" at bottom, were intended to be issued Mar. 21, 1963, but were not placed in use.

Coffee A5

**1963, July 1    Perf. 11½**

| | | | | |
|---|---|---|---|---|
| 27 | A5 | 10c violet bl & brn | .20 | .20 |
| 28 | A5 | 20c slate & yellow | .20 | .20 |
| 29 | A5 | 30c vermilion & grn | .20 | .20 |
| 30 | A5 | 40c dp green & brown | .20 | .20 |
| 31 | A5 | 1fr maroon & yellow | .20 | .20 |
| 32 | A5 | 4fr dk green & green | .65 | .40 |
| 33 | A5 | 4fr red & brown | .20 | .20 |
| 34 | A5 | 7fr yellow grn & yellow | .95 | .60 |
| 35 | A5 | 10fr violet & green | .20 | .20 |
| | | Nos. 27-35 (9) | 2.30 | 2.00 |

Designs: 10c, 40c, 4fr, Coffee. 20c, 1fr, 7fr, Bananas. 30c, 2fr, 10fr, Tea.

Post Horn and Pigeon — A6

**1963, Oct. 25    Photo.    Perf. 11½**

| | | | | |
|---|---|---|---|---|
| 37 | A6 | 50c ultra & rose | .20 | .20 |
| 38 | A6 | 1.50fr brown & blue | .50 | .40 |
| 39 | A6 | 3fr dp plum & gray | .20 | .20 |
| 40 | A6 | 20fr green & yellow | .35 | .20 |
| | | Nos. 37-40 (4) | 1.25 | 1.00 |

Rwanda's admission to the UPU, Apr. 6.

Scales, UN Emblem and Flame A7

**1963, Dec. 10    Unwmk.    Perf. 11½**

| | | | | |
|---|---|---|---|---|
| 41 | A7 | 5fr crimson | .20 | .20 |
| 42 | A7 | 6fr brt purple | .50 | .30 |
| 43 | A7 | 10fr brt blue | .90 | .70 |
| | | Nos. 41-43 (3) | | |

15th anniversary of the Universal Declaration of Human Rights.

Children's Clinic — A8

Designs: 20c, 7fr, Laboratory examination. 40c, 30c, 10fr, Physician examining infant. 60c, Litter bearers, horiz.

**1963, Dec. 30    Photo.**

| | | | | |
|---|---|---|---|---|
| 44 | A8 | 10c yel org, red & brn blk | .20 | .20 |
| 45 | A8 | 20c grn, red & brn blk | .20 | .20 |
| 46 | A8 | 30c bl, red & brn blk | .20 | .20 |
| 47 | A8 | 40c red lil, red & blk | .25 | .20 |
| 48 | A8 | 2fr bl grn, red & brn & blk | .60 | .40 |
| 49 | A8 | 7fr ultra, rod & blk | .25 | .20 |
| 50 | A8 | 10fr red brn, red & brn | .25 | .20 |
| 51 | A8 | 20fr dp org, red & brn | .50 | 1.80 |
| | | Nos. 44-51 (8) | 2.45 | 1.80 |

Centenary of the International Red Cross.

Map of Rwanda and Woman at Water Pump — A9

**1964, May 4    Unwmk.    Perf. 11½**

| | | | | |
|---|---|---|---|---|
| 52 | A9 | 3fr lt grn, dk brn & ultra | .20 | .20 |
| 53 | A9 | 7fr pink, dk brn & ultra | .30 | .20 |
| 54 | A9 | 10fr yel, dk brn & ultra | .45 | .30 |
| | | Nos. 52-54 (3) | .95 | .70 |

**Souvenir Sheet**
**Imperf**

| | | | | |
|---|---|---|---|---|
| 54A | A9 | 25fr lilac, bl, brn & blk | 6.00 | 6.00 |

UN 4th World Meteorological Day, Mar. 23.

First anniversary of independence.

Ruanda-Urundi Nos. 138-150, 153 Overprinted "REPUBLIQUE RWANDAISE." Some Surcharged, in Silver and Black

Buffaloes A10

Designs: 10c, 20c, 30c, Buffaloes. 40c, 2fr, Black-and-white colobus (monkey). 50c, 7.50fr, Impalas. 1fr, Mountain gorilla. 3fr, 4fr, 8fr, African elephants. 5fr, 10fr, Eland and zebras. 20fr, Leopard. 50fr, Lions. 40c, 1fr and 2fr are vertical.

**1964, June 29    Photo.    Perf. 11½**
**Size: 33x23mm, 23x33mm**

| | | | | |
|---|---|---|---|---|
| 55 | A10 | 10c on 20c gray, ap grn & blk | .20 | .20 |
| 56 | A10 | 20c blk, gray & ap grn | .20 | .20 |
| 57 | A10 | 30c on 1.50fr blk, grn | .20 | .20 |
| 58 | A10 | 40c mag, blk & gray grn | .20 | .20 |
| 59 | A10 | 50c grn, org yel & brn | .20 | .20 |
| 60 | A10 | 1fr ultra, blk & brn | .25 | .25 |
| 61 | A10 | 4fr on 3.50fr grnsh bl, ind & brn | .25 | .35 |
| 62 | A10 | 3fr brn, dl yel, car & blk | .25 | .35 |
| 63 | A10 | 4fr on 3.50fr on 3fr brn, dp car & blk | .45 | |
| 64 | A10 | 5fr brn, dl yel, grn & blk | .35 | .20 |
| 65 | A10 | 7.50fr on 6.50fr red, org yel & brn | .80 | |
| 66 | A10 | 8fr blue, mag & blk | 5.25 | 2.75 |
| 67 | A10 | 10fr brn, dl yel, brt pink & blk | 1.10 | .20 |
| | | Size: 45x26½mm | | |
| 68 | A10 | 20fr hn brn, ocher & blk | 1.75 | .75 |
| 69 | A10 | 50fr dp blue & brown | 2.75 | 2.25 |
| | | Nos. 55-69 (15) | 14.30 | 8.15 |

Inverted overprints/surcharges exist.

Basketball — A12

Boy with Crutch and Gatagara Home — A11

Designs: 40c, 8fr, Girls with sewing machines, horiz. 4fr, 10fr, Girl on crutches, map of Rwanda and Gatagara Home.

**1964, Nov. 10    Photo.    Perf. 11½**

| | | | | |
|---|---|---|---|---|
| 70 | A11 | 10c lilac blk brn | .20 | .20 |
| 71 | A11 | 40c blue & black | .20 | .20 |
| 72 | A11 | 4fr org red & blk brn | .20 | .20 |
| 73 | A11 | 7fr yel grn & blk brn | .45 | .20 |
| 74 | A11 | 8fr bister & blk brn | 1.50 | .60 |
| 75 | A11 | 10fr magenta & blk brn | .50 | .20 |
| | | Nos. 70-75 (6) | 3.05 | 1.60 |

Gatagara Home for handicapped children.

Quill, Books, Radical and Retort — A13

**1964, Dec. 8    Litho.    Perf. 13½**
Sport: 10c, 4fr, Runner, horiz. 30c, 20fr, High jump, horiz. 40c, 50fr, Soccer.
**Size: 26x38mm**

| | | | | |
|---|---|---|---|---|
| 76 | A12 | 10c grn, sl & dk grn | .20 | .20 |
| 77 | A12 | 20c pink, sl & rose red | .20 | .20 |
| 78 | A12 | 30c lt grn, sl & grn | .20 | .20 |
| 79 | A12 | 40c buff, sl & blk | .20 | .20 |
| 80 | A12 | 4fr vio gray, sl & vio | .20 | .20 |
| 81 | A12 | 5fr pale grn, sl & yel | .20 | .20 |
| 82 | A12 | 8fr pale lil, sl & red lil | 1.75 | 1.25 |
| 83 | A12 | 20fr gray, sl & dk gray | .50 | .35 |
| a. | | Souvenir sheet of 4 | 5.50 | 5.50 |
| | | Nos. 76-83 (8) | 4.10 | 3.30 |

18th Olympic Games, Tokyo, Oct. 10-25. No. 83a contains 4 stamps (10fr, soccer; 20fr, high jump; 40fr, runner). Size of stamps: 28x38mm.

**African Postal Union Issue**
Common Design Type
Common Design Type pictured following the introduction.

**1963, Sept. 8    Unwmk.    Perf. 12½**

| | | | | |
|---|---|---|---|---|
| 36 | CD114 | 14fr black, ocher & red | .60 | .50 |

## Medical School and Student with Microscope — A14

30c, 10fr, Scales, hand, staff of Mercury and globe. 40c, 12fr, View of University.

**1965, Feb. 22    Engr.    Perf. 11½**

| | | | | |
|---|---|---|---|---|
| 84 | A13 | 10c multicolored | .20 | .20 |
| 85 | A14 | 20c multicolored | .20 | .20 |
| 86 | A13 | 30c multicolored | .20 | .20 |
| 87 | A14 | 40c multicolored | .20 | .20 |
| 88 | A14 | 5fr multicolored | .20 | .20 |
| 89 | A14 | 7fr multicolored | .75 | .60 |
| 90 | A13 | 10fr multicolored | .75 | .60 |
| 91 | A14 | 12fr multicolored | 2.20 | 2.00 |

National University of Rwanda at Butare.
Nos. 84-91 (8)

## Abraham Lincoln, Death Cent. A15

**1965, Apr. 15    Photo.    Perf. 13½**

| | | | | |
|---|---|---|---|---|
| 92 | A15 | 10c emerald & dk red | .20 | .20 |
| 93 | A15 | 20c red brn & dk bl | .20 | .20 |
| 94 | A15 | 30c brt violet & red | .20 | .20 |
| 95 | A15 | 40c brt grnsh bl & red | .20 | .20 |
| 96 | A15 | 9fr orange bl & pur | .50 | .35 |
| 97 | A15 | 40fr black & brt grn | 2.60 | 1.60 |

Nos. 92-97 (6)

### Souvenir Sheet

| | | | | |
|---|---|---|---|---|
| 98 | A15 | 50fr red lilac & red | 2.50 | 2.50 |

Nos. 92-96 exist without figure of value.

Zebras A17

Marabous — A16

**1965, Apr. 28    Photo.    Perf. 11½**

Size: 32x23mm

| | | | | |
|---|---|---|---|---|
| 99 | A16 | 10c multicolored | 1.40 | .35 |
| 100 | A16 | 20c multicolored | .20 | .20 |
| 101 | A16 | 30c multicolored | .20 | .20 |
| 102 | A16 | 40c multicolored | .20 | .20 |
| 103 | A16 | 1fr multicolored | .50 | .35 |
| 104 | A16 | 3fr multicolored | .50 | .35 |
| 105 | A16 | 5fr multicolored | 5.00 | 2.00 |
| 106 | A16 | 10fr multicolored | .45 | .35 |

Size: 45x26mm

| | | | | |
|---|---|---|---|---|
| 107 | A17 | 40fr multicolored | 3.25 | .35 |
| 108 | A17 | 100fr multicolored | 11.90 | 4.45 |

Nos. 99-108 (10)
Kagera National Park publicity.

## Telstar and ITU Emblem A18

Designs: 40c, 50fr, Syncom satellite. 60fr, old and new communications equipment.

**1965    Unwmk.    Perf. 13½**

| | | | | |
|---|---|---|---|---|
| 109 | A18 | 10c red brn, ultra & car | .20 | .20 |
| 110 | A18 | 40c violet, emer & yel | .20 | .20 |
| 111 | A18 | 4.50fr blk, car & dk bl | 1.10 | .40 |
| 112 | A18 | 50fr dk brn, yel grn & brt grn | .20 | .20 |

Nos. 109-112 (4)    1.25  .20

### Souvenir Sheet

| | | | | |
|---|---|---|---|---|
| 113 | A18 | 60fr blk brn, org brn & bl | 2.75 | 1.00 |

ITU, cent. Issued: #113, 7/19; others, 5/17.

## Papilio Bromius Chrapkowskii Suffert — A19

**1965-66**

| | | | | |
|---|---|---|---|---|
| 114 | A19 | 10c black & yellow | .20 | .20 |
| 115 | A19 | 15c black & dp org ('66) | .20 | .20 |
| 116 | A19 | 20c black & lilac ('66) | .20 | .20 |
| 117 | A19 | 30c black & red lil | .20 | .20 |
| 118 | A19 | 35c dk brn & dk bl ('66) | .20 | .20 |
| 119 | A19 | 40c black & Prus bl | .25 | .20 |
| 120 | A19 | 1.50fr black & grn ('66) | .35 | .20 |
| 121 | A19 | 3fr dk brn & ol grn ('66) | .20 | .20 |
| 122 | A19 | 4fr black & red brn | 4.00 | 1.40 |
| 123 | A19 | 10fr black & pur ('66) | 2.75 | 1.75 |
| 124 | A19 | 50fr black & blk | .35 | .20 |
| 125 | A19 | 100fr blk brn & bl ('66) | 4.50 | 1.25 |

Nos. 114-125 (12)    15.85  7.40

The 15c, 20c, 40c, 1.50fr, 10fr and 50fr are horizontal.

Various butterflies and moths in natural colors.

## Cattle, ICY Emblem and Map of Africa — A20

**1965, Oct. 25    Unwmk.    Perf. 12**

| | | | | |
|---|---|---|---|---|
| 126 | A20 | 10c brt grn & | .20 | .20 |
| 127 | A20 | 40c ultra, red brn & | .20 | .20 |
| 128 | A20 | 4.50fr brt grn, yel & brn | 1.00 | .35 |
| 129 | A20 | 45fr rose claret | .90 | .25 |

Nos. 126-129 (4)    2.30  1.00

Map of Africa and 40c, Tree & lake. 4.50fr, Gazelle under tree. 45fr, Mount Ruwenzori.

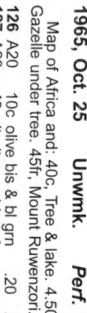

## John F. Kennedy (1917-1963) — A21

**1965, Nov. 22    Photo.    Perf. 11½**

| | | | | |
|---|---|---|---|---|
| 130 | A21 | 10c brt grn & dk brn | .20 | .20 |
| 131 | A21 | 20c brt pink & dk brn | .20 | .20 |
| 132 | A21 | 50c dk blue & dk brn | .20 | .20 |
| 133 | A21 | 1fr gray ol & dk brn | .20 | .20 |
| 134 | A21 | 8fr violet & dk brn | 1.60 | 1.00 |
| 135 | A21 | 50fr gray & dk brn | 1.25 | .80 |

Nos. 130-135 (6)    3.65  2.60

### Souvenir Sheet

| | | | | |
|---|---|---|---|---|
| 136 | | Sheet of 2 | 9.00 | 9.00 |
| a. | A21 | 40fr org & dk brown | 4.25 | 4.25 |
| b. | A21 | 60fr ultra & dark brown | 4.75 | 4.75 |

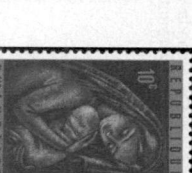

## Madonna — A22

**1965, Dec. 20**

| | | | | |
|---|---|---|---|---|
| 137 | A22 | 10c gold & dk green | .20 | .20 |
| 138 | A22 | 40c gold & dk brn red | .20 | .20 |
| 139 | A22 | 50c gold & dk blue | .60 | .45 |
| 140 | A22 | 4fr gold & slate | .60 | .20 |
| 141 | A22 | 6fr gold & violet | .30 | .30 |
| 142 | A22 | 30fr gold & dk brown | .50 | .40 |

Nos. 137-142 (6)    2.00  1.65
Christmas.

## Father Joseph Damien and Lepers — A23

**1966, Jan. 31    Perf. 11½**

| | | | | |
|---|---|---|---|---|
| 143 | A23 | 10c ultra & red brn | .20 | .20 |
| 144 | A23 | 40c red & vio bl | .20 | .20 |
| 145 | A23 | 4.50fr slate & brn grn | .20 | .20 |
| 146 | A23 | 45fr brn brn | 1.50 | .80 |

Nos. 143-146 (4)    2.10  1.40

Issued for World Leprosy Day.

Designs: 40c, 45fr, Dr. Albert Schweitzer and Hospital, Lambarene.

## Pope Paul VI, St. Peter's, UN Headquarters and Statue of Liberty — A24

**1966, Feb. 28    Photo.    Perf. 12**

| | | | | |
|---|---|---|---|---|
| 147 | A24 | 10c henna brn & slate | .20 | .20 |
| 148 | A24 | 40c brt blue & slate | .20 | .20 |
| 149 | A24 | 4.50fr lilac & slate | 1.25 | .65 |
| 150 | A24 | 50fr brt green & slate | 1.00 | .30 |

Nos. 147-150 (4)    2.65  1.35

Visit of Pope Paul VI to the UN, New York City, Oct. 4, 1965.

Design: 40c, 50fr, Pope Paul VI, Papal arms and UN emblem.

## Globe Thistle — A25

**1966, Mar. 14    Photo.    Perf. 11½**

Granite Paper

| | | | | |
|---|---|---|---|---|
| 151 | A25 | 10c lt blue & multi | .20 | .20 |
| 152 | A25 | 20c orange & multi | .20 | .20 |
| 153 | A25 | 30c car rose & multi | .20 | .20 |
| 154 | A25 | 40c green & multi | .20 | .20 |
| 155 | A25 | 1fr multicolored | .20 | .20 |
| 156 | A25 | 3fr indigo & multi | .20 | .20 |
| 157 | A25 | 8fr violet & dk brn | .20 | .20 |
| 158 | A25 | 10fr blue grn & multi | 4.25 | 1.75 |
| 159 | A25 | 40fr brown & multi | 1.00 | .45 |

Flowers: 20c, Blood lily. 30c, Natal plum. 1fr, Tulip tree. 3fr, Rendle orchid. 5fr, Aloe. 10fr, Ammocharis tinneana. 40fr, Coral tree. 100fr, Caper. (20c, 40c, 1fr, 3fr, 5fr, 10fr are vertical).

## Opening of WHO Headquarters, Geneva — A26

| | | | | |
|---|---|---|---|---|
| 160 | A25 | 100fr dk bl grn & multi | 2.50 | 1.25 |
| a. | | Miniature sheet | 6.25 | 6.25 |

No. 160a contains one 100fr stamp in changed color, bright blue and multicolored.

**1966, May 1    Litho.    Perf. 12½x12**

| | | | | |
|---|---|---|---|---|
| 161 | A26 | 2fr lt olive green | .20 | .20 |
| 162 | A26 | 3fr vermilion | .20 | .20 |
| 163 | A26 | 5fr violet blue | .60 | .60 |

Nos. 161-163 (3)    9.20  4.85

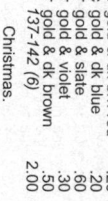

Soccer — A27

## Mother and Child, Planes Dropping Bombs — A28

**1966, May 30    Photo.    Perf. 15x14**

| | | | | |
|---|---|---|---|---|
| 164 | A27 | 10c dl grn, ultra & blk | .20 | .20 |
| 165 | A27 | 20c crimson, grn & blk | .20 | .20 |
| 166 | A27 | 30c bl, brt rose lil & blk | .20 | .20 |
| 167 | A27 | 40c yel bis, grn & blk | .20 | .20 |
| 168 | A27 | 9fr gray, red lil & blk | .25 | .20 |
| 169 | A27 | 50fr rose lil, Prus bl & blk | .75 | .60 |

Nos. 164-169 (6)    1.80  1.60

National Youth Sports Program.

20c, 9fr, Basketball. 30c, 50fr, Volleyball.

A29

**1966, June 29    Design and Inscription Black and Red**

| | | | | |
|---|---|---|---|---|
| 170 | A28 | 20c rose lilac | .20 | .20 |
| 171 | A28 | 30c yellow green | .20 | .20 |
| 172 | A28 | 50c lt ultra | .20 | .20 |
| 173 | A28 | 6fr yellow | .20 | .20 |
| 174 | A28 | 15fr blue green | .50 | .30 |
| 175 | A28 | 18fr lilac | 1.80 | 1.30 |

Nos. 170-175 (6)

**Perf. 13½**

Campaign against nuclear weapons.

A30

# RWANDA

Global soccer ball.

**1966, July — Perf. 11½**

| | | | | |
|---|---|---|---|---|
| 176 | A29 | 20c org & indigo | .20 | .20 |
| 177 | A29 | 20c org & indigo | .20 | .20 |
| 178 | A29 | 30c lilac & indigo | .20 | .20 |
| 179 | A29 | 50c brt rose & indigo | .35 | .35 |
| 180 | A29 | 12fr lt vio brn & ind | 1.50 | .35 |
| 181 | A29 | 25fr ultra & indigo | 1.75 | 1.00 |
| | | Nos. 176-181 (6) | 4.20 | 2.25 |

World Soccer Cup Championship. Wembley, England, July 11-30.

**1966, Oct. 24 — Engr. — Perf. 14**

Designs: 10c, Mikeno Volcano and crested shrike, horiz. 40c, Nyamilanga Falls. 4.50fr, Gahinga and Muhabura volcanoes and lobelias, horiz. 55fr, Rusumu Falls.

| | | | | |
|---|---|---|---|---|
| 182 | A30 | 10c green | .25 | .20 |
| 183 | A30 | 40c brown carmine | .35 | .20 |
| 184 | A30 | 4.50fr violet blue | .55 | .35 |
| 185 | A30 | 55fr red lilac | .65 | .35 |
| | | Nos. 182-185 (4) | 1.80 | 1.10 |

UNESCO Emblem, African Artifacts and Musical Clef — A31

UNESCO 20th Anniv.: 30c, 10fr, Hands holding primer showing giraffe and zebra. 50c, 15fr, Atom symbol and power drill. 1fr, 50fr, Submerged sphinxes and sailboat.

**1966, Nov. 4 — Photo. — Perf. 12**

| | | | | |
|---|---|---|---|---|
| 186 | A31 | 10c brt rose & dk bl | .20 | .20 |
| 187 | A31 | 30c brt rose & blk | .20 | .20 |
| 188 | A31 | 50c grnsh blue & blk | .20 | .20 |
| 189 | A31 | 1fr ocher & blk | .20 | .20 |
| 190 | A31 | 5fr yellow grn & blk | .25 | .20 |
| 191 | A31 | 10fr brown & blk | .35 | .30 |
| 192 | A31 | 15fr red lilac & dk bl | .40 | .30 |
| 193 | A31 | 50fr dull bl & blk | .45 | .35 |
| | | Nos. 186-193 (8) | 2.10 | 1.80 |

Rock Python — A32

Snakes: 20c, 20fr, Jameson's mamba. 30c, 3fr, Rock python. 50c, Gabon viper. 1fr, Black-lipped spitting cobra. 5fr, African sand snake. 7fr, Egg-eating snake. (20c, 50c, 3fr and 20fr are horizontal.)

**1967, Jan. 30 — Photo. — Perf. 11½**

| | | | | |
|---|---|---|---|---|
| 194 | A32 | 20c red & black | .20 | .20 |
| 195 | A32 | 30c dk brn & yel | .20 | .20 |
| 196 | A32 | 50c yel grn & multi | .20 | .20 |
| 197 | A32 | 1fr lt lil, blk & bis | .25 | .20 |
| 198 | A32 | 3fr lt vio, dk brn & yel | .35 | .20 |
| 199 | A32 | 5fr yellow & multi | .35 | .30 |
| 200 | A32 | 20fr pale pink & multi | 1.50 | .90 |
| 201 | A32 | 70fr pale vio, brn & blk | 2.25 | 1.00 |
| | | Nos. 194-201 (8) | 5.30 | 3.10 |

Ntaruka Hydroelectric Station and Tea Flowers — A33

Designs: 30c, 25fr, Transformer and chrysanthemums (pyrethrum). 50c, 50fr, Sluice and coffee.

**1967, Mar. 6 — Photo. — Perf. 13½**

| | | | | |
|---|---|---|---|---|
| 202 | A33 | 20c maroon & dp bl | .20 | .20 |
| 203 | A33 | 30c black & red brn | .20 | .20 |
| 204 | A33 | 50c brown & violet | .20 | .20 |
| 205 | A33 | 4fr dk grn & dp plum | .30 | .30 |
| 206 | A33 | 18fr brt rose & indigo | .75 | .50 |
| 207 | A33 | 25fr ultra & indigo | 1.85 | 1.60 |
| | | Nos. 202-207 (6) | | |

Ntaruka Hydroelectric Station.

## Souvenir Sheets

NAPLES 1967
SEPTIEME EXPOSITION DU TIMBRE-POSTE «EUROPA»
SEPTIEME SALON PHILATELIQUE DES ETATS AFRICAINS

Cogwheels — A34

**1967, Apr. 15 — Engr. — Perf. 11½**

| | | | | |
|---|---|---|---|---|
| 208 | A34 | 100fr dk red brown | 3.50 | 3.50 |
| 209 | A34 | 100fr brt rose lilac | 3.50 | 3.50 |

7th "Europa" Phil. Exhib. and the Philatelic Salon of African States, Naples, Apr. 8-16.

## Souvenir Sheet

REPUBLIQUE RWANDAISE 180fr
EXPOSITION UNIVERSELLE ET INTERNATIONALE DE 1967
MONTREAL - CANADA

African Dancers and EXPO '67 Emblem — A35

**1967, Apr. 28 — Perf. 11½**

| | | | | |
|---|---|---|---|---|
| 210 | A35 | 180fr dark purple | 3.50 | 3.50 |

EXPO '67, Intl. Exhib., Montreal, Apr. 28-Oct. 27.

A similar imperf. sheet has the stamp in violet brown.

St. Martin, by Van Dyck and Caritas Emblem — A36

Paintings: 40c, 15fr, Rebecca at the Well, by Murillo, horiz. 60c, 18fr, St. Christopher, by Dierick Bouts. 80c, 26fr, Job and his Friends, by Il Calabrese (Mattia Preti), horiz.

**1967, May 8 — Photo. — Perf. 13x11, 11x13**

**Black Inscription on Gold Panel**

| | | | | |
|---|---|---|---|---|
| 211 | A36 | 20c dark purple | .20 | .20 |
| 212 | A36 | 40c dark green | .20 | .20 |
| 213 | A36 | 60c rose carmine | .20 | .20 |
| 214 | A36 | 80c deep blue | .25 | .20 |
| 215 | A36 | 3fr redsh brown | .70 | .35 |
| 216 | A36 | 15fr orange ver | .25 | .25 |
| 217 | A36 | 18fr olive grn | .40 | .30 |
| 218 | A36 | 26fr dk carmine rose | 2.45 | 1.85 |
| | | Nos. 211-218 (8) | | |

Issued to publicize the work of Caritas-Rwanda, Catholic welfare organization.

Round Table Emblem and Zebra — A37

Round Table Emblem and: 40c, Elephant. 60c, Cape buffalo. 80c, Antelope. 18fr, Wheat. 100fr, Palm tree.

**1967, July 31 — Photo. — Perf. 14**

| | | | | |
|---|---|---|---|---|
| 219 | A37 | 20c gold & multi | .20 | .20 |
| 220 | A37 | 40c gold & multi | .20 | .20 |
| 221 | A37 | 60c gold & multi | .20 | .20 |
| 222 | A37 | 80c gold & multi | .20 | .20 |
| 223 | A37 | 18fr gold & multi | .30 | .20 |
| 224 | A37 | 100fr gold & multi | 1.40 | .65 |
| | | Nos. 219-224 (6) | 2.50 | 1.65 |

Rwanda Table No. 9 of Kigali, a member of the Intl. Round Tables Assoc.

EXPO '67 Emblem, Africa Place and Dancers and Drummers — A38

EXPO '67 Emblem, Africa Place and: 30c, 3fr, Drum and vessels. 50c, 40fr, Two dancers. 1fr, 34fr, Spears, shields and bow.

**1967, Aug. 10 — Photo. — Perf. 12**

| | | | | |
|---|---|---|---|---|
| 225 | A38 | 20c brt blue & sepia | .20 | .20 |
| 226 | A38 | 30c brt rose bl & sepia | .20 | .20 |
| 227 | A38 | 50c orange & sepia | .20 | .20 |
| 228 | A38 | 1fr green & sepia | .20 | .20 |
| 229 | A38 | 3fr violet & sepia | .20 | .20 |
| 230 | A38 | 15fr emerald & sepia | .40 | .30 |
| 231 | A38 | 34fr rose red & sepia | .55 | .40 |
| 232 | A38 | 40fr grnsh brn & sepia | | |
| | | Nos. 225-232 (8) | 2.15 | 1.90 |

Lions Emblem, Globe and Zebra — A39

**1967, Oct. 16 — Photo. — Perf. 13½**

| | | | | |
|---|---|---|---|---|
| 233 | A39 | 20c lilac, bl & blk | .20 | .20 |
| 234 | A39 | 80c lilac, bl & blk | .20 | .20 |
| 235 | A39 | 1fr rose car, bl & blk | .20 | .20 |
| 236 | A39 | 3fr bister, bl & blk | .20 | .20 |
| 237 | A39 | 10fr ultra, bl & blk | .25 | .20 |
| 238 | A39 | 50fr yel grn, bl & blk | 1.25 | .65 |
| | | Nos. 233-238 (6) | 2.35 | 1.65 |

50th anniversary of Lions International.

Woodland Kingfisher — A40

Birds: 20c, Red bishop, vert. 60c, Red-billed quelea, vert. 80c, Double-toothed barbet. 3fr, Pin-tailed whydah, vert. 3fr, Solitary cuckoo. 18fr, Green wood hoopoe, vert. 25fr, Blue-collared bee-eater. 80fr, Regal sunbird, vert. 100fr, Red-shouldered widowbird.

**1967, Dec. 18 — Perf. 11½**

| | | | | |
|---|---|---|---|---|
| 239 | A40 | 20c multicolored | .20 | .20 |
| 240 | A40 | 40c multicolored | .20 | .20 |
| 241 | A40 | 60c multicolored | .20 | .20 |
| 242 | A40 | 80c multicolored | .40 | .30 |
| 243 | A40 | 3fr multicolored | .75 | .60 |
| 244 | A40 | 18fr multicolored | .75 | .60 |
| 245 | A40 | 25fr multicolored | 1.00 | .65 |
| 246 | A40 | 80fr multicolored | 2.75 | 1.50 |
| 247 | A40 | 100fr multicolored | 3.75 | 2.00 |
| 248 | A40 | 100fr multicolored | 9.85 | 6.15 |
| | | Nos. 239-248 (10) | | |

## Souvenir Sheet

X^es JEUX OLYMPIQUES D'HIVER
REPUBLIQUE RWANDAISE 50f
GRENOBLE 1968

Ski Jump, Speed Skating — A41

**1968, Feb. 12 — Photo. — Perf. 11½**

| | | | | |
|---|---|---|---|---|
| 249 | | Sheet of 2 | 5.00 | 5.00 |
| a. | A41 | 50fr blk, blk & grn (skier) | 1.75 | 1.75 |
| b. | A41 | 50fr grn, blk & bl (skater) | 1.75 | 1.75 |
| c. | | Souv. sheet of 2, #249a at right | 5.00 | 5.00 |

10th Winter Olympic Games, Grenoble, France, Feb. 6-18.

MEXICO 68 20c

Runner, Mexican Sculpture and Architecture — A42

Sport and Mexican Art: 40c, Hammer throw, pyramid and animal head. 60c, Hurdler and sculpture. 80c, Javelin and sculpture.

**1968, May 27 — Photo. — Perf. 11½**

| | | | | |
|---|---|---|---|---|
| 250 | A42 | 20c ultra & multi | .20 | .20 |
| 251 | A42 | 40c multicolored | .20 | .20 |
| 252 | A42 | 60c lilac & multi | .25 | .25 |
| 253 | A42 | 80c orange & multi | .85 | .85 |
| | | Nos. 250-253 (4) | | |

19th Olympic Games, Mexico City, 10/12-27.

## Souvenir Sheet

XIX JEUX OLYMPIQUES
REPUBLIQUE RWANDAISE

19th Olympic Games, Mexico City — A43

**1967, May 27 — Granite Paper — Perf. 11½**

| | | | | |
|---|---|---|---|---|
| 254 | A43 | Sheet of 6, #a-f. | 7.25 | 7.25 |

a, 8fr, Soccer. b, 10fr, Mexican horseman, cactus. c, 12fr, Field hockey. d, 18fr, Cathedral, Mexico City. e, 20fr, Boxing. f, 30fr, Modern buildings, musical instruments, vase.

Three sets of circular gold "medal" overprints with black inscriptions were applied to the six stamps of No. 254 to honor 18 Olympic winners. Issued Dec. 12, 1968. Value $10.

## 1968, July 29 — Engr. — Perf. 13½
Souvenir Sheet

255 A44 100fr sepia 2.10 1.50

Rev. Dr. Martin Luther King, Jr. (1929-68),
American civil rights leader. See No. 406.

Martin Luther King, Jr. — A44

---

## 1968, Sept. 9 — Litho. — Perf. 13

256 A45 20c lilac & multi .20 .20
257 A45 40c multicolored .20 .20
258 A45 60c bl grn & multi .20 .20
259 A45 80c multicolored .20 .20
260 A45 2fr brt yellow & multi .20 .20
261 A45 3fr multicolored .20 .20
262 A45 18fr multicolored .30 .20
263 A45 25fr gray & multi .40 .20
264 A45 80c gray & multi 1.75 .90
265 A45 100fr multicolored 1.90 .90
265a A45 multicolored 5.55 3.15

Flowers: 40c, Pharaoh's scepter. 60c,
Flower of traveler's-tree. 80c, Costus afer. 2fr,
Banana tree flower. 3fr, Flower and fruit of
papaw tree. 18fr, Clerodendron. 25fr, 3wet
potato flower. 80fr, Baobab tree flower. 100fr,
Passion flower.

Diaphant
Orchid — A45

---

## Designs: 40c, Judo and "Tokyo 1964." 60c, Fencing and "Rome 1960." 80c, High jump and "Berlin 1936." 38fr, Women's diving and "London 1908 and 1948." 60fr, Weight lifting and "Paris 1900 and 1924."

Nos. 266-271 (6)

19th Olympic Games, Mexico City, 10/12-27.

Equestrian and "Mexico 1968" A46

## 1968, Oct. 24 — Litho. — Perf. 14x13

266 A46 20c orange & multi .20 .20
267 A46 40c grnsh bl & sepia .20 .20
268 A46 60c car rose & sepia .20 .20
269 A46 80c ultra & sepia .55 .25
270 A46 38fr red & sepia .55 .25
271 A46 60fr emerald & sepia 2.35 1.55

---

Souvenir Sheet

## Algeria — A47

Tuareg,
Algeria — A47

African National Costumes: 40c, Musicians,
Upper Volta. 60c, Senegalese women. 70c,
Gifts of Rwanda going to market. 8fr, Young
married couple from Morocco. 20fr, Nigerian
officials in state dress. 40fr, Man and women
from Zambia. 50fr, Man and woman from
Kenya.

---

## 1968, Nov. 4 — Litho. — Perf. 13

272 A47 30c multicolored .20 .20
273 A47 40c multicolored .20 .20
274 A47 60c multicolored .20 .20
275 A47 70c multicolored .20 .20
276 A47 20fr multicolored .20 .20
277 A47 8fr multicolored .35 .20
278 A47 40fr multicolored .75 .30
279 A47 50fr multicolored .85 .50
Nos. 272-279 (8) 2.90 2.00

---

## 1968, Dec. 16 — Engr. — Perf. 11½
280 A48 100fr green 3.50 3.50

Christmas.

See Nos. 309, 389, 422, 494, 564, 611, 713,
787, 848, 894.

Nativity, by Giorgione — A48

Souvenir Sheet

---

## 1969, Mar. 31 — Photo. — Perf. 13

281 A49 20c gold & multi .20 .20
282 A49 40c gold & multi .20 .20
283 A49 60c gold & multi .20 .20
284 A49 80c gold & multi 1.40 1.40
285 A49 2fr gold & multi .20 .20
286 A49 6fr gold & multi 1.40 1.40
a. Souvenir sheet, 75fr 4.95 3.80

Paintings and Music: 20c, Angels' Concert,
by van Eyck. 40c, Angels' Concert, by Matthias Grunewald. 60c, No. 283a, Singing Boy,
by Frans Hals. 80c, Lute Player, by Gerard
Terborch. 2fr, The Fifer, by Manet. 6fr, No.
286a, Young Girls at the Piano, by Renoir.

Nos. 281-286, C6-C7 (8)

Singing Boy,
by Frans
Hals — A49

---

## African Headdresses: 40c, Ovambo woman, South West Africa. 60c, Guinean man and Congolese woman. 80c, Dagger dancer, Guinean forest area. 8fr, Mohammedan Niger-ians. 20fr, Luba dancer, Kabondo, Congo. 40fr, Senegalese and Gambian women. 80fr,

## 1969, May 29 — Litho. — Perf. 13

287 A50 20c multicolored .20 .20
288 A50 40c multicolored .20 .20
289 A50 60c multicolored .20 .20
290 A50 80c multicolored .20 .20
291 A50 8fr multicolored .25 .20
292 A50 20fr multicolored .35 .20
293 A50 40fr multicolored .85 .35
294 A50 80fr multicolored 1.90 .60
Nos. 287-294 (8) 4.15 2.15

See #398-405. For overprints see #550-557.

Tuareg
Men — A50

---

## 1969, Oct. 9 — Engr. — Perf. 11½
Souvenir Sheet

297 A52 100fr blue gray 3.50 3.50

See note after Mali No. C80. See No. 407.

First Man on the Moon — A52

---

## The Moneylender and his Wife, by Quentin Massys — A51

Design: 70fr, The Moneylender and his
Wife, by Marinus van Reymerswaele.

## 1969, Sept. 10 — Photo. — Perf. 13
295 A51 30fr silver & multi .60 .40
296 A51 70fr gold & multi 1.40 1.00

5th anniv. of the African Development Bank.
Printed in sheets of 20 stamps and 20 labels
with commemorative inscription.

For overprints see Nos. 612-613.

---

## 1969, Nov. 24 — Photo. — Perf. 13
Flowers In Natural Colors

298 A53 20c gold, blue & blk .20 .20
299 A53 40c gold, yel grn & blk .20 .20
300 A53 60c gold, green & blk .20 .20
301 A53 80c gold, pink & blk .20 .20
302 A53 3fr gold, orange & blk .20 .20
303 A53 75fr gold, yel & blk 2.25 .65

Medicinal Plants and Health Emblem: 40c,
Aloe. 60c, Cola. 80c, Coca. 3fr, Hagenia abis-
sinica. 75fr, Cassia. 80fr, Cinchona. 100fr,
Tephrosia.

Camomile and
Health
Emblem — A53

Worker with Pickaxe
and Flag — A54

---

## Souvenir Sheet
1969, Dec. 15 — Engr. — Perf. 11½
309 A48 100fr ultra 2.75 2.75

Design: "Holy Night" (detail), by Correggio.

Christmas Type of 1968

---

## 1969, Nov. — Photo. — Perf. 11½
304 A53 80fr gold, lilac & blk 2.75 .80
305 A53 100fr gold, dl yel & blk 3.00 1.10
Nos. 298-305 (8) 9.00 3.55

306 A54 6fr brt pink & multi .25 .20
307 A54 18fr ultra & multi .50 .30
308 A54 40fr brown & multi .85 .50
Nos. 306-308 (3) 1.60 1.00

10th anniversary of independence.
For overprints see Nos. 608-610.

B1.

---

## Paintings of Napoleon Bonaparte (1769-1821): 40c, Decorating Soldier before Tilsit, by Jean Baptiste Debret. 60c, Addressing Troops at Augsburg, by Claude Gauthérot. 80c, First Consul, by Jean Auguste Ingres. 8fr, Battle of Marengo, by Jacques Auguste Pajou. 20fr, Napoleon Meeting Emperor Francis II, by Antoine Jean Gros. 40fr, Gen. Bonaparte at Arcole, by Gros. 80fr, Coronation, by David.

## 1969, Dec. 29 — Photo. — Perf. 13½
318 A56 20c gold & multi .20 .20
319 A56 40c gold & multi .20 .20
320 A56 60c gold & multi .20 .20
321 A56 80c gold & multi .20 .20
322 A56 8fr gold & multi .30 .20
323 A56 20fr gold & multi 1.40 .50
324 A56 40fr gold & multi 2.50 1.00
325 A56 80fr gold & multi 5.45 2.80
Nos. 318-325 (8)

Napoleon
Crossing St.
Bernard, by
Jacques L.
David — A56

---

## Paintings: 20c, Quarry Worker, by Oscar Bonnevalle, horiz. 40c, The Plower, by Peter Brueghel, horiz. 60c, Fisherman, by Constantin Meunier. 80c, Slipway, Ostende, by Jean van Noten, horiz. 10fr, The Forge of Vulcan, by Velasquez, horiz. 50fr, "Hiercheuse" (woman shoveling coal), by Meunier. 70fr, Miner, by Pierre Paulus.

## 1969, Dec. 22 — Photo.
310 A55 20c gold & multi .20 .20
311 A55 40c gold & multi .20 .20
312 A55 60c gold & multi .20 .20
313 A55 80c gold & multi .20 .20
314 A55 10fr gold & multi .25 .20
315 A55 10fr gold & multi 1.25 .40
316 A55 50fr gold & multi 1.60 .60
317 A55 70fr gold & multi 4.15 2.10
Nos. 310-317 (8)

ILO, 50th anniversary.

The Cook, by
Pierre
Aertsen — A55

---

## Epsom Derby, by Gericault — A57

Paintings of Horses: 40c, Horses Emerging from the Sea, by Delacroix. 60c, Charles V at Muhlberg, by Titian, vert. 80c, Amateur Jockeys, by Edgar Degas, 8fr, Horsemen at Rest, by Philips Wouwerman. 20fr, Imperial Guards Officer, by Géricault, vert. 40fr, Friends of the Desert, by Oscar Bonnevalle. 80fr, Two Horses (detail from the Prodigal Son), by Rubens.

**1970, Mar. 31    Photo.    Perf. 13½**

| | | | |
|---|---|---|---|
| 326 | A57 | 20c gold & multi | .20 .20 |
| 327 | A57 | 40c gold & multi | .20 .20 |
| 328 | A57 | 60c gold & multi | .20 .20 |
| 329 | A57 | 80c gold & multi | .20 .20 |
| 330 | A57 | 3fr gold & multi | .20 .20 |
| 331 | A57 | 8fr gold & multi | .20 .35 |
| 332 | A57 | 20fr gold & multi | .60 .65 |
| 333 | A57 | 40fr gold & multi | 2.00 2.00 |

Nos. 326-333 (8)    4.60 2.20

### Souvenir Sheet

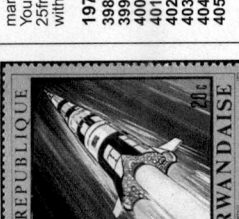

Fleet in Bay of Naples, by Peter Brueghel, the Elder—A58

**1970, May 2    Engr.    Perf. 11½**
334 A58 100fr brt rose lilac    7.25 7.25

10th Europa Phil. Exhib., Naples, Italy, May 2-10.

Copies of No. 334 were trimmed to 68x58mm and overprinted in silver or gold "NAPLES 1973" on the stamp, and "Salon Philatelique des Etats Africains / Exposition du Timbre Poste Europa" in October, 1973.

### Soccer and Mexican Decorations A59

Designs: Various scenes from soccer game and pre-Columbian decorations.

**1970, June 15    Photo.    Perf. 13**

| | | | |
|---|---|---|---|
| 335 | A59 | 20c gold & multi | .20 .20 |
| 336 | A59 | 30c gold & multi | .20 .20 |
| 337 | A59 | 50c gold & multi | .20 .20 |
| 338 | A59 | 3fr gold & multi | .20 .20 |
| 339 | A59 | 6fr gold & multi | .20 .20 |
| 340 | A59 | 18fr gold & multi | .45 .45 |
| 341 | A59 | 30fr gold & multi | .65 .70 |
| 342 | A59 | 90fr gold & multi | 1.60 1.70 |

Nos. 335-342 (8)    3.70 2.30

9th World Soccer Championships for the Jules Rimet Cup, Mexico City, 5/30-6/21.

### Tharaka Meru Woman, East Africa—A60

**1970, June 1    Litho.**

African National Costumes: 30c, Musician with wooden flute, Niger. 50c, Woman water carrier, Tunisia. 3fr, Strolling troubadour "Griot," North Nigeria. 5fr, Quipongos women, Angola. 50fr,

Man at prayer, Mauritania. 90fr, Sinehatiali dance costumes, Ivory Coast.

| | | | |
|---|---|---|---|
| 343 | A60 | 20c multi | .20 .20 |
| 344 | A60 | 30c multi | .20 .20 |
| 345 | A60 | 50c multi | .20 .20 |
| 346 | A60 | 1fr multi | .20 .20 |
| 347 | A60 | 3fr multi | .20 .20 |
| 348 | A60 | 5fr multi | .20 .40 |
| 349 | A60 | 50fr multi | 1.50 .70 |
| 350 | A60 | 90fr multi | 3.60 2.30 |

Nos. 343-350 (8)

For overprints and surcharges see Nos. 693-698, B2-B3.

### Flower Arrangement, Peacock, EXPO '70 Emblem—A61

EXPO Emblem and: 30c, Torii and Camellias, by Yukihiko Yasuda. 50c, Kabuki character and Woman Playing Samisen, by Nampu Katayama. 1fr, Tower of the Sun, and Warrior Riding into Water. 3fr, Pavilion and Buddhist deity. 5fr, Pagoda and modern painting by Shuho Yamakawa. 20fr, Japanese inscription "Omatsuri" and Osaka Castle. 70fr, EXPO '70 emblem and Warrior on Horseback.

**1970, Aug. 24    Photo.    Perf. 13**

| | | | |
|---|---|---|---|
| 351 | A61 | 20c gold & multi | .20 .20 |
| 352 | A61 | 30c gold & multi | .20 .20 |
| 353 | A61 | 50c gold & multi | .20 .20 |
| 354 | A61 | 1fr gold & multi | .20 .20 |
| 355 | A61 | 3fr gold & multi | .20 .20 |
| 356 | A61 | 5fr gold & multi | .20 .30 |
| 357 | A61 | 20fr gold & multi | .50 .50 |
| 358 | A61 | 70fr gold & multi | 2.70 2.00 |

Nos. 351-358 (8)

EXPO '70 International Exhibition, Osaka, Japan, Mar. 15-Sept. 13.

### Young Mountain Gorillas—A62

Various Gorillas. 40c, 80c, 2fr, 100fr are vert.

**1970, Sept. 7**

| | | | |
|---|---|---|---|
| 359 | A62 | 20c olive & blk | .20 .20 |
| 360 | A62 | 40c brt rose lil & blk | .20 .20 |
| 361 | A62 | 60c blue, brn & blk | .20 .25 |
| 362 | A62 | 80c org brn & blk | .75 .25 |
| 363 | A62 | 1fr dp car & blk | 1.00 .30 |
| 364 | A62 | 2fr black & multi | 2.25 .50 |
| 365 | A62 | 15fr sepia & blk | 6.00 2.50 |
| 366 | A62 | 100fr brt bl & blk | 10.80 4.35 |

Nos. 359-366 (8)

### Pierre J. Pelletier and Joseph B. Caventou A63

Designs: 20c, Cinchona flower and bark. 80c, Quinine powder and pharmacological vessels. 1fr, Anopheles mosquito. 3fr, Malaria patient and nurse. 25fr, "Malaria" (mosquito).

**1970, Oct. 27    Photo.    Perf. 13**

| | | | |
|---|---|---|---|
| 367 | A63 | 20c silver & multi | .20 .20 |
| 368 | A63 | 80c silver & multi | .20 .20 |
| 369 | A63 | 1fr silver & multi | .25 .25 |
| 370 | A63 | 3fr silver & multi | .60 .45 |
| 371 | A63 | 25fr silver & multi | 1.40 1.45 |
| 372 | A63 | 70fr silver & multi | 2.80 1.90 |

Nos. 367-372 (6)

150th anniv. of the discovery of quinine by Pierre Joseph Pelletier (1788-1842) and Joseph Bienaimé Caventou (1795-1877), French pharmacologists.

### Apollo Spaceship A64

Apollo Spaceship: 30c, Second stage separation. 50c, Spaceship over moon surface. 1fr, Landing module and astronauts on moon. 3fr, Take-off from moon. 5fr, Return to earth. 10fr, Final separation of nose cone. 80fr, Splashdown.

**1970, Nov. 23    Photo.    Perf. 13**

| | | | |
|---|---|---|---|
| 373 | A64 | 20c silver & multi | .20 .20 |
| 374 | A64 | 30c silver & multi | .20 .20 |
| 375 | A64 | 50c silver & multi | .20 .20 |
| 376 | A64 | 1fr silver & multi | .20 .20 |
| 377 | A64 | 3fr silver & multi | .20 .20 |
| 378 | A64 | 5fr silver & multi | .20 .20 |
| 379 | A64 | 10fr silver & multi | 2.25 .90 |
| 380 | A64 | 80fr silver & multi | 3.65 2.30 |

Nos. 373-380 (8)

Conquest of space.

### Franklin D. Roosevelt and Brassocattleya Olympia Alba—A65

Portraits of Roosevelt and various orchids.

**1970, Dec. 21    Photo.    Perf. 13**

| | | | |
|---|---|---|---|
| 381 | A65 | 20c blue, blk & brn | .20 .20 |
| 382 | A65 | 3uc car rose, blk & brn | .20 .20 |
| 383 | A65 | 60c rh orn, blk & brn | .20 .20 |
| 384 | A65 | 1fr green, blk & brn | .20 .20 |
| 385 | A65 | 2fr maroon, blk & grn | .20 .20 |
| 386 | A65 | 6fr lilac & multi | .30 .30 |
| 387 | A65 | 30fr bl, blk & sl grn | .65 .30 |
| 388 | A65 | 60fr lil rose, blk & sl grn | 1.50 .50 |

Nos. 381-388 (8)    3.35 2.00

Pres. Roosevelt, 25th death anniv.

### Christmas Type of 1968

#### Souvenir Sheet

Design: 100fr, Adoration of the Shephords, by José de Ribera, vert.

**1970, Dec. 24    Engr.    Perf. 11½**
389 A48 100fr Prus blue    2.75 2.75

### Pope Paul VI—A66

Popes: 20c, John XXIII, 1958-1963. 30c, Pius XII, 1939-1958. 40c, Pius XI, 1922-39. 1fr, Benedict XV, 1914-22. 18fr, St. Pius X, 1903-14. 20fr, Leo XIII, 1878-1903. 60fr, Pius IX, 1846-78.

**1970, Dec. 31    Photo.    Perf. 13**

| | | | |
|---|---|---|---|
| 390 | A66 | 10c dk brn | .20 .20 |
| 391 | A66 | 20c gold & dk brn | .20 .20 |
| 392 | A66 | 30c gold & dp claret | .20 .20 |
| 393 | A66 | 40c gold & indigo | .20 .20 |
| 394 | A66 | 18fr gold & dk pur | .55 .25 |
| 395 | A66 | 20fr gold & purple | .55 .25 |
| 396 | A66 | 60fr gold & org brn | .65 .45 |
| 397 | A66 | 60fr gold & blk brn | 1.60 .45 |

Nos. 390-397 (8)    3.85 1.90

Centenary of Vatican I, Ecumenical Council of the Roman Catholic Church, 1869-70. For overprints, see Nos. 644-651.

### Headdress Type of 1969

African Headdresses: 20c, Rendille woman. 30c, Young Toubou woman, Chad. 50c, Peul

---

man, Niger. 1fr, Young Masai man, Kenya. 5fr, Young Peul girl, Niger. 18fr, Rwanda woman. 25fr, Man, Mauritania. 50fr, Rwanda women with pearl necklaces.

**1971, Feb. 15    Litho.    Perf. 13**

| | | | |
|---|---|---|---|
| 398 | A50 | 20c multi | .20 .20 |
| 399 | A50 | 30c multi | .20 .20 |
| 400 | A50 | 50c multi | .20 .20 |
| 401 | A50 | 1fr multi | .20 .20 |
| 402 | A50 | 5fr multi | .20 .20 |
| 403 | A50 | 18fr multi | .40 .40 |
| 404 | A50 | 25fr multi | .60 .70 |
| 405 | A50 | 50fr multi | 1.40 .35 |

Nos. 398-405 (8)    3.40 1.75

### M. L. King Type of 1968

#### Souvenir Sheet

Design: 100fr, Charles de Gaulle (1890-1970), President of France.

**1971, Mar. 15    Engr.    Perf. 13½**
406 A44 100fr ultra    3.00 3.00

### Astronaut Type of 1969 inscribed in Dark Violet with Emblem and: "APOLLO / 14 / SHEPARD / ROOSA / MITCHELL"

#### Souvenir Sheet

**1971, Apr. 15    Engr.    Perf. 11½**
407 A52 100fr brown orange    7.25 7.25

Apollo 14 US moon landing, Jan. 31-Feb. 9.

### Beethoven, by Christian Horneman A67

Beethoven Portraits: 30c, Joseph Stieler. 50c, by Ferdinand Schimon. 3fr, by H. Bost. 50c, by W. Fassbender. 90fr, Beethoven's Funeral Procession, by Leopold Stöber.

**1971, July 5    Photo.    Perf. 13**

| | | | |
|---|---|---|---|
| 408 | A67 | 20c gold & multi | .20 .20 |
| 409 | A67 | 30c gold & multi | .20 .20 |
| 410 | A67 | 50c gold & multi | .20 .20 |
| 411 | A67 | 3fr gold & multi | .20 .20 |
| 412 | A67 | 6fr gold & multi | .30 .30 |
| 413 | A67 | 90fr gold & multi | 1.75 1.75 |

Nos. 408-413 (6)    2.85 1.75

Ludwig van Beethoven (1770-1827), composer.

### Equestrian—A68

Olympic Sports: 30c, Runner at start. 50c, Basketball. 1fr, High jump. 8fr, Boxing. 10fr, Pole vault. 20fr, Wrestling. 60fr, Gymnastics (rings).

**1971, Oct. 25    Photo.    Perf. 13**

| | | | |
|---|---|---|---|
| 414 | A68 | 20c gold & black | .20 .20 |
| 415 | A68 | 30c gold & dp rose lil | .20 .20 |
| 416 | A68 | 50c gold & vio bl | .20 .20 |
| 417 | A68 | 1fr gold & dp grn | .20 .20 |
| 418 | A68 | 8fr gold & henna brn | .20 .20 |
| 419 | A68 | 10fr gold & purple | .20 .30 |
| 420 | A68 | 20fr gold & dp brn | .30 .30 |
| 421 | A68 | 60fr gold & Prus bl | .75 .40 |

Nos. 414-421 (8)    2.25 1.80

20th Summer Olympic Games, Munich, Aug. 26-Sept. 10, 1972.

### Christmas Type of 1968

#### Souvenir Sheet

100fr, Nativity, by Anthony van Dyck, vert.

**1971, Dec. 20    Engr.    Perf. 11½**
422 A48 100fr indigo    3.00 3.00

Adam by
Dürer — A69

Paintings by Albrecht Dürer (1471-1528), German painter and engraver: 30c, Eve. 50c, Hieronymus Holzschuher, Portrait. 1fr, Lamentation of Christ. 3fr, Madonna with the Pear. 5fr, St. Eustace. 20fr, Sts. Paul and Mark. 70fr, Self-portrait. 1500.

**1971, Dec. 31**  **Photo.**  **Perf. 13**

| | | | | |
|---|---|---|---|---|
| 423 | A69 | 20c | gold & multi | .20 | .20 |
| 424 | A69 | 30c | gold & multi | .20 | .20 |
| 425 | A69 | 50c | gold & multi | .20 | .20 |
| 426 | A69 | 1fr | gold & multi | .20 | .20 |
| 427 | A69 | 3fr | gold & multi | .20 | .20 |
| 428 | A69 | 5fr | gold & multi | .20 | .20 |
| 429 | A69 | 20fr | gold & multi | .40 | .40 |
| 430 | A69 | 70fr | gold & multi | 1.40 | .90 |
| | | | | Nos. 423-430 (8) | 3.00 | 2.30 |

A 600fr on gold foil honoring Apollo 15 was issued Jan. 15, 1972. Value $90.

Guardsmen Exercising — A70

National Guard Emblem and: 6fr, Loading supplies. 15fr, Helicopter ambulance. 25fr, Health Service for civilians. 50fr, Guardsman and map of Rwanda, vert.

**1972, Feb. 7**  **Perf. 13½x14, 14x13½**

| | | | | |
|---|---|---|---|---|
| 431 | A70 | 4fr | org & multi | .20 | .20 |
| 432 | A70 | 6fr | yellow & multi | .20 | .20 |
| 433 | A70 | 15fr | lt blue & multi | .65 | .25 |
| 434 | A70 | 25fr | red & multi | 1.10 | .60 |
| 435 | A70 | 50fr | multicolored | 2.35 | 1.45 |
| | | | Nos. 431-435 (5) | | |

"The National Guard serving the nation." For overprints see Nos. 559-563.

Ice Hockey, Sapporo Olympics Emblem A71

**1972, Feb. 12**  **Perf. 13x13½**

| | | | | |
|---|---|---|---|---|
| 436 | A71 | 20c | shown | .20 | .20 |
| 437 | A71 | 30c | Speed skating | .20 | .20 |
| 438 | A71 | 50c | Ski jump | .20 | .20 |
| 439 | A71 | 1fr | Men's figure skating | .20 | .20 |
| 440 | A71 | 6fr | Cross-country skiing | .20 | .20 |
| 441 | A71 | 12fr | Slalom | .20 | .20 |
| 442 | A71 | 20fr | Bobsledding | .45 | .25 |
| 443 | A71 | 60fr | Downhill skiing | .90 | .20 |
| | | | Nos. 431-443 (8) | 3.10 | 2.35 |

11th Winter Olympic Games, Sapporo, Japan, Feb. 3-13.

Antelopes and Cercopithecus — A72

**1972, Mar. 20**  **Photo.**  **Perf. 13**

| | | | | |
|---|---|---|---|---|
| 444 | A72 | 20c | shown | .20 | .20 |
| 445 | A72 | 30c | Buffaloes | .20 | .20 |
| 446 | A72 | 50c | Zebras | .20 | .20 |
| 447 | A72 | 1fr | Rhinoceroses | .20 | .20 |
| 448 | A72 | 2fr | Wart hogs | .20 | .20 |
| 449 | A72 | 6fr | Hippopotami | .20 | .20 |
| 450 | A72 | 18fr | Hyenas | .80 | .20 |
| 451 | A72 | 32fr | Guinea fowl | 1.50 | .75 |
| 452 | A72 | 60fr | Antelopes | 2.50 | 1.40 |
| 453 | A72 | 80fr | Lions | 3.00 | 2.00 |
| | | | Nos. 444-453 (10) | 9.00 | 5.55 |

Akagera National Park.

A73

Family raising flag of Rwanda.

**1972, Apr. 4**  **Perf. 13x12½**

| | | | | |
|---|---|---|---|---|
| 454 | A73 | 6fr | dk red & multi | .20 | .20 |
| 455 | A73 | 18fr | green & multi | .40 | .20 |
| 456 | A73 | 60fr | brown & multi | 1.25 | .70 |
| | | | Nos. 454-456 (3) | 1.85 | 1.10 |

10th anniversary of the Referendum establishing Republic of Rwanda.

A74

**1972, May 17**  **Photo.**  **Perf. 13**

Birds: 20c, Common Waxbills and Hibiscus. 30c, Collared sunbird. 50c, Variable sunbird. 1fr, Greater double-collared sunbird. 4fr, Ruwenzori puff-back flycatcher. 6fr, Red-billed fire finch. 10fr, Scarlet-chested sunbird. 18fr, Red-headed quelea. 60fr, Black-headed gonolek. 100fr, African golden oriole.

| | | | | |
|---|---|---|---|---|
| 457 | A74 | 20c | dk grn & multi | .20 | .20 |
| 458 | A74 | 30c | buff & multi | .20 | .20 |
| 459 | A74 | 50c | yellow & multi | .20 | .20 |
| 460 | A74 | 1fr | lt blue & multi | .20 | .20 |
| 461 | A74 | 4fr | dl rose & multi | .20 | .20 |
| 462 | A74 | 6fr | lilac rose & multi | .20 | .20 |
| 463 | A74 | 10fr | pink & multi | .20 | .20 |
| 464 | A74 | 18fr | gray & multi | .80 | .20 |
| 465 | A74 | 60fr | multicolored | 2.75 | 1.00 |
| 466 | A74 | 100fr | violet & multi | 3.75 | 2.25 |
| | | | Nos. 457-466 (10) | 8.70 | 4.85 |

Belgica '72 Emblem, King Baudouin, Queen Fabiola, Pres. and Mrs. Kayibanda — A75

**1972, June 24**  **Photo.**  **Perf. 13**

**Size: 37x34mm**

| | | | | |
|---|---|---|---|---|
| 467 | A75 | 18fr | Rwanda landscape | .50 | .20 |
| 468 | A75 | 22fr | Old houses, Bruges | .65 | .20 |

**Size: 50x34mm**

| | | | | |
|---|---|---|---|---|
| 469 | A75 | 40fr | shown | 2.25 | .40 |
| a. | | Strip of 3, #467-469 | 4.75 | 4.75 |

Belgica '72 Int'l Phil. Exhib., Brussels, June 24-July 9.

Munchen
Equestrian, Olympic Emblems A77

Stadium, TV Tower and: 30c, Hockey. 50c, Soccer. 1fr, Broad jump. 6fr, Bicycling. 18fr, Yachting. 30fr, Hurdles. 44fr, Gymnastics. women's.

**1972, Aug. 16**  **Photo.**  **Perf. 14**

| | | | | |
|---|---|---|---|---|
| 478 | A77 | 20c | dk brn & gold | .20 | .20 |
| 479 | A77 | 30c | vio bl & gold | .20 | .20 |
| 480 | A77 | 50c | gold & gold | .20 | .20 |
| 481 | A77 | 1fr | black & gold | .20 | .20 |
| 482 | A77 | 6fr | dp claret & gold | .20 | .20 |
| 483 | A77 | 18fr | brown & gold | .35 | .20 |
| 484 | A77 | 30fr | dk vio & gold | .65 | .30 |
| 485 | A77 | 44fr | Prus bl & gold | .85 | .40 |
| | | | Nos. 478-485 (8) | 2.85 | 1.90 |

20th Olympic Games, Munich, 8/26-9/11.

Relay (Sport) and UN Emblem A78

**1972, Oct. 23**  **Photo.**  **Perf. 13**

| | | | | |
|---|---|---|---|---|
| 486 | A78 | 20c | shown | .20 | .20 |
| 487 | A78 | 30c | Musicians | .20 | .20 |
| 488 | A78 | 50c | Dancers | .20 | .20 |
| 489 | A78 | 1fr | Operating room | .20 | .20 |
| 490 | A78 | 6fr | Weaver & painter | .20 | .20 |
| 491 | A78 | 18fr | Classroom | .20 | .20 |
| 492 | A78 | 24fr | Laboratory | .55 | .25 |
| 493 | A78 | 50fr | Hands of 4 races reaching for equality | 1.00 | .55 |
| | | | Nos. 486-493 (8) | 2.75 | 2.00 |

Fight against racism.

Christmas Type of 1968
Souvenir Sheet

**1972, Dec. 11**  **Perf. 11½**

| | | | |
|---|---|---|---|
| 494 | A48 | 100fr red brown | 3.00 | 3.00 |

Design: 100fr, Adoration of the Shepherds, by Jacob Jordaens, vert.

Pres. Kayibanda Addressing Meeting — A76

Pres. Grégoire Kayibanda: 30c, promoting officers of National Guard. 50c, with wife and children. 6fr, casting vote. 10fr, with wife and dignitaries at Feast of Justice. 15fr, with Cabinet and members of Assembly. 18fr, taking oath of office. 50fr, Portrait, vert.

**1972, July 4**

| | | | | |
|---|---|---|---|---|
| 470 | A76 | 20c | gold & slate grn | .20 | .20 |
| 471 | A76 | 30c | gold & dk pur | .20 | .20 |
| 472 | A76 | 50c | gold & choc | .20 | .20 |
| 473 | A76 | 6fr | gold & Prus bl | .20 | .20 |
| 474 | A76 | 10fr | gold & dk pur | .30 | .20 |
| 475 | A76 | 15fr | gold & dk bl | .30 | .20 |
| 476 | A76 | 18fr | gold & brn | .40 | .20 |
| 477 | A76 | 50fr | gold & Prus bl | 1.00 | .60 |
| | | | Nos. 470-477 (8) | 2.70 | 2.00 |

10th anniversary of independence.

Phymateus Brunneri — A79

Various insects: 30c, 1fr, 6fr, 22fr, 100fr, vert.

**1973, Jan. 31**  **Photo.**  **Perf. 13**

| | | | | |
|---|---|---|---|---|
| 495 | A79 | 20c | multi | .20 | .20 |
| 496 | A79 | 30c | multi | .20 | .20 |
| 497 | A79 | 50c | multi | .20 | .20 |
| 498 | A79 | 1fr | multi | .20 | .20 |
| 499 | A79 | 2fr | multi | .25 | .20 |
| 500 | A79 | 6fr | multi | .70 | .35 |
| 501 | A79 | 18fr | multi | .70 | .35 |
| 502 | A79 | 22fr | multi | .75 | .50 |
| 503 | A79 | 60fr | multi | 2.75 | 1.50 |
| 504 | A79 | 100fr | multi | 4.00 | 2.00 |
| | | | Nos. 495-504 (10) | 9.60 | 5.30 |

**Souvenir Sheet**

| | | | |
|---|---|---|---|
| 505 | A79 | 80fr like 20c | 6.00 | 6.00 |

No. 505 contains one stamp 43½x33½mm.

Emile Zola,
by Edouard Manet — A80

Paintings Connected with Reading, and Book Year Emblem: 30c, Rembrandt's Mother. 50c, St. Jerome Removing Thorn from Lion's Paw, by El Greco. 2fr, Apostles Peter and Paul, by Colantonio. 1fr, Virgin and Child with Book, by Roger van der Weyden. 6fr, St. Jerome in his Cell, by Antonella da Messina. 40fr, St. Barbara, by Master of Flemalle. No. 513, Don Quixote, by Otto Bonevalle. No. 514, Pres. Kayibanda reading book.

**1973, Mar. 12**  **Photo.**  **Perf. 13**

| | | | | |
|---|---|---|---|---|
| 506 | A80 | 20c | gold & multi | .20 | .20 |
| 507 | A80 | 30c | gold & multi | .20 | .20 |
| 508 | A80 | 50c | gold & multi | .20 | .20 |
| 509 | A80 | 1fr | gold & multi | .20 | .20 |
| 510 | A80 | 6fr | gold & multi | .20 | .20 |
| 511 | A80 | 40fr | gold & multi | .30 | .30 |
| 512 | A80 | 40fr | gold & multi | 1.75 | .75 |
| 513 | A80 | 100fr | gold & multi | 3.65 | 2.25 |
| | | | Nos. 506-513 (8) | | |

**Souvenir Sheet**

**Perf. 14**

| | | | |
|---|---|---|---|
| 514 | A80 | 100fr gold, bl & ind | 3.00 | 3.00 |

International Book Year.

Longombe
A81

Rubens and Isabella Brandt, by Rubens — A82

Musical instruments of Central & West Africa.

**1973, Apr. 9    Photo.    Perf. 13½**

| | | | | |
|---|---|---|---|---|
| 515 | A81 | 20c | shown | .20 .20 |
| 516 | A81 | 30c | Horn | .20 .20 |
| 517 | A81 | 50c | Xylophone | .20 .20 |
| 518 | A81 | 1fr | Harp | .20 .20 |
| 519 | A81 | 4fr | Alur horns | |
| 520 | A81 | 6fr | Drum, bells and horn | .20 .20 |
| 521 | A81 | 18fr | Large drums (Ngoma) | .35 .20 |
| 522 | A81 | 90fr | Toba | 1.75 .80 |
| | | | Nos. 515-522 (8) | 3.30 2.20 |

**1973, May 11**

Paintings from Old Pinakothek, Munich (IBRA Emblem and): 30c, Young Man, by Cranach. 50c, Woman Peeling Turnips, by Chardin. 1fr, The Abduction of Leucippa's Daughters, by Rubens. 2fr, Virgin and Child, by Filippo Lippi. 6fr, Boys Eating Fruit, by Murillo. 40fr, The Lovesick Woman, by Jan Steen. No. 530, Jesus Stripped of His Garments, by El Greco. No. 531, Oswalt Krehl, by Dürer.

| | | | | |
|---|---|---|---|---|
| 523 | A82 | 20c | gold & multi | .20 .20 |
| 524 | A82 | 30c | gold & multi | .20 .20 |
| 525 | A82 | 50c | gold & multi | .20 .20 |
| 526 | A82 | 1fr | gold & multi | .20 .20 |
| 527 | A82 | 2fr | gold & multi | .20 .20 |
| 528 | A82 | 6fr | gold & multi | .20 .20 |
| 529 | A82 | 40fr | gold & multi | .70 .35 |
| 530 | A82 | 50fr | gold & multi | 1.90 .80 |
| | | | Nos. 523-530 (8) | 3.80 2.35 |

**Souvenir Sheet**

| | | | | |
|---|---|---|---|---|
| 531 | A82 | 100fr | gold & multi | 3.00 3.00 |

IBRA München 1973 Intl. Phil. Exhib., Munich, May 11-20. #531 contains one 40x56mm stamp.

Map of Africa and Doves — A83

Design: 94fr, Map of Africa and hands.

**1973, July 23    Photo.    Perf. 13½**

| | | | | |
|---|---|---|---|---|
| 532 | A83 | 6fr | gold & multi | .25 .20 |
| 533 | A83 | 94fr | gold & multi | 2.00 1.50 |

Org. for African Unity, 10th anniv. For overprints see Nos. 895-896.

Nos. 298-303 Overprinted in Blue, Black, Green or Brown. "SECHERESSE / SOLIDARITE AFRICAINE"

**1973, Aug. 23    Photo.    Perf. 13**

| | | | | |
|---|---|---|---|---|
| 534 | A53 | 20c | multi (Bl) | .20 .20 |
| 535 | A53 | 40c | multi (Bk) | .20 .20 |
| 536 | A53 | 60c | multi (G) | .20 .20 |
| 537 | A53 | 80c | multi (G) | .20 .20 |
| 538 | A53 | 3fr | multi (G) | .20 .20 |
| 539 | A53 | 75fr | multi (Br) | 1.50 .90 |
| | | | Nos. 534-539,B1 (7) | 5.00 4.15 |

African solidarity in drought emergency.

**African Postal Union Issue**
**Common Design Type**

**1973, Sept. 12    Engr.    Perf. 13**

| | | | | |
|---|---|---|---|---|
| 540 | CD137 | 100fr | dp brn, bl & brn | 2.50 1.60 |

Six-lined Distichodus — A84

African Fish: 30c, Little triggerfish. 50c, Spotted upside-down catfish. 1fr, Nile mouthbreeder. 2fr, African lungfish. 6fr, Pareutropius mandevillei. 40fr, Congo characin. 100fr, like 20c. 150fr, Julidochromis ornatus.

**1973, Sept. 3    Photo.    Perf. 13**

| | | | | |
|---|---|---|---|---|
| 541 | A84 | 20c | gold & multi | .20 .20 |
| 542 | A84 | 30c | gold & multi | .20 .20 |
| 543 | A84 | 50c | gold & multi | .20 .20 |
| 544 | A84 | 1fr | gold & multi | .20 .20 |
| 545 | A84 | 2fr | gold & multi | .20 .20 |
| 546 | A84 | 6fr | gold & multi | .20 .20 |
| 547 | A84 | 40fr | gold & multi | 1.25 .50 |
| 548 | A84 | 150fr | gold & multi | 4.50 2.50 |
| | | | Nos. 541-548 (8) | 6.95 4.20 |

**Souvenir Sheet**

| | | | | |
|---|---|---|---|---|
| 549 | A84 | 100fr | gold & multi | 5.00 5.00 |

No. 549 contains one stamp 48x29mm.

Nos. 398-405 Overprinted in Black, Silver, Green or Blue

**1973, Sept. 15    Litho.**

| | | | | |
|---|---|---|---|---|
| 550 | A50 | 20c | multi (Bk) | .20 .20 |
| 551 | A50 | 30c | multi (S) | .20 .20 |
| 552 | A50 | 50c | multi (G) | .20 .20 |
| 553 | A50 | 1fr | multi (G) | .20 .20 |
| 554 | A50 | 5fr | multi (Bk) | .20 .20 |
| 555 | A50 | 18fr | multi (Bk) | .40 .25 |
| 556 | A50 | 25fr | multi (Bl) | .55 .25 |
| 557 | A50 | 50fr | multi (Bl) | 1.40 .95 |
| | | | Nos. 550-557 (8) | 3.35 2.00 |

Africa Weeks, Brussels, Sept. 15-30, 1973. On the 30c, 1fr and 25fr the text of the overprint is horizontal.

**1973, Oct. 31    Perf. 13½x14, 14x13½    Photo.**

| | | | | |
|---|---|---|---|---|
| 559 | A70 | 4fr | dp org & multi | .20 .20 |
| 560 | A70 | 6fr | yellow & multi | .20 .20 |
| 561 | A70 | 1fr | lilac & multi | .40 .30 |
| 562 | A70 | 25fr | red & multi | .70 .40 |
| 563 | A70 | 50fr | multicolored | 1.50 1.90 |
| | | | Nos. 559-563 (5) | 3.00 1.90 |

25th anniv. of the Universal Declaration of Human Rights.

**Christmas Type of 1968**
**Souvenir Sheet**

Adoration of the Shepherds, by Guido Reni.

**1973, Dec. 15    Engr.    Perf. 11½**

| | | | | |
|---|---|---|---|---|
| 564 | A48 | 100fr | brt violet | 3.00 3.00 |

Copernicus and Astrolabe — A85

Pres. Juvénal Habyarimana — A86

Designs: 30c, 18fr, 100fr, Portrait. 50c, 20c, Copernicus and heliocentric system. 1fr, like 20c.

**1973, Dec. 26    Photo.    Perf. 13**

| | | | | |
|---|---|---|---|---|
| 565 | A85 | 20c | silver & multi | .20 .20 |
| 566 | A85 | 30c | silver & multi | .20 .20 |
| 567 | A85 | 50c | silver & multi | .20 .20 |
| 568 | A85 | 1fr | gold & multi | .20 .20 |
| 569 | A85 | 18fr | gold & multi | .20 .20 |
| 570 | A85 | 80fr | gold & multi | 1.75 .80 |
| | | | Nos. 565-570 (6) | 2.75 1.80 |

**Souvenir Sheet**

| | | | | |
|---|---|---|---|---|
| 571 | A85 | 100fr | gold & multi | 3.25 3.25 |

Nicolaus Copernicus (1473-1543).

**1974, Apr. 8    Photo.    Perf. 11½**
**Black Inscriptions**

| | | | | |
|---|---|---|---|---|
| 572 | A86 | 1fr | bister & sepia | .20 .20 |
| 573 | A86 | 2fr | ultra & sepia | .20 .20 |
| 574 | A86 | 5fr | rose red & sep | .20 .20 |
| 575 | A86 | 6fr | grnsh bl & sep | .20 .20 |
| 576 | A86 | 26fr | lilac & sepia | .45 .30 |
| 577 | A86 | 60fr | ol grn & sepia | 1.25 .65 |
| | | | Nos. 572-577 (6) | 2.50 1.75 |

**Souvenir Sheet**
Christ Between the Thieves (Detail), by Rubens — A87

**1974, Apr. 12    Engr.    Perf. 11½**

| | | | | |
|---|---|---|---|---|
| 578 | A87 | 100fr | sepia | 7.25 7.25 |

Easter.

Yugoslavia-Zaire Soccer Game — A88

Games' emblem and soccer games.

**1974, July 6    Photo.    Perf. 13½**

| | | | | |
|---|---|---|---|---|
| 579 | A88 | 20c | shown | .20 .20 |
| 580 | A88 | 40c | Netherlands-Sweden | .20 |
| 581 | A88 | 60c | Germany (Fed.)-Australia | .20 .20 |
| 582 | A88 | 80c | Haiti-Argentina | .20 .20 |
| 583 | A88 | 2fr | Brazil-Scotland | .20 .20 |
| 584 | A88 | 40fr | Bulgaria-Uruguay | .20 .20 |
| 585 | A88 | 40fr | Italy-Poland | 1.00 .40 |
| 586 | A88 | 50fr | Chile-Germany (DDR) | 1.50 .65 |
| | | | Nos. 579-586 (8) | 3.70 2.25 |

World Cup Soccer Championship, Munich, June 13-July 7.

Marconi's Laboratory Yacht "Elletra" — A89

Designs: 30c, Marconi and steamer "Carlo Alberto". 50c, Marconi's wireless apparatus and telecommunications satellites. 4fr, Marconi and globes connected by communications waves. 15fr, Marconi's radio, and radar. 60fr, Marconi and transmitter at Poldhu, Cornwall. 50fr, like 20c.

**1974, Aug. 19    Photo.    Perf. 13½**

| | | | | |
|---|---|---|---|---|
| 587 | A89 | 20c | violet, blk & grn | .20 .20 |
| 588 | A89 | 30c | green, blk & vio | .20 .20 |
| 589 | A89 | 50c | yellow, blk & lil | .20 .20 |
| 590 | A89 | 4fr | salmon, blk & bl | .20 .20 |
| 591 | A89 | 35fr | lilac, blk & yel | .60 .40 |
| 592 | A89 | 60fr | blue, blk & brnz | 2.65 1.90 |
| | | | Nos. 587-592 (6) | |

**Souvenir Sheet**

| | | | | |
|---|---|---|---|---|
| 593 | A89 | 50fr | gold, blk & lt bl | 1.75 1.75 |

Guglielmo Marconi (1874-1937), Italian electrical engineer and inventor.

The Flute Player, by J. Leyster — A90

Messenger Monk — A91

Paintings: 20c, Diane de Poitiers, Fontainebleau School. 50c, Virgin and Child, by David. 1fr, Triumph of Venus, by Boucher. 10fr, Seated Harlequin, by Picasso. 18fr, Virgin and Child, 15th century. 20fr, Beheading of St. John, by Hans Fries. 50fr, Daughter of Andersdotter, by J. F. Höckert.

**1974, Sept. 23    Photo.    Perf. 14x13**

| | | | | |
|---|---|---|---|---|
| 594 | A90 | 20c | gold & multi | .20 .20 |
| 595 | A90 | 30c | gold & multi | .20 .20 |
| 596 | A90 | 50c | gold & multi | .20 .20 |
| 597 | A90 | 1fr | gold & multi | .20 .20 |
| 598 | A90 | 10fr | gold & multi | .20 .20 |
| 599 | A90 | 18fr | gold & multi | .30 .20 |
| 600 | A90 | 20fr | gold & multi | .35 .20 |
| 601 | A90 | 50fr | gold & multi | 1.00 .60 |
| | | | Nos. 594-601 (8) | 2.65 2.00 |

INTERNABA 74 Intl. Phil. Exhib., Basel, June 7-10, and Stockholmia 74, Intl. Phil. Exhib., Stockholm, Sept. 21-29. Six multicolored souvenir sheets exist containing two 15fr designs each in various combinations of designs of Nos. 594-601. One souvenir sheet of four 25fr stamps exists with designs of Nos. 595, 597, 599 and 601.

**1974, Oct. 9    Perf. 14**

UPU Emblem and Messengers: 30c, Inca. 50c, Morocco. 1fr, India. 18fr, Polynesia. 80fr, Rwanda.

| | | | | |
|---|---|---|---|---|
| 602 | A91 | 20c | gold & multi | .20 .20 |
| 603 | A91 | 30c | gold & multi | .20 .20 |
| 604 | A91 | 50c | gold & multi | .20 .20 |
| 605 | A91 | 1fr | gold & multi | .20 .20 |
| 606 | A91 | 18fr | gold & multi | .40 .35 |
| 607 | A91 | 80fr | gold & multi | 1.60 1.60 |
| | | | Nos. 602-607 (6) | 2.80 2.75 |

Centenary of Universal Postal Union.

Nos. 306-308 Overprinted

15th anniversary of independence.

**Christmas Type of 1968**
**Souvenir Sheet**

Adoration of the Kings, by Joos van Cleve.

**1974, Dec. 16    Photo.    Perf. 11½**

| | | | | |
|---|---|---|---|---|
| 608 | A54 | 6fr | brt pink & multi | 4.75 4.25 |
| 609 | A54 | 18fr | ultra & multi | 4.75 4.25 |
| 610 | A54 | 40fr | brn & multi | 4.75 4.25 |
| | | | Nos. 608-610 (3) | 14.25 12.75 |

**1974, Dec. 23    Engr.    Perf. 11½**

| | | | | |
|---|---|---|---|---|
| 611 | A48 | 100fr | slate green | 6.25 6.25 |

Nos. 295-296 Overprinted: "1974 / 10e Anniversaire"

**1974, Dec. 30 — Photo. — Perf. 13**

| | | | |
|---|---|---|---|
| 612 | A51 | 30fr sil & multi | .85 .85 |
| 613 | A51 | 70fr gold & multi | 1.60 1.60 |

African Development Bank, 10th anniversary.

Uganda Kob — A92

**1975, Mar. 17 — Photo. — Perf. 13**

| | | | |
|---|---|---|---|
| 614 | A92 | 20c multi | .20 .20 |
| 615 | A92 | 30c multi | .20 .20 |
| 616 | A92 | 50c multi | .20 .20 |
| 617 | A92 | 4fr multi | .20 .20 |
| 618 | A92 | 4fr multi | .20 .20 |
| 619 | A92 | 10fr multi | .20 .20 |
| 620 | A92 | 34fr multi | 1.00 1.00 |
| 621 | A92 | 100fr multi | 4.00 4.00 |
| | | Nos. 614-621 (8) | 6.20 6.20 |

Antelopes: 30c, Bongos, horiz. 50c, Rwanda antelopes. 1fr, Young sitatungas, horiz. 4fr, Greater kudus. 10fr, Impalas, horiz. 34fr, Waterbuck. 60fr, Impalas. 60fr, Greater kudu. 100fr, Derby's elands, horiz.

**Miniature Sheets**

| | | | |
|---|---|---|---|
| 622 | A92 | 40fr multi | 11.20 11.20 |
| 623 | A92 | 60fr multi | 6.20 6.20 |

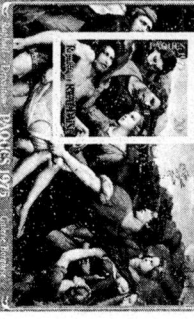

The Burial of Jesus, by Raphael — A93

**Souvenir Sheets**

**1975, Apr. 1 — Photo. — Perf. 13x14**

| | | | |
|---|---|---|---|
| 624 | A93 | 20fr shown | 2.10 2.10 |
| 625 | A93 | 30fr Pietà, by Cranach the Elder | 2.10 2.10 |
| 626 | A93 | 50fr by van der Weyden | 2.10 2.10 |
| 627 | A93 | 100fr by Bellini | 8.40 8.40 |

See Nos. 624-627 (4)

Easter. Size of stamps: 40x52mm.

Prince Balthazar Charles, by Velazquez — A94

Paintings: 30fr, Infanta Margaret of Austria, by Velazquez. 50fr, The Divine Shepherd, by Murillo. 100fr, Francisco Goya, by V. Lopez y Portana.

España 75 Intl. Phil. Exhib., Madrid, Apr. 4-13. Size of stamps: 38x48mm. See Nos. 642-643. For overprints see Nos. 844-847.

**1975, Apr. 4 — Photo. — Perf. 13**

| | | | |
|---|---|---|---|
| 628 | A94 | 20fr multi | 2.25 2.25 |
| 629 | A94 | 30fr multi | 2.25 2.25 |
| 630 | A94 | 50fr multi | 2.25 2.25 |
| 631 | A94 | 100fr multi | 9.00 9.00 |
| | | Nos. 628-631 (4) | 9.00 |

Pyrethrum (Insect Powder) — A95

**1975, Apr. 14 — Photo. — Perf. 13**

| | | | |
|---|---|---|---|
| 632 | A95 | 20c shown | .20 .20 |
| 633 | A95 | 30c Tea | .20 .20 |
| 634 | A95 | 50c Coffee (beans and pan) | .20 .20 |
| 635 | A95 | 4fr Bananas | .20 .20 |
| 636 | A95 | 10fr Corn | .20 .20 |
| 637 | A95 | 12fr Sorghum | .20 .20 |
| 638 | A95 | 26fr Rice | .50 .50 |
| 639 | A95 | 47fr Coffee (workers and beans) | 1.25 .45 |
| | | Nos. 632-639 (8) | 2.95 1.90 |

**Souvenir Sheets**

**Perf. 13½**

| | | | |
|---|---|---|---|
| 640 | A95 | 25fr like 50c | 1.25 1.26 |
| 641 | A95 | 75fr like 4/fr | 2.75 2.75 |

Year of Agriculture and 10th anniversary of Office for Industrialized Cultivation.

**Painting Type of 1975**

**Souvenir Sheets**

**1975, June 6 — Photo. — Perf. 13**

| | | | |
|---|---|---|---|
| 642 | A94 | 75fr multi | 4.00 4.00 |
| 643 | A94 | 125fr multi | 5.50 5.50 |

75fr, Louis XIV, by Hyacinthe Rigaud. 125fr, Cavalry Officer, by Jean Gericault.

ARPHILA 75, Intl. Philatelic Exhibition, Paris, June 6-16. Size of stamps: 38x48mm.

Nos. 390-397 Overprinted: "1975 / ANNÉE / SAINTE"

**1975, June 23 — Photo. — Perf. 13**

| | | | |
|---|---|---|---|
| 644 | A66 | 10c gold & dk brn | .20 .20 |
| 645 | A66 | 20c gold & dk grn | .20 .20 |
| 646 | A66 | 30c gold & dk claret | .20 .20 |
| 647 | A66 | 40c gold & indigo | .20 .20 |
| 648 | A66 | 1fr gold & dk pur | .20 .20 |
| 649 | A66 | 18fr gold & purple | .30 .30 |
| 650 | A66 | 20fr gold & org brn | .45 .45 |
| 651 | A66 | 60fr gold & blk brn | 1.60 1.60 |
| | | Nos. 644-651 (8) | 3.35 2.25 |

Holy Year 1975.

White Pelicans — A96

**1975, June 20 — Photo. — Perf. 13**

| | | | |
|---|---|---|---|
| 652 | A96 | 20c shown | .20 .20 |
| 653 | A96 | 30c Malachite kingfisher | .20 .20 |
| 654 | A96 | 50c Saddle-billed storks | .20 .20 |
| 655 | A96 | 1fr Goliath herons | .20 .20 |
| 656 | A96 | 4fr African jacana | .20 .20 |
| 657 | A96 | 10fr African anhingas | .20 .20 |
| 658 | A96 | 34fr Sacred ibis | 1.25 .75 |
| 659 | A96 | 80fr Hartlaub ducks | 3.00 1.25 |
| | | Nos. 652-659 (8) | 5.45 3.20 |

Designs: African birds.

**Miniature Sheets**

| | | | |
|---|---|---|---|
| 660 | A96 | 40fr Flamingoes | 8.00 8.00 |
| 661 | A96 | 80fr Crowned cranes | 10.00 10.00 |

Globe Representing Races and WPY Emblem — A97

The Bath, by Mary Cassatt and IWY Emblem — A98

World Population Year: 26fr, Population graph and emblem. 34fr, Globe with open door and emblem.

**1975, Sept. 1 — Photo. — Perf. 13½x13**

| | | | |
|---|---|---|---|
| 662 | A97 | 20fr dp bl & multi | .50 .50 |
| 663 | A97 | 26fr dl red brn & multi | .60 .25 |
| 664 | A97 | 34fr yel & multi | 1.90 .80 |
| | | Nos. 662-664 (3) | |

IWY Emblem and: 30c, Mother and Infant with Milk Jug, by Julius Gari Melchers. 50c, Woman in laboratory. 1fr, Water Carrier, by Goya. 8fr, Rwanda woman cotton picker. 12fr, Scientist with microscope. 18fr, Mother and child. 25fr, Empress Josephine, by Pierre-Paul Prud'hon. 40fr, Madame Vigée-Lebrun and Daughter, self-portrait. 60fr, Woman carrying child on back and water jug on head.

**1975, Sept. 15 — Photo. — Perf. 13**

| | | | |
|---|---|---|---|
| 665 | A98 | 20c gold & multi | .20 .20 |
| 666 | A98 | 30c gold & multi | .20 .20 |
| 667 | A98 | 50c gold & dk grn | .20 .20 |
| 668 | A98 | 1fr gold & multi | .20 .20 |
| 669 | A98 | 8fr gold & multi | .20 .20 |
| 670 | A98 | 12fr gold & multi | .35 .35 |
| 671 | A98 | 18fr gold & multi | .60 .60 |
| 672 | A98 | 60fr gold & multi | 2.95 2.00 |
| | | Nos. 665-672 (8) | |

**Souvenir Sheets**

**Perf. 13½**

| | | | |
|---|---|---|---|
| 673 | A98 | 25fr multi | 45.00 45.00 |
| 674 | A98 | 40fr multi | 45.00 45.00 |

International Women's Year. Nos. 673-674, each contain one stamp 37x49mm.

Owl, Quill and Book — A99

**1975, Sept. 29 — Photo. — Perf. 13**

| | | | |
|---|---|---|---|
| 675 | A99 | 20c pur & multi | .20 .20 |
| 676 | A99 | 30c ultra & multi | .20 .20 |
| 677 | A99 | 1.50fr lilac & multi | .20 .20 |
| 678 | A99 | 18fr blue & multi | .30 .30 |
| 679 | A99 | 26fr olive & multi | .45 .25 |
| 680 | A99 | 34fr blue & multi | .75 .35 |
| | | Nos. 675-680 (6) | 2.10 1.40 |

National Univ. of Rwanda, 10th anniv.

**Painting Type of 1975**

**Souvenir Sheets**

Paintings by Jan Vermeer (1632-1675): 20fr, Man and Woman Drinking Wine. 30fr, Young Woman Reading Letter. 50fr, Painter in his Studio. 100fr, Young Woman Playing Virginal.

Waterhole and Impatiens Stuhlmannii — A100

**1975, Oct. 13 — Photo. — Perf. 13x14**

| | | | |
|---|---|---|---|
| 681 | A93 | 20fr multi | 2.40 2.40 |
| 682 | A93 | 30fr multi | 2.40 2.40 |
| 683 | A93 | 40fr multi | 2.40 2.40 |
| 684 | A93 | 100fr multi | 9.60 9.60 |

Size of stamps: 40x52mm.

**1975, Oct. 25 — Photo. — Perf. 13**

| | | | |
|---|---|---|---|
| 685 | A100 | 20c blk & multi | .20 .20 |
| 686 | A100 | 30c blk & multi | .20 .20 |
| 687 | A100 | 50c blk & multi | .20 .20 |
| 688 | A100 | 1fr blk & multi | .20 .20 |
| 689 | A100 | 8fr blk & multi | .20 .20 |
| 690 | A100 | 10fr blk & multi | .65 .65 |
| 691 | A100 | 18fr blk & multi | .65 .65 |
| 692 | A100 | 100fr blk & multi | 4.10 3.20 |
| | | Nos. 685-692 (8) | |

Designs: 30c, Antelopes, zebras, candelabra cactus. 50c, Brush fire, and tapinanthus prunifolius. 5fr, Bulera Lake and Egyptian white lotus. 10fr, Erosion prevention and protea madiensis. 26fr, Marsh and melanthera brownei. 8fr, Landscape, lobelias and senecons. 100fr, Sabyinyo Volcano and polystachya kermesina.

Nature protection.

For overprints see Nos. 001-808.

Nos. 343-348 Overprinted

**1975, Nov. 10 — Litho. — Perf. 13**

| | | | |
|---|---|---|---|
| 693 | A60 | 20c multi | .20 .20 |
| 694 | A60 | 30c multi | .20 .20 |
| 695 | A60 | 50c multi | .20 .20 |
| 696 | A60 | 1fr multi | .20 .20 |
| 697 | A60 | 3fr multi | .20 .20 |
| 698 | A60 | 5fr multi | 5.35 3.70 |
| | | Nos. 693-698,B2-B3 (8) | |

African solidarity in drought emergency.

Fork-lift Truck on Airfield A101

**1975, Dec. 1 — Photo. — Wmk. JEZ Multiple (368) — Perf. 14x13½**

| | | | |
|---|---|---|---|
| 699 | A101 | 20c gold & multi | .20 .20 |
| 700 | A101 | 30c gold & multi | .20 .20 |
| 701 | A101 | 50c gold & multi | .20 .20 |
| 702 | A101 | 10fr gold & multi | .45 .25 |
| 703 | A101 | 35fr gold & multi | .60 .60 |
| 704 | A101 | 54fr gold & multi | 1.00 .55 |
| | | Nos. 699-704 (6) | 2.40 1.70 |

Designs: 30c, Coffee packing plant. 50c, Engineering plant. 10fr, Farmer with hoe, vert. 35fr, Coffee pickers, vert. 54fr, Mechanized harvester.

**Basket Carrier and Themabelga Emblem — A102**

Themabelga Emblem and: 30c, Warrior with shield and spear. 50c, Woman with beads. 1fr, Indian woman. 5fr, Male dancer with painted body. 7fr, Woman carrying child on back. 35fr, Male dancer with spear. 51fr, Female dancers.

**1975, Dec. 8    Unwmk.    Perf. 13½**

```
705 A102 20c  blk & multi      .20   .20
706 A102 30c  blk & multi      .20   .20
707 A102 50c  blk & multi      .20   .20
708 A102 1fr  blk & multi      .20   .20
709 A102 5fr  blk & multi      .20   .20
710 A102 7fr  blk & multi      .65   .60
711 A102 35fr blk & multi     1.00  1.00
712 A102 51fr blk & multi     2.85  2.00
   Nos. 705-712 (8)
```

THEMABELGA Intl. Topical Philatelic Exhibition, Brussels, Dec. 13-21.

**Christmas Type of 1968**

Adoration of the Kings, by Peter Paul Rubens.

**1975, Dec. 22    Engr.    Perf. 11½**

```
713 A48 100fr brt rose lil    4.50  4.50
```

**Dr. Schweitzer, Keyboard, Score — A103**

Albert Schweitzer and: 30c, 5fr, Lambaréné Hospital. 50c, 10fr, Organ pipes from Strassbourg organ, and score. 1fr, 80fr, Dr. Schweitzer's house, Lambaréné. 3fr, like 20c.

**1976, Jan. 30    Photo.    Perf. 13½**

```
714 A103 20c  maroon & pur     .20   .20
715 A103 30c  grn & pur        .20   .20
716 A103 50c  brn org & pur    .20   .20
717 A103 1fr  red lil & pur    .20   .20
718 A103 3fr  vio bl & pur     .20   .20
719 A103 5fr  brn & pur        .20   .20
720 A103 10fr bl & pur         .50   .50
721 A103 80fr ver & pur       2.90  2.00
   Nos. 714-721 (8)
```

World Leprosy Day.

For overprints see Nos. 788-795.

**Surrender at Yorktown — A104**

American Bicentennial (Paintings): 30c, Presentation of Captured Colors at Yorktown. 1fr, Washington Instruction at Valley Forge. 50c, Washington Studying British Warship. 18fr, Washington Boarding British Warship. 26fr, Washington Studying Battle Plans at Night. 34fr, Washington Firing Cannon. 40fr, Washington Crossing the Delaware. 100fr, Sailing Ship "Bonhomme Richard," vert.

**1976, Mar. 22    Photo.    Perf. 13x13½**

```
722 A104 20c  gold & multi     .20   .20
723 A104 30c  gold & multi     .20   .20
724 A104 50c  gold & multi     .20   .20
725 A104 1fr  gold & multi     .20   .20
726 A104 18fr gold & multi     .45   .20
727 A104 26fr gold & multi     .50   .50
728 A104 34fr gold & multi     .75   .35
729 A104 40fr gold & multi     .80   .45
   Nos. 722-729 (8)           3.30  2.00
```

**Souvenir Sheet**

**Perf. 13½**

```
730 A104 100fr gold & multi   3.50  3.50
```

See Nos. 754-761.

**Sister Yohana, First Nun — A105**

30c, Abdon Sabakati, one of first converts. 50c, Father Alphonse Brard, first Superior of Save Mission. 4fr, Abbot Balthazar Gafuku, one of first priests. 10fr, Msgr. Bigirumwami, first bishop. 25fr, Save Church, horiz. 60fr, Kabgayi Cathedral, horiz.

**1976, Apr. 26    Perf. 13x13½, 13½x13    Photo.**

```
731 A105 20c  multi            .20   .20
732 A105 30c  multi            .20   .20
733 A105 50c  multi            .20   .20
734 A105 4fr  multi            .20   .20
735 A105 10fr multi            .20   .20
736 A105 25fr multi            .45   .25
737 A105 60fr multi           1.00   .60
   Nos. 731-737 (7)           2.45  1.85
```

50th anniv. of the Roman Catholic Church of Rwanda.

**Yachting — A106**

Montreal Games Emblem and: 30c, Steeplechase. 50c, Long jump. 1fr, Hockey. 10fr, Swimming. 18fr, Soccer. 29fr, Boxing. 51fr, Vaulting.

**1976, May 24    Photo.    Perf. 13x13½**

```
738 A106 20c  gray & dk car    .20   .20
739 A106 30c  gray & Prus bl   .20   .20
740 A106 50c  gray & blkt      .20   .20
741 A106 1fr  gray & pur       .20   .20
742 A106 10fr gray & ultra     .25   .20
743 A106 18fr gray & brn       .35   .35
744 A106 29fr gray & blk       .60   .30
745 A106 51fr gray & slate grn .90   .50
   Nos. 738-745 (8)           2.90  2.00
```

21st Olympic Games, Montreal, Canada, July 17-Aug. 1.

**First Message, Manual Switchboard — A107**

Designs: 30c, Telephone, 1876 and interested crowd. 50c, Telephone c. 1900, and woman making a call. 1fr, Business telephone exchange, c. 1905. 4fr, "Candlestick" phone, globe and A. G. Bell. 8fr, Dial phone and Rwandan man making call. 26fr, Telephone, 1876, satellite and radar. 60fr, Push-button telephone, Rwandan international switchboard operator.

**1976, June 21    Photo.    Perf. 14**

```
746 A107 20c  dl red & multi       .20   .20
747 A107 30c  grnsh bl & indigo    .20   .20
748 A107 50c  brn bl & indigo      .20   .20
749 A107 1fr  org & multi          .20   .20
750 A107 4fr  lilac & indigo       .25   .20
751 A107 8fr  grn & indigo         .50   .25
752 A107 26fr dl red & indigo     1.10   .55
753 A107 60fr vio & indigo        2.80  2.00
   Nos. 746-753 (8)
```

Centenary of first telephone call by Alexander Graham Bell, Mar. 10, 1876.

**Soccer, Montreal Olympic Emblem — A108**

30c, Shooting. 50c, Woman canoeing. 1fr, Gymnast. 10fr, Weight lifting. 12fr, Diving. 26fr, Equestrian. 50fr, Shot put.

**1976, July 4    Perf. 13x13½**

```
754 A108 20c  silver & multi   .20   .20
755 A108 30c  silver & multi   .20   .20
756 A108 50c  silver & multi   .20   .20
757 A108 1fr  silver & multi   .20   .20
758 A108 10fr silver & multi   .35   .35
759 A108 12fr silver & multi   .65   .30
760 A108 26fr silver & multi   .70   .40
761 A108 50fr silver & multi
   Nos. 754-761 (8)           3.00  2.00
```

Independence Day.

**1976, Aug. 1    Photo.    Perf. 13½x13**

```
762 A108 20c  multi            .20   .20
763 A108 30c  multi            .20   .20
764 A108 50c  multi            .20   .20
765 A108 1fr  multi            .20   .20
766 A108 12fr multi            .20   .20
767 A108 26fr multi            .30   .30
768 A108 40fr multi            .50   .50
769 A108 50fr multi           1.50   .50
   Nos. 762-769 (8)           3.20  2.00
```

**Souvenir Sheet**

Various phases of hurdles race, horiz.

```
770    Sheet of 4            4.00  4.00
  a. A108 20fr Start         .45   .45
  b. A108 30fr Sprint        .70   .70
  c. A108 40fr Hurdle        .90   .90
  d. A108 60fr Finish       1.50  1.50
```

21st Olympic Games, Montreal, Canada, July 17-Aug. 1.

**Apollo and Soyuz Take-offs, Project Emblem A109**

Designs: 30c, Soyuz in space. 50c, Apollo in space. 1fr, Apollo. 2fr, Spacecraft before docking. 12fr, Spacecraft after docking. 30fr, Astronauts visiting in docked spacecraft. 54fr, Apollo splashdown.

**1976, Oct. 29    Photo.    Perf. 13½x14**

```
771 A109 20c  multi            .20   .20
772 A109 30c  multi            .20   .20
773 A109 50c  multi            .20   .20
774 A109 1fr  multi            .20   .20
775 A109 2fr  multi            .20   .20
776 A109 12fr multi            .35   .30
777 A109 30fr multi           1.50  1.25
778 A109 54fr multi           2.25  2.00
   Nos. 771-778 (8)           5.10  4.55
```

Apollo Soyuz space test program (Russo-American cooperation), July 1975. For overprints see Nos. 836-843.

**Eulophia Cucullata — A110**

Orchids: 30c, Eulophia streptopetala. 50c, Disa Stairsii. 1fr, Aerangis kotschyana. 10fr, Eulophia abyssinica. 12fr, Bonatea steudneri. 26fr, Ansellia gigantea. 50fr, Eulophia angolensis.

**1976, Nov. 22    Photo.    Perf. 14x13½**

```
779 A110 20c  silver & multi   .20   .20
780 A110 30c  multi            .20   .20
781 A110 50c  multi            .20   .20
782 A110 1fr  multi            .20   .20
783 A110 10fr multi            .25   .25
784 A110 12fr multi            .45   .25
785 A110 26fr multi           1.40   .40
786 A110 50fr multi           2.50   .75
   Nos. 779-786 (8)           5.35  2.40
```

**Christmas Type of 1968**

**Souvenir Sheet**

Design: Nativity, by Francois Boucher.

**1976, Dec. 20    Engr.    Perf. 11½**

```
787 A48 100fr brt ultra       4.25  4.25
```

**Nos. 714-721 Overprinted: "JOURNEE / MONDIALE / 1977"**

**1977, Jan. 29    Photo.    Perf. 13½**

```
788 A103 20c  mar & pur        .20   .20
789 A103 30c  grn & pur        .20   .20
790 A103 50c  brn org & pur    .20   .20
791 A103 1fr  red lil & pur    .20   .20
792 A103 3fr  vio bl & pur     .20   .20
793 A103 5fr  brn & pur        .20   .20
794 A103 10fr bl & pur         .25   .80
795 A103 80fr ver & pur       1.40   .80
   Nos. 788-795 (8)           2.85  2.20
```

World Leprosy Day.

**Hands and Symbols of Learning — A111**

**1977, Feb. 7    Litho.    Perf. 12½**

Designs: 26fr, Hands and symbols of science. 64fr, Hands and symbols of industry.

```
796 A111 10fr multi            .20   .20
797 A111 26fr multi            .55   .40
798 A111 64fr multi            .95   .75
   Nos. 796-798 (3)           1.70  1.35
```

10th Summit Conference of the African and Malagasy Union, Kigali, 1976.

**Souvenir Sheets**

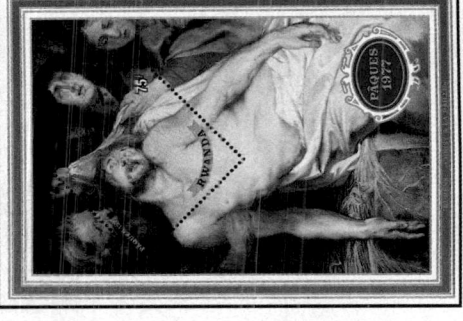

**Descent from the Cross, by Rubens — A112**

Easter: 25fr, Crucifixion, by Rubens.

**1977, Apr. 27    Photo.    Perf. 13**

```
799 A112 25fr multi           4.25  4.25
800 A112 75fr multi           5.25  5.25
```

Size of stamp: 40x40mm.

**Nos. 685-692 Overprinted**

**1977, May 2**

```
801 A100 20c  blk & multi      .20   .20
802 A100 30c  blk & multi      .20   .20
803 A100 50c  blk & multi      .20   .20
804 A100 5fr  blk & multi      .20   .20
```

Type of 1976 Overprinted in Silver with Bicentennial Emblem and "Independence Day"

Designs as before.

805 A100 8fr blk & multi .35 .20
806 A100 10fr blk & multi .35 .20
807 A100 26fr blk & multi 1.00 .45
808 A100 100fr blk & multi 1.90
   Nos. 801-808 (8) 5.75 3.55

World Water Conference.

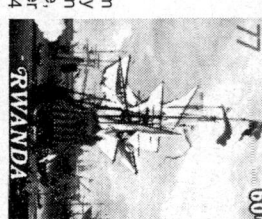

Roman Fire Tower, African Tom-tom — A113

ITU Emblem and: 30c, Chappe's optical telegraph and position. 50c, Morse telegraph and code. 1fr, Tug Goliath laying cable in English Channel. 4fr, Telephone, radio, television. 18fr, Kingsport (US space exploration ship), and Marots communications satellite. 26fr, Satellite tracking station and O.T.S. satellite. 50fr, Mariner II, Venus probe.

**1977, May 23**    Litho.    **Perf. 12½**
809 A113 20c multi .20 .20
810 A113 30c multi .20 .20
811 A113 50c multi .20 .20
812 A113 1fr multi .20 .20
813 A113 4fr multi .20 .20
814 A113 18fr multi .45 .20
815 A113 26fr multi .60 .30
816 A113 50fr multi 1.25 .60
   Nos. 809-816 (8) 3.30 2.10

World Telecommunications Day.

Amsterdam Harbor, by Willem van de Velde, the Younger A114

**1977, May 26**    Photo.
40fr, The Night Watch, by Rembrandt.
817 A114 40fr multi 2.75 2.75
818 A114 60fr multi 2.75 2.75

AMPHILEX '277 Intl. Philatelic Exhibition, Amsterdam, May 27-June 5. Size of stamp: 38x49mm.

## Souvenir Sheets

Road to Calvary, by Rubens — A115

**1977, June 13**    **Perf. 14**
819 A115 20c gold & multi .20 .20
820 A115 30c gold & multi .25 .20
821 A115 50c gold & multi .30 .20
822 A115 1fr gold & multi .35 .20
823 A115 4fr gold & multi .40 .20
824 A115 8fr gold & multi .45 .20
825 A115 26fr gold & multi .75 .20
826 A115 60fr gold & multi 1.75 .55
   Nos. 819-826 (8) 4.45 2.00

Paintings by Peter Paul Rubens (1577-1640). 30c, Judgment of Paris, horiz. 50c, Marie de Medicis. 1fr, Heads of Black Men, horiz. 4fr, Details from St. Ildefonso triptych. 8fr, Helene Fourment and her Children, horiz. 60fr, Helene Fourment.

Boy Scout Playing Flute — A118

**1977, Oct. 3**    Photo.    **Perf. 13**
844 A94 20fr multi .20 .20
845 A94 30fr multi .20 .20
846 A94 50fr multi .20 .20
847 A94 100fr multi .20 .20
   Nos. 844-847 (4)

ESPAMER '77, International Philatelic Exhibition, Barcelona, Oct. 7-13.

### Christmas Type of 1968
Souvenir Sheet
**1977, Dec. 12**    Engr.    **Perf. 13½**
848 A48 100fr violet blue 3.25 3.25

Marginal inscription typographed in red.

---

Souvenir Sheet

Viking on Mars — A116

**1977, June 27**    Photo.    **Perf. 13**
827 A116 100fr multi 25.00 25.00

US Viking landing on Mars, first anniv.

Crested Eagle — A117

Birds of Prey. 30c, Snake eagle. 50c, Fish eagle. 1fr, Monk vulture. 3fr, Red-tailed buzzard. 5fr, Yellow-beaked kite. 20fr, Swallow-tailed kite. 100fr, Bateleur.

**1977, Sept. 12**    Litho.    **Perf. 14**
828 A117 20c multi .20 .20
829 A117 30c multi .20 .20
830 A117 50c multi .20 .20
831 A117 1fr multi .20 .20
832 A117 3fr multi .20 .20
833 A117 5fr multi .20 .20
834 A117 20fr multi .50 .75
835 A117 100fr multi 2.00
   Nos. 828-835 (8)

## Souvenir Sheets

Nos. 771-778 Overprinted: "in memoriam / WERNHER VON BRAUN / 1912-1977"

**1977, Sept. 19**    Photo.    **Perf. 13½x14**
836 A109 20c multi .20 .20
837 A109 30c multi .20 .20
838 A109 50c multi .20 .20
839 A109 1fr multi .20 .20
840 A109 2fr multi .20 .20
841 A109 10fr multi .20 .20
842 A109 30fr multi 1.75 1.25
843 A109 54fr multi 2.25 2.25
   Nos. 836-843 (8) 6.20 4.70

Wernher von Braun (1912-1977), space and rocket expert.

## Souvenir Sheets

Nos. 628-631 Gold Embossed "ESPAMER '77" and ESPAMER Emblem

Euporus Strangulatus — A120

Coleoptera. 30c, Rhina afzelii, vert. 50c, Pentalobus palini. 3fr, Corynodes dejeani, vert. 10fr, Mecynorhina torquata. 15fr, Mecoceras rhombeus, vert. 20fr, Macrotoma serripes. 25fr, Neptunides stanleyi, vert. 26fr, Petrognatha gigas. 100fr, Eudicella gralli, vert.

**1978, May 22**    Litho.    **Perf. 14**
865 A120 20c multi .20 .20
866 A120 30c multi .20 .20
867 A120 50c multi .20 .20
868 A120 3fr multi .20 .20
869 A120 10fr multi .20 .20
870 A120 15fr multi .45 .25
871 A120 20fr multi .60 .40
872 A120 25fr multi .75 .40
873 A120 26fr multi .75 .40
874 A120 100fr multi 2.00 2.00
   Nos. 865-874 (10) 6.55 4.35

Crossing "River of Poverty" A121

**1978, May 29**    **Perf. 12½**
875 A121 4fr multi .20 .20
876 A121 10fr multi .20 .20
877 A121 26fr multi .50 .30
878 A121 60fr multi 1.25 .80
   Nos. 875-878 (4) 2.15 1.50

Emblem and: 10fr, 60fr. Men poling boat, facing right. 26fr, like 4fr.
Natl. Revolutionary Development Movement (M.R.N.D.).

---

Chimpanzees A119

Designs: 30c, Campfire. 50c, Bridge building. 1fr, Scouts with unit flag. 10fr, Map reading. 18fr, Boating. 26fr, Cooking. 44fr, Lord Baden-Powell.

**1978, Feb. 20**    Litho.    **Perf. 12½**
849 A118 20c yel grn & multi .20 .20
850 A118 30c blue & multi .20 .20
851 A118 50c lilac & multi .20 .20
852 A118 1fr blue & multi .20 .20
853 A118 10fr pink & multi .20 .25
854 A118 18fr lt grn & multi .65 .25
855 A118 26fr orange & multi 1.00 .45
856 A118 44fr salmon & multi 1.75 1.00
   Nos. 849-856 (8) 4.40 2.70

10th anniversary of Rwanda Boy Scouts.

Designs: 30c, Gorilla. 50c, Colobus monkey. 3fr, Galago. 10fr, Cercopithecus monkey (mone). 26fr, Potto. 60fr, Cercopithecus monkey (gruel). 150fr, Baboon.

**1978, Mar. 20**    Photo.    **Perf. 13½x13**
857 A119 20c multi .20 .20
858 A119 30c multi .20 .20
859 A119 50c multi .20 .20
860 A119 3fr multi .20 .20
861 A119 10fr multi .75 .20
862 A119 26fr multi 2.50 2.00
863 A119 60fr multi 5.00 4.00
864 A119 150fr multi 9.50 7.75
   Nos. 857-864 (8)

Wright Brothers' Flyer I — A123

History of Aviation: 30c, Santos Dumont and Canard 14, 1906. 50c, Henry Farman and Voisin No.1, 1908. 1fr, Jan Olieslaegers and Bleriot, 1910. 3fr, Marshal Balbo and Savoia S-17, 1919. 10fr, Charles Lindbergh and Spirit of St. Louis, 1927. 55fr, Hugo Junkers and Junkers JU52/3, 1932. 60fr, Igor Sikorsky and Sikorsky VS 300, 1939. 130fr, Concorde over New York.

**1978, Oct. 30**    Litho.    **Perf. 13½x14**
885 A123 20c multi .20 .20
886 A123 30c multi .20 .20
887 A123 50c multi .20 .20
888 A123 1fr multi .20 .20
889 A123 3fr multi .20 .20
890 A123 10fr multi .70 .70
891 A123 55fr multi 1.10 .70
892 A123 60fr multi 1.25 .80
   Nos. 885-892 (8) 3.55 2.70

### Souvenir Sheet
**Perf. 13x13½**
893 A123 130fr multi 3.50 3.50

No. 893 contains one stamp 47x35mm.

### Christmas Type of 1968
Souvenir Sheet
Design: 200fr, Adoration of the Kings, by Albrecht Dürer, vert.
**1978, Dec. 11**    Engr.    **Perf. 11½**
894 A48 200fr brown 5.25 5.25

Nos. 532-533, Overprinted "1963" / "1978" in Black or Blue
**1978, Dec. 18**    Photo.    **Perf. 13½**
895 A83 6fr multi (Bk) .20 .20
896 A83 94fr multi (Bl) 1.90 1.25

---

Soccer, Rinet Cup, Flags of Netherlands and Peru — A122

11th World cup, Argentina, June 1-25. (Various Soccer Scenes and Flags of): 30c, (Sweden & Spain). 50c, (Scotland & Iran). 10fr, (many & Tunisia). 3fr, (Italy & Hungary). 10fr, (Brazil and Austria). 34fr, (Poland & Mexico). 100fr, (Argentina & France).

**1978, June 19**    **Perf. 13**
879 A122 20c multi .20 .20
879A A122 30c multi .20 .20
879B A122 50c multi .20 .20
880 A122 3fr multi .20 .20
881 A122 10fr multi .40 .20
882 A122 34fr multi 1.00 .40
883 A122 100fr multi 2.75 1.25
884 A122 100fr multi 4.95 2.85
   Nos. 879-884 (8)

Goats A124

**1978, Dec. 28**    Litho.    **Perf. 14**
897 A124 20c multi .20 .20
898 A124 30c multi .20 .20
899 A124 50c multi .20 .20
900 A124 3fr multi .20 .20
901 A124 5fr multi .50 .20
902 A124 15fr multi .50 .35

20c, Ducks, vert. 50c, Cock and chickens, vert. 4fr, Rabbits. 5fr, Pigs, vert. 15fr, Turkey. 50fr, Sheep and cattle, vert. 75fr, Bull.

## Souvenir Sheet

**Amalfi Coast, by Giacinto Gigante — A136**

**1980, Apr. 28    Photo.    Perf. 13½**

974 A136 200fr multi — 5.75 2.50

20th Int'l. Philatelic Exhibition, Europa '80, Naples, Apr. 26-May 4.

**Geaster Mushroom A137**

**1980, July 21    Photo.    Perf. 13½**

| No. | Type | Denom / Desc | | |
|---|---|---|---|---|
| 975 | A137 | 20c shown | .20 | .20 |
| 976 | A137 | 30c Lentinus atrobrunneus | .30 | .20 |
| 977 | A137 | 50c Gomphus stereoides | .40 | .20 |
| 978 | A137 | 4fr Cantharellus cibarius | .50 | .20 |
| 979 | A137 | 10fr Stilbothamnium dybowskii | .60 | .20 |
| 980 | A137 | 15fr Xeromphalina tenulipes | 1.75 | .50 |
| 981 | A137 | 70fr Podoscypha elegans | 6.00 | 1.75 |
| 982 | A137 | 100fr Mycena | 8.50 | 3.00 |
|  |  |  | 18.25 | 6.25 |

Nos. 975-982 (8)

**Still Life, by Renoir — A138**

Impressionist Painters: 30c, 26fr, At the Theater, by Toulouse-Lautrec, vert. 50c, 10fr, Seaside Garden, by Monet. 4fr, Mother and Child, by Mary Cassatt. 5fr, Starry Night, by Van Gogh. 10fr, Dancers at their Toilet, by Degas, vert. 50fr, The Card Players, by Cezanne. 70fr, Tahitian Women, by Gauguin, vert. 75fr, like 20c. 100fr, In the Park, by Seurat.

**1980, Aug. 4    Litho.    Perf. 14**

| No. | Type | Denom | | |
|---|---|---|---|---|
| 983 | A130 | 20c multi | .20 | .20 |
| 984 | A138 | 30c multi | .20 | .20 |
| 985 | A138 | 50c multi | .20 | .20 |
| 986 | A138 | 4fr multi | .20 | .20 |
| a. | | Sheet of 2, 26fr | 1.75 | 1.75 |
| 987 | A138 | 5fr multi | .20 | .20 |
| a. | | Sheet of 2, 5fr | 2.00 | 2.00 |
| 988 | A138 | 10fr multi | .20 | .20 |
| a. | | Sheet of 2, 10fr, 70fr | 2.00 | 2.00 |
| 989 | A138 | 50fr multi | 1.40 | .50 |
| a. | | Sheet of 2, 50fr, 10fr | 1.75 | 1.75 |
| 990 | A138 | 70fr multi | 1.60 | .70 |
| 991 | A138 | 100fr multi | 2.25 | 1.00 |
|  |  |  | 6.45 | 3.40 |

Nos. 983-991 (9)

---

**First Footstep on Moon, Spacecraft A133**

Spacecraft and Moon Exploration: 1.50fr, Descent onto lunar surface. 8fr, American flag. 30fr, Solar panels. 50fr, Gathering soil samples. 60fr, Adjusting sun screen. 200fr, Landing craft.

**1980, Jan. 31    Photo.    Perf. 13x13, 13½**

| No. | Type | Denom | | |
|---|---|---|---|---|
| 951 | A133 | 50c multi | .20 | .20 |
| 952 | A133 | 1.50fr multi | .20 | .20 |
| 953 | A133 | 8fr multi | .20 | .30 |
| 954 | A133 | 30fr multi | .70 | .30 |
| 955 | A133 | 50fr multi | .70 | .60 |
| 956 | A133 | 60fr multi | 1.40 | .60 |
|  |  |  | 4.20 | 2.00 |

Nos. 951-956 (6)

**Souvenir Sheet**

957 A133 200fr multi — 5.25 5.25

Apollo 11 moon landing, 10th anniv. (1979).

**Globe, Butare Chicago Club Emblems A134**

Rotary Int'l, 75th Anniv. (Globe, Emblems of Butare ur Kigali Clubs and): 30c, San Francisco, 1908. 50c, Chicago, 1910. 4fr, Buffalo, 1911. 15fr, London, 1911. 20fr, Glasgow, 1912. 50fr, Bristol, 1917. 60fr, Rotary Int'l, 1980.

**1980, Feb. 23    Litho.    Perf. 13**

| No. | Type | Denom | | |
|---|---|---|---|---|
| 958 | A134 | 20c multi | .20 | .20 |
| 959 | A134 | 30c multi | .20 | .20 |
| 960 | A134 | 50c multi | .20 | .20 |
| 961 | A134 | 4fr multi | .00 | .71 |
| 962 | A134 | 15fr multi | .40 | .50 |
| 963 | A134 | 20fr multi | 1.00 | .50 |
| 964 | A134 | 50fr multi | 1.00 | 1.00 |
| 965 | A134 | 60fr multi | 1.25 | .60 |
|  |  |  | 3.75 | 2.30 |

Nos. 950-965 (8)

**Gymnast, Moscow '80 Emblem A135**

**1980, Mar. 10    Perf. 12½**

| No. | Type | Denom | | |
|---|---|---|---|---|
| 966 | A135 | 20c shown | .20 | .20 |
| 967 | A135 | 30c Basketball | .20 | .20 |
| 968 | A135 | 50c Bicycling | .20 | .20 |
| 969 | A135 | 3fr Boxing | .20 | .20 |
| 970 | A135 | 20fr Archery | .50 | .50 |
| 971 | A135 | 26fr Weight lifting | .65 | .65 |
| 972 | A135 | 50fr Javelin | 1.25 | .50 |
| 973 | A135 | 100fr Fencing | 2.50 | 2.75 |
|  |  |  | 5.70 | 2.75 |

Nos. 966-973 (8)

22nd Summer Olympic Games, Moscow, July 19-Aug. 3.

---

**Basket Weaving A129**

**1979, Dec. 3    Perf. 12½x13, 13x12½    Litho.**

| No. | Type | Denom / Desc | | |
|---|---|---|---|---|
| 926 | A129 | 50c shown | .20 | .20 |
| 927 | A129 | 1.50fr Wood carving, vert. | .20 | .20 |
| 928 | A129 | 2fr Metal working | .20 | .20 |
| 929 | A129 | 5fr Jewelry, vert. | .20 | .20 |
| 930 | A129 | 20fr Straw plaiting | .45 | .40 |
| 931 | A129 | 26fr Wall painting, vert. | .60 | .25 |
| 932 | A129 | 40fr Pottery | .90 | .40 |
| 933 | A129 | 100fr Smelting, vert. | 2.25 | 1.00 |
|  |  |  | 5.00 | 2.65 |

Nos. 926-933 (8)

**Souvenir Sheet**

**Children of Different Races, Christmas Tree — A130**

« Joyeux Noël pour tous les enfants du monde »

**1979, Dec. 24    Engr.    Perf. 12**

934 A130 200fr ultra & dp mag — 6.00 3.00

Christmas; Int'l. Year of the Child.

**German East Africa #N5, Hill A131**

Sir Rowland Hill (1795-1870), originator of penny postage, and Stamps of Ruanda-Urundi or: 30c, German East Africa #N23. 50c, German East Africa #NB9. 3fr, #25. 10fr, #42. 26fr, #123. 100fr, #28.

**1979, Dec. 31    Litho.    Perf. 14**

| No. | Type | Denom | | |
|---|---|---|---|---|
| 935 | A131 | 20c multi | .20 | .20 |
| 936 | A131 | 30c multi | .20 | .20 |
| 937 | A131 | 50c multi | .20 | .20 |
| 938 | A131 | 3fr multi | .20 | .20 |
| 939 | A131 | 10fr multi | .20 | .20 |
| 940 | A131 | 15fr multi | .25 | .25 |
| 941 | A131 | 26fr multi | .65 | .60 |
| 942 | A131 | 100fr multi | 2.50 | 1.00 |
|  |  |  | 5.65 | 2.85 |

Nos. 935-942 (8)

**Sarothrura Pulchra A132**

Birds of the Nyungwe Forest: 20c Ploceus alienus, vert. 30c, Regal sunbird, vert. 3fr, Tockus alboterminatus. 10fr, Pygmy owl, vert. 26fr, Emerald cuckoo. 60fr, Finch, vert. 100fr, Stepanoaetus coronatus, vert.

**1980, Jan. 7    Perf. 13½x13, 13x13½    Photo.**

| No. | Type | Denom | | |
|---|---|---|---|---|
| 943 | A132 | 20c multi | .20 | .20 |
| 944 | A132 | 30c multi | .20 | .20 |
| 945 | A132 | 50c multi | .20 | .20 |
| 946 | A132 | 3fr multi | .20 | .20 |
| 947 | A132 | 10fr multi | .40 | .40 |
| 948 | A132 | 20fr multi | 1.10 | .40 |
| 949 | A132 | 60fr multi | 2.40 | 1.00 |
| 950 | A132 | 100fr multi | 3.75 | 2.25 |
|  |  |  | 8.25 | 4.65 |

Nos. 943-950 (8)

---

903 A124 50fr multi — 1.75 1.00
904 A124 75fr multi — 2.25 1.75
        5.50 4.10

Nos. 897-904 (8)

Husbandry Year.

**Papilio Demodocus A125**

Butterflies: 30c, Precis octavia. 50c, Charaxes smaragdalis. 4fr, Charaxes guderiana. 15fr, Colotis evippe. 30fr, Danaus limniace. 50fr, Bybilia acheloia. 150fr, Utetheisa pulchella.

**1979, Feb. 19    Photo.    Perf. 14½**

| No. | Type | Denom | | |
|---|---|---|---|---|
| 905 | A125 | 20c multi | .20 | .20 |
| 906 | A125 | 30c multi | .25 | .25 |
| 907 | A125 | 50c multi | .25 | .25 |
| 908 | A125 | 4fr multi | .35 | .35 |
| 909 | A125 | 15fr multi | .60 | .40 |
| 910 | A125 | 30fr multi | 1.50 | .80 |
| 911 | A125 | 50fr multi | 2.25 | 2.50 |
| 912 | A125 | 150fr multi | 10.85 | 4.75 |

Nos. 905-912 (8)

**Euphorbia Grantii, Weavers A126**

Design: 60fr, Drummers and Intelsat IV-A.

**1979, June 8    Photo.    Perf. 13**

913 A126 40fr multi — .95 .55
914 A126 60fr multi — 1.50 .80

Philexafrique II, Libreville, Gabon, June 8-17.

**Entandrophragma Excelsum — A127**

Trees and Shrubs: 20c, Polyscias fulva. 50c, Ilex mitis. 4fr, Kigelia Africana. 20fr, Ficus thonningi. 50fr, Acacia Senegal. 110fr, Symphonia globulifera. 100fr, Acacia sieberana. 20c, 50c, 15fr, 50fr, vertical.

**1979, Aug. 27    Perf. 14**

| No. | Type | Denom | | |
|---|---|---|---|---|
| 915 | A127 | 20c multi | .20 | .20 |
| 916 | A127 | 30c multi | .20 | .20 |
| 917 | A127 | 50c multi | .20 | .20 |
| 918 | A127 | 4 fr multi | .20 | .20 |
| 919 | A127 | 15fr multi | .25 | .25 |
| 920 | A127 | 20fr multi | .35 | .35 |
| 921 | A127 | 50fr multi | .65 | .65 |
| 922 | A127 | 110fr multi | 2.50 | 1.50 |
|  |  |  | 5.60 | 3.40 |

Nos. 915-922 (8)

**Black and White Boys, IYC Emblem A128**

**1979, Nov. 19    Perf. 13½x13, 13x13½    Photo.**

| No. | Type | Denom | | |
|---|---|---|---|---|
| 923 | A128 | 100fr multi | 3.50 | 3.50 |
| a. | | Block of 8 | 5.25 | 5.25 |
| b. | | 26fr, any single | .65 | .35 |
| 924 | A128 | 42fr multi | 1.25 | .55 |

**Souvenir Sheet**

925 A128 100fr multi — 3.50 3.50

Int'l Year of the Child. No. 923 printed in sheets of 16 (4x4).

Souvenir Sheet

NOËL 1980

Virgin of the Harpies, by Andrea Del Sarto — A139

**1980, Dec. 22**
992  A139  200fr multi ........... 5.25  3.00
Christmas.

RWANDA 10F

Belgian War of Independence, Engraving — A140

**1980, Dec. 22  Photogravure and Engraved  Perf. 11½**

Belgian Independence Sesquicentennial:
Engravings of War of Independence.

**1980, Dec. 29  Litho.  Perf. 12½**
993  A140  20c  pale grn & brn .......... .20  .20
994  A140  30c  brn org & brn ........... .20  .20
995  A140  50c  lt bl & brn ............. .20  .20
996  A140  8fr  yel & brn .............. .20  .20
997  A140  10fr brt lil & brn .......... .40  .20
998  A140  20fr ap grn & brn .......... 1.40  .70
999  A140  40fr pink & brn ........... 2.50  1.25
1000 A140  90fr lem & brn ............ 4.55  2.80
Nos. 993-1000 (8)

Swamp Drainage — A141

20c

Soil Conservation Year.

**1980, Dec. 31  Photo.  Perf. 13½**
1001  A141  20c  shown ................. .20  .20
1002  A141  30c  Fertilizer shed ....... .20  .20
1003  A141  1.50fr Rice fields ......... .20  .20
1004  A141  8fr  Tree planting ......... .20  .20
1005  A141  10fr Terrace planting ...... .30  .20
1006  A141  40fr Farm buildings ....... 1.10  .55
1007  A141  90fr Bean cultivation ..... 2.50  1.25
1008  A141  100fr Tea cultivation ..... 4.20
Nos. 1001-1008 (8)

Rwanda  20c
PAVETTA RWANDENSIS

Pavetta Rwandensis — A142

**1981, Apr. 6  Photo.  Perf. 13½x13½**
1009  A142  20c  shown ................. .20  .20
1010  A142  30c  Cyrtorchis .......... .20  .20
1011  A142  50c  Pavonia urens ....... .20  .20
1012  A142  4fr  Cynorkis kass-
         nerana ...................... .20  .20
1013  A142  5fr  Gardenia
         ternifolia ................... .25  .20
1014  A142  10fr Leptactina
         platyphylia ................. .25  .20

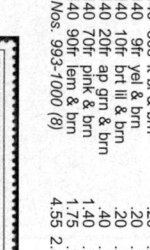

SOS VILLAGE D'ENFANTS  RWANDA  10f

Girl Knitting — A143

SOS Children's Village: Various children.

**1981, Apr. 27  Perf. 13**
1015  A142  20fr Lobelia petio-
         lata ......................... .50  .25
1016  A142  40fr Tapinanthus ........ .25  .25
1017  A142  70fr Impatiens
         niamniamen- .................
         sis .......................... 1.25  .75
1018  A142  150fr Dissotis
         rwandensis ................. 2.25  1.00
Nos. 1009-1018 (10)

SOS Children's Village: Various children.

**1981, Apr. 27  Perf. 13**
1019  A143  20c  multi ................. .20  .20
1020  A143  30c  multi ................. .20  .20
1021  A143  50c  multi ................. .20  .20
1022  A143  1fr  multi ................. .20  .20
1023  A143  8fr  multi ................. .20  .20
1024  A143  10fr multi ................. .25  .20
1025  A143  70fr multi ................ 1.50  .70
1026  A143  150fr multi .............. 3.25  1.50
Nos. 1019-1026 (8)

RWANDA  20c

Carolers, by Norman Rockwell — A144

Designs: Saturday Evening Post covers by
Norman Rockwell.

**1981, May 11  Litho.  Perf. 13½x14**
1027  A144  20c  multi ................. .20  .20
1028  A144  30c  multi ................. .20  .20
1029  A144  50c  multi ................. .20  .20
1030  A144  1fr  multi ................. .20  .20
1031  A144  8fr  multi ................. .20  .20
1032  A144  20fr multi ................. .75  .30
1033  A144  40fr multi ............... 1.50  .70
1034  A144  70fr multi ............... 2.40
Nos. 1027-1034 (8)

Cerval  A145

RWANDA  20c

Designs: Meat-eating animals.

**1981, June 29  Photo.  Perf. 13½x14**
1035  A145  20c  shown ................. .20  .20
1036  A145  30c  Jackals .............. .20  .20
1037  A145  2fr  Genet ................ .20  .20
1038  A145  2.50fr Banded mon-
         goose ....................... .20  .20
1039  A145  10fr Zorille .............. .20  .20
1040  A145  15fr White-
         cheeked otter ............... .40
1041  A145  70fr Golden
         cat ......................... 2.75  1.50
1042  A145  200fr Hunting dog,
         vert. ...................... 6.75  3.50
Nos. 1035-1042 (8)

RWANDA  20c

Drummer Sending Message — A146

**1981, Sept. 1  Litho.  Perf. 13**
1043  A146  20c  shown ................. .20  .20
1044  A146  30c  Map, communi-
         cation waves ................ .20  .20
1045  A146  2fr  Jet, radar
         screen ...................... .20  .20
1046  A146  2.50fr Satellite,
         teletype .................... .25  .20
1047  A146  10fr Dish antenna ....... .40  .20
1048  A146  15fr Ship, navigation
         devices ..................... .25  .20
1049  A146  70fr Helicopter ......... 1.75  .90
1050  A146  200fr Satellite with
         solar panels ............... 5.00  2.50
Nos. 1043-1050 (8)

RWANDA  20c

1500th Birth Anniv. of St. Benedict — A147

Paintings and Frescoes of St. Benedict:
20c, Leaving his Parents, Mt. Oliveto Monastery, Maggiore. 30c, Oldest portrait, 10th
cent., St. Chrisogone Church, Rome, vert.
50c, Portrait, Virgin of the Misericord polyp-
tich, Borgo San Sepolcro. 4fr, Giving the
Rules of the order to his Monks, Mt. Oliveto
Monastery. 5fr, Monks at their Meal, Mt.
Oliveto Monastery. 20fr, Portrait, 13th cent.,
Lower Chruch of the Holy Spirit, Subiaco, vert.
70fr, Our Lady in Glory with Sts. Gregory and
Benedict, San Gimignaio, vert. 100fr, Priest
Carrying Easter Meal to St. Benedict, by Jan
van Coninxloo, 16th cent.

**1981, Nov. 30  Photo.**
**Perf. 13½x13, 13x13½**
1051  A147  20c  multi ................. .20  .20
1052  A147  30c  multi ................. .20  .20
1053  A147  50c  multi ................. .20  .20
1054  A147  4fr  multi ................. .20  .20
1055  A147  5fr  multi ................. .20  .20
1056  A147  20fr multi ................. .45  .20
1057  A147  70fr multi ............... 1.50  .70
1058  A147  100fr multi .............. 2.00
Nos. 1051-1058 (8)

RWANDA  20c

Intl. Year of the Disabled — A148

**1981, Dec. 7  Litho.  Perf. 13**
1059  A148  20c  Painting ............. .20  .20
1060  A148  30c  Soccer .............. .20  .20
1061  A148  4.50fr Crocheting ......... .20  .20
1062  A148  5fr  Painting vase ........ .20  .20
1063  A148  10fr Sawing .............. .20  .20
1064  A148  60fr Sign language ...... 1.25  .65
1065  A148  70fr Doing puzzle ....... 1.40  .80
1066  A148  100fr Juggling .......... 2.00  1.10
Nos. 1059-1066 (8)

Souvenir Sheet

Noël 1981

Christmas — A149

**1981, Dec. 21  Photo. & Engr.  Perf. 13½**
1067  A149  200fr Adoration of the
         Kings, by van
         der Goes ................... 5.25  5.25

World Food Day, Oct. 16, 1981 — A151

RWANDA  20c

**1982, Jan. 25  Litho.  Perf. 13**
1068  A150  20c  Deer drinking ....... .20  .20
1069  A150  30c  Women carrying
         water, vert. ................ .20  .20
1070  A150  50c  Pipeline ............ .20  .20
1071  A150  10fr Filling pan, vert. .. .45  .25
1072  A150  15fr Drinking ........... .45  .25
1073  A150  70fr Mother, child,
         vert. ...................... 1.50  .75
1074  A150  100fr Lake pumping
         station, vert. ............. 5.00  2.90
Nos. 1068-1074 (7)

Natl. Rural Water Supply Year — A150

**1981, Dec. 28  Litho.  Perf. 12½**

**1982, Jan. 25  Litho.  Perf. 13**
1075  A151  20fr Cattle .............. .20  .20
1076  A151  30c  Bee ................. .20  .20
1077  A151  50c  Fish ................ .20  .20
1078  A151  8fr  Avocados ............ .20  .20
1079  A151  8fr  Boy eating ba-
         nana ....................... .20  .20
1080  A151  20fr Sorghum ............. .45  .20
1081  A151  70fr Vegetables ......... 1.50  .65
1082  A151  100fr Balanced diet .... 5.05  2.85
Nos. 1075-1082 (8)

RWANDA  20c

Hibiscus Berberidifolius — A152

**1982, June 14  Litho.  Perf. 13**
1083  A152  20c  shown ................. .20  .20
1084  A152  30c  Hypericum
         olatum, vert. ............... .20  .20
1085  A152  50c  Canarina ernini ...... .20  .20
1086  A152  4fr  Crocheting .......... .20  .20
1087  A152  10fr Polygala ruwen-
         oriensis ................... .20  .20
1088  A152  35fr Kniphofia grantii,
         vert. ...................... .20  .20
1089  A152  70fr Euphorbia cande-
         labrum, vert. .............. 1.00  .45
1090  A152  80fr Disa erubescens,
         vert. ...................... 2.00  .75
Nos. 1083-1090 (8)

RWANDA  20f

20th Anniv. of Independence — A153

**1982, June 28  Perf. 13**
1091  A153  10fr Flags .............. .20  .20
1092  A153  20fr Hands releasing
         doves ...................... .45  .30
1093  A153  30fr Flag, handshake ... 1.10  .65
1094  A153  200fr Govt. buildings .. 2.40  1.20
Nos. 1091-1094 (4)

## Local Trees — A165

**Litho. Perf. 13½x13**

**1984, Jan. 15**

| | | | | |
|---|---|---|---|---|
| 1167 | A165 | 20c Hagenia abyssinica | .20 | .20 |
| 1168 | A165 | 30c Dracaena steudneri | .20 | .20 |
| 1169 | A165 | 50c Phoenix reclinata | .20 | .20 |
| 1170 | A165 | 10fr Podocarpus milanjianus | .20 | .20 |
| 1171 | A165 | 19fr Entada abyssinica | .40 | .25 |
| 1172 | A165 | 70fr Parinari excelsa | .60 | .75 |
| 1173 | A165 | 100fr Newtonia buchananii | 2.00 | 1.00 |
| 1174 | A165 | 200fr Acacia gerrardi, vert. | 4.75 | 2.00 |
| | | Nos. 1167-1174 (8) | 10.95 | 4.80 |

## World Communications Year — A166

**1984, May 21 Litho. Perf. 12½**

| | | | | |
|---|---|---|---|---|
| 1175 | A166 | 20c Train | .20 | .20 |
| 1176 | A166 | 30c Ship | .20 | .20 |
| 1177 | A166 | 50c Radio | .20 | .20 |
| 1178 | A166 | 4.50fr Telephone | .20 | .20 |
| 1179 | A166 | 15fr Mail | .20 | .25 |
| 1180 | A166 | 50fr Jet | 1.25 | .50 |
| 1181 | A166 | 70fr Satellite, TV screen | 1.75 | .75 |
| 1182 | A166 | 100fr Satellite | 2.50 | 1.00 |
| | | Nos. 1175-1182 (8) | 6.50 | 3.25 |

## 1st Manned Flight Bicent. — A167

Historic flights: 20c, Le Martial, Sept. 19, 1783, 30c, La Montgolfiere, Nov. 21, 1783, and 50c, Charles and Robert, Dec. 1, 1783, and Blanchard, Mar. 2, 1784. 9fr, Jean-Pierre Blanchard and wife in balloon. 10fr, Blanchard and Jeffries, 1785. 50fr, E. Demuyter, 1937. 80fr, Propane gas balloons. 200fr, Abruzzo, Anderson and Newman, 1978.

**1984, June 4 Litho. Perf. 13**

| | | | | |
|---|---|---|---|---|
| 1183 | A167 | 20c multi | .20 | .20 |
| 1184 | A167 | 30c multi | .20 | .20 |
| 1185 | A167 | 50c multi | .20 | .20 |
| 1186 | A167 | 9fr multi | .20 | .20 |
| 1187 | A167 | 10fr multi | .25 | .50 |
| 1188 | A167 | 50fr multi | 1.25 | .80 |
| 1189 | A167 | 80fr multi | 1.75 | .80 |
| 1190 | A167 | 200fr multi | 4.50 | 2.00 |
| | | Nos. 1183-1190 (8) | 8.50 | 4.30 |

1984 Summer Olympics — A168

---

## A161

**1983, Feb. 14 Perf. 14½**

| | | | | |
|---|---|---|---|---|
| 1140 | A161 | 20c Driving cattle | .20 | .20 |
| 1141 | A161 | 30c Pineapple field | .20 | .20 |
| 1142 | A161 | 50c Interrupted ditching | .20 | .20 |
| 1143 | A161 | 9fr Hedges, ditches | .20 | .20 |
| 1144 | A161 | 10fr Reafforestation | .20 | .20 |
| 1145 | A161 | 20fr Anti erosion barriers | .40 | .20 |
| 1146 | A161 | 30fr Contour planting | .60 | .50 |
| 1147 | A161 | 50fr Terracing | 1.00 | .50 |
| 1148 | A161 | 60fr Protection of river banks | 1.25 | .60 |
| 1149 | A161 | 70fr Fallow, planted strips | 1.40 | .65 |
| | | Nos. 1140-1149 (10) | 5.65 | 3.25 |

For overprints & surcharges see #1247-1255.

Cardinal Cardijn (1882-1967) A162

Gorilla — A163

Young Catholic Workers Movement Activities. Inscribed 1982.

**1983, Feb. 22 Perf. 12½x13**

| | | | | |
|---|---|---|---|---|
| 1150 | A162 | 20c Feeding ducks | .20 | .20 |
| 1151 | A162 | 30c Harvesting bananas | .20 | .20 |
| 1152 | A162 | 50c Carrying melons | .20 | .20 |
| 1153 | A162 | 9fr Shoemakers | .25 | .25 |
| 1154 | A162 | 19fr Shoemakers | .50 | .50 |
| 1155 | A162 | 20fr Growing millet | .50 | .25 |
| 1156 | A162 | 70fr Embroidering | 1.75 | .75 |
| 1157 | A162 | 80fr shown | 2.00 | 1.00 |
| | | Nos. 1150-1157 (8) | 5.60 | 3.00 |

Various gorillas Nos. 1158-1163 horiz.

**1983, Mar. 14 Perf. 14**

| | | | | |
|---|---|---|---|---|
| 1158 | A163 | 20c multi | .20 | .20 |
| 1159 | A163 | 30c multi | .20 | .20 |
| 1160 | A163 | 9.50fr multi | .20 | .20 |
| 1161 | A163 | 10fr multi | .20 | .30 |
| 1162 | A163 | 20fr multi | 1.00 | 1.00 |
| 1163 | A163 | 30fr multi | 1.50 | .50 |
| 1164 | A163 | 60fr multi | 2.75 | 1.10 |
| 1165 | A163 | 70fr multi | 3.00 | 1.25 |
| | | Nos. 1158-1165 (8) | 9.05 | 3.95 |

**Souvenir Sheet**

RAPHAËL 1483 1520
NOËL
MADONNE DU GRAND DUC PALAIS PITTI-FLORENCE

The Granduca Madonna, by Raphael — A164

**1983, Dec. 19 Typo. & Engr. Perf. 11½**

| | | | | |
|---|---|---|---|---|
| 1166 | A164 | 200fr multi | 5.25 | 5.25 |

Christmas.

---

10th Anniv. of UN Conference on Human Environment — A158

**1982, Dec. 27 Litho. Perf. 14**

| | | | | |
|---|---|---|---|---|
| 1112 | A158 | 20c Elephants | .20 | .20 |
| 1113 | A158 | 30c Lion | .20 | .20 |
| 1114 | A158 | 50c Flower | .20 | .20 |
| 1115 | A158 | 4fr Deer | .20 | .20 |
| 1116 | A158 | 5fr Bull | .20 | .25 |
| 1117 | A158 | 10fr Flower, diff. | .20 | .25 |
| 1118 | A158 | 20fr Zebras | .55 | .75 |
| 1119 | A158 | 40fr Crowned cranes | 1.10 | .60 |
| 1120 | A158 | 50fr Bird | 1.25 | .75 |
| 1121 | A158 | 70fr Woman pouring coffee beans | 1.75 | 1.00 |
| | | Nos. 1112-1121 (10) | 5.85 | 3.80 |

Scouting Year A159

**1983, Jan. 17 Photo.**

| | | | | |
|---|---|---|---|---|
| 1122 | A159 | 20c Animal first aid | .20 | .20 |
| 1123 | A159 | 30c Camp | .20 | .20 |
| 1124 | A159 | 1.50fr Campfire | .20 | .20 |
| 1125 | A159 | 8fr Scout giving sign | .20 | .25 |
| 1126 | A159 | 10fr Knot | .20 | .50 |
| 1127 | A159 | 20fr Camp, diff. | 1.00 | 1.00 |
| 1128 | A159 | 70fr Chopping wood | 3.25 | 1.75 |
| 1129 | A159 | 90fr Sign, map | 3.75 | 2.00 |
| | | Nos. 1122-1129 (8) | 9.00 | 5.25 |

For overprints see Nos. 1234-1241.

Nectar-sucking Birds — A160

**1983, Jan. 31 Perf. 14x14½, 14½x14 Litho.**

| | | | | |
|---|---|---|---|---|
| 1130 | A160 | 20c Angola nectar bird | .20 | .20 |
| 1131 | A160 | 30c Royal nectar birds | .20 | .20 |
| 1132 | A160 | 50c Johnston's nectar bird | .20 | .20 |
| 1133 | A160 | 4fr Bronze nectar birds | .20 | .20 |
| 1134 | A160 | 5fr Collared souimangas | .20 | .20 |
| 1135 | A160 | 10fr Blue-headed nectar bird | .60 | .25 |
| 1136 | A160 | 20fr Purple-bellied nectar bird | .80 | .35 |
| 1137 | A160 | 40fr Copper nectar bird | 1.60 | .55 |
| 1138 | A160 | 50fr Olive-bellied nectar birds | 2.25 | .80 |
| 1139 | A160 | 70fr Red-breasted nectar bird | 3.00 | 1.10 |
| | | Nos. 1130-1139 (10) | | 4.05 |

---

1982 World Cup — A154

Designs: Various soccer players.

**1982, July 6 Perf. 14x14½**

| | | | | |
|---|---|---|---|---|
| 1095 | A154 | 20c multi | .20 | .20 |
| 1096 | A154 | 30c multi | .20 | .20 |
| 1097 | A154 | 1.50fr multi | .20 | .20 |
| 1098 | A154 | 8fr multi | .20 | .20 |
| 1099 | A154 | 10fr multi | .20 | .25 |
| 1100 | A154 | 20fr multi | .60 | .35 |
| 1101 | A154 | 70fr multi | 2.00 | .75 |
| 1102 | A154 | 90fr multi | 2.50 | 1.10 |
| | | Nos. 1095-1102 (8) | 6.10 | 3.20 |

TB Bacillus Centenary — A155

**1982, Nov. 22 Litho. Perf. 14½**

| | | | | |
|---|---|---|---|---|
| 1103 | A155 | 10fr Microscope, slide | .20 | .20 |
| 1104 | A155 | 20fr Serum, slide | .50 | 1.00 |
| 1105 | A155 | 70fr Lungs, slide | 2.50 | 1.75 |
| 1106 | A155 | 100fr Koch | 3.00 | 1.75 |
| | | Nos. 1103-1106 (4) | 6.20 | 3.15 |

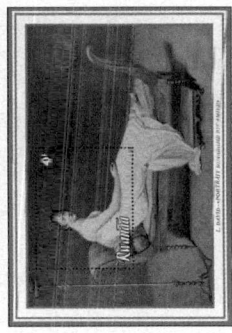

Madam Recamier, by David — A156

PHILEXFRANCE '82 Intl. Stamp Exhibition, Paris, June 11-21: No. 1108, St. Anne and Virgin and Child with Franciscan Monk, by H. van der Goes. No. 1109, Liberty Guiding the People, by Delacroix. No. 1110, Pygmalion, by P. Delvaux.

**Souvenir Sheets**

**1982, Dec. 11 Perf. 13½**

| | | | | |
|---|---|---|---|---|
| 1107 | A156 | 40fr multi | 2.10 | 2.10 |
| 1108 | A156 | 40fr multi | 2.10 | 2.10 |
| 1109 | A156 | 60fr multi | 2.10 | 2.10 |
| 1110 | A156 | 60fr multi | 2.10 | 2.10 |
| | | Nos. 1107-1110 (4) | 8.40 | 8.40 |

**Souvenir Sheet**

NOËL 1982
REPOS PENDANT LA FUITE - H.E. MILLO - 1618-1682 - ERMITAGE - LENINGRAD

Rest During the Flight to Egypt, by Murillo — A157

**1982, Dec. 20 Photo. & Engr. Perf.**

| | | | | |
|---|---|---|---|---|
| 1111 | A157 | 200fr carmine rose | 5.25 | 5.25 |

Christmas.

**1984, July 16**    **Perf. 14**

| 1191 | A168 | 20c Equestrian | .20 | .20 |
|---|---|---|---|---|
| 1192 | A168 | 30c Wind surfing | .20 | .20 |
| 1193 | A168 | 50c Soccer | .20 | .20 |
| 1194 | A168 | 9fr Swimming | .20 | .20 |
| 1195 | A168 | 10fr Field hockey | 1.25 | .50 |
| 1196 | A168 | 40fr Fencing | 1.25 | 1.50 |
| 1197 | A168 | 80fr Running | 2.50 | 1.00 |
| 1198 | A168 | 200fr Boxing | 5.00 | 2.00 |
| | | Nos. 1191-1198 (8) | 9.75 | 4.50 |

**Zebras and Buffaloes — A169**

**1984, Nov. 26**    **Litho.**    **Perf. 13**

| 1199 | A169 | 20c Zebra with colt | .20 | .20 |
|---|---|---|---|---|
| 1200 | A169 | 30c Buffalo with calf, vert. | .20 | .20 |
| 1201 | A169 | 50c Two zebras, vert. | .20 | .20 |
| 1202 | A169 | 9fr Zebras fighting | .20 | .20 |
| 1203 | A169 | 10fr Buffalo, vert. | .20 | .20 |
| 1204 | A169 | 80fr Zebra herd | 2.00 | 1.25 |
| 1205 | A169 | 100fr Zebra, vert. | 3.00 | 1.50 |
| 1206 | A169 | 200fr Buffalo | 12.50 | 6.75 |
| | | Nos. 1199-1206 (8) | | |

**Souvenir Sheet**

La Sainte Vierge adorant l'Enfant Jésus
LE CORRÈGE 1489-1534
Palais des Offices - Florence

**Christmas 1984 — A170**

**1984, Dec. 24**    **Typo. & Engr.**

| 1207 | A170 | 200fr Virgin and Child, by Correggio | 5.25 | 5.25 |
|---|---|---|---|---|

**Gorilla Gorilla Beringei — A171**

**1985, Mar. 25**    **Litho.**    **Perf. 13**

| 1208 | A171 | 10fr Adults and young | 2.50 | .75 |
|---|---|---|---|---|
| 1209 | A171 | 15fr Female holding young | 4.00 | 1.25 |
| 1210 | A171 | 25fr Female holding young | 7.50 | 2.50 |
| 1211 | A171 | 30fr Three adults | 9.00 | 3.50 |
| | | Nos. 1208-1211 (4) | 23.00 | 8.00 |

**Souvenir Sheet**    **Perf. 11½x12**

| 1212 | A171 | 200fr Baby climbing branch, vert. | 11.00 | 11.00 |
|---|---|---|---|---|

No. 1212 contains one 37x52mm stamp.

---

**Self-Sufficiency in Food Production — A172**

Designs: 20c, Raising chickens and turkeys. 30c, Pineapple harvest. 50c, Grain products. 9fr, Grain products. 10fr, Animal husbandry. 50fr, Sowing grain. 80fr, Food reserves. 100fr, Banana harvest.

**1985, Mar. 30**

| 1213 | A172 | 20c multi | .20 | .20 |
|---|---|---|---|---|
| 1214 | A172 | 30c multi | .20 | .20 |
| 1215 | A172 | 50c multi | .20 | .20 |
| 1216 | A172 | 9fr multi | .20 | .20 |
| 1217 | A172 | 10fr multi | .20 | .20 |
| 1218 | A172 | 50fr multi | .80 | .60 |
| 1219 | A172 | 80fr multi | 1.25 | .60 |
| 1220 | A172 | 100fr multi | 1.75 | .90 |
| | | Nos. 1213-1220 (8) | 4.80 | 2.90 |

**Natl. Redevelopment Movement, 10th Anniv. — A173**

**1985, July 5**

| 1221 | A173 | 10fr multi | .20 | .20 |
|---|---|---|---|---|
| 1222 | A173 | 30fr multi | .90 | .20 |
| 1223 | A173 | 70fr multi | 1.75 | .50 |
| | | Nos. 1221-1223 (3) | 2.85 | .90 |

**UN, 40th Anniv. A174**

**1985, July 25**

| 1224 | A174 | 50fr multi | 1.25 | .45 |
|---|---|---|---|---|
| 1225 | A174 | 100fr multi | 2.75 | .75 |

Illustrations of North American bird species by John J. Audubon.

**Audubon Birth Bicent. — A175**

**1985, Sept. 18**

| 1226 | A175 | 10fr Barn owl | .20 | .20 |
|---|---|---|---|---|
| 1227 | A175 | 20fr White-faced owl | .40 | .30 |
| 1228 | A175 | 40fr Red-breasted hummingbird | 2.00 | 1.00 |
| 1229 | A175 | 80fr Warbler | 4.00 | 1.75 |
| | | Nos. 1226-1229 (4) | 6.60 | 3.25 |

**Intl. Youth Year A176**

**1985, Oct. 14**    **Perf. 13½x14½**

| 1230 | A176 | 7fr Education and agriculture | .20 | .20 |
|---|---|---|---|---|
| 1231 | A176 | 9fr Bicycling | .20 | .20 |
| 1232 | A176 | 44fr Construction | 1.25 | .40 |
| 1233 | A176 | 80fr Schoolroom | 2.00 | .75 |
| | | Nos. 1230-1233 (4) | 3.65 | 1.55 |

Nos. 1122-1129 Ovptd. in Green or Rose Violet with the Girl Scout Trefoil and "1910/1985"

**Natl. Girl Scout Movement, 75th anniv.**

**1985, Nov. 25**

| 1234 | A159 | 20c multi | .20 | .20 |
|---|---|---|---|---|
| 1235 | A159 | 30c multi (RV) | .20 | .20 |
| 1236 | A159 | 1.50fr multi (RV) | .20 | .20 |
| 1237 | A159 | 8fr multi (RV) | .30 | .20 |
| 1238 | A159 | 20fr multi | .75 | .35 |
| 1239 | A159 | 50fr multi (RV) | 1.25 | .90 |
| 1240 | A159 | 70fr multi (RV) | 3.00 | 1.00 |
| 1241 | A159 | 90fr multi | 3.45 | .90 |
| | | Nos. 1234-1241 (8) | 9.35 | 3.75 |

**Souvenir Sheet**

**Adoration of the Magi, by Titian — A177**

**1985, Dec. 24**

| 1242 | A177 | 200fr violet | 5.00 | 5.00 |
|---|---|---|---|---|

Christmas.

**Photo. & Engr.**    **Perf. 11½**

---

**Transportation and Communication — A178**

**1986, Jan. 27**    **Litho.**    **Perf. 13**

| 1243 | A178 | 10fr Hand-canceling letters | .25 | .20 |
|---|---|---|---|---|
| 1244 | A178 | 30fr Articulated truck | .75 | .20 |
| 1245 | A178 | 40fr Kigali Satellite Station | 1.25 | .30 |

**Size: 52x34mm**

| 1246 | A178 | 80fr Kayibanda Airport, Kigali | 2.00 | .75 |
|---|---|---|---|---|
| | | Nos. 1243-1246 (4) | 4.25 | 1.45 |

Nos. 1141-1149 Surcharged or Ovptd. with Silver Bar and "ANNÉE 1986 / INTENSIFICATION AGRICOLE"

**1986, May 5**    **Litho.**    **Perf. 14½**

| 1247 | A161 | 9fr #143 | .20 | .20 |
|---|---|---|---|---|
| 1248 | A161 | 10fr on 30c #141 | .20 | .20 |
| 1249 | A161 | 10fr on 50c #142 | .20 | .20 |
| 1250 | A161 | 10fr shown | .20 | .20 |
| 1251 | A161 | 10fr like #144 | .60 | .20 |
| 1252 | A161 | 30fr like #145 | .60 | .20 |
| 1253 | A161 | 30fr like #146 | 1.00 | .75 |
| 1254 | A161 | 60fr #148 | 2.00 | 1.25 |
| 1255 | A161 | 70fr #149 | 2.50 | 1.75 |
| | | Nos. 1247-1255 (9) | 8.40 | 5.20 |

**Christmas, Intl. Peace Year — A181**

**1986, Dec. 24**    **Litho.**    **Perf. 13**

| 1270 | A181 | 10fr shown | .20 | .20 |
|---|---|---|---|---|
| 1271 | A181 | 15fr Dove, Earth | .50 | .25 |
| 1272 | A181 | 40fr like #141 | .90 | .90 |
| 1273 | A181 | 70fr like 15fr | 2.00 | 1.00 |
| | | Nos. 1270-1273 (4) | 3.60 | 1.75 |

**UN Child Survival Campaign A182**

**1987, Feb. 13**

| 1274 | A182 | 4fr Breast feeding | .20 | .20 |
|---|---|---|---|---|
| 1275 | A182 | 6fr Rehydration therapy | .20 | .20 |
| 1276 | A182 | 10fr Immunization | .20 | .20 |
| 1277 | A182 | 70fr Growth monitoring | 2.75 | .70 |
| | | Nos. 1274-1277 (4) | 3.35 | 1.30 |

---

**1986 World Cup Soccer Championships, Mexico — A179**

Various soccer plays, natl. flags.

**1986, June 16**    **Perf. 13**

| 1256 | A179 | 2fr Morocco, England | .20 | .20 |
|---|---|---|---|---|
| 1257 | A179 | 4fr Paraguay, Iraq | .20 | .20 |
| 1258 | A179 | 5fr Brazil, Spain | .20 | .20 |
| 1259 | A179 | 10fr Italy, Argentina | .50 | .20 |
| 1260 | A179 | 40fr Mexico, Belgium | 2.25 | 1.00 |
| 1261 | A179 | 45fr France, USSR | 2.50 | 1.50 |
| | | Nos. 1256-1261 (6) | 5.55 | 3.30 |

For overprints see Nos. 1360-1365.

**Akagera Natl. Park — A180**

**1986, Dec. 15**    **Litho.**    **Perf. 13**

| 1262 | A180 | 4fr Antelopes | .20 | .20 |
|---|---|---|---|---|
| 1263 | A180 | 7fr Shoebills | .20 | .20 |
| 1264 | A180 | 9fr Cape elands | .20 | .20 |
| 1265 | A180 | 10fr Giraffe | .20 | .20 |
| 1266 | A180 | 80fr Elephants | 3.75 | .90 |
| 1267 | A180 | 90fr Crocodiles | 4.25 | 1.10 |

**Size: 48x34mm**

| 1268 | A180 | 100fr Weaver birds | 4.50 | 2.00 |
|---|---|---|---|---|
| 1269 | A180 | 100fr Pelican, zebras | 4.50 | 2.00 |
| a. | | Pair, #1268-1269 + label | 9.00 | 4.00 |
| | | Nos. 1262-1269 (8) | 17.80 | 6.80 |

No. 1269a has continuous design.

## Year of Natl. Self-sufficiency in Food Production — A183

**1987, June 15**    Litho.    *Perf. 13*
| | | | | |
|---|---|---|---|---|
| 1278 | A183 | 5fr Farm | .20 | .20 |
| 1279 | A183 | 7fr Storing produce | .20 | .20 |
| 1280 | A183 | 40fr Boy carrying basket of fish, produce | .50 | .75 |
| 1281 | A183 | 60fr Tropical fruit | 1.50 | 1.65 |
| | | Nos. 1278-1281 (4) | 2.90 | 1.65 |

## Natl. Independence, 25th Anniv. — A184

10fr, Pres. Habyarimana, soldiers, farmers. 40fr, Pres. officiating government session. 70fr, Pres., Pope John Paul II. 100fr, Pres.

| | | | | |
|---|---|---|---|---|
| 1283 | A184 | 10fr multi | .25 | .20 |
| 1284 | A184 | 40fr multi | 1.40 | .60 |
| 1285 | A184 | 70fr multi | 2.50 | 1.25 |
| 1286 | A184 | 100fr multi, vert. | 3.25 | 1.75 |
| | | Nos. 1283-1286 (4) | 7.40 | 3.80 |

## Fruit — A185

**1987, Sept. 28**
| | | | | |
|---|---|---|---|---|
| 1287 | A185 | 10fr Bananas, vert. | .25 | .20 |
| 1288 | A185 | 40fr Pineapples | 1.10 | .45 |
| 1289 | A185 | 80fr Papayas | 2.25 | .90 |
| 1290 | A185 | 90fr Avocados | 2.50 | 1.25 |
| 1291 | A185 | 100fr Strawberries, vert. | 2.75 | 1.50 |
| | | Nos. 1287-1291 (5) | 8.80 | 4.30 |

## Leopards — A186

**1987, Nov. 18**    Litho.    *Perf. 13*
| | | | | |
|---|---|---|---|---|
| 1292 | A186 | 50fr Female, cub | 2.50 | .60 |
| 1293 | A186 | 50fr Three cubs | 2.50 | .60 |
| 1294 | A186 | 50fr Adult attacking gazelle | 2.50 | .60 |
| 1295 | A186 | 50fr In tree | 2.50 | .60 |
| 1296 | A186 | 50fr Leaping from tree | 2.50 | .60 |
| a. | | strip of 5, Nos. 1292-1296 | 12.50 | 12.50 |

## Intl. Year of the Volunteer — A187

**1987, Dec. 12**
| | | | | |
|---|---|---|---|---|
| 1297 | A187 | 5fr Constructing village water system | .20 | .20 |
| 1298 | A187 | 12fr Education, vert. | .30 | .25 |
| 1299 | A187 | 20fr Modern housing, vert. | .75 | .30 |
| 1300 | A187 | 60fr Animal husbandry, vert. | 2.00 | .75 |
| | | Nos. 1297-1300 (4) | 3.25 | 1.50 |

### Souvenir Sheet

NOËL 1987
LA VIERGE À L'ENFANT
FRA ANGELICO
(c. 1387 - 1455)
RIJKSMUSEUM - AMSTERDAM

## Virgin and Child, by Fra Angelico (c. 1387-1455) — A188

**1987, Dec. 24**    Engr.    *Perf. 11½*
| | | | | |
|---|---|---|---|---|
| 1301 | A188 | 200fr deep mag & dull blue | 5.00 | 5.00 |

Christmas.

## Maintenance of the Rural Economy Year — A189

**1988, June 13**    Litho.    *Perf. 13*
| | | | | |
|---|---|---|---|---|
| 1302 | A189 | 10fr Furniture store | .30 | .20 |
| 1303 | A189 | 40fr Daily form | 1.60 | .50 |
| 1304 | A189 | 60fr Produce market | 2.10 | .80 |
| 1305 | A189 | 80fr Fruit market | 5.00 | 2.50 |
| | | Nos. 1302-1305 (4) | | |

## Primates, Nyungwe Forest — A190

**1988, Sept. 15**    Litho.    *Perf. 13*
| | | | | |
|---|---|---|---|---|
| 1306 | A190 | 2fr Chimpanzee | .20 | .20 |
| 1307 | A190 | 3fr Black and white colobus | .25 | .20 |
| 1308 | A190 | 10fr Pygmy galago | .25 | .25 |
| 1309 | A190 | 90fr Cercopithecidae ascagne | 1.00 | |
| | | Nos. 1306-1309 (4) | 7.00 | 3.00 |
| | | | 8.45 | 3.65 |

## 1988 Summer Olympics, Seoul — A191

**1988, Sept. 19**
| | | | | |
|---|---|---|---|---|
| 1310 | A191 | 5fr Boxing | .20 | .20 |
| 1311 | A191 | 7fr Relay | .20 | .20 |
| 1312 | A191 | 8fr Table tennis | .20 | .20 |
| 1313 | A191 | 10fr Women's running | .75 | .20 |
| 1314 | A191 | 90fr Hurdles | 4.25 | 1.75 |
| | | Nos. 1310-1314 (5) | 5.60 | 2.55 |

## Organization of African Unity, 25th Anniv. — A192

**1988, Nov. 30**    Litho.    *Perf. 13*
| | | | | |
|---|---|---|---|---|
| 1315 | A192 | 5fr shown | .20 | .20 |
| 1316 | A192 | 7fr Handshake, map | .20 | .20 |
| 1317 | A192 | 8fr "OAU" in brick, map | .20 | .20 |
| 1318 | A192 | 90fr Slogan | 2.50 | 1.50 |
| | | Nos. 1315-1318 (4) | 3.10 | 2.10 |

### Souvenir Sheet

NOËL 1988
La Vierge à la soupe
VERONESE
1528 - 1588
Villa di Maser - Italie

## Detail of The Virgin and the Soup, by Paolo Veronese — A193

**1988, Dec. 23**    Engr.    *Perf. 13½*
| | | | | |
|---|---|---|---|---|
| 1319 | A193 | 200fr multicolored | 6.25 | 5.25 |

Christmas. Margin is typographed.

## Intl. Red Cross and Red Crescent Organizations, 125th Anniv. — A194

**1988, Dec. 30**    Litho.    *Perf. 13*
| | | | | |
|---|---|---|---|---|
| 1320 | A194 | 10fr Refugees | .25 | .20 |
| 1321 | A194 | 30fr First aid | .80 | .50 |
| 1322 | A194 | 40fr Elderly | 1.00 | .50 |
| 1323 | A194 | 100fr Travelling doctor | 2.60 | 1.25 |
| | | Nos. 1320-1323 (4) | 4.65 | 2.35 |

## Medicinal Plants — A195

**1989, Feb. 15**    Litho.    *Perf. 13*
| | | | | |
|---|---|---|---|---|
| 1324 | A195 | 5fr Plectranthus barbatus | .20 | .20 |
| 1325 | A195 | 10fr Tetradenia riparia | .40 | .25 |
| 1326 | A195 | 20fr Hygrophila auriculata | 1.25 | .40 |
| 1327 | A195 | 40fr Datura stramonium | 2.50 | .75 |
| 1328 | A195 | 50fr Pavetta ternifolia | 3.00 | 1.75 |
| | | Nos. 1324-1328 (5) | 7.35 | 3.35 |

## Interparliamentary Union, Cent. — A196

**1989, Oct. 20**    Litho.    *Perf. 13*
| | | | | |
|---|---|---|---|---|
| 1329 | A196 | 10fr shown | .30 | .30 |
| 1330 | A196 | 30fr Hills, lake | .85 | .50 |
| 1331 | A196 | 70fr Hills, stream | 2.10 | 1.10 |
| 1332 | A196 | 90fr Sun rays, hills | 2.75 | 1.50 |
| | | Nos. 1329-1332 (4) | 6.00 | 3.30 |

### Souvenir Sheet

NOËL 1989
L'Adoration des Mages
P.P. RUBENS
(1577-1640)
Musées Royaux des Beaux-Arts Bruxelles

## Christmas — A197

Adoration of the Magi by Rubens.

**1989, Dec. 29**    Engr.    *Perf. 11½*
| | | | | |
|---|---|---|---|---|
| 1333 | A197 | 100fr blk, red & grn | 5.00 | 5.00 |

## Rural Organization Year — A198

Designs: 10fr, Making pottery. 70fr, Carrying produce to market. 90fr, Firing clay pots. 100fr, Clearing land.

**1989, Dec. 29**    Litho.    *Perf. 13½x13*
| | | | | |
|---|---|---|---|---|
| 1334 | A198 | 10fr multi | .40 | .20 |
| 1335 | A198 | 70fr multi, vert. | 1.75 | 1.25 |
| 1336 | A198 | 90fr multi | 2.25 | 1.75 |
| 1337 | A198 | 200fr multi | 5.00 | 4.00 |
| | | Nos. 1334-1337 (4) | 9.40 | 7.20 |

## Revolution, 30th Anniv. (in 1989) — A199

Designs: 10fr, Improved living conditions. 60fr, Couple, farm tools. 70fr, Modernization. 100fr, Flag, map, native.

## 1990, Jan. 22 — Perf. 13

| 1338 | A199 | 10fr multi | .35 | .20 |
| 1339 | A199 | 60fr multi, vert. | 2.00 | 1.10 |
| 1340 | A199 | 70fr multi | 2.25 | 1.25 |
| 1341 | A199 | 100fr multi | 3.25 | 1.85 |

Nos. 1338-1341 (4)    7.85   4.40

Inscribed 1989.

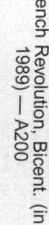

French Revolution, Bicent. (in 1989) — A200

Paintings of the Revolution: 10fr, Triumph of Marat by Boilly; 60fr, Rouget de Lisle singing La Marseillaise by Pils; 70fr, Oath of the Tennis Court; 100fr, Trial of Louis XVI by David.

### 1990, Jan. 22

| 1342 | A200 | 10fr multicolored | .20 | .20 |
| 1343 | A200 | 60fr multicolored | 2.00 | 1.10 |
| 1344 | A200 | 70fr multicolored | 2.25 | 1.25 |
| 1345 | A200 | 100fr multicolored | 3.25 | 1.90 |

Nos. 1342-1345 (4)    7.85   4.45

Inscribed 1989.

African Development Bank, 25th Anniv. (in 1989) — A201

### 1990, Feb. 22 — Perf. 13½x13

| 1346 | A201 | 10fr Building construction | .35 | .20 |
| 1347 | A201 | 20fr Harvesting | .70 | .45 |
| 1348 | A201 | 40fr Cultivation | 1.40 | .75 |
| 1349 | A201 | 90fr Building, truck, harvesters | 3.00 | 1.60 |

Nos. 1346-1349 (4)    5.45   3.00

Belgica '90, Intl. Philatelic Exhibition — A202

Illustration reduced.

### 1990, May 21 — Imperf.

| 1350 | A202 | 100fr Great Britain #1 | 3.50 | 1.75 |
| 1351 | A202 | 100fr Belgium #B1011 | 3.50 | 1.75 |
| 1352 | A202 | 100fr Rwanda #516 | 3.50 | 1.75 |

Nos. 1350-1352 (3)    10.50   5.25

Visit of Pope John Paul II A203

### 1990, Aug. 27 — Litho. — Perf. 13½x13

| 1353 | A203 | 10fr shown | 1.75 | .20 |
| 1354 | A203 | 70fr Holding crucifix | 11.00 | 1.25 |

### Souvenir Sheet — Perf. 11½

| 1355 | A203 | 100fr Hands together | 17.50 | 17.50 |

No. 1355 contains one 36x51mm stamp.

---

Designs: 10fr, Teacher seated at desk. 20fr, Teacher at blackboard. 50fr, Small outdoor class. 90fr, Large outdoor class.

### 1991, Jan. 25 — Litho. — Perf. 13½x13

| 1356 | A204 | 10fr multicolored | .20 | .20 |
| 1357 | A204 | 20fr multicolored | .55 | .25 |
| 1358 | A204 | 50fr multicolored | 1.25 | .55 |
| 1359 | A204 | 90fr multicolored | 2.50 | 1.00 |

Nos. 1356-1359 (4)    4.50   2.00

Intl. Literacy Year A204

Nos. 1256-1261 Ovptd. in Black on Silver

### 1990, May 25 — Litho. — Perf. 13

| 1360 | A179 | 2fr | .20 | .20 |
| 1361 | A179 | 4fr | .20 | .20 |
| 1362 | A179 | 5fr | .20 | .20 |
| 1363 | A179 | 10fr | .50 | .35 |
| 1364 | A179 | 40fr | 9.50 | 9.00 |
| 1365 | A179 | 45fr | 11.00 | 10.00 |

Nos. 1360-1365 (6)    21.60   19.95

on No. 1256 No. 1256
on No. 1257 No. 1257
on No. 1258 No. 1258
on No. 1259 No. 1259
on No. 1260 No. 1260
on No. 1261 No. 1261

Self-help Organizations — A205

### 1991, Jan. 25 — Litho. — Perf. 13½x13

| 1366 | A205 | 10fr Tool making | .30 | .20 |
| 1367 | A205 | 20fr Animal husbandry | .75 | .35 |
| 1368 | A205 | 50fr Textile manufacturing | 1.60 | .80 |
| 1369 | A205 | 90fr Road construction | 2.25 | 1.50 |

Nos. 1366-1369 (4)    4.90   2.85

Dated 1990.

Cardinal Lavigerie, Founder of the Order of White Fathers and Sisters, Death Cent. A206

5fr, Statue of Madonna. 15fr, One of the Order's nuns. 70fr, Group photo. 110fr, Cardinal Lavigerie.

### 1992, Oct. 1 — Litho. — Perf. 14

| 1370 | A206 | 5fr multi, vert. | .20 | .20 |
| 1371 | A206 | 15fr multi, vert. | .20 | .20 |
| 1372 | A206 | 70fr multi, vert. | 20.00 | 15.00 |
| 1373 | A206 | 110fr multi, vert. | 27.50 | 22.50 |

Nos. 1370-1373 (4)    47.90   37.90

1992 Summer Olympic Games, Barcelona A207

---

Designs: a, 20fr, Runners. b, 30fr, Swimmer. c, 90fr, Soccer players.

### 1993, Feb. 1

| 1374 | A207 | Sheet of 3, #a.-c. | 27.50 | 27.50 |

Protection of Vegetable Crops A208

Designs: 10fr, Removing parasites and weeds. 15fr, Spraying pesticides. 70fr, Zonocerus elegans on plants. 110fr, Phenacoccus manihoti.

### 1993, June 15 — Litho. — Perf. 14

| 1375 | A208 | 10fr multicolored | .20 | .20 |
| 1376 | A208 | 15fr multicolored | .20 | .20 |
| 1377 | A208 | 70fr multicolored | 17.50 | 17.50 |
| 1378 | A208 | 110fr multicolored | 27.50 | 27.50 |

Nos. 1375-1378 (4)    45.40   45.40

World Conference on Nutrition, Rome — A209

Designs: 15fr, Man fishing. 50fr, People at fruit market. 100fr, Man milking cow. 500fr, Mother breastfeeding.

### 1992, Dec. — Litho. — Perf. 14

| 1381 | A209 | 15fr multicolored | .20 | .20 |
| 1382 | A209 | 50fr multicolored | 2.75 | 2.75 |
| 1383 | A209 | 100fr multicolored | 4.50 | 4.50 |
| 1384 | A209 | 500fr multicolored | 22.50 | 22.50 |

Nos. 1381-1384 (4)    29.95   29.95

Wildlife A210

### 1998

| 1385 | A210 | 15fr Toad | .20 | .20 |
| 1386 | A210 | 100fr Snail | 1.50 | 1.50 |
| 1387 | A210 | 150fr Porcupine | 2.50 | 2.50 |
| 1388 | A210 | 300fr Chameleon | 4.75 | 4.75 |

a.   Souvenir sheet #1385-1388. Imperf. | 9.00 | 9.00 |

Nos. 1385-1388 (4)

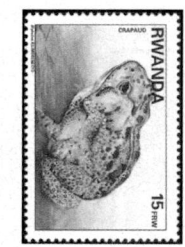

Plants A211

15fr, Opuntia. 100fr, Gloriosa superba. 150fr, Markhamia lutea. 300fr, Hagenia abyssinica.

### 1998 — Litho. — Perf. 14

| 1389 | A211 | 15fr multi, vert. | .20 | .20 |
| 1390 | A211 | 100fr multi, vert. | 1.50 | 1.50 |
| 1391 | A211 | 150fr multi, vert. | 2.50 | 2.50 |
| 1392 | A211 | 300fr multi, vert. | 4.75 | 4.75 |

a.   Souvenir sheet, #1389-1392, imperf. | 11.00 | 11.00 |

Nos. 1389-1392 (4)    8.95   8.95

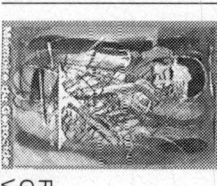

Remembrance of Genocide Victims — A212

### 1999 (?) — Litho. — Perf. 14

| 1392B | A212 | 20fr Map, coffins, horiz. | | |
| 1392C | A212 | 30fr Orphans, horiz. | | |
| 1393 | A212 | 200fr multicolored | | |
| 1394 | A212 | 400fr multicolored | | |

The editors suspect that more stamps were issued in this set, and would like to examine any examples.

Rwandan postal officials have declared "illegal" sets depicting: Millennium (eleven sheets of 9 with various subjects). Pornography (two sheets of 9). Chess (sheet of 9 unoverprinted, and also overprinted in Russian). Double-decker buses (sheet of 9). Butterflies (sheet of 9). Old automobiles (sheet of 9). Hot air balloons (sheet of 9). Motorcycle racing (sheet of 9). Trains (sheet of 9). Fungi (sheet of 6). Cats (sheet of 6). Roses (sheet of 6). Sheet of six stamps of various values depicting Wildlife Trusts (Snakes). Souvenir sheet of two 500fr stamps depicting Mother Teresa. Souvenir sheet of one 500fr stamp depicting Wildlife Trusts (Snakes).

---

## SEMI-POSTAL STAMPS

No. 305 Surcharged in Black and Overprinted in Brown: "SECHERESSE/SOLIDARITE AFRICAINE"

### 1973, Aug. 23 — Photo. — Perf. 13

| B1 | A53 | 100fr + 50fr multi | 2.50 | 2.25 |

African solidarity in drought emergency.

Nos. 349-350 Surcharged and Overprinted Like Nos. 693-698

### 1975, Nov. 10 — Litho. — Perf. 13

| B2 | A60 | 50fr + 25fr multi | 1.75 | 1.00 |
| B3 | A60 | 90fr + 25fr multi | 2.40 | 1.50 |

African solidarity in drought emergency.

---

## AIR POST STAMPS

### African Postal Union Issue, 1967
#### Common Design Type

### 1967, Sept. 18 — Engr. — Perf. 13

| C1 | CD124 | 6fr brown, rose d & gray | .20 | .20 |
| C2 | CD124 | 18fr brt lil, ol brn & plum | .40 | .30 |
| C3 | CD124 | 30fr green, dp bl & red | .65 | .50 |

Nos. C1-C3 (3)    1.25   1.00

African solidarity in drought emergency.

### PHILEXAFRIQUE Issue

Alexandre Lenoir, by Jacques L. David AP1

### 1968, Dec. 30 — Photo. — Perf. 12½

| C4 | AP1 | 100fr emerald & multi | 2.00 | .80 |

Issued to publicize PHILEXAFRIQUE, Philatelic exhibition in Abidjan, Feb. 14-23, 1969. Printed with alternating emerald label.

## RWANDA (continued)

### 2nd PHILEXAFRIQUE Issue

Ruanda-Urundi No. 123, Cowherd and Lake Victoria — AP2

**1969, Feb. 14      Litho.      Perf. 14**

| | | | |
|---|---|---|---|
| C5 | AP2 50fr multicolored | .90 | .80 |

Opening of PHILEXAFRIQUE, Abidjan, 2/14.

### Painting Type of Regular Issue

Paintings and Music: 50fr, The Music Lesson, by Fragonard. 100fr, Angels' Concert, by Memling, horiz.

**1969, Mar. 31      Photo.      Perf. 13**

| | | | |
|---|---|---|---|
| C6 | A49 50fr gold & multi | 1.25 | .60 |
| C7 | A49 100fr gold & multi | 2.50 | 2.00 |

### African Postal Union Issue, 1971
Common Design Type

Design: Woman and child of Rwanda and UAMPT Building, Brazzaville, Congo.

**1971, Nov. 13      Perf. 13x13½**

| | | | |
|---|---|---|---|
| C8 | CD135 100fr blue & multi | 1.75 | 1.75 |

No. C8 Overprinted in Red

**1973, Sept. 17   Photo.   Perf. 13x13½**

| | | | |
|---|---|---|---|
| C9 | CD135(a) 100fr multi | 3.00 | 3.00 |
| C10 | CD135(b) 100fr multi | 3.00 | 3.00 |
| a. | Pair, #C9-C10 | 6.00 | 6.00 |

3rd Conference of French-speaking countries, Liège, Sept. 15-Oct. 14. Overprints alternate checkerwise in same sheet.

Sassenage Castle, Grenoble — AP3

**1977, June 20   Litho.   Perf. 12½**

| | | | |
|---|---|---|---|
| C11 | AP3 50fr multi | 1.25 | 1.00 |

Intl. French Language Council, 10th anniv.

### Philexafrique II-Essen Issue
Common Design Types

Designs: No. C12, Okapi, Rwanda #239. No. C13, Woodpecker, Oldenburg #4.

**1978, Nov. 1   Litho.   Perf. 12½**

| | | | |
|---|---|---|---|
| C12 | CD138 30fr multi | 1.00 | 1.00 |
| C13 | CD139 30fr multi | 1.00 | 1.00 |
| a. | Pair, #C12-C13 | 2.00 | 2.00 |

## SAAR
sär

**LOCATION**—On the Franco-German border southeast of Luxembourg
**POP.**—1,400,000 (1959)
**AREA**—991 sq. mi.
**CAPITAL**—Saarbrücken

A former German territory, the Saar was administered by the League of Nations 1920-35. After a January 12, 1935, plebiscite, it returned to Germany, and the use of German stamps was resumed. After World War II, France occupied the Saar and later established a protectorate. The provisional semi-independent State of Saar was established Jan. 1, 1951. France returned the Saar to the German Federal Republic Jan. 1, 1957. Saar stamps were discontinued in 1959 and replaced by stamps of the German Federal Republic.

100 Pfennig = 1 Mark
100 Centimes = 1 Franc (1921)

> **Catalogue values for unused stamps in this country are for Never Hinged items, beginning with Scott 221 in the regular postage section, and Scott B85 in the semi-postal section.**

### Watermark

Wmk. 285 — Marbleized Pattern

### German Stamps of 1906-19 Overprinted

Overprinted

**1920, Jan. 30      Perf. 14, 14½      Wmk. 125**

| | | | | |
|---|---|---|---|---|
| 1 | A22 | 2pf gray | 1.10 | 3.75 |
| d. | | Double overprint | 1,750. | 2,400. |
| 2 | A22 | 2½pf gray | 8.50 | 25.00 |
| 3 | A16 | 3pf brown | .90 | 2.00 |
| 4 | A16 | 5pf green | .40 | .90 |
| f. | | Double overprint | 775.00 | 1,275. |
| 5 | A22 | 7½pf orange | .55 | 1.25 |
| 6 | A16 | 10pf carmine | .40 | .90 |
| d. | | Double overprint | 625.00 | 1,100. |
| 7 | A22 | 15pf dk violet | .40 | .90 |
| c. | | Double overprint | 700.00 | 1,250. |
| 8 | A16 | 20pf blue violet | .45 | .85 |
| c. | | Double overprint | 525.00 | 850.00 |
| 9 | A16 | 25pf org & blk, yel | 8.75 | 17.50 |
| 10 | A16 | 30pf org & blk, buff | 16.00 | 27.50 |
| 11 | A22 | 35pf red brown | .45 | .85 |
| 12 | A16 | 40pf lake & blk | .50 | .90 |
| 13 | A16 | 60pf pur & blk, buff | .50 | .85 |
| 14 | A16 | 60pf red violet | .50 | 1.10 |
| 15 | A16 | 75pf green & blk | .45 | .90 |
| 16 | A16 | 80pf green & blk, rose | 175.00 | 240.00 |

### Bavarian Stamps of 1914-16 Overprinted

Overprint forgeries exist.

**Inverted Overprint**

| | | | | |
|---|---|---|---|---|
| 1c | A22 | 2pf gray | 275.00 | 450.00 |
| 2c | A22 | 2½pf gray | 275.00 | 575.00 |
| 3c | A16 | 3pf brown | 275.00 | 500.00 |
| 4c | A16 | 5pf green | 525.00 | 700.00 |
| 6c | A22 | 7½pf orange | | 1,000. |
| 6d | A16 | 10pf carmine | 500.00 | 2,100. |
| 11c | A22 | 35pf red brown | 350.00 | 900.00 |
| 11d | A16 | 40pf org & blk, yel | 350.00 | 700.00 |
| 12c | A16 | 40pf lake & blk, buff | 425.00 | 700.00 |
| 15c | A16 | 60pf pur & blk, buff | 425.00 | 900.00 |
| 15d | A17 | 75pf green & black | 210.00 | 350.00 |
| 17a | A17 | 1m carmine rose | 625.00 | 1,250. |

**Wmk. 95      Perf. 14x14½**

**1920, Mar. 1**

| | | | | |
|---|---|---|---|---|
| 19 | A10 | 2pf gray | | 1.40 |
| 20 | A10 | 3pf brown | .65 | 1.75 |
| 21 | A10 | 5pf yellow grn | | 1.40 |
| a. | | Double overprint | 775.00 | 4,250. |
| 22 | A10 | 7½pf green | 70.65 | 575.00 |
| 23 | A10 | 10pf carmine | 27.50 | 1.40 |
| 24 | A10 | 15pf vermilion | .65 | 575.00 |
| a. | | Double overprint | .90 | 1.75 |
| 25 | A16 | 15pf carmine | 360.00 | 12.50 |
| 26 | A10 | 20pf blue | 6.25 | 1.40 |
| a. | | Double overprint | .55 | 14.00 |
| 27 | A10 | 25pf gray | 275.00 | 14.00 |
| 28 | A10 | 30pf orange | 10.00 | 2.10 |
| 30 | A10 | 40pf olive green | 5.75 | |
| 31 | A10 | 50pf red brown | 9.25 | 575.00 |
| a. | | Double overprint | 1.40 | 8.50 |
| 32 | A10 | 60pf dark green | 325.00 | |

Overprinted

**1m brown / 1m dark brown**

| | | | | |
|---|---|---|---|---|
| 35 | A11 | 1m brown | 17.50 | 32.50 |
| 36 | A11 | 7m violet | 14.00 | 27.50 |
| 37 | A11 | 3m scarlet | 52.50 | 125.00 |
| | | Nos. 35-37 (3) | 162.50 | 297.50 |

**Perf. 11½**

| | | | | |
|---|---|---|---|---|
| 38 | A12 | 5m deep blue | 575.00 | 775.00 |
| 39 | A12 | 10m yellow green | 110.00 | 200.00 |
| a. | | Double overprint | 2,800. | 7,000. |

Nos. 19, 20 and 22 were not officially issued, but were available for postage. Examples are known legitimately used on cover. The 20m type A12 was also overprinted in small quantity. Overprint forgeries exist.

### German Stamps of 1906-20 Overprinted

Overprinted

**1920, Mar. 26      Wmk. 125      Perf. 14, 14½**

| | | | | |
|---|---|---|---|---|
| 41 | A16 | 5pf green | .20 | .40 |
| 42 | A16 | 5pf red brown | .40 | .70 |
| 43 | A16 | 8pf orange | .35 | .40 |
| 44 | A16 | 15pf dk violet | .40 | .40 |
| 46 | A16 | 20pf blue violet | .40 | .40 |
| 47 | A16 | 30pf org & blk | .40 | .40 |
| 48 | A16 | 30pf org & blk, buff | .30 | .65 |
| a. | | Double overprint | | |
| 49 | A16 | 30pf dull blue | .65 | .50 |
| 50 | A16 | 40pf lake & blk | .20 | .40 |

### Germany No. 90 Surcharged in Black

| | | | | |
|---|---|---|---|---|
| 51 | A16 | 40pf carmine rose | .90 | .65 |
| 52 | A16 | 50pf pur & blk, buff | .20 | .40 |
| a. | | Double overprint | 65.00 | 325.00 |
| 53 | A16 | 60pf red violet | .40 | .40 |
| 54 | A16 | 75pf green & blk | .65 | .40 |
| a. | | Double overprint | 95.00 | 325.00 |
| 55 | A17 | 1.25m green | 1.25 | 1.10 |
| 56 | A17 | 1.50m yellow brn | 1.25 | 1.10 |
| 57 | A21 | 2.50m lilac rose | 3.25 | 10.00 |
| 58 | A16 | 4m black & rose | 7.00 | 20.00 |
| a. | | Double overprint | | |
| | | Nos. 41-58 (18) | 17.85 | 38.60 |

On No. 57 the overprint is placed vertically at each side of the stamp. Counterfeit overprints exist.

**Inverted Overprint**

| | | | | |
|---|---|---|---|---|
| 41a | A16 | 5pf green | 15.00 | 140.00 |
| 43a | A16 | 10pf carmine | 15.00 | 300.00 |
| 44a | A16 | 10pf orange | 14.00 | |
| 45a | A16 | 15pf dark violet | 25.00 | 210.00 |
| 46a | A16 | 20pf blue violet | 25.00 | |
| 48b | A16 | 30pf org & blk | | |
| 50a | A16 | 40pf lake & blk | | 225.00 |
| 52b | A16 | 50pf pur & blk, buff | | |
| 53a | A16 | 60pf red violet | 70.00 | |
| 54b | A16 | 75pf green & black | 110.00 | |
| 55a | A17 | 1.25m green | 90.00 | |
| 56a | A17 | 1.50m yellow brown | 90.00 | |

### Germany No. 120 Surcharged

**1921, Feb.**

| | | | | |
|---|---|---|---|---|
| 65 | A16 | 20pf on 75pf grn & blk | | 1.00 |
| a. | | Inverted surcharge | | |
| b. | | Double surcharge | | |
| 66 | A22 | 5m on 15pf vio brn | 4.50 | 13.00 |
| 67 | A22 | 10m on 15pf vio brn | 5.50 | 17.00 |
| | | | 10.35 | 31.00 |

Forgeries exist of Nos. 66-67.

Minor at Work — A4
Old Mill near Mettlach — A3
Entrance to Reden Mine — A5
Saar River Traffic — A6
Saar River near Mettlach — A7
Slag Pile at Völklingen — A8

730 SAAR

SAARGEBIET
50
Signal Bridge, Saarbrücken — A9

SAARGEBIET
60
Church at Mettlach — A10

SAARGEBIET
80
"Old Bridge," Saarbrücken A11

SAARGEBIET
1
Cable Railway at Ferne — A12

SAARGEBIET
1.25 MARK
Colliery Shafthead — A13

SAARGEBIET
2 M
Saarbrücken City Hall — A14

SAARGEBIET
3
Pottery at Mettlach — A15

SAARGEBIET
5 M
St. Ludwig's Cathedral — A16

SAARGEBIET
10
Presidential Residence, Saarbrücken A17

SAARGEBIET
25
Burbach Steelworks, Dillingen A18

**1921 Unwmk. Typo. *Perf. 12½***

| | | | | |
|---|---|---|---|---|
| **68** | A3 | 5pf ol grn & vio | .30 | *.35* |
| *a.* | | Tête bêche pair | 6.25 | *17.50* |
| *c.* | | Center inverted | 52.50 | 190.00 |
| **69** | A4 | 10pf org & ultra | .30 | *.35* |
| **70** | A5 | 20pf grn & slate | .30 | *.70* |
| *a.* | | Tête bêche pair | 10.50 | *35.00* |
| *c.* | | Perf. 10½ | 19.00 | *190.00* |
| *d.* | | As "c," tête bêche pair | 175.00 | *525.00* |
| **71** | A6 | 25pf brn & dk bl | .35 | *.70* |
| *a.* | | Tête bêche pair | 12.50 | *35.00* |
| **72** | A7 | 30pf gray grn & brn | .35 | *.55* |
| *a.* | | Tête bêche pair | 21.00 | *62.50* |
| *c.* | | 30pf ol grn & blk | 2.10 | *17.50* |
| *d.* | | As "c," tête bêche pair | 19.00 | *65.00* |
| *e.* | | As "c," imperf., pair | 95.00 | |
| **73** | A8 | 40pf vermilion | .35 | .35 |
| *a.* | | Tête bêche pair | 32.50 | *70.00* |
| **74** | A9 | 50pf gray & blk | .85 | *3.50* |
| **75** | A10 | 60pf red & dk brn | 1.40 | *2.75* |
| **76** | A11 | 80pf deep blue | .65 | *.90* |
| *a.* | | Tête bêche pair | 35.00 | *100.00* |
| **77** | A12 | 1m lt red & blk | .70 | *1.40* |
| *a.* | | 1m grn & blk | *625.00* | |
| **78** | A13 | 1.25m lt brn & dk grn | .85 | *1.75* |
| **79** | A14 | 2m red & black | 2.10 | *3.50* |
| **80** | A15 | 3m brn & dk ol | 2.75 | *7.75* |
| *a.* | | Center inverted | 92.50 | |
| **81** | A16 | 5m yellow & vio | 8.50 | *20.00* |
| **82** | A17 | 10m grn & red brn | 10.50 | *21.00* |
| **83** | A18 | 25m ultra, red & blk | 30.00 | *62.50* |
| | | *Nos. 68-83 (16)* | 60.25 | *128.05* |

Values for tête bêche are for vertical pair. Horizontal pairs sell for about twice as much.

The ultramarine ink on No. 69 appears to be brown where it overlays the orange.

Exist imperf. but were not regularly issued.

Nos. 70-83 Surcharged in Red, Blue or Black

a 
SAARGEBIET
5 cent.

b 
SAARGEBIET
1 Fr.

c 
SAARGEBIET
5 FRANKEN

**1921, May 1**

| | | | | |
|---|---|---|---|---|
| **85** | A5(a) | 3c on 20pf (R) | .35 | .40 |
| *a.* | | Tête bêche pair | 5.25 | *27.50* |
| *b.* | | Inverted surcharge | 100.00 | |
| *d.* | | Perf. 10½ | 5.25 | *100.00* |
| *e.* | | As "d," tête bêche pair | 22.50 | |
| **86** | A6(a) | 5c on 25pf (R) | .35 | .35 |
| *a.* | | Tête bêche pair | 95.00 | *350.00* |
| **87** | A7(a) | 10c on 30pf (Bl) | .35 | .35 |
| *a.* | | Tête bêche pair | 5.00 | *22.50* |
| *b.* | | Inverted surcharge | 110.00 | *375.00* |
| *c.* | | Double surcharge | 100.00 | *425.00* |
| **88** | A8(a) | 15c on 40pf (Bk) | .45 | .40 |
| *a.* | | Tête bêche pair | 95.00 | *325.00* |
| *b.* | | Inverted surcharge | 110.00 | *375.00* |
| **89** | A9(a) | 20c on 50pf (R) | .35 | .35 |
| **90** | A10(a) | 25c on 60pf (Bl) | .45 | .35 |
| **91** | A11(a) | 30c on 80pf (Bk) | 1.40 | .90 |
| *a.* | | Tête bêche pair | 13.00 | *52.50* |
| *c.* | | Inverted surcharge | 140.00 | *525.00* |
| *d.* | | Double surcharge | *150.00* | *525.00* |
| **92** | A12(a) | 40c on 1m (Bl) | 1.75 | .40 |
| *a.* | | Inverted surcharge | 140.00 | *375.00* |
| *b.* | | Double surcharge | 150.00 | *525.00* |
| **93** | A13(a) | 50c on 1.25m (Bk) | 2.75 | .90 |
| *a.* | | Double surcharge | 275.00 | *825.00* |
| *b.* | | Perf. 10½ | 72.50 | *125.00* |
| **94** | A14(a) | 75c on 2m (Bl) | 2.75 | 1.25 |
| *a.* | | Inverted surcharge | 125.00 | |
| **95** | A15(b) | 1fr on 3m (Bl) | 3.25 | 2.10 |
| **96** | A16(b) | 2fr on 5m (Bl) | 12.50 | 5.50 |
| **97** | A17(b) | 3fr on 10m (Bk) | 15.00 | *22.50* |
| *b.* | | Double surcharge | 190.00 | *700.00* |
| **98** | A18(c) | 5fr on 25m (Bl) | 17.00 | *32.50* |
| | | *Nos. 85-98 (14)* | 58.70 | *68.25* |

In these surcharges the period is occasionally missing and there are various wrong font and defective letters.

Values for tête bêche are for vertical pairs. Horizontal pairs sell for about twice as much.

Nos. 85-89, 91, 93, 97-98 exist imperf. but were not regularly issued.

SAARGEBIET
3
Cable Railway, Ferne — A19

SAARGEBIET
5 cent
Miner at Work — A20

SAARGEBIET
10
"Old Bridge," Saarbrücken A21

SAARGEBIET
Cent 20 Cent
Saarbrücken City Hall — A22

SAARGEBIET
30
Slag Pile at Völklingen A23

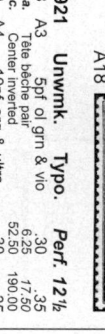

SAARGEBIET
Cent 40 Cent
Pottery at Mettlach — A24

SAARGEBIET
Cent 50 Cent
Saar River Traffic — A25

SAARGEBIET
Fr 1 Fr
St. Ludwig's Cathedral A26

SAARGEBIET
Fr 2 Fr
Colliery Shafthead A27

SAARGEBIET
3
Mettlach Church — A28

SAARGEBIET
Fr 5 Fr
Burbach Steelworks, Dillingen A29

***Perf. 12½x13½, 13½x12½***

**1922-23 Typo.**

| | | | | |
|---|---|---|---|---|
| **99** | A19 | 3c ol grn & straw | .35 | *.55* |
| **100** | A20 | 5c orange & blk | .35 | .35 |
| **101** | A21 | 10c blue green | .35 | .35 |
| **102** | A19 | 15c deep brown | 1.00 | .35 |
| **103** | A19 | 15c orange ('23) | 2.10 | .35 |
| **104** | A22 | 20c dk bl & lem | 10.50 | .35 |
| **105** | A22 | 20c brt bl & straw ('23) | 3.50 | .35 |
| **106** | A22 | 25c red & yellow | 3.75 | 1.75 |
| **107** | A22 | 25c mag & straw ('23) | 2.10 | .35 |
| **108** | A23 | 30c carmine & yel | 1.75 | 1.75 |
| **109** | A24 | 40c brown & yel | .85 | .35 |
| **110** | A25 | 50c dk bl & straw | .85 | .35 |
| **111** | A24 | 75c dp grn & straw | 10.50 | *17.50* |
| **112** | A24 | 75c blk & straw ('23) | 27.50 | 2.75 |
| **113** | A26 | 1fr brown red | 2.10 | .70 |
| **114** | A27 | 2fr deep violet | 3.25 | 2.50 |
| **115** | A28 | 3fr org & dk grn | 14.50 | 5.50 |
| **116** | A29 | 5fr brn & red brn | 14.50 | *40.00* |
| | | *Nos. 99-116 (18)* | 99.80 | *76.15* |

Nos. 99-116 exist imperforate but were not regularly issued.

For overprints see Nos. O1-O15.

10
SAARGEBIET
Madonna of Blieskastel — A30

**1925, Apr. 9 Photo. *Perf. 13½x12½***

**Size: 23x27mm**

| | | | | |
|---|---|---|---|---|
| **118** | A30 | 45c lake brown | 2.50 | *3.50* |

**Size: 31½x36mm**

***Perf. 12***

| | | | | |
|---|---|---|---|---|
| **119** | A30 | 10fr black brown | 14.00 | *77.50* |

Nos. 118-119 exist imperf. but were not regularly issued.

For overprint see No. 154.

SAARGEBIET
10
Market Fountain, St. Johann — A31

SAARGEBIET
15
View of Saar Valley A32

SAARGEBIET
60
Colliery Shafthead A35

SAARGEBIET
1.50
Burbach Steelworks A36

Designs: 15c, 75c, View of Saar Valley. 20c, 40c, 90c, Scene from Saarlouis fortifications. 25c, 50c, Tholey Abbey.

**1927-32 *Perf. 13½***

| | | | | |
|---|---|---|---|---|
| **120** | A31 | 10c deep brown | .65 | .30 |
| **121** | A32 | 15c olive black | .35 | *.90* |
| **122** | A32 | 20c brown orange | .35 | .30 |
| **123** | A32 | 25c bluish slate | .65 | .30 |
| **124** | A31 | 30c olive green | .85 | .30 |
| **125** | A32 | 40c olive brown | .65 | .30 |
| **126** | A32 | 50c magenta | .85 | .30 |
| **127** | A35 | 60c red org ('30) | 3.00 | .50 |
| **128** | A32 | 75c brown violet | .65 | .30 |
| **129** | A35 | 80c red orange | 2.75 | *8.25* |
| **130** | A32 | 90c deep red ('32) | 7.25 | *16.00* |
| **131** | A35 | 1fr violet | 2.40 | .30 |
| **132** | A36 | 1.50fr sapphire | 4.25 | .35 |
| **133** | A36 | 2fr brown red | 5.00 | .35 |
| **134** | A36 | 3fr dk olive grn | 10.00 | 1.10 |
| **135** | A36 | 5fr deep brown | 10.50 | 6.25 |
| | | *Nos. 120-135 (16)* | 50.15 | *36.10* |

For surcharges and overprints see Nos. 136-153, O16-O26.

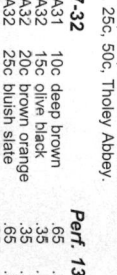

Nos. 126 and 129 Surcharged

SAARGEBIET
60 cent.

**1930-34**

| | | | | |
|---|---|---|---|---|
| **136** | A32 | 40c on 50c mag ('34) | 1.10 | *1.25* |
| **137** | A35 | 60c on 80c red orange | 1.75 | *2.10* |

St. Peter — A55

Peter Wust — A54

**1950, Apr. 3** — **Perf. 13**
221 A54 15fr carmine rose ... 11.50 5.00
Wust (1884-1940), Catholic philosopher.

**1950, June 29** — *Engr.*
222 A55 12fr deep green ... 3.00 8.50
223 A55 15fr red brown ... 4.50 8.50
224 A55 25fr blue ... 7.50 18.00
Nos. 222-224 (3) ... 15.00 35.00
Holy Year, 1950.

Street in Ottweiler — A56

**1950, July 10** — *Photo.* — **Perf. 13x13½**
225 A56 10fr orange brown ... 4.00 7.00
Reopening of Ottweiler, 400th anniv.

Symbols of the Council of Europe A57

**1950, Aug. 8** — **Perf. 13½**
226 A57 25fr deep blue ... 32.50 10.50
Issued to commemorate the Saar's admission to the Council of Europe. See No. C12.

Post Rider and Guard — A62

**1951, Apr. 29** — *Engr.* — **Perf. 13**
227 A62 15fr dk violet brn ... 6.50 17.00
Issued to publicize Stamp Day, 1951.

---

199 A44 20fr henna brn ... 3.00 .80
200 A44 50fr blue blk ... 6.50 2.75
Nos. 188-200 (13) ... 16.65 9.45
Set, never hinged ... 32.50

Map of the Saar A45

**1948, Dec. 15** — *Photo.* — **Perf. 13½x13**
201 A45 10fr dark red ... .60 2.40
202 A45 25fr deep blue ... 1.00 3.25
Set, never hinged ... 3.50
French Protectorate establishment, 1st anniv.

Caduceus, Microscope, Bunsen Burner and Book — A46

**Perf. 13x13½**
2.50 .45
7.00
Issued to honor Saar University.

Ludwig van Beethoven A47

**1949, Apr. 2** — **Perf. 13x13½**
203 A46 15fr carmine ... 2.50 .45
Never hinged ... 7.00
Issued to honor Saar University.

Laborer Using Spade — A51

Saarbrücken — A52

Designs: 10c, Building trades. 1fr, 3fr, Coars, factories. 5fr, Dumping mine waste. 6fr, Coal mine interior. 8fr, Communications symbols. 12fr, Emblem of printing. 15fr, Pottery. 20fr, Blast furnace workcl. 45fr, Rock formation "Great Boot." 60fr, Reden Colliery. Landsweiler. 100fr, View of Welbelskirchen.

**1949-51** — *Unwmk.* — **Perf. 13x13½**
204 A47 10c violet brn ... .20 1.75
205 A47 60c gray ('51) ... .20 1.75
206 A47 1fr carmine lake ... .45 .35
207 A47 3fr brown ('51) ... 2.75 .35
208 A47 5fr dp violet ('50) ... .45 .35
209 A47 6fr Prus grn ('51) ... 4.25 .35
210 A47 8fr olive grn ('51) ... .70 .30
211 A47 10fr orange ('50) ... 4.25 .35
212 A47 12fr dk green ... 5.75 .30
213 A47 15fr red ('50) ... 2.25 .30
214 A47 18fr brn car ('51) ... 1.10 4.50

**Perf. 13½**
215 A51 20fr gray ('50) ... .70 .25
216 A51 25fr violet blue ... 8.50 .30
217 A52 30fr red brown ('51) ... 1.40 .50
218 A51 45fr rose lake ('51) ... 5.75 .45
219 A51 60fr deep grn ('51) ... 2.75 1.75
220 A51 100fr brown ... 4.25 2.10
Nos. 204-220 (17) ... 42.95 15.85
Set, never hinged ... 125.00

> Catalogue values for unused stamps in this section, from this point to the end of the section, are for Never Hinged items.

---

**1947** — Types of 1947 — **Wmk. 285**
172 A37 12pf olive green ... .20 .45
173 A39 45pf crimson ... .20 11.00
174 A40 75pf brt blue ... .20 .35
Set, never hinged ... .55 11.80
Nos. 172-174 (3)
Nos. 172-174 exist imperf.

Types of 1947 Surcharged with New Value, Bars and Ornament in Black or Red

**1947, Nov. 27** — *Unwmk.*

**Printing II**
175 A37 10c on 2pf gray ... .20 .50
176 A37 60c on 3pf org ... .20 .90
177 A37 1fr on 10pf rose vio ... .20 .50
178 A37 2fr on 12pf ol grn ... .65 1.25
179 A38 3fr on 15pf brn ... .20 1.25
180 A38 4fr on 16pf ultra ... .20 7.00
181 A38 5fr on 20pf brn rose ... .20 .90
182 A38 6fr on 24pf dp brn org ... .20 .55
183 A39 9fr on 30pf lt ol grn ... .20 11.50
184 A39 10fr on 50pf bl vio (R) ... .40 17.50
185 A40 14fr on 60pf violet ... .45 11.50
186 A41 20fr on 84pf brn ... .35 18.00
187 A42 50fr on 1m gray grn ... 1.25 18.00
Nos. 175-187 (13) ... 89.35
Set, never hinged ... 4.75

**Printing I**
175a A37 10c on 2pf gray ... 325.00
176a A37 60c on 3pf orange ... 25.00 700.00
177a A37 1fr on 10pf rose ... 2.10 14.00
178a A37 2fr on 12pf ol grn. wmk. ... .65 3.50
      285
179a A37 3fr on 15pf brnwu ... 2,000.
180a A38 4fr on 16pf ultra ... 6.25 700.00
181a A38 5fr on 20pf brn rose ... 700.00 3,500.
182a A38 6fr on 24pf dp brn org ... .20 11.50
183a A39 9fr on 30pf lt ol grn ... 37.50 700.00
184a A39 10fr on 50pf bl vio (R) ... 125.00 1,200.
185a A40 14fr on 60pf violet ... 77.50 850.00
186a A41 20fr on 84pf brown ... 1.40 7.00
187a A42 50fr on 1m gray grn ... 25.00 300.00
Nos. 175a-187a (13) ... 1,925. 12,711.

Printing I was surcharged on Nos. 155-171. The crossbar of the A's in SAAR is high on the 10c, 60c, 1fr, 2fr, 9fr and 10fr; numeral "1" has no base serif on the 3fr and 4fr; wide space between vignette and SAAR panel; 1m inscribed "M."

Printing II was surcharged on a special printing of the basic stamps, with details of design that differ on each denomination. The "A" crossbar is low on 10c, 60c, 1fr, 2fr, 9fr, 10fr; numeral "1" has base serif on 3fr and 4fr; narrow space between vignette and SAAR panel; 1m inscribed "1M."
Inverted surcharges exist on Nos. 175-187 and 175a-187a.

**French Protectorate**

Colliery Shafthead — A44

2fr, 3fr, Worker. 4fr, 5fr, Girl gathering wheat. 6fr, 9fr, Miner. 14fr, Smelting. 20fr, Reconstruction. 50fr, Mettlach Abbey portal.

**Perf. 14x13, 13**

Clasped Hands — A43

**1948, Apr. 1** — *Engr.* — *Unwmk.*
188 A43 10c henna brn ... .35 1.75
189 A43 60c dk Prus grn ... .35 1.75
190 A43 1fr brown blk ... .20 .20
191 A43 2fr rose car ... .20 .20
192 A43 3fr black brn ... .20 .20
193 A43 4fr red ... .20 .20
194 A43 5fr red violet ... .20 .20
195 A43 6fr henna brown ... .20 .20
196 A43 9fr dk Prus grn ... .25 .20
197 A44 10fr dark blue ... 1.25 .20
198 A44 14fr dk vio brn ... 1.60 .80

---

**Plebiscite Issue**
Stamps of 1925-32 Overprinted in Various Colors

VOLKSABSTIMMUNG 1935

**Perf. 13½, 13½x13, 13x13½**

**1934, Nov. 1**
139 A31 10c brown (Br) ... .35 .45
140 A32 15c black grn (G) ... .35 .45
141 A32 20c brown org (Bl) ... .55 1.25
142 A32 25c bluish sl (B) ... .55 .45
143 A31 30c olive grn (G) ... .35 .45
144 A32 40c olive brn (G) ... .35 .65
145 A32 50c magenta (R) ... .65 1.10
146 A32 60c red orge (G) ... .65 .45
147 A32 75c brown vio (V) ... .65 1.25
148 A32 90c deep red (R) ... .65 1.25
149 A35 1fr violet (V) ... .65 1.40
150 A35 1.50fr sapphire (Bl) ... 1.10 2.75
151 A36 2fr brown red (R) ... 1.40 3.75
152 A36 3fr dk ol grn (G) ... 2.50 7.00
153 A36 5fr brown (Br) ... 15.00 27.50

**Size: 31½x36mm**
**Perf. 12**
154 A30 10fr black brn (Br) ... 21.00 52.50
Nos. 139-154 (16) ... 46.65 103.45

**French Administration**

Steel Workers A38

Mettlach Abbey — A40

Marshal Ney — A41

Miner A37

Harvesting Sugar Beets — A39

Saar River near Mettlach A42

**1947** — *Unwmk.* — *Photo.* — **Perf. 14**
155 A37 2pf gray ... .20 .35
156 A37 3pf orange ... .20 .45
157 A37 6pf dk Prus grn ... .20 .35
158 A37 8pf scarlet ... .20 .35
159 A37 10pf rose violet ... .20 5.50
160 A38 16pf ultra ... .20 .35
161 A38 16pf ... .20 .35
162 A38 20pf brown rose ... .20 .35
163 A38 24pf brown org ... .40 .35
164 A39 25pf cerise ... .20 .35
165 A39 40pf orange brn ... .20 .70
166 A39 50pf olive grn ... .20 .70
167 A39 60pf violet ... .40 18.00
168 A40 60pf blue violet ... .40 13.00
169 A40 80pf dp orange ... .20 .35
170 A41 84pf brown ... .20 .35
171 A42 1m gray green ... .20 .45
Set, never hinged ... 61.90
Nos. 155-171 (17) ... 4.00
Nos. 155-162, 164-171 exist imperf.

"Agriculture and Industry" and Fair Emblem — A63

**1951, May 12 Photo. Perf. 13x13½**
228 A63 15fr dk gray grn 2.50 4.25
1951 Fair at Saarbrücken.

Tower of Mittelbexbach and Flowers — A67

**1951, June 9 Engr. Perf. 13**
229 A67 15fr dark green 2.50 1.50
Exhibition of Gardens & Flowers, Bexbach, 1951.

Refugees — A68

Globe & Stylized Fair Building — A69

**1952, May 2 Unwmk. Perf. 13**
230 A68 15fr bright red 3.25 1.25
231 A69 15fr red brown 2.10 1.25
Issued to honor the Red Cross.
1952 Fair at Saarbrücken.

**1952, Apr. 26**

Ludwig's Gymnasium A71

Mine Shafts A70

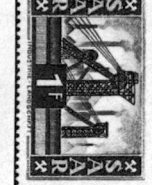
General Post Office A72

**1952-55 Engr.**
232 A70 1fr dk bl grn ('53) .20 .20
233 A71 2fr purple ('53) .20 .20
234 A72 3fr car rose ('53) .20 .20
235 A72 5fr dk grn (no inscription) .20
236 A72 5fr dk grn (no inscription) 4.25 .20

237 A70 6fr vio brn ol ('54) .35 .20
238 A71 10fr brn ol ('53) .35 .20
239 A72 12fr green ('53) .35 .20
240 A70 12fr brn car ('55) .65 .20
241 A70 15fr blk brn (no inscription) .20

242 A70 15fr blk brn ("Industrie-Land-schaft") ('53) 7.00
243 A72 18fr dp car ('55) 3.25 .30
244 A72 30fr ultra ('55) 2.50 .20
245 A73 500fr brn car ('53) 14.00 57.50
For overprints see Nos. 257-259.
Nos. 232-245 (14) 34.45 64.80

**1953, Mar. 23**
246 A74 15fr dark ultra 1.90 1.40
1953 Fair at Saarbrücken.

Bavarian and Prussian Postillions A75

**1953, May 3**
247 A75 15fr deep blue 3.25 11.50
Stamp Day.

Fountain and Fair Buildings — A76

**1954, Apr. 10**
248 A76 15fr deep green 1.90 .85
1954 International Fair at Saarbrücken.

Post Coach and Post Bus of 1920 — A77

**1954, May 9 Engr.**
249 A77 15fr red 3.50 10.50
Stamp Day, May 9, 1954.

Designs: 10fr, 15fr, Sistine Madonna, Raphael. 15fr, Madonna and Child with pearl, Durer.

Madonna and Child, Holbein A78

**1954, Aug. 14**
250 A78 5fr deep carmine .85 1.40
251 A78 10fr dark green 1.00 1.75
252 A78 15fr dp violet bl 3.25 6.40
Nos. 250-252 (3)
Centenary of the promulgation of the Dogma of the Immaculate Conception.

Cyclist and Flag — A79

**1955, Feb. 28 Photo. Perf. 13x13½**
253 A79 15fr multicolored .35 .65
World championship cross country bicycle race.

**1955, Feb. 28**
254 A80 15fr orange brown .35 .65
Rotary International, 50th anniversary.

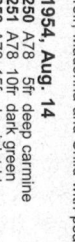
Symbols of Industry and Rotary Emblem — A80

Flags of Participating Nations — A81

**1955, Apr. 18 Photo. Perf. 13x13½**
255 A81 15fr multicolored .35 .65
1955 International Fair at Saarbrücken.

Postman at Illingen A82

**1955, May 8 Unwmk. Engr. Perf. 13**
256 A82 15fr deep claret .70 1.40
Issued to publicize Stamp Day, 1955.

Nos. 242-244 Overprinted "VOLKSBEFRAGUNG 1955"
**1955, Oct. 22**
257 A70 15fr deep carmine .20 .55
258 A72 18fr dk rose brn .30 .35
259 A72 30fr ultra .45 .55
Nos. 257-259 (3) .95 1.45
Plebiscite, Oct. 23, 1955.

Symbols of Industry and the Fair A83

**1956, Apr. 14 Photo. Perf. 11½**
260 A83 15fr dk brn red & yel grn .30 .65
Intl. Fair at Saarbrücken, Apr. 14-29, 1956.

Granite Paper

**1956, May 6**
261 A84 15fr grn & grnish bl .30 .65
Stamp Day.

Radio Tower, Saarbrücken A84

**German Administration**

Arms of Saar — A85

**1957, Jan. 1 Litho. Perf. 13x13½ Wmk. 304**
262 A85 15fr brick red & blue .20 .30
Return of the Saar to Germany.

Pres. Theodor Heuss — A86

**1957 Typo. Perf. 14**
**Size: 18x22mm**
263 A86 1(fr) brt green .20 .20
264 A86 2(fr) brt violet .20 .20
265 A86 3(fr) violet brn .20 .20
266 A86 4(fr) bister brown .30 .20
267 A86 5(fr) red violet .20 .20
268 A86 5(fr) olive green .20 .20
269 A86 10(fr) gray .20 .20
270 A86 10(fr) deep orange .20 .30
271 A86 12(fr) gray .20 .20
272 A86 15(fr) lt blue green .55 .20
273 A86 25(fr) carmine rose .55 2.10
**Engr.**
**Size: 24x29mm**
274 A86 30(fr) pale purple .35 .70
275 A86 45(fr) gray olive 1.00 2.50
276 A86 45(fr) violet brn 1.00 1.10
277 A86 60(fr) dull rose 1.40 2.75
278 A86 70(fr) red orange 2.50 4.25
279 A86 80(fr) olive green .85 3.25
280 A86 90(fr) dark gray 2.50 5.75
281 A86 100(fr) dk carmine 2.10 7.00
282 A86 200(fr) violet 5.75 22.50
Nos. 263-282 (20) 20.25 55.25
See Nos. 289-308.

Steel Industry — A87

Reconstruction of St. Ludwig's Cathedral A73

3fr. 18fr. Bridge, building, 6fr. Transporter bridge, Mettlach. 30fr, Saar University Library.

"SM" Monogram A74

Nos. B1-B4
Overprinted

**1927, Oct. 1**

| | | | | |
|---|---|---|---|---|
| B5 | SP1 | 20c + 20c dk ol grn | 10.50 | 25.00 |
| B6 | SP1 | 40c + 40c dk brn | 10.50 | 17.50 |
| B7 | SP1 | 50c + 50c red org | 8.50 | 55.00 |
| B8 | SP4 | 1.50fr + 1.50fr brt bl | 16.00 | 122.50 |
| | | *Nos. B5-B8 (4)* | 45.50 | |

"Almsgiving" by
Schiestl
SP6

"The Blind
Beggar" by
Dyckmans
SP5

"Charity" by
Raphael — SP7

**1928, Dec. 23**

Photo.

| | | | | |
|---|---|---|---|---|
| B9 | SP5 | 40c (+40c) blk | 10.50 | 65.00 |
| B10 | SP5 | 50c (+50c) brown rose | 10.50 | 65.00 |
| B11 | SP5 | 1fr (+1fr) dl vio | 10.50 | 65.00 |
| B12 | SP6 | 1.50fr (+1.50fr) cob bl | 13.00 | 92.50 |
| B13 | SP6 | 2fr (+2fr) red brn | 13.00 | 125.00 |
| B14 | SP6 | 3fr (+3fr) dk ol grn | 325.00 | |
| B15 | SP7 | 10fr (+10fr) dk brn | 393.00 | 3,600. |
| | | *Nos. B9-B15 (7)* | | |

"St. Ottilia" by
Feuerstein
SP9

"Orphaned" by
Kaulbach
SP8

"Madonna" by
Ferruzzio — SP10

**1929, Dec. 22**

| | | | | |
|---|---|---|---|---|
| B16 | SP8 | 40c (+15c) ol grn | 1.90 | 5.00 |
| B17 | SP8 | 50c (+20c) cop red | 4.00 | 8.50 |
| B18 | SP8 | 1fr (+50c) vio brn | 4.00 | 10.00 |
| B19 | SP9 | 1.50fr (+75c) Prus bl | 4.00 | 10.00 |

---

Jakob
Fugger — A98

**Perf. 13x13½**

Old and New
City Hall and
Burbach
Mill — A99

**1959, Mar. 6**    **Wmk. 304**    .20    .35

319 A98 15fr dk red & blk
500th anniv. of the birth of Jakob Fugger the
Rich, businessman and banker.

**1959, Apr. 1**    **Engr.**    **Perf. 14x13½**    .20    .35

320 A99 15fr light blue
Greater Saarbrücken, 50th anniversary.

Hands Holding
Merchandise
A100

Alexander von
Humboldt    A101

**Litho.**

**1959, Apr. 1**    .20    .35

321 A100 15fr deep rose
1959 Fair at Saarbrucken.

**1959, May 6**    **Engr.**    **Perf. 13½x14**    .20    .40

322 A101 15fr blue
Cent. of the death of Alexander von Humboldt, naturalist and geographer.

## SEMI-POSTAL STAMPS

Maternity Nurse
with
Child — SP4

Red Cross Dog
Leading Blind
Man — SP1

Designs: #B2, Nurse and invalid. #B3, Children getting drink at spring.

**1926, Oct. 25**    **Photo.**    **Unwmk.**

| | | | | |
|---|---|---|---|---|
| B1 | SP1 | 20c + 20c dk ol grn | 7.00 | 15.00 |
| B2 | SP1 | 40c + 40c dk brn | 7.00 | 15.00 |
| B3 | SP1 | 50c + 50c red org | 7.00 | 14.00 |
| B4 | SP4 | 1.50fr + 1.50fr brt bl | 17.00 | 45.00 |
| | | *Nos. B1-B4 (4)* | 38.00 | 89.00 |

---

Merzig Arms
and St. Peter's
Church — A88

**1957, Apr. 20**    **Litho.**    **Wmk. 304**    .20    .30

284 A87 15fr gray & magenta
The 1957 Fair at Saarbrücken.

**1957, May 25**    **Perf. 14**    .20    .30

285 A88 15fr blue
Centenary of the town of Merzig.

"United
Europe" — A89

**Lithographed; Tree Embossed**
**Perf. 14x13½**    **Unwmk.**

**1957, Sept. 16**    .35    .85
.75    1.00

286 A89 20fr orange & yel
287 A89 35fr violet & pink
Europa, publicizing a united Europe for
peace and prosperity.

"Prevent Forest
Fires" — A92

**1958, Mar. 5**    **Perf. 14**    .20    .40

311 A92 15fr brt red & blk
Issued to aid in the prevention of forest fires.

Rudolf
Diesel
A93

**1958, Mar. 18**    **Engr.**    .20    .35

312 A93 12fr dk blue grn
Centenary of the birth of Rudolf Diesel,
inventor.

Fair Emblem and
City Hall,
Saarbrücken
A94

View of
Homburg
A95

**1958, Apr. 10**    **Litho.**    **Perf. 11**    .20    .35

313 A94 15fr dull rose
1958 Fair at Saarbrücken.

**1958, June 14**    **Engr.**    **Wmk. 304**    .20    .35

314 A95 15fr gray green
400th anniversary of Homburg.

Turner Emblem
A96

Herman Schulze-
Delitzsch
A97

**1958, July 21**    **Litho.**    **Perf. 13½x14**    .20    .35

315 A96 12fr gray, blk & dl grn
150 years of German Gymnastics and the
1958 Gynastic Festival.

**1958, Aug. 29**    **Engr.**    **Wmk. 304**    .20    .35

316 A97 12fr yellow green
150th anniv. of the birth of Schultze-
Delitzsch, founder of German trade
organizations.

Common Design Types
pictured following the introduction.

**Europa Issue, 1958**
Common Design Type

**1958, Sept. 13**    **Litho.**

**Size: 24½x30mm**

317 CD1 12fr yellow grn & bl    .50    .85
318 CD1 30fr lt blue & red    .65    1.60
Issued to show the European Postal Union
at the service of European integration.

---

Merzig Arms and
St. Peter's
Church — A88

**1957, Apr. 20**    **Perf. 13x13½**    **Litho.**    **Wmk. 304**    .20    .30
**1957, May 25**    **Perf. 14**    .20    .30

Carrier
Pigeons — A90

**1957, Oct. 5**    **Litho.**    **Wmk. 304**    **Perf. 14**    .20    .30

288 A90 15fr dp carmine & blk
Intl. Letter Writing Week, Oct. 6-12.

Redrawn Type of 1957; "F" added after
denomination

**1957**    **Wmk. 304**    **Perf. 14**

**Size: 18x22mm**

| | | | | |
|---|---|---|---|---|
| 289 | A86 | 1fr gray green | .20 | .20 |
| 290 | A86 | 3fr blue | .20 | .20 |
| 291 | A86 | 5fr olive | .20 | .20 |
| 292 | A86 | 6fr lt brown | .20 | .45 |
| 293 | A86 | 10fr violet | .20 | .20 |
| 294 | A86 | 12fr brown org | .20 | .20 |
| 295 | A86 | 15fr dull green | .35 | .20 |
| 296 | A86 | 18fr gray | 1.75 | 4.25 |
| 297 | A86 | 3fr lt olive grn | 1.10 | 3.00 |
| 298 | A86 | 25fr orange brn | .35 | .35 |
| 299 | A86 | 30fr rose lilac | .85 | .35 |
| 300 | A86 | 35fr brown | 2.10 | 3.00 |
| 301 | A86 | 45fr lt blue grn | 1.75 | 3.50 |
| 302 | A86 | 50fr dk red brown | .85 | 1.75 |
| 303 | A86 | 70fr brt green | 4.25 | 5.00 |
| 304 | A86 | 80fr chalky blue | 2.10 | 4.50 |
| 305 | A86 | 90fr rose carmine | 5.00 | 5.75 |

**Engr.**

**Size: 24x29mm**

| | | | | |
|---|---|---|---|---|
| 306 | A86 | 100fr orange | 3.50 | 6.25 |
| 307 | A86 | 200fr green | 7.75 | 22.50 |
| 308 | A86 | 300fr blue | 8.50 | 25.00 |
| | | *Nos. 289-308 (20)* | 41.40 | 86.85 |

"Max and
Moritz" — A91

Design: 15fr, Wilhelm Busch.

**1958, Jan. 9**    **Perf. 13½x13**    **Litho.**    **Wmk. 304**    .20    .20

309 A91 12fr lt ol grn & blk
310 A91 15fr red & black    .20    .40
Death of Wilhelm Busch, humorist, 50th
anniv.

**VOLKSHILFE**
"The Safety-Man" SP11

Nos. B16-B22

| | | |
|---|---|---|
| B20 | SP9 | 2fr (+1fr) car — 4.00 10.00 |
| B21 | SP9 | 3fr (+2fr) sl grn — 7.00 22.50 |
| B22 | SP10 | 10fr (+8fr) blk — 42.50 125.00 |
| Nos. B16-B22 (7) | | 67.40 191.00 |

"The Good Samaritan" SP12

"In the Window" — SP13

**1931, Jan. 20**

| | | |
|---|---|---|
| B23 | SP11 | 40c (+15c) — 7.00 22.50 |
| B24 | SP11 | 60c (+20c) — 7.00 22.50 |
| B25 | SP12 | 1fr (+50c) — 7.00 42.50 |
| B26 | SP12 | 1.50fr (+75c) — 10.50 42.50 |
| B27 | SP12 | 2fr (+1fr) — 10.50 42.50 |
| B28 | SP12 | 3fr (+2fr) — 17.50 42.50 |
| B29 | SP13 | 10fr (+10fr) — 85.00 250.00 |
| Nos. B23-B29 (7) | | 144.50 465.00 |

St. Martin of Tours — SP14

**1931, Dec. 23**

| | | |
|---|---|---|
| B30 | SP14 | 40c (+15c) — 7.00 |
| B31 | SP14 | 60c (+20c) — 7.00 |
| B32 | SP14 | 1fr (+50c) — 7.00 |
| B33 | SP14 | 1.50fr (+75c) — 11.50 32.50 |
| B34 | SP14 | 2fr (+1fr) — 11.50 32.50 |
| B35 | SP14 | 3fr (+2fr) — 14.00 |
| B36 | SP14 | 5fr (+5fr) — 25.00 85.00 |
| Nos. B30-B36 (7) | | 85.00 300.00 / 184.00 600.00 |

#B33-B35, Charity. #B36, The Widow's Mite.

**VOLKSHILFE SAARGEBIET**
Ruins at Kirkel — SP17

Illingen Castle, Kerpen SP23

**1932, Dec. 20**

| | | |
|---|---|---|
| B37 | SP17 | 40c (+15c) — 8.50 20.00 |
| B38 | SP17 | 60c (+20c) — 8.50 20.00 |
| B39 | SP17 | 1fr (+50c) — 13.00 35.00 |
| B40 | SP17 | 1.50fr (+75c) — 17.50 42.50 |
| B41 | SP17 | 2fr (+1fr) — 17.50 50.00 |

Designs: 60c, Church at Blie. 1fr, Castle Ottweiler. 1.50fr, Church of St. Michael, Saarbrucken. 2fr, Statue of St. Wendel. 3fr, Church of St. John, Saarbrucken.

---

**1933, June 1**
Scene of Neunkirchen Disaster — SP24

| | | |
|---|---|---|
| B42 | SP17 | 3fr (+2fr) — 50.00 160.00 |
| B43 | SP23 | 5fr (+5fr) — 110.00 250.00 |
| Nos. B37-B43 (7) | | 225.00 577.50 |
| B44 | SP24 | 60c (+60c) org — 14.00 17.50 |
| B45 | SP24 | 3fr (+3fr) red — 32.50 65.00 |
| B46 | SP24 | 5fr (+5fr) org brn — 32.50 65.00 |
| Nos. B44-B46 (3) | | 79.00 147.50 |

The surtax was for the aid of victims of the explosion at Neunkirchen, Feb. 10.

"Love" — SP25

**1934, Mar. 15** Photo.

| | | |
|---|---|---|
| B47 | SP25 | 40c (+15c) blk — 4.50 14.00 |
| B48 | SP25 | 60c (+20c) red — 4.50 14.00 |
| B49 | SP25 | 1fr (+50c) dl vio — 4.50 14.00 |
| B50 | SP25 | 1.50fr (+75c) blue — 6.50 14.00 |
| B51 | SP25 | 2fr (+1fr) car — 11.50 32.50 |
| B52 | SP25 | 3fr (+2fr) ol grn — 10.00 32.50 |
| B53 | SP25 | 5fr (+5fr) rose red — 11.50 32.50 |
| Nos. B47-B53 (7) | | 29.00 77.50 / 220.50 |

Designs: 60c, "Anxiety." 1fr, "Peace." 1.50fr, "Welfare." 3fr, "Truth." 5fr, Figure on Tomb of Duchess Elizabeth of Lorraine. "Solace," 2fr.

Nos. B47-B53 Overprinted like Nos. 139-154 in Various Colors Reading up

| | | |
|---|---|---|
| B54 | SP25 | 40c (+15c) (Br) — 3.25 13.00 |
| B55 | SP25 | 60c (+20c) (R) — 3.25 14.00 |
| B56 | SP25 | 1fr (+50c) (R) — 4.50 14.00 |
| B57 | SP25 | 1.50fr (+75c) (Bl) — 6.50 14.00 |
| B58 | SP25 | 2fr (+1fr) (R) — 10.00 25.00 |
| B59 | SP25 | 3fr (+2fr) (G) — 9.25 25.00 |
| B60 | SP25 | 5fr (+5fr) (Br) — 13.50 35.00 |
| Nos. B54-B60 (7) | | 55.75 177.00 |

**French Protectorate**

SP32

Various Flood Scenes — SP33

**1934, Dec. 1** Perf. 13x13½

| | | |
|---|---|---|
| B61 | SP32 | 5fr + 5fr dl grn — 1.60 30.00 |
| B62 | SP33 | 6fr + 6fr dk vio — 1.60 30.00 |
| B63 | SP33 | 12fr + 8fr red — 2.40 30.00 |
| B64 | SP33 | 18fr + 12fr bl — 2.75 42.50 |
| a. | | Souv. sheet of 4, #B61- — 175.00 |
| | | Never hinged — 425.00 |
| Nos. B61-B64,CB1 (5) | | 20.35 337.50 |
| | | Set, never hinged — 40.00 |

B64, imperf. Never hinged — 1,700.
Souv. sheet of 4, #B61.

**1948, Oct. 12** Inscribed "Hochwasser-Hilfe 1947-48"

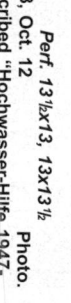
HOCHWASSER-HILFE 1947-48

The surtax was for flood relief.

---

8fr +5f VOLKSHILFE

Mare and Foal SP35

**1949, Jan. 11** Hikers approaching Weisskirchen Hostel.
Perf. 13½x13

| | | |
|---|---|---|
| B65 | SP34 | 8fr + 10fr dk grn — 1.10 90.00 |
| B66 | SP34 | 15fr + 5fr brn red — 5.00 90.00 |
| | | Set, never hinged |

The surtax aided youth hostels.
#B66, Hikers approaching Weisskirchen Hostel.

Hikers and Ludweiler Hostel SP34

**1949, Sept. 25**
Design: No. B68, Jumpers.
Perf. 13½

| | | |
|---|---|---|
| B67 | SP35 | 15fr + 5fr brn red — 5.25 29.00 |
| B68 | SP35 | 25fr + 15fr blue — 7.00 32.50 |
| | | Set, never hinged — 25.00 |

Day of the Horse, Sept. 25, 1949.

Detail from "Moses Striking the Rock" — SP36

**1949, Dec. 20** Engr.
#B70, "Christ at the Pool of Bethesda." #B71, "The Sick Child." #B72, "St. Thomas of Villeneuve." #B73, Madonna of Blieskastel.
Perf. 13

| | | |
|---|---|---|
| B69 | SP36 | 8fr + 2fr indigo — 3.25 35.00 |
| B70 | SP36 | 10fr + 4fr grn — 4.50 40.00 |
| B71 | SP36 | 12fr + 3fr dk grn — 6.50 70.00 |
| B72 | SP36 | 15fr + 5fr brn lake — 9.25 125.00 |
| B73 | SP36 | 50fr + 20fr choc — 17.00 200.00 |
| Nos. B69-B73 (5) | | 40.50 472.50 / 82.50 |

---

**1950, Apr. 3** Photo. Perf. 13x13½

| | | |
|---|---|---|
| B74 | SP37 | 15fr + 5fr car rose — 11.50 70.00 |
| | | Never hinged |

Adolph Kolping — SP37

Relief for the Hungry — SP38

**1950, Apr. 28** Engraved and Typographed Perf. 13

| | | |
|---|---|---|
| B75 | SP38 | 25fr + 10fr dk brn — 12.00 55.00 |
| | | Never hinged |

Stagecoach — SP39

TAG DER BRIEFMARKE 1950

**1950, Apr. 22** Engr.

| | | |
|---|---|---|
| B76 | SP39 | 15fr + 5fr brn red & dk brn — 30.00 100.00 / 60.00 |
| | | Never hinged |

Lutwinus Seeking Admission to Abbey SP40

**1950, Nov. 10** Unwmk. Perf. 13

| | | |
|---|---|---|
| B77 | SP40 | 8fr + 2fr brn car — 3.00 29.00 |
| B78 | SP40 | 12fr + 3fr dk grn — 3.00 29.00 |
| B79 | SP40 | 15fr + 5fr car — 3.50 45.00 |
| B80 | SP40 | 25fr + 10fr blue — 6.00 65.00 |
| B81 | SP40 | 50fr + 20fr brn car — 8.50 110.00 |
| Nos. B77-B81 (5) | | 24.00 278.00 |
| | | Set, never hinged — 47.50 |

Designs: 12fr+3fr, Lutwinus Building Mettlach Abbey. 15fr+5fr, Lutwinus as Abbot. 25fr+10fr, Bishop Lutwinus at Rheims. 50fr+20fr, Aid to the poor and sick.
The surtax was for public assistance.

Mother and Child — SP41

John Calvin and Martin Luther — SP42

**1951, Apr. 28**

| | | |
|---|---|---|
| B82 | SP41 | 25fr + 10fr dk grn & car — 8.50 55.00 |
| B83 | SP42 | 15fr + 5fr blk brn — .90 5.25 / 1.75 |
| | | Never hinged |

Reformation in Saar, 375th anniv.
The surtax was for the Red Cross.

"Mother" — SP43

Runner with Torch — SP44

**1951, Nov. 3**

| | | |
|---|---|---|
| B84 | SP43 | 12fr + 3fr dk grn — 2.50 17.00 |
| B85 | SP43 | 15fr + 5fr pur — 2.50 17.00 |
| B86 | SP43 | 18fr + 7fr dk red — 5.00 17.50 |
| B87 | SP43 | 30fr + 10fr dp grn — 5.00 32.50 |
| B88 | SP43 | 50fr + 20fr blk brn — 10.00 62.50 |
| Nos. B84-B88 (5) | | 23.00 146.50 |
| | | Set, never hinged — 45.00 |

Designs: 15fr+5fr, "Sisters of Charity." 18fr+7fr, "Before the Theater." 30fr+10fr, "The Good Samaritan." 50fr+20fr, "St. Martin and Beggar."

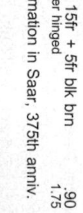

**1952, Mar. 29** Unwmk. Perf. 13

| | | |
|---|---|---|
| B89 | SP44 | 15fr + 5fr dp grn — 5.25 10.50 |
| B90 | SP44 | 30fr + 5fr dp bl — 5.25 12.50 |

XV Olympic Games, Helsinki, 1952.
30fr+5fr, Hand with olive branch, and globe.

Catalogue values for unused stamps in this section, from this point to the end of the section, are for Never Hinged items.

**Postrider Delivering Mail SP45**

**1952, Mar. 30**
B91 SP45 30fr + 10fr dark blue    8.50  25.00
Stamp Day, Mar. 29, 1952.

**Count Stroganoff as a Boy — SP46**

**1952, Nov. 3**
B92 SP46 15fr + 5fr dk brn    2.75  .50
B93 SP46 18fr + 7fr brn lake    4.50  13.00
B94 SP46 30fr + 10fr dp bl    5.75  14.00
Nos. B92-B94 (3)    13.00  35.50
Portraits: 18fr+7fr, The Holy Shepherd by Murillo. 30fr+10fr, Portrait of a Boy by Georg Melchior Kraus.
The surtax was for child welfare.

**Henri Dunant — SP47**

**Cross in Red**

**1953, May 3**
B95 SP47 15fr + 6fr blk brn    1.90  6.00

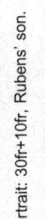

**Clarice Strozzi by Titian — SP48**

**Children of Rubens SP49**

**1953, Nov. 16**
B96 SP48 15fr + 5fr purple    1.75  5.00
B97 SP49 18fr + 7fr dp claret    1.75  5.25
B98 SP48 30fr + 10fr dp ol grn    4.00  8.50
Nos. B96-B98 (3)    7.50  18.75
Portrait: 30fr+10fr, Rubens' son.
The surtax was for child welfare.

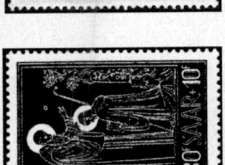

**St. Benedict Blessing St. Maurus — SP50**

**Child and Cross — SP51**

**1953, Dec. 18    Litho.**
B99 SP50 30fr + 10fr black    1.90  7.00
The surtax was for the abbey at Tholey.

**Engr.**
**1954, May 10**
B100 SP51 15fr + 5fr chocolate    2.10  5.75
The surtax was for the Red Cross.

**Street Urchin with Melon, Murillo — SP52**

**1954, Nov. 15    Engr.**
B101 SP52 5fr + 3fr red    .70  1.00
B102 SP52 10fr + 5fr dk grn    .70  1.10
B103 SP52 15fr + 7fr purple    .85  1.75
Nos. B101-B103 (3)    2.25  3.85
Paintings: 10fr+5fr, Maria de Medici, Bronzino. 15fr+7fr, Baron Emil von Maucler, Dietrich.
The surtax was for child welfare.

**Nurse Holding Baby — SP53**

**Perf. 13x13½    Photo.    Unwmk.**
**1955, May 5**
B104 SP53 15fr + 5fr blk & red    .50  .90
The surtax was for the Red Cross.

**Dürer's Mother, Age 63 — SP54    Perf. 13    Engr.**
**1955, Dec. 10**
B105 SP54 5fr + 3fr dk grn    .40  .70
B106 SP54 10fr + 5fr ol grn    .70  1.25
B107 SP54 15fr + 7fr ol bis    1.00  1.75
Nos. B105-B107 (3)    2.10  3.70
Etchings by Dürer: 10fr+5fr, Praying hands. 15fr+7fr, Old man of Antwerp.
The surtax was for public assistance.

**First Aid Station, Saarbrücken, 1870 — SP55**

**1956, May 7**
B108 SP55 15fr + 5fr dk grn    .30  .65
The surtax was for the Red Cross.

**"Victor of Benevent" SP56**

**Winterberg Monument SP57**

**1956, July 25    Unwmk.    Perf. 13**
B109 SP56 12fr + 3fr dk yel grn & bl grn    .50  .65
B110 SP56 15fr + 5fr brn vio & brn    .50  .65
Melbourne Olympics, 11/22-12/8/56.

**1956, Oct. 29**
B111 SP57 5fr + 2fr green    .20  .20
B112 SP57 12fr + 3fr red lilac    .20  .45
B113 SP57 15fr + 5fr brown    .60  1.20
Nos. B111-B113 (3)
The surtax was for the rebuilding of monuments.

**"La Belle Ferronnière" by da Vinci — SP58**

**1956, Dec. 10**
B114 SP58 5fr + 3fr brt blue    .20  .20
B115 SP58 10fr + 5fr deep claret    .20  .44
B116 SP58 15fr + 7fr dark green    .60  1.40
Nos. B114-B116 (3)    .75
Designs: 10fr + 5fr, "Family van Berchem," by Frans Floris. (Detail: Woman playing Spinet.)
The surtax was for charitable works.

**German Administration**

**Miner with Drill — SP59**

**1957, Oct. 1    Wmk. 304    Litho.**
6fr+4fr, Miner. 15fr+7fr, Miner and conveyor. 30fr+10fr, Miner and coal elevator.
B117 SP59 6fr + 4fr bis brn & blk    .20  .20
B118 SP59 12fr + 6fr blk & yel grn    .20  .30
B119 SP59 15fr + 7fr blk & red    .30  .35
B120 SP59 30fr + 10fr blk & bl    .65  1.50
Nos. B117-B120 (4)    1.05
The surtax was to finance young peoples' study trip to Berlin.

**"The Fox who Stole the Goose" — SP60**

**1958, Apr. 1    Wmk. 304    Perf. 14**
15fr+7fr, "A Hunter from the Palatinate."
B121 SP60 12fr + 6fr brn red, grn & blk    .20  .20
B122 SP60 15fr + 7fr grn, red, blk & gray    .20  .35
The surtax was to finance young peoples' study trip to Berlin.

**Dairy Maid SP62**

**Friedrich Wilhelm Raiffeisen SP61**

Designs: 15fr+7fr, Girl picking grapes. 30fr+10fr, Farmer with pitchfork.

**1958, Oct. 1    Wmk. 304    Perf. 14**
B123 SP61 6fr + 4fr gldn brn & dk brn    .20  .20
B124 SP62 12fr + 6fr grn, red & yel    .20  .20
B125 SP62 15fr + 7fr red, yel & bl    .35  .45
B126 SP62 30fr + 10fr bl & ocher    .45  .55
Nos. B123-B126 (4)    1.20  1.40

## AIR POST STAMPS

**Airplane over Saarbrücken — AP1**

**1928, Sept. 19    Unwmk.    Perf. 13½    Photo.**
C1 AP1 50c brown red    3.50  3.00
C2 AP1 1fr dark violet    5.75  3.50
For overprints see Nos. C5, C7.

**Saarbrücken Airport and Church of St. Arnual — AP2**

**1932, Apr. 30**
C3 AP2 60c orange red    5.75  4.25
C4 AP2 5fr dark brown    40.00  85.00
For overprints see Nos. C6, C8.

**Nos. C1-C4 Overprinted like Nos. 139-154 in Various Colors**

**1934, Nov. 1    Perf. 13½, 13½x13**
C5 AP1 50c brn red (R)    6.50  6.50
C6 AP1 60c org red (O)    3.00  2.50
C7 AP1 1fr dk vio (V)    5.00  8.50
C8 AP1 5fr dk brn (Br)    17.25  11.50
Nos. C5-C8 (4)    29.00

**French Protectorate**

**Shadow of Plane over Saar River AP3**

**1948, Apr. 1    Unwmk.    Engr.    Perf. 13**
C9 AP3 25fr red    1.75  3.00
C10 AP3 50fr dk Prus grn    1.10  1.50
C11 AP3 200fr rose car    10.50  32.50
Nos. C9-C11 (3)    13.35  37.00
Set, never hinged

**Symbols of the Council of Europe AP4**

## SAAR

**1950, Aug. 8**  Photo.  Perf. 13½
C12 AP4 200fr red brown ... 125.00 225.00
a. Never hinged ... 190.00

Saar's admission to the Council of Europe.

### AIR POST SEMI-POSTAL STAMP

**French Protectorate**

Flood Scene — SPAP1

**1948, Oct. 12**  Photo.  Perf. 13½x13
CB1 SPAP1 25fr + 25fr sep ... 12.00 200.00
a. Souvenir sheet of 1 ... 175.00
  Never hinged ... 425.00
  Never hinged ... 1,700.

The surtax was for flood relief.

### OFFICIAL STAMPS

DIENSTMARKE / SAARGEBIET / DIENSTMARKE

Regular Issue of 1922-1923 Overprinted Diagonally in Red or Blue

**1922-19**
O1 A19 3c ol grn & straw (R) ... .70 27.50

**Perf. 12½x13½, 13½x12½  Unwmk.**
O2 A20 5c org & blk (R) ... .35 .35
O3 A21 10c bl grn (R) ... .35 .30
O4 A19 10c bl grn (Bl) ... .35 .30
O5 A19 15c org (Bl) ... .35 .45
O6 A22 20c dk bl & lem (R) ('23) ... .35 .30
O7 A22 20c brt bl & straw (R) ... .35 .45
O8 A22 25c red & yel (R) ... 2.10 .45
O9 A22 25c mag & straw (Bl) ... 3.00 .85
O10 A23 30c car & yel ('23) ... 2.10
O11 A24 40c brn & yel (Bl) ... .45 .45
O12 A24 50c dk bl & straw (R) ... .45 .30
O13 A24 75c dp grn & straw (R) ... 16.00 25.00
O14 A24 75c blk & straw (R) ... 4.25 2.10
O15c A26 1fr brn red (Bl) ... 41.40 61.05

Nos. O1-O15c (15)

Inverted overprints exist on 10c, 20c, 30c, 50c, 1fr. Double overprints exist on #O4, O6, 1fr.

Regular Issue of 1927-30 Overprinted in Various Colors

**1927-34**
O19 A31 10c dp brn (Bl) ... 1.75 .30
O16 A31 15c ol blk (Bl) ('34) ... 1.75 .70
O17 A32 15c ol brn (Bl) ('34) ... 6.00
O18 A32 20c brn org (Bk) ... .35

**Perf. 13½**
O23 A35 60c red org (Bk) ... .30 .35
O22b A32 50c mag (Bl) ... 3.50 .35
O21b A32 40c ol brn (C) ... 1.75 .30
O20a A31 30c ol brn (C) ... 5.75
O20b A31 25c bluish sl ('31) ... 1.75 .30
O24b A32 75c brn vio ('30) ... 1.10
O25b A35 1fr brn vio (RO) ... 2.10
O25c A36 2fr brn red (Bl) ... 2.10
O26b A36 2fr brn red (Bl) ... 21.75 17.95

The overprint exists in two types; at a 32 degree angle, applied to O20-O22, O24-O26

in 1927, and at a 23-25 degree angle, applied to all values 1929/1934. The less expensive varieties are listed. For detailed listings, see the Scott Classic Specialized Catalogue.
The overprint on Nos. O16 and O20 is known only inverted. Nos. O21-O26 exist with double overprint.

**French Protectorate**

Arms — O1

**1949, Oct. 1**  Engr.  Perf. 14x13
O27 O1 10c deep carmine ... .20 17.00
O28 O1 30c blue black ... .20 20.00
O29 O1 1fr Prus green ... .20 .90
O30 O1 2fr orange red ... .50 1.10
O31 O1 5fr blue ... .65 .90
O32 O1 10fr black ... .30 .90
O33 O1 12fr red violet ... .65 3.00
O34 O1 15fr indigo ... .90 10.00
O35 O1 20fr green ... .65 1.10
O36 O1 30fr violet rose ... .50 4.25
O37 O1 50fr purple ... .50 3.50
O38 O1 100fr red brown ... 1.00 10.55
Nos. O27-O38 (12) ... 29.00 250.00 310.55
Set, never hinged ... 36.00 140.00

## ST. CHRISTOPHER

săn̄t 'kris-tə-fər

No. 7 Surcharged and Handstamp Surcharged in Black

No. 9 Bisected and Handstamp Surcharged in Black

 Italfenny — No. 19

 4d — No. 19

LOCATION — Island in the West Indies, southeast of Puerto Rico
GOVT. — A Presidency of the Leeward Islands Colony
AREA — 68 sq. mi.
POP. — 18,578 (estimated)
CAPITAL — Basseterre

Stamps of St. Christopher were discontinued in 1890 and replaced by issues, inscribed "St. Kitts-Nevis" or "St. Christopher-Nevis-Anguilla," see St. Kitts-Nevis.

12 Pence = 1 Shilling

Queen Victoria — A1

**1870, Apr. 1  Wmk. Crown and C C (1)  Typo.  Perf. 12½**
1 A1 1p dull rose ... 92.50 50.00
2 A1 1p lilac rose ... 140.00 30.00
3 A1 6p green ... 307.50 88.75
Nos. 1-3 (3)

**1875-79  Perf. 14**
4 A1 1p rose ... 75.00 8.00
a. Half used as ½p on cover ... 8.00
5 A1 2½p red brown ('79) ... 1,850.
6 A1 4p blue ('79) ... 210.00 16.00
7 A1 6p green ... 60.00 6.00
a. Horiz. pair, imperf. vert.
Nos. 4-7 (4) ... 545.00 305.00

**1882-90  Wmk. Crown and C A (2)**
8 A1 ½p green ... 1.75 1.75
9 A1 1p rose ... 1.50 2.50
a. Half used as ½p on cover
10 A1 1p lilac rose ... 575.00 72.50
a. Diagonal half used as ½p on cover
11 A1 2½p red brown ... 190.00 65.00
12 A1 2½p deep red brown ('84) ... 200.00 70.00
13 A1 2½p ultra ('84) ... 2.10 2.10
14 A1 4p blue ... 475.00 27.50
15 A1 6p gray ('84) ... 1.50 1.10
16 A1 6p olive brn ('90) ... 100.00 375.00
a. 1sh bright mauve ('90) ... 92.50 75.00
Nos. 8-16 (9) ... 1,436. 622.35

For surcharges see Nos. 17, 21-23.

 ONE PENNY — No. 20

**1885, Mar.**
**1884-86  Wmk. 1**
17 A1 ½p on half of 1p ... 27.50 45.00
a. Inverted surcharge ... 250.00 125.00
b. Unsevered pair ... 125.00
c. As "c," one surcharge invert-ed
d. As "c," one surcharge invert
e. Double surcharge ... 450.00 325.00

18 A1 1p on 6p green ('86) ... 22.50 32.50
a. Inverted surcharge ... 7,250.
19 A1 4p on 6p green ... 1,500.
a. Period after "PENNE" ... 57.50
b. Double surcharge ... 2,300.
20 A1 4p on 6p green ('86) ... 50.00 100.00
a. Without period after "d" ... 210.00 300.00
b. Double surcharge ... 1,850. 1,950.
Nos. 18-20 (3) ... 147.50 190.00

The line through original value on Nos. 18 and 20 was added by hand. Value for No. 18b is for stamp with pen cancellation or with violet handstamp (revenue cancels).

 ONE PENNY — No. 22

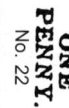 ONE PENNY — No. 23

ONE PENNY — No. 21

**1887-88  Wmk. 2**
21 A1 1p on ½p green ... 40.00 47.50
22 A1 1p on 2½p ('88) ... 70.00 70.00
a. Inverted surcharge ... 13,500.
23 A1 1p on 2½p ('88) ... 17,500. 11,500.
 ... 7,750.
 ... 17,500. 11,500.

Nos. 18, 21 and 23 all have the same type of One Penny surcharge. The line through the original value on Nos. 21 and 22 were added by hand. No. 23 probably is a sheet that was missed when the bars were added. Antigua No. 18 was used in St. Christopher in 1890. It is canceled "A12" instead of "A02." Values: used $140, on cover $850.

### POSTAL FISCAL ISSUES

St. Kitts Nos. 22 and 28 Overprinted "REVENUE" Horizontally and "Saint Christopher" Diagonally

**1883**
AR1 A5 1p violet ... 290.00
AR2 A5 6p green ... 77.50 140.00

Stamps of St. Christopher Ovptd. "SAINT KITTS / NEVIS / REVENUE" in 3 Lines

**1885**
AR3 A1 1p rose ... 2.50 15.00
AR4 A1 3p violet ... 15.00 67.50
AR5 A1 6p orange brown ... 9.25 52.50
AR6 A1 1sh olive ... 2.75 45.00

Other values exist with the above overprints but were not available for postal purposes.

# ST. HELENA

sānt 'he-lə-nə

LOCATION—Island in the Atlantic Ocean, 1,200 miles west of Angola
GOVT.—British Crown Colony
AREA—47 sq. mi.
POP.—7,145 (?) (1999 est.)
CAPITAL—Jamestown

12 Pence = 1 Shilling
20 Shillings = 1 Pound
100 Pence = 1 Pound (1971)

> **Catalogue values for unused stamps in this country are for Never Hinged items, beginning with Scott 128 in the regular postage section, Scott B1 in the semi-postal section and Scott J1 in the postage due section.**

Values for unused stamps are for examples with original gum as defined in the catalogue introduction. Very fine examples of Nos. 2-7, 11-39a and 47-47b will have perforations touching the design on one or more sides due to the narrow spacing of the stamps on the plates. Stamps with perfs clear of the design on all four sides are scarce and will command higher prices.

**Watermark**

Wmk. 6 — Star

Queen Victoria — A1

**1856, Jan. Wmk. 6 Engr. Imperf.**
1 A1 6p blue — 575.00 210.00
For types surcharged see Nos. 8-39, 47.

**1861 Clean-Cut Perf. 14 to 15½**
2 A1 6p blue — 2,000. 325.00

**1863 Rough Perf. 14 to 15½**
2B A1 6p blue — 450.00 150.00

**1871-74 Wmk. 1 Perf. 12½**
3 A1 6p dull blue — 750.00 110.00
4 A1 6p ultra (74) — 425.00 92.50

**1879 Perf. 14x12½**
5 A1 6p blue — 400.00 55.00

**1889 Perf. 14**
6 A1 6p gray blue — 425.00 57.50

**1889 Wmk. Crown and C A (2)**
7 A1 6p gray — 21.00 5.50

Type of 1856 Surcharged

**1863 Wmk. 1**
**Long Bar, 16, 17, 18 or 19mm Imperf.**
8 A1(a) 1p on 6p brown red (surch. 17mm) — 125.00 190.00
a. Double surcharge — 5,750. 3,500.
b. Surcharge omitted — 17,500.
9 A1(a) 1p on 6p brown red (surch.) — 140.00 200.00

**1864-73 Perf. 12½**
10 A1(a) 4p on 6p carmine — 50.00 27.50
b. Double surcharge — 8,000.
11 A1(a) 1p on 6p brn red (71) — 97.50 20.00
a. Blue black surcharge — 1,150.
12 A1(b) 1p on 6p brn red — 97.50 625.00
a. Blue black surcharge — 4,500.
13 A1(b) 2p on 6p yel (73) — 100.00
a. Blue black surcharge — 2,600.
14 A1(b) 3p on 6p dk vio (73) — 150.00
a. Double surcharge
15 A1(b) 4p on 6p car (73) — 62.50 100.00
a. Double surcharge — 6,250.
16 A1(b) 1sh on 6p grn (bar 16 to 17mm) — 55.00
17 A1(b) 1sh on 6p dp grn (bar 18mm)(73) — 30.00 300.00
a. Double surcharge — 22,500.

**1868 Short Bar, 14 or 15mm**
18 A1(a) 1p on 6p brn red — 160.00 57.50
a. Imperf., pair — 5,250.
b. Double surcharge
19 A1(b) 2p on 6p yellow — 190.00 70.00
a. Imperf. — 10,500.
20 A1(b) 3p on 6p dk vio — 87.50 57.50
a. Imperf., pair — 1,900.
21 A1(b) 4p on 6p car (words 18mm) — 100.00 55.00
a. Double surcharge
b. Imperf — 10,500.
22 A1(b) 4p on 6p violet (words 19mm) — 210.00 140.00
a. Words double, 18mm and 19mm — 23,000.
b. Imperf. — 10,500.
23 A1(a) 1sh on 6p yel grn (words 16mm) — 625.00 150.00
a. Double surcharge — 15,000.
b. Pair, one without surcharge
c. Imperf — 13,500.
24 A1(d) 5sh on 6p org — 52.50 70.00
No. 22 exists with surcharge omitted.

**1882 Perf. 14x12½**
25 A1(a) 1p on 6p brown red — 80.00 17.50
26 A1(a) 2p on 6p yellow — 100.00 57.50
27 A1(b) 3p on 6p violet — 210.00 80.00
28 A1(b) 4p on 6p carmine — 110.00 62.50

**1883 Perf. 14**
29 A1(a) 1p on 6p brown red — 92.50 19.00
30 A1(a) 2p on 6p yellow — 110.00 32.50
31 A1(a) 1sh on 6p yel grn — 22.50 12.50

**1882 Perf. 14x12½**
32 A1(b) 1sh on 6p dp grn — 625.00 24.00

**1884-94 Wmk. 2 Perf. 14**
33 A1(b) ½p on 6p grn — 8.75 16.00
a. ½p on 6p emer., blurred print (words 17mm)(84) — 11.50 16.00
b. Double surcharge — 1,250. 1,350.
34 A1(b) ½p on 6p grn (words 15mm)(94) — 625.00 24.00
a. Double surcharge
35 A1(a) 1p on 6p red (87) — 2.40 2.75
36 A1(b) 2p on 6p yel (94) — 2.40 4.50
37 A1(b) 3p on 6p dp vio (87) — 2.40 7.25
a. 3p on 6p red violet — 7.25 10.50
b. Double surcharge, #37a — 5.00 6,500.
c. Double surcharge, #37 — 9,250. 10,000.
38 A1(b) 4p on 6p pale brn (words 16½mm;90) — 25.00 17.00
a. 4p on 6p dk brn (words 17mm;94) — 21.00 25.00
b. With thin bar below thick one — 625.00

**1894 Long Bar, 18mm**
39 A1(b) 1sh on 6p yel grn — 50.00 25.00
a. Double surcharge — 4,750.
See note after No. 47.

Queen Victoria — A3

**1890-97 Typo. Perf. 14**
40 A3 ½p green (97) — 3.25 6.25
41 A3 1p rose (96) — 16.00 1.75
42 A3 1½p red brn & grn — 5.25 8.00
43 A3 2p yellow (96) — 5.75 14.00
44 A3 2½p ultra (96) — 13.50 14.00
45 A3 5p violet (96) — 12.50 32.50
46 A3 10p brown (96) — 27.50 70.00
Nos. 40-46 (7) — 83.75 146.50

Type of 1856 Surcharged

**1893 Engr. Wmk. 2**
47 A1 2½p on 6p blue — 3.00 5.75
a. Double surcharge — 10,500.
b. Double impression — 9,250.

In 1905 remainders of Nos. 34-47 were sold by the postal officials. They are canceled with bars, arranged in the shape of diamonds, in purple ink. No such cancellation was ever used on the island and the stamps so canceled are of slight value. With this cancellation removed, these remainders are sometimes offered as unused. Some have been recanceled with a false dated postmark.

King Edward VII — A5

**1902 Typo. Wmk. 2**
48 A5 ½p green — 1.75 2.75
49 A5 1p carmine rose — 7.25 .85

Government House — A6

"The Wharf" — A7

A8

**1903, June Wmk. 1**
50 A6 ½p gray grn & brn — 2.40 3.50
51 A7 1p carmine & blk — 1.75 .50
52 A6 2p ol grn & blk — 7.75 1.50
53 A6 8p brown & blk — 24.00 35.00
54 A6 1sh org buff & blk — 55.00 45.00
55 A7 2sh violet & blk — 115.90 90.00
Nos. 50-55 (6) — 115.90 175.50

**1908, May Wmk. 3**
56 A8 2½p ultra — 1.75 1.75
57 A8 4p black & red, yel — 3.50 19.00
58 A8 6p dull violet — 5.00 16.00
Nos. 56-58 (3) — 10.25 36.75

**Wmk. 2**
60 A8 10sh grn & red, grn — 210.00 300.00
Nos. 57 and 58 exist on both ordinary and chalky paper; No. 56 on ordinary and No. 60 on chalky paper.

Government House — A9

"The Wharf" — A10

**1912-16 Ordinary Paper Wmk. 3**
61 A10 ½p green & blk — 2.50 11.00
62 A10 1p carmine & blk — 5.00 2.00
a. 1p scarlet & black (16) — 12.50 22.50
63 A10 1p orange & blk — 3.75 6.50
64 A9 2p gray & black — 4.75 2.00
65 A10 2½p vio & blk, yel — 3.75 5.50
66 A9 3p vio & blk, yel — 7.50 55.00
67 A10 8p dull vio & blk — 9.50 37.50
68 A9 1sh black, green — 42.50 85.00
69 A10 2sh ultra & blk, bl — 57.50 140.00
70 A10 3sh violet & blk — 140.50 350.50
Nos. 61-70 (10)
See Nos. 75-77.

A12

A11 Die I

For description of dies I and II see back of this section of the Catalogue.

**1912 Chalky Paper**
71 A11 4p black & red, yel — 12.50 26.00
72 A11 6p dull vio & red vio — 4.50 5.50

**1913 Ordinary Paper**
73 A12 4p black & red, yel — 9.00 3.00
74 A12 6p dull vio & red vio — 15.00 30.00

**1922 Wmk. 4**
75 A10 1p green — 2.00 30.00
76 A10 1½p rose red — 11.00 30.00
77 A9 3p ultra — 20.00 62.50
Nos. 75-77 (3) — 33.00 122.50

Badge of the Colony — A13

**1922-27 Chalky Paper Wmk. 4**
79 A13 ½p black & gray — 2.50 2.50
80 A13 1p grn & blk — 2.75 1.75
81 A13 1½p rose red — 3.00 14.50
82 A13 2p pale gray & gray — 4.00 4.50
83 A13 3p ultra — 2.25 4.50
84 A13 5p red & grn, emer — 3.25 6.00
85 A13 6p red vio & blk — 5.00 9.00

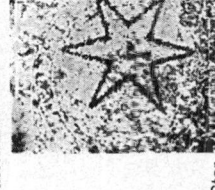

| | | | | | |
|---|---|---|---|---|---|
| 86 | A13 | 8p | violet & blk | 4.00 | 7.50 |
| 87 | A13 | 1sh | dk brn & blk | 7.25 | 10.50 |
| 88 | A13 | 1sh6p | grn & blk, *emer* | 17.00 | 50.00 |
| 89 | A13 | 2sh | ultra & vio, *bl* | 19.00 | 45.00 |
| 90 | A13 | 2sh6p | car & blk, *yel* | 16.00 | 62.50 |
| 91 | A13 | 5sh | grn & blk, *yel* | 42.50 | 82.50 |
| 92 | A13 | 7sh6p | orange & blk | 85.00 | 140.00 |
| 93 | A13 | 10sh | ol grn & blk | 125.00 | 190.00 |
| 94 | A13 | 15sh | vio & blk, *bl* | 925.00 | 1,700. |
| | *Nos. 79-93 (15)* | | | 338.50 | 628.50 |

Nos. 88, 90, and 91 are on ordinary paper.

**Wmk. 3**

**Chalky Paper**

| | | | | | |
|---|---|---|---|---|---|
| 95 | A13 | 4p | black, *yel* | 12.50 | 6.75 |
| 96 | A13 | 1sh6p | bl grn & blk, *grn* | 25.00 | 60.00 |
| 97 | A13 | 2sh6p | car & blk, *yel* | 30.00 | 62.50 |
| 98 | A13 | 5sh | grn & blk, *yel* | 42.50 | 100.00 |
| 99 | A13 | £1 | red vio & blk, *red* | 450.00 | 500.00 |
| | *Nos. 95-99 (5)* | | | 560.00 | 729.25 |

Issued: ½p, 1½p, 2p, 3p, 4p, 8p, 2/23; 5p, #88-91, 1927; others, 6/22.

### Centenary Issue

Lot and Lot's Wife — A14

Plantation; Queen Victoria and Kings William IV, Edward VII, George V A15

Map of the Colony A16

Quay, Jamestown A17

View of James Valley — A18

View of Jamestown A19

View of Mundens A20

St. Helena — A21

View of High Knoll — A22

Badge of the Colony A23

**Perf. 12**

**1934, Apr. 23 Engr. Wmk. 4**

| | | | | | |
|---|---|---|---|---|---|
| 101 | A14 | ½p | dk vio & blk | 1.25 | 1.00 |
| 102 | A15 | 1p | green & blk | .80 | 1.00 |
| 103 | A16 | 1½p | red & blk | 3.00 | 4.00 |
| 104 | A17 | 2p | orange & blk | 2.75 | 1.50 |
| 105 | A18 | 3p | blue & blk | 1.75 | 5.50 |
| 106 | A19 | 6p | lt blue & blk | 4.00 | 3.75 |
| 107 | A20 | 1sh | dk brn & blk | 8.00 | 22.50 |
| 108 | A21 | 2sh6p | car & blk | 42.50 | 60.00 |
| 109 | A22 | 5sh | choc & blk | 92.50 | 100.00 |
| 110 | A23 | 10sh | red vio & black | 250.00 | 325.00 |
| | *Nos. 101-110 (10)* | | | 406.55 | 524.25 |
| | Set, never hinged | | | 600.00 | |

Common Design Types pictured following the introduction.

### Silver Jubilee Issue

Common Design Type

**1935, May 6 Perf. 13½x14**

| | | | | | |
|---|---|---|---|---|---|
| 111 | CD301 | 1½p | car & dk blue | .75 | 5.75 |
| 112 | CD301 | 2p | gray blk & ultra | 1.50 | 1.00 |
| 113 | CD301 | 6p | indigo & grn | 7.00 | 3.50 |
| 114 | CD301 | 1sh | brt vio & ind | 10.00 | 15.00 |
| | *Nos. 111-114 (4)* | | | 19.25 | 25.25 |
| | Set, never hinged | | | 37.50 | |

### Coronation Issue

Common Design Type

**1937, May 19**

| | | | | | |
|---|---|---|---|---|---|
| 115 | CD302 | 1p | deep green | .40 | .75 |
| 116 | CD302 | 2p | deep orange | .35 | .50 |
| 117 | CD302 | 3p | bright ultra | .50 | .50 |
| | *Nos. 115-117 (3)* | | | 1.25 | 1.75 |
| | Set, never hinged | | | 2.00 | |

Badge of the Colony — A24

**1938-40 Perf. 12½**

| | | | | | |
|---|---|---|---|---|---|
| 118 | A24 | ½p | purple | .20 | .75 |
| 119 | A24 | 1p | dp green | 5.00 | 2.40 |
| 119A | A24 | 1p | org yel ('40) | .20 | .30 |
| 120 | A24 | 1½p | carmine | .20 | .40 |
| 121 | A24 | 2p | orange | .20 | .20 |
| 122 | A24 | 3p | ultra | 45.00 | 20.00 |
| 122A | A24 | 3p | gray ('40) | .20 | .30 |
| 122B | A24 | 4p | ultra ('40) | 1.10 | .85 |
| 123 | A24 | 6p | gray blue | 1.10 | 1.25 |
| 123A | A24 | 8p | olive ('40) | 1.75 | 1.00 |
| 124 | A24 | 1sh | sepia | 1.10 | .35 |
| 125 | A24 | 2sh6p | deep claret | 9.00 | 6.75 |
| 126 | A24 | 5sh | brown | 10.00 | 12.50 |
| 127 | A24 | 10sh | violet | 10.00 | 18.00 |
| | *Nos. 118-127 (14)* | | | 85.05 | 65.05 |
| | Set, never hinged | | | 160.00 | |

Issue dates: May 12, 1938, July 8, 1940.
See Nos. 136-138.

**Catalogue values for unused stamps in this section, from this point to the end of the section, are for Never Hinged items.**

### Peace Issue

Common Design Type

**Perf. 13½x14**

**1946, Oct. 21 Wmk. 4 Engr.**

| | | | | | |
|---|---|---|---|---|---|
| 128 | CD303 | 2p | deep orange | .30 | .30 |
| 129 | CD303 | 4p | deep blue | .40 | .30 |

### Silver Wedding Issue

Common Design Types

**1948, Oct. 20 Photo. Perf. 14x14½**

| | | | | | |
|---|---|---|---|---|---|
| 130 | CD304 | 3p | black | .30 | .30 |

**Engr.; Name Typo.**

**Perf. 11½x11**

| | | | | | |
|---|---|---|---|---|---|
| 131 | CD305 | 10sh | blue violet | 26.00 | 37.50 |

### UPU Issue

Common Design Types

**Engr.; Name Typo. on 4p, 6p**

**1949, Oct. 10 Perf. 13½, 11x11½**

| | | | | | |
|---|---|---|---|---|---|
| 132 | CD306 | 3p | rose carmine | .25 | 1.00 |
| 133 | CD307 | 4p | indigo | 3.25 | 1.50 |
| 134 | CD308 | 6p | olive | .50 | 1.75 |
| 135 | CD309 | 1sh | slate | .40 | 1.25 |
| | *Nos. 132-135 (4)* | | | 4.40 | 5.50 |

George VI Type of 1938

**1949, Nov. 1 Engr. Perf. 12½**

**Center in Black**

| | | | | | |
|---|---|---|---|---|---|
| 136 | A24 | 1p | blue green | 1.00 | 1.50 |
| 137 | A24 | 1½p | carmine rose | 1.00 | 1.50 |
| 138 | A24 | 2p | carmine | 1.00 | 1.50 |
| | *Nos. 136-138 (3)* | | | 3.00 | 4.50 |

### Coronation Issue

Common Design Type

**1953, June 2 Perf. 13½x13**

| | | | | | |
|---|---|---|---|---|---|
| 139 | CD312 | 3p | purple & black | 1.25 | 1.25 |

Badge of the Colony A25

A26

A27

Designs: 1p, Flax plantation. 1½p, Heart-shaped waterfall. 2p, Lace making. 2½p, Drying flax. 3p, Wire bird. 4p, Flagstaff and barn. 6p, Donkeys carrying flax. 7p, Map. 1sh, Entrance, government offices. 2sh 6p, Cutting flax. 5sh, Jamestown. 10sh, Longwood house.

**1953, Aug. 4 Perf. 13½x14, 14x13½**

**Center and Denomination in Black**

| | | | | | |
|---|---|---|---|---|---|
| 140 | A25 | ½p | emerald | .40 | .20 |
| 141 | A25 | 1p | dark green | .20 | .20 |
| 142 | A26 | 1½p | red violet | 1.90 | .70 |
| 143 | A25 | 2p | rose lake | .55 | .25 |
| 144 | A25 | 2½p | red | .45 | .40 |
| 145 | A25 | 3p | brown | 3.75 | .40 |
| 146 | A25 | 4p | deep blue | .45 | .50 |
| 147 | A25 | 6p | purple | .45 | .40 |
| 148 | A25 | 7p | gray | .75 | 1.40 |
| 149 | A25 | 1sh | dk car rose | .45 | .50 |
| 150 | A25 | 2sh 6p | violet | 14.50 | 5.25 |
| 151 | A25 | 5sh | chocolate | 19.00 | 11.00 |
| 152 | A25 | 10sh | orange | 45.00 | 30.00 |
| | *Nos. 140-152 (13)* | | | 87.85 | 51.20 |

**Perf. 11½**

**1956, Jan. 3 Wmk. 4 Engr.**

| | | | | | |
|---|---|---|---|---|---|
| 153 | A27 | 3p | dk car rose & blue | .20 | .20 |
| 154 | A27 | 4p | redsh brown & blue | .35 | .35 |
| 155 | A27 | 6p | purple & blue | .55 | .55 |
| | *Nos. 153-155 (3)* | | | 1.10 | 1.10 |

Cent. of the 1st St. Helena postage stamp.

Arms of East India Company A28

Designs: 6p, Dutton's ship "London" off James Bay. 1sh, Memorial stone from fort built by Governor Dutton.

**Perf. 12½x13**

**1959, May 5 Wmk. 314**

| | | | | | |
|---|---|---|---|---|---|
| 156 | A28 | 3p | rose & black | .20 | .20 |
| 157 | A28 | 6p | gray & yellow green | .45 | .45 |
| 158 | A28 | 1sh | orange & black | .65 | .65 |
| | *Nos. 156-158 (3)* | | | 1.30 | 1.30 |

300th anniv. of the landing of Capt. John Dutton on St. Helena and of the 1st settlement.

Cape Canary A29

Elizabeth II A30

Queen and Prince Andrew A31

Designs: 1p, Cunning fish, horiz. 2p, Brittle starfish, horiz. 4½p, Redwood flower. 6p, Red fody (Madagascar weaver). 7p, Trumpetfish, horiz. 10p, Keeled feather starfish, horiz. 1sh, Gumwood flowers. 1sh6p, Fairy tern. 2sh6p, Orange starfish, horiz. 5sh, Night-blooming cereus. 10sh, Deepwater bull's-eye, horiz.

**Perf. 11½x12, 12x11½**

**1961, Dec. 12 Photo. Wmk. 314**

| | | | | | |
|---|---|---|---|---|---|
| 159 | A29 | 1p | multicolored | .20 | .20 |
| 160 | A29 | 1½p | multicolored | .25 | .20 |
| 161 | A29 | 2p | gray & red | .20 | .20 |
| 162 | A30 | 3p | dk blue, rose & grnsh blue | .50 | .40 |
| 163 | A29 | 4½p | slate, brn & grn | .65 | .40 |
| 164 | A29 | 6p | cit, brn & dp car | 2.50 | .45 |
| 165 | A29 | 7p | vio, blk & red brn | .50 | .45 |
| 166 | A29 | 10p | blue & dp cl | .90 | .75 |
| 167 | A29 | 1sh | red brn, grn & yel | .90 | .75 |
| 168 | A29 | 1sh6p | gray bl & blk | 6.50 | 2.00 |
| 169 | A29 | 2sh6p | grnsh bl, yel & red | 5.00 | 3.25 |
| 170 | A29 | 5sh | grn, brn & yel | 9.75 | 4.75 |
| 171 | A29 | 10sh | gray bl, blk & sal | 13.50 | 11.00 |

**Perf. 14x14½**

| | | | | | |
|---|---|---|---|---|---|
| 172 | A31 | £1 | turq blue & choc | 26.00 | 25.00 |
| | *Nos. 159-172 (14)* | | | 67.35 | 49.80 |

For overprints see Nos. 176-179.

### Freedom from Hunger Issue

Common Design Type

**1963, Apr. 4 Perf. 14x14½**

| | | | | | |
|---|---|---|---|---|---|
| 173 | CD314 | 1sh6p | ultra | 3.00 | 2.50 |

### Red Cross Centenary Issue

Common Design Type

**Wmk. 314**

**1963, Sept. 2 Litho. Perf. 13**

| | | | | | |
|---|---|---|---|---|---|
| 174 | CD315 | 3p | black & red | .30 | .30 |
| 175 | CD315 | 1sh6p | ultra & red | 3.50 | 3.50 |

Nos. 159, 162, 164 and 168 Overprinted: "FIRST LOCAL POST / 4th JANUARY 1965"

***Perf. 11½x12, 12x11½***

**1965, Jan. 4 Photo. Wmk. 314**
**176** A29 1p multicolored .20 .20
**177** A30 3p dk bl, rose & grnsh bl .20 .20
**178** A29 6p cit, brn & dp car .25 .20
**179** A29 1sh6p gray blue & blk .35 .20
*Nos. 176-179 (4)* 1.00 .80

Establishment of the 1st internal postal service on the island.

**ITU Issue**
Common Design Type

***Perf. 11x11½***

**1965, May 17 Litho. Wmk. 314**
**180** CD317 3p ultra & gray .30 .30
**181** CD317 6p red lil & blue grn .70 .30

**Intl. Cooperation Year Issue**
Common Design Type

**1965, Oct. 25 Litho. *Perf. 14½***
**182** CD318 1p blue grn & claret .20 .20
**183** CD318 6p lt violet & green 1.00 .20

**Churchill Memorial Issue**
Common Design Type

**1966, Jan. 24 Photo. *Perf. 14***
**Design in Black, Gold and Carmine Rose**
**184** CD319 1p bright blue .20 .20
**185** CD319 3p green .40 .40
**186** CD319 6p brown .55 .55
**187** CD319 1sh6p violet .85 .85
*Nos. 184-187 (4)* 2.00 2.00

**World Cup Soccer Issue**
Common Design Type

**1966, July 1 Litho. *Perf. 14***
**188** CD321 3p multicolored .40 .30
**189** CD321 6p multicolored 1.00 .30

**WHO Headquarters Issue**
Common Design Type

**1966, Sept. 20 Litho. *Perf. 14***
**190** CD322 3p multicolored 1.00 .20
**191** CD322 1sh6p multicolored 2.75 1.50

**UNESCO Anniversary Issue**
Common Design Type

**1966, Dec. 1 Litho. *Perf. 14***
**192** CD323 3p "Education" .55 .50
**193** CD323 6p "Science" 1.10 .90
**194** CD323 1sh6p "Culture" 4.00 3.75
*Nos. 192-194 (3)* 5.65 5.15

Badge of St. Helena — A32

***Perf. 14½x14***

**1967, May 5 Photo. Wmk. 314**
**195** A32 1sh dk grn & multi .30 .30
**196** A32 2sh6p blue & multi .70 .70
**a.** Carmine omitted 450.00

St. Helena's New Constitution.

The Great Fire of London A33

3p, Three-master Charles. 6p, Boats bringing new settlers to shore. 1sh6p, Settlers at work.

***Perf. 13½x13***

**1967, Sept. 4 Engr. Wmk. 314**
**197** A33 1p black & carmine .20 .20
**198** A33 3p black & vio blue .20 .20
**199** A33 6p black & dull violet .20 .20
**200** A33 1sh6p black & ol green .30 .20
*Nos. 197-200 (4)* .90 .80

Tercentenary of the arrival of settlers from London after the Great Fire of Sept. 2-4, 1666.

Maps of Tristan da Cunha and St. Helena A34

Designs: 8p, 2sh3p, Maps of St. Helena and Tristan da Cunha.

***Perf. 14x14½***

**1968, June 4 Photo. Wmk. 314**
**Maps in Sepia**
**201** A34 4p dp red lilac .20 .20
**202** A34 8p olive .20 .25
**203** A34 1sh9p deep ultra .20 .35
**204** A34 2sh3p Prus blue .25 .35
*Nos. 201-204 (4)* .85 1.15

30th anniv. of Tristan da Cunha as a Dependency of St. Helena.

Sir Hudson Lowe A35

1sh6p, 2sh6p, Sir George Bingham.

***Perf. 13½x13***

**1968, Sept. 4 Litho. Wmk. 314**
**205** A35 3p multicolored .20 .20
**206** A35 9p multicolored .20 .20
**207** A35 1sh6p multicolored .20 .20
**208** A35 2sh6p multicolored .30 .30
*Nos. 205-208 (4)* .90 .90

Abolition of slavery in St. Helena, 150th anniv.

Road Construction — A36

Designs: 1p, Electricity development. 1½p, Dentist. 2p, Pest control. 3p, Apartment houses in Jamestown. 4p, Pasture and livestock improvement. 6p, School children listening to broadcast. 8p, Country cottages. 10p, New school buildings. 1sh, Reforestation. 1sh6p, Heavy lift crane. 2sh6p, Playing children in Lady Field Children's Home. 5sh, Agricultural training. 10sh, Ward in New General Hospital. £1, Lifeboat "John Dutton."

**Wmk. 314**

**1968, Nov. 4 Litho. *Perf. 13½***
**209** A36 ½p multicolored .20 .20
**210** A36 1p multicolored .20 .20
**211** A36 1½p multicolored .20 .20
**212** A36 2p multicolored .20 .20
**213** A36 3p multicolored .20 .20
**214** A36 4p multicolored .20 .20
**215** A36 6p multicolored .20 .25
**216** A36 8p multicolored .25 .30
**217** A36 10p multicolored .30 .50
**218** A36 1sh multicolored .40 .70
**219** A36 1sh6p multicolored .50 .85
**220** A36 2sh6p multicolored .95 1.60
**221** A36 5sh multicolored 1.60 2.75
**222** A36 10sh multicolored 3.25 5.50
**223** A36 £1 multicolored 8.50 14.50
*Nos. 209-223 (15)* 17.15 28.15

See Nos. 244-256.

Brig Perseverance, 1819 — A37

Ships: 8p, M.S. Dane, 1857. 1sh9p, S.S. Llandovery Castle, 1925. 2sh3p, M.S. Good Hope Castle, 1969.

**1969, Apr. 19 Litho. *Perf. 13½***
**224** A37 4p violet & multi .30 .30
**225** A37 8p ocher & multi .45 .45
**226** A37 1sh9p ver & multi .60 .60
**227** A37 2sh3p dk blue & multi .65 .65
*Nos. 224-227 (4)* 2.00 2.00

Issued in recognition of St. Helena's dependence on sea mail.

Surgeon and Officer (Light Company) 20th Foot, 1816 — A38

British Uniforms: 6p, Warrant Officer and Drummer, 53rd Foot, 1815. 1sh8p, Drum Major, 66th Foot, 1816, and Royal Artillery Officer, 1820. 2sh6p, Private 91st Foot and 2nd Corporal, Royal Sappers and Miners, 1832.

***Perf. 14x14½***

**1969, Sept. 3 Litho. Wmk. 314**
**228** A38 6p red & multi .50 .50
**229** A38 8p blue & multi .65 .65
**230** A38 1sh8p green & multi .65 .65
**231** A38 2sh6p gray & multi .65 .65
*Nos. 228-231 (4)* 2.45 2.45

Charles Dickens, "The Pickwick Papers" A39

Dickens and: 8p, "Oliver Twist." 1sh6p, "Martin Chuzzlewit." 2sh6p, "Bleak House."

***Perf. 13½x13***

**1970, June 9 Litho. Wmk. 314**
**232** A39 4p dk brown & multi .20 .20
**233** A39 8p slate & multi .40 .20
**234** A39 1sh6p multicolored .65 .25
**235** A39 2sh6p multicolored 1.40 .35
*Nos. 232-235 (4)* 2.65 1.00

Charles Dickens (1812-70), English novelist.

Mouth to Mouth Resuscitation — A40

Centenary of British Red Cross Society: 9p, Girl in wheelchair and nurse. 1sh9p, First aid. 2sh3p, British Red Cross Society emblem.

**1970, Sept. 15 *Perf. 14½***
**236** A40 6p bister, red & blk .20 .20
**237** A40 9p lt blue grn, red & blk .20 .20
**238** A40 1sh9p gray, red & blk .25 .20
**239** A40 2sh3p pale vio, red & blk .35 .30
*Nos. 236-239 (4)* 1.00 .90

A41

A42

Regimental Emblems: 4p, Officer's Shako Plate, 20th Foot, 1812-16. 9p, Officer's breast plate, 66th Foot, before 1818. 1sh3p, Officer's full dress shako, 91st Foot, 1816. 2sh11p, Ensign's shako, 53rd Foot, 1815.

**Wmk. 314**

**1970, Nov. 2 Litho. *Perf. 14½***
**240** A41 4p multicolored .20 .20
**241** A41 9p red & multi .40 .40
**242** A41 1sh3p dk gray & multi .65 .65
**243** A41 2sh11p dk gray grn & multi 1.00 1.00
*Nos. 240-243 (4)* 2.25 2.25

See Nos. 263-270, 273-276.

Type of 1968
"P" instead of "d"

**1971, Feb. 15 Litho. *Perf. 13½***
**244** A36 ½p like #210 .20 .20
**245** A36 1p like #211 .20 .20
**246** A36 1½p like #212 .20 .20
**247** A36 2p like #213 .30 .30
**a.** Perf. 14½ ('75) .55 .55
**248** A36 2½p like #214 .35 .35
**249** A36 3½p like #215 .45 .45
**250** A36 4½p like #216 .55 .55
**251** A36 5p like #217 .70 .70
**252** A36 7½p like #218 .90 .90
**253** A36 10p like #219 1.00 1.00
**254** A36 12½p like #220 1.40 1.40
**255** A36 25p like #221 2.75 2.75
**256** A36 50p like #222 12.50 12.50
*Nos. 244-256 (13)* 21.50 21.50

The paper of Nos. 244-256 is thinner than the paper of Nos. 209-223 and No. 223 (£1) has been reprinted in slightly different colors.

***Perf. 14x14½***

**1971, Apr. 5 Litho. Wmk. 314**

St. Helena, from Italian Miniature, 1460

**257** A42 2p violet blue & multi .20 .20
**258** A42 5p multicolored .25 .25
**259** A42 7½p multicolored .40 .40
**260** A42 12½p olive & multi .65 .65
*Nos. 257-260 (4)* 1.50 1.50

Easter 1971.

Napoleon, after J. L. David, and Tomb in St. Helena A43

34p, Napoleon, by Hippolyte Paul Delaroche.

**1971, May 5 *Perf. 13½***
**261** A43 2p multicolored .25 .20
**262** A43 34p multicolored 2.75 2.10

Sesquicentennial of the death of Napoleon Bonaparte (1769-1821).

**Military Type of 1970**

1½p, Sword Hilt, Artillery Private, 1815. 4p, Baker rifle, socket bayonet, c. 1816. 6p, Infantry officer's sword hilt, 1822. 22½p, Baker rifle, light sword bayonet, c. 1823.

**1971, Nov. 10 *Perf. 14½***
**263** A41 1½p green & multi .75 .20
**264** A41 4p gray & multi 1.00 .35
**265** A41 6p purple & multi 1.00 .45
**266** A41 22½p multicolored 1.75 1.50
*Nos. 263-266 (4)* 4.50 2.50

# ST. HELENA

## 1972, June 19
Designs: 2p, Royal Sappers and Miners breastplate, 1823. 5p, Infantry sergeant's pike, 1830. 7½p, Royal Artillery officer's breastplate, 1830. 12½p, English military pistol, 1800.

267 A41 2p multicolored .50 .50
268 A41 5p plum & black .75 .50
269 A41 7½p dp blue & multi 1.00 .60
270 A41 12½p olive & multi 3.25 3.30
Nos. 267-270 (4)

## Silver Wedding Issue, 1972
### Common Design Type
Design: Queen Elizabeth II, Prince Philip, St. Helena plover and white fairy tern.

**1972, Nov. 20 Photo. Perf. 14x14½**
271 CD324 2p si grn & multi .35
272 CD324 16p rose brn & multi .75

## Military Type of 1970
Designs: 2p, Shako, 53rd Foot, 1815. 5p, Band and Drums sword hilt, 1830. 7½p, Royal Sappers and Miners officers' hat, 1830. 12½p, General's sword hilt, 1831.

**1973, Sept. 20 Litho. Perf. 14½**
273 A41 2p dull brown & multi .85 .50
274 A41 5p multicolored 1.00 1.00
275 A41 7½p olive grn & multi 1.00 1.25
276 A41 12½p lilac & multi 1.75 1.50
Nos. 273-276 (4) 5.00 4.25

## Princess Anne's Wedding Issue
### Common Design Type
**1973, Nov. 14 Wmk. 314 Perf. 14**
277 CD325 2p multicolored .20 .20
278 CD325 18p multicolored .30 .30

## Westminster and Claudine Beached During Storm, 1849 — A45

Designs: 4p, East Indiaman True Briton, 1790. 6p, General Goddard in action off St. Helena, 1795. 22½p, East Indiaman Kent burning in Bay of Biscay, 1825.

**1973, Dec. 17 Litho. Wmk. 314**
279 A45 1½p multicolored .25 .45
280 A45 4p multicolored .45 .70
281 A45 6p multicolored .45 .70
282 A45 22½p multicolored 2.10 2.25
Nos. 279-282 (4) 3.25 4.10

Tercentenary of the East India Company Charter.

## UPU Emblem, Ships — A46
**1974, Oct. 15 Perf. 14½x14**
283 A46 5p blue & multi .80 .80
284 A46 25p red & multi 1.00 1.25
a. Souvenir sheet of 2, #283-284
Design: 25p, UPU emblem and letters.

Centenary of Universal Postal Union.

## Churchill and Blenheim Palace — A47

**1974, Nov. 30 Wmk. 373 Perf. 14½**
285 A47 5p black & multi .20 .20
286 A47 25p black & multi .80 .80
a. Souvenir sheet of 2, #285-286 1.00 2.00
Design: 25p, Churchill, Tower Bridge & Thames.

Sir Winston Churchill (1874-1965).

## Capt. Cook and Jamestown — A48

Design: 5p, Capt. Cook and "Resolution," vert.

**1975, July 14 Perf. 14x13½, 13½x14**
287 A48 5p multicolored 1.25 .35
288 A48 25p multicolored 2.10 .75

Return of Capt. James Cook to St. Helena, bicent.

## Mellissia Begonifolia — A49

Designs: 5p, Mellissius adumbratus (insect). 12p, Aegialitis St. Helena (bird), horiz. 25p, Scorpaenia mellissii (fish), horiz.

**1975, Oct. 20 Wmk. 373 Perf. 13**
289 A49 2p gray & multi .20 .20
290 A49 5p gray & multi .25 .25
291 A49 12p gray & multi .60 .60
292 A49 25p gray & multi .70 .70
Nos. 289-292 (4) 1.75 1.75

Centenary of the publication of "St. Helena," by John Charles Melliss.

## Pound Note — A50

**1976, Apr. 15 Wmk. 314 Perf. 13½**
293 A50 8p claret & multi .35 .35
294 A50 33p multicolored .90 .90
Design: 33p, 5-pound note.

First issue of St. Helena bank notes.

## St. Helena No. 8 — A51

**1976, May 4 Litho. Wmk. 373**
### Perf. 13½x14, 14x13½
295 A51 5p buff, brown & blk .20 .20
296 A51 8p lt grn, grn & blk .25 .25
297 A51 25p multicolored .55 .80
Nos. 295-297 (3) 1.00 1.25

Designs: 8p, St. Helena No. 80, vert. 25p, Freighter Good Hope Castle.

Festival of stamps 1976. See Tristan da Cunha #208a for souvenir sheet that contains one each of Ascension #214, St. Helena #297 and Tristan da Cunha #208.

## High Knoll, by Capt. Barnett — A52
**1976, Nov. 28 Wmk. 373 Perf. 14**

Views on St. Helena, lithographs: 3p, Friar Rock, by G. H. Bellasis, 1815. 5p, Column Lot, by Bellasis. 6p, Sandy Bay Valley, by H. Salt, 1809. 8p, View from Castle terrace, by Bellasis. 9p, The Briars, 1815. 10p, Plantation House, by J. Wathen, 1821. 15p, Longwood House, by Wathen, 1821. 18p, St. Paul's Church, by Vincent Brooks. 20p, St. James's Valley, by Capt. Hastings, 1815. 40p, St. Matthew's Church, Longwood, by Brooks. £1, St. Helena and sailing ship, by Bellasis. £2, Sugar Loaf Hill, by Wathen, 1821.

### Size: 38½x25mm
298 A52 1p multicolored .20 .85
299 A52 3p multicolored .20 .85
300 A52 5p multicolored .20 .85
301 A52 6p multicolored .20 .85
302 A52 8p multicolored .20 .85
303 A52 9p multicolored .20 .85
304 A52 10p multicolored .20 .85
305 A52 15p multicolored .55 .55
306 A52 18p multicolored .45 1.00
307 A52 20p multicolored .65 .85
308 A52 40p multicolored .85 1.50

### Size: 47½x35mm
### Perf. 13½
309 A52 £1 multicolored 2.25 3.00
310 A52 £2 multicolored 4.50 5.00
Nos. 298-310 (13) 10.50 17.50

Issue dates: 1p, 3p, 5p, 8p, 10p, 18p, 20p, 40p, £1, Sept. 28; others Nov. 23. For overprints see Nos. 376-377. 1p, 10p and £2 reissued inscribed 1982.

## Royal Party Leaving St. Helena, 1947 — A53

15p, Queen's scepter, dove. 26p, Prince Philip paying homage to the Queen.

**1977, Feb. 7 Wmk. 373 Perf. 13**
311 A53 8p multicolored .20 .20
312 A53 15p multicolored .25 .30
313 A53 26p multicolored .50 .50
Nos. 311-313 (3) .75 1.00

25th anniv. of the reign of Elizabeth II.

## Halley's Comet, Bayeux Tapestry — A54
**1977, Aug. 23 Litho. Perf. 14**
314 A54 5p multicolored .45 .45
315 A54 8p multicolored .55 .55
316 A54 27p multicolored 1.25 1.25
Nos. 314-316 (3) 2.25 2.25

Designs: 8p, 17th cent. sextant. 27p, Edmund Halley and Halley's Mount, St. Helena.

Edmund Halley's visit to St. Helena, 300th anniv.

## Elizabeth II Coronation Anniversary Issue
### Common Design Types
### Souvenir Sheet
**1978, June 2 Litho. Unwmk. Perf. 15**
317 Sheet of 6 1.75 1.75
a. CD326 25p Black dragon of Ulster .30 .30
b. CD327 25p Elizabeth II .30 .30
c. CD328 25p Sea Lion .30 .30

No. 317 contains 2 se-tenant strips of Nos. 317a-317c, separated by horizontal gutter.

## St. Helena, 17th Century Engraving — A55

Designs: 5p, 9p, 15p, Various Chinese porcelain and other utensils salvaged from wreck. 8p, Bronze cannon. 20p, Dutch East Indiaman.

**1978, Aug. 14 Wmk. 373 Perf. 14½**
318 A55 5p multicolored .20 .20
319 A55 8p multicolored .20 .20
320 A55 9p multicolored .25 .25
321 A55 15p multicolored .30 .30
322 A55 20p multicolored .35 .35
323 A55 50p multicolored .50 .50
Nos. 318-323 (6) 1.80 1.80

Wreck of the Witte Leeuw, 1613.

## "Discovery" — A56

Capt. Cook's voyages: 8p, Cook's portable observatory. 12p, Pharnaceum acidum (plant), after sketch by Joseph Banks. 25p, Capt. Cook, after Flaxman/Wedgwood medallion.

**1979, Feb. 19 Litho. Perf. 11**
324 A56 3p multicolored .20 .20
325 A56 8p multicolored .30 .30
326 A56 12p multicolored .50 .45
### Litho.; Embossed
327 A56 25p multicolored 1.00 .85
Nos. 324-327 (4) 2.00 1.75

## St. Helena No. 176 — A57

**1979, Aug. 20 Litho. Perf. 14**
328 A57 5p multi, vert. .20 .20
329 A57 8p multi .20 .20
330 A57 20p multi .30 .30
331 A57 32p multi .40 .40
Nos. 328-331 (4) 1.10 1.10

Designs: 5p, Rowland Hill and his signature. 20p, St. Helena No. 8. 32p, St. Helena No. 49.

Sir Rowland Hill (1795-1879), originator of penny postage.

## Seale's Chart, 1823 — A58

**1979, Dec. 10 Litho. Perf. 14**
332 A58 5p multi .20 .20
333 A58 8p multi .20 .20
334 A58 50p multi, vert. .60 .60
Nos. 332-334 (3) 1.00 1.00

Designs: 8p, Jamestown & Inclined Plane, 1829. 50p, Inclined Plane (stairs), 1979.

Inclined Plane, 150th anniversary.

## 1980, Feb. 23 — A59

Tomb of Napoleon I, 1848 — A59

Empress Eugenie: 8p, Landing at St. Helena. 62p, Visiting Napoleon's tomb.

**1980, Feb. 23  Litho.  Perf. 14½**
335 A59 5p multicolored .20 .20
336 A59 8p multicolored 1.10 1.10
337 A59 62p multicolored 1.50 1.50
a. Souvenir sheet of 3, #335-337 1.50 1.50
Nos. 335-337 (3)

Visit of Empress Eugenie (widow of Napoleon III) to St. Helena, centenary.

East Indiaman, London 1980 Emblem — A60

**1980, May 6  Litho.  Perf. 14½**
338 A60 5p shown .20 .20
339 A60 8p "Dolphin" postal stone .20 .20
340 A60 47p Jamestown postal stone .70 .70
a. Souvenir sheet of 3, #338-340 1.10 1.10
Nos. 338-340 (3)

London 1980 Intl. Stamp Exhib., May 6-14.

### Queen Mother Elizabeth Birthday Issue
Common Design Type

**1980, Aug. 18  Litho.  Perf. 14**
341 CD330 24p multicolored .50 .50

The Briars, 1815 — A61

**1980, Nov. 17  Litho.  Perf. 14**
342 A61 9p shown .25 .25
343 A61 30p Wellington, by Goya, vert. .70 .70

Duke of Wellington's visit to St. Helena, 175th anniv. Nos. 342-343 issued in sheets of 10 with gutter giving historical background.

Redwood Flower A62

**1981, Jan. 5  Perf. 13½**
344 A62 5p shown .20 .20
345 A62 8p Old father-live-forever .20 .20
346 A62 15p Gumwood .45 .45
347 A62 27p Black cabbage 1.10 1.10
Nos. 344-347 (4)

John Thornton's Map of St. Helena, 1700 — A63

## 1981, May 22 — A63

**1981, May 22  Litho.  Perf. 14½**
348 A63 5p Reinel Portolan Chart, 1530 .20 .20
349 A63 8p St. Helena, 1815 .40 .40
350 A63 20p St. Helena, 1815 .40 .40
351 A63 30p St. Helena, 1817 .60 .60
Nos. 348-351 (4) 1.40 1.40

**Souvenir Sheet**
352 A63 24p Gastaldi's map of Africa, 16th cent. .65 .65

### Royal Wedding Issue
Common Design Type

**1981, July 22  Wmk. 373  Litho.**
353 CD331 14p Bouquet .20 .20
354 CD331 29p Charles .45 .45
355 CD331 32p Couple .45 .45
Nos. 353-355 (3) 1.10 1.10

Traffic Guards Taking Oath — A65

**1981, Sept. 10  Litho.  Perf. 14**
356 A64 7p shown .20 .20
357 A64 14p Cypraea spurca sanctahelenae .30 .30
358 A64 25p Janthina janthina .75 .75
359 A64 53p Pinna rudis 1.40 1.40
Nos. 356-359 (4) 2.65 2.65

Charonia Variegata — A64

**1981, Nov. 5**
360 A65 7p shown .20 .20
361 A65 11p Posting signs .20 .20
362 A65 25p Animal care .50 .50
363 A65 59p Duke of Edinburgh 1.00 1.00
Nos. 360-363 (4) 1.90 1.90

Duke of Edinburgh's Awards, 25th anniv.

St. Helena Dragonfly — A66

**1982, Jan. 4  Litho.  Perf. 14½**
364 A66 7p shown .20 .20
365 A66 10p Burchell's beetle .25 .25
366 A66 10p Cockroach wasp .60 .60
367 A66 32p Earwig .85 .85
Nos. 364-367 (4) 1.90 1.90
See Nos. 386-389.

Sesquicentennial of Charles Darwin's Visit — A67

**1982, Apr. 19  Litho.  Perf. 14**
368 A67 7p Portrait .20 .20
369 A67 14p Flagstaff Hill, hammer .45 .45
370 A67 25p Ring-necked pheasants .70 .70
371 A67 29p Beagle .85 .85
Nos. 368-371 (4) 2.20 2.20

### Princess Diana Issue
Common Design Type

**1982, July 1  Litho.  Perf. 14**
372 CD333 7p Arms .20 .20
373 CD333 11p Diana .35 .35
374 CD333 19p Honeymoon .90 .90
375 CD333 55p Portrait 1.75 1.75
Nos. 372-375 (4) 3.20 3.20

## Nos. 305, 307 Overprinted:
"1st PARTICIPATION / COMMONWEALTH GAMES 1982"

**1982, Oct. 25  Litho.  Perf. 14**
376 A52 15p multicolored .30 .30
377 A52 26p multicolored .60 .60

Scouting Year A68

**1982, Nov. 29**
378 A68 3p Baden-Powell, vert. .20 .20
379 A68 11p Campfire .25 .25
380 A68 29p Canon Walcott, vert. .60 .60
381 A68 59p Thompsons Wood camp 1.25 1.25
Nos. 378-381 (4) 2.30 2.30

Coastline from Jamestown — A69

**1983, Jan.**
382 A69 7p King and Queen Rocks, vert. .20 .20
383 A69 11p Turk's Cap, vert. .25 .25
384 A69 29p Munden's Point .60 .60
385 A69 55p Munden's Point 1.10 1.10
Nos. 382-385 (4) 2.15 2.15

Insect Type of 1982

**1983, Apr. 22  Litho.  Perf. 14½**
386 A66 11p Death's-head hawk-moth .25 .25
387 A66 15p Saddid-shore bug .35 .35
388 A66 29p Click beetle .55 .55
389 A66 59p Weevil 1.25 1.25
Nos. 386-389 (4) 2.40 2.40

Local Fungi A70

**1983, June 16  Wmk. 373  Litho.  Perf. 14**
390 A70 11p Coriolus versicolor, vert. .25 .25
391 A70 15p Pluteus brun-neisucus, vert. .35 .35
392 A70 29p Polyporus induratus .70 .70
393 A70 59p Coprinus angulatus, vert. 1.25 1.25
Nos. 390-393 (4) 2.55 2.55

Local Birds — A71

Christmas 1983 — A72

## 1983, Sept. 12 — A71

**1983, Sept. 12  Litho.  Perf. 14x14½**
394 A71 7p Padda oryzivora .30 .20
395 A71 15p Foudia madagascariensis .65 .40
396 A71 33p Estrilda astrild 1.40 .90
397 A71 59p Serinus flaviventris 2.40 1.60
Nos. 394-397 (4) 4.75 3.10

**Souvenir Sheet**
**1983, Oct. 17  Litho.  Perf. 14x13½**
Stained Glass, Parish Church of St. Michael.
398 Sheet of 10 4.00 3.00
a. A72 10p multicolored .25 .25
b. A72 15p multicolored .45 .35
Sheet contains strips of 5 of 10p and 15p with center margin telling St. Helena story. See Nos. 424-427, 442-445.

150th Anniv. of the Colony — A73

**1984, Jan. 3  Litho.  Perf. 14**
399 A73 3p No. 101 .20 .20
400 A73 3p No. 102 .20 .20
401 A73 6p No. 103 .20 .20
402 A73 8p No. 104 .20 .25
403 A73 11p No. 105 .25 .25
404 A73 15p No. 106 .35 .35
405 A73 29p No. 107 .65 .65
406 A73 33p No. 110 .70 .70
407 A73 59p No. 110 1.10 1.10
408 A73 £1 No. 108 2.00 2.00
409 A73 £2 New coat of arms 4.25 4.25
Nos. 399-409 (11) 10.10 10.10

Visit of Prince Andrew A74

**1984, Apr. 4  Litho.**
410 A74 11p Andrew, Invincible .30 .30
411 A74 60p Andrew, Herald 1.50 1.50

### Lloyd's List Issue
Common Design Type

**1984, May  Perf. 14½x14**
412 CD335 10p Andrew, 1814 .25 .25
413 CD335 18p Solomon's facade .40 .40
414 CD335 25p Lloyd's Coffee House .60 .60
415 CD335 50p Papanui, 1898 1.25 1.25
Nos. 412-415 (4) 2.50 2.50

New Coin Issue A75

**1984, July**
416 A75 10p Donkey .25 .25
417 A75 15p Wire bird .40 .40
418 A75 29p Yellowfin tuna .80 .80
419 A75 50p Arum lily 1.40 1.40
Nos. 416-419 (4) 2.85 2.85

Centenary of Salvation Army in St. Helena — A76

**1984, Sept.  Litho.  Wmk. 373**
420 A76 7p Secretary Rebecca Fuller, vert. .20 .20
421 A76 11p Meals on Wheels service .35 .35
422 A76 25p Jamestown SA Hall .70 .70

423 A76 60p Hymn playing, clock tower ... 1.75 1.75
Nos. 420-423 (4) ... 3.00 3.00

**1984, Nov. 9**
**Stained Glass Windows Type of 1983**

424 A72 6p St. Helena visits prisoners ... .20 .20
425 A72 10p Betrothal of St. Helena ... .30 .30
426 A72 15p Marriage of St. Helena & Constantius ... .40 .40
427 A72 33p Birth of Constantine ... .90 .90
Nos. 424-427 (4) ... 1.80 1.80

**Queen Mother 85th Birthday Issue**
**Common Design Type**

**1985, June 7**    **Perf. 14½x14**

428 CD336 11p Portrait, age 2 ... .20 .20
429 CD336 15p Queen Mother, Elizabeth II ... .35 .35
430 CD336 29p Attending ballet, Covent Garden ... .65 .65
431 CD336 55p Holding Prince Henry ... 1.40 1.40
Nos. 428-431 (4) ... 2.65 2.65

**Souvenir Sheet**

432 CD336 70p Queen Mother and Ford V8 Pilot ... 3.00 2.25

**1985, July 12**   **Perf. 13x13½**   **Wmk. 384**

433 A70 7p Rock bullseye ... .20 .20
434 A78 11p Mackerel ... .25 .25
435 A78 15p Skipjack tuna ... .50 .50
436 A78 33p Yellowfin tuna ... 1.25 1.25
437 A78 50p Noddy tern ... 1.75 1.75
Nos. 433-437 (5) ... 4.00 4.00

**Marine Life—A78**

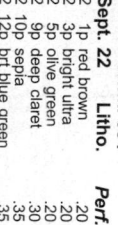

**1985, Sept. 2**   **Perf. 14**   **Wmk. 384**

438 A79 11p John Audubon, vert. ... .35 .35
439 A79 15p Common gallinule ... .45 .45
440 A79 25p Tropic bird ... .80 .80
441 A79 60p Noddy tern ... 2.00 2.00
Nos. 438-441 (4) ... 3.60 3.60

**Audubon Birth Bicent. A79**

Portrait of naturalist and his illustrations of American bird species.

**1985, Oct. 14**   **Perf. 13x13½**   **Wmk. 384**

442 A72 7p multicolored ... .20 .20
443 A72 10p multicolored ... .30 .30
444 A72 15p multicolored ... .45 .45
445 A72 60p multicolored ... 1.75 1.75
Nos. 442-445 (4) ... 2.70 2.70

**Stained Glass Windows Type of 1983**

Christmas: 7p, St. Helena journeys to the Holy Land. 10p, Zambres slays the bull. 15p, The bull restored to life, conversion of St. Helena. 60p, Resurrection of the corpse, the true cross identified.

**1986, Jan. 7**   **Perf. 13x13½**   **Wmk. 384**

446 A80 10p multicolored ... .30 .30
447 A80 11p multicolored ... .30 .30
448 A80 25p multicolored ... .70 .70

**Society Banners A80**

Designs: 10p, Church Provident Society for Women. 11p, Working Men's Christian Assoc. 25p, Church Benefit Society for Children. Assoc. Mechanics & Friendly Benefit Society. 33p, Ancient Order of Foresters.

449 A80 29p multicolored ... .80 .80
450 A80 33p multicolored ... .90 .90
Nos. 446-450 (5) ... 3.00 3.00

**1986, Apr. 21**
**Queen Elizabeth II 60th Birthday**
**Common Design Type**

**Perf. 14½**

451 CD337 10p scarlet, blk & sil ... .25 .25
452 CD337 15p ultra & multi ... .40 .40
453 CD337 20p green, blk & sil ... .50 .50
454 CD337 50p violet & multi ... 1.25 1.25
455 CD337 65p rose vio & multi ... 1.60 1.60
Nos. 451-455 (5) ... 4.00 4.00

For overprints see Nos. 488-492.

Designs: 10p, Making 21st birthday broadcast, royal tour of South Africa, 1947. 15p, In robes of state, Throne Room, Buckingham Palace, Silver Jubilee, 1977. 20p, Onboard HMS Implacable, en route to South Africa, 1947. 50p, State visit to US, 1976. 65p, Visiting Crown Agents' offices, 1983.

**1986, May 15**   **Wmk. 373**   **Perf. 14½**

456 A81 9p multicolored ... .50 .50
457 A81 12p multicolored ... .60 .60
458 A81 20p multicolored ... 1.00 1.00
459 A81 65p multicolored ... 1.90 1.90
Nos. 456-459 (4) ... 3.70 3.70

**Halley's Comet—A81**

Designs: 9p, Site of Halley's observatory on St. Helena. 12p, Edmond Halley, astronomer. 20p, Halley's planisphere of the southern stars. 65p, Voyage to St. Helena on the Unity.

**Royal Wedding Issue, 1986**
**Common Design Type**

in dress uniform at parade.

**1986, July 23**   **Wmk. 384**   **Litho.**   **Perf. 14**

460 CD338 10p multicolored ... .20 .20
461 CD338 40p multicolored ... .90 .90

Designs: 10p, Informal portrait. 40p, Andrew

**Explorers and Ships—A82**

**1986, Sept. 22**   **Wmk. 384**   **Perf. 14½**

462 A82 1p red brown ... .20 .20
463 A82 3p bright ultra ... .20 .20
464 A82 5p olive green ... .20 .20
465 A82 9p deep claret ... .30 .45
466 A82 10p sepia ... .35 .55
467 A82 12p brt blue green ... .35 .55
468 A82 15p brown lake ... .45 .75
469 A82 20p brown green ... .60 1.00
470 A82 25p sapphire ... .75 1.25
471 A82 40p red brown ... 1.00 2.10
472 A82 60p red brown ... 1.25 3.00
473 A82 £1 Prussian blue ... 1.75 5.25
474 A82 £2 bright violet ... 3.00 10.50
Nos. 462-474 (13) ... 15.40 26.00

Designs: 1p, James Ross (1800-62). Erebus. 3p, Robert FitzRoy (1805-65), Beagle. 5p, Adam Johann von Krusenstern (1770-1846), Nadezhda, Russia. 9p, William Bligh (1754-1817), Resolution. 10p, Otto von Kotzebue (1786-1846) Rurik, Germany. 12p, Philip Carteret (1639-82), Swallow. 12p, Thomas Cavendish (c.1560-92) Desire. 20p, Louis-Antoine de Bougainville (1729-1811), La Boudeuse, France. 25p, Fyodor Petrovitch Litke (1797-1882), Seniavin, Russia. 40p, Louis Isidore Duperrey (1786-1865), La Coquille, France. 60p, John Byron (1723-86), Dolphin. £1, James Cook, Endeavour. £2, Jules Dumont d'Urville (1790-1842), L'Astrolabe, France.

**1987, Feb. 16**   **Wmk. 373**   **Perf. 14**

475 A83 9p multicolored ... .75 .75
476 A83 13p multicolored ... 1.10 1.10
477 A83 38p multicolored ... 3.25 3.25
478 A83 45p multicolored ... 3.75 3.75
Nos. 475-478 (4) ... 8.85 8.85

**Ships of Royal Visitors A83**

Portraits and vessels: 9p, Prince Edward, HMS Repulse, 1925. 13p, King George VI, HMS Vanguard, 1947. 38p, Prince Philip, HMY Britannia, 1957. 45p, Prince Andrew, HMS Herald, 1984.

**1987, Aug. 3**   **Perf. 14½x14**

479 A84 9p St. Helena tea plant ... .60 .60
480 A84 13p Baby's toes ... .90 .90
481 A84 38p Salad plant ... 2.50 2.50
482 A84 45p Scrubwood ... 3.00 3.00
Nos. 479-482 (4) ... 7.00 7.00

**Rare Plants—A84**

**1987, Oct. 24**   **Wmk. 384**   **Litho.**   **Perf. 14**

483 A85 9p Lesser rorqual ... .75 .75
484 A85 13p Risso's dolphin ... 1.10 1.10
485 A85 45p Sperm whale ... 4.00 4.00
486 A85 60p Euphrosyne dolphin ... 5.75 5.75
Nos. 483-486 (4) ... 11.60 11.60

**Souvenir Sheet**

487 A85 75p Humpback whale ... 9.00 9.00

**Marine Mammals A85**

**1987, Dec. 9**   **Wmk. 384**   **Litho.**   **Perf. 14½**

Nos. 451-455 Ovptd. "40TH WEDDING ANNIVERSARY" in Silver.

488 CD337 10p scarlet, blk & sil ... .25 .25
489 CD337 15p ultra & multi ... .35 .35
490 CD337 20p green, blk & sil ... .55 .55
491 CD337 50p violet & multi ... 1.25 1.25
492 CD337 65p rose vio & multi ... 1.60 1.60
Nos. 488-492 (5) ... 4.00 4.00

**1988, Mar. 1**   **Wmk. 384**   **Litho.**   **Perf. 14½**

493 A86 9p multicolored ... 2.25 2.25
494 A86 13p multicolored ... 3.00 3.00
495 A86 45p multicolored ... 6.50 6.50
496 A86 60p multicolored ... 6.75 6.75
Nos. 493-496 (4) ... 16.75 16.75

**Australia Bicentennial A86**

Ships and signatures: 9p, HMS Defence, 1691, and William Dampier. 13p, HMS Resolution, 1775, and James Cook. 45p, HMS Providence, 1792, and William Bligh. 60p, HMS Beagle, 1836, and Charles Darwin.

**1988, Oct. 11**   **Wmk. 384**   **Perf. 14**

497 A87 5p multicolored ... .20 .20
498 A87 20p multicolored ... .65 .65
499 A87 38p multicolored ... 1.25 1.25
500 A87 60p multicolored ... 1.90 1.90
Nos. 497-500 (4) ... 4.00 4.00

**Christmas—A87**

Religious paintings by unknown artists: 5p, The Holy Family with Child. 20p, Madonna. 38p, The Holy Family with St. John. 60p, The Holy Virgin with the Child.

**1988, Nov. 1**   **Wmk. 384**   **Litho.**   **Perf. 14**

501 CD341 9p multi ... .40 .40
502 CD341 20p multi, horiz. ... 1.00 1.00
503 CD341 45p multi, horiz. ... 2.50 2.50
504 CD341 60p multi, horiz. ... 3.00 3.00
Nos. 501-504 (4) ... 7.00 7.00

**Lloyds of London 300th Anniv.**
**Common Design Type**

Designs: 9p, Underwriting room, 1886. 20p, Edinburgh Castle. 45p, Bosun Bird. 60p, Spangereid on fire off St. Helena, 1920.

**1989, Jan. 6**   **Wmk. 384**   **Perf. 14**

505 A88 9p St. Helena lobelia ... 1.00 1.00
506 A88 20p Ebony ... 2.10 2.10
507 A88 45p Large bellflower ... 2.75 2.75
508 A88 60p She cabbage tree ... 6.25 6.25
Nos. 505-508 (4) ... 

**Rare Plants—A88**

**1989, June 5**   **Litho.**   **Perf. 14**

509 Strip of 5 ... 7.75 7.75
a. A89 9p multicolored ... .45 .45
b. A89 9p multicolored
c. A89 13p multicolored
d. A89 45p multicolored
e. A89 60p multicolored

**Flags and Military Uniforms, 1815—A89**

Designs: 9p, Soldier, 53rd Foot. 13p, Officer, 53rd Foot. 20p, Royal marine. 45p, Officer, 66th Foot. 60p, Soldier, 66th Foot.

**1989, July 7**   **Litho.**   **Perf. 14**

Nos. 509a-509e Overprinted

510 Strip of 5 ... 8.25 8.25
a. A89 9p multicolored ... .50 .50
b. A89 13p multicolored ... .70 .70

## 1990, May 3 — Wmk. 373

| | | | | |
|---|---|---|---|---|
| 528 | A94 | 13p shown | .65 | .65 |
| 529 | A94 | 20p multicolored | 1.10 | 1.10 |
| 530 | A94 | 38p multicolored | 2.00 | 2.00 |
| 531 | A94 | 45p multicolored | 2.25 | 2.25 |
| | | Nos. 528-531 (4) | 6.00 | 6.00 |

Stamp World London '90, 150th anniv. of the Penny Black.

## Queen Mother, 90th Birthday
### Common Design Types

**1990, Aug. 4 — Wmk. 384 — Perf. 14x15**

| | | | | |
|---|---|---|---|---|
| 532 | CD343 | 25p As Duchess of York, 1923 | 1.25 | 1.25 |

**Perf. 14½**

| | | | | |
|---|---|---|---|---|
| 533 | CD344 | £1 Visiting communal feeding center, 1940 | 4.25 | 4.25 |

## Telecommunications — A95

**1990, July 28 — Wmk. 373 — Perf. 11**

| | | | | |
|---|---|---|---|---|
| 534 | A95 | Block of 4 | 4.25 | 4.25 |
| | | a.-d. 20p any single | 1.00 | 1.00 |

### Dane, 1857 — A96

**1990, Sept. 13 — Perf. 14½**

| | | | | |
|---|---|---|---|---|
| 535 | A96 | 13p multicolored | 1.25 | 1.25 |
| 536 | A96 | 20p multicolored | 2.10 | 2.10 |
| 537 | A96 | 38p multicolored | 4.00 | 4.00 |
| 538 | A96 | 45p multicolored | 4.50 | 4.50 |
| | | Nos. 535-538 (4) | 11.85 | 11.85 |

**Souvenir Sheet**

| | | | | |
|---|---|---|---|---|
| 539 | A96 | £1 multicolored | 12.50 | 12.50 |

See Ascension Nos. 493-497, Tristan da Cunha Nos. 482-486.

## Removal of Napoleon's Body from St. Helena, 150th Anniv. — A98

Designs: 13p, Funeral cortege, Jamestown wharf. 20p, Moving coffin to *Belle Poule*, James Bay. 38p, Transfer of coffin from *Belle Poule* to *Normandie*, Cherbourg. 45p, Napoleon's Tomb, St. Helena.

**1990, Dec. 15 — Wmk. 373 — Perf. 14**

| | | | | |
|---|---|---|---|---|
| 545 | A98 | 13p green & black | 1.10 | 1.10 |
| 546 | A98 | 20p blue & black | 2.00 | 2.00 |
| 547 | A98 | 38p violet & black | 3.50 | 3.50 |
| 548 | A98 | 45p multicolored | 4.25 | 4.25 |
| | | Nos. 545-548 (4) | 10.85 | 10.85 |

A99

Military Uniforms 1897: 13p, Officer, Leicestershire Regiment. 15p, Officer, York and Lancaster Regiment. 20p, Color Sergeant, Leicestershire Regiment. 30p, Drummer/Flautist, York and Lancaster Regiment. 45p, Lance Corporal, York and Lancaster Regiment.

**1991, May 2**

| | | | | |
|---|---|---|---|---|
| 549 | A99 | 13p multicolored | 1.25 | 1.25 |
| 550 | A99 | 15p multicolored | 1.25 | 1.25 |
| 551 | A99 | 20p multicolored | 1.75 | 1.75 |
| 552 | A99 | 30p multicolored | 3.50 | 3.50 |
| 553 | A99 | 45p multicolored | 4.00 | 4.00 |
| | | Nos. 549-553 (5) | 11.75 | 11.75 |

## Elizabeth & Philip, Birthdays
### Common Design Types

**1991, July 1 — Wmk. 384 — Perf. 14½**

| | | | | |
|---|---|---|---|---|
| 554 | CD345 | 25p multicolored | 1.25 | 1.25 |
| 555 | CD346 | 25p multicolored | 1.25 | 1.25 |
| | | a. Pair, #554-555 + label | 2.75 | 2.75 |

**1991, Nov. 2 — Wmk. 373 — Perf. 14**

Christmas (Paintings): 10p, Madonna and Child, Titian. 13p, Holy Family, Mengs. 20p, Madonna and Child, Dyce. 38p, Two Trinities, Murillo. 45p, Virgin and Child, Bellini.

| | | | | |
|---|---|---|---|---|
| 556 | A100 | 10p multicolored | .80 | .80 |
| 557 | A100 | 13p multicolored | 1.10 | 1.10 |
| 558 | A100 | 20p multicolored | 1.60 | 1.60 |
| 559 | A100 | 38p multicolored | 3.25 | 3.25 |
| 560 | A100 | 45p multicolored | 4.00 | 4.00 |
| | | Nos. 556-560 (5) | 10.75 | 10.75 |

### Phila Nippon '91 — A101

Motorcycles: 13p, Matchless 346cc (ohv), 1950. 20p, Triumph Tiger 100, 500cc, 1947. 38p, Honda CD 175cc, 1967. 45p, Yamaha DTE 400, 1976. 65p, Suzuki RM 250cc, 1984.

## 1991, Nov. 16 — Perf. 14x14½ — Litho. — Wmk. 384

| | | | | |
|---|---|---|---|---|
| 561 | A101 | 13p multicolored | 1.10 | 1.10 |
| 562 | A101 | 20p multicolored | 2.10 | 2.10 |
| 563 | A101 | 38p multicolored | 3.50 | 3.50 |
| 564 | A101 | 45p multicolored | 4.00 | 4.00 |
| | | Nos. 561-564 (4) | 10.70 | 10.70 |

**Souvenir Sheet**

| | | | | |
|---|---|---|---|---|
| 565 | A101 | 65p multicolored | 11.00 | 11.00 |

### Discovery of America, 500th Anniv. — A102

**1992, Jan. 24 — Litho. — Wmk. 373 — Perf. 14**

| | | | | |
|---|---|---|---|---|
| 566 | A102 | 15p STV Eye of the Wind | 1.60 | 1.60 |
| 567 | A102 | 25p STV Soren Larsen | 2.75 | 2.75 |
| 568 | A102 | 35p Santa Maria, Nina & Pinta | 3.75 | 3.75 |
| 569 | A102 | 50p Columbus, Santa Maria | 4.75 | 4.75 |
| | | Nos. 566-569 (4) | 12.85 | 12.85 |

World Columbian Stamp Expo '92, Chicago and Genoa '92 Intl. Philatelic Exhibitions.

## Queen Elizabeth II's Accession to the Throne, 40th Anniv.
### Common Design Type

**1992, Feb. 6**

| | | | | |
|---|---|---|---|---|
| 570 | CD349 | 11p multicolored | .45 | .45 |
| 571 | CD349 | 15p multicolored | .60 | .60 |
| 572 | CD349 | 25p multicolored | 1.10 | 1.10 |
| 573 | CD349 | 35p multicolored | 1.60 | 1.60 |
| 574 | CD349 | 50p multicolored | 2.25 | 2.25 |
| | | Nos. 570-574 (5) | 6.00 | 6.00 |

### Liberation of Falkland Islands, 10th Anniv. — A103

Designs: No. 579a, 13p + 3p, like No. 575. b, 20p + 4p, like No. 576. c, 38p + 8p, like No. 577. d, 45p + 9p, like No. 578.

**1992, June 12**

| | | | | |
|---|---|---|---|---|
| 575 | A103 | 13p HMS Ledbury | .85 | .85 |
| 576 | A103 | 20p HMS Brecon | 1.25 | 1.25 |
| 577 | A103 | 38p RMS St. Helena | 2.50 | 2.50 |
| 578 | A103 | 45p First mail drop, 1982 | 3.00 | 3.00 |
| | | Nos. 575-578 (4) | 7.60 | 7.60 |

**Souvenir Sheet**

| | | | | |
|---|---|---|---|---|
| 579 | A103 | Sheet of 4, #a.-d. | 7.50 | 7.50 |

Surtax for Soldiers', Sailors' and Airmens' Families Association.

## Christmas — A104

**1992, Oct. 12 — Wmk. 384**

| | | | | |
|---|---|---|---|---|
| 580 | A104 | 13p multicolored | 1.40 | 1.40 |
| 581 | A104 | 15p multicolored | 1.50 | 1.50 |
| 582 | A104 | 20p multicolored | 2.00 | 2.00 |
| 583 | A104 | 45p multicolored | 4.50 | 4.50 |
| | | Nos. 580-583 (4) | 9.40 | 9.40 |

Children in scenes from Nativity plays: 13p, Angel, shepherds. 15p, Magi, shepherds. 20p, Joseph, Mary. 45p, Nativity scene.

---

| | | | | |
|---|---|---|---|---|
| c. | A88 | 20p multicolored | 1.10 | 1.10 |
| d. | A88 | 45p multicolored | 2.40 | 2.40 |
| e. | A88 | 60p multicolored | 3.25 | 3.25 |

PHILEXFRANCE '89.

## New Central (Prince Andrew) School A90

**1989, Aug. 24 — Perf. 14½**

| | | | | |
|---|---|---|---|---|
| 511 | A90 | 13p Agriculture | .85 | .85 |
| 512 | A90 | 20p Literacy | 1.25 | 1.25 |
| 513 | A90 | 25p Building exterior | 1.60 | 1.60 |
| 514 | A90 | 60p Campus | 4.00 | 4.00 |
| | | Nos. 511-514 (4) | 7.70 | 7.70 |

## Christmas — A91

10p, The Madonna with the Pear, by Dürer. 20p, The Holy Family Under the Apple Tree, by Rubens. 45p, The Virgin in the Meadow, by Raphael. 60p, The Holy Family with Saint John, by Raphael.

**1989, Oct. 10 — Wmk. 373 — Perf. 14**

| | | | | |
|---|---|---|---|---|
| 515 | A91 | 10p multicolored | .60 | .60 |
| 516 | A91 | 20p multicolored | 1.25 | 1.25 |
| 517 | A91 | 45p multicolored | 2.75 | 2.75 |
| 518 | A91 | 60p multicolored | 3.50 | 3.50 |
| | | Nos. 515-518 (4) | 8.10 | 8.10 |

## Early Vehicles A92

**1989, Dec. 1 — Wmk. 384 — Perf. 14½**

| | | | | |
|---|---|---|---|---|
| 519 | A92 | 9p 1930 Chevrolet | .65 | .65 |
| 520 | A92 | 20p 1929 Austin Seven | 1.40 | 1.40 |
| 521 | A92 | 45p 1929 Morris Cowley | 3.00 | 3.00 |
| 522 | A92 | 60p 1932 Sunbeam | 4.25 | 4.25 |
| | | Nos. 519-522 (4) | 9.30 | 9.30 |

**Souvenir Sheet**

| | | | | |
|---|---|---|---|---|
| 523 | A92 | £1 Ford Model A | 9.75 | 9.75 |

## Farm Animals — A93

**1990, Feb. 1 — Litho. — Perf. 14**

| | | | | |
|---|---|---|---|---|
| 524 | A93 | 9p Sheep | .50 | .50 |
| 525 | A93 | 13p Pigs | .70 | .70 |
| 526 | A93 | 45p Cow, calf | 2.50 | 2.50 |
| 527 | A93 | 60p Geese | 3.50 | 3.50 |
| | | Nos. 524-527 (4) | 7.20 | 7.20 |

## Christmas — A97

Parish Churches.

**1990, Oct. 18**

| | | | | |
|---|---|---|---|---|
| 540 | A97 | 10p Baptist Chapel, Sandy Bay | .45 | .45 |
| 541 | A97 | 13p St. Martin in the Hills | .60 | .60 |
| 542 | A97 | 20p St. Helena and the Cross | .85 | .85 |
| 543 | A97 | 38p St. James Church | 1.90 | 1.90 |
| 544 | A97 | 45p St. Paul's Church | 5.80 | 5.80 |
| | | Nos. 540-544 (5) | | |

### Great Britain No. 2 A94

Exhibition emblem and: 20p, Great Britain No. 1. 38p, Mail delivery to branch p.o. 45p, Main p.o., mail van.

## Anniversaries — A105

**1992, Dec. 4    Wmk. 373    Perf. 14½**

| | | | |
|---|---|---|---|
| 584 | A105 | 13p multicolored | 1.00 1.00 |
| 585 | A105 | 20p multicolored | 1.75 1.75 |
| 586 | A105 | 38p multicolored | 3.25 3.25 |
| 587 | A105 | 45p multicolored | 3.75 3.75 |
| | | Nos. 584-587 (4) | 9.75 9.75 |

Designs: 13p, Man broadcasting at radio station, 20p, Scouts marching in parade, 38p, Breadfruit, HMS Providence, 1792, 45p, Governor Colonel Brooke, Plantation House.

Radio St. Helena, 25th anniv. (#584). Scouting on St. Helena, 75th anniv. (#585). Captain Bligh's visit, 200th anniv. (#586). Plantation House, 200th anniv. (#587).

## Flowers — A106

**1993, Mar. 19    Litho.    Perf. 14½x14**

| | | | |
|---|---|---|---|
| 588 | A106 | 9p Moses in the bulrush | .75 .75 |
| 589 | A106 | 13p Periwinkle | 1.25 1.25 |
| 590 | A106 | 20p Everlasting flower | 1.75 1.75 |
| 591 | A106 | 38p Cigar plant | 3.25 3.25 |
| 592 | A106 | 45p Lobelia erinus | 3.75 3.75 |
| | | Nos. 588-592 (6) | 10.75 10.75 |

See Nos. 635-640.

## Wirebird A107

**1993, Aug. 16    Wmk. 373    Litho.    Perf. 13½**

| | | | |
|---|---|---|---|
| 593 | A107 | 3p Adult with eggs | .45 .45 |
| 594 | A107 | 5p Male, brooding | .45 .45 |
| 595 | A107 | 12p Downy young, adult | .75 .75 |
| 596 | A107 | 25p Two immature birds | 1.90 1.90 |
| 597 | A107 | 40p Adult in flight | 2.00 2.00 |
| 598 | A107 | 45p Immature bird | 4.00 4.00 |
| | | Nos. 593-598 (6) | 12.10 12.10 |

## Birds A108

**1993, Aug. 26**

| | | | |
|---|---|---|---|
| 599 | A108 | 1p Swainson's canary | .25 .25 |
| 600 | A108 | 3p Chuckar partridge | .25 .25 |
| 601 | A108 | 11p Pigeon | .30 .30 |
| 602 | A108 | 12p Waxbill | .40 .45 |
| 603 | A108 | 15p Common myna | .45 .45 |
| 604 | A108 | 18p Java sparrow | .55 .65 |
| 605 | A108 | 25p Red-billed tropicbird | .85 1.00 |
| 606 | A108 | 35p Madeiran storm petrel | 1.10 1.40 |
| 607 | A108 | 75p Madagascar fody | 2.50 2.50 |
| 608 | A108 | £1 Common fairy tern | 3.50 3.50 |
| a. | | Souvenir sheet of 1, Common fairy tern | 3.50 4.25 |

| | | | |
|---|---|---|---|
| 609 | A108 | £2 Southern giant petrel | 6.75 8.25 |
| 610 | A108 | £5 Wirebird | 18.00 21.00 |
| | | Nos. 599-604, 607, 610 (12) | 34.90 41.75 |

No. 607a for Hong Kong '97, 610 are vert. No. 607a for Hong Kong '97. Issued: 2/3/97. See No. 691.

## Christmas — A109

**1993, Oct. 1    Perf. 13½x14**

| | | | |
|---|---|---|---|
| 611 | A109 | 12p multicolored | .80 .80 |
| 612 | A109 | 15p multicolored | 1.00 1.00 |
| 613 | A109 | 18p multicolored | 1.10 1.10 |
| 614 | A109 | 25p multicolored | 1.60 1.60 |
| 615 | A109 | 60p multicolored | 4.00 4.00 |
| | | Nos. 611-615 (5) | 8.50 8.50 |

Toys: 12p, Teddy bear, soccer ball, 15p, Sailboat, doll, 18p, Paint palette, rocking horse, 25p, Kite, airplane, 60p, Guitar, roller skates.

## Flowers — A110

Photographs: No. 616a, Arum lily. No. 617a, Ebony. No. 618a, Shell ginger. Nos. 616b-618b: Child's painting of same flower as in "a."

**1994, Jan. 6    Wmk. 373    Perf. 14**

| | | | |
|---|---|---|---|
| 616 | A110 | 12p multicolored Pair, #a.-b. | 1.25 1.25 |
| 617 | A110 | 25p multicolored Pair, #a.-b. | 2.50 2.50 |
| 618 | A110 | 35p multicolored Pair, #a.-b. | 3.50 3.50 |

## Pets — A111

Designs: 12p, Abyssinian guinea pig, 25p, Common tabby cat, 53p, Plain white, black rabbits, 60p, Golden labrador.

**1994, Feb. 18    Wmk. 373    Perf. 14½**

| | | | |
|---|---|---|---|
| 619 | A111 | 12p multicolored | .90 .90 |
| 620 | A111 | 25p multicolored | 1.90 1.90 |
| 621 | A111 | 53p multicolored | 4.00 4.00 |
| 622 | A111 | 60p multicolored | 4.25 4.25 |
| | | Nos. 619-622 (4) | 11.05 11.05 |

## Fish — A112

Designs: 12p, Springer's blenny, 25p, Bastard five finger, 53p, Deepwater gurnard, 60p, Green fish.

**1994, June 6    Wmk. 384    Perf. 14**

| | | | |
|---|---|---|---|
| 623 | A112 | 12p multicolored | .85 .85 |
| 624 | A112 | 25p multicolored | 1.75 1.75 |
| 625 | A112 | 53p multicolored | 4.25 4.25 |
| 626 | A112 | 60p multicolored | 4.25 4.25 |
| | | Nos. 623-626 (4) | 10.85 10.85 |

Hong Kong '94.

## Butterflies A113

**1994, Aug. 9    Wmk. 373**

| | | | |
|---|---|---|---|
| 627 | A113 | 12p Lampides boeticus | .75 .75 |
| 628 | A113 | 25p Cynthia cardui | 1.60 1.60 |
| 629 | A113 | 53p Hypolimnas bolina | 3.50 3.50 |
| 630 | A113 | 60p Danaus chrysippus | 3.75 3.75 |
| | | Nos. 627-630 (4) | 9.60 9.60 |

## Christmas Carols — A114

Designs: 12p, "Silent night, holy night...", 15p, "While shepherds watched...", 38p, "We three kings...", 25p, "Away in a manger...", 60p, "Angels from the realms of glory."

**1994, Oct. 6    Wmk. 384    Litho.    Perf. 14½**

| | | | |
|---|---|---|---|
| 631 | A114 | 12p multicolored | .75 .75 |
| 632 | A114 | 15p multicolored | .95 .95 |
| 633 | A114 | 25p multicolored | 1.50 1.50 |
| 634 | A114 | 38p multicolored | 2.40 2.40 |
| 635 | A114 | 60p multicolored | 3.75 3.75 |
| | | Nos. 631-635 (5) | 9.35 9.35 |

## Flower Type of 1993

**1994, Dec. 15    Litho.    Perf. 14½**

| | | | |
|---|---|---|---|
| 636 | A106 | 12p Honeysuckle | .50 .50 |
| 637 | A106 | 15p Gobblegreen | .65 .65 |
| 638 | A106 | 25p African lily | 1.00 1.00 |
| 639 | A106 | 38p Prince of Wales feathers | 1.60 1.60 |
| 640 | A106 | 60p St. Johns lily | 2.50 2.50 |
| | | Nos. 636-640 (5) | 6.25 6.25 |

## Emergency Services — A115

Designs: 12p, Police, rural patrol, 25p, Fire engine, 53p, Inshore rescue craft, 60p, Ambulance.

**1995, Feb. 2    Wmk. 384    Litho.    Perf. 14**

| | | | |
|---|---|---|---|
| 641 | A115 | 12p Fire engine | .50 .50 |
| 642 | A115 | 25p Inshore rescue craft | .85 .85 |
| 643 | A115 | 53p Police, rural patrol | 1.90 1.90 |
| 644 | A115 | 60p Ambulance | 4.50 4.50 |
| | | Nos. 641-644 (4) | 11.00 11.00 |

## Harpers Earth Dam Project A116

**1995, Apr. 6    Wmk. 373    Litho.    Perf. 14½**

| | | | |
|---|---|---|---|
| 645 | A116 | 25p Strip of 5, #a.-e. | 6.00 6.00 |

No. 645 is a continuous design.

Designs: a, Site clearance. b, Earthworks in progress. c, Laying the outlet pipe. d, Revetment block protection. e, Completed dam, June 1994.

## End of World War II, 50th Anniv.
### Common Design Types

Designs: No. 646, C.S. Lady Denison-Pender. No. 647, HMS Dragon. No. 648, RFA Darkdale. No. 649, HMS Hermes. No. 650, St. Helena Rifles on parade. No. 651, Gov. Maj. W.J. Bain Gray during Victory Parade. No. 652, 6-inch gun, Ladder Hill. No. 653, Signal Station, flag hoist signalling VICTORY.

**1995, May 8    Wmk. 373    Perf. 14**

| | | | |
|---|---|---|---|
| 646 | CD351 | 12p multicolored | .20 .20 |
| 647 | CD351 | 5p multicolored | .20 .20 |
| a. | | #646-647, Pair | .45 .40 |
| 648 | CD351 | 12p multicolored | 1.00 1.00 |
| 649 | CD351 | 12p multicolored | .40 .40 |
| a. | | #648-649, Pair | 2.25 2.25 |
| 650 | CD351 | 25p multicolored | 1.90 1.90 |
| 651 | CD351 | 25p multicolored | .75 .75 |
| a. | | #650-651, Pair | 4.25 4.25 |
| 652 | CD351 | 53p multicolored | 4.00 4.00 |
| 653 | CD351 | 53p multicolored | 1.65 1.65 |
| a. | | #652-653, Pair | 8.75 8.75 |
| | | Nos. 646-653 (8) | 14.20 |

### Souvenir Sheet

| | | | |
|---|---|---|---|
| 654 | CD352 | £1 multicolored | 6.50 6.50 |

No. 654, Reverse of War Medal 1939-45.

## Invertebrates — A117

Designs: 12p, Blushing snail, 25p, Golden sail spider, 53p, Spiky yellow woodlouse, 60p, St. Helena shore crab. £1, Giant earwig.

**1995, Aug. 29    Wmk. 373    Perf. 14**

| | | | |
|---|---|---|---|
| 655 | A117 | 12p multicolored | .90 .90 |
| 656 | A117 | 25p multicolored | 1.90 1.90 |
| 657 | A117 | 53p multicolored | 4.00 4.00 |
| 658 | A117 | 60p multicolored | 4.50 4.50 |
| | | Nos. 655-658 (4) | 11.30 11.30 |

### Souvenir Sheet

| | | | |
|---|---|---|---|
| 659 | A117 | £1 multicolored | 8.00 8.00 |

## Orchids — A118

Designs: a, Epidendrum ibaguense. b, Vanda Miss Joaquim.

**1995, Sept. 1    Perf. 14½x14**

| | | | |
|---|---|---|---|
| 660 | A118 | 50p Sheet of 2, #a.-b. | 8.25 8.25 |

Singapore '95.

## Christmas A119

Children's drawings: 12p, Christmas Eve in Jamestown. 15p, Santa, musicians. 25p, Party at Blue Hill Community Center. 38p, Santa walking in Jamestown. 60p, RMS St. Helena.

**1995, Oct. 17    Litho.    Perf. 14½x14½**

| | | | |
|---|---|---|---|
| 661 | A119 | 12p multicolored | .50 .50 |
| 662 | A119 | 15p multicolored | .60 .60 |
| 663 | A119 | 25p multicolored | 1.00 1.00 |
| 664 | A119 | 38p multicolored | 1.60 1.60 |
| 665 | A119 | 60p multicolored | 2.50 2.50 |
| | | Nos. 661-665 (5) | 6.20 6.20 |

## Union Castle Mail Ships A120

**1996, Jan. 8    Wmk. 384    Litho.    Perf. 14**

| | | | |
|---|---|---|---|
| 666 | A120 | 12p Walmer Castle, 1915 | 1.00 1.00 |
| 667 | A120 | 25p Llangibby Castle, 1934 | 2.00 2.00 |

668 A120 53p Stirling Castle, 1940 ... 4.50 4.50
669 A120 60p Pendennis Castle, 1965 ... 4.75 4.75
... 12.25 12.25
See Nos. 666-710.

**Radio, Cent. A121**

Designs: 60p. Telecommunications equipment on St. Helena. £1. Marconi aboard yacht, Elettra.

Wmk. 373   **Litho.**   **Perf. 13½**
**1996, Mar. 28**
670 A121 60p multicolored ... 3.00 3.00
671 A121 £1 multicolored ... 5.25 5.25

**Queen Elizabeth II, 70th Birthday**
Common Design Type

Various portraits of Queen, scenes of St. Helena: 15p. Jamestown. 25p. Prince Andrew School. 53p. Castle entrance. 60p. Plantation house. £1.50, Queen wearing tiara, formal dress.

Wmk. 384   **Litho.**   **Perf. 14x14½**
**1996, Apr. 22**
672 CD354 15p multicolored ... .75 .75
673 CD354 25p multicolored ... 1.25 1.25
674 CD354 53p multicolored ... 2.50 2.00
675 CD354 60p multicolored ... 3.00 3.00
Nos. 672-675 (4) ... 7.50 7.00

**Souvenir Sheet**
676 CD354 £1.50 multicolored ... 7.00 7.00

**CAPEX '96 A122**

Postal transport: 12p. Mail airlifted to HMS Protector, 1964. 25p. First local post delivery, motorscooter, 1965. 53p. Mail unloaded at Wideawake Airfield, Ascension Island. 60p. Mail received at St. Helena.
£1, LMS Jubilee Class 4-6-0 locomotive No. 5624 "St. Helena."

Wmk. 384   **Litho.**   **Perf. 14**
**1996, June 8**
677 A122 12p multicolored ... .50 .50
678 A122 25p multicolored ... 1.10 1.10
679 A122 53p multicolored ... 2.25 2.25
680 A122 60p multicolored ... 2.50 2.50
Nos. 677-680 (4) ... 6.35 6.35

**Souvenir Sheet**
681 A122 £1 multicolored ... 6.25 6.25

**Napoleonic Sites A123**

Wmk. 373   **Litho.**   **Perf. 14½**
**1996, Aug. 12**
682 A123 12p Mr. Porteous' House ... .65 .65
683 A123 25p Briars Pavillion ... 1.40 1.40
684 A123 53p Longwood House ... 2.75 2.75
685 A123 60p Napoleon's Tomb ... 3.25 3.25
Nos. 682-685 (4) ... 8.05 8.05

**Christmas A124**

Flowers: 12p. Frangipani. 15p. Bougainvillaea. 25p. Jacaranda. £1. Pink periwinkle.

Wmk. 373   **Litho.**   **Perf. 14½**
**1996, Oct. 1**
686 A124 12p multicolored ... .60 .60
687 A124 15p multicolored ... .75 .75
688 A124 25p multicolored ... 1.25 1.25
689 A124 £1 multicolored ... 4.75 4.75
Nos. 686-689 (4) ... 7.35 7.35

**Endemic Plants — A125**

Designs: a. Black cabbage tree. b. Whitewood. c, Tree fern. d, Dwarf jellico. e, Lobelia. f, Dogwood.

Wmk. 373   **Litho.**   **Perf. 14½x14**
**1997, Jan. 17**
690 A125 25p Sheet of 6, #a.-f. ... 7.75 7.75

**Bird Type of 1993**
**Souvenir Sheet**

Wmk. 373   **Litho.**   **Perf. 14½**
**1997, June 20**
691 A108 75p like No. 610 ... 3.50 3.50
Return of Hong Kong to China, July 1, 1997.

**Discovery of St. Helena, 500th Anniv. (in 2002) — A126**

Discovery by Joao da Nova, May 21, 1502. 20p, 1st inhabitant, Don Fernando Lopez, 1515. 30p, Landing by Thomas Cavendish, 1588. 80p, Ship, Royal Merchant, 1591.

**Perf. 14**
**1997, May 29**
692 A126 20p multicolored ... 1.10 1.10
693 A126 25p multicolored ... 1.50 1.50
694 A126 30p multicolored ... 1.60 1.60
695 A126 80p multicolored ... 4.25 4.45
Nos. 692-695 (4) ... 8.45 8.45

See Nos. 712-715, 736-739, 755-758.

**Queen Elizabeth II and Prince Philip, 50th Wedding Anniv. — A127**

#696, Queen, Prince coming down steps, royal visit, 1947. #697, Wedding portrait. #698, Wedding portrait, diff. #699, Queen receiving flowers, royal visit, 1947. #700, Royal visit, 1957. #701, Queen, Prince waving from balcony on wedding day.
£1.50, Queen, Prince riding in open carriage.

Wmk. 384   **Litho.**   **Perf. 13½**
**1997, July 10**
696 A127 10p multicolored ... .55 .55
697 A127 10p multicolored ... .55 .55
a. A127 Pair, #696-697 ... 1.00 1.00
698 A127 15p multicolored ... .85 .85
699 A127 15p multicolored ... .85 .85
a. A127 Pair, #698-699 ... 1.50 1.50
700 A127 50p multicolored ... 2.75 2.75
701 A127 50p multicolored ... 2.75 2.75
a. A127 Pair, #700-701 ... 5.00 5.00
Nos. 696-701 (6) ... 8.30 8.30

**Souvenir Sheet**   **Perf. 14x14½**
702 A127 £1.50 multi. horiz. ... 8.00 8.00

**Christmas — A128**

Wmk. 384   **Litho.**   **Perf. 13½x14**
**1997, Sept. 29**
703 A128 15p Flowers ... .65 .65
704 A128 20p Calligraphy ... .90 .90
705 A128 40p Camping ... 1.60 1.60
706 A128 75p Entertaining ... 3.25 3.25
Nos. 703-706 (4) ... 6.40 6.40

Duke of Edinburgh's Award in St. Helena, 25th anniv.

**Union Castle Mail Ships Type of 1996**

Wmk. 384   **Litho.**   **Perf. 14**
**1998, Jan. 2**
707 A120 20p Avondale Castle, 1900 ... 1.25 1.25
708 A120 25p Dunnottar Castle, 1936 ... 1.60 1.60
709 A120 30p Llandovery Castle, 1943 ... 2.00 1.25
710 A120 80p Good Hope Castle, 1977 ... 5.00 5.00
Nos. 707-710 (4) ... 9.85 9.10

**Diana, Princess of Wales (1961-97)**
Common Design Type

a, Wearing hat. b, In white pin-striped suit jacket. c, In green jacket. d, Wearing choker necklace.

Wmk. 373   **Litho.**   **Perf. 14½x14**
**1998, Apr. 4**
711 CD355 30p Sheet of 4, #a.-d. ... 4.75 4.75

No. 711 sold for £1.20 + 20p, with surtax from international sales being donated to Princess Diana Memorial Fund and surtax from national sales being donated to designated local charity.

**Discovery of St. Helena, 500th Anniv., Type of 1997**

17th Century events, horiz.: 20p, Fortifying and planting, 1659. 25p, Dutch invasion, 1672. 30p, English recapture, 1673. 80p, Royal Charter, 1673.

Wmk. 384   **Litho.**   **Perf. 14**
**1998, July 2**   **Size: 39x26mm**
712 A126 20p multicolored ... .90 .90
713 A126 25p multicolored ... 1.10 1.10
714 A126 30p multicolored ... 1.50 1.50
715 A126 80p multicolored ... 3.50 3.50
Nos. 712-715 (4) ... 7.00 7.00

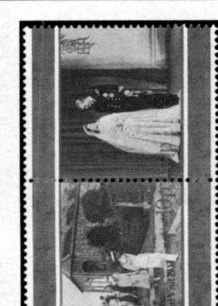

**Maritime Heritage — A129**

Ships: 10p, HMS Desire, 1588. 15p, Dutch ship, "White Leeuw," 1602. 20p, HMS Swallow, "White Lion," 1751. 25p, HMS Endeavour, 1771. 30p, HMS Dolphin, 1792. 35p, HMS Providence, 1792. 35p, HMS St. Helena, 1815. 40p, HMS Northumberland, 1815. 50p, Russian brig, "Rurik," 1815. 75p, HMS Erebus, 1826. 80p, Pole junk, "Keying," 1847. £2, La Belle Poule, 1840. £5, HMS Rattlesnake, 1861.

Wmk. 373   **Litho.**   **Perf. 13½x14**
**1998, Aug. 25**
716 A129 10p multicolored ... .45 .55
717 A129 15p multicolored ... .60 .70
718 A129 20p multicolored ... .75 .90
719 A129 25p multicolored ... .90 1.10
720 A129 30p multicolored ... 1.25 1.50
721 A129 35p multicolored ... 1.40 1.60
722 A129 40p multicolored ... 1.50 1.90
723 A129 50p multicolored ... 1.90 2.25
724 A129 75p multicolored ... 2.75 3.50
725 A129 80p multicolored ... 3.00 3.50
726 A129 £2 multicolored ... 7.50 9.00
727 A129 £5 multicolored ... 18.00 22.50
Nos. 716-727 (12) ... 40.25 49.00

**Christmas A130**

Island crafts: 15p. Metal work. 20p. Wood turning. 30p. Inlaid woodwork. 85p. Hessian and seedwork.

**Perf. 14**
**1998, Sept. 28**
728 A130 15p multicolored ... .60 .60
729 A130 20p multicolored ... .75 .75
730 A130 30p multicolored ... 1.25 1.25
731 A130 85p multicolored ... 3.25 3.25
Nos. 728-731 (4) ... 5.85 5.85

**Souvenir Sheet**

AUSTRALIA 99 WORLD STAMP EXPO

**H. M. Bark Endeavour at Anchor, 1771 — A131**

Illustration reduced.

Wmk. 373   **Litho.**   **Perf. 13½x14**
**1999, Mar. 5**
732 A131 £1.50 multicolored ... 9.25 9.25
Australia '99 World Stamp Expo.

**Wedding of Prince Edward and Sophie Rhys-Jones**
Common Design Type

Wmk. 384   **Litho.**   **Perf. 13½x14**
**1999, June 15**
733 CD356 30p Separate portraits ... 1.00 1.00
734 CD356 £1.50 Couple ... 6.25 6.25

**Souvenir Sheet**

**PhilexFrance '99, World Philatelic Exhibition — A132**

Illustration reduced.

**Perf. 14**
**1999, July 2**
735 A132 £1.50 #261 ... 8.00 8.00

**Discovery of St. Helena, 500th Anniv. Type of 1997**

Designs, horiz.: 20p, Jamestown fortification. 25p, First safe roadway up Ladder Hill, 1718. 30p, Governor Skottowe with Captain Cook. 80p, Presentation of sword of honor to Governor Brooke, 1799.

Wmk. 373   **Litho.**   **Perf. 14½x14**
**1999, July 12**
736 A126 20p multicolored ... 1.10 .95
737 A126 25p multicolored ... 1.40 1.25
738 A126 30p multicolored ... 1.75 1.50
739 A126 80p multicolored ... 4.50 5.00
Nos. 736-739 (4) ... 8.75 8.70

**Queen Mother's Century**
Common Design Type

Queen Mother: 15p, With King George VI visiting St. Helena. 20p, With King George VI inspecting bomb damage at Buckingham Palace. 30p, With Prince Andrew, 97th birthday. 80p, As commandant-in-chief of Royal Air Force Central Flying School.
£1.50, With family at coronation of King George VI.

**Wmk. 384**

**1999, Sept. 3 Litho. *Perf. 13½***

**740** CD358 15p multicolored .70 .70
**741** CD358 25p multicolored 1.25 1.25
**742** CD358 30p multicolored 1.50 1.50
**743** CD358 80p multicolored 4.00 4.00
*Nos. 740-743 (4)* 7.45 7.45

**Souvenir Sheet**

**744** CD358 £1.50 multicolored 7.50 7.50

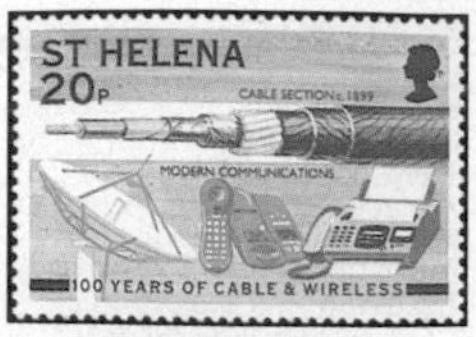
ST HELENA
20p
CABLE SECTION 1899
MODERN COMMUNICATIONS
100 YEARS OF CABLE & WIRELESS

Cable & Wireless, Cent. A133

**Wmk. 373**

**1999, Nov. 26 Litho. *Perf. 14***

**745** A133 20p Cable, communication equipment 1.10 1.10
**746** A133 25p CS Seine 1.25 1.25
**747** A133 30p CS Anglia 1.60 1.60
**748** A133 80p Headquarters 4.50 4.50
*Nos. 745-748 (4)* 8.45 8.45

Souvenir Sheet

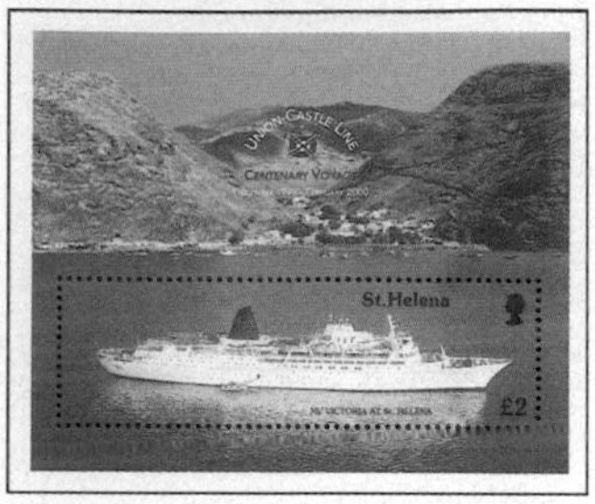
St.Helena
£2

Union-Castle Line Centenary Voyage — A134

**1999, Dec. 23 *Perf. 13x13¾***

**749** A134 £2 multicolored 10.50 10.50

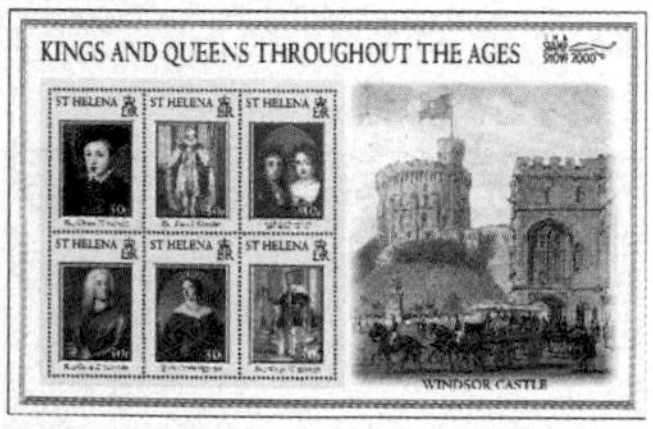
KINGS AND QUEENS THROUGHOUT THE AGES
WINDSOR CASTLE

British Monarchs — A135

Designs: a, Edward VI. b, James I. c, William III, Mary II. d, George II. e, Victoria. f, George VI.

**Wmk. 373**

**2000, Feb. 29 Litho. *Perf. 14***

**750** A135 30p Sheet of 6, #a.-f. 6.75 6.75

The Stamp Show 2000, London.

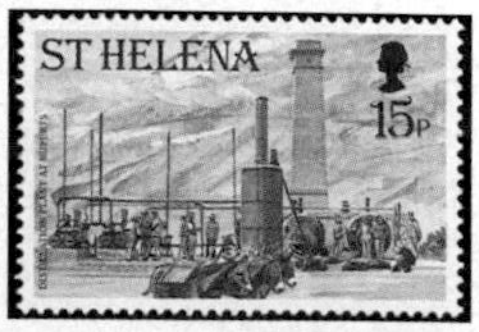
ST HELENA
15p

Boer War, Cent. A136

Designs: 15p, Distillation plant, Ruperts. 25p, Camp, Broadbottom. 30p, Committee of Boer prisoners. 80p, Boer General Piet Cronjé, prisoner at Kent Cottage.

**Wmk. 373**

**2000, Apr. 10 Litho. *Perf. 14***

**751-754** A136 Set of 4 7.50 7.50

**Discovery of St. Helena, 500th Anniv. Type of 1997**

Designs: 20p, Withdrawal of the East India Company, 1833, horiz. 25p, Abolition of slavery, 1832, horiz. 30p, Napoleon arrives in 1815, departs in 1840, horiz. 80p, Chief Dinizulu, 1890, horiz.

**2000, May 23 Wmk. 373 *Perf. 13¾***

**755-758** A126 Set of 4 6.25 6.25

Souvenir Sheet

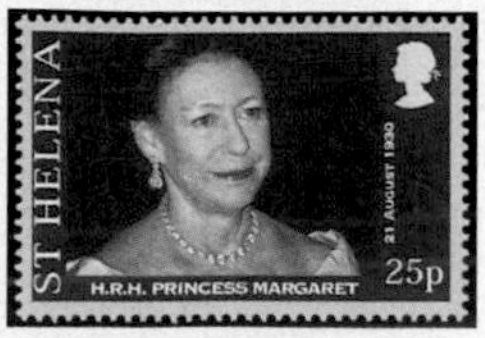
ST HELENA
H.R.H. PRINCESS MARGARET
21 AUGUST 1930
25p

Royal Birthdays A137

No. 759: a, Princess Margaret, 70th birthday. b, Prince Andrew, 40th birthday. c, Prince William, 18th birthday. d, Princess Anne, 50th birthday. e, Queen Mother, 100th birthday.

**2000, Aug. 4 Wmk. 384 *Perf. 14***

**759** Sheet of 5 9.50 9.50
*a.-d.* A137 25p Any single 1.40 1.40
*e.* A137 50p multi 2.75 2.75

No. 759e is 42x56mm.

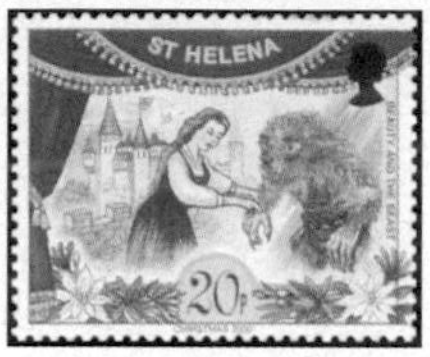
ST HELENA
20p

Christmas Pantomimes A138

a, Beauty and the Beast. b, Puss in Boots. c, Little Red Riding Hood. d, Jack and the Beanstalk. e, Snow White and the Seven Dwarfs.

**Wmk. 373**

**2000, Oct. 10 Litho. *Perf. 13***

**760** Strip of 5 5.25 5.25
*a.-e.* A138 20p Any single .75 .75

Souvenir Sheet

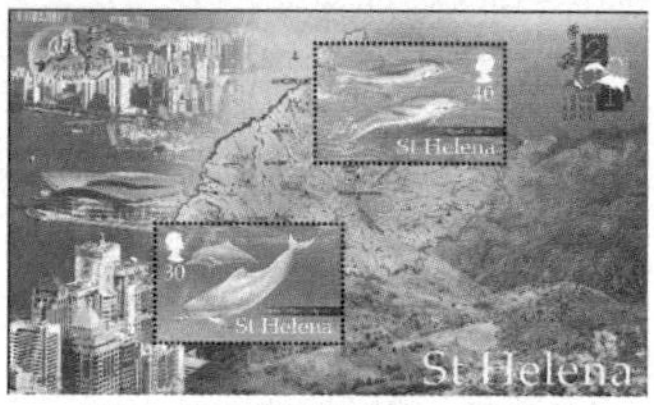
St Helena
St Helena
St Helena

New Year 2001 (Year of the Snake) — A139

No. 761: a, 30p, Chinese white dolphin. b, 40p, Striped dolphin.
Illustration reduced.

**Wmk. 373**

**2001, Feb. 1 Litho. *Perf. 14½***

**761** A139 Sheet of 2, #a-b 5.75 5.75

Hong Kong 2001 Stamp Exhibition.

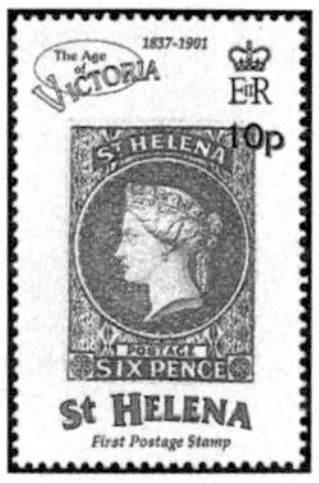
The Age of Victoria
1837-1901
10p
SIX PENCE
St HELENA
First Postage Stamp

Age of Victoria — A140

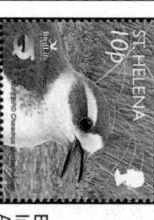

Designs: 10p, St. Helena #1. 15p, Visit of HMS Beagle, 1836. 20p, Jamestown, horiz. 25p, Queen Victoria, horiz. 30p, Diamond Jubilee, horiz. 50p, Lewis Carroll.

£1.50, Coffee receives award at the Great Exhibition.

**Wmk. 373**

**2001, May 24 Litho. *Perf. 14***

**762-767** A140 Set of 6 9.00 9.00

**Souvenir Sheet**

**768** A140 £1.50 multi 9.00 9.00

**Discovery of St. Helena, 500th Anniv. Type of 1997**

Designs, horiz.: 20p, World Wars I and II. 25p, Schools. 30p, Flax industry. 80p, RMS St. Helena.

**2001, June 19 *Perf. 14x14¾***

**769-772** A126 Set of 4 8.50 8.50

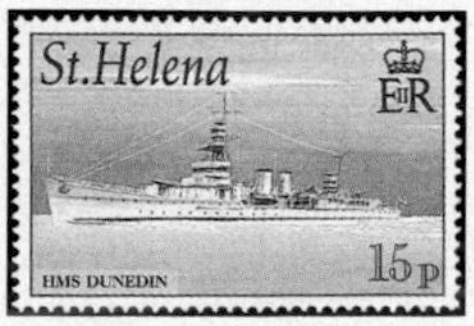
St.Helena
HMS DUNEDIN
15p

World War II Royal Navy Ships A141

HMS: 15p, Dunedin. 20p, Repulse. 25p, Nelson. 30p, Exmoor. 40p, Eagle. 50p, Milford.

**2001, Sept. 20 *Perf. 14***

**773-778** A141 Set of 6 11.25 11.25

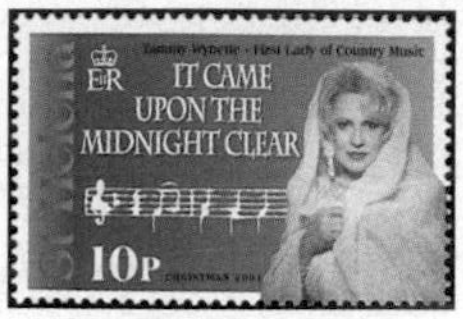
IT CAME UPON THE MIDNIGHT CLEAR
10p

Tammy Wynette (1942-98), American Singer A142

Wynette and Christmas carols: 10p, It Came Upon a Midnight Clear. 15p, Joy to the World. 20p, Away in the Manger. 30p, Silent Night.

**Wmk. 373**

**2001, Oct. 11 Litho. *Perf. 14***

**779-782** A142 Set of 4 4.75 4.75

**Souvenir Sheet**

**783** A142 £1.50 Portrait, vert. 7.50 7.50

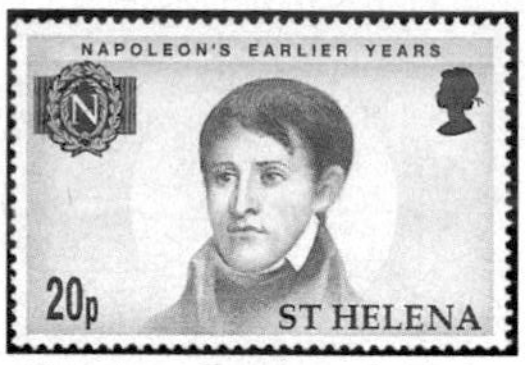
NAPOLEON'S EARLIER YEARS
20p
ST HELENA

Napoleon Bonaparte's Early Years — A143

Napoleon: 20p, As young man. 25p, At military school. 30p, At dance. 80p, With family.

**2001, Nov. 1 *Perf. 13¾x14***

**784-787** A143 Set of 4 9.00 9.00

**Reign Of Queen Elizabeth II, 50th Anniv. Issue**

Common Design Type

Designs: Nos. 788, 792a, 20p, Princess Elizabeth with Princess Margaret. Nos. 789, 792b, 25p, Wearing tiara. Nos. 790, 792c, 30p, With Princes Andrew and Edward, 1967. Nos. 791, 792d, 80p, In 1999. No. 792e, 50p, 1955 portrait by Annigoni (38x50mm).

***Perf. 14¼x14½, 13¾ (#792e)***

**2002, Feb. 6 Litho. Wmk. 373**

**With Gold Frames**

**788-791** CD360 Set of 4 6.25 6.25

**Souvenir Sheet**

**Without Gold Frames**

**792** CD360 Sheet of 5, #a-e 8.25 8.25

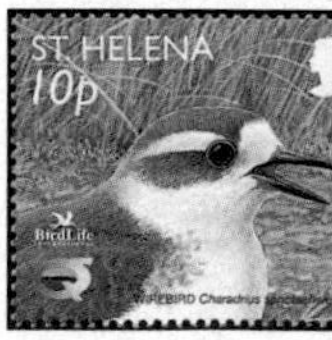
ST HELENA
10p

Birdlife International A144

Wirebird: 10p, With beak open. 15p, Running, vert. 25p, Looking left with beak closed, vert. 30p, In flight. 80p, Looking right with beak closed.

***Perf. 14¼x13¾, 13¾x14¼***

**2002, Apr. 15 Litho.**

**793** A144 10p multi .60 .60
*a.* Perf. 14¼ .50 .50
**794** A144 15p multi .95 .95
*a.* Perf. 14¼ .75 .75
**795** A144 30p multi 1.60 1.60
*a.* Perf. 14¼ 1.25 1.25
**796** A144 80p multi 4.25 4.25
*a.* Perf. 14¼ 3.50 3.50
*Nos. 793-796 (4)* 7.40 7.40

**Souvenir Sheet**

***Perf. 14¼***

**797** A144 Sheet, #793a-796a, 797a 7.50 7.50
*a.* 25p multi .95 .95

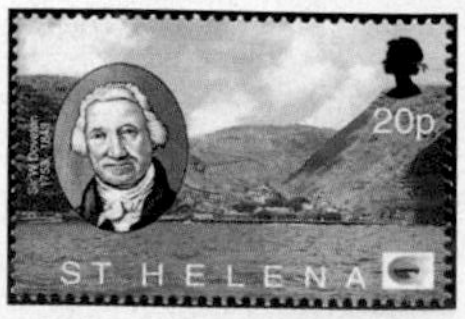
20p
ST HELENA

Discovery of St. Helena, 500th Anniv. A145

View of island and: 20p, Sir William W. Doveton (1753-1843), council member, military officer. 25p, Canon Lawrence C. Walcott (1880-1951). 30p, Governor Hudson R. Janisch (1824-84). 80p, Dr. Wilberforce J. J. Arnold (1867-1925), colonial surgeon.

**Wmk. 373**

**2002, May 21 Litho. *Perf. 14***

**798-801** A145 Set of 4 7.50 7.50

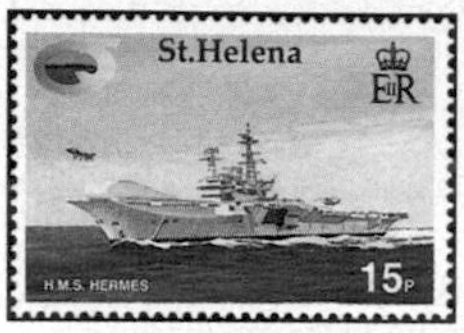
St.Helena
H.M.S. HERMES
15p

Ships of the Falkland Islands War A146

Designs: 15p, HMS Hermes. 20p, HMS Leeds Castle. 25p, HMS Intrepid. 30p, HMS Glasgow. 40p, RMS St. Helena, HMS Brecon, HMS Ledbury. 50p, HMS Courageous.

**Wmk. 373**

**2002, June 14 Litho. *Perf. 14***

**802-807** A146 Set of 6 6.75 6.75

**Queen Mother Elizabeth (1900-2002)**

Common Design Type

Designs: 20p, Holding baby (black and white photograph). 25p, Wearing red hat. 30p, As young woman, without hat (black and white photograph). 50p, Wearing blue hat.

No. 812: a, 35p, Without hat, diff. (black and white photo). b, £1, Wearing blue hat and scarf.

**Wmk. 373**

**2002, Aug. 5 Litho. *Perf. 14¼***

**With Purple Frames**

**808-811** CD361 Set of 4 5.75 5.75

**Souvenir Sheet**

**Without Purple Frames**

***Perf. 14½x14¼***

**812** CD361 Sheet of 2, #a-b 6.75 6.75

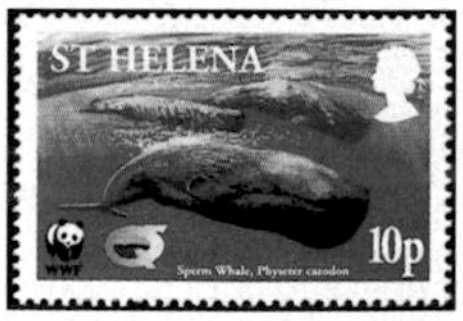
ST HELENA
10p

Worldwide Fund for Nature (WWF) A147

Sperm whales: 10p, Three underwater. 15p, One surfacing. 20p, Two underwater. 30p, One with tail out of water.

**Wmk. 373**

**2002, Oct. 3 Litho. *Perf. 14***

**813-816** A147 Set of 4 3.60 3.60
*816a* Strip of 4, #813-816 3.60 3.60

Souvenir Sheet

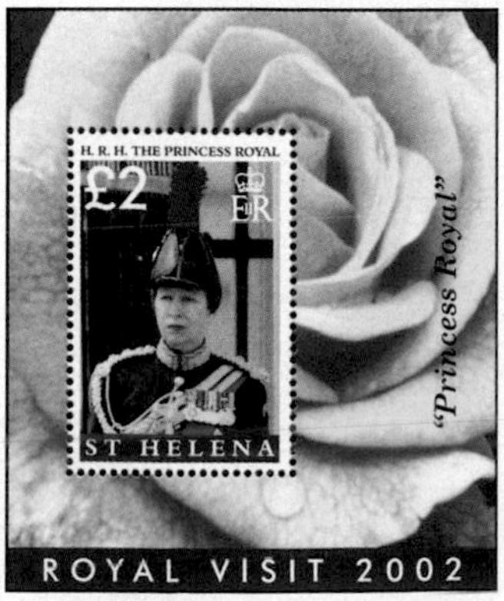
H. R. H. THE PRINCESS ROYAL
£2
ST HELENA
"Princess Royal"
ROYAL VISIT 2002

Visit of Princess Royal (Princess Anne) — A148

**Wmk. 373**

**2002, Nov. 15 Litho. *Perf. 14***
**817** A148 £2 multi 7.50 7.50

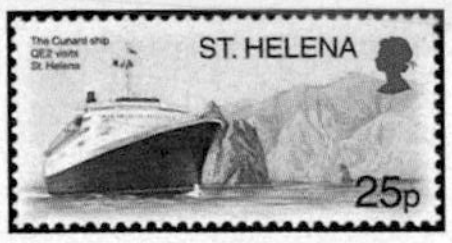

Tourism A149

Design: No. 818, Ship Queen Elizabeth 2 visits St. Helena.
No. 819: a, Plantation House. b, RMS St. Helena in Jamestown harbor. c, Napoleon's Tomb, Briars Pavilion. d, Ebony flower, Diana's Peak. e, Wirebird, Napoleon's House. f, Broadway House. g, St. Helena Golf Course. h, St. Helena Yacht Club. i, Sport fishing. j, Diving Club. k, St. Helena Heritage Society Museum.

***Perf. 13½x13¼***

**2003, Apr. 8 Litho. Wmk. 373**
**818** A149 25p multi .95 .95
**819** A149 25p Sheet of 12, #a-k, 818 + 4 labels 11.50 11.50

**Head of Queen Elizabeth II**
Common Design Type

**Wmk. 373**

**2003, June 2 Litho. *Perf. 13¾***
**820** CD362 £2.50 multi 9.50 9.50

**Coronation of Queen Elizabeth II, 50th Anniv.**
Common Design Type

Designs: Nos. 821, 823a, 30p, Queen with scepter. Nos. 822, 824b, 50p, Queen in carriage.

***Perf. 14¼x14½***

**2003, June 2 Litho. Wmk. 373**
**Vignettes Framed, Red Background**
**821-822** CD363 Set of 2 3.00 3.00

**Souvenir Sheet**
**Vignettes Without Frame, Purple Panel**
**823** CD363 Sheet of 2, #a-b 3.00 3.00

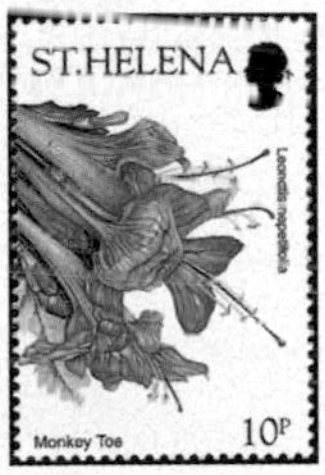

Wild Flowers — A150

Designs: 10p, Monkey toe. 15p, Buddleia madagascariensis. 20p, Lady's petticoat. 25p, Fuchsia boliviana. 30p, Tallowvine. 40p, Elderberry. 50p Yellow pops. 75p, Lucky leaf. 80p, Ginger. £1, Lily shot. £2, Waxy ginger. £5, Lantana camara.

**Wmk. 373**

**2003, July 10 Litho. *Perf. 14***
**824** A150 10p multi .45 .45
**825** A150 15p multi .60 .60
**826** A150 20p multi .80 .80
**827** A150 25p multi 1.00 1.00
**828** A150 30p multi 1.25 1.25
**829** A150 40p multi 1.50 2.75
**830** A150 50p multi 2.00 2.00
**831** A150 75p multi 3.00 3.00
**832** A150 80p multi 3.25 3.25
**833** A150 £1 multi 4.00 4.00
**834** A150 £2 multi 8.00 8.00
**835** A150 £5 multi 20.00 20.00
*Nos. 824-835 (12)* 45.85 47.10

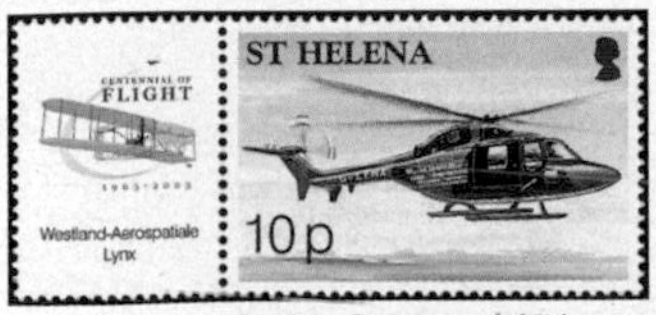

Powered Flight, Cent. — A151

Designs: 10p, Westland-Aerospatiale Lynx Helicopter. 15p, Douglas C-124 Globemaster. 20p, British Aerospace Nimrod AEW Mk3. 25p, Lockheed C-130 Hercules. 30p, Lockheed Tristar. 50p, Wright Flyer.
£1.80, Supermarine Walrus.
Illustration reduced.

**2003, Aug. 12 *Perf. 373***
**Stamp + Label**
**836-841** A151 Set of 6 6.75 6.75

**Souvenir Sheet**
**842** A151 £1.80 multi 7.50 7.50

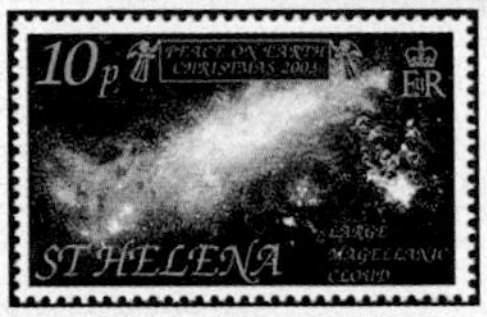

Christmas — A152

Astronomical photos: 10p, Large Magellanic Cloud. 15p, Small Magellanic Cloud. 20p, Omega Centauri. 25p, Eta Carinae. 30p, Southern Cross.

**Wmk. 373**

**2003, Oct. 3 Litho. *Perf. 13½***
**843-847** A152 Set of 5 3.75 3.75

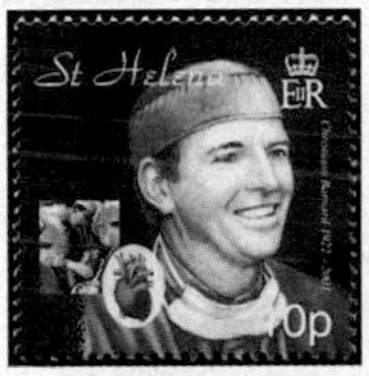

Medical Pioneers A153

Designs: 10p, Christiaan Barnard (1922-2001). 25p, Marie Curie (1867-1934). 30p, Louis Pasteur (1822-95). 50p, Sir Alexander Fleming (1881-1955).

**Wmk. 373**

**2004, Mar. 19 Litho. *Perf. 14¼***
**848-851** A153 Set of 4 4.75 4.75

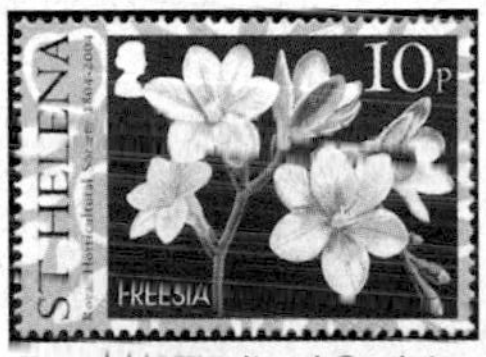

Royal Horticultural Society, Bicent. — A154

Flowers: 10p, Freesia. 15p, Bottle brush. 30p, Ebony. 50p, Olive.
£1, Maurandya.

**Wmk. 373**

**2004, May 25 Litho. *Perf. 14***
**852-855** A154 Set of 4 4.00 4.00

**Souvenir Sheet**
**856** A154 £1 multi 3.75 3.75

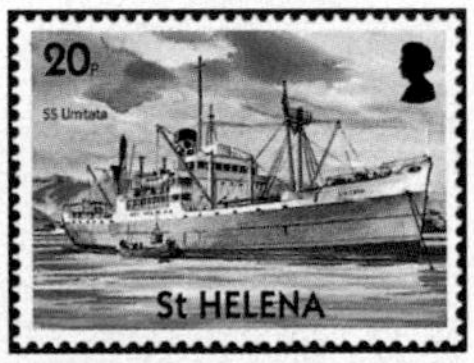

Merchant Ships A155

Designs: 20p, SS Umtata. 30p, SS Umzinto. 50p, SS Umtali. 80p, SS Umbilo.

**Wmk. 373**

**2004, Nov. 4 Litho. *Perf. 13¼***
**857-860** A155 Set of 4 6.75 6.75

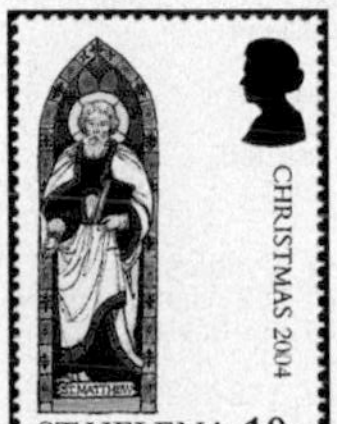

Christmas — A156

Stained-glass windows: 10p, St. Matthew. 15p, St. John. 20p, St. Peter. 30p, St. James. 50p, St. Paul.

**Wmk. 373**

**2004, Oct. 5 Litho. *Perf. 14***
**861-865** A156 Set of 5 4.50 4.50

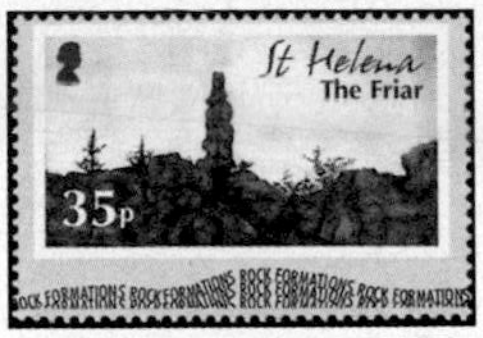

Rock Formations — A157

**Wmk. 373**

**2005, Jan. 14 Litho. *Perf. 14***
**866** Horiz. strip of 4 8.50 8.50
*a.* A157 35p The Friar 1.25 1.25
*b.* A157 40p Sugar Loaf 1.50 1.50
*c.* A157 50p The Turk's Cap 1.90 1.90
*d.* A157 £1 Lot's Wife 3.75 3.75

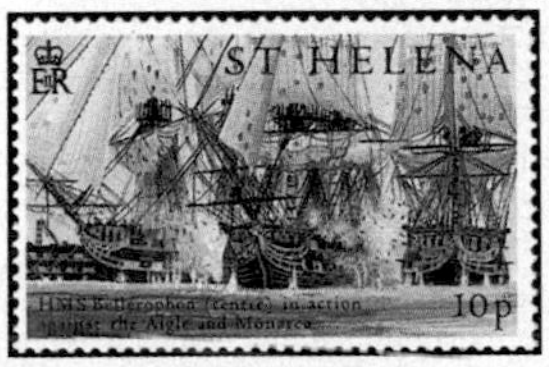

Battle of Trafalgar, Bicent. — A158

Designs: 10p, HMS Bellerophon in action against the Aigle and Monarca. 20p, British 18-pounder naval pattern cannon. 30p, HMS Victory. 50p, Royal Navy first lieutenant, 1805, vert. 60p, HMS Conqueror, vert. 80p, Portrait of Admiral Horatio Nelson, vert.
No. 873, vert.: a, Portrait of Admiral Cuthbert Collingwood. b, HMS Royal Sovereign.

**Wmk. 373, Unwmkd. (30p)**

**2005, May 10 Litho. *Perf. 13½***
**867-872** A158 Set of 6 9.50 9.50

**Souvenir Sheet**
**873** A158 75p Sheet of 2, #a-b 5.75 5.75

No. 869 has particles of wood from the HMS Victory embedded in the areas covered by a thermographic process that produces a raised, shiny effect.

Miniature Sheet

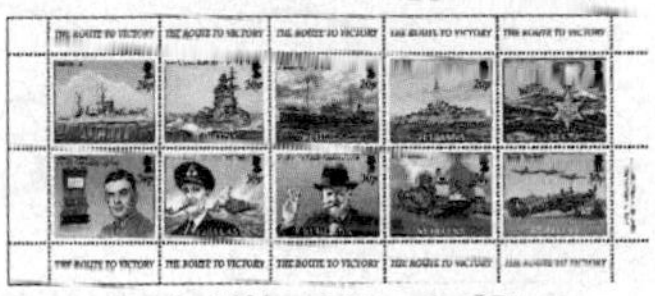
End of World War II, 60th Anniv. — A159

No. 874: a, 20p, HMS Milford. b, 20p, HMS Nelson. c, 20p, RFA Darkdale. d, 20p, HMS St. Helena. e, 20p, Ship and Atlantic Star Medal. f, 30p, Codebreaker Alan M. Turing and Enigma code machine. g, 30p, Capt. Johnnie Walker, HMS Starling. h, 30p, British Prime Minister Winston Churchill. i, 30p, Churchill infantry tank. j, 30p, Hawker Hurricanes.

**Wmk. 373**

**2005, July 15 Litho. *Perf. 13¾***
**874** A159 Shhet of 10, #a-j 9.00 9.00

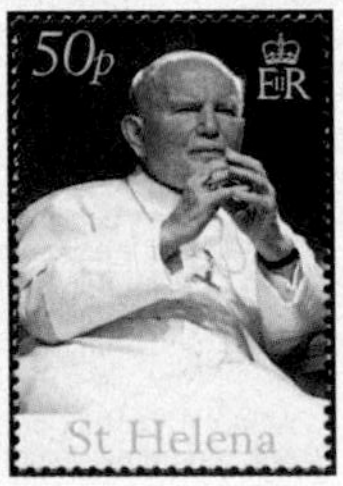

Pope John Paul II (1920-2005) A160

**Wmk. 373**

**2005, Aug. 31 Litho. *Perf. 14***
**875** A160 50p multi 1.90 1.90

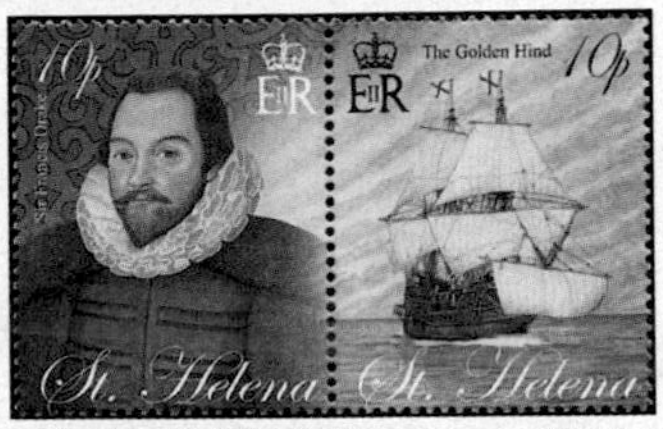

England's Elizabethan Era — A161

No. 876, 10p: a, Sir Francis Drake. b, Golden Hind.
No. 877, 15p: a, Sir Walter Raleigh. b, Ark Royal.
No. 878, 25p: a, Queen Elizabeth I. b, Spanish Armada.
No. 879, £1: a, William Shakespeare. b, Old Globe Theater.
Illustration reduced.

**2005, Sept. 7 *Perf. 13¾***
**Horiz. Pairs, #a-b**
**876-879** A161 Set of 4 11.00 11.00

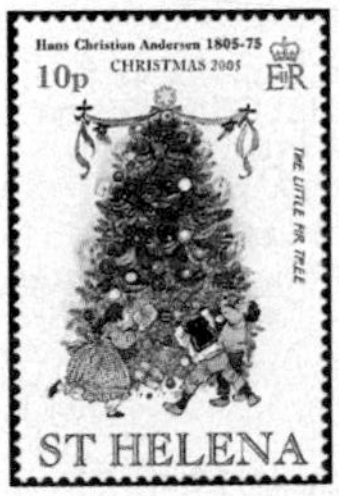

Christmas — A162

Stories by Hans Christian Andersen (1805-75): 10p, The Little Fir Tree. 25p, The Ugly Duckling. 30p, The Snow Queen. £1, The Little Mermaid.

**Wmk. 373**

**2005, Oct. 4 Litho. *Perf. 14***
**880-883** A162 Set of 4 6.00 6.00

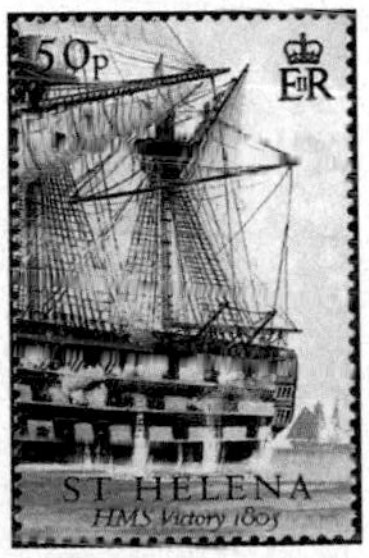

Battle of Trafalgar, Bicent. — A163

Designs: 50p, HMS Victory. 80p, Ships in battle, horiz. £1.20, Admiral Horatio Nelson.

**2005, Oct. 18 Unwmk. *Perf. 13¼***
**884-886** A163 Set of 3 9.00 9.00

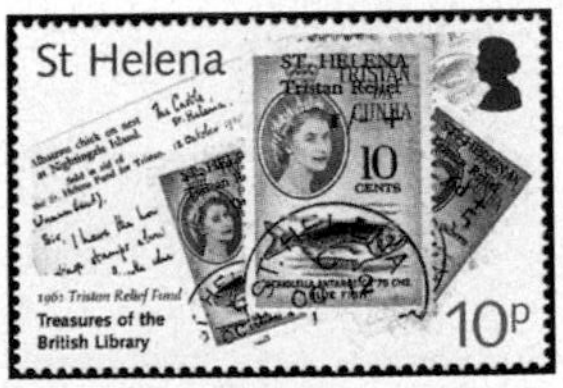

Stamps in the British Library Collection — A164

Designs: 10p, St. Helena #B2-B4. 20p, Cape of Good Hope #6. 25p, US #C3a. 30p, St. Helena #1. 80p, Great Britain #1. £1.20, Mauritius #2.
£2, Like 30p.

***Perf. 14¼x14¾***

**2006, Jan. 16 Litho. Wmk. 373**
**887-892** A164 Set of 6 10.00 10.00

**Souvenir Sheet**
**893** A164 £2 multi 7.00 7.00

St. Helena postage stamps, 150th anniv. (Nos. 890, 893).

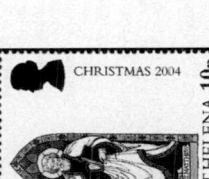

## ST. HELENA

**2006, Feb. 6**    **Unwmk.**    **Perf. 14**

| | | | | |
|---|---|---|---|---|
| 894-897 | A165 | Set of 4 | 8.50 | 8.50 |
| 897a | | Souvenir sheet #894-897 | 8.50 | 8.50 |

Europa Stamps, 50th Anniv. A165

Designs: 10p, Five stars, European Union flag. 30p, Five stars, letter. 80p, Four stars, ball. £1.20, Star painting stamp, three stars in circle.

### SEMI-POSTAL STAMPS

Catalogue values for unused stamps in this section are for Never Hinged items.

**1961, Oct. 12**    **Wmk. 314**    **Perf. 12½x13**

Tristan da Cunha Nos. 46, 49-51 Overprinted "ST. HELENA / Tristan Relief" and Surcharged with New Value and "+"

Engr.

| | | | | |
|---|---|---|---|---|
| B1 | A3 | 2½c + 3p | 575.00 | 600.00 |
| B2 | A3 | 5c + 6p | 600.00 | 700.00 |
| B3 | A3 | 7½c + 9p | 700.00 | 775.00 |
| B4 | A3 | 10c + 1sh | 775.00 | 2,650.00 |
| | | Nos. B1-B4 (4) | 2,650.00 | |

Withdrawn from sale Oct. 19.

### POSTAGE DUE STAMPS

Catalogue values for unused stamps in this section are for Never Hinged items.

Map—D1

**1986, June 9**    **Litho.**    **Perf. 15x14**

Background Color    Wmk. 384

| | | | | |
|---|---|---|---|---|
| J1 | D1 | 1p tan | .20 | .45 |
| J2 | D1 | 2p orange | .20 | .45 |
| J3 | D1 | 5p vermilion | .20 | .45 |
| J4 | D1 | 7p violet | .20 | .45 |
| J5 | D1 | 10p chalky blue | .55 | .55 |
| J6 | D1 | 25p dull yellow grn | .65 | 1.40 |
| | | Nos. J1-J6 (6) | 1.70 | 3.75 |

### WAR TAX STAMPS

**1916**    **Wmk. 3**    **Perf. 14**

| | | | | |
|---|---|---|---|---|
| MR1 | A10 | 1p + 1p scarlet & blk | 1.75 | 3.50 |
| a. | | Double surcharge | | 8,500. |

No. 62a Surcharged

---

## ST. KITTS

sänt 'kits

LOCATION — West Indies southeast of Puerto Rico

GOVT. — With Nevis, Associated State in British Commonwealth

AREA — 65 sq. mi.

POP. — 31,824 (1991)

CAPITAL — Basseterre

See St. Christopher for stamps used in St. Kitts until 1890. From 1890 until 1903, stamps of the Leeward Islands were used. From 1903 stamps of St. Kitts-Nevis and Leeward Islands were used concurrently. See St. Kitts-Nevis for stamps used through June 22, 1980, after which St. Kitts and Nevis pursued separate postal administrations.

100 Cents = 1 Dollar

### WAR TAX STAMPS

**1919**

| | | | | |
|---|---|---|---|---|
| MR2 | A10 | 1p + 1p carmine & blk | 1.50 | 4.75 |

No. 62 Surcharged

Ships A2

Watermark   Wmk. 380 — "POST OFFICE"

**1980, June 23**    **Perf. 14½x14**    **Litho.**    **Wmk. 373**

St. Kitts-Nevis Nos. 357-369 Ovptd.

| | | | | |
|---|---|---|---|---|
| 25 | A61 | 5c multicolored | .20 | .20 |
| 26 | A61 | 10c multicolored | .20 | .20 |
| 27 | A61 | 12c multicolored | .50 | .50 |
| 28 | A61 | 15c multicolored | .20 | .20 |
| 29 | A61 | 25c multicolored | .20 | .20 |
| 30 | A61 | 30c multicolored | .20 | .20 |
| 31 | A61 | 40c multicolored | .20 | .20 |
| 32 | A61 | 45c multicolored | .45 | .20 |
| 33 | A61 | 50c multicolored | .20 | .20 |
| 34 | A61 | 50c multicolored | .20 | .20 |
| 35 | A61 | 55c multicolored | .20 | .20 |
| 36 | A61 | $1 multicolored | .75 | 1.00 |
| 37 | A61 | $5 multicolored | 1.25 | 1.25 |
| | | Nos. 25-37 (13) | 4.75 | 5.65 |

**1980, Aug. 8**    **Perf. 13½**

| | | | | |
|---|---|---|---|---|
| 38 | A2 | 4c HMS Vanguard, 1762 | .20 | .20 |
| 39 | A2 | 10c HMS Boreas, 1787 | .20 | .20 |
| 40 | A2 | 30c HMS Druid, 1827 | .20 | .20 |
| 41 | A2 | 55c HMS Winchester, 1831 | .45 | .30 |
| 42 | A2 | $1.50 Philosopher, 1857 | .65 | .40 |
| 43 | A2 | S.S. Contractor, 1930 | 1.90 | 1.50 |
| | | Nos. 38-43 (6) | | |

Nos. 38-43 not issued without overprint. The 4c, and possibly others, exist without the overprint.

Queen Mother, 80th Birthday — A3

**1980, Sept. 4**    **Perf. 14**

| | | | | |
|---|---|---|---|---|
| 44 | A3 | $2 multicolored | .45 | .45 |

Christmas — A4

**1980, Nov. 10**    **Perf. 14½**

| | | | | |
|---|---|---|---|---|
| 45 | A4 | 5c Magi following star | .20 | .20 |
| 46 | A4 | 15c Shepherds, star | .20 | .20 |
| 47 | A4 | 30c Bethlehem, star | .50 | .50 |
| 48 | A4 | $4 Adoration of the Magi | 1.10 | 1.10 |
| | | Nos. 45-48 (4) | | |

Birds — A5

**1981**    **Wmk. 373**    **Perf. 13½x14**

Size: 38x25mm    Perf. 14

| | | | | |
|---|---|---|---|---|
| 49 | A5 | 1c Frigatebird | .20 | .20 |
| 50 | A5 | 4c Rusty-tailed flycatcher | .20 | .20 |
| 51 | A5 | 5c Purple-throated carib | .20 | .20 |
| 52 | A5 | 8c Purple martin | .20 | .20 |
| 53 | A5 | 10c Yellow-crowned night heron | .20 | .20 |
| 54 | A5 | 45c Black-faced grass-quit | .30 | .30 |
| 55 | A5 | 15c Bananaquit | .20 | .20 |
| 56 | A5 | Scaly-breasted thrasher | .20 | .20 |
| 57 | A5 | 25c Grey Kingbird | .50 | .50 |
| 58 | A5 | 30c Green-throated carib | .20 | .20 |
| 59 | A5 | 40c Ruddy turnstone | .20 | .30 |
| 60 | A5 | 45c Burrowing owl | .30 | .30 |
| 61 | A5 | 50c Cattle egret | .40 | .40 |
| 62 | A5 | 50c Brown pelican | .40 | .40 |
| 63 | A5 | $1 Lesser Antillean bullfinch | .40 | .40 |
| 64 | A5 | $2.50 Zenaida dove | .80 | .80 |
| 65 | A5 | $5 Sparrow hawk | 2.00 | 2.00 |
| 66 | A5 | $10 Antillean crested hummingbird | 4.00 | 4.00 |
| | | Nos. 49-66 (18) | 7.75 | 7.75 |
| | | | 18.05 | 18.05 |

Issued: #51, 54-66, Feb. 5; others, May 30. Nos. 49-66 exist with "1982" imprint. The 1981 set has no imprint.

For overprints see Nos. 112-122.

Military Uniforms — A6

Prince Charles and Lady Diana — A6b

**1981, June 23**    **Perf. 14**

| | | | | |
|---|---|---|---|---|
| 67 | A6 | 5c multi | .20 | .20 |
| 68 | A6 | 30c multi | .20 | .20 |
| 69 | A6 | 55c multi | .30 | .30 |
| 70 | A6 | 55c multi | .30 | .30 |
| 71 | A6 | 55c multi ('83) | .45 | .45 |
| 72 | A6 | 30c multi ('83) | .30 | .30 |
| 73 | A6 | $2.50 multi ('83) | 1.45 | 1.25 |
| 74 | A6 | $2.50 multi ('83) | 3.00 | 3.00 |
| | | Nos. 67-74 (8) | | |

Battalion Company officer, 45th Regiment, 1796-7. No. 70, Officer, 15th Regiment, c. 1780. No. 71, No. 70, Officer, 9th Regiment, 1790. No. 72, Light Company officer, 5th Regiment, c. 1822. No. 73, Grenadier, 38th Regiment, c. 1751. No. 74, Battalion Company officer, 11th Regiment, c. 1804.

Issued: 3/5/81; 5/25/81; 5/25/83.

Prince Charles and Lady Diana — A6b

Prince Charles, Lady Diana, Royal Yacht Charlotte A6a

**1981, June 23**    **Perf. 14**

Illustration A6b is greatly reduced.

| | | | | |
|---|---|---|---|---|
| 75 | A6a | 55c Saudadoes | .20 | .20 |
| 76 | A6a | 55c Couple | .20 | .20 |
| a. | | Bkt. pane of 4, perf. 12½x12, unwmkd. | | .90 |
| 77 | A6a | $2.50 The Royal George | | .90 |
| 78 | A6a | $2.50 like 55c | 2.00 | 2.00 |
| a. | | Bklt. pane of 2, perf. 12½x12, unwmkd. | | |
| 79 | A6a | $4 HMY Britannia | 1.40 | 1.40 |
| 80 | A6a | $4 like 55c | 1.40 | 1.40 |
| | | Nos. 75-80 (6) | 5.00 | 5.00 |

Souvenir Sheet

**1981, Dec. 14**    **Perf. 12½x12**

Wedding of Prince Charles and Lady Diana

| | | | | |
|---|---|---|---|---|
| 81 | A6b | $5 like 55c | 2.75 | 2.75 |

Spencer. Nos. 76a, 78a issued Nov. 19, 1981.

Nat'l. Girl Guide Movement, 50th Anniv. — A7

**1981, Sept. 21**    **Perf. 14½**

Designs: 5c, Miriam Pickard, 1st Guide commissioner. 30c, Lady Baden-Powell's visit, 1964. 55c, Visit of Princess Alice, 1960. $2, Thinking-Day Parade, 1980s.

| | | | | |
|---|---|---|---|---|
| 82 | A7 | 5c multicolored | .20 | .20 |
| 83 | A7 | 30c multicolored | .20 | .20 |
| 84 | A7 | 55c multicolored | .70 | .70 |
| 85 | A7 | $2 multicolored | 1.30 | 1.30 |
| | | Nos. 82-85 (4) | | |

Christmas — A8

**1981, Nov. 30**

Stained-glass windows.

Designs: 5c Annunciation. 30c Nativity, baptism. 55c Last supper, crucifixion.

| | | | | |
|---|---|---|---|---|
| 86 | A8 | 5c multicolored | .20 | .20 |
| 87 | A8 | 30c multicolored | .20 | .20 |
| 88 | A8 | 55c multicolored | .20 | .20 |

| 89 | A8 | $3 | Appearance before Apostles, ascension to heaven | .80 | .80 |
| | | | | 1.40 | 1.40 |

*Nos. 86-89 (4)*

**Brimstone Hill Siege, Bicent. — A9**

**1982, Mar. 15**

| 90 | A9 | 15c | Adm. Samuel Hood | .20 | .20 |
| 91 | A9 | 55c | Marquis de Bouille | .30 | .30 |

**Souvenir Sheet**

| 92 | A9 | $5 | Battle scene | 2.00 | 2.00 |

No. 92 has multicolored margin picturing battle scene. Size: 96x71mm.

**21st Birthday of Princess Diana, July 1 — A10**

15c, Alexandra of Denmark, Princess of Wales, 1863. 55c, Paternal arms of Wales. $6, Diana.

**1982, June 22    Perf. 13½x14**

| 93 | A10 | 15c | multicolored | .20 | .20 |
| 94 | A10 | 55c | multicolored | .30 | .30 |
| 95 | A10 | $6 | multicolored | 2.50 | 2.50 |

*Nos. 93-95 (3)    3.00 3.00*

**Nos. 93-95 Ovptd. ROYAL BABY**

**1982, July 12**

| 96 | A10 | 15c | multicolored | .20 | .20 |
| 97 | A10 | 55c | multicolored | .30 | .30 |
| 98 | A10 | $6 | multicolored | 2.50 | 2.50 |

*3.00 3.00*

Birth of Prince William of Wales.

**Scouting, 75th Anniv. — A11**

Merit badges.

**1982, Aug. 18    Perf. 14x13½**

| 99 | A11 | 5c | Nature | .20 | .20 |
| 100 | A11 | 55c | Rescue | .30 | .30 |
| 101 | A11 | $2 | First aid | 1.60 | 1.60 |

*Nos. 99-101 (3)*

**Christmas — A12**

Children's drawings.

**1982, Oct. 20**

| 102 | A12 | 5c | shown | .20 | .20 |
| 103 | A12 | 15c | Nativity | .20 | .20 |
| 104 | A12 | 55c | Three Kings | .30 | .30 |
| 105 | A12 | $1.10 | Annunciation | .90 | .90 |

*Nos. 102-105 (4)*

**A13**

Commonwealth Day: 55c, Cruise ship Stella Oceanis docked. $2, RMS Queen Elizabeth 2 anchored in harbor off St. Kitts.

**1983, Mar. 14    Perf. 14**

| 106 | A13 | 55c | multicolored | .20 | .20 |
| 107 | A13 | $2 | multicolored | .45 | .45 |

**Boys' Brigade, Cent. — A14**

Designs: 10c, Sir William Smith, founder. 45c, Brigade members outside Sandy Point Methodist Church. 50c, Drummers. $3, Badge.

**1983, July 27**

| 108 | A14 | 10c | multicolored | .35 | .35 |
| 109 | A14 | 45c | multicolored | .55 | .55 |
| 110 | A14 | 50c | multicolored | .55 | .55 |
| 111 | A14 | $3 | multicolored | .95 | .95 |

*Nos. 108-111 (4)    2.40 2.40*

**Nos. 51, 55-59 and 62-66 Ovptd.**

**1983, Sept. 19**

| 112 | A5(a) | 5c | multicolored | .20 | .20 |
| a. | | | Local overprint | 2.25 | 2.25 |
| 113 | A5(b) | 15c | multicolored | .20 | .20 |
| 114 | A5(b) | 20c | multicolored | .20 | .20 |
| 115 | A5(b) | 25c | multicolored | .20 | .20 |
| 116 | A5(b) | 30c | multicolored | .25 | .25 |
| 117 | A5(b) | 40c | multicolored | .25 | .25 |
| 118 | A5(b) | 55c | multicolored | .50 | .50 |
| 119 | A5(b) | $1 | multicolored | .90 | .90 |
| 120 | A5(b) | $2.50 | multicolored | 2.40 | 2.40 |
| 121 | A5(b) | $5 | multicolored | 4.50 | 4.50 |
| 122 | A5(b) | $10 | multicolored | 9.00 | 9.00 |

*Nos. 112-122 (11)    18.55 18.55*

Nos. 113-122 have "1982" imprint. Nos. 113, 116, 118-122 exist without imprint. No. 112 is without imprint. No. 112 with imprint is twice the value. "Set" of eight stamps without imprints sell for approximately $60. No. 112a has serifed letters and reads up and on imprinted stamp. Exists reading up and without imprint.

**Manned Flight Bicent. — A15**

Designs: 10c, *Montgolfiere,* 1783, vert. 45c, Sikorsky *Russian Knight,* 1913. 50c, Lockheed TriStar. $2.50, Bell XS-1, 1947.

**1983, Sept. 28    Wmk. 380**

| 123 | A15 | 10c | multicolored | .20 | .20 |
| 124 | A15 | 45c | multicolored | .20 | .20 |
| 125 | A15 | 50c | multicolored | .40 | .40 |
| 126 | A15 | $2.50 | multicolored | 1.50 | 1.50 |
| a. | | | Souvenir sheet of 4, #123-126 | 1.00 | 1.00 |

*Nos. 123-126 (4)*

1st Flight of a 4-engine aircraft, May 1913 (45c); 1st manned supersonic aircraft, 1947 ($2.50).

**Christmas — A16**

**1983, Nov. 7**

| 127 | A16 | 15c | shown | .20 | .20 |
| 128 | A16 | 30c | Shepherds | .20 | .20 |
| 129 | A16 | 55c | Mary, Joseph | .20 | .20 |
| 130 | A16 | $2.50 | Nativity | .30 | .30 |
| a. | | | Souvenir sheet of 4, #127-130 | 1.00 | 1.00 |

*Nos. 127-130 (4)    .90 .90*

**Batik Art A17**

**1984-85**

| 131 | A17 | 15c | Country bus | .20 | .20 |
| 132 | A17 | 40c | Donkey cart | .30 | .30 |
| 133 | A17 | 45c | Parrot, vert. | .20 | .20 |
| 134 | A17 | 50c | Man under palm tree, vert. | .20 | .20 |
| 135 | A17 | 60c | Rum shop, cyclist | .55 | .55 |
| 136 | A17 | $1.50 | Fruit seller, vert. | .35 | .50 |
| 137 | A17 | $3 | Butterflies, vert. | .65 | 1.25 |
| 138 | A17 | $3 | S.V. Polynesia | 1.40 | 1.75 |

*Nos. 131-138 (8)    3.85 4.50*

Issued: 15c, 40c, 60c, #138, 2/6/85; others, 1/30/84.

**Marine Life A18**

**1984, July 4**

| 139 | A18 | 5c | Cushion star | .20 | .20 |
| 140 | A18 | 10c | Rough file shell | .20 | .20 |
| a. | | | Wmk. 384 ('86) | | |

| 141 | A18 | 15c | Red-lined cleaning shrimp | .20 | .20 |
| 142 | A18 | 20c | Bristleworm | .20 | .20 |
| 143 | A18 | 25c | Flamingo tongue | .25 | .20 |
| 144 | A18 | 30c | Christmas tree worm | .55 | .55 |
| 145 | A18 | 40c | Pink-tipped anemone | .65 | .65 |
| 146 | A18 | 50c | Smallmouth grunt | .80 | .80 |
| 147 | A18 | 60c | Glasseye snapper | 1.10 | 1.10 |
| a. | | | Wmk. 384 ('88) | 1.40 | 1.40 |
| 148 | A18 | 75c | Reef squirrelfish | 1.40 | 1.40 |
| 149 | A18 | $1 | Sea fans, flamefish | 1.60 | 1.60 |
| 150 | A18 | $2.50 | Reef butterfly-fish | 4.00 | 4.25 |
| 151 | A18 | $5 | Black soldierfish | 8.25 | 8.75 |
| a. | | | Wmk. 384 ('88) | 10.50 | 11.00 |
| 152 | A18 | $10 | Cocoa damselfish | 17.00 | 18.00 |
| a. | | | Wmk. 384 ('88) | 22.50 | 24.00 |

*Nos. 139-152 (14)    36.40 38.10*

#140a has "1986" imprint; also exists with "1988" imprint. #147a, 151a, 152a have "1988" imprint.

**4-H in St. Kitts, 25th Anniv. A19**

**1984, Aug. 15**

| 153 | A19 | 30c | Agriculture | .20 | .20 |
| 154 | A19 | $1.10 | Pledge, flag, youths | .40 | .40 |
| 155 | A19 | $1.10 | Animal husbandry | .65 | .65 |
| 156 | A19 | $3 | Parade | 1.25 | 1.25 |

*Nos. 153-156 (4)    2.50 2.50*

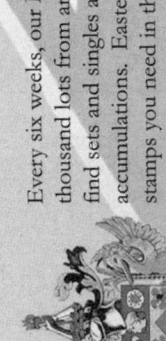

**1st Anniv. of Independence — A20**

15c, Construction of Royal St. Kitts Hotel. 30c, Folk dancers. $1.10, O Land of Beauty, vert. $3, Sea, palm trees, map, vert.

**1984, Sept. 18**

| 157 | A20 | 15c | multicolored | .20 | .20 |
| 158 | A20 | 30c | multicolored | .25 | .25 |
| 159 | A20 | $1.10 | multicolored | .55 | .55 |
| 160 | A20 | $3 | multicolored | 1.25 | 1.25 |

*Nos. 157-160 (4)    2.25 2.25*

ST. KITTS

St. Kitts 10c

Christmas 1984

**1984, Nov. 1**
Christmas — A21

| | | |
|---|---|---|
| 161 | A21 15c Opening gifts | .20 .20 |
| 162 | A21 60c Caroling | .55 .55 |
| 163 | A21 $1 Nativity | .80 .80 |
| 164 | A21 $2 Leaving church | 1.60 1.60 |
| | Nos. 161-164 (4) | 3.15 3.15 |

St. Kitts 15c Christmas 1985

St. Kitts 10 Christmas 1985

Ships — A22

**1985, Mar. 27** — *Perf. 13½x14*

| | | |
|---|---|---|
| 165 | A22 40c Tropic Jade | .75 .75 |
| 166 | A22 $1.20 Atlantic Clipper | 2.25 2.25 |
| 167 | A22 $2 M.V. Cunard Countess | 3.50 3.50 |
| 168 | A22 $2 Mandalay | 3.50 3.50 |
| | | 10.00 10.00 |

Mt. Olive Masonic Lodge, 150th Anniv. — A23

**1985, Nov. 9** — *Perf. 15*

| | | |
|---|---|---|
| 169 | A23 15c multicolored | .60 .60 |
| 170 | A23 75c multicolored | 1.40 1.40 |
| 171 | A23 $1.20 multicolored | 1.40 1.40 |
| 172 | A23 $3 multicolored | 2.10 2.10 |
| | Nos. 169-172 (4) | 5.50 5.50 |

Designs: 15c, James Derrick Cardin (1871-1954); 75c, Lodge banner, $1.20, Compass, Bible, square, horiz. $3, Charter, 1835.

Sir Francis Drake to St. Christopher

**1985, Nov. 27** — *Unwmk.*

| | | |
|---|---|---|
| 173 | A24 10c Map of St. Kitts | .35 .35 |
| 174 | A24 40c Golden Hind | .65 .65 |
| 175 | A24 60c Sir Francis Drake | .65 .65 |
| 176 | A24 $3 Drake's shield of arms | .85 2.75 |
| | Nos. 173-176 (4) | 2.50 4.40 |

Visit of Sir Francis Drake to St. Kitts, 400th anniv.

Queen Elizabeth II, 60th Birthday — A25

**1986, July 9** — *Perf. 14*

| | | |
|---|---|---|
| 177 | A25 10c multicolored | .20 .20 |
| 178 | A25 20c multicolored | .20 .20 |
| 179 | A25 40c multicolored | .45 .45 |
| 180 | A25 $3 multicolored | 3.85 3.85 |
| | Nos. 177-180 (4) | 3.00 3.00 |

Designs: 10c, With Prince Philip. 20c, Walking with government officials. 40c, Riding horse in parade. $3, Portrait.

For overprints see Nos. 185-188.

**Common Design Types** pictured following the introduction.

**Royal Wedding Issue, 1986**
Common Design Type

Designs: 15c, Prince Andrew and Sarah Ferguson, formal engagement announcement. $2.50, Prince Andrew in military dress uniform.

**1986, July 23** — *Perf. 14½x14*

| | | |
|---|---|---|
| 181 | CD338 15c multicolored | .20 .20 |
| 182 | CD338 $2.50 multicolored | 1.25 1.25 |

St. Kitts 15c Agriculture Exhibition 1986

Agriculture Exhibition — A26

**1986, Sept. 18** — *Wmk. 384*

| | | |
|---|---|---|
| 183 | A26 15c multicolored | .20 .20 |
| 184 | A26 $1.20 multicolored | 1.25 1.25 |

Nos. 177-180 Ovptd. "40th ANNIVERSARY / U.N. WEEK 19-26 OCT." in Gold

**1986, Oct. 22** — *Unwmk.* — *Perf. 13½x14*

| | | |
|---|---|---|
| 185 | A25 10c multicolored | .20 .20 |
| 186 | A25 20c multicolored | .20 .20 |
| 187 | A25 40c multicolored | .35 .35 |
| 188 | A25 $3 multicolored | 2.40 2.40 |
| | Nos. 185-188 (4) | 3.15 3.15 |

St. Kitts 40c Auguste Bartholdi — A28

THE CENTENARY OF THE DEDICATION

28 October, 1886
OF THE STATUE OF LIBERTY

St. Kitts $3.50

Statue of Liberty, Cent. — A29

World Wildlife Fund — A27

Various green monkeys, Cercopithecus aethiops sabaeus.

**1986, Dec. 1**

| | | |
|---|---|---|
| 189 | A27 15c multi. | 4.00 4.00 |
| 190 | A27 20c multi. diff. | 4.50 4.50 |
| 191 | A27 40c multi. diff. | 9.00 9.00 |
| 192 | A27 $1 multi. diff. | 9.50 8.25 |
| | Nos. 189-192 (4) | 27.00 14.05 |

**1986, Dec. 1**

| | | |
|---|---|---|
| 193 | A28 40c shown | .30 .30 |

**1986, Dec. 17** — *Perf. 14x14½, 14½x14*

| | | |
|---|---|---|
| 194 | A28 60c Torch, head, 1876-78 | .45 .45 |
| 195 | A28 $1.50 Warship Isere, France | 1.00 1.25 |
| 196 | A28 $3 Delivering statue, 1884 | 2.50 2.50 |
| | Nos. 193-196 (4) | 3.00 4.50 |

| | | |
|---|---|---|
| 197 | A29 $3.50 Head | 2.75 2.75 |

Souvenir Sheet

Nos. 194-195 horiz.

St. Kitts 15c Sugar Cane Industry

British and French Uniforms — A30

Sugar Cane Industry — A31

Designs: No. 198, Officer, East Norfolk Regiment, 1792. No. 199, Officer, De Neustrie Regiment, 1779. No. 200, Sergeant, Third Foot the Buffs, 1801. No. 201, Artillery officer, 1812. No. 202, Private, Light Company, 5th Foot Regiment, 1778. No. 203, Grenadier, Line Infantry, 1796.

**1987, Feb. 25** — *Perf. 14½*

| | | |
|---|---|---|
| 198 | A30 15c multicolored | .60 .60 |
| 199 | A30 15c multicolored | .60 .20 |
| 200 | A30 40c multicolored | 1.25 .55 |
| 201 | A30 40c multicolored | 1.25 .55 |
| 202 | A30 $2 multicolored | 2.10 2.75 |
| 203 | A30 $2 multicolored | 2.10 2.75 |
| a. | Souvenir sheet of 6, #198-203 | 9.25 9.25 |
| | Nos. 198-203 (6) | 7.90 7.00 |

St. Kitts 15c Officer E. Norfolk Regt. 1792

**1987, Apr. 15** — *Perf. 14*

No. 204: a. Warehouse. b. Barns. c. Steam plant. e. Field hands.
No. 205a, Locomotive. b. Locomotive and tender. c. Open cars. d. Empty and loaded cars; tractor. e. Loading sugar cane.

| | | |
|---|---|---|
| 204 | Strip of 5 | 1.25 1.25 |
| a.-e. | A31 15c any single | .20 .20 |
| 205 | Strip of 5 | 2.75 2.75 |
| a.-e. | A31 75c any single | .45 .45 |

St Kitts 15c Fungi — A33

Visiting Aircraft — A32

**1987, June 24** — *Wmk. 373*

| | | |
|---|---|---|
| 206 | A32 40c L-1011-500 Tri-Star | .60 .60 |
| 207 | A32 60c BAe Super 748 | .60 .60 |
| 208 | A32 $1.20 DHC-6 Twin Otter | 2.10 2.10 |
| 209 | A32 $3 Aerospatiale ATR-42 | 4.75 4.75 |
| | Nos. 206-209 (4) | 8.45 8.45 |

**1987, Aug. 26** — *Wmk. 384* — *Perf. 14*

| | | |
|---|---|---|
| 210 | A33 15c Hygrocybe occidentalis | 1.25 .75 |
| 211 | A33 40c Marasmius haematocephalus | 2.00 .50 |
| 212 | A33 $1.20 Psilocybe cubensis | 4.25 3.00 |
| 213 | A33 $2 Hygrocybe acutoconica | 5.50 3.75 |
| 214 | A33 $3 Boletellus cubensis | 6.50 5.00 |
| | Nos. 210-214 (5) | 19.50 13.00 |

Carnival Clowns — A34

**1987, Oct. 28** — *Perf. 14½*

| | | |
|---|---|---|
| 215 | A34 15c multi | .25 .25 |
| 216 | A34 60c multi. diff. | .65 .65 |
| 217 | A34 $1 multi. diff. | 1.60 1.60 |
| 218 | A34 $3 multi. diff. | 3.50 3.50 |
| | Nos. 215-218 (4) | 6.00 6.00 |

Christmas 1987. See Nos. 235-238.

St. Kitts 15c Independence
Independence, 5th Anniv. — A38

St Kitts 40c L.I.C.A.
Leeward Islands Cricket Tournament, 75th Anniv. — A37

Flowers — A35

**1988, Jan. 20** — *Wmk. 373*

| | | |
|---|---|---|
| 219 | A35 15c Ixora | .20 .20 |
| 220 | A35 40c Shrimp plant | .55 .55 |
| 221 | A35 $1 Poinsettia | 1.25 1.25 |
| 222 | A35 $3 Honolulu rose | 4.00 4.00 |
| | Nos. 219-222 (4) | 6.00 6.00 |

Tourism — A36

**1988, Apr. 20** — *Wmk. 373*

| | | |
|---|---|---|
| 223 | A36 60c Ft. Thomas Hotel | 1.10 1.10 |
| 224 | A36 60c Fairview Inn | 1.10 1.10 |
| 225 | A36 60c Frigate Bay Beach Hotel | 1.10 1.10 |
| 226 | A36 60c Ocean Terrace Inn | 1.10 1.10 |
| 227 | A36 $3 The Golden Lemon on Royal St. Kitts Casino and Jack Tar Village | 3.00 3.00 |
| 228 | A36 $3 | 3.00 3.00 |
| 229 | A36 $3 Rawlins Plantation Hotel and Restaurant | 3.00 3.00 |
| | Nos. 223-229 (7) | 13.40 13.40 |

See Nos. 239-244.

Designs: 40c, Leeward Islands Cricket Assoc. emblem, ball and wicket. $3, Cricket match at Warner Park.

**1988, July 13** — *Perf. 13x13½*

| | | |
|---|---|---|
| 230 | A37 40c multicolored | 1.75 .30 |
| 231 | A37 $3 multicolored | 4.50 3.75 |

## Natl. Census — A51

## Flowers — A50

**Perf. 14x13½, 13½x14 Litho. Wmk. 373**
**1991, May 8**

| | | | | |
|---|---|---|---|---|
| 312 | A50 | 10c White periwinkle, horiz. | .50 | .50 |
| 313 | A50 | 40c Pink oleander, horiz. | 1.10 | 1.10 |
| 314 | A50 | 60c Pink periwinkle | 1.50 | 1.50 |
| 315 | A50 | $2 White oleander | 4.75 | 4.75 |
| | | Nos. 312-315 (4) | 7.85 | 7.85 |

**1991, May 13 Wmk. 384 Perf. 14**

| | | | | |
|---|---|---|---|---|
| 316 | A51 | 15c multicolored | .25 | .25 |
| 317 | A51 | $2.40 multicolored | 3.75 | 3.75 |

### Elizabeth & Philip, Birthdays
### Common Design Types
**Wmk. 384**
**1991, June 17 Litho. Perf. 14½**

| | | | | |
|---|---|---|---|---|
| 318 | CD346 | $1.20 multicolored | 1.00 | 1.00 |
| 319 | CD345 | $1.80 multicolored | 1.75 | 1.75 |
| a. | | Pair, #318-319 + label | 2.75 | 2.75 |

## Fish — A52

 10c

**Perf. 14 Wmk. 373**
**1991, Aug. 28**

| | | | | |
|---|---|---|---|---|
| 320 | A52 | 10c Nassau grouper | .50 | .50 |
| 321 | A52 | 60c Hogfish | 1.40 | 1.40 |
| 322 | A52 | $1 Red hind | 2.25 | 2.25 |
| 323 | A52 | $3 Parrotfish | 6.50 | 6.50 |
| | | Nos. 320-323 (4) | 10.00 | 10.66 |

### University of the West Indies — A53

Designs: 15c, Chancellor Sir Shridath Ramphal, School of Continuing Studies, St. Kitts. 50c, Administration Bldg., Cave Hill Campus, Barbados. $1, Engineering Bldg., St. Augustine Campus, Trinidad & Tobago. $3, Ramphal, Mona Campus, Jamaica.

**Wmk. 384 Perf. 14**
**1991, Sept. 25**

| | | | | |
|---|---|---|---|---|
| 324 | A53 | 15c multicolored | .35 | .35 |
| 325 | A53 | 50c multicolored | .80 | .80 |
| 326 | A53 | $1 multicolored | 1.75 | 1.75 |
| 327 | A53 | $3 multicolored | 5.00 | 5.00 |
| | | Nos. 324-327 (4) | 7.90 | 7.90 |

## Christmas — A54

Various scenes of traditional play, "The Bull."

**1991, Nov. 6 Wmk. 6**

| | | | | |
|---|---|---|---|---|
| 328 | A54 | 10c multicolored | .40 | .40 |
| 329 | A54 | 15c multicolored | .40 | .40 |
| 330 | A54 | 60c multicolored | 1.10 | 1.10 |
| 331 | A54 | $3 multicolored | 5.50 | 5.50 |
| | | Nos. 328-331 (4) | 7.40 | 7.40 |

---

## Cannon on Brimstone Hill, 300th Anniv. — A46

15c, 40c, View of Brimstone Hill. 60c, Fort Charles under bombardment. $3, Men firing cannon.

**Perf. 14 Wmk. 384**
**1990, June 30**

| | | | | |
|---|---|---|---|---|
| 285 | A46 | 15c multicolored | .20 | .20 |
| 286 | A46 | 40c multicolored | .65 | .65 |
| 287 | A46 | 60c multicolored | .90 | .90 |
| | | Pair | 5.50 | 5.50 |
| 288 | A46 | 60c multicolored | 4.50 | 4.50 |
| b. | | A46 $3 multicolored | 7.25 | 7.25 |
| | | Nos. 285-288 (4) | | |

No. 288 has a continuous design.

### Souvenir Sheet
### Battle of Britain, 50th Anniv. — A47

**1990, Sept. 15**

| | | | | |
|---|---|---|---|---|
| 289 | | Sheet of 2 | 26.00 | 26.00 |
| a.-b. | A47 | $3 any single | 12.00 | 12.00 |

## Ships — A48

 10c

**Perf. 14 Wmk. 373**
**1990, Oct. 10**

| | | | | |
|---|---|---|---|---|
| 294 | A48 | 10c Romney | .20 | .20 |
| 295 | A48 | 15c Baralt | .20 | .20 |
| 296 | A48 | 20c Wear | .20 | .20 |
| 297 | A48 | 25c Sunmount | .20 | .20 |
| 298 | A48 | 40c Inanda | .20 | .20 |
| 299 | A48 | 50c Alcoa Partner | 1.00 | 1.00 |
| 300 | A48 | 60c Dominica | .75 | .75 |
| 301 | A48 | 80c CCM Provence | 1.25 | 1.25 |
| 302 | A48 | $1 Director | 1.25 | 1.25 |
| 303 | A48 | $1.20 Typical barque, 1860-1880 | 1.60 | 1.60 |
| 304 | A48 | $2 Chignecto | 2.75 | 2.75 |
| 305 | A48 | $3 Berbice | 4.50 | 4.50 |
| a. | | Souvenir sheet of 1 | 6.50 | 6.50 |
| 306 | A48 | $5 Vamos | 11.00 | 11.00 |
| 307 | A48 | $10 Federal Maple | 31.90 | 28.90 |
| | | Nos. 294-307 (14) | | |

No. 305a issued 2/3/97 for Hong Kong '97.

## Christmas — A49

 * CHRISTMAS 1990 * 10c

**Perf. 14**
**1990, Nov. 14**

Traditional games.

| | | | | |
|---|---|---|---|---|
| 308 | A49 | 10c Single fork | .20 | .20 |
| 309 | A49 | 15c Double fork | .35 | .35 |
| 310 | A49 | 60c Boulder breaking | 2.75 | 2.75 |
| 311 | A49 | $3 Run up | 3.50 | 3.50 |
| | | Nos. 308-311 (4) | | |

---

**1988, Sept. 19 Wmk. 384 Perf. 14½**

Designs: 15c, Natl. flag. 60c, Natl. coat of arms. $5, Princess Margaret presenting the Nevis Constitution Order to Prime Minister Simmonds, Sept. 19, 1983.

| | | | | |
|---|---|---|---|---|
| 232 | A38 | 15c shown | .70 | .30 |
| 233 | A38 | 60c multicolored | 1.60 | 1.40 |

### Souvenir Sheet

| | | | | |
|---|---|---|---|---|
| 234 | A38 | $5 multicolored | 5.00 | 5.00 |

### Christmas Type of 1987

Carnival clowns.

**1988, Nov. 2 Wmk. 373**

| | | | | |
|---|---|---|---|---|
| 235 | A34 | 15c multi | .20 | .20 |
| 236 | A34 | 40c multi, diff. | .45 | .45 |
| 237 | A34 | 80c multi, diff. | 1.90 | 1.90 |
| 238 | A34 | $3 multi, diff. | 2.75 | 2.75 |
| | | Nos. 235-238 (4) | | |

### Tourism Type of 1988

**1989, Jan. 25 Wmk. 384 Litho. Perf. 14**

| | | | | |
|---|---|---|---|---|
| 239 | A36 | 20c Old Colonial House | .20 | .20 |
| 240 | A36 | 20c Georgian House | .20 | .20 |
| 241 | A36 | $1 Romney Manor | 1.10 | .75 |
| 242 | A36 | $1 Lavington Great House | 1.10 | .75 |
| 243 | A36 | $2 Treasury Building | 1.50 | 1.50 |
| 244 | A36 | $2 Government House | 1.50 | 1.50 |
| | | Nos. 239-244 (6) | 5.60 | 4.90 |

### Intl. Red Cross and Red Crescent Organizations, 125th Anniv. (in 1988) — A39

40c

**Perf. 14x14½ Litho. Wmk. 384**
**1989, May 8**

| | | | | |
|---|---|---|---|---|
| 245 | A39 | 40c shown | .25 | .25 |
| 246 | A39 | $1 Ambulance | .90 | .90 |
| 247 | A39 | $3 Anniv. emblem | 2.75 | 2.75 |
| | | Nos. 245-247 (3) | 3.90 | 3.90 |

### Moon Landing, 20th Anniv.
### Common Design Type

 40c

Apollo 13: 10c, Lunar rover at Taurus Littrow landing site. 20c, Fred W. Haise Jr., John L. Swigert Jr., and James A. Lovell Jr. $1, Mission emblem. $2, Splashdown in the South Pacific. $5, Buzz Aldrin disembarking from the lunar module, Apollo 11 mission.

**Perf. 14**
**1989, July 20**
**Size of Nos. 249-250: 29x29mm**

| | | | | |
|---|---|---|---|---|
| 248 | CD342 | 10c multicolored | .20 | .20 |
| 249 | CD342 | 20c multicolored | .20 | .20 |
| 250 | CD342 | $1 multicolored | 1.25 | 1.25 |
| 251 | CD342 | $2 multicolored | 2.50 | 2.50 |
| | | Nos. 248-251 (4) | 4.15 | 4.15 |

### Souvenir Sheet

| | | | | |
|---|---|---|---|---|
| 252 | CD342 | $5 multicolored | 6.50 | 6.50 |

---

### Discovery of America, 500th Anniv. (in 1992) — A42

 15c

**Perf. 15x14**
**1989**

| | | | | |
|---|---|---|---|---|
| 255 | A41 | 10c purple & blk | .20 | .25 |
| 256 | A41 | 15c red & blk | .25 | .20 |
| 257 | A41 | 20c org brn & blk | .25 | .25 |
| 259 | A41 | 40c bister & blk | .60 | .25 |
| 261 | A41 | 60c blue & blk | .80 | .50 |
| 265 | A41 | $1 green & blk | 1.40 | .90 |
| | | Nos. 255-265 (6) | 3.50 | 2.30 |

This is an expanding set. Numbers will change if neccessary.

Designs: 15c, Galleon passing St. Kitts during Columbus's 2nd voyage, 1493. 80c, Coat of arms and map of 4th voyage. $1, Navigational instruments, c. 1500. $5, Exploration of Cuba and Hispaniola during Columbus's 2nd voyage, 1493-1496.

**Perf. 14 Wmk. 384**
**1989, Nov. 8**

| | | | | |
|---|---|---|---|---|
| 269 | A42 | 15c multicolored | 2.10 | .30 |
| 270 | A42 | 80c multicolored | 4.00 | 2.00 |
| 271 | A42 | $1 multicolored | 4.00 | 2.00 |
| 272 | A42 | $5 multicolored | 11.50 | 11.00 |
| | | Nos. 269-272 (4) | 21.60 | 15.30 |

### World Stamp Expo '89 — A43

 15c

Exhibition emblem, flags and: 15c, Poinciana tree. 40c, Ft. George Citadel, Brimstone Hill. $1, Light Company private, 5th Foot Regiment, 1778. $3, St. George's Anglican Church.

**Wmk. 373**
**1989, Nov. 17**

| | | | | |
|---|---|---|---|---|
| 273 | A43 | 15c multicolored | .20 | .20 |
| 274 | A43 | 40c multicolored | .65 | .65 |
| 275 | A43 | $1 multicolored | 1.90 | 1.90 |
| 276 | A43 | $3 multicolored | 5.25 | 5.25 |
| | | Nos. 273-276 (4) | 8.00 | 8.00 |

### Butterflies — A45

15c

15c, Junonia evarete. 40c, Anartia jatrophae. 60c, Heliconius charitonius. $3, Biblis hyperia.

**Perf. 13½ Wmk. 373 Litho.**
**1990, June 6**

| | | | | |
|---|---|---|---|---|
| 277 | A45 | 15c multicolored | 1.00 | .75 |
| 278 | A45 | 40c multicolored | 1.50 | 1.50 |
| 279 | A45 | 60c multicolored | 2.25 | 2.25 |
| 280 | A45 | $3 multicolored | 10.50 | 10.50 |
| | | Nos. 277-280 (4) | 15.25 | 15.00 |

**Nos. 277-280 with EXPO '90 Emblem Added to Design**
**1990, June 6**

| | | | | |
|---|---|---|---|---|
| 281 | A45 | 15c multicolored | .70 | .70 |
| 282 | A45 | 40c multicolored | 1.40 | 1.40 |
| 283 | A45 | 60c multicolored | 2.25 | 2.25 |
| 284 | A45 | $3 multicolored | 11.50 | 11.50 |
| | | Nos. 281-284 (4) | 15.85 | 15.85 |

Expo '90, International Garden and Greenery Exposition, Osaka, Japan.

### Conflict on the Champ-de-Mars — A40

**1989, July 7**

| | | | | |
|---|---|---|---|---|
| 253 | A40 | $5 multicolored | 5.50 | 5.50 |

PHILEXFRANCE '89, French revolution bicent.

### Outline Map of St. Kitts — A41

## Queen Elizabeth II's Accession to the Throne, 40th Anniv.

Common Design Type

**1992, Feb. 6**     **Wmk. 384**

| 332 | CD349 | 10c | multicolored | .25 | .25 |
| 333 | CD349 | 40c | multicolored | .55 | .55 |
| 334 | CD349 | 60c | multicolored | .80 | .80 |
| 335 | CD349 | $1 | multicolored | 1.40 | 1.40 |

**Wmk. 373**

| 336 | CD349 | $3 | multicolored | 4.00 | 4.00 |
| | | | Nos. 332-336 (5) | 7.00 | 7.00 |

A57

ST KITTS 25c

**1992, May 8**     **Litho.**     **Wmk. 373**

Perf. 13½x14

| 337 | A55 | 10c | multicolored | .50 | .50 |
| 338 | A55 | 20c | multicolored | .50 | .50 |
| 339 | A55 | 50c | multicolored | 1.75 | 1.75 |
| 340 | A55 | $2.40 | multicolored | 6.00 | 6.00 |
| | | | Nos. 337-340 (4) | 8.75 | 8.75 |

10c, Map of St. Kitts & Nevis, 20c, St. Kitts & Nevis flag, 50c, Red Cross House, St. Kitts, $2.40, Jean-Henri Dunant, founder of Red Cross.

CHRISTMAS 1992
ST KITTS 20c
A58

**1992, July 6**

Perf. 13

| 341 | A56 | $1 | Coming ashore | 2.10 | .90 |
| 342 | A56 | $2 | Natives, ships | 4.00 | 1.75 |

Discovery of America, 500th Anniv. — A56

Organization of East Caribbean States.

Designs: 25c, Fountain, Independence Square. 50c, Berkeley Memorial drinking fountain and clock. 80c, Sir Thomas Warner's tomb. $2, War Memorial.

**1992, Aug. 19**

Perf. 12½x13

| 343 | A57 | 25c | multicolored | .20 | .20 |
| 344 | A57 | 50c | multicolored | .50 | .50 |
| 345 | A57 | 80c | multicolored | .90 | .90 |
| 346 | A57 | $2 | multicolored | 2.10 | 2.10 |
| | | | Nos. 343-346 (4) | 3.70 | 3.70 |

**1992, Oct. 28**     **Wmk. 384**     **Perf. 14½**

Christmas — A58

Stained glass windows: 20c, Mary and Joseph. 25c, Shepherds. 80c, Three Wise Men. $3, Mary, Joseph and Christ Child.

| 347 | A58 | 20c | multicolored | .20 | .20 |
| 348 | A58 | 25c | multicolored | .20 | .20 |
| 349 | A58 | 80c | multicolored | .75 | .75 |
| 350 | A58 | $3 | multicolored | 3.25 | 3.25 |
| | | | Nos. 347-350 (4) | 4.40 | 4.40 |

## Royal Air Force, 75th Anniv.

Common Design Type

Designs: 25c, Short Singapore III. 50c, Bristol Beaufort. 80c, Westland Whirlwind. $1.60, English Electric Canberra.

Designs: 25c, Short Singapore III. 50c, Bristol Beaufort. 80c, Westland Whirlwind. $1.60, English Electric Canberra. No. 355a, Handley Page 0/400. b, Fairey Long Range Monoplane. c, Vickers Wellesley. d, Sepecat Jaguar.

---

**1993, Apr. 1**     **Wmk. 373**     **Litho.**

Perf. 14

| 351 | CD350 | 25c | multicolored | .70 | .70 |
| 352 | CD350 | 50c | multicolored | 1.50 | 1.50 |
| 353 | CD350 | $1.60 | multicolored | 4.75 | 4.75 |
| 354 | CD350 | $2 | multicolored | 9.20 | 9.20 |
| | | | Nos. 351-354 (4) | | |

**Miniature Sheet**

| 355 | CD350 | $2 | Sheet of 4, | 14.50 | 14.50 |
| | | | #a.-d. | | |

50c
St. KITTS

Diocese of the Northeastern Caribbean and Aruba, 150th Anniv. — A59

**1993, May 21**     **Litho.**     **Wmk. 384**

Perf. 13½x14, 14x13½

| 356 | A59 | 25c | multicolored | .30 | .30 |
| 357 | A59 | 50c | multicolored | .80 | .80 |
| 358 | A59 | 80c | multicolored | 1.40 | 1.40 |
| 359 | A59 | $2 | multicolored | 3.50 | 3.50 |
| | | | Nos. 356-359 (4) | 6.00 | 6.00 |

Designs: 25c, Diocesan Conference. Basseterre, horiz. 50c, Cathedral of St. John the Divine. 80c, Diocesan coat of arms and motto, horiz. $2, First Bishop, Right Reverend Daniel G. Davis.

## Coronation of Queen Elizabeth II, 40th Anniv. — A60

**1993, June 2**     **Perf. 14½x14**

| 360 | A60 | 10c | multicolored | .45 | .45 |
| 361 | A60 | 25c | multicolored | .60 | .60 |
| 362 | A60 | 80c | multicolored | 1.50 | 1.50 |
| 363 | A60 | $2 | multicolored | 3.25 | 3.25 |
| | | | Nos. 360-363 (4) | 5.80 | 5.80 |

Royal regalia and stamps of St. Kitts-Nevis: 10c, Eagle-shaped ampulla, #119. 25c, Anointing spoon, #334. 80c, Tassels, #333. $2, Staff of Scepter with the Cross, #354a-354c.

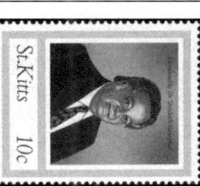

80c
CENTENARY OF THE GIRLS' BRIGADE INTERNATIONAL
ST.KITTS

Girls' Brigade Intl. Cent. — A61

**1993, July 1**

Perf. 13½x14

| 364 | A61 | 80c | Flags | 1.50 | 1.50 |
| 365 | A61 | $3 | Badge, coat of arms | 5.75 | 5.75 |

ST.KITTS
INTL. INDEPENDENCE OF

Independence, 10th Anniv. — A62

**1993, Sept. 10**     **Wmk. 373**     **Litho.**

Perf. 14

| 366 | A62 | 20c | multicolored | .20 | .20 |
| 367 | A62 | 80c | multicolored | 1.25 | 1.25 |
| 368 | A62 | $3 | multicolored | 4.75 | 4.75 |
| | | | Nos. 366-368 (3) | 6.20 | 6.20 |

Designs: 20c, Flag, map of St. Kitts and Nevis, plane, ship and island scenes. 80c, Natl. arms, independence emblem. $3, Natl. arms, map.

---

**1993, Nov. 16**     **Wmk. 373**     **Litho.**

Perf. 13½x14

| 369 | A63 | 25c | Roselia | .50 | .50 |
| 370 | A63 | 50c | Poinsettia | .75 | .75 |
| 371 | A63 | $1.60 | Snow on the Mountain | 2.50 | 2.50 |
| | | | Nos. 369-371 (3) | 3.75 | 3.75 |

Christmas — A63

ST.KITTS 25c

Prehistoric Aquatic Reptiles — A64

**1994, Feb. 18**     **Litho.**     **Wmk. 384**

Perf. 14

| 372 | A64 | $1.20 | Liopleurodon. d, Hydrotherosaurus. | 9.75 | 9.75 |
| 373 | A64 | $1.20 | Strip of 5 #a.-e. #372 ovptd. with Hong Kong '94 emblem | 9.75 | 9.75 |

Designs: a, Mesosaurus. b, Placodus. c, Caretta. e, Hydrotherosaurus.

ST. KITTS $10

Treasury Building, Cent. — A65

**Souvenir Sheet**

**1994, Mar. 21**     **Wmk. 373**     **Litho.**

Perf. 13½

| 374 | A65 | $10 | multicolored | 12.00 | 12.00 |

St.Kitts 10c

Order of the Caribbean Community A66

First award recipients: Nos. 375a, 376a, Sir Shridath Ramphal, statesman, Guyana. Nos. 375b, 376b, Emblem of the Order. Nos. 375c, 376c, Derek Walcott, writer, St. Lucia. Nos. 375d, 376d, William Demas, economist, Trinidad and Tobago.

**1994, July 13**     **Wmk. 373**     **Litho.**

Perf. 14

| 375 | A66 | 10c | Strip of 5, #a, b, c, | .85 | .85 |
| 376 | A66 | $1 | Strip of 5, #a, b, c, | 7.75 | 7.75 |

CARICOM, 20th anniv. (#375b, 376b).

Christmas 1994
ST KITTS 25c
A67

**1994, Oct. 31**

Perf. 13½x13

| 377 | A67 | 25c | Carol singing | .20 | .20 |
| 378 | A67 | 25c | Opening presents | .20 | .20 |
| 379 | A67 | 60c | Carnival | .85 | .85 |
| 380 | A67 | $2.50 | Nativity | 2.75 | 2.75 |
| | | | Nos. 377-380 (4) | 4.00 | 4.00 |

---

**1995, Feb. 27**     **Wmk. 373**     **Litho.**

Perf. 14

| 381 | A68 | 10c | shown | .65 | .65 |
| 382 | A68 | 40c | On beach | .90 | .90 |
| 383 | A68 | $1 | Laying eggs | 1.00 | 1.00 |
| 384 | A68 | $1 | Hatchlings | 1.40 | 1.40 |
| | | | Strip of 4, #381-384 | 4.25 | 4.25 |

Green Turtle
A68

WWF
ST.KITTS 10c

First St. Kitts Postage Stamp, 125th Anniv. — A69

**1995, Apr. 10**     **Wmk. 373**     **Litho.**

Perf. 13½

| 385 | A69 | 25c | multicolored | .25 | .25 |
| 386 | A69 | 40c | multicolored | .95 | .95 |
| 387 | A69 | 50c | multicolored | 3.00 | 3.00 |
| 388 | A69 | $3 | multicolored | 3.50 | 3.50 |
| | | | Nos. 385-388 (4) | 7.70 | 7.70 |

St. Christopher #1 at left and: 25c, St. Christopher #1. 80c, St. Kitts-Nevis #72. $2.50, St. Kitts-Nevis #91. $3, St. Kitts-Nevis #119.

## End of World War II, 50th Anniv.

Common Design Types

Designs: 20c, Caribbean Regiment, North Africa. 50c, TBM Avengers on anti-submarine patrol. $2, Spitfire Mk.Vb. $8, US destroyer escort on anti-submarine duty. $3, Reverse of War Medal 1939-45.

**1995, May 8**     **Wmk. 373**     **Litho.**

Perf. 13½

| 389 | CD351 | 20c | multicolored | .25 | .25 |
| 390 | CD351 | 50c | multicolored | .65 | .65 |
| 391 | CD351 | $2 | multicolored | 2.75 | 2.75 |
| 392 | CD351 | $8 | multicolored | 10.50 | 10.50 |
| | | | Nos. 389-392 (4) | 14.15 | 14.15 |

**Souvenir Sheet**

Perf. 14

| 393 | CD352 | $3 | multicolored | 6.75 | 6.75 |

ST. KITTS 10c
SKANTEL TELECOMMUNICATIONS

SKANTEL, 10th Anniv. — A70

Designs: 10c, Satellite transmission. 25c, Telephones, computer. $2, Transmission tower, satellite dish. $3, Satellite dish silhouetted against sun.

**1995, Sept. 27**

Perf. 13½x14

| 394 | A70 | 10c | multicolored | .20 | .20 |
| 395 | A70 | 25c | multicolored | .35 | .35 |
| 396 | A70 | $2 | multicolored | 2.75 | 2.75 |
| 397 | A70 | $3 | multicolored | 4.25 | 4.25 |
| | | | Nos. 394-397 (4) | 7.55 | 7.55 |

## UN, 50th Anniv.

Common Design Type

Designs: 40c, Energy, clean environment. 50c, Coastal, ocean resources. $1.60, Solid waste management. $2.50, Forestry reserves.

**1995, Oct. 24**

Perf. 13½x13

| 398 | CD353 | 40c | multicolored | .65 | .65 |
| 399 | CD353 | 50c | multicolored | .65 | .65 |
| 400 | CD353 | $1.60 | multicolored | 2.00 | 2.00 |
| 401 | CD353 | $2.50 | multicolored | 3.25 | 3.25 |
| | | | Nos. 398-401 (4) | 6.40 | 6.40 |

---

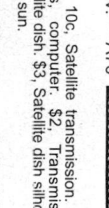

**FAO, 50th Anniv. — A71**

Designs: 25c, Vegetables. 50c, Glazed carrots, West Indian peas & rice. 80c, Tania, Cassava plants. $1.50, Waterfall, Green Hill Mountain.

**1995, Nov. 13**    *Perf. 13½*
| | | | | |
|---|---|---|---|---|
| 402 | A71 | 25c multicolored | .20 | .20 |
| 403 | A71 | 50c multicolored | .65 | .65 |
| 404 | A71 | 80c multicolored | .95 | .95 |
| 405 | A71 | $1.50 multicolored | 1.75 | 1.75 |
| | | *Nos. 402-405 (4)* | 3.55 | 3.56 |

**Sea Shells — A72**

a, Flame helmet. b, Triton's trumpet. c, King helmet. d, True tulip. e, Queen conch.

**1996, Jan. 10**   Wmk. 373   *Perf. 13*
406   A72   $1.50 Strip of 5, #a.-e.    8.50 8.50

Leeward Islands LMS Jubilee Class 4-6-0 Locomotives: 10c, No. 45614. $10, No. 5614.

**1996, June 8**   Wmk. 373 *Perf. 13½x14*
407   A73   10c multicolored    .65 .65

**Souvenir Sheet**   *Perf. 14x15*
408   A73   $10 multicolored    9.75 9.75
No. 408 is 48x31mm.

A74

A75

Modern Olympic Games, Cent.: 10c, Runner, St. Kitts & Nevis flag. 25c, High jumper, US flag. 80c, Runner, Olympic flag. $3, Athens Games poster, 1896.
$6, Olympic torch.

---

**Christmas 1997** — A76

**1996, June 30**   Wmk. 384   Litho.   *Perf. 14*
| | | | | |
|---|---|---|---|---|
| 409 | A74 | 10c multicolored | .20 | .20 |
| 410 | A74 | 25c multicolored | .20 | .20 |
| 411 | A74 | 80c multicolored | .75 | .75 |
| 412 | A74 | $3 multicolored | 2.75 | 2.75 |
| | | *Nos. 409-412 (4)* | 3.90 | 3.90 |

**Souvenir Sheet**
413   A74   $6 multicolored    5.50 5.50
Olymphilex '96 (#413).

**1996, Nov. 1**    **Wmk. 373**

Defense Force, Cent.: 10c, Volunteer rifleman, 1896. 50c, Mounted infantry, 1911. $2, Bandsman, 1940-60. $2.50, Modern uniform, 1996.
| | | | | |
|---|---|---|---|---|
| 414 | A75 | 10c multicolored | .20 | .20 |
| 415 | A75 | 50c multicolored | .55 | .55 |
| 416 | A75 | $2 multicolored | 2.10 | 2.10 |
| 417 | A75 | $2.50 multicolored | 2.50 | 2.50 |
| | | *Nos. 414-417 (4)* | 5.35 | 5.35 |

Paintings: 15c, Holy Virgin and Child, by Anais Colin, 1844. 25c, Holy Family, After Rubens. 50c, Madonna with the Goldfinch, by Krause on porcelain after Raphael, 1507. 80c, Madonna in Throne with Angels, by unknown Spanish, 17th cent.

**1996, Dec. 9**
| | | | | |
|---|---|---|---|---|
| 418 | A76 | 15c multicolored | .25 | .20 |
| 419 | A76 | 25c multicolored | .35 | .20 |
| 420 | A76 | 50c multicolored | .80 | .65 |
| 421 | A76 | 80c multicolored | 1.10 | 1.10 |
| | | *Nos. 418-421 (4)* | 2.50 | 2.15 |

Fish — A77

a, Princess parrot fish. b, Yellowbelly hamlet. c, Coney. d, Clown wrasse. e, Doctor fish. f, Squirrelfish. g, Queen angelfish h, Spanish hogfish. i, Red hind. j, Red grouper. k, Yellowtail snapper. l, Mutton hamlet.

**1997, Apr. 24**    *Perf. 13½*   13.00 13.00
422   A77   $1 Sheet of 12, #a.-l.

Queen Elizabeth II and Prince Philip, 50th Wedding Anniv. — A78

Designs: No. 423, Queen. No. 424, Prince Philip. No. 425, Queen riding with Royal Guard. No. 426, Prince riding in carriage. No. 427, Prince Philip. No. 427r, Early photo of Queen, Prince. No. 428, Prince riding horse.
Queen, Prince riding in open carriage, horiz.

**1997, July 10**   Wmk. 373   Litho.   *Perf. 13½*
| | | | | |
|---|---|---|---|---|
| 423 | A78 | 10c multicolored | .55 | .55 |
| 424 | A78 | 10c multicolored | .55 | .55 |
| a. | | Pair, #423-424 | 1.25 | 1.25 |
| 425 | A78 | 25c multicolored | .85 | .85 |
| 426 | A78 | 25c multicolored | .85 | .85 |
| a. | | Pair, #425-426 | 1.75 | 1.75 |
| 427 | A78 | $3 multicolored | 3.00 | 3.00 |
| 428 | A78 | $3 multicolored | 3.00 | 3.00 |
| a. | | Pair, #42/-428 | 6.50 | 6.50 |
| | | *Nos. 423-428 (6)* | 8.80 | 8.80 |

**Souvenir Sheet**   *Perf. 14x14½*
429   A78   $6 multicolored    9.50 9.50

---

**Christmas — A79**

Churches: No. 430, Zion Moravian. No. 431, Wesley Methodist. $1.50, St. Georges Anglican. $15, Co-Cathedral of the Immaculate Conception.

**1997, Oct. 31**   Litho.    **Wmk. 384**   *Perf. 13½x14*
| | | | | |
|---|---|---|---|---|
| 430 | A79 | 10c multi | .20 | .20 |
| 431 | A79 | 10c multi | .20 | .20 |
| 432 | A79 | $1.50 multi, vert. | 1.40 | 1.40 |
| 433 | A79 | $15 multi, vert. | 12.50 | 12.50 |
| | | *Nos. 430-433 (4)* | 14.30 | 14.30 |

Natl. Heroes' Day — A80

#434, Robert L. Bradshaw (1916-78), 1st premier of St. Kitts, Nevis, & Anguilla. #435, Joseph N. France, trade unionist. #436, C.A. Paul Southwell (1913-79), 1st chief minister of St. Kitts, Nevis, & Anguilla. $3, France, Bradshaw, & Southwell.

**1997, Sept. 16**    *Perf. 13½*
| | | | | |
|---|---|---|---|---|
| 434 | A80 | 25c multi, vert. | .20 | .20 |
| 435 | A80 | 25c multi, vert. | .20 | .20 |
| 436 | A80 | 25c multi, vert. | .20 | .20 |
| 437 | A80 | $3 multi | 2.40 | 2.40 |
| | | *Nos. 434-437 (4)* | 3.00 | 3.00 |

**Diana, Princess of Wales (1961-97)**
Common Design Type

#438: a, like #437A. b, Wearing red jacket c, Wearing white dress. d, Holding flowers.

**1998, Mar. 31**   Litho. *Perf. 14½x14*
437A   CD355   30c Wearing    .40 .40
white hat

**Sheet of 4**
438   CD355   $1.00 Sheet of 4, #a.-d.    5.25 5.25

No. 438 sold for $6.40 + 90c, with surtax from international sales being donated to Princess Diana Memorial Fund and surtax from national sales being donated to designated local charity.

Butterflies — A81

Designs: 10c, Common long-tail skipper. 15c, White peacock. 25c, Caribbean buckeye. 30c, Red rim. 40c, Cassius blue. 50c, Flambeau. 60c, Lucas's blue. 90c, Cloudless sulphur. $1, Monarch. $1.20, Fiery skipper. $1.60, Zebra. $3, Southern dagger tail. $5, Polydamus swallowtail. $10, Tropical checkered skipper.

**1997, Dec. 29**   Litho.   **Wmk. 373**
*Perf. 14½x14½*
| | | | | |
|---|---|---|---|---|
| 439 | A81 | 10c multicolored | .20 | .20 |
| a. | | "S" in "Proteus" to left of midline of leaf above | | |
| 440 | A81 | 15c multicolored | .20 | .20 |
| 441 | A81 | 25c multicolored | .30 | .30 |
| 442 | A81 | 30c multicolored | .35 | .35 |
| 443 | A81 | 40c multicolored | .35 | .35 |
| 444 | A81 | 50c multicolored | .60 | .60 |
| 445 | A81 | 60c multicolored | .75 | .75 |
| 446 | A81 | 90c multicolored | 1.00 | 1.00 |
| 447 | A81 | $1 multicolored | 1.00 | 1.00 |
| 448 | A81 | $1.20 multicolored | 1.25 | 1.25 |
| 449 | A81 | $1.60 multicolored | 1.60 | 1.60 |
| 450 | A81 | $3 multicolored | 3.00 | 3.00 |
| a. | | "S" in "S" same size as numeral | | |
| 451 | A81 | $5 multicolored | 5.00 | 5.00 |
| a. | | Inscribed "Polydamus" | 5.50 | 5.50 |

---

University of West Indies, 50th Anniv. — A82

452   A81   $10 multicolored    10.00 10.00
a.   "S" in "S" same size as numeral    11.00 11.00
   *Nos. 439-452 (14)*    25.35 25.35
Nos. 439a, 450a, 451a and 452a have other minor design differences.

**Carnival Santa — A83**

**1998, July 20**   Litho.   **Wmk. 373**
453   A82   80c shown    .80 .80
454   A82   $2 Arms, mortarboard    2.00 2.00

**1998, Oct. 30**   Wmk. 373   Litho.   *Perf. 14*
455   A83   80c shown    .70 .70
456   A83   $1.20 With two dancers    1.10 1.10

UPU, 125th Anniv. — A84

**1999, Mar. 5**   Wmk. 373   Litho.   *Perf. 14*
457   A84   30c shown    .35 .35
458   A84   90c Map of St. Kitts    1.00 1.00

Birds of the Eastern Caribbean — A85

Designs: a, Caribbean martin. b, Spotted sandpiper. c, Sooty tern. d, Red-tailed hawk. e, Trembler. f, Belted kingfisher. g, Black-billed duck. h, Yellow warbler. i, Blue-headed hummingbird. j, Antillean euphonia. k, Fulvous whistling duck. l, Mangrove cuckoo. m, Carib grackle. n, Caribbean elaenia. o, Common ground dove. p, Forest thrush.

**1999, Apr. 27**   Wmk. 373   Litho.   *Perf. 14*
459   A85   80c Sheet of 16, #a.-    14.00 14.00
IBRA '99.

**1st Manned Moon Landing, 30th Anniv.**
Common Design Type

Designs: 80c, Lift-off. 90c, In lunar orbit. $1, Aldrin deploying scientific equipment. $1.20, Heat shield burns on re-entry.
$10, Earth as seen from moon.

**1999, July 20**   Litho.    **Wmk. 384**
*Perf. 14x13¾*
| | | | | |
|---|---|---|---|---|
| 460 | CD357 | 80c multicolored | .90 | .90 |
| 461 | CD357 | 90c multicolored | 1.00 | 1.00 |
| 462 | CD357 | $1 multicolored | 1.10 | 1.10 |
| 463 | CD357 | $1.20 multicolored | 1.40 | 1.40 |
| | | *Nos. 460-463 (4)* | 4.40 | 4.40 |

**Souvenir Sheet**   *Perf. 14*
464   CD357   $10 multicolored    9.50 9.50
No. 464 contains one 40mm circular stamp.

**Christmas — A86**

**1999, Oct. 29    Wmk. 373    Litho.    Perf. 13¾**

| | | | |
|---|---|---|---|
| 465 | A86 | 10c shown | .20 .20 |
| 466 | A86 | 30c 3 musicians | .20 .20 |
| 467 | A86 | 80c 6 musicians | .70 .70 |
| 468 | A86 | $2 4 musicians, diff. | 1.90 1.90 |
| | | Nos. 465-468 (4) | 3.00 3.00 |

**Children's Drawings Celebrating the Millennium — A87**

**1999, Dec. 29    Litho.    Perf. 14**

| | | | |
|---|---|---|---|
| 469 | A87 | 10c by Adam Taylor | .35 .35 |
| 470 | A87 | 30c by Travis Liburd | .35 .35 |
| 471 | A87 | 50c by Darren Moses | .90 .90 |
| 472 | A87 | $1 by Pierre Liburd | 3.20 3.20 |
| | | Nos. 469-472 (4) | |

**Carifesta VII — A88**

Designs: 30c, Festival participants. 90c, Emblem. $1.20, Dancer, vert.

**2000, Aug. 30    Wmk. 373    Litho.**

| | | | |
|---|---|---|---|
| 473 | A88 | 30c multi | .25 .25 |
| 474 | A88 | 90c multi | .85 .85 |
| 475 | A88 | $1.20 multi | 1.25 1.25 |
| | | Nos. 473-475 (3) | 2.35 2.35 |

**Railroads in American Civil War — A89**

No. 476, $1.20, horiz.: a, Engine 133. b, Engine 150. e, Doctor Thompson. f, Engine 156.

No. 477, $1.20, horiz.: a, Governor Nye. b, Engine 31. c, C. A. Henry. d, Engine 152. e, Engine 116. f, Job Terry.

No. 478, $1.60, horiz.: a, Dover. b, Scout. c, Baltimore & Ohio Railroad locomotive. d, John M. Forbes. e, Edward Kidder. f, William W. Wright.

No. 479, $1.60, horiz.: a, Engine 83. b, General. c, Engine 38. d, Texas. e, Engine 162. f, Christopher Adams, Jr.

No. 480, $5, Ulysses S. Grant. No. 481, $5, George B. McClellan. No. 482, $5, Herman Haupt. No. 483, $5, Robert E. Lee.

**2001, Feb. 19    Unwmk.    Perf. 14**

**Sheets of 6, #a-f**

| | | | |
|---|---|---|---|
| 476-479 | A89 | Set of 4 | 25.00 25.00 |
| | | Souvenir Sheets | |
| 480-483 | A89 | Set of 4 | 32.00 32.00 |

---

**Flora & Fauna — A90**

No. 484, $1.20 — Flowers: a, Heliconia. b, Anthurium. c, Oncidium splendidum. d, Trumpet creeper. e, Bird of paradise. f, Hibiscus.

No. 485, $1.20: a, Bananaquit. b, Anthurium (hills and clouds in background). c, Common dolphin. d, Horse mushroom. e, Green anole. f, Monarch butterfly.

No. 486, $1.60 — Birds: a, Laughing gull. b, Sooty tern. c, White-tailed tropicbird. d, Painted bunting. e, Belted kingfisher. f, Yellow-bellied sapsucker.

No. 487, $1.60 — Butterflies: a, Figure-of-eight. b, Banded king shoemaker. c, Orange theope. d, Grecian shoemaker. e, Clorinde. f, Small lace-wing.

No. 488, $1.60, horiz.: a, Beaugregory. b, Banded butterflyfish. c, Cherubfish. d, Rock beauty. e, Red snapper. f, Leatherback turtle.

No. 489, $5, Leachilus carinatus. No. 489, $5, Iguana, horiz. No. 490, $5, Ruby-throated hummingbird, horiz. No. 491, $5, Common morpho, horiz.

No. 493, $5, Redband parrotfish, horiz.

**2001, Mar. 12    Perf. 14**

**Sheets of 6, #a-f**

| | | | |
|---|---|---|---|
| 484-488 | A90 | Set of 5 | 32.25 32.25 |
| | | Souvenir Sheets | |
| 489-493 | A90 | Set of 5 | 26.25 26.25 |

Compare No. 490 with No. 520.

**2001 Census — A91**

Designs: 30c, People in house. $3, People, barn, silos.

**2001, Apr. 18    Litho.    Perf. 14½x14¼**

| | | | |
|---|---|---|---|
| 494-495 | A91 | Set of 2 | 3.25 3.25 |

**Population & Housing Census May 2001**

---

**Caribbean Flowers**

**2001, Apr. 26    Perf. 14**

| | | | |
|---|---|---|---|
| 496 | A92 | $2 Sheet of 4, #a-d | 8.50 8.50 |
| | | Souvenir Sheet | |
| 497 | A92 | $5 black | 6.25 6.25 |

No. 496 contains four 28x42mm stamps.

**Queen Victoria (1819-1901) — A92**

No. 496: a, At coronation. b, In wedding gown. c, With Prince Albert visiting wounded Crimean War veterans. d, With Prince Albert, 1854.

$5, Wearing crown.

---

**Monet Paintings — A93**

No. 498, horiz.: a, On the Coast of Trouville. b, Vétheuil in Summer. c, Field of Yellow Iris Near Giverny. d, Coastiguard's Cottage at Varengeville.

$5, Poplars on the Banks of the Epte, Seen From the Marshes.

**2001, July 16    Perf. 13¾**

| | | | |
|---|---|---|---|
| 498 | A93 | $2 Sheet of 4, #a-d | 9.50 9.50 |
| | | Souvenir Sheet | |
| 499 | A93 | $5 multi | 5.75 5.75 |

---

**Giuseppe Verdi (1813-1901), Opera Composer — A94**

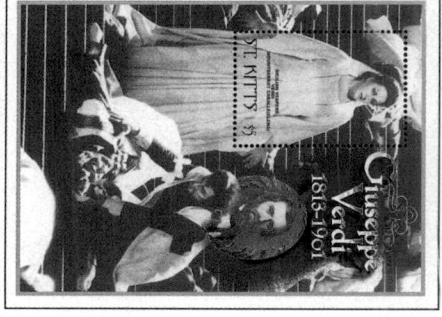

No. 500 — Scenes from the Sicilian Vespers: a, French soldiers in Palermo (all standing). b, French soldiers in Palermo (some seated). c, Costume design. d, Sicilian people and French soldiers.

$5, Montserrat Caballé.

**2001, July 16    Perf. 14**

| | | | |
|---|---|---|---|
| 500 | A94 | $2 Sheet of 4, #a-d | 8.50 8.50 |
| | | Souvenir Sheet | |
| 501 | A94 | $5 multi | 5.75 5.75 |

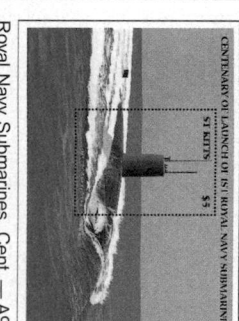

**Royal Navy Submarines, Cent. — A95**

No. 502, horiz.: a, A Class submarine. b, HMS Dreadnaught battleship. c, HMS Amethyst. d, HMS Barnham. e, HMS Exeter. f, HMS Eagle.

$5, HMS Dreadnaught submarine.

**2001, July 16    Perf. 14**

| | | | |
|---|---|---|---|
| 502 | A95 | $1.40 Sheet of 6, #a-f | 11.50 11.50 |
| | | Souvenir Sheet | |
| 503 | A95 | $5 multi | 7.50 7.50 |

No. 502 contains six 42x28mm stamps.

---

**Queen Elizabeth II, 75th Birthday — A96**

No. 504: a, In blue hat, holding flowers. b, In flowered hat, looking right. c, In blue hat and coat. d, In flowered hat, looking left.

$5, On horse.

**2001, July 16    Perf. 14**

| | | | |
|---|---|---|---|
| 504 | A96 | $2 Sheet of 4, #a-d | 8.50 8.50 |
| | | Souvenir Sheet | |
| 505 | A96 | $5 multi | 5.75 5.75 |

---

**Phila Nippon '01, Japan — A97**

Woodcuts: 50c, Hatsufunedayu as a Tatebina, by Shigenobu. Yamagawa 80c, Samurai Kodenji as Tsuyu No Mae, by Kiyonobu I. $1, Senya Nakamura as Tokonatsu, by Kiyomasu I. $1.60, Sumida River, by Shunsho. $2, Wrestler, Kuemon Yoba, by Shun-ei. $3, Two Actors in Roles, by Kiyonobu Torii I. $5, Full Length Actor Protraits, by Shun-ei.

**2001, July 16    Perf. 12x12¼**

| | | | |
|---|---|---|---|
| 506-511 | A97 | Set of 6 | 9.00 9.00 |
| | | Souvenir Sheet | |
| 512 | A97 | $5 multi | 5.75 5.75 |

---

**Mao Zedong (1893-1976) — A98**

No. 514: a, In 1926. b, In 1945 (green background). c, In 1945 (lilac background). $3, Undated picture.

**2001, July 16    Litho.    Perf. 13¾**

| | | | |
|---|---|---|---|
| 513 | A98 | $2 Sheet of 3, #a-c | 6.75 6.75 |
| | | Souvenir Sheet | |
| 514 | A98 | $3 multi | 4.75 4.75 |

Amerigo Vespucci studied cosmography, astronomy, and philosophy at the University of Pisa

St. Kitts $6

AMERIGO VESPUCCI ITALIAN EXPLORER 1454-1512

Amerigo Vespucci (1454-1512), Explorer — A108

No. 541, horiz.: a, Vespucci with feathered hat. b, 1507 World map by Martin Waldseemüller. c, Vespucci with beard. $6, Vespucci with bald head.

**2002, June 17**    **Perf. 13¼x13½**
541 A108 $3 Sheet of 3, #a-c   6.75 6.75
        **Souvenir Sheet**
        **Perf. 13½x13¼**
542 A108 $6 multi       5.75 5.75

St. Kitts 10¢

St. Kitts 30¢ KIM COLLINS

Kim Collins, Sprinter A109

Collins: 30c, Running. 90c, Wearing 2001 IAAF bronze medal.

**2002, July 2**
543-544 A109   Set of 2    2.50 2.50

Christmas A110

**Perf. 14**

**2002, Oct. 14**    **Litho.**
Fruits: 10c, Soursop. 80c, Passion fruit. $1, Sugar apple. $2, Custard apple.
545-548 A110   Set of 4    3.00 3.00

H.M. THE QUEEN MOTHER   St. Kitts $2
H.M. THE QUEEN MOTHER   St. Kitts $2

Queen Mother Elizabeth (1900-2002) — A111

No. 549: a, Wearing green dress. b, Wearing yellow dress and hat.

**2002, Nov. 18**   **Litho.**   **Perf. 14**
549 A111 $2 Pair, #a-b    3.00 3.00
No. 549 printed in sheets containing 2 pairs.

---

St. Kitts $6 MOUNTAINS

INTERNATIONAL YEAR OF MOUNTAINS — A105

Intl. Year of Mountains — A105

No. 535: a, Mt. Sakura, Japan. b, Mount Assiniboine, Canada. c, Mt. Asgard, Canada. d, Bugaboo Spire, Canada. e, Mt. Owen, Wyoming.

**2002, June 17**   **Perf. 13¼x13½**
535 A105 $2 Sheet of 4, #a-d   6.00 6.00
        **Souvenir Sheet**
536 A105 $6 multi       5.75 5.75

2002 FIFA WORLD CUP KOREA JAPAN
St. Kitts $6   JIE M F L ROGER MILLA 1990   GREAT MOMENTS FROM THE PAST   CAMEROON 2 : COLOMBIA 1

2002 World Cup Soccer Championships, Japan and Korea — A106

No. 537 — World Cup trophy and: a, $1.65, Just Fontaine, French flag. b, $1.65, 1982 World Cup poster. c, $1.65, U.S. player and flag. d, $1.65, Swedish player and flag. e, $6, Daegu Sports Complex, Korea (55x41mm).

**2002, June 17**   **Perf. 13¼x13½**
537 A106   Sheet of 5, #a-e   9.50 9.50
        **Souvenir Sheet**
538 A106 $6 multi       5.75 5.75

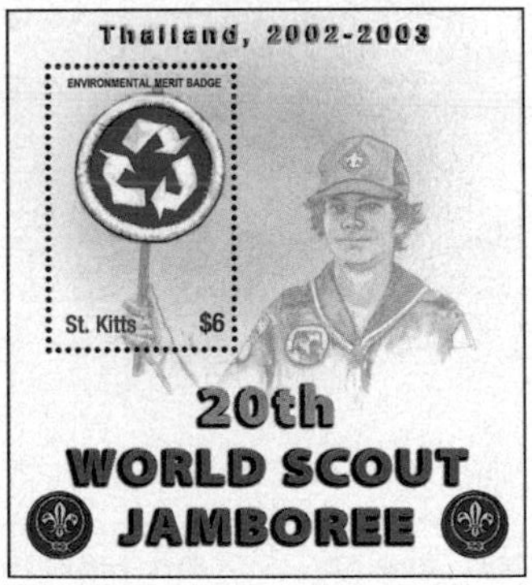

20th WORLD SCOUT JAMBOREE   Thailand, 2002-2003   ENVIRONMENTAL MERIT BADGE   St. Kitts $6

20th World Scout Jamboree, Thailand — A107

No. 539, horiz.: a, Scout sign. b, Scout with sword. 2. c, Council patch. d, Scout with sword.
$6, Environmental Studies merit badge.

**2002, June 17**   **Perf. 13¼x13½**
539 A107 $2 Sheet of 4, #a-d   6.00 6.00
        **Souvenir Sheet**
        **Perf. 13½x13¼**
540 A107 $6 multi       5.75 5.75

---

St. Kitts   GOLDEN JUBILEE - 6th February, 2002   50th Anniversary of the Accession to the throne of Her Majesty Queen Elizabeth II's Accession

Reign of Queen Elizabeth II, 50th Anniv. — A101

No. 529: a, Ceremonial coach. b, Prince Philip. c, Queen and Queen Mother. d, Queen wearing tiara.
$5, Queen and Prince Philip.

**2002, Feb. 6**   **Perf. 14¼**
529 A101 $2 Sheet of 4, #a-d   6.00 6.00
        **Souvenir Sheet**
530 A101 $5 multi       4.50 4.50

St. Kitts 80¢   UNITED WE STAND

United We Stand — A102

**Perf. 13½x13¼**

**2002, June 17**   **Litho.**
531 A102 80c multi     1.75 1.75
Printed in sheets of 4.

2002 Winter Olympics, Salt Lake City A103

Designs: No. 532, $3, Cross-country skiing. No. 533, $3, Alpine skiing.

**2002, June 17**   **Perf. 13¼x13½**
532-533 A103   Set of 2    5.00 5.00
533a   Souvenir sheet #532-533   5.00 5.00
        **Souvenir Sheet**

New Year 2002 (Year of the Horse) — A104

Details of Wen-Gi's Returning to Han, by Chang Yu: a, Horse and rider, dog. b, Group of horses and riders. c, Horse and rider, two attendants. d, Standard bearer on horse.

**2002, June 17**   **Perf. 12½**
534 A104 $1.60 Sheet of 4, #a-d   4.75 4.75

---

St. Kitts $5.00   Ruby-throated Hummingbird Archilochus colubris

Flora & Fauna — A99

No. 515, $1.20 — Birds: a. Trembler. b, White-tailed tropicbird. c, Red-footed booby. d, Red-legged thrush. e, Painted bunting. f, Bananaquit.
No. 516, $1.20 — Orchids: a, Maxillaria cucullata. b, Cattleya dowiana. c, Rossioglossum grande. d, Aspasia epidendroides. e, Lycaste skinneri. f, Cattleya percivaliana.
No. 517, $1.60 — Butterflies: a, Orangebarred sulphur. b, Giant swallowtail. c, Orange theope. d, Blue night. e, Grecian shoemaker. f, Cramer's mesene.
No. 518, $1.60 — Mushrooms: a, Pholiota spectabilis. b, Flammula penetrans. c, Ungulina marginata. d, Collybia iocephala. e, Amanita muscaria. f, Corinus comatus.
No. 519, $1.60, horiz. — Whales: a, Killer whale. b, Cuvier's beaked whale. c, Humpback whale. d, Sperm whale. e, Blue whale. f, Whale shark.
No. 520, $5, Ruby-throated hummingbird. No. 521, $5, Psychilis atropurpurea. No. 522, $5, Figure-of-eight butterfly. No. 523, $5, Lepiota procera. No. 524, $5, Sei whale, horiz.

**2001, Sept. 18**    **Perf. 14**
        **Sheets of 6, #a-f**
515-519 A99   Set of 5    32.50 32.50
        **Souvenir Sheets**
520-524 A99   Set of 5    26.25 26.25
Compare No. 520 with No. 490.

St. Kitts 10¢

Christmas and Carnival — A100

Designs: 10c, Angel, Christmas tree. 30c, Fireworks. 80c, Wreath, dove, bells, candy cane. $2, Steel drums.

**2001, Nov. 26**
525-528 A100   Set of 4    4.25 4.25

**First Non-stop Solo Transatlantic Flight, 75th Anniv. — A112**

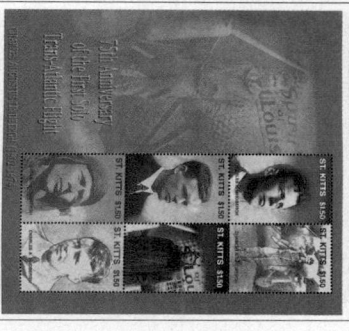

Charles Lindbergh: a, In suit, denomination in white. b, And Spirit of St. Louis, denomination in blue violet. c, In suit, looking right, denomination in blue violet. d, And Spirit of St. Louis, denomination in white. e, Wearing pilot's headgear. f, Wearing overcoat.

**2002, Nov. 18**
550 A112 $1.50 Sheet of 6, #a-f 6.75 6.75

---

**Princess Diana (1961-97) — A113**

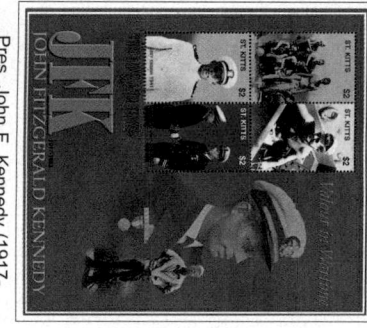

No. 551, $2: a, Wearing bulletproof vest. b, Wearing gray suit with pearls. c, Wearing yellow blouse. d, Wearing red dress and necklace.

No. 552, $2: a, Wearing white coat with purple piping. b, With hands clasped. c, Wearing red dress without necklace. d, Wearing white dress.

**2002, Nov. 18        Litho.**
551-552 A113    Sheets of 4, #a-d
          Set of 2          12.00 12.00

**JFK**
**JOHN FITZGERALD KENNEDY**

Pres. John F. Kennedy (1917-63) —A114

No. 553, $2: a, With sailors, Solomon Islands, 1942. b, On PT109, 1942. c, As Navy Ensign, 1941. d, Receiving medal for gallantry, 1944.
No. 554, $2: a, Peace Corps. b, Space program. c, Civil rights. d, Nuclear disarmament.

**2002, Nov. 18          Perf. 14**
553-554 A114    Sheets of 4, #a-d
          Set of 2          12.00 12.00

---

**New Year 2003 (Year of the Ram) — A115**

No. 555: a, Piebald ram. b, Ram with long coat. c, Ram sculpture, looking right.

**2003, Jan. 27        Perf. 14¼x13¾**
555 A115 $1 Vert. strip of 3, #a-c 2.25 2.25
No. 555 printed in sheets containing 2 strips.

**Celebrating 100 Years of Aviation**

**Powered Flight, Cent. — A116**

No. 556: a, Voisin LA5. b, Gotha G.V. c, Polikarpov I-16. d, Bell YFM-1.
$5, Bristol Blenheim 1.

**2003, June 17    Litho.    Perf. 14**
556 A116 $2 Sheet of 4, #a-d    6.00 6.00
557 A116 $5 multi            3.75 3.75
      Souvenir Sheet

**Tour de France Bicycle Race, Cent. — A117**

No. 558: a, Miguel Indurain, 1994. b, Indurain, 1995. c, Bjarne Riis, 1996. d, Jan Ullrich, 1997.
$5, Indurain, 1991-95.

**2003, June 17        Perf. 13½x13¾**
558 A117 $2 Sheet of 4, #a-d    6.00 6.00
559 A117 $5 multi            3.75 3.75
      Souvenir Sheet

---

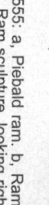

**Teddy Bears, Cent. — A118**

No. 560: a, Queen Victoria Bear. b, Teddy Roosevelt Bear. c, George Washington Bear. d, General Patton Bear.
$5, Buffalo Bill Bear.

**2003, June 17          Perf. 13¾**
560 A118 $2 Sheet of 4, #a-d    6.00 6.00
561 A118 $5 multi            3.75 3.75
      Souvenir Sheet

**Coronation of Queen Elizabeth II, 50th Anniv. — A119**

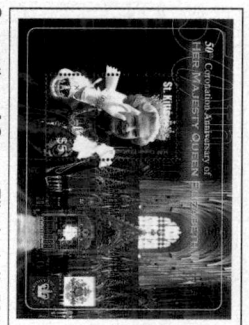

No. 562: a, Wearing tiara as young woman. b, Wearing tiara and red sash. c, Wearing tiara and blue sash.
$5, Queen waving.

**2003, June 17    Litho.    Perf. 14**
562 A119 $3 Sheet of 3, #a-c    6.75 6.75
563 A119 $5 multi            3.75 3.75
      Souvenir Sheet

**Caribbean Community, 30th Anniv. — A120**

**2003, June 23**
564 A120 30c multi           .25 .25

**Prince William, 21st Birthday — A121**

No. 565: a, As toddler, in jacket. b, As young boy, in striped shirt. c, Wearing sports shirt.
$5, As child, waving.

**2003, July 1**
565 A121 $3 Sheet of 3, #a-c    6.75 6.75
566 A121 $5 multi            3.75 3.75
      Souvenir Sheet

---

**Norman Rockwell Paintings of Boy Scouts from Boy Scout Calendars — A122**

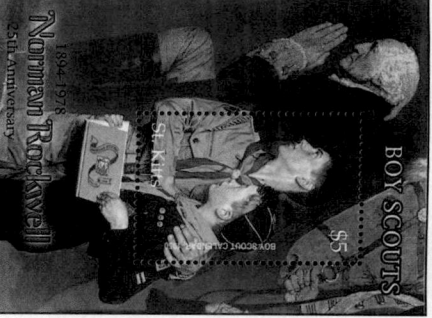

No. 567: a, Scout and Sailors, 1937. b, Scouts with Camping Gear, 1937. c, Boy and Dog at Window, 1968. d, Scout at Attention, 1932.
$5, Boy Scout and Cub Scout, 1950.

**2003, Aug. 18          Perf. 14**
567 A122 $2 Sheet of 4, #a-d    6.00 6.00
568 A122 $5 multi            3.75 3.75
      Souvenir Sheet

**Painting by Pablo Picasso — A123**

No. 569: a, Child with Wooden Horse. b, Child with a Ball. c, The Butterfly Catcher. d, Boy with a Lobster. e, Baby Wearing Polka Dot Dress. f, El Bobo. After Murillo.
$5, Untitled painting.

**2003, Aug. 18          Perf. 14**
569 A123 $1.60 Sheet of 4, #a-d  7.25 7.25
570 A123 $5 multi            3.75 3.75
      Souvenir Sheet
      Imperf.
No. 569 contains six 28x42mm stamps.

**Rembrandt Paintings — A124**

Designs: 50c, A Family Group. $1, Portrait of Cornelis Claesz Anslo and Aeltje Gerritsor Schouten, horiz. $1.60, Portrait of a Young Woman. $3, Man in Military Costume. $5, An Old Woman Reading. b, Hendrickje Stoffels. c, Rembrandt's Mother. d, Saskia. $5, Judas Returning the Thirty Pieces of Silver.

**2003, Aug. 18** *Perf. 14¼*
**571-574** A124 Set of 4 4.75 4.75
**575** A124 $2 Sheet of 4, #a-d 6.00 6.00

**Souvenir Sheet**

**576** A124 $5 multi 3.75 3.75

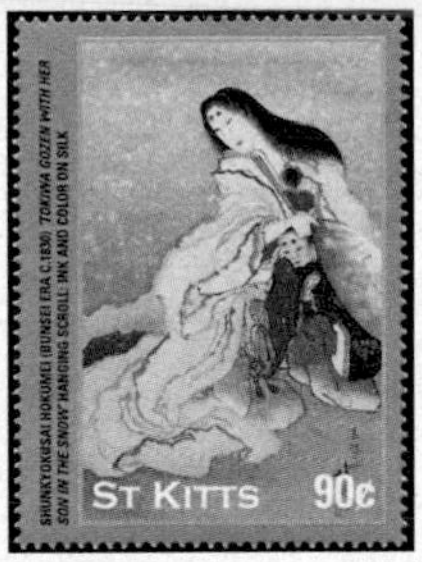


Japanese Art — A125

Designs: 90c, Tokiwa Gozen with Her Son in the Snow, by Hokumei Shunkyokusai. $1, Courtesan and Asahina, attributed to Choki Eishosai. $1.50, Parody of Sugawara No Michizane Seated on an Ox, by Toyokuni Utagawa. $3, Visiting a Flower Garden, by Kunisada Utagawa.

No. 581 — Akugenta Yoshihira, by Kunisada Utagawa: a, Man with bow. b, Man with sword at waist. c, Man holding scarf. d, Man with sword on shoulder.

$6, The Courtesan Katachino Under a Cherry Tree, by Toyoharu Utagawa.

**2003, Aug. 18**
**577-580** A125 Set of 4 4.75 4.75
**581** A125 $2 Sheet of 4, #a-d 6.00 6.00

**Souvenir Sheet**

**582** A125 $6 multi 4.50 4.50

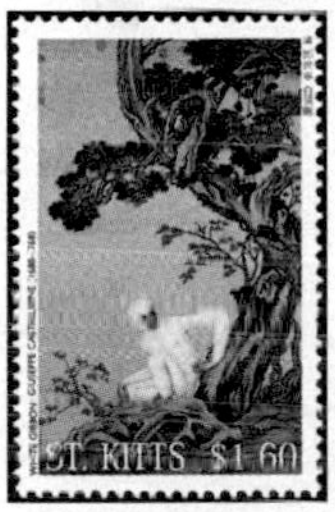


White Gibbon, by Giuseppe Castiglione A126

**2004, Jan. 15** *Perf. 13¾x13½*
**583** A126 $1.60 shown 1.25 1.25

**Souvenir Sheet**

*Perf. 13¼*

**584** A126 $3 Painting detail 2.25 2.25

New Year 2004 (Year of the Monkey). No. 583 printed in sheets of 4. No. 584 contains one 30x37mm stamp.

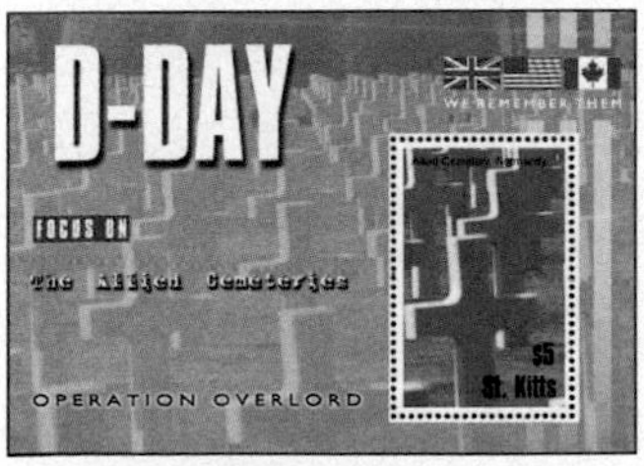


D-Day, 60th Anniv. — A127

No. 585, horiz.: a, 12th Panzer Division moves into position. b, German heavy tank. c, British and Germans clash (soldiers). d, British and Germans clash (soldiers, tank).

$5, Allied cemetery, Normandy.

**2004, Sept. 21** **Litho.** *Perf. 14*
**585** A127 $2 Sheet of 4, #a-d 6.00 6.00

**Souvenir Sheet**

**586** A127 $5 multi 3.75 3.75

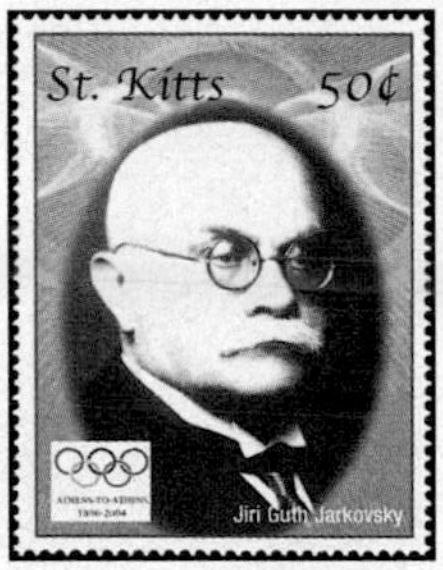


2004 Summer Olympics, Athens A128

Designs: 50c, Jiri Guth Jarkovsky, member of first International Olympic Committee. 90c, Poster for 1972 Munich Olympics. $1, Poster for 1900 Paris Olympics. $3, Sculpture of wrestlers.

**2004, Sept. 21** *Perf. 14¼*
**587-590** A128 Set of 4 4.00 4.00

**Souvenir Sheet**

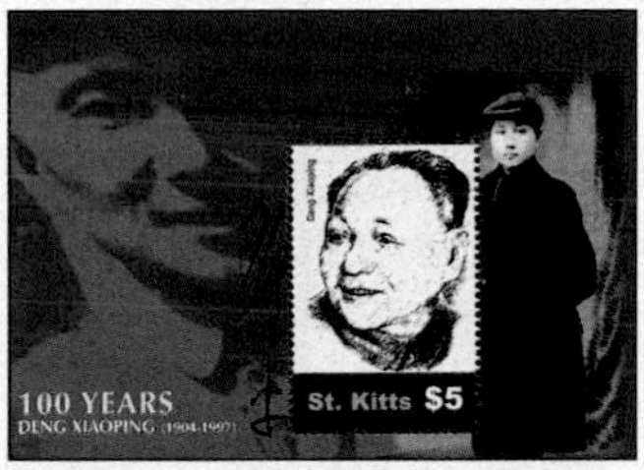


Deng Xiaoping (1904-97), Chinese Leader — A129

**2004, Sept. 21** **Litho.** *Perf. 14*
**591** A129 $5 multi 3.75 3.75

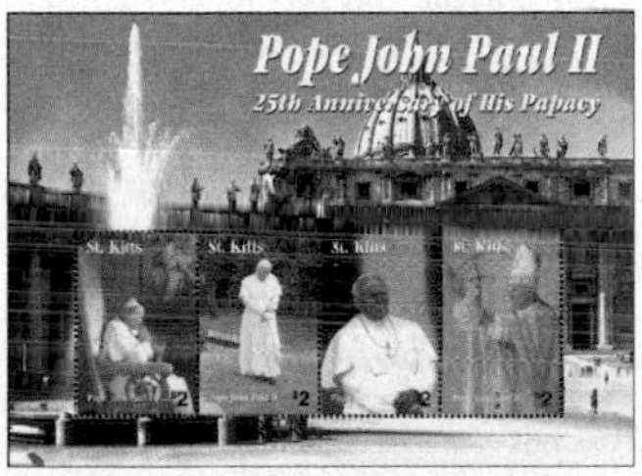


Election of Pope John Paul II, 25th Anniv. (in 2003) — A130

No. 592: a, Seated. b, Walking in garden. c, With arms clasped. d, Holding crucifix.

**2004, Sept. 21**
**592** A130 $2 Sheet of 4, #a-d 6.00 6.00

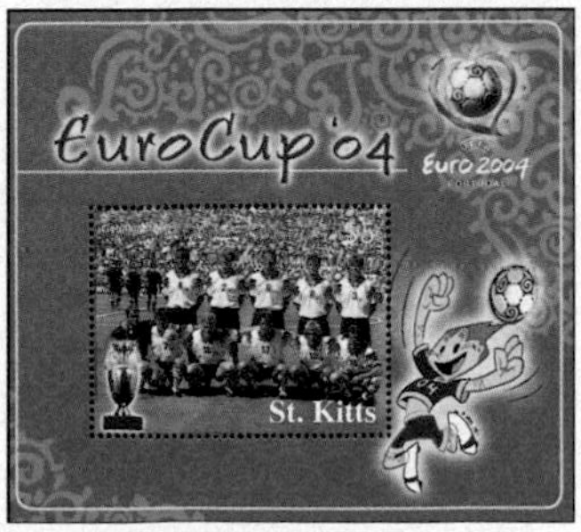


2004 European Soccer Championships, Portugal — A131

No. 593, vert.: a, Berti Vogts. b, Patrik Berger. c, Oliver Bierhoff. d, Empire Stadium.

$5, 1996 German team.

**2004, Sept. 21** *Perf. 14¼*
**593** A131 $2 Sheet of 4, #a-d 6.00 6.00

**Souvenir Sheet**

**594** A131 $5 multi 3.75 3.75

No. 593 contains four 28x42mm stamps.

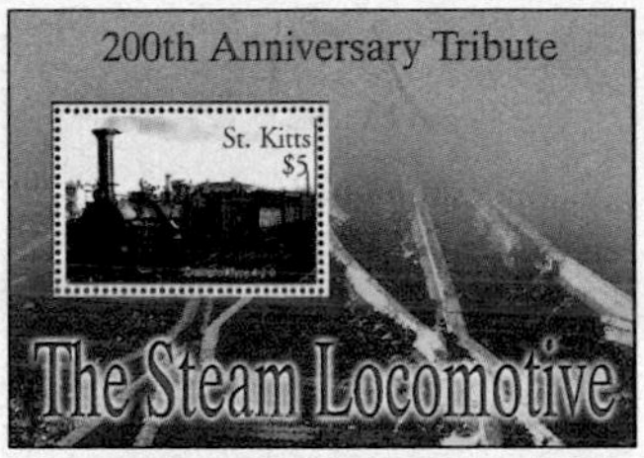


Locomotives, 200th Anniv. — A132

No. 595, $2: a, Italian State Railways Class 685 2-8-2. b, Swiss Federal Railways 4-6-0. c, BESA Class 4-6-0. d, Great Western City Class 4-4-0.

No. 596, $2: a, Northumbrian 0-2-2. b, Prince Class 2-2-2. c, Adler 2-2-2. d, L&NWR Webb Compound 2-4-0.

No. 597, $2: a, American Standard 4-4-0. b, New South Wales Government Class 79 4-4-0. c, Johnson Midland Single 4-2-2. d, Union Pacific FEF-3 Class 4-8-4.

No. 598, $5, Crampton Type 4-2-0. No. 599, $5, CN Class U-2 4-8-4. No. 600, $5, Baldwin 2-8-2, vert.

*Perf. 13¼x13½, 13½x13¼*

**2004, Sept. 21**

**Sheets of 4, #a-d**

**595-597** A132 Set of 3 18.00 18.00

**Souvenir Sheets**

**598-600** A132 Set of 3 11.50 11.50

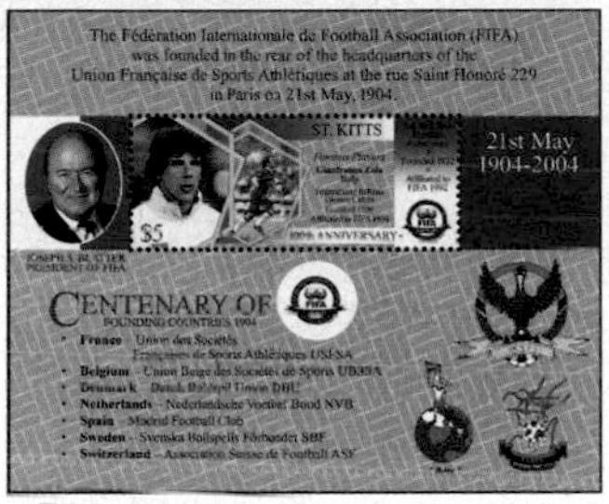


FIFA (Fédération Internationale de Football Association), Cent. — A133

No. 601: a, Demetrio Albertini. b, Romario. c, Gerd Muller. d, Danny Blanchflower.

$5, Gianfranco Zola.

**2004, Nov. 8** *Perf. 12¾x12½*
**601** A133 $2 Sheet of 4, #a-d 6.00 6.00

**Souvenir Sheet**

**602** A133 $5 multi 3.75 3.75

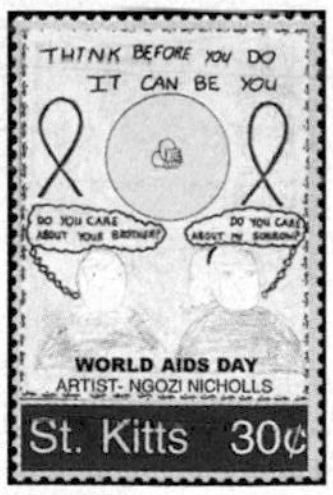


World AIDS Day — A134

Posters by: 30c, Ngozi Nicholls. 80c, Travis Liburd. 90c, Darren Kelly, horiz. $1, Shane Berry.

**2004, Dec. 1** *Perf. 14*
**603-606** A134 Set of 4 2.25 2.25

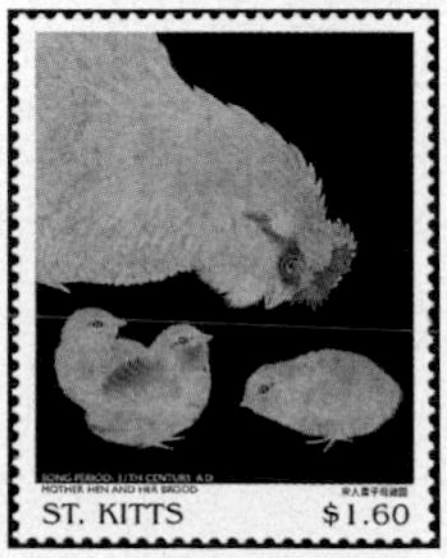


New Year 2005 (Year of the Rooster) A135

Mother Hen and Her Brood, by unknown artist: $1.60, Detail. $5, Entire painting.

**2005, Feb. 7** *Perf. 12*
**607** A135 $1.60 multi 1.25 1.25

**Souvenir Sheet**

**608** A135 $5 multi 3.75 3.75

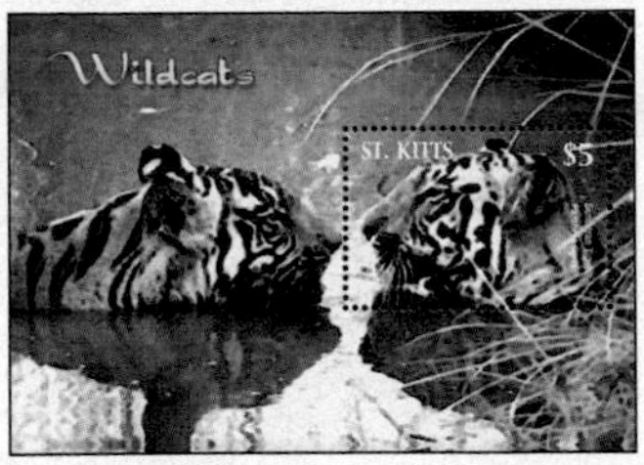


Wildcats — A136

No. 609, vert.: a, Ocelot. b, Bengal leopard. c, Tiger. d, Leopard.

$5, Sumatran tiger.

**2005, Feb. 7** *Perf. 12¾*
**609** A136 $2 Sheet of 4, #a-d 6.00 6.00

**Souvenir Sheet**

**610** A136 $5 multi 3.75 3.75

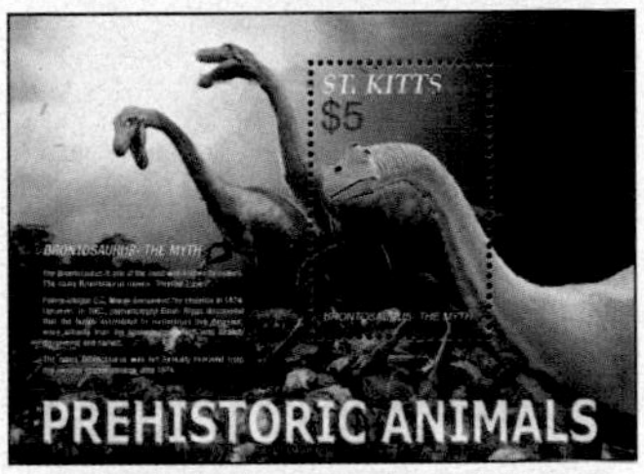


Prehistoric Animals — A137

No. 611, horiz.: a, Triceratops. b, Deinonychus. c, Apatosaurus.

No. 612, horiz.: a, Dimetrodon. b, Homalocephale. c, Stegosaurus.

No. 613, horiz.: a, Sabre-toothed tiger. b, Edmontosaurus. c, Tyrannosaurus rex.

No. 614, $5, Brontosaurus. No. 615, $5, Woolly mammoth. No. 616, $5, Andrewsarchus, horiz.

**2005, Feb. 7**
**611** A137 $3 Sheet of 3, #a-c 6.75 6.75
**612** A137 $3 Sheet of 3, #a-c 6.75 6.75
**613** A137 $3 Sheet of 3, #a-c 6.75 6.75

**Souvenir Sheet**

**614** A137 $5 multi 3.75 3.75
**615** A137 $5 multi 3.75 3.75
**616** A137 $5 multi 3.75 3.75

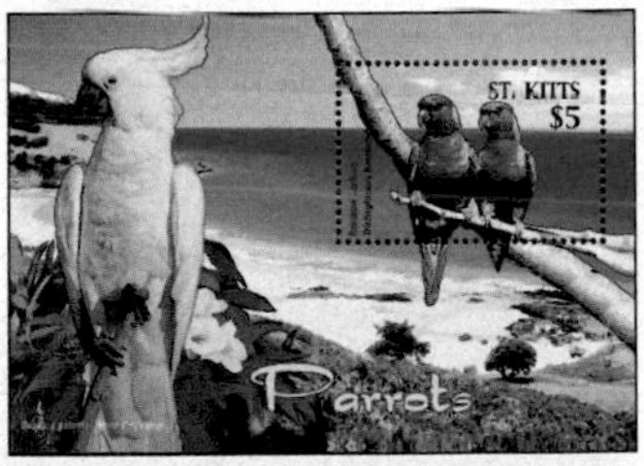


Parrots — A138

No. 617, vert.: a, Australian king parrot. b, Rose-breasted cockatoo. c, Pale-headed rosella. d, Eastern rosella.

$5, Rainbow lorikeets.

**2005, Feb. 7** **Litho.** *Perf. 12¾*
**617** A138 $2 Sheet of 4, #a-d 6.00 6.00

**Souvenir Sheet**

**618** A138 $5 multi 3.75 3.75

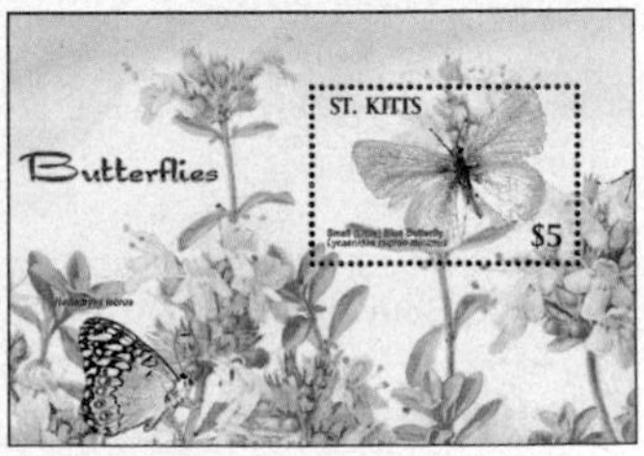


Insects and Butterflies — A139

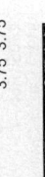

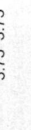

No. 619, vert.: a, Papilio demoleus. b, Ephemeroptera. c, Hamadryas februa. d, Aphylia caraiba.

**2005, Feb. 7**
619 A139 $2 Sheet of 4, #a-d   6.00 6.00

$5, Small blue butterfly.

**Souvenir Sheet**
620 A139 $5 multi   3.75 3.75

Designs: 25c. White-cheeked pintails. $1, Fulvous whistling ducks. $2, White-faced whistling duck. $3, Black-bellied whistling ducks.

**2005, Feb. 7**
621-624 A140 Set of 4   4.75 4.75

**Ducks — A140**

**25¢ St. Kitts**

**Souvenir Sheet**

Hans Christian Andersen (1805-75), Author — A142

No. 625: a, Beijing Rotary meeting. b, Sick man. c, Sick man and visitor.

**2005, May 11**
625 A141 $3 Sheet of 3, #a-c   6.75 6.75

No. 626 — Book covers: a, Hans Christian Andersen's Fairy Tales. b, The Emperor's New Clothes. c, The Nutcracker.

**2005, May 11**
626 A142 $3 Sheet of 3, #a-c   6.75 6.75

$5, The Emperor's New Clothes.

**Souvenir Sheet**
627 A142 $5 multi   3.75 3.75

Rotary International, Cent. — A141

**ROTARY — Celebrating 100 Years of Rotary — CHICAGO**

No. 630, $2: a, US Navy Hudson PDB-1 patrol bombomb. b, World War II combat. c, Gen. Dwight D. Eisenhower. d, Transporting German prisoners of war. e, Newspaper announcing Nazi surrender.

No. 631, $2: a, USS Arizona under attack. b, USS Arizona Captain Franklin Van Valkenburgh. c, Hiroshima atomic blast. d, Historic marker of first atomic bomb loading pit, Tinian Island. e, Memorial Cenotaph, Hiroshima Peace Park.

**2005, May 11**   **Litho.**
630-631 A144 Sheets of 5, #a-e   15.00 15.00

End of World War II, 60th Anniv. — A144

**VE DAY — 60th Anniversary**

No. 628, vert.: a, Verne. b, Sea monster attack. c, Rouguayrol. d, Modern Aqualung. $5, Atomic submarine.

**2005, May 11**
628 A143 $3 Sheet of 4, #a-d   6.00 6.00

$5, Atomic submarine.

**Souvenir Sheet**
629 A143 $5 multi   3.75 3.75

Jules Verne (1828-1905), Writer — A143

100th Anniversary of the Death of JULES VERNE — 20,000 Leagues Under the Sea $5

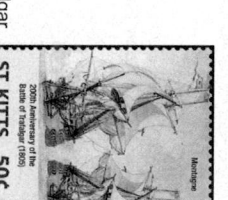

**ST. KITTS 50¢** — 200th Anniversary of the Battle of Trafalgar (1805) — Montagne

Battle of Trafalgar, Bicent. — A145

Ships: 50c. Montagne. 90c. San Jose. $2, Imperieuse. $3, San Nicolas.

**2005, May 11**
632-635 A145 Set of 4   5.00 5.00

$5, British Navy gun crew on HMS Victory.

**Souvenir Sheet**   **Perf. 12¾**
636 A145 $5 multi   3.75 3.75

**ST. KITTS $3 — POPE JOHN PAUL II & NELSON MANDELA**

Pope John Paul II (1920-2005) and Nelson Mandela — A146

**2005, July 19**   **Perf. 13½**
637 A146 $3 multi   2.25 2.25

Printed in sheets of 4.

Taipei 2005 Stamp Exhibition — A147

No. 638 — Various Chinese junks with denominations in: a, Red. b, Blue. c, Gray. d, Yellow orange.

**2005, Aug. 19**   **Perf. 14**
638 A147 $2 Sheet of 4, #a-d   6.00 6.00

**Souvenir Sheet**

Christmas — A148

**St. Kitts 30¢ — CHRISTMAS 2005 — VIRGIN AND CHILD FESTIVAL**

Paintings: 30c. Virgin and Child, by Gerard David. 50c. Virgin and Child, by David, diff. 90c. Virgin and Child, by David, diff. $2, Virgin and Child, by Bartolomeo Suardi Bramentine. $5, Nativity, by Martin Schongauer.

**2005, Dec. 6**   **Litho.**   **Perf. 13¾x13½**
639-642 A148   Set of 4   2.75 2.75

$5, Virgin and Child, by Martin Schongauer.

**Souvenir Sheet**
643 A148 $5 multi   3.75 3.75

## OFFICIAL STAMPS

Nos. 28-37 Ovptd. "OFFICIAL"
**Perf. 14½x14**
**1980, June 23**   **Litho.**   **Wmk. 373**

| No. | Type | Denom. | | |
|---|---|---|---|---|
| O1 | A61 | 15c multicolored | .20 | .20 |
| O2 | A61 | 25c multicolored | .20 | .20 |
| O3 | A61 | 30c multicolored | .20 | .20 |
| O4 | A61 | 40c multicolored | .20 | .20 |
| O5 | A61 | 45c multicolored | .20 | .20 |
| O6 | A61 | 50c multicolored | .20 | .20 |
| O7 | A61 | 55c multicolored | .20 | .20 |
| O8 | A61 | $1 multicolored | .30 | .30 |
| O9 | A61 | $5 multicolored | 1.50 | 1.50 |
| O10 | A61 | $10 multicolored | 2.75 | 2.75 |
| Nos. O1-O10 (10) | | | 5.95 | 5.95 |

**Unwmk.**

| No. | Type | Denom. | | |
|---|---|---|---|---|
| O1a | A61 | 15c multicolored | .25 | .20 |
| O2a | A61 | 25c | | .35 |
| O3a | A61 | 30c | .50 | |
| O4a | A61 | 40c | 11.50 | 10.75 |
| O7a | A61 | 55c | 1.75 | .55 |
| O8a | A61 | $1 | 1.25 | .55 |
| O9a | A61 | $5 | 3.75 | 4.00 |
| O10a | A61 | $10 | 5.75 | 5.75 |
| Nos. O2a-O10a (7) | | | 22.50 | 22.50 |

Nos. 55-66 Ovptd. "OFFICIAL"
**1981, Feb. 5**   **Perf. 14**

| No. | Type | Denom. | | |
|---|---|---|---|---|
| O11 | A5 | 15c multicolored | .20 | .20 |
| O12 | A5 | 20c multicolored | .20 | .20 |
| O13 | A5 | 25c multicolored | .20 | .20 |
| O14 | A5 | 30c multicolored | .25 | .20 |
| O15 | A5 | 40c multicolored | .40 | .20 |
| O16 | A5 | 45c multicolored | .45 | .25 |
| O17 | A5 | 50c multicolored | .45 | .25 |
| O18 | A5 | 55c multicolored | .55 | .30 |
| O19 | A5 | $1 multicolored | 1.00 | .55 |
| O20 | A5 | $2.50 multicolored | 2.00 | 1.50 |
| O21 | A5 | $5 multicolored | 3.75 | 3.00 |
| O22 | A5 | $10 multicolored | 6.75 | 6.00 |
| Nos. O11-O22 (12) | | | 16.25 | 13.00 |

**1983, Feb. 2**

| No. | Type | Denom. | | |
|---|---|---|---|---|
| O23 | A5 | 45c on $2.50 No. 77 | .25 | .25 |
| O24 | A66 | 45c on $2.50 No. 78 | .85 | .85 |
| O25 | A66 | 55c No. 75 | .25 | .25 |
| O26 | A67 | 55c No. 76 | .90 | .90 |
| O27 | A66 | $1.10 on $4 No. 79 (B) | .90 | .90 |
| O28 | A67 | $1.10 on $4 No. 80 (B) | 1.90 | 1.90 |
| Nos. O23-O28 (6) | | | 5.05 | 5.05 |

Nos. 75-80 Ovptd. or Surcharged "OFFICIAL" in Ultra or Black

Nos. 141-152 Ovptd. "OFFICIAL"
**1984, July 4**   **Wmk. 380**

| No. | Type | Denom. | | |
|---|---|---|---|---|
| O29 | A18 | 15c multicolored | .35 | .35 |
| O30 | A18 | 20c multicolored | .35 | .35 |
| O31 | A18 | 25c multicolored | .45 | .45 |
| O32 | A18 | 30c multicolored | .55 | .55 |
| O33 | A18 | 50c multicolored | .70 | .70 |
| O34 | A18 | 60c multicolored | .90 | .90 |
| O35 | A18 | 75c multicolored | 1.10 | 1.10 |
| O36 | A18 | $1 multicolored | 1.40 | 1.40 |
| O37 | A18 | $2.50 multicolored | 2.00 | 2.00 |
| O38 | A18 | $5 multicolored | 4.50 | 4.50 |
| O39 | A18 | $10 multicolored | 9.50 | 9.50 |
| O40 | A18 | multicolored | 18.00 | 18.00 |
| Nos. O29-O40 (12) | | | 39.80 | 39.80 |

## ST. KITTS-NEVIS

sānt 'kits-'nē-vəs

(St. Christopher-Nevis-Anguilla)

LOCATION — West Indies southeast of Puerto Rico
GOVT. — Associated State in British Commonwealth
AREA — 153 sq. mi.
POP. — 43,309, excluding Anguilla (1991)
CAPITAL — Basseterre, St. Kitts

St. Kitts-Nevis was one of the presidencies of the former Leeward Islands colony until it became a colony itself in 1956. In 1967 Britain granted internal self-government.

See "St. Christopher" for stamps used in St. Kitts before 1890. From 1890 until 1903, stamps of the Leeward Islands were used. From 1903 until 1956, stamps of St. Kitts-Nevis and Leeward Islands were used concurrently.

Starting in 1967, issues of Anguilla are listed under that heading. Starting in 1980 stamps inscribed St. Kitts or Nevis are listed under those headings.

12 Pence = 1 Shilling
20 Shillings = 1 Pound
100 Cents = 1 Dollar (1951)

**Catalogue values for unused stamps in this country are for Never Hinged items, beginning with Scott 91 in the regular postage section and Scott O1 in the officials section.**

Columbus Looking for Land — A1

Medicinal Spring — A2

**Wmk. Crown and C A (2)**

**1903** **Typo.** ***Perf. 14***
1 A1 ½p grn & vio 1.90 .75
2 A2 1p car & black 5.25 .20
3 A1 2p brn & vio 2.75 *12.00*
4 A1 2½p ultra & black 19.00 4.75
5 A2 3p org & green 14.50 *29.00*
6 A1 6p red violet & black 4.75 *37.50*
7 A1 1sh org & grn 6.75 *12.00*
8 A2 2sh blk & grn 13.50 *22.50*
9 A1 2sh6p violet & blk 20.00 *45.00*
10 A2 5sh ol grn & gray vio 60.00 *60.00*
*Nos. 1-10 (10)* 148.40 *223.70*

**1905-18** **Wmk. 3**
11 A1 ½p green & violet 6.25 *6.00*
12a A1 ½p dull bl grn ('16) .50 *1.75*
13 A2 1p carmine & blk 1.75 .30
14 A2 1p scarlet ('16) .75 .20
15 A1 2p brown & violet 6.75 8.50
16 A1 2½p ultra & blk 16.00 3.50
17 A1 2½p ultra 2.75 .60
18 A2 3p orange & green 3.00 3.00
19 A1 6p red vio & gray blk ('08) 6.25 *27.50*
a. 6p purple & gray ('08) 16.00 *27.50*
20 A1 1sh org & grn ('09) 4.00 *32.50*
21 A2 5sh ol grn & gray vio ('18) 35.00 *82.50*
*Nos. 11-21 (11)* 83.00 *166.35*

Nos. 13, 19a and 21 are on chalky paper only and Nos. 15, 18 and 20 are on both ordinary and chalky paper.

For stamp and type overprinted see #MR1-MR2.

King George V — A3

A4

**1920-22**

**Ordinary Paper**
24 A3 ½p green 4.00 *6.00*
25 A4 1p carmine 2.50 *6.50*
26 A3 1½p orange 1.40 *1.90*
27 A4 2p gray 3.25 *4.25*
28 A3 2½p ultramarine 2.25 *10.00*

**Chalky Paper**
29 A4 3p vio & dull vio, *yel* 1.90 *12.00*
30 A3 6p red vio & dull vio 4.00 *12.00*
31 A4 1sh blk, *gray grn* 4.00 *4.50*
32 A3 2sh ultra & dull vio, *blue* 15.00 *24.00*
33 A4 2sh 6p red & blk, *blue* 5.50 *32.50*
34 A3 5sh red & grn, *yel* 5.50 *45.00*
35 A4 10sh red & grn, *grn* 13.50 *52.50*
36 A3 £1 blk & vio, *red* ('22) 250.00 *325.00*
*Nos. 24-36 (13)* 312.80 *536.15*

**1921-29** **Wmk. 4**

**Ordinary Paper**
37 A3 ½p yel green 1.60 .90
38 A4 1p rose red .75 .25
39 A4 1p dp violet ('22) 4.00 1.00
40 A3 1½p rose red ('25) 2.75 *3.00*
41 A3 1½p fawn ('28) 1.10 [illegible]
42 A4 2p gray .65 *.65*
44 A3 2½p brown ('22) 2.40 *10.00*

**Chalky Paper**
43a A3 2½p ultra ('27) 1.75 *2.00*
45 A4 3p ultra ('22) 1.10 *4.50*
46 A4 3p vio & dull vio, *yel* .85 *5.00*
47 A3 6p red vio & dull vio ('24) 5.25 *6.25*
48 A4 1sh black, *grn* ('29) 4.25 *6.75*
49 A3 2sh ultra & vio, *bl* ('22) 8.75 *24.00*
50 A4 2sh6p red & blk, *bl* ('27) 17.00 *30.00*
51 A3 5sh red & grn, *yel* ('29) 45.00 *72.50*
*Nos. 37-51 (15)* 97.20 *167.15*

No. 43 exists on ordinary and chalky paper.

Caravel in Old Road Bay — A5

**1923** **Wmk. 4**
52 A5 ½p green & blk 2.50 *7.50*
53 A5 1p violet & blk 5.00 1.60
54 A5 1½p carmine & blk 5.00 *10.50*
55 A5 2p dk gray & blk 4.00 1.60
56 A5 2½p brown & blk 6.50 *35.00*
57 A5 3p ultra & blk 4.00 *16.00*
58 A5 6p red vio & blk 10.00 *35.00*
59 A5 1sh ol grn & blk 15.00 *35.00*
60 A5 2sh ultra & blk, *bl* 45.00 *62.50*
61 A5 2sh6p red & blk, *blue* 52.50 *77.50*
62 A5 10sh red & blk, *emer* 285.00 *400.00*

**Wmk. 3**
63 A5 5sh red & blk, *yel* 77.50 *175.00*
64 A5 £1 vio & blk, *red* 850.00 *1,450.*
*Nos. 52-63 (12)* 512.00 *857.20*

Tercentenary of the founding of the colony of St. Kitts (or St. Christopher).

Common Design Types pictured following the introduction.

**Silver Jubilee Issue**
Common Design Type
Inscribed "St. Christopher and Nevis"

***Perf. 11x12***
**1935, May 6** **Engr.** **Wmk. 4**
72 CD301 1p car & dk blue 1.00 *.75*
73 CD301 1½p gray blk & ultra .80 *.80*
74 CD301 2½p ultra & brown 1.00 .85
75 CD301 1sh brn vio & ind 5.75 *15.00*
*Nos. 72-75 (4)* 8.55 *17.40*
Set, never hinged 16.50

**Coronation Issue**
Common Design Type
Inscribed "St. Christopher and Nevis"

**1937, May 12** ***Perf. 13½x14***
76 CD302 1p carmine .30 .20
77 CD302 1½p brown .40 .20
78 CD302 2½p bright ultra .65 .85
*Nos. 76-78 (3)* 1.35 1.25
Set, never hinged 1.25

George VI A6

Medicinal Spring A7

Columbus Looking for Land — A8

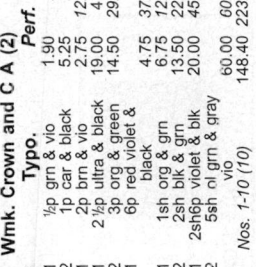

Map Showing Anguilla A9

***Perf. 13½x14 (A6, A9), 14 (A7, A8)***
**1938-48** **Typo.**
79 A6 ½p green .20 .20
80 A6 1p carmine 1.00 .50
81 A6 1½p orange .20 .30
82 A7 2p gray & car 1.00 1.25
83 A6 2½p ultra .75 .30
84 A7 3p car & pale lilac 20.00 4.00
85 A8 6p rose lil & dull grn 3.00 1.60
86 A7 1sh green & gray blk 2.75 .90
87 A7 2sh6p car & gray blk 7.50 4.00
88 A8 5sh car & dull grn 14.50 12.50

**Typo., Center Litho.**

**Chalky Paper**
89 A9 10sh brt ultra & blk 13.50 *20.00*
90 A9 £1 brown & blk 13.50 *24.00*
*Nos. 79-90 (12)* 77.90 *69.55*
Set, never hinged 87.50

Issued: ½, 1, 1½, 2½p, 8/15/38; 2p, 1941; 3, 6p, 2sh6p, 5sh, 1942; 1sh, 1943; 10sh, £1, 9/1/48.

For types overprinted see Nos. 99-104.

**1938, Aug. 15** ***Perf. 13x11½***
82a A7 2p 13.50 3.00
84a A7 3p 11.00 4.50
85a A8 6p 3.75 2.50
86a A7 1sh 7.50 1.75
87a A7 2sh6p 20.00 10.00
88a A8 5sh 37.50 *20.00*
*Nos. 82a-88a (6)* 93.25 *41.75*

**Catalogue values for unused stamps in this section, from this point to the end of the section, are for Never Hinged items.**

**Peace Issue**
Common Design Type
Inscribed "St. Kitts-Nevis"

**1946, Nov. 1** **Engr.** ***Perf. 13½x14***
91 CD303 1½p deep orange .20 .20
92 CD303 3p carmine .20 .20

**Silver Wedding Issue**
Common Design Types
Inscribed: "St. Kitts-Nevis"

**1949, Jan. 3** **Photo.** ***Perf. 14x14½***
93 CD304 2½p bright ultra .20 .20

**Engraved; Name Typographed**
***Perf. 11½x11***
94 CD305 5sh rose carmine 7.25 *4.75*

**UPU Issue**
Common Design Types
Inscribed: "St. Kitt's-Nevis"

**Engr.; Name Typo. on 3p, 6p**
**1949, Oct. 10** ***Perf. 13½, 11x11½***
95 CD306 2½p ultra .20 .20
96 CD307 3p deep carmine 1.50 1.25
97 CD308 6p red lilac .20 .50
98 CD309 1sh blue green .20 .35
*Nos. 95-98 (4)* 2.10 2.30

Types of 1938 Overprinted in Black or Carmine:

On A6

On A7-A8

***Perf. 13½x14, 13x12½***
**1950, Nov. 10** **Wmk. 4**
99 A6 1p carmine .20 .20
100 A6 1½p orange .20 .35
a. Wmk. 4a (error) *1,050.*
101 A6 2½p ultra .20 .20
102 A7 3p car & pale lilac .20 .65
103 A8 6p rose lil & dl grn .20 .20
104 A7 1sh grn & gray blk (C) .65 .25
*Nos. 99-104 (6)* 1.65 1.85

300th anniv. of the settlement of Anguilla.

**University Issue**
Common Design Types
Inscribed. "St. Kitts Nevis"

***Perf. 14x14½***
**1951, Feb. 16** **Engr.** **Wmk. 4**
105 CD310 3c org yel & gray blk .30 .20
106 CD311 12c red violet & aqua .30 1.25

### St. Christopher-Nevis-Anguilla

Bath House and Spa, Nevis — A10

Map — A11

Designs: 2c, Warner Park, St. Kitts. 4c, Brimstone Hill, St. Kitts. 5c, Nevis. 6c, Pinney's Beach, Nevis. 12c, Sir Thomas Warner's Tomb. 24c, Old Road Bay, St. Kitts. 48c, Picking Cotton. 60c, Treasury, St. Kitts. $1.20, Salt Pond, Anguilla. $4.80, Sugar Mill, St. Kitts.

**1952, June 14** ***Perf. 12½***
107 A10 1c ocher & dp grn .20 *1.25*
108 A10 2c emerald 1.10 *1.00*
109 A11 3c purple & red .30 *1.25*
110 A10 4c red .20 .20
111 A10 5c gray & ultra .30 .20
112 A10 6c deep ultra .30 .20
113 A11 12c redsh brn & dp blue 1.25 .20
114 A10 24c car & gray blk .30 .20
115 A10 48c vio brn & ol bister 2.25 *2.50*
116 A10 60c dp grn & och 2.10 *3.00*
117 A10 $1.20 dp ultra & dp green 7.25 3.00
118 A10 $4.80 car & emer 13.25 *19.00*
*Nos. 107-118 (12)* 28.80 32.00

### Coronation Issue
**Common Design Type**

**1953, June 2** — *Perf. 13½x13*
119  CD312  2c brt green & blk  .25  .20

Types of 1952 with Portrait of Queen Elizabeth II.

**1954-57** — *Engr.* — *Perf. 12½*

| No. | Type | Denom | | |
|---|---|---|---|---|
| 120 | A10 | ½c gray olive ('56) | .30 | .20 |
| 121 | A10 | 1c ocher & dp grn | .20 | .20 |
| a. | | Horiz. pair, imperf vert. | | |
| 122 | A10 | 3c emerald | .50 | .20 |
| 123 | A10 | 3c red | .65 | .20 |
| 124 | A10 | 4c purple & red | .20 | .20 |
| 125 | A10 | 5c gray & ultra | .20 | .20 |
| 126 | A10 | 6c deep ultra | .50 | .20 |
| 127 | A11 | 8c dark gray ('57) | 3.00 | .20 |
| 128 | A11 | 12c redsh brn & dp blue | .20 | .20 |
| 129 | A10 | 24c carmine & blk | .20 | .20 |
| 130 | A10 | 48c brn & ol bister | .40 | .75 |
| 131 | A10 | 60c dp grn & ocher | 6.25 | 3.50 |
| 132 | A10 | $1.20 dp ultra & dp green | 20.00 | 4.00 |
| 133 | A10 | $2.40 red org & blk | 11.50 | 12.50 |
| 134 | A10 | $4.80 car & emer | 58.80 | 35.25 |

Nos. 120-134 (15)

Issue dates: ½c, 24c-$1.20, $4.80, car & emer, 12/1/54; $2.40, 2/1/57; 7/3/56; 8c, 3/1/56; others, 3/1/57.

Alexander Hamilton and Nevis Scene A12

**1957, Jan. 11** — *Perf. 12½*
135  A12  24c dp ultra & yellow grn  .35  .20

Bicent. of the birth of Alexander Hamilton.

### West Indies Federation
**Common Design Type**

**1958, Apr. 22** — *Engr.* — *Wmk. 314* — *Perf. 11½x11*
136  CD313  3c green  .50  .50
137  CD313  6c blue  .85  .85
138  CD313  12c carmine rose  1.90  1.90
Nos. 136-138 (3)  3.25  3.25

Federation of the West Indies, Apr. 22, 1958.

Stamp of Nevis, 1861 A13

### Red Cross Centenary Issue
**Common Design Type**

**1961, July 15** — *Perf. 14*
139  A13  2c green & brown  .20  .20
140  A13  8c blue & pale brown  .20  .20
141  A13  12c carmine rose  .25  .25
142  A13  24c orange & green  .50  .50
Nos. 139-142 (4)  1.15  1.15

Centenary of the first stamps of Nevis.

Designs (Stamps of Nevis, 1861 issue): 8c, 4p stamp; 12c, 6p stamp; 24c, 1sh stamp.

New Lighthouse, Sombrero — A14

**1963, Sept. 2**
**Common Design Type**
*Litho.* — *Perf. 13*
143  CD315  3c black & red  .20  .20
144  CD315  12c ultra & red  .60  .60

Loading Sugar Cane, St. Kitts A15

**1963, Nov. 20** — *Photo.* — *Perf. 14*

| No. | Type | Denom | | |
|---|---|---|---|---|
| 145 | A15 | ½c blue & dk brn | .20 | .20 |
| 146 | A15 | 1c multicolored | .20 | .20 |
| 147 | A15 | 3c multicolored | .20 | .20 |
| 148 | A15 | 4c multicolored | .20 | .20 |
| a. | | Yellow omitted | 150.00 | |
| 149 | A15 | 5c multicolored | 2.00 | .20 |
| 150 | A15 | 6c multicolored | .20 | .20 |
| 151 | A15 | 10c multicolored | .20 | .20 |
| 152 | A15 | 12c multicolored | .20 | .20 |
| 153 | A15 | 15c multicolored | .20 | .20 |
| 154 | A15 | 24c multicolored | .40 | .20 |
| 155 | A15 | 25c multicolored | 1.00 | .35 |
| 156 | A15 | 50c multicolored | 1.00 | .90 |
| 157 | A15 | 60c multicolored | 2.00 | 1.00 |
| 158 | A15 | $1 multicolored | 2.00 | 2.50 |
| 159 | A15 | $2.50 multicolored | 2.50 | 3.00 |
| 160 | A15 | $5 multicolored | 5.50 | 4.50 |

Nos. 145-160 (16)  18.00  10.85

Designs: 2c, Pall Mall Square, Basseterre. 3c, Gateway, Brimstone Hill Fort, St. Kitts. 4c, Nelson's Spring, Nevis. 5c, Grammar School, St. Kitts. 6c, Mt. Misery Crater, St. Kitts. 10c, Hibiscus. 15c, Sea Island cotton, Nevis. 20c, Boat building, Anguilla. 25c, White-crowned pigeon. 60c, Alexander Hamilton. $1, Map of St. Kitts-Nevis. $2.50, Map of Anguilla. $5, Arms of St. Christopher-Nevis-Anguilla.

For overprints see Nos. 161-162.

**1964, Sept. 14**
161  A14  3c multicolored  .20  .20
162  A14  25c multicolored  .30  .30

Nos. 148 and 155 Overprinted: "ARTS / FESTIVAL / ST. KITTS / 1964"

### ITU Issue
**Common Design Type**

**1965, May 17** — *Litho.* — *Wmk. 314* — *Perf. 11x11½*
163  CD317  2c bister & rose red  .20  .20
164  CD317  50c grnsh blue & ol  .75  .75

### Int'l. Cooperation Year Issue
**Common Design Type**

**1965, Oct. 25** — *Perf. 14½*
165  CD318  2c blue grn & claret  .20  .20
166  CD318  25c lt violet & green  .45  .45

### Churchill Memorial Issue
**Design in Black, Gold and Carmine Rose**

**1966, Jan. 24** — *Photo.* — *Perf. 14*
167  CD319  ½c bright blue  .20  .20
168  CD319  3c green  .20  .20
169  CD319  15c brown  .30  .30
170  CD319  25c violet  .60  .60
Nos. 167-170 (4)  1.30  1.30

Charles Wesley, Cross and Palm — A18

### Royal Visit Issue
**Common Design Type**

**1966, Feb. 14** — *Litho.* — *Perf. 11x12*
171  CD320  3c violet blue  .20  .20
172  CD320  25c dk violet  .65  .65

### World Cup Soccer Issue
**Common Design Type**

**1966, July 1** — *Litho.* — *Perf. 14*
173  CD321  6c multicolored  .20  .20
174  CD321  25c multicolored  .50  .50

Festival Emblem With Dolphins — A16

**1966, Aug. 15** — *Unwmk.* — *Photo.* — *Perf. 14*
175  A16  3c gold, grn, yel & blk  .25  .25
176  A16  50c silver, grn, yel & blk  .30  .30

Arts Festival of 1966.

### WHO Headquarters Issue
**Common Design Type**

**1966, Sept. 20** — *Litho.* — *Perf. 14*
177  CD322  3c multicolored  .20  .20
178  CD322  40c multicolored  .40  .40

### UNESCO Anniversary Issue
**Common Design Type**

**1966, Dec. 1** — *Litho.* — *Perf. 14*
179  CD323  3c "Education"  .20  .20
180  CD323  6c "Science"  .50  .50
181  CD323  40c "Culture"  .90  .90
Nos. 179-181 (3)

Government Headquarters, Basseterre — A17

### Independent State

**1967, July 1** — *Photo.* — *Wmk. 314* — *Perf. 14½*
182  A17  3c multicolored  .20  .20
183  A17  10c multicolored  .20  .20
184  A17  25c multicolored  .30  .30
Nos. 182-184 (3)  .70  .70

Designs: 10c, Flag and map of Anguilla, St. Christopher and Nevis. 25c, Coat of Arms.

Achievement of independence, Feb. 27, 1967.

**1967, Dec. 1** — *Litho.* — *Perf. 13x13½*
185  A18  3c dp lilac, dp car & blk  .20  .20
186  A18  25c ultra, grnsh blue & blk  .30  .30
187  A18  40c ocher, yellow & blk  .70  .70
Nos. 185-187 (3)

3c, John Wesley. 40c, Thomas Coke.

Attainment of autonomy by the Methodist Church in the Caribbean and the Americas, and for the opening of headquarters near St. John's, Antigua, May 1967.

Cargo Ship and Plane A19

**1968, July 30** — *Litho.* — *Wmk. 314* — *Perf. 13½x13*
188  A19  25c multicolored  .25  .25
189  A19  50c brt blue & multi  .55  .55

Issued to publicize the organization of the Caribbean Free Trade Area, CARIFTA.

Martin Luther King, Jr. — A20

**1968, Sept. 30** — *Litho.* — *Wmk. 314* — *Perf. 12x12½*
190  A20  50c multicolored  .35  .35

Dr. Martin Luther King, Jr. (1929-68), American civil rights leader.

Mystical Nativity, by Botticelli — A21

**1968, Nov. 27** — *Photo.* — *Wmk. 314* — *Perf. 14½x14*
191  A21  12c brt violet & multi  .20  .20
192  A21  25c multicolored  .20  .20
193  A21  40c gray & multi  .30  .30
194  A21  50c crimson & multi  .90  .90
Nos. 191-194 (4)

Christmas (Paintings): 25c, 50c, The Adoration of the Magi, by Rubens. The 6c is misinscribed.

Snook A22

**1969, Feb. 25** — *Photo.* — *Wmk. 314* — *Perf. 14x14½*
195  A22  6c brt green & multi  .20  .20
196  A22  25c blue & multi  .25  .25
197  A22  40c gray blue & multi  .35  .35
198  A22  50c multicolored  .45  .45
Nos. 195-198 (4)  1.25  1.25

Fish: 12c, Needlefish (gar). 40c, Horse-eye jack. 50c, Red snapper. The 6c is misinscribed "tarpon."

Arms of Sir Thomas Warner and Map of Islands — A23

**1969, Sept. 1** — *Litho.* — *Perf. 13½*
199  A23  20c multicolored  .20  .20
200  A23  25c multicolored  .25  .25
201  A23  40c multicolored  .65  .65
Nos. 199-201 (3)

Designs: 25c, Warner's tomb in St. Kitts. 40c, Warner's commission from Charles I.

Issued in memory of Sir Thomas Warner, first Governor of St. Kitts-Nevis, Barbados and Montserrat.

Adoration of the Kings, by Jan Mostaert — A24

**1969, Nov. 17**    *Perf. 13½*

Christmas (Painting): 40c, 50c, Adoration of the Kings, by Geertgen tot Sint Jans.

| | | | |
|---|---|---|---|
| 202 | A24 | 10c olive & multi | .20 .20 |
| 203 | A24 | 25c violet & multi | .20 .20 |
| 204 | A24 | 40c yellow grn & multi | .20 .40 |
| 205 | A24 | 50c maroon & multi | .80 1.00 |

*Nos. 202-205 (4)*

Pip Meeting Convict, from "Great Expectations" — A27

**1970, May 1**   Litho.   **Wmk. 314**

*Perf. 13x13½, 13½x13*

| | | | |
|---|---|---|---|
| 223 | A27 | 4c gold, Prus blue & brn | .20 .20 |
| 224 | A27 | 20c gold, claret & brn | .20 .20 |
| 225 | A27 | 40c gold, olive & brn | .20 .40 |
| 226 | A27 | 40c dk blue, gold & brn | .80 1.00 |

*Nos. 223-226 (4)*

Designs: 20c, Miss Havisham from "Great Expectations." 25c, Dickens' birthplace, Portsmouth, vert. 40c, Charles Dickens, vert.

Charles Dickens (1812-70), English novelist.

Local Steel Band A28

**1970, Aug. 1**    *Perf. 13½*

| | | | |
|---|---|---|---|
| 227 | A28 | 20c multicolored | .20 .20 |
| 228 | A28 | 25c multicolored | .20 .20 |
| 229 | A28 | 40c multicolored | .60 .60 |

*Nos. 227-229 (3)*

25c, Local string band. 40c, "A Midsummer Night's Dream," 1963 performance.

Issued to publicize the 1970 Arts Festival.

Caravels, 16th Century A26

Pirates Burying Treasure, Frigate Bay — A25

Designs: 1c, English two-decker, 1650. 2c, Flags of England, Spain, France, Holland and Portugal. 3c, Hilt of 17th cent. rapier. 5c, Henry Morgan and fire boats. 6c, The pirate L'Ollonois and a carrack (pirate vessel). 10c, Smugglers' ship. 15c, Spanish 17th cent. piece of eight and map of Caribbean. 20c, Garrison and ship cannon and map of Spanish Main. 25c, Humphrey Cole's astrolabe. 1574. 50c, Flintlock pistol and map of Spanish Main. 60c, Dutch Flute (ship). $1, Capt. Bartholomew Roberts and document with death sentence for his crew. $2.50, Railing piece (small cannon), 17th cent. and map of Spanish Main. $5, Francis Drake, John Hawkins and ships. $10, Edward Teach (Blackbeard) and his capture.

**Wmk. 314 Upright (A25), Sideways (A26)**

**1970, Feb. 1**   Litho.   **Perf. 14**

| | | | |
|---|---|---|---|
| 206 | A25 | ½c multicolored | .20 .20 |
| 207 | A25 | 1c multicolored | .20 .20 |
| 208 | A25 | 2c multicolored | .35 .20 |
| 209 | A25 | 3c multicolored | .20 .20 |
| 210 | A26 | 4c multicolored | .20 .20 |
| 211 | A26 | 5c multicolored | .20 .20 |
| 212 | A26 | 6c multicolored | .35 .35 |
| 213 | A26 | 10c multicolored | .35 .35 |
| 214 | A25 | 15c *Hispanianism* | 2.25 .45 |
| 215 | A25 | 15c *Hispaniarum* | .80 .70 |
| 216 | A26 | 20c multicolored | .40 .20 |
| 217 | A25 | 25c multicolored | .45 .20 |
| 218 | A26 | 50c multicolored | .90 .85 |
| 219 | A26 | 60c multicolored | 2.25 .75 |
| 220 | A25 | $1 multicolored | 2.25 .75 |
| 221 | A26 | $2.50 multicolored | 3.00 3.00 |
| 222 | A26 | $5 multicolored | 16.50 12.75 |

*Nos. 206-222 (17)*

Coin inscription was misspelled on No. 214, corrected on No. 215 (issued Sept. 8).

**Wmk. 314 Sideways (A25), Upright (A26)**

**1973-74**

| | | | |
|---|---|---|---|
| 206a | A25 | ½c multicolored | .20 .75 |
| 208a | A25 | 2c multicolored | .20 .75 |
| 209a | A26 | 3c multicolored | .20 .75 |
| 211a | A26 | 4c multicolored | .30 .50 |
| 212a | A26 | 5c multicolored | .30 .50 |
| 212a | A26 | 10c multicolored | .45 .50 |
| 215a | A26 | 15c multicolored | .55 .75 |
| 216a | A26 | 20c multicolored | .65 .90 |
| 217a | A26 | 25c multicolored | .70 1.25 |
| 218a | A26 | 50c multicolored | 1.00 1.25 |
| 219a | A26 | $1 multicolored | 2.25 3.00 |
| 222A | A26 | $10 multi | 10.50 12.50 |

*Nos. 206a-220a,222A (12)*   24.30 23.65

Issue dates: $10, Nov. 16; others, Sept. 12.

**1975-77**    **Wmk. 373**

| | | | |
|---|---|---|---|
| 207b | A25 | 1c multi (77) | .20 .20 |
| 208b | A25 | 2c multi (76) | .20 .20 |
| 209b | A26 | 3c multicolored | .20 .35 |
| 211b | A26 | 4c multicolored | .80 .20 |
| 212b | A26 | 5c multi (76) | .20 .20 |
| 213b | A26 | 10c multi (77) | .35 .20 |
| 215b | A26 | 15c multi (76) | .20 .20 |
| 217b | A26 | 25c multicolored | 2.25 4.00 |
| 219b | A26 | 60c multi (77) | 1.40 1.40 |
| 220b | A25 | $1 multi (77) | 6.25 6.25 |

*Nos. 207b-220b (10)*   17.00 8.95

Monkey Fiddle A31

St.Christopher-Nevis-Anguilla

**1971, Mar. 1**    Litho.    *Perf. 14*

| | | | |
|---|---|---|---|
| 238 | A31 | ½c multicolored | .20 .20 |
| 239 | A31 | 20c multicolored | .20 .20 |
| 240 | A31 | 30c multicolored | .40 .60 |
| 241 | A31 | 50c multicolored | 1.00 1.20 |

*Nos. 238-241 (4)*

Flowers: 20c, Mountain violets. 30c, Morning glory. 50c, Fringed epidendrum.

Chateau de Poincy, St. Kitts — A32

**1971, June 1**    Litho.    **Wmk. 314**

| | | | |
|---|---|---|---|
| 242 | A32 | 20c green & multi | .20 .20 |
| 243 | A32 | 30c dull yellow & multi | .20 .20 |
| 244 | A32 | 50c brown & multi | .60 .60 |

*Nos. 242-244 (3)*

Designs: 20c, Royal poinciana. 50c, De Poincy's coat of arms, vert.

Philippe de Longvilliers de Poincy became first governor of French possessions in the Antilles in 1639.

East Yorks A33

**1971, Sept. 1**    *Perf. 14*

| | | | |
|---|---|---|---|
| 245 | A33 | ½c black & multi | .20 .20 |
| 246 | A33 | 20c black & multi | .35 .30 |
| 247 | A33 | 30c black & multi | .55 .45 |
| 248 | A33 | 50c black & multi | .90 .75 |

*Nos. 245-248 (4)*   2.00 1.70

Designs: 20c, Royal Artillery. 30c, French Infantry. 50c, Royal Scots.

Siege of Brimstone Hill, 1782.

St. Christopher No. 1 and St. Kitts Post Office, 1970 — A29

**1970, Sept. 14**    Litho.    **Wmk. 314**

*Perf. 14½*

| | | | |
|---|---|---|---|
| 230 | A29 | ½c groon & rose | .20 .20 |
| 231 | A29 | 20c vio bl, rose & grn | .20 .20 |
| 232 | A29 | 25c brown, rose & grn | .30 .30 |
| 233 | A29 | 50c black, grn & dk red | .90 .90 |

*Nos. 230-233 (4)*

Designs: 20c, 25c, St. Christopher Nos. 1 and 3. 50c, St. Christopher No. 3 and St. Kitts postmark, Sept. 2, 1871.

Centenary of stamps of St. Christopher.

**Festival of Arts 1970** A28a

**Perf. 13½**

| | | | |
|---|---|---|---|
| 227 | A28 | 20c multicolored | .20 .20 |
| | | | |

Madonna and Child, by Bergognone A35

Paintings: 20c, Adoration of the Kings, by Jacopo da Bassano, horiz. 25c, Adoration of the Shepherds, by Il Domenichino. 40c, Madonna and Child, by Fiorenzo di Lorenzo.

**1972, Oct. 2**   *Perf. 13½x14, 14x13½*

| | | | |
|---|---|---|---|
| 253 | A35 | 3c gray green & multi | .20 .20 |
| 254 | A35 | 20c deep plum & multi | .20 .20 |
| 255 | A35 | 25c sepia & multi | .25 .25 |
| 256 | A35 | 40c red & multi | .85 .85 |

*Nos. 253-256 (4)*

Christmas 1972.

**Silver Wedding Issue, 1972**
Common Design Type

Queen Elizabeth II, Prince Philip, pelicans.

**1972, Nov. 20**   Photo.   *Perf. 14x14½*

| | | | |
|---|---|---|---|
| 257 | CD324 | 4c car rose & multi | .25 .25 |
| 258 | CD324 | 25c ultra & multi | .35 .35 |

350th anniversary of the landing of Sir Thomas Warner at St. Kitts — A36

350TH ANNIVERSARY OF THE LANDING OF SIR THOMAS WARNER

**1973, Jan. 28**    Litho.    **Wmk. 314**

*Perf. 14x13½*

| | | | |
|---|---|---|---|
| 259 | A36 | 4c pink & multi | .20 .20 |
| 260 | A36 | 25c brown & multi | .25 .25 |
| 261 | A36 | 40c blue & multi | 1.00 1.00 |
| 262 | A36 | $2.50 multicolored | 1.65 1.65 |

*Nos. 259-262 (4)*

350th anniversary of the landing of Sir Thomas Warner at St. Kitts.

For overprints see Nos. 266-269.

Crucifixion, by Quentin Massys — A34

EASTER 1972

**1972, Apr. 1**    Litho.    **Wmk. 314**

*Perf. 14x13½*

| | | | |
|---|---|---|---|
| 249 | A34 | 4c brick red & multi | .20 .20 |
| 250 | A34 | 20c gray green & multi | .20 .20 |
| 251 | A34 | 30c dull blue & multi | .20 .20 |
| 252 | A34 | 40c lt brown & multi | .25 .25 |

*Nos. 249-252 (4)*   .85 .85

Easter 1972.

The Last Supper, by Juan de Juanes — A37

THE LAST SUPPER

**1973, Apr. 16**   Photo.   **Wmk. 314**

*Perf. 14x13½, 13½x14*

| | | | |
|---|---|---|---|
| 263 | A37 | 4c blue black & multi | .20 .20 |
| 264 | A37 | 25c multicolored | .85 .85 |
| 265 | A37 | $2.50 purple & multi | 1.25 1.25 |

*Nos. 263-265 (3)*

Easter (The Last Supper, by): 4c, Titian, vert. 25c, ascribed to Roberti, vert.

**VISIT OF H. H. THE PRINCE OF WALES 1973**

Nos. 259-262 Overprinted:

**1973, May 31**   Litho.   *Perf. 14x13½*

| | | | |
|---|---|---|---|
| 266 | A36 | 4c pink & multi | .20 .20 |
| 267 | A36 | 25c brown & multi | .85 .85 |
| 268 | A36 | 40c blue & multi | .40 .40 |
| 269 | A36 | $2.50 multicolored | 1.00 1.00 |

*Nos. 266-269 (4)*

Visit of Prince Charles, May 1973.

Holy Family, by Anthony van Dyck — A30

ST. CHRISTOPHER NEVIS ANGUILLA

**1970, Nov. 16**    *Perf. 14*

| | | | |
|---|---|---|---|
| 234 | A30 | 3c multicolored | .20 .20 |
| 235 | A30 | 20c ocher & multi | .20 .20 |
| 236 | A30 | 25c dull red & multi | .20 .20 |
| 237 | A30 | 40c green & multi | .80 .80 |

*Nos. 234-237 (4)*

Christmas: 3c, 40c, Adoration of the Shepherds, by Frans Floris.

St.Christopher-Nevis-Anguilla

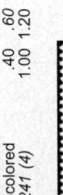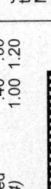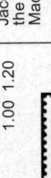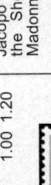

St. Christopher Nevis-Anguilla

Harbor Scene and St. Kitts-Nevis No. 3 — A38

**1973, Oct. 1    Litho.    Perf. 13½x14**

| | | | | |
|---|---|---|---|---|
| 270 | A38 | 4c salmon & multi | .20 | .20 |
| 271 | A38 | 25c lt blue & multi | .40 | .40 |
| 272 | A38 | 40c multicolored | .80 | .80 |
| 273 | A38 | $2.50 multicolored | 4.00 | 4.00 |
| a. | | Souvenir sheet of 4, #270-273 | 3.90 | 3.90 |

70th anniv. of 1st St. Kitts-Nevis stamps.

25c, Sugar mill and #2. 40c, Unloading of boat and #1. $2.50, Rock carvings and #5.

Princess Anne's Wedding Issue
Common Design Type

**1973, Nov. 14    Perf. 14**

| | | | | |
|---|---|---|---|---|
| 274 | CD325 | 25c brt green & multi | .20 | .20 |
| 275 | CD325 | 40c citron & multi | .20 | .20 |

Virgin and Child, by Murillo — A39

Christ Carrying Cross, by Sebastiano del Piombo — A40

Christmas (Paintings): 40c, Holy Family, by Anton Raphael Mengs. 60c, Holy Family, by Sassoferrato. $1, Holy Family, by Filippino Lippi, horiz.

**1973, Dec. 1    Litho.    Perf. 14x13½**

| | | | | |
|---|---|---|---|---|
| 276 | A39 | 4c brt blue & multi | .20 | .20 |
| 277 | A39 | 25c orange & multi | .20 | .20 |
| 278 | A39 | 40c multicolored | .25 | .25 |
| 279 | A39 | $1 multicolored | .35 | .35 |
| | | Nos. 276-279 (4) | 1.00 | 1.00 |

**1974, Apr. 8    Perf. 13**

| | | | | |
|---|---|---|---|---|
| 280 | A40 | 4c olive & multi | .20 | .20 |
| 281 | A40 | 25c lt blue & multi | .20 | .20 |
| 282 | A40 | 40c purple & multi | .20 | .20 |
| 283 | A40 | $2.50 gray & multi | 1.25 | 1.25 |
| | | Nos. 280-283 (4) | 1.85 | 1.85 |

Easter: 25c, Crucifixion, by Goya. 40c, Trinity, by Diego Ribera. $2.50, Burial of Christ, by Fra Bartolomeo, horiz.

University Center, St. Kitts, Chancellor Hugh Wooding — A41

**1974, June 1    Perf. 13½**

| | | | | |
|---|---|---|---|---|
| 284 | A41 | 10c blue & multi | .20 | .20 |
| 285 | A41 | $1 pink & multi | .50 | .50 |
| a. | | Souvenir sheet of 2, #284-285 | | |

University of the West Indies, 25th anniv.

---

St. Christopher Nevis Anguilla

Nurse Explaining Family Planning — A42

**1974, Aug. 5    Wmk. 314    Litho.    Perf. 14**

| | | | | |
|---|---|---|---|---|
| 286 | A42 | 4c blk, blue & brn | .20 | .20 |
| 287 | A42 | 25c multicolored | .20 | .20 |
| 288 | A42 | 40c multicolored | .30 | .30 |
| 289 | A42 | $2.50 lilac & multi | .90 | .90 |
| | | Nos. 286-289 (4) | | |

Family planning and World Population Week, Aug. 4-10.

Designs: 4c, Globe and hands reaching up, vert. 40c, Family, vert. $2.50, WPY emblem and scale balancing embryo and world.

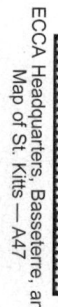

Churchill as Lieutenant, 21st Lancers — A43

Knight of the Garter — A44

**1974, Nov. 30**

| | | | | |
|---|---|---|---|---|
| 290 | A43 | 4c dull violet & multi | .20 | .20 |
| 291 | A43 | 25c yellow & multi | .20 | .20 |
| 292 | A44 | 40c lt blue & multi | .25 | .25 |
| 293 | A44 | 60c lt blue & multi | .25 | .25 |
| a. | | Souvenir sheet of 4, #290-293 | .90 | .90 |
| | | Nos. 290-293 (4) | .85 | .85 |

Designs: 25c, Churchill as Prime Minister. 60c, Churchill Statue, Parliament Square, London.

Sir Winston Churchill (1874-1965).

Souvenir Sheets

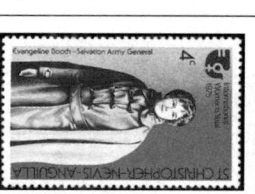

Boeing 747 over St. Kitts-Nevis — A45

**1974, Dec. 16    Perf. 14x13½**

| | | | | |
|---|---|---|---|---|
| 294 | A45 | 40c multicolored | .80 | .80 |
| 295 | A45 | 45c multicolored | 1.10 | 1.10 |

Opening of Golden Rock Intl. Airport.

---

The Last Supper, by Doré — A46

**1975, Mar. 24    Perf. 14½**

| | | | | |
|---|---|---|---|---|
| 296 | A46 | 4c ultra & multi | .20 | .20 |
| 297 | A46 | 25c ultra & multi | .20 | .20 |
| 298 | A46 | 40c bister & multi | .25 | .25 |
| 299 | A46 | $1 salmon pink & multi | .85 | .85 |
| | | Nos. 296-299 (4) | | |

Easter: 25c, Jesus mocked. 40c, Jesus falling beneath the Cross. $1, Raising the Cross. Designs based on Bible illustrations by Paul Gustave Doré (1833-1883).

ECCA Headquarters, Basseterre, and Map of St. Kitts — A47

**1975, June 2    Perf. 13½x14    Wmk. 373**

| | | | | |
|---|---|---|---|---|
| 300 | A47 | 12c orange & multi | .20 | .20 |
| 301 | A47 | 25c olive & multi | .20 | .20 |
| 302 | A47 | 40c vermilion & multi | .20 | .20 |
| 303 | A47 | 45c brt blue & multi | .20 | .20 |
| | | Nos. 300-303 (4) | .80 | .80 |

Designs: 25c, Specimen of $1 note, issued by ECCA. 40c, St. Kitts half dollar, 1801, and $4 coin, 1875. 45c, Nevis "9 dogs" coin, 1801, and 2c, 5c, coins, 1975.

East Caribbean Currency Authority Headquarters, Basseterre, opening.

Evangeline Booth, Salvation Army — A48

Colter Swinging Club — A49

**1975, Sept. 15    Litho.    Wmk. 314    Perf. 14x14½**

| | | | | |
|---|---|---|---|---|
| 304 | A48 | 4c orange brn & blk | .40 | .40 |
| 305 | A48 | 25c lilac pur & blk | .45 | .45 |
| 306 | A48 | 40c emerald & blk | .20 | .20 |
| 307 | A48 | $2.50 yellow brn & blk | 2.00 | 2.00 |
| | | Nos. 304-307 (4) | | |

Designs (IWY Emblem and): 25c, Sylvia Pankhurst, suffragette. 40c, Marie Curie, scientist. $2.50, Lady Annie Allen, teacher.

International Women's Year 1975.

**1975, Nov. 1    Perf. 14**

| | | | | |
|---|---|---|---|---|
| 308 | A49 | 4c rose red & blk | .90 | .20 |
| 309 | A49 | 25c yellow & blk | 1.25 | .20 |
| 310 | A49 | 40c emerald & blk | 1.75 | .45 |
| 311 | A49 | $1 blue & blk | 6.30 | 3.25 |
| | | Nos. 308-311 (4) | 5.35 | 5.20 |

Opening of Frigate Bay Golf Course.

---

St. Christopher Nevis-Anguilla

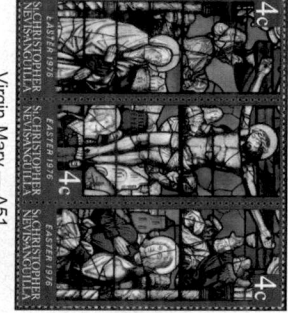

Virgin Mary — A51

St. Paul, by Sacchi Pier Francesco — A50

Christmas (Paintings, details): 40c, St. James, by Bonifazio di Pitati. 45c, St. John, by Pier Francesco Mola. $1, Virgin Mary, by Raphael.

**1975, Dec. 1    Litho.    Wmk. 373    Perf. 14**

| | | | | |
|---|---|---|---|---|
| 312 | A50 | 25c ultra & multi | .25 | .25 |
| 313 | A50 | 40c multicolored | .60 | .60 |
| 314 | A50 | 45c red brown & multi | .65 | .65 |
| 315 | A50 | $1 gold & multi | 1.50 | 1.50 |
| | | Nos. 312-315 (4) | 3.00 | 3.00 |

The Last Supper — A52

**1976, Apr. 14    Litho.    Wmk. 373    Perf. 14x13½**

| | | | | |
|---|---|---|---|---|
| 316 | A52 | 25c black & multi | .20 | .20 |
| 317 | A52 | 40c black & multi | .40 | .40 |
| 318 | A52 | $1 black & multi | .75 | .75 |
| a. | A51 | Triptych, #316-318 | | |

**Perf. 14½**

| | | | | |
|---|---|---|---|---|
| 319 | A52 | 25c black & multi | .25 | .25 |
| 320 | A52 | 40c black & multi | .40 | .40 |
| 321 | A52 | $1 black & multi | .75 | .75 |
| | | Nos. 319-321 (3) | 1.40 | 1.40 |

Easter 1976. No. 318a has continuous design.

Stained Glass Windows: No. 317, Christ on the Cross. No. 318, St. John. 40c, The Last Supper (different). $1, Baptism of Christ.

Map of West Indies, Bats, Wicket and Ball — A52a

Prudential Cup — A52b

# ST. KITTS-NEVIS

**1976, July 8** Unwmk. Litho. Perf. 14
| | | | |
|---|---|---|---|
| 322 | A52a | 12c lt blue & multi | .45 .35 |
| 323 | A52b | 40c lilac rose & blk | 1.40 1.00 |
| a. | | Souvenir sheet of 2, #322-323 | 6.00 6.00 |

World Cricket Cup, won by West Indies Team, 1975.

**Crispus Attucks and Boston Massacre — A53**

**1976, July 26** Litho. Wmk. 373
| | | | |
|---|---|---|---|
| 324 | A53 | 20c gray & multi | .20 .20 |
| 325 | A53 | 40c gray & multi | .25 .25 |
| 326 | A53 | 45c gray & multi | .25 .25 |
| 327 | A53 | $1 gray & multi | .50 .50 |
| | | Nos. 324-327 (4) | 1.20 1.20 |

American Bicentennial.
Designs: 40c, Alexander Hamilton and Battle of Yorktown. 45c, Thomas Jefferson and Declaration of Independence. $1, George Washington and Crossing of the Delaware.

**Estridge Mission A57**

**1977, Apr. 1** Wmk. 373 Litho. Perf. 14
| | | | |
|---|---|---|---|
| 335 | A56 | 25c yellow & multi | .20 .20 |
| 336 | A56 | 30c deep blue & multi | .20 .20 |
| 337 | A56 | 50c olive green & multi | .25 .25 |
| 338 | A56 | $1 red & multi | .85 .85 |
| | | Nos. 335-338 (4) | |

20c, Mission emblem. 40c, Basseterre Mission.

**1977, June 27** Litho. Perf. 12½
| | | | |
|---|---|---|---|
| 339 | A57 | 4c blue & black | .20 .20 |
| 340 | A57 | 20c multicolored | .20 .20 |
| 341 | A57 | 40c orange yel & blk | .60 .60 |
| | | Nos. 339-341 (3) | |

Bicentenary of Moravian Mission.

**Microscope, Flask, Syringe — A58**

**1977, Oct. 11** Litho. Perf. 14
| | | | |
|---|---|---|---|
| 342 | A58 | 3c multicolored | .20 .20 |
| 343 | A58 | 12c multicolored | .20 .20 |
| 344 | A58 | 20c multicolored | .20 .20 |
| 345 | A58 | $1 multicolored | 1.00 1.00 |
| | | Nos. 342-345 (4) | 1.60 1.60 |

12c, Blood, fat, nerve cells. 20c, Symbol of community participation. $1, Inoculation.
Pan American Health Organization, 75th anniversary (PAHO).

**Three Kings — A59**

**1977, Nov. 15** Wmk. 373 Litho.
| | | | |
|---|---|---|---|
| 346 | A59 | 4c multicolored | .20 .20 |
| 347 | A59 | 6c multicolored | .20 .20 |
| 348 | A59 | 40c multicolored | .30 .30 |
| 349 | A59 | $1 multicolored | .55 .55 |
| | | Nos. 346-349 (4) | 1.25 1.25 |

Christmas, Stained-glass Windows, Chartres Cathedral: 4c, Nativity, West Window. 40c, Virgin and Child. $1, Virgin and Child, Rose Window.

**Green Monkey and Young — A60**

**1978, Apr. 15** Wmk. 373 Litho. Perf. 14½
| | | | |
|---|---|---|---|
| 350 | A60 | 4c multicolored | .20 .20 |
| 351 | A60 | 5c multicolored | .60 .60 |
| 352 | A60 | 50c multicolored | 1.50 1.40 |
| 353 | A60 | $1.50 multicolored | 2.50 2.00 |
| | | Nos. 350-353 (4) | |

Green Monkeys: 5c, $1.50, Mother and young sitting on branch. 55c, like 4c.

## Elizabeth II Coronation Anniversary Issue
### Common Design Types
### Souvenir Sheet

**1978, Apr. 21** Unwmk. Litho. Perf. 15
| | | | |
|---|---|---|---|
| 354 | | Sheet of 6 | 1.00 1.00 |
| a. | CD326 | $1 Falcon of Edward III | .20 1.00 |
| b. | CD327 | $1 Elizabeth II | .20 .20 |
| c. | CD328 | $1 Pelican | .20 .20 |

No. 354 contains 2 se-tenant strips of Nos. 354a-354c, separated by horizontal gutter with commemorative and descriptive inscriptions and showing central part of coronation procession with coach.

**Tomatoes A61**

Designs: 2c, Defense Force band. 5c, Radio and TV station. 10c, Technical College. 12c, TV assembly plant. 15c, Sugar cane harvest. 25c, Craft Center. 30c, Cruise ship. 40c, Sea crab and lobster. 45c, Royal St. Kitts Hotel and golf course. 50c, Pinneys Beach. 55c, New Runway at Golden Rock. $1, Cotton pickers. $5, Brewery. $10, Pineapples and peanuts.

**1978, Sept. 8** Perf. 14½x14 Wmk. 373
| | | | |
|---|---|---|---|
| 355 | A61 | 1c multicolored | .20 .20 |
| 356 | A61 | 2c multicolored | .20 .20 |
| 357 | A61 | 5c multicolored | .20 .20 |
| 358 | A61 | 10c multicolored | .20 .20 |
| 359 | A61 | 12c multicolored | .20 .20 |
| 360 | A61 | 15c multicolored | .20 .20 |
| 361 | A61 | 25c multicolored | .20 .20 |
| 362 | A61 | 30c multicolored | .20 .20 |
| 363 | A61 | 40c multicolored | .20 .20 |
| 364 | A61 | 45c multicolored | .20 .20 |
| 365 | A61 | 50c multicolored | .35 .20 |
| 366 | A61 | 55c multicolored | .35 .35 |
| 367 | A61 | $1 multicolored | .70 .70 |
| 368 | A61 | $5 multicolored | .90 1.50 |
| 369 | A61 | $10 multicolored | 1.75 3.25 |
| | | Nos. 355-369 (15) | 9.60 7.45 |

For overprints see Nevis #100-112, O1-O10.

**Investiture — A62**

**King Bringing Gift — A63**

**1978, Oct. 9** Wmk. 373 Litho. Perf. 13½
| | | | |
|---|---|---|---|
| 370 | A62 | 4c multicolored | .20 .20 |
| 371 | A62 | 10c multicolored | .20 .20 |
| 372 | A62 | 25c multicolored | .30 .30 |
| 373 | A62 | 40c multicolored | .40 .40 |
| 374 | A62 | 50c multicolored | .60 .60 |
| 375 | A62 | 55c multicolored | .60 .60 |
| | | Nos. 370-375 (6) | 2.30 2.30 |

Designs: 10c, Map reading. 25c, Pitching tent. 40c, Cooking. 50c, First aid. 55c, Rev. W. A. Beckett, founder of Scouting in St. Kitts.
50th anniversary of St. Kitts-Nevis Scouting.

**Canna Coccinea — A64**

**1978, Dec. 1** Perf. 14x13½
Christmas: 15c, 30c, King bringing gift, diff. $2.25, Three Kings paying homage to Infant Jesus.
| | | | |
|---|---|---|---|
| 376 | A63 | 5c multicolored | .20 .20 |
| 377 | A63 | 15c multicolored | .20 .20 |
| 378 | A63 | 30c multicolored | .20 .20 |
| 379 | A63 | $2.25 multicolored | .40 .40 |
| | | Nos. 376-379 (4) | 1.00 1.00 |

Flowers: 30c, Heliconia bihai. 55c, Ruellia tuberosa. $1.50, Gesneria ventricosa.

**1979, Mar. 19** Perf. 14
| | | | |
|---|---|---|---|
| 380 | A64 | 5c multicolored | .20 .20 |
| 381 | A64 | 30c multicolored | .35 .35 |
| 382 | A64 | 55c multicolored | .45 .45 |
| 383 | A64 | $1.50 multicolored | .75 1.10 |
| | | Nos. 380-383 (4) | 1.75 2.10 |

See Nos. 393-396.

**Rowland Hill and St. Christopher No. 1 — A65**

Rowland Hill and: 15c, St. Kitts-Nevis #233. 50c, Great Britain #4. $2.50, St. Kitts-Nevis #64.

**1979, July 2** Litho. Perf. 14½
| | | | |
|---|---|---|---|
| 384 | A65 | 5c multicolored | .20 .20 |
| 385 | A65 | 15c multicolored | .20 .20 |
| 386 | A65 | 50c multicolored | .25 .25 |
| 387 | A65 | $2.50 multicolored | .45 .45 |
| | | Nos. 384-387 (4) | 1.10 1.10 |

Sir Rowland Hill (1795-1879), originator of penny postage.

**The Woodman's Daughter, by Millais — A66**

Paintings by John Everett Millais and IYC Emblem: 25c, Cherry Ripe. 30c, The Rescue, horiz. 55c, Bubbles. $1, Christ in the House of His Parents.

**1979, Nov. 12** Litho. Perf. 14
| | | | |
|---|---|---|---|
| 388 | A66 | 5c multicolored | .20 .20 |
| 389 | A66 | 25c multicolored | .25 .25 |
| 390 | A66 | 30c multicolored | .25 .25 |
| 391 | A66 | 55c multicolored | .30 .30 |
| | | Nos. 388-391 (4) | 1.00 1.00 |

**Souvenir Sheet**
| | | | |
|---|---|---|---|
| 392 | A66 | $1 multicolored | 1.00 1.00 |

Christmas 1979; Intl. Year of the Child.

**Flower Type of 1979**

Flowers: 4c, Clerodendrum aculeatum. 55c, Inga laurina. $1.50, Epidendrum difforme. $2, Salvia serontina.

**1980, Feb. 4** Litho. Perf. 14
| | | | |
|---|---|---|---|
| 393 | A64 | 4c multicolored | .35 .30 |
| 394 | A64 | 55c multicolored | .50 .30 |
| 395 | A64 | $1.50 multicolored | 1.40 1.25 |
| 396 | A64 | $2 multicolored | 1.25 1.75 |
| | | Nos. 393-396 (4) | 3.50 3.50 |

**Nativity, Sforza Book of Hours — A54**

**1976, Nov. 1** Perf. 14
| | | | |
|---|---|---|---|
| 328 | A54 | 20c purple & multi | .20 .20 |
| 329 | A54 | 40c dk blue & multi | .40 .40 |
| 330 | A54 | 45c multicolored | .40 .40 |
| 331 | A54 | $1 multicolored | 1.00 1.00 |
| | | Nos. 328-331 (4) | |

Christmas (Paintings): 40c, Virgin and Child, by Bernardino Pintoricchio. 45c, Our Lady of Good Child, by Ford Maddox Brown. $1, Christ Child, by Margaret W. Tarrant.

**Queen Planting Tree, 1966 Visit — A55**

**1977, Feb. 7** Litho. Perf. 14x13½
| | | | |
|---|---|---|---|
| 332 | A55 | 50c multicolored | .20 .20 |
| 333 | A55 | $1 multicolored | .60 .70 |
| 334 | A55 | $1.50 multicolored | .70 .70 |
| | | Nos. 332-334 (3) | |

Designs: 55c, The scepter. $1.50, Bishops paying homage to the Queen.
25th anniv. of the reign of Elizabeth II.

**Christ on the Cross, by Niccolo di Liberatore — A56**

Easter: 30c, Resurrection (imitator of Mantegna). 50c, Resurrection, by Ugolino, horiz. $1, Christ Rising from Tomb, by Gaudenzio.

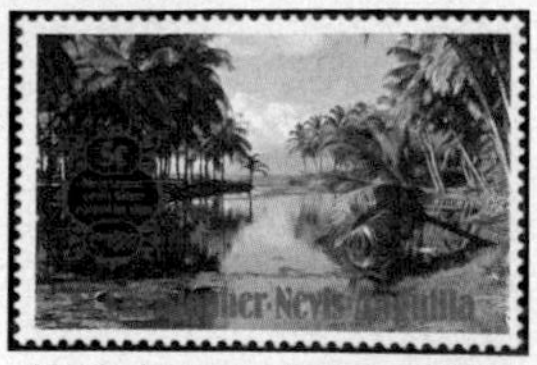

Nevis Lagoon, London 1980 Emblem — A67

**1980, May 6** **Litho.** *Perf. 13½*
**397** A67 5c shown .20 .20
**398** A67 30c Fig Tree Church, vert. .25 .20
**399** A67 55c Nisbet Plantation .40 .35
**400** A67 $3 Lord Nelson, by Fuger, vert. 2.25 1.90
*Nos. 397-400 (4)* 3.10 2.65

**Souvenir Sheet**

**401** A67 75c Nelson Falling, by D. Dighton 2.25 .75

London 80 Intl. Phil. Exhib., May 6-14; Lord Nelson, (1758-1805).

**WAR TAX STAMPS**

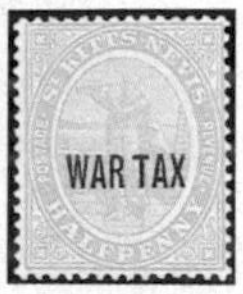
WAR TAX

No. 12 Overprinted

**1916** **Wmk. 3** *Perf. 14*
**MR1** A1 ½p green 1.00 .50

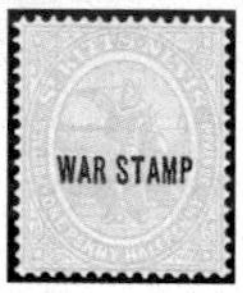
WAR STAMP

Type of 1905-18 Issue Overprinted

**1918**
**MR2** A1 1½p orange .80 .80

**OFFICIAL STAMPS**

**Catalogue values for unused stamps in this section are for Never Hinged items.**

Nos. 359, 361, 363-369 Overprinted: OFFICIAL

*Perf. 14½x14*

**1980** **Litho.** **Wmk. 373**
**O1** A61 12c multicolored 1.10 .90
**O2** A61 25c multicolored .20 .20
**O3** A61 40c multicolored .55 .50
**O4** A61 45c multicolored 2.25 2.00
**O5** A61 50c multicolored .40 .45
**O6** A61 55c multicolored 1.10 .40
**O7** A61 $1 multicolored 1.00 *2.25*
**O8** A61 $5 multicolored 1.10 *2.75*
**O9** A61 $10 multicolored 2.25 *4.00*
*Nos. O1-O9 (9)* 9.95 13.45

# ST. LUCIA

sānt 'lü-shə

LOCATION — Island in the West Indies, one of the Windward group
GOVT. — Independent state in British Commonwealth
AREA — 240 sq. mi.
POP. — 154,020 (1999 est.)
CAPITAL — Castries

The British colony of St. Lucia became an associated state March 1, 1967, and independent in 1979.

12 Pence = 1 Shilling
100 Cents = 1 Dollar (1949)

**Catalogue values for unused stamps in this country are for Never Hinged items, beginning with Scott 127 in the regular postage section, Scott C1 in the air post section, Scott J3 in the postage due section, and Scott O1 in the officials section.**

**Watermarks**

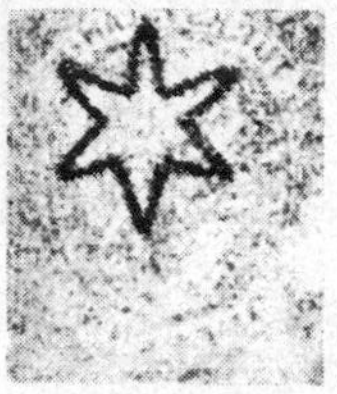

Wmk. 5 — Small Star

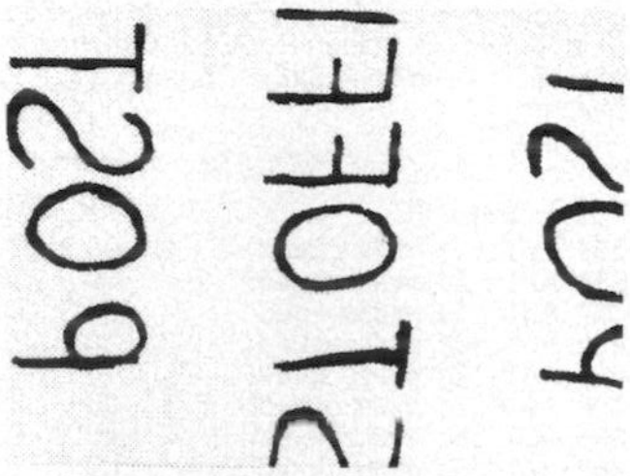

Wmk. 380 — "POST OFFICE"

Values for unused stamps are for examples with original gum as defined in the catalogue introduction. Very fine examples of Nos. 1-26 will have perforations touching the design on at least one side due to the narrow spacing of the stamps on the plates. Stamps with perfs clear of the framelines on all four sides are very scarce and will command higher prices.

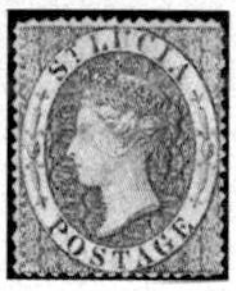

Queen Victoria — A1

*Perf. 14 to 16*

**1860, Dec. 18** **Engr.** **Wmk. 5**
**1** A1 (1p) rose red 100.00 75.00
*a.* Double impression *2,100.*
*b.* Horiz. pair, imperf vert. —
**2** A1 (4p) deep blue 240.00 175.00
*a.* Horiz. pair, imperf vert. —
**3** A1 (6p) green 325.00 225.00
*a.* Horiz. pair, imperf vert. —
*Nos. 1-3 (3)* 665.00 475.00

For types overprinted see #15, 17, 19-26.

**1863** **Wmk. 1** *Perf. 12½*
**4** A1 (1p) lake 77.50 *92.50*
**5** A1 (4p) slate blue 125.00 140.00
**6** A1 (6p) emerald 175.00 175.00
*Nos. 4-6 (3)* 377.50 407.50

Nos. 4-6 exist imperforate on stamp paper, from proof sheets.

**1864**
**7** A1 (1p) black 22.50 14.00
**8** A1 (4p) yellow 190.00 35.00
*a.* (4p) olive yellow 375.00 92.50
*b.* (4p) lemon yellow *1,750.*
**9** A1 (6p) violet 125.00 32.50
*a.* (6p) lilac 200.00 32.50
*b.* (6p) deep lilac 150.00 37.50
**10** A1 (1sh) red orange 250.00 29.00
*a.* (1sh) orange 350.00 29.00
*c.* Horiz. pair, imperf between —
*Nos. 7-10 (4)* 587.50 110.50

Nos. 7-10 exist imperforate on stamp paper, from proof sheets.

*Perf. 14*

**11** A1 (1p) deep black 27.50 17.50
*a.* Horiz. pair, imperf between —
**12** A1 (4p) yellow 110.00 21.00
*a.* (4p) olive yellow 300.00 97.50
**13** A1 (6p) pale lilac 110.00 21.00
*a.* (6p) deep lilac 110.00 35.00
*b.* (6p) violet 250.00 75.00
**14** A1 (1sh) deep orange 150.00 19.00
*a.* (1sh) orange 240.00 25.00
*Nos. 11-14 (4)* 397.50 78.50

Type of 1860 Surcharged in Black or Red:

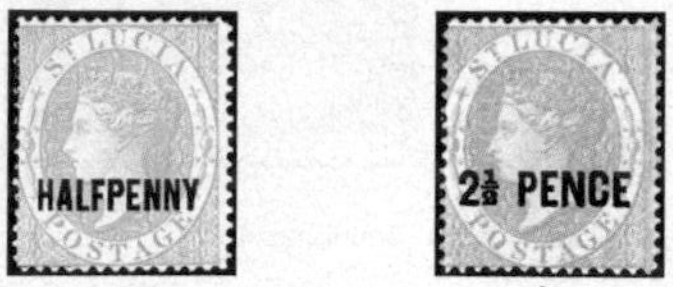
HALFPENNY
2½ PENCE

a b

**1881**
**15** A1(a) ½p green 70.00 *92.50*
**17** A1(b) 2½p scarlet 32.50 24.00

**1883-84** **Wmk. Crown and CA (2)**
**19** A1(a) ½p green 21.00 *30.00*
**20** A1(a) 1p black (R) 29.00 10.50
*a.* Half used as ½p on cover —
**21** A1(a) 4p yellow 300.00 20.00
**22** A1(a) 6p violet 30.00 29.00
**23** A1(a) 1sh orange 300.00 190.00
*Nos. 19-23 (5)* 680.00 279.50

**1884** *Perf. 12*
**24** A1(a) 4p yellow 300.00 32.50

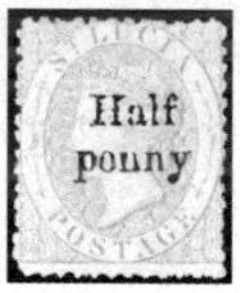
Half
penny

**1885** **Wmk. 1** *Perf. 12½*
**25** A1 ½p emerald 75.
**26** A1 6p slate blue 1,250.

Nos. 25 and 26 were prepared for use but not issued.

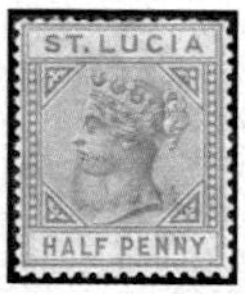

A5

Die B

For explanation of dies A and B see "Dies of British Colonial Stamps..." in the catalogue Table of Contents.

**1883-98** **Typo.** **Wmk. 2** *Perf. 14*
**27** A5 ½p green ('91) 2.40 1.00
*a.* Die A ('83) 8.75 4.50
**28** A5 1p rose (die A) ('83) 40.00 10.50
**29** A5 1p lilac ('91) 3.75 .30
*a.* Die A ('86) 7.50 *6.25*
*b.* Die A, imperf., pair 750.00
**30** A5 2p ultra & brn org ('98) 3.50 1.00
**31** A5 2½p ultra ('91) 4.75 1.00
*a.* Die A ('83) 42.50 2.25
**32** A5 3p lilac & grn ('91) 4.75 *6.25*
*a.* Die A ('86) 125.00 17.50
**33** A5 4p brown ('93) 3.00 *2.50*
*a.* Die A ('85) 32.50 1.40
*b.* Die A, imperf., pair 1,050.
**34** A5 6p vio (die A; '85) *300.00* *210.00*
*a.* Imperf., pair 1,800.
**35** A5 6p lil & bl (die A; '86) 4.25 *9.75*
*a.* Die B ('91) 27.50 27.50
**36** A5 1sh brn org (die A) ('85) 400.00 150.00
**37** A5 1sh lil & red ('91) 6.25 *5.75*
*a.* Die A ('86) 110.00 30.00
**38** A5 5sh lil & org ('91) 55.00 *140.00*
**39** A5 10sh lil & blk ('91) 97.50 *150.00*
*Nos. 27-39 (13)* 925.15 688.05

Nos. 32, 32a, 35a and 33a Surcharged in Black:

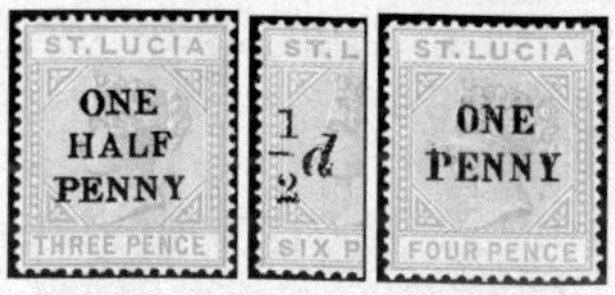
ONE HALF PENNY
½d
ONE PENNY

No. 40 No. 41 No. 42

**1892**
**40** A5 ½p on 3p lil & grn 80.00 25.00
*a.* Die A 150.00 80.00
*b.* Dbl. surch., die B 800.00 725.00
*c.* Invtd. surch., die B 2,000. 700.00
*d.* Triple surch., one on back *1,500.*
**41** A5 ½p on half of 6p lilac & blue 24.00 3.75
*a.* Slanting serif 210.00 150.00
*c.* Without the bar of "½" 225.00 160.00
*d.* "2" of "½" omitted 525.00 575.00
*e.* Surcharged sideways 1,250.
*f.* Double surcharge 625.00 625.00
*g.* Triple surcharge *1,150.*
**42** A5 1p on 4p brown 5.00 *4.00*
*b.* Double surcharge 225.00
*c.* Inverted surcharge 825.00 750.00
*Nos. 40-42 (3)* 109.00 32.75

No. 40 is found with wide or narrow "O" in "ONE," and large or small "A" in "HALF." The narrow "O" and small "A" varieties are worth about 3 times the normal No. 40.

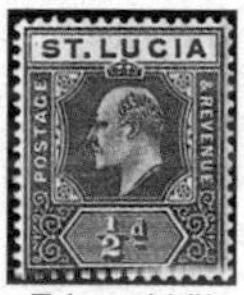

Edward VII
A9

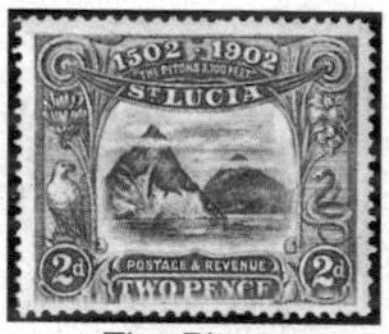

The Pitons
A10

Numerals of 3p, 6p, 1sh and 5sh of type A9 are in color on plain tablet.

**1902-03** **Typo.**
**43** A9 ½p violet & green 3.00 1.60
**44** A9 1p violet & car rose 5.25 .90
**46** A9 2½p violet & ultra 22.50 6.50
**47** A9 3p violet & yellow 6.25 *8.75*
**48** A9 1sh green & black 10.50 *30.00*
*Nos. 43-48 (5)* 47.50 *47.75*

**Wmk. 1 sideways**

**1902, Dec. 16** **Engr.**
**49** A10 2p brown & green 9.50 2.50

Fourth centenary of the discovery of the island by Columbus.

**1904-05** **Typo.** **Wmk. 3**
**50** A9 ½p violet & green 4.50 .60
**51** A9 1p violet & car rose 6.25 1.25
**52** A9 2½p violet & ultra 16.00 1.25
**53** A9 3p violet & yellow 6.25 3.25
**54** A9 6p vio & dp vio ('05) 16.00 *20.00*
**55** A9 1sh green & blk ('05) 32.50 26.00
**56** A9 5sh green & car ('05) 72.50 *175.00*
*Nos. 50-56 (7)* 154.00 227.35

#50, 51, 52, 54 are on both ordinary and chalky paper. #55 is on chalky paper only.

**1907-10**
**57** A9 ½p green 1.75 1.00
**58** A9 1p carmine 4.50 .30
**59** A9 2½p ultra 4.00 1.75

**Chalky Paper**

**60** A9 3p violet, *yel* ('09) 3.00 *12.50*
**61** A9 6p violet & red violet 8.75 *29.00*
*a.* 6p violet & dull vio ('10) 57.50 *72.50*
**62** A9 1sh black, *grn* ('09) 5.00 *8.25*
**63** A9 5sh green & red, *yel* 62.50 *72.50*
*Nos. 57-63 (7)* 89.50 *125.30*

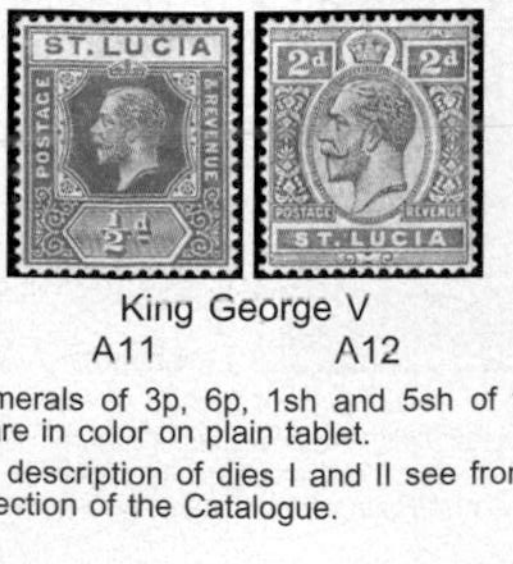

King George V
A11 A12

Numerals of 3p, 6p, 1sh and 5sh of type A11 are in color on plain tablet.

For description of dies I and II see front of this section of the Catalogue.

Die I

**1912-19**

**Ordinary Paper**

64 A11 ½p deep green .75 .50
65 A11 1p scarlet 3.75 .20
a. 1p carmine 2.00 .20
66 A12 2p gray ('13) 1.60 *4.50*
67 A11 2½p ultra 2.50 3.00

**Chalky Paper**

**Numeral on White Tablet**

68 A11 3p violet, *yel* 1.40 *2.50*
a. Die II 11.00 *42.50*
69 A11 6p vio & red vio 2.25 *12.00*
70 A11 1sh black, *green* 3.50 *5.25*
a. 1sh black, *bl grn, ol back* 8.25 *8.75*
71 A11 1sh fawn 10.50 *47.50*
72 A11 5sh green & red, *yel* 25.00 *77.50*
*Nos. 64-72 (9)* 51.25 *152.95*

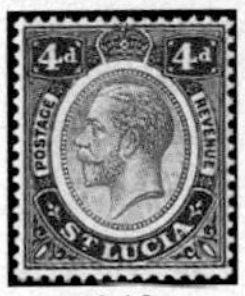
A13

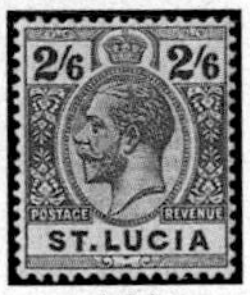
A14

**1913-14**

**Chalky Paper**

73 A13 4p scar & blk, *yel* 1.00 *2.25*
74 A14 2sh6p black & red, *bl* 24.00 *40.00*

**Surface-colored Paper**

75 A13 4p scar & blk, *yel* .75 *1.60*

Die II

**1921-24** **Wmk. 4**

**Ordinary Paper**

76 A11 ½p green .80 .50
77 A11 1p carmine 9.75 *15.00*
78 A11 1p dk brn ('22) 1.50 .20
79 A13 1½p rose red ('22) .75 *2.75*
80 A12 2p gray .75 .20
81 A11 2½p ultra 4.00 *2.75*
82 A11 2½p orange ('24) 11.50 *52.50*
83 A11 3p ultra ('22) 2.75 *11.50*

**Chalky Paper**

84 A11 3p violet, *yel* 1.25 *12.50*
85 A13 4p scar & blk, *yel* ('24) 1.25 *2.75*
86 A11 6p vio & red vio 2.00 *5.00*
87 A11 1sh fawn 2.50 *3.50*
88 A14 2sh6p blk & red, *bl* ('24) 19.00 *27.50*
89 A11 5sh grn & red, *yel* 50.00 *77.50*
*Nos. 76-89 (14)* 107.80 *214.15*

Common Design Types pictured following the introduction.

**Silver Jubilee Issue**

Common Design Type

**1935, May 6** **Engr.** ***Perf. 13½x14***

91 CD301 ½p green & blk .20 1.00
92 CD301 2p gray blk & ultra .50 1.00
93 CD301 2½p blue & brn 1.00 1.25
94 CD301 1sh brt vio & ind 7.75 *9.25*
*Nos. 91-94 (4)* 9.45 12.50
Set, never hinged 14.50

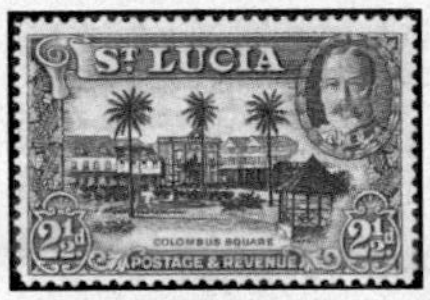
Columbus Square, Castries
A16

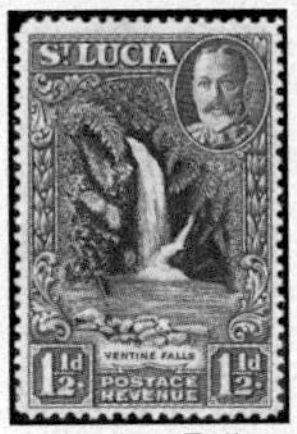
Ventine Falls
A17

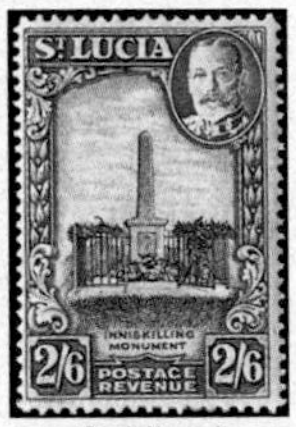
Soldiers' Monument
A19

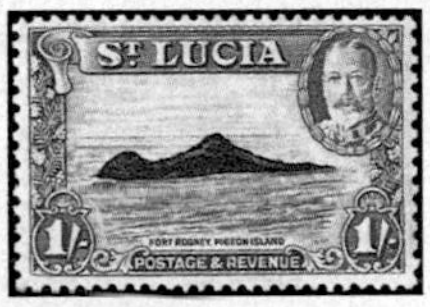
Fort Rodney, Pigeon Island
A18

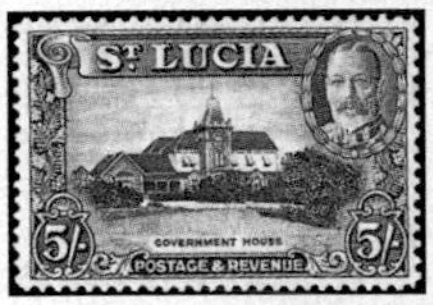
Government House
A20

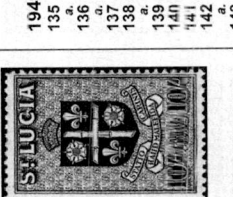

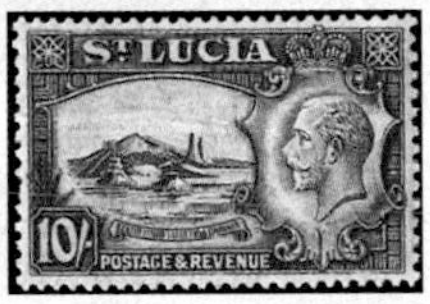
Seal of the Colony
A21

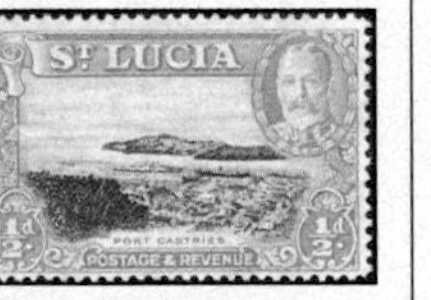
Port Castries
A15

**1936, Mar. 1** ***Perf. 14***

**Center in Black**

95 A15 ½p light green .30 .50
a. Perf. 13x12 2.50 *13.50*
96 A16 1p dark brown .40 .20
a. Perf. 13x12 3.00 2.75
97 A17 1½p carmine .60 .30
a. Perf. 12x13 7.75 2.50
98 A15 2p gray .55 .20
99 A16 2½p blue .55 .20
100 A17 3p dull green 1.40 .75
101 A15 4p brown .55 *1.00*
102 A16 6p orange 1.00 1.00
103 A18 1sh light blue, perf. 13x12 1.25 *2.50*
104 A19 2sh6p ultra 9.50 *14.50*
105 A20 5sh violet 10.00 *21.00*
106 A21 10sh car rose, perf. 13x12 52.50 *72.50*
*Nos. 95-106 (12)* 78.60 *114.65*
Set, never hinged 140.00

Nos. 95a, 96a and 97a are coils.
Issue date: Nos. 95a, 96a, Apr. 8.

**Coronation Issue**

Common Design Type

**1937, May 12** ***Perf. 11x11½***

107 CD302 1p dark purple .30 .35
108 CD302 1½p dark carmine .55 .20
109 CD302 2½p deep ultra .55 1.25
*Nos. 107-109 (3)* 1.40 1.80
Set, never hinged 1.25

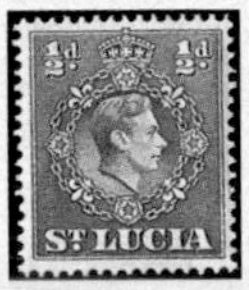
King George VI — A22

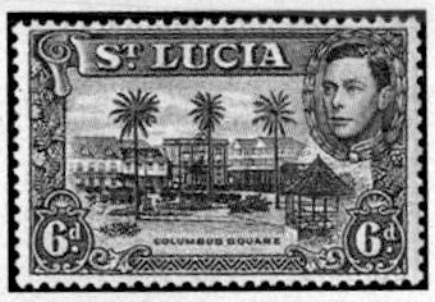
Columbus Square, Castries
A23

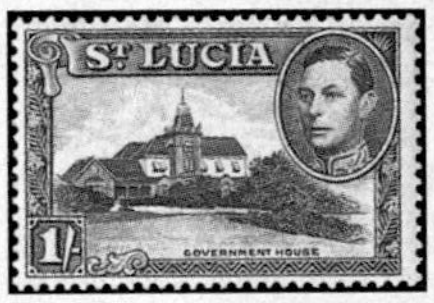
Government House
A24

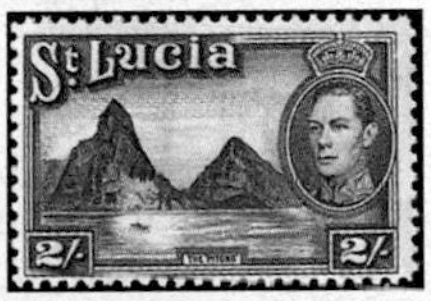
The Pitons
A25

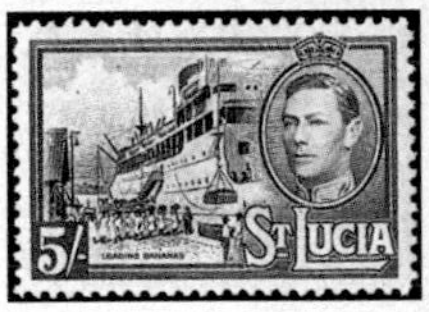
Loading Bananas
A26

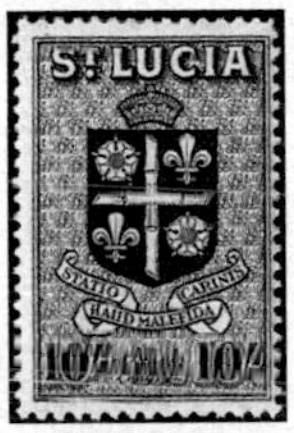
Arms of the Colony — A27

***Perf. 12½ (#110-111, 1½p-3½p, 8p, 3sh, 5sh, £1), 12 (6p, 1sh, 2sh, 10sh)***

**1938-48**

110 A22 ½p green ('43) .20 .20
a. Perf. 14½x14 1.40 .20
111 A22 1p deep violet .20 .20
a. Perf. 14½x14 1.60 .75
112 A22 1p red, Perf. 14½x14 ('47) .20 .20
a. Perf. 12½ .40 .20
113 A22 1½p carmine ('43) .70 1.00
a. Perf. 14½x14 1.25 .40
114 A22 2p gray ('43) .20 .20
a. Perf. 14½x14 2.00 *1.50*
115 A22 2½p ultra ('43) .20 .20
a. Perf. 14½x14 3.00 .20
116 A22 2½p violet ('47) .65 .20
117 A22 3p red org ('43) .20 .20
a. Perf. 14½x14 .80 .20
118 A22 3½p brt ultra ('47) .60 .20
119 A23 6p magenta ('48) 7.00 1.75
a. Perf. 13½ 2.00 .35
120 A22 8p choc ('46) 2.50 .30
121 A24 1sh lt brn ('48) .50 .20
a. Perf. 13½ .40 .30
122 A25 2sh red vio & sl bl 2.25 1.25
123 A22 3sh brt red vio ('46) 5.75 1.75
124 A26 5sh rose vio & blk 8.50 8.25
125 A27 10sh black, *yel* 5.75 *9.25*
126 A22 £1 sepia ('46) 7.50 8.25
*Nos. 110-126 (17)* 42.90 33.60
Set, never hinged 55.00

See Nos. 135-148.

**Catalogue values for unused stamps in this section, from this point to the end of the section, are for Never Hinged items.**

**Peace Issue**

Common Design Type

***Perf. 13½x14***

**1946, Oct. 8** **Wmk. 4** **Engr.**

127 CD303 1p lilac .20 .20
128 CD303 3½p deep blue .20 .20

**Silver Wedding Issue**

Common Design Types

**1948, Nov. 26** **Photo.** ***Perf. 14x14½***

129 CD304 1p scarlet .20 .20

**Engraved; Name Typographed**

***Perf. 11½x11***

130 CD305 £1 violet brown 16.00 35.00

**UPU Issue**

Common Design Types

**Engr.; Name Typo. on 6c, 12c.**

***Perf. 13½, 11x11½***

**1949, Oct. 10** **Wmk. 4**

131 CD306 5c violet .20 .60
132 CD307 6c deep orange 1.60 2.00
133 CD308 12c red lilac .20 .20
134 CD309 24c blue green .30 .20
*Nos. 131-134 (4)* 2.30 3.00

Types of 1938

Values in Cents and Dollars

**1949, Oct. 1** **Engr.** ***Perf. 12½***

135 A22 1c green .25 .20
a. Perf. 14 2.50 .40
136 A22 2c rose lilac 1.00 .20
a. Perf. 14½x14 2.50 1.00
137 A22 3c red 1.00 *1.75*
138 A22 4c gray .75 .20
a. Perf. 14½x14 *8,250.*
139 A22 5c violet 1.00 .20
140 A22 6c red orange .75 *2.75*
141 A22 7c ultra 3.00 *3.75*
142 A22 12c rose lake 5.75 *2.75*
a. Perf. 14½x14 ('50) 525.00 410.00
143 A22 16c brown 3.50 .50

***Perf 11½***

144 A27 24c Prus blue .50 .20
145 A27 48c olive green 1.60 1.25
146 A27 $1.20 purple 2.40 *8.25*
147 A27 $2.40 blue green 3.50 *17.50*
148 A27 $4.80 dark car rose 9.25 18.00
*Nos. 135-148 (14)* 34.25 57.50

Nos. 144 to 148 are of a type similar to A27, but with the denomination in the top corners and "St. Lucia" at the bottom.

For overprints see Nos. 152-155.

**University Issue**

Common Design Types

***Perf. 14x14½***

**1951, Feb. 16** **Wmk. 4**

149 CD310 3c red & gray black .45 .50
150 CD311 12c brn car & blk .65 .50

## Phoenix Rising from Burning Buildings — A28

**1951, June 19    Engr. & Typo.    Perf. 13½x13**

Reconstruction of Castries.

151   A28   12c deep blue & carmine    .25   1.00

**1951, Sept. 25    Engr.    Perf. 12½**

| | | | | |
|---|---|---|---|---|
| 152 | A22 | 2c rose lilac | .20 | .85 |
| 153 | A22 | 4c gray | .20 | .85 |
| 154 | A22 | 5c violet | .20 | .85 |
| 155 | A22 | 12c rose lilac | .75 | 2.90 |
| | | Nos. 152-155 (4) | 1.35 | 2.90 |

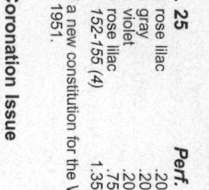 

Nos. 136, 138, 139 and 142 Overprinted in Black

Adoption of a new constitution for the Windward Islands, 1951.

## Coronation Issue — Common Design Type

**1953, June 2    Engr.    Perf. 13½x13**

156   CD312   3c carmine & black    .45   .45

## Queen Elizabeth II — A29

**1953-54    Engr.    Perf. 14½x14**

| | | | | |
|---|---|---|---|---|
| 157 | A29 | 1c green | .20 | .20 |
| 158 | A29 | 2c rose lilac | .20 | .20 |
| 159 | A29 | 3c red | .20 | .20 |
| 160 | A29 | 4c gray | .20 | .20 |
| 161 | A29 | 5c violet | .20 | .20 |
| 162 | A29 | 6c orange | .20 | .20 |
| 163 | A29 | 8c rose lake | .20 | .20 |
| 164 | A29 | 10c ultra | .35 | .20 |
| 165 | A29 | 15c brown | .35 | .20 |

## Arms of St. Lucia — A30

**Perf. 11x11½**

| | | | | |
|---|---|---|---|---|
| 166 | A30 | 25c green | .40 | .20 |
| 167 | A30 | 50c brown olive | .95 | .95 |
| 168 | A30 | $1 blue green | 4.50 | 2.25 |
| 169 | A30 | $2.50 dark car rose | 5.50 | 9.00 |
| | | Nos. 157-169 (13) | 17.00 | 17.00 |

Issued: 2c, 10/28; 4c, 1/7/54; 1c, 5c, 4/1/54; others, 9/2/54.

## West Indies Federation — Common Design Type

**1958, Apr. 22    Perf. 11½x11    Wmk. 314**

| | | | | |
|---|---|---|---|---|
| 170 | CD313 | 3c green | .35 | .20 |
| 171 | CD313 | 6c blue | .60 | .95 |
| 172 | CD313 | 12c carmine rose | .80 | .35 |
| | | Nos. 170-172 (3) | 1.75 | 1.50 |

16th Century Ship and Pitons — A31

---

## St. Lucia Stamp of 1860 — A32

**1960, Jan. 1    Engr.    Perf. 12½x13**

| | | | | |
|---|---|---|---|---|
| 173 | A32 | 8c carmine rose | .20 | .25 |
| 174 | A32 | 10c orange | .30 | .30 |
| 175 | A32 | 25c dark blue | .70 | .70 |
| | | Nos. 173-175 (3) | 1.25 | 1.25 |

Centenary of St. Lucia's first postage stamps.

**1960, Dec. 18    Engr.    Perf. 13½**

| | | | | |
|---|---|---|---|---|
| 176 | A32 | 5c ultra & red brown | .20 | .20 |
| 177 | A32 | 16c yel grn & blue blk | .65 | .30 |
| 178 | A32 | 25c carmine & green | 1.50 | 1.50 |
| | | Nos. 176-178 (3) | | |

Granting of new constitution.

## Freedom from Hunger Issue — Common Design Type

**1963, June 4    Photo.    Perf. 14x14½**

179   CD314   25c green    .60   .60

## Red Cross Centenary Issue — Common Design Type

**1963, Sept. 2    Litho.    Wmk. 314    Perf. 13**

| | | | | |
|---|---|---|---|---|
| 180 | CD315 | 4c black & red | .20 | .20 |
| 181 | CD315 | 25c ultra & red | 1.00 | 1.00 |

## Fishing Boats, Soufrière Bay — A35

**1964, Mar. 1    Photo.    Wmk. 314    Perf. 14½**

| | | | | |
|---|---|---|---|---|
| 182 | A33 | 1c dark car rose | .20 | .20 |
| 183 | A33 | 2c violet | .35 | .35 |
| 184 | A33 | 4c brt blue green | .35 | .35 |
| 185 | A33 | 5c slate blue | .35 | .35 |
| 186 | A33 | 6c brown | .45 | .60 |
| 187 | A34 | 8c lt blue & multi | .60 | .60 |
| 188 | A34 | 10c blue & multi | .20 | .20 |
| 189 | A35 | 12c multicolored | .40 | .75 |
| 190 | A35 | 15c blue & ocher | .25 | .20 |
| 191 | A35 | 25c multicolored | .40 | .20 |
| 192 | A35 | 35c dk blue & buff | .65 | .20 |
| 193 | A35 | 50c brt blue, blk & buff | .20 | .20 |
| 194 | A35 | $1 multicolored | 2.00 | .90 |
| 195 | A35 | $2.50 multicolored | 9.80 | 6.80 |
| | | Nos. 182-195 (14) | | |

Designs: 15c, Pigeon Island. 25c, Reduit Beach. 35c, Castries Harbor. 50c, The Pitons. $1, Vigie Beach, vert. $2.50, Queen Elizabeth II, close-up.

## Shakespeare Issue — Common Design Type

**1964, Apr. 23    Perf. 14x14½    Wmk. 314**

196   CD316   10c bright green    .40   .25

## ITU Issue — Common Design Type

**1965, May 17    Litho.    Perf. 11x11½    Wmk. 314**

| | | | | |
|---|---|---|---|---|
| 197 | CD317 | 2c red lilac & brt pink | .20 | .20 |
| 198 | CD317 | 50c lilac & yel grn | 1.30 | 1.30 |

---

## Int'l. Cooperation Year Issue — Common Design Type

**1965, Oct. 25    Wmk. 314    Perf. 14½**

| | | | | |
|---|---|---|---|---|
| 199 | CD318 | 1c blue grn & claret | .20 | .20 |
| 200 | CD318 | 25c lt violet & grn | .50 | .50 |

## Churchill Memorial Issue — Common Design Type

**1966, Jan. 24    Photo.    Perf. 14**

| | | | | |
|---|---|---|---|---|
| 201 | CD319 | 4c bright blue | .20 | .20 |
| 202 | CD319 | 6c green | .20 | .20 |
| 203 | CD319 | 25c brown | .40 | .40 |
| 204 | CD319 | 35c violet | .60 | .60 |
| | | Nos. 201-204 (4) | 1.40 | 1.40 |

## Royal Visit Issue — Common Design Type
### Design in Black, Gold and Carmine Rose

**1966, Feb. 4    Litho.    Perf. 11x12**

| | | | | |
|---|---|---|---|---|
| 205 | CD320 | 15c multicolored | .25 | .25 |
| 206 | CD320 | 25c dk carmine rose | .85 | .85 |

## World Cup Soccer Issue — Common Design Type

**1966, July 1    Litho.    Perf. 14**

| | | | | |
|---|---|---|---|---|
| 207 | CD321 | 4c multicolored | .25 | .25 |
| 208 | CD321 | 25c multicolored | .65 | .65 |

## WHO Headquarters Issue — Common Design Type

**1966, Sept. 20    Litho.    Perf. 14**

| | | | | |
|---|---|---|---|---|
| 209 | CD322 | 4c multicolored | .20 | .20 |
| 210 | CD322 | 25c multicolored | .40 | .30 |

## UNESCO Anniversary Issue — Common Design Type

**1966, Dec. 1    Litho.    Perf. 14**

| | | | | |
|---|---|---|---|---|
| 211 | CD323 | 4c "Education" | .20 | .20 |
| 212 | CD323 | 12c "Science" | .30 | .30 |
| 213 | CD323 | 25c "Culture" | 1.10 | 1.10 |
| | | Nos. 211-213 (3) | | |

## Associated State
Nos. 183, 185-194 Overprinted in Red: "STATEHOOD / 1st MARCH 1967"

**1967, Mar. 1    Photo.    Wmk. 314    Perf. 14½**

| | | | | |
|---|---|---|---|---|
| 215 | A33 | 2c violet | .30 | .30 |
| 216 | A33 | 5c slate blue | .20 | .20 |
| 217 | A33 | 6c brown | .20 | .20 |
| 218 | A34 | 8c lt blue & multi | .30 | .20 |
| 219 | A34 | 10c blue & multi | .40 | .20 |
| 220 | A35 | 12c multicolored | .50 | .50 |
| 221 | A35 | 15c blue & ocher | .40 | .40 |
| 222 | A35 | 25c multicolored | .90 | .50 |
| 223 | A35 | 35c dk blue & buff | .75 | .55 |
| 224 | A35 | 50c brt blue, blk & buff | .75 | .75 |
| 225 | A35 | $1 multicolored | 5.25 | 4.15 |
| | | Nos. 215-225 (11) | | |

The 1c and $2.50, similarly overprinted, were not sold to the public at the post office but were acknowledged belatedly (May 10) by the government and declared valid. The 1c, 6c and $2.50 overprints exist in black as well as red. No. 213 also exists with this overprint in black and in black.

---

**1967, Oct. 16    Wmk. 314    Perf. 14½**

| | | | | |
|---|---|---|---|---|
| 227 | A36 | 4c black, gold & multi | .20 | .20 |
| 228 | A36 | 25c multicolored | .30 | .20 |

Christmas 1967.

**1968, Mar. 8    Photo.    Wmk. 314    Perf. 14½x14**

| | | | | |
|---|---|---|---|---|
| 229 | A37 | 10c multicolored | .20 | .20 |
| 230 | A37 | 35c multicolored | .55 | .55 |

Visit of the Marylebone Cricket Club to the West Indies, Jan.-Feb. 1968.

## "Noli me Tangere" by Titian — A38

**1968, Mar. 25    Photo.    Perf. 14½**

| | | | | |
|---|---|---|---|---|
| 231 | A38 | 10c multicolored | .20 | .20 |
| 232 | A38 | 15c multicolored | .20 | .20 |
| 233 | A38 | 25c multicolored | .25 | .25 |
| 234 | A38 | 35c multicolored | .80 | .80 |
| | | Nos. 231-234 (4) | | |

Easter.

## Martin Luther King, Jr. — A39

**1968, July 4    Photo.    Wmk. 314    Perf. 13½x14**

| | | | | |
|---|---|---|---|---|
| 235 | A39 | 25c dp blue, blk & brn | .20 | .20 |
| 236 | A39 | 35c violet, blk & brn | .20 | .20 |
| | | Nos. 235-236 (2) | | |

Dr. Martin Luther King, Jr. (1929-68), American civil rights leader.

## Virgin and Child in Glory, by Murillo — A40

**1968, Oct. 17    Photo.    Wmk. 314    Perf. 14½x14**

| | | | | |
|---|---|---|---|---|
| 237 | A40 | 5c dark blue & multi | .20 | .20 |
| 238 | A40 | 10c multicolored | .20 | .20 |
| 239 | A40 | 25c red brown & multi | .25 | .25 |
| 240 | A40 | 35c deep blue & multi | .90 | .90 |
| | | Nos. 237-240 (4) | | |

Christmas: 10c, 35c, Virgin and Child, by Bartolomé E. Murillo.

## Purple-throated Carib — A41

**1969, Jan. 10    Litho.    Wmk. 314    Perf. 14½**

| | | | | |
|---|---|---|---|---|
| 241 | A41 | 10c multicolored | .55 | .55 |
| 242 | A41 | 15c multicolored | .70 | .70 |
| 243 | A41 | 25c multicolored | 1.00 | 1.00 |
| 244 | A41 | 35c multicolored | 1.25 | 1.25 |
| | | Nos. 241-244 (4) | 3.50 | 3.50 |

Birds: 15c, 35c, St. Lucia parrot.

## Cricket Batsman and Gov. Frederick Clarke — A37

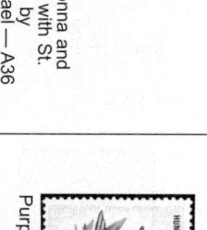

## Madonna and Child with St. John, by Raphael — A36

ST. LUCIA

## Ecce Homo, by Guido Reni — A42

Painting: 15c, 35c, The Resurrection, by Il Sodoma (Giovanni Antonio de Bazzi).

**1969, Mar. 20    Photo.    Wmk. 314    Perf. 14½x14**

| | | | |
|---|---|---|---|
| 245 | A42 | 10c purple & multi | .20 .20 |
| 246 | A42 | 15c green & multi | .20 .20 |
| 247 | A42 | 25c black & multi | .25 .25 |
| 248 | A42 | 35c ocher & multi | .90 .90 |

Nos. 245-248 (4)

Easter 1969.

## Map of Caribbean — A43

Design: 25c, 35c, Clasped hands and arrows with names of CARIFTA members.

**1969, May 29    Wmk. 314    Perf. 14**

| | | | |
|---|---|---|---|
| 249 | A43 | 5c violet blue & multi | .20 .20 |
| 250 | A43 | 10c deep plum & multi | .20 .20 |
| 251 | A43 | 25c green & multi | .20 .20 |
| 252 | A43 | 35c green & multi | .80 .80 |

Nos. 249-252 (4)

First anniversary of CARIFTA (Caribbean Free Trade Area).

## Silhouettes of Napoleon and Josephine — A44

**1969, Sept. 22    Photo.    Unwmk.    Perf. 14½x13**

**Gold Inscription; Gray and Brown Medallions**

| | | | |
|---|---|---|---|
| 253 | A44 | 15c dull blue | .20 .20 |
| 254 | A44 | 25c deep claret | .20 .20 |
| 255 | A44 | 35c deep green | .20 .50 |
| 256 | A44 | 50c yellow brown | .80 1.10 |

Nos. 253-256 (4)

Napoleon Bonaparte, 200th birth anniv.

## Madonna and Child, by Paul Delaroche — A45

Christmas: 10c, 35c, Holy Family, by Rubens.

**1969, Oct. 27    Photo.    Wmk. 314    Perf. 14½x14    Center Multicolored**

| | | | |
|---|---|---|---|
| 257 | A45 | 5c dp rose lil & gold | .20 .20 |
| 258 | A45 | 10c Prus blue & gold | .20 .20 |
| 259 | A45 | 25c maroon & gold | .25 .25 |
| 260 | A45 | 35c dp yel grn & gold | .90 .90 |

Nos. 257-260 (4)

## House of Assembly — A46

## Queen Elizabeth II, by A. C. Davidson-Houston — A47

2c, Roman Catholic Cathedral. 4c, Castries Boulevard. 5c, Castries Harbor. 6c, Sulphur springs. 10c, Vigie Airport. 12c, Reduit beach. 15c, Pigeon Island. 25c, The Pitons & sailboat. 35c, Marigot Bay. 50c, Diamond Waterfall. $1, St. Lucia flag & motto. $2.50, Coat of arms. $10, Map of St. Lucia.

**Wmk. 314 Sideways, Upright (#271-274)**

**1970-73    Litho.    Perf. 14½**

| | | | |
|---|---|---|---|
| 261 | A46 | 1c multicolored | .20 .20 |
| 262 | A46 | 2c multicolored | .20 .20 |
| | a. | Wmk. upright | .55 .55 |
| 263 | A46 | 4c multicolored | 1.10 1.00 |
| | a. | Wmk. upright | 1.00 1.00 |
| 264 | A46 | 5c multicolored | 1.75 1.75 |
| 265 | A46 | 6c multicolored | 1.40 |
| 266 | A46 | 10c multicolored | .20 .20 |
| 267 | A46 | 12c multicolored | .20 .20 |
| 268 | A46 | 15c multicolored | .20 .20 |
| 269 | A46 | 35c multicolored | .90 .90 |
| 270 | A46 | 50c multicolored | .45 .45 |
| 271 | A47 | $1 multicolored | .70 .70 |
| 272 | A47 | $2.50 multicolored | .45 1.75 |
| 273 | A47 | $5 multicolored | 1.40 3.75 |
| 274 | A47 | $10 multicolored | 6.00 8.50 |
| 274A | A47 | $10 multicolored | 16.00 17.50 |

Nos. 261-274, 274A (15)

Issued: #261-274, Feb. 1, 1970; #274A, Dec. 3, 1973; #262a, 263a, Mar. 15, 1974.

**1975, July 28    Wmk. 373**

| | | | |
|---|---|---|---|
| 263b | A46 | 5c multicolored | .65 1.90 |
| 264a | A46 | 6c multicolored | .85 .95 |
| 266a | A46 | 10c multicolored | 1.10 1.25 |
| 268a | A46 | 15c multicolored | 1.90 1.90 |

Nos. 263b-268a (4)    4.50 6.00

## The Three Marys at the Tomb, by Hogarth — A48

25c, The Sealing of the Tomb. $1, The Ascension. The designs are from the altarpiece painted by William Hogarth for the Church of St. Mary Redcliffe in Bristol, 1755-56.

**1970, Mar. 7    Litho.    Wmk. 314    Roulette 8½xPerf. 12½**

**Size: 27x54mm**

| | | | |
|---|---|---|---|
| 275 | A48 | 25c dark brown & multi | .20 .20 |
| 276 | A48 | 35c dark brown & multi | .20 .25 |

**Size: 38x54mm**

| | | | |
|---|---|---|---|
| 277 | A48 | $1 dark brown & multi | .35 .40 |
| | a. | Triptych (#275-277) | 1.75 1.75 |

Nos. 275-277 printed se-tenant in sheets of 30 (10 triptychs) with the center $1 stamp 10mm raised compared to the flanking 25c and 35c stamps.

Easter 1970.

## Charles Dickens and Characters from his Works — A49

**1970, June 8    Wmk. 314    Perf. 14**

| | | | |
|---|---|---|---|
| 278 | A49 | 1c brown & multi | .25 .25 |
| 279 | A49 | 25c Prus blue & multi | .25 .25 |
| 280 | A49 | 35c brown red & multi | .30 .30 |
| 281 | A49 | 50c red lilac & multi | .50 .60 |

Nos. 278-281 (4)    1.10 1.35

Charles Dickens (1812-70), English novelist.

## Nurse Holding Red Cross Emblem — A50

**1970, Aug. 18    Litho.    Wmk. 314    Perf. 14½x14**

| | | | |
|---|---|---|---|
| 282 | A50 | 10c multicolored | .20 .20 |
| 283 | A50 | 15c multicolored | .20 .20 |
| 284 | A50 | 25c buff & multi | .30 .30 |
| 285 | A50 | 35c multicolored | .40 .40 |

Nos. 282-285 (4)    1.10 1.10

15c, 35c, British, St. Lucia & Red Cross flags.

Centenary of British Red Cross Society.

## Madonna with the Lilies, by Luca della Robbia — A51

**1970, Nov. 16    Unwmk.    Perf. 11    Lithographed and Embossed**

| | | | |
|---|---|---|---|
| 286 | A51 | 5c dark blue & multi | .20 .20 |
| 287 | A51 | 10c violet blue & multi | .20 .20 |
| 288 | A51 | 35c car lake & multi | .35 .35 |
| 289 | A51 | 40c deep green & multi | .35 .35 |

Nos. 286-289 (4)    1.10 .95

Christmas 1970.

## Christ on the Cross, by Rubens — A52

**1971, Mar. 29    Litho.    Wmk. 314    Perf. 14x13½**

| | | | |
|---|---|---|---|
| 290 | A52 | 5c dull green & multi | .20 .20 |
| 291 | A52 | 10c dull red & multi | .20 .20 |
| 292 | A52 | 35c brt blue & multi | .35 .35 |
| 293 | A52 | 40c multicolored | .35 .35 |

Nos. 290-293 (4)    1.10 .95

Easter: 15c, 40c, Descent from the Cross, by Peter Paul Rubens.

## Moule à Chique Lighthouse — A53

Design: 25c, Beane Field Airport.

**1971, Apr. 30    Perf. 14½x14**

| | | | |
|---|---|---|---|
| 294 | A53 | 5c olive & multi | .30 .20 |
| 295 | A53 | 25c bister & multi | .60 .20 |

Opening of Beane Field Airport.

## View of Morne Fortune (Old Days) — A54

The "a" stamp shows an old print (as shown) and the "b" stamp a contemporary photograph of the same view (plain frame). 10c, Castries City. 25c, Pigeon Island. 50c, View from Government House.

**1971, Aug. 10    Litho.    Wmk. 314    Perf. 13½x14**

| | | | |
|---|---|---|---|
| 296 | A54 | 5c Pair, #a.-b. | .20 .20 |
| 297 | A54 | 10c Pair, #a.-b. | .55 .55 |
| 298 | A54 | 25c Pair, #a.-b. | 1.00 1.00 |
| 299 | A54 | 50c Pair, #a.-b. | 2.00 2.00 |

Nos. 296-299 (4)

## Virgin and Child, by Verrocchio — A55

Virgin and Child painted by: 10c, Paolo Morando. 35c, Giovanni Battista Cima. 40c, Andrea del Verrocchio.

**1971, Oct. 15    Perf. 14**

| | | | |
|---|---|---|---|
| 304 | A55 | 5c green & multi | .20 .20 |
| 305 | A55 | 10c brown & multi | .20 .20 |
| 306 | A55 | 35c ultra & multi | .25 .25 |
| 307 | A55 | 40c red & multi | .35 .35 |

Nos. 304-307 (4)    1.00 1.00

Christmas 1971.

## St. Lucia, School of Dolci, and Arms — A56

**1971, Dec. 13    Perf. 14x14½**

| | | | |
|---|---|---|---|
| 308 | A56 | 5c gray & multi | .20 .20 |
| 309 | A56 | 10c green & multi | .20 .20 |
| 310 | A56 | 25c tan & multi | .30 .30 |
| 311 | A56 | 50c lt blue & multi | .55 .55 |

Nos. 308-311 (4)    1.25 1.10

National Day.

## Lamentation, by Carracci — A57

**1972, Feb. 15    Wmk. 314**

| | | | |
|---|---|---|---|
| 312 | A57 | 10c lt violet & multi | .20 .20 |
| 313 | A57 | 25c ocher & multi | .25 .25 |
| 314 | A57 | 35c ultra & multi | .35 .50 |
| 315 | A57 | 50c lt green & multi | .50 .50 |

Nos. 312-315 (4)    1.25 1.10

Easter: 25c, 50c, Angels Weeping over Body of Jesus, by Guercino.

## Teachers' College and Science Building — A58

Opening of Morne Educational Complex.

15c, University Center and coat of arms. 25c, Secondary School. 35c, Technical College.

**1972, Apr. 18    Litho.    Perf. 14**
316 A58 5c multicolored .20 .20
317 A58 15c multicolored .20 .20
318 A58 25c multicolored .20 .20
319 A58 35c multicolored .80 .80
Nos. 316-319 (4)

## Steam Conveyance Co. Stamp and Map of St. Lucia — A59

Centenary of St. Lucia Steam Conveyance Co. Ltd. postal service.

**1972, June 22    Perf. 14½**
320 A59 5c yellow & multi .20 .20
321 A59 10c violet blue & multi .25 .20
322 A59 35c car rose & multi .70 .20
323 A59 50c emerald & multi 1.10 1.10
Nos. 320-323 (4)    2.25 1.70

Designs: 10c, Castries Harbor and 3c stamp. 35c, Soufriere Volcano and 1c stamp. 50c, One cent, 3c, 6c stamps.

## Holy Family, by Sebastiano Ricci — A60

**1972, Oct. 18    Common Design Type**
324 A60 5c dk brown & multi .20 .20
325 A60 10c green & multi .20 .20
326 A60 35c carmine & multi .35 .20
327 A60 40c dk blue & multi .80 .80
Nos. 324-327 (4)

Christmas 1972.

## Silver Wedding Issue, 1972
### Common Design Type

Design: Queen Elizabeth II, Prince Philip, St. Lucia coat of arms and St. Lucia parrot.

**1972, Nov.    Photo.    Perf. 14½x14**
328 CD324 15c car rose & multi .30 .30
329 CD324 35c olive & multi .30 .30

Weekday Headdress A61

Arms of St. Lucia A62

Women's Headdresses: 10c, For church wear. 25c, Unmarried girl. 50c, Formal occasions.

---

H.M.S. St. Lucia A63

**1973, Feb. 1    Wmk. 314    Perf. 13**
330 A61 5c multicolored .20 .20
331 A61 10c dark gray & multi .60 .60
332 A62 25c claret 14.00
333 A61 50c slate blue & multi .75 .75
Nos. 330-333 (4)    1.00 1.35

### Coil Stamps
**1973, Apr. 19    Litho.    Perf. 14½x14**
334 A62 5c gray olive .60 .60
335 A62 10c blue .60 .60
336 A62 25c multicolored 1.50 1.50
a. Watermark sideways (76)

Designs: Old Sailing ships.

**1973, May 24    Litho.    Perf. 13½x14**
337 A63 15c shown .20 .20
338 A63 35c "Prince of Wales" .35 .35
339 A63 35c "Oliph Blossom" .45 .45
340 A63 $1 "Rose" 1.00 1.00
a. Souv. sheet of 4, #337-340, perf. 15    2.10 2.10
Nos. 337-340 (4)    2.00 2.00

## Daliana Plantation and Flower — A64

**1973, July 26    Litho.    Perf. 14**
341 A64 15c multicolored .25 .20
342 A64 15c multicolored .25 .20
343 A64 35c multicolored .35 .20
344 A64 50c multicolored .85 .75
Nos. 341-344 (4)    1.65 1.35

Designs: 15c, Aerial spraying. 35c, Washing and packing bananas. 50c, Loading.
Banana industry.

---

## Madonna and Child, by Carlo Maratta — A65

**1973, Oct. 17    Litho.    Perf. 14x13½**
345 A65 5c citron & multi .20 .20
346 A65 15c ultra & multi .20 .20
347 A65 35c dp green & multi .35 .25
348 A65 50c red & multi 1.00 .85
Nos. 345-348 (4)

Christmas (Paintings): 15c, Virgin in the Meadow, by Raphael. 35c, Holy Family, by Angelo Bronzino. 50c, Madonna of the Pear, by Durer.

## Princess Anne's Wedding Issue
### Common Design Type

**1973, Nov. 14    Wmk. 314    Perf. 14**
349 CD325 40c gray green & multi .20 .20
350 CD325 50c lilac & multi .20 .20

## The Betrayal of Christ, by Ugolino — A66

---

## ST. LUCIA

Easter (Paintings by Ugolino, 14th Cent.): 35c, The Way to Calvary. 80c, Resurrection. $1, Descent from the Cross.

**1974, Apr. 1    Perf. 13½x13**
351 A66 5c multicolored .20 .20
352 A66 35c multicolored .25 .20
353 A66 80c multicolored .30 .30
354 A66 $1 multicolored 1.60 1.60
a. Souv. sheet of 4, #351-354    1.00 1.00
Nos. 351-354 (4)    .90

3 Escalins, 1798 — A67

Coins of Old St. Lucia.

**1974, May 20    Perf. 13½**
355 A67 15c lt olive & multi .25 .25
356 A67 35c multicolored .25 .25
357 A67 40c green & multi .35 .35
358 A67 $1 brown & multi 1.75 1.75
a. Souv. sheet of 4, #355-358    1.45 1.45
Nos. 355-358 (4)

Pieces of Eight 36c, 6 escudins, 1798, 40c, 2 livres 5 sols, 1813, $1, 6 livres 15 sols, 1813.

## Baron de Laborie, 1784 — A68

**1974, Aug. 29    Wmk. 314    Litho.    Perf. 14½**
359 A68 5c ocher & multi .20 .20
360 A68 35c brt blue & multi .20 .20
361 A68 80c violet & multi .25 .25
362 A68 $1 multicolored 1.00 1.00
a. Souv. sheet of 4, #359-362    .85 .85
Nos. 359-362 (4)

Portraits: 35c, Sir John Moore, Lieutenant Governor, 1796-97. 80c, Major General Sir Dudley St. Leger Hill, 1834-37. $1, Sir Frederick Joseph Clarke, 1967-71.
Past Governors of St. Lucia.

---

## Virgin and Child, by Verrocchio — A69

Christmas (Virgin and Child): 35c, by Andrea della Robbia. 80c, by Luca della Robbia. $1, by Antonio Rossellino.

**1974, Nov. 13    Wmk. 314    Perf. 13½**
363 A69 5c gray & multi .20 .20
364 A69 35c multicolored .20 .20
365 A69 80c pink & multi .20 .20
366 A69 $1 brown & multi 1.25 1.25
a. Souv. sheet of 4, #363-366    .85 .85
Nos. 363-366 (4)

## Churchill and Gen. Montgomery — A70

Design: $1, Churchill and Pres. Truman.

**1974, Nov. 30    Perf. 14**
367 A70 5c multicolored .20 .20
368 A70 $1 multicolored .40 .40

Sir Winston Churchill (1874-1965).

---

## Crucifixion, by Van der Weyden — A71

Easter: 35c, "Noli me Tangere," by Julio Romano. 80c, Crucifixion, by Fernando Gallego. $1, "Noli me Tangere," by Correggio.

**1975, Mar. 27    Wmk. 314    Perf. 14x13½**
369 A71 5c brown & multi .20 .20
370 A71 35c ultra & multi .25 .25
371 A71 80c red brown & multi .35 .35
372 A71 $1 green & multi 1.00 1.00
Nos. 369-372 (4)

Nativity — A72

Adoration of the Kings — A73

**1975, Dec.    Wmk. 314    Litho.    Perf. 14½**
373 A72 5c lilac rose & multi .20 .20
374 A73 10c yellow & multi .20 .20
375 A73 10c yellow & multi .20 .20
376 A73 10c yellow & multi .20 .20
a. Strip of 3, #374-376    .40 .40
377 A72 40c yellow & multi .85 .85
378 A72 $1 blue & multi 1.00 1.25
a. Souv. sheet of 3, #373, 377-378    2.05 2.05
Nos. 373-378 (6)

#375, Virgin & Child. #376, Adoration of the Shepherds. 40c, Nativity. $1, Virgin & Child with Sts. Catherine of Alexandria and Siena.
Christmas 1975.

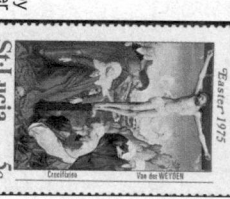

## "Hanna," First US Warship — A74

**1976, Jan. 26    Litho.    Perf. 14½    Unwmk.**
379-386 A74    Set of 8    6.00 3.50
386a    Souv. sheet of 4, #383-386, perf. 13    4.00 6.00

American Bicentennial.

Revolutionary Era Ships: 1c, "Prince of Orange," British packet. 2c, "Edward," British sloop. 5c, "Millem," British merchantman. 15c, "Surprise," Continental Navy lugger. 35c, "Serapis," British warship. 50c, "Randolph," first Continental Navy frigate. $1, "Alliance."

Laughing Gull — A75

Birds: 2c, Little blue heron. 4c, Belted kingfisher. 5c, St. Lucia parrot. 6c, St. Lucia oriole. 8c, Brown trembler. 10c, American kestrel. 12c, Red-billed tropic bird. 15c, Common gallinule. 25c, Brown noddy. 35c, Sooty tern. 50c, Osprey. $1, White-breasted thrasher. $5, St. Lucia black finch. $10, Red-necked pigeon. $10, Caribbean elaenia.

**Wmk. 314 (1c); 373 (others)**   **Litho.**

**1976, May 7**   **Perf. 14½**

| | | | | |
|---|---|---|---|---|
| 387 | A75 | 1c | gray & multi | .30 .30 |
| 388 | A75 | 2c | gray & multi | .30 .30 |
| 389 | A75 | 4c | gray & multi | .35 .35 |
| 390 | A75 | 5c | gray & multi | 1.75 1.00 |
| 391 | A75 | 6c | gray & multi | 1.25 1.00 |
| 392 | A75 | 8c | gray & multi | 1.25 1.00 |
| 393 | A75 | 10c | gray & multi | 1.40 1.75 |
| 394 | A75 | 12c | gray & multi | 1.90 2.40 |
| 395 | A75 | 15c | gray & multi | 1.25 1.75 |
| 396 | A75 | 25c | gray & multi | 1.75 1.25 |
| 397 | A75 | 35c | gray & multi | 3.00 3.25 |
| 398 | A75 | 50c | gray & multi | 6.00 6.25 |
| 399 | A75 | $1 | gray & multi | 3.75 6.75 |
| 400 | A75 | $2.50 | gray & multi | 4.25 7.25 |
| 401 | A75 | $5 | gray & multi | 6.75 7.75 |
| 402 | A75 | $10 | gray & multi | 45.00 37.50 |

Nos. 387-402 (16)

Map of West Indies, Bats, Wicket and Ball A75a

Prudential Cup — A75b

**1976, July 19**   **Unwmk.**   **Perf. 14**

| | | | | |
|---|---|---|---|---|
| 403 | A75a | 50c | lt blue & multi | 1.00 1.00 |
| 404 | A75b | $1 | lilac, rose & black | 2.00 2.00 |
| a. | | Souvenir sheet of 2, #403-404 | | 4.25 5.00 |

World Cricket Cup, won by West Indies Team, 1975.

Arms of H.M.S. Ceres — A76

Madonna and Child, by Murillo — A77

Coats of Arms of Royal Naval Ships: 20c, Pelican. 40c, Ganges. $2, Ariadne.

Paintings: 20c, Virgin and Child, by Lorenzo Costa. 50c, Madonna and Child, by Adriaen Isenbrandt. $2, Madonna and Child with St. John, by Murillo. $2.50, Like 10c.

**1976, Nov. 15**   **Litho.**   **Perf. 14½**

| | | | | |
|---|---|---|---|---|
| 409 | A77 | 10c | multicolored | .20 .20 |
| 410 | A77 | 15c | multicolored | .20 .20 |
| 411 | A77 | 50c | multicolored | .25 .25 |
| 412 | A77 | $2 | multicolored | .90 .90 |

Nos. 409-412 (4)   1.55 1.55

**Souvenir Sheet**

| | | | | |
|---|---|---|---|---|
| 413 | A77 | $2.50 | multicolored | 1.50 1.50 |

Christmas.

Elizabeth II, "Palms and Water" — A78

**1977, Feb. 7**   **Wmk. 373**   **Litho.**   **Perf. 14½**

| | | | | |
|---|---|---|---|---|
| 414 | A78 | 10c | multicolored | .20 .20 |
| 415 | A78 | 20c | multicolored | .20 .20 |
| 416 | A78 | 40c | multicolored | .25 .25 |
| 417 | A78 | $2 | multicolored | .40 .40 |

Nos. 414-417 (4)   1.00 1.00

**Souvenir Sheet**

| | | | | |
|---|---|---|---|---|
| 418 | A78 | $2.50 | multicolored | .75 1.50 |

25th anniv. of the reign of Elizabeth II.

Scouts of Tapion School — A79

1c, Sea Scouts, St. Mary's College. 2c, Scout giving oath. 10c, Tapion School Cub Scouts. 20c, Venture Scout, Soufrière. 50c, Scout from Gros Islet Division. $1, $2.50, Boat drill, St. Mary's College.

**1977, Oct. 17**   **Unwmk.**   **Perf. 15**

| | | | | |
|---|---|---|---|---|
| 419 | A79 | ½c | multicolored | .20 .20 |
| 420 | A79 | 1c | multicolored | .20 .20 |
| 421 | A79 | 2c | multicolored | .20 .20 |
| 422 | A79 | 10c | multicolored | .20 .20 |
| 423 | A79 | 20c | multicolored | .20 .20 |
| 424 | A79 | 50c | multicolored | .50 .50 |
| 425 | A79 | $1 | multicolored | 1.00 1.00 |

Nos. 419-425 (7)   2.50 2.50

**Souvenir Sheet**

| | | | | |
|---|---|---|---|---|
| 426 | A79 | $2.50 | multicolored | 2.00 2.00 |

6th Caribbean Boy Scout Jamboree, Kingston, Jamaica, Aug. 5-14.

Nativity, by Giotto — A80

**1977, Oct. 31**   **Litho.**   **Perf. 14**

Christmas (Virgin and Child by): 1c, Fra Angelico. 2c, El Greco. 20c, Caravaggio. 50c, Velazquez. $1, Tiepolo. $2.50, Adoration of the Kings, by Tiepolo.

427-433 A80 Set of 7   3.50 3.50

Suzanne Fourment in Velvet Hat, by Rubens — A81

Rubens Paintings: 35c, Rape of the Sabine Women (detail). 50c, Ludovicus Nonnius, portrait. $2.50, Minerva Protecting Pax from Mars (detail).

**1977, Nov. 28**   **Wmk. 373**   **Perf. 14x14½**   **Litho.**

| | | | | |
|---|---|---|---|---|
| 434 | A81 | 10c | multicolored | .20 .20 |
| 435 | A81 | 35c | multicolored | .30 .30 |
| 436 | A81 | 50c | multicolored | .30 .30 |
| 437 | A81 | $2.50 | multicolored | 1.60 1.60 |
| a. | | Souv. sheet, #434-437, perf. 15 | | 2.75 2.75 |

Nos. 434-437 (4)   2.30 2.30

Yeoman of the Guard and Life Guard A82

Peter Paul Rubens (1577-1640).

Dress Uniforms: 20c, Groom and coachman. 50c, Footman and postilion. $3, State trumpeter and herald. $5, Master of the Queen's House and Gentleman at Arms.

**1978, June 2**   **Unwmk.**   **Litho.**   **Perf. 14**

| | | | | |
|---|---|---|---|---|
| 438 | A82 | 15c | multicolored | .20 .20 |
| 439 | A82 | 20c | multicolored | .20 .20 |
| 440 | A82 | 50c | multicolored | .30 .30 |
| 441 | A82 | $3 | multicolored | 2.00 2.00 |

Nos. 438-441 (4)   2.70 2.70

**Souvenir Sheet**

| | | | | |
|---|---|---|---|---|
| 442 | A82 | $5 | multicolored | 3.00 3.00 |

25th anniv. of coronation of Elizabeth II. Nos. 438-441 exist in miniature sheets of 3 plus label, perf. 12.

Queen Angelfish A83

Tropical Fish: 20c, Four-eyed butterflyfish. 50c, French angelfish. $2, Yellowtail damselfish. $2.50, Rock beauty.

**1978, June 19**   **Litho.**   **Perf. 14½**

| | | | | |
|---|---|---|---|---|
| 443 | A83 | 10c | multicolored | .20 .20 |
| 444 | A83 | 20c | multicolored | .20 .20 |
| 445 | A83 | 50c | multicolored | .70 .70 |
| 446 | A83 | $2 | multicolored | 2.75 2.75 |

Nos. 443-446 (4)   3.85 3.85

**Souvenir Sheet**

| | | | | |
|---|---|---|---|---|
| 447 | A83 | $2.50 | multicolored | 4.00 4.00 |

French Grenadier, Map of Battle — A84

30c, British Grenadier & Bellin map of St. Lucia, 1762. 50c, British fleet opposing French landing & map of coast from Gros Islet to Cul-de-Sac. $2.50, Light infantrymen & Gen. James Grant.

**1978, Nov. 15**   **Litho.**   **Perf. 14**

| | | | | |
|---|---|---|---|---|
| 448 | A84 | 10c | multicolored | .20 .20 |
| 449 | A84 | 30c | multicolored | .35 .35 |
| 450 | A84 | 50c | multicolored | .60 .60 |
| 451 | A84 | $2.50 | multicolored | 3.00 3.00 |

Nos. 448-451 (4)   4.15 4.15

Bicent. of Battle of St. Lucia (Cul-de-Sac).

Annunciation A85

Christmas: 55c, 80c, Adoration of the Kings.

**1978, Dec. 4**   **Wmk. 373**   **Perf. 14x14½**

| | | | | |
|---|---|---|---|---|
| 452 | A85 | 30c | multicolored | .25 .25 |
| 453 | A85 | 35c | multicolored | .35 .35 |
| 454 | A85 | 55c | multicolored | .40 .40 |
| 455 | A85 | 80c | multicolored | .55 .55 |

Nos. 452-455 (4)   1.55 1.55

**Independent State**

Hewanorra Airport A86

Independence: 30c, New coat of arms. 50c, Government house and Allen Lewis, first Governor General. $2, Map of St. Lucia, French, St. Lucia and British flags.

**1979, Feb. 22**   **Litho.**   **Perf. 14**

| | | | | |
|---|---|---|---|---|
| 456 | A86 | 10c | multicolored | .20 .20 |
| 457 | A86 | 30c | multicolored | .20 .20 |
| 458 | A86 | 50c | multicolored | .30 .30 |
| 459 | A86 | $2 | multicolored | 1.25 1.25 |
| a. | | Souvenir sheet of 4, #456-459 | | 2.00 2.00 |

Nos. 456-459 (4)   1.95 1.95

Paul VI and John Paul I A87

Pope Paul VI and: 30c, Pres. Anwar Sadat of Egypt. 50c, Secretary General U Thant and UN emblem. 55c, Prime Minister Golda Meir of Israel. $2, Martin Luther King, Jr.

**1979, May 7**   **Litho.**   **Perf. 14**

| | | | | |
|---|---|---|---|---|
| 460 | A87 | 10c | multicolored | .20 .20 |
| 461 | A87 | 20c | multicolored | .25 .25 |
| 462 | A87 | 50c | multicolored | .40 .40 |
| 463 | A87 | 55c | multicolored | .45 .45 |
| 464 | A87 | $2 | multicolored | 1.75 1.75 |

Nos. 460-464 (5)   3.05 3.05

In memory of Popes Paul VI and John Paul I.

Jersey Cows A88

Agricultural Diversification: 35c, Fruits and vegetables. 50c, Waterfall (water conservation). $3, Coconuts, copra industry.

**1979, July 2**   **Litho.**   **Perf. 14**

| | | | | |
|---|---|---|---|---|
| 465 | A88 | 10c | multicolored | .20 .20 |
| 466 | A88 | 35c | multicolored | .30 .30 |
| 467 | A88 | 50c | multicolored | .40 .40 |
| 468 | A88 | $3 | multicolored | 2.50 2.50 |

Nos. 465-468 (4)   3.40 3.40

Lindbergh's Route over St. Lucia, Puerto Rico-Paramaribo — A89

**1979, Nov.**   **Litho.**   **Perf. 14**

| | | | | |
|---|---|---|---|---|
| 469 | A89 | 10c | Lindbergh, hydroplane | .20 .20 |
| 470 | A89 | 30c | shown | .25 .25 |
| 471 | A89 | 50c | Landing at La Toc | .40 .40 |
| 472 | A89 | $2 | Flight covers | 1.65 1.65 |

Nos. 469-472 (4)   2.50 2.50

Lindbergh's inaugural airmail flight (US-Guyana) via St. Lucia, 50th anniversary.

**Prince of Saxony, by Cranach the Elder — A90**

**1979, Dec. 17**    **Litho.**    **Perf. 14**

| | | | | |
|---|---|---|---|---|
| 473 | A90 | 10c multicolored | .20 | .20 |
| 474 | A90 | 50c multicolored | .40 | .40 |
| 475 | A90 | $2 multicolored | 1.65 | 1.65 |
| 476 | A90 | $2.50 multicolored | 2.00 | 2.00 |
| | | Nos. 473-476 (4) | 4.25 | 4.25 |

**Souvenir Sheet**

| 477 | A90 | $5 multicolored | 3.50 | 3.50 |
|---|---|---|---|---|

IYC (Emblem and): 50c, Infanta Margarita, by Velazquez; $2, Girl Playing Badminton, by Jean Baptiste Chardin. $2.50, Mary and Francis. Wilcox, by Stock. $5, Two Children, by Pablo Picasso.

A91

Maltese Cross Cancels and: 10c, Penny Post notice, 1839. 50c, Hill's original stamp design. $2, St. Lucia #1. $2.50, Penny Black. $5. Hill portrait.

**1979, Dec. 27**

| 478 | A91 | 10c multicolored | .20 | .20 |
|---|---|---|---|---|
| 479 | A91 | 50c multicolored | .40 | .40 |
| 480 | A91 | $2 multicolored | 1.25 | 1.25 |
| 481 | A91 | $2.50 multicolored | 1.50 | 1.50 |

**Souvenir Sheet**

| 482 | A91 | $5 multicolored | 3.00 | 3.00 |
|---|---|---|---|---|

Sir Rowland Hill (1793-1879), originator of penny postage. Nos. 478-481 also issued in sheets of 5 plus label, perf. 12x12½.

A92

St. Lucia Conveyance Co. Ltd. Stamp, 1873. A92a

London 1980 Emblem and Covers: 30c, "Assistance" 1p postmark, 1879, 50c, Postage due handstamp, 1929, $2. Postmarks on 1844 cover.

**1980, Jan. 14**

IYC Emblem, Virgin and Child, Virgin and Child by Bernardino Fungi. IYC: emblem. 50c, Giovanni Bellini.

| 483 | A92 | 10c multicolored | .20 | .20 |
|---|---|---|---|---|
| 484 | A92 | 50c multicolored | .40 | .40 |
| 485 | A92 | $2 multicolored | 1.65 | 1.65 |
| 486 | A92 | $2.50 multicolored | 2.00 | 2.00 |
| a. | | Souvenir sheet of 4, #483-486 | 4.50 | 4.50 |
| | | Nos. 483-486 (4) | 4.25 | 4.25 |

Christmas 1979: Intl. Year of the Child.

---

**1980, May 6**    **Wmk. 373**    **Litho.**    **Perf. 14**

| 487 | A92a | 10c multicolored | .20 | .20 |
|---|---|---|---|---|
| 488 | A92a | 30c multicolored | .35 | .35 |
| 489 | A92a | 30c multicolored | .35 | .35 |
| 490 | A92a | $2 multicolored | 1.40 | 1.40 |
| a. | | Souvenir sheet of 4, #487-490 | 2.50 | 2.50 |
| | | Nos. 487-490 (4) | 2.15 | 2.15 |

London 1980 Intl. Stamp Exhib., May 6-14.

**Int'l. Year of the Child — A93**

**1980, May 29**    **Litho.**    **Perf. 11**

| 491 | A93 | ½c Donald Duck spacewalking | .20 | .20 |
|---|---|---|---|---|
| 492 | A93 | 1c Donald Duck on rocket | .20 | .20 |
| 493 | A93 | 2c Minnie Mouse on moon | .20 | .20 |
| 494 | A93 | 3c Goofy hitch hiking | .20 | .20 |
| 495 | A93 | 4c Goofy on moon | .20 | .20 |
| 496 | A93 | 5c Pluto digging on moon | .20 | .20 |
| 497 | A93 | 10c Donald Duck, space creature | .20 | .20 |
| 498 | A93 | $2 Donald Duck padding satellite | .20 | .20 |
| 499 | A93 | $2.50 Mickey Mouse in lunar rover | .20 | .20 |
| | | Nos. 491-499 (9) | | |

**Souvenir Sheet**

| 500 | A93 | $5 Goofy on moon | 5.00 | 5.00 |
|---|---|---|---|---|

Space scenes. 1c, 4c, 5c, 10c, $2, $2.50 horiz.

**Queen Mother Elizabeth, 80th Birthday — A94**

**1980, Aug. 4**    **Litho.**    **Perf. 14**

| 501 | A94 | 10c multicolored | .20 | .20 |
|---|---|---|---|---|
| 502 | A94 | $2.50 multicolored | 1.75 | 1.75 |

**Souvenir Sheet**

| 503 | A94 | $3 multicolored | 2.00 | 2.00 |
|---|---|---|---|---|

HS-748 on Runway, St. Lucia Airport, Hewanorra — A95

**1980, Aug. 11**    **Wmk. 373**    **Litho.**    **Perf. 12½x12**

| 504 | A95 | 5c shown | .30 | .30 |
|---|---|---|---|---|
| 505 | A95 | 5c DC-10, St. Lucia Airport | .30 | .30 |
| 506 | A95 | 15c Bus, Castries | .30 | .30 |
| 507 | A95 | 20c Refrigerator ship | .30 | .30 |
| 508 | A95 | 25c Islander plane | .30 | .30 |
| 509 | A95 | 50c Pilot boat | .30 | .30 |
| 510 | A95 | 75c Cruise ship | .65 | .65 |
| 511 | A95 | $1 Lockheed Tristar, Piton Mountains | .90 | .90 |
| 512 | A95 | $2 Cargo ship | 1.75 | 2.40 |
| 513 | A95 | $5 Boeing 707 | 4.25 | 6.00 |
| 514 | A95 | $5 Boeing 707 | 1.75 | 2.40 |
| 515 | A95 | $10 Queen Elizabeth | 8.50 | 11.50 |
| a. | | | 18.25 | 24.25 |
| | | Nos. 504-515 (12) | | |

**1984, May 15**    **Wmk. 380**

| 507a | A95 | 20c | 2.25 | 2.25 |
|---|---|---|---|---|
| 508a | A95 | 20c | 2.25 | 2.25 |
| 509a | A95 | 30c | 2.75 | 2.75 |
| 512a | A95 | $1 | 2.00 | 2.00 |
| 513a | A95 | $2 | 7.00 | 7.00 |
| 514a | A95 | $2 | 14.00 | 14.00 |
| 515a | A95 | $10 | 35.00 | 35.00 |
| | | Nos. 507a-515a (6) | | |

For surcharges see Nos. 531-533.

---

**Shot Put, Moscow '80 Emblem — A96**

**1980, Sept. 22**    **Litho.**    **Perf. 14**

| 516 | A96 | 10c shown | .20 | .20 |
|---|---|---|---|---|
| 517 | A96 | 50c Swimming | .25 | .25 |
| 518 | A96 | $2 Weight lifting | 1.40 | 1.40 |
| 519 | A96 | $2.50 Gymnastics | 1.10 | 1.10 |
| | | Nos. 516-519 (4) | | |

**Souvenir Sheet**

| 520 | A96 | $5 Passing the torch | 2.75 | 2.75 |
|---|---|---|---|---|

22nd Summer Olympic Games, Moscow, July 19-Aug. 3.

A98

**1980, Sept. 30**    **Perf. 14**

| 521 | A97 | 10c Palms, coast at dusk | .20 | .20 |
|---|---|---|---|---|
| 522 | A97 | 50c Rocky shore | .25 | .25 |
| 523 | A97 | $2 Sand beach | 1.10 | 1.10 |
| 524 | A97 | $2.50 Pitons at sunset | 1.40 | 1.40 |
| | | Nos. 521-524 (4) | | |

**Souvenir Sheet**

| 525 | A97 | $5 Two-master | 2.75 | 2.75 |
|---|---|---|---|---|

A97

Rotary International, 75th Anniversary.

Nobel Prize Winners

**1980, Oct. 23**    **Litho.**    **Perf. 14**

| 526 | A98 | 10c multicolored | .20 | .20 |
|---|---|---|---|---|
| 527 | A98 | 50c multicolored | .30 | .30 |
| 528 | A98 | $2 multicolored | 1.25 | 1.25 |
| 529 | A98 | $2.50 multicolored | 1.65 | 1.65 |
| | | Nos. 526-529 (4) | | |

**Souvenir Sheet**

| 530 | A98 | $5 multicolored | 3.25 | 3.25 |
|---|---|---|---|---|

Nobel Prize Winners: 10c, Sir Arthur Lewis, Economics. 50c, Martin Luther King, Jr., peace, 1964. $2, Ralph Bunche, peace, 1950. $2.50, Albert Schweitzer, peace, 1952. $5, Albert Einstein, physics, 1921.

HURRICANE

**1980, Nov. 3**    **Litho.**    **Perf. 14½**    **Wmk. 380**

Nos. 506-507, 510 Surcharged:

| 531 | A95 | $1.50 on 15c multi | 1.50 | 1.50 |
|---|---|---|---|---|
| 532 | A95 | $1.50 on 30c multi | 1.50 | 1.50 |
| 533 | A95 | $1.50 on 50c multi | 1.50 | 1.50 |
| | | Nos. 531-533 (3) | 4.50 | 4.50 |

---

**Nativity, by Battista — A99**

**Angel and Citizens of St. Lucia — A100**

**1980, Dec. 1**    **Litho.**    **Perf. 14**

| 534 | A99 | 10c multicolored | .20 | .20 |
|---|---|---|---|---|
| 535 | A99 | 30c multicolored | .25 | .25 |
| 536 | A99 | $2 multicolored | 1.95 | 1.95 |
| | | Nos. 534-536 (3) | | |

**Souvenir Sheet**

| 537 | A100 | $1 shown | 2.00 | 2.00 |
|---|---|---|---|---|
| a. | | Sheet of 3 any single | .65 | .65 |

Christmas: 30c, Adoration of the Kings, by Bruegel the Elder. $2, Adoration of the Shepherds, by Murillo.

 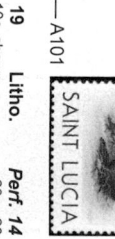

**Agouti — A101**

**1981, Jan. 19**    **Litho.**    **Perf. 14**

| 538 | A101 | 10c shown | .20 | .20 |
|---|---|---|---|---|
| 539 | A101 | 50c St. Lucia parrot | .40 | .40 |
| 540 | A101 | $2 Purple-throated carib | 1.50 | 1.50 |
| 541 | A101 | $2.50 Fiddler crab | 1.90 | 1.90 |
| | | Nos. 538-541 (4) | | |

**Souvenir Sheet**

| 542 | A101 | $5 Monarch butterfly | 4.00 | 4.00 |
|---|---|---|---|---|

A102

**1981, June 16**    **Litho.**    **Perf. 14**

**Royal Wedding Issue**
**Common Design Type**

| 543 | CD331 | 25c Couple | .20 | .20 |
|---|---|---|---|---|
| 544 | CD331 | 50c Clarence House | .30 | .30 |
| 545 | CD331 | $4 Charles | 2.50 | 2.50 |
| | | Nos. 543-545 (3) | 3.00 | 3.00 |

**Souvenir Sheet**

| 546 | CD331 | $5 Glass coach | 4.50 | 4.50 |
|---|---|---|---|---|

Nos. 543-545 also printed in sheets of 5 plus label, perf. 12, in changed colors.

| 549 | CD331 | | 8.75 | 8.75 |
|---|---|---|---|---|
| a. | | Booklet Pane of 1, $5, Couple | 3.50 | 3.50 |
| b. | | Pane of 6 (3x50c, Diana, 3x$2, Charles) | 5.25 | 5.25 |

## Picasso Birth Centenary

Picasso Birth Centenary: 30c, The Cock. 50c, Man with Ice Cream. 55c, Woman Dressing her Hair. $3, Seated Woman. $5, Night Fishing at Antibes.

**1981, May    Litho.    Perf. 14**

| | | | | |
|---|---|---|---|---|
| 550 | A102 | 30c multicolored | .20 | .20 |
| 551 | A102 | 50c multicolored | .35 | .35 |
| 552 | A102 | 55c multicolored | .40 | .40 |
| 553 | A102 | $3 multicolored | 2.00 | 2.00 |
| | | *Nos. 550-553 (4)* | 2.95 | 2.95 |

**Souvenir Sheet**

| | | | | |
|---|---|---|---|---|
| 554 | A102 | $5 multicolored | 4.00 | 4.00 |

A103

**1981, Sept. 28    Wmk. 373    Litho.    Perf. 14½**

| | | | | |
|---|---|---|---|---|
| 555 | A103 | 10c Industry | .20 | .20 |
| 556 | A103 | 35c Community service | .35 | .35 |
| 557 | A103 | 50c Hikers | .50 | .50 |
| 558 | A103 | $2.50 Duke of Edinburgh | 2.50 | 2.50 |
| | | *Nos. 555-558 (4)* | 3.55 | 3.55 |

Duke of Edinburgh's Awards, 25th anniv.

## Intl. Year of the Disabled — A104

**1981, Oct. 30    Litho.    Perf. 14**

| | | | | |
|---|---|---|---|---|
| 559 | A104 | 10c Louis Braille | .20 | .20 |
| 560 | A104 | 35c Sarah Bernhardt | .30 | .30 |
| 561 | A104 | $2 Joseph Pulitzer | 1.25 | 1.25 |
| 562 | A104 | $2.50 Henri de Toulouse Lautrec | 1.90 | 1.90 |
| | | *Nos. 559-562 (4)* | 3.45 | 3.45 |

**Souvenir Sheet**

| | | | | |
|---|---|---|---|---|
| 563 | A104 | $5 Franklin D. Roosevelt | 3.50 | 3.50 |

A105

Christmas: Adoration of the King Paintings.

**1981, Dec. 15    Litho.    Unwmk.**

| | | | | |
|---|---|---|---|---|
| 564 | A105 | 10c Sforza | .20 | .20 |
| 565 | A105 | 30c Gerard | .25 | .25 |
| 566 | A105 | 50c Orcana | 1.10 | 1.10 |
| 567 | A105 | $2.50 Foppa | 1.90 | 1.90 |
| | | *Nos. 564-567 (4)* | 3.45 | 3.45 |

A106

**1981, Dec. 29    Unwmk.**

| | | | | |
|---|---|---|---|---|
| 568 | A106 | 10c No. 1 | .20 | .20 |
| 569 | A106 | 30c No. 251 | .35 | .35 |
| 570 | A106 | 50c No. 459 | .55 | .55 |
| 571 | A106 | $2 UPU, St. Lucia flags | 2.25 | 2.25 |
| | | *Nos. 568-571 (4)* | 3.35 | 3.35 |

**Souvenir Sheets**

| | | | | |
|---|---|---|---|---|
| 572 | A106 | $5 GPO, Castries | 3.75 | 3.75 |

First anniv. of UPU membership.

A107

**1981, Dec. 11    Unwmk.    Litho.    Perf. 14**

1980s Decade for Women (Paintings of Women by Women): 10c, Fanny Travis Cochran, by Cecilia Beaux. 50c, Women with Dove, by Marie Laurencin. $2, Portrait of a Young Pupil of David $2.50, Self-portrait, by Rosalba Carriera. $5, Self-portrait, by Elisabeth Vigee-Le Brun.

| | | | | |
|---|---|---|---|---|
| 573 | A107 | 10c multicolored | .20 | .20 |
| 574 | A107 | 50c multicolored | .35 | .35 |
| 575 | A107 | $2 multicolored | 1.50 | 1.50 |
| 576 | A107 | $2.50 multicolored | 1.75 | 1.75 |
| | | *Nos. 573-576 (4)* | 3.80 | 3.80 |

**Souvenir Sheet**

| | | | | |
|---|---|---|---|---|
| 577 | A107 | $5 multicolored | 3.50 | 3.50 |

## 1982 World Cup Soccer — A108

Designs: Various soccer players.

**1982, Feb. 15    Litho.    Perf. 14½**

| | | | | |
|---|---|---|---|---|
| 578 | A108 | 10c multicolored | .25 | .25 |
| 579 | A108 | 50c multicolored | .60 | .60 |
| 580 | A108 | $2 multicolored | 2.40 | 2.40 |
| 581 | A108 | $2.50 multicolored | 3.00 | 3.00 |
| | | *Nos. 578-581 (4)* | 6.25 | 6.25 |

**Souvenir Sheet**

| | | | | |
|---|---|---|---|---|
| 582 | A108 | $5 multicolored | 3.50 | 3.50 |

## Battle of the Saints Bicentenary — A109

**1982, Apr. 13    Wmk. 373    Litho.    Perf. 14**

| | | | | |
|---|---|---|---|---|
| 583 | A109 | 10c Pigeon Isld. | .50 | .50 |
| 584 | A109 | 35c Battle | .80 | .80 |
| 585 | A109 | 50c Admirals Rodney, DeGrasse | 1.10 | 1.10 |
| 586 | A109 | $2.50 Map | 5.00 | 6.00 |
| | | | 7.40 | 7.40 |
| a. | | Souvenir sheet of 4, #583-586 | 9.25 | 9.25 |

*Nos. 583-586 (4)*

## Scouting Year — A110

**1982, Aug. 4    Litho.    Perf. 14**

| | | | | |
|---|---|---|---|---|
| 587 | A110 | 10c Map reading | .20 | .20 |
| 588 | A110 | 50c First aid | .45 | .45 |
| 589 | A110 | $1.50 Camping | 1.40 | 1.40 |
| 590 | A110 | $2.50 Campfire sing | 2.25 | 2.25 |
| | | *Nos. 587-590 (4)* | 4.30 | 4.30 |

## Princess Diana Issue

Common Design Type

**Perf. 14½x14**

| | | | | |
|---|---|---|---|---|
| 591 | CD332 | 10c Leeds Castle | .45 | .45 |
| 592 | CD332 | $2 Diana | 1.75 | 1.75 |
| 593 | CD332 | $4 Wedding | 3.50 | 3.50 |
| | | *Nos. 591-593 (3)* | 5.70 | 5.70 |

**Souvenir Sheet**

| | | | | |
|---|---|---|---|---|
| 594 | CD332 | $5 Diana, diff. | 5.50 | 5.50 |

## Christmas 1982 — A111

Paintings: 10c, Adoration of the Kings, by Brueghel the Elder. 30c, Nativity, by Lorenzo Costa. 50c, Virgin and Child, Fra Filippo Lippi. 80c, Adoration of the Shepherds, by Nicolas Poussin.

**1982, Nov. 10    Wmk. 373    Litho.    Perf. 14**

| | | | | |
|---|---|---|---|---|
| 595 | A111 | 10c multicolored | .25 | .25 |
| 596 | A111 | 30c multicolored | .35 | .35 |
| 597 | A111 | 50c multicolored | .55 | .55 |
| 598 | A111 | 80c multicolored | .85 | .85 |
| | | *Nos. 595-598 (4)* | 2.00 | 2.00 |

A111a

**1983, Mar. 14    Litho.**

| | | | | |
|---|---|---|---|---|
| 599 | A111a | 10c Twin Peaks | .20 | .20 |
| 600 | A111a | 30c Beach | .30 | .30 |
| 601 | A111a | 50c Banana harvester | .45 | .45 |
| 602 | A111a | $2 Flag | 1.75 | 1.75 |
| | | *Nos. 599-602 (4)* | 2.70 | 2.70 |

Commonwealth day.

## Crown Agents Sesquicentennial — A112

**1983, Apr. 1    Wmk. 373    Litho.    Perf. 14½**

| | | | | |
|---|---|---|---|---|
| 603 | A112 | 10c Headquarters, London | .20 | .20 |
| 604 | A112 | 15c Road construction | .20 | .20 |
| 605 | A112 | 50c Map | .40 | .40 |
| 606 | A112 | $2 First stamp | 1.65 | 1.65 |
| | | *Nos. 603-606 (4)* | 2.45 | 2.45 |

## World Communications Year — A113

**1983, July 12    Unwmk.    Litho.    Perf. 15**

| | | | | |
|---|---|---|---|---|
| 607 | A113 | 10c Shipboard inter-communication | .20 | .20 |
| 608 | A113 | 50c Satellite | .45 | .45 |
| 609 | A113 | $1.50 Air-to-air | 1.40 | 1.40 |
| 610 | A113 | $2.50 Computer communications | 2.25 | 2.25 |
| | | *Nos. 607-610 (4)* | 4.30 | 4.30 |

**Souvenir Sheet**

| | | | | |
|---|---|---|---|---|
| 611 | A113 | $5 Weather satellite | 4.25 | 4.25 |

## Coral Reef Fish — A114

**1983, Aug. 23    Litho.**

| | | | | |
|---|---|---|---|---|
| 612 | A114 | 10c Longspine squirrelfish | .20 | .20 |
| 613 | A114 | 50c Banded butterflyfish | .50 | .50 |
| 614 | A114 | $1.50 Blackbar soldierfish | 1.40 | 1.40 |
| 615 | A114 | $2.50 Yellowtail snappers | 2.25 | 2.25 |
| | | *Nos. 612-615 (4)* | 4.35 | 4.35 |

**Souvenir Sheet**

| | | | | |
|---|---|---|---|---|
| 616 | A114 | $5 Red hind | 4.50 | 4.50 |

For overprint see No. 800.

## Locomotives — A115

**1983, Oct. 13    Litho.    Unwmk.**

Se-tenant Pairs, #a.-b.

a. — Side and front views.

b. — Action scene.

| | | | | |
|---|---|---|---|---|
| 617 | A115 | 35c Princess Coronation | .45 | .45 |
| 618 | A115 | 35c Duke of Sutherland | .45 | .45 |
| 619 | A115 | 50c Leeds United | .60 | .60 |
| 620 | A115 | 50c Lord Nelson | .60 | .60 |
| 621 | A115 | $1 Bodmin | 1.25 | 1.25 |
| 622 | A115 | $1 Eton | 1.25 | 1.25 |
| 623 | A115 | $2 Flying Scotsman | 2.50 | 2.50 |
| 624 | A115 | $2 Stephenson's Rocket | 2.50 | 2.50 |
| | | *Nos. 617-624 (8)* | 9.60 | 9.60 |

See Nos. 674-679, 711-718, 774-777, 807-814.

## Virgin and Child Paintings by Raphael — A115a

**1983, Oct. 24    Wmk. 373    Litho.    Perf. 14**

| | | | | |
|---|---|---|---|---|
| 629 | A115a | 10c Niccolini-Cowper Madonna | .20 | .20 |
| 630 | A115a | 30c Holy Family with a Palm Tree | .20 | .20 |
| 631 | A115a | 60c Sistine Madonna | .30 | .30 |
| 632 | A115a | $5 Alba Madonna | 3.00 | 3.00 |
| | | *Nos. 629-632 (4)* | 3.70 | 3.70 |

Christmas.

## Battle of Waterloo, King George III — A116

#633a, 633b, shown. #634a, George III, diff. #634b, Kew Palace. #635a, Arms of Elizabeth II. #635b, Elizabeth I. #636a, Arms of George II. #636b, George III. #637a, Elizabeth I, diff. #637b, Hatfield Palace. #638a, Spanish Armada. #638b, Elizabeth, I, diff.

**1984, Mar. 13    Litho.    Unwmk.    Perf. 12½**

| | | | | |
|---|---|---|---|---|
| 633 | A116 | 5c Pair, #a.-b. | .20 | .20 |
| 634 | A116 | 5c Pair, #a.-b. | .20 | .20 |
| 635 | A116 | 35c Pair, #a.-b. | .40 | .40 |
| 636 | A116 | 60c Pair, #a.-b. | .60 | .60 |
| 637 | A116 | $2.50 Pair, #a.-b. | 1.00 | 1.00 |
| 638 | A116 | $2.50 Pair, #a.-b. | 2.50 | 2.50 |
| | | *Nos. 633-638 (6)* | 4.90 | 4.90 |

Unissued 30c, 50c, $1, $2.50 and $5 values became available with the liquidation of the printer.

## St. Lucia (continued)

**Local Architecture, 10c, vert.**
Colonial Building, Late 19th Cent. — A118

Logwood Tree and Blossom — A118a

**1984, Apr. 6  Perf. 14x13½, 13½x14  Wmk. 380**
- 645 A118  10c Buildings, mid-19th cent.  .20  .20
- 646 A118  45c shown  .35  .35
- 647 A118  65c Wooden chattel, early 20th cent.  .50  .50
- 648 A118  $2.50 Treasury, 1906  1.90  1.90

Nos. 645-648 (4)  2.95  2.95

For overprints see Nos. 796, 801.

**1984, June 12  Wmk. 380**
- 649 A118a  10c shown  .20  .20
- 650 A118a  45c Calabash  .35  .35
- 651 A118a  65c Gommier, vert.  .50  .50
- 652 A118a  $2.50 Rain tree  1.90  1.90

Nos. 649-652 (4)  2.95  2.95

For overprint see No. 802.

Automobiles — A119

**1984, June 25  Perf. 12½  Litho.  Unwmk.**
a. — Se-tenant Pairs, #a.-b.
b. — Side and front views.
- 653 A119  5c Bugatti 57SC, 1939  .20  .20
- 654 A119  10c Chevrolet Bel Air, 1957  .20  .20
- 655 A119  $1 Alfa Romeo, 1930  1.25  1.25
- 656 A119  $2.50 Duesenberg, 1932  3.00  3.00

Nos. 653-656 (4)  4.65  4.65

See Nos. 686-693, 739-742, 850-855.

Endangered Reptiles — A120

**1984, Aug. 8  Litho.  Perf. 14**
**Wmk. 380**
- 661 A120  10c Pygmy gecko  .20  .20
- 662 A120  45c Maria Isld. ground lizard  .35  .35

Leaders of the World, 1984
Olympics — A121

- 663 A120  65c Green iguana  .50  .50
- 664 A120  $2.50 Couresse snake  1.90  1.90

Nos. 661-664 (4)  2.95  2.95

For overprint see No. 797.

**1984, Sept. 21  Perf. 12½  Litho.  Unwmk.**
a. — Se-tenant Pairs, #a.-b.
b. — Action scene.
- 665 A121  5c Pair, #a.-b.  .20  .20
- 666 A121  10c Pair, #a.-b.  .20  .20
- 667 A121  65c Pair, #a.-b.  .50  .50
- 668 A121  $2.50 Pair, #a.-b.  3.00  3.00

Nos. 665-668 (4)  4.20  4.20

#665a, Volleyball; #665b, Volleyball, diff.; #666a, Women's hurdles; #666b, Men's hurdles; #667a, Showjumping; #667b, Dressage; #668a, Women's gymnastics; #668b, Men's gymnastics.

**Locomotive Type of 1983**
**1984, Sept. 21  Litho.  Perf. 12½  Unwmk.**
a. — Se-tenant Pairs, #a.-b.
b. — Action scene.
- 674 A115  1c TAW 2-6-2T, 1897  .20  .20
- 675 A115  15c Crocodile 1-C-C-1, 1920  .20  .20
- 670 A115  50c The Countess 0-6-0T, 1903  .55  .55
- 677 A115  75c Class GE6/6C.C..., 1921  .85  .85
- 678 A115  $1 Class P8, 4-6-0, 1906  .55  .55
- 679 A115  $2 Der Adler 2.2.2., 1835  2.25  2.25

Nos. 674-679 (6)  4.60  4.60

**Automobile Type of 1983**
**1984, Dec. 19  Litho.  Perf. 12½  Unwmk.**
a. — Se-tenant Pairs, #a.-b.
b. — Side and front views.
- 686 A119  10c Panhard and Levassor, 1889  .20  .20
- 687 A119  30c N.S.U. R0-80  .20  .20
- 688 A119  55c Abarth, Balbero, 1958  .35  .35
- 689 A119  65c TRV Vixen  .65  .65
- 690 A119  75c Ford Mustang Convertible, 1965  .75  .75
- 691 A119  $1 Ford Model T, 1914  .90  .90
- 692 A119  $2 Aston Martin DB3S, 1954  1.25  1.25
- 693 A119  $3 Chrysler Imperial CG, 1931  3.50  3.50

Nos. 686-693 (8)  10.10  10.10

150th Anniversary of the Abolition of Slavery
Abolition of Slavery, 150th Anniv. — A123

Christmas — A122

**1984, Oct. 31  Litho.  Wmk. 380  Perf. 14**
- 702 A122  10c Wine glass  .20  .20
- 703 A122  35c Altar  .30  .30
- 704 A122  55c Creche  .55  .55
- 705 A122  $3 Holy family, abstract  2.50  2.50
  - a. Souvenir sheet of 4, #702-705  3.50  3.50

Nos. 702-705 (4)  3.55  3.55

**Souvenir Sheet**
**1984, Dec. 12  Litho.  Perf. 14**
- 710 A123  Sheet of 4  5.00  5.00
  - a. A123 10c like No. 706  .20  .20
  - b. A123 35c like No. 707  .25  .25
  - c. A123 55c like No. 708  .40  .40
  - d. A123 $5 like No. 709  3.50  3.50

#710a-710d se-tenant in continuous design.

**1984, Dec. 12  Litho.**
- 706 A123  10c bright buff & blk  .20  .20
- 707 A123  35c bright buff & blk  .25  .25
- 708 A123  55c bright buff & blk  .40  .40
- 709 A123  $5 bright buff & blk  3.50  3.50

Nos. 706-709 (4)  4.35  4.35

Engraving details, Natl. Archives, Castries: 10c, Preparing manioc; 35c, Working with cassava flour; 55c, Cooking, twisting and drying tobacco; $5, Tobacco production, diff.

**Locomotive Type of 1983**
**1985, Feb. 4  Unwmk.  Perf. 12½**
a. — Se-tenant Pairs, #a.-b.
b. — Side and front views.
- 711 A115  5c J.N.R. Class C-53, 1928, Japan  .20  .20
- 712 A115  15c Heavy I, 1885, India  .20  .20
- 713 A115  35c QGR Class B18 ¼, 1926, Australia  .50  .50
- 714 A115  60c Glyndwr, 1923, U.K.  .80  .80
- 715 A115  75c Lion, 1838, U.K.  1.05  1.05
- 716 A115  $1 Coal Engine, 1873, U.K.  1.40  1.40
- 717 A115  $2 No. 2238 Class Q6, 1921, U.K.  2.50  2.50
- 718 A115  $2.50 Class H, 1920, U.K.  3.25  3.25

Nos. 711-718 (8)  9.90  9.90

Saint Lucia — Grenadier
Military Uniforms — A126

**Automobile Type of 1983**
**1985, Mar. 29  Se-tenant Pairs**
- 739 A119  15c 1940 Hudson Eight, US  .20  .20
- 740 A119  50c 1937 KdF, Ger.  .70  .70
- 741 A119  $1 1925 Kissel Goldbug, US  1.40  1.40
- 742 A119  $1.50 1973 Ferrari 246GTS, Italy  1.90  1.90

Nos. 739-742 (4)  4.20  4.20

**1985, May 7  Wmk. 380  Perf. 15**
Designs: 5c, Grenadier, 70th Foot Reg., c. 1775. 10c, Grenadier Co., Officer, 14th Foot Reg., 1780. 20c, Battalion Co., Officer, 46th Foot Reg., 1781. 25c, Officer, Royal Artillery Reg., c. 1782. 30c, Officer, Royal Engineers Corps., 1782. 35c, Battalion Co., Officer, 54th Foot Reg., 1782. 45c, Grenadier Co., Private, 14th Foot Reg., 1796. 50c, Gunner, Royal Artillery Reg., c. 1796. 65c, Private, 85th Foot Reg., c. 1796. 75c, Battalion Co., Private, 76th Foot Reg., c. 1796. 90c, Battalion Co., Private, 81st Foot Reg., 1796. $1, Sergeant, 74th (Highland) Foot Reg., 1796. $2.50, Private, Light Co., 93rd Foot Reg., 1850. $5, Battalion Co., Royal West India Reg., 1803. $15, Officer, Royal Artillery Reg., 1850.

| | | Unwmk. | |
|---|---|---|---|
| 747 A126 | 5c multicolored | .20 | .30 |
| 748 A126 | 10c multicolored | .20 | .40 |
| 749 A126 | 20c multicolored | .30 | .50 |
| 750 A126 | 25c multicolored | .30 | .50 |

Wmk. 384 ('88)

| 751 A126 | 30c multicolored | .40 | .60 |
|---|---|---|---|
| 752 A126 | 35c multicolored | .50 | .75 |
| 753 A126 | 45c multicolored | .50 | .75 |
| 754 A126 | 50c multicolored | .55 | 1.00 |
| 755 A126 | 65c multicolored | .65 | 1.40 |
| 756 A126 | 75c multicolored | .85 | 1.60 |
| 757 A126 | 90c multicolored | .90 | 1.90 |
| 758 A126 | $1 multicolored | 1.00 | 2.00 |
| 759 A126 | $2.50 multicolored | 2.00 | 6.25 |
| 760 A126 | $5 multicolored | 3.00 | 10.00 |
| 761 A126 | $15 multicolored | 17.00 | 26.00 |

Nos. 747-761 (15)  33.55  52.85

Nos. 749-750, 1989. See Nos. 876-879.

**1987**
| 747a A126 | 5c multicolored | .20 | .30 |
|---|---|---|---|
| 747b A126 | 10c multicolored | .20 | .40 |
| 748a A126 | 10c multicolored | .20 | .40 |
| 749a A126 | 20c multicolored | .30 | .50 |
| 751a A126 | 35c multicolored | .45 | .60 |
| 752a A126 | 45c multicolored | .45 | .60 |
| 760a A126 | $3 multicolored | 2.00 | 2.00 |

Nos. 747a-760a (7)  7.40  7.40

Issued: #747a-748a, 2/24; #751a-760a, 3/16. Dated 1986.

**1989**
| 747b A126 | 5c | .20 | .20 |
|---|---|---|---|
| 748b A126 | 10c | .20 | .20 |
| 749b A126 | 20c | .20 | .20 |

Wmk. 384

World War II Aircraft — A127

SAINT LUCIA 5c Messerschmitt 109-E

Girl Guides, 75th Anniv. — A124

**1985, Feb. 21  Wmk. 380  Perf. 14**
- 727 A124  10c multicolored  .35  .35
- 728 A124  35c multicolored  .55  .55
- 729 A124  60c multicolored  1.10  1.10
- 730 A124  $3 multicolored  5.00  5.00

Nos. 727-730 (4)  7.00  7.00

For overprint see No. 795.

Butterflies — A125

**1985, Feb. 28  Unwmk.  Perf. 12½**
- 731 A125  15c Pair, #a.-b.  .20  .20
- 732 A125  40c Pair, #a.-b.  .60  .60
- 733 A125  60c Pair, #a.-b.  .80  .80
- 734 A125  $3 Pair, #a.-b.  3.00  3.00

Nos. 731-734 (4)  4.60  4.60

#731a, Clossiana selene; #731b, Inachis io; #732a, Philaethria werneckei; #732b, Catagramma sorana; #733a, Kallima inachus; #733b, Hypanartia paullus; #734a, Morpho rhetenor helena; #734b, Ornithoptera meridionalis.

**1985, May 30 Unwmk. Perf. 12½**
Se-tenant Pairs, #a.-b.
a.— Action scene.
b.— Bottom, front and side views.

| | | | | |
|---|---|---|---|---|
| 762 | A127 | 5c Messerschmitt 109-E | .20 | .20 |
| 763 | A127 | 55c Avro 683 Lancaster Mark I Bomber | .75 | .75 |
| 764 | A127 | 60c North American P-51-D Mustang | .80 | .80 |
| 765 | A127 | $2 Supermarine Spitfire Mark II | 2.50 | 2.50 |
| | | | 4.25 | 4.25 |

Nos. 762-765 (4)

Nature Reserves A128

Saint Lucia 10c

**1985, June 20 Wmk. 380 Perf. 15**
Birds in habitats: 10c, Frigate bird, Frigate Island Sanctuary. 35c, Mangrove cuckoo, Savannes Bay, Scorpion Island. 65c, Yellow sandpiper, Maria Island. $3, Audubon's shearwater, Lapins Island.

| | | | | |
|---|---|---|---|---|
| 770 | A128 | 10c multicolored | .20 | .20 |
| 771 | A128 | 35c multicolored | .30 | .30 |
| 772 | A128 | 65c multicolored | .55 | .55 |
| 773 | A128 | $3 multicolored | 2.75 | 2.75 |
| | | | 3.80 | 3.80 |

Nos. 770-773 (4)

Locomotive Type of 1983
**1985, June 26 Unwmk. Perf. 12½**
Se-tenant Pairs, #a.-b.
a.— Side and front views.
b.— Action scene.

| | | | | |
|---|---|---|---|---|
| 774 | A115 | 10c No. 28 Tender engine, 1897, U.K. | .20 | .20 |
| 775 | A115 | 30c No. 1621 Class M, 1893, U.K. | .40 | .40 |
| 776 | A115 | 75c Class Dunalastair, 1896, U.K. | .95 | .95 |
| 777 | A116 | $2.50 Big Bertha No. 2290, 1910, U.K. | 3.00 | 3.00 |
| | | | 4.55 | 4.55 |

Nos. 774-777 (4)

SAINT LUCIA 40c — SAINT LUCIA 40c

Queen Mother, 85th Birthday — A129

#782a, 787a, Facing right. #782b, 787b, Facing right. #783a, Facing right. #783b, Facing left. #784a, 788a, Facing right. #784b, 788b, Facing front. #785a, Facing front. #785b, Facing left. #786a, Facing front. #786b, Facing left.

**1985, Aug. 16**

| | | | | |
|---|---|---|---|---|
| 782 | A129 | 40c Pair, #a.-b. | .60 | .60 |
| 783 | A129 | 75c Pair, #a.-b. | 1.10 | 1.10 |
| 784 | A129 | $1.10 Pair, #a.-b. | 1.60 | 1.60 |
| 785 | A129 | $1.75 Pair, #a.-b. | 2.25 | 2.25 |

Nos. 782-785 (4)

Souvenir Sheets of 2

| | | | | |
|---|---|---|---|---|
| 786 | A129 | $2 #a.-b. | 2.50 | 2.50 |
| 787 | A129 | $4 #a.-b. | 4.50 | 4.50 |
| 788 | A129 | $6 #a.-b. | 9.00 | 9.00 |

For overprints see No. 799.

=SAINT LUCIA= 10c International American Year of the Youth 1985

Intl. Youth Year — A130

SAINT LUCIA $5 — SAINT LUCIA $5
International Year of the Youth 1985

Abstracts, by Lyndon Samuel — A131

Illustrations by local artists: 10c, Youth playing banjo, by Wayne Whitfield. 45c, Riding tricycle, by Mark D. Maragh. 75c, Youth against landscape, by Bartholemew Eugene. $3.50, Abstract, by Lyndon Samuel.

**1985, Sept. 5 Wmk. 380 Perf. 15**

| | | | | |
|---|---|---|---|---|
| 791 | A130 | 10c multicolored | .20 | .20 |
| 792 | A130 | 45c multicolored | .40 | .40 |
| 793 | A130 | 75c multicolored | .75 | .75 |
| 794 | A130 | $3.50 multicolored | 3.00 | 3.00 |
| | | | 4.35 | 4.35 |

Nos. 791-794 (4)

Souvenir Sheet

| | | | | |
|---|---|---|---|---|
| 795 | A131 | $5 multicolored | 4.00 | 4.00 |

Intl. Youth Year.

Stamps of 1983-85 Ovptd. "CARIBBEAN ROYAL VISIT 1985" in Two or Three Lines

**1985, Nov. Perfs. as Before Wmk. as Before**

| | | | | |
|---|---|---|---|---|
| 796 | A124 | 35c #728 | 1.00 | 1.00 |
| 797 | A118 | 65c #647 | 1.75 | 1.75 |
| 798 | A120 | 65c #663 | 1.75 | 1.75 |
| 799 | A129 | $1.10 #784a-784b | 6.00 | 6.00 |
| 800 | A114 | $2.50 #615 | 6.50 | 6.50 |
| 801 | A118 | $2.50 #648 | 6.50 | 6.50 |
| 802 | A119 | $2.50 #652 | 6.50 | 6.50 |

Nos. 796-802 (7) 30.00 30.00

Saint Lucia 10c Pepe Jab — Christmas 1985

Masquerade Figures — A132

**1985, Dec. 23 Unwmk. Litho. Perf. 15**

| | | | | |
|---|---|---|---|---|
| 803 | A132 | 10c Papa Jab | .20 | .20 |
| 804 | A132 | 45c Paille Bananne | .35 | .35 |
| 805 | A132 | 65c Cheval Bois | .50 | .50 |

Nos. 803-805 (3) 1.05 1.05

Saint Lucia $4

Madonna and Child, by Dunstan St. Omer — A133

Miniature Sheet

| | | | | |
|---|---|---|---|---|
| 806 | A133 | $4 multi | 3.00 | 3.00 |

Christmas 1985.

Locomotive Type of 1983
**1986, Jan. 17 Perf. 12½x13**
Se-tenant Pairs, #a.-b.
a.— Side and front views.
b.— Action scene.

| | | | | |
|---|---|---|---|---|
| 807 | A115 | 5c 1983 MWCR Rack Loco Tip Top, US | .20 | .20 |
| 808 | A115 | 15c 1975 BR Class 87 Stephenson Bo-Bo, UK | .20 | .20 |
| 809 | A115 | 30c 1901 Class D No. 737, UK | .35 | .35 |
| 810 | A115 | 60c 1922 No. 13 2-Co-2, UK | .70 | .70 |
| 811 | A115 | 75c 1954 BR Class EM2 Electra Co-Co, UK | .85 | .85 |
| 812 | A115 | $1 1922 City of Newcastle, UK | 1.25 | 1.25 |
| 813 | A115 | $2.25 1930 DRG Von Kruckenberg, Propeller-driven Rail Car, Germany | 2.75 | 2.75 |
| 814 | A115 | $3 1893 JNR No. 860, Japan | 3.50 | 3.50 |
| | | | 9.80 | 9.80 |

Nos. 807-814 (8)

Miniature Sheets

ST LUCIA $4 ST LUCIA

Cook-out — A134

Designs: No. 823b, Scout sign. No. 824a, Wicker basket, weavings. No. 824b, Lady Olave Baden-Powell, Girl Guides founder.

**1986, Mar. 3 Litho. Perf. 13x12½**

| | | | | |
|---|---|---|---|---|
| 823 | | Sheet of 2 | 5.50 | 5.50 |
| | a.-b. | A134 $4 any single | 2.75 | 2.75 |
| 824 | | Sheet of 2 | 8.00 | 8.00 |
| | a.-b. | A134 $6 any single | 4.00 | 4.00 |

Scouting anniv., Girl Guides 75th anniv. Exist with plain or decorative border.

5c 60th BIRTHDAY OF HER MAJESTY QUEEN ELIZABETH II — Saint Lucia

A135

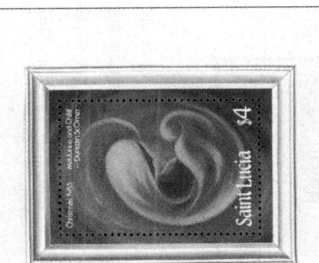
SAINT LUCIA 10c VISIT TO MARIAN HOME

Queen Elizabeth II, 60th Birthday — A136

Various photographs.

**Perf. 13x12½, 12½x13, 14x15 (A136)**
**1986**

| | | | | |
|---|---|---|---|---|
| 825 | A135 | 5c Pink hat | .20 | .20 |
| 826 | A136 | 10c Visiting Marian Home | .20 | .20 |
| 827 | A136 | 45c Mindoo Phillip Park speech | .30 | .30 |
| 828 | A136 | 50c Opening Leon Hess School | .35 | .35 |
| 829 | A135 | $1 Princess Elizabeth | .65 | .65 |
| 830 | A135 | $3.50 Blue hat | 2.25 | 2.25 |
| 831 | A136 | $5 Government House | 3.25 | 3.25 |
| 832 | A135 | $6 Canberra, 1982, vert. | 3.75 | 3.75 |

Nos. 825-832 (8) 10.95 10.95

Souvenir Sheets

| | | | | |
|---|---|---|---|---|
| 833 | A136 | $7 HMY Britannia, Castries Harbor | 5.50 | 5.50 |
| 834 | A135 | $8 Straw hat | 5.50 | 5.50 |

Issue dates: Nos. 825, 829-830, 832, Apr. 21; Nos. 826-828, 831, 833, June 14.

PAPAL VISIT JULY 1986 — Saint Lucia 55c

State Visit of Pope John Paul II — A137

**1986, July 7 Perf. 14x15, 15x14**

| | | | | |
|---|---|---|---|---|
| 835 | A137 | 55c Kissing the ground | 1.25 | 1.25 |
| 836 | A137 | 60c St. Joseph's Convent | 1.50 | 1.50 |
| 837 | A137 | 80c Cathedral, Castries | 2.00 | 2.00 |
| | | | 4.75 | 4.75 |

Nos. 835-837 (3)

Souvenir Sheet

| | | | | |
|---|---|---|---|---|
| 838 | A137 | $6 Pope | 10.50 | 10.50 |

Nos. 837-838 vert.

SAINT LUCIA — SAINT LUCIA
80c ROYAL WEDDING 1986 — 80c ROYAL WEDDING 1986

Wedding of Prince Andrew and Sarah Ferguson — A138

**1986, July 23 Perf. 12½**

| | | | | |
|---|---|---|---|---|
| 839 | A138 | 80c Pair, #a.-b. | 1.25 | 1.25 |
| 840 | A138 | $2 Pair, #a.-b. | 3.00 | 3.00 |

#839a, Sarah, vert. #839U, Andrew, vert. #840a, Couple. #840b, Andrew, Nancy Reagan.
#840a-840b show Westminster Abbey in LR.

25th Anniversary — PARTNERS IN PROGRESS 1983-1986 — Saint Lucia 80c

US Peace Corps in St. Lucia, 25th Anniv. — A139

**1986, Sept. 25 Litho. Perf. 14**

| | | | | |
|---|---|---|---|---|
| 843 | A139 | 80c Technical instruction | .60 | .60 |
| 844 | A139 | $2 Pres. Kennedy, corps emblem | 1.50 | 1.50 |
| 845 | A139 | $3.50 Natl. crests, corps emblem (3) | 2.60 | 2.60 |
| | | | 4.70 | 4.70 |

Nos. 843-845 (3)

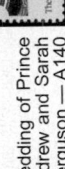
Saint Lucia 50c — The Royal Wedding 1986

Wedding of Prince Andrew and Sarah Ferguson — A140

## 1986, Oct. 15 — Perf. 15
### Souvenir Sheet
| | | | |
|---|---|---|---|
| 849A | A140 | $7 Andrew, Sarah | 5.25 5.25 |
| 846 | A140 | 50c Andrew | .40 .40 |
| 847 | A140 | 80c Sarah | .60 .60 |
| 848 | A140 | $1 At altar | .75 .75 |
| 849 | A140 | $3 In open carriage | 2.25 2.25 |
| | | Nos. 846-849 (4) | 4.00 4.00 |

## Automobile Type of 1983
## 1986, Oct. 23 Litho. — Perf. 12½x13
Se-tenant Pairs, #a.-b.
a. — Action scene.
b. — Side and front views.
| | | | |
|---|---|---|---|
| 850 | A119 | 20c 1969 AMC AMX, US | .20 |
| 851 | A119 | 50c 1912 Russo-Baltique, Russia | .60 .60 |
| 852 | A119 | 60c 1932 Lincoln KB, US | .70 .70 |
| 853 | A119 | $1 1933 Rolls Royce Phantom II Continental, UK | 1.25 1.25 |
| 854 | A119 | $1.50 1939 Buick Century, US | 1.75 1.75 |
| 855 | A119 | $3 1957 Chrysler 300 C, US | 3.50 3.50 |
| | | Nos. 850-855 (6) | 8.00 8.00 |

Chak-Chak Band — A141

Christmas A142

### Souvenir Sheet
| | | | |
|---|---|---|---|
| 866 | A141 | $10 Gros Islet | 7.50 7.50 |

## 1986, Nov. 7 — Perf. 15
| | | | |
|---|---|---|---|
| 862 | A141 | 15c shown | .20 .20 |
| 863 | A141 | 45c Folk dancing | .35 .35 |
| 864 | A141 | 80c Steel band | .60 .60 |
| 865 | A141 | $5 Limbo dancer | 3.75 3.75 |
| | | Nos. 862-865 (4) | 4.90 4.90 |

Churches: 10c, St. Ann Catholic, Mon Repos. 40c, St. Joseph the Worker Catholic, Gros Islet. 80c, Holy Trinity Anglican, Castries. $4, Our Lady of the Assumption Catholic, Soufriere, vert. $7, St. Lucy Catholic, Micoud.

## 1986, Nov. — Souvenir Sheet
| | | | |
|---|---|---|---|
| 867 | A142 | 10c multicolored | .20 .20 |
| 868 | A142 | 40c multicolored | .30 .30 |
| 869 | A142 | 80c multicolored | .60 .60 |
| 870 | A142 | $4 multicolored | 3.00 3.00 |
| | | Nos. 867-870 (4) | 4.10 4.10 |
| 871 | A142 | $7 multicolored | 5.25 5.25 |

Map of St. Lucia — A143

## 1987, Feb. 24 Litho. Wmk. 373 — Perf. 14x14½
| | | | |
|---|---|---|---|
| 872 | A143 | 5c beige & blk | .20 .20 |
| 873 | A143 | 10c pale yel grn & blk | .20 .20 |
| | | Wmk. 384 ('89) | |
| 874 | A143 | 45c orange & blk | .20 .20 |
| 875 | A143 | 50c pale violet & blk | .35 .35 |
| | | Nos. 872-875 (4) | 1.10 1.10 |

#872-873 exist inscribed 1988. #875 1989. Issued #872a, 873a, Apr. 12. See #937.

## Uniforms Type of 1985
Designs: 15c, Battalion company private, 2nd West India Regiment, 1803. 60c, Battalion company officer, 5th Regiment of Foot, 1778. 80c, Battalion company officer, 27th (or Inniskilling) Regiment of Foot, 1780. $20, Grenadier company private, 46th Regiment of Foot, 1778.

## 1988
| | | | |
|---|---|---|---|
| 876 | A126 | 15c multicolored | .20 .20 |
| 877 | A126 | 60c multicolored | .40 .40 |
| 878 | A126 | 80c multicolored | .55 .55 |
| 879 | A126 | $20 multicolored | 13.75 13.75 |
| | | Nos. 876-879 (4) | 14.90 14.90 |

Dated 1986. #876, 879 exist dated 1989.
| | | | |
|---|---|---|---|
| 876a | A126 | 15c | .20 .20 |
| 877a | A126 | 60c | .40 .40 |
| 878a | A126 | 80c | .55 .55 |
| 879a | A126 | $20 | 13.75 13.75 |
| | | Nos. 876a-879a (4) | 14.90 14.90 |

## 1987, Mar. 16 Unwmk. — Perf. 15

Statue of Liberty, Cent. — A145

Paintings (details) by unidentified artists.
## 1987, Nov. 30 Wmk. 384 — Perf. 15
| | | | |
|---|---|---|---|
| 897 | A149 | 15c The Holy Family | 45 45 |
| 898 | A149 | 50c Adoration of the Shepherds | .95 .95 |
| 899 | A149 | 60c Adoration of the Magi | 1.00 1.00 |
| 900 | A149 | 90c Madonna and Child | 1.60 1.60 |
| | | Nos. 897-900 (4) | 4.00 4.00 |

### Souvenir Sheet
| | | | |
|---|---|---|---|
| 901 | A149 | $6 Holy Family | 6.50 6.50 |

Christmas A149

## 1987, Apr. 29 Wmk. 373 — Perf. 14½
| | | | |
|---|---|---|---|
| 880 | A144 | 15c Statue, flags | .25 .25 |
| 881 | A144 | 80c Statue, ship | .70 .70 |
| 882 | A144 | $1 Statue, Concorde jet | .90 .90 |
| 883 | A144 | $5 Statue, flying boat | 4.50 4.50 |
| | | Nos. 880-883 (4) | 6.35 6.35 |

### Souvenir Sheet
| | | | |
|---|---|---|---|
| 884 | A145 | $6 Statue, New York City | 5.00 5.00 |

Maps, Surveying Instruments A147

First cadastral survey of St. Lucia.
## 1987, Aug. 31 Wmk. 384 Litho. — Perf. 14
| | | | |
|---|---|---|---|
| 888 | A147 | 15c 1775 | .50 .50 |
| 889 | A147 | 60c 1814 | 1.10 1.10 |
| 890 | A147 | 80c 1888 | 1.90 1.90 |
| 891 | A147 | $2.50 1987 | 4.75 4.75 |
| | | Nos. 888-891 (4) | 8.25 8.25 |

Victoria Hospital, Cent. — A148

## 1987, Nov. 4 Wmk. 384 Litho. — Perf. 14½
| | | | |
|---|---|---|---|
| 894 | A148 | $1 Pair, #a.-b. | 4.00 4.00 |
| 895 | A148 | $2 Pair, #a.-b. | 7.75 7.75 |

### Souvenir Sheet
| | | | |
|---|---|---|---|
| 896 | A148 | $4.50 Main gate, 1987 | 10.50 10.50 |

Nurse, hammock, 1913. #895a, Hospital, 1987. #895b, Hospital, 1887.

Designs: 15c, Ambulance, nurse, 1987. #894a, Ambulance, nurse. #894b, Nurse.

World Wildlife Fund — A150

Amazonian parrots, Amazona versicolor.
## 1987, Dec. 18 Wmk. 384 Litho. — Perf. 14
| | | | |
|---|---|---|---|
| 902 | A150 | 15c multi | 2.40 2.40 |
| 903 | A150 | 35c multi, diff. | 4.75 4.75 |
| 904 | A150 | 50c multi, diff. | 9.00 9.00 |
| 905 | A150 | $1 multi, diff. | 19.15 19.15 |
| | | Nos. 902-905 (4) | |

American Indian Artifacts — A151
## 1988, Feb. 12 Wmk. 384 Litho. — Perf. 14½
| | | | |
|---|---|---|---|
| 906 | A151 | 10c Carib clay zemi | .25 .25 |
| 907 | A151 | 30c Troumassee cylinder | .30 .30 |
| 908 | A151 | 80c Three-pointer stone | .70 .70 |
| 909 | A151 | $3.50 Dauphine petroglyph | 3.00 3.00 |
| | | Nos. 906-909 (4) | 4.25 4.25 |

## Lloyds of London, 300th Anniv. Common Design Type
## 1988, Sept. 15 — Perf. 14x13½ Wmk. 384
| | | | |
|---|---|---|---|
| 921 | A155 | Strip of 4 | 7.00 7.00 |
| a. | | 10c multicolored | .50 .50 |
| b. | | 30c multicolored | .50 .50 |
| c. | | 80c multicolored | 1.50 1.50 |
| d. | | $2.50 multicolored | 4.50 4.50 |

### Souvenir Sheet
| | | | |
|---|---|---|---|
| 922 | A155 | $5 multicolored | 5.00 5.00 |

Designs: 10c, San Francisco earthquake, 1906. 60c, Castries Harbor, horiz. 80c, Lady Nelson, sunk off Castries Harbor, 1942. $2.50, Castries on fire, 1948.

Tourism — A155

Lagoon and: 10c, Tourists, gourmet meal. 30c, Beverage, tourists. 80c, Tropical fruit. $2.50, Fish and chef. $5.50, Market. Illustration reduced.

## Cent. of the Methodist Church in St. Lucia — A154
## 1988, Aug. 15 Wmk. 384 Litho. — Perf. 14½
| | | | |
|---|---|---|---|
| 918 | A154 | 15c Altar window | .20 .20 |
| 919 | A154 | 60c Chancel | 1.40 1.40 |
| 920 | A154 | $3.50 Exterior | 3.40 3.40 |
| | | Nos. 918-920 (3) | |

Eastern Caribbean microwave communications system.
## 1988, June 10 Wmk. 384 Litho. — Perf. 14
| | | | |
|---|---|---|---|
| 914 | A153 | 15c multicolored | .25 .25 |
| 915 | A153 | 25c multicolored | .65 .65 |
| 916 | A153 | 80c multicolored | 2.10 2.10 |
| 917 | A153 | $5 multicolored | 3.25 3.25 |
| | | Nos. 914-917 (4) | |

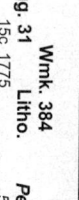

Cable and Wireless in St. Lucia, 50th Anniv. A153

## 1988, Apr. 29 — Perf. 15x14 Wmk. 373
| | | | |
|---|---|---|---|
| 910 | A152 | 10c Coins, banknotes | .50 .50 |
| 911 | A152 | 45c Branch in Castries | 1.00 1.00 |
| 912 | A152 | 45c like 45c | 1.25 1.25 |
| 913 | A152 | 80c Branch in Vieux Fort | 4.50 4.50 |
| | | Nos. 910-913 (4) | |

Designs: 15c, Antique and modern telephones. 80c, St. Lucia Teleport (satellite dish). $2.50, Map of St. Lucia. 25c, Rural telephone exchange.

## St. Lucia Cooperative Bank, 50th Anniv. — A152
## 1988, Oct. 17 Wmk. 373 Litho. — Perf. 14½
| | | | |
|---|---|---|---|
| 923 | A156 | 10c multicolored | .60 .60 |
| 924 | A156 | 45c multicolored | 1.40 1.40 |
| 925 | A156 | 80c multicolored | 1.90 1.90 |
| 926 | A156 | $2.50 multicolored | 5.75 5.75 |
| | | Nos. 923-926 (4) | 9.65 9.65 |

A156

Christmas: Flowers.
## 1988, Nov. 22 Wmk. 384 Litho. — Perf. 14½x14
| | | | |
|---|---|---|---|
| 927 | A156 | 15c Snow on the mountain | .50 .50 |
| 928 | A156 | 45c Christmas candle | .90 .90 |
| 929 | A156 | 60c Balisier | 1.10 1.10 |
| 930 | A156 | 80c Poinsettia | 1.50 1.50 |
| | | Nos. 927-930 (4) | 4.00 4.00 |

### Souvenir Sheet
| | | | |
|---|---|---|---|
| 931 | A156 | $5.50 Flower arrangement | 4.00 4.00 |

A157

## Left section

### 1989, Feb. 22 — Perf. 13½x13 — Wmk. 373

Natl. Independence, 10th Anniv.: 15c, Princess Alexandra presenting constitution to Prime Minister Compton. 80c, Sulfur springs geothermal well. $1, Sir Arthur Lewis Community College. $2.50, Pointe Seraphine tax-free shopping center. $5, Emblem.

| 932 | A157 | 15c | Nationhood | .20 | .20 |
|---|---|---|---|---|---|
| 933 | A157 | 80c | Development | .75 | .75 |
| 934 | A157 | $1 | Education | .90 | .90 |
| 935 | A157 | $2.50 | Progress | 2.40 | 2.40 |
| | | | | 4.25 | 4.25 |

Nos. 932-935 (4)

**Souvenir Sheet**

| 936 | A157 | $5 | With Confidence We Progress | 3.75 | 3.75 |
|---|---|---|---|---|---|

**Map Type of 1987**

### 1989, Mar. 17 — Litho. — Wmk. 373 — Perf. 14½x14

| 937 | A143 | $1 | scarlet & black | .75 | .75 |
|---|---|---|---|---|---|

**Indigenous Mushrooms A158**

### 1989, May 22 — Perf. 14½x14 — Litho. — Wmk. 384

| 938 | A158 | 15c | Geronema citrinum | .70 | .70 |
|---|---|---|---|---|---|
| 939 | A158 | 25c | Lepiota spiculata | .70 | .70 |
| 940 | A158 | 50c | Calocybe cyanocephala | 1.60 | 1.60 |
| 941 | A158 | $5 | Russula puiggarii | 15.00 | 15.00 |
| | | | | 18.00 | 18.00 |

Nos. 938-941 (4)

---

**Trees In Danger of Extinction — A162**

### 1990 — Wmk. 384 — Perf. 14

| 953 | A162 | 10c | Chinna | .20 | .20 |
|---|---|---|---|---|---|
| 954 | A162 | 15c | Latanier | .20 | .20 |
| 955 | A162 | 20c | Gwi gwi | .20 | .20 |
| 956 | A162 | 25c | L'encens | .20 | .20 |
| 957 | A162 | 50c | Bois lele | .45 | .45 |
| 958 | A162 | 80c | Bois d'amande | .70 | .70 |
| 959 | A162 | 95c | Mahot piman grand bois | .80 | .80 |
| 960 | A162 | $1 | Balata | .85 | .85 |
| 961 | A162 | $1.50 | Pencil cedar | 1.25 | 1.25 |
| 962 | A162 | $2.50 | Bois cendre | 2.00 | 2.00 |
| 963 | A162 | $5 | Lowye cannelle | 4.25 | 4.25 |
| 964 | A162 | $25 | Chalantier grand bois | 21.00 | 21.00 |
| | | | | 32.10 | 32.10 |

Nos. 953-964 (12)

Issued: 20c, 25c, 50c, $25, 2/21; 10c, 15c, 80c, $1.50, 4/12; 95c, $1, $2.50, $5, 6/25. For overprints see Nos. 971, O28-O39.

### 1992-95 — Wmk. 373

| 953a | A162 | 10c | | .50 | .50 |
|---|---|---|---|---|---|
| 954a | A162 | 15c | | .50 | .50 |
| 955a | A162 | 20c | (95) | .50 | .50 |
| 956a | A162 | 25c | (94) | 1.00 | 1.00 |
| 957a | A162 | 50c | | 3.00 | 3.00 |

Nos. 953a-957a (5)

#953a, 957a exist dated 1993; #953a, 954a, 957a; 1994; #955a, 1990.

---

**Centenary of St. Mary's College, Intl. Literary Year — A163**

Designs: 30c, Father Tapon, original building. 45c, Rev. Brother Collins, current building. 75c, Students in literacy class. $2, Door to knowledge, children.

### 1990, June 6 — Wmk. 373

| 965 | A163 | 30c | multicolored | .35 | .35 |
|---|---|---|---|---|---|
| 966 | A163 | 45c | multicolored | .55 | .55 |
| 967 | A163 | 75c | multicolored | .90 | .90 |
| 968 | A163 | $2 | multicolored | 2.40 | 2.40 |
| | | | | 4.20 | 4.20 |

Nos. 965-968 (4)

**Queen Mother, 90th Birthday**
**Common Design Types**

### 1990, Aug. 3 — Wmk. 384 — Perf. 14x15

| 969 | CD343 | 50c | Coronation, 1937 | .50 | .50 |
|---|---|---|---|---|---|

**Perf. 14½**

| 970 | CD344 | $5 | Arriving at theater, 1949 | 5.00 | 5.00 |
|---|---|---|---|---|---|

**No. 963 Overprinted**

**ST. LUCIA Endangered Trees**

### 1990, Aug. 13 — Perf. 14

| 971 | A162 | $5 | multicolored | 4.75 | 4.75 |
|---|---|---|---|---|---|

Intl. Garden and Greenery Exposition, Osaka, Japan.

---

## Middle section

**Christmas — A164**

**Butterflies — A166**

**Boats A165**

Paintings: 10c, Adoration of the Magi by Rubens. 30c, Adoration of the Shepherds by Murillo. 80c, Adoration of the Magi by Rubens, diff. $5, Adoration of the Shepherds by Champaigne.

### 1990, Dec. 3 — Perf. 14

| 972 | A164 | 10c | multicolored | .50 | .50 |
|---|---|---|---|---|---|
| 973 | A164 | 30c | multicolored | .65 | .65 |
| 974 | A164 | 80c | multicolored | 1.75 | 1.75 |
| 975 | A164 | $5 | multicolored | 9.75 | 9.75 |
| | | | | 12.65 | 12.65 |

Nos. 972-975 (4)

### 1991, Mar. 27 — Wmk. 373 — Perf. 14½

Various boats.

| 976 | A165 | 50c | multicolored | 1.00 | 1.00 |
|---|---|---|---|---|---|
| 977 | A165 | 80c | multicolored | 2.25 | 2.25 |
| 978 | A165 | $1 | multicolored | 2.75 | 2.75 |
| 979 | A165 | $2.50 | multicolored | 7.00 | 7.00 |
| | | | | 13.40 | 13.40 |

Nos. 976-979 (4)

**Souvenir Sheet**

| 980 | A165 | $5 | multicolored | 10.50 | 10.50 |
|---|---|---|---|---|---|

### 1991, Aug. 15 — Wmk. 373 — Litho. — Perf. 14

| 981 | A166 | 60c | Polydamas swallowtail | 2.10 | 2.10 |
|---|---|---|---|---|---|
| 982 | A166 | 80c | St. Christopher's hairstreak | 2.75 | 2.75 |
| 983 | A166 | $1 | St. Lucia mestra | 3.25 | 3.25 |
| 984 | A166 | $2.50 | Godman's hairstreak | 8.50 | 8.50 |
| | | | | 16.60 | 16.60 |

Nos. 981-984 (4)

**Christmas A167**

### 1991, Nov. 20 — Litho. — Wmk. 384 — Perf. 14x14½

| 985 | A167 | 10c | Jacmel Church | .35 | .35 |
|---|---|---|---|---|---|
| 986 | A167 | 15c | Red Madonna, vert. | .40 | .40 |
| 987 | A167 | 60c | Monchy Church | 1.25 | 1.25 |
| 988 | A167 | $5 | Blue Madonna, vert. | 7.25 | 7.25 |
| | | | | 9.25 | 9.25 |

Nos. 985-988 (4)

**Atlantic Rally for Cruisers A168**

---

## Right section

Designs: 60c, Cruisers crossing Atlantic, map. 80c, Cruisers tacking.

### 1991, Dec. 10 — Wmk. 384 — Perf. 14

| 989 | A168 | 60c | multicolored | 2.50 | 2.50 |
|---|---|---|---|---|---|
| 990 | A168 | 80c | multicolored | 3.25 | 3.25 |

**Discovery of America, 500th Anniv. — A169**

### 1992, July 6 — Wmk. 373 — Litho. — Perf. 13

| 991 | A169 | $1 | Coming ashore | 2.25 | 2.25 |
|---|---|---|---|---|---|
| 992 | A169 | $2 | Natives, ships | 4.75 | 4.75 |

Organization of East Caribbean States.

**Contact with New World A170**

**Perf. 13½**

| 993 | A170 | 15c | Amerindians | .60 | .60 |
|---|---|---|---|---|---|
| 994 | A170 | 40c | Juan de la Cosa, 1499 | .95 | .95 |
| 995 | A170 | 50c | Columbus, 1502 | 1.10 | 1.10 |
| 996 | A170 | $5 | Gimie, Dec. 13th | 10.50 | 10.50 |
| | | | | 13.15 | 13.15 |

Nos. 993-996 (4)

### 1992, Aug. 4

**Christmas A171**

Paintings: 10c, Virgin and Child, by Delaroche. 15c, The Holy Family, by Rubens. 60c, Virgin and Child, by Luini. 80c, Virgin and Child, by Sassoferrato.

### 1992, Nov. 9 — Wmk. 373 — Litho. — Perf. 14½

| 997 | A171 | 10c | multicolored | .90 | .90 |
|---|---|---|---|---|---|
| 998 | A171 | 15c | multicolored | .90 | .90 |
| 999 | A171 | 60c | multicolored | 1.90 | 1.90 |
| 1000 | A171 | 80c | multicolored | 2.50 | 2.50 |
| | | | | 6.20 | 6.20 |

Nos. 997-1000 (4)

**Anti-Drugs Campaign — A172**

### 1993, Feb. 1 — Litho. — Wmk. 373 — Perf. 13½x14

| 1001 | A172 | $5 | multicolored | 9.25 | 9.25 |
|---|---|---|---|---|---|

**Gros Piton from Delcer, Choiseul, by Dunstan St. Omer A173**

Paintings: 75c, Reduit Bay, by Derek Walcott. $5, Woman and Child at River, by Nancy Cole Auguste.

---

## Bottom section

**PHILEXFRANCE '89, French Revolution Bicent. — A159**

Views of St. Lucia announcement and text: 10c, Independence day announcement, vert. 60c, French revolutionary flag at Morne Fortune, 1791. $1, "Men are born and live free and equal in rights," vert. $3.50, Captain La Crosse's arrival at Gros Islet, 1792.

### 1989, July 14 — Wmk. 373 — Litho.

| 942 | A159 | 10c | multicolored | .75 | .75 |
|---|---|---|---|---|---|
| 943 | A159 | 60c | multicolored | 1.75 | 1.75 |
| 944 | A159 | $1 | multicolored | 2.50 | 2.50 |
| 945 | A159 | $3.50 | multicolored | 9.00 | 9.00 |
| | | | | 14.00 | 14.00 |

Nos. 942-945 (4)

**Intl. Red Cross, 125th Anniv. A160**

### 1989, Oct. 10 — Wmk. 384 — Perf. 14½

| 946 | A160 | 10c | Natl. headquarters | 1.75 | 1.75 |
|---|---|---|---|---|---|
| 947 | A160 | 80c | Seminar in Castries, 1987 | 2.75 | 3.50 |
| 948 | A160 | $1 | Ambulance | 8.00 | 8.00 |

Nos. 946-948 (3)

**Christmas Lanterns Shaped Like Buildings A161**

A174

**1993, Nov. 1**     **Wmk. 373**     **Perf. 13**
| | | | |
|---|---|---|---|
| 1002 | A173 | 20c multicolored | .50 .50 |
| 1003 | A173 | 75c multicolored | 1.00 1.00 |
| 1004 | A173 | $5 multicolored | 7.00 7.00 |
| | | Nos. 1002-1004 (3) | 8.50 8.50 |

Christmas
A174

Details of paintings: 15c, The Madonna and Child, by Murillo, 60c, The Annunciation, by Champagne.

**1993, Dec. 6**     **Perf. 14**
| | | | |
|---|---|---|---|
| 1005 | A174 | 15c multicolored | .50 .50 |
| 1006 | A174 | 60c multicolored | 1.10 1.10 |
| 1007 | A174 | 95c multicolored | 1.90 1.90 |
| | | Nos. 1005-1007 (3) | 3.50 3.50 |

Details of paintings: 15c, The Madonna and Child, by Van Dyck. 95c, The Annunciation, by Champagne.

A175

A176

**1994, July 25**     **Wmk. 373**     **Perf. 13**
| | | | |
|---|---|---|---|
| 1008 | A175 | 20c multicolored | .35 .35 |

Abolition of Slavery on St. Lucia, bicent.

**Souvenir Sheet**

**1994**     **Perf. 12½x13**
| | | | |
|---|---|---|---|
| 1009 | A175 | $5 multicolored | 8.00 8.00 |

**1994, Dec. 9**

Christmas (Flowers): 20c, Euphorbia pulcherrima. 75c, Heliconia rostrata. 95c, Alpinia purpurata. $5.50, Anthurium andreanum.
| | | | |
|---|---|---|---|
| 1010 | A176 | 20c multicolored | .30 .30 |
| 1011 | A176 | 75c multicolored | .80 .80 |
| 1012 | A176 | 95c multicolored | 1.00 1.00 |
| 1013 | A176 | $5.50 multicolored | 6.00 6.00 |
| | | Nos. 1010-1013 (4) | 8.10 8.10 |

**1995, Apr. 28**
| | | | |
|---|---|---|---|
| 1014 | A177 | 20c Map of island | 1.00 1.00 |
| 1015 | A177 | 75c Rebelling | 1.40 1.40 |
| 1016 | A177 | 95c Battle scene | 2.75 2.75 |

Battle of Rabot, Bicent.
A177

**Souvenir Sheet**

**1995**     **Perf. 13**
| | | | |
|---|---|---|---|
| 1017 | A177 | $5.50 Battle map | 5.50 5.50 |

**End of World War II, 50th Anniv.**

**Common Design Types**

Designs: 20c, ATS women in Britain. 75c, German U-boat off St. Lucia, Caribbean regiment, North Africa. $1.10, Presentation. $5.50, Reverse of War Medal 1939-45.
Spitfire Mk V.

---

**1995, May 8**     **Wmk. 373**     **Perf. 13½**
| | | | |
|---|---|---|---|
| 1018 | CD351 | 20c multicolored | .65 .65 |
| 1019 | CD351 | 75c multicolored | 1.75 1.75 |
| 1020 | CD351 | 95c multicolored | 2.25 2.25 |
| 1021 | CD351 | $1.10 multicolored | 2.50 2.50 |
| | | Nos. 1018-1021 (4) | 7.15 7.15 |

**UN, 50th Anniv.**

**Common Design Type**

10c, Puma helicopter. 65c, Renault truck. $1.35, Transall C160. $5, Douglas DC3.

**Souvenir Sheet**

**1995, Oct. 24**     **Wmk. 373**     **Perf. 14**
| | | | |
|---|---|---|---|
| 1022 | CD352 | $5.50 multicolored | 6.25 6.25 |

**1995, Oct. 24**     **Litho.**
| | | | |
|---|---|---|---|
| 1023 | CD353 | 10c multicolored | .30 .30 |
| 1025 | CD353 | 65c multicolored | .70 .70 |
| 1026 | CD353 | $1.35 multicolored | 1.40 1.40 |
| 1026 | CD353 | $5 multicolored | 5.25 5.25 |
| | | Nos. 1023-1026 (4) | 7.65 7.65 |

Christmas — A178

Flowers: 15c, Eranthemum nervosum. 70c, Bougainvillea. $1.10, Allamanda cathartica. $3, Hibiscus rosa sinensis.

**1995, Nov. 20**     **Wmk. 373**     **Perf. 13**
| | | | |
|---|---|---|---|
| 1027 | A178 | 15c multicolored | .25 .25 |
| 1028 | A178 | 70c multicolored | .65 .65 |
| 1029 | A178 | $1.10 multicolored | 1.00 1.00 |
| 1030 | A178 | $3 multicolored | 2.75 2.75 |
| | | Nos. 1027-1030 (4) | 4.65 4.65 |

Carnival — A179

Water — A180

**1996, Feb. 16**     **Wmk. 384**     **Perf. 13**
| | | | |
|---|---|---|---|
| 1031 | A179 | 20c Calypso king | .40 .40 |
| 1032 | A179 | 75c Carnival king | .95 .95 |
| 1033 | A179 | 95c Carnival band | 1.40 1.40 |
| 1034 | A179 | $3 Carnival queen | 4.25 4.25 |
| | | Nos. 1031-1034 (4) | 7.00 7.00 |

**1996, Mar. 5**     **Wmk. 373**
| | | | |
|---|---|---|---|
| 1035 | A180 | 20c Muddy stream | .25 .25 |
| 1036 | A180 | 65c Clear stream | .65 .65 |
| 1037 | A180 | $5 Modern dam | 4.75 4.75 |
| | | Nos. 1035-1037 (3) | 5.65 5.65 |

Tourism
A181

---

Designs: 65c, Market. 75c, Riding horses on beach. 95c, Outdoor wedding ceremony. $5, Annual Intl. Jazz Festival.

Modern Olympic Games, Cent.—A182

**1996, May 13**     **Wmk. 373**     **Perf. 14**
| | | | |
|---|---|---|---|
| 1038-1041 | A181 | Litho. Set of 4 | 7.25 7.25 |

10c, Early runner. #1042a, Modern runners. #1043a, Two sailboats. #1043b, Four sailboats.

**1996, July 19**     **Wmk. 373**     **Perf. 14**
| | | | |
|---|---|---|---|
| 1042 | A182 | 15c Pair, #a.-b. | .75 .75 |
| 1043 | A182 | 75c Pair, #a.-b. | 3.00 3.00 |

Nos. 1042-1043 have continuous designs.

Flags & Ships
A183

Flags, ship: 10c, Spanish Royal banner, 1502. Spanish caravel. 15c, Skull & crossbones, 1550, pirate carrack. 20c, Royal Netherlands, 1660, Dutch 80-gun ship. 25c, Union flag, 1739, Royal Navy 64-gun ship. 40c, French Imperial, 1750, French 74-gun ship. 50c, Martinique & St. Lucia, 1766, Royal Navy frigate Squadron. 65c, British Red Ensign, 1782, Battle of the Saints. 75c, British Blue Ensign, 1782, RN brig. 95c, French Tricolor, 1792, French 38-gun frigate. $1, British Union, 1801, West Indies Grand Fleet. $2.50, Confederate, 1861, CSA steam/sail armed cruiser. $5, Canada, 1915-19, Canadian V & W class destroyer. $10, US, 1942-48, Fletcher class destroyer. $25, National, cruise ship.

**1996-2002**     **Perf. 14x15**
| | | | | |
|---|---|---|---|---|
| 1046 | A183 | 10c multi | Wmk. 384 | .20 .20 |
| 1047 | A183 | 15c multi | Wmk. 373 | .20 .20 |
| 1048 | A183 | 20c multi | Wmk. 373 | .20 .20 |
| 1049 | A183 | 25c multi | Wmk. 373 | .20 .20 |
| 1050 | A183 | 40c multi | Wmk. 373 | .30 .30 |
| 1051 | A183 | 50c multi | Wmk. 373 | .40 .40 |
| 1052 | A183 | 55c multi | Wmk. 373 | .50 .50 |
| 1053 | A183 | 65c multi | Wmk. 373 | .50 .50 |
| 1054 | A183 | 75c multi | Wmk. 373 | .55 .55 |
| 1055 | A183 | 95c multi | Wmk. 373 | .70 .70 |
| 1056 | A183 | $1 multi | Wmk. 373 | .75 .75 |
| 1057 | A183 | $2.50 multi | | 1.85 1.85 |
| 1058 | A183 | $5 multi | | 3.75 3.75 |
| 1059 | A183 | $10 multi | | 7.50 7.50 |
| 1060 | A183 | $25 multi | | 18.75 18.75 |
| | | Nos. 1046-1060 (15) | | 36.25 36.25 |

#1046a-1048a, 1051a are inscribed "1998." Nos. 1053a, 1056a, 1059a are inscribed "2001." No. 1048a dated "2001." No. 1048a exists dated "2002" or "2004." Issued: 10c, 15c, 20c, 9/16/96; 25c, 55c, 65c, 75c, 95c, 9/16/96; 40c, 50c, $1, 11/18/96; $2.50, $5, $10, $25, 1/8/97; #1048a, 1047a, 1048a, 1051a, 7/12/98; #1053a, 1056a, 1059a, 4/2001. #1049a, 2002: No. 1054a, May 2003. No. 1048a exists dated "2000." No. 1046-1049 exist dated "2002." No. 1048a exists dated "2003."

---

Flowers: 20c, Cordia sebestena. 75c, Cryptostegia grandiflora. 95c, Hibiscus elatus. $5, Caularthron bicornutum.

Queen Elizabeth II and Prince Philip, 50th Wedding Anniv.—A185

**1997, July 10**     **Wmk. 384**     **Perf. 14½x14**
| | | | |
|---|---|---|---|
| 1068 | A185 | 75c Pair, #a.-b. | 1.75 1.75 |
| 1069 | A185 | 95c Pair, #a.-b. | 2.10 2.10 |
| 1070 | A185 | $1 Pair, #a.-b. | 2.40 2.40 |
| | | Nos. 1068-1070 (3) | 6.25 6.25 |

#1068a, Queen. #1068b, Queen with horses. #1069a, Prince. #1069b, Queen riding in carriage. #1070a, Queen, Prince. #1070b, Princess Anne riding horse. $5, Queen, Prince riding in open carriage, horiz.

**Souvenir Sheet**

**1997, July 14**     **Perf. 14x15**
| | | | |
|---|---|---|---|
| 1071 | A185 | $5 multicolored | 5.25 5.25 |

**1996, Dec. 1**     **Wmk. 384**     **Perf. 14**
| | | | |
|---|---|---|---|
| 1061- 1064 | A184 | Litho. Set of 4 | 7.25 7.25 |

Christmas—A184

Disasters — A186

20c, MV St. George capsizes, 1935. 55c, SS Belle of Bath founders. $1, SS Ethelgonda runs aground, 1897. $2.50, Hurricane devastation, 1817.

**1997, July 14**     **Perf. 14x15**
| | | | |
|---|---|---|---|
| 1072-1075 | A186 | Litho. Set of 4 | 6.25 6.25 |

Events of 1797—A187

Designs: 20c, Taking of Praslin. 55c, Battle of Dennery. 70c, Peace. $3, Brigands join 1st West India Regiment.

**1997, Aug. 15**     **Wmk. 373**     **Perf. 14**
| | | | |
|---|---|---|---|
| 1076-1079 | A187 | Litho. Set of 4 | 6.25 6.25 |

Christmas—A188

Church art: 20c, Roseau Church. 60c, Altarpiece, Regional Seminary, Trinidad. 95c, Our Lady of the Presentation, Trinidad. $5, The Four Days of Creation.

**1997, Dec. 1**     **Perf. 14x15**
| | | | |
|---|---|---|---|
| 1080-1083 | A188 | Litho. Set of 4 | 5.75 5.75 |

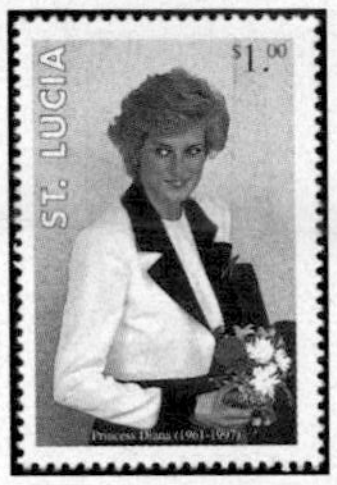

Diana, Princess of Wales (1961-97) — A189

**1998, Jan. 19 Litho. *Perf. 14***
**1084** A189 $1 multicolored .75 .75

No. 1084 was issued in sheets of 9.

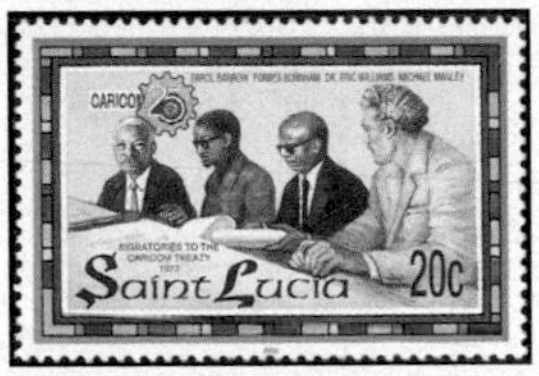

CARICOM, 25th Anniv. — A190

20c, Errol Barrow, Forbes Burnham, Dr. Eric Williams, Michael Manley signing CARICOM Treaty, 1973. 75c, CARICOM flag, St. Lucia Natl. flag.

**Wmk. 373**
**1998, July 1 Litho. *Perf. 13½***
**1085** A190 20c multicolored .20 .20
**1086** A190 75c multicolored .55 .55

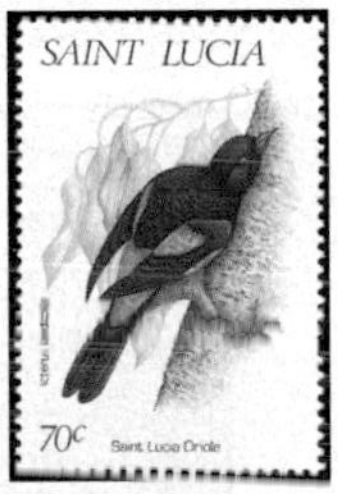

Birds — A191

Designs: 70c, St. Lucia oriole. 75c, Lesser Antillean pewee. 95c, Bridled quail dove. $1.10, Semper's warbler.

**1998, Oct. 23 Wmk. 373 *Perf. 14***
**1087-1090** A191 70c Set of 4 3.75 3.75

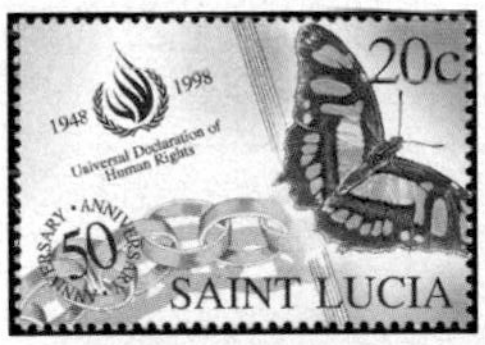

Universal Delcaration of Human Rights, 50th Anniv. — A192

Various butterflies, chains or rope.

**1998, Oct. 28**
**1091** A192 20c multicolored .30 .30
**1092** A192 65c multicolored .75 .75
**1093** A192 70c multicolored .85 .85
**1094** A192 $5 multicolored 5.50 5.50
*Nos. 1091-1094 (4)* 7.40 7.40

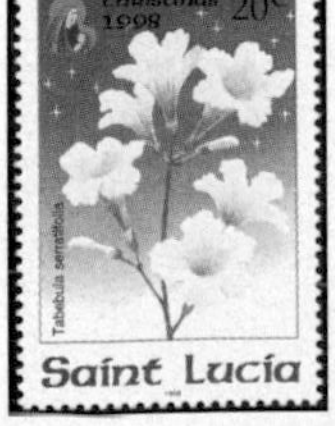

Christmas — A193

Flowers: 20c, Tabebuia serratifolia. 50c, Hibiscus sabdariffa. 95c, Euphorbia leucocephala. $2.50, Calliandra slaneae.

**Wmk. 373**
**1998, Nov. 27 Litho. *Perf. 14***
**1095-1098** A193 20c Set of 4 3.25 3.25

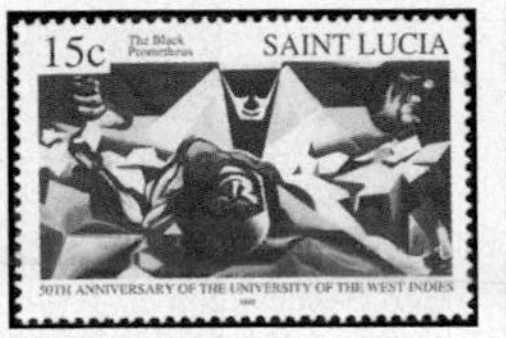

University of West Indies, 50th Anniv. A194

15c, The Black Prometheus. 75c, Sir Arthur Lewis, Sir Arthur Lewis College. $5, The Pitons.

**1998, Nov. 30**
**1099** A194 15c multicolored .20 .20
**1100** A194 75c multicolored .60 .60
**1101** A194 $5 multicolored 3.75 3.75
*Nos. 1099-1101 (3)* 4.55 4.55

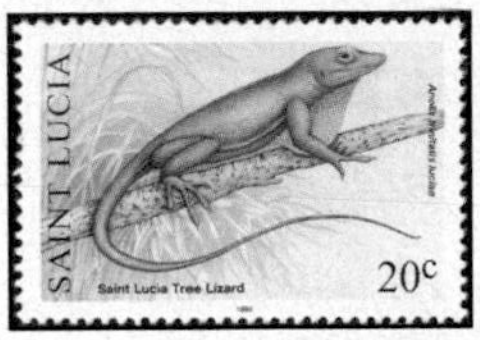

Wildlife A195

Designs: 20c, Saint Lucia tree lizard. 75c, Boa constrictor. 95c, Leatherback turtle. $5, Saint Lucia whiptail.

**Wmk. 373**
**1999, July 15 Litho. *Perf. 13½***
**1102-1105** A195 Set of 4 5.75 5.75

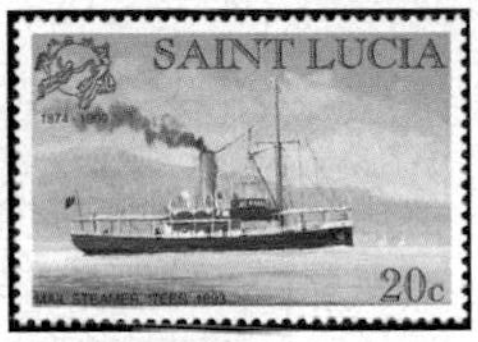

UPU, 125th Anniv. A196

**Wmk. 373**
**1999, Oct. 9 Litho. *Perf. 14***
**1106** A196 20c Mail steamer "Tees" .25 .25
**1107** A196 65c Sikorsky S.38 .60 .60
**1108** A196 95c Mail ship "Lady Drake" .80 .80
**1109** A196 $3 DC 10 2.50 2.50
*Nos. 1106-1109 (4)* 4.15 4.15

**Souvenir Sheet**
***Perf. 14¼***
**1110** A196 $5 Heinrich von Stephan 4.25 4.25

Stamp inscription on #1107 is misspelled. #1110 contains one 30x38mm stamp.

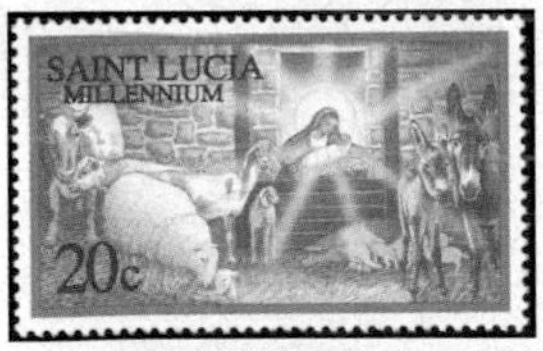

Christmas and Millennium — A197

Designs: 20c, Nativity. $1, Cathedral of the Immaculate Conception.

***Perf. 13¾x14***
**1999, Dec. 14 Litho. Wmk. 373**
**1111** A197 20c multi .20 .20
**1112** A197 $1 multi .70 .70

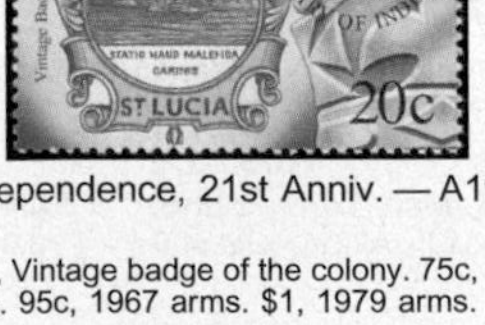

Independence, 21st Anniv. — A198

20c, Vintage badge of the colony. 75c, 1939 badge. 95c, 1967 arms. $1, 1979 arms.

***Perf. 14x13¾***
**2000, Feb. 29 Litho. Wmk. 373**
**1113** A198 20c multi .20 .20
**1114** A198 75c multi .55 .55
**1115** A198 95c multi .70 .70
**1116** A198 $1 multi .75 .75
*Nos. 1113-1116 (4)* 2.20 2.20

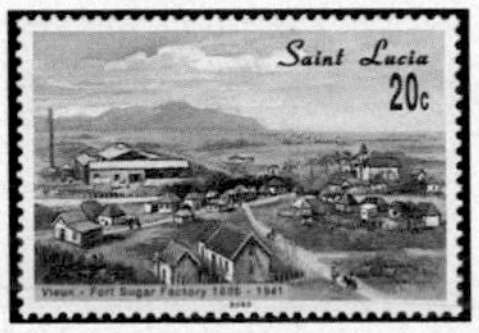

Historical Views A199

Designs: 20c, Fort sugar factory, 1886-1941. 60c, Coaling at Port Castries, 1885-1940. $1, Fort Rodney, Pigeon Island, 1780-1861. $5, Military hospital ruins, Pigeon Island, 1824-1861.

**Wmk. 373**
**2000, Sept. 4 Litho. *Perf. 14***
**1117-1120** A199 Set of 4 6.25 6.25

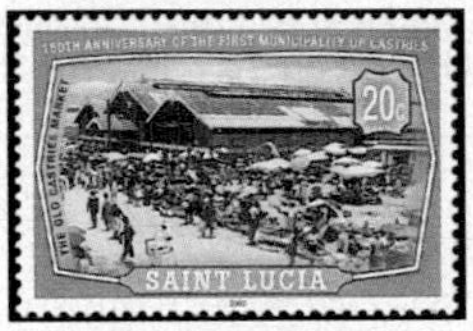

First Municipality of Castries, 150th Anniv. — A200

Designs: 20c, Old Castries Market. 75c, Central Library. 95c, Port Castries. $5, Mayors Henry H. Breen, Joseph Desir.

***Perf. 13¼x13½***
**2000, Oct. 9 Litho. Wmk. 373**
**1121-1124** A200 Set of 4 6.50 6.50

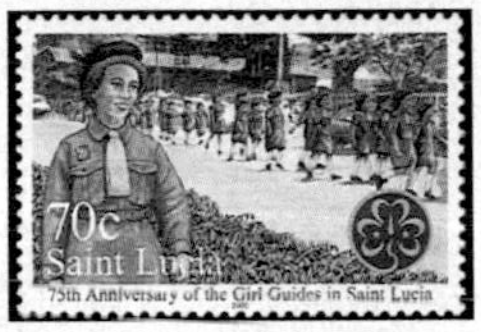

Girl Guides in St. Lucia, 75th Anniv. A201

Guides: 70c, Marching in brown uniforms. $1, Marching in blue uniforms. $2.50, At campground.

**2000, Oct. 16**
**1125-1127** A201 Set of 3 5.50 5.50

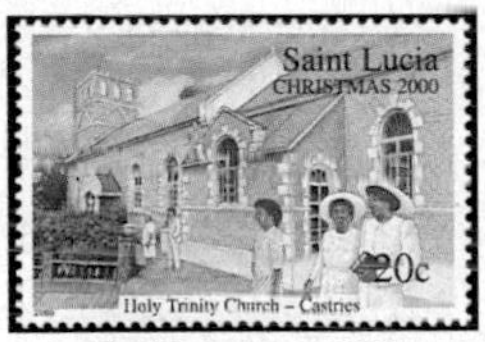

Christmas — A202

Churches: 20c, Holy Trinity, Castries. 50c, St. Paul's, Vieux-Fort. 95c, Christ, Soufriere. $2.50, Grace, River D'Oree.

**2000, Nov. 22 *Perf. 14***
**1128-1131** A202 Set of 4 5.25 5.25

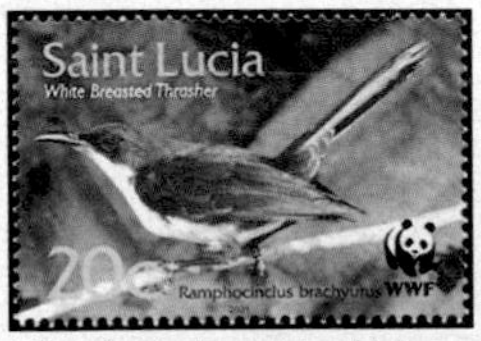

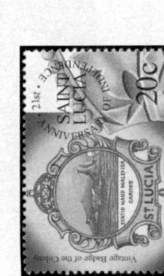

Worldwide Fund for Nature (WWF) — A203

Birds: #1132, 20c, White breasted thrasher. #1133, 20c, St. Lucia black finch. #1134, 95c, St. Lucia oriole. #1135, 95c, Forest thrush.

**Wmk. 373**
**2001, Jan. 2 Litho. *Perf. 14***
**1132-1135** A203 Set of 4 3.75 3.75
*1135a* Strip of 4, #1132-1135 3.75 3.75

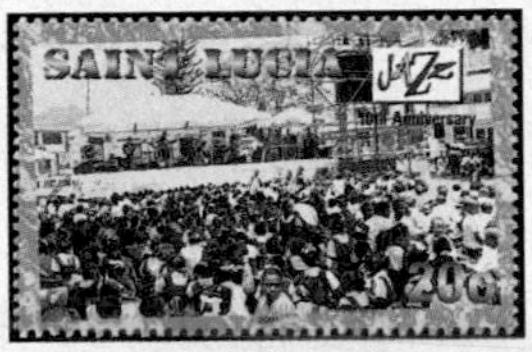

Jazz Festival, 10th Anniv. — A204

Designs: 20c, Crowd, stage. $1, Crowd, stage, ocean. $5, Musicians.

***Perf. 13¾x14***
**2001, May 3 Litho. Wmk. 373**
**1136-1138** A204 Set of 3 7.25 7.25

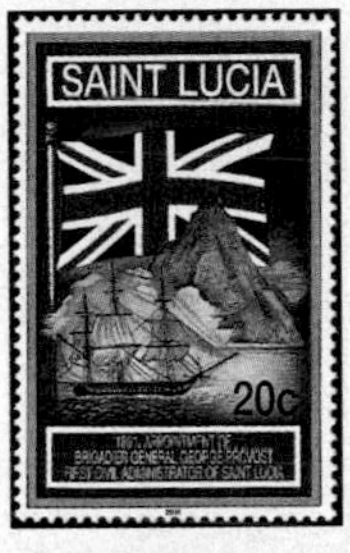

Civil Administration, Bicent. — A205

Designs: 20c, British flag, island, ship. 65c, French flag, Napoleon Bonaparte, signing of the Treaty of Amiens. $1.10, British flag, King George III, ships. $3, Island map, King George IV.

***Perf. 14x13¾***
**2001, Sept. 24 Litho. Unwmk.**
**1139-1142** A205 Set of 4 4.25 4.25

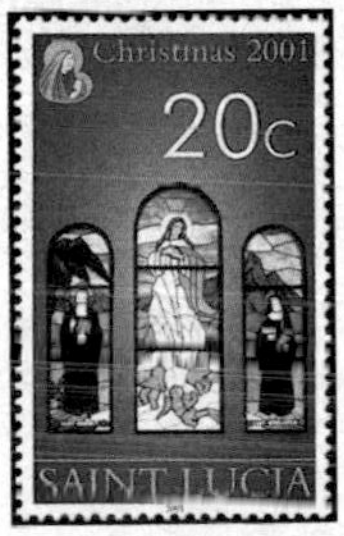

Christmas — A206

Various stained glass windows: 20c, 95c, $2.50

**2001, Dec. 7 Wmk. 373 *Perf. 13½***
**1143-1145** A206 Set of 3 4.25 4.25

**Reign Of Queen Elizabeth II, 50th Anniv. Issue**
Common Design Type

Designs: Nos. 1146, 1150a, 25c, Princess Elizabeth, 1927. Nos. 1147, 1150b, 65c, Wearing hat. Nos. 1148, 1150c, 75c, In 1947. Nos. 1149, 1150d, 95c, In 1996. No. 1150e, $5, 1955 portrait by Annigoni (38x50mm).

***Perf. 14¼x14½, 13¾ (#1150e)***
**2002, Feb. 6 Litho. Wmk. 373**
**With Gold Frames**
**1146-1149** CD360 Set of 4 3.75 3.75

**Souvenir Sheet**
**Without Gold Frames**
**1150** CD360 Sheet of 5, #a-e 5.75 5.75

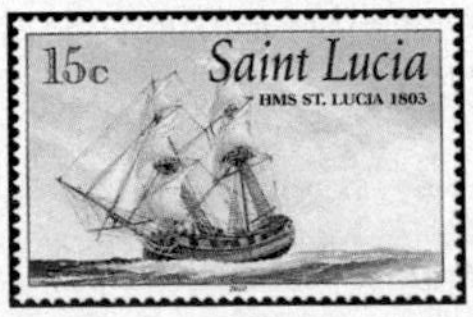

Royal Navy Ships A207

Designs: 15c, HMS St. Lucia, 1803. 75c, HMS Thetis, 1781. $1, HMS Berwick, 1903. $5, HMS Victory, 1805.

**Wmk. 373**
**2002, May 22 Litho. *Perf. 14***
**1151-1154** A207 Set of 4 5.25 5.25

**Queen Mother Elizabeth (1900-2002)**
Common Design Type

Designs: 50c, Holding baby (black and white photograph). 65c, Wearing red hat. 95c, Wearing hat (black and white photograph). $1, Wearing blue hat.
No. 1159: a, $2, Wearing tiara. b, $2, Wearing blue hat, diff.

*Perf. 13¾x14¼*
**2002, Aug. 5 Litho. Wmk. 373**
**With Purple Frames**
**1155-1158** CD361 Set of 4 3.75 3.75

**Souvenir Sheet**
**Without Purple Frames**
*Perf. 14½x14¼*
**1159** CD361 Sheet of 2, #a-b 6.75 6.75

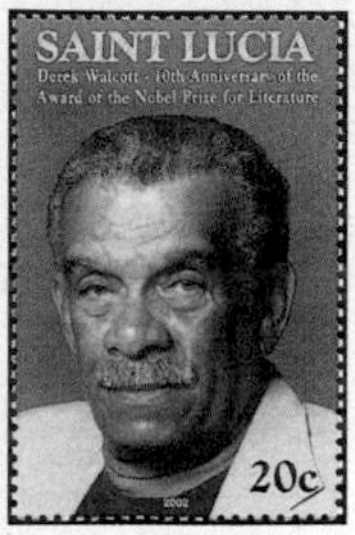

Awarding of Nobel Literature Prize to Derek Walcott, 10th Anniv. — A208

Designs: 20c, Walcott. 65c, Men and children, horiz. 70c, Women. $5, People in boat.

**Wmk. 373**
**2002, Oct. 11 Litho.** *Perf. 13¾*
**1160-1163** A208 Set of 4 6.00 6.00

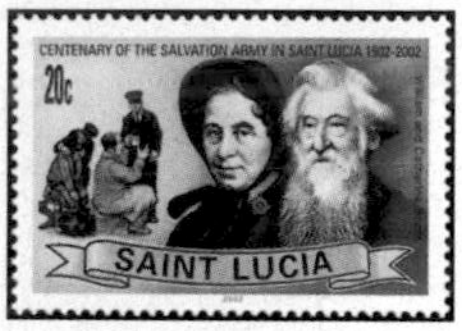

Salvation Army in St. Lucia, Cent. A209

Designs: 20c, William and Catherine Booth, Salvation Army workers. $1, Early Salvation Army officers in parade. $2.50, Salvation Army shield, "Blood and Fire" crest.

**Wmk. 373**
**2002, Nov. 27 Litho.** *Perf. 14*
**1164-1166** A209 Set of 3 4.25 4.25

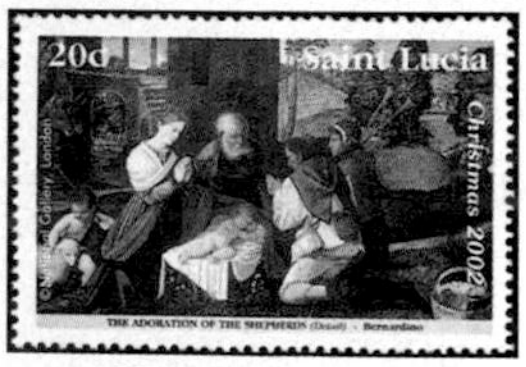

Christmas — A210

Paintings: 20c, Adoration of the Shepherds, by Bernardino. 50c, Adoration of the Kings, by Girolamo, vert. 75c, Adoration of the Kings, by Foppa, vert. $5, Adoration of the Shepherds, by the Le Nain Brothers.

**2002, Dec. 4** *Perf. 14x14¾, 14¾x14*
**1167-1170** A210 Set of 4 6.00 6.00

**Coronation of Queen Elizabeth II, 50th Anniv.**
Common Design Type

Designs: Nos. 1171, 20c, 1173b, Queen with crown. Nos. 1172, 75c, 1173a, Queen's carriage.

*Perf. 14¼x14½*
**2003, June 2 Litho. Wmk. 373**
**Vignettes Framed, Red Background**
**1171-1172** CD363 Set of 2 .75 .75

**Souvenir Sheet**
**Vignettes Without Frame, Purple Panel**
**1173** CD363 $2.50 Sheet of 2, #a-b 3.75 3.75

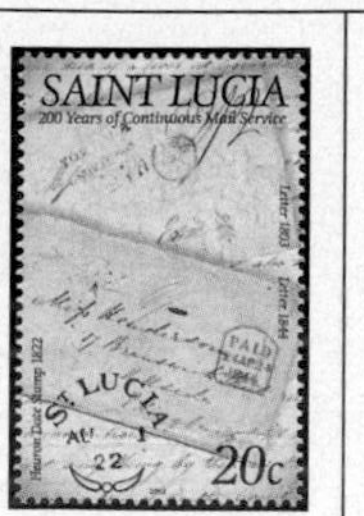

200 Years of Continuous Mail Service — A211

Designs: 20c, Letters from 1803 and 1844, 1822 fleuron postmark. 25c, St. Lucia #1-3. 65c, Map, mail ship Hewanorra. 75c, Post offices of 1900 and present time.

**Wmk. 373**
**2003, July 14 Litho.** *Perf. 14¼*
**1174-1177** A211 Set of 4 1.40 1.40

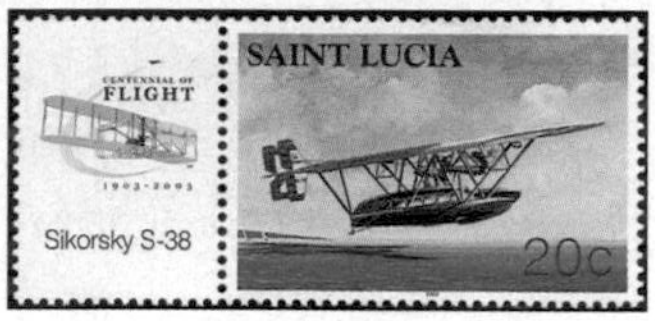

Powered Flight, Cent. — A212

Designs: 20c, Sikorsky S-38. 70c, Consolidated PBY-5A Catalina. $1, Lockheed Lodestar. $5, Spitfire Mk V "St. Lucia."
Illustration reduced.

*Perf. 13¼x13¾*
**2003, Nov. 28 Litho. Wmk. 373**
**Stamps + Labels**
**1178-1181** A212 Set of 4 5.25 5.25

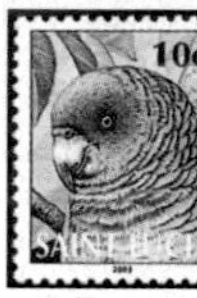

Parrot A213

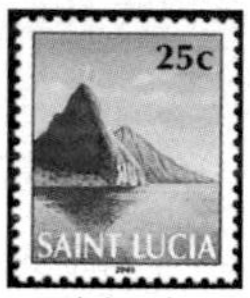

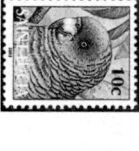

Island A214

**2003, Nov.** *Perf. 14x14¼*
**Coil Stamps**
**1182** A213 10c multi .20 .20
**1183** A214 25c multi .20 .20

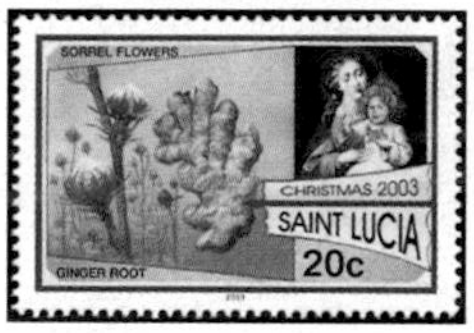

Christmas A215

Madonna and Child and: 20c, Sorrel flowers, ginger root. 75c, Sorrel drink, ginger ale. 95c, Masqueraders. $1, Christmas lanterns.

**2003, Dec. 2** *Perf. 14*
**1184-1187** A215 Set of 4 2.25 2.25

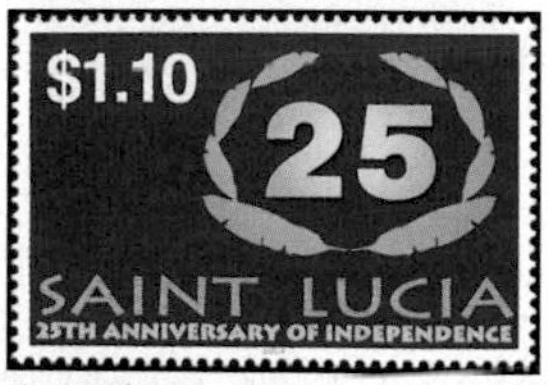

Independence, 25th Anniv. — A216

Designs: 20c, Flag raising ceremony, vert. 95c, People, book, airplane, ships, banana plant, vert. $1.10, "25" and leaves. $5, Harbor.

**2004, Feb. 20** *Perf. 13¾*
**1188-1191** A216 Set of 4 5.50 5.50

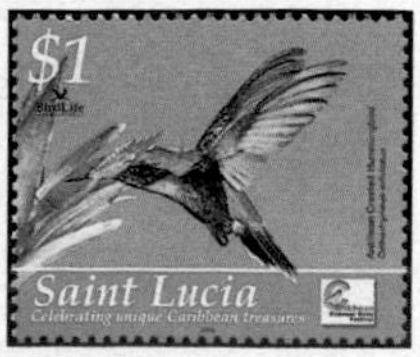

Caribbean Bird Festival A217

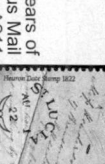

No. 1192: a, Antillean crested hummingbird. b, St. Lucia pewee. c, Purple-throated carib. d, Gray trembler. e, Rufous-throated solitaire. f, St. Lucia warbler. g, Antillean euphonia. h, Semper's warbler.

*Perf. 13¼x13*
**2004, June 30 Litho. Wmk. 373**
**1192** Block of 8 6.00 6.00
*a.-h.* A217 $1 Any single .75 .75

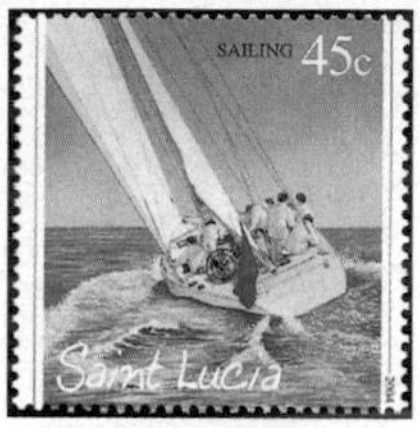

Tourism A218

Designs: 45c, Sailing. 65c, Horse riding. 70c, Scuba diving. $1, Walking.

**2004, Sept. 6** *Perf. 13¼*
**1193-1196** A218 Set of 4 2.10 2.10

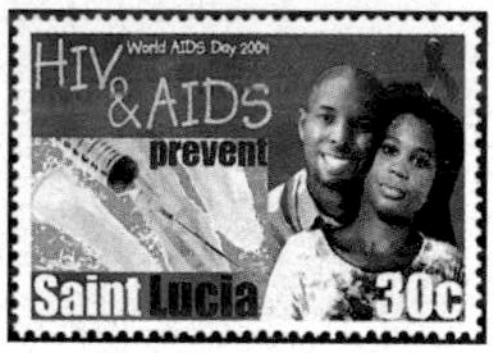

World AIDS Day A219

Designs: No. 1197, 30c, Condoms, syringe, couple. No. 1198, 30c, Children, woman.

**Wmk. 373**
**2004, Dec. 1 Litho.** *Perf. 14*
**1197-1198** A219 Set of 2 .45 .45

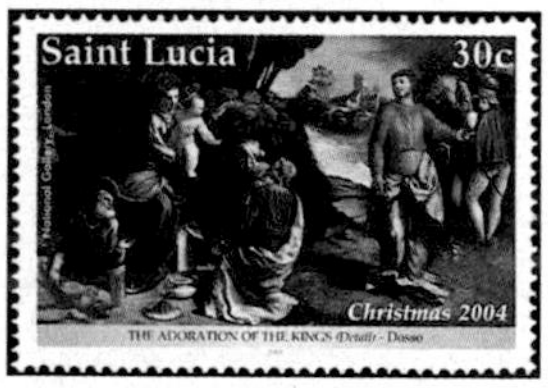

Christmas — A220

Painting details: 30c, Adoration of the Kings, by Dosso Dossi. 75c, Adoration of the Shepherds, by Nicolas Poussin, vert. 95c, Adoration of the Kings, by Joos van Wassenhove, vert. $1, Adoration of the Shepherds, by Carel Fabritius.

**2004, Dec. 14** *Perf. 14x14¾, 14¾x14*
**1199-1202** A220 Set of 4 2.25 2.25

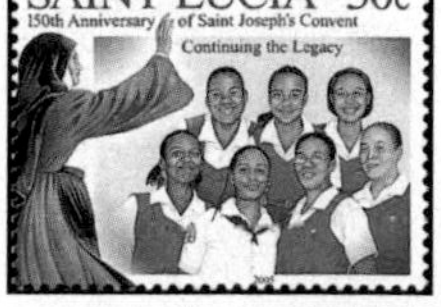

St. Joseph's Convent, 150th Anniv. A221

Nun and: 30c, Women. 95c, Convent and steps. $2.50, Building and street.

**Wmk. 373**
**2005, Mar. 14 Litho.** *Perf. 13¾*
**1203-1205** A221 Set of 3 3.00 3.00

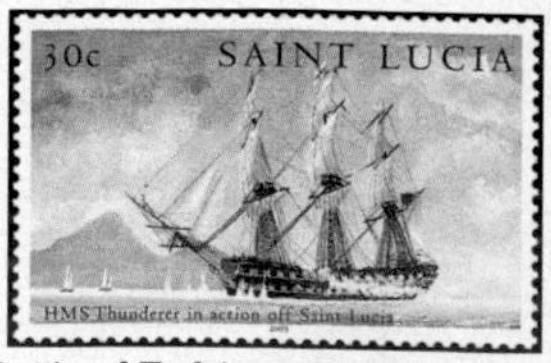

Battle of Trafalgar, Bicent. — A222

Designs: 30c, HMS Thunderer off St. Lucia. 75c, HMS Britannia in action against the Bucentaure. 95c, Admiral Horatio Nelson, vert. $5, HMS Victory.
$10, HMS Thunderer (44x44mm).

**Wmk. 373, Unwmkd. ($5)**
**2005, June 13 Litho.** *Perf. 13¼*
**1206-1209** A222 Set of 4 5.25 5.25

**Souvenir Sheet**
*Perf. 13¾*
**1210** A222 $10 multi 7.50 7.50

No. 1209 has particles of wood from the HMS Victory embedded in the areas covered by a thermographic process that produces a shiny, raised effect.

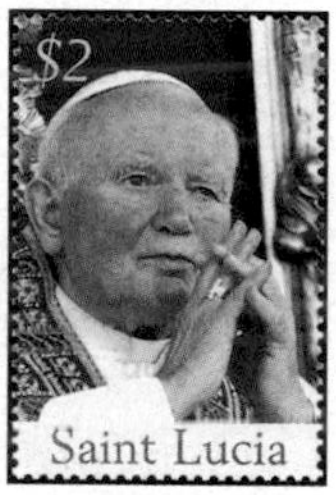

Pope John Paul II (1920 2005) A223

**2005, Aug. 29 Wmk. 373** *Perf. 14*
**1211** A223 $2 multi 1.50 1.50

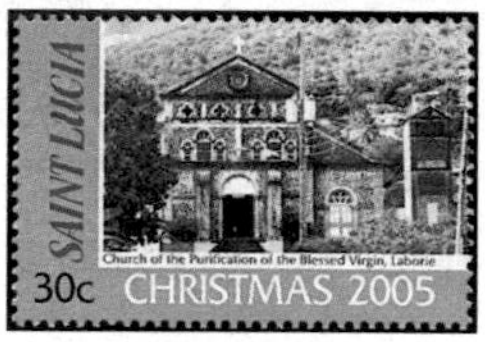

Christmas — A224

Designs: 30c, Church of the Purification of the Blessed Virgin, Castries. $5, Minor Basilica of the Immaculate Conception, Castries.

**Wmk. 373**
**2005, Nov. 28 Litho.** *Perf. 14*
**1212-1213** A224 Set of 2 4.00 4.00

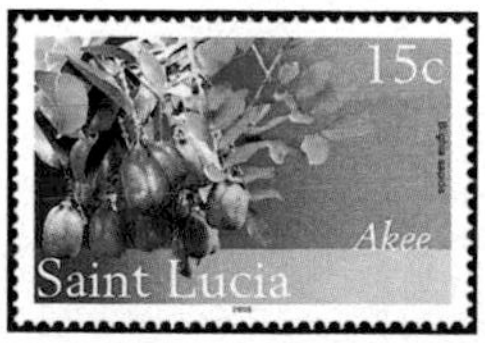

Fruits and Nuts A225

Designs: 15c, Blighia sapida. 20c, Solanum melongena. 25c, Mangifera indica. 30c, Coccoloba uvifera. 50c, Carica papaya. 55c, Spondias mombin. 65c, Chrysobalanus icaco. 70c, Artocarpus altilis. 75c, Annona reticulata. 95c, Psidium guajava. $1, Musa sp. $2.50, Manilkara achras. $5, Anacardium occidentale. $25, Mammea americana.

**2005, Dec. 5** *Perf. 14*

| | | | | | |
|---|---|---|---|---|---|
| **1214** | A225 | 15c | multi | .20 | .20 |
| **1215** | A225 | 20c | multi | .20 | .20 |
| **1216** | A225 | 25c | multi | .20 | .20 |
| **1217** | A225 | 30c | multi | .25 | .25 |
| **1218** | A225 | 50c | multi | .35 | .35 |
| **1219** | A225 | 55c | multi | .40 | .40 |
| **1220** | A225 | 65c | multi | .45 | .45 |
| **1221** | A225 | 70c | multi | .50 | .50 |
| **1222** | A225 | 75c | multi | .55 | .55 |
| **1223** | A225 | 95c | multi | .70 | .70 |
| **1224** | A225 | $1 | multi | .75 | .75 |
| **1225** | A225 | $2.50 | multi | 1.90 | 1.90 |
| **1226** | A225 | $5 | multi | 3.75 | 3.75 |
| **1227** | A225 | $25 | multi | 19.00 | 19.00 |
| | *Nos. 1214-1227 (14)* | | | 29.20 | 29.20 |

## ST. LUCIA (continued)

Art by Llewellyn Xavier — A226

Designs: 20c, Axe Head, 30c, Turtle, $2.50, Pre-Columbian Vase, $5, Pre-Columbian Zemi.

**2006, Mar. 15    Wmk. 373    Litho.    Perf. 12¾**

Set of 4

| | | | Unused | Used |
|---|---|---|---|---|
| 1228-1231 | A226 | | 6.00 | 6.00 |

### AIR POST STAMP

Catalogue values for unused stamps in this section are for Never Hinged items.

Map of St. Lucia — AP1

**1967, Mar. 1    Perf. 14½x14    Photo.    Unwmk.**

| | | | Unused | Used |
|---|---|---|---|---|
| C1 | AP1 | 15c blue | .40 | .40 |

St. Lucia's independence.

Exists imperf. and also in souvenir sheet.

### POSTAGE DUE STAMPS

D1

Type I — "No." 3mm wide (shown).
Type II — "No." 4mm wide.

**1931    Unwmk.    Rough Perf. 12    Typeset**

| | | | Unused | Used |
|---|---|---|---|---|
| J1 | D1 | 1p blk, gray bl, type I | 5.00 | 15.00 |
| a. | | Type II | 17.50 | 40.00 |
| J2 | D1 | 2p blk, yel, type I | 12.50 | 42.50 |
| a. | | Type II | 35.00 | 95.00 |
| b. | | Vertical pair, imperf. btwn. | 5,250. | |

The serial numbers are handstamped. Type II has round "o" and period. Type I has tall "o" and square period.

Catalogue values for unused stamps in this section, from this point to the end of the section, are for Never Hinged items.

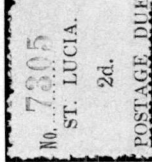

D2

**1933-47    Typo.    Wmk. 4    Perf. 14**

| | | | Unused | Used |
|---|---|---|---|---|
| J3 | D2 | 1p black | 5.00 | 6.25 |
| J4 | D2 | 2p black | 20.00 | 8.25 |
| J5 | D2 | 4p black ('47) | 5.75 | 42.50 |
| J6 | D2 | 8p black ('47) | 36.50 | 109.50 |

Nos. J3-J6 (4)

Issue date: June 28, 1947.

**1949, Oct. 1    Values in Cents**

| | | | Unused | Used |
|---|---|---|---|---|
| J7 | D2 | 2c black | .20 | 8.75 |
| J8 | D2 | 4c black | .30 | 11.00 |
| J9 | D2 | 8c black | 3.00 | 40.00 |
| J10 | D2 | 16c black | 4.75 | 112.25 |

Nos. J7-J10 (4)

Values are for examples on chalky paper, which were issued in 1952. Regular paper examples are worth more.

**Wmk. 4a (error)**

| | | Unused |
|---|---|---|
| J7a | 2c | 32.50 |
| J8a | 4c | 47.50 |
| J9a | 8c | 350.00 |
| J10a | 16c | 475.00 |

Nos. J7a-J10a (4)    905.00

In the 2c center the "c" is heavier and the period bigger.

Nos. J9-J12 exist with overprint "Statehood/1st Mar. '67" in red.

**1965, Mar. 9    Wmk. 314**

| | | | Unused | Used |
|---|---|---|---|---|
| J11 | D2 | 2c black | .50 | 6.50 |
| J12 | D2 | 4c black | .60 | 7.50 |

Arms of St. Lucia — D3

**1981, Aug. 4    Litho.    Wmk. 373**

| | | | Unused | Used |
|---|---|---|---|---|
| J13 | D3 | 5c red brown | .20 | .35 |
| J14 | D3 | 15c green | .20 | .40 |
| J15 | D3 | 25c deep orange | .40 | 1.00 |
| J16 | D3 | $1 dark blue | 1.05 | 2.15 |

Nos. J13-J16 (4)

**1990    Wmk. 384    Perf. 15x14**

| | | | Unused | Used |
|---|---|---|---|---|
| J17 | D3 | 5c red brown | .20 | .20 |
| J18 | D3 | 15c green | .20 | .20 |
| J19 | D3 | 25c deep orange | .60 | .75 |
| J20 | D3 | $1 dark blue | 1.20 | 1.35 |

Nos. J17-J20 (4)

### WAR TAX STAMPS

No. 65 Overprinted

**1916    Wmk. 3**

| | | | Unused | Used |
|---|---|---|---|---|
| MR1 | A11 | 1p scarlet | 10.50 | 10.50 |
| a. | | Double overprint | 450.00 | 450.00 |
| h. | | 1p carmine | 60.00 | 37.50 |

Overprinted

**Perf. 14**

| | | | Unused | Used |
|---|---|---|---|---|
| MR2 | A11 | 1p scarlet | 1.25 | .35 |

### OFFICIAL STAMPS

Catalogue values for unused stamps in this section are for Never Hinged items.

Nos. 504-515 Overprinted

**1983, Oct. 13    Litho.    Wmk. 373    Perf. 14½**

| | | | Unused | Used |
|---|---|---|---|---|
| O1 | A95 | 5c multicolored | .20 | .20 |
| O2 | A95 | 10c multicolored | .25 | .25 |
| O3 | A95 | 15c multicolored | .25 | .25 |
| O4 | A95 | 20c multicolored | .35 | .25 |
| O5 | A95 | 25c multicolored | .45 | .45 |
| O6 | A95 | 30c multicolored | .60 | .45 |
| O7 | A95 | 50c multicolored | .70 | .45 |
| O8 | A95 | 75c multicolored | .90 | .80 |
| O9 | A95 | $1 multicolored | 1.25 | 1.10 |
| O10 | A95 | $2 multicolored | 1.75 | 2.50 |
| O11 | A95 | $5 multicolored | 3.75 | 4.75 |
| O12 | A95 | $10 multicolored | 7.75 | 9.75 |

Nos. O1-O12 (12)    18.25    21.20

Nos. 747-761 Ovptd.

**1985, May 7    Litho.    Perf. 15**

| | | | Unused | Used |
|---|---|---|---|---|
| O13 | A126 | 5c multicolored | .60 | .60 |
| O14 | A126 | 10c multicolored | .60 | .60 |
| O15 | A126 | 20c multicolored | .70 | .70 |
| O16 | A126 | 25c multicolored | .70 | .70 |
| O17 | A126 | 30c multicolored | .80 | .80 |
| O18 | A126 | 35c multicolored | .90 | .90 |
| O19 | A126 | 45c multicolored | 1.00 | 1.00 |
| O20 | A126 | 50c multicolored | 1.00 | 1.00 |
| O21 | A126 | 65c multicolored | 1.25 | 1.25 |
| O22 | A126 | 75c multicolored | 1.25 | 1.25 |
| O23 | A126 | 90c multicolored | 1.40 | 1.40 |
| O24 | A126 | $1 multicolored | 1.75 | 1.75 |
| O25 | A126 | $2.50 multicolored | 2.75 | 2.75 |
| O26 | A126 | $5 multicolored | 4.00 | 4.00 |
| O27 | A126 | $15 multicolored | 8.75 | 8.75 |

Nos. O13-O27 (15)    27.45    27.45

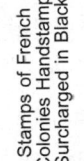

Nos. 953-964 Ovptd.

**1990, Feb. 21    Wmk. 384    Perf. 14**

| | | | Unused | Used |
|---|---|---|---|---|
| O28 | A162 | 10c multicolored | .20 | .20 |
| O29 | A162 | 15c multicolored | .20 | .20 |
| O30 | A162 | 20c multicolored | .20 | .20 |
| O31 | A162 | 25c multicolored | .30 | .30 |
| O32 | A162 | 50c multicolored | .40 | .40 |
| O33 | A162 | 80c multicolored | .50 | .50 |
| O34 | A162 | 95c multicolored | .50 | .50 |
| O35 | A162 | $1 multicolored | .95 | .95 |
| O36 | A162 | $1.50 multicolored | 1.50 | 1.50 |
| O37 | A162 | $2.50 multicolored | 2.75 | 2.75 |
| O38 | A162 | $5 multicolored | 13.50 | 13.50 |
| O39 | A162 | $25 multicolored | 21.20 | 21.20 |

Nos. O28-O39 (12)

Issued: 20c, 25c, 50c, $25, 2/21; 10c, 15c, 80c, $1.50, 4/12; 95c, $1, $2.50, $5, 6/25.

---

# STE.-MARIE DE MADAGASCAR

sänt-mə-rē-də-mad-ə-'gas-kär

LOCATION — An island off the east coast of Madagascar
GOVT. — French Possession
AREA — 64 sq. mi.
POP. — 8,000 (approx.)

In 1896 Ste.-Marie de Madagascar was attached to the colony of Madagascar for administrative purposes.

100 Centimes = 1 Franc

Navigation and Commerce — A1

**1894    Unwmk.    Typo.    Perf. 14x13½**

Name of Colony in Blue or Carmine

| | | | Unused | Used |
|---|---|---|---|---|
| 1 | A1 | 1c black, lil bl | .90 | .90 |
| 2 | A1 | 2c brown, buff | 1.40 | 1.40 |
| 3 | A1 | 4c claret, lavender | 3.25 | 3.25 |
| 4 | A1 | 5c green, grnsh | 9.25 | 7.75 |
| 5 | A1 | 10c black, lavender | 10.50 | 7.00 |
| 6 | A1 | 15c blue | 29.00 | 24.00 |
| 7 | A1 | 20c red, green | 21.00 | 17.00 |
| 8 | A1 | 25c black, rose | 20.00 | 13.50 |
| 9 | A1 | 30c brown, bister | 13.50 | 11.50 |
| 10 | A1 | 40c red, straw | 11.50 | 11.50 |
| 11 | A1 | 50c carmine, rose | 40.00 | 32.50 |
| 12 | A1 | 75c violet, org | 70.00 | 42.50 |
| 13 | A1 | 1fr brnz grn, straw | 40.00 | 29.00 |

Nos. 1-13 (13)    270.30    201.80

Perf. 13½x14 stamps are counterfeits.

These stamps were replaced by those of Madagascar.

---

# ST. PIERRE & MIQUELON

sānt-'pi,ə,r and 'mik-ə-,län

LOCATION — Two small groups of islands off the southern coast of Newfoundland
GOVT. — Formerly a French colony, now a Department of France
AREA — 93 sq. mi.
POP. — 6,966 (1999 est.)
CAPITAL — St. Pierre

The territory of St. Pierre and Miquelon became a Department of France in July 1976.

100 Centimes = 1 Franc
100 Cents = 1 Euro (2002)

Catalogue values for unused stamps in this country are for Never Hinged items, beginning with Scott 300 in the regular postage section, Scott B13 in the semi-postal section, Scott C1 in the air-post section, and Scott J68 in the postage due section.

Stamps of French Colonies Handstamp Surcharged in Black

**Imperf.**

**1885    Unwmk.**

| | | | Unused | Used |
|---|---|---|---|---|
| 1 | A8 | 05c on 40c ver, straw | 22.50 | 21.00 |
| 2 | A8 | 10c on 40c ver, straw | 92.50 | 39.00 |
| a. | | "M" inverted | 210.00 | 175.00 |
| 3 | A8 | 15c on 40c ver, straw | 29.00 | 22.50 |

Nos. 1-3 (3)    144.00    82.50

Nos. 2 and 3 exist with "SPM" 17mm wide instead of 15½mm. Nos. 1-3 exist with surcharge inverted and with it doubled.

Handstamp Surcharged in Black

(Surcharge types b, c, d)

**1885**

| | | | Unused | Used |
|---|---|---|---|---|
| 4 | A8 (b) | 05c on 35c | blk, yel | 110.00 | 77.50 |
| 5 | A8 (b) | 05c on 75c | car, rose | 290.00 | 210.00 |

**1885**

| | | | | |
|---|---|---|---|---|
| 6 | A8 (b) | 05c on 1fr brnz grn, | | |
| 7 | A8 (c) | 25c on 1fr brnz grn, | 22.50 | 21.00 |
| | a. | on 1fr brnz grn, | 10,500. | |
| 8 | A8 (d) | 25c on 1fr brnz straw | 2,250. | 2,100. |
| | a. | 25c on 1fr brnz straw | 1,600. | |

Nos. 7 and 8 exist with surcharge inverted, and with No. 7 vertical. No. 7 exists with surcharge inverted. No. 8 exists with "25" above "25" (the handstamping was done in two steps).

**1885**     **Perf. 14x13½**

| | | | | |
|---|---|---|---|---|
| 9 | A9 (c) | 5c on 2c brn, | 1,100. | |
| 10 | A15 | 10c black | 5,750. | 2,100. |
| | a. | 10c black | 925.00 | 1,100. |
| 11 | A9 (b) | 05c on 20c red, grn | 260.00 | |
| | a. | 05c on 20c red, grn | 29.00 | 29.00 |

No. 9 surcharge is always inverted. No. 10 exists with surcharge inverted.

**1886, Feb.**     **Typo.**     **Imperf.**

| | | | | |
|---|---|---|---|---|
| 12 | A9 (e) | 5c black | | 1,100. |
| 13 | A15 | 10c black | 5,750. | 2,100. |
| 14 | A15 | 15c black | 450.00 | 260.00 |
| | | Nos. 12-14 (3) | | 3,125. |

"P D" are the initials for "Payé a destination."
Excellent forgeries exist.

Stamps of French Colonies Surcharged in Black

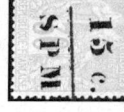

F D 5     15 c. SPM

**1891**     **Without Gum**

| | | | | |
|---|---|---|---|---|
| 15 | A9 (e) | 15c on 30c | 35.00 | 29.00 |
| 16 | A9 (e) | 15c on 35c | 210.00 | 175.00 |
| | a. | Inverted surcharge | 550.00 | 450.00 |
| 17 | A9 (e) | 15c on 35c blk, org | 600.00 | 525.00 |
| | a. | Inverted surcharge | 1,500. | 1,100. |
| 18 | A9 (e) | 15c on 40c red, straw | 1,250. | 1,600. |
| | a. | Inverted surcharge | 80.00 | 62.50 |
| | | | 175.00 | 175.00 |

e

**Perf. 14x13½**

**1891, Oct. 15**

| | | | | |
|---|---|---|---|---|
| 19 | A9 | 1c blk bl | 12.00 | 10.50 |
| 20 | A9 | 1c blk, lil bl (R) | 25.00 | 25.00 |
| | a. | Inverted overprint | 35.00 | 29.00 |
| 21 | A9 | 2c blk, lav | 11.50 | 10.00 |
| | a. | Inverted overprint | 21.00 | 21.00 |
| 22 | A9 | 2c blk, buff | 12.00 | 10.50 |
| | a. | Inverted overprint | 25.00 | 25.00 |
| 23 | A9 | 4c claret, | 24.00 | 24.00 |
| | a. | Inverted overprint | 57.50 | 57.50 |
| 24 | A9 | 4c claret, lav (R) | 25.00 | 25.00 |
| | a. | Inverted overprint | 57.50 | 57.50 |
| 25 | A9 | 5c grn, grnsh | 42.50 | 42.50 |
| | a. | Inverted overprint | 27.50 | 27.50 |
| 26 | A9 | 10c blk, lav | 12.00 | 10.50 |
| | a. | Double overprint | 95.00 | 95.00 |
| 27 | A9 | 15c blk, lav | 35.00 | 29.00 |
| | a. | Inverted overprint | 65.00 | 65.00 |
| 28 | A9 | 15c blue | 42.50 | 42.50 |
| | a. | Inverted overprint | 17.50 | 17.50 |
| 29 | A9 | 20c red, grn | 27.50 | 27.50 |
| | a. | Inverted overprint | 72.50 | 65.00 |
| 30 | A9 | 25c blk, rose | 29.00 | 25.00 |
| | a. | Inverted overprint | 100.00 | 22.50 |
| 31 | A9 | 30c brn, bis | 100.00 | 22.50 |
| 32 | A9 | 35c vio, org | 425.00 | 325.00 |
| 33 | A9 | 40c red, straw | 175.00 | 57.50 |
| 34 | A9 | 75c car, rose | 95.00 | 57.50 |
| | a. | Double surcharge | 160.00 | 150.00 |
| | | Inverted overprint | 85.00 | |

**1891-92**

| | | | | |
|---|---|---|---|---|
| 36 | A9 | 1c on 5c grn, grnsh | 9.00 | 8.50 |
| 37 | A9 | 1c on 10c blk, lav | 9.50 | 9.00 |
| 38 | A9 | 1c on 25c blk, rose | 9.00 | 9.00 |
| | a. | Inverted surcharge ('92) | | |
| 39 | A9 | 2c on 10c blk, lav | 9.00 | 8.50 |
| 40 | A9 | 4c on 20c red, grn | 92.50 | 7.75 |
| 41 | A9 | 4c on 25c blk, rose | 9.00 | |
| | a. | Double surcharge ('92) | 7.75 | 7.75 |
| 42 | A9 | 4c on 20c red, grn ('92) | | |
| 43 | A9 | 4c on 25c blk, rose ('92) | | |
| 44 | A9 | 4c on 30c brn, bis | 17.50 | 14.00 |
| 45 | A9 | 4c on 40c red, straw | 22.50 | 16.00 |
| | | Nos. 36-45 (10) | 106.00 | 94.00 |

See note after No. 35.

Surcharged in Black

**1891-92**

| | | | | |
|---|---|---|---|---|
| 35 | A9 | 1fr brnz grn, straw | 70.00 | 65.00 |
| | a. | Inverted overprint | 140.00 | 37.50 |
| | | | 1,041. | 876.00 |

Numerous varieties of mislettering occur in the preceding overprint: "S," "ST," "P," "M," "ON," or "=" missing; "S" instead of "ST," "P" instead of "ON"; "=" instead of "-." These varieties command double or triple values of normal stamps.

**1892, Nov. 4**     Surcharged

 j

| | | | | |
|---|---|---|---|---|
| 46 | A9 (k) | 1c on 5c grn, grnsh | 11.00 | 11.00 |
| 47 | A9 (k) | 2c on 5c grn, grnsh | 11.00 | 11.00 |
| 48 | A9 (k) | 4c on 5c grn, grnsh | 9.25 | 9.25 |
| 49 | A9 (k) | 10c on 25c blk, rose | 7.00 | 7.00 |
| 50 | A9 (k) | 15c on 25c blk, rose | 7.00 | 7.00 |
| 51 | A9 (k) | 4c on 25c blk, rose | 7.00 | 7.00 |
| | | Nos. 46-51 (6) | 52.25 | 52.25 |

See note after No. 35.

Postage Due Stamps of French Colonies Overprinted in Red

**1892, Dec. 1**     **Black Overprint**     **Imperf.**

| | | | | |
|---|---|---|---|---|
| 52 | D1 | 1c blk | 32.50 | 32.50 |
| 53 | D1 | 10c black | 32.50 | 32.50 |
| 54 | D1 | 20c black | 27.50 | 27.50 |
| 55 | D1 | 30c black | 27.50 | 22.50 |
| 56 | D1 | 60c black | 110.00 | 110.00 |
| 57 | D1 | 1fr brown | 150.00 | 150.00 |
| 58 | D1 | 2fr brown | 225.00 | 225.00 |
| 59 | D1 | 5fr brown | 400.00 | 400.00 |
| | | Nos. 52-59 (8) | 995.00 | 995.00 |

 k    Surcharged

**1909-30**

| | | | | |
|---|---|---|---|---|
| 79 | A17 | 1c org red & ol | .20 | .20 |
| 80 | A17 | 2c olive & bl | .20 | .20 |
| 81 | A17 | 4c grn & ol | .35 | .20 |
| 82 | A17 | 5c blk, grn & ol | .35 | .20 |
| 83 | A17 | 5c blk & ol grn ('22) | .80 | .20 |
| 84 | A17 | 10c car rose & blk ('22) | .35 | .35 |
| 85 | A17 | 10c brn & ol grn | .80 | .55 |
| 86 | A17 | 15c bister & mag | .40 | .40 |
| 86A | A17 | 15c dl vio & rose ('17) | .55 | .70 |
| 87 | A17 | 20c brn & vio | .55 | .20 |
| 88 | A18 | 25c bl grn & vio | .95 | .35 |
| 89 | A18 | 25c ol brn & bl grn | 3.25 | 1.60 |
| 90 | A18 | 30c org & vio brn | .95 | .95 |
| 91 | A18 | 30c rose & dull red ('22) | 1.75 | 1.40 |
| 92 | A18 | 30c brn & bl ('22) | 1.10 | 1.10 |
| 93 | A18 | 30c gray grn & bl ('25) | .95 | .95 |
| 94 | A18 | 35c ol grn & bl ('26) | .95 | .95 |
| 95 | A18 | 40c vio brn & olive | 2.90 | 1.60 |
| 96 | A18 | 45c grn & vio brn ('27) | 1.60 | 1.60 |
| 97 | A18 | 45c violet & ol grn | 1.40 | 1.10 |
| 98 | A18 | 50c ol & ol grn | .95 | .95 |
| 99 | A18 | 50c yel brn & mag ('22) | 1.10 | 1.10 |
| 100 | A18 | 60c dk bl & ver ('25) | .95 | .95 |
| 101 | A18 | 65c vio & red ('25) | 1.60 | 1.60 |
| 102 | A18 | 75c brown & olive ('28) | 1.40 | 1.10 |
| 103 | A18 | 90c brn red & org | 27.50 | 27.50 |
| 104 | A19 | 1fr blk & dp bl ('30) | 4.00 | 4.00 |
| 105 | A19 | 1.10fr org & org | 4.00 | 2.10 |
| 106 | A19 | 1.50fr blk & dp bl ('28) | 11.50 | 11.50 |
| 107 | A19 | 2fr violet & brn | 4.00 | 2.50 |
| 108 | A19 | 2fr violet & org ('30) | 13.00 | 13.00 |
| 109 | A19 | 5fr vio brn & ol | 13.00 | 13.00 |
| | | Nos. 79-109 (32) | 99.35 | 88.20 |

For overprints and surcharges see Nos. 121-131, 206C-206D, B1-B2, Q3-Q5.

 Fulmar Petrel A18

Fishing Schooner A19

 Fisherman A17

**1924-27**

| | | | | |
|---|---|---|---|---|
| 121 | A17 | 25c on 15c dl vio & rose ('25) | .35 | .35 |
| | a. | Double surcharge | 140.00 | |
| | b. | Triple surcharge | 140.00 | |
| 122 | A19 | 25c on 2fr vio & blk (Bl) | .50 | .50 |
| 123 | A19 | 25c on 5fr brn & ol (Bl) | .55 | .35 |
| 124 | A18 | 65c on 45c vio & brn (Bl) ('25) | 1.60 | 1.60 |
| | a. | Triple surcharge | 140.00 | |
| 125 | A18 | 85c on 75c brn & ol ('25) | 1.60 | 1.60 |
| 126 | A18 | 90c on 75c brn & red ('25) | .50 | .50 |
| 127 | A19 | 1.25fr on 1fr blk & ultra (R) ('26) | 2.25 | 2.10 |
| 128 | A19 | 1.50fr on 1fr ultra (R) ('27) | 2.90 | 2.90 |
| 129 | A19 | 3fr on 5fr dk bl ('27) | 2.90 | 2.90 |
| 130 | A19 | 10fr on 5fr red vio & ol ('27) | 4.00 | 4.00 |
| 131 | A19 | 20fr on 5fr vio & ver ('27) | 24.00 | 19.00 |
| | | Nos. 121-131 (11) | 59.00 | 58.70 |

Stamps and Types of 1909-17 Surcharged with New Value and Bars in Black, Blue (Bl) or Red

| | | | | |
|---|---|---|---|---|
| 115 | A16 | 5c on 30c brn, bis | .55 | .55 |
| 116 | A16 | 5c on 35c blk, yel (C) | 1.25 | .85 |
| 117 | A16 | 10c on 40c red, straw (C) | .85 | .85 |
| 118 | A16 | 10c on 50c car, rose | 1.25 | 1.25 |
| 119 | A16 | 10c on 75c dp vio, | .85 | .85 |
| 120 | A16 | 10c on 1fr brnz grn, org straw | 2.40 | 2.40 |
| | a. | 10c on 1fr brnz grn, straw | 3.50 | 3.50 |
| | | | 14.05 | 14.05 |

Two spacings between the surcharged numerals are found on Nos. 110 to 120.

| | | | | |
|---|---|---|---|---|
| 74 | A16 | 40c red, straw | 6.00 | 6.00 |
| 75 | A16 | 40c blk, bl ('00) | 37.50 | 30.00 |
| 76 | A16 | 50c car, az ('00) | 35.00 | 29.00 |
| 78 | A16 | 1fr brnz grn, straw | 24.00 | 16.00 |
| | | Nos. 60-78 (19) | 299.80 | 213.80 |

Perf. 13½x14 stamps are counterfeits. For stamps and overprints see Nos. 110-120, Q1-Q2.

**1892-1908**     **Typo.**     **Perf. 14x13½**

| | | | | |
|---|---|---|---|---|
| 60 | A16 | 1c blk, lil bl | .85 | .85 |
| 61 | A16 | 2c brn, buff | .95 | .95 |
| 62 | A16 | 4c claret, lav | 1.75 | 1.75 |
| 63 | A16 | 5c green, grnsh | 3.25 | 2.25 |
| 64 | A16 | 5c yel grn ('08) | 3.50 | 2.25 |
| 65 | A16 | 10c black, lav | 5.75 | 4.50 |
| 66 | A16 | 15c blue, quadrille paper ('00) | 12.00 | 4.00 |
| 67 | A16 | 15c red ('00) | 85.00 | |
| 68 | A16 | 15c gray, lt gray ('00) | 47.50 | |
| 69 | A16 | 20c red, grn | 21.00 | 17.50 |
| 70 | A16 | 25c black, rose | 10.00 | 2.25 |
| 71 | A16 | 25c blue ('00) | 15.00 | 10.50 |
| 72 | A16 | 30c brown, bis | 9.25 | 5.25 |
| 73 | A16 | 35c blk, yel ('06) | 5.75 | 5.25 |

Navigation and Commerce — A16

Stamps of 1892-1906 Surcharged in Carmine or Black

 05   n     10   o

**1912**

| | | | | |
|---|---|---|---|---|
| 110 | A16 | 5c on 2c brn, buff | .85 | .65 |
| 111 | A16 | 5c on 4c claret, lav | 2.25 | 2.25 |
| 112 | A16 | 5c on 5c blue (C) | .65 | .65 |
| 113 | A16 | 5c on 5c grn, grnsh ('08) | .55 | .55 |
| 114 | A16 | 5c on 25c blk, rose | .55 | .55 |

**1931, Apr. 13**     **Engr.**     **Perf. 12½**

Name of Country in Black

**Colonial Exposition Issue**     Common Design Types

| | | | | |
|---|---|---|---|---|
| 132 | CD70 | 40c deep green | 4.50 | 4.50 |
| 133 | CD71 | 50c violet | 4.50 | 4.50 |
| 134 | CD72 | 90c red orange | 4.50 | 4.50 |
| 135 | CD73 | 1.50fr dull blue | 4.50 | 4.50 |
| | | Nos. 132-135 (4) | 18.00 | 18.00 |

Common Design Types pictured following the introduction.

**1932-33**     **Perf. 13½x14, 14x13½**     **Typo.**

| | | | | |
|---|---|---|---|---|
| 136 | A20 | 1c brn brn & ultra | .20 | .20 |
| 137 | A21 | 2c blk & dk grn | .20 | .20 |
| 138 | A21 | 4c mag & dk brn | .20 | .20 |
| 139 | A22 | 5c vio & dk brn | .55 | .55 |
| 140 | A21 | 10c red brn & blk | .55 | .55 |

Fishing Steamer and Sea Gulls A22

Map and Fishermen — A20

Lighthouse and Fish — A21

**141** A21 15c dk blue & vio 1.10 1.10
**142** A20 20c blk & red org 1.40 1.40
**143** A20 25c lt vio & lt grn 1.40 1.40
**144** A22 30c ol grn & bl grn 1.40 1.40
**145** A22 40c dp bl & dk brn 1.40 1.40
**146** A21 45c ver & dp grn 1.40 1.40
**147** A21 50c dk brn & dk grn 1.40 1.40
**148** A22 65c ol brn & org 1.75 1.75
**149** A20 75c grn & red org 1.90 1.90
**150** A20 90c dull red & red 2.25 2.25
**151** A22 1fr org brn & org red 2.10 2.10
**152** A20 1.25fr dp bl & lake ('33) 2.10 2.10
**153** A20 1.50fr dp blue & blue 2.10 2.10
**154** A22 1.75fr blk & dk brn ('33) 2.40 2.40
**155** A22 2fr bl blk & Prus bl 9.25 9.25
**156** A21 3fr dp grn & dk brn 10.00 10.00
**157** A21 5fr brn red & dk brn 22.50 22.50
**158** A22 10fr dk grn & vio 60.00 60.00
**159** A20 20fr ver & dp grn 65.00 65.00
*Nos. 136-159 (24)* 192.55 192.55

For overprints and surcharges see Nos. 160-164, 207-221.

Nos. 147, 149, 153-154, 157 Overprinted in Black, Red or Blue

p

q

**1934, Oct. 18**
**160** A21(p) 50c (Bk) 3.50 3.50
**161** A20(q) 75c (Bk) 4.00 4.00
**162** A20(q) 1.50fr (Bk) 4.50 4.50
**163** A22(p) 1.75fr (R) 5.75 5.75
**164** A21(p) 5fr (Bl) 27.50 27.50
*Nos. 160-164 (5)* 45.25 45.25

400th anniv. of the landing of Jacques Cartier.

**Paris International Exposition Issue**
Common Design Types

**1937** *Perf. 13*
**165** CD74 20c deep violet 1.90 1.90
**166** CD75 30c dark green 1.90 1.90
**167** CD76 40c carmine rose 1.90 1.90
**168** CD77 50c dk brown & blue 1.90 1.90
**169** CD78 90c red 1.90 1.90
**170** CD79 1.50fr ultra 1.90 1.90
*Nos. 165-170 (6)* 11.40 11.40

**Colonial Arts Exhibition Issue**
Souvenir Sheet
Common Design Type

**1937** *Imperf.*
**171** CD78 3fr dark ultra 27.50 *35.00*

Dog Team A23

Port St. Pierre A24

Tortue Lighthouse A25

Soldiers' Bay at Langlade A26

**1938-40** **Photo.** *Perf. 13½x13*
**172** A23 2c dk blue green .20 .20
**173** A23 3c brown violet .20 .20
**174** A23 4c dk red violet .20 .20
**175** A23 5c carmine lake .20 .20
**176** A23 10c bister brown .20 .20
**177** A23 15c red violet .50 .50
**178** A23 20c blue violet .70 .70
**179** A23 25c Prus blue 2.10 2.10
**180** A24 30c dk red violet .50 .50
**181** A24 35c deep green .70 .70
**182** A24 40c slate blue ('40) .20 .20
**183** A24 45c dp grn ('40) .35 .35
*a.* Value omitted 77.50
**184** A24 50c carmine rose .70 .70
**185** A24 55c Prus blue 3.25 3.25
**186** A24 60c violet ('39) .50 .50
**187** A24 65c brown 5.00 5.00
**188** A24 70c org yel ('39) .55 .55
**189** A25 80c violet 1.25 1.25
**190** A25 90c ultra ('39) .70 .70
**191** A25 1fr brt pink 10.50 10.50
**192** A25 1fr pale ol grn ('40) .80 .80
**193** A25 1.25fr brt rose ('39) 1.75 1.75
**194** A25 1.40fr dk brown ('40) .95 .95
**195** A25 1.50fr blue green .95 .95
**196** A25 1.60fr rose violet ('40) .95 .95
**197** A25 1.75fr deep blue 2.90 2.90
**198** A26 2fr rose violet .70 .70
**199** A26 2.25fr brt blue ('39) .95 .95
**200** A26 2.50fr org yel ('40) .95 .95
**201** A26 3fr gray brown .85 .85
**202** A26 5fr henna brown .95 .95
**203** A26 10fr dk bl, *bluish* 1.40 1.40
**204** A26 20fr slate green 1.75 1.75
*Nos. 172-204 (33)* 44.35 44.35

For overprints and surcharges see Nos. 222-265, 260-299, B9-B10.

**New York World's Fair Issue**
Common Design Type

**1939, May 10** **Engr.** *Perf. 12½x12*
**205** CD82 1.25fr carmine lake 1.90 1.60
**206** CD82 2.25fr ultra 2.00 1.60

For overprints and surcharges see Nos. 256-259.

Lighthouse on Cliff — A27

**1941** **Engr.** *Perf. 12½x12*
**206A** A27 1fr dull lilac 1.40
**206B** A27 2.50fr blue 1.50

Nos. 206A-206B were issued by the Vichy government in France, but were not placed on sale in St. Pierre & Miquelon.
For surcharges, see B11-C12.

Free French Administration

The circumstances surrounding the overprinting and distribution of these stamps were most unusual. Practically all of the stamps issued in small quantities, with the exception of Nos. 260-299, were obtained by speculators within a few days after issue. At a later date, the remainders were taken over by the Free French Agency in Ottawa, Canada, by whom they were sold at a premium for the benefit of the Syndicat des Oeuvres Sociales. Large quantities appeared on the market in 1991, including many "errors." More may exist.

Excellent counterfeits of these surcharges and overprints are known.

Nos. 86 and 92 Overprinted in Black

a

**1942** **Unwmk.** *Perf. 14x13½*
**206C** A17 10c 1,250. 1,250.
**206D** A18 30c 1,250. 1,250.

The letters "F. N. F. L." are the initials of "Forces Navales Francaises Libres" or "Free French Naval Forces."

**Same Overprint in Black on Nos. 137-139, 145-148, 151, 154-155, 157**

**207** A21 2c 225.00 225.00
**208** A22 4c 55.00 55.00
**208A** A22 5c 825.00 825.00
**209** A22 40c 14.00 14.00
**210** A21 45c 175.00 175.00
**211** A21 50c 14.00 14.00
**212** A22 65c 45.00 45.00
**213** A22 1fr 375.00 375.00
**214** A22 1.75fr 14.00 14.00
**215** A22 2fr 17.50 17.50
**216** A22 5fr 350.00 350.00

Nos. 142, 149, 152-153 Overprinted in Black

*Perf. 13½x14*
**216A** A20 20c 400.00 400.00
**217** A20 75c 26.00 26.00
**218** A20 1.25fr 22.50 22.50
**218A** A20 1.50fr 525.00 525.00

**On Nos. 152, 149 Surcharged with New Value and Bars**

**219** A20 10fr on 1.25fr 46.00 46.00
**220** A20 20fr on 75c 52.50 52.50

No. 154 Surcharged in Red

*Perf. 14x13½*
**221** A22 5fr on 1.75fr 17.50 17.50

**Stamps of 1938-40 Overprinted type "a" in Black**

*Perf. 13½x13*
**222** A23 2c dk blue grn 440.00 440.00
**223** A23 3c brown vio 125.00 125.00
**224** A23 4c dk red vio 92.50 92.50
**225** A23 5c car lake 850.00 850.00
**226** A23 10c bister brn 14.00 14.00
**227** A23 15c red vio-let 1,575. 1,575.
**228** A23 20c blue vio-let 175.00 175.00
**229** A23 25c Prus blue 14.00 14.00
**230** A24 35c deep green 775.00 775.00
**231** A24 40c slate blue 17.50 17.50
**232** A24 45c deep green 17.50 17.50
**233** A24 55c Prus blue 9,250. 9,250.
**234** A24 60c violet 575.00 575.00
**235** A24 65c brown 21.00 21.00
**236** A24 70c or-ange yel 40.00 40.00
**237** A25 80c violet 440.00 440.00
**238** A25 90c ultra 17.50 17.50
**239** A25 1fr pale ol grn 21.00 21.00
**240** A25 1.25fr brt rose 20.00 20.00
**241** A25 1.40fr dark brown 17.50 17.50
**242** A25 1.50fr blue green 775.00 775.00
**243** A25 1.60fr rose vio-let 17.50 17.50
**244** A26 2fr rose vio-let 67.50 67.50
**245** A26 2.25fr brt blue 17.50 17.50
**246** A26 2.50fr or-ange yel 22.50 22.50
**247** A26 3fr gray brown *10,750.* *10,750.*
**248** A26 5fr hen-na brn *2,100.* *2,100.*
**248A** A26 20fr slate green 950.00 950.00

Nos. 176, 190 Surcharged in Black

**249** A23 20c on 10c 11.50 11.50
**250** A23 30c on 10c 9.25 9.25
**251** A25 60c on 90c 10.50 10.50
**252** A25 1.50fr on 90c 14.00 14.00
**253** A23 2.50fr on 10c 17.50 17.50
**254** A23 10fr on 10c 57.50 57.50
**255** A25 20fr on 90c 57.50 57.50
*Nos. 249-255 (7)* 177.75 177.75

**New York World's Fair Issue Overprinted type "a" in Black**

*Perf. 12½x12*
**256** CD82 1.25fr car lake 16.00 16.00
**257** CD82 2.25fr ultra 16.00 16.00

Nos. 205-206 Surcharged

**258** CD82 2.50fr on 1.25fr 17.50 17.50
**259** CD82 3fr on 2.25fr 17.50 17.50

Stamps of 1938-40 Overprinted in Carmine

**1941** *Perf. 13½x13*
**260** A23 10c bister brn 37.50 37.50
**261** A23 20c blue violet 35.00 35.00
**262** A23 25c Prus blue 39.00 39.00
**263** A24 40c slate blue 39.00 39.00
**264** A24 45c deep green 39.00 39.00
**265** A24 65c brown 39.00 39.00
**266** A24 70c orange yel 39.00 39.00
**267** A25 80c violet 39.00 39.00
**268** A25 90c ultra 39.00 39.00
**269** A25 1fr pale ol grn 39.00 39.00
**270** A25 1.25fr brt rose 39.00 39.00
**271** A25 1.40fr dk brown 39.00 39.00
**272** A25 1.60fr rose violet 42.50 42.50
**273** A25 1.75fr brt blue 42.50 42.50
**274** A26 2fr rose violet 45.00 45.00
**275** A26 2.25fr brt blue 45.00 45.00
**276** A26 2.50fr orange yel 45.00 45.00
**277** A26 3fr gray brown 45.00 45.00

**Same Surcharged in Carmine with New Values**

**278** A23 10fr on 10c bister brn 85.00 85.00
**279** A25 20fr on 90c ultra 85.00 85.00
*Nos. 260-279 (20)* 897.50 897.50

**Stamps of 1938-40 Overprinted in Black**

**280** A23 10c bister brn 60.00 60.00
**281** A23 20c blue violet 60.00 60.00
**282** A23 25c Prus blue 60.00 60.00
**283** A24 40c slate blue 60.00 60.00

| | | | | |
|---|---|---|---|---|
| 284 | A24 | 45c deep green | 60.00 | 60.00 |
| 285 | A24 | 65c brown | 60.00 | 60.00 |
| 286 | A24 | 70c orange yel | 60.00 | 60.00 |
| 287 | A24 | 80c violet | 60.00 | 60.00 |
| 288 | A24 | 90c ultra | 60.00 | 60.00 |
| 289 | A24 | 1fr pale ol grn | 60.00 | 60.00 |
| 291 | A25 | 1.25fr brt rose | 60.00 | 60.00 |
| 290 | A25 | 1.40fr dk brown | 60.00 | 60.00 |
| 292 | A25 | 1.60fr rose violet | 60.00 | 60.00 |
| 293 | A25 | 1.75fr brt blue | 775.00 | 775.00 |
| 294 | A26 | 2fr rose violet | 60.00 | 60.00 |
| 295 | A26 | 2.25fr brt blue | 60.00 | 60.00 |
| 296 | A26 | 2.50fr orange yel | 60.00 | 60.00 |
| 297 | A26 | 3fr gray | 60.00 | 60.00 |

## Same Surcharged in Black with New Values

| | | | | |
|---|---|---|---|---|
| 298 | A23 | 10fr on 10c bister brn | 140.00 | 140.00 |
| 299 | A25 | 20fr on 90c ul-tra | 160.00 | 160.00 |

Nos. 280-299 (20) 2,095. 2,095.

Christmas Day plebiscite ordered by Vice Admiral Emile Henri Muselier, commander of the Free French naval forces (Nos. 260-299).

### Types of 1938-40 Without RF

**1942 Photo. Perf. 13½**

| | | | | |
|---|---|---|---|---|
| 299A | A23 | 4c dk red vio | .35 | .35 |
| 299B | A23 | 15c red violet | 1.10 | 1.10 |
| 299C | A23 | 20c blue violet | 1.75 | 1.75 |
| 299D | A26 | 10fr dk blue | 2.10 | |
| 299E | A26 | 20fr rolive | 6.40 | |

Nos. 299A-299E (5)

Nos. 299A-299E were issued by the Vichy government in France, but were not placed on sale in St. Pierre & Miquelon.

> Catalogue values for unused stamps in this section, from this point to the end of the section, are for Never Hinged items.

St. Malo Fishing Schooner A28

**1942 Photo. Perf. 14x14½**

| | | | | |
|---|---|---|---|---|
| 300 | A28 | 5c dark blue | .20 | .20 |
| 301 | A28 | 10c dull pink | .20 | .20 |
| 302 | A28 | 25c brt green | .20 | .20 |
| 303 | A28 | 30c slate black | .20 | .20 |
| 304 | A28 | 40c brt ultra | .20 | .20 |
| 305 | A28 | 60c brnsh blue | .40 | .35 |
| 306 | A28 | 60c brown red | .40 | .35 |
| 307 | A28 | 1fr dark violet | .60 | .55 |
| 308 | A28 | 1.50fr brt red | 1.25 | 1.10 |
| 309 | A28 | 2fr brown | .75 | .65 |
| 310 | A28 | 2.50fr brt ultra | 1.25 | 1.10 |
| 311 | A28 | 4fr dk orange | .95 | .85 |
| 312 | A28 | 10fr dp plum | 1.40 | 1.25 |
| 313 | A28 | 20fr dark green | 10.05 | 9.10 |

Nos. 300-313 (14)

Nos. 300, 302, 309 Surcharged in Carmine or Black

### Eboue Issue

**1945 Common Design Type Engr. Perf. 13**

| | | | | |
|---|---|---|---|---|
| 314 | A28 | 50c on 5c (C) | .20 | .20 |
| 315 | A28 | 70c on 5c (C) | .20 | .20 |
| 316 | A28 | 80c on 5c (C) | .40 | .35 |
| 317 | A28 | 1.20fr on 5c (C) | .55 | .45 |
| 318 | A28 | 2.40fr on 25c | .55 | .55 |
| 319 | A28 | 3fr on 25c | .65 | .55 |
| 320 | A28 | 4.50fr on 25c | 1.25 | 1.00 |
| 321 | A28 | 15fr on 2.50fr (C) | 1.40 | 1.25 |

Nos. 314-321 (8) 5.20 4.45

### Common Design Issue

**1945 Engr. Perf. 13**

| | | | | |
|---|---|---|---|---|
| 322 | A28 | 2fr black | .85 | .75 |
| 323 | CD91 | 25fr Prussian green | 2.50 | 2.00 |

Nos. 322 and 323 exist imperforate.

Soldiers' Bay — A29

Fishing Industry Symbols A30

Fishermen A31

Weighing the Catch A32

Fishing Boat and Dinghy A33

Storm-swept Coast — A34

**1947, Oct. 6 Engr. Perf. 12½**

| | | | | |
|---|---|---|---|---|
| 324 | A29 | 10c chocolate | .20 | .20 |
| 325 | A29 | 30c violet | .20 | .20 |
| 326 | A29 | 40c rose lilac | .20 | .20 |
| 327 | A29 | 50c intense blue | .20 | .20 |
| 328 | A29 | 60c carmine | .85 | .70 |
| 329 | A30 | 80c brt ultra | .85 | .70 |
| 330 | A30 | 1fr dk green | .85 | .70 |
| 331 | A31 | 1.20fr blue grn | .75 | .55 |
| 332 | A31 | 1.50fr black | .75 | .55 |
| 333 | A31 | 3fr red brown | .75 | .55 |
| 334 | A32 | 3fr rose violet | 2.50 | 1.90 |
| 335 | A32 | 3.60fr brown org | 1.90 | 1.40 |
| 336 | A32 | 4fr sepia | 2.25 | 1.40 |
| 337 | A32 | 5fr orange | 2.25 | 1.90 |
| 338 | A33 | 5fr dp brown org | 2.25 | 1.90 |
| 339 | A33 | 6fr orange | 4.00 | 3.25 |
| 340 | A34 | 10fr Prus green | 4.00 | 2.50 |
| 341 | A34 | 15fr dk slate grn | 6.50 | 5.50 |
| 342 | A34 | 20fr vermilion | 6.50 | 4.25 |
| | A34 | 25fr dark blue | 35.75 | 27.80 |

Nos. 324-342 (19)

Imperforates
Most stamps of St. Pierre and Miquelon from 1947 onward exist imperforate in issued and trial colors, and also in small presentation sheets in issued colors.

Silver Fox — A35

**1952, Oct. 10 Engr. Unwmk. Perf. 13**

| | | | | |
|---|---|---|---|---|
| 343 | A35 | 8fr dk brown | 4.00 | 1.25 |
| 344 | A35 | 17fr blue | 5.25 | 2.00 |

### Military Medal Issue

**1952, Dec. 15 Common Design Type Engr. & Typo.**

| | | | | |
|---|---|---|---|---|
| 345 | CD101 | 8fr multicolored | 10.50 | 10.00 |

Fish Freezing Plant A36

**1955-56 Engr. Perf. 13**

| | | | | |
|---|---|---|---|---|
| 346 | A36 | 30c ultra & dk blue | .65 | .55 |
| 347 | A36 | 50c gray, blk & sepia | .65 | .55 |
| 348 | A36 | 3fr purple | 1.10 | 1.00 |
| 349 | A36 | 40fr Prussian blue | 2.75 | 2.25 |

Nos. 346-349 (4) 5.15 4.35

Issued: 40fr, July 4; others, Oct. 22, 1956.

Fish Freezer "Le Galantry" A37

### FIDES Issue

**1956, Mar. 15 Unwmk. Perf. 13x12½**

| | | | | |
|---|---|---|---|---|
| 350 | A37 | 15fr blk brn & chestnut | 4.50 | 2.75 |

See note in Common Design section after CD103.

Codfish A38

**1957, Nov. 4 Engr. Perf. 13**

| | | | | |
|---|---|---|---|---|
| 351 | A38 | 40c dk brn & grnsh bl | .45 | .35 |
| 352 | A38 | 1fr brown & green | .50 | .40 |
| 353 | A38 | 1fr indigo & dull blue | .85 | .70 |
| 354 | A38 | 4fr maroon, car & pur | 2.00 | 1.60 |
| 355 | A38 | 10fr grnsh bl, dk bl & brn | 6.05 | 4.80 |

Nos. 351-355 (5)

4fr, 10fr, Lighthouse and fishing fleet.

### Human Rights Issue

**1958, Dec. 10 Common Design Type Engr. Perf. 13**

| | | | | |
|---|---|---|---|---|
| 356 | CD105 | 20fr red brn & dk blue | 2.75 | 2.10 |

### Flower Issue

**1959, Jan. 28 Photo. Perf. 12½x12**

| | | | | |
|---|---|---|---|---|
| 357 | CD104 | 5fr Spruce | 3.25 | 1.60 |

Ice Hockey A39

**1959, Oct. 10 Engr. Perf. 13**

| | | | | |
|---|---|---|---|---|
| 358 | A39 | 20fr multicolored | 2.75 | 1.40 |

Mink A40

**1959, Oct. 7 Engr. Perf. 13**

| | | | | |
|---|---|---|---|---|
| 359 | A40 | 25fr ind, yel grn & brn | 3.75 | 2.00 |

Cypripedium Acaule — A41

**1962, Apr. 24 Unwmk. Perf. 13**

| | | | | |
|---|---|---|---|---|
| 360 | A41 | 25fr grn, org & car rose | 4.25 | 2.00 |
| 361 | A41 | 50fr grn & car lake | 6.50 | 2.75 |

Nos. 360-361, C24 (3) 22.75 8.25

Flower, 50fr, Calopogon pulchellus.

**1963, Mar. 4 Engr. Perf. 13**

Birds: 1fr, Rock ptarmigan. 2fr, Ringed plovers. 6fr, Blue-winged teal.

| | | | | |
|---|---|---|---|---|
| 362 | A42 | 50c blk, ultra & ocher | .70 | .45 |
| 363 | A42 | 1fr red brn, ultra & rose | 1.10 | .70 |
| 364 | A42 | 2fr blk, bl & bis | 1.40 | .70 |
| 365 | A42 | 6fr multicolored | 3.00 | 1.50 |

Nos. 362-365 (4) 6.20 3.35

Albert Calmette A43

**1963, Aug. 5 Engr. Perf. 13**

| | | | | |
|---|---|---|---|---|
| 366 | A43 | 30fr dk brn & dk blue | 10.00 | 5.50 |

Albert Calmette, bacteriologist, birth cent.

### Red Cross Centenary Issue

**1963, Sept. 2 Common Design Type Unwmk. Perf. 13**

| | | | | |
|---|---|---|---|---|
| 367 | CD113 | 25fr ultra, gray & car | 10.00 | 4.25 |

### Human Rights Issue

**1963, Dec. 10 Common Design Type Unwmk. Perf. 13**

| | | | | |
|---|---|---|---|---|
| 368 | CD117 | 20fr org, bl & dk brn | 6.00 | 2.75 |

### Philatec Issue

**1964, Apr. 4 Common Design Type Engr.**

| | | | | |
|---|---|---|---|---|
| 369 | CD118 | 60fr choc, grn & dk bl | 9.00 | 6.50 |

Rabbits A44

**1964, Sept. 28 Engr. Perf. 13**

| | | | | |
|---|---|---|---|---|
| 370 | A44 | 3fr shown | 1.75 | 1.10 |
| 371 | A44 | 4fr Fox | 1.75 | 1.00 |
| 372 | A44 | 5fr Roe deer | 3.75 | 2.00 |
| 373 | A44 | 34fr Charolais bull | 12.50 | 9.00 |

Nos. 370-373 (4) 19.75 10.20

Airport and Map of St. Pierre and Miquelon A45

**1967 Engr. Perf. 13**

| | | | | |
|---|---|---|---|---|
| 374 | A45 | 30fr ind, bl & dk red | 7.00 | 4.00 |
| 375 | A45 | 40fr sl grn, ol & dk red | 7.00 | 4.00 |
| 376 | A45 | 48fr dk red, brn & sl bl | 12.00 | 4.50 |

Nos. 374-376 (3) 26.00 12.50

Issued: 30fr, 10/23; 40fr, 11/20; 48fr, 9/25.

40fr. Television tube and tower; map. 48fr. Map of new harbor of St. Pierre.

Eider Ducks — A42

## WHO Anniversary Issue
Common Design Type
**1968, May 4** Engr. Perf. 13
377 CD126 10fr multicolored 10.00 6.50

René de Chateaubriand and Map of Islands — A46

Designs: 4fr, J. D. Cassini and map. 15fr, Prince de Joinville, Francois F. d'Orleans (1818-1900), ships and map. 25fr, Admiral Gauchet, World War I warship and map.

**1968, May 20** Photo. Perf. 12½x13
378 A46 4fr multicolored 4.25 2.75
379 A46 6fr multicolored 5.00 3.25
380 A46 15fr multicolored 8.25 4.25
381 A46 25fr multicolored 10.00 5.00
Nos. 378-381 (4) 27.50 15.25

## Human Rights Year Issue
Common Design Type
**1968, Aug. 10** Engr. Perf. 13
382 CD127 20fr bl, ver & org yel 8.00 4.25

Belle Rivière, Langlade A47

Design: 15fr, Debon Brouk, Langlade.

**1969, Apr. 30** Engr. Perf. 13
Size: 36x22mm
383 A47 5fr bl, slate grn & brn 3.75 2.00
384 A47 15fr brn, bl & dl grn 4.75 3.25
Nos. 383-384, C41-C42 (4) 46.00 22.25

Treasury A48

Designs: 25fr, Scientific and Technical Institute of Maritime Fishing. 30fr, Monument to seamen lost at sea. 60fr, St. Christopher College.

**1969, May 30** Engr. Perf. 13
385 A48 10fr brt bl, cl & blk 3.75 2.25
386 A48 25fr dk bl, brt bl & brn red 7.00 3.25
387 A48 30fr blue, grn & gray 8.25 5.00
388 A48 60fr brt bl, brn red & blk 13.50 7.00
Nos. 385-388 (4) 32.50 17.50

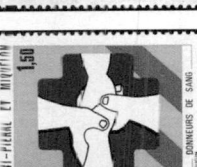

Ringed Seals A49

Designs: 3fr, Sperm whales. 4fr, Pilot whales. 6fr, Common dolphins.

**1969, Oct. 6** Engr. Perf. 13
389 A49 1fr lil, vio brn & red brn 2.50 1.40
390 A49 3fr bl grn, ind & red 2.50 1.40
391 A49 4fr ol, gray grn & mar 4.25 2.75
392 A49 6fr brt grn, pur & red 6.75 2.75
Nos. 389-392 (4) 16.00 8.30

L'Estoile and Granville, France A50

**1969, Oct. 13** Engr. Perf. 13
393 A50 34fr grn, mar & slate 14.00 7.50
394 A50 40fr brn red, lem & sl grn 22.50 7.50
395 A50 48fr multicolored 29.00 10.00
Nos. 393-395 (3) 65.50 25.00

Historic ships connecting St. Pierre and Miquelon with France.

## ILO Issue
Common Design Type
**1969, Nov. 24**
396 CD131 20fr org, gray & ocher 8.00 4.25

## UPU Headquarters Issue
Common Design Type
**1970, May 20** Engr. Perf. 13
397 CD133 25fr dk car, brt bl & brn 11.00 6.50
398 CD133 34fr maroon, brn & gray 16.00 7.00

Rowers and Globe A51

**1970, Oct. 13** Photo. Perf. 12½x12
399 A51 20fr lt grnsh bl & brn 15.00 6.00
World Rowing Championships, St. Catherine.

Blackberries A52

**1970, Oct. 20** Engr.
400 A52 3fr shown 1.25 1.00
401 A52 4fr Strawberries 1.25 1.25
402 A52 5fr Raspberries 2.00 1.25
403 A52 6fr Blueberries 3.50 1.50
Nos. 400-403 (4) 8.00 5.00

Ewe and Lamb A53

30fr, Animal quarantine station. 34fr, Charolais bull. 48fr, Refrigeration ship slaughterhouse.

**1970** Engr. Perf. 13
404 A53 15fr plum, grn & olive 9.00 3.50
405 A53 30fr sl, bis brn & ap grn 13.00 5.50
406 A53 34fr red lil, org brn & emer 22.50 7.00
407 A53 48fr multicolored 17.50 6.50
Nos. 404-407 (4) 62.00 22.50

Issue dates: 48fr, Nov. 10; others, Dec. 8.

Saint François d'Assise 1900 A54

Ships: 35fr, Sainte Jehanne, 1920. 40fr, L'Aventure, 1950. 80fr, Commandant Bourdais, 1970.

**1971, Aug. 25** Engr. Perf. 13
40fr, "La Jolie" & St. Jean de Luz, France, 1750. 48fr, "Le Juste" & La Rochelle, France, 1860.
408 A54 30fr Prus bl & hn 26.00 12.00
409 A54 35fr Prus bl, lt grn & ol brn 37.50 12.00
410 A54 40fr sl grn, bl & dk grn 42.50 9.00
411 A54 80fr dp grn, bl & blk 55.00 16.00
Nos. 408-411 (4) 161.00 49.00

Deep-sea fishing fleet.

"Aconit" and Map of Islands — A55

**1971, Sept. 27** Engr. Perf. 13
412 A55 22fr shown 25.00 7.50
413 A55 25fr Alysse 30.00 10.00
414 A55 50fr Mimosa 37.50 16.00
Nos. 412-414 (3) 92.50 33.50

Rallying of the Free French forces, 30th anniv.

Ship's Bell — A56

St. Pierre Museum: 46fr, Old chart and sextants, horiz.
**1971, Oct. 25** Photo. Perf. 12½x13
415 A56 20fr gray & multi 15.00 6.50
416 A56 46fr red brn & multi 30.00 10.00

## De Gaulle Issue
Common Design Type
Designs: 36fr, Gen. de Gaulle, 1940. Pres. de Gaulle, 1970.
**1971, Nov. 9** Engr. Perf. 13
417 CD134 35fr vermilion & blk 17.50 10.00
418 CD134 45fr vermilion & blk 25.00 11.50

Haddock A57

Fish: 3fr, Hippoglossoides platessoides. 5fr, Sebastes mentella. 10fr, Codfish.
**1972, Mar. 7** Engr. Perf. 13
419 A57 2fr vio bl, ind & pink 3.25 1.50
420 A57 3fr grn & gray olive 6.25 3.00
421 A57 5fr Prus bl & brick red 4.50 2.50
422 A57 10fr grn & slate grn 11.00 4.50
Nos. 419-422 (4) 25.00 11.50

Oldsquaws — A58

Birds: 10c, 70c, Puffins. 20c, 90c, Snow owl. 40c, like 6c. Identification of birds on oldsquaw and puffin stamps transposed.
**1973, Jan. 1** Engr. Perf. 13
423 A58 6c Prus bl, pur & brn 1.50 1.10
424 A58 10c Prus bl, blk & org 2.25 1.75
425 A58 20c ultra, bis & dk vio 2.75 2.25
426 A58 40c pur, sl grn & brn 5.00 2.75

427 A58 70c brt grn, blk & org 7.50 3.50
428 A58 90c Prus bl, bis & pur 9.00 5.50
Nos. 423-428 (6) 28.00 16.85

Indoor Swimming Pool — A59

Design: 1fr, Cultural Center of St. Pierre.
**1973, Sept. 25** Engr. Perf. 13
429 A59 60c brn, brt bl & dk car 5.50 3.50
430 A59 1fr bl grn, ocher & choc 8.00 4.75
Opening of Cultural Center of St. Pierre.

Map of Islands, Weather Balloon and Ship, WMO Emblem A60

**1974, Mar. 23** Engr. Perf. 13
431 A60 1.60fr multicolored 12.50 6.25
World Meteorological Day.

Gannet Holding Letter — A61

**1974, Oct. 9** Engr. Perf. 13
432 A61 70c multi 5.50 2.75
433 A61 90c red & multi 7.00 4.00
Centenary of Universal Postal Union.

Clasped Hands over Red Cross — A62

**1974, Oct. 15** Photo. Perf. 12½x13
434 A62 1.50fr multicolored 12.00 5.50
Honoring blood donors.

Hands Putting Money into Fish-shaped Bank — A63

**1974, Nov. 15** Engr. Perf. 13
435 A63 50c ocher & vio bl 6.25 4.00
St. Pierre Savings Bank centenary.

Church of St. Pierre and Seagulls A64

Designs: 10c, Church of Miquelon and fish. 20c, Church of Our Lady of the Sailors, and fishermen.
**1974, Dec. 9** Engr. Perf. 13
436 A64 6c multicolored 2.10 1.75
437 A64 10c multicolored 3.50 1.75
438 A64 20c multicolored 5.00 2.50
Nos. 436-438 (3) 10.60 5.50

Danaus Plexippus — A65

Design: 1fr. Vanessa atalanta, vert.

**1975, July 17      Litho.      Perf. 12½**
439   A65   1fr blue & multi                10.00   5.00
440   A65   1.20fr green & multi            15.00   5.00

Pottery — A66

**1975, Oct. 2      Engr.      Perf. 13**
441   A66   50c ol, brn & choc             4.00   3.50
442   A67   60c blue & dull yel            6.25   3.50

Local handicrafts.

Mother and Child, Wood Carving — A67

Pointe Plate Lighthouse and Murres A68

**1975, Oct. 21      Engr.      Perf. 13**
443   A68   6c vio bl, blk & lt grn        3.25   2.25
444   A68   10c lil rose, blk & dk ol      5.50   3.50
445   A68   20c blue, indigo & brn         8.25   6.75
                                          17.00  12.50

10c, Galantry lighthouse and Atlantic puffins. 20c, Cap Blanc lighthouse, whale and squid.

Georges Pompidou (1911-74), Pres. of France — A68a

**1976, Feb. 17      Engr.      Perf. 13**
446   A68a   1.10fr brown & slate          7.00   3.50

Georges Pompidou (1911-1974), President of France.

Washington and Lafayette, American Flag — A69

**1976, July 12      Photo.      Perf. 13**
447   A69   1fr multicolored              6.00   3.50

American Bicentennial.

Statue of Liberty, Cent. — A74

**1986, Feb. 4      Engr.      Perf. 13**
453   A915   5c dark green                .45   .20
454   A915   10c dull red                 .20   .20
455   A915   20c brt green                .25   .25
456   A915   30c orange                   .25   .25
457   A915   40c brown                    .20   .20
458   A915   50c lilac                    .20   .20
459   A915   1fr olive green              .45   .25
460   A915   1.80fr emerald               .90   .50
461   A915   2fr brt yellow grn           .90   .75
462   A915   2.20fr red                  1.00   .55
463   A915   3fr chocolate brn           1.25  1.00
464   A915   3.20fr sapphire             1.60  1.00
465   A915   4fr brt carmine             1.75  1.40
466   A915   5fr gray blue               2.25  1.00
467   A915   10fr purple                 4.50  2.75
                                        16.10 11.05

Nos. 453-467 (15)

France Nos. 1783-1784, 1786-1789, 1794, 1882, 1799, 1885, 1802, 1889, 1803-1804 and 1891 Ovptd. "SAINT PIERRE / ET / MIQUELON"

**1976, Oct. 5      Photo.      Perf. 13**
451   A72   1.20fr multicolored          10.00  3.50
452   A72   1.40fr multicolored          12.00  5.50

Fishing Vessels: 1.40f, Goelette.

Croix de Lorraine — A72

**1976, Sept. 7      Engr.      Perf. 13**
450   A71   2.20fr multicolored          8.50   5.00

Vigie Dam — A71

**1976, Aug. 10      Engr.      Perf. 13**
448   A70   70c multicolored             5.50   4.00
449   A70   2.50fr multicolored         12.00   5.00

21st Olympic Games, Montreal, Canada, July 17-Aug. 1.

70c, Basketball and maple leaf, vert.

Woman Swimmer and Maple Leaf — A70

Discovery of St. Pierre & Miquelon by Jacques Cartier, 450th Anniv. — A73

**1986, June 11      Engr.      Perf. 13**
476   A73   2.20fr sep, sage grn &        1.75   1.00
            redsh brn

**1987, May 16**
492   A79   5fr dp ultra, dk rose brn     2.75   2.00
            & brt bl

Transat Yacht Race, Lorient to St. Pierre to Lorient A79

**1987, Apr. 29      Engr.      Perf. 13**
491   A78   2.20fr brt bl, blk & dk       1.25   .90
            red brn

Dr. François Dunan (1884-1961), Clinic — A78

Hygrophorus Pratensis — A77

**1987-90      Engr.      Perf. 12½**
487   A77   shown                        2.00   1.25
488   A77   2.50fr Russula paludosa
489   A77   2.50fr Tricholoma vir-        1.50   .90
            gatum
            britz                        1.10   .90
490   A77   2.50fr Hydnum re-
            pandum                        1.10   .90
                                         5.70   3.95

Nos. 487-490 (4)

Issued: #487, Feb. 14; #488, Jan. 29, 1988; #489, Jan. 28, 1989; #490, Jan. 17, 1990.

**1986, Dec. 10      Litho.      Perf. 13**
486   A76   2.20fr multicolored          1.75   1.00

Christmas.

**1986-89      Engr.      Perf. 13**
478   A75   1fr bright red               .75   .30
479   A75   1.10fr brt orange            .60   .35
480   A75   1.30fr dark red              .75   .40
481   A75   1.40fr violet               1.00   .45
482   A75   1.50fr dark red              .75   .45
483   A75   1.50fr dark red              .90   .50
484   A75   1.60fr emerald grn           .90   .50
485   A75   1.70fr green                 .90   .55
                                        6.55   3.60

Nos. 478-485 (8)

Issued: 1fr, 10/22; 1.10fr, 1.50fr, 10/14/87; 1.30fr, 1.60fr, 8/7/88; #482, 1.70fr, 7/14/89.

Fishery Resources A75

Holy Family, Stained Glass by J. Balmet A76

**1986, July 4**
477   A74   2.50fr Statue, St. Pierre     2.00   1.25
            Harbor

Marine Slip, Cent. A81

**1987, June 20      Litho.      Perf. 13**
494   A81   2.50fr pale sal & dk red      1.75   1.10
            brn

Stern Trawler La Normande — A82

**1987-91      Photo.**
495   A82   3fr shown                    3.25   1.75
496   A82   3fr Le Marmouset             1.75   1.10
497   A82   3fr Tugboat Le Malabar       1.25   .95
498   A82   3fr St. Denis, St. Pierre    1.50   1.10
499   A82   3fr Cryos                    1.50   1.10
                                        9.25   6.15

Nos. 495-499 (5)

Issued: #495, 10/14; #496, 9/28/88; #497, 11/2/89; #498, 10/24/90; #499, 11/6/91. This is an expanding set. Numbers will change when complete.

**1987, May 29      Litho.      Perf. 12½x13**
493   A80   2.20fr dull ultra, gold &     2.00   .90
            scar

Visit of Pres. Mitterand A80

Voyage de François Mitterand, Président de la République.

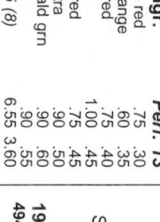

The Great Barachoise Nature Reserve — A84

**1987, Dec. 16      Engr.      Perf. 13x12½**
504   A84   3fr Horses, waterfowl         2.00   1.50
505   A84   3fr Waterfowl, seals          2.00   1.50
  a.   Pair 3fr Waterfowl + label         4.90   3.50

No. 505a is in continuous design.

St. Christopher and the Christ Child, Stained Glass Window and Scout Emblem — A83

**1987, Dec. 9      Litho.      Perf. 13**
503   A83   2.20fr multicolored          1.75   1.00

Christmas, Scout movement in St. Pierre & Miquelon, 50th anniv.

ST. PIERRE & MIQUELON

**1988, Nov. 2**
506 A84 2.20fr Ross Cove 1.50 .75
507 A84 13.70fr Cap Perce 5.50 4.75
a. Pair, #506-507 + label 8.50 8.50

No. 507a is in continuous design.

1988 Winter Olympics, Calgary — A86

**1988, Mar. 5 Engr. Perf. 13**
508 A86 5fr brt ultra & dark red 2.50 1.90

Louis Thomas (1887-1976), Photographer — A87

**1988, May 4 Engr. Perf. 13**
509 A87 2.20fr blk, dk ol bis & Prus bl 1.10 .70

France No. 2105 Overprinted "ST-PIERRE ET MIQUELON"

**1988, July 25 Engr. Perf. 13**
510 A1107 2.20fr ver, blk & violet blue 1.75 .75

The Nellie J. Banks was seized by Canada for carrying prohibited alcohol in 1938.

Seizure of Schooner Nellie J. Banks, 50th Anniv. A88

**1988, Aug. 7**
511 A88 2.50fr brn, vio blue & brt blue 1.75 .90

Christmas — A89

**1988, Dec. 17 Litho. Perf. 13**
512 A89 2.20fr multicolored 1.10 .90

Judo Competitions in St. Pierre & Miquelon, 25th Anniv. — A90

**1989, Mar. 4 Engr. Perf. 13**
513 A90 5fr brn org, blk & yel grn 2.50 1.60

French Revolution Bicent.; 40th Anniv. of the UN Declaration of Human Rights (in 1988) — A91

**1989 Engr. Perf. 12½x13**
514 A91 2.20fr Liberty 1.10 .75
515 A91 2.20fr Equality 1.10 .75
516 A91 2.20fr Fraternity 3.30 2.25

Issued: #514, 3/22; #515, 5/3; #516, 6/17.
Nos. 514-516 (3)

Souvenir Sheet

PHILEXFRANCE 89

French Revolution, Bicent. — A92

Designs: a, Bastille, liberty troo. b, Bastille, ship. c, Building, revolutionaries raising flag and liberty tree. d, Revolutionaries, building with open doors.

**1989, July 14 Engr. Perf. 13**
517 A92 Sheet of 4 + 2 labels 10.50 10.50
a.-d. 5fr any single 2.25 2.25

Designs: 2.20fr, Coastline, ships in harbor, girl in boat, fish. 13.70fr, Coastline, ships in harbor, boy flying kite from boat, map of Ile aux Marins.

Heritage of Ile aux Marins — A93

**1989, Sept. 9 Engr. Perf. 13x12½**
518 A93 2.20fr multi 1.50 .70
519 A93 13.70fr multi 5.50 4.25
a. Pair, #518-519 + label 8.25 8.25

Nos. 519a is in continuous design.

George Landry and Bank Emblem A95

**1989, Nov. 8 Engr. Perf. 13**
520 A95 2.20fr bl & golden brn 1.10 .75

Bank of the Islands, cent.

NOËL 89

Christmas — A96

**1989, Dec. 2 Litho. Perf. 13**
521 A96 2.20fr multicolored 1.10 .75

France Nos. 2179-2182, 2182A-2186, 2188-2189, 2191-2194, 2204B, 2331, 2333-2334, 2336-2339, 2342 Ovptd. "ST-PIERRE / ET / MIQUELON"

**1990-96 Engr. Perf. 13**
522 A116I 10c brn blk .20 .20
523 A116I 20c light grn .20 .20
524 A116I 50c bright vio .20 .20
525 A116I 1fr orange .35 .35
526 A116I 2fr apple grn .70 .70
527 A116I 2fr blue .90 .75
528 A116I 2.10fr green .90 .75
529 A116I 2.20fr green 1.00 .80
530 A116I 2.30fr red 1.00 .50
531 A116I 2.40fr emerald 1.10 .50
532 A116I 2.50fr red 1.10 1.10
533 A116I 2.70fr emerald 1.50 .75
534 A116I 3.20fr bright bl 1.50 .75
535 A116I 3.40fr blue 1.50 .75
536 A116I 3.50fr apple grn 1.50 .75
537 A116I 3.80fr brt pink 1.50 .75
538 A116I 3.80fr blue 1.50 .75
539 A116I 4fr brt lil rose 1.75 .75
540 A116I 4.20fr rose lilac 1.75 .75
541 A116I 4.40fr blue 1.75 1.00
542 A116I 4.50fr magenta 1.90 1.90
543 A116I 5fr dull blue 1.90 1.00
544 A116I 10fr violet 3.50 1.00
544A A116I (2.50fr) red .95 .50
Nos. 522-544A (24) 29.85 16.95

Booklet Stamps
Self-Adhesive
Die Cut

**545** A116I 2.50fr red 1.40 1.00
a. Booklet pane of 10 14.00
**545B** A116I (2.80fr) red 1.50 1.10
a. Booklet pane of 10 15.00

Issued: 2.30fr, 1/2/90; 10c, 2/5/90; 90c, 20c, 50c, 3.20fr, #537, 4/17/90; 1fr, 5fr, #526, 10fr, 7/16/90; #532, 2/8/92; 4.20fr, 12/21/91; 3.40fr, 4fr, 1/8/92; #545, 2/8/92; 4.40fr, #545B, #544A, 7/5/93; 2.40fr, 3.50fr, 10/6/93; #527, 8/17/94; #538, 2.70fr, 4.50fr, 6/12/96. 1/13/93; 10/4/96,

25 Kilometer Race of Miquelon A99

**1990, June 23**
549 A99 5fr Runner, map 2.10 1.75

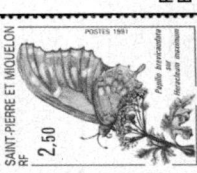

Micmac Canoe, 1875 A100

**1990, Aug. 15 Engr. Perf. 13x13½**
550 A100 2.50fr multicolored 1.25 .95

Views of St. Pierre — A101

Harbor scene.

**1990, Oct. 24 Engr. Perf. 13x12½**
551 A101 2.30fr bl, grn & brn 1.00 .50
552 A101 14.50fr bl, grn & brn 6.50 3.50
a. Pair, #551-552 + label 9.00 9.00

No. 552a is in continuous design.

Christmas — A103

**1990, Dec. 15 Litho.**
553 A103 2.30fr multicolored 1.10 .65

Papilio Brevicaudata A104

**1991-92 Litho. Perf. 13**
554 A104 2.50fr multicolored 1.25 .95

**Perf. 12**
555 A104 3.60fr Aeshna Eremita, Nuphar Variegatum 1.40 1.40

Issued: 2.50fr, Jan. 16; 3.60fr, Mar. 4, 1992. This is an expanding set. Numbers will change again if necessary.

Marine Tools, Sailing Ship A105

A97

**1990, June 18 Perf. 13**
546 A97 2.30fr Charles de Gaulle 1.10 .80

De Gaulle's call for French Resistance, 50th anniv.

A98

**1990, Nov. 22**
547 A98 1.70fr red, claret & blue .75 .70
548 A98 2.30fr red, claret & blue 1.25 .95
a. Pair, #547-548 + label 2.25 2.25

Scenic Views A106

**1991, Mar. 6**    **Litho. & Engr.**    **Perf. 13**
559   A105   1.40fr yellow & green   .75   .55
560   A105   1.70fr yellow & red   .90   .65

**1991, Apr. 17**    **Engr.**    **Perf. 13**
561   A106   1.70fr blue   .75   .65
562   A106   1.70fr blue   .75   .65
563   A106   1.70fr blue   .75   .65
564   A106   1.70fr blue   .75   .65
a.   Strip of 4, #561-564   3.00   3.00
565   A106   2.50fr red   1.25   .95
566   A106   2.50fr red   1.25   .95
567   A106   2.50fr red   1.25   .95
568   A106   2.50fr red   1.25   .95
a.   Strip of 4, #565-568   5.00   5.00
   Nos. 561-568 (8)   8.00   6.40

Designs: Nos. 548, 552, Saint Pierre. Nos. 549, 553, Ile aux Marins. Nos. 550, 554, Langlade. Nos. 551, 555, Miquelon.

Lyre Music Society, Cent. — A107
**1991, June 21**    **Engr.**    **Perf. 13**
569   A107   2.50fr multicolored   1.10   .85

Newfoundland Crossing by Rowboat "Los Gringos" — A108
**1991, Aug. 3**    **Engr.**    **Perf. 13x12½**
570   A108   2.50fr multicolored   1.10   .85

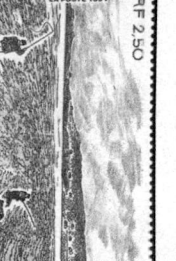

Basque Sports A109
**1991, Aug. 24**
571   A109   5fr red & green   2.10   1.75

Natural Heritage — A110
**1991, Oct. 18**    **Engr.**    **Perf. 13x12½**
572   A110   2.50fr multicolored   1.50   .90
573   A110   14.50fr multicolored   6.50   5.00
a.   Pair, #572-573 + label   8.50   8.50
2.50fr, Fishermen. 14.50fr, Shoreline, birds.
No. 573a is in continuous design.

---

Central Economic Cooperation Bank, 50th Anniv. — A111
**1991, Dec. 2**    **Engr.**    **Perf. 13x12½**
574   A111   2.50fr 1941 100fr note   1.10   1.00

Christmas A112
**1991, Dec. 21**    **Litho.**    **Perf. 13**
575   A112   2.50fr multicolored   1.10   .85
Christmas Day Plebiscite, 50th anniv.

Vice Admiral Emile Henri Muselier (1882-1965), Commander of Free French Naval Forces — A113
**1992, Jan. 8**    **Litho.**    **Perf. 13**
576   A113   2.50fr multicolored   1.50   .75

1992 Winter Olympics, Albertville A114
**1992, Feb. 8**    **Engr.**    **Perf. 13**
577   A114   5fr vio bl, blue & mag   2.10   1.90

Caulking Tools, Bow of Ship A115
**1992, Apr. 1**    **Litho. & Engr.**    **Perf. 13x12½**
578   A115   1.50fr pale bl gray & brn   .75   .45
579   A115   1.80fr pale bl gray & bl   .90   .45

Lighthouses — A116
**1992, July 8**    **Litho.**    **Perf. 13**
580   A116   2.50fr Strip of 4, #a.-d.   5.50   4.00
Designs: a, Galantry. b, Feu Rouge. c, Pointe-Plate. d, Ile Aux Marins.

---

Natural Heritage — A117
**1992, Sept. 9**    **Engr.**    **Perf. 13x12½**
581   A117   2.50fr Langlade   1.50   .75
582   A117   15.10fr Douisle Valley   7.50   3.75
a.   Pair, #581-582 + label   9.00   9.00
No. 582a is in continuous design. See Nos. 593-594, 605-606.

Discovery of America, 500th Anniv. — A118
**1992, Oct. 12**    **Photo. & Engr.**    **Perf. 13x12½**
583   A118   5.10fr multicolored   2.25   1.50

Le Baron de L'Esperance — A119
**1992, Nov. 18**    **Engr.**    **Perf. 13**
584   A119   2.50fr claret, brn & bl   1.25   .75

Christmas — A120
**1992, Dec. 9**    **Litho.**    **Perf. 13**
585   A120   2.50fr multicolored   1.25   .90

Commander R. Birot (1906-1942) — A121
**1993, Jan. 13**    **Engr.**    **Perf. 12**
586   A121   2.50fr multicolored   1.50   .90

Deep Sea Diving A122
**1993, Feb. 10**    **Engr.**    **Perf. 13**
587   A122   5fr multicolored   2.25   1.50

---

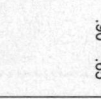

A124

Monochamus Scutellatus, Cichorium Intybus.
**1993, Mar. 10**    **Litho.**    **Perf. 13½x13**
588   A123   3.60fr multicolored   1.50   1.25
See No. 599.

A123

Natural Heritage — A117
**1993, Apr. 7**    **Litho.**    **Perf. 13½x13**
589   A124   1.50fr green & multi   .75   .55
590   A124   1.80fr red & multi   .90   .70
Slicing cod.

Move to the Magdalen Islands, Quebec, by Miquelon Residents, Bicent. — A125
**1993, June 9**    **Engr.**    **Perf. 13**
591   A125   5.10fr brn, bl & grn   2.10   1.50

Fish A126
**1993, July 30**    **Photo.**    **Perf. 13**
592   A126   2.80fr Strip of 4, #a.-d.   6.00   6.00
Designs: a, Capelin. b, Ray. c, Halibut (fletan). d, Toad fish (crapaud).

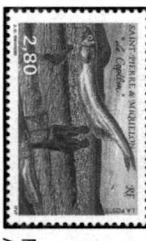

Nat. Heritage Type of 1992
**1993, Aug. 18**    **Engr.**    **Perf. 13x12½**
593   A117   2.80fr Miquelon   1.50   1.00
594   A117   16fr Otter pool   6.50   5.75
a.   Pair, #593-594 + label   9.00   9.00
No. 594a is a continuous design.

Commissioner's Residence — A127
**1993, Oct. 6**    **Engr.**    **Perf. 13**
595   A127   3.70fr multicolored   1.75   .90

## Christmas — A146

Design: 2.80fr, Toys in store window.

**1995, Nov. 22**   Litho.   *Perf. 13*
621  A146  2.80fr multicolored   1.50  1.00

## Charles de Gaulle (1890-1970) A147

**1995, Nov. 9**   Litho.   *Perf. 13x13½*
622  A147  14fr multicolored   6.00  5.00

## Commandant Jean Levasseur (1909-47) — A148

**1996, Jan. 10**   Litho.   *Perf. 13*
623  A148  2.80fr multicolored   1.50  1.25

## Boxing A149

**1996, Feb. 7**   Engr.   *Perf. 12x12½*
624  A149  5.10fr multicolored   2.50  2.25

## Plant Type of 1995

Design: Cladonia verticillata and polytrichum juniperinum.

**1996, Mar. 13**   Litho.   *Perf. 13*
625  A140  3.70fr multicolored   1.75  1.60

## Blacksmiths and Their Tools A150

**1996, Apr. 10**   Litho.
626  A150  1.50fr black & multi   .75  .65
627  A150  1.80fr red & multi   .85  .75

## Ship Type of 1994

Designs: a, Radar II. b, SPM Roro. c, Pinta. d, Pascal Anne.

**1996, July 10**   Litho.
628  Sheet of 4   6.00  6.00
a.-d. A134 3fr Any single   1.40  1.00

---

## A141

A140

Dicranum Scoparium & Cladonia Cristatella.

**1995, Mar. 8**   Litho.   *Perf. 13*
612  A140  3.70fr multicolored   1.60  1.50

Cooper and his tools.

**1995, Apr. 5**   Litho.   *Perf. 13½x13*
613  A141  1.50fr black & multi   .75  .65
614  A141  1.80fr red & multi   .90  .75

See Nos. 625, 635.

## Shellfish A142

a, Snail. b, Crab. c, Scallop. d, Lobster.

**1995, July 5**   Litho.   *Perf. 13*
616  Strip of 4   6.00  6.00
a.-d. A142 2.80fr any single   1.40  1.00

## Geological Mission — A143

Designs: 2.80fr, Rugged terrain along shoreline, diagram of mineral location, zircon. 16fr, Geological map, terrain.

**1995, Aug. 16**   Engr.   *Perf. 13x12½*
617  A117  2.80fr multicolored   1.50  1.00
618  A117  16fr multicolored   6.75  5.00
a. Pair, #617-618 + label   9.00  9.00

## Sister Cesarine (1845-1922), St. Joseph de Cluny — A144

**1995, Sept. 6**   Litho.   *Perf. 13*
619  A144  1.80fr multicolored   1.00  .75

## The Francoforum Public Building — A145

**1995, Oct. 4**   Engr.   *Perf. 13*
620  A145  3.70fr multicolored   1.75  1.00

---

## Souvenir Sheet

Ships A134

Designs: a, Miquelon. b, Isle of St. Pierre. c, St. George XII. d, St. Eugene IV.

**1994, July 6**   *Perf. 12*
604  Sheet of 4   7.50  7.50
a.-b. A134 2.80fr any single   1.25  1.25
c.-d. A134 3.70fr any single   1.75  1.75

See No. 628.

## Natural Heritage Type of 1992

**1994, Aug. 17**   Engr.   *Perf. 13*
605  A117  2.80fr Woods   1.50  1.10
606  A117  16fr "The Hat"   6.50  6.50
a. Pair, #605-606 + label   9.00  8.00

## Parochial School A135

**1994, Oct. 5**   Engr.   *Perf. 13*
607  A135  3.70fr multicolored   1.50  1.10

## Stamp Show A136

**1994, Oct. 15**
608  A136  3.70fr grn, yel & bl   1.75  1.10

## Christmas A137

**1994, Nov. 23**   Litho.   *Perf. 13*
609  A137  2.80fr multicolored   1.50  1.10

## Louis Pasteur (1822-95) A138

**1995, Jan. 11**   Litho.   *Perf. 13*
610  A138  2.80fr multicolored   1.50  1.10

## Triathlon A139

**1995, Feb. 8**   Engr.   *Perf. 12*
611  A139  5.10fr multicolored   2.25  2.00

---

## Christmas A128

**1993, Dec. 13**   Litho.   *Perf. 13*
596  A128  2.80fr multicolored   1.50  .95

## Commander Louis Blaison (1906-1942), Submarine Surcouf — A129

**1994, Jan. 12**   Litho.   *Perf. 13*
597  A129  2.80fr multicolored   1.50  .90

## Petanque World Championships — A130

**1994, Feb. 9**   Engr.   *Perf. 12½x12*
598  A130  5.10fr multicolored   2.25  1.75

## Insect and Flower Type of 1993

Cristalis tenax, taraxacum officinale, horiz.

**1994, Mar. 9**   Litho.   *Perf. 13x13½*
599  A123  3.70fr multicolored   1.75  1.25

## Drying Codfish, 1905 A131

**1994**   Litho.   *Perf. 13*
600  A131  1.50fr blk & bl grn   .75  .55
601  A131  1.80fr multicolored   1.00  .65

Issued: 1.50fr, 5/4/94; 1.80fr, 4/6/94.

## Women's Right to Vote, 50th Anniv. A132

**1994, Apr. 21**
602  A132  2.80fr multicolored   1.50  1.00

## Hospital Ship St. Pierre, Cent. A133

**1994, July 2**
603  A133  2.80fr multicolored   1.50  1.00

Aerial View of Miquelon — A151

**1996, Aug. 14** *Perf. 13x12½*
Engr.
629 A151 3fr multicolored 1.25 1.25
630 A151 15.50fr multicolored 6.50 6.50
a. Pair, #629-630 + label 7.75 7.75

Designs: 3fr, "Le Cap." mountains, buildings. 15.50fr, "Le Village," buildings.

Customs House, Cent. A152

**1996, Oct. 9** Engr. *Perf. 12½x13*
631 A152 3.80fr blue & black 1.50 1.50

Fall Stamp Show — A153

**1996, Nov. 6** Litho. *Perf. 13*
632 A153 1fr multicolored .50 .20

Christmas — A154

**1996, Nov. 20** Litho. *Perf. 13*
633 A154 3fr multicolored 1.50 1.25

Constant Colmay (1903-65) A155

**1997, Jan. 8** Litho. *Perf. 13*
634 A155 3fr multicolored 1.50 1.50

Flora and Fauna Type of 1995

Design: Phalacrocorax carbo, sedum rosea.

**1997, Mar. 12** Litho. *Perf. 13*
635 A140 3.80fr multicolored 1.50 1.50

Maritime Heritage A156

**1997, Apr. 9** Litho. *Perf. 13*
636 A156 1.70fr multicolored .75 .70
637 A156 2fr multicolored .90 .80

Designs: 1.70fr, Man in doorway of salt house. 2fr, Boat, naval architect's drawing.

Volleyball A157

**1997, Apr. 9** Litho. & Engr. *Perf. 12*
638 A157 5.20fr multicolored 2.10 2.10

Fish A158

**1997, July 9** Litho. *Perf. 13*
639 A158 3fr Strip of 4, #a.-d. 6.00 5.00
a. Shark. b. Salmon. c. Poule d'eau. d. Mackerel.

Bay, Headlands — A159

**1997, Aug. 13** Engr. *Perf. 13x12*
640 A159 3fr multicolored 1.50 1.00
641 A159 15.50fr multicolored 5.50 5.25
a. Pair #640-641 + label 7.00 6.25

3fr, Basque Cape. 15.50fr, Diamant.

"ST. PIERRE / ET / MIQUELON"
France Nos. 2589-2603 Ovptd.

**1997-98** Engr. *Perf. 13*
642 A409 10c brown .20 .20
643 A409 20c brt blue grn .20 .20
644 A409 50c purple .20 .20
645 A409 1fr bright blue .35 .35
646 A409 2fr bright org .70 .70
647 A409 2.70fr bright green .90 .90
648 A409 (3fr) red 1.00 1.00
649 A409 3.50fr apple green 1.25 1.25
650 A409 3.80fr blue 1.25 1.25
651 A409 4.20fr dark orange 1.50 1.50
652 A409 4.40fr blue 1.60 1.60
653 A409 4.50fr bright pink 1.60 1.60
654 A409 5fr brt grn bl 1.75 1.75
655 A409 6.70fr dark green 2.40 2.40
656 A409 10fr violet 3.50 3.50
Nos. 642-656 (15) 18.65 18.40

Issued: 2.70fr, (3fr), 3.80fr, 8/13/97; 10c, 20c, 50c, 3.50fr, 4.40fr, 10fr, 10/8/97; 1fr, 4.20fr, 4.50fr, 5fr, 6.70fr, 1/7/98. See No. 664 for self-adhesive (3fr).

Ice Workers A165

**1998, Apr. 8** Engr. *Perf. 13*
662 A165 1.70fr shown .75 .60
663 A165 2fr Cutting ice from lake .90 .75

"ST. PIERRE / ET / MIQUELON"
France Nos. 2604, 2620 Ovptd.

**1998, Apr. 8** Self-Adhesive
Die Cut x Serpentine Die Cut
Engr.
664 A1409 (3fr) red 1.25 1.00
a. Booklet pane of 10 12.50

No. 664a is a complete booklet. The peelable backing serves as a booklet cover. 2fr shown.

**1998, May 13** *Perf. 13*
665 A1424 3fr red & blue 1.25 1.00

Post Office Building A160

**1997, Oct. 8** Engr. *Perf. 13*
657 A160 3.80fr multicolored 1.50 1.40

Christmas — A161

**1997, Nov. 19** Litho. *Perf. 13*
658 A161 3fr multicolored 1.25 1.10

Houses A166

**1998, July 8** Litho. *Perf. 13*
666 A166 3fr Strip of 4, #a.-d. 5.00 5.00
a. Gray. b. Yellow, red roof. c. Pink, d, White, red roof.

French in North America — A167

**1998, Sept. 30** Engr. *Perf. 13x12½*
670 A167 3fr multicolored 1.25 1.10

Alain Savary (1918-88), Governor, Territorial Deputy A162

**1998, Jan. 7** Litho. *Perf. 13*
659 A162 3fr multicolored 1.25 1.10

1998 Winter Olympic Games, Nagano A163

**1998, Feb. 11** Engr. *Perf. 12*
660 A163 5.20fr Curling 2.10 1.90

Flora and Fauna A164

**1998, Mar. 11** Photo. *Perf. 13*
661 A164 3.80fr multicolored 1.50 1.40

France, 1998 World Cup Soccer Champions A169

**1998, Oct. 21** Litho. *Perf. 13*
673 A169 3fr multicolored 1.25 1.10

Cape Blue Natl. Park — A168

**1998, Sept. 30** *Perf. 13x12*
671 A168 3fr multicolored 1.25 1.25
672 A168 15.50fr multicolored 6.50 5.75
a. Pair #671-672 + label 8.00 8.00

Designs: 3fr, Point Plate Lighthouse, shoreline. 15.50fr, Cape Blue.

Memorial to War Dead — A170

**1998, Nov. 11** Engr.
674 A170 3.80fr multicolored 1.60 1.40

Christmas — A171

**1998, Nov. 18** Litho.
675 A171 3fr multicolored 1.25 1.10

Emile Letournel (1927-94), Orthopedic Surgeon, Traumatologist — A172

**1999, Jan. 6** Engr. *Perf. 13*
676 A172 3fr multicolored 1.25 1.10

Painting, "The Beach at Fisherman Island," by Patrick Guillaume — A173

**1999, Feb. 10** Litho.
677 A173 5.20fr multicolored 2.25 1.90

See No. 692.

**ST. PIERRE & MIQUELON**

---

**Whale Type of 2000**

Designs: 3fr, Orcinus orca. 5.70fr, Globicephala melaena.

2001, Jan. 24    Engr.    *Perf. 13x12¾*
702-703 A183   Set of 2    3.25   2.40

Landscape A190

0.79€ 5.20F

2001, Feb. 21   Litho.     *Perf. 13*
704 A190 5.20fr multi    2.00   1.40

**Plant Type of 1999**

2001, Mar. 21   Litho.     *Perf. 13*
705 A174 3.80fr Vaccinium ox-
    yoocos    1.25   1.00

1,70 F

Hay Gatherers A191

Denomination colors: 1.70fr, Red brown. 2fr, Lilac.

2001, Apr. 18
706-707 A191   Set of 2    1.25   .95

0,26 €

3.00 Г

Seasons A192

Designs: No. 708, 3fr, Autumn. No. 709, 3fr, Winter.

2001, June 20
708-709 A192   Set of 2    2.00   1.50

See Nos. 714-715.

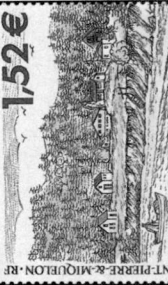

0,46 €     3.00 F

Vestibules — A193

No. 710: a, Guillou House. b, Jugan House. c, Ile-aux-Marins town hall. d, Vogé House.

2001, July 25
710    Horiz. strip of 4    4.00   4.00
   *a.-b.*   A193 3fr Any single    1.00   1.00

1,52 €

10,00F

Anse du Gouvernement — A194

Houses and: a, Boat. b, Rocks near shore.

2001, Sept. 12   Engr.    *Perf. 13x12¾*
711    Horiz. pair, #a-b, +
    central label    7.50   7.50
   *a.-b.*   A194 10fr Any single    3.25   3.25

---

Vignette colors: 1.70fr, Blue. 2fr, Brown.
              Engr.
              1.00   1.00

3.00

Millennium A185

2000, Apr. 5   Set of 2
694-695 A184

No. 696: a, Lobstermen on Newfoundland coast, 1904. b, Women on shore, 1905. c, World War I conscripts on ship Chicago, 1915. d, Soldiers in action at Souain Hill, 1915. e, Men walking on ice, 1923. f, Unloading cases of champagne to be smuggled to US, 1925. g, St. Pierre & Miquelon Pavilion at Colonial Exposition in Paris, 1931. h, Alcohol smugglers, 1933. i, Adm. Emile Muselier inspecting troops on ship Mimosa, 1942. j, World War II soldiers crossing bridge, 1945.

No. 697: a, Fishery employees, 1951. b, Fishing trawler, 1960. c, Visit of Gen. Charles de Gaulle, 1967. d, First television images, 1967. e, Port facilities, 1977. g, Resumption of stamp issuing, 1986. h, Voyage to Eric Tabarly, 1987. i, Exclusive Economic Zone, 1992. j, New airport, 1999.

              *Perf. 13x13¼*
2000         Litho.
696    Sheet of 10    12.50   12.50
   *a.-j.* A185 3fr Any single    1.25   1.25
697    Sheet of 10    7.50   7.50
   *a.-j.* A185 2fr Any single    .75   .75

Issue: No. 696, 6/21; No. 697, 12/6.

5.40

The Inger — A186

             *Port. 13x13¼*
2000, Oct. 4   Engr.
698 A186 5.40fr green    2.00   1.40

RF

15.50

Boathouses in November — A187

             *Perf. 13x12¼*
2000, Oct. 4        6.50   6.50
699    Pair + central label    1.00   1.00
   *a.*   A187 3fr Hill
   *b.*   A187 15.50fr Church    5.00   5.00

0,46 €

3,00

Christmas — A188

2000, Nov. 15   Litho.    *Perf. 13¼x13*
700 A188 3fr multi    1.00   .80

0,46 €

3,00F

New Year 2001 — A189

2001, Jan. 3   Litho.     *Perf. 13x12¾*
701 A189 3fr multi    1.25   .90

---

          *Perf. 13x12¼*   Engr.
1999, Aug. 11   Engr.
684 A178   3fr Cars, yield sign   1.00   1.00
685 A178 15.50fr Docked boats   5.50   5.50
   *a.*   Pair, #684-685 + label   6.50   6.50

Visit of Pres. Jacques Chirac, Sept. 1999 — A179

5.40

           *Perf. 13¼x13*
1999, Sept. 7   Litho.    1.00   1.00
686 A179 3fr multicolored

Archives A180

           *Perf. 13x12¾*
1999, Oct. 6   Engr.    1.75   1.75
687 A180 5.40fr deep rose lilac

RF   3.00 F 0,46 €

Christmas A181

1999, Nov. 17   Litho.    *Perf.*   1.00   .95
688 A181 3fr multi

3.00 0,46 € Saint Pierre-&-Miquelon-RF Postes

Year 2000 — A182

           *Perf. 13¼x13*
2000, Jan. 12   Litho.    1.00   .95
689 A182 3fr multi

3.00

Whales A183

Designs: 3fr, Megaptera novaeangliae. 5.70fr, Balaenoptera physalus.

2000, Jan. 26   Engr.     *Perf. 13x12¾*
690 A183     3fr blk & Prus bl   .95   .95
691 A183 5.70fr Prus grn & blk   1.90   1.90

**Painting Type of 1999**

2000, Feb. 9   Litho.     *Perf. 13*
692 A173 5.20fr Les Graves   1.75   1.50

**Plant Type of 1999**

2000, Mar. 8
693 A174 3.80fr Vaccinium vitis-
    idaea        1.10   1.10

1,70 0,46 € Postes 2000

Wood Gatherer A184

---

3.80 LaPlate-Bière

La Plate-Bière A174

1999, Mar. 10   Litho.    *Perf. 13*
678 A174 3.80fr Rubus
    chamaemorus    1.60   1.25

See No. 693.

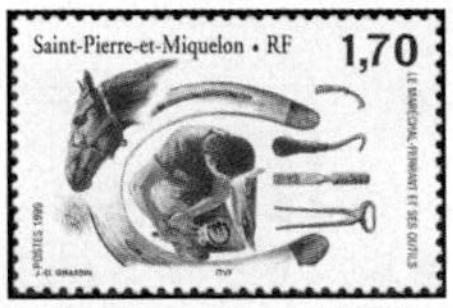

1,70

Horseshoeing — A175

1.70fr, Horse, blacksmith and his tools. 2fr, Applying horseshoes in blacksmith's shop.

1999, Apr. 7   Litho.     *Perf. 13*
679 A175 1.70fr multicolored   .75   .55
680 A175   2fr multicolored   .85   .65

France No. 2691 Ovptd. "ST. PIERRE / ET / MIQUELON"
              Engr.
1999, Apr. 7        1.00   1.00
681 A1470 3fr red & blue

Value is shown in both francs and euros on No. 681.

France No. 2691A Overprinted "ST. PIERRE / ET / MIQUELON"
*Die Cut x Serpentine Die Cut 7*
1999, Apr. 5        Engr.
         **Self-Adhesive**
              2.00   1.00
681A A1470 3fr red & blue
   *b.*   Booklet of 10    20.00

3,00 1885 1849 1909

First Stamps of France, 150th Anniv. A176

a, France #3, St. Pierre & Miquelon #9, 79. b, #145, 270. c, #C21, C36. d, #476, 676.

1999, June 23   Litho.     *Perf. 13*
682 A176 3fr Sheet of 4, #a.-d.   5.00   5.00

PhilexFrance '99, World Philatelic Exhibition.

3,00 le Bearn

Ships A177

a, Bearn. b, Pro Patria. c, Erminie. d, Colombier.

1999, July 7   Litho.     *Perf. 13x13½*
683 A177 3fr Sheet of 4, #a.-d.   5.00   5.00

3,00

General de Gaulle Place — A178

Saint Pierre Pointe Blanche — A195

**2001, Sept. 26**　　　**Litho.**　　**Perf. 13**
712 A195 5fr multi 　1.60 1.40

The Marie-Thérèse — A196

**2001, Sept. 26**　**Engr.**　**Perf. 13x13¼**
713 A196 5.40fr green 　2.00 1.40

Seasons Type of 2001

Summer.

**2001, Oct. 17**　　　**Litho.**　　**Perf. 13**
714-715 A192 　2.00 1.60
Set of 2

Designs: No. 714, 3fr, Spring. No. 715, 3fr, Summer.

Commander Jacques Pepin I ehailleur (1911-2000) A197

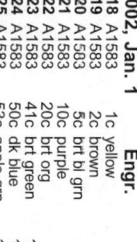

**2001, Nov. 14**
716 A197 3fr multi 　1.00 .80

Christmas — A198

**2001, Nov. 28**
717 A198 3fr multi 　1.25 .80

France Nos. 2849-2863 Overprinted

100 Cents = 1 Euro (€)

**2002, Jan. 1**　　　**Engr.**　　**Perf. 13**
718 A1583 1c yellow 　.20 .20
719 A1583 2c brown 　.20 .20
720 A1583 5c brt bl grn 　.20 .20
721 A1583 10c purple 　.25 .25
722 A1583 20c brt org 　.50 .50
723 A1583 41c brt green 　1.00 1.00
724 A1583 50c dk blue 　1.25 1.25
725 A1583 53c apple grn 　1.40 1.25
726 A1583 58c blue 　1.40 1.40
727 A1583 64c dark org 　1.60 1.50
728 A1583 67c brt blue 　1.75 1.50
729 A1583 69c brt pink 　1.75 1.60
730 A1583 €1 Prus blue 　2.50 2.40
731 A1583 €1.02 dk green 　2.75 2.50
732 A1583 €2 violet 　5.25 4.75
Nos. 718-732 (15) 　22.10 20.60

Introduction of the Euro A199

**2002, Jan. 30**　　　**Litho.**　　**Perf. 13**
733 A199 €1 multi 　2.50 2.40

Pinnipeds A200

**2002, Mar. 7**　**Engr.**　**Perf. 13¼**
734-735 A200 　3.50 3.25
Set of 2

Designs: 46c, Halichoerus grypus. 87c, Phoca vitulina.

Plant Type of 1999

**2002, Mar. 20**　　　**Litho.**　　**Perf. 13**
736 A174 58c Pomme de pré 　1.50 1.40

See Nos. 748-749.

Laranaga Farm, c. 1900 — A201

**2002, Mar. 20**　**Engr.**　**Perf. 13x12¾**
737 A201 79c green 　2.00 1.90

Net Mender A202

**2002, Apr. 15**　**Engr.**　**Perf. 13x13¼**
738-739 A202 　1.40 1.40
Set of 2

Colors: 26c, Orange brown. 30c, Blue.

West Point — A204

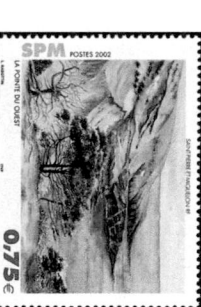

**2002, June 24**　　　**Litho.**　　**Perf. 13**
741 A204 75c multi 　2.00 1.75

Tiaude de Morue, Local Cod Dish — A205

**2002, July 10**
742 A205 50c multi 　1.25 1.25

France No. 2835 Overprinted "ST. PIERRE / ET / MIQUELON"

**2002, Sept. 11**　**Engr.**　**Perf. 13**
743 A1409 (46c) red 　1.10 1.10

Arctic Hare A206

**2002, Sept. 11**　　　**Litho.**　　**Perf. 13**
744 A206 46c multi 　1.25 1.10

The Troutpool — A207

**2002, Oct. 11**　**Engr.**　**Perf. 13x13¼**
745 A207 84c green 　2.25 2.00

Henry Cove — A208

**2002, Nov. 6**　**Engr.**　**Perf. 13x12¾**
746 A208 　10.50 10.50
a.-b. A208 €2 Either single 　5.25 5.25
Horiz. pair + central label

No. 208: a, Gull and islands. b, Aerial view of St. Pierre.

Christmas A209

**2002, Nov. 27**　　　**Litho.**　　**Perf. 13**
747 A209 46c multi 　1.25 1.10

Pinnipeds Type of 2002

**2003, Jan. 5**　**Engr.**　**Perf. 13¼**
748-749 A200 　3.50 3.25
Set of 2

Designs: 46c, Phoca groenlandica. 87c, Cystophora cristata.

Msgr. François Maurer (1922-2000) A210

**2003, Jan. 8**　　　**Litho.**　　**Perf. 13**
750 A210 46c multi 　1.25 1.10

Farm Type of 2002

**2003, Mar. 12**　**Engr.**　**Perf. 13x13¼**
751 A201 79c Capandeguy Farm, c. 1910 　2.00 1.75

France No. 2921 Overprinted Like No. 718

**2003**　　　**Engr.**　　**Perf. 13**
752 A1583 (41c) brt green 　1.10 .95
753 A1583 56c apple grn 　1.50 1.40
754 A1583 70c yellow grn 　2.00 1.75
755 A1583 75c bright blue 　2.00 1.75
756 A1583 90c dark blue 　2.40 2.10
757 A1583 €1.11 red lilac 　2.90 2.60
758 A1583 €1.90 violet brown 　4.50 4.50
Nos. 752-758 (7) 　16.65 14.90

Issued: (41c), 4/23. 58c, 70c, 75c, 90c, €1.11, €1.90, 9/24.

Blueberries — A211

**2003, Apr. 23**　　　**Litho.**　　**Perf. 13**
759 A211 75c multi 　2.00 1.75

Pulley Repairer A212

**2003, May 14**　**Engr.**　**Perf. 13**
760 A212 30c blue gray 　.80 .70

Intl. Congress on Traditional Architecture — A213

**2003, May 22**　**Engr.**　**Perf. 13x12¾**
761 A213 　10.50 10.50
a.-b. A213 €2 Either single 　5.25 5.25
Horiz. pair + central label

No. 761: a, Patrice, Jézéquel and Jugan houses. b, Notre-Dame des Marins Church, Borotra house.

ASSP Soccer Team, Cent. A214

**2003, Aug. 7**　　　**Litho.**　　**Perf. 13**
762 A214 50c multi 　1.25 1.25

Buck A215

**2003, Sept. 10**　　　**Perf. 13**
763 A215 50c multi 　1.25 1.25

Lions Club in St. Pierre & Miquelon, 50th Anniv. A216

**2003, Oct. 29**　　　**Litho.**　　**Perf. 13x13¼**
764 A216 50c multi 　1.25 1.25

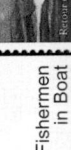
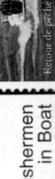

Fishermen in Boat — A223

Litho. *Perf. 13* .75 .75
**2004, May 12** A223 30c multi

Port of St. Pierre — A224

Engr. *Perf. 13x12¼* 10.00 10.00
**2004, June 26** 5.00 5.00
No. 774: a, Ships, denomination at right. b, Ships and dock, denomination at left.
774 Horiz. pair + central label
a.-b. A224 €2 Either single

Micmac Indians of Miquelon — A225

Litho. *Perf. 13* 1.25 1.25
**2004, July 17** A225 50c multi

No. 775 Overprinted

**2004, Aug. 14** 1.25 1.25
776 A225 50c multi

Red Fox A226

Litho. *Perf. 13* 1.25 1.25
**2004, Sept. 13** A226 50c multi
777

Dinner Table — A227

2.25 2.25
**2004, Sept. 13** 778 A227 90c multi

---

Henri Claireaux (1999-2001), Senator — A232

Engr. *Perf. 13x13¼* 1.40 1.40
**2005, Jan. 25** 804 A232 50c lilac

Allumette Cove — A233

Litho. *Perf. 13* 2.00 2.00
**2005, Feb. 16** 805 A233 75c multi

Marine Mammals Type of 2004
Designs: 53c, Delphinus delphis. €1.15, Lagenorhynchus albirostris.
Engr. *Perf. 13¼* 4.50 4.50
**2005, Mar. 9** Set of 2
806-807 A222

Horse Point Farm — A234

Engr. *Perf. 13x13¼* 2.40 2.40
**2005, Apr. 20** 808 A234 90c olive green

Fog, Clouds and Houses A235

Litho. *Perf. 13* .75 .75
**2005, May 11** 809 A235 30c multi

Seven Ponds Valley — A236

No. 810: a, Bird at left. b, Rabbit at right.
*Perf. 13x12¼* 9.75 9.75
**2005, June 14** 4.75 4.75
810 Horiz. pair + central label
a.-b. A236 €2 Either single

Variable Hare A237

Litho. *Perf. 13* 1.40 1.40
**2005, sept. 7** 811 A237 53c multi

---

Langlade Strawberry Preserves — A217

Litho. *Perf. 13* 1.25 1.25
**2003, Oct. 29** 765 A217 50c multi

The Afrique — A218

Engr. *Perf. 13x12¼* 2.40 2.10
**2003, Nov. 6** 766 A218 90c blue green

Christmas — A219

Litho. *Perf. 13* 1.25 1.25
**2003, Dec. 3** 767 A219 50c multi

Joseph Lehuenen (d. 2001), Historian, Mayor — A220

Engr. *Perf. 13x13¼* 1.25 1.25
**2004, Feb. 25** 768 A220 50c brown

Rodrigue Cove — A221

Litho. *Perf. 13* 1.90 1.90
**2004, Mar. 10** 769 A221 75c multi

Marine Mammals A222

*Perf. 13¼* 4.00 4.00
**2004, Mar. 24** Set of 2
770-771 A222
Designs: 50c, Lagenorhynchus acutus. €1.08, Phocoena phocoena.

Farm Type of 2002
Engr. *Perf. 13x12½* 2.25 2.25
**2004, Apr. 7** 772 A201 90c Ollivier Farm, c. 1920

---

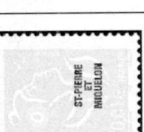

The Fulwood — A228

Engr. *Perf. 13x13¼* 2.00 2.00
**2004, Nov. 5** 779 A228 75c dark purple

Souvenir Sheet

Saint-Pierre-et-Miquelon

Les transporteurs
Ships — A229

No. 780: a, Cap Blanc. b, Lisabeth-C. c, Shamrock. d, Aldorna.
Litho. *Perf. 13* 5.50 5.50
**2004, Nov. 17** 780 A229 50c Sheet of 4, #a-d

SIAA Soccer Team, 50th Anniv. (in 2003) A230

0.44€
Litho. *Perf. 13* 1.25 1.25
**2004, Nov. 24** 781 A230 44c multi

Christmas — A231

*Perf. 13* 1.40 1.40
**2004, Dec. 8** 782 A231 50c multi

France Nos. 3066, 3068-3070, 3072, 3074-3075, 3077-3079, 3081 and 3083 Overprinted

Engr. *Perf. 13*
**2005**
| | | |
|---|---|---|
| 783 A1713 1c yellow | | .20 .20 |
| 784 A1713 5c brown black | | .20 .20 |
| 785 A1713 10c violet | | .25 .25 |
| 786 A1713 (45c) green | | 1.40 1.40 |
| 787 A1713 (50c) red | | 1.40 1.40 |
| 788 A1713 55c dark blue | | 1.50 1.50 |
| 789 A1713 58c olive green | | 1.50 1.50 |
| 790 A1713 64c dark green | | 1.75 1.75 |
| 791 A1713 70c dark green | | 1.90 1.90 |
| 792 A1713 75c light blue | | 2.00 2.00 |
| 793 A1713 82c fawn | | 2.25 2.25 |
| 794 A1713 90c dark blue | | 2.40 2.40 |
| 795 A1713 €1 orange | | 2.60 2.60 |
| 796 A1713 €1.11 red violet | | 3.00 3.00 |
| 797 A1713 €1.22 red violet | | 3.25 3.25 |
| 798 A1713 €1.90 chocolate | | 5.00 5.00 |
| 799 A1713 €1.98 chocolate | | 5.25 5.25 |
| Nos. 783-799 (17) | | 35.70 35.70 |

Booklet Stamp
Self-Adhesive
*Serpentine Die Cut 6¾ Vert.*
800 A1713 (50c) red 1.40 1.40
a. Booklet pane of 10 (on France #3083a) 14.00

Issued: Nos. 1c, 10c, (45c), (50c), 58c, 70c, 75c, 90c, €1, €1.11, €1.90, 1/12. 5c, 55c, 64c, 82c, €1.22, €1.98, 3/23. Face values shown for Nos. 786, 787 and 800 are those the stamps sold for on the day of issue.

**2005, Sept. 29**
812 A238 90c multi    2.25 2.25

Local Expression "Ben Vous Savez
Madame" — A238

**2005, Oct. 12    Engr.    Perf. 13x13¼**
813 A239 75c blue    1.90 1.90

The Transpacific — A239

**2005, Oct. 27    Litho.    Perf. 13**
814 A240 53c multi    1.40 1.40

Status as Territorial Collectivity, 20th
Anniv. — A240

**2005, Dec. 7**
815 A241 53c multi    1.25 1.25

Christmas
A241

Le pandrin de chioquette.

0.53€

**2006, Jan. 25**
816 A242 53c multi    1.25 1.25

Snow on Trees — A242

**2006, Feb. 8**
817 A243 53c multi    1.25 1.25

Sailors'
Festival — A243

**2006, Mar. 1**
818 A244 53c henna brn    1.25 1.25

Albert Pen (1935-
2003), President of
General
Council — A244

---

## SEMI-POSTAL STAMPS

Regular
Issue of
1909-17
Surcharged
in Red

**1915-17    Unwmk.    Perf. 14x13½**
B1 A17    10c + 5c car rose &
red    1.75 1.75
B2 A17    15c + 5c dl vio & rose
("17)    1.75 1.75

Surcharged
in Red

**1938, Oct. 24    Engr.    Perf. 13**
B3 CD80 1.25fr + 50c brt ultra    15.00 15.00

Curie Issue
Common Design Type

**1939, July 5    Photo.**
Name and Value Typo. in Black
B4 CD83    45c + 25c green    12.00 8.00
B5 CD83    70c + 30c brown    12.00 8.00
B6 CD83    90c + 35c red org    12.00 8.00
B7 CD83    1.25fr + 1fr rose    12.00 8.00
B8 CD83    2.25fr + 2fr blue    12.00 8.00

French Revolution Issue
Common Design Type

pink
60.00 40.00

Nos. B4-B8 (5)

Common Design Type and
national relief.

Sailor of Landing
Force — SP1

Dispatch
Boat "Ville
d'Ys"
SP2

**1941    Photo.    Perf. 13½**
B8A SP1    1fr + 1fr red    2.75 2.75
B8B SP1    1.50fr + 3fr maroon    2.75 2.75
B8C SP2    2.50fr + 1fr blue    2.75 2.75

Nos. B8A-B8C (3)    8.25

Nos. B8A-B8C were issued by the
government and were not placed on
sale in the colony.

**1942    Unwmk.    Perf. 13½x13**
B9 A25    1fr + 50c    57.50 52.50
B10 A26    2.50fr + 1fr    57.50 52.50

Petain Type of 1941
Surcharged in Black or Red

**1944    Engr.    Perf. 12½x12**
B11    50c + 1.50fr on 2.50fr deep
blue (R)    1.10
B12    + 2.50fr on 1fr violet    1.10

Colonial Development Fund.
Nos. B11-B12 were issued by the Vichy
government in France, but were not placed on
sale in St. Pierre & Miquelon.

Nos. 239, 246 With Additional
Surcharge in Carmine

+ 50 c
FRANCE
LIBRE
ŒUVRES
SOCIALES
+ 1f.

**1944**
B13 CD90 5fr + 20fr dp ultra    1.75 1.75

Red Cross Issue
Common Design Type

---

Catalogue values for unused
stamps in this section, from this
point to the end of the section, are
for **Never Hinged** items.

**1950, May 15    Engr.    Perf. 13**
B14 CD100 10fr + 2fr red brn
& red    11.00 10.00

Tropical Medicine Issue
Common Design Type

The surtax was for charitable work.

Surtax for the French Red Cross and

---

## AIR POST STAMPS

Catalogue values for unused
stamps in this section are for
**Never Hinged** items.

**1942, Aug. 17    Photo.    Unwmk.**
C1 CD87    1fr dark orange    .55 .45
C2 CD87    1fr bright red    .70 .55
C3 CD87    1.50fr olive grn    .55 .55
C4 CD87    5fr brown red    1.00 .80
C5 CD87    10fr black    1.25 1.00
C6 CD87    25fr ultra    1.25 1.00
C7 CD87    50fr dark green    2.25 1.75

Common Design Type
Perf. 14½x14

Nos. C1-C7 (7)    9.90 7.90

**1947, Oct. 6    AP4**
C12 CD96 20fr violet    1.90
C13 CD97 25fr chocolate    2.40
C14 CD98 50fr grnsh blk    2.90

Nos. C9-C14 (6)    10.60

Plane, Sailing Vessel and
Coast — AP2

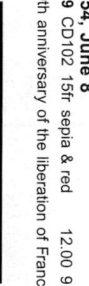

**1947, Oct. 6    AP4**
C15 AP2    50fr yel grn & rose    5.75 3.00
C16 AP3    100fr dk blue grn    10.00 5.00
C17 AP4    200fr bluish blk & brt    8.25

Nos. C15-C17 (3)    rose

**1949, Oct. 1    Engr.    Perf. 13**
C18 CD99 25fr multicolored    14.00 10.00

UPU Issue
Common Design Type

**1954, June 8**
C19 CD102 15fr sepia & red    12.00 9.00

Liberation Issue
Common Design Type

10th anniversary of the liberation of France.

**1946, June 6**
C9 CD93    5fr brown red    1.25 1.10
C10 CD94 10fr lilac rose    1.25 1.10
C11 CD95 15fr gray blk    1.90 1.60

Chad to Rhine Issue
Common Design Types

**1946, May 8    Engr.    Perf. 12½**
C8 CD92 8fr deep claret    1.75 1.40

Victory Issue
Common Design Type

**1950, May 15**
B14 CD100 10fr + 2fr red brn
& red    11.00 10.00

**1956, Oct. 22**
C20 AP6 500fr ultra & indigo    62.50 19.00

Plane over St. Pierre Harbor — AP6

**1957, Nov. 4    Unwmk.    Perf. 13**
C21 AP7    50fr gray, brn blk &
bl    40.00 19.00
C22 AP7 100fr black & gray    18.00 8.50

Dog and Village — AP7

Design: 100fr, Caravelle over archipelago.

## Band A

**Anchors and Torches — AP8**

1959, Sept. 14    Engr.    *Perf. 13*
C23 AP8 200fr dk pur, grn & cl    14.00 6.50

Approval of the constitution and the vote which confirmed the attachment of the Islands to France.

**Pitcher Plant — AP9**

1962, Apr. 24    Unwmk.    *Perf. 13*
C24 AP9 100fr green, org & car    12.00 3.50

**Gulf of St. Lawrence and Submarine "Surcouf" — AP10**

*Perf. 13½x12½*
C25 AP10 50fr dk red & bl    110.00 82.50

20th anniv. of St. Pierre & Miquelon's joining the Free French.

**Telstar Issue**
Common Design Type

1962, Nov. 22    Engr.    *Perf. 13*
C26 CD111 50fr Prus grn & bis    6.00 4.00

**Arrival of Governor Dangeac, 1763 — AP11**

1963, Aug. 5    Unwmk.    *Perf. 13*
C27 AP11 200fr dk bl, sl grn & brn    25.00 10.00

Bicentenary of the arrival of the first French governor.

**Jet Plane and Map of Maritime Provinces and New England — AP12**

1964, Sept. 28    Engr.    *Perf. 13*
C28 AP12 100fr choc & Prus bl    12.00 7.00

Inauguration of direct airmail service between St. Pierre and New York City.

**ITU Issue**
Common Design Type

1965, May 17
C29 CD120 40fr org brn, dk bl & lil rose    20.00 10.50

## Band B

**French Satellite A-1 Issue**
Common Design Type

Designs: 25fr, Diamant rocket and launching installations. 30fr, A-1 satellite.

1966, Jan. 24    Engr.    *Perf. 13*
C30 CD121 25fr dk brn, dk bl & rose cl    5.00 2.75
C31 CD121 30fr dk bl, rose cl & dk brn    3.50 2.75
a.   Strip of 2, #C30-C31 + label    12.00 12.00

**French Satellite D-1 Issue**
Common Design Type

1966, May 23    Engr.    *Perf. 13*
C32 CD122 48fr brt grn, ultra & rose claret    8.00 5.00

**Arrival of Settlers — AP13**

1966, June 22    Photo.    *Perf. 13*
C33 AP13 100fr multicolored    14.00 5.50

150th anniv. of the return of the islands of St. Pierre and Miquelon to France.

**Front Page of Official Journal and Printing Presses — AP14**

1966, Oct. 20    *Perf. 13*
C34 AP14 60fr dk bl, lake & dk pur    10.50 5.00

Centenary of the Government Printers and the Official Journal.

**Map of Islands, Old and New Fishing Vessels — AP15**

Design: 100fr, Cruiser Colbert, maps of Brest, St. Pierre and Miquelon.

1967, July 20    *Perf. 13*
C35 AP15 25fr dk bl, gray & crim    20.00 13.00
C36 AP15 100fr multicolored    35.00 25.00

Visit of President Charles de Gaulle.

**Speed Skater and Olympic Emblem — AP16**

60fr, Ice hockey goalkeeper.

## Band C

1968, Apr. 22    Photo.    *Perf. 13*
C37 AP16 50fr ultra & multi    8.00 3.25
C38 AP16 60fr green & multi    10.00 5.00

10th Winter Olympic Games, Grenoble, France, Feb. 6-18.

**War Memorial, St. Pierre — AP17**

1968, Nov. 11    Photo.    *Perf. 12½*
C39 AP17 500fr multicolored    25.00 15.00

World War I armistice, 50th anniv.

**Concorde Issue**
Common Design Type

1969, Apr. 17    Engr.    *Perf. 13*
C40 CD129 34fr dk brn & olive    30.00 10.00

Scenic Type of Regular Issue, 1969.

Designs: 50fr, Grazing horses, Miquelon. 100fr, Gathering driftwood on Mirande Beach, Miquelon.

1969, Apr. 30    Engr.    *Perf. 13*
    Size: 47½x27mm
C41 A47 50fr ultra, brn & olive    13.50 6.00
C42 A47 100fr dk brn, bl & sl    24.00 11.00

**L'Esperance Leaving Saint-Malo, 1600 — AP18**

1969, June 16    Engr.    *Perf. 13*
C43 AP18 200fr blk, grn & dk red    50.00 20.00

**Pierre Loti and Sailboats — AP19**

1969, June 23    Engr.    *Perf. 13*
C44 AP19 300fr lemon, choc & Prus bl    55.00 22.50

Loti (1850-1923), French novelist and naval officer.

**EXPO Emblem and "Mountains" by Yokoyama Taikan — AP20**

34fr, Geisha, rocket and EXPO emblem, vert.

1970, Sept. 8    Engr.    *Perf. 13*
C45 AP20 34fr dp cl, ol & ind    15.00 6.50
C46 AP20 85fr org, ind & car    30.00 14.00

EXPO 70 Intl. Exposition, Osaka, Japan, Mar. 15-Sept. 13.

## Band D

**Etienne François Duke of Choiseul and his Ships — AP21**

Designs: 50fr, Jacques Cartier, ship and landing party. 60fr, Sébastien Le Gonrad de Sourdeval, ships and map of islands.

1970, Nov. 25    Portrait in Lake
C47 AP21 25fr lilac & Prus bl    20.00 7.50
C48 AP21 50fr sl grn & red lil    35.00 9.00
C49 AP21 60fr red lil & sl grn    75.00 30.50
Nos. C47-C49 (3)

**De Gaulle, Cross of Lorraine, Sailor, Soldier, Coast Guard — AP22**

1972, June 18    Engr.    *Perf. 13*
C50 AP22 100fr lil, brn & grn    22.50 13.00

Charles de Gaulle (1890-1970), French pres.

**Louis Joseph de Montcalm — AP23**

Designs: 2fr, Louis de Buade Frontenac, vert. 4fr, Robert de La Salle.

1973, Jan. 1
C51 AP23 1.60fr multicolored    10.00 3.25
C52 AP23 2fr multicolored    12.50 5.50
C53 AP23 4fr multicolored    22.50 10.00
Nos. C51-C53 (3)    45.00 18.75

**Transall C 160 over St. Pierre — AP24**

1973, Oct. 16    Engr.    *Perf. 13*
C54 AP24 10fr multicolored    40.00 21.00

**Arms and Map of Islands, Fish and Bird — AP25**

1974, Nov. 5    Photo.    *Perf. 13*
C55 AP25 2fr gold & multi    16.00 5.50

**1974, Nov. 26** Engr.

C56 AP26 4fr multicolored 16.00 7.75

Nicolaus Copernicus (1473-1543), Polish astronomer.

Copernicus, Kepler, Newton and Einstein — AP26

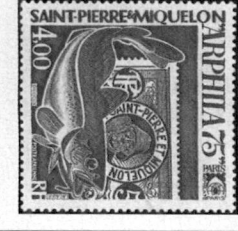

Type of 1909, Cod

**1975, Aug. 5** Engr. Perf. 13

C57 AP27 4fr ultra, red & indigo 20.00 8.00

ARPHILA '75, International Philatelic Exhibition, Paris, June 6-16.

**1975**, ARPHILA Emblem AP27

**1975, Nov. 18** Engr. Perf. 13

C58 AP28 1.90fr red, blue & vio 9.00 4.50

Pre-Olympic Year.

Judo, Maple Leaf, Olympic Rings AP28

**1976, Jan. 21** Engr. Perf. 13

C59 AP29 10fr red, blk & slate 30.00 14.00

1st commercial flight of supersonic jet Concorde from Paris to Rio, Jan. 21.

Concorde — AP29

A. G. Bell, Telephone and Satellite AP30

**1976, June 22** Litho. Perf. 12½

C60 AP30 5fr vio bl, org & red 8.00 5.50

Centenary of first telephone call by Alexander Graham Bell, Mar. 10, 1876.

---

Aircraft — AP31

**1987, June 30** Engr. — AP31

C61 AP31 5fr Hawker-Siddeley H.S. 748, 1987 1.90 1.25
C62 AP31 10fr Latecoere 522, 1939 3.50 2.25

Hindenburg — AP32

**1988-89** Engr. Perf. 13

C63 AP32 5fr multicolored 2.10 1.10
C64 AP32 10fr multicolored 3.25 2.10
C65 AP32 20fr multicolored 6.75 3.00
Nos. C63-C65 (3) 12.10 6.20

Issued: 20fr, May 31, 1989; others, June 22.

10fr, Douglas DC3, 1948-1988. 20fr, Piper Aztec.

Flying Flea, Bird — AP33

**1990, May 16** Engr. Perf. 13

C66 AP33 5fr multicolored 1.75 1.25

Piper Tomahawk — AP34

**1991, May 29** Perf. 13

C67 AP34 10fr multicolored 4.00 2.50

Radio-controlled Model Airplanes — AP35

**1992, May 6** Perf. 13

C68 AP35 20fr brown, red & org 8.00 5.00

Migratory Birds — AP36

**1993-97** Perf. 13x12½

C69 AP36 5fr Shearwater (Puffin) 1.90 1.25
C70 AP36 10fr Golden plover 3.75 2.00

Perf. 13x13½

C71 AP36 10fr Arctic Tern 4.25 3.50

Perf. 13

C72 AP36 15fr Courlis 6.25 4.50
C73 AP36 5fr Peregrine falcon, vert. 2.75 1.25

Issued: #C69-C70, 5/12; #C71, 5/10/95; #C72, 5/15/96; #C73, 5/28/97.

Nos. C69-C73 (5) 18.90 12.50

---

Bald Eagle — AP38

**1997, June 11**

C74 AP37 14fr blk, grn bl & brn 5.50 4.00

Disappearance of the Flight of Nungesser and Coli, 70th Anniv. — AP37

**1998-2001** Engr. Perf. 13

C74A AP38 5fr Buzzard 1.60 1.00
C75 AP38 10fr shown 3.50 3.00
C75A AP38 15fr Heron 3.75 2.75
C76 AP38 20fr Wild duck 7.25 5.50

Issued: 5fr, 12/13/00; 10fr, 5/23/01; 20fr, 5/5/99. 15fr, 5/6;

Puffin — AP39

**2002, Apr. 22** Perf. 13

C77 A203 €2.50 multi 6.50 6.00

Solan Goose — AP40

**2003, June 18** Engr. Perf. 13x12½

C78 AP40 €2.50 multi 6.50 5.75

Bustard — AP41

**2004, July 7** Perf. 13x13½

C79 AP41 €2.50 multi 6.25 6.25

---

Piping Plover — AP42

**2005, June 22** Perf. 13x12½

C80 AP42 €2.50 multi 6.00 6.00

## AIR POST SEMI-POSTAL STAMPS

Bringing Children to Hospital — SPAP1

**1942, June 22** Unwmk. Photo.
Perf. 13½x12½

CB1 SPAP1 1.50fr + 3.50fr green 3.50
CB2 SPAP1 2fr + 6fr brown 3.50

Native children's welfare fund.

Nos. CB1-CB2 were issued by the Vichy government in France, but were not placed on sale in St. Pierre & Miquelon.

**Colonial Education Fund**

Common Design Type

**1942, June 22**

CB3 CD6a 1.20fr + 1.80fr blue & red 4.25

No. CB3 was issued by the Vichy government in France, but was not placed on sale in St. Pierre & Miquelon.

## POSTAGE DUE STAMPS

Postage Due Stamps of French Colonies Overprinted in Red

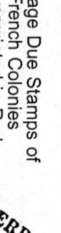
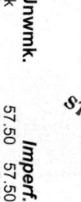

ST-PIERRE M-on

**1892** Unwmk. Imperf.

J1 D1 1c black 57.50 57.50
J2 D1 10c black 17.50 17.50
J3 D1 15c black 17.50 17.50
J4 D1 20c black 17.50 17.50
J5 D1 30c black 17.50 17.50
J6 D1 45c black 17.50 17.50
J7 D1 60c black 60.00 60.00

**Black Overprint**

J8 D1 1fr brown 150.00 150.00
J9 D1 2fr brown 150.00 150.00
Nos. J1-J9 (9) 505.00 505.00

These stamps exist with and without hyphen. See note after No. 59.

**1925-27** Perf. 14x13½

Postage Due Stamps of France, 1893-1924, Overprinted

J10 D2 5c blue .35 .35
J11 D2 10c dark brown .35 .35
J12 D2 20c olive green .55 .55
J13 D2 25c rose .55 .55
J14 D2 30c green .55 .55
J15 D2 45c blue green 1.25 1.25
J16 D2 50c brown vio 1.25 1.25
J17 D2 1fr red brn, straw 1.90 1.90
J18 D2 3fr magenta ('27) 9.25 9.25

# ST. PIERRE & MIQUELON

## SAINT-PIERRE -ET-MIQUELON

### 2 francs à percevoir

Surcharged

| | | | | Perf. 13 | |
|---|---|---|---|---|---|
| J19 | D2 | 60c on 50c buff | | 2.10 | 2.10 |
| J20 | D2 | 2fr on 1fr red | | 3.50 | 3.50 |
| | | Nos. J10-J20 (11) | | 23.30 | 23.30 |

For overprints and surcharge see Nos. J42-J46.

Newfoundland Dog — D3

**1932, Dec. 5**     **Typo.**

| | | | | | |
|---|---|---|---|---|---|
| J21 | D3 | 5c dk green & blk | | 1.10 | 1.10 |
| J22 | D3 | 10c green & blk | | 1.10 | 1.10 |
| J23 | D3 | 20c red & blk | | 1.40 | 1.40 |
| J24 | D3 | 25c red vio & blk | | 2.75 | 2.75 |
| J25 | D3 | 30c orange & blk | | 4.50 | 4.50 |
| J26 | D3 | 45c lt blue & blk | | 6.75 | 6.75 |
| J27 | D3 | 50c blue grn & blk | | 10.00 | 10.00 |
| J28 | D3 | 60c brt rose & blk | | 18.00 | 18.00 |
| J29 | D3 | 1fr yellow brn & blk | | 18.00 | 18.00 |
| J30 | D3 | 2fr dp violet & blk | | 27.50 | 27.50 |
| J31 | D3 | 3fr dk brown & blk | | 35.00 | 35.00 |
| | | Nos. J21-J31 (11) | | 109.50 | 109.50 |

For overprints see Nos. J48-J67.

Codfish — D4

**1938, Nov. 17**    **Photo.**    **Perf. 13**

| | | | | | |
|---|---|---|---|---|---|
| J32 | D4 | 5c gray black | | .20 | .20 |
| J33 | D4 | 10c dk red violet | | .20 | .20 |
| J34 | D4 | 15c slate green | | .20 | .20 |
| J35 | D4 | 20c deep blue | | .20 | .20 |
| J36 | D4 | 30c rose carmine | | .20 | .20 |
| J37 | D4 | 50c dk blue green | | .50 | .50 |
| J38 | D4 | 60c blue | | .80 | .80 |
| J39 | D4 | 1fr henna brown | | 1.40 | 1.40 |
| J40 | D4 | 2fr gray brown | | 2.50 | 2.50 |
| J41 | D4 | 3fr dp vio & blk | | 4.00 | 4.00 |
| | | Nos. J32-J41 (10) | | 10.35 | 10.35 |

**1942**    **Unwmk.**    **Perf. 14x13½**

| | | | | | |
|---|---|---|---|---|---|
| J42 | D3 | 25c red vio & blk | | 325.00 | 325.00 |
| J43 | D3 | 30c orange & blk | | 325.00 | 325.00 |
| J44 | D3 | 15c blue grn & blk | | 1,050. | 1,050. |
| J45 | D3 | 2fr dp vio & bl | | | |
| | | blk | | 45.00 | 45.00 |

Same Surcharged in Black

FRANCE LIBRE F.N.F.L.

No. J46

| | | | | |
|---|---|---|---|---|
| J46 | D3 | 3fr on 2fr vio & blk, "F.N.F.L." | | 17.50 17.50 |
| a. | With "F.N.F.L." omitted | | 29.00 29.00 |
| | Nos. J42-J46 (5) | | 1,762. 1,762. |

FRANCE LIBRE F.N.F.L.

No. J46a

Postage Due Stamps of NOËL 1941 F N F L
1938 Overprinted in Black

## PARCEL POST STAMPS

### COLIS POSTAUX

No. 65 Overprinted

**1901**    **Unwmk.**    **Perf. 14x13½**

| | | | | |
|---|---|---|---|---|
| Q1 | A16 | 10c black, lavender | 87.50 | 87.50 |
| a. | Inverted overprint | | | |

No. 66 Overprinted

| | | | | |
|---|---|---|---|---|
| Q2 | A16 | 10c red | 18.00 | 18.00 |

Nos. 84 and 87 Overprinted

Colis Postaux

| | | | | |
|---|---|---|---|---|
| | | | 2.75 | 2.75 |
| | | | 160.00 | |
| | | | 2.10 | 2.10 |
| | | | 125.00 | |

**1917-25**

| | | | | |
|---|---|---|---|---|
| Q3 | A17 | 10c | | |
| a. | Double overprint | | | |
| Q4 | A17 | 20c (25) | | |
| a. | Double overprint | | | |

### FRANCE LIBRE
### F. N. F. L.

No. Q4 with Additional Overprint in Black

**1942**

| | | | | |
|---|---|---|---|---|
| Q5 | A17 | 20c | 875.00 | 875.00 |

---

## ST. THOMAS AND PRINCE ISLANDS

sänt-'täm-as and 'prin,t,s 'i-lands

**Democratic Republic of Sao Tome and Principe**

**LOCATION**—Two islands in the Gulf of Guinea, 125 miles off the west coast of Africa

**GOVT.**—Republic

**AREA**—387 sq. mi.

**POP.**—154,878 (1999 est.)

**CAPITAL**—Sao Tome

This colony of Portugal became a province, later an overseas territory, and achieved independence on July 12, 1975.

1000 Reis = 1 Milreis
100 Centavos = 1 Escudo (1913)
100 Cents = 1 Dobra (1977)

Catalogue values for unused stamps in this country are for Never Hinged items, beginning with Scott 353 in the regular postage section, Scott J52 in the postage due section, and Scott RA4 in the postal tax section.

10 REIS: "1" has short serif at top.
Type I— "1" has short serif at top.
Type II— "1" has long serif at top.
40 REIS: "4" is broad.
Type I— "4" is broad.
Type II— "4" is narrow.

**1869-75**   **Unwmk.**   **Perf. 12½, 13½**   **Typo.**

| | | | | |
|---|---|---|---|---|
| 1 | A1 | 5r black, I | 2.00 | 1.90 |
| 2 | A1 | 10r yellow, I | 2.00 | 1.90 |
| | a. | Type II | 14.00 | 8.50 |
| 3 | A1 | 20r bister | 17.50 | 10.50 |
| 4 | A1 | 25r rose, I | 3.50 | 2.75 |
| | a. | Type II | 1.25 | 1.10 |
| 5 | A1 | 40r blue (75), I | 4.50 | 1.50 |
| | a. | Type II | 4.75 | 3.50 |
| 6 | A1 | 50r gray grn, II | 5.50 | 4.50 |
| | a. | Type I | 5.50 | 7.00 |
| 7 | A1 | 100r gray lilac | 9.00 | 7.00 |
| 8 | A1 | 200r red orange ('75) | 15.00 | 14.00 |
| 9 | A1 | 300r chocolate ('75) | 6.00 | 5.50 |
| | | | 6.25 | 6.25 |
| | | | 8.25 | 7.00 |
| | | Nos. 1-9 (9) | 57.00 | 43.50 |

**1881-85**

| | | | | |
|---|---|---|---|---|
| 10 | A1 | 10r gray grn, I | 8.00 | 6.75 |
| | a. | Type II | 9.50 | 6.00 |
| | b. | Perf. 13½ | 11.00 | 8.00 |
| 11 | A1 | 20r car rose ('85) | 3.50 | 3.00 |
| 12 | A1 | 25r violet, II | 2.25 | 1.75 |
| 13 | A1 | 40r yel buff, II | 5.00 | 4.00 |
| | a. | Perf. 13½ | 4.50 | 4.50 |
| 14 | A1 | 50r dk blue, I | 2.50 | 2.25 |
| | | Nos. 10-14 (5) | 21.25 | 17.75 |

For surcharges and overprints see Nos. 63-64, 129-129B, 154.

Nos. 1-14 have been reprinted on stout white paper, ungummed, with rough perforation 13½, also on ordinary paper with shiny white gum and clean-cut perforation 13½ with large holes.

Typo., Head Embossed

**1887**    **Perf. 12½, 13½**

| | | | | |
|---|---|---|---|---|
| 15 | A2 | 5r black | 3.75 | 2.50 |
| 16 | A2 | 10r green | 4.25 | 2.50 |
| 17 | A2 | 20r brt rose | 4.25 | 3.00 |
| | | Perf. 12½ | 55.00 | 55.00 |
| 18 | A2 | 25r violet | 4.25 | 1.60 |
| 19 | A2 | 40r brown | 4.25 | 2.25 |
| 20 | A2 | 50r blue | 4.25 | 2.50 |
| 21 | A2 | 100r yellow brn | 15.00 | 2.00 |
| 22 | A2 | 200r gray lilac | 15.00 | 10.50 |
| 23 | A2 | 300r orange | 15.00 | 10.50 |
| | | Nos. 15-23 (9) | 59.25 | 37.35 |

For surcharges and overprints see Nos. 24-26, 62, 65, 72, 130-131, 155-160, 204, 237.

Nos. 15, 16, 19, 21, 22, and 23 have been reprinted in paler colors than the originals, with white gum and cleancut perforation 13½. Value $1.50 each.

Nos. 16-17, 19 Surcharged:

| | | | | |
|---|---|---|---|---|
| 24 | A2(a) | 5r on 10r | 35.00 | 20.00 |
| 25 | A2(b) | 5r on 20r | 25.00 | 20.00 |
| 26 | A2(c) | 50r on 40r ('91) | 225.00 | 50.00 |
| | | Nos. 24-26 (3) | 285.00 | 90.00 |

Without Gum

**1889-91**

Varieties of Nos. 24-26, including inverted and double surcharges, "5" inverted, "Cinoc" and "Cinoc," were deliberately made and unofficially issued.

King Luiz — A2

Portuguese Crown — A1

King Carlos — A7

**1895**    **Typo.**    **Perf. 11½, 12½**

| | | | | |
|---|---|---|---|---|
| 27 | A6 | 5r yellow | .50 | .60 |
| 28 | A6 | 10r red lilac | 1.25 | 1.00 |
| 29 | A6 | 15r red brown | 1.40 | 1.10 |

---

## FRANCE LIBRE (continued)

Christmas Day plebiscite ordered by Vice Admiral Emile Henri Muselier, commander of the Free French naval forces.

Postage Due Stamps of 1938 Overprinted in Black

FRANCE LIBRE F.N.F.L.

**1942**

| | | | | Perf. 13 | |
|---|---|---|---|---|---|
| J48 | D4 | 5c gray black | | 17.50 | 17.50 |
| J49 | D4 | 10c dk red violet | | 17.50 | 17.50 |
| J50 | D4 | 15c slate green | | 17.50 | 17.50 |
| J51 | D4 | 20c deep blue | | 17.50 | 17.50 |
| J52 | D4 | 30c rose carmine | | 17.50 | 17.50 |
| J53 | D4 | 50c dk blue green | | 35.00 | 35.00 |
| J54 | D4 | 60c dark blue | | 70.00 | 90.00 |
| J55 | D4 | 1fr henna brown | | 82.50 | 82.50 |
| J56 | D4 | 2fr gray brown | | 90.00 | 90.00 |
| J57 | D4 | 3fr dull violet | | 100.00 | 100.00 |
| | | Nos. J48-J57 (10) | | 465.00 | 465.00 |

Postage Due Stamps of 1932 Overprinted in Black

FRANCE LIBRE F.N.F.L.

**1942**

| | | | | | |
|---|---|---|---|---|---|
| J58 | D4 | 5c gray black | | 40.00 | 40.00 |
| J59 | D4 | 10c dk red violet | | 7.75 | 7.75 |
| J60 | D4 | 15c slate green | | 7.75 | 7.75 |
| J61 | D4 | 20c orange & blk | | 7.75 | 7.75 |
| J62 | D4 | 30c rose carmine | | 7.75 | 7.75 |
| J63 | D4 | 50c dk blue green | | 8.50 | 8.50 |
| J64 | D4 | 60c dark blue | | 21.00 | 21.00 |
| J65 | D4 | 1fr henna brown | | 25.00 | 25.00 |
| J66 | D4 | 2fr gray brown | | 475.00 | 475.00 |
| J67 | D4 | 3fr dull violet | | 608.25 | 608.25 |
| | | Nos. J58-J67 (10) | | 608.25 | 608.25 |

Arms and Fishing Schooner — D5

**1947, Oct. b**    **Engr.**    **Perf. 13**

| | | | | | |
|---|---|---|---|---|---|
| J68 | D5 | 10c deep orange | | .20 | .20 |
| J69 | D5 | 30c deep ultra | | .20 | .20 |
| J70 | D5 | 50c dk blue green | | .35 | .35 |
| J71 | D5 | 1fr deep carmine | | .55 | .55 |
| J72 | D5 | 2fr dk green | | 1.40 | 1.40 |
| J73 | D5 | 3fr chocolate | | 1.40 | 1.40 |
| J74 | D5 | 4fr chocolate | | 1.60 | 1.60 |
| J75 | D5 | 5fr yellow green | | 2.00 | 2.00 |
| J76 | D5 | 10fr black brown | | 2.25 | 2.25 |
| J77 | D5 | 20fr orange red | | 10.45 | 10.45 |
| | | Nos. J68-J77 (10) | | | |

Newfoundland Dog — D6

**1973, Jan. 1**    **Engr.**    **Perf. 13**

| | | | | | |
|---|---|---|---|---|---|
| J78 | D6 | 2c brown & blk | | 1.00 | 1.00 |
| J79 | D6 | 10c purple & blk | | 1.40 | 1.40 |
| J80 | D6 | 20c grnsh brn & blk | | 2.25 | 2.25 |
| J81 | D6 | 30c dk car & blk | | 4.50 | 4.50 |
| J82 | D6 | 1fr blue & blk | | 11.00 | 11.00 |
| | | Nos. J78-J82 (5) | | 20.15 | 20.15 |

France Nos. J106-J115 Overprinted "ST - PIERRE ET MIQUELON" Reading Up in Red

**1986, Sept. 15**    **Engr.**    **Perf. 13**

| | | | | | |
|---|---|---|---|---|---|
| J83 | D8 | 10c multicolored | | .20 | .20 |
| J84 | D8 | 20c multicolored | | .20 | .20 |
| J85 | D8 | 30c multicolored | | .20 | .20 |
| J86 | D8 | 40c multicolored | | .20 | .20 |
| J87 | D8 | 50c multicolored | | .35 | .35 |
| J88 | D8 | 1fr multicolored | | .45 | .45 |
| J89 | D8 | 2fr multicolored | | .80 | .80 |
| J90 | D8 | 3fr multicolored | | 1.25 | 1.25 |
| J91 | D8 | 4fr multicolored | | 1.60 | 1.60 |
| J92 | D8 | 5fr multicolored | | 1.75 | 1.75 |
| | | Nos. J83-J92 (10) | | 7.00 | 7.00 |

Catalogue values for unused stamps in this section, from this point to the end of the section, are for Never Hinged items.

Colis Postaux

5, 25, 50 REIS:
Type I— "5" is upright.
Type II— "5" is slanting.

## 1898-1903
### Name and Value in Black except 500r
**Perf. 11½**

| 30 | A6 | 20r lavender | 1.50 | 1.10 |
|---|---|---|---|---|
| 31 | A6 | 25r green | | .75 |
| 32 | A6 | 50r light blue | 1.60 | .70 |

**Perf. 13½**

| 33 | A6 | 50r brown | 1.50 | |
|---|---|---|---|---|
| 34 | A6 | 75r rose | 3.75 | 3.25 |
| 35 | A6 | 100r yellow grn | 8.00 | 6.25 |
| 36 | A6 | 150r car, rose | 3.50 | 3.00 |
| 37 | A6 | 200r car, rose | 8.50 | 7.75 |
| 38 | A6 | 300r dk bl, sal | 45.55 | 37.00 |

Nos. 27-38 (12)

For surcharges and overprints see Nos. 73-84, 132-137, 159-165, 238-243, 262-264, 268-274.

## 1898-1903
### Name and Value in Black except 500r
**Perf. 11½**

| 39 | A7 | 2½r gray | .30 | .30 |
|---|---|---|---|---|
| 40 | A7 | 5r orange | .30 | .25 |
| 41 | A7 | 10r lt green | .40 | .30 |
| 42 | A7 | 15r brown | 2.00 | 1.75 |
| 43 | A7 | 20r gray grn ('03) | 1.10 | 1.10 |
| 44 | A7 | 25r gray violet | .90 | .25 |
| 45 | A7 | 25r sea green | .70 | .25 |
| 46 | A7 | 25r carmine ('03) | 1.10 | .30 |
| 47 | A7 | 50r brown ('03) | .30 | .30 |
| 48 | A7 | 50r blue | 4.50 | 4.50 |
| 49 | A7 | 65r brown ('03) | 1.10 | .90 |
| 50 | A7 | 75r rose | 10.00 | 9.00 |
| 51 | A7 | 75r red lilac ('03) | 6.50 | 6.50 |
| 52 | A7 | 80r brt lilac | 2.50 | 1.40 |
| 53 | A7 | 115r org brn, pink | 3.00 | 2.00 |
| 54 | A7 | 115r org brn, pink ('03) | | |
| 55 | A7 | 130r blk, straw ('03) | 8.00 | 8.00 |
| 56 | A7 | 150r brn, buff | 6.00 | 6.00 |
| 57 | A7 | 200r red lil, pnksh | 5.00 | 2.25 |
| 58 | A7 | 300r dk blue, rose | 8.00 | 5.00 |
| 59 | A7 | 400r dk bl, | 8.00 | 5.00 |
| 60 | A7 | 500r blk & red, straw('03) | 13.00 | 8.50 |
| 61 | A7 | 700r vio, yel/sh('01) | 16.00 | 12.00 |

Nos. 39-61 (23) 121.80 83.10

For overprints and surcharges see Nos. 86-105, 116-128, 138-153, 167-169, 244-249, 255-261, 265-267.

### Stamps of 1869-95
### Surcharged in Red or Black

## 1902
### On Stamp of 1887

| 62 | A2 | 130r on 5r blk (R) | 6.00 | 5.00 |
|---|---|---|---|---|
| a. | | Perf. 13½ | 32.50 | 32.50 |

### On Stamps of 1869

| 63 | A1 | 115r on 50r grn | 10.00 | 7.50 |
|---|---|---|---|---|
| 64 | A1 | 400r on 10r yel | 25.00 | 12.00 |
| a. | | Double surcharge | 75.00 | 50.00 |

### On Stamps of 1887

| 65 | A2 | 65r on 20r rose | 6.25 | 4.50 |
|---|---|---|---|---|
| 66 | A2 | 65r on 25r violet | 8.50 | 4.50 |
| a. | | Inverted surcharge | 4.50 | 4.00 |
| 67 | A2 | 65r on 100r yel brn | 4.50 | 4.00 |
| 68 | A2 | 115r on 10r blue grn | 4.50 | 25.00 |
| 69 | A2 | 115r on 15r blue grn | 4.50 | 4.75 |
| 70 | A2 | 400r on 200r orange | 6.00 | 5.00 |
| 71 | A2 | 400r on 300r gray lil | 6.00 | 7.00 |
| 72 | A2 | 400r on 50r blue | 14.00 | 12.00 |
| a. | | Perf. 13½ | 110.00 | 90.00 |

### On Stamps of 1895

| 73 | A6 | 65r on 5r yellow | 5.00 | 3.00 |
|---|---|---|---|---|
| 74 | A6 | 65r on 10r red vio | 5.00 | 3.00 |
| 75 | A6 | 65r on 15r choc | 5.00 | 3.00 |
| 76 | A6 | 65r on 20r lav | 5.00 | 3.00 |
| 77 | A6 | 115r on 25r grn | 5.00 | 3.00 |
| 78 | A6 | 115r on 50r brn rose | 5.00 | 3.00 |
| 79 | A6 | 115r on 200r bl, bl | 5.00 | 3.00 |
| 80 | A6 | 115r on 75r car, | 5.00 | 3.00 |
| 81 | A6 | 130r on 100r brn. | 5.00 | 3.00 |
| a. | | Double surcharge | | |
| 82 | A6 | 130r on 30r sal | 5.00 | 3.00 |
| 83 | A6 | 400r on 300r bl blue | 5.00 | 3.00 |
| a. | | Perf. 13½ | 2.00 | 1.60 |
| 84 | A6 | 400r on 80r yel grn | | 1.50 |

### On Newspaper Stamp No. P12

| 85 | N3 | 400r on 2½r brown | 1.10 | .95 |
|---|---|---|---|---|
| a. | | Double surcharge | 147.45 | 103.65 |

Nos. 62-85 (24)

Reprints of Nos. 63, 64, 67, 71, and 72 have shiny white gum and clean-cut perf. 13½.

## 1902
### Stamps of 1898
### Overprinted

| 86 | A7 | 15r brown | 2.00 | 1.50 |
|---|---|---|---|---|
| 87 | A7 | 25r sea green | 2.25 | 1.25 |
| 88 | A7 | 50r blue | 2.25 | 1.25 |
| 89 | A7 | 75r rose | 3.50 | 1.75 |

Nos. 86-89 (4)

## 1905
### No. 49 Surcharged in Black

| 90 | A7 | 50r on 65r dull blue | 3.25 | 2.75 |
|---|---|---|---|---|

### Stamps of 1898-1903
### Overprinted in Carmine or Green

| 91 | A7 | 2½r gray | .25 | .20 |
|---|---|---|---|---|
| 92 | A7 | 5r orange | .25 | .20 |
| 93 | A7 | 10r lt green | .25 | .20 |
| 94 | A7 | 15r gray green | .25 | .20 |
| 95 | A7 | 25r gray violet | .60 | .20 |
| 96 | A7 | 25r carmine (G) | .25 | .20 |
| 97 | A7 | 50r brown | .30 | .20 |

## 1911
| 98 | A7 | 2½r gray | 15.00 | 11.00 |
|---|---|---|---|---|
| a. | | Inverted overprint | | |
| 99 | A7 | 10r brt dk bl, bl | .25 | .20 |
| 100 | A7 | 15r org brn, pink | 17.50 | 14.00 |
| a. | | Inverted overprint | | |
| 101 | A7 | 130r brown, straw | 1.50 | .95 |
| 102 | A7 | 200r red lil, pnksh | 6.00 | 4.25 |
| 103 | A7 | 400r dull blue, straw | 2.00 | 1.00 |
| 104 | A7 | 500r blk & red, bl | 2.00 | 1.00 |
| 105 | A7 | 700r violet, yel/sh | 18.30 | 11.25 |

Nos. 91-105 (15)

### King Manuel II — A8
**Perf. 11½, 12**

## 1912
### Overprinted in Carmine or Green

| 106 | A8 | 2½r violet | 16.00 | 16.00 |
|---|---|---|---|---|
| a. | | Double overprint | 25.00 | |
| 107 | A8 | 5r black | .20 | .20 |
| a. | | Double overprint, one inverted | | |
| 108 | A8 | 10r gray green | .20 | .20 |
| 109 | A8 | 20r carmine (G) | 1.00 | 1.00 |
| 110 | A8 | 25r violet brn | .60 | .45 |
| 111 | A8 | 50r dk blue | .90 | .55 |
| 112 | A8 | 75r bister brn | .55 | .55 |
| 113 | A8 | 100r brn, lt grn | 1.10 | .90 |
| 114 | A8 | 200r dk grn, sal | 2.00 | 1.40 |
| 115 | A8 | 300r dk grn, azure | 2.00 | 2.00 |
| a. | | Double overprint | 8.80 | 6.80 |

Nos. 106-115 (10)

## 1913
### Stamps of 1898-1903
### Overprinted in Black

| 116 | A7 | 2½r gray | 1.00 | 1.00 |
|---|---|---|---|---|
| a. | | Inverted overprint | 12.00 | 12.00 |
| 117 | A7 | 5r orange | 21.40 | 12.00 |
| a. | | Double overprint | 22.50 | 17.50 |
| 118 | A7 | 15r gray green | 75.00 | |
| 119 | A7 | 20r gray violet | 1.50 | 1.50 |
| a. | | Inverted overprint | | |
| 120 | A7 | 25r carmine | 4.50 | 4.50 |
| b. | | Double overprint | | |

### On Stamps of 1898-1903

| 121 | A7 | 75r red lilac | 5.00 | 5.00 |
|---|---|---|---|---|
| 122 | A7 | 100r bl, bluish | 8.50 | 7.50 |
| 123 | A7 | 115r org brn, pink | 37.50 | 35.00 |
| a. | | Double overprint | | |
| 124 | A7 | 130r brn, straw | 13.00 | 13.00 |
| 125 | A7 | 200r red lil, pnksh | 13.00 | 13.00 |
| 126 | A7 | 400r dl bl, straw | 14.00 | 12.50 |
| 127 | A7 | 500r blk & red, | | |
| 128 | A7 | 700r vio, yel/sh | 35.00 | 42.50 |

Nos. 116-128 (13)

### On Provisional Issue of 1902

| 129 | A1 | 115r on 50r grn | 110.00 | 85.00 |
|---|---|---|---|---|
| a. | | Inverted overprint | | |
| 130 | A1 | 400r on 10r yel | 600.00 | 500.00 |
| 131 | A2 | 65r on 20r rose | 2.50 | 2.00 |
| 132 | A6 | 130r on 75r rose | 2.25 | 2.00 |
| a. | | Inverted overprint | 75.00 | |
| 133 | A6 | 115r on 25r grn | 20.00 | |
| 134 | A6 | 115r on 50r brn, | | |
| 135 | A6 | 130r on 30r sal | 40.00 | |
| 136 | A6 | 400r on 300r bl bl | 4.00 | 4.00 |
| a. | | Perf. 13½ | 20.00 | 10.00 |
| 137 | A6 | 400r on 80r yel | | |

### Same Overprint on Nos. 86, 88, 90

| 138 | A7 | 15r brown | 2.00 | 1.75 |
|---|---|---|---|---|
| 139 | A7 | 50r blue | 2.25 | 2.25 |
| 140 | A7 | 50r on 65r dl bl | 16.00 | 16.00 |

Nos. 138-140 (3) 20.25 15.75

No. 123-125, 130-131 and 137 were issued without gum.

### Stamps of 1898-1905
### Overprinted in Black

## 1913
### On Stamps of 1898-1903

| 141 | A7 | 2½r gray | .60 | .50 |
|---|---|---|---|---|
| a. | | Double overprint | 11.00 | |
| 142 | A7 | 15r gray green | 30.00 | |
| 143 | A7 | 15r brown | 27.50 | 22.50 |
| 144 | A7 | 20r gray violet | 1.50 | 1.50 |
| 145 | A7 | 25r carmine | 25.00 | |
| 146 | A7 | 50r brown | 2.75 | 2.25 |
| 147 | A7 | 75r red lilac | 2.25 | 27.50 |
| a. | | Inverted overprint | | |
| 148 | A7 | 100r blue, bl | 8.00 | 8.00 |
| 149 | A7 | 115r org brn, pink | 25.00 | |
| 150 | A7 | 130r brown, straw | 2.50 | 1.75 |
| 151 | A7 | 400r dull bl, straw | 10.00 | 8.00 |
| 152 | A7 | 500r blk & red, | 8.50 | 8.00 |
| 153 | A7 | 700r violet, yel/sh | 9.00 | 8.50 |

### On Provisional Issue of 1902

| 154 | A1 | 115r on 50r green | 200.00 | 150.00 |
|---|---|---|---|---|
| 155 | A1 | 115r on 10r grn | 250.00 | 125.00 |
| 156 | A2 | 65r on 20r rose | 2.50 | 2.25 |
| 157 | A6 | 400r on 300r org | 250.00 | 125.00 |
| 158 | A6 | 400r on 5r blk | 200.00 | 90.00 |
| 159 | A6 | 130r on 75r rose | 2.00 | 1.75 |
| 160 | A6 | 115r on 25r green | | |

### Same Overprint on Nos. 86, 88, 90

| 161 | A6 | 115r on 200r bl, bl | 2.50 | 2.25 |
|---|---|---|---|---|
| 162 | A6 | 130r on 30r sal | 2.50 | 2.25 |
| 163 | A6 | 130r on 100r brn. | 2.00 | 1.75 |
| 164 | A6 | 400r on 50r bl bl | 3.50 | 3.00 |
| a. | | "REPUBLICA" inverted | | |
| 165 | A6 | 400r on 80r yel grn | 3.00 | 6.00 |
| 166 | N3 | 400r on 2½r brn | | |

### Same Overprint on Nos. 86, 88, 90

| 167 | A7 | 15r brown | 1.50 | 1.25 |
|---|---|---|---|---|
| 168 | A7 | 50r blue | 1.50 | 1.25 |
| 169 | A7 | 50r on 65r dull bl | 1.50 | 1.25 |

Nos. 167-169 (3) 5.25 4.00

Most of Nos. 141-169 were issued without gum.

For surcharges see Nos. 250-253, 281-282.

## 1902
### Stamps of 1898
### Overprinted

### Preceding Issues Overprinted in Carmine

### On Stamps of Macao

| 170 | CD20 | ¼c on ⅛a bl grn | 1.60 | 1.40 |
|---|---|---|---|---|
| 171 | CD21 | ¼c on ¼a bl grn | 1.60 | 1.40 |
| 172 | CD22 | 1c on 2a red vio | 1.40 | 1.25 |
| 173 | CD22 | 1c on 5r red | 1.10 | 1.10 |
| 174 | CD24 | 5c on 10r red vio | 1.10 | 1.10 |
| 175 | CD24 | 5c on 8a dk gl | 1.90 | 1.90 |
| 176 | CD26 | 10c on 12a vio brn | 1.90 | 1.90 |
| 177 | CD27 | 10c on 24a bister | 9.00 | 9.00 |

Nos. 170-177 (8)

### On Stamps of Portuguese Africa

| 178 | CD20 | ¼c on ½a bl grn | 1.10 | 1.10 |
|---|---|---|---|---|
| 179 | CD21 | ¼c on 5r red | 1.10 | 1.10 |
| 180 | CD21 | 1c on 10r red vio | 30.00 | |
| 181 | CD23 | 2½c on 75r vio brn | | |
| 182 | CD24 | 5c on 50r dk bl | | |
| 183 | CD25 | 7½c on 16a bis brn | 1.40 | 1.10 |
| 184 | CD26 | 10c on 150r bister | 1.10 | 1.10 |
| 185 | CD27 | 15c on 150r bister | 1.40 | 1.10 |

Nos. 178-185 (8)

### On Stamps of Timor

| 186 | CD20 | ¼c on ⅛a bl grn | 1.25 | 1.10 |
|---|---|---|---|---|
| 187 | CD21 | ¼c on ¼a bl grn | 1.40 | 1.25 |
| 188 | CD22 | 1c on 2a red vio | 1.40 | 1.25 |
| 189 | CD23 | 2½c on ¼a yel grn | 1.75 | 1.60 |
| 190 | CD24 | 5c on 8a dk bl | 2.50 | 2.50 |
| 191 | CD25 | 10c on 16a brn | 1.40 | 1.40 |
| 192 | CD26 | 10c on 16a bis brn | 2.50 | 2.50 |
| 193 | CD27 | 15c on 24a bister | 37.85 | 34.30 |

Nos. 186-193 (8)

### Vasco da Gama Issue of Various Portuguese Colonies Surcharged as Above

### On Provisional Issue of 1902

## 1914-26  Typo.  Perf. 12x11½, 15x14
### Name and Value in Black
### Ceres — A9

| 194 | A9 | ¼c olive brown | .20 | .20 |
|---|---|---|---|---|
| 195 | A9 | ½c yellow brn | .50 | .40 |
| 196 | A9 | 1c yellow grn ('22) | .30 | .20 |
| 197 | A9 | 1½c lilac brn | .20 | .20 |
| 198 | A9 | 2c ultra ('22) | .45 | .35 |
| 199 | A9 | 2c carmine | .30 | .20 |
| 200 | A9 | 2½c gray ('26) | .25 | .20 |
| 201 | A9 | 3c orange | .25 | .20 |
| 202 | A9 | 4c orange ('22) | .20 | .20 |
| 203 | A9 | 4½c gray ('22) | .25 | .25 |
| 204 | A9 | 5c deep blue | .40 | .35 |
| 205 | A9 | 5c brt blue ('22) | .45 | .40 |
| 206 | A9 | 6c choc ('22) | .25 | .25 |
| 207 | A9 | 7c ultra ('22) | .30 | .20 |
| 208 | A9 | 7½c yellow brn | .25 | .20 |
| 209 | A9 | 8c slate | .25 | .20 |
| 210 | A9 | 8c yellow brn | .40 | .25 |
| 211 | A9 | 9c blue green ('22) | .50 | .40 |
| 212 | A9 | 10c orange brn | .50 | .25 |
| 213 | A9 | 12c blue green ('22) | .40 | .25 |
| 214 | A9 | 15c plum | .50 | .40 |
| 215 | A9 | 15c yellow green | 1.00 | .75 |
| 216 | A9 | 16c gray ('22) | 3.00 | 2.00 |
| 217 | A9 | 20c choc ('26) | .75 | .40 |
| 218 | A9 | 24c brown, grn | 1.75 | 1.40 |
| 219 | A9 | 25c gray grn ('22) | 1.40 | .30 |
| 220 | A9 | 30c carmine rose | 1.40 | .30 |
| 221 | A9 | 30c carmine, pink | 1.75 | .75 |
| 222 | A9 | 40c turq bl ('22) | 4.00 | 3.00 |
| 223 | A9 | 40c brn rose ('22) | | |
| 224 | A9 | 50c lt violet ('26) | .40 | .30 |
| 225 | A9 | 50c blue ('22) | .40 | .40 |
| 226 | A9 | 60c rose ('26) | 1.60 | .75 |
| 227 | A9 | 80c brt rose ('22) | 4.00 | 1.60 |
| 228 | A9 | 1e pale rose ('22) | 2.50 | 1.60 |
| 229 | A9 | 1e pale rose ('26) | 1.50 | 1.10 |
| 230 | A9 | 2e pale grn ('22) | 2.75 | 1.75 |
| 231 | A9 | 2½c dk violet ('22) | 11.50 | 14.00 |
| 232 | A9 | 5e buff ('26) | 60.00 | 40.00 |
| 233 | A9 | 10e pink ('26) | 19.00 | 14.00 |
| | A9 | 20e pale turq ('26) | 127.80 | 87.25 |

Nos. 194-233 (40)

Perforation and paper variations command a premium for some of Nos. 194-233.

### Common Design Types pictured following the introduction.

## 1915
### On Provisional Issue of 1902
| | | | | |
|---|---|---|---|---|
| 234 | A2 | 115r on 10r green | 1.75 | 1.60 |
| 235 | A2 | 115r on 300r org | 1.75 | 1.75 |
| 236 | A2 | 130r on 5r black | 4.00 | 2.75 |
| 237 | A2 | 200r on 200r gray III | 1.40 | 1.25 |
| 238 | A6 | 115r on 25r green | .60 | .40 |
| 239 | A6 | 115r on 150r car, rose | .60 | .40 |
| 240 | A6 | 115r on 200r bl, bl | .60 | .40 |
| 241 | A6 | 130r on 75r rose | .60 | .40 |
| 242 | A6 | 130r on 100r brn, yel | 1.10 | 1.25 |
| 243 | A6 | 130r on 300r bl, ssl | 1.00 | .75 |

### Same Overprint on Nos. 88 and 90
| | | | | |
|---|---|---|---|---|
| 244 | A7 | 50r blue | .70 | .55 |
| 245 | A7 | 50r on 65r dull bl | 14.80 | 12.05 |

Nos. 234-245 (12)

Nos. 238-243
Surcharged in Blue or Red

**Without Gum**

## 1923
| | | | | |
|---|---|---|---|---|
| 268 | A6 | 10c on 115r on 25r (Bl) | .70 | .50 |
| 269 | A6 | 10c on 115r on 150r (Bl) | .70 | .50 |
| 270 | A6 | 10c on 115r on 200r (R) | .70 | .50 |
| 271 | A6 | 10c on 115r on 25r green | .70 | .50 |
| 272 | A6 | 10c on 130r on 75r (Bl) | .70 | .50 |
| 273 | A6 | 10c on 130r on 300r (R) | 4.20 | 3.00 |

Nos. 268-273 (6)

Nos. 268-273 are usually stained and discolored.

No. 86 Overprinted in Blue and Surcharged in Black

## 1919
| | | | | |
|---|---|---|---|---|
| 246 | A7 | 2½c on 15r brown | .60 | .55 |

No. 91 Surcharged in Black

| | | | | |
|---|---|---|---|---|
| 247 | A7 | ½c on 2½r gray | 3.00 | 2.75 |
| 248 | A7 | 1c on 2½r gray | 2.25 | 2.50 |
| 249 | A7 | 2½c on 2½r gray | 1.10 | .65 |

No. 194 Surcharged in Blue

| | | | | |
|---|---|---|---|---|
| 250 | A9 | ½c on ¼c ol brn | 2.00 | 1.75 |
| 251 | A9 | 2c on ¼c ol brn | 2.25 | 1.90 |
| 252 | A9 | 2½c on ¼c ol brn | 5.00 | |

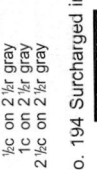

No. 201 Surcharged in Black

| | | | | |
|---|---|---|---|---|
| 253 | A9 | 4c on 2½r lt vio | .90 | .75 |

Nos. 246-253 (8)  18.10  15.35

Nos. 246-253 were issued without gum.

Stamps of 1898-1905 Overprinted in Green or Red

## 1920
### On Stamps of 1898-1903
| | | | | |
|---|---|---|---|---|
| 255 | A7 | 75r red lilac (G) | | .50 |
| 256 | A7 | 100r blue, blue (R) | .55 | |
| 257 | A7 | 115r org brn, pink (G) | .80 | .75 |
| 258 | A7 | 130r brn, straw (G) | 2.00 | 1.40 |
| 259 | A7 | 200r red lil, prnksh (G) | 80.00 | 50.00 |
| 260 | A7 | 500r blk, & red, gray (G) | 2.00 | 1.00 |
| 261 | A7 | 700r vio, yelsh (G) | 1.50 | 1.25 |

### On Stamps of 1902
| | | | | |
|---|---|---|---|---|
| 262 | A6 | 115r on 25r grn (R) | 1.00 | .60 |
| 263 | A6 | 115r on 200r bl, bl (G) | 1.00 | 1.50 |
| 264 | A6 | 130r on 75r rose (G) | 2.00 | |

### On Nos. 88-89
| | | | | |
|---|---|---|---|---|
| 265 | A7 | 50r blue (G) | 1.50 | 1.10 |
| 266 | A7 | 75r rose (G) | 10.00 | 7.00 |

### On No. 90
| | | | | |
|---|---|---|---|---|
| 267 | A7 | 50r on 65r dl bl (R) | 12.00 | 7.00 |

Nos. 255-257,259-267 (12)  36.85  24.10

Nos. 84-85 Surcharged

## 1925
| | | | | |
|---|---|---|---|---|
| 274 | A6 | 40c on 400r on 80r yel grn | .90 | .45 |
| 275 | N3 | 40c on 400r on 2½r brn | .90 | .45 |

Nos. 228 and 230 Surcharged

## 1931
| | | | | |
|---|---|---|---|---|
| 281 | A9 | 70c on 1e pale rose | 2.00 | 1.25 |
| 282 | A9 | 1.40e on 2e dk vio | 2.75 | 2.50 |

Ceres — A11

**Perf. 12x11½**
**Typo.   Wmk. 232**

## 1934
| | | | | |
|---|---|---|---|---|
| 283 | A11 | 1c bister | .20 | .20 |
| 284 | A11 | 5c olive brown | .20 | .20 |
| 285 | A11 | 10c violet | .20 | .20 |
| 286 | A11 | 15c black | .20 | .20 |
| 287 | A11 | 20c gray | .20 | .20 |
| 288 | A11 | 30c dk green | .20 | .20 |
| 289 | A11 | 40c rod orange | .35 | .35 |
| 290 | A11 | 45c brt blue | .35 | .35 |
| 291 | A11 | 50c brown | .35 | .35 |
| 292 | A11 | 60c olive grn | .35 | .35 |
| 293 | A11 | 70c brown org | .35 | .35 |
| 294 | A11 | 80c emerald | .65 | .45 |
| 295 | A11 | 85c deep rose | .75 | |
| 296 | A11 | 1e maroon | 1.75 | 1.40 |
| 297 | A11 | 1.40e blue | 1.75 | |
| 298 | A11 | 2e dk violet | 2.50 | 2.50 |
| 299 | A11 | 5e apple green | 5.50 | 4.00 |
| 300 | A11 | 10e olive bister | 9.50 | |
| 301 | A11 | 20e orange | 32.50 | 17.00 |
| | | | 56.15 | 30.70 |

Nos. 283-301 (19)

Common Design Types
Inscribed "S. Tomé"

## 1938   Unwmk.   Perf. 13½x13
### Name and Value in Black
| | | | | |
|---|---|---|---|---|
| 302 | CD34 | 1c gray green | .20 | .20 |
| 303 | CD34 | 5c orange brown | .20 | .20 |
| 304 | CD34 | 10c dk carmine | .20 | .20 |
| 305 | CD34 | 15c dk violet brn | .20 | .20 |
| 306 | CD34 | 20c slate | .20 | .20 |
| 307 | CD35 | 30c rose violet | .20 | .20 |
| 308 | CD35 | 35c brt green | .20 | .20 |
| 309 | CD35 | 40c brown | .20 | .20 |
| 310 | CD35 | 50c brt red vio | .20 | .20 |
| 311 | CD36 | 60c gray black | .20 | .20 |
| 312 | CD36 | 70c brown violet | .25 | .20 |
| 313 | CD36 | 80c orange | .60 | .45 |
| 314 | CD36 | 1e red | 1.10 | .60 |
| 315 | CD37 | 1.75e blue | 1.25 | |
| 316 | CD37 | 2e brown car | 2.75 | |
| 317 | CD37 | 5e olive green | 8.00 | 3.00 |
| 318 | CD38 | 10e blue violet | 17.00 | 5.00 |
| 319 | CD38 | 20e red brown | 46.80 | 18.55 |

Nos. 302-319 (18)

Marble Column and Portuguese Arms with Cross — A12

Common Design Types
Inscribed "S. Tomé e Principe"

## 1938   Perf. 12½
| | | | | |
|---|---|---|---|---|
| 320 | A12 | 80c blue green | 2.00 | 1.00 |
| 321 | A12 | 1.75e deep blue | 7.75 | 3.00 |
| 322 | A12 | 20e brown | 30.00 | 12.50 |
| | | | 39.75 | 16.50 |

Nos. 320-322 (3)

Visit of the President of Portugal in 1938.

## 1939   Perf. 13½x13
### Name and Value in Black
| | | | | |
|---|---|---|---|---|
| 323 | CD34 | 1c gray grn | .20 | .20 |
| 324 | CD34 | 5c orange brn | .20 | .20 |
| 325 | CD34 | 10c dk carmine | .20 | .20 |
| 326 | CD34 | 15c dk vio brn | .20 | .20 |
| 327 | CD34 | 20c slate | .20 | .20 |
| 328 | CD35 | 30c rose violet | .20 | .20 |
| 329 | CD35 | 35c brt green | .20 | .20 |
| 330 | CD35 | 40c brown | .35 | .20 |
| 331 | CD35 | 50c brt red vio | .35 | .20 |
| 332 | CD36 | 60c gray black | .45 | .20 |
| 333 | CD36 | 70c brown violet | .45 | .20 |
| 334 | CD36 | 80c orange | .65 | .45 |
| 335 | CD36 | 1e red | 1.10 | .45 |
| 336 | CD37 | 1.75e blue | 1.75 | 1.10 |
| 337 | CD37 | 2e brown car | 4.50 | 2.00 |
| 338 | CD37 | 5e olive green | 6.50 | 3.00 |
| 339 | CD38 | 10e blue violet | 11.00 | 4.00 |
| 340 | CD38 | 20e red brown | 28.80 | 13.40 |

Nos. 323-340 (18)

Cola Nuts — A13

UPU Symbols — A14

Designs: 5c, Cola Nuts. 10c, Breadfruit. 30c, Annona. 50c, Cacao pods. 1e, Coffee. 1.75e, Dendem. 2e, Avocado. 5e, Pineapple. 10e, Mango. 20e, Coconuts.

## 1948   Litho.   Perf. 14½
| | | | | |
|---|---|---|---|---|
| 341 | A13 | 5c black & yellow | .30 | .30 |
| 342 | A13 | 10c black & buff | .40 | .40 |
| 343 | A13 | 30c indigo & yellow | 1.25 | .25 |
| 344 | A13 | 50c brown & yellow | 1.50 | 1.25 |
| 345 | A13 | 1e red & rose | 1.50 | 1.00 |
| 346 | A13 | 1.75e blue & gray | 1.75 | |
| 347 | A13 | 2e black & gray | 3.25 | |
| 348 | A13 | 5e brown & lil rose | 4.00 | 3.00 |
| 349 | A13 | 10e black & pink | 4.00 | |
| 350 | A13 | 20e black & gray | 7.00 | 7.50 |
| | | | 90.00 | 41.10 |

Nos. 341-350 (10)
a. Sheet of 10, #341-350  90.00

No. 350a sold for 42.50 escudos.

### Lady of Fatima Issue
Common Design Type

## 1948, Dec.   Unwmk.
| | | | | |
|---|---|---|---|---|
| 351 | CD40 | 50c purple | 5.25 | 4.50 |

> Catalogue values for unused stamps in this section, from this point to the end of the section, are for Never Hinged items.

## 1949   Unwmk.   Perf. 14
| | | | | |
|---|---|---|---|---|
| 352 | A14 | 3.50e black & gray | 8.00 | 3.50 |

UPU, 75th anniv.

### Holy Year Issue
Common Design Types

## 1950   Perf. 13x13½
| | | | | |
|---|---|---|---|---|
| 353 | CD41 | 2.60e blue | 2.40 | 1.50 |
| 354 | CD42 | 4e orange | 3.50 | 2.10 |

### Holy Year Extension Issue
Common Design Type

## 1951   Perf. 14
| | | | | |
|---|---|---|---|---|
| 355 | CD43 | 4e indigo & bl gray + label | 2.00 | 1.00 |

Stamp without label attached sells for less.

### Medical Congress Issue
Common Design Type

## 1952   Perf. 13½
| | | | | |
|---|---|---|---|---|
| 356 | CD44 | 10c Clinic | .30 | .30 |

Jeronymos Convent A16

Joao de Santarem — A15

Portraits: 30c, Pero Escobar. 50c, Fernao de Po 1e, Alvaro Esteves. 2e, Lopo Gonçalves. 3.50e, Martim Fernandes.

## 1952   Unwmk.   Litho.   Perf. 14
### Centers Multicolored
| | | | | |
|---|---|---|---|---|
| 357 | A15 | 10c cream & choc | .20 | .20 |
| 358 | A15 | 30c pale grn & dk grn | .20 | .20 |
| 359 | A15 | 50c gray & dk gray | .20 | .20 |
| 360 | A15 | 1e gray bl & dk bl | .60 | .20 |
| 361 | A15 | 2e lil gray & vio brn | .60 | .20 |
| 362 | A15 | 3.50e buff & choc | 2.25 | 1.20 |

Nos. 357-362 (6)

For overprints and surcharges see Nos. 423, 425, 428-429, 432, 450-457, 474-481.

## 1953   Perf. 13x13½
| | | | | |
|---|---|---|---|---|
| 363 | A16 | 10c dk brown & gray | .20 | .20 |
| 364 | A18 | 50c brn org & org | .50 | .40 |
| 365 | A18 | 3e blue blk & gray blk | 2.70 | 1.40 |

Nos. 363-365 (3)

Exhib. of Sacred Missionary Art, Lisbon, 1951.

### Stamp Centenary Issue

Stamp of Portugal and Arms of Colonies — A17

## 1953   Photo.   Perf. 13
| | | | | |
|---|---|---|---|---|
| 366 | A17 | 50c multicolored | 1.00 | .60 |

Centenary of Portugal's first postage stamps.

### Presidential Visit Issue

Map and Plane — A18

## 1954   Typo. & Litho.   Perf. 13½
| | | | | |
|---|---|---|---|---|
| 367 | A18 | 15c blk, bl, red & grn | .20 | .20 |
| 368 | A18 | 5e brown, green & red | 1.10 | .80 |

Visit of Pres. Francisco H. C. Lopes.

### Sao Paulo Issue
Common Design Type

## 1954   Litho.
| | | | | |
|---|---|---|---|---|
| 369 | A46 | 2.50e bl, gray bl & blk | .55 | .35 |

## Fair Emblem, Globe and Arms — A19

**1958**    Unwmk.    **Perf. 12x11½**
370 A19 2.50e multicolored   .60 .50
World's Fair at Brussels.

## Tropical Medicine Congress Issue

Design: Cassia occidentalis.
Common Design Type

**1958**    **Perf. 13½**
371 CD47 5e pale grn, brn, yel, grn & red   2.25 1.75

Compass Rose — A20

Going to Church — A21

**1960**
373 A21 1.50e multicolored   .40 .30
10th anniv. of the Commission for Technical Co-operation in Africa South of the Sahara (C.C.T.A.).

**1960**
372 A20 1½e gray & multi   .60 .50
500th death anniv. of Prince Henry the Navigator.

## Sports Issue

Common Design Type

**1962, Jan. 18**    Litho.    **Perf. 13½**
374 CD48 50c gray green   .20 .20
  a. "$50 CORREIOS" omitted   50.00
375 CD48 1e lt lilac   .60 .25
376 CD48 1.50e salmon   .65 .35
376 CD48 2e blue   .75 .35
378 CD48 2.50e dark blue   1.00 .50
379 CD48 20e gray green   3.00 1.60
379 CD48 20e dark blue   6.20 3.15
Nos. 374-379 (6)

Sports: 50c, Angling. 1e, Gymnast on rings. 1.50e, Handball. 2e, Sailing. 2.50e, Sprinting. 20e, Skin diving.

## Multicolored Design

On No. 374a, the blue impression, including imprint, is missing.
For overprint see No. 449.

## Anti-Malaria Issue

Design: Anopheles gambiae.
Common Design Type

**1962**    Unwmk.    **Perf. 13½**
380 CD49 2.50e multicolored   1.10 .80

## Airline Anniversary Issue

Common Design Type

**1963**    Unwmk.    **Perf. 14½**
381 CD50 1.50e pale blue & multi   .60 .50

## National Overseas Bank Issue

Design: Francisco de Oliveira Chamico.
Common Design Type

**1964, May 16**    **Perf. 13½**
382 CD51 2.50e multicolored   .70 .50

## ITU Issue

Common Design Type

**1965, May 17**    Litho.    **Perf. 14½**
383 CD52 2.50e tan & multi   1.50 1.00

---

Infantry Officer, 1788 — A22

35c, Sergeant with pike, 1788. 40c, Corporal with pike, 1788. 1e, Private with musket, 1788. 2.50e, Artillery officer, 1806. 5e, Private, 1811. 7.50e, Private, 1833. 10e, Lancer officer, 1834.

**1965, Aug. 24**    Litho.    **Perf. 13½**
384 A22 20c multicolored   .20 .20
385 A22 35c multicolored   .20 .20
386 A22 40c multicolored   .30 .20
387 A22 1e multicolored   .50 .20
388 A22 2.50e multicolored   1.10 .50
389 A22 5e multicolored   1.60 1.25
390 A22 7.50e multicolored   2.00 1.90
391 A22 10e multicolored   2.50 2.00
Nos. 384-391 (8)   9.00 6.75

For overprints and surcharges see Nos. 424, 426-427, 435, 458-463, 482-485, 489-490.

## National Revolution Issue

Design: 4e, Arts and Crafts School and Anti-Tuberculosis Dispensary.
Common Design Type

**1966, May 28**    Litho.    **Perf. 11½**
392 CD53 4e multicolored   .75 .50

## Navy Club Issue

Designs: 1.50e, Capt. Campos Rodrigues and ironclad corvette Vasco da Gama. 2.50e, Dr. Aires Kopke, microscope and tsetse fly.
Common Design Type

**1967, Jan. 31**    Litho.    **Perf. 13**
393 CD54 1.50e multicolored   1.10 .50
394 CD54 2.50e multicolored   1.60 .75

Cabral Medal, from St. Jerome's Convent A24

Valinhos Shrine, Children and Apparition A23

**1967, May 13**    Litho.    **Perf. 12½x13**
395 A23 2.50e multicolored   .30 .25
50th anniv. of the apparition of the Virgin Mary to 3 shepherd children, Lucia dos Santos, Francisco and Jacinta Marto, at Fatima.

**1968, Apr. 22**    Litho.    **Perf. 14**
396 A24 1.50e blue & multi   .50 .30
500th birth anniv. of Pedro Alvares Cabral, navigator who took possession of Brazil for Portugal.

## Admiral Coutinho Issue

Design: 2e, Adm. Coutinho, Cago Coutinho Island and monument, vert.
Common Design Type

**1969, Feb. 17**    Litho.    **Perf. 14**
397 CD55 2e multicolored   .50 .35

---

Vasco da Gama's Fleet — A25

Manuel Portal of Guarda Episcopal See — A26

**1969, Aug. 29**    Litho.    **Perf. 14**
398 A25 2.50e multicolored   .75 .50
Vasco da Gama (1469-1524), navigator.

## Administration Reform Issue

Common Design Type

**1969, Sept. 25**    Litho.    **Perf. 14**
399 CD56 2.50e multicolored   .50 .35

**1969, Dec. 1**    Litho.    **Perf. 14**
400 A26 4e multicolored   .50 .35
500th birth anniv. of King Manuel I.
For overprint see No. 430.

Pero Escobar, Joao de Santarem and Map of Islands — A27

Pres. Américo Rodrigues Thomaz — A28

**1970, Jan. 25**    Litho.    **Perf. 12½**
401 A27 2.50e lt blue & multi   .35 .30
500th anniv. of the discovery of St. Thomas and Prince Islands.

**1970**    Litho.    **Perf. 12½**
402 A28 2.50e multicolored   .35 .30
Visit of Pres. Américo Rodrigues Thomaz of Portugal.

## Marshal Carmona Issue

Common Design Type

**1970, Nov. 15**    Litho.    **Perf. 14**
403 CD57 5e multicolored   .75 .55
Antonio Oscar Carmona in dress uniform.

Coffee Plant and Stamps — A29

Descent from the Cross — A30

**1970, Dec.**    **Perf. 13½**
Designs: 1.50e, Postal Administration Building and stamp No. 1, horiz. 2.50e, Cathedral of St. Thomas and stamp No. 2.
404 A29 1e multicolored   .25 .20
405 A29 1.50e multicolored   .35 .20
406 A29 2.50e multicolored   .60 .20
Nos. 404-406 (3)   1.20 .60
Centenary of St. Thomas and Prince Islands postage stamps.

**1972, May 25**    Litho.    **Perf. 13**
407 A30 20e lilac & multi   2.50 1.90
4th centenary of publication of The Lusiads by Luiz Camoens.

---

## Olympic Games Issue

Common Design Type
Track and javelin, Olympic emblem.

**1972, June 20**    **Perf. 14x13½**
408 CD59 1.50e multicolored   .35 .25

## Lisbon-Rio de Janeiro Flight Issue

Design: 2.50e, "Lusitania" flying over warship at St. Peter Rocks.
Common Design Type

**1972, Sept. 20**    Litho.    **Perf. 13½**
409 CD60 2.50e multicolored   .35 .25

## WMO Centenary Issue

Common Design Type

**1973, Dec. 15**    Litho.    **Perf. 13**
410 CD61 5e dull grn & multi   .60 .50
For overprint see No. 434.

Flags of Portugal and St. Thomas & Prince A31

## Republic

Man and Woman with St. Thomas & Prince Flag A32

**1975, July 12**    Litho.    **Perf. 13½**
411 A31 3e gray & multi   .20 .20
412 A31 10e yellow & multi   .90 .40
413 A31 20e lt blue & multi   1.60 .90
414 A31 50e salmon & multi   3.75 1.50
Nos. 411-414 (4)   6.45 3.00
Argel Agreement, granting independence, Argel, Sept. 26, 1974.
For overprints see Nos. 411-414.

**1975, Dec. 21**    Litho.    **Perf. 13½**
415 A32 1.50e pink & multi   .20 .20
416 A32 4e multicolored   .30 .20
417 A32 7.50e org & multi   .40 .40
418 A32 20e lt blue & multi   .60 .60
419 A32 50e ocher & multi   2.25 1.50
Nos. 415-419 (5)   4.35 3.25
Proclamation of Independence, 12/7/75.

**1975, Dec. 21**    Litho.    **Perf. 13½**
420 A33 1e ocher & multi   .20 .20
421 A33 1.50e multicolored   .30 .20
422 A33 2.50e orange & multi   .70 .60
Nos. 420-422 (3)
National Reconstruction Fund.

Chart and Hand — A33

Stamps of 1952-1973 Overprinted

Rep. Democr. 12-7-75

**1977**    Litho.    **Perf. 13½, 14, 13**
423 A15 10c multi (#357)   .20 .20
424 A22 20c multi (#384)   .20 .20
425 A15 20c multi (#358)   .35 .35
426 A22 35c multi (#385)   .20 .20
427 A22 40c multi (#386)   .40 .40
428 A15 50c multi (#359)   .50 .50

República Democrática
DE SÃO TOMÉ E PRÍNCIPE

Pres. Manuel Pinto da Costa and Flag — A34

**1977, Jan.** **Perf. 13½**
437  A34  2e  yellow & multi  .20  .20
438  A34  3.50e  blue & multi  .40  .20
439  A34  4.50e  red & multi  .55  .20
440  A34  12.50e  multicolored  .90  .40
        Nos. 437-440 (4)  2.05  1.00

1st anniversary of independence.

Some of the sets that follow may not have been issued by the government.

429  A15  1e  multi (#360)
430  CD56  multi (#399)
431  A27  2.50e  multi (#401)
432  A15  3.50e  multi (#362)
433  A26  4e  multi (#410)
434  CD61  5e  multi (#390)
435  A22  7.50e  multi (#372)
        Nos. 423-436 (14)  9.00

The 10c, 30c, 50c, 1e, 3.50e, 10e issued with glassine interleaving stuck to back.

---

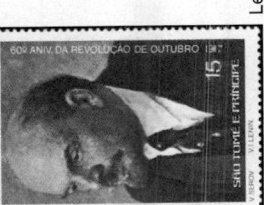

Ludwig van Beethoven — A36

Designs: a, 20e, Miniature, 1802, by C. Hornemann. b, 30e, Life mask, 1812, by F. Klein. c, 50e, Portrait, 1818, by Ferdinand Schimon.

**1977, June 28**  **Perf. 13½**
448  A36  Strip of 3, #a.-c.  13.50
        For overprint see No. 617.

No. 379 Ovptd. "Rep. Democr. / 12-7-77"

**1977, July 12**
449  CD48  20e  multicolored  75.00

Pairs of Nos. 358-359, 357, 362, 384-386 Overprinted Alternately in Black

---

Peter Paul Rubens (1577-1640), Painter — A35

Details from or entire paintings: 1e (60x44mm), Diana and Calixto, horiz. 5e (60x36mm), The Judgement of Paris, horiz. 10e (60x28mm), Diana and her Nymphs Surprised by Fauns, horiz. 15e (40x64mm), Andromeda and Perseus. 20e (40x64mm), The Banquet of Tereo. 50e (32x64mm), Fortuna.

No. 447a, 20e, (30x40mm) like #445. No. 447b, 75e, (40x30mm) The Banquet of Tereo, diff.

**1977, June 28**  **Perf. 13½**
441  A35  1e  multicolored
442  A35  5e  multicolored
443  A35  10e  multicolored
444  A35  15e  multicolored
445  A35  20e  multicolored
446  A35  50e  multicolored
        Nos. 441-446 (6)  13.50

**Souvenir Sheet**
**Perf. 14**
447  A35  Sheet of 2, #a.-b.  13.50

See type A40 for Rubens stamps without "$" in denomination.

---

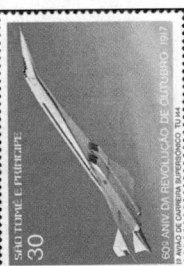

Lenin — A38

---

Russian Supersonic Plane — A39

Designs: 40d, Rowing crew. 50d, Cosmonaut Yuri A. Gagarin.

**1977, Dec.**  **Perf. 13½x14, 14x13½**
465  A38  15d  multicolored  2.00
466  A39  30d  multicolored  4.00
467  A39  40d  multicolored  5.25
468  A38  50d  red & black  6.50
        Sheet of 4, #465-468  27.50
    a.  Sheet of 4, #465-468 (4)  17.75

60th anniv. of Russian October Revolution. For overprints see Nos. 592-595.

---

CENTENÁRIO
1874 — 1974
UPU
MEMBRO
1877 — 1977
1977
a

b

**1977, Oct. 19**  **Litho.**  **Perf. 14, 13½**
450  A16(a)  2e  on 30c multi
451  A15(b)  3e  on 30c multi
452  A15(a)  5e  on 50c multi
453  A15(b)  5e  on 50c multi
454  A15(a)  10e  on 10c multi
455  A15(b)  10e  on 10c multi
456  A15(a)  15e  on 3.50e multi
457  A15(b)  15e  on 3.50e multi
458  A22(a)  20e  on 20c multi
459  A22(b)  20e  on 20c multi
460  A22(a)  35e  on 35c multi
461  A22(b)  35e  on 35c multi
462  A22(a)  40e  on 40c multi
463  A22(b)  40e  on 40c multi
        Nos. 450-463 (14)  27.50

Centenary of membership in UPU. Overprints "a" and "b" alternate in sheets. Nos. 450-457 issued with glassine interleaving stuck to back.

These overprints exist in red on Nos. 452-453, 458-463 and on 1e on 10c, 3.50e and 30e on 30c. Value, set $150.

---

Paintings by Rubens — A40

Designs: 5d, 70d, Madonna and Standing Child. 10d, Holy Family. 25d, Holy Family, diff. 50d, Madonna and Child.

**1977, Dec.**  **Perf. 13½, 13½x14 (50d)**
    **Size: 31x47mm**
469  A40  5d  multicolored
470  A40  10d  multicolored
471  A40  25d  multicolored
472  A40  40d  multicolored  27.50
473  A40  70d  multicolored  35.00
    a.  Sheet of 4, #469-471, #473  35.00
        Nos. 469-473 (4)

---

Mao Tse-tung (1893-1976), Chairman, People's Republic of China — A37

**1977, Dec.**  **Litho.**  **Perf. 13½x14**
464  A37  50d  multicolored  9.00
    a.  Souvenir sheet  9.00
        For overprint see No. 597.

---

#475

#479

#477
c

Pairs of Nos. 357-359, 362, 384-385 Surcharged

---

#481

#483, 485

**1978, May 25**  **Perf. 14½, 13½**
474  A15  3d  on 30c #358
475  A15  3d  on 30c #358
476  A15 (a)  5d  on 50c #359
477  A15  5d  on 50c #359
    a.  Pair, #474-475
478  A15 (a)  10d  on 10c #357
479  A15  10d  on 10c #357
    a.  Pair, #476-477
480  A15 (a)  15d  on 3.50e #362
481  A15  15d  on 3.50e #362
    a.  Pair, #478-479
482  A22 (a)  20d  on 20c #384
483  A22  20d  on 20c #384
    a.  Pair, #480-481
484  A22 (a)  35d  on 35c #385
485  A22  35d  on 35c #385
    a.  Pair, #482-483
    a.  Pair, #484-485
        Nos. 474-485 (12)  20.00

Overprints for each denomination alternate on sheet. Nos. 474-481 issued with glassine interleaving stuck to back.

---

Flag of St. Thomas and Prince Islands — A41

Designs: Nos. 487, 487a, Map of Islands, vert. No. 488, Coat of arms, vert.

**1978, July 12**  **Perf. 14x13½, 13½x14**
486  A41  5d  multi  .40
487  A41  5d  multi  .40
    a.  Souvenir sheet, 50d  12.50
488  A41  5d  multi  1.25
        Strip of 3, #486-488  .40

Third anniversary of independence. Printed in sheets of 9. No. 487a contains one imperf. stamp.

---

No. 306 Surcharged

1975  40  3°  ANIV. DA ENTRADA NA ONU  1975/1978
1978  40

**1978, Sept. 3**  **Litho.**  **Perf. 13½**
489  A22  40d  on 40e #386
490  A22  40d  on 40e #386 (2)  6.75
        Nos. 489-490 (2)

Membership in United Nations, 3rd anniv.

**Miniature Sheets**

#491: b, Still Life, by Matisse. c, Barbaric Tales, by Gauguin. d, Portrait of Armand Roulin, by Van Gogh. e, Abstract, by Georges Braque.

Tahitian Women with Fan, by Paul Gauguin A42

**ST. THOMAS AND PRINCE ISLANDS**

---

#492: a, 20d, like #491c. b, 30d, Horsemen on the Beach, by Gauguin.

**1978, Nov. 1** **Perf. 14**

491 A42 10d Sheet of 9, #e., 2 each #a.-d. 20.00

**Imperf**

492 A42 Sheet of 3, #491a, 492a-492b 10.00

Intl. Philatelic Exhibition, Essen. No. 492 has simulated perfs and exists with green margin and without simulated perfs and stamps in different order.

Miniature Sheet of 12

UPU, Centennial — A43

**1978, Nov. 1** **Perf. 14**

493 A43 #a.-d., 2 ea.
a.-d. 5d any single
e.-h. 15d any single 45.00

Souvenir Sheet

494 A43 50d multicolored 27.50

For overprint see No. 706.

Designs: Nos. 493, Emblem, yellow & black. b, Emblem, green & black. c, Emblem, blue & black. d, Emblem, red & black. e, Concorde, balloon. f, Sailing ship, satellite. g, Monorail, stagecoach. h, Dirigible, steam locomotive. 50d, like #487g.

Miniature Sheets

1º ANIVERSÁRIO DA INTRODUÇÃO DA NOVA MOEDA "DOBRA" 8.9.77

New Currency, 1st Anniv. — A44

**1978, Dec. 15** **Perf. 13½**

495 A44 5d #e., 2 each #a.-d.
496 A44 8d #e., 2 each #a.-d.
a.-d. 16.00

Nos. 495-496 (2)

Obverse and reverse of bank notes: #a, 1000d. b, 50d. c, 5000d. d, 1000d. e, Obverse of 50c. 1d, 2d, 5d, 10d, 20d coins.

Db 3

World Cup Soccer Championships, Argentina — A45

**1978, Dec. 15** **Perf. 14**

497 A45 3d Block of 4, #a.-d.
498 A45 25d Strip of 3, #a.-c. 27.50

Nos. 497-498 (2)

Various soccer plays: No. 497a, Two players in yellow shirts, one in blue. b, Two players in blue shirts, one in white. c, Six players, referee. d, Two players, one in red. No. 498a, Seven players. b, Two players at goal. c, Six players.

Souvenir sheets of one exist.

---

Overprinted with Names of Winning Countries

No. 499b, ITALIA, 1934/38. c, BRASIL, 1958/62/70. d, ALEMANIA 1954/74. INGLATERRA / 1966. b, Venecdores 1978 / 1o ARGENTINA / 1966. b, Venecdores 1978 / 1o HOLANDA / 3o BRASIL. c, ARGENTINA 1978.

**1979, June 1** **Litho.** **Perf. 14**

499 A45 3d Block of 4, #a.-d.
500 A45 25d Strip of 3, #a.-c. 11.50

Souvenir sheets of one exist.
Nos. 499-500

Flowers — A46

**1979, June 8** **Perf. 15, 15x14½ (#503), 14½x15 (#505)**

501 A46 50c multicolored
502 A47 1d multicolored
503 A47 8d multicolored
504 A46 10d multicolored
505 A47 11d Block of 4, #a.-d.
506 A47 25d multicolored
Nos. 501-506 (12) 21.00

Souvenir Sheets

507 A46 50d multicolored 13.50

**Imperf**

508 A47 50d multicolored 10.50

No. 508 contains one 30x46mm stamp with simulated perforations.

Designs: 50c, Charaxes odysseus. 1d, Crinum giganteum. No. 503a, Quisqualis indica. b, Tecoma stans. c, Nerium oleander. d, Pyrostegia venusta. 10d, Hypolimnas salmacis thomensis. No. 505a, Charaxes monteiri. male. b, Charaxes monteiri, female. c, Papilio leonidas thomasius. d, Crenis boisduvali insularis. 25d, Asystasia gangetica. No. 507, Charaxes varanes defixivata. No. 508, Hibiscus mutabilis.

Butterflies — A47

Db 25

Sir Rowland Hill, 1795-1879 — A50

**1979, Sept. 15** **Perf. 14**

518 A50 25d DC-3 Dakota
519 A50 25d Graf Zeppelin, vert. 22.50

1st Air Mail Flight, Lisbon to St. Thomas & Prince, 30th anniv. (#518), Brasiliana '79 Intl. Philatelic Exhibition and 18th UPU Congress (#519).

See Nos. 528-533 for other stamps inscribed "Historia da Aviancao." For overprint see No. 700.

---

Intl. Year of the Child A49

**1979, July 6**

513 A49 1d multicolored
514 A49 7d multicolored
515 A49 14d multicolored
516 A49 17d multicolored

**Size: 100x100mm**

517 A49 50d multicolored
Nos. 513-517 (5)

**Imperf**

40.00

Souvenir Sheets

Designs: 1d, Child's painting of bird. 7d, Young Pioneers. 14d, Children coloring on paper. 17d, Children eating fruit. 50d, Children from different countries joining hands.

History of Aviation A52

**1979, Dec. 21**

528 A52 50c Wright Flyer I
529 A52 1d Sikorsky VS 300
530 A52 5d Spirit of St. Louis
531 A52 7d Dornier DO X
532 A52 8d Santa Cruz Fairey III D
533 A52 17d Space Shuttle
Nos. 528-533 (6) 11.50

Souvenir Sheet inscribed "Historia da Aviancao."
See No. 518 for souvenir sheet inscribed "Historia da Aviancao."

30º ANIVERSARIO DO 1º VOO POSTAL S. TOME-LISBOA 21/AGOSTO/1949

History of Navigation A53

**1979, Dec. 21**

534 A53 50c Caravel, 1460
535 A53 1d Portuguese galleon, 1560
536 A53 3d Sao Gabriel, 1497
537 A53 5d Caravelao Navio Dos
538 A53 8d Caravel Redonda, 1512
539 A53 25d Galley Fusta, 1540
Nos. 534-539 (6) 11.50

**Size: 129x98mm**

540 A53 25d Map of St. Thomas & Prince, 1602

**Imperf**

11.50

---

511 A48 14d Syncom, 1963
512 A48 17d Symphony, 1975
a. Pair, #511-512 + label 6.75

Intl. Advisory Council on Radio Communications (CCIR), 50th anniv. (#510).

Db 0.50

Db 1

Int'l Year of the Child A49

**1979, July 6** **Perf. 13**

509 A48 1d shown
510 A48 1d CCIR emblem
a. Pair, #509-510 + label

Intl. Communications Day — A48

**Imperf**

**Perf. 13**

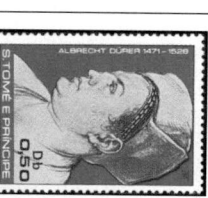

Db 0.50

ALBRECHT DÜRER 1471-1528

Albrecht Durer, 450th Death Anniv. — A51

Portraits: No. 520, Willibald Pirckheimer. No. 521, Portrait of a Negro. 1d, Portrait of a Young Man, facing right. 7d, Adolescent boy. 8d, The Negress Catherine. No. 524, Girl with Braided Hair. No. 526, Self-portrait as a Boy. No. 527, Feast of the Holy Family.

**1979**

**Background Color**

520 A51 50c blue green
521 A51 50c orange
522 A51 1d blue
523 A51 7d brown
524 A51 8d red
525 A51 25d lilac
Nos. 520-525 (6) 13.50

**Perf. 14**

---

526 A51 25d III, buff & blk
527 A51 25d blk, III & buff 22.50

Souvenir Sheets
**Perf. 13½x14**

Christmas, Intl. Year of the Child (#527). No. 527 contains one 35x50mm stamp issued. Nov. 29 (#527), No. 527, Dec. 25. For overprint see No. 591.

Db 1

S. TOMÉ E PRINCIPE
HISTORIA DA AVIACAO

History of Aviation A52

**1979, Dec. 21** **Perf. 15**

Souvenir Sheets

---

547 A54 25d Treron S. thomae 15.00

No. 546 is airmail.

Souvenir Sheet
**Perf. 14½**

Birds — A54

**1979, Dec. 21**

541 A54 50c Serinus rufobrunneus
542 A54 50c Euplectes aureus
543 A54 1d Alcedo leucogaster nais
544 A54 7d Dreptes thomensis
545 A54 8d Textor grandis
546 A54 100d Speirops lugubris
Nos. 541-546 (6) 22.50

**Perf. 14**

Db 0.50

---

Db 0.50

Fish A55

Crassibarbus
"Vusala"

Fish — A55

**1979, Dec. 28**    Perf. 14
548 A55 50c Cypselurus lineatus
549 A55 1d Canthidermis maculatus
550 A55 5d Diodon hystrix
551 A55 7d Ostracion tricornis
552 A55 8d Rhinecanthus aculeatus
553 A55 50d Chaetodon striatus    18.00
Souvenir Sheet    Perf. 14½
Nos. 548-553 (6)
554 A55 25d Holocentrus axensionis    16.00
No. 553 is airmail.

## Balloons — A56

Designs: 50c, Blanchard, 1784. 1d, Lunardi II, 1785. 3d, Von Lutgendorf, 1786. 7d, Wise "Atlantic," 1859. 8d, Salomon Anree "The Eagle," 1896. No. 560, Stratospheric balloon of Prof. Piccard, 1931. No. 560A, Indoor demonstration of hot air balloon, 1709, horiz.

**1979, Dec. 28**    Perf. 15
555 A56 50c multicolored
556 A56 1d multicolored
557 A56 3d multicolored
558 A56 7d multicolored
559 A56 8d multicolored
560 A56 25d multicolored
Souvenir Sheet    Perf. 14
Nos. 555-560 (6)    11.50
560A A56 25d multicolored    12.50
No. 560A contains one 50x38mm stamp.

## Dirigibles A57

Designs: 50c, Dupuy de Lome, 1872. 1d, Paul Hanlein, 1872. 3d, Gaston brothers, 1882. 7d, Willows II, 1909. 8d, Ville do Lucerne, 1910. 17d, Mayfly, 1910.

**1979, Dec. 28**    Perf. 15
561 A57 50c multicolored
562 A57 1d multicolored
563 A57 3d multicolored
564 A57 7d multicolored
565 A57 8d multicolored
566 A57 17d multicolored
Nos. 561-566 (6)    10.50

## 1980 Olympics, Lake Placid & Moscow A58

Olympic Venues: 50c, Lake Placid, 1980. Nos. 568, 572a, Mexico City, 1968. Nos. 569, 572b, Munich, 1972. Nos. 570, 572c, Montreal, 1976. Nos. 571, 572d, Moscow, 1980.

**1980, June 13**    Litho.    Perf. 15
567 A58 50c multicolored
568 A58 1d multicolored
569 A58 11d multicolored
570 A58 11d multicolored
571 A58 11d multicolored    11.50
Souvenir Sheet
572 A58 7d Sheet of 4, #a.-d.    10.50

## Proclamation Type of 1975 and Sir Rowland Hill (1795-1879) — A59

Sir Rowland Hill and: 50c, #1. 1d, #415. 8d, #411. No. 571. 8d, #449. No. 572. #418.

**1980, June 1**    Perf. 15
573 A59 50c multicolored
574 A59 1d multicolored
575 A59 8d multicolored
576 A59 20d multicolored
Nos. 573-576 (4)    10.00
Souvenir Sheet    Imperf
577 A32 20d multicolored    12.50
No. 577 contains one 38x32mm stamp with simulated perforations.

## Moon Landing, 10th Anniv. (in 1979) A60

50c, Launch of Apollo 11, vert. 1d, Astronaut on lunar module ladder, vert. 14d, Setting up research experiments. 17d, Astronauts, 25d, Command module during re-entry.

**1980, June 13**    Perf. 15
578 A60 50c multicolored
579 A60 1d multicolored
580 A60 14d multicolored
581 A60 17d multicolored
Nos. 578-581 (4)    15.00
Souvenir Sheet
582 A60 25d multicolored    13.50

## Independence, 5th Anniv. — A61

Miniature Sheet    Perf. 13

#583: a, US #1283B. b, Venezuela #C942. c, Russia #3710. d, India #676. e, T. E. Lawrence (1888-1935). f, Ghana #106. g, Russia #2486. h, Algeria #624. i, Cape Verde #366. k, Mozambique #617. l, Angola #601. 25d, King Amador.

**1980, July 12**    Perf. 13
583 A61 5d Sheet of 12, #a.-l. + 13 labels    13.50

**1980, Dec. 25**    Perf. 14
584 A61 25d multicolored    12.50
No. 584 contains one 35x50mm stamp. For overprint see No. 596.

No. 527 Ovprtd. "1980" on Stamp and Intl. Year of the Child emblem in Sheet Margin

**1980, Dec. 25**
591 A51 25d on No. 527    22.50
Christmas.

Nos. 465-468a Overprinted in Black or Silver

**1981, Feb. 2**    Perf. 13½x14, 14x13½
592 A38 15d on #465 (S)
593 A39 30d on #466 (S)
594 A39 40d on #467
595 A38 50d on #468    50.00
   a. on No. 468a    22.50
Nos. 592-595 (4)

No. 584 Ovprtd. with UN and Intl. Year of the Child emblems and Three Inscriptions

**1981, Feb. 2**    Perf. 14
596 A61 25d on No. 584    29.00

Nos. 464-464a Ovptd. in Silver and Black "UNIAO / SOVIETICA / VENCEDORA / 1980" with Olympic emblem and "JOGOS OLIMPICOS DE MOSCOVO 1980"

**1981, May 15**    Perf. 13½x14
597 A37 50d on #464    9.00
   a. on #464a    9.00

## Mammals — A65

**1981, May 22**    Perf. 14
598 A65 50c Crocidura thomensis
599 A65 50c Mustela nivalis
600 A65 1d Viverra civetta
601 A65 7d Hippopsideros fuliginosus
602 A65 8d Rattus norvegicus
603 A65 14d Eidolon helvum
Nos. 598-603 (6)    10.50
Souvenir Sheet    Perf. 14½
604 A65 25d Cercopithecus mona    24.00

## Shells — A66

No. 611: a, 10d, Bolinus cornutus, diff. b, 15d, Conus genuanus.

**1981, May 22**    Perf. 14
605 A66 50c Haxaplex hoplites
606 A66 50c Bolinus cornutus
607 A66 1d Cassis tessellata
608 A66 1.50d Harpa doris
609 A66 11d Strombus latus
610 A66 17d Cymbium glans
Nos. 605-610 (6)    10.50
Souvenir Sheet    Perf. 14½
611 A66 Sheet of 2, #a.-    22.50
   b.

## Johann Wolfgang von Goethe (1749-1832), Poet — A67

Design: 75d, Goethe in the Roman Campagna, by Johann Heinrich W. Tischbein.

**1981, Nov. 14**    Perf. 14
612 A67 25d multicolored    3.50
Souvenir Sheet
613 A67 75d multicolored    8.00
PHILATELIA '81, Frankfurt/Main, Germany.

## Tito — A68

Perf. 12½x13

**1981, Nov. 14**
614 A68 17d Wearing glasses    3.50
615 A68 17d shown    2.50
   a. Sheet of 2, #614-615 (2)    6.75
Souvenir Sheet    Perf. 14x13½
616 A68 75d In uniform    6.75
Nos. 614-615 issued in sheets of 4 each plus label. For overprints see Nos. 644-646.

No. 448 Ovprtd. in White

Wedding of Prince Charles and Lady Diana. On No. 617 the white overprint was applied by a thermographic process producing a shiny, raised effect. Overprint exists in gold, $35 value.

**1981, Nov. 28**    Perf. 13½
617 A36 Strip of 3, #a.-c.    20.00

## World Chess Championships — A69

Chess pieces: 50c, No. 618, Egyptian. No. 619, Two Chinese, green. No. 620, Two Chinese, red. No. 621, English. No. 622, Indian. No. 623, Scandinavian. 75d, Khmer.

No. 624: a, Anatoly Karpov. b, Victor Korchnoi.

**1981, Nov. 28    Litho.    Perf. 14**
618 A69 1.50d multicolored
619 A69 1.50d multicolored
620 A69 1.50d multicolored
621 A69 1.50d multicolored
622 A69 30d multicolored
623 A69 30d multicolored
624 A69 30d multicolored
   Pair, #a.-b.
   Nos. 618-624 (7) 18.00

**Souvenir Sheet**
625 A69 75d multicolored 22.50

Nos. 618-623 exist in souvenir sheets of one. No. 624 exists in souvenir sheet with simulated perfs. Nos. 618-625 exist imperf.

No. 624 Ovptd. in red "ANATOLIJ KARPOV / Campeao Mundial / de Xadrez 1981"

**1981, Dec. 10    Perf. 14**
627 A69 30d Pair, #a.-b. 14.00

Exists in souvenir sheet with simulated perfs or imperf.

Pablo Picasso — A70

Paintings: No. 629: a, The Old and the New Year. b, Young Woman. b, Child with Dove. c, Paul as Pierrot with Flowers. d, Francoise, Claude, and Paloma.
No. 630: a, Girl. b, Girl with Doll. 75d, Father, Mother and Child.

**1981, Dec. 10    Perf. 14x13½**
628 A70 14d multicolored
629 A70 17d Strip of 4, #a.-d.
630 A70 20d multicolored
   Nos. 628-630 (3) 15.00

**Souvenir Sheet    Perf. 13½**
631 A70 75d multicolored 15.00

Intl. Year of the Child (#628, 631). No. 630 is airmail. Nos. 628, 629a-629d, 630a-630b exist in souvenir sheets of one. No. 631 contains one 50x60mm stamp. See Nos. 663-685.

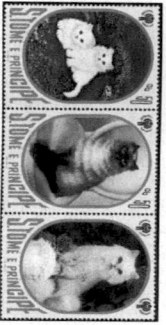

Paintings: No. 632: a, Girl with Dog, by Thomas Gainsborough. b, Miss Bowles, by Sir Joshua Reynolds. c, Sympathy, by Sir Master Simpson, by Devis. e, Two Boys with Dogs, by Gainsborough.
No. 633: a, Girl feeding cat. b, Girl wearing cat mask. c, White cat. d, Cat wearing red bonnet. e, Girl teaching cat to read.
No. 634: a, Boy and Dog, by Picasso. b, Clipper, by Picasso.
No. 635: a, Two white cats. b, Himalayan cat.

**1981, Dec. 30    Perf. 14**
632 A71 1.50d Strip of 5, #a.-e. 1.50
633 A71 1.50d Strip of 5, #a.-e. 1.50
634 A71 50d Pair, #a.-b. 10.00
635 A71 50d Pair, #a.-b. + label 10.00
   Nos. 632-635 (14) 15.00

**Souvenir Sheets    Perf. 13½**
636 A71 75d Girl with dog 10.00
637 A71 75d Girl with cat 10.00

Nos. 636-637 contain one 30x40mm stamp.

2nd Central Africa Games, Luanda, Angola — A73

No. 638: a, Shot put. b, Discus. c, High jump. d, Javelin.
50d, Team handball. 75d, Runner.

**1981, Dec. 30    Perf. 13½x14**
638 A73 17d Strip of 4, a.-d.
639 A73 50d multicolored
   Nos. 638-639 (5) 11.50

**Souvenir Sheet**
640 A73 75d multicolored 7.00

World Food Day — A74

No. 641: a, Ananas sativus. b, Colocasia esculenta. c, Artocarpus altilis.
No. 642: a, Mangifera indica. b, Theobroma cacao. c, Coffea arabica. 75d, Musa sapientum.

**1981, Dec. 30    Perf. 13½x14**
641 A74 11d Strip of 3, #a.-c.
642 A74 30d Strip of 3, #a.-c.
   Nos. 641-642 (6) 12.50

**Souvenir Sheet**
643 A74 75d multicolored 8.00

World Cup Soccer Championships, Spain — A75

**1982, May 25**
644 A68 17d on #614
645 A68 17d on #615
   a. On #615a
   Nos. 644-645 (2) 8.00

**Souvenir Sheet    Perf. 14**
646 A68 75d on #616 8.00

Nos. 614-616 Ovptd. in Black

Emblem and: No. 647: a, Goalie in blue shirt jumping to catch ball. b, Two players, yellow, red shirts. c, Two players, black shirts. d, Goalie in green shirtcatching ball.
No. 648: a, Player dribbling. b, Goalie facing opponent.
No. 649: a, Goalie catching ball from emblem in front of goal. No. 650: Like #649 with continuous design.

**1982, June 21    Perf. 13½x14**
647 A75 15d Strip of 4, #a.-d.
648 A75 25d Pair, #a.-b.
   Nos. 647-648 (6) 12.50

**Souvenir Sheets**
649 A75 75d multicolored
650 A75 75d multicolored
   Nos. 649-650 (2) 21.00

Nos. 648a-648b are airmail. Nos. 647a-647d, 648a-648b exist in souvenir sheets of one.

Transportation: No. 651, Steam locomotive. TGV train. No. 652, Propeller plane and Concorde.

**1982, June 21    Perf. 12½x13**
651 A76 15d multicolored 15.00
652 A76 Souv. sheet of 2, #651-652 12.00
   Nos. 651-652 (2)

PHILEXFRANCE '82.

Robert Koch, discovery of tuberculosis bacillus, cent. — A77

**1982, July 31**
653 A77 25d multicolored 6.00

Goethe, 150th Anniv. of Death — A78

**1982, July 31    Perf. 13½x12½**
654 A78 50d multicolored 7.25

**Souvenir Sheet**
655 A78 10d like #654 13.50

**1982, July 31    Perf. 12½x13**
656 A79 10d multicolored
657 A79 10d Sheet of 2, purple & multi
657A A79 10d Sheet of 2, #657A
   Nos. 656-657 (2) 6.00
   6.75
   7.50

Princess Diana, 21st birthday. No. 657A exists with red violet inscriptions and different central flower.

**1982, July 31**
658 A80 15d multicolored
659 A80 30d multicolored
   a. Souv. sheet, #658-659 + label
   Nos. 658-659 (2) 13.50
   5.00

Boy Scouts, 75th Anniv.: 15d, Cape of Good Hope #178-179. 30d, Lord Baden-Powell, founder of Boy Scouts.
Nos. 658-659 exits in sheets of 4 each plus label.

Caricatures by Picasso — #660: a, Musicians. b, Stravinsky.

Igor Stravinsky (1882-1971), composer.

**1982, July 31**
660 A81 30d Pair, #a.-b. 5.00

**Souvenir Sheet**
661 A81 5d like #660b 13.50

George Washington, 250th Anniv. of Birth: Nos. 662, 663b, Washington, by Gilbert Stuart. Nos. 662-663, 663c, Washington, by Roy Lichtenstein.

**1982, July 31**
662 A82 30d multicolored
663 A82 30d blk & pink
   Nos. 662-663 (2) 5.00

**Souvenir Sheet**
663A A82 5d Sheet of 2, #b.-c. 13.50

Dinosaurs — A83

**1982, Nov. 30    Perf. 14x13½**
664 A83 6d Parasaurolophus
665 A83 16d Stegosaurus
666 A83 16d Triceratops
667 A83 16d Brontosaurus
668 A83 16d Tyrannosaurus rex
669 A83 50d Dimetrodon
   Nos. 664-669 (6) 16.00

**Souvenir Sheet**
a, 25d, Pteranodon. b, 50d, Stenopterygius.
670 A83 Sheet of 2, #a.-b. 12.50
Charles Darwin, cent. of death (#670).

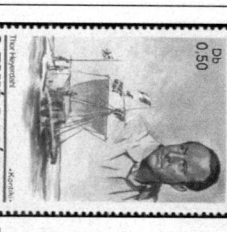

Explorers — A84

## Automobiles — A92

#709: a, Renault, 1912. b, Rover Phaeton, 1907.
#710: a, Morris, 1913. b, Delage, 1910.
#711: a, Mercedes Benz, 1927. b, Mercedes Coupe, 1936.
#712: a, Mercedes Cabriolet, 1924. b, Mercedes Simplex, 1902.
75d, Peugeot Daimler, 1894.

**1983, Dec. 28**     *Perf. 14x13½*
709 A92 12d Pair, #a.-b.
710 A92 12d Pair, #a.-b.
711 A92 20d Pair, #a.-b.
712 A92 20d Pair, #a.-b.   14.00

**Souvenir Sheet**
713 A92 75d multicolored   11.50

Nos. 709-712 exist as souvenir sheets. No. 713 contains one 50x41mm stamp.

## Medicinal Plants — A93

**1983, Dec. 28**     *Perf. 13½*
714 A93 50c Cymbopogon citratus
715 A93 1d Adenoplus breviflorus
716 A93 5.50d Bryophillum pinnatum
717 A93 15.50d Buchholzia coriacea
718 A93 16d Hiliotropium indicum
719 A93 20d Mimosa pigra
720 A93 40d Piparonia nal-lucila
721 A93 50d Achyranthes aspera
    Nos. 714-721 (8)   18.00

## 1984 Olympics, Sarajevo and Los Angeles A94

#722, Pairs' figure skating.
#723: a, Downhill skiing. b, Speed skating. c, Ski jumping.
#724, Equestrian.
#725: a, Cycling. b, Rowing. c, Hurdling.
#726: a, Bobsled. b, Women's archery.

**1983, Dec. 29**     *Perf. 13½x14*
722 A94 16d multicolored
723 A94 16d Strip of 3, #a.-c.
724 A94 18d multicolored
725 A94 18d Strip of 3, #a.-c.   15.00

**Souvenir Sheet**
726 A94 30d Sheet of 2, #a.-b.   8.50

Souvenir sheets of 2 exist containing Nos. 722 and 723b, 723a and 723c, 724 and 725b, 725a and 725c.

---

## No. 519 Overprinted with Various Designs

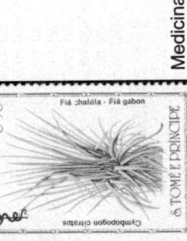

**1983, July 29**   **Litho.**   *Perf. 14*

**Souvenir Sheet**
700 A50 25d multicolored   50.00
    BRASILIANA '83.

## First Manned Flight, Bicent. — A90

No. 701: a, Wright Flyer No. 1, 1903. b, Alcock & Brown Vickers Vimy, 1919.
No. 702: a, Bleriot monoplane, 1909. b, Boeing 747, 1983.
No. 703: a, Graf Zeppelin, 1929. b, Pierre Tetu-Brissy, 60d, Flight of Vincent Lunardi's second balloon, vert.

**1983, Sept. 16**     *Perf. 14x13½*
701 A90 18d Pair, #a.-b.
702 A90 18d Pair, #a.-b.
703 A90 20d Pair, #a.-b.
704 A90 20d multicolored   17.00
    Nos. 701-704 (7)

**Souvenir Sheet**     *Perf. 13½x14*
705 A90 60d multicolored   0.50

Individual stamps from Nos. 701-704 exist in souvenir sheets of 1. Value of 4 $50.

Nos. 493e, 493a, 493e (#706a) and 493g, 493c, 493g (#706b) Ovptd. in Gold with UPU and Philatelic Salon Emblems and:
"SALON DER PHILATELIE ZUM / XIX WELTPOSTKONGRESS / HAMBURG 1984" Across Strips of Three Stamps

Nos. 493f, 493b, 493f (#706c) 493h, 493d, 493h (#706d) Ovptd. in Gold with UPU and Philatelic Salon Emblems and:
"19TH CONGRESSO DA / UNIAO POSTAL UNIVERSAL / HAMBURGO 1984" Across Strips of Three Stamps

**1983, Dec. 24**     *Perf. 14*
706 A43   Sheet of 12, #a.-d.   32.50

Overprint is 91x30mm. Exists imperf with silver overprint.

## Christmas — A91

Paintings: No. 707, Madonna of the Promenade, 1518, by Raphael. No. 708, Virgin of Guadalupe, 1959, by Salavador Dali.

**1983, Dec. 24**     *Perf. 12½x13*
707 A91 30d multicolored
708 A91 30d multicolored   6.75
    Nos. 707-708 (2)

Nos. 707-708 exist in souvenir sheets of 1.

---

## Easter — A88

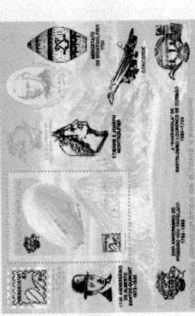

Paintings: No. 690: a, St. Catherine, by Raphael. b, St. Margaret, by Raphael.
No. 691: a, Young Man with a Pointed Beard, by Rembrandt. b, Portrait of a Young Woman, by Rembrandt.
No. 692: a, Rondo (Dance of the Italian Peasants), by Rubens, horiz. b, The Garden of Love, by Rubens, horiz.
No. 693, Samson and Delilah, by Rubens.
No. 694, Descent from the Cross, by Rubens.
No. 695: a, Elevation of the Cross, by Rembrandt. b, Descent from the Cross, by Rembrandt.
Nos. 696a, 697, The Crucifixion, by Raphael. Nos. 696b, 698, The Transfiguration, by Raphael.

**1983, May 9**   *Perf. 13½x14, 14x13½*
690 A88 16d Pair, #a.-b.
691 A88 16d Pair, #a.-b.
692 A88 16d Pair, #a.-b.
693 A88 18d multicolored
694 A88 18d multicolored
695 A88 18d Pair, #a.-b.
696 A88 10d Pair, #a.-b.   25.00
    Nos. 690-696 (12)

**Souvenir Sheets**
697 A88 18d vio & multi   10.00
698 A88 18d multicolored   10.00

Souvenir sheets containing Nos. 690-690b, 691a-691b, 692a-692b, 693, 694, 695a-695b exist.

## Santos-Dumont dirigibles

Santos-Dumont dirigibles: No. 699a, #5. b, #14 with airplane.

**1983, July 29**   **Litho.**   *Perf. 13½*
699 A89 25d Pair, #a.-b.   5.00
    First manned flight, bicent.

---

## Departure of Marco Polo from Venice — A85

Explorers and their ships: 50c, Thor Heyerdahl, Kon-tiki.
No. 672: a, Magellan, Carrack. b, Drake, Golden Hind. c, Columbus, Santa Maria. d, Leif Eriksson, Viking longship.
50d, Capt. Cook, Endeavour.

**1982, Dec. 21**     **Litho.**
671 A84 50c multicolored
672 A84 18d Strip of 4, #a.-d.
673 A84 50d multicolored   13.50
    Nos. 671-673 (6)

**Souvenir Sheet**
674 A85 75d multicolored   15.00

Nos. 411-414 Ovptd. with Assembly Emblem and
"2o ANIVERSARIO DA 1a ASSEMBLEIA DA J.M.L.S.T.P." in Silver

**1982, Dec. 24**     *Perf. 13½x14*
675 A31 3d on #411
676 A31 10d on #412
677 A31 20d on #413
678 A31 50d on #414   10.00
    Nos. 675-678 (4)

## MLSTP 3rd Assembly A86

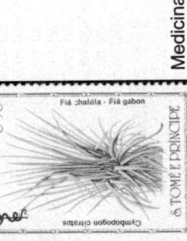

**1982, Dec. 24**     *Perf. 13½x14*
679 A86 8d bl & multi
680 A86 12d brn org & multi
681 A86 16d brn org & multi
682 A86 30d red lilac & multi   6.75
    Nos. 679-682 (4)

## Picasso Painting Type of 1981

Designs: No. 683a, Lola. b, Aunt Pepa. c, Mother. d, Lola with Mantilla.
No. 684: a, Corina Romeu. b, The Aperitif. 75d, Holy Family in Egypt, horiz.

**1982, Dec. 24**
683 A70 18d Strip of 4, #a.-d.
684 A70 25d Pair, #a.-b.   14.00
    Nos. 683-684 (6)

**Souvenir Sheet**     *Perf. 14x13½*
685 A70 75d multicolored   30.00

Intl. Women's Year (#683-684) Christmas (#685).

---

## 1982, Dec. 31   *Perf. 14x13½*
686 A87 9d multicolored
687 A87 16d Strip of 4, #a.-d.
688 A87 50d multicolored   12.50
    Nos. 686-688 (6)

**Souvenir Sheet**
689 A87 75d multicolored   10.00

## Locomotives — A87

9d, Class 231K, France, 1941.
No. 687: a, 1st steam locomotive, Great Britain, 1825. b, Class 59, Africa, 1947. c, William Mason, US, 1850. d, Mallard, Great Britain, 1938.
50d, Henschel, Portugal, 1929. 75d, Locomotive barn, Swindon, Great Britain.

## Birds — A95

50c. Spermestes cucullatus. 1d. Xanthophi-
lus princeps. 1.50d. Thomasophantes sanc-
tithomae. 2d. Quelea erythrops. 3d. Textor
velatus peixotoi. 4d. Anabathmis hartlaubii.
5.50d. Serinus mozambicus santhome. 7d.
Estrilda astrild angolensis. 10d. Horizorhinus
dohrni. 11d. Zosterops ficedulinus. 12d. Prinia
molleri. 14d. Chrysococcyx cupreus insu-
larum. 15.50d. Halcyon malimbicus dryas.
16d. Turdus olivaceofuscus. 17d. Oriolus cras-
sirostris. 18.50d. Dicrurus modestus. 20d.
Columba thomensis. 25d. Stigmatopelia senegalensis thome. 30d. Chaetura thomensis.
42d. Onychognatus fulgidus. 46d. Lam-
protornis ornatus. 100d. Tyto alba thomensis.

**1983, Dec. 30**    **Perf. 13½**
727 A95 50c. multi
728 A95 1d multi
729 A95 1.50d multi
730 A95 2d multi
731 A95 3d multi
732 A95 4d multi
733 A95 5.50d multi
734 A95 7d multi
735 A95 10d multi

**Size: 30x43mm**
736 A95 11d multi
737 A95 12d multi
738 A95 14d multi
739 A95 15.50d multi
740 A95 16d multi
741 A95 17d multi
742 A95 18.50d multi
743 A95 20d multi
744 A95 25d multi

**Size: 31x47mm**    **Perf. 13½x14**
745 A95 30d multi
746 A95 42d multi
747 A95 46d multi
748 A95 100d multi
Nos. 727-748 (22)    50.00

**Souvenir Sheet**

## ESPANA '84, Madrid — A96

Paintings: a, 15.50d, Paulo Riding Donkey,
by Picasso. b, 16d, Abstract, by Miro. c,
18.50d, My Wife in the Nude, by Dali.

**1984, Apr. 27**    **Perf. 13½x14**
749 A96 Sheet of 3, #a.-c.    6.00

## LUBRAPEX '84, Lisbon — A97

Children's drawings: 16d. Children watching
play. 30d. Adults.

**1984, May 9**    **Perf. 13½**
750 A97 16d multicolored
751 A97 30d multicolored
Nos. 750-751 (2)    5.00

## Int'l. Maritime Organization, 25th Anniv. — A98

Ships: Nos. 752a, 753a, Phoenix, 1869.
752b, 753b, Hamburg, 1893. 752c, 753c,
Prince Heinrich, 1900.
No. 754: a, Leopold, 1840. b, Stadt Schaff-
hausen, 1851. c, Crown Prince, 1890. d, St.
Gallen, 1905.
No. 755: a, Elise, 1816. b, De Zeeuw, 1824.
c, Friedrich Wilhelm, 1827. d, Packet Hansa.
No. 756: a, Savannah, 1818. b, Chaperone,
1884. c, Alida, 1847. d, City of Worcester,
1881.
No. 757, Ferry, Lombard Bridge, Hamburg,
c. 1900. No. 758, Train, coaches on bridge,
1880, vert. No. 759, Windmill, bridge, vert. No.
760, Queen of the West. No. 761, Bremen.
No. 762, Union.

**1984, June 19**    **Litho.**    **Perf. 14x13½**
752 A98 50c Strip of 3, #a.-c.
753 A98 50c Strip of 3, #a.-c.
754 A98 7d Piece of 4, #a.-d.
  e. Souv. sheet of 2, #754a-754b
  f. Souv. sheet of 2, #754c-754d
755 A98 8d Piece of 4, #a.-d.
  e. Souv. sheet of 2, #755a-755b
  f. Souv. sheet of 2, #755c-755d
756 A98 15.50d Piece of 4, #a.-d.
  e. Souv. sheet of 2, #756a-756b
  f. Souv. sheet of 2, #756c-756d
Nos. 752-756 (5)    27.50
Nos. 754e-754f, 755e-755f,
756e-756f (6)    80.00

**Souvenir Sheets**
**Perf. 14x13½, 13½x14**
757 A98 10d multicolored
758 A98 10d multicolored
759 A98 10d multicolored
760 A98 15d multicolored
761 A98 15d multicolored
762 A98 15d multicolored
Nos. 757-762 (6)    75.00

Nos. 757-759 exist imperf. in different colors,
each. Nos. 760-762 contain one 60x33mm stamp
each. Nos. 753a-753c have UPU and
additionally inscribed "PARTICIPACAO DE S.
TOME E PRINCIPE / NO CONGRESSO DA
U.P.U. EM HAMBURGO."
Sheets containing Nos. 754-756 contain
one label.

## Natl. Campaign Against Malaria — A99

**1984, Sept. 30**    **Perf. 13½**
764 A99 8d Malaria victim
765 A99 16d Mosquito, DDT,
  vert.
766 A99 30d Exterminator, vert.
Nos. 764-766 (3)    8.00

## A100

World Food Day, 8d, Emblem, animals, produce. 16d, Silhouette, animals. 46d, Plowed
field, produce. 30d, Tractor, field, produce,
horiz.

**1984, Oct. 16**
767 A100 8d multicolored
768 A100 16d multicolored
769 A100 46d multicolored
Nos. 767-769 (3)    6.75

**Souvenir Sheet**
770 A100 30d multicolored    4.00

## Mushrooms — A101

Mushrooms: 10d, Coprinus micaceus. 20d,
Amanita rubescens. 30d, Armillariella mellea.
50d, Hygrophorus chrysodon, horiz.

**1984, Nov. 5**
771 A101 10d multicolored
772 A101 20d multicolored
773 A101 30d multicolored
Nos. 771-773 (3)    20.00

**Souvenir Sheet**
774 A101 50d multicolored    20.00

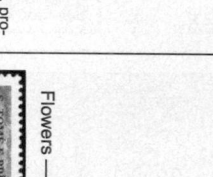

## Christmas — A102

Designs: 30d, Candles, offering, stable.
50d, Stable, Holy Family, Kings.

**1984, Dec. 25**
775 A102 30d multicolored    3.25

**Souvenir Sheet**
776 A102 50d multicolored    5.25
No. 776 contains one 60x40mm stamp.

## Conference of Portuguese Territories in Africa — A103

**1985, Feb. 14**
777 A103 25d multicolored    2.75

## Reinstatement of Flights from Lisbon to St. Thomas, 1st Anniv. — A104

Designs: 25d, Douglas DC-3, map of northwest Africa. 30d, Air Portugal Douglas DC-8.
50d, Fokker Friendship.

**1985, Dec. 6**    **Litho.**    **Perf. 13½**
778 A104 25d multicolored
779 A104 30d multicolored
Nos. 778-779 (2)    5.75

**Souvenir Sheet**
779A A104 50d multicolored    9.00

## Flowers — A105

**1985, Dec. 30**    **Perf. 11½x12**
780 A105 16d Flowering cactus
781 A105 20d Sunflower
782 A105 30d Porcelain rose
Nos. 780-782 (3)    5.75

## Mushrooms — A106

**1986, Sept. 18**    **Perf. 13½**
783 A106 6d Fistulina hepatica
784 A106 25d Collybia
  butyracea
785 A106 30d Entoloma
  clypeatum
Nos. 783-785 (3)    6.25

**Souvenir Sheet**
786 A106 75d Cogumelos II    10.00
No. 786 exists with margins trimmed on four
sides removing the control number.

## World Cup Soccer, Mexico — A107

#787: a, Top of trophy. b, Bottom of trophy.
c, Interior of stadium. d, Exterior of stadium.

**1986, Oct. 1**
787 A107 25d Sheet of 4, #a.-d.    11.50
For overprints see Nos. 818-818A.

## 1988 Summer Olympics, Seoul — A108

**Miniature Sheet**

Seoul Olympic Games emblem, and: No.
788a, Map of North Korea. b, Torch. c,
Olympic flag, map of South Korea. d, Text.

**1986, Oct. 2**
788 A108 25d Sheet of 4, #a.-d.    18.00

ST. THOMAS AND PRINCE ISLANDS

REPÚBLICA DEMOCRÁTICA DE S. TOMÉ PRINCIPE
PESCA ARTESANAL

XI EXPOSIÇÃO FILATÉLICA
LUSO-BRASILEIRA "LUBRAPEX '86"

LUBRAPEX '86, Brazil — A112

Exhibition emblem and: No. 796a, 1d, Line fisherman on shore. b, 1d, Line fisherman in boat. c, 2d, Net fisherman. d, 46d, Couple trap fishing, lobster.

**1987, Jan. 15**
796  A112  Sheet of 4, #a.+2 labels  5.00

ANO INTERNACIONAL DA PAZ

Intl. Peace Year — A113

Designs: 8d, Mahatma Gandhi. 10d, Martin Luther King, Jr. 10d, Perl Gmnn. Intl. Peace Year, UN, UNESCO, Olympic emblems and Nobel Peace Prize medal. 20d, Albert Luthuli. 75d, Peace Dove, by Picasso.

**1987, Jan. 15**
797  A113  8d  blk & pur
798  A113  10d  blk, blk & grn
799  A113  16d  multicolored
800  A113  20d  multicolored  8.00
  Nos. 797-800 (4)
  Souvenir Sheet
801  A113  75d multicolored  7.00

Christmas 1986 — A114

Paintings by Albrecht Durer: No. 802a, 50c, Virgin and Child. b, 1d, Madonna of the Carnation. c, 16d, Virgin and Child, diff. d, 20d, The Nativity. 75d, Madonna of the Goldfinch.

**1987, Jan. 15**
802  A114  Strip of 4, #a.-d.  6.00
  Souvenir Sheet
803  A114  75d multicolored  10.00

Db 1  S. TOMÉ E PRINCIPE

Fauna and Flora — A115

Birds: a, 1d, Agapornis fischeri. b, 2d, Psittacula krameri. c, 10d, Psittacus erithacus. d, 20d, Agapornis personata psittacidae.

---

Flowers: e, 1d, Passiflora caerulea. f, 2d, Oncidium nubigenum. g, 10d, Helicontia wagneriana. h, 20d, Guzmania liguiata. Butterflies: i, 1d, Aglais urticae. j, 2d, Pieris brassicae. k, 10d, Fabriciana niobe. l, 20d, Zerynthia polyxena.
Dogs: m, 1d, Sanshu. n, 2d, Hamilton-stovare. o, 10d, Gran spitz. p, 20d, Chow-chow.

**1987, Oct. 15**  *Perf. 14x13½*
804  A115  Sheet of 16, #a.-p.  20.00

Sports Institute, 10th Anniv. — A116

No. 805: a, 50c, Three athletes. b, 20d, Map of St. Thomas and Prince, torchbearers. c, 30d, Volleyball, soccer, team handball and basketball players.

**1987, Oct. 30**
805  A116  Strip of 3, #a.-c.  4.50
  Souvenir Sheet  *Perf. 13½x14*
806  A116  50d  Sheet of 1 + label  6.25
  Miniature Sheet

Y LOS LEGADOS DO DESTENIMENTO NA AMÉRICA

Discovery of America, 500th Anniv. (in 1992) — A117

Emblem and: No. 807: a, 15d, Columbus with globe, map and arms. b, 20d, Battle between Spanish galleon and pirate ship. c, 20d, Columbus landing in New World. 100d, Model ship, horiz.

**1987, Nov. 3**  *Perf. 13½x14*
807  A117  Sheet of 3, #a.-c. + 3 labels  9.00
  Souvenir Sheet  *Perf. 14x13½*
808  A117  100d multicolored  10.00

Mushrooms — A118

Designs: No. 809a, 6d, Calocybe ionides. b, 25d, Hygrophorus coccineus. c, 30d, Boletus versipellis. 35d, Morchella vulgaris, vert.

**1987, Nov. 10**  *Perf. 14x13½*
809  A118  Strip of 3, #a.-c.  5.75
  Souvenir Sheet  *Perf. 13½x14*
810  A118  35d multicolored  6.00

---

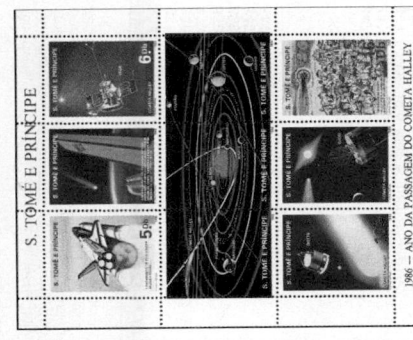

S. TOMÉ E PRINCIPE  Db 5
S. TOMÉ E PRINCIPE  Db 10
S. TOMÉ E PRINCIPE  Db 20

Locomotives — A119

No. 811: a, 5d, Jung, Germany. b, 10d, Mikado 2413. c, 20d, Baldwin, 1920. 50d, Pamplona Railroad Station, 1900.

**1987, Dec. 1**  *Litho.*  *Perf. 14x13½*
811  A119  Strip of 3, #a.-c.  7.50
  Souvenir Sheet
812  A119  50d multicolored  6.25

NATAL 87  S. TOMÉ E PRINCIPE

Christmas — A120

Paintings of Virgin and Child by: No. 813a, 1d, Botticelli. b, 5d, Murillo. c, 15d, Raphael. d, 20d, Memling.

**1987, Dec. 20**  *Perf. 13½x14*
813  A120  Sheet of 4, #a.-d.  4.00
  Souvenir Sheet  *Perf. 14x13½*
814  A120  50d multicolored  6.25

AUSTRALIA 1987-88  WORLD JAMBOREE

World Boy Scout Jamboree, Australia, 1987-88 — A121

**1987, Dec. 30**  *Perf. 14x13½*
815  A121  50c multicolored  3.00

---

S. TOMÉ E PRINCIPE

1986 — ANO DA PASSAGEM DO COMETA HALLEY

Halley's Comet — A109

Designs: No. 789a, 5d, Challenger space shuttle, 1st launch. b, 6d, Vega probe. c, 10d, Giotto probe. d, 16d, Comet over Nuremberg, A.D. 684.
90d, Comet, Giotto probe, horiz.

**1986, Oct. 27**
789  A109  Sheet of 4, #a.-d.+5 labels  10.00
  Souvenir Sheet
790  A109  90d multicolored  10.00

S. TOMÉ E PRINCIPE

Automobiles — A110

Designs: No. 791a, 60c, Columbia Manument, Barcelona. b, 6d, Fire engine ladder truck. c, 1900. c, 16d, Fire engine. c, 1900. d, 30d, Fiat 18 BL Red Cross ambulance, c. 1916.

**1986, Nov. 1**
791  A110  Sheet of 4, #a.-d.+5 labels  10.00

Railway Stations and Signals — A111

Designs: 50c, London Bridge Station, 1900. 6d, 100-300 meter warning signs. 20d, Signal lamp. 50d, St. Thomas & Prince Station.

**1986, Nov. 2**  *Perf. 13½*
792  A111  50c  multicolored  6.00
793  A111  6d  multicolored
794  A111  20d  multicolored
  Nos. 792-794 (3)
  Souvenir Sheet
795  A111  50d multicolored  7.00

## Russian October Revolution, 70th Anniv. — A122

**1988**
816 A122 25d Lenin addressing revolutionaries 2.25

*S. TOMÉ E PRINCIPE*

Souvenir Sheet

**Perf. 12**

*Lubrapex '88 — A123*

**1988, May**
817 A123 80d Trolley 6.00

**Perf. 14x13½**

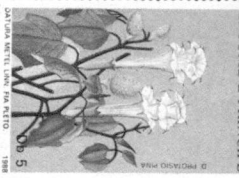

*Medicinal Plants — A123a*

Nos. 787a-787d Ovptd. "CAMPEONATO MUNDIAL / DE FUTEBOL MEXICO '86 / ALEMANHA / SUBCAMPIAO" or Same with "ARGENTINA / CAMPIAO" Instead in Gold (#818A) Across Four Stamps

**1988, Aug. 15**

**Perf. 13½**
818 A107 25d Block of 4 (S) 25.00
818A A107 25d Block of 4 (G) 25.00

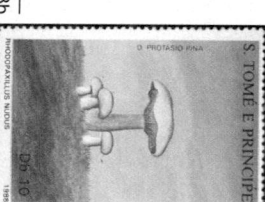

*S. TOMÉ E PRINCIPE*

Mushrooms — A123b

Medicinal plants: No. 819a, 5d, Datura metel. b, 5d, Salaconia. c, 5d, Cassia occidentalis. d, 10d, Solanum ovigerum. e, 20d, Leonotis nepetifolia.
Mushrooms: No. 820a, 10d, Rhodopaxillus nudus. b, 10d, Volvaria volvacea. c, 10d, Psaliota bispora. d, 10d, Pleurotus ostreatus. e, 20d, Clitocybe geotropa.

**1988, Oct. 26**

**Perf. 13½x14**
819 A123a 35d 6.75
820 A123a 35d 9.00

**Souvenir Sheets**
821 A123a 35d Hiersas durero 6.25
822 A123b 35d Mushroom on wood 6.25

## Passenger Trains — A123c

*CAMINHOS DE FERRO*

Miniature Sheets of 4

No. 823, a, Swiss Federal Class RE 6/6, left. b, Class RE 6/6, right. No. 824: a, Japan Nat. Class EF 81, left. b, Class EF 81, right. No. 825: a, German Electric E 18, 1930, left. b, E 18, 1930, right.

**1988, Nov. 4**

**Perf. 14x13½**
823 A123c 10d 2 ea #a-b. + 2 labels
824 A123c 10d 2 ea #a-b. + 2 labels
825 A123c 10d 2 ea #a-b. + 2 labels
*Nos. 823-825 (12)* 18.00

**Souvenir Sheet**
826 A123c 60d multicolored 9.00

## Butterflies — A123d

*S. TOMÉ E PRINCIPE*

Various flowers and: No. 827a, White and brown spotted butterfly. b, Dark brown and white butterfly, flower stigma pointing down. c, Brown and white butterfly, flower stigma pointing down.

**1988, Nov. 25**

**Perf. 13½x14**
827 A123d 10d Strip of 3, #a-c. 4.50
*50d, Brown, white and orange butterfly.*

**Souvenir Sheet**
828 A123d 50d multicolored 8.50

*S. TOMÉ E PRINCIPE*

Ferdinand von Zeppelin (1838-1917) — A123e

## Berlin, 750th Anniv. — A123f

*S. TOMÉ E PRINCIPE*

No. 829: a, Sailing ship, dirigible L23. b, Dirigibles flying over British merchant ships. c, Rendezvous of zeppelin with Russian ice breaker Malygin. No. 830: a, Airship Le Jeune at mooring pad, Paris, 1903, vert. b, von Zeppelin, vert.

**1988, Nov. 25**

**Perf. 14x13½, 13½x14**
829 A123e 10d Strip of 3, #a-c. 16.00
830 A123e 10d Pair, #a-b.
*(5)*

**Souvenir Sheet**
831 A123f 50d multicolored 9.00

*Db 10  S. TOMÉ E PRINCIPE*

Natl. Arms — A123g

## Automatic Telephone Exchange Linking the Islands, 1st Anniv. — A123h

*S. TOMÉ E PRINCIPE*

**1988, Dec. 15**

**Perf. 13½**
832 A123g 10d multicolored 2.00
833 A123h 25d multicolored 3.25

## Olympics Games, Seoul, Barcelona and Albertville — A123i

*S. TOMÉ E PRINCIPE  Db 5*

*ITALIA'90  Db 5*

World Cup Soccer Championships, Italy, 1990 — A123

#834, View of Barcelona, Cobi. #835, Barcelona Games emblem. #836, Gold medal from 1988 Seoul games. #837, Emblems of 1988 & 1992 games. #838, Bear on skis,

Albertville, 1992. #839, Soccer ball. #840, Italy '90 Championships emblem. #841, World Cup Trophy. #842, Transfer of Olympic flag during Seoul closing ceremony. No. 843, Olympic pins. #844, like #838. #845, Soccer balls as hemispheres of globe.

**1988, Dec. 15 Perf. 14x13½, 13½x14**
834 A123i 5d multi 10.00
835 A123i 5d multi 10.00
836 A123i 5d multi. vert.
837 A123i 5d multi. vert.
838 A123i 5d grn & multi
839 A123i 5d multi
840 A123i 5d multi. vert.
841 A123i 5d multi. vert.
*(8)* 14.00
842 A123j 50d multi
843 A123j 50d multi
844 A123j 50d blue & multi 10.00
845 A123j 50d multi 10.00

**Souvenir Sheets**
*Nos. 834-841* 14.00

No. 842 exists with Olympic emblems in gold or silver. No. 845 exists with marginal inscriptions in gold or silver. See Nos. 876-877 for souvenir sheets similar in design to No. 840.

Int'l. Boy Scout Jamboree, Australia, 1987-88 — A123k

#846: a, Campfire. b, 3cout emblem, pitched tents, flag. c, Scout emblem, tent flaps, flag, axe. 110d, Trefoil center point, horiz.

**1988, Dec. 15**

**Perf. 14x13½**
846 A123k 10d Strip of 3, #a-c. 6.75

**Souvenir Sheet**
847 A123k 110d multicolored 25.00

*S. TOMÉ E PRINCIPE*

Int'l. Red Cross, 125th Anniv. — A123m

No. 848: a, 50c, Patient in hospital. b, 5d, Transporting victims. c, 20d, Instructing workers. 50d, Early mail train, horiz.

**1988, Dec. 15**

**Perf. 14x13½**
848 A123m 10d Strip of 3, #a-c. 9.00

**Souvenir Sheet**
849 A123m 50d multicolored 10.50

*S. TOMÉ E PRINCIPE  NATAL'88*

Christmas — A123n

Miniature Sheet

#850: a, 10d, Madonna and Child with St. Anthony Abbot and the Infant Baptism, by Titian. b, 10d, Madonna and Child with St. Catherine and a Rabbit, by Titian. c, 10d, Nativity Scene, by Rubens. d, 30d, Adoration of the Magi, by Rubens. 50d, The Annunciation (detail), by Titian, vert.

**1988, Dec. 23** — *Perf. 14x13½* — 9.00
850 A123n Sheet of 4, #a.-d. 9.00
**Souvenir Sheet**
*Perf. 13½x14*
851 A123n 50d multicolored 7.50
Titian, 500th anniv. of birth. Country name does not appear on No. 850d.

**French Revolution, Bicent. — A123o**
Designs: No. 852, Eiffel Tower, Concorde, stylized doves, flag. No. 853 Eiffel Tower, flag, stylized doves. No. 854, Eiffel Tower, flag, stylized doves, TGV train, vert. 50d, TGV train.
*Perf. 14x13½, 13½x14*
**1989, July 14** — **Litho.**
852 A123o 10d multicolored
853 A123o 10d multicolored
854 A123o 10d multicolored
Nos. 852-854 (3) 4.50
**Souvenir Sheet**
*Perf. 13½x14*
855 A123o 50d multicolored 6.25

S. TOMÉ E PRÍNCIPE Db 10

---

S. TOMÉ E PRÍNCIPE Db 0.50 — PROTASIO PINA

**Fruit — A123p**
**1989, Sept. 15** — *Perf. 14x13½*
856 A123p 50c Chapu-chapu
857 A123p 1d Guava
858 A123p 5d Mango
859 A123p 10d Carambola
860 A123p 25d Nona
861 A123p 50d Avacado
862 A123p 50d Cajamanga
*Perf. 14x13½*
863 A123p 60d Jackfruit
864 A123p 100d Cacao
865 A123p 250d Bananas
866 A123p 500d Papaya
Nos. 856-866 (11) 21.00
**Souvenir Sheet**
*Perf. 13½x14*
867 A123p 1000d Pomegranate 22.50
Nos. 863-866 are horiz.

---

S. TOMÉ E PRÍNCIPE Db 20

**Hummingbirds — A124**
Designs: No. 871, Topaza bella, Sappho sparganura, vert. No. 872, Petasophores anais. No. 873, Lophornis adorabilis, Chalcostigma herrani, vert. 50d, Oreotrochilus chimborazo.
**1989, Oct. 15** — *Perf. 13½x14, 14x13½*
871 A124 20d multicolored
872 A124 20d multicolored
873 A124 20d multicolored
Nos. 871-873 (3) 5.25
**Souvenir Sheet**
*Perf. 14x13½*
874 A124 50d multicolored 5.25

**Miniature Sheet**

**1990 World Cup Soccer Championships, Italy — A125**
Program covers: No. 875, a, 10d, Globe and soccer ball, 1962. b, 10d, Foot kicking ball, 1950. c, 10d, Abstract design, 1982. d, 20d, Player kicking ball, 1934.
No. 876: a, Character emblem, horiz. b, USA 04, horiz. 50d, like #876a, horiz.
*Perf. 13½x14*
**1989, Oct. 24**
875 A125 Block of 4, #a.-d. 7.50
**Souvenir Sheets**
*Perf. 14x13½*
876 A125 25d blue & multi
877 A125 50d blue & multi
Nos. 876-877 (2) 15.00

---

S. TOMÉ E PRÍNCIPE

**Orchids — A123q**
Designs: No. 868, Dendrobium phalaenopsis. No. 869, Catteleya granulosa. 50d, Diothonea imbricata and maxillaria eburnea.
**1989, Oct. 15** — *Perf. 13½x14*
868 A123q 20d multicolored
869 A123q 20d multicolored
Nos. 868-869 (2) 4.00
**Souvenir Sheet**
870 A123q 50d multicolored 5.25

---

S. TOMÉ E PRÍNCIPE Db 20

**Locomotives — A127**
**1989, Oct. 27** — *Perf. 14x13½, 13½x14*
884 A127 20d Japan
885 A127 20d Philippines
886 A127 20d Spain, vert.
887 A127 20d India
888 A127 20d Asia
Nos. 884-888 (5) 10.50
**Souvenir Sheets**
889 A127 50d Garratt, Africa
890 A127 50d Trans-Gabon, vert.
Nos. 889-890 (2) 18.00
Nos. 884-888 exist in souvenir sheets of one.

---

S. TOMÉ E PRÍNCIPE Db 20

**Ships A128**
#891, Merchant ships at sea, 16th cent. #892, Caravels, merchant ships in harbor, 16th cent. #893, 3 merchant ships at sea, 18th cent. #894, War ships, 18th cent. #895, 4 merchant ships, 18th cent. #896, Passenger liner, Port of Hamburg. #897, German sailing ship, 17th cent.
**1989, Oct. 27** — *Perf. 14x13½*
891 A128 20d multicolored
892 A128 20d multicolored
893 A128 20d multicolored
894 A128 20d multicolored
895 A128 20d multicolored
Nos. 891-895 (5) 10.50
**Souvenir Sheets**
*Perf. 13½x14*
896 A128 50d multicolored 6.00
897 A128 50d multi, vert. 6.00
Discovery of America, 500th anniv., in 1992 (#891-895) and Hamburg, 800th anniv. (#891-897).
Nos. 891-895 exist in souvenir sheets of one. Value for 4 sheets, $15.

---

S. TOMÉ E PRÍNCIPE

**1992 Summer Olympics, Barcelona — A126**
**1989, Oct. 24** — *Perf. 13½x14, 14x13½*
878 A126 5d Tennis, vert.
879 A126 5d Basketball, vert.
880 A126 5d Running
881 A126 35d Baseball, vert.
Nos. 878-881 (4) 10.50
**Souvenir Sheet**
*Perf. 14x13½*
882 A126 50d Sailing
883 A126 50d Mosaic
Nos. 878-881 exist in souvenir sheets of one. Value for 4 sheets, $22.50. No country name on souvenir sheet of one of No. 878.

---

S. TOMÉ E PRÍNCIPE Db 2...

**Butterflies A129**
**1989, Dec. 20** — *Perf. 13½x14*
898 A129 20d Tree bark
899 A129 20d Leaves
900 A129 20d Flowers
901 A129 20d Bird
902 A129 20d Blades of grass
Nos. 898-902 (5) 10.50
**Souvenir Sheet**
903 A129 100d yel, brn & multi 10.50
Nos. 898-902 exist in souvenir sheets of one. Value for 4 sheets, $18.

---

**25° ANIVERSÁRIO BANCO AFRICANO DE DESENVOLVIMENTO**

Db 25
S. TOMÉ E PRÍNCIPE

**African Development Bank, 25th Anniv. — A130**
*Perf. 13½x14*
**1989, Dec. 20**
904 A130 25d blk, lt bl & grn 3.25

S. TOMÉ E PRÍNCIPE Db 60

**World Telecommunications Day — A131**
*Perf. 14x13½*
**1989, Dec. 20**
905 A131 60d multicolored 5.00
**Souvenir Sheet**
*Perf. 13½x14*
906 A131 100d Early Bird satellite, vert. 10.00

S. TOMÉ E PRÍNCIPE Db 25

**Christmas A132**
Paintings: No. 907, Adoration of the Magi (detail), by Durer. No. 908, Young Virgin Mary, by Titian. No. 909, Adoration of the King, by Kubens. No. 910, Cistino Madonna, by Raphael. 100d, Madonna and Child Surrounded by Garland and Boy Angels, by Rubens.
**1989, Dec. 23** — *Perf. 13½x14*
907 A132 25d multicolored
908 A132 25d multicolored
909 A132 25d multicolored
910 A132 25d multicolored
Nos. 907-910 (4) 10.50
**Souvenir Sheet**
911 A132 100d multicolored 10.50
Nos. 907-910 exist in souvenir sheets of one. Value for 4 sheets, $13.50.

---

**Expedition of Sir Arthur Eddington to St. Thomas and Prince, 70th Anniv. A133**

Designs: No. 912, Albert Einstein with Eddington. No. 913, Locomotive on Prince Island. No. 914, Roca Sundy railway station.
**1990** — **Litho.** — *Perf. 13½*
912 A133 60d multicolored
913 A133 60d multicolored
914 A133 60d multicolored
Nos. 912-914 (3) 16.00
a. Souvenir sheet of 3, #912-914 22.50 16.00

## Souvenir Sheet

**1990, July 12**    **Perf. 13½**
916 A134 50d Sheet of 3, #a.-c.    14.00

Independence, 15th Anniv. — A134

Designs: a, Map, arms. b, Map, birds carrying envelope. c, Flag.

Orchids — A135

**1990, Sept. 15**    **Litho.**    **Perf. 13½**
917 A135 20d Eulophia guineensis
918 A135 20d Ancistrochilus
919 A135 20d Oeceoclades maculata
920 A135 20d Vanilla imperialis
921 A135 20d Ansellia africana
Nos. 917-921 (5)    10.00

922 A135 50d Angraecum distichum, horiz.
923 A135 50d Polystachya affinis, horiz.
Nos. 922-923 (2)    10.00

Souvenir Sheets    **Perf. 14x13½**

Expo '90, Intl. Garden and Greenery Exposition, Osaka.

## S. TOMÉ E PRÍNCIPE

Db 5

Locomotives — A136

**1990, Sept. 28**    **Perf. 14x13½**
924 A136 5d Bohemia, 1923-41
925 A136 20d W. Germany, 1951-56
926 A136 25d Mallet, 1896-1903
927 A136 25d Russia, 1927-30
928 A136 25d England, 1927-30
Nos. 924-928 (5)    10.00

Souvenir Sheets
929 A136 50d Camden-Amboy, 1834-38    6.00
930 A136 50d Stockton-Darlington, 1825    6.00

## Souvenir Sheet

**1990, Oct. 7**
931 A137 300d Armas Castle    20.00

Iberoamericana '90 Philatelic Exposition — A137

1990 World Cup Soccer Championships, Italy — A138

**1990, Oct. 15**    **Perf. 13½**
932 A138 25d multicolored
933 A138 25d multicolored
934 A138 25d multicolored
935 A138 25d multicolored
Nos. 932-935 (4)    10.00

936 A138 50d multi, horiz.
937 A138 50d multi, horiz.
Nos. 936-937 (2)    10.00

Souvenir Sheets    **Perf. 14x13½**

#932, German team with World Cup Trophy. #933, 2 players with ball. #934, 3 players with ball. #935, Italian player. #936, U.S. Soccer Federation emblem and team members. #937, World Cup Trophy.

Mushrooms A139

S. TOMÉ E PRÍNCIPE
Db 20

**1990, Nov. 2**    **Perf. 13½x14**
938 A139 20d Boletus aereus
939 A139 20d Coprinus micaceus
940 A139 20d Pholiota spectabilis
941 A139 20d Krombholzia aurantiaca
942 A139 20d Stropharia aeruginosa
Nos. 938-942 (5)    10.00

943 A139 50d Hypholoma capnoides
944 A139 50d Pleurotus ostreatus
Nos. 943-944 (2)    12.00

Souvenir Sheets    **Perf. 14x13½**

Nos. 943-944 horiz. See Nos. 1014-1020.

Butterflies — A140

S. TOMÉ E PRÍNCIPE
Db 25

## Souvenir Sheet

NATAL - 1990
Db 25

**1990, Nov. 2**    **Perf. 14x13½, 13½x14**
945 A140 15d Megistanis baeotus
946 A140 15d Ascia vanillae
947 A140 15d Danaus chrysippus
948 A140 15d Morpho menelaus
949 A140 15d Papilio rutulus, vert.
950 A140 25d Papilio paradisea, vert.
Nos. 945-950 (6)    10.00

Souvenir Sheets
951 A140 50d Parnassius clodius, vert.
952 A140 50d Papilio macmaon, vert.
Nos. 951-952 (2)    15.00

Presenting Gifts to the Newborn King — A141

**1990, Nov. 30**    **Perf. 13½x14**
953 A141 25d multicolored
954 A141 25d multicolored
955 A141 25d multicolored
956 A141 25d multicolored
Nos. 953-956 (4)    10.00

957 A141 50d multicolored
958 A141 50d multicolored
Nos. 957-958 (2)    10.00

Souvenir Sheets    **Perf. 14x13½**

Christmas: No. 954, Nativity scene. No. 955, Adoration of the Magi. No. 956, Flight into Egypt. No. 957, Adoration of the Magi. No. 958, Portrait of Artist's Daughter Clara (detail), by Rubens, horiz.
Death of Rubens, 350th anniv. (#958).

Anniversaries and Events A142

S. TOMÉ E PRÍNCIPE
Db 20

**1990, Dec. 15**
959 A142 20d shown

Souvenir Sheets    **Perf. 13½x14**
**Perf. 14x13½, 13½x14 (#962, 964)**
960 A142 50d Oath of Confederation
961 A142 50d Pointed roof
962 A142 50d William Tell statue, vert.
963 A142 50d Brandenburg Gate
964 A142 50d Penny Black, vert.
965 A142 100d bank note
Nos. 960-965 (6)    30.00

Swiss Confederation, 700th anniv. (#960); Brandenburg Gate, 200th anniv. (#963); First postage stamp, 150th anniv. (#964); Independence of St. Thomas and Prince, 15th anniv. (#965).

Paintings — A143

S. TOMÉ E PRÍNCIPE
Db 20

**1990, Dec. 15**    **Perf. 14x13½, 13½x14**
966 A143 10d multi
967 A143 10d multi, vert.
968 A143 10d multi, vert.
969 A143 10d multi, vert.
970 A143 10d multi, vert.
971 A143 10d multi, vert.
972 A143 20d multi
973 A143 25d multi
974 A143 25d multi
Nos. 966-974 (9)    15.00

Souvenir Sheets    **Perf. 13½x14**
975 A143 50d multi, vert.    8.00
976 A143 50d multi, vert.    8.00
977 A143 50d multi, vert.    8.00

Designs: #966, The Bathers, by Renoir. #967, Girl Holding Mirror for Nude, by Picasso. #968, Nude, by Rubens. #969, Descent from the Cross (detail), by Rubens. #970, Nude, by Titian. #971, Landscape, by Durer. #972, Rowboats, by Van Gogh. #973, Nymphs, by Titian. #974, Bather, by Titian. #975, Postman Joseph Roulin (detail), by Van Gogh. #976, The Abduction of the Daughters of Leucippus, by Rubens. #977, Nude, by Titian, diff.
See No. 958 for other souvenir sheet for Rubens death anniv.

## S. TOMÉ E PRÍNCIPE

Db 1

Flora and Fauna — A144

**1991, Feb. 2**    **Perf. 14x13½**
978 A144 1d multicolored
979 A144 1d multicolored
980 A144 5d multicolored
981 A144 10d multicolored
982 A144 50d multicolored
983 A144 70d multicolored
984 A144 75d multicolored
985 A144 75d multicolored
986 A144 80d multicolored
987 A144 100d multicolored
988 A144 250d multicolored
989 A144 500d multicolored
Nos. 978-989 (12)    18.00

Souvenir Sheets    **Perf. 13½x14**
990 A144 500d Orchid, vert.    9.00
991 A144 500d Rose, vert.    9.00
See Nos. 1054l-1054L.

Designs: 1d, Gecko. 5d, Cobra. 10d, No. 980, Sea turtle. No. 981, Fresh water turtle. No. 982, Civet. 70d, Civet in tree. No. 983, 75d, Civet with young. No. 985, Civet in tree. No. 984, Psittacus erithacus: 80d, In tree. 100d, On branch with wings spread, vert. 250d, Feeding young, vert. No. 989, Three in flight, vert.

## S. TOMÉ E PRÍNCIPE

Db 75

Locomotives — A145

**1991, May 7**    **Perf. 14x13½, 13½x14**
992 A145 75d shown
993 A145 75d North America, vert.
994 A145 75d Germany, vert.
995 A145 75d New Delhi, vert.
996 A145 75d Brazil, vert.
997 A145 200d Two leaving terminal
Nos. 992-997 (6)    7.50

Souvenir Sheets
998 A145 500d Engine 120, vert.    7.00
999 A145 500d Engine 151-001    7.00

**Birds — A146**

**Perf. 13½x14**

**1991, July 8**
1000  A146  75d  Psittacula kuh-lii
1001  A146  75d  Plyodolophus rosaceus
1002  A146  75d  Falco tinnuncu-lus
1003  A146  75d  Platycercus palliceps
1004  A146  200d  Marcrocercus aracanga
  Nos. 1000-1004 (5)   8.00

**Souvenir Sheets**
1005  A146  500d  Ramphastos culmenatus
1006  A146  500d  Strix nyctea   22.50
  Nos. 1005-1006 (2)

Db 75

**Paintings**
A117

50d, Venus and Cupid, by Titian. #1008, Horse's Head (detail), by Rubens. #1009, Child's Tara (detail), by Rubens. 100d, Spanish Woman, by Picasso. 200d, Man with Christian Flag, by Titian. #1012, Study of a Negro, by Rubens. #1013, Madonna and Child, by Raphael.

**1991, July 31**
1007  A117  50d  multicolored
1008  A117  75d  multicolored
1009  A117  75d  multicolored
1010  A117  100d  multicolored
1011  A117  200d  multicolored
  Nos. 1007-1011 (5)   8.00

**Souvenir Sheets**
1012  A117  500d  multicolored   8.00
1013  A117  500d  multicolored   16.00
  Nos. 1012-1013 (2)

**Mushroom Type of 1990**

**1991, Aug. 30**
1014  A139  50d  Clitocybe geotropa
1015  A139  50d  Lepiota procera
1016  A139  75d  Boletus granulatus
1017  A139  125d  Coprinus comatus
1018  A139  200d  Amanita rubescens
  Nos. 1014-1018 (5)   8.00

**Souvenir Sheets**
1019  A139  500d  Armillariella mellea

**Perf. 14x13½**
1020  A139  500d  Nictalis parasitica, horiz.   16.00
  Nos. 1019-1020 (2)

**Flowers**
A148

Db 50

---

#1022, Zan tedeschia elliotiana. #1023, Cyrtanthes pohliana. #1024, Phalaenopsis lueddemanniana. #1025, Haemanthus katharinae. 500d, Arundina graminifolia.

**1991, Sept. 9   Perf. 13½x14**
1021  A148  50d  shown
1022  A148  75d  multicolored
1023  A148  100d  multicolored
1024  A148  100d  multicolored
1025  A148  200d  multicolored
  Nos. 1021-1025 (5)   8.00

**Souvenir Sheet**
1026  A148  500d  multicolored   8.00

**Iberoamericano '92 Intl. Philatelic Exhibition — A149**

**1991, Oct. 11   Litho.   Perf. 14x13½**
1027  A149  800d  multicolored   7.00

**Discovery of America, 500th Anniv. — A150**
(in 1992)

Db 15

**1991, Oct. 12   Perf. 13½x14**
1028  A150  50d  Columbus
1029  A150  50d  Sailing ship
1030  A150  50d  Sailing ship, diff.
1031  A150  125d  Landing in New World
1032  A150  200d  Pointing the way
  Nos. 1028-1032 (5)   10.00

**Souvenir Sheet   Perf. 14x13½**
1033  A150  500d  Columbus' fleet, horiz.   10.00

S. TOMÉ E PRÍNCIPE
Db 125

**Butterflies — A151**

**1991, Oct. 16   Perf. 14x13½**
1034  A151  125d  Limentis popul
1035  A151  125d  Pavon inachis io
  Nos. 1034-1035 (2)   8.00

**Souvenir Sheet   Perf. 13½x14**
1036  A151  500d  Zerynthia polyxena   8.00
  Phila Nippon '91.

---

**1991, Nov. 15   Perf. 14x13½**
1037  A151  125d  Macaon papilio machaon
1038  A151  125d  Gran pavon
1039  A151  125d  Pavon inachis io, diff.
1040  A151  125d  Artia caja   8.00
  Nos. 1037-1040 (4)

**Souvenir Sheet   Perf. 13½x14**
1041  A151  500d  Unnamed butterfly, vert.   8.00
  Christmas.

S. TOMÉ E PRÍNCIPE
Db 25

**Landmarks — A152**

Landmarks of France: No. 1042, Ile de France, vert. No. 1043, Chenonceau Castle. No. 1044, Azay-le-Rideau Castle. No. 1045, Chambord Castle. No. 1046, Chaumont Castle. No. 1047, Fountainebleau Palace.

**Perf. 13½x14, 14x13½**
1042-1047  A152  25d  Set of 6   8.00

**Souvenir Sheet**
1048  A152  500d  Paris map, 1615   7.50
  French National Exposition.

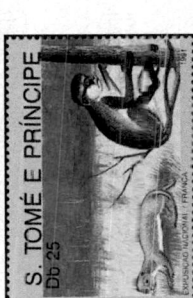

S. TOMÉ E PRÍNCIPE
Db 25

**Fauna — A153**

Animals and birds: a. Weasel, monkey. b, Civet, rats. c, Goat, cow. d, Rabbits, wildcat. e, Parrot, black bird. f, White bird, multicolored bird.

**1991, Nov. 15   Perf. 14x13½**
1049  A153  25d  Sheet of 0, #e.   8.00
  French National Exposition.

S. TOMÉ E PRÍNCIPE
Db 3000

**Express Mail Service from St. Thomas and Prince — A154**

**1991   Litho.   Perf. 14**
1050  A154  3000d  multicolored   18.00

**Souvenir Sheets**

NAGANO
NOMINAÇÃO DA SEDE OLÍMPICA

S. TOMÉ E PRÍNCIPE

**1991 Intl. Olympic Committee Session, Birmingham — A154a**

Designs: No. 1050A, IOC emblem, Birmingham Session. No. 1050B, 1998 Winter Olympics emblem, Nagano. No. 1050C, 1998 Winter Olympics mascot.

---

**1992   Litho.   Perf. 14**
1050A  A154a  800d  multi
1050B  A154a  800d  multi
1050C  A154a  800d  multi   32.50
  Nos. 1050A-1050C (3)

**Souvenir Sheet**

IBEREX '91
BEREX 91

**IBEREX '91 — A154b**

**1992**
1050D  A154b  800d  multi   10.00

**Souvenir Sheets**

S. TOMÉ E PRÍNCIPE

**1992 Winter Olympics, Albertville — A154c**

**1992**
1050E  A154c  50d  Olympic medals, Set of 4, a.-d.   40.00

No. 1050E exists as four souvenir sheets with pictures of different medalists in sheet margins: a., Blanca Fernandez, Spain; b., Alberto Tomba, Italy, c., Mark Kirchner, Germany; d., Torgny Mogren, Norway.

S. TOMÉ E PRÍNCIPE
Db 50

**1992 Summer Olympics, Barcelona A154d**

View of earth from space with: No. 1050F, High jumper. No. 1050G, Roller hockey player. No. 1050H, Equestrian. No. 1050I, Kayaker. No. 1050J, Weight lifter. No. 1050K, Archer. No. 1050L, Michael Jordan, horiz.

**1992**
1050F-1050K  A154d  50d  Set of 6   8.50

**Souvenir Sheet**
1050L  A154d  50d  multicolored   8.00

S. TOMÉ E PRÍNCIPE
WWF
450 CENTIMOS DBs.
ORCINUS ORCA

**Whales — A155**

**1992   Litho.   Perf. 14**

Designs: No. 1051, Orcinus orca. No. 1052, Orcinus orca, two under water. No. 1053, Pseudoraca crassidens. No. 1054, Pseudoraca crassidens, three under water.

**1992**
1051-1054  A155  450d  Set of 4   20.00
  World Wildlife Fund.

1992 Ano da visita de S.S. Papa J. Paulo II

S. TOMÉ E PRÍNCIPE

Visit of Pope John Paul II — A155a

75d, Leccinum ocabrum, 100d, Amanita spissa, horiz, 125d, Strugliomyces floccopus, 200d, Suillus luteus, 500d, Agaricus siluaticus, #1061, Amanita pantherma, horiz, #1062, Agaricus campestre.

**1992, Sept. 5** **Souvenir Sheets** **Perf. 14**
| | | | |
|---|---|---|---|
| 1056 | A157 | 75d multicolored | |
| 1057 | A157 | 100d multicolored | |
| 1058 | A157 | 125d multicolored | |
| 1059 | A157 | 200d multicolored | |
| 1060 | A157 | 500d multicolored | |
| | | Nos. 1056-1060 (5) | 10.00 |
| 1061 | A157 | 1000d multicolored | |
| 1062 | A157 | 1000d multicolored | |
| | | Nos. 1061-1062 (2) | 22.50 |

c, Flags, Pope, d, Church with two steeples, e, Church, diff. f, Pope, vert. g, Church, blue sky, vert. h, Church, closer view, vert.

**1992, Apr. 19** **Litho.** **Perf. 14**
**Sheets of 4**
| | | |
|---|---|---|
| 1054A | A155a | 200d #d.-g, 2 |
| | | #c |
| 1054B | A155a | 200d #g.-h., 2 |
| | | #f |
| | | Set | 20.00 |

Flora and Fauna Type of 1991

Designs: No. 1054I, 1000d, Brown & white bird, vert. No. 1054J, 1500d, Yellow flower, vert. No. 1054K, 2000d, Red flower, vert. No. 1054L, 2500d, Black bird, vert.

**1992, Apr. 19**
| | | |
|---|---|---|
| 1054I-1054L | A1440 Set of 4 | 35.00 |

Birds — A158

Designs: 75d, Paradisea regie, rupicole. 100d, Trogon paradisea, 200d, Pavecnictus. 500d, Ramphatos apotla, 2004. Paradisea apotla, 2004, Pavecrictotus. 500d, No. 1069, Picus major.

**1992, Sept. 15** **Perf. 14**
| | | | |
|---|---|---|---|
| 1063 | A158 | 75d multicolored | |
| 1064 | A158 | 100d multicolored | |
| 1065 | A158 | 125d multicolored | |
| 1066 | A158 | 200d multicolored | |
| 1067 | A158 | 500d multicolored | |
| | | Nos. 1063-1067 (5) | 8.00 |

**Souvenir Sheets** **Perf. 13½x14**
| | | | |
|---|---|---|---|
| 1068 | A158 | 1000d multicolored | |
| 1069 | A158 | 1000d multicolored | |
| | | Nos. 1068-1069 (2) | 20.00 |

UN Conference on Environmental Development, Rio — A155b

**1992, June 6** **Litho.** **Perf. 14**
| | | |
|---|---|---|
| 1054M-1054Q | A155b | |
| | | Set of 5 | 15.00 |

**Souvenir Sheets**
| | |
|---|---|
| 1054R-1054S | A155b 800d multi 15.00 |

S. TOMÉ E PRÍNCIPE

Db 75

Paradisea regie
Pipra rupicole

S. TOMÉ E PRÍNCIPE

Db 75

Olymphilex '92 — A156

**1992, June 6** **Litho.** **Perf. 14**
| | | |
|---|---|---|
| 1054M-1054Q | A155b | |

S. TOMÉ E PRÍNCIPE

Jogos Olimpicos de Verão
BARCELONA
92

**1992, July 29**
| | | | |
|---|---|---|---|
| 1055 | A156 | 300d Sheet of 3, #a.-c. | 11.50 |

Olympic athletes: a, Women's running. b, Women's gymnastics. c, Earvin "Magic" Johnson.

S. TOMÉ E PRÍNCIPE

Db 75

Mushrooms
A157

Db 75

**1992, Oct. 18**
75d, Chelonia purpurea, 100d, Hoetera philocteles, 125d, Attacus pavonia major, 200d, Ornithoptera urvilliana, 500d, Acheron- tia atropos, No. 1083, Peridrornia amphinome, vert. No. 1084, Urania riphacus, vert.

**Perf. 14x13½**
| | | | |
|---|---|---|---|
| 1078 | A161 | 75d multicolored | |
| 1079 | A161 | 100d multicolored | |
| 1080 | A161 | 125d multicolored | |
| 1081 | A161 | 200d multicolored | |
| 1082 | A161 | 500d multicolored | |
| | | Nos. 1078-1082 (5) | 8.00 |

**Souvenir Sheets** **Perf. 13½x14**
| | | | |
|---|---|---|---|
| 1083 | A161 | 1000d multicolored | |
| 1084 | A161 | 1000d multicolored | |
| | | Nos. 1083-1084 (2) | 16.00 |

Db 50

S. TOMÉ E PRÍNCIPE

WIN LYMPEG

1992, 1996 Summer Olympics, Barcelona and Atlanta — A162

**1992, Oct. 1** **Litho.** **Perf. 14**
| | | | |
|---|---|---|---|
| 1085 | A162 | 50d multicolored | |
| 1086 | A162 | 300d multicolored | |
| 1087 | A162 | 300d multicolored | |
| 1088 | A162 | 300d multicolored | |
| 1089 | A162 | 300d multicolored | |
| 1090 | A162 | 300d multicolored | |
| 1091 | A162 | 300d multicolored | |
| 1092 | A162 | 300d multicolored | |
| 1093 | A162 | 300d multicolored | |
| | | Set. Nos. | |
| | | 1085-1093 | |
| | | (9) | 20.00 |

50d, Wind surfing #1086, Wrestling, #1087, Women's 4x100 meters relay, #1088, Swim- ming. #1089, Equestrian, vert. #1090, Field hockey, #1091, Men's 4x100 meters relay, vert. #1092, Mascots for Barcelona and Atlanta, #1093, Opening ceremony, Barcelona.

#1094, Atlanta '96, Emblem, vert. #1095, Archer lighting Olympic Flame with flaming arrow, vert. #1096, Transfer of Olympic Flag, closing ceremony, vert. #1097, Gymnastics. #1098, Tennis players.

**Souvenir Sheets**
| | | | |
|---|---|---|---|
| 1094 | A162 | 800d multicolored | 10.00 |
| 1095 | A162 | 1000d multicolored | 8.00 |
| 1096 | A162 | 1000d multicolored | 8.00 |

**Perf. 13½**
| | | | |
|---|---|---|---|
| 1097 | A162 | 1000d multicolored | 7.25 |

**Perf. 14**
| | | | |
|---|---|---|---|
| 1098 | A162 | 1000d multicolored | 7.25 |

Db 50

MARCELO da VEIGA

S. TOMÉ E PRÍNCIPE

Marcelo da Veiga (1892-1976), Writer — A159

**1992, Oct. 3**
| | | |
|---|---|---|
| 1070 | A159 | Sheet of 4, #a.-d. | 3.50 |

Designs: a, 10d. b, 40d. c, 50d. d, 100d.

COMBOIOS

S. TOMÉ E PRÍNCIPE

Db 75

Locomotives — A160

**1992, Oct. 3** **Perf. 14x13½**
| | | | |
|---|---|---|---|
| 1071 | A160 | 75d black | |
| 1072 | A160 | 100d black | |
| 1073 | A160 | 125d black | |
| 1074 | A160 | 200d black | |
| 1075 | A160 | 500d black | |
| | | Nos. 1071-1075 (5) | 8.00 |

**Souvenir Sheets** **Perf. 13½**
| | | | |
|---|---|---|---|
| 1076 | A160 | 1000d black | |
| 1077 | A160 | 1000d black | |
| | | Nos. 1076-1077 (2) | 16.00 |

Designs: 75d, 100d, 125d, 200d, 500d, Vari- ous locomotives. No. 1076, Steam train arriv- ing at station. No. 1077, Engineer, stoker in locomotive cab.

S. TOMÉ E PRÍNCIPE

Db 500

FUCINHO DE PORCO

Flowers
A164

**1993, May 26** **Litho.** **Perf. 14**
| | | | |
|---|---|---|---|
| 1099-1103 | A163 | 500d Set of 5 | 12.00 |

**Souvenir Sheet**
| | | | |
|---|---|---|---|
| 1104 | A163 | 2000d multi | 18.00 |

Designs: No. 1099, White butterfly, No. 1100, Black and orange butterfly, No. 1101, Pink flower, black, white, red and blue butter- fly. No. 1102, Black and white butterfly on right side of flower stem. No. 1103, Yellow and black butterfly, 2000d, Iris flower, black butter- fly wing, horiz.

**1993, June 18**
| | | | |
|---|---|---|---|
| 1105 | A164 | 500d Fucinho de porco | |
| 1106 | A164 | 500d Heliconia | |
| 1107 | A164 | 500d Gravo nacion- al | |
| 1108 | A164 | 500d Tremessura | |
| 1109 | A164 | 500d Anturius | |
| | | Nos. 1105-1109 (6) | 18.00 |

**Souvenir Sheet**
| | | | |
|---|---|---|---|
| 1110 | A164 | 2000d Girassol | 14.00 |

Butterflies and Moths — A161

UC CLA

Db 100

S. TOMÉ E PRÍNCIPE

Union of Portuguese Speaking Capitals A165

**1993, July 30**
| | | | |
|---|---|---|---|
| 1111 | A165 | Sheet of 9, #a.-i. | 18.00 |

Designs: a, 100d, Emblem. b, 150d, Grotto. c, 200d, Statue of Christ the Redeemer, Rio de Janeiro. d, 250d, Skyscraper. e, 250d, Monument. f, 300d, Building with pointed domed roof. g, 350d, Municipal building. h, 400d, Square tower. i, 500d, Residence, flag, truck.

S. TOMÉ E PRÍNCIPE

Db 500

BORBOLETAS

Butterflies
A163

**1992, Oct. 3**
(same as above)

S. TOMÉ E PRÍNCIPE

Db 500

Birds — A166

**1993, June 15** **Litho.** **Perf. 14**
| | | | |
|---|---|---|---|
| 1112-1116 | A166 | 500d Set of 5 | 18.50 |

**Souvenir Sheet**
| | | | |
|---|---|---|---|
| 1117 | A166 | 1000d multi | 7.50 |

Designs: No. 1112, Cecla, No. 1113, Sui- sui. No. 1114, Falcon. No. 1115, Parrot. No. 1116, Heron. No. 1117, Macaw, toucan, horiz. Brasiliana '93.

S. TOMÉ E PRÍNCIPE

Db 500

CECA
1993

Dinosaurs — A167

#1118, Lystrosaurus. No. #1119, Patagosaurus. #1120, Shonisaurus Ictiosaurus, vert. #1121, Dilophosaurus, vert. #1122, Dicraeosaurus, vert. #123, Tyrannosaurus rex, vert.

**1993, July 21**
1118-1123  A167  500d  Set of 6  22.50
**Souvenir Sheets**
1124  A167  1000d  Protoavis
1125  A167  1000d  Brachiosaurus  15.00
Nos. 1124-1125 (2)

Mushrooms A168

**1993, May 25**  **Litho.**  **Perf. 14**
1126-1130  A168  800d  Set of 5  20.00
**Souvenir Sheets**
1131-1132  A168  2000d  Set of 2  20.00

#1126, Agrocybe aegerita. #1127, Psalliota arvensis. #1128, Coprinus comatus. #1129, Hygrophorus psittacinus. #1130, Amanita caesarea. #1131, Ramaria aurea. #1132, Pluteus murinus, horiz.

Locomotives — A169

#1133-1137, Various views of small diesel locomotive.
#1138-1139, Various steam locomotives, vert.

**1993, June 16**
1133-1137  A169  800d  Set of 5  27.50
**Souvenir Sheets**
1138-1139  A169  2000d  Set of 2  27.50

1994 World Cup Soccer Championships, U.S. — A170

Designs: No. 1140, Team photo. No. 1141, Players in white uniforms. No. 1142, Two players in yellow uniforms, player in red, white and blue uniform. No. 1143, Players with yellow shirts and green shorts celebrating. No. 1144, Two players in red and white uniforms, one player in red, white and blue uniform. No. 1145, Player in yellow and blue uniform, player in red, white and blue uniform. No. 1146, Two players and official. No. 1147, Two players, vert. No. 1148, Fans, faces painted as flags. No. 1149, Stylized player.

---

**1993, July 6**
1140-1147  A170  800d  Set of 8  32.50
**Souvenir Sheets**
1148-1149  A170  2000d  Set of 2  20.00

UPU Congress — A171

**1993, Aug. 16**
1150  A171  1000d shown  6.00
**Souvenir Sheet**
1151  A171  2000d  Ship  10.00

1996 Summer Olympics, Atlanta — A172

#1152, Fencing. #1153, Women's running. #1154, Water polo. #1155, Soccer. #1156, Men's running. #1157, Boxing. #1158, Wrestling. #1159, High jump. #1160, Shooting, vert. #1161, Sailing, vert. #1162, Equestrian, vert. #1163, Kayak, vert.

**1993, Oct. 19**  **Litho.**  **Perf. 13½x14**
1152-1159  A172  800d  Set of 8  40.00
**Souvenir Sheets**
1160-1163  A172  2000d  multi  10.00

1994 World Cup Soccer Championships, U.S. — A173

**1994, Jan. 12**  **Perf. 14**
1164  A173  500d  blk, bl & red  3.00
Issued in miniature sheets of 4.

Movie Stars — A174

#1165a, James Dean. b, Bette Davis. c, Elvis Presley. d, Humphrey Bogart. e, John Lennon. h, Audrey Hepburn.
#1166a-1166i, Various portraits of Elvis Presley.
#1167a-1167i, Various portraits of Marilyn Monroe.
#1168, James Dean, diff. #1169, Elvis Presley, diff #1169A, Marilyn Monroe.

**1994, Feb. 15**
1165  A174  10d  #a.-h.  5.00
1166-1167  A174  10d  #a.-i.  5.00

---

**Souvenir Sheets**
1168-1169  A174  50d  multi  5.00
1169A  A174  2000d  multi  15.00
Souvenir Sheet

Sydney 2000 — A175

**1994, June 8**
1170  A175  3000d multicolored  15.00

Signing of Argel Accord, 20th Anniv. A175a

**1994**  **Litho.**  **Perf. 14**
1170A  A175a  250d multi  20.00

Nos. 860, 979 Surcharged

d

Nos. 856, 979 Surcharged

e

**Methods and Perfs as Before**
**1995, Mar. 2**
1170B  A123p(d)  100d  on 25d
1170D  A123p(e)  350d  on 50c  #860
1170E  A123p(e)  350d  on 50c  #856
1170F  A144(e)  350d  on 1d
1170I  A144(d)  400d  on 5d  #978
1170J  A144(e)  400d  on 5d  #979
                              #979

Numbers have been reserved for additional surcharges. The editors would like to examine any examples.

Butterflies A176

---

#1171, Timeleoa maqulata-formosana. #1172, Morfho cypris. #1173, Thais polixena. #1174, Argema moenas. #1175, Leptocircus megus-emius. 2000d, Armandia lidderdalei.

**1995, May 10**  **Litho.**  **Perf. 14**
1171-1175  A176  1200d  Set of 5  16.00
**Souvenir Sheet**
1176  A176  2000d  multi  8.00

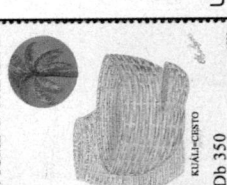

Flowering Fruits, Orchids A177

Flowering fruits: No. #1177, 350d, Pessego. #1178, 370d, Untue. #1179, 380d, Pitanga. #1180, 800d, Morango. #1181, 1000d, Izaquente.
Orchids: No. 1182, Max. houtteana. No. 1183, Max. marginata.

**1995, June 6**
1177-1181  A177  Set of 5  16.00
**Souvenir Sheets**
1182-1183  A177  2000d each  16.00

Mushrooms A179

Designs: No. 1185, Lactarius deliciosus. No. 1186, Marasmius oreades. No. 1187, Boletus edulis. No. 1188, Boletus aurantiacus. No. 1189, Lepiota procera. No. 1190, Cortinarius praestans.
No. 1191, Chantharellus cibarius. No. 1102, Lycoperdon pyriforme, horiz.

**1995, Nov. 2**  **Litho.**  **Perf. 14**
1185-1190  A179  1000d  Set of 6  16.00
**Souvenir Sheets**
1191-1192  A179  2000d each  16.00

Traditional handicrafts made from palm leaves: No. 1193, 350d, Baskets. No. 1194, 350d, Brooms. No. 1195, 400d, Lamp shades. No. 1196, 500d, Klissakil, mussuá. No. 1197, 500d, Pávu. No. 1198, 1000d, Vámplégá.

**1995, June 20**  **Litho.**  **Perf. 13½x14**
1193-1198  A180  Set of 6  8.00

UN, 50th Anniv. — A180

## Trains—A181

**1995, July 24** **Perf. 14x13½, 13½x14**
1199-1204 A181 1000d Set of 6 25.00
**Souvenir Sheets**
1205-1206 A181 2000d multi 21.00
See Nos. 1280-1286.

Locomotives: No. 1199, Steam, "#100." No. 1200, Steam, "#778." No. 1201, G. Thommen steam. No. 1202, Steam "#119." Vert. No. 1203, Mt. Washington cog railway; vert. No. 1205, Electric train on snow-covered mountain, vert. No. 1206, Electric train car with door open, vert.

## Dogs & Cats—A182

**1995, Aug. 12** **Perf. 14**
1207-1208 A182 1000d Sheets of 9, #a.-i. 50.00
1209-1212 A182 2000d Sheets of 9, #a.-i. multicolored 45.00

No. 1207: Various dogs, b, d, f, h, vert. No. 1208: Various cats b, d, f, h, vert. No. 1209, St. Bernard, German shepherd. No. 1210, Beagle, vert. No. 1211, Cat, kittens. No. 1212, Kitten on top of mother, vert.

HOMENAGEM AO CINEMA

**New Year 1996 (Year of the Rat) A183**

**1995, Oct. 28**
1213 A183 100d Sheet of 9, #a.-i. 6.00

Various species of rats, mice.

## Motion Pictures, Cent.—A184

Movie posters from: No. 1214: a, Gone with the Wind. b, Stagecoach. c, Tarzan and His Mate. d, Oregon Trail. e, The Oklahoma Kid. f,

King Kong: g, A Lady Fights Back, h, Steamboat Around the Bend. i, Wee Willie Winkie. Indian chief.

**1995, May 10** **Litho.** **Perf. 14**
1214 A184 1000d Sheet of 9, #a.-i. 16.00
1215, Bring 'Em Back Alive. No. 1216 Indian chief.
**Souvenir Sheets**
1215-1216 A184 2000d multi 16.00

CAVALOS

## Horses—A185

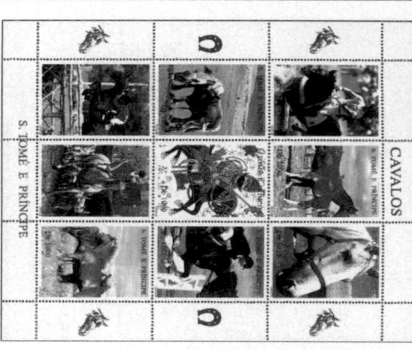

**1995, May 16**
1217 A185 1000d Sheet of 9, #a.-i. 16.00
**Souvenir Sheets**
1218-1219 A185 2000d multi 16.00

Designs: No. 1217, Various horses. No. 1218, Painting of Indian on horse, wild horses, horiz. No. 1219, City scene, horses, carriage, horiz. Nos. 1218-1219 each contain one 50x35mm stamp.

## Souvenir Sheet

Illustration reduced.
**1995, July 2** **Perf. 13½x14**
1220 A186 2000d multicolored 8.00

**Euro '96, European Soccer Championships, Great Britain—A186**

S. TOMÉ E PRÍNCIPE

## Souvenir Sheet

**Protection of World's Endangered Species—A187**

## Mushrooms—A188

**1995, Nov. 2**
1222 A188 1000d Sheet of 9, #a.-i. 16.00
**Souvenir Sheets**
1223-1224 A188 2000d multi 16.00

Designs: No. 1222a, Xerocomus rubellus. b, Rozites caperata. c, Cortinarius violaceus. d, Pholiota flammans. e, Lactarius volemus. f, Cortinarius (yellow). g, Cartinarius (blue). h, Higroforo. i, Boletus chrysenteron. No. 1223, Amanita muscaria, vert. No. 1224, Russula cyanoxantha, vert.

**1995, July 6** **Perf. 14**
1221 A187 2000d multicolored 8.00

PINTURAS

## Details or Entire Paintings—A189

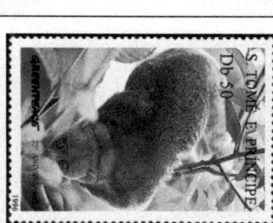

No. 1225: a, Aurora and Cefalo. b, Madonna and Child with St. John as a Boy. c, Romulus and Remus. d, Lamentation over the Dead Christ. e, Vison of All Saints Day. f, Perseus and Andromeda. g, The Scent. h, The Encounter in Lyon. i, The Art School of Rubens-Bildern. No. 1226, Statue of Ceres. No. 1227, Flight into Egypt, horiz. All but #1225g (Jan Brueghel the Elder) and 1225i are by Rubens.

**1995, Sept. 27** **Litho.** **Perf. 14**
1225 A189 1000d Sheet of 9, #a.-i. 20.00
**Souvenir Sheets**
1226-1227 A189 2000d each 10.00

## Souvenir Sheet

**Greenpeace, 25th Anniv.—A190**

Designs: No. 1237, Potto. No. 1238, Iguana. No. 1239, Tiger. No. 1240, Lion. 500d, Elephant, horiz.

**1996, Aug. 5** **Litho.** **Perf. 14**
1237-1240 A190 50d Set of 4 20.00
**Souvenir Sheet**
1241 A190 50d multicolored 6.00

## Dogs & Cats—A191

**1995, Aug. 12** **Litho.** **Perf. 14**
1242-1243 A191 1000d Sheets of 9, #a.-i., ea 22.50
**Souvenir Sheets**
1244-1250 A191 2000d each 16.00

Nos. 1242a-1242i: Various pictures of dogs with cats, kittens. Nos. 1243a-1243i, vert. Various close-up pictures of different breeds of dogs. No. 1244, woman's pet. No. 1245, Bird, woman's pet. No. 1246, Two kittens. No. 1247, Collie, vert. No. 1248, Poodle, vert. No. 1249, Pit bull terrier, vert. No. 1250, Brown and white terrier, vert.

## Orchids A192

**1995, Sept. 12**
1251 A192 1000d Sheet of 9, #a.-i. 16.00
**Souvenir Sheets**
1252-1253 A192 2000d multi 16.00

No. 1251: a, Findlayanum. b, Stan. c, Cruentum. d, Trpla suavis. e, Lowianum. f, Gratiosissimum. g, Cyrtorchis monteiras. h, Sarcanthus birmanicus. i, Loddigesii. No. 1252, Barkeria Skinneri. No. 1253, Dendrobium nobile.

## Paintings, Drawings by Durer, Rubens—A193

NATAL 95

Designs: No. 1254, Soldier on Horseback, by Durer, vert. No. 1255, Archangel St. Michael Slaying Satan, by Rubens, vert. No. 1256, Nursing Madonna in Half Length, by Durer, vert. No. 1257, Head of a Deer, by Durer, vert. No. 1258, View of Innsbruck from the North, by Durer. No. 1259, Madonna Nursing on a Grassy Bench, by Durer, vert. No. 1260, Helene Fourment and Her Children, by Rubens, vert. No. 1261, Adam and Eve, by Rubens. No. 1262, A Young Hare by Durer, vert. No. 1263, Mills on a River Bank, by Durer. No. 1264, Holy Family with a Basket, by Rubens, vert. No. 1265, The Annunciation, by Rubens, vert.

**1995, Dec. 16** **Litho.** **Perf. 14**
1254-1261 A193 750d Set of 8 20.00
**Souvenir Sheets**
1262-1265 A193 2000d each 20.00
Christmas.

**Methods and Perfs as Before**

**1997, Apr. 16**
1307A A144 1000d on 250d multi ... 25.00

Diana, Princess of Wales (1961-97) — A202

No. 1308: Various portraits, vert. 100d, Diana taking with her sons (in sheet margin), vert. 500d, Portrait. Diana, Mother Teresa (in sheet margin), vert.

**1997    Litho.    Perf. 14**
1308 A202   10d  Sheet of 9, #a.-i. ... 4.00

**Souvenir Sheets**
**Perf. 13½x14, 14x13½**
1309 A202  100d multicolored ... 6.00
1310 A202  500d gold & multi ... 8.00
1311 A202 2000d gold & multi ... 16.00

Issued: #1308, 100d, 500d, 10/15/97; 2000d, 10/20/97.

Michael Schumacher, World Champion Formula I Driver — A203

Illustration reduced.

**1997, Dec. 12    Perf. 14**
1312 A203 500d multicolored ... 10.00

Souvenir Sheets

S. TOMÉ E PRÍNCIPE

Titanic — A205

Designs: No. 1319, 2000d, Captain and Titanic (multicolored). No. 1320, 2000d, Captain and Titanic (black).

**1998, July 1    Litho.    Perf. 14x13¾**
1319-1320 A205 ... Set of 2

Numbers are reserved for two additional items in this set. The editors would like to examine two examples.

---

Nos. 736-737, 744, 746, 748
Surcharged
in Blue or Black

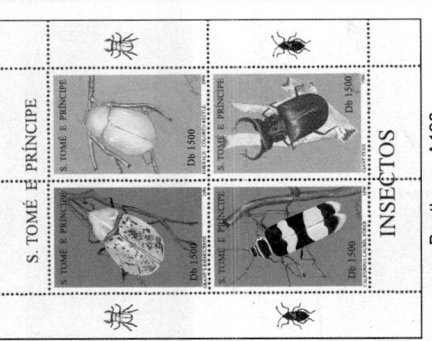

**Perfs. & Printing Methods as Before**
**1996?**
1295  A123p  350d on 1d #857
1295A A123p  400d on 5d #858
1295D A133  500d on 60d #914
1296  A95  1000d on 11d #736 (BI)
1297  A95  1000d on 12d #737 (BI)
1298  A95  1000d on 42d #746 (BI)
1299  A95  2500d on 100d #744 (BI)
1300  A95  2500d on 100d #748 (BI)

Set ... 250.00

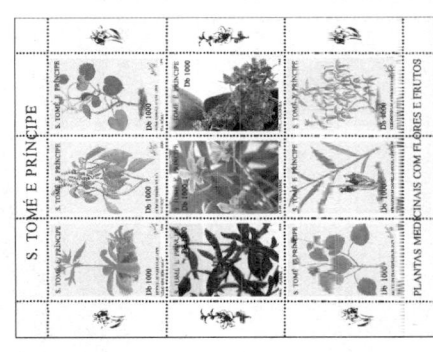

Musicians, Musical Instruments A200

"The Beatles" — #1301: a, John Lennon. b, Paul McCartney. c, George Harrison. d, Ringo Starr. Traditional instruments — #1302: a, Animal horn. b, Flutes. c, Tambourine, drum, sticks. d, Canza.

**1996, Nov. 19    Litho.    Perf. 13½x14**
**Sheets of 4**
1301-1302 A200 1500d #a.-d., ea ... 18.00

**Souvenir Sheets**
1303-1304 A200 2000d each ... 10.00

Fish A201

#1305: a, Sailfish. b, Barracuda. c, Cod. d, Atlantic mackerel. #1306, Bluefin tuna. #1307, Squirrelfish.

**1996, Dec. 10    Perf. 14x13½**
1305 A201 1500d  Sheet of 4, #a.-d. ... 18.00

**Souvenir Sheets**
1306-1307 A201 2000d each ... 10.00

No. 988
Surcharged in
Dark Blue

---

INSECTOS

Beetles — A198

#1287: a, Grant's rhinoceros. b, Emerald-colored. c, California laurel borer. d, Giant stag.  Maple borer. #1288, Maple borer. #1289, Arizona june.

**1996, Nov. 7    Perf. 13½x14**
1287 A198 1500d  Sheet of 4, #a.-d. ... 18.00

**Souvenir Sheets**
1288-1289 A198 2000d each ... 10.00

Plants, Orchids — A199

No. 1290: a, Eryngium foetidum. b, Ocimum viride. c, Piper umbellatum. d, Phal. mariae. e, Odm. chiriquense. f, Phal. gigantea. g, Abutilon grandiflorum. h, Aframomium danielli. i, Chenopodium ambrosiodes. No. 1291, Crinum jacus. No. 1292, Oncoba spinosa forsk. No. 1293, Z. mackai. No. 1294, Aspasia principissa.

**1996, Oct. 14**
1290 A199 1000d  Sheet of 9, #a.-i. ... 25.00

**Souvenir Sheets**
1291-1294 A199 2000d each ... 10.00

Nos. 857-858 Surcharged

---

ST. THOMAS AND PRINCE ISLANDS

Independence, 20th Anniv. — A194

**1996, July 12    Litho.    Perf. 13½**
1266 A194  350d multicolored ... 5.00

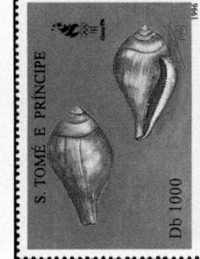

Various shells.

**1996, Jan. 10    Litho.    Perf. 14**
1267-1271 A195 1000d multicolored ... 16.00

**Souvenir Sheet**
1272 A195 2000d multicolored ... 16.00

1996 Summer Olympic Games, Atlanta — A195

Anniversaries and Events — A196

**1996, Aug. 2    Perf. 14x13½**
1273 A196  500d multicolored ... 6.00

UNICEF, 50th anniv., Alfred Nobel, 150th anniv. of birth, Phila-Seoul 96, KOREA 2002, 1996 Summer Olympic Games, Atlanta.

UNESCO A197

Butterflies: No. 1274, Papilio weiskei. No. 1275, Heliconius melpomene. No. 1276, Papilio arcas-mylotes. No. 1277, Mesomenia cresus. No. 1278, Catagramma lyca-satrana. No. 1279, Lemonius sudias.

**1996, Sept. 10    Perf. 13½x14**
1274-1278 A197 1000d  Set of 5 ... 16.00

**Souvenir Sheet**
1279 A197 2000d multicolored ... 10.00

Train Type of 1995

No. 1280, SNCF. No. 1281, CN. No. 1282, White locomotive. No. 1283, Green locomotive. No. 1284, Train in city. No. 1285, Modern train. No. 1286, Old train.

**1996, Oct. 7    Perf. 14**
1280-1284 A181 1000d  Set of 5 ... 16.00

**Souvenir Sheets**
1285-1286 A181 2000d each ... 20.00

## Expo '98, Lisbon — A206

Sea around the islands: No. 1326, Man fishing from shore. No. 1327, Man in small sailboat, sharks in water below. No. 1328, Flying fish. No. 1329, Diver connecting line on sea bottom. No. 1330, Man paddling boat, turtle, fish below. Map of St. Thomas & Prince, vert. 8000d, Map of St. Thomas & Prince, vert.

**1998**    Litho.    *Perf. 14*
1326-1330 A206 3500d Set of 5   16.00

**Souvenir Sheet**
1331 A206 8000d multicolored   20.00

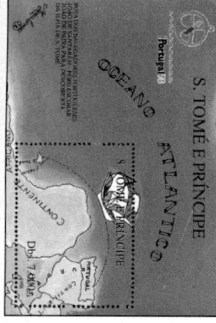

## 2nd AICEP Philatelic Exhibition — A207

Traditional food: No. 1333, Feijão de coco, coconuts. No. 1334, Molho no fogo, fish, fruit, wine. No. 1335, Calulu, fruits, vegetables, wine. No. 1336, Izaquente de açucar, sugar beet. 7000d, Pot cooking over open fire, vert.

**1998, Aug. 1**    *Perf. 14x13¾*
1332-1336 A207 3500d Set of 5   16.00

**Souvenir Sheet**
1337 A207 7000d multicolored   20.00

 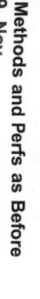

## Portugal 98 Stamp Exhibition — A210

**1998, Sept. 4**   Litho.   *Perf. 14x13¾*
1342 A210 7000d Ship on map   15.00

Two stamps were issued with the souvenir sheet. The editors would like to examine them.

**Methods and Perfs as Before**

Nos. 728, 735, 739 Surcharged

**1999, Nov.**
1361 A95 5000d on 15.50d   10.00   10.00
1362 A95 7000d on 10d #735   15.00   15.00
   #739
1363 A95 10,000d on 1d #728   20.00   20.00
Nos. 1361-1363 (3)   45.00   45.00

---

## Christmas — A211

Designs: Nos. 1364, 1367, 5000d, Adoration of the Shepherds. Nos. 1365, 1368, 6000d. Presentation of Jesus in the Temple. Nos. 1366, 1369, 10,000d, Flight into Egypt.

**1999, Dec. 23**   Litho.   *Perf. 12¾x13*
1364-1366 A211 Set of 3   6.50   6.50

**Souvenir Sheets**
1367-1369 A211 Set of 3   6.50   6.50

Stamps on Nos. 1367-1369 have continuous designs.

## Independence, 25th Anniv. — A213

No. 1371: a, 5000d, Mountain, bird. b, 6000d, Stylized mountains, birds, flag. c, 7000d, Mountains, '25', flag. d, 10,000d, Mountain, bird, diff.

**2000, July 12**   Litho.   *Perf. 12¾*
1371 A213 Sheet of 4, #a-f   6.75   6.75

## Holy Year 2000 — A216

Designs: No. 1381a, 3000d, God, the Father. No. 1381b, 5000d, St. Anne, Virgin Mary, infant Jesus. No. 1378, St. Thomas. No. 1381d, 6000d, cross. Nos. 1379, 1381e, 7000d, Processional cross. Nos. 1380, 1381f, 8000d, Cathedral.

**2000, Dec. 21**   *Perf. 12¾*

**With "Natal 2000" Inscription**
1378-1380 A216 Set of 3   6.00   6.00

**Without "Natal 2000" Inscription**
1381 A216 Sheet of 6, #a-f   11.50   11.50
   1381a-g.
   1381b, 1381d-1381e, perf. 12

---

**2000, Oct. 6**   *Perf. 12¾*
1377 A215 15,000d multi   3.25   3.25

## España 2000 Intl. Philatelic Exhibition — A215

**Souvenir Sheet**

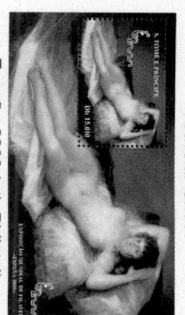 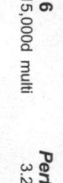 

**2000, Oct. 6**   *Perf. 12¾*
1377 A215 15,000d multi   3.25   3.25

## Souvenir Sheet

## Worldwide Fund for Nature (WWF) A220

**2001, Oct.**   *Perf. 12¾*
1400-1403 A220 Set of 4   4.75   4.75

Lepidochelys olivacea: 3500d, One swimming. 5000d, Two swimming. 6000d, Three leaving water. 7500d, Three hatchlings in sand.

Nos. 1400-1403 were each issued in sheets of four. The margin of each of the four stamps on the sheets differs. See also No. 1431.

## Famous Men — A221

**2002**   Litho.   *Perf. 13¼*
1404-1407 A221 Set of 4   14.00   14.00

Designs: No. 1404, 15,000d, Charlie Chaplin (1889-1977), comedian. No. 1405, 15,000d, Louis Armstrong (1900-71), musician. No. 1406, 15,000d, Walt Disney (1901-66), film producer, vert. No. 1407, 15,000d, Giuseppe Verdi (1813-1901), composer, vert.

Issued: No. 1404, 3/11; No. 1405, 3/12; No. 1406, 3/13; No. 1407, 3/14.

---

## 2000 Summer Olympics, Sydney — A214

Olympic rings and: 5000d, Runner, stadium, kangaroos, bird. 7000d, Runner, Sydney Opera House, kangaroos, emu. 15,000d, Sydney Harbour Bridge, Opera House, kangaroo, horiz.

**2000, Sept. 14**   Litho.   *Perf. 12¾*
1374-1375 A214 Set of 2   4.00   4.00

**Souvenir Sheet**   *Perf. 13*
1376 A214 15,000d multi   5.00   5.00

**Methods & Perfs as Before**

Nos. 746, 748 Surcharged

**2000, Aug. 7**
1372 A95 5000d on 42d multi   1.60   1.60
1373 A95 5000d on 100d multi   1.60   1.60

## Rosa de Porcellana A218

Flower in: Nos. 1391, 5000d, 1393a, 7000d, Pink. Nos. 1392, 5000d, 1393b, 8000d, Red.

**2001, Apr. 12**   Litho.   *Perf. 13¾x14*
1391-1392 A218 Set of 2   2.75   2.75

**Souvenir Sheet**
1393 A218 Sheet of 2, #a-b   4.00   4.00

## Butterflies A219

**2001, July 15**   *Perf. 13¼x13½*
1394-1397 A219 Set of 4   5.75   5.75

**Souvenir Sheets**
1398 A219 Sheet of 4, #a-d   5.75   5.75
1399 A219 15,000d multi   4.00   4.00

Designs: No. 1394, 3500d, Graphium leonidas (brown frame). No. 1395, 5000d, Acraea newtoni (bright red frame). No. 1396, 6000d, Papilio bromius (bright red frame). No. 1397, 7500d, Papilio dardanos (brown frame). No. 1398: a, 3500d, Graphium leonidas (orange frame). b, 5000d, Acraea newtoni (dark red frame). c, 6000d, Papilio bromius (dark red frame). d, 7500d, Papilio dardanos (orange frame). 15,000d, Euchloron megaera serrei.

## Insects A222

**2002, Mar. 15**   *Perf. 13¼x13½*
1408-1411 A222 Set of 4   5.25   5.25

**Souvenir Sheet**

Designs: No. 1408, 5000d, Euchroea clementi. No. 1409, 5000d, Dicranorrhina derbyana. No. 1410, 50000d, Polybothris sumptuosa gutata. 8000d, Polybothris sumptuosa gemma.

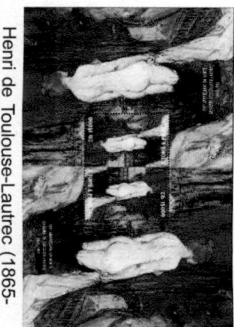

## Henri de Toulouse-Lautrec (1865-1901), Painter — A223

**2002, Mar. 16**   *Perf. 13¼x13¼x13¼x Rouletted*
1412 A223 15,000d Sheet of 2   7.00   7.00

Stamps in souvenir are tete-beche. The rouletting continues through the selvage allowing the sheet to be broken up into two half-sheets.

ST. THOMAS AND PRINCE ISLANDS

Souvenir Sheets

**Chinese Zodiac Animals — A224**

No. 1413, 15,000d: a, Rat. b, Tiger. c, Ox. d, Rabbit.
No. 1414, 15,000d: a, Dragon. b, Horse. c, Snake. d, Goat.
No. 1416, 15,000d: a, Monkey. b, Dog. c, Cock. d, Pig.

**2002**

| | | | | Perf. |
|---|---|---|---|---|
| 1413-1415 | A224 | Set of 3 | | 42.50 42.50 |

Each sheet was rouletted into quadrants.

In Remembrance of Sept. 11, 2001 Terrorist Attacks — A225

**Perf. 13½x13¼**

| | | With White Frame | |
|---|---|---|---|
| 2002, May 27 | | | |
| 1416 | A225 | 5000d multi | 1.25 1.25 |

**Souvenir Sheet**
**Without White Frame**

| 1417 | A225 | 15,000d multi | 3.50 3.50 |

No. 1417 contains one 40x51mm stamp.

Souvenir Sheet

**Barcelona Architecture of Antonio Gaudi — A226**

No. 1418: a, 7000d, Casa Battló (dark brown building, 27x41mm). b, 7000d, Casa Mila (light building, 27x41mm). c, 20,000d, Church of Sagrada Familia (29x47mm).

**Perf. 13½x13¼, 13¼ (#1418c)**

| 2002, Sept. 28 | | | |
|---|---|---|---|
| 1418 | A226 | Sheet, #a-c | 7.75 7.75 |

A column of rouletting separates the sheet into two halves, one containing Nos. 1418a-1418b, and the other containing No. 1418c. An additional column of rouletting is found at the left side of the half sheet containing No. 1418c.

---

**Perf. 13½x13¼** **Litho.**

| | | | | 6.00 6.00 |
|---|---|---|---|---|
| 2002, Nov. 19 | A227 | Set of 4 | | |

**Souvenir Sheet**

| 1419-1422 | | | | |
| 1424 | A227 | 20,000d multi | 4.50 4.50 |

A number has been reserved for an additional item in this set.

**Birds — A228**

Designs: 1000d, Nectarinia newtonii. 7000d, Prinior molleri. 9000d, Neospiza concolor. 10,000d, Lanius newtoni. 20,000d, Otus hartlaubi.

**Perf. 13½x13¼** **Litho.**

| | | | | 6.00 6.00 |
|---|---|---|---|---|
| 2002, Nov. 20 | | | | |
| 1425-1428 | A228 | Set of 4 | | |
| 1428a | | Souvenir sheet, #1425-1428 | | 6.00 6.00 |

**Souvenir Sheet**

| 1429 | A228 | 20,000d multi | 4.50 4.50 |

Miniature Sheet

**Circus Animals — A229**

No. 1430: a, 2000d, Horses (30x40mm). b, 6000d, Chimpanzees (30x40mm). c, 9000d, Seals (30x40mm). d, 10,000d, Tigers (30x40mm). e, 20,000d, Elephants (60x80mm).

**Perf. 13½x13** | |
|---|---|
| 2002, Nov. 22 | |
| 1430 | A229 | Sheet of 5, #a-e | 10.50 10.50 |

A column of rouletting separates the sheet into two halves, one containing Nos. 1430a-1430d and the other containing No. 1430e.

**Worldwide Fund for Nature Type of 2001**

**Souvenir Sheet**

No. 1431 — Lepidochelys olivacea: a, 6000d, Two swimming. b, 6000d, Three hatchlings in sand. c, 7000d, One swimming. d, 7000d, Three leaving water.

**Perf. 13½x13¼**

| 2002, Dec. 31 | | | |
|---|---|---|---|
| 1431 | A220 | Sheet of 4, #a-d | 6.00 6.00 |

---

Souvenir Sheet

**The Last Supper, by Leonardo da Vinci — A231**

**Perf. 13½x13¼**

| 2003, Apr. 17 | | | | 5.75 5.75 |
|---|---|---|---|---|
| 1435 | A231 | 25,000d multi | | |

Easter.

**Crustaceans — A232**

Designs: Nos. 1436, 1440a, 3500d, Coenobita perlatus. Nos. 1437, 1440b, 7000d, Carcinus maenas. Nos. 1438, 1440c, 8000d, Uca tetragonnn. Nos. 1439, 1440d, 9000d, Ovalipes ocellatus.
20,000d, Panulirus pencillatus.

**Perf. 13¼x13½**

| | | With White Frames | | |
|---|---|---|---|---|
| 2003, Apr. 24 | A232 | | | |
| 1436-1439 | A232 | | 6.25 6.25 |

**Without White Frames**

| 1440 | A232 | Sheet of 4, #a-d | | 6.25 6.25 |

**Souvenir Sheet**

| 1441 | A232 | 20,000d multi | | 4.50 4.50 |

**Vincent van Gogh (1853-90), Painter — A233**

Paintings: No. 1442, 6000d, Young Peasant Woman with Straw Hat Sitting in the Wheat, 1890. No. 1443, 6000d, Head of a Peasant Woman with White Cap, 1885. No. 1444, 7000d, Patience Escalier. No. 1445, 7000d, Charles Elzéard Trabuc.
No. 1446 — Self-portraits from: a, 6000d, 1886 (head at left). b, 6000d, 1886 (head at right). c, 7000d, 1888. d, 7000d, 1889.

**2003, May 30** **Litho.** **Perf. 13½x13**

| 1442-1445 | A233 | Set of 4 | | 5.75 5.75 |
|---|---|---|---|---|

**Souvenir Sheet**

| 1446 | A233 | Sheet of 4, #a-d | | 5.75 5.75 |

---

**Space Travelers — A230**

Designs: 6000d, Laika. 7000d, Yuri Gagarin. 8000d, Dennis Tito.

**Perf. 13x13¼**

| 2003, Feb. 20 | | | | 4.75 4.75 |
|---|---|---|---|---|
| 1432-1434 | A230 | Set of 3 | | |
| 1434a | | Souvenir sheet, #1432-1434, perf. 12½x12¾ | | 4.75 4.75 |

**Skull With Burning Cigarette, by Vincent van Gogh — A234**

**2003, May 31** | | | |
|---|---|---|---|
| 1447 | A234 | 7000d multi | 1.60 1.60 |

WHO anti-smoking campaign.

---

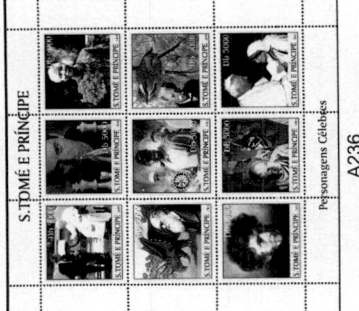

A235

Personagens Célebres

A236

Personagens Célebres

A237

Personagens Célebres

**Famous People — A237**

No. 1448: a, Lord Robert Baden-Powell, dogs. b, Pres. George W. Bush, rescue workers. c, Pope John Paul II, Galileo. d, Astronaut Neil Armstrong, Russian cosmonaut. e, Vincent van Gogh self-portrait and painting. f, Louis Pasteur, cat. g, Sir Alexander Fleming, mushrooms. h, Elvis Presley on motorcycle, automobile. i, Walt Disney, dog.
No. 1449: a, Pope John Paul II, Pres. George W. Bush. b, Male chess player. c, Nelson Mandela, mineral. d, Charles Darwin, dinosaur. e, Tiger Woods, Rotary emblem. f, Dr. Albert Schweitzer, bird. g, Hector Berlioz. h, Pablo Picasso and painting. i, Pope John Paul II and Mother Teresa.
No. 1450: a, Pope John Paul II and UN Secretary General Kofi Annan. b, Formula 1 race car driver and car. c, Lady Olave Baden-Powell, cat. d, Female chess player. e, Sir Rowland Hill, train. f, Rotary emblem, Lions emblem and founders. g, Henri Dunant, Princess Diana. h, Paul Gauguin and painting. i, Pope John Paul II, Princess Diana.

**2003** **Litho.** **Perf. 12¾x13¼**

| 1448 | A235 | 5000d | Sheet of 9, #a-i | 10.00 10.00 |
|---|---|---|---|---|
| 1449 | A236 | 5000d | Sheet of 9, #a-i | 10.00 10.00 |
| 1450 | A237 | 5000d | Sheet of 9, #a-i | 30.00 30.00 |

Nos. 1448-1450 (3)

Each stamp exists in a souvenir sheet of 1.

---

**Orchids — A227**

Designs: 2000d, Phalus mannil. 6000d, Cyrtorchis arcuata. 9000d, Calanthe sylvatica. 10,000d, Bulbophyllum iizae. 20,000d, Bulbophyllum saltatorium.

## Reign of Pope John Paul II, 25th Anniv. — A241

Various photographs of Pope John Paul II.

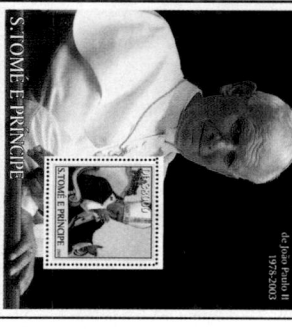 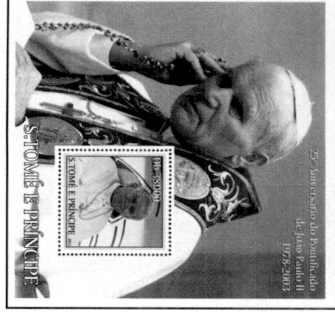 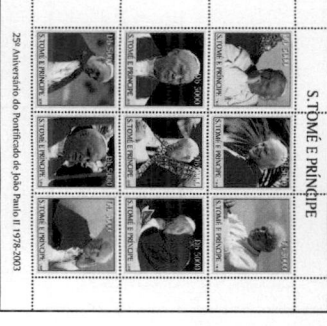  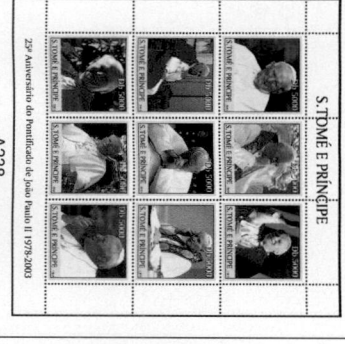

**2003**

| | | | | |
|---|---|---|---|---|
| **1451** | A238 | 5000d Sheet of 9, | 10.00 | 10.00 |
| | | #a-i | 10.00 | |
| **1452** | A239 | 5000d Sheet of 9, | 10.00 | 10.00 |
| | | #a-i | 10.00 | |
| | | **Souvenir Sheets** | | |
| **1453** | A240 | 38,000d multi | 8.50 | 8.50 |
| **1454** | A241 | 38,000d multi | 8.50 | 8.50 |

## Marilyn Monroe (1926-62), Actress — A245

Various Marilyn Monroe photographs and magazine covers.

**2003**

| | | | | |
|---|---|---|---|---|
| **1455** | A242 | 5000d Sheet of 9, | 10.00 | 10.00 |
| | | #a-i | 10.00 | |
| **1456** | A243 | 5000d Sheet of 9, | 10.00 | 10.00 |
| | | #a-i | 10.00 | |
| | | **Souvenir Sheets** | | |
| **1457** | A244 | 38,000d multi | 8.50 | 8.50 |
| **1458** | A245 | 38,000d multi | 8.50 | 8.50 |

## Ancient Egyptian Monuments — A249

Various photographs.

  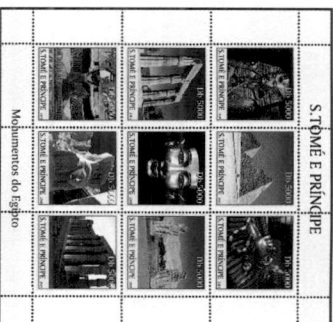 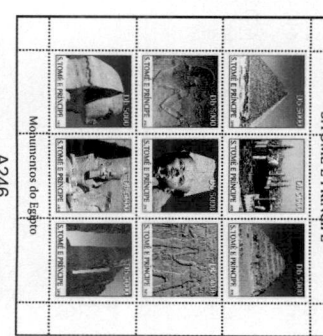

**2003**

| | | | | |
|---|---|---|---|---|
| **1459** | A246 | 5000d Sheet of 9, | 10.00 | 10.00 |
| | | #a-i | 10.00 | |
| **1460** | A247 | 5000d Sheet of 9, | 10.00 | 10.00 |
| | | #a-i | 10.00 | |
| | | **Souvenir Sheets** | | |
| **1461** | A248 | 38,000d multi | 8.50 | 8.50 |
| **1462** | A249 | 38,000d multi | 8.50 | 8.50 |

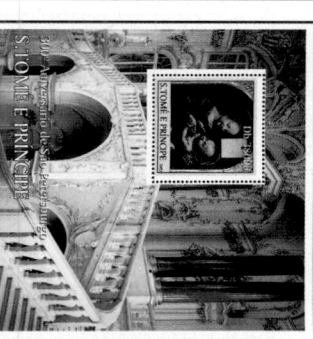 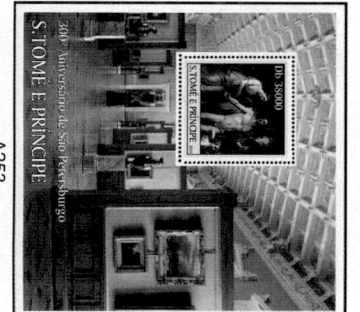 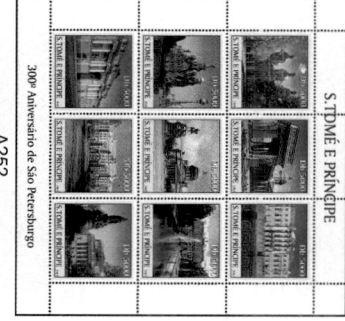  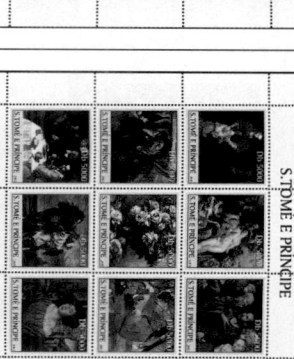

300º Aniversário de São Petersburgo

# ST. THOMAS AND PRINCE ISLANDS

**S. TOMÉ E PRÍNCIPE**

St. Petersburg, Russia, 300th Anniv. — A255

Various unnamed paintings or buildings.

**2003**
| | | | |
|---|---|---|---|
| 1463 | A250 | 5000d | Sheet of 9, #a-i | 10.00 | 10.00 |
| 1464 | A251 | 5000d | Sheet of 9, #a-i | 10.00 | 10.00 |
| 1465 | A252 | 5000d | Sheet of 9, #a-i | 10.00 | 10.00 |
| | | | Nos. 1463-1465 (3) | 30.00 | 30.00 |

**Souvenir Sheets**
| | | | |
|---|---|---|---|
| 1466 | A253 | 38,000d multi | 8.50 | 8.50 |
| 1467 | A254 | 38,000d multi | 8.50 | 8.50 |
| 1468 | A255 | 38,000d multi | 8.50 | 8.50 |

Fire Vehicles — A259

Nos. 1469 — Various pictures of volcanoes and minerals: a, 1000d, With firefighter. b, 2000d, Without firefighter. c, 3000d, With firefighter. d, 5000d, Without firefighter. e,

---

6000d, With firefighter. f, 15,000d, Without firefighter.

Nos. 1470 — Various pictures of volcanoes and minerals: a, 1000d, Without firefighter. b, 2000d, With firefighter. c, 3000d, Without firefighter. d, 5000d, With firefighter. e, 6000d, Without firefighter. f, 15,000d, With firefighter. Without firefighter. — Various fire vehicles: a, 1000d. b, 2000d. c, 3000d. d, 5000d. e, 6000d. f, 15,000d.

*Perf. 12¾x13¼, 13¼x12¾ (#1474)*
| | | | | |
|---|---|---|---|---|
| 1469 | A256 | Sheet of 6, #a-f | 7.25 | 7.25 |
| 1470 | A257 | Sheet of 6, #a-f | 7.25 | 7.25 |
| 1471 | A258 | Sheet of 6, #a-f | 7.25 | 7.25 |
| 1472 | A259 | Sheet of 6, #a-f | 7.25 | 7.25 |
| | | Nos. 1469-1472 (4) | 29.00 | 29.00 |

**Souvenir Sheets**
| | | | |
|---|---|---|---|
| 1473 | A256 | 38,000d multi | 8.50 | 8.50 |
| 1474 | A257 | 38,000d multi | 8.50 | 8.50 |
| 1475 | A258 | 38,000d multi | 8.50 | 8.50 |
| 1476 | A259 | 38,000d multi | 8.50 | 8.50 |

Marilyn Monroe and Orchids — A263

No. 1481 — Monroe and orchids: a, 1000d, Phalaenopsis amabilis. b, 2000d, Rhynchostylis retusa. c, 3000d, Phalaenopsis stuartiana. d, 5000d, Rhynchostylis gigantea. e, 6000d, Vanda coerulea. f, 15,000d, Trichoglottis brachiata.

**2003**
| | | | | |
|---|---|---|---|---|
| 1479 | A262 | Sheet of 6, #a-f | 7.25 | 7.25 |

**Souvenir Sheet**
| | | | |
|---|---|---|---|
| 1480 | A262 | 38,000d multi | 8.50 | 8.50 |

---

**S.TOMÉ E PRÍNCIPE**

A260

**S. TOMÉ E PRÍNCIPE**

Red Cross Emblem and Dogs — A261

No. 1477 — Red Cross emblem and various dogs: a, 1000d. b, 2000d. c, 3000d. d, 5000d. e, 6000d. f, 15,000d.

*Perf. 12¾x13¼, 13¼x12¾ (#1478)*

**2003**
| | | | | |
|---|---|---|---|---|
| 1477 | A260 | Sheet of 6, #a-f | 7.25 | 7.25 |

**Souvenir Sheet**
| | | | |
|---|---|---|---|
| 1478 | A261 | 38,000d multi | 8.50 | 8.50 |

Pope John Paul II and Orchids — A262

No. 1479 — Pope and orchids: a, 1000d, Phalaenopsis bellina. b, 2000d, Rhynchostylis monachica. c, 3000d, Vanda bensonii. d, 5000d, Paphiopedilum hirsutissimum. e, 6000d, Liparis latifolia. f, 15,000d, Trichoglottis seidenfadenii.
38,000d, Like #1479a.

---

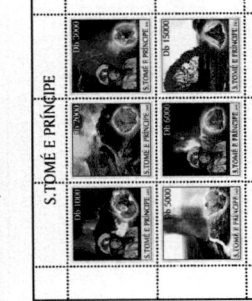

**S.TOMÉ E PRÍNCIPE**

**2003**
| | | | | |
|---|---|---|---|---|
| 1481 | A263 | Sheet of 6, #a-f | 7.25 | 7.25 |

**Souvenir Sheet**
| | | | |
|---|---|---|---|
| 1482 | A263 | 38,000d multi | 8.50 | 8.50 |

Birds and Concorde — A264

No. 1483 — Concorde and penguins: a, 1000d. b, 2000d. c, 3000d. d, 5000d. e, 6000d. f, 15,000d.

No. 1484 — Birds: a, 1000d, Lybius torquatus, and Concorde. b, 2000d, Prinia subflava, and Concorde. c, 3000d, Tockus erythrorhynchus, and Concorde. d, 5000d, Poicephalus meyeri. e, 6000d, Uraeginthus angolensis, and Concorde. f, 15,000d, Lanarius atrococcineus.

No. 1485, 38,000d, Like #1483e. No. 1486, 38,000d, Like #1484c.

**2003**
| | | | | |
|---|---|---|---|---|
| 1483-1484 | A264 | Set of 2 | 14.50 | 14.50 |

**Souvenir Sheets**
| | | | |
|---|---|---|---|
| 1485-1486 | A264 | Set of 2 | 17.00 | 17.00 |

---

**S.TOMÉ E PRÍNCIPE**

Birds — A265

No. 1487 — Various pheasants: a, 1000d. b, 2000d. c, 3000d. d, 5000d. e, 6000d. f, 15,000d.

No. 1488 — Birds and orchids: a, Polytelis alexandrae, Dendrochilum wenzelii. b, Neophena splendida, Dendrobium sulcatum. c, Pyrrhura calliptera, Dendrobium nobile. d, Aratinga jandaya, Cymbidium lowianum. e, Melopsittacus undulatus, Dendrobium bullenianum. f, Psittacula himalayana, Chiloschista parishii.

No. 1489, 38,000d, Like #1487a, with Bangkok 2003 Jamboree emblem added. No. 1490, 38,000d, Like #1488b, with Bangkok 2003 Jamboree emblem added. See illustration A266 for stamps showing Bangkok 2003 Jamboree emblem.

**2003**
| | | | | |
|---|---|---|---|---|
| 1487 | A265 | Set of 2 | 7.25 | 7.25 |

---

**2003**
| | | | | | |
|---|---|---|---|---|---|
| 1488 | A265 | 10,000d | Sheet of 6, #a-f | 13.50 | 13.50 |

**Souvenir Sheets**
| | | | |
|---|---|---|---|
| 1489-1490 | A266 | Set of 2 | 17.00 | 17.00 |

Bangkok 2003 Scout Jamboree Emblem and Birds, Orchids, Mushrooms, Insects or Butterflies — A266

No. 1491 — Emblem and various fighting roosters: a, 1000d. b, 2000d. c, 3000d. d, 5000d. e, 6000d. f, 15,000d.

No. 1492 — Emblem and unnamed water birds or orchids: a, 1000d, Bird in flight. b, 2000d, Aerides odorata. c, 3000d, Two birds at nest. d, 5000d, Aerides roaea. e, 6000d, Two birds. f, 15,000d, Aerides quinquevulnera.

No. 1493 — Emblem and mushrooms and orchids: a, 1000d, Xerocomus cubtomentosus, Aerides quinquevulnera. b, 2000d, Suillus placidus, Suillus variegatus. c, 3000d, Suillus granulatus, Dendrobium bullenianum. d, 5000d, Boletus edulis, Coelogyne mooreana. e, 6000d, Tylopilus felleus, Dendrobium crumenatum. f, 15,000d, Russula cyanoxantha. Catoneplehe nunili.

No. 1494 — Emblem, wasp and mushrooms: a, 1000d, Boletus edulis f. betulicola. b, 2000d, Boletus edulis f. pinicola. c, 3000d, Boletus appendiculatus. d, 5000d, Boletus fechtneri. e, 6000d, Boletus luridus. f, 15,000d, Boletus impolitus.

No. 1495 — Emblem, mushroom and butterfly: a, 1000d, Russula nigricans, Papilio demoleus. b, 2000d, Lactarius volemus, Libythea geoffroyi. c, 3000d, Russula cyanoxantha, Ascocentrum garayi, Gomphidius roseus, Doxocopa cherubina. e, 6000d, Russula integra, Dione juno. f, 15,000d, Agaricus bisporus, Philaethria.

No. 1496, 38,000d, Like #1491a. No. 1497, 38,000d, Like #1492f. No. 1498, 38,000d, Like #1493d. No. 1499, 38,000d, Like #1494a. No. 1500, 38,000d, Like #1495f.

**2003**
| | | | |
|---|---|---|---|
| 1491-1495 | A266 | Set of 5 | 37.50 | 37.50 |

**Souvenir Sheets**
| | | | |
|---|---|---|---|
| 1496-1499 | A266 | Set of 4 | 35.00 | 35.00 |

See Nos. 1480-1400 for additional souvenir sheets with Jamboree emblem.

---

**S. TOMÉ E PRÍNCIPE**

Jamboree Tailandia 2002

Lord Robert Baden-Powell and Songbirds — A267

**S. TOMÉ E PRÍNCIPE**

Jamboree Tailandia 2002

Lord Robert Baden-Powell and Cats, Dogs, Butterflies or Owls — A268

No. 1500 — Lord Baden-Powell and unnamed songbirds: a, 1000d. b, 2000d. c, 3000d. d, 5000d. e, 6000d. f, 15,000d.

No. 1501 — Lord Baden-Powell and unnamed cats or dogs: a, 1000d, Cat. b,

---

**S. TOMÉ E PRÍNCIPE**

2000d, Cat, diff. c, 3000d, Cat, diff. d, 5000d, Dog, e, 6000d, Dog, diff.
No. 1502 — Lord Baden-Powell and butterflies: a, 1000d, Lycaena dispar, b, 2000d, Papilio macheon. c, 3000d, Cethosia biblis d, 5000d, Netrocoryne repanda, e, 6000d, Eupackardia calleta, f, 15,000d, Gangara thyrsis.
No. 1503 — Lord Baden-Powell and owls: a, 1000d, Bubo lacteus, b, 2000d, Asio capensis, c, 3000d, Strix woodfordii, d, 5000d, Strix butleri, e, 6000d, Otus insularis, f, 15,000d, Glaucidium perlatum.

**2003**
| | | | | |
|---|---|---|---|---|
| 1500 | A267 | Sheet of 6, #a-f | 7.25 | 7.25 |
| 1501 | A268 | Sheet of 6, #a-f | 7.25 | 7.25 |
| 1502 | A268 | Sheet of 6, #a-f | 7.25 | 7.25 |
| 1503 | A268 | Sheet of 6, #a-f | 7.25 | 7.25 |
| | | Nos. 1500-1503 (4) | 29.00 | 29.00 |

**Souvenir Sheets**
| | | | | |
|---|---|---|---|---|
| 1504 | A267 | 38,000d multi | 8.50 | 8.50 |
| 1505 | A268 | 38,000d multi | 8.50 | 8.50 |
| 1506 | A268 | 38,000d multi | 8.50 | 8.50 |
| 1507 | A268 | 38,000d multi | 8.50 | 8.50 |

No. 1504, 38,000d, Like #1500c. No. 1505, 38,000d, Like #1501e. No. 1506, 38,000d, Like #1502c. No. 1507, 38,000d, Like #1503a.

A269

### Lady Olave Baden-Powell and Pandas — A270

No. 1508 — Lady Baden-Powell and various pandas: a, 1000d. b, 2000d. c, 3000d. d, 5000d. e, 6000d. f, 15,000d.

**2003**
| | | | | |
|---|---|---|---|---|
| 1508 | A269 | Sheet of 6, #a-f | 7.25 | 7.25 |

**Souvenir Sheet**
| | | | | |
|---|---|---|---|---|
| 1509 | A270 | 38,000d multi | 8.50 | 8.50 |

### Scouting Emblem and Cats or Prehistoric Animals and Minerals — A271

No. 1510 — Scouting emblem and various cats: a, 1000d. b, 2000d. c, 3000d. d, 5000d. e, 6000d. f, 15,000d.
No. 1511 — Scouting emblem, unnamed minerals and prehistoric animals: a, 1000d, Corythosaurus causurus. b, 2000d, Compsognathus. c, 3000d, Edaphosaurus. d, 5000d, Monoclonius. e, 6000d, Rhamphorhynchus. f, 15,000d, Stegosaurus.

**2003**
| | | | | |
|---|---|---|---|---|
| 1510 | A271 | Sheet of 6, #a-f | 7.25 | 7.25 |
| 1511 | A271 | Sheet of 6, #a-f | 7.25 | 7.25 |

**Souvenir Sheet**
| | | | | |
|---|---|---|---|---|
| 1512 | A271 | 38,000d multi | 8.50 | 8.50 |

See No. 1522.

### Rotary Emblem and Roses — A272

No. 1508 — Rotary emblem and various roses: a, 1000d. b, 2000d. c, 3000d. d, 5000d. e, 6000d. f, 15,000d.

**2003**
| | | | | |
|---|---|---|---|---|
| 1513 | A272 | Sheet of 6, #a-f | 7.25 | 7.25 |

**Souvenir Sheet**
| | | | | |
|---|---|---|---|---|
| 1514 | A272 | 38,000d multi | 8.50 | 8.50 |

No. 1508, 38,000d, Like #1513e.

A274

### Rotary or Lions Emblems and Pinnipeds or Birds — A273

No. 1515 — Various pinnipeds and: a, 1000d, Rotary emblem. b, 2000d, Lions emblem. c, 3000d, Rotary emblem. d, 5000d, Lions emblem. e, 6000d, Rotary emblem. f, 15,000d, Lions emblem.
No. 1516: a, 1000d, Rotary emblem, Polemaetus bellicosus. b, 2000d, Lions emblem, Aquila verreauxi. c, 3000d, Rotary emblem, Circus aeruginosus. d, 5000d, Lions emblem, Aquila nipalensis. e, 6000d, Rotary emblem, Hieraetus fasciatus. f, 15,000d, Lions emblem, Aquila pomarina.

**2003**
| | | | | |
|---|---|---|---|---|
| 1515-1516 | A273 | Sheets of 6, #a-f | 14.50 | 14.50 |
| | | Set of 2 | | |

**Souvenir Sheets**
| | | | | |
|---|---|---|---|---|
| 1517-1518 | A273 | Set of 2 | 17.00 | 17.00 |

No. 1517, 38,000d, Like #1515a. No. 1518, 38,000d, Like #1516b.

A275

### Dogs and Cats — A277

No. 1519: a, 1000d, Dog. b, 2000d, Dog, Dogs. c, 3000d, Dog. d, 5000d, Cat, diff. e, 6000d, Dog, diff.
No. 1520: a, 1000d, Dog, Dogs, diff. b, 2000d, Cat, diff. c, 3000d, Dogs, diff. d, 5000d, Cat, diff. e, 6000d, Dog, diff. f, 15,000d, Cat, diff.

**2003**
| | | | | |
|---|---|---|---|---|
| 1519 | A274 | Sheet of 6, #a-f | 7.25 | 7.25 |
| 1520 | A275 | Sheet of 6, #a-f | 7.25 | 7.25 |

**Souvenir Sheets**
| | | | | |
|---|---|---|---|---|
| 1521 | A276 | 38,000d multi | 8.50 | 8.50 |
| 1522 | A277 | 38,000d multi | 8.50 | 8.50 |
| 1523 | A275 | 38,000d multi | 8.50 | 8.50 |

No. 1523, Like #1520e.

A276

### Sled Dogs — A278

No. 1508 — Various sled dogs: a, 1000d. b, 2000d. c, 3000d. d, 5000d. e, 6000d. f, 15,000d.

**2003**
| | | | | |
|---|---|---|---|---|
| 1524 | A278 | Sheet of 6, #a-f | 7.25 | 7.25 |

**Souvenir Sheet**
| | | | | |
|---|---|---|---|---|
| 1525 | A278 | 38,000d multi | 8.50 | 8.50 |

No. 1508, 38,000d, Like #1524b.

### Dolphins — A279

No. 1526 — Various dolphins: a, 1000d. b, 2000d. c, 3000d. d, 5000d. e, 6000d. f, 15,000d.

**2003**
| | | | | |
|---|---|---|---|---|
| 1526 | A279 | Sheet of 6, #a-f | 7.25 | 7.25 |

### Rams — A280

Various rams.

**2003**
| | | | | |
|---|---|---|---|---|
| 1527 | A280 | 7000d Sheet of 6, #a-f | 9.50 | 9.50 |

### Hot Air Balloons and Zeppelins — A281

No. 1528: a, 1000d, Balloon. b, 2000d, Zeppelin. c, 3000d, Balloon, diff. d, 5000d, Moored Zeppelin. e, 6000d, Balloon, diff. f, 15,000d, Zeppelin cockpit.

**2003**
| | | | | |
|---|---|---|---|---|
| 1528 | A281 | Sheet of 6, #a-f | 7.25 | 7.25 |

**Souvenir Sheet**
| | | | | |
|---|---|---|---|---|
| 1529 | A281 | 38,000d multi | 8.50 | 8.50 |

No. 1528, 38,000d, Like #1528e.

### Aviation, Cent. — A282

No. 1530 — Various military aircraft: a, 1000d, Helicopter. b, 2000d, Helicopter, diff. d, 5000d, Airplane. e, 6000d, Helicopter, diff. f, 15,000d, Airplane.

**2003**
| | | | | |
|---|---|---|---|---|
| 1530 | A282 | Sheet of 6, #a-f | 7.25 | 7.25 |

**Souvenir Sheet**
| | | | | |
|---|---|---|---|---|
| 1531 | A282 | 38,000d multi | 8.50 | 8.50 |

No. 1530, 38,000d, Like #1530c.

### Apollo 11 — A283

ST. THOMAS AND PRINCE ISLANDS

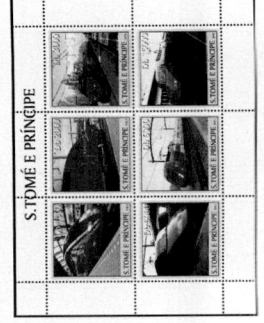

A296 — A301 (top row sheets)

A297
A298
A299
A300
A301

Formula 1 Racing — A292

Formula 1 Racing — A293

Motorcycle Racing — A294

No. 1547: a, 1000d, Car 4x. b, 2000d, Cars 12 and 21. c, 3000d, Cars 46, 54 and 42. d, 5000d, Cars 11, 37 and 4. e, 6000d, Southside Fina car. f, 15,000d, Car 16.

No. 1548: a, 1000d, Two cars. b, 2000d, Two drivers holding trophies. c, 3000d, Car. d, 5000d, Two drivers with champagne bottles. e, 6000d, Car. diff. f, 15,000d, Three drivers.

No. 1549: a, 1000d, Red car with Marlboro wing. b, 2000d, Yellow car with Benson & Hedges wing. c, 3000d, Red car, driver with arms raised. e, 6000d, Blue and yellow car. f, 15,000d, Black, red and white car, diff.

No. 1550: a, Yellow motorcycle without number. b, Green motorcycle #1. c, Motorcycle #26. d, White motorcycle #1. e, Motorcycle #9. f, Motoroyalo #21.

No. 1551, Like #1548a. No. 1552, Like #1549c.

**2003**

| | | | |
|---|---|---|---|
| 1547 | A291 | Sheet of 6, #a-f | 7.25 7.25 |
| 1548 | A292 | Sheet of 6, #a-f | 7.25 7.25 |
| 1549 | A293 | Sheet of 6, #a-f | 7.25 7.25 |
| 1550 | A294 | Sheet of 6, #a-f | 13.50 13.50 |
| | | 10,000d Sheet of 6, #a-f | 35.25 35.25 |

**Souvenir Sheets**

*Nos. 1547-1550 (4)*

| | | | |
|---|---|---|---|
| 1551 | A292 | 38,000d multi | 8.50 8.50 |
| 1552 | A293 | 38,000d multi | 8.50 8.50 |

A295

**2003**

Sheet of 6, #a-f  7.25 7.25

**Souvenir Sheet**

1539 A287
1540 A287 38,000d multi  8.50 8.50

Tractor Trailer Trucks — A288

No. 1541 — Trucks with cabs in: a, 1000d, Red. b, 2000d, Blue. c, 3000d, Red, diff. d, 5000d, White. e, 6000d, Black. f, 15,000d, Purple.
38,000d, Like #1542a.

**2003**

1541 A288  Sheet of 6, #a-f  7.25 7.25

**Souvenir Sheet**

1542 A288  38,000d multi  8.50 8.50

Volkswagen Beetles — A289

Mercedes-Benz Automobiles — A290

No. 1543: a, 1000d. b, 2000d. c, 3000d. d, 5000d. e, 6000d. f, 15,000d.
No. 1544: a, 1000d. b, 2000d. c, 3000d. d, 5000d. e, 6000d. f, 15,000d.
No. 1545, Like #1543d. No. 1546, Like #1544d.

**2003**

| | | | |
|---|---|---|---|
| 1543 | A289 | Sheet of 6, #a-f | 7.25 7.25 |
| 1544 | A290 | Sheet of 6, #a-f | 7.25 7.25 |

**Souvenir Sheets**

1545 A289  38,000d multi  8.50 8.50
1546 A290  38,000d multi  8.50 8.50

Auto Racing — A291

Space — A284

Concorde and Spacecraft — A285

Deceased Crew of Space Shuttle Columbia — A286

No. 1532: a, 1000d, Astronaut Edwin Aldrin. b, 2000d, Lift-off. c, 3000d, Crew in capsule. d, 5000d, Retrieval of crew at sea. e, 6000d, Astronauts Neil Armstrong, Michael Collins and Aldrin. f, 15,000d, Astronaut on Moon.

No. 1533: a, 1000d, Astronaut, vehicle and structures on planet. c, 3000d, Intl. Space Station. d, 5000d, Astronauts working in outer space. e, 6000d, Untethered astronaut. f, 15,000d, Lift-off of rocket.

No. 1534: a, 1000d, Concorde. b, 2000d, Lift-off of Space Shuttle, diff. c, 3000d, Concorde, diff. d, 5000d, Intl. Space Station. e, 6000d, Concorde on runway. f, 15,000d, Space Shuttle in outer space.

No. 1535, Like #1532e. No. 1536, Like #1533c. No. 1537, Like #1534b.

**2003**

| | | | |
|---|---|---|---|
| 1532 | A283 | Sheet of 6, #a-f | 7.25 7.25 |
| 1533 | A284 | Sheet of 6, #a-f | 7.25 7.25 |
| 1534 | A285 | Sheet of 6, #a-f | 21.75 21.75 |

*Nos. 1532-1534 (3)*

**Souvenir Sheets**

| | | | |
|---|---|---|---|
| 1535 | A283 | 38,000d multi | 8.50 8.50 |
| 1536 | A284 | 38,000d multi | 8.50 8.50 |
| 1537 | A285 | 38,000d multi | 8.50 8.50 |
| 1538 | A286 | 38,000d multi | 8.50 8.50 |

Tandem Bicycles — A287

No. 1539 — Various tandem bicycles and riders: a, 1000d. b, 2000d. c, 3000d. d, 5000d. e, 6000d. f, 15,000d.
38,000d, Like #1539a.

## S. TÔMÉ E PRÍNCIPE

### A302

### A303

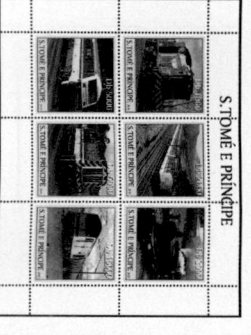

### A306

**2003**

1574 A306 Sheet of 6, #a-f ........ 7.25 7.25

**2004 Summer Olympics, Athens — A306**

No. 1574 — Various rowing teams: a. 10000d. b. 2000d. c. 3000d. d. 5000d. e. 6000d. f. 15,000d. 38,000d. Like #1574b.

**Souvenir Sheet**

1575 A306 38,000d multi .......... 8.50 8.50

---

**2003**

1573 A305 7000d Sheet of 6, #a-f .... 9.50 9.50

Various ships.

**Ships — A305**

**Trains — A304**

Nos. 1553-1562 — Various trains: a. 10000d. b. 2000d. c. 3000d. d. 5000d. e. 6000d. f. 15,000d.
No. 1563. Like #1553d. No. 1564. Like #1554c. No. 1565. Like #1555f. No. 1566. Like #1556d. No. 1557a. No. 1558b. No. 1569. Like #1559f. No. 1570. Like #1560b. No. 1571. Like #1561c. No. 1572. Like #1562d.

**Souvenir Sheets**

**2003**

| 1553 | A295 | 38,000d multi | Sheet of 6, #a-f | 7.25 | 7.25 |
|------|------|---------------|------------------|------|------|
| 1554 | A296 | 38,000d multi | Sheet of 6, #a-f | 7.25 | 7.25 |
| 1555 | A297 | 38,000d multi | Sheet of 6, #a-f | 7.25 | 7.25 |
| 1556 | A298 | 38,000d multi | Sheet of 6, #a-f | 7.25 | 7.25 |
| 1557 | A299 | 38,000d multi | Sheet of 6, #a-f | 7.25 | 7.25 |
| 1558 | A300 | 38,000d multi | Sheet of 6, #a-f | 7.25 | 7.25 |
| 1559 | A301 | 38,000d multi | Sheet of 6, #a-f | 7.25 | 7.25 |
| 1560 | A302 | 38,000d multi | Sheet of 6, #a-f | 7.25 | 7.25 |
| 1561 | A303 | 38,000d multi | Sheet of 6, #a-f | 7.25 | 7.25 |
| 1562 | A304 | 38,000d multi | Sheet of 6, #a-f | 8.50 | 8.50 |

Nos. 1553-1562 (10) .... 72.50 72.50

---

## AIR POST STAMPS

**1938**

Common Design Type
Inscribed "S. Tomé"

Name and Value in Black

**Perf. 13½x13**

| C1 | CD39 | 10c red orange | 30.00 | .50 |
|----|------|----------------|-------|-----|
| C2 | CD39 | 20c purple | 22.50 | .50 |
| C3 | CD39 | 50c orange | 15.00 | 11.00 |
| C4 | CD39 | 1e ultra | 1.50 | 1.25 |
| C5 | CD39 | 2e lilac brown | 3.00 | .50 |
| C6 | CD39 | 1e deep ultra | 3.75 | 3.00 |
| C7 | CD39 | 5e red brown | 5.75 | 4.00 |
| C8 | CD39 | 5e dark green | 6.50 | 6.50 |
| C9 | CD39 | 10e rose carmine | 84.00 | 63.25 |

Nos. C1-C9 (9)

**1939**

Name and Value Typo. in Black

**Engr.**  **Unwmk.**

| C10 | CD39 | 10c scarlet | .50 | .25 |
|-----|------|-------------|-----|-----|
| C11 | CD39 | 20c purple | .50 | .25 |
| C12 | CD39 | 30c purple | .50 | .25 |
| C13 | CD39 | 1e lilac brown | .50 | .25 |
| C14 | CD39 | 2e lilac brown | .50 | .25 |
| C15 | CD39 | 3e dark green | 1.50 | 1.25 |
| C16 | CD39 | 5e red brown | 2.00 | 1.50 |
| C17 | CD39 | 9e rose carmine | 5.00 | 2.50 |
| C18 | CD39 | 10e magenta | 6.00 | 2.50 |

Nos. C10-C18 (9) .... 19.50 10.10

No. C16 exists with overprint "Exposicao International de Nova York, 1939-1940" and Trylon and Perisphere.

---

## POSTAGE DUE STAMPS

**1904**

Name and Value Typo. in Black

**Unwmk.**  **Typo.**  **Perf. 12**

"S. Thomé" — D1

| J1 | D1 | 5r yellow green | .55 | .55 |
|----|----|-----------------|-----|-----|
| J2 | D1 | 10r slate | .65 | .65 |
| J3 | D1 | 20r yellow brown | .65 | .65 |
| J4 | D1 | 30r orange | 1.00 | .65 |
| J5 | D1 | 50r gray brown | 1.75 | 1.40 |
| J6 | D1 | 60r red brown | 2.25 | 1.60 |
| J7 | D1 | 100r red lilac | 3.00 | 1.75 |
| J8 | D1 | 130r dull blue | 4.50 | 3.00 |
| J9 | D1 | 200r carmine | 4.50 | 3.50 |
| J10 | D1 | 500r gray violet | 26.60 | 19.00 |

Nos. J1-J10 (10)

**1911**

Overprinted in Carmine or Green

| J11 | D1 | 5r yellow green | .25 | .25 |
|-----|----|-----------------|-----|-----|
| J12 | D1 | 10r slate | .25 | .25 |
| J13 | D1 | 20r yellow brown | .25 | .25 |

**AIR POST STAMPS**

**1913**

Overprinted "Republica" in Italic Capitals like Regular Issue in Green

No. J5 Overprinted "Republica" in Italic Capitals like Regular Issue in Green

**1920**

J41 D1 50r gray brn .... 40.00 35.00

**Without Gum**

**1913**

| J31 | D1 | 5r yellow green | 3.00 | 3.00 |
|-----|----|-----------------|------|------|
| a. | | Inverted overprint | 40.00 | 40.00 |
| J32 | D1 | 10r slate | 3.00 | 3.00 |
| J33 | D1 | 20r yellow brown | 3.00 | 3.00 |
| a. | | Inverted overprint | 40.00 | 40.00 |
| J34 | D1 | 30r orange | 3.00 | 3.00 |
| J35 | D1 | 50r gray brown | 3.00 | 3.00 |
| a. | | Inverted overprint | 40.00 | 40.00 |
| J36 | D1 | 60r red brown | 4.00 | 4.00 |
| J37 | D1 | 100r red lilac | 4.00 | 4.00 |
| J38 | D1 | 130r dull blue | 4.00 | 4.00 |
| J39 | D1 | 200r carmine | 6.00 | 6.00 |
| J40 | D1 | 500r gray violet | 17.00 | 15.00 |

Nos. J31-J40 (10) .... 52.00 49.00

---

**1921**

**Typo.**  **Perf. 11½**

"S. Tomé" — D2

| J42 | D2 | ½c yellow green | .20 | .20 |
|-----|----|-----------------|-----|-----|
| J43 | D2 | 1c slate | .20 | .20 |
| J44 | D2 | 2c yellow brown | .20 | .20 |
| J45 | D2 | 3c orange brown | .20 | .20 |
| J46 | D2 | 5c gray brown | .20 | .20 |
| J47 | D2 | 6c lt brown | .20 | .20 |
| J48 | D2 | 10c red violet | .25 | .25 |
| J49 | D2 | 13c red brown | .25 | .25 |
| J50 | D2 | 50c dull blue | .35 | .40 |
| J51 | D2 | 50c carmine | 2.25 | 2.20 |

Nos. J42-J51 (10)

In each sheet one stamp is inscribed "S. Thomé" instead of "S. Tomé." Value, set of 10, $60.

Catalogue values for unused stamps in this section, from this point to the end of the section, are for Never Hinged items.

**1952**

Numeral in Red, Frame Multicolored

Common Design Type

**Photo. & Typo.**

**Unwmk.**  **Perf. 14**

| J52 | CD45 | 10c chocolate | .30 | .30 |
|-----|------|---------------|-----|-----|
| J53 | CD45 | 30c red brown | .30 | .30 |
| J54 | CD45 | 50c dark blue | .50 | .50 |
| J55 | CD45 | 1e dark blue | .50 | .50 |
| J56 | CD45 | 5e black brown | .75 | .75 |
| J57 | CD45 | 5e olive green | 2.00 | 2.00 |

Nos. J52-J57 (6) .... 4.15 4.15

---

## ST. THOMAS AND PRINCE ISLANDS

**1913**

Nos. J1-J10 Overprinted in Black

| J21 | D1 | 30r orange | .25 | .25 |
|-----|----|------------|-----|-----|
| J15 | D1 | 50r gray brown | .25 | .25 |
| J16 | D1 | 60r red brown | .55 | .55 |
| J17 | D1 | 100r red lilac | .55 | .55 |
| J18 | D1 | 130r dull blue | .70 | .70 |
| J19 | D1 | 130r dull blue | .70 | .70 |
| J20 | D1 | 200r carmine violet (G) | .70 | .70 |
| | D1 | 500r gray violet | 1.10 | 1.10 |

Nos. J11-J20 (10) .... 5.00 5.00

**1911**

Overprinted in Black

Nos. J1-J10

| J21 | D1 | 5r yellow green | 3.75 | 3.75 |
|-----|----|-----------------|------|------|
| J22 | D1 | 10r slate | 5.00 | 4.50 |
| J23 | D1 | 20r yellow brown | 2.50 | 2.50 |
| J24 | D1 | 30r orange | 2.50 | 2.50 |
| J25 | D1 | 50r gray brown | 3.00 | 3.00 |
| J26 | D1 | 60r red brown | 3.00 | 3.00 |
| J27 | D1 | 100r red lilac | 4.00 | 4.00 |
| J28 | D1 | 130r dull blue | 35.00 | 35.00 |
| a. | | Inverted overprint | 70.00 | 70.00 |
| J29 | D1 | 200r carmine | 50.00 | 50.00 |
| a. | | Inverted overprint | 70.00 | 70.00 |
| J30 | D1 | 500r gray violet | 75.00 | 40.00 |
| a. | | Inverted overprint | 184.25 | 147.75 |

Nos. J21-J30 (10)

**Without Gum**

---

## NEWSPAPER STAMPS

### N1

### N2

### N3

**1892**

Perf. 11½, 12½ and 13½

**Without Gum**  **Unwmk.**

**Black Surcharge**

| P1 | N1 | 2½r on 10r green | 95.00 | 55.00 |
|----|----|------------------|-------|-------|
| P2 | N1 | 2½r on 20r rose | 125.00 | 57.50 |
| P3 | N1 | 2½r on 10r green | 57.50 | 57.50 |
| P4 | N1 | 2½r on 20r rose | 125.00 | 57.50 |

Nos. P1-P4 (4) .... 470.00 227.50

**Green Surcharge**

| P5 | N1 | 2½r on 5r black | 67.50 | 30.00 |
|----|----|-----------------|-------|-------|
| P6 | N1 | 2½r on 10r green | 57.50 | 57.50 |
| P7 | N1 | 2½r on 20r rose | 60.00 | 60.00 |
| P8 | N1 | 2½r on 10r green | 125.00 | 62.50 |
| P9 | N1 | 2½r on 20r rose | 125.00 | 62.50 |
| P10 | N1 | 2½r on 10r rose | 125.00 | 62.50 |

Nos. P5-P10 (5) .... 567.50 287.50

Both surcharges exist on No. 18 in green.

**1893**

**Typo.**  **Perf. 11½, 13½**

P12 N3 2½r brown .... .45 .40

For surcharges and overprints see Nos. 85, 166, 275, P13.

**1899**

P13 N3 2½r brown .... 25.00 16.00

**Without Gum**

No. P12 Overprinted Type "d" in Blue

---

## POSTAL TAX STAMPS

**1925**

Pombal Issue

Common Design Types

**Unwmk.**  **Perf. 12½**

| RA1 | CD28 | 15c orange & black | .45 | .45 |
|-----|------|--------------------|-----|-----|
| RA2 | CD29 | 15c orange & black | .45 | .45 |
| RA3 | CD30 | 15c orange & black | .45 | .45 |

Nos. RA1-RA3 (3) .... 1.35 1.35

**1948-58**

Denomination in Black

**Typo.**  **Perf. 12x11½**

| RA4 | PT1 | 50c yellow grn | 4.00 | 1.10 |
|-----|-----|----------------|------|------|
| RA5 | PT1 | 1e carmine rose | 4.25 | 1.10 |
| RA6 | PT1 | 1e emerald ('58) | 1.75 | 1.75 |
| RA7 | PT1 | 1.50e bister brown | 2.50 | 1.90 |

Nos. RA4-RA7 (4) .... 12.50 5.25

Certain revenue stamps (5e, 6e, 7e, 8e and other denominations) were surcharged in 1946 "Assistencia," 2 bars and new values (1e or 1.50e) and used as postal tax stamps.

Denominations of 2e and up were used only for revenue purposes. No. RA6 lacks "Colonia de" below coat of arms.

Catalogue values for unused stamps in this section, from this point to the end of the section, are for Never Hinged items.

Type of 1958 Surcharged

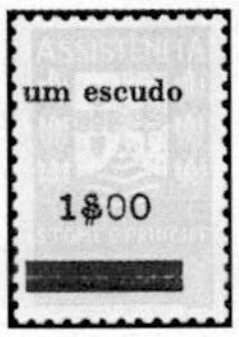

m

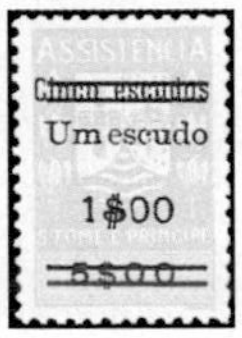

n

**1964-65** **Typo.** ***Perf. 12x11½***
**RA8** PT1(m) 1e on 5e org yel 12.00 12.00
**RA9** PT1(n) 1e on 5e org yel ('65) 4.50 4.50

The basic 5e orange yellow does not carry the words "Colonia de."

No. RA6 Surcharged: "Um escudo"

**1965**
**RA10** PT1 1e emerald 2.00 2.00

Type of 1948 Surcharged

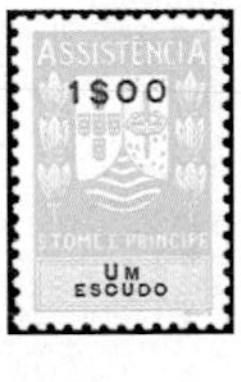


**1965** **Typo.** ***Perf. 12x11½***
**RA11** PT1 1e emerald .40 .40

## POSTAL TAX DUE STAMPS

**Pombal Issue**
Common Design Types

**1925** **Unwmk.** ***Perf. 12½***
**RAJ1** CD28 30c orange & black .75 .75
**RAJ2** CD29 30c orange & black .75 .75
**RAJ3** CD30 30c orange & black .75 .75
*Nos. RAJ1-RAJ3 (3)* 2.25 2.25

# ST VINCENT

sānt ˈvint-sənt

LOCATION — Island in the West Indies
GOVT. — Independent state in the British Commonwealth
AREA — 150 sq. mi.
POP. — 120,519 (1999 est.)
CAPITAL — Kingstown

The British colony of St. Vincent became an associated state in 1969 and independent in 1979.

12 Pence = 1 Shilling
20 Shillings = 1 Pound
100 Cents = 1 Dollar (1949)

**Catalogue values for unused stamps in this country are for Never Hinged items, beginning with Scott 152 in the regular postage section, Scott B1 in the semi-postal section, and Scott O1 in the officials section.**

Values for unused stamps are for examples with original gum as defined in the catalogue introduction. Early stamps were spaced extremely narrowly on the plates, and the perforations were applied irregularly.

Therefore, very fine examples of Nos. 1-28, 30-39 will have perforations that cut into the design slightly on one or more sides.

Also, very fine examples of Nos. 40-53, 55-60 will have perforations touching the design on at least one side.

These stamps with perfs clear of the design on all four sides, especially Nos. 1-28, 30-39, are extremely scarce and command substantially higher prices.

**Watermark**

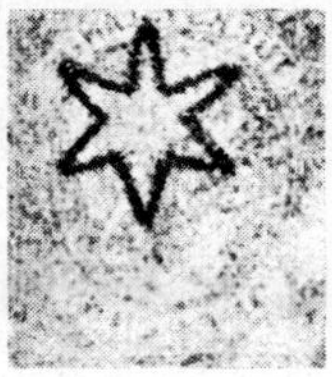

Wmk. 5 — Small Star

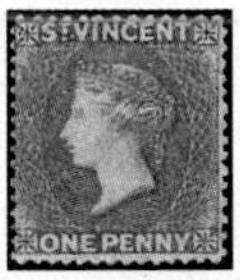


Queen Victoria — A1

**1861** **Engr.** **Unwmk.** ***Perf. 14 to 16***
**1** A1 1p rose *50.00* 15.00
*a.* Imperf., pair 275.00
*c.* Horiz. pair, imperf. vert. 325.00
**1B** A1 6p yellow green *7,250.* 250.00

Perfs on Nos. 1-1B are not clean cut. See Nos. 2-3 for rough perfs.

**1862-66** ***Rough Perf. 14 to 16***
**2** A1 1p rose 45.00 14.50
*a.* Horiz. pair, imperf. vert. 400.00
**3** A1 6p dark green 60.00 19.00
*a.* Imperf., pair 950.00
*b.* Horiz. pair, imperf. between 5,250. *5,750.*
**4** A1 1sh slate ('66) 325.00 150.00
*Nos. 2-4 (3)* 430.00 183.50

**1863-69** ***Perf. 11 to 13***
**5** A1 1p rose 37.50 17.00
**6** A1 4p blue ('66) 300.00 125.00
*a.* Horiz. pair, imperf. vert.
**7** A1 4p orange ('69) 375.00 175.00
**8** A1 6p deep green 225.00 82.50
**8A** A1 1sh slate ('66) *2,100.* 1,000.
**9** A1 1sh indigo ('69) 350.00 100.00
**10** A1 1sh brown ('69) 500.00 175.00

***Perf. 11 to 13x14 to 16***
**11** A1 1p rose *3,600.* 1,250.
**12** A1 1sh slate 250.00 140.00

***Rough Perf. 14 to 16***
**1871-78** **Wmk. 5**
**13** A1 1p black 55.00 12.50
*a.* Vert. pair, imperf. btwn. *8,000.*
**14** A1 6p dk blue green 300.00 77.50

***Clean-Cut Perf. 14 to 16***
**14A** A1 1p black 50.00 9.00
**14B** A1 6p dp bl grn 700.00 50.00
*c.* 6p dull blue green 1,000. 52.50
**15** A1 6p pale yel green ('78) 700.00 30.00
**15A** A1 1sh vermilion ('77) *13,500.*

For surcharge see No. 30.

***Perf. 11 to 13***
**16** A1 4p dk bl ('77) 500.00 100.00
**17** A1 1sh deep rose ('72) 800.00 150.00
**18** A1 1sh claret ('75) 650.00 275.00

***Perf. 11 to 13x14 to 16***
**20** A1 1p black 72.50 10.00
*a.* Horiz. pair, imperf. btwn. *7,500.*
**21** A1 6p pale yel grn ('77) 625.00 55.00
**22** A1 1sh lilac rose ('72) *5,500.* 375.00
**23** A1 1sh vermilion ('77) 1,000. 95.00
*a.* Horiz. pair, imperf. vert.

See Nos. 25-28A, 36-39, 42-53. For surcharges see Nos. 30, 32-33, 40, 55-60.

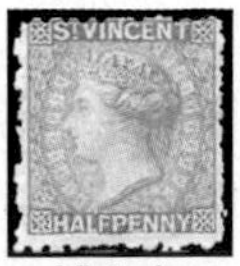


Victoria
A2

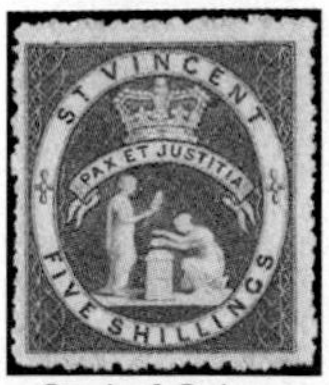


Seal of Colony
A3

**1880-81** ***Perf. 11 to 13***
**24** A2 ½p orange ('81) 8.00 4.25
**25** A1 1p gray green 150.00 4.25
**26** A1 1p drab ('81) 575.00 9.50
**27** A1 4p ultra ('81) 1,350. 125.00
*a.* Horiz. pair, imperf. btwn.
**28** A1 6p yellow green 425.00 77.50
**28A** A1 1sh vermilion 725.00 60.00
**29** A3 5sh rose 1,250. 1,350.

No. 29 is valued well centered with design well clear of the perfs.

See #35, 41, 54, 598. For surcharges see #31-33.

No. 14B Bisected and Surcharged in Red

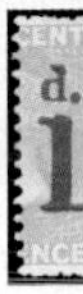


**1880, May** ***Perf. 14 to 16***
**30** A1 1p on half of 6p 475.00 350.00
*a.* Unsevered pair 1,250. 900.00

No. 28 Bisected and Surcharged in Red

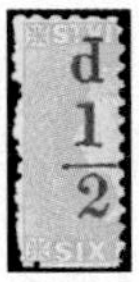


**1881, Sept. 1**
**31** A1 ½p on half of 6p yel grn ('81) 175. 175.
*a.* Unsevered pair 450. 450.
*b.* "1" with straight top 900.
*c.* Without fraction bar, pair, #31, 31c 4,250. *4,750.*

Nos. 28 and 28A Surcharged in Black:

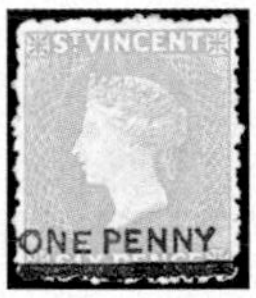

c

d

**1881, Nov.** ***Perf. 11 to 13***
**32** A1(c) 1p on 6p yel green 500. 350.
**33** A1(d) 4p on 1sh ver 1,550. 825.

**1883-84** **Wmk. 2** ***Perf. 12***
**35** A2 ½p green ('84) 85.00 27.50
**36** A1 4p ultra 425.00 25.00
**37** A1 4p dull blue ('04) 1,100. 275.00
**38** A1 6p yellow grn 175.00 325.00
**39** A1 1sh orange ver 125.00 57.50
*a.* Imperf., pair

The ½p orange, 1p rose red, 1p milky blue and 5sh carmine lake were never placed in use. Some authorities believe them to be color trials.

Nos. 35-60 may be found watermarked with single straight line. This is from the frame which encloses each group of 60 watermark designs.

Type of A1 Surcharged in Black

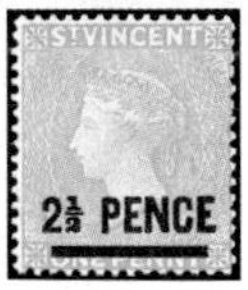

e

**1883** ***Perf. 14***
**40** A1 2½p on 1p lake 10.00 1.75

**1883-97**
**41** A2 ½p green ('85) 1.10 .65
**42** A1 1p drab 50.00 2.10
**43** A1 1p rose red ('85) 1.75 1.00
**44** A1 1p pink ('86) 5.00 1.90
**45** A1 2½p brt blue ('97) 4.25 1.90
**46** A1 4p ultra 450.00 40.00
**47** A1 4p red brown ('85) 950.00 25.00
**48** A1 4p lake brn ('86) 62.50 1.50
**49** A1 4p yellow ('93) 1.75 8.25
*a.* 4p olive yellow 350.00 350.00
**50** A1 5p gray brn ('97) 6.00 *22.50*
**51** A1 6p violet ('88) 150.00 *175.00*
**52** A1 6p red violet ('91) 2.50 *13.50*
**53** A1 1sh org ver ('91) 6.00 12.00
**54** A3 5sh car lake ('88) 30.00 *55.00*

Grading footnote after No. 29 applies equally to Nos. 54-54a.

For other shades, see the *Scott Classic Catalogue.*

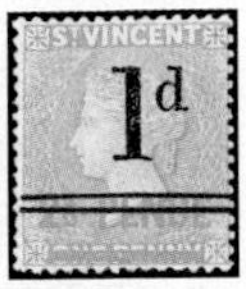


No. 40 Resurcharged in Black

**1885, Mar.**
**55** A1 1p on 2½p on 1p lake 24.00 17.50

Copies with 3-bar cancel are proofs.

Stamps of Type A1 Surcharged in Black or Violet:

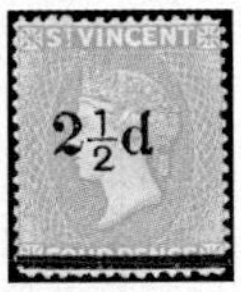

g

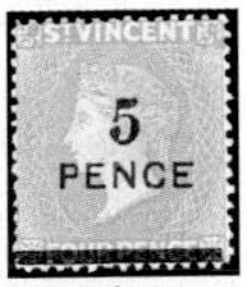

h

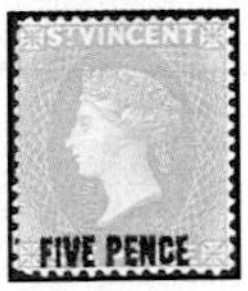

i

**1890-91**
**56** A1(e) 2½p on 1p brt blue 1.60 .40
*a.* 2½p on 1p milky blue 25.00 6.00
*b.* 2½p on 1p gray blue 20.00 .75
**57** A1(g) 2½p on 4p vio brn ('90) 87.50 *125.00*
*a.* Without fraction bar 400.00 *450.00*

**1892-93**
**58** A1(h) 5p on 4p lake brn (V) 20.00 *32.50*
**59** A1(j) 5p on 6p dp lake ('93) 1.10 *1.90*
*a.* 5p on 6p carmine lake 22.50 *32.50*
*b.* Double surcharge 5,000. 3,250.

**1897**
**60** A1(j) 3p on 1p lilac 6.00 *19.00*

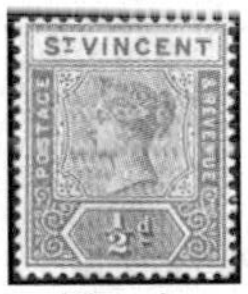


Victoria
A13

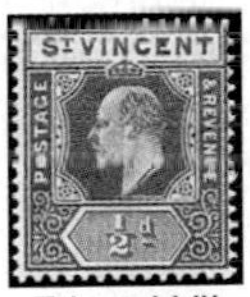


Edward VII
A14

Numerals of 1sh and 5sh, type A13, and of 2p, 1sh, 5sh and £1, type A14, are in color on plain tablet.

**1898** **Typo.** ***Perf. 14***
**62** A13 ½p lilac & grn 3.00 2.75
**63** A13 1p lil & car rose 5.00 1.10
**64** A13 2½p lilac & ultra 4.50 2.25
**65** A13 3p lilac & ol grn 4.50 *14.50*
**66** A13 4p lilac & org 4.50 *19.00*
**67** A13 5p lilac & blk 7.75 *14.50*
**68** A13 6p lilac & brn 14.50 *37.50*
**69** A13 1sh grn & car rose 14.50 *52.50*
**70** A13 5sh green & ultra 82.50 *150.00*
*Nos. 62-70 (9)* 140.75 *294.10*

**1902**
**71** A14 ½p violet & green 3.00 .75
**72** A14 1p vio & car rose 4.75 .35
**73** A14 2p violet & black 2.75 2.50
**74** A14 2½p violet & ultra 5.50 3.75
**75** A14 3p violet & ol grn 5.50 3.25
**76** A14 6p violet & brn 12.00 *32.50*
**77** A14 1sh grn & car rose 26.00 *60.00*
**78** A14 2sh green & violet 27.50 *60.00*
**79** A14 5sh green & ultra 77.50 *140.00*
*Nos. 71-79 (9)* 164.50 *303.10*

**1904-11** **Wmk. 3**

**Chalky Paper**
**82** A14 ½p vio & grn 1.40 1.40
**83** A14 1p vio & car rose 22.50 1.75
**84** A14 2½p vio & ultra 17.50 *47.50*
**85** A14 6p vio & brn 17.50 *47.50*
**86** A14 1sh grn & car rose 12.50 *52.50*
**87** A14 2sh vio & bl, *bl* 25.00 *47.50*
**88** A14 5sh grn & red, *yel* 19.00 *55.00*
**89** A14 £1 vio & blk, *red* 300.00 *350.00*
*Nos. 82-88 (7)* 115.40 *253.15*

#82, 83 and 86 also exist on ordinary paper.

Issued: 1p, 1904, ½p, 6p, 1905; 2½p, 1906; 1sh, 1908; 2sh, 5sh, 1909; £1, July 22, 1911.

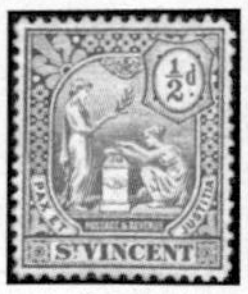
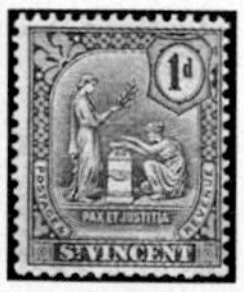

"Peace and Justice"
A15 A16

**1907** **Engr.**

**Ordinary Paper**

**90** A15 ½p yellow green 3.50 2.50
**91** A15 1p carmine 3.75 .25
**92** A15 2p orange 1.60 7.25
**93** A15 2½p ultra 30.00 10.00
**94** A15 3p dark violet 8.75 16.00
*Nos. 90-94 (5)* 47.60 36.00

**1909**

**Without Dot under "d"**

**95** A16 1p carmine 1.40 .40
**96** A16 6p red violet 6.00 35.00
**97** A16 1sh black, *green* 4.75 9.25
*Nos. 95-97 (3)* 12.15 44.65

**1909-11**

**With Dot under "d"**

**98** A16 ½p yellow grn ('10) 1.60 .65
**99** A16 1p carmine 1.60 .25
**100** A16 2p gray ('11) 4.50 9.25
**101** A16 2½p ultra 8.75 3.75
**102** A16 3p violet, *yel* 2.75 7.75
**103** A16 6p red violet 11.00 5.50
*Nos. 98-103 (6)* 30.20 27.15

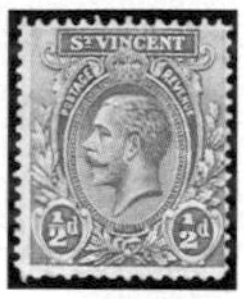

King George V — A17

**1913-14** ***Perf. 14***

**104** A17 ½p gray green .80 .25
**105** A17 1p carmine .90 .85
**106** A17 2p gray 3.25 32.50
**107** A17 2½p ultra .55 .80
**108** A17 3p violet, *yellow* .90 5.50
**109** A17 4p red, *yellow* .90 2.25
**110** A17 5p olive green 2.50 15.00
**111** A17 6p claret 2.25 5.00
**112** A17 1sh black, *green* 1.60 4.00
**113** A17 1sh bister ('14) 4.50 25.00
**114** A16 2sh vio & ultra 5.25 27.50
**115** A16 5sh dk grn & car 14.50 52.50
**116** A16 £1 black & vio 92.50 175.00
*Nos. 104-116 (13)* 130.40 346.15

Issued: 5p, 11/7; #113, 5/1/14; others, 1/1/13.

For overprints see Nos. MR1-MR2.

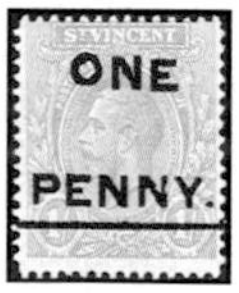

No. 112 Surcharged in Carmine

**1915**

**117** A17 1p on 1sh black, *grn* 8.25 29.00
*a.* "PENNY" & bar double 750.00 750.00
*b.* Without period 14.00
*c.* "ONE" omitted 1,000. 900.00
*d.* "ONE" double 750.00

Space between surcharge lines varies from 8 to 10mm.

**1921-32** **Wmk. 4**

**118** A17 ½p green 1.90 .35
**119** A17 1p rose red 1.10 .90
**120** A17 1½p yel brn ('32) 3.50 .20
**121** A17 2p gray 2.75 .90
**122** A17 2½p ultra ('26) 1.40 1.10
**123** A17 3p ultra 1.10 6.50
**124** A17 3p vio, *yel* ('27) 1.10 1.60
**125** A17 4p red, *yel* ('30) 1.90 6.50
**126** A17 5p olive green 1.10 7.25
**127** A17 6p claret ('27) 1.60 3.75
**128** A17 1sh bister 3.50 19.00
**129** A16 2sh brn vio & ultra 8.25 14.50
**130** A16 5sh dk grn & car 20.00 35.00
**131** A16 £1 blk & vio ('28) 92.50 125.00
*Nos. 118-131 (14)* 141.70 222.55

Common Design Types pictured following the introduction.

**Silver Jubilee Issue**

Common Design Type

**1935, May 6** ***Perf. 11x12***

**134** CD301 1p car & dk blue .55 2.50
**135** CD301 1½p gray blk & ultra 1.40 4.00
**136** CD301 2½p ultra & brn 2.50 4.00
**137** CD301 1sh brn vio & ind 2.75 4.00
*Nos. 134-137 (4)* 7.20 14.50
Set, never hinged 13.50

**Coronation Issue**

Common Design Type

**1937, May 12** ***Perf. 11x11½***

**138** CD302 1p dark purple .20 .40
**139** CD302 1½p dark carmine .25 .40
**140** CD302 2½p deep ultra .30 1.25
*Nos. 138-140 (3)* .75 2.05
Set, never hinged 1.25

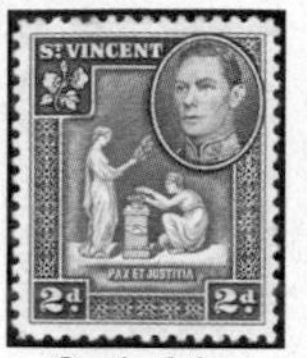

Seal of the Colony — A18

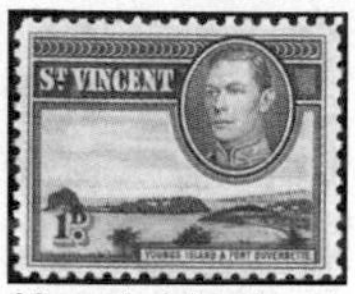

Young's Island and Fort Duvernette — A19

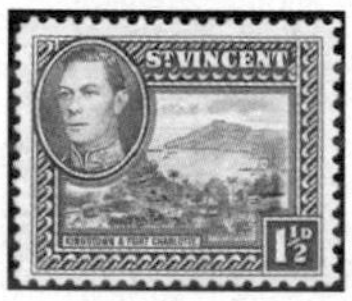

Kingstown and Fort Charlotte — A20

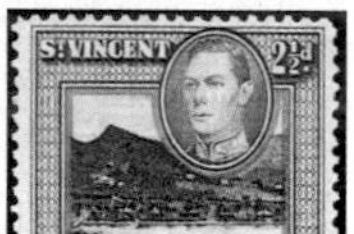

Villa Beach — A21

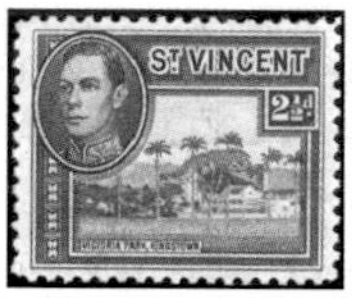

Victoria Park, Kingstown — A22

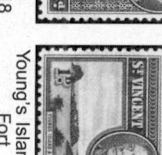

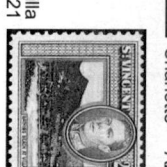

**1938-47** **Wmk. 4** ***Perf. 12***

**141** A18 ½p grn & brt bl .20 .20
**142** A19 1p claret & blue .20 .20
**143** A20 1½p scar & lt grn .20 .20
**144** A18 2p black & green .30 .20
**145** A21 2½p pck bl & ind .20 .20
**145A** A22 2½p choc & grn ('47) .20 .20
**146** A18 3p dk vio & org .20 .20
**146A** A21 3½p dp bl grn & ind ('47) .35 1.50
**147** A18 6p claret & blk .60 .25
**148** A22 1sh green & vio .60 .45
**149** A18 2sh dk vio & brt blue 4.50 .85
**149A** A18 2sh6p dp bl & org brn ('47) .80 3.75
**150** A18 5sh dk grn & car 7.50 2.75
**150A** A18 10sh choc & dp vio ('47) 3.00 10.00
**151** A18 £1 black & vio 11.00 16.00
*Nos. 141-151 (15)* 29.85 36.95
Set, never hinged 50.00

Issue date: Mar. 11, 1938.
See Nos. 156-169, 180-184.

**Catalogue values for unused stamps in this section, from this point to the end of the section, are for Never Hinged items.**

**Peace Issue**

Common Design Type

**1946, Oct. 15** **Engr.** ***Perf. 13½x14***

**152** CD303 1½p carmine .20 .20
**153** CD303 3½p deep blue .20 .20

**Silver Wedding Issue**

Common Design Types

**1948, Nov. 30** **Photo.** ***Perf. 14x14½***

**154** CD304 1½p scarlet .20 .20

**Engraved; Name Typographed**

***Perf. 11½x11***

**155** CD305 £1 red violet 25.00 25.00

Types of 1938

**1949, Mar. 26** **Engr.** ***Perf. 12***

**156** A18 1c grn & brt bl .20 1.75
**157** A19 2c claret & bl .20 .50
**158** A20 3c scar & lt grn .55 .95
**159** A18 4c gray blk & grn .40 .20
**160** A22 5c choc & grn .20 .20
**161** A18 6c dk vio & org .55 1.20
**162** A21 7c pck blue & ind 5.25 1.40
**163** A18 12c claret & blk .50 .20
**164** A22 24c green & vio .50 .55
**165** A18 48c dk vio & brt bl 2.75 2.75
**166** A18 60c dp bl & org brn 2.00 3.75
**167** A18 $1.20 dk grn & car 4.75 4.75
**168** A18 $2.40 choc & dp vio 6.75 9.25
**169** A18 $4.80 gray blk & vio 12.50 19.00
*Nos. 156-169 (14)* 37.10 46.45

For overprints see Nos. 176-179.

**UPU Issue**

Common Design Types

**Engr.; Name Typo. on 6c, 12c**

***Perf. 13½, 11x11½***

**1949, Oct. 10** **Wmk. 4**

**170** CD306 5c blue .20 .20
**171** CD307 6c dp rose violet .45 .90
**172** CD308 12c red lilac .25 .90
**173** CD309 24c blue green 1.00 .25
*Nos. 170-173 (4)* 1.90 2.25

**University Issue**

Common Design Types

**1951, Feb. 16** **Engr.** ***Perf. 14x14½***

**174** CD310 3c red & blue green .60 .60
**175** CD311 12c rose lilac & blk .60 1.10

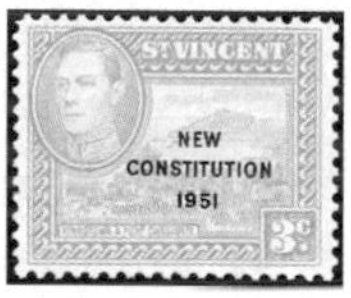

Nos. 158-160 and 163 Overprinted in Black

**1951, Sept. 21** ***Perf. 12***

**176** A20 3c scarlet & lt grn .20 1.25
**177** A18 4c gray blk & grn .20 .30
**178** A22 5c chocolate & grn .20 .30
**179** A18 12c claret & blk .60 .60
*Nos. 176-179 (4)* 1.20 2.45

Adoption of a new constitution for the Windward Islands, 1951.

Type of 1938-47

**1952**

**180** A18 1c gray black & green .20 .20
**181** A18 3c dk violet & orange .20 .20
**182** A18 4c green & brt blue .20 .20
**183** A20 6c scarlet & dp green .20 .20
**184** A21 10c peacock blue & indigo .35 .35
*Nos. 180-184 (5)* 1.15 1.15

**Coronation Issue**

Common Design Type

**1953, June 2** ***Perf. 13½x13***

**185** CD312 4c dk green & blk .70 .50

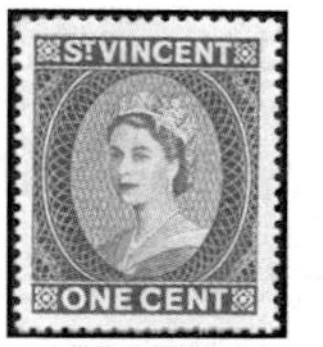

Elizabeth II — A23

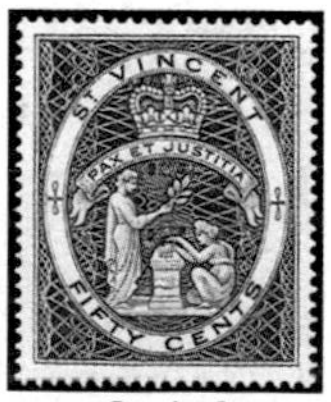

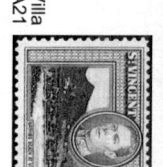

Seal of Colony — A24

***Perf. 13x14***

**1955, Sept. 16** **Wmk. 4** **Engr.**

**186** A23 1c orange .20 .20
**187** A23 2c violet blue .20 .20
**188** A23 3c gray .20 .20
**189** A23 4c dk red brown .20 .20
**190** A23 5c scarlet .20 .20
**191** A23 10c purple .25 .20
**192** A23 15c deep blue .40 .40
**193** A23 20c green .50 .20
**194** A23 25c brown black .90 .20

***Perf. 14***

**195** A24 50c chocolate 5.50 1.90
**196** A24 $1 dull green 8.75 1.25
**197** A24 $2.50 deep blue 9.00 9.00
*Nos. 186-197 (12)* 26.30 14.15

**West Indies Federation**

Common Design Type

***Perf. 11½x11***

**1958, Apr. 22** **Wmk. 314**

**198** CD313 3c green .30 .25
**199** CD313 6c blue .40 .50
**200** CD313 12c carmine rose .80 1.00
*Nos. 198-200 (3)* 1.50 1.75

**Freedom from Hunger Issue**

Common Design Type

**1963, June 4** **Photo.** ***Perf. 14x14½***

**201** CD314 8c lilac .90 .50

**Red Cross Centenary Issue**

Common Design Type

**1963, Sept. 2** **Litho.** ***Perf. 13***

**202** CD315 4c black & red .25 .20
**203** CD315 8c ultra & red .65 .65

Types of 1955

***Perf. 13x14***

**1964-65** **Wmk. 314** **Engr.**

**205** A23 1c orange .20 .20
**206** A23 2c violet blue .20 .20
**207** A23 3c gray .55 .60
**208** A23 5c scarlet .30 .30
**209** A23 10c purple .45 .45
*a.* Perf. 12½ .25 .25
**210** A23 15c deep blue .90 .80
*a.* Perf. 12½ .45 .30
**211** A23 20c green .70 .75
*a.* Perf. 12½ 7.50 2.00
**212** A23 25c brown black 1.25 1.35
*a.* Perf. 12½ 1.10 .85

***Perf. 14***

**213** A24 50c chocolate ('65) 5.25 5.50
*a.* Perf. 12½ 5.00 7.00
*Nos. 205-213 (9)* 9.80 10.15

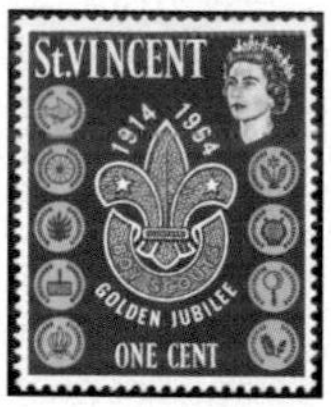

Scout Emblem and Merit Badges — A25

**1964, Nov. 23** **Litho.** ***Perf. 14***

**216** A25 1c dk brn & brt yel grn .20 .20
**217** A25 4c dk red brn & brt bl .20 .20
**218** A25 20c dk violet & orange .35 .20
**219** A25 50c green & red .65 .40
*Nos. 216-219 (4)* 1.40 1.00

Boy Scouts of St. Vincent, 50th anniv.

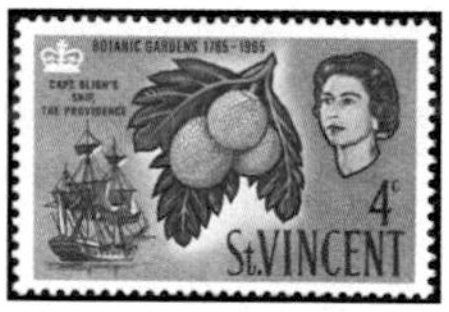

Breadfruit and Capt. Bligh's Ship "Providence" — A26

Designs: 1c, Tropical fruit. 25c, Doric temple and pond, vert. 40c, Blooming talipot palm and Doric temple, vert.

***Perf. 14½x13½, 13½x14½***

**1965, Mar. 23** **Photo.** **Wmk. 314**

**220** A26 1c dk green & multi .20 .20
**221** A26 4c lt & dk brn grn & yel .20 .20
**222** A26 25c blue, grn & bister .25 .20
**223** A26 40c dk blue & multi .50 .75
*Nos. 220-223 (4)* 1.15 1.35

Bicentenary of the Botanic Gardens.

**ITU Issue**

Common Design Type

**1965, May 17** **Litho.** ***Perf. 11x11½***

**224** CD317 4c blue & yel grn .20 .20
**225** CD317 48c yellow & orange .80 .70

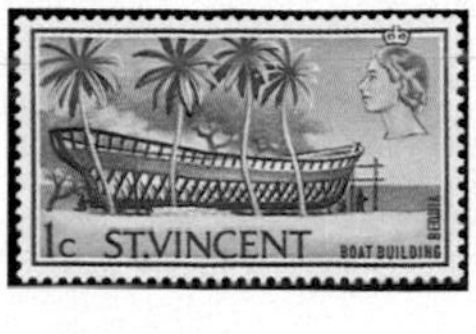

Boat Building, Bequia A27

DHC6
Twin Otter
A37

20th anniv. of regular air services: 8c, Grumman Goose amphibian. 10c, Hawker Siddeley 748. 25c, Douglas DC-3.

**1970, Mar. 13    Litho.    Wmk. 314**

| | | | |
|---|---|---|---|
| 295 | A37 | 5c | lt blue & multi | .20 | .20 |
| 296 | A37 | 8c | lt green & multi | .20 | .20 |
| 297 | A37 | 10c | pink & multi | .40 | .25 |
| 298 | A37 | 25c | yellow & multi | 1.00 | .65 |
| | | | *Nos. 295-298 (4)* | 1.80 | 1.30 |

Nurse and Children
A38

Red Cross and: 5c, First aid. 12c, Volunteers. 25c, Blood transfusion.

**1970, June 1    Photo.    Perf. 14**

| | | | |
|---|---|---|---|
| 299 | A38 | 3c | blue & multi | .20 | .20 |
| 300 | A38 | 5c | yellow & multi | .20 | .20 |
| 301 | A38 | 12c | lt green & multi | .30 | .30 |
| 302 | A38 | 25c | pale salmon & multi | .60 | .55 |
| | | | *Nos. 299-302 (4)* | 1.30 | 1.15 |

Centenary of British Red Cross Society.

St. George's Cathedral — A39

Doeigno: ¼c, ½c, Angel and Twin Marys at the Tomb, stained glass window, vert. 25c, St. George's Cathedral, front view, vert. 35c, Interior with altar.

**1970, Sept. 7    Litho.    Wmk. 314**

| | | | |
|---|---|---|---|
| 303 | A39 | ¼c | multicolored | .20 | .20 |
| 304 | A39 | 5c | multicolored | .20 | .20 |
| 305 | A39 | 25c | multicolored | .25 | .20 |
| 306 | A39 | 35c | multicolored | .30 | .25 |
| 307 | A39 | 50c | multicolored | .35 | .30 |
| | | | *Nos. 303-307 (5)* | 1.35 | 1.15 |

St. George's Anglican Cathedral, 150th anniv.

Virgin and Child, by Giovanni Bellini — A40

Christmas: 25c, 50c, Adoration of the Shepherds, by Louis Le Nain, horiz.

**1970, Nov. 23    Litho.    Wmk. 314**

| | | | |
|---|---|---|---|
| 308 | A40 | 8c | brt violet & multi | .20 | .20 |
| 309 | A40 | 8c | crimson & multi | .20 | .20 |
| 310 | A40 | 35c | yellow grn & multi | .25 | .25 |
| 311 | A40 | 50c | sapphire & multi | .40 | .30 |
| | | | *Nos. 308-311 (4)* | 1.05 | .90 |

Post Office and St. Vincent No. 1B — A41

---

"Strength in Unity" — A34

5c, 25c, Map of the Caribbean, vert.

**1969, July 1    Perf. 13½x13, 13x13½    Litho.**

| | | | |
|---|---|---|---|
| 272 | A34 | 2c | orange, yel & blk | .20 | .20 |
| 273 | A34 | 5c | lilac & multi | .20 | .20 |
| 274 | A34 | 8c | emerald, yel & blk | .20 | .20 |
| 275 | A34 | 25c | blue & multi | .50 | .30 |
| | | | *Nos. 272-275 (4)* | 1.10 | .90 |

1st anniv. of CARIFTA (Caribbean Free Trade Area.)

Flag and Arms of St. Vincent — A35

Designs: 10c, Uprising of 1795. 50c, Government House.

**1969, Oct. 27    Photo.    Wmk. 314**

| | | | |
|---|---|---|---|
| 276 | A35 | 4c | deep ultra & multi | .20 | .20 |
| 277 | A35 | 10c | olive & multi | .20 | .20 |
| 278 | A35 | 50c | orange, gray & blk | .65 | .50 |
| | | | *Nos. 276-278 (3)* | 1.05 | .90 |

Green Heron
A36

Birds: ¼c, House wren, vert. 2c, Bullfinches. 3c, St. Vincent parrots. 4c, St. Vincent solitaire, vert. 6c, Scalynecked pigeon, vert. 6c, Bananaquits. 8c, Purple-throated Carib. 10c, Mangrove cuckoo, vert. 12c, Black hawk, vert. 20c, Bare-eyed thrush. 25c, Hooded tanager. 50c, Blue-hooded euphonia. $1, Barn owl, vert. $2.50, Yellow-bellied elaenia, vert. $5, Ruddy quail-dove.

**Wmk. 314 Upright on ¼c, 4c, 5c, 10c, 12c, 50c, $5, Sideways on Others**

**1970, Jan. 12    Photo.    Perf. 14**

| | | | |
|---|---|---|---|
| 279 | A36 | ¼c | multicolored | .20 | .20 |
| 280 | A36 | 1c | multicolored | .20 | .20 |
| 281 | A36 | 2c | multicolored | .20 | .20 |
| 282 | A36 | 3c | multicolored | .20 | .20 |
| 283 | A36 | 4c | multicolored | .40 | .20 |
| 284 | A36 | 4c | multicolored | 1.25 | .65 |
| 285 | A36 | 6c | multicolored | .40 | .35 |
| 286 | A36 | 8c | multicolored | .45 | .35 |
| 287 | A36 | 10c | multicolored | .45 | .25 |
| 288 | A36 | 12c | multicolored | .60 | .40 |
| 289 | A36 | 20c | multicolored | .80 | .50 |
| 290 | A36 | 25c | multicolored | .80 | .55 |
| 291 | A36 | 50c | multicolored | 1.25 | .75 |
| 292 | A36 | $1 | multicolored | 3.25 | 1.50 |
| 293 | A36 | $2.50 | multicolored | 6.50 | 4.00 |
| 294 | A36 | $5 | multicolored | 16.00 | 10.00 |
| | | | *Nos. 279-294 (16)* | 32.70 | 20.25 |

See #379-381. For surcharges see #364-366.

**Wmk. 314 Upright on 2c, 3c, 6c, 20c, Sideways on Others**

**1973**

| | | | |
|---|---|---|---|
| 281a | A36 | 2c | multicolored | .35 | .40 |
| 282a | A36 | 3c | multicolored | .35 | .35 |
| 283a | A36 | 4c | multicolored | .50 | .40 |
| 284a | A36 | 6c | multicolored | .50 | .55 |
| 285a | A36 | 8c | multicolored | .50 | .55 |
| 286a | A36 | 10c | multicolored | .75 | .55 |
| 287a | A36 | 20c | multicolored | .85 | .55 |
| 288a | A36 | 50c | multicolored | 4.00 | 3.00 |
| | | | *Nos. 281a-289a (8)* | | |

---

Woman Carrying Bananas — A28

Designs: 2c, Friendship Beach, Bequia. 3c, Terminal building. 5c, Crater Lake. 6c, Rock carvings, Carib Stone. 8c, Arrowroot. 10c, Owia saltpond. 12c, Ship at deep water wharf. 20c, Sea Island cotton. 25c, Map of St. Vincent and neighboring Islands. 50c, Breadfruit. $1, Baleine Falls. $2.50, St. Vincent parrot. $5, Coat of arms.

**1965-67    Perf. 14x13½, 13½x14    Photo.    Wmk. 314**

| | | | |
|---|---|---|---|
| 226 | A27 | 1c | (BEQUIA) | .20 | .75 |
| 226A | A27 | 1c | (BEQUIA) | .60 | .35 |
| 227 | A27 | 2c | lt ultra, grn, yel & red | .20 | .20 |
| 228 | A27 | 3c | red, yel & brn | .40 | .20 |
| 229 | A28 | 4c | brown, ultra & yel | .75 | .35 |
| | | a. | Wmkd. sideways | .50 | .20 |
| 230 | A27 | 5c | pur, bl, yel & gray | .20 | .20 |
| 231 | A28 | 6c | sl grn, yel & gray | .20 | .30 |
| 232 | A28 | 8c | pur, yel & grn | .20 | .40 |
| 233 | A27 | 10c | org brn, yel & bluish grn | .40 | .20 |
| 234 | A27 | 12c | grnish bl, yel & pink | .65 | .20 |
| 235 | A28 | 20c | brt yel, grn, pur & brn | .40 | .20 |
| 236 | A27 | 25c | ultra, grn & vio blue | .20 | .20 |
| 237 | A28 | 50c | grn, yel & bl | .45 | .45 |
| 238 | A27 | $1 | vio bl, lt grm & dk sl grn | .45 | .45 |
| 239 | A28 | $2.50 | pale lilac & multi | 4.00 | 4.00 |
| 240 | A28 | $5 | dull vio blue & multi | 18.50 | 8.00 |
| | | | | 4.25 | 10.00 |
| | | | *Nos. 226-240 (16)* | 32.05 | 22.10 |

Issued: #226A, 8/8/67; others, 8/16/65. For overprint see No. 270.

**Churchill Memorial Issue**
**Common Design Type**

**1966, Jan. 24    Perf. 14**

**Design in Black, Gold and Carmine Rose**

| | | | |
|---|---|---|---|
| 241 | CD319 | 1c | bright blue | .20 | .20 |
| 242 | CD319 | 4c | green | .20 | .20 |
| 243 | CD319 | 20c | brown | .40 | .40 |
| 244 | CD319 | 25c | violet | .75 | .75 |
| | | | *Nos. 241-244 (4)* | 1.55 | 1.55 |

**Royal Visit Issue**
**Common Design Type**

**1966, Feb. 4    Litho.    Perf. 11x12**
**Portrait in Black**

| | | | |
|---|---|---|---|
| 245 | CD320 | 4c | violet blue | .50 | .20 |
| 246 | CD320 | 25c | dk carmine rose | 2.50 | 1.50 |

**WHO Headquarters Issue**
**Common Design Type**

**1966, Sept. 20    Litho.    Perf. 14**

| | | | |
|---|---|---|---|
| 247 | CD322 | 4c | multicolored | .20 | .20 |
| 248 | CD322 | 25c | multicolored | 1.00 | .75 |

**UNESCO Anniversary Issue**
**Common Design Type**

**1966, Dec. 1    Litho.    Perf. 14**

| | | | |
|---|---|---|---|
| 249 | CD323 | 4c | "Education" | .20 | .20 |
| 250 | CD323 | 8c | "Science" | .50 | .50 |
| 251 | CD323 | 25c | "Culture" | 1.50 | .75 |
| | | | *Nos. 249-251 (3)* | 2.20 | 1.15 |

View of Mt. Coke Area
A29

Designs: 8c, Kingstown Methodist Church. 25c, First license to perform marriage, May 15, 1867. 35c, Arms of Conference of the Methodist Church in the Caribbean and the Americas.

---

**1967, Dec. 1    Perf. 14x14½    Photo.    Wmk. 314**

| | | | |
|---|---|---|---|
| 252 | A29 | 2c | multicolored | .20 | .20 |
| 253 | A29 | 8c | multicolored | .20 | .20 |
| 254 | A29 | 25c | multicolored | .25 | .20 |
| 255 | A29 | 35c | multicolored | .30 | .30 |
| | | | *Nos. 252-255 (4)* | .95 | .80 |

Attainment of autonomy by the Methodist Church in the Caribbean and the Americas, and opening of headquarters near St. John's, Antigua, May 1967.
For overprints see Nos. 268-269, 271.

Caribbean Meteorological Institute, Barbados — A30

**1968, June 28    Perf. 14x14½    Photo.    Wmk. 314**

| | | | |
|---|---|---|---|
| 256 | A30 | 4c | cerise & multi | .20 | .20 |
| 257 | A30 | 25c | vermilion & multi | .25 | .20 |
| 258 | A30 | 35c | violet blue & multi | .65 | .60 |
| | | | *Nos. 256-258 (3)* | | |

Issued for World Meteorological Day.

Martin Luther King, Jr. and Cotton Pickers
A31

**1968, Aug. 28    Perf. 13½x13    Litho.    Wmk. 314**

| | | | |
|---|---|---|---|
| 259 | A31 | 5c | violet & multi | .25 | .25 |
| 260 | A31 | 25c | gray & multi | .35 | .25 |
| 261 | A31 | 35c | brown red & multi | .80 | .70 |
| | | | *Nos. 259-261 (3)* | | |

Dr. Martin Luther King, Jr. (1929-68), American civil rights leader.

Scales of Justice and Human Rights Flame — A32

3c, Speaker addressing demonstrators, horiz.

**1968, Nov. 1    Perf. 13x14, 14x13    Photo.    Unwmk.**

| | | | |
|---|---|---|---|
| 262 | A32 | 3c | orange & multi | .20 | .20 |
| 263 | A32 | 35c | grnsh blue & vio blue | .35 | .20 |

International Human Rights Year.

Carnival Costume — A33

5c, Sketch of a steel bandsman. 8c, Revelers, horiz. 25c, Queen of Bands & attendants.

**1969, Feb. 17    Litho.    Perf. 14½**

| | | | |
|---|---|---|---|
| 264 | A33 | 1c | multicolored | .20 | .20 |
| 265 | A33 | 5c | red & dark brown | .20 | .20 |
| 266 | A33 | 8c | multicolored | .40 | .20 |
| 267 | A33 | 25c | multicolored | 1.00 | .85 |
| | | | *Nos. 264-267 (4)* | | |

St. Vincent Carnival celebration, Feb. 17.

Nos. 252-253, 236 and 255 Overprinted: "METHODIST / CONFERENCE / MAY / 1969"

**1969, May 14    Perf. 14x14½, 13½x14    Photo.    Wmk. 314**

| | | | |
|---|---|---|---|
| 268 | A29 | 2c | multicolored | .20 | .20 |
| 269 | A29 | 8c | multicolored | .25 | .20 |
| 270 | A28 | 25c | multicolored | 1.50 | 2.00 |
| 271 | A29 | 35c | multicolored | 2.10 | 2.60 |

1st Caribbean Methodist Conf. held outside Antigua.

New Post Office and: 4c, $1, St. Vincent No.
1, 25c, as 2c.

**1971, Mar. 29**          **Perf. 14½x14**
312  A41  2c violet & multi          .20  .20
313  A41  4c olive & multi           .20  .20
314  A41  25c brown org & multi      .65  .50
315  A41  $1 lt green & multi       1.25  1.10
  Nos. 312-315 (4)

110th anniv. of 1st stamps of St. Vincent.

National Trust Emblem, Fish and
Birds — A42

Designs: 30c, 45c, Cannon at Ft. Charlotte.

**1971, Aug. 4    Litho.    Wmk. 314**
316  A42  12c emerald & multi       .20  .20
317  A42  30c lt blue & multi       .40  .35
318  A42  40c brt pink & multi      .80  .40
319  A42  45c black & multi         .80  .60
  Nos. 316-319 (4)                 2.00  1.55

Publicity for the National Trust (for conservation of wild life and historic buildings).

Holy Family with Angels (detail), by
Pietro da Cortona
A43

Christmas: 5c, 25c, Madonna Appearing to
St. Anthony, by Domenico Tiepolo, vert.

**1971, Oct. 6    Perf. 14x14½, 14½x14**
320  A43  5c rose & multi          .20  .20
321  A43  10c lt green & multi     .20  .20
322  A43  25c lt blue & multi      .75  .55
323  A43  $1 yellow & multi       1.35  1.15

Careening
A44

**1971, Nov. 25          Perf. 14x13½**
324  A44  1c dp ver & multi         .20  .20
325  A44  5c blue & multi           .20  .20
326  A44  6c yel grn & multi        .35  .20
327  A44  15c org brn & multi       .35  .35
328  A44  20c yellow & multi        .40  .30
329  A44  50c blue, blk & plum     1.00  .85
  a.  Souvenir sheet of 6, #324-329  13.00  13.00
  Nos. 324-329 (6)                  2.35  2.00

The Grenadines of St. Vincent tourist issue.

Grenadier
Company
Private,
1764 — A45

Designs: 5c, 20c, Seine fishermen. 6c, 50c,
Map of Grenadines. 15c, as 1c.

---

Designs: 30c, Battalion Company officer,
1772. 50c, Grenadier Company private, 1772.

**1972, Feb. 14          Perf. 14x13½**
330  A45  12c gray violet & multi   .75  .60
331  A45  30c gray blue & multi    2.00  1.50
332  A45  50c dark gray & multi    2.75  2.75
  Nos. 330-332 (3)                 6.25  4.85

Breadnut — A46

**1972, May 16    Litho.    Perf. 14x13½**
333  A46  3c shown                  .20  .20
334  A46  5c Papaya                 .20  .20
335  A46  12c Rose apples           .40  .30
336  A46  25c Mangoes              1.10  .75
  Nos. 333-336 (4)                 1.90  1.45

Flowers of St.
Vincent — A47

Sir Charles Brisbane, Arms of St.
Vincent — A48

**1972, July 31    Litho.    Perf. 13½x13**
337  A47  1c Candlestick Cassia     .20  .20
338  A47  30c Lobster claw          .35  .35
339  A47  40c White trumpet         .40  .35
340  A47  $1 Flowers, Soufriere
           tree                    1.10  .75
  Nos. 337-340 (4)                 2.05  1.60

Bicentenary of the birth of Sir Charles Brisbane, naval hero, governor of St. Vincent.

**1972, Sept. 29    Wmk. 314    Perf. 13½**
341  A48  20c yel, brn & gold       .45  .35
342  A48  30c lilac & multi         .45  .40
343  A48  $1 multicolored          1.75  1.50
  a.  Souvenir sheet of 3, #341-343  6.00  6.00
  Nos. 341-343 (3)                 2.65  2.25

Silver Wedding Issue, 1972
Common Design Type

Design: Queen Elizabeth II, Prince Philip,
arrowroot plant, breadfruit foliage and fruit.

**1972, Nov. 20    Photo.    Perf. 14x14½**
344  CD324  30c rose brn & multi    .20  .20
345  CD324  $1 multicolored         .45  .30

Columbus Sighting St. Vincent — A49

12c, Caribs watching Columbus' ships. 30c,
Christopher Columbus. 50c, Santa Maria.

---

**1973, Jan. 18          Litho.    Perf. 13**
346  A49  5c multicolored           .20  .25
347  A49  12c multicolored          .35  .25
348  A49  30c multicolored         1.10  .75
349  A49  50c multicolored         2.25  2.00
  Nos. 346-349 (4)                 3.90  3.25

475th anniversary of Columbus's Third Voyage to the West Indies.

The Last Supper — A50

**1973, Apr. 19    Litho.    Wmk. 314**
350  A50  15c red & multi           .20  .25
351  A50  60c red & multi           .30  .30
352  A50  $1 red & multi           1.00  1.00
  a.  Strip of 3, #350-352          .55  .55

Easter.

William Wilberforce and Slave Auction
Poster — A51

40c, Slaves working on sugar plantation.
50c, Wilberforce & medal commemorating 1st
anniversary of abolition of slavery.

**1973, July 11          Perf. 14x13½**
353  A51  30c multicolored          .20  .20
354  A51  40c multicolored          .25  .20
355  A51  50c multicolored          .45  .45
  Nos. 353-355 (3)                  .90  .75

140th anniv of the death of William Wilberforce (1759-1833), member of British Parliament who fought for abolition of slavery.

21st ANNIVERSARY of the
INTERNATIONAL PLANNED
PARENTHOOD FEDERATION

Families — A52

Design: 40c, Families and "IPPF."

**1973, Oct. 3          Perf. 14½**
356  A52  12c multicolored          .20  .20
357  A52  40c multicolored          .50  .35

Intl. Planned Parenthood Assoc., 21st anniv.

Princess Anne's Wedding Issue
Common Design Type

**1973, Nov. 14          Perf. 14**
358  CD325  50c slate & multi       .20  .20
359  CD325  70c gray green & multi  .25  .20

---

**1973, Dec. 13    Perf. 14x14, 14x14½**
360  A53  5c multicolored           .20  .20
361  A53  10c multicolored          .20  .20
362  A53  30c multicolored          .40  .20
363  A53  $1 multicolored          1.00  .85
  Nos. 360-363 (4)

University of the West Indies, 25th anniv.

Administration Buildings, Mona
University — A53

Designs: 10c, University Center, Kingstown.
30c, Mona University, aerial view. $1, Coat of
arms of University of West Indies.

**1973, Dec. 15    Photo.    Perf. 14**
364  A36  30c on 50c multi        10.75  .30
365  A36  40c on 8c multi           .45  .30
366  A36  $10 on $1 multi         11.50  9.00
  Nos. 364-366 (3)                22.50

Nos. 291, 286 and 292 Surcharged

The position of the surcharge and shape of
obliterating bars differs on each denomination.

Easter: 30c, Descent from the Cross. 40c,
Pietá, $1, Resurrection. Designs are from
sculptures in Victoria and Albert Museum,
London, and Provincial Museum, Valladolid
(40c).

Descent from the
Cross — A54

**1974, Apr. 10    Litho.    Perf. 13½x13**
367  A54  5c multicolored           .20  .20
368  A54  30c multicolored          .30  .20
369  A54  40c multicolored          .30  .20
370  A54  $1 multicolored          .90  .80
  Nos. 367-370 (4)

"Istra"
A55

**1974, June 28          Perf. 14½**
371  A55  15c shown                 .20  .20
372  A55  20c multicolored          .35  .20
373  A55  30c "Oceanic"             .60  .20
374  A55  $1 "Alexander Pushkin"   1.00  .60
  a.  Souvenir sheet of 4, #371-374  1.75  1.25
  Nos. 371-374 (4)

Cruise ships visiting Kingstown.

Arrows
Circling
UPU
Emblem
A56

UPU, cont.: 12c, Post horn and globe. 60c,
Target over map of islands. 90c, Goode's
map projection.

Centenary of Universal Postal Union

ST. VINCENT

## 1974, July 25 — Perf. 14½
375 A56 5c violet & multi .20 .20
376 A56 12c ocher, green & blue .20 .25
377 A56 60c blue green & multi .50 .40
378 A56 90c red & multi 1.20 1.05

### Bird Type of 1970
Birds: 30c, Royal tern. 40c, Brown pelican, vert. $10, Magnificent frigate bird, vert.

### Wmk. 314 Sideways on 40c, $10, Upright on 30c
1974, Aug. 29 — Litho. — Perf. 14½
379 A36 30c multicolored 2.00 .75
380 A36 40c multicolored 2.00 .75
381 A36 $10 multicolored 13.00 10.00
Nos. 379-381 (3) 17.00 11.50

### Scout Emblem and Badges — A57

1974, Oct. 9 — Wmk. 314 — Perf. 13½x14
385 A57 10c lilac & multi .20 .20
386 A57 25c bister & multi .25 .20
387 A57 45c gray & multi .40 .30
388 A57 $1 multicolored .80 .60
Nos. 385-388 (4) 1.65 1.30

St. Vincent Day Scouts, 60th anniversary.

### Churchill as Prime Minister — A58

25c ST. VINCENT

Designs (Churchill as): 35c, Lord Warden of the Cinque Ports. 45c, First Lord of the Admiralty. $1, Royal Air Force officer.

1974, Nov. 28 — Perf. 14½x14
389 A58 25c multicolored .20 .20
390 A58 35c multicolored .20 .20
391 A58 45c multicolored .20 .20
392 A58 $1 multicolored .40 .30
Nos. 389-392 (4) 1.00 .90

Sir Winston Churchill (1874-1965), birth centenary. Sheets of 30 in 2 panes of 15 with inscribed gutter between.

A59 / A60

1974, Dec. 5 — Perf. 12x12½
393 A59 3c like 8c .20 .20
394 A59 3c like 35c .20 .20
395 A60 3c like 45c .20 .20
396 A60 3c like $1 .20 .20
a. Strip of 4, #393-396
397 A59 8c Shepherds .20 .20
398 A59 35c Virgin, Child and Star .20 .20
399 A60 45c St. Joseph, Ass & Ox .25 .30
400 A60 $1 Three Kings 1.95 1.70
Nos. 393-400 (8)

Christmas. Nos. 396a, 397-400 have continuous picture.

### Giant Mask and Dancers — A61

Designs: 15c, Pineapple dancers. 25c, Giant bouquet. 35c, Girl dancers. 45c, Butterfly dancers. $1.25, Sun and moon dancers and float.

1975, Feb. 7 — Wmk. 314 — Perf. 14
401 A61 1c multicolored .20 .20
a. Bkt. pane of 2 + label .25
b. Bkt. pane of 3, #401, 403, 405 .60
402 A61 15c multicolored 1.50 .20
a. Bkt. pane of 3, #402, 404, 406 1.50
403 A61 25c multicolored .20 .20
404 A61 35c multicolored .20 .20
405 A61 45c multicolored .50 .35
406 A61 $1.25 multicolored 1.75 1.25
a. Souvenir sheet of 6, #401-406 1.50 1.35
Nos. 401-406 (6)

Kingstown carnival 1975.

### French Angelfish — A62

Designs: Fish and whales.

Two types of $2.50:
I — Line to fish's mouth.
II — Line removed (1976).

1975, Apr. 10 — Wmk. 373 — Litho. — Perf. 14
407 A62 1c shown .20 .20
408 A62 2c Spotfin butterflyfish .20
409 A62 3c Horse-eyed jack .20
410 A62 4c Mackerel .20
411 A62 5c French grunts .20
412 A62 8c Spotted goatfish .20 .20
413 A62 9c Dollyhooa .20
414 A62 10c Sperm whale .20
415 A62 12c Humpback whale .20 .20
416 A62 15c Cowfish .20 .20
417 A62 20c Queen angelfish .35
418 A62 25c Princess parrotfish .30 .25
419 A62 35c Red hind .36 .25
420 A62 45c Atlantic flying fish .60 .35
421 A62 50c Porkfish .60 .45
422 A62 $1 Queen triggerfish .70 .50
423 A62 $2.50 Sailfish, type I 1.50 1.10
a. Type II 3.25 2.25
424 A62 $5 Dolphinfish 3.00 4.50
425 A62 $10 Blue marlin 12.00 9.25
Nos. 407-425 (19) 28.45 21.05

The 4c, 10c, 20c, $1, were reissued with "1976" below design; 1c, 2c, 3c, 5c, 6c, 8c, 12c, 50c, $10, with "1977" below design; 10c with "1978" below design.
No. 423a issued 7/12/76.
See #472-474. For surcharges and overprints see #463-464, 499-500, 502-503, 572-581, 584-586.

### Cutting Bananas — A63

Banana Industry: 35c, La Croix packing station. 45c, Women cleaning and packing bananas. 70c, Freighter loading bananas.

## 1975, June 26 — Wmk. 314 — Perf. 14
426 A63 25c blue & multi .20 .20
427 A63 35c blue & multi .20 .20
428 A63 45c carmine & multi .25 .30
429 A63 70c carmine & multi .40 .30
Nos. 426-429 (4) 1.05 .90

### Snorkel Diving — A64

15c ST. VINCENT — SNORKEL DIVING

Designs: 20c, Aquaduct Golf Course. 35c, Steel band at Mariner's Inn. 45c, Sunbathing at Young Island. $1.25, Yachting marina.

1975, July 31 — Wmk. 373 — Litho. — Perf. 13½
430 A64 15c multicolored .25 .20
431 A64 20c multicolored .50 .50
432 A64 35c multicolored .75 .30
433 A64 45c multicolored 2.00 1.00
434 A64 $1.25 multicolored 4.25 2.30
Nos. 430-434 (5)

Tourist publicity.

### Presidents Washington, John Adams, Jefferson and Madison — A65

U.S. Presidents: 1c, Monroe, John Quincy Adams, Jackson, Van Buren. 1½c, Wm. Harrison, Tyler, Polk, Taylor. 5c, Fillmore, Pierce, Buchanan, Lincoln. 10c, Johnson, Grant, Hayes, Garfield. 25c, Arthur, Cleveland, Benjamin Harrison, McKinley. 35c, Theodore Roosevelt, Taft, Wilson, Harding. 45c, Coolidge, Hoover, Franklin D. Roosevelt, Truman. $1, Eisenhower, Kennedy, Lyndon B. Johnson, Nixon. $2, Ford and White House.

1975, Sept. 11 — Unwmk. — Perf. 14½
435 A65 ½c violet & blk .20 .20
436 A65 1c green & black .20 .20
437 A65 1½c rose lilac & blk .20 .20
438 A65 5c yellow grn & blk .20 .20
439 A65 10c ultra & blk .20 .20
440 A65 25c ocher & blk .25 .25
441 A65 35c brt blue & blk .20 .20
442 A65 45c carmine & blk .20 .20
443 A65 $1 orange & blk .30 .25
444 A65 $2 lt olive & blk .60 .45
a. Souvenir sheet of 10, #435-444 + 2 labels 2.75 2.75
Nos. 435-444 (10) 2.50 2.30

Bicentenary of American Independence. Each issued in sheets of 10 stamps and 2 labels picturing the White House, Capitol, Mt. Vernon, etc.

### Nativity — A66

8 cents — St. Vincent — Christmas 1975

#445a, 8c, Star of Bethlehem. #445b, 45c, Shepherds. #445c, $1, Kings. #445d, 35c, Nativity.

## 1975, Dec. 4 — Wmk. 314 — Litho. — Perf. 14
### Se-tenant Pairs, #a.-b.
a. — Top stamp.
b. — Bottom stamp.
445 A66 3c Triangular block of 4, #a.-b. .45 .45
446 A66 8c Pair, #a.-b. .20 .20
447 A66 35c Pair, #a.-b. .30 .30
448 A66 45c Pair, #a.-b. .35 .35
449 A66 70c Pair, #a.-b. .65 .60
Nos. 445-449 (5) 2.00 1.75

Christmas. No. 445 has continuous design.

### Carnival Costumes — A68

ST. VINCENT — KINGSTOWN CARNIVAL 76

Designs: 2c, Humpty-Dumpty people. 5c, Smiling faces (masks). 35c, Dragon worshippers. 45c, Duck costume. $1.25, Bumble bee dance.

1976, Feb. 19 — Perf. 13x13½ — Litho.
457 A68 1c carmine & multi .20 .20
a. Bkt. pane of 2, #457-458 + label 1.75
458 A68 2c black & multi .20 .20
a. Bkt. pane of 3, #458-460 .50
459 A68 5c lt blue & multi .20 .20
460 A68 35c lt blue & multi .50 .50
a. Bkt. pane of 3, #460-462 1.75
461 A68 45c black & multi .25 .20
462 A68 $1.25 carmine & multi .50 .30
Nos. 457-462 (6) 1.55 1.30

Kingstown carnival 1976.

### Nos. 409 and 421 Surcharged with New Value and Bar

1976, Apr. 8 — Wmk. 314 — Perf. 14
463 A62 70c on 3c multi .65 1.00
464 A62 90c on 50c multi .65 1.25

### Yellow Hibiscus and Blue-headed Hummingbird A69
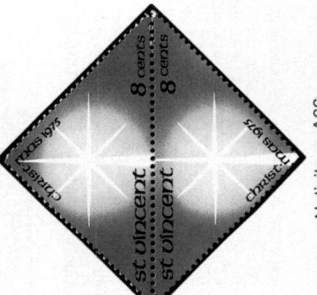

Designs: 10c, Single pink hibiscus and crested hummingbird. 35c, Single white hibiscus and purple-throated carib. 45c, Common red hibiscus and blue-headed hummingbird. $1.25, Single peach hibiscus and green-throated carib.

1976, May 20 — Litho. — Wmk. 373
465 A69 5c multicolored .20 .20
466 A69 10c multicolored .40 .30
467 A69 35c multicolored 1.25 1.00
468 A69 45c multicolored 2.00 1.50
469 A69 $1.25 multicolored 6.00 3.75
Nos. 465-469 (5) 9.85 6.75

### Map of West Indies, Bats, Wicket and Ball A69a

15c ST. VINCENT

### Prudential Cup — A69b

45c St. VINCENT

ST. VINCENT

ST. VINCENT

## Fish Type of 1975

| | | | |
|---|---|---|---|
| **1976, Sept. 16** | | **Unwmk.** | **Perf. 14** |
| 470 | A69a | 15¢ tt blue & multi | .60 .30 |
| 471 | A69b | 45¢ lilac rose & blk | 1.40 1.00 |

World Cricket Cup, won by West Indies Team, 1975.

| | | | |
|---|---|---|---|
| **1976, Oct. 14** | | **Wmk. 373** | **Perf. 14** |
| 472 | A62 | 15¢ Skipjack | .20 .20 |
| 473 | A62 | 70¢ Albacore | .65 .65 |
| 474 | A62 | 90¢ Pompano | .75 .75 |
| | | Nos. 472-474 (3) | 1.60 1.60 |

For overprints see Nos. 501, 582-583.

The 15¢ exists dated "1977." See No. 508.

St. Mary's R.C. Church, Kingstown — A70

| | | | |
|---|---|---|---|
| **1976, Nov. 18** | | **Litho.** | **Perf. 14** |
| 475 | A70 | 35¢ multicolored | .20 .20 |
| 476 | A70 | 45¢ multicolored | .55 .55 |
| 477 | A70 | 50¢ multicolored | .20 .20 |
| 478 | A70 | $1 multicolored | 1.15 1.15 |
| | | Nos. 475-478 (4) | |

Christmas: 45¢, Anglican Church, Georgetown; 50¢, Methodist Church, Georgetown; $1.25, St. George's Anglican Cathedral, Kingstown.

Barrancoid Pot-stand, c. 450 A.D. — A71

5¢

| | | | |
|---|---|---|---|
| **1976, Dec. 16** | | | **Perf. 13½** |
| 479 | A71 | 5¢ multicolored | .20 .20 |
| 480 | A71 | 45¢ multicolored | .20 .20 |
| 481 | A71 | 70¢ multicolored | .30 .30 |
| 482 | A71 | $1 multicolored | .40 .40 |
| | | Nos. 479-482 (4) | 1.10 1.10 |

Designs (National Trust Emblem and): 45¢, National Museum. 70¢, Carib stone head, c. 1510. $1, Ciboney petroglyph, c. 4000 B.C.

Carib Indian art and establishment of National Museum in Botanical Gardens, Kingstown.

Kings William I, Henry I, Stephen A72

½¢

St. Vincent

| | | | |
|---|---|---|---|
| **1977, Feb. 7** | | **Wmk. 373** | **Perf. 13½** |
| 483 | A72 | ½¢ multicolored | .20 .20 |
| a. | | Bklt. pane of 4, #483-486 | 2.25 |
| 484 | A72 | 1¢ multicolored | .20 .20 |
| 485 | A72 | 1½¢ multicolored | .20 .20 |
| 486 | A72 | 2¢ multicolored | .20 .20 |
| 487 | A72 | 5¢ multicolored | .20 .20 |
| a. | | Bklt. pane of 4, #487-490 | 2.25 |
| 488 | A72 | 10¢ multicolored | .20 .20 |
| 489 | A72 | 25¢ multicolored | .20 .20 |
| 490 | A72 | 35¢ multicolored | .20 .20 |
| 491 | A72 | 75¢ multicolored | .25 .20 |
| 492 | A72 | $1 multicolored | .25 .20 |
| 493 | A72 | $2 multicolored | .40 .20 |
| 494 | A72 | $5 multicolored | 1.25 2.25 |
| a. | | Souv. sheet of 12, #483-494, perf. 14½x14 | 2.65 2.40 |

Kings and Queens of England: 1¢, Henry II. Richard I, John, Henry III. 1½¢, Edward I, II. III. Richard II. 2¢, Henry IV, V, VI. Edward IV, V. 5¢, Edward V, Richard III, Henry VII, VIII. 10¢, Edward VI, Lady Jane Grey, Mary I, Elizabeth I. 25¢, James I, Charles I, Charles II. 35¢, William III, Mary II, Anne, George I. 45¢, George II, III. 75¢, William IV, Victoria. $1, Edward VII, George V, Edward VIII. $2, Elizabeth II, coronation. George VI, Elizabeth II.

25th anniv. of the reign of Elizabeth II.

Nos. 483-494 (12)

Nos. 483a, 487a and 491a are unwmkd.

---

Bishop Alfred P. Berkeley, Bishop's Miters — A73

35¢        35¢

| | | | |
|---|---|---|---|
| **1977, May 12** | | **Wmk. 373** | |
| 495 | A73 | 15¢ multicolored | .20 .20 |
| 496 | A73 | 35¢ multicolored | .40 .20 |
| 497 | A73 | 45¢ multicolored | .40 .50 |
| 498 | A73 | $1.25 multicolored | 1.00 1.10 |
| | | Nos. 495-498 (4) | |

15¢, Grant of Arms to Bishopric, 1951, & names of former Bishops, 45¢, Coat of arms & map of Diocese. $1.25, Interior of St. George's Anglican Cathedral & Bishop G. C. M. Woodroffe.

Diocese of the Windward Islands, centenary.

Girl Guide and Emblem — A74

| | | | |
|---|---|---|---|
| **1977, June 2** | | **Litho.** | **Perf. 14** |
| 499 | A62 | 5¢ multi | .20 .20 |
| 500 | A62 | 10¢ multi (R) | .20 .20 |
| 501 | A62 | 15¢ multi (R) | .20 .20 |
| 502 | A62 | 20¢ multi (R) | .20 .20 |
| 503 | A62 | $1 multi | .65 .65 |
| | | Nos. 499-503 (5) | 1.45 1.45 |

Nos. 411, 414, 472, 417, 422 Overprinted in Black or Red: "CARNIVAL 1977/JUNE 25TH - JULY 5TH"

St. Vincent Carnival, June 25-July 5. 5¢, 15¢ dated "1977"; 10¢, 20¢, $1 "1976."

5¢ Girl Guides Golden Jubilee

"While Shepherds Watched" A75

| | | | |
|---|---|---|---|
| **1977, Sept. 1** | | **Wmk. 373** | **Perf. 13½** |
| 504 | A74 | 5¢ multicolored | .20 .20 |
| 505 | A74 | 15¢ multicolored | .20 .20 |
| 506 | A74 | 50¢ multicolored | .20 .20 |
| 507 | A74 | $2 multicolored | 1.00 1.25 |
| | | Nos. 504-507 (4) | |

Designs: 15¢, Early Guide's uniform, Ranger, Brownie and Guide. 20¢, Guide uniforms, 1917 and 1977. $2, Lady Baden-Powell, World Chief Guide, 1930-1977.

St. Vincent Girl Guides, 50th anniversary.

No. 494 with Additional Inscription: "CARIBEAN / VISIT 1977"

| | | | |
|---|---|---|---|
| **1977, Oct. 27** | | | |
| 508 | A72 | $2 multicolored | 1.00 1.00 |

Caribbean visit of Queen Elizabeth II.

| | | | |
|---|---|---|---|
| **1977, Nov.** | | **Litho.** | **Perf. 13x11** |

Christmas: 10¢, "Fear not" said He. 15¢, David's Town. 25¢, The Heavenly Babe. 50¢,

"Christmas 1977"

St. Vincent Christmas 1977        5¢

---

Map of St. Vincent — A76

40¢

| | | | |
|---|---|---|---|
| **1977-78** | | **Wmk. 373** | **Perf. 14½x14** |
| 509 | A75 | 5¢ buff & multi | .20 .20 |
| 510 | A75 | 10¢ buff & multi | .20 .20 |
| 511 | A75 | 15¢ buff & multi | .20 .20 |
| 512 | A75 | 40¢ buff & multi | .20 .20 |
| 513 | A75 | 50¢ buff & multi | .30 .30 |
| 514 | A75 | $1.25 buff & multi | .50 .50 |
| a. | | Souv. sheet, #509-514, perf. 13½ | 1.00 1.25 |
| | | Nos. 509-574 (6) | 1.30 1.50 |

Thus Spake and Seraph, $1.25, All Glory be to God.

| | | | |
|---|---|---|---|
| **1977-78** | | **Litho.** | **Wmk. 373** |
| 515 | A76 | 20¢ dk bl & lt bl ('78) | .20 .20 |
| 516 | A76 | 40¢ salmon & black | .30 .30 |
| 517 | A76 | 40¢ ocher, sal & ocher ('78) | .25 .25 |
| | | Nos. 515-517 (3) | .75 .75 |

Issued: #516, 11/30; #515, 517, 1/31. For types surcharged see Nos. B1-B4.

Painted Lady and Bougainvillea — A77

5¢

| | | | |
|---|---|---|---|
| **1978, Apr. 6** | | **Litho.** | **Perf. 14** |
| 523 | A77 | 5¢ multicolored | .20 .20 |
| 524 | A77 | 25¢ multicolored | .35 .20 |
| 525 | A77 | 40¢ multicolored | .45 .20 |
| 526 | A77 | 50¢ multicolored | .50 .20 |
| 527 | A77 | $1.25 multicolored | 1.00 .60 |
| | | Nos. 523-527 (5) | 2.50 1.40 |

Butterflies and Bougainvillea: 25¢, Silver spot. 40¢, Red anartia. 50¢, Mimic. $1.25, Giant hairstreak.

Westminster Abbey — A78

40¢ St. Vincent

| | | | |
|---|---|---|---|
| **1978, June 2** | | **Litho.** | **Perf. 13x13½** |
| 528 | A78 | 40¢ multicolored | .20 .20 |
| 529 | A78 | 50¢ multicolored | .20 .20 |
| 530 | A78 | 40¢ multicolored | .20 .20 |
| 531 | A78 | $1 multicolored | .20 .20 |
| a. | | Souv. sheet, #528-531, perf. 13½x14 | .75 1.00 |
| | | Nos. 528-531 (4) | .80 .80 |

25th anniv. of coronation of Queen Elizabeth II. Nos. 528-531 issued in booklet panes of 10. #528-531 also exist in sheets of two.

Cathedral: 50¢, Gloucester. $1.25, Durham. $2.50, Exeter.

Rotary Emblem A79

ST.VINCENT 40¢

| | | | |
|---|---|---|---|
| **1978, July 13** | | **Wmk. 373** | **Perf. 14½** |
| 532 | A79 | 40¢ brown & multi | .20 .20 |
| 533 | A79 | 50¢ dark green & multi | .35 .35 |
| 534 | A79 | $1 crimson & multi | .75 .75 |
| | | Nos. 532-534 (3) | |

Emblems: 50¢, Lions Intl. $1, Jaycees.

Service clubs aiding in development of St. Vincent.

---

Design: 40¢, Flags of St. Vincent and Ontario, teacher pointing to board, vert.

ST. VINCENT $2

Flags of Ontario and St. Vincent, Teacher A80

| | | | |
|---|---|---|---|
| **1978, Sept. 7** | | **Litho.** | **Perf. 14** |
| 535 | A80 | 40¢ multicolored | .20 .20 |
| 536 | A80 | $2 multicolored | .45 .60 |

School to School Project between children of Ontario, Canada, and St. Vincent, 10th anniversary.

Arnos Vale Airport A81

| | | | |
|---|---|---|---|
| **1978, Oct. 19** | | | **Perf. 14½** |
| 537 | A81 | 10¢ multicolored | .20 .20 |
| 538 | A81 | 40¢ multicolored | .40 .40 |
| 539 | A81 | 50¢ multicolored | .40 .40 |
| 540 | A81 | $1.25 multicolored | 1.00 1.00 |
| | | Nos. 537-540 (4) | |

75th anniversary of 1st powered flight. For overprint see No. 568.

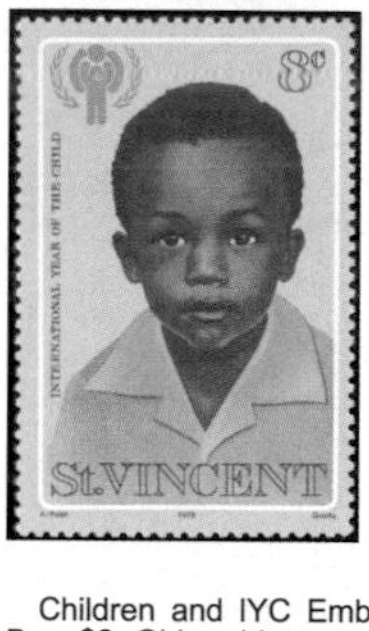

40¢, Wilbur Wright landing Flyer I. 50¢, Flyer I airborne. $1.25, Orville Wright and Flyer I.

Vincentian Boy, IYC Emblem — A82

St. VINCENT 8¢

| | | | |
|---|---|---|---|
| **1979, Feb. 14** | | **Litho.** | **Perf. 14x13½** |
| 541 | A82 | 8¢ multicolored | .20 .20 |
| 542 | A82 | 20¢ multicolored | .20 .20 |
| 543 | A82 | 50¢ multicolored | .40 .40 |
| 544 | A82 | $2 multicolored | 1.00 1.00 |
| | | Nos. 541-544 (4) | |

Children and IYC Emblem: 20¢, Girl. 50¢, Boy. $2, Girl and boy.

International Year of the Child.

Rowland Hill A83

ST.VINCENT

| | | | |
|---|---|---|---|
| **1979, May 31** | | **Litho.** | **Perf. 14** |
| 545 | A83 | 40¢ multicolored | .60 .60 |
| 546 | A83 | 50¢ multicolored | .60 .60 |
| 547 | A83 | $3 multicolored | 1.75 1.75 |
| a. | | Souvenir sheet of 6 | 1.00 1.00 |
| | | Nos. 545-547 (3) | |

Sir Rowland Hill (1795-1879), originator of penny postage.

No. 547a contains Nos. 545-547 and Nos. 560, 561 and 565.

50¢, Great Britain #1-2. $3, St. Vincent #1-1B.

Buccament Cancellations, Map of St. Vincent — A84

## Prince Charles, Lady Diana, Royal Yacht Charlotte — A94a

Prince Charles and Lady Diana — A94b

Illustration A94b is reduced.

**1981, July 13 — Wmk. 380 — Litho. — Perf. 14**

| 627 | A94a | 60c Couple, Isabella | .20 | .20 |
|---|---|---|---|---|
| a. | | Bklt. pane of 4, perf. 12 | .60 | |
| 628 | A94b | 60c Couple | .20 | .20 |
| 629 | A94a | $2.50 Alberta | .70 | .70 |
| 630 | A94a | $2.50 like #628 | .70 | .70 |
| a. | | Bklt. pane of 2, perf. 12 | 1.00 | |
| 631 | A94a | $4 Britannia | 1.25 | 1.25 |
| 632 | A94b | $4 like #628 | 1.25 | 1.25 |
| a. | A94b | | 4.30 | 4.30 |

Nos. 627-632 (6)

Royal wedding. Each denomination issued in sheets of 7 (6 type A94a, 1 type A94b). For surcharges and overprints see Nos. 891-892, O1-O6.

### Souvenir Sheet

**1981 — Litho. — Perf. 12**

| 632A | A95b | $5 Couple | 1.40 | 1.40 |
|---|---|---|---|---|

## Kingstown General Post Office — A95

**1981, Sept. 1 — Wmk. 373 — Litho. — Perf. 14**

| 633 | A95 | $2 Pair, #a-b. | 1.10 | 1.75 |
|---|---|---|---|---|

UPU membership centenary.

## First Anniv. of UN Membership — A96

**1981, Sept. 1 — Wmk. 373 — Litho. — Perf. 14**

| 634A | A96 | $1.50 Flags | .35 | .35 |
|---|---|---|---|---|
| 634B | A96 | $2.50 Prime Minister Cato | .55 | .55 |

## "The People that Walked in Darkness . . ." — A97

**1981, Nov. 19 — Litho. — Perf. 12**

| 635 | A97 | 50c shown | .20 | .20 |
|---|---|---|---|---|
| 636 | A97 | 60c Angel | .20 | .20 |
| 637 | A97 | $1 "My soul . . ." | .25 | .25 |
| 638 | A97 | $2 Flight into Egypt | .50 | .50 |
| a. | | Souvenir sheet of 4, #635-638 | 1.25 | 1.50 |

Nos. 635-638 (4) 1.15 1.15

Christmas. For surcharge see No. 674.

---

## Agouti — A91

**1980, Aug. 7 — Perf. 13½**

| 604 | A90 | 10c shown | .20 | .20 |
|---|---|---|---|---|
| 605 | A90 | 60c Bicycling | .25 | .25 |
| 606 | A90 | 80c Women's basketball | .40 | 1.00 |

Sport for all.

| 607 | A90 | $2.50 Boxing | 1.25 | 1.75 |
|---|---|---|---|---|

For surcharges see Nos. B5-B8.

**1980, Oct. 2 — Litho. — Perf. 14x14½**

| 608 | A91 | 25c shown | .20 | .20 |
|---|---|---|---|---|
| 609 | A91 | 50c Giant toad | .60 | .60 |
| 610 | A91 | $2 Mongoose | 1.00 | 1.00 |

Nos. 608-610 (3)

## Map of North Atlantic showing St. Vincent — A92

Maps showing St. Vincent: 10c, World. $1, Caribbean. $2, St. Vincent, sail boats, plane.

**1980, Dec. 4 — Litho. — Perf. 13½x14**

| 611 | A92 | 10c multicolored | .20 | .20 |
|---|---|---|---|---|
| 612 | A92 | 50c multicolored | .20 | .20 |
| 613 | A92 | $1 multicolored | .30 | .30 |
| 614 | A92 | $2 multicolored | .55 | .80 |
| a. | | Souv. sheet of 1, perf. 14 | 1.25 | .90 |

Nos. 611-614 (4)

## Ville de Paris in Battle of the Saints, 1782 — A93

**1981, Feb. 19 — Wmk. 373 — Litho. — Perf. 14**

| 615 | A93 | 50c shown | .45 | .25 |
|---|---|---|---|---|
| 616 | A93 | 60c Ramillies lost in storm, 1782 | .55 | .40 |
| 617 | A93 | $1.50 Providence, 1793 | 1.25 | 1.60 |
| 618 | A93 | $2 Mail Packet Dee, 1840 | 1.75 | 2.00 |

Nos. 615-618 (4) 4.00 4.25

## A94

#619a, Arrowroot processing. #619b, Arrowroot cultivation. #620a, Banana packing plant. #620b, Banana cultivation. #621a, Copra drying frames. #621b, Coconut plantation. #622a, Cocoa beans. #622b, Cocoa cultivation.

**1981, May 21 — Wmk. 373 — Litho. — Perf. 14**

| 619 | A94 | 25c Pair, #a-b. | .20 | .60 |
|---|---|---|---|---|
| 620 | A94 | 50c Pair, #a-b. | .45 | .60 |
| 621 | A94 | $1 Pair, #a-b. | .65 | 1.00 |
| 622 | A94 | $2 Pair, #a-b. | 1.75 | 2.40 |

Nos. 619-622 (4)

---

Cancellations and location of village.

**1979, Sept. 1 — Perf. 14 — Litho.**

| 548 | A84 | 1c shown | .20 | .20 |
|---|---|---|---|---|
| 549 | A84 | 2c Sion Hill | .20 | .20 |
| 550 | A84 | 3c Cumberland | .20 | .20 |
| 551 | A84 | 4c Questelles | .20 | .20 |
| 552 | A84 | 5c Layou | .20 | .20 |
| 553 | A84 | 6c New Ground | .20 | .20 |
| 554 | A84 | 8c Mesopotamia | .20 | .20 |
| 555 | A84 | 12c Troumaca | .20 | .20 |
| 556 | A84 | 15c Arnos Vale | .20 | .20 |
| 557 | A84 | 15c Stubbs | .20 | .20 |
| 558 | A84 | 20c Orange Hill | .30 | .30 |
| 559 | A84 | 25c Calliaqua | .30 | .30 |
| 560 | A84 | 40c Edinboro | .30 | .30 |
| 561 | A84 | 50c Colonarie | .30 | .30 |
| 562 | A84 | 80c Babou St. Vincent | .45 | .30 |
| 563 | A84 | $1 Chateaubelair | .45 | .45 |
| 564 | A84 | $2 Kingstown | .55 | .70 |
| 565 | A84 | $3 Barrouallie | .65 | 1.00 |
| 566 | A84 | $5 Georgetown | .90 | 1.75 |
| 567 | A84 | $10 Kingstown | 7.75 | 3.00 |

Nos. 548-567 (20) 1.75 10.00

See No. 547a.

The 5c, 10c, 25c reissued inscribed 1982. Singles of #562-564 from #601a are inscribed 1980.

## No. 537 Overprinted in Red: "ST. VINCENT AND THE GRENADINES AIR SERVICE 1979"

**1979, Aug. 6 — Litho. — Perf. 14½**

| 568 | A81 | 10c multicolored | .20 | .20 |
|---|---|---|---|---|

St. Vincent and Grenadines air service inauguration.

---

## Oleander and Wasp — A87

| 590 | A86 | 40c multicolored | .20 | .20 |
|---|---|---|---|---|
| 591 | A86 | 50c multicolored | .30 | .30 |
| 592 | A86 | $2 multicolored | 1.00 | 1.25 |
| a. | | Souvenir sheet of 6, #587-592 | 1.30 | 1.30 |

Nos. 587-592 (6)

Christmas.

Oleander and Insects: 10c, Beetle. 25c, Praying mantis. 50c, Green guava beetle. $2, Citrus weevil.

**1979, Dec. 13 — Litho. — Perf. 14**

| 593 | A87 | 5c multicolored | .20 | .20 |
|---|---|---|---|---|
| 594 | A87 | 10c multicolored | .20 | .20 |
| 595 | A87 | 25c multicolored | .20 | .20 |
| 596 | A87 | 50c multicolored | .20 | .20 |
| 597 | A87 | $2 multicolored | .50 | 1.30 |

Nos. 593-597 (5)

## Type of 1880 Souvenir Sheet

**1980, Feb. 28 — Litho. — Perf. 14x13½**

| 598 | | Sheet of 3 | 1.00 | 1.00 |
|---|---|---|---|---|
| a. | A3 | 50c dark green | .30 | .30 |
| b. | A3 | $1 dark green | .60 | .60 |
| c. | A3 | $2 dark blue | 1.30 | 1.30 |

Coat of arms stamps centenary; London 1980 Intl. Stamp Exhibition, May 6-14.

## London '80 Intl. Stamp Exhibition, May 6-14 — A88

**1980, Apr. 24 — Litho. — Perf. 14**

| 599 | A88 | 80c Queen Elizabeth II | .20 | .20 |
|---|---|---|---|---|
| 600 | A88 | $1 GB #297, SV #190 | .25 | .25 |
| 601 | A88 | 80c Unissued stamp, 1971 | .55 | .55 |
| a. | | Souv. sheet, #562-564, 599-601 | 1.00 | 1.00 |

Nos. 599-601 (3)

## Steel Band — A89

a, shown. b, Drummers, dancers.

**1980, June 12 — Litho. — Perf. 14**

| 602 | A89 | 20c Pair, #a-b. | .35 | .75 |
|---|---|---|---|---|

Kingstown Carnival, July 7-8.

## Soccer, Olympic Rings — A90

---

## Independent State

St. Vincent Flag, Ixora Ixora Coccinea AUJ

Designs: 50c, House of Assembly. Ixora stricta. 80c, Prime Minister R. Milton Cato.

**1979, Oct. 27 — Perf. 12½x12**

| 569 | A85 | 20c multi + label | .20 | .20 |
|---|---|---|---|---|
| 570 | A85 | 50c multi + label | .25 | .25 |
| 571 | A85 | 80c multi + label | .40 | .25 |

Nos. 569-571 (3)

Independence of St. Vincent.

Nos. 407, 410-416, 418, 421, 473-474, 422-423, 425 Overprinted in Black: "INDEPENDENCE 1979"

**1979, Oct. 27 — Litho. — Perf. 14½**

| 572 | A62 | 1c multicolored | .20 | .20 |
|---|---|---|---|---|
| 573 | A62 | 4c multicolored | .20 | .20 |
| 574 | A62 | 5c multicolored | .20 | .20 |
| 575 | A62 | 6c multicolored | .20 | .20 |
| 576 | A62 | 8c multicolored | .20 | .20 |
| 577 | A62 | 10c multicolored | .20 | .20 |
| 578 | A62 | 12c multicolored | .25 | .20 |
| 579 | A62 | 15c multicolored | .25 | .20 |
| 580 | A62 | 25c multicolored | .25 | .20 |
| 581 | A62 | 50c multicolored | .40 | .40 |
| 582 | A62 | 70c multicolored | .70 | .35 |
| 583 | A62 | 90c multicolored | .70 | .40 |
| 584 | A62 | $1 multicolored | .70 | .40 |
| 585 | A62 | $2.50 multicolored | 1.10 | 1.00 |
| 586 | A62 | $10 multicolored | 2.50 | 3.75 |

Nos. 572-586 (15) 8.00 8.00

## Silent Night Text, Virgin and Child — A86

Silent Night Text and: 20c, Infant Jesus. 25c, Shepherds. 40c, Angel. 50c, Angels holding Jesus. $2, Nativity.

**1979, Nov. 1 — Litho. — Perf. 13½x14**

| 587 | A86 | 10c multicolored | .20 | .20 |
|---|---|---|---|---|
| 588 | A86 | 20c multicolored | .20 | .20 |
| 589 | A86 | 25c multicolored | .20 | .20 |

# ST. VINCENT

**Re-introduction of Sugar Industry, First Anniv. — A98**

**1982, Apr. 5**    **Litho.**    **Perf. 14**
| | | | |
|---|---|---|---|
| 639 | A98 | 50c Boilers | .20 .20 |
| 640 | A98 | 60c Drying plant | .25 .25 |
| 641 | A98 | $1.50 Gearwheels | .50 .50 |
| 642 | A98 | $2 Loading sugar cane | .90 .90 |

Nos. 639-642 (4)   1.85 1.85

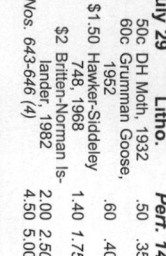

**50th Anniv. of Airmail Service — A99**

**1982, July 29**    **Litho.**    **Perf. 14**
| | | | |
|---|---|---|---|
| 643 | A99 | 50c DH Moth, 1932 | .50 .35 |
| 644 | A99 | 60c Grumman Goose, 1982 | .60 .40 |
| 645 | A99 | $1.50 Hawker-Siddeley 748, 1968 | 1.40 1.75 |
| 646 | A99 | $2 Britten-Norman Islander, 1982 | 2.00 2.50 |

Nos. 643-646 (4)   4.50 5.00

**75th ANNIVERSARY OF SCOUTING 1907-1982**

**1982, June**    **Wmk. 380**
Litho.   **Perf. 14**
| | | | |
|---|---|---|---|
| 647 | A99a | 50c Augusta of Saxe, 1736 | .35 .35 |
| 648 | A99a | 60c Saxe arms | .40 .40 |
| 649 | A99a | $6 Diana | 2.00 2.00 |

Nos. 647-649 (3)   2.75 2.75

For overprints see Nos. 647-649

**21st Birthday of Princess Diana, July 1 — A99a**

**21st Birthday**

**1982, July 15**    **Wmk. 373**
Litho.   **Perf. 14**
| | | | |
|---|---|---|---|
| 650 | A100 | 50c Emblem | .75 1.00 |
| 651 | A100 | $2.50 "75" | 1.25 1.75 |

For overprints see Nos. 652-654 (3)

**1982, July**
| | | | |
|---|---|---|---|
| 652 | A99a | 50c multicolored | .20 .20 |
| 653 | A99a | 60c multicolored | .20 .30 |
| 654 | A99a | $6 multicolored | .85 1.25 |

Birth of Prince William of Wales, June 21.

**ST. VINCENT CARNIVAL 1982 50c**

**Carnival A101**

**1982, July**    **Wmk. 380**
"ROYAL BABY" Overprinted:
| | | | |
|---|---|---|---|
| | | | 1.25 1.85 |

For overprints see Nos. 890, 893.

---

**1982, June 10**    **Litho.**    **Perf. 13½**
| | | | |
|---|---|---|---|
| 655 | A101 | 50c Butterfly float | .25 .25 |
| 656 | A101 | 60c Angel dancer, vert. | .30 .30 |
| 657 | A101 | $1.50 Winged dancer, vert. | .70 .70 |
| 658 | A101 | $2 Eagle float | 1.00 1.00 |

Nos. 655-658 (4)   2.25 2.25

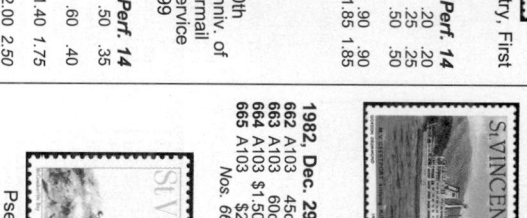

**Cruise Ships A103**

**1982, Dec. 29**    **Wmk. 373**
Litho.   **Perf. 14**
| | | | |
|---|---|---|---|
| 662 | A103 | 45c Geestport | .35 .35 |
| 663 | A103 | 45c Stella Oceanis | .45 .45 |
| 664 | A103 | $1.50 Victoria | 1.10 1.10 |
| 665 | A103 | $2 QE 2 | 1.50 1.50 |

Nos. 662-665 (4)   3.40 3.40

**Pseudocorynactis caribbeorum**

**Pseudocorynactis Caribbeorum — A104**

Sea Horses and Anemones, 60c, $1.50, $2 vert.

**1983, Jan. 12**    **Wmk. 373**
Litho.   **Perf. 12**
| | | | |
|---|---|---|---|
| 666 | A104 | 50c shown | .90 .90 |
| 667 | A104 | 60c Actinoporus elegans | 1.10 1.10 |
| 668 | A104 | $1.50 Arachnanthus nocturnus | 1.90 1.90 |
| 669 | A104 | $2 Hippocampus reidi | 2.10 2.10 |

Nos. 666-669 (4)   6.00 6.00

For overprint see No. 886.

**Commonwealth Day — A104a**

**1983, Mar. 14**    **Wmk. 373**
Litho.   **Perf. 14**
| | | | |
|---|---|---|---|
| 670 | A104a | 45c Map | .30 .30 |
| 671 | A104a | 45c Flag | .40 .40 |
| 672 | A104a | $1.50 Prime Minister Cato | .65 .65 |
| 673 | A104a | $2 Banana industry | .90 .90 |

Nos. 670-673 (4)   2.25 2.25

**Commonwealth Day 45c**

**1983, Apr. 26**    **Wmk. 373**
No. 635 Surcharged
| | | | |
|---|---|---|---|
| 674 | A97 | 45c on 50c multi | .45 .35 |

**A104b**

**1983, July 6**    **Wmk. 373**
Litho.   **Perf. 12**
| | | | |
|---|---|---|---|
| 675 | A104b | 45c Handshake | .20 .30 |
| 676 | A104b | 60c Emblem | .25 .30 |
| 677 | A104b | $1.50 Map | .55 .75 |
| 678 | A104b | $2 Flags | 1.00 1.25 |

Nos. 675-678 (4)   2.00 2.65

10th anniv. of Chaguaramas (Caribbean Free Trade Assoc.)

**St. Vincent, Fort Duvernette 35c**

**Fort Duvernette A108**

---

**1983, Oct. 6**    **Wmk. 373**
Litho.   **Perf. 12x11½**
| | | | |
|---|---|---|---|
| 679 | A105 | 45c Founder William A. Smith | .25 .25 |
| 680 | A105 | 60c Boy, officer | .25 .35 |
| 681 | A105 | $1.50 Emblem | .90 .90 |
| 682 | A105 | $2 Community service | 1.25 1.25 |

Nos. 679-682 (4)   2.75 2.75

Boys' Brigade, cent. For overprint see #887.

**CHRISTMAS 1983 ST. VINCENT 10c**

**Christmas — A106**

**1983, Nov. 15**    **Wmk. 373**
Litho.   **Perf. 12**
| | | | |
|---|---|---|---|
| 683 | A106 | 10c Shepherds at Watch | .20 .20 |
| 684 | A106 | 50c The Angel of the Lord | .30 .30 |
| 685 | A106 | $1.50 A Glorious Light | 1.00 1.10 |
| 686 | A106 | $2.40 At the Manger | 1.75 1.75 |

a.   Souvenir sheet of 4, #683-686   3.25 3.25

Nos. 683-686 (4)   3.35 3.35

**1908 FORD MODEL T 10c**   **1908 FORD MODEL T 10c**

**Classic Cars A107**

**1983, Nov. 9**    **Litho.**    **Perf. 12½**
Se-tenant Pairs, #a.-b.
a. — Side and front views.

| | | | |
|---|---|---|---|
| 687 | A107 | 10c Ford Model T | .20 .20 |
| 688 | A107 | 60c Supercharged Cord | .20 .20 |
| 689 | A107 | $1.50 Mercedes Benz | .40 .40 |
| 690 | A107 | $2 Citroen Open Tourer | .40 .40 |
| 691 | A107 | $2 Ferrari Boxer | .40 .40 |
| 692 | A107 | $2 Rolls-Royce Phantom | 2.00 2.00 |

Nos. 687-692 (6)

See #773-777, 815-822, 906-911.

---

**World War I Battle Scene, King George V — A110**

**1c KINGS & QUEENS ST. VINCENT 1c**

**1984, Apr. 25**    **Litho.**    **Perf. 13x12½**
Se-tenant Pairs, #a.-b.
a. — Action scene.
b. — Side and front views.

| | | | |
|---|---|---|---|
| 731 | A110 | 1c Pair, #a.-b. | .20 .20 |
| 732 | A110 | 5c Pair, #a.-b. | .20 .20 |
| 733 | A110 | 60c Pair, #a.-b. | .35 .35 |
| 734 | A110 | 75c Pair, #a.-b. | .35 .35 |
| 735 | A110 | $1 Pair, #a.-b. | .35 .35 |
| 736 | A110 | $4 Pair, #a.-b. | .80 .80 |

Nos. 731-736 (6)   2.25 2.25

#732a, Battle of Bannockburn. #732b, Edward II. #733a, George V. #733b, York Cottage, Sandringham. #734a, Edward II. #734b, Berkeley Castle. #735a, Arms of Edward II. #735b, Edward II. #736a, Arms of George V. #736b, George V.

**World War I Battle Scene, King George V — A110**

**1984, Apr. 2**    **Wmk. 373**
**Flowering Trees — A109**

| | | | |
|---|---|---|---|
| 719 | A109 | 5c White frangipani | .20 .20 |
| 720 | A109 | 10c Genip | .20 .20 |
| 721 | A109 | 15c Immortelle | .20 .20 |
| 722 | A109 | 20c Pink poui | .20 .20 |
| 723 | A109 | 35c Buttercup | .25 .25 |
| 724 | A109 | 45c Sandbox | .25 .25 |
| 725 | A109 | 50c Locust | .25 .25 |
| 726 | A109 | 75c Colville's glory | .35 .35 |
| 727 | A109 | $1 Lignum vitae | .55 .55 |
| 728 | A109 | $2 Golden shower | 1.00 1.00 |
| 729 | A109 | $5 Angelin | 3.50 7.00 |
| 730 | A109 | $10 Roucou | 7.25 7.00 |

Nos. 719-730 (12)   15.35 22.70

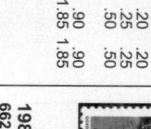

**35c St. Vincent**

**Carnival A112**

**1984, June 25**    **Wmk. 380**
Litho.   **Perf. 14**
| | | | |
|---|---|---|---|
| 743 | A112 | 35c Musical fantasy | .20 .20 |
| 744 | A112 | 45c African woman | .25 .25 |
| 745 | A112 | $1 Market woman | .65 .65 |
| 746 | A112 | $3 Carib hieroglyph | 3.10 3.10 |

Nos. 743-746 (4)  

**Locomotives Type of 1985**
**1984, July 27**    **Litho.**    **Perf. 12½**
Se-tenant Pairs, #a.-b.
a. — Action scene.
b. — Side and front views.

| | | | |
|---|---|---|---|
| 747 | A120 | 1c Liberation Class 141R, 1945 | .20 .20 |
| 748 | A120 | 2c Dreadnought Class 50, 1967 | .20 .20 |
| 749 | A120 | 3c No. 242A1, 1946 | .20 .20 |
| 750 | A120 | 50c Dean Goods, 1883 | .50 .50 |
| 751 | A120 | 75c Hetton Colliery, 1822 | .50 .50 |
| 752 | A120 | $1 Penydarren, 1804 | .50 .50 |

**Locomotives Type of 1985**
**1983, Dec. 8**    **Litho.**    **Perf. 12½x13**
Se-tenant Pairs, #a.-b.
a. — Action scene.
b. — Side and front views.

| | | | |
|---|---|---|---|
| 699 | A120 | 10c King Henry VIII | .20 .20 |
| 700 | A120 | 10c Royal Scots Greys | .20 .20 |
| 701 | A120 | 25c Hagley Hall | .20 .20 |
| 702 | A120 | 25c Sir Lancelot | .35 .35 |
| 703 | A120 | 60c B12 Class | .35 .35 |
| 704 | A120 | 75c No. 1000 Deeley Compound | .35 .35 |
| 705 | A120 | $2.50 Cheshire | .45 .45 |
| 706 | A120 | $3 Bulleid Austerity | .55 .55 |

Nos. 699-706 (8)   2.65 2.65

## Queen Mother, 85th Birthday — A122

#861a, 867a, Facing right. #861b, 867b,
#866b, Facing left. #862a, 866a, Facing right. #862b,
866b, Facing left. #863a, Facing right. #863b,
Facing left. #864a, Facing front. #864b, Facing
left. #865a, Facing right. #865b, Facing front.

**1985**
| No. | Type | | | | |
|---|---|---|---|---|---|
| 861 | A122 | 35c | Pair, #a.-b. | .20 | .20 |
| 862 | A122 | 85c | Pair, #a.-b. | .20 | .20 |
| 863 | A122 | $1 | Pair, #a.-b. | .35 | .35 |
| 864 | A122 | $1.20 | Pair, #a.-b. | .35 | .35 |
| | A122 | $1.60 | Pair, #a.-b. | 1.10 | 1.10 |

**Souvenir Sheets of 2**
| 865 | A122 | $2.10 | #a.-b. | 1.00 | 1.00 |
|---|---|---|---|---|---|
| 866 | A122 | $3.50 | #a.-b. | 3.75 | 3.75 |
| 867 | A122 | $6 | #a.-b. | 6.25 | 6.25 |
| | | Nos. 865-867 (3) | | 11.00 | 11.00 |

Issued: #861-865, 8/9; #866-867, 12/19.
For overprints see No. 888.

## Elvis Presley (1935-77), American Entertainer — A123

#874a, 878a. In concert. #874b, 878b. Fac-
ing front. #875a, 879a. In concert. #875b,
879b. Facing left. #876a, 880a. In concert.
#876b, 880b. Facing front. #877a, 881a.
Wearing leather jacket. #877b, 881b. Facing
left.

**1985, Aug. 16**
| 874 | A123 | 10c | Pair, #a.-b. | .60 | .60 |
|---|---|---|---|---|---|
| 875 | A123 | 60c | Pair, #a.-b. | .90 | .90 |
| 876 | A123 | $1 | Pair, #a.-b. | 1.60 | 1.60 |
| 877 | A123 | $5 | Pair, #a.-b. | 4.00 | 4.00 |

**Souvenir Sheets of 4**
| 878 | A123 | 30c | #a.-b. | 1.25 | 1.25 |
|---|---|---|---|---|---|
| 879 | A123 | 50c | #a.-b. | 1.90 | 1.90 |
| 880 | A123 | $1.50 | #a.-b. | 5.75 | 5.75 |
| 881 | A123 | $4.50 | #a.-b. | 24.90 | 24.90 |
| | | Nos. 878-881 (4) | | | |

Nos. 878-881 contain two of each stamp.
Two $4 "stamps" were not issued.
For other Presley souvenir sheet see No.
1567. For overprints see Nos. 1009-1016.

## Flour Milling A124

**1985, Oct. 17 — Wmk. 373 — Perf. 15**
| 882 | A124 | 20c | Conveyor from elevators | .20 | .20 |
|---|---|---|---|---|---|
| 883 | A124 | 30c | Roller mills | .20 | .20 |
| 884 | A121 | 75c | Office | .55 | .55 |
| 885 | A124 | $3 | Bran finishers | 2.25 | 2.25 |
| | | Nos. 882-885 (4) | | 3.20 | 3.20 |

Nos. 667, 680, 862, 650, 631-632, 651
Ovptd. "CARIBBEAN / ROYAL VISIT /
-1985," or Surcharged with 3 Black
Bars and New Value in Black

**1985, Oct. 27 — Perfs. as Before**
| 886 | A104 | 60c | multi | 1.90 | 1.90 |
|---|---|---|---|---|---|
| 887 | A105 | 60c | multi | 1.90 | 1.90 |
| 888 | A122 | 85c | Pair, #a.-b. | 6.00 | 6.00 |
| 890 | A100 | $1.60 on $4 | | 5.50 | 5.50 |
| 891 | A94a | $1.60 on $4 | multi | 5.50 | 5.50 |
| 892 | A94b | $1.60 on $4 | | 5.50 | 5.50 |
| 893 | A100 | $2.50 | multi | 8.50 | 8.50 |
| | | Nos. 886-893 (7) | | 34.55 | 34.55 |

---

## Herbs and Spices — A119

**1985, Apr. 22 — Perf. 14**
| 829 | A119 | 25c | Pepper | .20 | .20 |
|---|---|---|---|---|---|
| 830 | A119 | 35c | Sweet marjoram | .20 | .20 |
| 831 | A119 | $1 | Nutmeg | .50 | .50 |
| 832 | A119 | $3 | Ginger | 1.90 | 1.90 |
| | | Nos. 829-832 (4) | | | |

## Locomotives of the United Kingdom — A120

**1985, Apr. 26 — Perf. 12½**
Se-tenant Pairs, #a.-b.
a. — Side and front views.
b. — Action scene.

| 833 | A120 | 1c | 1913 Glen Douglas | .20 | .20 |
|---|---|---|---|---|---|
| 834 | A120 | 10c | 1872 Fenchurch Terrier | .20 | .20 |
| 835 | A120 | 40c | 1870 No. 1 Stirling Single | .30 | .30 |
| 836 | A120 | 60c | 1866 No. 15RA Class | .30 | .30 |
| 837 | A120 | $1 | 1893 No. 103 Class Jones Goods | .50 | .50 |
| 838 | A120 | $2.50 | 1908 Great Bear | .80 | .80 |
| | | Nos. 833-838 (6) | | 2.30 | 2.30 |

See #699-706, 747-754, 787-790, 849-854,
961-964.

## Traditional Instruments — A121

**1985, May 16 — Perf. 15**
| 845 | A121 | 25c | Bamboo flute | .20 | .20 |
|---|---|---|---|---|---|
| 846 | A121 | 35c | Quatro | .25 | .25 |
| 847 | A121 | $1 | Bamboo base, vert. | .55 | .55 |
| 848 | A121 | $2 | Goat-skin drum, vert. | 1.10 | 1.10 |
| a. | | Sheet of 4, #845-848 | | 2.25 | 2.25 |
| | | Nos. 845-848 (4) | | 2.10 | 2.10 |

## Locomotives Type of 1985

**1985, June 27 — Perf. 12½**
Se-tenant Pairs, #a.-b.
a. — Side and front views.
b. — Action scene.

| 849 | A120 | 5c | 1874 Loch, U.K. | .20 | .20 |
|---|---|---|---|---|---|
| 850 | A120 | 30c | 1919 Class 47XX, U.K. | .30 | .30 |
| 851 | A120 | 60c | 1876 P.L.M. Class 121, France | .40 | .40 |
| 852 | A120 | 75c | 1927 D.R.G. Class 24, Germany | .40 | .40 |
| 853 | A120 | $1 | 1889 No. 1008, U.K. | .55 | .55 |
| 854 | A120 | $2.50 | 1926 S.R. Class PS-4, US | .65 | .65 |
| | | Nos. 849-854 (6) | | 2.50 | 2.50 |

---

## Cricket Players — A116

**1985, Jan. 7 — Litho. — Perf. 12½**
Se-tenant Pairs, #a.-b.

| 795 | A116 | 5c | N.S. Taylor, portrait | .20 | .20 |
|---|---|---|---|---|---|
| 796 | A116 | 35c | T.W. Graveney with bat | .40 | .40 |
| 797 | A116 | 50c | R.G.D. Willis at wicket | .60 | .60 |
| 798 | A116 | $3 | S.D. Fletcher at wicket | 3.50 | 3.50 |
| | | Nos. 795-798 (4) | | 4.70 | 4.70 |

## Orchids — A117

**1985, Jan. 31 — Litho. — Perf. 14**
| 803 | A117 | 35c | Epidendrum ciliare | .20 | .20 |
|---|---|---|---|---|---|
| 804 | A117 | 45c | Ionopsis utricularioides | .30 | .30 |
| 805 | A117 | $1 | Epidendrum secundum | .60 | .60 |
| 806 | A117 | $3 | Oncidium altissimum | 1.25 | 1.25 |
| | | Nos. 803-806 (4) | | 2.35 | 2.35 |

## Audubon Birth Bicent. — A118

Illustrations of North American bird species
by artist/naturalist John J. Audubon: #807a,
Brown pelican. #807b, Green heron. #808a,
Pileated woodpecker. #808b, Common flicker.
#809a, Painted bunting. #809b, White-winged
crossbill. #810a, Red-shouldered hawk.
#810b, Crested caracara.

**1985, Feb. 7 — Litho. — Perf. 12½**
| 807 | A118 | 15c | Pair, #a.-b. | .20 | .20 |
|---|---|---|---|---|---|
| 808 | A118 | 40c | Pair, #a.-b. | .45 | .45 |
| 809 | A118 | 60c | Pair, #a.-b. | .90 | .90 |
| 810 | A118 | $2.25 | Pair, #a.-b. | 2.00 | 2.00 |
| | | Nos. 807-810 (4) | | | |

## Car Type of 1983

1c, 1937 Lancia Aprilia, Italy. 25c, 1922
Essex Coach, US. 55c, 1973 Pontiac Firebird
Trans Am, US. 60c, 1950 Nash Rambler, US.
$1, 1961 Ferrari Tipo 156, Italy. $1.50, 1967
Eagle-Weslake Type 58, US. $2, 1953 Cun-
ningham C-5R, US.

**1985**
a. — Side and front views.
b. — Action scene.

| 815-821 | A107 | Set of 7 pairs | | 2.10 | 2.10 |
|---|---|---|---|---|---|

**Souvenir Sheet of 4**
| 822 | A107 | #a.-d. | | 2.25 | 2.25 |
|---|---|---|---|---|---|

#822 contains a pair of $4 stamps like #820
(#a.-b.), and a pair of $5 stamps like #819
(#c.-d.).
Issued: 1c, 55c; $2, 3/11; others, 6/7.

---

| 753 | A120 | $2 | Novelty, 1829 | .70 | .70 |
|---|---|---|---|---|---|
| 754 | A120 | $3 | Class 44, 1925 | 3.50 | 3.50 |
| | | Nos. 747-754 (8) | | | |

## Slavery Abolition Sesquicentennial — A113

**1984, Aug. 1 — Litho. — Perf. 14**
| 761 | A113 | 35c | Hoeing | .20 | .20 |
|---|---|---|---|---|---|
| 762 | A113 | 45c | Gathering sugar cane | .25 | .25 |
| 763 | A113 | $1 | Cutting sugar cane | .65 | .65 |
| 764 | A113 | $3 | Abolitionist William Wilberforce | 2.00 | 2.00 |
| | | Nos. 761-764 (4) | | 3.10 | 3.10 |

## 1984 Summer Olympics — A114

#765a, Judo. #765b, Weight lifting. #766a,
Bicycling (facing left). #766b, Bicycling (facing
right). #767a, Swimming (back stroke). #767b,
Dreast stroke. #768a, Running (start). #768b,
Running (finish).

**1984, Aug. 30 — Unwmk. — Perf. 12½**
Se-tenant Pairs, #a.-b.
a. — Side and front views.
b. — Action scene.

| 765 | A114 | 1c | Pair, #a.-b. | .20 | .20 |
|---|---|---|---|---|---|
| 766 | A114 | 3c | Pair, #a.-b. | .20 | .20 |
| 767 | A114 | 60c | Pair, #a.-b. | .50 | .50 |
| 768 | A114 | $3 | Pair, #a.-b. | 2.50 | 2.50 |
| | | Nos. 765-768 (4) | | 3.40 | 3.40 |

## Car Type of 1983

**1984, Oct. 22 — Litho. — Perf. 12½**
Se-tenant Pairs, #a.-b.
a. — Side and front views.
b. — Action scene.

| 773 | A107 | 5c | Austin-Healey Sprite, 1958 | .20 | .20 |
|---|---|---|---|---|---|
| 774 | A107 | 20c | Maserati, 1971 | .25 | .25 |
| 775 | A107 | 55c | Pontiac GTO, 1964 | .40 | .40 |
| 776 | A107 | $1.50 | Jaguar, 1957 | .50 | .50 |
| 777 | A107 | $2.50 | Ferrari, 1970 | .65 | .65 |
| | | Nos. 773-777 (5) | | 2.00 | 2.00 |

## Military Uniforms — A115

**1984, Nov. 12 — Wmk. 380 — Perf. 14**
| 783 | A115 | 45c | Grenadier, 1773 | .30 | .30 |
|---|---|---|---|---|---|
| 784 | A115 | 60c | Grenadier, 1775 | .45 | .45 |
| 785 | A115 | $1.50 | Grenadier, 1768 | 1.15 | 1.15 |
| 786 | A115 | $3 | Battalion Co. Officer, 1780 | 1.50 | 1.50 |
| | | Nos. 783-786 (4) | | 3.40 | 3.40 |

## Locomotives Type of 1985

**1984, Nov. 21 — Litho. — Perf. 12½x13**
Se-tenant Pairs, #a.-b.
a. — Side and front views.
b. — Action scene.

| 787 | A120 | 5c | 1954 R.R. Class 20, Zimbabwe | .20 | .20 |
|---|---|---|---|---|---|
| 788 | A120 | 40c | 1928 Southern Maid, U.K. | .35 | .35 |
| 789 | A120 | 75c | 1911 Prince of Wales, U.K. | .35 | .35 |
| 790 | A120 | $2.50 | 1935 D.R.G. Class 05, Germany | 1.10 | 1.10 |
| | | Nos. 787-790 (4) | | 2.00 | 2.00 |

Michael Jackson (b. 1960), American
Entertainer — A125

#894a, Portrait. #894b, On stage. #895a,
Singing. #895b, Portrait. #896a, Black jacket.
#896b, Red jacket. #897a, Portrait. #897b,
Wearing white glove.

**1985, Dec. 2**                    **Perf. 12½**
894  A125  60c  Pair, #a.-b.           .60    .60
895  A125  $1   Pair, #a.-b.          1.00   1.00
896  A125  $1.50 Pair, #a.-b.         1.90   1.90
897  A125  $2   Pair, #a.-b.          2.50   2.50
        Nos. 894-897 (4)              9.10   9.10

**Souvenir Sheets of 4**
**Perf. 13x12½**
898  A125  45c  #a.-b.                 .90    .90
899  A125  90c  #a.-b.                1.90   1.90
900  A125  $1.50 #a.-b.               3.00   3.00
901  A125  $4   #a.-b.                8.25   8.25

#898-901 contain two of each stamp.

Christmas
A126

Children's drawings: 25c, Serenade, 75c,
Poinsettia. $2.50, Jesus, Our Master.

**1985, Dec. 9    Wmk. 373    Perf. 14**
903  A126  25c  multicolored           .20    .20
904  A126  75c  multicolored           .55    .55
905  A126  $2.50 multicolored         1.90   1.90
        Nos. 903-905 (3)              2.65   2.65

Car Type of 1983

30c, 1916 Cadillac Type 53, US. 45c, 1939
Triumph Dolomite, UK. 60c, 1972 Panther J-
72, UK. 90c, 1967 Ferrari 275 GTB/4, Italy.
$1.50, 1953 Packard Caribbean, US. $2.50,
1931 Bugatti Type 41 Royale, France.

**1986, Jan. 27                    Perf. 12½**
    a. — Action scene.
    b. — Side and front views.
906-911 A107  Set of 6 pairs         7.50   7.50

Halley's
Comet
A127

**1986, Apr. 14    Litho.    Perf. 15**
918  A127  45c  shown                  .35    .35
919  A127  60c  Edmond Halley          .45    .45
920  A127  75c  Newton's reflector
                telescope              .55    .55
921  A127  $3   Local astronomer      2.25   2.25
    a.  Souvenir sheet of 4, #918-921 3.60   3.60
        Nos. 918-921 (4)              3.60   3.60

---

Souvenir Sheets of 2

Discovery of America, 500th Anniv.
(1992) — A130

Scouting Movement, 75th
Anniv. — A127a

American flag & Girl Guides or Boy Scouts
emblem and: #922b, Scout sign, handshake.
#922c, Paintbrushes, pallet. #922d, Knots.
#922e, Lord Baden-Powell.

**1986, Feb. 25    Litho.    Perf. 13x12½**
922  A127a  $5  #b.-c.                4.50   4.50
922A A127a  $6  #d.-e.                5.50   5.50

"Capex '87" overprints on this issue were
not authorized.

Elizabeth II
at Victoria
Park
A129

Elizabeth II Wearing Crown
Jewels — A128

**1986, Apr. 21    Wmk. 373    Perf. 12½**
923  A128  10c  multicolored           .20    .20
924  A128  45c  multicolored           .55    .55
925  A128  90c  multicolored          1.00   1.00
926  A128  $2.50 multicolored         3.00   3.00
        Nos. 923-926 (4)              4.75   4.75

**Souvenir Sheet**
927  A128  $10 multicolored           7.25   7.25

Various portraits.

**1986, June 14    Wmk. 373    Perf. 15x14**
928  A129  10c  multicolored           .20    .20
929  A129  45c  multicolored           .55    .55
930  A129  60c  multicolored           .60    .60
931  A129  75c  multicolored           .75    .75
        Nos. 928-931 (4)              2.10   2.10

**Souvenir Sheet**
932  A129  $3  multicolored           2.50   2.50
        Queen Elizabeth II, 60th birthday.

---

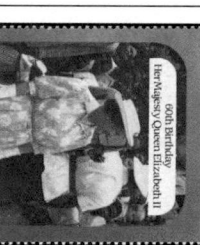

Discovery of America, 500th Anniv.
(1992) — A130

#936a, Fleet. #936b, Columbus. #937a, At
Spanish, Court. #937b, Ferdinand, Isabella.
#938a, Fruit, Santa Maria. #938b, Fruit.

**1986, Jan. 23    Litho.    Perf. 12½**
936  A130  60c  Pair, #a.-b.          2.25   2.25
937  A130  $1.50 Pair, #a.-b.         4.00   4.00
938  A130  $2.75 Pair, #a.-b.         7.15   7.15
        Nos. 936-938 (3)

**Souvenir Sheet**
939  A130  $6  Columbus, diff.        4.50   4.50

1986 World Cup Soccer
Championships, Mexico — A131

**1986, May 7    Litho.    Perf. 15**
940  A131  1c  Emblem                  .40    .40
941  A131  2c  Mexico                  .20    .20
942  A131  5c  Scotland                .20    .20
943  A131  5c  Mexico, diff.           .20    .20
944  A131  10c Spain vs. Scot-
               land                    .20    .20
945  A131  30c England vs.
               USSR                    .20    .20
946  A131  45c Spain vs.
               France                  .30    .30
947  A131  $1  England vs. Italy       .60    .60

**Size: 56x36mm    Perf. 13½**
948  A131  75c Mexico                  .95    .95
949  A131  $2  Scotland               1.25   1.25
950  A131  $4  England                2.50   2.50
951  A131  $5  England                3.00   3.00
        Nos. 940-951 (12)             9.25   9.25

**1986, July 7    Souvenir Sheets**
952  A131  $1.50 like #950            1.50   1.50
953  A131  $1.50 like #941            1.40   1.40
954  A131  $1.50 like #949            1.50   1.50
955  A131  $2.50 like #948            1.60   1.60
956  A131  $3  like #946              1.60   1.60
957  A131  $5.50 like #951            3.50   3.50
        Nos. 952-957 (6)              9.90   9.90
    Nos. 941-944, 946-947, vert.
    Nos. 952-957 (6)

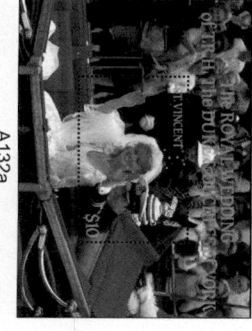

A132a

Wedding of Prince Andrew and Sarah
Ferguson — A132

#958a, Andrew. #958b, Sarah. #959a,
Andrew, horiz. #959b, Andrew, Nancy Reagan, horiz.

**1986, Sept.**
968  A133  10c multicolored            .40    .40
969  A133  60c Pithecellobium
               saman                  1.00   1.00

Trees — A133    Perf. 14

970  A133  75c Tabebuia pallida       1.25   1.25
971  A133  $3  Andira inermis         4.75   4.75
        Nos. 968-971 (4)              7.40   7.40

---

Locomotives Type of 1985

Designs: 30c, 1926 JNR ABT Rack & Adhe-
sion Class ED41 BZZ, Japan. 50c, 1883 Chicago RR Exposition, The Judge, 1A Type, US.
$1, 1973 BM & LPRR E60C Co-Co, US. $3,
1972 GM (EMD) SD40-2 Co-Co, US.

**1986, July    Perf. 12½x13**
    a. — Side and front views.
    b. — Action scene.
961  A120  30c Pair, #a.-b.            .30    .30
962  A120  50c Pair, #a.-b.            .45    .45
963  A120  $1  Pair, #a.-b.            .60    .60
964  A120  $3  Pair, #a.-b.           2.35   2.35
        Nos. 961-964 (4)

A number of unissued items,
imperfs, part perfs., missing color varieties, etc., were made available when
the Format International inventory was
liquidated.

Illustration A132a reduced.

**1986    Litho.    Perf. 12½x13, 13x12½**
958  A132  60c Pair, #a.-b.            .70    .70
959  A132  $2  Pair, #a.-b.           2.50   2.50
960  A132a $10 In coach               9.20   9.20
        Nos. 958-960 (3)

Issued: $10, Nov.; others, July 23.
For overprints see Nos. 976-977.

---

St. Vincent Cadet Force, 50th anniv., and
Girls' High School, 75th anniv.

**1986, Sept. 30**
972  A134  45c Cadet Force em-
               blem, vert.            .40    .40
973  A134  60c Grimble Building,
               GHS                    .50    .50
974  A134  75c GHS class             1.25   1.25
975  A134  $2  Cadets in formation   1.75   1.75
        Nos. 972-975 (4)             3.90   3.90

St. Vincent Cadet Force, 50th anniv., and
Girls' High School, 75th anniv.

Anniversaries — A134

The Legend of King Arthur — A134a

Nos. 958-959 Overprinted
"Congratulations to T.R.H. The Duke &
Duchess of York" in Silver

**1986, Oct.    Perf. 12½x13, 13x12½**
976  A132  60c Pair, #a.-b.            .90    .90
977  A132  $2  Pair, #a.-b.           3.00   3.00

Stamps of the same denomination also exist
printed tete-beche.

Litho.

**1986, Nov. 3** — **Perf. 14**

| | | | | |
|---|---|---|---|---|
| 979 | A134a | 30c King Arthur | .30 | .30 |
| 979A | A134a | 45c Merlin raises Arthur | .45 | .45 |
| 979B | A134a | 60c Arthur pulls Excalibur from stone | .50 | .50 |
| 979C | A134a | 75c Camelot | .65 | .65 |
| 979D | A134a | $1 Lady of the Lake | .90 | .90 |
| 979E | A134a | $1.50 Knights of the Round Table | 1.25 | 1.25 |
| 979F | A134a | $2 Holy Grail | 1.75 | 1.75 |
| 979G | A134a | $5 Sir Lancelot | 4.50 | 4.50 |
| | | Nos. 979-979G (8) | 10.30 | 10.30 |

A134b

Statue of Liberty, Cent. — A135

Various views of the statue.

**1986, Nov. 26** — **Litho.** — **Perf. 14**

| | | | | |
|---|---|---|---|---|
| 980 | A134b | 15c multicolored | .20 | .20 |
| 980A | A134b | 25c multicolored | .20 | .20 |
| 980B | A134b | 40c multicolored | .25 | .25 |
| 980C | A134b | 45c multicolored | .35 | .35 |
| 980D | A134b | 55c multicolored | .50 | .50 |
| 980E | A134b | 75c multicolored | .60 | .60 |
| 980F | A134b | $1 multicolored | 1.10 | 1.10 |
| 980G | A134b | $1.75 multicolored | 1.25 | 1.25 |
| 980H | A134b | $2.50 multicolored | 1.65 | 1.65 |
| 980I | A134b | multicolored | 1.90 | 1.90 |
| | | Nos. 980-980I (10) | 8.00 | 8.00 |

Souvenir Sheets

| | | | | |
|---|---|---|---|---|
| 981 | A135 | $3.50 multicolored | 2.25 | 2.25 |
| 982 | A135 | $4 multicolored | 2.50 | 2.50 |
| 983 | A135 | $5 multicolored | 3.00 | 3.00 |

Fresh-water Fishing — A136

#984a, Tri tri fishing. #984b, Tri tri. #985a. Crayfishing. #985b, Crayfish.

**1986, Dec. 10** — **Perf. 15**

| | | | | |
|---|---|---|---|---|
| 984 | A136 | 75c Pair, #a.-b. | 1.10 | 1.10 |
| 985 | A136 | $1.50 Pair, #a.-b. | 2.25 | 2.25 |

1987 Wimbledon Tennis Championships A137

Natl. Child Survival Campaign A138

**1987, June 22** — **Perf. 13x12½**

| | | | | |
|---|---|---|---|---|
| 988 | A137 | 40c Hana Mandlikova | .25 | .25 |
| 989 | A137 | 60c Yannick Noah | .35 | .35 |
| 990 | A137 | 80c Ivan Lendl | .50 | .50 |
| 991 | A137 | $1 Chris Evert Lloyd | .60 | .60 |
| 992 | A137 | $1.25 Steffi Graf | .75 | .75 |
| 993 | A137 | $1.50 John McEnroe | .95 | .95 |
| 994 | A137 | $1.75 Martina Navratilova | 1.10 | 1.10 |
| 995 | A137 | $2 Boris Becker | 1.25 | 1.25 |
| | | Nos. 988-995 (8) | 5.75 | 5.75 |

Souvenir Sheet

| | | | | |
|---|---|---|---|---|
| 996 | | Sheet of 2 | 3.50 | 3.50 |
| a. | A137 | $2.25 like $2 | 1.75 | 1.75 |
| b. | A137 | $2.25 like $1.75 | 1.75 | 1.75 |

**1987, June 10** — **Perf. 14x14½**

| | | | | |
|---|---|---|---|---|
| 997 | A138 | 10c Growth monitoring | .20 | .20 |
| 998 | A138 | 50c Oral rehydration therapy | .40 | .40 |
| 999 | A138 | 75c Breast-feeding | .60 | .60 |
| 1000 | A138 | $1 Universal immunization | .75 | .75 |
| | | Nos. 997-1000 (4) | 1.95 | 1.95 |

For overprints see Nos. 1040-1043.

Carnival, 10th Anniv. A139

Designs: 20c, Queen of the Bands, Miss Prima Donna 1986, 45c, Donna Young, Miss Carival 1985. 55c, M. Haydock, Miss. St. Vincent and the Grenadines 1986. $3.70, Spirit of I lope Year 1986.

**1987, June 29** — **Perf. 12½x13**

| | | | | |
|---|---|---|---|---|
| 1001 | A139 | 20c multicolored | .20 | .20 |
| 1002 | A139 | 45c multicolored | .35 | .35 |
| 1003 | A139 | bbc multicolored | .40 | .40 |
| 1004 | A139 | $3.70 multicolored | 2.75 | 2.75 |
| | | Nos. 1001-1004 (4) | 3.70 | 3.70 |

Nos. 874-881 Overprinted "THE KING OF ROCK AND ROLL LIVES FOREVER. AUGUST 16TH" and "1977-1987" (Nos. 1009-1012) or "TENTH ANNIVERSARY" (Nos. 1013-1016)

**1987, Aug. 26** — **Litho.** — **Perf. 12½**

| | | | | |
|---|---|---|---|---|
| 1009 | A123 | 10c Pair, #a.-b. | .20 | .20 |
| 1010 | A123 | 60c Pair, #a.-b. | .80 | .80 |
| 1011 | A123 | $1 Pair, #a.-b. | 1.25 | 1.25 |
| 1012 | A123 | $5 Pair, #a.-b. | 6.50 | 6.50 |
| | | Nos. 1009-1012 (4) | 8.75 | 8.75 |

Souvenir Sheets of 4

| | | | | |
|---|---|---|---|---|
| 1013 | A123 | 30c #a.-b. | .90 | .90 |
| 1014 | A123 | 50c #a.-b. | 1.50 | 1.50 |
| 1015 | A123 | $1.50 #a.-b. | 4.50 | 4.50 |
| 1016 | A123 | $4.50 #a.-b. | 13.00 | 13.00 |

Nos. 1013-1016 contain two of each stamp.

Portrait of Queen Victoria, 1841, by R. Thorburn A140

Portraits and photographs: 75c, Elizabeth and Charles, 1948. $1, Coronation, 1953. $2.50, Duke of Edinburgh, 1948. $5, Elizabeth, c. 1980. $6, Elizabeth and Charles, 1948, diff.

**1987, Nov. 20** — **Litho.** — **Perf. 12½x13**

| | | | | |
|---|---|---|---|---|
| 1017 | A140 | 15c multicolored | .20 | .20 |
| 1018 | A140 | 75c multicolored | .45 | .45 |
| 1019 | A140 | $1 multicolored | .60 | .60 |
| 1020 | A140 | $2.50 multicolored | 1.50 | 1.50 |
| 1021 | A140 | $5 multicolored | 3.00 | 3.00 |
| | | Nos. 1017-1021 (5) | 5.75 | 5.75 |

Souvenir Sheet

| | | | | |
|---|---|---|---|---|
| 1022 | A140 | $6 multicolored | 4.50 | 4.50 |

Sesquicentennial of Queen Victoria's accession to the throne, wedding of Queen Elizabeth II and Prince Philip, 40th anniv.

Nos. 997-1000 Ovptd. "WORLD POPULATION / 5 BILLION / 11TH JULY 1987"

**1987, July 11** — **Litho.** — **Perf. 14x14½**

| | | | | |
|---|---|---|---|---|
| 1040 | A138 | 10c on No. 997 | .20 | .20 |
| 1041 | A138 | 50c on No. 998 | .40 | .40 |
| 1042 | A138 | 75c on No. 999 | .60 | .60 |
| 1043 | A138 | $1 on No. 1000 | .75 | .75 |
| | | Nos. 1040-1043 (4) | 1.95 | 1.95 |

Automobile Centenary — A143

Automotive pioneers and vehicles: $1, $3, Carl Benz (1844-1929) and the Velocipede, patented 1886. $2, No. 1049, Enzo Ferrari (b. 1898) and 1966 Ferrari Dino 206SP. $4, $6, Charles Rolls (1877-1910), Sir Henry Royce (1863-1933) and 1907 Rolls Royce Silver Ghost. No. 1047, $8, Henry Ford (1863-1947) and Model T Ford.

**1987, Dec. 4** — **Perf. 13x12½**

| | | | | |
|---|---|---|---|---|
| 1044 | A143 | $1 multicolored | .65 | .65 |
| 1045 | A143 | $3 multicolored | 1.10 | 1.10 |
| 1046 | A143 | $4 multicolored | 2.25 | 2.25 |
| 1047 | A143 | $5 multicolored | 3.00 | 3.00 |
| | | Nos. 1044-1047 (4) | 7.00 | 7.00 |

Souvenir Sheets

| | | | | |
|---|---|---|---|---|
| 1048 | A143 | $3 like No. 1044 | 2.25 | 2.25 |
| 1049 | A143 | $5 like No. 1045 | 3.75 | 3.75 |
| 1050 | A143 | $6 like No. 1046 | 4.50 | 4.50 |
| 1051 | A143 | $8 like No. 1047 | 6.00 | 6.00 |
| | | Nos. 1048-1051 (4) | 16.50 | 16.50 |

Soccer Teams — A144

**1987, Dec. 4**

| | | | | |
|---|---|---|---|---|
| 1052 | A144 | $2 Derby County | 1.60 | 1.60 |
| 1053 | A144 | $2 Leeds United | 1.60 | 1.60 |
| 1054 | A144 | $2 Tottenham Hotspur | 1.60 | 1.60 |
| 1055 | A144 | $2 Manchester United | 1.60 | 1.60 |
| 1056 | A144 | $2 Everton | 1.60 | 1.60 |
| 1057 | A144 | $2 Liverpool | 1.60 | 1.60 |
| 1058 | A144 | $2 Portsmouth | 1.60 | 1.60 |
| 1059 | A144 | $2 Arsenal | 12.80 | 12.80 |
| | | Nos. 1052-1059 (8) | 12.80 | 12.80 |

A145

A Christmas Carol, by Charles Dickens (1812-1870) — A147

Portrait of Dickens as left page of book (Nos. 1061a-1064a) and various scenes from novels as right page of book (Nos. 1061b-1064b).

**1987, Dec. 17** — **Horiz. Pairs, #a.-b.** — **Perf. 14x14½**

| | | | | |
|---|---|---|---|---|
| 1061 | A145 | 6c Mr. Fezziwig's Ball | .35 | .35 |
| 1062 | A145 | 25c Ghost of Christmases to Come | .70 | .70 |
| 1063 | A145 | 50c The Cratchits | 1.25 | 1.25 |
| 1064 | A145 | 75c Carolers | 1.90 | 1.90 |
| | | Nos. 1061-1064 (4) | 4.20 | 4.20 |

Souvenir Sheet

| | | | | |
|---|---|---|---|---|
| 1065 | A147 | $5 Reading book to children | 3.75 | 3.75 |

Eastern Caribbean Currency — A148

Various Eastern Caribbean coins (Nos. 1069-1081) and banknotes (Nos. 1082-1086) in denominations equaling that of the stamp on which they are pictured.

**1987-89** — **Litho.** — **Perf. 15**

| | | | | |
|---|---|---|---|---|
| 1069 | A148 | 5c multicolored | .20 | .20 |
| 1070 | A148 | 5c multicolored | .20 | .20 |
| 1071 | A148 | 10c multicolored | .20 | .20 |
| 1072 | A148 | 15c multicolored | .20 | .20 |
| 1073 | A148 | 15c multicolored | .20 | .20 |
| 1074 | A148 | 20c multicolored | .20 | .20 |
| 1075 | A148 | 25c multicolored | .20 | .20 |
| 1076 | A148 | 30c multicolored | .25 | .25 |
| 1077 | A148 | 35c multicolored | .30 | .30 |
| 1078 | A148 | 45c multicolored | .35 | .35 |
| 1079 | A148 | 50c multicolored | .40 | .40 |
| 1080 | A148 | 65c multicolored | .50 | .50 |
| 1081 | A148 | 75c multicolored | .60 | .60 |
| 1082 | A148 | $1 multi, horiz. | .75 | .75 |
| 1083 | A148 | $1 multi, horiz. | 1.50 | 1.50 |
| 1084 | A148 | $3 multi, horiz. | 2.25 | 2.25 |
| 1085 | A148 | $5 multi, horiz. | 3.75 | 3.75 |
| 1086 | A148 | $10 multi, horiz. | 7.50 | 7.50 |

**Perf. 14**

| | | | | |
|---|---|---|---|---|
| 1086A | A148 | $20 multi, horiz. (19) | 15.00 | 15.00 |
| | | Nos. 1069-1086A (19) | 34.55 | 34.55 |

Issued: $20, Nov. 7, 1989; others, Dec. 11.

**1991** — **Perf. 12**

| | | | | |
|---|---|---|---|---|
| 1071a | A148 | 10c | .20 | .20 |
| 1073a | A148 | 15c | .20 | .20 |
| 1074a | A148 | 20c | .20 | .20 |
| 1078a | A148 | 45c | .35 | .35 |
| 1079a | A148 | 50c | .45 | .45 |
| 1080a | A148 | 65c | .55 | .55 |
| 1081a | A148 | 75c | .70 | .70 |
| 1082a | A148 | $1 | 1.40 | 1.40 |
| 1083a | A148 | $3 | 3.50 | 3.50 |
| 1085a | A148 | $5 | 8.05 | 8.05 |
| | | Nos. 1071a-1085a (11) | | |

This perf. may not have been issued in St. Vincent.

## US Constitution Bicentennial — A149

| | | | |
|---|---|---|---|
| 10711 | A148 | 10c | .20 .20 |
| 10731 | A148 | 15c | .20 .20 |
| 10741 | A148 | 20c | .20 .20 |
| 10751 | A148 | 25c | .30 .30 |
| 10761 | A148 | 35c | .30 .30 |
| 10781 | A148 | 40c | .30 .30 |
| 10791 | A148 | 45c | .45 .45 |
| 10801 | A148 | 50c | .45 .45 |
| 10811 | A148 | 55c | .55 .55 |
| 10821 | A148 | 65c | .55 .55 |
| 10831 | A148 | 70c | .70 .70 |
| 10841 | A148 | $1 | 1.40 1.40 |
| 10851 | A148 | $2 | 3.50 3.50 |
| 10851 | A148 | $5 | 8.05 8.05 |

Nos. 10711b-10856b (11)

Christopher Columbus's fleet: 15c, Santa Maria. 75c, Nina and Pinta. $1, Hour glass, compass. $1.50, Columbus planting flag of Spain on American soil. $3, Arawak natives. $4, Parrot, hummingbird, corn, pineapple, eggs. $5, $6, Columbus, Spanish royal coat of arms and caravel.

**1988, Jan. 11**    **Perf. 14x14**

| | | | |
|---|---|---|---|
| 1087 | A149 | 15c multicolored | .20 .20 |
| 1088 | A149 | 75c multicolored | .60 .60 |
| 1089 | A149 | $1 multicolored | 1.25 1.25 |
| 1090 | A149 | $1.50 multicolored | 1.25 1.25 |
| 1091 | A149 | $3 multicolored | 2.25 2.25 |
| 1092 | A149 | $4 multicolored | 3.00 3.00 |

Nos. 1087-1092 (6)   8.05 8.05

**Souvenir Sheets**
**Perf. 14x14½, 14½x14**

| | | | |
|---|---|---|---|
| 1093 | A149 | $5 multicolored | 3.75 3.75 |
| 1093A | A149 | $6 multicolored | 4.50 4.50 |

US Constitution, bicent.; 500th anniv. of the discovery of America (in 1992).

**1988, Feb. 15**    **Perf. 14**

| | | | |
|---|---|---|---|
| 1094 | A150 | 45c multicolored | .35 .35 |

See No. 1298.

Brown Pelican — A150

A151

**1988, Feb. 22**    **Litho.**    **Perf. 15**

| | | | |
|---|---|---|---|
| 1095 | A151 | 10c Windsurfing, diff., vert. | .20 .20 |
| 1096 | A151 | 45c Scuba diving, vert. | .35 .35 |

Tourism — A152

| | | | |
|---|---|---|---|
| 1097 | A151 | 65c shown | .50 .50 |
| 1098 | A151 | $5 Chartered ship | 3.75 3.75 |

Nos. 1095-1098 (4)   4.80 4.80

**Souvenir Sheet**
**Perf. 13x12½**

| | | | |
|---|---|---|---|
| 1099 | A152 | $10 shown | 7.50 7.50 |

---

## Cricket Players A156

**1988, July 29**    **Litho.**    **Perf. 14½x14**

| | | | |
|---|---|---|---|
| 1108 | A156 | 15c D.K. Lillee | .20 .20 |
| 1109 | A156 | 50c G.A. Gooch | .40 .40 |
| 1110 | A156 | 75c R.N. Kapil Dev | .60 .60 |
| 1111 | A156 | $1 S.M. Gavaskar | .75 .75 |
| 1112 | A156 | $1.50 M.W. Gatting | .75 .75 |
| 1113 | A156 | $2.50 Imran Khan | 1.15 1.15 |
| 1114 | A156 | $2 I.T. Botham | 1.90 1.90 |
| 1115 | A156 | $4 I.V.A. Richards | 3.00 3.00 |

Nos. 1108-1115 (8)   10.25 10.25

A souvenir sheet containing a $2 stamp like No. 1115 and a $3.50 stamp like No. 1114 was not issued by the post office.

**1988, July 29**    **Litho.**    **Perf. 12½**

| | | | |
|---|---|---|---|
| 1100 | A153 | 15c multicolored | .20 .20 |
| 1101 | A153 | 50c multicolored | .45 .45 |
| 1102 | A153 | 75c multicolored | 1.00 1.00 |
| 1103 | A153 | $1 multicolored | 1.25 1.25 |
| 1104 | A153 | $3.50 multicolored | 2.00 2.00 |
| 1105 | A153 | $5 multicolored | 3.00 3.00 |

Nos. 1100-1105 (6)   7.90 7.90

16th cent. ships and artifacts: 15c, Nuestra Senora del Rosario, Spanish Chivalric Cross. 75c, Ark Royal, Armada medal. $1.50, English fleet, 16th cent. navigational instrument. $2, Dismasted galleon, cannon balls. $3.50, English fireships among the Armada. $5, Revenge, Drake's drum. $8, Shoreline sentries awaiting the outcome of the battle.

**Souvenir Sheet**

| | | | |
|---|---|---|---|
| 1106 | A154 | $8 multicolored | 5.00 5.00 |

Destruction of the Spanish Armada by the English, 400th Anniv. — A154

A153

400th Anniversary of the Armada

## Christmas — A159

Walt Disney characters: 1c, Minnie Mouse in freight car. 2c, Morty and Ferdy in open rail car. 3c, Chip 'n Dale in open boxcar. 4c, Huey, Dewey, Louie and reindeer. 5c, Donald and Daisy Duck aboard dining car. 10c, Gramma Duck conducting chorus including Scrooge McDuck. $1, Goofy and Clarabelle Cow. $5, No. 1127, Mickey Mouse in locomotive. $6, Santa Claus in caboose. No. 1129, Mickey, Minnie Mouse and nephews in train station, vert. No. 1130, Characters riding carousel, vert.

**1988, Dec. 23**    **Litho.**    **Perf. 14x13½, 13½x14**

| | | | |
|---|---|---|---|
| 1121-1128 | A159 | Set of 8 | 11.50 11.50 |

**Souvenir Sheets**

| | | | |
|---|---|---|---|
| 1129-1130 | A159 | $5 Set of 2 | 11.50 11.50 |

---

## 1988 Summer Olympics, Seoul A158

**1988, Dec. 7**    **Litho.**    **Perf. 14**

| | | | |
|---|---|---|---|
| 1116 | A158 | 10c Running | .20 .20 |
| 1117 | A158 | 50c Long jump, vert. | .40 .40 |
| 1118 | A158 | $1 Triple jump | .75 .75 |
| 1119 | A158 | $5 Boxing, vert. | 3.75 3.75 |

Nos. 1116-1119 (4)   5.10 5.10

**Souvenir Sheet**

| | | | |
|---|---|---|---|
| 1120 | A158 | $10 Torch | 7.50 7.50 |

1st Participation of St. Vincent athletes in the Olympics. For overprints see Nos. 1346-1351.

 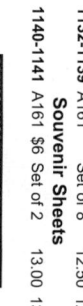

Designs: 10c, Harry James (1916-83). 15c, Sidney Bechet (1897-1959). 25c, Benny Goodman (1909-86). 35c, Django Reinhardt (1910-53). 50c, Lester Young (1909-59). 90c, Gene Krupa (1909-73). $3, Louis Armstrong (1900-71). $4, Duke Ellington (1899-1974). $5, Billie Holiday (1915-59).

Entertainers of the Jazz and Big Band Eras — A162

**1989, Feb. 7**    **Litho.**    **Perf. 14**

| | | | |
|---|---|---|---|
| 1132-1139 | A161 | Set of 8 | 12.50 12.50 |

**Souvenir Sheets**

| | | | |
|---|---|---|---|
| 1140-1141 | A161 | $6 Set of 2 | 13.00 13.00 |

Exhibition emblem and Walt Disney characters: 1c, Mickey Mouse as snake charmer, Minnie Mouse as dancer. 2c, Goofy tossing rings at a chowsingha antelope. 3c, Mickey, Minnie, blue peacock. 5c, Goofy and Mickey as miners, Briolette diamond. 10c, Goofy as count presenting Orloff Diamond to Catherine the Great of Russia. 25c, Goofy as Regent Diamond and Donald Duck as Napoleon (portrait) in the Louvre. $4, Minnie as Queen Victoria, Mickey as King Albert, crown bearing the Kohinoor Diamond. $5, Minnie and Goofy on safari. No. 1140, Mickey as Nehru, riding an elephant. No. 1141, Mickey as postman delivering Hope Diamond to the Smithsonian Institute.

India '89, Jan. 20-29, New Delhi — A161

**1988, Dec. 7**    **Litho.**    **Perf. 14**

| | | | |
|---|---|---|---|
| 1131 | A160 | $2 multicolored | 2.00 2.00 |

Babe Ruth (1895-1948), American Baseball Star — A160

**1989, Apr. 3**    **Litho.**    **Perf. 14**

| | | | |
|---|---|---|---|
| 1142-1149 | A162 | Set of 8 | 11.00 11.00 |

**Souvenir Sheets**

| | | | |
|---|---|---|---|
| 1150-1151 | A162 | $5 Set of 2 | 12.00 12.00 |

Holiday misspelled "Holliday" on No. 1151.

### Miniature Sheet
### Noah's Ark — A163

Designs: a, Clouds, 2 birds at right. b, Rainbow, 4 clouds. c, Ark. d, Rainbow, 3 clouds. e, Clouds, 2 birds at left. f, African elephant facing right. g, Elephant facing forward. h, Leaves on tree branch. i, Kangaroos. j, Hummingbird facing left, flower. k, Lions. l, White-tailed deer. m, Koala at right. n, Koala at left. o, Hummingbird facing right, flower. p, Flower, toucan facing left. q, Toucan facing right. r, Camels. s, Giraffes. t, Sheep. u, Ladybugs. v, Butterfly (UR). w, Butterfly (LL). x, Snakes. y, Dragonflies.

**1989, Apr. 10**    **Perf. 14**

| | | | |
|---|---|---|---|
| 1152 a.-y. | A163 | 40c any single | .30 .30 |
| 1152 | | Sheet of 25 | 14.50 14.50 |

---

Paintings by Titian: 5c, Baptism of Christ. 30c, Temptation of Christ. 45c, Ecce Homo. 65c, Noli Me Tangere. 75c, Christ Carrying the Cross. $1, Christ Crowned with Thorns. $4, Lamentation Over Christ. $5, The Entombment. No. 1161, Pieta. No. 1162, The Deposition.

Easter A164

**1989, Apr. 17**    **Perf. 13½x14**

| | | | |
|---|---|---|---|
| 1153-1160 | A164 | Set of 8 | 13.50 13.50 |

**Souvenir Sheets**

| | | | |
|---|---|---|---|
| 1161-1162 | A164 | $6 Set of 2 | 12.50 12.50 |

Designs: 15c, Mercury cosmonaut. 35c, non-Soviet cosmonaut, 1978. $1, CNES Hermes space plane, France. $3, ESA emblem. 60c, Vladimir Remek of Czechoslovakia, 1st non-Soviet cosmonaut.

15c, Recovery of astronaut L. Gordon Cooper, Mercury 9/Faith 7 mission. 35c, Satellite transmission of Martin Luther King's civil rights march address, 1963. 40c, US shuttle STS-7, 1st use of Canadarm; deployment & recovery of a W. German free-flying experiment platform. 50c, Satellite transmission of Pope John XXIII (1881-1963) blessing crowd at the Vatican. $4, Ulf Merbold, W. Germany, 1st non-American astronaut, 1983.

Telstar II and Cooperation in Space — A165

#1171, Launch of Telstar II, 5/7/63. #1172, 1975 Apollo-Soyuz mission members shaking hands.

**1989, Apr. 26    Litho.    Perf. 14**
1163-1170 A165    Set of 8    12.00 12.00
**Souvenir Sheets**
1171-1172 A165 $5 Set of 2    10.00 10.00

**Cruise Ships — A166**

**1989, Apr. 21    Litho.    Perf. 14**
1173 A166 10c Ile de France    .40 .40
1174 A166 40c Liberte    .60 .60
1175 A166 50c Mauretania    .80 .80
1176 A166 75c France    1.10 1.10
1177 A166 $1 Aquitania    1.50 1.50
1178 A166 $2 United States    3.00 3.00
1179 A166 $3 Olympic    4.25 4.25
1180 A166 $4 Queen Elizabeth    5.75 5.75
Nos. 1173-1180 (8)    17.40 17.40
**Souvenir Sheets**
1181 A166 $6 Queen Mary    8.50 8.50
1182 A166 $6 QE 2    8.50 8.50
Nos. 1181-1182 contain 84x28mm stamps. For overprints see Nos. 1352-1361.

**1988 World Series — A167**
Designs: a. Dodgers emblem and players celebrating victory. b. Emblems of the Dodgers and the Oakland Athletics.

**1989, May 3    Litho.    Perf. 14x13½**
1183    Sheet of 2    5.75 5.75
a.-b. A167 $2 any single    1.50 1.50

**World Wildlife Fund, St. Vincent Parrots A168**

**1989, Apr. 5    Perf. 14**
1184 A168 10c Parrot's head    .55 .55
1185 A168 20c Parrot's wing span    .55 .55
1186 A169 25c Mistletoe bird    .55 .55
1187 A168 40c Parrot feeding,    .85 .85
1188 A168 70c Parrot on rock, vert.    1.40 1.40
**Indigenous Birds — A169**
1189 A169 75c Crab hawk    1.75 1.75
1190 A169 $1 Coucou    4.25 4.25
1191 A169 $3 Prince bird    6.00 6.00
Nos. 1184-1191 (8)    15.90 15.90
**Souvenir Sheets**
1192 A169 $5 Doctor bird    4.25 4.25
1193 A169 $5 Soufrieres, vert.    4.25 4.25

**Fan Paintings — A170**
By Hiroshige unless otherwise stated: 10c, Autumn Flowers in Front of the Full Moon. 40c, Hibiscus. 50c, Iris. 75c, Morning Glories. $1, Dancing Swallows. $2, Sparrow and Bamboo. $3, Yellow Bird and Cotton Rose. $4, Judos Chrysanthemums in a deep ravine in China. No. 1202, Rural Cottages in Spring, by Sotatsu. No. 1203, The Six Immortal Poets Portrayed as Cats, by Kuniyoshi.

**1989, July 6    Litho.    Perf. 14x13½**
1194-1201 A170    Set of 8    11.00 11.00
**Souvenir Sheets**
1202-1203 A170 $6 Set of 2    11.00 11.00
Hirohito (1901-89) and enthronement of Akihito as emperor of Japan.

**First Moon Landing, 20th Anniv. A171**
Apollo 11 Mission: 35c, Columbia command module. 75c, Lunar module Eagle landing. $1, Rocket launch. No. 1207a, Buzz Aldrin conducting solar wind experiments. No. 1207b, Lunar module on plain. No. 1207c, Earthrise. No. 1207d, Neil Armstrong. No. 1208, Separation of lunar and command modules. No. 1209a, Command module. No. 1209b, Lunar module. $6, Armstrong preparing to take man's 1st step onto the Moon.

**1989, Sept. 11    Perf. 14**
1204 A171 35c multicolored    .40 .30
1205 A171 75c multicolored    1.00 .55
1206 A171 $1 multicolored    1.10 .75
1207    Strip of 4    .75
a.-d. A171 $2 any single    .75 1.50
1208 A171 $3 multicolored    3.25 3.25
Nos. 1204-1208 (5)    14.50 13.60
**Souvenir Sheets**
1209    Sheet of 2    6.50 6.50
a.-b. A171 $3 any single    2.25 2.25
1210 A171 $6 multicolored    6.50 6.50
No. 1207 has continuous design.

**Players Elected to the Baseball Hall of Fame — A172**

**1989 All-Star Game, July 11, Anaheim, California — A173**

**Rookies of the Year, Most Valuable Players and Cy Young Award Winners A175**

**1989, July 23    Litho.    Perf. 14**
1211 A172 $2 Cobb, 1936    1.50 1.50
1212 A172 $2 Mays, 1979    1.50 1.50
1213 A172 $2 Musial, 1969    1.50 1.50
1214 A172 $2 Bench, 1989    1.50 1.50
1215 A172 $2 Banks, 1977    1.50 1.50
1216 A172 $2 Schoendienst, 1989    1.50 1.50
1217 A172 $2 Gehrig, 1939    1.50 1.50
1218 A172 $2 Robinson, 1962    1.50 1.50
1219 A172 $2 Feller, 1962    1.50 1.50
1220 A172 $2 Williams, 1966    1.50 1.50
1221 A172 $2 Yastrzemski, 1989    1.50 1.50
1222 A172 $2 Kaline, 1980    1.50 1.50
Nos. 1211-1222 (12)    18.00 18.00
"Yastrzemski" is misspelled on No. 1221.

Size: 116x82mm
**1989    Imperf    Perf. 13**
1223 A173 $5 multicolored    5.75 5.75

**1989    Embossed    Perf. 13**
No. 1223A, Johnny Bench. No. 1223B, Carl Yastrzemski, 1961. c, Randy Johnson, 1989. No. 1223C, Ernie Banks. No. 1223D, Jerome Walton. No. 1223E, Al Kaline. No. 1223F, Ty Cobb. No. 1223G, Ted Williams. No. 1223H, Red Schoendienst. No. 1223I, Jackie Robinson. No. 1223J, Lou Gehrig. No. 1223K, Bob Feller. No. 1223L, Stan Musial.
1223A-1223L A173a $20 Set of 12, gold

**Miniature Sheets**
No. 1224: a, Dante Bichette, 1989. b, Carl Yastrzemski, 1961. c, Randy Johnson, 1989. d, Jerome Walton. e, Ramon Martinez, 1989. f, Ken Hill, 1989. g, Tom McCarthy, 1989. h, Gaylord Perry, 1963. i, John Smoltz, 1989.
No. 1225: a, Bob Milacki, 1989. b, Babe Ruth, 1915. c, Jim Abbott, 1989. d, Gary Sheffield, 1989. e, Gregg Jeffries, 1989. f, Kevin Brown, 1989. g, Cris Carpenter, 1989. h, Johnny Bench, 1968. i, Ken Griffey Jr., 1989. No. 1226: a, Chris Sabo, 1988 Natl. League Rookie of the Year. b, Walt Weiss, 1988 American League Rookie of the Year. c, Willie Mays, 1951 Rookie of the Year. d, Kirk Gibson, 1988 Natl. League Most Valuable Player. e, Ted Williams, Most Valuable Player of 1946 and 1949. f, Jose Canseco, 1988 American League Most Valuable Player. g, Gaylord Perry, Cy Young winner for 1972 and 1978. h, Orel Hershiser, 1988 National League Cy Young winner. i, Frank Viola, 1988 American League Cy Young winner.

1224    Sheet of 9    5.00 5.00
a.-i. A174 60c any single    .50 .50

**Baseball Hall of Fame Members — A173a**

**Rookies and Team Emblems A174**

1225    Sheet of 9    5.00 5.00
a.-i. A174 60c any single    .50 .50
1226    Sheet of 9    5.00 5.00
a.-i. A175 60c any single    .50 .50
For surcharges see Nos. B9-B11.

**French Revolution Bicent. PHILEXFRANCE '89 — A176**
French governors and ships.

**1989, July 7    Litho.    Perf. 13½x14**
1227 A176 30c Goelette    .65 .65
1228 A176 55c Corvette    1.00 1.00
1229 A176 75c Fregate 36    1.60 1.60
1230 A176 $1 Vaisseau 74    2.00 2.00
1231 A176 $3 Ville de Paris    6.00 6.00
Nos. 1227-1231 (5)    11.25 11.25
**Souvenir Sheet**
1232 A176 $6 Map    6.00 6.00

**Miniature Sheet**

**Discovery of the New World, 500th Anniv. (in 1992) — A177**
Designs: a, Map of Florida, queen conch and West Indian purpura. b, Caribbean reef fish. c, Sperm whale. d, Columbus's fleet. e, Cuba, Isle of Pines, remora. f, The Bahamas, Turks & Caicos Isls. g, Navigational instruments. h, Sea monster. i, Kemp's Ridley turtle, Cayman Isls. j, Jamaica, parts of Cuba and Hispaniola, magnificent frigatebird. k, Cayman manatee, Hispaniola, Puerto Rico, Virgin Isls. l, Caribbean Monk seal, Anguilla and Caribbean isls. m, Mayan chief, galleon, dugout canoe. n, Masked boobies. o, Venezuelan village on pilings and the Netherlands Antilles. p, Atlantic wing oyster, lion's paw scallop, St. Vincent, Grenada, Trinidad & Tobago, Barbados. q, Panama, great hammerhead and maku sharks. r, Brown pelican, Colombia, Hyacinthine macaw. s, Venezuela, Indian bow and spear hunters. t, Capuchin and squirrel monkeys.

**1989, Aug. 31    Perf. 14**
1233 A177    Sheet of 20    17.50 17.50
a.-t. 50c any single    .70 .70

**Major League Baseball: Los Angeles Dodgers — A178**

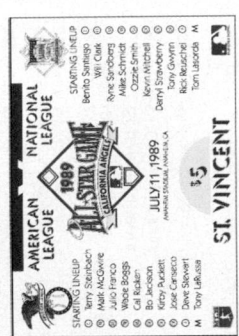

No. 1234: a, Jay Howell, Alejandro Pena. b, Mike Davis, Kirk Gibson. c, Fernando Valenzuela, John Shelby. d, Jeff Hamilton, Franklin Stubbs. e, Dodger Stadium. f, Ray Searage, John Tudor. g, Mike Sharperson, Mickey Hatcher. h, Coaches Amalfitano, Cresse, Ferguson, Hines, Mota, Perranoski, Russell. i, John Wetteland, Ramon Martinez. No. 1235: a, Tim Belcher, Tim Crews. b, Orel Hershiser, Mike Morgan. c, Mike Scioscia, Rick Dempsey. d, Dave Anderson, Alfredo Griffin. e, Team emblem. f, Kal Daniels, Mike Marshall. g, Eddie Murray, Willie Randolph. h, Manager Tom Lasorda, Jose Gonzalez. i, Lenny Harris, Chris Gwynn, Billy Bean.

Ty Cobb $2 / $5 ST. VINCENT 1989 All-Star Game, July 11, Anaheim, California — A173

**1989, Sept. 23**    **Perf. 12½**
1990 World Cup Soccer
Championships, Italy — A179

| 1234 | A179 | 10c | shown | 7.50 | 7.50 |
| 1236 | A179 | 10c | | .65 | .65 |
| 1237 | A179 | 55c | Youth soccer | 7.50 | 7.50 |

a.-t. Sheet of 9
a.-t. A178 60c any single .65 .65

**1989, Oct. 16**    **Litho.**    **Perf. 14**
1990 World Cup Soccer
Championships, Italy—A179

| 1238 | A179 | $1 | Nat. team | 1.25 | 1.25 |
| 1239 | A179 | $5 | Trophy winners | 6.25 | 6.25 |

Nos. 1236-1239 (4)    8.50 8.50

**Souvenir Sheets**

| 1240 | A179 | $6 | Youth soccer team | 7.50 | 7.50 |
| 1241 | A179 | $6 | Nat. team, diff. | 7.50 | 7.50 |

See Nos. 1344-1345.

St. Vincent

**1989, Nov. 1**
Fauna and Flora
A180

| 1242 | A180 | 65c | St. Vincent parrot | .90 | .90 |
| 1243 | A180 | 75c | Whistling warbler | 1.10 | 1.10 |
| 1244 | A180 | 75c | Black snake | 7.00 | 7.00 |

Nos. 1242-1244 (3)    9.00 9.00

**Souvenir Sheet**

| 1245 | A180 | $6 | Volcano plant, vert. | 6.75 | 6.75 |

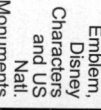

ST. VINCENT   6c

Little Yellow Butterfly, St. V., No. 1248

**1989, Oct. 16**    **Perf. 14x14½, 14½x14**
Butterflies
A181

| 1246 | A181 | 6c | Little yellow | .30 | .30 |
| 1247 | A181 | 10c | Orion | .30 | .20 |
| 1248 | A181 | 15c | American painted lady | .30 | .20 |
| 1249 | A181 | 75c | Cassius blue | .95 | .60 |
| 1250 | A181 | $1 | Polydamas swallowtail | 1.20 | 1.20 |
| 1251 | A181 | $2 | Guaraguao | 2.40 | 2.40 |
| 1252 | A181 | $3 | The Queen | 3.50 | 3.50 |
| 1253 | A181 | $5 | Royal blue | 5.00 | 3.50 |

Nos. 1246-1253 (8)    14.95 14.30

**Souvenir Sheets**

| 1254 | A181 | $6 | Monarch | 6.50 | 6.50 |
| 1255 | A181 | $6 | Barred sulphur | 6.50 | 6.50 |

ST. VINCENT   4c

Designs: 1c, Seagull Monument, Washington, DC. 3c, Crazy Horse Memorial, SD. 4c, Uncle Sam Wilson, Troy, NY. 5c, Benjamin Franklin Natl. Memorial, Philadelphia, PA. 10c, Statue of George Washington, Federal Hall, NY. $3, John F. Kennedy's birthplace, Brookline, MA. $6, George Washington's home, Mount Vernon, VA. No. 1264, Mt. Rushmore, SD. No. 1265, Stone Mountain, GA.

Exhibition Emblem, Disney Characters and US Natl. Monuments
A182

**1989, Nov. 30**    **Sheets of 9**    **Perf. 12½**

| 1267 | A184 | 30c | #a.-j. | 3.50 | 3.50 |
| 1268 | A184 | 30c | #a.-j. | 3.50 | 3.50 |
| 1269 | A184 | 30c | #a.-j. | 3.50 | 3.50 |
| 1270 | A184 | 30c | #a.-j. | 3.50 | 3.50 |
| 1271 | A184 | 30c | #a.-j. | 3.50 | 3.50 |
| 1272 | A184 | 30c | #a.-j. | 3.50 | 3.50 |
| 1273 | A184 | 30c | #a.-j. | 3.50 | 3.50 |
| 1274 | A184 | 30c | #a.-j. | 3.50 | 3.50 |
| 1275 | A184 | 30c | #a.-j. | 3.50 | 3.50 |

No. 1268d is incorrectly inscribed "Finger." Cochrane is misspelled "Cochpane" on No. 1272d.
No. 1272d was also issued in sheets of 9.

Players, owners and commissioner.
No. 1267: a. Early Wynn. b. Cecil Cooper. c. Joe DiMaggio. d. Kevin Mitchell. e. Tom Browning. f. Bobby Witt. g. Tim Wallach. h. Bob Gibson. i. Steve Garvey.
No. 1268: a. Mike Marshall. b. Tom Seaver. c. Bob Milacki. d. Dave Smith. e. Robin Roberts. f. Kent Hrbek. g. Bill Veeck, owner. h. Carmelo Martinez. i. Rogers Hornsby.
No. 1270: a. Barry Bonds. b. Jim Palmer. c. Lou Boudreau. d. Ernie Whitt. e. Jose Canseco. f. Ken Griffey, Jr. g. Johnny Vander Meer. h. Kevin Seitzer. i. Dave Dravecky.
No. 1271: a. Glenn Davis. b. Nolan Ryan. c. Hank Greenberg. d. Richie Allen. e. Dave Righetti. f. Jim Abbott. g. Harold Reynolds. h. Dennis Martinez. i. Rod Carew.
No. 1272: a. Joe Morgan. b. Tony Fernandez. c. Ozzie Guillen. d. Mike Greenwell. e. Cochrane. h. Willie McGee. i. Von Hayes.
No. 1273: a. Frank White. b. Brook Jacoby. c. Boog Powell. d. Will Clark. e. Ray Knight, owner. f. Fred McGriff. g. Willie Stargell. h. John Smoltz. i. B.J. Surhoff.
No. 1274: a. Keith Hernandez. b. Eddie Mathews. c. Tom Paciorek. d. Alan Trammell. e. Greg Maddux. f. Ruben Sierra. g. Tony Oliva. h. Chris Bosio. i. Orel Hershiser.
No. 1275: a. Casey Stengel. b. Jim Rice. c. Reggie Jackson. d. Jerome Walton. e. Bob Knepper. f. Andres Galarraga. g. Christy Mathewson. h. Willie Wilson. i. Ralph Kiner.

Major League Baseball — A184

ST. VINCENT 30c
CHICAGO WHITE SOX
EARLY WYNN
U.S. BASEBALL SERIES 2

**1989, Nov. 17**    **Perf. 13½x14**
| 1256-1263 | A182 | | Set of 8 | 14.00 | 14.00 |

**Souvenir Sheets**
| 1264-1265 | A182 | $5 | Set of 2 | 15.00 | 15.00 |

World Stamp Expo '89.

ST. VINCENT $5

**1989, Nov. 17**    **Litho.**    **Perf. 14**
The Washington Monument, Washington, DC—A183

| 1266 | A183 | $5 | multicolored | 3.75 | 3.75 |

**Miniature Sheets**
World Stamp Expo '89.

St. Vincent 35c

**1989, Dec. 20**    **Perf. 14**
Boy Scouts and Girl Guides — A187

| 1278 | A186 | 65c | multicolored | .75 | .75 |

**1989, Dec. 20**    **Perf. 14**
| 1279 | A186 | $10 | multicolored | 9.00 | 9.00 |

Independence, 10th anniv.

**1989, Dec. 20**    **Perf. 14**
Lord or Lady Baden-Powell and various scouts or girl guides.

| 1280 | A187 | 35c | Boy's modern uniform | .70 | .70 |
| 1281 | A187 | 35c | Guide, ranger, brownie | .70 | .70 |
| 1282 | A187 | 55c | Boy's old uniform | .95 | .95 |
| 1283 | A187 | 55c | Mrs. Jackson | .95 | .95 |
| 1284 | A187 | $2 | 75th anniv. emblem | 3.50 | 3.50 |
| 1285 | A187 | $2 | Mrs. Russell | 3.50 | 3.50 |

Nos. 1280-1285 (6)    10.30 10.30

**Souvenir Sheets**

| 1286 | A187 | $5 | Canoeing, merit badges | 7.00 | 7.00 |
| 1287 | A187 | $5 | Flag-raising, Camp Yourumei, 1985 | 7.00 | 7.00 |

St. Vincent 65c
10th Anniversary of INDEPENDENCE

**1989, Nov. 30**    **Litho.**    **Perf. 12½**
| 1276 | | Sheet of 9 | 13.50 | 13.50 |
| a.-t. | A185 | $2 any single | 1.50 | 1.50 |

Achievements of Nolan Ryan,
American Baseball Player—A185

Portrait and inscriptions: a. 383 League-leading strikeouts, 1973. b. No hitter, Kansas City Royals, May 15, 1973. c. No hitter, Detroit Tigers, July 15, 1973. d. No hitter, Minnesota Twins, Sept. 28, 1974. e. No hitter, Baltimore Orioles, June 1, 1975. f. No hitter, Los Angeles Dodgers, Sept. 26, 1981. g. Won 100+ games in both leagues. h. Struck out 200+ batters in 13 seasons. i. 5000th Strikeout, Aug. 22, 1989, Arlington, Texas.

For overprints see Nos. 1336-1337.

ST. VINCENT

**1990, Mar. 5**    **Litho.**    **Perf. 14**
Lions Intl.
of St. Vincent, 25th Anniv. (in 1989)
A189

| 1303-1307 | A189 | | Set of 5 | 8.25 | 8.25 |

Services: 10c, Scholarships for the blind, vert. 65c, Free textbooks. 75c, Health education (diabetes). $2, Blood sugar testing machines. $4, Publishing and distribution of pamphlets on drug abuse.

World War II
A190

**1990, Apr. 2**    **Perf. 14x13½**
| 1308-1317 | A190 | | Set of 10 | 18.00 | 18.00 |

**Souvenir Sheet**
| 1318 | A190 | $6 | multi | 8.50 | 8.50 |

Historic events: 5c, Defeat of the Graf Spee, 12/13-17/39. 10c, Charles De Gaulle calls the French Resistance to arms, 6/18/40. 15c, The British drive the Italian army out of Egypt, 12/15/40. 25c, US destroyer Reuben James torpedoed off Iceland, 10/31/41. 30c, MacArthur becomes allied supreme commander of the southwest Pacific, 4/18/42. 40c, US forces attack Corregidor, 2/16/45. 55c, HMS King George V engages the Bismarck, 5/27/41. 75c, US fleet enters Tokyo Harbor, 8/27/45. $5, Russian takeover of Berlin completed, 5/2/45. $6, #1317, Battle of the Philippine Sea, 6/18/44. #1318, Battle of the Java Sea, 2/28/42.

150th ANNIVERSARY
OF THE PENNY BLACK
St. Vincent
POSTAGE
4c

Penny Black, 150th Anniv.—A191

**1990, May 3**    **Litho.**    **Perf. 14x15**
| 1319 | A191 | $2 | "NK" | 2.50 | 2.50 |

Great Britain No. 1 (various plate positions).

**ST. VINCENT**

St. Vincent 65c

Coat of Arms, No. 570 — A186

**1989, Dec. 20**    **Perf. 14**

**Miniature Sheet**

Nolan Ryan
383 LEAGUE LEADING STRIKEOUTS, 1973
St. Vincent $2

**1989, Dec. 20**
Christmas — A188

Paintings by Da Vinci and Botticelli: 10c, The Adoration of the Magi (holy family), by Botticelli. 25c, The Adoration of the Magi (with nesses), 30c, The Madonna of the Magnificat, by Botticelli. 40c, The Annunciation, by Da Vinci. 55c, The Annunciation (angel), by Da Vinci. #1296, The Annunciation (Madonna), $5, #1294, 65c, The Madonna of the Carnation, by Da Vinci. 75c, The Virgin and Child with St. Anne and St. John the Baptist, by Da Vinci. The Annunciation, by Da Vinci. #1297, The Adoration of the Magi, by Botticelli.

**Bird Type of 1988**
| 1298 | A150 | 55c | St. Vincent parrot | .40 | .40 |

**1989, July 31**    **Litho.**    **Perf. 15x14**

| 1288-1295 | A188 | | Set of 8 | 13.00 | 13.00 |

**Souvenir Sheets**
| 1296-1297 | A188 | $5 | Set of 2 | 9.50 | 9.50 |

**1989, Dec. 20**    **Perf. 14**

CHRISTMAS 1989
10c
ST. VINCENT

Christmas — A188

**Souvenir Sheet**

| | | | | | |
|---|---|---|---|---|---|
| 1320 | A191 | $4 "AB" | | 5.00 | 5.00 |
| 1321 | A191 | $6 Simulated #1, "SV" | | 7.50 | 7.50 |

Watt Disney characters in British military uniforms: 5c, Donald Duck as 18th cent. Admiral. 10c, Huey as Bugler, 68th Light Infantry, 1854. 15c, Minnie Mouse as Drummer, 1st Irish Guards, 1900. 25c, Goofy as Lance Corporal, Seaforth Highlanders, 1944. $1, Mickey Mouse as officer, 58th Regiment, 1879, 1881. $2, Donald Duck as officer, Royal Engineers, 1813. $4, Mickey Mouse as Drum Major, 1914. $5, Goofy as Pipe Sergeant, 1918. No. 1330, Scrooge as Company Clerk and Goofy as King's Lifeguard of Foot. No. 1331, Mickey Mouse as British Grenadier.

Stamp World London '90 — A192

**1990, May  Litho.  Perf. 13½x14**

| | | | | |
|---|---|---|---|---|
| 1322-1329 | A192 | Set of 8 | 19.00 | 19.00 |

**Souvenir Sheets**

| | | | | |
|---|---|---|---|---|
| 1330-1331 | A192 | $6 Set of 2 | 14.50 | 14.50 |

A193

**1990, July 5**

| | | | | |
|---|---|---|---|---|
| 1332 | | $2 In robes | 2.00 | 2.00 |
| 1333 | | $2 Queen Mother signing book | 2.00 | 2.00 |
| 1334 | | $2 In robes | 4.65 | 4.65 |
| a. | A193 Strip of 3, #1332-1334 | | 6.00 | 6.00 |

*Nos. 1332-1334 (3)*

**Souvenir Sheet**

| | | | | |
|---|---|---|---|---|
| 1335 | A194 | $6 Like No. 1334 | 5.25 | 5.25 |

**No. 1276 Overprinted**
Miniature Sheets

a

b

**1990, July 23  Litho.  Perf. 12½**

| | | | | |
|---|---|---|---|---|
| 1336 | A185a | $2 #1336a-1336i | 13.50 | 13.50 |
| 1337 | A185b | $2 #1337a-1337i | 13.50 | 13.50 |

World Cup Soccer Championships, Italy — A195

Players from participating countries.

**1990, Sept. 24  Litho.  Perf. 14**

| | | | | |
|---|---|---|---|---|
| 1338 | A195 | 10c Argentina | .40 | .20 |
| 1339 | A195 | 75c Colombia | 1.10 | 1.10 |
| 1340 | A195 | $1 Uruguay | 1.50 | 1.50 |
| 1341 | A195 | $5 Belgium | 7.50 | 7.50 |
| | | | 10.50 | 10.30 |

*Nos. 1338-1341 (4)*

**Souvenir Sheets**

| | | | | |
|---|---|---|---|---|
| 1342 | A195 | $6 Brazil | 6.50 | 6.50 |
| 1343 | A195 | $6 West Germany | 6.50 | 6.50 |

**Dodger Baseball Type of 1989**

No. 1344: a, Hubie Brooks, Orel Hershiser. b, Manager Tom Lasorda, Tim Crews. c, Fernando Valenzuela, Eddie Murray. d, Kal Daniels, Jose Gonzalez. e, Dodger centennial emblem. f, Chris Gwynn, Jeff Hamilton. g, Kirk Gibson, Rick Dempsey. h, Jim Gott, Alfredo Griffin. i, Coaches, Ron Perranoski, Bill Russell, Joe Ferguson, Joe Amalfitano, Mark Cresse, Ben Hines, Manny Mota.
No. 1345: a, Mickey Hatcher, Jay Howell. b, Juan Samuel, Mike Scioscia. c, Lenny Harris, Mike Hartley. d, Ramon Martinez, Mike Morgan. e, Dodger Stadium. f, Stan Javier, Don Aase. g, Ray Searage, Mike Sharperson. h, Tim Belcher, Pat Perry. i, Dave Walsh, Jose Vizcaino, Jim Neidlinger, Jose Offerman, Carlos Hernandez.

**Hyphen-hole roulette 7**

**1990, Sept. 21**

| | | | | |
|---|---|---|---|---|
| 1344 | | Sheet of 9 | 7.25 | 7.25 |
| a.-i. | A178 60c any single | | .40 | .40 |
| 1345 | | Sheet of 9 | 7.25 | 7.25 |
| a.-i. | A178 60c any single | | .40 | .40 |

*Nos. 1116-1120 Ovprtd. or Similarly*

**Perf. 14**

| | | | | |
|---|---|---|---|---|
| 1346 | A158 | 10c shown | .30 | .30 |
| 1347 | A158 | 50c "CARL / LEWIS / U.S.A." | .60 | .60 |
| 1348 | A158 | $1 "HRISTO / MARKOV / BULGARIA" | 1.10 | 1.10 |
| 1349 | A158 | $5 "HENRY / MASKE / E. GERMANY" | 5.50 | 5.50 |
| | | | 7.50 | 7.50 |

*Nos. 1346-1349 (4)*

**Souvenir Sheets**

| | | | | |
|---|---|---|---|---|
| 1350 | A158 | $10 USSR, US medals | 7.50 | 7.50 |
| 1351 | A158 | $10 South Korea, Spain medals | 7.50 | 7.50 |

Orchids — A196

Designs: 10c, Dendrophylax funalis. Dimeranda emarginata. 15c, Epidendrum elongatum. 45c, Comparettia falcata. 60c, Brassia maculata. $2, Cyrtopodium punctatum. $4, Encyclia cordigera. $2, Cyrtopodium punctatum. No. 1370, Ionopsis utricularioides. No. 1371, Vanilla planifolia.

**1990, Nov. 23**

| | | | | |
|---|---|---|---|---|
| 1362-1369 | A196 | Set of 8 | 14.00 | 14.00 |

**Souvenir Sheets**

| | | | | |
|---|---|---|---|---|
| 1370-1371 | A196 | $6 Set of 2 | 12.50 | 12.50 |

Christmas 1990 — A197

Details from paintings by Rubens: 10c, Miraculous Draught of Fishes. 45c, $2, Crowning of Holy Katherine. 50c, St. Ives of Treguier. 65c, Allegory of Eternity. $1, $4, St. Bavo Receives Monastic Habit of Ghent. $5, St. Ives of Communion of St. Francis. #1380, St. Ives of Treguier (entire). #1381, Allegory of Eternity. #1382, St. Bavo Receives Monastic Habit of Ghent, horiz. #1383, The Miraculous Draft of Fishes, horiz.

**1990, Dec. 3  Litho.  Perf. 14**

| | | | | |
|---|---|---|---|---|
| 1372-1379 | A197 | Set of 8 | 14.00 | 14.00 |

**Souvenir Sheets**

| | | | | |
|---|---|---|---|---|
| 1380-1383 | A197 | $6 Set of 4 | 18.00 | 18.00 |

Miniature Sheet

Intl. Literacy Year A198

Canterbury Tales: a, Geoffrey Chaucer (1342-1400), author. b, "When April with his showers sweet..." c, "When Zephyr also has..." d, "And many little birds make melody..." e, "And palmers to go seeking out strange strands..." f, Quill pen, open book. g, Bluebird in tree. h, Trees, rider's head with white hair. i, Banner on staff. j, Town. k, Rider's head, diff. l, Blackbird in tree. m, Old monk. n, Horse, rider. o, Nun, monk carrying banner. p, Monks. q, White horse, rider. r, Black horse, rider. s, Squirrel. t, Rooster. u, Chickens. v, Rabbit. w, Butterfly. x, Mouse.

**1990, Dec. 12  Perf. 13½**

| | | | | |
|---|---|---|---|---|
| 1384 | | Sheet of 24 | 18.00 | 18.00 |
| a.-x. | A198 40c any single | | | .30 |

Vincent Van Gogh (1853-1890), Painter — A198a

Self-Portraits.

**1990, Dec. 17  Litho.  Perf. 13**

| | | | | |
|---|---|---|---|---|
| 1385 | A198a | 1c 1889 | .30 | .30 |
| 1386 | A198a | 5c 1886 | .30 | .30 |
| 1387 | A198a | 10c 1888, with hat & pipe | .30 | .30 |
| 1388 | A198a | 15c 1888, painting | .30 | .30 |
| a. | Strip of 4, #1385-1388 | | .50 | .50 |
| 1389 | A198a | 20c 1887 | .50 | .50 |
| 1390 | A198a | 45c 1889, diff. | .55 | .55 |
| 1391 | A198a | $5 1889, with bandaged ear | 5.75 | 5.75 |
| 1392 | A198a | $6 1887, with straw hat | 7.00 | 7.00 |
| a. | Strip of 4, #1389-1392 | | 14.50 | 14.50 |
| | | | 14.80 | 14.80 |

*Nos. 1385-1392 (8)*

Hummel Figurines — A199

**1990, Dec. 30  Litho.  Perf. 14**

| | | | | |
|---|---|---|---|---|
| 1393 | A199 | 10c Photographer | .30 | .20 |
| 1394 | A199 | 15c Boy with ladder & pipe | .30 | .20 |
| 1395 | A199 | 40c Boy & man | .40 | .30 |
| 1396 | A199 | 60c Boy answering telephone | .60 | .45 |
| 1396A | A199 | $1 Bootmaker | .95 | .70 |
| 1396B | A199 | $2 Artist | 2.00 | 2.00 |
| 1397 | A199 | $4 Waiter | 4.00 | 4.00 |
| a. | Sheet of 4, 15c, 40c, $2, $4 | | 6.75 | 6.75 |
| 1398 | A199 | $5 Mailman | 6.75 | 6.75 |
| a. | Sheet of 4, 10c, 60c, $1, $5 | | 12.55 | 11.85 |

*Nos. 1393-1398 (8)*

Souvenir Sheets

**25th ANNIVERSARY SUPER BOWL**

Super Bowl Highlights — A200

Designs: Nos. 1400-1424, 1425-1449. Super Bowl I (1967) through Super Bowl XXV (1991). Nos. 1425-1449 picture Super Bowl Program Covers. Nos. 1443, 1449 horiz.

**1991, Jan. 15  Litho.  Perf. 13½x14**

| | | | | |
|---|---|---|---|---|
| 1400-1424 | A200 | Set of 25 | 32.00 | 32.00 |

**Size: 99x125mm**

**Imperf**

| | | | | |
|---|---|---|---|---|
| 1425-1449 | A200 | $2 Set of 25 | 60.00 | 60.00 |

Nos. 1400-1423 contain two 50c stamps printed with continuous design showing game highlights. No. 1424 contains three 50c stamps showing AFC and NFC team helmets and the Vince Lombardi Trophy.

ST. VINCENT

## Miniature Sheets

Discovery of America, 500th Anniv. (in 1992) — A201

No. 1450: a, 1c. US #230, b, 2c, US #232, d, 4c. US #233, e, 8, $10. Sailing ship, parrot, f, 5c. US #236, i, 10c. US #237.
No. 1451: a, 15c. US #238, b, 30c. US #239, c, 50c. US #240, d, $1, US #241, e, $10. Compass rose, sailing ship, f, $2, US #242, g, $3, US #243, h, $4, US #244, i, $5, US #245. Ship's figurehead.
No. 1452. Bow of sailing ship. No. 1453. Ship's figurehead.

**1991, Mar. 18    Litho.    Perf. 14**

| | | |
|---|---|---|
| 1450 A201 | #1450a-1450i | 9.50 9.50 |
| 1451 A201 | #1451a-1451i | 24.00 24.00 |

**Souvenir Sheets**

| | | |
|---|---|---|
| 1452 A201 | $6 multicolored | 7.25 7.25 |
| 1453 A201 | $6 multicolored | 7.25 7.25 |

Nos. 1452-1453 each contain one 38x31mm stamp.

Jetsons, The Movie — A202

**1991, Mar. 25    Sheets of 9**

| | | |
|---|---|---|
| 1454-1462 A202 | Set of 9 | 16.25 16.25 |

**Souvenir Sheets    Perf. 13½**

| | | |
|---|---|---|
| 1463-1464 A202 | $6 multicolored | 13.00 13.00 |

Hanna-Barbera characters: 5c. Cosmo Spacely, vert. 20c, Elroy, Judy, Astro, Jane & George Jetson, vert. 45c, Judy, Apollo Blue, vert. 50c. Mr. Spacely, George, vert. 60c, George, sprocket factory. $1, Apollo Blue, Judy, Elroy and Grungees. $2, Jane and George in Grungee cavern. $4, George, Elroy, Jane and Little Grungee, vert. $5, Jetsons leaving for Earth, vert. No. 1463, Jetsons in sprocket factory. No. 1464, Jetsons traveling to Orbiting Ore Asteroid.

The Flintstones Enjoy Sports — A203

**1991, Mar. 25**

| | | |
|---|---|---|
| 1465 A203 | 10c Boxing | .20 .20 |
| 1466 A203 | 15c Soccer | .35 .35 |
| 1467 A203 | 20c Rowing | .60 .35 |
| 1468 A203 | 55c Dinosaur riding | .70 .70 |
| 1469 A203 | $1 Basketball | 1.10 .70 |
| 1470 A203 | $2 Wrestling | 2.50 2.00 |
| 1471 A203 | $4 Tennis | 5.00 2.00 |
| 1472 A203 | $5 Cycling | 6.25 6.25 |
| | Nos. 1465-1472 (8) | 16.85 15.10 |

**Souvenir Sheets**

| | | |
|---|---|---|
| 1473 A203 | $6 Baseball, batting | 7.25 7.25 |
| 1474 A203 | $6 Baseball, sliding home | 7.25 7.25 |

Royal Family Birthday, Anniversary
Common Design Type

**1991, July    Litho.    Perf. 14**

| | | |
|---|---|---|
| 1485 CD347 | 5c multicolored | .20 .20 |
| 1486 CD347 | 20c multicolored | .40 .20 |
| 1487 CD347 | 25c multicolored | .40 .20 |
| 1488 CD347 | 60c multicolored | .80 .50 |
| 1489 CD347 | $1 multicolored | 1.25 .75 |
| 1490 CD347 | $2 multicolored | 2.40 2.40 |
| 1491 CD347 | $4 multicolored | 4.75 4.75 |
| 1492 CD347 | $5 multicolored | 6.00 6.00 |
| | Nos. 1485-1492 (8) | 16.20 15.00 |

**Souvenir Sheets**

| | | |
|---|---|---|
| 1493 CD347 | $5 Elizabeth, Philip | 6.75 6.75 |
| 1494 CD347 | $5 Charles, Diana, sons | 6.75 6.75 |

20c, 25c, $1. Nos. 1492, 1494, Charles and Diana. 10th wedding anniversary. Others, Queen Elizabeth II, 65th birthday.

Japanese Trains
A205

Designs: No. 1495a, D51 steam locomotive. b, 9600 steam locomotive. c, Chrysanthemum emblem. d, Passenger coach. e, C57 steam locomotive. f, Oil tank car. g, C53 steam locomotive. h, First steam locomotive. No. 1496a, Class 181 electric train, b, EH-10 electric locomotive. c, Special Express emblem. d, Sendai City Class 1 trolley e, Class 485 electric train. f, Sendai City trolley street cleaner. g, Hakari bullet train. h, ED-11 electric locomotive. i, EF-66 electric locomotive. No. 1497, C55 steam locomotive, vert. No. 1498, Series 400 electric train. No. 1499, C62 steam locomotive, vert. No. 1500, Super Hitachi electric train, vert.

**1991, Aug. 12    Litho.    Perf. 14x13½**

| | | |
|---|---|---|
| 1495 A205 | 75c Sheet of 9, #a.-i. | 7.50 7.50 |
| 1496 A205 | $1 Sheet of 9, #a.-i. | 10.50 10.50 |

**Souvenir Sheets    Perf. 13x13½**

| | | |
|---|---|---|
| 1497 A205 | $6 multicolored | 8.00 8.00 |
| 1498 A205 | $6 multicolored | 8.00 8.00 |
| 1499 A205 | $6 multicolored | 8.00 8.00 |
| 1500 A205 | $6 multicolored | 8.00 8.00 |

Phila Nippon '91. Nos. 1497-1500 each contain 27x44mm or 44x27mm stamps.

Entertainers
A206

## Miniature Sheets

Madonna, Various portraits of Italian entertainers: #1502a, Marcello Mastroianni, b, Sophia Loren, c, Mario Lanza canini (1867-1957), f, Anna Magnani (1908-73), g, Giancarlo Giannini, e, Arturo Toscanini (1867-1957), i, Enrico Caruso (1873-1921).

**1991, Aug. 22    Perf. 13**

| | | |
|---|---|---|
| 1501 A206 | $1 Sheet of 9, #a.- | 13.75 13.75 |
| 1502 A206 | $1 Sheet of 9, #a.- | 10.00 10.00 |
| 1503 A206 | $1 +2c, Sheet of 9, #a.-i. | 12.00 12.00 |

**Souvenir Sheets    Perf. 12x13**

| | | |
|---|---|---|
| 1504 A206 | $6 Madonna | 12.50 12.50 |
| 1505 A206 | $6 Luciano Pavarotti, horiz. | 9.50 9.50 |

No. 1503 is semi-postal with surtax going to the Spirit Foundation. No. 1504 contains one 28x42mm stamp. Compare with No. 1505. See Nos. 1642-1643.

Int'l. Literacy Year — A207

Walt Disney characters in "The Prince and the Pauper": 5c, Pauper pals. 10c. Princely boredom. 15c. The valet. 25c. Look alikes. 60c. Trading places. 75c. How to be a prince. 80c. Food for the populace. $1, Captain's plot. $2, Doomed in the dungeon. $3, Looking for a way out. $4, A Goofy jailbreak. $5, Long live the real prince. No. 1518, Crowning the wrong guy. No. 1519, Mickey meets the captain of the guard. No. 1520, Real prince arrives. No. 1521, Seize the guard.

**1991, Nov. 18    Perf. 14x13½**

| | | |
|---|---|---|
| 1506-1517 A207 | Set of 12 | 18.00 18.00 |

**Souvenir Sheets    Perf. 14x13½**

| | | |
|---|---|---|
| 1518-1521 A207 | $6 Set of 4 | 23.00 23.00 |

Wolfgang Amadeus Mozart, Death Bicent. A210

Designs: $1. Scene from "Marriage of Figaro." $3. Scene from "The Clemency of Titus." $4. Portrait of Mozart, vert.

**1991, Nov. 18    Litho.    Perf. 14**

| | | |
|---|---|---|
| 1543 A210 | $1 multicolored | 1.25 1.25 |
| 1544 A210 | $3 multicolored | 3.50 3.50 |

**Souvenir Sheet**

| | | |
|---|---|---|
| 1545 A210 | $4 multicolored | 4.25 4.25 |

17th World Scout Jamboree, Korea — A211

Designs: 65c, Adventure tales around camp fire, vert. $1.50, British defenses at Mateking, 1900. Cape of Good Hope. $3.50, Scouts scuba diving, queen angelfish.

**1991, Nov. 18    Litho.    Perf. 14**

| | | |
|---|---|---|
| 1546 A211 | 65c multicolored | .50 .50 |
| 1547 A211 | $1.50 multicolored | 1.15 1.15 |
| 1548 A211 | $3.50 multicolored | 2.65 2.65 |
| | Nos. 1546-1548 (3) | 4.30 4.30 |

**Souvenir Sheet**

| | | |
|---|---|---|
| 1549 A211 | $5 multicolored | 3.75 3.75 |

Charles de Gaulle, Birth Cent. A212

De Gaulle and: 10c. Free French Forces, 1944. 45c, Churchill, 1944. 75c, Liberation of Paris, 1944.

**1991, Nov. 18    Litho.    Perf. 14**

| | | |
|---|---|---|
| 1550 A212 | 10c multicolored | .60 .60 |
| 1551 A212 | 45c multicolored | 1.00 1.00 |
| 1552 A212 | 75c multicolored | 1.60 1.60 |
| | Nos. 1550-1552 (3) | 3.20 3.20 |

**Souvenir Sheet**

| | | |
|---|---|---|
| 1553 A212 | $5 Portrait | 3.75 3.75 |

Anniversaries and Events — A213

Designs: No. 1554, Woman, flag, map. No. 1555, Steam locomotive. $1.65, Otto Lilienthal, glider in flight. No. 1557, Gottfried Wilhelm Liebniz, mathematician. No. 1558, Street warfare.

**1991, Nov. 18**

| | | |
|---|---|---|
| 1554 A213 | 10c multicolored | 3.00 3.00 |
| 1555 A213 | $1.50 multicolored | 3.25 3.25 |
| 1556 A213 | $1.65 multicolored | 3.75 3.75 |
| 1557 A213 | $2 multicolored | 4.25 4.25 |
| 1558 A213 | $5 multicolored | 4.25 4.25 |
| | Nos. 1554-1558 (5) | 19.00 19.00 |

Swiss Confederation, 700th anniv. (#1554). Trans-Siberian Railway, 100th anniv. (#1555). First glider flight, cent. (#1556). City of Hanover, 750th anniv. (#1557). Fall of Kiev, Sept. 19, 1941 (#1558).

Miniature Sheets

5c, Sanger 2. 10c, Magellan probe, 1990. 25c, Buran space shuttle. 75c, American space station. $1, Mars mission, 21st century. $2, Hubble space telescope, 1990. $4, Salling ship to Mars. $5, Crat satellite, 2000. $6, Sailing ship, Island hopping. #1484, Sailing ship returning home.

**1991, May 13**

| | | |
|---|---|---|
| 1475-1482 A204 | Set of 8 | 14.25 14.25 |

**Souvenir Sheets**

| | | |
|---|---|---|
| 1483-1484 A204 | $6 Set of 2 | 14.50 14.50 |

Discovery of America, 500th anniv. (in 1992).

Voyages of Discovery A204

Prince and the Pauper
A207

Madonna
Entertainers
A206

Brandenburg Gate, Bicent. — A209

50c, Demonstrator with sign. 75c, Soldiers at Berlin Wall. 90c, German flag, shadows on wall. $1, Pres. Gorbachev and Pres. Bush shaking hands. $4, Coat of Arms of Berlin.

**1991, Nov. 18    Litho.    Perf. 14**

| | | |
|---|---|---|
| 1538-1541 A209 | Set of 4 | 4.25 4.25 |

**Souvenir Sheet**

| | | |
|---|---|---|
| 1542 | A209 $4 multi | 4.25 4.25 |

**ST. VINCENT**

## Miniature Sheet

Heroes of Pearl Harbor A214

Congressional Medal of Honor recipients: a, Myrvyn S. Bennion. b, George H. Cannon. c, John W. Finn. d, Francis C. Flaherty. e, Samuel G. Fuqua. f, Edwin J. Hill. g, Herbert C. Jones. h, Isaac C. Kidd. i, Jackson C. Pharris. j, Thomas J. Reeves. k, Donald K. Ross. l, Robert R. Scott. m, Franklin Van Valkenburgh. n, James R. Ward. o, Cassin Young.

**1991, Nov. 18**      Perf. 14½x15
| | | | |
|---|---|---|---|
| 1559 A214 | $1 Sheet of 15, #a.-o. | 19.00 | 19.00 |

## Miniature Sheets
**Famous People — A215**

Golfers — #1560: a, Player. b, Faldo. c, Ballesteros. d, Hogan. e, Nicklaus. f, Norman. g, Olazabal. h, Bobby Jones.

Statesmen and historical events — #1561: a, Hans-Dietrich Genscher, German Foreign Minister, winged victory symbol. b, Destruction of Berlin Wall. c, Charles de Gaulle delivering radio appeal. Winston Churchill, de Gaulle. d, Dwight D. Eisenhower, de Gaulle, Normandy invasion. e, Brandenburg Gate. f, German Chancellor Helmut Kohl, mayors of East, West Berlin. g, De Gaulle and Konrad Adenauer. h, George Washington and Lafayette, De Gaulle and John F. Kennedy.

Chess masters — #1562: a, Francois Andre Danican Philidor. b, Adolph Anderssen. c, Wilhelm Steinitz. d, Alexander Alekhine. e, Boris Spassky. f, Bobby Fischer. g, Anatoly Karpov. h, Garri Kasparov.

Nobel Prize winners — #1563: a, Einstein, physics. b, Roentgen, physics. c, William Shockley, physics. d, Charles Townes, physics. e, Lev Landau, physics. f, Marconi, physics. g, Willard Libby, chemistry. h, Ernest Lawrence, physics.

Entertainers — #1564: a, Michael Jackson. b, Madonna. c, Elvis Presley. d, David Bowie. e, Prince. f, Frank Sinatra. g, George Michael. h, Mick Jagger.

Nos. 1565-1567 each contain one 27x43mm stamp. See Nos. 1642-1643, 1729-1730 for more Elvis Presley stamps.

No. 1565, Roosevelt, de Gaulle, Churchill at Morocco Conf., 1943. No. 1566, Madonna. No. 1567, Elvis Presley.

**1991, Nov. 25**    Litho.
**Sheets of 8**
| | | | |
|---|---|---|---|
| 1560 A215 | $1 #a-h. | 16.00 | 16.00 |
| 1561 A215 | $1 #a-h. | 11.50 | 14.50 |
| 1562 A215 | $1 #a-h. | 12.00 | 12.00 |
| 1563 A215 | $1 #a-h. | 13.50 | 13.50 |
| 1564 A215 | $2 #a-h. | 18.00 | 18.00 |

**Souvenir Sheets**
**Perf. 14**
| | | | |
|---|---|---|---|
| 1565 A215 | $6 multicolored | 7.50 | 7.50 |
| 1566 A215 | $6 multicolored | 6.00 | 6.00 |
| 1567 A215 | $6 multicolored | 6.00 | 6.00 |

## Walt Disney Christmas Cards A216

Designs and year of issue: 10c, Goofy, Mickey and Pluto decorating Christmas tree, 1982. 45c, Mickey, reindeer, 1980. 55c, Christmas tree ornament, 1970. 75c, Baby duck holding 1944 sign, 1943. $1.50, Characters papering globe with greetings, 1941. $2, Lady and the Tramp beside Christmas tree, 1986. $4, Donald, Goofy, Mickey, and Pluto reciting "Night Before Christmas," 1977. $5, Mickey in doorway of Snow White's Castle, 1965. No. 1577a, People from around the world, 1966. No. 1577, Mickey in balloon basket with people of different countries, 1966.

**1991, Dec. 23**     Perf. 13½x14
| | | | |
|---|---|---|---|
| 1568-1575 A216 | Set of 8 | 14.25 | 14.25 |

**Souvenir Sheets**
| | | | |
|---|---|---|---|
| 1576-1577 A216 | $6 Set of 2 | 16.00 | 16.00 |

## Environmental Preservation — A217

**1992, Jan.**    Litho.    Perf. 14
| | | | |
|---|---|---|---|
| 1578 A217 | 10c Kings Hill | .30 | .30 |
| 1579 A217 | 55c Tree planting | .65 | .65 |
| 1580 A217 | 75c Botanical Gardens | .95 | .95 |
| 1581 A217 | $2 Kings Hill Project | 2.25 | 2.25 |
| Nos. 1578-1581 (4) | | 4.15 | 4.15 |

## Queen Elizabeth II's Accession to the Throne, 40th Anniv.
**Common Design Type**

**1992, Feb. 6**
| | | | |
|---|---|---|---|
| 1582 CD348 | 10c multicolored | .20 | .20 |
| 1583 CD348 | 20c multicolored | .20 | .20 |
| 1584 CD348 | $1 multicolored | .75 | .75 |
| 1585 CD348 | $5 multicolored | 4.90 | 4.90 |
| Nos. 1582-1585 (4) | | | |

**Souvenir Sheets**
| | | | |
|---|---|---|---|
| 1586 CD348 | $6 Queen, beach | 5.75 | 5.75 |
| 1587 CD348 | $6 Queen, harbor | 5.75 | 5.75 |

Queen Elizabeth II's Accession to the Throne, 40th Anniv. A217a

**Embossed Without Gum**    Perf. 12

Designs: No. 1587A, Queen Elizabeth II. No. 1587B, King George VI.

**1993, Mar. 2**    Embossed Without Gum
| | | | |
|---|---|---|---|
| 1587A A217a | $5 gold | | |
| 1587B A217a | $5 gold | | |

**1992 Winter Olympics, Albertville — A218**
**1992 Summer Olympics, Barcelona — A219**

**1992, Apr. 21**    Litho.    Perf. 14
| | | | |
|---|---|---|---|
| 1588 A218 | 10c Women's luge, horiz. | .20 | .20 |
| 1589 A218 | 15c Women's figure skating | .20 | .20 |
| 1590 A218 | 25c Two-man bobsled, horiz. | .20 | .20 |
| 1591 A218 | 30c Mogul skiing | .30 | .30 |
| 1592 A218 | 45c Nordic combined, horiz. | .40 | .40 |
| 1593 A218 | 55c Ski jump, horiz. | .45 | .45 |
| 1594 A218 | 75c Giant slalom, horiz. | .65 | .65 |
| 1595 A218 | $1.50 Women's slalom | 1.25 | 1.25 |
| 1596 A218 | $5 Ice hockey, horiz. | 4.25 | 4.25 |
| 1597 A218 | $8 Biathlon, horiz. | 6.50 | 6.50 |
| Nos. 1588-1597 (10) | | 14.40 | 14.40 |

**Souvenir Sheets**
| | | | |
|---|---|---|---|
| 1598 A218 | $6 Downhill skiing | 7.50 | 7.50 |
| 1599 A218 | $6 Speed skating | 7.50 | 7.50 |

**1992, Apr. 21**

10c, Women's synchronized swimming duet, horiz. 15c, High jump. 25c, Small-bore rifle, horiz. 30c, 200-meter run. 45c, Judo. 55c, 200-meter freestyle swimming, horiz. 75c, Javelin. $1.50, Pursuit cycling. $5, Boxing. $8, Women's basketball. #1610, Tennis. #1611, Board sailing.

| | | | |
|---|---|---|---|
| 1600-1609 A219 | Set of 10 | 17.00 | 17.00 |

**Souvenir Sheets**
| | | | |
|---|---|---|---|
| 1610-1611 A219 | $15 Set of 2 | 27.50 | 27.50 |

## World Columbian Stamp Expo '92, Chicago — A220

Walt Disney characters visiting Chicago area landmarks: 10c, Mickey, Pluto at Picasso Sculpture. 50c, Mickey, Donald admiring Frank Lloyd Wright's Robie House. $1, Gus Gander at Calder Sculpture in Sears Tower. $5, Pluto in Buckingham Memorial Fountain. No. 1616, Mickey painting Minnie at Chicago Art Institute, vert.

**1992, Apr.**    Litho.    Perf. 14x13½
| | | | |
|---|---|---|---|
| 1612-1615 A220 | Set of 4 | 7.50 | 7.50 |

**Souvenir Sheet**
**Perf. 13½x14**
| | | | |
|---|---|---|---|
| 1616 A220 | $6 multi | 8.75 | 8.75 |

## Granada '92 — A221

Walt Disney characters from "The Three Little Pigs" in Spanish military uniforms: 15c, Big Bad Wolf as General of Spanish Moors. 40c, Pig as Captain of Spanish infantry. $2, Pig in Spanish armor, c. 1580. $4, Pig as Spaniard of rank, c. 1550. $6, Little Pig resisting wolf from castle built of stone.

**1992, Apr. 28**    Perf. 13½x14
| | | | |
|---|---|---|---|
| 1622-1625 A221 | Set of 4 | 7.50 | 7.50 |

**Souvenir Sheet**
| | | | |
|---|---|---|---|
| 1626 A221 | $6 multi | 6.75 | 6.75 |

## Discovery of America, 500th Anniv. A222

**1992, May 22**    Litho.    Perf. 14
| | | | |
|---|---|---|---|
| 1632 A222 | 5c Nina | .35 | .35 |
| 1633 A222 | 10c Pinta | .35 | .35 |
| 1634 A222 | 45c Santa Maria | .60 | .60 |
| 1635 A222 | 55c Leaving Palos, Spain | .70 | .70 |
| 1636 A222 | $4 Columbus, vert. | 5.25 | 5.25 |
| 1637 A222 | $5 Columbus' arms, vert. | 6.50 | 6.50 |
| Nos. 1632-1637 (6) | | 13.75 | 13.75 |

**Souvenir Sheet**
| | | | |
|---|---|---|---|
| 1638 A222 | $6 Map, vert. | 7.00 | 7.00 |
| 1639 A222 | $6 Sailing ship, vert. | 7.00 | 7.00 |

World Columbian Stamp Expo '92, Chicago. Nos. 1638-1639 contain one 42x57mm stamp.

## Bonnie Blair, US Olympic Speed Skating Champion A223

Designs: No. 1641a, Skating around corner. b, Portrait holding skates. c, On straightaway.

**1992, May 25**    Perf. 13½
| | | | |
|---|---|---|---|
| 1640 A223 | $3 multicolored | 4.25 | 4.25 |

**Souvenir Sheet**
| | | | |
|---|---|---|---|
| 1641 A223 | $2 Sheet of 3, #a.-c. | 7.25 | 7.25 |

World Columbian Stamp Expo '92. No. 1641b is 48x60mm.

## Entertainers Type of 1991
**Miniature Sheet**

Various portraits of Elvis Presley.

**1992, May 25**    Perf. 13½x14
| | | | |
|---|---|---|---|
| 1642 A206 | $1 Sheet of 9, #a.-i. | 13.75 | 13.75 |

**Souvenir Sheet**
**Perf. 14**
| | | | |
|---|---|---|---|
| 1643 A206 | $6 multicolored | 10.50 | 10.50 |

No. 1643 contains one 28x43mm stamp. See Nos. 1729-1730.

## Hummingbirds A224

**1992, June 15**    Perf. 14
| | | | |
|---|---|---|---|
| 1644 A224 | 5c Rufous-breasted hermit | .25 | .25 |
| 1645 A224 | 15c Hispaniolan emerald | .25 | .25 |
| 1646 A224 | 45c Green-throated carib | .45 | .35 |
| 1647 A224 | 55c Jamaican mango | .40 | .50 |
| 1648 A224 | 65c Vervain | .55 | .65 |
| 1649 A224 | 75c Purple-throated carib | .75 | .58 |
| 1650 A224 | 90c Green mango | .90 | .70 |
| 1651 A224 | $1 Bee | 1.10 | .80 |
| 1652 A224 | $2 Cuban emerald | 2.00 | 2.00 |
| 1653 A224 | $3 Puerto Rican emerald | 2.50 | 2.50 |
| 1654 A224 | $4 Antillean mango | 4.00 | 4.00 |
| 1655 A224 | $5 Streamertail | 5.00 | 5.00 |
| Nos. 1644-1655 (12) | | 18.40 | 17.33 |

**Souvenir Sheets**
| | | | |
|---|---|---|---|
| 1656 A224 | $6 Antillean crested | 6.00 | 6.00 |
| 1657 A224 | $6 Bahama woodstar | 6.00 | 6.00 |
| 1658 A224 | $6 Blue-headed | 6.00 | 6.00 |

Genoa '92 Intl. Philatelic Exhibition.

## Butterflies A225

5c, Dull astraptes. 10c, White peacock. 35c, Tropic queen. 45c, Polydamas swallowtail.

55c, West Indian buckeye, 65c, Long-tailed skipper. 75c, Tropical checkered skipper. $1, Crimson-banded black. $2, Barred sulphur. $3, Cassius blue. $4, Florida duskywing. $5, Malachite. No. 1671, Cloudless giant sulphur. No. 1672, Julia. No. 1673, Zebra longwing. 5c, 35c, 45c, 65c, $1, $2, $5, #1671 vert.

**1992, June 15**
**1659-1670 A225**   Set of 12   19.00  19.00
Souvenir Sheets
**1671-1673 A225**  $6  Set of 3
Genoa '92.                     18.00  18.00

A226

A227

Medicinal Plants: No. 1674a, Coral vine. b, Cocoplum. c, Angel's trumpet. d, Lime. e, White ginger. f, Pussley. g, Sea grape. h, Indian mulberry. i, Plantain. j, Lignum vitae. k, Periwinkle. l, Guava.

**1992, July 22    Litho.      Perf. 14**
Miniature Sheet of 12
**1674 A226**  75c  #a.-l.           15.00  15.00
Souvenir Sheets
**1675 A226**  $6  Aloe              6.00   6.00
**1676 A226**  $6  Clove tree        6.00   6.00
**1677 A226**  $6  Wild sage         6.00   6.00

**1992, July 2    Litho.      Perf. 14**

Mushrooms: 10c, Collybia subpruinosa. 15c, Gerronema citrinum. 20c, Amanita antillana. 45c, Dermoloma atrobrunneum. 50c, Inopilus maculosus. 65c, Pulveroboletus brachyspermus. 75c, Mycena violacella. $1, Xeroconus brasiliensis. $2, Amanita ingrata. $3, Leptonia caeruleocapitata. $4, Limacella myochroa. $5, Inopilus magnificus. No. 1690, Limacella guttata. No. 1691, Amanita agglutinata. No. 1692, Trogia buccinalis.

**1678-1689 A227**   Set of 12   19.00  19.00
Souvenir Sheets
**1690-1692 A227**  $6  Set of 3   18.00  18.00

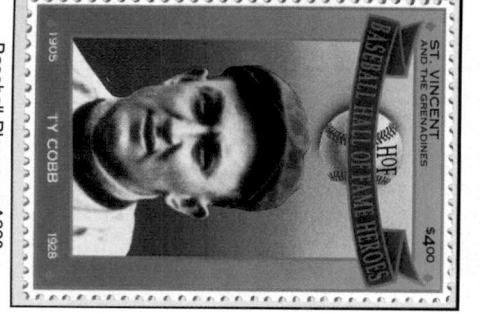

1992
Miniature Sheet of 12

**1992, Aug. 5    Litho.      Imperf.**
Self-Adhesive
Size: 64x89mm
**1693-1704 A228**  $4  Set of 12   36.00

Designs: #1693, Ty Cobb. #1694, Dizzy Dean. #1695, Bob Feller. #1696, Whitey Ford. #1697, Lou Gehrig. #1698, Rogers Hornsby. #1699, Mel Ott. #1700, Satchel Paige. #1701, Babe Ruth. #1702, Casey Stengel. #1703, Honus Wagner. #1704, Cy Young.

**1992, Aug. 5    Litho.      Imperf.**
Self-Adhesive
Baseball Players — A228

Nos. 1693-1704 printed on thin card and distributed in boxed sets. To affix stamps, backing containing player's statistics must be removed.

1992 Winter Olympic Gold Medalists, Albertville. No. 1705a, Kristi Yamaguchi, US. women's figure skating. b, Pernilla Wiberg, Sweden, women's giant slalom. c, Lyubov Yegorova, Unified Team, women's 10-kilometer cross country. e, Finn Christian-Jagge, Norway, men's slalom. f, Kerrin Lee-Gartner, Canada, women's downhill. g, Viktor Petrenko, Russia, men's figure skating.

No. 1706a, Kristi Yamaguchi, US. women's figure skating. b, Fabrice Guy, France, men's combined nordic. c, Patrick Ortlieb, Austria, men's downhill. d, Vegard Ulvang, Norway, cross country. e, Edgar Grospiron, France, freestyle mogul skiing. f, Kjetil-Andre Aamodt, Norway, super giant slalom. g, Alberto Tomba, Italy, men's giant slalom.

No. 1707a, Kristi Yamaguchi, US. women's figure skating. b, Steffania Belmondo, Italy, women's 30-kilometer cross country. No. 1708, Alberto Tomba, diff.

**1992, Aug. 10    Litho.      Perf. 14**
Sheets of 7
**1705 A229**  $1  #a.-g. + label   8.50   8.50
**1706 A229**  $1  #a.-g. + label   8.50   8.50
Souvenir Sheets
**1707 A229**  $6  multicolored     6.75   6.75
**1708 A229**  $6  multicolored     6.75   6.75

**1992    Litho.      Perf. 14½**
**1709 A230**  $1  Coming ashore    1.90   1.90
**1710 A230**  $2  Natives, ships   3.75   3.75

Discovery of America, 500th anniv. Organization of East Caribbean States.

A229

A230

Details or entire paintings of The Nativity by: 10c, Hospitality Refused to the Virgin Mary and Joseph, by Jan Metsys. 40c, Albrecht Durer. 45c, The Nativity, by Geertgen Tot Sint Jans. 50c, The Nativity, by Tintoretto. 65c, Follower of Jan Joest Calcar. 65c, Workshop of Fra Angelico. 75c, Filippino Lippi. $1, Filippino Lippi. $2, Petrus Christus. $3, Edward Burne-Jones. $4, Giotto. $5, The Birth of Christ, by Domenico Ghirlandaio. No. 1725, Nativity, by Jean Fouquet. No. 1726, Sandro Botticelli. No. 1727, Gerard Horenbout.

**1992, Nov.    Litho.      Perf. 13½x14**
**1713-1724 A232**   Set of 12   17.50  17.50
Souvenir Sheets
**1725-1727 A232**  $6  Set of 3   18.50  18.50

Jacob Javits Convention Center, NYC — A233

**1992, Oct. 28    Litho.      Perf. 14**
**1728 A233**  $6  multicolored     7.00   7.00
Postage Stamp Mega Event '92, NYC.

No. 1642 Inscribed Vertically
"15th Anniversary"

Nos. 1564, 1567 (in margin) Inscribed or Ovptd. "15th Anniversary" and "Elvis Presley's Death / August 16, 1977"

**1992, Dec. 15    Litho.      Perf. 14**
**1729 A206**  $1  Sheet of 9,
                    #a.-i.         15.00  15.00
**Perf. 14½**
**1729J A215**  $2  Sheet of 8,
                    #k.-r.         21.50  21.50
**Perf. 14**
**1730 A215**  $6  Souv. sheet     15.00  15.00

Walt Disney movies: #1711a, Pinocchio. b, Alice in Wonderland. c, Bambi. d, Cinderella. e, Snow White and the Seven Dwarfs. f, Peter Pan.

**1992**
**1711 A231**  $1  Sheet of 6, #a.-
                    f.             11.50  11.50
Souvenir Sheet
**Perf. 12½**
**1712 A231**  $5  Mickey Mouse      9.50   9.50

Opening of Euro Disney — A231

Miniature Sheet

Player, year inducted: No. 1733, Roberto Clemente, 1973. No. 1734, Hank Aaron, 1982. No. 1735, Tom Seaver, 1992.

**1992, Dec. 21**
1992 Summer Olympics, Barcelona.

**1992, Nov. 9    Litho.      Perf. 14**
**1731 A234**  $5  Howard Johnson    3.75   3.75
**1732 A234**  $5  Don Mattingly     3.75   3.75

Baseball
Players — A234

Members of
Baseball Hall
Fame — A235

**1992, Dec. 21    Litho.      Perf. 14**
**1733 A235**  $2  multicolored      3.00   3.00
**1734 A235**  $2  multicolored      3.00   3.00
**1735 A235**  $2  multicolored      3.00   3.00
Nos. 1733-1735 (3)                  9.00   9.00

Fishing
Industry
A236

**1992, Nov.**
**1736 A236**  5c  Fishing with rods   .25   .25
**1737 A236**  10c  Inside fishing
                    complex           .25   .25

Christmas 1992
Christmas
A232

Anniversaries and Events: 10c, Globe and UN emblem. 45c, Zeppelin Viktoria Luise over Kiel Regatta, 1912. 45c, Zeppelin. 65c, vert. 65c, Food products. No. 1749, America's Cup Trophy and Bill Koch, skipper of America 3. No. 1750, Konrad Adenauer, German flag. No. 1751, Adenauer, diff. No. 1752, Snow leopard. $1.50, Caribbean manatee. $2, Humpback whale. No. 1755, Adenauer, patient having eye exam. No. 1756, Adenauer, Pope John XXIII. $5, Michael Schumacher, race car. $6, Count Zeppelin's first airship over Lake Constance, 1900. No. 1761, Gondola of Graf Zeppelin.

A241

A240

Michael Schumacher
Belgium Grand Prix '92
A239

US
Olympic
Basketball
"Dream
Team"
A238

**1992, Dec. 22    Litho.      Perf. 14**
**1744 A238**  $2  Sheet of 6, #a.-f.   9.00   9.00
**1745 A238**  $2  Sheet of 6, #a.-f.   9.00   9.00
1992 Summer Olympics, Barcelona.

#1744: a, Scottie Pippen. b, Earvin "Magic" Johnson. c, Larry Bird. d, Christian Laettner. e, Karl Malone. f, David Robinson. #1745: a, Michael Jordan. b, Charles Barkley. c, John Stockton. d, Chris Mullin. e, Clyde Drexler. f, Patrick Ewing.

Children's paintings: 10c, Island coastline. 40c, Four people standing on islands. 45c, Four people standing on beach.

**1992, Nov.    Litho.      Perf. 14**
**1740 A237**  10c  multicolored      .65   .20
**1741 A237**  40c  multicolored      .95   .30
**1742 A237**  45c  multicolored     1.10   .35
Nos. 1740-1742 (3)                   2.70   .85

Miniature Sheets
A237

Uniting
the
Windward
Islands
A237

**1738 A236**  50c  Landing the catch  .50   .50
**1739 A236**  $5  Fishing with nets  4.50  4.50
Nos. 1736-1739 (4)                   5.50  5.50

ST. VINCENT

Formula I race car. No. 1763, Sailing ship, steam packet. No. 1764, Adenauer at podium. No. 1765, Woolly spider monkey. No. 1765A, People waving to plane during Berlin airlift.

**1992-93** **Litho.** *Perf. 14*

| | | | | | |
|---|---|---|---|---|---|
| **1746** | A239 | 10c multi | .20 | .20 |
| **1747** | A239 | 45c multi | 5.50 | 5.50 |
| **1748** | A242 | 65c multi | 1.50 | 1.50 |
| **1749** | A239 | 75c multi | 1.25 | 1.25 |
| **1750** | A239 | 75c multi | 8.00 | 8.00 |
| **1751** | A239 | $1 multi | 8.00 | 8.00 |
| **1752** | A239 | $1 multi | 7.50 | 7.50 |
| **1753** | A239 | $1.50 multi | 7.50 | 7.50 |
| **1754** | A239 | $2 multi | 7.50 | 7.50 |
| **1755** | A239 | $3 multi | 2.25 | 2.25 |
| **1756** | A239 | $3 multi | 4.50 | 4.50 |
| **1757** | A239 | $4 multi | 3.00 | 3.00 |
| **1758** | A239 | $4 multi | 3.00 | 3.00 |
| **1759** | A240 | $5 multi | 5.50 | 5.50 |
| **1760** | A239 | $6 multi | 5.50 | 5.50 |
| | *Nos. 1746-1760 (15)* | | 70.70 | 70.70 |

**Souvenir Sheets**

| | | | | |
|---|---|---|---|---|
| **1761** | A239 | $6 multi | 5.50 | 5.50 |
| **1762** | A240 | $6 multi | 5.50 | 5.50 |
| **1763** | A241 | $6 multi | 4.50 | 4.50 |
| **1764** | A239 | $6 multi | 4.50 | 4.50 |
| **1765** | A239 | $6 multi | 4.50 | 4.50 |
| **1765A** | A239 | $6 multi | 4.50 | 4.50 |

UN Intl. Space Year (#1746, 1757). Count Zeppelin, 75th anniv. of death (#1747, 1760-1761). Intl. Conference on Nutrition, Rome (#1748). America's Cup yacht race (#1749). Konrad Adenauer, 25th death anniv. (#1750-1751, 1755, 1758, 1764). Earth Summit, Rio de Janeiro (#1752-1754, 1765). Lions Intl., 75th anniv. (#1756). Belgian Grand Prix (#1759, 1762). Discovery of America, 500th anniv. (#1763). Konrad Adenauer, 75th death anniv. (#1765A).

Issued: #1747, 1759-1762, Dec; #1763, 10/28/92; #1746, 1749, 1750-1751, 1755-1758, 1764, Dec; #1752-1754, 1765, Dec. 15; #1765A, 6/30/93.

A243

A244

Care Bears Promote Conservation: 75c, Bear, stork. $2, Bear riding in hot air balloon, horiz.

**1992, Dec.** **Litho.** *Perf. 14*

**1766** A243 75c multicolored 1.25 1.25

**Souvenir Sheet**

**1767** A243 $2 multicolored 2.25 2.25

**1993** **Litho.** *Perf. 14*

Elvis Presley (1935-1977): b, Portrait. c, With guitar. d, With microphone.

**1767A** A244 $1 Strip of 3, #b.-d. 2.75 2.75

Printed in sheets of 9 stamps.

Walt Disney's Beauty and the Beast — A245

Designs: 2c, Gaston. 3c, Belle and her father, Maurice. 5c, Lumiere, Mrs. Potts and Cogsworth. 10c, Philippe. 15c, Beast and Lumiere. 20c, Lumiere and Feather Duster.

No. 1774a, Belle and Gaston. b, Maurice. c, The Beast. d, Mrs. Potts. e, Belle and the Enchanted Vase. f, Belle discovers an Enchanted Rose. g, Belle with wounded Beast. h, Belle. i, Household objects alarmed.

No. 1774k, Belle and Chip. l, Lumiere. m, Cogsworth. n, Armoire. o, Belle and Beast. p, Feather Duster. q, Footstool. r, Belle. All vert.

No. 1775, Belle reading, vert. No. 1776, Lumiere, diff., vert. No. 1776A, Lumiere, Mrs. Potts. No. 1776B, Belle, lake and castle, vert. No. 1776C, The Beast, vert.

*Perf. 14x13½, 13½x14*

**1992, Dec. 15** **Litho.**

| | | | | | |
|---|---|---|---|---|---|
| **1768** | A245 | 2c multicolored | .20 | .20 |
| **1769** | A245 | 3c multicolored | .20 | .20 |
| **1770** | A245 | 5c multicolored | .20 | .20 |
| **1771** | A245 | 10c multicolored | .20 | .20 |
| **1772** | A245 | 15c multicolored | .20 | .20 |
| **1773** | A245 | 20c multicolored | .20 | .20 |
| | *Nos. 1768-1773 (6)* | | 1.20 | 1.20 |

**Miniature Sheets of 9, 8**

| | | | | |
|---|---|---|---|---|
| **1774** | A245 | 60c #a.-i. | 7.50 | 7.50 |
| **1774J** | A245 | 60c #k.-r. | 7.50 | 7.50 |

**Souvenir Sheets**

| | | | | |
|---|---|---|---|---|
| **1775** | A245 | $6 multicolored | 6.75 | 6.75 |
| **1776** | A245 | $6 multicolored | 6.75 | 6.75 |
| **1776A** | A245 | $6 multicolored | 6.75 | 6.75 |
| **1776B** | A245 | $6 multicolored | 6.75 | 6.75 |
| **1776C** | A245 | $6 multicolored | 6.75 | 6.75 |

Louvre Museum, Bicent. A246

Details or entire paintings by Jean-Auguste-Dominique Ingres: No. 1777a, Louis-Francois Bertin. b, The Apotheosis of Homer. c, Joan of Arc. d, The Composer Cherubini with the Muse of Lyric Poetry. e, Mlle Caroline Riviere. f, Oedipus Answers the Sphinx's Riddle. g, Madame Marcotte. h, Mademoiselle Caroline Riviere.

Details or entire paintings by Jean Louis Andre Theodore Gericault (1791-1824): No. 1778a, The Woman with Gambling Mania. b, Head of a White Horse. c, Wounded Cuirassier. d, An Officer of the Cavalry. e, The Vendean. f, The Raft of the Medusa. g-h, The Horse Market (left, right).

Details or entire paintings by Nicolas Poussin (1594-1665): No. 1779a-1779b, The Arcadian Shepherds (left, right). c, Ecstasy of Paul. d-e, The Inspiration of the Poet (left, right). f-g, St. John Baptizing (left, right). h, The Miracle of St. Francis Xavier.

Details or entire paintings by Eustache Le Sueur (1616-1655): No. 1780a-1780b, Melpomene, Erato & Polyhymnia (left, right). By Poussin: c, Christ and Woman Taken in Adultery. d, Spring. e, Autumn. f-h, The Plague of Asdod (left, center, right).

No. 1781a, The Beggars, by Pieter Brueghel, the Elder (1520-1569). b, The Luncheon, by Francois Boucher (1703-1770). c, Louis Guene, Royal Violinist, by Francois Dumont (1751-1831). d, The Virgin of Chancellor Rolin, by Jan Van Eyck. e, Conversation in the Park, by Thomas Gainsborough. f, Lady Alston, by Gainsborough. g, Mariana Waldstein, by Francisco de Goya. h, Ferdinand Guillemardet, by Goya.

No. 1782, The Grand Odalisque, horiz. No. 1783, The Dressing Room of Esther, by Theodore Chasseriau (1819-1856). No. 1784, Liberty Guiding the People, by Eugene Delecroix (1798-1863), horiz.

**1993, Apr. 19** *Perf. 12x12½*

**Sheets of 8**

| | | | | | |
|---|---|---|---|---|---|
| **1777** | A246 | $1 #a.-h. + label | 7.00 | 7.00 |
| **1778** | A246 | $1 #a.-h. + label | 7.00 | 7.00 |
| **1779** | A246 | $1 #a.-h. + label | 7.00 | 7.00 |
| **1780** | A246 | $1 #a.-h. + label | 7.00 | 7.00 |
| **1781** | A246 | $1 #a.-h. + label | 7.00 | 7.00 |

**Souvenir Sheets**

*Perf. 14½*

| | | | | |
|---|---|---|---|---|
| **1782** | A246 | $6 multicolored | 6.50 | 6.50 |
| **1783** | A246 | $6 multicolored | 6.50 | 6.50 |
| **1784** | A246 | $6 multicolored | 6.50 | 6.50 |

Nos. 1783-1784 each contain a 55x88mm or 88x55mm stamp.

Paintings on Nos. 1777d and 1777h were switched.

Numbers have been reserved for two additional souvenir sheets in this set.

Miniature Sheets

A247

A247a

Scenes from Disney Animated Films — A247b

Symphony Hour (1942): No. 1787a, Maestro Mickey. b, Goofy plays a mean horn. c, On first bass with Clara Cluck. d, Stringing along with Clarabelle. e, Donald on drums. f, Clarabelle all fiddled out. g, Donald drumming up trouble. h, Goofy's sour notes. i, Mickey's moment.

Clock Cleaners (1937): No. 1788a, Goofy gets in gear. b, Donald on the mainspring. c, Donald in the works. d, Mickey's fine-feathered friend. e, Stork with bundle of joy. f, Father Time. g, Goofy, Mickey leaping upward. h, Donald, Goofy, Mickey out of gear. i, Donald, Goofy, Mickey with headaches.

The Art of Skiing (1941): No. 1789a, The ultimate back scratcher. b, Striking a pose. c, And we're off. d, Divided he stands. e, A real twister. f, Hangin' in there. g, Over the hill. h, At the peak of his form. i, Up a tree.

Orphan's Benefit (1941): No. 1790a, Mickey introduces Donald. b, Donald recites "Little Boy Blue." c, Orphan mischief. d, Clara Cluck, singing sensation. e, Goofy's debut with Clarabelle. f, Encore for Clara and Mickey. g, A Bronx cheer. h, Donald blows his stack. i, Donald's final bow.

Thru the Mirror (1936): No. 1791a, Mickey steps thru the looking glass. b, Mickey finds a tasty treat. c, Mickey's nutty effect. d, Hats off to Mickey. e, What a card, Mickey. f, Mickey dancing with the Queen Hearts. g, A real two-faced opponent. h, Mickey with a pen mightier than a sword. i, Mickey awake at last.

The Small One: No. 1791k, Morning comes in Nazareth. l, Good morning, small one. m, Too old to keep. n, Heatbroken. o, Nazareth markplace. p, Auction mockery. q, Off the auction block. r, Lonely and dejected. s, Happy and useful again.

The Three Little Pigs (1933): No. 1792a, Fifer Pig building house of straw. b, Fiddler Pig building house of sticks. c, Practical Pig building house of bricks. d, The Big Bad Wolf. e, Wolf scaring two lazy pigs. f, Wolf blowing down staw house. g, Wolf in sheep's clothing. h, Wolf blowing down twig house. i, Wolf huffs and puffs at brick house.

How to Play Football (1944): No. 1792k, Cheerleaders. l, Here comes the team. m, In the huddle. n, Who's got the ball? o, Who, me coach? p, Half-time pep talk. q, Another down, and out. r, Only a little injury. s, Up and at 'em.

Rescue Rangers: No. 1793a, Special agents. b, Chip 'n Dale, ready for action. c, Chip 'n Dale on stakeout. d, Gadget in gear. e, Gadget and Monterey Jack rescue Zipper. f, Zipper confers with Monterey Jack. g, Zipper zaps fat cat. h, Team work. i, Innovative Gadget.

Darkwing Duck: No. 1793k, Darkwing Duck. l, Launchpad McQuack. m, Gosalyn. n, Honker Muddlefoot. o, Tank Muddlefoot. p, Herb & Binkie Muddlefoot. q, Drake Mallard, aka Darkwing Duck. r, Darkwing Duck logo.

No. 1794, Bird's-eye-view of Goofy. No. 1795, Mickey and Macaroni enjoying applause. No. 1796, On the edge of Goofyness. No. 1797, Gonged-out Goofy.

No. 1798, Film poster for Art of Skiing with Goofy slaloming down mountain. No. 1799, Goofy home in bed at last.

No. 1800, Caveman ballet. No. 1801, Mickey tickles the ivories.

No. 1802, Mickey's true reflection. No. 1803, Mickey hopping home.

No. 1804, Hard Work in Nazareth. No. 1805, Finding a buyer in Nazareth.

No. 1806, Animator's sketch of little pig and brick house. No. 1807, Little pigs playing and singing at piano, vert.

No. 1807A, Goofy demonstrating how to score touchdown. No. 1807B, Goofy shouting "Hooray for the team," vert.

No. 1807C, Gadget at controls of Ranger plane, vert. No. 1807D, Dale, vert.

No. 1807E, Quarterjack. No. 1807F, Darkwing Duck and Launchpad to the rescue in Ratcatcher.

*Perf. 14x13½, 13½x14*

**1992, Dec. 15** **Litho.**

**Sheets of 9 or 8 (#1793J)**

| | | | | |
|---|---|---|---|---|
| **1787** | A247 | 60c #a.-i. | 7.50 | 7.50 |
| **1788** | A247 | 60c #a.-i. | 7.50 | 7.50 |
| **1789** | A247 | 60c #a.-i. | 7.50 | 7.50 |
| **1790** | A247 | 60c #a.-i. | 7.50 | 7.50 |
| **1791** | A247 | 60c #a.-i. | 7.50 | 7.50 |
| **1791J** | A247a | 60c #k.-s. | 7.50 | 7.50 |
| **1792** | A247 | 60c #a.-i. | 7.50 | 7.50 |
| **1792J** | A247 | 60c #k.-s. | 7.50 | 7.50 |
| **1793** | A247a | 60c #a.-i. | 7.50 | 7.50 |
| **1793J** | A247b | 60c #k.-r. | 7.50 | 7.50 |

**Souvenir Sheets**

| | | | | |
|---|---|---|---|---|
| **1794** | A247 | $6 multicolored | 5.75 | 5.75 |
| **1795** | A247 | $6 multicolored | 5.75 | 5.75 |
| **1796** | A247 | $6 multicolored | 5.75 | 5.75 |
| **1797** | A247 | $6 multicolored | 5.75 | 5.75 |
| **1798** | A247 | $6 multicolored | 5.75 | 5.75 |
| **1799** | A247 | $6 multicolored | 5.75 | 5.75 |
| **1800** | A247 | $6 multicolored | 5.75 | 5.75 |
| **1801** | A247 | $6 multicolored | 5.75 | 5.75 |
| **1802** | A247 | $6 multicolored | 5.75 | 5.75 |
| **1803** | A247 | $6 multicolored | 5.75 | 5.75 |
| **1804** | A247a | $6 multicolored | 5.75 | 5.75 |
| **1805** | A247a | $6 multicolored | 5.75 | 5.75 |
| **1806** | A247 | $6 multicolored | 5.75 | 5.75 |
| **1807** | A247 | $6 multicolored | 5.75 | 5.75 |
| **1807A** | A247 | $6 multicolored | 5.75 | 5.75 |
| **1807B** | A247 | $6 multicolored | 5.75 | 5.75 |
| **1807C** | A247a | $6 multicolored | 5.75 | 5.75 |
| **1807D** | A247a | $6 multicolored | 5.75 | 5.75 |
| **1807E** | A247b | $6 multicolored | 5.75 | 5.75 |
| **1807F** | A247b | $6 multicolored | 5.75 | 5.75 |

See Nos. 2144-2146 for 30c & $3 stamps.

Fish A248

**1993, Apr. 1** **Litho.** *Perf. 14*

| | | | | | |
|---|---|---|---|---|---|
| **1808** | A248 | 5c | Sergeant major | .30 | .30 |
| **1809** | A248 | 10c | Rainbow parrotfish | .30 | .30 |
| **1810** | A248 | 55c | Hogfish | .55 | .40 |
| **1811** | A248 | 75c | Porkfish | .85 | .60 |
| **1812** | A248 | $1 | Spotfin butterflyfish | 1.00 | .75 |
| **1813** | A248 | $2 | Trunkfish | 2.10 | 2.10 |
| **1814** | A248 | $4 | Queen triggerfish | 4.25 | 4.25 |
| **1815** | A248 | $5 | Queen angelfish | 4.25 | 4.25 |
| | *Nos. 1808-1815 (8)* | | | 13.60 | 12.95 |

**Souvenir Sheets**

| | | | | | |
|---|---|---|---|---|---|
| **1816** | A248 | $6 | Bigeye, vert. | 6.25 | 6.25 |
| **1817** | A248 | $6 | Smallmouth grunt, vert. | 6.25 | 6.25 |

Birds — A249

Seashells — A250

Designs: 10c, Brown pelican. 25c, Red-necked grebe, horiz. 45c, Belted kingfisher, horiz. 55c, Yellow-bellied sapsucker. $1, Great blue heron. $2, Crab hawk, horiz. $4, Yellow warbler. $5, Northern oriole, horiz. No. 1826, White ibises, map, horiz. No. 1827, Blue-winged teal, map, horiz.

ST. VINCENT

## 1993, Apr. 1        Litho.        Perf. 14
1818-1825  A249  Set of 8        14.50  14.50

**Souvenir Sheets**
1826-1827  A249  $6  Set of 2        15.00  15.00

## 1993, May 24        Litho.        Perf. 14

10c. Hexagonal murex. 15c. Caribbean vase. 30c. Measled cowrie. 45c. Dyson's keyhole limpet. 50c. Atlantic hairy triton. 65c. Orange-banded marginella. 75c. Bleeding tooth. $1. Pink conch. $2. Hawk-wing conch. $3. Music volute. $4. Alphabet cone. $5. Antillean cone. #1840, Flame auger. #1841, Netted olive. #1842, Wide-mouthed purpura.

1828-1839  A250        18.50  18.50

**Souvenir Sheets**
1840-1842  A250  $6  Set of 3        18.00  18.00

St. VINCENT $1

Yujiro Ishihara, Actor
A251

### Miniature Sheet

## 1993, May 24        Litho.        Perf. 13½x14
1843  A251  Sheet of 9  #a.-i.        11.00  11.00

**Souvenir Sheets**
1844  A251  Sheet of 4, #a.-d.        6.25  6.25

**Stamp Size: 32x41mm**
1845  A251  Sheet of 4, #a.-d.        6.25  6.25

**Stamp Size: 60x41mm**
1846  A251  Sheet of 3, #a.-c.        7.50  7.50
1847  A251  Sheet of 3, #a.-c.        9.75  9.75

St. Vincent & the Grenadines
$1

**Automobiles**
A252

Various portraits: No. 1843a. $1. b. 55c. c, $1. d. 55c. e, 55c. f, 55c. g, $1. h, 55c. i, $1. $1. 1845a. 55c. b. $1. c, $2. d. $2. No. 1846a. 55c. b. $2. c, $4. d. $4. No. 1847a. 55c. b. $4. c, $4.

## 1993, May        Litho.        Perf. 14
1848-1851  A252  Set of 4        10.50  10.50

**Souvenir Sheets**
1852-1853  A252  $6  Set of 2        12.00  12.00

$1. 1932 Ford V8. 1915 Ford Model T. Henry Ford's 1st car. $2. Benz 540K, 1928. Benz Stuttgart, 1908. Benz Racer. $3. 1911 Blitzen Benz, 1905 Benz Tourenwagen, 1894 Benz. $4. 1935 Ford, 1903 Ford A Runabout, 1913 Ford Model T Tourer. #1852, Karl Benz. #1853, Henry Ford.

First Benz motor. cent. (#1848, 1851, 1853). First Ford motor car. cent. (#1849-1850, 1852).

---

### Miniature Sheet

ST. VINCENT & The Grenadines
Coronation Anniversary 1953-1993
45¢

Coronation of Queen Elizabeth II, 40th Anniv.
A253

## 1993, June 2        Litho.        Perf. 13½x14
1854  A253  Sheet, 2 ea #a.-d.        13.50  13.50

**Souvenir Sheet**
1855  A253  $6  multicolored        6.50  6.50

No. 1855 contains one 28x42mm stamp.

a, 45c. Official coronation photograph. b, 65c. Opening Parliament, 1960s. c, $2, Coronation ceremony, 1953. d, $4, Queen with her dog, 1970s.

No. 1855, Portrait of Queen as a child.

Adelpys annulata
St. Vincent & the Grenadines
50c

Moths — A254

## 1993, June 14        Litho.        Perf. 14
1856  A254  10c  Erynnis ello        .20  .20
1857  A254  $1  Erynnis tan-        1.00  1.00
1858  A254  50c  Aellopos talus        .50  .50
1859  A254  65c  Erynnis alope        .60  .60
1860  A254  75c  Manduca rustica        .75  .75
1861  A254  $1  Xylophanes pluto        .85  .85
1862  A254  $2  Hyles lineata        1.10  1.10
1863  A254  $4  Pseudosphinx tetrio        2.25  2.25
1864  A254  $5  Protambulyx strigilis        4.50  4.50
1864A A254  $6  Xylophanes tersa        5.75  5.75

**Souvenir Sheets**
Nos. 1856-1863 (8)        16.00  16.00

Uethelsa ornatrix        6.00  6.00
A255        6.00  6.00

St. Vincent & The Grenadines
50¢

Supermarine Spitfire Mk I F, R.A.F.

St. Vincent & The Grenadines
$1
Dr. Hugo Eckener 1868-1954

St. Vincent & the Grenadines

**Aviation Anniversaries — A257**

50c. Supermarine Spitfire, 1931, Hugo Eckener, balloon. Zeppelin over Egypt. #1866, Graf Zeppelin over New York, 1928. Eckener, Graf Zeppelin over Tokyo, 1929. Eckener, Graf Walnut State Prison, balloon lifting off. #1872, Hawker Hurricane. $1873, Blanchard's Balloon. #1874, Blanchard's Balloon.

#1867, Jean Pierre Blanchard, balloon.

---

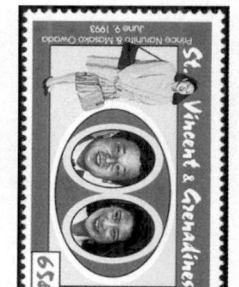

St. Vincent & the Grenadines
45¢
Prince Naruhito & Masako Owada June 9, 1993

George Washington. #1868, De Havilland Mosquito. No. 1869, Eckener, Graf Zeppelin over New York, 1928. $3. Eckener, Graf Zeppelin over Tokyo. $4. Eckener, Graf Walnut State Prison, balloon lifting off. #1872, Hawker Hurricane. $1873, Blanchard's Balloon.

Royal Air Force, 75th anniv. (#1865, 1868 1872). Dr. Hugo Eckener, 125th anniv. of birth (#1866, 1869-1870, 1873). First US balloon flight, bicent. (#1867, 1871). Tokyo spelled incorrectly on No. 1870.

## 1993, June        Litho.        Perf. 14
1865  A255  50c  multi        .90  .90
1866  A256  $1  multi        1.60  1.60
1867  A257  $1  multi        1.60  1.60
1868  A255  $2  multi        3.25  3.25
1869  A256  $2  multi        3.25  3.25
1870  A257  $4  multi        6.50  6.50
1871  A256  $4  multi, vert.        6.50  6.50
1872  A255  50c  multi        .90  .90
1873  A256  $1  multi, vert.        5.50  5.50
1874  A257  $4  multi, vert.        5.50  5.50

**Souvenir Sheets**
Nos. 1865-1871 (7)        22.10  22.10

Two values and a souvenir sheet commemorating the Wedding of Japan's Crown Prince Naruhito and Masako Owada were printed in 1993 but not accepted by the St. Vincent post office. Scott value $5, Souvenir Sheet $5.50.

## 1994 Winter Olympics, Lillehammer, Norway — A259

ST. VINCENT & the GRENADINES  45¢

## 1993, June 30        Litho.        Perf. 14
1878  A259  45c  multicolored        .50  .50
1879  A259  $5  multicolored        5.00  5.00

**Souvenir Sheet**
1880  A259  $6  multicolored        6.00  6.00

Designs: 45c. Marc Girardelli, silver medalist, giant slalom, 1992. $5, Paul Accola, downhill, 1992. $6, Thommy Moe, downhill, 1992.

---

ST. VINCENT & THE GRENADINES  45¢
Massacre in Korea, 1951

**Picasso (1881-1973) — A260**

## 1993, June 30        Litho.
1881  A260  45c  multicolored        .50  .50
1882  A260  $1  multicolored        1.00  1.00
1883  A260  $4  multicolored        4.00  4.00

**Souvenir Sheet**
1884  A260  $6  multicolored        6.00  6.00

Paintings: 45c. Massacre in Korea, 1951. $1. Family of Saltimbanques, 1905. $4, La Joie de Vivre, 1946. $6, Woman Eating a Melon and Boy Writing, 1965, vert.

---

St. Vincent & the Grenadines
$5
Galileo Galilei

George Washington, De Havilland Mosquito... etc.

**Copernicus — A262**

45c. Astronomical instrument. $4, Space shuttle lift-off. $6, Copernicus.

## 1993, June 30        Litho.        Perf. 14
1885  A261  45c  multicolored        .50  .50
1886  A261  $5  multicolored        5.25  5.25

**Souvenir Sheet**
1887  A261  $6  multicolored        6.00  6.00

1888  A262  45c  multicolored        .60  .60
1889  A262  $4  multicolored        5.00  5.00

**Souvenir Sheet**
1890  A262  $6  multicolored        6.00  6.00

1891-1894  A263  Set of 4        3.00  3.00

European Royalty: 45c. Johannes, Gloria, Thurn & Taxis. 65c, Johannes, Thurn & Taxis family. $1, Princess Stephanie of Monaco. $2, Gloria Thurn & Taxis.

---

St. Vincent & the Grenadines

**Inauguration of Pres. William J. Clinton — A264**

## 1993, June 30        Litho.
1895  A264  $5  multicolored        5.50  5.50

**Souvenir Sheet**
1896  A264  $6  multicolored        6.00  6.00

Designs: $5, Bill Clinton, children. $6, Clinton wearing cowboy hat, vert.

---

Polska '93
A265

## 1993, June 30        Litho.
1897  A265  $6  multicolored        5.75  5.75
1898  A265  Pair, #a.-b.        3.75  3.75

**Souvenir Sheet**
1899  A265  $6  multicolored        6.00  6.00

#1897, Bogusz Church. Gozlin. #1898a, $1, Deux Tetes (Man), by S.I. Witkiewicz, 1920, vert. #1898b, $3, Deux Tetes (Woman), vert. No. 1899, Dancing, by Wladyslaw Roguski, vert.

1994 World Cup Soccer Qualifying A266

St. Vincent vs: 5c, Mexico. 10c, Honduras. 65c, Costa Rica. $5, St. Vincent goalkeeper.

**1993, Sept. 2**
**1900-1903** A266 Set of 4 6.75 6.75

Cooperation with Japan — A267

Designs: 10c, Fish delivery van. 50c, Fish aggregation device, vert. 75c, Trawler. $5, Fish complex.

**1993, Sept. 2**
**1904-1907** A267 Set of 4 7.00 7.00

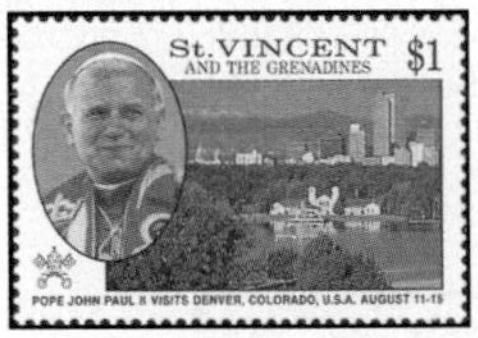


Pope John Paul II's Visit to Denver, CO A268

Design: $6, Pope, Denver skyline, diff.

**1993, Aug. 13**
**1908** A268 $1 multicolored 1.50 1.50

**Souvenir Sheet**

**1909** A268 $6 multicolored 7.00 7.00

No. 1908 issued in sheets of 9.

Miniature Sheet

Corvette, 40th Anniv. — A269

Corvettes: a, 1953. b, 1993, c, 1958, d, 1960. e, "40," Corvette emblem (no car). f, 1961. g, 1963. h, 1968, i, 1973. j, 1975. k, 1982. l, 1984.

**1993, Aug. 13** ***Perf. 14x13½***
**1910** A269 $1 Sheet of 12, #a.-l. 13.50 13.50

Taipei '93 — A270

Designs: 5c, Yellow Crane Mansion, Wuchang. 10c, Front gate, Chung Cheng Ceremonial Arch, Taiwan. 20c, Marble Peifang, Ming 13 Tombs, Beijing. 45c, Jinxing Den, Beijing. 55c, Forbidden City, Beijing. 75c, Tachih, the Martyr's Shrine, Taiwan. No. 1917, Praying Hall, Xinjiang, Gaochang. No. 1918, Chih Kan Tower, Taiwan. $2, Taihu Lake, Jiangsu. $4, Chengde, Hebei, Pula Si. No. 1921, Kaohsiung, Cheng Ching Lake, Taiwan. No. 1922, Great Wall.

Chinese paintings — #1923: a, Street in Macao, China, by George Chinnery. b, Pair of Birds on Cherry Branch. c, Yellow Dragon Cave, by Patrick Procktor. d, Great Wall of China, by William Simpson. e, Dutch Folly Fort Off Conton, by Chinnery. f, Forbidden City, by Procktor.

Chinese silk paintings: No. 1924a, Rhododendron. b, Irises and bees. c, Easter lily. d, Poinsettia. e, Peach and cherry blossoms. f, Weeping cherry and yellow bird.

Chinese kites — #1925: a, Dragon and tiger fighting. b, Two immortals. c, Five boys playing round a general. d, Zheng Chenggong. e, Nezha stirs up the sea. f, Immortal maiden He.

No. 1926, Giant Buddha, Longmen Caves, Luoyang, Hunan. No. 1927, Guardian and Celestial King, Longmen Caves, Hunan, vert. No. 1928, Giant Buddha, Yungang Caves, Datong, Shanxi, vert.

**1993, Aug. 16 Litho.** ***Perf. 14x13½***
**1911-1922** A270 Set of 12 15.00 15.00

**Miniature Sheets of 6**

**1923** A270 $1.50 #a.-f. 6.75 6.75
**1924** A270 $1.50 #a.-f. 6.75 6.75
**1925** A270 $1.50 #a.-f. 6.75 6.75

**Souvenir Sheets**

**1926** A270 $6 multicolored 6.50 6.50

***Perf. 13½x14***

**1927** A270 $6 multicolored 6.50 6.50
**1928** A270 $6 multicolored 6.50 6.50

No. 1925e issued missing "St." in country name. Some sheets of No. 1925 may have been withdrawn from sale after discovery of error.

### With Bangkok '93 Emblem

Designs: 5c, Phra Nakhon Khiri (Rama V's Palace), vert. 10c, Grand Palace, Bangkok. 20c, Rama IX Park, Bangkok. 45c, Phra Prang Sam Yot, Lop Buri. 55c, Dusit Maha Prasad, vert. 75c, Phimai Khmer architecture, Pak Tong Chai. No. 1935, Burmese style Chedi, Mae Hong Son. No. 1936, Antechamber, Central Prang, Prasat Hin Phimai. $2, Brick chedi on laterite base, Si Thep, vert. $4, Isan's Phanom Rung, Korat, vert. No. 1939, Phu Khau Thong, the Golden Mount, Bangkok. No. 1940, Islands, Ang Thong.

Thai Buddha sculpture — #1941: a, Interior of Wat Hua Kuang Lampang, vert. b, Wat Yai Suwannaram, vert. c, Phra Buddha Sihing, City Hall Chapel, vert. d, Wat Ko Keo Suttharam, vert. e, U Thong B image, Wat Ratburana crypt, vert. f, Sri Sakyamuni Wat Suthat, vert.

No. 1942a-1942f: Various details from Mural at Buddhaisawan Chapel.

Thai painting — #1943: a, Untitled, by Arunothai Somsakul. b, Mural at Wat Rajapradit. c, Mural at Wat Phumin (detail). d, Serenity, by Surasit Souakong. e, Scenes of early Bangkok mural (detail). f, Ramayana.

No. 1944, Roof detail of Dusit Mahaprasad, vert. No. 1945, Standing Buddha, Hua Hin, vert. No. 1946, Masked dance.

***Perf. 13½x14, 14x13½***

**1993, Aug. 16 Litho.**
**1929-1940** A270 5c Set of 12 15.00 15.00

**Miniature Sheets of 6**

**1941** A270 $1.50 #a.-f. 6.75 6.75
**1942** A270 $1.50 #a.-f. 6.75 6.75
**1943** A270 $1.50 #a.-f. 6.75 6.75

**Souvenir Sheets**

**1944** A270 $6 multicolored 6.50 6.50
**1945** A270 $6 multicolored 6.50 6.50
**1946** A270 $6 multicolored 6.50 6.50

### With Indopex '93 Emblem

Indopex '93 emblem with designs: 5c, Local landmark, Gedung site, 1920. 10c, Masjid Jamik Mosque, Sumenep. 20c, Bromo Caldera, seen from Penanjakan. 45c, Kudus Mosque, Java. 55c, Kampung Naga. 75c, Lower level of Borobudur. No. 1953, Dieng Temple, Dieng Plateau. No. 1954, Temple 1, Gedung Songo group, Semarang. $2, Istana Bogor, 1856. $4, Taman Sari complex, Yogyakarta. $5, #1957, Landscape near Mt. Sumbing, Central Java. $5, #1958, King Adityawarman's Palace, Batusangar.

Paintings — #1959: a, Female Coolies, by Djoko Pekik. b, Family Outing, by Sudjana Kerton. c, My Family, by Pekik. d, Javanese Dancers, by Arthur Melville. e, Leisure Time, by Kerton. f, In the Garden of Eden, by Agus Djaja.

#1960: a, Tayubon, by Pekik. b, Three Dancers, by Nyoman Gunarsa. c, Nursing Neighbor's Baby, by Hendra Gunawan. d, Imagining within a Dialogue, by Sagito. e, Three Balinese Mask Dancers, by Anton H. f, Three Prostitutes, by Gunawan.

Masks — #1961: a, Hanuman. b, Subali/Sugnwa. c, Kumbakarna. d, Sangut. e, Jatayu. f, Rawana.

No. 1962, Relief of Sudamala story, Mt. Lawu. No. 1963, Plaque, 9th Cent., Banyumas, Central Java. No. 1964, Panel from Ramayana reliefs, vert.

**1993, Aug. 16 Litho.** ***Perf. 14x13½***
**1947-1958** A270 Set of 12 15.00 15.00

**Minature Sheets of 6**

**1959** A270 $1.50 #a.-f. 6.75 6.75
**1960** A270 $1.50 #a.-f. 6.75 6.75
**1961** A270 $1.50 #a.-f. 6.75 6.75

**Souvenir Sheets**

**1962** A270 $6 multicolored 6.50 6.50
**1963** A270 $6 multicolored 6.50 6.50

***Perf. 13½x14***

**1964** A270 $6 multicolored 6.50 6.50

Reggie Jackson, Selection to Baseball Hall of Fame — A271

**1993, Oct. 4** ***Perf. 14***
**1965** A271 $2 multicolored 2.00 2.00

Christmas A272

Details or entire woodcut, The Adoration of the Magi, by Durer: 10c, 35c, 40c, $5.

Details or entire paintings by Rubens: 50c, Holy Family with Saint Francis. 55c, 65c, Adoration of the Shepherds. $1, Holy Family.

No. 1974, The Adoration of the Magi, by Durer, horiz. No. 1975, Holy Family with St. Elizabeth & St. John, by Rubens.

***Perf. 13½x14, 14x13½***

**1993, Nov. 18**
**1966-1973** A272 Set of 8 9.00 9.00

**Souvenir Sheets**

**1974-1975** A272 $6 each 12.50 12.50

Miniature Sheet

Legends of Country Music A273

Various portraits of: a, f, l, Roy Acuff. b, g, j, Patsy Cline. c, h, i, Jim Reeves. d, e, k, Hank Williams, Sr.

**1994, Jan. 17 Litho.** ***Perf. 13½x14***
**1976** A273 $1 Sheet of 12, #a.-l. 12.50 12.50

Mickey's Portrait Gallery A274

Mickey Mouse as: 5c, Aviator. 10c, Foreign Legionnaire. 15c, Frontiersman. 20c, Best Pals, Mickey, Goofy, Donald. 35c, Horace, Clarabelle. 50c, Minnie, Frankie, Figuro. 75c, Donald, Pluto today. 80c, Party boy Mickey. 85c, Best Friends, Minnie, Daisy. 95c, Mickey's Girl, Minnie. $1, Cool forties Mickey. $1.50, Mickey, "Howdy!", 1950. $2, Totally Mickey. $3, Minnie, Mickey. $4, Congratulations Mickey, birthday cake. $5, Uncle Sam.

No. 1993, Donald Duck, early photo of Mickey, horiz. No. 1994, Minnie disco dancing, horiz. No. 1995, Mickey photographing nephews, horiz. No. 1996, Pluto, Mickey looking at wall of photos.

**1994, May 5 Litho.** ***Perf. 13½x14***
**1977-1992** A274 Set of 16 26.00 26.00

**Souvenir Sheets**

***Perf. 14x13½***

**1993-1996** A274 $6 Set of 4 30.00 30.00

Breadfruit — A275 Intl. Year of the Family — A276

**1994, Jan. Litho.** ***Perf. 13½x14***
**1997** A275 10c Planting .20 .20
**1998** A275 45c Captain Bligh, plant .70 .70
**1999** A275 65c Fruit sliced .60 .60
**2000** A275 $5 Fruit on branch 5.50 5.50
*Nos. 1997-2000 (4)* 7.00 7.00

**1994, Jan.** ***Perf. 14x13½, 13½x14***
**2001** A276 10c Outing .20 .20
**2002** A276 50c Praying in church .50 .50
**2003** A276 65c Working in garden .65 .65
**2004** A276 75c Jogging .70 .70
**2005** A276 $1 Portrait 1.05 1.05
**2006** A276 $2 Running on beach 2.10 2.10
*Nos. 2001-2006 (6)* 5.20 5.20

Nos. 2001-2004, 2006 are horiz.

Library Service, Cent. A277

**1994, Jan.** ***Perf. 14x13½***
**2007** A277 5c Mobile library .20 .20
**2008** A277 10c Old public library .20 .20
**2009** A277 $1 Family education .90 .90
**2010** A277 $1 Younger, older men .90 .90
*Nos. 2007-2010 (4)* 2.20 2.20

Barbra Streisand, 1993 MGM Grand Garden Concert — A278

A278a

Illustration A278a reduced.

**1994, Jan.**
**2011** A278 $2 multicolored 1.75 1.75

**Embossed**
***Perf. 12***

**2011A** A278a $20 gold

No. 2011 issued in sheets of 9.

ST. VINCENT
& the Grenadines
40¢
HONG KONG '94
STAMP EXPOSITION
18-21 FEB., 1994
Hong Kong Harbor
A279

St. Vincent & The Grenadines 40¢
A280

Plate, Bird on a Flowering Spray, Qianlong.
St Vincent & the Grenadines 50c
Hong Kong '94 — A281

St. VINCENT & the GRENADINES
$1.50
Hong Kong '94 — A282

Stamps, 19th cent. painting of Hong Kong Harbor: #2012a, Hong Kong #626, ship under sail. #2012b, Ship at anchor, #1548.

Porcelain ware, Qing Dynasty — #2013: a, Bowl with bamboo & sparrows. b, Bowl with flowers of four seasons. c, Bowl with lotus pool & dragon. d, Bowl with landscape. e, Shar-Pei puppies in bowl (not antiquity). f, Covered bowl with dragon & pearls.

Chinese dragon boat races — #2014: a, Dragon boats. b, Tapestry of dragon races. c, Dragon race. d, Dragon boats, diff. e, Chinese crested dog. f, Dragon boats, 4 banners above boats.

Chinese junks — #2015: a, Junk, Hong Kong Island. b, Junk with white sails in harbor. c, Junk with inscription on stern, Hong Kong Island. d, Junk KLN B/G. e, Chow dog, junk. f, Junk with red, white sails, Hong Kong Island.

Chinese seed stitch purses — #2016: a, Vases, fruit on pink purse. b, Peonies, butterflies. c, Vase, fruit on dark blue purse. d, Vases, fruit on light blue purse. e, Fu-dog. f, Flowers.

Chineses pottery — #2017: a, Plate, bird on flowering spray, Qianlong. b, Large dish, Kangxi. c, Egshell plate, cocks on rocky ground, Yongzheng. d, Gladen dish decorated with Qilin curicorn, Yuan. e, Porcelain pug dog. f, Dish with Dutch ship, Uryburg, Qianlong.

Ceramic figures, Qing Dynasty, vert — #2018: a, Waterdropper. b, Two women playing chess. c, Liu-Hai. d, Laughing twins. e, Seated hound. f, Louhan (Ma Ming).

#2019, Dr. Sun Yat-sen. #2020, Chiang Kai-shek.

Dinosaurs — #2021: a, Triceratops. b, Unidentified, vert. c, Apatosaurus (d). d, Stegosaurus, vert.

**1994, Feb. 18** ***Perf. 14***

| | | | | |
|---|---|---|---|---|
| **2012** | A279 | 40c Pair, #a.-b. | .85 | .85 |

**Miniature Sheets of 6**

| | | | | |
|---|---|---|---|---|
| **2013** | A280 | 40c #a.-f. | 2.25 | 2.25 |
| **2014** | A280 | 40c #a.-f. | 2.25 | 2.25 |
| **2015** | A280 | 45c #a.-f. | 2.40 | 2.40 |
| **2016** | A280 | 45c #a.-f. | 2.40 | 2.40 |
| **2017** | A281 | 50c #a.-f. | 2.75 | 2.75 |

***Perf. 13***

| | | | | |
|---|---|---|---|---|
| **2018** | A280 | 50c #a.-f. | 4.00 | 4.00 |

**Souvenir Sheets**

| | | | | |
|---|---|---|---|---|
| **2019** | A281 | $2 multicolored | 1.50 | 1.50 |
| **2020** | A281 | $2 multicolored | 1.50 | 1.50 |
| **2021** | A282 | $1.50 Sheet of 4, #a.-d. | 4.50 | 4.50 |

No. 2012 issued in sheets of 10 stamps and has a continuous design.

Portions of the design on No. 2021 have been applied by a thermographic process producing a shiny, raised effect.

New Year 1994 (Year of the Dog) (#2013e, 2014e, 2015e, 2016e, 2017e, 2018e). Hong Kong '94 (#2018, 2021).

Miniature Sheet

St. Vincent
and the grenadines
Blue Flasher
50¢
Hong Kong '94 — A283

Butterflies: a, Blue flasher. b, Tiger swallowtail. c, Lustrous copper. d, Tailed copper. e, Blue copper. f, Ruddy copper. g, Viceroy. h, California sister. i, Mourning cloak. j, Red passion flower. k, Small flambeau. l, Blue wave. m, Chiricahua metalmark. n, Monarch. o, Anise swallowtail. p, Buckeye.

**1994, Feb. 18** **Litho.** ***Perf. 14½***

| | | | | |
|---|---|---|---|---|
| **2022** | A283 | 50c Sheet of 16, #a.-p. | 11.50 | 11.50 |

JUVENTUS F.C.
Franco CAUSIO
St.Vincent & the Grenadines $1
A284

St.Vincent & the Grenadines
10¢
Epidendrum ibaguense
A285

Players: No. 2023, Causio. No. 2024, Tardelli. No. 2025, Rossi. No. 2026, Bettega. No. 2027, Platini, Baggio. No. 2028, Cabrini. No. 2029, Scirea. No. 2030, Furino. No. 2031, Kohler. No. 2032, Zoff. No. 2033, Gentile.

$6, Three European Cups won by team, horiz.

**1994, Mar. 22** **Litho.** ***Perf. 14***

| | | | | |
|---|---|---|---|---|
| **2023-2033** | A284 | $1 Set of 11 | 11.25 | 11.25 |

**Souvenir Sheet**

| | | | | |
|---|---|---|---|---|
| **2034** | A284 | $6 multicolored | 6.00 | 6.00 |

Juventus football (soccer) club of Turin.

**1994, Apr. 6** **Litho.** ***Perf. 14***

Orchids: 10c, Epidendrum ibaguense. 25c, Ionopsis utricularioides. 50c, Brassavola cucullata. 65c, Enclyclia cochleata. $1, Liparis nervosa. $2, Vanilla phaeantha. $4, Elleanthus cephalotus. $5, Isochilus linearis.

No. 2043, Rodriguezia lanceolata. No. 2044, Eulophia alta.

| | | | | |
|---|---|---|---|---|
| **2035-2042** | A285 | Set of 8 | 15.00 | 15.00 |

**Souvenir Sheets**

| | | | | |
|---|---|---|---|---|
| **2043-2044** | A285 | $6 each | 12.50 | 12.50 |

ST. VINCENT
AND THE GRENADINES
75c
Protoavis
A286

ST. VINCENT
75c
DIMORPHODON
Dinosaurs — A287

#2045: a, Protoavis (e). b, Pteranodon. c, Quetzalcoatlus (b). d, Lesothosaurus (a, c, e-h). e, Hetrodontosaurus. f, Archaeopteryx (b, e). g, Cearadactylus (f). h, Anchisaurus.

No. 2046: a, Dimorphodon (e). b, Camarasaurus (e, f). c, Spinosaurus (b). d, Allosaurus (a-c, e-h). e, Rhamphorhynchus (a). f, Pteranodon (b). g, Eudimorphodon (c). h, Ornithomimus.

No. 2047: a, Dimorphodon (b). b, Pterodactylus (a). c, Rhamphorhynchus (b). d, Pteranodon. e, Gallimimus. f, Setgosaurus. g, Acanthopholis. h, Trachodon (g). i, Thecodonti (j). j, Ankylosaurus (i). k, Compsognathus. l, Protoceratops.

No. 2048: a, Hesperonis. b, Mesosaurus. c, Plesiosaurus. d, Squalicorax (a). e, Tylosaurus (d, g). f, Plesiosoar. g, Stenopterygius ichthyosaurus (j). h, Stenosaurus (f). i, Eurhinosaurus longirostris (e, f, h, l). j, Cryptocleidus oxoniensis. k, Caturus (h, i, j, l). l, Protostega (k).

No. 2049: a, Quetzalcoatlus. b, Diplodocus (a). c, Spinosaurus (f, g). d, Apatosaurus (c). e, Ornitholestes. f, Lesothosaurus (e). g, Trachodon. h, Protoavis. i, Oviraptor. j, Coelophysis (i). k, Ornitholestes (j). l, Archaeopteryx.

No. 2050, horiz: a, Albertosaurus. b, Chasmosaurus (c). c, Brachiosaurus. d, Coelophysis (e). e, Deinonychus (d). f, Anatosaurus. g, Iguanodon. h, Baryonyx. i, Steneosaurus. j, Nanotyrannus. k, Camptosaurus (j). l, Camarasaurus.

No. 2051, Tyrannosaurus rex. No. 2052: Triceratops, horiz. No. 2053, Pteranodon, diplodocus carnegii, horiz. No. 2054, Styracosaurus.

**1994, Apr. 20** **Litho.** ***Perf. 14***

| | | | | |
|---|---|---|---|---|
| **2045** | A286 | 75c Sheet of 8, #a.-h. | 6.75 | 6.75 |
| **2046** | A286 | 75c Sheet of 8, #a.-h. | 6.75 | 6.75 |

**Miniature Sheets of 12**

| | | | | |
|---|---|---|---|---|
| **2047-2050** | A287 | 75c #a.-l, each | 8.50 | 8.50 |

**Souvenir Sheets**

| | | | | |
|---|---|---|---|---|
| **2051** | A286 | $6 multi | 6.25 | 6.25 |
| **2052-2054** | A287 | $6 each | 6.25 | 6.25 |

No. 2048 is horiz.

**Entertainers Type of 1991**
Miniature Sheet

Various portraits of Marilyn Monroe.

**1994, May 16** ***Perf. 13½***

| | | | | |
|---|---|---|---|---|
| **2055** | A206 | $1 Sheet of 9, #a.-i. | 10.00 | 10.00 |

COLOMBIA
ST. VINCENT AND THE GRENADINES 50c
1994 World Cup Soccer Championships, US — A288

Team photos: #2056, Colombia. #2057, Romania. #2058, Switzerland. #2059, US. #2060, Brazil. #2061, Cameroon. #2062, Russia. #2063, Sweden. #2064, Bolivia. #2065, Germany. #2066, South Korea. #2067, Spain. #2068, Argentina. #2069, Bulgaria. #2070, Greece. #2071, Nigeria. #2072, Ireland. #2073, Italy. #2074, Mexico. #2075, Norway. #2076, Belgium. #2077, Holland. #2078, Morocco. #2079, Saudi Arabia.

**1994** ***Perf. 13½***

| | | | | |
|---|---|---|---|---|
| **2056-2079** | A288 | 50c Set of 24 | 14.00 | 14.00 |

Miniature Sheets of 9

St. Vincent & Grenadines
$1
FRED L. WHIPPLE
First Manned Moon Landing, 25th Anniv. A289

Famous men, aviation & space scenes: No. 2080a, Fred L. Whipple, Halley's Comet. b, Robert G. Gilruth, Gemini 12. c, George E. Mueller, Ed White walking in space during Gemini 4. d, Charles A. Berry, Johnsville Centrifuge. e, Christopher C. Kraft, Jr., Apollo 4 reentry. f, James A. Van Allen, Explorer I, Van Allen Radiation Belts. g, Robert H. Goddard, Goddard Liquid Fuel Rocket, 1926. h, James E. Webb, Spirit of '76 flight. i, Rocco A. Patrone, Apollo 8 coming home.

No. 2081: a, Walter R. Dornberger, missile launch, 1942. b, Alexander Lippisch, Wolfgang Spate's ME-163B. c, Kurt H. Debus, A4b Launch, 1945. d, Hermann Oberth, Oberth's Spaceship, 1923. e, Hanna Reitsch, Reichenberg (type 2) Piloted Bomb. f, Ernst Stuhlinger, Explorer I, 2nd stage ignition. g, Werner von Braun, Rocket Powered He112. h, Arthur Rudolph, Rudolph Rocket Motor, 1934. i, Willy Ley, Rocket Airplane, Greenwood Lake NY.

No. 2082, Hogler N. Toftoy. No. 2083, Eberhardt Rees.

**1994, July 12** ***Perf. 14***

| | | | | |
|---|---|---|---|---|
| **2080-2081** | A289 | $1 #a.-i, each | 9.00 | 9.00 |

**Souvenir Sheets**

| | | | | |
|---|---|---|---|---|
| **2082-2083** | A289 | $6 each | 6.25 | 6.25 |

Nos. 2082-2083 each contain one 50x38mm stamp.

ST. VINCENT & THE GRENADINES 40c
D-Day, 50th Anniv. A290

Designs: 40c, Supply armada. $5, Beached cargo ship unloads supplies.

$6, Liberty ship.

**1994, July 19** **Litho.** ***Perf. 14***

| | | | | |
|---|---|---|---|---|
| **2084** | A290 | 40c multicolored | .40 | .40 |
| **2085** | A290 | $5 multicolored | 4.75 | 4.75 |

**Souvenir Sheet**

| | | | | |
|---|---|---|---|---|
| **2086** | A290 | $6 multicolored | 5.25 | 5.25 |

ST. VINCENT &
10¢
Yorkshire Terrier
THE GRENADINES
New Year 1994 (Year of the Dog) — A291

Designs: 10c, Yorkshire terrier. 25c, Yorkshire terrier, diff. 50c, Golden retriever. 65c, Bernese mountain dog. $1, Vorstehhund. $2, Tibetan terrier. $4, West highland terrier. $5, Shih tzu.

No. 2095a, Pomeranian. b, English springer spaniel. c, Bearded collie. d, Irish wolfhound. e, Pekingese. f, Irish setter. g, Old English sheepdog. h, Basset hound. i, Cavalier King Charles spaniel. j, Kleiner munsterlander. k, Shetland sheepdog. l, Dachshund.

No. 2096, Afghan hound. No. 2097, German shepherd.

**1994, July 21**

| | | | | |
|---|---|---|---|---|
| **2087-2094** | A291 | Set of 8 | 10.00 | 10.00 |

**Miniature Sheet of 12**

| | | | | |
|---|---|---|---|---|
| **2095** | A291 | 50c #a.-l. | 4.50 | 4.50 |

**Souvenir Sheets**

| | | | | |
|---|---|---|---|---|
| **2096-2097** | A291 | $6 each | 4.50 | 4.50 |

No. 2150, $1, Airplanes, ICAO emblem. No. 2151, $1, J.F. Mitchell Airport, Bequia.

**1994, Dec. 1**    **Litho.**    **Perf. 14**
2147-2151 A302 Set of 5    4.00 4.00

Miniature Sheets of 9

Cats — A303

Parrots — A304

WHITE-EARED CONURE
Weight 2.3oz (65g)
Length 80in (25cm)

Cats: No. 2152a, Snowshoe. b. Abyssinian. c. Ocicat. d. Tiffany (e. h). e. Russian blue. f. Siamese. g. Bi-color. h. Malayan. i. Manx.
Parrots: No. 2153a, Mealy Amazon. b. Nanday conure. c. Black-headed caique. d. Scarlet macaw (g). e. Red-masked conure. f. Blue-headed parrot. g. Hyacinth macaw. h. Sun conure. i. Blue & yellow macaw.

**1995, Apr. 25**    **Litho.**    **Perf. 14**
2152-2153 A303 $1    11.00 11.00

**Souvenir Sheets**
2154 A304 $5 multicolored    6.2b   6.25
2155 A304 $6 multicolored    7.50   7.50

MASTER BOOBY
Sula dactylatra

Birds — A306

World Wildlife Fund, masked booby: No. 2156: a. One standing. b. Two birds. c. One nesting. d. One stretching wings.
No. 2157: a. Greater egret. b. Roseate spoonbill. c. Ring-billed gull. d. Ruddy quail-dove. e. Royal tern. f. Killdeer. g. Osprey. h. Frigatebird. i. Masked booby. j. Green-backed heron. k. Cormorant. l. Brown pelican.
No. 2158, Flamingo, vert. No. 2159, Purple gallinule, vert.

**1995, May 2**
2156 A305 75c Strip of 4, #a.-d.    3.00 3.00

**Miniature Sheet of 12**
2157 A306 75c #a.-l.    9.50 9.50

**Souvenir Sheets**
2158 A306 $5 multicolored    4.25 4.25
2159 A306 $6 multicolored    5.75 5.75

No. 2156 is a continuous design and was issued in sheets of 3.

ST. VINCENT & THE GRENADINES

VE Day, 50th Anniv. — A307

No. 2159A. a, b, Douglas Devastator. c, Doolittle's B25 leads raid on Tokyo. d, Curtis Helldiver. e, USS Yorktown. f, USS Wasp. g, USS Lexington sinks.

---

Team photos: No. 2123a, Kashima Antlers. b, JEF United. c, Red Diamonds. d, Verdy Yomiuri. e, Nissan FC Yokohama Marinos. f, AS Flugels. g, Bellmare. h, Shimizu S-pulse. i, Jubilo Iwata. j, Nogoya Grampus Eight. k, Panasonic Gamba Osaka. l, Sanfrecce Hiroshima FC.
Jubilo Iwata, action scenes: Nos. 2124a, c-d, 55c. b, e, $1.50. f, $3, Team picture.
Red Diamonds, action scenes: Nos. 2125a, c-d, 55c. b, e, $1.50. f, $3, Team pictue.
Nissan FC Yokohama Marinos, action scenes: Nos. 2126a, c-d, 55c. b, e, $1.50. f, $3, Team picture.
Verdy Yomiuri, action scenes: Nos. 2127a, c-d, 55c. b, e, $1.50. f, $3, Team picture.
Nagoya Grampus eight, action scenes: Nos. 2128a, c-d, 55c. b, e, $1.50. f, $3, Team picture.
Kashima Antlers, action scenes: Nos. 2129a, c-d, 55c. b, e, $1.50. f, $3, Team picture.
JEF United, action scenes: Nos. 2130a, c-d, 55c. b, e, $1.50. f, $3, Team picture.
AS Flugels, action scenes: Nos. 2131a, c-d, 55c. b, e, $1.50. f, $3, Team picture.
Bellmare, action scenes: Noa. 2132a, c-d, 55c. b, e, $1.50. f, $3, Team picture.
Sanfrecce Hiroshima FC, action scenes: Nos. 2133a, c-d, 55c. b, e, $1.50. f, $3, Team picture.
Shimizu S-pulse, action scenes: Nos. 2134a, c-d, 55c. b, e, $1.50. f, $3, Team picture.
Panasonic Gamba Isajam, action scenes: Nos. 2135a, c-d, 55c. b, e, $1.50. f, $3, Team picture.
League All-Stars: No. 2136a, $1.50. League emblem. b, 55c, Shigetatsu Matsunaga. c, 55c, Masami Ihara. d, $1.50, Takumi Horiike. e, 55c, Shunzoh Ohno. f, 55c, Luiz Carlos Pereira. g, 55c, Tetsuji Hashiratani. h, 55c, Carlos Alberto Souza Dos Santos. i, 55c, Rui Ramos. j, 55c, Yasuto Honda. k, 55c, Kazuyoshi Miura. l, $1.50, Ramon Angel Diaz.

**1994, July 1**    **Perf. 14x13½**
2123 A300 #a.-l.    11.00 11.00
2124-2135 A300 #a.-f., each    5.75 5.75

**Perf. 13½x14**
2136 A300 #a.-l., vert.    11.00 11.00

Christmas A301

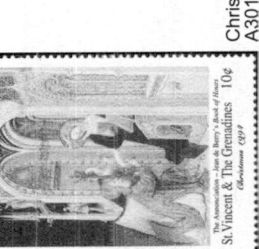

The Annunciation — from de Barry's Book of Hours
(Chrétienne CLF-8

Illustrations from Book of Hours, by Jean de Berry: 10c, The Annunciation, angel kneeling. 45c, The Visitation. 60c, The Nativity. 65c, The Purification of the Virgin. 75c, Presentation of Jesus in the Temple. $5, Flight into Egypt. $6, Adoration of the Magi.

**1994**    **Litho.**    **Perf. 13½x14**
2137-2142 A301 Set of 6    9.50 9.50

**Souvenir Sheet**
2143 A301 $6 multicolored    7.50 7.50

**Miniature Sheet with New Denominations and Added Inscription**

Nos. 1792, 1806-1807 with New Denominations and Added Inscription

**1995, Jan. 24**    **Perf. 14x13½**
2144 A247 30c Sheet of 9, #a.-i.    5.25 5.25

**Souvenir Sheets**
2145 A247 $3 multi (#1806)    3.25 3.25
2146 A247 $3 multi (#1807)    3.25 3.25

Nos. 2144-2146 are inscribed with emblem for "New Year 1995, Year of the Pig."

---

**ST. VINCENT**

Souvenir Sheets    **Perf. 14**
2115-2116 A295 $4 each    3.75 3.75

Miniature Sheet of 9

Star Trek, The Next Generation, 7th Anniv. — A297

A297a

Designs: No. 2117a, Capt. Picard. b, Cmdr. Riker. c, Lt. Cmdr. Data. d, Lt. Worf. e, Cast members. f, Dr. Crusher. g, Lt. Yar, Lt. Worf. h, Q. i, Counselor Troi.
$10, Cast members, horiz.
$20, Starship Enterprise, Capt. Picard. Illustration A297a reduced.

**1994, June 27**    **Litho.**    **Perf. 14x13½**
2117 A297 $2 #a.-i.    16.00 16.00

**Souvenir Sheet**    **Perf. 14x14½**
2118 A297 $10 multicolored    10.00 10.00

No. 2117e exists in sheets of 9. No. 2118 contains one 60x40mm stamp.

**Litho. & Embossed**
**1994, May**    **Perf. 9**
2118A A297a $20 gold & multi

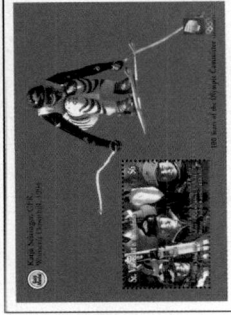

Intl. Year of the Family A298

**1994**    **Perf. 14**
2119 A298 75c multicolored    .95 .95

Order of the Caribbean Community — A299

First award recipients: $1, Sir Shridath Ramphal, statesman, Guyana, vert. $2, Derek Walcott, writer, St. Lucia, vert. $5, William Demas, economist, Trinidad and Tobago.

**1994, Sept. 1**
2120-2122 A299 Set of 3    8.00 8.00

Miniature Sheets of 6 or 12

Japanese Soccer — A300

---

ST. VINCENT AND THE GRENADINES

English Touring Cricket, Cent. — A292

Designs: 10c, M.R. Ramprakash, England. 30c, P.V. Simmons, W. Indies. $2, Sir. G. St. A. Sobers, W. Indies, vert.
$3, Firsh English team, 1895.

**1994, July 25**
2098-2100 A292 Set of 3    3.25 3.25

**Souvenir Sheet**
2101 A293 $3 multicolored    3.50 3.50

A293

Intl. Olympic Committee, Cent. — A294

Designs: 45c, Peter Frennel, German Democratic Republic, 20k walk, 1972. 50c, Kijung Son, Japan, marathon, 1936. 75c, Jesse Owens, US, 100-, 200-meters, 1936. $1, Greg Louganis, US, diving, 1984, 1988. $2, Katja Seizinger, Germany, women's downhill, 1994.

**1994, July 25**    **Set of 4**
2102-2105 A293    3.00 3.00

**Souvenir Sheet**
2106 A294 $6 multicolored    6.00 6.00

PHILAKOREA '94    A296

Designs: 10c, Oryon Waterfall. 45c, Outside Pyongyang Indoor Sports Stadium, horiz. 65c, Pombong, Ch'onhwadae. 75c, Uisangdae, Naksansa. $1, Buddha of the Sokkuram Grotto, Kyangju, horiz. $2, Moksogwon, horiz. Nos. 2113a-2113h, Various letter pictures. eight panel screen, 18th cent. Choson Dynasty.
Letter pictures, 19th cent. Choson Dynasty: No. 2114a, Fish. No. 2114b, Birds. Nos. 2114c-2114d, Various bookshelf pictures. Nos. 2114e-2114g, Various designs from six-panel screen.
No. 2115, Hunting scene, embroidery on silk, Choson Dynasty, horiz. No. 2116, Chongdong Mirukbul.

**1994, July 25**    **Set of 6**    **Perf. 14**
2107-2112 A295    9.00 9.00

**Miniature Sheets of 8**    **Perf. 13½**
2113-2114 A296 50c #a.-h.    7.25 7.25

---

ICAO, 50th Anniv. — A302

St. Vincent

Designs: 10c, Bequia Airport. 65c, Union Island. 75c, Liat B-100, E.T. Joshua Airport.

St. Vincent & the Grenadines $1.50

No. 2160: a, US First Army nears the Rhine. b, Last V2 rocket fired at London, Mar. 1945. c, 8th Air Force B24 Liberators devastate industrial Germany. d, French Army advances on Strasbourg. e, Gloster Meteor, first jet aircraft to enter squadron service. f, Berlin burns from both air and ground bombardments. g, Soviet tanks on Unter Den Linden near Brandenburg Gate. h, European war is won. No. 2161, Pilot in cockpit of Allied bomber. No. 2161A, Ships in Pacific, sunset.

**1995, May 8 — Litho. — Perf. 14**

| | | | |
|---|---|---|---|
| 2159A | A307 $2 | #b-g + label | 11.50 11.50 |
| 2160 | A307 $2 | #a-h + label | 15.50 15.50 |

**Souvenir Sheets**

| | | | |
|---|---|---|---|
| 2161-2161A | A307 $6 each | | 7.50 7.50 |

No. 2161 contains one 57x43mm stamp.

A308

**1995, May 5**

| | | | |
|---|---|---|---|
| 2162 | A308 $2 Strip of 3, #a-c. | | 5.25 5.25 |
| 2163 | A308 $6 multicolored | | 5.25 5.25 |

**Souvenir Sheet**

No. 2162 is a continuous design and was issued in miniature sheets of 3.

UN, 50th anniv.: a, Globe, dove. b, Lady Liberty. c, UN Headquarters. $6, Child.

A309

**1995, May 5**

18th World Scout Jamboree, Holland: $1, Natl. Scout flag. $4, Lord Baden Powell, $5, Scout handshake. No. 2167, Scout sign. No. 2168, Scout salute.

**1995**

| | | | |
|---|---|---|---|
| 2164-2166 | A309 Set of 3 | | 8.75 8.75 |
| 2167-2168 | A309 $6 each | | 5.75 5.75 |

**Souvenir Sheets**

Yalta Conference, 50th Anniv. A310

**1995, May 8 — Litho. — Perf. 14**

| | | | |
|---|---|---|---|
| 2169 | A310 $1 multicolored | | 1.75 1.75 |

**Litho. & Embossed — Perf. 9**

| | | | |
|---|---|---|---|
| 2169A | A310 $50 gold & multi | | 27.50 27.50 |

No. 2169 was issued in sheets of 9.
$50, like #2169. Illustration reduced.

---

New Year 1995 (Year of the Boar) — A311

**1995, May 8**

| | | | |
|---|---|---|---|
| 2170 | A311 75c Strip of 3, #a-c. | | 2.50 2.50 |

**Souvenir Sheet**

| | | | |
|---|---|---|---|
| 2171 | A311 $2 multicolored | | 2.50 2.50 |

No. 2170 was issued in sheets of 3.
Stylized boars: a, blue green & multi. b, brown & multi. c, red & multi. $2, Two boars, horiz.

FAO, 50th Anniv. — A312

**1995, May 8**

| | | | |
|---|---|---|---|
| 2172 | A312 $2 Strip of 3, #a-c. | | 5.25 5.25 |

**Souvenir Sheet**

| | | | |
|---|---|---|---|
| 2173 | A312 $6 multicolored | | 5.25 5.25 |

No. 2172 is a continuous design and was issued in sheets of 3.

Designs: a, Girl holding plate, woman with bowl. b, Stirring pot of food. c, Working in fields of grain. $6, Infant.

Rotary Intl, 90th Anniv. A313

**1995, May 8**

| | | | |
|---|---|---|---|
| 2174 | A313 $5 multicolored | | 4.50 4.50 |

**Souvenir Sheet**

| | | | |
|---|---|---|---|
| 2175 | A313 $6 multicolored | | 5.25 5.25 |

Designs: $5, Paul Harris, Rotary emblem. $6, St. Vincent flag, Rotary emblem.

Queen Mother, 95th Birthday A314

**1995, May 8 — Perf. 13½x14**

| | | | |
|---|---|---|---|
| 2176 | A314 $1.50 Block or strip of 4, #a-d. | | 5.25 5.25 |

**Souvenir Sheet**

| | | | |
|---|---|---|---|
| 2177 | A314 $6 multicolored | | 5.25 5.25 |

Designs: a, Drawing. b, Wearing blue hat. c, Formal portrait. d, Wearing lavender outfit. $6, Wearing crown jewels, yellow dress.

No. 2176 was issued in sheet of 2. In 2002, sheets of Nos. 2176 and 2177 were overprinted "In Memoriam — 1900-2002" in margin.

---

Miniature Sheets

Marine Life A315

**1995, May 23 — Perf. 14**

| | | | |
|---|---|---|---|
| 2178 | A315 90c Sheet of 9, #a-i. | | 7.50 7.50 |
| 2179 | A315 $1 Sheet of 4, #a-d. | | 5.00 5.00 |

**Souvenir Sheets**

| | | | |
|---|---|---|---|
| 2180-2181 | A315 $6 each | | 6.50 6.50 |

No. 2180, Physalia physalis, vert. No. 2181, Sea anemones, vert.

No. 2178, vert.: a, Humpback whale (b, d, e, f, j). b, Green turtle (c). c, Bottlenose dolphin (f, j). d, Monk seal (e). e, Krill. f, Blue shark. g, Striped pork fish. h, Chaelodon sedentarius (e, g). i, Ship wreck, bottom of sea. No. 2179: a, Pomacanthus leucostictus (b). b, Pomacanthus arcuatus (d). c, Micros-pathodon chrysurus (d). d, Chaetodon capistratus.

A316a

1995 Special Olympics World Games, Connecticut A316

**1995, July 6 — Perf. 9**

| | | | |
|---|---|---|---|
| 2182 | A316 $1 blk, yel & bl | | 1.10 1.10 |

**Embossed**

| | | | |
|---|---|---|---|
| 2182A | A316a $20 gold | | |

No. 2182 issued in sheets of 9.
Illustration A316a reduced.

1995 IAAF World Track & Field Championships, Gothenburg & 1996 Summer Olympics, Atlanta — A317

**1995, July 31 — Litho. — Perf. 14**

| | | | |
|---|---|---|---|
| 2183 | A317 $1 #a-f. | | 4.50 4.50 |

**Miniature Sheet of 6**

No. 2183: a, Ingrid Kristiansen, Norway. b, Trine Hattestad, Norway. c, Grete Waitz, Norway. d, Vebjorn Rodal, Norway. e, Geir Moen, Norway. f, Steinar Hoen, Norway. horiz.

---

A318

A319

**1995, Aug. 4**

| | | | |
|---|---|---|---|
| 2184-2187 | A318 Set of 4 | | 6.75 6.75 |

WHO, UNICEF Baby Friendly Program.
Designs: 15c, Breast, bowl of food, horiz. 20c, Expressing milk, cup, spoon. 90c, Drawing of mother breastfeeding child, by Picasso. $5, Mother, child, olive wreath.

**1995, Aug. 8**

| | | | |
|---|---|---|---|
| 2188-2192 | A319 Set of 5 | | 1.90 1.90 |

Caribbean Development Bank, 25th anniv.
Designs: 10c, Leeward Coast, horiz. 15c, Feeder roads project, horiz. 25c, Anthurium andraeanum, horiz. 50c, Coconut palm. 65c, Housing scene, Fairhall, horiz.

Fudo Myoou (God of Fire), Woodprint, by Shunichi Kadowaki — A320

**1995, July 1 — Litho. — Perf. 14**

| | | | |
|---|---|---|---|
| 2193 | A320 $1.40 multicolored | | 1.25 1.25 |

A321

Nolan Ryan, Baseball Player — A322

Designs: No. 2194, Nolan Ryan Foundation emblem. No. 2195, Emblem of major league All Star Game, Arlington, TX. Portraits of Ryan: No. 2196a, In Rangers' cap. b, With western hat, dog. c, In Texas Rangers' cap. d, Throwing football. e, With son. f, Laughing, without hat. g, With family. h, Wearing Houston Astros cap. No. 2197a: a, "34" on front. b, Looking left. c, Looking left. d, After pitch looking forward. e, After pitch looking left. f, With bloody lip. g, Ready to pitch ball. h, Holding up cap. $6, Being carried by team mates. $30, Ready to pitch (illustration reduced).

**1995, Aug. 1**

| | | | |
|---|---|---|---|
| 2194 | A321 $1 multicolored | | .75 .75 |
| 2195 | A321 $1 multicolored | | .75 .75 |

a. | A321 $1 Pair, #2194-2195 | | 1.50 1.50 |

**Miniature Sheets of 9**

| | | | |
|---|---|---|---|
| 2196 | A321 $1 #a-h. + #2194 | | 12.00 12.00 |
| 2197 | A321 $1 #a-h. + #2195 | | 12.00 12.00 |

**Souvenir Sheet**

| | | | |
|---|---|---|---|
| 2198 | A321 $6 multicolored | | 5.25 5.25 |

**Litho. & Embossed — Perf. 9**

| | | | |
|---|---|---|---|
| 2199 | A322 $30 gold & multi | | |

Nos. 2194-2195 were issued in sheets containing 5 #2194, 4 #2195.

## ST. VINCENT

Disney Christmas — A331

Antique Disney toys: 1c, Lionel Santa car. 2c, Mickey Mouse "Choo Choo." 3c, Minnie Mouse pram. 5c, Mickey Mouse circus pull toy. 10c, Mickey, Pluto wind-up cart. 25c, Mickey Mouse mechanical motorcycle. $3, Lionel's Mickey Mouse handcar. $5, Casey Jr. Disneyland Express.
No. 2239, Silver Link, Mickey the Stoker. No. 2240, Mickey, Streamliner Engine.

**1995, Dec. 7**     **Perf. 13½x14**
2231-2238 A331 Set of 8   14.50 14.50
**Souvenir Sheets**
2239-2240 A331 $6 each   7.25 7.25

Crotons
A331a

Codiaeum variegatum: 10c, Mons florin. 15c, Prince of Monaco. 20c, Craigii. 40c, Gloriosum. 50c, Ebureum. vert. 60c, Volutum ramshorn. 70c, Narrenii. vert. 90c, Undutatum. vert. $1. Caribbean. $1.10, Gloriosa. $1.40, Katonii. $2, Appleleaf. $5, Tapestry. $10, Cornutum. $20, Puntatum aureum.

**1996, Jan. 1**   **Litho.**   **Perf. 14**

| | | | |
|---|---|---|---|
| 2240A | A331a | 10c multi | .20 .20 |
| 2240B | A331a | 15c multi | .20 .20 |
| 2240C | A331a | 20c multi | .20 .20 |
| 2240D | A331a | 40c multi | .30 .30 |
| 2240E | A331a | 50c multi | .40 .40 |
| 2240F | A331a | 60c multi | .45 .45 |
| 2240G | A331a | 70c multi | .55 .55 |
| 2240H | A331a | 90c multi | .70 .70 |
| 2240I | A331a | $1 multi | .75 .75 |
| 2240J | A331a | $1.10 multi | .85 .85 |
| 2240K | A331a | $1.40 multi | 1.00 1.00 |
| 2240L | A331a | $2 multi | 1.50 1.50 |
| 2240M | A331a | $5 multi | 3.75 3.75 |
| 2240N | A331a | $10 multi | 7.50 7.50 |
| 2240O | A331a | $20 multi | 15.00 15.00 |
| Nos. 2240A-2240O (15) | | | 33.35 33.35 |

New Year 1996 (Year of the Rat) — A332

Stylized rats, Chinese inscriptions within checkered squares, #2241-2242: a, lilac & multi. b, orange & multi. c, pink & multi. $2, orange, green & black.

**1996, Jan. 2**   **Litho.**   **Perf. 14½**
2241 A332 75c Strip of 3, #a.-c.   1.75 1.75
**Miniature Sheet**
2242 A332 $1 Sheet of 3, #a.-c.   2.25 2.25
**Souvenir Sheet**
2243 A332 $2 multicolored   1.50 1.50

No. 2241 was issued in sheets of 9 stamps.

Miniature Sheets of 9

A333

---

h, Jean-Paul Sartre, literature, 1964. i, Aleksandr Solzhenitsyn, literature, 1970. j, Hermann Staudinger, chemistry, 1953. k, Igor Tamm, physics, 1958. l, Samuel Beckett, literature, 1969.
No. 2221, Adolf Windaus, chemistry, 1928. No. 2222, Hideki Yukawa, physics, 1949. No. 2223, Bertha von Suttner, peace, 1905. No. 2224, Karl Landsteiner, medicine, 1930.

**1995, Oct. 2**   **Litho.**   **Perf. 14**
2217-2220 A327 $1 #a.-i., each   11.50 11.50
**Souvenir Sheets**
2221-2224 A327 $6 each   6.50 6.50

Classic Cars A328

No. 2225: a, 1931 Duesenberg Model J. b, 1913. Sleeve-valve Minerva. c, 1933 Delage D.8. SS. d, 1931-32 Bugatti Royale, Coupe De Ville chassis 41111. e, 1926 Rolls Royce 7668CC Phantom 1 Landauette. f, 1927 Mercedes Benz S26/120/180 PS.
$5, Hispano-Suiza Type H6B tulipwood-bodied roadster by Neuport.

**1995, Oct. 3**
2225 A328 $1.50 Sheet of 6, #a.-f.   7.75 7.75
**Souvenir Sheet**
2226 A328 $5 multicolored   7.00 7.00

Singapore '95 (#2225). No. 2226 contains one 85x28mm stamp.

Miniature Sheet

Sierra Club, Cent. — A329

#2227: a, Gray wolf in front of trees. b, Gray wolf pup. c, Gray wolf up close. d, Hawaiian goose. e, Two Hawaiian geese. f, Jaguar. g, Lion-tailed macaque. h, Sand cat. i, Three sand cats.
#2228, horiz.: a, Orangutan swinging from tree. b, Orangutan facing forward. c, Orangutan close up. d, Jaguar on rock. e, Jaguar up close. f, Sand cats. g, Hawaiian goose. h, Three lion-tailed macaques. i, Lion-tailed macaque.

**1995, Dec. 1**   **Litho.**   **Perf. 14**
2227 A329 $1 Sheet of 9, #a.-i.   9.00 9.00
2228 A329 $1 Sheet of 9, #a.-i.   9.00 9.00

Miniature Sheet

Natural Wonders of the World A330

No. 2229: a, Nile River. b, Yangtze River. c, Niagara Falls. d, Victoria Falls. e, Grand Canyon, US. f, Sahara Desert, Algeria. g, Kilimanjaro, Tanzania. h, Amazon river. No. 2230, Haleakala Crater, Hawaii.

**1995, Dec. 1**
2229 A330 $1.10 Sheet of 8, #a.-h.   9.50 9.50
**Souvenir Sheet**
2230 A330 $6 multicolored   6.75 6.75

---

2206-2210 A325 $1 #a.-i., each   8.00 8.00
**Souvenir Sheets**
2211-2214 A325 $6 each   6.50 6.50

No. 2208 has serifs in lettering. No. 2209 has pink lettering.

Elvis Presley — A325a

$30, Marilyn Monroe. Illustration reduced.

**1995**   **Litho. & Embossed**   **Perf. 9**
2214A A325a $20 gold & multi   24.00 24.00
2214B A325a $30 gold & multi   36.00 36.00

Miniature Sheet

Passenger Trains — A326

Designs: No. 2215a, German Federal Railway E14-03, high speed four car electric. b, Tres Grande Vitesse (TGV), Franco. c, British Railways Class 87 electric. d, Beijing locomotive, Railways of the People's Republic of China. e, American Amtrak turbo. f, Swedish State Railways class RC4 electric.
$6, Eurostar.

**1995, Oct. 3**   **Perf. 14**
2215 A326 $1.50 Sheet of 6, #a.-f.   7.75 7.75
**Souvenir Sheet**
2216 A326 $6 multicolored   8.50 8.50

No. 2216 contains one 85x28mm stamp.

Miniature Sheets of 12

Nobel Prize Fund Established, Cent. — A327

Recipients: No. 2217a, Heinrich Böll, literature, 1972. b, Walther Bothe, physics, 1954. c, Richard Kuhn, chemistry, 1938. d, Hermann Hesse, literature, 1946. e, Knut Hamsun, literature, 1920. f, Konrad Lorenz, medicine, 1973. g, Thomas Mann, literature, 1929. h, Fridtjof Nansen, peace, 1922. i, Fritz Pregl, chemistry, 1923. j, Christian Lange, peace, 1921. k, Otto Loewi, medicine, 1936. l, Erwin Schrödinger, physics, 1933.
No. 2218: a, Giosue Carducci, literature, 1906. b, Wladyslaw Reymont, literature, 1924. c, Ivan Bunin, literature, 1933. d, Pavel Cherenkov, physics, 1958. e, Ivan Pavlov, medicine, 1904. f, Pyotr Kapitza, physics, 1978. g, Lev Landau, physics, 1962. h, Daniel Bovet, medicine, 1957. i, Henryk Sienkiewicz, literature, 1905. j, Aleksandr Prokhorov, physics, 1964. k, Julius Wagner von Jauregg, medicine, 1927. l, Grazia Deledda, literature, 1926.
No. 2219: a, Bjornstjerne Bjornson, literature, 1903. b, Frank Kellogg, peace, 1929. c, Gustav Hertz, physics, 1925. d, Har Gobind Khorana, medicine, 1968. e, Kenichi Fukui, chemistry, 1981. f, Henry Kissinger, peace, 1973. g, Martin Luther King, Jr., peace, 1964. h, Odd Hassel, chemistry, 1969. i, Polykarp Kusch, physics, 1955. j, Ragnar Frisch, economics, 1969. k, Willis E. Lamb, Jr., physics, 1955. l, Sigrid Undset, literature, 1928.
No. 2220: a, Robert Barany, medicine, 1914. b, Ernest Walton, physics, 1951. c, Alfred Fried, peace, 1911. d, James Franck, medicine, 1956. f, Yasunari Kawabata, literature, 1968. g, Wolfgang Pauli, physics, 1945.

---

Miniature Sheets of 6 or 8

1996 Summer Olympics, Atlanta — A323

No. 2200: a, Jean Shiley, US. b, Ruth Fuchs, Germany. c, Alessandro Andrei, Italy. d, Dorando Pietri, Italy. e, Heide Rosendahl, Germany. f, Mitsuoki Watanabe, Japan. g, Yasuhiro Yamashita, Japan. h, Dick Fosbury, US.
No. 2201: a, Long jump. b, Hurdles. c, Sprint. d, Marathon. e, Gymnastics. f, Rowing. No. 2202, Magic Johnson. No. 2203, Swimmer's hand, horiz.

**1995, Aug. 24**   **Litho.**   **Perf. 14**
2200 A323 $1 #a.-h.   7.00 7.00
2201 A323 $2 #a.-f.   10.50 10.50
**Souvenir Sheets**
2202-2203 A323 $5 each   6.00 6.00

Miniature Sheet

Stars of American League Baseball A324

#2204, Different portraits of: a, e, i, Frank Thomas, Chicago White Sox. b, f-g, Cal Ripken, Jr., Baltimore Orioles. c-d, h, Ken Griffey, Jr., Seattle Mariners.
No. 2204J, Ken Griffey, Jr. No. 2204K, Cal Ripken, Jr., Frank Thomas.

**1995, Sept. 6**   **Litho.**   **Perf. 14**
2204 A324 Sheet of 9, #a.-i.   8.50 8.50

A324a

**Litho. & Embossed**   **Perf. 9**
2204J-2204L A324a $30 Set of 3, gold & multi

Miniature Sheets of 6 or 9

Entertainers A325

#2205-2206: Portraits of Elvis Presley. #2207: Portraits of John Lennon. #2208-2210: Portraits of Marilyn Monroe. #2211, Presley, diff. #2212, Lennon, diff. #2213, Monroe, in black. #2214, Monroe, in red.

**1995, Sept. 18**   **Perf. 13½x14**
2205 A325 $1 #a.-f.   7.00 7.00

## Star Trek, 30th Anniv. — A333a

St. Vincent & The Grenadines $30

#2244: a. Spock. b. Kirk. c. Uhura. d. Sulu. e. Starship Enterprise. f. Kirk, Spock. g. Scott. h. Kirk, McCoy, Spock. i. Chekov.
#2245: a. Spock holding up hand in Vulcan greeting. b. Kirk, Spock in "A Piece of the Action." c. Captain Kirk. d. Kirk, "The Trouble with Tribbles." e. Crew, "City on the Edge of Forever." f. Uhura, Sulu. "Mirror, Mirror." g. exterior. i. Khan, "Space Seed." h. Building Romulans. "Balance of Terror." h. Building
$30, Spock, Kirk, McCoy, Scott, Starship Enterprise.
$6, Spock, Uhura

**1996, Jan. 4**

| | | | | |
|---|---|---|---|---|
| 2246 A333 $6 multicolored | | | | |

**Litho. & Embossed    Perf. 9**

2246A A333a $6 multicolored

**Miniature Sheets**

**Perf. 13½x14**

| | | | |
|---|---|---|---|
| 2246 A333a $30 gold & multi | | 4.50 | 4.50 |
| 2244-2245 A333 $1 #a-i, each | | 7.50 | 7.50 |

Illustration A333a reduced.

---

## Disney Characters in Various Occupations — A334

St. Vincent and the Grenadines
10¢  STAMP DEALER

Merchants: No. 2247: a. Stamp dealer. b. supermarket. c. Car salesman. d. Florist. e. Fast food carhop. f. Street vendor. g. Gift shop. h. Hobby shop owner. i. Bakery.
Transport workers: No. 2248: a. Delivery service. b. Truck driver. c. Airplane crew. d. Railroad men. e. Bus driver. f. Tour guide. g. Messenger service. h. Trolley conductor. i. Air traffic controller.
Law & order: No. 2249: a. Postal inspector. b. Traffic cop. c. Private detectives. d. Highway patrol. e. Justice of the peace. f. Security guard. g. Judge and lawyer. h. Sheriff. i. Court stenographer.
School of education: No. 2250: a. Classroom teacher. b. Nursery school teacher. c. Band teacher. d. Electronic teacher. e. School psychologist. f. School principal. g. Professor. h. Graduate.
Scientists: No. 2251: a. Paleontologist. b. Archaeologist. c. Inventor. d. Astronaut. e. Chemist. f. Engineer. g. Computer graphics. h. Astronomer. i. Zoologist.
Sports professionals: No. 2252: a. Basketball player. b. Referee. c. Track coach. d. Ice skater. e. Golfer and caddy. f. Sportscaster. g. Tennis champs. h. Football coach. i. Race car driver.
Sea & shore workers: No. 2253: a. Ship builders. b. Fisherman. c. Pearl diver. d. Underwater photographer. e. Bait & tackle shop owner. f. Bathing suit covergirls. g. Marine life painter. h. Lifeguard. i. Lighthouse keeper.
No. 2254, Donald in ice cream parlor. No. 2255, Goofy as an oceanographer. No. 2256, Grandma, Grandpa, Daisy Duck as jury. vert. No. 2257, Donald as deep sea treasure hunter. vert. No. 2258, Minnie as librarian. vert. No. 2259, Mickey, ducks, as cheerleaders. vert. No. 2260, Mickey as seaman. vert.

**1996, Jan. 8    Perf. 14x13½, 13½x14**

**Souvenir Sheet**

**Sheets of 9 or 8**

| | | | |
|---|---|---|---|
| 2247 A334 10c #a-i. | | 1.25 | 1.25 |
| 2248 A334 10c #a-i. | | 6.00 | 6.00 |
| 2249 A334 75c #a-i. | | 8.50 | 8.50 |
| 2250 A334 90c #a-i. | | 10.50 | 10.50 |
| 2251 A334 95c #a-i. | | 11.00 | 11.00 |
| 2252 A334 $1.10 #a-h. | | 11.50 | 11.50 |
| 2253 A334 $1.20 #a-i. | | 14.00 | 14.00 |

**1996, Jan. 8**

**Souvenir Sheets**

| | | | |
|---|---|---|---|
| 2254-2260 A334 $6 each | | 4.50 | 4.50 |

#2248-2253 exist in sheets of 7 or 8 10c stamps + label. The label replaced the following stamps: #2248e, 2249e, 2250e, 2251e, vert.

---

**ST. VINCENT**

No. 2268E, Jordan as basketball player. Illustration reduced.

2252d, 2253e, 2268e. The sheets had limited release on Dec. 3, 1996.

**Miniature Sheets**

Moses Striking Rock Detail   Bucksnort
St. Vincent & The Grenadines  75¢

## Paintings from Metropolitan Museum of Art — A335

Details or entire paintings, artist: No. 2261a, Moses Striking Rock, by Bloemaert. b. The Last Communion, by Caravaggio. d. Francesco Sassetti y Son, by Ghirlandaio. e. Pepito Costa y Bunells, by Goya. f. Saint Andrew, by Martini. g. The Nativity, by a follower of van der Weyden. h. Christ Blessing, by Solario.
By Cézanne: No. 2262a, Madame Cézanne. b. Still Life with Apples and Pears. c. Man in a Straw Hat. d. Still Life with a Ginger Jar. e. Madame Cézanne in a Red Dress. f. Still Life, diff. i. The Card Players.
No. 2263a, Bullfight, by Goya. b. Portrait of a Man, by Frans Hals. c. Mother and Son, by Sully. d. Portrait of a Young Man, by Menling. e. Matilde Stoughton de Jaudenes, by Stuart. f. Josef de Jaudenes y Nebot, by Stuart. g. Mont Sainte-Victoire, by Cézanne. h. Gardanne, by Cézanne. i. The Empress Eugenie, by Winterhalter.
No. 2264a, The Dissolute Household, by Steen. b. Portrait of Gerard de Lairesse, by Rembrandt. c. Juan de Pareja, by Velázquez. d. Curiosity, by G. Ter Borch. e. The Companions of Rinaldo, by Poussin. f. Don Gaspar de Guzman, by Velázquez. g. Merry Company on a Terrace, by Steen. h. Pilate Washing Hands, by Rembrandt. i. Portrait of a Man, by Van Dyck.
j. In red jersey. k. In white jersey.
No. 2265, Hagar in Wilderness, by Corot. Courbet. No. 2266, Young Ladies from the Village, by Courbet. No. 2267, Two Young Peasant Women, by Pissarro. No. 2268, Allegory of the Planets and Continents, by Tiepolo.

**1996, Feb. 1    Litho.    Perf. 14**

**Sheets of 8 or 9**

| | | | |
|---|---|---|---|
| 2261 A335 75c #a-h.+label | | 4.50 | 4.50 |
| 2262 A335 90c #a-i. | | 6.00 | 6.00 |
| 2263 A335 $1 #a-i. | | 6.75 | 6.75 |
| 2264 A335 $1.10 #a-i. | | 7.50 | 7.50 |

**Souvenir Sheets**

| | | | |
|---|---|---|---|
| 2265-2268 A335 $6 each | | 4.50 | 4.50 |

Nos. 2265-2268 each contain one 8x53mm stamp.

---

## Michael Jordan, Basketball Player — A335a

St. Vincent The Grenadines  $2.00

**1996, Apr. 17    Litho.**

**Perf. 14, Imperf. (#2268Ac)**

| | | | | |
|---|---|---|---|---|
| 2268A A335a $6 | | | | |
| #c. A335a $2 shown | | 29.00 | 29.00 | |
| c. A335a $6 Portrait up close | | 4.50 | 4.50 | |

No. 2268Ac is 68x100mm and has simulated perforations.

## Michael Jordan, Basketball Player, Baseball Player — A335b

St. Vincent & The Grenadines  $30

**Litho. & Embossed    Perf. 9**

**1996, Apr. 17**

| | |
|---|---|
| 2268D A335b $30 gold & multi | |
| 2268E A335b $30 gold & multi | |

---

## Joe Montana, Football Player — A335c

St. Vincent The Grenadines  $2.00

**1996, Apr. 17    Litho.**

**Perf. 14, Imperf. (#2268Fh)**

**Sheet of 17, 16 #g, 1**

| | | | |
|---|---|---|---|
| 2268F A335c $2 shown | | 29.00 | 29.00 |
| #h A335c $6 | | 1.50 | 1.50 |
| h. A335c $6 In action | | 4.50 | 4.50 |

No. 2268Fh is 68x100mm and has simulated perforations.

## Joe Montana, Football Player — A335d

**1996, Apr. 17    Sheet of 2**

2268I A335d $15 #j-k. gold & multi

---

## Lou Gehrig and Cal Ripken, Jr., Baseball Ironmen — A336

**1995**

**Litho. & Embossed    Perf. 9**

2269 A336 $30 gold & multi

Illustration reduced.

---

## Star Wars Trilogy — A338

#2269: b. In Space Bar. c. Luke, Emperor. d. X-Wing Fighter. e. Star Destroyers. f. Cloud City. g. Speeders on Forest Moon.
Nos. 2270, 2273a, Darth Vader, "Star Wars," 1977. Nos. 2271, 2273c, Darth Vader, "The Empire Strikes Back," 1980. Nos. 2272, 2273b, Yoda, "Return of the Jedi," 1983. Nos. 2274, Darth Vader, "Star Wars," 1977. troopers. No. 2275, Yoda, "Return of the Jedi," 1983. Storm No. 2276, Storm Trooper, "The Empire Strikes Back," 1980.

**1996, Mar. 19    Litho.    Perf. 14**

2269A A336a #b-9.

**Self-Adhesive**

**Serpentine Die Cut 6**

| | | | |
|---|---|---|---|
| 2270 A337 $1 sil & multi | | 3.00 | 3.00 |
| 2271 A337 $1 sil & multi | | 3.00 | 3.00 |
| 2272 A337 $1 sil & multi | | 3.00 | 3.00 |

**Serpentine Die Cut 9**

**Souvenir Sheet**

| | | | |
|---|---|---|---|
| 2273 A338 $2 Sheet of 3. #a-c. | | 9.50 | 9.50 |

**Litho. & Embossed    Perf. 9**

2274-2276 A337 $30 gold & multi

Nos. 2270-2272 were issued in sheets of 3 each arranged in alternating order.
Nos. 2274-2276 also exist in silver & multi. Issued: Nos. 2274-2276, 11/18/95; others 3/19/96.

---

St. Vincent and the Grenadines

A337

©1996 Lucasfilm Ltd.
St. Vincent The Grenadines  35¢

A336a

---

## Butterflies — A339

St. Vincent & The Grenadines  70¢

**1996, Apr. 15    Litho.    Perf. 14**

| | | | |
|---|---|---|---|
| 2277-2280 A339 Set of 4 | | 4.00 | 4.00 |
| 2281 A339 90c Sheet of 9, #a-i. | | 7.00 | 7.00 |

**Souvenir Sheets**

| | | | |
|---|---|---|---|
| 2282 A339 $5 multicolored | | 4.25 | 4.25 |
| 2283 A339 $6 multicolored | | 5.25 | 5.25 |

Designs: 70c, Anteos menippe. $1, Eunica alcmena tarricina. $1.10, Doxocopa lavinia. $2, Tithorea harmonia.
No. 2281: a. Papilio lycophron. b. Prepona buckleyana. c. Parides agavus. d. Papilio dymena. e. Euryades duponchelii. f. Diaethria cacicus. g. Orimba jansoni. h. Polystichtis siaka. i. Papilio machaonides.
$5, Adelpha abia. $6, Themone pais.

---

## Queen Elizabeth II, 70th Birthday — A340

$2  $2  $2

**1996, June 12    Litho.    Perf. 13½x14**

| | | | |
|---|---|---|---|
| 2284 A340 $2 Strip of 3, #a-c. | | 5.50 | 5.50 |

**Souvenir Sheet**

**Perf. 14x13½**

| | | | |
|---|---|---|---|
| 2285 A340 $6 multicolored | | 5.50 | 5.50 |

No. 2284 was issued in sheets of 9 stamps.
Designs: a. Portrait. b. In robes of Order of the Garter. c. Wearing red coat, hat. $6, Waving from balcony, horiz.

**Birds A341**

Designs: 60c, Coereba flaveola. $1, Myadestes genibarbis. $1.10, Tangara cucullata. $2, Eulampis jugularis.

No. 2290: a, Progne subis. b, Buteo platypterus. c, Phaethon lepturus. d, Himantopus himantopus. e, Sterna anaethetus. f, Euphonia musica. g, Arenaria interpres. h, Sericotes holosericeus. i, Nyctanassa violacea.

$5, Dendrocygna autumnalis, vert. $6, Amazona guildingii.

1996, July 11    **Perf. 14**
2286-2289 A341   Set of 4, vert.   4.00 4.00
    **Miniature Sheet**
2290 A341   $1 Sheet of 9, #a.-i.   7.50 7.50
    **Souvenir Sheets**
2291 A341   $5 multi, vert.   4.25 4.25
2292 A341   $6 multi, vert.   5.25 5.25

**Radio, Cent. A342**

Entertainers: 60c, Walter Winchell. $1, Fred Allen. $1.10, Hedda Hopper. $2, Eve Arden. $6, Major Bowes.

1996, July 11    **Perf. 13½x14**
2293-2296 A342   Set of 4   4.25 4.25
    **Souvenir Sheet**
2297 A042   $6 multicolored   6.00 6.00

**UNICEF, 50th Anniv. A343**

Designs: $1, Boy raising arm. $1.10, Children reading. $2, Girl, microscope. $5, Boy.

1996, July 11    **Litho. Perf. 12**
2298-2300 A343   Set of 3   3.25 3.25
    **Souvenir Sheet**
2301 A343   $5 multicolored   3.80 3.80

**Chinese Animated Films — A344**

Nos. 2302, 2304: Various characters from "Uproar in Heaven." Nos. 2303, 2305: Various characters from "Nezha Conquers the Dragon King."

1996, May 10    **Litho. Perf. 12**
    **Strips of 5**
2302-2303 A344   15c #a.-e., each   1.75 1.75
    **Souvenir Sheets**
2304-2305 A344   75c vert, each   2.00 2.00
Nos. 2302-2303 each were issued in a sheet of 10 stamps. CHINA '96, 9th Asian Intl. Philatelic Exhibition.

**Fish A348**

Designs: 70c, French angelfish. 90c, Redspotted hawkfish. $1.10, Montefiore Windmill. $2, Shrine of the Book. $5, Jerusalem of Gold.

No. 2333: a, Barred hamlet. b, Flamefish. c, Longsnout butterflyfish. d, Fairy basslet. e, Redtail parrotfish. f, Blackbar soldierfish. g, Threespot damselfish. h, Candy basslet. i, Spotfin hogfish.

No. 2334: a, Equetus lanceolatus. b, Acanthurus coeruleus. c, Lutjanus analis. d, Hippocampus hudsonius. e, Serranus annularis. f, Squatina dumerili. g, Muraena miliaris. h, Bolbometopon bicolor. i, Tritonium nodiferum.

$5, Queen triggerfish. $6, Blue marlin.

1996, Aug. 10    **Perf. 14**
2329-2332 A348   Set of 4   3.60 3.60
    **Sheets of 9**
2333-2334 A348   $1 #a.-i., each   6.75 6.75
    **Souvenir Sheets**
2335 A348   $5 multicolored   3.75 3.75
2336 A348   $6 multicolored   4.50 4.50

**1996 Summer Olympic Games, Atlanta A346**

20c, Maurice King, weight lifter, vert. 70c, Eswort Coombs, 400-meter relay, vert. No. 2312, 90c, Runners, Olympia. No. 2313, 90c, Pamenos Ballantyne, Benedict Ballantyne, runners, vert. $1, London landmarks, 1908 Olympics, Great Britain. No. 2315, $1.10, Rodney "Chang" Jack, soccer player, vert. No. 2316, $1.10, Dorando Pietri, marathon runner, London, 1908, vert. $2, Yachting.

Past winners, event: No. 2318, vert: a, Vitaly Shcherbo, gymnastics. b, Fu Mingxia, diving. c, Wilma Rudolph, track & field. d, Rafer Johnson, decathlon. e, Teofilo Stevenson, boxing. f, Babe Didrikson, track & field. g, Kyoko Iwasaki, swimming. h, Yoo Namkyu, table tennis. i, Michael Gross, swimming.

No. 2319: a, Chuhei Nambu, triple jump. b, Duncan McNaughton, high jump. c, Jack Kelly, single sculls. d, Larbie Joyner-Kersee, heptathlon. e, Tyrell Biggs, boxing. f, Larisa Latynina, gymnastics. g, Bob Garrett, discus. h, Paavo Nurmi, 5000-meters. i, Eric Lemming, javelin.

No. 2320: a, Yasuhiro Yamashita, judo. b, Peter Rono, 1500-meters. c, Aleksandr Kourlovitch, weight lifting. d, Juha Tiainen, hammer throw. e, Sergei Bubka, pole vault. f, Q. F. Newall, women's archery. g, Nadia Comaneci, gymnastics. h, Carl Lewis, long jump. i, Bob Mathias, decathlon.

Sporting events, vert.: No. 2321a, Women's archery. b, Gymnastics. c, Basketball. d, Soccer. e, Water polo. f, Baseball. g, Kayak. h, Fencing. i, Cycling.

No. 2322, Olympic Torch. No. 2323, Carl Lewis, runner, vert. No. 2324, Alexander Ditiatin, gymnastics, 1980. No. 2325, Hannes Kolehmainen, marathon runner.

1996, July 19
2310-2317 A346   Set of 8   7.00 7.00
    **Sheets of 9**
2318-2321 A346   $1 #a.-i., each   7.75 7.75
    **Souvenir Sheets**
2322-2325 A346   $5 each   3.75 3.75
St. Vincent Olympic Committee (#2310-2311, 2313, 2315).

Designs: 70c, French angelfish. 90c, Redspotted hawkfish. $1.10, Spiny puffer. $2, Gray triggerfish.

**Disney's "The Hunchback of Notre Dame" A347**

No. 2326: a, Quasimodo. b, Phoebus. c, Laverne, Hugo. d, Clopin. e, Frollo. f, Esmeralda. g, Victor. h, Djali.
No. 2327, Esmeralda, Quasimodo, horiz. No. 2328, Esmeralda, Phoebus, horiz.

1996, July 25    **Perf. 13½x14**
2326 A347   $1 Sheet of 8, #a.-h.   6.00 6.00
    **Souvenir Sheets**
    **Perf. 14X13½**
2327-2328 A347   $6 each   4.50 4.50

**Flowers A349**

70c, Beloperone guttata. $1, Epidendrum elongatum. $1.10, Pettrea volubilis. $2, Oncidium altrissimum.

No. 2341: a, Datura candida. b, Amherstia nobilis. c, Ipomoea acuminata. d, Bougainvillea glabra. e, Cassia alata. f, Cordia sebestena. g, Upuntia dilenii. h, Cryptostegia grandiflora. i, Rodriguezia lanceolata.

No. 2342, Acalypha hispida. No. 2343, Hibiscus rosa-sinensis.

1996, Aug. 15    Set of 4
2337-2340 A349     3.60 3.60
2341 A349   90c Sheet of 9, #a.-i.   6.00 6.00
    **Souvenir Sheets**
    **Perf. 14x13½**
2342 A349   $5 multicolored   3.75 3.75
2343 A349   $5 multicolored   3.75 3.75

**John F. Kennedy (1917-63) — A350**

No. 2344a: As young boy. b, Proclamation to send man to the moon. c, With Caroline, Jackie. d, Inauguration. e, Giving speech. f, On PT 109. g, With Jackie. h, Funeral procession, portrait. i, Guard, Eternal Flame.

No. 2345: a, With family on yacht. b, On yacht. c, On yacht holding sail. d, "JFK", portrait. e, Talking to astronauts in space. f, Younger picture in uniform. g, Portrait. h, Riding in motorcade. i, Giving speech, US flag.

No. 2346: a, Up close picture. b, In front of house at Hyannis Port. c, Memorial plaque, picture. d, Photograph among crowd. e, Portrait, flag. f, Rocket, portrait. g, Signing document. h, Martin Luther King, John F. Kennedy, Robert F. Kennedy. i, Painting looking down toward microphones.

No. 2347: a, Photograph with Jacqueline greeting people. b, Formal oval-shaped portrait. c, Photograph. d, With family. e, Space capsule, painting. f, Addressing UN. g, In rocking chair, h, Seated at desk, dignitaries. i, Holding telephone, map.

1996, Aug.    **Sheets of 9**
2344-2347 A350   $1 #a.-i., each   6.75 6.75

**Ships A351**

No. 2348: a, SS Doric, 1923, Great Britain. b, SS Nerissa, 1926, Great Britain. c, SS Howick Hall, 1910, Great Britain. d, SS Jervis Bay, 1922, Great Britain. e, SS Vauban, 1912, Great Britain. f, MV Orinoco, 1928, Germany. No. 2349: a, SS Lady Rodney, 1929, Canada. b, SS Empress of Russia, 1913, Canada. c, SS Providence, 1914, France. d, SS Reina Victori-Eugenia, 1913, Spain. e, SS Balmoral Castle, 1910, Great Britain. f, SS Tivives, 1911, US.
No. 2350, SS Imperator, 1913, Germany. No. 2351, SS Aquitania, 1914, Great Britain.

1996, Sept. 5    **Perf. 14**
    **Sheets of 6**
2348-2349 A351   $1.10 #a.-f., ea   5.00 5.00
    **Souvenir Sheets**
2350-2351 A351   $6 each   4.50 4.50

**Elvis Presley's 1st "Hit" Year, 40th Anniv. A352**

Various portraits.

1996, Sept. 8    **Perf. 13½x14**
2352 A352   $2 Sheet of 9, #a.-i.   9.00 9.00

**Richard Petty, NASCAR Driving Champion — A353**

a, 1990 Pontiac. b, Richard Petty. c, 1972 Plymouth. d, 1974 Dodge. e, 1970 Plymouth Superbird. $6, 1996 STP 25th Anniversary Pontiac.

1996, Sept. 26    **Perf. 14**
2353 A353   $2 Sheet of 4, #a.-d.   6.00 6.00
    **Souvenir Sheets**
2354 A353   $5 multicolored   3.75 3.75
2355 A353   $6 multicolored   4.50 4.50
No. 2354 contains one 85x28mm stamp.

**Sandy Koufax, Baseball Pitcher — A354**

A354a

No. 2356: a.-c., Various action shots.

Illustration A354a reduced.

**1996, Sept. 26**

**Perf. 14, Imperf. (#2356d)**

| | | | | |
|---|---|---|---|---|
| 2356 | | Sheet of 17 | | |
| a.-c. | A354 | $2 each | 28.50 | 28.50 |
| | A354 | $2 each | 1.50 | 1.50 |
| d. | A354 | $6 Portrait | 4.50 | 4.50 |

**Perf. 9**

**Litho. & Embossed**

| | | | |
|---|---|---|---|
| 2356E | A354a | $30 gold & multi | |

No. 2356 contains 6 #2356a, 5 each #2356b, 2356c and 1 #2356d. No. 2356d is 70x103mm and has simulated perforations.

Cadet Force, 60th Anniv. — A355

Insignia and: 70c, 2nd Lt. D.S. Cozier, founder. 90c, Cozier, first Lt cadets, 1936.

**1996, Oct. 23   Litho.   Perf. 14x13½**

| | | | | |
|---|---|---|---|---|
| 2357 | A355 | 70c multicolored | .55 | .55 |
| 2358 | A355 | 90c multicolored | .70 | .70 |

Christmas A356

Details or entire paintings: 70c, Virgin and Child, by Memling. 90c, St. Anthony, by Memling. $1, Madonna and Child, by Bouts. $1.10, Virgin and Child, by Lorenzo Lotto. $2, St. Roch, by Lotto. $5, St. Sebastian, by Lotto. No. 2365, Virgin and Child with St. Roch and St. Sebastian, by Lotto. No. 2366, Virgin and Child with a Donor, by Memling.

**1996, Nov. 14   Perf. 13½x14**

| | | | | |
|---|---|---|---|---|
| 2359-2364 | A356 | Set of 6 | 3.75 | 3.75 |
| 2365-2366 | A356 | $5 each | 8.00 | 8.00 |

Souvenir Sheets

Sylvester Stallone in Movie "Rocky IV" — A358

**1996   Litho.   Perf. 14**

| | | | | |
|---|---|---|---|---|
| 2373 | A358 | $2 Sheet of 3 | 4.50 | 4.50 |

 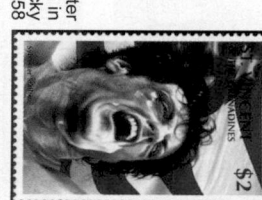 

A359

New Year 1997 (Year of the Ox) — A359a

Stylized oxen, Chinese inscriptions within checkered squares: Nos. 2374a, 2375a, pale orange, pale lilac & black. Nos. 2374b, 2375b, green, violet & black. Nos. 2374c, 2375c, tan, pink & black.

Illustration A359a reduced.

**1997, Jan. 2**

| | | | | |
|---|---|---|---|---|
| 2374 | A359 | 75c Strip of 3, #a.-c. | 1.70 | 1.70 |
| 2375 | A359 | $1 Sheet of 3, #a.-c. | 2.25 | 2.25 |

**Souvenir Sheet**

| | | | |
|---|---|---|---|
| 2376 | A359 | $2 orange, yellow & blk | |

**Perf. 9**

**Litho. & Embossed**

| | | | | |
|---|---|---|---|---|
| 2376A | A359a | $30 gold & multi | 1.50 | 1.50 |

No. 2374 was issued in sheets of 9 stamps.

Mickey Mantle (1931-95), baseball player. Illustration A361 reduced.

**1997, Jan. 23   Perf. 14, Imperf. (#2379b)**

| | | | | |
|---|---|---|---|---|
| 2379 | | Sheet of 17, 16 | | |
| a. | A361 | $2 shown | 28.50 | 28.50 |
| b. | A361 | $6 Portrait holding bat | 4.50 | 4.50 |

**Litho. & Embossed**

**Perf. 9**

| | | | |
|---|---|---|---|
| 2379C | A361a | $30 gold & multi | |

No. 2379b is 70x100mm.

Hong Kong Changeover — A364

Flags of Great Britain, Peoples' Republic of China and panoramic view of Hong Kong: Nos. 2382a-2382e, In daytime. Nos. 2382f-2382j, At night.

Market scene: No. 2383: a, Vendors, corner of building. b, People strolling. c, Man choosing items to purchase.

Buddhist religious ceremony: No. 2384: a, Fruit, incense pot, torch. b, Monk at fire. c, Flower.

Lantern ceremony: No. 2385: a, Boy, girl. b, Couple on bridge. c, Girls with lanterns.

Illustration A364a reduced.

**1997, Feb. 12   Perf. 14**

| | | | | |
|---|---|---|---|---|
| 2382 | A364 | 90c Sheet of 10, #a.-j. | 6.75 | 6.75 |

**Perf. 13   Sheets of 3**

| | | | | |
|---|---|---|---|---|
| 2383-2385 | A364 | $2 #a.-c., ea | 4.50 | 4.50 |

**Litho. & Embossed**

**Perf. 9**

| | | | |
|---|---|---|---|
| 2385D | A364a | $30 gold & multi | |

Hong Kong '97.

Nos. 2383-2385 each contain 3 35x26mm stamps.

Designs: Various scenes from film. No. 2370, Quasimodo. Phoebus. No. 2371, Esmeralda, Phoebus, Quasimodo, citizens, vert. No. 2372,

Disney's "The Hunchback of Notre Dame"—A357

**1996, Dec. 12   Litho.   Perf. 14x13½**

| | | | | |
|---|---|---|---|---|
| 2367 | A357 | 10c Single vert. | .45 | .45 |

**Perf. 13½x14**

| | | | | |
|---|---|---|---|---|
| 2368 | A357 | 30c Sheet of 9, #a.-i. | 2.00 | 2.00 |
| 2369 | A357 | $1 Sheet of 9, #a.-i. | 6.75 | 6.75 |

**Souvenir Sheets**

| | | | | |
|---|---|---|---|---|
| 2370-2372 | A357 | $6 each | 4.50 | 4.50 |

Star Trek Voyager A360

No. 2377: a, Lt Tuvak. b, Kes. c, Lt. Paris. d, The Doctor. e, Capt. Janeway. f, Lt. Torres. g, Neelix. h, Ens. Kim. i, Cdr. Chakotay.

**1997, Jan. 23   Litho.   Perf. 14**

| | | | | |
|---|---|---|---|---|
| 2377 | A360 | $2 Sheet of 9, #a.- | 13.50 | 13.50 |

**Souvenir Sheet**

| | | | | |
|---|---|---|---|---|
| 2378 | A360 | $2 multicolored | 4.50 | 4.50 |

No. 2378 contains one 29x47mm stamp.

Black Baseball Players: a, Frank Robinson. b, Satchel Paige. c, Billy Williams. d, Reggie Jackson. e, Roberto Clemente. f, Ernie Banks. g, Hank Aaron. h, Roy Campanella. i, Willie McCovey. j, Monte Irvin. k, Willie Stargell. l, Rod Carew. m, Ferguson Jenkins. n, Bob Gibson. o, Lou Brock. p, Joe Morgan. q, Jackie Robinson.

**1997, Jan. 23   Perf. 14x14½, Imperf. (#2380q)**

| | | | | |
|---|---|---|---|---|
| 2380 | | Sheet of 17 | 16.50 | 16.50 |
| a.-p. | A362 | $1 each | .75 | .75 |
| q. | A362 | $6 Portrait | 4.50 | 4.50 |

No. 2380q is 66x100mm and has simulated perforations.

Chongqing Dazu Stone Carving—A363

Souvenir Sheet

Illustration reduced.

**1996, May 20   Litho.   Perf. 12**

| | | | | |
|---|---|---|---|---|
| 2381 | A363 | $2 multicolored | 1.50 | 1.50 |

No. 2381 was not available until March 1997.

UNESCO, 50th Anniv. — A365

World Heritage Sites: 70c, Lord Howe Islands, Australia, vert. 90c, Uluru-Kata Tjuta Nat'l. Park, Australia, vert. $1, Kakadu Nat'l. Park, Australia, vert. $2, Te Wahipounamu, New Zealand, vert. $5, Tongariro Nat'l. Park, New Zealand.

Various sites in Greece, vert - #2392: a, Monastery of Rossanou, Meteora. b, f, h, Painted ceiling, interior, Mount Athos Monastery. c, Monastery Osios Varlaam, Meteora. d, Ruins in Athens. e, Museum of the Acropolis. g, Mount Athos.

Various sites in Japan, vert - #2393: a, Himeji-Jo. b, Temple Lake, Gardens, Kyoto. c, Kyoto. d, Buddhist Temple of Ninna-ji. e, View of city of Himeji-Jo. f, Forest, Shirakami-Sanchi. g, h, Forest, Yakushima.

Various sites in Italy, vert - #2394: a, City of San Gimignano, Italy. b, Cathedral of Santa Maria Asunta, Pisa, Italy. c, Cathedral of Santa Maria Fiore, Florence, Italy. d, Archaeological site, Valley of the Boyne, Ireland. e, Church of Saint-Savin-Sur-Gartempe, France. f, g, h, City of Bath, England.

No. 2395: a, Trinidad, Valley de los Ingenios, Cuba. b, City of Zacatecas, Mexico. c, Lima, Peru. d, Ruins of Monastery, Paraguay. e, Mayan Ruins, Copan, Honduras.

Various sites in China - No. 2396: a, Palace, Wudang Mountains, Hubei Province. b, Cave Sanctuaries, Mogao. c, House, Palace, Taklamakan. d, e, Great Wall.

Nos. 2397a-2397e: Various sites in Quedlinberg, Germany.

No. 2398, Wailing Wall, Jerusalem. No. 2400, Oasis, Dunbuang, China. No. 2401, Oasis, Dunbuang, China. No. 2402, Himeji-Jo, Japan. No. 2403, Great Wall, China. No. 2404, City of Venice, Italy.

No. 2473: a, Snow leopard. b, Polar bear. c, d, Isle Royale Natl. Park. e, f, Denali Natl. Park. g, h, i, Joshua Tree Natl. Park. No. 2474, vert: a, b, c, Mountain gorilla. d, e, Snow leopard. f, g, Polar bear. h, Denali Natl. Park. i, Isle Royale Nat. Park.

Sierra Club, Cent. A380

**1997, July 24** *Perf. 14¹⁄₂x14, 14x14¹⁄₂*
2467-2472 A379 Set of 6    3.30 3.30

Vincy Mas Carnival, 20th Anniv. A379

10c, Mardi Gras Band, "Cinemas." 20c, Queen of the Bands, J. Ballantyne. 50c, Queen of the Bands, "Conquistadore." 90c, Starlift Steel Bands, "Conquistadore." $2, Frankie McIntosh, musical arranger, vert.

**1997, Aug. 26** *Perf. 14x13¹⁄₂, 13¹⁄₂x14*    Litho.
2453-2458 A378   Set of 6    4.25 4.25
    **Sheets of 8 + Label**
2459-2462 A378 $1 multicolored, vert. No. 2466, Mario Kempes, Argentina, vert. No. 2466, Paulao, Angola.

    **Souvenir Sheets**
2463-2466 A378 $5 each    3.75 3.75

Players: 70c, Beckenbauer, W. Germany. 90c, Moore, England. $1, Lato, Poland. $1.10, Pele, Brazil. $2, Maier, W. Germany. $10, Eusebio, Portugal.

Scenes from England's victory, 1966: No. 2459: a, Stadium. b, c, d, e, f, h, Various action scenes. g, Coming from field, holding trophy. Action scenes from various finals: No 2460: a, c, Argentina. W. Germany, 1986. b, e, England. W. Germany, 1966. d, Italy, W. Germany, 1982. f, g, Argentina, Holland, 1978. h, W. Germany, Holland, 1974.
Players, vert.: No. 2461: a, Borgkamp, Holland. b, Seaman, England. c, Schmeichel, Denmark. d, Ince, England. e, Futre, Portugal. f, Ravanelli, Italy. g, Keane, Ireland. h, Gascoigne, England.
Action scenes from Argentina v Holland, 1978, vert.: No. 2462: a-h.
No. 2463, Ally McCoist, Scotland, vert. No. 2464, Salvatori Schillaci, Italy, vert. No. 2465, Mario Kempes, Argentina, vert. No. 2466, Paulao, Angola.

Mother Goose — A376

Scenes showing "Old Sultan:" No. 2444: a, With woman, man. b, On hillside. c, With wolf. No. 2446, Man. Old Sultan, girl.
Scenes from "The Cobbler and the Elves:" No. 2445: a, Cobbler. b, Elves. c, Cobbler holding elf. No. 2448, Elf.
No. 2448, Curly-Locks sewing.

**1997, June 3** *Perf. 13¹⁄₂x14*
2444-2445 A375 $2 #a.-c., each    4.50 4.50
    **Souvenir Sheets**
2446-2447 A375 $5 each    3.75 3.75
    *Perf. 14*
2448 A376 $5 multicolored    3.75 3.75

Numbers have been reserved for two additional souvenir sheets with this set.

Grimm's Fairy Tales A375

**1997, June 3**   Litho.
2442 A374 $2 multicolored    1.50 1.50
2443 A374 $2 multicolored    1.50 1.50

Designs: No. 2442, Chabad's Children of Chernobyl. No. 2443, UNESCO.

**1997, June 20**   Litho.
2451 A377 90c multicolored    .70 .70
2452 A377 $5 multicolored    3.75 3.75

Designs: 90c, Alphonso Theodore Roberts (1937-96), vert. $5, Arnos Vale Playing field.

Inaugural Cricket Test, Arnos Vale — A377

1998 World Cup Soccer Championships, France — A378

**1997, June 20**   *Perf. 13¹⁄₂x14, 14x13¹⁄₂*

Heinrich von Stephan (1831-97) A373

Portraits of Von Stephan and: a, Bicycle postman, India, 1800's. b, UPU emblem. c, Zebu-drawn post carriage, Indochina. $5, Post rider, Indochina.

**1997, June 3**
2440 A373 $2 Sheet of 3, #a.-c.    4.50 4.50
    **Souvenir Sheet**
2441 A373 $5 gray brown    3.75 3.75
    PACIFIC 97.

Chernobyl Disaster, 10th Anniv. A374

Children of Chernobyl — A decade later 1986-1996

Paintings by Hiroshige (1797-1858) A371

No. 2435: a, Furukawa River, Hiroo. b, Chiyogaike Pond, Meguro. c, New Fuji, Meguro. d, Moon-Viewing Point. c, Ushimachi, Takanawa. f, Original Fuji, Meguro. No. 2436, Gotenyama, Shinagawa. No. 2437, Shinagawa Susaki.

**1997, June 3**   *Perf. 13¹⁄₂x14*
2435 A371 $1.50 Sheet of 6, #a.- f.    6.75 6.75
    **Souvenir Sheets**
2436-2437 A371 $5 each    4.50 4.50

Paul Harris (1868-1947), Founder of Rotary Intl. — A372

$2, World Community Service, blankets from Japan donated to Thai children, Harris. $5, Rotary Intl. Pres. Luis Vincente Giay, US Pres. Jimmy Carter, Rotary award recipient.

**1997, June 3**
2438 A372 $2 multicolored    1.50 1.50
    **Souvenir Sheet**
2439 A372 $5 multicolored    3.75 3.75

Jackie Robinson (1919-72) A369

A369a

Illustration A369a reduced.

*Serpentine Die Cut 7*

**1997, Jan. 23**   Litho.
    **Self-Adhesive**
2432 A369 $1 multicolored    .75 .75
    *Litho. & Embossed*
    *Perf. 9*
2432A A369a $30 gold & multi   

No. 2432 was issued in sheets of 3 and was not available until June 1997.

Queen Elizabeth II, Prince Philip, 50th Wedding Anniv. A370

No. 2433: a, Queen. b, Royal arms. c, Portrait of Queen, Prince. d, Queen, Prince, crowd. e, Buckingham Palace. f, Prince. g, Queen seated in wedding gown, crown.

**1997, June 3**   Litho.    *Perf. 14*
2433 A370 $1.10 Sheet of 6, #a.- f.    5.00 5.00
    **Souvenir Sheet**
2434 A370 $5 multicolored    3.75 3.75

**1997, Mar. 24**   *Perf. 13¹⁄₂x14, 14x13¹⁄₂*    Litho.
    **Sheets of 8 + Label**
2386-2391 A365 $1.10 #a.-h., ea    8.00 8.00
2392-2394 A365 $1.10 #a.-h., ea    6.60 6.60
    **Sheets of 5 + Label**
2395-2397 A365 $1.50 #a.-e., ea    5.75 5.75
    **Souvenir Sheets**
2398-2404 A365 $5 each    3.75 3.75

Telecommunications in St. Vincent, 125th Anniv. — A366

Designs: 5c, Microwave radio relay tower, Dorsetshire Hill. 10c, Cable & wireless headquarters, Kingstown. 90c, Blackburnian warbler. 20c, Microwave relay tower, vert. 35c, Cable & wireless complex, Arnos Vale. 50c, Cable & wireless tower, Mt. St. Andrew. 70c, Cable ship. 90c, Eastern telecommunication network, 1872. $1.10, Telegraph map of world, 1876.

No. 2420: 5c, Microwave radio relay tower, Dorsetshire Hill. 10c, Cable & wireless headquarters. 90c, Blackburnian warbler. 20c, Microwave relay tower, vert. 35c, Cable & wireless complex, Arnos Vale. 50c, Cable & wireless tower, Mt. St. Andrew. 70c, Cable ship. 90c, Eastern telecommunication network, 1872. $1.10, Telegraph map of world, 1876.

**1997, Apr. 3**   *Perf. 14x14¹⁄₂, 14¹⁄₂x14*    Litho.
2405-2412 A366   Set of 8    3.00 3.00

Birds of the World — A367

Water Birds — A368

Designs: 90c, Swallow-tailed gull. 70c, Belted kingfisher. 90c, Blackburnian warbler. $1.10, Blue tit. $2, Chaffinch. $5, Ruddy turnstone.
No. 2419: a, Blue grosbeak. b, Bananaquit. c, Cedar waxwing. d, Ovenbird. e, Hooded warbler. f, Flicker.
No. 2420: a, Song thrush. b, Robin. c, Blackbird. d, Great spotted woodpecker. e, Wren. f, Kingfisher.
No. 2421, St. Vincent parrot. No. 2422, Tawny owl.

**1997, Apr. 7**   *Perf. 14*
2413-2418 A367   Set of 6    7.75 7.75
2419 A367 $1 Sheet of 6, #a.-f.    4.50 4.50
2420 A367 $2 Sheet of 6, #a.-f.    9.00 9.00
    **Souvenir Sheets**
2421-2422 A367 $5 each    3.75 3.75

**1997, Apr. 7**   *Perf. 15*

Designs: 70c, Mandarin duck, horiz. 90c, Green heron, horiz. $1, Drake ringed teal, horiz. $1.10, Blue-footed booby, horiz. $2, Australian jacana. $5, Reddish egret.
No. 2429: a, Crested auklet. b, Adelie penguins. c, Pigeon guillemot. d, Adelie penguins. e, Rockhopper penguin. f, Emperor penguin.
No. 2430, Snowy egrets, horiz. No. 2431, Flamingos, horiz.

2423-2428 A368   Set of 6    8.00 8.00
2429 A368 $1.10 Sheet of 6, #a.- f.    5.00 5.00
    **Souvenir Sheet**
2430-2431 A368 $5 each    3.75 3.75

ST. VINCENT

No. 2475, vert: a, b, c, Sifaka. d, e, Peregrine falcon. f, Galapagos tortoise. g, h, African Rain Forest. i, China's Yellow Mountains.

No. 2476: a, b, c, Galapagos tortoise. d, e, f, Peregrine falcon. g, h, African Rain Forest. i, China's Yellow Mountains.

No. 2477: a, Mountain lion. b, c, Siberian tiger. d, Red wolf. e, Black bear. f, i, Wolong Natl. Reserve. g, h, Belize Rain Forest.

No. 2478, vert: a, Siberian tiger. b, Mountain lion. d, e, Black bear. f, g, Red wolf. h, Belize Rain Forest. i, Wolong Natl. Reserve.

No. 2479, vert: a, b, c, Indri. d, e, Gopher tortoise. f, g, Black-footed ferret. h, Haleakala Natl. Park. i, Grand Teton Natl. Park.

No. 2480: a, Black-footed ferret. b, Gopher tortoise. c, d, Grand Teton Natl. Park. e, f, Haleakala Natl. Park. g, h, i, Madagascar Rain Forest.

Scenes in Olympic Natl. Park: No. 2481, Lake, trees. No. 2482, Mountain summit. No. 2483, Snow-topped mountains.

**1997, Sept. 18**

| | | | **Perf. 14** |
|---|---|---|---|
| 2473 | A380 | 20c | 1.40 1.40 |
| 2474 | A380 | 40c | 2.75 2.75 |
| 2475 | A380 | 50c | 3.40 3.40 |
| 2476 | A380 | 60c | 4.00 4.00 |
| 2477 | A380 | 70c | 4.75 4.75 |
| 2478 | A380 | 90c | 6.00 6.00 |
| 2479 | A380 | $1 | 6.75 6.75 |
| 2480 | A380 | $1.10 | 7.50 7.50 |

**Souvenir Sheets**

2481-2483 A380 $5 each 3.75 3.75

Various portraits: No. 2484, Dark brown. No. 2485, Dark blue. No. 2486, Black. No. 2487, Deng Xiaoping, Zhuo Lin, horiz.

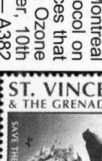

Deng Xiaoping (1904-97), Chinese Leader — A381

**1997, June 3** **Litho. Perf. 14**

**Sheets of 4**

2484-2486 A381 $2 #a.-d., each 6.00 6.00

**Souvenir Sheet**

2487 A381 $5 multicolored 3.75 3.75

Montreal Protocol on Substances that Deplete Ozone Layer, 10th Anniv. — A382

**1997, Sept. 16**

2488 A382 90c multicolored .70 .70

A383

A384

Orchids: 90c, Rhyncholaelia digbyana. $1, Laeliocattleya. $2, Rhyncholaelia. $2, Phalaenopsis.

---

No. 2493: a, Eulophia speciosa. b, Aerangis rhodosticta. c, Angraecum infundibularea. d, Calanthe sylvatica. e, Phalaenopsis mariae. f, Paphiopedilum insigne. g, Dendrobium nobile. h, Aerangis kotschyana. i, Cyrtorchis chailluana.

No. 2494, Brassavola nodosa. No. 2495, Sanguine broughtonia.

**1997, Sept. 18**

2494-2495 A383 $5 each contain one 51x38mm stamp.

**Souvenir Sheets**

2489-2492 A383 Set of 4 3.75 3.75
2493 A383 $1 Sheet of 9, #a.-i. 6.75 6.75

**1997**

Close-up portraits: No. 2496: a, Wearing tiara. b, Black dress. c, Blue dress. d, Denomination in black.

No. 2497: a, White collar. b, Sleeveless. c, Black dress, holding flowers. d, Blue collar, flowers.

No. 2498, Blue dress. No. 2499, White collar.

Diana, Princess of Wales (1961-97).

**Sheets of 4**

2496-2497 A384 $2 #a.-d., each 6.00 6.00

**Souvenir Sheets**

2498-2499 A384 $6 each 3.75 3.75

Sections of the ship: a, 1st funnel. b, 2nd, 3rd funnels. c, 4th funnel. d, Upper decks. e, Stern.

Sinking of RMS Titanic, 85th Anniv. — A385

**1997, Nov. 5** **Litho. Perf. 14**

2500 A385 $1 Sheet of 5, #a.-e. 3.75 3.75

1997 Inductions, Rock & Roll Hall of Fame, Cleveland, OH: $1, Exterior view. $1.50, Stylized guitar, "the house that rock built."

A386

**1997, Nov. 5**

2501 A386 $1 multicolored .75 .75
2502 A386 $1.50 multicolored 1.15 1.15

Nos. 2501-2502 were each issued in sheets of 8.

A387

"The Doors" album covers: 90c, Morrison Hotel, 1970. 95c, Waiting for the Sun, 1968. $1, L.A. Woman, 1971. $1.10, The Soft Parade, 1969. $1.20, Strange Days, 1967. $1.50, The Doors, 1967.

**1997, Nov. 5**

2503-2508 A387 Set of 6 5.00 5.00

Nos. 2503-2508 were each issued in sheets of 8.

---

Opera singers: No. 2509: a, Lily Pons (1904-76). b, Donizetti's "Lucia Di Lammermoor," Lily Pons. c, Bellini's "I Puritani," Maria Callas. d, Callas (1923-77). e, Beverly Sills (b. 1929). f, Puccini's "Daughter of the Regiment," Sills. g, Schoenberg's "Erwartung," Jessye Norman. h, Norman (b.1945).

No. 2510: a, Enrico Caruso (1873-1921). b, Verdi's "Rigoletto," Caruso. c, "The Seven Hills of Rome," Mario Lanza. d, Lanza (1921-59). e, Luciano Pavarotti (b. 1935). f, Donizetti's "Elixer of Love," Pavarotti. g, Puccini's "Tosca," Placido Domingo. h, Domingo (b. 1941).

No. 2511: a, Constantin Brancusi (1876-1957). b, "The New Born," Brancusi, 1920. c, "Four Elements," Alexander Calder, 1962. d, Calder (1898-1976). e, Isamu Noguchi (1904-88). f, "Dodge Fountain," Noguchi, 1975. g, "The Shuttlecock," Claes Oldenburg, 1994. h, Oldenburg (b. 1929).

**1997, Nov. 5**

**Sheets of 8**

2509-2511 A388 $1.10 #a.-h., ea 6.50 6.50

Size: Nos. 2509a-2509c, 2509f-2509g, 2510b-2510c, 2510f-2510g, 2511b-2511c, 2511f-2511g, 53x38mm.

20th Cent. Artists — A388

Christmas A389

Paintings (entire or details), or sculptures: 60c, The Sistine Madonna, by Raphael. 70c, Angel, by Edward Burne-Jones. 90c, Cupid, by Etienne-Maurice Flaconet. $1, Saint Michael, by Hubert Gerhard. $1.10, Apollo and the Horse, by Tiepolo. $2, Madonna in a Garland of Flowers, by Rubens and Bruegel the Elder.

No. 2518, The Sacrifice of Isaac, by Tiepolo, horiz. No. 2519, Madonna in a Garland of Flowers, by Rubens and Bruegel the Elder.

**1997, Nov. 26**

2512-2517 A389 Set of 6 6.25 6.25

**Souvenir Sheets**

2518-2519 A389 $5 each 3.75 3.75

Stylized tigers, Chinese inscriptions within checkered squares: No. 2520: a, light brown & pale olive. b, tan & gray. c, pink & pale violet.

New Year 1998 (Year of the Tiger) — A390

**1998, Jan. 5** **Perf. 14½**

2520 A390 $1 Sheet of 3, #a.-c. 2.25 2.25

**Souvenir Sheet**

2521 A390 $2 multicolored 1.50 1.50

---

Cooperative Foundation for Natl. Development Aid A391

Designs: 20c, Children going to school. 90c, People working in field. Credit Union office, vert. $1.10, Industry, ship at dock.

**1998, Jan. 5** **Perf. 13⅓**

2522-2524 A391 Set of 3 2.10 2.10

Jazz Entertainers — A392

Designs: a, King Oliver. b, Louis Armstrong. c, Sidney Bechet. d, Nick Larocca. e, Louis Prima. f, Buddy Bolden.

**1998, Feb. 2** **Perf. 14x13½**

2525 A392 $1 Sheet of 6, #a.-f. 4.50 4.50

1998 Winter Olympic Games, Nagano A393

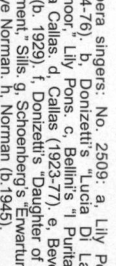

Designs, horiz: 70c, Ice hockey. 70c, Bobsled. $2, Pairs figure skating. $2, Medalists: No. 2530: a, Bjorn Daehlie. b, Gillis Grafstrom. c, Sonja Henie. d, Ingemar Stenmark. e, Christian Jagge. f, Tomas Gustafson. g, Johann Olav Koss. h, Thomas Wassberg.

Olympic rings in background: No. 2531: a, Downhill skier. b, Woman figure skater. c, Ski jumper. d, Speed skater. e, 4-Man bobsled team. f, Cross country skier.

Olympic flame in background: No. 2532: a, Downhill skier. b, Bobsled. c, Ski jumper. d, Slalom skier. e, Luge. f, Biathlon.

No. 2533, Slalom skiing. No. 2534, Hockey player, horiz.

**1998, Feb. 2** **Perf. 14**

2526-2529 A393 Set of 4 4.50 4.50
2530 A393 $1.10 Sheet of 8, #a.-h. 6.50 6.50

**Sheets of 6**

2531-2532 A393 $1.50 #a.-f., ea 6.75 6.75

**Souvenir Sheets**

2533-2534 A393 $5 each 3.75 3.75

Butterflies A395

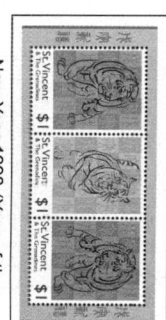

20c, Amarynthis meneria. 50c, Papilio polyxenes. 70c, Emesis fatima, vert. $1, Anartia amathea.

No. 2539, vert: a, Heliconius erato. b, Danaus plexippus. c, Papilio phorcas. d, Morpho peleides. e, Pandoriana pandora. f, Basilarchia astyanax. g, Vanessa cardui. h, Colobura dirce. i, Heraclides cresphontes.

No. 2540, Colias eurytheme. No. 2541, Everes comyntas.

**1998, Feb. 23** **Perf. 13½**

2535-2538 A395 Set of 4 1.80 1.80
2539 A395 $1 Sheet of 9, #a.-i. 6.75 6.75

**Souvenir Sheets**

2540-2541 A395 $6 each 4.50 4.50

ST. VINCENT

Endangered Fauna — A396

50c, Anegada rock iguana. 70c, Jamaican swallowtail. 90c, Blossom bat. $1, Solenodon. $1.10, Hawksbill turtle. $2, West Indian whistling duck.

No. 2548: a, Roseate spoonbill. b, Golden swallow. c, Short-snouted spinner dolphin. d, Queen conch. e, West Indian manatee. f, Loggerhead turtle.

No. 2549: a, Magnificent frigatebird. b, Humpback whale. c, Southern dagger-tail. d, St. Lucia whiptail. e, St. Lucia oriole. f, Green turtle.

No. 2550, St. Vincent parrot. No. 2551, Antiguan racer.

**1998, Feb. 23**     *Perf. 13*
2542-2547 A396   Set of 6    4.75   4.75

**Sheets of 6**
2548-2549 A396 $1.10 #a.-f., ea   5.00   5.00

**Souvenir Sheets**
2550-2551 A396 $6 each    3.75   3.75

Mushrooms
A397

Designs: 10c, Gymnopilus spectabilis. 20c, Entoloma lividum. 70c, Pholiota flammans. 90c, Panaeolus semiovatus. $1, Stropharia rugosoannulata. $1.10, Tricholoma sulphureum.

No. 2558: a, Amanita caesarea. b, Amanita muscaria. c, Amanita ovoidea. d, Amanita phalloides. e, Amanitopsis inaurata. f, Amanitopsis vaginata. g, Psalliota campestris. h, Russula virescens.

No. 2559: a, Coprinus picaceus. b, Stropharia umbonatescens. c, Hebeloma crustuliniforme, figure-of-eight butterfly. d, Cortinarius collinitus. e, Cortinarius violaceus, common dotted butterfly. f, Cortinarius armillatus. g, Inocloma aurantium. h, Russula virescens. i, Clitocybe infundibuliformis.

No. 2560, Hygrocybe conica. No. 2561, Amanita caesarea.

**1998, Mar. 23**     *Perf. 13½*
2552-2557 A397   Set of 6    3.00   3.00
2558 A397 $1 Sheet of 9, #a.-i.   6.75   6.75
2559 A397 $1.10 Sheet of 9, #a.-   7.50   7.50
   i.

**Souvenir Sheets**
2560-2561 A397 $6 each    4.50   4.50

Mickey Mouse, 70th Birthday — A398

Designs: 2c, Wake up, Mickey. 3c, Morning run. 4c, Getting ready. 5c, Eating breakfast. 10c, School "daze." 65c, Time out for play. $3, Volunteer worker. $4, A date with Minnie. $5, Ready for bed.

Weekly hi-lites from "Mickey Mouse Club," vert: a, The opening march. b, Monday, fun with music day. c, Tuesday, guest star day. d, Wednesday, anything can happen day. e, Thursday, circus day. f, Friday, talent round up day.

Mickey Mouse: No. 2572, Reading, vert. No. 2573, Playing piano, vert. No. 2574, Blowing trumpet. No. 2575, On the Internet, vert.

---

**1998, Mar. 23**   *Perf. 14x13½, 13½x14*   **Litho.**
2562-2570 A398   Set of 9    9.75   9.75
2571 A398 $1.10 Sheet of 6, #a.-   5.00   5.00
   f.

**Souvenir Sheets**
2572 A398 $5 multicolored   3.75   3.75
2573-2575 A398 $6 each    4.50   4.50

Winnie the Pooh — A399

Scenes from animated films: a, Pooh looking out window. b, Eeyore, Kanga, Roo. c, Pooh getting honey from tree. d, Rabbit, Pooh stuck in entrance to Rabbit's house. e, Christopher Robin pulling Pooh from Rabbit's house, Owl. f, Piglet sweeping leaves. g, Pooh sleeping. h, Eeyore. i, Tigger on top of Pooh.

No. 2577, Tigger, Pooh, Piglet.

**1998, Mar. 23**   *Perf. 14x13½*
2576 A399 $1 Sheet of 9, #a.-i.   6.75   6.75

**Souvenir Sheet**
2577 A399 $6 multicolored    4.50   4.50

Dogs — A400

Designs: 70c, Australian terrier. 90c, Bull mastiff. $1.10, Pomeranian. $2, Dandie dinmont terrier.

No. 2582, horiz: a, Tyrolean hunting dog. b, Papillon. c, Fox terriers. d, Bernese mountain dog. e, King Charles spaniel. f, German sheepdog.

No. 2583, horiz: a, Beagle. b, German shepherd. c, Pointer. d, Vizsla. e, Bulldog. f, Shetland sheepdogs.

No. 2584, Scottish terrier, wooden deck, grass. No. 2585, Scottish terrier, glass, trees.

**1998, Apr. 21**     *Perf. 14*
2578-2581 A400   Set of 4    3.50   3.50

**Sheets of 6**
2582-2583 A400 $1.10 #a.-f., ea   5.00   5.00

**Souvenir Sheets**
2584-2585 A400 $6 each    4.50   4.50

Trains
A401

10c, LMS Bahamas No. 5596. 20c, Ex-Mza 1400. 50c, Mallard. 70c, Monarch 0-4-4 OT.

**1998, May 19**     **Litho.**   *Perf. 13½*
2586-2588 A345   Set of 3    3.25   3.25

**Souvenir Sheet**
2589 A345 $5 multicolored   3.75   3.75

No. 2589 contains overprint "ISRAEL 98 - WORLD STAMP EXHIBITION / TEL-AVIV 13-21 MAY 1998" in sheet margin.

Nos. 2306-2309 Ovptd.

**1998, May 19**     **Litho.**   *Perf. 13½*
2578-2581 A400   Set of 4    3.50   3.50

---

90c, Big Chief. $1.10, Duchess of Rutland LMS No. 6228.

No. 2596: a, Hadrian Flyer. b, Highland Jones Goods No. 103. c, Blackmore Vale No. 34023. d, Wainwright SECR No. 27. e, Stephney Brighton Terrier. f, RENFE Freight train No. 040 2184. g, Calbourne No. 24. h, Clun Castle 1950.

No. 2597: a, Ancient Holmes J36 060. b, Patentee 2-2-2. c, Kingfisher. d, St. Pierre No. 23. e, SAR Class 19r-4-8-2. f, SAR 6J 4-6-0. g, Evening Star No. 92220. h, Old No. 1.

No. 2598, King George V No. 6000 BR. No. 2599, Caledonia.

**1998, June 2**     **Litho.**   *Perf. 14*
2590-2595 A401   Set of 6    2.60   2.60

**Sheets of 8**
2596-2597 A401 $1.10 #a.-h., ea   6.75   6.75

**Souvenir Sheets**
2598-2599 A401 $5 each    3.75   3.75

UNESCO
Intl. Year
of the
Ocean
A402

Marine life: 70c, Beluga whale. 90c, Atlantic manta. $1.10, Forceps butterfly fish, copperband butterfly fish, moorish idol. $2, Octopus.

No. 2604, vert: a, Harlequin wrasse. b, Blue sturgeon fish. c, Spotted trunkfish. d, Regal angelfish. e, Porcupine fish. f, Clownfish, damselfish. g, Lion fish. h, Moray eel. i, French angelfish.

No. 2605, vert: a, Lemonpeel angelfish. b, Narwhal. c, Panther grouper. d, Fur seal. e, Spiny boxfish. f, Loggerhead turtle. g, Opah. h, Clown triggerfish. i, Bighead searobin. No. 2606, Seahorse, vert. No. 2607, Australian sea dragon, vert.

**1998, July 1**
2600-2603 A402   Set of 4    3.50   3.50

**Sheets of 9**
2604-2605 A402 $1 #a.-i., each   6.75   6.75

**Souvenir Sheets**
2606-2607 A402 $5 each    3.75   3.75

Birds
A403

50c, Cock of the rock, vert. 60c, Quetzal, vert. 70c, Wood stork, vert. No. 2611, 90c, St. Vincent parrot, vert. No. 2612, 90c, Toucan. $1, Greater bird of paradise. $1.10, Sunbittern. $2, Green honeycreeper.

#2616, vert.: a, Racquet-tailed motmot. b, Red-billed quelea. c, Leadbeater's cockatoo. d, Scarlet macaw. e, Bare-throated bellbird. f, Tucaman Amazon parrot. g, Black-lored red tanager. h, Fig parrot. i, St. Vincent Amazon parrot. j, Peach-faced love birds. k, Blue fronted Amazon parrot. l, Yellow billed Amazon parrot.

No. 2617, Hyacinth macaw, vert. No. 2618, Blue-headed hummingbird, vert.

**1998, June 16**     **Litho.**   *Perf. 14*
2608-2615 A403   Set of 8    5.75   5.75

**Sheet of 12**
2616 A403 90c Sheet of 12, #a.-l.   8.25   8.25

**Souvenir Sheets**
2617-2618 A403 $5 each    3.75   3.75

No. 2611 has different style of lettering.

Diana, Princess of Wales (1961-97) — A404

#2619, Diana in orange jacket. #2620, Diana in blue blouse. Illustration reduced.

---

**Litho. & Embossed**   *Die Cut 7½*

**1998, Aug. 1**
2619 A404 $20 gold & multi
2620 A404 $20 gold & multi

CARICOM, 25th Anniv. — A405

**1998, July 4**   **Litho.**   *Perf. 13½*
2621 A405 $1 multicolored    .75   .75

Enzo Ferrari (1898-1988), Automobile Manufacturer — A406

Classic Ferraris — #2622: a, 365 GTS. b, Testarossa. c, 365 GT4 BB. $6, Dino 206 GT.

**1998, Sept. 15**   **Litho.**   *Perf. 14*
2622 A406 $2 Sheet of 3, #a.-c.   4.50   4.50

**Souvenir Sheet**
2623 A406 $6 multicolored    4.50   4.50

No. 2623 contains one 91x35mm stamp.

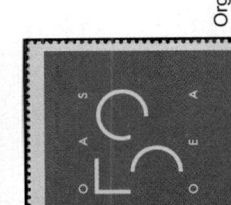

Paintings by Pablo Picasso (1881-1973) — A407

Designs: $1.10, Landscape, 1972. No. 2625, $2, The Kiss, 1969. No. 2626, $2, The Death of the Female Torero, 1933. $5, Flute Player, 1962, vert.

**1998, Sept. 15**   *Perf. 14½*
2624-2020 A407   Set of 3    1.00   4.00

**Souvenir Sheet**
2627 A407 $5 multicolored    3.75   3.75

Organization
of American
States, 50th
Anniv.
A408

**1998, Sept. 15**   **Litho.**   *Perf. 13½*
2628 A408 $1 multicolored   .75   .75

Diana, Princess
of Wales (1961-
97)
A409

**1998, Sept. 15**   *Perf. 14½*
2629 A409 $1.10 multicolored   .85   .85

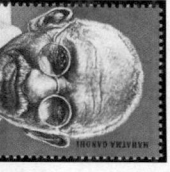

Mahatma Gandhi
(1869-1948)
A411

**Souvenir Sheet**
**Self-Adhesive**
**Serpentine Die Cut Perf. 11½**
**Size: 53x65mm**

2630 A409 $8 Diana, buildings 
No. 2629 was issued in sheets of 6. Soaking in water may affect the image of No. 2630.

$5, Seated at table with officials, horiz.

**1998, Sept. 15** **Perf. 14**
2631 A411 $1 shown .75 .75

**Souvenir Sheet**
2632 A411 $5 multicolored 3.75 3.75
No. 2631 was issued in sheets of 4.

Royal Air Force, 80th Anniv. A412

$2

No. 2633: a. AEW1 AWACS. b. BAe Eurofighter EF2000. c, d. BAe Hawk T1A.

No. 2634: a. Two Sepcat Jaguar GR1s. b. Panavia Tornado F3. c. Three BAe Harrier GR7s. d. Panavia Tornado F3 IDV.

No. 2635. Mosquito, Eurofighter, No. 2636, Hawk's head, hawk, biplane. No. 2637, Biplane, hawk in flight. No. 2638, Vulcan B2, Eurofighter.

**1998, Sept. 15** **Perf. 14**
2633-2634 A412 $2 #a-.d., each 6.00 6.00
**Sheets of 4**
2635-2638 A412 $6 each 4.50 4.50

1998 World Scout Jamboree, Chile — A413

**Souvenir Sheet**
2639 A413 $2 Sheet of 3, #a-.c. 4.50 4.50

No. 2639: a. Astronaut John Glenn receives Silver Buffalo award, 1965. b. Herb Shriner learns knot tying at 1960 Natl. Jamboree. c. "Ready to go" Boy Scouts break camp, 1940's. vert.

**1998, Sept. 15**
Ancient Order of Foresters Friendly Society, Court Morning Star 2298, Cent. — A414

The Royal Air Force 80. Anniversary

2640 A413 $5 multicolored 3.75 3.75

Designs: 10c. Bro. H.E.A. Daisley, PCR. 20c, R.N. Jack, PCR. 50c, Woman, man shaking hands, emblem. 70c, Symbol of recognition. 90c, Morning Star Court's headquarters.

**1998, Oct. 29** **Litho.** **Perf. 13½**
2641-2645 A414 Set of 5 1.75 1.75

---

RMS Titanic — A415

Illustration reduced.

**1998, Oct. 29** **Die Cut 7½**
2646 A415 $20 gold **Embossed**

Christmas
A418

Domestic cats: 20c, Bi-color longhair. 50c, Korat. 60c, Seal-point Siamese. 70c, Red self longhair. 90c, Black longhair. $1.10, Red tabby exotic shorthair.

No. 2653, Seal-point colorpoint. No. 2654, Tortoiseshell shorthair.

**1998, Dec.** **Litho.** **Perf. 14**
2647-2652 A418 Set of 6 3.00 3.00
**Souvenir Sheets**
2653-2654 A418 $5 each 3.75 3.75

ST. VINCENT & THE GRENADINES
$1.10
A419

No. 2655: a. Woman playing flute. b. Hildegard holding tablets. c. Woman playing violin. d, Pope Eugenius. e, Bingen, site of Hildegard's convent. f, Portrait.

**1998, Dec. 15** **Litho.** **Perf. 14**
2655 A419 $1.10 Sheet of 6, #a-f. 5.00 5.00

**Souvenir Sheet**
2656 A419 $5 multicolored 3.75 3.75
Hildegard von Bingen (1098?-1179).

A420

Stylized rabbits: a. Looking right. b. Looking forward. c, Looking left.

**1999, Jan. 4** **Litho.** **Perf. 14½**
2657 A420 $1 Sheet of 3, #a-.c. 2.25 2.25
**Souvenir Sheet**
2658 A420 $2 multicolored 1.50 1.50
New Year 1999 (Year of the Rabbit).

---

Queen Elizabeth II and Prince Philip, 50th Wedding Anniv. (in 1997) — A421

Illustration reduced.

**1999, Jan. 5** **Litho. & Embossed**
**Die Cut Perf. 6**
2659 A421 $20 gold & multi **Without Gum**

Disney Characters in Winter Sports A422

$1.10

Wearing checkered outfits — #2660: a. Minnie. b. Mickey. c, Goofy. d, Donald. e, Mickey (goggles on head). f, Daisy.

Wearing brightly-colored outfits — # 2661: a, Daisy. b, Mickey. c, Mickey, Goofy. d, Goofy. e, Minnie. f, Donald.

Wearing red, purple & yellow — #2002: a, Mickey. b, Goofy. c, Donald. d, Goofy, Mickey. e, Goofy (arms over head). f, Minnie.

No. 2663, Mickey in checkered outfit. No. 2664, Goofy eating ice cream cone, Mickey, horiz. No. 2665, Mickey in red, purple & yellow.

**1999, Jan. 21** **Litho.** **Perf. 13½x14**
2660-2662 A422 $1.10 #a-.f. **Sheets of 6**
each 5.00 5.00
**Souvenir Sheets**
2663-2665 A422 $5 each 3.75 3.75
Mickey Mouse, 70th anniv.

World Championship Wrestling A423

Designs: a. Hollywood Hogan. b, Sting. c, Randy Savage. d, the Giant. e, Kevin Nash. f, Bill Goldberg.

**1999, Jan. 25** **Litho.** **Perf. 13**
2666 A423 70c Sheet of 8, #a-.h. 4.25 4.25

Australia '99, World Stamp Expo A424

70¢

Prehistoric animals: 70c, Plateosaurus. 90c, Euoplocephalus. $1.10, Dilophosaurus. $1.40, Dilophosaurus.

No. 2671: a. Struthiomimus. b. Indricotherium. c, Giant moa. d. Deinonychus. e. Sabre tooth cat. f, Dawn horse. g, Peltacosaurus. h, Giant ground sloth. i, Wooly rhinoceros. j. Mosasaur. k, Mastodon. l, Syndoceras. m, Glyptodon. n, Archaeopteryx. o, Dimetrodon. p. Stegosaurus. q, Archaeopteryx. b, Pteranodon. c, Archaeopteryx. d, Dimetrodon. e, Iguanodon. f, Triceratops. g, Rhamphorhynchus. h, Pteranodon. i, Tyrannosaurus. j. Ichthyosaurus. k, Plesiosaurus. l, Herperonis, mammoth, vert.

**1999, Mar. 1** **Litho.** **Perf. 14**
2667-2670 A424 Set of 4 4.25 4.25
**Sheets of 12**
2671 A424 70c #a-.l. 6.50 6.50
As #2671, imperf.
2672 A424 90c #a-.l. 8.25 8.25
As #2672, imperf.

Designs: 10c, Acacia tree, elephant. 20c, Green turtle, coconut palm. 25c, Mangrove tree, white ibis. 50c, Tiger swallowtail, ironweed. 70c, Eastern box turtle, jack-in-the-pulpit, vert. 90c, Praying mantis, milkweed, vert. $1.10, Zebra finch, bottle brush, vert. $1.40, No. 2683, vert: a, Red tailed hawk, octillo. b, Morning dove, organ pipe cactus. c, Saguaro cactus. e, Octillo, puma. f, Organ pipe cactus, gray fox. g, Coyote, prickly pear cactus. h, Saguaro cactus, gila woodpecker. i, Collared lizard, barrel cactus. j. Cowblinder cactus, gila monster. k, Hedgehog cactus, roadrunner. l, Saguaro cactus, jack rabbit. No. 2684, vert: a, Strangler fig, basilisk lizard. b, Macaw, kapok trees. c, Cecropia tree, howler monkey. d, Cecropia tree, toucan. e, Arrow poison frog, bromiliad. f, Rattlesnake orchid, heliconius phyllis. g, Tree fern, bat eating hawk. h, Jaguar, tillandsia. i, Margay, sierra palm. j, Lesser bird of paradise, aristolchia. k, Parides, erythrina. l, Fer-de-lance, zebra plant.

No. 2685, Alligator, water lilies. No. 2686, Ruiolis, hummingbird.

**1999, Apr. 12** **Litho.** **Perf. 14**
2673-2674 A424 $5 each 3.75 3.75
imperf, each 3.75 3.75
**Souvenir Sheets**
2675-2682 A425 Set of 8 3.75 3.75
**Sheets of 8**
2683-2684 A425 70c #a-.l., each 6.50 6.50
**Souvenir Sheets**
2685-2686 A425 $5 each 3.75 3.75

$1.00

'N Sync, Musical Group—A427

Designs: 60c, Montgolfier balloon, 1783, vert. 70c, Lilienthal glider, 1894. 90c, Zeppelin, $1, Wright brothers, 1903.

No. 2691: a. DH-4 bomber. b, Sopwith Camel. c, Sopwith Dove. d, Jeannin Stahl Taube. e, Fokker DR-1 triplane. f, Albatros Diva. g, Sopwith Pup. h, Spad XIII Smith IV.

No. 2692: a, M-130 Clipper. b, DC-3, 1937. c, Beech Staggerwing CVR FT C-17L. d, Hughes H-1 racer. e, Gee Bee Model R-1, 1932. f, Lockheed Sirius Tingmissartoq. g, Fokker T-2, 1923. h, Curtiss CW-16E Floatplane.

No. 2693, Bleriot XI crossing English Channel, 1914. No. 2694, Le Bandy airship, 1903.

Aviation History A426

70¢

**1999, Apr. 26** **Litho.** **Perf. 12½**
2687-2690 A426 Set of 4 2.50 2.50
**Sheets of 8**
2691-2692 A426 $1.10 #a-.h, ea 6.75 6.75
**Souvenir Sheets**
2693-2694 A426 $5 each 3.75 3.75

**1999, May 4** **Litho.** **Perf. 12½**
2695 A427 $1 multicolored .75 .75
No. 2695 was issued in sheets of 8.

History of Space Exploration, 1609-2000 — A428

Designs: 20c, Galileo, 1609. 50c, Konstantin Tsiolkovsky, 1903. 70c, Robert H. Goddard, 1926. 90c, Sir Isaac Newton, 1668, vert.
No. 2700: a, Luna 9, 1959. b, Soyuz 11, 1971. c, Mir Space Station, 1996. d, Sputnik 1, 1957. e, Apollo 4, 1967. f, Bruce McCandless, 1984. g, Sir William Herschel, telescope, 1781. h, John Glenn, 1962. i, Space Shuttle Columbia, 1981.
No. 2701, vert: a, Yuri Gargarin, 1962. b, Lunar Rover, 1971. c, Mariner 10, 1974-75. d, Laika, 1957. e, Neil A. Armstrong, 1969. f, Skylab Space Station, 1973. g, German V-2 Rocket, 1942. h, Gemini 4, 1965. i, Hubble Telescope, 1990.
No. 2702, vert: a, Explorer, 1958. b, Lunokhod Explorer, 1970. c, Viking Lander, 1975. d, R7 Rocket, 1957. e, Edward H. White, 1965. f, Salyut 1, 1971. g, World's oldest observatory, Freedom 7, 1961. i, Ariane Rocket, 1980's.
No. 2703, Atlantis docking with Space Station Mir, 1995. No. 2704, Saturn V, 1969, vert.

**1999, May 6**    **Perf. 14**
2696-2699 A428    Set of 4    1.75 1.75
     **Sheets of 9**
2700-2702 A428 $1 #a.-i., each   6.75 6.75
     **Souvenir Sheets**
2703-2704 A428 $5 each    3.75 3.75

Johann Wolfgang von Goethe (1749-1832), Poet — A430

No. 2709: a, Faust Dying in the Arms of the Lemures. b, Portraits of Goethe, Friederich von Schiller (1759-1805). c, The Immortal Spirit of Faust is Carried Aloft.
No. 2710: a, Faust and Helena with Their Son, Euphonon. b, Mephistopheles Leading the Lemures to Faust.
No. 2711, The Immortal soul of Faust, vert. No. 2712, Portrait of Goethe, vert.

**1999, June 25**    **Litho.**
     **Sheets of 3**
2709 A430 $3 #a.-c.    6.75 6.75
2710 A430 $3 #a.-b. + #2709b   6.75 6.75
     **Souvenir Sheets**
2711-2712 A430 $5 each    3.75 3.75

Paintings, by Hokusai (1760-1849) A431

#2713: a, Landscape with a Hundred Bridges (large mountain). b, Sea Life (turtle, head LL). c, Landscape with a Hundred Bridges (large bridge in center). d, A View of Aoigaoka Waterfall in Edo. e, Sea Life (crab).
#2714: a, Admiring the Irises at Yatsuhashi, f, Women on the Beach at Enoshima.
#2714: a, Admiring the Irises at Yatsuhashi (large tree). b, Sea Life (turtle, head UL). c, Admiring the Irises at Yatsuhashi (head of bridge). d, Pilgrims Bathing in Roben Waterfall. e, Sea Life (turtle, head UR). f, Farmers Crossing a Suspension Bridge.
#2715, In the Horse Washing Waterfall. #2716, A Fisherman at Kajikazawa.

**1999, June 25**    **Perf. 13¾**
     **Sheets of 6**
2713-2714 A431 $1.10 #a.-f., ea   5.00 5.00
     **Souvenir Sheet**
2715-2716 A431    $5 each    3.75 3.75

Wedding of Prince Edward and Sophie Rhys-Jones A432

No. 2717: a, Edward. b, Sophie, Edward. c, Sophie.

**1999, June 19**    **Litho.**    **Perf. 13½**
2717 A432 $3 Sheet of 3, #a.-c.   6.75 6.75
     **Souvenir Sheet**
2718 A432 $6 multicolored    4.50 4.50

IBRA '99, World Philatelic Exhibition, Nuremberg — A433

Design: $1, Krauss-Maffei V-200 diesel locomotive, Germany, 1852. Illustration reduced.

A 90c value was issued.

**1999, June 25**
2720 A433 $1 multicolored    .75 .75

PhilexFrance '99, World Philatelic Exhibition — A434

Locomotives: No. 2721, Pacific, 1930's. No. 2722, Quadrt, electric hight-speed, 1940. Illustration reduced.

**1999, June 25**    **Perf. 13¾**
2721-2722 A434 $6 each    4.50 4.50

Children — #2723: a, Tyreek Isaacs. b, Fredique Isaacs. c, Jerome Burke III. d, Kellisha Roberts.
#2724: a, Girl with braided hair. b, Girl wearing hat. c, Girl holding kitten.
$5, Girl with bow in hair.

**1999, June 25**    **Perf. 14**
2723 A435 90c Sheet of 4, #a.-d.   2.75 2.75

**2724** A435    $3    Sheet of 3, #a.-c.   6.75 6.75
     **Souvenir Sheet**
2725 A435    $5 multicolored    3.75 3.75

UN Convention on Rights of the Child, 10th anniv.

**1999, June 25**
Intl. Year of Older Persons — No. 2726: a, I.M. Pei. b, Billy Graham. c, Barbara Cartland. d, Mike Wallace. e, Jeanne Moreau. f, B.B. King. g, Elie Wiesel. h, Arthur Miller. i, Colin Powell. j, Jack Palance. k, Neil Simon. l, Eartha Kitt.
No. 2727: a, Thomas M. Saunders J.P. b, Mother Sarah Baptiste, M.B.E. c, Sir Sydney Gun-Munro MD, KF, GCMG. d, Dr. Earle Kirby, JP, OBE.

2726 A436   70c Sheet of 12,    6.25 6.25
     #a.-l.
2727 A436 $1.10 Sheet of 4, #a.-   3.25 3.25
     d.

World Teachers' Day — A437

No. 2728: a, Henry Alphaeus Robertson. b, Yvonne C. E. Francis-Gibson. c, Edna Peters. d, Christopher Wilberforce Prescod.

**1999, Oct. 5**    **Litho.**    **Perf. 14¾**
2728 A437 $2 Sheet of 4, #a.-d.   6.00 6.00

A4JU

Queen Mother (b. 1900) — A439

No. 2729: a, In 1909. b, With King George VI, Princess Elizabeth, 1930. c, At Badminton, 1977. d, In 1983.
$6, In 1987. $20, Close-up.
     **Gold Frames**
**1999, Oct. 18**    **Litho.**    **Perf. 14**
2729 A438 $2 Sheet of 4, #a.-d.,   6.00 6.00
     + label
     **Souvenir Sheet**
       **Perf. 13¾**
2730 A438 $6 multicolored    4.50 4.50
No. 2730 contains one 38x50mm stamp. See Nos. 3010-3011.

Christmas A440

Designs: 20c, The Resurrection, by Albrecht Dürer. 50c, Christ in Limbo, by Dürer. 70c, Christ Falling on the Way to Calvary, by Raphael. 90c, St. Ildefonso with the Madonna and Child, by Peter Paul Rubens. $5, The Crucifixion, by Raphael.
$6, The Sistine Madonna, by Raphael.

**1999, Nov. 22**    **Litho.**    **Perf. 13¾**
2732-2736 A440    Set of 5    5.50 5.50
     **Souvenir Sheet**
2737 A440 $6 multicolored    4.50 4.50

UPU, 125th Anniv. A441

Designs: a, Mail coach. b, Intercontinental sea mail. c, Concorde.

**1999, Dec. 7**    **Perf. 14**
2738 A441 $3 Sheet of 3, #a.-c.   6.75 6.75

Paintings A442

Various paintings making up a photomosalc of the Mona Lisa.

**1999, Dec. 7**    **Perf. 13¾**
2739 A442 $1.10 Sheet of 8,    6.50 6.50
     #a.-h.
See #2744, 2816.

A443

Millennium: No. 2740, Clyde Tombaugh discovers Pluto, 1930. —
No. 2741 — Highlights of the 1930s: a, Mahatma Gandhi's Salt March, 1930. b, Like #2740, with colored margin. c, Empire State Building opens, 1931. d, Spain becomes a republic, 1931. e, Franklin D. Roosevelt launches New Deal, 1933. f, Reichstag burns in Germany, 1933. g, Mao Zedong leads China's revolution, 1934. h, Spanish Civil War led by Francisco Franco, 1936. i, Edward VIII abdicates, 1936. j, Diego Rivera, 50th birthday, 1936. k, Golden Gate Bridge opens, 1937. l, First atomic reaction achieved, 1939. m, World War II begins, 1939. n, Television debuts at New York World's Fair, 1939. o,

     **Litho. & Embossed**
**1999, Aug. 4**    **Die Cut 9x8¾**
     **Size: 55x93mm**
2731 A439 $20 gold & multi

Selection of Dalai Lama, 1939, p. Hindenburg explodes, 1937 (60x40mm). q. Igor Sikorsky builds first practical helicopter, 1939.

No. 2742 — Sculptures by: a. Elizabeth Murray. b. Alexander Calder. c. Charles William Moss. d. Gaston Lachaise. e. Claes Oldenburg. f. Louise Bourgeois. g. Duane Hanson. h. Brancusi. i. David Smith. j. Dan Flavin. k. Boccioni. l. George Segal. m. Lucas Samaras. n. Marcel Duchamp. o. Isamu Noguchi. p. Donald Judd (60x40mm). q. Louise Nevelson.

**1999, Dec. 7    Litho.    Perf. 13¼x13**
2740  A443  60c multicolored            .45   .45

Inscription on No. 2742e is misspelled. A number has been reserved for an additional sheet in this set.
See No. 2764.

**Sheets of 17**
**1999, Dec. 31    Litho.    Perf. 13¾**
2744  A442  $1 Sheet of 8, #a.-h.   6.00  6.00

**Painting Type of 1999**

Various flowers making up a photomosaic of Princess Diana.

**Perf. 12¾x12½**
2741  A443  60c #a.-q. + label       7.50  7.50
2742  A443  60c #a.-q. + label       7.50  7.50

A444

Marine Life — A445

High Hat

ST. VINCENT & THE GRENADINES

Equetus acuminatus

50c

**2000, Feb. 5    Litho.    Perf. 14¾**

New Year 2000 (Year of the Dragon). Background colors - No. 2745: a. Blue and red lilac. b. Salmon pink and olive. c. Brick red and lilac rose.

2745  A444  $2 Sheet of 3, #a.-c.   4.50  4.50

**Souvenir Sheet**
2746  A444  $4 multi               3.00  3.00

50c. High hat. 90c. Spotfin hogfish. Royal gramma. $2. Queen angelfish.

No. 2751: a. Sergeant major. b. Hawksbill turtle, whale's tail. c. Two horse-eyed jacks, rear of turtle. d. Two horse-eyed jacks, head of humpback whale. e. Three horse-eyed jacks, head of Common dolphins. f. Black-cap gramma. g. Three horse-eyed jacks, with Latin inscription. h. French grunts, no Latin inscription. k. Sea horse. i. Southern stingray, dolphin. k. Barracuda. j. Bottlenosed French grunt. m. French grunts, no Latin inscription. n. Indigo hamlet. o. Basking shark. p. Nassau grouper. q. Nurse shark, ribbonfish. r. Southern stingray. s. Southern stingray, blue shark. t. Spanish hogfish.
No. 2752, Rock beauties. No. 2753, Banded butterflyfish.

**2000, Feb. 28    Litho.    Perf. 14**
2747-2750  A445   Set of 4        3.25  3.25
**Sheet of 20**
2751  A445  50c #a.-t.            7.50  7.50
**Souvenir Sheets**
2752-2753  A445   $5 each         3.75  3.75

ST. VINCENT & THE GRENADINES

Fish
A446

10¢

Starlight Parrotfish
Thalassoma bifasciatum

10c. Stoplight parrotfish. 20c. Spotfin hogfish. 70c. Beaugregory. 90c. Porkfish. $1. Barred hamlet. $1.40. Queen triggerfish.
No. 2760: a. French angelfish. b. Smooth trunkfish. c. Sargassum triggerfish. d. Indigo hamlet. e. Yellowheaded jawfish. f. Peppermint bass.

No. 2761: a. Porcupine fish. b. Blue tang. c. Bluehead wrasse. d. Juvenile queen angelfish. e. Sea horse. f. Small mouth grunt. No. 2762, Pygmy angelfish. No. 2763, Foureye butterflyfish.

**2000, Feb. 28    Perf. 14**
2754-2759  A446   Set of 6       3.25  3.25
**Sheets of 6, #a.-f.**
2760-2761  A446  $1.10 each      5.00  5.00
**Souvenir Sheets**
2762-2763  A446   $5 each        3.75  3.75

**Millennium Type of 1999**

Highlights of 1900-1950: a. Sigmund Freud publishes "Interpretation of Dreams." b. First long distance wireless transmission. c. First powered airplane flight. d. Einstein proposes theory of relativity. e. Henry Ford unveils Model T. f. Alfred Wegener develops theory of continental drift. g. World War I begins. h. 1917 Russian revolution. i. James Joyce publishes "Ulysses." j. Alexander Fleming discovers penicillin. k. Edwin Hubble determines universe is expanding. l. Mao Zedong leads "Long March." m. Alan Turing develops theory of digital computing. n. Discovery of fission. o. World War II begins. p. Allied leaders meet at Yalta. q. Mahatma Gandhi and Jawaharlal Nehru celebrate India's independence. r. Invention of the transistor.

**2000, Mar. 13    Perf. 12½**
2764  A443  20c Sheet of 18, a.-r.   2.75  2.75
            + label

Date on No. 2764a is incorrect.

Paintings of Anthony Van Dyck
A447

ST. VINCENT & THE GRENADINES

$1

ANTHONY VAN DYCK

No. 2765: a. Robert Rich, 2nd Earl of Warwick. b. James Stuart, Duke of Lennox and Richmond. c. Sir John Suckling. d. Sir Robert Shirley. e. Teresia, Lady Shirley. f. Thomas Wentworth, 1st Earl of Strafford.
No. 2766: a. Thomas Wentworth, Earl of Strafford, in Armor. b. Lady Anne Carr, Countess of Bedford. c. Portrait of a Member of the Charles Family. d. Thomas Howard, 2nd Earl of Arundel. e. Diana Cecil, Countess of Oxford. f. The Violincellist.
No. 2767: a. The Apostle Peter. b. St. Matthew. c. St. James the Greater. d. St. Bartholomew. e. The Apostle Thomas. f. The Apostle Jude (Thaddeus).
No. 2768: a. The Vision of St. Anthony. b. The Mystic Marriage of St. Catherine. c. The Vision of the Blessed Herman Joseph. d. Madonna and Child Enthroned with Sts. Rosalie, Peter and Paul. e. St. Rosalie Interceding for the Plague-stricken of Palermo. f. Francesco Orero in Adoration of the Crucifixion in the Presence of Sts. Frances and Bernard.
No. 2769, William Feilding, 1st Earl of Denbigh. No. 2770, The Mystic Marriage of St. Catherine. No. 2771, St. Augustine in Ecstasy, horiz.

**2000, Apr. 10    Litho.    Perf. 13¾**
**Sheets of 6, #a.-f.**
2765-2768  A447  $1 each         4.50  4.50
**Souvenir Sheets**
2769-2771  A447  $5 each         3.75  3.75

ST. VINCENT & THE GRENADINES

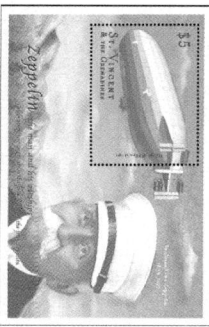

Orchids
70¢

Brassavola nodosa

Orchids
A448

Designs: 70c. Brassavola nodosa. 90c. Bletia purpurea. $1.40, Brassavola cucullata. $5, Oeceoclades maculata. b. Cyrtopodium punctatum. c. Oncidium urophyllum. d. Oececlades maculata. e. Vanilla planifolia. d. Isolhilus linearis. e. Ionopsis utricularioides. f. Nidema boothii.
No. 2776, vert.: a. Cyrtopodium punctatum. b. Dendrophylax funalis. c. Dichaea hystricina. d. Cyrtopodium andersonii. e. Epidendrum secundum. f. Dimerandra emarginata.

Prince William, 18th Birthday — A449

ST. VINCENT
18th Birthday, 21st June 2000

HRH Prince William — 18th Birthday

$5

No. 2777, vert.: a. Brassavola cordata. b. Brassia caudata. c. Broughtonia sanguinea. d. Comparettia falcata. e. Clowesia rosea. f. Caularthron bicornutum.
No. 2778, Neocongiauxia hexaptera, vert. No. 2779, Epidendrum altissimum, vert.

**2000, May 25    Litho.    Perf. 14**
2772-2774  A448  $1.50 each      2.25  2.25
**Sheets of 6, #a.-f.**
2775-2777  A448  $1.50 each      6.75  6.75
**Souvenir Sheets**
2778-2779  A448   $5 each        3.75  3.75

The Stamp Show 2000, London.

No. 2780: a. Wearing checked suit. b. Wearing scarf. c. Wearing solid suit. d. Wearing sweater. e. Wearing suit with boutonniere.
$5, Wearing suit with boutonniere.

**2000, June 21    Litho.    Perf. 14**
2780  A449  $1.40 Sheet of 4,            4.25  4.25
            #a-d
**Souvenir Sheet**
2781  A449  $5 multi    Perf. 13¾  3.75  3.75

No. 2780 contains four 28x42mm stamps.

100th Test Match at Lord's Ground — A450

ST. VINCENT & THE GRENADINES

WEST INDIES TOUR 2000

Ian Allen

10c. Ian Allen. 20c. T. Michael Findlay. $1.10, Winston Davis. $1.40, Nixon McLean. $5, Lord's Ground, horiz.

**2000, June 26    Perf. 14**
2782-2785  A450   Set of 4       2.10  2.10
**Souvenir Sheet**
2786  A450  $5 multi    Perf. 13¾  3.75  3.75

First Zeppelin Flight, Cent. — A451

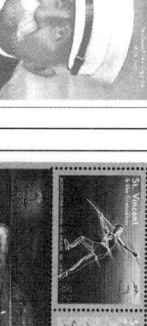

Zeppelin

ST. VINCENT & THE GRENADINES

$5

No. 2787: a. LZ-6. b, LZ-127. c, LZ-129.
Illustration reduced.

**2000, June 26**
2787  A451  $3 Sheet of 3, #a-c  6.75  6.75
**Souvenir Sheet**
2788  A451  $5 multi            3.75  3.75

No. 2787 contains 39x24mm stamps.

Berlin Film Festival, 50th Anniv. — A452

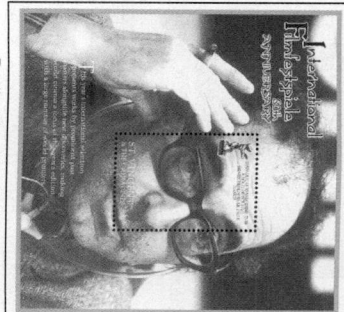

International Filmfestspiele Berlin

No. 2789: a. Pane, Amore e Fantasia. b. Richard III. c. Smultronstället (Wild Strawberries). d. The Defiant Ones. e. The Living Desert. f. A Bout de Souffle.
$5, Jean-Luc Godard.
Illustration reduced.

**2000, June 26**
2789  A452  $1.40 Sheet of 6, #a-f  6.25  6.25
**Souvenir Sheet**
2790  A452  $5 multi            3.75  3.75

Space — A453

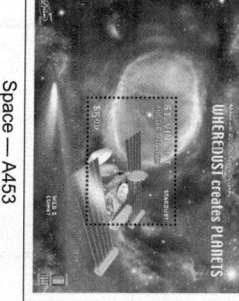

ST. VINCENT & THE GRENADINES

WHEREDUST creates PLANETS

$35

No. 2791: a. Comet Hale-Bopp, Calisto, Galileo probe. c. Ulysses probe. d, Pioneer 11. e, Voyager 1. f, Pioneer 10.
No. 2792: a, Voyager 2. b, Pioneer 11. Project. c, Voyager 1, purple background. d, Oort cloud. e, Pluto, Kuiper Express. f, Voayger 2 near Neptune.
No. 2793: a, Cassini probe b. Pioneer 11. c, Voyager 1, green background. d, Huygens. e, Deep Space IV Champollion. f, Voyager 2.
No. 2794, Stardust. No. 2795, Pluto Project, diff.
Illustration reduced.

**2000, June 26**
**Sheets of 6, #a-f**
2791-2793  A453  $1.50 each      6.75  6.75
**Souvenir Sheets**
2794-2795  A453   $5 each        3.75  3.75

World Stamp Expo 2000, Anaheim.

2000 Summer Olympics, Sydney — A454

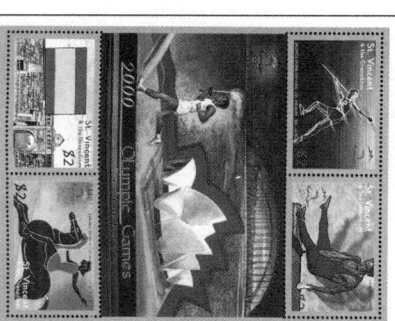

2000 Olympic Games

St. Vincent

$2

No. 2796: a. Mildred Didrikson. b. Pommel horse. c. Barcelona Stadium and Spanish flag. d. Ancient Greek horse racing.

Illustration reduced.

## Albert Einstein (1879-1955) — A455

No. 2797: a. Wearing green sweater. b. Wearing blue sweater. c. Wearing black sweater.
Illustration reduced.

**2000, June 26**
2797 A455 $2 Sheet of 3, #a-c    4.50 4.50

**2000, June 26**
2796 A454 $2 Sheet of 4, #a-d    6.00 6.00

## Public Railways, 175th Anniv. — A456

No. 2798: a. Locomotion No. 1, George Stephenson. b. John Bull.
Illustration reduced.

**2000, July 6    Perf. 12x12¼**
2798 A456 $3 Sheet of 2, #a-b    4.50 4.50

## Mario Andretti, Automobile Racer — A457

No. 2799: a. In car, without helmet. b. In white racing uniform. c. With hands in front of face. d. In car, with helmet. e. In white, standing in front of car. f. With trophy. g. In red racing uniform. h. Close-up.
Illustration reduced.

**2000, July 6    Perf. 12x12¼**
2799 A457 $1.10 Sheet of 8, #a-h    6.50 6.50

**Souvenir Sheet    Perf. 13¾**
2800 A457 $5 multi    3.75 3.75

---

## Souvenir Sheets

## Monty Python's Flying Circus, 30th Anniv. (in 1999) — A458

No. 2801: a. Michael Palin. b. Eric Idle. c, John Cleese. d. Graham Chapman. e. Terry Gilliam. f. Terry Jones.
Illustration reduced.

**2000, July 6    Perf. 12x12¼**
2801 A458 $1.40 Sheet of 6, #a-f    6.25 6.25

## Jazz — A459

No. 2802: a. Clarinetist. b. Pianist. c. Trumpeter. d. Guitarist. e. Bassist. f. Saxophonist.
Illustration reduced.

**2000, July 6    Perf. 14**
2802 A459 $1.40 Sheet of 6, #a-f    6.25 6.25

## Female Recording Groups of the 1960s — A460

No. 2803. Portraits of the members of The Chantels (green background). No. 2804, Portraits of the members of The Marvelettes (blue background)

**2000, July 6    Sheets of 5, #a-e**
2803-2804 A460 $1.40 each    5.25 5.25

## Barbara Taylor Bradford, Writer — A461

Illustration reduced.

**2000, July 6**
2805 A461 $5 multi

---

## Betty Boop — A462

No. 2806: a. As Jill, with Jack. b. With three blind mice. c. Jumping over candlestick. d. As fiddler in Hey, Diddle, Diddle. e. On back of Mother Goose. f. As Little Miss Muffet. g. With three cats. h. As candlestick maker, with butcher and baker. i. As Little Jack Horner.
No. 2807, As the Woman Who Lived In a Shoe. No. 2808, As Little Bo Peep.
Illustration reduced.

**2000, July 6    Perf. 13¾**
2806 A462 $1 Sheet of 9 #a-i    6.75 6.75

**Souvenir Sheets**
2807-2808 A462 $5 each    3.75 3.75

## Artifacts A463

Goblet / Monkey

Designs: 20c, Goblet. 50c, Goose. 70c, Boley and calabash. $1, Flat iron.

**2000, Aug. 21    Litho.    Perf. 14**
2809-2812 A463    Set of 4    1.75 1.75

## Flowers — A464

No. 2813: a. Pink ginger lily. b. Thumbergia grandiflora. c. Red ginger lily. d. Madagascar jasmine. e. Cluster palm. f. Red torch lily. g. Salvia splendens. h. Balsam apple. i. Rostrata. No. 2814, Red flamingo. No. 2815, Balsam apple, horiz.
Illustration reduced.

**2000, Aug. 21**
2813 A464 90c Sheet of 9, #a-i    6.00 6.00

**Souvenir Sheet**
2814-2815 A464 $5 Set of 2    7.50 7.50

## Paintings Type of 1999

Various pictures of flowers making up a photomosaic of the Queen Mother.

**2000, Sept. 5    Perf. 13¾**
2816 A442 $1 Sheet of 8, #a-h, imperf.    6.00 6.00
i.  As No. 2816, imperf.    6.00 6.00

---

## Magician David Copperfield — A465

No. 2817: a. Head of Copperfield. b. Copperfield's body, c. Copperfield's body vanishing. d. Copperfield's body vanished.

**2000, July 6    Perf. 14**
2817 A465b $1.40 Sheet of 4,    4.25 4.25
#a-d    4.25 4.25

## Local Musicians — A466

Designs: No. 2818, $1.40, Horn player with striped shirt. No. 2819, $1.40, Horn player, diff. No. 2820, $1.40, Pianist. No. 2821, $1.40, Fiddler.

**2000, Oct. 16    Litho.    Perf. 14**
2818-2821 A466    Set of 4    4.25 4.25

## Blues Musicians — A467

No. 2822, $1.40: a. Bessie Smith. b. Willie Dixon. c. Gertrude "Ma" Rainey. d. W. C. Handy. e. Leadbelly. f. Big Bill Broonzy. No. 2823, $1.40: a. Ida Cox. b. Lonnie Johnson. c. Muddy Waters. d. T-Bone Walker. e. Howlin' Wolf. f. Sister Rosetta Tharpe. No. 2824, Robert Johnson. No. 2825, Billie Holiday.
Illustration reduced.

**2000, Oct. 16**

**Sheets of 6, #a-f**
2822-2823 A467    Set of 2    12.50 12.50

**Souvenir Sheets**
2824-2825 A467    Set of 2    7.50 7.50

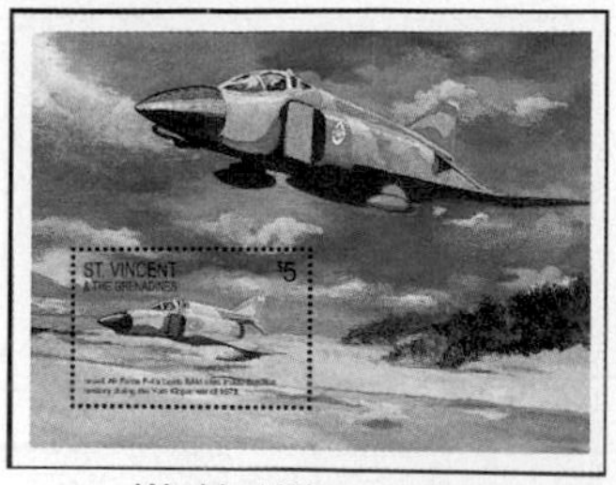

World at War — A468

No. 2826: a, USS Shaw explodes at Pearl Harbor. b, B-24s bomb Ploesti oil fields. c, Soviet T-34 tank moves towards Berlin. d, USS New Jersey off coast of North Korea. e, F-86 Sabre over North Korea. f, USS Enterprise off the Indochina coast. g, B-52 over Viet Nam. h, M-113 tank in Viet Nam.

No. 2827: a, Israeli F-4 Phantoms in action in Six-day War. b, Egyptian T-72 tank destroyed, Six-day War. c, Egyptian SAM-6 missiles, Yom Kippur War. d, Israeli M-48 tanks in desert, Yom Kippur War. e, HMS Hermes, Falkland Islands War. f, British AV-8 harriers in action, Falkland Islands War. g, Iraqi Scud missile launcher in desert, Gulf War. h, M1-A1 Abrams tanks in desert, Gulf War.

No. 2828, Israeli F-4s bomb SAM sites, Yom Kippur War. No. 2829 B-52 bomber, Pershing II missile.

Illustration reduced.

**2000, Oct. 16**

**Sheets of 8, #a-h**

**2826-2827** A468 $1 Set of 2 12.00 12.00

**Souvenir Sheets**

**2828-2829** A468 $5 Set of 2 7.50 7.50

No. 2829 contains one 56x42mm stamp.

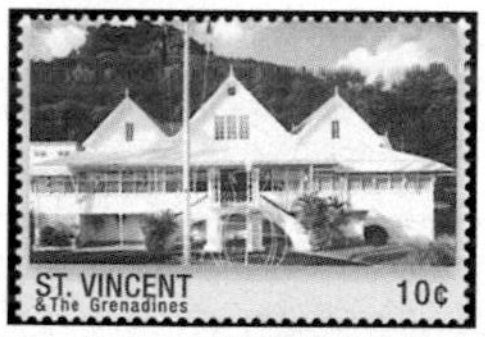


Independence, 21st Anniv. — A469

Designs: 10c, Government House. 15c, First session of Parliament, 1998. 50c, House of Assembly. $2, Financial Complex.

**2000, Oct. 27 Litho. *Perf. 14***

**2830-2833** A469 Set of 4 2.00 2.00

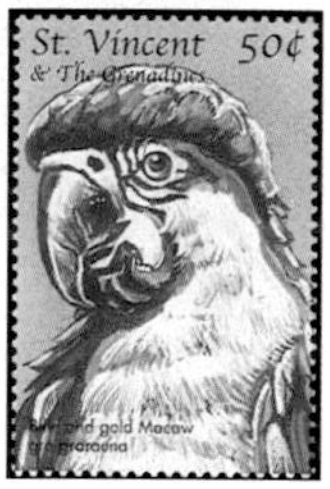


Birds — A470

Designs: 50c, Blue and gold macaw. 90c, English fallow budgerigar. $1, Barraband parakeet. $2, Dominat pied blue.

No. 2838, $2: a, English short-faced tumbler. b, Diamond dove. c, Norwich cropper.

No. 2839, $2: a, Scarlet macaw. b, Blue-fronted Amazon. c, Button's macaw.

No. 2840, $2: a, Stafford canary. b, Masked lovebird. c, Parisian full canary.

No. 2841, $2, horiz.: a, Canada goose. b, Mandarin duck. c, Gouldian finch.

No. 2842, $5, Common peafowl, horiz. No. 2843, $5, Budgerigar, horiz.

**2000, Nov. 15**

**2834-2837** A470 Set of 4 3.25 3.25

**Sheets of 3, #a-c**

**2838-2841** A470 Set of 4 18.00 18.00

**Souvenir Sheets**

**2842-2843** A470 Set of 2 7.50 7.50

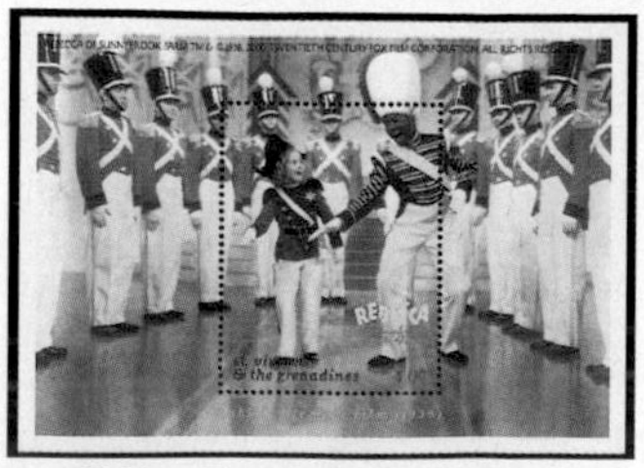

Shirley Temple in Rebecca of Sunnybrook Farm — A471

No. 2844, horiz.: a, With man in dark suit. b, With man and woman. c, With woman wearing glasses. d, with blonde woman. e, With man in white hat. f, With three women.

No. 2845: a, At microphone, wearing checked coat and hat. b, Wearing straw hat. c, At microphone, no hat. d, With woman wearing glasses.

No. 2846, With Bill Robinson.

**2000, Nov. 29 *Perf. 13¾***

**Sheets of 6 and 4**

**2844** A471 90c #a-f 4.00 4.00
**2845** A471 $1.10 #a-d 3.25 3.25

**Souvenir Sheet**

**2846** A471 $1.10 multi .85 .85

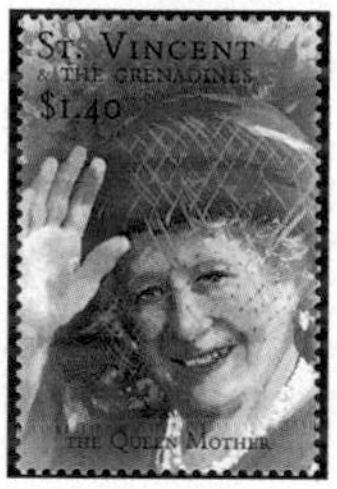


Queen Mother, 100th Birthday — A472

**2000, Sept. 5 Litho. *Perf. 14***

**2847** A472 $1.40 multi 1.00 1.00

Printed in sheets of 6.

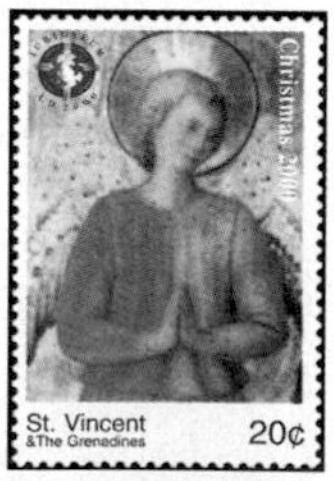


Christmas — A473

20c, Angel looking right. 70c, Two angels, orange background. 90c, Two angels, blue background. #2851, $5, Angel looking left.

No. 2852, Angel, yellow background.

**2000, Dec. 7**

**2848-2851** A473 Set of 4 5.00 5.00

**Souvenir Sheet**

**2852** A473 $5 multi 3.75 3.75

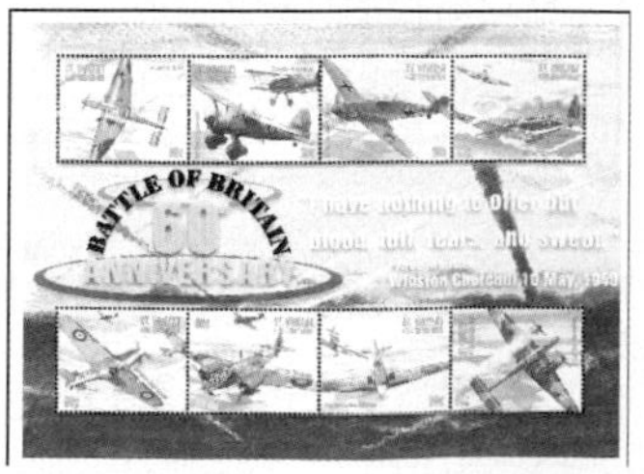

Battle of Britain, 60th Anniv. — A474

No. 2853, 90c: a, Junkers Ju87. b, Two Gloster Gladiators flying left. c, Messerschmitt BF109. d, Heinkel He111 bomber, British fighter. e, Three Hawker Hurricanes. f, Two Bristol Blenheims. g, Two Supermarine Spitfires and ground. h, Messerschmitt BF110.

No. 2854, 90c: a, Two Spitfires, flying left. b, Spitfire. c, Dornier DO217. d, Two Gladiators flying right. e, Four Hurricanes. f, Junkers Ju87 Stuka. g, Two Spitfires flying right. h, Junkers Ju88.

#2855, $5, Spitfire. #2856, $5, Hurricane.

Illustration reduced.

**2000, Dec. 18 *Perf. 14¼x14½***

**Sheets of 8, #a-h**

**2853-2854** A474 Set of 2 10.50 10.50

**Souvenir Sheets**

***Perf. 14¼***

**2855-2856** A474 Set of 2 7.50 7.50

New Year 2001 (Year of the Snake) — A475

No. 2857: a, Blue and light blue background. b, Purple and pink background. c, Green and light green background.

**2001, Jan. 2 Litho. *Perf. 13x13¼***

**2857** A475 $1 Sheet of 3, #a-c 2.25 2.25

**Souvenir Sheet**

**2858** A475 $2 shown 1.50 1.50

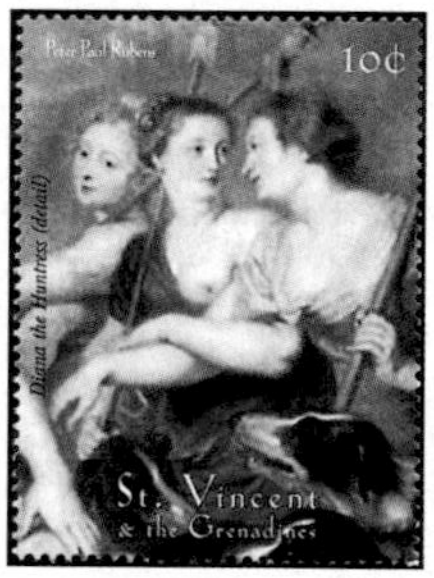


Paintings of Peter Paul Rubens in the Prado A476

Designs: 10c, Three women and dog from Diana the Huntress. 90c, Adoration of the Magi. $1, Woman and two dogs from Diana the Huntress.

No. 2862, $2: a, Heraclitus, the Mournful Philosopher. b, Heraclitus, close-up. c, Anne of Austria, Queen of France, close-up. d, Anne of Austria.

No. 2863, $2: a, Prometheus Carrying Fire. b, Vulcan Forging Jupiter's Thunderbolt. c, Saturn Devouring One of His Sons. d, Polyphemus.

No. 2864, $2: a, St. Matthias. b, The Death of Seneca. c, Maria de'Medici, Queen of France. d, Achilles Discovered by Ulysses.

No. 2865, $5, The Judgment of Solomon. No. 2866, $5, The Holy Family with St. Anne.

**2001, Jan. 2 *Perf. 13¾***

**2859-2861** A476 Set of 3 1.50 1.50

**Sheets of 4, #a-d**

**2862-2864** A476 Set of 3 18.00 18.00

**Souvenir Sheets**

**2865-2866** A476 Set of 2 7.50 7.50

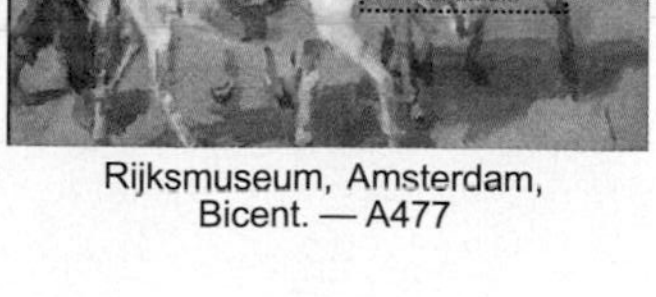

Rijksmuseum, Amsterdam, Bicent. — A477

No. 2867, $1.40: a, The Spendthrift, by Thomas Asselijn. b, The Art Gallery of Jan Gildermeester Jansz, by Adriaan de Lelie. c, The Rampoortje, by Wouter Johannes van Troostwijk. d, Winter Landscape, by Barend Cornelis Koekkoek. e, Man with white head-dress from The Procuress, by Dirck van Baburen. f, Man and woman from The Procuress.

No. 2868, $1.40: a, A Music Party, by Rembrandt. b, Rutger Jan Schimmelpennick and Family, by Pierre Paul Prud'hon. c, Tobit and Anna With a Kid, by Rembrandt. d, The Syndics of the Amsterdam Goldsmiths' Guild, by Thomas de Keyser. e, Portrait of a Lady, by de Keyser. f, Marriage Portrait of Isaac Massa and Beatrix van der Laen, by Frans Hals.

No. 2869, $1.40: a, The Concert, by Hendrick ter Brugghen. b, Vertumnus and Pomona, by Paulus Moreelse. c, Standing couple from Dignified Couples Courting, by Willem Buytewech. d, The Sick Woman, by Jan Steen. e, Seated couple from Dignified Couples Courting. f, Don Ramón Satué, by Francisco de Goya.

No. 2870, $5, Donkey Riding on the Beach, by Isaac Lazarus Israels. No. 2871, $5, The Stone Bridge, by Rembrandt, horiz. No. 2872, $5, Child with Dead Peacocks, by Rembrandt, horiz.

**2001, Jan. 15 *Perf. 13¾***

**Sheets of 6, #a-f**

**2867-2869** A477 Set of 3 19.00 19.00

**Souvenir Sheets**

**2870-2872** A477 Set of 3 11.00 11.00

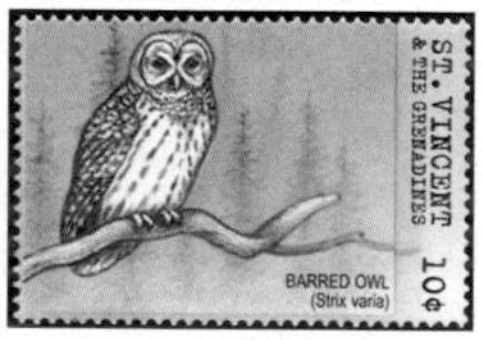


Birds of Prey A478

Designs: 10c, Barred owl. No. 2874, 90c, Lammergeier. $1, California condor. $2, Mississippi kite.

No. 2877, 90c: a, Crested caracara. b, Boreal owl. c, Harpy eagle. d, Oriental bay owl. e, Hawk owl. f, Laughing falcon.

No. 2878, $1.10: a, Bateleur. b, Hobby. c, Osprey. d, Goshawk. e, African fish eagle. f, Egyptian vulture.

No. 2879, $5, Great gray owl. No. 2880, $5, American kestrel.

**2001, Feb. 13 *Perf. 14***

**2873-2876** A478 Set of 4 3.00 3.00

**Sheets of 6, #a-f**

**2877-2878** A478 Set of 2 9.00 9.00

**Souvenir Sheets**

**2879-2880** A478 Set of 2 7.50 7.50

Hong Kong 2001 Stamp Exhibition (Nos. 2877-2880).

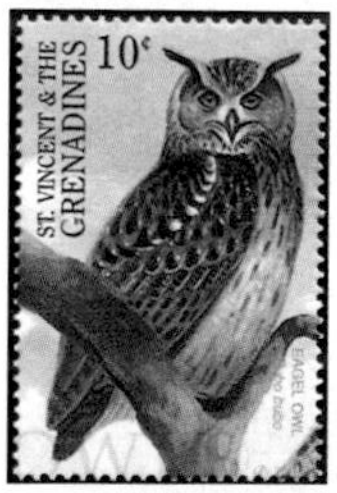


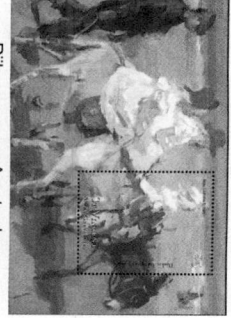

Owls — A479

Designs: 10c, Eagle. 20c, Barn. 50c, Great gray. 70c, Long-eared. 90c, Tawny. $1, Hawk.

No. 2887, horiz.: a, Ural. b, Tengmalm's. c, Marsh. d, Brown fish. e, Little. f, Short-eared.

No. 2888, $5, Hume's. No. 2889, $5, Snowy.

**2001, Feb. 13**

**2881-2886** A479 Set of 6 2.50 2.50
**2887** A479 $1.40 Sheet of 6, #a-f 6.25 6.25

**Souvenir Sheets**

**2888-2889** A479 Set of 2 7.50 7.50

## Pokémon — A480

Season's Greetings 2000

No. 2890: a, Kadabra. b, Spearow. c, Kakuna. d, Koffing. e, Tentacruel. f, Cloyster.

**2001, Feb. 13**    *Perf. 13¾*
2890 A480 90c Sheet of 6, #a-f   4.00 4.00
**Souvenir Sheet**
2891 A480 $3 Meowth   2.25 2.25

## UN Women's Human Rights Campaign — A481

Winnin. 90c, With bird and flunu. $1, With necklace.

**2001, Mar. 8**    *Perf. 14*
2892-2893 A481 Set of 2   1.40 1.40

## Mushrooms — A482

Designs: 20c, Amanita fulva. 90c, Hygrophorus speciosus. $1.10, Amanita phalloides. $2, Cantharellus cibarius.

No. 2898, $1.40: a, Amanita muscaria. b, Boletus zelleri. c, Coprinus picaceus. d, Stropharia aeruginosa. e, Lepista nuda. f, Hygrophorus coricus.

No. 2899, $1.40: a, Lactarius deliciosus. b, Hygrophorus psittacinus. c, Tricholomopsis rutilans. d, Hygrophorus coccineus. e, Collybia iocephala. f, Gyromitra esculenta.

No. 2900, $1.40: a, Lactarius peckii. b, Lactarius rufus. c, Cortinarius elatior. d, Boletus luridus. e, Russula cyanoxantha. f, Craterellus cornopioioles.

No. 2901, $5, Cyathus olla. No. 2902, $5, Lycoperdon pyriforme, horiz. No. 2903, $5, Pleurotus ostreatus, horiz.

**Perf. 13½x13¾, 13½x13½**
**2001, Mar. 15**
2894-2897 A482 Set of 4   3.25 3.25
**Sheets of 6, #a-f**
2898-2900 A482 Set of 3   19.00 19.00
**Souvenir Sheets**
2901-2903 A482 Set of 3   11.00 11.00

## Butterflies and Moths — A486

Designs: No. 2904, 10c, Tiger. No. 2905, 20c, Figure-of-eight. No. 2906, 50c, Mosaic. No. 2907, 90c, Monarch. No. 2908, $1, Blue-green reflector. No. 2909, $2, Blue tharops. No. 2910, 10c, Eunica alemena. No. 2911, 70c, Euphaedra merion. No. 2912, 90c, Prepona praeneste. No. 2913, $1, Gold-banded forester.

No. 2914, 20c, Ancycluris formosissima. No. 2915, 50c, Callicore cynosura. No. 2916, 70c, Nessaea obrinus. No. 2917, $2, Eunica alemena.

No. 2918, 90c: a, Orange theope. b, Blue night. c, Small lace-wing. d, Grecian shoemaker. e, Clorinde. f, Orange-barred sulphur.

No. 2919, $1.10: a, Atala. b, Giant swallowtail. c, Banded king shoemaker. d, White peacock. e, Cramer's mesene. f, Polydamas swallowtail.

No. 2920, 90c: a, Cepora aspasia. b, Morpho aega. c, Mazuca amoeva. d, Beautiful tiger. e, Gold-drop helicopsis. f, Esmerelda.

No. 2921, $1.10: a, Lilac nymph. b, Ruddy dagger wing. c, Tiger pierid. d, Orange forester. e, Prepona deiphile. f, Phoebus avellaneda.

No. 2922, $1: a, Calisthenia salvinii flying downward. b, Puriciania vaninka. c, Melanitis. d, Diachria aurelia. e, Pensamia doriplanil. f, Cramer's mesene. g, Calisthenia salvinii flying upward. h, Carpella districata

No. 2923, $1: a, Euphaedra heuphron. b, Milionia grandis. c, Ruddy dagger wiry. d, Bocotus bacotus. e, Cream spot tiger moth. f, Yellow tiger moth. g, Baorisa hiroglyphica. h, Jersey tiger.

No. 2924, $5, Small flambeau. No. 2925, $5, Common morpho, vert. No. 2926, $5, Heliconius sapho. No. 2927, $5 Ornate moth. No. 2928, $5, Hewitson's blue hair streak. No. 2929, $5, Anaxita drucei.

**Perf. 13½x13½, 13½x13¾**    **Litho.**
**2001, Mar. 22**
2904-2909 A484 Set of 6   3.50 3.50
2910-2913 A485 Set of 4   2.00 2.00
2914-2917 A486 Set of 4   2.50 2.50
**Sheets of 6, #a-f**
2918-2919 A484   9.00 9.00
2920-2921 A485   9.00 9.00
**Sheets of 8, #a-h**
2922-2923 A486   12.00 12.00
**Souvenir Sheets**
2924-2925 A484   7.50 7.50
2926-2927 A485   7.50 7.50
2928-2929 A486   7.50 7.50

## Giuseppe Verdi (1813-1901), Opera Composer — A487

No. 2930: a, Mario Del Monico, Raina Kabaivanska in Othello. b, 1898 Costume design for Iago. c, 1898 costume design for Othello. d, Anna Tomowa-Sintow as Desdemona.
$5, Nicolai Ghiaurov in Othello.

**2001, June 12**    **Litho.**    *Perf. 14*
2930 A487 $2 Sheet of 4, #a-d   6.00 6.00
**Souvenir Sheet**
2931 A487 $5 multi   3.75 3.75

## Toulouse-Lautrec Paintings — A488

No. 2932: a, Portrait of Comtesse Adéleame Zoé de Toulouse-Lautrec. b, Carmen. c, Madame Lily Grenier.
$5, Jane Avril.

**2001, June 12**    *Perf. 13¾*
2932 A488 $3 Sheet of 3, #a-c   6.75 6.75
**Souvenir Sheet**
2933 A488 $5 multi   3.75 3.75

## Mao Zedong (1893-1976) — A489

No. 2934: a, In 1924. b, In 1938. c, In 1945.
$5, Undated portrait.

**2001, June 12**    *Perf. 13¾*
2934 A489 $2 Sheet of 3, #a-c   4.50 4.50
**Souvenir Sheet**
2935 A489 $5 multi   3.75 3.75

## Queen Victoria (1819-1901) — A490

No. 2936: a, As young lady in dark blue dress. b, In white dress. c, With flowers in hair. d, Wearing crown. e, Wearing black dress, facing forward. f, With gray hair.
$5, Sky in background.

**2001, June 12**    *Perf. 14*
2936 A490 $1.10 Sheet of 6, #a-f   5.00 5.00
**Souvenir Sheet**
   *Perf. 13¾*
2937 A490 $5 multi   3.75 3.75
No. 2936 contains six 28x42mm stamps.

## Queen Elizabeth II, 75th Birthday — A491

No. 2938: a, With gray hat. b, In gray jacket, no hat. c, In dark blue dress. d, Wearing tiara. e, With blue hat. f, With green hat.
$5, In uniform.

**2001, June 12**    *Perf. 14*
2938 A491 $1.10 Sheet of 6, #a-f   5.00 5.00
**Souvenir Sheet**
   *Perf. 13¾*
2939 A491 $5 multi   3.75 3.75
No. 2938 contains six 28x42mm stamps.

## Monet Paintings — A492

Designs: No. 2940, $2, Venice at Dusk (shown). No. 2941, $2, Regatta at Argenteuil. No. 2942, $2, Grain Stacks, End of Summer, Evening Effect. No. 2943, $2, Impression, Sunrise.
$5, Parisians Enjoying the Parc Monceau, vert.

**2001, June 12**    *Perf. 13¾*
2940-2943 A492 Set of 4   6.00 6.00
**Souvenir Sheet**
2944 A492 $5 multi   3.75 3.75

## Phila Nippon '01, Japan — A493

Designs: 10c, The Courtesan Sumimoto of the Okanaya, by Koryusai Isoda. 15c, Oiran at Shinto Shrine — Shotenyama, by Kiyonaga. No. 2947, 20c, Two Girls on a Veranda, by Kiyonaga. No. 2948, 20c, Rooster, from A Variety of Birds, by Hoen Nishiyama, horiz. 50c, On Banks of the Sumida, by Kiyonaga. 70c, Three ducks, from A Variety of Birds,

horiz., 90c. Seven ducks, from A Variety of Birds, horiz. b, \$1. Three pigeons and other birds from A Variety of Birds, horiz. c, \$1.10. Two birds, from A Variety of Birds, horiz. \$2. Five birds, from A Variety of Birds.

No. 2955, \$1.40 — Paintings by Eishi: a, Toriwagi, Geisha of Kanaya, Writing. b, Courtesan Preparing for Doll Festival. c, Two Court Ladies in a Garden. d, Lady With a Lute.

No. 2956, \$1.40 — Portraits by Sharaku: a, Onji Otani II as Edohei. b, Yakko Ko Hanshiro Iwai IV. c, Kikunojo Segawa. d, Komazo Ichikawa II.

No. 2957, \$1.40 — Paintings by Harunobu Suzuki: a, 6 Tama Rivers, Girls by Lespedeza Bush in Moonlight. b, Warming Sake with Maple Leaves. c, Young Samurai on Horseback. d, 6 Tama Rivers, Ide No Tamagawa.

No. 2958, \$1.40 — Paintings by Harunobu Suzuki: a, Girl on River Bank. b, Horseman Guided by Peasant Girl. c, Komachi Praying for Rain. d, Washing Clothes in the Stream.

No. 2959, \$5. Peasants Ferried Across Sumida, by Hokkei No. 2960, \$5 Shadows on the Shoji, by Kikugawa. No. 2961, \$5, Boy Spying on Lovers, by Suzuki. No. 2962, \$5, Tayu Komurasaki and Hanamurasaki of the Kado Tamaya, by Masanobu Kitao. No. 2963, \$5, Gathering Lotus Flowers, by Suzuki.

**2001, June 12**    **Litho.**    **Perf. 13¾**
2945-2954 A493   Set of 10    5.25   5.25
Sheets of 4, #a-d
2955-2958 A493   Set of 4    17.00 17.00
    Souvenir Sheets
2959-2963 A493   Set of 5    19.00 19.00

"The Intimidator"—Dale Earnhardt

Dale Earnhardt (1951-2001), Stock Car Racer — A494

**2001, July 16**
2964 A494   \$2 Sheet of 6, #a-f +    9.00 9.00
    label
Printed in sheets of 4.

ST. VINCENT & THE GRENADINES
MAMMOTH
10c

Dinosaurs and Prehistoric Animals — A496

Designs: 10c, Mammoth. 20c, Pinacosaurus. No. 2968, 90c, Oviraptor. \$1, Centrosaurus. No. 2970, \$1.40, Protoceratops. \$2, Bactrosaurus.

"The Dominator"—Dale Earnhardt

Designs: a, Dale Earnhardt, Jr. b, Dale and phy. c, Dale and Dale. d, Dale with trophy. b, Dale and Dale, Jr. embracing. f, Dale Jr. with trophy.

ROYAL WEDDING
\$5
ST.VINCENT & The Grenadines

Wedding of Norwegian Prince Haakon and Mette-Marie Tjessem Hoiby — A495

**2001, Aug. 1**
2965 A495   \$5 multi    3.75 3.75
Printed in sheets of 4.

2002 FIFA WORLD CUP
KOREA JAPAN
Seoul World Cup Stadium

2002 World Cup Soccer Championships, Japan and Korea — A498

Players and flags — No. 2981, \$1.40: a, Hong Myung-Bo, Korea. b, Hidetoshi Nakata, Japan. c, Ronaldo, Brazil. d, Paolo Maldini, Italy. e, Peter Schmeichel, Denmark. f, Raul Blanco, Spain.
No. 2982, \$1.40: a, Kim Bong Soo, Korea. b, Masami Ihara, Japan. c, Marcel Desailly, France. d, David Beckham, England. e, Carlos Valderrama, Colombia. f, George Popescu, Romania.
No. 2983, \$5, Seoul World Cup Stadium. No. 2984, \$5, International Yokohama Stadium.

**2001, Nov. 29**
2981-2982 A498   Set of 6, #a-f
    Sheets of 6, #a-f
2981-2982 A498   Set of 2    12.50 12.50
    Souvenir Sheets
2983-2984 A498   Set of 2    7.50 7.50
Nos. 2983-2984 each contain one 63x31mm stamp.

Photomosaic of Queen Elizabeth II—A497

St. Vincent & The Grenadines
\$1

**2001, Nov. 12**    **Perf. 14**
2980 A497   \$1 multi    .75 .75
Printed in sheets of 8.

No. 2972, 90c: a, Saltasaurus. b, Apatosaurus. c, Brachiosaurus. d, Troodon. e, Deinonychus. f, Segnosaurus.
No. 2973, 90c: a, Iguanodon. b, Hypacrosaurus. c, Ceratosaurus. d, Hypsilophodon. e, Herrerasaurus. f, Velociraptor.
No. 2974, \$1.40: a, Pteranodon. b, Archaeopteryx. c, Eudimorphodon. d, Shonisaurus. e, Elasmosaurus. f, Kronosaurus.
No. 2975, \$1.40: a, Allosaurus. b, Dilophosaurus. c, Lambeosaurus. d, Coelophysis. e, Ornitholestes. f, Eustreptospondylus.
No. 2976, \$5, Stegosaurus. No. 2977, \$5, Triceratops. No. 2978, \$5, Parasaurolophus, vert. No. 2979, \$5, Tyrannosaurus, vert.

**2001, Oct. 15**    **Litho.**    **Perf. 13¾**
2966-2971 A496   Set of 6    4.25 4.25
    Sheets of 4, #a-f
2972-2975 A496   Set of 4    21.00 21.00
    Souvenir Sheets
    Perf. 13¾
2976-2979 A496   Set of 4    15.00 15.00
Nos. 2976-2977 each contain one 50x38mm stamp; Nos. 2978-2979 each contain one 36x50mm stamp.

PEARL HARBOR
60TH ANNIVERSARY OF THE ATTACK ON PEARL HARBOR DECEMBER 7, 1941

Attack on Pearl Harbor, 60th Anniv. — A499

No. 2985, \$1.40, horiz.: a, Japanese bombing Pearl Harbor. b, Japanese pilot ties on a hachimaki. c, Emperor Hirohito. d, Japanese Adm. Isoroku Yamamoto. e, Japanese fighter planes from aircraft carrier Akagi. f, Japanese Zero plane.
No. 2986, \$1.40, horiz.: a, Japanese fighter from the Kaga over Ewa Marine Base. b, Hero Dorie Miller downing four Japanese planes. c, Battleship USS Nevada sinking. d, American sailors struggle on the USS Oklahoma. e, Japanese plane takes off from the Akagi. f, Rescue during bombing.
No. 2987, \$5, Dorie Miller receiving navy Cross from Adm. Chester Nimitz. No. 2988, \$5, Second wave of attack at Wheeler Field, horiz.

**2001, Dec. 7**
2985-2986 A499   Set of 2    12.50 12.50
    Souvenir Sheets
2987-2988 A499   Set of 2    7.50 7.50

JOHN FITZGERALD KENNEDY 1917-1963
ST. VINCENT
\$5

Pres. John F. Kennedy — A500

Pres. Kennedy — No. 2989, \$1.40: a, With John, Jr. b, With Jacqueline (red dress). c, With Caroline. d, With family, 1963. e, With Jacqueline, at sea. f, With Jacqueline (white dress).
No. 2990, \$1.40: a, At 1956 Democratic Convention. b, Campaigning with Jacqueline, 1959. c, At White House, 1960. d, With brother Robert. e, Announcing Cuban blockade, 1962. f, John Jr. saluting father's casket.
No. 2991, \$5, Portrait with violet background. No. 2992, \$5, Portrait with green background.

**2001, Dec. 7**
2989-2990 A500   Set of 2    12.50 12.50
    Sheets of 6, #a-f
2989-2990 A500   Set of 2    12.50 12.50
    Souvenir Sheets
2991-2992 A500   Set of 2    7.50 7.50

PRINCESS DIANA
40TH ANNIVERSARY OF HER BIRTHDAY (1961-1997)
\$5
PRINCESS DIANA

Princess Diana (1961-97) — A501

Flowers and Diana: a, In gray suit. b, In pink dress. c, With tiara.
\$5. With tiara and high-necked gown.

**2001, Dec. 7**
2993 A501   \$1.40 Sheet, 2 each    6.25 6.25
     #a-c
    Souvenir Sheet
2994 A501   \$5 multi    3.75 3.75

CROKER'S FROTHER
St. Vincent & Grenadines
70c

Moths
A502

Designs: 70c, Croker's frother. 90c, Virgin tiger moth. \$1, Leopard moth. \$2, Fiery campylotes.
No. 2999, \$1.40: a, Buff-tip. b, Elephant hawkmoth. c, Streaked sphinx. d, Cizara hawkmoth. e, Eyespot anthelid. f, Boisduval's autumnal moth.
No. 3000, \$1.40: a, Eyespot anthelid. b, Collenette's variegated browntail. c, Common epicoma moth. d, Staudinger's longtail. e, Green silver lines. f, Salt marsh moth.
No. 3001, \$5, Gypsy moth. No. 3002, Orizaba silkmoth caterpillar.

**2001, Dec. 10**
2995-2998 A502   Set of 4    3.50 3.50
    Sheets of 6, #a-f
2999-3000 A502   Set of 2    12.50 12.50
    Souvenir Sheets
3001-3002 A502   Set of 2    7.50 7.50

ST. VINCENT
10c

Christmas — A503

Paintings: 10c, Madonna and Child, by Francesco Guardi. 20c, The Immaculate Conception, by Giovanni Battista Tiepolo. 70c, Adoration of the Magi by Tiepolo. 90c, The Virgin, by Tintoretto. \$1.10, The Annunciation, by Veronese. \$1.40 Madonna della Quaglia, by Antonio Pisanello.
No. 3010: a, In 1909. b, With King George, Princess Elizabeth, 1930. c, At Badminton, Neri, by Tiepolo.

**2001, Dec. 12**
3003-3008 A503   Set of 6    3.25 3.25
    Souvenir Sheet
3009 A503   \$5 multi    3.75 3.75

**Queen Mother Type of 1999 Redrawn**

No. 3010: a, In 1909. b, With King George, Princess Elizabeth, 1930. c, At Badminton, 1977. d, In 1983.
\$6, In 1987.

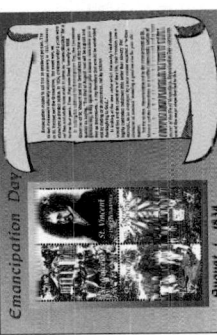

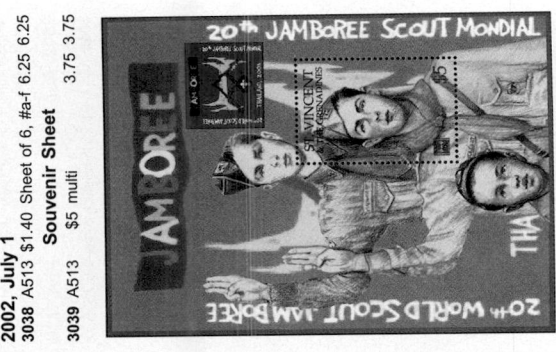

## 20th World Scout Jamboree, Thailand — A514

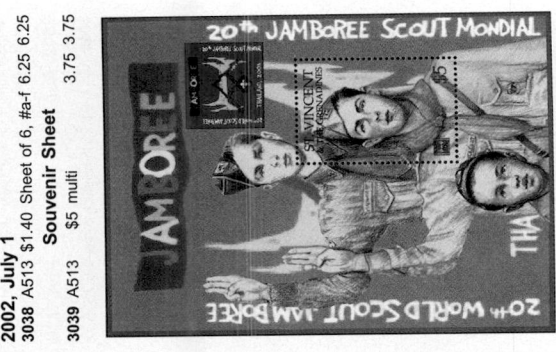

**2002, July 1**
3038 A513 $1.40 Sheet of 6, #a-f 6.25 6.25
**Souvenir Sheet**
3039 A513 $5 multi 3.75 3.75

No. 3040, horiz.: a, Scout with kudu horn. b, Scouts breaking camp. c, Daniel Beard and Lord Robert Baden-Powell. No. 3041, Scout.

**Perf. 13¼x13½**
**2002, July 1**
3040 A514 $5 Sheet of 3, #a-c 11.50 11.50
**Souvenir Sheet**
**Perf. 13½x13½**
3041 A514 $5 multi 3.75 3.75

## Emancipation Day, 168th Anniv. — A515

No. 3042: a, Crowd near fence. b, Lieutenant and Governor of St. Vincent. c, Black couple dancing, white couple. d, Allegory of freedom.

**Perf. 14**
**2002, Aug. 1**
3042 A515 $2 Sheet of 4, #a-d 6.00 6.00

## 2002 Winter Olympics, Salt Lake City — A516

Designs: No. 3043, $3, Biathlon. No. 3044, $3, Freestyle skiing.

**Perf. 13¼x13½**
**2002, July 1 Litho.**
3043-3044 A516 Set of 2 4.50 4.50
3044a Souvenir sheet, #3043-3044 4.50 4.50

## Elvis Presley (1935-77) — A517

Designs: $1, With red background. No. 3046: a, Playing guitar. b, In Army uniform. c, In suit, with guitar strap. d, With vertically striped shirt, looking left. e, In horizontally

---

## Pan-American Health Organization, Cent. — A510

Designs: 20c, Anniversary emblem, vert. 70c, Dr. Gideon Cordice, vert. 90c, Dr. Arthur Cecil Cyrus, vert. $1.10, Headquarters, Christ Church, Barbados.

**Perf. 14**
**2002, Apr. 8 Set of 4**
3026-3029 A510 2.25 2.25

## Vincy Mas, 25th Anniv. — A511

Designs: 10c, Section of the Bands. 20c, Cocktail, the Blue Dragon, horiz. 70c, Safari, Snake in the Grass. 90c, Bridgette Creese, 2001 Calypso Monarch. $1.10, Heat Wave, horiz. $1.40, Sion Hill Steel Orchestra, horiz.

**Perf. 14**
**2002, June 15 Litho.**
3030-3035 A511 Set of 6 3.25 3.25

## Intl. Year of Ecotourism — A512

No. 3036: a, Butterfly. b, Manatee. c, Deer. d, Plant.

**Perf. 13½x13¼**
**2002, July 1**
3036 A512 $2 Sheet of 4, #a-d 6.00 6.00
**Souvenir Sheet**
3037 A512 $6 multi 4.50 4.50

## Intl. Year of Mountains — A513

No. 3038: a, Mt. Ararat, Turkey. b, Mt. Ama Dablem, Nepal. c, Mt. Cook, New Zealand. d, Mt. Kilimanjaro, Tanzania. e, Mt. Kenya, Kenya. f, Giant's Castle, South Africa. $5, Mt. Aconcagua, Argentina.

---

No. 3019, $5, Blue night butterfly. No. 3020, $5, Brown pelican, vert.

**Litho. Perf. 14**
**2001, Dec. 10**
**Sheets of 6, #a-f**
3017-3018 A506 Set of 2 12.50 12.50
**Souvenir Sheets**
3019-3020 A506 Set of 2 7.50 7.50

## Baseball Player Cal Ripken, Jr. — A507

No. 3021: a, Hitting ball. b, Running. c, Without hat. d, Batting (orange shirt). e, Holding trophy. f, Waving hat. g, Greeting fans (68x56mm).

**Perf. 13¼**
**2001, Dec. 27**
3021 A507 $2 Sheet of 7, #a-g 10.50 10.50
**Souvenir Sheet**
**Perf. 13x13¼**
3022 A507 $6 multi 4.50 4.50
No. 3022 contains one 36x56mm stamp.

## United We Stand — A508

**Perf. 14**
**2001, Dec. 28**
3023 A508 $2 multi 1.50 1.50

## Reign of Queen Elizabeth II, 50th Anniv. — A509

No. 3024: a, With Prince Philip. b, With Princess Margaret. c, Wearing blue dress. d, In wedding gown.

**Perf. 14½**
**2002, Apr. 8 Litho.**
3024 A509 $2 Sheet of 4, #a-d 6.00 6.00
**Souvenir Sheet**
3025 A509 $5 multi 3.75 3.75

---

**Perf. 14**
**2001, Dec. 13**
**Yellow Orange Frames**
3010 A438 $2 Sheet of 4, #a-d, + 6.00 6.00
label
**Souvenir Sheet**
**Perf. 13¾**
3011 A438 $6 multi 4.50 4.50

Queen Mother's 101st birthday. No. 3010 contains one 38x50mm stamp with a greener background than that found on No. 2730. Sheet margins of Nos. 3010-3011 lack embossing and gold arms and frames found on Nos. 2729-2730.

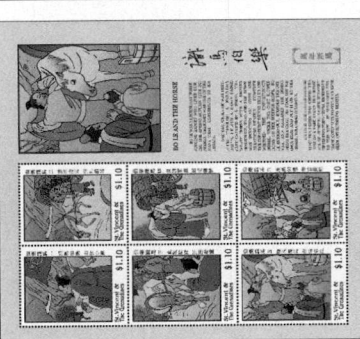

## New Year 2002 (Year of the Horse) — A504

Scenes from Bo Le and the Horse: a, Man pointing at horse. b, Horse pulling cart. c, Horse snorting. d, Horse drinking. e, Man putting robe on horse. f, Horse rearing.

**Perf. 13¾**
**2001, Dec. 17**
3012 A504 $1.10 Sheet of 6, #a-f 5.00 5.00

## Tourism — A505

Designs: 20c, Vermont Nature Trails. 70c, Tamarind Beach Hotel, horiz. 90c, Tobago Cays, horiz. $1.10, Trinity Falls.

**Perf. 14**
**2001, Dec. 31**
**Stamps + labels**
3013-3016 A505 Set of 4 2.25 2.25

## Fauna — A506

No. 3017, $1.40, vert.: a, Bumble bee. b, Green darner dragonfly. c, Small lace-wing. d, Black widow spider. e, Praying mantis. f, Firefly.
No. 3018, $1.40: a, Caspian tern. b, Whitetailed tropicbird. c, Black-necked stilt. d, Blackbellied plover. e, Black-winged stilt. f, Ruddy turnstone.

striped shirt. f, In vertically striped shirt, looking forward.

**2002, Aug. 19** ***Perf. 13¾***

| | | | | |
|---|---|---|---|---|
| **3045** A517 | $1 multi | | .75 | .75 |
| **3046** A517 | $1.25 Sheet of 6, #a-f | | 5.75 | 5.75 |

No. 3045 printed in sheets of nine.

Souvenir Sheet

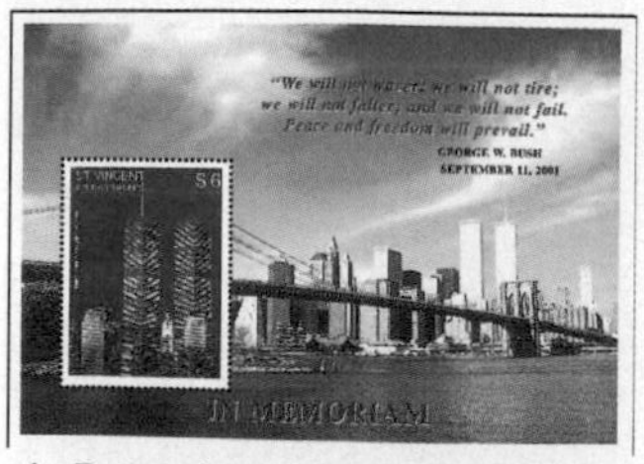
"We will not waver, we will not tire; we will not falter, and we will not fail. Peace and freedom will prevail."
GEORGE W. BUSH
SEPTEMBER 11, 2001
IN MEMORIAM

In Remembrance of Sept. 11, 2001 Terrorist Attacks — A518

**2002, Sept. 11** ***Perf. 13¾***

**3047** A518 $6 multi 4.50 4.50

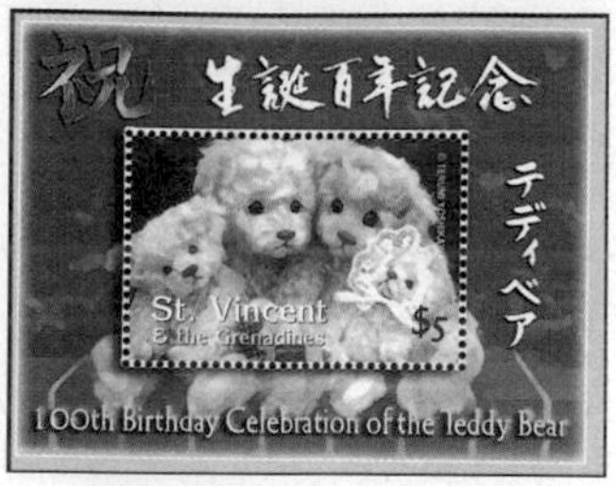
100th Birthday Celebration of the Teddy Bear

Teddy Bears, Cent. — A519

No. 3048, $2, vert.: a, Cowboy bear. b, Fisherman bear. c, Camper bear. d, Hiker bear.
No. 3049, $2, vert.: a, Bear in kimono. b, Two bears. c, Bear with hair ribbon, baby bear. d, Bear with sunglasses.
No. 3050, vert.: a, Bear with red dress and cap. b, Bear with bonnet. c, Bear with strapless dress. d, Bear with dress with red ruffled collar. e, Bear with blue dress with ribbon.
No. 3051, $5, Four bears by Terumi Yoshikawa. No. 3052, $5, Four bears by Tomoko Suenaga.

**2002, Sept. 23** ***Perf. 13¾ (#3048), 14***

**Sheets of 4, #a-d**

| | | | |
|---|---|---|---|
| **3048-3049** A519 | Set of 2 | 12.00 | 12.00 |
| **3050** A519 | $2 Sheet of 5, #a-e | 7.50 | 7.50 |

**Souvenir Sheets**

| | | | |
|---|---|---|---|
| **3051-3052** A519 | Set of 2 | 7.50 | 7.50 |

No. 3048 contains four 38x50mm stamps.

Souvenir Sheets

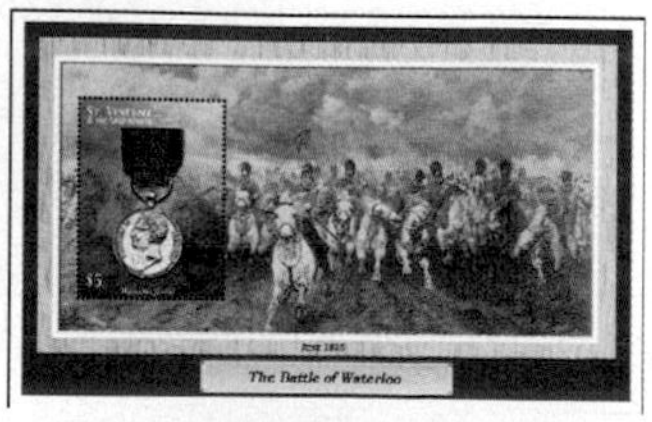
The Battle of Waterloo

British Military Medals — A520

Designs: No. 3053, $5, Waterloo Medal. No. 3054, $5, South African War Medal. No. 3055, $5, Queen's South Africa Medal. No. 3056, $5, 1914-15 Star. No. 3057, $5, British War Medal.

**2002, Oct. 7** ***Perf. 14¼***

**3053-3057** A520 Set of 5 19.00 19.00

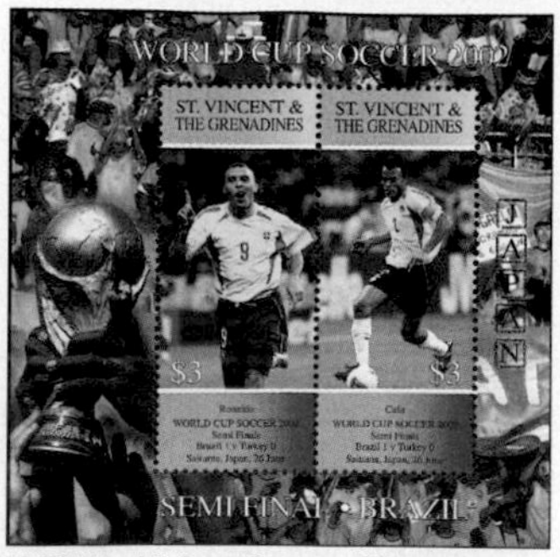
WORLD CUP SOCCER 2002
ST. VINCENT & THE GRENADINES
SEMI FINAL • BRAZIL

2002 World Cup Soccer Championship Semifinals, Japan and Korea — A521

No. 3058, $1.40: a, Kleberson and Emre Belozoglu. b, Cafu. c, Roberto Carlos. d, Yildiray Basturk. e, Tugay Kerimoglu and Rivaldo. f, Bulent.
No. 3059, $1.40: a, Ji Sung Park and Dietmar Hamann. b, Miroslav Klose and Tae Young Kim. c, Chong Gug Song and Christoph Metzelder. d, Tae Young Kim and Gerald Asamoah. e, Torsten Frings and Ji Sung Park. f, Oliver Neuville and Tae Young Kim.
No. 3060, $3: a, Ronaldo. b, Cafu, diff.
No. 3061, $3: a, Michael Ballack. b, Oliver Kahn.
No. 3062, $3: a, Bulent, diff. b, Yildiray Basturk, diff.
No. 3063, $3: a, Tae Young Kim. b, Du Ri Cha.

**2002, Nov. 4** ***Perf. 13¼***

**Sheets of 6, #a-f**

| | | | |
|---|---|---|---|
| **3058-3059** A521 | Set of 2 | 12.50 | 12.50 |

**Souvenir Sheets of 2, #a-b**

| | | | |
|---|---|---|---|
| **3060-3063** A521 | Set of 4 | 18.00 | 18.00 |

**Shirley Temple Movie Type of 2000**

Temple in "Dimples" No. 3046, horiz.: a, Embracing man. b, Conducting musicians. c, Seated, in blue dress. d, On stage with actors in black-face. e, Head on pillow. f, With woman, holding plate.
No. 3047: a, Standing on barrel. b, In green dress. c, Adjusting man's ascot. d, With seated woman.
$5, Dancing with man in black face.

**2002, Oct. 28** ***Perf. 14¼***

| | | | |
|---|---|---|---|
| **3064** A471 | $1.40 Sheet of 6, #a-f | 6.25 | 6.25 |
| **3065** A471 | $2 Sheet of 4, #a-d | 6.00 | 6.00 |

**Souvenir Sheet**

| | | | |
|---|---|---|---|
| **3066** A471 | $5 multi | 3.75 | 3.75 |

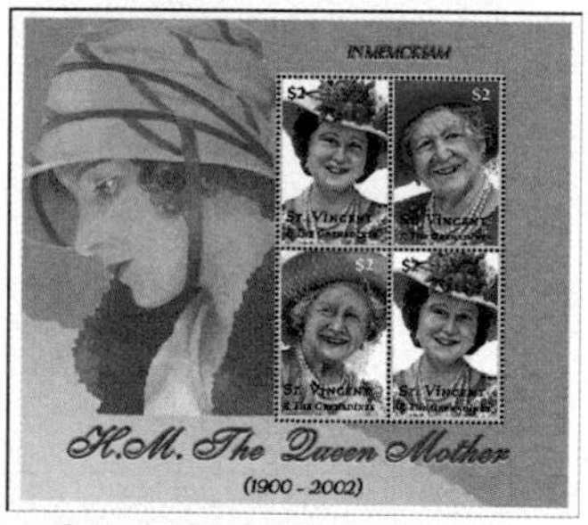
IN MEMORIAM
H.M. The Queen Mother
(1900 - 2002)

Queen Mother Elizabeth (1900-2002) — A522

No. 3067: a, Wearing blue hat and dress. b, Wearing purple hat, dress and corsage. c, Wearing flowered hat.

**2002, Nov. 9** **Litho.** ***Perf. 14***

**3067** A522 $2 Sheet of 4, #a-b, 2 #c 6.00 6.00

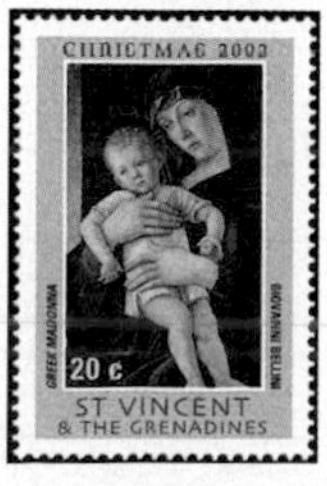
CHRISTMAS 2002
20c
ST. VINCENT & THE GRENADINES

Christmas — A523

Designs: 20c, Greek Madonna, by Giovanni Bellini. 90c, Kneeling Agostino Barbarigo, by Bellini. $1.10, Presentation of Jesus in the Temple, by Perugino. $1.40, Madonna and Child with the Infant St. John, by Perugino. $1.50, San Giobbe Altarpiece, by Bellini.
$5, Madonna and Child with Saints John the Baptist and Sebastian, by Perugino, horiz.

**2002, Nov. 18**

| | | | |
|---|---|---|---|
| **3068-3072** A523 | Set of 5 | 4.00 | 4.00 |

**Souvenir Sheet**

| | | | |
|---|---|---|---|
| **3073** A523 | $5 multi | 3.75 | 3.75 |

Souvenir Sheets

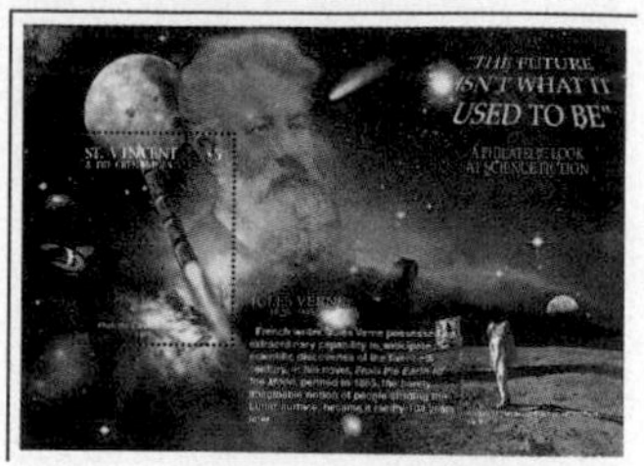
"THE FUTURE ISN'T WHAT IT USED TO BE"

Science Fiction — A524

Designs: No. 3074, $5, From the Earth to the Moon, by Jules Verne. No. 3075, $5, The War of the Worlds, by H. G. Wells. No. 3076, $5, The Time Machine, by Wells.

**2002, Dec. 2** ***Perf. 13¾***

**3074-3076** A524 Set of 3 11.50 11.50

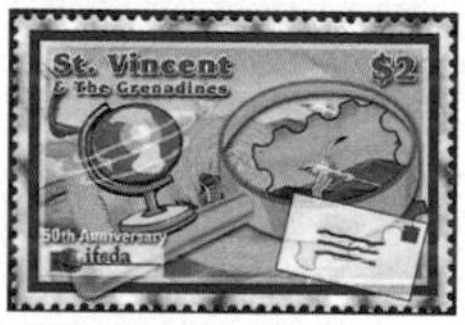
St. Vincent & The Grenadines
$2

Intl. Federation of Stamp Dealers Associations, 50th Anniv. — A525

**2003, Feb. 16** ***Perf. 14***

**3077** A525 $2 multi 1.50 1.50

**British Military Medals Type of 2002**

Souvenir Sheets

Designs: No. 3078, $5, Victoria Medal. No. 3079, $5, Atlantic Star. No. 3080, $5, 1939-45 Star. No. 3081, $5, Africa Star.

**2003, Jan. 27** ***Perf. 13¼***

**3078-3081** A520 Set of 4 15.00 15.00

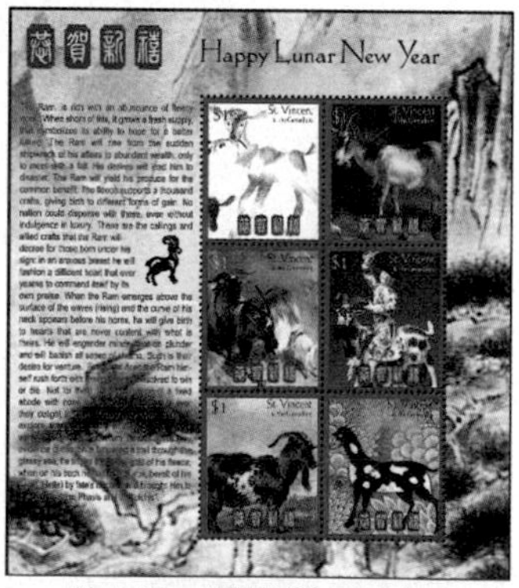
Happy Lunar New Year

New Year 2003 (Year of the Ram) — A526

No. 3082: a, Goat with gray collar. b, Goat facing left. c, Goats and kid. d, Man on goat. e, Goat facing right. f, Goat with piebald coat (flora in background).

**2003, Feb. 1** ***Perf. 14¼x13¾***

**3082** A526 $1 Sheet of 6, #a-f 4.50 4.50

Miniature Sheet

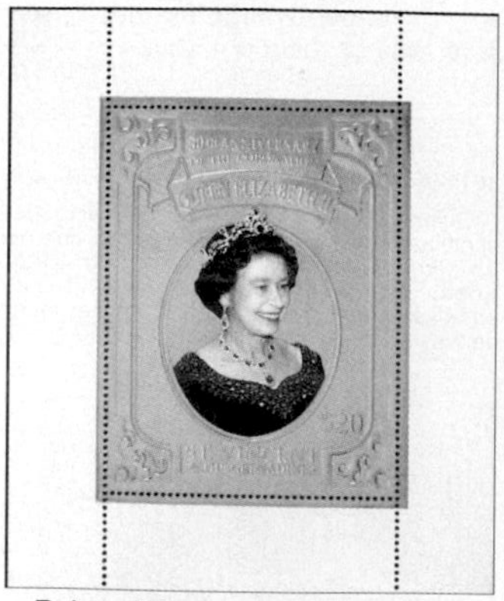

Reign of Queen Elizabeth II, 50th Anniv. (in 2002) — A527

**Litho. & Embossed**

**2003, Feb. 24** ***Perf. 13¼x13***

**3083** A527 $20 gold & multi 15.00 15.00

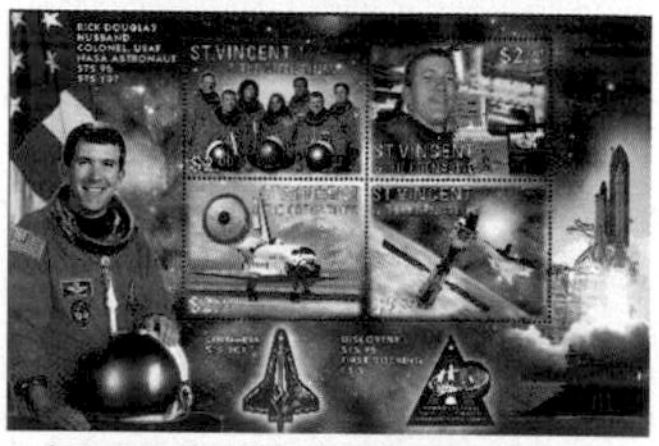

Astronauts Killed in Space Shuttle Columbia Accident — A528

No. 3084, $2 — Col. Rick D. Husband: a, Crew photo (green sky). b, Husband, interior of shuttle. c, Shuttle landing. d, Shuttle and space station.
No. 3085, $2 — Commander William C. McCool: a, Crew photo (tan sky). b, McCool in airplane cockpit. c, McCool, interior of shuttle. d, Shuttle in flight, comet.
No. 3086, $2 — Capt. David M. Brown: a, Crew photo (cloudy sky). b, Shuttle being moved to launch pad. c, Shuttle orbiting earth. d, Brown, interior of shuttle.

**2003, Apr. 7** **Litho.** ***Perf. 14¼***

**Sheets of 4, #a-d**

**3084-3086** A528 Set of 3 18.00 18.00

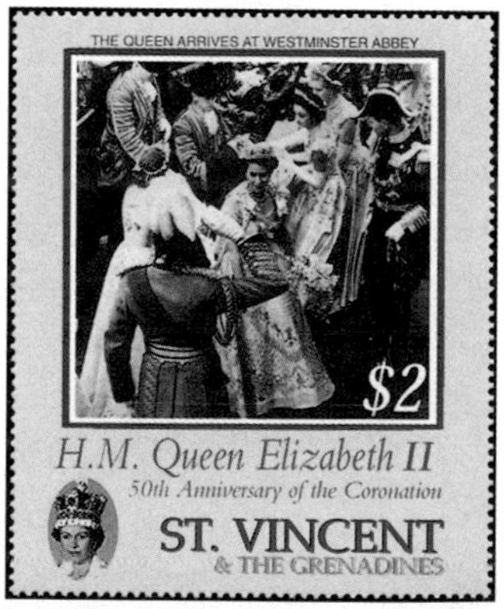
THE QUEEN ARRIVES AT WESTMINSTER ABBEY
$2
H.M. Queen Elizabeth II
50th Anniversary of the Coronation
ST. VINCENT
& THE GRENADINES

Coronation of Queen Elizabeth II, 50th Anniv. — A529

Designs: No. 3087, $2, Queen arrives at Westminster Abbey. No. 3088, $2, Queen seated in Chair of Estate. No. 3089, $2, Queen's first progress along the nave. No. 3090, $2, Queen leaving Buckingham Palace. No. 3091, $2, Queen and Duke of Edinburgh in state coach. No. 3092, $2, Gold state coach. No. 3093, $2, Westminster Abbey.
$5, Queen's portrait.

**2003, Feb. 26** **Litho.** ***Perf. 13¼***

**3087-3093** A529 Set of 7 10.50 10.50

**Souvenir Sheet**

***Perf. 14¼***

**3094** A529 $5 multi 3.75 3.75

No. 3094 contains one 38x50mm stamp.

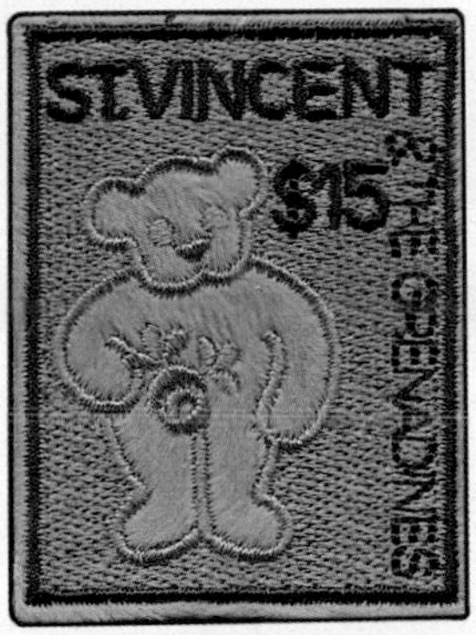
ST.VINCENT
$15
& THE GRENADINES
Teddy Bear A530

**2003, Apr. 30 Embroidered** ***Imperf.***
**Self-Adhesive**

**3095** A530 $15 multi 11.50 11.50

Issued in sheets of 4.

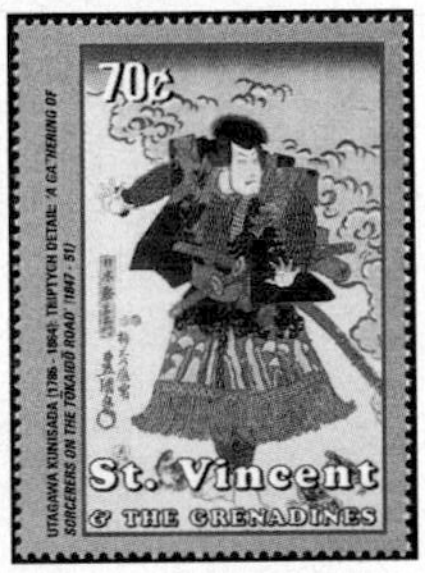
70¢
St. Vincent
& THE GRENADINES
Japanese Art — A531

Designs: 70c, A Gathering of Sorcerers on the Tokaido Road (detail), by Kunisada Utagawa. $1.10, Kiyohime and the Moon, by Chikanobu Yoshu. $1.10, A Gathering of Sorcerers on the Tokaido Road (detail), by Kunisada Utagawa, diff. $3, A Gathering of Sorcerers on the Tokaido Road (detail), by Kunisada Utagawa, diff.

No. 3100: a, Snake Mountain, by Kuniyoshi Utagawa. b, Sadanobu and Oni, by Yoshitoshi Tsukioka. c, Shoki, by Tsukioka. d, The Nightly Weeping Rock, by Kuniyoshi Utagawa.

$5, The Ghosts of Matahachi and Kikuno, by Kunisada Utagawa.

**2003, Apr. 30 Litho.** ***Perf. 14¼***
**3096-3099** A531 Set of 4 4.75 4.75
**3100** A531 $2 Sheet of 4, #a-d 6.00 6.00

**Souvenir Sheet**

**3101** A531 $5 multi 3.75 3.75

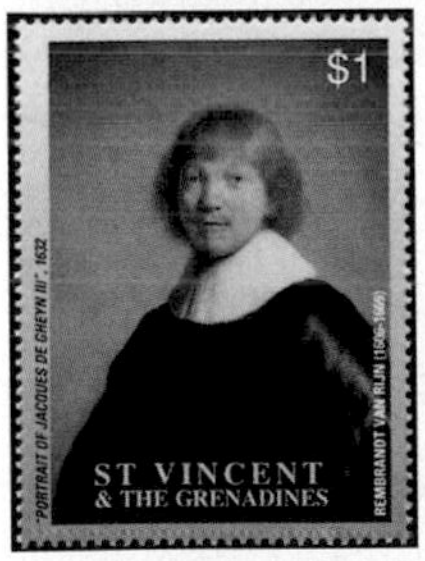
$1
ST VINCENT
& THE GRENADINES
Rembrandt Paintings A532

Designs: $1, Portrait of Jacques de Gheyn III. $1.10, Young Man in a Black Beret. $1.40, Hendrickje Stoffels. No. 3105, $2, The Polish Rider, horiz.

No. 3106, $2: a, Belthazzar Sees the Writing on the Wall. b, Portrait of a Young Man. c, Jacob Blessing the Sons of Joseph. d, King Uzziah Stricken with Leprosy.

$5, The Stoning of St. Stephen.

**2003, Apr. 30**
**3102-3105** A532 Set of 4 4.25 4.25
**3106** A532 $2 Sheet of 4, #a-d 6.00 6.00

**Souvenir Sheet**

**3107** A532 $5 multi 3.75 3.75

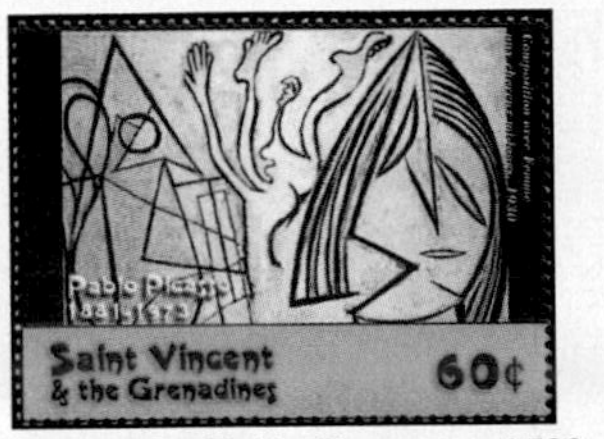
Saint Vincent
& the Grenadines
60¢
Paintings By Pablo Picasso — A533

Designs: 60c, Composition: Woman with Half-Length Hair. 70c, Sister of the Artist, vert. 90c, Maternity, vert. $1, Bearded Man's Head, vert. $1.10, Two Seated Children (Claude and Paloma), vert. $1.40, Woman with a Blue Lace Collar.

No. 3114: a, Corrida. b, Mandolin, Pitcher and Bottle. c, The Painter and Model. d, Reclining Woman Sleeping Under a Lamp.

No. 3115, Reclining Nude. No. 3116, Spanish Woman Against an Orange Background, vert.

**2003, Apr. 30** ***Perf. 14¼***
**3108-3113** A533 Set of 6 4.25 4.25
**3114** A533 $2 Sheet of 4, #a-d 6.00 6.00

***Imperf***
**Size: 103x82mm**

**3115** A533 $5 multi 3.75 3.75

**Size: 82x105mm**

**3116** A533 $5 multi 3.75 3.75

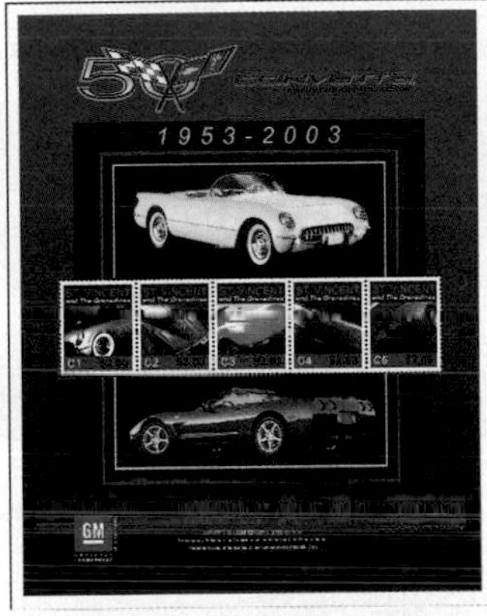
1953-2003
Corvette Automobiles, 50th Anniv. — A534

No. 3117: a, C1. b, C2. c, C3. d, C4. e, C5.
No. 3118: a, 1953 Corvette. b, 2003 Corvette.

**2003, May 5** ***Perf. 13¼***
**3117** A534 $2 Sheet of 5, #a-e 7.50 7.50

***Perf. 14¼***

**3118** A534 $3 Sheet of 2, #a-b 4.50 4.50

No. 3118 contains two 50x38mm stamps.

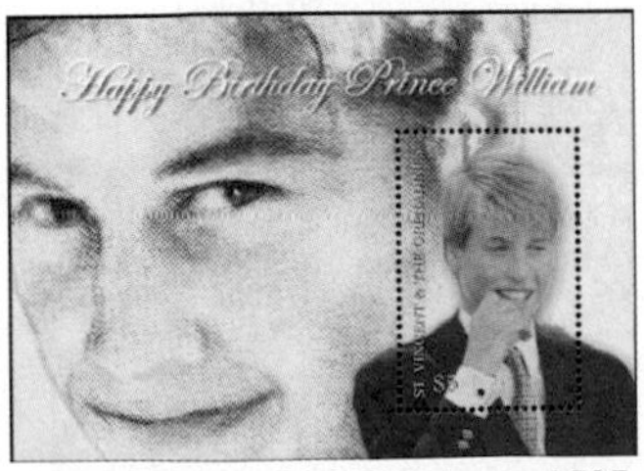
Happy Birthday Prince William
Prince William, 21st Birthday — A535

No. 3119: a, Wearing suit. b, Wearing polo jersey. c, Wearing blue shirt.

$5, Wearing suit and tie.

**2003, May 13** ***Perf. 14***
**3119** A535 $3 Sheet of 3, #a-c 6.75 6.75

**Souvenir Sheet**

**3120** A535 $5 multi 3.75 3.75

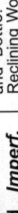

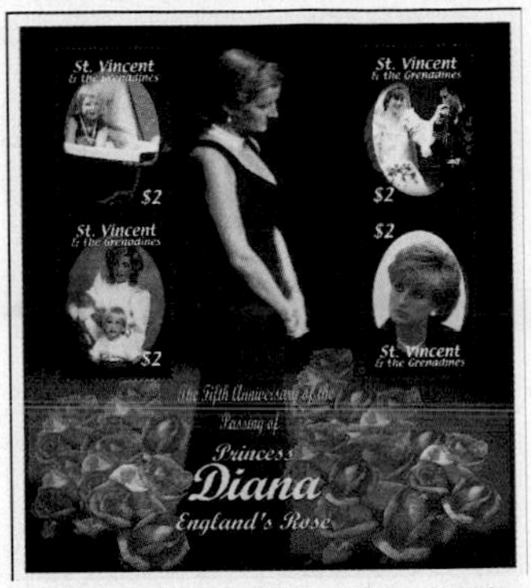
Princess
Diana
England's Rose
Princess Diana (1961-97) — A536

No. 3121, $2 (vignettes in ovals): a, As child in baby carriage. b, With Prince Charles on wedding day. c, With Princes William and Harry. d, In purple jacket.

No. 3122, $2 (white background): a, Wearing tiara. b, Wearing white gown. c, Wearing purple sweater. d, Wearing lilac dress.

**2003, May 26** **Sheets of 4, #a-d**
**3121-3122** A536 Set of 2 12.00 12.00

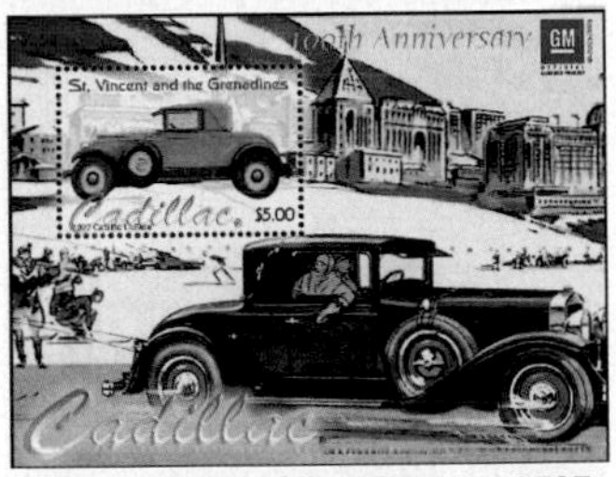
St. Vincent and the Grenadines
Cadillac
$5.00
Cadillac
Cadillac Automobiles, Cent. — A537

No. 3123: a, 1953 Eldorado. b, 2002 Eldorado. c, 1967 Eldorado. d, 1962 Series 62.

$5, 1927 LaSalle.

**2003, July 1** ***Perf. 13¼x13¾***
**3123** A537 $2 Sheet of 4, #a-d 6.00 6.00

**Souvenir Sheet**

**3124** A537 $5 multi 3.75 3.75

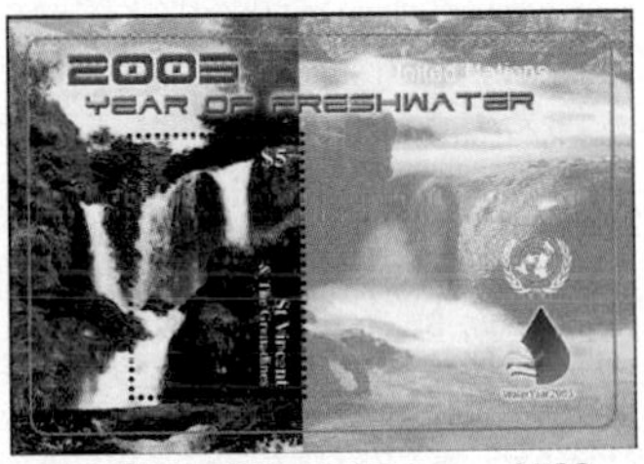
2003
YEAR OF FRESHWATER
Intl. Year of Fresh Water — A538

No. 3125: a, Owia Salt Pond. b, The Soufriere. c, Falls of Baleine.

$5, Trinity Falls.

**2003, July 1** ***Perf. 13½***
**3125** A538 $3 Sheet of 3, #a-c 6.75 6.75

**Souvenir Sheet**

**3126** A538 $5 multi 3.75 3.75

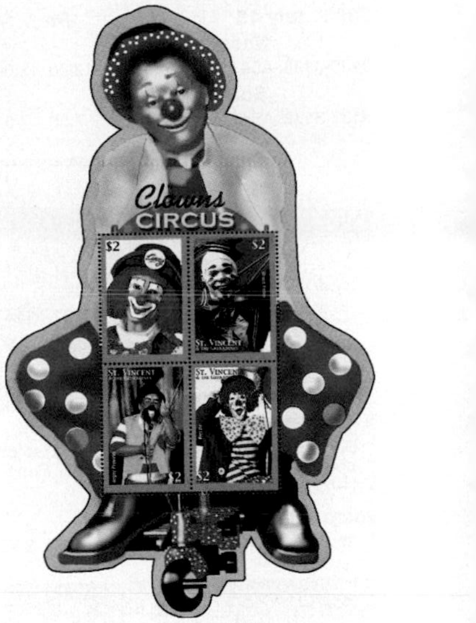
Clowns
CIRCUS
Circus — A539

No. 3127, $2: a, Linny. b, Bruce Feiler. c, Segey Provirin. d, Weezle.

No. 3128, $2: a, Mermaids. b, Robert Wolf. c, Elbrus Pilev's Group. d, Stinky.

**2003, July 1** ***Perf. 14***

**Sheets of 4, #a-d**

**3127-3128** A539 Set of 2 12.00 12.00

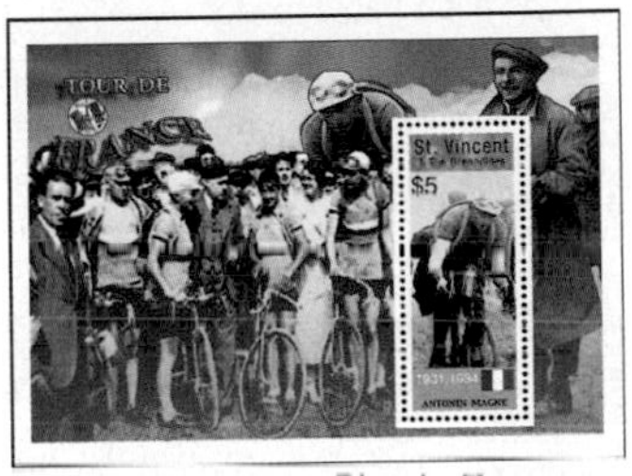
St. Vincent
$5
Tour de France Bicycle Race, Cent. — A540

No. 3129: a, Antonin Magne, 1931. b, André Leducq, 1932. c, Georges Speicher, 1933. d, Magne, 1934.

No. 3130: a, Romain Maes, 1935. b, Sylvére Maes, 1936. c, Roger Lapebie, 1937. d, Gino Bartali, 1938.

No. 3131. a, Sylvére Maes, 1939. b, Jean Lazaridés, 1946. c, Jean Robic, 1947. d, Bartali, 1948.

No. 3132, $5, Magne, 1931, 1934. No. 3133, $5, Fausto Coppi, 1949. No. 3134, $5, Ferdinand Kubler, 1950.

**2003, July 1** ***Perf. 13¼***

**Sheets of 4, #a-d**

**3129-3131** A540 Set of 3 18.00 18.00

**Souvenir Sheets**

**3132-3134** A570 Set of 3 11.50 11.50

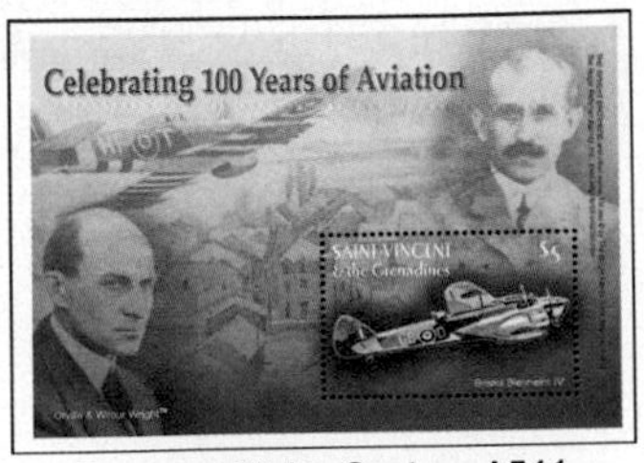
Celebrating 100 Years of Aviation
SAINT VINCENT
& the Grenadines
$5
Powered Flight, Cent. — A541

No. 3135, $2: a, Handley Page Heyford. b, Heinkel He-111B. c, Gloster Gauntlet. d, Curtiss BF2C-1.

No. 3136, $2: a, Mitsubishi A6M Reisen. b, Dewoitine D520. c, Messerschmitt Bf 109E. d, Republic Thunderbolt.

No. 3137, $5, Bristol Blenheim IV. No. 3138, $5, Fairey Flycatcher.

**2003, July 15** **Perf. 14**

3135-3136 A541 Set of 2 **Sheets of 4, #a-d**
3137-3138 A541 Set of 2 **Souvenir Sheets**

Designs: 70c, Chief musicians, 90c, District temple. $1, Christmas Kettle Appeal Fund. $1.10, Headquarters, horiz.

Salvation Army in St. Vincent, Cent. — A542

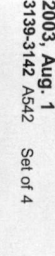

**2003, Aug. 1**
3139-3142 A542 Set of 4 7.50 7.50

2.75 2.75

No. 3143: a, Gen. Richard B. Meyers. b, Lt. Gen. David McKiernan. c, Lt. Gen. Michael Moseley. d, Vice Admiral Timothy Keating. e, Lt. Gen. Jay Garner. f, Gen. Tommy R. Franks. g, Lt. Gen. Earl B. Hailston. h, Gen. John Jumper.

No. 3144: a, Private Jessica Lynch. b, Gen. Franks. c, Specre gunship. d, Stryker vehicle. e, USS Constellation. f, USS Kitty Hawk.

Operation Iraqi Freedom — A543

**2003, Aug. 25** **Perf. 14¼**
3143 A543 $1 **Sheet of 8, #a-h** 6.00 6.00
3144 A543 $1.50 **Sheet of 6, #a-f** 6.75 6.75

A544

Marvel Comic Book Characters — A546

No. 3145 — Spiderman: a, Shooting cable from one arm. b, Grasping two cables. c, Grasping one cable. d, Climbing on building.

No. 3146: a — The Incredible Hulk: a, Close-up of face, denomination at UR. b, Fire in background, denomination at UL. c, Like "a," denomination at UR. d, Like "a," denomination at UL.

No. 3147 $2 — The Incredible Hulk: a, Punching ground. b, Grasping. c, Showing fists. d, Punching rocks.

No. 3148, $2 — X-Men United: a, Night-crawler. b, Professor X. c, Iceman. d, Rogue.
No. 3149, $2 — X-Men United: a, Magneto.
b, Mystique. c, Stryker. d, Lady Deathstrike.
No. 3150, $2 — X-Men United: a, Jean Grey. b, Storm. c, Wolverine. d, Cyclops.

**2003, Sept. 10** **Perf. 13¼**
3145 A544 $2 **Sheet of 4, #a-d** 6.00 6.00
**Sheets of 4, #a-d**
3146-3147 A545 Set of 2 12.00 12.00
3148-3150 A546 Set of 3 18.00 18.00

PRE-HISTORIC ANIMALS

$5

Prehistoric Animals — A547

No. 3151: $2, horiz.: a, Daspletosaurus. b, Utahraptor. c, Scutellosaurus. d, Scelidosaurus.
No. 3152: $2, horiz.: a, Syntarsus. b, Velociraptor. c, Mononikus. d, Massospondylus.
No. 3153, $5, Pterodactylus. No. 3154, $5, Giganotosaurus.

**2003, Nov. 5** **Perf. 13¾**
**Sheets of 4, #a-d**
3151-3152 A547 Set of 2 12.00 12.00
3153-3154 A547 Set of 2 7.50 7.50
**Souvenir Sheets**
**Perf. 13¾x13¾**

X-MEN UNITED

A545

Laela lobata

Cats — A548

Dogs — A549

Designs: 50c, British Shorthair, $1, Burmese. $1.40, American Shorthair, $3, Havana Brown.
No. 3159: a, Ocicat. b, Manx. c, Somali. d, Angora.
$5, Abyssinian.

**2003, Nov. 5** **Perf. 14**
3155-3158 A548 Set of 4 4.50 4.50
3159 A548 $2 **Sheet of 4, #a-d** 6.00 6.00
**Souvenir Sheet**
3160 A548 $5 multi 3.75 3.75

Designs: 10c, Chihuahua. 20c, Bulldog. 60c, Weimaraner. No. 3164, $5, Dalmatian.
No. 3165: a, Dachshund. b, Collie. c, Springer spaniel. d, Hamilton hound.
No. 3166, $5, Golden retriever.

**2003, Nov. 5**
3161-3164 A549 Set of 4 4.50 4.50
3165 A549 $2 **Sheet of 4, #a-d** 6.00 6.00
**Souvenir Sheet**
3166 A549 $5 multi 3.75 3.75

Orchids — A550

Laelia lobata 40¢

Marine Life — A551

Designs: 40c, Laelia lobata. 90c, Miltoniopsis phalaenopsis. $1, Phalaenopsis violacea. $3, Trichopilia fragrans.
No. 3171: a, Masdevallia uniflora. b, Laelia flava. c, Barkeria lindleyana. d, Laelia tenebrosa.
$5, Cattleya lawrenceana.

**2003, Nov. 5**
3167-3170 A550 Set of 4 4.00 4.00
3171 A550 $2 **Sheet of 4, #a-d** 6.00 6.00
**Souvenir Sheet**
3172 A550 $5 multi 3.75 3.75

Designs: 70c, Lutjanus kasmira. 90c, Chaetodon collare. $1.10, Istiophorus platypterus. No. 3176, $2, Pomacanthidae.
No. 3177, $2: a, Equetus lanceolatus. b, Hypoplectrus guttavarius. c, Pomacentridae. d, Cichlidae.
$5, Dolphins.

**2003, Nov. 5**
3173-3176 A551 Set of 4 3.50 3.50
3177 A551 $2 **Sheet of 4, #a-d** 6.00 6.00
**Souvenir Sheet**
3178 A551 $5 multi 3.75 3.75

3rd PRIZE

ST. VINCENT 70¢

Children's contest-winning art by: 70c, Andrew Gonsalves. 90c, Adam Gravel, vert. $1.10, Georgia Gravel.

Christmas — A552

**2003, Nov. 5** **Perf. 14¼**
3179-3181 A552 Set of 3 2.00 2.00

PLAYBOY'S FIFTIETH ANNIVERSARY

Playboy Magazine, 50th Anniv. — A553

Magazine covers depicting: a, Marilyn Monroe. b, Playboy emblem. c, Rabbit and kisses. d, Woman with legs above head. e, Woman licking stamp. f, 50th Anniversary emblem.

**2003, Dec. 1** **Litho.** **Perf. 14**
3182 A553 $1.50 **Sheet of 6, #a-f** 6.75 6.75

Ma Yüan (1160-1235)

Ma Yuan (1160-1235), Painter — A554

No. 3183: a, Apricot Blossoms. b, Peach Blossoms. c, Unnamed painting, denomination at left. d, Unnamed painting, denomination at right.
$5, On a Mountain Path in Spring.
No. 3183 contains four 40x30mm stamps.

**2004, Jan. 30** **Perf. 13½x13½**
3183 A554 $2 **Sheet of 4, #a-d** 6.00 6.00
**Imperf**
3184 A554 $5 multi 3.75 3.75

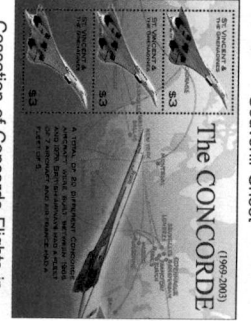
The CONCORDE (1969-2003)

Cessation of Concorde Flights in 2003 — A555

Concorde over map showing: a, Anchorage. b, Los Angeles. c, South Pacific (no cities named).

**2004, Feb. 16** **Perf. 13½x13½**
3185 A555 $3 **Sheet of 3, #a-c** 6.75 6.75

**Souvenir Sheet**

St.Vincent & The Grenadines $1.40

New Year 2004 (Year of the Monkey) — A556

**2004, Jan. 15** **Litho.** **Perf. 13½x13**
3186 A556 $1.40 buff, lt brn & blk 1.10 1.10
**Souvenir Sheet**
3187 A556 $3 pink, brn & blk 2.25 2.25

No. 3186 printed in sheets of 4.

## ST. VINCENT

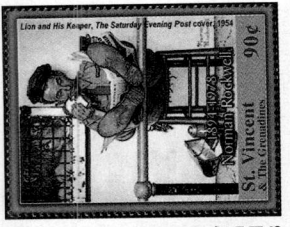

A557

### Marilyn Monroe (1926-62), Actress — A558

No. 3188: a, Sepia-toned portrait. b, Wearing blue dress. c, Wearing white dress. d, Wearing black dress.
No. 3189: a, Wearing round white earrings. b, With hand showing. c, Wearing no earrings. d, Wearing different earrings.

2004, May 3    **Perf. 14**
3188 A557 $2 Sheet of 4, #a-d    6.00 6.00
**Perf. 13½x13¼**
3189 A558 $2 Sheet of 4, #a-d    6.00 6.00

### European Soccer Championships, Portugal — A559

No. 3190, vert.: a, Roger Lemerre. b, Marco Delvecchio. c, David Trezeguet. d, De Kuip Stadium. $5, 2000 French team.

2004, May 17    **Perf. 13½x13¼**
3190 A559 $2 Sheet of 4, #a-d    6.00 6.00
**Souvenir Sheet**
**Perf. 13¼**
3191 A559 $5 multi    3.75 3.75
No. 3190 contains four 28x42mm stamps.

2004 Summer Olympics, Athens A560

Designs: 70c, Pierre de Coubertin, first Intl. Olympic Committee Secretary General. $1, Pin from 1904 St. Louis Olympics. $1.40,

---

Water Polo, 1936 Berlin Olympics, horiz. $3, Greek amphora.

2004, June 17    **Perf. 14¼**
3192-3195 A560 Set of 4    4.75 4.75

### Babe Ruth (1895-1948), Baseball Player — A561

No. 3196: a, Facing right. b, Facing forward. c, Leaning on bat. d, Swinging bat.

2004, July 1    **Perf. 13½x13¼**
3196 A561 $2 Sheet of 4, #a-d    6.00 6.00

### D-Day, 60th Anniv. A562

Designs: 70c, Air Chief Marshal Sir Trafford Leigh-Mallory. 90c, Lt. Col. Maureen Gara. $1, Gen. Omar Bradley. $1.10, Jean Valentine. $1.40, Jack Culshaw. $1.50, Gen. Dwight D. Eisenhower.
No. 3203, $2: a, British land on Gold Beach. b, British Infantry land on Gold Beach. c, Canadians at Juno Beach. d, Canadians land at Juno Beach.
No. 3204, $2: a, Rangers take Pointe du Hoc. b, Rangers hold Pointe du Hoc. c, Invasion announced to press. d, British liberate Hermanville.
No. 3205, $5, Soldiers prepare to board assault landing craft. No. 3206, $5, Code breaking team at work.

2004, July 19    **Perf. 14**
**Stamp + Label (#3197-3202)**
3197-3202 A562 Set of 6    5.00 5.00
**Sheets of 4, #a-d**
3203-3204 A562 Set of 2    12.00 12.00
**Souvenir Sheets**
3205-3206 A562 Set of 2    7.50 7.50

### General Employees' Cooperative Credit Union — A563

Designs: 70c, GECCU children. 90c, GECCU Building. $1.10, Calvin Nicholls, vert. $1.40, Bertrand Neehall, vert.

2004, Sept. 15    **Litho.**
3207-3210 A563 Set of 4    3.25 3.25

---

### Pres. Ronald Reagan (1911-2004) A564

No. 3211: a, Portrait. b, With flag. c, At microphone.

2004, Oct. 13    **Perf. 13½x13¼**
3211    3.25 3.25
a.-c. A564 $1.40 Any single    1.00 1.00
Printed in sheets containing two strips.

### Railroads, 200th Anniv. — A565

No. 3212, $2: a, 1911 0-6-0 Standard, Boston & Maine. b, AG locomotive. c, BA 101 Antigua locomotive. d, Aster 1449.
No. 3213, $2: a, Narrow gauge locomotive W12. b, Gambler. LNV9701 4-4-0 NG. c, No. 4 Snowdon. d, Hiawatha 3-1.
No. 3214, $2: a, CO1604-1. b, CP steam locomotive N135. c, 6042-6. d, F1 narrow gauge 0-4-0T.
No. 3215, $5, NAT2A 01-06-00. No. 3216, $5, Union Pacific 044. No. 3217, $5, Holy War 1, vert.

2004, Oct. 13    **Perf. 14**
**Sheets of 4, #a-d**
3212-3214 A565 Set of 3    18.00 18.00
**Souvenir Sheets**
3215-3217 A565 Set of 3    11.50 11.50

### Independence, 25th Anniv. — A566

Designs: 10c, Halliman DeShong. 20c, Winston Davis, cricket player. 70c, Miss Carnival 2003. No. 3221, 70c, Flag, horiz. No. 3222, 70c, Pamenoa Ballantyne, runner, horiz. No. 3223, 90c, Carl "Blazer" Williams. No. 3224, 90c, Breadfruit, horiz. No. 3225, 90c, Rodney "Chang" Jack, soccer player, horiz. $1.10, St. Vincent parrot. No. 3227, $5, Capt. Hugh Mulzac. No. 3228, $5, George McIntosh, political leader. No. 3229, $5, E. T. Joshua, chief, national hero. No. 3230, $10, Joseph Chatoyer, Carib chief, national hero. No. 3231, $10, Robert Milton Cato, politician.

2004, Oct. 25
3218-3231 A566 Set of 14    31.00 31.00

### FIFA (Fédération Internationale de Football Association), Cent. — A567

No. 3232: a, David Ginola. b, Paul Scholes. c, Jurgen Kohler. d, Ian Rush. $5, Alan Shearer.

2004, Oct. 27    **Perf. 12¾x12½**
3232 A567 $2 Sheet of 4, #a-d    6.00 6.00
**Souvenir Sheet**
3233 A567 $5 multi    3.75 3.75

---

### Paintings by Norman Rockwell A568

Designs: 90c, Lion and His Keeper. $1, Weighing In. $1.40, The Young Lawyer. $2, The Bodybuilder. $5, Triple Self-portrait.

2004, Oct. 29    **Perf. 14¼**
3234-3237 A568 Set of 4    4.00 4.00
**Imperf    Size: 66x88mm**
3238 A568 $5 multi    3.75 3.75

### Various St. Vincent and St. Vincent Grenadines Stamps Surcharged

SURCHARGE TYPES ON ST. VINCENT STAMPS:
10c on 47c #1071l — Type 1: "4" without bottom serif "0" same thickness. Type 2: "4" with bottom serif "0" thin at top and bottom.
10c on 65c #1080h and 10c on 75c #1081b Type 1: "1" with bottom serif, "0" thin at top and bottom. Type 2: "1" without bottom serif "0" same thickness.
20c on 60c #726 — Type 1: New denomination at lower left with small "c." Type 2: New denomination at upper left, with cent sign. Type 3: New denomination below obliterator and approximately 6mm to left of it, with small "c." Type 4: New denomination below obliterator and approximately 16mm to left of it, with small "c."
20c on 75c #984a-984b horiz. pair — Type 1: Small "c." Type 2: Cent sign.
20c on $1.25 #527 — Type 1: New denomination to left of round obliterator, with raised "c" at lower left, round obliterator with cent sign and serifed "2." Type 2: New denomination at lower left, round obliterator with cent sign and serifed "2." Type 3: New denomination below square obliterator, unserifed "2" and "c."
20c on $2 #638 — Type 1: New denomination to right and below obliterator, with serifed "2" and small "c" with ball. Type 2: New denomination to right of obliterator, with unserifed "2" and small "c" without ball.
20c on $2 #665 — Type 1: New denomination at left, with small "c" with ball and serifed "2." Type 2: New denomination close to obliterator at left, with small "c" without ball and unserifed "2."
20c on $2 #975 — Type 1: Cent sign. Type 2: Small "c."
20c on $3.70 #1004 — Type 1: New denomination at upper left, with serifed "2," "0" thin at top and bottom. Type 2: New denomination at upper right with unserifed "2," "0" same thickness.

SURCHARGE TYPES ON ST. VINCENT GRENADINES STAMPS:
20c on 75c #511 — Type 1: Cent sign. Type 2: Small "c."
20c on 75c #593 — Type 1: New denomination at lower left, below obliterator, with cent sign. Type 2: New denomination to right of obliterator, with small "c."
20c on $1.50 #277 — Type 1: New denomination at top center, with small "c." Type 2: New denomination at lower left, with cent sign.
20c on $2 #186 — Type 1: New denomination to left of obliterator, with small "c." Type 2: New denomination at upper left, with cent sign.
20c on $2.50 #265 — Type 1: Unserified "2," small "c" even with base of numerals. Type 2: Serifed "2," raised small "c."

## Methods, Perfs and Watermarks As Before

### 1994 (?)-2004

#### On St. Vincent Stamps

| No. | Type | Description |
|---|---|---|
| 3239 | A36 | 10c on 2c #281 |
| 3240 | A148 | 10c on 6c #1070 |
| 3241 | A148 | 10c on 12c #1072 |
| 3242 | A148 | 10c on 15c |
| 3243 | A36 | 10c on 25c #290 |
| 3244 | A148 | 10c on 25c #1073b |
| a. | | #1075b |
| 3245 | A112 | 10c on 35c #743 |
| 3246 | A148 | 10c on 35c #1077 |
| 3247 | A109 | 10c on 45c #1077 |
| 3248 | A148 | 10c on 45c #725 |
| 3249 | A148 | 10c on 45c #1078, Type 1 |
| a.1 | | On #1078b (perf. 14), Type 2 |
| a.2 | | On #1078b, Type |
| 3250 | A151 | 10c on 45c #1096 |
| 3251 | A98 | 10c on 60c #640 |
| 3252 | A104a | 10c on 60c #671 |
| 3253 | A104b | 10c on 60c #676 |
| 3254 | A148 | 10c on 65c #1080b, Type 1 |
| 3255 | A148 | 10c on 65c #1080b, Type 2 |
| 3256 | A71 | 10c on 70c #481 |
| 3257 | A148 | 10c on 75c #1081b, Type 1 |
| 3257A | A148 | 10c on 75c #1081b, Type 2 |
| 3258 | A109 | 10c on $1 #728 |
| 3259 | A77 | 10c on $1.25 #527 |
| 3260 | A98 | 10c on $1.50 #641 |
| 3261 | A105 | 10c on $1.50 #681 |
| 3262 | A162 | 10c on 45c #1096 |
| 3263 | A105 | 10c on $1.50 #544 |
| 3264 | A90 | 10c on 90c #607 |
| 3266 | A36 | 10c on 1c #337 |
| 3267 | A47 | 10c on #1061a-1061b horiz. |
| 3268 | A126 | 10c on 25c #903 |
| 3273 | A113 | 20c on 35c #761 |
| 3274 | A162 | 20c on 45c #1145 |
| 3275 | A105 | 20c on 45c #679 |
| 3277 | A105 | 20c on 45c #1096 |
| 3278 | A90 | 20c on 60c #605 |
| 3279 | A98 | 20c on 60c #616 |
| 3280 | A104 | 20c on 60c #636 |
| 3281 | A104 | 20c on 60c #640 |
| 3282 | A104 | 20c on 60c #667 |
| 3283 | A104b | 20c on 60c #676 |
| 3284 | A105 | 20c on 60c #680 |
| 3285 | A109 | 20c on 60c #726, Type 1 |
| 3286 | A109 | 20c on 60c #726, Type 2 |
| 3287 | A109 | 20c on 60c #726, Type 3 |
| 3288 | A109 | 20c on 60c #726, Type 4 |
| 3289 | A115 | 20c on 70c #784 |
| 3290 | A71 | 20c on 70c #481 |
| 3292 | A136 | 20c on 75c #984a-984b horiz. pair, Type 1 |
| 3293 | A136 | 20c on 20c 984b horiz. pair, Type 2 |
| 3294 | A126 | 20c on 25c #903 |
| 3295 | A138 | 20c on 35c #761 |
| 3296 | A75 | 20c on 35c #1145 |
| 3297 | A94 | 20c on 45c #679 |
| 3298 | A97 | 20c on 45c #1096 |
| 3299 | A121 | 20c on 62b pair |
| 3302 | A64 | 20c on $1 #637 |
| 3303 | A70 | 20c on $1 #622a- |
| 3304 | A73 | 20c on 70c #481 |
| 3306 | A77 | 20c on 75c #498 |
| 3307 | A77 | 20c on $1.25 #527, Type 1 |
| 3308 | A77 | 20c on $1.25 #527, Type 2 |
| 3310 | A103 | 20c on $1.50 #664 |
| 3311 | A104 | 20c on $1.50 #668 |
| 3313 | A105 | 20c on $1.50 #681 |
| 3314 | A105 | 20c on $1.50 #677 |
| 3316 | A115 | 20c on $1.50 #785 |
| 3317 | A136 | 20c on $1.50 #974 |
| 3318 | A93 | 20c on $1.50 horiz. pair |
| 3320 | A97 | 20c on $2 #638, Type 1 |
| 3321 | A97 | 20c on $2 #638, Type 2 |
| 3322 | A98 | 20c on $2 #642 |
| 3324 | A103 | 20c on $2 #665, Type 1 |
| 3325 | A103 | 20c on $2 #665, Type 2 |
| 3326 | A104 | 20c on $2 #669 |
| 3327 | A104b | 20c on $2 #678 |
| 3328 | A105 | 20c on $2 #682 |
| 3329 | A115 | 20c on $2 #86 |

#### On St. Vincent Grenadines Stamps

| No. | Type | Description |
|---|---|---|
| 3330 | A134 | 20c on $2 #975, Type 1 |
| 3331 | A134 | 20c on $2 #975, Type 2 |
| a. | | Horiz. pair, #3330-3331 |
| 3333 | A126 | 20c on 1c #33 |
| 3334 | A108 | 20c on $2.50 #905 |
| 3337 | A113 | 20c on $3 #718 |
| 3338 | A117 | 20c on $3 #764 |
| 3339 | A119 | 20c on $3 #806 |
| 3342 | A139 | 20c on $3 #832 |
| 3343 | A139 | 20c on $3.70 #1004, Type 1 |
| 3345 | A189 | 20c on $4 #1307, Type 2 |

#### On St. Vincent Grenadines Stamps

| No. | Type | Description |
|---|---|---|
| 3346 | G3 | 10c on 1c #33 |
| 3347 | G16 | 10c on 6c #133 |
| 3348 | G16 | 10c on 6c #138 |
| 3349 | G35 | 10c on 35c #433 |
| 3350 | G33 | 10c on 45c #271 |
| 3351 | G33 | 10c on 45c #297 |
| 3352 | G20 | 10c on 45c #185 |
| 3353 | A90 | 10c on 45c #192 |
| 3354 | A106 | 10c on $1 #435 |
| 3355 | G32 | 10c on $1 #278 |
| 3356 | G35 | 10c on 35c #469 |
| 3358 | G39 | 10c on 35c #484 |
| 3359 | G31 | 10c on 45c #470 |
| 3360 | G31 | 10c on 45c #561 |
| 3361 | G35 | 10c on 50c #71 |
| 3362 | G45 | 10c on 60c #272 |
| 3364 | G7 | 10c on 75c #511, Type 1 |
| 3366 | G41 | 10c on 75c #511, Type 2 |
| 3367 | A41 | 20c on 75c #511 |
| 3368 | G50 | 20c on 75c #588 |
| 3369 | G51 | 20c on 75c #593, Type 1 |
| 3370 | G51 | 20c on 75c #593, Type 2 |
| a. | | Horiz. pair, #3366-3367 |
| 3371 | G20 | 20c on 90c #185 |
| 3372 | G7 | 20c on $2 #72 |
| 3374 | G17 | 20c on $2 #242 |
| 3375 | G46 | 20c on $1.25 #160 |
| 3376 | G31 | 20c on $1.50 #566 |
| 3377 | A97 | 20c on $1.50 #264 |
| 3378 | G31 | 20c on $1.50 #273 |
| 3379 | G32 | 20c on $1.50 #277, Type 1 |
| 3381 | A76 | 20c on $2 #128, Type 2 |
| 3383 | G20 | 20c on $2 #186, Type 1 |
| 3384 | G20 | 20c on $2 #186, Type 2 |
| 3385 | G21 | 20c on $2 #198 |
| 3386 | G27 | 20c on $2 #242 |
| 3387 | G32 | 20c on $2 #278 |
| 3390 | A97 | 20c on $2.50 |
| 3391 | A97 | 20c on $2.50 #265, Type 1 |
| 3392 | A82 | 20c on $3 #179, Type 2 |
| 3394 | G35 | 20c on $3 #436 |
| 3395 | G37 | 20c on $3 #475 |
| 3396 | G39 | 20c on $3 #487 |
| 3397 | G43 | 20c on $3 #536 |
| 3399 | G59 | 20c on $3 #692 |
| 3400 | G50 | 20c on $3.50 #589 |
| 3401 | G45 | 20c on $4 #563 |

These surcharges were printed from the mid-1990s to 2004, with the bulk created from 1999 to 2004. Issue dates are not certain as the stamps were available for both revenue and postal use. Numbers are reserved for stamps that printer's records indicate were been surcharged. Additional stamps may also have been surcharged.

These stamps were not available through the philatelic agency, but could be bought at post offices, as well as Treasury offices and other locations throughout the country where revenue stamps were used, including retail stores.

The surcharged Grenadines issues were not necessarily sent only to the Grenadines for sale there.

Nos. 3246, 3249a, 3254, 3255, 3257A, 3263, 3347, 3349, 3351, and 3354, which are currently known only with revenue cancels, may also have been used postally.

The shape of the obliterators and the location of new denominations varies.

On No. 3240, the original denomination is obliterated with a marker. No. 3275 is known only with a double surcharge.

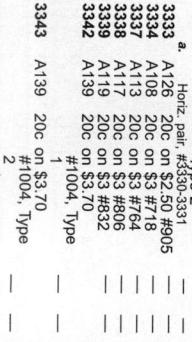
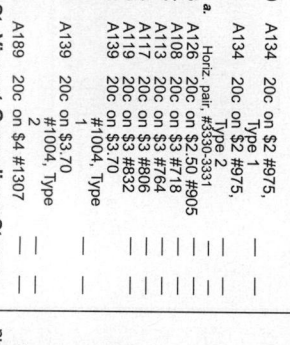

The item illustrated above is a revenue stamp, though it lacks any revenue stamp inscription. 10c on 20c, 20c, 50c, $5 and $60 stamps of this design also exist. Some of these revenue stamps also have been used on mail as they were available for sale to the public at the same locations as the surcharged stamps listed above. Non-governmental vendors of these stamps were lax in notifying stamp purchasers that the stamps were intended for revenue use only.

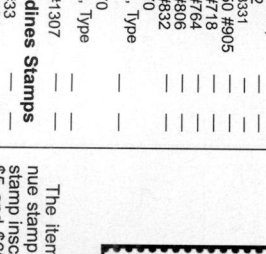

Queen Juliana of the Netherlands (1909-2004)
A569

**2004, Aug. 25  Litho.  Perf. 13¼**

| 3405 | A569 | $2 multi | 1.50 | 1.50 |
|---|---|---|---|---|

Printed in sheets of 6.

National Soccer Team — A570

**2004, Oct. 27**

| 3406 | A570 | 70c multi | **Perf. 12** | |
|---|---|---|---|---|
| | | | .55 | .55 |

Paintings in the Hermitage, St. Petersburg, Russia
A571

Designs: 10c, Head of a Young Girl, by Jean-Baptiste Greuze. 20c, Two Actresses, by Jean-Baptiste Santerre. 40c, An Allegory of History, by José de Ribera. 60c, A Young Woman Trying on Earrings, by Rembrandt. The Girlhood of the Virgin, by Francisco Zurbarán. No. 3412, $5, ... c, Landscape with Terrace and Cascade, by Robert. e, A Shepherdess, by Jan Siberecht. f, Landscape with Waterfall, by Robert. No. 3414, $1.40: a, Landscape with Obelisk, by Hubert Robert. b, At the Hermit's, by Robert. c, Landscape with Ruins, by Robert, d, Count N. D. Guriev, by Jean Auguste-Dominque Ingres. f, Portrait of an Actor, by Domenico Fetti.

Bonaparte on the Bridge at Arcole, by Baron Antoine-Jean Gros. d, A Young Man with a Glove, by Frans Hals. e, Portrait of General Alexei Yermolov, by George Dawe. f, A Scholar, by Rembrandt. No. 3415, The Bean King, by Jacob Jordaens, horiz. No. 3416, Three Men at a Table, by Diego Velázquez. No. 3417, Family Portrait, by Cornelis de Vos, horiz.

**2004, Nov. 1  Perf. 14¼**

| 3407-3412 | A571 | Set of 6 | 6.25 | 6.25 |
|---|---|---|---|---|
| 3413-3414 | A571 | Sheets of 6, #a-f Set of 2 | 13.00 | 13.00 |

**Imperf**

| 3415 | A571 | $5 multi | 3.75 | 3.75 |
|---|---|---|---|---|
| | | Size: 98x72mm | | |
| 3416 | A571 | $5 multi | 3.75 | 3.75 |
| | | Size: 78x83mm | | |
| 3417 | A571 | $5 multi | 3.75 | 3.75 |
| | | Size: 88x76mm | | |

National Basketball Association Players — A572

**2004-05  Perf. 14**

| 3418-3423 | A572 | Set of 6 | 5.25 | 5.25 |
|---|---|---|---|---|

Issued: No. 3418, 11/2; Nos. 3419-3420, 11/3; No. 3421, 11/9; Nos. 3422-3423, 2/10/05.

Designs: No. 3418, 75c, Gary Payton, Los Angeles Lakers. No. 3419, 75c, Lebron James, Cleveland Cavaliers. No. 3420, 75c, Adonal Foyle, Golden State Warriors. No. 3421, 75c, Peja Stojakovic, Sacramento Kings. No. 3422, 75c, Kirk Hinrich, Chicago Bulls. $3, Steve Francis, Houston Rockets.

Battle of Trafalgar Bicent. — A573

**2004, Nov. 25  Perf. 14¼**

| 3424-3427 | A573 | Set of 4 | 4.50 | 4.50 |
|---|---|---|---|---|

**Souvenir Sheets**

| 3428-3429 | A573 | Set of 2 | 7.50 | 7.50 |
|---|---|---|---|---|

Designs: 50c, Captain Thomas Masterman Hardy. $1, Napoleon Bonaparte. $1.50, Admiral Lord Horatio Nelson. $3, Admiral Cuthbert Collingwood. No. 3428, $5, The Nelson touch. No. 3429, $5, H.M.S. Victory.

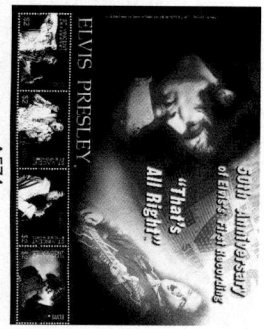

A574

# ELVIS PRESLEY

Elvis Presley (1935-77) — A575

No. 3430: a, Country name at UL reading across, denomination at R. b, Country name at R, denomination at LL. c, Country name at R, denomination at LR. d, Country name at L reading up, denomination at LL.
No. 3431 — Denomination color: a, Green. b, Blue. c, Red. d, Purple.

**2004, Nov. 25**    *Perf. 13¼x13½*
3430 A574 $2 Sheet of 4, #a-d   6.00 6.00
     *Perf. 13½x13¼*
3431 A575 $2 Sheet of 4, #a-d   6.00 6.00
     **Souvenir Sheet**

Deng Xiaoping (1904-97), Chinese Leader — Ab/6

**2004, Dec. 6**    *Perf. 14*
3432 A576 $5 multi   3.75 3.75

Subway Systems — A577

No. 3433 — New York City subway: a, 1953 subway token. b, 23rd Street IRT kiosk. c, 1935 Subway car Hi-V 3398. d, 1936 subway car R6 1208 interior. e, Construction of Harlem River Tunnel, 1904. f, Underground construction, early 1900s. g, Hoppers, above ground construction, early 1900s. h, Workers on scaffold, above ground construction early 1900s.
No. 3434: a, $1.40 — Subway cars from: a, Moscow Metro. b, Tokyo Metro. c, Mexico City Metro. d, Paris Metro. e, Hong Kong MTR. f, Prague Metro.
No. 3435: $1.40 — London Underground: a, Thames Tunnel, 1859. b, City & South London Railway locomotives, 1890. c, East London line. d, Piccadilly line. e, Victoria line. f, Jubilee line.
No. 3436, $5, A Train, New York City. No. 3437, $5, Train in station, London Underground. No. 3438, $5, 1992 Tube, Central line, London.

---

Christmas A578

**2004, Dec. 13**    *Perf. 13½x13½*
3433 A577 $1 Sheet of 8, #a-h   6.00 6.00
3434-3435   Set of 2   13.00 13.00
     **Souvenir Sheets**
3436-3438 A577   Set of 3   11.50 11.50

Paintings by Norman Rockwell: 70c, Santa's Helpers. 90c, Tiny Tim (detail). $1.10, Department Store Santa. $3, The Muggleton Stage Coach.

**2004, Dec. 13**    *Perf. 12*
3439-3442 A578   Set of 4   4.25 4.25
     *Imperf*
     **Size: 64x84mm**
3443 A578 $5 multi   3.75 3.75

New Year 2005 (Year of the Rooster) — A579

**2005, Jan. 26**    *Perf. 12*
3444 A579 75c multi   .55 .55
Issued in sheets of 3.

     **Miniature Sheet**

World Peace — A580

No. 3445: a, Mahatma Gandhi. b, Elie Wiesel. c, Rigoberta Menchu.

**2005, Jan. 26**    *Perf. 14*
3445 A580 $3 Sheet of 3, #a-c   6.75 6.75

Intl. Year of Rice (in 2004) — A581

No. 3446, horiz.: a, Oxen pulling plow. b, Man and child harvesting rice. c, Man and field.
$5, Child with bowl of rice.

**2005, Jan. 26**    **Souvenir Sheet**
3446 A581 $3 Sheet of 3, #a-c   6.75 6.75
3447 A581 $5 multi   3.75 3.75

---

     **Souvenir Sheet**

Rotary International, Cent. — A582

No. 3448: a, Jehanzeb Khan, polio victim. b, Dr. Jonas Salk. c, Child receiving polio vaccination.

**2005, Apr. 4**    *Litho.*    *Perf. 14*
3448 A582 $3 Sheet of 3, #a-c   6.75 6.75

Wedding of Prince Charles and Camilla Parker Bowles — A583

Various photos of couple with oval color of:
No. 3449, $2, Blue. No. 3450, $2, Red violet. No. 3451, $2, Purple, horiz.

**2005, Apr. 9**    *Perf. 13½*
3449-3451 A583   Set of 3   4.50 4.50

Vatican City No. 63 — A584

Pope John Paul II (1920-2005) — A585

**2005, June 1**    *Perf. 13x13¼*
3452 A584 70c multi   .55 .55
     *Perf. 13½*
3453 A585 $3 multi   2.25 2.25
No. 3452 issued in sheets of 12; No. 3453, in sheets of 6.

---

     **Souvenir Sheet**

Maimonides (1135-1204), Philosopher — A586

No. 3454 — Statue of Maimonides with frame in: a, Yellow. b, Yellow and black.

**2005, June 7**    *Perf. 12*
3454 A586 $2 Vert. pair, #a-b   3.00 3.00
Printed in sheets containing two pairs.

Expo 2005, Aichi, Japan — A587

No. 3455 — Woolly mammoth with country name in: a, Red. b, Black. c, White.

**2005, June 7**    *Perf. 12¾*
3455 A587 $3 Sheet of 3, #a-c   6.75 6.75

Fish A588

Designs: $1, Red Irish lord. $1.10, Deep sea anglerfish. $1.40, Viperfish. $2, Lionfish. $5, Gulper eel.

**2005, June 7**
3456-3459 A587   Set of 4   4.25 4.25
     **Souvenir Sheet**
3460 A588 $5 multi   3.75 3.75

Bats — A589

No. 3461: a, Mexican long-tongued bat. b, Wahlberg's fruit bat. c, Common vampire bat. d, False vampire bat. e, Horseshoe bat. f, Spear-nosed long-tongued bat. $5, Greater long-nosed bat.

**2005, June 7**
3461 A589 $1.60 Sheet of 6, #a-f   7.25 7.25
     **Souvenir Sheet**
3462 A589 $5 multi   3.75 3.75

## 200TH ANNIVERSARY

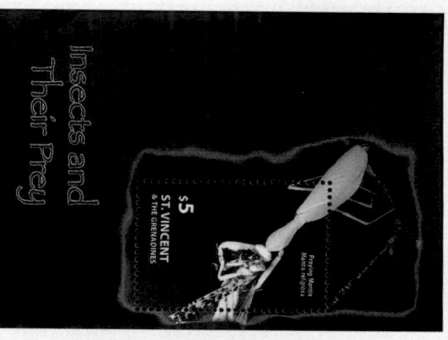

Friedrich von Schiller (1759-1805), Writer — A592

No. 3467 — Schiller: a, At desk. b, Facing right. c, Facing left.

## Insects and Their Prey

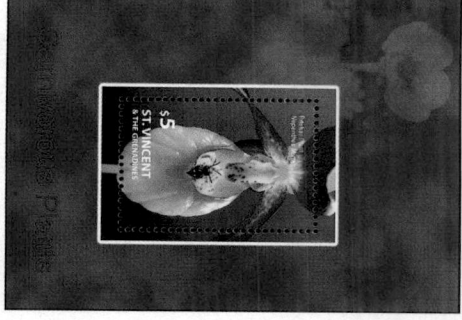

### Insects and Spiders — A590

No. 3463: a, Field-digger wasp. b, Water spider. c, Yellow crab spider. d, Mantid. $5, Praying mantis.

**2005, June 7**

| | | | | |
|---|---|---|---|---|
| 3463 | A590 | $2 Sheet of 4, #a-d | 6.00 | 6.00 |

**Souvenir Sheet**

| | | | | |
|---|---|---|---|---|
| 3464 | A590 | $5 multi | 3.75 | 3.75 |

### Carnivorous Plants — A591

No. 3465: a, Butterwort, denomination in black. b, Common sundew. c, Venus's flytrap. d, Butterwort, denomination in white. $5, Pitcher plant.

**2005, June 7**

| | | | | |
|---|---|---|---|---|
| 3465 | A591 | $2 Sheet of 4, #a-d | 6.00 | 6.00 |

**Souvenir Sheet**

| | | | | |
|---|---|---|---|---|
| 3466 | A591 | $5 multi | 3.75 | 3.75 |

$5, Facing right, diff.

**2005, June 7**

| | | | | |
|---|---|---|---|---|
| 3467 | A592 | $3 Sheet of 3, #a-c | 6.75 | 6.75 |
| 3468 | A592 | $5 multi | 3.75 | 3.75 |

**Souvenir Sheet**

## Hans Christian Andersen

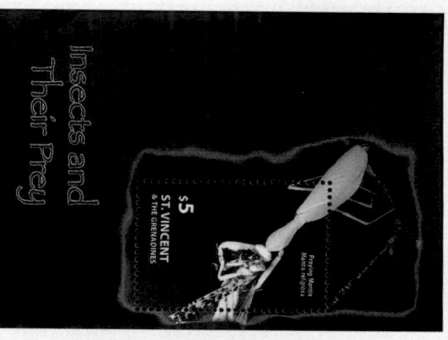

Hans Christian Andersen (1805-75), Author — A593

No. 3469: a, The Brave Tin Soldier. b, The Top and Ball. c, Ole-Luk-Ole, the Dream-God. $5, The Snow Queen.

**2005, June 7**    **Perf. 12¼**

| | | | | |
|---|---|---|---|---|
| 3469 | A593 | $3 Sheet of 3, #a-c | 6.75 | 6.75 |

**Souvenir Sheet**    **Perf. 12½x12¾**

| | | | | |
|---|---|---|---|---|
| 3470 | A593 | $5 multi | 3.75 | 3.75 |

No. 3469 contains three 43x32mm stamps.

## Jules Verne

Jules Verne (1828-1905), Writer — A594

No. 3471, $2 — Around the World in 80 Days: a, Princess Aouda. b, Characters in train windows. c, Phileas Fogg. d, Passepartout.
No. 3472, $2 — 20,000 Leagues Under the Sea: a, Mariner using sextant. b, Captain at ship's wheel. c, Sea monster at window. d, Men in diving suits.
No. 3473, $5, Hot air balloon. No. 3474, $5, Helicopter.

**2005, June 7**    **Perf. 12¾**

| | | | | |
|---|---|---|---|---|
| 3471-3472 | A594 | Set of 2 | 12.00 | 12.00 |

**Souvenir Sheets**

| | | | | |
|---|---|---|---|---|
| 3473-3474 | A594 | Set of 2 | 7.50 | 7.50 |

## End of World War II

End of World War II, 60th Anniv. — A595

No. 3475, $2, horiz.: a, USSR T34-85 tank. b, German Tiger tank. c, USA LVT(A)-1. d, Great Britain Cruiser tank Mk VI.
No. 3476, $2, horiz.: a, SBD-3 Dauntless. b, Mitsubishi Zero A6M5. c, USS Hornet.
No. 3477, $5, Winston Churchill. No. 3478, $5, Gen. Douglas MacArthur signing Japanese surrender instrument, horiz.

**2005, June 7**    **Perf. 12¾**

| | | | | |
|---|---|---|---|---|
| 3475-3476 | A595 | Sheets of 4, #a-d | 12.00 | 12.00 |

**Souvenir Sheets**

| | | | | |
|---|---|---|---|---|
| 3477-3478 | A595 | Set of 2 | 7.50 | 7.50 |

## Taipei 2005 Stamp Exhibition

Taipei 2005 Stamp Exhibition — A596

No. 3479: a, Panda. b, Formosan rock monkey. c, Formosan black bear. d, Formosan sika deer.

**2005, Aug. 5**    **Perf. 14**

| | | | | |
|---|---|---|---|---|
| 3479 | A596 | $2 Sheet of 4, #a-d | 6.00 | 6.00 |

Souvenir Sheet

## SEMI-POSTAL STAMPS

Catalogue values for unused stamps in this section are for Never Hinged items.

Map Type of 1977-78 Overprinted: "SOUFRIERE / RELIEF / FUND 1979" and New Values, "10c+5c" etc.

**1979**    **Wmk. 373**    **Litho. and Typo.**    **Perf. 14½x14**

| | | | | |
|---|---|---|---|---|
| B1 | A76 | 10c + 5c multi | .20 | .20 |
| B2 | A76 | 50c + 25c multi | .35 | .35 |
| B3 | A76 | $1 + 50c multi | .70 | .70 |
| B4 | A76 | $2 + $1 multi | 1.40 | 1.40 |
| | | Nos. B1-B4 (4) | 2.65 | 2.65 |

The surtax was for victims of the eruption of Mt. Soufriere.

**1980, Aug. 7**    **Litho.**    **Perf. 13½**

| | | | | |
|---|---|---|---|---|
| B5 | A76 | 10c + 50c multi | .30 | .30 |
| B6 | A76 | 50c + 50c multi | .55 | .55 |
| B7 | A90 | 80c + 50c multi | .65 | .65 |
| B8 | A90 | $2.50 + 50c multi | 1.50 | 1.50 |
| | | Nos. B5-B8 (4) | 3.00 | 3.00 |

Surtax was for victims of Hurricane Allen.

Nos. 604-607 Surcharged: "HURRICANE / RELIEF / 50c"

**1989, Nov. 17**    **Litho.**    **Perf. 13½x14**

| | | | | |
|---|---|---|---|---|
| B9 | A174 | 60c +10c #1224a-1224i | 7.00 | 7.00 |
| | | Sheet of 9 | | |
| B10 | A174 | 60c +10c #1225a-1225i | 7.00 | 7.00 |
| | | Sheet of 9 | | |
| B11 | A175 | 60c +10c #1226a-1226i | 7.00 | 7.00 |
| | | Sheet of 9 | | |

Nos. 1224-1226 Surcharged "CALIF EARTHQUAKE RELIEF" on 1 or 2 Lines and "+10c".

## WAR TAX STAMPS

No. 105 Overprinted

**1916**    **Wmk. 3**    **Perf. 14**

| | | | | |
|---|---|---|---|---|
| MR1 | A17 | 1p car., type III | 3.25 | 13.50 |
| | a. | Double ovpt., type III | 250.00 | 250.00 |
| | b. | 1p carmine, type I | 5.50 | 9.25 |
| | c. | Comma after "STAMP", type I | | |
| | d. | Double overprint, type I | 8.76 | 17.50 |
| | e. | 1p carmine, type II | 175.00 | 175.00 |
| | | | 87.50 | 87.50 |

Type I — Words 2 to 2½mm apart.
Type II — Words 1½mm apart.
Type III — Words 3½mm apart.

## OFFICIAL STAMPS

Catalogue values for unused stamps in this section are for Never Hinged items.

**1982, Nov.**    **Litho.**    **Perf. 14**

| | | | | |
|---|---|---|---|---|
| O1 | A94a | 60c Couple, Isabella | .30 | .30 |
| O2 | A94b | 60c Couple | .30 | .30 |
| O3 | A94a | $2.50 Couple, Alberta | 1.25 | 1.25 |
| O4 | A94b | $2.50 Couple | 1.25 | 1.25 |
| O5 | A94a | $4 Couple, Britannia | 1.75 | 1.75 |
| O6 | A94b | $4 Couple | 1.75 | 1.75 |
| | | Nos. O1-O6 (6) | 5.90 | 5.90 |

Nos. 627-632 Ovptd. "OFFICIAL".

Overprinted

| | | | | |
|---|---|---|---|---|
| MR2 | A17 | 1p carmine | .35 | .90 |

# ST. VINCENT GRENADINES

sănt vĭn̩t-sənt grə-nä-də

LOCATION — Group of islands south of St. Vincent

CAPITAL — None

St. Vincent's portion of the Grenadines includes Bequia, Canouan, Mustique, Union and a number of smaller islands.

> **Catalogue values for unused stamps in this area are for Never Hinged items.**

All stamps are designs of St. Vincent unless otherwise noted or illustrated. See St. Vincent Nos. 324-329a for six stamps and a souvenir sheet issued in 1971 inscribed "The Grenadines of St. Vincent."

## Princess Anne's Wedding Issue
### Common Design Type

**1973, Nov. 14    Litho.    Perf. 14**

| | | | | |
|---|---|---|---|---|
| 1 | CD325 | 25c green & multi | .20 | .20 |
| 2 | CD325 | $1 org brn & multi | .50 | .50 |

Common Design Types pictured following the introduction.

## Bird Type of 1970 and St. Vincent
### Nos. 281a-285a, 287a-289a
### Overprinted

a     h

**1974    Photo.    Wmk. 314    Perf. 14**

| | | | | |
|---|---|---|---|---|
| 3 | A36(a) | 1c multicolored | .20 | .20 |
| 4 | A36(a) | 2c multicolored | .40 | .40 |
| 5 | A36(b) | 2½c multicolored | .40 | .40 |
| 6 | A36(a) | 3c multicolored | .40 | .40 |
| 7 | A36(a) | 3r multicolored | .40 | .40 |
| 8 | A36(a) | 4c multicolored | .40 | .40 |
| 9 | A36(a) | 5c multicolored | .20 | .20 |
| 10 | A36(a) | 6c multicolored | .20 | .20 |
| 11 | A36(a) | 8c multicolored | .20 | .20 |
| 12 | A36(a) | 12c multicolored | .20 | .20 |
| 13 | A36(a) | 15c multicolored | .25 | .25 |
| 14 | A36(a) | 20c multicolored | .40 | .40 |
| 15 | A36(a) | 25c multicolored | .45 | .45 |
| 16 | A36(a) | 50c multicolored | .80 | .85 |
| 17 | A36(a) | $1 multicolored | 1.25 | 1.10 |
| 18 | A36(a) | $2.50 multicolored | 2.25 | 2.00 |
| 19 | A36(a) | $5 multicolored | 9.00 | 7.50 |

Nos. 3-19 (17)

Nos. 8-9, 12-13, 17-18 vert.
Issue dates: #5, 7, June 7; others, Apr. 24.

### Maps of Islands — G1

**1974, May 9    Litho.    Wmk. 314**

| | | | | |
|---|---|---|---|---|
| 20 | G1 | 5c Bequia | .20 | .20 |
| 21 | G1 | 15c Prune | .20 | .20 |
| 22 | G1 | 20c Mayreau | .20 | .20 |
| 23 | G1 | 30c Mustique | .20 | .20 |

**Perf. 13x12½**

| | | | | |
|---|---|---|---|---|
| 24 | G1 | 40c Union | .20 | .20 |
| 24A | G1 | $1 Canouan | 1.20 | 1.20 |

Nos. 20-24A (6)

No. 20 has no inscription at bottom. No. 84 is dated "1976." See Nos. 84-111.

## UPU Type of 1974

2c, Arrows circling UPU emblem. 15c, Post horn, globe. 40c, Target over map of islands, hand canceler. $1, Goode's map projection.

**1974, July 25    Litho.    Perf. 14½**

| | | | | |
|---|---|---|---|---|
| 25-28 | A56 | Set of 4 | .85 | .80 |

### Bequia Island — G2

**1974**

| | | | | |
|---|---|---|---|---|
| 29-32 | G2 | Set of 4 | .85 | .80 |

Designs: 5c, Boat building. 30c, Careening at Port Elizabeth. 35c, Admiralty Bay. $1, Fishing Boat Race.

### Shells — G3

**1974-76    Wmk. 373**

| | | | | |
|---|---|---|---|---|
| 33-51 | C3 | Set of 19 | 19.00 | 19.00 |

Designs: 1c, Atlantic thorny oyster. 2c, Zigzag scallop. 3c, Reticulated helmet. 4c, Music volute. 5c, Amber pen shell. 6c, Angular triton. 8c, Flame helmet. 10c, Caribbean olive. 12c, Common sundial. 15c, Glory of the atlantic cone. 20c, Flame auger. 25c, King venus. 36c, Long-spined star-shell. 45c, Speckled tellin. 50c, Rooster tail conch. $1, Green star-shell. $2.50, Incomparable cone. $5, Rough file clam. $10, Measled cowrie.

Issued: #33-50, 11/27/74; #51, 7/12/76. #36-40, 43, 45, 47-48, exist dated "1976." #40, 42-45, 49-50 dated "1977."

## Churchill Type

Churchill as: 5c, Prime Minister. 40c, Lord Warden of the Cinque Ports. 50c, First Lord of the Admiralty. $1, Royal Air Force officer.

**1974, Nov. 28    Set of 4**

| | | | | |
|---|---|---|---|---|
| 52-55 | A58 | Set of 4 | .90 | .90 |

### Mustique Island — G4

**1975, Feb. 27    Wmk. 373**

| | | | | |
|---|---|---|---|---|
| 56 | G4 | 5c Cotton House | .20 | .20 |
| 57 | G4 | 35c Blue Waters, Endeavour | .20 | .20 |
| 58 | G4 | 45c Endeavour Bay | .35 | .35 |
| 59 | G4 | $1 Gelliceaux Bay | .95 | .95 |

Nos. 56-59 (4)

### Butterflies — G5

**1975, May 15    Perf. 14**

| | | | | |
|---|---|---|---|---|
| 60 | G5 | 5c Soldier martinique | .40 | .40 |
| 61 | G5 | 5c Silver-spotted flambeau | | |
| 62 | G5 | 35c Gold rim | .55 | .55 |
| 63 | G5 | 45c Bright blue, Donkey's eye | 1.30 | 1.30 |
| 64 | G5 | $1 Biscuit | 2.00 | 2.00 |

Nos. 60-64 (5)    5.25  5.25

### Views of Petit St. Vincent — G6

**1975, July 24    Perf. 14½**

| | | | | |
|---|---|---|---|---|
| 65 | G6 | 5c Resort pavilion | .20 | .20 |
| 66 | G6 | 35c Jetty | .20 | .20 |
| 67 | G6 | 45c Harbor | .35 | .35 |
| 68 | G6 | $1 Sailing in coral lagoon | .95 | .95 |

Nos. 65-68 (4)

### Christmas — G7

Island churches: 5c, Ecumenical Church, Union. 10c, Catholic Church, Mustique. 25c, Catholic Church, Bequia. $1, Anglican Church, Bequia.

**1975, Nov. 20    Wmk. 314**

| | | | | |
|---|---|---|---|---|
| 69-72 | G7 | Set of 4 | .90 | .90 |

### Union Island — G8

**1976, Feb. 26    Wmk. 373**

| | | | | |
|---|---|---|---|---|
| 73 | G8 | 5c Sunset | .20 | .20 |
| 74 | G8 | 35c Customs and post office | .30 | .30 |
| 75 | G8 | 45c Anglican Church | .30 | .30 |
| 76 | G8 | $1 Mail boat | .90 | .90 |

Nos. 73-76 (4)

### Staghorn Coral — G9

**1976, May 13    Perf. 14½**

| | | | | |
|---|---|---|---|---|
| 77 | G9 | 5c shown | .20 | .20 |
| 78 | C9 | 35c Elkhorn coral | .25 | .25 |
| 79 | G9 | 45c Pillar coral | .25 | .25 |
| 80 | G9 | $1 Brain coral | 1.10 | .85 |

Nos. 77-80 (4)

### US Bicentennial Coins — G10

**1976, July 15    Perf. 13½**

| | | | | |
|---|---|---|---|---|
| 81 | G10 | 25c Washington quarter | .20 | .20 |
| 82 | G10 | 50c Kennedy half dollar | .30 | .30 |
| 83 | G10 | $1 Eisenhower dollar | .70 | .70 |

Nos. 81-83 (3)

## St. Vincent Grenadines Map Type
### Bequia Island

**1976, Sept. 23    Litho.    Perf. 14**

| | | | | |
|---|---|---|---|---|
| 84 | G1 | 5c grn, brt grn & blk | .20 | .20 |
| 85 | G1 | 10c multicolored | .20 | .20 |
| a. | | Bkt. pane of 3, 2 #84, 85 | .35 | .35 |
| 86 | G1 | 35c multicolored | .40 | .40 |
| 87 | G1 | 45c multicolored | .60 | .60 |
| a. | | Bkt. pane of 3, 2 #85, 86 | .85 | .85 |
| b. | | Bkt. pane of 3, 2 #86, 87 | | |

Nos. 84-87 (4)

For previous 5c see No. 20.

### Canouan Island

**1976, Sept. 23**

| | | | | |
|---|---|---|---|---|
| 88 | G1 | 5c multicolored | .20 | .20 |
| 89 | G1 | 10c multicolored | .20 | .20 |
| a. | | Bkt. pane of 3, 2 #88, 89 | .35 | .35 |
| 90 | G1 | 35c multicolored | .40 | .40 |
| 91 | G1 | 45c multicolored | .60 | .60 |
| a. | | Bkt. pane of 3, 2 #89, 90 | .85 | .85 |
| b. | | Bkt. pane of 3, 2 #90, 91 | | |

Nos. 88-91 (4)

### Mayreau Island

**1976, Sept. 23**

| | | | | |
|---|---|---|---|---|
| 92 | G1 | 5c multicolored | .20 | .20 |
| 93 | G1 | 10c multicolored | .20 | .20 |
| a. | | Bkt. pane of 3, 2 #92, 93 | .35 | .35 |
| 94 | G1 | 35c multicolored | .40 | .40 |
| 95 | G1 | 45c multicolored | .60 | .60 |
| a. | | Bkt. pane of 3, 2 #92-93, 95 | .85 | .85 |
| b. | | Bkt. pane of 3, 2 #94, 95 | | |

Nos. 92-95 (4)

### Mustique Island

**1976, Sept. 23**

| | | | | |
|---|---|---|---|---|
| 96 | G1 | 5c multicolored | .20 | .20 |
| 97 | G1 | 10c multicolored | .20 | .20 |
| a. | | Bkt. pane of 3, 2 #96, 97 | .35 | .35 |
| 98 | G1 | 35c multicolored | .40 | .40 |
| 99 | G1 | 45c multicolored | .60 | .60 |
| a. | | Bkt. pane of 3, 2 #96-97, 99 | .85 | .85 |
| b. | | Bkt. pane of 3, 2 #98, 99 | | |

Nos. 96-99 (4)

### Petit St. Vincent

**1976, Sept. 23**

| | | | | |
|---|---|---|---|---|
| 100 | G1 | 5c multicolored | .20 | .20 |
| 101 | G1 | 10c multicolored | .20 | .20 |
| a. | | Bkt. pane of 3, 2 #100-101, 103 | .35 | .35 |
| 102 | G1 | 35c multicolored | .40 | .40 |
| 103 | G1 | 45c multicolored | .60 | .60 |
| a. | | Bkt. pane of 3, 2 #101, 102 | .85 | .85 |
| b. | | Bkt. pane of 3, 2 #102, 103 | | |

Nos. 100-103 (4)

### Prune Island

**1976, Sept. 23**

| | | | | |
|---|---|---|---|---|
| 104 | G1 | 5c multicolored | .20 | .20 |
| 105 | G1 | 10c multicolored | .20 | .20 |
| a. | | Bkt. pane of 3, 2 #104, 105 | .35 | .35 |
| 106 | G1 | 35c multicolored | .40 | .40 |
| 107 | G1 | 45c multicolored | .60 | .60 |
| a. | | Bkt. pane of 3, 2 #105, 106 | .85 | .85 |
| b. | | Bkt. pane of 3, 2 #106, 107 | | |

Nos. 104-107 (4)

### Union Island

**1976, Sept. 23**

| | | | | |
|---|---|---|---|---|
| 108 | G1 | 5c multicolored | .20 | .20 |
| 109 | G1 | 10c multicolored | .20 | .20 |
| a. | | Bkt. pane of 3, 2 #108, 109 | .35 | .35 |
| 110 | G1 | 35c multicolored | .40 | .40 |
| 111 | G1 | 45c multicolored | .60 | .60 |
| a. | | Bkt. pane of 3, 2 #108-109, 111 | .85 | .85 |
| b. | | Bkt. pane of 3, 2 #110, 111 | | |

Nos. 108-111 (4)

### Mayreau Island — G11

Designs: 5c, Station Hill school, post office. 35c, Church at Old Wall. 45c, Cruiser at anchor, La Souciere. $1, Saline Bay.

**1976, Dec. 3**

| | | | | |
|---|---|---|---|---|
| 112-115 | G11 | Set of 4 | .70 | .50 |

### Queen Elizabeth II, Silver Jubilee — G12

Coins: 25c, Coronation Crown. 50c, Silver Wedding Crown. $1, Silver Jubilee Crown.

**1977, Mar. 3**

| | | | | |
|---|---|---|---|---|
| 116-118 | G12 | Set of 3 | .50 | .40 |

**Fiddler Crab G13**

**1977, May 19** **Perf. 13½**
| | | | |
|---|---|---|---|
| 119 | G13 | 5c shown | .20 .20 |
| 120 | G13 | 35c Ghost crab | .30 .30 |
| 121 | G13 | 50c Blue crab | .30 .30 |
| 122 | G13 | $1.25 Spiny lobster | 1.40 1.40 |
| | | Nos. 119-122 (4) | |

**GRENADINES OF St.VINCENT** — Prune Island G14

**1977, Aug. 25**
| | | | |
|---|---|---|---|
| 123 | G14 | 5c Snorkel diving | .20 .20 |
| 124 | G14 | 35c Palm Island Resort | .20 .20 |
| 125 | G14 | 45c Casuarina Beach | .20 .20 |
| 126 | G14 | $1 Palm Island Beach Club | .90 .90 |
| | | Nos. 123-126 (4) | |

**Map Type of 1977 Overprinted**

ROYAL VISIT MUSTIQUE 1952-1977

SILVER JUBILEE 30TH OCTOBER 1977

**1977, Oct. 31** **Perf. 14½x14**
| | | Wmk. 314 | |
|---|---|---|---|
| 127 | A76 | 40c multicolored (R) | .20 .20 |
| 128 | A76 | $2 multicolored (B) | .60 .60 |

Canouan Island G15

**Grenadines of St.Vincent**

**1977, Dec. 8** **Wmk. 373** **Perf. 14½**
| | | | |
|---|---|---|---|
| 129 | G15 | 5c Clinic, Charlestown | .20 .20 |
| 130 | G15 | 35c Town Jetty, Charlestown | .20 .20 |
| 131 | G15 | 45c Mailboat, Charlestown | .20 .20 |
| 132 | G15 | $1 Grand Bay | .35 .35 |
| | | Nos. 129-132 (4) | .95 .95 |

Birds and Eggs G16

1c. Tropical Mockingbird. 2c. Mangrove cuckoo. 3c. Osprey. 4c. Smooth billed ani. 5c. House wren. 6c. Bananaquit. 8c. Carib grackle. 10c. Yellow bellied elaenia. 12c. Collared plover. 15c. Cattle egret. 20c. Red footed booby. 25c. Red-billed tropic bird. 40c. Royal tern. 50c. Rusty tailed flycatcher. 80c. Purple gallinule. $1. Broad winged hawk. $2. Common ground dove. $3. Laughing gull. $5. Brown noddy. $10. Grey kingbird.

**1978, May 11** **Perf. 13x12**
| | | | |
|---|---|---|---|
| 133-152 | G16 | Set of 20 | 18.00 18.00 |

Elizabeth II Coronation Anniv. Type

Cathedrals.

#139, 143, 149 exist imprinted "1979." #137-138, 140, 142, 144 imprinted "1980." Nos. 147-148 imprinted "1979" are from No. 175a. Nos. 145-146, 150 imprinted "1980" are from No. 189a.

For surcharge see No. 266.

---

**Turtles G17**

**1978, June 2** **Perf. 13½**
| | | | |
|---|---|---|---|
| 153 | A78 | 5c Worcester | .20 .20 |
| 154 | A78 | 40c Coventry | .25 .25 |
| 155 | A78 | 50c Winchester | .25 .25 |
| 156 | A78 | $3 Chester | .70 .70 |
| a. | | Souv. sheet of 4, perf. 14 | |
| | | Nos. 153-156 (4) | |

**GREEN TURTLE** — Grenadines of St.Vincent G17

**1978, July 20** **Perf. 14**
| | | | |
|---|---|---|---|
| 157 | G17 | 5c Green turtle | .20 .20 |
| 158 | G17 | 40c Hawksbill turtle | .50 .50 |
| 159 | G17 | 50c Leatherback turtle | 1.40 1.40 |
| 160 | G17 | $1.25 Loggerhead turtle | 2.30 2.30 |
| | | Nos. 157-160 (4) | |

Christmas scenes and verses from the carol "We Three Kings of Orient Are".

**1978, Nov. 2** Christmas G18
| | | | |
|---|---|---|---|
| 161 | G18 | 5c Three kings following star | .20 .20 |
| 162 | G18 | 10c Gold | .20 .20 |
| 163 | G18 | 25c Frankincense | .20 .20 |
| 164 | G18 | 50c Myrrh | .35 .35 |
| 165 | G18 | $2 With infant Jesus | 1.15 1.15 |
| a. | | Souvenir sheet of 5 + label, #161-165 | |
| | | Nos. 161-165 (5) | |

**1979** Sailing Yachts — G19
| | | | |
|---|---|---|---|
| 166 | G19 | 5c multicolored | .20 .20 |
| 167 | G19 | 40c multi, diff. | .20 .20 |
| 168 | G19 | 50c multi, diff. | .20 .20 |
| 169 | G19 | $2 multi, diff. | .75 .75 |
| | | Nos. 166-169 (4) | 1.35 1.35 |

**THE GRENADINES OF St. VINCENT** — Regatta 1979

**Sir Rowland Hill Type of 1979**

Designs: 80c, Sir Rowland Hill. $1, Great Britain Types A1 and A5 with "A10" (kingstown, St. Vincent) cancel. $2, St. Vincent #41 & 43 with Bequia cancel.

**1979, May 31** **Perf. 13x12**
| | | | |
|---|---|---|---|
| 173 | A83 | 80c multicolored | .20 .20 |
| 174 | A83 | $1 multicolored | .20 .20 |
| 175 | A83 | $2 multicolored | .40 .40 |
| a. | | Souv. sheet, #173-175, 147-149 | |
| | | Nos. 173-175 (3) | .85 .85 |

**Wildlife Type of 1980**

**1979, Mar. 8** **Perf. 14½**
| | | | |
|---|---|---|---|
| 170 | A91 | 20c Green iguana | .20 .20 |
| 171 | A91 | 40c Manicou | .25 .25 |
| 172 | A91 | $2 Red-legged tortoise | .85 .85 |
| | | Nos. 170-172 (3) | 1.25 1.25 |

IYC Type of 1979

Children and IYC emblem: 6c, Girl. $1, Boy, diff. $3, Girl and boy.

**1979, Oct. 24** **Perf. 14x13½**
| | | | |
|---|---|---|---|
| 176 | A82 | 6c multicolored | .20 .20 |
| 177 | A82 | 40c multicolored | .20 .20 |
| 178 | A82 | $1 multicolored | .50 .50 |
| 179 | A82 | $3 multicolored | 1.10 1.10 |
| | | Nos. 176-179 (4) | |

---

**Independence Type of 1979**

Designs: 5c, National flag, Ixora salici-folia. 40c, House of Assembly, Ixora odorata. $1, Prime Minister R. Milton Cato, Ixora jayanica.

**1979, Oct. 27** **Perf. 12½x12**
| | | | |
|---|---|---|---|
| 180-182 | A85 | Set of 3 | .75 .75 |

Printed se-tenant with label inscribed "Independence of St. Vincent and the Grenadines."

**FALSE KILLER WHALE** — False Killer Whale G20 — Grenadines of St.Vincent

**1979, Jan. 25** **Perf. 14**
| | | | |
|---|---|---|---|
| 183 | G20 | 10c shown | .90 .90 |
| 184 | G20 | 50c Spinner dolphin | 1.00 1.00 |
| 185 | G20 | 90c Bottle nosed dolphin | 1.20 1.20 |
| 186 | G20 | $2 Blackfish | 3.50 3.50 |
| | | Nos. 183-186 (4) | 6.60 6.60 |

**London '80 Type**

**1980, Apr. 24** **Perf. 13x12**
| | | | |
|---|---|---|---|
| 187 | A88 | 40c Queen Elizabeth II | .20 .20 |
| 188 | A88 | 50c St. Vincent #227 | .20 .20 |
| 189 | A88 | $3 #1-2 | .60 .60 |
| a. | | Souvenir sheet of 6, #187-189, 145-146, 150 | 2.75 2.50 |
| | | Nos. 187-189 (3) | 1.00 1.00 |

**Olympics Type of 1980**

**1980, Aug. 7** **Perf. 13½**
| | | | |
|---|---|---|---|
| 190 | A90 | 25c Running | .20 .20 |
| 191 | A90 | 50c Sailing | .20 .20 |
| 192 | A90 | $1 Long jump | .40 .40 |
| 193 | A90 | $2 Swimming | 1.00 1.00 |
| a. | | Souvenir sheet of 6, #187-189, 150 | |
| | | Nos. 190-193 (4) | |

**1980, Nov. 13** **Perf. 14**
| | | | |
|---|---|---|---|
| 194 | G21 | 5c multicolored | .20 .20 |
| 195 | G21 | 10c multicolored | .20 .20 |
| 196 | G21 | 50c multicolored | .20 .20 |
| 197 | G21 | 60c multicolored | .20 .20 |
| 198 | G21 | $2 multicolored | .85 .85 |
| a. | | Souvenir sheet of 5 + label, #194-198 | 1.05 1.05 |
| | | Nos. 194-198 (5) | 1.25 |

Scenes and verse from the carol "De Bornes Day." — Christmas G21

**Grenadines OF St.VINCENT** — Bequia Island G22

**1981, Feb. 19** **Perf. 14½**
| | | | |
|---|---|---|---|
| 199 | G22 | 50c P.O., Port Elizabeth | .20 .20 |
| 200 | G22 | 50c Moonhole | .20 .20 |
| 201 | G22 | $1.50 Fishing boats, Admiralty Bay | .30 .30 |
| 202 | G22 | $2 Friendship Rose at jetty | .45 .45 |
| | | Nos. 199-202 (4) | 1.15 1.15 |

---

**Maps by R. Ottens, c. 1765—G23**

Maps: Nos. 204, 206 by J. Parsons, 1861. No. 208, by T. Jefferys, 1763.

**1981, Apr. 2** **Perf. 14**
| | | | |
|---|---|---|---|
| 203 | A94a | 50c Ins. Cannaouan | .30 .30 |
| 204 | G23 | Pair, #203-204 | .30 .30 |
| 205 | A94a | 50c Cannaouan Island | .30 .30 |
| 206 | G23 | Pair, #205-206 | .30 .30 |
| 207 | A94a | 50c Ins. Mustiquois | .50 .50 |
| 208 | G23 | Pair, #207-208 | .50 .50 |
| | | Nos. 203-208 (6) | 2.20 2.20 |

**Royal Wedding Types**

**1981, July 17** **Wmk. 380**
| | | | |
|---|---|---|---|
| 209 | A94a | 50c Couple, the Mary | .20 .20 |
| 210 | A94b | 50c Couple, diff. | .60 .60 |
| 211 | A94a | $3 Couple, the Alexandra | .90 .90 |
| 212 | A94b | $3 like #210 | .90 .90 |
| 213 | A94a | $3.50 Couple, a, perf. 12 | 2.00 2.00 |
| 214 | A94b | $3.60 like #210 | |
| a. | | Pair, #207-208 | |
| | | Nos. 209-214 (6) | |

Each denomination issued in sheets of 7 (6 type A94a, 1 type A94b). For surcharges see Nos. 507-508.

**1981**
| | | | |
|---|---|---|---|
| 215 | A94b | $5 like #210 | 1.00 1.00 |

**Souvenir Sheet** **Perf. 12**
| | | | |
|---|---|---|---|
| 218-221 | | | |

**BLACKJACK** — Bar Jack G25 — 10c Grenadines of St.Vincent

**1981, Oct. 9** **Wmk. 373** **Perf. 14**
| | | | |
|---|---|---|---|
| 218 | G25 | 10c shown | .20 .20 |
| 219 | G25 | 50c Tarpon | .35 .35 |
| 220 | G25 | 60c Cobia | .45 .45 |
| 221 | G25 | $2 Blue marlin | 2.10 2.10 |
| | | Nos. 218-221 (4) | |

**Ships G26**

**HMS EXPERIMENT**

**1982, Jan. 28** **Perf. 14x13½**
| | | | |
|---|---|---|---|
| 222 | G26 | 1c Experiment | .20 .20 |
| 223 | G26 | 3c Lady Nelson | .20 .20 |
| 224 | G26 | 5c Daisy | .20 .20 |
| 225 | G26 | 6c Carib canoe | .20 .20 |
| 226 | G26 | 15c Hairoun Star | .35 .35 |
| 227 | G26 | 15c Jupiter | .45 .45 |
| 228 | G26 | 20c Christina | .45 .45 |
| 229 | G26 | 25c Orinoco | .60 .60 |
| 230 | G26 | 30c Lively | .60 .60 |
| 231 | G26 | 60c Denmark | .60 .60 |
| 232 | G26 | 60c Alabama | .85 .85 |
| 233 | G26 | 75c Santa Maria | .95 .95 |
| 234 | G26 | $1 Baffin | 1.10 1.10 |
| 235 | G26 | QE 2 | 1.20 1.20 |
| 236 | G26 | $3 Britannia | 1.75 1.75 |
| 237 | G26 | $5 Geeststar | 1.75 1.75 |
| 238 | G26 | $10 Grenadines Star | 15.60 15.60 |
| | | Nos. 222-238 (17) | |

For overprint see No. 509.

**1982, Apr. 5** *Perf. 14*
239 G27 10c Prickly pear fruit .20 .20
240 G27 50c Flower buds .35 .35
241 G27 $1 Flower .60 .60
242 G27 $2 Cactus 1.50 1.50
Nos. 239-242 (4) 2.65 2.65

**Princess Diana Type of 1980**
**1982, July 1** **Wmk. 380** *Perf. 14*
243 A99a 50c Anne Neville .20 .20
244 A99a 60c Arms of Anne Neville .20 .20
245 A99a $6 Diana, Princess of Wales .60 .60
1.00 1.00
Nos. 243-245 (3)

For overprints see Nos. 248-262.

**1982, July 1** **Wmk. 373** *Perf. 14½*
246 G29 $1.50 Old, new uniforms .60 .60
247 G29 $2.50 Lord Baden-Powell 1.00 1.00

75th anniversary of Boy Scouts.

**Nos. 243-245 Ovptd.**
**"ROYAL BABY / BEQUIA"**
**1982, July 19** **Wmk. 380** *Perf. 14*
248 A99a 50c multicolored .20 .20
249 A99a 60c multicolored .20 .20
250 A99a $6 multicolored .60 .60
1.00 1.00
Nos. 248-250 (3)

**"ROYAL BABY / CANOUAN"**
**1982, July 19**
251 A99a 50c multicolored .20 .20
252 A99a 60c multicolored .20 .20
253 A99a $6 multicolored .60 .60
1.00 1.00
Nos. 251-253 (3)

**"ROYAL BABY / MAYREAU"**
**1982, July 19**
254 A99a 50c multicolored .20 .20
255 A99a 60c multicolored .20 .20
256 A99a $6 multicolored .60 .60
1.00 1.00
Nos. 254-256 (3)

**"ROYAL BABY / MUSTIQUE"**
**1982, July 19**
257 A99a 50c multicolored .20 .20
258 A99a 60c multicolored .20 .20
259 A99a $6 multicolored .60 .60
1.00 1.00
Nos. 257-259 (3)

**"ROYAL BABY / UNION"**
**1982, July 19**
260 A99a 50c multicolored .20 .20
261 A99a 60c multicolored .20 .20
262 A99a $6 multicolored .60 .60
1.00 1.00
Nos. 260-262 (3)

**Christmas Type of 1981**
**1982, Nov. 18** *Perf. 13½*
263 A97 10c Mary and Joseph at inn .20 .20
264 A97 $1.50 Animals of stable .45 .45
265 A97 $2.50 Nativity .60 .60
a. Souvenir sheet of 3, #263-265 1.10 1.10
1.25 1.25

---

Old Coinage — G33

**1983, Dec. 1** **Wmk. 373** *Perf. 14*
291 G33 20c Quarter and half dollar, 1797 .20 .20
292 G33 45c Nine bitts, 1811-14 .20 .20
293 G33 75c Six and twelve bitts, 1811-14 .25 .25
294 G33 $3 Sixty six shillings, 1798 .85 .85
1.50 1.50
Nos. 291-294 (4)

**Locomotives Type of 1985**
**1984-87** **Litho.** **Unwmk.** *Perf. 12½*
Se-tenant Pairs, #a.-b.
a. — Side and front views.
b. — Action scene.
295 A120 1c 1948 Class C62, Japan .20 .20
296 A120 1c 1898 P.L.M. Grosse C, France .20 .20
297 A120 5c 1892 Class D13, US .20 .20
298 A120 5c 1903 Class V, UK .20 .20
299 A120 10c 1980 Class 253, UK .30 .30
300 A120 10c 1968 Class 581, Japan .40 .40
301 A120 10c 1874 1001 Class, UK .40 .40
302 A120 10c 1977 Class 142, DDR .45 .45
303 A120 15c 1899 T-9 Class, UK .25 .25
304 A120 15c 1932 Class C12, Japan .25 .25
305 A120 15c 1897 Class T15, Japan .30 .30
306 A120 20c 1808 Catch-me-who-can, UK .30 .30
307 A120 35c 1900 Claud Hamilton Class, UK .40 .40
308 A120 35c 1948 Class E10, Japan .30 .30
309 A120 35c 1947 Consolidation Class, UK .25 .25
310 A120 40c 1936 Class 231, Algeria .45 .45
311 A120 40c 1927 Class 1P, UK .55 .55
312 A120 40c 1979 Class 120, Germany .70 .70
313 A120 45c 1941 Class J, US .35 .35
314 A120 45c 1900 Class 13, UK .40 .40
315 A120 45c 1913 Glieve Gullion Class S, UK .55 .55
316 A120 50c 1950 Class A3, UK .85 .85
317 A120 50c 1954 Class X, Australia .85 .85
318 A120 60c 1885 Class D16, US .45 .45
319 A120 60c 1904 J. B. Earle, UK .50 .50
320 A120 60c 1879 Halesworth, UK .40 .40
321 A120 60c 1930 Class V1, UK .85 .85
322 A120 60c 1986 Class 59, UK .85 .85
323 A120 70c 1935 Class E18, Germany .60 .60
324 A120 75c 1923 Class D50, Japan .50 .50
325 A120 75c 1859 Problem Class, UK .85 .85
326 A120 75c 1958 Class 40, UK .85 .85
327 A120 75c 1875 Class A, US .90 .90
328 A120 $1 1907 Star Class, British .50 .50
329 A120 $1 1898 Lyn, UK .55 .55
330 A120 $1 1961 Western Class, UK .50 .50
331 A120 $1 1958 Warship Class 42, UK .85 .85
332 A120 $1 1831 Samson Type, US .90 .90
333 A120 $1.20 1854 Hayes, US .90 .90
334 A120 $1.25 1902 Class P-69, US .85 .85
335 A120 $1.50 1865 Talyllyn, UK .55 .55
336 A120 $1.50 1899 Drummond's Bug, UK .50 .50
337 A120 $1.50 1913 Class 60-3 Shay, US 1.10 1.10
338 A120 $1.50 1938 Class H1-d, Canada 1.10 1.10
339 A120 $2 1890 Class 2120, Japan 1.25 1.25
340 A120 $2 1951 Clan Class, UK .60 .60

---

No. 146 Surcharged
**1983, Apr. 26** **Wmk. 373**
266 G16 45c on 50c multicolored .35 .35

Union Island G30
**1983, May 12** *Perf. 13½*
267 G30 50c Power Station, Clifton .20 .20
268 G30 60c Sunrise, Clifton Harbor .20 .20
269 G30 $1.50 School, Ashton .45 .45
270 G30 $2 Frigate Rock, Conch Shell Beach .65 .65
1.50 1.50
Nos. 267-270 (4)

Treaty of Versailles, Bicent. — G31
**1983, Sept. 15** *Perf. 14½x14*
271 G31 45c British warship .20 .20
272 G31 60c American warship .30 .30
273 G31 $1.50 US troops, flag .65 .65
274 C31 $2 British troops in battle .95 .95
2.10 2.10
Nos. 271-274 (4)

200 Years of Manned Flight G32
**1983, Sept. 15** *Perf. 14*
275 G32 45c multicolored .20 .20
276 G32 60c multicolored .20 .20
277 G32 $1.50 multicolored .45 .45
278 G32 $2 multicolored .65 .65
1.50 1.50
Nos. 275-278 (4)

Designs: 45c, Montgolfier balloon 1783, vert. 60c, Ayres Turbo-thrush Commander. $1.50, Lebaudy "1" dirigible. $2, Space shuttle Columbia.

**British Monarch Type of 1984**
#279a, Arms of Henry VIII. #279b, Henry VIII. #280a, Arms of James I. #280b, James I. #281a, Henry VIII. #281b, Hampton Court. #282a, James I. #282b, Edinburgh Castle. #283a, Mary Rose. #283b, Henry VIII, Portsmouth harbor. #284a, Gunpowder Plot. #284b, James I & Gunpowder Plot.
**1983, Oct. 25** **Unwmk.** *Perf. 12½*
279 A110 60c Pair, #a.-b. .30 .30
280 A110 60c Pair, #a.-b. .30 .30
281 A110 75c Pair, #a.-b. .30 .30
282 A110 75c Pair, #a.-b. .30 .30
283 A110 $2.50 Pair, #a.-b. .90 .90
284 A110 $2.50 Pair, #a.-b. .90 .90
a. Souvenir sheet of 6 3.00 3.00
Nos. 279-284 (6)

---

341 A120 $2 1934 Pioneer Zephyr, US 1.25 1.25
342 A120 $2.50 1948 Blue Peter, UK .75 .75
343 A120 $2.50 1874 Class Beattie Well Tank, UK 2.00 2.00
344 A120 $3 1906 Cardean, UK .65 .65
345 A120 $3 1840 Fire Fly, UK 1.25 1.25
346 A120 $3 1884 Class 1.75 1.75
a. Souvenir sheet of 4, #324, 345 .60 .60
32.20 32.20
Nos. 295-346 (52)

Issued: #297, 299, 303, 307, 313, 318, 328, 342, 3/15/84; #295, 298, 306, 308, 319, 329, 335, 344, 10/9/84; #296, 304, 324, 345, 1/31/85; #300, 310, 315, 343, 5/17/85; #309, 323, 333, 339, 9/16/85; #305, 314, 320, 325, 330, 336, 340, 346, 3/14/86; #301, 311, 316, 321, 326, 331, 334, 337, 5/5/87; #302, 312, 317, 322, 327, 332, 338, 341, 8/26/87.

Spotted Eagle Ray G34
**1984, Apr. 26** **Wmk. 380** **Litho.** *Perf. 14*
399 G34 45c shown .20 .20
400 G34 60c Queen trigger fish .20 .20
401 G34 $1.50 White spotted file fish .50 .50
402 G34 $2 Schoolmaster fish .70 .70
1.60 1.60
For overprint see No. 504.
Nos. 399-402 (4)

**Cricket Players Type of 1985**
**1984-85** **Unwmk.** *Perf. 12½*
Pairs, #a.-b.
403 A116 1c R. A. Woolmer, portrait .20 .20
404 A116 3c K. S. Ranjitsinhji, portrait .20 .20
405 A116 5o W. R. Hammond, in action .20 .20
406 A116 5c S. F. Barnes, portrait .20 .20
407 A116 30c D. L. Underwood, in action .30 .30
408 A116 30c R. Peel, in action .25 .25
409 A116 55c M. D. Moxon, in action .25 .25
410 A118 60c W. C. Grace, portrait .40 .40
411 A116 60c L. Potter, portrait .40 .40
412 A116 $1 E. A. E. Baptiste, portrait .40 .40
413 A118 $1 H. Larwood, in action .30 .30
414 A116 $2 A. P. E. Knott, portrait .45 .45
415 A116 $2 Yorkshire & Kent county cricket clubs .40 .40
416 A116 $2.50 Sir John Berry Hobbs, portrait .45 .45
417 A116 $3 L. E. G. Ames, in action .60 .60
4.85 4.85
Nos. 403-417 (15)

Size of stamps in No. 415: 58x38mm.
Issued: #403, 407, 410, 412, 414, 417, 8/16/84; #406, 408, 413, 416, 11/2/84; #409, 411, 415, 2/22/85.

Canouan Island G35
**1984, Sept. 3** **Wmk. 380**
433 G35 35c Junior secondary school .20 .20
434 G35 45c Police station .20 .20
435 G35 $1 Post office .45 .45
436 G35 $3 Anglican church 1.25 1.25
2.10 2.10
Nos. 433-436 (4)

Night-blooming Flowers — G36

## Car Type of 1983

**1984, Oct. 15**

| | | | | |
|---|---|---|---|---|
| 437 | G36 | 5c Lady of the night | .20 | .20 |
| 438 | G36 | 35c Four o'clock | .35 | .35 |
| 439 | G36 | 75c Mother-in-law's tongue | .60 | .60 |
| 440 | G36 | $3 Queen of the night | 3.85 | 3.85 |

Nos. 437-440 (4)

**1984-86**

a. — Side and front views.
b. — Action scene.

Se-tenant Pairs, #a.-b.

**Unwmk.**    **Perf. 12½**

| | | | | |
|---|---|---|---|---|
| 441 | A107 | 5c 1959 Facel Vega, France | .20 | .20 |
| 442 | A107 | 5c 1903 Winton, Britain | .20 | .20 |
| 443 | A107 | 15c 1914 Mercedes-Benz, Germany | .20 | .20 |
| 444 | A107 | 25c 1936 BMW, Germany | .20 | .20 |
| 445 | A107 | 45c 1954 Rolls Royce, Britain | .20 | .20 |
| 446 | A107 | 50c 1934 Frazer Nash, Britain | .20 | .20 |
| 447 | A107 | 60c 1931 Invicta, Britain | .30 | .30 |
| 448 | A107 | 60c 1974 Lamborghini, Italy | .30 | .30 |
| 449 | A107 | $1 1959 Daimler, Britain | .30 | .30 |
| 450 | A107 | $1 1932 Marmon, US | .30 | .30 |
| 451 | A107 | $1.50 1966 Brabham, Britain | .30 | .30 |
| 452 | A107 | $1.75 1060 Lotus Ford, US | .30 | .30 |
| 453 | A107 | $3 1949 Repco, Britain | .30 | .30 |
| 454 | A107 | $3 1927 Delage, France | .50 | .50 |

Nos. 441-454 (14)

Issued: #441, 444, 446, 450, 452, 454, 2/20/86 not inscribed "Leaders of the World."

Stamps issued 2/20/86; #442, 447, 449, 451, 4/9/85; #443, 445, 448, 453, 11/28/84; 450, 452, 454, 2/20/86.

## Christmas Type of 1983

**1984, Dec. 3**   **Wmk. 380**   **Litho.**   **Perf. 14½**

| | | | | |
|---|---|---|---|---|
| 469 | A106 | 20c Three wise men, star | .20 | .20 |
| 470 | A106 | 45c Journeying to Bethlehem | .20 | .20 |
| 471 | A106 | $3 Presenting gifts | .60 | .60 |
| a. | | Souvenir sheet of 3, #469-471 | 1.40 | 1.40 |

Nos. 469-471 (3)

Shellfish G37

**1985, Feb. 11**

| | | | | |
|---|---|---|---|---|
| 472 | G37 | 25c Caribbean king crab | .25 | .25 |
| 473 | G37 | 60c Queen conch | .40 | .40 |
| 474 | G37 | $1 West sea urchin | .50 | .50 |
| 475 | G37 | $3 White sea urchin shell | .95 | .95 |

Nos. 472-475 (4)   2.10   2.10

Flowers — G38

#476a, Cypripedium calceolus. #476b, Gentiana asclepiadea. #477a, Clianthus formosus. #477b, Celmisia coriacea. #478a, Erythronium americanum. #478b, Laelia anceps. #479a, Leucadendron discolor. #479b, Meconopsis horridula.

**1985, Mar. 13**   **Unwmk.**   **Perf. 12½**

| | | | | |
|---|---|---|---|---|
| 476 | G38 | 5c Pair, #a.-b. | .20 | .20 |
| 477 | G38 | 35c Pair, #a.-b. | .30 | .30 |
| 478 | G38 | 60c Pair, #a.-b. | .30 | .30 |
| 479 | G38 | $2 Pair, #a.-b. | .70 | .70 |

Nos. 476-479 (4)   1.50   1.50

Water Sports G39

**1985, May 9**   **Wmk. 380**   **Perf. 14**

| | | | | |
|---|---|---|---|---|
| 484 | G39 | 35c Windsurfing | .25 | .25 |
| 485 | G39 | 45c Water skiing | .25 | .25 |
| 486 | G39 | 75c Scuba diving | .50 | .50 |
| 487 | G39 | $3 Deep sea fishing | 1.25 | 1.25 |

Nos. 484-487 (4)

Tourism.

Fruits and Blossoms G40

**1985, June 24**   **Perf. 15**

| | | | | |
|---|---|---|---|---|
| 488 | G40 | 30c Passion fruit | .20 | .20 |
| 489 | G40 | 40c Guava | .40 | .40 |
| 490 | G40 | 75c Sapodilla | .40 | .40 |
| 491 | G40 | $1 Mango | 1.10 | 1.10 |
| a. | | Souvenir sheet of 4, #488-491, perf. 14½x15 | 2.75 | 2.75 |

Nos. 488-491 (4)   2.30   2.30

For overprint see No. 503.

## Queen Mother Type of 1985

**1985, July 31**   **Unwmk.**   **Perf. 12½**

| | | | | |
|---|---|---|---|---|
| 496 | A122 | 40c Pair, #a.-b. | .20 | .20 |
| 497 | A122 | 75c Pair, #a.-b. | .35 | .35 |
| 498 | A122 | $1.10 Pair, #a.-b. | .35 | .35 |
| 499 | A122 | $1.75 Pair, #a.-b. | 1.25 | 1.25 |

Nos. 496-499 (4)

#496a, Facing right. #496b, Facing forward. #497a, Facing right. #497b, Facing left. #498a, Facing right. #498b, Facing forward. #499a, Facing forward, As girl facing right. #499b, Facing left. #500a, As girl facing left. #500b, Facing left.

**Souvenir Sheet of 2**

| | | | | |
|---|---|---|---|---|
| 500 | A122 | $2 Pair, #a.-b. | .85 | .85 |

Souvenir sheets containing two $4 or two $5 stamps exist.

Nos. 213-214, 236, 399, 488, and 496-497 Overprinted or Surcharged "CARIBBEAN ROYAL VISIT 1985" in 1, 2 or 3 Lines

Traditional Dances G41

**1985, Oct. 27**   **Perfs., Wmks. as Before**

| | | | | |
|---|---|---|---|---|
| 503 | G40 | 30c On #488 | 1.30 | 1.30 |
| 504 | G40 | 45c On #399 | 1.70 | 1.70 |
| 505 | A122 | $1.10 On #496 | 3.00 | 3.00 |
| 506 | A122 | $1.10 On #497 | 3.00 | 3.00 |
| 507 | A94A | $1.50 On #213 | 3.25 | 3.25 |
| 508 | A94b | $1.50 On $3.50, #214 | 24.00 | 24.00 |
| 509 | G26 | $3 On $3.50, #236 | 40.00 | 40.00 |

Nos. 503-509 (7)

**1985, Dec. 16**   **Unwmk.**   **Perf. 15**

| | | | | |
|---|---|---|---|---|
| 510 | G41 | 45c Donkey man | .20 | .20 |
| 511 | G41 | 75c Cake dance, vert. | .30 | .30 |
| 512 | G41 | $1 Bois-bois man, vert. | .45 | .45 |
| 513 | G41 | $2 Maypole dance | .85 | .85 |

Nos. 510-513 (4)   1.80   1.80

## Queen Elizabeth II 60th Birthday Type

5c, Elizabeth II. $1, At Princess Anne's christening. $4, As Princess. $6, In Canberra, 1982, vert. $8, Elizabeth II with crown.

**1986**

| | | | | |
|---|---|---|---|---|
| 538 | A132 | 60c Pair, #a.-b. | .40 | .40 |
| 540 | A132 | $2 Pair, #a.-b. | 1.25 | 1.25 |

**Souvenir Sheet**

| | | | | |
|---|---|---|---|---|
| 541 | A132a | $8 Andrew, Sarah, in coach | 4.00 | 4.00 |

Issued: #539-540, July 18; #541, Oct. 15.

## Royal Wedding Type of 1986

#539a, Sarah, Diana. #539b, Andrew. #540a, Anne, Andrew, Charles, Margaret, horiz. #540b, Sarah, Andrew, horiz.

Nos. 539-540 Ovptd. in Silver "Congratulations to TRH The Duke & Duchess of York" in 3 Lines

**1986, Oct. 15**

| | | | | |
|---|---|---|---|---|
| 542 | A132 | 60c Pair, #a.-b. | .60 | .60 |
| 543 | A132 | $2 Pair, #a.-b. | 2.25 | 2.25 |

**1986, Apr. 21**   **Perf. 12½**

514-517 A128 Set of 4   2.75   2.75

**Souvenir Sheet**

518 A128 $8 multi   3.25   3.25

## Statue of Liberty Type

Souvenir Sheets

Each stamp shows different views of Statue of Liberty and a different US president in the margin.

Handicrafts — G41a

**1986, Apr. 22**   **Wmk. 380**   **Litho.**   **Perf. 15**

| | | | | |
|---|---|---|---|---|
| 519 | G41a | 10c Dolls | .20 | .20 |
| 520 | G41a | 60c Basketwork | .20 | .20 |
| 521 | G41a | $1 Scrimshaw | .35 | .35 |
| 522 | G41a | $3 Model boat | 1.10 | 1.10 |

Nos. 519-522 (4)   1.85   1.85

## World Cup Soccer Championship, Mexico — G42

**1986, May 7**   **Perf. 12½, 15 (#525-528)**   **Unwmk.**

| | | | | |
|---|---|---|---|---|
| 523 | G42 | 1c Uruguayan team | .20 | .20 |
| 524 | G42 | 10c Polish team | .20 | .20 |
| 525 | G42 | 10c Bulgarian player | .35 | .35 |
| 526 | G42 | 45c Iraqi player | .40 | .40 |
| 527 | G42 | 75c S. Korean player | 1.00 | 1.00 |
| 528 | G42 | $1.50 N. Ireland player | 1.10 | 1.10 |
| 529 | G42 | $4 Portuguese team | 1.40 | 1.40 |
| 530 | G42 | $5 Canadian team | 6.15 | 6.15 |

Nos. 523-530 (8)

**Souvenir Sheets**

| | | | | |
|---|---|---|---|---|
| 531 | G42 | $1 like #529 | .50 | .50 |
| 532 | G42 | $3 like #523 | 1.50 | 1.50 |

Size: Nos. 525-528, 25x40mm.

## Fungi — G43

**1986, May 23**   **Wmk. 380**   **Litho.**   **Perf. 14**

| | | | | |
|---|---|---|---|---|
| 533 | G43 | 45c Marasmius pallescens | 2.75 | 2.75 |
| 534 | G43 | 60c Leucocoprinus fragilissimus | 3.00 | 3.00 |
| 535 | G43 | 75c Hygrocybe occidentalis | 3.25 | 3.25 |
| 536 | G43 | $3 Xeromocomus hypoxanthus | 18.50 | 18.50 |

Nos. 533-536 (4)

## Dragonflies — G44

**1986, Nov. 19**   **Perf. 15**

546 G44 45c Brachymesia furcata   .20   .20

**1986, Nov. 26**   **Perf. 14**

| | | | | |
|---|---|---|---|---|
| 547 | G44 | 60c Lepthemis vesiculosa | .25 | .25 |
| 548 | G44 | 75c Perithemis domitta | .30 | .30 |
| 549 | G44 | $2.50 Tramea abdominalis, vert. | .95 | .95 |

Nos. 546-549 (4)   1.70   1.70

**1986, Nov. 19**   **Perf. 14**

| | | | | |
|---|---|---|---|---|
| 550 | A135 | $1.50 multicolored | .60 | .60 |
| 551 | A135 | $1.75 multicolored | .70 | .70 |
| 552 | A135 | 60c multicolored | .80 | .80 |
| 553 | A135 | $2.50 multicolored | 1.00 | 1.00 |
| 554 | A135 | $2.50 multicolored | 1.00 | 1.00 |
| 555 | A135 | $3.50 multicolored | 1.40 | 1.40 |
| 556 | A135 | $6 multicolored | 1.90 | 1.90 |
| 557 | A135 | $6 multicolored | 2.25 | 2.25 |
| 558 | A135 | multicolored | 3.25 | 3.25 |

Nos. 550-558 (9)   13.00   13.00

## Birds of Prey — G45

**1986, Nov. 26**   **Perf. 12½**

| | | | | |
|---|---|---|---|---|
| 560 | G45 | 10c Sparrow hawk | .75 | .75 |
| 561 | G45 | 45c Black hawk | 1.25 | 1.25 |
| 562 | G45 | 45c Duck hawk | 1.50 | 1.50 |
| 563 | G45 | $4 Fish hawk | 13.50 | 13.50 |

Nos. 560-563 (4)

## Christmas — G46

**1986, Nov. 26**

| | | | | |
|---|---|---|---|---|
| 564 | G46 | 45c Santa playing drums | .25 | .25 |
| 565 | G46 | 60c Santa wind surfing | .30 | .30 |
| 566 | G46 | $1.25 Santa water skiing | .80 | .80 |
| 567 | G46 | $2 Santa limbo dancing | 1.25 | 1.25 |
| a. | | Souvenir sheet of 4, #564-567 | 2.60 | 2.60 |

Nos. 564-567 (4)

## Queen Elizabeth II, 40th Wedding Anniv. Type of 1987

**1987, Oct. 15**   **Litho.**   **Perf. 12½**

| | | | | |
|---|---|---|---|---|
| 568 | A140 | 15c Elizabeth, Charles | .20 | .20 |
| 569 | A140 | 45c Victoria, Albert | .20 | .20 |
| 570 | A140 | $1.50 Elizabeth, Philip | .55 | .55 |
| 571 | A140 | $3 Elizabeth, Philip, diff. | 1.10 | 1.10 |
| 572 | A140 | $4 Elizabeth, portrait | 1.50 | 1.50 |
| a. | | Souvenir sheet of 4, #568-571 | 1.50 | 1.50 |

**Souvenir Sheet**

573 A140 $6 Elizabeth as Princess   2.50   2.50

Nos. 568-572 (5)   3.55   3.55

Victoria's accession to the throne, 150th anniv.

## Marine Life G48

**1987, Dec. 17**    **Perf. 15**
| | | | | |
|---|---|---|---|---|
| 574 | G48 | 45c | Banded coral shrimp | .30 .30 |
| 575 | G48 | 50c | Arrow crab, flamingo tongue | .40 .40 |
| 576 | G48 | 65c | Cardinal fish | .50 .50 |
| 577 | G48 | $5 | Moray eel | 4.00 4.00 |
| | | | Nos. 574-577 (4) | 5.20 5.20 |

**Souvenir Sheet**
| 578 | G48 | $5 | Puffer fish | 3.25 3.25 |
|---|---|---|---|---|

## Great Explorers G52

Designs: 15c, Vitus Bering and the St. Peter. 75c, Bering and pancake ice. $1, David Livingstone and the Ma-Robert. $2, Livingstone meeting Henry M. Stanley. $3, John Speke (1827-1864) and Sir Richard Burton (1821-1890) welcomed at Tabori. $3.50, Speke, Burton at Lake Victoria. $4, Crewman of Christopher Columbus spotting land. $4.50, Columbus, exchange of gifts. $5, Sextant. $6, Columbus' ship landing in Bahamas, 1492.

**1988, July 29**    **Perf. 14**
| 596-603 | G52 | Set of 8 | 4.50 4.50 |
|---|---|---|---|

**Souvenir Sheets**
| 604 | G52 | $5 multi | 2.00 2.00 |
|---|---|---|---|
| 605 | G52 | $6 multi | 2.25 2.25 |

Nos. 602-603, 605 picture 500th anniversary discovery of America emblem.

A number of unissued items, imperfs, part perfs., missing color varieties, etc., were made available when the Format International inventory was liquidated.

## America's Cup Yachts — G49

**1988, Mar. 31**    **Perf. 12½**
| | | | | |
|---|---|---|---|---|
| 579 | G49 | 5c | Australia IV | .20 .20 |
| 580 | G49 | 65c | Crusader II | .25 .25 |
| 581 | G49 | 75c | New Zealand K27 | .30 .30 |
| 582 | G49 | $2 | Italia | .85 .85 |
| 583 | G49 | $4 | White Crusader | 1.75 1.75 |
| 584 | G49 | $5 | Stars and Stripes | 2.25 2.25 |
| | | | Nos. 579-584 (6) | 5.60 5.60 |

**Souvenir Sheet**
| 585 | G49 | $1 Champosa V | .80 .80 |
|---|---|---|---|

## Bequia Regatta G50

**1988, Mar. 31**    **Perf. 12½**
| | | | | |
|---|---|---|---|---|
| 586 | G50 | 5c | Seine boats | .20 .20 |
| 587 | G50 | 50c | Friendship Rose | .20 .20 |
| 588 | G50 | 75c | Fishing boats | .30 .30 |
| 589 | G60 | $3.50 | Yacht racing | 1.50 1.50 |
| | | | Nos. 586-589 (4) | 2.20 2.20 |

**Souvenir Sheet**
| 590 | G50 | $8 Port Elizabeth | 5.25 5.25 |
|---|---|---|---|

## Cricketers — G53

**1988, July 29**    **Perf. 15**
| | | | | |
|---|---|---|---|---|
| 606 | G53 | 20c | A. I. Razvi | .20 .20 |
| 607 | G53 | 45c | R. J. Hadlee | .25 .25 |
| 608 | G53 | 75c | M. D. Crowe | .50 .50 |
| 609 | G53 | $1.25 | C. H. Lloyd | .80 .80 |
| 610 | G53 | $1.50 | A. R. Boarder | .95 .95 |
| 611 | G53 | $2 | M. D. Marshall | 1.25 1.25 |
| 612 | G53 | $2.50 | C. A. Hick | 1.50 1.50 |
| 613 | G53 | $3.50 | C. G. Greenidge, horiz. | 2.25 2.25 |
| | | | Nos. 606-613 (8) | 7.70 7.70 |

A $3 souvenir sheet in the design of the $2 stamp was not a postal issue according to the St. Vincent P.O. Value $6.

## Tennis Type of 1987

**1988, July 29**    **Perf. 12½**
| | | | | |
|---|---|---|---|---|
| 614 | A137 | 15c | Pam Shriver, horiz. | .20 .20 |
| 615 | A137 | 50c | Kevin Curran | .20 .20 |
| 616 | A137 | 75c | Wendy Turnbull | .30 .30 |
| 617 | A137 | $1 | Evonne Cawley | .40 .40 |
| 618 | A137 | $1.50 | Ilie Nastase, horiz. | .60 .60 |
| 619 | A137 | $2 | Billie Jean King | .80 .80 |
| 620 | A137 | $3 | Bjorn Borg | 1.25 1.25 |
| 621 | A137 | $3.50 | Virginia Wade | 1.40 1.40 |
| | | | Nos. 614-621 (8) | 5.15 5.15 |

**Souvenir Sheet**
| 622 | A137 | Sheet of 2 | 2.75 2.75 |
|---|---|---|---|
| a. | A137 | $2.25 Stefan Edberg | 1.25 1.25 |
| b. | A137 | $2.25 Steffi Graf | 1.25 1.25 |

No. 616 inscribed "Turnball" in error.

## Tourism — G51

**1988, May 26**    **Perf. 14x13½**
| | | | | |
|---|---|---|---|---|
| 591 | G51 | 15c | multicolored | .20 .20 |
| 592 | G51 | 65c | multi, diff. | .25 .25 |
| 593 | G51 | 75c | multi, diff. | .30 .30 |
| 594 | G51 | $5 | multi, diff. | 2.00 2.00 |
| | | | Nos. 591-594 (4) | 2.75 2.75 |

**Souvenir Sheet**
| 595 | G51 | $10 Waterfall, vert. | 6.00 6.00 |
|---|---|---|---|

No. 595 contains one 35x56mm stamp.

Aircraft of Mustique Airways, Genadine Tours.

---

**1989, Feb. 7**    **Perf. 14x13½**
| | | | | |
|---|---|---|---|---|
| 623 | G54 | 1c | Fatehpur Sikri | .20 .20 |
| 624 | G54 | 2c | Palace on Wheels | .20 .20 |
| 625 | G54 | 3c | Old fort, Delhi | .20 .20 |
| 626 | G54 | 5c | Pinjore Gardens | .20 .20 |
| 627 | G54 | 10c | Taj Mahal | .20 .20 |
| 628 | G54 | 25c | Chandni Chowk | .20 .20 |
| 629 | G54 | $4 | Agra Fort, Jaipur | 3.75 3.75 |
| 630 | G54 | $5 | Gandhi Memorial | 5.50 5.50 |
| | | | Nos. 623-630 (8) | 10.45 10.45 |

**Souvenir Sheets**
| 631 | G54 | $4 | Qutab Minar, vert. | 7.25 7.25 |
|---|---|---|---|---|
| 632 | G54 | $6 | Palace of the Winds | 7.25 7.25 |

## Japanese Art Type

Paintings: 5c, The View at Yotsuya, by Hokusai. 30c, Landscape at Ochanomizu, by Hokuju. 45c, Itabashi, by Eisen. 65c, Early Summer Rain, by Kunisada. 75c, High Noon at Kasumigaseki, by Kuniyoshi. $1, The Yoshiwara Embankment by Moonlight, by Kuniyoshi. $4, The Bridge of Boats at Sano, by Hokusai. $5, Lingering Snow on Mount Hira, by Kunitora. No. 641, Colossus of Rhodes, by Kunitora. No. 642, Shinobazu Pond, by Kokan.

**1989, July 6**    **Perf. 14x13½**
| 633-640 | A170 | Set of 8 | 13.50 13.50 |
|---|---|---|---|

**Souvenir Sheets**
| 641 | A170 | $6 multicolored | 6.00 6.00 |
|---|---|---|---|
| 642 | A170 | $6 multicolored | 6.00 6.00 |

Miniature Sheet

## 1990 World Cup Soccer Championships, Italy — G55

Soccer players and landmarks: a Mt. Vesuvius. b, The Colosseum. c, Venice. d, Roman Forum. e, Leaning Tower of Pisa. f, Florence. g, The Vatican. h, The Pantheon.

**1989, July 10**    **Perf. 14**
| 643 | | Sheet of 8 | 15.00 15.00 |
|---|---|---|---|
| a.-h. | G55 | $1.50 any single | 1.75 1.75 |

## Discovery of America 500th Anniv. Type of Antigua & Barbuda

UPAE emblem and American Indians: 25c, Smoking tobacco. 75c, Rolling tobacco. $1, Body painting. No. 647a, Starting campfire. No. 647b, Woman drinking from bowl. No. 647c, Woman frying grain or corn patties. No. 647d, Adult resting in hammock using stone mortar and pestle. $4, Smoothing wood. No. 649, Chief. No. 650, Fishing with bow and arrow.

**1989, Oct. 2**    **Litho.**    **Perf. 14**
| | | | | |
|---|---|---|---|---|
| 644 | A196 | 25c | multicolored | .20 .20 |
| 645 | A196 | 75c | multicolored | .80 .80 |
| 646 | A196 | $1 | multicolored | 1.00 1.00 |
| 647 | A196 | | Strip of 4 | 6.00 6.00 |
| a.-d. | A196 | $1.50 | any single | 1.50 1.50 |
| 648 | A196 | $4 | multicolored | 4.00 4.00 |
| | | | Nos. 644-648 (5) | 12.00 12.00 |

**Souvenir Sheets**
| 649 | A196 | $6 multicolored | 6.25 6.25 |
|---|---|---|---|
| 650 | A196 | $6 multicolored | 6.25 6.25 |

No. 647 has continuous design.

## 1st Moon Landing Type

Designs: 5c Columbia command module. 40c, Neil Armstrong saluting flag on the Moon. 55c, Command module over Moon. 65c, Eagle liftoff from Moon. 70c, Eagle on the Moon. $1, Command module re-entering Earth's atmosphere. $3, Apollo 11 mission emblem. $5, Armstrong and Buzz Aldrin walking on the Moon. No. 659, Apollo 11 launch, vert. No. 660, Splashdown.

**1989, Oct. 2**    **Perf. 14**
| 651-658 | A171 | Set of 8 | 16.00 16.00 |
|---|---|---|---|

**Souvenir Sheets**
| 659 | A171 | $6 multi, vert. | 6.50 6.50 |
|---|---|---|---|
| 660 | A171 | $6 multi | 6.50 6.50 |

India '89, International Stamp Exhibition, New Dehli — G54

Disney characters and sites in India.

---

## Butterflies G56

*5c Southern Dagger Tail*

**1989, Oct. 16**    **Litho.**    **Perf. 14x14½**
| | | | | |
|---|---|---|---|---|
| 661 | G56 | 5c | Southern dagger tail | .30 .30 |
| 662 | G56 | 30c | Androgeus swallowtail | .60 .60 |
| 663 | G56 | 45c | Clench's hairstreak | .85 .85 |
| 664 | G56 | 65c | Buckeye | 1.25 1.25 |
| 665 | G56 | 75c | Venezuelan sulphur | 1.50 1.50 |
| 666 | G56 | $1 | Mimic | 1.90 1.90 |
| 667 | G56 | $4 | Common longtail skipper | 7.25 7.25 |
| 668 | G56 | $5 | Carribean buckeye | 9.00 9.00 |
| | | | Nos. 661-668 (8) | 22.65 22.65 |

**Souvenir Sheets**
| 669 | G56 | $6 | Flambeau | 11.00 11.00 |
|---|---|---|---|---|
| 670 | G56 | $6 | Queen, large orange sulphur, Ramsden's giant white | 11.00 11.00 |

## Flora — G57

**1989, Nov. 1**    **Litho.**    **Perf. 14**
| | | | | |
|---|---|---|---|---|
| 671 | G57 | 80c | Solanum urens | 1.25 1.25 |
| 672 | G57 | $1.25 | Passiflora andersonii | 2.00 2.00 |
| 673 | G57 | $1.65 | Miconia andersonii | 2.75 2.75 |
| 674 | G57 | $1.85 | Pitcairnia sulphurea | 3.00 3.00 |
| | | | Nos. 671-674 (4) | |

## Christmas — G58

Walt Disney characters and classic automobiles.

**1989, Dec. 20**    **Perf. 14x13½, 13½x14**
| | | | | |
|---|---|---|---|---|
| 675 | G58 | 5c | 1907 Rolls-Royce | .20 .20 |
| 676 | G58 | 10c | 1897 Stanley Steamer | .20 .20 |
| 677 | G58 | 15c | 1904 Darracq | .20 .20 |
| 678 | G58 | 45c | 1914 Detroit Electric Coupe | .50 .50 |
| 679 | G58 | 55c | 1896 Ford | .65 .65 |
| 680 | G58 | $2 | 1904 REO Runabout | 2.25 2.25 |
| 681 | G58 | $3 | 1899 Winton Mail Truck | 3.50 3.50 |
| 682 | G58 | $5 | 1893 Duryea Car | 6.00 6.00 |
| | | | Nos. 675-682 (8) | 13.50 13.50 |

**Souvenir Sheets**
| 683 | G58 | $6 | 1912 Pope-Hartford | 8.00 8.00 |
|---|---|---|---|---|
| 684 | G58 | $6 | 1908 Buick Model 10 | 8.00 8.00 |

Nos. 683-684 vert.

Battles of World War II G59

872 ST. VINCENT GRENADINES

10c, 1st Battle of Narvik, 4/10/40. 15c, Allies land at Anzio, 1/22/44. 20c, Battle of Midway, 6/4/42. 45c, Allies launch offensive on Gustav Line, 5/11/44. 55c, Allies take over zones in Berlin, 7/3/45. 65c, Battle of the Atlantic, 3/1-20/43. 90c, Allies launch final phase of North African Campaign, 4/22/43. $3, US forces land on Guam, 7/21/44. $5, US 7th Army meets the 3rd Army across the Rhine, 3/26/45. #694, Battle of Leyte Gulf, 10/23/44. #695, The Dambusters Raid, 5/16/43.

**1990, Apr. 2 Litho. *Perf. 14***

**685-694** G59 Set of 10 22.00 22.00

**Souvenir Sheet**

**695** G59 $6 multi 10.50 10.50

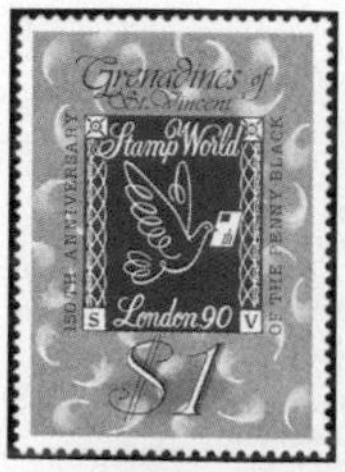
Grenadines of St. Vincent
Stamp World
London 90
$1

Penny Black, 150th Anniv. — G60

$1, Stamp World London '90 emblem. $5, Negative image of the Penny Black. $6, Penny Black with non-existent letters.

**1990, May 3 *Perf. 14x15***

**696** G60 $1 pale rose & blk 1.50 1.50
**697** G60 $5 pale violet & blk 6.75 6.75

**Souvenir Sheet**

**698** G60 $6 dull blue & blk 7.50 7.50

Stamp World London '90.

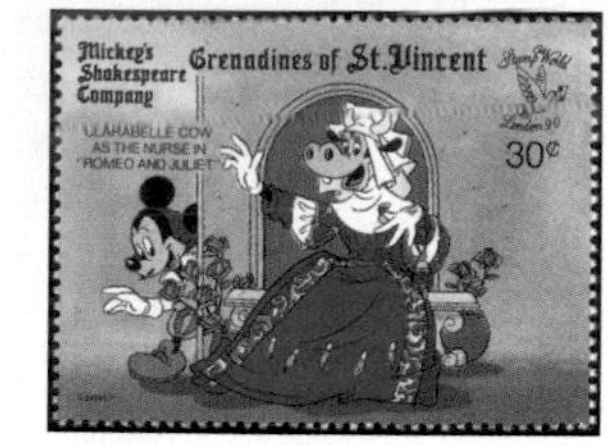
Grenadines of St. Vincent
30c

Disney Characters Portraying Shakespearian Roles — G61

Designs: 20c, Goofy as Marc Antony in "Julius Caesar." 30c, Clarabelle Cow as nurse in "Romeo and Juliet." 45c, Pete as Falstaff in "Henry IV." 50c, Minnie Mouse as Portia in "The Merchant of Venice." $1, Donald Duck holding head of Yorick in "Hamlet." $2, Daisy Duck as Ophelia in "Hamlet." $4, Donald and Daisy Duck as Benedick and Beatrice in "Much Ado About Nothing." $5, Minnie Mouse and Donald Duck as Katherine and Petruchio in "The Taming of the Shrew." No. 707, Mickey and Minnie Mouse portraying Romeo and Juliet. No. 708, Clarabelle Cow as Titania in "A Midsummer Night's Dream."

**1990, May *Perf. 14x13½***

**699-706** G61 Set of 8 16.00 16.00

**Souvenir Sheets**

**707** G61 $6 multi 8.00 8.00
**708** G61 $6 multi 8.00 8.00

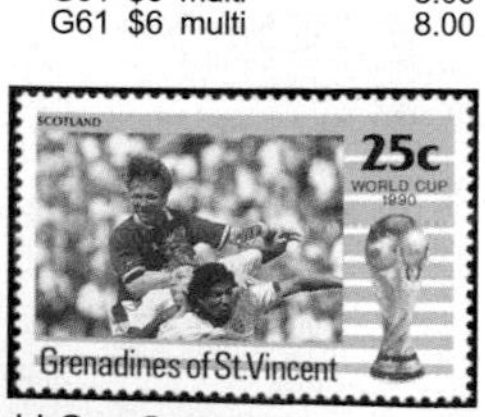
25c
Grenadines of St.Vincent

World Cup Soccer Championships, Italy — G62

World Cup Trophy and players from participating countries.

**1990, Sept. 24 Litho. *Perf. 14***

**709** G62 25c Scotland .40 .40
**710** G62 50c Egypt .90 .90
**711** G62 $2 Austria 3.25 3.25
**712** G62 $4 United States 6.50 6.50
*Nos. 709-712 (4)* 11.05 11.05

**Souvenir Sheets**

**713** G62 $6 Holland 8.50 8.50
**714** G62 $6 England 8.50 8.50

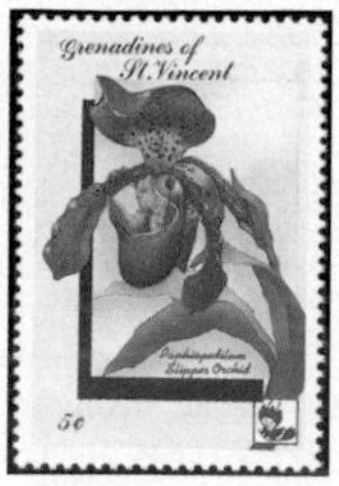
Grenadines of St. Vincent
5c

Orchids — G63

Designs: 5c, Paphiopedilum. 25c, Dendrobium phalaenopsis, Cymbidium. 30c, Miltonia candida. 50c, Epidendrum ibaguense, Cymbidium Elliot Rogers. $1, Rossioglassum grande. $2, Phalaenopsis Elisa Chang Lou, Masdevallia coccinea. $4, Cypripedium accale, Cypripedium calceolus. $5, Orchis spectabilis. No. 723, Epidendrum ibaguense, Phalaenopsis. No. 724, Dendrobium anosmum.

**1990, Nov. 23 Litho. *Perf. 14***

**715-722** G63 Set of 8 18.50 18.50

**Souvenir Sheets**

**723** G63 $6 multi 11.00 11.00
**724** G63 $6 multi 11.00 11.00

Expo '90, Intl. Garden and Greenery Exposition, Osaka, Japan.

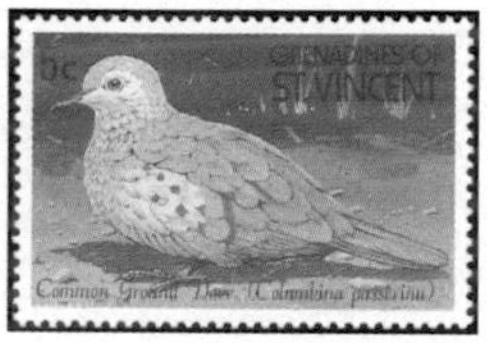
GRENADINES OF ST.VINCENT

Birds G64

**1990, Nov. 20**

**725** G64 5c Common ground dove .30 .30
**726** G64 25c Purple martin .30 .30
**727** G64 45c Painted bunting .50 .50
**728** G64 55c Blue-hooded euphonia .55 .55
**729** G64 75c Blue-gray tanager .80 .80
**730** G64 $1 Red-eyed vireo 1.10 1.10
**731** G64 $2 Palm chat 2.25 2.25
**732** G64 $3 North American jacana 3.25 3.25
**733** G64 $4 Green-throated carib 4.50 4.50
**734** G64 $5 St. Vincent parrot 5.50 5.50
*Nos. 725-734 (10)* 19.05 19.05

**Souvenir Sheets**

**735** Sheet of 2 6.50 6.50
*a.* G64 $3 Bananaquit 3.25 3.25
*b.* G64 $3 Magnificent frigatebird 3.25 3.25
**736** G64 $6 Red-legged honeycreeper 6.50 6.50

**Queen Mother 90th Birthday Type**

Photographs: Nos. 737a-737i, From 1900-1929. Nos. 738a-738i, From 1930-1959. Nos. 739a-739i, From 1960-1989. Nos. 740-748, Enlarged photographs used for Nos. 737-739.

**1991, Feb. 14 Litho. *Perf. 14***

**Miniature Sheets of 9, #a.-i.**

**737** A193 $2 blue & multi 15.00 15.00
**738** A193 $2 pink & multi 15.00 15.00
**739** A193 $2 green & multi 15.00 15.00

**Souvenir Sheets**

**740** A193 $5 like #737a 4.25 4.25
**741** A193 $5 like #737f 4.25 4.25
**742** A193 $5 like #737h 4.25 4.25
**743** A193 $5 like #738b 4.25 4.25
**744** A193 $5 like #738f 4.25 4.25
**745** A193 $5 like #738g 4.25 4.25
**746** A193 $5 like #739b 4.25 4.25
**747** A193 $5 like #739d 4.25 4.25
**748** A193 $5 like #739h 4.25 4.25

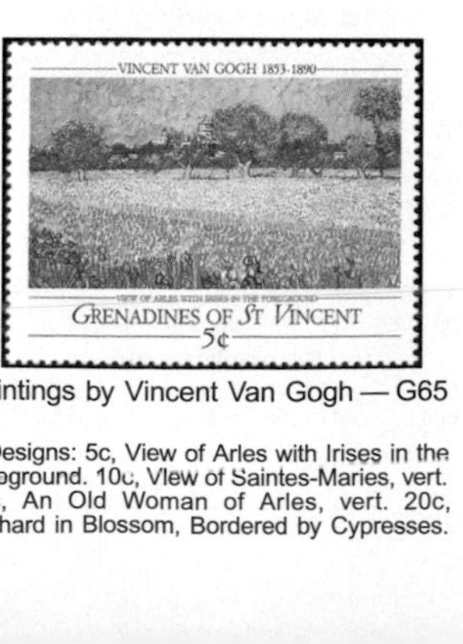
VINCENT VAN GOGH 1853-1890
GRENADINES OF ST VINCENT
5c

Paintings by Vincent Van Gogh — G65

Designs: 5c, View of Arles with Irises in the Foreground. 10c, View of Saintes-Maries, vert. 15c, An Old Woman of Arles, vert. 20c, Orchard in Blossom, Bordered by Cypresses. 25c, Three White Cottages in Saintes-Maries. 35c, Boats at Saintes-Maries-De-La-Mer. 40c, Interior of a Restaurant in Arles. 45c, Peasant Woman, vert. 55c, Self-Portrait, Sept. 1888, vert. 60c, A Pork Butcher's Shop Seen From a Window, vert. 75c, The Night Cafe in Arles. $1, Portrait of Milliet, Second Lieutenant of the Zouaves, vert. $2, The Cafe Terrace on the Place Du Forum Arles, at Night, vert. $3, The Zouave, vert. $4, Two Lovers (Fragment), vert. No. 764, Still Life: Blue Enamel Coffeepot, Earthenware and Fruit. No. 765, Street in Saintes-Maries. No. 766, A Lane Near Arles. No. 767, Harvest at La Crau, with Montmajour in the Background. No. 768, The Sower.

**1991, June 10 Litho. *Perf. 13½***

**749-764** G65 Set of 16 26.00 26.00

**Size: 102x76mm**

***Imperf***

**765-766** G65 $5 Set of 2 11.00 11.00
**767-768** G65 $6 Set of 2 15.00 15.00

**Royal Family Birthday, Anniversary**

Common Design Type

**1991, July 5 Litho. *Perf. 14***

**769** CD347 10c multicolored .30 .30
**770** CD347 15c multicolored .30 .30
**771** CD347 40c multicolored .50 .50
**772** CD347 50c multicolored .70 .70
**773** CD347 $1 multicolored 1.30 1.30
**774** CD347 $2 multicolored 2.50 2.50
**775** CD347 $4 multicolored 5.00 5.00
**776** CD347 $5 multicolored 6.50 6.50
*Nos. 769-776 (8)* 17.10 17.10

**Souvenir Sheets**

**777** CD347 $5 Henry, William, Charles, Diana 7.50 7.50
**778** CD347 $5 Elizabeth, Andrew, Philip 5.50 5.50

10c, 50c, $1, Nos. 776-777, Charles and Diana, 10th wedding anniversary. Others, Queen Elizabeth II, 65th birthday.

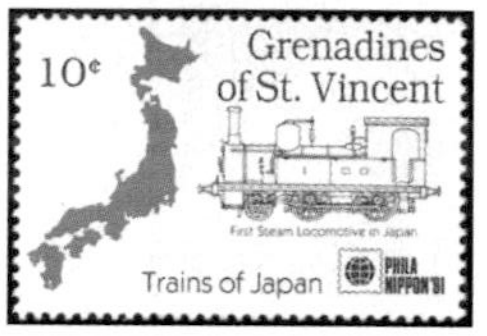
10c
Grenadines of St. Vincent
Trains of Japan
PHILA NIPPON '91

Phila Nippon '91 G66

Japanese locomotives: 10c, First Japanese steam. 25c, First American steam locomotive in Japan. 35c, Class 8620 steam. 50c, C53 steam. $1, DD-51 diesel. $2, RF 22327 electric. $4, EF-55 electric. $5, EF-58 electric. No. 787, Class 9600 steam, vert. No. 788, Class 4100 steam, vert. No. 789, C57 steam, vert. No. 790, C62 steam, vert.

**1991, Aug. 12 Litho. *Perf. 14x13½***

**779-786** G66 Set of 8 19.00 19.00

**Souvenir Sheets**

***Perf. 12x13***

**787-790** G66 $6 Set of 4 24.00 24.00

**Brandenburg Gate Type**

Designs: 45c, Brandenburg Gate and Soviet Pres. Mikhail Gorbachev. 65c, Sign. 80c, Statue, soldier escaping through barbed wire. No. 794, Berlin police insignia. No. 795, Berlin coat of arms.

**1991, Nov. 18 Litho. *Perf. 14***

**791** A209 45c multicolored .80 .80
**792** A209 65c multicolored 1.10 1.10
**793** A209 80c multicolored 1.40 1.40
*Nos. 791-793 (3)* 3.30 3.30

**Souvenir Sheets**

**794** A209 $5 multicolored 4.50 4.50
**795** A209 $5 multicolored 4.50 4.50

**Wolfgang Amadeus Mozart Type**

Portrait of Mozart and: $1, Scene from "Abduction from the Seraglio." $3, Dresden, 1749. No. 799, Portrait, vert. No. 800, Bust, vert.

**1991, Nov. 18 Litho. *Perf. 14***

**797** A210 $1 multicolored 1.40 1.40
**798** A210 $3 multicolored 4.00 4.00

**Souvenir Sheets**

**799** A210 $5 multicolored 4.75 4.75
**800** A210 $5 multicolored 4.75 4.75

**Boy Scout Type**

Designs: $2, Scout delivering mail and Czechoslovakian (local) scout stamp. $4, Cog train, Boy Scouts on Mt. Snowdon, Wales, vert. Nos. 803-804, Emblem of World Scout Jamboree, Korea.

**1991, Nov. 18 Litho. *Perf. 14***

**801** A211 $2 multicolored 2.40 2.40
**802** A211 $4 multicolored 4.75 4.75

**Souvenir Sheets**

**803** A211 $5 tan & multi 4.75 4.75
**804** A211 $5 violet blue & multi 4.75 4.75

Lord Robert Baden-Powell, 50th death anniv. and 17th World Scout Jamboree, Korea.

**De Gaulle Type**

Designs: 60c, De Gaulle in Djibouti, 1959. No. 807, In military uniform, vert. No. 808, Portrait as President.

**1991, Nov. 18 Litho. *Perf. 14***

**806** A212 60c 1.75 1.75

**Souvenir Sheets**

**807** A212 $5 multicolored 4.75 4.75
**808** A212 $5 multicolored 4.75 4.75

A number has been reserved for additional value in this set.

**Anniversaries and Events Type**

Designs: $1.50, Otto Lilienthal, aviation pioneer. No. 810, Train in winter, vert. No. 811, Trans-Siberian Express Sign. No. 812, Man and woman celebrating. No. 813, Woman and man wearing hats. No. 814, Georg Ludwig Friedrich Laves, architect of Hoftheater, Hanover. No. 815, Locomotive, Trans-Siberian Railway, vert. No. 816, Cantonal arms of Appenzell and Thurgau. No. 817, Hanover, 750th anniv.

**1991, Nov. 18 Litho. *Perf. 14***

**809** A213 $1.50 multicolored 3.75 3.75
**810** A213 $1.75 multicolored 3.50 3.50
**811** A213 $1.75 multicolored 3.50 3.50
**812** A213 $2 multicolored 1.75 1.75
**813** A213 $2 multicolored 1.75 1.75
**814** A213 $2 multicolored 3.75 3.75
*Nos. 809-814 (6)* 18.00 18.00

**Souvenir Sheets**

**815** A213 $5 multicolored 7.50 7.50
**816** A213 $5 multicolored 6.75 6.75
**817** A213 $5 multicolored 5.75 5.75

First glider flight, cent. (#809). Trans-Siberian Railway, cent. (#810-811, 815). Swiss Confederation, 700th anniv. (#812-813, 816). City of Hanover, 750th anniv. (#814, 817). No. 815 contains one 42x58mm stamp.

**Pearl Harbor Type of 1991**

Miniature Sheet

Designs: a, Japanese submarines and aircraft leave Truk to attack Pearl Harbor. b, Japanese flagship, Akagi. c, Nakajima B5N2 Kate, attack leader. d, Torpedo bombers attack battleship row. e, Ford Island Naval Air Station. f, Doris Miller earns Navy Cross. g, USS West Virginia and USS Tennessee ablaze. h, USS Arizona destroyed. i, USS New Orleans. j, Pres. Roosevelt declares war.

**1991, Nov. 18 *Perf. 14½x15***

**818** A214 $1 Sheet of 10, #a.-j. 25.00 25.00

**Disney Christmas Card Type**

Card design and year of issue: 10c, Mickey in sleigh pulled by Pluto, 1974. 55c, Donald, Pluto, and Mickey watching marching band, 1961. 65c, Greeting with stars, 1942. 75c, Mickey, Donald watch Merlin create a snowman, 1963. $1.50, Mickey placing wreath on door, 1958. $2, Mickey as Santa beside fireplace, 1957. $4, Mickey manipulating "Pinnochio" for friends. $5, Prince Charming and Cinderella dancing beside Christmas tree, 1987. No. 827, Snow White, 1957, vert. No. 828, Santa riding World War II bomber, 1942, vert.

**1991, Nov. 18 *Perf. 14x13½,13½x14***

**819-826** A216 Set of 8 18.00 18.00

**Souvenir Sheets**

**827-828** A216 $6 Set of 2 9.00 9.00

Nos. 819-826 are horiz.

**Queen Elizabeth II's Accession to the Throne, 40th Anniv.**

Common Design Type

**1992, Feb. 6 Litho. *Perf. 14***

**829** CD348 15c multicolored .30 .30
**830** CD348 45c multicolored .50 .50
**831** CD348 $2 multicolored 2.25 2.25
**832** CD348 $4 multicolored 4.50 4.50
*Nos. 829-832 (4)* 7.55 7.55

**Souvenir Sheets**

**833** CD348 $6 Queen at left, beach 6.50 6.50
**834** CD348 $6 Queen at right, building 6.50 6.50

### World Columbian Stamp Expo Type

Walt Disney characters as famous Chicagoans: 10c, Mickey as Walt Disney walking past birthplace. 50c, Donald Duck and nephews sleeping in George Pullman's railway cars. $1, Daisy Duck as Jane Addams in front of Hull House. $5, Mickey as Carl Sandburg. No. 839, Grandma McDuck as Mrs. O'Leary with her cow, vert.

**1992, Apr. Litho. *Perf. 14x13½***
**835** A220 10c multicolored .35 .35
**836** A220 50c multicolored .65 .65
**837** A220 $1 multicolored 1.40 1.40
**838** A220 $5 multicolored 7.25 7.25
*Nos. 835-838 (4)* 9.65 9.65

**Souvenir Sheet**
***Perf. 13½x14***
**839** A220 $6 multicolored 8.50 8.50

Nos. 840-844 have not been used.

### Granada '92 Type

Walt Disney characters as Spanish explorers in New World: 15c, Aztec King Goofy giving treasure to Big Pete as Hernando Cortes. 40c, Mickey as Hernando de Soto discovering Mississippi River. $2, Goofy as Vasco Nunez de Balboa discovering Pacific Ocean. $4, Donald Duck as Francisco Coronado discovering Rio Grande. $6, Mickey as Ponce de Leon discovering Fountain of Youth.

**1992, Apr. *Perf. 14x13½***
**845** A221 15c multicolored .35 .35
**846** A221 40c multicolored .65 .65
**847** A221 $2 multicolored 1.40 1.40
**848** A221 $4 multicolored 7.25 7.25
*Nos. 845-848 (4)* 9.65 9.65

**Souvenir Sheet**
***Perf. 13½x14***
**849** A221 $6 multicolored 8.50 8.50

Nos. 850-854 have not been used.

### Discovery of America, 500th Anniv. Type

10c, King Ferdinand & Queen Isabella. 45c, Santa Maria & Nina in Acul Bay, Haiti. 55c, Santa Maria, vert. $2, Columbus' fleet departing Canary Islands, vert. $4, Sinking of Santa Maria off Hispanola. $5, Nina and Pinta returning to Spain. #861, Columbus' fleet during night storm. #862, Columbus landing on San Salvador.

**1992, May 22 Litho. *Perf. 14***
**855-860** A222 Set of 6 11.50 11.50

**Souvenir Sheets**
**861-862** A222 $6 Set of 2 11.50 11.50

World Columbian Stamp Expo '92, Chicago.

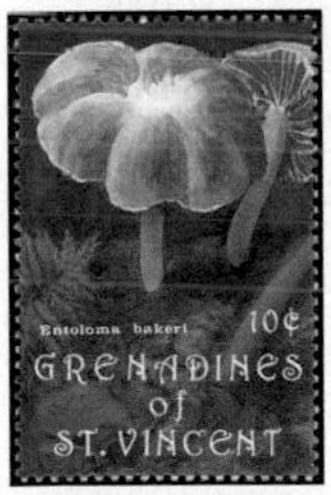


Mushrooms — G67

Designs: 10c, Entoloma bakeri. 15c, Hydropus paraensis. 20c, Leucopaxillus gracillimus. 45c, Hygrotrama dennisianum. 50c, Leucoagaricus hortensis. 65c, Pyrrhoglossum pyrrhum. 75c, Amanita craeoderma. $1, Lentinus bertieri. $2, Dennisiomyces griseus. $3, Xerulina asprata. $4, Hygrocybe acutoconica. $5, Lepiota spiculata. No. 879, Pluteus crysophlebius. No. 880, Lepiota volvatua. No. 881, Amanita lilloi.

**1992, July 2**
**867-878** G67 Set of 12 26.00 26.00

**Souvenir Sheets**
**879-881** G67 $6 each 7.50 7.50

### Butterfly Type of 1992

15c, Nymphalidae paulogramma 20c, Heliconius cydno. 30c, Ithomiidae eutresis hypereia. 45c, Eurytides Columbus koll, vert. 55c, Papilio ascolius. 75c, Anaea pasibula. 80c, Heliconius doris. $1, Nymphalidae persisama pitheas. $2, Nymphalidae batesia hypochlora. $3, Heliconius erato. $4, Elzunia cassandrina. $5, Ithomiidae sais. #894, Pieridae dismorphia orise. #895, Nymphalidae podotricha. #896, Oleria tigilla.

**1992, June 15 Litho. *Perf. 14***
**882-893** A225 Set of 12 25.00 25.00

**Souvenir Sheets**
**894-896** A225 $6 Set of 3 17.50 17.50

Genoa '92.

### Hummingbirds Type of 1992

5c, Antillean crested, female, horiz. 10c, Blue-tailed emerald, female. 35c, Antillean mango, male, horiz. 45c, Antillean mango, female, horiz. 55c, Green-throated carib, horiz. 65c, Green violet-ear. 75c, Blue-tailed emerald, male, horiz. $1, Purple throated carib. $2, Copper-rumped, horiz. $3, Rufous-breasted hermit. $4, Antillean crested, male. $5, Green breasted mango, male. #909, Blue-tailed emerald. #910, Antillean mango, diff. #911, Antillean crested, male, diff.

**1992, July 7 Litho. *Perf. 14***
**897-908** A224 Set of 12 25.00 25.00

**Souvenir Sheets**
**909-911** A224 $6 Set of 3 21.00 21.00

Genoa '92.

### Discovery of America Type

**1992 Litho. *Perf. 14½***
**912** A230 $1 Coming ashore 1.50 1.50
**913** A230 $2 Natives, ships 3.00 3.00

Organization of East Caribbean States.

### Summer Olympics Type

10c, Volleyball, vert. 15c, Men's floor exercise. 25c, Cross-country skiing, vert. 30c, 110-meter hurdles. 45c, 120-meter ski jump. 55c, Women's 4x100-meter relay, vert. 75c, Triple jump, vert. 80c, Mogul skiing, vert. $1, 100-meter butterfly. $2, Tornado class yachting. $3, Decathlon. $5, Equestrian jumping. #926, Ice hockey. #927, Single luge. #928, Soccer.

**1992, Apr. 21 Litho. *Perf. 14***
**914** A219 10c multicolored .20 .20
**915** A219 15c multicolored .20 .20
**916** A218 25c multicolored .20 .20
**917** A219 30c multicolored .35 .35
**918** A218 45c multicolored .55 .55
**919** A219 55c multicolored .65 .65
**920** A219 75c multicolored 1.00 1.00
**921** A218 80c multicolored 1.00 1.00
**922** A219 $1 multicolored 1.15 1.15
**923** A219 $2 multicolored 2.40 2.40
**924** A219 $3 multicolored 3.50 3.50
**925** A219 $5 multicolored 6.25 6.25
*Nos. 914-925 (12)* 17.45 17.45

**Souvenir Sheets**
**926** A218 $6 multicolored 6.75 6.75
**927** A218 $6 multicolored 6.75 6.75
**928** A219 $6 multicolored 6.75 6.75

### Christmas Art Type

Details or entire paintings: 10c, Our Lady with St. Roch & St. Anthony of Padua, by Giorgione. 40c, St. Anthony of Padua, by Master of the Emboridered Leaf. 45c, Madonna & Child in a Landscape, by Orazio Gentileschi. 50c, Madonna & Child with St. Anne, by Leonardo da Vinci. 55c, The Holy Family, by Giuseppe Maria Crespi. 65c, Madonna & Child, by Andrea Del Sarto. 75c, Madonna & Child with Sts. Lawrence & Julian, by Gentile da Fabriano. $1, Virgin & Child, by School of Parma. $2, Madonna with the Iris in the style of Durer. $3, Virgin & Child with St. Jerome & St. Dominic, by Filippino Lippi. $4, Rapolano Madonna, by Ambrogio Lorenzetti. $5, The Virgin & Child with Angels in a Garden with a Rose Hedge, by Stefano da Verona. #941, Virgin & Child with St. John the Baptist, by Botticelli. #942, Madonna & Child with St. Anne, by Leonardo da Vinci. #943, Madonna & Child with Grapes, by Lucas Cranach the Elder.

**1992, Nov. Litho. *Perf. 13½x14***
**929-940** A232 Set of 12 20.00 20.00

**Souvenir Sheets**
**941-943** A232 $6 Set of 3 18.50 18.50

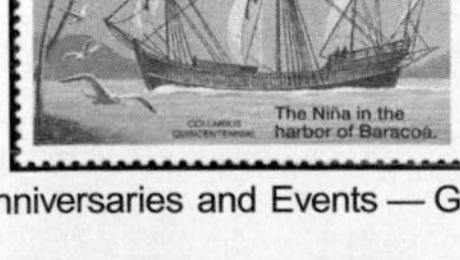


Anniversaries and Events — G68

Designs: 10c, Nina in the harbor of Baracoa. No. 948, Columbus' fleet at sea. No. 949, America 3, US and Il Moro, Italy. No. 945, Zeppelin LZ3, 1907. No. 946, Blind man with guide dog, vert. No. 947, Guide dog. No. 950, German flag, natl. arms, Konrad Adenauer. No. 951, Hands breaking bread, vert. $2, Mars, Voyager 2. $3, Berlin airlift, Adenauer. No. 954, Wolfgang Amadeus Mozart, Constanze, vert. No. 955, Adenauer, Cologne after World War II. No. 956, Zeppelin LZ 37 shot down over England, World War I. $5, Buildings in Germany, Adenauer. No. 958, Scene from "Don Giovanni," vert. No. 959, Columbus looking through telescope. No. 960, Count Ferdinand von Zeppelin, facing right. No. 960A, Count Ferdinand von Zeppelin, facing left. No. 961, Mars Observer. No. 962, Adenauer with hand on face, vert. No. 963, Adenauer, diff.

**1992, Dec. *Perf. 14***
**944** G68 10c multicolored 1.00 1.00
**945** G68 75c multicolored 1.00 1.00
**946** G68 75c multicolored 2.75 2.75
**947** G68 75c multicolored 2.75 2.75
**948** G68 $1 multicolored 3.50 3.50
**949** G68 $1 multicolored 2.50 2.50
**950** G68 $1 multicolored 1.50 1.50
**951** G68 $1 multicolored 3.25 3.25
**952** G68 $2 multicolored 4.25 4.25
**953** G68 $3 multicolored 3.00 3.00
**954** G68 $4 multicolored 4.75 4.75
**955** G68 $4 multicolored 4.50 4.50
**956** G68 $4 multicolored 4.50 4.50
**957** G68 $5 multicolored 4.50 4.50
*Nos. 944-957 (14)* 43.75 43.75

**Souvenir Sheets**
**958-963** G68 $6 each 5.75 5.75

Discovery of America, 500th anniv. (#944, 948, 959). Count Zeppelin, 75th death anniv. (#945, 956, 960-960A). Lions Intl., 75th anniv. (#946-947). Konrad Adenauer, 25th death anniv. (#950, 953, 955, 957, 962-963).America's Cup yacht race (#949). Intl. Conference on Nutrition, Rome (#951). Intl. Space Year (#952, 961). Wolfgang Amadeus Mozart, bicent. of death (in 1991) (#954, 958).

Issued: #945, 956, 960-960A, 12/15; others, Dec.

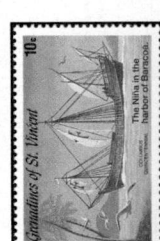

Miniature Sheets

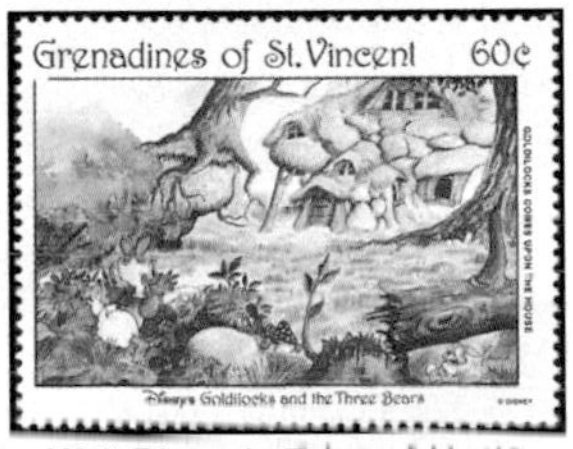


Walt Disney's Tales of Uncle Scrooge — G69

Goldilocks (Daisy Duck) and the Three Bears: No. 964a, Comes upon the house. b, Finds three bowls of soup. c, Finds three chairs. d, Ventures upstairs. e, Tries Papa Bear's bed. f, Falls asleep in Baby Bear's bed. g, The Three Bears return home. h, Baby Bear finds Goldilocks in his bed. i, Goldilocks awakens.

No. 970, The Three Bears in the forest, vert. No. 971, Goldilocks runs home.

The Princess (Minnie Mouse) and the Pea: No. 965a, Prince Mickey in search of a bride. b, Princess Minnie caught in a storm. c, Queen Clarbelle meets the princess. d, Royal family entertains Princess Minnie. e, Queen places a pea on the mattress. f, Mattresses upon mattresses. g, Princess Minnie at her bed-chamber. h, Princess Minnie very tired the next morning. i, A true princess for a real prince.

No. 972, Prince Mickey's useless search for a true princess. No. 973, Mickey's royal family lived happily ever after.

Little Red Riding Hood (Minnie Mouse): No. 966a, Off to Grandmother's. b, Stopping for flowers. c, Followed by the wolf. d, Frightened by the wolf. e, Wolf charges into Grandmother's house. f, Little Red Riding Hood at Grandmother's door. g, "What big teeth you have." h, Calling woodsman for help. i, Woodsman to the rescue.

No. 974, Little Riding Hood on the way to Grandmother's, vert. No. 975, A happy ending.

Hop O'-My-Thumb (Mickey, Minnie, family): No. 967a, Poor woodcutter without food for his children. b, Pebbles to find way back. c, Sadly leaving children's forest. d, Surveying from tree top. e, Ogress sends boys to bed. f, Ogre and his magic seven-league boots. g, Ogre chasing boys. h, Taking the magic seven-league boots. i, Running to Royal Palace.

No. 976, Boy of woodcutter with bag over shoulder. No. 977, Woodcutter's family reunited.

Pied Piper of Hamelin (Donald, Mickey and friends): No. 968a, Mayor (Donald) offers reward. b, Piper Mickey accepts the challenge. c, Piper leads rats to the river. d, Piper promises revenge. Children follow Piper outside village gates. f, Mayor and townspeople watch from above. g, Children follow Piper through countryside. h, Children pass through the cavern. i, All closed off from Hamelin, except for one.

No. 978, Pied Piper leading rats past town square. No. 979, Piper Mickey encouraging children in land of sweets, vert.

Puss in Boots (Goofy, Donald and friends): No. 969a, Gift for the king. b, Puss brings Marquis of Carabas to bathe in river. c, Puss calls for king's help. d, King introduces his daughter (Daisy Duck). e, Puss and reapers. f, Puss received by the Ogre. g, Ogre changed into a lion. h, Ogre changed into a mouse. i, Puss shows off Marquis' castle.

No. 980, Miller's estate, Donald with cat, Puss, donkey. No. 981, Marriage of Marquis of Carabis to daughter of the king, vert.

***Perf. 14x13½, 13½x14***
**1992, Dec. 15 Litho.**
**964** G69 60c Sheet of 9, #a.-i. 6.75 6.75
**965** G69 60c Sheet of 9, #a.-i. 6.75 6.75
**966** G69 60c Sheet of 9, #a.-i. 6.75 6.75
**967** G69 60c Sheet of 9, #a.-i. 6.75 6.75
**968** G69 60c Sheet of 9, #a.-i. 6.75 6.75
**969** G69 60c Sheet of 9, #a.-i. 6.75 6.75

**Souvenir Sheets**
***Perf. 13½x14, 14x13½***
**970-981** G69 $6 each 5.50 5.50

### Disney Animated Films Type
Miniature Sheets

Duck Tales (Donald Duck and family): No. 982: a, Scrooge McDuck, Launchpad. b, Scrooge reads treasure map. c, Collie Baba's treasure revealed. d, Webby finds magic lamp. e, Genie and new masters. f, Webby gets her wish. g, Scrooge McDuck, Genie. h, Retrieving the magic lamp. i, Villain Merlock, Genie.

No. 984, Webby's tea party, vert. No. 985, Treasure of the lost lamp, vert.

Darkwing Duck: No. 983: a, Darkwing Duck. b, Tuskerninni. c, Megavolt. d, Bushroot. e, Steelbeak. f, Eggman. g, Agent Gryzlikoff. h, Director J. Gander Hooter.

No. 985A, Gosalyn. No. 985B, Honker, horiz.

***Perf. 14x13½, 13½x14***
**1992, Dec. 15 Litho.**
**982** A247a 60c Sheet of 9, #a.-i. 7.00 7.00
**983** A247b 60c Sheet of 8, #a.-h. 6.50 6.50

**Souvenir Sheets**
**984** A247a $6 multicolored 5.50 5.50
**985** A247a $6 multicolored 5.50 5.50
**985A** A247b $6 multicolored 5.50 5.50
**985B** A247b $6 multicolored 5.50 5.50

Miniature Sheets

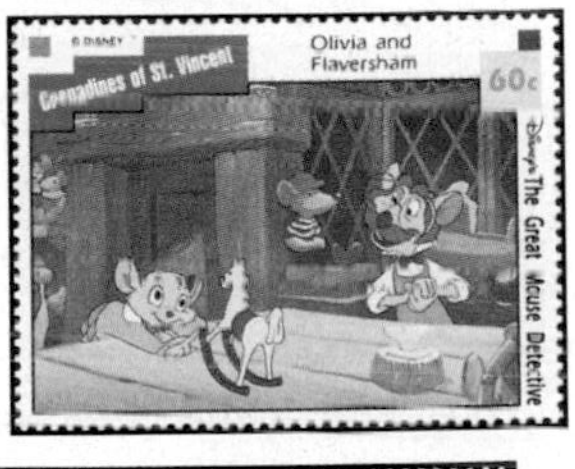


G71

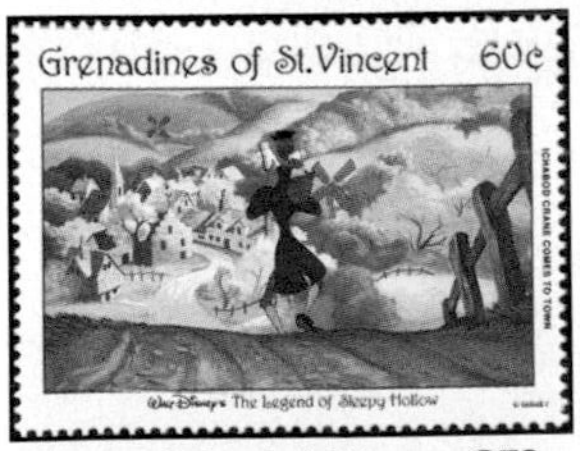


Disney Animated Films — G72

The Great Mouse Detective: No. 986: a, Olivia and Flaversham. b, Olivia's mechanical mouse. c, Ratigan's evil scheme. d, Ratigan and Mechanical Mouse Queen. e, Fidget pens ransom note. f, Basil studies clues. g, Fidget holds Olivia captive. h, Ratigan in disguise. i, Basil and Dr. Dawson, crime stoppers.

Oliver & Company: No. 987: a, Dodger. b, Oliver. c, Dodger and Oliver. d, Oliver introduced to the Company. e, Oliver meets Fagin. f, Fagin's bedtime story hour. g, Oliver sleeping with Dodger. h, Fagin's trike. i, Georgette and Tito.

The Legend of Sleepy Hollow: No. 988: a, Ichabod Crane comes to town. b, Ichabod meets Katrina Van Tassel. c, Schoolmaster Ichabod Crane. d, Ichabod and rival, Brom Bones. e, Ichabod and Katrina at Halloween dance. f, Ichabod is scared of ghosts. g, Ichabod in Sleepy Hollow. h, Ichabod and his horse. i, Meeting the Headless Horseman.

No. 989, Detective Basil holding pipe. No. 990, Detective Basil holding magnifying glass. No. 991, Oliver. No. 992, Oliver and kittens.

No. 993, Ichabod Crane, children praying, vert. No. 994, Headless Horseman.

*Perf. 14x13½, 13½x14*

**1992, Dec. 15** Litho.

**986** G71 60c Sheet of 9, #a.-i. 6.75 6.75
**987** G71 60c Sheet of 9, #a.-i. 6.75 6.75
**988** G72 60c Sheet of 9, #a.-i. 6.75 6.75

**Souvenir Sheets**

**989-994** G71 $6 each 5.50 5.50

**Elvis Presley Type of 1993**

Designs: a, Portrait. b, With guitar. c, With microphone.

**1993** Litho. *Perf. 14*

**1001** A244 $1 Strip of 3, #a.-c. 3.25 3.25

Printed in sheets of 9 stamps.

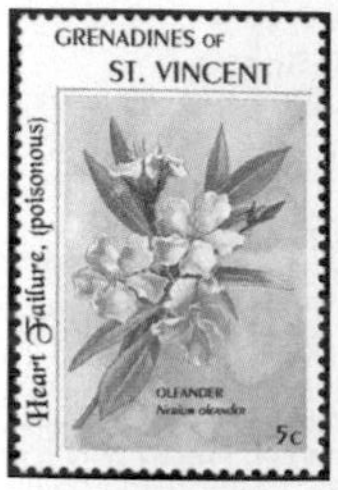
GRENADINES OF
ST. VINCENT
Heart Failure, (poisonous)
OLEANDER
5c

Medicinal Plants — G73

Designs: 5c, Oleander. 10c, Beach morning glory. 30c, Calabash. 45c, Porita tree. 55c, Cashew. 75c, Prickly pear. $1, Shell ginger. $1.50, Avocado. $2, Mango. $3, Blood flower. $4, Sugar apple. $5, Barbados lily.

**1994, May 20** Litho. *Perf. 13½x13*

**1002-1013** G73 Set of 12 20.00 20.00

## SEMI-POSTAL STAMPS

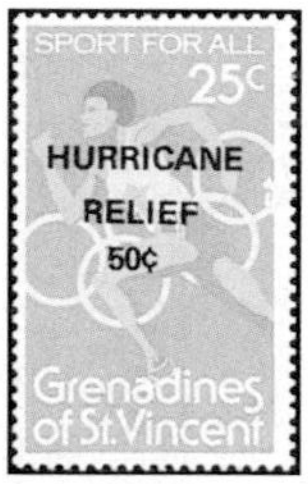
SPORT FOR ALL
25c
HURRICANE
RELIEF
50¢
Grenadines
of St.Vincent

Nos. 190-193 Surcharged

**1980, Aug. 7** Litho. *Perf. 13½*

**B1** A90 25c + 50c Running .20 .20
**B2** A90 50c + 50c Sailing .20 .20
**B3** A90 $1 + 50c Long jump .20 .20
**B4** A90 $2 + 50c Swimming .35 .35
*Nos. B1-B4 (4)* .95 .95

## OFFICIAL STAMPS

Nos. 209-214 Ovptd. "OFFICIAL"

**1982, Oct. 11**

**O1** A66 50c on No. 209 .20 .20
**O2** A67 50c on No. 210 .20 .20
**O3** A66 $3 on No. 211 .90 .90
**O4** A67 $3 on No. 212 .90 .90
**O5** A66 $3.50 on No. 213 1.10 1.10
**O6** A67 $3.50 on No. 214 1.10 1.10
*Nos. O1-O6 (6)* 4.40 4.40

# BEQUIA

All stamps are types of St. Vincent ("A" illustration letter), St. Vincent Grenadines ("G" illustration letter) or Bequia ("B" illustration letter).

**"Island" issues are listed separately beginning in 1984. See St. Vincent Grenadines Nos. 84-111, 248-262 for earlier issues.**

**Locomotive Type of 1985**

**1984-87 Litho. Unwmk.** *Perf. 12½*

**Se-tenant Pairs, #a.-b.**

**a. — Side and front views.**

**b. — Action scene.**

**1** A120 1c 1942 Challenger Class, US .20 .20
**2** A120 1c 1908 S3/6, Germany .20 .20
**3** A120 5c 1944 2900 Class, US .20 .20
**4** A120 5c 1903 Jersey Lily, UK .20 .20
**5** A120 10c 1882 Gladstone Class, UK .20 .20
**6** A120 10c 1909 Thundersley, UK .20 .20
**7** A120 15c 1860 Ser Class 118, UK .20 .20
**8** A120 25c 1893 No. 999 NY Central & Hudson River, US .20 .20
**9** A120 25c 1921 Class G2, UK .20 .20
**10** A120 25c 1902 Jr. Class 6400, Japan .20 .20
**11** A120 25c 1877 Class G3, Germany .20 .20
**12** A120 35c 1945 Niagara Class, US .25 .25
**13** A120 35c 1938 Manor Class, UK .25 .25
**14** A120 40c 1880 Class D VI, Germany .25 .25
**15** A120 45c 1914 K4 Class, US .30 .30
**16** A120 50c 1960 Class U25B, US .35 .35
**17** A120 55c 1921 Stephenson, UK .40 .40
**18** A120 55c 1909 Class H4, US .40 .40
**19** A120 60c 1922 Baltic, UK .40 .40
**20** A120 60c 1903 J.R. 4500, Japan .40 .40
**21** A120 60c 1915 Class LS .40 .40
**22** A120 75c 1841 Borsig, Germany .50 .50
**23** A120 75c 1943 Royal Scot, UK .50 .50
**24** A120 75c 1961 Krauss-Maffei, US .50 .50
**25** A120 $1 1928 River IRT, UK .70 .70
**26** A120 $1 1890 Electric, UK .70 .70
**27** A120 $1 1934 A.E.C., UK .70 .70
**28** A120 $1.50 1929 No. 10000, UK 1.00 1.00
**29** A120 $2 1904 City Class, UK 1.40 1.40
**30** A120 $2 1901 No. 737, UK 1.40 1.40
**31** A120 $2 1847 Cornwall, UK 1.40 1.40
**32** A120 $2.50 1938 Duke Dog Class, UK 1.75 1.75
**33** A120 $2.50 1881 Ella, UK 1.75 1.75
**34** A120 $3 1910 George V Class, UK 2.00 2.00
*Nos. 1-34 (34)* 19.90 19.90

Issued: #1, 3, 5, 8, 12, 15, 28-29, 2/22/84; #2, 4, 6, 13, 22, 25, 32, 34, 11/26/84; #9, 17, 19, 30, 2/1/85; #10, 18, 20, 23, 26, 33, 8/14/85; #7, 11, 14, 16, 21, 24, 27, 31, 11/16/87.

Stamps issued 11/16/87 are not inscribed "Leaders of the World."

St. Vincent Grenadines Nos. 222-238 Ovptd. "BEQUIA"

*Perf. 14x13½*

**1984, Aug. 23** Wmk. 373

**69** G26 1c on No. 222 .20 .20
**70** G26 3c on No. 223 .20 .20
**71** G26 5c on No. 224 .20 .20
**72** G26 6c on No. 225 .20 .20
**73** G26 10c on No. 226 .20 .20
**74** G26 15c on No. 227 .20 .20
**75** G26 20c on No. 228 .20 .20
**76** G26 25c on No. 229 .20 .20
**77** G26 30c on No. 230 .20 .20
**78** G26 50c on No. 231 .40 .40
**79** G26 60c on No. 232 .55 .55
**80** G26 75c on No. 233 .70 .70
**81** G26 $1 on No. 234 .90 .90
**82** G26 $2 on No. 235 1.75 1.75
**83** G26 $3 on No. 236 2.75 2.75
**84** G26 $5 on No. 237 4.50 4.50
**85** G26 $10 on No. 238 9.50 9.50
*Nos. 69-85 (17)* 22.85 22.85

**Car Type of 1983**

**1984-87 Unwmk.** *Perf. 12½*

**Se-tenant Pairs, #a.-b.**

**a. — Side and front views.**

**b. — Action scene.**

**86** A107 5c 1953 Cadillac, US .20 .20
**87** A107 5c 1932 Fiat, Italy .20 .20
**88** A107 5c 1968 Excalibur, US .20 .20
**89** A107 5c 1952 Hudson, US .20 .20
**90** A107 10c 1924 Leyand, UK .20 .20
**91** A107 20c 1911 Marmon, US .20 .20
**92** A107 20c 1950 Alfa Romeo, Italy .20 .20
**93** A107 20c 1968 Ford Escort, UK .20 .20
**94** A107 20c 1939 Maserati 8 CTF, Italy .20 .20
**95** A107 25c 1963 Ford, UK .20 .20
**96** A107 25c 1958 Vanwall, UK .20 .20
**97** A107 25c 1910 Stanley, US .20 .20
**98** A107 35c 1948 Ford Wagon, US .25 .25
**99** A107 40c 1936 Auto Union, Germany .30 .30
**100** A107 45c 1907 Chadwick, US .35 .35
**101** A107 50c 1924 Lanchester, UK .40 .40
**102** A107 50c 1957 Austin-Healy, UK .40 .40
**103** A107 60c 1935 Brewster-Ford, US .45 .45
**104** A107 60c 1942 Willys Jeep, US .45 .45
**105** A107 65c 1929 Isotta, Italy .50 .50
**106** A107 75c 1940 Lincoln, US .60 .60
**107** A107 75c 1964 Bluebird II, UK .60 .60
**108** A107 75c 1948 Moore-Offenhauser, US .60 .60
**109** A107 75c 1936 Ford, UK .60 .60
**110** A107 80c 1936 Mercedes Benz, Germany .65 .65
**111** A107 90c 1928 Mercedes Benz SSK, Germany .70 .70
**112** A107 $1 1907 Rolls Royce, UK .75 .75
**113** A107 $1 1955 Citroen, France .75 .75
**114** A107 $1 1936 Fiat, Italy .75 .75
**115** A107 $1 1922 Dusenberg, US .75 .75
**116** A107 $1 1957 Pontiac Bonneville, US .75 .75
**117** A107 $1.25 1916 Hudson Super Six, US 1.00 1.00
**118** A107 $1.25 1977 Coyote Ford, US 1.00 1.00
**119** A107 $1.50 1960 Porsche, Germany 1.25 1.25
**120** A107 $1.50 1970 Plymouth, US 1.25 1.25
**121** A107 $1.75 1933 Stutz, US 1.35 1.35
**122** A107 $2 1910 Benz-Blitzen, Germany 1.60 1.60
**123** A107 $2 1933 Napier Railton, UK 1.60 1.60
**124** A107 $2.50 1978 BMW, Germany 2.00 2.00
**125** A107 $3 1912 Hispano Suiza, Spain 2.40 2.40
**126** A107 $3 1954 Mercedes Benz, Germany 2.40 2.40
**127** A107 $3 1927 Stutz Black Hawk, US 2.40 2.40
*Nos. 86-127 (42)* 31.25 31.25

Issued: #86, 99, 112, 119, 9/14; #87, 90-91, 95, 106, 113, 124-125, 12/19; #88, 96, 101, 114, 117, 122, 6/25/85; #92, 100, 120, 123, 9/26/85; #97, 102, 105, 107, 115, 126, 1/29/86; #93, 103, 108, 111, 116, 127, 12/23/86; #89, 94, 98, 104, 109-110, 118, 121, 7/22/87.

Beginning on Sept. 26, 1985, this issue is not inscribed "Leaders of the World."

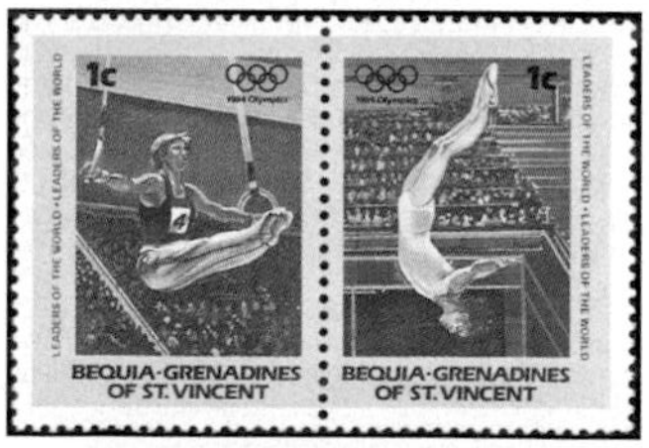
1c
1c
BEQUIA-GRENADINES OF ST. VINCENT
BEQUIA-GRENADINES OF ST. VINCENT

1984 Summer Olympics — B1

#170a, Men's gymnastics. #170b, Women's gymnastics. #171a, Men's javelin. #171b, Women's javelin. #172a, Women's basketball. #172b, Men's basketball. #173a, Women's long jump. #173b, Men's long jump.

**1984, Sept. 14** *Perf. 12½*

**170** B1 1c Pair, #a.-b. .20 .20
**171** B1 10c Pair, #a.-b. .20 .20
**172** B1 60c Pair, #a.-b. .50 .50
**173** B1 $3 Pair, #a.-b. 2.25 2.25
*Nos. 170-173 (4)* 3.15 3.15

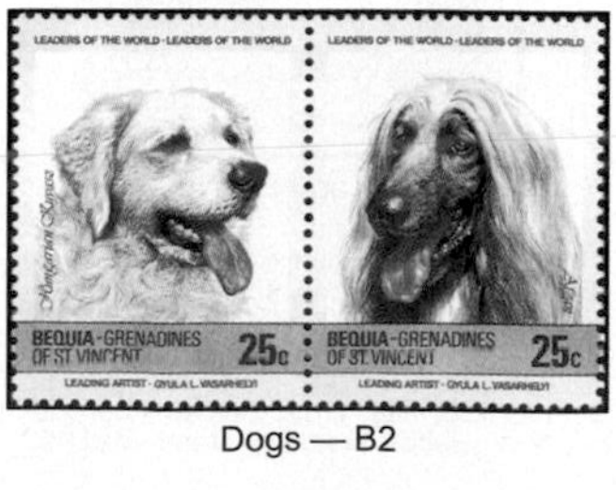
BEQUIA-GRENADINES OF ST VINCENT
25c
BEQUIA-GRENADINES OF ST VINCENT
25c

Dogs — B2

#178a, Hungarian Kuvasz. #178b, Afghan. #179a, Whippet. #179b, Bloodhound. #180a, Cavalier King Charles Spaniel. #180b, German Shepherd. #181a, Pekinese. #181b, Golden Retriever.

**1985, Mar. 14** *Perf. 12½*

**178** B2 25c Pair, #a.-b. .25 .25
**179** B2 35c Pair, #a.-b. .50 .50
**180** B2 55c Pair, #a.-b. .75 .75
**181** B2 $2 Pair, #a.-b. 2.75 2.75
*Nos. 178-181 (4)* 4.25 4.25

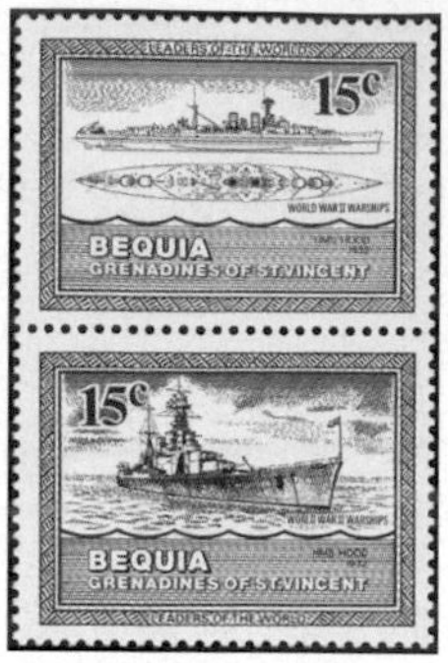
15c
BEQUIA
GRENADINES OF ST. VINCENT
15c
BEQUIA
GRENADINES OF ST. VINCENT

World War II Warships B3

**1985, Apr. 29** *Perf. 12½*

**Se-tenant Pairs, #a.-b.**

**a.-Side and top views.**

**b.-Action scene.**

**186** B3 15c HMS Hood .50 .50
**187** B3 50c HMS Duke of York 1.10 1.10
**188** B3 $1 KM Admiral Graf Spee 1.50 1.50
**189** B3 $1.50 USS Nevada 2.50 2.50
*Nos. 186-189 (4)* 5.60 5.60

**St. Vincent Grenadines Flower Type**

#194a, Primula veris. #194b, Pulsatilla vulgaris. #195a, Lapageria rosea. #195b, Romneya coulteri. #196a, Anigozanthos manglesii. #196b, Metrosideros collina. #197a, Protea laurifolia. #197b, Thunbergia grandiflora.

**1985, May 31** *Perf. 12½*

**194** G38 10c Pair, #a.-b. .20 .20
**195** G38 20c Pair, #a.-b. .20 .20
**196** G38 70c Pair, #a.-b. .50 .50
**197** G38 $2.50 Pair, #a.-b. 1.75 1.75
*Nos. 194-197 (4)* 2.65 2.65

**Queen Mother Type of 1985**

Hat: #206a, 212a, Blue. #206b, 212b, Violet. #207a, 211a, Blue. #207b, 211b, Tiara. #208a, Blue. #208b, White. #209a, Blue. #209b, Pink. #210a, Hat. #210b, Tiara.

**1985, Aug. 29** *Perf. 12½*

**206** A122 20c Pair, #a.-b. .25 .25
**207** A122 65c Pair, #a.-b. .75 .75
**208** A122 $1.35 Pair, #a.-b. 1.50 1.50
**209** A122 $1.80 Pair, #a.-b. 2.10 2.10
*Nos. 206-209 (4)* 4.60 4.60

**Souvenir Sheets of 2**

**210** A122 $2.05 #a.-b. 2.00 2.00
**211** A122 $3.50 #a.-b. 3.50 3.50
**212** A122 $6 #a.-b. 6.00 6.00

**Queen Elizabeth II Type of 1986**

Various portraits.

**1986, Apr. 21**

**213** A128 5c multicolored .20 .20
**214** A128 75c multicolored .30 .30
**215** A128 $2 multicolored .80 .80
**216** A128 $8 multicolored, vert. 3.25 3.25
*Nos. 213-216 (4)* 4.55 4.55

**Souvenir Sheet**

**217** A128 $10 multicolored 4.00 4.00

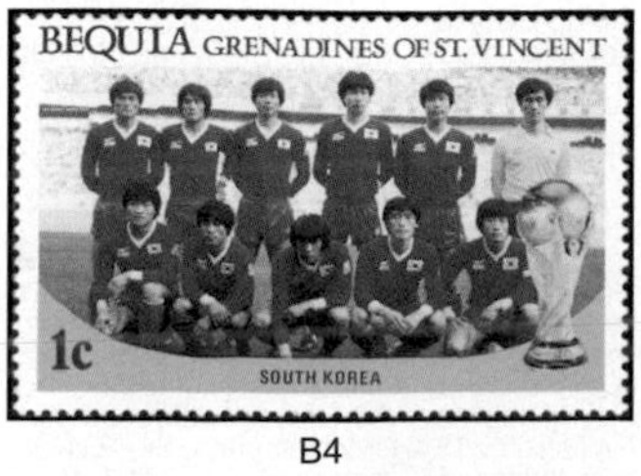
BEQUIA GRENADINES OF ST. VINCENT
1c
SOUTH KOREA

B4

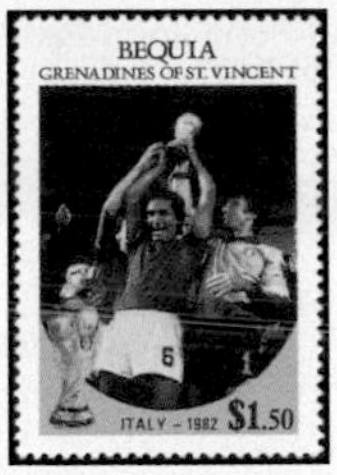


World Cup Soccer Championships, Mexico, 1986 — B5

**1986 July 3** — *Perf. 12½, 15 (B5)*

218 B4 1c South Korean team .20 .20
219 B4 2c Iraqi team .20 .20
220 B4 5c Algerian team .20 .20
221 B4 10c Bulgaria vs. France .20 .20
222 B5 45c Belgium .20 .20
223 B4 60c Danish team .30 .30
224 B4 75c Italy vs. W. Germany .35 .35
225 B4 $1.50 USSR vs. England .65 .65
226 B5 $1.50 Italy, 1982 champions .65 .65
227 B5 $2 W. Germany .95 .95
228 B5 $3.50 N. Ireland 1.65 1.65
229 B4 $6 England 2.75 2.75
*Nos. 218-229 (12)* 8.30 8.30

**Souvenir Sheets**

230 B4 $1 like No. 219 .45 .45
231 B4 $1.75 like No. 221 .85 .85

### Royal Wedding Type of 1986

**1986, July 15** — *Perf. 12½x13, 13x12½*

232 A132 60c Andrew .35 .35
233 A132 60c Andrew in helicopter .35 .35
234 A132 $2 Andrew in crowd 1.00 1.00
235 A132 $2 Andrew, Sarah 1.00 1.00
*Nos. 232-235 (4)* 2.70 2.70

**Souvenir Sheet**

236 A132a $8 Andrew, Sarah in coach 4.50 4.50

Nos. 234-235 horiz.

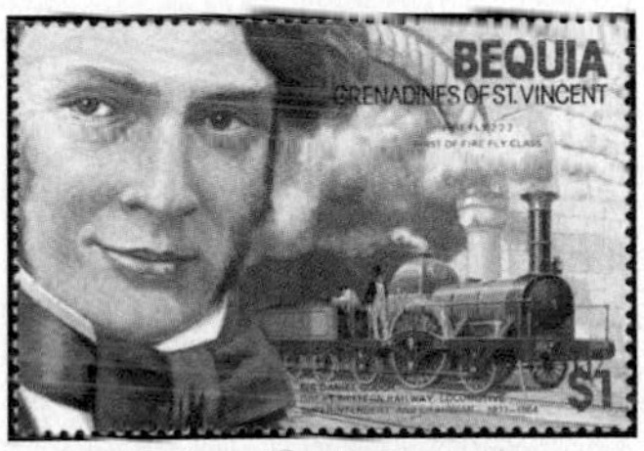


Railway Engineers and Locomotives — B6

Designs: $1, Sir Daniel Gooch, Fire Fly Class, 1840. $2.50, Sir Nigel Gresley, A4 Class, 1938. $3, Sir William Stanier, Coronation Class, 1937. $4, Oliver V. S. Bulleid, Battle of Britain Class, 1946.

**1986, Sept. 30** — *Perf. 13x12½*

237-240 B6 Set of 4 5.00 5.00

Nos. 232-235 Ovptd. "Congratulations to TRH The Duke & Duchess of York" in 3 Lines

**1986** — *Perf. 12½x13, 13x12½*

241 A132 60c on No. 232 1.00 1.00
242 A132 60c on No. 233 1.00 1.00
243 A132 $2 on No. 234 3.25 3.25
244 A132 $2 on No. 235 3.25 3.25
*Nos. 241-244 (4)* 8.50 8.50

### Royalty Portrait Type

Portraits and photographs: 15c, Queen Victoria, 1841. 75c, Elizabeth, Charles, 1948. $1, Coronation, 1953. $2.50, Duke of Edinburgh, 1948. $5, Elizabeth c. 1980. $6, Elizabeth, Charles, 1948, diff.

**1987, Oct. 15** — *Perf. 12½x13*

245-249 A140 Set of 5 3.50 3.50

**Souvenir Sheet**

250 A140 $6 multi 3.75 3.75

### Great Explorers Type of St. Vincent Grenadines

Designs: 15c, Gokstad, ship of Leif Eriksson (c. 1000). 50c, Eriksson and bearing dial. $1.75, The Mathew, ship of John Cabot. $2, Cabot, quadrant. $2.50, The Trinidad, ship of Ferdinand Magellan. $3, Arms, portrait of Christopher Columbus. $3.50, Columbus' ship Santa Maria. $4, Magellan, globe. $5, Anchor, long boat, ship.

**1988, July 11** — **Litho.** — *Perf. 14*

251-258 G52 Set of 8 11.75 11.75

**Souvenir Sheet**

259 G52 $5 multi 3.50 3.50

### Tennis Type of 1987

**1988, July 29** — *Perf. 13x13½*

260 A137 15c Anders Jarryd .20 .20
261 A137 45c Anne Hobbs .25 .25
262 A137 80c Jimmy Connors .50 .50
263 A137 $1.25 Carling Bassett .75 .75
264 A137 $1.75 Stefan Edberg, horiz. 1.00 1.00
265 A137 $2.00 Gabriela Sabatini, horiz. 1.20 1.20
266 A137 $2.50 Mats Wilander 1.50 1.50
267 A137 $3.00 Pat Cash 1.80 1.80
*Nos. 260-267 (8)* 7.20 7.20

No. 263 inscribed "Carlene Basset" instead of "Carling Bassett."
An unissued souvenir sheet exists.

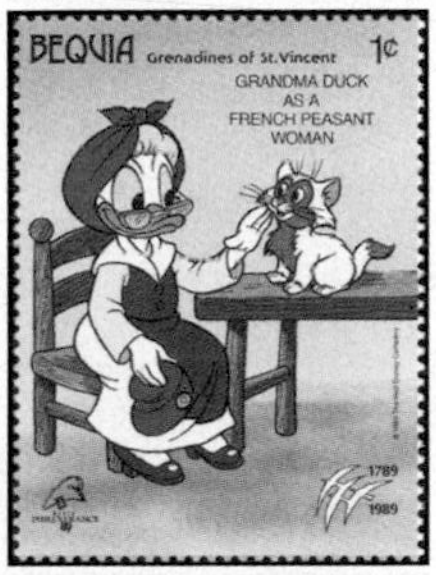


French Revolution Bicentennial B7

1c, Grandma Duck as French peasant woman. 2c, Donald & Daisy celebrating liberty. 3c, Minnie as Marie Antoinette. 4c, Clarabelle & patriotic chair. 5c, Goofy in Republican citizen's costume. 10c, Mickey & Donald planting liberty tree. $5, #274, Horace taking Tennis Court Oath. $6, Grand Master Mason McDuck. #276, Dancing the Carmagnole. #277, Philosophers at Cafe La Procope.

**1989, July 7** — *Perf. 13½x14*

268-275 B7 Set of 8 11.25 11.25

**Souvenir Sheets**

276-277 B7 $5 Set of 2 10.00 10.00

### Anniversaries and Events Type

$5, Otto Lililienthal, aviation pioneer.

**1991, Nov. 18** — **Litho.** — *Perf. 14*

278 A213 $5 multicolored 6.00 6.00

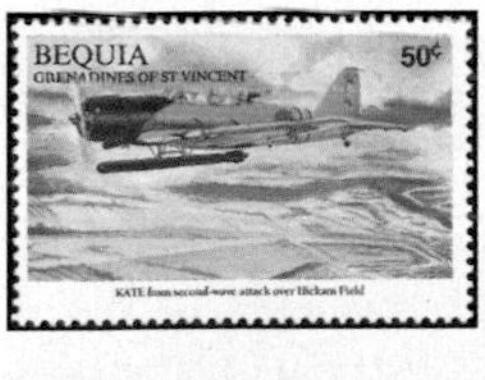


Japanese Attack on Pearl Harbor, 50th Anniv. B8

Designs: 50c, Kate from second-wave over Hickam Field. $1, B17 sights Zeros in Pearl Harbor attack. $5, Firefighters rescue sailors from blazing USS Tennessee.

**1991, Nov. 18**

287 B8 50c multicolored .50 .50
288 B8 $1 multicolored 1.50 1.50

**Souvenir Sheet**

289 B8 $5 multicolored 4.75 4.75

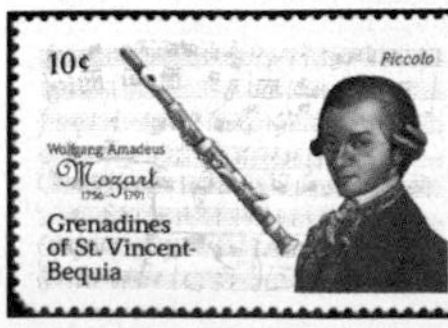


Wolfgang Amadeus Mozart, Death Bicentennial — B9

Mozart and: 10c, Piccolo. 75c, Piano. $4, Violotta.
No. 293, Mozart's last composition, Lacrimosa from the Requiem Mass. No. 294, Bronze of Mozart by Adrien-Etienne Gaudez, vert. No. 295, Score of opening of the "Paris" symphony, K297.

**1991** — **Litho.** — *Perf. 14*

290-292 B9 Set of 3 6.75 6.75

**Souvenir Sheets**

293-295 B9 $6 Set of 3 21.00 21.00

Nos. 293-295 each contain one 57x42mm or 42x57mm stamp.

### Boy Scout Type

50c, Lord Baden-Powell, killick hitch knot. $1, Baden-Powell, clove hitch knot. $2, Drawing of Boy Scout by Baden-Powell, vert. $3, American 1st Class Scout badge, vert. $6, Baden-Powell, Lark's head knot.

**1991**

296-299 A211 Set of 4 9.25 9.25

**Souvenir Sheet**

300 A211 $6 multicolored 8.00 8.00

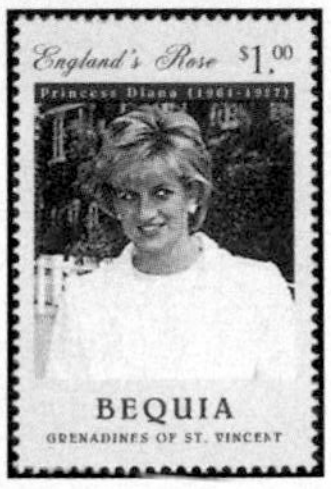


Diana, Princess of Wales, (1961-97) — B10

**1997, Dec. 10** — **Litho.** — *Perf. 14*

301 B10 $1 multicolored 2.00 2.00

No. 301 was issued in sheets of 6.

### Paintings Type of 1999

Various pictures of flowers making up a photomosaic of the Queen Mother.

**2000, Sept. 5** — *Perf. 13¾*

302 A442 $1 Sheet of 8, #a-h 6.00 6.00
*i.* As No. 302, imperf. 6.00 6.00

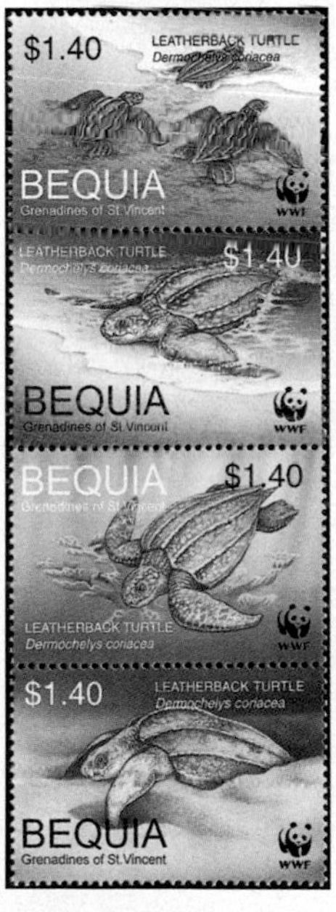


Worldwide Fund for Nature (WWF) B11

Leatherback turtle: a, Three on beach. b, One coming ashore. c, One in water. d, One digging nest.

**2001, Dec. 10** — **Litho.** — *Perf. 14*

303 B11 $1.40 Vert or horiz. strip of 4, #a-d 4.25 4.25

### Queen Elizabeth II, 50th Anniv. of Reign Type of 2002

No. 304: a, Without hat. b, Wearing tiara. c, Wearing scarf. d, With Prince Philip and baby. $2, Wearing scarf, diff.

**2002, June 17** — **Litho.** — *Perf. 14¼*

304 A509 80c Sheet of 4, #a-d 2.40 2.40

**Souvenir Sheet**

305 A509 $2 multi 1.50 1.50

### United We Stand Type of 2001

**2002, Nov. 4** — *Perf. 14*

306 A508 $2 multi 1.50 1.50

Printed in sheets of 4.

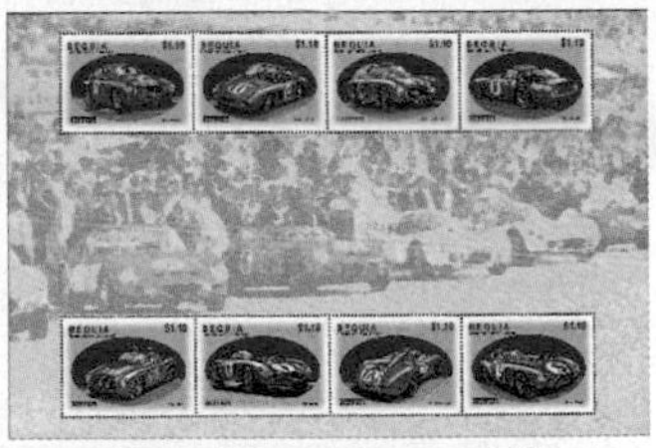

Ferrari Race Cars — B12

No. 307: a, 1953 250MM. b, 1962 330LM. c, 1952 340 Mexico. d, 1963 330LM. e, 1952 225S. f, 1956 500TR. g, 1954 750 Monza. h, 1954 375 Plus.

**2002, June 10** — **Litho.** — *Perf. 13¾*

307 B12 $1.10 Sheet of 8, #a-h 6.75 6.75

### Elvis Presley Type of 2002

**2002, Aug. 19**

308 A517 $1 multi .75 .75

Printed in sheets of 9.

### Shirley Temple Movie Type of 2000

No. 309, horiz. — Scenes from *Captain January* of Temple with: a, Man at table. b, Woman. c, Two men annd bird with bow. d, Boy and teacher. e, Two men at table. f, Three men in boat.
No. 310: a, Man with beard. b, Three men. c, Two men and doll. d, With man, dancing.
$5, With sailors.

**2002, Aug. 19**

309 A471 $1.40 Sheet of 6, #a-f 6.25 6.25
310 A471 $2 Sheet of 4, #a-d 6.00 6.00

**Souvenir Sheet**

311 A471 $5 multi 3.75 3.75

Sheet margins are dated "2003."

### Queen Mother Elizabeth Type of 2002

No. 312: a, Wearing yellow dress. b, Wearing red dress.

**2002, Nov. 4** — *Perf. 14*

312 A522 $2 Pair, #a-b 3.00 3.00

No. 312 printed in sheets containing 2 pairs.

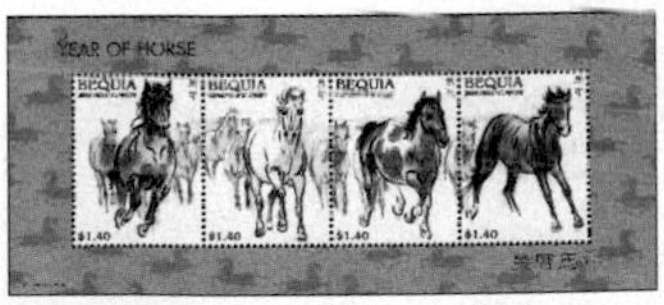


Year of the Horse — B13

No. 313: a, Black horse in foreground, front feet raised. b, White horse in foreground. c, Piebald horse in foreground. d, Black horse in foreground, front feet not raised.

**2002, Dec. 17** — *Perf. 13¼x13*

313 B13 $1.40 Sheet of 4, #a-d 4.25 4.25

### Teddy Bears Type of 2002

No. 314, $2 — Bears from Germany: a, Balloon pilot bear. b, Bear in lederhosen. c, Bear in pants and ice skates. d, Bear in skirt and ice skates.
No. 315, $2 — Bears from Italy: a, Bear with feathered hat, standing in gondola. b, Bear with cap, seated on gondola. c, Bear with umbrella. d, Gondolier bear.

**2003, Jan. 27** — *Perf. 13½x13¼*

**Sheets of 4, #a-d**

314-315 A519 Set of 2 12.00 12.00

### Year of the Ram Type of 2003

No. 316: a, Ram with white horns and beard, denomination at right. b, Ram with black horns, denomination at left. c, Ram with dark horns, denomination at right. d, Ram with white horns, denomination at left. e, Ram with leg raised. f, Ram with horns with lines, denomination at left.

**2003, Feb. 1** — *Perf. 14¼x13¾*

316 A526 $1 Sheet of 6, #a-f 4.50 4.50

## Princess Diana Type of 2003

No. 317, $2: a. Wearing pink hat. b. Wearing gray dress. c. Wearing white blouse. d. Wearing checked pants.

No. 318, $2: a. Wearing red blouse. b. Wearing white hat. c. Wearing black dress. b. Wearing black dress. c. Wearing white blouse, holding flowers.

**2003, May 26**   Litho.   **Perf. 13½**

317-318 A536   Sheets of 4, #a-d   12.00 12.00

## Corvette Type of 2003

No. 319: a. 1957 convertible. b. 1964 Sting Ray. c. 1954 convertible. d. 1989. $5, 1988.

**2003, July 1**   **Perf. 13½x13½**

319 A534 $2 Sheet of 4, #a-d   6.00 6.00

320 A534 $5 multi   Souvenir Sheet   3.75 3.75

## Pres. John F. Kennedy (1917-63) — B14

40th anniversary of the Death of John F. Kennedy. Born in 1917, JFK became the 35th President of the United States of America.

No. 321: a. Denomination at UL, name at right. b. Denomination at UL, name at left. c. Denomination at UR, name at left. d. Denomination at UR, name at right.

**2003, Aug. 25**   **Perf. 14**

321 B14 $2 Sheet of 4, #a-d   6.00 6.00

## Elvis Presley (1935-77) — B15

No. 322: a. Silhouette. b. Holding guitar.

**2003, Dec. 1**   Litho.   **Perf. 13½**

322 B15 90c. Sheet #322a, 8 #322b   6.25 6.25

## Birds — B16

Designs: 90c, Stripe-headed tanager. $1, Violaceous trogon. $1.40, Barn owl. $2, Green jay. $5, Montezuma oropendola.

**2003, Dec. 1**   **Perf. 13½**

323-326 B16   Set of 4   4.00 4.00

327 B16 $5 multi   Souvenir Sheet   3.75 3.75

## (Romping Monkeys) — B17

Romping Monkeys, by unknown painter: $1.40, Detail. $3, Entire painting.

New Year 2004 (Year of the Monkey) — B17

**2004, Jan. 15**   Litho.   **Perf. 13¾**

328 B17 $1.40 multi   1.10 1.10

Souvenir Sheet

329 B17 $3 multi   2.25 2.25

## Paintings by Pablo Picasso (1881-1973) — B18

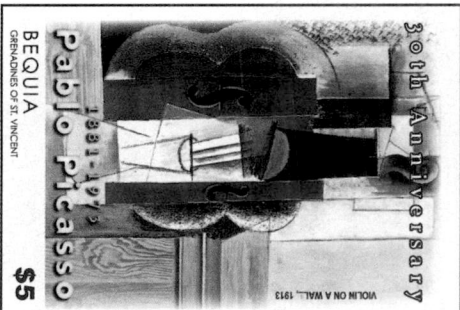

30th Anniversary 1881–1973 — Pablo Picasso — $5 — VIOLIN ON A WALL, 1913

No. 330: a. Bust of a Woman with Self-Portrait. b. Jacqueline in a Turkish Jacket. c. Françoise in an Armchair. d. Still Life on a Pedestal Table. $5, Violin on a Wall.

**2004, Apr. 30**   **Perf. 14¾**

330 B18 $2 Sheet of 4, #a-d   3.75 3.75

No. 330 contains four 38x51mm stamps.

Souvenir Sheet

331 B18 $5 multi   6.00 6.00

## Marilyn Monroe Type of 2004

**2004, May 3**   **Perf. 14**

332 A558 70c multi   .55 .55

Printed in sheets of 12.

## Babe Ruth Type of 2004

*Imperf*

**2004, July 1**   **Perf. 13¾**

333 A561 70c multi   .55 .55

Printed in sheets of 12.

## Ancient Greece — B19

BEQUIA Grenadines of St. Vincent — PALACE OF MINOS, ISLAND OF CRETE — 30¢

Designs: 30c, Palace of Minos, Crete. 70c, Apollo's Temple, Delphi. 90c, Statue of Zeus, Olympia. $1.40, Bust of Aphrodite. $2, Bust of Socrates. $3, Parthenon. $5, Panathenaic Stadium, Athens.

**2004, Aug. 16**   **Perf. 14**

334-339 B19   Set of 6   6.25 6.25

340 B19 $5 multi   Souvenir Sheet   3.75 3.75

## Ronald Reagan Type of 2004

No. 341, horiz.: a. Reagan with wife, Nancy. b. Reagan with George H. W. Bush.

**2004, Oct. 13**   **Perf. 13½**

341 A564   Horiz. pair   2.10 2.10

a.-b. Either single   1.00 1.00

No. 341 printed in sheets containing three each #341a-341b.

## Railroads Type of 2004

No. 342, $2: a. GN 2507 Class P 2-4-8-2. b. Great Northern 2507. c. Great Northern. d. ...

No. 343, $2: a. LMS 2MT 2-6-2 T. b. Green Arrow. c. LMS Stainer Class 5MT 4-6-0. d. Liner Class A4 Sir Nigel Gresley.

No. 344, $2: a. Barclay 0-4-0 Saddle tank. b. Beyer Peacock. c. BR Class 4MT 2-6-0. d. Dampflok 109.

No. 345, $2: a. British Railways 2-6-4 T. b. Caledonian Railway 0-4-4 T. c. Evening Star. d. Southern Railway Carolina Special.

No. 346, $5, Pakistan Railways SPS 4-4-0. No. 347, $5, Norwegian State Railway. No. 348, $5, Russell Hunslet 2-6-2 T. No. 349, $5, North British Railway 0-6-0.

**2004, Dec. 13**   **Perf. 14¼x14, 14 (#344, 348)**

342-345 A565   Sheets of 4, #a-d   24.00 24.00

Souvenir Sheets

346-349 A565   Set of 4   15.00 15.00

## Christmas — B20

BEQUIA Grenadines of St. Vincent — Christmas 2004 — MADONNA OF PORT LLIGAT — 55¢

Paintings: 55c, Madonna of Port Lligat, by Salvador Dali. 90c, Madonna and Child, by Barolome Esteban Murillo. $1, Madonna and Child, by Jan van Eyck. $4, Madonna and Child, by Giovanni Bellini. $5, Madonna and Child, by Caravaggio.

**2004, Dec. 13**   **Perf. 12**

350-353 B20   Set of 4   5.00 5.00

Souvenir Sheet

354 B20 $6 multi   4.50 4.50

## End of World War II, 60th Anniv. — B21

The Route to Victory — SINKING OF THE BISMARCK

Paintings: No. 355, $2 — Sinking of the Bismarck, 1941: a. Bismarck, Map. b. Aircraft make ready for flight. c. The Bismarck getting pounded by British Navy. d. The Bismarck goes down.

No. 356, $2 — Liberation of Paris: a. Allied troops enter Paris. b. The end of German occupation. c. Allied troops help supply people of Paris. d. Victory at last.

No. 357, $5, Bismarck. No. 358, $5, General De Gaulle returns.

**2005, May 9**   Litho.   **Perf. 13½**

355-356 B21   Sheets of 4, #a-d   12.00 12.00

Souvenir Sheets

357-358 B21   Set of 2   7.50 7.50

## Vatican Stamp and Pope John Paul II Types of 2005

BEQUIA Grenadines of St. Vincent — 90¢

No. 359: Vatican #64, Pope and crowd, horiz.

**2005, June 1**   **Perf. 13½x13¼**

359 A584 70c multi   .55 .55

360 A585 $4 multi   3.00 3.00

No. 359 printed in sheets of 12; No. 360, in sheets of 4.

## Moths — B22

Designs: 90c, Pericallia galactina. $1, Automeris io draudtiana. $1.40, Anthina suraka. $2, Bunaea alcinoe. $5, Rothschildia erycina nigrescens.

**2005, July 26**   **Perf. 12¾**

361-364 B22   Set of 4   4.00 4.00

365 B22 $5 multi   Souvenir Sheet   3.75 3.75

## Flowers — B23

BEQUIA — FLOWERS OF THE CARIBBEAN — $5

No. 366, horiz.: a. Anthurium acropolis. b. Anthurium andreaenum. c. Gloxinia avanti. d. Heliconia psittacorum choconiana. c. Gloxinia avanti. d. Dendrobium dearei.

**2005, June 26**   **Perf. ...**

366 B23 $2 Sheet of 4, #a-d   6.00 6.00

Souvenir Sheet

367 B23 $5 multi   3.75 3.75

## Marine Life — B24

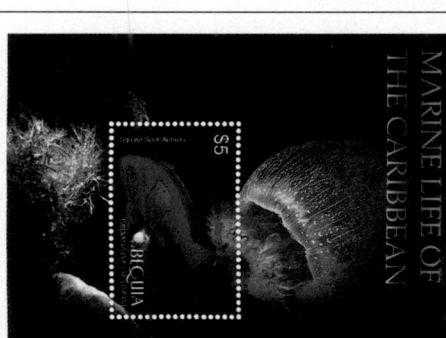

BEQUIA — MARINE LIFE OF THE CARIBBEAN — $5

No. 368: a, Hermissenda crassicornis. b, Chromodoris leopardus. c, Chromodoris kuniei. d, Coryphella verrucosa.
$5, Square spot anthias.

**2005, June 26**
**368** B24 $2 Sheet of 4, #a-d 6.00 6.00

**Souvenir Sheet**

**369** B24 $5 multi 3.75 3.75

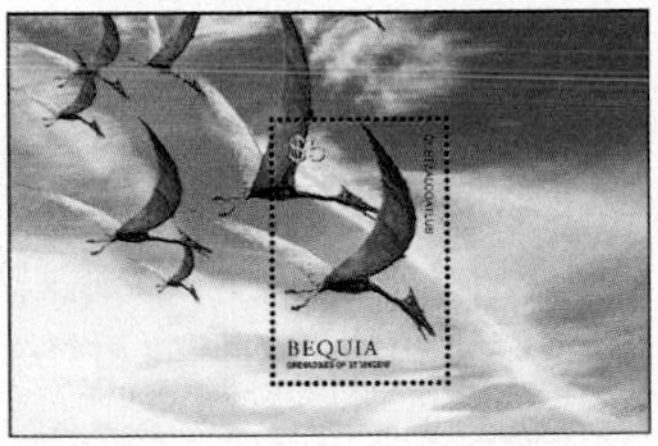


Prehistoric Animals — B25

No. 370, $2: a, Tenontosaurus. b, Gorgosaurus. c, Psittacosaurus. d, Parasaurolophus.
No. 371, $2, horiz.: a, Brachiosaurus. b, Seismosaurus. c, Struthiomimus. d, Oviraptor.
No. 372, $2, horiz.: a, Argentinosaurus. b, Triceratops. c, Ankylosaurus. d, Stegosaurus.
No. 373, $5, Quetzalcoatlus. No. 374, $5, Mammoth. No. 375, $5, Pteranodon, horiz.

**2005, Sept. 1** ***Perf. 14***

**Sheets of 4, #a-d**

**370-372** B25 Set of 3 18.00 18.00

**Souvenir Sheets**

**373-375** B25 Set of 3 11.50 11.50

## CANOUAN

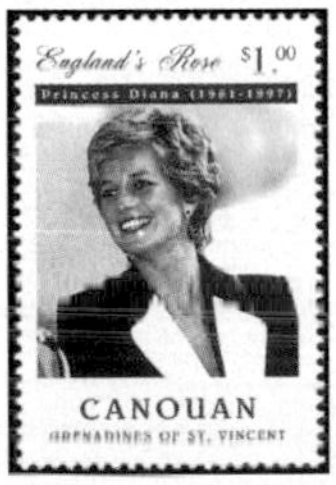


Diana, Princess of Wales (1961-97) — C1

**1997** **Litho.** ***Perf. 14***
**1** C1 $1 multicolored .75 .75

Issued in sheets of 6.
See Mustique No. 1.

**Queen Mother Type of 2000 Inscribed "Canouan"**

**2000, Sept. 5** **Litho.** ***Perf. 14***
**2** A472 $1.40 multi 1.00 1.00

Issued in sheets of 6.

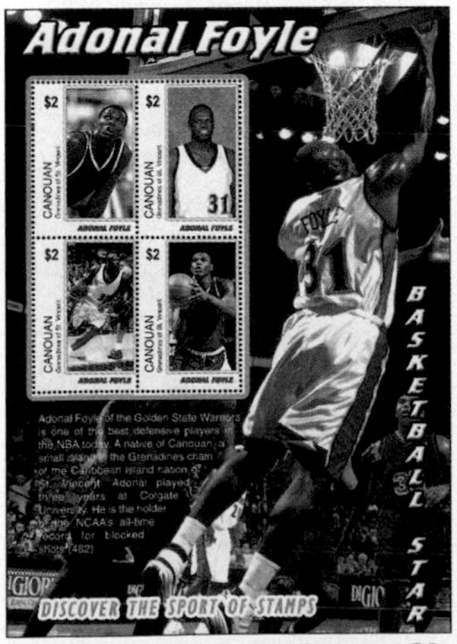


Adonal Foyle, Basketball Player — C2

No. 3, $2 — White backgrounds with yellow frames around vignettes: a, Black uniform. b, White uniform. c, Dribbling basketball. d, Shooting basketball.
No. 4, $2 — Black backgrounds with no frames around vignettes: a, Blocking shot. b, Overhead view of dunk shot. c, Leaping near basket. d, Leaping near basket and three opponents in blue uniforms.
No. 5, $2 — Black backgrounds with white frames around vignette: a, Guarding opponent. b, Shooting basketball. c, Wearing glasses. d, Blocking shot.
No. 6, $2 — White backgrounds with no frames around vingettes: a, Overhead view of rebound. b, Blocking shot. c, Lay-up shot, crowd in background. d, Lay-up shot, court in background.

**2003, Feb. 13** **Litho.** ***Perf. 14***

**Sheets of 4, #a-d**

**3-6** C2 Set of 4 24.00 24.00

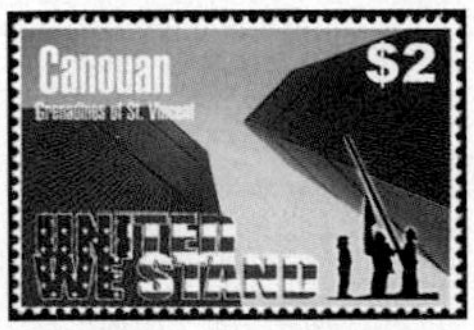


United We Stand C3

**2003, Aug. 25**
**7** C3 $2 multi 1.50 1.50

Printed in sheets of 4.

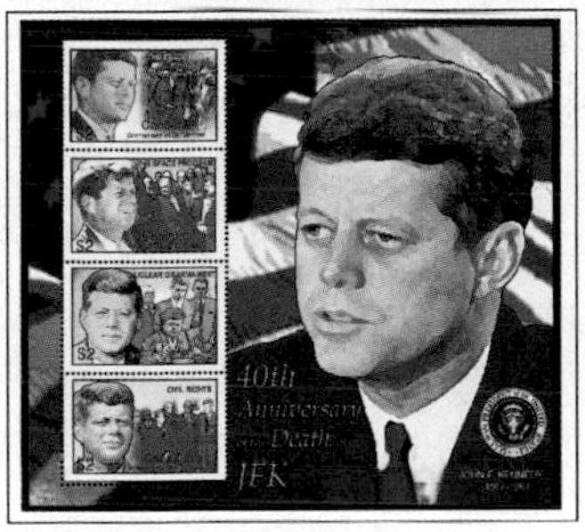

Pres. John F. Kennedy (1917-63) — C4

No. 8: a, Peace Corps. b, Space program. c, Nuclear disarmament. d, Civil rights.

**2003, Aug. 25**
**8** C4 $2 Sheet of 4, #a-d 6.00 6.00

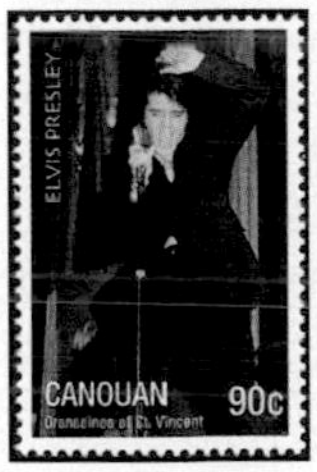


Elvis Presley (1935-77) — C5

**2003, Dec. 1** ***Perf. 13½x13¼***
**9** C5 90c multi .70 .70

Printed in sheets of 9.

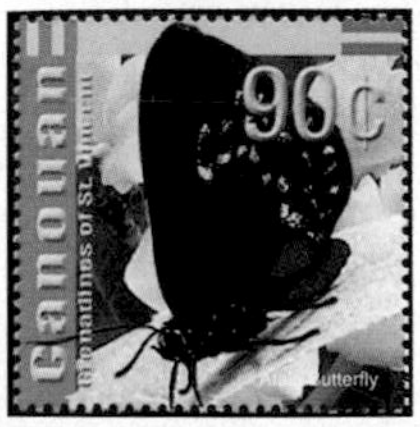


Butterflies C6

Designs: 90c, Atala. $1, Calico uranus. $1.40, Ceuptychia. $2, Aphrissa statira.
$5, Phoebis sennae.

**2003, Dec. 1** ***Perf. 13¼***
**10-13** C6 Set of 4 4.00 4.00

**Souvenir Sheet**

**14** C6 $5 multi 3.75 3.75

**Pope John Paul II Type of 2005**

**2005, June 1** **Litho.** ***Perf. 12½x12¾***
**15** A585 $2 multi 1.50 1.50

Printed in sheets of 4.

## MUSTIQUE

All stamps are designs of St. Vincent ("A" illustration letter) or Canouan ("C" illustration letter) unless otherwise illustrated.

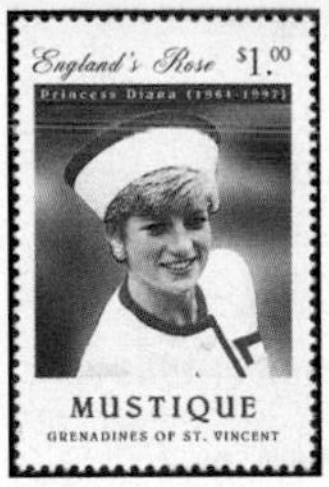


Diana, Princess of Wales (1961-97) — M1

**1997** **Litho.** ***Perf. 14***
**1** M1 $1 multicolored .75 .75

Issued in sheets of 6.
See Canouan No. 1.

**Paintings Type of 1999**

Various pictures of flowers making up a photomosaic of the Queen Mother. Stamps inscribed "Mustique."

**2000, Sept. 5** ***Perf. 13¾***
**2** A442 $1 Sheet of 8, #a-h 6.00 6.00
*i.* As No. 1017, imperf. 6.00 6.00

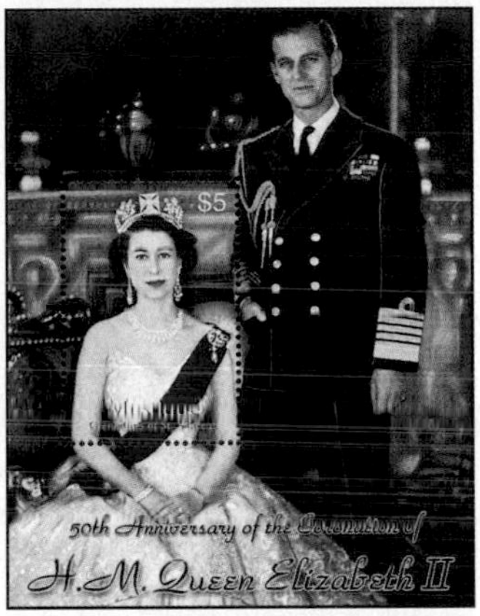


Coronation of Queen Elizabeth II, 50th Anniv. — M2

No. 3: a, Wearing yellow hat. b, Wearing blue dress. c, Wearing tiara.
$5, Wearing crown.

**2003, Feb. 26** **Litho.** ***Perf. 14***
**3** M2 $3 Sheet of 3, #a-c 6.75 6.75

**Souvenir Sheet**

**4** M2 $5 multi 3.75 3.75

**Prince William, 21st Birthday Type of 2003**

No. 5: a, Looking right. b, Wearing ski cap and goggles. c, Looking down.
$5, Wearing suit.

**2003, May 13**
**5** A535 $3 Sheet of 3, #a-c 6.75 6.75

**Souvenir Sheet**

**6** A535 $5 multi 3.75 3.75

**Corvette Type of 2003**

No. 7: a, 1960 Shark. b, 1988. c, 1956 convertible. d, 1967.
$5, 1964 Sting Ray convertible.

**2003, July 1** ***Perf. 13¼x13½***
**7** A534 $2 Sheet of 4, #a-d 6.00 6.00

**Souvenir Sheet**

**8** A534 $5 multi 3.75 3.75

**Cadillac Type of 2003**

No. 9: a, 1978 Seville. b, 1927 La Salle. c, 1953 Eldorado. d, 2002 Seville.
$5, 1961 Sedan de Ville.

**2003, July 1**
**9** A537 $2 Sheet of 4, #a-d 6.00 6.00

**Souvenir Sheet**

**10** A537 $5 multi 3.75 3.75

**Circus Type of 2003**

No. 11: a, Josaphine. b, Korolev Group (girl and monkey). c, Korolev Group (monkey). d, Zebra.

**2003, July 1** ***Perf. 14***
**11** A539 $2 Sheet of 4, #a-d 6.00 6.00

**Kennedy Type of Canouan**

No. 12: a, On Solomon Islands, 1943. b, On PT 109, 1942. c, Senate campaign, 1952. d, Recieving medal for gallantry, 1944.

**2003, Aug. 25**
**12** C4 $2 Sheet of 4, #a-d 6.00 6.00

**United We Stand Type of Canouan**

**2003, Sept. 8**
**13** C5 $2 multi 1.50 1.50

Printed in sheets of 4.

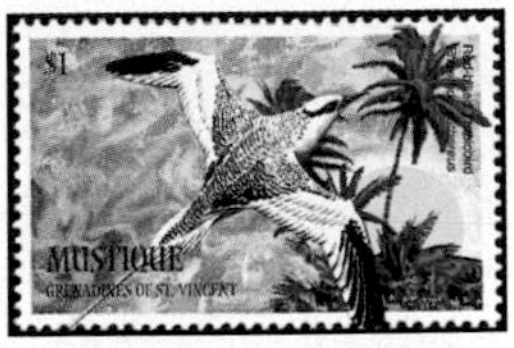


Birds M3

Designs: $1, Red-billed tropicbird. $1.10, Bananaquit. $1.40, Belted kingfisher. $2, Ruby-throated hummingbird.
$5, Brown pelican, vert.

**2003, Nov. 5** ***Perf. 13½x13¾***
**14-17** M3 Set of 4 4.25 4.25

**Souvenir Sheet**

***Perf. 13¾x13½***

**18** M3 $5 multi 3.75 3.75

**Elvis Presley Type of Canouan**

**2003, Dec. 1** ***Perf. 13½x13¼***
**19** C5 90c multi .70 .70

Printed in sheets of 9.

**Pope John Paul II Type of 2005**

**2005, June 1** **Litho.** ***Perf. 12½x12¾***
**20** A585 $2 multi 1.50 1.50

Printed in sheets of 4.

## UNION ISLAND

All stamps are types of St. Vincent ("A" illustration letter), St. Vincent Grenadines ("G" illustration letter) or Union ("U" illustration letter).

**"Island" issues are listed separately beginning in 1984. See St. Vincent Grenadines Nos. 84-111, 248-262 for earlier issues.**

**British Monarch Type of 1984**

#1a, Battle of Hastings. #1b, William the Conqueror. #2a, William the Conqueror. #2b, Abbaye Aux Dames. #3a, Skirmish at Dunbar. #3b, Charles II. #4a, Arms of William the Conqueror. #4b, William the Conqueror. #5a, Charles II. #5b, St. James Palace. #6a, Arms of Charles II. #6b, Charles II, Great Fire of London.

***Perf. 12½***

**1984, Mar. 29** **Litho.** **Unwmk.**

| | | | | | |
|---|---|---|---|---|---|
| **1** | A110 | 1c Pair, #a.-b. | .20 | .20 |
| **2** | A111 | 5c Pair, #a.-b. | .20 | .20 |
| **3** | A110 | 10c Pair, #a.-b. | .20 | .20 |
| **4** | A110 | 20c Pair, #a.-b. | .20 | .20 |
| **5** | A111 | 60c Pair, #a.-b. | .50 | .50 |
| **6** | A111 | $3 Pair, #a.-b. | 2.25 | 2.25 |
| | | *Nos. 1-6 (6)* | 3.55 | 3.55 |

**Locomotives Type of 1985**

**1984-87** ***Perf. 12½***

**Se-tenant Pairs, #a.-b.**

**a. — Side and front views.**

**b. — Action scene.**

| | | | | |
|---|---|---|---|---|
| **13** | A120 | 5c 1813 Puffing Billy, UK | .20 | .20 |
| **14** | A120 | 5c 1911 Class 9N, UK | .20 | .20 |
| **15** | A120 | 5c 1882 Class Skye Bogie, UK | .20 | .20 |

| | | | |
|---|---|---|---|
| 16 | A120 | 10c 1912 Class G8, Germany | .20 |
| 17 | A120 | 15c 1954 Class 65,10, Germany | .20 |
| 18 | A120 | 15c 1900 Castle Class, US | .20 |
| 19 | A120 | 15c 1887 Spinner Class 25, UK | .20 |
| 20 | A120 | 15c 1951 Fell #10100, UK | .20 |
| 21 | A120 | 20c 1942 Class 42, Germany | .20 |
| 22 | A120 | 20c 1951 Class 5MT, UK | .20 |
| 23 | A120 | 25c 1929 P.O. Rebuilt Class 3500, France | .20 |
| 24 | A120 | 25c 1886 Class 123, UK | .20 |
| 25 | A120 | 30c 1976 Class 56, UK | .25 |
| 26 | A120 | 30c 1897 Class G5, US | .25 |
| 27 | A120 | 40c 1947 9400 Class, US | .30 |
| 28 | A120 | 45c 1888 Sir Theodore, UK | .35 |
| 29 | A120 | 45c 1929 Class Z, UK | .35 |
| 30 | A120 | 45c 1896 Atlantic City RR, US | .35 |
| 31 | A120 | 50c 1906 45xx Class, UK | .35 |
| 32 | A120 | 50c 1912 Class D15, UK | .40 |
| 33 | A120 | 50c 1938 Class U4-b, Canada | .40 |
| 34 | A120 | 60c 1812 Prince Regent, UK | .45 |
| 35 | A120 | 60c 1920 Butler Henderson, UK | .45 |
| 36 | A120 | 60c 1889 Eldin, UK | .45 |
| 37 | A120 | 60c 1934 7200 Class, US | .45 |
| 38 | A120 | 75c 1911 Class C, UK | .45 |
| 39 | A120 | 75c 1938 Class C, Australia | .45 |
| 40 | A120 | 75c 1879 Sir Haydn, UK | .60 |
| 41 | A120 | $1 1904 Class H-20, US | .60 |
| 42 | A120 | $1 1883 Class Y14, UK | .60 |
| 43 | A120 | 75c 1915 River Class, UK | .60 |
| 44 | A120 | $1 1936 D51 Class, GG1, US | .60 |
| 45 | A120 | $1 1837 L&B Bury, UK | .75 |
| 46 | A120 | $1 1903 Class 900, UK | .75 |
| 47 | A120 | $1 1904 Class H-20, US | .75 |
| 48 | A120 | $1 1905 Class L, UK | .75 |
| 49 | A120 | $1.50 1952 Class 4, US | .75 |
| 50 | A120 | $1.50 1837 Campbell's 8-Wheeler, US | 1.10 |
| 51 | A120 | $1.50 1934 Class GG1, US | 1.10 |
| 52 | A120 | $1.50 1924 Class 01, Germany | 1.10 |
| 53 | A120 | $2 1920 Gordon Highlander, UK | 1.50 |
| 54 | A120 | $2 1969 Metroliner Railcar, US | 1.50 |
| 55 | A120 | $2 1951 Class GP7, US | 1.50 |
| 56 | A120 | $2 1873 Hardwicke Precedent Class, UK | 1.50 |
| 57 | A120 | $2.50 1899 Highflyer Class, UK | 1.75 |
| 58 | A120 | $3 1925 Class U1, UK | 2.25 |
| 59 | A120 | $3 1880 Class 7100, Japan | 2.25 |
| 60 | A120 | $3 1972 Gas Turbine Prototype, France | 2.25 |

Nos. 13-60 (48) ... 34.00 34.00

St. Vincent Grenadines #13, 34, 44, 52, 8/9/84; #14, 16, 21, 23, 39, 45, 56, 58, 12/18/84; #15, 31, 35, 53, 3/25/85; #17, 25, 28, 36, 40, 49, 57, 59, 1/3/86; #18, 29, 33, 37, 41, 55, 60, 12/23/86; #19, 24, 27, 32, 38, 42, 47, 55, 9/87; #20, 22, 26, 30, 43, 48, 51, 124/87. Beginning on Jan. 31, 1986, this issue is not inscribed "Leaders of the World."

**1984, Aug. 23    Perf. 14x13½**

Leaders of the World — UNION ISLAND Overprinted "UNION ISLAND" on Nos. 222-238

**Wmk. 373**

| | | | |
|---|---|---|---|
| 109 | G26 | 1c on No. 222 | .20 .20 |
| 110 | G26 | 3c on No. 223 | .20 .20 |
| 111 | G26 | 5c on No. 224 | .20 .20 |
| 112 | G26 | 6c on No. 225 | .20 .20 |
| 113 | G26 | 10c on No. 226 | .20 .20 |
| 114 | G26 | 15c on No. 227 | .20 .20 |
| 115 | G26 | 50c on No. 230 | .25 .25 |
| 116 | G26 | 50c on No. 231 | .25 .25 |
| 117 | G26 | 50c on No. 232 | .25 .25 |
| 118 | G26 | 75c on No. 233 | .55 .55 |
| 119 | G26 | 75c on No. 234 | .55 .55 |
| 120 | G26 | 75c on No. 235 | .55 .55 |
| 121 | G26 | $1 on No. 236 | 1.00 1.00 |
| 122 | G26 | $2 on No. 237 | 2.00 2.00 |
| 123 | G26 | $3 on No. 238 | 2.75 2.75 |

**1984, Nov.    Perf. 12½**

Cricket Players Type of 1985 Unwmk. Pairs, #a.-b.

| | | | |
|---|---|---|---|
| 124 | G26 | $5 on No. 237 | 4.75 4.75 |
| 125 | G26 | $10 on No. 238 | 9.00 9.00 |

Nos. 109-125 (17) ... 23.00 23.00

**Classic Car Type of 1983**

**1985-86    Perf. 12½**

Se-tenant Pairs, #a.-b.
a. — Side and front views.
b. — Action scene.

| | | | |
|---|---|---|---|
| 126 | A116 | 10c G. W. Johnson | .20 .20 |
| 127 | A116 | 10c G. S. N. Hartley | .20 .20 |
| 128 | A116 | 55c R. M. Ellison | .25 .25 |
| 129 | A116 | 55c C. S. Cowdrey | .50 .50 |
| 130 | A116 | 60c K. Sharp | .60 .60 |
| 131 | A116 | 75c M. C. Cowdrey, in action | .70 .70 |
| 132 | A116 | $1.50 G. R. Dilley, in action | 1.50 1.50 |
| 133 | A116 | $3 R. Illingworth, in action | 2.75 2.75 |

Nos. 126-133 (8) ... 6.70 6.70

| | | | |
|---|---|---|---|
| 142 | A107 | 1c 1963 Lancia, Italy | .20 |
| 143 | A107 | 5c 1895 Duryea, US | .20 |
| 144 | A107 | 10c 1970 Datsun, Japan | .20 |
| 145 | A107 | 10c 1962 BRM, Japan | .20 |
| 146 | A107 | 50c 1927 Amilcar, France | .35 |
| 147 | A107 | 55c 1929 Duesenberg, US | .40 |
| 148 | A107 | 60c 1913 Peugeot, France | .50 |
| 149 | A107 | 60c 1938 Lagonda, UK | .50 |
| 150 | A107 | 60c 1924 Fiat, Italy | .50 |
| 151 | A107 | 75c 1957 Alfa Romeo, Italy | .50 |
| 152 | A107 | 75c 1957 Panhard, France | .60 |
| 153 | A107 | 75c 1954 Porsche, Germany | .60 |
| 154 | A107 | 90c 1904 Darracq, France | .70 |
| 155 | A107 | $1 1927 Daimler, US | .85 |
| 156 | A107 | $1 1949 Oldsmobile, US | .85 |
| 157 | A107 | $1 1934 Chrysler, US | .85 |
| 158 | A107 | $1.50 1965 MG, UK | 1.25 |
| 159 | A107 | $1.50 1922 Fiat, Italy | 1.25 |
| 160 | A107 | $1.50 1934 Bugatti, France | 1.25 |
| 161 | A107 | $2 1963 Mercer, US | 1.60 |
| 162 | A107 | $2.50 1917 Locomobile, US | 2.00 |
| 163 | A107 | $3 1928 Ford, US | 2.50 |

Nos. 142-163 (22) ... 17.95 17.95

Issued: #142, 146, 151, 162, 1/4/85; #143, 148, 155, 158, 5/20/85; #144, 147, 149, 152, 154, 156, 159, 161, 7/15/85; #145, 150, 153, 157, 160, 163, 7/30/86.

Beginning on 7/30/86, this issue is not inscribed "Leaders of the World."

Birds — U1

UNION ISLAND 15c

| | | | |
|---|---|---|---|
| 186 | U1 | 15c Hooded warbler | .20 .20 |
| 187 | U1 | 50c Song sparrow | .40 .40 |
| 188 | U1 | $1 Scarlet tanager | .80 .80 |
| 189 | U1 | $1.50 Merlin | 1.25 1.25 |

**1985, Feb.    Perf. 12½**

Nos. 186-189 (4) ... 2.65 2.65

#186a, Hooded warbler. #186b, Carolina wren. #187a, Song sparrow. #187b, Black-headed grosbeak. #188a, Scarlet tanager. #188b, Lazuli bunting. #189a, Sharp-shinned hawk. #189b, Merlin.

**Queen Mother Type of 1985**

85th birthday — Hats: #206a, Mortarboard. #206b, Blue. #207a, Turquoise. #207b, Blue. #208a, 212a. Without hat. #208b, 212b. White. #209a, 211a, White hat, violet feathers. #209b, 211b, Blue. #210a, Crown, Hat.

| | | | |
|---|---|---|---|
| 194 | U2 | 10c Pair, #a.-b. | .20 .20 |
| 195 | U2 | 15c Pair, #a.-b. | .20 .20 |
| 196 | U2 | 75c Pair, #a.-b. | 1.60 1.60 |
| 197 | U2 | $2 Pair, #a.-b. | 2.60 2.60 |

**1985, Apr. 15**

Nos. 194-197 (4)

| | | | |
|---|---|---|---|
| 206 | A122 | 55c Pair, #a.-b. | .50 .50 |
| 207 | A122 | 70c Pair, #a.-b. | .60 .60 |
| 208 | A122 | $1 Pair, #a.-b. | .90 .90 |
| 209 | A122 | $1.70 Pair, #a.-b. | 1.60 1.60 |

**1985, Aug. 19**

Nos. 206-209 (4)

**Souvenir Sheets of 2**

| | | | |
|---|---|---|---|
| 210 | A122 | $1.95 #a.-b. | 2.50 2.50 |
| 211 | A122 | $2.85 #a.-b. | 3.60 3.60 |
| 212 | A122 | $7 | 6.50 6.50 |

Nos. 206-209 (4)

**Elizabeth II 60th Birthday Type of 1986**

Designs: 10c, Wearing scarf. 60c, Riding clothes. $2, Wearing crown and jewels. $8, In clothes. $10, Holding flowers.

| | | | |
|---|---|---|---|
| 213-216 | A128 | 10c Set of 4 | 4.50 4.50 |

**1986, Apr. 21**

**Souvenir Sheet**

217 | A128 | $10 multi | 4.75 4.75

Butterflies — U2

| | | | |
|---|---|---|---|
| 230 | A132 | $2 Sarah Ferguson | 1.00 1.00 |
| 231 | A132 | $4 Andrew, Andrew | 2.70 2.70 |

Nos. 228-231 (4)

**Prince Andrew Royal Wedding Type**

**1986, July 15    Perf. 12½x13, 13x12½**

| | | | |
|---|---|---|---|
| 228 | A132 | 60c on No. 228 | .35 .35 |
| 229 | A132 | 60c Andrew, with cap | .35 .35 |

"CONGRATULATIONS TO T.R.H. THE DUKE & DUCHESS OF YORK" in 3 Lines

Nos. 228-231 Overprinted in Silver

| | | | |
|---|---|---|---|
| 232 | A132 | 60c on No. 228 | 1.00 1.00 |
| 233 | A132 | 60c on No. 229 | 1.00 1.00 |
| 234 | A132 | 60c on No. 230 | 3.00 3.00 |
| 235 | A132 | $2 on No. 231 | 3.00 3.00 |

Nos. 232-235 (4)

**1986, Oct.**

Nos. 236-240 (5)

**Queen Elizabeth II Wedding Anniv. Type of St. Vincent Grenadines**

**1987, Oct. 15    Perf. 12½**

| | | | |
|---|---|---|---|
| 236 | G47 | 15c like No. 568 | .20 .20 |
| 237 | G47 | 45c like No. 569 | .25 .25 |
| 238 | G47 | $1.50 like No. 571 | .70 .70 |
| 239 | G47 | $4 like No. 572 | 1.40 1.40 |
| 240 | G47 | like No. 572 | 1.75 1.75 |

World Cup Soccer Championships, Mexico — U4

UNION ISLAND WORLD CUP-MEXICO 1986 30c

U3

| | | | |
|---|---|---|---|
| 218 | U3 | 10c Moroccan team | .20 .20 |
| 219 | U3 | 10c Argentinian team | .20 .20 |
| 220 | U3 | 30c Algerian player | .20 .20 |
| 221 | U3 | 75c Hungarian team | .30 .30 |
| 222 | U3 | $1 Russian team | .45 .45 |
| 223 | U3 | $2.50 Belgian player | 1.10 1.10 |
| 224 | U3 | $3 French player | 1.25 1.25 |
| 225 | U4 | $6 W. German player | 6.20 6.20 |

**1986, May 7    Perf. 12½ (U3), 15 (U4)**

Nos. 218-225 (8)

**Souvenir Sheets**

| | | | |
|---|---|---|---|
| 226 | U3 | $1.85 like No. 222 | 2.50 2.50 |
| 227 | U4 | $6 like No. 219 | 2.50 2.50 |

Souvenir sheets contain one 60x40mm stamp.

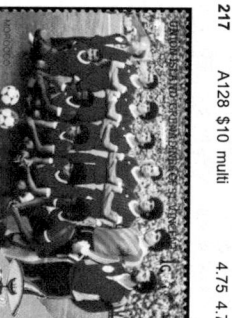

Diana, Princess of Wales (1961-97) — U6

UNION ISLAND England's Rose $1.

**1997    Perf. 14**

251 | U6 | $1 multicolored | 2.00 2.00

No. 251 was issued in sheets of 6.

**Paintings Type of 1999**

Various pictures making up a photomosaic of the Queen Mother.

**2000, Sept. 5    Perf. 13¾**

252 | A442 | $1 Sheet of 9, #a-i | 6.00 6.00
l. As No. 252, imperf. | 6.00

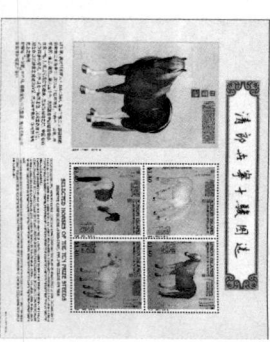

New Year 2002 (Year of the Horse) — U7

Disney characters in various French vehicles: 1c, 1893 Peugeot. 2c, 1090-91 Panhard-Levassor. 3c, 1893 Renault. 4c, 1919 Citroen. 5c, 1878 La Mancelle. 10c, 1891 De Dion Bouton Quadricycle. 55c, 1896 Leon Bollee Trike. No. 248, 1911 Brasier Coupe. No. 249, 1911 Brasier Coupe. No. 250, 1769, Cugnot's artillery tractor.

**1989, July 7    Perf. 14x13½**

241-250 | U5 | Set of 10 ... 18.00 18.00

PHILEXFRANCE '89.

UNION ISLAND 1c

U5

Horse paintings by Giuseppe Castiglione: a, White horse with head down. b, Brown horse. c, Piebald horse. d, White horse with head up.

**2001, Dec. 17** **Litho.** ***Perf. 12¾***
**253** U7 $1.40 Sheet of 4, #a-d 4.25 4.25

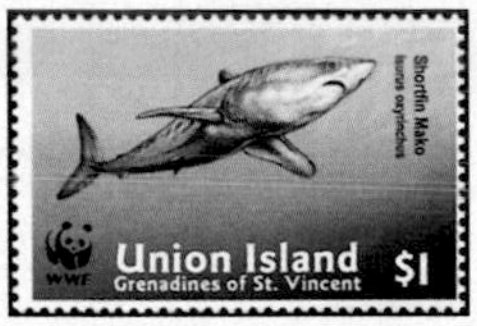
Shortfin Mako
Union Island $1
Grenadines of St. Vincent

Worldwide Fund for Nature (WWF) U8

Shortfin mako shark: a, View of underside. b, Side view. c, Pair of sharks. d, Shark at surface.

**2002, Nov. 1** ***Perf. 14***
**254** Horiz. or vert. strip 3.00 3.00
***a.-d.*** U8 $1 Any single .75 .75
***e.*** Souvenir sheet of 4, #a-d 3.00 3.00

### United We Stand Type of 2001

**2002, Nov. 4**
**255** A508 $1.40 multi 1.10 1.10

Printed in sheets of 4.

### Queen Mother Elizabeth Type of 2002

No. 256: a, Wearing purple hat. b, Wearing green hat. c, Wearing pink hat.

**2002, Nov. 4** **Litho.** ***Perf. 14***
**256** A522 $2 Sheet of 4, #a-b, 2 #c 6.00 6.00

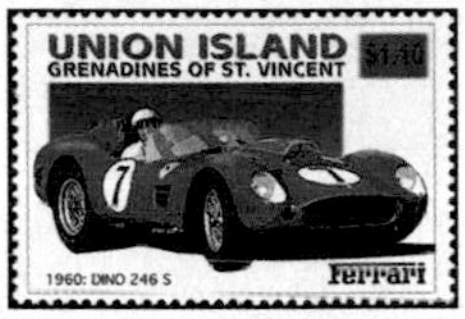
UNION ISLAND
GRENADINES OF ST. VINCENT
$1.10
Ferrari

Ferrari Automobiles — U9

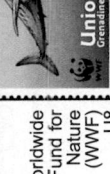

Designs: No. 257, $1.10, 1960 Dino 246S No. 258, $1.10, 1962 248SP. No. 259, $1.10, 1966 330GTC-GTS. No. 260, $1.10, 1967 Dino 206GT. No. 261, $1.10, 1984 Testarossa. No. 262, $1.10, 1989 348TB-TS. No. 263, $1.10, 2002 Enzo Ferrari. No. 264, $1.10, 2002 360 Challenge.

**2002, Dec. 9**
**257-264** U9 Set of 8 6.75 6.75

### Teddy Bears Type of 2002

No. 265, $2 — Bears from Britain: a, Palace Guard bear. b, Bear with crown. c, Bear with bowler hat. d, Beefeater bear.

No. 266, $2 — Bears from Holland: a, Artist bear. b, Bear with black hat. c, Bears in wagon. d, Bear with overalls and checked shirt.

**2003, Jan. 27** ***Perf. 13½x13¼***
**Sheets of 4, #a-d**
**265-266** A519 Set of 2 12.00 12.00

### Year of the Ram Type of 2003

No. 267 — Color of ram: a, Red violet. b, Red. c, Yellow green. d, Violet. e, Brown. f, Blue green.

**2003, Jan. 27** ***Perf. 14¼x13¾***
**267** A526 $1 Sheet of 6, #a-f 4.50 4.50

### Princess Diana Type of 2003

No. 268: a, Wearing pink hat, holding roses. b, Wearing lilac dress and necklace. c, Wearing red hat. d, With hand on chin. e, Wearing pink blouse, holding flowers. d, Wearing blue dress.

No. 269, horiz.: a, Children's Cancer Hospital. b, Meeting with AIDS patients. c, Conference on eating disorders. d, Red Cross child feeding center.

**2003, May 26** **Litho.** ***Perf. 14***
**268** A536 $1.40 Sheet of 6, #a-f 6.25 6.25
**269** A536 $2 Sheet of 4, #a-d 6.00 6.00

### Kennedy Type of Bequia

No. 270: a, Denomination at UL, name at right. b, Denomination at UL, name at left. c, Denomination at UR, name at left. d, Denomination at UR, name at right.

**2003, Aug. 25**
**270** B14 $2 Sheet of 4, #a-d 6.00 6.00

### Elvis Presley Type of Bequia

No. 271 — Color of illustration: a, Brown. b, Dark blue. c, Green. d, Purple. e, Yellow brown. f, Red violet. g, Sepia. h, Bright blue. i, Red brown.

**2003, Dec. 1** ***Perf. 13½***
**271** B15 90c Sheet of 9, #a-i 6.25 6.25

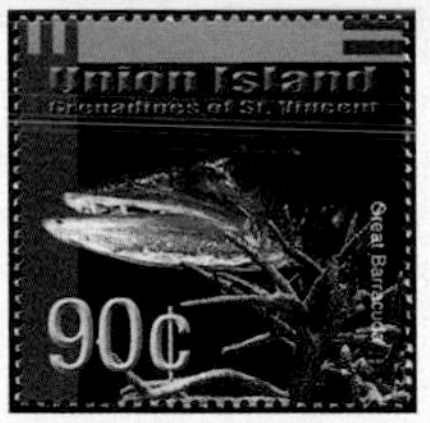
Union Island
Grenadines of St. Vincent
90¢

Fish — U10

Designs: 90c, Great barracuda. $1, French angelfish. $1.40, Reef shark. $2, Tarpon. $5, Queen angelfish.

**2003, Dec. 1** ***Perf. 13¼***
**272-275** U10 Set of 4 4.00 4.00

**Souvenir Sheet**

**276** U10 $5 multi 3.75 3.75

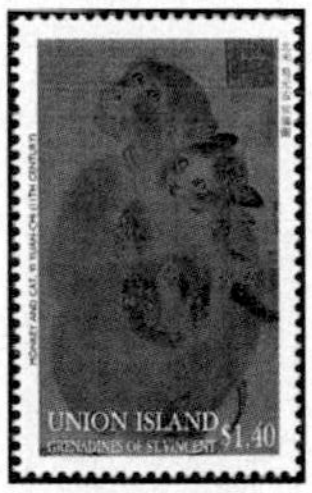
UNION ISLAND
$1.40

Detail from Monkey and Cat, by Yi Yuan-Chi — U11

**2004, Jan. 15** ***Perf. 13½***
**277** U11 $1.40 shown 1.10 1.10

**Souvenir Sheet**
***Perf. 13¾***

**278** U11 $3 Entire painting 2.25 2.25

New Year 2004 (Year of the Monkey). No. 277 printed in sheets of 4. No. 278 contains one 58x35mm stamp.

### Marilyn Monroe Type of 2004

Monroe and: No. 279, 75c, Denomination in blue. No. 280, 75c, Denomination in red.

**2004, May 3** **Litho.** ***Perf. 13½***
**279-280** A558 Set of 2 1.10 1.10

Each stamp printed in sheets of 10.

### Ronald Reagan Type of 2004

Reagan and denomination color of: a, Red. b, White. c, Blue.

**2004, Oct. 13**
**281** Vert. strip of 3 3.25 3.25
***a.-c.*** A564 $1.40 Any single 1.00 1.00

Printed in sheets containing two strips.

### Babe Ruth Type of 2004

**2004, Nov. 25** ***Perf. 14***
**282** A561 75c multi .55 .55

Printed in sheets of 10.

Miniature Sheet

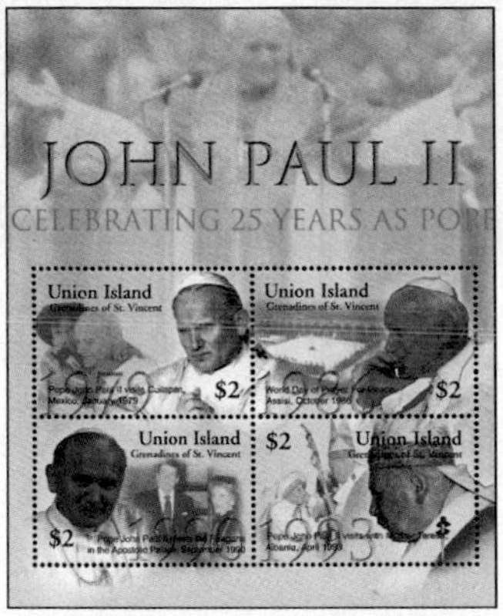
JOHN PAUL II
Union Island
$2

Election of Pope John Paul II, 25th Anniv. (in 2003) — U12

Pope John Paul II: a, With child, Cuilapan, Mexico, 1979. b, At World Day of Prayer for Peace, Assisi, Italy, 1986. c, With Ronald and Nancy Reagan, 1990. d, Visiting Mother Teresa, 1993.

**2005, Jan. 26** ***Perf. 14***
**283** U12 $2 Sheet of 4, #a-d 6.00 6.00

### Basketball Players Type of 2004-05

Designs: No. 284, 90c, Mike Bibby, Sacramento Kings. No. 285, 90c, Reggie Miller, Indiana Pacers. No. 286, 90c, Alonzo Mourning, Miami Heat. No. 287, 90c, Paul Pierce, Boston Celtics. No. 288, 90c, Jim Jackson, Phoenix Suns.

No. 289: a, New Jersey Nets emblem. b, Jason Kidd, New Jersey Nets.

**2005, Feb. 10** **Litho.** ***Perf. 14***
**284-288** A572 Set of 5 3.50 3.50

**Miniature Sheet**

**289** A572 90c Sheet of 12, 2 #289a, 10 #289b 8.25 8.25

Nos. 284-288 each printed in sheets of 12.

### Vatican Stamp and Pope John Paul II Types of 2005

Designs: 70c, Vatican #64. $3, Pope holding Bible, horiz.

**2005, June 1** ***Perf. 13x13¼***
**290** A584 70c multi .55 .55

***Perf. 13¼x13½***

**291** A585 $3 multi 2.25 2.25

No. 290 printed in sheets of 12; No. 291, in sheets of 6.

### Railroads Type of 2004

No. 292, $1: a, British Rail intercity high-speed train. b, British-built Edwardian Mogul, Paraguay. c, Fireless locomotive, Ludlow jute mill, Calcutta. d, Welders working on Wisconsin Central. e, Serving breakfast on British intercity train. f, Pacific locomotive, Pulgaon-Avri line, India. g, Locomotive shed laborers, Wankaner, India. h, British Rail train driver with head out of window. i, British Rail train driver at controls.

No. 293, $1: a, Southern Pacific Bullied Pacific "Blackmore Vale." b, Bagnall 0-4-0ST on Assam coalfield. c, Orenstein & Koppel 0-8-0T, Java. d, Baldwin 0-6-6-0 Compound Mallet, Philippines. e, Coal loads on C&I sub, Illinois. f, Class 37 on China Clay, Cornwall. g, BNSF stack train, New Mexico. h, China Railways QJ 2-10-2 near Anshan. i, Kitson 0-6-2 at Suraya Sugar Mill, India.

No. 294, $5, Amtrak Coast Starlight, California. No. 295, $5, Glacier Express.

**2005, June 7** ***Perf. 12¾***
**Sheets of 9, #a-i**
**292-293** A565 Set of 2 13.50 13.50

**Souvenir Sheets**

**294-295** A565 Set of 2 7.50 7.50

## EL SALVADOR

'el-sal-və-ˌdor

LOCATION — On the Pacific coast of Central America, between Guatemala, Honduras and the Gulf of Fonseca
GOVT. — Republic
AREA — 8,236 sq. mi.
POP. — 5,839,079 (1999 est.)
CAPITAL — San Salvador

8 Reales = 100 Centavos = 1 Peso
100 Centavos = 1 Colón

**Catalogue values for unused stamps in this country are for Never Hinged items, beginning with Scott 589 in the regular postage section, Scott C85 in the airpost section, and Scott O362 in the official section.**

### Watermarks

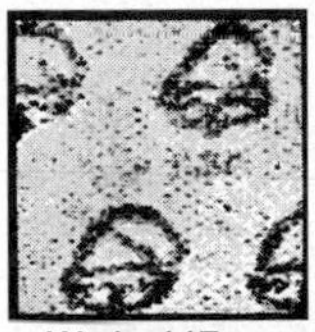

Wmk. 117 — Liberty Cap

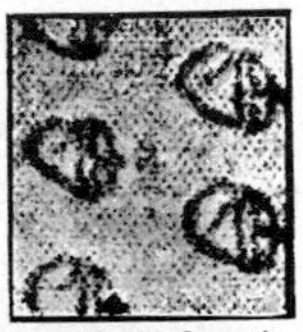

Position of wmk. on reprints

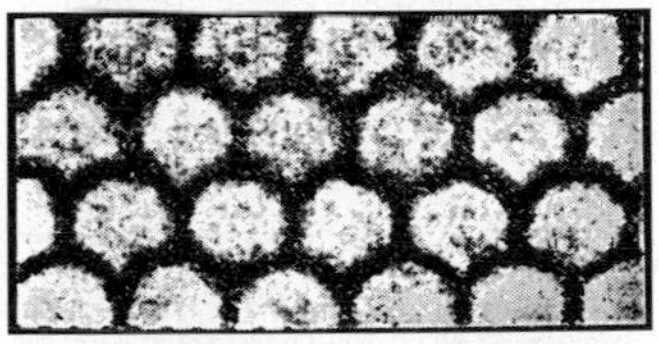

Wmk. 172 — Honeycomb

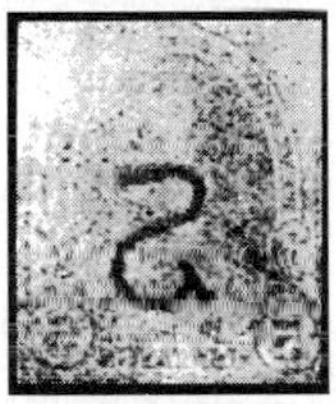

Wmk. 173 — S

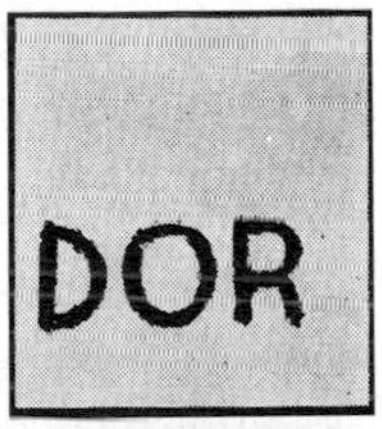
DOR

Wmk. 240 — REPUBLICA DE EL SALVADOR in Sheet

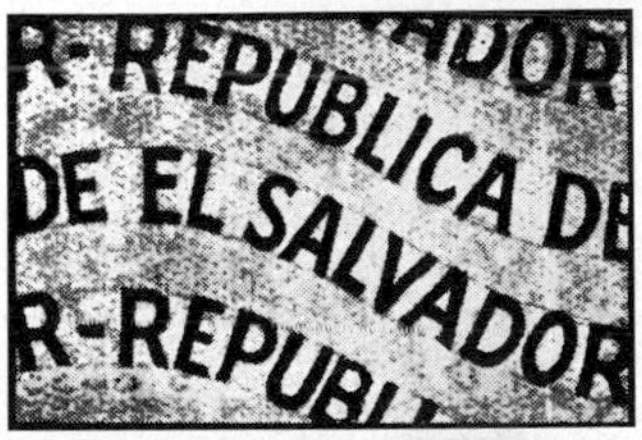
REPUBLICA
DE EL SALVADOR

Wmk. 269 — REPUBLICA DE EL SALVADOR

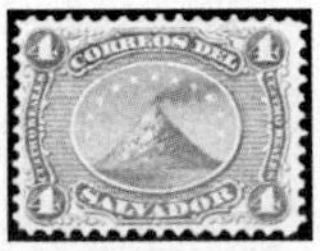

Volcano San Miguel — A1

**1867** **Unwmk.** **Engr.** ***Perf. 12***

| | | | | |
|---|---|---|---|---|
| **1** | A1 | ½r blue | .55 | *.70* |
| **2** | A1 | 1r red | .55 | .55 |
| **3** | A1 | 2r green | 2.40 | *2.75* |
| **4** | A1 | 4r bister | 4.50 | 3.50 |
| | | *Nos. 1-4 (4)* | 8.00 | 7.50 |

Nos. 1-4 when overprinted "Contra Sello" and shield with 14 stars, are telegraph stamps. For similar overprint see Nos. 5-12.

Counterfeits exist.

Nos. 1-4 Handstamped

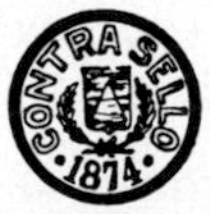


**1874**

| | | | | |
|---|---|---|---|---|
| **5** | A1 | ½r blue | 6.50 | 3.50 |
| **6** | A1 | 1r red | 6.50 | 3.50 |
| **7** | A1 | 2r green | 6.50 | 3.50 |
| **8** | A1 | 4r bister | 19.00 | 17.50 |
| | | *Nos. 5-8 (4)* | 38.50 | 28.00 |

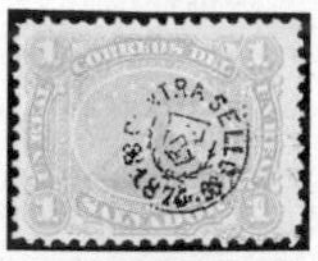

Nos. 1-4 Handstamped

| | | | | |
|---|---|---|---|---|
| **9** | A1 | ½r blue | 3.75 | 2.00 |
| **10** | A1 | 1r red | 3.75 | 2.00 |
| **11** | A1 | 2r green | 3.75 | 2.00 |
| **12** | A1 | 4r bister | 7.50 | 5.00 |
| | | *Nos. 9-12 (4)* | 18.75 | 11.00 |

The overprints on Nos. 5-12 exist double. Counterfeits are plentiful.

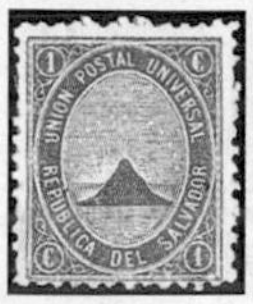

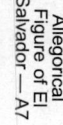

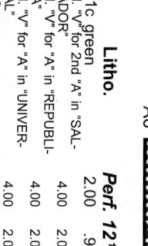

Coat of Arms
A2 A3

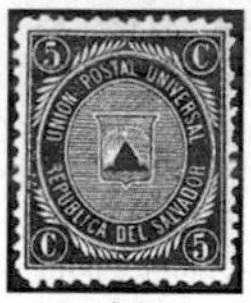
A4

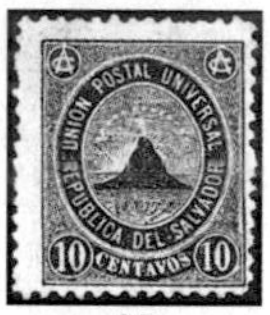
A5

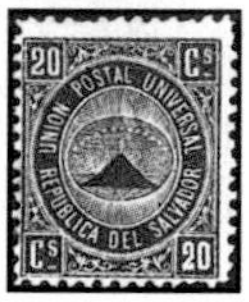
A6

**1879** **Litho.** ***Perf. 12½***

| | | | | |
|---|---|---|---|---|
| **13** | A2 | 1c green | 2.00 | .90 |
| *a.* | | Invtd. "V" for 2nd "A" in "SALVADOR" | 4.00 | 2.00 |
| *b.* | | Invtd. "V" for "A" in "REPUBLICA" | 4.00 | 2.00 |
| *c.* | | Invtd. "V" for "A" in "UNIVERSAL" | 4.00 | 2.00 |
| **14** | A3 | 2c rose | 2.75 | 1.50 |
| *a.* | | Invtd. scroll in upper left corner | 8.00 | 5.00 |
| **15** | A4 | 5c blue | 5.00 | 1.25 |
| *a.* | | 5c ultra | 8.00 | 4.00 |
| **16** | A5 | 10c black | 10.00 | 3.50 |
| **17** | A6 | 20c violet | 16.00 | 10.00 |
| | | *Nos. 13-17 (5)* | 35.75 | 17.15 |

There are fifteen varieties of the 1c and 2c, twenty-five of the 5c and five each of the 10 and 20c.

In 1881 the 1c, 2c and 5c were redrawn, the 1c in fifteen varieties and the 2c and 5c in five varieties each.

No. 15 comes in a number of shades from light to dark blue.

These stamps, when overprinted "Contra sello" and arms, are telegraph stamps.

Counterfeits of No. 14 exist.

For overprints see Nos. 25D-25E, 28A-28C.

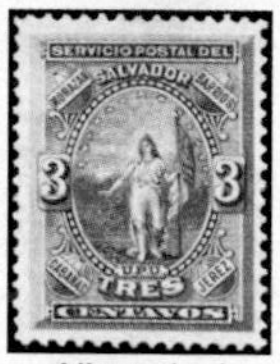
Allegorical Figure of El Salvador — A7

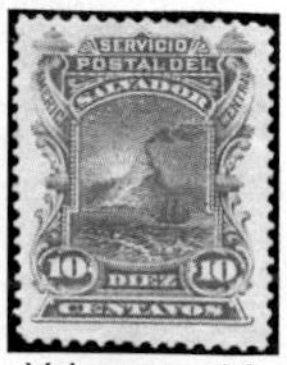
Volcano — A8

**1887** **Engr.** ***Perf. 12***

| | | | | |
|---|---|---|---|---|
| **18** | A7 | 3c brown | .40 | .20 |
| *a.* | | Imperf., pair | 2.50 | 2.50 |
| **19** | A8 | 10c orange | 3.00 | .90 |

For surcharges and overprints see Nos. 25, 26C-28, 30-32.

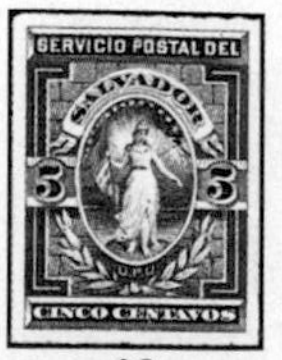
A9

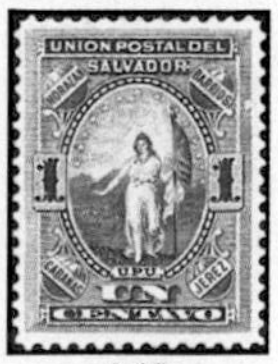
A10

**1888** ***Rouletted***

| | | | | |
|---|---|---|---|---|
| **20** | A9 | 5c deep blue | .40 | .35 |

For overprints see Nos. 35-36.

**1889** ***Perf. 12***

| | | | | |
|---|---|---|---|---|
| **21** | A10 | 1c green | .20 | |
| **22** | A10 | 2c scarlet | .20 | |

**Same Overprinted with Heavy Bar Obliterating "UNION POSTAL DEL"**

| | | | | |
|---|---|---|---|---|
| **23** | A10 | 1c green | .30 | .25 |
| **24** | A10 | 2c scarlet | .30 | |

Nos. 21, 22 and 24 were never placed in use.

For overprints see Nos. 26, 29.

No. 18 Surcharged

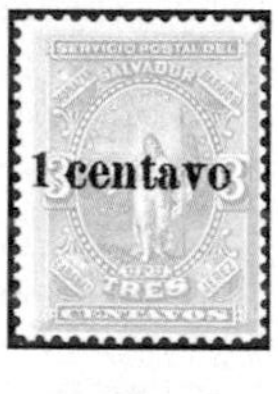


Type I — thick numerals, heavy serifs.
Type II — thin numerals, straight serifs.

| | | | | |
|---|---|---|---|---|
| **25** | A7 | 1c on 3c brn, type II | .65 | .50 |
| *a.* | | Double surcharge | 1.50 | |
| *b.* | | Triple surcharge | 3.50 | |
| *c.* | | Type I | .65 | |

The 1c on 2c scarlet is bogus.

Handstamped

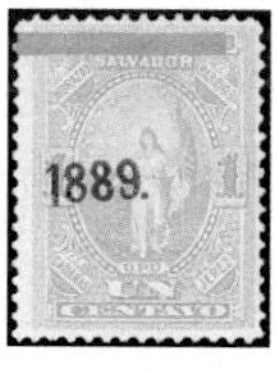


**1889**

**Violet Handstamp**

| | | | | |
|---|---|---|---|---|
| **25D** | A2 | 1c green | 12.50 | 12.50 |
| **25E** | A6 | 20c violet | 30.00 | 30.00 |
| **26** | A10 | 1c green, #23 | 1.00 | .90 |
| **26C** | A7 | 1c on 3c, #27 | 20.00 | 20.00 |
| **27** | A7 | 3c brown | 1.00 | .90 |
| **28** | A8 | 10c orange | 5.00 | 4.00 |

**Black Handstamp**

| | | | | |
|---|---|---|---|---|
| **28A** | A2 | 1c green | 15.00 | 14.00 |
| **28B** | A3 | 2c rose | 17.50 | 17.50 |
| **28C** | A6 | 20c violet | 30.00 | 30.00 |
| **29** | A10 | 1c green, #23 | 1.25 | 1.00 |
| **30** | A7 | 3c brown | 1.25 | 1.00 |
| **31** | A7 | 1c on 3c, #27 | 17.50 | 17.50 |
| **32** | A8 | 10c orange | 4.50 | 3.50 |

***Rouletted***

**Black Handstamp**

| | | | | |
|---|---|---|---|---|
| **35** | A9 | 5c deep blue | 1.25 | .75 |

**Violet Handstamp**

| | | | | |
|---|---|---|---|---|
| **36** | A9 | 5c deep blue | 1.25 | .75 |

The 1889 handstamps as usual, are found double, inverted, etc. Counterfeits are plentiful.

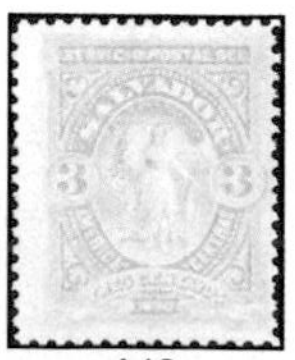
A13

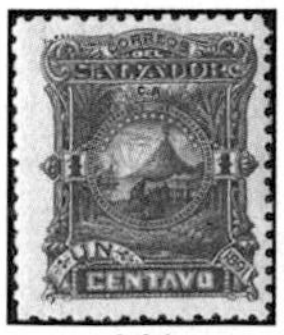
A14

**1890** **Engr.** ***Perf. 12***

| | | | | |
|---|---|---|---|---|
| **38** | A13 | 1c green | .20 | .20 |
| **39** | A13 | 2c bister brown | .20 | .20 |
| **40** | A13 | 3c yellow | .20 | .20 |
| **41** | A13 | 5c blue | .20 | .20 |
| **42** | A13 | 10c violet | .20 | .20 |
| **43** | A13 | 20c orange | .25 | .20 |
| **44** | A13 | 25c red | .90 | *1.00* |
| **45** | A13 | 50c claret | .50 | *.65* |
| **46** | A13 | 1p carmine | .75 | *1.50* |
| | | *Nos. 38-46 (9)* | 3.40 | *4.35* |

**The issues of 1890 to 1899 inclusive were printed by the Hamilton Bank Note Co., New York, to the order of N. F. Seebeck, who held a contract for stamps with the government of El Salvador. This contract gave the right to make reprints of the stamps and such were subsequently made in some instances, as will be found noted in italic type.**

**Used values of 1890-1899 issues are for stamps with genuine cancellations applied while the stamps were valid. Various counterfeit cancellations exist.**

**1891**

| | | | | |
|---|---|---|---|---|
| **47** | A14 | 1c vermilion | .20 | .20 |
| **48** | A14 | 2c yellow green | .20 | .20 |
| **49** | A14 | 3c violet | .20 | .20 |
| **50** | A14 | 5c carmine lake | 1.00 | *2.00* |
| **51** | A14 | 10c blue | .20 | .20 |
| **52** | A14 | 11c violet | .20 | .20 |
| **53** | A14 | 20c green | .20 | *.30* |
| **54** | A14 | 25c yellow brown | .20 | *.40* |
| **55** | A14 | 50c dark blue | .20 | *.90* |
| **56** | A14 | 1p dark brown | .20 | *1.50* |
| | | *Nos. 47-56 (10)* | 2.80 | *6.10* |

For surcharges see Nos. 57-59.

*Nos. 47 and 56 have been reprinted in thick toned paper with dark gum.*

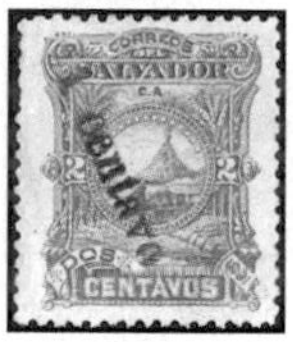
A15

Nos. 48, 49 Surcharged in Black or Violet:

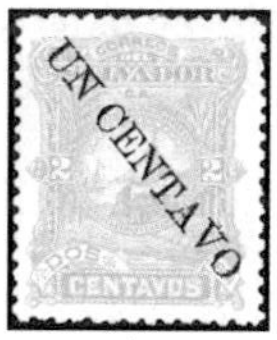

b

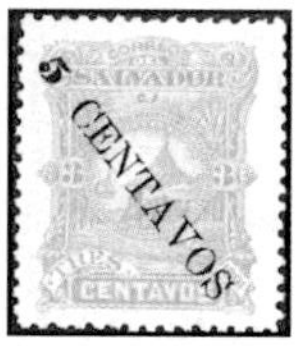

c

**1891**

| | | | | |
|---|---|---|---|---|
| **57** | A15 | 1c on 2c yellow grn | 2.25 | 2.00 |
| *a.* | | Inverted surcharge | 4.00 | |
| **58** | A14 (b) | 1c on 2c yellow grn | 1.60 | 1.40 |
| **59** | A14 (c) | 5c on 3c violet | 4.00 | 3.25 |
| | | *Nos. 57-59 (3)* | 7.85 | 6.65 |

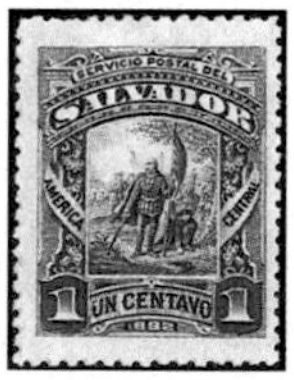
Landing of Columbus — A18

**1892** **Engr.**

| | | | | |
|---|---|---|---|---|
| **60** | A18 | 1c blue green | .35 | .20 |
| **61** | A18 | 2c orange brown | .35 | .20 |
| **62** | A18 | 3c ultra | .35 | .20 |
| **63** | A18 | 5c gray | .35 | .20 |
| **64** | A18 | 10c vermilion | .35 | .20 |
| **65** | A18 | 11c brown | .35 | .35 |
| **66** | A18 | 20c orange | .35 | .35 |
| **67** | A18 | 25c maroon | .35 | *.55* |
| **68** | A18 | 50c yellow | .35 | *1.10* |
| **69** | A18 | 1p carmine lake | .35 | *1.90* |
| | | *Nos. 60-69 (10)* | 3.50 | *5.25* |

400th anniversary of the discovery of America by Columbus.

Nos. 63, 66-67 Surcharged

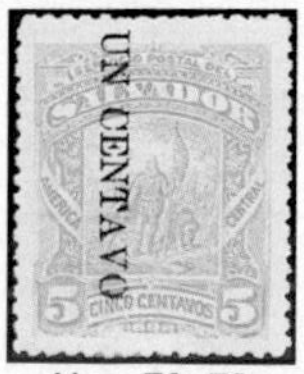

Nos. 70, 72

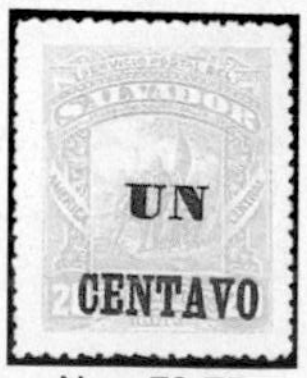

Nos. 73-75

Surcharged in Black, Red or Yellow

**1892**

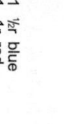

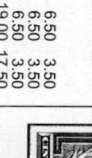

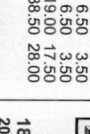

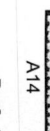

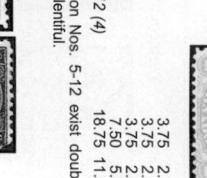

| | | | | |
|---|---|---|---|---|
| **70** | A18 | 1c on 5c gray (Bk) (down) | 1.00 | .65 |
| *a.* | | Surcharge reading up | 1.75 | 1.10 |
| **72** | A18 | 1c on 5c gray (R) (up) | 1.00 | .80 |
| *a.* | | Surcharge reading down | | |
| **73** | A18 | 1c on 20c org (Bk) | 1.50 | .75 |
| *a.* | | Inverted surcharge | 3.50 | 2.50 |
| *b.* | | "V" of "CENTAVO" inverted | 3.50 | 2.50 |
| | | *Nos. 70-73 (3)* | 3.50 | 2.20 |

**Similar Surcharge in Yellow or Blue, "centavo" in lower case letters**

| | | | | |
|---|---|---|---|---|
| **74** | A18 | 1c on 25c mar (Y) | 1.50 | 1.25 |
| *a.* | | Inverted surcharge | 2.50 | 2.50 |
| **75** | A18 | 1c on 25c mar (Bl) | *200.00* | *200.00* |
| *a.* | | Double surcharge (Bl + Bk) | *225.00* | *225.00* |

Counterfeits exist of Nos. 75 and 75a. Nos. 75, 75a have been questioned.

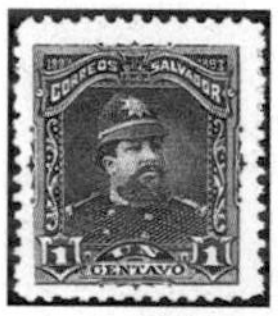
Pres. Carlos Ezeta — A21

**1893** **Engr.**

| | | | | |
|---|---|---|---|---|
| **76** | A21 | 1c blue | .20 | .20 |
| **77** | A21 | 2c brown red | .20 | .20 |
| **78** | A21 | 3c purple | .20 | .20 |
| **79** | A21 | 5c deep brown | .20 | .20 |
| **80** | A21 | 10c orange brown | .20 | .20 |
| **81** | A21 | 11c vermilion | .25 | *.25* |
| **82** | A21 | 20c green | .25 | *.30* |
| **83** | A21 | 25c dk olive gray | .25 | *.40* |
| **84** | A21 | 50c red orange | .25 | *.50* |
| **85** | A21 | 1p black | .30 | *.75* |
| | | *Nos. 76-85 (10)* | 2.30 | *3.20* |

For surcharge see No. 89.

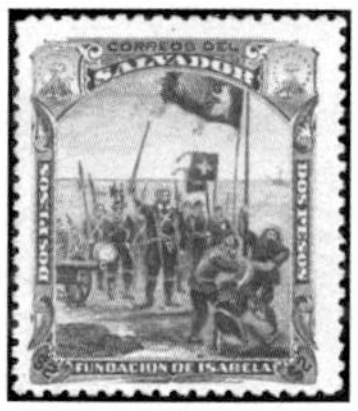
Founding City of Isabela — A22

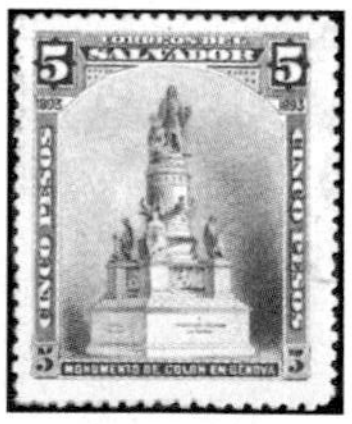
Columbus Statue, Genoa — A23

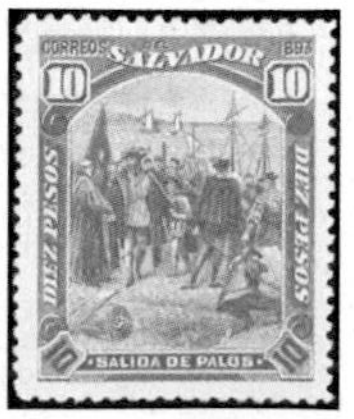
Departure from Palos — A24

**1893**

| | | | | |
|---|---|---|---|---|
| **86** | A22 | 2p green | .75 | — |
| **87** | A23 | 5p violet | .75 | |
| **88** | A24 | 10p orange | .75 | |
| | | *Nos. 86-88 (3)* | 2.25 | |

Discoveries by Columbus. No. 86 is known on cover, but experts are not positive that Nos. 87 and 88 were postally used.

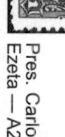

No. 77 Surcharged "UN CENTAVO"

**1893**

| | | | | |
|---|---|---|---|---|
| **89** | A21 | 1c on 2c brown red | .50 | .40 |
| *a.* | | "CENTNVO" | 3.00 | 2.50 |

Liberty — A26

Columbus before Council of Salamanca A27

Columbus Protecting Indian Hostages A28

Columbus Received by Ferdinand and Isabella A29

**1894, Jan.**

| | | | | |
|---|---|---|---|---|
| **91** | A26 | 1c brown | .20 | .20 |
| **92** | A26 | 2c blue | .20 | .20 |
| **93** | A26 | 3c maroon | .20 | .20 |
| **94** | A26 | 5c orange brn | .20 | .20 |
| **95** | A26 | 10c violet | .20 | .20 |
| **96** | A26 | 11c vermilion | .20 | .25 |
| **97** | A26 | 20c dark blue | .20 | .30 |
| **98** | A26 | 25c orange | .20 | .40 |
| **99** | A26 | 50c black | .20 | .65 |
| **100** | A26 | 1p slate blue | .20 | .90 |
| **101** | A27 | 2p deep blue | .75 | |
| **102** | A28 | 5p carmine lake | .75 | |
| **103** | A29 | 10p deep brown | .75 | |
| | | *Nos. 91-103 (13)* | 4.25 | |
| | | *Nos. 91-100 (10)* | | *3.50* |

Nos. 101-103 for the discoveries by Columbus. Experts are not positive that these were postally used.

No. 96 Surcharged

**1894, Dec.**

| | | | | |
|---|---|---|---|---|
| **104** | A26 | 1c on 11c vermilion | 1.50 | .65 |
| *a.* | | "Ccntavo" | *40.00* | *40.00* |
| *b.* | | Double surcharge | | |

Coat of Arms
A31 A32

Arms Overprint in Second Color
Various Frames

**1895, Jan. 1**

| | | | | |
|---|---|---|---|---|
| **105** | A31 | 1c olive & green | .20 | .20 |
| **106** | A31 | 2c dk green & bl | .20 | .20 |
| *a.* | | 2c dark green & green | 1.00 | .85 |
| **107** | A31 | 3c brown & brown | .20 | .20 |
| **108** | A31 | 5c blue & brown | .20 | .20 |
| **109** | A31 | 10c orange & brn | .20 | *.25* |
| **110** | A31 | 12c magenta & brn | .20 | *.30* |
| **111** | A31 | 15c ver & ver | .20 | *.35* |
| **112** | A31 | 20c yellow & brn | .20 | *.40* |
| *a.* | | Inverted overprint | 2.00 | |
| **113** | A31 | 24c violet & brn | .20 | *.45* |
| **114** | A31 | 30c dp blue & blue | .20 | *.50* |
| **115** | A31 | 50c carmine & brn | .20 | *.65* |
| **116** | A31 | 1p black & brn | .20 | *.90* |
| | | *Nos. 105-116 (12)* | 2.40 | *4.60* |

As printed, Nos. 105-116 portrayed Gen. Antonio Ezeta, brother of Pres. Carlos Ezeta. Before issuance, Ezeta's overthrow caused the government to obliterate his features with the national arms overprint. The 3c, 10c, 30c exist without overprint. Value $1 each.

*Reprints of 2c are in dark yellow green on thick paper. Value 20 cents.*

Various Frames

**1895** **Engr.** ***Perf. 12***

| | | | | |
|---|---|---|---|---|
| **117** | A32 | 1c olive | .55 | .50 |
| **118** | A32 | 2c dk blue grn | .20 | .20 |
| **119** | A32 | 3c brown | .20 | .20 |
| **120** | A32 | 5c blue | .20 | .20 |
| **121** | A32 | 10c orange | .65 | .30 |
| **122** | A32 | 12c claret | .65 | .30 |
| **123** | A32 | 15c vermilion | .20 | *.30* |
| **124** | A32 | 20c deep green | .20 | *.50* |
| **125** | A32 | 24c violet | .20 | *.50* |
| **126** | A32 | 30c deep blue | .20 | *.45* |
| **127** | A32 | 50c carmine lake | 1.25 | *1.25* |
| **128** | A32 | 1p gray black | 1.50 | *1.75* |
| | | *Nos. 117-128 (12)* | 6.00 | *6.45* |

*The reprints are on thicker paper than the originals, and many of the shades differ. Value 15c each.*

Nos. 122, 124-126 Surcharged in Black or Red:

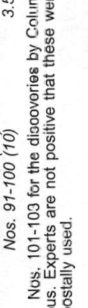

**1895**

| | | | | |
|---|---|---|---|---|
| **129** | A32 | 1c on 12c claret (Bk) | 1.00 | .90 |
| **130** | A32 | 1c on 24c violet | 1.00 | .90 |
| **131** | A32 | 1c on 30c dp blue | 1.00 | .90 |
| **132** | A32 | 2c on 20c dp green | 1.00 | .90 |
| **133** | A32 | 3c on 30c dp blue | 1.25 | 1.10 |
| *a.* | | Double surcharge | 4.50 | |
| | | *Nos. 129-133 (5)* | 5.25 | 4.70 |

"Peace" — A45

**1896, Jan. 1** **Engr.** **Unwmk.**

| | | | | |
|---|---|---|---|---|
| **134** | A45 | 1c blue | .20 | .20 |
| **135** | A45 | 2c dark brown | .20 | .20 |
| **136** | A45 | 3c blue green | .20 | .20 |
| **137** | A45 | 5c brown olive | .20 | .20 |
| **138** | A45 | 10c yellow | .20 | .20 |
| **139** | A45 | 12c dark blue | .75 | .90 |
| **140** | A45 | 15c brt ultra | .20 | *.20* |
| *a.* | | 15c light violet | 1.10 | *2.00* |
| **141** | A45 | 20c magenta | .65 | .50 |
| **142** | A45 | 24c vermilion | .20 | *.25* |
| **143** | A45 | 30c orange | .20 | *.40* |
| **144** | A45 | 50c black brn | .20 | *.50* |
| **145** | A45 | 1p rose lake | .20 | *.90* |
| | | *Nos. 134-145 (12)* | 3.40 | *4.65* |

The frames of Nos. 134-145 differ slightly on each denomination.

For overprints see Nos. O1-O12, O37-O48.

**Wmk. 117**

| | | | | |
|---|---|---|---|---|
| **145B** | A45 | 2c dark brown | .20 | .20 |

*The 1c, 2c, 12c, 20c, 30c, 50c and 1p on unwatermarked paper and the 2c on watermarked have been reprinted. The paper is thicker than that of the originals and the shades are different. The watermark is always upright on original stamps of Salvador, sideways on the reprints. Value 15c each.*

Coat of Arms — A46

"White House" — A47

Locomotive A48

Mt. San Miguel A49

Ocean Steamship
A50 A51

Post Office A52

Lake Ilopango A53

Atehausillas Waterfall A54

Coat of Arms A55

Coat of Arms A56

Columbus A57

**1896**

| | | | | |
|---|---|---|---|---|
| **146** | A46 | 1c emerald | .20 | .20 |
| **147** | A47 | 2c lake | .20 | .20 |
| **148** | A48 | 3c yellow brn | .20 | .20 |
| **149** | A49 | 5c deep blue | .20 | .20 |
| **150** | A50 | 10c brown | .20 | .20 |
| **151** | A51 | 12c slate | .20 | *.20* |
| **152** | A52 | 15c blue green | .20 | .25 |
| **153** | A53 | 20c carmine rose | .20 | *.30* |
| **154** | A54 | 24c violet | .20 | *.40* |
| **155** | A55 | 30c deep green | .20 | .40 |
| **156** | A56 | 50c orange | .20 | *.40* |
| **157** | A57 | 100c dark blue | .20 | *.90* |
| | | *Nos. 146-157 (12)* | 2.40 | *3.85* |

Nos. 146-157 exist imperf.

**Unwmk.**

| | | | | |
|---|---|---|---|---|
| **157B** | A46 | 1c emerald | .20 | .20 |
| **157C** | A47 | 2c lake | .20 | .20 |
| **157D** | A48 | 3c yellow brn | .20 | .20 |
| **157E** | A49 | 5c deep blue | .20 | .20 |
| **157F** | A50 | 10c brown | .20 | .20 |
| **157G** | A51 | 12c slate | .20 | .20 |
| **157I** | A52 | 15c blue green | .25 | .20 |
| **157J** | A53 | 20c carmine rose | .20 | *.45* |
| **157K** | A54 | 24c violet | .50 | *.80* |
| **157M** | A55 | 30c deep green | .20 | *.55* |
| **157N** | A56 | 50c orange | .20 | *.55* |
| **157O** | A57 | 100c dark blue | .20 | *1.00* |
| | | *Nos. 157B-157O (12)* | 2.75 | *4.75* |

See Nos. 159-170L. For surcharges and overprints see Nos. 158, 158D, 171-174C, O13-O36, O49-O72, O79-O126.

*The 15c, 30c, 50c and 100c have been reprinted on watermarked and the 1c, 2c, 3c, 5c, 12c, 20c, 24c and 100c on unwatermarked paper. The papers of the reprints are thicker than those of the originals and the shades are different. Value, set of 12, $1.20.*

Black Surcharge on Nos. 154, 157K

**1896** **Wmk. 117**

| | | | | |
|---|---|---|---|---|
| **158** | A54 | 15c on 24c violet | 4.00 | 4.00 |
| *a.* | | Double surcharge | | |
| *b.* | | Inverted surcharge | 8.50 | |

**Unwmk.**

| | | | | |
|---|---|---|---|---|
| **158D** | A54 | 15c on 24c violet | 4.00 | 3.00 |

Exist spelled "Qnince."

Types of 1896

**1897** **Engr.** **Wmk. 117**

| | | | | |
|---|---|---|---|---|
| **159** | A46 | 1c scarlet | *.20* | *.20* |
| **160** | A47 | 2c yellow grn | .20 | .20 |
| **161** | A48 | 3c bister brn | .20 | .20 |
| **162** | A49 | 5c orange | .20 | .20 |
| **163** | A50 | 10c blue grn | .20 | .20 |
| **164** | A51 | 12c blue | .40 | .30 |
| **165** | A52 | 15c black | 2.50 | 2.00 |
| **166** | A53 | 20c slate | .20 | .20 |
| **167** | A54 | 24c yellow | .20 | .25 |
| **168** | A55 | 30c rose | .20 | .20 |
| **169** | A56 | 50c violet | .20 | .50 |
| **170** | A57 | 100c brown lake | 2.50 | 2.00 |
| | | *Nos. 159-170 (12)* | 7.20 | 6.45 |

**Unwmk.**

| | | | | |
|---|---|---|---|---|
| **170A** | A46 | 1c scarlet | .20 | .20 |
| **170B** | A47 | 2c yellow grn | .20 | .20 |
| **170C** | A48 | 3c bister brn | .20 | .20 |
| **170D** | A49 | 5c orange | .20 | .20 |
| **170E** | A50 | 10c blue grn | .75 | .50 |
| **170F** | A51 | 12c blue | .75 | .75 |
| **170G** | A52 | 15c black | 2.00 | 2.00 |
| **170H** | A53 | 20c slate | .20 | *.25* |
| **170I** | A54 | 24c yellow | .20 | *.50* |
| **170J** | A55 | 30c rose | 1.90 | 1.25 |
| **170K** | A56 | 50c violet | .90 | .90 |
| **170L** | A57 | 100c brown lake | 6.25 | 6.25 |
| | | *Nos. 170A-170L (12)* | 13.75 | 13.20 |

*The 1c, 2c, 3c, 5c, 12c, 15c, 50c and 100c have been reprinted on watermarked and the entire issue on unwatermarked paper. The papers of the reprints are thicker than those of the originals. Value, set of 20, $2.*

Surcharged in Red or Black

**1897** **Wmk. 117**

| | | | | |
|---|---|---|---|---|
| **171** | A54 | 13c on 24c yel (R) | 2.50 | 2.50 |
| **172** | A55 | 13c on 30c rose (Bk) | 2.50 | 2.50 |
| **173** | A56 | 13c on 50c vio (Bk) | 2.50 | 2.50 |
| **174** | A57 | 13c on 100c brn lake (Bk) | 2.50 | 2.50 |

**Unwmk.**

| | | | | |
|---|---|---|---|---|
| **174A** | A54 | 13c on 24c yel (R) | 2.50 | 2.50 |
| **174B** | A55 | 13c on 30c rose (Bk) | 2.50 | 2.50 |
| **174C** | A56 | 13c on 50c vio (Bk) | 2.50 | 2.50 |
| | | *Nos. 171-174C (7)* | 17.50 | 17.50 |

Coat of Arms of "Republic of Central America" — A59

ONE CENTAVO:
Originals: The mountains are outlined in red and blue. The sea is represented by short red and dark blue lines on a light blue background.
*Reprints: The mountains are outlined in red only. The sea is printed in green and dark blue, much blurred.*

FIVE CENTAVOS:
Originals: The sea is represented by horizontal and diagonal lines of dark blue on a light blue background.
*Reprints: The sea is printed in green and dark blue, much blurred. The inscription in gold is in thicker letters.*

**1897** **Litho.**

| | | | | |
|---|---|---|---|---|
| **175** | A59 | 1c bl, gold, rose & grn | .50 | *1.50* |
| **176** | A59 | 5c rose, gold, bl & grn | .50 | *1.50* |

Forming of the "Republic of Central America."

For overprints see Nos. O73-O76.

*Stamps of type A59 formerly listed as "Type II" are now known to be reprints.*

EL SALVADOR

Allegory of Central
American Union — A60

### 1898

| | | | | |
|---|---|---|---|---|
| 177 | A60 | 1c orange ver | .20 | .20 |
| 178 | A60 | 2c rose | .20 | .20 |
| 179 | A60 | 3c pale yel grn | .20 | .20 |
| 180 | A60 | 5c blue | .20 | .20 |
| 181 | A60 | 10c blue green | .20 | .20 |
| 182 | A60 | 12c violet | .20 | .20 |
| 183 | A60 | 13c brown lake | .20 | .20 |
| 184 | A60 | 20c deep blue | .20 | .20 |
| 185 | A60 | 24c deep blue | .20 | .35 |
| 186 | A60 | 26c deep ultra | .20 | .40 |
| 187 | A60 | 50c bister brn | .20 | .75 |
| 188 | A60 | 1p yellow | .40 | 1.00 |
| | | Nos. 177-188 (12) | 2.40 | 4.25 |

**Engr.** **Wmk. 117**

No. 180 Overprinted
Vertically, up or down
in Black, Violet, Red,
Magenta and Yellow

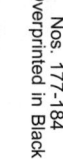

Tránsito
Territorial

No. 180 Overprinted
used in 1899-1900.

### 1899

| | | | | |
|---|---|---|---|---|
| 189 | A60 | 5c blue grn (Bk) | 7.50 | 6.25 |
| | | Italic 3rd "r" in "Territorial" | 12.50 | 12.50 |
| | a. | Double ovpt. (Bk + Y) | 37.50 | 37.50 |
| 190 | A60 | 5c blue grn (R) | 82.50 | 82.50 |
| 191 | A60 | 5c blue grn (V) | 70.00 | 70.00 |
| 191A | A60 | 5c blue grn (M) | 75.00 | 75.00 |
| 191B | A60 | 5c blue grn (Y) | 305.00 | 303.75 |
| | | Nos. 189-191B (5) | | |

Counterfeits exist.

Nos. 177-184
Overprinted in Black

Counterfeits exist of the "wheel" overprint
used in 1899-1900.

Inscribed: "Estado de El Salvador"

| **Ceres** | | **Unwmk.** | **Litho.** | **Perf. 12** |
|---|---|---|---|---|
| ("Estado") — A61 | | | | |
| 192 | A61 | 1c orange ver | 1.00 | .50 |
| 193 | A61 | 2c rose | 1.25 | 1.00 |
| 194 | A61 | 3c pale yel grn | 1.25 | .50 |
| 195 | A61 | 5c blue green | 2.00 | 1.25 |
| 196 | A61 | 10c gray blue | 2.00 | 2.00 |
| 197 | A61 | 12c violet | 3.25 | 2.50 |
| 198 | A61 | 13c brown lake | 3.25 | 2.00 |
| 198A | A61 | 5c blue grn | — | — |
| | | Nos. 192-198 (7) | 13.25 | 8.25 |

For overprints and surcharges see Nos.
189-198A, 224-241, 269A-269B, O129-O142,
210-223, 242-252D, O143-O185.

For overprints and surcharges see Nos.
189-198A, 224-241, 269A-269B, O129-O142,
210-223, 242-252D, O143-O185.
#208-209 were probably not placed in use.

Same, Overprinted

**Red Overprint**

| 210 | A61 | 1c brown | 50.00 | 32.50 |
|---|---|---|---|---|

**Blue Overprint**

| 211 | A61 | 1c brown | .50 | .20 |
| 212 | A61 | 10c brown org | .50 | .20 |
| 212A | A61 | 10c chocolate | 5.00 | 3.50 |

**Black Overprint**

| 213 | A61 | 1c brown | .50 | .20 |
| 214 | A61 | 2c gray grn | .75 | .20 |
| 215 | A61 | 3c blue | .75 | .20 |
| 216 | A61 | 5c light blue | .20 | .20 |
| 217 | A61 | 10c chocolate | .35 | .20 |
| 218 | A61 | 12c dark green | .50 | .20 |
| 219 | A61 | 13c pale rose | 1.00 | .65 |
| 220 | A61 | 24c light blue | 1.10 | .50 |
| 221 | A61 | 26c car rose | 12.50 | 10.00 |
| 222 | A61 | 50c orange red | 3.25 | 2.00 |
| 223 | A61 | 100c violet | 3.25 | 3.25 |
| | | Nos. 213-223 (11) | 27.45 | 20.20 |

"Wheel" overprint exists double and triple.

No. 177 Handstamped

| 225 | A60 | 1c orange ver | 15.00 | 15.00 |

No. 177 Overprinted

**1900**

| 224 | A60 | 1c orange ver | 1.00 | 1.00 |

**Wmk. 117**

Stamps of 1898
Surcharged in Black

**1 centavo**

### 1900

| 226 | A60 | 1c on 10c gray | 5.00 | 4.25 |
| 227 | A60 | 1c on 13c brn blue | 7.50 | 6.50 |
| | a. | "eentavo" | | |
| 228 | A60 | 2c on 12c vio | 275.00 | |
| 229 | A60 | 2c on 13c brn lake | 30.00 | |
| 230 | A60 | 5c on 20c dp blue | 2.00 | 1.75 |
| | a. | Inverted surcharge | 3.25 | 2.75 |
| | b. | "1900" omitted | 5.00 | 4.00 |
| 230B | A60 | 2c on 26c bis brn | 2.00 | 2.00 |
| 231 | A60 | 2c on 26c bis brn | 37.50 | 37.50 |
| 232 | A60 | 3c on 50c org | 35.00 | 35.00 |
| | a. | Inverted surcharge | | |
| 233 | A60 | 5c on 12c vio | 10.00 | 10.00 |
| 234 | A60 | 5c on 24c ultra | 11.00 | 11.00 |
| | a. | "eentavo" | | |
| 235 | A60 | 5c on 26c bis brn | 37.50 | 37.50 |
| 236 | A60 | 5c on 1p yel | 15.00 | 15.00 |
| | a. | Inverted surcharge | | |

With Additional Overprint in
Black

| 237 | | | 2.50 | 2.50 |
| | a. | "eentavo" vio | 2.50 | |
| | b. | Inverted surcharge | 8.00 | |
| | c. | "centavos" (plural) | 75.00 | |
| | d. | "1900" omitted | | |
| 238 | A60 | 2c on 12c brn lake | 42.50 | 42.50 |
| 239 | A60 | 3c on 26c bis brn | 67.50 | 67.50 |

Inscribed: "Republica de El Salvador"

Handstamped in Violet or
Black

**Ceres**
("Republica") — A63

There are two varieties of the 1c, type A63,
one with the word "centavo" in the middle of
the label (#253, 263, 270, 299, 305, 326), the
other with "centavo" nearer the left end than
the right (#270, 299, 305, 326).
The stamps of type A63 are found in a great
variety of shades. Stamps of type A63 without
handstamp were not regularly issued.

| **1900** | | | | |
|---|---|---|---|---|
| 242 | A61 | 1c on 13c dp rose | .40 | .40 |
| | a. | "eentavo" | 1.00 | .75 |
| | b. | Inverted surcharge | 1.50 | .75 |
| | c. | "1 centavo 1" | 4.50 | 3.00 |
| | d. | Double surcharge | | |
| 243 | A61 | 2c on 12c dk grn | 1.75 | 1.25 |
| | a. | "eentavo" | 3.00 | 2.50 |
| 244 | A61 | 2c on 13c dp rose | 1.00 | .75 |
| | a. | "eentavo" | 1.00 | 1.25 |
| | b. | Inverted surcharge | 2.00 | 1.40 |
| 245 | A61 | 3c on 12c dk grn | 3.00 | |
| | a. | Double surcharge | 3.00 | |
| | b. | Inverted surcharge | 3.00 | |
| | c. | Double surcharge | 4.00 | |
| | | Nos. 242-245 (4) | 4.15 | 3.25 |

Same Surcharge on Stamps of 1899
Without Wheel

With Additional Overprint in
Black

| 246 | A61 | 1c on 2c gray | .25 | .20 |
| | a. | "eentavo" | | .66 |
| | b. | Inverted eurahcrgo | 3.00 | |
| 247 | A61 | 1c on 13c dp | 1.00 | .85 |
| | | rose | | |
| 248 | A61 | 2c on 12c dk | 1.40 | 1.00 |
| | a. | "eentavo" grn | 1.25 | |
| | b. | Double surcharge | | |
| 249 | A61 | 2c on 13c dp | 1.40 | .90 |
| | a. | "eentavo" grn | 1.50 | 1.25 |
| | b. | Inverted surcharge | 2.50 | 2.25 |
| 250 | A61 | 3c on 12c dk | 42.50 | |
| | | rose | | |
| 251 | A61 | 5c on 24c lt bl | 2.50 | 1.25 |
| | a. | Inverted surcharge | 4.00 | 4.00 |
| 252 | A61 | 5c on 26c car | 1.10 | 1.00 |
| | a. | "1 centavo 1" | 2.50 | 1.50 |
| | b. | Inverted surcharge | 4.00 | 1.50 |
| 252D | A61 | 5c on 1c on 26c | 7.65 | 5.20 |
| | | car rose | | |

Counterfeits exist of the surcharges on Nos.
242-252D and the "wheel" overprint on Nos.
246-252D.

Stamps of 1900
Overpriced in Black

| **1903** | | **Engr.** | **Perf. 14, 14½** | |
|---|---|---|---|---|
| | | | | **Wmk. 173** |
| 283 | A64 | 1c green | .35 | .20 |
| 284 | A64 | 2c carmine | .35 | .20 |
| 285 | A64 | 3c rose | .80 | .50 |
| 286 | A64 | 5c dark blue | .35 | .20 |
| 287 | A64 | 10c dull violet | .40 | .20 |
| 288 | A64 | 12c slate | 2.50 | .40 |
| 289 | A64 | 13c red brown | 2.50 | 1.25 |
| 290 | A64 | 24c scarlet | 2.50 | 1.25 |
| 291 | A64 | 50c yellow brn | 3.75 | 2.50 |
| 292 | A64 | 100c grnsh blue | 13.00 | 7.45 |
| 293 | A64 | 13c yel brown | 6.00 | 4.65 |
| | | Nos. 283-293 (11) | | |

For surcharges and overprint see Nos. 312-
316, 318-325, O253.

Morazán
Monument — A64

Stamps of 1900 with Shield in Black
Overprinted:

**1905** **1905**

(5¾x13½mm) — (5x14¾mm)
a b

## 1905

**(4½x16mm) — c**    **1905**    *Perf. 12*

**(4½x13½mm) — d**    **1905**

**(5x14½mm) — e**    **1905**

**1905-06**   **Unwmk.**   *Perf. 12*

### Blue Overprint
| | | | |
|---|---|---|---|
| 293A | A63 (a) | 2c rose | 3.00 |
| 294 | A63 (a) | 3c gray blk | 4.00 |
| 295 | A63 (a) | 5c blue | 4.50  3.00 |

*a.* Without shield

### Purple Overprint
| | | | |
|---|---|---|---|
| 296 | A63 (b) | 3c gray blk (Shield in pur) | 4.00 |
| 296A | A63 (b) | 5c bl (Shield in pue) | 4.50 |
| 297 | A63 (b) | 3c gray blk | 3.25  3.00 |
| 298 | A63 (b) | 5c blue | 6.00  4.50 |
| | | | 4.00  3.00 |

### Black Overprint
| | | | |
|---|---|---|---|
| 298A | A63 (b) | 5c blue | |

### Blue Overprint
| | | | |
|---|---|---|---|
| 299 | A63 (c) | 1c green | 6.50  3.00 |
| 299B | A63 (c) | 2c rose | .40  .35 |

*c.* "1905" vert.   .80

| | | | |
|---|---|---|---|
| 300 | A63 (c) | 5c blue | 1.25  .60 |
| 301 | A63 (c) | 10c deep blue | .75  .60 |

### Black Overprint
| | | | |
|---|---|---|---|
| 302 | A63 (c) | 2c rose | 1.50 |
| 303 | A63 (c) | 5c blue | 12.50  12.50 |
| 304 | A63 (c) | 10c deep blue | 6.00  3.50 |

### Blue Overprint
| | | | |
|---|---|---|---|
| 305 | A63 (d) | 1c green | 7.00  6.50 |
| 306 | A63 (d) | 2c rose, ovpt. vert. | 1.50 |

*a.* Overprint horiz.   6.00

| | | | |
|---|---|---|---|
| 306B | A63 (d) | 3c gray black | 7.00  1.75 |
| 307 | A63 (d) | 5c blue | 2.50  1.00 |

### Blue Overprint
| | | | |
|---|---|---|---|
| 311 | AC3 (e) | 2c roso | 4.00  2.00 |

*a.* Without shield   6.50  3.00

### Black Overprint
| | | | |
|---|---|---|---|
| 311B | A63 (e) | 5c blue | 20.00  19.00 |
| | | 10c blue | 106.90  76.80 |

These overprints are found double, inverted, omitted, etc. Counterfeits exist.

**Regular Issue of 1903 with New Values:**

| | | | |
|---|---|---|---|
| 312 | A64 (f) | 1c on 2c car | .25 |

*a.* Double surcharge   3.00

### Red Surcharge
| | | | |
|---|---|---|---|
| 312B | A64 (g) | 5c on 12c slate | .75  .50 |

*b.* Double surcharge
*c.* Black surcharge   3.50  3.50
*d.* As 'd, double surcharge

### Blue Handstamped Surcharge
| | | | |
|---|---|---|---|
| 313 | A64 (h) | 1c on 2c car | .25  .20 |
| 314 | A64 (h) | 1c on 10c vio | |
| 315 | A64 (h) | 1c on 12c sl ('06) | 1.00  .50 |
| 316 | A64 (h) | 1c on 13c red brm | 4.00  3.25 |

---

## No. 271 with Handstamped Surcharge in Blue

**Unwmk.**

| | | | |
|---|---|---|---|
| 317 | A63 (h) | 1c on 2c rose | 42.50  37.50 |
| | | | 49.10  42.40 |

*Nos. 312-317 (7)*

The "h" is handstamped in strips of four stamps each differing from the others in the size of the upper figures of value and in the letters of the word "CENTAVO." particularly in the size of the "N" and the "O" of that word. The surcharge is known inverted, double, etc.

**Regular Issue of 1903 with Handstamped Surcharge:**

i   **5 5 5**   j   **5 5 5**   k

**Wmk. 173**

### Red Handstamped Surcharge
| | | | |
|---|---|---|---|
| 318 | A64 (i) | 5c on 12c slate | 3.00  1.50 |
| 319 | A64 (i) | 5c on 12c slate | 3.00  1.75 |

*a.* Blue surcharge

### Blue Handstamped Surcharge
| | | | |
|---|---|---|---|
| 320 | A64 (k) | 5c on 12c slate | 2.50  1.75 |
| | | | 8.50  5.00 |

*Nos. 318-320 (3)*

One or more of the numerals in the handstamped surcharges on Nos. 318, 319 and 320 are frequently omitted, inverted, etc.

**Surcharged:**

l   **6 6**

 m

**6CENTAVOS**   l

### Blue Handstamped Surcharge
| | | | |
|---|---|---|---|
| 321 | A64 (l) | 6c on 12c slate | .50  .30 |
| 322 | A64 (l) | 6c on 13c red brm | 1.00  .40 |

### Red Handstamped Surcharge
| | | | |
|---|---|---|---|
| 323 | A64 (l) | 6c on 12c slate | 17.50  12.00 |

Type "l" is handstamped in strips of four varieties, differing in the size of the numerals and letters. The surcharge is known double and inverted.

### Black Surcharge
| | | | |
|---|---|---|---|
| 324 | A64 (m) | 1c on 12c red brn | 1.50  1.00 |

*a.* Double surcharge   4.00  3.00
*b.* Right "1" & dot omitted
*c.* Both numerals omitted

| | | | |
|---|---|---|---|
| 325 | A64 (m) | 3c on 13c red brm | .50  .40 |

Counterfeits of Nos. 326-335 abound.

**01905**   n

## Stamps of 1900, with Shield in Black, Overprinted — n

**1905**   **Unwmk.**

### Blue Overprint
| | | | |
|---|---|---|---|
| 326 | A63 (n) | 1c green | 7.00  3.25 |

*a.* Inverted overprint

| | | | |
|---|---|---|---|
| 327 | A63 (n) | 2c rose | 3.25  3.25 |

*a.* Vertical overprint   5.00

| | | | |
|---|---|---|---|
| 327B | A63 (n) | 3c black | 9.00  5.00 |
| 328 | A63 (n) | 5c blue | 30.00  27.50 |
| 328A | A63 (n) | 10c deep blue | 12.50  10.00 |

### Black Overprint
| | | | |
|---|---|---|---|
| 328A | A63 (n) | 10c deep blue | 7.50  4.50 |
| | | (6) | 66.25  53.00 |

Counterfeits of Nos. 326-335 abound.

---

## Stamps of 1900, with Shield in Black Surcharged or Overprinted:

**1906**   **5**   **1906**

o   **2 2**   p   **1906**   q

### 1906 — Blue and Black Surcharge
| | | | |
|---|---|---|---|
| 329 | A63 (o) | 2c on 26c brn | 2.50 |
| 330 | A63 (o) | 3c on 26c brn org | .50  7.50 |

*a.* "2" & dot double   .40
| | | | |
|---|---|---|---|
| | | | 4.00  3.25 |
| | | | 7.50 |
| 331 | A63 (o) | 3c on 26c brn | 2.50 |

### Black Surcharge or Overprint
*a.* Disks & numerals omitted
*b.* "3" and disks double
*c.* "1906" omitted

| | | | |
|---|---|---|---|
| 333 | A63 (p) | 10c deep blue | 4.00  3.75 |
| 334 | A63 (p) | 10c deep blue | 3.50  3.50 |
| 334A | A63 (p) | 26c brown org | 22.50  20.00 |

*a.* "1906" in black

### No. 257 Overprinted in Black
| | | | |
|---|---|---|---|
| 335 | A63 (q) | 10c dp bl (Shield in violet) | 17.50  15.00 |

*a.* Overprint type "p"   55.00  48.40

*Nos. 329-335 (7)*

There are numerous varieties of these surcharges and overprints.

**Nos. 336-338 Overprinted in Black**

**1907**

| | | | |
|---|---|---|---|
| 349 | A65 | 1c green & blk | .25  .20 |

*a.* Shield in red   3.50

| | | | |
|---|---|---|---|
| 350 | A65 | 2c red & blk | .25  .20 |

*a.* Shield in red   3.50

| | | | |
|---|---|---|---|
| 351 | A65 | 3c yellow & blk | .75  .60 |

*Nos. 349-351 (3)*

Reprints of Nos. 349 to 351 have the same characteristics as the reprints of the preceding issue. Value, set of 3, 15c.

---

**Pres. Pedro José Escalón — A65**

**1906**   **Engr.**   *Perf. 11½*

**Glazed Paper**
| | | | |
|---|---|---|---|
| 336 | A65 | 1c green & blk | .20  .20 |
| 337 | A65 | Thin paper | .75  .20 |
| 338 | A65 | 2c red & blk | .20  .20 |
| 339 | A65 | 3c yellow & blk | .20  .20 |
| | | 5c ultra & blk | .20  .20 |

*a.* 5c dark blue & black   .20

| | | | |
|---|---|---|---|
| 340 | A65 | 6c carmine & blk | .20  .20 |
| 341 | A65 | 10c violet & blk | .20  .20 |
| 342 | A65 | 12c violet & blk | .20  .20 |
| 343 | A65 | 13c dk brn & blk | .35  .35 |
| 345 | A65 | 24c carmine & blk | .35  .35 |
| 346 | A65 | 26c choc & blk | .35  .45 |
| 347 | A65 | 50c yellow & blk | .45 |
| 348 | A65 | 100c blue & blk | 3.00  3.00 |
| | | | 5.65  5.75 |

*Nos. 336-348 (12)*

All values of this set are known imperforate but are not believed to have been issued in this condition.

See Nos. O263-O272. For overprints and surcharges see Nos. 349-354.

The entire set has been reprinted. The shades of the reprints differ from those of the originals, the paper is thicker and the perforation 12. Value, set of 12, $1.20.

---

## Stamps of 1906 Surcharged with Shield and

| | | | |
|---|---|---|---|
| 352 | A65 | 1c on 5c ultra & blk | .20  .20 |
| | | 1c on 5c dark blue & black | .35  .35 |

*a.* Inverted surcharge   .45  .45
*b.* Double surcharge

| | | | |
|---|---|---|---|
| 352D | A65 | 1c on 6c rose & blk | 1.25  1.25 |

*e.* Double surcharge   2.00  1.00

| | | | |
|---|---|---|---|
| 353 | A65 | 2c on 6c rose & blk | .50  .35 |
| 354 | A65 | 10c on 6c rose & blk | 2.90  1.75 |

*Nos. 352-354 (4)*

The above surcharges are frequently found with the shield double, inverted, or otherwise misplaced.

---

**National Palace — A66**

**Overprinted with Shield in Black**

**1907**   **Engr.**   **Unwmk.**

**Paper with or without colored dots**
| | | | |
|---|---|---|---|
| 355 | A66 | 1c green & blk | .20  .20 |
| 356 | A66 | 2c red & blk | .20  .20 |
| 357 | A66 | 3c blue & blk | .20  .20 |
| 358 | A66 | 5c blue & blk | .20  .20 |

*a.* 5c ultramarine & black

| | | | |
|---|---|---|---|
| 359 | A66 | 6c ver & blk | .20  .20 |

*a.* Shield in red   3.25

| | | | |
|---|---|---|---|
| 360 | A66 | 10c violet & blk | .20  .20 |
| 361 | A66 | 12c violet & blk | .20  .20 |
| 362 | A66 | 13c sepia & blk | .20  .20 |
| 363 | A66 | 24c rose & blk | .30  .30 |
| 364 | A66 | 26c yel brn & blk | .30  .35 |
| 365 | A66 | 50c orange & blk | .50  .50 |
| | | 50c yellow & black | 3.60 |
| 366 | A66 | 100c turq bl & blk | 1.00  .50 |
| | | | 3.60  2.85 |

*Nos. 355-366 (12)*

Most values exist without shield, also with shield inverted, double, and otherwise misprinted. Many of these were never sold to the public.

See 2nd footnote following No. 421.

See Nos. 369-373, 397-401. For surcharges and overprints see Nos. 367-369A, 374-77, 414-421, 443-444, J71-J74, J76-J80, O329-O331.

---

**UN CENTAVO**

## No. 356 With Additional Surcharge in Black

**1908**

| | | | |
|---|---|---|---|
| 367 | A66 | 1c on 2c red & blk | 19.00  17.50 |
| | | | 27.50  25.00 |

*a.* Double surcharge
*b.* Inverted surcharge
*c.* Double surcharge, one inverted
*d.* Red surcharge

**Same Surcharged in Black or Red**

| | | | |
|---|---|---|---|
| 368 | A66 | 1c on 2c | .25  .25 |
| 368A | A66 | 1c on 2c (R) | 1.00  1.00 |
| | | | .50  .50 |

Counterfeits exist of the surcharges on Nos. 368-368A.

**Type of 1907**

**1909**   **Engr.**   **Wmk. 172**

| | | | |
|---|---|---|---|
| 369 | A66 | 1c green & blk | .20  .20 |
| 370 | A66 | 2c rose & blk | .20  .25 |
| 371 | A66 | 3c yellow & blk | .25  .25 |
| 372 | A66 | 5c blue & blk | .20  .20 |
| 373 | A66 | 10c violet & blk | .30  1.00 |

*Nos. 369-373 (5)*   1.20  1.00

The note after No. 366 will apply here also.

*(Bottom margin stamp images — f: UN CENTAVO, g: 5 CENTAVOS, h: 1 CENTAVO 1)*

1821
15 septiembre
1909

Nos. 355, 369 Overprinted in Red

**1909, Sept.** **Unwmk.**
**374** A66 1c green & blk 2.25 1.10
*a.* Inverted overprint 10.00

**Wmk. 172**
**375** A66 1c green & blk 1.75 1.40
*a.* Inverted overprint

88th anniv. of El Salvador's independence.

2
CENTAVOS
1909

Nos. 362, 364 Surcharged

**1909** **Unwmk.**
**376** A66 2c on 13c sep & blk 1.50 1.25
*a.* Inverted surcharge
**377** A66 3c on 26c yel brn & blk 1.75 1.40
*a.* Inverted surcharge

A67

A68

Design: Pres. Fernando Figueroa.

**1910** **Engr.** **Wmk. 172**
**378** A67 1c sepia & blk .20 .20
**379** A67 2c dk grn & blk .20 .20
**380** A67 3c orange & blk .20 .20
**381** A67 4c carmine & blk .20 .20
*a.* 4c scarlet & black .20 .20
**382** A67 5c purple & blk .20 .20
**383** A67 6c scarlet & blk .20 .20
**384** A67 10c purple & blk .20 .20
**385** A67 12c dp bl & blk .20 .20
**386** A67 17c ol grn & blk .20 .20
**387** A67 19c brn red & blk .20 .20
**388** A67 29c choc & blk .20 .20
**389** A67 50c yellow & blk .20 .20
**390** A67 100c turq bl & blk .20 .20
*Nos. 378-390 (13)* 2.60 2.60

**1911** **Unwmk.**

5c, José Matías Delgado. 6c, Manuel José Arce. 12c, Centenary Monument.

**Paper with colored dots**
**391** A68 5c dp blue & brn .20 .20
**392** A68 6c orange & brn .20 .20
**393** A68 12c violet & brn .20 .20

**Wmk. 172**
**394** A68 5c dp blue & brn .20 .20
**395** A68 6c orange & brn .20 .20
**396** A68 12c violet & brn .20 .20
*Nos. 391-396 (6)* 1.20 1.20

Centenary of the insurrection of 1811.

Palace Type of 1907 without Shield

**1911**
**Paper without colored dots**
**397** A66 1c scarlet .20 .20
**398** A66 2c chocolate .30 .30
*a.* Paper with brown dots
**399** A66 13c deep green .20 .20
**400** A66 24c yellow .20 .20
**401** A66 50c dark brown .20 .20
*Nos. 397-401 (5)* 1.10 1.10

José Matías Delgado — A71

Manuel José Arce — A72

Francisco Morazán A73

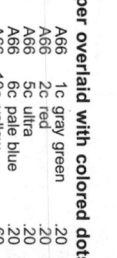

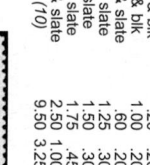

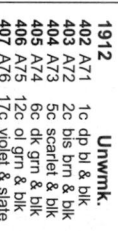

Rafael Campo A74

Trinidad Cabañas A75

Monument of Gerardo Barrios A76

Centenary Monument A77

National Palace A78

Rosales Hospital — A79

Coat of Arms — A80

**1912** **Unwmk.** ***Perf. 12***
**402** A71 1c dp bl & blk .20 .20
**403** A72 2c bis brn & blk .25 .20
**404** A73 5c scarlet & blk .25 .20
**405** A74 6c dk grn & blk .20 .20
**406** A75 12c ol grn & blk 1.00 .20
**407** A76 17c violet & slate .60 .20
**408** A77 19c scar & slate 1.25 .30
**409** A78 29c org & slate 1.50 .30
**410** A79 50c blue & slate 1.75 .45
**411** A80 1col black & slate 2.50 1.00
*Nos. 402-411 (10)* 9.50 3.25

Juan Manuel Rodríguez A81

Pres. Manuel E. Araujo A82

**1914** ***Perf. 11½***
**412** A81 10c orange & brn 2.50 .75
**413** A82 25c purple & brn 2.50 .75

Type of 1907 without Shield Overprinted in Black

1915

**1915**
**Paper overlaid with colored dots**
**414** A66 1c gray green .20 .20
**415** A66 2c red .20 .20
**416** A66 5c ultra .20 .20
**417** A66 6c pale blue .20 .20
**418** A66 10c yellow .60 .30
**419** A66 12c brown .50 .20
**420** A66 50c violet .20 .20
**421** A66 100c black brn 1.40 1.40
*Nos. 414-421 (8)* 3.50 2.90

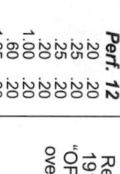

Varieties such as center omitted, center double, center inverted, imperforate exist with or without date, date inverted, date double, etc., but are believed to be entirely unofficial.

Preceding the stamps with the "1915" overprint a quantity of stamps of this type was overprinted with the letter "S." Evidence is lacking that they were ever placed in use. The issue was demonetized in 1916.

National Theater — A83

Various frames.

**1916** **Engr.** ***Perf. 12***
**431** A83 1c deep green .20 .20
**432** A83 2c vermilion .20 .20
**433** A83 5c deep blue .20 .20
**434** A83 6c gray violet .25 .20
**435** A83 10c black brn .25 .20
**436** A83 12c violet 2.50 .50
**437** A83 17c orange .35 .20
**438** A83 25c dk brown .80 .20
**439** A83 29c black 5.00 .75
**440** A83 50c slate 2.50 1.50
*Nos. 431-440 (10)* 12.25 4.15

Watermarked letters which occasionally appear are from the papermaker's name.

For surcharges and overprints see Nos. 450-455, 457-466, O332-O341.

Nos. O324-O325 with "OFICIAL" Barred out in Black

**1917**
**441** O3 2c red .45 .45
*a.* Double bar
**442** O3 5c ultramarine .50 .35
*a.* Double bar

1915
OFICIAL
CORRIENTE

Regular Issue of 1915 Overprinted "OFICIAL" and Re-overprinted In Red

**443** A66 6c pale blue .65 .50
*a.* Double bar
**444** A66 12c brown .85 .65
*a.* Double bar
*b.* "CORRIENTE" inverted

**Same Overprint in Red On Nos. O323-O327**
**445** O3 1c gray green 1.75 1.25
*a.* "CORRIENTE" inverted
*b.* Double bar
*c.* "CORRIENTE" omitted
**446** O3 2c red 1.75 1.25
*a.* Double bar
**447** O3 5c ultra 9.00 6.00
*a.* Double bar, both in black
**448** O3 10c yellow 1.00 .50
*a.* Double bar
*b.* "OFICIAL" and bar omitted
**449** O3 50c violet .50 .50
*a.* Double bar
*Nos. 443-449 (7)* 15.50 10.65

Nos. O334-O335 Overprinted or Surcharged in Red:

Corriente
a

1
CORRIENTE
Un Centavo
b

**450** A83 (a) 5c deep blue 1.50 1.00
*a.* "CORRIENTE" double
**451** A83 (b) 1c on 6c gray vio 1.00 .75
*a.* "CORRIERTE"
*b.* "CORRIENRE" 5.00
*c.* "CORRIENTE" double

1
1 CENTAVO 1

No. 434 Surcharged in Black

**1918**
**452** A83 1c on 6c gray vio 1.75 1.00
*a.* Double surcharge
*b.* Inverted surcharge

No. 434 Surcharged in Black

1
1 Centavo 1

**1918**
**453** A83 1c on 6c gray vio 1.50 .75
*a.* "Centado" 2.25 1.50
*b.* Double surcharge 2.50 1.75
*c.* Inverted surcharge

No. 434 Surcharged in Black or Red

1
1 CENTAVO 1

**454** A83 1c on 6c gray vio 4.00 3.25
*a.* Double surcharge
*b.* Inverted surcharge 5.00 5.00
**455** A83 1c on 6c gray vio (R) 4.00 3.25
*a.* Double surcharge
*b.* Inverted surcharge 5.00 5.00
*Nos. 454-455 (2)* 8.00 6.50

Counterfeits exist of Nos. 454-455.

Pres. Carlos Meléndez — A85

**1919** **Engr.**
**456** A85 1col dk blue & blk .50 .50

For surcharge see No. 467.

No. 437 Surcharged in Black

1
1 Centavo 1

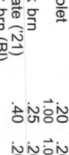

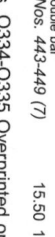

**1919**
**457** A83 1c on 17c orange .25 .25
*a.* Inverted surcharge 1.00 1.00
*b.* Double surcharge 1.00 1.00

Nos. 435-436, 438, 440 Surcharged in Black or Blue

1
1 Centavo 1

2
2 centavos 2

VALE
5 Centavos

6
SEIS

**1920-21**
**458** A83 1c on 12c violet .20 .20
*a.* Double surcharge 1.00 1.00
**459** A83 2c on 10c dk brn .25 .20
**460** A83 5c on 50c slate ('21) .40 .20
**461** A83 6c on 25c dk brn (Bl) ('21) .40 .20

## Top stamp designs

National Gymnasium — A107
Daniel Hernández Monument — A106
Atlacatl — A108
Conspiracy of 1811 — A109
Map of Central America — A111
Bridge over Lempa River — A110
Balsam Tree — A112
Tulla Serra — A114
Columbus at La Rábida — A115
Coat of Arms — A116

**Photogravure; Engraved (35c, 1col)**
*Perf. 12½; 14 (35c, 1col)*

**1924-25**

| | | | | |
|---|---|---|---|---|
| 495 | A106 | 1c red violet | .20 | .20 |
| 496 | A107 | 2c dark red | .25 | .25 |
| 497 | A108 | 3c chocolate | .20 | .20 |
| 498 | A109 | 5c olive blk | .20 | .20 |
| 499 | A110 | 6c grnsh blue | .25 | .20 |
| 500 | A111 | 10c orange | .60 | .20 |
| a. | | "ATLANT CO" | 5.50 | 5.50 |
| 501 | A112 | 20c deep green | 1.00 | .25 |
| 502 | A114 | 35c scar & grn | 1.50 | .35 |
| 503 | A115 | 50c orange brown | 2.00 | .30 |
| 504 | A116 | 1col grn & vio (25) | 3.00 | .30 |
| | | Nos. 495-504 (10) | 10.20 | 2.40 |

For overprints and surcharges see Nos. 510-511, 520-534, 585, C1-C10, C19, O350-O361, RA1-RA4.

**No. 480 Surcharged in Red**

*Perf. 12*

**1925, Aug.**

| | | | | |
|---|---|---|---|---|
| 506 | A100 | 2c on 60c violet | 1.25 | 1.25 |

City of San Salvador, 400th anniv.
The variety with dates in black is an essay.

---

## No. 475 Surcharged in Red

**1923**

| | | | | |
|---|---|---|---|---|
| 485 | A95 | 10c on 2c black | .50 | .20 |

José Simeón Cañas y Villacorta — A102

**Engr.** *Perf. 11½*

**1923**

| | | | | |
|---|---|---|---|---|
| 486 | A102 | 5c blue | .50 | .30 |

Centenary of abolition of slavery.
For surcharge see No. 571.

**Nos. 479, 481 Surcharged in Red or Black**

*Perf. 12*

**1924**

| | | | | |
|---|---|---|---|---|
| 487 | A99 | 1c on 25c ol grn (R) | .20 | .20 |
| a. | | Numeral at right inverted | | |
| b. | | Double surcharge | | |
| 488 | A99 | 2c on 25c ol grn (R) | .20 | .20 |
| 489 | A99 | 20c on 25c ol grn (R) | .50 | .25 |
| 490 | A101 | 20c on 1col blk brn (Bk) | .65 | .35 |
| | | | 1.55 | 1.00 |
| | | Nos. 487-490 (4) | | |

**Nos. 476, 478 Surcharged:**

**1924**

| | | | | |
|---|---|---|---|---|
| 491 | A96 | 1c on 5c orange (Bk) | .35 | .20 |
| 492 | A98 | 6c on 10c dp bl (R) | .35 | .20 |

Nos. 491-492 exist with double surcharge. A stamp similar to No. 492 but with surcharge "6 centavos 6" is an essay.

**No. 476 Surcharged**

**1924**

| | | | | |
|---|---|---|---|---|
| 493 | A96 | 2c on 5c orange | .40 | .35 |
| a. | | Top ornament omitted | 2.00 | 2.00 |
| | | Nos. 491-493 (3) | 1.10 | .75 |

**No. 480 Surcharged:**

**Red Surcharge**

**1924**

| | | | | |
|---|---|---|---|---|
| 494 | A100 | 5c on 60c violet | 4.25 | 3.75 |
| a. | | "1781" for "1874" | 10.00 | 8.75 |
| b. | | "1934" for "1924" | 10.00 | 8.75 |

Universal Postal Union, 50th anniversary.
This stamp with black surcharge is an essay. Copies have been passed through the post.

---

Confederation Coin — A96
Delgado Addressing Crowd — A97
Francisco Morazán — A99
Coat of Arms of Confederation — A98
Columbus — A101
Independence Monument — A100

**Engr.** *Perf. 12*

**1921**

| | | | | |
|---|---|---|---|---|
| 474 | A94 | 1c green | .25 | .20 |
| 475 | A95 | 2c black | .25 | .20 |
| 476 | A96 | 5c orange | .50 | .20 |
| 477 | A97 | 6c carmine rose | .50 | .50 |
| 478 | A98 | 10c dccp bluc | 2.50 | .50 |
| 479 | A99 | 25c olive grn | 6.00 | .75 |
| 480 | A100 | 60c violet | 10.00 | 2.45 |
| 481 | A101 | 1col black brn | 21.00 | 2.45 |
| | | Nos. 474-481 (8) | | |

For overprints and surcharges see Nos. 481A-485, 487-494, 506, O342-O349.

**Nos. 474-477 Overprinted in Red, Black or Blue**

**1921**

| | | | | |
|---|---|---|---|---|
| 481A | A94 (a) | 1c green (R) | 5.00 | 5.00 |
| 481B | A95 (a) | 2c black (Bk) | 5.00 | 4.00 |
| 481C | A96 (b) | 5c orange (Bl) | 5.00 | 4.00 |
| 481D | A97 (b) | 6c car rose (Bl) | 20.00 | 16.00 |
| | | Nos. 481A-481D (4) | | |

Centenary of independence.

**No. 477 Surcharged:**

**1923**

| | | | | |
|---|---|---|---|---|
| 482 | A97 (a) | 5c on 6c | .35 | .20 |
| 483 | A97 (b) | 5c on 6c | .30 | .25 |
| 484 | A97 | 20c on 6c | .35 | .65 |
| | | Nos. 482-484 (3) | | |

Nos. 482-484 exist with double surcharge.

---

## Same Surch. in Black on No. O337

| | | | | |
|---|---|---|---|---|
| 462 | A83 | 1c on 12c violet | 1.00 | 1.00 |
| a. | | Double surcharge | 2.25 | 1.80 |
| | | Nos. 458-462 (5) | | |

No. 460 surcharged in yellow and 461 surcharged in red are essays.
No. 462 is due to some sheets of Official Stamps being mixed with the ordinary 12c stamps at the time of surcharging. The error stamps were sold to the public and used for ordinary postage.

**Surcharged in Red, Blue or Black:**

**15c Types:**

15  15  15  15
I   II  III  IV

**Engr.**

**1921**

| | | | | |
|---|---|---|---|---|
| 463 | A83 | 15c on 29c blk (III) ('21) | 1.00 | .40 |
| a. | | Double surcharge | 2.00 | |
| b. | | Type I | 1.50 | .75 |
| c. | | Type IV | 2.50 | |
| 464 | A83 | 26c on 29c blk (Bl) | 1.00 | .60 |
| a. | | Double surcharge | | |
| 466 | A83 | 35c on 50c slate (Bk) | 1.00 | .60 |
| 467 | A85 | 60c on 1col dk bl & blk (R) | .30 | .25 |
| | | | 3.30 | 1.85 |
| | | Nos. 463-467 (4) | | |

Surcharge on No. 464 differs from 16c illustration in that bar at bottom extends across stamp and denomination includes "cts." One stamp in each row of ten of No. 464 has the "t" of "cts" inverted and one stamp in ninth row of No. 466 has the letters "c" in "cinco" larger than the normal.
Setting for No. 467 includes three types of numerals and "CENTAVOS" measuring from 16mm to 20mm wide.
No. 464 surcharged in green or yellow and the 35c on 29c black are essays.

A93

**1921**

| | | | | |
|---|---|---|---|---|
| 468 | A93 | 1c on 1c ol grn | .20 | .20 |
| a. | | Double surcharge | | .75 |
| 469 | A93 | 1c on 5c yellow | .20 | .20 |
| a. | | Inverted surcharge | | |
| 470 | A93 | 1c on 10c blue | .20 | .20 |
| a. | | Double surcharge | | .50 |
| 471 | A93 | 1c on 25c green | .20 | .20 |
| 472 | A93 | 1c on 50c olive | .20 | .20 |
| a. | | Double surcharge | | |
| 473 | A93 | 1c on 1p gray blk | 1.20 | 1.20 |
| a. | | Double surcharge | | |
| | | Nos. 468-473 (6) | | |

The frame of No. 473 differs slightly from the illustration.
Setting includes many wrong font letters and numerals.

Manuel José Arce — A95
Francisco Menéndez — A94

## 1925
**Photo.** **Perf. 12½**

View of San Salvador — A118

| | | | | |
|---|---|---|---|---|
| 507 | A118 | 1c blue | .65 | .65 |
| 508 | A118 | 2c deep green | .65 | .65 |
| 509 | A118 | 3c Mahogany red | 1.95 | 1.95 |
| | | Nos. 507-509 (3) | | |

#506-509 for the 4th centenary of the founding of the City of San Salvador.

## 1928, July 17

510 A111 3c on 10c orange .75 .50

Industrial Exhibition, Santa Ana, July 1928.

Black Surcharge

## 1928

511 A109 1c on 5c olive black .25 .20
a. "ATLANT CO" .40 .25
a. Bar instead of top left "1"

Red Surcharge

## 1929
**Litho.** **Perf. 11½**

### Portraits in Dark Brown

| | | | | |
|---|---|---|---|---|
| 512 | A121 | 1c dull violet | .35 | .35 |
| 513 | A121 | 3c brown | 11.50 | 11.50 |
| a. | | Center inverted | 35.00 | |
| 514 | A121 | 5c gray grn | .35 | .35 |
| a. | | Center inverted | 35.00 | |
| 515 | A121 | 10c orange | 1.40 | 1.00 |
| | | Nos. 512-515 (4) | | |

Pres. Pío Romero Bosque, Salvador, and Pres. Lázaro Chacón, Guatemala A121

Opening of the international railroad connecting El Salvador and Guatemala. Nos. 512-515 exist imperforate. No. 512 in the colors of No. 515.

## 1930, Dec. 3

Tomb of Menéndez A122

| | | | | |
|---|---|---|---|---|
| 516 | A122 | 1c violet | 3.00 | 3.00 |
| 517 | A122 | 3c brown | 3.00 | 2.50 |
| 518 | A122 | 5c dark green | 3.00 | 2.50 |
| 519 | A122 | 10c yellow grn | 12.00 | 10.00 |
| | | Nos. 516-519 (4) | | |

Centenary of the birth of General Francisco Menéndez.

## 1932
Stamps of 1924-25 Issue Overprinted

**Perf. 12½, 14**

| | | | | |
|---|---|---|---|---|
| 520 | A106 | 1c deep violet | .20 | .20 |
| 521 | A107 | 2c dark red | .20 | .20 |
| 522 | A108 | 3c chocolate | .30 | .20 |
| 523 | A109 | 5c deep blue | .35 | .20 |
| 524 | A110 | 6c deep blue | .20 | .20 |
| 525 | A111 | 10c orange | 1.00 | .20 |
| a. | | "ATLANT CO" | 6.25 | |
| 526 | A112 | 20c deep green | 7.50 | .90 |
| 527 | A114 | 35c scar & grn | 1.50 | .75 |
| 528 | A115 | 50c orange brown | 3.00 | 1.00 |
| 529 | A116 | 1col green & vio | 14.10 | 5.65 |
| | | Nos. 520-529 (10) | | |

Values are for the overprint measuring 7½x3mm. It is found in two other sizes: 7½x3mm and 8x3mm.

## 1934

| | | | | |
|---|---|---|---|---|
| 530 | A109 | 2(c) on 5c grnsh blk | .25 | .20 |
| a. | | Double surcharge | | |
| 531 | A111 | 3(c) on 10c org (Bk) | 4.00 | 4.00 |
| a. | | "ATLANT CO" | | |
| 532 | A115 | 2(c) on 50c | .30 | .20 |
| 533 | A116 | 8(c) on 1col | 3.00 | |
| 534 | A114 | 15(c) on 35c | .30 | .20 |
| | | Nos. 530-534 (5) | 1.25 | 1.00 |

Types of 1924-25 Surcharged with New Values in Red or Black

Nos. 503, 504, 502 Surcharged with New Values in Black

Police Barracks — A123

## 1934-35
**Litho.** **Perf. 12½**

| | | | | |
|---|---|---|---|---|
| 535 | A123 | 2c gray brn, type I | .20 | .20 |
| a. | | 2c brown; type II | | |
| 536 | A123 | 5c car, type II | .20 | .20 |
| 537 | A123 | 8c lt ultra, type II | 2.10 | 1.75 |
| | | Nos. 535-537, C33-C35 (6) | | |

Two types of the 2c:
Type I — The clouds have heavy lines of shading.
Type II — The lines of shading have been removed from the clouds.

Discus Thrower A124

## 1935, Mar. 16
**Engr.** **Unwmk.**

| | | | | |
|---|---|---|---|---|
| 538 | A124 | 2c carmine | 2.00 | 2.00 |
| 539 | A124 | 8c blue | 2.00 | 1.90 |
| 540 | A124 | 10c orange yel | 2.75 | 2.00 |
| 541 | A124 | 15c bister | 3.25 | 2.25 |
| 542 | A124 | 37c green | 4.00 | 3.25 |
| | | Nos. 538-542, C36-C40 (10) | 50.50 | 39.30 |

3rd Central American Games.

**Wmk. 240**

## 1935, June 27
**Engr.** **Unwmk.**

| | | | | |
|---|---|---|---|---|
| 543 | A124 | 5c carmine | 3.50 | |
| 544 | A124 | 8c blue | 5.00 | 2.00 |
| 545 | A124 | 10c orange yel | 5.00 | 2.00 |
| 546 | A124 | 15c bister | 5.00 | 2.50 |
| 547 | A124 | 37c green | 8.00 | |
| | | Nos. 543-547, C41-C45 (10) | 68.00 | 43.25 |

Same Overprinted in Black

HABILITADO

## 1935, Oct. 26
**Litho.** **Wmk. 240**

Flag of El Salvador A125

| | | | | |
|---|---|---|---|---|
| 548 | A125 | 1c gray blue | .20 | .20 |
| 549 | A125 | 2c black brn | .20 | .20 |
| 550 | A125 | 3c plum | .20 | .20 |
| 551 | A125 | 5c rose carmine | .25 | .20 |
| 552 | A125 | 8c ultra | .30 | .20 |
| 553 | A125 | 15c fawn | .40 | .25 |
| | | Nos. 548-553, C46 (7) | 2.05 | 1.50 |

Tree of San Vicente A126

| | | | | |
|---|---|---|---|---|
| 554 | A126 | 2c black brn | .50 | .25 |
| 555 | A126 | 5c dk blue grn | .50 | .35 |
| 556 | A126 | 5c rose red | .50 | .35 |
| 557 | A126 | 8c dark blue | .50 | .40 |
| 558 | A126 | 15c brown | .50 | .50 |
| | | Nos. 554-558, C47-C51 (10) | 6.50 | 5.30 |

Tercentenary of San Vicente.

## 1935, Dec. 26
Numerals in Black, Tree in Yellow Green

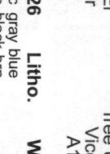

## 1935, Dec.
**Engr.** **Unwmk.**

Dr. Tomás G. Palomo — A131

Doroteo Vasconcelos A129

Volcano of Izalco — A127

Wharf at Cutuco — A128

Parade Ground A130

Coffee at Pier — A133

Sugar Mill — A132

Gathering Balsam — A134

| | | | | |
|---|---|---|---|---|
| 559 | A127 | 1c deep violet | .20 | .20 |
| 561 | A129 | 3c green | .20 | .20 |
| 562 | A130 | 5c carmine | .20 | .20 |
| 563 | A131 | 8c dull blue | .20 | .20 |
| 564 | A132 | 10c orange | .20 | .20 |
| 565 | A133 | 15c dk olive bis | .40 | .20 |

Pres. Manuel E. Araujo — A135

Map of Flags of US and El Salvador — A136

## 1938, Apr. 21
Engraved and Lithographed
**Perf. 12**

572 A136 8c multicolored .65 .50

US Constitution, 150th anniv. See #C61.

## 1938
No. 560 Surcharged with New Value in Black

573 A128 1c on 2c chestnut .20 .20

**Perf. 12½**

## 1938
Stamps of 1935 Surcharged with New Value in Black

No. 486 Surcharged with New Value in Red

571 A102 3c on 5c blue .25 .25

**Perf. 11½**

Centenary of the death of José Simeón Cañas, liberator of slaves in Latin America.

## 1938
**Perf. 12½**

| | | | | |
|---|---|---|---|---|
| 566 | A134 | 50c indigo | 2.00 | 1.25 |
| 567 | A135 | 1col black | 5.00 | 3.00 |
| | | Nos. 559-567 (9) | 8.85 | 5.65 |

## 1938

| | | | | |
|---|---|---|---|---|
| 568 | A130 | 1c on 5c carmine | .20 | .20 |
| 569 | A132 | 3c on 10c orange | .20 | .20 |
| 570 | A133 | 8c on 15c dk ol bis | .60 | .60 |
| | | Nos. 568-570 (3) | | |

Paper has faint imprint "El Salvador" on face. For surcharges and overprint see Nos. 568-570, 573, 583-584, C52.

## 1938-39
**Engr.** **Perf. 12**

Indian Sugar Mill — A137

| | | | | |
|---|---|---|---|---|
| 574 | A137 | 1c dark violet | .20 | .20 |
| 575 | A137 | 2c dark green | .20 | .20 |
| 576 | A137 | 3c dark brown | .25 | .20 |
| 578 | A137 | 8c scarlet | 1.25 | .20 |
| 579 | A137 | 10c yel org ('39) | .20 | .20 |
| 580 | A137 | 20c bis brn ('39) | 1.75 | .20 |
| 581 | A137 | 50c bis brn ('39) | 2.25 | .45 |
| 582 | A137 | 1col dull blk ('39) | 2.00 | .75 |
| | | Nos. 574-582 (39) | 10.15 | 2.60 |

Designs: 2c, Indian women washing. 3c, Izote flower. 5c, Indian plowing. 8c, Champion cow. 10c, Extracting balsam. 20c, Maquilishuat in bloom. 1col, Post Office, San Salvador.
For surcharges & overprints see #591-592, C96.

## 1939, Sept. 25
**Engr.** **Perf. 12½, 14**

| | | | | |
|---|---|---|---|---|
| 583 | A134 | 8c on 50c indigo | .30 | .20 |
| 584 | A135 | 10c on 1col blk | .45 | .20 |
| 585 | A116 | 50c on 1col grn & vio | 3.50 | 2.50 |
| | | Nos. 583-585 (3) | 2.75 | 2.10 |

Battle of San Pedro Perulapán, 100th anniv.

Nos. 566-567, 504 Surcharged in Red

**1940, Mar. 1**          **Perf. 12½**
586 A146 8c dk bl, lt bl & blk          5.50   1.75
          24.00  14.00

Sir Rowland
Hill — A146

Postage stamp centenary.

Gen. Juan José
Canas — A150

**1945, June 9**
590 A150 8c blue          .40   .20

No. 575 Surcharged in Black

591 A137(a) 1(c) on 2c dk grn          .20   .20
592 A137(b) 1(c) on 2c dk grn ('46)          .20   .20

Lake of Ilopango
A151

**1944, Mar. 1**          Perf. 12½
586 A146

**1947, Feb. 25**          **Perf. 12½**
605 A163 8c deep blue          .30   .20
          3.00  2.00
Nos. 605,C108-C110 (4)

Manuel José
Arce — A163

**1948, Feb. 25**

President Roosevelt Presenting
Awards for Distinguished
Service — A164

President
Franklin D.
Roosevelt
A165

A166

Designs: 8c, Pres. and Mrs. Roosevelt. 15c,
Mackenzie King, Roosevelt and Winston
Churchill. 20c, Roosevelt and Cordell Hull.
50c, Funeral of Pres. Roosevelt.

**1948, Apr. 12**
**Various Frames; Center in Black**
606 A164 5c dk bl          .20   .20
607 A164 8c green          .20   .20
608 A165 12c violet          .20   .20
609 A164 15c vermilion          .25   .20
610 A164 20c car lake          .30   .20
611 A164 50c gray          .70   .45
          10.85  7.45
Nos. 606-611,C111-C117 (13)

**Souvenir Sheet**
**Perf. 13½**
612 A166 1col ol grn & brn          2.25  1.50
3rd anniv. of the death of F. D. Roosevelt.

Torch and
Winged
Letter
A167

**1949, Oct. 9**          **Perf. 12½**  **Unwmk.**     **Engr.**
613 A167 8c blue          .65   .40
Nos. 613,C122-C124 (4)          16.00  12.30
75th anniv. of the UPU.

Wreath and
Open
Book — A169

**1949, Dec. 15     Litho.     Perf. 10½**
614 A168 8c blue          .30   .25
Nos. 614,C125-C129 (6)          6.50  5.00
Revolution of Dec. 14, 1948, 1st anniv.

Workman and
Soldier Holding
Torch — A168

**1952, Feb. 14     Perf. 11½     Photo.     Unwmk.**
**Wreath in Dark Green**
615 A169 1c yel grn          .20   .20
616 A169 2c magenta          .20   .20
617 A169 5c brn red          .20   .20
618 A169 10c yellow          .20   .20
619 A169 20c gray grn          .20   .20
620 A169 1col dp car          1.00   .75
Nos. 615-620,C134-C141 (14)          8.70  5.75
Constitution of 1950.

Nos. 598, 600, 603 Surcharged
with New Values in Various Colors
**1952-53     Perf. 12½     Wmk. 240**
621 A154 2c on 3c vio (C)          .20   .20
622 A154 3c on 8c dp bl (C)          .20   .20
623 A154 3c on 8c dp bl (G)          .20   .20
624 A154 5c on 8c dp bl (O)          .20   .20
625 A154 5c on 8c dp bl (Bk)          .20   .20
626 A154 10c on 50c blk (O)          1.20  1.20
(53)
Nos. 621-626 (6)

Nos. C106 and C107 Surcharged and
"AEREO" Obliterated in Various Colors
**1952-53     Wmk. 240**
627 AP31 2c on 12c choc (Bl)          .20   .20
628 AP32 2c on 14c bl (R)          .20   .20
(53)
629 AP31 5c on 12c choc (Bl)          .20   .20
630 AP32 10c on 14c dk bl (C)          .80   .80
Nos. 627-630 (4)

José
Marti — A170

**1953, Feb. 27     Litho.     Perf. 10½     Unwmk.**
631 A170 1c rose red          .25   .20
632 A170 2c bl grn          .25   .20
633 A170 10c dk vio          2.60  1.35
Nos. 631-633,C142-C144 (6)
José Marti, Cuban patriot, birth cent.

No. 598
Overprinted
in Carmine

**1953, June 19     Perf. 12½**
634 A154 3c violet          .20   .20
4th. Pan-American Congress of Social
Medicine, San Salvador, April 16-19, 1953.
See #C146.

Signing of Act
of
Independence
A171

**1942, Nov. 23     Wmk. 269     Perf. 14     Engr.**
587 A147 8c deep blue          .50   .20

**Souvenir Sheet**
**Import**
**Without Gum**
**Lilac Tinted Paper**
588 A148 Sheet of 4          15.00  15.00
a.   8c deep blue          3.75   3.75
b.   30c red orange          3.75   3.75
Nos. 587-588 commemorate the first
Eucharistic Congress of Salvador. See No.
C85.
No. 588 contains two No. 587 and two No.
C85, imperf.

Statue of Christ and San Salvador
Cathedral — A147

**Catalogue values for unused
stamps in this section, from this
point to the end of the section, are
for Never Hinged items.**

Ceiba Tree
A152

Water
Carriers — A153

**1946-47     Litho.     Wmk. 240**
593 A151 1c blue ('47)          .25   .20
594 A152 2c lt bl grn ('47)          .25   .20
595 A153 5c carmine          .75   .60
Nos. 593-595 (3)

Isidro Menéndez
A154

2c, Cristano Salazar. 3c, Juan Bertis. 5c,
Francisco Duenas. 8c, Ramon Belloso. 10c,
Jose Presentacion Trigueros. 20c, Salvador
Rodriguez Gonzalez. 50c, Francisco Cas-
taneda. 1col, David Castro.

**1947     Unwmk.     Engr.     Perf. 12**
596 A154 1c car rose          .20   .20
597 A154 2c dp org          .20   .20
598 A154 3c violet          .20   .20
599 A154 5c slate gray          .20   .20
600 A154 8c dp bl          .20   .20
601 A154 10c bis brn          .30   .20
602 A154 20c green          .65   .30
603 A154 50c black          1.40   .40
604 A154 1col scarlet          3.55  2.10
Nos. 596-604 (9)
For surcharges and overprints see Nos.
621-626, 634, C118-C120, O362-O368.

Cuscatlán Bridge, Pan-American
Highway — A149

**Arms Overprint at Right in Carmine**
**1944, Nov. 24     Unwmk.     Perf. 12½**
589 A149 8c dk blue & blk          .25   .20
See No. C92.

## 1953, Sept. 15 — Litho. — Perf. 11½
### Capt. Gen. Gerardo Barrios — A172

| 635 | A171 | 1c rose pink | .20 | .20 |
|---|---|---|---|---|
| 636 | A171 | 2c dp bl grn | .20 | .20 |
| 637 | A171 | 3c purple | .20 | .20 |
| 638 | A171 | 5c green | .20 | .20 |
| 639 | A171 | 7c lt brn | .20 | .20 |
| 640 | A171 | 10c ocher | .20 | .20 |
| 641 | A171 | 20c blue | .60 | .20 |
| 642 | A171 | 50c green | .80 | .20 |
| 643 | A171 | 1col gray | 1.60 | .90 |

Nos. 635-643,C147-C150 (13) — 5.75 3.70

Act of Independence, Sept. 15, 1821.

### Black Overprint ("C de C")

Portrait, (facing left), Francisco Morazan.

| 644 | A172 | 1c green | .20 | .20 |
|---|---|---|---|---|
| 645 | A172 | 2c blue | .20 | .20 |
| 646 | A172 | 3c green | .20 | .20 |
| 647 | A172 | 5c carmine | .20 | .20 |
| 648 | A172 | 7c blue | .20 | .20 |
| 649 | A172 | 10c carmine | .20 | .20 |
| 650 | A172 | 20c violet | .25 | .20 |
| 651 | A172 | 22c violet | .40 | .20 |

Nos. 644-651 (8) — 1.90 1.60

The overprint "C de C" is a control indicating the overprint occurs twice in this "Tribunal of Accounts." A double entry of this denomination.
For overprint see No. 729.

### 1953, Dec. 1 — Perf. 11½
3c, 7c, 10c, 22c.

Coastal Bridge A173

Motherland and Liberty A174

Census Allegory — A175

Balboa Park — A176

## 1954, June 1 — Unwmk. — Photo.

| 652 | A173 | 1c car rose & brn | .20 | .20 |
|---|---|---|---|---|
| 653 | AP43 | 1c ol & bl gray | .20 | .20 |
| 654 | A173 | 1c pur & pale lil | .20 | .20 |
| 655 | A173 | 2c yel grn & lt gray | .20 | .20 |
| 656 | A174 | 2c car lake | .20 | .20 |
| 657 | A175 | 2c org red | .20 | .20 |
| 658 | AP44 | 3c car lake | .20 | .20 |
| 659 | A173 | 3c org | .20 | .20 |
| 660 | A174 | 3c maroon | .20 | .20 |
| 661 | A175 | 5c emerald | .20 | .20 |
| 662 | AP44 | 5c red vio & vio | .20 | .20 |
| 663 | A176 | 7c magenta & buff | .20 | .20 |
| 664 | AP45 | 7c bl grn & gray bl | .20 | .20 |
| 665 | A174 | 7c dp bl & bl | .20 | .20 |
| 666 | A175 | 10c car lake | .20 | .20 |
| 667 | A176 | 10c red, dk brn & bl | .20 | .20 |
| 668 | A174 | 20c org & cr | .20 | .20 |
| 669 | A173 | 20c dk bl grn | .20 | .20 |
| 670 | A176 | 22c gray & brn | .30 | .25 |
| 671 | A173 | 50c dk gray vio | .30 | .30 |
| 672 | AP46 | 1col brn org, dk brn | 1.25 | .75 |
| 673 | A173 | 1col brt bl & bl | .50 | .50 |

Nos. 652-673 (22) — 5.40

695 A173 1col brt bl & bl — 7.15

Nos. 652-673,C151-C165 (37) — 17.15 10.55

For surcharges & overprints see #692-693, 736, C193.

Designs: Nos. 654, 655, National Palace. Nos. 659, 665, Izalco Volcano. Nos. 660, 661, Guayabo dam. No. 666, Lake Ilopango. Nos. 670, 673, Housing development. Lake Ilopango. Nos. 670, 673, Coast guard boat. No. 671, Modern highway.

## 1955, Dec. 20 — Wmk. 269 — Engr. — Perf. 12½
### Capt. Gen. Gerardo Barrios — A177

| 674 | A177 | 1c red | .20 | .20 |
|---|---|---|---|---|
| 675 | A177 | 2c yel grn | .30 | .25 |
| 676 | A177 | 3c vio bl | .30 | .25 |
| 677 | A177 | 20c violet | 1.70 | 1.50 |

Nos. 674-677,C166-C167 (6)

### 1956, June 20 — Litho. — Perf. 13½

| 678 | A178 | 3c bis grn | .20 | .20 |
|---|---|---|---|---|
| 679 | A178 | 5c red org | .20 | .20 |
| 680 | A178 | 5c red org | 1.60 | 1.00 |
| 681 | A178 | 2col dk red | 6.70 | 4.30 |

Nos. 678-681,C168-C172 (9)

Centenary of Santa Ana Department.
For overprint see No. C187.

Coffee Picker — A178

### 1956, Sept. 14

| 682 | A179 | 2c blue | .20 | .20 |
|---|---|---|---|---|
| 683 | A179 | 7c rose red | .30 | .25 |
| 684 | A179 | 50c yel brn | .50 | .20 |

Nos. 682-684,C173-C178 (9) — 3.25 2.60

Map of Chalatenango — A179

Centenary of Chalatenango Department (in 1955).
For surcharge see No. 694.

### 1957, Jan. 3 — Wmk. 269 — Engr. — Perf. 12½

| 685 | A180 | 1c rose red | .20 | .20 |
|---|---|---|---|---|
| 686 | A180 | 2c green | .20 | .20 |
| 687 | A180 | 3c violet | .30 | .20 |
| 688 | A180 | 7c red org | .35 | .20 |
| 689 | A180 | 10c ultra | .35 | .20 |
| 690 | A180 | 60c pale brn | .65 | .35 |
| 691 | A180 | 1col dl red | 5.50 | 3.70 |

Nos. 685-691,C179-C183 (12)

Coat of Arms of Nueva San Salvador — A180

Centenary of the founding of the city of Nueva San Salvador (Santa Tecla). For surcharges and overprints see Nos. 695-696, 706, 713, C194-C195, C197-C199.

### 1957 — Unwmk. — Photo. — Perf. 11½

| 692 | A173 | 6c on 7c bl grn & gray | .30 | .30 |
|---|---|---|---|---|
| 693 | A173 | 6c on 7c org brn & gray | .30 | .30 |

Nos. 664-665, 683 and 688 Surcharged with New Value in Black

### 1957 — Litho. — Perf. 13½

694 A179 6c on 7c rose red — .20 .20

## 1955, Dec. 20 — Wmk. 269 (El Salvador Intercontinental Hotel — A181)

### 1957-58 — Wmk. 269 — Engr. — Perf. 12½

| 695 | A180 | 5c on 7c red org ('58) | .25 | .20 |
|---|---|---|---|---|
| 696 | A180 | 6c on 7c red org | 1.35 | 1.20 |

Nos. 692-696 (5)

### 1958, June 28 — Unwmk. — Photo. — Perf. 11½
### El Salvador Intercontinental Hotel — A181
Vignette in Green, Dark Blue & Red — Granite Paper

| 697 | A181 | 3c brown | .20 | .20 |
|---|---|---|---|---|
| 698 | A181 | 6c crim rose | .20 | .20 |
| 699 | A181 | 15c brt grn | .20 | .20 |
| 700 | A181 | 20c brt grn | .30 | .20 |
| 701 | A181 | 30c lilac | .40 | .20 |
| 702 | A181 | 30c brt yel grn | 1.50 | 1.25 |

Nos. 697-702 (6)

## 1959, Dec. 14 — Granite Paper
### Presidents Eisenhower and Lemus and Flags — A182
Design in Ultramarine, Dark Brown, Light Brown and Red

| 703 | A182 | 3c pink | .20 | .20 |
|---|---|---|---|---|
| 704 | A182 | 6c green | .20 | .20 |
| 705 | A182 | 10c crimson | 1.45 | 1.20 |

Nos. 703-705,C184-C186 (6)

Visit of Pres. José M. Lemus of El Salvador to the US, Mar. 9-21.

### 1960 — Wmk. 269 — Engr. — Perf. 12½

706 A180 2c green — .20 .20

No. 686 Overprinted: "5 Enero 1960 XX Aniversario Fundación Sociedad Filatélica de El Salvador"

Philatelic Association of El Salvador, 20th anniv.

## 1960, Dec. — Photo. — Perf. 12½
### Multicolored Centers; Granite Paper

| 707 | A183 | 3c scarlet | .20 | .20 |
|---|---|---|---|---|
| 708 | A183 | 15c brt pur | .20 | .20 |
| 709 | A183 | 25c brt yel grn | .20 | .20 |
| 710 | A183 | 30c Prus bl | .25 | .20 |
| 711 | A183 | 40c olive | .35 | .25 |
| 712 | A183 | 80c olive | .75 | .25 |

Nos. 707-712 (6) — 2.00 1.80

Apartment Houses A183

Issued to publicize the erection of multifamily housing projects in 1958.
For surcharges see Nos. 730, 733.

### 1960 — Wmk. 269 — Engr. — Perf. 12½

713 A180 1c on 2c grn — .20 .20

No. 686 Surcharged with New Value

Poinsettia — A184

## 1960, Dec. — Unwmk. — Photo. — Perf. 11½
### Granite Paper
Design in Slate Green, Red and Yellow

| 714 | A184 | 3c yellow | .20 | .20 |
|---|---|---|---|---|
| 715 | A184 | 6c salmon | .20 | .20 |
| 716 | A184 | 10c grnsh bl | .30 | .20 |
| 717 | A184 | 15c pale vio bl | .30 | .20 |

Nos. 714-717,C188-C191 (8) — 2.85 1.80

### Miniature Sheet
Design in Slate Green, Red and Yellow

718 A184 40c silver — 1.00 1.00

Nos. 718 and C192 exist with overprints for: 1 — 1st Central American Philatelic Cong., July, 1961. 2 — Death of General Barrios, 96th anniv. 3 — Cent. of city of Anuachapan. 4 — Football (soccer) games. 5 — 4th Latin American Cong. of Pathological Anatomy, Dec. 1963. 6 — Alliance for Progress, 2nd anniv.
For surcharge see No. C196.

Fathers Nicolas, Vicente and Manuel Aguilar A185

## 1961, Nov. 5 — Unwmk. — Photo. — Perf. 11½

| 719 | A185 | 6c brt pink & dk brn | .20 | .20 |
|---|---|---|---|---|
| 720 | A185 | 10c bl & dk brn | .20 | .20 |
| 721 | A185 | 5c pale brn & dk ol | .20 | .20 |
| 722 | A185 | 6c brt pink & dk brn | .20 | .20 |
| 723 | A185 | 10c bl & dk brn | .20 | .20 |
| 724 | A185 | 20c vio & dk brn | .40 | .20 |
| 725 | A185 | 30c brt bl & vio | .40 | .20 |
| 726 | A185 | 30c brt bl & dk brn | .75 | .20 |
| 727 | A185 | 50c bl grn & sep | .75 | .40 |
| 728 | A185 | 80c brn & ultra | 4.25 | 2.75 |

Nos. 719-728 (10)

Designs: 5c, 6c, Manuel José Arce, José Matías Delgado and Juan Manuel Rodríguez. 10c, 20c, Pedro Pablo Castillo, Domingo Antonio de Lara and Santiago José Celis. 50c, 80c, Monument to the Fathers, Plaza Libertad.

Sesquicentennial of the first cry for independence in Central America. For surcharges and overprints see Nos. 731-732, 734-735, 737, 760, 769, 776.

## 1962, Dec. 21 — Litho. — Perf. 11½

729 A172 22c violet — .28 .20

Nos. 729,C193-C195 (4) — 2.78 1.95

3rd Central American Industrial Exposition.
No. 651 Overprinted: "III Exposición Industrial Centroamericana Diciembre de 1962"

### 1962-63 — Photo.
Surcharged
Nos. 708, 726-728 and 673

| 730 | A183 | 6c on 15c ('63) | .25 | .20 |
|---|---|---|---|---|
| 731 | A186 | 6c on 40c ('63) | .25 | .20 |
| 732 | A186 | 6c on 20c ('63) | .25 | .20 |
| 733 | A183 | 6c on 15c ('63) | .30 | .20 |
| 734 | A186 | 10c on 15c | .30 | .20 |
| 735 | A186 | 10c on 50c ('63) | .30 | .20 |
| 736 | A173 | 10c on 1col ('63) | 1.95 | 1.40 |

Nos. 730-736 (7)

Surcharge includes bars on Nos. 731-734, 736; dot on Nos. 730, 735.

Coyote A187

### 1963, Mar. 21

737 A186 40c brn org & sepia — .70 .40

FAO "Freedom from Hunger" campaign.

No. 726 Overprinted in Arc: "CAMPAÑA MUNDIAL CONTRA EL HAMBRE"

Christ on
Globe — A188

2c, Spider monkey, vert. 3c, Raccoon, 5c,
King vulture, vert. 6c, Brown coati. 10c,
Kinkajou.

**1963** **Photo.** **Perf. 11½**
| | | | |
|---|---|---|---|
| 738 | A187 | 1c lil, blk, ocher & brn | .20 .20 |
| 739 | A187 | 2c lt grn & blk | .20 .20 |
| 740 | A187 | 3c fawn, dk brn & buff | .20 .20 |
| 741 | A187 | 5c gray grn, ind, red & buff | .20 .20 |
| 742 | A187 | 6c rose lil, blk, brn & buff | .20 .20 |
| 743 | A187 | 10c lt bl, brn & buff | .20 .20 |

2nd Natl. Eucharistic Cong., San Salvador,
Apr. 16-19.

**1964-65** **Perf. 12x11½**
| | | | |
|---|---|---|---|
| 744 | A188 | 6c bl & brn | .20 .20 |
| 745 | A188 | 10c bl & bis | .90 .80 |

**Miniature Sheets**

*Imperf*
| | | | |
|---|---|---|---|
| 746 | A188 | 60c bl & brt pur | 1.00 .60 |
| a. | Marginal ovpt. La Union | | 1.25 1.25 |
| b. | Marginal ovpt. Usulutan | | 1.25 1.25 |
| c. | Marginal ovpt. La Libertad | | 1.25 1.25 |

Nos. 746a, 746b and 746c commemorate
the centenaries of the Departments of La
Union, Usulután and La Libertad.
Issued: No. 744-746, Apr. 16, 1964; #746a-
746b, June 22, 1965; #746c, Jan. 28, 1965.
See #C210. For overprints see #C232,
C238.

Pres. John
F. Kennedy
A189

**1964, Nov. 22** **Unwmk.**
| | | | |
|---|---|---|---|
| 747 | A189 | 6c buff & blk | .20 .20 |
| 748 | A189 | 10c tan & blk | .20 .20 |
| 749 | A189 | 50c pink & blk | .50 .25 |

Nos. 747-749,C211-C213 (6) 1.75 1.25

**Miniature Sheet**

*Imperf*
| | | | |
|---|---|---|---|
| 750 | A189 | 70c dp grn & blk | 1.00 1.00 |

President John F. Kennedy (1917-1963).
For overprints & surcharge see #798, 843,
C269.

---

**1965, Apr. 27** **Photo.** **Perf. 11½x12**
**Design in Brown and Gold**
| | | | |
|---|---|---|---|
| 757 | A191 | 5c dp yel | .20 .20 |
| 758 | A191 | 6c dp rose | .25 .20 |
| 759 | A191 | 10c gray | .25 .20 |

Nos. 757-759,C221-C223 (6) 1.40 1.20

International Cooperation Year.

No. 728 Overprinted in Red: "1er.
Centenario Muerte / Cap. Gral.
Gerardo Barrios / 1865 1965 / 29 de
Agosto"

**1965** **Unwmk.**
| | | | |
|---|---|---|---|
| 760 | A186 | 80c gray & ultra | .65 .50 |
| a. | "Garl." instead of "Gral." | | 1.00 1.00 |

Capt. Gen. Gerardo Barrios, death cent.

Gavidia
A192

Fair
Emblem — A193

**1965, Sept. 24** **Photo.** **Perf. 11½x12**
**Portrait in Natural Colors** **Unwmk.**
| | | | |
|---|---|---|---|
| 761 | A192 | 2c blk & rose vio | .20 .20 |
| 762 | A192 | 3c blk & org | .20 .20 |
| 763 | A192 | 6c blk & lt ultra | .20 .20 |

Nos. 761-763,C224-C226 (6) 2.30 1.50

Francisco Antonio Gavidia, philosopher.
For surcharges see Nos. 852-853.

No. 759 Overprinted in Carmine:
"1865 / 12 de Octubre / 1965 / Dr.
Manuel Enrique Araujo"

**1965, Oct. 12**
| | | | |
|---|---|---|---|
| 764 | A191 | 10c brn, gray & gold | .20 .20 |

Centenary of the birth of Manuel Enrique
Araujo, president of Salvador, 1911-1913. See
No. C227.

**1965, Nov. 5** **Photo.** **Perf. 12x11½**
| | | | |
|---|---|---|---|
| 765 | A193 | 6c yel & multi | .20 .20 |
| 766 | A193 | 10c multi | .20 .20 |
| 767 | A193 | 20c pink & multi | .20 .20 |

Nos. 765-767,C228-C230 (6) 4.70 3.45

Intl. Fair of El Salvador, Nov. 5-Dec. 4.
For overprints and surcharge see Nos. 784,
C246, C311, C323.

WHO Headquarters, Geneva — A194

**1966, May 20** **Photo.** **Unwmk.**
| | | | |
|---|---|---|---|
| 768 | A194 | 15c beige & multi | .20 .20 |

Inauguration of WHO Headquarters,
Geneva. See No. C231. For overprints and
surcharges see Nos. 778, 783, 864, C242,
C245, C322.

No. 728 Overprinted in Red: "Mes de
Commemoracion / Civica de la
Independencia / Centroamericana / 19
Sept. / 1821 1966"

**1966, Sept. 19** **Photo.** **Perf. 11½**
| | | | |
|---|---|---|---|
| 769 | A186 | 80c gray & ultra | .50 .50 |

Month of civic commemoration of Central
American independence.

---

UNESCO
Emblem
A195

**1966, Nov. 4** **Unwmk.** **Perf. 12**
| | | | |
|---|---|---|---|
| 770 | A195 | 20c gray, blk & vio bl | .20 .20 |
| 771 | A195 | 1col multi, blk & vio bl | .85 .40 |

Nos. 770-771,C233-C234 (4) 2.95 1.80

20th anniv. of UNESCO.
For surcharges see Nos. 853a, C352.

Map of
Central
America,
Flags and
Cogwheels
A196

**1966, Nov. 27** **Litho.** **Perf. 12**
| | | | |
|---|---|---|---|
| 772 | A196 | 6c multi | .20 .20 |
| 773 | A196 | 10c multi | .30 1.15 |

Nos. 772-773,C235-C237 (5) 1.30 1.15

2nd Intl. Fair of El Salvador, Nov. 5-27.

José Simeon Cañas Pleading for
Indian Slaves — A197

**1967, Feb. 18** **Litho.** **Perf. 11½**
| | | | |
|---|---|---|---|
| 774 | A197 | 6c yel & multi | .20 .20 |
| 775 | A197 | 10c lil roso & multi | .20 .20 |

Nos. 774-775,C239-C240 (4) 1.15 .95

Father José Simeon Cañas y Villacorta,
D.D. (1767-1838), emancipator of the Central
American slaves.
For surcharges see #841A-842, 891, C403-
C405.

No. 726 Overprinted in Red: "XV
Convención de Clubes / de Leones,
Región de / El Salvador-11 y 12 / de
Marzo de 1967"

**1967** **Photo.**
| | | | |
|---|---|---|---|
| 776 | A186 | 40c brn org & sepia | .50 .25 |

Issued to publicize the 15th Convention of
Lions Clubs of El Salvador, March 11-12.

Volcano
San Miguel
A198

**1967, Apr. 14** **Photo.** **Perf. 13**
| | | | |
|---|---|---|---|
| 777 | A198 | 70c lt rose lilac & brn | 1.00 .60 |

Centenary of stamps of El Salvador.
See No. C241. For surcharges see Nos.
841, C320, C350.

No. 768 Overprinted in Red: "VIII
CONGRESO / CENTROAMERICANO
DE / FARMACIA Y BIOQUIMICA / 5 di
11 Noviembre de 1967"

**1967, Oct. 26** **Photo.** **Perf. 12x11½**
| | | | |
|---|---|---|---|
| 778 | A194 | 15c multi | .20 .20 |

8th Central American Congress for Pharmacy and Biochemistry. See No. C242.

---

No. 751 Overprinted in Red: "I Juegos
/ Centroamericanos y del / Caribe de
Basquetbol / 25 Nov. al 3 Dic. 1967"

**1967, Nov. 15**
| | | | |
|---|---|---|---|
| 779 | A190 | 3c dl grn, brn, yel & org | .20 .20 |

First Central American and Caribbean Basketball Games, 11/25-12/3. See #C243.

No. 757 Overprinted in Carmine:
"1968 / AÑO INTERNACIONAL DE /
LOS DERECHOS HUMANOS"

**1968, Jan. 2** **Photo.** **Perf. 11½x12**
| | | | |
|---|---|---|---|
| 780 | A191 | 5c dp yel, brn & gold | .20 .20 |

Intl. Human Rights Year. See #C244.

Weather
Map, Satellite
and WMO
Emblem
A199

**1968, Mar. 25** **Photo.** **Perf. 11½x12**
| | | | |
|---|---|---|---|
| 781 | A199 | 1c multi | .20 .20 |
| 782 | A199 | 30c multi | .30 .20 |

World Meteorological Day, Mar. 25.

No. 768 Overprinted in Red: "1968 /
XX ANIVERSARIO DE LA /
ORGANIZACION MUNDIAL / DE LA
SALUD"

**1968, Apr. 7** **Perf. 12x11½**
| | | | |
|---|---|---|---|
| 783 | A194 | 15c multi | .20 .20 |

20th anniv. of WHO. See No. C245.

No. 765 Overprinted in Red: "1968 /
Año / del Sistema / del Crédito /
Rural"

**1968, May 6** **Photo.** **Perf. 12x11½**
| | | | |
|---|---|---|---|
| 784 | A193 | 6c yellow & multi | .20 .20 |

Rural credit system. See No. C246.

Alberto
Masferrer
A200

Scouts Helping to
Build — A201

**1968, June 22** **Litho.** **Perf. 12x11½**
| | | | |
|---|---|---|---|
| 785 | A200 | 5c multi | .20 .20 |
| 786 | A200 | 6c multi | .20 .20 |
| 787 | A200 | 25c vio & multi | .30 .20 |

Nos. 785-787,C247-C248 (5) 1.10 1.00

Centenary of the birth of Alberto Masferrer,
philosopher and scholar.
For surcharges and overprints see Nos.
819, 843A, 890, C297.

**1968, July 26** **Litho.** **Perf. 12**
| | | | |
|---|---|---|---|
| 788 | A201 | 25c multi | .20 .20 |

Issued to publicize the 7th Inter-American
Boy Scout Conference. July-Aug., 1968.
See No. C249.

Water
Lily — A190

ICY Emblem
A191

Map of Central America, Flags and Presidents of US, Costa Rica, Salvador, Guatemala, Honduras and Nicaragua — A202

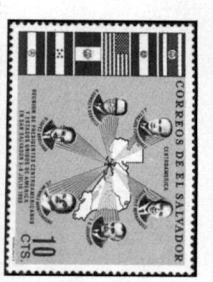

**1968, Dec. 5** **Litho.** **Perf. 14½**
789 A202 10c tan & multi .20 .20
790 A202 15c multi .20 .20
Nos. 789-790,C260-C261 (4) 1.35 1.10

Meeting of Pres. Lyndon B. Johnson with the presidents of the Central American republics (J. J. Trejos, Costa Rica; Fidel Sanchez Hernandez, Salvador; J. C. Mendez Montenegro, Guatemala; Osvaldo Lopez Arellano, Honduras; Anastasio Somoza Debayle, Nicaragua), San Salvador, July 5-8, 1968.

Red Cross Activities A204

**1969** **Litho.** **Perf. 14½**
791 A203 5c bluish lil, blk & yel .20 .20
Nos. 791-794,C252-C255 (8) 11.50 7.35

Various Butterflies.

Helionius Charithonius — A203

**1969** **Perf. 12**
792 A203 10c beige & multi .20 .20
793 A203 30c lt grn & multi .25 .20
794 A203 50c tan & multi .40 .30
Nos. 796-797,C256-C258 (6) 5.00 3.80

For surcharge see No. C259.

50th anniv. of the League of Red Cross Societies.

**1969** **Litho.** **Perf. 12**
795 A204 10c lt bl & multi .20 .20
796 A204 20c pink & multi .20 .20
797 A204 40c lil & multi .25 .20

No. 749 Overprinted in Green:
"Alunizaje / Apolo-11 / 21 Julio / 1969"

**1969, Sept.** **Photo.** **Perf. 11½x12**
798 A189 50c pink & blk .40 .30

Man's first landing on the moon, July 20, 1969. The same overprint in red brown and pictures of the landing module and the astronauts on the moon were applied to the margin of No. 750. See No. C259.

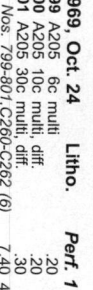

Social Security Hospital A205

**1969, Oct. 24** **Litho.** **Perf. 11½**
799 A205 6c multi .20 .20
800 A205 10c multi; diff. .30 .20
801 A205 30c multi; diff. .60 .20
Nos. 799-801,C260-C262 (6) 7.40 4.60

For surcharges see Nos. 857, C355.

---

ILO Emblem — A206

**1969** **Litho.** **Perf. 13**
802 A206 10c yel & multi .20 .20

50th anniv. of the ILO. See No. C263.

Chorros Spa A207

Views: 40c, Jaltepeque Bay, 80c, Fountains, Amapulapa Spa.

**1969, Dec. 19** **Photo.** **Perf. 12x11½**
803 A207 10c blk & multi .20 .20
804 A207 40c blk & multi .30 .25
805 A207 80c blk & multi .65 .30
Nos. 803-805,C264-C266 (6) 2.15 1.75

Tourism.

Euchroma Gigantea — A208

Insects: 25c, Grasshopper. 30c, Digger wasp.

**1970, Feb. 24** **Litho.** **Perf. 11½x11**
806 A208 5c lt bl & multi .20 .20
807 A208 20c dl yel & multi .45 .20
808 A208 30c dl rose & multi .55 .20
Nos. 806-808,C267-C269 (6) 15.50 5.10

For surcharges see Nos. C371-C373.

Map and Arms of Salvador, National Unity Emblem A209

**1970, Apr. 14** **Litho.** **Perf. 14**
809 A209 10c yel & multi .20 .20
810 A209 40c pink & multi .70 .20
Nos. 809-810,C270-C271 (4) 1.70 1.00

Salvador's support of universal human rights. For overprints and surcharge see Nos. 823, C301, C402.

Soldiers with Flag A210

**1970, May 7** Design: 30c, Anti-aircraft gun.
811 A210 10c green & multi .20 .20
812 A210 30c lemon & multi .30 .20
Nos. 811-812,C272-C274 (5) 1.50 1.00

Issued for Army Day, May 7.

---

National Lottery Headquarters A211

**1970, July 15** **Litho.** **Perf. 12**
813 A211 20c lt vio & multi .20 .20

National Lottery centenary. See No. C291.

UN and Education Year Emblems A212

**1970, Sept. 11** **Litho.** **Perf. 12**
814 A212 50c multi .40 .20
815 A212 1col multi .85 .45
Nos. 814-815,C292-C293 (4) 3.05 1.85

Issued for International Education Year.

Map of Salvador, Globe and Cogwheels A213

**1970, Oct. 28** **Litho.** **Perf. 12**
816 A213 5c pink & multi .20 .20
817 A213 10c buff & multi .20 .20
Nos. 816-817,C294-C295 (4) 1.00 .80

4th International Fair, San Salvador.

Beethoven — A214

**1971, Feb. 22** **Litho.** **Perf. 13½**
818 A214 50c ol, brn & yel .50 .20

Second International Music Festival. See No. C296. For overprint see No. 833.

No. 787 Overprinted: "Año / del Centenario de la / Biblioteca Nacional / 1970"

**1970, Nov. 25** **Perf. 12x11½**
819 A200 25c vio & multi .20 .20

Cent. of the National Library. See No. C297.

---

Maria Elena Sol — A215

**1971, Apr. 1** **Litho.** **Perf. 14**
820 A215 10c lt grn & multi .20 .20
821 A215 30c multi .20 .20
Nos. 820-821,C298-C299 (4) 1.05 .90

Maria Elena Sol, Miss World Tourism, 1970-71. For overprint see No. 832.

**1971, May 10** **Litho.** **Perf. 14**
822 A216 10c salmon & vio brn .20 .20

Mother's Day, 1971. See No. C300.

Pietà, by Michelangelo A216

No. 810 Overprinted in Red

**1971, July 6** **Litho.** **Perf. 14**
823 A209 40c pink & multi .35 .20

National Police, 104th anniv. See #C301.

Tiger Sharks — A217

**1971, July 28**
824 A217 10c shown .20 .20
825 A217 40c Swordfish .20 .20
Nos. 824-825,C302-C303 (4) 1.25 1.15

Declaration of Independence — A218

Designs: Various sections of Declaration of Independence of Central America.

**1971** **Perf. 13½x13**
826 A218 5c yel grn & blk .20 .20
827 A218 10c brt rose & blk .20 .20
828 A218 15c dp org & blk .20 .20
829 A218 20c dp red lil & blk .20 .20
Nos. 826-829,C304-C307 (8) 2.15 1.80

Sesquicentennial of independence of Central America. For overprints see Nos. C321, C347.

Izalco Church A219

**1971, Aug. 21** **Litho.** **Perf. 13½x13½**
830 A219 20c blk & multi .20 .20
831 A219 30c pur & multi .30 .20
Nos. 830-831,C308-C309 (4) 1.25 .95

Design: 30c, Sonsonate Church.

No. 821 Overprinted in Carmine:
"1972 Año de Turismo / de las Américas"

**1972, Nov. 15** **Litho.** **Perf. 14**
832 A215 30c multi .20 .20

Tourist Year of the Americas, 1972.

EL SALVADOR

## Map of Americas and El Salvador, Trophy A229

**1975, June 25**   **Litho.**   *Perf. 12½*
859 A229 10c red org & multi   .20 .20
860 A229 40c yel & multi   .25 .25
Nos. 859-860,C360-C361 (4)   1.15 1.05
El Salvador, site of 1975 Miss Universe Contest.

Claudia Lars, Poet, and IWY Emblem — A230
**1975, Sept. 4**   **Litho.**   *Perf. 12½*
861 A230 10c yel & bl blk   .20 .20
Nos. 861,C362-C363 (3)   .60 .60
Intl. Women's Year 1975.

## Nurses Attending Patient A231

**1975, Oct. 24**   **Litho.**   *Perf. 12½*
862 A231 10c lt grn & multi   .20 .20
Nurses' Day. See No. C364. For overprint see No. 868.

Congress Emblem — A232
**1975, Nov. 19**   **Litho.**   *Perf. 12½*
863 A232 10c yel & multi   .20 .20
15th Conference of Inter American Federation of Securities Enterprises, San Salvador, Nov. 16-20. See No. C365.

No. 768 Overprinted in Red: "XVI / CONGRESO MEDICO / CENTROAMERICANO / SAN SALVADOR, / EL SALVADOR, / DIC. 10-13, 1975"
**1975, Nov. 26**   **Photo.**   *Perf. 12x11½*
864 A194 15c beige & multi   .20 .20
16th Central American Medical Congress, San Salvador, Dec. 10-13.

## Flags of Participants, Arms of Salvador A233

**1975, Nov. 28**   **Litho.**   *Perf. 12½*
865 A233 15c blk & multi   .20 .20
866 A233 50c brn & multi   .85 .80
Nos. 865-866,C366-C367 (4)
8th Ibero-Latin-American Dermatological Congress, San Salvador, Nov. 28-Dec. 3.

---

No. 763 Surcharged

**1974, Oct. 14**   **Photo.**   *Perf. 11½x12*
852 A192 5c on 6c multi   .20 .20
12th Central American and Caribbean Chess Tournament, Oct. 1974.

Nos. 762 and 771 Surcharged

**1974-75**   *Perf. 11½x12, 12*
853 A192 10c on 3c multi   .20 .20
853A A195 25c on 1col multi (75)   .20 .20
Bar and surcharge on one line on No. 853A. Issued: #853, Dec. 19; #853A, Jan. 13.

UPU Emblem A226
**1975, Jan. 22**   **Litho.**   *Perf. 13*
854 A226 10c bl & multi   .20 .20
855 A226 60c bl & multi   .90 .90
Nos. 854-855,C356-C357 (4)
Cent. of UPU.

## Acajutla Harbor A227

**1975, Feb. 17**
856 A227 10c blue & multi   .20 .20
See No. C358.

No. 799 Surcharged

**1975**   **Litho.**   *Perf. 11½*
857 A205 5c on 6c multi   .20 .20

Central Post Office, San Salvador A228
**1975, Apr. 25**   **Litho.**   *Perf. 13*
858 A228 10c bl & multi   .20 .20
See No. C359.

---

Nos. 747 and 786 Surcharged:

**1974**   **Photo.**   *Perf. 11½x12*
843 A189 5c on 6c buff & blk   .20 .20
  **Litho.**   *Perf. 12x11½*
843A A200 5c on 6c multi   .20 .20
No. 843A has one obliterating rectangle and sans-serif "5." Issued: #843, Apr. 22; #843A, June 21.

Rehabilitation Institute Emblem A222
**1974, Apr. 30**   **Litho.**   *Perf. 13*
844 A222 10c multi   .20 .20
10th anniversary of the Salvador Rehabilitation Institute. See No. C324.

INTERPOL Headquarters, Saint-Cloud, France — A223
**1974, Sept. 2**   **Litho.**   *Perf. 12½*
845 A223 10c multi   .20 .20
50th anniv. of Intl. Criminal Police Organization (INTERPOL). See No. C341.

UN and FAO Emblems A224
**1974, Sept. 2**   **Litho.**   *Perf. 12½*
846 A224 10c bl, dk bl & gold   .20 .20
World Food Program, 10th anniv. See #C342.

25c Silver Coin, 1914 A225
**1974, Nov. 19**   **Litho.**   *Perf. 12½x13*
848 A225 10c shown   .20 .20
849 A225 15c 50c silver, 1953   .20 .20
850 A225 25c 25c silver, 1943   .20 .20
851 A225 30c 1c copper, 1892   .20 .20
Nos. 848-851,C343-C346 (8)   2.30 1.80

---

No. 818 Overprinted in Red
**1973, Feb. 5**   **Litho.**   *Perf. 13½*
833 A214 50c ol, brn & yel   .25 .20
3rd Intl. Music Festival, Feb. 9-25. See No. C313.

Lions International Emblem A220
**1973, Feb. 20**   **Litho.**   *Perf. 13*
834 A220 10c pink & multi   .20 .20
835 A220 25c lt bl & multi   .90 .80
Nos. 834-835,C314-C315 (4)
31st Lions International District "D" Convention, San Salvador, May 1972.

No. 812 Overprinted: "1923 1973 / 50 AÑOS FUNDACION / FUERZA AEREA"
**1973, Mar. 20**   **Litho.**   *Perf. 12*
836 A210 30c lem & multi   .20 .20
50th anniversary of Salvadorian Air Force.

Hurdling A221
**1973, May 21**   **Litho.**   *Perf. 13*
837 A221 5c shown   .20 .20
838 A221 10c High jump   .20 .20
839 A221 25c Running   .20 .20
840 A221 60c Pole vault   .30 .25
Nos. 837-840,C316-C319 (8)   6.35 2.85
20th Olympic Games, Munich, Aug. 26-Sept. 11, 1972.

No. 777 Surcharged:

**1973, Dec.**   **Photo.**   *Perf. 13*
841 A198 10c on 70c multi   .20 .20
See No. C320.

Nos. 774, C240 Surcharged with New Value and Overprinted "1823-1973 / 150 Aniversario Liberación / Esclavos en Centroamérica"
**1973-74**   **Litho.**   *Perf. 11½*
841A A197 5c on 6c multi ('74)   .20 .20
842 A197 10c on 45c multi   .20 .20
Sesquicentennial of the liberation of the slaves in Central America. On No. 841A two bars cover old denomination. On No. 842 "Aereo" is obliterated with a bar and old denomination with two bars.

**1975, Dec. 18    Litho.    Perf. 13½**
867   A234   10c dull red & maroon    .20   .20

7th Latin American Charity Congress, San Salvador, Nov. 1971. See No. C268.

No. 862 Overprinted: "III CONGRESO / ENFERMERIA / CENCAMEX 76"

**1976, May 10    Litho.    Perf. 12½**
868   A231   10c lt grn & multi    .20   .20

CENCAMEX 76, 3rd Nurses' Congress.

Map of El Salvador
A235

**1976, May 18**
869   A235   10c vio bl & multi    .20   .20

10th Congress of Revenue Collectors (Centro Interamericano de Administradores Tributarios, CIAT), San Salvador, May 16-22. See No. C382.

Flags of Salvador and US, Torch, Map of Americas
A236

The Spirit of '76, by Archibald M. Willard — A237

**1976, June 30    Litho.**
870   A236   10c yel & multi    .20   .20
871   A237   40c multi    .20   .20
Nos. 870-871,C383-C384 (4)    4.35   3.10

American Bicentennial.

Post-classical Vase, San Salvador
A239

Crocodylus Acutus — Lagarto

American Crocodile — A238

**1976, Sept. 23    Litho.    Perf. 12½**
872   A238   10c shown    .20   .20
873   A238   20c Green Iguana    .25   .25
874   A238   30c Iguana    1.65   1.50
Nos. 872-874,C385-C387 (6)

---

Map of El Salvador
Tazumal.

Pre-Columbian Art: 15c, Brazier with classical head, Tazumal. 40c, Vase with classical head, Tazumal.

**1976, Oct. 11    Litho.    Perf. 12½**
875   A239   10c multi    .20   .20
876   A239   15c multi    .30   .30
877   A239   40c multi    .30   .30
Nos. 875-877,C388-C390 (6)    1.85   1.55

For overprint see No. C429.

Fair Emblem
A240

**1976, Oct. 25    Litho.    Perf. 12½**
878   A240   10c multi    .20   .20
879   A240   30c multi    .25   .25
Nos. 878-879,C391-C392 (4)    1.20   1.05

7th Intl. Fair, Nov. 5-22.

Child under Christmas Tree — A241

**1976, Dec. 16    Litho.    Perf. 11**
880   A241   10c yel & multi    .20   .20
881   A241   15c buff & multi    .20   .20
882   A241   30c vio & multi    .25   .25
883   A241   40c pink & multi    .30   .30
Nos. 880-883,C393-C396 (8)    2.65   2.10

Christmas 1976.

Rotary Emblem, Map of Salvador
A242

**1977, June 20    Litho.    Perf. 11**
884   A242   10c multi    .20   .20
885   A242   15c multi    .20   .20
Nos. 884-885,C397-C398 (4)    1.40   1.10

San Salvador Rotary Club, 50th anniversary.

Cerron Grande Hydroelectric Station — A243

Designs: No. 887, 15c, Central sugar refinery. Jiboa, 30c, Radar station, Izalco, vert.

**1977, June 29    Perf. 12½**
886   A243   10c multi    .20   .20
887   A243   10c multi    .20   .20
888   A243   15c multi    .25   .20
889   A243   30c multi    .25   .20
Nos. 886-889,C399-C401 (7)    2.05   1.60

Industrial development. Nos. 886-889 have colorless overprint in multiple rows: GOBIERNO DEL SALVADOR.

Nos. 785 and 774 Surcharged with New Value and Bar

**1977, June 30    Perf. 12x11½, 11½**
890   A200   15c on 2c multi    .20   .20
891   A197   25c on 6c multi    .20   .20

---

Microphone, ASDER Emblem — A244

**1977, Sept. 14    Litho.    Perf. 12½**
892   A244   10c multi    .20   .20
893   A244   15c multi    .80   .80
Nos. 892-893,C406-C407 (4)    .80   .80

Broadcasting in El Salvador, 50th anniversary (Asociación Salvadoreño de Empresa Radio).

Wooden Drum
A245

Design: 10c, Flute and recorder.

**1978, Aug. 29    Litho.    Perf. 12½**
894   A245   5c multi    .20   .20
895   A245   10c multi    .20   .20
Nos. 894-895,C433-C435 (5)    1.60   1.20

For surcharge see No. C492.

"Man and Engineering"
A246

**1978, Sept. 12    Litho.    Perf. 13½**
896   A246   10c multi    .20   .20

4th National Engineers' Congress, San Salvador, Sept. 18-23. See No. C436.

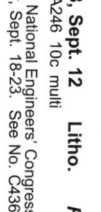

Izalco Station
A247

**1978, Sept. 14**
897   A247   10c multi

Inauguration of Izalco satellite earth station, Sept. 15, 1978. See No. C437.

Fair Emblem
A248

**1978, Oct. 30    Litho.    Perf. 12½**
898   A248   10c multi    .20   .20
899   A248   20c multi    .20   .20
Nos. 898-899,C440-C441 (4)    .80   .80

8th Intl. Fair, Nov. 3-20.

---

Henri Dunant, Red Cross Emblem
A249

**1978, Oct. 30    Perf. 11**
900   A249   10c multi    .20   .20

Henri Dunant (1828-1910), founder of the Red Cross. See No. C442.

World Map and Cotton Boll
A250

**1978, Nov. 22    Perf. 12½**
901   A250   15c multi    .20   .20

Intl. Cotton Consulting Committee, 37th Meeting, San Salvador, 11/27-12/2. See #C443.

Nativity, Stained glass Window
A251

**1978, Dec. 5    Litho.    Perf. 12½**
902   A251   10c multi    .20   .20
903   A251   15c multi    1.40   1.10
Nos. 902-903,C444-C445 (4)

Christmas 1978.

Athenaeum Coat of Arms — A252

**1978, Dec. 20    Litho.    Perf. 14**
904   A252   5c multi    .25   .20

Millennium of Castilian language. See No. C446.

Postal Service and UPU Emblems
A253

**1979, Apr. 2    Litho.    Perf. 14**
905   A253   10c multi    .20   .20

Centenary of Salvador's membership in Universal Postal Union. See No. C447.

A270

Children, Dove and Star — A264

**1980, Nov. 26    Litho.    Perf. 14**
931  A269  15c multi         .20  .20
932  A269  20c multi         .20  .20
Nos. 931-932,C479-C480 (4)  1.40  1.05
Corporation of Auditors, 50th anniv.

**1980, Dec. 5    Litho.    Perf. 14**
933  A270  5c multi          .20  .20
934  A270  10c multi         .20  .20
Nos. 933-934,C481-C482 (4)  1.10  .90
Christmas.

A271

A272

Dental association emblems.

**1981, June 18    Litho.    Perf. 14**
935  A271  15c lt yel grn & blk   .20  .20
Dental Society of Salvador, 50th anniv.; Odontological Federation of Central America and Panama, 25th anniv. See No. C494.

**1981, Aug. 14    Litho.    Perf. 14x14½**
936  A272  10c multi         .20  .20
Nos. 936,C489-C490 (3)      1.20  1.60
Design: Hands reading braille book.
Intl. Year of the Disabled.

A273

A274

**1981, Aug. 28    Litho.    Perf. 14x14½**
937  A273  10c multi         .20  .20
Roberto Quinonez Natl. Agriculture College, 25th anniv. See No. C499.

**1981, Sept. 16    Litho.    Perf. 14x14½**
938  A274  10c multi         .20  .20
World Food Day. See No. C500.

1981 World Cup Preliminaries — A275

---

Cogwheel around Map of Americas
A259

**1979, Oct. 19    Litho.    Perf. 14½x14**
915  A259  10c multi         .20  .20
8th COPIMERA Congress (Mechanical, Electrical and Allied Trade Engineers), San Salvador, Oct. 22-27. See No. C462.

Children of Various Races, IYC Emblem
A260

Children and Nurses, IYC Emblem
A261

**1979, Oct. 29    Perf. 14x14½, 11½x14**
916  A260  10c multi         .20  .20
917  A261  15c multi         .20  .20
International Year of the Child.

Map of Central and South America, Congress Emblem — A262

**1979, Nov. 1    Litho.    Perf. 14½x14**
918  A262  10c multi         .20  .20
5th Latin American Clinical Biochemistry Cong., San Salvador, 11/5-10. See #C465.

Coffee Bushes in Bloom, Coffee Association Emblem
A263

**1979, Dec. 18    Perf. 14x14½, 14½x14**
919  A263  10c multi         .20  .20
920  A263  30c multi         .25  .25
921  A263  40c multi         .30  .30
Nos. 919-921,C466-C468 (6)  2.55  1.95
Salvador Coffee Assoc., 50th Anniv.: 30c, Planting coffee bushes; vert. 40c, Coffee berries.

---

**1979, Dec. 18    Litho.    Perf. 14½x14**
922  A264  10c multi         .20  .20
Christmas 1979.

Hoof and Mouth Disease Prevention
A265

**1980, June 3    Litho.    Perf. 14½x14**
923  A265  10c multi         .20  .20
See No. C469.

Anadara Grandis
A266

**1980, Aug. 12    Perf. 14x14½**
924  A266  10c shown         .20  .20
925  A266  30c Ostrea iridescens   .25  .25
926  A266  40c Turltella leucus-toria   .30  .30
Nos. 924-926,C470-C473 (7)  2.45  2.10

Quetzal (Pharomachrus mocino) — A267

**1980, Sept. 10    Litho.    Perf. 14x14½**
927  A267  10c shown         .20  .20
928  A267  20c Penelopina nigra   .20  .20
Nos. 927-928,C474-C476 (5)  1.60  1.25

Local Snakes
A268

**1980, Nov. 12    Litho.    Perf. 14x14½**
929  A268  10c Tree snake     .20  .20
930  A268  20c Water snake    .20  .20
Nos. 929-930,C477-C478 (4)  1.00  .85

A269

---

"75," Health Organization and WHO Emblems — A254

**1979, Apr. 7    Perf. 14x14½**
906  A254  10c multi         .20  .20
Pan-American Health Organization, 75th anniversary. See No. C448.

Flame and Pillars — A255

**1979, May 25    Litho.    Perf. 12½**
907  A255  10c multi         .20  .20
908  A255  15c multi         .25  .25
Nos. 907-908,C449-C450 (4)  1.40  1.10
Social Security 5-year plan, 1978-1982.

Pope John Paul II, Map of Americas
A256

**1979, July 12    Litho.    Perf. 14½x14**
909  A256  10c multi         .20  .20
910  A256  20c multi         .20  .20
Nos. 909-910,C454-C455 (4)  4.90  3.20

Mastodon
A257

**1979, Sept. 7    Perf. 14**
911  A257  10c shown         .20  .20
912  A257  20c Saber-toothed tiger   .20  .20
913  A257  30c Toxodon       .25  .25
Nos. 911-913,C458-C460 (6)  2.65  2.05

Salvador Flag, José Aberiz and Proclamation
A258

**1979, Sept. 14    Litho.    Perf. 14½x14**
914  A258  10c multi         .20  .20
National anthem centenary. See No. C461.

**1981, Nov. 27    Litho.    Perf. 14x14½**
939  A275  10c shown    .20  .20
940  A275  40c Cup soccer ball, flags    .30  .25
Nos. 939-940,C505-C506 (4)    1.30  1.05

**1981, Dec. 17    Litho.    Perf. 14**
941  A276  10c multi    .20  .20
Salvador Lyceum (High School), 100th Anniv. — A276
See No. C507.

Pre-Columbian Stone Sculptures
A277

**1982, Jan. 22    Litho.    Perf. 14**
942  A277  10c Axe with bird's head    .20  .20
943  A277  20c Sun disc    .20  .20
944  A277  40c Stele Carving with effigy    .30  .30
Nos. 942-944,C508-C510 (6)    1.80  1.55

**1982, Mar. 17    Litho.    Perf. 14½x14**
945  A278  10c shown    .20  .20
946  A278  30c Girl Scout helping woman    .25  .25
Nos. 945-946,C511-C512 (4)    1.05  .90
Scouting Year — A278

**1982, May 7    Litho.    Perf. 14½x13½**
947  A279  10c multi    .20  .20
See No. C514.
Armed Forces
A279

**1982, July 14    Perf. 14x14½**
948  A280  10c Team, emblem    .20  .20
Nos. 948,C518-C520 (4)    2.50  1.75
1982 World Cup
A280

---

**1982, Oct. 14    Litho.    Perf. 14**
949  A281  10c multi    .20  .20
See No. C524.
10th International Fair — A281

**1982, Dec. 14    Litho.    Perf. 14**
950  A282  5c multi    .20  .20
See No. C528.
Christmas 1982 — A282

Dancers, Pre-Columbian Ceramic Design — A283

**1983, Feb. 18    Litho.    Perf. 14**
951  A283  10c shown    .20  .20
952  A283  20c Sower    .20  .20
953  A283  25c Flying Man    .20  .20
954  A283  60c Hunters    .50  .50
955  A283  60c Hunters, diff.    .50  .50
a.    Pair, #954-955    1.00  1.00
956  A283  1col Procession    .80  .80
957  A283  1col Procession, diff.    .80  .80
a.    Pair, #956-957    1.60  1.60
Nos. 951-957 (7)    3.20  3.20
Nos. 953-957 airmail. #955a, 957a have continuous designs.

Visit of Pope John Paul II — A284

**1983, Mar. 4    Litho.    Perf. 14**
958  A284  25c shown    .20  .20
959  A284  60c Monument to the Divine Savior, Pope    .50  .40

Salvadoran Air Force, 50th Anniv. — A285

**1983, Mar. 24    Litho.    Perf. 14**
960  A285  10c Ricardo Aberle    .20  .20
961  A285  10c Air Force Emblem    .20  .20
962  A285  10c Enrico Massi    .20  .20
a.    Strip of 3, #960-962    .60  .60
963  A285  10c Juan Ramon Munes    .20  .20
964  A285  10c American Air Force Cooperation Emblem    .20  .20
965  A285  10c Belisario Salazar    .20  .20
a.    Strip of 3, #963-965    .60  .60
Nos. 960 or 963 at left and two Nos. 962 or 965 at right.
Arranged se-tenant horizontally with two Nos. 960 or 963 at left and two Nos. 962 or 965 at right.

---

Local butterflies.

**1983, May 31    Litho.    Perf. 14**
966  A286  5c Papilio torquatus    .50  .50
967  A286  5c Metamorphia stereiles    .20  .20
a.    Pair    .60  .60
968  A286  10c Papilio torquatus, diff.    .20  .20
a.    Pair    .60  .60
969  A286  15c Prepona brooksiana    .75  .75
a.    Pair    .75  .75
970  A286  15c Caligo aireus    .20  .20
a.    Pair    .25  .25
    25c Morpho peleides    1.25  1.25
a.    Pair    1.25  1.25
    25c Dismorphia praxinoe    .25  .25
a.    Pair    .25  .25
    50c Morpho polyphemus    2.40  2.40
a.    Pair    .45  .45
    50c Metamorphia epaphus    .45  .45
Nos. 966-970 (5)    5.50  5.50

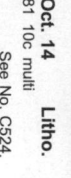
A286

**1983, June 23    Litho.    Perf. 14**
971  A287  75c multi    .60  .50
Simon Bolivar, 200th birth anniv.
A287

**1983, July 21    Litho.    Perf. 14**
972  A288  10c Dr. Jose Mendoza, college emblem    .20  .20
Salvador Medical College, 40th anniv.
A288

A289

**1983, Oct. 30    Perf. 13½x14, 14x13½**
973  A289  10c multi    .20  .20
974  A289  50c multi, horiz.    .40  .40
Centenary of David J. Guzman national museum. 50c airmail.
A289

---

San Salvador. 25c, 50c airmail.
10c, Gen. Juan Jose Canas, Francisco Duenas (organizers of 1st natl. telegraph service), Morse Key, 1870. 25c, Mailman delivering letters. 50c, Post Office sorting center,

**1983, Nov. 23    Perf. 14x13½, 13½x14**
975  A290  10c multi    .20  .20
976  A290  25c multi, vert.    .40  .30
977  A290  50c multi    .80  .70
Nos. 975-977 (3)    .20  .20

**1983, Nov. 30    Perf. 13½x14, 14x13½**
978  A291  10c Dove over globe    .20  .20
979  A291  25c Creche figures, horiz.    .20  .20
A291

**1983, Dec. 13**
980  A292  10c Vehicle exhaust    .20  .20
981  A292  15c Fig tree    .20  .20
982  A292  25c Rodent    .60  .60
Nos. 980-982 (3)
Environmental protection. 15c, 25c airmail.
A292

Philatelists' Day
A293

**1984, Jan. 5    Perf. 14x13½**
983  A293  10c No. 1    .20  .20
Corn — A294

**1984, Feb. 21    Litho.    Perf. 14½x14**
984  A294  10c shown    .20  .20
985  A294  15c Cotton    .20  .20
986  A294  25c Coffee beans    .20  .20
987  A294  25c Sugar cane    .20  .20
988  A294  75c Beans    .30  .25
989  A294  1col Agave    .40  .30
990  A294  5col Balsam    2.00  1.50
Nos. 984-990 (7)    3.50  2.85

Caluco Church, Sonsonate
A295

**1984, Mar. 30    Perf. 14x13½**
991  A295  5c shown    .20  .20
992  A295  10c Salcoatitan, Sonsonate    .20  .20

World Communications Year — A290

## 993–996

- 993 A295 15c Huizucar, La Libertad ... .20 .20
- 994 A295 25c Santo Domingo, Sonsonate ... .20 .20
- 995 A295 50c Pilar, Sonsonate ... .30 .25
- 996 A295 75c Nahuizalco, Sonsonate ... 1.30 1.25

Nos. 991–996 (6)

Nos. 993–996 airmail.

## Central Reserve Bank of Salvador, 50th Anniv. A296

**1984, July 17    Litho.    Perf. 14x14½**

- 997 A296 10c First reserve note ... .20 .20
- 998 A296 25c Bank, 1959 ... .20 .20

25c airmail.

## 1984 Summer Olympics A297

**1984, July 20    Perf. 14x13½, 13½x14**

- 999 A297 10c Boxing ... .20 .20
- 1000 A297 25c Running, vert. ... .20 .20
- 1001 A297 40c Bicycling ... .25 .20
- 1002 A297 50c Swimming ... .35 .25
- 1003 A297 75c Judo, vert. ... .45 .25
- 1004 A297 1col Pierre de Coubertin ... .55 .30

Nos. 999–1004 (6) ... 2.00 1.35

Nos. 1000–1004 airmail. For surcharge see No. C536A.

## Govt. Printing Office Building Opening A298

**1984, July 27    Perf. 14x14½**

- 1005 A298 10c multi ... .20 .20

## 5th of November Hydroelectric Plant — A299

Designs: 55c, Cerron Grande Plant, 70c, Ahuachapan Geothermal Plant. 90c, Mural. 15th of September Plant. 7c, 90c, 2 col airmail.

**1984, Sept. 13    Litho.    Perf. 14x14½**

- 1006 A299 20c multi ... .20 .20
- 1007 A299 55c multi ... .25 .20
- 1008 A299 70c multi ... .35 .25
- 1009 A299 90c multi ... .50 .30
- 1010 A299 2col multi ... 1.00 .60

Nos. 1006–1010 (5) ... 2.30 1.55

## Boys Playing Marbles A300

**Perf. 14½x14**

- 1011 A300 55c Spinning top ... .25 .20
- 1012 A300 70c Flying kite ... .40 .25
- 1013 A300 90c Top, diff. ... .50 .30
- 1014 A300 2col ... .95 .60

Nos. 1011–1014 (4) ... 2.10 1.35

## 11th International Fair — A301

**1984, Oct. 31    Litho.    Perf. 14x14½**

- 1015 A301 25c shown ... .20 .20
- 1016 A301 70c Fairgrounds ... .30 .25

70c airmail.

## Los Chorros Tourist Center A302

**1984, Nov. 23    Litho.    Perf. 14½x14**

- 1017 A302 15c shown ... .20 .20
- 1018 A302 25c Plaza las Americas ... .30 .20
- 1019 A302 70c El Salvador International Airport ... .40 .20
- 1020 A302 90c El Tunco Beach ... .35 .30
- 1021 A302 2col Sihuatehuacan Tourist Center ... .95 .60

Nos. 1017–1021 (5) ... 2.20 1.50

## The Paper of Papers, 1979, by Roberto A. Galicia (b. 1945) A002a

Paintings by natl. artists: 20c, The White Nun, 1939, by Salvador Salazar Arrue (b. 1899), vert. 70c, Supreme Elegy to Masferrer, 1968, by Antonio G. Ponce (b. 1938), vert. 90c, Transmutation, 1979, by Armando Solis (b. 1940). 2 col, Figures at Theater, 1959, by Carlos Canas (b. 1924), vert.

**1984, Dec. 10    Litho.    Perf. 14**

- 1021A A302a 20c multi ... .20 .20
- 1021B A302a 55c multi ... .25 .20
- 1021C A302a 70c multi ... .40 .25
- 1021D A302a 90c multi ... .50 .25
- 1021E A302a 2col multi ... .95 .60

Nos. 1021A–1021E (5) ... 2.30 1.50

Nos. 1021B–1021E are airmail. 70c and 2col issued with overprinted silver bar and corrected inscription in black; copies exist without overprint.

## Christmas 1984 — A303

**1984, Dec. 19    Litho.**

- 1022 A303 25c Glass ornament ... .20 .20
- 1023 A303 70c Ornaments, dove ... .35 .25

No. 1023 airmail.

## Birds — A304

**1984, Dec. 21    Litho.    Perf. 14½x14**

- 1024 A304 15c Lepidocolaptes affinis ... .20 .20
- 1025 A304 25c Spodiornis rusticus barrileriensis ... .30 .20
- 1026 A304 55c Claravis mondetoura ... .40 .20
- 1027 A304 70c Hylomanes momotula ... .50 .25
- 1028 A304 90c Xenotriccus calizonus ... .60 .30
- 1029 A304 1col Cardellina rubrifrons ... .70 .35

Nos. 1024–1029 (6) ... 2.70 1.50

Nos. 1026–1029 airmail.

## Salvador Bank Centenary A305

**1985, Feb. 6    Litho.    Perf. 14**

- 1030 A305 25c Stock certificate ... .20 .20

## Mortgage Bank, 50th Anniv. — A306

**1985, Feb. 20    Litho.    Perf. 14**

- 1031 A306 25c Mortgage ... .20 .20

## Intl. Youth Year A307

**1985, Feb. 28    Litho.    Perf. 14**

- 1032 A307 25c IYY emblem ... .20 .20
- 1033 A307 55c Woodcrafting ... .35 .20
- 1034 A307 70c Professions symbolized ... .45 .25
- 1035 A307 1.50col Youths marching ... .75 .45

Nos. 1032–1035 (4) ... 1.75 1.10

Nos. 1033–1035 airmail.

## Archaeology A308

**1985, Mar. 6    Litho.    Perf. 14½x14**

- 1036 A308 15c Pre-classical figure ... .20 .20
- 1037 A308 20c Engraved vase ... .25 .20
- 1038 A308 55c Post-classical ceramic ... .30 .20
- 1039 A308 55c Post-classical figure ... .40 .20
- 1040 A308 70c Late post-classical deity ... .50 .25
- 1041 A308 1col Late post-classical figure ... .60 .30

Nos. 1036–1041 (6) ... 2.20 1.35

**Souvenir Sheet**

**Rouletted 13½**

- 1042 A308 2col Tazumal ruins, horiz. ... 1.25 .60

Nos. 1039–1041 airmail. No. 1042 has enlargement of stamp design in margin.

## Natl. Red Cross, Cent. A309

**1985, Mar. 13    Litho.    Perf. 14**

- 1043 A309 25c Anniv. emblem vert. ... .20 .20
- 1044 A309 55c Sea rescue ... .25 .25
- 1045 A309 70c Blood donation service ... .40 .20
- 1046 A309 90c First aid, ambulance, vert. ... .50 .25

Nos. 1043–1046 (4) ... 1.40 .85

Nos. 1044–1046 are airmail.

## Agriculture Type of 1984

**Perf. 14½x14**

1985

- 1047 A294 55c Cotton ... .20 .20
- 1048 A294 70c Corn ... .25 .20
- 1049 A294 90c Sugar cane ... .35 .25
- 1050 A294 2col Beans ... .75 .60
- 1051 A294 10col Agave ... 4.00 3.00

Nos. 1047–1051 (5) ... 5.55 4.25

Issued: 55c, 70c, 90c, 4/4; 2col, 10col, 9/4.

## Child Survival A310

Children's drawings.

**1985, May 3    Litho.    Perf. 14x14½**

- 1052 A310 25c Hand, houses ... .20 .20
- 1053 A310 55c House, children ... .30 .20
- 1054 A310 70c Boy, girl holding hands ... .40 .30
- 1055 A310 90c Oral vaccination ... .50 .30

Nos. 1052–1055 (4) ... 1.40 .90

Nos. 1053–1055 are airmail.

## Salvador Army A311

**1985, May 17**

- 1056 A311 25c Map ... .20 .20
- 1057 A311 70c Recruit, natl. flag ... .40 .20

No. 1057 is airmail.

## Inauguration of Pres. Duarte, 1st Anniv. — A312

**Perf. 14**

**1985, June 28    Perf. 14½x14**

- 1058 A312 25c Flag, laurel, book ... .20 .20
- 1059 A312 70c Article I, Constitution ... .25 .20

**Inter-American Development Bank, 25th Anniv. — A313**

25c, Central Hydro-electric Dam, power station. 70c, Map of Salvador, 1col, Natl. arms.

**1985, July 5**     **Perf. 14x13½**
| | | | | |
|---|---|---|---|---|
| 1060 | A313 | 25c multi | .20 | .20 |
| 1061 | A313 | 70c multi | .40 | .20 |
| 1062 | A313 | 1col multi | .50 | .30 |
| | | | 1.10 | .70 |

Nos. 1060-1062 (3)
Nos. 1061-1062 are airmail.

Fish
A314

**1985, Sept. 30**     **Perf. 14x14½**
| | | | | |
|---|---|---|---|---|
| 1064 | A314 | 25c Cichlasoma trimaculatum | .20 | .20 |
| 1065 | A314 | 55c Rhamdia guatemalensis | .20 | .20 |
| 1066 | A314 | 70c Poecilia sphenops | .25 | .20 |
| 1067 | A314 | 90c Cichlasoma nigrofasciatum | .35 | .30 |
| 1068 | A314 | 1col Astyanax fasciatus | .40 | .30 |
| 1069 | A314 | 1.50col Dormitator latifrons | .60 | .40 |
| | | | 2.00 | 1.60 |

Nos. 1064-1069 (6)
Nos. 1065-1069 are airmail.

**1985, Oct. 16**     **Perf. 14½x14**
| | | | | |
|---|---|---|---|---|
| 1070 | A315 | 20c Cornucopia | .20 | .20 |
| 1071 | A315 | 40c Centeotl, Nahuat god of corn | .20 | .20 |

UNFAO, 40th Anniv. — A315

Dragonflies
A316

**1985, Dec. 9**     **Perf. 14x14½**
| | | | | |
|---|---|---|---|---|
| 1072 | A316 | 25c multi | .20 | .20 |
| 1073 | A316 | 55c multi | .25 | .20 |
| 1074 | A316 | 70c multi | .35 | .20 |
| 1075 | A316 | 90c multi | .40 | .30 |
| 1076 | A316 | 1col multi | .50 | .30 |
| 1077 | A316 | 1.50col multi | .70 | .40 |
| | | | 2.40 | 1.60 |

Nos. 1072-1077 (6)
25c, Corduiegaster godmani mclachlan. 55c, Libellula herculea karsch. 70c, Cora marina selys. 90c, Aeshna cornigera braver. 1col, Mecistogaster ornata rambur. 1.50col, Hetaerina smaragdalis de marmels.

For surcharge see No. C544.
Nos. 1073-1077 are airmail.

---

Summer, 1984, by Roberto Huezo (b.1947)
A317

Paintings by natl. artists: 25c, Profiles, vert., 1978, by Rosa Mena Valenzuela (b. 1924). 70c, The Deliverance, 1984, by Fernando Llort (b. 1949). 90c, Making Tamale, 1975, by Pedro A. Garcia (b. 1930). 1col, Warm Presence, 1984, by Miguel A. Orellana (b. 1929), vert.

**1985, Dec. 18**     **Perf. 14**
| | | | | |
|---|---|---|---|---|
| 1078 | A317 | 25c multi | .20 | .20 |
| 1079 | A317 | 55c multi | .25 | .20 |
| 1080 | A317 | 70c multi | .35 | .25 |
| 1081 | A317 | 90c multi | .40 | .30 |
| 1082 | A317 | 1col multi | 1.40 | 1.15 |

Nos. 1078-1082 (5)
Nos. 1079-1082 are airmail.

San Vincente de Austria y Lorenzana City, 350th Anniv.
A318

**1985, Dec. 20**     **Perf. 14**
| | | | | |
|---|---|---|---|---|
| 1083 | A318 | 15c multi | .20 | .20 |
| 1084 | A318 | 20c Cathedral | .20 | .20 |

Intl. Peace Year 1986 — A319

**1986, Feb. 21**     **Perf. 14**
| | | | | |
|---|---|---|---|---|
| 1085 | A319 | 15c multi | .20 | .20 |
| 1086 | A319 | 70c multi | .50 | .40 |

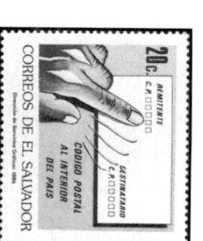

Postal Code Inauguration — A320

**1986, Mar. 14**     **Litho.**     **Perf. 14x14½**
| | | | | |
|---|---|---|---|---|
| 1087 | A320 | 20c Domestic mail | .20 | .20 |
| 1088 | A320 | 25c Intl mail | .20 | .20 |

Radio El Salvador, 60th Anniv.
A321

**1986, Mar. 21**
| | | | | |
|---|---|---|---|---|
| 1089 | A321 | 25c Microphone | .20 | .20 |
| 1090 | A321 | 70c Map | .50 | .40 |

No. 1090 is airmail.

---

Mammals
A322

**1986, May 30**     **Litho.**     **Perf. 14x14½**
| | | | | |
|---|---|---|---|---|
| 1091 | A322 | 15c Felis wiedii | .20 | .20 |
| 1092 | A322 | 20c Tamandua tetradactyla | .20 | .20 |
| 1093 | A322 | 70c Dasypus novemcinctus | .80 | .60 |
| 1094 | A322 | 2col Pecari tajacu | 1.60 | 1.25 |
| | | | 2.80 | 2.25 |

Nos. 1091-1094 (4)
Nos. 1093-1094 are airmail.

1986 World Cup Soccer Championships, Mexico — A323

Designs: 70c, Flags, mascot, 1col, Players, Soccer Cup, vert. 2col, Natl. flag, player dribbling, vert. 5col, Goal, emblem.

**1986, June 6**     **Perf. 14x14½, 14½x14**
| | | | | |
|---|---|---|---|---|
| 1095 | A323 | 70c multi | .55 | .40 |
| 1096 | A323 | 1col multi | .80 | .60 |
| 1097 | A323 | 2col multi | 1.60 | 1.25 |
| 1098 | A323 | 5col multi | 4.00 | 3.00 |
| | | | 6.95 | 5.25 |

Nos. 1095-1098 (4)

Teachers — A324

**1986, June 30**     **Litho.**     **Perf. 14½x14**
| | | | | |
|---|---|---|---|---|
| 1099 | A324 | 20c Dario Gonzalez | .20 | .20 |
| 1100 | A324 | 20c Valero Lecha | .20 | .20 |
| 1101 | A324 | 40c Marcelino G. Flamenco | .35 | .35 |
| a. | | Pair, #1099-1100 | | |
| 1102 | A324 | 40c Camilo Campos | .25 | .20 |
| a. | | Pair, #1101-1102 | .70 | .70 |
| 1103 | A324 | 70c Saul Flores | .35 | .35 |
| 1104 | A324 | 70c Jorge Larde | .25 | .25 |
| a. | | Pair, #1103-1104 | | |
| 1105 | A324 | 1col Francisco Moran | 1.10 | 1.10 |
| 1106 | A324 | 1col Mercedes M. De Luarca | .50 | .50 |
| a. | | Pair, #1105-1106 | 1.75 | 1.75 |
| | | | 2.60 | 2.00 |

Nos. 1099-1106 (8)
Nos. 1103-1106 are airmail.

---

Flowers
A327

**1986, Sept. 30**     **Perf. 14**
| | | | | |
|---|---|---|---|---|
| 1114 | A327 | 20c Spathiphyllum phryllifolium, vert. | .20 | .20 |
| 1115 | A327 | 25c Asclepias curassavica | .20 | .20 |
| 1116 | A327 | 70c Tagetes tenuifolia, vert. | .40 | .25 |
| 1117 | A327 | 1col Ipomoea tiliacea, vert. | 1.10 | .80 |
| | | | .50 | .35 |

Nos. 1115-1117 (3)
Nos. 1116-1117 are airmail.

World Food Day
A326

**1986, Oct. 30**     **Litho.**     **Perf. 14x14½**
| | | | | |
|---|---|---|---|---|
| 1113 | A326 | 20c multi | .20 | .20 |

Christmas
A328

**1986, Dec. 10**
| | | | | |
|---|---|---|---|---|
| 1118 | A328 | 25c Candles, vert. | .20 | .20 |
| 1119 | A328 | 70c Doves | .30 | .25 |

No. 1119 is airmail.

Crafts
A329

**1986, Dec. 18**
| | | | | |
|---|---|---|---|---|
| 1120 | A329 | 25c Basket-making | .20 | .20 |
| 1121 | A329 | 55c Ceramicware | .25 | .20 |
| 1122 | A329 | 70c Guitars, vert. | .30 | .25 |
| 1123 | A329 | 1col Baskets, diff. | .50 | .35 |
| | | | 1.25 | 1.00 |

Nos. 1120-1123 (4)

Christmas
A330

Paintings: 25c, Church, by Mario Araujo Rajo, vert. 70c, Landscape, by Francisco Reyes.

**1986, Dec. 22**     **Litho.**
| | | | | |
|---|---|---|---|---|
| 1124 | A330 | 25c multi | .20 | .20 |
| 1125 | A330 | 70c multi | .30 | .25 |

No. 1125 is airmail.

---

**1986, July 23**     **Litho.**     **Perf. 13½**
| | | | | |
|---|---|---|---|---|
| 1107 | A325 | 25c org & brn | .20 | .20 |
| 1108 | A325 | 55c grn, org & brn | .25 | .20 |
| 1109 | A325 | 70c pale gray, org | .25 | .20 |
| 1110 | A325 | 90c pale yel, org & brn | .30 | .25 |
| 1111 | A325 | 1col pale grn, org & brn | .45 | .30 |
| 1112 | A325 | 1.50col pale pink, org & brn | .70 | .50 |
| | | | 2.40 | 1.80 |

Pre-Hispanic Ceramic Seal, Cara Sucia, Ahuachapan, Tlaloc Culture (300 B.C.-A.D. 1200) — A325

Nos. 1107-1112 (6)
Nos. 1108-1112 are airmail.

## Promotion of Philately A331

**1987, Mar. 10  Litho.  Perf. 14½x14**
1126 A331 25c multi .20 .20

## Intl. Aid Following Earthquake, Oct. 10, 1986 — A332

**1987, Mar. 25**
1127 A332 15c multi .20 .20
1128 A332 70c multi .30 .25
1129 A332 1.50col multi .70 .50
1130 A332 5col multi 2.40 1.75
a. Nos. 1127-1130 (4) 3.60 2.70

## Orchids — A333

**Perf. 14½x14**
**1987, June 8  Litho.**
1131 A333 20c Maxillaria tenuifolia .20 .20
1132 A333 20c Ponthieva maculata .20 .20
a. Pair, #1131-1132 .40 .40
1133 A333 20c Meiracyllium trinasutum .25 .20
1134 A333 25c Encyclia vagans .25 .20
1135 A333 70c Encyclia cochleata .36 .50
1136 A333 70c Maxillaria atrata .35 .25
a. Pair, #1135-1136 1.25 1.25
1137 A333 1.50col Sobralia xantholeuca .70 .50
1138 A333 1.50col Encyclia microcharis .70 .50
a. Pair, #1137-1138 2.75 2.75
b. Pair, #1135-1136 3.00 2.30
#1133-1138 horiz. #1135-1138 (8) are airmail.

## Teachers — A334

Designs: No. 1139, C. de Jesus Alas, music. No. 1140, Luis Edmundo Vasquez, medicine. No. 1141, David Rosales, law. No. 1142, Guillermo Trigueros, medicine. No. 1143, Manuel Farfan Castro, history. No. 1144, In Sol, voice. No. 1145, Carlos Arturo Imendia, primary education. No. 1146, Benjamin Orozco, chemistry.

**Perf. 14½x14**
**1987, June 30  Litho.**
1139 A334 15c greenish blue & blk .20 .20
1140 A334 15c greenish blue & blk .20 .20
a. Pair, #1139-1140 .35 .35
1141 A334 20c beige & blk .20 .20
1142 A334 20c beige & blk .20 .20
a. Pair, #1141-1142 .35 .35
1143 A334 70c yel org & blk .35 .35
1144 A334 70c yel org & blk .35 .35
a. Pair, #143-1144 1.10 1.10
1145 A334 1.50col lt blue grn & blk .70 .50
1146 A334 1.50col lt blue grn & blk .70 .50
a. Pair, #1145-1146 2.50 2.50
Nos. 1139-1146 are airmail.

## 10th Pan American Games, Indianapolis — A335

**Perf. 14½x14, 14x14½**
**1987, July 31**
1147 A335 20c Emblem. vert. .20 .20
1148 A335 20c Table tennis. vert. .25 .25
1149 A335 25c Wrestling .20 .20
1150 A335 25c Fencing .30 .30
a. Pair, #1149-1150 .35 .25
1151 A335 70c Softball .35 .25
1152 A335 70c Equestrian .80 .80
a. Pair, #1151-1152 2.40 1.75
1153 A335 5col Weight lifting. vert. 2.40 1.75
1154 A335 5col Hurdling. vert. 6.00 6.00
a. Pair, #1153-1154 6.30 4.80
Nos. 1149-1153 are horizontal. Nos. 1151-1154 are airmail.

## Prior Nicolas Aguilar (1742-1818) A336

Famous men: 20c, Domingo Antonio de Lara (1783-1814), aviation pioneer. 70c, president Juan Manuel Rodrigucs (1771-1837), who abolished slavery. 1.50col, Pedro Pablo Castillo (1780-1814), patriot.

**Perf. 14½x14**
**1987, Sept. 11  Litho.**
1155 A336 15c multi .20 .20
1156 A336 20c multi .20 .20
1157 A336 70c multi .30 .25
1158 A336 1.50col multi .70 .50
a. Nos. 1155-1158 (4) 1.40 1.15
Nos. 1157-1158 are airmail.

## World Food Day A337

**Perf. 14x14½**
**1987, Oct. 16**
1159 A337 50c multi .25 .20

## Paintings by Salarrue A338

**Perf. 14½x14, 14x14½**
**1987, Nov. 30**
1160 A338 25c Self-portrait .20 .20
1161 A338 70c Lake .30 .25
#1161 is airmail. See #1186-1189.

## Christmas 1987 A339

25c, Virgin of Perpetual Sorrow, stained-glass window. 70c, The Three Magi, figurines.

**Perf. 14x14½**
**1987, Nov. 18**
1162 A339 25c multi .20 .20
1163 A339 70c multi .30 .25
No. 1163 is airmail.

## Pre-Columbian Musical Instruments — A340

Designs: 20c, Pottery drum worn around neck. No. 1165, Frieze picturing pre-Columbian musicians, from a Salua culture ceramic vase, c. 700-800 A.D. (left side). vert. No. 1166, Frieze (right side). vert. 1.50col, Conch shell trumpet.

**Perf. 14x14½, 14½x14**
**1987, Dec. 14  Litho.**
1164 A340 20c multi .20 .20
1165 A340 70c multi .30 .25
1166 A340 70c multi .30 .55
a. Pair, #165-1166 .65 .70
1167 A340 1.50col multi 1.50 1.20
a. Pair, #1164-1167 (4)
Nos. 1165-1167 are airmail. No. 1166a has a continuous design.

## Promotion of Philately A341

**Perf. 14**
**1088, Jan. 20  Litho.**
1168 A341 25c multi .20 .20

## Young Entrepreneurs of El Salvador — A342

**Perf. 14x14½**
**1988**
1169 A342 25c multi .20 .20

## St. John Bosco (1815-88) A343

## Environmental Protection — A344

**Perf. 14x14½**
**1988, Mar. 15  Litho.**
1170 A343 20c multi .20 .20

## 1988, June 3  Litho.  Perf. 14x14½

1171 A344 20c Forests .20 .20
1172 A344 70c Forests and rivers .35 .30
No. 1172 is airmail.

## 1988-1992 Summer Olympics, Seoul and Barcelona A345

**1988, Aug. 31  Litho.  Perf. 13½**
1173 A345 1col High jump .50 .20
1174 A345 1col Javelin .50 .20
1175 A345 1col Shooting .50 .20
1176 A345 1col Wrestling .50 .20
1177 A345 1col Basketball .50 .20
a. Strip of 5, #1173-1177
b. Min. sheets of 5 + 5 labels

**Souvenir Sheets**
1178 A345 2col Torch

Printed in sheets of 10 containing 2 each
No. 1177b exists in 2 forms: 1st contains labels picturing 1988 Summer Games emblem or character trademark; 2nd contains labels picturing the 1992 Summer Games emblem or character trademark.
No. 1178 exists in 2 forms: 1st contains 1988 Games emblem; 2nd 1992 Games emblem.
Some, or all, of this issue seem not to have been available to the public.

## World Food Day A346

**1988, Oct. 11  Litho.**
1179 A346 20c multi .20 .20

## 13th Intl. Fair, Nov. 23-Dec. 11 — A347

**Perf. 14x14½**
**1988, Oct. 25**
1180 A347 70c multi .35 .30

## Child Protection A348

**Perf. 14½x14**
**1988, Nov. 10**
1181 A348 15c Flying kite .20 .20
1182 A348 20c Child hugging adult's leg .20 .20

## Christmas A349

Paintings by Titian: 25c, Virgin and Child with the Young St. John and St. Anthony. 70c, Virgin and Child with the Young St. John and St. Anthony. 70c,

Virgin and Child in Glory with St. Francis and St. Alvise, vert.

**1988, Nov. 15**
1183 A349 25c multi .20 .20
1184 A349 70c multi .35 .30

70c is airmail.

Return to Moral Values
A350

**1988, Nov. 22** **Perf. 14½x14**
1185 A350 25c multi .20 .20

Art Type of 1987

Paintings by Salvadoran artists: 40c, *Esperanza de los Soles*, by Victor Rodriguez Preza. 1col, *Shepherd's Song*, by Luis Angel Salinas, horiz. 2col, *Children*, by Julio Hernandez Aleman, horiz. 5col, *El Niño de Las Alcancias*, by Camilo Minero. Nos. 1187-1189 are airmail.

**1988, Nov. 30** **Perf. 14½x14, 14½x14½**
1186 A338 40c multi .20 .20
1187 A338 1col multi .50 .40
1188 A338 2col multi 1.00 .75
1189 A338 5col multi 2.50 1.90
Nos. 1186-1189 (4) 4.20 3.25

A351

Discovery of America, 500th Anniv. (in 1992) — A352

Ruins and artifacts: a, El Tazumul. b, Multicolored footed bowl. c, San Andres. d, Two-color censer. e, Sihuatan. f, Carved head of the God of Lluvia. g, Cara Sucia. h, Man-shaped pear-shaped vase. i, San Lorenzo. j, Multicolored vase. 2col, Christopher Columbus.

**1988, Dec. 9** **Perf. 14½x14, 14½x14½**
1192 A353 25c Family, map, emblem, vert. .20 .20
1193 A353 70c shown .35 .30

70c is airmail.

**1988, Dec. 21** **Perf. 14x14½**
1190 A351 1col any single .50 .40

*Souvenir Sheet*

*Roulette 13½*

1191 A352 2col vermilion 1.00 .75

UN Declaration of Human Rights, 40th Anniv. A353

---

World Wildlife Fund — A354

Felines: a, *Felis wiedii* laying on tree branch. b, *Felis wiedii* sitting on branch. c, *Felis pardalis* laying in brush. d, *Felis pardalis* standing on tree branch.

**1988** **Perf. 14½x14**
1194 A354 25c any single 11.50 11.50
1195 A354 25c any single 4.50 4.50
1196 A355 55c any single 5.00 2.50
  a-d. Strip of 4

World Meteorological Organization, 40th Anniv. — A355

Meteorology in El Salvador, cent.

**1989, Feb. 3** **Litho.** **Perf. 14½x14**
1195 A355 15c shown .20 .20
1196 A355 20c Wind gauge .20 .20

Promotion of Philately A356

**1989, Mar. 15** **Litho.** **Perf. 14½x14**
1197 A356 25c Philatelic Soc. emblem .20 .20

See No. 1230.

Nat'l. Fire Brigade, 106th Anniv. A357

**1989, June 19** **Litho.**
1198 A357 25c Fire truck .20 .20
1199 A357 70c Firemen .35 .30

French Revolution, Bicent. A358

**1989, July 12** **Perf. 14x14½**
1200 A358 90c anniv emblem .45 .35
1201 A358 1col Storming of the Bastille .50 .40

*Souvenir Sheet*

1206 A362 25c multi .20 .20

**1989, July 26**
Demographic Assoc., 27th Anniv. — A362

Signing Act of Independence — A361

**1989, Sept. 1** **Perf. 14x14½**
1204 A361 25c shown .20 .20
1205 A361 70c Flag, nat'l seal, heroes .30 .20

Nat'l. independence, 168th anniv. No. 1205 is airmail.

Statues of Queen Isabella and Christopher Columbus — A360

**1989, May 31** **Litho.** **Perf. 14x14½**
1202 A359 50c any single 1.75 1.75

Designs: a, #88. b, #101. c, #86. d, #102. e, #87. f, #103.

*Miniature Sheet*

*Rouletted 13½*

1203 A360 2col shown 1.50 1.50

Discovery of America, 500th anniv. (in 1992). No. 1203 exists in two forms: margin pictures Nat'l. Palace with either emblem or anniv. emblem and "92" at lower right.

Souvenir Sheets

Stamps on Stamps A359

Beatification of Marcellin Champagnat, Founder of the Marist Brothers Order — A364

**1989, Sept. 28**
1213 A364 20c multicolored .20 .20

**1989, Sept. 1** **Litho.** **Perf. 14x14½**
1207 A363 20c shown .20 .20
1208 A363 20c multicolored .20 .20
  a. Pair, #1207-1208 .20
1209 A363 25c multicolored .20 .20
1210 A363 25c multicolored .20 .20
  a. Pair, #1209-1210 .25
1211 A363 55c multicolored .25 .20
1212 A363 1col multicolored 1.55 1.35
Nos. 1207-1212 (6) 1.55 1.35

UPAE emblem and pre-Columbian artifacts: 25c, *The Cultivator*, rock painting. 70c, Ceramic urn.

America Issue A365

**1989, Oct. 12**
1214 A365 25c multicolored .20 .20
1215 A365 70c multicolored .35 .30

World Food Day A366

**1989, Oct. 16** **Perf. 14½x14½, 14½x14** **Litho.**
1216 A366 15c shown .20 .20
1217 A366 55c Aspects of agriculture, vert. .30 .20

Children's Rights A367

**1989, Oct. 26** **Litho.** **Perf. 14½x14**
1218 A367 25c multicolored .20 .20

Creche Figures A368

**1989, Dec. 1** **Perf. 14½x14½**
1219 A368 25c shown .20 .20
1220 A368 70c Holy Family, diff. .35 .30

Christmas.

1990 World Cup Soccer Championships, Italy — A363

Soccer ball, flags of Salvador and: No. 1207, US No. 1208, Guatemala. No. 1209, Costa Rica No. 1210, Trinidad & Tobago. 55c, Trinidad & Tobago, Guatemala, US, Costa Rica. 1col, Soccer ball, Cuscatlan Stadium.

**1989, Dec. 20**

## Birds of Prey — A369

**Perf. 14½x14, 14x14½**

| 1221 | A369 | 70c | Sarcoramphus papa | .35 | .30 |
|---|---|---|---|---|---|
| 1222 | A369 | 1col | Polyborus plancus | .50 | .40 |
| 1223 | A369 | 2col | Accipiter striatus | 1.00 | .75 |
| 1224 | A369 | 10col | Glaucidium brasilianum | 5.00 | 3.75 |
| | | | Nos. 1221-1224 (4) | 6.85 | 5.20 |

Nos. 1221 and 1223 vert.

Tax Court, 50th Anniv. — A370

**1990, Jan. 12    Litho.    Perf. 14x14½**

| 1225 | A370 | 50c | multicolored | .20 | .20 |
|---|---|---|---|---|---|

Lord Baden-Powell, 133rd Birth Anniv. — A371

**1990, Feb. 23    Perf. 14½x14**

| 1226 | A371 | 25c | multicolored | .20 | .20 |
|---|---|---|---|---|---|

Intl. Women's Day — A372

**1990, Mar. 8    Litho.    Perf. 14x14½**

| 1227 | A372 | 25c | multicolored | .20 | .20 |
|---|---|---|---|---|---|

Type of 1989 and

Hour Glass — A373

**1990    Perf. 14½x14**

| 1228 | A373 | 25c | multicolored | .20 | .20 |
|---|---|---|---|---|---|
| 1229 | A373 | 55c | multicolored | .20 | .20 |

**Souvenir Sheet**
**Rouletted 13½ with Simulated Perfs.**

| 1230 | A356 | 2col | blk & pale blue | .80 | .60 |
|---|---|---|---|---|---|

Philatelic Soc., 50th anniv. Nos. 1229-1230 are airmail.

## Fight Against Addictions — A375

**Perf. 14½x14**

**1990, Apr. 26**

| 1231 | A375 | 20c | Alcohol | .20 | .20 |
|---|---|---|---|---|---|
| 1232 | A375 | 25c | Smoking | .60 | .40 |
| 1233 | A375 | 1.50col | Drugs | 1.00 | .80 |
| | | | Nos. 1231-1233 (3) | | |

No. 1233 is airmail.

La Prensa, 75th Anniv. — A376

**1990, May 14    Litho.    Perf. 14½x14**

| 1234 | A376 | 15c | multicolored | .20 | .20 |
|---|---|---|---|---|---|
| 1235 | A376 | 25c | "75", newspaper | .20 | .20 |

## World Cup Soccer Championships, Italy — A378

A377

Soccer player and flags of: No. 1236, Argentina, USSR, Cameroun, Romania. No. 1237, Italy, US, Austria, Czechoslovakia. No. 1238, Brazil, Costa Rica, Sweden, Scotland. No. 1239, Germany, United Arab Emirates, Yugoslavia, Colombia. No. 1240, Belgium, Spain, Korea, Uruguay. No. 1241, England, Netherlands, Ireland, Egypt.

**1990, June 15    Perf. 14x14½**

| 1236 | A377 | 55c | multicolored | .25 | .20 |
|---|---|---|---|---|---|
| 1237 | A377 | 55c | multicolored | .25 | .20 |
| 1238 | A377 | 70c | multicolored | .35 | .25 |
| 1239 | A377 | 70c | multicolored | .35 | .25 |
| 1240 | A377 | 1col | multicolored | .50 | .40 |
| 1241 | A377 | 1col | multicolored | .50 | .40 |
| 1242 | A378 | 1.50col | multicolored | .80 | .55 |
| | | | Nos. 1236-1242 (7) | 3.00 | 2.25 |

For surcharge see No. 1245.

Christopher Columbus — A379

## Columbus, Map — A380

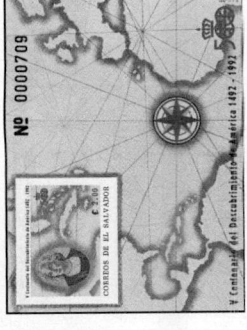

Stained glass window: b, Queen Isabella. c, Columbus' window. b, Queen Isabella. c, Columbus' Arms. d, Discovery of America 500th anniv. emblem. e, One boat of Columbus' fleet. f, Two boats.

**1990, July 30    Litho.    Perf. 14**

**Miniature Sheet**

| 1243 | A379 | Sheet of 6 | 5.00 | 5.00 |
|---|---|---|---|---|
| a.-f. | | 1col any single | .50 | .40 |

**Souvenir Sheet**
**Rouletted 13 1/2**

| 1244 | A380 | 2col | multicolored | 1.50 | 1.50 |
|---|---|---|---|---|---|

See Nos. 1283-1284.

No. 1239 Surcharged in Black

## World Summit for Children — A381

**1991, Feb.    Litho.    Perf. 14x14½**

| 1245 | A377 | 90c on 700 multi | .45 | .25 |
|---|---|---|---|---|

**1990, Sept. 25    Perf. 14½x14**

| 1246 | A381 | 5col blk, gold & dk bl | 2.75 | 2.00 |
|---|---|---|---|---|

## First Postage Stamps, 150th Anniv. — A382

a, Sir Rowland Hill. b, Penny Black. c, No. 21. d, Central Post Office. e, No. C124.

**1990, Oct. 5    Litho.    Perf. 14**

| 1247 | | Sheet of 5 + label | 8.00 | 8.00 |
|---|---|---|---|---|
| a.-e. | A382 | 2col any single | .95 | .70 |

## World Food Day — A383

**1990, Oct. 16    Litho.    Perf. 14**

| 1248 | A383 | 5col multicolored | 2.40 | 1.75 |
|---|---|---|---|---|

## San Salvador Electric Light Co., Cent. — A384

**1990, Oct. 30**

| 1249 | A384 | 20c | shown | .20 | .20 |
|---|---|---|---|---|---|
| 1250 | A384 | 90c | Lineman, power lines | .45 | .35 |

## America Issue — A385

**1990, Oct. 11    Litho.    Perf. 14x14½**

| 1251 | A385 | 25c | Chichontepec Volcano | .20 | .20 |
|---|---|---|---|---|---|
| 1252 | A385 | 70c | Lake Coatepeque | .35 | .25 |

## Chamber of Commerce, 75th Anniv. — A386

**1990, Nov. 22**

| 1253 | A386 | ₡1 ool blk, gold & bl | .50 | .35 |
|---|---|---|---|---|

## Traffic Safety — A387

Design: 40c, Interaction, horiz

**1990, Nov. 13**

| 1254 | A387 | 25c | multicolored | .20 | .20 |
|---|---|---|---|---|---|
| 1255 | A387 | 40c | multicolored | .20 | .20 |

## Butterflies — A388

**Perf. 14x14½, 14½x14**

**1990, Nov. 28**

| 1256 | A388 | 15c | Eurytides calliste | .50 | .20 |
|---|---|---|---|---|---|
| 1257 | A388 | 25c | Papilio garamas americas | .50 | .20 |
| 1258 | A388 | 25c | Papilio garamas | .50 | .20 |
| 1259 | A388 | 55c | Hypanartia godmani | .75 | .20 |
| 1260 | A388 | 70c | Anaea excellens | .90 | .30 |
| 1261 | A388 | 1col | Papilio pilumnus | 1.25 | .40 |
| | | | Nos. 1256-1261 (6) | 4.40 | 1.50 |

**Souvenir Sheet**
**Roulette 13½**

| 1262 | A388 | 2col | Anaea proserpina | 3.00 | 3.00 |
|---|---|---|---|---|---|

Nos. 1259-1261 are vert.

# EL SALVADOR

**1991, Feb. 27**   **Litho.**   **Perf. 14½x14**

University of El Salvador, 150th Anniv. — A389

| | | | | |
|---|---|---|---|---|
| 1263 | A389 | 25c shown | .20 | .20 |
| 1264 | A389 | 70c Sun, footprints, hand | .35 | .30 |
| 1265 | A389 | 1.50col Dove, globe | .75 | .65 |
| | | Nos. 1263-1265 (3) | 1.30 | 1.15 |

**1990, Dec. 7**   **Perf. 14x14½, 14½x14**

Christmas A390

| | | | | |
|---|---|---|---|---|
| 1266 | A390 | 25c shown | .20 | .20 |
| 1267 | A390 | 70c Nativity, vert. | .35 | .30 |

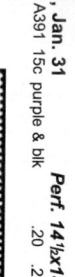

**1991, Jan. 31**   **Litho.**   **Perf. 14½x14**

Month of the Elderly A391

| | | | | |
|---|---|---|---|---|
| 1268 | A391 | 15c purple & blk | .20 | .20 |

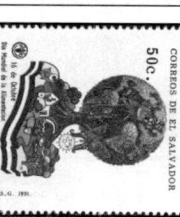 

Restoration of Santa Ana Theater A392

**1991, Apr. 12**   **Litho.**   **Perf. 14**

| | | | | |
|---|---|---|---|---|
| 1269 | A392 | 20c Interior | .35 | .30 |
| 1270 | A392 | 70c Exterior | .30 | |

Amphibians — A393

Designs: 25c, Smilisca baudinii. 70c, Eleutherodactylus rugulosus. 1col, Plectrohyla guatemalensis. 1.50col, Agalychnis moreletii.

**1991, May 29**   **Litho.**   **Perf. 14x14½**

| | | | | |
|---|---|---|---|---|
| 1271 | A393 | 25c multicolored | .25 | .20 |
| 1272 | A393 | 70c multicolored | .45 | .30 |
| 1273 | A393 | 1col multicolored | .65 | .40 |
| 1274 | A393 | 1.50col multicolored | 1.00 | .65 |
| | | Nos. 1271-1274 (4) | 2.35 | 1.55 |

Aid for Children's Village A394

Designs: 90c, Children playing outdoors.

**1991, June 21**   **Litho.**   **Perf. 14x14½**

| | | | | |
|---|---|---|---|---|
| 1275 | A394 | 20c multicolored | .20 | .20 |
| 1276 | A394 | 90c multicolored | .40 | .35 |

United Family A395

**1991, June 28**   **Litho.**   **Perf. 14x14½**

| | | | | |
|---|---|---|---|---|
| 1277 | A395 | 50c multicolored | .25 | .20 |

Birds — A396

 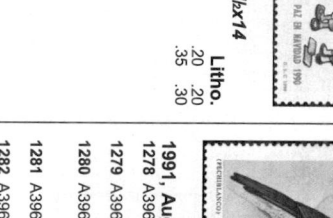

**1991, Aug. 30**   **Litho.**

| | | | | |
|---|---|---|---|---|
| 1278 | A396 | 20c Melanotis hypoleucus | .30 | .20 |
| 1279 | A396 | 25c Agelaius phoeniceus | .30 | .20 |
| 1280 | A396 | 70c Campylorhynchus rufinucha | .50 | .30 |
| 1281 | A396 | 1col Cissilopha melanocyanea | .60 | .40 |
| 1282 | A396 | 5col Chiroxiphia linearis | 2.75 | 1.75 |
| | | Nos. 1278-1282 (5) | 4.45 | 2.85 |

Discovery of America, 500th Anniv. Type of 1990

No. 1283: a, Hourglass, chart. b, Chart, ship's sails. c, Sailing ship near Florida. d, Corner of chart, ships. e, Compass rose, "500" emblem. No. 1284, Sail, landfall.

**1991, Sept. 16**   **Litho.**   **Perf. 14**

| | | | | |
|---|---|---|---|---|
| 1283 | A379 | 1col Sheet of 6, #a.-f. | 4.50 | 4.50 |

Miniature Sheet

| | | | | |
|---|---|---|---|---|
| 1284 | A380 | 2col multicolored | 1.50 | 1.50 |

Souvenir Sheet

Rouletted 6½

America Issue A397

**1991, Oct. 11**   **Litho.**   **Perf. 14x14½**

| | | | | |
|---|---|---|---|---|
| 1285 | A397 | 25c multicolored | .20 | .20 |
| 1286 | A397 | 70c multicolored | .35 | .30 |

Designs: 25c, Battle of Acaxual. 70c, First missionaries in Cuzcatlan.

World Food Day — A398

**1991, Oct. 16**   **Litho.**   **Perf. 14½x14**

| | | | | |
|---|---|---|---|---|
| 1287 | A398 | 50c multicolored | .25 | .20 |

Wolfgang Amadeus Mozart, Death Bicent. A399

**1991, Oct. 23**   **Litho.**   **Perf. 14½x14**

| | | | | |
|---|---|---|---|---|
| 1288 | A399 | 1col multicolored | .50 | .40 |

Christmas A400

**1991, Nov. 13**   **Litho.**   **Perf. 14½x14, 14x14½**

| | | | | |
|---|---|---|---|---|
| 1289 | A400 | 25c Nativity scene, vert. | .20 | .20 |
| 1290 | A400 | 70c Children singing | .40 | .30 |

Total Solar Eclipse, July 11 — A401

**1991, Dec. 17**   **Perf. 14½x14**

| | | | | |
|---|---|---|---|---|
| 1291 | A401 | 70c shown | .40 | .30 |
| 1292 | A401 | Pair, #1291-1292 | 1.25 | 1.25 |
| a. | A401 | 70c Eastern El Salvador | .40 | .30 |

No. 1292a has continous design.

Red Cross Life Guards A402

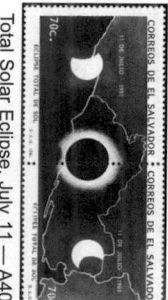

**1992, Feb. 28**   **Litho.**   **Perf. 14x14½**

| | | | | |
|---|---|---|---|---|
| 1293 | A402 | 3col Rescue | 1.50 | 1.10 |
| 1294 | A402 | 4.50col Swimming competition | 2.25 | 1.70 |

Lions Clubs in El Salvador, 50th Anniv. — A403

**1992, Mar. 13**   **Perf. 14x14½**

| | | | | |
|---|---|---|---|---|
| 1295 | A403 | 90c multicolored | .50 | .35 |

Protect the Environment A404

Designs: 60c, Man riding bicycle. 80c, Children walking outdoors. 90c, Clean water. 2.20col, Sower in field. 1.60col, Recycling center. 10col, Natural foods. 5col, Recycling center. 10col, Conservation of trees and nature. 25col, Wildlife protection.

**1992, Apr. 6**   **Litho.**   **Perf. 14½x14**

| | | | | |
|---|---|---|---|---|
| 1298 | A404 | 60c multi | .30 | .25 |
| 1299 | A404 | 80c multi | .40 | .30 |
| 1300 | A404 | 90c multi | .45 | .30 |
| 1301 | A404 | 1.60col multi | .80 | .60 |
| 1302 | A404 | 2.20col multi | 1.10 | .85 |
| 1303 | A404 | 3col multi | 1.50 | 1.10 |
| 1304 | A404 | 5col multi | 2.50 | 1.90 |
| 1305 | A404 | 5.00col multi | 3.75 | |
| 1306 | A404 | 10col multi | 12.50 | 9.50 |
| 1307 | A404 | 25col multi | 24.10 | 18.25 |
| | | Nos. 1298-1307 (8) | | |

Physicians A405

80c, Dr. Roberto Orellana Valdes. 1col, Dr. Carlos Gonzalez Bonilla. 1.60col, Dr. Andres Gonzalo Funes. 2.20col, Dr. Joaquin Coto.

**1992, Apr. 30**   **Litho.**   **Perf. 14½x14**

| | | | | |
|---|---|---|---|---|
| 1308 | A405 | 80c multicolored | .40 | .40 |
| 1309 | A405 | 1col multicolored | .50 | .40 |
| 1310 | A405 | 1.60col multicolored | .80 | .60 |
| 1311 | A405 | 2.20col multicolored | 1.10 | .85 |
| | | Nos. 1308-1311 (4) | 2.80 | 2.15 |

This is an expanding set. Numbers may change.

Women's Auxiliary of St. Vincent de Paul Society, Cent. — A406

**1992, Mar. 10**   **Litho.**   **Perf. 14½x14**

| | | | | |
|---|---|---|---|---|
| 1312 | A406 | 80c multicolored | .45 | .40 |

Population and Housing Census A407

80c, Globe showing location of El Salvador.

**1992, June 29**   **Litho.**   **Perf. 14½x14**

| | | | | |
|---|---|---|---|---|
| 1313 | A407 | 60c multicolored | .35 | .30 |
| 1314 | A407 | 80c multicolored | .45 | .40 |

1992 Summer Olympics, Barcelona A408

**1992, July 17**   **Litho.**   **Perf. 14½x14**

| | | | | |
|---|---|---|---|---|
| 1315 | A408 | 60c Hammer throw | .45 | .30 |
| 1316 | A408 | 80c Volleyball | .55 | .40 |
| 1317 | A408 | 90c Shot put | .60 | .60 |
| 1318 | A408 | 2.20col Long jump | 1.50 | .90 |
| 1319 | A408 | 3col Vault | 2.25 | .85 |
| 1320 | A408 | 5col Balance beam | 3.50 | 1.50 |
| | | Nos. 1315-1320 (6) | 9.15 | 4.30 |

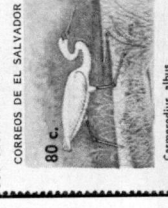

**Perf. 14x14½**

**1993, Jan. 15**    **Litho.**
| | | | |
|---|---|---|---|
| 1337 | A419 | 50c multicolored | .45 .20 |
| 1338 | A419 | 70c multicolored | .55 .20 |
| 1339 | A419 | 1col multicolored | 1.10 .30 |
| 1340 | A419 | 3col multicolored | 2.25 .85 |
| 1341 | A419 | 4.50col multicolored | 3.25 1.25 |
| | | Nos. 1337-1341 (5) | 7.60 2.80 |

**Month of the Elderly A420**

Design: 2.20col, Boy, old man holding tree.

**1993, Jan. 27**
| | | | |
|---|---|---|---|
| 1342 | A420 | 80c black | .45 .25 |
| 1343 | A420 | 2.20col multicolored | 1.25 .60 |

**Agape Social Welfare Organization — A421**

Designs: a, Divine Providence Church. b, People, symbols of love and peace.

**Perf. 14x14½**

**1993, Mar. 4**    **Litho.**
| | | | |
|---|---|---|---|
| 1344 | A421 | 1col Pair, #a.-b. | 1.00 1.00 |

**Secretary's Day A422**

**Perf. 14x14½**

**1993, Apr. 26**    **Litho.**
| | | | |
|---|---|---|---|
| 1345 | A422 | 1col multicolored | .55 .25 |

**Benjamin Bloom Children's Hospital A423**

**Perf. 14x14½**

**1993, June 18**    **Litho.**
| | | | |
|---|---|---|---|
| 1346 | A423 | 5col multicolored | 2.50 1.10 |

**Visit by Mexican President Carlos Salinas de Gortari A424**

**Perf. 14x14½**

**1993, July 14**
| | | | |
|---|---|---|---|
| 1347 | A424 | 2.20col multicolored | 1.10 .50 |

---

**Simon Bolivar A409**

**1992, July 24**
| | | | |
|---|---|---|---|
| 1321 | A409 | 2.20col multicolored | 1.25 .65 |

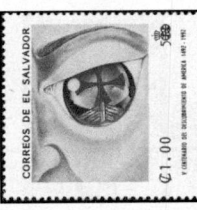

**A410**

**1992, Aug. 28**    **Litho.**    **Perf. 14x14½**
| | | | |
|---|---|---|---|
| 1322 | A410 | 1col multicolored | .75 .30 |
| 1323 | A410 | 1col multicolored | .75 .30 |

**Perf. 14½x14**
| | | | |
|---|---|---|---|
| 1324 | A410 | 1col multicolored | .75 .30 |
| 1325 | A410 | 1col multicolored | .75 .30 |
| a. | | Min. sheet, 2 each #1322-1325 | 6.00 2.40 |
| | | Nos. 1322-1325 (4) | 3.00 1.20 |

**Souvenir Sheet**

**Rouletted 13½**
| | | | |
|---|---|---|---|
| 1326 | A411 | 3col multicolored | 2.50 2.50 |

**Discovery of America, 500th Anniv. — A411**

Designs: No. 1322, European and Amerindian faces. No. 1323, Ship in person's eye. No. 1324, Ship at sea. No. 1325, Satellite over Earth. 3col, Cross, Indian pyramid.

**Immigrants to El Salvador A412**

Designs: No. 1327, Feet walking over map. No. 1328, Footprints leading to map.

**1992, Sept. 16**    **Litho.**    **Perf. 14x14½**
| | | | |
|---|---|---|---|
| 1327 | A412 | 2.20col multicolored | 1.10 .60 |
| 1328 | A412 | 2.20col multicolored | 1.10 .60 |
| a. | | Pair, #1327-1328 | 3.00 |

**General Francisco Morazan (1792-1842) A413**

**Perf. 14½x14**

**1992, Sept. 28**
| | | | |
|---|---|---|---|
| 1329 | A413 | 1col multicolored | .60 .30 |

---

**Association of Salvadoran Broadcasters A414**

**1992, Oct. 3**
| | | | |
|---|---|---|---|
| 1330 | A414 | 2.20col multicolored | 1.10 .60 |

Salvadoran Radio Day, Intl. Radio Day.

**Discovery of America, 500th Anniv. A415**

**Perf. 14x14½**

**1992, Oct. 13**    **Litho.**
| | | | |
|---|---|---|---|
| 1331 | A415 | 80c Indian artifacts | .45 .25 |
| 1332 | A415 | 2.20col Map, ship | 1.25 .60 |

**Exflina '92 — A416**

**Perf. 14x14½**

**1992, Oct. 22**
| | | | |
|---|---|---|---|
| 1333 | A416 | 5col multicolored | 3.50 1.40 |

Discovery of America, 500th Anniv.

**Peace in El Salvador A417**

**1992, Oct. 30**
| | | | |
|---|---|---|---|
| 1334 | A417 | 50c black, blue & yellow | .30 .20 |

**Christmas A418**

**Perf. 14x14½, 14½x14**    **Litho.**

**1992, Nov. 23**
| | | | |
|---|---|---|---|
| 1335 | A418 | 80c shown | .65 .25 |
| 1336 | A418 | 2.20col Nativity, vert. | 1.50 .60 |

**Wildlife A419**

Designs: 50c, Tapirus bairdii. 70c, Chironectes minimus. 1col, Eira barbara. 3col, Felis yagouaroundi. 4.50col, Odocoileus virginianus.

---

**Aquatic Birds A425**

**Perf. 14x14½**

**1993, Sept. 28**    **Litho.**
| | | | |
|---|---|---|---|
| 1348 | A425 | 80c Casmerodius albus | .40 .20 |
| 1349 | A425 | 1col Mycteria americana | .55 .20 |
| 1350 | A425 | 2.20col Ardea herodias | 1.00 .25 |
| 1351 | A425 | 5col Ajaja ajaja | 2.40 .60 |
| | | Nos. 1348-1351 (4) | 4.35 1.25 |

**Pharmacy Review Commission, Cent. — A426**

**1993, Oct. 6**
| | | | |
|---|---|---|---|
| 1352 | A426 | 80c multicolored | .45 .20 |

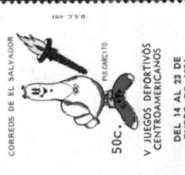

**America Issue A427**

Endangered species: 80c, Dasyprocta punctata. 2.20col, Procyon lotor.

**Perf. 14x14½**

**1993, Oct. 11**    **Litho.**
| | | | |
|---|---|---|---|
| 1353 | A427 | 80c multicolored | .40 .20 |
| 1354 | A427 | 2.20col multicolored | .95 .25 |

**Fifth Central America Games A428**

50c, Mascot, torch. 1.60col, Emblem. 2.20col, Mascot, map of Central America. 4.50col, Map of El Salvador, mascot.

**Perf. 14½x14, 14x14½**    **Litho.**

**1993, Oct. 29**
| | | | |
|---|---|---|---|
| 1355 | A428 | 50c multi | .40 .20 |
| 1356 | A428 | 1.60col multi | .85 .20 |
| 1357 | A428 | 2.20col multi, horiz. | 1.00 .25 |
| 1358 | A428 | 4.50col multi, horiz. | 2.10 .50 |
| | | Nos. 1355-1358 (4) | 4.35 1.15 |

**Miniature Sheet**

**Medicinal Plants — A429**

Designs: a, Solanum mammosum. b, Hamelia patens. c, Tridex procumbens. d, Calea urticifolia. e, Ageratum conyzoides. f, Pluchea odorata.

**Perf. 14½x14**

**1993, Dec. 10**    **Litho.**
| | | | |
|---|---|---|---|
| 1359 | A429 | 1col Sheet of 6, #a.-f. | 3.00 .65 |

**1993, Nov. 23** **Perf. 14x14½**
1360 A430 80c Holy Family .30 .20
1361 A430 2.20col Nativity Scene .85 .40
Christmas A430

**1993, Nov. 30**
1362 A431 2.20col multicolored .40
Alberto Masferrer (1868-1932),
Writer — A431

**1994, Feb. 28** **Litho.**
1363 A432 2.20col multicolored 1.10 .40
Intl. Year of the Family — A432

**1994, Apr. 27** **Perf. 14**
1364 A433 1col shown .50 .20
1365 A433 1col Hospital building .50 .20
Military Hospital, Cent. A433

City of Santa Ana, Cent. — A434

**1994, Apr. 29** **Perf. 14**
1366 A434 60c multicolored .35 .20
1367 A434 80c multicolored .40 .20

Designs: 60c, Arms of Department of Santa Ana. 80c, Inscription honoring heroic deeds of 44 patriots.

**1994 World Cup Soccer Championships, US — A435**

Soccer plays, flags from: 60c, Romania, Colombia, Switzerland, US. 80c, Sweden, Cameroun, Russia, Brazil. 1col, South Korea.

---

**1994, June 6** **Litho.**
1368 A435 60c multicolored .45 .20
1369 A435 80c multicolored .55 .20
1370 A435 1col multicolored .55 .25
1371 A435 2.20col multicolored 1.00 .25
1372 A435 4.50col multicolored 2.25 .55
1373 A435 5col multicolored 2.40 .55
Nos. 1368-1373 (6) 7.10 1.90

Spain, Bolivia, Germany, Nigeria, Greece, Argentina, Norway, Ireland, Italy, Netherlands, Morocco, Belgium. 2.20col, Mexico, 4.50col, Saudi Arabia.

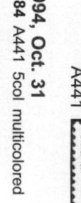

**1994, June 24** **Litho.**
1374 A436 2.20col multicolored 1.00 .25
Plaza of Sovereign Military Order of Malta A436

Traditions A437

**1994, June 30**
1375 A437 1col multicolored .45 .20
1376 A437 2.20col multicolored 1.00 .25

Designs: 1col, Tiger and deer dance. 2.20col, Spotted bull dance.

Nutritional Plants — A438

**1994, Aug. 29** **Litho.**
1377 A438 70c Capsicum annuum .50 .20
1378 A438 80c Theobroma cacao .50 .20
1379 A438 1col Ipomoea batatas .60 .20
1380 A438 5col Chamaedorea tepejilote 2.50 .55
Nos. 1377-1380 (4) 4.10 1.15

Postal Transport Vehicles A439

**1994, Oct. 11** **Perf. 14**
1381 A439 80c Jeep .40 .20
1382 A439 2.20col Train 1.10 .55
America issue.

**1994, Oct. 26**
1383 A440 80c multicolored .40 .20
22nd Bicycle Race of El Salvador A440

---

**1994, Oct. 31**
1384 A441 5col multicolored 2.50 1.25
16th Intl. Fair of El Salvador A441

**1994, Nov. 16**
1385 A442 80c shown .40 .20
1386 A442 2.20col Magi, Christ child 1.10 .55
Christmas A442

Beetles A443

**1994, Dec. 16** **Litho.**
1387 A443 80c Cotinis mutabilis .35 .20
1388 A443 1col Phyllophaga .45 .20
1389 A443 2.20col Galota 1.10 .30
1390 A443 5col Callipogon barbatus 2.50 .60
Nos. 1387-1390 (4) 4.40 1.30

Ceramic Treasures
Archeological Site — A445

**1995, Mar. 24** **Litho.**
1391 A444 70c shown .40 .20
1392 A444 1col "40" emblem .45 .20
Salvadoran Culture Center, 40th Anniv. — A444

**1995, Apr. 26** **Litho.** **Perf. 14½x14**
1393 A445 60c multicolored .30 .20
1394 A445 70c multicolored .30 .20
1395 A445 80c multicolored .40 .25
1396 A445 2.20col multicolored 1.10 .55
1397 A445 4.50col multicolored 2.25 1.25
1398 A445 5col multicolored 2.75 1.25
Nos. 1393-1398 (6) 7.50 3.70

Designs: 60c, Cup. 70c, Three-footed earthen pot. 80c, Two-handled jar. 2.20col, Long-necked jar. 4.50col, Excavation structure #3. 5col, Excavation structure #4.

---

Orchids A451

**1995, Aug. 30** **Perf. 14x14½**
1404 A450 50c multicolored .25 .20
1405 A450 60c multicolored .30 .20
1406 A450 80c multicolored .40 .25
1407 A450 5col multicolored 2.75 1.25
Nos. 1404-1407 (4) 4.40 2.20

Designs: 50c, Los Almendros Beach, Sonsonate. 60c, Green Lagoon, Apaneca. 2.20col, Guerrero Beach, La Union. 5col, Usulutan Volcano.

**1995, Aug. 16** **Litho.** **Perf. 14½x14**
1403 A449 80c multicolored 1.10 .55
FAO, 50th Anniv. — A449

Tourism A450

El Salvador A450

---

**1995, July 7** **Litho.** **Perf. 14**
1400 A447 80c multicolored .40 .20
1401 A447 2.20col multicolored 1.10 .55
Central America, SA, 80th Anniv. — A447

Designs: 80c, Insuring the future of children. 2.20col, Child wearing costume.

Sacred Heart College, Cent. A448

**1995, July 26**
1402 A448 80c multicolored .40 .20

**1995, May 19**
1399 A446 80c multicolored .45 .25
Fr. Isidro Menendez (1795-1858), Physician A446

EL SALVADOR

#1408, Pleurothallis glandulosa. #1409, Pleurothallis grobyi. #1410, Pleurothallis fuegii. #1411, Lemboglossum stellatum. #1412, Lepanthes inaequalis. #1413, Pleurothallis hirsuta. #1414, Hexadesmia micrantha. #1415, Pleurothallis segoviense. #1416, Stelis aprica. #1417, Platystele stenostachya. #1418, Stelis barbata. #1419, Pleurothallis schiedeli.

**1995, Sept. 28 Litho. Perf. 14½x14**

| 1408 | A451 | 60c multicolored | .40 | .20 |
|---|---|---|---|---|
| 1409 | A451 | 60c multicolored | .40 | .20 |
| a. | | Pair, #1408-1409 | .80 | .30 |
| 1410 | A451 | 70c multicolored | .55 | .25 |
| 1411 | A451 | 70c multicolored | .55 | .25 |
| 1412 | A451 | 70c multicolored | .75 | .30 |
| 1413 | A451 | 70c multicolored | .75 | .30 |
| 1414 | A451 | 1col multicolored | .75 | .30 |
| 1415 | A451 | 1col multicolored | 2.10 | .80 |
| 1416 | A451 | 3col multicolored | | 1.25 |
| 1417 | A451 | 4.50col multicolored | 3.25 | 1.25 |
| a. | | Pair, #1416-1417 | 6.50 | 2.50 |
| 1418 | A451 | 5col multicolored | 3.75 | 1.40 |
| 1419 | A451 | 5col multicolored | 3.75 | 1.40 |
| | | Nos. 1408-1419 (12) | 21.60 | 8.30 |

**America Issue — A452**

Martins: 80c, Chloroceryle aenea. 2.20col, Chloroceryle americana.

**1995, Oct. 11**

| 1420 | A452 | 80c multicolored | .50 | .20 |
|---|---|---|---|---|
| 1421 | A452 | 2.20col multicolored | 1.50 | .60 |

**UN, 50th Anniv. — A453**

Design: 2.20col, Hands of different races holding UN emblem, "50."

**1995, Oct. 23**

| 1422 | A453 | 80c multicolored | .50 | .20 |
|---|---|---|---|---|
| 1423 | A453 | 2.20col multicolored | 1.50 | .60 |

**Christmas A454**

**1995, Nov. 17 Litho. Perf. 14½x14**

| 1424 | A454 | 80c shown | .50 | .20 |
|---|---|---|---|---|
| 1425 | A454 | 2.20col Families, clock tower | 1.50 | .60 |

**Fauna A455**

Designs: a, Bubo virginianus. b, Potos flavus. c, Porthidium godmani. d, Felis pardalis flavus. e, Dellatis bifurcata. f, Felis concolor (h). g, Mazama americana. h, Leptophobia aripa. i, Bolitoglossa salvinii. j, Eugenes fulgens (h. i).

**Perf. 14x14½**

**1995, Nov. 24**

| 1426 | A455 | 80c Sheet of 10, #a.-j. | 6.00 | 6.00 |
|---|---|---|---|---|

**Independence, 174th Anniv. — A456**

Designs: 80c, Natl. arms, export products, money, textile workers, pharmaceuticals. 25col, Crates of products leaving El Salvador.

**Perf. 14½x14**

**1995, Sept. 14**

| 1427 | A456 | 80c shown | .40 | .20 |
|---|---|---|---|---|
| 1428 | A456 | 25col multicolored | 13.00 | 7.50 |

**2nd Visit of Pope John Paul II — A457**

5.40col, Pope John Paul II, Metropolitan Cathedral.

**1996, Feb. 8 Litho. Perf. 14½x14**

| 1429 | A457 | 1.50col multicolored | 1.00 | .45 |
|---|---|---|---|---|
| 1430 | A457 | 5.40col multicolored | 4.00 | 1.60 |

**ANTEL, Telecommunications Workers' Day — A458**

1.50col, Satellite dish, hand holding cable fibers. 5col, Three globes, telephone receiver.

**Perf. 14x14½, 14½x14**

**1996, Apr. 27**

| 1431 | A458 | 1.50col multi | .90 | .45 |
|---|---|---|---|---|
| 1432 | A458 | 5col multi, vert. | 3.00 | 1.50 |

**City of San Salvador, 450th Anniv. A459**

Designs: 2.50col, Spanish meeting natives. 2.70col, Diego de Holguin, first mayor, mission. 3.30col, Old National Palace. 4col, Heroe's Boulevard, modern view of city.

**Perf. 14x14½**

**1996, Mar. 27 Litho.**

| 1433 | A459 | 2.50col multicolored | 1.50 | .80 |
|---|---|---|---|---|
| 1434 | A459 | 2.70col multicolored | 1.75 | .85 |
| 1435 | A459 | 3.30col multicolored | 2.00 | 1.00 |
| 1436 | A459 | 4col multicolored | 2.50 | 1.25 |
| | | Nos. 1433-1436 (4) | 7.75 | 3.90 |

**Natl. Artists, Entertainers A460**

Designs: 1col, Rey Avila (1929-95). 1.50col, Maria Teresa Moreira (1934-95). 2.70col, Francisco Antonio Lara (1900-88). 4col, Carlos Alverez Pineda (1928-93).

**1996, May 17 Litho. Perf. 14½x14**

| 1437 | A460 | 1col multicolored | .60 | .30 |
|---|---|---|---|---|
| 1438 | A460 | 1.50col multicolored | .90 | .45 |
| 1439 | A460 | 2.70col multicolored | 1.50 | .75 |
| 1440 | A460 | 4col multicolored | 2.25 | 1.10 |
| | | Nos. 1437-1440 (4) | 5.25 | 2.60 |

**YSKL Radio, 40th Anniv. A461**

**Perf. 14x14½**

**1996, May 24**

| 1441 | A461 | 1.40col multicolored | .85 | .40 |
|---|---|---|---|---|

**1996 Summer Olympic Games, Atlanta A462**

Early Greek athletes: 1.50col, Discus thrower. 3col, Jumper. 4col, Wrestlers. 5col, Javelin thrower.

**Perf. 14**

**1996, July 3 Litho.**

| 1442 | A462 | 1.50col multicolored | .90 | .45 |
|---|---|---|---|---|
| 1443 | A462 | 3col multicolored | 1.75 | .90 |
| 1444 | A462 | 4col multicolored | 2.40 | 1.25 |
| 1445 | A462 | 5col multicolored | 3.00 | 1.50 |
| | | Nos. 1442-1445 (4) | 8.05 | 4.10 |

**Birds A463**

Designs: a, Pheucticus ludovicianus. b, Tyrannus forficatus. c, Dendroica petechia. d, Falco sparverius. e, Icterus galbula.

**Perf. 14½x14**

**1996, Aug. 9 Litho.**

| 1446 | A463 | 1.50col Strip of 5, #a.-e. | 4.50 | 2.25 |
|---|---|---|---|---|

**Diario de Hoy Newspaper, 60th Anniv. — A464**

**Perf. 14½x14**

**1996, Sept. 20**

| 1447 | A464 | 5.20col multicolored | 3.00 | 1.50 |
|---|---|---|---|---|

**Channel 2 Television Station, 30th Anniv. — A465**

**Perf. 14½x14**

**1996, Sept. 27**

| 1448 | A465 | 10col multicolored | 5.75 | 3.00 |
|---|---|---|---|---|

**UNICEF, 50th Anniv. A466**

**Perf. 14x14½**

**1996, Oct. 4**

| 1449 | A466 | 1col multicolored | .60 | .30 |
|---|---|---|---|---|

**Traditional Costumes A467**

America issue: 1.50col, Blouse, short flannel skirt, Nahuizalco. 4col, Blouse, long skirt, Panchimalco.

**Perf. 14½x14**

**1996, Oct. 11**

| 1450 | A467 | 1.50col multicolored | 1.25 | .45 |
|---|---|---|---|---|
| 1451 | A467 | 4col multicolored | 2.75 | 1.10 |

**Christmas A468**

Designs: 2.50col, Night scene of homes, Christmas tree, church. 4col, Day scene of people celebrating outside homes, church.

**Perf. 14½x14**

**1996, Nov. 28**

| 1452 | A468 | 2.50col multicolored | 1.60 | 1.10 |
|---|---|---|---|---|
| 1453 | A468 | 4col multicolored | 2.25 | 1.10 |

**Constitution Day — A469**

**Litho. Perf. 14½x14**

**1996, Dec. 19**

| 1454 | A469 | 1col multicolored | .60 | .30 |
|---|---|---|---|---|

**Marine Life — A470**

a, Nasolamia velox. b, Scomberomorus sierra. c, Delphinus delphis. d, Eretmochelys imbricata. e, Epinephelus labriformis. f, Pomacanthus zonipectus. g, Scarus perrico. h, Hippocampus ingens.

**Litho.**

**1996, Dec. 17**

| 1455 | A470 | 1col Sheet of 8, #a.-h. | 6.00 | 6.00 |
|---|---|---|---|---|

**1996, Dec. 5** **Litho.** **Perf. 14x14½**
1456 A471 1col multicolored .60 .30

Jerusalem, 3000th Anniv. A471

**1997, Feb. 6** **Litho.** **Perf. 14x14½**
1457 A472 10col multicolored 5.75 3.00

El Mundo Newspaper, 30th Anniv. A472

**1997, Feb. 21**
1458 A473 4col multicolored 2.25 1.25

Exfilna '97 — A473

Carmelite Order of San Jose, 80th Anniv. A474

**1997, Mar. 19**
1459 A474 1col multicolored .60 .30

Design: Mother Clara Maria of Jesus Quiros.

**1997, Apr. 10** **Perf. 14½x14**
1460 A475 25col multicolored 14.50 7.25

American School, 50th Anniv. — A475

**1997, May 28** **Litho.** **Perf. 14x14½**
1461 A476 1.50col Sheet of 4, #a.-d. 5.00 5.00
1462 A476 4col multicolored 2.25 2.25

Souvenir Sheet
Rouletted 13½

No. 1461: a. Annona diversifolia. b. Ana-cardium occidentale. c, Cucumis melo. d, Pouteria mammosa.

Design: Carica papaya.

Tropical Fruit A476

 (Anona diversifolia, ¢1.50)

 (Escuela Americana, ¢25.00)

---

**1997, Aug. 15** **Litho.** **Perf. 14**
1463 A476a 4col multicolored 2.25 1.10

Lions Club in El Salvador, 55th Anniv. A476a

 (El Salvador ¢4.00)

**1997, Aug. 28** **Litho.** **Perf. 14**
1464 A477 1.50col shown .90 .45
1465 A477 4col multicolored 2.25 1.10

Montreal Protocol on Substances that Deplete Ozone Layer, 10th Anniv. — A477

Inter-American Water Day (#1465).

No. 1464: Boy drinking water.

**1997, Sept. 26** **Litho.** **Perf. 14**
1466 A478 4col multicolored 2.25 1.10

Miguel de Cervantes Saavedra (1547-1616), Writer — A478

 (¢4.00)

**1997, Sept. 10** **Litho.** **Perf. 14x14½**
1467 A479 2.50col multicolored 1.40 .70
1468 A479 5.20col multicolored 2.75 1.40

Independence Day — A479

No. 1467: Flag, children, dove.

 (¢2.50 15 de Septiembre)

**1997, Oct. 3** **Perf. 14½x14**
1469 A480 1.50col multicolored 1.25 .50

Scouting in El Salvador, 75th Anniv. — A480

 (¢1.50)

Life of a Postman A481

 (El Cartero AMERICA ¢1.00)

América issue: 1col; Postman delivering mail. 4col; Postman on motor scooter, dog.

---

**1997, Oct. 10** **Litho.** **Perf. 14½x14**
1470 A481 1col multicolored .60 .30
1471 A481 4col multicolored 2.40 1.25

**1997, Oct. 28** **Perf. 14x14½**
1472 A482 10col multicolored 5.75 3.00

ACES (Automobile Club of El Salvador), 26th Anniv. A482

 (¢10.00 ¢26)

**1997, Nov. 20** **Litho.** **Perf. 14**
1473 A483 1.50col multicolored 1.25 .50
1474 A483 1.50col multicolored 1.25 .50
a. A483 Pair, #1473-1474 2.50 2.50

Christmas — A483

Children's paintings: No. 1473, Outdoor scene. No. 1474, Indoor scene.

 (Navidad 97 ¢1.50)

Salesian Order in El Salvador, Cent. A484

 (El Salvador ¢1.50 100 AÑOS SALESIANOS)

**1997, Dec. 6** **Perf. 14**
1475 A484 1.50col Sheet of 6, #a.-f. 4.00 4.00

Designs: a, Map, St. John Bosco (1715-88). b, St. Cecilia College. c, San Jose College, priest. d, Ricaldone, students working with machinery. e, Maria Auxiliadora Church. f, City of St. John Bosco, students working with electronic equipment.

**1997, Dec. 17** **Litho.**
1476 A485 2.50col Sheet of 6, #a.-f. 4.50 2.25

Antique Automobiles — A485

Designs: a, 1946 Standard. b, 1954 Chrysler. c, 1954 Jaguar. d, 1930 Ford. e, 1953 Mercedes Benz. f, 1956 Porsche.

 (¢2.50 1946)

St. Joseph Missionaries, 125th Anniv. — A486

 (JOSEFINOS 125 ANIVERSARIO ¢1.00)

**1998, Jan. 23** **Litho.** **Perf. 14**
1477 A486 1col multicolored .30 .20
1478 A486 4col multicolored 1.25 .60

1col, Image, Church of St. Joseph, Anuachapan. 4col, Jose M. Vilaseca, Cesarea España.

---

**1998, Mar. 17** **Litho.** **Perf. 14½x14**
1479 A487 10col multicolored 3.50 1.50

New Intl. Airport A487

 (El Salvador ¢10.00)

**1998, May 29** **Litho.** **Perf. 14½x14**
1480 A488 4col multicolored 1.25 .60

Organization of American States, 50th Anniv. — A488

 (OEA El Salvador ¢4.00)

1998 World Cup Soccer Championships, France — A489

 (Francia 98 El Salvador ¢1.50)

**1998, May 13** **Perf. 14**
1481 A489 1.50col Strip of 4, #a.-d. 3.00 3.00

Souvenir Sheet
Rouletted 13½
1482 A489 4col multicolored 2.25 2.25

Soccer player, Paris landmarks: a, Sacre Coeur. b, Eiffel Tower. c, Louvre. d, Notre Dame.

4col, Soccer ball, Arc d'Triumphe, horiz.

El Salvador, 1997 Champions of the 6th Central American Games A490

 (El Salvador ¢1.50 El Salvador Campeón 1997 VI Juegos Centroamericanos)

**1998, July 17** **Litho.** **Perf. 14**
1483 A490 1.50col multicolored .45 .20
1484 A490 1.50col multicolored .45 .20
1485 A490 1.50col multicolored .45 .20
1486 A490 1.50col multicolored .45 .20
Nos. 1483-1486 (4) 1.80 .80

Designs inside medals: No. 1483, Women's gymnastics, weight lifting, judo. No. 1484, Discus, volleyball, women's basketball. No. 1485, Swimming, tennis, water polo. No. 1486, Gymnastics, wrestling, shooting.

Dr. Jose Gustavo Guerrero (1876-1958), President of the World Court — A491

 (El Salvador ¢1.00 DR. JOSE GUSTAVO GUERRERO NBC!Ø: 26-JUNIO-1876)

**1998, July 22** **Litho.** **Perf. 14**
1487 A491 1col multicolored .25 .20

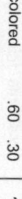

18th International Fair — A492

**1998, Aug. 28**
1488 A492 4col multicolored    1.25   .60

Painting of the Death of Manuel José Arce, Soldier, Politician A493

**1998, Sept. 1**
1489 A493 4col multicolored    4.00   4.00

*Archilochus colubris*

Hummingbirds and Flowers — A494

a, Archilochus colubris. b, Amazilia rutila. c, Hylocharis eliciae. d, Colibri thalassinus. e, Campylopterus hemileucurus. f, Lampornis amethystinus.

**1998, Sept. 7**
1490 A494 1.50col   Sheet of 6, #a.-f.    4.00   4.00

House Social Fund, 25th Anniv. — A495

**1998, Sept. 29**    **Litho.**    **Perf. 14**
1491 A495 10col multicolored    3.50   1.75

*AMERICA*

Famous Women A497

**1998, Oct. 2**
1492 A496 1.50col multicolored    .45   .25

America issue: 1col, Alice Lardé de Venturino. 4col, María de Baratta.

---

**1998, Oct. 12**
1493 A497 1col multicolored    .30   .20
1494 A497 4col multicolored    1.25   .65

Christmas A498

Children's drawings: 1col, Clock tower, nativity scene. 4col, Pageant players as angels, Holy Family parading to church, nativity scene.

**1998, Nov. 24**    **Litho.**
1495 A498 1col multicolored    .30   .20
1496 A498 4col multicolored    1.25   .60

World Stamp Day A499

**1998, Nov. 27**    **Perf. 14**
1497 A499 1col multicolored    .35   .20

Salvadoran Air Force, 75th Anniv. — A500

Designs: a, C47T transport plane. b, IH-300 helicopter. c, UH-1H helicopter. d, Dragonfly bomber.

**1998, Dec. 1**    **Litho.**    **Perf. 14½**
1498 A500 1.50col   Strip of 4, #a.-d.    2.50   2.50

Traditional Foods A501

Designs: a, Ensalada de papaya y pacaya. b, Sopa de mondongo. c, Camarones en alhuaiste. d, Buñuelos en miel de panela. e, Refresco de ensalada. f, Ensalada de aguacate. g, Sopa de arroz aguado con chipilín. h, Plato típico salvadoreño. i, Empanadas de plátano. j, Horchata.

**1998, Dec. 9**    **Litho.**    **Perf. 14**
1499 A501 1.50col   Block of 10, #a.-j.    6.00   6.00

Roberto D'Aubisson Signing New Constitution, 1983 — A502

**1998, Dec. 15**    **Litho.**    **Perf. 14x14½**
1503 A502 25col multicolored    7.25   3.50

---

First Natl. Topical Philatelic Exhibition A503

Salvador Railway Company Steamship Service.

**1999, Feb. 19**    **Litho.**    **Perf. 14**
1504 A503 2.50col multicolored    1.00   .40

Introduction of Television, 40th Anniv. — A504

**1999, Feb. 24**
1505 A504 4col multicolored    .90   .45

European Union Cooperation with El Salvador — A505

**1999, May 7**    **Litho.**    **Perf. 14x14½**
1506 A505 5.20col shown    1.50   .75
1507 A505 10col Hands clasped    3.00   1.50

Water Birds A506

No. 1508: a, Gallinula chloropus. b, Porphyrula martinica. c, Portirallus maculatus. d, Anas discors. e, Dendrocygna autumnalis. f, Fulica americana. g, Jacana spinosa. h, Perzana carolina. i, Aramus guarauna. j, Oxyura dominica.

**1999, Apr. 22**    **Perf. 14x14½**
1508 A506 1col   Block of 10, #a.-j.    4.00   4.00

Souvenir Sheet
*Rouletted 8¾*
1509 A506 4col multicolored    1.50   1.50

*Glossophaga soricina*

Bats A507

Designs: a, Glossophaga soricina. b, Desmodus rotundus. c, Noctilio leporinus. d, Vampyrum spectrum. e, Ectophilla alba. f, Myotis nigricans.

**1999, June 30**    **Litho.**    **Perf. 14x14½**
1510 A507 1.50col   Sheet of 6, #a.-f.    4.00   4.00

---

Visit of US Pres. William J. Clinton — A508

Designs: a, Seals, flags of El Salvador, US. b, Pres. Francisco Flores of El Salvador, Pres. Clinton.

**1999, May 19**    **Perf. 14½**
1511 A508 5col   Pair, #a.-b.    3.00   1.50

Quality Control Institute, 20th Anniv. — A509

**1999, May 20**    **Perf. 14½**
1512 A509 5.40col multicolored    1.60   .80

Geothermic Energy A510

**1999, July 16**    **Litho.**    **Perf. 14x14½**
1513 A510 1col   Drilling tower    .30   .20
1514 A510 4col   Power station    1.25   .60

Exports A511

**1999, July 21**    **Perf. 14½x14**
1515 A511 4col multicolored    1.25   .60

Salvadoran Journalists' Association A512

**1999, July 30**    **Perf. 14x14½**
1516 A512 1.50col multicolored    .45   .25

Cattleya Orchids A513

Designs: a, Skinneri var. alba. b, Skinneri var. coerulea. c, Skinneri. d, Guatemalensis. e, Aurantiaca var. flava. f, Aurantiaca.

**1999, Aug. 25**
1517 A513 1.50col   Sheet of 6, #a.-f. + 4 labels    4.00   4.00

HOMENAJE A TOÑO SALAZAR

Toño Salazar, Caricaturist
A514

**1999, Aug. 31**
1518 A514 1.50col Strip of 5, #a-e. 3.50 3.50

Designs: a, Self-portrait. b, Claudia Lars. d, Francisco Gavidia. e, Miguel Angel Asturias.

FUERZA ARMADA DE EL SALVADOR

Central American Nutrition Institute
A515

**1999, Sept. 14    Litho.    Perf. 14½x14½**
1519 A515 5.20col Children, food 1.40 .70
1520 A515 5.40col Food 1.50 .75

Armed Forces, 175th Anniv. — A516

**1999, Sept. 24**
1521 A516 1col Gens. Arce & Barrios .30 .20
1522 A516 1.50col Soldier, flag .45 .20

**1999, Oct. 8    Perf. 14½x14**
1523 A517 10col multicolored 2.75 1.40

Int. Year of Older Persons — A517

AMERICA '99

America Issue. A New Millennium Without Arms — A518

**1999, Oct. 12**
1524 A518 1col Dove, children .30 .20
1525 A518 4col "No Guns" sign 1.10 .55

UPU, 125th Anniv. — A519

**1999, Oct. 22**
1526 A519 4col Pair, #a-b. 3.50 3.50

Designs: a, UPU emblem. b, Mail, jeep, ship, airplane, computer.

CORREOS DE EL SALVADOR

A520

**1999, Nov. 4**
1527 A520 1.50col Pair, #a-b. 1.00 .45
1528 A520 4col Pair, #a-b. 3.00 1.10

Paintings by — #1527: a, Delmy Guandique. b, Margarita Orellana — #1528: a, Lolly Sandoval. b, José Francisco Guadrón.

Christmas — A520

cheje

Woodpeckers
A522

**1999, Nov. 24    Litho.    Perf. 14½x14**
1529 A521 25col multi 7.00 3.50

Inter-American Development Bank, 40th Anniv. — A521

Designs: a, Melanerpes aurifrons. b, Piculus rubiginosus. c, Sphyrapicus varius. d, Dryocopus lineatus. e, Melanerpes formicivorus.

**1999, Dec. 3**
1530 A522 1.50col Vert. strip of 5, #a-e. 3.50 3.50

Salvadoreños 2000

Millennium
A524

**1999, Dec. 7**
1531 A523 10col multi 3.25 1.50

Salvadoran Coffee Assoc., 70th Anniv. — A523

ASOCIACION CAFETALERA DE EL SALVADOR

**2000, Jan. 6    Perf. 14½x14**
1532 A524 1.50col multi .60 .20

Portal de Acceso

El Imposible Natl. Park — A528

**2000**    **Sheets of 4    Perf. 14½x14¼**
1536 A527 1.50col #a-d. 2.00 2.00
1537 A527 1.50col #a-d+2 labels 2.00 2.00

Issued: #1536, 3/16; #1537, 6/16.
No. 1536 includes two labels.

#1536: a, El Tazumal Mayan pyramid. b, Christopher Columbus and ships. c, Spanish soldier, native. d, Independence.
#1537: a, Salvadoran White House, 1920. b, Shoppers at street market, 1920. c, Trolley and Nuevo Mundo Hotel, 1924. d, Automobiles on South 2nd Avenue, San Salvador, 1924.

Millennium
A527

**2000, Feb. 10**
1535 A526 1col multi .50 .20

Faith and Happiness Foundation, 30th Anniv. — A526

Trains
A532

No. 1542: a, Baldwin locomotive Philadelphia 58441. b, General Electric locomotive series, 65k-15. c, Train car. d, Presidential coach car.

**2000, Aug. 3**
1542 A532 Vert. strip of 4 a-d. 2.50 2.50
.45 .20

El Renacer de Una Patria

Fireman's Foundation, 25th Anniv. — A525

Designs: 2.50col, Fireman rescuing child. 25col, Emblem.

**2000, Jan. 17    Litho.    Perf. 14½x14**
1533 A525 2.50col multi .70 .35
1534 A525 25col multi 7.00 3.50

La Prensa Grafica, 85th Anniv. — A529

**2000, May 9**
1539 A529 5col multi 1.75 .90

Champagnat

Canonization of Marcelino Champagnat (1789-1840) — A530

**2000, June 2**
1540 A530 10col multi 2.75 1.40

2000 Summer Olympics, Sydney — A531

No. 1541: a, Runners. b, Gymnast. c, High jumper. d, Weight lifter. e, Fencer. f, Cyclist. g, Swimmer. h, Shooter. i, Archer. j, Judo.

**2000, July 20    Perf. 14½x14¼**
1541 A531 1col Any single 4.50 4.50
Sheet of 10 a-j. .35 .20

World Post Day — A533

**2000, Oct. 9    Litho.    Perf. 14½x14¼**
1543 A533 5col multi 1.75 1.00

CORREOS DE El Salvador

**2000, Apr. 28**
1538 A528 1col Any single
a-t. Sheet of 20 5.50 2.75
.25 .20

No. 1538: a, Gate. b, Ocelot (tigrillo). c, Paca (tepezcuintle). d, Venado River waterfalls. e, Black curassow (pajuil). f, Tree with yellow leaves. g, Orchid (flor de encarnación). h, Honeycreeper (torogoz). i, Bird with purple head (siete colores). j, Vegetation near cliff. k, Interpretation center. l, Bird with black and yellow plumage (payasito). m, Frog. n, Mushrooms (hongos). o, Red flower (guaco de tierra). p, Green toucan. q, Hillside foliage. r, Agouti (cotuza). s, Ant bear (oso hormiguero). t, Cascades of El Imposible.

Navidad 2000

Christmas Tree Ornaments
A534

EL SALVADOR

Central American Parliament, 10th Anniv. (in 2001) — A549

**2002, Sep. 13**  
1567 A549 25col multi — 18.00 10.00

Pan-American Health Organization, Cent. — A550

No. 1568: a, Headquarters, Washington, DC. b, Emblem and "100." Illustration reduced.

**2002, Oct. 18 Litho. Perf. 14½x14**  
1568 A550 2.70col Horiz. pair,  
    #a-b — 4.00 2.10

Tourism — A551

No. 1569, 1col: a, Forest, Pilatario Volcano. b, Jiquilisco Bay. No. 1570, 4col: a, Joya de Cerén Archaeological Site. b, Juayua, Sonsonate Department.

**2002, Dec. 6 Vert. Pairs, #a-b**  
1569-1570 A551 — 8.00 4.00

America Issue — Youth, Education, and Literacy — A552

Designs: 1col, Stylized person, book, block. 1.50col, Teacher and students.

**2002, Nov. 26 Set of 2**  
1571-1572 A552 — 2.00 1.00

Scouting in El Salvador, 80th Anniv. — A553

**Perf. 14½x14**  
1573 A553 2.70col multi — 2.00 1.10

---

Designs: No. 1558, 2.50col, Dove and sun. No. 1559, 2.50col, UN emblem and handshake. No. 1560: a, 2.50col, Dove with olive branch flying over village. b, 2.50col, Dove, flag.

**2002, May 15 Perf. 14½x14**  
1558-1559 A544 Set of 2 — 3.50 2.00  
**Souvenir Sheet**  
**Rouletted Irregularly**  
1560 A544 Sheet of 2, #a-b — 3.50 3.50

19th Central American and Caribbean Games — A545

No. 1561: a, Montage of athletes. b, Bicycle race. c, Children's drawing of various athletes. d, Gymnast. 4col, Mascots.

**2002, June 13 Perf. 14½x14**  
1561 Vert. strip of 4 — 3.00 3.00  
  a.-d. A545 1col Any single — .65 .40  
**Souvenir Sheet**  
**Rouletted Irregularly**  
1562 A545 4col multi — 3.00 3.00

A546

2002 World Cup Soccer Championships, Japan and Korea — A547

No. 1563 — Various Korean World Cup stadia and flags of countries in Group: a, A. b, B. c, C. d, D. No. 1564 — Various Japanese World Cup stadia and flags of countries in Group: a, E. b, F. c, G. d, H. 4col, Flag of winning team, Brazil.

**2002, July 11 Perf. 14½x14**  
1563 Vert. strip of 4 — 2.75 2.75  
  a.-d. A546 1col Any single — .65 .40  
1564 Vert. strip of 4 — 5.25 5.25  
  a.-d. A546 1.50col Any single — 1.00 .60  
**Souvenir Sheet**  
**Rouletted Irregularly**  
1565 A547 4col multi — 3.00 3.00

Natl. Academy of Public Security, 10th Anniv. — A548

**2002, Sep. 6 Litho. Perf. 14½x14**  
1566 A548 1col multi — .75 .40

---

St. Vincent de Paul Children's Home, 125th Anniv. A539

**2001, Oct. 26**  
1551 A539 4col multi — 1.60 .90

Mushrooms A540

No. 1552: a, Lactaius indigo. b, Pleurotus ostreatus. c, Ramaria sp. d, Clavaria vermicularis. No. 1553: a, Amanita muscaria. b, Phillipsia sp. c, Russula emetica. d, Geastrum triplex.

**2001, Dec. 20 Perf. 14½x14**  
1552 Horiz. strip of 4 — 4.25 4.25  
  a.-d. A540 1.50col Any single — 12.00 12.00  
1553 Horiz. strip of 4 — 12.00 12.00  
  a.-d. A540 4col Any single — 2.75 1.60

St. Josemaria Escrivá de Balaguer (1902-75), Founder of Opus Dei — A541

Nakaguei and 1col, Plowed field. bcol, People and computers.

**2002, Apr. 26 Litho. Perf. 14½x14**  
1554-1555 A541 Set of 2 — 4.50 2.50

San Miguel Lions Club, 51st Anniv. — A542

**2002, July 31**  
1556 A542 5col multi — 3.50 2.00

Rosales National Hospital, Cent. — A543

**2002, June 28**  
1557 A543 10col multi — 7.25 4.00

Peace Accords, 10th Anniv. — A544

---

No. 1544: a, Snowman. b, Bells. c, Striped pendants. d, Candy cane. e, Candles. f, Sleigh. g, Gifts. h, Santa Claus. i, Santa's hat. j, Santa's boot.

**2000, Nov. 9**  
1544 Block of 10 — 6.00 6.00  
  a.-j. A534 1col Any single — .50 .20

Art by Expatriates A535

Art by: a, Roberto Mejía Ruiz. b, Alex Cuchilla. c, Nicolas Fredy Shi Quán. d, José Bernardo Pacheco. e, Oscar Soles.

**2000, Dec. 4 Perf. 14x14½**  
1545 Horiz. strip of 5 — 15.00 15.00  
  a.-e. A535 4col Any single — 2.50 1.50

Pets A536

No. 1546: a, 1.50col, Dogs. b, 1.50col, Dog and cat. No. 1547: a, 2.50col, Parakeets. b, 2.50col, Dogs, diff.

**2001, Feb. 28 Litho. Perf. 14x14½**  
**Vert. Pairs, #a-b**  
1546-1547 A536 Set of 2 — 5.00 5.00

Starting with Nos. 1546-1547, stamps also show denominations in US dollars.

Saburo Hirao Park, 25th Anniv. A537

Designs: 5col, Playground. 25col, Bridge in gardens.

**2001, Mar. 14 Set of 2**  
1548-1549 A537 — 20.00 11.00

Claudia Lars (1899-1974), Salvadoran Writer, and Federico Proaño (1848-94), Ecuadoran Writer — A538

**2001, Aug. 28 Litho. Perf. 14x14½**  
1550 A538 10col multi — 4.00 2.25

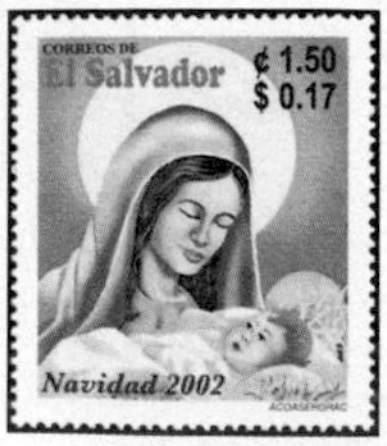


Christmas A554

Infant Jesus and: 1.50col, Mary. 2.50col, Joseph.

**2002, Nov. 29**
**1574-1575** A554 Set of 2 3.00 1.60

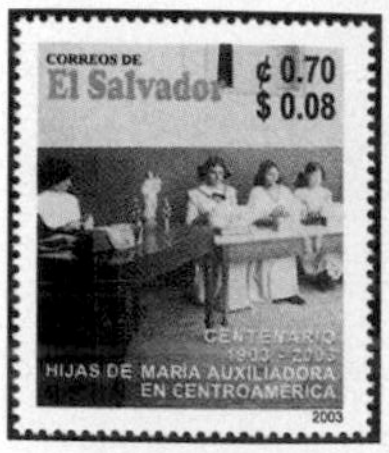


Daughters of Our Lady Help of Christians (Salesian Sisters) in Central America, Cent. — A555

Designs: 70c, Girls, nun in classroom. 1.50col, Statue of Madonna and Child.

**2003, May 26 Litho.** ***Perf. 14¼x14***
**1576-1577** A555 Set of 2 1.75 .90

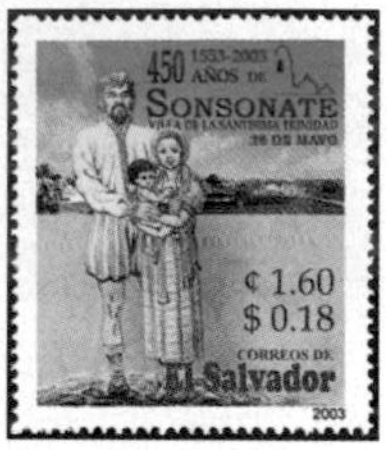


Town of Sonsonate, 450th Anniv. — A556

**2003, May 28**
**1578** A556 1.60col multi 1.25 .65

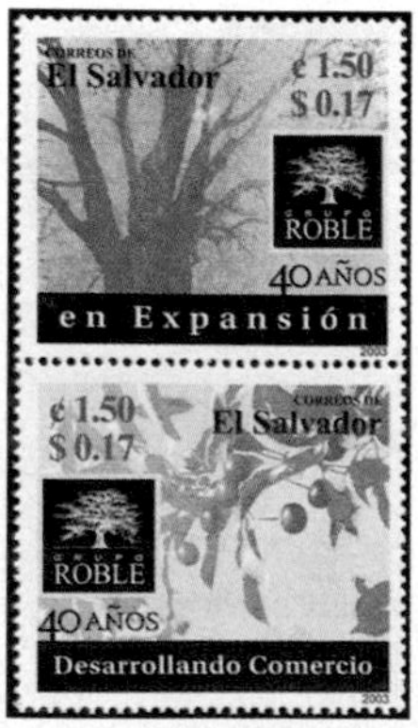


Grupo Roble, 40th Anniv. A557

No. 1579: a, Tree without leaves. b, Cherries on branch.
4col, Bird and nest.

**2003, July 18** ***Perf. 14x14¼***
**1579** A557 1.50col Vert. pair, #a-b 2.25 1.25

**Souvenir Sheet**
***Rouletted 12¾x13½***
**1580** A557 4col multi 3.00 3.00

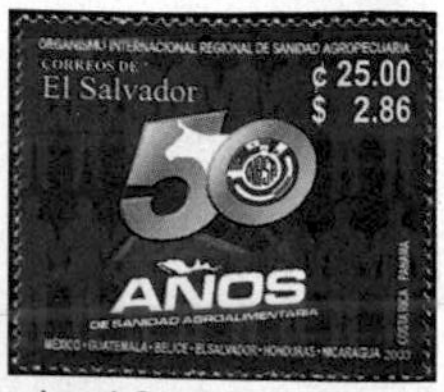


Regional Sanitary Agricultural Organization, 50th Anniv. — A558

**2003, July 25** ***Perf. 14x14¼***
**1581** A558 25col multi 18.00 10.00

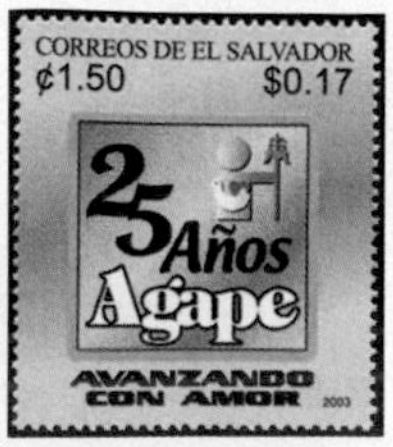


Agape Ministries in El Salvador, 25th Anniv. — A559

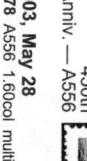

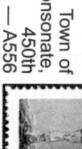

**2003, Aug. 25** ***Perf. 14¼x14***
**1582** A559 1.50col multi 1.10 .60

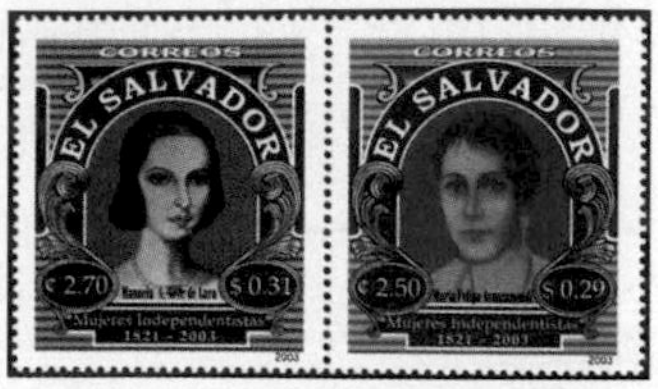


A560

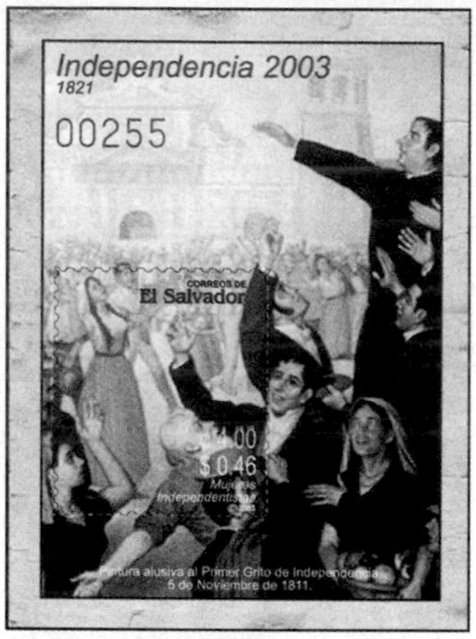


Independence, 182nd Anniv. — A561

No. 1583: a, 2.50col, Maria Felipa Aranzamendi y Aguiar. b, 2.70col, Manuela Antonia Arce de Lara.
4col, Cry for Independence, Nov. 5, 1811.
Illustration A560 reduced.

**2003, Sept. 30** ***Perf. 14¼x14***
**1583** A560 Horiz. pair, #a-b 4.00 4.00

**Souvenir Sheet**
***Rouletted 13½x13¼***
**1584** A561 4col multi 3.00 3.00

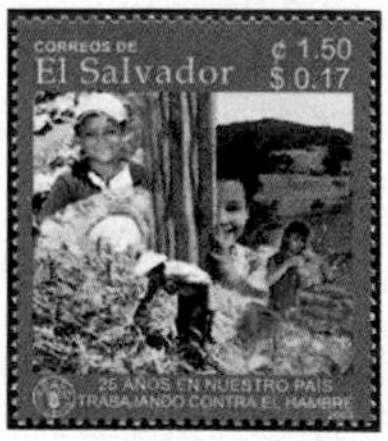


FAO in El Salvador, 25th Anniv. — A562

Designs: 1.50col, Children, farmers.
4col, Child, farmer, food preparation workers.

**2003, Oct. 8** ***Perf. 14¼x14***
**1585** A562 1.50col multi 1.10 .60

**Souvenir Sheet**
***Rouletted 13¼x13¾***
**1586** A562 4col multi 3.00 3.00

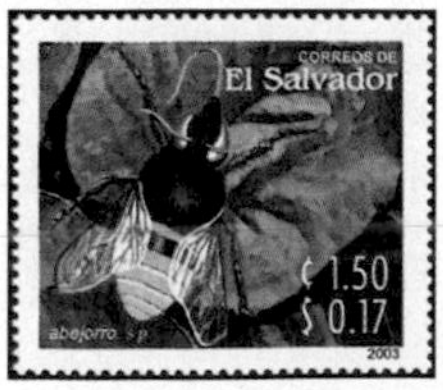


Insects and Flowers A563

No. 1587: a, Abejorro sp. b, Chrysina quetzalcoatli. c, Anartia fatima. d, Manduca sp. e, Manduca sexta. f, Tabebuia chrysantha. g, Alpinia purpurata. h, Tecoma stans. i, Tabebuia rosea. j, Passiflora edulis.
4col, Anartia fatima, Tabebuia rosea, vert.

**2003, Oct. 23** ***Perf. 14x14¼***
**1587** Block of 10 12.00 12.00
***a.-j.*** A563 1.50col Any single 1.00 .60

**Souvenir Sheet**
***Rouletted 13¼x13¾***
**1588** A563 4col multi 3.00 3.00

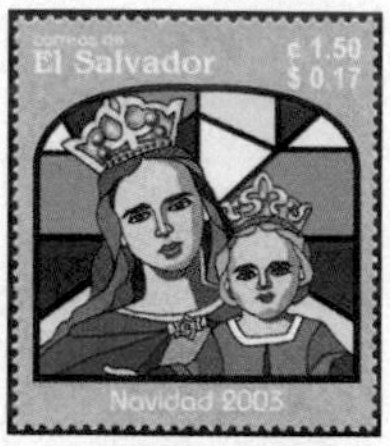


Christmas A564

Designs: 1.50col, Madonna and Child. 4col, Holy Family.

**2003, Nov. 7** ***Perf. 14¼x14***
**1589-1590** A564 Set of 2 4.00 2.25

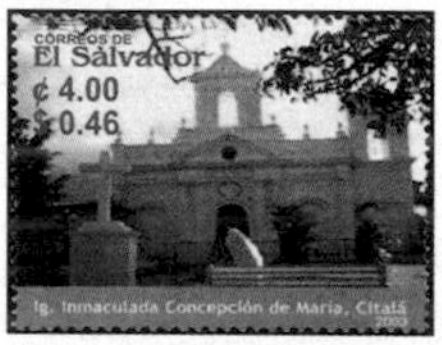


Churches A565

No. 1591: a, Church of the Immaculate Conception, Citalá. b, St. James the Apostle Church, Chalchuapa. c, St. Peter the Apostle Church, Metapán. d, Our Lady of Santa Ana Church, Chapeltique. e, St. James the Apostle Church, Conchagua.
5col, Calvary Church, San Salvador, vert.

**2003, Nov. 14** ***Perf. 14x14¼***
**1591** Horiz. strip of 5 12.00 12.00
***a.-e.*** A565 4col Any single 2.25 1.25

**Souvenir Sheet**
***Rouletted 13¼x13¾***
**1592** A565 5col multi 2.75 2.75

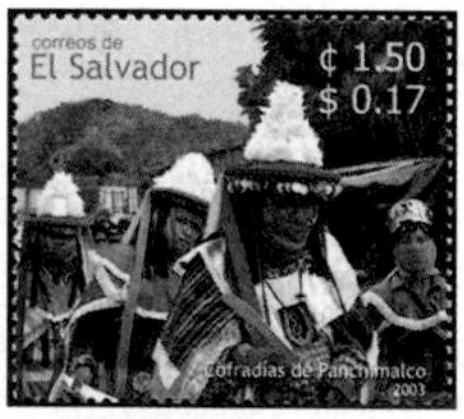


Tourism A566

No. 1593: a, Brotherhood of Panchimalco. b, Church cupola, Juayúa. c, Shalpa Beach, La Libertad. d, Tazumal Ruins.

**2003, Dec. 10** ***Perf. 14x14¼***
**1593** Vert. strip of 4 4.50 4.50
***a.-d.*** A566 1.50col Any single 1.00 .60

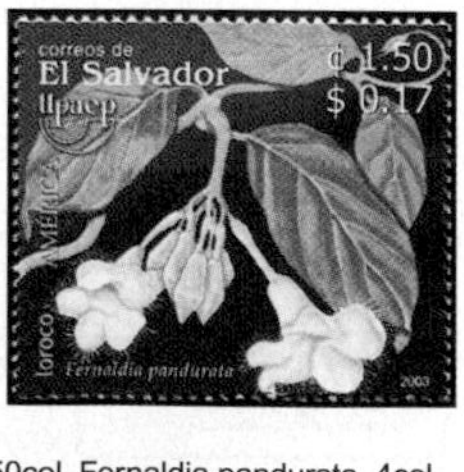


America Issue - Flora and Fauna A567

Designs: 1.50col, Fernaldia pandurata. 4col, Lepidophyma smithii.

**2003, Dec. 19**
**1594-1595** A567 Set of 2 4.00 2.25

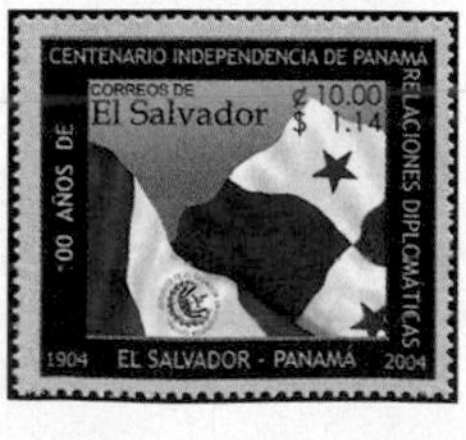


El Salvador — Panama Diplomatic Relations, Cent. A568

Designs: 10col, Flags of El Salvador and Panama. 25col, Flags, ship in dock.

**2004, Feb. 17 Litho.** ***Perf. 14x14¼***
**1596-1597** A568 Set of 2 8.00 4.00

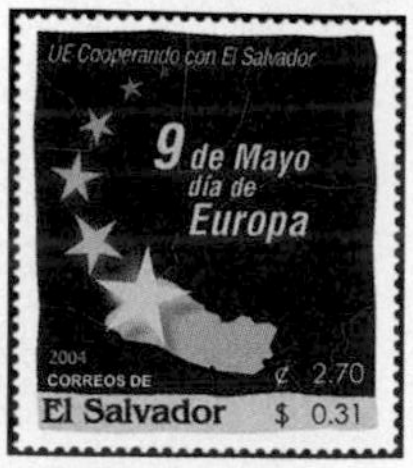


Salvadoran Cooperation With European Union — A569

Stars and map of: 2.70col, Central America. 5col, Europe.

**2004, May 13** ***Perf. 14¼x14***
**1598-1599** A569 Set of 2 1.75 .90

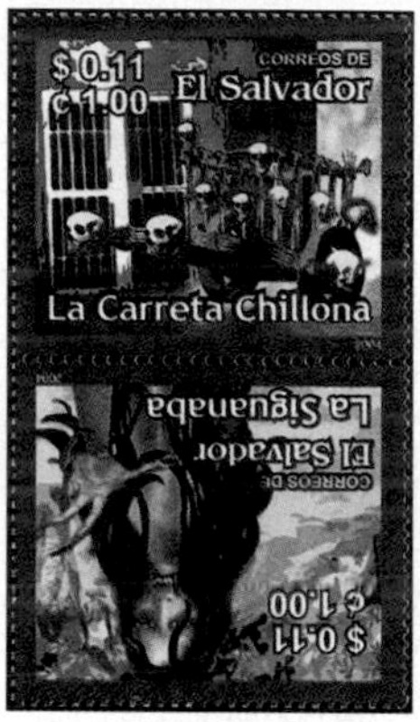


Legends A570

No. 1600, 1col: a, La Carreta Chillona. b, La Siguanaba.
No. 1601, 1.60col: a, Justo Juez de la Noche. b, El Cipitío.

**2004, June 30** ***Perf. 14x14¼***
**Vert. Tete-beche Pairs, #a-b**
**1600-1601** A570 Set of 2 1.25 .60

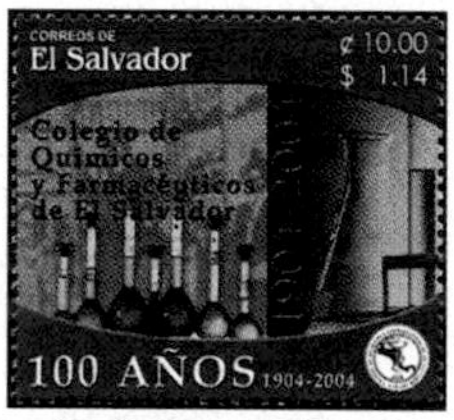


El Salvador College of Chemistry and Pharmaceuticals, Cent. — A571

**2004, Sept. 17**
**1602** A571 10col multi 2.40 1.25

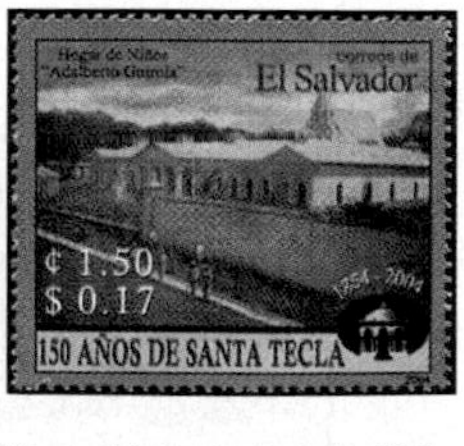


Santa Tecla (Nueva San Salvador), 150th Anniv. A572

Designs: 1.50col, Adalberto Guirola Children's Home. 4col, Second Avenue.

**2004, Oct. 14**
**1603-1604** A572 Set of 2 1.25 .60

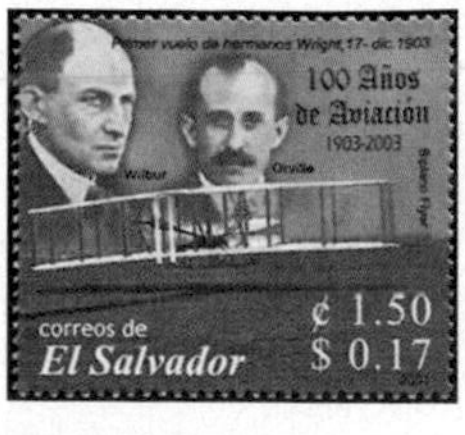


Powered Flight, Cent. (in 2003) A573

No. 1605: a, Wilbur and Orville Wright, Wright Flyer. b, Alberto Santos-Dumont, 14-Bis. c, Louis Blériot, Blériot XI. d, Glenn Curtiss, Curtiss JN-4D Jenny. e, Hugo Junkers, Junkers J.1.

No. 1606: a, Charles Lindbergh, Spirit of St. Louis. b, Amelia Earhart, Lockheed Vega. c, Chuck Yeager, Bell X-1. d, Robert Withe, X-15. e, Dick Rutan and Jeana Yeager, Voyager.

No. 1607, Wilbur and Orville Wright, Wright Flyer, vert.

**2004, Nov. 5** *Perf. 14x14¼*

| | | | |
|---|---|---|---|
| **1605** | Horiz. strip of 5 | 1.75 | .85 |
| *a.-e.* | A573 1.50col Any single | .35 | .20 |
| **1606** | Horiz. strip of 5 | 4.75 | 2.40 |
| *a.-e.* | A573 4col Any single | .95 | .45 |

**Souvenir Sheet**

***Rouletted Irregularly***

**1607** A573 4col multi .95 .45

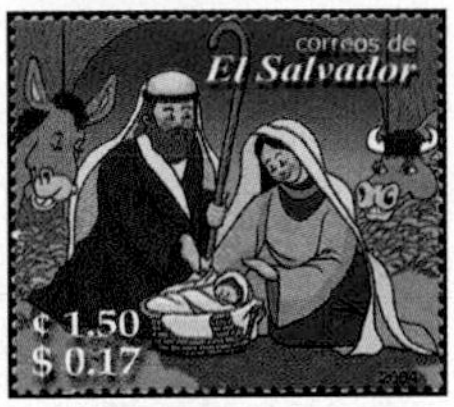

Christmas A574

Designs: 1.50col, Holy Family. 2.50col, Shepherd and sheep. 4col, Magi. 5col, Flight into Egypt.

**2004, Dec. 7 Litho.** *Perf. 14x14¼*

**1608-1611** A574 Set of 4 3.00 1.50

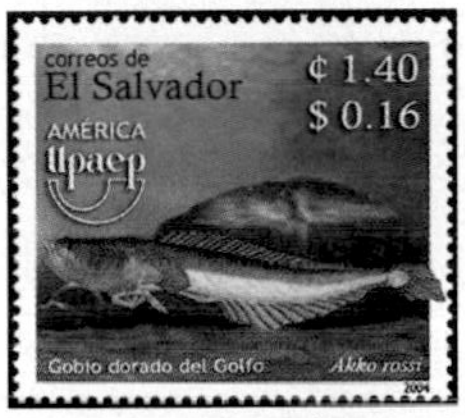

America Issue - Environmental Protection — A575

Marine life: 1.40col, Akko rossi. 2.20col, Chromodoris sphoni.

**2004, Dec. 17**

| | | | |
|---|---|---|---|
| **1612-1613** A575 | Set of 2 | .85 | .40 |
| *1613a* | Tete-beche pair, #1612-1613 | .85 | .40 |

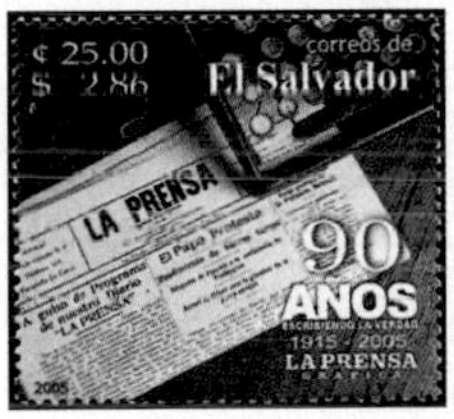

La Prensa Newspaper, 90th Anniv. A576

**2005, Apr. 7**

**1614** A576 25col multi 5.75 3.00

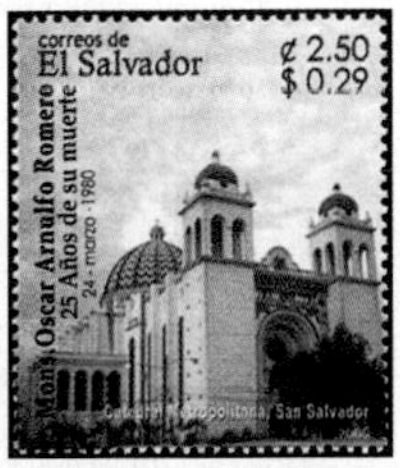

Assassination of Archbishop Oscar Romero, 25th Anniv. — A577

Designs: 2.50col, Metropolitan Cathedral, San Salvador. 5col, Romero (1917-80).

**2005, Apr. 23** *Perf. 14¼x14*

**1615-1616** A577 Set of 2 1.75 .85

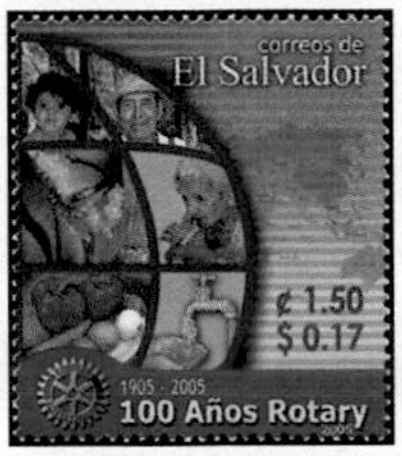

Rotary International, Cent. — A578

**2005, June 15** *Perf. 14¼x14*

**1617** A578 1.50col shown .35 .20

**Souvenir Sheet**

***Rouletted Irregularly***

**1618** A578 4col Children .95 .45

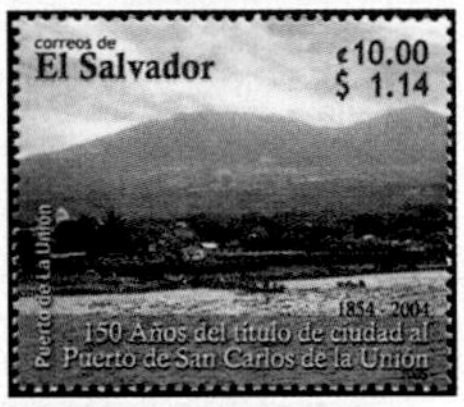

Puerto de San Carlos de la Unión, 150th Anniv. A579

**2005, July 27** *Perf. 14x14¼*

**1619** A579 10col shown 2.40 1.25

**Souvenir Sheet**

***Rouletted Irregularly***

**1620** A579 4col Pirigallo Island .95 .45

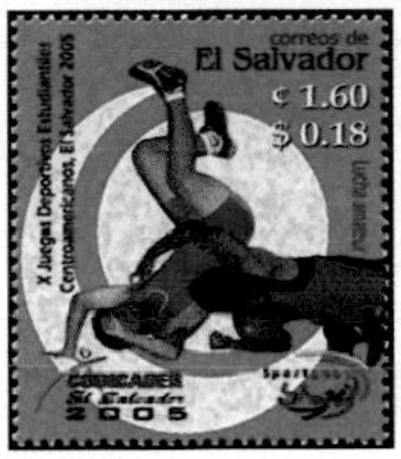

Tenth Central American Students' Games A580

Designs: 1.60col, Wrestling. 2.20col, High jump. 2.70col, Karate. No. 1624, 4col, Rollerblading.

No. 1625, 4col, Karate, high jump and wrestling.

**2005, Sept. 14 Litho.** *Perf. 14¼x14*

**1621-1624** A580 Set of 4 2.40 1.25

**Souvenir Sheet**

***Rouletted 11x10¾x10x10½***

**1625** A580 4col multi .95 .45

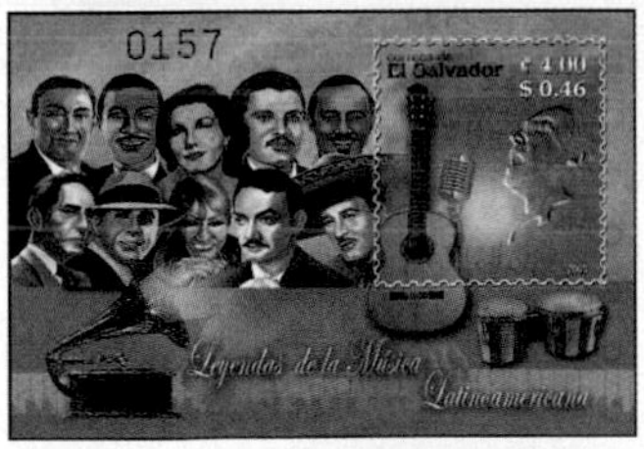

Latin American Musicians — A581

No. 1626: a, Agustín Lara (1897-1970), composer, Mexico. b, Pedro Infante (1917-57), singer, Mexico. c, Libertad Lamarque (1906-2000), singer, Argentina. d, Carlos Gardel (1890-1936), singer, Argentina. e, Celia Cruz (1924-2003), singer, Cuba. f, Damaso Pérez Prado (1916-89), composer, Cuba. g, Daniel Santos (1916-92), song writer, Puerto Rico. h, Pedro Vargas (1908-89), singer, Mexico. i, Beny Moré (1919-63), singer, Cuba. j, Jorge Negrete (1911-53), singer, Mexico.

4col, Singer, microphone and guitar.

**2005, Oct. 11** *Perf. 14¼x14*

**1626** A581 1.50col Sheet of 10, #a-j 3.50 1.75

**Souvenir Sheet**

***Rouletted 11x10¾***

**1627** A581 4col multi .95 .45

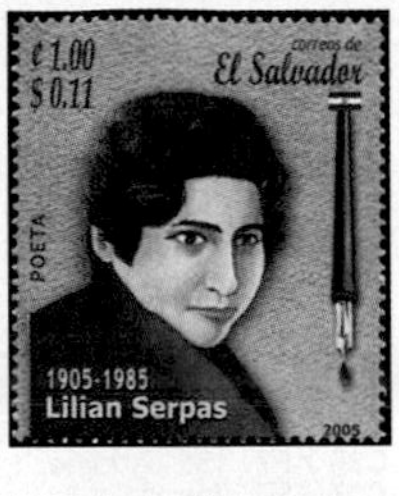

Writers A582

Designs: No. 1628, 1col, Lilian Serpas (1905-85), poet. No. 1629, 1col, Oswaldo Escobar Velado (1919-61), poet. No. 1630, 4col, Alvaro Menendez Leal (1931-2000), dramatist. No. 1631, 4col, Roque Dalton (1935-75), poet. No. 1632, 5col, Pedro Geoffroy Rivas (1908-79), poet. No. 1633, 5col, Italo Lopez Vallecillos (1932-86), poet.

**2005, Oct. 20** *Perf. 14¼x14*

**1628-1633** A582 Set of 6 4.75 2.40

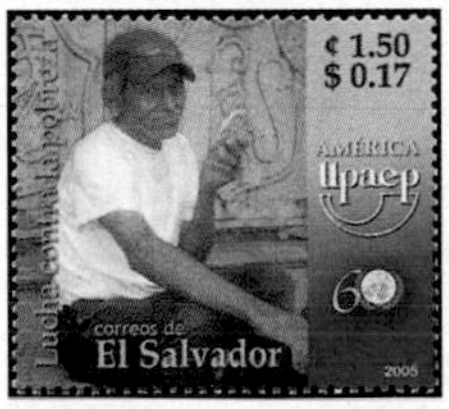

America Issue - Fight Against Poverty A583

Designs: 1.50col, Man holding food. 4col, Children and shack.

**2005, Nov. 25** *Perf. 14x14¼*

**1634-1635** A583 Set of 2 1.25 .65

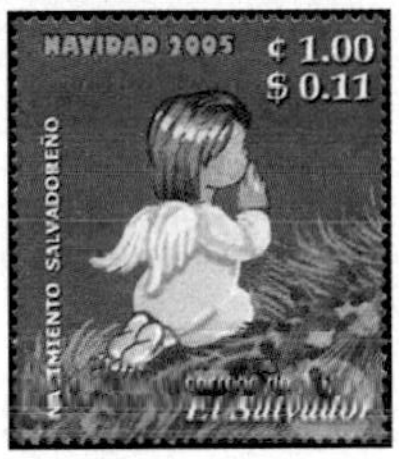

Christmas A584

No. 1636 — Creche figures: a, Praying angel. b, Chicken and left half of star. c, Rooster and right half of star. d, Angel with horn. e, Donkey. f, Mary and Jesus. g, Joseph and two sheep. h, Cow. i, Camel with red saddle cloth and Magus. j, Camel without saddle and Magus. k, Camel with blue saddle cloth and Magus. l, Shepherd and three sheep. m, Woman, table and pot. n, Man and oxcart. o, Musicians. p, Bride, groom and church. q, Dog and kneeling woman. r, Sheep and shepherd holding lamb. s, Women with water jugs. t, Birds.

**2005, Nov. 30** *Perf. 14¼x14*

| | | | |
|---|---|---|---|
| **1636** | Sheet of 20 | 4.50 | 2.25 |
| *a.-t.* | A584 1col Any single | .20 | .20 |

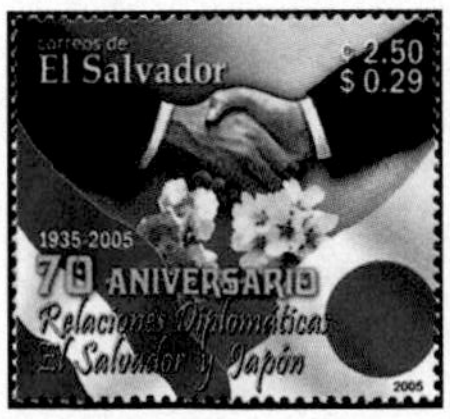

Diplomatic Relations Between El Salvador and Japan, 70th Anniv. A585

Designs: 2.50col, Flags of El Salvador and Japan, flowers, men shaking hands. 9col, Airport, medical worker and highway.

**2005, Dec. 20** *Perf. 14x14¼*

**1637-1638** A585 Set of 2 2.75 1.40

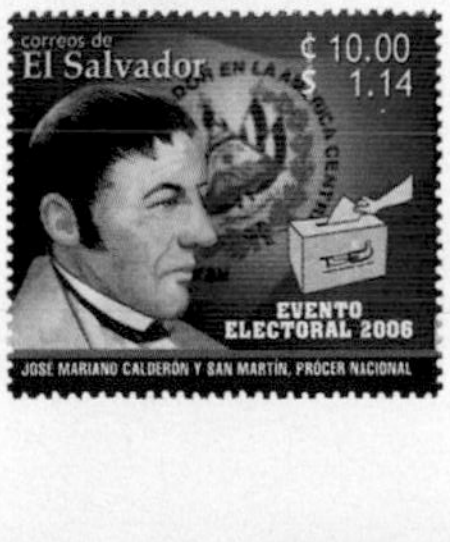

2006 Elections A586

Ballot box, flag and: 10col, José Mariano Calderón y San Martín. 25col, Miguel José de Castro y Lara.

**2006**

**1639-1640** A586 Set of 2 8.00 4.00

## AIR POST STAMPS

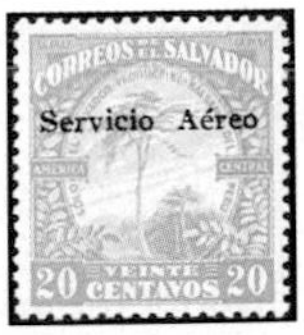

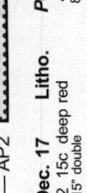

Regular Issue of 1924-25 Overprinted in Black or Red

First Printing.

15c on 10c: "15 QUINCE 15" measures 22½mm.

20c: Shows on the back of the stamp an albino impression of the 50c surcharge.

25c on 35c: Original value canceled by a long and short bar.

40c on 50c: Only one printing.

50c on 1col: Surcharge in dull orange red.

*Perf. 12½, 14*

**1929, Dec. 28** **Unwmk.**

| | | | | |
|---|---|---|---|---|
| **C1** | A112 20c dp green (Bk) | 3.25 | 3.25 |
| *a.* | Red overprint | 600.00 | 600.00 |

Counterfeits exist of No. C1a.

**With Additional Surcharge of New Values and Bars in Black or Red**

| | | | |
|---|---|---|---|
| **C3** | A111 15c on 10c orange | .50 | .50 |
| *a.* | "ALTANT CO" | 14.00 | 14.00 |
| **C4** | A114 25c on 35c scar & grn | 1.25 | 1.25 |
| *a.* | Bars inverted | 7.50 | 7.50 |
| **C5** | A115 40c on 50c org brn | .50 | .35 |
| **C6** | A116 50c on 1col grn & vio (R) | 8.00 | 6.50 |
| | *Nos. C1-C6 (5)* | 13.50 | 11.85 |

Second Printing.

15c on 10d: "15 QUINCE 15" measures 20½mm.

20c: Has not the albino impression on the back of the stamp.

25c on 35c: Original value cancelled by two bars of equal length.

50c on 1col: Surcharge in carmine rose.

**1930, Jan. 10**

| | | | |
|---|---|---|---|
| **C7** | A112 20c deep green | .45 | .45 |
| **C8** | A111 15c on 10c org | .45 | .45 |
| *a.* | "ATLANT CO" | 17.50 | |
| *b.* | Double surcharge | 10.00 | |
| *c.* | As "a," double surcharge | 75.00 | |
| *d.* | Pair, one without surcharge | 175.00 | |
| **C9** | A114 25c on 35c scar & grn | .40 | .40 |
| **C10** | A116 50c on 1col grn & vio (C) | .90 | .90 |
| *a.* | Without bars over "UN COLON" | 2.50 | |
| *b.* | As "a," without block over "1" | 2.50 | |
| | *Nos. C7-C10 (4)* | 2.20 | 2.20 |

Numerous wrong font and defective letters exist in both printings of the surcharges.

No. C10 with black surcharge is bogus.

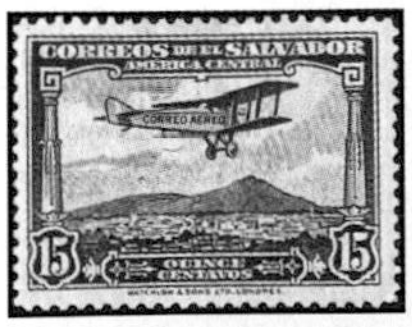

Mail Plane over San Salvador AP1

**1930, Sept. 15 Engr.** *Perf. 12½*

| | | | |
|---|---|---|---|
| **C11** | AP1 15c deep red | .20 | .20 |
| **C12** | AP1 20c emerald | .20 | .20 |
| **C13** | AP1 25c brown violet | .20 | .20 |
| **C14** | AP1 40c ultra | .30 | .20 |
| | *Nos. C11-C14 (4)* | .90 | .80 |

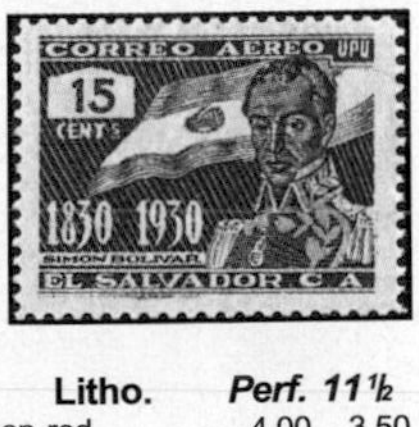

Simón Bolivar — AP2

**1930, Dec. 17 Litho.** *Perf. 11½*

| | | | |
|---|---|---|---|
| **C15** | AP2 15c deep red | 4.00 | 3.50 |
| *a.* | "15" double | 82.50 | |

Centenary of death of Simón Bolívar. Counterfeits of Nos. C15-C18 exist.

| | | |
|---|---|---|
| C16 | AP2 20c emerald | 4.00 3.50 |
| C17 | AP2 25c brown violet | 4.00 3.50 |
| a. | Vert. pair, imperf. btwn. | 110.00 |
| C18 | AP2 40c dp ultra | 16.00 14.00 |
| a. | Imperf. pair, imperf. pair | 16.00 14.00 |

Nos. C15-C18 (4) 16.00 14.00

**1931, June 29    Engr.    Perf. 14**
C19 A116 1col green & vio    3.25 2.00

No. 504 Overprinted in Red

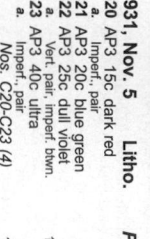

**1931. Nov. 5    Litho.    Perf. 11½**
Tower of La Merced Church — AP3

| | | |
|---|---|---|
| C20 | AP3 15c dark red | 3.00 2.25 |
| C21 | AP3 20c blue green | 3.00 2.25 |
| a. | Imperf. pair | 50.00 |
| C22 | AP3 25c dull violet | 3.00 2.25 |
| a. | AP3 25c dull vio & grn | 110.00 |
| C23 | AP3 40c ultra & grn | 3.00 2.25 |
| a. | Imperf. pair | 60.00 |

Nos. C20-C23 (4)    9.00

120th anniv. of the 1st movement toward the political independence of El Salvador. In the tower of La Merced Church hangs the bell which José Matías Delgado–called the Father of his Country–rang to initiate the movement for liberty.

**1932, Nov. 12    Wmk. 271    Perf. 12½**
José Matías Delgado AP4
Airplane and Caravels of Columbus AP5

| | | |
|---|---|---|
| C24 | AP4 15c dull red & vio | .75 .75 |
| C25 | AP4 20c blue grn & bl | 1.00 1.00 |
| C26 | AP4 25c dull violet | 1.00 1.00 |
| C27 | AP4 40c ultra | 1.25 1.20 |

Nos. C24-C27 (4)    4.00 4.00

**1933, Oct. 12    Wmk. 240    Perf. 13**

| | | |
|---|---|---|
| C28 | AP5 15c red orange | 1.25 1.00 |
| C29 | AP5 20c blue green | 1.40 1.00 |
| C30 | AP5 25c lilac | 2.00 1.40 |
| C31 | AP5 40c ultra | 2.00 1.40 |
| C32 | AP5 1col black | 9.25 6.60 |

Nos. C28-C32 (5)

1st centenary of the death of Father José Matías Delgado, who is known as the Father of El Salvadoran Political Emancipation. Nos. C24-C27 show each cheek without shading in the 72nd stamp of each sheet.

**1934, Dec. 16    Police Barracks Type    Perf. 12½**

| | | |
|---|---|---|
| C33 | A123 25c lilac | .25 .20 |
| C34 | A123 30c brown | .40 .30 |
| C35 | A123 1col black | 42.50 |

Nos. C33-C35 (3)    1.50 1.15

---

**1935, Mar. 16    Engr.    Unwmk.**
Runner AP7

| | | |
|---|---|---|
| C36 | AP7 15c carmine | 3.25 3.00 |
| C37 | AP7 25c violet | 3.25 3.00 |
| C38 | AP7 30c brown | 2.75 2.25 |
| C39 | AP7 55c blue | 16.00 11.00 |
| C40 | AP7 1col black | 11.00 11.00 |

Nos. C36-C40 (5)    36.25 28.25

Third Central American Games. For overprints and surcharge see Nos. C41-C45, C53.

**1935, June 27    Same Overprinted in Black**
HABILITADO

| | | |
|---|---|---|
| C41 | AP7 15c carmine | 1.75 |
| C42 | AP7 25c violet | 3.00 1.75 |
| C43 | AP7 30c brown | 3.00 1.75 |
| C44 | AP7 55c blue | 22.50 17.50 |
| C45 | AP7 1col black | 41.50 30.25 |

Nos. C41-C45 (5)

**1935, Oct. 26    Litho.    Wmk. 240**
Flag of El Salvador Type
C46 A125 30c black brown    .50 .25

**1935, Dec. 26    Perf. 12½**
Tree of San Vicente Type
Numerals in Black, Tree in Yellow Green

| | | |
|---|---|---|
| C47 | A126 10c orange | .80 .70 |
| C48 | A126 15c brown | .80 .70 |
| C49 | A126 20c dk blue grn | .80 .70 |
| C50 | A126 25c dark purple | .80 .70 |
| C51 | A126 30c black brown | 4.00 3.50 |

Nos. C47-C51 (5)

Tercentenary of San Vicente.

No. 565 Overprinted in Red

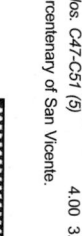

**1937    Engr.    Unwmk.**
C52 A133 15c dk olive bis    .35 .25
a. Double overprint    25.00

**1937**
No. C44 Surcharged in Red
Panchimalco Church — AP10

C53 AP7 30c on 55c blue    2.00 .75

**1937, Dec. 3    Engr.    Perf. 12**

| | | |
|---|---|---|
| C54 | AP10 15c orange yel | .25 .20 |
| C55 | AP10 20c green | .25 .20 |
| C56 | AP10 25c violet | .25 .20 |
| C57 | AP10 30c brown | .25 .20 |
| C58 | AP10 40c brown | .25 .20 |

---

US Constitution Type of Regular Issue
**1938, Apr. 22    Engr. & Litho.**

| | | |
|---|---|---|
| C59 | AP10 1col black | .90 .25 |
| C60 | AP10 5col rose carmine | 5.40 3.55 |

Nos. C54-C60 (7)    3.25 2.25

**1938, Aug. 18    Engr.**
José Simeón Cañas y Villacorta — AP12

| | | |
|---|---|---|
| C61 | A136 30c multicolored | .60 .50 |
| C62 | AP12 15c orange | .90 .85 |
| C63 | AP12 20c brt green | 1.10 .85 |
| C64 | AP12 30c redsh brown | 1.10 .85 |
| C65 | AP12 1col black | 3.75 2.75 |

Nos. C62-C65 (4)    6.85 5.30

José Simeón Cañas y Villacorta (1767-1838), liberator of slaves in Central America.

**1939, Apr. 14    Perf. 12½**
Golden Gate Bridge, San Francisco Bay — AP13

| | | |
|---|---|---|
| C66 | AP13 15c dull yel & blk | .25 .20 |
| C67 | AP13 30c dk brown & blk | .30 .20 |
| C68 | AP13 40c dk blue & blk | .40 .25 |

Nos. C66-C68 (3)    .95 .65

Golden Gate Intl. Exposition, San Francisco. For surcharges see Nos. C86-C91.

**1940, Mar. 1    Engr.**
Sir Rowland Hill Type

| | | |
|---|---|---|
| C69 | A146 30c dk brn, buff & blk | 5.00 1.75 |
| C70 | A146 80c org red & blk | 13.50 10.50 |

Centenary of the postage stamp, first postmarked Feb. 29 were predated. Covers postmarked Feb. 29 were predated. Actual first day was Mar. 1.

---

**1940, Nov. 27**
Coffee Tree with Ripe Berries — AP17

| | | |
|---|---|---|
| C73 | AP16 15c yellow orange | 1.00 .20 |
| C74 | AP16 20c deep green | 1.25 .40 |
| C75 | AP16 25c dark violet | 1.50 .40 |
| C76 | AP16 30c copper brown | 2.00 .45 |
| C77 | AP17 1col black | 6.00 1.00 |

Nos. C73-C77 (5)    11.75 1.45

Juan Lindo, Gen. Francisco Mallespín and New National University of El Salvador — AP18

**1941, Feb. 16    Perf. 12½**

| | | |
|---|---|---|
| C78 | AP18 20c dk grn & rose | .80 .50 |
| C79 | AP18 40c ind & brn org | .80 .50 |
| C80 | AP18 60c dl pur & brn | .80 .50 |
| C81 | AP18 80c hn brn & dk bl | 2.00 1.40 |
| C82 | AP18 1col black & org | 2.00 1.40 |
| C83 | AP18 2col yel org & rose | 8.40 5.70 |

Nos. C78-C83 (6)    9.25 9.25
a. Min. sheet of 5, #C78-C83, perf. 11½    9.25

Centenary of University of El Salvador. Stamps from No. C83a, perf. 11½, sell for about the same values as the perf. 12½ stamps.

Designs (portraits changed): 40c, 80c, Narciso Monterey and Antonio José Canas. 60c, 1col, Isidro Menéndez and Chrisanto Salazar.

**Catalogue values for unused stamps in this section, from this point to the end of the section, are for Never Hinged items.**

---

**1940, May 22    Perf. 12**
Map of the Americas, Figure of Peace, Plane — AP15

| | | |
|---|---|---|
| C71 | AP15 30c brown & blue | .25 .20 |
| C72 | AP15 80c dk rose & blk | .50 .40 |

Pan American Union, 50th anniversary.

**1942, Nov. 25    Wmk. 269    Engr.    Perf. 14**
Map of El Salvador AP20

C85 AP20 30c red orange    .50 .30
a. Horiz. pair, imperf. between    100.00

1st Eucharistic Cong. of El Salvador. See #588.

**1943    Unwmk.    Perf. 12½**
Coffee Tree in Bloom — AP16

Nos. C66 to C68 Surcharged with New Values in Dark Carmine

| | | |
|---|---|---|
| C86 | AP13 15c on 15c dl yel & blk | .30 .20 |
| C87 | AP13 20c on 30c dk brn & blk | |
| C88 | AP13 25c on 40c dk bl & blk | .40 .30 |

Nos. C86-C88 (3)    1.35 1.00

## Arce Type of Regular Issue

Engr.   Unwmk.

**1948, Feb. 26**

| | | | |
|---|---|---|---|
| C108 | A163 | 12c green | .20 .20 |
| C109 | A163 | 14c rose carmine | 2.25 1.40 |
| C110 | A163 | 1col violet | 2.70 1.80 |
| | | Nos. C108-C110 (3) | |

Cent. of the death of Manuel José Arce (1783-1847). "Father of Independence" and 1st pres. of the Federation of Central America.

## Roosevelt Types of Regular Issue

Designs: 12c, Pres. Franklin D. Roosevelt. 14c, Pres. Roosevelt presenting awards for distinguished service. 20c, Roosevelt and Cordell Hull. 25c, Pres. and Mrs. Roosevelt. 1col, Mackenzie King, Roosevelt and Winston Churchill. 2col, Funeral of Pres. Roosevelt. 4col, Pres. and Mrs. Roosevelt.

**1948, Apr. 12**   Engr.   Perf. 12½

### Various Frames, Center in Black

| | | | |
|---|---|---|---|
| C111 | A165 | 12c green | .35 .25 |
| C112 | A164 | 14c olive | .35 .25 |
| C113 | A164 | 20c chocolate | .35 .25 |
| C114 | A164 | 25c carmine | .35 .25 |
| C115 | A164 | 1col violet brn | 1.35 .75 |
| C116 | A164 | 2col blue violet | 2.25 1.25 |
| | | Nos. C111-C116 (6) | 5.00 3.00 |

### Souvenir Sheet

Perf. 13½

| | | | |
|---|---|---|---|
| C117 | A166 | 4col gray & brn | 4.00 3.00 |

Aéreo

**Nos. 599, 601 and 604 Overprinted in Carmine or Black**

**1948, Sept. 7**   Perf. 12½

| | | | |
|---|---|---|---|
| C118 | A154 | 5c slate gray | .20 .20 |
| C119 | A154 | 10c bister brown | 1.20 .50 |
| C120 | A154 | 1col scarlet (Bk) | 1.60 .90 |
| | | Nos. C118-C120 (3) | |

**No. C99 Surcharged in Black**

**1949, July 23**

| | | | |
|---|---|---|---|
| C121 | AP26 | 10(c) on 30c rose car | .20 .20 |

## UPU Type of Regular Issue

**1949, Oct. 9**   Engr.   Perf. 12½

| | | | |
|---|---|---|---|
| C122 | A167 | 5c brown | .35 .20 |
| C123 | A167 | 10c black | .60 .50 |
| C124 | A167 | 1col purple | 14.50 11.50 |
| | | | 15.35 11.90 |
| | | Nos. C122-C124 (3) | |

Flag and Arms of El Salvador — AP38

**1949, Dec. 15**   Perf. 10½

### Flag and Arms in Blue, Yellow and Green

| | | | |
|---|---|---|---|
| C125 | AP38 | 5c ocher | .20 .20 |
| C126 | AP38 | 10c dk green | 20.00 |
| b. | | Yellow omitted | |
| C127 | AP38 | 15c violet | .55 .40 |
| C128 | AP38 | 1col rose | 5.00 3.75 |
| C129 | AP38 | 5col red violet | 6.20 4.75 |
| | | Nos. C125-C129 (5) | |

1st anniv. of the Revolution of 12/14/48.

Isabella I of Spain — AP39

Flag, Torch and Scroll — AP40

Litho.   Unwmk.

### Background in Ultramarine, Red and Yellow

**1951, Apr. 28**   Perf. 11½

| | | | |
|---|---|---|---|
| C130 | AP39 | 10c green | .30 .20 |
| C131 | AP39 | 20c purple | .25 .20 |
| C132 | AP39 | 40c rose carmine | 25.00 |
| a. | | Horiz. pair, imperf. between | .35 .50 |
| C133 | AP39 | 1col black brown | 1.25 .50 |
| | | | 2.20 1.10 |

500th anniv. of the birth of Queen Isabella I of Spain. Nos. C130-C133 exist imperforate.

**1952, Feb. 14**   Photo.   Perf. 11½

### Flag in Blue

| | | | |
|---|---|---|---|
| C134 | AP40 | 10c brt blue | .20 .20 |
| C135 | AP40 | 15c chocolate | .20 .20 |
| C136 | AP40 | 20c deep blue | .20 .20 |
| C137 | AP40 | 25c gray | .25 .20 |
| C138 | AP40 | 40c purple | .35 .20 |
| C139 | AP40 | 1col red orange | .70 .35 |
| C140 | AP40 | 2col orange brn | 2.40 1.75 |
| C141 | AP40 | 5col violet blk | 2.40 .90 |
| | | | 6.70 4.00 |

Constitution of 1950.

## Marti Type of Regular Issue Inscribed "Aéreo"

**1953, Feb. 27**   Litho.   Perf. 10½

| | | | |
|---|---|---|---|
| C142 | A170 | 10c dk purple | .25 .20 |
| C143 | A170 | 20c dull brown | .35 .20 |
| C144 | A170 | 1col dull orange | 1.25 .35 |
| | | | 1.85 .75 |
| | | Nos. C142-C144 (3) | |

**No. C95 Surcharged "C 0.20" and Obliterations in Red**

**1953, Mar. 20**   Perf. 12½

| | | | |
|---|---|---|---|
| C145 | AP24 | 20c on 25c dl vio | .30 .20 |

No. C95 Overprinted in Carmine

**1953, June 19**

| | | | |
|---|---|---|---|
| C146 | AP24 | 25c dull violet | .40 .20 |

See note after No. 634.

Bell Tower, La Merced Church AP42

**1953, Sept. 15**   Perf. 11½

| | | | |
|---|---|---|---|
| C147 | AP42 | 5c rose pink | .20 .20 |
| C148 | AP42 | 10c dp blue grn | .20 .20 |
| C149 | AP42 | 20c blue | .50 .50 |
| C150 | AP42 | 1col purple | 1.55 1.10 |
| | | Nos. C147-C150 (4) | |

132nd anniv. of the Act of Independence, Sept. 15, 1821.

Postage Types and

Fishing Boats — AP43

ODECA Officials and Flag AP46

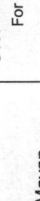

Gen. Manuel José Arce — AP44

---

Municipal Children's Garden, San Salvador AP27

Civil Aeronautics School, Ilopango Airport AP28

Unwmk.

**1946, May 1**

| | | | |
|---|---|---|---|
| C99 | AP26 | 30c rose carmine | .20 .20 |
| C100 | AP27 | 40c deep ultra | .20 .20 |
| C101 | AP28 | 1col black | .85 .30 |
| | | | 1.25 .70 |

For surcharge see No. C121.

Alberto Masferrer — AP29

**1946, July 19**   Litho.   Wmk. 240

| | | | |
|---|---|---|---|
| C102 | AP29 | 12c carmine | .20 .20 |
| C103 | AP29 | 14c dull green | 12.50 |
| a. | | Imperf., pair | |

## Souvenir Sheets

AP30

Designs: 40c, Charles I of Spain. 60c, Juan Manuel Rodriguez. 1col, Arms of San Salvador. 2col, Flag of El Salvador.

Perf. 12, Imperf.

**1946, Nov. 8**   Engr.   Unwmk.

| | | | |
|---|---|---|---|
| C104 | AP30 | Sheet of 4 | 3.00 3.00 |
| a. | | 40c brown | .50 .50 |
| b. | | 60c carmine | .50 .50 |
| c. | | 1col green | .50 .50 |
| d. | | 2col ultramarine | .50 .50 |

4th cent. of San Salvador's city charter. The imperf. sheets are without gum.

Juan Ramon Uriarte — AP25

Felipe Soto — AP31

Alfredo Espino — AP32

**1946, Jan. 1**   Typo.   Wmk. 240

| | | | |
|---|---|---|---|
| C97 | AP25 | 12c dark blue | .20 .20 |
| C98 | AP25 | 14c deep orange | .20 .20 |

**1947, Sept. 11**   Litho.   Perf. 12½

| | | | |
|---|---|---|---|
| C106 | AP31 | 12c chocolate | .20 .20 |
| C107 | AP32 | 14c dark blue | .20 .20 |

For surcharges see Nos. 627-630.

Mayan Pyramid, St. Andrés Plantation AP26

---

Nos. C66 to C68 Surcharged with New Values in Dark Carmine

**1944**

| | | | |
|---|---|---|---|
| C89 | AP13 | 15c on 15c dl yel & blk | .30 .20 |
| C90 | AP13 | 20c on 30c dk brn & blk | .50 .30 |
| C91 | AP13 | 25c on 40c dk bl & blk | .65 .30 |
| | | | 1.45 .80 |

## Bridge Type of Regular Issue Arms Overprint at Right in Blue Violet

Engr.

**1944, Nov. 24**

| | | | |
|---|---|---|---|
| C92 | A149 | 30c crim rose & blk | .30 .20 |

No. C92 exists without overprint, but was not issued in that form.

Presidential Palace AP22

National Palace AP24

National Theater AP23

**1944, Dec. 22**   Perf. 12½

| | | | |
|---|---|---|---|
| C93 | AP22 | 15c red violet | .20 .20 |
| C94 | AP23 | 20c dk blue grn | .20 .20 |
| C95 | AP24 | 25c dull green | .60 .60 |
| | | Nos. C93-C95 (3) | |

For surcharge and overprint see Nos. C145-C146.

No. 582 Overprinted in Red

Aéreo

**1945, Aug. 23**   Perf. 12

| | | | |
|---|---|---|---|
| C96 | A137 | 1col black | .60 .20 |

#C155, National Palace. #C157, Coast guard boat. #C158, Lake Ilopango. #C160, Guayabo dam. #C161, Housing development. #C162, Modern highway. #C164, Izalco volcano.

*Perf. 11½*

**1954, June 1 Unwmk. Photo.**

**C151** AP43 5c org brn & cr .20 .20
**C152** A175 5c brt carmine .20 .20
**C153** AP44 10c gray blue .25 .20
**C154** A176 10c pur & lt brn .25 .20
**C155** AP43 10c ol & bl gray .25 .20
**C156** AP46 10c bl grn, dk grn & bl .25 .20
**C157** AP43 10c rose carmine .30 .20
**C158** AP43 15c dk gray .35 .20
**C159** A173 20c pur & gray .40 .20
**C160** AP46 25c bl grn & bl .45 .20
**C161** AP46 30c mag & sal .50 .20
**C162** A176 40c brt org & brn .60 .25
**C163** A174 80c red brown 1.40 .90
**C164** AP43 1col magenta & sal 1.60 .90
**C165** A174 2col orange 3.00 .90
*Nos. C151-C165 (15)* 10.00 5.15

### Barrios Type of Regular Issue

**Wmk. 269**

**1955, Dec. 20 Engr. *Perf. 12½***

**C166** A177 20c brown .25 .25
**C167** A177 30c dp red lilac .30 .25

### Santa Ana Type of Regular Issue

*Perf. 13½*

**1956, June 20 Unwmk. Litho.**

**C168** A178 5c orange brown .20 .20
**C169** A178 10c green .20 .20
**C170** A178 40c red lilac .25 .20
**C171** A178 80c emerald .60 .35
**C172** A178 5col gray blue 3.25 1.75
*Nos. C168-C172 (5)* 4.50 2.70

For overprint see No. C187.

### Chalatenango Type of Regular Issue

**1956, Sept. 14**

**C173** A179 10c brt rose .20 .20
**C174** A179 15c orange .20 .20
**C175** A179 20c lt olive grn .20 .20
**C176** A179 25c dull purple .30 .20
**C177** A179 50c orange brn .50 .40
**C178** A179 1col brt vio bl .85 .65
*Nos. C173-C178 (6)* 2.25 1.85

### Nueva San Salvador Type

**Wmk. 269**

**1957, Jan. 3 Engr. *Perf. 12½***

**C179** A180 10c pink .20 .20
**C180** A180 20c dull red .20 .20
**C181** A180 50c pale org red .30 .20
**C182** A180 1col lt green .75 .35
**C183** A180 2col orange red 1.90 1.00
*Nos. C179-C183 (5)* 3.35 1.95

For overprints see Nos. C195, C198.

### Lemus' Visit Type of Regular Issue

*Perf. 11½*

**1959, Dec. 14 Unwmk. Photo.**

**Granite Paper**

**Design in Ultramarine, Dark Brown Light Brown and Red**

**C184** A182 15c red .20 .20
**C185** A182 20c green .25 .20
**C186** A182 30c carmine .30 .20
*Nos. C184-C186 (3)* .75 .60

No. C169 Overprinted in Red: "ANO MUNDIAL DE LOS REFUGIADOS 1959-1960"

**1960, Apr. 7 Litho. *Perf. 13½***

**C187** A178 10c green .25 .20

World Refugee Year, 7/1/59-6/30/60.

### Poinsettia Type of Regular Issue

*Perf. 11½*

**1960, Dec. 17 Unwmk. Photo.**

**Granite Paper**

**Design in Slate Green, Red and Yellow**

**C188** A184 20c rose lilac .35 .20
**C189** A184 30c gray .35 .20
**C190** A184 40c light gray .45 .20
**C191** A184 50c salmon pink .70 .40
*Nos. C188-C191 (4)* 1.85 1.00

**Miniature Sheet**

*Imperf*

**C192** A184 60c gold 1.00 1.00

See note after No. 718.
For surcharge see No. C196.

Nos. 672, 691 and C183 Overprinted: "III Exposición Industrial Centroamericana Diciembre de 1962" with "AEREO" Added on Nos. 672, 691

**1962, Dec. 21 *Perf. 11½, 12½***

**C193** A174 1col brn org, dk brn & bl 1.00 .75
**C194** A180 1col dull red .50 .35
**C195** A180 2col orange red 1.00 .65
*Nos. C193-C195 (3)* 2.50 1.75

3rd Central American Industrial Exposition.
For surcharges see Nos. C197, C199.

Nos. C189, C194, C182 and C195 Surcharged

**1963**

**C196** A184 10c on 30c multi .20 .20
**C197** A180 10c on 1col dl red .20 .20
**C198** A180 10c on 1col lt grn 1.10 .25
**C199** A180 10c on 2col org red 1.10 .25
*Nos. C196-C199 (4)* 2.60 .90

Surcharges include: "X" on No. C196; two dots and bar at bottom on No. C197. Heavy bar at bottom on No. C198. On No. C199, the four-line "Exposition" overprint is lower than on No. C195.

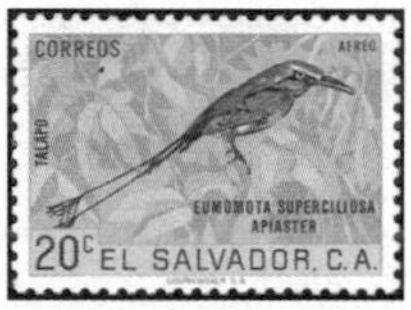


Turquoise-browed Motmot — AP49

Birds: 5c, King vulture (vert., like No. 741). 6c, Yellow-headed parrot, vert. 10c, Spotted-breasted oriole. 30c, Greattailed grackle. 40c, Great curassow, vert. 50c, Magpie-jay. 80c, Golden-fronted woodpecker, vert.

**1963 Unwmk. Photo. *Perf. 11½***

**Birds in Natural Colors**

**C200** AP49 5c gray grn & blk .20 .20
**C201** AP49 6c tan & blue .20 .20
**C202** AP49 10c lt bl & blk .20 .20
**C203** AP49 20c gray & brn .25 .20
**C204** AP49 30c ol bis & blk .35 .20
**C205** AP49 40c pale & dk vio .50 .20
**C206** AP49 50c lt grn & blk .55 .25
**C207** AP49 80c vio bl & blk 1.00 .55
*Nos. C200-C207 (8)* 3.25 2.00

### Eucharistic Congress Type

**1964-65 *Perf. 12x11½***

**C208** A188 10c slate grn & bl .25 .20
**C209** A188 25c red & blue .25 .20

**Miniature Sheets**

*Imperf*

**C210** A188 80c blue & green 1.00 1.00
*a.* Marginal ovpt. La Union 1.00 1.00
*b.* Marginal ovpt. Usulutan 1.00 1.00
*c.* Marginal ovpt. La Libertad .85 .85

See note after No. 746.
Issued: #C208-C210, Apr. 16, 1964; #C210a-C210b, June 22, 1965; #210c, Jan. 28, 1965.
For overprints see Nos. C232, C238.

### Kennedy Type of Regular Issue

**1964, Nov. 22 *Perf. 11½x12***

**C211** A189 15c gray & blk .20 .20
**C212** A189 20c sage grn & blk .25 .20
**C213** A189 40c yellow & blk .40 .20
*Nos. C211-C213 (3)* .85 .60

**Miniature Sheet**

*Imperf*

**C214** A189 80c grnsh bl & blk 1.00 .75

For overprint see No. C259.

### Flower Type of Regular Issue

**1965, Jan. 6 Photo. *Perf. 12x11½***

**C215** A190 10c Rose .20 .20
**C216** A190 15c Platanillo .20 .20
**C217** A190 25c San Jose .20 .20
**C218** A190 40c Hibiscus .25 .20
**C219** A190 45c Veranera .40 .20
**C220** A190 70c Fire flower .55 .30
*Nos. C215-C220 (6)* 1.80 1.30

For overprint and surcharges see Nos. C243, C348-C349.

### ICY Type of Regular Issue

*Perf. 11½x12*

**1965, Apr. 27 Photo. Unwmk.**

**Design in Brown and Gold**

**C221** A191 15c light blue .20 .20
**C222** A191 30c dull lilac .20 .20
**C223** A191 50c ocher .30 .20
*Nos. C221-C223 (3)* .70 .60

For overprints see Nos. C227, C244, C312.

### Gavidia Type of Regular Issue

**1965, Sept. 24 Photo. Unwmk.**

**Portraits in Natural Colors**

**C224** A192 10c black & green .20 .20
**C225** A192 20c black & bister .25 .20
**C226** A192 1col black & rose 1.25 .50
*Nos. C224-C226 (3)* 1.70 .90

No. C223 Overprinted in Green: "1865 / 12 de Octubre / 1965 / Dr. Manuel Enrique Araujo"

**1965, Oct. 12 *Perf. 11½x12***

**C227** A191 50c brn, ocher & gold .45 .40

See note after No. 764.

### Fair Type of Regular Issue

**1965, Nov. 5 *Perf. 12x11½***

**C228** A193 20c blue & multi .20 .20
**C229** A193 80c multi .65 .40
**C230** A193 5col multi 3.25 2.25
*Nos. C228-C230 (3)* 4.10 2.85

For overprint see No. C311.

### WHO Type of Regular Issue

**1966, May 20 Photo. Unwmk.**

**C231** A194 50c multicolored .40 .20

For overprints see Nos. C242, C245.

No. C209 Overprinted in Dark Green: "1816 1966 / 150 años / Nacimiento / San Juan Bosco"

**1966, Sept. 3 Photo. *Perf. 12x11½***

**C232** A188 25c red & blue .30 .25

150th anniv. of the birth of St. John Bosco (1815-88), Italian priest, founder of the Salesian Fathers and Daughters of Mary.

### UNESCO Type of Regular Issue

**1966, Nov. 4 Photo. *Perf. 12***

**C233** A195 30c tan, blk & vio bl .30 .20
**C234** A195 2col emer, blk & vio bl 1.60 1.00

For surcharge see No. C352.

### Fair Type of Regular Issue

**1966, Nov. 27 Litho. *Perf. 12***

**C235** A196 15c multicolored .20 .20
**C236** A196 20c multicolored .20 .20
**C237** A196 60c multicolored .50 .35
*Nos. C235-C237 (3)* .90 .75

No. C209 Overprinted: "IX-Congreso / Interamericano / de Educacion / Católica / 4 Enero 1967"

**1967, Jan. 4 Photo. *Perf. 12x11½***

**C238** A188 25c red & blue .30 .25

Issued to publicize the 9th Inter-American Congress for Catholic Education.

### Cañas Type of Regular Issue

**1967, Feb. 18 Litho. *Perf. 11½***

**C239** A197 5c multicolored .20 .20
**C240** A197 45c lt bl & multi .55 .35

For surcharges see Nos. C403-C405.

### Volcano Type of Regular Issue

**1967, Apr. 14 Photo. *Perf. 13***

**C241** A198 50c ol gray & brn .50 .25

For surcharges see Nos. C320, C350

No. C231 Overprinted in Red: "VIII CONGRESO / CENTROAMERICANO DE / FARMACIA & B10QUIMICA / 5 di 11 Noviembre de 1967"

**1967, Oct. 26 Photo. *Perf. 12x11½***

**C242** A194 50c multicolored .45 .40

Issued to publicize the 8th Central American Congress for Pharmacy and Biochemistry.

No. C217 Overprinted in Red: "I Juegos / Centroamericanos y del / Caribe de Basquetbol / 25 Nov. al 3 Dic. 1967"

**1967, Nov. 15**

**C243** A190 25c bl, yel & grn .25 .25

First Central American and Caribbean Basketball Games, Nov. 25-Dec. 3.

No. C222 Overprinted in Carmine: "1968 / AÑO INTERNACIONAL DE / LOS DERECHOS HUMANOS"

**1968, Jan. 2 Photo. *Perf. 11½x12***

**C244** A191 30c dl lil, brn & gold .40 .30

International Human Rights Year 1968.

No. C231 Overprinted in Red: "1968 / XX ANIVERSARIO DE LA / ORGANIZACION MUNDIAL / DE LA SALUD"

**1968, Apr. 7 *Perf. 12x11½***

**C245** A194 50c multicolored .50 .50

20th anniv. of WHO.

No. C229 Overprinted in Red: "1968 / Año / del Sistema / del Crédito / Rural"

**1968, May 6 Photo. *Perf. 12x11½***

**C246** A193 80c multicolored .65 .50

Rural credit system.

### Masferrer Type of Regular Issue

**1968, June 22 Litho. *Perf. 12x11½***

**C247** A200 5c brown & multi .20 .20
**C248** A200 15c green & multi .20 .20

For overprint see No. C297.

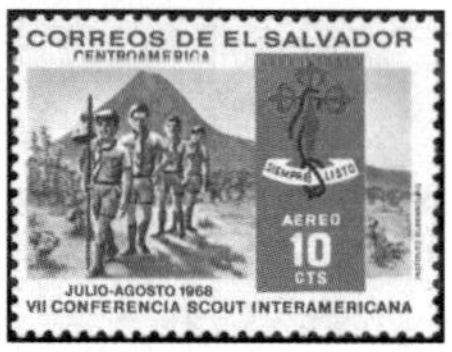


Scouts Hiking AP50

**1968, July 26 Litho. *Perf. 12***

**C249** AP50 10c multicolored .20 .20

Issued to publicize the 7th Inter-American Boy Scout Conference, July-Aug., 1968.

### Presidents' Meeting Type

**1968, Dec. 5 Litho. *Perf. 14½***

**C250** A202 20c salmon & multi .20 .20
**C251** A202 1col lt blue & multi .75 .50

### Butterfly Type of Regular Issue

Designs: Various butterflies.

**1969 Litho. *Perf. 12***

**C252** A203 20c multi .20 .20
**C253** A203 1col multi .65 .35
**C254** A203 2col multi 1.60 1.00
**C255** A203 10col gray & multi 8.00 5.00
*Nos. C252-C255 (4)* 10.45 6.55

For surcharge see No. C353.

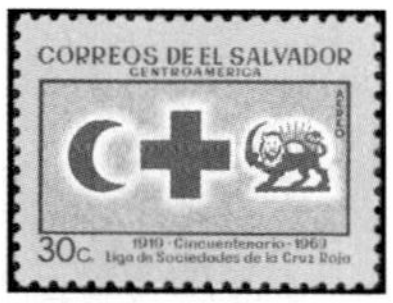


Red Cross, Crescent and Lion and Sun Emblems AP51

**1969 Litho. *Perf. 11***

**C256** AP51 30c yellow & multi .25 .20
**C257** AP51 1col multicolored .85 .50
**C258** AP51 4col multicolored 3.25 2.50
*Nos. C256-C258 (3)* 4.35 3.20

League of Red Cross Societies, 50th anniv.
For surcharges see Nos. C351, C354.

No. C213 Overprinted in Green: "Alunizaje / Apolo-11 / 21 Julio / 1969"

**1969, Sept. Photo. *Perf. 11½x12***

**C259** A189 40c yellow & blk .30 .30

Man's 1st landing on the moon, July 20, 1969. See note after US No. C76.

The same overprint in red brown and pictures of the landing module and the astronauts on the moon were applied to the margin of No. C214.

## Hospital Type of Regular Issue
Benjamin Bloom Children's Hospital.

**1969, Oct. 24**  **Litho.**  *Perf. 11½*
| | | | |
|---|---|---|---|
| C260 | A205 | 1col multi | .85 .50 |
| C261 | A205 | 2col multi | 1.60 1.00 |
| C262 | A205 | 5col multi | 6.70 4.00 |
| | | Nos. C260-C262 (3) | |

For surcharge see No. C355.

## ILO Type of Regular Issue
**1969**  **Litho.**  *Perf. 13*
| | | | |
|---|---|---|---|
| C263 | A206 | 50c lt bl & multi | .40 .20 |

## Tourist Type of Regular Issue
Views: 20c, Devil's Gate. 35c, Ichanmichen Spa. 60c, Aerial view of Acajutla Harbor.

**1969, Dec. 19**  **Photo.**  *Perf. 12x11½*
| | | | |
|---|---|---|---|
| C264 | A207 | 20c black & multi | .20 .20 |
| C265 | A207 | 35c black & multi | .30 .20 |
| C266 | A207 | 60c black & multi | .50 .40 |
| | | Nos. C264-C266 (3) | 1.00 .80 |

## Insect Type of Regular Issue, 1970
**1970, Feb. 24**  **Litho.**  *Perf. 11½x11*
| | | | |
|---|---|---|---|
| C267 | A208 | 2col Bee | 3.00 1.00 |
| C268 | A208 | 3col Elaterida | 4.75 1.50 |
| C269 | A208 | 4col Praying mantis | 6.25 2.00 |
| | | Nos. C267-C269 (3) | 14.00 4.50 |

For surcharges see Nos. C371-C373.

## Human Rights Type of Regular Issue
20c, 80c, Map and arms of Salvador and National Unity emblem similar to A209, but vert.

**1970, Apr. 14**  **Litho.**  *Perf. 14*
| | | | |
|---|---|---|---|
| C270 | A209 | 20c blue & multi | .20 .20 |
| C271 | A209 | 80c blue & multi | .80 .40 |

For overprint & surcharge see #C301, C402.

## Army Type of Regular Issue
Designs: 20c, Fighter plane. 40c, Gun and crew. 50c, Patrol boat.

**1970, May 7**  **Perf. 12**
| | | | |
|---|---|---|---|
| C272 | A210 | 20c gray & multi | .20 .20 |
| C273 | A210 | 40c green & multi | .35 .20 |
| C274 | A210 | 50c blue & multi | .45 .20 |
| | | Nos. C272-C274 (3) | 1.00 .60 |

For overprint see No. C310.

Brazilian Team, Jules Rimet Cup — AP52

Soccer teams and Jules Rimet Cup.

**1970, May 25**  **Litho.**  *Perf. 12*
| | | | |
|---|---|---|---|
| C275 | AP52 | 1col Belgium | 1.10 .65 |
| C276 | AP52 | 1col Brazil | 1.10 .65 |
| C277 | AP52 | 1col Bulgaria | 2.00 1.00 |
| C278 | AP52 | 1col Czechoslovakia | 1.10 .65 |
| C279 | AP52 | 1col Germany (Fed. Rep.) | 1.10 .65 |
| C280 | AP52 | 1col Britain | 1.10 .65 |
| C281 | AP52 | 1col Israel | 1.10 .65 |
| C282 | AP52 | 1col Italy | 1.10 .65 |
| C283 | AP52 | 1col Mexico | 1.10 .65 |
| C284 | AP52 | 1col Morocco | 1.10 .65 |
| C285 | AP52 | 1col Peru | 1.10 .65 |
| C286 | AP52 | 1col Romania | 1.10 .65 |
| C287 | AP52 | 1col Russia | 1.10 .65 |
| C288 | AP52 | 1col Salvador | 1.10 .65 |
| C289 | AP52 | 1col Sweden | 1.10 .65 |
| C290 | AP52 | 1col Uruguay | 1.10 .65 |
| | | Nos. C275-C290 (16) | 18.50 10.75 |

9th World Soccer Championships for the Jules Rimet Cup, Mexico City, 5/30-6/21/70.

## Lottery Type of Regular Issue
**1970, July 15**  **Litho.**  *Perf. 12*
| | | | |
|---|---|---|---|
| C291 | A211 | 80c multi | .65 .25 |

## Education Year Type of Regular Issue
**1970, Sept. 11**  **Litho.**  *Perf. 12*
| | | | |
|---|---|---|---|
| C292 | A212 | 20c pink & multi | .20 .20 |
| C293 | A212 | 2col buff & multi | 1.60 1.00 |

## Fair Type of Regular Issue
**1970, Oct. 28**  **Litho.**  *Perf. 12*
| | | | |
|---|---|---|---|
| C294 | A213 | 20c multi | .25 .20 |
| C295 | A213 | 30c yel & multi | .35 .20 |

## Music Type of Regular Issue
Johann Sebastian Bach, harp, horn, music.

**1971, Feb. 22**  **Litho.**  *Perf. 13½*
| | | | |
|---|---|---|---|
| C296 | A214 | 40c gray & multi | .40 .20 |

For overprint see No. C313.

No. C247 Overprinted: "Año / del Centenario de la / Biblioteca Nacional / 1970"

**1970, Nov. 25**
| | | | |
|---|---|---|---|
| C297 | A200 | 5c brn & multi | .20 .20 |

## Miss Tourism Type of Regular Issue
**1971, Apr. 1**  **Litho.**  *Perf. 14*
| | | | |
|---|---|---|---|
| C298 | A215 | 20c lil & multi | .20 .20 |
| C299 | A215 | 60c gray & multi | .45 .30 |

## Pietà Type of Regular Issue
**1971, May 10**
| | | | |
|---|---|---|---|
| C300 | A216 | 40c lt yel grn & vio brn | .30 .20 |

No. C270 Overprinted in Red Like No. 823

**1971, July 6**  **Litho.**  *Perf. 13½*
| | | | |
|---|---|---|---|
| C301 | A209 | 20c bl & multi | .20 .20 |

## Fish Type of Regular Issue
30c, Smalltooth sawfish. 1col, Atlantic sailfish.

**1971, July 28**
| | | | |
|---|---|---|---|
| C302 | A217 | 30c lilac & multi | .20 .25 |
| C303 | A217 | 1col multi | .65 .50 |

## Independence Type of Regular Issue
Designs: Various sections of Declaration of Independence of Central America.

**1971**  **Litho.**  *Perf. 13½x13*
| | | | |
|---|---|---|---|
| C304 | A218 | 30c bl & blk | .20 .20 |
| C305 | A218 | 40c brn & blk | .30 .20 |
| C306 | A218 | 50c yel & blk | .35 .35 |
| C307 | A218 | 60c gray & blk | .50 .35 |
| | a. | Souvenir sheet of 8 | 1.75 1.60 |
| | | Nos. C304-C307 (4) | 1.35 1.00 |

a. No. C307a contains 8 stamps with simulated perforations similar to Nos. 826-829, C304-C307.

For overprints see Nos. C311, C347.

## Church Type of Regular Issue
15c, Metapan Church. 70c, Panchimalco Church.

**1971, Aug. 21**  **Litho.**  *Perf. 13½x13*
| | | | |
|---|---|---|---|
| C308 | A219 | 15c ol & multi | .20 .20 |
| C309 | A219 | 70c multi | .55 .35 |

No. C274 Overprinted in Red

**1971, Oct. 12**  **Litho.**  *Perf. 12*
| | | | |
|---|---|---|---|
| C310 | A210 | 50c bl & multi | .40 .30 |

National Navy, 20th anniversary.

No. C229 Overprinted: "V Feria / Internacional / 3-20 Noviembre / de 1972"

**1972, Nov. 3**  **Photo.**  *Perf. 12x11½*
| | | | |
|---|---|---|---|
| C311 | A193 | 80c multi | .90 .50 |

5th Intl. Fair, El Salvador, Nov. 3-20.

No. C223 Overprinted in Red

"1972 - XXX Aniversario Creación Instituto Interamericano de Ciencias Agrícolas"

30th anniversary of the Inter-American institute for Agricultural Sciences.

**1972, Nov. 30**  **Photo.**  *Perf. 11½x12*
| | | | |
|---|---|---|---|
| C312 | A191 | 50c ocher, brn & gold | .40 .30 |

No. C296 Overprinted

**1973, Feb. 5**  **Litho.**  *Perf. 13½*
| | | | |
|---|---|---|---|
| C313 | A214 | 40c gray & multi | .30 .25 |

3rd International Music Festival, Feb. 9-29.

## Lions Type of Regular Issue
Designs: 20c, 40c, Map of El Salvador and Lions International Emblem.

**1973, Feb. 20**  **Litho.**  *Perf. 13*
| | | | |
|---|---|---|---|
| C314 | A220 | 20c gray & multi | .20 .20 |
| C315 | A220 | 40c multi | .30 .20 |

## Olympic Type of Regular Issue
Designs: 20c, Javelin, women's. 80c, Discus, women's. 1col, Hammer throw. 2col, Shot put.

**1973, May 21**  **Litho.**  *Perf. 13*
| | | | |
|---|---|---|---|
| C316 | A221 | 20c lt grn & multi | .20 .20 |
| C317 | A221 | 80c sal & multi | .45 .20 |
| C318 | A221 | 1col ultra & multi | 1.00 .35 |
| C319 | A221 | 2col multi | 2.75 .90 |
| | | Nos. C316-C319 (4) | 5.45 2.00 |

No. C241 Surcharged Like No. 841

**1973, Dec.**  **Photo.**  *Perf. 13*
| | | | |
|---|---|---|---|
| C320 | A198 | 25c on 50c multi | .20 .20 |

No. C307a Overprinted: "Centenario / Ciudad / Santiago de Maria / 1874 1974"

Souvenir Sheet

**1974, Mar. 7**  **Imperf.**
| | | | |
|---|---|---|---|
| C321 | A218 | Sheet of 8 | 1.00 1.00 |

Centenary of the City Santiago de Maria. The overprint is so arranged that each line appears on a different pair of stamps.

No. C231 Surcharged in Red

**1974, Apr. 22**  **Photo.**  *Perf. 12x11½*
| | | | |
|---|---|---|---|
| C322 | A194 | 25c on 50c multi | .20 .20 |

No. C229 Surcharged

**1974, Apr. 24**  **Photo.**  *Perf. 12x11½*
| | | | |
|---|---|---|---|
| C323 | A193 | 10c on 80c multi | .20 .20 |

## Rehabilitation Type
**1974, Apr. 30**  **Litho.**  *Perf. 13*
| | | | |
|---|---|---|---|
| C324 | A222 | 25c multi | .20 .20 |

Nos. C275-C290 Overprinted "ALEMANIA 1974"

**1974, June 4**  **Litho.**  *Perf. 12*
| | | | |
|---|---|---|---|
| C325 | AP52 | 1col Belgium | .90 .50 |
| C326 | AP52 | 1col Brazil | .90 .50 |
| C327 | AP52 | 1col Bulgaria | .90 .50 |
| C328 | AP52 | 1col Czech. | .90 .50 |
| C329 | AP52 | 1col Germany | .90 .50 |
| C330 | AP52 | 1col Britain | .90 .50 |
| C331 | AP52 | 1col Israel | .90 .50 |
| C332 | AP52 | 1col Italy | .90 .50 |
| C333 | AP52 | 1col Mexico | .90 .50 |
| C334 | AP52 | 1col Morocco | .90 .50 |
| C335 | AP52 | 1col Peru | .90 .50 |
| C336 | AP52 | 1col Romania | .90 .50 |
| C337 | AP52 | 1col Russia | .90 .50 |
| C338 | AP52 | 1col Salvador | .90 .50 |
| C339 | AP52 | 1col Sweden | .90 .50 |
| C340 | AP52 | 1col Uruguay | .90 .50 |
| | | Nos. C325-C340 (16) | 14.40 8.00 |

World Cup Soccer Championship, Munich, June 13-July 7.

## INTERPOL Type of 1974
**1974, Sept. 2**  **Litho.**  *Perf. 12½*
| | | | |
|---|---|---|---|
| C341 | A223 | 25c multi | .20 .20 |

## FAO Type of 1974
**1974, Sept. 2**  **Litho.**  *Perf. 12½*
| | | | |
|---|---|---|---|
| C342 | A224 | 25c bl, dk bl & gold | .20 .20 |

## Coin Type of 1974
**1974, Nov. 19**  **Litho.**  *Perf. 12½x13*
| | | | |
|---|---|---|---|
| C343 | A225 | 20c 1p silver, 1892 | .20 .20 |
| C344 | A225 | 40c silver, 1828 | .30 .20 |
| C345 | A225 | 50c 20p gold, 1892 | .50 .25 |
| C346 | A225 | 60c 20col gold, 1925 | .60 .35 |
| | | Nos. C343-C346 (4) | 1.60 1.00 |

No. C307a Overprinted: "X ASAMBLEA GENERAL DE LA CONFERENCIA / INTERAMERICANA / DE SEGURIDAD SOCIAL Y XX / REUNION DEL COMITE PERMANENTE INTERAMERICANO / DE SEGURIDAD SOCIAL 24 NOVIEMBRE 1974"

Souvenir Sheet

**1974, Nov. 18**  **Litho.**  **Imperf.**
| | | | |
|---|---|---|---|
| C347 | A218 | Sheet of 8 | 1.75 1.75 |

Social Security Conference, El Salvador, Nov. 24-30. The overprint is so arranged that each line appears on a different pair of stamps.

Issues of 1965-69 Surcharged

a

b

# EL SALVADOR

IWY
Emblem — AP53

Map of South
America,
Argentina '78
Emblem
AP59

Caularthron
Bilamellatum
AP55

Symbolic
Chessboard and
Emblem — AP56

Softball,
Bat and
Globes
AP60

UNICEF
Emblem — AP54

**1974-75**

| | | | |
|---|---|---|---|
| C348 | A190(a) | 1c on 45c #C219 | .20 |
| C349 | A190.(a) | 1c on 70c #C220 | .20 |
| C350 | A198(b) | 10c on 10c #C224 | .20 |
| C351 | A198(b) | 10c on 50c #C241 | .20 |
| C352 | A195(c) | 25c on 1col #C257 | .20 |
| C353 | A203(d) | 25c on 2col #C254 | .30 |

No. C353 has new value at left and 6 vertical bars. No. C355 has 7 vertical bars.

| | | | |
|---|---|---|---|
| C354 | AP51(d) | 25c on 4col #C258 | .20 |
| C355 | A205(d) | 25c on 5col #C262 | .20 |

Nos. C348-C355 (8) 1.70 1.60

**Women's Year Type and**

**1975, June 25** Litho. Perf. 13

| | | |
|---|---|---|
| C359 | A228 | 25c bl & multi | .20 .20 |
| C360 | A229 | 25c multi | .20 .20 |
| C361 | A229 | 60c lil & multi | .50 .40 |

**Miss Universe Type of 1975**

**1975, Apr. 25** Litho. Perf. 12½

| | | |
|---|---|---|
| C358 | A227 | 15c bl & multi | .20 .20 |

**Acajutla Harbor Type of 1975**

**1975, Feb. 17** Perf. 13

| | | |
|---|---|---|
| C357 | A226 | 30c bl & multi | .25 .20 |
| C356 | A226 | 25c bl & multi | .20 .20 |

**Post Office Type of 1975**

**1975, Jan. 22** Litho. Perf. 13

**UPU Type of 1975**

**1975, Sept. 4** Litho. Perf. 12½

| | | |
|---|---|---|
| C362 | A230 | 15c bl & blk | .20 .20 |
| C363 | AP53 | 25c yel grn & blk | .20 .20 |

International Women's Year 1975.

**Nurse Type of 1975**

**1975, Oct. 24** Litho. Perf. 12½

| | | |
|---|---|---|
| C364 | A231 | 25c lt blue & multi | .20 .20 |

**Printers' Congress Type**

**1975, Nov. 19** Litho. Perf. 12½

| | | |
|---|---|---|
| C365 | A232 | 30c green & multi | .20 .20 |

**Dermatologists' Congress Type**

**1975, Nov. 28** Litho. Perf. 12½

| | | |
|---|---|---|
| C366 | A233 | 20c blue & multi | .20 .20 |
| C367 | A233 | 30c red & multi | .25 .20 |

**Caritas Type of 1975**

**1975, Dec. 18** Litho. Perf. 13½

| | | |
|---|---|---|
| C368 | A234 | 20c bl & vio bl | .20 .20 |

**1975, Dec. 18**

| | | |
|---|---|---|
| C369 | AP54 | 15c lt grn & sil | .20 .20 |
| C370 | AP54 | 20c dl rose & sil | .20 .20 |

UNICEF, 25th anniv. (in 1971).

Nos. C267-C269 Surcharged

**1976, Jan. 14** Perf. 11½x11

| | | |
|---|---|---|
| C371 | A208 | 25c on 2col multi | .60 .60 |
| C372 | A208 | 25c on 3col multi | .20 .20 |
| C373 | A208 | 25c on 4col multi | .20 .20 |

Nos. C371-C373 (3)

Designs: Orchids.

**1976, Feb. 19** Litho. Perf. 12½

| | | |
|---|---|---|
| C374 | AP55 | 25c shown | .25 .20 |
| C375 | AP55 | 25c Oncidium oli- | |
| | | ganthum | .25 .20 |
| C376 | AP55 | 25c Epidendrum radi- | |
| | | cans | .25 .20 |
| C377 | AP55 | 25c Epidendrum | |
| | | vitellinum | .25 .20 |
| C378 | AP55 | 25c Cyrtopodium | |
| | | punctatum | .25 .20 |
| C379 | AP55 | 25c Pleurothallis | |
| | | schiedei | .25 .20 |
| C380 | AP55 | 25c Lycaste cruenta | .25 .20 |
| C381 | AP55 | 25c Spiranthes speci- | |
| | | osa | .25 .20 |

Nos. C374-C381 (8) 2.00 1.60

**CIAT Type of 1976**

**1976, May 18** Litho. Perf. 12½

| | | |
|---|---|---|
| C382 | A235 | 50c org & multi | .40 .20 |

**Bicentennial Types of 1976**

**1976, June 30** Litho. Perf. 12½

| | | |
|---|---|---|
| C383 | A236 | 25c multi | .20 .20 |
| C384 | A237 | 50c multi | .50 .45 |

Nos. C385-C387 (3)

**Reptile Type of 1976**

**1976, Sept. 23** Litho. Perf. 12½

| | | |
|---|---|---|
| C385 | A238 | 15c multi | .20 .20 |
| C386 | A238 | 25c multi | .25 .20 |
| C387 | A238 | 60c multi | 1.00 .85 |

Reptiles: 15c, Green fence lizard. 25c,
Basilisk. 60c, Star lizard.

**Archaeology Type of 1976**

**1976, Oct. 11** Litho. Perf. 12½

| | | |
|---|---|---|
| C388 | A239 | 25c multi | .20 .20 |
| C389 | A239 | 50c multi | .40 .25 |
| C390 | A239 | 70c multi | .55 .40 |

Nos. C388-C390 (3) 1.15 .85

Pre-Columbian Art: 25c, Brazier with pre-
classical head, El Trapiche. 50c, Kettle with
pre-classical head, Atiquizaya. 70c, Classical
whistling vase, Tazumal.

For overprint see No. C429.

**Fair Type of 1976**

**1976, Oct. 25** Litho. Perf. 12½

| | | |
|---|---|---|
| C391 | A240 | 25c multi | .20 .20 |
| C392 | A240 | 70c yel & multi | .55 .40 |

**Christmas Type of 1976**

**1976, Dec. 14** Litho. Perf. 11

| | | |
|---|---|---|
| C393 | A241 | 25c bl & multi | .20 .20 |
| C394 | A241 | 50c multi | .40 .25 |
| C395 | A241 | 60c multi | .50 .30 |
| C396 | A241 | 75c red & multi | .60 .40 |

Nos. C393-C396 (4) 1.70 1.15

**Rotary Type of 1977**

**1977, June 20** Litho. Perf. 11

| | | |
|---|---|---|
| C397 | A242 | 25c multi | .20 .20 |
| C398 | A242 | 1col multi | .80 .50 |

Nos. C399-C401 have colorless overprint in
multiple rows: GOBIERNO DEL SALVADOR.

**1977, June 29** Perf. 12½

| | | |
|---|---|---|
| C399 | A243 | 25c multi | .20 .20 |
| C400 | A243 | 50c multi | .40 .20 |
| C401 | A243 | 75c multi | 1.20 .80 |

Nos. C399-C401 (3)

Designs: 25c, Radar station, Izalco (vert.).
50c, Central sugar refinery, Jiboa. 75c, Cerron Grande hydroelectric station.

**Industrial Type of 1977**

Nos. C271 and C239 Surcharged with
New Value and Bar

**1977** Perf. 14, 11½

| | | |
|---|---|---|
| C402 | A209 | 25c on 80c multi | .20 .20 |
| C403 | A197 | 30c on 5c multi | .25 .20 |
| C404 | A197 | 40c on 5c multi | .30 .20 |
| C405 | A197 | 50c on 5c multi | .40 .25 |

Nos. C402-C405 (4) 1.15 .85

**Broadcasting Type of 1977**

**1977, Sept. 14** Litho. Perf. 14

| | | |
|---|---|---|
| C406 | A244 | 20c multi | .20 .20 |
| C407 | A244 | 25c multi | .20 .20 |

**1977, Oct. 20** Litho. Perf. 11

| | | |
|---|---|---|
| C408 | A256 | 25c multi | .20 .20 |
| C409 | AP56 | 50c multi | .40 .25 |

El Salvador's victory in International Chess
Olympiad, Tripoli, Libya, Oct. 24-Nov. 15,
1976.

**1977, Nov. 16** Litho. Perf. 16

| | | |
|---|---|---|
| C410 | AP57 | 10c shown | .20 .20 |
| C411 | AP57 | 10c Basketball | .20 .20 |
| C412 | AP57 | 15c shown | .20 .20 |
| C413 | AP57 | 15c Javelin | .20 .20 |
| C414 | AP57 | 20c Weight lifting | .20 .20 |
| C415 | AP57 | 20c Volleyball | .20 .20 |
| C416 | AP57 | 25c shown | .20 .20 |
| C417 | AP57 | 25c Baseball | .20 .20 |
| C418 | AP58 | 25c Softball | .20 .20 |
| C419 | AP58 | 30c Swimming | .25 .20 |
| C420 | AP58 | 30c Fencing | .35 .20 |
| C421 | AP58 | 40c Bicycling | .35 .25 |
| C422 | AP58 | 50c Rifle shooting | .45 .25 |
| C423 | AP58 | 60c Judo | .55 .30 |
| C424 | AP58 | 75c Women's tennis | .55 .30 |
| C425 | AP58 | 75c Wrestling | .65 .35 |
| C426 | AP58 | 90c Equestrian hur- | |
| | | dles | .70 .40 |
| C427 | AP58 | 1col Woman gymnast | .90 .50 |

Nos. C410-C427 (18) 8.35 5.60

**Size: 100x119mm**

| | | |
|---|---|---|
| C428 | AP57 | 5col Games' poster | 4.00 4.00 |

2nd Central American Olympic Games, San
Salvador, Nov. 25-Dec. 4.

No. C390 Overprinted in Red:
"CENTENARIO / CIUDAD DE /
CHALCHUAPA / 1878-1978"

**1978, Feb. 13** Litho. Perf. 12½

| | | |
|---|---|---|
| C429 | A239 | 70c multi | .55 .55 |

Centenary of Chalchuapa.

**1978, Oct. 30** Litho. Perf. 12½

| | | |
|---|---|---|
| C438 | AP60 | 25c pink & multi | .20 .20 |
| C439 | AP60 | 1col yel & multi | .80 .50 |

**Fair Type, 1978**

**1978, Oct. 30** Litho. Perf. 12½

| | | |
|---|---|---|
| C440 | A248 | 15c multi | .20 .20 |
| C441 | A248 | 25c multi | .20 .20 |

4th World Softball Championship for
Women, San Salvador, Oct. 13-22.

**Red Cross Type, 1978**

**1978, Oct. 30** Litho. Perf. 11

| | | |
|---|---|---|
| C442 | A249 | 25c multi | .20 .20 |

**Cotton Conference Type, 1978**

**1978, Nov. 22** Litho. Perf. 12½

| | | |
|---|---|---|
| C443 | A250 | 40c multi | .30 .20 |

**Christmas Type, 1978**

**1978, Dec. 5** Litho. Perf. 12½

| | | |
|---|---|---|
| C444 | A251 | 15c multi | .20 .20 |
| C445 | A251 | 1col multi | .80 .50 |

**Atheneum Type 1978**

**1978, Dec. 20** Litho. Perf. 14

| | | |
|---|---|---|
| C446 | A252 | 25c multi | .20 .20 |

**Health Organization Type**

**1979, Apr. 7** Litho. Perf. 14x14½

| | | |
|---|---|---|
| C448 | A254 | 25c multi | .20 .20 |

**UPU Type of 1979**

**1979, Apr. 2** Litho. Perf. 14

| | | |
|---|---|---|
| C447 | A253 | 75c multi | .60 .40 |

**Social Security Type of 1979**

**1979, May 25** Litho. Perf. 12½

| | | |
|---|---|---|
| C449 | A255 | 25c multi | .20 .20 |
| C450 | A255 | 1col multi | .80 .50 |

**Musical Instrument Type**

**1978, Aug. 29** Litho. Perf. 12½

| | | |
|---|---|---|
| C433 | A245 | 25c multi | .20 .20 |
| C434 | A245 | 50c multi | .40 .20 |
| C435 | A245 | 80c multi | .60 .40 |

Nos. C433-C435 (3) 1.20 .80

Designs: 25c, Drum, vert. 50c, Hollow rat-
tles. 80c, Xylophone.

For surcharge see No. C492.

**Engineering Type of 1978**

**1978, Sept. 12** Litho. Perf. 13½

| | | |
|---|---|---|
| C436 | A246 | 25c multi | .20 .20 |

**Izalco Station Type of 1978**

**1978, Sept. 14** Litho. Perf. 12½

| | | |
|---|---|---|
| C437 | A247 | 75c multi | .60 .40 |

**1978, Aug. 15** Litho. Perf. 11

| | | |
|---|---|---|
| C430 | AP59 | 25c multi | .50 .20 |
| C431 | AP59 | 60c multi | 4.00 3.00 |
| C432 | AP59 | 75c multi | 4.70 3.60 |

Nos. C430-C432 (3)

11th World Cup Soccer Championship,
Argentina, June 1-25.

Boxing
AP58

Soccer
AP57

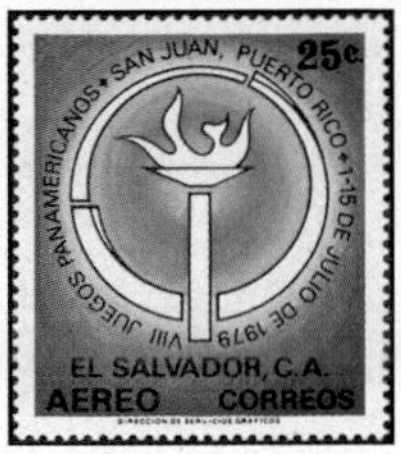


Games Emblem AP61

**1979, July 12 Litho. *Perf. 14½x14***

C451 AP61 25c multi .20 .20
C452 AP61 40c multi .30 .20
C453 AP61 70c multi .50 .40
*Nos. C451-C453 (3)* 1.00 .80

8th Pan American Games, Puerto Rico, July 1-15.
For surcharge see No. C493.

**Pope John Paul II Type of 1979**

60c, 5col, Pope John Paul II & pyramid.

**1979, July 12**

C454 A256 60c multi, horiz. .50 .30
C455 A256 5col multi, horiz. 4.00 2.50

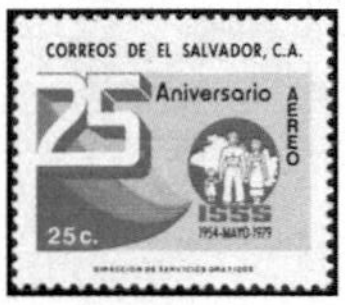


"25," Family and Map of Salvador — AP62

**1979, May 14 Litho. *Perf. 14x14½***

C456 AP62 25c blk & bl .20 .20
C457 AP62 60c blk & lil rose .50 .35

Social Security, 25th anniversary.

**Pre-Historic Animal Type**

**1979, Sept. 7 Litho. *Perf. 14***

C458 A257 15c Mammoth .20 .20
C459 A257 25c Giant anteater, vert. .20 .20
C460 A257 2 col Hyenas 1.60 1.00
*Nos. C458-C460 (3)* 2.00 1.40

**National Anthem Type, 1979**

**1979, Sept. 14 *Perf. 14½x14***

C461 A258 40c Jose Aberiz, score .30 .20

**COPIMERA Type, 1979**

**1979, Oct. 19 Litho. *Perf. 14½x14***

C462 A259 50c multi .40 .25

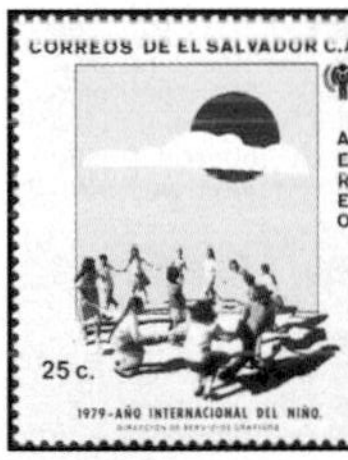


Circle Dance, IYC Emblem AP63

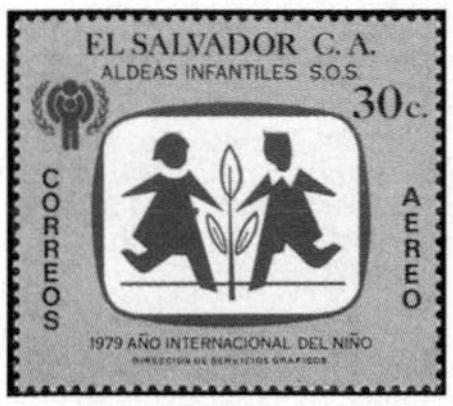


Children's Village and IYC Emblems AP64

**1979, Oct. 29 *Perf. 14½x14, 14x14½***

C463 AP63 25c multi .20 .20
C464 AP64 30c vio & blk .25 .20

International Year of the Child.

**Biochemistry Type of 1979**

**1979, Nov. 1 Litho. *Perf. 14½x14***

C465 A262 25c multi .20 .20

**Coffee Type of 1979**

Designs: 50c, Picking coffee. 75, Drying coffee beans. 1col, Coffee export.

**1979, Dec. 18 *Perf. 14x14½, 14½x14***

C466 A263 50c multi .40 .25
C467 A263 75c multi .60 .40
C468 A263 1 col multi .80 .55
*Nos. C466-C468 (3)* 1.80 1.20

**Hoof and Mouth Disease Type**

**1980, June 3 Litho. *Perf. 14½x14***

C469 A265 60c multi .50 .30

**Shell Type of 1980**

**1980, Aug. 12 *Perf. 14x14½***

C470 A266 15c *Hexaplex regius* .20 .20
C471 A266 25c *Polinices helicoides* .20 .20
C472 A266 75c *Jenneria pustulata* .50 .40
C473 A266 1 col *Pitar lupanaria* .80 .55
*Nos. C470-C473 (4)* 1.70 1.35

**Birds Type**

**1980, Sept. 10 Litho. *Perf. 14x14½***

C474 A267 25c Aulacorhynchus prasinus .20 .20
C475 A267 50c Strix varia fulvescens .40 .25
C476 A267 75c Myadestes unicolor .60 .40
*Nos. C474-C476 (3)* 1.20 .85

**Snake Type of 1980**

**1980, Nov. 12 Litho. *Perf. 14x14½***

C477 A268 25c Rattlesnake .20 .20
C478 A268 50c Coral snake .40 .25

**Auditors Type**

**1980, Nov. 26 Litho. *Perf. 14***

C479 A269 50c multi .40 .25
C480 A269 75c multi .60 .40

**Christmas Type**

**1980, Dec. 5 Litho. *Perf. 14***

C481 A270 25c multi .20 .20
C482 A270 60c multi .50 .30

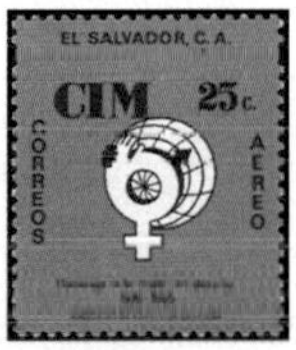


Intl. Women's Decade, 1976-85 — AP65

**1981, Jan. 30 *Perf. 14½x14***

C483 AP65 25c olive green & blk .20 .20
C484 AP65 1 col orange & black .80 .50

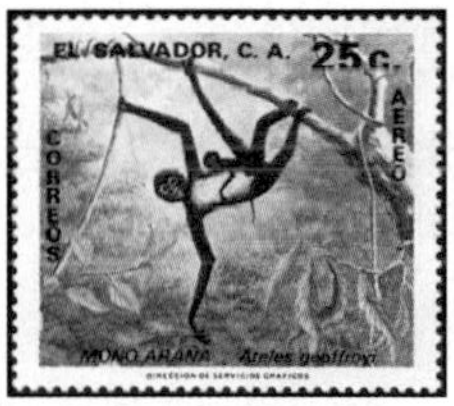


Protected Animals AP66

**1981, Mar. 20 Litho. *Perf. 14x14½***

C485 AP66 25c Ateles geoffroyi .20 .20
C486 AP66 40c Lepisosteus tropicus .30 .20
C487 AP66 50c Iguana iguana .40 .25
C488 AP66 60c Eretmochelys imbricata .50 .35
C489 AP66 75c Spizaetus ornatus .60 .40
*Nos. C485-C489 (5)* 2.00 1.40

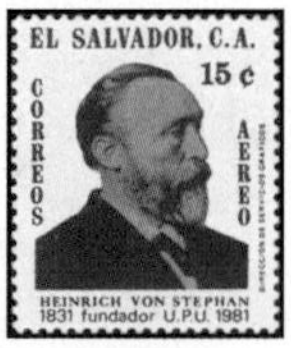


Heinrich von Stephan, 150th Birth Anniv. — AP67

**1981, May 18 Litho. *Perf. 14½x14***

C490 AP67 15c multi .20 .20
C491 AP67 2 col multi 1.60 1.00

Nos. C435, C453 Surcharged

***Perf. 12½, 14½x14***

**1981, May 18 Litho.**

C492 A245 50c on 80c, #C435 .40 .25
C493 AP61 1 col on 70c, #C453 .80 .55

**Dental Associations Type**

**1981, June 18 Litho. *Perf. 14***

C494 A271 5 col bl & blk 7.00 3.00

**IYD Type of 1981**

**1981, Aug. 14 Litho. *Perf. 14x14½***

C495 A272 25c like #936 .20 .20
C496 A272 50c Emblem .40 .25
C497 A272 75c like #936 .60 .40
C498 A272 1 col like # C496 .80 .55
*Nos. C495-C498 (4)* 2.00 1.40

**Quinonez Type**

**1981, Aug. 28 Litho. *Perf. 14x14½***

C499 A273 50c multi .40 .25

**World Food Day Type**

**1981, Sept. 16 Litho. *Perf. 14x14½***

C500 A274 25c multi .20 .20

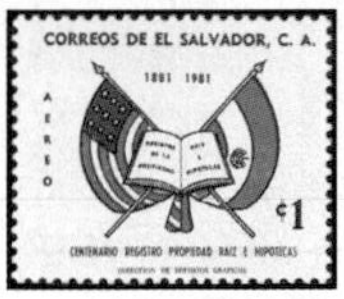


Land Registry Office, 100th Anniv. — AP68

**1981, Oct. 30 Litho. *Perf. 14x14½***

C501 AP68 1 col multi .80 .55

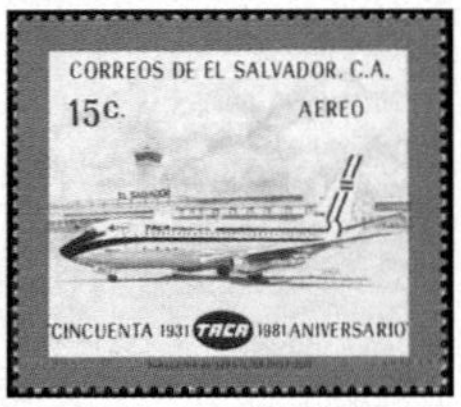


TACA Airlines, 50th Anniv. AP69

**1981, Nov. 10 Litho. *Perf. 14***

C502 AP69 15c multi .20 .20
C503 AP69 25c multi .20 .20
C504 AP69 75c multi .60 .40
*Nos. C502-C504 (3)* 1.00 .80

**World Cup Preliminaries Type**

**1981, Nov. 27 Litho. *Perf. 14x14½***

C505 A275 25c Like No. 939 .20 .20
C506 A275 75c Like No. 940 .60 .40

**Lyceum Type**

**1981, Dec. 17 Litho. *Perf. 14***

C507 A276 25c multi .20 .20

**Sculptures Type**

**1982, Jan. 22 Litho. *Perf. 14***

C508 A277 25c Palm leaf with effigy .20 .20
C509 A277 30c Jaguar mask .25 .20
C510 A277 80c Mayan flint carving .65 .45
*Nos. C508-C510 (3)* 1.10 .85

**Scouting Year Type of 1982**

**1982, Mar. 17 Litho. *Perf. 14½x14***

C511 A278 25c Baden-Powell .20 .20
C512 A278 50c Girl Scout, emblem .40 .25

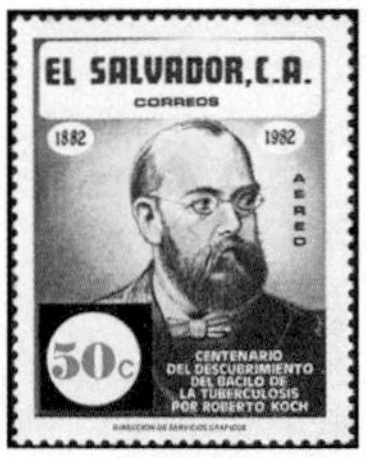


TB Bacillus Cent. — AP70

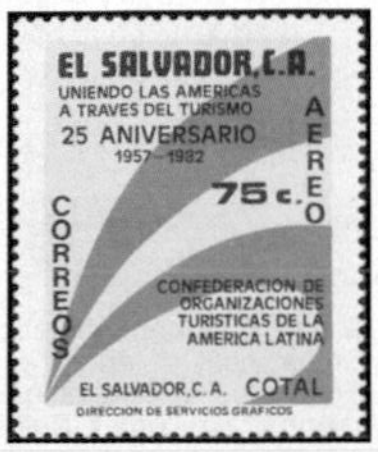


Symbolic Design — AP71

**1982, Mar. 24 *Perf. 14***

C513 AP70 50c multi .40 .25

**Armed Forces Type of 1982**

**1982, May 7 Litho. *Perf. 14x13½***

C514 A279 25c multi .20 .20

**1982, May 14 *Perf. 14***

C515 AP71 75c multi .60 .40

25th anniv. of Latin-American Tourist Org. Confederation (COTAL).

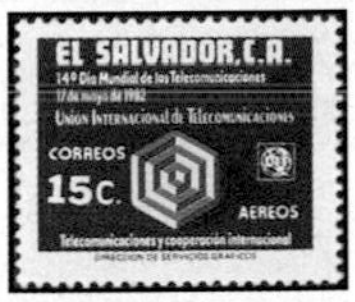


14th World Telecommunications Day — AP72

**1982, May 17 *Perf. 14x14½***

C516 AP72 15c multi .20 .20
C517 AP72 2col multi 1.60 1.00

**World Cup Type of 1982**

**1982, July 14**

C518 A280 25c Team, emblem .20 .20
C519 A280 60c Map, cup .50 .35

**Size: 67x47mm**

***Perf. 11½***

C520 A280 2col Team, emblem, diff. 1.60 1.00

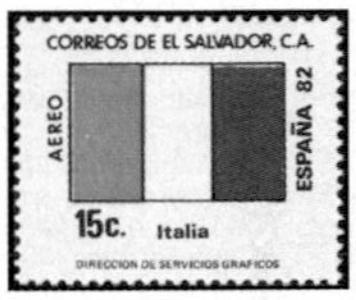


1982 World Cup — AP73

Flags or Arms of Participating Countries; #C521a, C522a, Italy. #C521b, C522c, Germany. #C521c, C522e, Argentina. #C521d, C522m, England. #C521e, C522o, Spain. #C521f, C522q, Brazil. #C521g, C522b, Poland. #C521h, C522d, Algeria. #C521i, C522f, Belgium. #C521j, C522n, France. #C521k, C522p, Honduras. #C521l, C522r, Russia. #C521m, C522g, Peru. #C521n, C522i, Chile. #C521o, C522k, Hungary. #C521p, C522s, Czechoslovakia. #C521q, C522u, Yugoslavia. #C521r, C522w, Scotland. #C521s, C522h, Cameroun. #C521t, C522j, Austria. #C521u, C522l, Salvador. #C521v, C522t, Kuwait. #C521w, C522v, Ireland. #C521x, C522x, New Zealand.

**1982, Aug. 26**

C521 Sheet of 24 4.50
*a.-x.* AP73 15c Flags .20 .20
C522 Sheet of 24 7.50
*a.-x.* AP73 25c Arms .25 .20

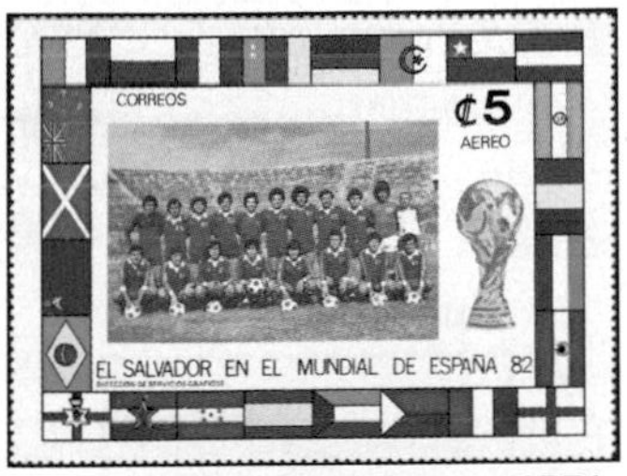


Salvador Team, Cup, Flags — AP74

**1982, Aug. 26 Litho. *Perf. 11½***

C523 AP74 5col multi 4.00 2.50

**International Fair Type**

**1982, Oct. 14 Litho. *Perf. 14***

C524 A281 15c multi .20 .20

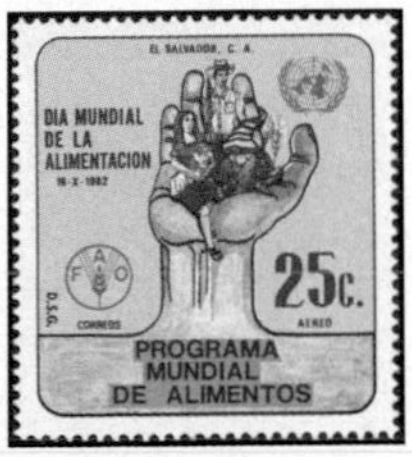


World Food Day — AP75

**1982, Oct. 21 Litho. *Perf. 14***

C525 AP75 25c multi .20 .20

## St. Francis of Assisi, 800th Birth Anniv. AP76

**1982, Nov. 10**   **Litho.**   **Perf. 14**
C526 AP76 1col multi   .80 .60

## Natl. Labor Campaign AP77

**1982, Nov. 30**   **Litho.**   **Perf. 14x14½**
C527 AP77 50c multi   .40 .25

## Christmas Type

**1982, Dec. 14**   **Litho.**   **Perf. 14**
C528 A282 25c multi, horiz.   .20 .20

## Salvadoran Paintings AP78

**1983, Oct. 18**   **Perf. 14x13½, 13½x14**   **Litho.**

#C529, The Pottery of Paleca, by Miguel Ortiz Villacorta. #C530, The Rural School, by Luis Caceres Madrid. #C531, To the Wash, by Julia Diaz. #C532, "La Pancha" by Jose Mejia Vides. #C533, Boats Near The Beach, by Raul Elas Reyes. #C534, The Muleteers, by Canjura.

C529 AP78 20c multi   .20 .20
C530 AP78 25c multi   .55 .55
  a. Pair, #C529-C530   .60 .40
C531 AP78 75c multi, vert.   .60 .40
C532 AP78 75c multi, vert.   1.75 1.75
  a. Pair, #C531-C532   .80 .55
C533 AP78 1col multi, vert.   .80 .55
C534 AP78 1col multi, vert.   2.50 2.50
  a. Pair, #C533-C534   3.20 2.30
Nos. C529-C534 (6)

## Fishing Industry AP79

**1983, Dec. 20**   **Litho.**   **Perf. 14½x14**
C535 AP79 25c Fisherman   .25 .20
C536 AP79 75c Feeding fish   .75 .40

## No. 999 Surcharged

**1985, Apr. 10**   **Litho.**   **Perf. 14**
C536A A297 1col on 10c multi   .80 .50

---

## Natl. Constitution, Cent. — AP80

**1986, Aug. 29**   **Litho.**   **Perf. 14**
C537 AP80 1col multi   .50 .35

## Hugo Lindo (1917-1985), Writer — AP81

**1986, Nov. 10**   **Litho.**   **Perf. 14½x14**
C538 AP81 1col multi   .50 .35

## Central American Economic Integration Bank, 25th Anniv. AP82

**1986, Nov. 20**
C539 AP82 1.50col multi   .70 .50

## 12th Intl. Fair, Feb. 14-Mar. 1 AP83

**1987, Jan. 20**   **Litho.**   **Perf. 14½x14**
C540 AP83 70c multi   .35 .25

## Intl. Year of Shelter for the Homeless AP84

**1987, July 15**   **Perf. 14x14½, 14½x14**   **Litho.**
C541 AP84 70c shown   .35 .25
C542 AP84 1col Emblem, vert.   .45 .35

## Discovery of America, 500th Anniv. (in 1992) AP85

**1987, Dec. 21**   **Litho.**   **Perf. 14**
C543 AP85 1col any single   .45 .35
  a.-j. Sheet of 10   8.50 8.50

15th cent. map of the Americas (details) and: a. Ferdinand. b. Isabella. c. Caribbean. d. Ships. e. coat of arms. f. Base of flagstaff. g. Pre-Columbian statue. h, Compass. i, Anniv. emblem. j, Columbus rose.

---

**1988, Oct. 28**   **Litho.**   **Perf. 14x14½**
C544 A316 5col on 90c multi   2.50 1.75
PRENFIL '88, Nov. 25-Dec. 2, Buenos Aire.

## Organization of American States 18th General Assembly, Nov. 14-19 — AP86

**1988, Nov. 19**
C545 AP86 70c multi   .40 .30

## Handicapped Soccer Championships — AP87

**1990, May 2**   **Litho.**   **Perf. 14½x14**
C546 AP87 70c multicolored   .35 .25

---

# ACKNOWLEDGMENT OF RECEIPT STAMPS

## Gen. Rafael Antonio Gutiérrez — R1

**1897**   **Engr.**   **Wmk. 117**   **Perf. 12**
F1 R1 10c dark blue   125.00
F2 R1 10c brown lake   .20
**Unwmk.**
F3 R1 10c dark blue   .20
F4 R1 10c brown lake   .20

Nos. F1 and F3 were probably not placed in use without the overprint "FRANQUEO OFICIAL" (Nos. O127-O128). The reprints are on thick unwatermarked paper. Value, set of 2, 16c.

---

# REGISTRATION STAMPS

---

## POSTAGE DUE STAMPS

### No. 1075 Surcharged

**1897**   **Engr.**   **Wmk. 117**   **Perf. 12**
H1 AR1 5c dark green   .20
**Unwmk.**
H2 AR1 5c dark green   .20

No. H2 has been reprinted on thick paper. Value 15c.

D1

**1895**   **Unwmk.**   **Engr.**   **Perf. 12**
J1 D1 1c olive green   .20 .20
J2 D1 2c olive green   .20 .20
J3 D1 3c olive green   .20 .20
J4 D1 5c olive green   .20 .25
J5 D1 10c olive green   .20 .25
J6 D1 15c olive green   .20 .30
J7 D1 25c olive green   .20 .35
J8 D1 50c olive green   1.60 1.65
Nos. J1-J8 (8)

**1896**   **Unwmk.**
J9 D1 1c red   .20 .20
J10 D1 2c red   .20 .20
J11 D1 3c red   .20 .20
J12 D1 5c red   .20 .25
J13 D1 10c red   .25 .25
J14 D1 15c red   .25 .30
J15 D1 25c red   .30 .35
J16 D1 50c red   2.00 2.10
Nos. J9-J16 (8)

**1897**   **Wmk. 117**
J17 D1 1c red   .20
J18 D1 2c red   .20
J19 D1 3c red   .20
J20 D1 5c red   .20
J21 D1 10c red   .20
J22 D1 15c red   .20
J23 D1 25c red   .20
J24 D1 50c red   1.60
Nos. J17-J24 (8)

Nos. J17-J24 exist imperforate.

**1897**
J25 D1 1c deep blue   .20
J26 D1 2c deep blue   .20
J27 D1 3c deep blue   .20
J28 D1 5c deep blue   .20
J29 D1 10c deep blue   .20
J30 D1 15c deep blue   .20
J31 D1 25c deep blue   .20
J32 D1 50c deep blue   1.60
Nos. J25-J32 (8)

**1898**   **Unwmk.**
J33 D1 1c violet   .20
J34 D1 2c violet   .20
J35 D1 3c violet   .20
J36 D1 5c violet   .20
J37 D1 10c violet   .20
J38 D1 15c violet   .20
J39 D1 25c violet   .20
J40 D1 50c violet   1.60
Nos. J33-J40 (8)

Reprints of Nos. J1 to J40 are on thick paper, often in the wrong shades and usually with the impression somewhat blurred. Value, set of 40, $2, watermarked or unwatermarked.

**1899**   **Wmk. 117 Sideways**
J41 D1 1c orange   .20
J42 D1 2c orange   .20
J43 D1 3c orange   .20
J44 D1 5c orange   .20
J45 D1 10c orange   .20
J46 D1 15c orange   .20
J47 D1 25c orange   .20
J48 D1 50c orange   1.60
Nos. J41-J48 (8)

**Unwmk.**
J49 D1 1c orange   .20
J50 D1 2c orange   .20
J51 D1 3c orange   .20
J52 D1 5c orange   .20
J53 D1 10c orange   .20
J54 D1 15c orange   .20
J55 D1 25c orange   .20
J56 D1 50c orange   1.60
Nos. J49-J56 (8)

**Thick Porous Paper**
Nos. J41-J56 were probably not put in use without the wheel overprint.

See Nos. J9-J56. For overprints see Nos. J57-J64, O186-O214.

AR1

## OFFICIAL STAMPS

**Overprint Types**

a

### Nos. 134-157O Overprinted Type a

**Perf. 12**
**1896 — Unwmk.**

| No. | Type | Value | Price |
|---|---|---|---|
| O1 | A45 | 1c blue | .20 |
| O2 | A45 | 2c dk brown | .20 |
| | | a. Double overprint | |
| O3 | A45 | 3c blue grn | .30 |
| O4 | A45 | 5c brown ol | .20 |
| O5 | A45 | 10c yellow | .20 |
| O6 | A45 | 12c dk blue | .20 |
| O7 | A45 | 15c blue | .20 |
| O8 | A45 | 20c magenta | .30 |
| O9 | A45 | 24c vermilion | .20 |
| O10 | A45 | 30c orange | .30 |
| O11 | A45 | 50c black brn | .20 |
| O12 | A45 | 1p rose lake | 2.70 |

Nos. O1-O12 (12)

*The 1c has been reprinted on thick unwatermarked paper. Value 15c.*

**Wmk. 117**

| O13 | A46 | 1c emerald | .20 |
|---|---|---|---|
| O14 | A47 | 2c lake | .20 |
| O15 | A48 | 3c yellow brn | .20 |
| O16 | A49 | 5c dp blue | 1.00 |
| O17 | A50 | 10c brown | .20 |
| | | a. Inverted overprint | 1.25 |
| O18 | A51 | 12c slate | .20 |
| O19 | A52 | 15c blue grn | .20 |
| O20 | A53 | 20c car rose | .20 |
| | | a. Inverted overprint | |
| O21 | A54 | 24c violet | .20 |
| O22 | A55 | 30c dp green | .20 |
| O23 | A56 | 50c orange | .20 |
| O24 | A57 | 100c dk blue | 2.40 |

Nos. O13-O24 (12)

**Unwmk.**

| O25 | A46 | 1c emerald | .20 |
|---|---|---|---|
| | | a. Double overprint | |
| O26 | A47 | 2c lake | .20 |
| O27 | A48 | 3c yellow brn | .20 |
| O28 | A49 | 5c dp blue | .85 |
| O29 | A50 | 10c brown | .20 |
| O30 | A51 | 12c slate | .20 |
| O31 | A52 | 15c blue grn | .20 |
| O32 | A53 | 20c car rose | .20 |
| | | a. Inverted overprint | |
| O34 | A54 | 24c violet | .40 |
| O35 | A56 | 50c orange | 1.10 |
| O36 | A57 | 100c dk blue | 4.80 |

Nos. O25-O36 (12)

*The 3, 5, 10, 12, 15, 20, 24, 30 and 100c have been reprinted on thick unwatermarked paper and the 15c, 50c and 100c on thick watermarked paper. Value, set of 12, $1.20.*

### Nos. 134-145 Handstamped Type b in Black or Violet

b

**1896**

| O37 | A45 | 1c blue | 7.50 |
|---|---|---|---|
| O38 | A45 | 2c dk brown | 7.50 |
| O39 | A45 | 3c blue green | 7.50 |
| O40 | A45 | 5c brown olive | 8.75 |
| O41 | A45 | 10c yellow | 11.50 |
| O42 | A45 | 15c blue violet | 11.50 |
| O43 | A45 | 15c blue violet | 11.50 |
| O44 | A45 | 20c magenta | 11.50 |
| O45 | A45 | 24c vermilion | 11.50 |
| O46 | A45 | 30c orange | 15.00 |
| O47 | A45 | 50c black brown | 15.00 |
| O48 | A45 | 100c rose lake | 126.25 |

Nos. O37-O48 (12)

*Reprints of the 1c and 2c on thick paper exist with this handstamp. Value, set of 2, 20c.*

### Nos. 146-157F, 157I-157O, 158D Handstamped Type b in Black or Violet

**Wmk. 117**
**1896**

| O49 | A46 | 1c emerald | 6.25 |
|---|---|---|---|
| O50 | A47 | 2c lake | 6.25 |
| O51 | A48 | 3c yellow brn | 6.25 |
| O52 | A49 | 5c deep blue | 6.25 |
| O53 | A50 | 10c brown | 6.25 |
| O54 | A51 | 12c slate | 10.00 |
| O55 | A52 | 15c blue green | 11.50 |
| O56 | A53 | 20c carmine rose | 11.50 |
| O57 | A54 | 24c violet | 11.50 |
| O58 | A55 | 30c deep green | 11.50 |
| O59 | A56 | 50c orange | 11.50 |
| O60 | A57 | 100c dark blue | 110.25 |

Nos. O49-O60 (12)

**Unwmk.**

| O61 | A46 | 1c emerald | 6.25 |
|---|---|---|---|
| O62 | A47 | 2c lake | 6.25 |
| O63 | A48 | 3c yellow brn | 6.25 |
| O64 | A49 | 5c deep blue | 8.75 |
| O65 | A50 | 10c brown | 11.50 |
| O66 | A51 | 12c blue green | 11.50 |
| O67 | A52 | 15c on 24c vio | 11.50 |
| O68 | A53 | 20c carmine rose | 11.50 |
| O69 | A54 | 24c violet | 11.50 |
| O70 | A55 | 30c deep green | 12.50 |
| O71 | A56 | 50c orange | 12.50 |
| O72 | A57 | 100c dark blue | 116.25 |

Nos. O61-O72 (12)

### Nos. 175-176 Overprinted Type a in Black

**1897**

| O73 | A59 | 1c bl, gold, rose & grn | .25 |
|---|---|---|---|
| O74 | A59 | 5c rose, gold, bl & grn | .25 |

*These stamps were probably not officially issued.*

### Nos. 175-176 Handstamped Type b in Black or Violet

**1900**

| O75 | A59 | 1c bl, gold, rose & grn | 17.50 |
|---|---|---|---|
| O76 | A59 | 5c rose, gold, bl & grn | 17.50 |

### Nos. 159-170L Overprinted Type a in Black

**Wmk. 117**
**1897**

| O79 | A46 | 1c scarlet | .20 |
|---|---|---|---|
| O80 | A47 | 2c yellow green | 1.25 |
| O81 | A48 | 3c bister brown | .50 |
| O82 | A49 | 5c orange | .20 |
| O83 | A50 | 10c blue green | .25 |
| O84 | A51 | 12c blue | .25 |
| O85 | A52 | 15c black | .20 |
| O86 | A53 | 20c slate | .20 |
| O87 | A54 | 24c yellow | .20 |
| | | a. Inverted overprint | |
| O89 | A56 | 50c rose | 1.00 |
| O90 | A57 | 100c brown lake | 6.75 |

Nos. O79-O90 (12)

**Unwmk.**

| O91 | A46 | 1c scarlet | .20 |
|---|---|---|---|
| O92 | A47 | 2c yellow green | .30 |
| O93 | A48 | 3c bister brown | .20 |
| O94 | A49 | 5c orange | .65 |
| O95 | A50 | 10c blue green | .65 |
| O96 | A51 | 12c blue | .75 |
| O97 | A52 | 15c black | .20 |
| O98 | A53 | 20c slate | .35 |
| O99 | A54 | 24c yellow | .35 |
| O100 | A55 | 30c rose | .20 |
| O101 | A56 | 50c violet | .65 |
| O102 | A57 | 100c brown lake | 4.60 |

Nos. O91-O102 (12)

*All values have been reprinted on thick paper without watermark and the 1c, 12c, 15c and 100c on thick paper with watermark. Value, set of 16, $1.60.*

### Nos. 159-170L Handstamped Type b in Violet or Black

**Wmk. 117**
**1897**

| O103 | A46 | 1c scarlet | 7.50 |
|---|---|---|---|
| O104 | A47 | 2c yellow green | 7.50 |
| O105 | A48 | 3c bister brown | 7.50 |
| O106 | A49 | 5c orange | 8.75 |
| O107 | A50 | 10c blue green | 8.75 |
| O108 | A51 | 12c blue | 11.50 |
| O109 | A52 | 15c black | 11.50 |
| O110 | A53 | 20c slate | 11.50 |
| O111 | A54 | 24c yellow | 11.50 |
| O112 | A55 | 30c rose | 15.00 |
| O113 | A56 | 50c violet | 15.00 |
| O114 | A57 | 100c brown lake | 126.25 |

Nos. O103-O114 (12)

**Unwmk.**

| O115 | A46 | 1c scarlet | 7.50 |
|---|---|---|---|
| O116 | A47 | 2c yellow green | 7.50 |
| O117 | A48 | 3c bister brn | 7.50 |
| O118 | A49 | 5c orange | 7.50 |
| O119 | A50 | 10c blue green | |
| O120 | A51 | 12c blue | |
| O122 | A53 | 20c slate | |
| O123 | A54 | 24c yellow | 2.40 |

*Forged overprints exist of Nos. O37-O78, O103-O126 and of the higher valued stamps of O141-O214.*

### Nos. F1, F3 Overprinted Type a in Red

**Wmk. 117**
**1898**

| O124 | A55 | 30c rose | 15.00 |
|---|---|---|---|
| O125 | A56 | 50c violet | 17.50 |
| O126 | A57 | 100c brown lake | |

| O127 | R1 | 10c dark blue | .20 |
|---|---|---|---|

**Unwmk.**

| O128 | R1 | 10c dark blue | .20 |
|---|---|---|---|

*The reprints are on thick paper. Value 15c. Originals of the 10c brown lake Registration Stamp and the 5c Acknowledgment of Receipt stamp are believed not to have been issued with the "FRANQUEO OFICIAL" overprint. They are believed to exist only as reprints.*

### Nos. 177-188 Overprinted Type a

**Wmk. 117**
**1898**

| O129 | A60 | 1c orange ver | .20 |
|---|---|---|---|
| O130 | A60 | 2c rose | .20 |
| O131 | A60 | 3c pale yel grn | 1.40 |
| O132 | A60 | 5c blue green | .20 |
| O133 | A60 | 10c gray blue | .20 |
| O134 | A60 | 12c violet | 1.40 |
| O135 | A60 | 13c brown lake | .20 |
| O136 | A60 | 20c deep blue | .20 |
| O137 | A60 | 24c ultra | .20 |
| O138 | A60 | 26c bister brn | .20 |
| O139 | A60 | 50c orange | .20 |
| O140 | A60 | 1c yellow | 4.80 |

Nos. O129-O140 (12)

*Reprints of the above set are on thick paper. Value, set of 12, $1.20, with or without watermark.*

### No. 177 Handstamped Type b in Violet

| O141 | A60 | 1c orange ver | 30.00 |
|---|---|---|---|

### No. O141 with Additional Overprint Type c in Black

c

*Type "c" is called the "wheel" overprint.*

| O142 | A60 | 1c orange ver | .50 |
|---|---|---|---|

*Counterfeits exist of the "wheel" overprint.*

### Nos. 204-205, 207 and 209 Overprinted Type a

**1899 — Unwmk.**

| O143 | A61 | 12c dark green | .35 |
|---|---|---|---|
| O144 | A61 | 13c deep rose | .35 |
| O145 | A61 | 26c carmino rose | .35 |
| O146 | A61 | 100c violet | 1.00 |

### Nos. O143-O144 Punched With Twelve Small Holes

| O147 | A61 | 12c dark green | .65 |
|---|---|---|---|
| O148 | A61 | 13c deep rose | |

*Official stamps punched with twelve small holes were issued and used for ordinary postage.*

### Nos. 199-209 Overprinted

d

**1899**

**Blue Overprint**

| O149 | A61 | 1c brown | .20 |
|---|---|---|---|
| O150 | A61 | 2c gray green | .20 |
| O151 | A61 | 3c blue | .20 |
| O152 | A61 | 5c brown orange | .20 |
| O153 | A61 | 10c chocolate | .20 |
| O154 | A61 | 12c deep rose | .20 |
| O155 | A61 | 26c carmine rose | .20 |
| O156 | A61 | 50c orange red | .20 |
| O157 | A61 | 100c violet | .20 |

**Black Overprint**

| O158 | A61 | 3c blue | .20 |
|---|---|---|---|
| O159 | A61 | 13c dark green | .20 |
| O160 | A61 | 24c lt blue | 2.40 |

Nos. O149-O160 (12)

*#O149-O160 were probably not placed in use.*

---

### Nos. J49-J56 Overprinted in Black

**1900**

| J57 | D1 | 1c orange | .50 |
|---|---|---|---|
| J58 | D1 | 2c orange | .50 |
| J59 | D1 | 3c orange | .50 |
| J60 | D1 | 5c orange | .75 |
| J61 | D1 | 10c orange | 1.00 |
| J62 | D1 | 15c orange | 1.25 |
| J63 | D1 | 25c orange | 1.50 |
| J64 | D1 | 50c orange | 7.00 |

Nos. J57-J64 (8)

See note after No. 198A.

### Morazán Monument — D2

**1903 — Perf. 14, 14½ — Wmk. 173**
**Engr.**

| J65 | D2 | 1c yellow green | 1.75 | 1.00 |
|---|---|---|---|---|
| J66 | D2 | 2c carmine | 2.75 | 1.50 |
| J67 | D2 | 3c orange | 2.75 | 1.50 |
| J68 | D2 | 5c dark blue | 2.75 | 1.50 |
| J69 | D2 | 10c dull violet | 2.75 | 1.50 |
| J70 | D2 | 25c blue green | 15.50 | 8.50 |

Nos. J65-J70 (6)

### Nos. 355, 356, 358 and 360 Overprinted

**Perf. 11½**
**1908 — Unwmk.**

| J71 | A66 | 1c yellow green | .40 | .35 |
|---|---|---|---|---|
| J72 | A66 | 2c red & blk | .30 | .25 |
| J73 | A66 | 5c blue & blk | .75 | .50 |
| J74 | A66 | 10c violet & blk | 1.10 | 1.00 |

Nos. J71-J75 (5)

**Same Overprint on No. O275**

| J75 | O3 | 2c yellow & blk | .75 | .50 |
|---|---|---|---|---|
| | | | 3.30 | 2.75 |

### Nos. 355-358, 360 Overprinted

| J76 | A66 | 1c green & blk | .25 | .25 |
|---|---|---|---|---|
| J77 | A66 | 2c red & blk | .30 | .30 |
| J78 | A66 | 3c yellow & blk | .35 | .35 |
| J79 | A66 | 5c blue & blk | .50 | 1.00 |
| J80 | A66 | 10c violet & blk | 2.40 | 2.40 |

Nos. J76-J80 (5)

*It is now believed that stamps of type A66, on paper with Honeycomb watermark, do not exist with genuine overprints of the types used for Nos. J71-J80.*

### Pres. Fernando Figueroa — D3

**1910 — Engr. — Wmk. 172**

| J81 | D3 | 1c sepia & blk | .20 | .20 |
|---|---|---|---|---|
| J82 | D3 | 2c dk grn & blk | .20 | .20 |
| J83 | D3 | 3c orange & blk | .20 | .20 |
| J84 | D3 | 4c scarlet & blk | .20 | .20 |
| J85 | D3 | 5c purple & blk | .20 | .20 |
| J86 | D3 | 12c deep blue & blk | .20 | .20 |
| J87 | D3 | 24c brown red & blk | 1.40 | 1.40 |

Nos. J81-J87 (7)

**With Additional Overprint Type c in Black**

| | | | | |
|---|---|---|---|---|
| O161 | A61 | 1c brown | .40 | .35 |
| O162 | A61 | 2c gray green | .60 | .50 |
| O163 | A61 | 3c blue | .40 | .35 |
| O164 | A61 | 5c brown org | .40 | .35 |
| O165 | A61 | 10c chocolate | .50 | .40 |
| O166 | A61 | 12c dark green | 1.00 | .85 |
| O167 | A61 | 13c deep rose | | |
| O168 | A61 | 24c lt blue | 15.00 | 15.00 |
| O169 | A61 | 26c carmine rose | 1.00 | .60 |
| O170 | A61 | 50c orange red | 1.00 | .85 |
| O171 | A61 | 100c violet | 1.25 | .85 |

Nos. O161-O165,O167-O171 (10)   21.55   20.10

Nos. O149-O155, O159-O160 Punched With Twelve Small Holes

e

It is stated that Nos. O172-O214 inclusive were issued for ordinary postage and not for use as official stamps.

Nos. O161-O167, O169 Overprinted Type c in Black

| | | | | |
|---|---|---|---|---|
| O180 | A61 | 1c brown | 2.75 | 1.00 |
| O181 | A61 | 3c blue | 3.25 | 1.00 |
| O182 | A61 | 5c brown org | | |
| O182A | A61 | 10c chocolate | | |
| O182B | A61 | 12c dark green | | |
| O183 | A61 | 24c lt blue | | |
| O184 | A61 | 26c carmine rose | | |

**Black Overprint**

| | | | | |
|---|---|---|---|---|
| O172 | A61 | 1c brown | 2.75 | 1.00 |
| O173 | A61 | 2c gray green | 3.25 | 1.00 |
| O174 | A61 | 3c blue | 4.50 | 3.75 |
| O175 | A61 | 5c brown org | 3.00 | 3.75 |
| O176 | A61 | 10c chocolate | 7.50 | 5.00 |
| O177 | A61 | 12c dark green | 7.50 | 3.75 |
| O177A | A61 | 13c deep rose | | |
| O178 | A61 | 24c lt blue | | |
| O179 | A61 | 26c carmine rose | | |

**Blue Overprint**

Nos. O172-O177,O178-O179 (8)   11.50   57.00

Nos. O186-O189, O194-O189, O191-O193 Overprinted Type c in Black

O185 A61 100c violet

Nos. J49-J56 Overprinted Type a in Black

Overprinted Types a and e in Black

**1900**

Nos. O186-O189 Overprinted Type c in Black

| | | | | |
|---|---|---|---|---|
| O186 | D1 | 1c orange | | 22.50 |
| O187 | D1 | 3c orange | | 22.50 |
| O188 | D1 | 5c orange | | 22.50 |
| O189 | D1 | 10c orange | | 22.50 |

Nos. O186-O189 Punched With Twelve Small Holes

| | | | | |
|---|---|---|---|---|
| O194 | D1 | 1c orange | | 35.00 |
| O195 | D1 | 3c orange | | 35.00 |
| O196 | D1 | 5c orange | | 35.00 |
| O197 | D1 | 10c orange | | 35.00 |
| O198 | D1 | 15c orange | | 50.00 |
| O199 | D1 | 25c orange | | 50.00 |
| O200 | D1 | 50c orange | | 262.50 |
| O191 | D1 | 15c orange | | 50.00 |
| O192 | D1 | 25c orange | | 50.00 |
| O193 | D1 | 50c orange | | 140.00 |

Nos. O201-O204 Overprinted Type c in Black

| | | | | |
|---|---|---|---|---|
| O201 | O1 | 1c orange | | 35.00 |
| O202 | O1 | 3c orange | | 35.00 |
| O203 | O1 | 5c orange | | 35.00 |
| O204 | O1 | 24c orange | | 140.00 |

Nos. O201-O204 (4)   12.50

Overprinted Type a in Violet and Type c in Black

| | | | | |
|---|---|---|---|---|
| O205 | D1 | 1c orange | | 9.00 |
| O206 | D1 | 3c orange | | 6.50 |
| O207 | D1 | 5c orange | | 6.50 |
| O208 | D1 | 10c orange | | 6.50 |

Overprinted Type a in Black

| | | | | |
|---|---|---|---|---|
| O209 | D1 | 2c orange | | 12.50 |
| O210 | D1 | 3c orange | | |
| a. | | Inverted overprint | | |
| O211 | D1 | 10c orange | | 3.00 |

---

Nos. O161-O165,O167-O171 Handstamped Type e Punched With Twelve Small Holes

| | | | | |
|---|---|---|---|---|
| O178 | A61 | 26c carmine rose | | |
| O177A | A61 | 24c lt blue | | |
| O177 | A61 | 13c deep rose | | |
| O176 | A61 | 12c dark green | | |
| O175 | A61 | 10c chocolate | | |
| O174 | A61 | 5c brown org | | |
| O173 | A61 | 3c blue | | |
| O172 | A61 | 2c gray green | | |

See note after No. O48.

**Type of Regular Issue of 1900 Overprinted Type a in Black**

| | | | | |
|---|---|---|---|---|
| O212 | D1 | 1c orange | 9.00 | 7.50 |
| a. | | Inverted overprint | | |
| O213 | D1 | 2c orange | 9.00 | 7.50 |
| a. | | Inverted overprint | | |
| O214 | D1 | 3c orange | 27.00 | 24.00 |

Nos. O212-O214 (3)

Nos. O186-O188 Handstamped Type e in Violet

Nos. O272-O214 (3)

**1903**

| | | | | |
|---|---|---|---|---|
| O223 | A63 | 1c lt green | 22.50 | |
| O224 | A63 | 2c rose | 27.50 | |
| O225 | A63 | 3c gray black | 17.50 | |
| a. | | Inverted overprint | | |
| O226 | A63 | 10c blue | 17.50 | |
| O227 | A63 | 12c yellow brn | | |
| O228 | A63 | 13c yellow grn | 45.00 | |
| O229 | A63 | 24c gray black | 45.00 | |
| O230 | A63 | 26c yellow brn | 32.50 | |
| O231 | A63 | 50c yellow brn | 30.00 | |
| O232 | A63 | 50c dull rose | | .00 |

Nos. O223-O224, O231-O232 Overprinted in Violet

**Overprinted in Black**

| | | | | |
|---|---|---|---|---|
| O233 | A63 | 1c lt green | 4.75 | 4.00 |
| O234 | A63 | 2c rose | | 25.00 |
| a. | | "FRANQUEO OFICIAL" invtd. | | |
| O235 | A63 | 26c yellow brown | .50 | .50 |
| O236 | A63 | 50c dull rose | .75 | .55 |

Nos. O223, O225-O220, O232 Overprinted in Black

f

g

**Violet Overprint**

O242 A63 50c dull rose   10.00

The shield overprinted on No. O242 is of the type on No. O212.

| | | | | |
|---|---|---|---|---|
| O237 | A63 | 1c lt green | 5.00 | 5.00 |
| O238 | A63 | 3c gray green | — | 40.00 |
| O239 | A63 | 5c blue | | |
| O240 | A63 | 10c blue | | |
| O241 | A63 | 12c yellow green | | |

**1903**

**Wmk. 173**   **Perf. 14, 14½**

| | | | | |
|---|---|---|---|---|
| O243 | O1 | 1c yellow green | .45 | .25 |
| O244 | O1 | 2c carmine | .45 | .20 |
| O245 | O1 | 3c orange | 1.40 | .85 |
| O246 | O1 | 5c dark blue | .70 | .35 |
| O247 | O1 | 10c dull violet | .70 | .35 |
| O248 | O1 | 15c red brown | .70 | .35 |
| O249 | O1 | 15c yellow brown | 5.00 | 1.75 |
| O250 | O1 | 24c scarlet | .45 | .35 |
| O251 | O1 | 50c bister | .70 | .35 |
| O252 | O1 | 100c grnsh blue | 11.00 | 5.40 |

Nos. O243-O252 (10)

For surcharges see Nos. O254-O257.

O1

**1904**

O253 A64 3c orange   35.00

No. 285 Handstamped Type b in Black

Nos. O243-O252 Overprinted Type c in Black

**1906**

c

**National Palace — O3**

Escalón — O2

**1906**

| | | | | |
|---|---|---|---|---|
| O260 | A63(c) | 3c gray black | 11.25 | 10.00 |
| O261 | A63(c) | 3c gray black | 1.00 | 1.00 |
| a. | | Overprint "1906" in blk | | |
| O262 | A63(d) | 3c gray black | 1.40 | 1.25 |

Nos. O260-O262 (3)   13.90   12.25

**1906**

| | | | | |
|---|---|---|---|---|
| O263 | O2 | 1c green & blk | .20 | .20 |
| O264 | O2 | 2c carmine & blk | .20 | .20 |
| O265 | O2 | 3c yellow & blk | .20 | .20 |
| O266 | O2 | 5c blue & blk | .20 | .20 |
| O267 | O2 | 10c violet & blk | .20 | .30 |
| O268 | O2 | 13c dk brown & blk | .20 | .20 |
| O269 | O2 | 15c red org & blk | .20 | .20 |
| O270 | O2 | 24c carmine & blk | .20 | .20 |
| O271 | O2 | 50c orange & blk | .25 | .20 |
| O272 | O2 | 100c dk blue & blk | .35 | .65 |

Nos. O263-O272 (10)   2.15   4.35

The centers of these stamps are also found in blue black.

Nos. O263 to O272 have been reprinted. The shades differ, the paper is thicker and the perforation 12. Value, set of 10, 50c.

**Engr.**

| | | |
|---|---|---|
| O258 | A63(a) | 3c gray black |
| O259 | A63(b) | 3c gray black |

Nos. O224-O225 Overprinted in Blue

**1905**

a

b

**Unwmk.**

| | | | | |
|---|---|---|---|---|
| O254 | O1 | 2c on 5c dark blue | 3.25 | 2.75 |
| O255 | O1 | 3c on 5c dark blue | | |
| a. | | Double surcharge | | |
| O256 | O1 | 3c on 10c dl vio | .85 | .70 |
| a. | | 3c on 13c red brn | | |

No. O225 Overprinted in Black

A 2c surcharge of this type exists on No. O247.

Nos. O246-O248 Surcharged in Black

**1905**

Regular Issue, Type A63. Overprinted or Surcharged:

| | | | | |
|---|---|---|---|---|
| O292 | O3 | 100c turq blue & blk | 3.00 | |
| O291 | O3 | 50c yellow & blk | 2.50 | |
| O290 | O3 | 24c rose & blk | 2.00 | |
| O289 | O3 | 15c pale brn & blk | 1.50 | |
| O288 | O3 | 13c violet & blk | 1.25 | |
| O287 | O3 | 10c violet & blk | 1.25 | |
| O286 | O3 | 5c blue & blk | 1.25 | |

Nos. O283-O292 (10)   15.85

Pres. Figueroa — O4

**1910**

**Engr.**   **Wmk. 172**

| | | | | |
|---|---|---|---|---|
| O293 | O4 | 2c dk green & blk | .20 | |
| O294 | O4 | 3c orange & blk | .20 | |
| O295 | O4 | 4c scarlet & blk | .20 | |
| O296 | O4 | 4c carmine & blk | .20 | |
| O297 | O4 | 5c purple & blk | .20 | |
| O298 | O4 | 6c scarlet & blk | .20 | |
| O299 | O4 | 10c purple & blk | .20 | |
| O300 | O4 | 12c dp blue & blk | .20 | |
| O301 | O4 | 13c olive grn & blk | .20 | |
| O302 | O4 | 19c brn red & blk | .20 | |
| O303 | O4 | 25c choc & blk | .20 | |
| O304 | O4 | 50c yellow & blk | 2.40 | 2.40 |

Nos. O293-O304 (12)

**Regular Issue, Type A63, Overprinted in Blue**

**OFICIAL**

a

**OFICIAL 3**

b

**OFICIAL UN COLÓN**

c

**1911**

**Unwmk.**

| | | | | |
|---|---|---|---|---|
| O305 | A63(a) | 1c lt green | .20 | |
| O306 | A63(a) | 3c on 13c yel brn | .20 | |
| O307 | A63(a) | 3c on 10c dp brn | .20 | |
| O308 | A63(a) | 10c dp blue | .20 | |
| O309 | A63(a) | 10c deep blue | .20 | |
| O310 | A63(a) | 12c lt green | .20 | |
| O311 | A63(b) | 50c on 10c dp bl | .20 | |
| O312 | A63(c) | 1col on 13c yel brn | 1.60 | 1.60 |

Nos. O305-O312 (8)   1.60

**1908**

| | | | | |
|---|---|---|---|---|
| O273 | O3 | 1c green & blk | .20 | .20 |
| O274 | O3 | 2c red & blk | .20 | .20 |
| O275 | O3 | 3c yellow & blk | .20 | .20 |
| O276 | O3 | 5c blue & blk | .20 | .20 |
| O277 | O3 | 10c violet & blk | .20 | .20 |
| O278 | O3 | 13c violet & blk | .20 | .20 |
| O279 | O3 | 15c pale brn & blk | .20 | .20 |
| O280 | O3 | 24c rose & blk | .20 | .20 |
| O281 | O3 | 50c yellow & blk | .20 | .20 |
| O282 | O3 | 100c turq blue & blk | 2.00 | 2.00 |

Nos. O273-O282 (10)

For overprints see Nos. 441-442, 445-449, J75, O283-O292, O323-O328.

Nos. O273-O282 Overprinted Type g in Black

| | | |
|---|---|---|
| O283 | O3 | 1c green & blk |
| O284 | O3 | 2c red & blk |
| O285 | O3 | 3c yellow & blk |

**1914**

**Typo.**   **Perf. 11½**

**Background in Green, Shield and "Provisional" in Black**

| | | | | |
|---|---|---|---|---|
| O313 | A63(a) | 2c yellow brn | .20 | |
| O314 | O5 | 2c yellow brn | .20 | |
| O315 | O5 | 5c dark blue | .20 | |
| O316 | O5 | 10c red | .20 | |
| O317 | O5 | 12c green | .20 | |
| O318 | O5 | 17c violet | .20 | |
| O319 | O5 | 50c brown | .20 | |
| O320 | O5 | 100c dull rose | 1.60 | 1.60 |

Nos. O313-O320 (8)

Stamps of this issue are known imperforate or with parts of the design omitted or misplaced. These varieties were not regularly issued.

O5

O6

**1914**

**Typo.**

| | | | | |
|---|---|---|---|---|
| O321 | O6 | 2c blue green | .20 | .20 |
| O322 | O6 | 3c orange | .20 | .20 |

Type of Official Stamps of 1908 With Two Overprints

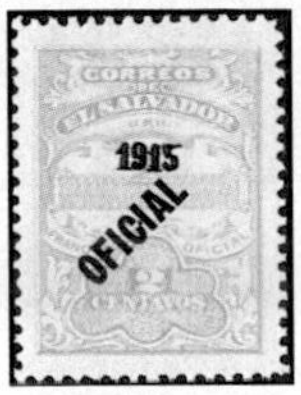

**1915**
**O323** O3 1c gray green .30 .25
*a.* "1915" double
*b.* "OFICIAL" inverted
**O324** O3 2c red .30 .25
**O325** O3 5c ultra .30 .25
**O326** O3 10c yellow .30 .25
*a.* Date omitted
**O327** O3 50c violet .55 .50
**O328** O3 100c black brown 1.25 1.00
*Nos. O323-O328 (6)* 3.00 2.50

### Same Overprint on #414, 417, 429

**O329** A66 1c gray green 1.60 1.60
**O330** A66 6c pale blue .50 .40
*a.* 6c ultramarine
**O331** A66 12c brown .60 .60
*Nos. O329-O330 (2)* 2.10 2.00

# O323-O327, O329-O331 exist imperf.
Nos. O329-O331 exist with "OFICIAL" inverted and double. See note after No. 421.

Nos. 431-440 Overprinted in Blue or Red

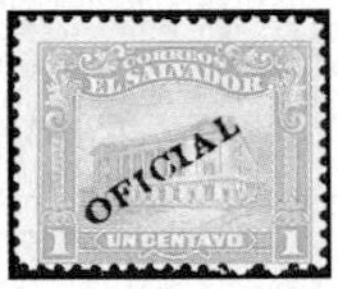

**1916**
**O332** A83 1c deep green .20 .20
**O333** A83 2c vermilion .35 .20
**O334** A83 5c dp blue (R) .25 .20
**O335** A83 6c gray vio (R) .20 .20
**O336** A83 10c black brown .20 .20
**O337** A83 12c violet .40 .25
**O338** A83 17c orange .20 .20
**O339** A83 25c dark brown .20 .20
**O340** A83 29c black (R) .20 .20
**O341** A83 50c slate (R) .20 .20
*Nos. O332-O341 (10)* 2.40 2.05

Nos. 474-481 Overprinted

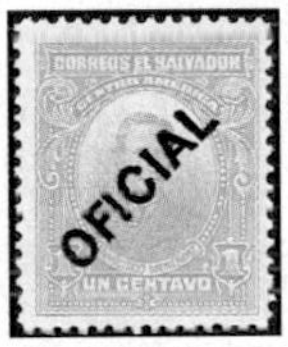
a

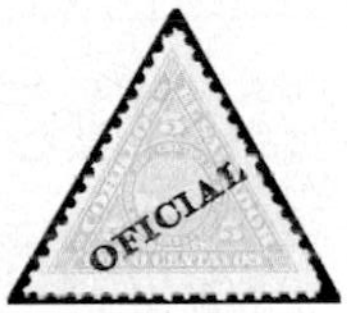
b

**1921**
**O342** A94(a) 1c green .20 .20
**O343** A95(a) 2c black .20 .20
*a.* Inverted overprint
**O344** A96(b) 5c orange .20 .20
**O345** A97(a) 6c carmine rose .20 .20
**O346** A98(a) 10c deep blue .20 .20
**O347** A99(a) 25c olive green .50 .25
**O348** A100(a) 60c violet .60 .50
**O349** A101(a) 1col black brown .65 .65
*Nos. O342-O349 (8)* 2.75 2.40

Nos. 498 and 500 Overprinted in Black or Red

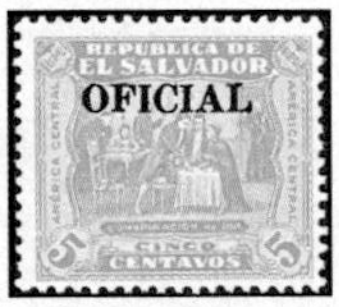

**1925**
**O350** A109 5c olive black .35 .20
**O351** A111 10c orange (R) .50 .20
*a.* "ATLANT CO" 7.50 6.25

Inverted overprints exist.

Regular Issue of 1924-25 Overprinted in Black or Red

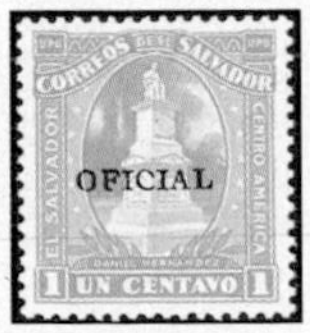

**1927**
**O352** A106 1c red violet .20 .20
**O353** A107 2c dark red .40 .25
**O354** A109 5c olive blk (R) .40 .25
**O355** A110 6c dp blue (R) 3.00 2.50
**O356** A111 10c orange .50 .30
*a.* "ATLANT CO" 12.50 11.50
**O357** A116 1col grn & vio (R) 1.50 1.00
*Nos. O352-O357 (6)* 6.00 4.50

Inverted overprints exist on 1c, 2c, 5c, 10c.

Regular Issue of 1924-25 Overprinted in Black

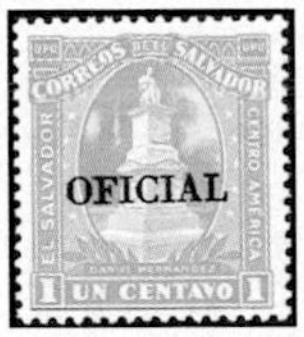

**1932** *Perf. 12½*
**O358** A106 1c deep violet .20 .20
**O359** A107 2c dark red .40 .20
**O360** A109 5c olive black .20 .20
**O361** A111 10c orange .70 .30
*a.* "ATLANT CO" 14.00 12.50
*Nos. O358-O361 (4)* 1.50 .90

**Catalogue values for unused stamps in this section, from this point to the end of the section, are for Never Hinged items.**

Regular Issue of 1947 Overprinted in Black or Red

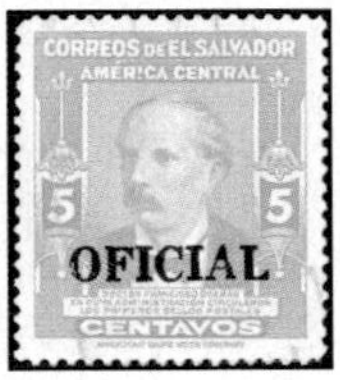

**1948** **Unwmk.** **Engr.** *Perf. 12*
**O362** A154 1c car rose 65.00 22.50
**O363** A154 2c deep org 65.00 22.50
**O364** A154 5c slate gray (R) 65.00 22.50
**O365** A154 10c bis brn (R) 65.00 22.50
**O366** A154 20c green (R) 65.00 22.50
**O367** A154 50c black (R) 65.00 22.50
*Nos. O362-O367 (6)* 390.00 135.00

No. 602 Surcharged in Carmine and Black

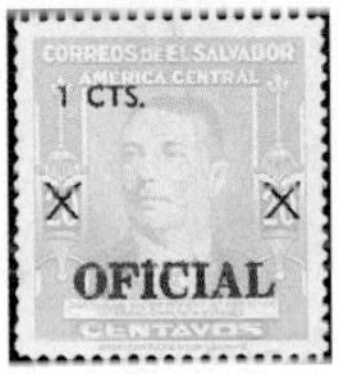

**1964(?)**
**O368** A154 1c on 20c green

The X's are black, the rest carmine.

### PARCEL POST STAMPS

Mercury
PP1

**1895** **Unwmk.** **Engr.** *Perf. 12*
**Q1** PP1 5c brown orange .25
**Q2** PP1 10c dark blue .25
**Q3** PP1 15c red .25
**Q4** PP1 20c orange .25
**Q5** PP1 50c blue green .25
*Nos. Q1-Q5 (5)* 1.25

### POSTAL TAX STAMPS

Nos. 503, 501 Surcharged

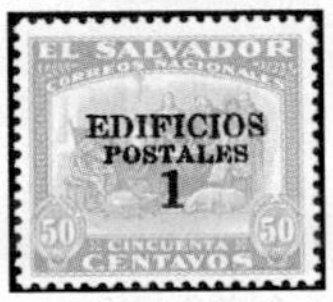

**1931** **Unwmk.** *Perf. 12½*
**RA1** A115 1c on 50c org brn .20 .20
*a.* Double surcharge 2.00 2.00
**RA2** A112 2c on 20c dp grn .20 .20

Nos. 501, 503 Surcharged

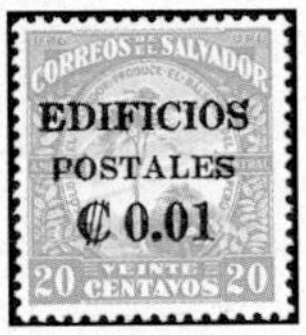

**RA3** A112 1c on 20c dp grn .20 .20
**RA4** A115 2c on 50c org brn .20 .20
*a.* Without period in "0.02" 1.25

The use of these stamps was obligatory, in addition to the regular postage, on letters and other postal matter. The money obtained from their sale was to be used to erect a new post office in San Salvador.

## SAMOA

sə-'mō-ə

(Western Samoa)

LOCATION — Archipelago in the south Pacific Ocean, east of Fiji
GOVT. — Independent state; former territory mandated by New Zealand
AREA — 1,093 sq. mi.
POP. — 161,298 (1991)
CAPITAL — Apia

In 1861-99, Samoa was an independent kingdom under the influence of the US, to which the harbor of Pago Pago had been ceded, and that of Great Britain and Germany. In 1898 a disturbance arose, resulting in the withdrawal of Great Britain, and the partitioning of the islands between Germany and the US. Early in World War I the islands under German domination were occupied by New Zealand troops and in 1920 the League of Nations declared them a mandate to New Zealand. Western Samoa became independent Jan. 1, 1962.

12 Pence = 1 Shilling
20 Shillings = 1 Pound
100 Pfennig = 1 Mark (1900)
100 Sene (Cents) = 1 Tala (Dollar) (1967)

**Catalogue values for unused stamps in this country are for Never Hinged items, beginning with Scott 191 in the regular postage section, Scott B1 in the semi-postal section and Scott C1 in the air post section.**

### Watermarks

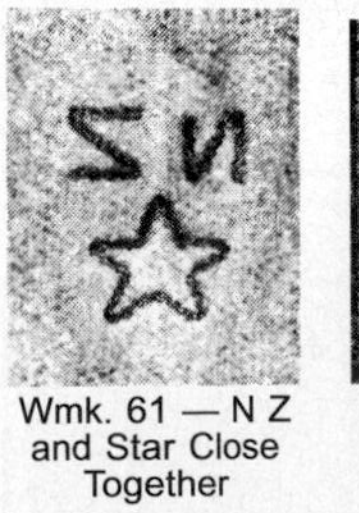
Wmk. 61 — N Z and Star Close Together

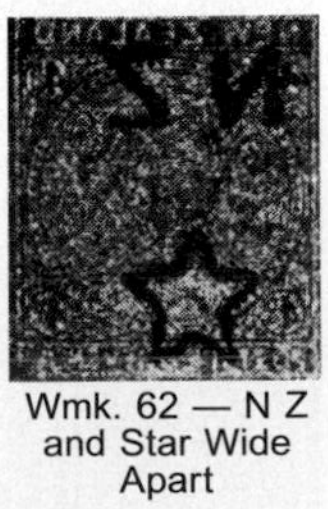
Wmk. 62 — N Z and Star Wide Apart

On watermark 61 the margins of the sheets are watermarked "NEW ZEALAND POSTAGE" and parts of the double-lined letters of these words are frequently found on the stamps. It occasionally happens that a stamp shows no watermark whatever.

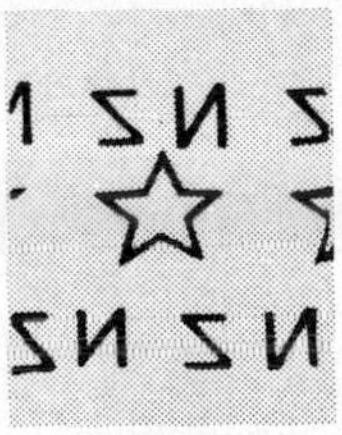
Wmk. 253 — Multiple N Z and Star

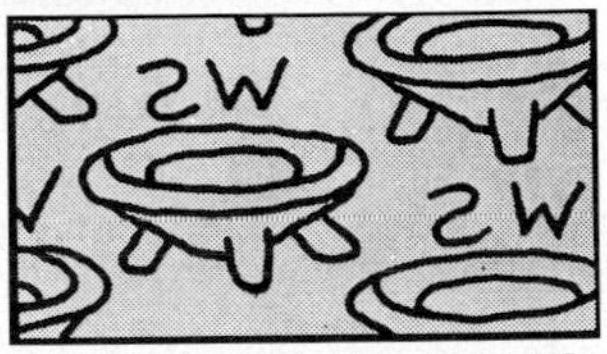
Wmk. 355 — Kava Bowl and WS, Multiple

### Issues of the Kingdom

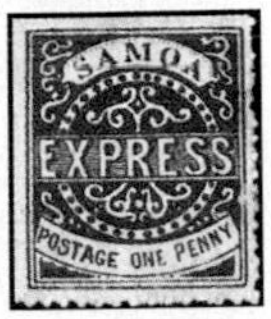
A1

Type I — Line above "X" is usually unbroken. Dots over "SAMOA" are uniform and evenly spaced. Upper right serif of "M" is horizontal.
Type II — Line above "X" is usually broken. Small dot near upper right serif of "M."
Type III — Line above "X" roughly retouched. Upper right serif of "M" bends down (joined to dot).
Type IV — Speck of color on curved line below center of "M."

*Perf. 11¾, 12½*
**1877-82** **Litho.** **Unwmk.**
**1** A1 1p blue (III), Perf 11¾ ('79) 32.50
**1a** A1 1p sky blue (III) ('79) 350.00 *140.00*
**2** A1 2p lilac rose (IV) ('82) 25.00
**3c** A1 3p vermilion (I) 300.00 *350.00*
**3d** A1 3p vermilion, rough perfs (III), Perf 11¾ 65.00
**4** A1 6p lilac (III) ('79) 600.00 200.00
**4c** A1 6p violet (III), Perf 11¾ ('79) 55.00 *100.00*
**5** A1 9p yel brn (IV) ('80) 80.00 *160.00*
**6** A1 1sh org yel (II) ('78) 125.00 125.00
**6c** A1 1sh golden yellow (II), Perf 11¾ ('79) 75.00 *400.00*
**7** A1 2sh deep brown (III) ('79) 450.00 *500.00*
**7d** A1 2sh dp brn (III), Perf 11¾ ('79) 200.00
**8** A1 5sh emerald green (III) ('79) 2,500. 1,000.
**8a** A1 5sh yel green (III), Perf 11¾ ('79) 550.00

Values are for the least expensive varieties. For detailed listings, see the *Scott Classic Specialized Catalogue.*

The 1p often has a period after "PENNY." The 2p was never placed in use since the Samoa Express service was discontinued late in 1881.

Imperforates of this issue are proofs.

Sheets of the first issue were not perforated around the outer sides. All values except the 2p were printed in sheets of 10 (2x5). The 1p, 3p and 6p type I and the 1p type III were also printed in sheets of 20 (4x5), and six stamps on each of these sheets were perforated all around. These are the only varieties of the original stamps which have not one or two imperforate edges. The 2p was printed in sheets of 21 (3x7) and five stamps in the second row were perforated all around. The 2p was also reprinted in sheets of 40, which are much more common than the sheets of 21.

*Reprints are of type IV and nearly always perforated on all sides. They have a spot of*

*color at the edge of the panel below the "M." This spot is not on any originals except the 9p, the original of which may be distinguished by having a rough blind perf. 12. The 2p does show a spot of color.*

Forgeries exist.

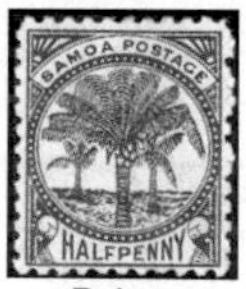
Palms
A2

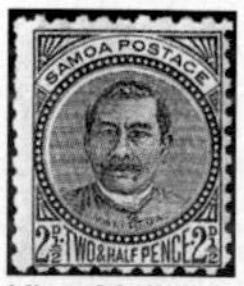
King Malietoa Laupepa
A3

**Perf. 11, 12x11½ (#14, 17a), 12½ (#16, 18)**

**1886-1900 Typo. Wmk. 62**

**9d** A2 ½p brown vio 2.00 *10.00*
**10** A2 ½p dull bl grn ('99) 2.00 *40.00*
**11f** A2 1p bluish green ('97) 2.00 *10.00*
**12** A2 1p red brown 2.00 *20.00*
**13g** A2 2p br yellow ('97) 2.00 *20.00*
**14** A3 2½p rose ('92) 100.00 10.00
**14b** A3 2½p rose 2.00 *40.00*
**15** A3 2½p blk, perf. 10x11 ('96) 1.50 *3.00*
**16** A2 4p blue ('86) 20.00 20.00
**16f** A2 4p dp blue ('00) 2.00 *100.00*
**17a** A2 6p maroon ('90) 40.00 10.00
**17e** A2 6p maroon ('00) 2.00 *100.00*
**18** A2 1sh rose carmine ('86) 20.00 10.00
*a.* Perf 12½, diagonal half used on cover ('95) *300.00*
**18g** A2 1sh carmine ('00) 2.00
**19h** A2 2sh6p dp purple ('98) 5.00 *20.00*
*i.* Vert. pair, imperf. btwn. 500.00

Three forms of watermark 62 are found on stamps of type A2:

1 — Wide "N Z" and wide star, 6mm apart (used 1886-87).

2 — Wide "N Z" and narrow star, 4mm apart (1890).

3 — Narrow "NZ" and narrow star, 7mm apart (1890-1900). The 2½p has only the 3rd form.

Nos. 9-19 exist in various printings, perf 11, 12½ and 12x11½. Values are for the least expensive varieties. For detailed listings, see the *Scott Classic Specialized Catalogue*.

For surcharges or overprints on stamps or types of design A2 see Nos. 20-22, 24-38.

No. 16b Handstamp Surcharged in Black or Red:

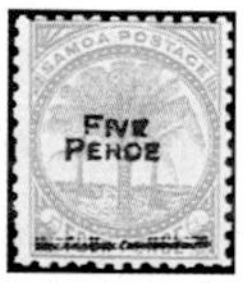
a

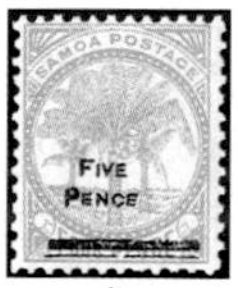
b

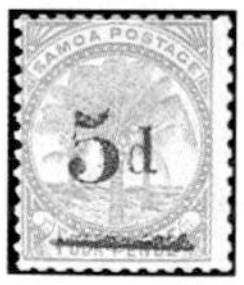
c

**1893 Perf. 12x11½**

**20** A2(a) 5p on 4p blue (#16c) 40.00 —
*a.* On 4p deep blue (#16b) 100.00 100.00
**21** A2(b) 5p on 4p blue (#16c) 40.00 *100.00*
*a.* On 4p deep blue (#16b) 100.00 100.00
**22** A2(c) 5p on 4p blue (#16c) (R) 10.00 *20.00*
*a.* On 4p deep blue (#16b) 10.00 *40.00*
*Nos. 20-22 (3)* 90.00 *120.00*

As the surcharges on Nos. 20-21 were handstamped in two steps and on No. 22 in three steps, various varieties exist.

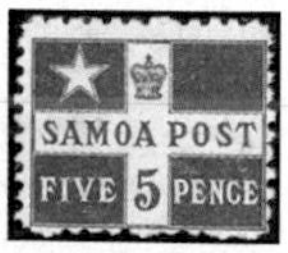
Flag Design — A7

**1894-95 Typo. Perf. 11½x12**

**23** A7 5p vermilion 20.00 10.00
*a.* Perf. 11 ('95) 100.00 20.00

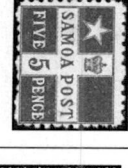

Types of 1887-1895 Surcharged in Blue, Black, Red or Green:

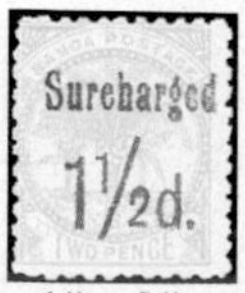
1½p, 2½p

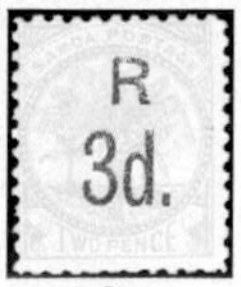
3p

### Handstamped Surcharges

**1895 Perf. 11**

**24** A2 1½p on 2p orange (Bl) 20.00 *10.00*
*a.* 1½p on 2p brn org, perf 12x11½ (Bl) 40.00 20.00
*b.* 1½p on 2p yellow, "2" ends with vertical stroke 5.00 *20.00*
**25** A2 3p on 2p orange (Bk) 5.00 5.00
*a.* 3p on 2p brn org, perf. 12x11½ (Bk) 40.00 40.00
*b.* 3p on 2p org yellow (Bk) 2.00 40.00
*c.* Vert. pair, imperf. btwn. 500.00

### Typographed Surcharges (#26 Handstamped)

**1898-1900 Perf. 11**

**26** A2 2½p on 1sh rose (Bk), hand-stamped surcharge 10.00 *20.00*
*a.* As #26, double surcharge 100.00 100.00
*b.* 2½p, typo surcharge 5.00 *40.00*
**27** A2 2½p on 2sh6p vio (Bk) 5.00 *40.00*
**28** A2 2½p on 1p bl grn (R) 2.00 *40.00*
*a.* Inverted surcharge 200.00 *200.00*
**29** A2 2½p on 1sh rose car (R) 5.00 *40.00*
**30** A2 3p on 2p dp red org (G) 10.00 20.00
*Nos. 26-30 (5)* 32.00 160.00

No. 30 was a reissue, available for postage. The surcharge is not as tall as the 3p surcharge illustrated, which is the surcharge on No. 25.

Stamps of 1886-99 Overprinted in Red or Blue

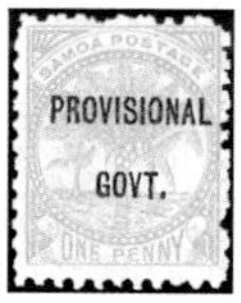

**1899**

**31** A2 ½p dull bl green (R) 2.00 *20.00*
**32** A2 1p red brown (Bl) 2.00 *20.00*
**33** A2 2p br orange (R) 2.00 *20.00*
*a.* 2p deep ocher 2.00 *40.00*
**34** A2 4p blue (R) 2.00 *40.00*
**35** A7 5p dp scarlet (Bl) 2.00 *20.00*
**36** A2 6p maroon (Bl) 2.00 *20.00*
**37** A2 1sh rose car (Bl) 2.00 *40.00*
**38** A2 2sh6p mauve (R) 2.00 *40.00*
*Nos. 31-38 (8)* 16.00 *220.00*

In 1900 the Samoan islands were partitioned between the US and Germany. The part which became American has since used US stamps.

### Issued under German Dominion

Stamps of Germany Overprinted

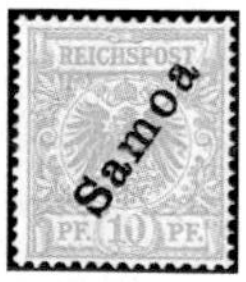

**1900 Unwmk. Perf. 13½x14½**

**51** A10 3pf dark brown 6.50 *8.75*
**52** A10 5pf green 8.00 *11.50*
**53** A11 10pf carmine 6.50 *11.50*
**54** A11 20pf ultra 12.50 *20.00*
**55** A11 25pf orange 26.00 *52.50*
**56** A11 50pf red brown 26.00 *50.00*
*Nos. 51-56 (6)* 85.50 *154.25*

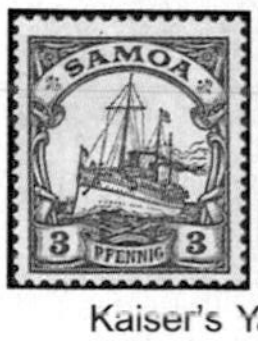
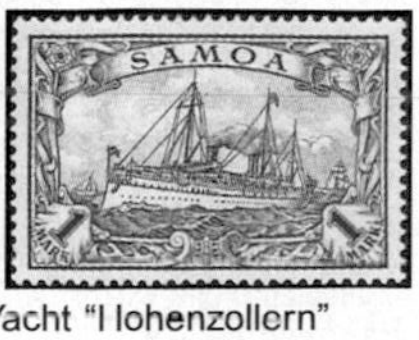
Kaiser's Yacht "Hohenzollern"
A12 A13

**1900 Typo. Perf. 14**

**57** A12 3pf brown .70 .75
**58** A12 5pf green .70 .75
**59** A12 10pf carmine .70 .75
**60** A12 20pf ultra .70 *1.50*
**61** A12 25pf org & blk, *yel* .75 *8.00*
**62** A12 30pf org & blk, *sal* 1.00 *7.00*
**63** A12 40pf lake & blk 1.00 *8.00*
**64** A12 50pf pur & blk, *sal* 1.00 *8.75*
**65** A12 80pf lake & blk, *rose* 1.90 *20.00*

**Engr.**

**66** A13 1m carmine 2.40 *40.00*
**67** A13 2m blue 3.25 *65.00*
**68** A13 3m black vio 4.75 *100.00*
**69** A13 5m slate & car 95.00 *350.00*
*Nos. 57-69 (13)* 113.85 *610.50*

**1915 Wmk. 125 Typo. Perf. 14**

**70** A12 3pf brown .65
**71** A12 5pf green .90
**72** A12 10pf carmine .90

**Perf. 14½x14**

**Engr.**

**73** A13 5m slate & car 14.50

Nos. 70-73 were never put in use.

### Issued under British Dominion

#57-69 Surcharged:

On A12

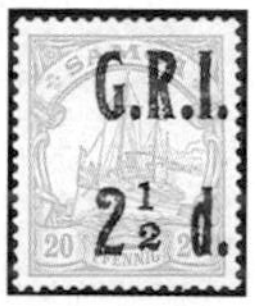

On A13

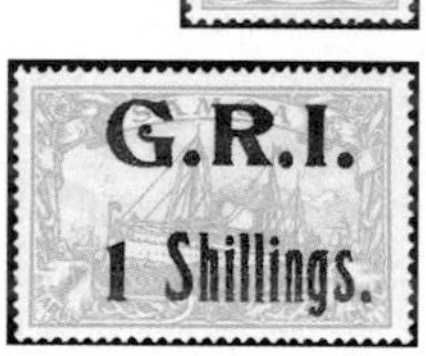

**1914 Unwmk. Perf. 14**

**101** A12 ½p on 3pf brown 22.50 9.00
*a.* Double surcharge 600.00 450.00
*b.* Fraction bar omitted 50.00 30.00
*c.* Comma after "I" 550.00 375.00
**102** A12 ½p on 5pf green 45.00 10.00
*a.* Double surcharge 600.00 450.00
*b.* Fraction bar omitted 110.00 55.00
*d.* Comma after "I" 325.00 225.00
**103** A12 1p on 10pf car 90.00 40.00
*a.* Double surcharge 600.00 450.00
**104** A12 2½p on 20pf ultra 35.00 10.00
*a.* Fraction bar omitted 70.00 37.50
*b.* Inverted surcharge 725.00 650.00
*c.* Double surcharge 600.00 500.00
*d.* Commas after "I" 375.00 310.00
**105** A12 3p on 25pf org & blk, *yel* 50.00 40.00
*a.* Double surcharge 700.00 550.00
*b.* Comma after "I" 4,000. 800.00
**106** A12 4p on 30pf org & blk, *sal* 100.00 62.50
**107** A12 5p on 40pf lake & blk 100.00 70.00
**108** A12 6p on 50pf pur & blk, *sal* 60.00 35.00
*a.* Inverted "9" for "6" 165.00 110.00
*b.* Double surcharge 750.00 700.00
**109** A12 9p on 80pf lake & blk, *rose* 200.00 100.00

**Perf. 14½x14**

**110** A13 1sh on 1m car ("1 Shillings.") 3,000. *3,500.*
*a.* "1 Shilling." *9,500.* *7,000.*
**111** A13 2sh on 2m blue 3,000. 2,750.
**112** A13 3sh on 3m blk vio 1,200. 1,000.
*a.* Double surcharge *7,500.* *8,500.*
**113** A13 5sh on 5m slate & car 1,000. 900.00

G.R.I. stands for Georgius Rex Imperator.

The 3d on 30pf and 4d on 40pf were produced at a later time.

Stamps of New Zealand Overprinted in Red or Blue:

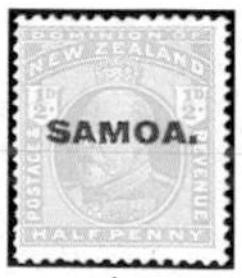
k

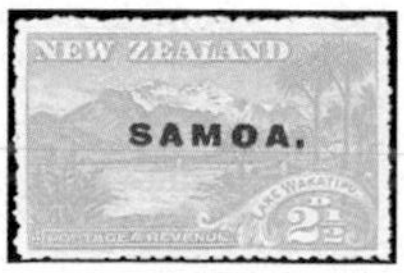
m

**Perf. 14, 14x13½, 14x14½**

**1914, Sept. 29 Wmk. 61**

**114** A41(k) ½p yel grn (R) .60 .25
**115** A42(k) 1p carmine .60 .20
**116** A41(k) 2p mauve (R) .75 *.80*
**117** A22(m) 2½p blue (R) 1.40 *1.50*
**118** A41(k) 6p car rose, perf. 14x14½ 1.40 *1.50*
*a.* Perf. 14x13½ 17.00 20.00
**119** A41(k) 1sh vermilion 4.25 *13.50*
*Nos. 114-119 (6)* 9.00 *17.75*

Overprinted Type "m"

**1914-25 Perf. 14, 14½x14**

**120** PF1 2sh blue (R) 5.50 *7.00*
**121** PF1 2sh6p brown (Bl) 5.00 *8.50*
**122** PF1 3sh vio (R) ('22) 13.50 *40.00*
**123** PF1 5sh green (R) 12.00 *11.00*
**124** PF1 10sh red brn (Bl) 20.00 *27.50*
**125** PF2 £1 rose (Bl) 55.00 *50.00*
**126** PF2 £2 vio (R) ('25) 400.00
*Nos. 120-126 (7)* 511.00
*Nos. 120-125 (6)* *144.00*

Postal use of the £2 is questioned.

Overprinted Type "k"

**Perf. 14x13½, 14x14½**

**1916-19 Typo.**

**127** A43 ½p yellow grn (R) .50 *.60*
**128** A47 1½p gray blk (R) ('17) .40 .20
**129** A47 1½p brn org (R) ('19) .30 .25
**130** A43 2p yellow (R) ('18) 1.25 .20
**131** A43 3p chocolate (Bl) 1.25 *9.50*

**Engr.**

**132** A44 2½p dull blue (R) .55 .25
**133** A45 3p violet brn (Bl) .50 *.75*
**134** A45 6p carmine rose (Bl) 1.50 *2.25*
**135** A45 1sh vermilion (Bl) 1.75 1.00
*Nos. 127-135 (9)* 8.00 15.00

Overprinted Type "k"

On New Zealand Victory Issue of 1919

**1920, June Perf. 14**

**136** A48 ½p yellow grn (R) 4.25 *10.00*
**137** A49 1p carmine (Bl) 3.00 *10.00*
**138** A50 1½p brown org (R) 1.60 *9.25*
**139** A51 3p black brn (Bl) 8.75 *9.00*
**140** A52 6p purple (R) 5.00 *7.50*
**141** A53 1sh vermilion (Bl) 14.50 11.00
*Nos. 136-141 (6)* 37.10 56.75

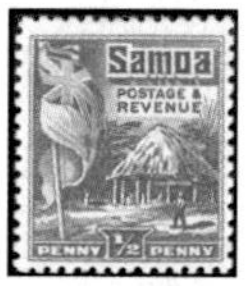
British Flag and Samoan House — A22

**1921, Dec. 23 Engr. Perf. 14x13½**

**142** A22 ½p green 4.50 *2.00*
*a.* Perf. 14x14½ 1.75 *20.00*
**143** A22 1p lake 5.00 .50
*a.* Perf. 14x14½ 2.75 2.00
**144** A22 1½p orange brn, perf. 14x14½ 9.50 *8.25*
*a.* Perf. 14x13½ 4.00 *37.50*
**145** A22 2p yel, perf. 14x14½ 11.50 2.00
*a.* Perf. 14x13½ 5.00 *7.00*
**146** A22 2½p dull blue 2.00 *6.75*
**147** A22 3p dark brown 2.00 *5.00*
**148** A22 4p violet 2.00 *4.00*
**149** A22 5p brt blue 2.00 *7.00*
**150** A22 6p carmine rose 2.00 *6.50*
**151** A22 8p red brown 2.25 *10.00*
**152** A22 9p olive green 2.50 *27.00*
**153** A22 1sh vermilion 2.25 *24.00*
*Nos. 142-153 (12)* 47.50 *103.00*

For overprints see Nos. 163-165.

New Zealand Nos. 182-183 Overprinted Type "m" in Red

**1926-27 Perf. 14½x14**

**154** A56 2sh dark blue 5.00 *12.00*
*a.* 2sh blue ('27) 10.00 *35.00*
**155** A56 3sh deep violet 11.00 *30.00*
*a.* 3sh violet ('27) 45.00 *75.00*

Issued: 2sh, Nov.; 3sh, Oct.; #154a, 155a, 11/10.

New Zealand Postal-Fiscal Stamps, Overprinted Type "m" in Blue or Red

**1932, Aug. Perf. 14**

**156** PF5 2sh6p brown 15.00 *35.00*
**157** PF5 5sh green (R) 22.50 *37.50*
**158** PF5 10sh lake 45.00 *80.00*
**159** PF5 £1 pink 55.00 *100.00*
**160** PF5 £2 violet (R) *650.00*
**161** PF5 £5 dk bl (R) *1,600.*
*Nos. 156-159 (4)* 137.50 *252.50*

See Nos. 175-180, 195-202, 216-219.

**Silver Jubilee Issue**

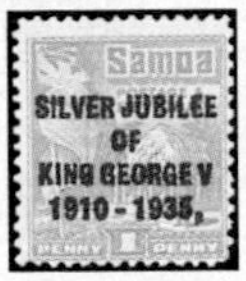

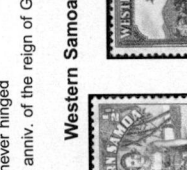

Stamps of 1921 Overprinted in Black

**1935, May 7** *Perf. 14x13½*

**163** A22 1p lake .40 *.50*
**a.** Perf. 14x14½ 92.50 *175.00*
**164** A22 2½p dull blue .75 *1.25*
**165** A22 6p carmine rose 3.00 *5.50*
*Nos. 163-165 (3)* 4.15 7.25
Set, never hinged 8.50

25th anniv. of the reign of George V.

**Western Samoa**

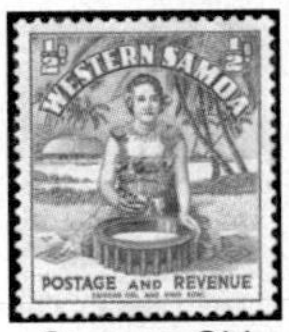

Samoan Girl and Kava Bowl — A23

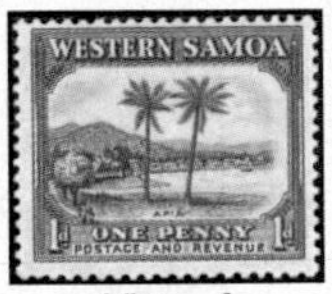

View of Apia — A24

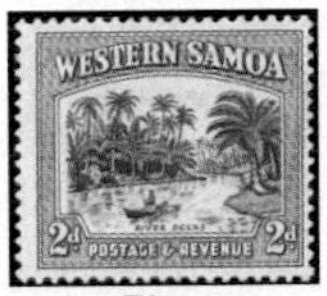

River Scene — A25

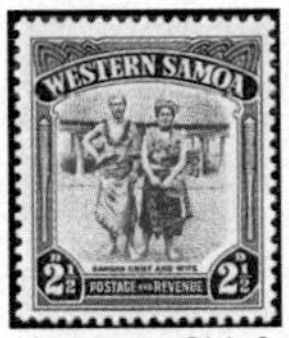

Samoan Chief and Wife — A26

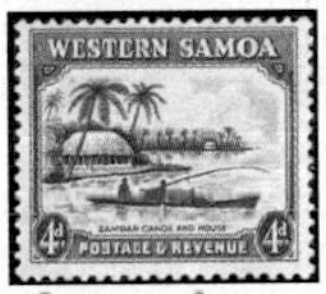

Samoan Canoe and House — A27

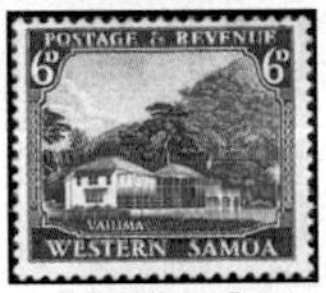

"Vailima," Stevenson's Home — A28

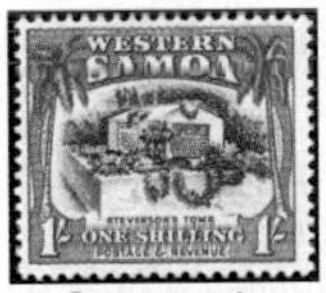

Stevenson's Tomb — A29

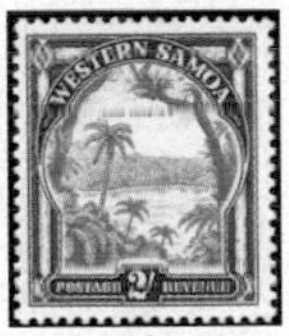

Lake Lanuto'o — A30

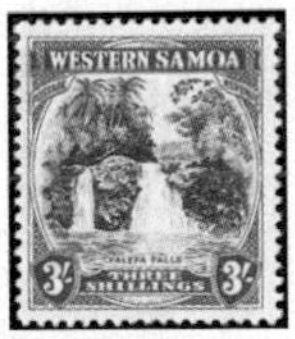

Falefa Falls — A31

*Perf. 14x13½, 13½x14*

**1935, Aug. 7** Engr. Wmk. 61

**166** A23 ½p yellow grn .20 .40
**167** A24 1p car lake & blk .20 .20
**168** A25 2p red org & blk, perf. 14 2.75 2.50
**a.** Perf. 13½x14 3.50 *4.00*
**169** A26 2½p dp blue & blk .25 .25
**170** A27 4p blk brn & dk gray .50 .50
**171** A28 6p plum .70 .50
**172** A29 1sh brown & violet .50 .80
**173** A30 2sh red brn & yel grn 1.00 1.25
**174** A31 3sh org brn & brt bl 1.75 *3.00*
*Nos. 166-174 (9)* 7.85 9.40
Set, never hinged 16.00

See Nos. 186-188.

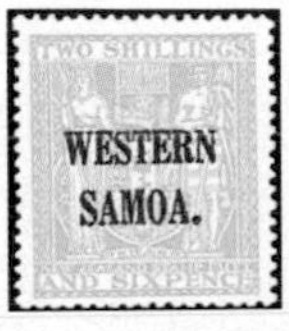

Postal-Fiscal Stamps of New Zealand Overprinted in Blue or Carmine

**1935** *Perf. 14*

**175** PF5 2sh6p brown 7.00 *18.00*
**176** PF5 5sh green 13.50 *25.00*
**177** PF5 10sh dp carmine 62.50 *85.00*
**178** PF5 £1 pink 62.50 *110.00*
**179** PF5 £2 violet (C) 180.00 *400.00*
**180** PF5 £5 dk bl (C) 250.00 *525.00*
*Nos. 175-180 (6)* 575.50 *1,163.*

See Nos. 195-202, 216-219.

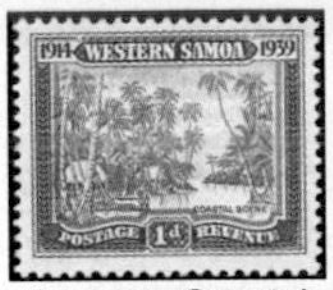

Samoan Coastal Village — A32

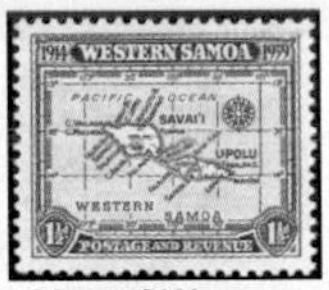

Map of Western Samoa — A33

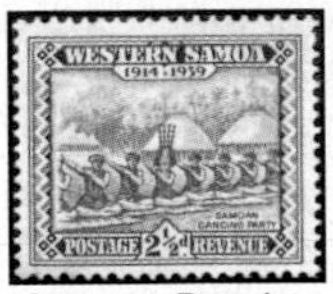

Samoan Dancing Party A34

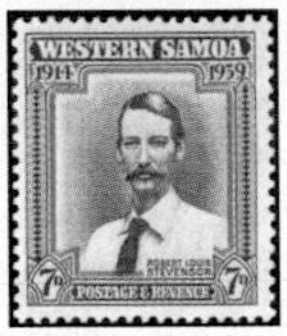

Robert Louis Stevenson A35

*Perf. 13½x14*

**1939, Aug. 29** Engr. Wmk. 253

**181** A32 1p scar & olive .60 .35
**182** A33 1½p copper brn & bl 1.00 .90
**183** A34 2½p dk blue & brn 1.00 1.00

*Perf. 14x13½*

**184** A35 7p dp sl grn & vio 3.50 3.00
*Nos. 181-184 (4)* 6.10 5.25
Set, never hinged 11.00

25th anniv. of New Zealand's control of the mandated territory of Western Samoa.

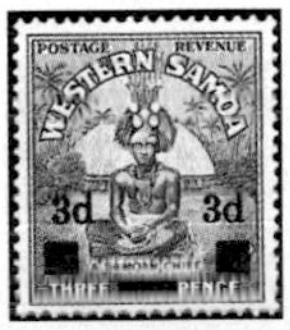

Samoan Chief — A36

**1940, Sept. 2** *Perf. 14x13½*

**185** A36 3p on 1½p brown .60 .30
Never hinged .75

Issued only with surcharge. Examples without surcharge are from printer's archives.

Types of 1935 and A37

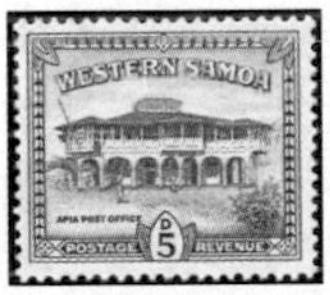

Apia Post Office — A37

**1944-49** Wmk. 253 *Perf. 14*

**186** A23 ½p yellow green .30 16.50
**187** A25 2p red orange & blk 1.50 5.00
**188** A26 2½p dp blue & blk ('48) 2.50 27.50

*Perf. 13½x14*

**189** A37 5p dp ultra & ol brn ('49) 1.00 .75
*Nos. 186-189 (4)* 5.30 49.75
Set, never hinged 11.00

Issue date: 5p, June 8.

**Catalogue values for unused stamps in this section, from this point to the end of the section, are for Never Hinged items.**

**Peace Issue**

New Zealand Nos. 248, 250, 254, and 255 Overprinted in Black or Blue

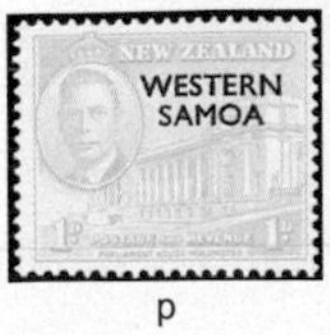

p

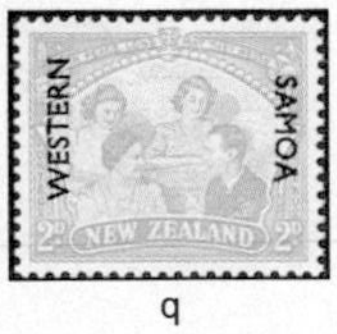

q

**1946, June 1** *Perf. 13x13½, 13½x13*

**191** A94(p) 1p emerald .25 .20
**192** A96(q) 2p rose violet (Bl) .25 .20
**193** A100(p) 6p org red & red brn .30 .20
**194** A101(p) 8p brn lake & blk (Bl) .30 .20
*Nos. 191-194 (4)* 1.10 .80

Stamps and Type of New Zealand, 1931-50 Overprinted Like Nos. 175-180 in Blue or Carmine

**1945-50** Wmk. 253 *Perf. 14*

**195** PF5 2sh6p brown 4.00 *10.00*
**196** PF5 5sh green 6.50 *12.00*
**197** PF5 10sh car ('48) 19.00 17.00
**198** PF5 £1 pink ('48) 75.00 *125.00*
**199** PF5 30sh choc ('48) 125.00 *200.00*
**200** PF5 £2 violet (C) 140.00 *225.00*
**201** PF5 £3 lt grn ('50) 175.00 *300.00*
**202** PF5 £5 dk bl (C) ('50) 300.00 *400.00*

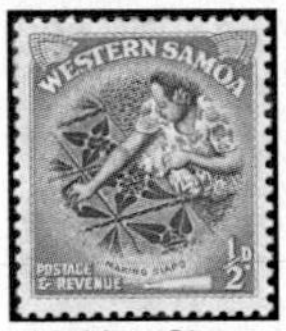

Making Siapo Cloth — A38

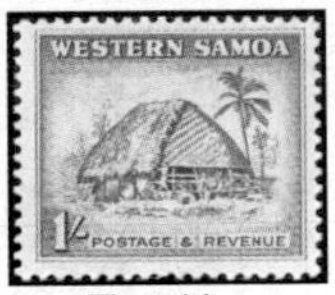

Thatching Hut — A40

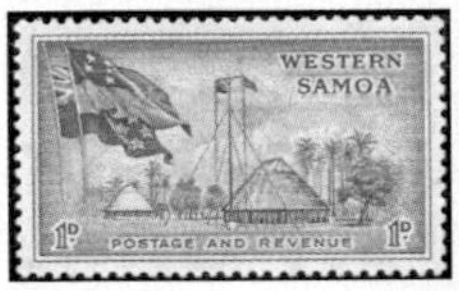

Western Samoa and New Zealand Flags, Village A39

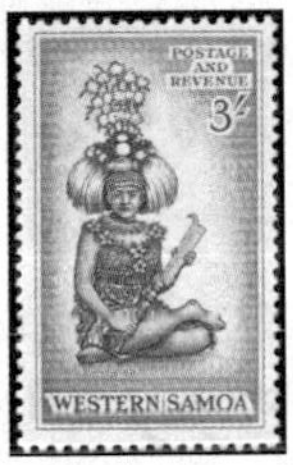

Samoan Chieftainess — A41

Designs: 2p, Western Samoa seal. 3p, Aleisa Falls (actually Malifa Falls). 5p, Manumea (tooth-billed pigeon). 6p, Fishing canoe. 8p, Harvesting cacao. 2sh, Preparing copra.

*Perf. 13, 13½x13*

**1952, Mar. 10** Engr. Wmk. 253

**203** A38 ½p org brn & claret .20 *1.60*
**204** A39 1p green & olive .20 .20
**205** A38 2p deep carmine .20 .20
**206** A39 3p indigo & blue .45 .25
**207** A38 5p dk grn & org brn 6.50 .75
**208** A39 6p dp rose pink & bl .80 .25
**209** A39 8p rose carmine .35 .30
**210** A40 1sh blue & brown .20 .25
**211** A39 2sh yellow brown 1.10 .50
**212** A41 3sh ol gray & vio brn 2.75 3.25
*Nos. 203-212 (10)* 12.75 7.55

**Coronation Issue**

Types of New Zealand 1953

**1953, May 25** Photo. *Perf. 14x14½*

**214** A113 2p brown .50 .50
**215** A114 6p slate black 1.25 1.25

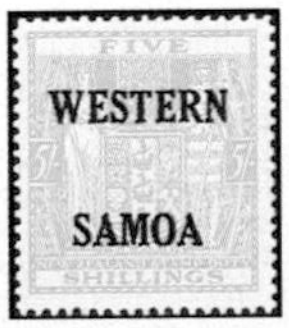

Type of New Zealand 1944-52 Overprinted in Blue or Carmine

Wmk. 253

**1955, Nov. 14** Typo. *Perf. 14*

**216** PF5 5sh yellow green 11.00 *16.00*
**217** PF5 10sh carmine rose 11.00 *21.00*
**218** PF5 £1 dull rose 18.00 *30.00*
**219** PF5 £2 violet (C) 85.00 *125.00*
*Nos. 216-219 (4)* 125.00 *192.00*

Redrawn Types of 1952 and

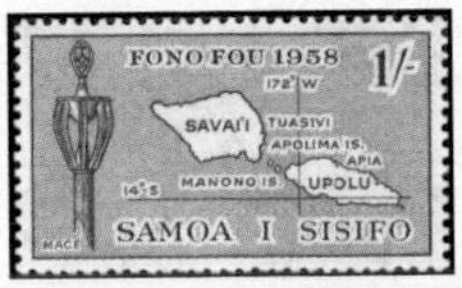

Map of Western Samoa and Mace A42

Designs: 4p, as 1p. 6p, as 2p.

Inscribed: "Fono Fou 1958" and "Samoa I Sisifo"

*Perf. 13½x13, 13*

**1958, Mar. 21** Engr. Wmk. 253

**220** A39 4p rose carmine .20 .20
**221** A38 6p dull purple .20 .20
**222** A42 1sh light violet blue .70 .30
*Nos. 220-222 (3)* 1.10 .70

**Independent State**

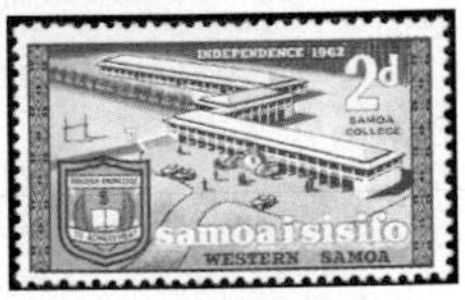

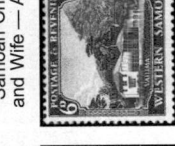

Samoa College A43

Designs: 1p, Woman holding ceremonial mat, vert. 3p, Public Library. 4p, Fono House (Parliament). 6p, Map of Western Samoa, ship and plane. 8p, Faleolo airport. 1sh, Talking chief with fly whisk, vert. 1sh3p, Government House, Vailima. 2sh6p, Flag of Western Samoa. 5sh, State Seal.

Wmk. 253

**1962, July 2** Litho. *Perf. 13½*

**223** A43 1p car & brown .20 .20
**224** A43 2p org, lt grn, red & brown .20 .20
**225** A43 3p blue, grn & brn .20 .20
**226** A43 4p dk grn, bl & car .35 .35
**227** A43 6p yel, grn & ultra .45 .45
**228** A43 8p blue & emerald .55 .55
**229** A43 1sh brt grn & brn .85 .85
**230** A43 1sh3p blue & emerald 1.10 1.10
**231** A43 2sh6p vio blue & red 1.65 1.65
**232** A43 5sh olive gray, red & dk blue 4.00 4.00
*Nos. 223-232 (10)* 9.55 9.55

Western Samoa's independence. See #242-247.

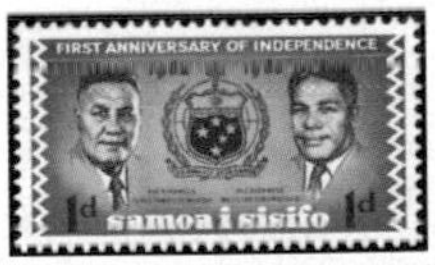

Tupua Tamasese Mea'ole, Malietoa Tanumafili II and Seal — A44

**1963, Oct. 1** Photo. *Perf. 14*

**233** A44 1p green & blk .20 .20
**234** A44 4p dull blue & blk .20 .20
**235** A44 8p carmine rose & blk .20 .20
**236** A44 2sh orange & blk .20 .20
*Nos. 233-236 (4)* .80 .80

First anniversary of independence.

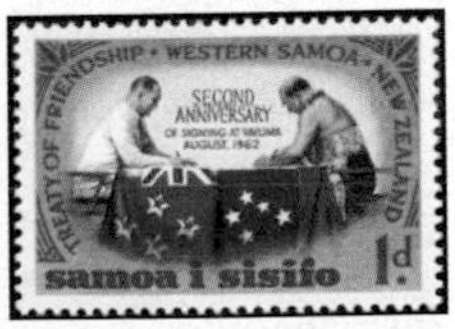

Signing of Western Samoa-New Zealand Friendship Treaty A45

**1964, Sept. 1** Unwmk. *Perf. 13½*

**237** A45 1p multicolored .20 .20
**238** A45 8p multicolored .20 .20
**239** A45 2sh multicolored .25 .20
**240** A45 3sh multicolored .25 *.35*
*Nos. 237-240 (4)* .90 .95

2nd anniv. of the signing of the Treaty of Friendship between Western Samoa and New Zealand. Signers: J. B. Wright, N. Z. High Commissioner for Western Pacific, and Fiame Mata'afa, Prime Minister of Western Samoa.

Type of 1962

Wmk. 355

**1965, Oct. 4** Litho. *Perf. 13½*

**242** A43 1p carmine & brn .40 *1.00*
**243** A43 3p blue, grn & brn 37.50 8.00
**244** A43 4p dk grn, bl & car .40 *1.00*
**245** A43 6p yel, grn & ultra .50 .45

SAMOA

246 A43 8p blue & emerald .55 .20
247 A43 1sh brt green & brn .70 1.00
Nos. 242-247 (6) 40.05 11.65
For surcharge see No. B1.

Aerial View
of Deep-
Sea Wharf
A46

8p, 2sh, View of Apia harbor & deep-sea
wharf.

**1966, Mar. 2** **Photo.** **Perf. 13½**
251 A46 1p multicolored .20 .20
252 A46 8p multicolored .30 .30
253 A46 2sh multicolored .30 .25
254 A46 3sh multicolored .50 .35
Nos. 251-254 (4) 1.20 1.00

Opening of Western Samoa's first deep-sea
wharf at Apia.

Inauguration of WHO Headquarters,
Geneva — A47

Design: 8p, 1sh, WHO building and flag.

**1966, July 4** **Wmk. 355**
255 A47 3p gray, ultra & bister .35 .35
256 A47 4p multicolored .45 .45
257 A47 6p lt olive grn, pur & grn .55 .55
258 A47 1sh multicolored .50 .50
Nos. 255-258 (4) 2.85 2.85

Tuatagaloa
L.S.,
Minister of
Justice
A48

Designs: 8p, F.C.F. Nelson, Minister of
Works, Marine and Civil Aviation. 3sh,
To'omata T. L., Minister of Lands. 3sh,
Fa'alava'au Galu, Minister of Post Office,
Radio and Broadcasting.

**1967, Jan. 16** **Photo.** **Wmk. 355**
259 A48 3p violet & sepia .20 .20
260 A48 8p blue & sepia .20 .20
261 A48 2sh olive & sepia .30 .30
262 A48 3sh lilac rose & sepia .50 .50
Nos. 259-262 (4) 1.20 1.20

Fifth anniversary of Independence.

Wattled Honey-Eater — A50

**1967, May 16** **Perf. 14½**
263 A49 8p multicolored .30 .30
264 A49 1sh multicolored .40 .40

Centenary of Mulinu'u as Government Seat.

Samoan
Fales,
1900, and
Fly Whisk
A49

Samoa i Sisifo

CENTENARY OF MULINU'U AS THE SEAT OF GOVERNMENT

1sh, Fono House (Parliament) and mace.

Designs: 4p, 1sh, WHO building and flag.

---

pigeon, 50s, Island thrush, $1, Samoan fantail.
$2, Mao (gymnomyza samoensis), $4,
Samoan white-eye (zosterops samoensis).

**1967, July 10** **Photo.** **Wmk. 355**
Birds in Natural Colors
Size: 37x24mm
265 A50 1s black & lt brown .20 .20
266 A50 2s lt ultra, blk & brn .20 .20

267 A50 3s blk, lt brn & emer .20 .20
268 A50 5s lilac, blk & vio bl .20 .20
269 A50 7s blk, vio bl & gray .20 .20
270 A50 10s Prus blue & blk .20 .20
271 A50 20s dk gray & blue .50 .50
272 A50 50s pink, blk & dk grn 2.00 .50
273 A50 50s brn, blk & lt grn 1.00 .50
274 A50 $1 yellow & black 2.00 .75

**1969**
274A A50 $2 blk & lt grnsh bl 4.25 8.00
274B A50 $4 dp orange & blk 2.50 42.50
62.45 54.80
Nos. 265-274B (½) 62.45 54.80
For surcharge see No. 294.

Designs: 7s, Leprosarium. 20s, Mobile X-
ray unit. 25s, Apia Hospital.

**1967, Dec. 1** **Litho.** **Perf. 14**
275 A51 3s multicolored .20 .20
276 A51 7s multicolored .40 .40
277 A51 20s multicolored .50 .50
278 A51 25s multicolored 1.30 1.30
Nos. 275-278 (4)

South Pacific Health Service.

Child
Care
A51

SAMOA I SISIFO

Thomas
Trood
A52

Portraits: 7s, Dr. Wilhelm Solf. 20s, John C.
Williams. 25s, Fritz Marquardt.

**1968, Jan. 1** **Unwmk.** **Perf. 13½**
279 A52 3s multicolored .20 .20
280 A52 7s multicolored .40 .30
281 A52 20s multicolored .40 .30
282 A52 25s multicolored 1.10 1.10
Nos. 279-282 (4)

Sixth anniversary of independence.

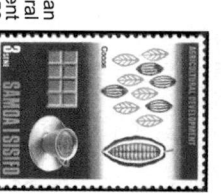

Samoan
Agricultural
Development
A53

**1968, Feb. 15** **Photo.** **Perf. 13x12½**
283 A53 3s Cocoa .20 .20
284 A53 5s Breadfruit .20 .20
285 A53 10s Copra .30 .30
286 A53 20s Bananas .40 .40
Nos. 283-286 (4) 1.10 1.10

Curio
Vendors,
Pago
Pago
A54

20s, Palm trees at the shore. 25s, A'Umi
Beach.

---

**1968, Apr. 22** **Photo.** **Perf. 14½x14**
287 A54 7s multicolored .20 .20
288 A54 20s multicolored .35 .35
289 A54 25s multicolored .40 .40
Nos. 287-289 (3)

South Pacific Commission, 21st anniv.

Bougainville and Compass
Rose — A55

Designs: 3s, Map showing Western Samoa
Archipelago and Bougainville's route. 20s,
Bougainville. 25s, Bougainville's ships La
Boudeuse and L'Etoile.

**1968, June 10** **Litho.** **Perf. 14**
290 A55 3s brt blue & blk .50 .50
291 A55 7s ocher & blk .20 .20
292 A55 20s grnsh blk, brt rose .20 .20
& grn
293 A55 25s brt lil, vio, blk & org 1.55 1.55
Nos. 290-293 (4)

200th anniv. of the visit of Louis Antoine de
Bougainville (1729-1811) to Samoa.

No. 270 Surcharged with New Value,
Three Bars and:
"1928-1968"

KINGSFORD-SMITH / TRANSPACIFIC
FLIGHT

**1968, June 13** **Photo.** **Perf. 14x14½**
294 A50 20s on 10s multicolored .35 .35

40th anniv. of the 1st Transpacific flight
under Capt. Charles Kingsford-Smith (Oakland, CA to Brisbane, Australia, via Honolulu
and Fiji).

Human
Rights
Flame
and
Globe
A56

**1968, Aug. 26** **Photo.** **Perf. 14½x14**
295 A56 7s multicolored .20 .20
296 A56 20s multicolored .35 .35
297 A56 25s multicolored .45 .45
Nos. 295-297 (3) 1.00 1.00

International Human Rights Year, 1968.

SAMOA I SISIFO

Martin Luther
King, Jr. — A57

**1968, Sept. 23** **Litho.** **Perf. 14**
298 A57 7s green & black .20 .20
299 A57 20s brt rose lil & blk .40 .40

Rev. Dr. Martin Luther King, Jr. (1929-68),
American civil rights leader.

Polynesian
Madonna — A58

**1968, Oct. 12** **Wmk. 355**
300 A58 1s olive & multi .20 .20
301 A58 3s multicolored .20 .20
302 A58 20s crimson & multi .20 .20
303 A58 30s dp orange & multi .40 .40
Nos. 300-303 (4) 1.00 1.00

Christmas 1968.

---

**1969, Jan. 20** **Unwmk.** **Perf. 14**
304 A59 2s brt blue & multi .45 .45
305 A59 7s multicolored .70 .70
306 A59 20s yellow & multi 1.25 1.25
307 A59 30s multicolored 1.60 1.60
Nos. 304-307 (4) 4.00 4.00

Seventh anniversary of independence.

Frangipani — A59

Flowers: 7s, Chinese hibiscus. 20s,
Red ginger. 30s, Cananium odoratum.

R. L. Stevenson and Silver from
"Treasure Island" — A60

Robert Louis Stevenson and: 7s, Stewart
and Balfour on the moor from "Kidnapped."
20s, "Doctor Jekyll and Mr. Hyde." 22s, Archie
Weir and Christiana Elliot from "Weir of
Hermiston."

**1969, Apr. 21** **Litho.** **Perf. 14x13½**
308 A60 3s gray & multi .40 .40
309 A60 7s gray & multi .60 .60
310 A60 20s gray & multi .60 .60
311 A60 22s gray & multi 2.00 2.00
Nos. 308-311 (4) 2.00 2.00

75th anniv. of the death of Robert Louis Stevenson, who is buried in Samoa.

SAMOA I SISIFO

Weight Lifting — A61

**1969, July 21** **Photo.** **Perf. 13½x13**
312 A61 3s shown .20 .30
313 A61 20s Sailing .30 .30
314 A61 25s Boxing .90 .90
Nos. 312-314 (3)

3rd Pacific Games, Port Moresby, Papua
and New Guinea, Aug. 13-23.

SAMOA HONOURS U.S. MOON ASTRONAUTS

American Astronaut on Moon,
Splashdown and Map of Samoan
Islands — A62

**1969, July 24** **Photo.**
315 A62 7s red, blk, silver & grn .20 .20
316 A62 20s car, blk, sil & ultra .40 .40

US astronauts. See note after US No. C76.

---

Birds of Western Samoa: 2s, Pacific pigeon.
3s, Samoan starling. 5s, Samoan broadbill.
7s, Red-headed parrot finch. 10s, Purple
swamp hen. 20s, Barn owl. 25s, Tooth-billed

SAMOA

Asau Wharf, Savaii — A75

Designs: 8s, Parliament Building. 10s, Mothers' Center. 22s, Portraits of Tupua Tamasese Mea'ole and Malietoa Tanumafili II, and view of Vailima.

**1972, Jan. 10    Litho.    Wmk. 355    Perf. 13x13½**

| 357 | A75 | 1s bright pink & multi | .20 | .20 |
|---|---|---|---|---|
| 358 | A75 | 8s lilac & multi | .20 | .25 |
| 359 | A75 | 10s green & multi | .25 | .25 |
| 360 | A75 | 22s multicolored | .60 | .60 |
| | | Nos. 357-360 (4) | 1.25 | 1.25 |

10th anniversary of independence.

---

Commission Members' Flags — A76

Designs: 7s, Atoafouvale Misimoa, Secretary-General, 1970-71 and Commission flag. 8s, Headquarters Building, Noumea, New Caledonia, horiz. 10s, Flag of Samoa, flag and map of South Pacific Commission area, horiz.

**1972, Mar. 17    Perf. 11x11½, 13½x11**

| 361 | A76 | 3s ultra & multi | .20 | .20 |
|---|---|---|---|---|
| 362 | A76 | 7s yellow, black & ultra | .25 | .25 |
| 363 | A76 | 8s multicolored | .30 | .30 |
| 364 | A76 | 10s lt green & multi | .35 | .35 |
| | | Nos. 361-364 (4) | 1.10 | 1.10 |

South Pacific Commission, 25th anniv.

---

Sunset and Ships — A77

Designs: 8s, Sailing ships Arend, Thienhoven and Africaansche Galey in storm. 10s, Outlijger canoe and Roggeveen's ships. 30s, Hemispheres with exploration route and map of Samoan Islands. All horiz.

**1972, June 14    Size: 85x25mm**

| 365 | A77 | 2s car rose & multi | .20 | .20 |
|---|---|---|---|---|
| 366 | A77 | 3s violet blue & multi | .40 | .30 |
| 367 | A77 | 10s ultra & multi | .45 | .40 |

**Size: 85x25mm**

| 368 | A77 | 30s ocher & multi | 1.75 | 1.10 |
|---|---|---|---|---|
| | | Nos. 365-368 (4) | 2.80 | 2.00 |

250th anniv. of Jacob Roggeveen's Pacific voyage and discovery of Samoa in June 1722.

---

Bull Conch A78

**1972-75    Litho.    Size: 41x24mm    Perf. 14½**

| 369 | A78 | 1s shown | .25 | .25 |
|---|---|---|---|---|
| 370 | A78 | 2s Rhinoceros beetle | .25 | .25 |
| 371 | A78 | 4s Skipjack (fish) | .25 | 1.00 |
| 372 | A78 | 4s Painted crab | .25 | .25 |
| 373 | A78 | 5s Butterflyfish | .30 | .25 |
| 374 | A78 | 7s Samoan monarch | 1.50 | .75 |
| 375 | A78 | 10s Triton shell | 2.00 | .75 |

---

Souvenir Sheet

Longboat in Apia Harbor, Samoa #3 and US #3 — A70

**1971, Mar. 12    Photo.    Perf. 11½**

Granite Paper

| 343 | A70 | 70s blue & multi | 2.40 | 2.40 |

INTERPEX, 13th Intl. Stamp Exhib., NYC, Mar. 12-14.

---

Siva Dance A71

Tourist Publicity: 7s, Samoan cricket game. 8s, Hideaway Resort Hotel. 10s, Aggie Grey and Aggie's Hotel.

**1971, Aug. 9    Wmk. 355    Litho.    Perf. 14**

| 344 | A71 | 5s orange brn & multi | .50 | .50 |
|---|---|---|---|---|
| 345 | A71 | 7s orange brn & multi | 1.00 | .60 |
| 346 | A71 | 8s orange brn & multi | 1.00 | .45 |
| 347 | A71 | 10s orange brn & multi | 1.00 | .75 |
| | | Nos. 344-347 (4) | 3.50 | 2.00 |

---

A73

Samoan Legends, carved by Sven Ortquist: 3s, Queen Salamasina. 8s, Lu and his sacred hens (Samoa). 10s, God Tagaloa fishing Samoan islands of Upolu and Savaii from the sea. 22s, Mt. Vaea and Pool of Tears.

A72

**1971, Sept. 20    Perf. 14x13½**

| 348 | A72 | 3s dark violet & multi | .20 | .20 |
|---|---|---|---|---|
| 349 | A72 | 8s multicolored | .20 | .20 |
| 350 | A72 | 10s dark blue & multi | .25 | .25 |
| 351 | A72 | 22s dark blue & multi | .65 | .55 |
| | | Nos. 348-351 (4) | 1.30 | 1.15 |

See Nos. 399-402.

---

**1971, Oct. 4    Perf. 14x13½**

Christmas: 2s, 3s, Virgin and Child, by Giovanni Bellini. 20c, 30c, Virgin and Child with St. Anne and St. John the Baptist, by Leonardo da Vinci.

| 352 | A73 | 2s blue & multi | .20 | .20 |
|---|---|---|---|---|
| 353 | A73 | 3s black & multi | .20 | .20 |
| 354 | A73 | 20s yellow & multi | .55 | .65 |
| 355 | A73 | 30s dark red & multi | .65 | .65 |
| | | Nos. 352-355 (4) | 1.60 | 1.60 |

---

Samoan Islands, Scales of Justice A74

**1972, Jan. 10    Photo.    Perf. 11½x12**

| 356 | A74 | 10s light blue & multi | .40 | .35 |

1st So. Pacific Judicial Conf., Samoa, Jan. 1972.

---

"Peace for the World" by Frances B. Eccles — A67

Designs: 1s, Kendal's chronometer and Cook's sextant. 20s, Capt. Cook bust, in profile. 30s, Capt. Cook, island scene and "Endeavour," horiz.

**1970, Sept. 14    Litho.    Wmk. 355    Perf. 14x14½    Size: 25x41mm**

| 329 | A66 | 1s silver, dp car & blk | .35 | .25 |
|---|---|---|---|---|
| 330 | A66 | 2s multicolored | .60 | .40 |
| 331 | A66 | 20s gold, black & ultra | 1.40 | 1.00 |

**Perf. 14½x14    Size: 83x25mm**

| 332 | A66 | 30s multicolored | 3.00 | 2.00 |
|---|---|---|---|---|
| | | Nos. 329-332 (4) | 5.35 | 3.65 |

Bicentenary of Capt. James Cook's exploration of South Pacific.

---

**1970, Oct. 26    Photo.    Perf. 13½    Unwmk.**

Christmas: 3s, Samoan coat of arms and Holy Family, by Werner Erich Jahnke. 20s, Samoan Mother and Child, by F. B. Eccles. 30s, Prince of Peace, by Sister Melane Fe'ao.

| 333 | A67 | 2s gold & multi | .20 | .20 |
|---|---|---|---|---|
| 334 | A67 | 3s gold & multi | .20 | .20 |
| 335 | A67 | 20s gold & multi | .50 | .40 |
| 336 | A67 | 30s gold & multi | .70 | .60 |
| a. | | Souvenir sheet of 4, #333-336 | 1.60 | 1.40 |
| | | Nos. 333-336 (4) | 2.25 | 2.25 |

---

Pope Paul VI A68

**1970, Nov. 29    Litho.    Wmk. 355    Perf. 14**

| 337 | A68 | 8s Prus blue & black | .20 | .20 |
|---|---|---|---|---|
| 338 | A68 | 20s deep plum & black | .45 | .35 |

Visit of Pope Paul VI, Nov. 29, 1970.

---

Lumberjack A69

**1971, Feb. 1    Litho.    Perf. 14x13½, 13½x14    Unwmk.**

Designs: 8s, Woman and tractor in clearing, horiz. 20s, Log and saw carrier, horiz. 22s, Logging and ship.

| 339 | A69 | 3s multicolored | .20 | .20 |
|---|---|---|---|---|
| 340 | A69 | 8s multicolored | .30 | .20 |
| 341 | A69 | 20s multicolored | .60 | .30 |
| 342 | A69 | 22s multicolored | .75 | .40 |
| | | Nos. 339-342 (4) | 1.85 | 1.10 |

Development of the timber industry on Savaii Island by the American Timber Company of Potlatch.

---

Holy Family by El Greco A63

Christmas (Paintings): 1s, Virgin and Child, by Murillo. 20s, Nativity by El Greco. 30s, Virgin and Child (from Adoration of the Kings), by Velazquez.

**1969, Oct. 13    Unwmk.    Perf. 14**

| 317 | A63 | 1s gold, red & multi | .20 | .20 |
|---|---|---|---|---|
| 318 | A63 | 3s gold, red & multi | .35 | .35 |
| 319 | A63 | 20s gold, red & multi | .55 | .55 |
| 320 | A63 | 30s gold, red & multi | 2.00 | 2.00 |
| a. | | Souvenir sheet of 4, #317-320 | 1.30 | 1.30 |
| | | Nos. 317-320 (4) | | |

---

Seventh Day Adventists' Sanatorium, Apia — A64

7s, Father Louis Violette, R. C. Cathedral, Apia. 20s, Church of Latter Day Saints (Mormon), Tuasivi, Safotulafai, vert. 22s, John Williams, London Missionary Soc. Church, Sapapali'i.

**1970, Jan. 19    Litho.    Wmk. 355**

| 321 | A64 | 2s brown, blk & gray | .20 | .20 |
|---|---|---|---|---|
| 322 | A64 | 7s violet, blk & bister | .20 | .20 |
| 323 | A64 | 10s rose, blk & lt violet | .35 | .35 |
| 324 | A64 | 22s olive, blk & bistor | .40 | .40 |
| | | Nos. 321-324 (4) | 1.15 | 1.15 |

Eighth anniversary of independence.

---

U.S.S. Nipsic A65

Designs: 5s, Wreck of German ship Adler. 10s, British ship Calliope in storm. 20s, Apia after hurricane.

**1970, Apr. 27    Perf. 13½x14**

| 325 | A65 | 5s multicolored | .40 | .30 |
|---|---|---|---|---|
| 326 | A65 | 7s multicolored | .50 | .35 |
| 327 | A65 | 10s multicolored | .85 | .60 |
| 328 | A65 | 20s multicolored | 1.60 | 1.10 |
| | | Nos. 325-328 (4) | 3.35 | 2.35 |

The great Apia hurricane of 1889.

| 376 | A78 | 20s | Jewel beetle | 1.00 | .25 |
| 377 | A78 | 50s | Spiny lobster | 1.50 | 2.00 |

**Size: 29x45mm**

**Perf. 14x13½**

| 378 | A78 | $1 | Hawk moth | 6.00 | 4.75 |
| 378A | A78 | $2 | Green turtle | 5.50 | 2.75 |
| 378B | A78 | $4 | Black marlin | 5.25 | 7.00 |
| 378C | A78 | $5 | Green tree liz- | | |
| | | | ard | 7.00 | 10.00 |
| | | Nos. 369-378C (13) | | 31.05 | 30.25 |

Issued: 1s-$1, Oct. 18, 1972; $2, June 18, 1973; $4, Mar. 27, 1974, $5, June 30, 1975.

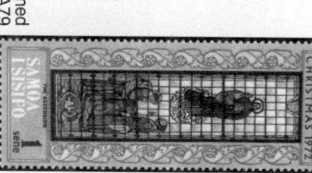

CHRISTMAS 1972

SAMOA I SISIFO 1 SENE

Ascension, Stained
Glass Window — A79

Stained Glass Windows in Apia Churches:
4s, Virgin and Child. 10s, St. Andrew blessing
Samoan canoe. 30s, The Good Shepherd.

**1972, Nov. 1　　Perf. 14x14½**

| 379 | A79 | 1s | ocher & multi | .20 | .25 |
| 380 | A79 | 4s | gray & multi | .30 | .30 |
| 381 | A79 | 10s | dull green & multi | .90 | .90 |
| 382 | A79 | 30s | blue & multi | 2.25 | 2.25 |
| a. | | Souvenir sheet of 4, #379-382 | | 1.60 | 1.60 |

Christmas.

BOY SCOUT MOVEMENT

SAMOA I SISIFO 2 SENE

Boy Scouts of Samoa.

Scouts
Saluting
Flag,
Emblems
A80

**1973, Jan. 29　　Wmk. 355**

| 383 | A80 | 2s | shown | .20 | .20 |
| 384 | A80 | 3s | First aid | .20 | .20 |
| 385 | A80 | 4s | Pitching tent | .40 | .40 |
| 386 | A80 | 20s | Action song | 1.80 | 1.80 |
| | | Nos. 383-386 (4) | | | |

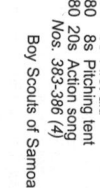

SAMOA I SISIFO 2 SENE

**1973, Aug. 20　　Perf. 14x13½**

| 387 | A81 | 2s | green & multi | .20 | .20 |
| 388 | A81 | 8s | multicolored | .25 | .25 |
| 389 | A81 | 20s | brown & multi | .55 | .55 |
| 390 | A81 | 22s | vermilion & multi | .65 | .65 |
| | | Nos. 387-390 (4) | | 1.65 | 1.65 |

WHO, 25th anniv.: 8s, Baby clinic. 20s, Filariasis research. 22s, Family welfare.

Apia General
Hospital — A81

"A Prince is
Born," by
Jahnke — A82

**1973, Oct. 15　　Litho.　　Perf. 14**

| 391 | A82 | 3s | blue & multi | .20 | .20 |
| 392 | A82 | 4s | purple & multi | .30 | .30 |
| 393 | A82 | 10s | red & multi | .95 | .95 |
| 394 | A82 | 30s | blue & multi | 2.00 | 2.00 |
| a. | | Souvenir sheet of 4, #391-394 | | 1.65 | 1.65 |

Christmas: 4s, "Star of Hope," by Fiasili Keil. 10s, "Mother and Child," by Ernesto Coter. 30s, "The Light of the World," by Coter.

---

SAMOA I SISIFO 8 SENE

10th British Commonwealth Games, Christchurch, New Zealand, Jan. 24-Feb. 2.

Boxing
and
Games'
Emblem
A83

**1974, Jan. 24　　Wmk. 355**

| 395 | A83 | 8s | shown | .20 | .20 |
| 396 | A83 | 10s | Weight lifting | .30 | .30 |
| 397 | A83 | 20s | Lawn bowling | .65 | .65 |
| 398 | A83 | 30s | Lawn bowling | .90 | .90 |
| | | Nos. 395-398 (4) | | 2.05 | 2.05 |

Legends Type of 1971

Samoan Legends, Wood Carvings by Sven Ortquist: 2s, Tigilau and dove. 8s, Pili with his sons and famous fish net. 20s, The girl Sina and the eel which became the coconut tree. 30s, Nafanua who returned from the spirit world to free her village.

**1974, Aug. 13　　Wmk. 355　　Perf. 14**

| 399 | A72 | 2s | lemon & multi | .20 | .20 |
| 400 | A72 | 8s | rose red & multi | .65 | .65 |
| 401 | A72 | 20s | yellow grn & multi | .95 | .95 |
| 402 | A72 | 30s | lt violet & multi | 2.00 | 2.00 |
| | | Nos. 399-402 (4) | | | |

SAMOA I SISIFO 8 SENE

Faleolo Airport — A84

Designs: 20s, Apia Wharf. 22s, Early post office, Apia. 50s, William Willis, raft "Age Unlimited" and route from Callao, Peru, to Tully, Western Samoa.

**1974, Sept. 4　　Unwmk.**

**Size: 47x29mm**

| 403 | A84 | 8s | multicolored | .20 | .20 |
| 404 | A84 | 20s | multicolored | .45 | .45 |
| 405 | A84 | 22s | multicolored | .60 | .60 |

**Size: 86x29mm**

| 406 | A84 | 50s | multicolored | 1.25 | 1.25 |
| | | Souvenir sheet of 1, perf. 13 | | 1.75 | 1.75 |
| | | Nos. 403-406 (4) | | 2.50 | 2.50 |

Cent. of UPU. The 8s is inscribed "Air Mail," 20s, "Sea Mail", 22s, "Raft Mail."

SAMOA I SISIFO 3 SENE

Holy Family, by Sebastiano — A85

Christmas: 4s, Virgin and Child with Saints, by Lotto. 10s, Virgin and Child with St. John, by Titian. 30s, Adoration of the Shepherds, by Rubens.

**1974, Nov. 18　　Litho.　　Perf. 13x13½**

| 407 | A85 | 3s | ocher & multi | .20 | .20 |
| 408 | A85 | 4s | fawn & multi | .25 | .25 |
| 409 | A85 | 10s | dull green & multi | .80 | .80 |
| 410 | A85 | 30s | blue & multi | 1.40 | 1.40 |
| a. | | Souvenir sheet of 4, #407-410 | | 1.45 | 1.45 |

Samoa I Sisifo

Winged
Passion
Flower
A86

**1976, Jan. 20　　Litho.**

**Perf. 13½x14**

| 428 | A90 | 7s | salmon & multi | .20 | .20 |
| 429 | A90 | 8s | green & multi | .25 | .25 |
| 430 | A90 | 20s | lilac & multi | .60 | .60 |
| 431 | A90 | 22s | blue & multi | .65 | .65 |

20s, Gardenias, vert. 22s, Lecythidaceae, vert. 30s, Malay apple.

---

SAMOA I SISIFO 8 SENE

Joyita
Loading at
Apia
A87

17th INTERPEX Phil. Exhib., NYC, 3/14-16.

**1975, Mar. 14　　Photo.　　Perf. 13**

| 415 | A87 | 1s | multicolored | .20 | .20 |
| 416 | A87 | 8s | multicolored | .45 | .45 |
| 417 | A87 | 20s | multicolored | 1.25 | 1.25 |
| 418 | A87 | 22s | multicolored | 1.55 | 1.55 |
| 419 | A87 | 50s | multicolored | 2.65 | 2.65 |
| a. | | Souvenir sheet of 5, #415-419 | | 2.75 | 2.75 |

Designs: 8s, Joyita, Samoa and Tokelau Islands. 20s, Joyita sinking. Oct. 1955. 22s, Rafts in storm. 50s, Plane discovering wreck.

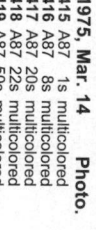

SAMOA I SISIFO 8 SENE

Pate
Drum — A88

Mother and Child,
by Meleane
Fe'ao — A89

**1975, Sept. 30　　Litho.　　Perf. 14½x14**

| 420 | A88 | 8s | shown | .50 | .50 |
| 421 | A88 | 20s | Lali drum | .50 | .50 |
| 422 | A88 | 22s | Logo drum | .55 | .55 |
| 423 | A88 | 30s | Pu shell horn | .75 | .75 |
| | | Nos. 420-423 (4) | | 2.00 | 2.00 |

Christmas (Paintings): 4s, Christ Child and Samoan flag, by Polataia Tuigamala. 10s, "A Star is Born," by Iosua Toafa. 30s, Mother and Child, by Ernesto Coter.

**1975, Nov. 25　　Litho.　　Wmk. 355**

| 424 | A89 | 3s | shown | .20 | .20 |
| 425 | A89 | 4s | multicolored | .20 | .20 |
| 426 | A89 | 10s | multicolored | .75 | .75 |
| 427 | A89 | 30s | multicolored | 1.40 | 1.40 |
| a. | | Souvenir sheet of 4, #424-427 | | | |

SAMOA I SISIFO 7 SENE

BICENTENARY OF INDEPENDENCE

THE BOSTON MASSACRE 1770

Boston
Massacre, by Paul
Revere — A90

8s, Declaration of Independence, by John Trumbull. 20s, The Sinking of the Bonhomme Richard, by J. L. G. Ferris. 22s, Wm. Pitt Addressing House of Commons, by R. A. Hickel. 50s, Battle of Princeton, by William Mercer.

---

SAMOA I SISIFO 10 SENE

Mullet
Fishing
A91

Bicentenary of American Independence.

**1976, Apr. 27　　Litho.　　Perf. 14½**

| 432 | A90 | 50s | yellow & multi | 1.50 | 1.50 |
| a. | | Souvenir sheet of 5, #428-432 + label | | 3.20 | 3.20 |
| | | Nos. 428-432 (5) | | | |

| 433 | A91 | 10s | shown | .20 | .20 |
| 434 | A91 | 12s | Fish traps | .25 | .25 |
| 435 | A91 | 20s | Fishermen | .45 | .45 |
| 436 | A91 | 50s | Net fishing | 1.90 | 1.90 |
| | | Nos. 433-436 (4) | | 1.00 | 1.00 |

INTERPHIL 1976

Samoan $100 Gold Coin with Paul
Revere and US Map — A92

**1976, May 29　　Unwmk.**

**Photo.　　Perf. 13**

| 437 | A92 | $1 | green & gold | 3.00 | 3.00 |

American Bicentennial and Interphil 76 Intl. Phil. Exhib., Philadelphia, PA, May 29-June 6.

SAMOA I SISIFO 10 SENE

1976 OLYMPICS

Boxing
A93

**1976, June 21　　Litho.**

**Perf. 14½x14**

| 438 | A93 | 10s | black & multi | .20 | .20 |
| 439 | A93 | 12s | dark brown & multi | .25 | .25 |
| 440 | A93 | 22s | dark purple & multi | .45 | .45 |
| 441 | A93 | 30s | dark blue & multi | 1.10 | 1.10 |
| | | Nos. 438-441 (4) | | 2.00 | 2.00 |

21st Olympic Games, Montreal, Canada, July 17-Aug. 1.

12s, Wrestling. 22s, Javelin. 50s, Weight lifting.

Mary and
Joseph on Road
to Bethlehem
A94

**1976, Oct. 18　　Litho.　　Perf. 14x13½**

| 442 | A94 | 3s | multicolored | .20 | .20 |
| 443 | A94 | 4s | multicolored | .20 | .20 |
| 444 | A94 | 5s | multicolored | .45 | .45 |
| 445 | A94 | 22s | multicolored | 2.10 | 2.10 |
| a. | | Souvenir sheet of 4, #442-445 | | 2.50 | 2.50 |
| | | Nos. 442-445 (4) | | 1.25 | 1.25 |

Christmas 1976: 5s, Nativity. 50s, Adoration of the Kings.

**Presentation of the Spurs of Chivalry — A95**

Designs: 12s, Queen and view of Apia. 32s, Royal Yacht Britannia and Queen. 50s, Queen leaving Westminster Abbey.

**1977, Feb. 11     Wmk. 355     Perf. 13½x14**

| | | | | |
|---|---|---|---|---|
| 446 | A95 | 12s multicolored | .20 | .20 |
| 447 | A95 | 26s multicolored | .35 | .35 |
| 448 | A95 | 32s multicolored | .55 | .55 |
| 449 | A95 | 50s multicolored | .85 | .85 |
| a. | | Souvenir sheet of 4, #446-449 (4) | 1.95 | 1.95 |

25th anniv. of the reign of Elizabeth II.

**Lindbergh and Spirit of St. Louis A96**

Designs: 22s, Map of transatlantic route and plane. 24s, Spirit of St. Louis in flight. 26s, Spirit of St. Louis taking off.

**1977, May 20     Litho.     Perf. 14**

| | | | | |
|---|---|---|---|---|
| 450 | A96 | 22s multicolored | .35 | .35 |
| 451 | A96 | 24s multicolored | .40 | .40 |
| 452 | A96 | 26s multicolored | .45 | .45 |
| 453 | A96 | 50s multicolored | .85 | .85 |
| a. | | Souvenir sheet of 4, #450-453 (4) | 2.05 | 2.05 |

Charles A. Lindbergh's solo transatlantic flight from New York to Paris, 50th anniv.

**Apia Automatic Telephone Exchange — A97**

Designs: 13s, Mulinuu radio terminal. 26s, Old wall and new dial telephones. 50s, Global communications (2 telephones and globe).

**1977, July 11     Litho.     Perf. 14**

| | | | | |
|---|---|---|---|---|
| 454 | A97 | 13s multicolored | .20 | .20 |
| 455 | A97 | 13s multicolored | .20 | .20 |
| 456 | A97 | 26s multicolored | .45 | .45 |
| 457 | A97 | 50s multicolored | .80 | .80 |
| a. | | Souvenir sheet of 4, #454-457 (4) | 1.65 | 1.65 |

Telecommunications.

**Samoa No. 3 and First Mail Notice — A98**

13s, Samoa #4 & 1881 cover. 26s, Samoa #1 & Chief Post Office, Apia. 50s, Samoa #4 & schooner "Energy," which carried 1st mail.

**1977, Aug. 29     Wmk. 355     Perf. 13½**

| | | | | |
|---|---|---|---|---|
| 458 | A98 | 12s multicolored | .20 | .20 |
| 459 | A98 | 13s multicolored | .20 | .20 |
| 460 | A98 | 26s multicolored | .40 | .40 |
| 461 | A98 | 50s multicolored | .80 | .80 |
| | | Nos. 458-461 (4) | 1.60 | 1.60 |

Samoan postage stamp centenary.

**Nativity — A99**

Christmas: 6s, People bringing gifts to Holy Family in Samoan hut. 26s, Virgin and Child. 50s, Stars over Christ Child.

**1977, Oct. 11     Litho.     Perf. 14**

| | | | | |
|---|---|---|---|---|
| 462 | A99 | 4s multicolored | .20 | .20 |
| 463 | A99 | 26s multicolored | .35 | .35 |
| 464 | A99 | 26s multicolored | 1.25 | 1.25 |
| 465 | A99 | 50s multicolored | 2.00 | 2.00 |
| a. | | Souvenir sheet of 4, #462-465 (4) | 2.00 | 2.00 |

**Polynesian Airlines' Boeing 737 — A100**

Aviation Progress: 24s, Kitty Hawk. 26s, Kingsford-Smith Fokker. 50s, Concorde.

**1978, Mar. 21     Litho.     Perf. 14**

| | | | | |
|---|---|---|---|---|
| 466 | A100 | 12s multicolored | .20 | .20 |
| 467 | A100 | 24s multicolored | .45 | .45 |
| 468 | A100 | 26s multicolored | .50 | .50 |
| 469 | A100 | 50s multicolored | .95 | .95 |
| a. | | Souvenir sheet of 4, #466-469, perf. 13½ (4) | 2.10 | 2.10 |
| | | Nos. 466-469 (4) | 2.10 | 2.10 |

**Turtle Hatchery, Aleipata — A101**

$1, Hawksbill turtle & Wildlife Fund emblem.

**1978, Apr. 14     Wmk. 355     Perf. 14½**

| | | | | |
|---|---|---|---|---|
| 470 | A101 | 24s multicolored | 4.50 | 1.50 |
| 471 | A101 | $1 multicolored | 15.00 | 5.00 |

Project to replenish endangered hawksbill turtles.

**Common Design Types** pictured following the introduction.

**Elizabeth II Coronation Anniversary Issue**

**Souvenir Sheet**

**Common Design Types**

**1978, Apr. 21     Unwmk.     Perf. 15**

| | | | | |
|---|---|---|---|---|
| 472 | | Sheet of 6 | 3.00 | 3.00 |
| a. | | CD326 26s King's lion | .45 | .45 |
| b. | | CD327 26s Elizabeth II | .45 | .45 |
| c. | | CD328 26s Pacific pigeon | .45 | .45 |

No. 472 contains 2 se-tenant strips of Nos. 472a-472c, separated by horizontal gutter with commemorative and descriptive inscriptions and showing central part of coronation procession with coach.

**Canadian and Samoan Flags — A102**

**Souvenir Sheet**

A104

**1978, June 9     Wmk. 355     Litho.     Perf. 14½**

| | | | | |
|---|---|---|---|---|
| 473 | A102 | $1 multicolored | 2.25 | 2.25 |

CAPEX Canadian Intl. Phil. Exhib., Toronto, June 9-18.

**Capt. James Cook — A103**

Designs: 24s, Cook's cottage, now in Melbourne, Australia. 26s, Old drawbridge over River Esk, Whitby, 1766-1833. 50s, Resolution and map of Hawaiian Islands.

**1978, Aug. 28     Litho.     Perf. 14½x14**

| | | | | |
|---|---|---|---|---|
| 474 | A103 | 12s multicolored | .25 | .25 |
| 475 | A103 | 24s multicolored | .55 | .55 |
| 476 | A103 | 26s multicolored | .70 | .70 |
| 477 | A103 | 50s multicolored | 1.40 | 1.40 |
| | | Nos. 474-477 (4) | 2.90 | 2.90 |

A105

Cowrie Shells: 1s, Thick-edged Cowrie. 2s, Isabella cowrie. 3s, Money cowrie. 4s, Eroded cowrie. 6s, Honey cowrie. 7s, Banded cowrie. 10s, Globe cowrie. 11s, Mole cowrie. 12s, Children's cowrie. 13s, Flag cone. 14s, Soldier cone. 24s, Cloth-of-gold cone. 26s, Lettered cone. 50s, Tiled cone. $1, Black marble cone. $2, Marlin-spike auger. $3, Scorpion spider conch. $5, Common harp.

**1978-80     Photo.     Unwmk.     Perf. 12½**

**Size: 31x24mm**

**Granite Paper**

| | | | | |
|---|---|---|---|---|
| 478 | A104 | 1s multicolored | .20 | .20 |
| 479 | A104 | 2s multicolored | .20 | .20 |
| 480 | A104 | 3s multicolored | .20 | .20 |
| 481 | A104 | 4s multicolored | .20 | .20 |
| 482 | A104 | 6s multicolored | .20 | .20 |
| 483 | A104 | 7s multicolored | .20 | .20 |
| 484 | A104 | 10s multicolored | .20 | .20 |
| 485 | A104 | 11s multicolored | .20 | .20 |
| 486 | A104 | 12s multicolored | .20 | .20 |
| 487 | A104 | 13s multicolored | .20 | .20 |
| 488 | A104 | 14s multicolored | .25 | .25 |
| 489 | A104 | 24s multicolored | .25 | .25 |
| 490 | A104 | 26s multicolored | .45 | .45 |
| 491 | A104 | 50s multicolored | .45 | .45 |
| 492 | A104 | $1 multicolored | .90 | .90 |

**Perf. 11½**

**Size: 36x26mm**

| | | | | |
|---|---|---|---|---|
| 493 | A104 | $2 multi (79) | 1.75 | 1.75 |
| 494 | A104 | $3 multi (79) | 3.00 | 3.00 |
| 494A | A104 | $5 multi ('80) | 7.50 | 7.50 |
| a. | | Souvenir sheet of 4, #478-494A (18) | 16.30 | 16.30 |

Issue dates: 1s-12s, Sept. 15. 13s-$1, Nov. 20. $2, $3, July 18. $5, Aug. 26.

**1978, Nov. 6     Wmk. 355     Litho.     Perf. 14**

Works by Dürer: 4s, The Virgin in Glory. 6s, Nativity. 26s, Adoration of the Kings. 50s, Annunciation.

| | | | | |
|---|---|---|---|---|
| 495 | A105 | 4s lt brown & blk | .20 | .20 |
| 496 | A105 | 6s grnsh blue & blk | .40 | .40 |
| 497 | A105 | 26s violet blue & blk | .40 | .40 |
| 498 | A105 | 50s purple & blk | .80 | .80 |
| a. | | Souvenir sheet of 4, #495-498 (4) | 1.75 | 1.75 |
| | | Nos. 495-498 (4) | 1.60 | 1.60 |

Christmas and for 450th death anniv. of Albrecht Dürer.


**Boy Carrying Coconuts A106**

Designs: 24s, Children leaving church on White Sunday. 26s, Children pumping water. 50s, Girl playing ukulele.

**1979, Apr. 10     Litho.     Perf. 14**

| | | | | |
|---|---|---|---|---|
| 499 | A106 | 12s multicolored | .20 | .20 |
| 500 | A106 | 24s multicolored | .40 | .40 |
| 501 | A106 | 26s multicolored | .45 | .45 |
| 502 | A106 | 50s multicolored | .95 | .95 |
| | | Nos. 499-502 (4) | 2.00 | 2.00 |

International Year of the Child.

**Charles W. Morgan A107**

**1979, May 29     Litho.     Perf. 13½**

| | | | | |
|---|---|---|---|---|
| 503 | A107 | 12s multicolored | .30 | .30 |
| 504 | A107 | 14s multicolored | .40 | .40 |
| 505 | A107 | 24s James T. Arnold | .65 | .65 |
| 506 | A107 | 50s Splendid | 1.40 | 1.40 |
| | | Nos. 503-506 (4) | 2.75 | 2.75 |

See Nos. 521-524, 543-546.

**Saturn V Launch — A108**

Designs: 14c, Landing module and astronaut on moon, horiz. 24s, Earth seen from moon. 26s, Astronaut on moon, horiz. 50s, Command Lunar and command modules. $1, Command module after splashdown, horiz.

**Perf. 14½x14, 14x14½     Wmk. 355**

**1979, June 20     Litho.     Perf. 12½**

| | | | | |
|---|---|---|---|---|
| 507 | A108 | 12s multicolored | .20 | .20 |
| 508 | A108 | 14s multicolored | .30 | .30 |
| 509 | A108 | 24s multicolored | .35 | .35 |
| 510 | A108 | 26s multicolored | .65 | .65 |
| 511 | A108 | 50s multicolored | 1.40 | 1.40 |
| 512 | A108 | $1 multicolored | 1.75 | 1.75 |
| a. | | Souvenir sheet | 3.10 | 3.10 |
| | | Nos. 507-512 (6) | | |

1st moon landing, 10th anniv.

**1979, Aug. 27     Perf. 14**

24s, Great Britain #2 with Maltese Cross postmark. 26s, Penny Black and Rowland Hill. $1, Great Britain #2 and Hill statue.

| | | | | |
|---|---|---|---|---|
| 513 | A109 | 12s multicolored | .20 | .20 |
| 514 | A109 | 24s multicolored | .25 | .25 |
| 515 | A109 | 26s multicolored | .30 | .30 |
| 516 | A109 | $1 multicolored | 1.10 | 1.10 |
| a. | | Souvenir sheet of 4, #513-516 (4) | 1.90 | 1.90 |
| | | Nos. 513-516 (4) | 1.85 | 1.85 |

Sir Rowland Hill (1795-1879), originator of penny postage.

**Anglican Church, Apia A110**

Samoan Churches: 6s, Congregational Christian Church, Leulumoega. 26s, Methodist Church, Piula. 50s, Protestant Church, Apia.

**1979, Oct. 22     Photo.     Perf. 12x11½**

| | | | | |
|---|---|---|---|---|
| 517 | A110 | 4s lt blue & blk | .20 | .20 |
| 518 | A110 | 6s lt yellow grn & blk | .20 | .20 |
| 519 | A110 | 26s dull yellow & blk | .40 | .40 |

520 A110 50s It lilac & blk .75 .75
a. Souvenir sheet of 4, #517-520 1.40 1.40
Nos. 517-520 (4) 1.55 1.55
Christmas.

**Ship Type of 1979**

1980, Jan. 22 Wmk. 355 Perf. 14 Litho.
521 A107 12s William Hamilton .25 .25
522 A107 14s California .30 .30
523 A107 24s Liverpool II .55 .55
524 A107 50s Two Brothers 1.10 1.10
Nos. 521-524 (4) 2.20 2.20

Map of Samoan Islands, Rotary Emblem A111

1980, Mar. 26 Photo. Perf. 14
525 A111 12s shown .50 .20
526 A112 13s shown .40 .60
527 A112 14s German flag, Dr. Wilhelm Solf, plaque .90 .20
528 A113 24s shown .90 .40
529 A113 26s Williams Memorial, Savaii .75 .50
530 A111 50s Emblem, Paul P. Harris, founder 1.25 1.50
Nos. 525-530 (6) 4.70 3.40

Rotary Intl., 75th anniv. (A111); arrival of Williams, missionary in Samoa, 150th anniv. (13s, 26s); raising of the German flag, 150th anniv. (14s, 24s).

Flag-raising Memorial — A113
Missionary Flag, John Williams, Plaque — A112

**Souvenir Sheet**

1980, May 6 Wmk. 355 Litho. Perf. 14
531 A114 $1 multicolored 2.00 2.00

Village and Long Boat — A114

**Queen Mother Elizabeth Birthday Issue**
**Common Design Type**
1980, Aug. 4 Litho.
532 CD330 50s multicolored .70 .70

---

**Souvenir Sheet**
Samoa No. 239, ZEAPEX Emblem — A115

1980, Aug. 23 Litho. Unwmk.
533 A115 $1 multicolored 2.00 2.00

ZEAPEX '80, New Zealand International Stamp Exhibition, Auckland, Aug. 23-31.

Afiamalu Satellite Earth Station A116

1980, Sept. 17 Litho. Granite Paper Perf. 11½
534 A116 12s multicolored .20 .20
535 A116 14s multicolored .20 .20
536 A116 24s multicolored .30 .30
537 A116 50s multicolored .70 .70
Nos. 534-537 (4) 1.40 1.40

**Souvenir Sheet**

1980, Sept. 29 Litho. Imperf.
538 A116 $2 multicolored 2.25 2.25

14s, Station, diff. 24s, Station, map of Samoa. 50s, Satellite sending waves to earth. $2, Samoa #536, Sydpex '80 emblem.
Sydpex '80 Natl. Phil. Exhib., Sydney.

**Ship Type of 1979**

1980, Oct. 28 Wmk. 355 Litho. Perf. 14
539 A117 8s multicolored .20 .20
540 A117 18s multicolored .30 .30
541 A117 27s multicolored .50 .50
542 A117 50s multicolored 1.40 1.40
a. Souvenir sheet of 4, #539-542 1.95 1.95
Nos. 539-542 (4) 1.20 1.20

Christmas (Paintings by Local Artists): 14s, Nativity, by Pasila Feata. 50s, Yuletide, by R.P. Alono.

The Savior, by John Poynton — A117

1981, Jan. 26 Ship Type of 1979 Perf. 14
543 A107 12s Ocean .25 .25
544 A107 18s Horatio .40 .40
545 A107 27s Calliope .60 .60
546 A107 32s Calypso .70 .70
Nos. 543-546 (4) 1.95 1.95

1981, Apr. 29 Wmk. 355 Litho. Perf. 14
547 A118 12s shown .25 .25
548 A118 13s Inauguration .20 .20
549 A118 27s Pres. & Mrs. Roosevelt .25 .25
550 A110 32s Atlantic convoy (Lend Lease Bill) .30 .30
551 A118 38s With stamp collection .35 .35
552 A118 $1 Campobello House .85 .85
Nos. 547-552 (6) 2.15 2.15

IYD: Scenes of Franklin D. Roosevelt.

Pres. Franklin Roosevelt and Hyde Park Home A118

---

Tusitala — A119
Hotel — A119

1981, June 29 Litho. Perf. 14½x14
553 A119 12s shown .20 .20
554 A119 18s Apia Harbor .30 .30
555 A119 27s Aggie Grey's Hotel .35 .35
556 A119 32s Ceremonial kava preparation .60 .60
557 A119 54s Piula Pool 1.65 1.65
Nos. 553-557 (5)

**Royal Wedding Issue**
**Common Design Type**
1981, July 22 Wmk. 355 Litho. Perf. 14
558 CD331 18s Bouquet .20 .20
559 CD331 32s Charles .65 .65
560 CD331 $1 Couple 1.05 1.05
Nos. 558-560 (3)

Tattooing Instruments A120

1981, Sept. 29 Litho. Perf. 13½x14
561 Strip of 4 1.75 1.75
a. A120 12s shown .20 .20
b. A120 18s 1st stage .30 .30
c. A120 27s Later stage
d. A120 $1 Tattooed man 1.10 1.10

Christmas — A121

1981, Nov. 30 Litho. Perf. 13½
562 A121 11s Milo tree blossom .20 .20
563 A121 15s Copper leaf .20 .20
564 A121 23s Yellow allamanda .25 .25
565 A121 23s Mango blossom 1.10 1.10
a. Souvenir sheet of 4, #562-565 2.25 2.25
Nos. 562-565 (4) 1.75 1.75

**Souvenir Sheet**
Christmas — A122
Philatokyo '81 Intl. Stamp Exhibition — A122

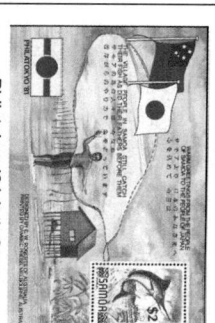

1981, Oct. 9 Litho. Perf. 14x13½
566 A122 $2 multicolored 2.25 2.25

250th Birth Anniv. of George Washington A123

---

20th Anniv. of Independence — A124

1982, Feb. 26 Litho. Perf. 14
567 A123 23s Pistol .25 .25
568 A123 23s Mt. Vernon .30 .30
569 A123 34s Portrait .45 .45
Nos. 567-569 (3)

**Souvenir Sheet**
570 A123 $1 Taking oath 1.25 1.25

1982, May 24 Litho. Perf. 13½x14
571 A124 18s Freighter Forum Samoa .50 .50
572 A124 23s Jet, routes 1.40 1.40
573 A124 25s Natl. Provident Fund building .55 .55
574 A124 $1 Intl. subscriber dialling system 2.00 2.00
Nos. 571-574 (4) 3.50 3.50

Scouting Year A125

1982, July 20 Wmk. 355 Perf. 14½
575 A125 5s Map reading .20 .20
576 A125 38s Salute .65 .65
577 A125 44s Rope bridge .75 .75
578 A125 $1 Troop 1.90 1.90
a. Souvenir sheet 3.00 3.00
Nos. 575-578 (4)

No. 578a contains one stamp similar to No. 578, 48x36mm.

12th Commonwealth Games, Brisbane, Australia, Sept. 30-Oct. 9 — A126

1982, Sept. 20 Wmk. 373 Perf. 14x14½
579 A126 23s Boxing .25 .25
580 A126 25s Hurdles .30 .30
581 A126 34s Weightlifting .40 .40
582 A126 $1 Lawn bowling 1.95 1.95
Nos. 579-582 (4)

**Christmas A127**

1982, Nov. 15 Litho. Wmk. 355
583 A127 11s multicolored .20 .20
584 A127 15s multicolored .30 .30
585 A127 38s multicolored .50 .50
586 A127 $1 multicolored 1.95 1.95
a. Souvenir sheet of 4, #583-586 2.00 2.00
Nos. 583-586 (4) 1.10 1.10

Children's Drawings: 11s, Flight into Egypt diff. 38s; $1, Virgin and Child, diff.

Commonwealth Day — A128

## SAMOA

**1983, Feb. 23  Perf. 13½x14  Wmk. 373**

| 587 | A128 | 14s Map | .20 | .20 |
|---|---|---|---|---|
| 588 | A128 | 29s Flag | .35 | .35 |
| 589 | A128 | 43s Harvesting copra | .50 | .50 |
| 590 | A128 | $1 Malietoa Tanumafili II | 1.10 | 1.10 |
| | | *Nos. 587-590 (4)* | 2.15 | 2.15 |

### Manned Flight Bicentenary and 50th Anniv. of Douglas Aircraft — A129

a, DC-1. b, DC-2. c, DC-3. d, DC-4. e, DC-5. f, DC-6. g, DC-7. h, DC-8. i, DC-9. j, DC-10.

**1983, June 7  Wmk. 373  Litho.**

| 591 | | Sheet of 10 | 6.75 | 6.75 |
|---|---|---|---|---|
| a.-j. | A129 | 32s any single | .65 | .65 |

### 7th South Pacific Games, Apia — A130

**1983, Aug. 29  Litho.  Perf. 14x14½**

| 592 | A130 | 8s Pole vault | .45 | .45 |
|---|---|---|---|---|
| 593 | A130 | 15s Basketball | .55 | .55 |
| 594 | A130 | 25c Tennis | .70 | .70 |
| 595 | A130 | 32s Weightlifting | 1.00 | 1.00 |
| 596 | A130 | 46s Boxing | 1.50 | 1.50 |
| 597 | A130 | 46s Soccer | 1.50 | 1.50 |
| 598 | A130 | 48s Golf | 1.75 | 1.75 |
| 599 | A130 | 56s Rugby | 1.90 | 1.90 |
| | | *Nos. 592-600 (8)* | 8.05 | 8.05 |

### Local Fruit — A131

**1983-84  Wmk. 373  Litho.  Perf. 14x13½**

| 600 | A131 | 1s Limes | .40 | .40 |
|---|---|---|---|---|
| 601 | A131 | 2s Star fruit | .40 | .40 |
| 602 | A131 | 3s Mangosteen | .40 | .40 |
| 603 | A131 | 4s Lychee | .40 | .40 |
| 604 | A131 | 7s Passion fruit | .40 | .40 |
| 605 | A131 | 8s Mangoes | .40 | .40 |
| 606 | A131 | 11s Papaya | .40 | .40 |
| 607 | A131 | 13s Pineapple | .45 | .45 |
| 608 | A131 | 14s Breadfruit | .45 | .45 |
| 609 | A131 | 15s Bananas | .45 | .45 |
| 610 | A131 | 21s Cashew nut | .50 | .50 |
| 611 | A131 | 25s Guava | .60 | .60 |
| 612 | A131 | 32s Water Melon | .70 | .70 |
| 613 | A131 | 48s Sasalapa | 1.10 | 1.10 |
| 614 | A131 | 56s Avocado | 1.25 | 1.25 |
| 615 | A131 | $1 Coconut | 2.25 | 2.25 |

**Perf. 13½**

| 616 | A131 | $2 Apples ('84) | 4.50 | 4.50 |
|---|---|---|---|---|
| 617 | A131 | $4 Grapefruit ('84) | 9.00 | 9.00 |
| 618 | A131 | $5 Oranges ('84) | 11.00 | 11.00 |
| | | *Nos. 600-618 (19)* | 35.00 | 35.00 |

Issued: 1s-15s, 9/28; 21s-$1, 11/30; $2-$5, 4/11. For overprint see No. 628.

### Boys' Brigade Centenary — A132

Miniature Sheet

**1983, Oct. 10  Perf. 14½**

| 619 | A132 | $1 multicolored | 3.50 | 3.50 |
|---|---|---|---|---|

### Togitogiga Falls, Upolu — A133

**1984, Feb. 15  Wmk. 373  Litho.  Perf. 14**

| 620 | A133 | 25s shown | .45 | .45 |
|---|---|---|---|---|
| 621 | A133 | 32s Flag | .55 | .55 |
| 622 | A133 | 48s Mulinu'u Point, Upolu | .80 | .80 |
| 623 | A133 | 56s Nu'utele Isld. | .95 | .95 |
| | | *Nos. 620-623 (4)* | 2.75 | 2.75 |

### Lloyd's List Issue
Common Design Type

**1984, May 24  Litho.  Wmk. 373  Perf. 14½x14**

| 624 | CD335 | 32s Apia Harbor | .30 | .30 |
|---|---|---|---|---|
| 625 | CD335 | 48s Apia hurricane, 1889 | .50 | .50 |
| 626 | CD335 | 60s Forum Samoa | .60 | .60 |
| 627 | CD335 | $1 Matua | 1.00 | 1.00 |
| | | *Nos. 624-627 (4)* | 2.40 | 2.40 |

**No. 615 Overprinted: "19th U.P.U. CONGRESS / HAMBURG 1984"**

**1984, June 7  Perf. 14x13½**

| 628 | A131 | $1 multicolored | 1.75 | 1.75 |
|---|---|---|---|---|

### Los Angeles Coliseum — A134

**1984, June 26  Litho.  Perf. 14½**

| 629 | A134 | 25s shown | .25 | .25 |
|---|---|---|---|---|
| 630 | A134 | 32s Weightlifting | .35 | .35 |
| 631 | A134 | 48s Boxing | .55 | .55 |
| 632 | A134 | $1 Running | 1.10 | 1.10 |
| a. | | Souvenir sheet of 4, #629-632 | 2.25 | 2.25 |
| | | *Nos. 629-632 (4)* | 2.25 | 2.25 |

1984 Summer Olympics and Samoa's first Olympic participation.

Souvenir Sheet

### Ausipex '84 — A135

**1984, Sept. 21  Litho.  Perf. 14**

| 633 | A135 | $2.50 Nomad N24 | 6.75 | 6.75 |
|---|---|---|---|---|

### Christmas — A136

The Three Virtues, by Raphael.

**1984, Nov. 7  Perf. 14½x14**

| 634 | A136 | 24s Faith | .45 | .45 |
|---|---|---|---|---|
| 635 | A136 | 35s Hope | .55 | .55 |
| 636 | A136 | $1 Charity | 1.75 | 1.75 |
| a. | | Souvenir sheet of 3, #634-636 | 4.00 | 4.00 |
| | | *Nos. 634-636 (3)* | 2.75 | 2.75 |

### Orchids — A137

**1985, Jan. 23  Unwmk.  Litho.  Perf. 14**

| 637 | A137 | 48s Dendrobium biflorum | .75 | .45 |
|---|---|---|---|---|
| 638 | A137 | 56s Dendrobium vaupelianum kraenzl | 1.00 | 1.00 |
| 639 | A137 | 67s Glomera montana | 1.25 | 1.25 |
| 640 | A137 | $1 Spathoglottis plicata | 1.75 | 1.75 |
| | | *Nos. 637-640 (4)* | 4.75 | 4.45 |

### Vintage Automobiles — A138

**1985, Mar. 26  Wmk. 373  Litho.  Perf. 14**

| 641 | A138 | 48s Ford Model A, 1903 | 1.25 | 1.25 |
|---|---|---|---|---|
| 642 | A138 | 56s Chevrolet Tourer, 1912 | 1.50 | 1.50 |
| 643 | A138 | 67s Morris Oxford, 1913 | 1.75 | 1.75 |
| 644 | A138 | $1 Austin Seven, 1923 | 2.75 | 2.75 |
| | | *Nos. 641-644 (4)* | 7.25 | 7.25 |

### Fungi — A139

**1985, Apr. 17  Litho.  Perf. 14½**

| 645 | A139 | 48s Dictyophora indusiata | 1.75 | 1.75 |
|---|---|---|---|---|
| 646 | A139 | 56s Ganoderma tornatum | 2.00 | 2.00 |
| 647 | A130 | 67s Mycena chlorophos | 2.25 | 2.25 |
| 648 | A139 | $1 Mycobonia flava | 3.50 | 3.50 |
| | | *Nos. 645-648 (4)* | 9.50 | 9.50 |

### Queen Mother 85th Birthday
Common Design Type

**1985, June 7  Litho.  Perf. 14½x14**

| 649 | CD336 | 32s Photo., age 9 | .40 | .40 |
|---|---|---|---|---|
| 650 | CD336 | 48s With Prince William at christening of Prince Henry | .65 | .65 |
| 651 | CD336 | 56s At Liverpool street station | .80 | .80 |
| 652 | CD336 | $1 Holding Prince Henry | 1.40 | 1.40 |
| | | *Nos. 649-652 (4)* | 3.25 | 3.25 |

**Souvenir Sheet**

| 653 | CD336 | $2 Arriving at Tattenham corner station | 4.25 | 4.25 |
|---|---|---|---|---|

Souvenir Sheet

### EXPO '85, Tsukuba, Japan — A140

**1985, Aug. 26  Unwmk.  Litho.  Perf. 14**

| 654 | A140 | $2 Emblem, elevation map | 2.50 | 2.50 |
|---|---|---|---|---|

### Int'l. Youth Year — A141

Portions of world map and: a, Emblem, map of No. America, Europe and Africa. b, Hands reaching high. c, Arms reaching, hands limp. d, Hands clenched. e, Emblem and map of Africa, Asia and Europe.

**1985, Sept. 18**

| 655 | | Strip of 5 | 2.75 | 2.75 |
|---|---|---|---|---|
| a.-e. | A141 | 60s any single | .55 | .55 |

### Christmas — A142

Illustrations by Millicent Sowerby from A Child's Garden of Verses, by Robert Louis Stevenson.

**1985, Nov. 5  Unwmk.  Perf. 14x14½**

| 656 | A142 | 32s System | .30 | .30 |
|---|---|---|---|---|
| 657 | A142 | 48s Time to Rise | .40 | .40 |
| 658 | A142 | 56s Auntie's skirts | .50 | .50 |
| 659 | A142 | $1 Good Children | .90 | .90 |
| a. | | Souvenir sheet of 4, #656-659 | 2.50 | 2.50 |
| | | *Nos. 656-659 (4)* | 2.10 | 2.10 |

### Butterflies — A143

**1986, Feb. 13  Wmk. 384  Perf. 14½**

| 660 | A143 | 25s Hypolimnas bolina inconstans | .40 | .40 |
|---|---|---|---|---|
| 661 | A143 | 32s Anapheis java sparrman | .50 | .50 |
| 662 | A143 | 48s Deudorix epijarbas doris | .70 | .70 |
| 663 | A143 | 56s Badamia exclamationis | .85 | .85 |
| 664 | A143 | 60s Tirumala hamata mellitula | 1.00 | 1.00 |
| 665 | A143 | $1 Catochrysops taitensis | 1.75 | 1.75 |
| | | *Nos. 660-665 (6)* | 5.20 | 5.20 |

### Halley's Comet — A144

## 1986, Mar. 24

Designs: 32s, Comet over Apia, 48s, Edmond Halley, astronomer, 60s, Comet orbiting the Earth, $2, Giotto space probe under construction at British Aerospace.

| | | | | |
|---|---|---|---|---|
| 666 | A144 | 32s multicolored | .30 | .30 |
| 667 | A144 | 48s multicolored | .40 | .40 |
| 668 | A144 | 60s multicolored | .55 | .55 |
| 669 | A144 | $2 multicolored | 1.75 | 1.75 |

Nos. 666-669 (4)  3.00 3.00

## Queen Elizabeth II 60th Birthday
### Common Design Type

Designs: 32s, Engagement to the Duke of Edinburgh, 1947, 48s, State visit to US, 1976, 56s, Attending outdoor ceremony, Apia, 1977, 67s, At Badminton Horse Trials, 1978, $2, Visiting Crown Agents offices, 1983.

## 1986, Apr. 21

| | | | | |
|---|---|---|---|---|
| 670 | CD337 | 32s scarlet, blk & sil | .30 | .30 |
| 671 | CD337 | 48s ultra & multi | .40 | .40 |
| 672 | CD337 | 56s green & multi | .50 | .50 |
| 673 | CD337 | 67s violet & multi | .60 | .60 |
| 674 | CD337 | $2 rose violet & multi | 1.75 | 1.75 |

Nos. 670-674 (5)  3.55 3.55

## 1986, May 22

| | | | | |
|---|---|---|---|---|
| 675 | A145 | 48s USS Vincennes | .40 | .40 |
| 676 | A145 | 56s Sikorsky S-42 | .50 | .50 |
| 677 | A145 | 60s USS Swan | .55 | .55 |
| 678 | A145 | $2 Apollo 10 splashdown | 1.75 | 1.75 |

Nos. 675-678 (4)  3.20 3.20

### Souvenir Sheet
AMERIPEX '86, Chicago, May 22-June 1 — A145

## 1986, Aug. 4

679 A146 $3 multicolored  5.25 5.25

STAMPEX '86, Adelaide, Aug. 4-10.

Vailima, Estate of Novelist Robert Louis Stevenson, Upolu Is. — A146

Fish A147

US Peace Corps in Samoa, 25th Anniv. A148

## 1986, Aug. 13  Unwmk.  Litho.  Perf. 14

| | | | | |
|---|---|---|---|---|
| 680 | A147 | 32s Spotted grouper | .70 | .70 |
| 681 | A147 | 48s Sabel squirrelfish | .95 | .95 |
| 682 | A147 | 56s Lunartail grouper | 1.10 | 1.10 |
| 683 | A147 | 67s Longtail snapper | 1.50 | 1.50 |
| 684 | A147 | $1 Berndt's soldierfish | 2.25 | 2.25 |

Nos. 680-684 (5)  6.50 6.50

## 1986, Dec. 1  Perf. 14½

Statesmen: Vaai Kolone of Samoa, Ronald Reagan of US and: 45s, Fiame Mata'afa, John F. Kennedy (1961) and Parliament House, 60s, Jules Grevy, Grover Cleveland (1886) and the Statue of Liberty.

| | | | | |
|---|---|---|---|---|
| 685 | A148 | 45s multicolored | .40 | .40 |
| 686 | A148 | 60s multicolored | .55 | .55 |
| a. | | Souvenir sheet of 2, #685-686 | 3.75 | 3.75 |

Christmas, Statue of Liberty, cent.

## 1987, Feb. 16  Perf. 14x14½  Litho.

| | | | | |
|---|---|---|---|---|
| 687 | A149 | 15s Map, hibiscus | .20 | .20 |
| 688 | A149 | 45s Parliament | .65 | .65 |
| 689 | A149 | 60s Rowing race, 1987 | .80 | .80 |
| 690 | A149 | 70s Dove | .90 | .90 |
| 691 | A149 | $2 Prime minister, flag | 2.50 | 2.50 |

Nos. 687-691 (5)  5.05 5.05

Natl. Independence, 25th Anniv. — A149

## 1987, Mar. 31

Marine Life A150

| | | | | |
|---|---|---|---|---|
| 692 | A150 | 45s Gulper | .50 | .50 |
| 693 | A150 | 56s Hatchet-fish | .75 | .75 |
| 694 | A150 | 70s Angler | .90 | .90 |
| 695 | A150 | $2 Gulper, diff. | 2.00 | 2.00 |

Nos. 692-695 (4)  4.15 4.15

### Souvenir Sheet

## 1987, June 13  Perf. 14½

696 A151 $3 Logger, construction workers  2.75 2.75

CAPEX '87 — A151

## 1987, July 29  Perf. 14

| | | | | |
|---|---|---|---|---|
| 697 | A152 | 45s Lefaga Beach, Upolu | .65 | .65 |
| 698 | A152 | 60s Vaisala Beach, Savaii | .85 | .85 |
| 699 | A152 | 70s Solosolo Beach, Upolu | 1.00 | 1.00 |
| 700 | A152 | $2 Neiafu Beach, Savaii | 3.00 | 3.00 |

Nos. 697-700 (4)  5.50 5.50

Landscapes — A152

## 1987, Sept. 30  Litho.  Perf. 14½

| | | | | |
|---|---|---|---|---|
| 701 | A153 | 40s multicolored | .50 | .50 |
| 702 | A153 | 45s multicolored | .60 | .60 |
| 703 | A153 | 80s multicolored | 1.00 | 1.00 |
| 704 | A153 | $2 multicolored | 2.40 | 2.40 |
| a. | | Souvenir sheet of 1 | 4.50 | 4.50 |

Nos. 701-704 (4)  4.50 4.50

Explorers of the Pacific: 40s, Abel Tasman (c. 1603-1659), Dutch navigator, discovered Tasmania, 1642. 45s, James Cook. 80s, Count Louis-Antoine de Bougainville (1729-1811), French navigator, discovered Bougainville Is., largest of the Solomon Isls., 1768. $2, Comte de La Perouse (1741-1788), French navigator, discovered La Perouse Strait.

Australia Bicentennial A153

## Natl. Independence, 25th Anniv. — A149

## No. 704a Ovptd. with HAFNIA '87 Emblem in Scarlet

### 1987, Oct. 16

705 A153 $2 multicolored  3.25 3.25

## Christmas 1987 — A154

### 1987, Nov. 30  Perf. 14

| | | | | |
|---|---|---|---|---|
| 706 | A154 | 40s Christmas tree | .45 | .45 |
| 707 | A154 | 45s Going to church | .60 | .60 |
| 708 | A154 | 80s Bamboo fire-gun | .65 | .65 |
| 709 | A154 | $2 Going home | 2.70 | 2.70 |

Nos. 706-709 (4)  1.00 1.00

## Australia Bicentennial A155

### 1988, Jan. 27  Perf. 14½

| | | | | |
|---|---|---|---|---|
| 710 | A155 | 45s any single | 1.10 | 1.10 |
| a.-e. | | Strip of 5 | 5.75 | 5.75 |

a, Samoan natl. crest, Australia Post emblem. b, Two jets, postal airmail. d, Jet, van, postman. c, Loading van. e, Congratulatory aerogramme.

## Faleolo Intl. Airport A156

### 1988, Mar. 24  Perf. 13x13½  Litho.  Unwmk.

| | | | | |
|---|---|---|---|---|
| 711 | A156 | 40s Terminal, Boeing 727 | .70 | .70 |
| 712 | A156 | 45s Boeing 727, Fuatino | .80 | .80 |
| 713 | A156 | 60s So. Pacific Is. N43SP, terminal | 1.10 | 1.10 |
| 714 | A156 | 70s Air New Zealand Boeing 737 | 1.25 | 1.25 |
| 715 | A156 | 80s Hawaiian Air DC-9, Tower, jet | 1.40 | 1.40 |
| 716 | A156 | $1 VIP house | 1.75 | 1.75 |

Nos. 711-716 (6)  7.00 7.00

## 1988, Apr. 27  Perf. 14½

| | | | | |
|---|---|---|---|---|
| 717 | A157 | 45s Island village display | .75 | .75 |
| 718 | A157 | 70s EXPO complex, monorail and flags | 1.25 | 1.25 |
| 719 | A157 | $2 Map | 3.25 | 3.25 |

Nos. 717-719 (3)  5.25 5.25

EXPO '88, Brisbane, Australia A157

## Souvenir Sheet
Arrival of the Latter Day Saints in Samoa, Cent. — A158

### 1988, June 9  Litho.  Perf. 13½

720 A158 $3 The Temple, Apia  3.00 3.00

## 1988 Summer Olympics, Seoul — A159

### 1988, Aug. 10  Litho.  Perf. 14

| | | | | |
|---|---|---|---|---|
| 721 | A159 | 15s Running | .20 | .20 |
| 722 | A159 | 60s Weight lifting | .60 | .60 |
| 723 | A159 | 80s Boxing | .80 | .80 |
| 724 | A159 | $2 Olympic Stadium | 2.00 | 2.00 |
| a. | | Souvenir sheet of 4, #721-724 | 3.60 | 3.60 |

Nos. 721-724 (4)  3.60 3.60

## Birds — A160

### 1988-89  Unwmk.  Litho.  Perf. 13½

| | | | | |
|---|---|---|---|---|
| 725 | A160 | 10s Polynesian triller | .25 | .25 |
| 726 | A160 | 15s Samoan wood rail | .20 | .20 |
| 727 | A160 | 20s Flat-billed kingfisher | .25 | .25 |
| 728 | A160 | 25s Samoan fantail | .30 | .30 |
| 729 | A160 | 35s Scarlet robin | .40 | .40 |
| 730 | A160 | 40s Mao | .45 | .45 |
| 731 | A160 | 50s Cardinal honeyeater | .55 | .55 |
| 732 | A160 | 65s Samoan whistler | .70 | .70 |
| 733 | A160 | 75s Many-colored fruit dove | .85 | .85 |
| 734 | A160 | 85s White-throated pigeon | .90 | .90 |

**Size: 45x39mm**

| | | | | |
|---|---|---|---|---|
| 735 | A160 | 75s Silver gull | .85 | .85 |
| 736 | A160 | 85s Great frigatebird | .90 | .90 |
| 737 | A160 | 90s Eastern reef heron | .95 | .95 |
| 738 | A160 | $3 Short-tailed albatross | 3.50 | 3.50 |
| 739 | A160 | $10 Common fairy tern | 10.50 | 10.50 |
| 740 | A160 | $20 Shy albatross | 21.00 | 21.00 |

Nos. 725-740 (16)  42.50 42.50

Issue dates: #725-734, 8/17/88; #735-738, 2/28/89; #739-740, 7/31/89.

## Conservation — A161

### 1988, Oct. 25  Perf. 14

| | | | | |
|---|---|---|---|---|
| 741 | A161 | 15s Forests, vert. | .50 | .50 |
| 742 | A161 | 40s Culture, vert. | 1.00 | 1.00 |
| 743 | A161 | 45s Wildlife, vert. | 1.10 | 1.10 |
| 744 | A161 | 50s Water, vert. | 1.25 | 1.25 |

## Souvenir Sheet

**1991 Rugby World Cup — A175**

**Perf. 14½**

**1991, Oct. 12    Litho.**
792  A175  $5 multicolored    11.50  11.50

## Christmas
A176

Orchids and Christmas carols: 20s, O Come All Ye Faithful. 60s, Joy to the World. 75s, Hark! the Herald Angels Sing. $4, We Wish You a Merry Christmas.

**Perf. 14½**

**1991, Oct. 31    Litho.**
793  A176  20s multicolored    .30  .30
794  A176  60s multicolored    .95  .95
795  A176  75s multicolored    1.25  1.25
796  A176  $4 multicolored     6.25  6.25
*Nos. 793-796 (4)*             8.75  8.75

**Phila Nippon '91 — A177**

Samoan hawkmoth: 60s, I larae convolvuli. 75s, Gnathothibus erotus. 75s, Hippotion celerio. $3, Cephonodes armatus.

**Perf. 13½x14**

**1991, Nov. 16**
797  A177  60s multicolored    1.25  1.25
798  A177  75s multicolored    1.50  1.50
799  A177  75s multicolored    1.75  1.75
800  A177  $3 multicolored     6.00  6.00
*Nos. 797-800 (4)*             10.50  10.50

See Nos. 815-818, 836-840.

**Independence, 30th Anniv. — A178**

**Perf. 14**

**1992, Jan. 8    Litho.**
801  A178  50s Honor guard     .75  .75
802  A178  65s Siva scene      1.00  1.00
803  A178  $1 Parade float     1.50  1.50
804  A178  $3 Raising flag     5.00  5.00
*Nos. 801-804 (4)*             8.25  8.25

**Queen Elizabeth II's Accession to the Throne, 40th Anniv.**
Common Design Type

**1992, Feb. 6    Wmk. 384    Perf. 14**
805  CD349  20s multicolored   .30  .30
806  CD349  60s multicolored   .85  .85
807  CD349  75s multicolored   1.10  1.10
808  CD349  85s multicolored   1.25  1.25
*Nos. 805-808 (4)*

**Wmk. 373**
809  CD349  $3 multicolored    4.50  4.50
*Nos. 805-809 (5)*             8.00  8.00

---

**Perf. 14**

**1990, July 30    Litho.**
776  A170  18s Visitors Bureau    .25  .25
777  A170  50s Samoa Village Resorts    .65  .65
778  A170  65s Aggies Hotel    .85  .85
779  A170  $3 Tusitala Hotel    3.75  3.75
*Nos. 776-779 (4)*             5.50  5.50

## Souvenir Sheet

**No. 240, Exhibition Emblem — A171**

**Perf. 13**

**1990, Aug. 24    Litho.**
780  A171  $3 multicolored    4.75  4.75
World Stamp Exhib. New Zealand 1990.

## Christmas — A172

Paintings of Madonna and Child.

**Perf. 12½**

**1990, Oct. 31**
781  A172  18s Bellini    .45  .45
782  A172  18s Bouts    .95  .95
783  A172  66o Correggio    1.10  1.10
784  A172  $3 Cima    5.50  5.50
*Nos. 781-784 (4)*    8.00  8.00

The 55s is "The School of Love," not "Madonna of the Basket."

**UN Development Program, 40th Anniv. — A173**

**Perf. 13½**

**1990, Nov. 26**
785  A173  $3 multicolored    4.25  4.25

## Parrots
A174

**Perf. 13½**

**1991, Apr. 8    Litho.**
786  A174  18s Black-capped lory    .40  .40
787  A174  50s Eclectus parrot    1.10  1.10
788  A174  65s Scarlet macaw    1.50  1.50
789  A174  $3 Palm cockatoo    6.50  6.50
*Nos. 786-789 (4)*    9.50  9.50

**Elizabeth & Philip, Birthdays**
Common Design Types

**1991, June 17    Wmk. 384    Litho.    Perf. 14½**
790  CD346  75s multicolored    1.10  1.10
791  CD345  $2 multicolored    3.00  3.00
*a.* Pair, #790-791 + label    4.25

---

**Perf. 14**

**1989, July 20    Wmk. 384    Perf. 14**
Size of Nos. 761-762: 29x29mm
760  CD342  18s multicolored    .30  .30
761  CD342  50s multicolored    .75  .75
762  CD342  65s multicolored    .95  .95
763  CD342  $2 multicolored    3.00  3.00
*Nos. 760-763 (4)*    5.00  5.00

## Souvenir Sheet
764  CD342  $3 multicolored    4.00  4.00
"Roosa" is misspelled on No. 761.

## Christmas
A166

**Perf. 13½x13**

**1989, Nov. 1    Litho.    Unwmk.**
765  A166  18s Joseph and Mary    .40  .40
766  A166  50s Shepherds    .95  .95
767  A166  66o Animals    1.10  1.10
768  A166  $2 Three kings    3.75  3.75
*Nos. 765-768 (4)*    6.20  6.20

## Local Transport — A167

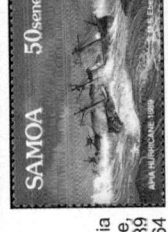

Designs: 18s, Pao pao (outrigger canoe). 55s, Fautasi (longboat). 60s, Polynesian Airlines propeller plane. $3, Lady Samoa ferry.

**Perf. 14x15**

**1990, Jan. 31    Unwmk.**
769  A167  18s multicolored    .40  .40
770  A167  55s multicolored    1.10  1.10
771  A167  60s multicolored    1.25  1.25
772  A167  $3 multicolored    6.25  6.25
*Nos. 769-772 (4)*    9.00  9.00

**Otto von Bismarck, Brandenburg Gate — A168**

**Perf. 14x13½**

**1990, May 3**
773  A168  75s shown    2.00  2.00
774  A168  $3 SMS Adler    10.00  10.00
*a.* Pair, #773-774    7.25  7.25

Opening of the Berlin Wall, 1989, and cent. of the Treaty of Berlin (in 1989). No. 774a has a continuous design.

**Great Britain No. 1 and Alexandra Palace — A169**

Illustration reduced.

**1990, May 3**
775  A169  $3 multicolored    3.75  3.75
Stamp World London '90 and 150th anniv. of the Penny Black.

## Tourism
A170

---

**Christmas**
A162

745  A161  60s Marine resources    1.40  1.40
746  A161  $1 Land and soil    2.25  2.25
*Nos. 741-746 (6)*    7.50  7.50

## Orchids — A163

Designs: 15s, 40s, Congregational Church of Jesus, Apia. 40s, Roman Catholic Church, Leauvaa. 45s, Congregational Christian Church, Moataa. $2, Baha'i Temple, Vailima.

**Perf. 14x14½**

**1988, Nov. 14    Litho.    Unwmk.**
747  A162  15s multicolored    .20  .20
748  A162  40s multicolored    .50  .50
749  A162  45s multicolored    .55  .55
750  A162  $2 multicolored    2.25  2.25
*Nos. 747-750 (4)*    3.50  3.50
*a.* Souvenir sheet of 4, #747-750    3.75  3.75

**Perf. 14**

**1989, Jan. 31    Litho.**
751  A163  15s Phaius flavus    .20  .20
752  A163  45s Calanthe triplicata    .65  .65
753  A163  60s Luisia teretifolia    .85  .85
754  A163  $3 Dendrobium mohlianum    4.50  4.50
*Nos. 751-754 (4)*    6.20  6.20

## Apia Hurricane, 1889
A164

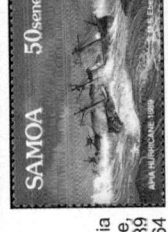

**Litho.    Unwmk.**
**1989, Mar. 16**
755    Strip of 4    7.25  7.25
*a.* A164  50s SMS Eber    .90  .90
*b.* A164  65s SMS Olga    1.10  1.10
*c.* A164  65s SMS Calliope    1.50  1.50
*d.* A164  89s SMS Vandalia    3.50  3.50
*e.* A164  $2 SMS Trenton    .75  .75
*Nos. 756-759 (4)*

World Stamp Expo '89.
#755e, Issued Nov. 1 / is wmk. 355.

**Intl. Red Cross and Red Crescent Organizations, 125th Anniv. — A165**

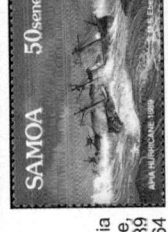

**Perf. 14½x14**

**1989, May 15**
756  A165  50s Youths in parade    .45  .45
757  A165  65s Blood donation    .60  .60
758  A165  $1 First Aid    .70  .70
759  A165  $3 Volunteers    2.75  2.75
*Nos. 756-759 (4)*    4.50  4.50

**Moon Landing, 20th Anniv.**
Common Design Type

Apollo 14: 18s, Saturn-Apollo vehicle and mobile launcher. 50s, Alan Shepard, Stuart Roosa and Edgar Mitchell. 65s, Mission emblem. $2, Tracks of the modularised equipment transporter. $3, Buzz Aldrin and American flag raised on the Moon, Apollo 11 mission.

## Discovery of America, 500th Anniv. — A179

**1992, Apr. 17**     Unwmk.     **Perf. 14½**

**Souvenir Sheet**

810 A179 $4 No. 1     5.00   5.00

World Columbian Stamp Expo '92, Granada '92 and Genoa '92 Philatelic Exhibitions.

---

**1992, July 28**     Wmk. 373     **Perf. 14**

1992 Summer Olympics, Barcelona — A180

| 811 | A180 | 60s | Weight lifting | .85 | .85 |
| 812 | A180 | 75s | Boxing | 1.25 | 1.25 |
| 813 | A180 | 85s | Running | 1.40 | 1.40 |
| 814 | A180 | $3 | Stadium, statue | 4.75 | 4.75 |
| | | | Nos. 811-814 (4) | 8.25 | 8.25 |

---

**1992, Oct. 28**     Litho.     **Perf. 14**

Christmas Type of 1991

| 815 | A176 | 50s | multicolored | .65 | .65 |
| 816 | A176 | 60s | multicolored | .70 | .70 |
| 817 | A176 | 75s | multicolored | .90 | .90 |
| 818 | A176 | $4 | multicolored | 4.75 | 4.75 |
| | | | Nos. 815-818 (4) | 7.25 | 7.25 |

Christmas carol, orchid: 50s, "God rest you, merry gentlemen...," liparis layardii. 60s, "While shepherds watched...," corymborkis veratrifolia. 75s, "Away in a manger...," phaius flavus. $4, "O little town...," bulbophyllum longifolium.

---

Fish A182

**1993, Mar. 17**     Litho.     **Perf. 13½x14**

| 819 | A182 | 60s | Batfish | .90 | .90 |
| 820 | A182 | 75s | Lined surgeonfish | 1.10 | 1.10 |
| 821 | A182 | $1 | Red-tail snapper | 1.50 | 1.50 |
| 822 | A182 | $3 | Long-nosed emperor | 4.75 | 4.75 |
| | | | Nos. 819-822 (4) | 8.25 | 8.25 |

---

**1993, May 12**     **Perf. 13½x14**

World Cup Seven-a-Side Rugby Championships, Scotland — A183

| 823 | A183 | 60s | multi | 1.50 | 1.50 |
| 824 | A183 | 75s | multi. vert. | 1.75 | 1.75 |
| 825 | A183 | 85s | multi. vert. | 2.00 | 2.00 |
| 826 | A183 | $3 | multi. vert. | 6.25 | 6.25 |
| | | | Nos. 823-826 (4) | 11.50 | 11.50 |

60s, Team performing traditional dance. 75c, Two players. 85c, Player. $3, Edinburgh Castle.

---

Bats A184

**1993, June 10**     **Perf. 14x14½**

| 827 | A184 | 20s | Two hanging | 1.25 | 1.25 |
| 828 | A184 | 50s | Two flying | 2.75 | 2.75 |
| 829 | A184 | 60s | Three flying | 3.25 | 3.25 |
| 830 | A184 | 75s | One on flower | 9.50 | 9.50 |
| | | | Nos. 827-830 (4) | | |

World Wildlife Fund.

---

Taipei '93 Asian Intl. Invitation Stamp Exhibition — A185

**1993, Aug. 16**     Litho.     **Perf. 14**

**Souvenir Sheet**

831 A185 $5 multicolored     8.75   8.75

Illustration reduced.

---

World Post Day A186

**1993, Oct. 8**     Litho.     **Perf. 14½**

| 832 | A186 | 60s | multicolored | .75 | .75 |
| 833 | A186 | 75s | multicolored | .90 | .90 |
| 834 | A186 | 85s | multicolored | 1.10 | 1.10 |
| 835 | A186 | $4 | multicolored | 5.00 | 5.00 |
| | | | Nos. 832-835 (4) | 7.75 | 7.75 |

Designs: 60s, Globe, letter, flowers. 75s, Customers at Post Office. 85s, Black, white hands exchanging letter. $4, Globe, national flags, letter.

---

**1993, Nov. 1**     Litho.     **Perf. 14½**

Christmas Type of 1991

| 836 | A176 | 20s | multicolored | .45 | .45 |
| 837 | A176 | 60s | multicolored | .95 | .95 |
| 838 | A176 | 75s | multicolored | 1.10 | 1.10 |
| 839 | A176 | $1.50 | multicolored | 2.25 | 2.25 |
| 840 | A176 | $3 | multicolored | 4.50 | 4.50 |
| | | | Nos. 836-840 (5) | 9.25 | 9.25 |

Flowers, Christmas carol: 20s, "Silent Night, Holy Night!..." 60s, "As with gladness men of old..." 75s, "Mary had a Baby, Yes Lord..." $1.50, "Once in Royal David's City..." $3, "Angels, from the realms of Glory..."

---

Corals A187

**1994, Feb. 18**     Litho.     **Perf. 14**

| 841 | A187 | 20s | Acropora listeri | .30 | .30 |
| 842 | A187 | 60s | Acropora polystoma | .70 | .70 |
| 843 | A187 | 90s | Acropora listeri | 1.00 | 1.00 |
| 844 | A187 | $4 | Acropora grandis | 4.75 | 4.75 |
| | | | Nos. 841-844 (4) | 6.75 | 6.75 |

**1994, Feb. 18**     Unwmk.

Ovptd. with Hong Kong '94 Emblem

| 845 | A187 | 20s | on #841 | .30 | .30 |
| 846 | A187 | 60s | on #842 | .70 | .70 |
| 847 | A187 | 90s | on #843 | 1.25 | 1.25 |
| 848 | A187 | $4 | on #844 | 5.00 | 5.00 |
| | | | Nos. 845-848 (4) | 7.25 | 7.25 |

---

Manu Samoa Rugby Team A188

**1994, Apr. 11**     Litho.     **Perf. 14**

| 849 | A188 | 70s | multicolored | .90 | .90 |
| 850 | A188 | 90s | multicolored | 1.10 | 1.10 |
| 851 | A188 | 95s | multicolored | 1.25 | 1.25 |
| 852 | A188 | $4 | multicolored | 5.00 | 5.00 |
| | | | Nos. 849-852 (4) | 8.25 | 8.25 |

Designs: 70s, Management. 90s, Test match with Wales. 95s, Test match with New Zealand. $4, Apia Park Stadium.

---

PHILAKOREA '94 — A189

**1994, Aug. 16**     Litho.     **Perf. 13**

**Souvenir Sheet**

853 A189 $5 multicolored     6.50   6.50

Butterflies: $5. White caper, glasswing. Illustration reduced.

---

Teuila Tourism Festival A190

**1994, Sept. 22**     Litho.     **Perf. 13½**

| 854 | A190 | 70s | Singers | .90 | .90 |
| 855 | A190 | 90s | Fire dancer | 1.10 | 1.10 |
| 856 | A190 | 95s | Parade float | 1.25 | 1.25 |
| 857 | A190 | $4 | Police band | 5.50 | 5.50 |
| | | | Nos. 854-857 (4) | 8.75 | 8.75 |

---

A191 — CENTENARY OF THE DEATH OF ROBERT LOUIS STEVENSON

**1994, Nov. 21**     **Perf. 14**

| 858 | A191 | 70s | Schooner Equator | .85 | .85 |
| 859 | A191 | 90s | Portrait | 1.00 | 1.00 |
| 860 | A191 | $1.20 | Tomb, Mount Vaea | 1.40 | 1.40 |
| 861 | A191 | $4 | Vailima House, horiz. | 5.00 | 5.00 |
| | | | Nos. 858-861 (4) | 8.25 | 8.25 |

Robert Louis Stevenson (1850-94), writer.

---

A192

**1994, Nov. 30**     **Perf. 14½x13**

| 862 | A192 | 70s | multicolored | .75 | .75 |
| 863 | A192 | 90s | multicolored | 1.10 | 1.10 |
| 864 | A192 | 95s | multicolored | 1.40 | 1.40 |
| 865 | A192 | $4 | multicolored | 4.50 | 4.50 |
| | | | Nos. 862-865 (4) | 7.75 | 7.75 |

Children's Christmas paintings: 70s, Father Greetings. 90s, Nativity. $1.20, Picnic. $4,

---

Scenic Views A193

**1995**     Litho.     **Perf. 14½x13**

| 866 | A193 | 5s | multicolored | .20 | .20 |
| 867 | A193 | 10s | multicolored | .20 | .20 |
| 868 | A193 | 30s | multicolored | .25 | .25 |
| 871 | A193 | 50s | multicolored | .40 | .40 |
| 874 | A193 | 70s | multicolored | .55 | .55 |
| 876 | A193 | 80s | multicolored | .55 | .55 |
| 877 | A193 | 90s | multicolored | .65 | .65 |
| 878 | A193 | 95s | multicolored | .70 | .70 |
| 879 | A193 | $1 | multicolored | .80 | .80 |
| 880 | A193 | $4 | multicolored | 5.00 | 5.00 |
| | | | Nos. 866-880 (10) | | |

Designs: 5s, Lotofaga Beach, Aleipata. 10s, Nuutele Island. 30s, Satuiatua, Savaii. 50s, Sinalele. Aleipata. 60s, Paradise Beach. 70s, Lefaga. Houses, Piula Cave. 80s, Taga blowholes. 90s, View from east coast road. 95s, Canoes. $1, Leulumoega. $4, Parliament Building.

Issued: Nos. 866-867, 871, 874-880, 3/29/95. This is an expanding set. Numbers may change.

---

**1995, May 25**     Litho.     **Perf. 14x13½**

1995 World Rugby Cup Championships, South Africa — A194

| 886 | A194 | 70s | multicolored | .70 | .70 |
| 887 | A194 | 90s | multicolored | .95 | .95 |
| 888 | A194 | $1 | multicolored | 1.10 | 1.10 |
| 889 | A194 | $4 | multicolored | 4.50 | 4.50 |
| | | | Nos. 886-889 (4) | 7.25 | 7.25 |

Designs: 70s, Players under age 12. 90s, Secondary Schools' rugby teams. $1, Manu Samoa test match with New Zealand. $4, Ellis Park Stadium, Johannesburg.

---

End of World War II, 50th Anniv.
Common Design Types

**1995, May 31**     Litho.     **Perf. 13½**

| 890 | CD351 | 70s | multicolored | 1.25 | 1.25 |
| 891 | CD351 | 90s | multicolored | 1.50 | 1.50 |
| 892 | CD351 | 95s | multicolored | 1.75 | 1.75 |
| 893 | CD351 | $3 | multicolored | 5.50 | 5.50 |
| | | | Nos. 890-893 (4) | 10.00 | 10.00 |

**Souvenir Sheet**

894 CD352 $4 multicolored     6.00   6.00

Designs: 70s, OS2U Kingfisher over Faleolo Air Base. 90s, F4U Corsair, Faleolo Air Base. 95s, US troops landing on Samoan beach. $4, US Reverse of War Medal 1939-45.

---

Year of the Sea Turtle — A195

**1995, Aug. 24**     Litho.     **Perf. 13x13½**

| 895 | A195 | 70s | Leatherback | .70 | .70 |
| 896 | A195 | 90s | Loggerhead | .95 | .95 |
| 897 | A195 | $1 | Green turtle | 1.10 | 1.10 |
| 898 | A195 | $4 | Pacific Ridley | 4.50 | 4.50 |
| | | | Nos. 895-898 (4) | 7.25 | 7.25 |

Greenpeace, 26th Anniv. — A207

Dolphins: 50s, #947a, Jumping out of water. 60s, #947b, Two swimming right. 70s, #947c, Two facing front. $1, #947d, With mouth open out of water.

**1997, Sept. 17   Litho.   Perf. 13½x14**

| | | | | |
|---|---|---|---|---|
| 943 | A207 | 50s multicolored | .60 | .60 |
| 944 | A207 | 60s multicolored | .80 | .80 |
| 945 | A207 | 70s multicolored | .95 | .95 |
| 946 | A207 | $1 multicolored | 1.25 | 1.25 |
| | | | 3.60 | 3.60 |

**Miniature Sheet**

947   A207   $1.25   Sheet of 4, #a.-d.   4.50   4.50

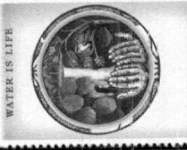

Christmas
A208

**1997, Nov. 26   Litho.   Perf. 14**

| | | | | |
|---|---|---|---|---|
| 948 | A208 | 70s Bells | .70 | .70 |
| 949 | A208 | 80s Ornament | .80 | .80 |
| 950 | A208 | $2 Candle | 1.75 | 1.75 |
| 951 | A208 | $3 Star | 2.75 | 2.75 |
| | | | 6.00 | 6.00 |

Nos. 948-951 (4)

Mangroves
A209

Bruguiera gymnorrhiza: 70s, Fruit on trees. 80s, Saplings. $2, Roots. $4, Tree at water's edge.

**1998, Feb. 26   Litho.   Perf. 13½**

| | | | | |
|---|---|---|---|---|
| 952 | A209 | 70s multicolored | .60 | .60 |
| 953 | A209 | 80s multicolored | .65 | .65 |
| 954 | A209 | $2 multicolored | 1.50 | 1.50 |
| 955 | A209 | $4 multicolored | 3.25 | 3.25 |
| | | | 6.00 | 6.00 |

Nos. 952-955 (4)

**Diana, Princess of Wales (1961-97)**
Common Design Type

#956: a, Up close portrait. b, Wearing checkered jacket. c, In red dress. d, Holding flowers.

**Perf. 14½x14**

**1998, Mar. 31   Litho.   Unwmk.**

955A   CD355   50s like #956a   1.00   1.00

**Sheet of 4**

956   CD355   $1.40   #a.-d.   12.75   12.75

No. 956 sold for $5.60 + 75c, with surtax from international sales being donated to the Princess Diana Memorial Fund and surtax from national sales being donated to designated local charity.

**Royal Air Force, 80th Anniversary**
Common Design Type of 1993
Re-Inscribed

70s, Westland Wallace. 80s, Hawker Fury. $2, Vickers Varsity. $5, BAC Jet Provost. No. 961: a, Norman-Thompson N.T.2b. b, Nieuport 27 Scout. c, Miles Magister. d, Bristol Bombay.

**1998, Apr. 1   Perf. 13½**

| | | | | |
|---|---|---|---|---|
| 957 | CD350 | 70s multicolored | .80 | .80 |
| 958 | CD350 | 80s multicolored | .85 | .85 |
| 959 | CD350 | $2 multicolored | 2.10 | 2.10 |
| 960 | CD350 | $5 multicolored | 5.00 | 5.00 |
| | | | 8.75 | 8.75 |

**Miniature Sheet**

961   CD350   $2   Sheet of 4, #a.-d.   8.00   8.00

---

Souvenir Sheet

Child receiving injection. $4, Mothers, children playing.

**Perf. 14**

**1996, Oct. 24   Litho.**

| | | | | |
|---|---|---|---|---|
| 929 | A203 | 70s multicolored | .75 | .75 |
| 930 | A203 | 90s multicolored | .85 | .85 |
| 931 | A203 | $1 multicolored | .90 | .90 |
| 932 | A203 | $4 multicolored | 3.75 | 3.75 |
| | | | 6.25 | 6.25 |

Nos. 929-932 (4)

**Souvenir Sheet**

Many-Colored Fruit Dove — A204

**Perf. 14**

**1997, Feb. 3   Litho.**

933   A204   $3 multicolored   3.00   3.00

Illustration reduced.

Hong Kong '97. See No. 962.

Souvenir Sheet

PACIFIC 97.

1st US Postage Stamps, 150th Anniv. 1st Samoan Postage Stamps, 120th Anniv. — A205

**Perf. 14½**

**1997, May 29   Litho.**

934   A205   $5   US #1, Samoa #1   4.25   4.25

Phaius Tankervilleae Type of 1995
Souvenir Shoot
Wmk. 373

**Perf. 14½**

**1997, June 20   Litho.**

935   A196   $2.50 multicolored   2.50   2.50

Return of Hong Kong to China, July 1, 1997.

Queen Elizabeth
II & Prince Philip,
50th Wedding
Anniv. — A206

#936, Queen. #937, Prince at reins of team, Royal Windsor Horse Show, 1996. #938, Queen, horse. #939, Prince laughing, horse show, 1995. #940, Zara Philips, Balmoral 1993. Prince Philip. #941, Queen, Prince William.

**1997, July 10   Unwmk.   Perf. 13**

| | | | | |
|---|---|---|---|---|
| 936 | A206 | 70s multicolored | 1.10 | 1.10 |
| 937 | A206 | 70s multicolored | 1.10 | 1.10 |
| a. | | Pair, #936-937 | 2.25 | 2.25 |
| 938 | A206 | 90s multicolored | 1.25 | 1.25 |
| 939 | A206 | 90s multicolored | 1.25 | 1.25 |
| a. | | Pair, #938-939 | 2.50 | 2.50 |
| 940 | A206 | $1 multicolored | 1.50 | 1.50 |
| 941 | A206 | $1 multicolored | 1.50 | 1.50 |
| a. | | Pair, #940-941 | 3.00 | 3.00 |
| | | | 7.70 | 7.70 |

Nos. 936-941 (6)

**Souvenir Sheet**

942   A206   $5 multicolored   6.50   6.50

---

**Perf. 14½   Litho.   Unwmk.**

**1996, Apr. 22**

| | | | | |
|---|---|---|---|---|
| 912 | CD354 | 70s multicolored | .75 | .75 |
| 913 | CD354 | 90s multicolored | 1.00 | 1.00 |
| 914 | CD354 | $1 multicolored | 1.00 | 1.00 |
| 915 | CD354 | $3 multicolored | 3.00 | 3.00 |
| | | | 5.75 | 5.75 |

Nos. 912-915 (4)

**Souvenir Sheet**

916   CD354   $5 multicolored   5.75   5.75

**Souvenir Sheet**

Moon Festival — A199

**Perf. 14**

**1996, May 18   Litho.**

917   A199   $2.50 multicolored   3.50   3.50

CHINA '96.

Illustration reduced.

Souvenir Sheet

63rd Session of African-Carribean-Pacific-European Union Council of Ministers — A200

**Perf. 13½**

**1996, June 19   Litho.**

918   A200   $5 multicolored   5.50   5.50

Illustration reduced.

A202

**Perf. 13½**

**1996, July 15   Litho.**

| | | | | |
|---|---|---|---|---|
| 919 | A201 | 60s Logo | .80 | .80 |
| 920 | A201 | 90s Running | 1.10 | 1.10 |
| 921 | A201 | $1 Boxing | 1.10 | 1.10 |
| 922 | A201 | $4 Javelin | 4.50 | 4.50 |
| | | | 7.50 | 7.50 |

Nos. 919-922 (4)

1996 Summer Olympic Games, Atlanta.

A201

**Perf. 14**

**1996, Sept. 13   Litho.**

| | | | | |
|---|---|---|---|---|
| 923 | A202 | 60s Logo | .65 | .65 |
| 924 | A202 | 70s Pottery | .70 | .70 |
| 925 | A202 | 80s Stained glass | .80 | .80 |
| 926 | A202 | 90s Dancing | .90 | .90 |
| 927 | A202 | $1 Wood carving | .95 | .95 |
| 928 | A202 | $4 Samoan chief | 3.75 | 3.25 |
| | | | 7.75 | 7.25 |

Nos. 923-928 (6)

7th Pacific Festival of Arts, Apia.

UNICEF, 50th Anniv. — A203

70s, Children in doctor's waiting room. 90s, Children in hospital undergoing treatment. $1,

---

Souvenir Sheet

Singapore '95 — A196

**1995, Sept. 1   Perf. 14**

899   A196   $5   Phaius tankervilleae   6.25   6.25

See No. 935.

**UN, 50th Anniv.**
Common Design Type

70s, Mobile hospital. 90s, Bell Sioux helicopter. $1, Bell 212 helicopter. $4, RNZAF Andover.

**Unwmk.**

**1995, Oct. 24   Litho.**

| | | | | |
|---|---|---|---|---|
| 900 | CD353 | 70s multicolored | 1.00 | 1.00 |
| 901 | CD353 | 90s multicolored | 1.40 | 1.40 |
| 902 | CD353 | $1 multicolored | 1.60 | 1.60 |
| 903 | CD353 | $4 multicolored | 6.00 | 6.00 |
| | | | 10.00 | 10.00 |

Nos. 900-903 (4)

A197

CHRISTMAS 1995

A198

**Perf. 14½**

**1995, Nov. 15**

| | | | | |
|---|---|---|---|---|
| 904 | A197 | 25s Madonna & Child | .30 | .30 |
| 905 | A197 | 70s Wise Man | .75 | .75 |
| 906 | A197 | 90s Wise Man, diff. | .95 | .95 |
| 907 | A197 | $5 Wise Man, diff. | 5.50 | 5.50 |
| | | | 7.50 | 7.50 |

Nos. 904-907 (4)

Christmas.

WATER IS LIFE

SAMOA 70s

**Perf. 14**

**1996, Jan. 26   Litho.**

| | | | | |
|---|---|---|---|---|
| 908 | A198 | 70s multicolored | .70 | .70 |
| 909 | A198 | 90s multicolored | .90 | .90 |
| 910 | A198 | $2 multicolored | 1.90 | 1.90 |
| 911 | A198 | $4 multicolored | 3.75 | 3.75 |
| | | | 7.25 | 7.25 |

Nos. 908-911 (4)

Importance of Water: 70s, Waterfall, bird, woman, hands. 90s, Girl standing under fountain, "WATER FOR LIFE." $2, Outline of person's head containing tree, birds, waterfall, girl. $4, Community receiving water from protected watersheds.

**Queen Elizabeth II, 70th Birthday**
Common Design Type

Various portraits of Queen, Samoan scenes: 70s, Apia, Main Street. 90s, Nelafu beach. $1, Official residence of Head of State. $3, Parliament Building. $5, Queen wearing tiara, formal dress.

## Many-Colored Fruit Dove Type of 1997

**1998, Sept. 1**    **Litho.**    **Perf. 14**
962 A204 25s multicolored .20 .20

## Christmas Ornaments — A210

**1998, Nov. 16**    **Litho.**    **Perf. 14**
963 A210 70s Star .60 .60
964 A210 $1.05 Bell .90 .90
965 A210 $1.40 Ball 1.25 1.25
966 A210 $5 Cross 4.25 4.25
Nos. 963-966 (4) 7.00 7.00

Australia '99, World Stamp Expo — A211

Boats: 70s, Dugout canoe. 90s, Tasman's ships Heemskerck & Zeehaen, 1642, $1.05, HMS Resolution, HMS Adventure, 1773, $6, New Zealand scow schooner, 1880.

**1999, Mar. 19**    **Litho.**    **Perf. 14**
967 A211 70s multicolored .70 .70
968 A211 90s multicolored .85 .85
969 A211 $1.05 multicolored 1.00 1.00
970 A211 $6 multicolored 5.50 5.50
Nos. 967-970 (4) 8.05 8.05

## Wedding of Prince Edward and Sophia Rhys-Jones

Common Design Type

**1999, June 19**    **Litho.**    **Perf. 14**
971 CD356 $1.50 Separate portraits 1.00 1.00
972 CD356 $6 Couple 4.00 4.00

## 1st Manned Moon Landing, 30th Anniv.

Common Design Type

70s, Lift-off. 90s, Lunar module separates from Service module. $3, Aldrin deploys solar wind experiment. $5, Parachutes open. $5, Earth as seen from moon.

**1999, July 20**    **Litho.**    **Wmk. 384**
   **Perf. 14x13¾**
973 CD357 70s multicolored .50 .50
974 CD357 90s multicolored .75 .75
975 CD357 $3 multicolored 2.25 2.25
976 CD357 $5 multicolored 4.00 4.00
Nos. 973-976 (4) 7.50 7.50

**Souvenir Sheet**    **Perf. 14**
977 CD357 $5 multicolored 4.75 4.75
No. 977 contains one 40mm circular stamp.

## Queen Mother's Century

Common Design Type

Queen Mother. 70s, Talking to tenants of bombed apartments, 1940. 90s, At garden party, South Africa. $2, Reviewing scouts at Windsor. $6, With Princess Eugenie, 98th birthday. $5, With film showing Charlie Chaplin.

**1999, Aug. 24**    **Litho.**    **Unwmk.**
   **Perf. 13½**
978 CD358 70s multicolored .65 .65
979 CD358 90s multicolored .75 .75
980 CD358 $2 multicolored 1.60 1.60
981 CD358 $2 multicolored 1.60 1.60
Nos. 978-981 (4) 4.50 4.50

**Souvenir Sheet**    **Perf. 14**
982 CD358 $5 multicolored 4.00 4.00

## Christmas and Millennium — A212

**1999, Nov. 30**    **Litho.**    **Perf. 13½x13¾**    **Unwmk.**
983 A212 70s Hibiscus .55 .55
984 A212 90s Poinsettia .70 .70
985 A212 $2 Christmas cactus 1.50 1.50
986 A212 $6 Flag, Southern Cross 4.25 4.25
Nos. 983-986 (4) 7.00 7.00

## Millennium — A213

**2000, Jan. 1**    **Unwmk.**    **Litho.**    **Perf. 14**
987 A213 70s shown .80 .80
988 A213 70s Rocks .80 .80
a. Pair #987-988 2.00 2.00

## Sesame Street — A214

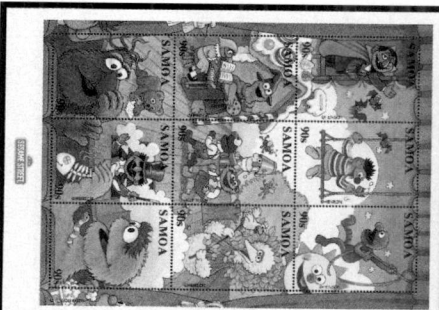

No. 989: a, The Count. b, Ernie. c, Grover. d, Cookie Monster and Prairie Dawn. e, Ernie and Zoe. f, Big Bird. g, Telly. h, Magician. i, Oscar the Grouch.

**2000, Mar. 22**    **Litho.**    **Perf. 14½x14¾**
989 A214 90s Sheet of 9, #a-i 5.50 5.50

**Souvenir Sheet**
990 A214 $3 multi 2.25 2.25
$3, Cookie Monster. Illustration reduced.

## Fire Dancers — A215

Various dancers. Denominations: 25s, 50s, 90s, $1, $4.

**2001, Sept. 3**    **Litho.**    **Perf. 13x13¾**
991-995 A215 Set of 5 5.00 5.00

## Serpentine Die Cut

## Butterflies — A216

**2001, Dec. 12**    **Self-Adhesive**    **Litho.**
996    Horiz. strip of 5    6.00
a. A216 70s Vagrans egista .50 .50
b. A216 $1.20 Jamides bochus .85 .85
c. A216 $1.40 Papilio godeffroy 1.00 1.00
d. A216 $2 Achraea andromacha 1.40 1.40
e. A216 $3 Eurema hecabe 2.25 2.25

## Int'l. Year of Ecotourism — A217

Designs: 60s, Snorkelers. 95s, Kayakers. $1.90, Village, children, craftsman. $3, Bird watchers.

**2002, Feb. 27**    **Litho.**    **Perf. 13¾**
997-1000 A217 Set of 4 6.00 6.00
1000a   Horiz strip of 4, #997-1000 + central label   6.00

## Independence, 40th Anniv. — A218

Flag and. 25s, Buses, cricket player, huts. 70s, Natives. 95s, Flower, woman, ship, airplane, woman using telephone. $5, Flower, buildings, rugby player, inspection of troops.

**2002, June 1**    **Litho.**    **Perf. 13¾**
1001-1004 A218 Set of 4 7.25 7.25
1004a   Souvenir sheet of 1, #1004   3.00 3.00

## People and Their Activities — A219

Designs: 5s, Woman holding fish. 10s, Family. 20s, Men carrying baskets. 25s, Two boys smiling. 35s, Woman, girl and flowers. 50s, Toddler and adult. 60s, Male dancer. 70s, Female dancer. 80s, Woman laughing. 90s, Group of women. 95s, Two women with flowers in hair. $1, Boy in stream of water. $1.20, Child smiling. $1.85, Man smiling. $10, People at church.

**2002, Aug. 1**    **Litho.**    **Perf. 13x13¾**
1005 A219 5s multi .20 .20
1006 A219 10s multi .20 .20
1007 A219 20s multi .20 .20
1008 A219 25s multi .20 .20
1009 A219 35s multi .20 .20
1010 A219 50s multi .30 .30
1011 A219 60s multi .30 .30
1012 A219 70s multi .35 .35
1013 A219 80s multi .45 .45
1014 A219 90s multi .50 .50
1015 A219 95s multi .55 .55
1016 A219 $1 multi .60 .60
1018 A219 $1.20 multi .70 .70
1017 A219 $1.85 multi 1.10 1.10
1019 A219 $10 multi 5.75 5.75
Nos. 1005-1019 (15) 11.70 11.70

## Scenic Views — A220

**2002, Sept. 18**
Designs: 95s, Family on beach. $1.20, Man and woman on rock. $1.40, Woman in ocean. $2, Waterfall.

   **Perf. 14x14¾**
1020-1023 A220 Set of 4 4.00 4.00
1023a   Souvenir sheet #1021, 1023   2.50 2.50

## Ginger Flowers — A221

Designs: 25s, Alpinia purpurata. $1.05, Alpinia samoensis. $1.20, Hedychium flavescens. $4, Etlingera cevuga.

**2002, Nov. 20**    **Litho.**    **Perf. 13½**
1024-1027 A221 Set of 4 6.00 6.00

## Decorated Buses — A222

Inscriptions on buses: 25s, Return to Paradise. 70s, Misiieti Fetu. 90s, Jungle Boys. 95s, Sun Rise Transport. $4, Laifoni.

**2003, Jan. 22**    **Self-Adhesive**    **Serpentine Die Cut**    **Litho.**
1028-1032 A222 Set of 5 5.50 5.50

## Marine Protected Areas — A223

Designs: 25s, Aleipata. $5, Safata.

**2003, Mar. 19**    **Litho.**    **Perf. 13½x13¾**
1033-1034 A223 Set of 2 4.50 4.50

## Artists and Their Works — A224

Artists: 25s, Vanya Taule'alo. 70s, Michel Tuffery. 90s, Momoe von Reiche. $1, Fatu Feu'u. $4, Lily Laita.

| | | | |
|---|---|---|---|
| **2003, May 7** | **Litho.** | | ***Perf. 13*** |
| **1035-1039** A224 | Set of 5 | 5.50 | 5.50 |

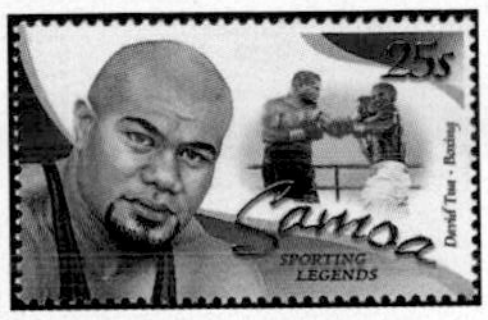


Sports Stars A225

Designs: 25s, David Tua, boxer. 70s, Beatrice Faumuina, discus. 90s, Michael Jones, rugby. 95s, Rita Fatialofa, netball. $4, Jesse Sapolu, football.

| | | | |
|---|---|---|---|
| **2003, July 16** | | | ***Perf. 13½*** |
| **1040-1044** A225 | Set of 5 | 6.00 | 6.00 |

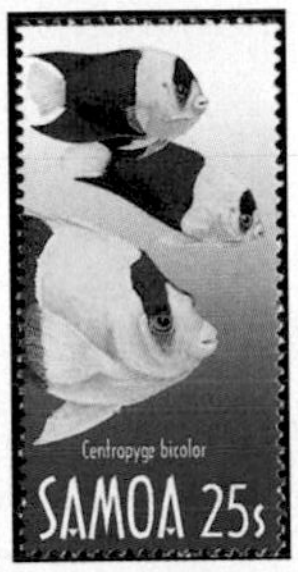


Angelfish — A226

Designs: 25s, Centropyge bicolor. 60s, Centropyge loriculus. 90s, Pygoplites diacanthus. $5, Pomocanthus imperator.

| | | | |
|---|---|---|---|
| **2003, Sept. 10** | | | ***Perf. 13x13¼*** |
| **1045-1048** A226 | Set of 4 | 5.50 | 5.50 |
| *1048a* | Souvenir sheet of 1 | 6.50 | 6.50 |

Flowers — A227

Designs: 70s, Heliconia caribaea. 80s, Heliconia psittacorum. 90s, Hibiscus rosa-sinensis. $4, Plumeria rubra.

| | | | |
|---|---|---|---|
| ***Perf. 12¾x13¼*** | | | |
| **2004, Mar. 26** | | | **Litho.** |
| **1049-1052** A227 | Set of 4 | 6.50 | 6.50 |

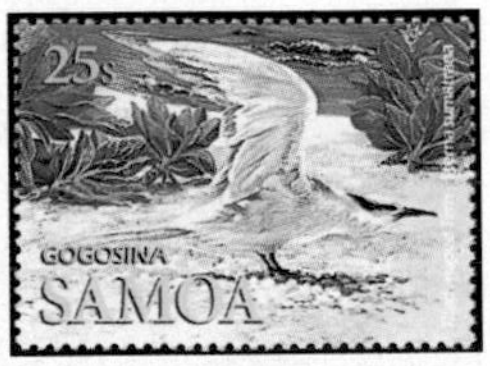


Birds A228

Designs: 25s, Black-naped tern. 60s, Crested tern. 70s, Common noddy, vert. 90s, Lesser frigatebird, vert. $4, Reef heron.

| | | | |
|---|---|---|---|
| **2004, June 16** | **Litho.** | | ***Perf. 13¼*** |
| **1053-1057** A228 | Set of 5 | 6.50 | 6.50 |
| *1057a* | Souvenir sheet, #1053-1057 | 6.50 | 6.50 |

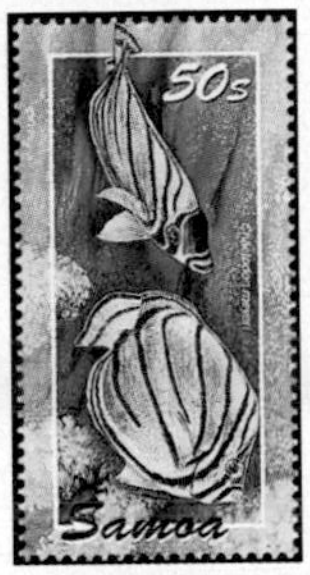


Butterflyfish — A229

Designs: 50s, Chaetodon meyeri. 90s, Chaetodon punctatofasciatus, horiz. $1, Chaetodon ephippium, horiz. $4, Chaetodon flavirostris.

| | | | |
|---|---|---|---|
| ***Perf. 14¼x14, 14x14¼*** | | | |
| **2004, Sept. 29** | | | **Litho.** |
| **1058-1061** A229 | Set of 4 | 6.50 | 6.50 |
| *1061a* | Souvenir sheet of 1 | 5.50 | 5.50 |

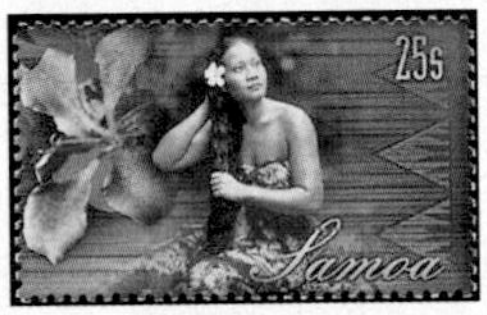


Women and Flowers A230

Various women and: 25s, Pink flower. 70s, Red flowers, vert. 90s, White flowers. $4, Orange flowers, vert.

| | | | |
|---|---|---|---|
| **2004, Dec. 15** | **Litho.** | | ***Perf. 13¼*** |
| **1062-1065** A230 | Set of 4 | 4.50 | 4.50 |

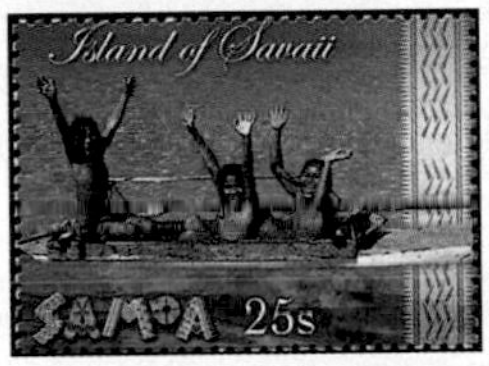


Scenes From Savaii Island A231

Designs: 25s, Children in small boat. 70s, Women, building. 90s, Women on rope bridge, vert. $4, Coastline, vert.

| | | | |
|---|---|---|---|
| **2005, Feb. 17** | **Litho.** | | ***Perf. 13¼*** |
| **1066-1069** A231 | Set of 4 | 4.50 | 4.50 |

Souvenir Sheet

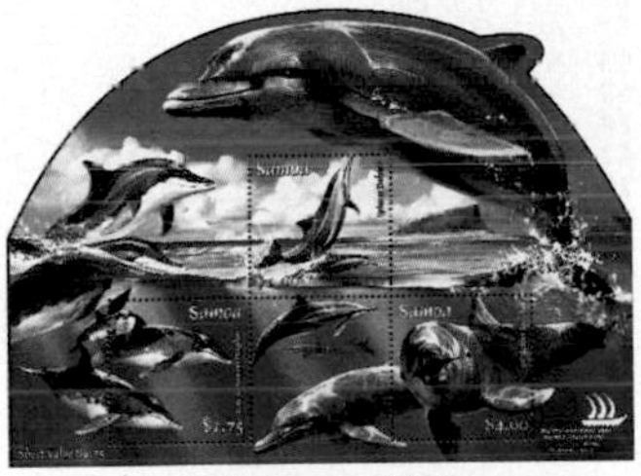

Dolphins — A232

No. 1070: a, $1, Spinner dolphin. b, $1.75, Rough-toothed dolphin. c, $4, Bottlenose dolphin.

| | | | |
|---|---|---|---|
| **2005, Apr. 21** | **Litho.** | | ***Perf. 13¼*** |
| **1070** A232 | Sheet of 3, #a-c | 5.25 | 5.25 |

Pacific Explorer 2005 World Stamp Expo, Sydney.

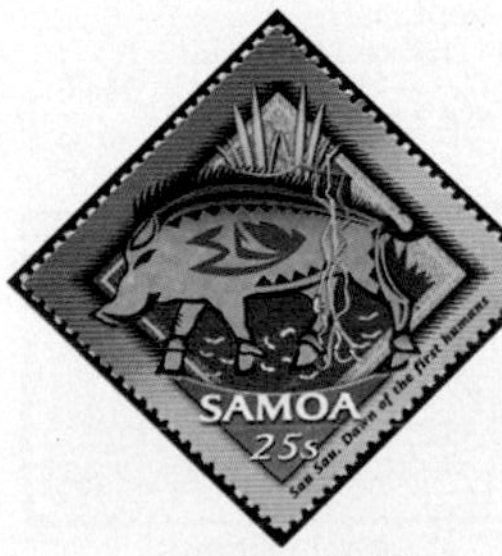


Legends — A233

Designs: 25s, Sau Sau, Dawn of the First Humans. 70s, Tuimanu'a and the Flying Fox. 90s, Fonuea and Salofa Escape Famine. $4, Patea, the Sea Demon.

| | | | |
|---|---|---|---|
| **2005, Sept. 28** | **Litho.** | | ***Perf. 13¼*** |
| **1071-1074** A233 | Set of 4 | 4.50 | 4.50 |

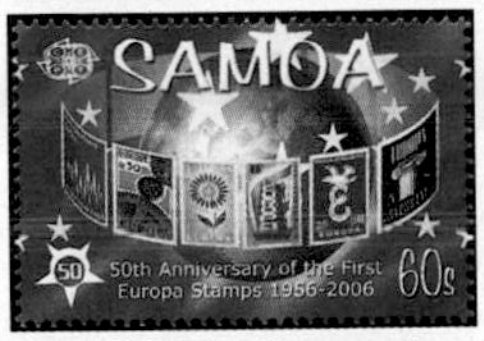


European Philatelic Cooperation, 50th Anniv. (in 2006) — A234

Globe, CEPT emblem, stars and various Europa stamps: 60s, $3, $4, $10.

| | | | |
|---|---|---|---|
| **2005, Dec. 7** | | | ***Perf. 14*** |
| **1075-1078** A234 | Set of 4 | 13.00 | 13.00 |
| *1078a* | Souvenir sheet, #1075-1078 | 13.00 | 13.00 |

Europa stamps, 50th anniv. (in 2006).

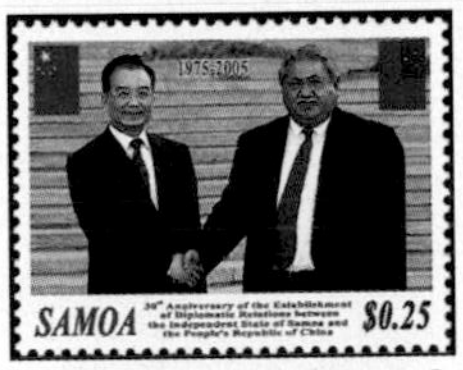


Diplomatic Relations Between Samoa and People's Republic of China, 30th Anniv. A235

Designs: 25s, Chinese and Samoan representatives and flags. 50s, Building. $1, Wooden bowl. $4, Chinese astronauts.

| | | | |
|---|---|---|---|
| **2005, Nov. 6** | **Litho.** | | ***Perf. 13x13¼*** |
| **1079-1082** A235 | Set of 4 | 4.25 | 4.25 |

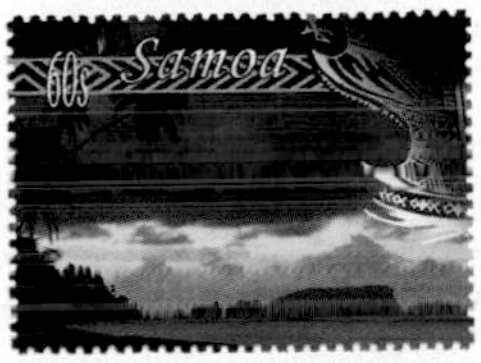


Sunsets A236

Various sunsets: 60s, 90s, $1, $4.

| | | | |
|---|---|---|---|
| **2006, Feb. 15** | | | ***Perf. 13¼*** |
| **1083-1086** A236 | Set of 4 | 4.75 | 4.75 |

## SEMI-POSTAL STAMP

**Catalogue values for unused stamps in this section are for Never Hinged items.**

No. 246 Surcharged: "HURRICANE RELIEF / 6d"

**Wmk. 355**

| | | | |
|---|---|---|---|
| **1966, Sept. 1** | **Litho.** | | ***Perf. 13½*** |
| **B1** A43 8p + 6p blue & emerald | | .25 | .25 |

Surtax for aid to plantations destroyed by the hurricane of Jan. 29, 1966.

## AIR POST STAMPS

**Catalogue values for unused stamps in this section are for Never Hinged items.**

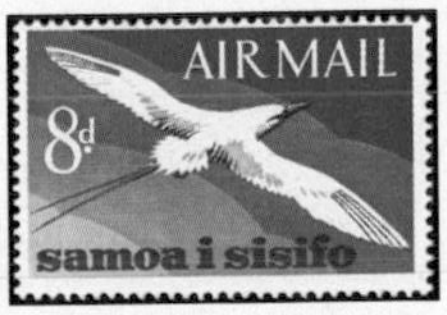


Red-tailed Tropic Bird — AP1

**Wmk. 355**

| | | | |
|---|---|---|---|
| **1965, Dec. 29** | **Photo.** | | ***Perf. 14½*** |
| **C1** AP1 8p shown | | .25 | .25 |
| **C2** AP1 2sh Flying fish | | .65 | .65 |

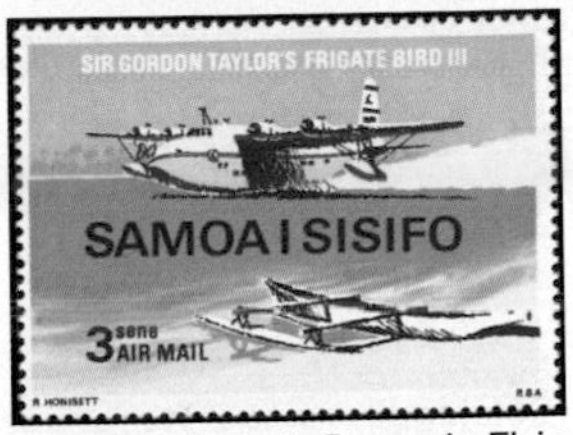


Sir Gordon Taylor's Bermuda Flying Boat "Frigate Bird III" — AP2

Designs: 7s, Polynesian Airlines DC-3. 20s, Pan American Airways "Samoan Clipper." 30s, Air Samoa Britten-Norman "Islander."

| | | | |
|---|---|---|---|
| ***Perf. 13½x13*** | | | |
| **1970, July 27** | **Photo.** | | **Unwmk.** |
| **C3** AP2 3s multicolored | | .70 | .20 |
| **C4** AP2 7s multicolored | | 1.00 | .20 |
| **C5** AP2 20s multicolored | | 1.25 | .90 |
| **C6** AP2 30s multicolored | | 1.25 | 1.00 |
| *Nos. C3-C6 (4)* | | 4.20 | 2.30 |

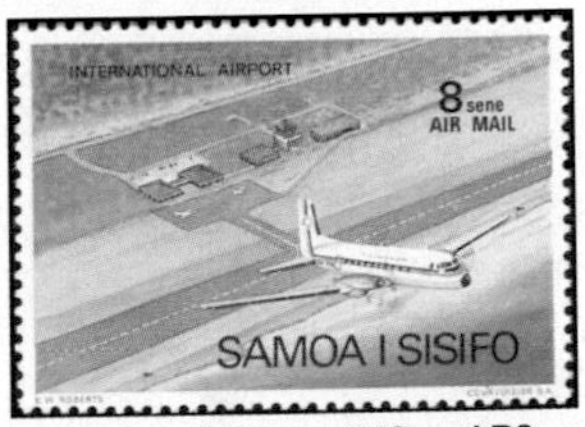


Hawker Siddeley 748 — AP3

Planes at Faleolo Airport: 10s, Hawker Siddeley 748 in the air. 12s, Hawker Siddeley 748 on ground. 22s, DAO 1-11 planes on ground.

| | | | |
|---|---|---|---|
| **1973, Mar. 9** | | | ***Perf. 11½*** |
| **Granite Paper** | | | |
| **C7** AP3 8s multicolored | | .55 | .55 |
| **C8** AP3 10s multicolored | | .75 | .75 |
| **C9** AP3 12s multicolored | | .80 | .80 |
| **C10** AP3 22s multicolored | | 1.50 | 1.50 |
| *Nos. C7-C10 (4)* | | 3.60 | 3.60 |

# SAN MARINO

ˌsan mə-ˈrē-ˌnō

LOCATION — Eastern Italy, about 20 miles inland from the Adriatic Sea
GOVT. — Republic
AREA — 24.1 sq. mi.
POP. — 25,061 (1999 est.)
CAPITAL — San Marino

100 Centesimi = 1 Lira
100 Cents = 1 Euro (2002)

**Catalogue values for unused stamps in this country are for Never Hinged items, beginning with Scott 412 in the regular postage section, Scott B39 in the semi-postal section, Scott C97 in the airpost section, Scott E26 in the special delivery section, and Scott Q40 in the parcel post section.**

**Watermarks**

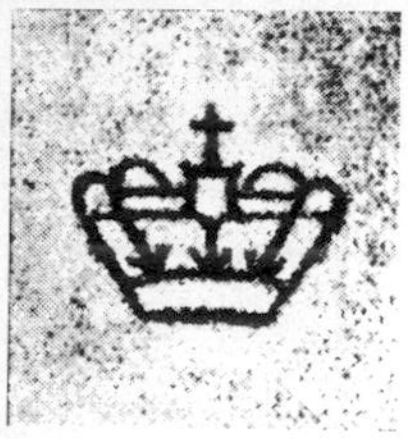
Wmk. 140 — Crown

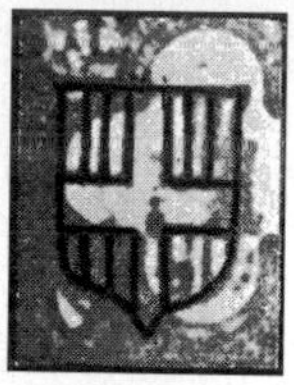
Wmk. 174 — Coat of Arms

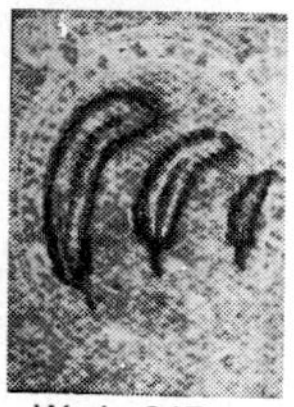
Wmk. 217 — Three Plumes

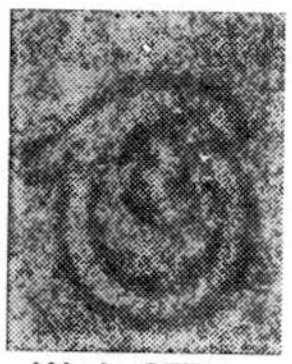
Wmk. 277 — Winged Wheel

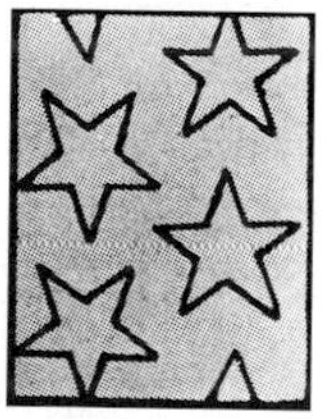
Wmk. 303 — Multiple Stars

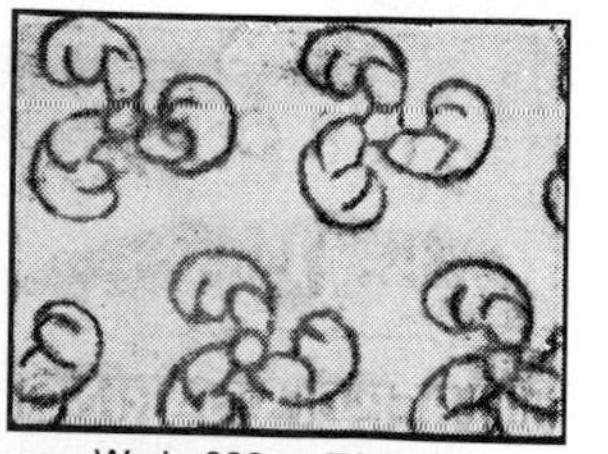
Wmk. 339 — Triskelion

Nos. 1-28 were spaced very narrowly on the plates, so that perforations often cut into the design on one or two sides. Values are for stamps with perforations clear of the design. Examples with perfs cutting in the design sell for less, while examples with four clear, full margins sell for substantially more than the values shown.

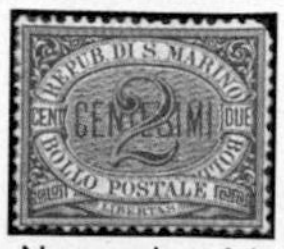
Numeral — A1

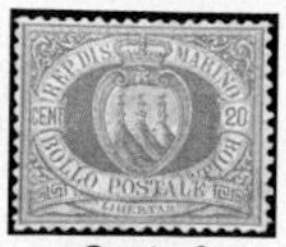
Coat of Arms — A2

**1877-99 Typo. Wmk. 140 *Perf. 14***

| | | | | |
|---|---|---|---|---|
| **1** | A1 | 2c green | 20.00 | 7.00 |
| **2** | A1 | 2c blue ('94) | 10.00 | 7.00 |
| **3** | A1 | 2c claret ('95) | 8.25 | 8.50 |
| **4** | A2 | 5c orange ('90) | 110.00 | 17.50 |
| **5** | A2 | 5c olive grn ('92) | 5.50 | 1.75 |
| **6** | A2 | 5c green ('99) | 5.50 | 3.50 |
| **7** | A2 | 10c ultra | 175.00 | 27.50 |
| *a.* | | 10c blue ('90) | 625.00 | 100.00 |
| **8** | A2 | 10c dk green ('92) | 5.50 | 4.25 |
| **9** | A2 | 10c claret ('99) | 5.50 | 2.50 |
| **10** | A2 | 15c claret ('94) | 125.00 | 55.00 |
| **11** | A2 | 20c vermilion | 25.00 | 7.00 |
| **12** | A2 | 20c lilac ('95) | 5.50 | 5.50 |
| **13** | A2 | 25c maroon ('90) | 110.00 | 27.50 |
| **14** | A2 | 25c blue ('99) | 5.50 | 5.50 |
| **15** | A2 | 30c brown | 700.00 | 70.00 |
| **16** | A2 | 30c org yel ('92) | 5.50 | 7.00 |
| **17** | A2 | 40c violet | 700.00 | 70.00 |
| **18** | A2 | 40c dk brown ('92) | 5.50 | 7.00 |
| **19** | A2 | 45c gray grn ('92) | 5.50 | 7.00 |
| **20** | A2 | 65c red brown ('92) | 5.50 | 7.00 |
| **21** | A2 | 1 l car & yel ('92) | 1,400. | 500.00 |
| **22** | A2 | 1 l lt blue ('95) | 1,250. | 400.00 |
| **23** | A2 | 2 l brn & yel ('94) | 62.50 | 62.50 |
| **24** | A2 | 5 l vio & grn ('94) | 150.00 | 175.00 |

See Nos. 911-915.

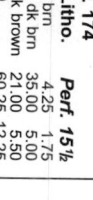

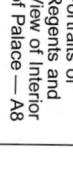

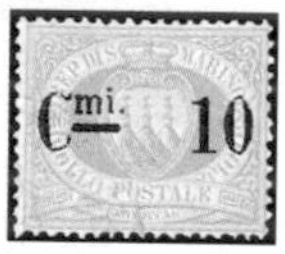
Nos. 7a, 15, 11 Surcharged in Black

**1892**

| | | | | |
|---|---|---|---|---|
| **25** | A2 | 5c on 10c blue | 62.50 | 17.00 |
| *a.* | | Inverted surcharge | 70.00 | 21.00 |
| *b.* | | 5c on 10c ultramarine | *32,000.* | *6,000.* |
| *c.* | | As "b," inverted surcharge | — | — |
| *d.* | | Double surcharge, one inverted | — | — |
| *e.* | | Pair, one without surcharge | 1,250. | |
| *e.* | | Pair, one without surcharge, surcharge inverted | 1,250. | |
| **26** | A2 | 5c on 30c brown | 225.00 | 70.00 |
| *a.* | | Inverted surcharge | 275.00 | 82.50 |
| *b.* | | Double surch., one inverted | 275.00 | 110.00 |
| *c.* | | Double invtd. surcharge | 275.00 | 110.00 |
| **27** | A2 | 10c on 20c ver | 47.50 | 8.25 |
| *a.* | | Inverted surcharge | 55.00 | 12.50 |
| *b.* | | Double surch., one inverted | 62.50 | 17.50 |
| *c.* | | Double surcharge | 62.50 | 17.50 |
| | | *Nos. 25-27 (3)* | 335.00 | 95.25 |

Ten to twelve varieties of each surcharge.

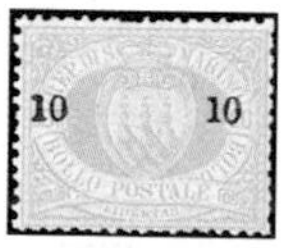
No. 11 Surcharged

| | | | | |
|---|---|---|---|---|
| **28** | A2 | 10c on 20c ver | 225.00 | 12.50 |

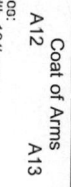

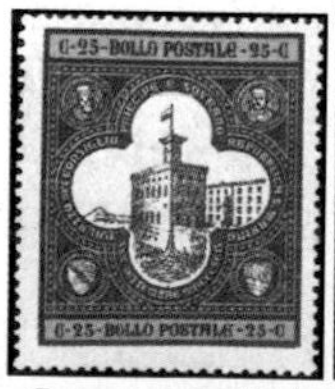
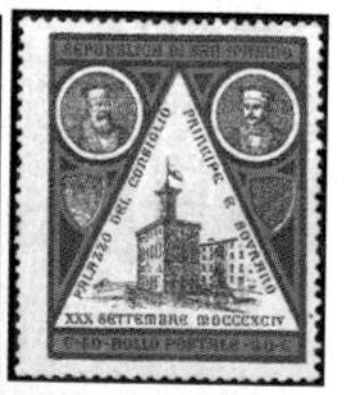
Government Palace and Portraits of Regents, Tonnini and Marcucci
A6 A7

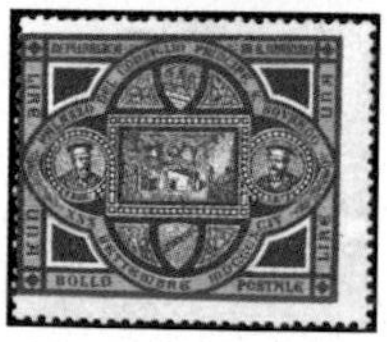
Portraits of Regents and View of Interior of Palace — A8

**Wmk. 174**

**1894, Sept. 30 Litho. *Perf. 15½***

| | | | | |
|---|---|---|---|---|
| **29** | A6 | 25c blue & dk brn | 4.25 | 1.75 |
| **30** | A7 | 50c dull red & dk brn | 35.00 | 5.00 |
| **31** | A8 | 1 l green & dk brown | 21.00 | 5.50 |
| | | *Nos. 29-31 (3)* | 60.25 | 12.25 |

Opening of the new Government Palace and the installation of the new Regents.

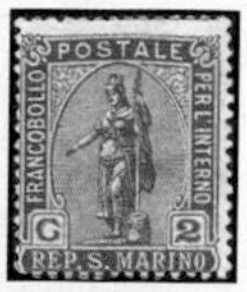
Statue of Liberty — A9

**Wmk. 140**

**1899-1922 Typo. *Perf. 14***

| | | | | |
|---|---|---|---|---|
| **32** | A9 | 2c brown | 2.00 | 1.40 |
| **33** | A9 | 2c claret ('22) | .45 | .20 |
| **34** | A9 | 5c brown org | 5.00 | 3.00 |
| **35** | A9 | 5c olive grn ('22) | .45 | .40 |
| **36** | A9 | 10c brown org ('22) | .45 | .40 |
| **37** | A9 | 20c dp brown ('22) | .45 | .40 |
| **38** | A9 | 25c ultra ('22) | 1.00 | 1.00 |
| **39** | A9 | 45c red brown ('22) | 2.00 | 2.00 |
| | | *Nos. 32-39 (8)* | 11.80 | 8.80 |

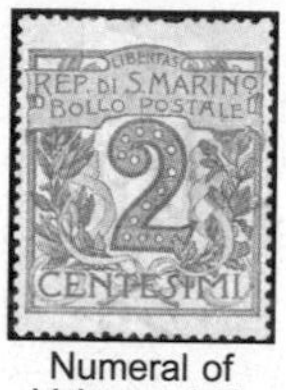
Numeral of Value — A10

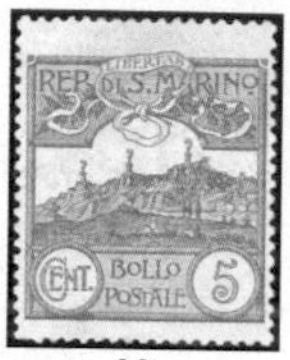
Mt. Titano — A11

**1903-25 *Perf. 14, 14½x14***

| | | | | |
|---|---|---|---|---|
| **40** | A10 | 2c violet | 9.00 | 4.25 |
| **41** | A10 | 2c org brn ('21) | .50 | .50 |
| **42** | A11 | 5c blue grn | 4.25 | 1.80 |
| **43** | A11 | 5c olive grn ('21) | .50 | .50 |
| **44** | A11 | 5c red brn ('25) | .20 | .20 |
| **45** | A11 | 10c claret | 4.25 | 1.80 |
| **46** | A11 | 10c brown org ('21) | .50 | .50 |
| **47** | A11 | 10c olive grn ('25) | .20 | .20 |
| **48** | A11 | 15c blue grn ('22) | .50 | .50 |
| **49** | A11 | 15c brown vio ('25) | .20 | .20 |
| **50** | A11 | 20c brown orange | 125.00 | 25.00 |
| **51** | A11 | 20c brown ('21) | .50 | .50 |
| **52** | A11 | 20c blue grn ('25) | .20 | .20 |
| **53** | A11 | 25c blue | 9.25 | 4.25 |
| **54** | A11 | 25c gray ('21) | .50 | .50 |
| **55** | A11 | 25c violet ('25) | .20 | .20 |
| **56** | A11 | 30c brown red | 4.25 | *5.25* |
| **57** | A11 | 30c claret ('21) | .50 | .50 |
| **58** | A11 | 30c orange ('25) | 10.50 | 1.60 |
| **59** | A11 | 40c orange red | 8.75 | 6.50 |
| **60** | A11 | 40c dp rose ('21) | .50 | .50 |
| **61** | A11 | 40c brown ('25) | .20 | .20 |
| **62** | A11 | 45c yellow | 6.50 | 6.50 |
| **63** | A11 | 50c brown vio ('23) | 1.25 | *1.80* |
| **64** | A11 | 50c gray blk ('25) | .20 | .20 |
| **65** | A11 | 60c brown red ('25) | .60 | .30 |
| **66** | A11 | 65c chocolate | 6.50 | 6.50 |
| **67** | A11 | 80c blue ('21) | 2.50 | 2.50 |
| **68** | A11 | 90c brown ('23) | 2.50 | 2.50 |
| **69** | A11 | 1 l olive green | 19.00 | 11.50 |
| **70** | A11 | 1 l ultra ('21) | .50 | .50 |
| **71** | A11 | 1 l lt blue ('25) | .60 | .25 |
| **72** | A11 | 2 l violet | 750.00 | 160.00 |
| **73** | A11 | 2 l orange ('21) | 12.50 | 12.50 |
| **74** | A11 | 2 l lt green ('25) | 4.25 | 4.25 |
| **75** | A11 | 5 l slate | 140.00 | 110.00 |
| **76** | A11 | 5 l ultra ('25) | 12.50 | 12.00 |
| | | *Nos. 40-76 (37)* | 1,139. | 386.95 |

For overprints and surcharges see Nos. 77, 93-96, 103, 107, 188-189, B1-B2, E2, E4.

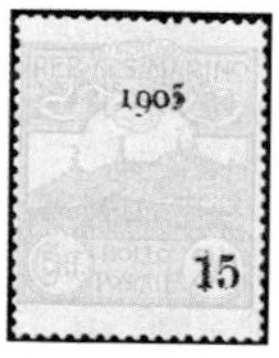
No. 50 Surcharged

**1905, Sept. 1**

| | | | | |
|---|---|---|---|---|
| **77** | A11 | 15c on 20c brown org | 11.00 | 3.75 |
| *a.* | | Large 5 in 1905 on level with 9 | 57.50 | 27.50 |

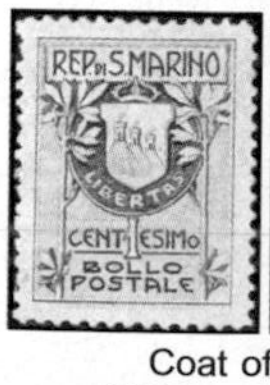
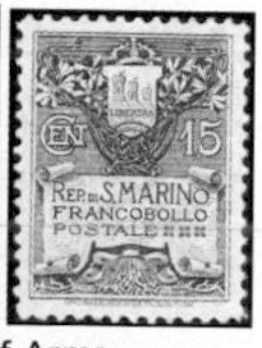
Coat of Arms
A12 A13

Two typos:
I — Width 18½mm.
II — Width 19mm.

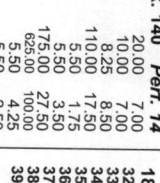

**1907-10 Unwmk. Engr. *Perf. 12***

| | | | | |
|---|---|---|---|---|
| **78** | A12 | 1c brown, II ('10) | 3.75 | .70 |
| *a.* | | Type I | 6.25 | 1.00 |
| **79** | A13 | 15c gray, I | 17.50 | 3.00 |
| *a.* | | Type II ('10) | 190.00 | 19.00 |

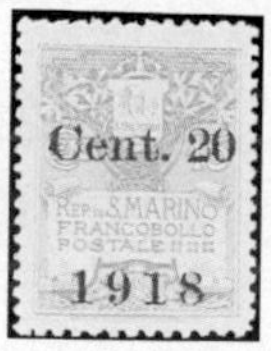
No. 79a Surcharged in Brown

**1918, Mar. 15**

| | | | | |
|---|---|---|---|---|
| **80** | A13 | 20c on 15c gray | 3.75 | 1.90 |

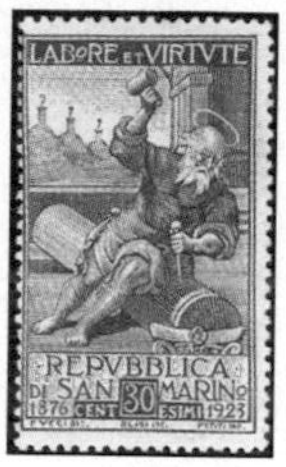
St. Marinus — A14

***Perf. 14½x14, 14x14½***

**1923, Aug. 11 Typo. Wmk. 140**

| | | | | |
|---|---|---|---|---|
| **81** | A14 | 30c dark brown | .75 | .75 |

San Marino Intl. Exhib. of 1923. Proceeds from the sale of this stamp went to a mutual aid society.

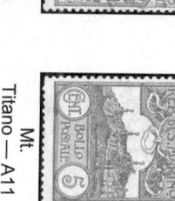

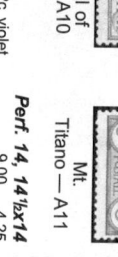

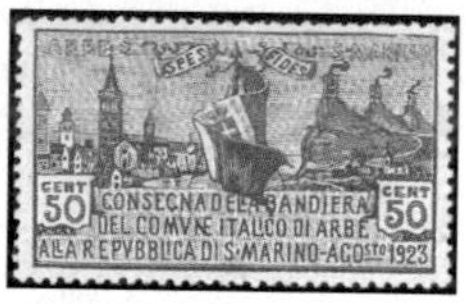
Italian Flag and Views of Arbe and Mt. Titano
A15

**1923, Aug. 6**

| | | | | |
|---|---|---|---|---|
| **82** | A15 | 50c olive green | .75 | .75 |

Presentation to San Marino of the Italian flag which had flown over the island of Arbe, the birthplace of the founder of San Marino. Inscribed on back: "V. Moraldi dis. Blasi inc. Petiti impr.-Roma."

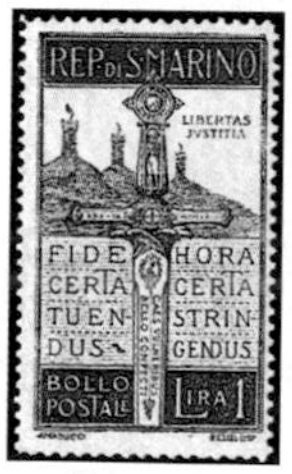
Mt. Titano and Sword — A16

**1923, Sept. 29 *Perf. 14x14½***

| | | | | |
|---|---|---|---|---|
| **83** | A16 | 1 l dark brown | 15.00 | 15.00 |

In honor of the San Marino Volunteers who were killed or wounded in WWI.

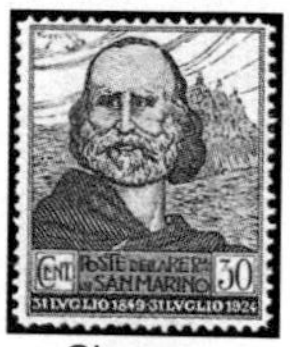
Giuseppe Garibaldi
A17

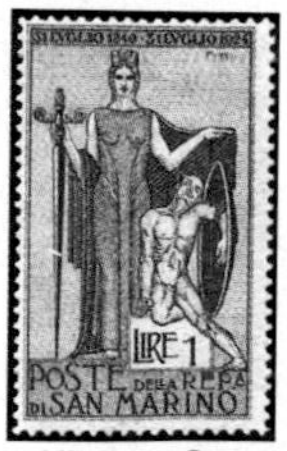
Allegory-San Marino Sheltering Garibaldi
A18

**1924, Sept. 25 *Perf. 14***

| | | | | |
|---|---|---|---|---|
| **84** | A17 | 30c dark violet | 2.50 | 2.50 |
| **85** | A17 | 50c olive brown | 2.60 | 2.60 |
| **86** | A17 | 60c dull red | 3.00 | 3.00 |

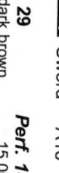

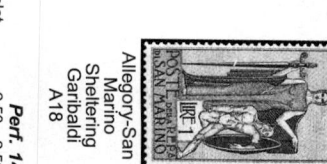

87 A18 1 l deep blue 5.25 5.25
88 A18 2 l gray green 6.50 6.50
19.85 19.85
*Nos. 84-88 (5)*

75th anniv. of Garibaldi's taking refuge in San Marino.

**Semi-Postal Stamps of 1918 Surcharged with New Values and Bars**

**1924, Oct. 9**
89 SP2 30c on 45c yel brn & blk .90 .90

Surcharged

---

**1927, Mar. 10 Unwmk. Perf. 11**
104 A19 1.25 l on 1 l 4.25 4.25
105 A19 2.50 l on 2 l 8.00 8.00
106 A19 3 l on 3 l 37.50 37.50
49.75 49.75
*Nos. 104-106 (3)*

Type of Special Delivery Stamp of 1923 Surcharged

**1927, Sept. 15 Wmk. 140 Perf. 14**
107 A11 1.75 l on 50c on 25c 1.10 1.10

The 50c on 25c violet was not issued without 1.75-lire surcharge.

War Memorial A21

**1927, Sept. 28 Unwmk. Engr. Perf. 12**
108 A21 50c brown violet 1.60 1.60
109 A21 1 l blue 2.25 2.25
110 A21 1 l gray 22.00 22.00
25.85 25.85
*Nos. 108-110 (3)*

Erection of a cenotaph in memory of the San Marino volunteers in WWI.

---

**1926, July 1**
93 A11 75c on 80c blue 1.25 1.25
94 A11 1.20 l on 90c brown 1.25 1.25
95 A11 1.25 l on 90c brown (K) 2.75 2.75
96 A11 2.50 l on 80c blue (R) 6.00 6.00
11.25 11.25
*Nos. 93-96 (4)*

For surcharges see Nos. 104-106, 181-182.

Antonio Onofri — A19

A20

**1926, July 29 Unwmk. Engr. Perf. 11**
97 A19 10c dk blue & blk .20 .20
98 A19 20c olive grn & blk .45 .45
99 A19 45c dk vio & blk .30 .30
100 A19 65c green & blk .30 .30
101 A19 1 l orange & blk 3.50 3.50
102 A19 2 l red vio & blk 8.25 8.25
*Nos. 97-102 (6)*

Special Delivery Stamp No. E2 surcharged with New Value and Bars

**1926, Nov. 25 Wmk. 140 Perf. 14½x14**
103 A20 1.85 l on 60c violet .50 .50

Nos. 101 and 102 Surcharged

---

**1928, Jan. 2**
111 A22 50c red 18.00 4.25
112 A22 1.20 l lp blue 7.25 6.50
113 A22 1.25 l dk brown 7.25 6.50
114 A22 5 l dull violet 24.00 19.00
56.50 36.25
*Nos. 111-114 (4)*

7th centenary of the death of St. Francis of Assisi.
For surcharges see Nos. 183-184.

Design: 250, 51, Death of St. Francis.

Capuchin Church and Convent A22

Government Palace A25

The Rocca (State Prison) A24

Statue of Liberty — A26

**1929-35 Wmk. 217**
115 A24 5c vio brn & ultra 1.50 .60
116 A24 10c lt gray & red vio .60
117 A24 15c dp org & emer 1.90 .90
118 A24 20c dk bl & org red 1.50 .60
119 A24 25c grn & gray blk 1.50 .60
120 A24 30c grn & red vio 1.50 .60
121 A24 50c red vio & ol gray 1.50 .60
122 A24 75c dp red & gray blk 1.50 .60
123 A24 1 l dk brn & emer 1.50 .60
124 A25 1.25 l dk blue & blk 1.50 .60
125 A25 1.75 l green & org 3.50 1.50
126 A25 2 l bl gray & red 1.90 .90

---

127 A25 2.50 l car rose & ultra 1.90 .90
128 A25 3 l dp org & bl 1.90 .90
129 A25 3.70 l ol blk & red brn ('35)
130 A26 5 l dk vio & dk grn 1.90 1.90
131 A26 10 l bis brn & dk bl 2.75 2.00
132 A26 15 l green & red 7.75 6.50
133 A26 20 l dk bl & red vio 57.50 45.00
275.00 230.00
*Nos. 115-133 (19)* 369.50 294.90

General Post Office — A27

San Marino-Rimini Electric Railway — A28

**1932, Feb. 4**
134 A27 20c blue green 5.50 5.50
135 A27 50c dark red 9.00 9.50
136 A27 1.25 l dark blue 14.00 50.00
137 A27 1.75 l dark brown 225.00 100.00
138 A27 2.75 l dark violet 100.00 22.50
388.00 187.50
*Nos. 134-138 (5)*

Opening of new General Post Office.
For surcharges see Nos. 151-160.

**1932, June 11**
139 A28 20c deep green 1.90 1.90
140 A28 50c dark red 2.50 2.50
141 A28 1.25 l dark blue 7.75 7.75
142 A28 5 l deep brown 62.50 55.00
74.65 67.15
*Nos. 139-142 (4)*

Opening of the new electric railway between San Marino and Rimini.

Giuseppe Garibaldi — A29

Garibaldi's Arrival at San Marino — A30

**1932, July 30**
143 A29 10c violet brown 2.50 .85
144 A29 20c violet 2.50 .85
145 A29 25c green 2.50 .85
146 A29 75c yellow brn 5.25 2.60
147 A30 75c dark red 6.75 5.00
148 A30 1.25 l dark blue 12.50 10.50
149 A30 2.75 l brown org 37.50 26.00
150 A30 5 l olive green 240.00 240.00
309.50 286.65
*Nos. 143-150 (8)*

Garibaldi (1807-1882), Italian patriot.

Nos. 138 and 137 Surcharged

---

**1933, May 27**
151 A27 25c on 2.75 l 5.25 5.25
152 A27 50c on 1.75 l 10.50 10.50
153 A27 75c on 2.75 l 22.50 22.50
154 A27 1.25 l on 1.75 l 275.00 275.00
313.25 313.25
*Nos. 151-154 (4)*

Convention of philatelists, San Marino, May 28.

Nos. 134-137 Surcharged in Black

**1934, Apr. 12**
155 A27 25c on 1.25 l 1.60 1.60
156 A27 50c on 1.75 l 3.25 3.25
157 A27 75c on 50c 7.00 7.00
158 A27 1.25 l on 20c 26.00 26.00
37.85 37.85
*Nos. 155-158 (4)*

San Marino's participation (with a philatelic pavilion) in the 15th annual Trade Fair at Milan, Apr. 12-27.

Nos. 136 and 138 Surcharged Wheel and New Value

**1934, Apr. 12**
159 A27 3.70 l on 1.25 l 55.00 55.00
160 A27 3.70 l on 2.75 l 67.50 67.50

Ascent to Mt. Titano A31

## 1935, Feb. 7 — Unwmk. Engr. Perf. 14

| No. | Type | Description | | |
|---|---|---|---|---|
| 161 | A31 | 5c choc & blk | .40 | .40 |
| 162 | A31 | 10c dk vio & blk | .40 | .40 |
| 163 | A31 | 20c orange & blk | .40 | .40 |
| 164 | A31 | 25c green & blk | .40 | .40 |
| 165 | A31 | 50c olive bis & blk | .40 | .40 |
| 166 | A31 | 75c brown red & blk | 3.50 | 3.50 |
| 167 | A31 | 1.25l blue & blk | 12.50 | 12.50 |

Nos. 161-167 (7)

12th anniv. of the founding of the Fascist Movement.

## 1935, Apr. 15 — Wmk. 217 Perf. 12

Melchiorre Delfico—A32

Statue of Delfico—A33

Center in Black

| No. | Type | Description | | |
|---|---|---|---|---|
| 169 | A32 | 5c brown lake | .85 | .65 |
| 170 | A32 | 7½c lt brown | .85 | .65 |
| 171 | A32 | 10c dk blue grn | .85 | .65 |
| 172 | A32 | 15c rose carmine | 11.00 | 3.50 |
| 173 | A32 | 20c orange | 1.90 | 1.40 |
| 174 | A32 | 25c green | 1.90 | 1.40 |
| 175 | A32 | 30c dull violet | 1.90 | 1.40 |
| 176 | A32 | 50c olive green | 3.50 | 3.50 |
| 177 | A32 | 75c red | 10.50 | 8.00 |
| 178 | A32 | 1.25l dark blue | 47.50 | 37.50 |
| 179 | A33 | 1.50l dk brown | 57.50 | 60.00 |
| 180 | A33 | 1.75l dk brown org | 121.25 | 121.15 |

Nos. 169-180 (12)

For surcharges see Nos. 202, 277.

Melchiorre Delfico (1744-1835), historian.

## 1936 — Unwmk. Perf. 11

| No. | Type | Description | | |
|---|---|---|---|---|
| 181 | A19 | 80c on 45c dk vio & blk | 2.50 | 2.50 |
| 182 | A19 | 80c on 65c grn & blk | 2.50 | 2.50 |

Perf. 12

| 183 | A22 | 2.05l on 1.25l | 7.50 | 7.50 |
|---|---|---|---|---|
| 184 | A22 | 2.75l on 2.50l | 24.00 | 24.00 |

Nos. 181-184 (4) 36.50 36.50

Issued: #181-182, 4/14; #183-184, 8/23.

L. 2,05

Nos. 99-100 Surcharged in Black

Nos. 112-113 Surcharged in Black

## 1936 — Souvenir Sheet

ANNO 1937 - 1636 d. FR

## 1937, Aug. 23 — Engr. Wmk. 217

185 A34 5l steel blue 10.00 10.00

Design from Base of Roman Column—A34

Unveiling of the Roman Column at San Marino. The date "1636 d. F. R." means the 1,636th year since the founding of the republic.

No. 185 was privately surcharged "+ 10 L 1941."

## 1938, Apr. 7 — Wmk. 217 Perf. 13

| 186 | A35 | 3l dark blue | 1.25 | 1.25 |
|---|---|---|---|---|
| 187 | A35 | 5l rose red | 15.00 | 15.00 |

Abraham Lincoln—A35

Dedication of a Lincoln bust, Sept. 3, 1937.

## Souvenir Sheets

REPVBBLICA DI SAN MARINO
3 SETTEMBRE 1937 - 1636 d.F.R.

## 1941 — Wmk. 140 Perf. 14

| 188 | A11 | 10c on 15c brown vio | .25 | .25 |
|---|---|---|---|---|
| 189 | A11 | 10c on 30c brown org | 1.00 | 1.00 |

No. 49 and Type of 1925 Surcharged with New Value in Black

## 1942 — Photo.

Harbor of Arbe A37

Flags of Italy and San Marino—A36

| No. | Type | Description | | |
|---|---|---|---|---|
| 190 | A36 | 10c yel brn & brn org | .25 | .25 |
| 191 | A36 | 15c brn & red brn | .25 | .25 |
| 192 | A36 | 20c gray grn & gray blk | .25 | .25 |
| 193 | A36 | 25c green & blue | .25 | .25 |
| 194 | A36 | 50c brn red & brn | .25 | .25 |
| 195 | A36 | 75c red & gray blk | .25 | .25 |
| 196 | A37 | 1.25l brn & grnsh bl | .50 | .50 |
| 197 | A37 | 1.75l bis brn & gray bl | .25 | .25 |
| 198 | A37 | 2.75l brn & gray bl | .50 | .50 |
| 199 | A37 | 5l green & brown | 4.50 | 4.50 |

Nos. 190-199 (10) 7.00 7.00

Return of the Italian flag to Arbe.

## 1942, July 30

200 A36 30c on 10c .20 .20

No. 192 Surcharged with New Value and Bars in Black

## 1942, Sept. 14

201 A36 30c on 20c .20 .20

No. 190 Surcharged in Black

## 1942, Sept. 28 — Wmk. 217 Perf. 12

202 A33 20l on 75c red & blk 12.00 12.00

No. 177 Surcharged with New Value in Black

GIORNATA FILATELICA
3 AGOSTO 1942 [16]l d. F.R.]
RIMINI - SAN MARINO
C. 30

## 1942 — Souvenir Sheet

No. 190 Surcharged in Black

## 1943, Apr. 12 — Wmk. 140 Photo. Perf. 14

Printing Press and Newspaper A38

Newspapers A39

| No. | Type | Description | | |
|---|---|---|---|---|
| 203 | A38 | 10c deep green | .25 | .25 |
| 204 | A38 | 15c deep green | .25 | .25 |
| 205 | A38 | 20c bister | .25 | .25 |
| 206 | A38 | 20c dk orange brn | .25 | .25 |
| 207 | A38 | 30c dk rose vio | .25 | .25 |
| 208 | A38 | 75c red orange | .25 | .25 |
| 209 | A38 | 1l blue | 1.00 | 1.00 |
| 210 | A39 | 1.75l deep violet | .25 | .25 |
| 211 | A39 | 5l slate | .25 | .25 |
| 212 | A39 | 10l dark brown | 7.50 | 7.50 |

Nos. 203-212 (10)

## 1943, July 1

| 213 | A38 | 30c dk rose vio | .20 | .20 |
|---|---|---|---|---|
| 214 | A38 | 50c blue black | .20 | .20 |

Nos. 206 and 207 Overprinted in Red

Rimini-San Marino Stamp Day, July 5.

## 1943, Aug. 27

Overprinted in Black: "28 LVGLIO 1943 1642 F. R."

| No. | Type | Description | | |
|---|---|---|---|---|
| 215 | A40 | 5c brown | .20 | .20 |
| 216 | A40 | 10c orange red | .20 | .20 |
| 217 | A40 | 15c ultra | .20 | .20 |
| 218 | A40 | 25c deep green | .20 | .20 |
| 219 | A40 | 30c brown carmine | .20 | .20 |
| 220 | A40 | 50c deep violet | .20 | .20 |
| 221 | A40 | 75c car rose | .20 | .20 |
| 222 | A40 | 1.25l sapphire | .20 | .20 |
| 223 | A41 | 1.25l red org | .45 | .45 |
| 224 | A41 | 2.75l dk red brn | .45 | .45 |
| 225 | A41 | 5l green | .45 | .45 |
| 226 | A41 | 10l violet | .75 | .75 |
| 227 | A41 | 20l slate blue | 1.90 | 1.90 |

Nos. 215-227,C26-C33 (21) 11.10 11.10

This series was prepared for the 20th anniv. of fascism, but as Mussolini was overthrown July 25, 1943, it was overprinted for the downfall of fascism.

Overprint on Nos. 222-227 adds "d." before "F. R."

Exist without overprint. Value of set $16.

## 1943, Aug. 27

Overprinted "Governo Provvisorio" in Black

| No. | Type | Description | | |
|---|---|---|---|---|
| 228 | A42 | 5c brown | .25 | .25 |
| 229 | A42 | 10c orange red | .25 | .25 |
| 230 | A42 | 15c ultra | .25 | .25 |
| 231 | A42 | 25c deep green | .25 | .25 |
| 232 | A42 | 30c brown carmine | .25 | .25 |
| 233 | A42 | 50c deep violet | .25 | .25 |
| 234 | A42 | 75c carmine rose | .25 | .25 |
| 235 | A43 | 1.25l sapphire | .25 | .25 |
| 236 | A43 | 1.75l red orange | .75 | .75 |
| 237 | A43 | 5l slate blue | 2.00 | 2.00 |
| 238 | A43 | 20l slate blue | 10.00 | 10.00 |

Nos. 228-238,C34-C39 (17)

A42, A43

## 1945, Mar. 15 — Perf. 14, Imperf. Photo.

239 A44 Sheet of 3

| | | | Never hinged | |
|---|---|---|---|---|
| 239 | A44 | | 90.00 70.00 | 125.00 70.00 |
| a. | | 10l dull rose | 20.00 | 20.00 |
| b. | | 15l dull green | 20.00 | 20.00 |
| c. | | 25l dull red brown | 20.00 | 20.00 |

Government Palace—A45

Sheets contain a papermaker's watermark, "Hammermill Bond. Made in U.S.A."

Nos. 239, 241 and C40 were issued to commemorate the 50th anniv. of the reconstruction of the Government Palace.

A44

## 1945, Mar. 15 — Wmk. 140 Perf. 14

241 A45 25l brown violet 4.50 4.50 / 9.25

Never hinged

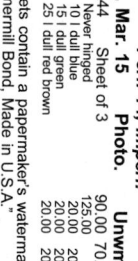 

## Coat of Arms of Faetano—A46

Coats of Arms: 20c, 60c, 25 l, Montegiardino. 40c, 5 l, 50 l, 80c, Serravalle.

## 1945-46 — Wmk. 277

| 242 | A46 | 10c dark blue | .20 | .20 |
|---|---|---|---|---|
| 243 | A46 | 20c vermilion | .20 | .20 |
| 244 | A46 | 40c deep orange | .20 | .20 |

## San Marino (continued — A46 series)

| No. | Type | Description | Unused | Used |
|---|---|---|---|---|
| 245 | A46 | 60c slate black | .20 | .20 |
| 246 | A46 | 80c dark green | .20 | .20 |
| 247 | A46 | 1 l dk car rose | .20 | .20 |
| 248 | A46 | 2 l chestnut | .20 | .20 |
| 249 | A46 | 3 l deep violet | .20 | .20 |
| 250 | A46 | 4 l red org ('46) | .20 | .20 |
| 250A | A46 | | .25 | .25 |
| 251 | A46 | 15 l dark brown | .25 | .25 |
| 251A | A46 | 15 l dp brown ('46) | 1.25 | 1.00 |

**Lithographed and Engraved**
**Size: 22x27mm**

| No. | Type | Description | Unused | Used |
|---|---|---|---|---|
| 252 | A46 | 10 l brt red & brown | 1.25 | 1.00 |
| 253 | A46 | 20 l brt red & ultra | 3.50 | 2.75 |
| 254 | A46 | 20 l org brn & ultra ('46) | 7.00 | 5.50 |
| | | | 300.00 | |
| a. | | Vert. pair, imperf. btwn. | 425.00 | |
| | | Never hinged | | |
| 255 | A46 | 25 l hn brn & ultra ('46) | 6.25 | 5.00 |

**Size: 22x27mm**

| No. | Type | Description | Unused | Used |
|---|---|---|---|---|
| 256 | A46 | 50 l ol brn & ultra | 9.25 | 7.50 |
| | | | 30.75 | 25.00 |
| | | Nos. 242-256 (17) | 57.50 | |
| | | Set, never hinged | | |

Nos. 252-256 are in sheets of 10 (2x5). Values: No. 252, 254-255, $60 each. No. 253, $90. No. 256, $200.
For surcharges see Nos. 258-259, B26.

**"Dawn of New Hope" — A52**

**Engr. & Litho.**

| | | **1946** **Unwmk.** | | **Perf. 14** |
|---|---|---|---|---|
| 257 | A52 | 100 l dull yel & brn vio | 6.25 | 6.25 |
| j. | | Vert. pair, imperf. btwn. | 12.50 | |
| | | Never hinged | 350.00 | |
| | | Never hinged | 525.00 | |

UN Relief and Rehabilitation Administration. Sheets of 10 with blue coat of arms in top margin.

**Franklin D. Roosevelt and Flags of San Marino and U3 — A52a**

Designs: 1 l, 50 l, Quotation on Liberty, from Franklin D. Roosevelt. 2 l, 100 l, Roosevelt portrait, vert. 5 l, 15 l, Roosevelt and flags (as shown).

**1947, May 3** **Wmk. 277** **Photo.** **Perf. 14**

| No. | Type | Description | Unused | Used |
|---|---|---|---|---|
| 257A | A52a | 1 l bister & brn | .20 | .20 |
| 257B | A52a | 2 l blue & sepia | .20 | .20 |
| 257C | A52a | 5 l violet & multi | .20 | .20 |
| 257D | A52a | 15 l green & multi | .25 | .25 |
| 257E | A52a | 50 l vermilion & brn | .40 / .70 | .40 / .70 |
| 257F | A52a | 100 l violet & sepia | 20.80 | 17.20 |
| | | | 37.50 | |
| | | Nos. 257A-257F,C51A-C51H (14) | | |
| | | Set, never hinged | | |

For surcharges see #257G-257C, C51I-C51K.

**1947, June 16**

| No. | Type | Description | Unused | Used |
|---|---|---|---|---|
| 257G | A52a | 3 l on 1 l | .25 | .25 |
| 257H | A52a | 4 l on 2 l | .25 | .25 |
| 257I | A52a | 6 l on 5 l | 1.50 | 1.50 |
| | | Nos. 257G-257I,C51I-C51K (6) | 3.25 | |
| | | Set, never hinged | | |

**No. 250A Surcharged with New Value in Black**

**1947, June 16** **Wmk. 277**

| 258 | A46 | 6(l) on 4 l red org | .20 | .20 |
|---|---|---|---|---|
| | | Never hinged | | |

---

**No. 250A Surcharged in Black**

| 259 | A46 | 21 l on 4 l red org | .55 | .50 |
|---|---|---|---|---|
| | | Never hinged | 1.10 | |

**"St. Marinus Raising the Republic" by Girolamo Batoni — A53**

**Wmk. 217**
**1947, July 18** **Engr.** **Perf. 12**

| No. | Type | Description | Unused | Used |
|---|---|---|---|---|
| 260 | A53 | 1 l brt grn & vio | .20 | .20 |
| 261 | A53 | 2 l purple & olive | .20 | .20 |
| 262 | A53 | 4 l vio brn & dk bl grn | .20 | .20 |
| 263 | A53 | 10 l org & bl blk | .20 | .20 |
| 264 | A53 | 25 l carmine & purple | .55 | .50 |
| 265 | A53 | 50 l dk bl grn & brn | 12.50 / 16.25 | 11.00 / 14.50 |
| | | Nos. 260-265,C52-C53 (8) | 32.50 | |
| | | Set, never hinged | | |

For overprints and surcharges see Nos. 294-295, B27-B38, C56.

**United States 1847 Stamp A54**
**United States Stamps of 1847 and 1869 A55**
**A56**

**1947, Dec. 24** **Wmk. 277** **Photo.** **Perf. 14**

| No. | Type | Description | Unused | Used |
|---|---|---|---|---|
| 266 | A54 | 5 l red vio & dk brn | .20 | .20 |
| 267 | A55 | 3 l sl gray, dp ultra & car | .20 | .20 |
| 268 | A54 | 6 l dp bl & dk gray grn | .25 | .25 |
| 269 | A56 | 15 l vio, dp ultra & car | .25 | .25 |
| 270 | A55 | 35 l dk brn, dp ultra & car | 1.00 | 1.00 |
| 271 | A56 | 100 l sl grn, dp ultra & car | 9.85 | 8.35 |
| | | | 19.00 | |
| | | Nos. 266-271,C55 (7) | | |
| | | Set, never hinged | | |

1st United States postage stamps.

**Laborer and San Marino Flag A57**

**1948, June 3** **Engr.**

| No. | Type | Description | Unused | Used |
|---|---|---|---|---|
| 272 | A57 | 5 l brown | .20 | .20 |
| 273 | A57 | 8 l green | .20 | .20 |
| 274 | A57 | 30 l crimson | .30 | .30 |
| 275 | A57 | 50 l red brn & rose lil | .80 | .75 |
| 276 | A57 | 100 l dk bl & dp vio | 30.00 / 31.40 | 30.00 / 31.35 |
| | | Nos. 272-276 (5) | 62.50 | |
| | | Set, never hinged | | |

See Nos. 373-374.

---

**No. 172 Surcharged with New Value and Ornaments in Black**

**1948** **Wmk. 217** **Perf. 12**

| 277 | A32 | 100 l on 15c | 37.50 | 37.50 |
|---|---|---|---|---|
| | | Never hinged | 70.00 | |

**Government Palace — A58**
**Mt. Titano, Distant View — A59**

Various Views of San Marino.

**1949-50** **Wmk. 277** **Photo.** **Perf. 14**

| No. | Type | Description | Unused | Used |
|---|---|---|---|---|
| 278 | A58 | 1 l black & blue | .20 | .20 |
| 279 | A58 | 2 l violet & car | .20 | .20 |
| 280 | A58 | 3 l violet & ultra | .20 | .20 |
| 281 | A58 | 4 l black & vio | .20 | .20 |
| 282 | A58 | 5 l violet & brn | .20 | .20 |
| 283 | A58 | 6 l dp blue & sep | .55 | .55 |
| 284 | A59 | 8 l blk brn & yel brn | .55 | .30 |
| 285 | A59 | 10 l brn blk & bl | .30 | .20 |
| 286 | A59 | 12 l brt rose & bl | .40 | .20 |
| 287 | A58 | 15 l vio & brt rose | 1.10 | .60 |
| 288 | A58 | 20 l dp bl & brn ('50) | 3.25 | 1.10 |
| 289 | A58 | 35 l green & violet | 9.50 | 1.40 |
| 290 | A58 | 50 l brt rose & yel brn | 6.25 | 3.75 |
| 291 | A58 | 55 l dp bl & dl grn ('50) | 3.25 | 1.10 |

**Perf. 14x13½**
**Engr.**

| 292 | A59 | 100 l blk brn & dk grn | 37.50 | 25.00 |
|---|---|---|---|---|
| 293 | A59 | 200 l dp blue & brn | 108.10 | 137.15 |
| | | Nos. 278-293 (16) | 325.00 | |
| | | Set, never hinged | | |

**Nos. 260 and 261 Overprinted in Black**

San Marino-Riccione Stamp Day, June 28.

**1949, June 28** **Wmk. 217**

| 294 | A53 | 1 l brt green & vio | .20 | .20 |
|---|---|---|---|---|
| 295 | A53 | 2 l purple & olive | .60 | .60 |
| | | Set, never hinged | | |

**Francesco Nullo — A60**

1 l, 20 l, Francesco Nullo. 2 l, 5 l, Anita Garibaldi. 3 l, 50 l, Giuseppe Garibaldi. 4 l, 15 l, Ugo Bassi.

**1949, July 31** **Wmk. 277** **Photo.** **Perf. 14**
**Size: 22x28mm**

| No. | Type | Description | Unused | Used |
|---|---|---|---|---|
| 296 | A60 | 1 l blk & car lake | .20 | .20 |
| 297 | A60 | 2 l red brn & blue | .20 | .20 |
| 298 | A60 | 3 l car lake & dk grn | .20 | .20 |
| 299 | A60 | 4 l violet & dk brn | .20 | .20 |

**Size: 26½x36½mm**

| No. | Type | Description | Unused | Used |
|---|---|---|---|---|
| 300 | A60 | 5 l purple & dk brn | .60 | .60 |
| 301 | A60 | 15 l car lake & gray bl | .60 | .60 |
| 302 | A60 | 20 l violet & car lake | 1.00 | 1.00 |
| 303 | A60 | 50 l red brn & violet | 8.35 | |
| | | Nos. 296-303, #AIR POST STAMPS (13) | 21.60 / 41.50 | 21.60 |
| | | Set, never hinged | | |

Centenary of Garibaldi's escape to San Marino.
See Nos. C57-C61, 404-410.

---

**Stagecoach on Road from San Marino — A61**

**Engr.**

**1949, Dec. 29**

| 304 | A61 | 100 l blue & gray vio | 7.75 | 7.75 |
|---|---|---|---|---|
| | | Never hinged | 16.00 | |
| | | Sheet of 6 | 200.00 | |
| | | Never hinged | 250.00 | |

UPU, 75th anniversary.

A62 — A63a — A63

**Perf. 13½x14, 14x13½**
**Engr.**

**Sky and Cross in Carmine**

**1951, Mar. 15**

| No. | Type | Description | Unused | Used |
|---|---|---|---|---|
| 305 | A62 | 25 l dk brn & red vin | 4.75 | 4.75 |
| 306 | A63 | 75 l org brn & dk brn | 6.25 | 6.25 |
| 307 | A63a | 100 l dk brn & gray blk | 7.75 / 18.75 | 7.75 / 18.75 |
| | | Nos. 305-307 (3) | 37.50 | |
| | | Set, never hinged | | |

Issued to honor the San Marino Red Cross.

**Christopher Columbus A64**

Designs: 2 l, 25 l, Columbus on his ship. 3 l, 10 l, 20 l, Landing of Columbus. 4 l, 15 l, 80 l, Pioneers trading with Indians. 5 l, 200 l, Columbus and map of Americas.

**1952, Jan. 28** **Photo.** **Perf. 14**

| No. | Type | Description | Unused | Used |
|---|---|---|---|---|
| 308 | A64 | 2 l brn org & dk grn | .20 | .20 |
| 309 | A64 | 3 l violet & dk brn | .20 | .20 |
| 310 | A64 | 4 l blue & org | .20 | .20 |
| 311 | A64 | 5 l grn & dk bl | .20 | .20 |
| 312 | A64 | 10 l dk brown & dk bl | .30 | .30 |
| 313 | A64 | 15 l carmine & blk | .45 | .45 |

**Engr.**

| 314 | A64 | 20 l dp bl & dk bl grn | .65 | .65 |
|---|---|---|---|---|
| 315 | A64 | 20 l dp bl & dk bl grn | .95 | .95 |
| 316 | A64 | 25 l vio brn & blk | 4.00 | 4.00 |
| 317 | A64 | 60 l choc & vio bl | 5.50 | 5.50 |

**Type of 1952 in New Colors Overprinted in Black or Red**

| 318 | A64 | 80 l gray & blk | 17.50 | 17.50 |
|---|---|---|---|---|
| 319 | A64 | 200 l Prus grn & dp ultra | 17.50 | 17.50 |
| | | Set, never hinged | 32.50 | 32.50 |
| | | Nos. 308-319,C80 (13) | 81.65 | 81.65 |

Issued to honor Christopher Columbus.

**1952, June 29**    **Photo.**

| 320 | A64 | 1 l vio & dk brn | .20 | .20 |
|---|---|---|---|---|
| 321 | A64 | 2 l carmine & blk | .20 | .20 |
| 322 | A64 | 3 l grn & dk grn (R) | .20 | .20 |
| 323 | A64 | 4 l blk & blk | .20 | .20 |
| 324 | A64 | 5 l purple & vio | .20 | .25 |
| 325 | A64 | 10 l bl & org brn (R) | .60 | .65 |
| 326 | A64 | 15 l org brn & blue | .20 | .20 |
| | | Set, never hinged | 2.10 | 1.90 |
| | | Nos. 320-326,C81 (8) | 28.75 | 28.60 |
| | | | 57.50 | 28.60 |

4th Int'l Sample Fair of Trieste.

Discobolus — A65

Tennis A66

Model Airplane — A67

**1953, Apr. 20**   **Wmk. 277**   **Perf. 14**

| 327 | A65 | 1 l dk brn & blk | .20 | .20 |
|---|---|---|---|---|
| 328 | A66 | 2 l black & brown | .20 | .20 |
| 329 | A65 | 3 l blk & grnsh brn | .20 | .20 |
| 330 | A66 | 4 l dk & brt bl | .20 | .20 |
| 331 | A66 | 5 l dk brn & vio | .20 | .20 |
| 332 | A67 | 10 l dp blue & blk | .20 | .20 |
| 333 | A66 | 25 l blk & dk grn | 1.25 | 1.25 |
| 334 | A67 | 100 l dk brn & slate | 4.75 | 4.75 |
| | | Set, never hinged | 39.75 | 39.75 |
| | | | 75.00 | |

Designs: 3 l, Runner. 4 l, Cyclist. 5 l, Soccer. 25 l, Shooting. 100 l, Roller skating.

See No. 438.

Narcissus A68

**1953, Aug. 24**

| 335 | A66 | 100 l grn & dk grn | 10.00 | 10.00 |
|---|---|---|---|---|
| | | | | 20.00 |

San Marino-Riccione Stamp Day, Aug. 24.

**Type of 1953 Overprinted in Black**

CIORNATA FILATELICA S. MARINO - RICCIONE 24 AGOSTO 1953

See No. 438.

Walking Racer — A69

Fencing A70

**1953, Dec. 28**   **Photo.**

| 336 | A68 | 1 l multicolored | .20 | .20 |
|---|---|---|---|---|
| 337 | A68 | 2 l multicolored | .20 | .20 |
| 338 | A68 | 3 l multicolored | .20 | .20 |
| 339 | A68 | 4 l multicolored | .20 | .20 |
| 340 | A68 | 5 l multicolored | .20 | .20 |
| 341 | A68 | 10 l multicolored | .20 | .20 |
| 342 | A68 | 25 l multicolored | 1.50 | 1.50 |
| 343 | A68 | 80 l multicolored | 15.00 | 9.00 |
| 344 | A68 | 100 l multicolored | 9.00 | 9.00 |
| | | Set, never hinged | 26.70 | 26.70 |
| | | Nos. 336-344 (9) | 52.50 | |

Flowers: 2 l, Tulips. 3 l, Oleanders. 4 l, Cornflowers. 5 l, Cyclamen. 10 l, Geraniums. 80 l, Irises. 25 l, Cyclamen. 100 l, Roses.

A71

A72

**1954-55**   **Engr.**

| 345 | A69 | 1 l violet & cer | .20 | .20 |
|---|---|---|---|---|
| 346 | A70 | 2 l dk grn & vio | .20 | .20 |
| 347 | A70 | 3 l brn & brn org | .20 | .20 |
| 348 | A69 | 4 l dk brn & grn | .20 | .20 |
| 349 | A70 | 5 l dk grn & dk | .20 | .20 |
| 350 | A70 | 8 l lil rose & pur | .20 | .20 |
| 351 | A70 | 10 l black & crim | .25 | .25 |
| 352 | A69 | 25 l bl & dk grn | .20 | .25 |
| 353 | A69 | 80 l dk & bl grn | .70 | .70 |
| 354 | A69 | 200 l violet & brn | 2.75 | 2.75 |
| | | | 39.75 | |

**Photo.**   **Wmk. 277**

| 355 | A69 | 250 l multi | 22.50 | 22.50 |
|---|---|---|---|---|
| | | Sheet of 4 (#355) | 160.00 | 160.00 |
| | | Nos. 345-355 (11) | 27.60 | 27.60 |
| | | | 55.00 | |

Sports: 3 l, Boxing. 4 l, 200 l, 250 l, Gymnastics. 5 l, Motorcycling. 8 l, Javelin-throwing. 12 l, Automobiling. 25 l, Wrestling. 80 l, Walking racer.

**Perf. 12½x13**

**1954, Dec. 16**   **Perf. 13x13½**

| 356 | A71 | 20 l choc & blue | .20 | .20 |
|---|---|---|---|---|
| 357 | A71 | 60 l car & dk grn | .40 | .40 |
| | | Set, never hinged | 1.15 | 1.15 |
| | | | 2.25 | |

Liberty statue and Government palace.

Murata Nuova Bridge — A73

View of La Rocca — A74

**1955, Aug. 27**   **Wmk. 303**   **Perf. 14**

| 358 | A72 | 100 l gray blk & bl | 1.60 | 1.60 |
|---|---|---|---|---|
| | | Never hinged | 3.25 | |

7th San Marino-Riccione Stamp Fair. See No. 385.

Designs: 15 l, Government Palace.

Design: 15 l, Government Palace.

**1955, Nov. 15**   **Perf. 14**
**Size: 22x27½mm; 27½x22mm**

| 359 | A73 | 5 l blue & brown | .20 | .20 |
|---|---|---|---|---|
| 360 | A74 | 10 l org & bl grn | .20 | .20 |
| 361 | A73 | 15 l Prus grn & car | .20 | .20 |
| 362 | A73 | 25 l dk brn & vio | .20 | .20 |
| 363 | A74 | 35 l vio & red car | 1.00 | 1.00 |
| | | Set, never hinged | 1.50 | |
| | | Nos. 359-363 (5) | .75 | |

See Nos. 386-388, 636-638.

Views: 3 l, Gate tower. 20 l, Covered Market of Borgo Maggiore. 125 l, View from South Bastion.

Skier A76

**1955, Dec. 15**   **Wmk. 303**   **Perf. 14**

| 364 | A75 | 1 l brown & yellow | .20 | .20 |
|---|---|---|---|---|
| 365 | A76 | 2 l brt blue & red | .20 | .20 |
| 366 | A75 | 3 l bk brn & lt brn | .20 | .20 |
| 367 | A76 | 4 l brown & green | .20 | .20 |
| 368 | A76 | 5 l ultra & green | .20 | .20 |
| 369 | A/b | 10 l ultra & pink | .20 | .20 |
| 370 | A76 | 25 l gray blk & red | .40 | .40 |
| 371 | A76 | 50 l brown & indigo | 1.10 | 1.10 |
| 372 | A76 | 100 l blk & Prus grn | 3.25 | 3.25 |
| | | Set, never hinged | 18.45 | 18.45 |
| | | Nos. 364-372,C96 (10) | 35.00 | |

3 l, 50 l, Tobogganing. 4 l, Skier going downhill. 5 l, 100 l, Ice Hockey player. 10 l, Girl ice skater.

7th Winter Olympic Games at Cortina d'Ampezzo, Jan. 26-Feb. 5, 1956. For surcharge see No. C96.

Ice Skater — A75

**Type of 1948 Inscribed: "50th Anniversario Arengo 25 Marzo 1906"**

**1956, Mar. 24**   **Wmk. 303**   **Perf. 14**

| 373 | A57 | 50 l sapphire | 4.00 | 5.00 |
|---|---|---|---|---|
| | | Never hinged | 7.50 | |

50th anniv. of the meeting of the heads of families (Arengo), the beginning of the democratic era in San Marino.

**Type of 1948 Inscribed: "Assistenza Invernale"**

**1956, Mar. 24**   **Photo.**

| 374 | A57 | 50 l dark green | 4.00 | 5.00 |
|---|---|---|---|---|
| | | Never hinged | 7.50 | |

Issued to publicize the Winterhelp charity.

Pointer and Arms A77

**1956, June 8**   **Wmk. 303**   **Perf. 14**

| 375 | A77 | 1 l ultra & brown | .20 | .20 |
|---|---|---|---|---|
| 376 | A77 | 2 l car lake & bl | | |
| 377 | A77 | 3 l gray | .20 | .20 |
| 378 | A77 | 4 l ultra & brown | .20 | .20 |
| 379 | A77 | 5 l grnsh bl & gray | .20 | .20 |
| 380 | A77 | 10 l car lake & dk brn | .20 | .20 |
| 381 | A77 | 25 l dk blue & brown | .20 | .20 |
| 382 | A77 | 60 l car lake & multi | 3.00 | 3.00 |
| 383 | A77 | 80 l car lake & multi | 3.50 | 3.50 |
| 384 | A77 | 100 l dk blue & multi | 4.50 | 4.50 |
| | | Set, never hinged | 15.70 | 18.95 |
| | | Nos. 375-384 (10) | 40.00 | |

Dogs: 2 l, Russian greyhound. 3 l, Sheepdog. 4 l, English greyhound. 5 l, Boxer. 10 l, Great Dane. 25 l, Irish setter. 60 l, German shepherd. 80 l, Scotch collie. 100 l, Hunting hound.

**1956**   **Perf. 14**
**Size: 26x36mm; 36x26mm**

| 385 | A72 | 100 l brown & bl grn | .75 | .95 |
|---|---|---|---|---|
| | | Never hinged | 1.50 | |

8th San Marino-Riccione Stamp Fair.

**Sailboat Type of 1955**   **Wmk. 303**

| 386 | A74 | 20 l blue & brown | .25 | .25 |
|---|---|---|---|---|
| 387 | A73 | 80 l vio & red car | .95 | .95 |
| 388 | A74 | 100 l org & bl grn | 2.70 | 2.70 |
| | | Set, never hinged | 5.50 | |
| | | Nos. 386-388 (3) | | |

"Congresso Internaz. Periti Filatelici San Marino-Salsomaggiore 6-8 Ottobre 1956."

**Types of 1955 with added inscription:**

Int'l Philatelic Cong., San Marino, 10/6-8.

Street and Borgo Maggiore Church — A78

Hospital Street — A79

**1956, Oct. 6**   **Perf. 14**
**Size: 22x28mm**

| 389 | A78 | 2 l dk grn & rose red | .20 | .20 |
|---|---|---|---|---|
| 390 | A79 | 10 l blue & brown | .20 | .20 |
| 391 | A78 | 20 l dk blue green | .45 | .45 |
| 392 | A79 | 60 l brn & blue vio | .50 | .50 |

**Engr.**

| 393 | A78 | 125 l dk blue & blk | 1.30 | 1.30 |
|---|---|---|---|---|
| | | Set, never hinged | 2.00 | 1.35 |
| | | Nos. 389-393 (5) | | |

See Nos. 473-476, 633-635.

Daisies and View of San Marino — A80

**Type of 1949 Inscribed: "Commemorazione 150 Nascita G. Garibaldi."**

**1957, Aug. 31**   **Photo.**   **Perf. 14**
**Flowers in Natural Colors**

| 394 | A80 | 1 l dk vio blue | .20 | .20 |
|---|---|---|---|---|
| 395 | A80 | 2 l dk vio blue | .20 | .20 |
| 396 | A80 | 3 l dk vio blue | .20 | .20 |
| 397 | A80 | 4 l dk vio blue | .20 | .20 |
| 398 | A80 | 5 l dk vio blue | .20 | .20 |
| 399 | A80 | 10 l blue, buff & lilac | .20 | .20 |
| 400 | A80 | 25 l blue, red & lilac | .25 | .30 |
| 401 | A80 | 60 l blue, yel & dl red | .25 | .30 |
| 402 | A80 | 80 l blue & dl red brn | .75 | 1.25 |
| 403 | A80 | 100 l blue, yel & dl red brn | 2.80 | 3.60 |
| | | Set, never hinged | 4.00 | |
| | | Nos. 394-403 (10) | | |

Flowers: 2 l, Primrose. 3 l, Lily. 4 l, Orchid. 5 l, Lily of the Valley. 10 l, Poppy. 25 l, Pansy. 60 l, Gladiolus. 80 l, Wild Rose. 100 l, Anemone.

**Type of 1949 Inscribed:**

Portraits: 2 l, 50 l, Anita Garibaldi. 3 l, 25 l, Francesco Nullo. 5 l, 100 l, Giuseppe Garibaldi. 15 l, Ugo Bassi.

**1957, May 9**   **Photo.**   **Wmk. 303**

**1957, Dec. 12**   **Wmk. 303**   **Perf. 14**
**Size: 22x28mm**

| 404 | A60 | 2 l vio & dull red | .20 | .20 |
|---|---|---|---|---|
| 405 | A60 | 3 l lake & blue | .20 | .20 |
| 406 | A60 | 5 l brn & ol gray | .20 | .20 |

## Size: 26½x37mm

| | | | | |
|---|---|---|---|---|
| 407 | A60 | 1 l blue & vio | .20 | .20 |
| 408 | A60 | 25 l green & dk gray | .20 | .20 |
| 409 | A60 | 50 l violet & brn | .60 | .95 |
| 410 | A60 | 100 l brown & vio | 2.20 | 2.90 |

Set, never hinged  3.25

Nos. 404-410 are printed se-tenant. Birth of Giuseppe Garibaldi, 150th anniv.

**Panoramic View A81**

**1958, Feb. 27    Engr.    Perf. 14**

| | | | | |
|---|---|---|---|---|
| 411 | A81 | 500 l green & blk | 55.00 | 55.00 |
| | | Never hinged | 500.00 | |
| | | Sheet of 6 | 500.00 | |
| | | Never hinged | 575.00 | |

**Catalogue values for unused stamps in this section, from this point to the end of the section, are for Never Hinged items.**

**Fair Emblem and San Marino Peaks — A82**

**1958, Apr. 12    Photo.    Perf. 14**

| | | | | |
|---|---|---|---|---|
| 412 | A82 | 40 l yel green & brn | .20 | .20 |
| 413 | A82 | 60 l brt blue & mar | .20 | .20 |

World's Fair, Brussels, Apr. 17-Oct. 19.

**Madonna and Fair Entrance A83**

**1958, Apr. 12**

| | | | | |
|---|---|---|---|---|
| 414 | A83 | 15 l yellow, grn & bl | .20 | .20 |
| 415 | A83 | 60 l green & rose red | .55 | .80 |
| | | Nos. 414-415,C97 (3) | 2.35 | 2.25 |

San Marino's 10th participation in the Milan Fair.

Design: 60 l, View of Fair Grounds.

**Wheat — A84**

**1958, Aug. 30    Wmk. 303    Perf. 14**

| | | | | |
|---|---|---|---|---|
| 416 | A84 | 1 l dk blue & yel org | .20 | .20 |
| 417 | A84 | 2 l dk grn & red org | .20 | .20 |
| 418 | A84 | 3 l blue & ocher | .20 | .20 |
| 419 | A84 | 4 l green & rose car | .20 | .20 |
| 420 | A84 | 5 l blue, yel & grn | .20 | .20 |
| 421 | A84 | 25 l ultra & brn org | .25 | .20 |
| 422 | A84 | 40 l multicolored | .40 | .40 |
| 423 | A84 | 60 l multicolored | .25 | .20 |
| 424 | A84 | 80 l multicolored | 1.10 | .45 |
| 425 | A84 | 125 l bl, grn & org ver | 3.50 | 1.75 |
| | | Nos. 416-425 (10) | 6.20 | 3.80 |

**Bay and Stamp of Naples A85**

**Photo.**

| | | | | |
|---|---|---|---|---|
| 426 | A85 | 25 l lilac & red brn | .25 | .20 |

Cent. of the stamps of Naples. See No. C100.

**Pierre de Coubertin — A86**

**1959, May 19    Wmk. 303    Perf. 14**

| | | | | |
|---|---|---|---|---|
| 427 | A86 | 1 l brn org & blk | .20 | .20 |
| 428 | A86 | 3 l lilac & gray brn | .20 | .20 |
| 429 | A86 | 5 l blue & dk grm | .20 | .20 |
| 430 | A86 | 30 l violet & blk | .20 | .20 |
| 431 | A86 | 60 l dk grn & gray brn | .20 | .20 |
| 432 | A86 | 80 l car rose & dp grn | .45 | 2.05 |
| | | Nos. 427-432,C106 (7) | 4.45 | 2.05 |

Leaders of the Olympic movement; 1960 Olympic Games, Rome. See Nos. 1060-1062.

**Lincoln and his Praise of San Marino, May 7, 1861 A87**

**1959, July 1    Perf. 14**

| | | | | |
|---|---|---|---|---|
| 433 | A87 | 5 l brown & blk | .20 | .20 |
| 434 | A87 | 10 l blue grn & ultra | .20 | .20 |
| 435 | A87 | 15 l gray & green | .20 | .20 |

**Perf. 13x13½    Engr.**

| | | | | |
|---|---|---|---|---|
| 436 | A87 | 70 l violet | .45 | .45 |
| | | Nos. 433-436,C108 (5) | 3.45 | 3.15 |

Birth sesquicentennial of Abraham Lincoln.

**Arch of Augustus, Rimini, and Romagna ½b Stamp A88**

**1959, Aug. 29    Photo.    Perf. 14**

| | | | | |
|---|---|---|---|---|
| 437 | A88 | 30 l black & brown | .20 | .20 |

Centenary of the first stamps of Romagna. See No. C109.

**Type of 1953 Inscribed: "Universiade Torino"**

**1959, Aug. 29    Wmk. 303    Perf. 14**

| | | | | |
|---|---|---|---|---|
| 438 | A65 | 30 l red orange | .60 | .40 |

Turin University Sports Meet, 8/27-9/6.

**Messina Cathedral Portal and Stamp of Sicily 1859 — A89**

**1959, Oct. 16**

| | | | | |
|---|---|---|---|---|
| 439 | A89 | 1 l ocher & dk brn | .20 | .20 |
| 440 | A89 | 2 l olive & dk red | .20 | .20 |
| 441 | A89 | 3 l blue & slate | .20 | .20 |
| 442 | A89 | 4 l red & brown | .20 | .20 |
| 443 | A89 | 5 l dull bl & rose lil | .20 | .20 |
| 444 | A89 | 25 l multicolored | .25 | .25 |
| 445 | A89 | 60 l multicolored | 2.15 | 2.00 |

Nos. 439-445,C110 (8)

Stamp of Sicily and: 2 l, Greek temple, Selinus. 3 l, Erice Church. 4 l, Temple of Concordia, Agrigento. 5 l, Ruins of Castor and Pollux Temple, Agrigento. 25 l, San Giovanni degli Eremiti Church. 60 l, Greek theater, Taormina, horiz.

Centenary of stamps of Sicily.

**Golden Oriole A90**

**Nightingale — A91**

**Shot Put — A92**

Birds: 3 l, Woodcock. 4 l, Hoopoe. 5 l, Red-legged partridge. 10 l, Goldfinch. 25 l, European Kingfisher. 80 l, Ringnecked pheasant. 110 l, Green woodpecker. 110 l, Red-breasted flycatcher.

**1960, Jan. 28    Photo.    Wmk. 303**

**Centers in Natural Colors    Perf. 14**

| | | | | |
|---|---|---|---|---|
| 446 | A90 | 1 l blue | .20 | .20 |
| 447 | A91 | 2 l green & red | .20 | .20 |
| 448 | A90 | 3 l green & red | .20 | .20 |
| 449 | A91 | 4 l dk green & red | .20 | .20 |
| 450 | A90 | 5 l dark green | .20 | .20 |
| 451 | A91 | 10 l blue & red | .20 | .20 |
| 452 | A90 | 25 l gmsh blue | .40 | .20 |
| 453 | A91 | 60 l blue & red | 1.10 | 1.00 |
| 454 | A91 | 80 l Prus blue & red | 2.00 | 1.90 |
| 455 | A91 | 110 l blue & red | 10.00 | 2.25 |
| | | Nos. 446-455 (10) | 14.70 | 6.55 |

Sports: 2 l, Gymnastics. 3 l, Walking. 4 l, Boxing. 5 l, Fencing, horiz. 10 l, Rowing, horiz. 15 l, Hockey, horiz. 25 l, Bicycling. 60 l, Soccer. 110 l, Equestrian, horiz.

**1960, May 23    Wmk. 303    Perf. 14**

| | | | | |
|---|---|---|---|---|
| 456 | A92 | 1 l car rose & vio | .20 | .20 |
| 457 | A92 | 2 l brn ol & pur | .20 | .20 |
| 458 | A92 | 4 l rose red & brn | .20 | .20 |
| 459 | A92 | 5 l brown & blue | .20 | .20 |
| 460 | A92 | 10 l red brn & bl | .20 | .20 |
| 461 | A92 | 15 l emer & lilac | .20 | .20 |
| 462 | A92 | 25 l bl grn & org | .20 | .20 |
| 463 | A92 | 60 l dp grn & org | .30 | .20 |
| 464 | A92 | 110 l emer, red & blk | .30 | .30 |
| 465 | A92 | emer red & blk | 5.50 | 5.50 |
| | | Nos. 456-465,C111-C114 (14) | 3.00 | 2.80 |

Set of 3 souvenir sheets

17th Olympic Games, Rome, 8/25-9/11.

Souvenir sheets are: (1.) Sheet of 4, one each of 1 l, 2 l, 3 l and 60 l, all printed in deep

green and brown. (2.) Sheet of 4, one each of 4 l and 10 l plus a 20 l and 40 l in designs of Nos. C111-C112 but without "Posta Aerea" inscribed-all 4 printed in rose red and brown. (3.) Sheet of 6, one each of 5 l, 15 l, 25 l and 110 l plus an 80 l and 125 l in designs of Nos. C113-C14 but without "Posta Aerea"- all 6 printed in emerald and brown.

**Mt. Titano — A93**

**Founder Melvin Jones and Lions Headquarters — A94**

60 l, Government Palace and statue of Liberty. 115 l, Clarence L. Sturm, president. 150 l, Finis E. Davis, vice president.

**1960, July 1    Photo.    Wmk. 303**

| | | | | |
|---|---|---|---|---|
| 466 | A93 | 30 l red brn & dk bl | .20 | .50 |
| 467 | A94 | 45 l bl vio & bis brn | .20 | .50 |
| 468 | A93 | 60 l dull rose & bl | .20 | .50 |
| 469 | A94 | 115 l green & blk | .50 | .50 |
| 470 | A94 | 150 l brn & dk bl | 3.50 | 2.75 |
| | | Nos. 466-470,C115 (6) | 9.90 | 8.15 |

Lions Intl.; founding of the Lions Club of San Marino.

**Beach of Riccione and San Marino Peaks A95**

**1960, Aug. 27    multicolored**

| | | | | |
|---|---|---|---|---|
| 471 | A95 | 30 l multicolored | .35 | .20 |

12th San Marino-Riccione Stamp Day, Aug. 27. See No. C116.

**Boy with Basket of Fruit, by Caravaggio — A96**

**1960, Dec. 29    Wmk. 303    Perf. 14**

| | | | | |
|---|---|---|---|---|
| 472 | A96 | 200 l multicolored | 6.50 | 4.75 |

350th anniversary of the death of Michelangelo da Caravaggio (Merisi), painter.

**Types of 1957**

Views: 1 l, Hospital street. 4 l, Government building. 80 l, Gate tower. 115 l, Covered market of Borgo Maggiore.

**1961, Feb. 16    Perf. 14**

| | | | | |
|---|---|---|---|---|
| 473 | A79 | 1 l dk blue grn | .20 | .20 |
| 474 | A74 | 4 l dk blue & blk | .20 | .20 |
| 475 | A78 | 30 l brt vio & brn | .40 | .20 |
| 476 | A78 | 115 l brown & blue | 1.00 | .80 |

Nos. 473-476 (4)

**Hunting Roebuck A97**

## 1961, May 4    Wmk. 303    Photo.    Perf. 14

Hunting Scenes (16th-18th century): 2 l, Falconer, vert. 3 l, Wild boar hunt. 4 l, Duck shooting with crossbow. 5 l, Stag hunt. 10 l, Mounted falconer, vert. 30 l, Hunter with horn and dogs. 60 l, Hunter with rifle and dog, vert. 70 l, Hunter and beater. 115 l, Duck hunt.

| 477 | A97 | 1 l | lil rose & vio bl | .20 | .20 |
|---|---|---|---|---|---|
| 478 | A97 | 2 l | gray, dk red & bl | .20 | .20 |
| 479 | A97 | 3 l | red org, brn & blk | .20 | .20 |
| 480 | A97 | 4 l | lt bl, red & blk | .20 | .20 |
| 481 | A97 | 5 l | yellow grn & blk | .20 | .20 |
| 482 | A97 | 10 l | org, blk, brn & vio | .20 | .20 |
| 483 | A97 | 30 l | yel, bl, brn & blk | .20 | .20 |
| 484 | A97 | 60 l | ocher, brn, blk & red | .25 | .25 |
| 485 | A97 | 70 l | green, blk & car | .40 | .40 |
| 486 | A97 | 115 l | brt pink, blk & dk bl | 2.25 | 2.25 |

Nos. 477-486 (10)

Mt. Titano and Cancelled Stamp of Sardinia, 1862 — A98

Cent. of Independence Phil. Exhib., Turin, 1961.

## 1961, Sept. 5    Wmk. 303    Perf. 13
### Photogravure and Embossed

| 487 | A98 | 30 l | multicolored | .50 | .50 |
|---|---|---|---|---|---|
| 488 | A98 | 70 l | multicolored | 1.00 | 1.00 |
| 489 | A98 | 200 l | multicolored | 2.00 | 2.00 |

Nos. 487-489 (3)

View of San Marino A99

## 1961, Oct. 20    Wmk. 339    Photo.    Perf. 13

| 490 | A99 | 500 l | brn & blue | 42.50 | 15.00 |
|---|---|---|---|---|---|
|  |  | Sheet of 6 grn |  | 300.00 | 150.00 |

### Europa Issue, 1961

King Enzo's Palace and Neptune Fountain, Bologna — A100

Views of Bologna: 70 l, Loggia dei Mercanti. 100 l, Two Towers.

## 1961, Nov. 25    Wmk. 339    Perf. 14

| 491 | A100 | 30 l | grnsh bl & blk | .20 | .20 |
|---|---|---|---|---|---|
| 492 | A100 | 70 l | dk ol grn & blk | .20 | .20 |
| 493 | A100 | 100 l | red brown & blk | .20 | .60 |

Nos. 491-493 (3)

Duryea, 1892 A101

Automobiles (pre-1910): 2 l, Panhard-Levassor. 3 l, Peugeot. 4 l, Decauville. 5 l, Fiat, vert. 10 l, Napier. 30 l, White, vert. 50 l, Daimler. 5 l, Wolseley. 25 l, Benz. 25 l, Renault, vert. 100 l, Isotta Fraschini. 115 l, Bianchi. 150 l, Alfa.

## 1962, Jan. 23    Wmk. 303    Perf. 14

Historic Planes (1907-1910): 2 l, Ernest Archdeacon. 3 l, Albert and Emile Bonnet-Labranche. 4 l, Glenn Curtiss. 5 l, Farman. 10 l, Louis Bleriot. 30 l, Hubert Latham. 60 l, Alberto Santos Dumont. 70 l, Alliott Verdon Roe. 115 l, Faccioli.

Wright Plane, 1904 A102

| 494 | A101 | 1 l | red brn & bl | .20 | .20 |
|---|---|---|---|---|---|
| 495 | A101 | 2 l | ultra & org brn | .20 | .20 |
| 496 | A101 | 3 l | black & ultra | .20 | .20 |
| 497 | A101 | 4 l | gray & dk ocher | .20 | .20 |
| 498 | A101 | 5 l | black & org | .20 | .20 |
| 499 | A101 | 10 l | violet & org | .20 | .20 |
| 500 | A101 | 15 l | black & org | .20 | .20 |
| 501 | A101 | 25 l | gray & org | .20 | .20 |
| 502 | A101 | 30 l | black & ocher | .20 | .20 |
| 503 | A101 | 50 l | black & brt pink | .20 | .20 |
| 504 | A101 | 60 l | black, gray & grn | .20 | .20 |
| 505 | A101 | 70 l | black, yel & car | .20 | .20 |
| 506 | A101 | 100 l | black, org & bl grn | .30 | .30 |
| 507 | A101 | 115 l | bl, org & dl grn | .30 | .30 |
| 508 | A101 | 150 l | multicolored | 3.10 | 3.10 |

Nos. 494-508 (15)

## 1962, Apr. 4    Wmk. 339    Photo.    Perf. 14

| 509 | A102 | 1 l | blk & dull yel | .20 | .20 |
|---|---|---|---|---|---|
| 510 | A102 | 2 l | red brn & gray | .20 | .20 |
| 511 | A102 | 3 l | red brn & grn | .20 | .20 |
| 512 | A102 | 4 l | brown & blk | .20 | .20 |
| 513 | A102 | 5 l | magenta & blue | .20 | .20 |
| 514 | A102 | 10 l | ocher & bl grn | .20 | .20 |
| 515 | A102 | 30 l | ocher & ultra | .20 | .20 |
| 516 | A102 | 70 l | ocher & bl grn | .40 | .40 |
| 517 | A102 | 115 l | dp orange & ocher | 2.50 | 2.50 |
| 518 | A102 | 115 l | blk, grn & ocher | 2.50 | 2.50 |

Nos. 509-518 (10)

## 1962, June 14    Wmk. 339    Perf. 14

Mountaineer Descending A103

Designs: 2 l, View of Sassolungo. 3 l, Mt. Titano. 4 l, Three Peaks of Javaredo. 5 l, Matterhorn. 15 l, Skier on downhill run. 30 l, Climbing an overhang. 40 l, Cutting steps in ice. 85 l, Giant's Tooth. 115 l, Mt. Titano.

| 519 | A103 | 1 l | bis brn & blk | .20 | .20 |
|---|---|---|---|---|---|
| 520 | A103 | 2 l | Prus grn & blk | .20 | .20 |
| 521 | A103 | 3 l | lilac & blk | .20 | .20 |
| 522 | A103 | 4 l | brt bl & blk | .20 | .20 |
| 523 | A103 | 5 l | dp org & blk | .20 | .20 |
| 524 | A103 | 15 l | org yel & blk | .20 | .20 |
| 525 | A103 | 30 l | ocher & blk | .20 | .20 |
| 526 | A103 | 40 l | carmine & blk | .20 | .20 |
| 527 | A103 | 85 l | lt green & blk | .20 | .20 |
| 528 | A103 | 115 l | vio bl & blk | 2.00 | 2.00 |

Nos. 519-528 (10)

Hunter with Dog A104

Modern Hunting Scenes: 2 l, Hound master on horseback, vert. 3 l, Duck hunt. 4 l, Stag hunt. 5 l, Partridge hunt. 15 l, Lapwing (hunt). 50 l, Wild duck hunt. 70 l, Duck hunt from boat. 100 l, Boar hunt. 150 l, Pheasant hunt, vert.

## 1962, Aug. 25    Photo.    Perf. 14

| 529 | A104 | 2 l | brown & blk | .20 | .20 |
|---|---|---|---|---|---|
| 530 | A104 | 3 l | brn & org | .20 | .20 |
| 531 | A104 | 4 l | blk & Prus bl | .20 | .20 |
| 532 | A104 | 5 l | blk & brown | .20 | .20 |
| 533 | A104 | 15 l | blk & yel grn | .20 | .20 |
| 534 | A104 | 50 l | blk & org | .20 | .20 |
| 535 | A104 | 70 l | brn & red brn | .20 | .20 |
| 536 | A104 | 100 l | brn, dp grn & blk | .20 | .20 |

## 1962, Oct. 25    Wmk. 339    Perf. 14

Egyptian Cargo Ship A106

Ancient Ships: 2 l, Greece, 2nd Cent. B.C. 3 l, Roman galley, 2nd Cent. 4 l, Vikings, 10th Cent. 5 l, "Santa Maria," 1492. 10 l, Cypriote galleon, "Santa Maria," 1637. 30 l, Galley, 1600. 60 l, Sovereign of the Seas, 1637, vert. 70 l, Danish ship, 1750. vert. 115 l, Frigate, 1850.

| 537 | A104 | 100 l | blk, brick red & sep | .20 | .20 |
|---|---|---|---|---|---|
| 538 | A104 | 150 l | grn, lil & blk | .20 | .20 |

Nos. 529-538 (10)

Mt. Titano and "Europa" A105

## 1962, Oct. 25    Wmk. 339    Perf. 14

| 539 | A105 | 200 l | gray & car | 1.50 | 1.25 |
|---|---|---|---|---|---|
|  |  | Sheet of 6 |  | 10.00 | 10.00 |

### Europa Issue, 1962

## 1963, Jan. 10

| 540 | A106 | 1 l | blue & org yel | .20 | .20 |
|---|---|---|---|---|---|
| 541 | A106 | 2 l | mag, tan & brn | .20 | .20 |
| 542 | A106 | 3 l | brown & lil rose | .20 | .20 |
| 543 | A106 | 4 l | vio brn & grn | .20 | .20 |
| 544 | A106 | 5 l | brown & yellow | .20 | .20 |
| 545 | A106 | 10 l | brn & brt yel grn | .20 | .20 |
| 546 | A106 | 30 l | bis, bl & sep | .30 | .30 |
| 547 | A106 | 60 l | lt vio bl & dl red | .40 | .45 |
| 548 | A106 | 70 l | blk, gray & dl red | .40 | .40 |
| 549 | A106 | 115 l | blk, brn & gray bl | 5.00 | 3.75 |

Nos. 540-549 (10)

Lady with Veil, by Raphael — A107

Paintings by Raphael: 70 l, Self-portrait. 100 l, St. Barbara from Sistine Madonna. 200 l, Portrait of a Young Woman (Maddalena Strozzi).

## 1963, Mar. 28    Size: 26½x37mm    Perf. 14

| 550 | A107 | 30 l | multicolored | .20 | .20 |
|---|---|---|---|---|---|
| 551 | A107 | 70 l | multicolored | .25 | .25 |
| 552 | A107 | 100 l | multicolored | .35 | .20 |

### Size: 26½x44mm

| 553 | A107 | 200 l | multicolored | 1.00 | .80 |
|---|---|---|---|---|---|

Nos. 550-553 (4)

Jousting with "Saracen," Arezzo — A108

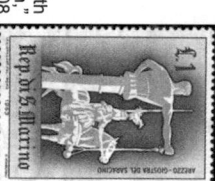

Medieval "Knightly Games": 2 l, French knights, horiz. 3 l, Crossbow contest. 4 l, English knight receiving lance, horiz. 5 l, Tournament, Florence. 10 l, "Jousting with 'Quintana,'" Ascoli Piceno. 30 l, "Jousting with 'Quintana,'" Foligno, horiz. 60 l, Race through Siena. 70 l, Tournament, Malpaga, horiz. 115 l, Knights challenging.

## 1963, June 22    Wmk. 339    Perf. 14

| 554 | A108 | 2 l | lilac rose | .20 | .20 |
|---|---|---|---|---|---|
| 555 | A108 | 3 l | slate | .20 | .20 |
| 556 | A108 | 4 l | violet | .20 | .20 |
| 557 | A108 | 5 l | rose violet | .20 | .20 |
| 558 | A108 | 10 l | ... | .20 | .20 |
| 559 | A108 | 30 l | dull green | .20 | .20 |
| 560 | A108 | 60 l | red brown | .20 | .20 |
| 561 | A108 | 70 l | Prus green | .20 | .20 |
| 562 | A108 | 115 l | brown | .20 | .20 |
| 563 | A108 | 115 l | black | 2.00 | 2.00 |

Nos. 554-563 (10)

Butterfly — A109

### Europa Issue, 1963

## 1963, Aug. 31    Wmk. 339    Photo.    Perf. 14

Various butterflies.

| 564 | A109 | 25 l | multicolored | .20 | .20 |
|---|---|---|---|---|---|
| 565 | A109 | 30 l | multicolored | .20 | .20 |
| 566 | A109 | 60 l | multicolored | .20 | .20 |
| 567 | A109 | 70 l | multicolored | .25 | .20 |
| 568 | A109 | 115 l | multicolored | .55 | .35 |

Nos. 564-568 (5)

St. Marinus Statue, Government Palace — A110

## 1963, Aug. 31

| 569 | A110 | 100 l | shown | 1.40 | 1.15 |
|---|---|---|---|---|---|
| 570 | A110 | 100 l | Modern fountain | .20 | .20 |

San Marino-Riccione Stamp Fair.

Flag and "E" — A111

### Europa Issue, 1963

## 1963, Sept. 21    Wmk. 339    Perf. 14

| 571 | A111 | 200 l | blue & brn org | .60 | .50 |
|---|---|---|---|---|---|

Women's Hurdles A112

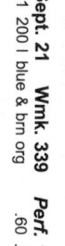

Sports: 2 l, Pole vaulting, vert. 3 l, Women's relay race. 4 l, Men's high jump. 5 l, Soccer. 10 l, Women's high jump. 30 l, Women's javelin throw. 60 l, Women's discus throw, vert. 60 l, Women's javelin throw. 70 l, Water polo. 115 l, Hammer throw.

## 1963, Sept. 21

| 572 | A112 | 1 l | org & red brn | .20 | .20 |
|---|---|---|---|---|---|
| 573 | A112 | 2 l | lt grn & dk brn | .20 | .20 |
| 574 | A112 | 3 l | bl & dk brn | .20 | .20 |
| 575 | A112 | 4 l | dp & dk brn | .20 | .20 |
| 576 | A112 | 5 l | red & dk brn | .20 | .20 |
| 577 | A112 | 10 l | lil rose & claret | .20 | .20 |
| 578 | A112 | 30 l | gray & red brn | .20 | .20 |
| 579 | A112 | 60 l | brt yel & dk brn | .20 | .20 |
| 580 | A112 | 70 l | brt grn & dk brn | .20 | .20 |
| 581 | A112 | 115 l | grn & dk brn | 2.00 | 2.00 |

Nos. 572-581 (10)

Modern Pentathlon A113

Publicity for 1964 Olympic Games.

# SAN MARINO

**Inscribed "Tokio, 1964"**

Designs: 1 l, Runner, vert. 2 l, Woman gymnast, vert. 4 l, Basketball, vert. 5 l, Dual rowing. 15 l, Broad jumper. 30 l, Swimmer racing dive. 70 l, Woman sprinter. 120 l, Bicycle racers, vert. 150 l, Fencers, vert.

1964, June 25    Wmk. 339    Perf. 14
582 A113 1 l brn & yel grn .20 .20
583 A113 2 l blk & red brn .20 .20
584 A113 3 l blk & brown .20 .20
585 A113 4 l blk & org red .20 .20
586 A113 5 l blk & brt bl .20 .20
587 A113 15 l blk brn & org .20 .20
588 A113 30 l dk vio & bl .20 .20
589 A113 70 l red brn & grn .20 .20
590 A113 120 l brn & brt bl .20 .20
591 A113 150 l blk & crimson 2.00 2.00
Nos. 582-591 (10)

18th Olympic Games, Tokyo, Oct. 10-25.

**Same Inscribed "Verso Tokio"**

1964, June 25    Photo.
592 A113 30 l indigo & lilac .20 .20
593 A113 70 l brn & Prus grn .20 .20

"Verso Tokyo" Stamp Exhibition at Rimini, Italy, June 25-July 6.

**Murray-Blenkinsop Locomotive, 1812 — A114**

History of Locomotive: 2 l, Puffing Billy, 1813. 3 l, Locomotion I, 1825. 4 l, Rocket, 1829. 5 l, Lion, 1838. 15 l, Bayard, 1839. 20 l, Crampton, 1849. 50 l, Little England, 1851. 90 l, Spitfire, c. 1860. 110 l, Rogers, c. 1865.

1964, Aug. 29    Wmk. 339    Perf. 14
594 A114 1 l blk & buff .20 .20
595 A114 2 l blk & green .20 .20
596 A114 3 l blk & rose lilac .20 .20
597 A114 4 l blk & yellow .20 .20
598 A114 5 l blk & salmon .20 .20
599 A114 15 l blk & yel grn .20 .20
600 A114 20 l blk & dp pink .20 .20
601 A114 50 l blk & pale bl .20 .20
602 A114 90 l blk & yel org .20 .20
603 A114 110 l blk & brt bl .20 .20
Nos. 594-603 (10)

**Baseball Players A115**

1964, Aug. 29    Photo.
604 A115 30 l shown .20 .20
605 A115 70 l Pitcher .20 .20

8th European Baseball Championship, Milan.

**Europa Issue, 1964**

"E" and Globe A116

1964, Oct. 15    Wmk. 339    Perf. 14
606 A116 200 l dk blue & red 2.25 1.00

**President John F. Kennedy (1917-1963) — A117**

130 l, Kennedy and American flag, vert.

**Start of Bicycle Race from Government Palace — A118**

1964, Nov. 22    Photo.
607 A118 70 l multicolored .20 .20
608 A117 130 l multicolored .20 .20

**Rooks on Chessboard A120**

**Brontosaurus — A119**

Designs: 70 l, Cyclists (going right) and view of San Marino. 200 l, Cyclists (going left) and view of San Marino.

1965, May 15    Photo.    Wmk. 339
609 A118 30 l sepia .20 .20
610 A118 70 l deep claret .20 .20
611 A118 200 l rose red .60 .60

48th Bicycle Tour of Italy.

1965, June 30    Wmk. 339    Perf. 14

Dinosaurs: 2 l, Brachiosaurus, vert. 3 l, Pteranodon. 4 l, Elasmosaurus. 5 l, Tyrannosaurus. 10 l, Stegosaurus. 75 l, Thaumatosaurus victor. 100 l, Iguanodon. 200 l, Triceratops.

612 A119 1 l dk brn & emer .20 .20
613 A119 2 l blk & sl bl .20 .20
614 A119 3 l sl grn, ol grn & yel .20 .20
615 A119 4 l brn & slate bl .20 .20
616 A119 5 l claret & grn .20 .20
617 A119 10 l dk brn & grn .20 .20
618 A119 75 l dk bl & bl grn .30 .30
619 A119 100 l green & claret .30 .30
620 A119 200 l brown & grn .35 .35
Nos. 612-620 (9) 2.25 2.25

**Europa Issue, 1965**

1965, Aug. 28    Photo.    Perf. 14
621 A120 200 l brown & multi 1.25 .65

**Dante by Gustave Doré A121**

1965, Nov. 20    Engr.    Perf. 14x14½

**Center in Brown Black**
622 A121 1 l indigo .20 .20
623 A121 90 l car rose .80 .80
624 A121 130 l red brown .80 .80
625 A121 140 l ultra .80 .80
Nos. 622-625 (4)

Doré's Illustrations for Divina Commedia: 90 l, Charon ferrying boat across Acheron. 130 l, Eagle carrying Dante from Purgatory to Paradise. 140 l, Dante with Beatrice examined by Sts. Peter, James and John on faith.

Dante Alighieri (1265-1321), poet.

**Stylized Peaks, Flags of Italy and San Marino A122**

1965, Nov. 25    Photo.    Perf. 14
626 A122 115 l grn, red, ocher & bl .20 .20

Visit of Giuseppe Saragat, president of Italy.

**Trotter A123**

Horses: 20 l, Cross Country, vert. 40 l, Hurdling. 70 l, Gallop. 90 l, Steeplechase. 170 l, Polo, vert.

1966, Feb. 28    Photo.    Wmk. 339    Perf. 14x13, 13x14
627 A123 10 l multicolored .20 .20
628 A123 20 l multicolored .20 .20
629 A123 40 l multicolored .20 .20
630 A123 70 l multicolored .20 .20
631 A123 90 l multicolored .20 .20
632 A123 170 l multicolored 1.20 1.20
Nos. 627-632 (6)

**Scenic Types of 1955-57**

5 l, Hospital Street. 10 l, Gate tower. 15 l, View from South Bastion. 40 l, Murata Nuova Bridge. 90 l, View of La Rocca. 140 l, Government Palace.

1966, Mar. 29    Wmk. 339    Perf. 14
633 A79 5 l blue & brn .20 .20
634 A78 10 l dk sl grn & bl grn .20 .20
635 A78 15 l dk brn & vio .20 .20
636 A73 40 l dk pur & brick red .20 .20
637 A74 90 l blk & dull bl .20 .20
638 A74 140 l violet & org 1.20 1.20
Nos. 633-638 (6)

**"Bella" by Titian A124**

Titian Paintings: 90 l, 100 l, Details from "The Education of Love." 170 l, Detail from "Sacred and Profane Love."

1966, June 16    Wmk. 339    Perf. 14
639 A124 40 l multicolored .20 .20
640 A124 90 l multicolored .80 .80
641 A124 100 l multicolored .80 .80
642 A124 170 l multicolored .80 .80
Nos. 639-642 (4)

**Stone Bass A125**

Fish: 2 l, Cuckoo wrasse. 3 l, Dolphin. 4 l, John Dory. 5 l, Octopus, vert. 10 l, Orange scorpionfish. 40 l, Electric ray, vert. 90 l, Jellyfish, vert. 115 l, Sea Horse, vert. 130 l, Dentex.

1966, Aug. 27    Photo.    Perf. 14x13½, 13½x14    Wmk. 339
643 A125 1 l multicolored .20 .20
644 A125 2 l multicolored .20 .20
645 A125 3 l multicolored .20 .20
646 A125 4 l multicolored .20 .20
647 A125 5 l multicolored .20 .20
648 A125 10 l multicolored .20 .20
649 A125 40 l multicolored .20 .20
650 A125 90 l multicolored .80 .80
651 A125 115 l multicolored .20 .20
652 A125 130 l multicolored 2.00 2.00
Nos. 643-652 (10)

**Europa Issue, 1966**

Our Lady of Europe A126

1966, Sept. 24    Wmk. 339    Perf. 14
653 A126 200 l multicolored .35 .25

**Peony and Mt. Titano — A127**

Flowers and Various Views of Mt. Titano: 10 l, Pyrenean poppy. 20 l, Purple nettle. 40 l, Day lily. 140 l, Gentian. 170 l, Thistle.

1967, Jan. 12    Wmk. 339    Photo.
654 A127 5 l multicolored .20 .20
655 A127 10 l multicolored .20 .20
656 A127 15 l multicolored .20 .20
657 A127 20 l multicolored .20 .20
658 A127 40 l multicolored .20 .20
659 A127 140 l multicolored 1.40 1.40
660 A127 170 l multicolored 1.40 1.40
Nos. 654-660 (7)

**St. Marinus — A128**

**The Return of the Prodigal Son — A129**

Design: 170 l, St. Francis. The paintings are by Giovanni Francesco Barbieri (1591-1666).

1967, Mar. 16    Wmk. 339    Photo.    Perf. 14
661 A128 40 l multicolored .20 .20
662 A128 190 l multicolored .20 .20
663 A129 170 l multicolored .40 .40
a. Strip of 3, #661-663
Nos. 661-663 (3)

**Map Showing Members of CEPT — A130**

Amanita
Caesarea —A131

**1967, May 5** **Wmk. 339** **Perf. 14**
664 A130 200 l sl grn & brn org .85 .45

**1967, June 15** **Photo.** **Perf. 14**
Various Mushrooms.
665 A131 5 l multicolored .20 .20
666 A131 15 l multicolored .20 .20
667 A131 40 l multicolored .20 .20
668 A131 40 l multicolored .20 .20
669 A131 50 l multicolored .20 .20
670 A131 170 l multicolored 1.20 1.20
Nos. 665-670 (6)

Amiens
Cathedral
A132

**Europa Issue, 1967**

**1967, Sept. 21** **Wmk. 339** **Perf. 14**
671 A132 20 l dk vio, bister .20 .20
672 A132 40 l slate grn, bis .20 .20
673 A132 80 l slate gn, bis .20 .20
674 A132 90 l sepia, bis .20 .20
675 A132 170 l deep plum, bis 1.00 1.00
Nos. 671-675 (5)

Designs: 40 l, Siena Cathedral. 80 l, Toledo
Cathedral. 90 l, Salisbury Cathedral. 170 l,
Cologne Cathedral.

Crucifix of
Santa
Croce, by
Cimabue
A133

**1967, Dec. 5** **Wmk. 339** **Perf. 15**
676 A133 300 l brn & vio blue .40 .40

The Crucifix of Santa Croce, by Giovanni
Cimabue (1240-1302), was severely damaged
in the Florentine flood of Nov. 1966.

Coat of
Arms —A134

**1968, Mar. 14** **Perf. 13x13½**
**Litho.** **Wmk. 339**
677 A134 2 l multi .20 .20

Coats of Arms: 3 l, Penna Rossa. 5 l,
Fiorentina. 10 l, Montecerreto. 25 l, Serravalle.
35 l, Montegiardino. 50 l, Faetano. 90 l, Borgo
Maggiore. 180 l, Montelupo. 500 l, State arms
of San Marino.

678 A134 3 l multi .20 .20
679 A134 5 l multi .20 .20
680 A134 10 l multi .20 .20
681 A134 25 l multi .20 .20
682 A134 35 l multi .20 .20
683 A134 50 l multi .20 .20
684 A134 90 l multi .20 .20
685 A134 180 l multi .25 .20
686 A134 500 l multi (10) 2.50 2.00
Nos. 677-686 (10)

---

Common Design Types
pictured following the introduction.

**Europa Issue, 1968**
**1968, Apr. 29** Common Design Type
**Engr.** **Perf. 14x13½**
687 CD11 250 l claret brown .75 .35

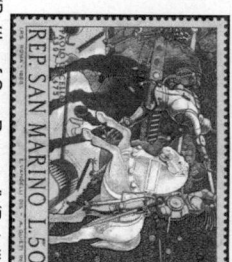

"Battle of San Romano" (Detail), by
Paolo Uccello —A135

**1968, June 14** **Wmk. 339** **Perf. 14**
688 A135 50 l pale lil & blk .20 .20
689 A135 90 l pale lil & blk,
vert. .20 .20
690 A135 130 l pale lil & blk .20 .20
691 A135 230 l pale pink & blk .90 .90
Nos. 688-691 (4)

Designs: Details from "The Battle of San
Romano," by Paolo Uccello (1397-1475).

**Photogravure and Engraved**

The Mystic
Nativity, by
Botticelli,
Detail
A136

**1968, Dec. 5** **Wmk. 339** **Perf. 14**
692 A136 50 l dark blue .20 .20
693 A136 90 l deep claret .25 .25
694 A136 180 l sepia .65 .65
Nos. 692-694 (3)

Christmas.

"Peace" by
Lorenzetti
A137

**1969, Feb. 13** **Wmk. 339**
**Engr.** **Perf. 14**
695 A137 50 l dark blue .20 .20
696 A137 80 l brown .20 .20
697 A137 90 l dk blue vio .25 .25
698 A137 180 l magenta .85 .85
Nos. 695-698 (4)

Designs: 80 l, "Justice." 90 l, "Moderation."
180 l, View of Siena. 14th century, horiz. All
designs are from the "Good Government" frescoes by Ambrogio Lorenzetti in the Town Hall
of Siena.

---

**Europa Issue, 1969**
**1969, Apr. 28** Common Design Type
**Engr.** **Perf. 14x13**
**Size: 37x27mm**
699 A138 50 l multicolored .20 .20
700 A138 90 l multicolored .20 .20

Designs: 90 l, Old Soldier, by Bramante.
Designs are from murals in the Pinakotheke of
Brear, Milan.

Young Soldier, by Bramante —A138

**1969, Apr. 28** **Photo.** **Perf. 14**
701 CD12 50 l dull green .35 .20
702 CD12 180 l rose claret .40 .25

Bramante (1444-1514), Italian architect and
painter.

Charabanc
A139

**1969, June 25** **Perf. 14½x14**
**Photo.** **Unwmk.**
703 A139 5 l blk, ocher & dk bl .20 .20
704 A139 10 l blk, grn & pur .20 .20
705 A139 25 l blk grn, pink &
brn .20 .20
706 A139 40 l ind, lil & lt brn .20 .20
707 A139 50 l blk, dk yel & dk bl .20 .20
708 A139 90 l blk, yel grn & brn .20 .20
709 A139 180 l multi 1.45 1.45
Nos. 703-709 (7)

Coaches, 19th Century: 10 l, Barouche. 25
l, Private drag. 40 l, Hansom cab. 50 l, Curri-
cle. 90 l, Wagonette. 180 l, Spider phaeton.

Pier at
Rimini
A140

**1969, Sept. 17** **Unwmk.**
710 A140 20 l multicolored .20 .20
711 A140 180 l multicolored .25 .25
712 A140 200 l multicolored .70 .70
Nos. 710-712 (3)

Paintings by R. Viola: 20 l, Mt. Titano. 200 l,
Pier at Riccione, horiz.

**1969, Dec. 10** **Perf. 13½x14**
**Engr.** **Wmk. 339**
713 A141 20 l dl pur & sal .20 .20
714 A141 180 l dl pur & lt grn .25 .25
715 A141 200 l dp pur & bis .70 .70
Nos. 713-715 (3)

Designs: 180 l, "Hope" by Raphael.
"Charity" by Raphael.

---

Signs of
the Zodiac
A142

**1970, Feb. 18** **Perf. 14x13½**
**Photo.** **Unwmk.**
716 A142 1 l Aries .20 .20
717 A142 2 l Taurus .20 .20
718 A142 3 l Gemini .20 .20
719 A142 4 l Cancer .20 .20
720 A142 5 l Leo .20 .20
721 A142 15 l Virgo .20 .20
722 A142 20 l Libra .20 .20
723 A142 50 l Scorpio .20 .20
724 A142 70 l Sagittarius .20 .20
725 A142 90 l Capricorn .20 .20
726 A142 100 l Aquarius .25 .25
727 A142 180 l Pisces 2.45 2.45
Nos. 716-727 (12)

Fleet in Bay of Naples, by Peter
Brueghel, the Elder —A143

**1970, Apr. 30** **Unwmk.**
728 A143 230 l multi .30 .30

10th Europa Phil. Exhib., Naples, May 2-10.

**Europa Issue, 1970**
**1970, Apr. 30** Common Design Type
**Photo.** **Perf. 14x13½**
**Size: 36x27mm**
729 CD13 90 l brt grn & red .50 .25
730 CD13 180 l ocher & red .60 .30

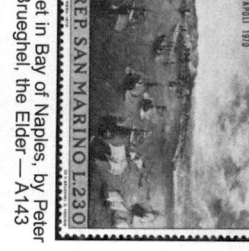

St. Francis' Gate
and Rotary
Emblem —A144

**1970, June 25** **Photo.** **Perf. 13½x14**
**Size: 26½x37½mm**
731 A144 180 l multi .25 .25
732 A144 220 l multi .30 .30

65th anniv. of Rotary Intl.; 10th anniv. of the
San Marino Rotary Club.

Woman with Mandolin, by
Tiepolo —A145

**1970, Sept. 10** **Unwmk.** **Perf. 14**
**Size: 56x37½mm**
733 A145 50 l multi .20 .20
734 A145 180 l multi .25 .25
735 A145 220 l multi .30 .30
a. Strip of 3, #733-735 .65 .65

Paintings by Tiepolo: 180 l, Woman with
Parrot. 220 l, Rinaldo and Armida Surprised,
horiz.

Giambattista Tiepolo (1696-1770), Venetian
painter.

Black
Pete — A146

**1970, Dec. 22**    **Perf. 13x14, 14x13**    **Photo.**

| 736 | A146 | 1 l | multi | .20 | .20 |
|-----|------|-----|-------|-----|-----|
| 737 | A146 | 2 l | multi | .20 | .20 |
| 738 | A146 | 3 l | multi | .20 | .20 |
| 739 | A146 | 4 l | multi | .20 | .20 |
| 740 | A146 | 5 l | multi | .20 | .20 |
| 741 | A146 | 10 l | multi | .20 | .20 |
| 742 | A146 | 15 l | multi | .20 | .20 |
| 743 | A146 | 50 l | multi | .20 | .20 |
| 744 | A146 | 90 l | multi | 3.50 | 3.50 |
| 745 | A147 | 220 l | multi | 5.30 | 5.30 |

*Nos. 736-745 (10)*

Disney Characters: 2 l, Gyro Gearloose. 3 l, Pluto. 4 l, Minnie Mouse. 5 l, Donald Duck. 10 l, Goofy. 15 l, Scrooge McDuck. 50 l, Huey, Louey and Dewey. 90 l, Mickey Mouse.

Walt Disney (1901-66), cartoonist & film maker.

Customhouse Dock, by
Canaletto — A148

**1971, Mar. 23**    **Unwmk.**    **Perf. 14**

| 746 | A148 | 20 l | multi | .20 | .20 |
|-----|------|------|-------|-----|-----|
| 747 | A148 | 180 l | multi | .25 | .25 |
| 748 | A148 | 200 l | multi | .85 | .85 |

*Nos. 746-748 (3)*

Paintings by Canaletto: 180 l, Grand Canal between Balbi Palace and Rialto Bridge. 200 l, St. Mark's and Doges' Palace.

Save Venice campaign.

**Europa Issue, 1971**
Common Design Type

**1971, May 29**    **Perf. 13½x14**
**Size: 27½x23mm**

| 749 | CD14 | 50 l | org & blue | .35 | .25 |
|-----|------|------|------------|-----|-----|
| 750 | CD14 | 90 l | blue & org | .45 | .30 |

Congress Emblem and Hall, San
Marino Flag — A149

**1971, May 29**    **Photo.**    **Perf. 12**

| 751 | A149 | 20 l | violet & multi | .20 | .20 |
|-----|------|------|----------------|-----|-----|
| 752 | A149 | 90 l | olive & multi | .25 | .25 |
| 753 | A149 | 180 l | multi | .65 | .65 |

*Nos. 751-753 (3)*

Design: 90 l, Detail from Government Palace door, Congress and San Marino emblems, vert.

Italian Philatelic Press Union Congress, San Marino, May 29-30.

---

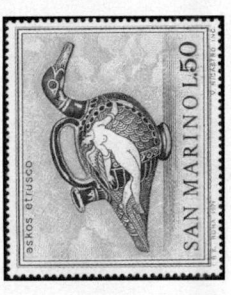

Duck-shaped Jug with Flying
Lasa — A150

Etruscan Art, 6th-3rd Centuries B.C.: 80 l, Head of Mercury, vert. 90 l, Sarcophagus of a married couple, vert. 180 l, Chimera.

**1971, Sept. 16**    **Photo. & Engr.**    **Perf. 14**

| 754 | A150 | 50 l | blk & org | .20 | .20 |
|-----|------|------|-----------|-----|-----|
| 755 | A150 | 80 l | blk & lt grn | .20 | .20 |
| 756 | A150 | 90 l | blk & lt blu | .20 | .20 |
| 757 | A150 | 180 l | blk & org | .25 | .85 |

*Nos. 754-757 (4)*

Tiger Lily
A151

**1971, Dec. 2**    **Photo.**

| 758 | A151 | 1 l | shown | .20 | .20 |
|-----|------|-----|-------|-----|-----|
| 759 | A151 | 2 l | Phlox | .20 | .20 |
| 760 | A151 | 3 l | Carnations | .20 | .20 |
| 761 | A151 | 4 l | Globe flowers | .20 | .20 |
| 762 | A151 | 5 l | Thistles | .20 | .20 |
| 763 | A151 | 10 l | Peonies | .20 | .20 |
| 764 | A151 | 15 l | Hellebore | .20 | .20 |
| 765 | A151 | 50 l | Anemones | .20 | .20 |
| 766 | A151 | 90 l | Gaillardia | .30 | .30 |
| 767 | A151 | 220 l | Asters | 2.10 | 2.10 |

*Nos. 758-767 (10)*

**1972, Feb. 23**    **Perf. 14, 13x14 (180 l)**

Details from La Primavera, by Sandro Botticelli: 180 l, Three Graces. 220 l, Spring.

**Sizes: 50 l, 220 l, 21x37mm;
180 l, 27x37mm**

| 768 | A152 | 50 l | gold & multi | .20 | .20 |
|-----|------|------|--------------|-----|-----|
| 769 | A152 | 180 l | gold & multi | .40 | .40 |
| 770 | A152 | 220 l | gold & multi | .85 | .85 |

*Nos. 768-770 (3)*

**Europa Issue 1972**
Common Design Type

**1972, Apr. 27**    **Perf. 11½**
**Granite Paper**
**Size: 22½x33mm**

| 771 | CD15 | 50 l | org & multi | .35 | .20 |
|-----|------|------|-------------|-----|-----|
| 772 | CD15 | 90 l | lt bl & multi | .40 | .25 |

St. Marinus
Taming
Bear
A153

**1972, Apr. 27**    **Photo. & Engr.**    **Perf. 14**

| 773 | A153 | 25 l | dl yel & blk | .20 | .20 |
|-----|------|------|--------------|-----|-----|
| 774 | A153 | 55 l | sal pink & blk | .20 | .20 |
| 775 | A153 | 100 l | dl bl & blk | .20 | .20 |
| 776 | A153 | 130 l | citron & blk | .80 | .80 |

*Nos. 773-776 (4)*

Designs: 55 l, Donna Felicissima asking St. Marinus for mercy for her sons. 100 l, St. Felicissima turning archers to stone. 130 l, Felicissima giving mountains to St. Marinus to establish Republic.

Allegories of San Marino after 16th century paintings.

---

Italian House
Sparrow — A154

**1972, June 30**    **Photo.**
**Granite Paper**    **Perf. 11½**

| 777 | A154 | 1 l | shown | .20 | .20 |
|-----|------|-----|-------|-----|-----|
| 778 | A154 | 2 l | Firecrest | .20 | .20 |
| 779 | A154 | 3 l | Blue tit | .20 | .20 |
| 780 | A154 | 4 l | Ortolan bunting | .20 | .20 |
| 781 | A154 | 5 l | White-spotted bluethroat | .20 | .20 |
| 782 | A154 | 10 l | Bullfinch | .20 | .20 |
| 783 | A154 | 25 l | Linnet | .20 | .20 |
| 784 | A154 | 50 l | Black-eared wheatear | .20 | .20 |
| 785 | A154 | 90 l | Sardinian warbler | .25 | .25 |
| 786 | A154 | 220 l | Greenfinch | 2.05 | 2.05 |

*Nos. 777-786 (10)*

Young Man,
Heart,
Emblem — A155

Italian Philatelic
Federation
Emblem — A156

**1972, Aug. 26**    **Perf. 13½x14, 14x13½**

| 787 | A155 | 50 l | lt bl & multi | .20 | .20 |
|-----|------|------|---------------|-----|-----|
| 788 | A155 | 90 l | ocher & multi | .20 | .20 |

World Heart Month.

Design: 90 l, Heart disease victim, horiz.

**1972, Aug. 26**    **Perf. 13½x14**

| 789 | A156 | 25 l | gold & ultra | .20 | .20 |

Honoring veterans of Philately.

5c Coin,
1864
A157

Coins: 10 l, 10c coin, 1935. 15 l, 1 lira, 1906. 20 l, 5 lire, 1898. 25 l, 5 lire, 1937. 50 l, 10 lire, 1932. 55 l, 20 lire, 1938. 220 l, 20 lire, 1925.

**1972, Dec. 15**    **Litho.**    **Perf. 12½x13**

| 790 | A157 | 5 l | gray, blk & brn | .20 | .20 |
|-----|------|-----|-----------------|-----|-----|
| 791 | A157 | 10 l | org, blk & sil | .20 | .20 |
| 792 | A157 | 15 l | brt rose, blk & sil | .20 | .20 |
| 793 | A157 | 20 l | lt, blk & sil | .20 | .20 |
| 794 | A157 | 25 l | vio, blk & sil | .20 | .20 |
| 795 | A157 | 50 l | brt bl, blk & sil | .20 | .20 |
| 796 | A157 | 55 l | ocher, blk & gold | .30 | .30 |
| 797 | A157 | 220 l | emer, blk & gold | 1.70 | 1.70 |

*Nos. 790-797 (8)*

New York, 1673 — A158

300 l, View of New York from East River, 1973.

---

**1973, Mar. 9**    **Photo.**
**Granite Paper**    **Perf. 11½**

| 798 | 200 l | bis, och & ol grn | .25 | .25 |
|-----|-------|-------------------|-----|-----|
| 799 | 300 l | bl, lil & blk | .45 | .45 |
| a. | A158 | Pair, #798-799 | .70 | .70 |

New York, 300th anniv. Printed checkerwise.

Rotary Press,
San Marino
Towers — A159

Gymnasts and
Olympic
Rings — A160

**1973, May 10**    **Photo.**    **Perf. 13x14**

| 800 | A159 | 50 l | multi | .20 | .20 |

Tourist Press Congress, San Marino.

**1973, May 10**    **Unwmk.**

| 801 | A160 | 100 l | grn & multi | .20 | .20 |

5th Youth Games.

**Europa Issue 1973**
Common Design Type

**1973, May 10**    **Perf. 11½**
**Size: 32½x23mm**

| 802 | CD16 | 20 l | salmon & multi | .40 | .25 |
|-----|------|------|----------------|-----|-----|
| 803 | CD16 | 180 l | lt bl & multi | .60 | .35 |

Grapes — A161

**1973, July 11**    **Photo.**    **Perf. 11½**

| 804 | A161 | 1 l | shown | .20 | .20 |
|-----|------|-----|-------|-----|-----|
| 805 | A161 | 2 l | Tangerines | .20 | .20 |
| 806 | A161 | 3 l | Apples | .20 | .20 |
| 807 | A161 | 4 l | Plums | .20 | .20 |
| 808 | A161 | 5 l | Strawberries | .20 | .20 |
| 809 | A161 | 10 l | Pears | .20 | .20 |
| 810 | A161 | 25 l | Cherries | .20 | .20 |
| 811 | A161 | 50 l | Pomegranate | .20 | .20 |
| 812 | A161 | 90 l | Apricots | .30 | .30 |
| 813 | A161 | 220 l | Peaches | 2.10 | 2.10 |

*Nos. 804-813 (10)*

Arc-en-Ciel, France — A162

Famous Aircraft: 55 l, Macchi Castoldi, Italy. 60 l, Antonov, USSR. 90 l, Spirit of St. Louis, US. 220 l, Handley Page, Great Britain.

**1973, Aug. 31**    **Photo.**    **Perf. 14x13½**

| 814 | A162 | 25 l | ocher, vio bl & gold | .20 | .20 |
|-----|------|------|----------------------|-----|-----|
| 815 | A162 | 55 l | gray, vio bl & gold | .20 | .20 |
| 816 | A162 | 60 l | rose, vio bl & gold | .20 | .20 |
| 817 | A162 | 90 l | lem, vio bl & gold | 1.10 | 1.10 |
| 818 | A162 | 220 l | org, vio bl & gold | 1.10 | 1.10 |

*Nos. 814-818 (5)*

Crossbowman, Serravalle Castle — A163

Attendants, by Gentile Fabriano — A164

Designs: 10 l, Crossbowman, Pennarossa Castle, 15 l, Drummer, Montegiardino Castle, 20 l, Trumpeter, Fiorentino Castle, 30 l, Crossbowman, Borga Maggiore Castle, 50 l, Crossbowman, Faetano, Guaita Castle, 80 l, Crossbowman, Montelupo Castle.

**1973, Nov. 7    Photo.    Perf. 13½**

| | | | | |
|---|---|---|---|---|
| 819 | A163 | 5 l | black & multi | .20 .20 |
| 820 | A163 | 10 l | black & multi | .20 .20 |
| 821 | A163 | 15 l | black & multi | .20 .20 |
| 822 | A163 | 15 l | black & multi | .20 .20 |
| 823 | A163 | 40 l | black & multi | .20 .20 |
| 824 | A163 | 50 l | black & multi | .20 .20 |
| 825 | A163 | 50 l | black & multi | .20 .20 |
| 826 | A163 | 80 l | black & multi | .25 .20 |
| 827 | A163 | 200 l | black & multi | 1.85 1.85 |

Nos. 819-827 (9)

San Marino victorse in the Crossbow Tournament, Massa Marittima, July 15, 1973.

Shield, 16th Century A165

**1973, Dec. 19    Photo.    Perf. 11½**

| | | | | |
|---|---|---|---|---|
| 828 | A164 | 5 l | shown | .20 .20 |
| 829 | A164 | 30 l | King | .20 .20 |
| 830 | A164 | 115 l | King | .35 .35 |
| 831 | A164 | 250 l | Horses | .95 .95 |

Nos. 828-831 (4)

Christmas: Details from Adoration of the Kings, by Gentile Fabriano (1370-1427).

Head of Woman, by Emilio Greco — A166

16th Century Armor: 5 l, Round shield, 10 l, German full armor, 15 l, Helmet with intricate etching, 20 l, Horse's head armor "Massimiliano," 30 l, Decorated helmet with Sphinx statuette on top, 50 l, Pommeled sword and gauntlets, 80 l, Sparrow-beaked helmet, 250 l, Sforza round shield.

**1974, Mar. 12    Engr. & Litho.    Perf. 13**

| | | | | |
|---|---|---|---|---|
| 832 | A165 | 5 l | blk, lt grn & buff | .20 .20 |
| 833 | A165 | 10 l | blk, grn & bl | .20 .20 |
| 834 | A165 | 15 l | blk, bl & ultra | .20 .20 |
| 835 | A165 | 30 l | blk, tan & bl | .20 .20 |
| 836 | A165 | 30 l | blk & lt bl | .20 .20 |
| 837 | A165 | 50 l | blk, rose & ultra | .20 .20 |
| 838 | A165 | 80 l | blk, gray & yel | .20 .20 |
| 839 | A165 | 250 l | blk & yel & grn | .35 .35 |

Nos. 832-839 (8)   1.75 1.75

**1974, May 9    Engr. & Litho.    Perf. 13x14**

| | | | | |
|---|---|---|---|---|
| 840 | A166 | 100 l | buff & blk | .60 .50 |
| 841 | A166 | 200 l | pale grn & blk | 1.00 .60 |

Europa: 200 l, Nude, by Emilio Greco (head shown on 100 l).

Yachts at Riccione and San Marino — A167

**1974, July 18    Photo.    Granite Paper    Perf. 11½**

| | | | | |
|---|---|---|---|---|
| 842 | A167 | 50 l | ultra & multi | .20 .20 |

26th San Marino-Riccione Stamp Day.

Arms of Lucia — A168

Coats of arms of participating cities.

**1974, July 18    Perf. 12**

| | | | | |
|---|---|---|---|---|
| 843 | A168 | 15 l | shown | .45 .45 |
| 844 | A168 | 20 l | Massa Marittima | .45 .45 |
| 845 | A168 | 50 l | San Marino | .45 .45 |
| 846 | A168 | 115 l | Gubbio | .45 .45 |
| 847 | A168 | 300 l | Lucca | 2.25 2.25 |
| a. | | | Strip of 5, #843-847 | 2.25 2.25 |

9th Crossbow Tournament, San Marino.

UPU Emblem — A169

**1974, Oct. 9    Photo.    Perf. 11½**

| | | | | |
|---|---|---|---|---|
| 848 | A169 | 50 l | multi | .20 .20 |
| 849 | A169 | 90 l | grn & multi | .20 .20 |

Centenary of Universal Postal Union.

Mt. Titano and Hymn by Tommaseo A170

Niccolo Tommaseo A171

**1974, Dec. 12    Photo.    Perf. 13½x14**

| | | | | |
|---|---|---|---|---|
| 850 | A170 | 50 l | lt grn, blk & red | .20 .20 |
| 851 | A171 | 150 l | yel, grn & blk | .20 .20 |

Tommaseo (1802-1874), Italian writer.

Virgin and Child, 14th Century Wood Panel — A172

**1974, Dec. 12    Photo.    Perf. 11½**

| | | | | |
|---|---|---|---|---|
| 852 | A172 | 250 l | gold & multi | .35 .35 |

Christmas.

"Refuge in San Marino" — A173

**1975, Feb. 20    Photo.    Perf. 13½x14**

| | | | | |
|---|---|---|---|---|
| 853 | A173 | 50 l | multi | .20 .20 |

Flight of 100,000 refugees from Romagna to San Marino, 30th anniversary.

Musicians, from Leopard Tomb, Tarquinia — A174

**1975, Feb. 20    Litho. & Engr.    Perf. 14**

| | | | | |
|---|---|---|---|---|
| 854 | A174 | 30 l | multi | .20 .20 |
| 855 | A174 | 30 l | multi | .20 .20 |
| 856 | A174 | 180 l | multi | .25 .25 |
| 857 | A174 | 220 l | multi | .30 .30 |

Nos. 854-857 (4)   .95 .95

Etruscan Art: 30 l, Chariot race, from Tomb on the Hill, Chiusi, 180 l, Achilles and Troilus, from Bulls' Tomb, Tarquinia, 220 l, Dancers, from Triclinium Tomb, Tarquinia.

St. Marinus, by Guercino (Francesco Barbieri) A176

**Europa Issue 1975**

**1975, May 14    Photo.    Granite Paper    Perf. 11½**

| | | | | |
|---|---|---|---|---|
| 858 | A175 | 100 l | multi | .55 .25 |
| 859 | A176 | 200 l | multi | .75 .35 |

The Lamentation, by Giotto — A177

Frescoes by Giotto (details): 40 l, Mary and Jesus (Flight into Egypt), 50 l, Heads of four angels (Flight into Egypt), 100 l, Mary Magdalene (Noli Me Tangere), horiz., 500 l, Angel and the elect (Last Judgment), horiz.

**1975, July 10    Photo.    Granite Paper    Perf. 11½**

| | | | | |
|---|---|---|---|---|
| 860 | A177 | 10 l | gold & multi | .20 .20 |
| 861 | A177 | 40 l | gold & multi | .20 .20 |
| 862 | A177 | 50 l | gold & multi | .20 .20 |
| 863 | A177 | 100 l | gold & multi | .20 .20 |
| 864 | A177 | 500 l | gold & multi | .65 .65 |

Nos. 860-864 (5)   1.45 1.45

Holy Year.

Tokyo, 1835, Woodcut by Hiroshige — A178

300 l, Tokyo, Business District, 1975.

**1975, Sept. 5    Photo.    Granite Paper    Perf. 11½**

| | | | | |
|---|---|---|---|---|
| 865 | A178 | 200 l | multi | .25 .25 |
| 866 | A178 | 300 l | multi | .40 .40 |
| a. | | | Pair, #865-866 | .65 .65 |

Printed checkerwise.

Aphrodite A179

**1975, Sept. 19    Photo.    Perf. 11½**

| | | | | |
|---|---|---|---|---|
| 867 | A179 | 50 l | vio, blk & gray | .20 .20 |

Europa 75 Philatelic Exhibition, Naples.

Multiple Crosses A180

**1975, Sept. 19    Photo.    Perf. 11½**

| | | | | |
|---|---|---|---|---|
| 868 | A180 | 100 l | blk, dp org & vio | .20 .20 |

EUROCOPHAR Intl. Pharmaceutical Cong.

Christmas — A181

**1975, Dec. 3    Photo.    Granite Paper    Perf. 11½**

| | | | | |
|---|---|---|---|---|
| 869 | A181 | 50 l | multi | .20 .20 |
| 870 | A181 | 100 l | multi | .20 .20 |
| 871 | A181 | 250 l | multi | .75 .75 |
| a. | | | Strip of 3, #869-871 | |

Christmas: Paintings by Michelangelo: 50 l, Angel, 100 l, Head of Virgin, 250 l, Doni Madonna.

Woman on Balcony, by Gentilini — A183

230 l, Woman (same as right head on 150 l) & IWY emblem, by Franco Gentilini.

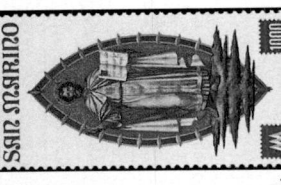

Two Women, by Gentilini — A184

**1975, Dec. 3** **Granite Paper**
| | | | | |
|---|---|---|---|---|
| 872 | A183 | 70 l | bl & multi | .20 .20 |
| 873 | A184 | 150 l | multi | .30 .30 |
| 874 | A183 | 230 l | multi | .70 .70 |

*Nos. 872-874 (3)*

International Women's Year.

Modesty, by Emilio Greco — A185

"Civic Virtues": 20 l, Temperance. 50 l, Fortitude. 100 l, Altruism. 150 l, Prudence. 220 l, Justice. 250 l, Justice. 300 l, Faith. 500 l, Honesty. 1000 l, Industry. Designs show drawings of women's heads by Emilio Greco.

**1976, Mar. 4** **Photo.** *Perf. 11½*
**Granite Paper**
| | | | | |
|---|---|---|---|---|
| 875 | A185 | 10 l | buff & blk | .20 .20 |
| 876 | A185 | 20 l | pink & blk | .20 .20 |
| 877 | A185 | 50 l | grnsh & blk | .20 .20 |
| 878 | A185 | 100 l | salmon & blk | .20 .20 |
| 879 | A185 | 150 l | lilac & blk | .20 .20 |
| 880 | A185 | 220 l | gray & blk | .30 .30 |
| 881 | A185 | 250 l | yel & multi | .35 .35 |
| 882 | A185 | 300 l | gray & blk | .40 .40 |
| 883 | A185 | 500 l | yel & blk | .65 .65 |
| 884 | A185 | 1000 l | yel & blk | 1.25 1.25 |

*Nos. 875-884 (10)* 3.96 3.95

See Nos. 900-905, 931-933.

Capitol, Washington, D.C. — A186

Arms of San Marino and: 150 l, Statue of Liberty. 180 l, Independence Hall, Philadelphia.

**1976, May 29** **Photo.** *Perf. 11½*
| | | | | |
|---|---|---|---|---|
| 885 | A186 | 70 l | multi | .20 .20 |
| 886 | A186 | 150 l | multi | .25 .25 |
| 887 | A186 | 180 l | multi | .65 .65 |

*Nos. 885-887 (3)*

American Bicentennial.

Montreal Olympic Games Emblem A187

**1976, May 29**
888 A187 150 l crimson & blk .20 .20

21st Olympic Games, Montreal, Canada, 7/17-8/1.

Decorated Plate — A188

Europa: 180 l, Seal of San Marino.

**1976, July 8** **Photo.** *Perf. 11½*
**Granite Paper**
| | | | | |
|---|---|---|---|---|
| 889 | A188 | 150 l | multi | .50 .25 |
| 890 | A188 | 180 l | bl, sil & blk | .60 .35 |

"Unity" — A189

"Peaks of San Marino" — A190

**1976, July 8** *Perf. 13½x14*
891 A189 150 l vio blk, yel & red .20 .20

United Mutual Aid Society, centenary.

ITALIA 76

**1976, Oct. 14** **Photo.** *Perf. 13x14*
892 A190 150 l blk & multi .25 .25

ITALIA 76 Intl. Phil. Exhib., Milan, 10/14-24.

Children and UNESCO Emblem A191

**1976, Oct. 14** *Perf. 11½*
**Granite Paper**
| | | | | |
|---|---|---|---|---|
| 893 | A191 | 180 l | multi | .25 .25 |
| 894 | A191 | 220 l | multi | .30 .30 |

UNESCO, 30th anniv.

Christmas — A192

Design: 150 l, Annunciation (detail), by Titian. 300 l, Virgin and Child, by Titian.

**1976, Dec. 15** **Litho. & Engr.** *Perf. 13x14*
| | | | | |
|---|---|---|---|---|
| 895 | A192 | 150 l | multi | .20 .20 |
| 896 | A192 | 300 l | multi | .45 .45 |

*a. A192 Pair, #895-896* .60 .60

Exhibition Emblem A193

**1977, Jan. 28** **Photo.** *Perf. 11½*
**Granite Paper**
| | | | | |
|---|---|---|---|---|
| 897 | A193 | 80 l | multi | .20 .20 |
| 898 | A193 | 170 l | multi | .25 .25 |
| 899 | A193 | 200 l | multi | .90 .90 |

*Nos. 897-899,C133 (4)*

San Marino 77 Phil. Exhib.

**Civic Virtues Type of 1976**

70 l, Fortitude. 90 l, Prudence. 120 l, Altruism. 160 l, Temperance. 170 l, Hope. 320 l, Faith.

**1977, Apr. 14** **Photo.** *Perf. 11½*
**Granite Paper**
| | | | | |
|---|---|---|---|---|
| 900 | A185 | 70 l | pink & blk | .20 .20 |
| 901 | A185 | 90 l | buff & blk | .20 .20 |
| 902 | A185 | 120 l | lt bl & blk | .20 .20 |
| 903 | A185 | 160 l | lt grn & blk | .20 .20 |
| 904 | A185 | 170 l | cream & blk | .40 .40 |
| 905 | A185 | 320 l | lil & blk | 1.40 1.40 |

*Nos. 900-905 (6)*

San Marino, after Ghirlandaio A194

Europa: 200 l, San Marino, detail from painting by Guercino.

**1977, Apr. 14** *Perf. 13x14*
**Granite Paper**
| | | | | |
|---|---|---|---|---|
| 906 | A194 | 170 l | multi | .75 .35 |
| 907 | A194 | 200 l | multi | .75 .35 |

Vertical Flying Machine, by da Vinci — A195

**1977, June 6** **Litho. & Engr.** *Perf. 13x14*
908 A195 120 l multi .20 .20

Centenary of Enrico Forlanini's experiments with vertical flight.

University Square, Bucharest, 1877 — A196

Design: 400 l, National Theater and Intercontinental Hotel, 1977.

**1977, June 6** **Photo.** *Perf. 11½*
**Granite Paper**
| | | | | |
|---|---|---|---|---|
| 909 | 200 l | bis & multi | .30 .30 |
| 910 | 400 l | lt bl & multi | .50 .50 |

*a. A196 Pair, #909-910* .80 .80

Centenary of Romanian independence. Printed checkerwise.

Type A2 of 1877 — A197

**1977, June 15** **Engr.** *Perf. 15x14½*
| | | | | |
|---|---|---|---|---|
| 911 | A197 | 40 l | slate grn | .20 .20 |
| 912 | A197 | 70 l | deep blue | .20 .20 |
| 913 | A197 | 170 l | red | .20 .20 |
| 914 | A197 | 500 l | brown | .65 .65 |
| 915 | A197 | 1000 l | purple | 1.25 1.25 |

*Nos. 911-915 (5)* 2.50 2.50

Centenary of San Marino stamps.

St. Marinus, by Retrosi — A198

Medicinal Plants — A199

**Souvenir Sheet**

**1977, Aug. 28** **Photo.** *Perf. 11½*
**Granite Paper**
916 A198 Sheet of 5 7.50 7.50
*a. 1000 l single stamp* 1.25 1.25

Centenary of San Marino stamps; San Marino 77 Phil. Exhib., Aug. 28-Sept. 4.

Congress of Italian Pharmacists' Union. Design shows high mallow, tilia, camomile, borage, centaury and juniper.

**1977, Oct. 19** **Photo.** *Perf. 11½*
917 A199 170 l multi .20 .20

Woman Attacked by Octopus, Emblem A200

World Rheumatism Year.

**1977, Oct. 19**
918 A200 200 l multi .25 .25

Virgin Mary — A201

San Francisco Gate — A202

Christmas: 230 l, Palm, olive and star. 300 l, Angel.

**1977, Dec. 5** **Photo.** **Perf. 11½**
919 A201 170 l sil, gray & blk .20 .20
920 A201 230 l sil, gray & blk .30 .30
921 A201 300 l sil, gray & blk .40 .40
a. Strip of 3, #919-921 .90 .90

Baseball Player and Diamond — A203

**1978, May 30** **Photo.** **Perf. 11½**
922 A202 170 l lt bl & dk bl .75 .30
923 A202 200 l buff & brn 1.00 .40

Europa: 200 l, Ripa Gate.

**1978, May 30**
924 A203 90 l multi .20 .20
925 A203 120 l multi .20 .20

World Baseball Championships.

**1978, May 30**
926 A204 320 l multi .40 .40

Fight against hypertension.

Feather, WHO Emblem — A204

ITU Emblem, Waves Coming from 3 Peaks — A205

**1978, July 26** **Photo.** **Perf. 11½**
927 A205 10 l car & yel .20 .20
928 A205 200 l vio bl & lt bl .25 .25

Membership in ITU.

Seagull and Falcon, 3 Peaks A206

**1978, July 26**
929 A206 120 l multi .20 .20
930 A206 170 l multi .20 .20

30th San Marino-Riccione Stamp Day.

### Civic Virtues Type of 1976

Drawings by Emilio Greco: 5 l, Wisdom, 35 l, Love, 2000 l, Faithfulness.

**1978, Sept. 28** **Photo.**
**Granite Paper** **Perf. 11½**
931 A185 5 l lt vio & blk .20 .20
932 A185 35 l gray & blk .20 .20
933 A185 2000 l yel & blk 2.50 2.50
Nos. 931-933 (3) 2.90 2.90

Christmas A207

**1978, Dec. 6** **Photo.** **Perf. 14x13½**
941 A207 10 l Holly leaves .20 .20
942 A207 120 l Stars .20 .20
943 A207 170 l Snowflakes .60 .60
Nos. 941-943 (3) .60 .60

---

Globe and Woman Holding Torch — A208

**1978, Dec. 6**
944 A208 200 l multi .25 .25

Universal Declaration of Human Rights, 30th anniversary.

First San Marino Autobus, 1915 A209

**1979, Mar. 29** **Photo.** **Perf. 11½x12**
945 A209 170 l multi 1.25 .50
946 A209 220 l multi 1.50 .75

Europa: 220 l, Mail coach, 1895.

Albert Einstein (1879-1955), Theoretical Physicist — A210

**1979, Mar. 29**
947 A210 120 l gray, lt & dk brn .20 .20

Maigret — A212

**1979, July 12** **Litho.** **Perf. 14x13**
948 A211 120 l multi .20 .20

14th Crossbow Tournament.

San Marino Crossbow Federation Emblem — A211

**1979, July 12** **Litho. & Engr.** **Perf. 13x14**
949 A212 10 l multi .20 .20
950 A212 80 l multi .20 .20
951 A212 150 l multi .20 .20
952 A212 170 l multi .20 .20
953 A212 220 l multi .35 .35
Nos. 949-953 (5) 1.15 1.15

Fictional Detectives: 80 l, Perry Mason, 150 l, Nero Wolfe, 170 l, Ellery Queen, 220 l, Sherlock Holmes.

Girl Holding Bird — A213

---

**1979, Sept. 6** **Litho.** **Perf. 11½**
954 A213 20 l multi .20 .20
955 A213 120 l multi .20 .20
956 A213 170 l multi .30 .25
957 A213 220 l multi .45 .20
958 A213 350 l multi 1.35 1.25
Nos. 954-958 (5)

IYC Emblem, Paintings by Marina Busignani: 120 l, 170 l, 220 l, Children and birds, diff. 350 l, Mother nursing child.

St. Apollonia, 15th Century Woodcut — A214

**1979, Sept. 6**
959 A214 170 l multi .20 .20

13th Biennial Intl. Congress of Stomatology.

Waterskier A215

**1979, Sept. 6** **Photo.**
960 A215 150 l multi .20 .20

European Waterskiing Championship.

Chestnut Tree, Deer — A216

**1979, Oct. 25** **Photo.** **Perf. 11½**
961 A216 5 l multi .20 .20
962 A216 10 l multi .20 .20
963 A216 35 l multi .20 .20
964 A216 50 l multi .20 .20
965 A216 70 l multi .20 .20
966 A216 80 l multi .20 .20
967 A216 100 l multi .20 .20
968 A216 120 l multi .20 .20
969 A216 150 l multi .20 .20
970 A216 170 l multi 2.00 2.00
Nos. 961-970 (10)

Protected Trees and Animals or Birds: 10 l, Cedar of Lebanon, falcon, 35 l, Dogwood, racoon, 50 l, Banyan, tiger, 70 l, Umbrella pine, hoopoe, 90 l, Siberian spruce, marten, 100 l, Eucalyptus, koala bear, 120 l, Date palm, camel, 150 l, Sugar maple, beaver, 170 l, Adansonia, elephant.

---

Disturbing Muses, by Giorgio de Chirico — A218

**1979, Dec.**
975 A218 40 l shown .20 .20
976 A218 150 l Ancient horses .20 .20
977 A218 170 l Self-portrait .60 .60
Nos. 975-977 (3)

Giorgio de Chirico, Italian surrealist painter.

St. Benedict, 15th Century Fresco — A219

**1980, Mar. 27** **Photo.** **Perf. 12x11½**
978 A219 170 l multi .20 .20

St. Benedict of Nursia, 1500th birth anniversary.

Fight Against Cigarette Smoking — A220

**1980, Mar. 27**
979 A220 120 l multi .20 .20
980 A220 220 l multi .25 .25
981 A220 520 l multi .65 .65
Nos. 979-981 (3) 1.10 1.10

Designs: Sketches of smokers and cigarettes by Giuliana Consilvio.

Naples, 17th Century Engraving A221

**1980, Mar. 27** **Perf. 14x13½**
982 A221 170 l multi .25 .25

20th Intl. Phil. Exhib., Europa '80, Naples, Apr. 26-May 4.

View of London, 1850 — A222

**1980, May 8** **Perf. 11½x12**
983 A222 200 l shown .25 .25
984 A222 400 l London, 1980 .50 .50
Nos. 983-984 .75 .75

London 1980 Intl. Stamp Exhib., May 6-14. Printed checkerwise.

See Nos. 1001-1002, 1032-1033, 1054-1055, 1069-1070, 1098-1099, 1110-1111, 1141-1142, 1339-1340.

---

Holy Family, by Antonio Alberto de Ferrara, 15th Century Fresco A217

**1979, Dec. 6** **Photo.** **Perf. 12**
971 A217 80 l multi .20 .20
972 A217 170 l multi .20 .20
973 A217 220 l multi .30 .30
974 A217 320 l multi .40 .40
Nos. 971-974 (4) 1.10 1.10

Christmas (de Ferrara Fresco): 80 l, St. Joseph, 170 l, Infant Jesus, 220 l, One of the Three Kings.

# SAN MARINO

A228

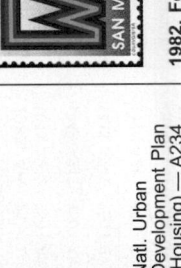

A223

A224

Europa: 170 l, Giovanbattista Belluzzi (1506-54), military architect. 220 l, Antonio Orafo (1460-1552), goldsmith and jeweler.

**1980, May 8**    **Perf. 11½**
985 A223 170 l multi    .85 .30
986 A223 220 l multi    1.40 .35

**1980, July 7**    **Photo.**
**Granite Paper**    **Perf. 11½**
987 A224 70 l Bicycling    .20 .20
988 A224 90 l Basketball    .20 .20
989 A224 170 l Running    .45 .45
990 A224 350 l Gymnast    .60 .60
991 A224 450 l High jump    1.65 1.65
   Nos. 987-991 (5)

22nd Summer Olympic Games, Moscow, July 19-Aug. 3.

Weight Lifting
A226

Ancient Fortifications
A225

World Tourism Conf., Manila, Sept. 27.

**1980, Sept. 18**    **Perf. 13½x14**
992 A225 220 l multi    .25 .25

**1980, Sept. 18**    **Photo.**    **Perf. 14x13½**
993 A226 170 l multi    .20 .20

European Junior Weight Lifting Championship, Sept.

Robert Stolz, "Philatelic Waltz" Score — A227

**1980, Sept. 18**    **Photo. & Engr.**    **Perf. 14**
994 A227 120 l lt bl & blk    .20 .20

Robert Stolz (1880-1975) composer.

Annunciation by Del Sarto (Details): 250 l, Virgin Mary. 500 l, Angel.

**1980, Dec. 11**    **Perf. 13½**
995 A228 180 l multi    .25 .25
996 A228 250 l multi    .40 .40
997 A228 500 l multi    .70 .70
   Nos. 995-997 (3)    1.35 1.35

Christmas; 450th death anniv. of Del Sarto.

---

St. Joseph's Eve Bonfire — A229

**Europa Issue 1981**
**1981, Mar. 24**    **Photo.**
**Granite Paper**    **Perf. 12**
998 A229 200 l shown    .60 .45
999 A229 300 l San Marino Day fireworks    1.40 .65

**1981, May 15**    **Photo.**
**Granite Paper**    **Perf. 11½**
1000 A230 300 l multi    .40 .40

Intl. Year of the Disabled — A230

**Exhibition Type of 1980**
St. Charles' Square, Vienna, by Jakob Alt, 1817.

**1981, May 15**    **Granite Paper**
1001 A222 200 l shown    .25 .25
1002 A222 300 l Vienna, 1981    .40 .40
   a. Pair, #1001-1002    .65 .65

WIPA '81 Intl. Phil. Exhib., Vienna, 5/22-31.

Woman Playing Flute — A232

Grand Prix Motorcycle Race — A233

Drawings based on Roman sculptures.

**1981, July 10**    **Photo.**    **Perf. 11½**
**Granite Paper**
1003 A232 300 l shown    .35 .35
1004 A232 550 l Soldier    .70 .70
1005 A232 1500 l Shepherd    1.90 1.90
   a. Souv. sheet of 3, #1003-1005    4.00 4.00

Virgil's birth bimillennium. No. 1005a has continuous design.

**1981, July 10**    **Litho.**    **Perf. 14x15**
1006 A233 200 l multi    .25 .25

---

Natl. Urban Development Plan (Housing) — A234

**1981, Sept. 22**    **Photo.**
**Granite Paper**
1007 A234 20 l shown    .20 .20
1008 A234 80 l Parks    .20 .20
1009 A234 400 l Energy plants    .50 .50
   Nos. 1007-1009 (3)    .90 .90

European Junior Judo Championship, Oct. 30-Nov. 1 — A235

**1981, Sept. 22**    **Photo.**    **Perf. 11½**
**Granite Paper**
1010 A235 300 l multi    .40 .40

World Food Day — A236

**1981, Oct. 23**    **Granite Paper**
1011 A236 300 l multi    .40 .40

A237

A238

Designs: 150 l, Child Holding a Dove, by Pablo Picasso (1881-1973). 200 l, Homage to Picasso, by Renato Guttuso.

**1981, Oct. 23**    **Granite Paper**
1012 A237 150 l multi    .20 .20
1013 A237 200 l multi    .25 .25

**1981, Dec. 15**    **Photo. & Engr.**    **Perf. 13½**
1014 A238 200 l multi    .25 .25
1015 A238 300 l multi    .40 .40
1016 A238 600 l multi    .75 .75
   Nos. 1014-1016 (3)    1.40 1.40

Christmas; 500th Birth Anniv. of Benvenuto Tisi da Garofalo. Adoration of the Kings and St. Bartholomew): 200 l, One of the Three Kings with Goblet, by Garofalo. 300 l, King with a Jar. 600 l, Virgin and Child.

---

Postal Stationery Centenary A239

**1982, Feb. 19**    **Photo.**    **Perf. 12**
1017 A239 200 l multi    .25 .25

Savings Bank Centenary A240

**1982, Feb. 19**
1018 A240 300 l multi    .40 .40

Europa 1982 — A241

Designs: 300 l, Convocation of the Assembly of Heads of Families, 1906. 450 l, Napoleon's Treaty of Friendship offer, 1797.

**1982, Apr. 21**    **Photo.**    **Perf. 11½**
**Granite Paper**
1019 A241 300 l multi    3.25 1.60
1020 A241 450 l multi    4.75 2.25

Archimedes
A242

800th Birth Anniv. of St. Francis of Assisi
A243

**1982, Apr. 21**    **Photo.**    **Perf. 14x13½**
1021 A242 20 l shown    .20 .20
1022 A242 30 l Copernicus    .20 .20
1023 A242 40 l Newton    .20 .20
1024 A242 50 l Lavoisier    .20 .20
1025 A242 60 l Marie Curie    .20 .20
1026 A242 100 l Robert Koch    .20 .20

**Litho. & Engr.**
1027 A242 200 l Thomas Edison    .25 .25
1028 A242 300 l Guglielmo Marconi    .40 .40
1029 A242 450 l Hippocrates    .60 .60

**Engr.**
1030 A242 5000 l Galileo    6.25 6.25
   Nos. 1021-1030 (10)    8.70 8.70

See Nos. 1041-1046.

**1982, June 10**
1031 A243 200 l multi    .25 .25

**Exhibition Type of 1980**
**1982, June 10**    **Photo.**
1032 A222 300 l Notre Dame, 1806    .40 .40
1033 A222 450 l 1982    .60 .60
   a. Pair, #1032-1033    1.00 1.00

PHILEXFRANCE '82 Stamp Exhibition, Paris, June 11-21.

## Visit of Pope John Paul II — A245

**1982, Aug. 29    Litho.    Perf. 13½x14**
1034  A245  900 l multi    1.10  1.10

## Natl. Flags of ASCAT Members — A246

**1982, Sept. 1    Photo.    Perf. 11½**
Granite Paper
1035  A246  300 l multi    .40  .40

Inaugural Meeting of ASCAT (Assoc. of Editors of Philatelic Catalogues), 1977.

A247

A248

**1982, Sept. 1    Perf. 11½**
1036  A247  700 l blk & red    .90  .90

15th Amnesty Intl. Congress, Rimini, Italy, Sept. 9-15.

**1982, Dec. 15    Photo. & Engr.    Perf. 13½**
1037  A248  200 l Angel    .25  .25
1038  A248  300 l Virgin and Child    .40  .40
1039  A248  450 l Angel, diff.    .60  .60
Nos. 1037-1039 (3)    1.25  1.25

Christmas: Paintings by Gregorio Scitian (1900-85).

## Secondary School Centenary A249

A249

## Auguste Piccard — A251

## 3rd Formula One Grand Prix A250

**1983, Feb. 24    Photo.    Perf. 13½x14**
1040  A249  300 l Begni Building    .35  .35

## Scientist Type of 1982    Perf. 14x13½

**1983, Apr. 21**
1041  A242  150 l Alexander Fleming    .20  .20
1042  A242  250 l Alessandro Volta    .35  .35
1043  A242  350 l Evangelista Torricelli    .45  .45
1044  A242  400 l Carolus Lin- naeus    .45  .45
1045  A242  1000 l Pythagoras    1.25  1.25
1046  A242  1400 l Leonardo da Vinci    1.75  1.75
Nos. 1041-1046 (6)    4.50  4.50

## Flag-wavers Group, 2nd Anniv. — A257

**1983, Apr. 20    Photo. & Engr.    Perf. 14x13½**
1047  A250  50 l multi    .20  .20
1048  A250  350 l multi    .45  .45

Paintings, Raphael (1483-1520): 300 l, Our Lady of the Grand Duke; 400 l, Our Goldfinch; 500 l, Our Lady of the Chair.

**1983, Apr. 20    Granite Paper    Perf. 14x13½**
1049  A251  400 l Aerostat    2.50  1.50
1050  A251  500 l Bathyscaph    3.75  2.25

Europa. Piccard (1884-1962), Swiss scientist.

## World Communications Year — A252

**1983, Apr. 20    Perf. 12x11½**
1052  A252  500 l Ham radio opera- tor    .50  .50

## Manned Flight Bicentenary A253

**1983, Apr. 28    Engr.    Perf. 14x13**
1051  A252  400 l Mailman    .45  .45

## Exhibition Type of 1980    Perf. 13½x14

**1983, May 22**
1053  A253  500 l Montgolfiere, 1783    .65  .65

## Lithographed and Engraved    Perf. 13½x14

**1983, July 29    Photo.    Granite Paper    Perf. 11½x12**
1054  A222  400 l 1845    .50  .50
1055  A222  1400 l 1983    1.75  1.75
a.  Pair, #1054-1055    2.25  2.25

BRASILIANA '83 Intl. Stamp Show, Rio de Janeiro, July 29-Aug. 7.

Designs: Botafogo Bay and Monte Corcovado, Rio de Janeiro.

## 20th Anniv. of World Food Program A255

**1983, Sept. 29    Photo.    Perf. 14x13½**
1056  A255  500 l multi    .50  .50

## Christmas A256

## Olympic Type of 1959    Perf. 14x13½

**1983, Dec. 1**
1057  A256  300 l multi    .40  .40
1058  A256  400 l multi    .55  .55
1059  A256  500 l multi    .70  .70
a.  Strip of 3, #1057-1059    1.75  1.75

IOC Presidents: 300 l, Demetrius Vikelas, 1894-96; 400 l, Lord Killanin; 550 l, Antonio Samaranch, 1984.

**1984, Feb. 8    Photo.    Perf. 14x13½**
1060  A86  300 l multi    .40  .40
1061  A86  400 l multi    .50  .50
1062  A86  550 l multi    .70  .70
Nos. 1060-1062 (3)    1.60  1.60

## Litho. & Engr.    Perf. 13x14

**1984, Apr. 27**
1063  A257  300 l Flag    .40  .40
1064  A257  400 l Flags    .50  .50

## Europa (1959-1984) A258

**1984, Apr. 27    Granite Paper    Perf. 11½**
1065  A258  400 l multi    2.75  1.00
1066  A258  550 l multi    3.75  1.50

## Exhibition Type of 1980

**1984, June 14    Photo.    Perf. 13½x14**
1067  A259  450 l multi    .60  .60

Motorcross Grand Prix, Baldasserona.

A260

## Souvenir Sheet

**1984, June 14    Litho.    Perf. 13x14**
1068  Sheet of 2    2.00  2.00
a.  A260  550 l Man    .70  .70
b.  A260  1000 l Woman    1.25  1.25

1984 Summer Olympics.

A259

## Exhibition Type of 1980

**1984, Sept. 21    Photo.    Granite Paper    Perf. 11½**
1069  A222  1500 l 1839    1.90  1.90
1070  A222  2000 l 1984    2.50  2.50
a.  Pair, #1069-1070    4.50  4.50

Ausipex '84: Views of Melbourne. Se-tenant.

## Visit of Italian Pres. Pertini A262

**1984, Oct. 20    Photo.    Perf. 14x13½**
1071  A262  1950 l multi    2.50  2.50

## Christmas — A264

**1984, Dec. 5    Litho.    Perf. 13½x14**

Details of Madonna of San Girolamo by Correggio, 1527.

1078  A264  400 l multi    .65  .65
1079  A264  450 l multi    .70  .70
1080  A264  550 l multi    .90  .90
a.  Strip of 3, #1078-1080    2.25  2.25

## School and Philately — A263

Sketches by Jacovitti.

**1984, Oct. 30    Perf. 13½x14**
1072  A263  100 l Universe    .20  .20
1073  A263  100 l Evolution    .20  .20
1074  A263  150 l Environment    .20  .20
1075  A263  200 l Mankind    .25  .25
1076  A263  450 l Science    .60  .60
1077  A263  550 l Philosophy    .70  .70
Nos. 1072-1077 (6)    2.15  2.15

## Composers and Music — A265

**1985, Mar. 18    Photo.    Perf. 12**
1081  A265  450 l ocher & gray blk    2.50  1.10
1082  A265  600 l yel grn & gray blk    3.50  1.40

Europa: 450 l, Johann Sebastian Bach (1685-1750), Toccata and Fugue; 600 l, Vincenzo Bellini (1801-1835), Norma.

## Olympiad of the Small States, May 23-26 — A266

**1985, May 16    Litho.    Perf. 13½x14**
1083  A266  50 l Diving    .20  .20
1084  A266  350 l Running    .45  .45
1085  A266  400 l Rifle shooting    .50  .50
1086  A266  450 l Cycling    .60  .60
1087  A266  600 l Handball    .75  .75
Nos. 1083-1087 (5)    2.50  2.50

Sportphilex '85: Natl. Olympic Committee and Sportphilex '85 emblems, flags of Andorra, Cyprus, Iceland, Liechtenstein, Luxembourg, Malta, Monaco, San Marino.

# SAN MARINO

**Emigration A267**

**Intl. Youth Year — A268**

**1985, May 16**
1088 A267 600 l Birds migrating .75 .75

**Photo.** *Perf. 12*
**Granite Paper**
1089 A268 400 l Boy, dove .50 .50
1090 A268 600 l Girl, dove, horse .75 .75

**Helsinki Conference, 10th Anniv. — A269**

**City Hall, by Renzo Bonelli, Camora lens — A270**

**1985, June 24** *Perf. 13½x14*
1091 A269 600 l Sapling, sunburst, clouds .75 .75

*Perf. 13½x14½*
1092 A270 450 l multi .60 .60
Intl. Fed. of Photographic Art, 18th Congress.

**World Angling Championships, Arno River, Florence, Sept. 14-15 — A271**

**1985, Sept. 11 Photo.** *Perf. 14½x15*
1093 A271 600 l Hooked fish .75 .75

Alessandro Manzoni (1785-1873), Novelist & Poet — A272

19th century engravings from Manzoni's I Promessi Sposi (1825-27): 400 l, Don Abbondio encounters Don Rodrigo's henchmen. 450 l, The attempt to force the curate to perform a dubious marriage ceremony. 600 l, The Plague at Milan.

**1985, Sept. 11 Engr.** *Perf. 14x13½*
1094 A272 400 l multi .50 .50
1095 A272 450 l multi .60 .60
1096 A272 600 l multi .75 .75
*Nos. 1094-1096 (3)* 1.85 1.85

**Intl. Feline Fed. Congress A273**

Mosaic detail: Cat, Natl. Museum, Naples.

**1985, Oct. 25 Photo.** *Perf. 12*
**Granite Paper**
1097 A273 600 l multi .75 .75

**Exhibition Type of 1980**

ITALIA '85: Views of the Colosseum, Rome.

**1985, Oct. 25 Photo.** *Perf. 11½x12*
**Granite Paper**
1098 A222 1000 l multi 1.25 1.25
1099 A222 1500 l multi 1.90 1.90
a. Pair, #1098-1099 3.25 3.25

**Christmas A275**

**1985, Dec. 3 Photo. & Engr.** *Perf. 14*
1100 A275 400 l Angel .55 .55
1101 A275 450 l Mother and Child .60 .60
1102 A275 600 l Angel, diff. .80 .80
a. Strip of 3, #1100-1102 1.90 1.90

**Hospital, Cailungo A2/6**

**1986, Mar. 6 Photo.** *Perf. 12x11½*
1103 A276 450 l multi .60 .60
1104 A276 650 l multi .85 .85
Natl. social security org., ISS, 30th anniv., and World Health Day.

**Halley's Comet — A277**

Designs: 550 l, Giotto space probe. 1000 l, Adoration of the Magi, by Giotto (1276-1337).

**1986, Mar. 6 Photo.** *Perf. 11½x12*
1105 A277 550 l multi .70 .70
1106 A277 1000 l multi 1.25 1.25

**Deer — A278**

**3rd Veterans World Table Tennis Championships A279**

**Europa Issue 1986**

**1986, May 22 Photo.** *Perf. 13½x14*
1107 A278 550 l shown 10.00 7.50
1108 A278 650 l Falcon 15.00 10.00

**Engr.**
1109 A279 450 l multicolored .60 .60

**AMERIPEX '86, Chicago, May 22-June 1 — A280**

Views of Old Water Tower, Chicago: 2000 l, Lithograph, 1870, by Charles Shober. 3000 l, Photograph, 1986.

*Perf. 11½x12* **Unwmk.**
1110 A280 2000 l multi 2.50 2.50
1111 A280 3000 l multi 3.75 3.75
a. Pair, #1110-1111 6.25 6.25

**Intl. Peace Year — A281**

**1986, May 22 Photo.** *Perf. 11½x12*
1112 A281 550 l multi .70 .70

**Terra Cotta Statuary, Tomb of Emperor Qin Shi Huang Di (259-210 B.C.) — A282**

**Souvenir Sheet**

**1986, July 10 Litho. & Engr.** *Perf. 13½*
1113 Sheet of 3 4.50 4.50
a. A282 550 l Bearded man .70 .70
b. A282 650 l Horse, horiz. .85 .85
c. A282 2000 l Bearded man, diff. 2.75 2.75
Normalization of diplomatic relations with the People's Republic of China, 15th anniv.

**UNICEF, 40th Anniv. — A283**

**European Boccie Championships A284**

**1986, Sept. 16 Photo.** *Perf. 12*
1114 A283 650 l multi .85 .85

*Perf. 14x15*
1115 A284 550 l multi .70 .70

**Choral Society, 25th Anniv. — A285**

**Christmas A286**

Painting (detail): Apollo Dancing with the Muses, by Giulio Romano (1492-1546).

**1986, Sept. 16 Photo. & Engr.** *Perf. 14*
1116 A285 450 l multi .60 .60

Design: Oil on wood triptych, 15th cent. by Hans Memling (1435-1494), Kunsthistorisches Museum, Vienna.

**1986, Nov. 26**
1117 A286 450 l St. John the Baptist .80 .80
1118 A286 550 l Virgin and Child .95 .95
1119 A286 650 l St. John the Evangelist 1.25 1.25
a. Strip of 3, #1117-1119 3.00 3.00

**Europa Issue 1987**

**Our Lady of Consolation Church, Borgomaggiore A287**

Church designed by Giovanni Michelucci, architect; 600 l, Architect's sketch of interior. 700 l, Actual interior.

**1987, Mar. 12 Photo.** *Perf. 12*
1120 A287 600 l multi 8.50 5.00
1121 A287 700 l multi 13.00 6.50

## Motoring Events — A288

**1987, Mar. 12**    **Perf. 11½**

Designs: 500 l, 80th anniv., Peking-Paris Race. 600 l, 15th anniv., Mille Miglia Race. 700 l, 60th anniv., San Marino Rally.

| | | | | |
|---|---|---|---|---|
| 1122 | A288 | 500 l multi | .65 | .65 |
| 1123 | A288 | 600 l multi | .75 | .75 |
| 1124 | A288 | 700 l multi | .90 | .90 |
| Nos. 1122-1124 (3) | | | 2.30 | 2.30 |

### Sculptures, Open-air Museum — A289

**1987, June 13**    **Perf. 14½x13½**

| | | | | |
|---|---|---|---|---|
| 1125 | A289 | 50 l Reffi | .20 | .20 |
| 1126 | A289 | 100 l Busignani | .20 | .20 |
| 1127 | A289 | 200 l Bini | .30 | .30 |
| 1128 | A289 | 300 l Guglianu | .40 | .40 |
| 1129 | A289 | 300 l Berti | .40 | .40 |
| 1130 | A289 | 500 l Crocetti | .55 | .55 |
| 1131 | A289 | 600 l Berti, diff. | .70 | .70 |
| 1132 | A289 | 1000 l Messina | .80 | .80 |
| 1133 | A289 | 1000 l Minguzzi | 1.40 | 1.40 |
| 1134 | A289 | 2000 l Greco | 3.00 | 3.00 |
| 1135 | A289 | 10000 l Sassu | | |
| | | Nos. 1125-1134 (10) | 21.05 | 21.05 |

### — A290

**1987, June 13**    **Granite Paper**

| | | | | |
|---|---|---|---|---|
| 1135 | A290 | 500 l multi | .65 | .65 |
| 1136 | A290 | 600 l multi | .75 | .75 |

Abstract works: 500 l, Dal Diario del Brasile-foresta Vergine, by Emilio Vedova. 600 l, Invenzione Cromatica con Brio, by Corrado Cagli.

### Air Club of San Marino Ultra-lightweight Aircraft — A291

**1987, June 13**    **Perf. 11½**

| | | | | |
|---|---|---|---|---|
| 1137 | A291 | 600 l multi | .75 | .75 |

### — A292

**1987, Aug. 2**    **Photo.**

| | | | | |
|---|---|---|---|---|
| 1138 | A292 | 500 l Gandhi | .65 | .65 |

Mahatma Gandhi bust.

### — A293

**1987, Aug. 29**    **Granite Paper**

| | | | | |
|---|---|---|---|---|
| 1139 | A293 | 600 l Olympic emblem, athlete | .90 | .90 |

OLYMPHILEX '87, Rome.

### Seventh Natl. Art Biennale — A290

First Representation of San Marino at the Mediterranean Games, Syria, Sept. 11-15.

| | | | | |
|---|---|---|---|---|
| 1140 | A294 | 700 l ultra, blk & red | .90 | .90 |

### — A294

**1987, Aug. 29**    **Perf. 12**

### Exhibition Type of 1980

HAFNIA '87: Views of Copenhagen (1836-1986), as seen from the Round Tower.

**1987, Oct. 16**    **Photo.**    **Perf. 11½x12**

| | | | | |
|---|---|---|---|---|
| 1141 | A222 | 1200 l multi | 1.90 | 1.90 |
| 1142 | A222 | 2200 l multi, diff. | 3.50 | 3.50 |
| a. | | Pair, #1141-1142 | 5.50 | 5.50 |

### Christmas — A296

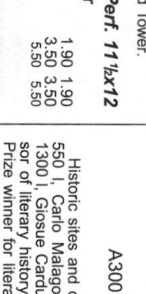

### Granite Paper

| | | | | |
|---|---|---|---|---|
| 1143 | A296 | 600 l multi | 1.10 | 1.10 |
| 1144 | A296 | 600 l multi | 1.10 | 1.10 |
| 1145 | A296 | 600 l multi | 1.10 | 1.10 |
| a. | | Strip of 3, #1143-1145 | 3.50 | 3.50 |

Details from Triptych of Cortona and The Annunciation, by Fra Angelico (c. 1400-1455), Diocesan Museum of Cortona: No. 1143, Angel. No. 1144, Madonna. and child. No. 1145, Saint. Printed se-tenant.

### High Speed Train — A297

**1987, Nov. 12**    **Photo. & Engr.**    **Perf. 13½**

| | | | | |
|---|---|---|---|---|
| 1146 | A297 | 600 l shown | 5.50 | 4.50 |
| 1147 | A297 | 700 l Fiber optics | 9.25 | 5.00 |

### Promote Stamp Collecting — A298

**1988, Mar. 17**    **Photo.**    **Perf. 11½**

| | | | | |
|---|---|---|---|---|
| 1148 | A298 | 50 l multi | .20 | .20 |
| 1149 | A298 | 150 l multi | .20 | .20 |
| 1150 | A298 | 300 l multi | .40 | .40 |

Stamps, cancellations, covers: 50 l, Nos. 81, B25 and 859. 150 l, No. C11. 300 l, Nos. 349 and 1006. 350 l, Nos. 944 and 1031. 1000 l, Nos. 303, 1081 and 308.

### Europa Issue 1988

**1988, Mar. 17**    **Granite Paper**    **Perf. 12**

| | | | | |
|---|---|---|---|---|
| 1151 | A298 | 350 l multi | .50 | .50 |
| 1152 | A298 | 1000 l multi | 1.40 | 1.40 |
| | | Nos. 1148-1152 (5) | 2.70 | 2.70 |

### — A299

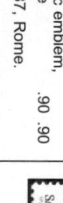

| | | | | |
|---|---|---|---|---|
| 1153 | A299 | 550 l multi | .70 | .70 |
| 1154 | A299 | 650 l multi | .85 | .85 |
| 1155 | A299 | 1300 l multi | 1.60 | 1.60 |
| 1156 | A299 | 1700 l multi | 2.25 | 2.25 |
| | | Nos. 1153-1156 (4) | 5.40 | 5.40 |

Historic sites and distinguished professors: 550 l, Carlo Malagola. 650 l, Pietro Ellero. 1300 l, Giosue Carducci (1835-1907), professor of literary history, 1861-1904, and Nobel Prize winner for literature, 1906. 1700 l, Giovanni Pascoli (1855-1912), lyric poet, Pascoli's successor as professor at Bologna.

Bologna University, 900th anniv.

**1988, May 7**    **Photo.**    **Perf. 13½x14**

### — A300

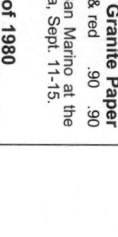

| | | | | |
|---|---|---|---|---|
| 1157 | A300 | 300 l multi | .40 | .40 |
| 1158 | A300 | 900 l multi | 1.25 | 1.25 |
| 1159 | A300 | 1200 l multi | 1.75 | 1.75 |
| | | Nos. 1157-1159 (3) | 3.40 | 3.40 |

Posters from Fellini Films: 300 l, La Strada. 900 l, La Dolce Vita. 1200 l, Amarcord.

Federico Fellini, Italian film director and winner of the 1988 San Marino Prize. See Nos. 1187-1189, 1202-1204.

**1988, July 8**    **Photo.**    **Perf. 13½x14**

### Mt. Titano and Sand Dunes of the Adriatic Coast — A301

**1988, July 8**    **Perf. 14x13½**

| | | | | |
|---|---|---|---|---|
| 1160 | A301 | 750 l multi | .95 | .95 |

40th Stamp Fair, Riccione.

### Souvenir Sheet

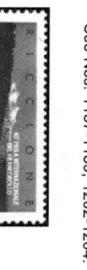

### 1988 Summer Olympics, Seoul — A302

**1988, Sept. 19**    **Photo.**    **Perf. 13½x14**

| | | | | |
|---|---|---|---|---|
| 1161 | A302 | Sheet of 3 | 3.50 | 3.50 |
| a. | | 650 l Running | .85 | .85 |
| b. | | 750 l Hurdles | .95 | .95 |
| c. | | 1300 l Gymnastics | 1.60 | 1.60 |

### Kurhaus Scheveningen, The Hague — A304

**1988, Oct. 18**    **Photo.**    **Perf. 11½x12**

### Granite Paper

| | | | | |
|---|---|---|---|---|
| 1166 | A304 | 1600 l shown | 2.00 | 2.00 |
| 1167 | A304 | 3000 l | 3.75 | 3.75 |
| a. | | Pair, #1166-1167 | 5.75 | 5.75 |

FILACEPT '88, Holland.

### Intl. AIDS Congress, San Marino, Oct. 10-14 — A303

**1988, Sept. 19**    **Perf. 14x13½**

| | | | | |
|---|---|---|---|---|
| 1162 | A303 | 250 l shown | .35 | .35 |
| 1163 | A303 | 350 l "AIDS" | .45 | .45 |
| 1164 | A303 | 650 l Virus, knot | .85 | .85 |
| 1165 | A303 | 1000 l Newspaper | 1.25 | 1.25 |
| | | Nos. 1162-1165 (4) | 2.90 | 2.90 |

### Christmas — A305

**1988, Dec. 9**    **Photo.**    **Perf. 13½**

**Size of No. 1169: 21x40mm**

| | | | | |
|---|---|---|---|---|
| 1168 | A305 | 650 l multi | 1.00 | 1.00 |
| 1169 | A305 | 650 l multi | 1.00 | 1.00 |
| 1170 | A305 | 650 l multi | 1.00 | 1.00 |
| a. | | Strip of 3, #1168-1170 | 3.00 | 3.00 |

Paintings by Melozzo da Forli (1438-1494): No. 1168, Angel with Violin, Vatican Art Gallery. No. 1169, Angel of the Annunciation, Uffizi Gallery, Florence. No. 1170, Angel with Lute, Vatican Art Gallery.

### Children's Games — A306

### Europa Issue 1989

### Souvenir Sheet

**1989, Mar. 31**    **Photo.**    **Perf. 13½x14**

| | | | | |
|---|---|---|---|---|
| 1171 | A302 | Sheet of 2 | 32.50 | 30.00 |
| a. | | A306 650 l Sledding | 12.50 | 11.00 |
| b. | | A306 750 l Hopscotch | 12.50 | 11.00 |

### Nature Conservation — A307

Illustrations by contest-winning youth: 200 l, Federica Sparagna. 500 l, Giovanni Monteduro. 650 l, Rosa Mannarino.

**1989, Mar. 31    Perf. 14x13½**
1172 A307 200 l multi   .25 .25
1173 A307 500 l multi   .65 .65
1174 A307 650 l multi   .85 .85
Nos. 1172-1174 (3)   1.75 1.75

**Sporting Anniversaries and Events — A308**

**1989, May 13    Photo.    Perf. 12**
**Granite Paper**
1175 A308 650 l Olympics   .85 .85
1176 A308 750 l Soccer   .95 .95
1177 A308 800 l Tennis   1.10 1.10
1178 A308 1300 l Car racing   1.60 1.60
Nos. 1175-1178 (4)   4.50 4.50

Natl. Olympic Committee, 30th anniv. (650 l); admission of San Marino Soccer Federation to the UEFA and FIFA (750 l); San Marino '89, the tennis grand prix (850 l); Grand Prix of San Marino, Imola (1300 l).

**Stamp Collecting Type of 1988**
Covers and canceled stamps (postal history): 100 l, 1977. 200 l, No. 916a with Iserravalle cancel, Sept. 1, 1977. 200 l, No. 1151 with Montegiardino cancel, May 3, 1986. 400 l, Italy No. 47 canceled on San Marino parcel card #422, 1895. 500 l, Type SP3 essay proposed by Martin Riester di Parigi, March 1865. 1000 l, Stampless cover, 1862.

**1989, May 13    Granite Paper**
1179 A298 100 l multi   .20 .20
1180 A298 200 l multi   .25 .25
1181 A298 400 l multi   .50 .50
1182 A298 500 l multi   .60 .60
1183 A298 1000 l multi   1.25 1.25
Nos. 1179-1183 (5)   2.80 2.80

**French Revolution, Bicent. — A309**

**1989, July 7    Litho.    Perf. 12½x13**
1184 A309 700 l The Tennis Court Oath   .80 .80
1185 A309 1000 l Arrest of Louis XVI   1.25 1.25
1186 A309 1800 l Napoleon   2.25 2.25
Nos. 1184-1186 (3)   4.30 4.30

**Show Business Type of 1988**
Scenes from: 1200 l, Marguerite et Armand. 1500 l, Apollon Musagete. 1700 l, Valentino.

**1989, Sept. 18    Photo.    Perf. 13½x14**
1187 A300 1200 l multi   1.60 1.60
1188 A300 1500 l multi   2.00 2.00
1189 A300 1700 l multi   2.40 2.40
Nos. 1187-1189 (3)   6.00 6.00

Rudolf Nureyev, Russian ballet dancer and winner of the 1989 San Marino Prize.

**Exhibition Type of 1988**
Views of The Capitol, Washington, DC: 2000 l, in 1850. 2500 l, in 1989.

**1989, Nov. 17    Photo.    Perf. 11½**
**Granite Paper**
1190 A304 2000 l multi   2.50 2.50
1191 A304 2500 l multi   3.25 3.25
a.   Pair, #1190-1191   5.75 5.75
World Stamp Expo '89.

A310

Christmas: Panels from a Polyptych, c. 1540, by Coda Studio of Rimini, in the Church of the Servants of Mary, Valdragone.

**1989, Nov. 17**
Size of No. 1193: 50x40mm
**Granite Paper**
1192 A310 650 l Angel   .90 .90
1193 A310 650 l Holy family   .90 .90
1194 A310 650 l Praying Madonna   .90 .90
a.   A310 Strip of 3, #1192-1194   2.75 2.75

A311

Europa: Post offices.
**1990, Feb. 22    Photo.    Perf. 13½x14**
**Granite Paper**
1195 A311 700 l Palazzetto delle Poste, 1842   1.50 1.10
1196 A311 800 l Dogana   2.00 1.40

A312

Design: *The Martyrdom of Saint Agatha,* by Giambattista Tiepolo, and occupation force departing by the Porta del Loco.

**1990, Feb. 22    Granite Paper    Perf. 12**
1197 A312 3500 l multicolored   4.50 4.50

Liberation from Cardinal Alberoni's occupation force, 250th anniv.

A313

European Tourism Year: No. 1198, The republic pinpointed on a map of Italy. No. 1199, San Marino atop Mt. Titano in proximity to other cities in the region. No. 1200, Rocca Guaita, San Marino.

**1990, Mar. 23    Photo.    Perf. 11½x12**
**Granite Paper**
1198 A313 600 l shown   .75 .75
1199 A313 600 l multicolored   .75 .75
1200 A313 600 l multicolored   .75 .75
Nos. 1198-1200 (3)   2.25 2.25

**Souvenir Sheet**
See Nos. 1209a, 1260-1262.

1990 World Cup Soccer Championships, Italy — A314

Various athletes: a, Germany. b, Italy. c, Great Britain. d, Uruguay. e, Brazil. f, Argentina.

**Show Business Type of 1988**
Scenes from: 600 l, *Hamlet.* 700 l, *Richard III.* 1500 l, *Marathon Man.*

**1990, Mar. 23    Sheet of 6    Perf. 13½x14**
1201 A314 700 l   5.50 5.50
a.-f.   700 l any single   .90 .90

**1990, May 3    Photo.    Perf. 13½x14**
1202 A315 600 l multi   .90 .90
1203 A315 700 l multi   1.00 1.00
1204 A315 1500 l multi   2.10 2.10
Nos. 1202-1204 (3)   4.00 4.00

Sir Laurence Olivier (1907-1989), British actor, winner of the 1990 San Marino Prize. Name misspelled "Lawrence" on the stamps.

President of Italy, State Visit A315

Statue of Saint Marinus — A316

**1990, June 11    Litho.    Perf. 13x12½**
1205 A316 600 l multicolored   .75 .75

#1207, Liberty statue. #1208, Government Palace. #1209, Flag of San Marino.

**1990, June 11    Photo.    Perf. 11½**
**Granite Paper**
**Booklet Stamps**
1206 A316 50 l multicolored   .20 .20
1207 A316 50 l multicolored   .20 .20
1208 A316 50 l multicolored   .20 .20
1209 A316 50 l multicolored   .20 .20
a.   Bklt. pane of 7, #1196-1200, perf. 11½ vert., #1206-1209 (4)   2.80 2.80
Nos. 1206-1209 (4)   .80 .80

See Nos. 1256-1259.

Discovery of America, 500th Anniv. (in 1992) A317

**1990, Sept. 6    Litho.    Perf. 13x12½**
1210 A317 1500 l Artifacts, map   1.90 1.90
1211 A317 2000 l Native plants, map   2.50 2.50
See Nos. 1230-1231.

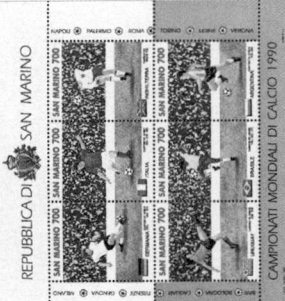

Flora and Fauna A319

Pinocchio, by Carlo Collodi (1826-1890) A318

Cartoon style drawings from Pinocchio.

**1990, Sept. 6    Photo.    Perf. 11½x12**
**Granite Paper**
1212 A318 250 l shown   .35 .35
1213 A318 400 l Geppetto   .50 .50
1214 A318 450 l Blue fairy   .60 .60
1215 A318 500 l Cat & wolf   .75 .75
Nos. 1212-1215 (4)   2.20 2.20

**1990, Oct. 31    Photo.    Perf. 14x13½**
Designs: 200 l, Papilio machaon, Ephedra major. 300 l, Apodemus coryli, Corylus avellana. 500 l, Eliomys quercinus, Quercus ilex.

1000 l, Lacerta viridis, Ophrys bertolonii. 2000 l, Regulus ignicapillus, Pinus nigra.
1216 A319 200 l multicolored   .25 .25
1217 A319 300 l multicolored   .40 .40
1218 A319 500 l multicolored   .65 .65
1219 A319 1000 l multicolored   1.25 1.25
1220 A319 2000 l multicolored   2.50 2.50
Nos. 1216-1220 (5)   5.05 5.05

A320

Christmas: Cuciniello Crib, San Martino Museum of Naples.

**1990, Oct. 31    Perf. 11½**
**Granite Paper**
1221 A320 750 l shown   1.50 1.50
1222 A320 750 l Nativity, diff.   1.50 1.50
a.   Pair, #1221-1222   3.00 3.00

A321

**1991, Feb. 12    Photo.    Perf. 13½x14**
1223 A321 750 l Ariane 4 rocket   5.00 5.00
1224 A321 800 l FRS-1 satellite   5.00 5.00
Europa.

**Stamp Collecting Type of 1988**
Areas of philately: 100 l, Stamp store. 150 l, Clubs. 200 l, Exhibitions. 450 l, Albums, catalogues. 1500 l, Magazines, books.

**1991, Feb. 12    Granite Paper**
1225 A298 100 l multicolored   .20 .20
1226 A298 150 l multicolored   .20 .20
1227 A298 200 l multicolored   .30 .30
1228 A298 450 l multicolored   .60 .60
1229 A298 1500 l multicolored   1.90 1.90
Nos. 1225-1229 (5)   3.20 3.20

Italian Philatelic Press Union, 25th anniv. (No. 1229).

**Discovery of America Type**

**1991, Mar. 22    Litho.    Perf. 13x12½**
1230 A317 750 l Map, instruments   .95 .95
1231 A317 3000 l Columbus' fleet   3.75 3.75

1992 Summer Olympics, Barcelona A323

Olympic torch relay.

**1991, Mar. 22    Perf. 15x14**
1232 A323 400 l Athens   .50 .50
1233 A323 600 l Barcelona   .75 .75
1234 A323 2000 l Barcelona   2.50 2.50
Nos. 1232-1234 (3)   3.75 3.75

## Basketball, Cent. — A324

**1991, June 4** **Photo.** **Perf. 13½x14**
| | | | | |
|---|---|---|---|---|
| 1235 | A324 | 650 l | multicolored | .85 | .85 |
| 1236 | A324 | 750 l | multicolored | .95 | .95 |

Designs: 750 l, James Naismith (1861-1939), creator of basketball, players.

## Fauna — A325

**1991, June 4** **Photo.** **Perf. 14x13½**
| 1237 | A325 | 500 l | House cat | .65 | .65 |
|---|---|---|---|---|---|
| 1238 | A325 | 550 l | Hamster on wheel | .70 | .70 |
| 1239 | A325 | 750 l | Great Dane, poodle | .95 | .95 |
| 1240 | A325 | 1000 l | Tropical fish | 1.25 | 1.25 |
| 1241 | A325 | 1200 l | Birds in cage | 1.50 | 1.50 |
| | | | Nos. 1237-1241 (5) | 5.05 | 5.05 |

See Nos. 1251-1255.

## Children's Day.

**1991, Sept. 24** **Photo.** **Perf. 14x13½**
| 1242 | A326 | 750 l | multicolored | 1.10 | 1.10 |
|---|---|---|---|---|---|

"James Clerk Maxwell (1831-1879), Physicist — A326

Radio, cent. (in 1995).
See Nos. 1263, 1279, 1300.

## Souvenir Sheet

**1991, Sept. 24** **Litho.**
| 1243 | A327 | 1500 l | Sheet of 3, #a.-c. | 5.00 | 5.00 |
|---|---|---|---|---|---|

## Birth of New Europe — A327

Designs: No. 1243a, Dove, broken chains, Brandenburg Gate. b, Pres. Gorbachev, rainbow, Pres. Bush. c, Flower, broken barbed wire, map.

## La Rocca fortress — A328

**1991, Nov. 13** **Litho.** **Perf. 14½**
| 1244 | A328 | 600 l | multicolored | .75 | .75 |
|---|---|---|---|---|---|
| 1245 | A328 | 750 l | multicolored | .95 | .95 |
| 1246 | A328 | 1200 l | multicolored | 1.50 | 1.50 |
| | | | Nos. 1244-1246 (3) | 3.20 | 3.20 |

Christmas: Diff. winter views of 10th cent.
No. 1246 is airmail.

---

## Gioacchino Rossini (1792-1868), Composer — A329

**1992, Feb. 3** **Photo.** **Perf. 14x13½**
| 1247 | A329 | 750 l | multicolored | .95 | .95 |
|---|---|---|---|---|---|
| 1248 | A329 | 1200 l | multicolored | 1.50 | 1.50 |

Designs: 750 l, Bianca e Falliero, Rossini opera festival 1989. 1200 l, The Barber of Seville, La Scala 1982-83.

## Discovery of America, 500th Anniv. — A330

**1992, Feb. 3** **Litho.** **Perf. 12**
| 1249 | A330 | 1500 l | multicolored | 1.90 | 1.90 |
|---|---|---|---|---|---|
| 1250 | A330 | 2000 l | multicolored | 2.50 | 2.50 |

Designs: 1500 l, Columbus, ships at anchor, natives. 2000 l, Map of voyages.

## Fauna Type of 1991

**1992, Mar. 26** **Litho.** **Perf. 13½**
| 1251 | A325 | 50 l | Roses | .20 | .20 |
|---|---|---|---|---|---|
| 1252 | A325 | 200 l | House plant | .25 | .25 |
| 1253 | A325 | 300 l | Orchids | .40 | .40 |
| 1254 | A325 | 450 l | Cacti | .60 | .60 |
| 1255 | A325 | 5000 l | Geraniums | 6.25 | 6.25 |
| | | | Nos. 1251-1255 (5) | 7.70 | 7.70 |

Flora.

## Tourism Types of 1990

**1992, Mar. 26** **Perf. 14½x13½**
| 1256 | A313 | 600 l | multicolored | .95 | .95 |
|---|---|---|---|---|---|
| 1257 | A313 | 600 l | multicolored | .95 | .95 |
| 1258 | A313 | 600 l | multicolored | .95 | .95 |
| 1259 | A316 | 50 l | multicolored | .20 | .20 |

**Perf. 13½ Vert.**
| 1260 | A316 | 50 l | multicolored | .20 | .20 |
|---|---|---|---|---|---|
| 1261 | A316 | 50 l | multicolored | .20 | .20 |
| 1262 | A316 | 50 l | multicolored | .20 | .20 |
| a. | | | Bkl. pane of 7, #1256-1262+1a-bel | 3.50 | |

Designs: No. 1256, Crossbowman. No. 1257, Tennis player. No. 1258, Motorcyclist. No. 1259, Race car. No. 1260, Couple in moonlight. No. 1261, Man in restaurant. No. 1262, Woman reading beneath umbrella.

## Physicist Type of 1991

**1992, Mar. 26** **Photo.** **Perf. 14x13½**
| 1263 | A326 | 750 l | multicolored | 1.10 | 1.10 |
|---|---|---|---|---|---|

Radio, cent. (in 1995).

## Granite Paper

**1992, May 22** **Photo.** **Perf. 12x11½**
| 1264 | A331 | 750 l | Globe, ship at sea | 2.10 | 2.10 |
|---|---|---|---|---|---|
| 1265 | A331 | 850 l | Ship in egg | 2.40 | 2.40 |

Discovery of America, 500th Anniv. — A331

Europa.

---

## Mushrooms — A333

**1992, May 22** **Litho.** **Perf. 14**
| 1266 | A332 | 1250 l | Sheet of 4, #a.-d. | 8.00 | 8.00 |
|---|---|---|---|---|---|

1992 Summer Olympics, Barcelona — A332

a, Soccer. b, Shooting. c, Swimming. d, Running.

**1992, Sept. 18** **Photo.** **Perf. 11½x12**
| 1267 | A333 | 50 l | multicolored | .90 | .90 |
|---|---|---|---|---|---|
| 1268 | A333 | 250 l | any single | .45 | .45 |
| a.-b. | | | Pair | 1.10 | 1.10 |
| 1269 | A333 | 350 l | any single | .55 | .55 |
| a.-b. | | | Pair | 1.10 | 1.10 |

Granite Paper

Designs: Nos. 1267, Poisonous mushrooms. No. 1268a, Edible mushrooms in bowl. No. 1268b, Edible mushrooms on table.

## Admission to the UN — A334

**1992, Sept. 18** **Litho.** **Perf. 12x12½**
| 1269 | A334 | Pair | | 2.50 | 2.50 |
|---|---|---|---|---|---|
| 1270 | A334 | 1000 l | any single | 1.25 | 1.25 |

Designs: a, Arms of San Marino, buildings. b, UN emblem, buildings.

## The Sacred Conversation, by Piero della Francesca (1420-1492) — A335

**1992, Nov. 16** **Litho.** **Perf. 14½**
| 1270 | A335 | 750 l | Triptych | 2.50 | 2.50 |
|---|---|---|---|---|---|
| a.-c. | | | any single | 1.25 | 1.25 |

Christmas: a, Entire painting. b, Detail of faces. c, Detail of dome.

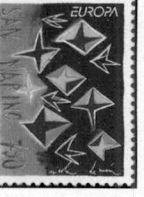

## Contemporary Art — A336

---

Paintings: 750 l, Stars, by Nicola de Maria. 850 l, Abstract face, by Mimmo Paladino.

**1993, Jan. 29** **Litho.** **Perf. 11½**
| 1271 | A336 | 750 l | multicolored | .95 | .95 |
|---|---|---|---|---|---|
| 1272 | A336 | 850 l | multicolored | 1.10 | 1.10 |

Europa.

## 1993 Sporting Events — A337

**1993, Jan. 29** **Perf. 13½x14**
| 1273 | A337 | 300 l | Tennis | .40 | .40 |
|---|---|---|---|---|---|
| 1274 | A337 | 400 l | Cross-country skiing | .50 | .50 |
| 1275 | A337 | 550 l | Women running | .70 | .70 |
| 1276 | A337 | 600 l | Fisherman | .75 | .75 |
| 1277 | A337 | 700 l | Men running | .90 | .90 |
| 1278 | A337 | 1300 l | Sailboat, runners | 1.60 | 1.60 |
| | | | Nos. 1273-1278 (6) | 4.85 | 4.85 |

No. 1273, Youth Games. No. 1274-1275, European Youth Olympic Days. No. 1276, World Championships for Freshwater Angling Clubs, Ostellato, Italy. No. 1277, Games of Small European Countries, Malta. No. 1278, Mediterranean Games, Rousillon, France.

## Physicists Type of 1991

**1993, Mar. 26** **Photo.** **Perf. 14x13½**
| 1279 | A326 | 750 l | multicolored | 1.00 | 1.00 |
|---|---|---|---|---|---|

Radio, cent. (in 1995).

## Souvenir Sheet

Design: 750 l, Édouard Branly (1844-1940).

## Inauguration of State Television — A338

**1993, Mar. 26** **Litho.** **Perf. 13½**
| 1280 | A338 | Sheet of 3 | | 7.50 | 7.50 |
|---|---|---|---|---|---|
| a.-c. | | A338 | 2000 l | any single | 2.50 | 2.50 |

Designs: a, 100-meter finals, World Track Championships, Tokyo, 1991. b, San Marino. c, Neil Armstrong on moon, 1969.

Soaking may affect the hologram on #1280b.

## Butterflies — A339

**1993, May 26** **Litho.** **Perf. 14x15**
| 1281 | A339 | 250 l | Iphiclides podalirius | .40 | .40 |
|---|---|---|---|---|---|
| 1282 | A339 | 250 l | Colias crocea | .40 | .40 |
| 1283 | A339 | 250 l | Nymphalis antiopa | .40 | .40 |
| 1284 | A339 | 250 l | Melitaea cinxia | .40 | .40 |
| a. | | | Block or strip of 4, #1281-1284 | 1.60 | 1.60 |

World Wildlife Fund.

**Miniature Sheet**

United Europe — A340

Village of Europe: No. 1285a, Denmark. b, England. c, Ireland. d, Luxembourg. e, Germany. f, Netherlands. g, Belgium. h, Portugal. i, Italy. j, Spain. k, France. l, Greece.

**1993, May 26** Perf. 13½x14
1285 A340 750 l Sheet of 12 11.50 11.50
  a. Any single, #a.-l. .95 .95

Famous Men A341

Designs: 550 l, Carlo Goldoni (1707-93), playwright, vert. 650 l, Horace (65-8 BC), poet and satirist. 850 l, Claudio Monteverdi (1567-1643), composer. 1850 l, Guy de Maupassant (1850-93), writer.

**1993, Sept. 17** Litho. Perf. 13½x14
1286 A341 550 l multicolored .70 .70
1287 A341 650 l multicolored .85 .85
1288 A341 850 l multicolored 1.10 1.10
1289 A341 1850 l multicolored 2.40 2.40
  Nos. 1286-1289 (4) 5.05 5.05

Christmas A342

Designs: 600 l, San Marino in winter, vert. Paintings by Gerard van Honthorst: 750 l, Adoration of the Child. 850 l, Adoration of the Shepherds, vert.

**1993, Nov. 12** Litho. Perf. 14½
1290 A342 600 l multicolored .75 .75
1291 A342 750 l multicolored .95 .95
1292 A342 850 l multicolored 1.10 1.10
  Nos. 1290-1292 (3) 2.80 2.80

10th Intl. Dog Show A343

Designs: 350 l, Dachshund. 400 l, Afghan hound. 450 l, Belgian tervueren shepherd dog. 500 l, Boston terrier. 550 l, Mastiff. 600 l, Alaskan malamute.

**1994, Jan. 31** Litho. Perf. 15x14
1293 A343 350 l multicolored .45 .45
1294 A343 400 l multicolored .50 .50
1295 A343 450 l multicolored .60 .60
1296 A343 500 l multicolored .65 .65
1297 A343 550 l multicolored .70 .70
1298 A343 600 l multicolored .75 .75
  Nos. 1293-1298 (6) 3.65 3.65

**Souvenir Sheet**

1994 Winter Olympics, Lillehammer — A344

a, 90-meter ski jump. b, Downhill skiing. c, Giant slalom skiing. d, Pairs figure skating.

**1994, Jan. 31** Perf. 13½
1299 A344 750 l 2 each #a.-d. 6.50 6.50

**Physicists Type of 1991**

Aleksandr Stepanovich Popov (1859-1905).

**1994, Mar. 11** Photo. Perf. 14x13½
1300 A326 750 l multicolored 1.10 1.10
  Radio cent. (in 1995).

Gardens — A345

**1994, Mar. 11** Litho. Perf. 13
1301 A345 100 l Gate .20 .20
1302 A345 200 l Grape arbor .25 .25
1303 A345 300 l Well .40 .40
1304 A345 450 l Gazebo .60 .60
1305 A345 1850 l Pond 2.40 2.40
  Nos. 1301-1305 (5) 3.85 3.85

Intl. Olympic Committee, Cent. A346

**1994, Mar. 11** Photo. Perf. 14x13½
1306 A346 600 l multicolored .80 .80

A347

A348

Various soccer plays: a, Two players, one with #8 on shirt. b, Player in blue shirt kicking ball upward. c, Player heading ball. d, Players, one with #6 on shirt. e, Goal keeper.

**1994, May 23** Litho. Perf. 14
1307 A347 600 l Strip of 5, #a.-e. 3.75 3.75
  1994 World Cup Soccer Championships, US. No. 1307 has a continuous design.

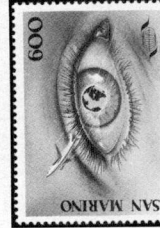

Europa (Ulysses spacecraft) and: 750 l, Flight path around Sun and Jupiter. 850 l, Sun.

**1994, May 23**
1308 A348 750 l multicolored .95 .95
1309 A348 850 l multicolored 1.10 1.10

Inauguration of Government Building, Cent. — A349

Designs: 150 l, Exterior in shade, vert. 600 l, Exterior in sunshine, vert. 650 l, Clock tower. 1000 l, Interior.

**1994, Sept. 30** Perf. 13½x13, 13x13½ Litho.
1310 A349 150 l multicolored .20 .20
1311 A349 600 l multicolored .75 .75
1312 A349 650 l multicolored .85 .85
1313 A349 1000 l multicolored 1.25 1.25
  Nos. 1310-1313 (4) 3.05 3.05

Dedication of St. Mark's Basilica, 900th Anniv. A350

**1994, Oct. 8** Photo. Perf. 13½x13
1314 A350 750 l multicolored 1.10 1.10
  a. Souvenir sheet of 2, tete beche 2.25 2.25

No. 1314 printed with se-tenant label. No. 1314a contains No. 1314 and Italy No. 2003. Only No. 1314 was valid for postage in San Marino.

Touring Club of Italy, Cent. — A351

Vehicles traveling on road in middle of flower field: a, Traffic cop, bus. b, Tandem tanker truck. c, Sailboat, volcano. d, Truck loaded with animals, camper, fish in lake.

**1994, Nov. 18** Litho. Perf. 14x13½
1315 Block of 4 5.00 5.00
  a.-d. A351 1000 l any single 1.25 1.25
  No. 1315 is a continuous design.

A352

A353

The Enthroned Madonna and Child with Saints, by Giovanni Santi (1440-1494) (Christmas): 600 l, Drummer, piper. 750 l, Madonna and Child. 850 l, Piper, harpist.

**1994, Nov. 18** Perf. 14x15
1316 A352 600 l multicolored .75 .75
1317 A352 750 l multicolored .95 .95
1318 A352 850 l multicolored 1.10 1.10
  Nos. 1316-1318 (3) 2.80 2.80

**Sporting Events**

**1995, Feb. 10** Photo. Perf. 13x14
1319 A353 100 l Cycling .20 .20
1320 A353 500 l Volleyball .65 .65
1321 A353 650 l Speed skater .85 .85
1322 A353 850 l Runner 1.10 1.10
  Nos. 1319-1322 (4) 2.80 2.80

Sporting Events of 1995: Junior World Cycling Championships, Forli, San Marino (#1319). Volleyball, cent. (#1320). Men's Speed Skating World Championships, Baselga di Pine, Italy (#1321). World Track & Field Championships, Goteborg, Sweden (#1322).

European Nature Conservation Year — A354

Nature scenes with flowers, water: a, Snails, dragonfly, fish. b, Frog, snake. c, Ladybugs, butterfly. d, Ducklings, frog. e, Ducks, snail.

**1995, Feb. 10**
1323 A354 600 l Strip of 5, #a.-e. 3.75 3.75
  No. 1323 is a continuous design.

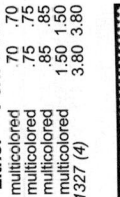

UN, 50th Anniv. — A355

Designs: 550 l, UN emblem surrounded by people. 600 l, Emblem in center of rose. 650 l, Hourglass shaped from halves of globe. 1200 l, "50," Emblem, rainbow.

**1995, Mar. 24** Litho. Perf. 14x15
1324 A355 550 l multicolored .70 .70
1325 A355 600 l multicolored .75 .75
1326 A355 650 l multicolored .85 .85
1327 A355 1200 l multicolored 1.50 1.50
  Nos. 1324-1327 (4) 3.80 3.80

Peace & Freedom A356

**1995, Mar. 24** Perf. 15x14
1328 A356 750 l shown .95 .95
1329 A356 850 l Sheep, meadow 1.10 1.10
  Europa.

World Tourism Organization, 20th Anniv. — A357

Designs: 750 l, Mt. Titano encircled by five colored lines symbolizing continents. 850 l, Airplane over globe. 1200 l, Five lines encircling earth.

**1995, May 5**   **Litho.**   **Perf. 15x14**
| 1330 | A357 | 600 l | multicolored | .75 | .75 |
|---|---|---|---|---|---|
| 1331 | A357 | 750 l | multicolored | .95 | .95 |
| 1332 | A357 | 850 l | multicolored | 1.10 | 1.10 |
| 1333 | A357 | 1200 l | multicolored | 1.50 | 1.50 |
| | | Nos. 1330-1333 (4) | | 4.30 | 4.30 |

### Santa Croce Basilica, Florence, 700th Anniv. — A358

1200 l, Detail from fresco, The Legend of the True Cross, by Agnolo Gaddi, facade of the basilica. 1250 l, Painting, The Madonna and Child with Saints, by Andrea della Robbia, Santa Croce Cloister, Pazzi Chapel.

**1995, May 5**   **Litho.**   **Perf. 15x14**
| 1334 | A358 | 1200 l | multicolored | 1.50 | 1.50 |
|---|---|---|---|---|---|
| 1335 | A358 | 1250 l | multicolored | 1.60 | 1.60 |

### Radio, Cent. — A359

Designs: No. 1336, Stations on radio dial. No. 1337, Guglielmo Marconi (1874-1937), transmitting equipment.

**1995, June 8**   **Litho.**   **Perf. 14**
| 1336 | A359 | 850 l | multicolored | 1.10 | 1.10 |
|---|---|---|---|---|---|
| 1337 | A359 | 850 l | multicolored | 1.10 | 1.10 |
| a. | | Pair, Nos. 1336-1337 | | 2.25 | 2.25 |

Printed in sheets of 10 stamps. See Germany #1900, Ireland #973-974, Italy #2038-2039, Vatican City #978-979.

### Motion Picture, Cent. — A360

Different frames from films: The General: a, 1. b, 2. c, 3. d, 4. Il Gattopardo: e, 1. f, 2. g, 3. h, 4. Allegro Non Troppo: i, 1. j, 2. k, 3. l, 4. Braveheart: m, 1. n, 2. o, 3. p, 4.

**1995, Sept. 14**   **Litho.**   **Perf. 15x14**
| 1338 | A360 | 250 l | any single | .35 | .35 |
|---|---|---|---|---|---|
| a.-p. | | Sheet of 16 | | 5.75 | 5.75 |

### Exhibition Type of 1980

Qianmen complex of Zhengyangmen Rostrum, Embrasured Watchtower, Beijing: No. 1339. In 1914. No. 1340. In 1995.

**1995, Sept. 14**   **Perf. 14**
| 1339 | A222 | 1500 l | multicolored | 1.90 | 1.90 |
|---|---|---|---|---|---|
| 1340 | A222 | 1500 l | multicolored | 1.90 | 1.90 |
| a. | | Pair, #1339-1340 | | 4.00 | 4.00 |

Beijing '95.

**1995, Nov. 6**   **Litho.**   **Perf. 14x15**
| 1341 | A361 | 650 l | multicolored | .85 | .85 |
|---|---|---|---|---|---|

Designs: 650 l, The Annunciation.

### Neri of Rimini, 14th Cent. Artist — A361

### Christmas — A362

Designs: a, Santa, sleigh, reindeer. b, Children, Christmas tree. c, Nativity, star.

**1995, Nov. 6**   **Litho.**   **Perf. 14x15**
| 1342 | A362 | 750 l | any single | 1.00 | 1.00 |
|---|---|---|---|---|---|
| a.-c. | | Strip of 3 | | 3.00 | 3.00 |

No. 1342 is a continuous design.

### Express Mail Service — A363

**1995, Nov. 6**   **Litho.**   **Perf. 15x14**
| 1343 | A363 | 6000 l | multicolored | 7.50 | 7.50 |
|---|---|---|---|---|---|

**1996, Feb. 12**   **Litho.**   **Perf. 14x15**
| 1344 | A364 | 100 l | Discus | .20 | .20 |
|---|---|---|---|---|---|
| 1345 | A364 | 500 l | Wrestling | .65 | .65 |
| 1346 | A364 | 650 l | Athletics | .85 | .85 |
| 1347 | A364 | 1500 l | Javelin | 1.90 | 1.90 |
| 1348 | A364 | 2500 l | Running | 3.25 | 3.25 |
| | | Nos. 1344-1348 (5) | | 6.85 | 6.85 |

1996 Summer Olympics, Atlanta.

**1996, Mar. 22**   **Photo.**   **Perf. 12**
| 1349 | A365 | 750 l | multicolored | 1.10 | 1.10 |
|---|---|---|---|---|---|

**Granite Paper**

Europa.

Portrait of Mother Teresa of Calcutta, by Gina Lollobrigida.

### China '96 Philatelic Exhibition, Beijing, — A366

**1996, Mar. 22**   **Perf. 14x13½**
| 1350 | A366 | 1250 l | multicolored | 1.60 | 1.60 |
|---|---|---|---|---|---|

Marco Polo's return from China, 700th anniv. (in 1995). See Italy No. 2070.

### Nature World Exhibition — A367

Photographs of wildlife: 50 l, Dolphin. 100 l, Frog. 150 l, Penguins. 1000 l, Butterfly. 3000 l, Ducks.

**1996, Mar. 22**   **Granite Paper**   **Perf. 12**
| 1351 | A367 | 50 l | multicolored | .20 | .20 |
|---|---|---|---|---|---|
| 1352 | A367 | 100 l | multicolored | .20 | .20 |
| 1353 | A367 | 150 l | multicolored | .20 | .20 |
| 1354 | A367 | 1000 l | multicolored | 1.25 | 1.25 |
| 1355 | A367 | 3000 l | multicolored | 3.75 | 3.75 |
| | | Nos. 1351-1355 (5) | | 5.60 | 5.60 |

### China-San Marino Relations, 25th Anniv. — A368

#1356, Great Wall of China. #1357, Wall surrounding Mount Titano, San Marino.

**1996, May 6**   **Litho.**   **Perf. 12**
| 1356 | A368 | 750 l | multicolored | .95 | .95 |
|---|---|---|---|---|---|
| 1357 | A368 | 750 l | multicolored | .95 | .95 |
| a. | | Pair, Nos. 1356-1357 | | 1.90 | 1.90 |
| b. | | Souvenir sheet, No. 1357a | | 2.00 | 2.00 |

No. 1357a is a continuous design. See People's Republic of China Nos. 2675-2676.

### Medieval Days Celebration — A369

Festival activities: No. 1358, Woman weaving yarn, vert. No. 1359, Potter, vert. No. 1360, Woman making brushes, vert. No. 1361, Man playing checkers, vert. No. 1362, Group blowing trumpets. No. 1363, Group holding banners. No. 1364, Men seated with crossbows. No. 1365, Street performers.

**1996, May 6**   **Perf. 14 on 2 Sides**   **Litho. & Photo.**

**Booklet Stamps**
| 1358 | A369 | 750 l | multicolored | .95 | .95 |
|---|---|---|---|---|---|
| 1359 | A369 | 750 l | multicolored | .95 | .95 |
| 1360 | A369 | 750 l | multicolored | .95 | .95 |
| 1361 | A369 | 750 l | multicolored | .95 | .95 |
| 1362 | A369 | 750 l | multicolored | .95 | .95 |
| 1363 | A369 | 750 l | multicolored | .95 | .95 |
| 1364 | A369 | 750 l | multicolored | .95 | .95 |
| 1365 | A369 | 750 l | multicolored | .95 | .95 |
| a. | | Booklet pane, #1358-1365 | | 7.75 | |
| | | Complete booklet, #1365a | | 7.75 | |

**1996, May 25**   **Litho.**   **Perf. 14x13½**
| 1366 | A370 | 2000 l | shown | 2.50 | 2.50 |
|---|---|---|---|---|---|

### Festival Bar — A370

### History of Italian Songs — A371

Singer, allegory of song: a, Enrico Caruso, "Pioveva." b, Armando Gill, "O Sole Mio." c, Ettore Petrolini, "Gastone." d, Vittorio de Sica, "Parlami D'Amore Marui." e, Odoardo Spadaro, "La Porti un Bacione a Firenze." f, Alberto Rabagliati, "O Mia Bela Madonina." g, Beniamino Gigli, "Mamma." h, Claudio Villa, "Luna Rossa." i, Secondo Casadei, "Romagna Mia." j, Renato Rascel, "Arrivederci Roma." k, Fred Buscaglione, "Guarda Che Luna." l, Domenico Modugno, "Nel Blu Dipinto di Blu."

**1996, May 25**   **Litho.**   **Perf. 14x13½**
| 1367 | A371 | 750 l | Sheet of 12, #a.-l. | 11.50 | 11.50 |
|---|---|---|---|---|---|

**Photo.**   **Granite Paper**   **Perf. 12x11½**

### Gazzetta Dello Sport, Cent. — A372

**1996, May 25**   **Granite Paper**   **Perf. 12**
| 1368 | A372 | 1850 l | multicolored | 2.40 | 2.40 |
|---|---|---|---|---|---|

### UNICEF, 50th Anniv. — A373

**1996, Sept. 20**   **Photo.**   **Perf. 12**
| 1369 | A373 | 550 l | Hen, chicks | .70 | .70 |
|---|---|---|---|---|---|
| 1370 | A373 | 1000 l | Baby birds | 1.25 | 1.25 |

### UNESCO, 50th Anniv. — A374

World Heritage Sites: 450 l, Yellowstone Natl. Park, U.S. 500 l, Prehistoric caves, Vézère Valley, France. 650 l, Old town center, San Gimignano, Italy. 1450 l, Church of the Wies Pilgrimage, Germany.

**1996, Sept. 20**   **Granite Paper**
| 1371 | A374 | 450 l | multicolored | .60 | .60 |
|---|---|---|---|---|---|
| 1372 | A374 | 500 l | multicolored | .65 | .65 |
| 1373 | A374 | 650 l | multicolored | .85 | .85 |
| 1374 | A374 | 1450 l | multicolored | 1.90 | 1.90 |
| | | Nos. 1371-1374 (4) | | 4.00 | 4.00 |

### Christmas — A375

Scenes looking through windows of a home: a, Playing game underneath Christmas tree. b, Tags draped from holly branch. c, Girl reading book, Santa in sleigh. d, Christmas tree. e, Fruits, candles, nuts. f, Streaking star, snowflakes. g, Toys. h, Presents. i, Santa Claus puppet. j, Nativity. k, Mistletoe. l, Stocking hung by fireplace. m, Family eating, drinking. n, Christmas tree, silhouettes of mother, father, wreath. o, Wreath, silhouettes of children and grandmother, snowman. p, Calendar, champagne bottle popping cork.

**1996, Nov. 8**   **Photo.**   **Perf. 14½**
| 1375 | A375 | 750 l | Sheet of 16, #a.-p. | 16.00 | 16.00 |
|---|---|---|---|---|---|

## Souvenir Sheet

View from harbor: a, 1897. b, 1997.

**1997, Feb. 12**   **Litho.**   **Perf. 12½**
| | | | | |
|---|---|---|---|---|
| 1376 | A376 | 750 l | Sheet of 2, #a.-b. | 2.00 | 2.00 |

Hong Kong — A376

## World Alpine Skiing Championships, Sestrière, Italy — A377

**1997, Feb. 12**   **Granite Paper**   **Perf. 12**
| | | | | |
|---|---|---|---|---|
| 1377 | A377 | 1000 l | Block of 4, #a.-d. | 5.00 | 5.00 |

No. 1377 is a continuous design.

Scene of people skiing on mountain: a, Skier jumping left. b, Ski lift, bird in sky. c, Coming down mountain, sleigh. d, Coming down mountain, Sestrière Sign.

## San Marino Townships (Castelli) A378

**1997, Mar. 21**   **Photo.**   **Granite Paper**   **Perf. 12**
| | | | | | |
|---|---|---|---|---|---|
| 1378 | A378 | 100 l | Acquaviva | .20 | .20 |
| 1379 | A378 | 200 l | Borgomaggiore | .25 | .25 |
| 1380 | A378 | 250 l | Chiesanuova | .35 | .35 |
| 1381 | A378 | 400 l | Domagnano | .50 | .50 |
| 1382 | A378 | 500 l | Faetano | .65 | .65 |
| 1383 | A378 | 550 l | Fiorentino | .70 | .70 |
| 1384 | A378 | 650 l | Montegiardino | .85 | .85 |
| 1385 | A378 | 800 l | Serravalle | .95 | .95 |
| 1386 | A378 | 5000 l | San Marino | 6.25 | 6.25 |
| | | Nos. 1378-1386 (9) | | 10.70 | 10.70 |

## Stories and Legends — A379

St. Marinus, Mt. Titano: 650 l, St. Marinus talking to bear that killed the mule. 750 l, Mother begging St. Marinus to forgive her son for trying to kill him.

**1997, Mar. 21**   **Granite Paper**
| | | | | |
|---|---|---|---|---|
| 1387 | A379 | 650 l | multicolored | .85 | .85 |
| 1388 | A379 | 750 l | multicolored | .95 | .95 |

Europa.

## Sporting Events A380

500 l, Giro d'Italia cycling event. 550 l, 10th Tennis Intl. 750 l, Formula 1 San Marino Grand Prix. 850 l, Bowls (pétanque) World Championship. 1000 l, Motorcross 250cc World Championship. 1250 l, Mille Miglia classic car spectacle.

**1997, May 19**   **Photo.**   **Perf. 12**
| | | | | |
|---|---|---|---|---|
| 1389 | A380 | 500 l | multicolored | .65 | .65 |
| 1390 | A380 | 550 l | multicolored | .70 | .70 |
| 1391 | A380 | 750 l | multicolored | .95 | .95 |
| 1392 | A380 | 850 l | multicolored | 1.10 | 1.10 |
| 1393 | A380 | 1000 l | multicolored | 1.25 | 1.25 |
| 1394 | A380 | 1250 l | multicolored | 1.60 | 1.60 |
| 1395 | A380 | 1500 l | multicolored | 1.90 | 1.90 |
| | | Nos. 1389-1395 (7) | | 8.15 | 8.15 |

## 5th Intl. Symposium on UFO's and Associated Phenomena A381

**1997, May 19**   **Granite Paper**
| | | | | |
|---|---|---|---|---|
| 1396 | A381 | 750 l | multicolored | .95 | .95 |

## Trees — A382

50 l, Pinus pinea. 800 l, Quercus pubescens. 1800 l, Juglans regia. 2000 l, Pinus communis.

**1997, June 27**   **Photo.**   **Perf. 12**
| | | | | |
|---|---|---|---|---|
| 1397 | A382 | 50 l | multicolored | .20 | .20 |
| 1398 | A382 | 800 l | multicolored | 1.00 | 1.00 |
| 1399 | A382 | 1800 l | multicolored | 2.25 | 2.25 |
| 1400 | A382 | 2000 l | multicolored | 2.50 | 2.50 |
| | | Nos. 1397-1400 (4) | | 5.95 | 5.95 |

## First Stamps of San Marino, 120th Anniv. — A383

Designs: No. 1401, G. Battista Barbavara di Gravellona, director general of Sardinian Post Office. No. 1402, Enrico Repettati, chief engraver for Officina Carte Valori, Turin. No. 1403, Otto Bickel, German stamp dealer, promoter of San Marino-Philatelist. No. 1404, Alfredo Reffi, San Marino stamp dealer, publisher of post cards, stamp catalogue.

**1997, June 27**   **Perf. 11½**
| | | | | |
|---|---|---|---|---|
| 1401 | A383 | 800 l | multicolored | 1.00 | 1.00 |
| 1402 | A383 | 800 l | multicolored | 1.00 | 1.00 |
| 1403 | A383 | 800 l | multicolored | 1.00 | 1.00 |
| 1404 | A383 | 800 l | multicolored | 1.00 | 1.00 |
| a. | | Strip of 4, #1401-1404 | | 4.00 | 4.00 |

## Beatification of Bartolomeo Maria Dal Monte (1726-78) A384

**1997, Sept. 18**   **Photo.**   **Granite Paper**   **Perf. 12**
| | | | | |
|---|---|---|---|---|
| 1405 | A384 | 800 l | multicolored | .90 | .90 |

## Italian Comic Book Characters A385

Designs: a, "Quadratino," by Antonio Rubino. b, "Signor Bonaventura," by Sergio Tofano. c, "Kit Carson," by Rino Albertarelli. d, "Cocco Bill," by Benito Jacovitti. e, "Tex Willer," by Gian Luigi Bonelli and Aurelio Galleppini. f, "Diabolik," by Angela and Luciana Giussani and Franco Paludetti. g, "Valentina," by Guido Crepax. h, "Corto Maltese," by Hugo Pratt. i, "Sturmtruppen," by Franco Bonvicini. j, "Alan Ford," by Max Bunker. k, "Lupo Alberto," by Guido Silvestri. l, "Pimpa," by Francesco Tullio Altan. m, "Bobo," by Sergio Staino. n, "Zanardi," by Andrea Pazienza. o, "Martin Mystère," by Alfredo Castelli and Giancarlo Alessandrini. p, "Dylan Dog," by Tiziano Sclavi and Angelo Stano.

**1997, Sept. 18**   **Granite Paper**   **Sheet of 16**
| | | | | |
|---|---|---|---|---|
| 1406 | A385 | 800 l | #a.-p. | 16.00 | 16.00 |

## Adoration of the Magi, by Giorgio Vasari (1511-74) — A386

**1997, Nov. 14**   **Photo.**   **Granite Paper**   **Perf. 12**
| | | | | |
|---|---|---|---|---|
| 1407 | A386 | 800 l | multicolored | 1.00 | 1.00 |

## Volunteer Service, Solidarity A387

Designs: 550 l, St. Francis of Assisi, doves. 650 l, Mariele Ventre, children. 800 l, Children circling hands around world, Zecchino d'Oro song festival.

**1997, Nov. 14**   **Granite Paper**
| | | | | |
|---|---|---|---|---|
| 1408 | A387 | 550 l | multicolored | .70 | .70 |
| 1409 | A387 | 650 l | multicolored | .85 | .85 |
| 1410 | A387 | 800 l | multicolored | 1.00 | 1.00 |
| | | Nos. 1408-1410 (3) | | 2.55 | 2.55 |

## Volkswagen Beetle A388

Designs: a, Maggiolino (old Beetle). b, Golf I. c, New Beetle. d, Golf IV.

**1997, Nov. 14**   **Granite Paper**
| | | | | |
|---|---|---|---|---|
| 1411 | A388 | 800 l | Sheet of 4, #a.-d. | 4.25 | 4.25 |

No. 1411 was issued with attached entry form for drawing to win a new Beetle car. Entry form is rouletted at top to separate from bottom of sheet. Values are for sheets with entry form attached.

## Ferrari's Formula 1 Race Cars, 50th Anniv. — A389

Model number, year: a, 125S, 1947. b, 500F2, 1952. c, 801, 1956. d, 246 Dino, 1958. e, 156, 1961. f, 158, 1964. g, 312T, 1975. h, 312T4, 1979. i, 126C, 1981. j, 156/85, 1985. k, 639, 1989. l, F310, 1996.

**1998, Feb. 11**   **Litho.**   **Perf. 13**
| | | | | |
|---|---|---|---|---|
| 1412 | A389 | 800 l | Sheet of 12, #a.-l. | 12.00 | 12.00 |

A390

A391

6th World Day of the Sick: 1500 l, Rainbow pulled over earth by dove.

**1998, Feb. 11**
| | | | | |
|---|---|---|---|---|
| 1413 | A390 | 650 l | shown | .85 | .85 |
| 1414 | A390 | 1500 l | multicolored | 1.90 | 1.90 |

Europa (Natl. Feasts and Festivals): 650 l, Installation of the Captains Regent. 1200 l, Feast Day of the Republic's Patron Saint.

**1998, Mar. 31**   **Litho.**   **Perf. 14x15**
| | | | | |
|---|---|---|---|---|
| 1415 | A391 | 650 l | multicolored | .85 | .85 |
| 1416 | A391 | 1200 l | multicolored | 1.50 | 1.50 |

## Giacomo Leopardi (1798-1837), Poet — A392

Words from poem, illustration: 550 l, "The Infinite," 1819, hedges, hill. 650 l, "A Village Saturday," 1829, woman walking. 900 l, "Nocturne of a Wandering Asian Shepherd," 1822-30, man looking at moon. 2000 l, "To Sylvia," woman's face.

**1998, Mar. 31**   **Perf. 15x14**
| | | | | |
|---|---|---|---|---|
| 1417 | A392 | 550 l | multicolored | .70 | .70 |
| 1418 | A392 | 650 l | multicolored | .85 | .85 |
| 1419 | A392 | 900 l | multicolored | 1.10 | 1.10 |
| 1420 | A392 | 2000 l | multicolored | 2.50 | 2.50 |
| | | Nos. 1417-1420 (4) | | 5.15 | 5.15 |

## 1998 World Cup Soccer Championships, France — A393

SAN MARINO

**1998, May 28    Photo.    Perf. 11½x12**

Soccer players: 650 l, At goal, 800 l, In black & yellow. 900 l, In red, in black & blue.

| | | | |
|---|---|---|---|
| 1421 | A393 | 650 l multicolored | .85 | .85 |
| 1422 | A393 | 800 l multicolored | 3.50 | |
| a. | Booklet pane of 4 | | 1.00 | 1.00 |
| 1423 | A393 | 900 l multicolored | 4.00 | |
| a. | Booklet pane of 4 | | 1.10 | 1.10 |
| | Complete booklet, #1421a, | | 4.50 | |
| | 1422a, 1423a | | 12.00 | |
| | Nos. 1421-1423 (3) | | 2.95 | 2.95 |

Emigration — A394

**1998, May 28**

Designs: a, Launch of US space shuttle. b, Shuttle in orbit, flag of San Marino. c, Earth, space shuttle.

Souvenir Sheet

San Marino Natl. Flag in Space — A395

**1998, May 28    Granite Paper**

| | | | |
|---|---|---|---|
| 1424 | A394 | 800 l multicolored | 1.00 | 1.00 |
| 1425 | A394 | 1500 l multicolored | 1.90 | 1.90 |

A396

**1998, May 28    Granite Paper**

| | | | |
|---|---|---|---|
| 1426 | A395 | 2000 l Sheet of 3, | | |
| | | #a.-c. | 7.50 | 7.50 |

**1998, Aug. 28    Photo.    Perf. 12x11½**

| | | | |
|---|---|---|---|
| 1427 | A396 | 800 l multicolored | 1.00 | 1.00 |
| 1428 | A396 | 1500 l multicolored | 1.90 | 1.90 |

A397

**1998, Aug. 28    Granite Paper    Perf. 14½**

Science Fiction: a, Twenty Thousand Leagues Under the Sea, by Jules Verne (1828-1905). b, War of the Worlds, by H.G. Wells (1866-1946). c, Brave New World, by Aldous Huxley (1894-1963). d, 1984, by George Orwell (1903-50). e, Chronicles of the Galaxy, by Isaac Asimov (1920-92). f, City without End, by Clifford D. Simak (1904-88). g, The Seventh Victim, by Robert Sheckley (b. 1928). h, The Space Merchants, by Frederik Pohl (b. 1919) and C.M. Kornbluth (1923-58). j, Neighbors from the Middle Ages, by Roberto Vacca (b. 1927). k, Stranger in a Strange Land, by Robert Heinlein (1907-88). l, A Clockwork Orange, by Anthony Burgess (1917-93). m, Drowned World, by James G. Ballard (b. 1930). n, Dune, by Frank Herbert (1920-86). o, 2001, A Space Odyssey, by Arthur Clarke (b. 1917). p, Blade Runner (Do Androids Dream of Electric Sheep), by Philip K. Dick (1928-82).

**1998, Aug. 28    Granite Paper    Perf. 12x11½**

| | | | |
|---|---|---|---|
| 1432 | A400 | 900 l Woman | 1.10 | 1.10 |
| 1433 | A400 | 900 l Man | 1.10 | 1.10 |
| a. | Pair, #1432-1433 | | 2.25 | 2.25 |

Universal Declaration of Human Rights, 50th Anniv. No. 1433a is a continuous design.

A399

**1998, Oct. 23    Granite Paper    Perf. 12x11½**

Christmas tree made up of different races, Christmas (Children of different races, gifts): a, Boy running left, star on tree. b, Child, from tropical region, star on tree. c, Child, rabbit, bottom of tree. d, Dog, girl, bottom of tree.

| | | | |
|---|---|---|---|
| 1431 | A399 | 800 l Block of 4, #a.- | | |
| | | d. | 4.00 | 4.00 |

No. 1431 is a continuous design.

**1998, Oct. 23    Granite Paper**

| | | | |
|---|---|---|---|
| 1434 | A401 | 1800 l multicolored | 2.25 | 2.25 |

A402

**1998, Oct. 23    Granite Paper**

Italia '98: Statue, "Giri," by Emilio Greco.

Riccione 1998, Intl. Stamp Fair. 800 l, Sun, sail on boat as canceled stamp. 1500 l, Dolphin diving through canceled stamp.

1999 World Cycling Championships, Veneto, Italy — A406

Beginning with No. 1435 denominations are shown in euros and lira. For listing purposes we are showing the face value in lira.

Italia '98
A398

**1998, Oct. 23    Photo.    Perf. 14**

| | | | |
|---|---|---|---|
| 1429 | A397 | 800 l Sheet of | | |
| | | 16, #a.-p. | 16.00 | 16.00 |

See Italy No. 2265, Vatican City No. 1085.

**1998, Oct. 23    Photo.    Perf. 14**

| | | | |
|---|---|---|---|
| 1430 | A398 | 800 l Pope John Paul | | |
| | | II | 1.00 | 1.00 |

A400

**1999, Feb. 12    Granite Paper**

1999 World Hang Gliding Championships, Italy: 800 l, Hand using feather to write in sky. 1800 l, Man on glider, holding balloon.

| | | | |
|---|---|---|---|
| 1435 | A402 | 800 l multicolored | 1.10 | 1.10 |
| 1436 | A402 | 1800 l multicolored | 2.40 | 2.40 |

Operas in San Marino, 400th Anniv. — A403

**1999, Feb. 12    Litho.    Perf. 13½x13**

Opera, composer: a, "L'incoronazione di Poppea," by Monteverdi. b, "Dido and Aeneas," by Purcell. c, "Orpheus and Euridice," by Gluck. d, "Don Giovanni," by Mozart. e, "The Barber of Seville," by Rossini. f, "Norma," by Bellini. g, "Aida," by Verdi. j, "Faust," by Gounod. j, "Carmen," by Bizet. k, "The Ring of the Nibelungen," by Wagner. l, "Boris Godonov," by Mussorgski. m, "Tosca," by Puccini. n, "Love for Three Oranges," by Prokofiev. o, "Porgy and Bess," by Gershwin. p, "West Side Story," by Bernstein.

| | | | |
|---|---|---|---|
| 1437 | A403 | 800 l Sheet of 16, | | |
| | | #a.-p. | 17.00 | 17.00 |

**1999, Feb. 12    Sheet of 16    Perf. 13½x13½**

Bonsai '99, San Marino Bonsai Exhibition
A404

**1999, Mar. 27    Litho.    Perf. 13x13½**

50 l, Pinus mugo. 300 l, Olea europaea. 350 l, Pinus silvestris. 500 l, Quercus robar.

| | | | |
|---|---|---|---|
| 1438 | A404 | 50 l multicolored | .20 | .20 |
| 1439 | A404 | 300 l multicolored | .40 | .40 |
| 1440 | A404 | 350 l multicolored | .45 | .45 |
| 1441 | A404 | 500 l multicolored | .65 | .65 |
| | Nos. 1438-1441 (4) | | 1.70 | 1.70 |

Europa: 650 l, Walled enclosure, Cesta tower. 1250 l, Eastern slopes, fortress tower.

| | | | |
|---|---|---|---|
| 1442 | A405 | 650 l multicolored | .85 | .85 |
| 1443 | A405 | 1250 l multicolored | 1.60 | 1.60 |

Mount Titano Natl. Park
A405

**1999, Mar. 27    Granite Paper**

| | | | |
|---|---|---|---|
| 1444 | A406 | 900 l Building, em- | | |
| | | blem | 1.10 | 1.10 |
| 1445 | A406 | 3000 l Colosseum, | | |
| | | emblem | 3.75 | 3.75 |

Fauna of San Marino
A411

**1999, June 5**

| | | | |
|---|---|---|---|
| 1455 | A411 | 500 l Lepus | | |
| | | europaeus | .65 | .65 |
| 1456 | A411 | 650 l Sciurus vul- | | |
| | | garis | .85 | .85 |
| 1457 | A411 | 1100 l Meles meles | 1.40 | 1.40 |
| 1458 | A411 | 1250 l Vulpes vulpes | 1.60 | 1.60 |
| 1459 | A411 | 1850 l Hystrix cristata | 2.40 | 2.40 |
| | Nos. 1455-1459 (5) | | 6.90 | 6.90 |

Holy Year 2000
A410

**1999, June 5**

650 l, Map of route of 15th cent. European pilgrims, Canterbury Cathedral. 800 l, Fresco of priest blessing pilgrim, 11th cent. Cathedral. 900 l, Fresco of hospice welcoming pilgrims, 15th cent. Duomo de Pavia. 1250 l, Bas-relief of pilgrims on the road, Cathedral of Fidenza, 12th cent. 1500 l, View of Rome from Monte Mario, by Sir Charles Eastlake. St. Peter's Basilica, Rome.

| | | | |
|---|---|---|---|
| 1450 | A410 | 650 l multicolored | .85 | .85 |
| 1451 | A410 | 800 l multicolored | 1.00 | 1.00 |
| 1452 | A410 | 900 l multicolored | 1.10 | 1.10 |
| 1453 | A410 | 1250 l multicolored | 1.60 | 1.60 |
| 1454 | A410 | 1500 l multicolored | 1.90 | 1.90 |
| | Nos. 1450-1454 (5) | | 6.45 | 6.45 |

**1999, May 12    Litho.    Perf. 13x13¼**

800 l, Text from original UPU Treaty, Swiss Parliament Building, Bern. 3000 l, World map highlighting UPU's 22 founding countries.

| | | | |
|---|---|---|---|
| 1448 | A409 | 800 l multicolored | 1.00 | 1.00 |
| 1449 | A409 | 3000 l multicolored | 4.50 | 4.50 |

UPU, 125th Anniv.
A409

Council of Europe, 50th Anniv. — A408

**1999, May 12    Perf. 13¼x13**

| | | | |
|---|---|---|---|
| 1446 | A407 | 1250 l multicolored | 1.60 | 1.60 |
| 1447 | A408 | 1300 l multicolored | 1.60 | 1.60 |

2nd Roman Republic, Garibaldi's Escape to San Marino, 150th Anniv. — A407

**1999, May 12    Litho.    Perf. 13½x13**

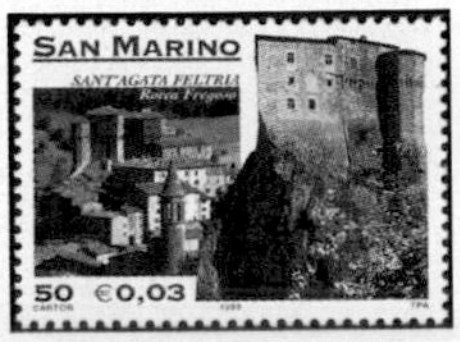


Architecture — A412

Designs: 50 l, Sant'Agata Feltria, Rocca Fregosa. 250 l, San Leo, Rocca Feltresca. 650 l, Urbino, Ducal Palace. 1300 l, Sassocorvaro, Rocca Ubaldinesca. 6000 l, Montale and Rocca towers, San Marino.

**1999, Sept. 20 Litho.** ***Perf. 13x13¼***

| | | | | |
|---|---|---|---|---|
| **1460** A412 | 50 l multicolored | .20 | .20 |
| **1461** A412 | 250 l multicolored | .35 | .35 |
| **1462** A412 | 650 l multicolored | .85 | .85 |
| **1463** A412 | 1300 l multicolored | 1.60 | 1.60 |
| **1464** A412 | 6000 l multicolored | 7.50 | 7.50 |
| | *Nos. 1460-1464 (5)* | 10.50 | 10.50 |

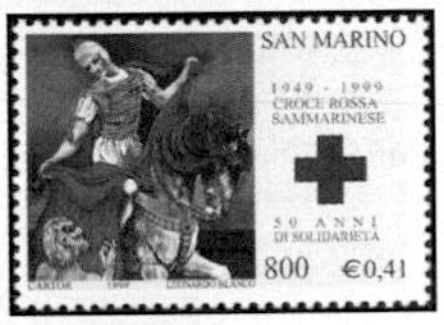


San Marino Red Cross, 50th Anniv. A413

**1999, Sept. 20**
**1465** A413 800 l St. Martin of Tours 1.00 1.00

Souvenir Sheet

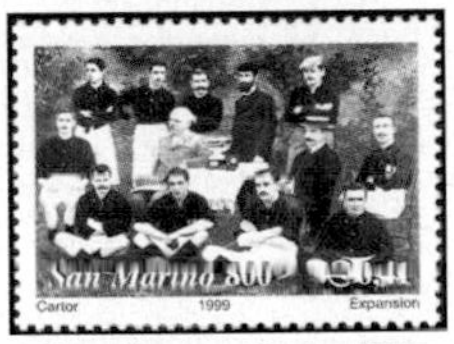

Milan Soccer Club, 100th Anniv. — A414

Designs: a, 1901 team, trophy on table. b, Players Gren, Nordahl and Liedholm. c, 1963 team, black and white photograph. d, 1990 team, white shirts. e, 1994 team, hanging banners. f, 1999 team, player holding trophy.

**1999, Sept. 20**
**1466** A414 800 l Sheet of 6, #a.-f. 6.25 6.25

Souvenir Sheet

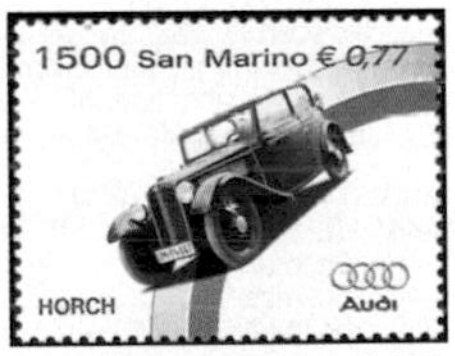


Audi Automobiles — A415

Designs: a, Horch. b, Audi TT. c, Audi A8. d, Auto Union.

**1999, Nov. 5 Litho.** ***Perf. 13x13¼***
**1467** A415 1500 l Sheet of 4, #a.-d. 7.75 7.75

No. 1467 was issued with attached entry form for drawing to win a new Audi A3 car. Entry form is rouletted at top to separate from bottom of sheet. Values are for sheets with entry form attached.

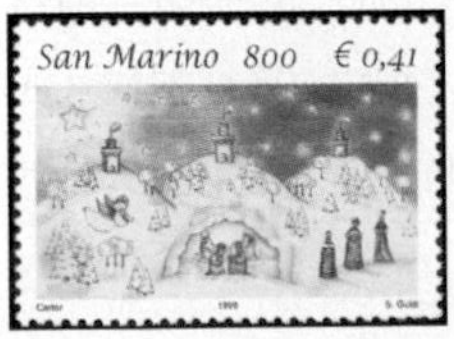


Christmas A416

**1999, Nov. 5**
**1468** A416 800 l multicolored 1.00 1.00

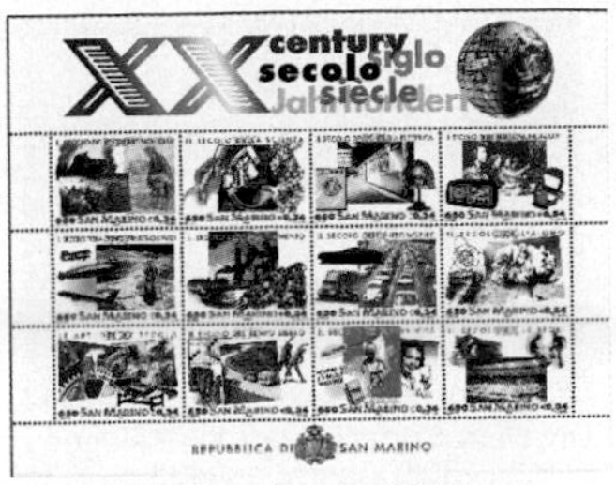

Millennium — A417

Designs: a, Tank, soldiers and refugees of World Wars. b, Syringe and vial, MRI machine, DNA molecule. c, Washing machine, subway, Tiffany lamp. d, Radio, telephone operators, person at computer. e, Airplanes, airship, astronaut on moon. f, Pollution. g, Automobiles and truck. h, Atomic diagram, nuclear submarine, mushroom cloud. i, Charlie Chaplin in "Modern Times," comic strip, chair. j, Crossword puzzle, art gallery visitors, car and trailer, people exercising. k, Advertisements and slogans. l, Cyclist, soccer players, stadium.

**2000, Feb. 2 Litho.** ***Perf. 13x13¼***
**1469** A417 650 l Sheet of 12, #a.-l. 10.50 10.50

Souvenir Sheet

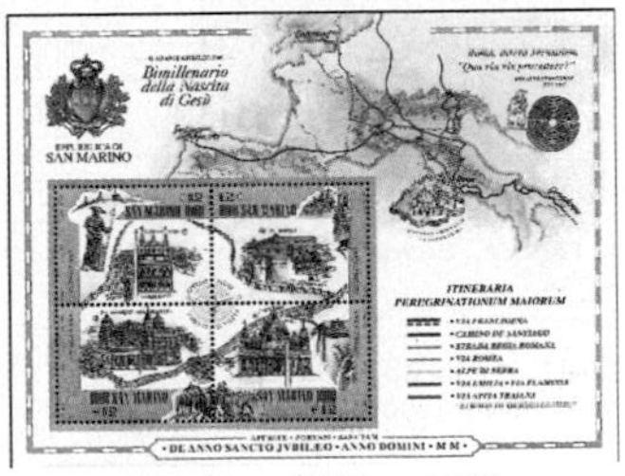

Holy Year 2000 — A410

Designs: a, St. John Lateran Basilica, St. Marinus and Mt. Titano. b, Basilica of St. Paul, statue of St. Marinus, the Rocca. c, Basilica of St. Mary Major, Basilica of San Marino. d, St. Peter's Basilica, St. Marinus.

**2000, Feb. 2**
**1470** A418 1000 l Sheet of 4, #a.-d. 5.00 5.00

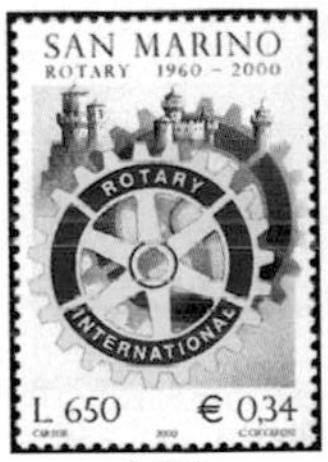


A419

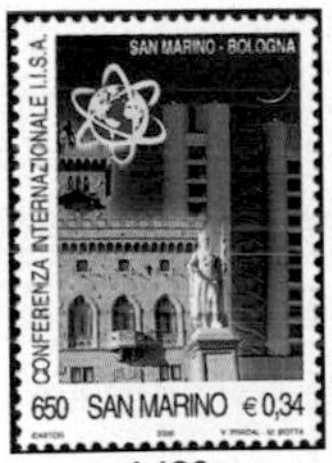


A420

Designs: 650 l, Rotary emblem and towers. 800 l, Palace, coat of arms, Statue of Liberty, Rotary emblem.

**2000, Apr. 27 Litho.** ***Perf. 13¼x13***

| | | | |
|---|---|---|---|
| **1471** A419 650 l multi | .85 | .85 |
| **1472** A419 800 l multi | 1.00 | 1.00 |

Rotary Club of San Marino, 40th anniv.

**2000, Apr. 27**

Bologna, European City of Culture: 650 l, Government Palace and Statue of Liberty, San Marino, and Fiera Towers, Bologna. 800 l, Marconi's workbench, radio antenna, Bologna buildings. 1200 l, Microchip, drums, keyboards, Bologna buildings. 1500 l, Still Life, by Giorgio Morandi, antique books, Bologna buildings.

| | | | |
|---|---|---|---|
| **1473** A420 650 l multi | .85 | .85 |
| **1474** A420 800 l multi | 1.00 | 1.00 |
| **1475** A420 1200 l multi | 1.50 | 1.50 |
| **1476** A420 1500 l multi | 1.90 | 1.90 |
| *Nos. 1473-1476 (4)* | 5.25 | 5.25 |

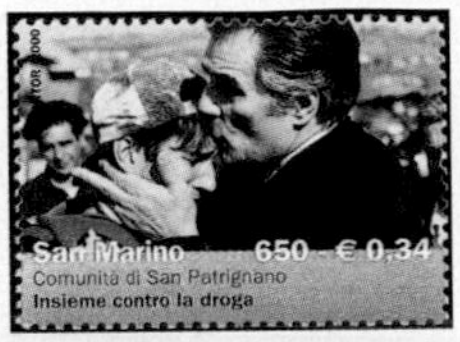


Community of San Patrignano's Fight Against Drug Abuse — A421

Designs: 650 l, Vincenzo Muccioli, community's founder. 1200 l, Rainbow emblem. 2400 l, Muccioli and community residents.

**2000, Apr. 27** ***Perf. 13x13¼***

| | | | |
|---|---|---|---|
| **1477** A421 650 l multi | .85 | .85 |
| **1478** A421 1200 l multi | 1.50 | 1.50 |
| **1479** A421 2400 l multi | 3.00 | 3.00 |
| *Nos. 1477-1479 (3)* | 5.35 | 5.35 |

**Europa, 2000**

Common Design Type

**2000, Apr. 27** ***Perf. 13¼x13***
**1480** CD17 800 l multi 1.00 1.00

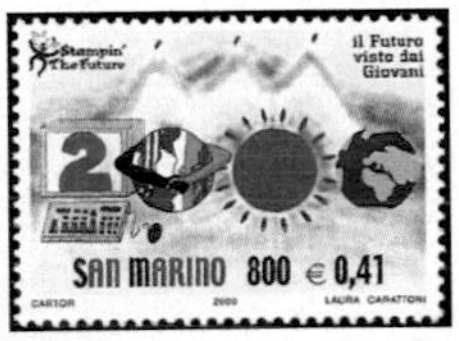


Stampin' the Future Children's Stamp Design Contest Winner A422

**2000, May 31** ***Perf. 13x13¼***
**1481** A422 800 l multi 1.00 1.00

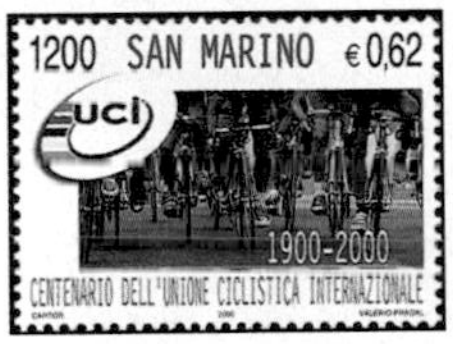


Intl. Cycling Union, Cent. A423

**2000, May 31**
**1482** A423 1200 l multi 1.50 1.50

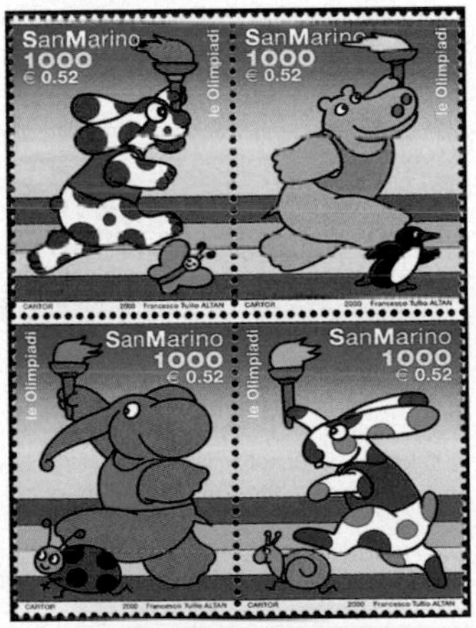


2000 Summer Olympics, Sydney — A424

Designs: a, Dog, butterfly. b, Hippopotamus, penguin. c, Elephant, ladybug. d, Rabbit, snail. Illustration reduced.

**2000, May 31** ***Perf. 13¼x13***
**1483** A424 1000 l Block of 4, #a-d 5.00 5.00

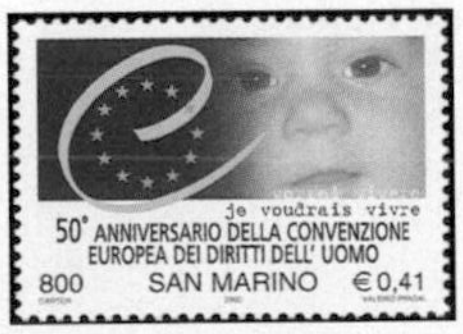


European Convention on Human Rights, 50th Anniv. A425

**2000, Sept. 15 Litho.** ***Perf. 13x13¼***
**1484** A425 800 l multi 1.00 1.00

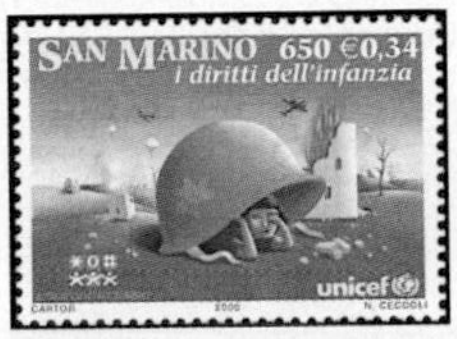


Intl. Rights of the Child Convention, 10th Anniv. A426

Child: 650 l, And army helmet. 800 l, In corner of room. 1200 l, As flower. 1500 l, With book.

**2000, Sept. 15**
**1485-1488** A426 Set of 4 5.50 5.50

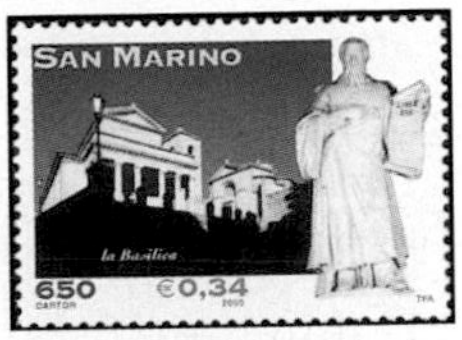


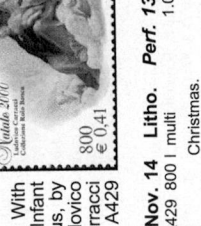

Art of the Montefeltro A427

650 l, Basilica of San Marino, Statue of St. Marinus, by Adamo Tadolini. 800 l, Santa Maria d'Antico Church, Madonna and Child statue, by Luca Della Robbia. 1000 l, San Lorenzo Church, church door. 1500 l, Interior and exterior of San Leo Church. 1800 l, Frescoes, Santuario Madonna della Grazie.

**2000, Sept. 15**
**1489-1493** A427 Set of 5 7.50 7.50

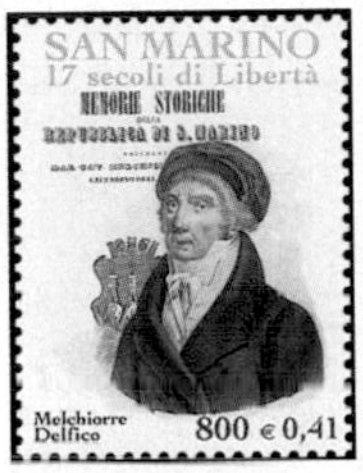


Republic of San Marino, 1700th Anniv. — A428

No. 1494: a, Melchiorre Delfico (1744-1835), historian. b, Giuseppe Garibaldi. c, Abraham Lincoln. d, World War II refugees. e, Jewels from Treasure of Domagnano. f, Map after 1643 war. g, Napoleon Bonaparte's offer to extend territory. h, Arengo of 1906. i, Child's head. j, Young man's head. k, Woman's head. l, Old man's head. m, St. Marinus, by Francesco Manzocchi di Forli, left half of arms. n, Right half of arms, St. Marinus, work attributed to Ghirlandaio. o, St. Marinus, by School of Guercino (blue denomination at top). p, St. Marinus in Glory, by anonymous artist. q, Double throne of Regents. r, Republican statutes, 17th cent. s, Palace Guards on parade. t, Flags of San Marino and other countries.

**2000, Nov. 14 Photo.** ***Perf. 11¾***

| | | | |
|---|---|---|---|
| **1494** | Souvenir booklet | 25.00 | |
| *a.-l.* | A428 800 l Any single | 1.00 | 1.00 |
| *m.-t.* | A428 1200 l Any single | 1.50 | 1.50 |
| *u.* | Booklet pane, #1494a-1494d | 4.00 | |
| *v.* | Booklet pane, #1494e-1494h | 4.00 | |
| *w.* | Booklet pane, #1494i-1494l | 4.00 | |
| *x.* | Booklet pane, #1494m-1494p | 6.00 | |
| *y.* | Booklet pane, #1494q-1494t | 6.00 | |

No. 1494 includes an 800 l postal card.

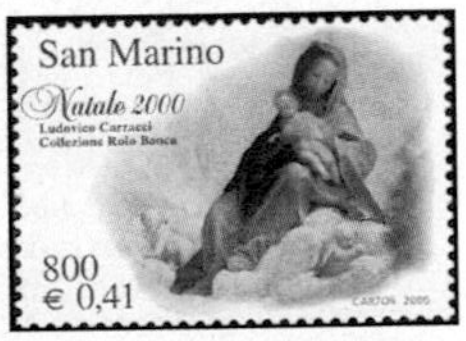


Virgin With the Infant Jesus, by Ludovico Carracci A429

**2000, Nov. 14 Litho.** ***Perf. 13x13½***
**1495** A429 800 l multi 1.00 1.00

Christmas.

Souvenir Sheet

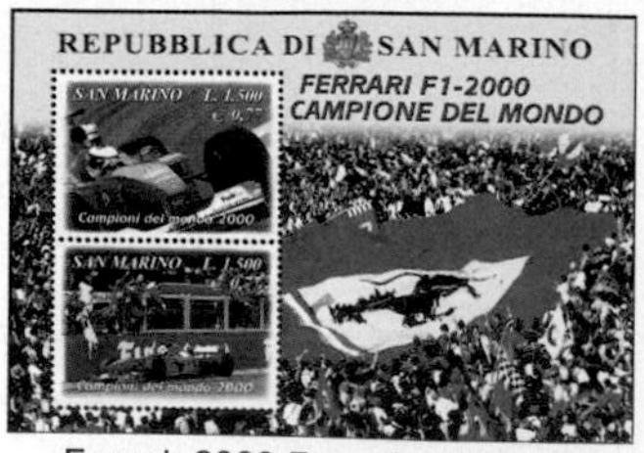
REPUBBLICA DI SAN MARINO
FERRARI F1-2000
CAMPIONE DEL MONDO

Ferrari, 2000 Formula 1 Racing Champion — A430

a, Car on track. b, Car, track wall.

**2001, Jan. 10**
**1496** A430 1500 l #a-b 4.00 4.00

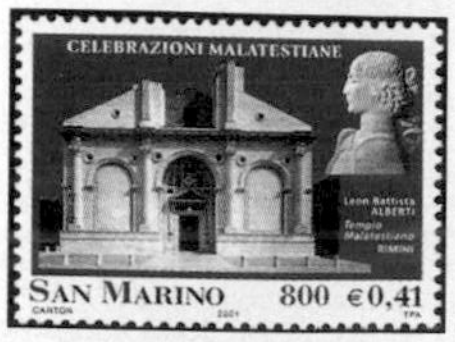
CELEBRAZIONI MALATESTIANE
SAN MARINO 800 €0,41

Heritage of the Malatesta Family A431

Sigismondo Malatesta and: 800 l, Malatestian Temple, by Leon Battista Alberti. 1200 l, Pieta by Giovanni Bellini.

**2001, Feb. 19 Litho.** ***Perf. 13x13¼***
**1497-1498** A431 Set of 2 2.75 2.75

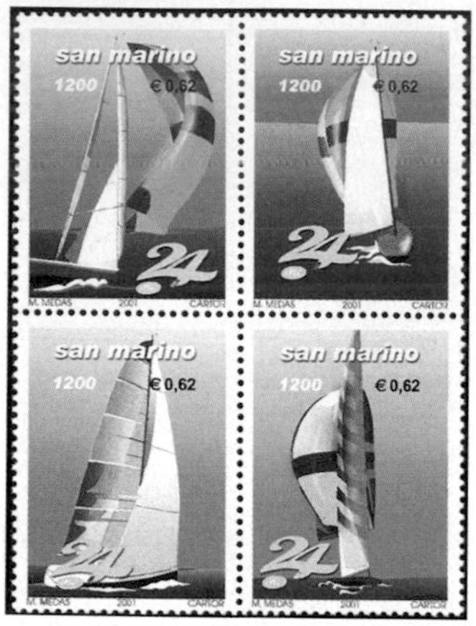
san marino
1200
€0,62
24

24 Hours of San Marino Regatta — A432

Hull colors: a, Green. b, Orange. c, Black. d, Brown.

**2001, Feb. 19** ***Perf. 13¼x13***
**1499** A432 1200 l Block or strip of 4, #a-d 6.25 6.25

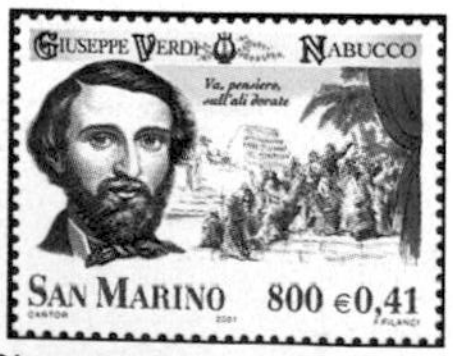
GIUSEPPE VERDI
NABUCCO
SAN MARINO 800 €0,41

Giuseppe Verdi (1813-1901), Composer — A433

Verdi and scenes from operas: a, Nabucco. b, Ernani. c, Rigoletto. d, Il Trovatore. e, La Traviata. f, I Vespri Siciliani. g, Un Ballo in Maschera. h, La Forza del Destino. i, Don Carlos. j, Aida. k, Otello. l, Falstaff.

**2001, Feb. 19** ***Perf. 13x13¼***
**1500** Sheet of 12 12.50 12.50
***a.-l.*** A433 800 l Any single 1.00 1.00

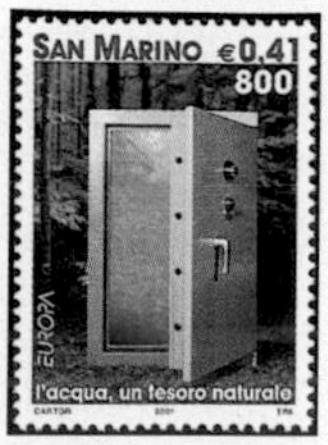
SAN MARINO €0,41
800
EUROPA
l'acqua, un tesoro naturale

Europa — A434

Designs: 800 l, Safe in forest. 1200 l, Faucet on mountain.

**2001, Apr. 17 Litho.** ***Perf. 13¼x13***
**1501-1502** A434 Set of 2 2.50 2.50

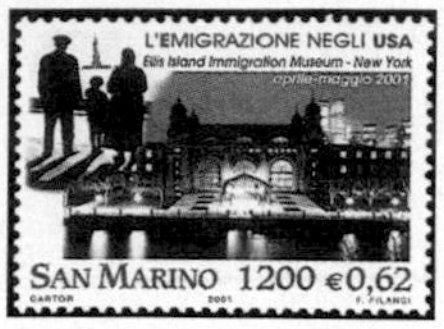
L'EMIGRAZIONE NEGLI USA
SAN MARINO 1200 €0,62

Emigration to the US — A435

Immigrants viewing Statue of Liberty and: 1200 l, Ellis Island Immigration Museum, New York. 2400 l, San Marino Social Club, Detroit.

**2001, Apr. 17** ***Perf. 13x13¼***
**1503-1504** A435 Set of 2 4.00 4.00

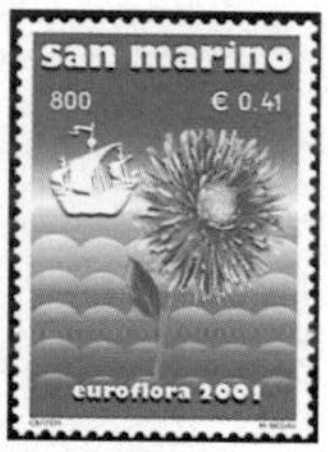
san marino
800
€ 0.41
euroflora 2001

Euroflora 2001, Genoa — A436

Designs: 800 l, Dahlia variabilis, ship. 1200 l, Zantedeschia aethiopica, ship. 1500 l, Helen Troubel rose, ship. 2400 l, Amaryllis hippeastrum, Lanterna.

**2001, Apr. 17** ***Perf. 13¼x13***
**1505-1508** A436 Set of 4 7.50 7.50

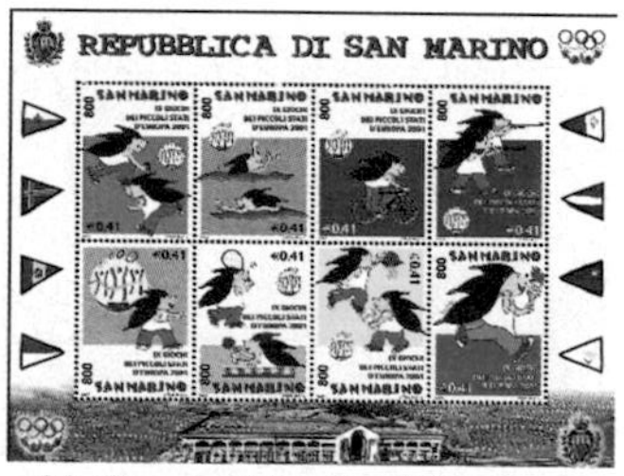
REPUBBLICA DI SAN MARINO

9th Games of the Small European States — A437

No. 1509: a, Bocce, running. b, Swimming. c, Cycling. d, Shooting. e, Judo. f, Tennis, table tennis. g, Basketball and volleyball. h, Mascot carrying torch.

**2001, Apr. 17**
**1509** A437 800 l Sheet of 8, #a-h 8.25 8.25

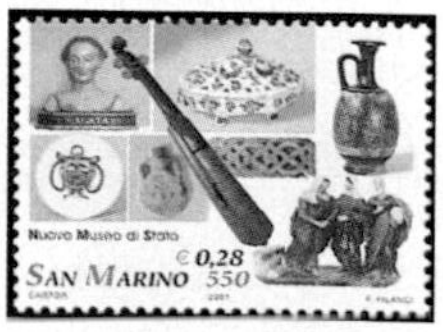
Nuovo Museo di Stato
SAN MARINO €0,28 550

Opening of New State Museum A438

Various holdings: 550 l, 800 l, 1500 l, 2000 l.

**2001, June 23** ***Perf. 13x13¼***
**1510-1513** A438 Set of 4 6.25 6.25

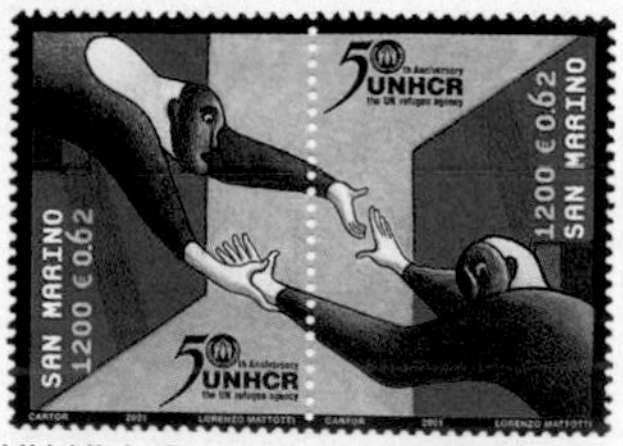
SAN MARINO
1200 €0,62
UNHCR

UN High Commisioner for Refugees, 50th Anniv. — A439

No. 1514: a, Emblem at bottom. b, Emblem at top.

**2001, June 23** ***Perf. 13¼x13***
**1514** A439 1200 l Horiz. pair, #a-b 3.75 3.75

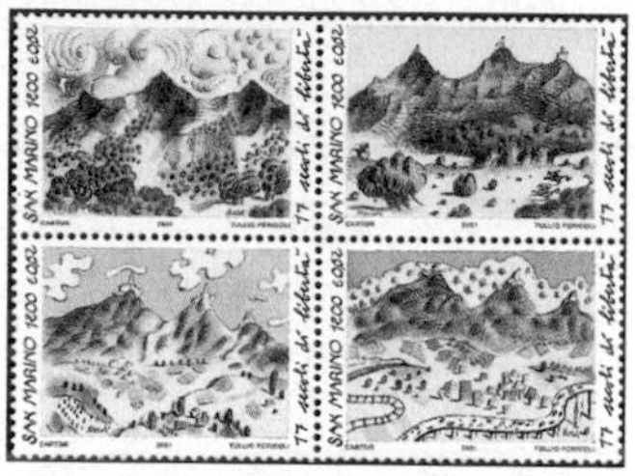

Foundation of the Republic, 1700th Anniv. — A440

No. 1515: a, Uninhabited land. b, People on horses. c, Small community. d, Town with highway.
Illustration reduced.

**2001, June 23** ***Perf. 13x13¼***
**1515** A440 1200 l Block of 4, #a-d 6.25 6.25

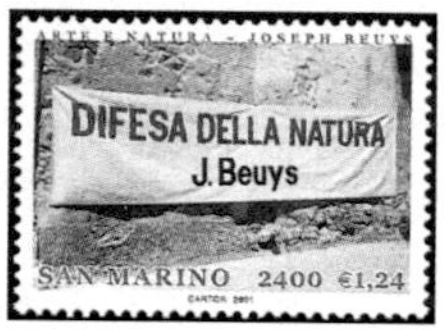
DIFESA DELLA NATURA
J.Beuys
SAN MARINO 2400 €1,24

Homage to Artist Joseph Beuys A441

**2001, Sept. 10**
**1516** A441 2400 l multi 3.00 3.00

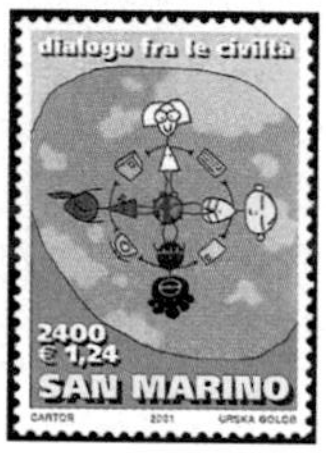
dialogo fra le civiltà
2400
€1,24
SAN MARINO

Year of Dialogue Among Civilizations A442

**2001, Sept. 10** ***Perf. 13¼x13***
**1517** A442 2400 l multi 3.00 3.00

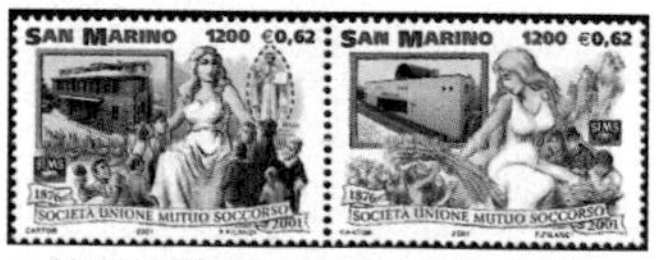
SAN MARINO 1200 €0,62
SOCIETÀ UNIONE MUTUO SOCCORSO

United Mutual Aid Society, 125th Anniv. — A443

Allegory of assistance and: a, Old building. b, Modern building.
Illustration reduced.

**2001, Sept. 10** ***Perf. 13x13¼***
**1518** A443 1200 l Horiz. pair, #a-b 3.75 3.75

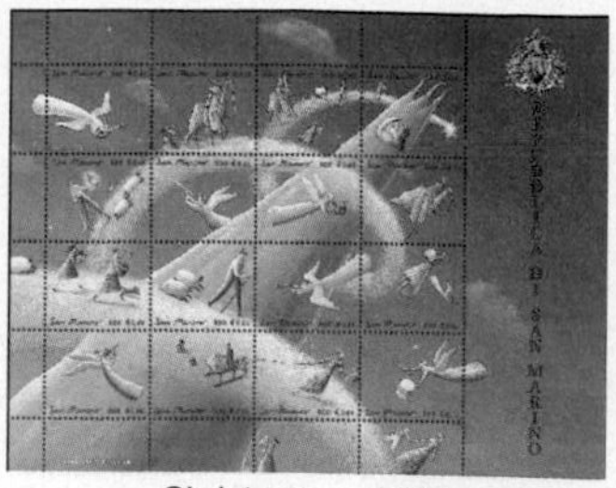

Christmas — A444

No. 1519: a, Angel with lute. b, Woman with basket, Magus on camel. c, Magus on camel, shepherd with sheep, woman with gift. d, Man with gift, castles, star, Holy Family. e, Man with lantern, goose, chicken, sheep. f, Angel with long, thin-mouthed, horn. g, Angel with harp. h, Magus on camel. i, Two women with baskets, dog. j, Shepherd with two sheep. k, Angel with short, wide-mouthed horn. l, Woman with gift, angel with horn. m, Angel with violin. n, Man, sleigh, gifts. o, Woman with gift, pulling sleigh. p, Angel with drum.

**2001, Oct. 18 Litho.** ***Perf. 13***
**1519** A444 800 l Sheet of 16, #a-p 17.00 17.00

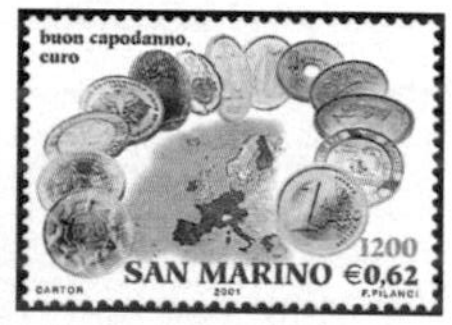
buon capodanno. euro
1200
SAN MARINO €0,62

Introduction of the Euro (in 2002) A445

Map of Europe and: 1200 l, Coins of various countries, 1-euro coin. 2400 l, Banknotes of various countries, 100-euro banknote.

**2001, Oct. 18** ***Perf. 13x13¼***
**1520-1521** A445 Set of 2 4.50 4.50

100 Cents = 1 Euro (€)

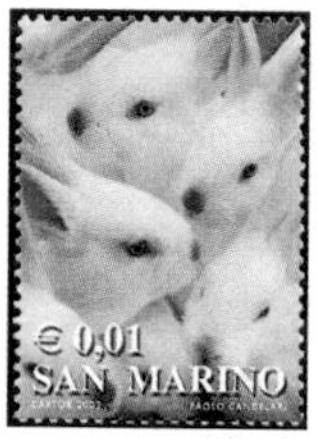
€ 0,01
SAN MARINO

A446

Designs: 1c, Rabbits. 2c, Sunset over San Marino. 5c, Cactus. 10c, Field of grain. 25c, Aerial view of alpine landscape. 50c, Wet olive branches. €1, Sparrows. €5, Baby.

**2002, Jan. 16 Litho.** ***Perf. 13¼x13***

| | | | | | |
|---|---|---|---|---|---|
| **1522** | A446 | 1c | multi | .20 | .20 |
| **1523** | A446 | 2c | multi | .20 | .20 |
| **1524** | A446 | 5c | multi | .20 | .20 |
| **1525** | A446 | 10c | multi | .25 | .25 |
| **1526** | A446 | 25c | multi | .60 | .60 |
| **1527** | A446 | 50c | multi | 1.25 | 1.25 |
| **1528** | A446 | €1 | multi | 2.50 | 2.50 |
| **1529** | A446 | €5 | multi | 12.50 | 12.50 |
| | *Nos. 1522-1529 (8)* | | | 17.70 | 17.70 |

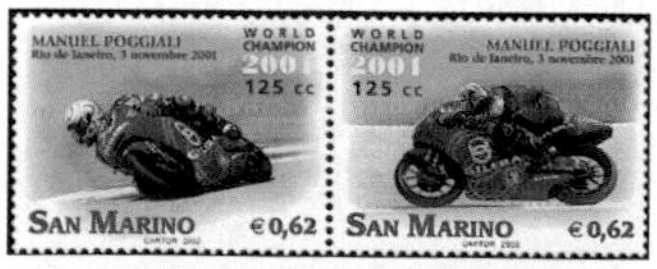
MANUEL POGGIALI
WORLD CHAMPION
2001
125 cc
SAN MARINO €0,62

Manuel Poggiali, 2001 World 125cc Class Motorcycling Champion — A447

No. 1530: a, "2001" at UR. b, "2001" at UL.
Illustration reduced.

**2002, Jan. 16** ***Perf. 13x13¼***
**1530** A447 62c Horiz. pair, #a-b 3.00 3.00

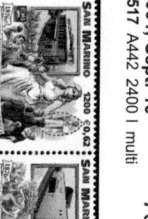

SAN MARINO

**2002 Winter Olympics, Salt Lake City — A448**

No. 1531: a, Dog skiing. b, Hippopotamus skating. c, Rabbit skiing. d, Elephant playing ice hockey.

**2002, Jan. 16** *Perf. 13½x13¼*
1531 A448 41c Block of 4, #a-d    4.00 4.00

**Maastricht Treaty, 10th Anniv. — A452**

**2002, June 3    Litho.    *Perf. 13x13¼***
1537 A452 €1.24 multi    3.00 3.00

**Intl. Year of Mountains — A453**

No. 1538: a, Clouds at and above level of Mt. Titano. b, Clouds below Mt. Titano. c, Mt. Titano with no clouds. Illustration reduced.

**2002, June 3    *Perf. 13¼x13***
1538 A453 41c Horiz. strip of 3,    3.00 3.00
#a-c

**Souvenir Sheet**

No. 1539: a, Parts of #1, 7. b, Parts of #7, 11. c, Parts of #11, 15. d, Parts of #15, 17.

**2002, June 3    *Perf. 13¼***
1539 A454 €1.24 Sheet of 4,    12.00 12.00
#a-d

**San Marino Postage Stamps, 125th Anniv. — A454**

**Europa — A449**

Designs: 36c, Lion tamer, clown, trapeze artist, tightwalker 62c, Trapeze artist, horse act, clown, acrobat.

**2002, Mar. 22    Litho.    *Perf. 13¼x13***
1532-1533 A449    Set of 2    2.40 2.40

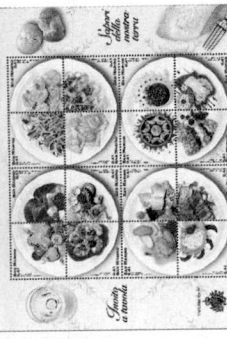

**Priority Mail A450**

Designs: 62c, Cyclist. €1.24, Hurdler.

**2002, Mar. 22    *Perf. 13x13¼***
1534-1535 A450    Set of 2    4.50 4.50

**Stamp + Etiquette**

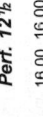 

**2002, Sept. 19**
1540-1541 A455    Set of 2    2.40 2.40

**Intl. Amateur Radio Conference A455**

Emblems of San Marino and International Amateur Radio Associations, Morse code and map in: 36c, Green. 62c, Orange.

**2002 World Cup Soccer Championships, Japan and Korea — A451**

Scenes from Italian team's victorious matches in: a, 1934. b, 1938. c, 1970. d, 1982. e, 1990. f, 1994.

**2002, Mar. 22**
1536 A451 41c Sheet of 6, #a-f    6.00 6.00

**Craftsmen — A456**

Designs: 26c, Blacksmith. 36c, Broom maker. 41c, Chair mender. 77c, Scribe. €1.24, Knife grinder. €1.55, Charcoal maker.

**2002, Sept. 19**
1542-1547 A456    Set of 6    11.50 11.50

---

**Souvenir Sheet**

**Tourist Attractions — A457**

No. 1548: a, Public Palace (30x52mm). b, Guaita (First Tower), buildings at bottom (45x30mm). c, Cesta and Montale (Second and Third Towers) (45x30mm). d, Basilica del Santo (building with steps at left (45x30mm). e, Cappucini Church (building with steps at center) (45x30mm). f, Gate of San Francesco (40x40mm).

**2002, Sept. 19    *Perf. 12½***
1548 A457 62c Sheet of 6, #a-f    9.00 9.00

**Greetings — A458**

Designs: No. 1549, 41c, "Da mi basia mille." No. 1550, 41c, "Hello." No. 1551, 41c, "Best Wishes." No. 1552, 41c, "Eh! Ci sono anch'io." No. 1553, 41c, "?????!!!!!" No. 1554, 41c, "Sorry."

**2002, Oct. 31    *Perf. 13¼x13***
1549-1554 A458    Set of 6    6.00 6.00

**Christmas — A459**

No. 1555: a, Baby's hands grasping adult's hands. b, Baby looking up towards mother. c, Baby breastfeeding. d, Mother and baby asleep. e, Hands cradling baby. f, Baby and mother in blanket. g, Mother kissing baby. h, Mother showing open mouth to baby. i, Baby on mother's shoulder. j, Mother smiling at baby. k, Mother nuzzling baby's hand. l, Two babies.

**2002, Oct. 31    *Perf. 12½***
1555 A459 41c Sheet of 12,    12.00 12.00
#a-l

**Girolamo Fracastoro (1478-1553), Physician and Verona, Italy — A463**

**2003, Mar. 18    Litho.    *Perf. 13x13¼***
1561 A463 77c multi    1.75 1.75
100th Veronafil Philatelic Exhibition, Verona, Italy.

**Paintings — A460**

Designs: 52c, Woman with Mango, by Paul Gauguin (1848-1903). 62c, Wheatfield with Flight of Crows, by Vincent Van Gogh (1853-90). €1.55, Portrait of a Young Woman, by Il Parmigianino (1503-40).

**2003, Jan. 24    Litho.    *Perf. 13½x13***
1556-1558 A460    Set of 3    6.50 6.50

---

**2003 World Nordic Skiing Championships, Val di Fiemme, Italy — A461**

No. 1559: a, Skiers #4, 13. b, Skier #37. c, Skiers #6, 7.

**2003, Jan. 24**
1559 A461 77c Sheet of 3, #a-c    5.75 5.75

**Cuisine — A462**

No. 1560: a, Artichoke and mushroom salad. b, Prosciutto, sausage and cheese. c, Spaghetti with chopped tomatoes. d, Tortellini with ham. e, Shrimp. f, Octopus. g, Ravioli. h, Fettucini with tomato sauce. i, Breast of fowl. j, Fish, shrimp and salad greens. k, Dessert with red sauce in starburst design. l, Dessert with yellow sauce. m, Salad with cherry tomato garnish. n, Meat on bed of vegetables. o, Dessert with raspberry, grape and whipped cream garnishes. p, Custard in shell with lines of chocolate sauce.

**2003, Jan. 24    *Perf. 12½***
1560 A462 41c Sheet of 16,    16.00 16.00
#a-p

**Europa — A464**

Poster art by: 28c, Armando Testa. 77c, Henri de Toulouse-Lautrec.

**2003, Mar. 18**
1562-1563 A464    Set of 2    2.50 2.50

**Race Horses — A465**

Designs: 11c, Molvedo. 15c, Tornese. 26c, Ribot. €1.55, Varenne.

**2003, Mar. 18**
**1564-1567** A465 Set of 4 4.50 4.50

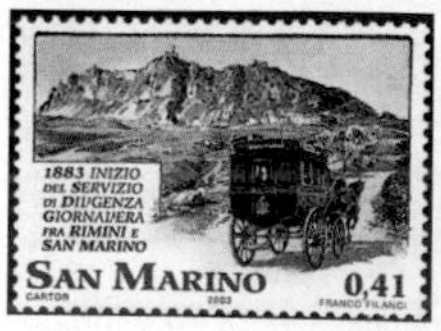

Start of Stagecoach Mail Service, 120th Anniv. A466

Designs: 41c, Stagecoach going to Rimini. 77c, Stagecoach drawn by four horses.

**2003, June 7** ***Perf. 13x13¼***
**1568-1569** A466 Set of 2 2.75 2.75

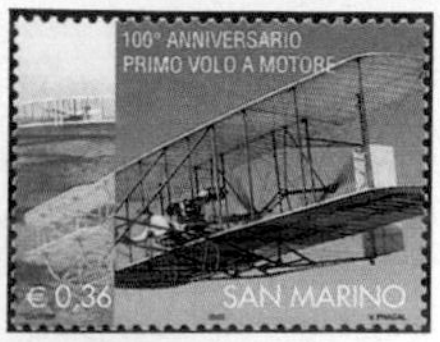

Powered Flight, Cent. A467

Designs: 36c, Wright Flyer. 41c, Bleriot XI. 62c, Aermacchi MB339. 77c, Italian 313th Acrobatic Training Group (Frecce Tricolori).

**2003, June 7**
**1570-1573** A467 Set of 4 5.00 5.00

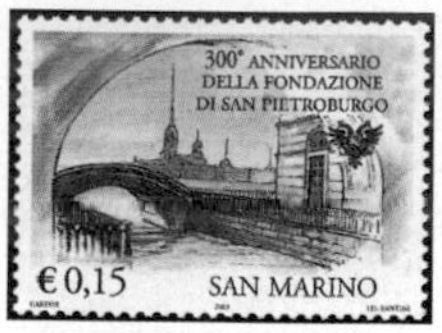

St. Petersburg, Russia, 300th Anniv. A468

Designs: 15c, Bridge across Winter Canal, Fortress, Cathedral of Sts. Peter and Paul. 26c, Architect Bartolomeo Francesco Rastrelli, Opera House. 36c, View of city from Trinity Bridge. 41c, Aleksandr Pushkin. 77c, Empress Catherine II (the Great). €1.55, Czar Peter I (the Great).

**2003, June 7**
**1574-1579** A468 Set of 6 8.25 8.25

Souvenir Sheet

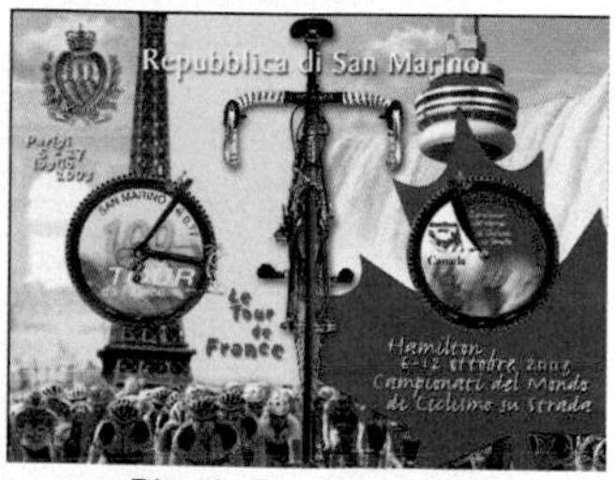

Bicycle Races — A469

No. 1580: a, Tour de France, cent. b, 2003 Road Cycling World Championships, Hamilton, Ont., Canada.

**2003, June 7** ***Perf.***
**1580** A469 77c Sheet of 2, #a-b 3.75 3.75

No. 1580 contains two 38mm diameter stamps.

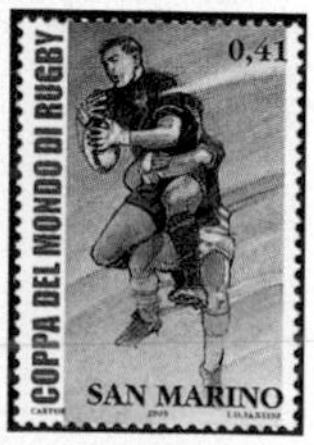

2003 Rugby World Cup, Australia — A470

Various rugby players: 41c, 62c, 77c, €1.55.

**2003, Sept. 15 Litho. *Perf. 13¼x13***
**1581-1584** A470 Set of 4 7.75 7.75

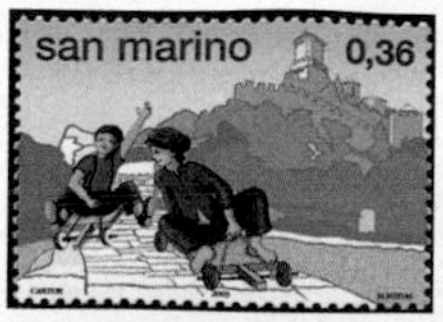

Children's Games A471

Designs: 36c, Cart racing. 41c, Blind man's buff. 62c, Hoop rolling. 77c, Marbles. €1.24, Handkerchief game. €1.55, Tug-of-war.

**2003, Sept. 15** ***Perf. 13x13¼***
**1585-1590** A471 Set of 6 11.50 11.50

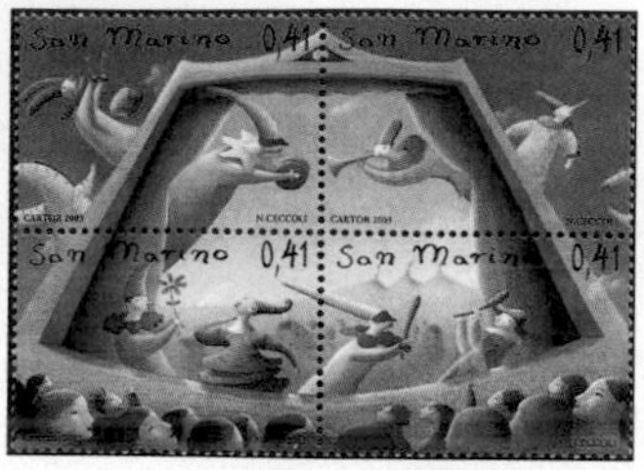

Puppetry — A472

No. 1591: a, Puppets with drum and cymbals. b, Puppet with horn. c, Audience, puppet with flower. d, Audience, puppets with sticks.

Illustration reduced.

**2003, Sept. 15**
**1591** A472 41c Block of 4, #a-d 3.75 3.75

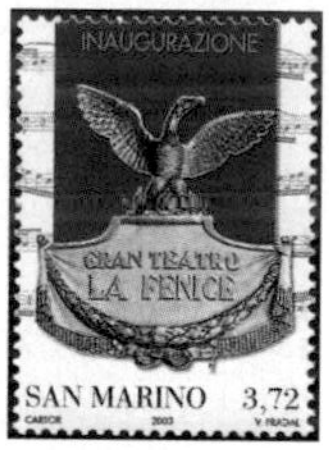

Reconstruction of La Fenice Theater, Venice — A473

**Litho. & Embossed**

**2003, Oct. 24** ***Perf. 13¼x13***
**1592** A473 €3.72 multi 8.75 8.75

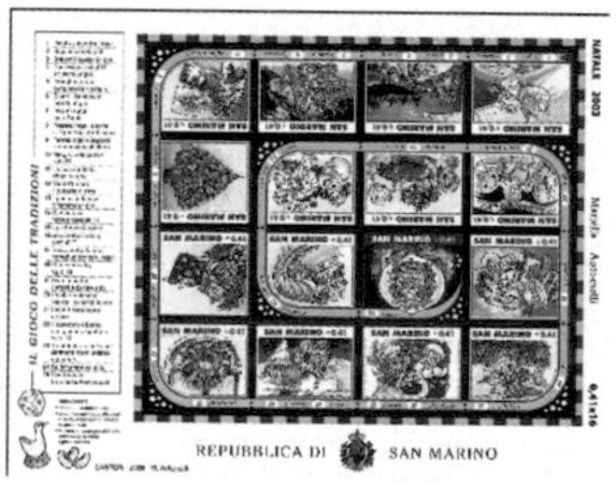

Christmas — A474

No. 1593: a, Christmas cards. b, Holy Family c, Shepherds and Magi. d, Angel. e, Christmas tree, vert. f, Girl and games. g, Children, fruit and cake. h, Carolers. i, Stocking on Christmas tree, vert. j, Cornucopia. k, Arms of San Marino. l, Girl, toys and gift, vert. m, Wreath. n, Boy, sled and snowman. o, Santa Claus. p, Children, toys and Christmas tree.

**2003, Oct. 24 Litho.** ***Perf. 13½***
**1593** A474 41c Sheet of 16, #a-p 15.00 15.00

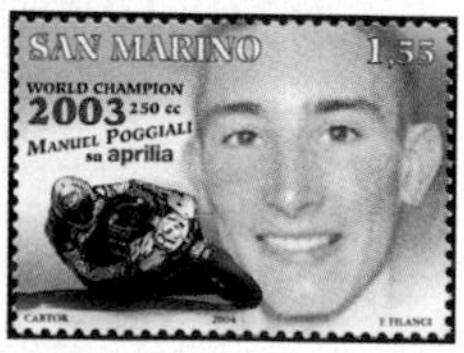

Manuel Poggiali, 2003 250cc Motorcycle World Champion A475

**2004, Feb. 6 Litho.** ***Perf. 13x13¼***
**1594** A475 €1.55 multi 4.00 4.00

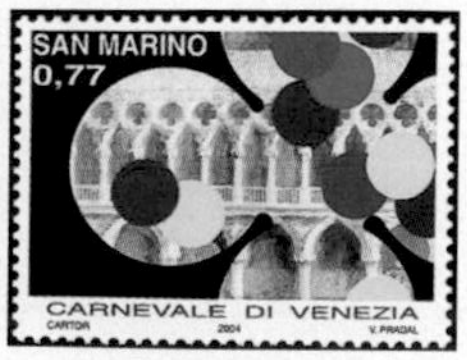

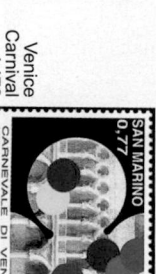

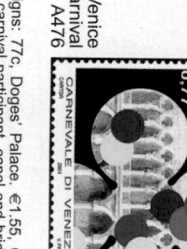

Venice Carnival A476

Designs: 77c, Doges' Palace. €1.55, Costumed carnival participant, canal and bridge.

**2004, Feb. 6**
**1595-1596** A476 Set of 2 6.00 6.00

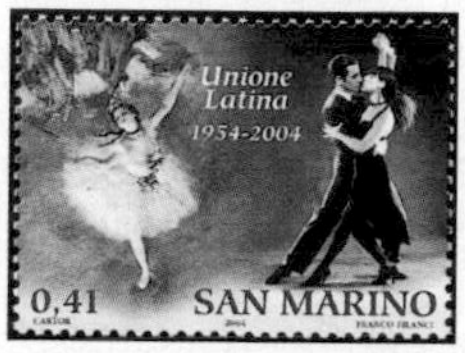

Latin Union, 50th Anniv. A477

Designs: 41c, Ballerina, by Edgar Degas, tango dancers. 77c, Illustration from *Don Quixote*, scene from *Dona Flor and Her Two Husbands*. €1.55, Susanna and the Elders, by Tintoretto, and Sunday Afternoon, by Fernando Botero.

**2004, Feb. 6**
**1597-1599** A477 Set of 3 7.00 7.00

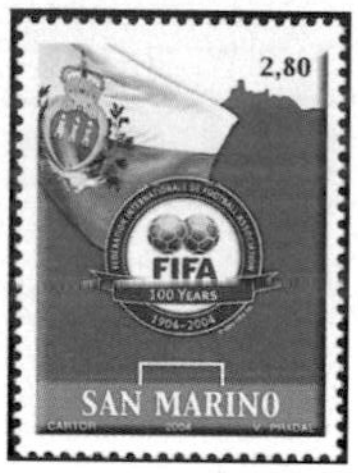

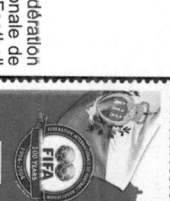

FIFA (Fédération Internationale de Football Association), Cent. — A478

**2004, Apr. 16 Litho.** ***Perf. 13¼x13***
**1600** A478 €2.80 multi 6.75 6.75

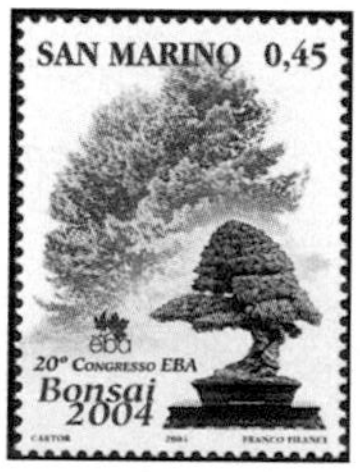

European Bonsai Association, 20th Convention A479

Trees and: 45c, Black Japanese pine bonsai, by Kunjo Kobayashi. 60c, Dwarf pine bonsai, by Pius Notter.

**2004, Apr. 16**
**1601-1602** A479 Set of 2 2.50 2.50

Souvenir Sheet

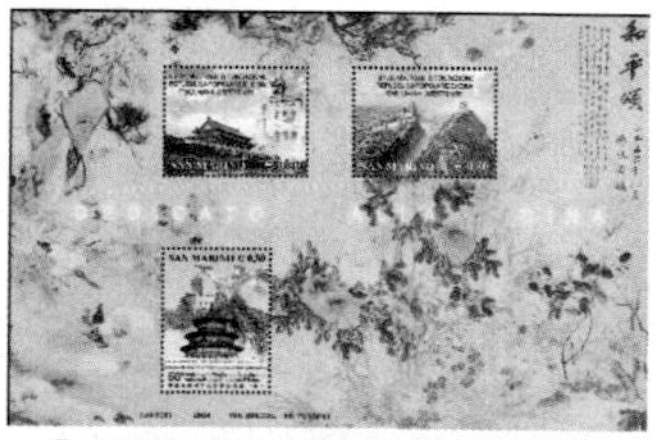

People's Republic of China, 55th Anniv. — A480

No. 1603: a, Tien-an-men Palace, Beijing, and Government Palace, San Marino. b, Mount San Marino, Great Wall of China. c, Tower of San Marino, Pagoda of the Temple of Heaven, Peace Statue, vert.

***Perf. 13x13¼, 13¼x13 (#1603c)***
**2004, Apr. 16**
**1603** A480 80c Sheet of 3, #a-c 5.75 5.75

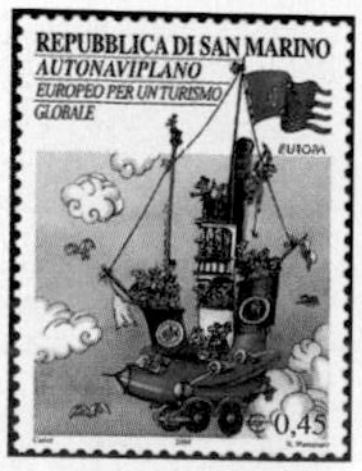

Europa — A481

Fantasy vacation vehicles made up of: 45c, Automobile, airplane and boat. 80c, Boat, camper, train and bus.

***Perf. 13¼x13, 13x13¼***
**2004, May 21 Litho.**
**1604-1605** A481 Set of 2 3.00 3.00

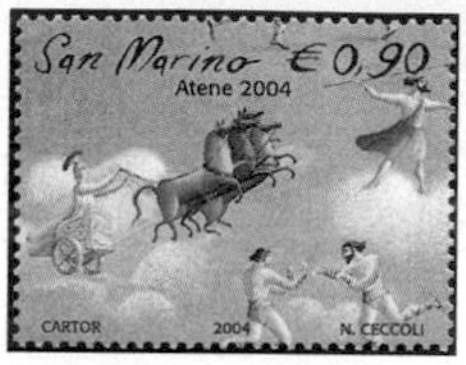

2004 Summer Olympics, Athens A482

No. 1606: a, Chariot, boxers, javelin thrower. b, Discus thrower, wrestlers, torch bearer. c, Relay race runner, cyclist, golfer. d, Tennis player, weight lifter, gymnasts.

**2004, May 21** ***Perf. 13x13¼***
**1606** Horiz. strip of 4 8.75 8.75
***a.-d.*** A482 90c Any single 2.10 2.10

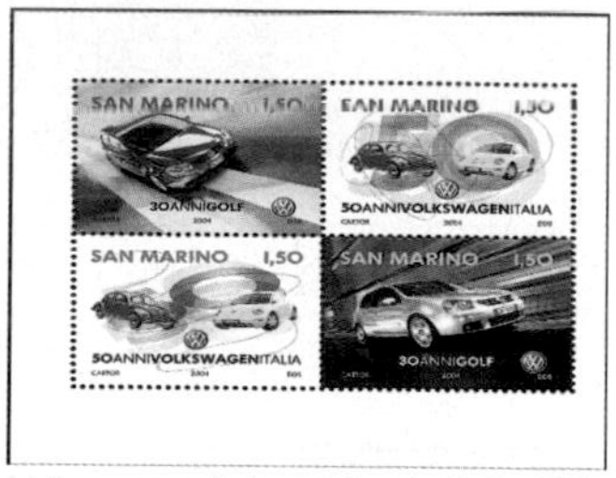

Volkswagen Automobiles in Italy, 50th Anniv. — A483

No. 1607: a, Blue Volkswagen Golf. b, Old and new Volkswagen Beetles, blue denomination. c, Old and new Volkswagen Beetles, green denomination. d, Silver Volkswagen Golf.

**2004, May 21** ***Perf. 13x13¼***
**1607** A483 Booklet pane of 4 14.50 —
***a.-d.*** €1.50 Any single 3.50 3.50
Complete booklet, #1607 14.50

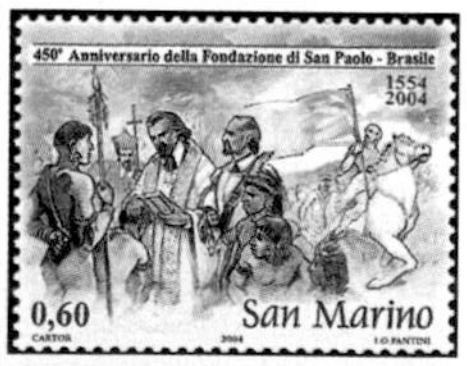

Sao Paolo, Brazil, 450th Anniv. A484

Designs: 60c, Founding of city by Jesuits Manuel de Nobrega and José Anchieta. 80c, Mario de Andrade, artist, Antonio Alcantara Machado, writer, and Municipal Theater. €1.40, City skyline, monastery building.

**2004, Aug. 20**
**1608-1610** A484 Set of 3 7.00 7.00

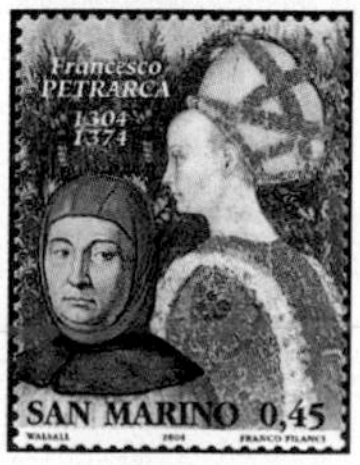

Writers — A485

Miniature Sheet

Il Teatro di Revista

Musical Theater — A500

No. 1652: a, Erminio Macario in *Made in Italy.* b, Wanda Osiris in *Gran Baraonda.* c, Toto in *A Prescindere.* d, Anna Magnani in *Volumeide.* e, Aldo Fabrizzi in *Rugantino.* f, Nino Taranto in *Napoli che Ride.* h, Delia Scala in *Il Della Scala Show.* i, Tino Scotti in *Ghe Pensi Mi.* j, Carlo Dapporto in *Giove in Doppiopetto.*

**2005, June 4**
1652 A500 45c Sheet of 10, #a-j ..... 11.00 11.00

Giovanni Pascoli (1855-1912), Poet — A501

Giovanni Pascoli (1855-1912).

**Perf. 13x13**

**2005, Aug. 26**
1653-1656 A501 Set of 4 ..... 9.75 9.75

Poetry and: 36c, Kite and child. 45c, Mt. Titano. €1, Tower and horse. €2, Pascoli and church bell tower.

Venice Gondola Regatta A502

Designs: €1.40, Statues of angel and devil as racing gondoliers. €2, Gondolier, vert.

**Perf. 13x13¼, 13½x13** **Litho.**

**2005, Aug. 26**
1657-1658 A502 Set of 2 ..... 8.50 8.50

Miniature Sheet

REPUBLICA DI SAN MARINO

Italian Wine Bottle Labels — A503

Grandi Vini Italiani

---

Race cars and: 1c, Juan Manuel Fangio. 4c, Niki Lauda. 5c, John Surtees. 45c, Michael Schumacher. 62c, Ferrari emblem. €1.50, Alberto Ascari.

**2005, Feb. 28**
1628-1633 A494 Set of 6 ..... 7.25 7.25

 SAN MARINO 0,62

Europa — A495

Designs: 62c, Bread. €1.20, Wine.

**Perf. 13¼x13**

**2005, Apr. 25** **Litho.**
1634-1635 A495 Set of 2 ..... 4.75 4.75

 SAN MARINO 0,36

78th Annual Reunion of Italian Alpine Troops — A496

Soldier: 36c, Climbing mountain. 45c, Picking flower. 62c, Assisting mother and child. €1, With other soldiers at reunion.

**2005, Apr. 25**
1636-1639 A496 Set of 4 ..... 6.25 6.25

 SAN MARINO 0.36

Uniformed Militia — A497

Designs: 36c, Officer with saber, Third Tower. 45c, Soldier with musket, Second Tower. 62c, Standard bearer, Palazzo Pubblico. €1.50, Officer with saber, member of Military Band, First Tower.

**Perf. 13¼x14**

**2005, Apr. 25**
1640-1643 A497 Set of 4 ..... 7.75 7.75

 SAN MARINO 0.36

History of Mail Service A498

Designs: 36c, Courier, ship, train. 45c, Man reading letter. 60c, Men reading letter. 62c, Man and woman.

**Perf. 13¼x13¼**

**2005, June 4**
1644-1647 A498 Set of 4 ..... 5.00 5.00

 SAN MARINO 0.36

Coins A499

Designs: 36c, 1864 copper 5-centisimi coin. 45c, 1898 silver 5-lire coin. €1, Gold 10 and 20-lire coins, euro coins. €2.20, Euro coins.

**2005, June 4**
1648-1651 A499 Set of 4 ..... 9.75 9.75

---

Souvenir Sheet

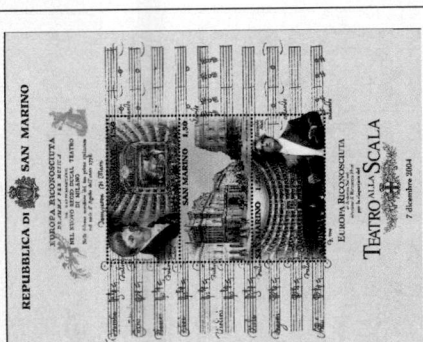

REPUBLICA DI SAN MARINO

TEATRO ALLA SCALA

Reopening of La Scala Theater, Milan — A490

No. 1623: a, Composer Antonio Saliere, theater's stage. b, Theater's facade. c, Conductor Riccardo Muti, audience.

**Perf. 13¼**

**2004, Nov. 12**
1623 A490 €1.50 Sheet of 3, #a-c ..... 12.00 12.00

SAN MARINO 0,36

Dec. 26, 2004 Tsunami Relief A491

**Perf. 13½x13¼** **Litho.**

**2005, Feb. 28**
1624 A491 €1.50 multi ..... 4.00 4.00

Profits from the sale of this stamp went to charities involved with tsunami relief.

SAN MARINO 2,20

Intl. Weight Lifting Federation, Cent. — A492

**Perf. 13¼x13**

**2005, Feb. 28**
1625 A492 €2.20 multi ..... 6.00 6.00

SAN MARINO

2004 Beatification of Alberto Marvelli — A493

Designs: 90c, Marvelli assisting injured man. €1.80, Marvelli, Pope John Paul II, Loreto Basilica.

**2005, Feb. 28**
1626-1627 A493 Set of 2 ..... 7.25 7.25

 SAN MARINO 0,01

Ferrari Race Cars — A494

CAMPIONE DEL MONDO

---

Designs: 45c, Petrarch (1304-74). €1.50, Oscar Wilde (1854-1900). €2.20, Anton Chekhov (1860-1904).

**Perf. 13¼x13**

**2004, Aug. 20** Set of 3
1611-1613 A485 ..... 10.50 10.50

 san marino 0,45

Fairy Tales — A486

Designs: 45c, Hansel and Gretel. 60c, Little Red Riding Hood. 80c, Pinocchio. €1, Puss in Boots.

**2004, Aug. 20** Set of 4
1614-1617 A486 ..... 7.00 7.00

Souvenir Sheet

REPUBLICA DI SAN MARINO

meeting

Meeting of Rimini, 25th Anniv. — A487

No. 1618: a, Man with tie, two men with construction helmets. b, Woman wearing glasses, child, woman. c, Child, woman and man. d, Priest, rabbi and man.

**Perf. 13½**

**2004, Aug. 20**
1618 A487 €1 Sheet of 4, #a-d ..... 10.00 10.00

SAN MARINO

Christmas — A488

No. 1619 — Angels and: a, Musical instruments. b, Bag of toys. c, Christmas tree. d, Cornucopia and "2005."

**Perf. 13¼x13**

**2004, Nov. 12**
1619 A488 60c Block of 4, #a-d ..... 6.25 6.25

Paintings A489

SAN MARINO 0,45

Designs: 45c, Rebecca at the Well, by Giovanni Battista Piazzetta (1682-1754). €1.40, Piazza Navona, by Scipione Gino Bonichi (1904-33). €1.70, The Persistence of Memory, by Salvador Dali (1904-89).

**Perf. 14¾x14¼**

**2004, Nov. 12** Set of 3
1620-1622 A489 ..... 9.25 9.25

---

No. 1659: a, Ferrari Brut. b, Amarone della Valpolicella. c, Canevel. d, Biondi-Santi. e, Vecchioflorio. f, Fazi Battaglia. g, Sassicaia, vert. h, Piano di Monte Vergine del Feudi di San Gregorio, vert. i, Schioppetto, vert. j, Barolo, vert.

**2005, Aug. 26**
1659  A503  45c  Sheet of 10, #a-j  11.50  11.50

**Perf. 13x13¼, 13¼x13 (vert. stamps)**

Dahlia — A504
1660  A504  (45c) multi  1.10  1.10

**2005, Nov. 17**
**Coil Stamp**
**Self-Adhesive**  **Photo.**
**Serpentine Die Cut 6¾ Vert.**

Pope Clement XIV (1705-74) — A505
1661-1662  A505  Set of 2  4.25  4.25

Designs: 80c, Wearing monk's habit and cardinal's biretta. €1, Giving blessing.

**2005, Nov. 17**  **Litho.**  **Perf. 13x13¼**
1663-1666  A506  Set of 4  7.75  7.75

Artists and Writers — A506

Designs: 36c, Baptistry door panel by Lorenzo Ghiberti (1378-1455), sculptor, 62c. The Annunciation, by Fra Angelico (c. 1400-1455), €1, Jules Verne (1828-1905), writer. €1.30, Hans Christian Andersen (1805-75), writer.

**2005, Nov. 17**
Set of 4  7.75  7.75

---

Christmas A507

Designs: 62c, Annunciation Family. €2.20, Adoration of the Magi. €1.55, Holy

**2005, Nov. 17**  **Perf. 13x13¼**
1667-1669  A507  Set of 3  10.50  10.50

2004 Winter Olympics, Turin — A508

No. 1670 — Ski slope with: a, American flag at left. b, Eagle and airplane at right. c, Finish line. d, Skaters at right. Illustration reduced.

**2006, Feb. 1**  **Perf. 12½x12¾**
1670  A508  45c  Block of 4, #a-d  4.50  4.50

Christopher Columbus (1451-1506), Explorer — A509

Columbus and: 90c, Native American.

**2006, Feb. 1**  **Perf. 13x13¼**
1671-1672  A509  Set of 2  6.50  6.50

€1.80, Ship and globe.

Assembly of the Patriarchs, Cent. — A510

Assembled patriarchs and: 45c, Government Palace, 62c, Statue of Liberty, €1.50, Basilica.

**2006, Feb. 1**  **Perf. 13½x13**
1673-1675  A510  Set of 3  6.25  6.25

---

## SEMI-POSTAL STAMPS

Regular Issue of 1903 Surcharged:

**1917, Dec. 15**  **Wmk. 140**  **Perf. 14**
B1  A10(a)  25c on 2c violet  5.00  4.00
a
B2  A11(b)  50c on 2 l violet  25.00  20.00
b

The surtax was used for workers' houses.
See No. CB1.

No. 256 Surcharged in Red "L. 10"

Coat of Arms SP3

**1923, Sept. 20**  **Engr.**
B18  SP3  5c + 5c olive grn  .30  .20
B19  SP3  10c + 5c orange  .30  .20
B20  SP3  15c + 5c dk green  .30  .20
B21  SP3  25c + 5c brn lake  2.25  2.25
B22  SP3  40c + 5c vio brn  1.25  .20
B23  SP3  50c + 5c gray  1.50  .20
B24  SP4  1 l + 5c blk & bl  9.70  8.30
Nos. B18-B24 (7)

Liberty SP4

**1944, Apr. 25**  **Wmk. 140**  **Photo.**  **Perf. 14**
St. Marinus SP5
B25  SP5  20 l + 10 l gldn brn  1.60  1.60
  Sheet of 8  3.25
  Never hinged  40.0
Never hinged

**1946, Aug. 24**  **Unwmk.**
B26  A46  50 l + 10 l  11.00  11.00
  Sheet of 10  22.50
  Never hinged  575.00  575.00

Air Post Types of 1946 Surcharged "CONVEGNO FILATELICO / 30 NOVEMBRE 1946 / + LIRE 25" (or "LIRE 50") in Red or Violet

**1946, Nov. 30**  **Wmk. 277**
B26A  AP6  3 l + 25 l dk brn (R)  .65  .50
B26B  AP8  5 l + 25 l red org  .50  .50
B26C  AP6  10 l + 50 l ultra (R)  .65  .50
Set, never hinged
Nos. B26A-B26C (3)

Inscription "Posta Aerea" does not appear on these stamps.

Third Philatelic Day, Rimini. The surtax was for the exhibition.

**1947, Nov. 13**  **Wmk. 217**  **Perf. 12**
B27  A53  1 l + 1 l brn grn & vio  .20  .20
B28  A53  1 l + 2 l brn grn & vio  .20  .20
B29  A53  1 l + 3 l brn grn & vio  .20  .20
B30  A53  1 l + 4 l brn grn & vio  .20  .20
B31  A53  1 l + 5 l brt grn & vio  .20  1.00
a.  Strip of 5, #B27-B31
Surcharged on No. 261
B32  A53  2 l + 1 l pur & olive  .20  .20
B33  A53  2 l + 2 l pur & olive  .20  .20
B34  A53  2 l + 3 l pur & olive  .20  .20
B35  A53  2 l + 4 l pur & olive  .20  .20

---

View of San Marino SP2

**1918, June 1**  **Typo.**
B3  SP1  2c dl vio & blk  .70  .70
B4  SP1  5c bl grn & blk  .70  .70
B5  SP1  10c lake & blk  .70  .70
B6  SP1  20c brn org & blk  .70  .70
B7  SP1  25c ultra & blk  .70  .70
B8  SP1  45c yel brn & blk  .70  .70
B9  SP1  1 l bl grn & blk  8.25  8.25
B10  SP2  2 l vio & blk  7.75  7.75
B11  SP2  3 l claret & blk  27.95  27.95
Nos. B3-B11 (9)

These stamps were sold at an advance of 5c each over face value, the receipts from that source being devoted to the support of a hospital for Italian soldiers.
For surcharges see Nos. 89-92.

Statue of Liberty — SP1

**Overprinted**

Nos. B6-B8 Overprinted

**1918, Dec. 12**
B12  SP1  20c brn org & blk  1.25  1.25
B13  SP1  25c ultra & blk  1.40  1.40
B14  SP1  45c yel brn & blk  1.25  1.25

3 Novembre 1918 Overprinted

B15  SP2  1 l blue grn & blk  3.25  3.25
B16  SP2  2 l violet & blk  7.00  7.00
B17  SP2  3 l claret & blk  6.50  6.50
Nos. B12-B17 (6)  21.45  20.00

No. 260 Surcharged in Black

Celebration of Italian Victory over Austria. Inverted overprints were privately produced.

# SAN MARINO

B36 A53 2 l + 5 l pur & olive .20 .20 / 1.00
 a. Strip of 5, #B32-B36 1.00

**Surcharged on No. 262**

B37 A53 4 l + 1 l 1.60 1.60
B38 A53 4 l + 2 l 1.60 1.60
 a. Pair, #B37-B38 11.00 11.00
Nos. B27-B38 (12) 5.20 5.20
Set, never hinged 8.00

Surcharges on Nos. B27-B38 are arranged consecutively, changing from ascending to descending order of denomination on alternate rows in the sheet.

> Catalogue values for unused stamps in this section, from this point to the end of the section, are for Never Hinged items.

**1982, Dec. 15 Photo. Perf. 11½**
B39 SP6 300 l + 100 l multi .40 .40
Surcharge was for refugee support.

Refugee Boy — SP6

## AIR POST STAMPS

View of San Marino AP1

**1931, June 11 Wmk. 217 Engr. Perf. 12**
C1 AP1 50c blue grn 5.00 5.00
C2 AP1 80c org 5.00 5.00
C3 AP1 1 l bister brn 1.75 1.75
C4 AP1 1 l brt violet 1.75 1.75
C5 AP1 2.60 l Prus bl 21.00 21.00
C6 AP1 5 l dk gray 21.00 21.00
C7 AP1 5 l olive grn 1.75 1.75
C8 AP1 7.70 l dk orange 21.00 21.00
C9 AP1 9 l dp orange 5.00 5.00
C10 AP1 10 l dk blue 225.00 225.00
Nos. C1-C10 (10) 292.25 292.25
Exist imperf.

**Graf Zeppelin Issue**
Stamps of Type AP1 Surcharged in Blue or Black

**1933, Apr. 28**
C11 AP1 3 l on 50c org 1.60 45.00
C12 AP1 5 l on 80c ol grn 30.00 45.00
C13 AP1 10 l on 1 l dk bl 30.00 55.00
 (Bk) 30.00 67.50
C14 AP1 12 l on 2 l yel brn 30.00 75.00
C15 AP1 15 l on 2.60 l dl red (Bk) 30.00 87.50
C16 AP1 20 l on 3 l bl grn 151.60 375.00
Nos. C11-C16 (6)
Exist imperf.

**1936, Apr. 14**
C17 AP1 75c on 50c blue 1.25 1.25 / grn 6.00 6.00
C18 AP1 75c on 80c red 1.25 1.25 / 6.00 6.00

Nos. C5 and C6 Surcharged with New Value and Bars

**1941, Jan. 12**
C19 AP1 10 l on 2.60 l 60.00 60.00
C20 AP1 10 l on 35 l 15.00 15.00

View of Arbe — AP2

**1942, Mar. 16 Wmk. 140 Photo. Perf. 14**
C21 AP2 25c brn & gray blk .20 .20
C22 AP2 50c grn & brn .20 .20
C23 AP2 75c gray bl & red brn .25 .25
C24 AP2 1 l ocher & black 3.00 3.00
C25 AP2 5 l bis brn & bl 3.85 3.85
Nos. C21-C25 (5)

Return of the Italian flag to Arbe.

Gulls and San Marino Skyline AP6

Plane and View of San Marino AP7

Plane over Globe AP9

**1945, Mar. 15 Photo.**
C40 AP5 25 l bister brn 4.50 4.50 / 9.25
See note after No. 239.

**Photo, Engr. (20 l, 50 l) Perf. 14**
**1946-47 Unwmk.**
C41 AP6 25c blue blk .20 .20
C42 AP7 75c red org .20 .20
C43 AP6 1 l brown .20 .20
C44 AP7 1 l dull green .20 .20
C45 AP7 3 l violet .20 .20
C46 AP6 5 l violet blue .20 .20
C47 AP6 10 l crimson .20 .20
C48 AP8 20 l brown lake 1.25 1.25
C49 AP8 35 l orange red 3.75 3.75
C50 AP8 50 l dk yellow grn 5.50 5.50
C51 AP9 100 l sepia ('47) 6.25 6.00
 13.65 12.90 / 20.00
Nos. C41-C51 (11)
Set, never hinged

Some values exist imperforate.

Issue dates: 35 l, Nov. 3, 1946; 100 l, Mar. 27, 1947; others, Aug. 8, 1946.
For surcharges and overprint see Nos. B26A-B26C, C54.

**Roosevelt Type of Regular Issue, 1947**
F. D. Roosevelt and: 1 l, 3 l l, 50 l, Eagle. 2 l, 20 l, 100 l, San Marino arms. 5 l, 200 l, Flags of San Marino and US, vert.

**1947, May 3 Wmk. 277 Photo. Perf. 14**
C51A A52a 1 l dp ultra & .20 .20
C51B A52a 2 l org red & sep .20 .20
C51C A52a 5 l multicolored .20 .20
C51D A52a 20 l choc & sep .40 .40
C51E A52a 31 l org red & sep .40 .40
C51F A52a 50 l dk car & sep .70 .70
C51G A52a 100 l bl & sepia 3.00 1.40
C51H A52a 200 l multicolored 14.00 12.00
 18.90 15.30
Nos. C51A-C51H (8)
Set, never hinged 35.00
Nos. C51A-C51E, C51H exist imperf. Value, set $105.

**1947, June 16**
C51I A52a 3 l on 1 l dp ultra & sep .25 .25
C51J A52a 4 l on 2 l org red & sep .25 .25
C51K A52a 6 l on 5 l multicolored .25 .25
Nos. C51I-C51K (3) .75 .75

Nos. C51A-C51C Surcharged

**St. Marinus Type of Regular Issue, 1947**
**1947, July 18 Wmk. 217 Engr. Perf. 12**
Center in Bright Blue
C52 A53 25 l deep orange .80 .70
C53 A53 50 l red brown 1.60 1.50
Set, never hinged 4.75

No. C51 Overprinted in Red

Planes over Mt. Titano — AP8

Government Palace — AP5

US No. 1 and Mt. Titano AP11

**1947, July 18 Unwmk. Perf. 14**
C54 AP9 100 l sepia .50 .70
 a. Double overprint 90.00
 b. Inverted overprint 150.00 150.00
 Never hinged .80
 Never hinged 90.00
 Never hinged 150.00
Rimini Phil. Exhib., July 18-20.

**1947, Dec. 24 Wmk. 277 Engr. Perf. 14**
C55 AP11 100 l dk pur & dk brn 7.00 5.50
 Never hinged 14.00
 Never hinged 200.00
 Sheet of 10 1,500.
1st US postage stamps, cent.

No. 264 Surcharged "POSTA AEREA" and New Value in Black

**1948, Oct. 9 Wmk. 217 Perf. 12**
C56 A53 200 l on 25 l 17.50 17.50
 17.50 1.50

Giuseppe and Anita Garibaldi Entering San Marino — AP12

**1949, June 28 Wmk. 277 Photo. Size: 27½x22mm**
C57 AP12 2 l brn red & ultra .20 .20
C58 AP12 3 l dk green & sepia .20 .20
C59 AP12 5 l dk bl grn & ultra .20 .20
Size: 37x22mm
C60 AP12 20 l dk green & vio 1.90 1.90
C61 AP12 65 l grnsh blk & gray blk 6.50 6.50
 9.00 9.00
Nos. C57-C61 (5) 17.50
Set, never hinged

Garibaldi's escape to San Marino, cent.

Stagecoach on Road from San Marino AP13

**1950, Feb. 9 Engr. Perf. 14**
C62 AP13 200 l deep blue 1.10 1.10
 Never hinged 1.60
 2.40
 Never hinged 3.25
 a. As "a," sheet of 6 27.50 27.50
 Never hinged 27.50
 b. Imperf ('51) 12.50 12.50
 As "b," sheet of 6 140.00 140.00

UPU, 75th anniv. #C62 was issued in sheets of 25. #C62a & C62b in sheets of 6. See #C75.

AP14

AP15

Nos. C1 and C2 Surcharged

POSTA AEREA — AP16

**1950, Apr. 12** — Various Views of San Marino.  
**Photo. Perf. 14**  
Size: 27½x21½mm, 21½x27½mm  
C63 AP14 2 l vio & dp ... .20 .20  
C64 AP14 3 l blue & grn ... .20 .20  
C65 AP15 5 l brm blk & brown ... .20 .20  
C66 AP14 10 l grnsh blk & rose red ... .20 .20  
C67 AP14 15 l grnsh blk & bl ... .90 .45  
Size: 36x26½mm, 26½x36mm  
C68 AP15 55 l dk bl & dp ... .75 .30  
C69 AP14 100 l car & gray ... 13.00 9.25  
C70 AP15 250 l violet & brn ... 42.50 26.00  
C71 AP16 500 l bl, dk grn & vio brn ... 42.50 62.50  
Nos. C63-C71 (9) ... 110.25 110.60  
Set, never hinged ... 225.00

See No. C78. For overprints and surcharges see Nos. C72-C74, C76, C79.

**Types of 1950 Overprinted in Black, Blue or Brown**

**1950, Apr. 12 — New Colors; Sizes as Before** — **Photo.**  
C72 AP15 5 l dp bl & dp grn ... .20 .20  
C73 AP14 15 l car & gray (Bl) ... .40 .40  
C74 AP15 55 l vio & brn (Brn) ... 2.75 2.75  
Nos. C72-C74 (3) ... 3.35 3.35  
**Engr.**  
a. ... 4.75  
Set, never hinged

The overprint is arranged differently on each denomination.

See No. C78. For overprints and surcharges see Nos. C72-C74, C76, C79.

**Stagecoach Type of 1950**  
**1951, Jan. 31 Engr. Perf. 13½x14**  
C75 AP13 300 l rose brown & brown ... 16.00 16.00  
Never hinged ... 22.50  
Sheet of 6 ... 140.00  
Never hinged ... 160.00  
Imperf. ... 228.00  
Sheet of 6 ... 350.00  
Never hinged ... 625.00  
... 2,100.  
Never hinged ... 3,750.

No. C71 Surcharged in Black "Giornata Filatelica San Marino-Riccione 20-8-1951," New Value and Bars

San Marino's participation in the 28th Intl. Fair at Milan, Apr., 1950.

**1951, Aug. 20 Photo. Perf. 14**  
C76 AP16 300 l on 500 l ... 24.00 24.00  
Never hinged ... 47.50

**Flag and Plane — AP17**

**1951, Nov. 22 Engr. Perf. 13½x14 Wmk. 277**  
C77 AP17 1000 l multi ... 325.00 325.00  
Sheet of 6 ... 4,250.  
Never hinged ... 4,250.

**Type of 1950**  
**1951, Apr. 28**  
Size: 36x26½mm  
**Photo. Perf. 14**  
C78 AP16 500 l dk grn & brn ... 80.00 80.00  
Never hinged ... 160.00  
Sheet of 6 ... 1,500.  
Never hinged ... 1,200.

---

**1951, Dec. 6**  
C79 AP15 100 l on 250 l ... 2.50 2.50  
Never hinged ... 4.50

Issued to raise funds for flood victims in northern Italy.

No. C70 Surcharged in Black

**1952, Jan. 28**  
C80 AP18 200 l dk bl & blk ... 19.00 19.00  
Never hinged ... 37.50

Issued to honor Christopher Columbus.

Columbus, Globe, Statue of Liberty and Buildings — AP18

**1952, June 29**  
C81 AP18 200 l blk brn & choc 25.00 25.00  
Never hinged ... 50.00

4th Intl. Sample Fair of Trieste.

**Type of 1952 Overprinted in Red**

FIERA DI TRIESTE 1952

GIORNATA FILATELICA — Cyclamen — AP19

**1952, Aug. 25 Photo. Perf. 10x14**  
C82 AP19 1 l pur & lil rose ... .20 .20  
C83 AP19 2 l blue & bl grn ... .20 .20  
C84 AP19 3 l dk brn & red ... .20 .20  
**Perf. 14**  
C85 AP20 5 l rose lil & brn ... .20 .20  
C86 AP20 25 l vio & bl grn ... .20 .20  
C87 AP20 200 l multicolored ... 27.50 27.50  
Sheet of 6, #C87 ... 560.00 560.00  
Nos. C82-C87 (6) ... 28.50 28.55  
Set, never hinged ... 57.50

2 l, As #C85-C87 with flowers omitted. 3 l, Rose.

Riccione Phil. Exhib., Aug. 25, 1952.

**Flowers and Seacoast — AP20**

GIORNATA FILATELICA SAN MARINO-RICCIONE 1952

REPUBBLICA AEREA SAN MARINO — Plane Making Photographic Survey — AP21

**1952, Nov. 17 Photo. Perf. 14**  
C88 AP21 25 l olive green ... .80 .80  
C89 AP21 75 l red brn & pur ... 2.75 2.75  
Nos. C82-C87 (6)  
Set, never hinged

75 l, Aerial survey, seen through window.

Aerial photographic survey of San Marino, 1952.

---

**1953, Apr. 20**  
C90 AP22 200 l brn & dk ... 32.50 32.50  
Never hinged ... 550.00  
Sheet of 6 ... 550.00

**Skier — AP22**

**1954, Apr. 5**  
C91 AP23 1000 l dp bl & dk brn ... 62.50 62.50  
Never hinged ... 575.00  
Sheet of 6 ... 625.00

Plane and Arms of San Marino — AP23

**Type of Regular Issue, 1954**  
**1954, Dec. 16 Photo. Perf. 13**  
C92 A71 120 l dk blue & red ... .55 .55  
Never hinged ... 1.10

REPUBBLICA di SAN MARINO — Hurdler AP25

**1955, June 26 Wmk. 303 Perf. 14**  
C93 AP25 80 l shown ... .70 .65  
C94 AP25 120 l Relay ... 1.00 .95  
San Marino's first Intl. Exhib. of Olympic Stamps, June.

POSTE AEREA — Ski Jumper AP26

**1955, Dec. 15**  
C95 AP26 200 l blk & red org 12.50 12.50  
Never hinged ... 25.00

7th Winter Olympic Games at Cortina d'Ampezzo, Jan. 26-Feb. 5, 1956.

No. 372 Overprinted in Upper Right Corner with Plane and "Posta Aerea"

**1956, Dec. 10**  
C96 A76 100 l blk & Prus grn ... .85 1.75  
Never hinged ... 1.75

---

REP. DI S. MARINO

**1958, Oct. 8 Photo. Perf. 14**  
C100 A85 125 l brn & red brn ... 1.25 1.25

Design: Bay of Naples and 50g stamp of Naples.

**Naples Stamps Type of Regular Issue**

POSTA AEREA — Sea Gull AP29

**1958, June 23 Wmk. 303 Engr. Perf. 13**  
C98 A28 200 l brn & dk blue ... 2.25 2.25  
C99 300 l magenta & vio ... 2.25 2.25  
a. Strip, Nos. C98, C99 + label ... 5.50 5.50  

Printed in sheets containing 20 each of Nos. C98 and C99 flanking a center label with San Marino coat of arms. Nos. C98 and C99 also come se-tenant in sheet.

**Skier AP22**

Design: 300 l, Road from Mt. Titano.

**View of San Marino — AP28**

**1959, Feb. 12**  
C101 AP29 5 l green & gray ... .20 .20  
C102 AP29 10 l blue & org brn ... .20 .20  
C103 AP29 15 l red & multi ... .20 .20  
C104 AP29 120 l rose red, yel & gray blk ... .70 .35  
C105 AP29 250 l dp grn, yel & brn ... 1.90 1.10  
Nos. C101-C105 (5) ... 3.20 2.05

Birds: 10 l, Falcon. 15 l, Mallard. 120 l, Stock dove. 250 l, Barn swallow.

Alitalia Viscount Over San Marino AP31

**1959, May 19 Wmk. 303 Engr. Perf. 13**  
C106 AP30 120 l sepia ... 3.25 .85

Pierre de Coubertin; 1960 Olympic Games in Rome.

**Pierre de Coubertin AP30**

**Lincoln Type of Regular Issue, 1959**  
**1959, June 3 Photo. Perf. 14**  
C107 AP31 120 l bright violet ... 1.10 1.10

First flight San Marino-Rimini-London.

Design: Abraham Lincoln and San Marino peaks.

**1959, July 1 Engr. Perf. 14**  
C108 A87 200 l dark blue ... 2.40 2.10

Design: Bologna view, 3b Romagna stamp.

**Romagna Stamps Type**

**1959, Aug. 29 Photo. Perf. 14**  
C109 A88 120 l blk & blue grn ... 1.60 1.10

Design: Fishing boats, Monte Pellegrino and 50g stamp of Sicily, horiz.

**Sicily Stamps Type**

**1959, Oct. 16**  
C110 A89 200 l multicolored ... .65 .60

**Catalogue values for unused stamps in this section, from this point to the end of the section, are for Never Hinged items.**

## Olympic Games Type

Sports: 20 l, Basketball. 40 l, Sprint race. 80 l, Swimming, horiz. 125 l, Target shooting, horiz.

**1960, May 23  Wmk. 303  Perf. 14**

| | | | | |
|---|---|---|---|---|
| C111 | A92 | 20 l lilac | .20 | .20 |
| C112 | A92 | 40 l bis brn & dk red | .20 | .20 |
| C113 | A92 | 80 l ultra & buff | .30 | .30 |
| C114 | A92 | 125 l ver & dk brn | .90 | .80 |

Nos. C111-C114 (4)

Souvenir sheets are valued and described below No. 465.

## Lions Intl. Type

Design: 200 l, Globe and Lions emblem.

**1960, July 1  Photo.**

C115 A94 200 l ol grn, brn & ultra  5.00  4.00

## 12th Stamp Fair Type

**1960, Aug. 27  Wmk. 303  Perf. 14**

C116 A95 125 l multicolored  1.10  1.00

Helicopter and Mt. Titano AP32

**1961, July 6  Engr.  Perf. 14**

C117 AP32 1000 l rose car  35.00  22.50
Sheet of 6  225.00  140.00

Tupolev TU-104A AP33

**1963-65  Wmk. 339  Photo.  Perf. 14**

| | | | | |
|---|---|---|---|---|
| C118 | AP33 | 5 l bl & vio brn | .20 | .20 |
| C119 | AP33 | 10 l org & dk bl | .20 | .20 |
| C120 | AP33 | 10 l viulet & leu | .20 | .20 |
| C121 | AP33 | 25 l violet & car | .20 | .20 |
| C122 | AP33 | 50 l grnsh bl & red | .20 | .20 |
| C123 | AP33 | 75 l emer & dp org | .20 | .20 |
| C124 | AP33 | 120 l vio bl & red | .20 | .20 |
| C125 | AP33 | 250 l brt yel & blk | .25 | .25 |
| C126 | AP33 | 300 l org & blk | .40 | .40 |

**Perf. 13**

| | | | | |
|---|---|---|---|---|
| C127 | AP33 | 500 l multicolored | 2.50 | 2.50 |
| | | Sheet of 4 | 14.00 | 14.00 |
| C128 | AP33 | 1000 l lil rose, ultra & yel | 1.60 | 1.60 |
| | | Sheet of 4 | 15.00 | 15.00 |

Nos. C118-C128 (11)  6.15  6.15

Planes: 10 l, Boeing 707, vert. 15 l, Douglas DC-8. 25 l, Boeing 707. 50 l, Vickers Viscount 837. 75 l, Caravelle, vert. 120 l, Vickers VC10. 500 l, Rolls Royce Dart turbo-prop. 1000 l, Boeing 707.

Issued: Nos. C118-C126, Dec. 5, 1963. No. C127, Mar. 4, 1965. No. C128, Mar. 12, 1964.

**1974, Oct. 9  Photo.**

Granite Paper

| | | | | |
|---|---|---|---|---|
| C130 | AP35 | 40 l multicolored | .20 | .20 |
| C131 | AP35 | 120 l multicolored | .20 | .20 |
| C132 | AP35 | 500 l multicolored | 1.05 | 1.05 |

Nos. C130-C132 (3)

50th anniversary of gliding in Italy.

## San Marino '77 Type of 1977

**1977, Jan. 28  Photo.  Perf. 11½**

C133 A193 200 l multicolored  .25  .25

Wright Brothers' Flyer A — AP36

**1978, Sept. 28  Photo.  Perf. 11½**

| | | | | |
|---|---|---|---|---|
| C134 | AP36 | 10 l multicolored | .20 | .20 |
| C135 | AP36 | 50 l multicolored | .20 | .20 |
| C136 | AP36 | 200 l multicolored | .65 | .65 |

Nos. C134-C136 (3)

75th anniversary of first powered flight.

## AIR POST SEMI-POSTAL STAMP

View of San Marino APSP1

**1944, Apr. 25  Wmk. 140  Photo.  Perf. 14**

CB1 APSP1 20 l + 10 l ol grn  1.60  1.60
Never hinged
Sheet of 8  40.00
Never hinged  80.00

The surtax was used for workers' houses.

## SPECIAL DELIVERY STAMPS

SD1

**1907, Apr. 25  Unwmk.  Engr.  Perf. 12**

E1 SD1 25c carmine  15.00  7.50

For surcharges see Nos. E3, E5.

## Type of Regular Issue of 1903 Overprinted

**1923, May 30  Perf. 14½x14  Wmk. 140**

E2 A11 60c violet  .50  .50

For surcharge see No. 103.

Mt. Titano and Flight Symbolized AP34

Glider AP35

**1972, Oct. 25  Unwmk.  Perf. 11½**

Granite Paper

C129 AP34 1000 l multi  1.25  .90

Designs: Each stamp shows a different type of air current in background.

---

## Type of 1907 Issue Surcharged

**1923, July 26  Perf. 14**

E3 SD1 60c on 25c carmine  .50  .50
  a. Vert. pair, imperf. between  125.00

No. E2 Surcharged

**Perf. 14½x14**

**1926, Nov. 25**

E4 A11 1.25 l on 60c violet  1.00  1.00

No. E3 Surcharged

**1927, Sept. 15**

E5 SD1 1.25 l on 60c on 25c  .50  .50
  a. Inverted surcharge  72.50
  b. Vert. pair, imperf. between  300.00
  c. Double surcharge  85.00

Statue of Liberty and View of San Marino — SU2

**Wmk. 217**

**1929, Aug. 29  Engr.  Perf. 12**

E6 SD2 1.25 l green  .20  .20

Overprinted in Red

E7 SD2 2.50 l deep blue  .60  .60

Arms of San Marino SD3

**1943, Sept.  Wmk. 140  Photo.  Perf. 14**

E8 SD3 1.25 l green  .20  .20
E9 SD3 2.50 l reddish orange  .20  .20

View of San Marino SD4

**1945-46  Photo.  Wmk. 140**

E12 SD4 2.50 l deep green  .20  .20
E13 SD4 5 l deep orange  .20  .20

Unwmk.

E14 SD4 5 l carmine rose  .70  .50

Pegasus SD5

**Wmk. 140**

---

**Wmk. 277  Engr.**

E15 SD4 10 l sapphire ('46)  1.75  1.25

**Unwmk.**

E16 SD5 30 l deep ultra ('46)  4.00  4.00
  6.85  6.15
  Nos. E12-E16 (5)

See Nos. E22-E23. For surcharges see Nos. E17-E21, E24-E25.

Nos. E14 and E15 Surcharged in Black

**1947  Perf. 14  Unwmk.**

E17 SD4 15 l on 5 l car rose  .25  .20

**Wmk. 277**

E18 SD4 15 l on 10 l saph  .25  .20

No. E16 Surcharged with New Value and Bars in Carmine

**Unwmk.**

**1947-48**

| | | | | |
|---|---|---|---|---|
| E19 | SD5 | 35 l on 30 l (48) | 18.00 | 18.00 |
| E20 | SD5 | 60 l on 30 l (48) | 3.00 | 3.00 |
| E21 | SD5 | 80 l on 30 l (48) | 8.50 | 10.00 |

Nos. E19-E21 (3)  29.50  31.00

Types of 1945-46

**1950, Dec. 11  Photo.  Wmk. 277**

E22 SD4 60 l rose brown  3.50  3.50
E23 SD5 80 l deep blue  3.50  3.50
Set, never hinged  21.00

Nos. E22-E23 Surcharged with New Value and Three Bars

**1957, Dec. 12  Perf. 14**

E24 SD4 7.5 l on 60 l rose brn  1.50  1.50
E25 SD5 100 l on 30 l dp blue  1.50  1.50
Set, never hinged  5.00

> **Catalogue values for unused stamps in this section, from this point to the end of the section, are for Never Hinged items.**

Crossbow SD6

Design: No. E27, "Espresso" at left; crossbow casts two shadows.

**1965, Aug. 28  Photo.  Wmk. 339**

E26 SD6 120 l on 75 l blk, gray & yel  .20  .20
E27 SD6 135 l on 100 l blk & org  .20  .20

Without Surcharge

Design: 80 l, 100 l, "Espresso" at left; crossbow casts two shadows.

**1966, Mar. 29**

| | | | | |
|---|---|---|---|---|
| E28 | SD6 | 75 l blk, gray & yel | .20 | .20 |
| E29 | SD6 | 80 l blk & lilac | .20 | .20 |
| E30 | SD6 | 100 l blk & orange | .60 | .60 |

Nos. E28-E30 (3)

## SEMI-POSTAL SPECIAL DELIVERY STAMP

SPSD1

**Wmk. 277  Engr.**

**1923, Sept. 20  Perf. 14**

EB1 SPSD1 60c + 5c brown red  .75  .75

## POSTAGE DUE STAMPS

D1

**Wmk. 140**

**1897-1920 Typo. *Perf. 14***

| | | | | |
|---|---|---|---|---|
| **J1** | D1 | 5c bl grn & dk brn | .20 | .20 |
| **J2** | D1 | 10c bl grn & dk brn | .20 | .20 |
| *a.* | | Numerals inverted | 125.00 | — |
| **J3** | D1 | 30c bl grn & dk brn | .75 | .75 |
| **J4** | D1 | 50c bl grn & dk brn | 1.25 | 1.25 |
| *a.* | | Numerals inverted | 125.00 | — |
| **J5** | D1 | 60c bl grn & dk brn | 10.50 | 5.50 |
| **J6** | D1 | 1 l claret & dk brn | 3.00 | 3.50 |
| **J7** | D1 | 3 l claret & brn ('20) | 10.50 | 11.00 |
| **J8** | D1 | 5 l claret & dk brn | 45.00 | 29.00 |
| **J9** | D1 | 10 l claret & dk brn | 16.00 | 16.00 |
| | | *Nos. J1-J9 (9)* | 87.40 | 67.40 |

See Nos. J10-J36. For surcharges see Nos. J37-J60, J64.

**1924**

| | | | | |
|---|---|---|---|---|
| **J10** | D1 | 5c rose & brown | .50 | .50 |
| **J11** | D1 | 10c rose & brown | .50 | .50 |
| **J12** | D1 | 30c rose & brown | .75 | .75 |
| **J13** | D1 | 50c rose & brown | 1.25 | 1.25 |
| **J14** | D1 | 60c rose & brown | 3.50 | 3.50 |
| **J15** | D1 | 1 l green & brown | 6.00 | 6.00 |
| **J16** | D1 | 3 l green & brown | 22.50 | 22.50 |
| **J17** | D1 | 5 l green & brown | 26.00 | 26.00 |
| **J18** | D1 | 10 l green & brown | 160.00 | 160.00 |
| | | *Nos. J10-J18 (9)* | 221.00 | 221.00 |

**1925-39 *Perf. 14***

| | | | | |
|---|---|---|---|---|
| **J19** | D1 | 5c blue & brn | .35 | .20 |
| *a.* | | Numerals inverted | 125.00 | — |
| **J20** | D1 | 10c blue & brn | .35 | .20 |
| *a.* | | Numerals inverted | 125.00 | — |
| **J21** | D1 | 15c blue & brn ('39) | .20 | .20 |
| **J22** | D1 | 20c blue & brn ('39) | .20 | .20 |
| **J23** | D1 | 25c blue & brn ('39) | .25 | .25 |
| **J24** | D1 | 30c blue & brn | .35 | .20 |
| **J25** | D1 | 40c blue & brn ('39) | 2.50 | 2.50 |
| **J26** | D1 | 50c blue & brn | .75 | .25 |
| *a.* | | Numerals inverted | 125.00 | — |
| **J27** | D1 | 60c blue & brn | 1.50 | .60 |
| **J28** | D1 | 1 l buff & brn | 3.00 | .50 |
| **J29** | D1 | 2 l buff & brn ('39) | 1.50 | 1.50 |
| **J30** | D1 | 3 l buff & brn | 50.00 | 22.50 |
| **J31** | D1 | 5 l buff & brn | 13.50 | 3.75 |
| **J32** | D1 | 10 l buff & brn | 18.00 | 9.75 |
| **J33** | D1 | 15 l buff & brn ('28) | 1.50 | .85 |
| **J34** | D1 | 25 l buff & brn ('28) | 27.50 | 16.00 |
| **J35** | D1 | 30 l buff & brn ('28) | 6.00 | 6.00 |
| **J36** | D1 | 50 l buff & brn ('28) | 7.25 | 6.75 |
| | | *Nos. J19-J36 (18)* | 134.70 | 72.20 |

Postage Due Stamps of 1925 Surcharged in Black and Silver

**1931, May 18**

| | | | | |
|---|---|---|---|---|
| **J37** | D1 | 15c on 5c bl & brn | .60 | .20 |
| **J38** | D1 | 15c on 10c bl & brn | .60 | .20 |
| **J39** | D1 | 15c on 30c bl & brn | .60 | .20 |
| **J40** | D1 | 20c on 5c bl & brn | .60 | .20 |
| **J41** | D1 | 20c on 10c bl & brn | .60 | .20 |
| **J42** | D1 | 20c on 30c bl & brn | .60 | .20 |
| **J43** | D1 | 25c on 5c bl & brn | 1.75 | .75 |
| **J44** | D1 | 25c on 10c bl & brn | 1.90 | .75 |
| **J45** | D1 | 25c on 30c bl & brn | 11.00 | 7.50 |
| **J46** | D1 | 40c on 5c bl & brn | 1.90 | .20 |
| **J47** | D1 | 40c on 10c bl & brn | 2.40 | .25 |
| **J48** | D1 | 40c on 30c bl & brn | 2.50 | .25 |
| **J49** | D1 | 2 l on 5c bl & brn | 45.00 | 30.00 |
| **J50** | D1 | 2 l on 10c bl & brn | 92.50 | 55.00 |
| **J51** | D1 | 2 l on 30c bl & brn | 60.00 | 45.00 |
| | | *Nos. J37-J51 (15)* | 222.55 | 140.90 |

Nos. J19, J24-J25, J30, J34, J33, J22 Surcharged in Black

***Perf. 14, 14½x14***

**1936-40 Wmk. 140**

| | | | | |
|---|---|---|---|---|
| **J52** | D1 | 10c on 5c ('38) | .65 | .50 |
| **J53** | D1 | 25c on 30c ('38) | 9.00 | 7.25 |
| **J54** | D1 | 50c on 5c ('37) | 9.25 | 7.25 |
| **J55** | D1 | 1 l on 30c | 35.00 | 5.50 |
| **J56** | D1 | 1 l on 40c ('40) | 6.25 | 3.75 |
| **J57** | D1 | 1 l on 3 l ('37) | 35.00 | 1.90 |
| **J58** | D1 | 1 l on 25 l ('39) | 70.00 | 12.00 |
| **J59** | D1 | 2 l on 15 l ('38) | 35.00 | 14.50 |
| **J60** | D1 | 3 l on 20c ('40) | 26.00 | 14.00 |
| | | *Nos. J52-J60 (9)* | 226.15 | 66.65 |

Coat of Arms — D6

**1939 Typo. *Perf. 14***

| | | | | |
|---|---|---|---|---|
| **J61** | D6 | 5c blue & brown | .20 | .20 |

Nos. J61 and J36 Surcharged with New Values and Bars

**1940-43**

| | | | | |
|---|---|---|---|---|
| **J62** | D6 | 10c on 5c | .25 | .20 |
| **J63** | D6 | 50c on 5c | 2.00 | .60 |
| **J64** | D1 | 25 l on 50 l ('43) | 2.75 | 1.75 |
| | | *Nos. J62-J64 (3)* | 5.00 | 2.55 |

Coat of Arms — D7

**Unwmk.**

**1945, June 7 Photo. *Perf. 14***

| | | | | |
|---|---|---|---|---|
| **J65** | D7 | 5c dk green | .20 | .20 |
| **J66** | D7 | 10c orange brn | .20 | .20 |
| **J67** | D7 | 15c rose red | .20 | .20 |
| **J68** | D7 | 20c dp ultra | .20 | .20 |
| **J69** | D7 | 25c dk purple | .20 | .20 |
| **J70** | D7 | 30c rose lake | .20 | .20 |
| **J71** | D7 | 40c bister | .20 | .20 |
| **J72** | D7 | 50c slate blk | .20 | .20 |
| **J73** | D7 | 60c chestnut | .20 | .20 |
| **J74** | D7 | 1 l dp orange | .20 | .20 |
| **J75** | D7 | 2 l carmine | .20 | .20 |
| **J76** | D7 | 5 l dull violet | .20 | .20 |
| **J77** | D7 | 10 l dark blue | .20 | .20 |
| **J78** | D7 | 20 l dark green | 4.50 | 4.00 |
| **J79** | D7 | 25 l red orange | 4.50 | 4.00 |
| **J80** | D7 | 50 l dark brown | 4.50 | 4.00 |
| | | *Nos. J65-J80 (16)* | 16.10 | 14.60 |

## PARCEL POST STAMPS

These stamps were used by affixing them to the way bill so that one half remained on it following the parcel, the other half staying on the receipt given the sender. Most used halves are right halves. Complete stamps were and are obtainable canceled, probably to order. Both unused and used values are for complete stamps.

PP1

**Engraved, Typographed**

**1928, Nov. 22 Unwmk. *Perf. 12***

**Pairs are imperforate between**

| | | | | |
|---|---|---|---|---|
| **Q1** | PP1 | 5c blk brn & bl | .20 | .20 |
| *a.* | | Imperf. | 40.00 | |
| **Q2** | PP1 | 10c dk bl & bl | .20 | .20 |
| **Q3** | PP1 | 20c gray blk & bl | .20 | .20 |
| *a.* | | Imperf. | 40.00 | |
| **Q4** | PP1 | 25c car & blue | .20 | .20 |
| **Q5** | PP1 | 30c ultra & blue | .20 | .20 |
| **Q6** | PP1 | 50c orange & bl | .20 | .20 |
| **Q7** | PP1 | 60c rose & blue | .20 | .20 |
| **Q8** | PP1 | 1 l violet & brn | .20 | .20 |
| *a.* | | Imperf. | 40.00 | |
| **Q9** | PP1 | 2 l green & brn | .60 | .60 |
| **Q10** | PP1 | 3 l bister & brn | .75 | .75 |
| **Q11** | PP1 | 4 l gray & brn | 1.00 | 1.00 |
| **Q12** | PP1 | 10 l rose lilac & brn | 2.40 | 2.40 |
| **Q13** | PP1 | 12 l red brn & brn | 8.50 | 8.50 |
| **Q14** | PP1 | 15 l olive grn & brn | 13.50 | 13.50 |
| *a.* | | Imperf. | 40.00 | |
| **Q15** | PP1 | 20 l brn vio & brn | 21.00 | 21.00 |
| | | *Nos. Q1-Q15 (15)* | 49.35 | 49.35 |

**Halves Used**

| | |
|---|---|
| Q1-Q8 | .20 |
| Q9-Q10 | .20 |
| Q11 | .20 |
| Q12 | .35 |
| Q13 | .65 |
| Q14 | 2.75 |
| Q15 | 3.00 |

**1945-46 Wmk. 140 *Perf. 14***

**Pairs are perforated between**

| | | | | |
|---|---|---|---|---|
| **Q16** | PP1 | 5c rose vio & red org | .20 | .20 |
| **Q17** | PP1 | 10c red org & blk | .20 | .20 |
| **Q18** | PP1 | 20c dark red & grn | .20 | .20 |
| **Q19** | PP1 | 25c yel & blk | .20 | .20 |
| **Q20** | PP1 | 30c red vio & org red | .20 | .20 |
| **Q21** | PP1 | 50c dull pur & blk | .20 | .20 |
| **Q22** | PP1 | 60c rose lake & blk | .20 | .20 |
| **Q23** | PP1 | 1 l brown & dp bl | .20 | .20 |
| **Q24** | PP1 | 2 l dk brn & dk bl | .20 | .20 |
| **Q25** | PP1 | 3 l olive brn & brn | .20 | .20 |
| **Q26** | PP1 | 4 l blue grn & brn | .20 | .20 |
| **Q27** | PP1 | 10 l bl blk & brt pur | .20 | .20 |
| **Q28** | PP1 | 12 l myr grn & dl bl | 3.00 | 1.40 |
| **Q29** | PP1 | 15 l green & purple | 1.90 | 1.40 |
| **Q30** | PP1 | 20 l rose lil & brn | 1.60 | 1.40 |
| **Q31** | PP1 | 25 l dp car & ultra ('46) | 29.00 | 20.00 |
| **Q32** | PP1 | 50 l yel & dp org ('46) | 45.00 | 29.00 |
| | | *Nos. Q16-Q32 (17)* | 82.90 | 55.60 |

**Halves Used**

| | |
|---|---|
| Q16-Q27 | .20 |
| Q28 | .20 |
| Q29 | .20 |
| Q30 | .20 |
| Q31 | .25 |
| Q32 | .50 |

Nos. Q32 and Q31 Surcharged with New Value and Wavy Lines in Black

**1948-50**

| | | | | |
|---|---|---|---|---|
| **Q33** | PP1 | 100 l on 50 l | 42.50 | 32.50 |
| | | Half, used | | 1.00 |
| **Q34** | PP1 | 200 l on 25 l ('50) | 140.00 | 90.00 |
| | | Half, used | | 1.00 |

**1953, Mar. 5 Wmk. 277 *Perf. 13½***

**Pairs Perforated Between**

| | | | | |
|---|---|---|---|---|
| **Q35** | PP1 | 10 l dk grn & rose lil | 24.00 | 8.50 |
| | | Half, used | | 1.00 |
| **Q36** | PP1 | 300 l pur & lake | 110.00 | 82.50 |
| | | Half, used | | 1.00 |

**1956 Wmk. 303 *Perf. 13½***

| | | | | |
|---|---|---|---|---|
| **Q37** | PP1 | 10 l gray & brt pur | .20 | .20 |
| | | Half, used | | .20 |
| **Q38** | PP1 | 50 l yel & dp org | .60 | .50 |
| | | Half, used | | .20 |

**No. Q38 Surcharged with New Value and Wavy Lines In Black**

| | | | | |
|---|---|---|---|---|
| **Q39** | PP1 | 100 l on 50 l | .40 | .40 |
| | | Half, used | | .25 |

**Catalogue values for unused stamps in this section, from this point to the end of the section, are for Never Hinged items.**

**1960-61**

| | | | | |
|---|---|---|---|---|
| **Q40** | PP1 | 300 l violet & brn | 35.00 | 24.00 |
| | | Half, used | | .50 |
| **Q41** | PP1 | 500 l dk brn & car ('61) | 1.50 | 1.50 |
| | | Half, used | | .20 |

**1965-72 Wmk. 339 *Perf. 13½***

**Pairs Perforated Between**

| | | | | |
|---|---|---|---|---|
| **Q42** | PP1 | 10 l gray & brt pur | .20 | .20 |
| **Q43** | PP1 | 50 l yel & red org | .20 | .20 |
| **Q44** | PP1 | 100 l on 50 l yel & red org | .50 | .50 |
| **Q45** | PP1 | 300 l violet & brown | .20 | .20 |
| **Q46** | PP1 | 500 l brn & red ('72) | 3.75 | 3.75 |
| **Q47** | PP1 | 1000 l bl grn & lt red brn ('67) | .50 | .50 |
| | | *Nos. Q42-Q47 (6)* | 5.35 | 5.35 |

**Halves Used**

| | |
|---|---|
| Q42-Q43 | .20 |
| Q44-Q45 | .20 |
| Q46 | .20 |
| Q47 | .45 |

# SARAWAK

sə-ˈrä-ˌwäˌk

LOCATION — Northwestern part of the island of Borneo, bordering on the South China Sea
GOVT. — Former British Crown Colony
AREA — 48,250 sq. mi. (approx.)
POP. — 1,954,300 (1997 est.)
CAPITAL — Kuching

The last ruling Raja, who retired in 1946 when he ceded Sarawak to the British Crown, was Sir Charles Vyner Brooke, an Englishman. He inherited the title from his father, Sir Charles Johnson Brooke, who in turn received it from his uncle, Sir James Brooke. The title of Raja was conferred on Sir James by Raja Muda Hassim after Sir James had aided him in subduing a rebellion. The title and right of succession were duly recognized by the Sultan of Brunei and by Great Britain.

Sarawak joined the Federation of Malaysia in 1963.

100 Cents = 1 Dollar

**Catalogue values for unused stamps in this country are for Never Hinged items, beginning with Scott 155.**

**Watermarks**

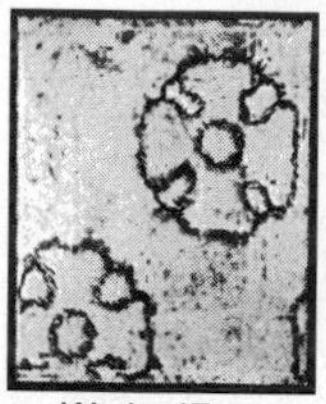

Wmk. 47 — Multiple Rosettes

Wmk. 71 — Rosette

Wmk. 231 — Oriental Crown

Unused examples of Nos. 1-7, 25 and 32-35 are valued without gum. Stamps with original gum are worth more.

Sir James Brooke — A1

Sir Charles Johnson Brooke — A2

**Unwmk.**

**1869, Mar. 1 Litho. *Perf. 11***

| | | | | |
|---|---|---|---|---|
| **1** | A1 | 3c brown, *yellow* | 50.00 | *225.00* |

**1871, Jan.**

| | | | | |
|---|---|---|---|---|
| **2** | A2 | 3c brown, *yellow* | 2.00 | *4.00* |
| *a.* | | Vertical pair, imperf between | *575.00* | |
| *b.* | | Horiz. pair, imperf between | *900.00* | |
| *c.* | | Period after "THREE" | 52.50 | *62.50* |

No. 2 surcharged "TWO CENTS" is believed to be bogus.

There are a number of lithographic flaws, including narrow A, "period" after THREE, etc.

Imperfs. of Nos. 1, 2 are proofs.

A papermaker's watermark, "LNL," usually appears once or twice in each pane.

For surcharges see Nos. 25, 32.

**1875, Jan. 1 *Perf. 12***

| | | | | |
|---|---|---|---|---|
| **3** | A2 | 2c gray lilac, *lilac* | 5.00 | *19.00* |
| **4** | A2 | 4c brown, *yellow* | 3.75 | 3.50 |
| *b.* | | Vertical pair, imperf between | *800.00* | |
| **5** | A2 | 6c green, *green* | 3.75 | *4.00* |
| **6** | A2 | 8c blue, *blue* | 3.75 | *4.00* |
| **7** | A2 | 12c red, *rose* | 7.50 | *7.50* |
| | | *Nos. 3-7 (5)* | 23.75 | *38.00* |

Nos. 3-7 have each five varieties of the words of value.

Imperfs are proofs.

A papermaker's watermark usually appears once or twice in each pane of Nos. 3-7, "LNT" on No. 5, "LNL" on others.

Some examples of No. 7 have the appearance of being on laid paper, but the lines are accidental and not constant within the sheets.

For surcharges see Nos. 33-35.

Sir Charles Johnson Brooke — A4

**1888-97 Typo. *Perf. 14***

**8** A4 1c lilac & blk ('92) 2.00 .55
**9** A4 2c lilac & rose 3.00 1.40
**10** A4 3c lilac & blue 3.25 *4.00*
**11** A4 4c lilac & yellow 18.00 *57.50*
**12** A4 5c lil & grn ('91) 13.00 2.50
**13** A4 6c lilac & brown 15.00 *62.50*
**14** A4 8c green & car 11.50 3.00
*a.* 8c green & rose ('97) 24.00 17.00
**15** A4 10c grn & vio ('91) 42.50 16.00
**16** A4 12c green & blue 10.00 *10.00*
**17** A4 16c gray grn & org ('97) 50.00 *80.00*
**18** A4 25c green & brown 47.50 *40.00*
**19** A4 32c gray grn & blk ('97) 35.00 *57.50*
**20** A4 50c gray green ('97) 45.00 *95.00*
**21** A4 $1 gray grn & blk ('97) 80.00 *85.00*
*Nos. 8-21 (14)* 375.75 *514.95*

No. 21 shows the numeral on white tablet.
Three higher values — $2, $5, $10 — were prepared but not issued. Value $750 each.
For surcharges see Nos. 22-24, 26-27.

Nos. 14 and 16 Surcharged in Black:

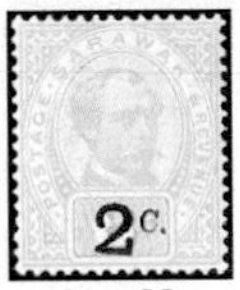
No. 22

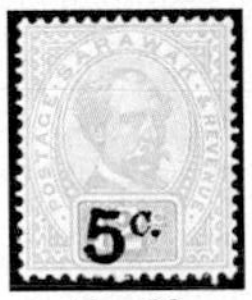
No. 23

No. 24 **5C.**

**1889-91**
**22** A4 2c on 8c 3.50 *5.75*
*a.* Double surcharge 450.00
*b.* Pair, one without surcharge 4,500.
*c.* Inverted surcharge 2,600.
**23** A4 5c on 12c ('91) 27.50 *50.00*
*a.* Double surcharge 1,100.
*b.* Pair, one without surcharge *8,000.*
*c.* No period after "C" 29.00 *50.00*
*d.* Without "C" 425.00 425.00
*e.* Double surch., one vert. 2,750.
**24** A4 5c on 12c ('91) 110.00 *175.00*
*a.* No period after "C" 100.00 *110.00*
*b.* Double surcharge 1,400.
*c.* "C" omitted 575.00 625.00

No. 2 Surcharged in Black

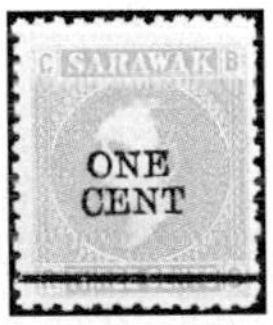

**1892, May 23 *Perf. 11***
**25** A2 1c on 3c brown, *yel* 1.60 *2.25*
*b.* Without bar 210.00
*c.* Period after "THREE" 40.00 *45.00*
*d.* Double surcharge 425.00 *450.00*
*e.* Vertical pair, imperf between *750.00*
*f.* Vertical pair, imperf horiz. *700.00*

Examples of No. 25b must be from the first printing, wherein the bar was applied after the surcharge. Examples of No. 25 with parts of the surcharge and/or bar omitted are stamps that had gum on the face prior to the surcharging operation. The ink was removed when the gum was washed off.

No. 10 Surcharged in Black:

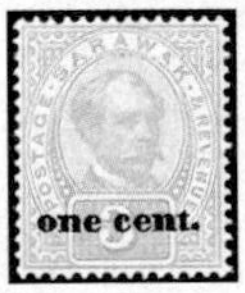
e

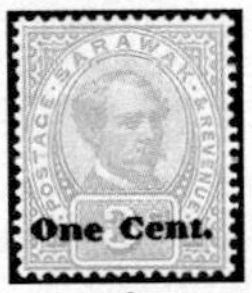
f

**1892 *Perf. 14***
**26** A4(e) 1c on 3c lilac & blue 3.50 *3.00*
*a.* No period after "cent" 175.00
**27** A4(f) 1c on 3c lil & bl 45.00 32.50
*b.* Double surcharge 625.00 500.00

Issued: #26, Feb.; #27, Jan. 12.

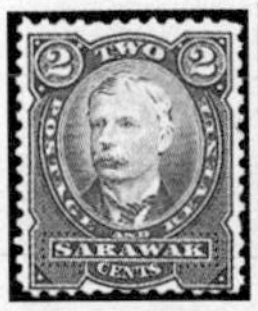
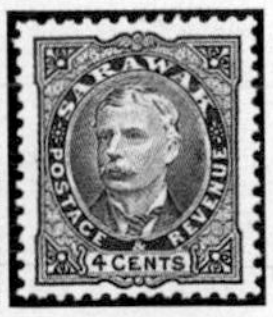
Sir Charles Johnson Brooke
A11 A12

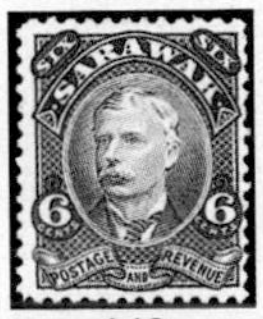
A13

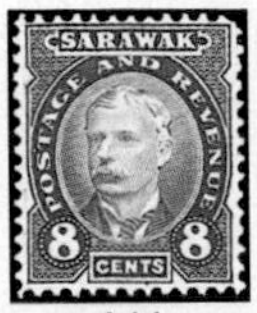
A14

**1895, Jan. 1 Engr. *Perf. 11½, 12***
**28** A11 2c red brown 8.50 *10.00*
*a.* Perf. 12½ 10.00 4.50
*b.* Vertical pair, imperf between *475.00*
*c.* Horiz. pair, imperf between *400.00*
*d.* As "a," horiz. pair, imperf between *500.00*
**29** A12 4c black 8.50 4.00
*a.* Horiz. pair, imperf between *625.00*
**30** A13 6c violet 9.75 *10.00*
**31** A14 8c deep green 30.00 7.00
*Nos. 28-31 (4)* 56.75 31.00

The 2c and 8c imperf are proofs. Perforated stamps of these designs in other colors are color trials, which exist surcharged with new values in pence. These surcharged varieties were used in trial printings of a British South African issue.

Stamps of 1871-75 Surcharged in Black or Red

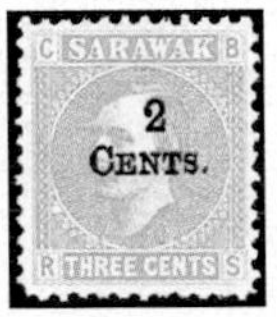

**1899 *Perf. 11***
**32** A2 2c on 3c brown, *yel* 2.00 *2.00*
*a.* Period after "THREE" 57.50 *62.50*
*b.* Vertical pair, imperf between *1,000.*

***Perf. 12***
**33** A2 2c on 12c red, *rose* 3.50 *3.50*
*a.* Inverted surcharge 900.00 *1,400.*
**34** A2 4c on 6c green, *grn* (R) 32.50 *67.50*
**35** A2 4c on 8c blue, *bl* (R) 5.00 *8.50*
*Nos. 32-35 (4)* 43.00 *81.50*

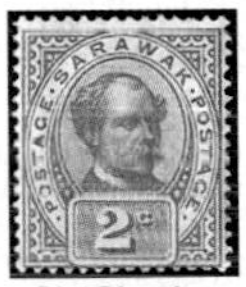
Sir Charles J. Brooke
A16

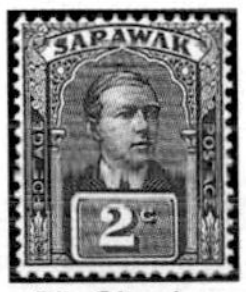
Sir Charles Vyner Brooke
A17

**1899-1908 Typo. *Perf. 14***
**36** A16 1c blue & car ('01) 1.40 *1.40*
**37** A16 2c gray green 2.25 1.00
**38** A16 3c dull violet ('08) 8.00 .75
**39** A16 4c analine car 8.00 2.75
**40** A16 8c yellow & black 2.00 .90
**41** A16 10c ultra 2.75 1.10
**42** A16 12c light violet 5.00 5.00
**43** A16 16c org brn & grn 3.00 2.00
**44** A16 20c brn ol & vio ('00) 6.25 4.00
**45** A16 25c brown & ultra 5.00 *5.75*
**46** A16 50c ol grn & rose 22.50 *27.50*
**47** A16 $1 rose & green 57.50 *125.00*
*Nos. 36-47 (12)* 123.65 *177.15*

A 5c was prepared but not issued. Value $13.50.
See the *Scott Classic Catalogue*, for listings of shades.

**1901 Wmk. 71**
**48** A16 2c gray green 29.00 16.00

**1918-23 Unwmk.**
**50** A17 1c slate bl & rose 2.50 *2.75*
**51** A17 2c deep green 2.90 1.75
**52** A17 2c violet ('23) 2.25 *3.00*
**53** A17 3c violet brown 3.75 3.00
**54** A17 3c deep grn ('22) 1.75 *1.40*
**55** A17 4c carmine rose 4.50 3.50
**56** A17 4c purple brn ('23) 1.75 .95
**57** A17 5c orange ('23) 2.00 1.00
**58** A17 6c lake brown ('22) 1.75 *1.60*
**59** A17 8c yellow & blk 14.00 *70.00*
**60** A17 8c car rose ('22) 5.00 *35.00*
**61** A17 10c ultra 3.50 3.50
*a.* 10c blue 3.50 3.50
**62** A17 10c black ('23) 2.25 *4.50*
**63** A17 12c violet 12.50 *30.00*
**64** A17 12c ultra ('22) 11.00 *21.00*
**65** A17 16c brn & blue grn 6.25 *8.50*
**66** A17 20c olive bis & vio 8.00 *7.50*
*a.* 20c olive green & violet 8.00 *7.50*
**67** A17 25c brown & blue 4.50 *14.00*
**68** A17 30c bis & gray ('22) 4.25 *4.75*

**69** A17 50c olive grn & rose 11.50 *17.00*
**70** A17 $1 car rose & grn 19.00 *32.50*
*Nos. 50-70 (21)* 124.90 *267.20*

In 1918 a supply of the 1c (No. 50) had the value tablet printed, by error, in slate blue instead of rose. It is officially stated that this stamp was never issued and had no franking power. Value $10.
The $1 denomination shows numeral of value in color on white tablet.

Nos. 61 and 63 Surcharged

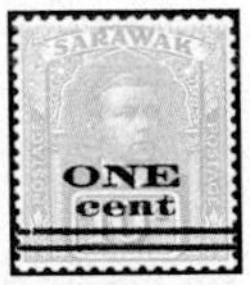

1st Printing — bars 1¼mm apart.
2nd Printing — Bars ¾mm apart.

**1923, Jan.**
**77** A17 1c on 10c ultra 11.00 *62.50*
*a.* "cnet" 400.00 *900.00*
*b.* Bars ¾mm apart 140.00 *400.00*
**78** A17 2c on 12c violet 7.50 *47.50*
*a.* Bars ¾mm apart 80.00 *225.00*

Type of 1918 Issue

**1928-29 Typo. Wmk. 47**
**79** A17 1c slate blue & rose 1.60 .40
**80** A17 2c dull violet 2.00 1.40
**81** A17 3c deep green 2.00 *5.75*
**82** A17 4c purple brown 1.75 .20
**83** A17 5c orange ('29) 2.50 5.75
**84** A17 6c brown lake 1.75 .35
**85** A17 8c carmine 3.75 *17.50*
**86** A17 10c black 2.00 1.40
**87** A17 12c ultra 3.75 *25.00*
**88** A17 16c dp brn & bl grn 3.75 *4.50*
**89** A17 20c dp olive & vio 3.75 *6.25*
**90** A17 25c dk brown & ultra 6.25 *9.75*
**91** A17 30c olive bis & gray 5.25 *11.50*
**92** A17 50c olive grn & rose 7.00 *15.00*
**93** A17 $1 car rose & grn 20.00 *27.50*
*Nos. 79-93 (15)* 67.10 *132.25*
Set, never hinged 145.00

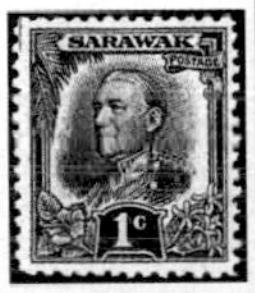
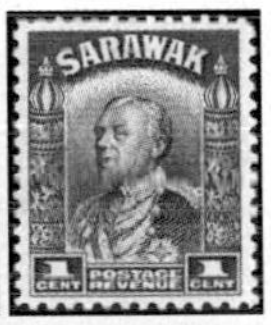
Sir Charles Vyner Brooke
A18 A19

**Wmk. 231**
**1932, Jan. 1 Engr. *Perf. 12½***
**94** A18 1c indigo .90 1.10
**95** A18 2c dark green 1.10 *1.75*
**96** A18 3c deep violet 4.00 1.10
**97** A18 4c deep orange 3.00 .85
**98** A18 5c brown lake 8.50 1.40
**99** A18 6c deep red 9.75 *11.00*
**100** A18 8c orange yel 7.50 *9.75*
**101** A18 10c black 2.50 *3.75*
**102** A18 12c violet blue 4.50 *11.00*
**103** A18 15c orange brown 8.00 *9.75*
**104** A18 20c violet & org 6.25 *9.00*
**105** A18 25c org brn & yel 15.00 *25.00*
**106** A18 30c org red & ol brn 11.00 *25.00*
**107** A18 50c olive grn & red 14.00 *15.00*
**108** A18 $1 car & green 25.00 *40.00*
*Nos. 94-108 (15)* 121.00 *165.45*

**1934-41 Unwmk. *Perf. 12***
**109** A19 1c brown violet 1.25 .20
**110** A19 2c blue green 1.50 .20
**111** A19 2c black ('41) 3.50 *1.75*
**112** A19 3c black 1.25 .20
**113** A19 3c blue grn ('41) 7.00 *5.00*
**114** A19 4c magenta 1.50 .20
**115** A19 5c violet 1.75 .20
**116** A19 6c deep rose 2.50 .70
**117** A19 6c red brn ('41) 7.00 *9.00*
**118** A19 8c red brown 2.25 .20
**119** A19 8c dp rose ('41) 7.75 .20
**120** A19 10c red 2.50 .45
**121** A19 12c deep ultra 3.00 .30
**122** A19 12c orange ('41) 5.50 *6.25*
**123** A19 15c orange 4.00 *12.00*
**124** A19 15c deep blue ('41) 8.25 *20.00*
**125** A19 20c dp rose & olive 4.00 1.10
**126** A19 25c orange & vio 4.00 *2.00*
**127** A19 30c vio & red brn 4.00 *3.25*
**128** A19 50c red & violet 4.50 1.00
**129** A19 $1 dk brn & red 1.75 1.00
**130** A19 $2 violet & mag 15.00 10.00
**131** A19 $3 blue grn & rose 29.00 *32.50*
**132** A19 $4 red & ultra 29.00 *50.00*
**133** A19 $5 red brn & red 32.50 *50.00*
**134** A19 $10 orange & blk 22.50 *57.50*
*Nos. 109-134 (26)* 206.75 *265.20*

Issue dates: May 1, 1934, Mar. 1, 1941.
For overprints see #135-154, 159-173, N1-N22.

Stamps of 1934-41 Overprinted in Black or Red

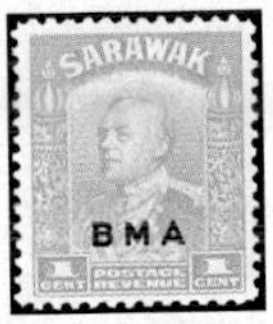

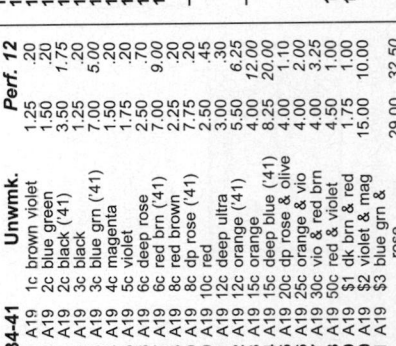

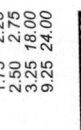

**1945, Dec. 17**
**135** A19 1c brown violet .75 .45
**136** A19 2c black (R) .75 *1.00*
**137** A19 3c blue green .75 *1.10*
**138** A19 4c magenta .75 .35
**139** A19 5c violet (R) 1.40 1.00
**140** A19 6c red brown 1.75 .90
**141** A19 8c deep rose 9.50 *13.50*
**142** A19 10c red .90 .80
**143** A19 12c orange 1.25 *4.25*
**144** A19 15c deep blue 2.25 .45
**145** A19 20c dp rose & ol 1.75 *2.50*
**146** A19 25c org & vio (R) 2.00 *3.00*
**147** A19 30c vio & red brn 4.50 *3.00*
**148** A19 50c red & violet .90 .40
**149** A19 $1 dk brn & red 1.75 1.40
**150** A19 $2 violet & mag 6.50 *11.00*
**151** A19 $3 bl grn & rose 12.50 *55.00*
**152** A19 $4 red & ultra 25.00 *45.00*
**153** A19 $5 red brn & red 140.00 *210.00*
**154** A19 $10 org & blk (R) 125.00 *225.00*
*Nos. 135-154 (20)* 339.95 *580.10*
Set, never hinged 550.00

**Catalogue values for unused stamps in this section, from this point to the end of the section, are for Never Hinged items.**

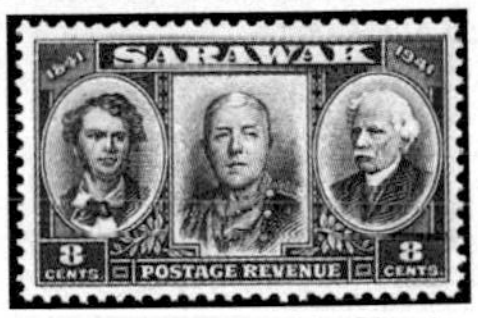
Sir James Brooke, Sir Charles V. Brooke and Sir Charles J. Brooke
A20

**1946, May 18**
**155** A20 8c dark carmine 1.75 1.00
**156** A20 15c dark blue 1.75 *2.25*
**157** A20 50c red & black 2.50 *2.75*
**158** A20 $1 sepia & black 3.25 *18.00*
*Nos. 155-158 (4)* 9.25 *24.00*

Type of 1934-41 Overprinted in Blue or Red

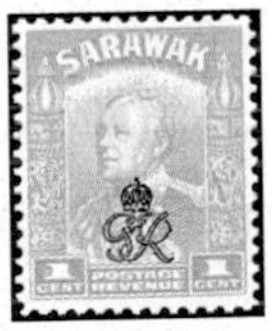

**1947, Apr. 16 Wmk. 4 *Perf. 12***
**159** A19 1c brown violet .20 .30
**160** A19 2c black (R) .20 .20
**161** A19 3c blue green (R) .20 .20
**162** A19 4c magenta .20 .20
**163** A19 6c red brown .30 *1.00*
**164** A19 8c deep rose .85 .20
**165** A19 10c red .30 .20
**166** A19 12c orange .30 *1.10*
**167** A19 15c deep blue (R) .30 .55
**168** A19 20c dp rose & ol (R) 2.25 .65
**169** A19 25c orange & vio (R) .60 .55
**170** A19 50c red & violet (R) .60 .75
**171** A19 $1 dk brown & red 1.10 *1.50*
**172** A19 $2 violet & magenta 2.00 *4.00*
**173** A19 $5 red brown & red 4.50 4.00
*Nos. 159-173 (15)* 13.90 15.40

Common Design Types pictured following the introduction.

**Silver Wedding Issue**
Common Design Types

**1948, Oct. 25 Photo. *Perf. 14x14½***
**174** CD304 8c scarlet .40 .40

**Engraved; Name Typographed**
***Perf. 11½x11***
**175** CD305 $5 light brown 40.00 *45.00*

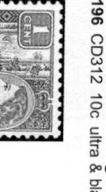

**UPU Issue**
Common Design Types
**Engr.; Name Typo. on 15c, 25c**
***Perf. 13½, 11x11½***

**1949, Oct. 10** **Wmk. 4**
**176** CD306 8c rose carmine 1.50 .60
**177** CD307 15c indigo 3.00 2.25
**178** CD308 25c green 2.10 1.50
**179** CD309 50c violet 2.10 *4.50*
*Nos. 176-179 (4)* 8.70 8.85

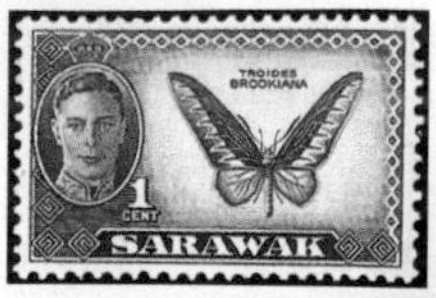
Troides Brookiana A21

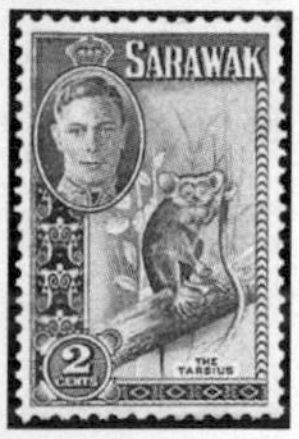
Western Tarsier — A22

Designs: 3c, Kayan tomb. 4c, Kayan girl and boy. 6c, Bead work. 8c, Dyak dancer. 10c, Scaly anteater. 12c, Kenyah boys. 15c, Fire making. 20c, Kelemantan rice barn. 25c, Pepper vines. 50c, Iban woman. $1, Kelabit smithy. $2, Map of Sarawak. $5, Arms of Sarawak.

***Perf. 11½x11, 11x11½***

**1950, Jan. 3** **Engr.**
**180** A21 1c black .45 .30
**181** A22 2c orange red .20 *.40*
**182** A22 3c green .25 *.60*
**183** A22 4c brown .25 .20
**184** A22 6c aquamarine .30 .20
**185** A21 8c red .25 .30
**186** A21 10c orange 1.25 *4.00*
**187** A21 12c purple 3.75 1.50
**188** A21 15c deep blue 2.50 .25
**189** A21 20c red org & brn 2.00 .50
**190** A21 25c carmine & grn 3.00 .60
**191** A22 50c purple & brn 4.00 .20
**192** A21 $1 dk brn & bl grn 22.50 4.00
**193** A21 $2 rose car & blue 30.00 15.00

**Engr. and Typo.**
**194** A21 $5 dp vio, blk, red & yel 20.00 15.00
*Nos. 180-194 (15)* 90.70 43.05

**1952, Feb. 1**
**195** A21 10c orange *(Map)* 1.75 .55

**Coronation Issue**
Common Design Type
**1953, June 3 Engr.** ***Perf. 13½x13***
**196** CD312 10c ultra & black 1.25 *1.50*

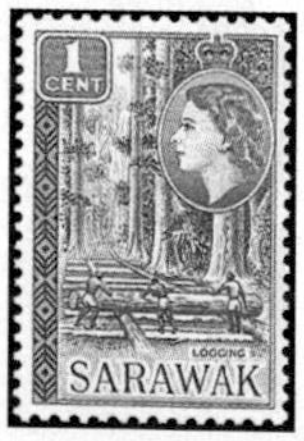
Logging — A23

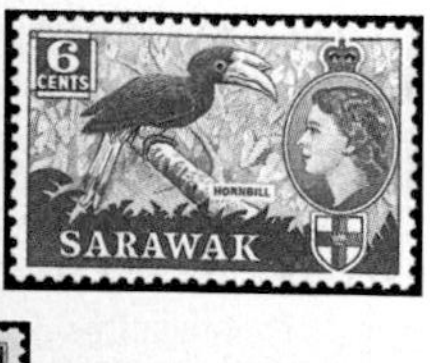
Hornbill A24

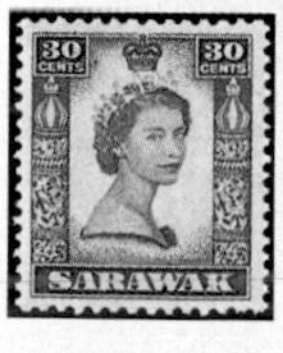
Elizabeth II — A25

Designs: 2c, Young Orangutan. 4c, Kayan Dancing. 8c, Shield with spears. 10c, Kenyah ceremonial carving. 12c, Barong Panau (sailboat). 15c, Turtles. 20c, Melanau basket making. 25c, Astana, Kuching (Governor's Residence). $1, $2, Queen Elizabeth II (Portrait like Fiji A39). $5, Arms.

***Perf. 11x11½, 11½x11, 12x12½ (A25)***

**1955-57** **Wmk. 4** **Engr.**
**197** A23 1c green .20 *.25*
**198** A23 2c red orange .35 *.50*
**199** A23 4c brown carmine .50 *.55*
**200** A24 6c greenish blue 3.50 2.50
**201** A24 8c rose red .30 .30
**202** A24 10c dark green .20 .20
**203** A24 12c purple 4.25 .50
**204** A24 15c ultra 1.25 .25
**205** A24 20c brown & olive 1.25 .20
**206** A24 25c brt green & brn 7.50 .25
**207** A25 30c violet & red brn 6.00 .25
**208** A25 50c car rose & blk 2.25 .30
**209** A25 $1 orange brn & grn 9.00 1.00
**210** A25 $2 green & violet 17.50 3.50

**Engr. and Typo.**
**211** A24 $5 dp vio, blk, red & yel 19.00 10.00
*Nos. 197-211 (15)* 73.05 20.55

Issued: 30c, 6/1/55; others, 10/1/57.
See Nos. 215-222.

**Freedom from Hunger Issue**
Common Design Type
***Perf. 14x14½***
**1963, June 4** **Photo.** **Wmk. 314**
**212** CD314 12c sepia 1.75 1.00

**STATE OF MALAYSIA**
Types of 1955-57
***Perf. 11x11½, 11½x11***

**1964-65** **Engr.** **Wmk. 314**
**215** A23 1c green .20 *.50*
**216** A23 2c red orange 1.00 *12.00*
**217** A24 6c green blue 6.25 *5.00*
**218** A24 10c dark green 1.50 1.00
**219** A24 12c purple 2.25 *10.00*
**220** A24 15c ultra 2.00 *15.00*
**221** A24 20c brown & olive 1.50 *2.00*
**222** A24 25c brt grn & brn 3.25 *5.00*
*Nos. 215-222 (8)* 17.95 *50.50*

Issued: 20c, 6/9/64; 2c, 15c, 8/17/65; others, 9/9/64.

Orchid Type of Johore (Malaysia), 1965, with State Crest

**Wmk. 338**
**1965, Nov. 15** **Photo.** ***Perf. 14½***
**Flowers in Natural Colors**
**228** A14 1c black & lt grnsh bl .20 *1.25*
**229** A14 2c black, red & gray .20 *2.00*
**230** A14 5c black & Prus blue .65 .20
**231** A14 6c black & lt lilac .85 *2.00*
**232** A14 10c black & lt ultra 1.20 .20
**233** A14 15c black, lil rose & grn 2.00 .20
**234** A14 20c black & brown 3.00 .50
*Nos. 228-234 (7)* 8.10 6.35

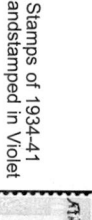

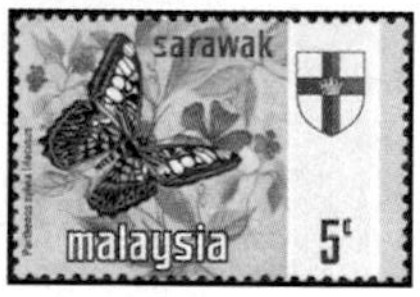
Clipper and State Crest — A26

***Perf. 13½x13***
**1971, Feb. 1** **Litho.** **Unwmk.**
**235** A26 1c Delias ninus .45 *1.60*
**236** A26 2c Danaus melanippus .55 *1.60*
**237** A26 5c Parthenos sylvia 1.60 .20
*a.* Booklet pane of 4 ('73) 5.00
**238** A26 6c Papilio demoleus 1.60 *2.00*
**239** A26 10c Hebomnia glaucippe 1.60 .20
*a.* Booklet pane of 4 ('73) 7.00
**240** A26 15c Precis orithya 2.50 .20
*a.* Booklet pane of 4 ('73) 10.00
**241** A26 20c Valeria valeria 2.50 1.10
*Nos. 235-241 (7)* 10.80 6.90

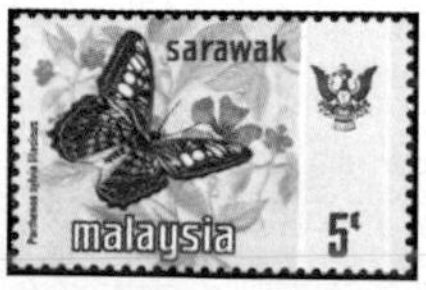
Clipper and New State Crest — A27

Changed Colors, Designs as Before

**1977-78** **Photo.** **Unwmk.**
**242** A27 1c multi ('78) 7.00 *8.00*
**243** A27 2c multi ('78) 18.00 *16.00*
**244** A27 5c multicolored 2.00 2.00
**245** A27 10c multicolored 1.25 .80
**246** A27 15c multicolored 2.00 .30
**247** A27 20c multi ('78) 6.50 5.75
*Nos. 242-247 (6)* 36.75 32.85

Flower Type of Johore, 1979, with State Crest

**1979, Apr. 30** **Wmk. 47** ***Perf. 14½***
**248** A16 1c multicolored .20 .20
**249** A16 2c multicolored .20 .20
**250** A16 5c multicolored .20 .20
**251** A16 10c multicolored .30 .20
**252** A16 15c multicolored .30 .20
**253** A16 20c multicolored .40 .20
**254** A16 25c multicolored .75 .25
*Nos. 248-254 (7)* 2.35 1.45

**1983-86** **Unwmk.**
*250a* A16 5c ('86) 1.00 1.25
*251a* A16 10c ('85) 1.00 1.10
*253a* A16 20c 1.00 1.10
*Nos. 250a-253a (3)* 3.00 3.45

Agriculture and State Arms Type of Johore
Shield Divided into 3 Parts of Different Colors

**Wmk. 388**
**1986, Oct. 25** **Litho.** ***Perf. 12***
**255** A19 1c multicolored .20 .20
**256** A19 2c multicolored .20 .20
**257** A19 5c multicolored .20 .20
**258** A19 10c multicolored .40 .20
**259** A19 15c multicolored .55 .20
**260** A19 20c multicolored .55 .20
**261** A19 30c multicolored 1.00 .20
*Nos. 255-261 (7)* 3.10 1.40

Agriculture and Arms Type of Johore
Yellow Shield Divided by Diagonal Bands of Black and Red

**1986-96** **Litho.** **Wmk. 388** ***Perf. 12***
**262** A19 1c multicolored .20 .20
**263** A19 2c multicolored .20 .20
*a.* Perf. 15x14½ 3.00
**264** A19 5c multicolored .20 .20
*a.* Perf 14 ('96) .90 .20
**265** A19 10c multicolored .20 .20
*a.* Perf. 14 ('95) 2.00
*b.* Perf. 15x14½ ('95) 2.00
*c.* Perf. 14x14½ ('96) 4.50 .35
**266** A19 15c multicolored .20 .20
**267** A19 20c multicolored .20 .20
**268** A19 30c multicolored .25 .20
*a.* Perf. 14 ('94) 1.75 .20
*b.* Perf. 15x14½ ('94) 4.00 .35
*c.* Perf. 14x14½ ('94) 4.25 .45
*Nos. 262-268 (7)* 1.45 1.40

**OCCUPATION STAMPS**

**Issued under Japanese Occupation**

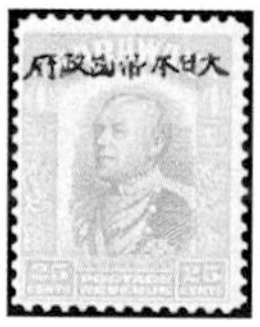
Stamps of 1934-41 Handstamped in Violet

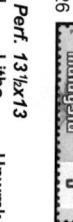

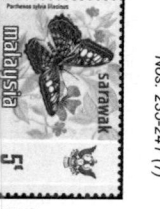

**1942** **Unwmk.** ***Perf. 12***
**N1** A19 1c brown violet 45.00 *60.00*
**N2** A19 2c blue green 100.00 *150.00*
**N3** A19 2c black 100.00 *90.00*
**N3A** A19 3c black 275.00 *275.00*
**N4** A19 3c blue green 60.00 *72.50*
**N5** A19 4c magenta 65.00 *80.00*
**N6** A19 5c violet 80.00 *72.50*
**N7** A19 6c deep rose 125.00 100.00
**N8** A19 6c red brown 80.00 *80.00*
**N8A** A19 8c red brown 260.00 *275.00*
**N9** A19 8c deep rose 110.00 *110.00*
**N10** A19 10c red 75.00 *75.00*
**N11** A19 12c deep ultra 165.00 140.00
**N12** A19 12c orange 165.00 150.00
**N12A** A19 15c orange 275.00 *275.00*
**N13** A19 15c deep blue 110.00 100.00
**N14** A19 20c dp rose & ol 60.00 *80.00*
**N15** A19 25c orange & vio 100.00 *80.00*
**N16** A19 30c violet & red brn 65.00 *80.00*
**N17** A19 50c red & violet 80.00 *80.00*
**N18** A19 $1 dk brown & red 100.00 *100.00*
**N19** A19 $2 violet & mag 200.00 *200.00*
**N19A** A19 $3 blue grn & rose *1,100.* *1,200.*
**N20** A19 $4 red & ultra 225.00 *260.00*
**N21** A19 $5 red brown & red 225.00 *260.00*
**N22** A19 $10 orange & blk 225.00 *260.00*
*Nos. N1-N22 (26)* *4,470.* *4,705.*

Stamps overprinted with Japanese characters in oval frame or between 2 vertical black lines were not for paying postage.

## SASENO

ˈsə-ˈzā-ˌnō

LOCATION — An island in the Adriatic Sea, lying at the entrance of Valona Bay, Albania.
GOVT. — Italian possession
AREA — 2 sq. mi.

Italy occupied this Albanian islet in 1914, and returned it to Albania in 1947.

100 Centesimi = 1 Lira

**Used values in italics are for postally used stamps. CTO's or stamps with fake cancels sell for about the same as unused, hinged stamps.**

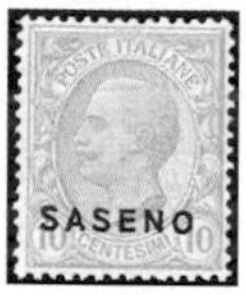
Italian Stamps of 1901-22 Overprinted

**1923** **Wmk. 140** ***Perf. 14***
**1** A48 10c claret 11.00 *20.00*
**2** A48 15c slate 11.00 *20.00*
**3** A50 20c brown orange 11.00 *20.00*
**4** A49 25c blue 11.00 *20.00*
**5** A49 30c yellow brown 11.00 *20.00*
**6** A49 50c violet 11.00 *20.00*
**7** A49 60c carmine 11.00 *20.00*
**8** A46 1 l brown & green 11.00 *20.00*
*a.* Double overprint 190.00
*Nos. 1-8 (8)* 88.00 *160.00*
Set, never hinged 200.00

Superseded by postage stamps of Italy.

## SAUDI ARABIA

ˈsau-dē ə-ˈrā-bē-ə

LOCATION — Southwestern Asia, on the Arabian Peninsula between the Red Sea and the Persian Gulf
GOVT. — Kingdom
AREA — 849,400 sq. mi.
POP. — 17,880,000 (1995 est.)
CAPITAL — Riyadh

In 1916 the Grand Sherif of Mecca declared the Sanjak of Hejaz independent of Turkish rule. In 1925, Ibn Saud, then Sultan of the Nejd, captured the Hejaz after a prolonged siege of Jedda, the last Hejaz stronghold.

The resulting Kingdom of the Hejaz and Nejd was renamed Saudi Arabia in 1932.

40 Paras = 1 Piaster = 1 Guerche (Garch, Qirsh)
11 Guerche = 1 Riyal (1928)
110 Guerche = 1 Sovereign (1931)
440 Guerche = 1 Sovereign (1952)
20 Piasters (Guerche) = 1 Riyal (1960)
100 Halalas = 1 Riyal (1976)

**Catalogue values for unused stamps in this country are for Never Hinged items, beginning with Scott 178 in the regular postage section, Scott C1 in the airpost section, Scott J28 in the postage due section, Scott O7 in official section, and Scott RA6 in the postal tax section.**

**Watermarks**

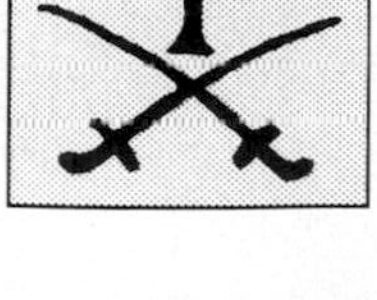
Wmk. 337 — Crossed Swords and Palm Tree

Watermark lines are thicker than the paper.

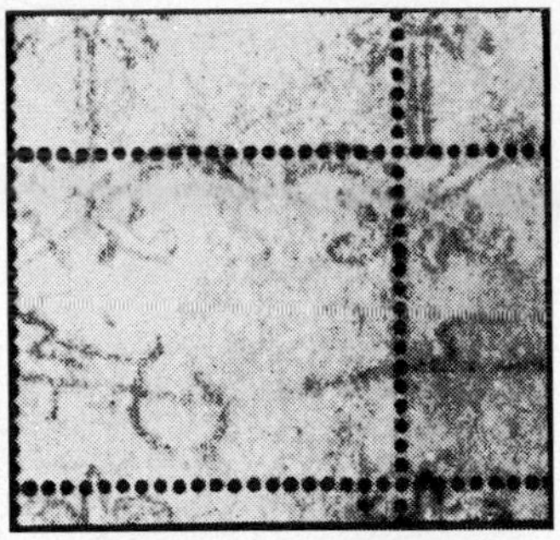

Wmk. 361 — Crossed Swords, Palm Tree and Arabic Inscription

## HEJAZ

### Sherifate of Mecca

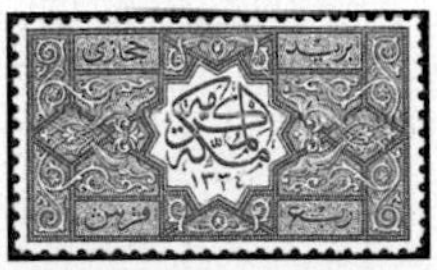

Adapted from Carved Door Panels of Mosque El Salih Talay, Cairo — A1

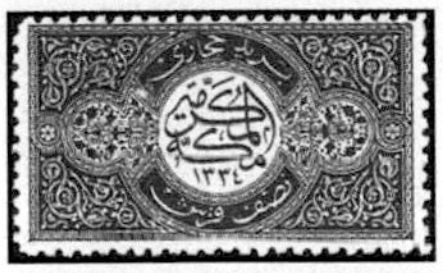

Taken from Page of Koran in Mosque of El Sultan Barquq, Cairo — A2

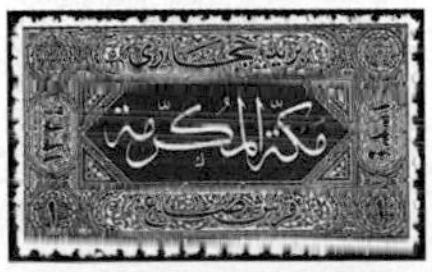

Taken from Details of an Ancient Prayer Niche in the Mosque of El Amri at Qus in Upper Egypt — A3

*Perf. 10, 12*

**1916, Oct.** **Unwmk.** **Typo.**

| | | | | |
|---|---|---|---|---|
| **L1** | A1 | ⅛pi green | 45.00 | 32.50 |
| **L2** | A2 | ¼pi red | 45.00 | 30.00 |
| *a.* | | Perf. 10 | 200.00 | 90.00 |
| **L3** | A3 | 1pi blue | 17.50 | 11.00 |
| *a.* | | Perf. 12 | 140.00 | 140.00 |
| *b.* | | Perf. 10x12 | | 775.00 |
| | | *Nos. L1-L3 (3)* | 107.50 | 73.50 |

Exist imperf. Forged perf. exist.

See Nos. L5-L7, L10-L12. For overprints see Nos. L16-L18, L26-L28, L52-L54, L57-L59, L61-L66, L67, L70-L72, L77-L81, 37.

Central Design Adapted from a Koran Design for a Tomb. Background is from Stone Carving on Entrance Arch to the Ministry of Wakfs — A4

**1916-17** ***Roulette 20***

| | | | | |
|---|---|---|---|---|
| **L4** | A4 | ⅛pi orange ('17) | 4.00 | 1.40 |
| **L5** | A1 | ¼pi green | 5.00 | 1.40 |
| **L6** | A2 | ½pi red | 8.00 | 1.40 |
| **L7** | A3 | 1pi blue | 8.50 | 1.40 |
| | | *Nos. L4-L7 (4)* | 25.50 | 5.60 |

See #L9. For overprints & surcharge see #L15a, L16c, L17b, L18d, L25, L51, L56, L69, 33.

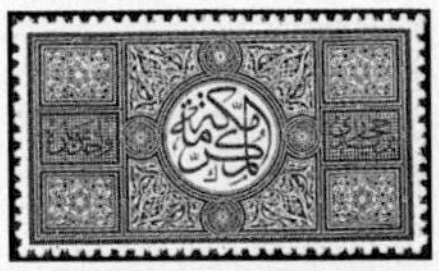

Adapted from Stucco Work above Entrance to Cairo R. R. Station A5

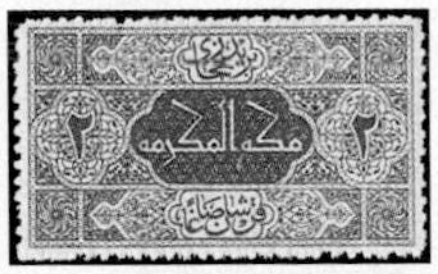

Adapted from First Page of the Koran of Sultan Farag — A6

**1917** ***Serrate Roulette 13***

| | | | | |
|---|---|---|---|---|
| **L8** | A5 | 1pa lilac brown | 3.25 | 1.40 |
| **L9** | A4 | ⅛pi orange | 3.75 | 1.40 |
| **L10** | A1 | ¼pi green | 4.25 | 1.40 |
| **L11** | A2 | ½pi red | 4.75 | 1.40 |
| **L12** | A3 | 1pi blue | 5.00 | 1.40 |
| **L13** | A6 | 2pi magenta | 20.00 | 9.00 |
| | | *Nos. L8-L13 (6)* | 41.00 | 16.00 |

Designs A1-A6 are inscribed "Hejaz Postage."

For overprints and surcharge see #L14-L31, L55-60, L62, L65--L75, L79a-81.

### Kingdom of the Hejaz

Stamps of 1917-18 Overprinted in Black, Red or Brown:

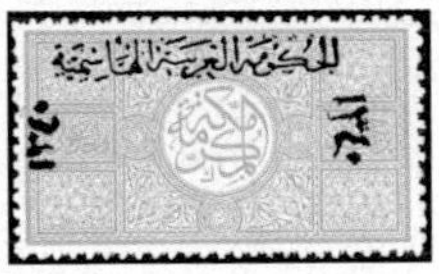

**1921, Dec. 21** ***Serrate Roulette 13***

| | | | | |
|---|---|---|---|---|
| **L14** | A5 | 1pa lilac brown | 30.00 | 14.00 |
| **L15** | A4 | ⅛pi orange | 57.50 | 16.00 |
| *a.* | | Inverted overprint | 90.00 | |
| *b.* | | Double overprint | 175.00 | |
| *c.* | | Roulette 20 | 650.00 | |
| *d.* | | As "c," invtd. overprint | 1,500. | *1,400.* |
| *e.* | | Double overprint, one inverted | 425.00 | |
| *f.* | | Double overprint, both inverted | 425.00 | |
| **L16** | A1 | ¼pi green | 12.50 | 5.50 |
| *a.* | | Inverted overprint | 90.00 | |
| *b.* | | Double overprint | 175.00 | |
| *c.* | | Roulette 20 | 650.00 | |
| *d.* | | As "c," invtd. overprint | 1,500. | |
| *e.* | | Double overprint, one inverted | 550.00 | |
| *f.* | | Double overprint, both inverted | 150.00 | |
| **L17** | A2 | ½pi red | 15.00 | 6.75 |
| *a.* | | Inverted overprint | 140.00 | 77.50 |
| *b.* | | Roulette 20 | 550.00 | |
| *c.* | | Double overprint | 425.00 | |
| *d* | | Double overprint, both inverted | 425.00 | |
| **L18** | A3 | 1pi blue (R) | 12.50 | 6.25 |
| *a.* | | Brown overprint | 25.00 | 18.00 |
| *b.* | | Black overprint | 32.50 | 27.50 |
| *c.* | | As "b," invtd. overprint | 350.00 | |
| *d.* | | Roulette 20 | 625.00 | |
| **L19** | A6 | 2pi magenta | 17.50 | 9.00 |
| *a.* | | Double overprint | — | |
| | | *Nos. L14-L19 (6)* | 145.00 | 57.50 |

Nos. L15-L17, L18b and L19 exist with date (1340) omitted at left or right side.

Some values exist with gold overprint.

Forgeries of Nos. L14-L23 abound.

No. L14 With Additional Surcharge:

a

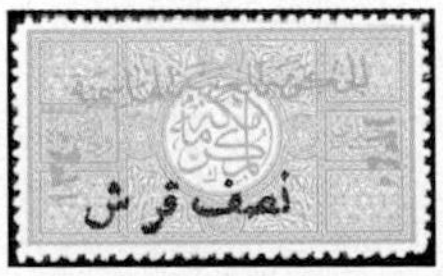

b

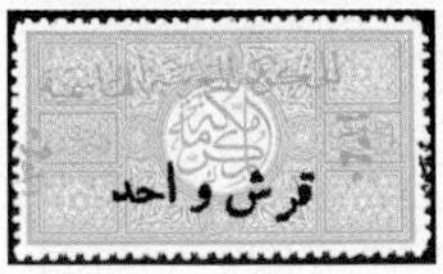

| | | | | |
|---|---|---|---|---|
| **L22** | A5(a) | ½pi on 1pa | 325.00 | 125.00 |
| **L23** | A5(b) | 1pi on 1pa | 325.00 | 125.00 |

Stamps of 1917-18 Overprinted in Black

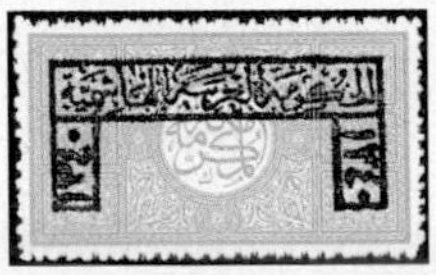

**1922, Jan. 7**

| | | | | |
|---|---|---|---|---|
| **L24** | A5 | 1pa lilac brown | 4.00 | 2.75 |
| *a.* | | Inverted overprint | 140.00 | |
| *b.* | | Double overprint | 90.00 | |
| *c.* | | Double ovpt., one inverted | 175.00 | |
| **L25** | A4 | ⅛pi orange | 10.00 | 6.25 |
| *a.* | | Inverted overprint | 90.00 | |
| *b.* | | Double ovpt., one inverted | 175.00 | |
| **L26** | A1 | ¼pi green | 4.50 | 2.75 |
| *a.* | | Inverted overprint | 90.00 | |
| *b.* | | Double ovpt., one inverted | 175.00 | |
| **L27** | A2 | ½pi red | 3.00 | 1.75 |
| *a.* | | Inverted overprint | 90.00 | |
| *b.* | | Double ovpt., one inverted | 175.00 | |
| **L28** | A3 | 1pi blue | 3.25 | .80 |
| *a.* | | Double overprint | 80.00 | |
| *b.* | | Inverted overprint | 140.00 | |
| **L29** | A6 | 2pi magenta | 7.50 | 5.50 |
| *a.* | | Double overprint | 140.00 | |

**With Additional Surcharge of New Value**

| | | | | |
|---|---|---|---|---|
| **L30** | A5(a) | ½pi on 1pa lil brn | 22.50 | 14.00 |
| **L31** | A5(b) | 1pi on 1pa lil brn | 3.00 | .90 |
| *a.* | | Inverted surcharge | 90.00 | |
| *b.* | | Double surcharge | 80.00 | |
| *c.* | | Dbl. surch., one invtd., ovpt. invtd. | | |
| *d.* | | Inverted overprint | 75.00 | |
| *e.* | | Inverted overprint and surcharge | 210.00 | |
| *f.* | | Inverted overprint, double surcharge | 210.00 | |
| *g.* | | Words of surcharge transposed | 200.00 | |
| *h.* | | Overprint and surcharge inverted, words of surcharge transposed | 400.00 | |
| *i.* | | Right hand character of surcharge inverted | 75.00 | |
| | | *Nos. L24-L31 (8)* | 57.75 | 34.70 |

The 1921 and 1922 overprints read: "The Government of Hashemite Arabia, 1340."

The overprint on No. L28 in red is bogus.

Forgeries abound.

Types A7 and A8

Very fine examples will be somewhat off center but perforations will be clear of the framelines.

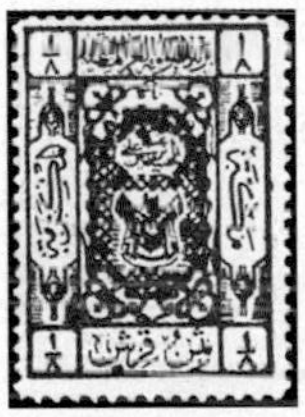

Arms of Sherif of Mecca — A7

**1922, Feb.** **Typo.** ***Perf. 11½***

| | | | | |
|---|---|---|---|---|
| **L32** | A7 | ⅛pi red brown | 2.25 | .45 |
| **L34** | A7 | ½pi red | 2.50 | .45 |
| **L35** | A7 | 1pi dark blue | 2.75 | .45 |
| **L36** | A7 | 1½pi violet | 3.00 | .45 |
| **L37** | A7 | 2pi orange | 4.00 | .45 |
| **L38** | A7 | 3pi olive brown | 3.25 | .45 |
| **L39** | A7 | 5pi olive green | 3.50 | .55 |
| | | *Nos. L32-L39 (7)* | 21.25 | 3.25 |

Numerous shades exist. Some values were printed in other colors in 1925 for handstamping by the Nejdi authorities in Mecca. These exist without handstamps.

Exist imperf.

Forgeries exist, usually perf. 11.

*Reprints of Nos. L32, L35 exist; paper and shades differ.*

See Nos. L48A-L49. For surcharges and overprints see Nos. L40-L48, L76, L82-L159, 7-20, 38A-48, 55A-58A, LJ11-LJ16, LJ26-LJ39, J1-J8, J10-J11, P1-P3, Jordan 64-72, 91, 103-120, J1-J17, O1.

Stamps of 1922 Surcharged with New Values in Arabic:

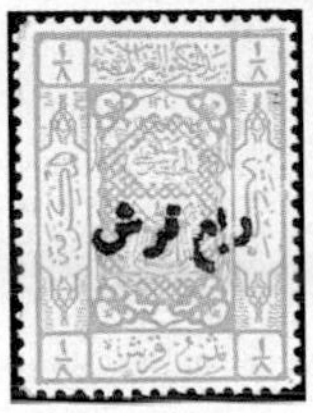

c

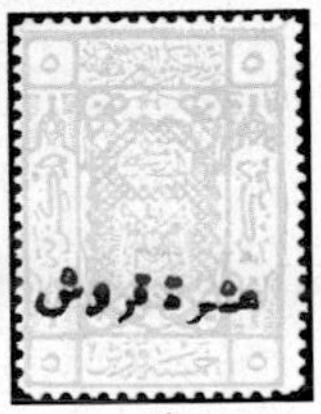

d

**1923**

| | | | | |
|---|---|---|---|---|
| **L40** | A7(c) | ¼pi on ⅛pi org brn | 35.00 | 32.50 |
| *a.* | | Double surcharge | | |
| *b.* | | Double inverted surcharge | | |
| *c.* | | Double surch., one invtd. | | |
| **L41** | A7(d) | 10pi on 5pi ol grn | 30.00 | 27.50 |
| *a.* | | Double surch., one invtd. | | |
| *b.* | | Inverted surcharge | | |

Forgeries exist.

**Caliphate Issue**

Stamps of 1922 Overprinted in Gold

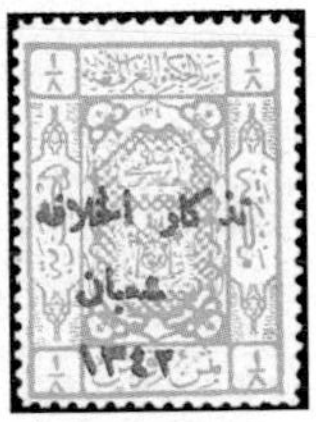

**1924**

| | | | |
|---|---|---|---|
| **L42** | A7 | ⅛pi orange brown | 4.75 |
| **L43** | A7 | ½pi red | 3.50 |
| **L44** | A7 | 1pi dark blue | 5.00 |
| *a.* | | Inverted overprint | 200.00 |
| **L45** | A7 | 1½pi violet | 4.75 |
| **L46** | A7 | 2pi orange | 4.50 |
| *a.* | | Inverted overprint | 200.00 |
| **L47** | A7 | 3pi olive brown | 5.00 |

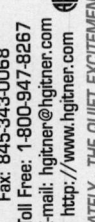

**L48** A7 5pi olive green 5.50
*a.* Inverted overprint 200.00
*Nos. L42-L48 (7)* 33.00

Assumption of the Caliphate by King Hussein in Mar., 1924. The overprint reads "In commemoration of the Caliphate, Shaaban, 1342."

The overprint was typographed in black and dusted with "gold" powder while wet. Inverted overprints on other values are forgeries. So-called black overprints are either forgeries or gold overprints with the gold rubbed off. No genuine black overprints are known.

The overprint is 18-20mm wide. The 1st setting of the ½p is 16mm.

Forgeries exist.

Nos. L43-L44, L46 exist with postage due overprint as on Nos. LJ11-LJ13.

Type of 1922 and

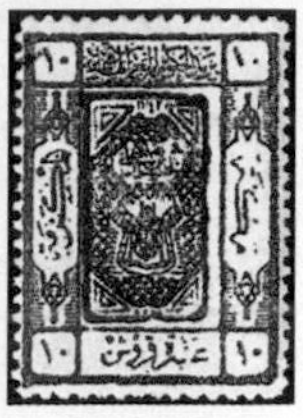

Arms of Sherif of Mecca — A8

**1924** ***Perf. 11½***

**L48A** A7 ¼pi yellow green 4.50 5.75
*b.* Tête bêche pair 27.50
**L49** A7 3pi brown red 10.00 9.00
*a.* 3pi dull red 3.00 4.50
**L50** A8 10pi vio & dk brn 5.00 4.50
*a.* Center inverted 55.00 55.00
*b.* Center omitted 67.50
*c.* 10pi purple & sepia 3.00 4.50
*Nos. L48A-L50 (3)* 19.50 19.25

Nos. L48A, L50, L50a exist imperf.

Several printings of Nos. L48A-L50 exist; paper and shades differ.

Forgeries exist, usually perf. 11.

For overprint see Nos. L76A, Jordan 121.

### Jedda Issues

Stamps of 1916-17 Overprinted

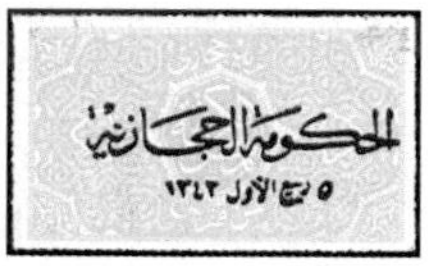

The control overprints on Nos. L51-L159 read: "Hukumat al Hejaziyeh, 5 Rabi al'awwal 1343"

(The Hejaz Government, October 4, 1924). This is the date of the accession of King Ali.

Counterfeits exist of all Jedda overprints.

Jedda issues were also used in Medina and Yambo.

**Used values for #L51-L186 and LJ17-LJ39 are for genuine cancels. Privately applied cancels exist for "Mekke" (Mecca, bilingual or all Arabic), Khartoum, Cairo, as well as for Jeddah. Many private cancels have wrong dates, some as early as 1916. These are worth half the used values.**

#### Red Overprint

**1925, Jan.** ***Roulette 20***

**L51** A4 ⅛pi orange 17.50 14.00
*a.* Inverted overprint 90.00
*b.* Ovptd. on face and back 175.00
*c.* Normal ovpt. on face, double ovpt. on back 200.00
**L52** A1 ¼pi green 17.50 14.00
*a.* Inverted overprint 60.00
*b.* Double overprint 55.00
*c.* Double overprint, one invtd. 140.00
**L53** A2 ½pi red 70.00 67.50
*a.* Inverted overprint 150.00
**L54** A3 1pi blue 35.00 32.50
*a.* Inverted overprint 140.00
*b.* Double ovpt., one invtd. 125.00
*Nos. L51-L53 (3)* 105.00 95.50

***Serrate Roulette 13***

**L55** A5 1pa lilac brown 15.00 12.50
*a.* Inverted overprint 67.50
*b.* Double overprint 60.00
*c.* Ovptd. on face and back 175.00
*d.* Normal ovpt. on face, double ovpt. on back 125.00
**L56** A4 ⅛pi orange 37.50 35.00
*a.* Inverted overprint 80.00
**L57** A1 ¼pi green 22.50 20.00
*a.* Pair, one without overprint 1,600.
*b.* Inverted overprint 45.00
*c.* Double ovpt., one inverted 275.00
**L58** A2 ½pi red 30.00 27.50
*a.* Inverted overprint 140.00
**L59** A3 1pi blue 35.00 32.50
*a.* Inverted overprint 100.00
**L60** A6 2pi magenta 40.00 35.00
*a.* Inverted overprint 140.00
*Nos. L55-L60 (6)* 180.00 162.50

#### Gold Overprint

***Roulette 20***

**L61** A1 ¼pi green, gold on red ovpt. 3,000.
*a.* Gold on blue ovpt. 3,750. 7,000.

***Serrate Roulette 13***

**L62** A1 ¼pi green, gold on red ovpt. 25.00 22.50
*a.* Inverted overprint 100.00

The overprint on No. L61 was typographed in red or blue (No. L62 only in red) and dusted with "gold" powder while wet.

#### Blue Overprint

***Roulette 20***

**L63** A1 ¼pi green 80.00 22.50
*a.* Inverted overprint 150.00
*b.* Ovptd. on face and back 175.00
**L64** A2 ½pi red, invtd. ovpt. 90.00 80.00
*a.* Upright overprint 140.00

***Serrate Roulette 13***

**L65** A1 ¼pi green 17.50 16.00
*a.* Inverted overprint 67.50
*b.* Vertical overprint 900.00
**L66** A2 ½pi red 30.00 27.50
*a.* Inverted overprint 90.00
**L66B** A6 2pi mag, invtd. ovpt. 1,400.

Blue overprint on Nos. L4, L8, L9 are bogus.

#### Same Overprint in Blue on Provisional Stamps of 1922 Overprinted on No. L17

**L67** A2 ½pi red 2,500.

#### Overprinted on Nos. L24-L29

**L68** A5 1pa lilac brn 175.00 160.00
**L69** A4 ⅛pi orange 2,500. 1,800.
*a.* Inverted overprint
**L70** A1 ¼pi green 70.00 65.00
*a.* Inverted overprint 725.00
**L71** A2 ½pi red 90.00 85.00
*a.* Inverted overprint 800.00
**L72** A3 1pi blue 110.00 110.00
**L73** A6 2pi magenta 160.00 160.00
*a.* Inverted overprint 1,400.

#### Same Overprint on Nos. L30 and L31

**L74** A5(a) ½pi on 1pa 95.00 90.00
**L75** A5(b) 1pi on 1pa 80.00 75.00
*a.* Inverted overprint 575.00

#### Same Overprint in Blue Vertically, Reading Up or Down, on Stamps of 1922-24

***Perf. 11½***

**L76** A7 ½pi red 900.00 900.00
**L76A** A8 10pi vio & dk brn 1,800. 1,800.

Nos. L5, L10 Overprinted Reading Up in Blue or Red (Overprint reads up in illustration)

***Roulette 20***

*L77a* A1 ¼pi green (Bl) 500.00 500.00
**L78** A1 ¼pi green (R) 450.00 450.00

***Serrate Roulette 13***

*L79a* A1 ¼pi green (Bl) 300.00 300.00
**L80** A1 ¼pi green (R) 60.00 60.00

#### Overprint Reading Down

***Roulette 20***

**L77** A1 ¼pi green (Bl) 175.00 175.00

***Serrate Roulette 13***

**L79** A1 ¼pi green (Bl) 90.00 90.00
*L80a* A1 ¼pi green (R) 200.00 200.00

Nos. L10, L32-L39, L48A, L49a, L50 Overprinted

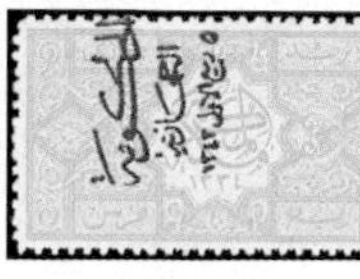

***Serrate Roulette 13***

#### Red Overprint (vertical)

**L81** A1 ¼pi green 1,200.

Overprint on No. L81 also exists horizontal and inverted.

***Perf. 11½***

#### Blue Overprint

**L82** A7 ⅛pi red brown 7.00 5.50
*a.* Inverted overprint 45.00
**L83** A7 ½pi red 8.50 7.25
*a.* Double overprint 67.50
*b.* Inverted overprint 45.00 45.00
*c.* Double ovpt., one invtd. 67.50
*d.* Overprint reading up
**L84** A7 1pi dark blue 350.00
*a.* Inverted overprint 350.00
**L85** A7 1½pi violet 12.50 11.00
*a.* Inverted overprint 45.00 45.00
**L86** A7 2pi orange 12.50 11.00
*a.* Double ovpt., one invtd. 67.50
*b.* Inverted overprint 45.00
*c.* Double overprint 67.50
**L87** A7 3pi olive brown 10.00 9.00
*a.* Inverted overprint 45.00
*b.* Double ovpt., one invtd. 67.50
*c.* Overprint reading up 160.00
*d.* Dbl. ovpt., both invtd. 90.00
**L88** A7 3pi dull red 12.50 11.00
*a.* Inverted overprint 45.00
*b.* Double ovpt., one invtd. 67.50
**L89** A7 5pi olive green 13.00 11.00
*a.* Inverted overprint 45.00

Some values exist in pairs, one without overprint.

#### Black Overprint

**L90** A7 ⅛pi red brown 50.00
*a.* Inverted overprint 140.00
**L91** A7 ½pi red 6.00 4.50
*a.* Inverted overprint 60.00
**L92** A7 1pi dark blue 350.00
*a.* Inverted overprint 350.00
**L93** A7 1½pi violet 15.00 12.00
*a.* Inverted overprint 67.50
**L94** A7 2pi orange 9.00 7.25
*a.* Inverted overprint 45.00
**L95** A7 3pi olive brown 7.00 5.50
*a.* Inverted overprint 67.50 67.50
**L96** A7 3pi dull red 9.00 7.25
*a.* Inverted overprint 45.00
**L97** A7 5pi olive green 11.00 9.00
*a.* Inverted overprint 45.00

#### Red Overprint

**L98** A7 ⅛pi red brn, invtd. 725.00
**L99** A7 ¼pi yellow grn 20.00 16.00
*a.* Tête bêche pair 62.50
*b.* Inverted overprint 45.00
*c.* Tête bêche pair, one with inverted overprint 75.00
**L100** A7 ½pi red 1,000. 500.00
*a.* Inverted overprint 1,000. 500.00
**L101** A7 1pi dark blue 10.00 8.00
*a.* Inverted overprint 45.00
*b.* Double ovpt., one invtd. 32.50
**L102** A7 1½pi violet 6.00 4.50
*a.* Inverted overprint 45.00
**L103** A7 2pi orange 15.00 12.00
*a.* Inverted overprint 45.00
*b.* Overprint reading up 160.00
**L104** A7 3pi olive brown 15.00 12.00
*a.* Inverted overprint 45.00
**L105** A7 3pi dull red, invtd. 1,500.
**L106** A7 5pi olive green 10.00 7.25
*a.* Inverted overprint 45.00
*b.* Overprint reading up
*c.* Overprint reading down
**L107** A8 10pi vio & dk brn 20.00 16.00
*a.* Inverted overprint 45.00
*b.* Center inverted 90.00
*c.* As "b," invtd. ovpt. 140.00

Nos. L98, L105 with normal overprint are fakes.

#### Gold Overprint

**L108** A7 ⅛pi red brown 30.00 27.50
**L109** A7 ½pi red 30.00 27.50
**L110** A7 1pi dark blue 35.00 27.50
**L111** A7 1½pi violet 110.00 110.00
**L112** A7 2pi orange 100.00 90.00
**L113** A7 3pi olive brown 40.00 35.00
**L114** A7 3pi dull red 120.00 100.00
**L115** A7 5pi olive green 95.00 85.00
*Nos. L108-L115 (8)* 560.00 502.50

Inverted overprints are forgeries.

#### Same Overprint on Nos. L42-L48

#### Blue Overprint

**L116** A7 ⅛pi red brown 45.00 42.50
*a.* Double ovpt., one invtd. 275.00
**L117** A7 ½pi red 85.00 80.00
**L118** A7 1pi dark blue 70.00 55.00
**L119** A7 1½pi violet 75.00 65.00
**L120** A7 2pi orange 275.00 275.00
*a.* Inverted overprint 425.00
**L121** A7 3pi olive brown 110.00 110.00
*a.* Inverted overprint 175.00
**L122** A7 5pi olive green 40.00 37.50
*a.* Inverted overprint 200.00
*Nos. L116-L122 (7)* 700.00 665.00

#### Black Overprint

**L123** A7 ⅛pi red brown 45.00 42.50
*a.* Inverted overprint 225.00
**L125** A7 1½pi violet 140.00 140.00
*a.* Inverted overprint 225.00
**L127** A7 3pi olive brown 110.00 110.00
*a.* Inverted overprint 225.00
**L128** A7 5pi olive green 140.00 140.00
*a.* Inverted overprint 225.00
*Nos. L123-L128 (4)* 435.00 432.50

#### Red Overprint

**L129** A7 1pi dark blue 100.00 90.00
**L130** A7 1½pi violet 110.00 110.00
**L131** A7 2pi orange 110.00 90.00
*Nos. L129-L131 (3)* 320.00 290.00

Overprints on stamps or in colors other than those listed are forgeries.

Stamps of 1922-24 Surcharged

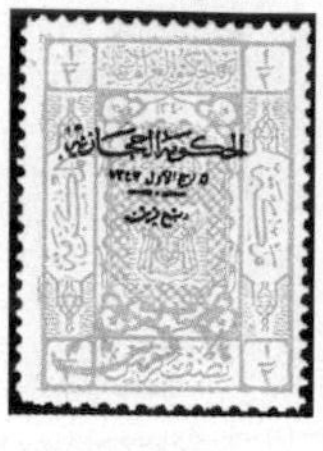

a

and Handstamp Surcharged

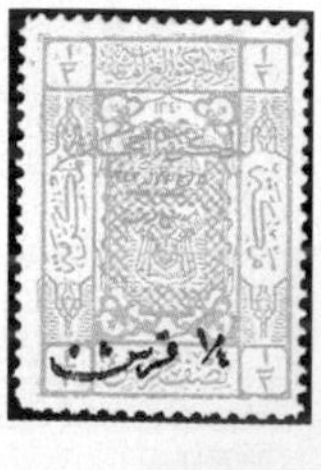

b — 1/4pi

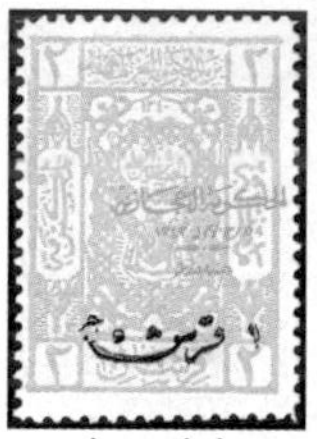

b — 1pi

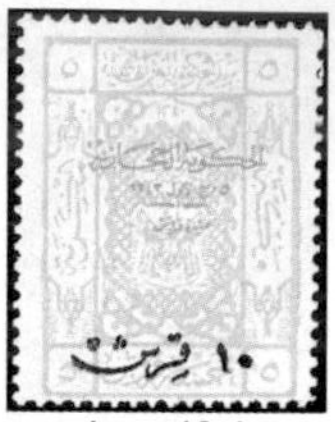

b — 10pi

**1925** **Litho.** ***Perf. 11½***

**L135** A7 ¼pi on ¼pi on ⅛pi red brn 50.00 47.50
*b.* 1pi on ¼pi on ⅛pi red brown
**L136** A7 ¼pi on ¼pi on ½pi red 35.00 30.00
*c.* 1pi on ¼pi on ½pi 55.00 55.00
**L138** A7 1pi on 1pi on 2pi orange 35.00 30.00
*a.* ¼pi on ¼pi on 2pi org 90.00
*b.* 10pi on 1pi on 2pi org 90.00
*c.* ¼pi on 1pi on 2pi org 45.00
*d.* 1pi on ¼pi on 2pi org 90.00
**L139** A7 1pi on 1pi on 3pi ol brn 25.00 22.50
**L140** A7 1pi on 1pi on 3pi dl red 40.00 35.00
*b.* ¼pi on 1pi on 3pi dl red
**L141** A7 10pi on 10pi on 5pi ol grn 20.00 16.00
*b.* 1pi on 10 pi on 5 pi
*Nos. L135-L141 (6)* 205.00 181.00

The printed surcharge (a) reads "The Hejaz Government. October 4, 1924." with new denomination in third line. This surcharge alone was used for the first issue (Nos. L135a-L141a). The new denomination was so small and indistinct that its equivalent in larger characters was soon added by handstamp (b) at bottom of each stamp for the second issue (Nos. L135-L141).

The handstamped surcharge (b) is found double, inverted, etc. It is also known in dark violet.

#### Without Handstamp "b"

*L135a* A7 ¼pi on ⅛pi red brn 90.00
*L136b* A7 ¼pi on ½pi red 90.00
*L138e* A7 1pi on 2pi orange 90.00
*L139a* A7 1pi on 3pi olive brn 90.00
*L140a* A7 1pi on 3pi dull red 90.00
*L141a* A7 10pi on 5pi olive grn 90.00
*Nos. L135a-L141a (6)* 540.00

Stamps of 1922-24 Surcharged

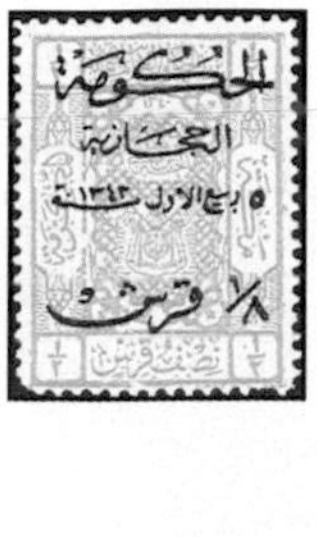

**Black Surcharge**

L142 A7 ⅛pi on ½pi red 9.00 7.25
a. Inverted surcharge 35.00
L143 A7 ¼pi on ½pi red 9.50 7.25
a. Inverted surcharge 35.00
L144 A7 1pi on ½pi red 10.50 7.25
a. Inverted surcharge 22.50
L145 A7 1pi on 1½pi vio 11.00 7.25
a. Inverted surcharge 32.50
L146 A7 1pi on 2pi org 9.00 7.25
a. "10pi" 77.50
b. Inverted surcharge 35.00
c. As "a," inverted surcharge 130.00
L147 A7 1pi on 3pi olive brn 10.00 7.25
a. "10pi" 67.50
b. Inverted surcharge 45.00
c. As "a," inverted surcharge 130.00
L148 A7 10pi on 5pi olive grn 17.50 14.00
a. Inverted surcharge 60.00
*Nos. L142-L148 (7)* 76.50 57.50

**Blue Surcharge**

L149 A7 ⅛pi on ½pi red 15.00 11.00
a. Inverted surcharge 60.00
b. Double surcharge 200.00
L150 A7 ¼pi on ½pi red 12.50 11.00
a. Inverted surcharge 45.00
L151 A7 1pi on ½pi red 12.50 11.00
a. Inverted surcharge 45.00
b. Double surcharge
L152 A7 1pi on 1½pi vio 15.00 11.00
a. Inverted surcharge 60.00
L153 A7 1pi on 2pi org 15.00 11.00
a. "10pi" 62.50
b. Inverted surcharge 60.00
L154 A7 1pi on 3pi olive brn 25.00 22.50
a. "10pi" 77.50
b. Inverted surcharge 62.50
L155 A7 10pi on 5pi olive grn 30.00 25.00
a. Inverted surcharge 55.00
*Nos. L149-L155 (7)* 125.00 102.50

**Red Surcharge**

L156 A7 1pi on 1½pi vio 25.00 22.50
a. Inverted surcharge 72.50
L157 A7 1pi on 2pi org 27.50 22.50
a. "10pi" 72.50
b. Inverted surcharge 72.50
L158 A7 1pi on 3pi olive brn 30.00 22.50
a. "10pi" 90.00
b. Inverted surcharge 72.50
L159 A7 10pi on 5pi olive grn 30.00 22.50
a. Inverted surcharge 72.50
*Nos. L156-L159 (4)* 112.50 90.00
*Nos. L142-L159 (18)* 314.00 250.00

The "10pi" surcharge is found inverted on Nos. L146a, L147a. The existence of genuine inverted "10pi" surcharges on Nos. L153a, L154a, L157a and L158a is in doubt.
The 10pi on 1½pi is bogus.

**King Ali Issue**

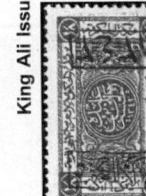

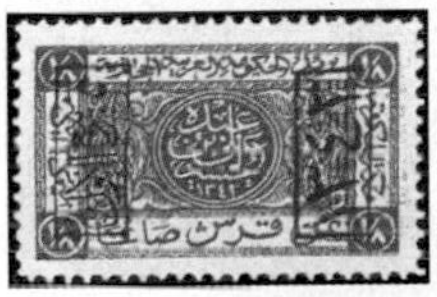
A9

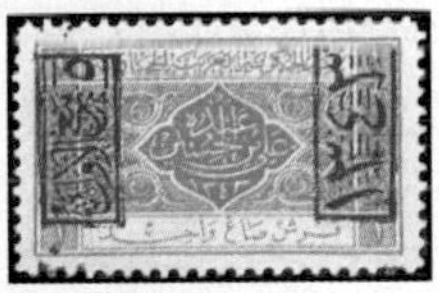
A10

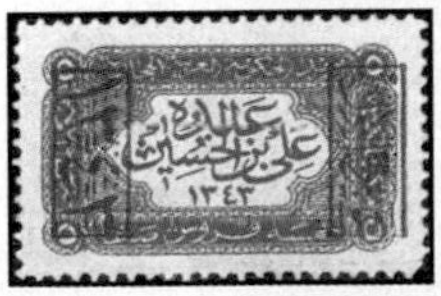
A11

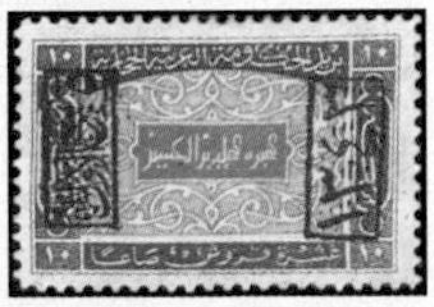
A12

**1925, May-June** *Perf. 11½*

**Black Overprint**

L160 A9 ⅛pi chocolate 2.00 1.50
L161 A9 ¼pi ultra 2.00 1.50
L162 A9 ½pi car rose 2.00 1.50
L163 A10 1pi yellow green 2.50 1.75
L164 A10 1½pi orange 2.50 1.75
L165 A10 2pi blue 3.00 2.25
L166 A11 3pi dark green 3.00 2.25
L167 A11 5pi orange brn 3.00 2.25
L168 A12 10pi red & green 5.00 4.50
a. Center inverted 67.50
*Nos. L160-L168 (9)* 25.00 19.25

**Red Overprint**

L169 A9 ⅛pi chocolate 3.50 2.75
L170 A9 ¼pi ultra 2.00 1.60
L171 A10 1pi yellow green 2.50 2.00
L172 A10 1½pi orange 2.50 2.00
L173 A10 2pi deep blue 3.00 2.50
L174 A11 3pi dark green 3.25 2.75
a. Horiz. pair, imperf. vert.
L175 A11 5pi org brn 3.50 2.75
L176 A12 10pi red & green 6.00 5.50
*Nos. L169-L176 (8)* 26.25 21.85

**Blue Overprint**

L177 A9 ⅛pi chocolate 2.25 1.75
L179 A9 ½pi car rose 2.25 1.75
L180 A10 1pi yellow green 2.25 1.75
L181 A10 1½pi orange 2.25 1.75
L182 A11 3pi dark green 2.25 1.75
L183 A11 5pi orange brn 6.25 5.50
L184 A12 10pi red & green 8.00 7.25
L185 A12 10pi red & org 275.00
*Nos. L177-L184 (7)* 25.50 21.50

**Without Overprint**

L186 A12 10pi red & green 7.50 6.75
a. Dbl. impression of center 90.00

The overprint in the tablets on Nos. L160-L185 reads: "5 Rabi al'awwal, 1343" (Oct. 5, 1924), the date of the accession of King Ali.
The tablet overprints vary slightly in size. Each is found reading upward or downward and at either side of the stamp. These control overprints were first applied in Jedda by the government press.
They were later made from new plates by the stamp printer in Cairo. In the Jedda overprint, the bar over the "0" figure extends to the left.

Some values exist with 13m or 15mm instead of 18mm between tablets. They sell for more. The lines of the Cairo overprinting are generally wider, but more lightly printed, usually appearing slightly grayish and the bar is at center right. The Cairo overprints are believed not to have been placed in use.
Imperforates exist.
Nos. L160-L168 are known with the overprints spaced as on type D3 and aligned horizontally.

Copies of those stamps (perforated or imperforate) without the overprint, except No. L186 were not regularly issued and not available for postage.
No. L185 exists only with Cairo overprint. Imperfs of No. L105 sell for much less than No. L185. Fake perfs have been added to the imperfs.
The ¼pi with blue overprint is bogus.
No. L186 in other colors are color trials.
For overprints see #58B-58D, Jordan 122-129.

## NEJDI ADMINISTRATION OF HEJAZ

Handstamped in Blue, Red, Black or Violet

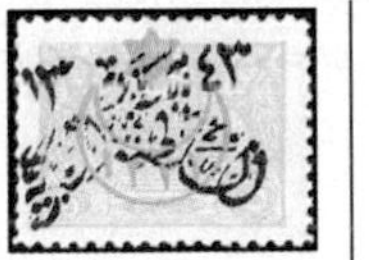

The overprint reads: "1343. Barid al Sultanat an Nejdia" (1925. Post of the Sultanate of Nejd).
The overprints on this and succeeding issues are handstamped and, as usual, are found double, inverted, etc. These variations are scarce.

**1925, Mar.-Apr. Unwmk.** *Perf. 12*

**On Stamp of Turkey, 1915, With Crescent and Star in Red**

1 A22 5pa ocher (Bl) 40.00 27.50
2 A22 5pa ocher (R) 25.00 20.00
3 A22 5pa ocher (Bk) 30.00 22.50
4 A22 5pa ocher (V) 25.00 18.00

**On Stamp of Turkey, 1913**

5 A28 10pa green (Bl) 22.50 16.00
6 A28 10pa green (R) 18.00 12.50

**On Stamps of Hejaz, 1922-24**
*Perf. 11½*

7 A7 ⅛pi red brn (R) 24.00 24.00
8 A7 ⅛pi red brn (Bk) 35.00 35.00
9 A7 ⅛pi red brn (V) 24.00 24.00
10 A7 ⅛pi car (R) 30.00 30.00
11 A7 ⅛pi car (Bk) 35.00 35.00
12 A7 ⅛pi car (V) 27.50 27.50
13 A7 ½pi red (Bl) 22.50 22.50
14 A7 ½pi red (V) 18.00 18.00
15 A7 1½pi vio (R) 24.00 24.00
16 A7 2pi yel buff (R) 57.50 57.50
a. 2pi orange (R) 35.00
17 A7 2pi yel buff (V) 57.50 57.50
a. 2pi orange (V) 32.50 32.50
18 A7 3pi brn red (Bl) 30.00 30.00
19 A7 3pi brn red (R) 22.50 22.50
20 A7 3pi brn red (V) 25.00 25.00

Many Hejaz stamps of the 1922 type were especially printed for this and following issues. The re-impressions are usually more clearly printed, in lighter shades than the 1922 stamps, and some are in new colors.
Counterfeits exist.

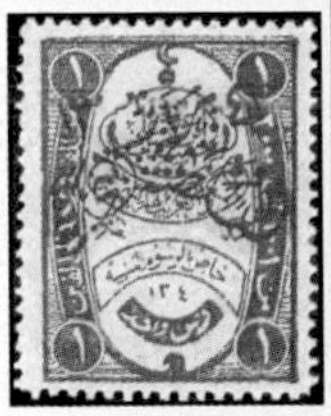
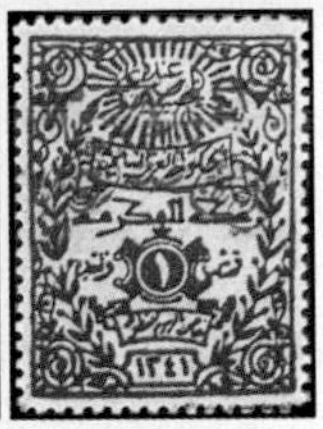
Arabic Inscriptions
R1 R2

**On Hejaz Bill Stamp**

22 R1 1pi violet (R) 15.00 15.00

**On Hejaz Notarial Stamps**

23 R2 1pi violet (R) 20.00 20.00
24 R2 2pi blue (R) 30.00 30.00
25 R2 2pi blue (V) 27.50 27.50

For overprint see No. 49.

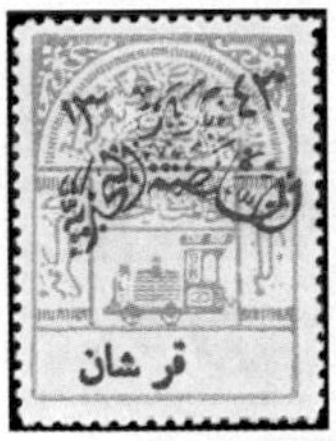
Locomotive — R3

**On Hejaz Railway Tax Stamps**

26 R3 1pi blue (R) 37.50 9.00
27 R3 2pi ocher (R) 45.00 14.00
28 R3 2pi ocher (V) 37.50 14.00
29 R3 3pi lilac (R) 40.00 20.00
*Nos. 1-20,22-29 (28)* 845.50 698.50

There are two types of the basic stamps. The difference is in the locomotive.
For overprints and surcharges see Nos. 34, 50-54, 55, 59-68, J12-J15.

**Pilgrimage Issue**

Various Stamps Handstamp Surcharged in Blue and Red in Types "a" and "b" and with Tablets with New Values

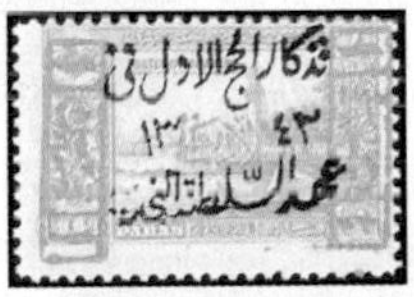
a

b

Surcharge "a" reads: "Tezkar al Hajj al Awwal Fi 'ahd al Sultanat al Nejdia, 1343" (Commemorating the first pilgrimage under the Nejdi Sultanate, 1925).
"b" reads: "Al Arba" (Wednesday.)

**1925, July 1** *Perf. 12*

**On Stamps of Turkey, 1913**

30 A28 1pi on 10pa grn (Bl & R) 75.00 55.00
31 A30 5pi on 1pi bl (Bl & R) 75.00 55.00

**On Stamps of Hejaz, 1917-18**
***Serrate Roulette 13***

32 A5 2pi on 1pa lil brn (R & Bl) 95.00 67.50
33 A4 4pi on ⅛pi org (R & Bl) 350.00 350.00

**On Hejaz Railway Tax Stamp**
***Perf. 11½***

34 R3 3pi lilac (Bl & R) 125.00 40.00
*Nos. 30-34 (5)* 720.00 567.50

No. 30 with handstamp "a" in black was a favor item. Nos. 30 and 33 with both handstamps in red is a forgery.

Handstamped in Blue, Red, Black or Violet

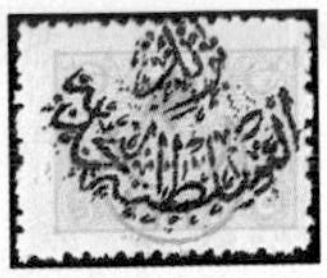

This overprint has practically the same meaning as that described over No. 1. The Mohammedan year (1343) is omitted.
**This handstamp is said to be in private hands at this time. Extreme caution is advised before buying rare items.**

**1925, July-Aug.** *Perf. 12*

**On Stamp of Turkey, 1915, with Crescent and Star in Red**

35 A22 5pa ocher (Bl) 24.00 24.00

**On Stamps of Turkey, 1913**

36 A28 10pa green (Bl) 20.00 20.00
a. Black overprint 85.00

**On Stamps of Hejaz, 1922 (Nos. L28-L29)**
***Serrate Roulette 13***

37 A3 1pi blue (R) 60.00 67.50
38 A6 2pi magenta (Bl) 60.00 67.50

**On Stamps of Hejaz, 1922-24**
***Perf. 11½***

38A A7 ⅛pi red brn (Bk) 4,250.
38B A7 ⅛pi red brn (Bl) 3,500.
39 A7 ½pi red (Bl) 10.00 10.00
a. Imperf., pair 22.50 22.50
39B A7 ½pi red (Bk) 18.00 18.00
c. Imperf., pair 37.50 37.50
40 A7 1pi gray vio (R) 29.00 29.00
a. 1pi black violet (R) 40.00
41 A7 1½pi dk red (Bk) 30.00 30.00
a. 1½pi brick red (Bk) 45.00
42 A7 2pi yel buff (Bl) 47.50 47.50
a. 2pi orange (Bl) 55.00 55.00
43 A7 2pi deep vio (Bl) 52.50 52.50
44 A7 3pi brown red (Bl) 30.00 30.00
45 A7 5pi scarlet (Bl) 37.50 37.50
*Nos. 35-38,39-45 (12)* 418.50 433.50

Overprint on Nos. 38A, 39B, 39C is blue-black.
**See note above No. 35.**

With Additional Surcharge of New Value Typo. in Black:

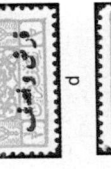

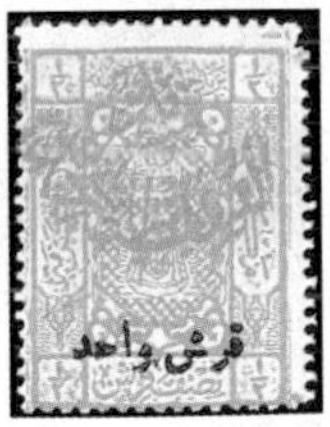
c

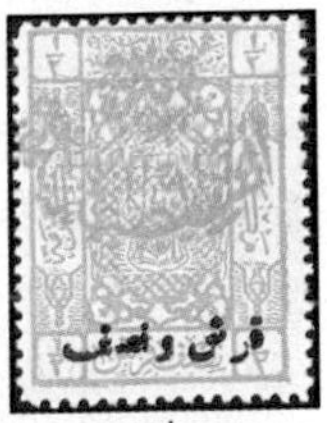
d

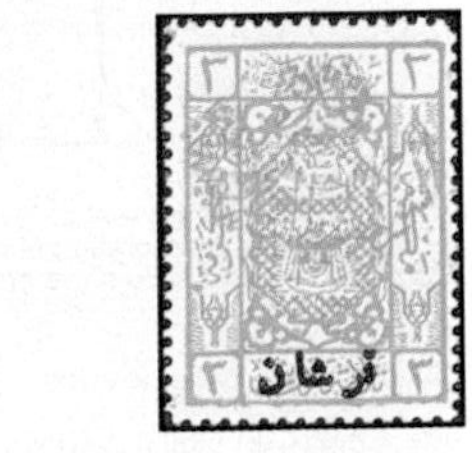
e

Color in parenthesis is that of overprint on basic stamp.

46 A7(c) 1pi on ½pi (Bl) 10.00 1.75
a. Imperf, pair 27.50
b. Ovpt. & surch. inverted
47 A7(d) 1½pi on ½pi (Bl) 15.00 7.25
a. Imperf., pair 27.50
b. Black overprint 18.00
48 A7(e) 2pi on 3pi (Bl) 16.00 16.00
*Nos. 46-48 (3)* 41.00 25.00

Several variations in type settings of "c," "d" and "e" exist, including inverted letters and values.

**On Hejaz Notarial Stamp**

49 R2 2pi blue (Bk) 20.00 20.00

**On Hejaz Railway Tax Stamps**

**50** R3 1pi blue (R) 25.00 25.00
**51** R3 1pi blue (Bk) 30.00 9.00
**52** R3 2pi ocher (Bl) 27.50 9.00
**53** R3 3pi lilac (Bl) 22.50 22.50
**54** R3 5pi green (Bl) 20.00 20.00
*Nos. 49-54 (6)* 145.00 105.50

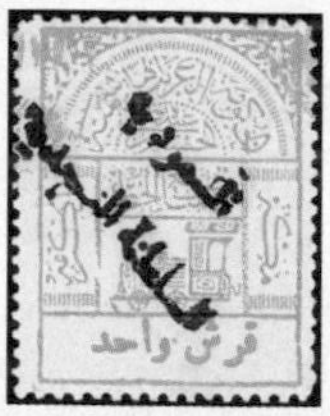

Hejaz Railway Tax Stamp Handstamped in Black

This overprint reads: "Al Saudia. — Al Sultanat al Nejdia." (The Saudi Sultanate of Nejd.)

**1925-26**
**55** R3 1pi blue — 175.00

**On Nos. L34, L36-L37, L41**

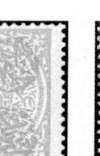

**55A** A7 ½ pi red — 325.00
**56** A7 1½pi violet — 350.00
*a.* Violet overprint — 325.00
**57** A7 2pi orange — 350.00
**57A** A7 10pi on 5pi ol grn — 325.00

**On Nos. L95 and L97**

**Color in parentheses is that of rectangular overprint on basic stamp**

**58** A7 3pi olive brn (Bk) — 350.00
**58A** A7 5pi olive grn (Bk) — 325.00

**On Nos. L162-L163, L173**

***Perf. 11½***

**58B** A9 ½pi car rose (Bk) — 325.00
**58C** A10 1pi yel grn (Bk) — 190.00
**58D** A10 2pi blue (R) — 325.00

Nos. 55-58D were provisionally issued at Medina after its capitulation.

This overprint exists on Nos. L160-L161, L164-L172, L174-L175, L180-L183. These 17 are known as bogus items, but may exist genuine.

Lithographed overprints are forgeries.

**Medina Issue**

Hejaz Railway Tax Stamps Handstamped

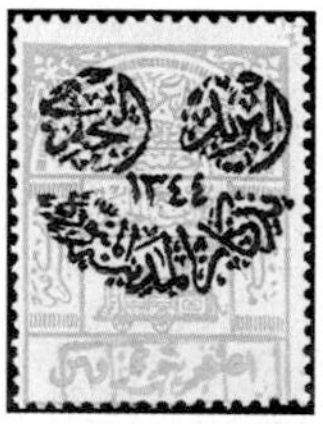

and Handstamp Surcharged in Various Colors

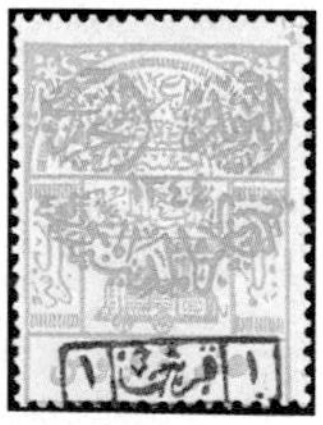

The large overprint reads: "The Nejdi Posts — 1344 — Commemorating Medina, the Illustrious." The tablet shows the new value.

**1925**
**59** R3 1pi on 10pi vio (Bk & V) 65.00 65.00
**60** R3 2pi on 50pi lt bl (R & Bl) 65.00 65.00
**61** R3 3pi on 100pi red brn (Bl & Bk) 65.00 65.00
**62** R3 4pi on 500pi dull red (Bl & Bk) 65.00 65.00
**63** R3 5pi on 1000pi dp red (Bl & Bk) 65.00 65.00
*Nos. 59-63 (5)* 325.00 325.00

**JEDDA ISSUE**

Hejaz Railway Tax Stamps Handstamped and Tablet with New Value in Various Colors

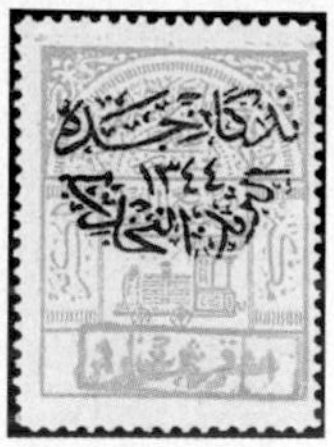

This handstamp reads: "Commemorating Jedda — 1344 — The Nejdi Posts."

**1925**
**64** R3 1pi on 10pi vio (Bk & Bl) 65.00 65.00
**65** R3 2pi on 50pi lt bl (R & Bk) 65.00 65.00
**66** R3 3pi on 100pi red brn (R & Bl) 65.00 65.00
**67** R3 4pi on 500pi dl red (Bk & Bl) 65.00 65.00
**68** R3 5pi on 1000pi dp red (Bk & Bl) 65.00 65.00
*Nos. 64-68 (5)* 325.00 325.00

Nos. 59-63 and 64-68 were prepared in anticipation of the surrender of Medina and Jedda.

**Kingdom of Hejaz-Nejd**

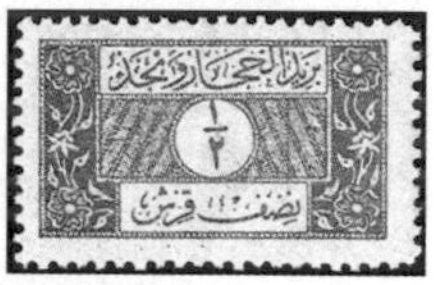

Arabic Inscriptions and Value — A1

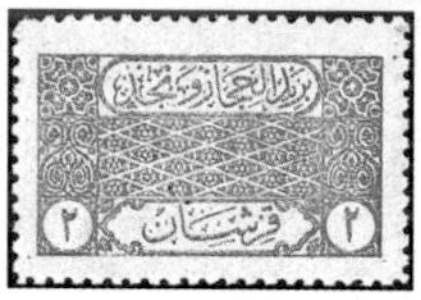

A2

Inscriptions in upper tablets: "Barid al Hejaz wa Nejd" (Posts of the Hejaz and Nejd)

**1926, Feb. Typo. Unwmk.** ***Perf. 11***
**69** A1 ¼pi violet 12.00 8.25
**70** A1 ½pi gray 12.00 8.25
**71** A1 1pi deep blue 15.00 10.00
**72** A2 2pi blue green 13.00 8.25
**73** A2 3pi carmine 15.00 9.00
**74** A2 5pi maroon 9.00 5.75
*Nos. 69-74 (6)* 76.00 49.50

Nos. 69-71, 74 exist imperf. Value, each $30.
Used values are for favor cancels.

**1926, Mar.** ***Perf. 11***
**75** A1 ¼pi orange 6.00 3.25
**76** A1 ½pi blue green 3.00 1.40
**77** A1 1pi carmine 2.00 1.10
**78** A2 2pi violet 3.00 1.40
**79** A2 3pi dark blue 3.00 1.40
**80** A2 5pi lt brown 6.00 3.25
*a.* 5pi olive brown
*Nos. 75-80 (6)* 23.00 11.80

Nos. 75-80 also exist with perf. 14, 14x11, 11x14 and imperf. All of these sell for 10 times the values quoted.

Counterfeits of types A1 and A2 are perf. 11½. They exist with and without overprints.

Types A1 and A2 in colors other than listed are proofs.

**Pan-Islamic Congress Issue**

Stamps of 1926 Handstamped

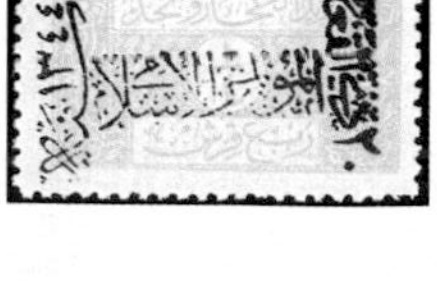

**1926** ***Perf. 11***
**92** A1 ¼pi orange 8.00 2.75
**93** A1 ½pi blue green 8.00 2.75
**94** A1 1pi carmine 8.00 2.75
**95** A2 2pi violet 8.00 2.75
**96** A2 3pi dark blue 8.00 2.75
**97** A2 5pi light brown 8.00 2.75
*Nos. 92-97 (6)* 48.00 16.50

The overprint reads: "al Mootamar al Islami 20 Zilkada, Sanat 1344." (The Islamic Congress, June 1, 1926.)

See counterfeit note after No. 80.

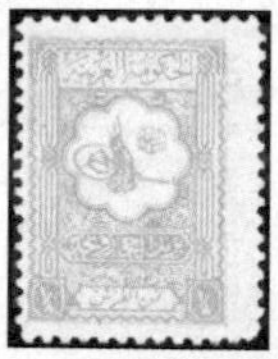

Tughra of King Abdul Aziz — A3

**1926-27 Typo.** ***Perf. 11½***
**98** A3 ⅛pi ocher 4.00 .45
**99** A3 ¼pi gray green 4.50 1.10
**100** A3 ½pi dull red 4.50 1.10
**101** A3 1pi deep violet 5.00 1.10
**102** A3 1½pi gray blue 13.00 1.75
**103** A3 3pi olive green 10.00 3.50
**104** A3 5pi brown orange 20.00 4.00
**105** A3 10pi dark brown 50.00 5.50
*Nos. 98-105 (8)* 111.00 18.50

Inscription at top reads: "Al Hukumat al Arabia" (The Arabian Government). Inscription below tughra reads: "Barid al Hejaz wa Nejd" (Post of the Hejaz and Nejd).

Stamps of 1926-27 Handstamped in Black or Red

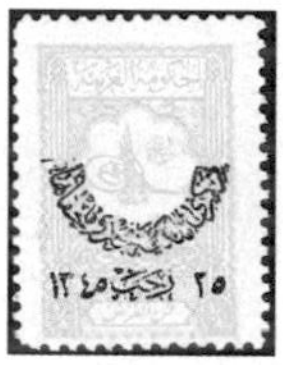

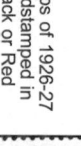

**1927**
**107** A3 ⅛pi ocher 12.00 4.50
**108** A3 ¼pi gray grn 12.00 4.50
**109** A3 ½pi dull red 12.00 4.50
**110** A3 1pi deep violet 12.00 4.50
**111** A3 1½pi gray bl (R) 12.00 4.50
**112** A3 3pi olive green 12.00 4.50
**113** A3 5pi brown orange 13.00 4.50
**114** A3 10pi dark brown 15.00 4.50
*Nos. 107-114 (8)* 100.00 36.00

The overprint reads: "In commemoration of the Kingdom of Nejd and Dependencies, 25th Rajab 1345."

Inverted varieties have not been authenticated.

Turkey No. 258 Surcharged in Violet

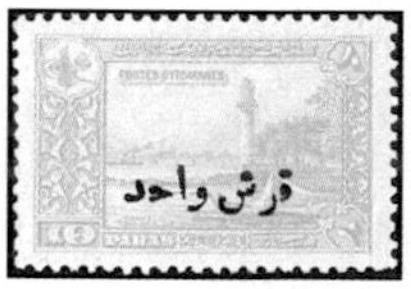

**1925** ***Perf. 12***
**115** A28 1g on 10pa green 175.00

Similar surcharges of 6g and 20g were made in red, but were not known to have been issued.

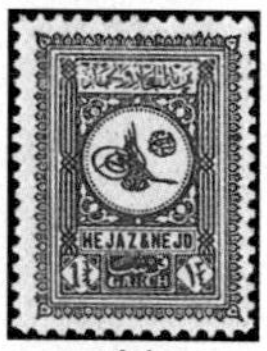

A4

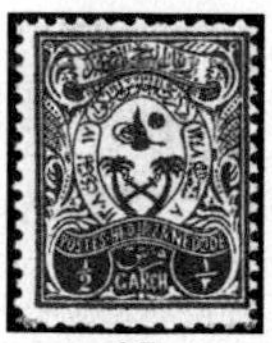

A5

**1929-30 Typo.** ***Perf. 11½***
**117** A4 1¾g gray blue 20.00 2.25
**119** A4 20g violet 25.00 5.00
**120** A4 30g green 40.00 11.00

**1930** ***Perf. 11, 11½***
**125** A5 ½g rose 16.00 2.75
**126** A5 1½g violet 16.00 1.75
**127** A5 1¾g ultra 16.00 2.25
**128** A5 3½g emerald 16.00 3.50

***Perf. 11***
**129** A5 5g black brown 25.00 5.50
*Nos. 125-129 (5)* 89.00 15.75

Anniversary of King Ibn Saud's accession to the throne of the Hejaz, January 8, 1926.

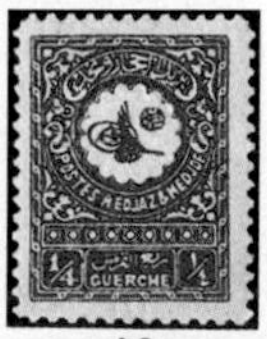

A6

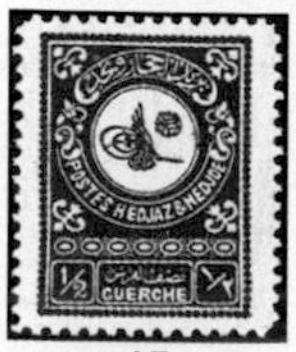

A7

**1931-32** ***Perf. 11½***
**130** A6 ⅛g ocher ('32) 15.00 2.25
**131** A6 ¼g blue green 15.00 1.75
**133** A6 1¾g ultra 25.00 2.25
*Nos. 130-133 (3)* 55.00 6.25

**1932** ***Perf. 11½***
**135** A7 ¼g blue green 10.00 1.75
*a.* Perf 11
**136** A7 ½g scarlet 25.00 2.75
*a.* Perf 11
**137** A7 2¼g ultra 47.50 4.50
*a.* Perf 11
*Nos. 135-137 (3)* 82.50 9.00

**Kingdom of Saudi Arabia**

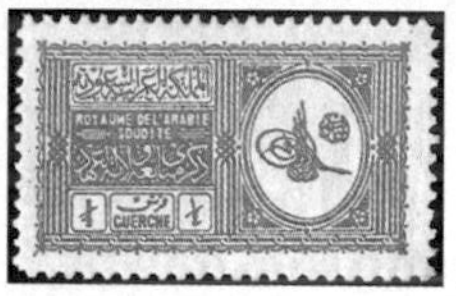

A8

**1934, Jan.** ***Perf. 11½, Imperf.***
**138** A8 ¼g yellow green 8.00 7.25
**139** A8 ½g red 8.00 7.25
**140** A8 1⅛g light blue 15.00 14.00
**141** A8 3g blue green 15.00 14.00
**142** A8 3½g ultra 27.50 5.50
**143** A8 5g yellow 35.00 27.50
**144** A8 10g red orange 65.00
**145** A8 20g bright violet 80.00
**146** A8 ¼s claret 160.00
**147** A8 30g dull violet 100.00
**148** A8 ½s chocolate 325.00
**149** A8 1s violet brown 700.00
*Nos. 138-149 (12)* 1,538.

Proclamation of Emir Saud as Heir Apparent of Arabia. Perf. and imperf. stamps were issued in equal quantities.

Favor cancels exist on Nos. 144-149.

Tughra of King Abdul Aziz — A9

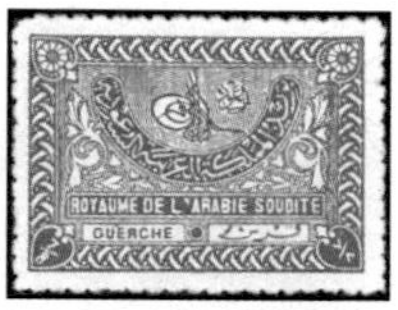

**1934-57** ***Perf. 11, 11½***
**159** A9 ⅛g yellow 4.00 .35
**160** A9 ¼g yellow grn 4.00 .35
**161** A9 ½g rose red ('43) 3.00 .20
*a.* ½g dark carmine 12.00 1.40
**162** A9 ⅞g lt blue ('56) 5.00 .45
**163** A9 1g blue green 4.00 .35
**164** A9 2g olive grn ('57) 7.00 1.75
*a.* 2g olive bister ('57) 25.00 7.25
**165** A9 2⅞g violet ('57) 5.00 .45
**166** A9 3g ultra ('38) 5.00 .20
*a.* 3g light blue 20.00 1.75
**167** A9 3½g lt ultra 27.50 1.75
**168** A9 5g orange 5.00 .45
**169** A9 10g violet 15.00 1.40
**170** A9 20g purple brn 25.00 .90
*a.* 20g purple black 25.00 2.25
**171** A9 100g red vio ('42) 70.00 4.00
**172** A9 200g vio brn ('42) 90.00 5.50
*Nos. 159-172 (14)* 269.50 18.10

The ½g has two types differing in position of the tughra.

No. 162 measures 31x22mm. No. 164 30½x21½mm. No. 165, 30½x22mm. No. 166 30x21mm. No. 171, 31x22mm. No. 172, 30½x21½mm. Rest of set, 29x20½mm. Grayish paper was used in 1946-49 printings.

No. 168 exists with pin-perf 6.

For overprint see No. J24.

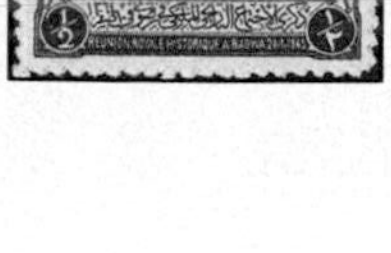

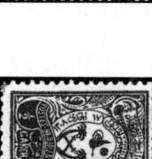

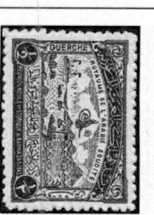

Yanbu Harbor near Radwa — A10

# SAUDI ARABIA

## 1945 Typo. Perf. 11½
173 A10 ½g brt carmine 7.00 .30
174 A10 3g lt ultra 9.00 1.00
175 A10 5g purple 25.00 1.25
176 A10 10g dk brown vio 96.00 5.55

Meeting of King Abdul Aziz and King Farouk of Egypt at Jebal Radwa, Saudi Arabia, Jan. 24, 1945.

**Catalogue values for unused stamps in this section, from this point to the end of the section, are for Never Hinged items.**

Arms of Saudi Arabia and Afghanistan A12

## 1950, Mar. Perf. 11
178 A12 ½g carmine 7.50 1.00
179 A12 3g violet blue 12.50 1.00

Visit of Zahir Shah of Afghanistan, March 1950. One 3g in each sheet inscribed POSTFS, value $45.

Old City Walls, Riyadh A13

## 1950 Center in Red Brown
180 A13 ½g magenta 5.25 .30
181 A13 1g lt blue 10.00 .70
182 A13 1g violet 15.00 .70
183 A13 5g vermilion 32.50 1.40
184 A13 10g green 60.00 3.50
a. Singular "guerche" in Arabic 450.00 52.50
122.75 6.20

50th lunar anniversary of King Ibn Saud's capture of Riyadh, Jan. 16, 1902. No. 184a: On the 3g, 5g and 10g the currency as expressed in the plural in both French (grouche) and Arabic. One stamp in each sheet of 20 (4x5), position 11, of the 10g shows the Arabic characters in the singular form of "guerche" as on the ½g and 1g.

Arms of Saudi Arabia and Jordan — A14

## 1951, Nov. Perf. 11
185 A14 ½g carmine 8.75 1.40
a. "BOYAUME" 250.00
186 A14 3g violet blue 13.50 2.10
a. "BOYAUME" 250.00

Visit of King Tallal of Jordan, Nov. 1951.

Bedouins and Train — A15

## 1952, June Engr. Perf. 12
187 A15 ½g redsh brown 9.75 1.50
188 A15 1g deep green 9.75 1.50
189 A15 3g violet 20.00 7.50
190 A15 10q rose pink 40.00 15.00
191 A15 20q blue 80.00 15.00
Nos. 187-191 (5) 159.50 26.50

Inaugural trip over the Saudi Government Railroad between Riyadh and Dammam.

---

## 1953, Feb. Typo. Perf. 11
192 A16 ½g carmine 5.25 1.00
193 A16 3g violet blue 10.50 1.60

Visit of President Camille Chamoun of Lebanon.

Arms of Saudi Arabia and Emblem of Pakistan A17

## 1953, Mar.
194 A17 ½g dark carmine 7.00 1.00
195 A17 3g violet blue 15.00 1.60

Visit of Gov.-Gen. Ghulam Mohammed of Pakistan.

Globe — A18a

## 1953, July Unwmk. Perf. 11
196 A18 ½g carmine 5.25 1.00
a. "GUERCHE" 76.00
197 A18 3g violet blue 16.00 1.60

Visit of King Hussein of Jordan, July, 1953.

## 1955, July Litho.
198 A18a ½g emerald 3.00 .50
199 A18a 3g violet 8.00 1.00
200 A18a 4g orange 11.50 2.50
Nos. 198-200 (3) 22.50 4.00

Founding of the Arab Postal Union, July 1, 1954.

Ministry of Communications Building, Riyadh — A19

## 1960, Apr. 12 Photo. Perf. 13
201 A19 2p bright blue .75 .20
202 A19 5p deep claret 1.50 .20
203 A19 10p dark green 4.00 .50
6.25 .90

Arab Postal Union Conference, at Riyadh, Apr. 11. Imperfs. exist.
Nos. 201-203 (3)

Arab League Center, Cairo A20

## 1960, Mar. 22 Perf. 13x13½
204 A20 2p dull grn & blk 2.00 .25

Opening of the Arab League Center and the Arab Postal Museum in Cairo. Exists imperf.

Radio Tower and Waves A21

---

## 1960, June 4
205 A21 2p red & black 2.10 .30
206 A21 5p brown blk & mar 3.25 .35
207 A21 10p bluish blk & ultra 5.50 .80
10.85 1.45

1st international radio station in Saudi Arabia. Imperfs. exist.
Nos. 205-207 (3)

Map of Palestine, Refugee Camp and WRY Emblem — A22

## 1960, Oct. 30 Litho. Perf. 13
208 A22 2p dark blue .35 .25
209 A22 8p lilac 1.10 .25
210 A22 10p green 1.80 .75

World Refugee Year, July 1, 1959-June 30, 1960. Imperfs. exist.
Nos. 208-210 (3)

Wadi Hanifa Dam, near Riyadh — A23

Gas-Oil Separating Plant, Buqqa — A24

Type I (Saud Cartouche) (Illustrated over No. 286)

## 1960-62 Unwmk. Photo. Perf. 14
### Size: 27⅛x22mm
211 A23 ½p bis brn & org 1.50 .25
212 A23 1p ol bis & pur 1.50 .25
213 A23 2p blue & sepia 1.50 .25
214 A23 4p sepia & blue 1.50 .25
215 A23 4p sepia & ocher 1.50 .25
216 A23 5p blk & dk violet 1.50 .25
217 A23 6p brn blk & car rose 1.60 .26
a. 6p black & carmine rose 1.75 .40
218 A23 7p red & gray ol 1.50 .35
219 A23 8p dk bl & brn blk 1.50 .35
220 A23 9p org brn & scar 1.75 .55
c. 9p yel brn & metallic red
221 A23 10p cmcr grn & mar (62) 2.10 .85
a. 10p blue green & maroon 4.25 .40
222 A23 20p brown & green 24.00 2.10
223 A23 50p black & brown 65.00 2.40
224 A23 75p brown & gray 60.00 2.75
225 A23 100p dk bl & grn bl 92.50 7.00
226 A23 200p lilac & green 262.50 17.75
Nos. 211-226 (16)

## 1960-61
227 A24 ½p maroon & org 1.25 .25
228 A24 1p blue & red org 1.25 .25
229 A24 2p ver & blue 1.25 .25
231 A24 3p lilac & brt grn 1.25 .25
232 A24 4p yel grn & lilac 1.25 .25
A24 5p dk gray & brn 1.25 .25
red
233 A24 6p brn org & dk red 1.25 .25
234 A24 7p vio & dull grn 1.25 .25
235 A24 8p blue grn & gray 1.25 .25
236 A24 9p ultra & sepia 4.00 .25
237 A24 10p dk blue & rose 2.10 .40
238 A24 20p org brn & blk 7.25 .55
239 A24 50p red & brn grn 21.00 1.60
240 A24 75p red & blk brn 32.50 3.25
241 A24 100p dk bl & red brn 50.00 3.00
242 A24 200p dk gray & ol grn 85.00 6.75
Nos. 227-242 (16) 213.10 18.05

Nearly all of Nos. 211-242 exist imperf, probably not regularly issued. See Nos. 258-273, 286-341, 393-450, 461-483.

---

Dammam Port — A25

## 1961, Aug. 16 Wmk. 337 Litho. Perf. 13
243 A25 3p lilac 1.60 .25
244 A25 6p light blue 2.25 .35
245 A25 8p dark green 3.75 .35
7.60 .95

Expansion of the port of Dammam. Imperf min. sheets of 4 were for presentation purposes and have no wmk. sideways. Value, set $425. Imperforate pairs or margined imperfs with upright watermark come from full sheets not perforated by the print shop.
Nos. 243-245 (3)

Globe, Radio and Telegraph A26

## 1961, Aug. 7 Perf. 13x13½ Photo. Unwmk.
246 A26 3p dull purple 1.50 .20
247 A26 6p gray black 3.50 .55
248 A26 8p brown 7.25 1.10

Arab Union of Telecommunications. Imperfs. exist.
Nos. 246-248 (3)

Malaria Eradication Emblem — A28

## 1962, Apr. 22 Wmk. 337 Perf. 13
249 A27 3p olive green 1.25 .25
250 A27 6p carmine rose 2.50 .35
251 A27 8p slate blue 4.00 .40
7.75 1.00

Arab League Week, Mar. 22-28.
Nos. 249-251 (3)

Imperforate or missing-color varieties of Nos. 249-285 and 344-353 were not regularly issued.

## 1962, May 7 Litho. Wmk. 337
252 A28 3p red org & blue 1.00 .25
253 A28 6p emerald & Prus bl 1.40 .30
254 A28 8p black & lil rose 2.25 .50
a. Souv. sheet of 3, #252-254, imperf. 22.50 22.50
Nos. 252-254 (3) 4.65 1.05

WHO drive to eradicate malaria. Nos. 252-254 are known unofficially overprinted with new dates only or with "AIR MAIL" and two plane silhouettes. A 4p exists as an essay.

Koran A29

## 1963, Mar. 12 Wmk. 337 Perf. 11
255 A29 2½p lilac rose & pink 1.00 .25
256 A29 7½p blue & pale grn 2.00 .40
257 A29 9½p green & gray 3.25 1.05
6.25 1.00

First anniversary of the Islamic Institute, Medina. A 3p exists as an essay. Copies of the 2½p exist with virtually all the pink background
Nos. 255-257 (3)

omitted. No copies are known with the pink completely omitted.

Dam Type of 1960 Redrawn
Type I (Saud Cartouche)

*Perf. 13½x13*

**1963-65 Wmk. 337 Litho.**

**Size: 28½x23mm**

**258** A23 ½p bis brn & org 10.00 .75

Nos. 258, 264-265 are widely spaced in the sheet, producing large margins.

*Perf. 14*

**Photo.**

**Size: 27½x22mm**

**259** A23 ½p bis brn & org ('65) 22.50 1.75
**260** A23 3p sepia & blue 9.00 .65
**261** A23 4p sepia & ocher ('64) 12.50 .80
**262** A23 5p black & dk vio 12.50 .80
**263** A23 20p dk car & grn 22.50 1.60
*Nos. 258-263 (6)* 89.00 6.35

A 1p was prepared but not issued. It is known only imperf.

Gas-Oil Plant Type of 1960 Redrawn
Type I (Saud Cartouche)

*Perf. 13½x13*

**1963-65 Wmk. 337 Litho.**

**Size: 28½x23mm**

**264** A24 ½p maroon & orange 12.00 1.10
**265** A24 1p blue & red org ('64) 6.00 .40

**Photo.**

*Perf. 14*

**Size: 27½x22mm**

**266** A24 ½p mar & org ('64) 10.00 .55
**267** A24 1p blue & red org 9.00 .40
**268** A24 3p lilac & brt grn 20.00 1.00
**269** A24 4p yel grn & lilac 12.50 .55
**270** A24 5p dk gray & brn red 12.50 .55
**271** A24 6p brn org & dk vio ('65) 17.00 .70
**272** A24 8p dull grn & blk 30.00 1.25
**273** A24 9p blue & sepia 30.00 1.60
*Nos. 264-273 (10)* 159.00 8.10

The 3p, 4p and 6p exist imperf.

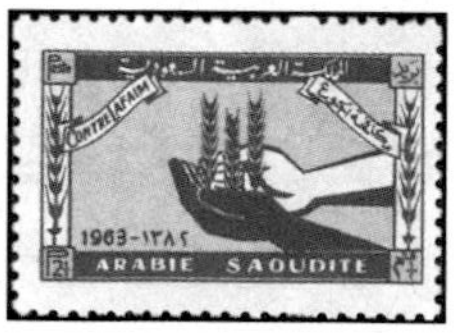

Hands Holding Wheat Emblem A30

**1963, Mar. 21 Litho.** *Perf. 11*

**274** A30 2½p lilac rose & rose 1.10 .25
**275** A30 7½p brt lilac & pink 1.10 .35
**276** A30 9p red brn & lt blue 2.50 .40
*Nos. 274-276 (3)* 4.70 1.00

FAO "Freedom from Hunger" campaign. The 3p imperf in various colors are essays.

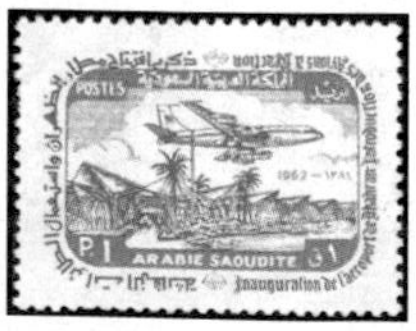

Jet over Dhahran Airport — A31

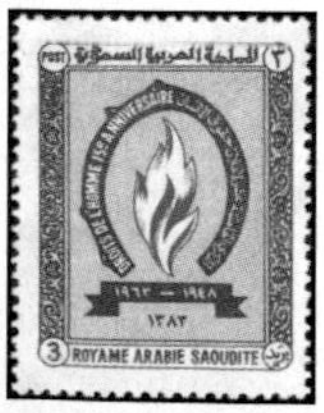

Flame — A32

**1963, July 27 Litho.** *Perf. 13*

**277** A31 1p blue gray & ocher 1.50 .30
**278** A31 3½p ultra & emer 3.00 .30
**279** A31 6p emerald & rose 5.25 .40
**a.** "Thahran" for "Dharan" in Arabic 8.75
**280** A31 7½p lilac rose & lt bl 5.25 .50
**281** A31 9½p ver & dull vio 7.50 .55
*Nos. 277-281 (5)* 22.50 2.05

Opening of the US-financed terminal of the Dhahran Airport and inauguration of international jet service

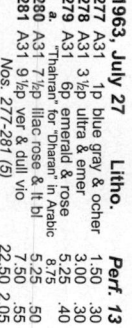

On No. 279a the misspelling consists of an omitted dot over character near top left in one horiz. row of five.

Nos. 277-281 with a second impression of the frame are forgeries.

**1964, Apr. Wmk. 337** *Perf. 13x13½*

**282** A32 3p lil, pink & Prus bl 3.25 .25
**283** A32 6p yel grn, lt bl & Prus bl 3.75 .30
**284** A32 9p brn, buff & Prus bl 8.25 .40
*Nos. 282-284 (3)* 15.25 .95

15th anniv. of the signing of the Universal Declaration of Human Rights.

The 3p in other colors is an essay.

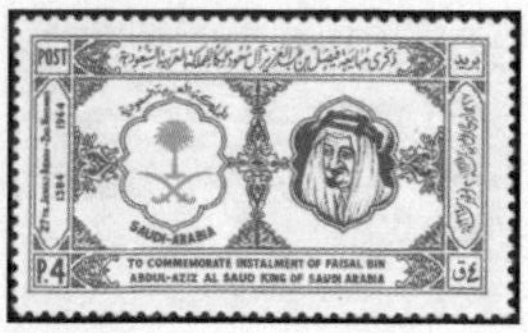

King Faisal and Arms of Saudi Arabia A33

**1964, Nov. Litho.** *Perf. 13*

**285** A33 4p dk blue & emerald 4.50 .25

Installation of Prince Faisal ibn Abdul Aziz as King, Nov. 2, 1964.

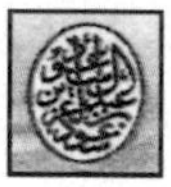

King Saud's Cartouche — Type I

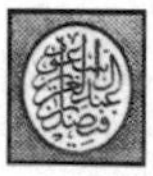

King Faisal's Cartouche — Type II

Redrawn Dam Type of 1960
Type I (Saud Cartouche)

**1965-70 Litho. Unwmk.** *Perf. 14*

**Size: 27x22mm**

**286** A23 1p ol bis & pur 27.50 1.40
**287** A23 2p dk blue & sep 5.25 .40
**288** A23 3p sepia & blue 4.00 .45
**289** A23 4p sepia & ocher 7.50 .45
**290** A23 5p blk & dk vio 6.75 .45
**291** A23 6p blk & car rose 16.00 .80
**292** A23 7p brown & gray 16.00 .45
**293** A23 8p dk bl & gray *90.00* 6.75
**294** A23 9p org brn & scar *82.50* 6.75
**295** A23 10p bl grn & mar *77.50* 4.25
**296** A23 11p red & yel grn 7.25 2.75
**297** A23 12p org & dk bl 7.25 .45
**298** A23 13p dk ol & rose 7.25 .50
**299** A23 14p org brn & yel grn 7.25 .50
**300** A23 15p sepia & gray grn 7.25 2.75
**301** A23 16p dk red & dl vio 9.00 .60
**302** A23 17p rose lil & dk bl 9.00 3.00
**303** A23 18p green & brt bl 9.00 .60
**304** A23 19p black & bister 12.00 .70
**305** A23 20p brn & grn 11.50 1.40
**306** A23 23p mar & lilac 9.75 2.75
**307** A23 24p ver & blue 12.00 .80
**308** A23 26p olive & yel 15.00 1.00
**309** A23 27p ultra & red brn 15.00 1.00
**310** A23 31p gray & dull bl 15.00 1.10
**311** A23 33p ol grn & lilac 15.00 1.10
**312** A23 100p dk bl & grnsh bl *450.00* *67.50*
**313** A23 200p dull lil & grn *450.00* *67.50*
*Nos. 286-313 (28)* *1,401.* *178.15*

A 50p exists but was never placed in use.

Issue years: 1966, 2p, 4p, 10p-20p, 1968, 6p-9p. 1970, 100p-200p.

Redrawn Gas-Oil Plant Type of 1960
Type I (Saud Cartouche)

**1964-70 Litho. Unwmk.**

**Size: 27x22mm**

**314** A24 1p bl & red org 7.25 .20
**315** A24 2p vermilion & bl 11.00 .20
**316** A24 3p lilac & brt grn 4.50 .20
**317** A24 4p yel grn & lilac 6.50 .20
**318** A24 5p dl gray vio & dk red brn 24.00 1.75
**319** A24 6p brn org & dk vio 50.00 4.50
**320** A24 7p vio & dull grn 27.50 1.75
**321** A24 8p bl grn & gray 6.00 .30
**322** A24 9p ultra & sepia 12.50 .70
**323** A24 10p dk blue & rose *325.00* 32.50
**324** A24 11p olive & org 4.00 .30
**325** A24 12p bister & grn 4.00 .30
**326** A24 13p rose red & dk bl 4.00 .35
**327** A24 14p vio & lt brown 5.50 .35
**328** A24 15p rose red & sep 6.00 .45
**329** A24 16p green & rose red 8.00 .45
**330** A24 17p car rose & red brn 12.50 1.40
**331** A24 18p gray & ultra 8.00 .55
**332** A24 19p brown & yel 8.00 .55
**333** A24 20p dull org & dk gray 27.50 1.75
**334** A24 23p orange & car 7.25 .65
**335** A24 24p emer & org yel 8.00 .70
**336** A24 26p lil & red brn 11.00 .70
**337** A24 27p ver & dk gray 11.00 .70
**338** A24 31p dull grn & car 19.00 1.40
**339** A24 33p red brn & gray 17.00 1.40
**340** A24 50p red brn & dull grn *325.00* *45.00*
**341** A24 200p dk gray & ol gray *325.00* *45.00*
*Nos. 314-341 (28)* *1,285.* *144.30*

A 100p exists but was never placed in use.

Issue years: 1965, 4p, 8p, 9p, 23p-33p. 1966, 1p, 2p, 5p, 11p-14p, 16p-20p. 1967, 15p. 1968, 6p, 7p. 1969, 50p. 1970, 200p. Others, 1964.

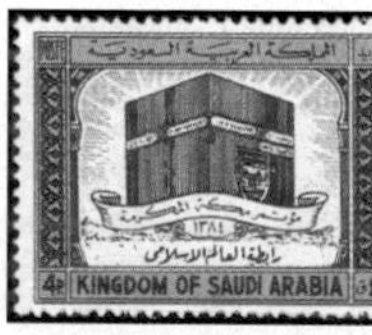

Holy Ka'aba, Mecca — A34

**1965, Apr. 17 Wmk. 337** *Perf. 13*

**344** A34 4p salmon & blk 4.00 .25
**345** A34 6p brt pink & blk 6.00 .30
**346** A34 10p yel grn & blk 8.25 .40
*Nos. 344-346 (3)* 18.25 .95

Mecca Conf. of the Moslem World League.

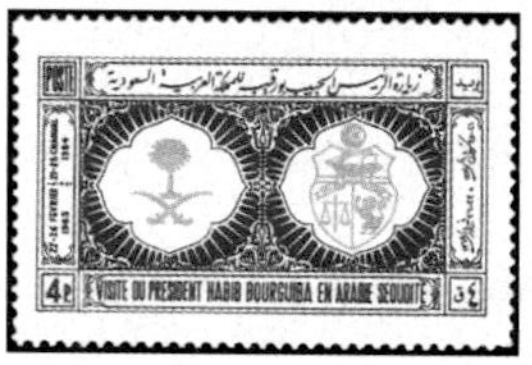

Arms of Saudi Arabia and Tunisia A35

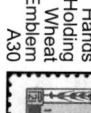

**1965, Apr. Litho.**

**347** A35 4p car rose & silver 3.25 .25
**348** A35 8p red lilac & silver 4.25 .40
**349** A35 10p ultra & silver 6.00 .40
*Nos. 347-349 (3)* 13.50 1.05

Visit of Pres. Habib Bourguiba of Tunisia, Feb. 22-26.

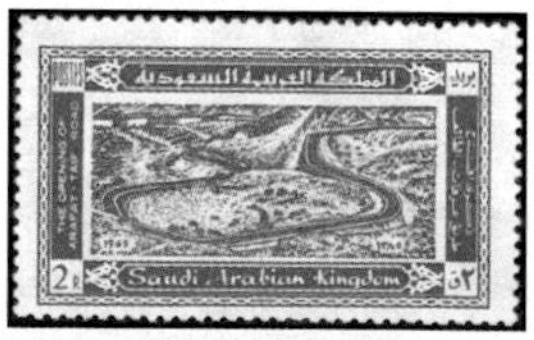

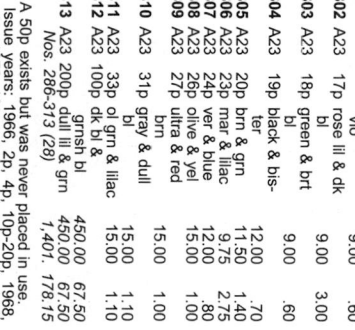

Highway, Hejaz Mountains — A36

**1965, June 2 Wmk. 337** *Perf. 13*

**350** A36 2p red & blk 2.00 .35
**351** A36 4p blue & blk 3.00 .40
**352** A36 6p lilac & blk 4.25 .55
**353** A36 8p brt green & blk 6.00 .65
*Nos. 350-353 (4)* 15.25 1.95

Opening of highway from Mecca to Tayif.

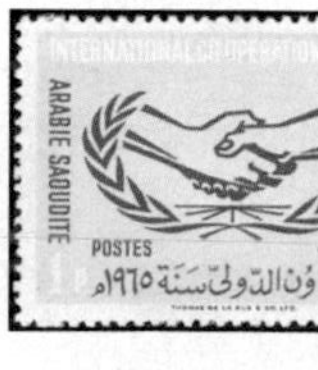

ICY Emblem A37

**1965, Nov. 13 Unwmk.** *Perf. 13*

**354** A37 1p yellow & dk brn 1.75 .25
**355** A37 2p orange & ol grn 1.75 .25
**356** A37 3p lt blue & gray 1.75 .25
**357** A37 4p yel grn & dk sl grn 1.75 .25
**358** A37 10p orange & magenta 4.25 .55
*Nos. 354-358 (5)* 11.25 1.55

International Cooperation Year, 1965.

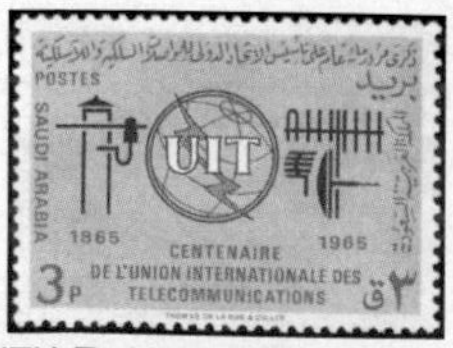

ITU Emblem, Old and New Communication Equipment — A38

**1965, Dec. 22 Litho.** *Perf. 13*

**359** A38 3p blue & blk 2.25 .20
**360** A38 4p lilac & dk grn 2.25 .20
**361** A38 8p emerald & dk brn 2.25 .40
**362** A38 10p dull org & dk grn 2.25 .40
*Nos. 359-362 (4)* 9.00 1.20

Centenary of the ITU.

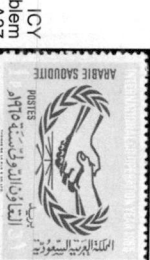

Library Aflame and Lamp A39

**1966, Jan. Litho.** *Perf. 12x12½*

**363** A39 1p orange 1.90 .20
**364** A39 2p dark red 1.90 .20
**365** A39 3p red violet 2.50 .20
**366** A39 4p violet 3.00 .20
**367** A39 5p lilac rose 4.50 .35
**368** A39 6p vermilion 9.50 .45
*Nos. 363-368 (6)* 23.30 1.60

Burning of the Library of Algiers, June 2, 1962. Nos. 363-368 were withdrawn from sale Jan. 26, 1966, due to incorrect Arabic inscriptions. Later some values were inadvertently again placed in use.

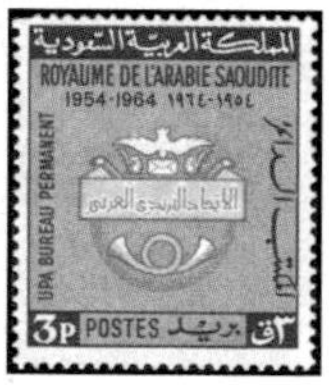

Arab Postal Union Emblem — A40

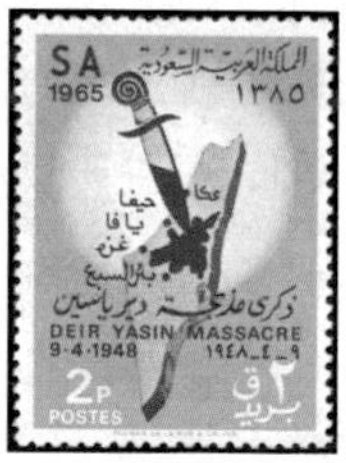

Dagger in Map of Palestine — A41

**1966, Mar. 15 Litho.** *Perf. 14*

**369** A40 3p dull pur & olive 1.10 .25
**370** A40 4p deep blue & olive 1.10 .25
**371** A40 6p maroon & olive 4.50 .30
**372** A40 7p deep green & olive 4.50 .45
*Nos. 369-372 (4)* 11.20 1.25

10th anniv. (in 1964) of the APU. Printed in sheets of two panes, so horizontal gutter pairs exist.

**1966, Mar. 19 Litho.** *Perf. 13*

**373** A41 2p yel grn & blk 1.75 .25
**374** A41 4p lt brown & blk 3.25 .25
**375** A41 6p dull blue & blk 4.50 .30
**376** A41 8p ocher & blk 6.75 .40
*Nos. 373-376 (4)* 16.25 1.20

Deir Yassin massacre, Apr. 9, 1948.

Emblems of World Boy Scout Conference and Saudi Arabian Scout Association
A42

**1966, Mar. 23** **Unwmk.**
**377** A42 4p yel, blk, grn & gray 4.50 .50
**378** A42 8p yel, blk, org & lt bl 4.50 .50
**379** A42 10p yel, blk, sal & bl 9.00 .75
*Nos. 377-379 (3)* 18.00 1.75

Arab League Rover Moot (Boy Scout Jamboree).

WHO Headquarters, Geneva, and Flag — A43

**1966, May** **Litho.** ***Perf. 13***
**380** A43 4p aqua & multi 1.25 .20
**381** A43 6p yel brn & multi 2.50 .30
**382** A43 10p pink & multi 5.25 .40
*Nos. 380-382 (3)* 9.00 .90

Opening of the WHO Headquarters, Geneva.

UNESCO Emblem — A44

**1966, Sept.** **Unwmk.** ***Perf. 12***
**383** A44 1p apple grn & multi 1.50 .25
**384** A44 2p dull org & multi 1.50 .25
**385** A44 3p lilac rose & multi 2.00 .25
**386** A44 4p pale green & multi 2.00 .25
**387** A44 10p gray & multi 3.00 .40
*Nos. 383-387 (5)* 10.00 1.40

20th anniv. of UNESCO.

Radio Tower, Telephone and Map of Arab Countries — A45

**1966, Nov. 7** **Litho.** ***Perf. 12½***
**Design in Black, Carmine & Yellow**
**388** A45 1p vio blue 1.90 .25
**389** A45 2p bluish lilac 1.90 .25
**390** A45 4p rose lilac 3.75 .25
**391** A45 6p lt olive grn 3.75 .35
**392** A45 7p gray green 4.75 .45
*Nos. 388-392 (5)* 16.05 1.55

Issued to publicize the 8th Congress of the Arab Telecommunications Union, Riyadh.

Redrawn Dam Type of 1960
Type II (Faisal Cartouche)
(Illustrated over No. 286)

**1966-76** **Litho.** **Unwmk.** ***Perf. 14***
**Size: 27x22mm**
**393** A23 1p ol bis & pur *160.00* *22.50*
**394** A23 2p dk blue & sep 19.00 1.50
**395** A23 3p blk & dk bl 11.00 .80
**396** A23 4p sepia & ocher 15.00 .40
**397** A23 5p blk & dk vio 40.00 7.50
**398** A23 6p blk & car rose 32.50 6.75
**399** A23 7p sepia & gray 18.00 1.75
**400** A23 8p dk bl & gray 11.00 .45
**401** A23 9p org brn & scar 7.50 .80
**402** A23 10p bl grn & mar 15.00 1.40
**403** A23 11p red & yel grn 11.00 1.40
**404** A23 12p org & dk bl 6.50 1.40
**405** A23 13p blk & rose 22.50 1.40
**406** A23 14p org brn & yel grn 19.00 1.40
**407** A23 15p sep & gray grn 19.00 1.75
**408** A23 16p dk red & dl vio 27.50 3.25
**409** A23 17p rose lil & dk bl 32.50 1.75
**410** A23 18p green & brt bl 22.50 2.50
**411** A23 19p black & bister 7.25 .80
**412** A23 20p brown & grn 72.50 *2.25*
**413** A23 23p maroon & lil *260.00* *4.50*
**414** A23 24p ver & blue 52.50 5.50
**415** A23 26p olive & yel 6.75 .70
**416** A23 27p ultra & red brn 7.75 .70
**417** A23 33p ol grn & lilac 42.50 2.25
**419** A23 50p black & brown *175.00* *35.00*
**420** A23 100p dk bl & grnsh bl *275.00* *45.00*
**421** A23 200p dull lilac & grn *275.00* *72.50*
*Nos. 393-421 (28)* *1,663.* *227.90*

A 31p has been reported.

Issue years: 1966, 1p. 1967, 2p, 10p. 1968, 3p, 4p, 6p, 7p, 20p; 1969, 5p, 8p. 1970, 9p, 23p; 1972, 12p, 15p, 16p. 1973, 11p; 1974, 17p, 50p-200p; 1975, 13p, 14p, 19p, 24p-33p; 1976, 18p.

Redrawn Gas-Oil Plant Type of 1960
Type II (Faisal Cartouche)

**1966-78** **Unwmk.**
**Size: 27x22mm**
**422** A24 1p bl & red org 35.00 *2.75*
**423** A24 2p ver & dull bl 7.00 .30
**424** A24 3p lilac & brt grn 14.00 .55
**425** A24 4p grn & dull lil 8.00 .30
**426** A24 5p dl gray vio & dk red brn 37.50 1.75
**427** A24 6p brn org & dull pur 24.00 3.50
**428** A24 7p vio & dull grn 32.50 1.75
**429** A24 8p bl grn & grnsh gray 5.50 .30
**430** A24 9p ultra & sep 3.75 .30
**431** A24 10p dk bl & rose 4.50 .55
**432** A24 11p olive & org 72.50 7.25
**433** A24 12p bister & grn 4.50 .70
**434** A24 13p rose red & dk bl 42.50 .30
**435** A24 14p vio & lt brn 40.00 2.25
**436** A24 15p car & sepia 10.50 .60
**437** A24 16p grn & rose red 14.00 .70
**438** A24 17p car rose & red brn 10.00 .55
**439** A24 18p gray & ultra 14.00 1.60
**440** A24 19p brown & yel 16.00 1.50
**441** A24 20p brn org & gray 12.00 1.50
**442** A24 23p orange & car 20.00 1.75
**443** A24 24p emer & org yel 9.00 .70
**444** A24 26p lilac & red brn *175.00*
**445** A24 27p ver & dk gray 35.00 3.50
**446** A24 31p green & rose car 11.00 .70
**447** A24 33p brown & gray 20.00 1.10
**448** A24 50p red brn & dl grn 350.00 *140.00*
**449** A24 100p dk bl & red brn 300.00 *40.00*
**450** A24 200p dk gray & ol gray 350.00 *57.50*
*Nos. 422-450 (29)* 1,677.

Issue years: 1967, 20p; 1968, 3p, 5p-9p, 15p, 16p; 1969, 100p; 1970, 11p, 14p, 200p; 1973, 13p, 18p, 24p; 1974, 19p, 50p; 1975, 12p, 17p, 27p-33p; 1978, 26p; others, 1966.

No. 442 with a double impression of the frame is a forgery.

Emblem of Saudi Arabian Scout Association
A46

Meteorological Instruments and WMO Emblem — A47

**1967, Mar. 28** **Litho.** ***Perf. 13½***
**Emblem in Green, Red, Yellow & Black**
**451** A46 1p dk blue & blk 2.25 .25
**452** A46 2p blue grn & blk 2.25 .25
**453** A46 3p lt blue & blk 3.50 .25
**454** A46 4p rose brn & blk 4.25 .25
**455** A46 10p brown & blk 9.75 .50
*Nos. 451-455 (5)* 22.00 1.50

2nd Arabic League Rover Moot, Mecca, March 13-28.

**1967, July** **Unwmk.** ***Perf. 13***
**456** A47 1p brt magenta 1.10 .25
**457** A47 2p violet 2.25 .25
**458** A47 3p olive 2.25 .25
**459** A47 4p blue green 7.00 .25
**460** A47 10p blue 9.75 .40
*Nos. 456-460 (5)* 22.35 1.40

Issued for World Meteorological Day.

Redrawn Dam Type of 1960
Type II (Faisal Cartouche)

**1968-76** **Wmk. 361** **Litho.** ***Perf. 14***
**461** A23 1p ol bis & pur ('71) *1,100.* *275.00*
**462** A23 2p dk blue & sep 30.00 *1.75*
**463** A23 3p blk & dk bl 20.00 *.95*
**464** A23 4p sepia & ocher 175.00 *30.00*
**465** A23 5p blk & dk vio 25.00 *1.75*
**466** A23 6p blk & car rose 24.00 *1.40*
**467** A23 7p sepia & gray 35.00 *2.75*
**468** A23 8p dk bl & gray 18.00 .90
**469** A23 9p org brn & ver 65.00 *6.25*
**470** A23 10p bl grn & mar 45.00 *3.50*
**471** A23 11p red & yel grn 55.00 *5.50*
**472** A23 12p org & sl bl 50.00 *4.50*
**473** A23 13p black & rose 67.50 *6.75*
*Nos. 462-473 (12)* 609.50 *66.00*

Issue years: 1968, 2p, 10p; 1969, 3p; 1970, 8p; 1971, 1p, 5p; 1972, 6p, 9p, 11p, 12p; 1973, 4p; 1974, 13p; 1976, 9p.

Redrawn Gas-Oil Plant Type of 1960
Type II (Faisal Cartouche)

**1968-76** ***Perf. 14***
**474** A24 1p bl & red org 9.50 .90
**475** A24 2p ver & dl bl 5.75 .45
**476** A24 4p grn & dl lil 72.50 *7.25*
**477** A24 5p dk brn & red brn ('73) 20.00 1.40
**478** A24 6p brn org & dk vio ('73) 25.00 1.75
**479** A24 9p dk bl & sep ('76) 40.00 3.50
**480** A24 10p dk bl & rose 8.50 .60
**481** A24 11p ol & org ('72) 30.00 1.75
**482** A24 12p bis & grn ('72) 32.50 2.75
**483** A24 23p org & car ('74) 55.00 2.75
*Nos. 474-483 (10)* 298.75 23.10

Map Showing Dammam to Jedda Road, and Dates — A48

**Wmk. 361**
**1968, Aug.** **Litho.** ***Perf. 14***
**484** A48 1p yellow & multi 1.50 .20
**485** A48 2p orange & multi 1.50 .20
**486** A48 3p multicolored 3.00 .20
**487** A48 4p multicolored 3.00 .20
**488** A48 10p multicolored 9.00 .40
*Nos. 484-488 (5)* 18.00 1.20

Issued to commemorate the completion of the trans-Saudi Arabia highway in 1967.

Several positions in the sheet have the dots representing Dammam and Riyadh omitted. Most had the dots added by pen before issuance.

Prophet's Mosque, Medina — A49

New Arcade, Mecca Mosque — A50

**Wmk. 361, 337 (#489, 493)**
**1968-76** **Litho.** ***Perf. 13½x14***
**Design A49**
**489** A49 1p org & grn ('70) 2.10 .30
**490** A49 2p red brn & grn, redrawn ('72) 3.50 .35
*a.* 2p red brn & grn, wmk. 337 6.25 .30
*b.* As "a," redrawn 175.00
**491** A49 3p vio & grn ('72) 3.25 .35
*a.* 3p vio & grn, wmk. 337 ('70) 2.75 .30
**492** A49 4p ocher & grn 3.50 .35
*a.* Redrawn ('71) 5.50 .45
*b.* 4p ocher & green, redrawn, wmk. 337 6.25
**493** A49 5p dp lil rose & grn ('71) 7.75 .90
**494** A49 6p blk & grn ('73) 9.75 .90
*a.* 6p gray & green ('76) 18.00 .90
**495** A49 10p brown & grn 12.00 .90
*a.* Redrawn 9.00
**496** A49 20p dk brn & grn ('70) 15.00 1.75
*a.* Redrawn 18.00
**497** A49 50p sepia & grn ('75) 19.00 5.75
**498** A49 100p dk bl & grn ('75) 15.00 4.50
**499** A49 200p red & grn ('75) 19.00 6.25
*Nos. 489-499 (11)* 109.85 22.30

See redrawn note following design A55. No. 494 exists imperf.

**Warning: Stamps of design A49 in other colors, double frames, inverted centers or centers omitted are forgeries. They are printed on sheet selvage.**

**1968-69** **Wmk. 361**
**500** A50 3p dp org & gray ('69) 350.00 90.00
**501** A50 4p green & gray 5.75 .45
**502** A50 10p mag & gray 8.25 .90

Expansion of Prophet's Mosque — A51

Madayin Saleh — A52

**1968-76** **Wmk. 361**
**503** A51 1p org & grn ('72) 4.50 .25
**504** A51 2p brn & grn ('72) 7.25 .25
**505** A51 3p blk & grn ('69) 6.25 .35
*b.* 3p gray & green ('76) 18.00 1.75
*c.* As No. 505, redrawn 4.50
**506** A51 4p org & grn ('70) 6.25 .45
*a.* Redrawn 4.50 .45
**507** A51 5p red & grn, redrawn ('74) 6.75 .75
**508** A51 6p Prus bl & grn ('72) 9.00 .90
**509** A51 8p rose red & grn ('76) 22.50 1.75
**510** A51 10p brn red & grn ('70) 8.25 .55
*b.* 10p org & grn, redrawn ('76) 18.00 .90
**511** A51 20p vio & grn ('74) 18.00 2.25
*Nos. 503-511 (9)* 88.75 7.50

**Wmk. 337**
*503a* A51 1p 5.00 .35
*504a* A51 2p ('70) 6.75 .35
*b.* As "a," redrawn 35.00
*505a* A51 3p ('71) 7.25 .70
*d.* As "a," redrawn —
*506b* A51 4p Redrawn ('72) 9.00
*507a* A51 5p ('70) 4.50 .45
*508a* A51 6p ('72) 6.25 .55
*510a* A51 10p ('70) 11.00 .60
*c.* As "a," redrawn 18.00
*511a* A51 20p ('72) 8.25 .70
*Nos. 503a-511a (8)* 58.00 3.70

See redrawn note following design A55.

**1968-75**
512 A52 2p ultra & bis brn ('70) 20.00 3.50
513 A52 4p dk & lt brown 5.00 .70
514 A52 7p org & lt brn ('75) 40.00 9.00
515 A52 10p sl grn & lt brn 12.50 1.75
516 A52 20p lil rose & brn 14.00 1.40
Nos. 512-516 (5) 91.50 16.35

Camels and Oil Derrick — A54

**Arabian Stallion — A53**
517 A53 4p mag & org brn .80
519 A53 10p blk & org brn 10.00 3.25
519 A53 14p bl & ocher ('71) 26.00 6.50
520 A53 20p ol grn & ocher 6.00
Nos. 517-520 (4) 58.25 12.55

**1969-71**
521 A54 4p dk pur & redsh brn ('71) 21.00 3.50
522 A54 10p ultra & hn brn 19.00 2.75

9.25 2.00

Holy Ka'aba, Mecca — A55

Original

Redrawn

On the original stamps the knob-shaped Arabic letter, located under the two square dots in the middle of the top panel, has a small central dot. The dot often is missing.

On the redrawn stamps the dot has been enlarged into a conspicuous irregular oval. The 3p also has a period added after the value and the 4p has the "4" under the "T" instead of the "S". There are other small differences.

Numeral & "Postage" on Gray Background, 8p on White

**1969-75**
523 A55 4p dp grn & blk ('70) 7.75 .70
a. Redrawn, value corner white ('74) 16.00 14.00
524 A55 6p dp lil rose & blk 14.00 1.75
b. Redrawn ('74)
525 A55 8p red & blk ('75) 4.50 .35
a. Redrawn, 8p red & blk ('75) 27.50 2.75
526 A55 10p org & blk ('69) 16.00 1.40
b. Redrawn, value corner white 16.00 1.40
a. Value corner white ('74) 18.00 1.75
Nos. 523-526 (4) 55.75 5.20

Rover Moot Badge — A56

**1969, Feb. 19 Perf. 13½x14 Litho. Wmk. 337**
607 A56 1p orange & multi 1.40 .20
608 A56 4p dull purple & multi 4.50 .20
609 A56 10p orange brn & multi 12.00 .65
Nos. 607-609 (3) 17.90 1.05
3rd Arab League Rover Moot, Mecca, Feb. 19-Mar. 3.

---

Traffic Light and Intersection — A57

**1969, Feb. Wmk. 361 Perf. 13½**
610 A57 3p dl bl, red & brt bl 2.25 .20
611 A57 4p org brn, red & gray 13.50 1.00
a. 3p dull blue, red & gray green 2.25 .20
612 A57 10p dl pur, red & gray grn 4.50 .50
Nos. 610-612 (3) 9.00 .90
Issued for Traffic Day.

WHO Emblem — A58

**1969, Oct. 20 Wmk. 337 Perf. 14**
613 A58 4p lt bl, vio bl & yel 10.00 .20
20th anniv. (in 1968) of WHO.

Islamic Conference Emblem — A59

**1970, Mar. 23 Litho. Wmk. 361**
614 A59 4p blue & black 2.75 .20
615 A59 10p yellow bis & blk 4.00 .40
Islamic Conference of Foreign Ministers, Jedda, March 1970.

Open Book and Satellite Earth Receiving Station — A60

**1970, Aug. 1 Litho. Wmk. 337**
616 A60 4p violet bl & multi 4.75 .20
617 A60 10p green & multi 9.50 .50
World Telecommunications Day.

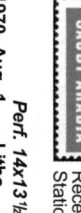
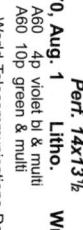

Steel Rolling Mill, Jedda A61

**1970, Oct. 26 Wmk. 337 Perf. 13½**
618 A61 3p yellow org & multi 2.75 .20
619 A61 4p violet & multi 4.25 .20
620 A61 10p brt green & multi 7.25 .50
Nos. 618-620 (3) 14.25 .90
Inauguration of 1st steel mill in Saudi Arabia.

Rover Moot Emblem — A62

**1971, Feb. Litho. Perf. 14**
621 A62 10p brt blue & multi 9.00 .70
4th Arab League Rover Moot, 1971.

Telecommunications Symbol — A63

**1971, May 17 Wmk. 337 Perf. 14**
622 A63 4p blue & blk 2.25 .20
623 A63 10p lilac & blk 5.00 .40
World Telecommunications Day.

University Minaret — A64

**1971, Aug. Wmk. 337; Wmk. 361 (4p) Litho. Perf. 14**
624 A64 3p brt green & black 1.75 .20
625 A64 4p brown & black 3.50 .50
626 A64 10p blue & black 6.50 .90
Nos. 624-626 (3) 11.75 .90
King Abdul Aziz National University.

Arab League Emblem — A65

**1971, Nov. Wmk. 337 Perf. 13½**
627 A65 10p multicolored 6.75 .40
Arab League Week.

Education Year Emblem — A66

**1971, Nov. Litho.**
628 A66 4p apple grn & brn red 5.75 .20
International Education Year 1970.

OPEC Emblem — A67

**1971, Dec. Litho. Perf. 14**
629 A67 4p light blue 6.75 .20
10th anniversary of OPEC (Organization of Petroleum Exporting Countries).

---

Globe A68

**1972, Aug. Wmk. 361 Perf. 14**
630 A68 4p multicolored 6.75 .20
4th World Telecommunications Day.

Telephone — A69

**1972, Oct. Wmk. 337, 361 (5p)**
631 A69 1p red, blk & grn 2.00 .20
632 A69 4p dk grn, blk & grn 2.00 .20
633 A69 5p blk, lilac & grn 3.75 .20
634 A69 10p tan, blk & grn 8.00 .40
Nos. 631-634 (4) 15.75 1.00
Inauguration of automatic telephone system (1969).

Writing Hand — A70

**1972, Sept. 8 Litho. Wmk. 361**
635 A70 10p multicolored 9.00 .40
World Literacy Day, Sept. 8.

Holy Ka'aba and Grand Mosque, Mecca A71

**1973**
636 A71 4p lt blue & multi 3.50 .20
637 A71 6p lilac & multi 7.00 .35
638 A71 10p salmon & multi 10.50 .60
Nos. 636-638 (3) 21.00 1.15
5th Arab League Rover Moot.
Rover Moot Emblem and: 4p, Prophet's Mosque, Medina. 10p, Plains of Arafat.

Globe and Map of Palestine A71a

**1973 Litho. Wmk. 361 Perf. 14**
639 A71a 4p black, yel & red 3.50 .20
640 A71a 10p blue, yel & red 7.25 .40
Palestine Week.

Leaf and Emblem — A72

**1973**
641 A72 4p yellow & multi     6.25 .30
International Hydrological Decade 1965-74.

Desalination Plant — A77

| | | **Perf. 14** | |
|---|---|---|---|
| 650 | A77 | 4p dp orange & bl | 2.10 | .20 |
| 651 | A77 | 6p emerald & vio | 4.50 | .25 |
| 652 | A77 | 10p rose red & blk | 6.75 | .50 |
| | | | 13.35 | .95 |

**1974, Sept. 3   Wmk. 361**
Nos. 650-652 (3)

Opening (in 1971) of sea water desalination plant, Jedda.

**1974, May 21**
648 A76 4p orange & multi    2.75 .25
649 A76 10p green & multi    11.00 .65
**Perf. 13½**
International Book Year, 1972.

King Faisal — A86

KSA 6th Islamic Conference of Foreign Ministers

Conference Emblem — A87

**1975, July 6   Unwmk.**
671 A86 4p green & rose brn   3.00 .30
672 A86 16p violet & green   3.75 .75
673 A86 23p dk green & vio   7.75 1.25
     14.50 2.30
Nos. 671-673 (3)
**Perf. 14**

**Miniature Sheet**
*Imperf*
674 A86 40p Prus bl & ocher   350.00
King Faisal ibn Abdul-Aziz Al Saud (1906-1975). Size of No. 674: 71x80mm.

**1975, July 11**
675 A87 10p rose brn & blk   5.50 .50
6th Islamic Conference of Foreign Ministers, Jedda, July 12.
**Perf. 14**

Holy Ka'aba, Globe, Clasped Hands — A89

Wheat and Sun — A88

**1975, Sept. 17   Litho.   Wmk. 361**
676 A88 4p lilac & multi   3.00 .20
677 A88 10p blue & multi   8.75 .40
Charity Society, 20th anniversary.

**1975, Sept. 17**
678 A89 4p olive bis & multi   7.75 .25
679 A89 10p orange & multi   16.00 .45
Conference of Moslem Organizations, Mecca, Apr. 6-10, 1974.
**Perf. 14**

A82

A84

A83

Red Crescent flower,

**1974, Dec. 17   Perf. 14x14½**
662 A82 4p gray & multi   1.90 .25
663 A82 6p lt green & multi   4.75 .50
664 A82 10p lt blue & multi   9.50 .95
     16.15 1.70
Nos. 662-664 (3)
Saudi Arabian Red Crescent Society, 10th anniversary (in 1973).

**1974, Dec. 23   Wmk. 361   Perf. 14**
665 A83 4p blue blk & multi   5.00 .20
666 A83 6p blue blk & multi   9.50 .35
667 A83 10p purple & multi   14.50 .60
     29.00 1.15
Nos. 665-667 (3)
Saudi Arabian scout emblem and minarets.
6th Arab League Rover Moot, Mecca.

**1974, Dec. 15**
659 A81 3p slate & multi   2.10 .20
660 A81 4p brown & multi   4.25 .25
661 A81 10p lilac & multi   11.50 .70
     17.85 1.15
Nos. 659-661 (3)
**Perf. 14**
King Faisal Military Cantonment, 1971.

A78

A79

**1974, Nov. 1**
653 A78 4p ocher & ultra   7.25 .20
654 A78 10p emerald & ultra   14.50 .50
50th anniversary (in 1973) of International Criminal Police Organization.

**1974, Oct. 26   Litho.   Wmk. 361**
655 A79 4p multicolored   7.25 .20
Arab Consultative Council for Postal Studies, 3rd session.

Design: INTERPOL emblem.

Anemometer and Weather Balloon with UN Emblem — A85

**1975, Mar. 31   Perf. 14x13½**
Design: Reading braille.
668 A84 4p multicolored   3.50 .25
669 A84 10p multicolored   8.50 .45
Day of the Blind.

**1975, May 8   Litho.   Wmk. 361   Perf. 13½x14**
670 A85 4p multicolored   9.00 .25
Centenary (in 1973) of International Meteorological Cooperation.

Arab Postal Union Emblem — A73

**1973, Dec.   Litho.**
642 A73 4p sepia & multi   4.75 .30
643 A73 10p purple & multi   10.50 .50
**Perf. 14**
25th anniversary (in 1971) of the Conference of Sofar, Lebanon, establishing the Arab Postal Union.

Balloons and Pacifier — A74

**1973, Dec.**
644 A74 4p lt blue & multi   8.00 .20
Universal Children's Day (stamp dated 1971).

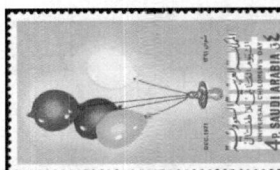

Arab Postal and UPU Emblems A75

**1974, July 7   Wmk. 361**
645 A75 3p yellow & multi   52.50 3.00
646 A75 4p rose & multi   52.50 5.75
647 A75 10p lt green & multi   52.50 8.75
     157.50 17.50
Nos. 645-647 (3)
Centenary of the Universal Postal Union.

UPU Headquarters, Bern — A80

**1974, Nov. 15   Perf. 13½**
656 A80 3p orange & multi   3.75 .25
657 A80 4p lilac & multi   6.25 .50
658 A80 10p blue & multi   8.75 1.25
     18.75 2.00
Nos. 656-658 (3)
Opening of new Universal Postal Union Headquarters, Bern, May 1970.

Tank, Planes, Rockets and Flame A81

Handshake and UNESCO Emblem — A76

## 1975, Sept. Litho. Unwmk.

Saudia Tri-Star and DC-3 — A90

| 680 | A90 | 4p buff & multi | 7.75 | .30 |
| 681 | A90 | 10p lt blue & multi | 16.00 | .55 |

Saudia, Saudi Arabian Airline, 30th anniversary.

Conference Centers in Mecca and Riyadh A91

## 1975, Sept.

| 682 | A91 | 10p multicolored | 11.00 | .55 |

Friday Mosque, Medina, and Juwatha Mosque, al-Hasa — A92

## 1975, Oct. 26 Litho. Unwmk.

| 683 | A92 | 4p green & multi | 6.25 | .30 |
| 684 | A92 | 10p vermilion & multi | 8.75 | .55 |

Ancient Islamic holy places.

FAO Emblem — A93

## 1975, Oct. 26 Litho.

| 685 | A93 | 4p gray & multi | 4.25 | .20 |
| 686 | A93 | 10p buff & multi | 13.50 | .55 |

World Food Program, 10th anniversary (in 1973). Stamps are dated 1973.

Conference Emblem — A94

## 1976, Mar. 20 Unwmk. Perf. 14

| 687 | A94 | 4p multicolored | 16.00 | .30 |

Islamic Solidarity Conference of Science and Technology.

---

## 1976, May 26 Litho. Perf. 14

Saudi Arabia Map, Transmission Tower, TV Screen — A95

| 688 | A95 | 4p multicolored | 21.00 | .30 |

Saudi Arabian television, 10th anniversary.

Grain, Atom, Symbol, Graph A96

## 1976, June 28 Litho. Perf. 14

| 689 | A96 | 20h yellow & multi | 4.25 | .30 |
| 690 | A96 | 50h yellow & multi | 7.25 | .60 |

Second Five-year Plan.

Holy Ka'aba A97

## 1976-79 Litho. Wmk. 361 Perf. 14

### Type II

Two types:

I — "White" minarets. Gray vignette.
II — Black minarets and vignette. Design redrawn, strengthened, darkened, clarified.

| 691 | A97 | 5h lilac & blk | .20 | .20 |
| 692 | A97 | 10h lt violet & blk | .20 | .20 |
| 693 | A97 | 15h salmon & blk | .35 | .20 |
| | | Type I | | |
| 694 | A97 | 20h lt bl & blk, II | .20 | .20 |
| | | Type I | | |
| 695 | A97 | 25h yellow & blk | 3.75 | .20 |
| 696 | A97 | 30h gray grn & blk | 5.00 | .20 |
| 697 | A97 | 35h bister & blk | 1.00 | .20 |
| 698 | A97 | 40h lt green & blk | 1.40 | .20 |
| | | Type I (77) | | |
| 699 | A97 | 45h dull rose & blk | 3.25 | .30 |
| 700 | A97 | 50h pink & blk | .80 | .20 |
| 703 | A97 | 65h gray blue & blk | 1.00 | .30 |
| 710 | A97 | 1r lt yel grn & blk | 1.10 | .20 |
| 711 | A97 | 2r green & black | 1.25 | .20 |
| | | | 1.75 | .20 |
| | | | 6.50 | .35 |
| | | Nos. 691-711 (13) | 22.60 | 2.75 |

No. 698 imperf exists as an issued error. Value, $110. Nos. 691-711 also exist as imperfs not regularly issued.

Issue years: 1976, 1977; 5h-15h, 25h-50h, 1r, 1978; 65h, 2r, 1979.

See Nos. 872-882, 961-968.

Quba Mosque, Medina, built 622 — A98

## 1976-77

| 719 | A98 | 20h orange & blk | 2.00 | .20 |
| 720 | A98 | 50h emer & lilac (77) | 3.75 | .20 |

Reissued in 1978 in different shades. No. 720 exists imperf as an issued error.

---

## 1976, July 17 Unwmk. Perf. 13½

Globe, Telephones, 1876 and 1976 A100

| 721 | A100 | 50h multicolored | 7.25 | .30 |

Centenary of first telephone call by Alexander Graham Bell, Mar. 10, 1876.

Arab Leaders A101

## 1976, Oct. 30 Litho. Perf. 14

| 722 | A101 | 20h ultra & emerald | 5.25 | .25 |

Arab Summit Conference, Riyadh, October. Leaders pictured: Pres. Elias Sarkis, Lebanon; Pres. Anwar Sadat, Egypt; Pres. Hafez al Assad, Syria; King Khalid, Saudi Arabia; Amir Sabah, Kuwait; Yasir Arafat, Palestine Liberation Organization chairman.

WHO Emblem and Eye A102

## 1976, Nov. 28 Litho. Perf. 14

| 723 | A102 | 20h multicolored | 11.00 | .20 |

World Health Day; Prevention of Blindness.

Holy Ka'aba — A103

## 1976, Nov. 28 Unwmk.

| 724 | A103 | 20h multicolored | 8.00 | .25 |

50th anniversary of installation of new covering of Holy Ka'aba, Mecca.

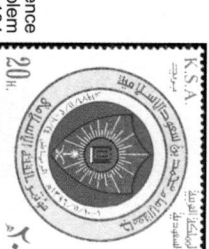

Conference Emblem A104

## 1977, Feb. 18 Unwmk. Litho.

| 725 | A104 | 20h multicolored | 8.00 | .20 |

Islamic Jurisprudence Conference, Riyadh, Oct. 24-Nov. 2, 1976.

---

## 1977, Feb. 25 Perf. 14

A105

| 726 | A105 | 4p multicolored | 7.25 | .20 |

25th anniversary (in 1974) of the founding of Sharia (Islamic Law) College, Mecca.

Design: Sharia College emblem.

A106

## 1977

| 727 | A106 | 20h dk brn & brt grn | 2.00 | .20 |
| a. | | Incorrect date | 17.50 | |
| 728 | A106 | 80h bl blk & brt grn | | .55 |
| a. | | Incorrect date | 17.50 | |

2nd anniversary of installation of King Khalid Ibn Abdul-Aziz. Nos. 727a-728a (illustrated), issued Mar. 3, have incorrect Arabic date in bottom panel, last characters of 2nd and 3rd rows identical. Stamps withdrawn after a few days and replaced Aug. 14 with corrected date; last characters in 3rd row changed to "ro".

Diesel Train and Map of Route A107

## 1977, May 23 Litho. Perf. 14

| 729 | A107 | 20h multicolored | 24.00 | .20 |

Dammam-Riyadh railroad, 25th anniversary.

Arabic Ornament and Names — A108

## 1977, Aug. 15 Litho. Perf. 14

| 730 | A108 | 20h, single stamp | 5.00 | .40 |
| a.-d. | | 20h, Block of 4 | 55.00 | 3.25 |

Designs (Names from Left to Right): UL, Malik Ben Anas (715-795); UR, Mohammad Ben Idris Al-Shafi'i (767-820); LL, Abu Hanifa an-Nu'man (699-767); LR, Ahmed Ben Hanbal (780-855).

Famous Imams (7th-9th centuries), founders of traditional schools of Islamic jurisprudence. Sheets of 60 stamps (15 blocks). No. 730 exists with a double impression of the blue color. Stamps with double impressions of the black color are forgeries.

Al Khafji Oil
Rig — A109

**1976-80**

<table>
<tr><td>731</td><td>A109</td><td>5h vio blue & org</td><td>.20</td><td>.20</td></tr>
<tr><td>732</td><td>A109</td><td>10h yel grn & org</td><td>.20</td><td>.20</td></tr>
<tr><td>733</td><td>A109</td><td>15h brown & org</td><td>.20</td><td>.20</td></tr>
<tr><td>734</td><td>A109</td><td>20h green & org</td><td>.20</td><td>.20</td></tr>
<tr><td>735</td><td>A109</td><td>25h dk pur & org</td><td>.20</td><td>.20</td></tr>
<tr><td>736</td><td>A109</td><td>30h blue & orange</td><td>.25</td><td>.20</td></tr>
<tr><td>737</td><td>A109</td><td>35h sepia & org</td><td>.30</td><td>.20</td></tr>
<tr><td>738</td><td>A109</td><td>40h mag & org</td><td>.30</td><td>.20</td></tr>
<tr><td>a.</td><td></td><td>40h dull purple (error)</td><td>175.00</td><td></td></tr>
<tr><td>739</td><td>A109</td><td>45h violet & orange</td><td>.35</td><td></td></tr>
<tr><td>740</td><td>A109</td><td>50h rose & orange</td><td>.45</td><td></td></tr>
<tr><td>741</td><td>A109</td><td>50h dull org & org (error)</td><td>67.50</td><td></td></tr>
<tr><td>743</td><td>A109</td><td>55h grnsh bl & org</td><td>20.00</td><td>6.75</td></tr>
<tr><td>744</td><td>A109</td><td>65h grnsh bl & org</td><td>1.10</td><td>3.50</td></tr>
<tr><td>750</td><td>A109</td><td>1r gray & orange</td><td>1.40</td><td>.35</td></tr>
<tr><td>751</td><td>A109</td><td>2r dk vio & org</td><td></td><td>.55</td></tr>
<tr><td></td><td></td><td></td><td>3.00</td><td>.90</td></tr>
<tr><td></td><td></td><td>('80)</td><td>28.15</td><td>7.30</td></tr>
</table>

Nos. 731-751 (14)

All values exist with extra dot in Arabic "Al Khafji." The 20h, 25h, 50h, 65h and 1r were retouched to remove the dot. Color of flame varies from light orange to vermilion. See Nos. 885-892.
No. 737 imperf exists as an issued error. Value, $275. Nos. 731-751 also exist as imperfs not regularly issued.

Mohenjo-Daro Ruins — A110 **Unwmk.**
**1977, Oct. 23    Litho.**    8.00  .35
761  A110  50h multicolored

UNESCO campaign to save Mohenjo Daro excavations in Pakistan.

Idrisi's World
Map, 1154 — A111

**1977, Nov. 1    Litho.    Perf. 14**
762  A111  20h multicolored    2.75  .30
763  A111  50h multicolored    5.50  .55

First International Symposium on Studies in the History of Arabia at the University of Riyadh, Apr. 23-26, 1977.

King Faisal Specialist Hospital,
Riyadh — A112

**1977, Nov. 13    Litho.    Unwmk.**
764  A112  20h multicolored    3.25  .25
765  A112  50h multicolored    5.25  .40

---

Conference
Emblem — A113

**1978, Jan. 24    Litho.    Perf. 14**
766  A113  20h vio blue & yel    4.25  .20

1st World Conf. on Moslem Education.

APU
Emblem,
Members'
Flags
A114

**1978, Jan. 21**
767  A114  20h multicolored    1.75  .20
768  A114  80h multicolored    3.75  .50

25th anniversary of Arab Postal Union.

Taif Abha Gizan Highway — A115

**1978, Oct. 15    Litho.    Perf. 14**
769  A115  20h multicolored    1.75  .20
770  A115  80h multicolored    3.75  .40

Inauguration of Taif-Abha-Gizan highway. No. 770 exists with black (road) missing and with black double.

Pilgrims, Mt. Arafat and Holy
Ka'aba — A116

**1978, Nov. 6    Litho.    Unwmk.**
771  A116  20h multicolored    1.75  .20
772  A116  80h multicolored    3.75  .40

Pilgrimage to Mecca.
No. 772 exists with inscriptions (black and blue colors) omitted.

Gulf Postal
Organization
Emblem — A117

**1979, Feb. 6    Litho.    Perf. 14**
773  A117  20h multicolored    1.40  .20
774  A117  50h multicolored    2.75  .30

1st Conf. of Gulf Postal Organization, Baghdad.

---

Saudi
Arabia No.
129, King
Abdul Aziz
ibn Saud
A118

**Unwmk.    Litho.    Perf. 14**
**1979, June 4**
775  A118  20h multicolored    1.50  .25
776  A118  50h multicolored    3.25  .25
777  A118  115h multicolored    5.25  .65
    10.00  1.05

**Souvenir Sheet**
**Imperf**
778  A118  100h multicolored    90.00

1st commemorative stamp, 50th anniv. No. 778 contains one stamp with simulated perforations. Size: 101x76mm.

Crown
Prince
Fahd
A119

**1979, June 25    Perf. 14**
779  A119  20h multicolored    2.00  .20
780  A119  50h multicolored    4.00  .30

Crown Prince Fahd ibn Abdul Aziz.

Dome of
the Rock,
Jerusalem
A120

**1979, July 2    Wmk. 361**
781  A120  20h multi (shades)    2.00  .30

No. 781 exists with inscriptions (green and mauve colors) omitted.
Imperfs. exist. See No. 866.

Gold Door, Holy
Ka'aba — A121

**1979, Oct. 13    Litho.    Perf. 14**
782  A121  20h multicolored    1.60  .20
783  A121  80h multicolored    3.25  .40

Installation of new gold doors. Imperfs. exist.

Pilgrims at Holy Ka'aba, Mecca
Mosque — A122

**1979, Oct. 27**
784  A122  20h multicolored    1.10  .20
785  A122  50h multicolored    2.75  .30

Pilgrimage to Mecca. Imperfs. exist.

---

Birds in Trees, IYC Emblem — A123

IYC Emblem and: 50h, Child's drawing.

**1980, Feb. 17    Litho.    Perf. 14**
786  A123  20h multicolored    9.50  .20
787  A123  50h multicolored    15.00  .30

Intl. Year of the Child (1979). Imperfs. exist.

King Abdul
Aziz ibn
Saud on
Horseback,
Saudi Flag
A124

**1980, Apr. 5    Litho.    Perf. 14**
788  A124  20h multicolored    1.50  .20
789  A124  80h multicolored    3.50  .35

Saudi Arabian Army, 80th anniv. (1979). Imperfs. exist.

Arab League,
35th Anniversary
A125

Smoke Entering
Lungs, WHO
Emblem — A127

International Bureau of Education,
50th Anniversary — A126

**1980, Apr. 27    Litho.    Perf. 14**
790  A125  20h multicolored    1.75  .20

Imperfs. exist.

**1980, May 4**
791  A126  50h multicolored    2.25  .30

Imperfs. exist.

**1980, May 20**
792  A127  20h shown    1.75  .20
793  A127  50h Cigarette, horiz.    4.25  .30

Anti-smoking campaign. Imperfs. exist.

20th
Anniversary
of OPEC
A128

Design: 50h, Workers holding OPEC emblem (Organization of Petroleum Exporting Countries).

**1980, Sept. 1**    Litho.
794 A128 20h multicolored   1.50 .20
795 A128 50h multi, vert.   2.75 .30

**1980, Oct. 18**
796 A129 20h multicolored   .90 .20
797 A129 50h multicolored   1.90 .30

Pilgrims Arriving at Jedda Airport
A129

Pilgrimage to Mecca.

Conference Emblem
A130

Third Islamic Summit Conference, Mecca.

Holy Ka'aba, Mecca
Mosque — A131

**1981, Jan. 26**    Litho.    Perf. 14
798 A130 20h shown   1.00 .20
799 A131 20h shown   1.00 .20
800 A131 20h multicolored   1.00 .20
801 A131 20h multicolored   1.00 .20

Nos. 798-801 (4)   4.00 .80

Medina, Prophet's Mosque, Jerusalem Dome of the Rock.

Hegira, 1500th Anniv.
A132

**1981, Jan. 25**
802 A132 20h multicolored   .70 .20
803 A132 50h multicolored   1.40 .25
804 A132 80h multicolored   4.85 .85

Nos. 802-804 (3)

**Souvenir Sheet**
805 A132 300h multicolored   110.00

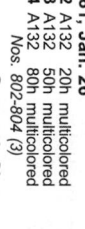

**1981, Feb. 21**
806 A133 20h multicolored   .70 .20
807 A133 80h multicolored   2.25 .40

Industry Week
A133

---

Line Graph and Telephone
A134

**1981, Feb. 28**
808 A134 20h shown   .40 .25
809 A135 80h shown   2.50 .45
810 A134 115h Earth satellite station   5.90 1.25

Map of Saudi Arabia, Microwave Tower
A135

**Souvenir Sheets**
811 A134 100h like #808   50.00
812 A135 100h like #809   50.00
813 A134 100h like #810   50.00

Nos. 808-810 (3)   3.00 .55

Ministry of Posts and Telecommunications achievements.

**1981, Apr. 2**    Litho.    Perf. 14
814 A135a 20h multicolored   .40 .20
815 A135a 65h multicolored   1.10 .40
816 A135a 80h multicolored   1.60 .40
817 A135a 115h multicolored   2.25 .65

Nos. 814-817 (4)   5.35 1.65

Arab City Day — A135a

**1981, Apr. 12**
818 A136 20h shown   .60 .20
819 A136 80h Plane over airport, diff.   2.50 .45

Jedda Airport Opening
A136

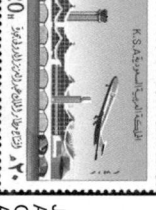

**1981, July 26**    Litho.    Perf. 14
820 A137 20h multicolored   2.10 .25
821 A137 80h multicolored   4.00 .40

Int'l Year of the Disabled — A138

1982 World Cup Soccer Preliminary Games — A137

---

Map of Saudi Arabia
A135

**1981, Aug. 5**
822 A138 20h Reading braille   1.75 .20
823 A138 50h Man weaving rug   2.75 .25

3rd Five-year Plan (1981-1985) — A139

**1981, Sept. 5**
824 A139 20h multicolored   1.45 .20

King Abdul Aziz, Map of Saudi Arabia
A140

**1981, Sept. 23**    Litho.    Perf. 14
825 A140 5h multicolored   .20 .20
826 A140 10h multicolored   .20 .20
827 A140 15h multicolored   .20 .20
828 A140 20h multicolored   .20 .20
829 A140 50h multicolored   .35 .20
830 A140 65h multicolored   .70 .30
831 A140 80h multicolored   1.00 .20
832 A140 115h multicolored   3.25 .60

Nos. 825-832 (8)   0.40 2.50

**Souvenir Sheet**    Imperf
833 A140 10r multicolored   90.00

50th anniv. of Kingdom; No. 833 shows king, map, document. Size: 100x75mm.

**1981, Oct. 7**
834 A141 20h multicolored   1.40 .20
835 A141 65h multicolored   2.75 .40

Pilgrimage to Mecca
A141

**1981, Oct. 16**
836 A142 20h multicolored   2.25 .40

World Food Day
A142

**1981, Nov. 10**    Litho.    Perf. 14
837 A143 20h multicolored   .70 .20
838 A143 80h multicolored   2.25 .45

2nd Session of the Gulf Cooperative Council Summit Conference, Riyadh, Nov. 10 — A143

---

King Saud University, 25th Anniv.
A144

**1982, Mar. 10**    Litho.    Perf. 14
839 A144 20h multicolored   .90 .25
840 A144 50h multicolored   1.90 .30

New Regional Postal Centers
A145

**1982, July 14**    Litho.    Perf. 14
841 A145 20h Riyadh P.O.   .40 .20
842 A145 65h Jedda   1.25 .35
843 A145 80h Dammam   1.60 .35
844 A145 115h Automated sort-ing   5.15 1.45

Nos. 841-844 (4)   1.90 .55

Four 300h souvenir sheets exist in same designs as Nos. 841-844 respectively. Value, $10 each.

Riyadh Television Center — A146

**1982, Sept. 4**
845 A146 20h multicolored   1.10 .20

25th Anniv. of King's Soccer Cup
A147

**1982, Sept. 8**
846 A147 20h multicolored   .85 .20
847 A147 65h multicolored   1.90 .35

30th Anniv. of Arab Postal Union
A148

**1982, Sept. 8**
848 A148 20h multicolored   .80 .20
849 A148 65h Emblem, vert.   1.90 .40

Pilgrimage to Mecca
A149

**1982, Sept. 26**
850 A149 20h multicolored   .80 .20
851 A149 50h multicolored   1.90 .40

## World Standards Day A150

**1982, Oct. 14** Litho. Perf. 12
852 A150 20h multicolored 1.50 .20

## World Food Day A151

**1982, Oct. 16**
853 A151 20h multicolored 1.25 .20

## Coronation of King Fahd, June 14, 1982 A152
## Installation of Crown Prince Abdullah, June 14, 1982 A153

**1983, Feb. 12** Litho. Perf. 14
854 A152 20h multicolored .35 .20
855 A152 20h multicolored .35 .20
856 A152 50h multicolored .70 .30
857 A153 50h multicolored .70 .30
858 A152 65h multicolored 1.10 .35
859 A153 65h multicolored 1.10 .35
860 A152 80h multicolored 1.10 .35
861 A163 80h multicolored 1.25 .40
862 A152 115h multicolored 1.90 .65
863 A153 115h multicolored 1.90 .65
10.60 3.80
Nos. 854-863 (10)
Two one-stamp souvenir sheets contain Nos. 862-863, perf. 12½. Value $250.

## 6th Anniv. of United Arab Shipping Co. — A154

Various freighters.
**1983, Aug. 9** Litho. Perf. 14
864 A154 20h multicolored .45 .20
865 A154 65h multicolored 2.00 .20

## Dome of the Rock, Jerusalem A155

**1983, Sept.** Wmk. 361 Perf. 12
866 A155 20h multicolored .65 .20
See No. 781.

## Opening of King Khalid International Airport — A158

## Pilgrimage to Mecca A156

**1983, Sept. 16** Litho. Perf. 14
867 A156 20h brt blue & multi .40 .20
868 A156 65h dk black & multi 1.40 .20

## World Communications Year — A157

**1983, Oct. 8** Litho. Perf. 14
869 A157 20h Post and UPU emblems .30 .20
870 A157 80h Telephone and ITU emblems 1.50 .30

## Holy Ka'ba Type of 1976
### Type II

Perf. 14x13½ Litho. Wmk. 361
Size: 26x21mm
**1982-86**
872 A97 10h lt vio & blk ('83) .20 .20
874 A97 20h lt blue & blk .20 .20
880 A97 50h pink & blk ('83) .45 .20
881 A97 65h gray bl & blk .60 .60
882 A97 1r lt yel grn & blk 1.40 1.40

Perf. 13½
874c A97 20h lt blue & blk .20 .20
880a A97 50h pink & blk ('83) .50 .45
881a A97 65h gray bl & blk .60 .60
882a A97 1r lt yel grn & blk 1.40 1.40

Perf. 12
872b A97 10h lt vio & blk .20 .20
873 A97 15h sal & blk ('85) .20 .20
874a A97 20h lt blue & blk ('84) .20 .20
880b A97 50h pink & blk ('00) HI HI
882b A97 1r lt yel grn & blk ('83) 1.40 1.40

Unwmk.
872a A97 10h lt vio & blk ('87) .20 .20
874d A97 20h lt blue & blk .20 .20
881c A97 65h gray bl & blk ('84) .60 .60
882c A97 1r lt yel grn & blk ('85) 1.40 1.40
Counterfeits of the 1r exist as perf. 11.

## Al Khafji Oil Rig Type of 1976

Perf. 14x13½ Litho. Wmk. 361
Size: 26x21mm
**1982-84**
885 A109 5h vio bl & org .20 .20
886 A109 10h yel grn & org .20 .20
887 A109 15h bis brn & org .20 .20
888 A109 20h green & org .20 .20
889 A109 25h dk pur & org ('00) .35 .35
890 A109 50h rose & org 2.75 .30
891a A109 65h sepia & orange .60 1.40
892 A109 1r gray & org .30 .30

Perf. 13½
885a A109 5h .20 .20
886a A109 10h .20 .20
887a A109 15h .20 .20
888a A109 20h .20 .20
890a A109 50h .20 .20
891 A109 65h sepia & org ('84) .35 .35
892a A109 1r .55 .30

Perf. 13½
**1983**
886b A109 10h .20 .20
887b A109 15h .20 .20
888b A109 20h .20 .20
889b A109 25h dk pur & org .30 .30
890b A109 50h .35 .35
892b A109 1r .45 .30

## World Food Day — A159

**1983, Nov. 16** Litho. Perf. 13½x14
893 A158 20h shown .50 .20
894 A158 65h blue & multi 1.60 .20

**1983, Nov. 29** Litho. Perf. 14
895 A159 20h Wheat, Irrigation, Silos 1.40 .20

## Aqsa Mosque, Jerusalem A160

**1983, Dec. 13** Litho. Perf. 14
896 A160 20h multicolored .55 .25

## Old and Modern Riyadh — A161

## Shohra Palace, Taif — A162

## Old and New Jedda (Waterfront) — A163

## Damman — A164

**1984-95** Litho. Wmk. 361 Perf. 12
897 A161 20h lilac rose & multi .20 .20
898 A162 20h Prus grn & multi .20 .20
899 A161 50h black & multi .20 .20
900 A162 50h brown & multi .30 .35

Unwmk.
901 A161 50h multicolored .45 .25
902 A162 50h multicolored .65 .35
903 A163 50h green & multi .90 .45
904 A164 50h green & multi .40 .25
905 A161 75h multicolored .65 .35
906 A162 75h multicolored .65 .35
907 A163 75h blue & multi .90 .45
908 A164 75h multicolored .60 .35
909 A161 150h pink & multi 1.50 .75
910 A162 150h pink & multi 1.50 .75
911 A163 150h green & multi 1.60 .75
911A A164 150h red lilac & multi 1.25 .60
12.40 6.60
Nos. 897-911A (16)

Issued: #897, 6/27/84; #898, 10/13/84; #899, 8/29/84; #900, 3/10/87; #910, 9/3/87; #902, 11/3/87; #909, 5/4/88; #903, 911, 1/31/89; #906, 1990; #901, 907, 1991; #904, 908, 911A, 1995.

## Estate Development Fund, 10th Anniv. — A165

Unwmk.
912 A165 20h multicolored .55 .25

## Opening of Solar Village, Al-near Al-Eyenah A166

**1984, July 28** Litho. Perf. 12
913 A166 20h multicolored .40 .20
914 A166 80h Stylized sun, solar panels 1.25 .30

Imperf
Size: 81x81mm
915 A166 100h like 20h 32.50
916 A166 100h like 80h 32.50

**1984, Aug. 14**

## Pilgrimage to Mecca — A167

Al-Kheef Mosque: 65h, Aerial view.
**1984, Sept. 4** Litho. Perf. 14
917 A167 20h brown & multi .50 .20
Perf. 12
918 A167 65h olive gray & multi 1.60 .20

## Participation of Saudi Arabian Soccer Team in 1984 Olympics — A168

**1984, Sept. 25** Litho. Perf. 12
919 A168 20h blue & multi 1.75 1.00
920 A168 115h green & multi 5.50 1.75
"Games" and "Olympiad" are misspelled on both stamps.

## World Food Day A169

Litho. Perf. 12
**1984, Oct. 16**
921 A169 20h multicolored .55 .25

SAUDI ARABIA

Beginning with Nos. 922-923 some issues are printed in sheets that have labels inscribed in Arabic. Generally there are from 2 to 6 labels per sheet. Stamps with label attached command a premium.

**90th Anniv. International Olympic Committee — A170**

**1984, Dec. 23    Litho.    Perf. 12**
922 A170 20h multicolored    .50 .40
923 A170 50h multicolored    3.00 .40

**Launch of ARABSAT — A171**

**1985, Feb. 9    Litho.    Perf. 12**
924 A171 20h ARABSAT, view of Earth    2.00 .20

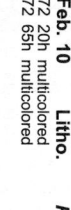

**7th Holy Koran Competition — A172**

**1985, Feb. 10    Litho.    Perf. 12**
925 A172 20h multicolored    .40 .20
926 A172 65h multicolored    1.10 .20

**4th Five-Year Development Plan, 1985-1990 — A173**

Portrait of King Fahd, industry emblems and: 20h, Dhahran Harbor, Jubail. 50h, Television tower, earth receiver, microwave tower. 65h, Agriculture. 80h, Harbor, Yanbu.

**1985, Mar. 23    Litho.    Perf. 13x12**
927 20h multicolored    .35 .20
928 50h multicolored    .90 .20
929 65h multicolored    1.10 .20
930 80h multicolored    1.25 .20
a. A173 Block of 4, #927-930    5.00 1.00

**Int'l. Youth Year — A174**

**1985, May 4    Perf. 12**
931 A174 20h multicolored    .35 .20
932 A174 80h multicolored    1.10 .30

**Self-sufficiency in Wheat Production — A175**

**1985, May 4**
933 A175 20h multicolored    .55 .25

**East-West Pipeline — A176**

**1985, June 9**
934 A176 20h Tanker loading berth, Yanbu    .50 .20
935 A176 65h Pipeline, map    1.50 .20

**Shuttle Launch — A177**

**Shuttle, Missions Emblem — A178**

**1985, July 7**
936 A177 20h multicolored    1.00 .50
937 A178 115h multicolored    5.00 .90

Prince Sultan Ibn Salman Al-Saud, 1st Arab-Moslem astronaut, on Discovery 51-G.

**UN. 40th Anniv. A179**

**1985, July 15**
938 A179 20h multicolored    .65 .25

**Highway, Map, Holy Ka'aba in Mecca to Prophet's Mosque in Medina — A180**

**1985, July 22**
939 A180 20h multicolored    .45 .25
940 A180 65h multicolored    1.10 .25
Mecca-Medina Highway opening, 10/11/84.

**Post Code Inauguration — A181**

**1985, July 24**
941 A181 20h Covers    .55 .25

**1984 Asian Soccer Cup Victory A182**

**1985, July 30**
942 A182 20h multicolored    .40 .30
943 A182 65h multicolored    1.00 .30
944 A182 115h multicolored    2.50 .55
Nos. 942-944 (3)    3.90 1.15

**Pilgrimage to Mecca — A183**

**1985, Aug. 25    Litho.    Perf. 12**
945 A183 10h multicolored    .25 .25
946 A183 15h multicolored    .25 .25
947 A183 20h multicolored    .35 .25
948 A183 65h multicolored    .85 .25
Nos. 945-948 (4)    1.70 1.00

**1st Gulf Olympics Day, Riyadh, May 2 A184**

**1985, Sept. 8**
949 A184 20h multicolored    .40 .20
950 A184 115h multicolored    1.90 .40

**World Food Day A185**

**1985, Oct. 16**
951 A185 20h multicolored    .80 .40
952 A185 65h multicolored    2.75 .40

**King Abdul Aziz, Masmak Fort and Horsemen — A186**

**1985, Dec. 1**
953 A186 15h multicolored    .25 .25
954 A186 20h multicolored    .25 .25
955 A186 65h multicolored    .85 .25
956 A186 80h multicolored    1.10 .30
Nos. 953-956 (4)    2.45 1.05

Int'l. Conference on the History of King Abdul Aziz Al-Sa'ud, Riyadh. An imperf. souvenir sheet showing smaller versions of Nos. 953-956 and the conference emblem exists. Sold for 10r.

**King Fahd Koran Publishing Center, Medina — A187**

**1985, Dec. 18**
957 A187 20h multicolored    .25 .25
958 A187 65h multicolored    1.25 .25

**OPEC, 25th Anniv. A188**

**1985, Dec. 24**
959 A188 20h multicolored    .30 .25
960 A188 65h multicolored    1.60 .25

**Holy Ka'aba Type of 1976 Type II**

**Booklet Stamps**

**Size: 29x19mm**

**1986, Feb. 17    Litho.    Perf. 12**
961 A97 10h lt vio & blk    6.75
a. Booklet pane of 4    30.00
965 A97 20h bluish grn & blk    11.00
968 A97 50h pink & black    22.50
a. Bklt. pane of 4, #961,2 #965, #968    50.00

Due to vending machine breakdowns, distribution of this set has been very limited. The government does have stocks of these stamps but they are not currently being sold.

A189

A191

## Saudi-Bahrain Highway Inauguration — A207

**Perf. 14**

**1986, Nov. 26**
1039 A207 20h any single — 2.25 .30
1.00 .20
a.-b. Strip of 2
Printed se-tenant in a continuous design.

## 1st Modern Olympic Games, Athens, 90th Anniv. — A208

**1986, Dec. 27**
1040 A208 20h multicolored — 1.00 .50
1041 A208 100h multicolored — 5.75 .90

## General Petroleum and Minerals Organization (Petromin), 25th Anniv. — A209

**Unwmk.** **Perf. 12**
**1987, Feb. 23 Litho.**
1042 A209 50h multicolored — 60 .30
1043 A209 100h multicolored — 1.25 .60

## Restoration and Expansion of Quba Mosque, Medina — A210

Design. View of mosque and model of expanded mosque.

**Unwmk.** **Perf. 12**
**1987, Mar. 21 Litho.**
1044 A210 50h multicolored — .70 .30
1045 A210 75h multicolored — 1.10 .40

## Vocational Training A211

Designs: a, Welding. b, Drill press operation. c, Lathe operation. d, Electrician.

**Unwmk.** **Perf. 12**
**1987, Apr. 8 Litho.**
1046 A211 50h any single — 6.25 6.25
1.25 .60
a.-d. Block of 4

---

## Saudi Universities

Imam Mohammed ibn Saud — A200
Umm al-Qura — A201
King Saud — A202
King Fahd Petroleum and Minerals — A203
King Faisal — A204
King Abdul Aziz — A205
Medina Islamic — A206

**1906-91**

| No. | Type | Denom | Color | | |
|---|---|---|---|---|---|
| 1009 | A200 | 15h | sage grn & blk | .20 | .20 |
| 1010 | A200 | 20h | ultra & black | .20 | .20 |
| 1011 | A200 | 50h | ultra & black | .40 | .25 |
| 1012 | A200 | 65h | brt bl & blk | .50 | .25 |
| 1013 | A200 | 75h | brt bl & blk | .65 | .35 |
| 1014 | A200 | 100h | rose & black | .70 | .35 |
| 1015 | A200 | 150h | rose cl & blk | 1.25 | .60 |
| 1016 | A201 | 50h | ultra & blk | .50 | .30 |
| 1017 | A201 | 65h | brt bl & blk | .65 | .35 |
| 1018 | A201 | 75h | brt bl & blk | .65 | .45 |
| 1019 | A201 | 100h | dull rose & blk | 1.00 | .50 |
| 1020 | A202 | 150h | rose cl & blk | 1.50 | .75 |
| 1021 | A202 | 50h | ultra & black | 1.55 | .30 |
| 1022 | A202 | 75h | brt bl & blk | .65 | .35 |
| 1023 | A202 | 100h | dull rose & blk | | |
| 1024 | A202 | 150h | rose cl & blk | 1.00 | .50 |
| 1025 | A203 | 50h | ultra & black | 1.40 | .65 |
| 1026 | A203 | 75h | brt bl & blk | .65 | .35 |
| 1027 | A203 | 150h | rose cl & blk | 1.25 | .60 |
| 1028 | A204 | 50h | ultra & black | .65 | .40 |
| 1029 | A204 | 75h | brt bl & blk | .65 | .35 |
| 1030 | A204 | 150h | rose cl & blk | 1.40 | .40 |
| 1031 | A205 | 50h | ultra & black | 1.40 | .25 |
| 1032 | A205 | 75h | brt bl & blk | .65 | .45 |
| 1033 | A205 | 150h | rose cl & blk | 1.40 | .65 |
| 1034 | A206 | 50h | ultra & black | 1.40 | .65 |
| 1035 | A206 | 75h | brt bl & blk | .45 | .35 |
| 1036 | A206 | 150h | rose cl & blk | .65 | .35 |
| | Nos. 1009-1036 (28) | | | 21.35 | 10.50 |

Issued: #1009-1010, 1012, 1014, 11/26; #1019, 3/29; #1023, 7/22; #1016, 1020, 8/8; #1015, 1029, 1031, 1036, 1/31/89; #1011, 1025, 1030, 1033, 2/25/89; #1017, 3/89; #1021, 1989; #1013, 1018, 1026, 1990; #1022, 1029, 1032, 1035, 1991.

---

989 A195 150h black & rose lilac — 1.60 .80
a. Perf. 13½x14 — 1.40 .70
990 A195 2r blk & vio blue — 1.75 .90
6.15 3.30
Nos. 984-990 (7)
Issued: 30h, 40h, 8/5; 75h, 150h, 7/30/90; 50h, 10/9/90; #987a, 6/13/92; #989a, 6/6/92; 2r, 4/99; #987B, 988, 9/21/96.
This is an expanding set. Numbers may change.

## Pilgrimage to Mecca — A196

Designs of: a, A116. b, A129. c, A156. d, A149. e, A141. f, A122. g, A183. h, A167.

**1986, Aug. 13 Litho.** **Perf. 12**
1002 A196 20h, any single — 18.00 18.00
a.-h. Block of 8

## Discovery of Oil, 50th Anniv. — A197

**1986, Sept. 16**
1003 A197 20h Well, refinery — .45 .20
1004 A197 65h Well, map — 1.40 .20
Because of difficulty in separation most copies have damaged perfs.

## World Food Day — A198

**1986, Oct. 18**
1005 A198 20h shown — .25 .25
1006 A198 115h Stylized plant — 1.25 .45

## Massacre of Palestinian Refugees, Sept. 17, 1982 — A199

**1986, Nov. 1 Litho.** **Perf. 12**
1007 A199 80h multicolored — .80 .40
1008 A199 115h multicolored — 1.25 .65

Definitive stamps generally do not have an official date of issue. Any dates shown probably reflect sales at the Riyadh or Dammam post offices only.

---

A190

**1986, Jan. 8 Litho.** **Perf. 12**
971 A189 20h multicolored — 1.10 .25
Intl. Peace Year.

**1986, Mar. 24** **Perf. 14, 12 (65h)**
972 A190 20h multicolored — .55 .20
973 A190 65h multicolored — 1.10 .20
Riyadh Municipality, 50th aAnniv.

**1986, Apr. 21** **Perf. 12**
974 A191 20h multicolored — .45 .20
975 A191 50h multicolored — .90 .20
UN child survival campaign.

## General Establishment for Electric Power, 10th Anniv. — A192

**1986, Apr. 26**
976 A192 20h multicolored — .30 .25
977 A192 65h multicolored — 1.25 .26

## Continental Maritime Cable Inauguration — A193

**1986, June 1 Litho.** **Perf. 12**
978 A193 20h multicolored — .55 .25
979 A193 50h multicolored — 1.10 .25

## Natl. Guard Housing Project, Riyadh, Inauguration — A194

**1986, July 19**
980 A194 20h multicolored — .35 .20
981 A194 65h multicolored — 1.10 .20

## Islamic Arch, Holy Ka'aba — A195

**1986-98 Litho.** **Perf. 12**
984 A195 30h blk & bluish grn — .20 .20
985 A195 40h black & lilac — .25 .20
A195 50h rose
986 A195 50h black & brt green — .65 .35
987 A195 75h black & Prus bl — .80 .40
a. Perf. 13½x14
987B A195 100h black & red — .65 .35
988 A195 100h blk & bl green — .90 .45

Cairo Exhibition
A212

A213

**1987, June 17**
**Unwmk.**   **Litho.**   **Perf. 12**
1047 A212 50h multicolored   .65   .35
1048 A212 75h multicolored   1.10   .45

Design: Desert fortifications in silhouette, Riyadh television tower, King Khalid Intl. Airport hangars and pyramid of Giza.

Inauguration of King Fahd Telecommunications Center, Jedda — A214

**1987, July 21**
1049 A214 50h multicolored   .65   .35
1050 A214 75h multicolored   1.10   .60

Afghan Resistance Movement
A215

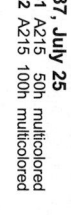

**1987, July 25**
1051 A215 50h multicolored   .35
1052 A215 100h multicolored   .60

Pilgrimage to Mecca — A216

**1987, Aug. 3**
1053 A216 50h multicolored   .35
1054 A216 75h multicolored   .45
1055 A216 100h multicolored   .65
  Nos. 1053-1055 (3)   1.45

Design: View of Ihram and Meqat Wadi Muhrim Mosque from Wadi Muhrim Meqat.

Home for Disabled Children, 1st Anniv. — A217

**1987, Oct. 3**
1056 A217 50h multicolored   .60   .30
1057 A217 75h multicolored   .90   .40

World Post Day — A218

**1987, Oct. 10**
1058 A218 50h multicolored   .60   .35
1059 A218 150h multicolored   1.60   .80

World Food Day
A219

**1987, Oct. 17**
1060 A219 50h multicolored   .70   .30
1061 A219 75h multicolored   1.10   .40

Social Welfare Society, 25th Anniv. — A220

**1987, Oct. 26**
1062 A220 50h multicolored   .75   .35
1063 A220 100h multicolored   1.40   .60

Dome of the Rock — A221

**1987, Dec. 5**
1064 A221 75h multicolored   1.75   .50
1065 A221 150h multicolored   3.50   .90

Restoration and Expansion of the Prophet's Mosque, Medina — A222

**1987, Dec. 15**   **Perf. 14**
1066 A222 50h multicolored   .70   .30
1067 A222 75h multicolored   1.00   .40
1068 A222 100h multicolored   2.00   .80
  Nos. 1066-1068 (3)   3.70   1.50
  An imperf. 300th souvenir sheet exists.

Battle of Hattin, 800th Anniv.
A223

**1987, Dec. 21**
1069 A223 75h multicolored   1.75   .40
1070 A223 150h multicolored   3.50   .90

Warriors in silhouette and Dome of the Rock.

Saladin's conquest of Jerusalem.

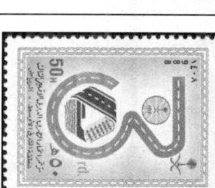

A224

A225

**1987, Dec. 26**
1071 A224 50h multicolored   .70   .35
1072 A224 75h multicolored   1.10   .45

8th session of the Supreme Council of the Gulf Cooperation Council.

A226

**1988, Feb. 13**   **Litho.**   **Perf. 12**
1073 A225 50h multicolored   .95   .50
1074 A225 75h multicolored   1.40   .70

3rd Regional Highways Conf. of the Middle East.

Inauguration of King Fahd Intl. Stadium — A227

**1988, Mar. 2**
1075 A226 50h multicolored   .75   .35
1076 A227 150h multicolored   2.25   .95

Blood Donation — A228

**1988, Apr. 13**   **Litho.**   **Perf. 12**
1077 A228 50h multicolored   .75   .35
1078 A228 75h multicolored   .95   .45

WHO, 40th Anniv. — A229

**1988, Apr. 7**
1079 A229 50h multicolored   .85   .35
1080 A229 75h multicolored   .95   .45

King Fahd, Custodian of the Holy Mosques — A230

King Fahd and mosques at Medina and Mecca.

**1988, Apr. 23**   **Litho.**   **Perf. 12**
1081 A230 50h multicolored   .50   .30
1082 A230 75h multicolored   .75   .40
1083 A230 150h multicolored   1.60   .75
  Nos. 1081-1083 (3)   2.85   1.45

A 75h souvenir sheet exists containing an enlarged version of No. 1082. Sold for 3r.

Environmental Protection
A231

**1988, June 5**
1084 A231 50h multicolored   .75   .30
1085 A231 75h multicolored   1.25   .45

Palestinian Uprising, Gaza and the West Bank
A232

**1988, July 10**
1086 A232 75h multicolored   1.25   .45
1087 A232 150h multicolored   2.25   .85

Pilgrimage to Mecca — A233

**1988, July 23**   **Litho.**   **Perf. 12**
1088 A233 50h multicolored   .95   .35
1089 A233 75h multicolored   1.40   .50

World Food Day
A234

**1988, Oct. 16**   **Litho.**   **Perf. 12**
1090 A234 50h multicolored   1.00   .40
1091 A234 75h multicolored   1.60   .60

**SAUDI ARABIA**

## Qiblatain Mosque Expansion — A235

**1988, Nov. 9**
| | | | |
|---|---|---|---|
| 1092 | A235 | 50h multicolored | .75 .30 |
| 1093 | A235 | 75h multicolored | 1.25 .45 |

## 5th World Youth Soccer Championships, Riyadh, Dammam, Jedda and Taif — A250

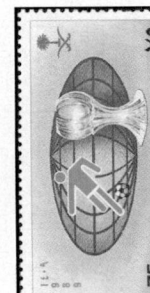

**1989, Feb. 16    Litho.    Perf. 12**
| | | | |
|---|---|---|---|
| 1094 | A250 | 75h multicolored | 1.40 .50 |
| 1095 | A250 | 150h multicolored | 2.50 1.00 |

## World Health Day — A251

**1989, Apr. 8    Litho.    Perf. 12**
| | | | |
|---|---|---|---|
| 1096 | A251 | 50h multicolored | .90 .30 |
| 1097 | A251 | 75h multicolored | 1.40 .45 |

## Sea Water Desalination Plant — A252

**1989, May 30    Litho.    Perf. 12**
| | | | |
|---|---|---|---|
| 1098 | A252 | 50h multicolored | .50 .30 |
| 1099 | A252 | 75h multicolored | .80 .45 |

## Proclamation of the State of Palestine, Nov. 15, 1988 — A253

**1989, June 6    Litho.    Perf. 12**
| | | | |
|---|---|---|---|
| 1100 | A253 | 50h multicolored | .65 .20 |
| 1101 | A253 | 75h multicolored | 1.00 .25 |

## Pilgrimage to Mecca — A254

Design: Al-Tan'eem Mosque, Mecca.

**1989, July 12    Litho.    Perf. 12**
| | | | |
|---|---|---|---|
| 1102 | A254 | 50h multicolored | .70 .20 |
| 1103 | A254 | 75h multicolored | 1.10 .30 |

## World Food Day A255

**1989, Oct. 16    Litho.    Perf. 12**
| | | | |
|---|---|---|---|
| 1104 | A255 | 75h multicolored | .55 .35 |
| 1105 | A255 | 150h multicolored | 1.10 .70 |

## Holy Mosque Expansion — A256

**1989, Dec. 30    Litho.    Perf. 12**
| | | | |
|---|---|---|---|
| 1106 | A256 | 50h multicolored | .65 .30 |
| 1107 | A256 | 75h multicolored | .90 .45 |
| 1108 | A256 | 150h multicolored | 1.75 .90 |
| | | Nos. 1106-1108 (3) | 3.30 1.65 |

An imperf souvenir sheet containing an enlarged version of design A256 exists. Sold for 6r.

## Youth Soccer Cup Championships A257

**1989, Dec. 20    Litho.**
| | | | |
|---|---|---|---|
| 1109 | A257 | 75h multicolored | .90 .40 |
| 1110 | A257 | 150h multicolored | 1.90 .85 |

## UNESCO World Literacy Year — A258

**1990, Jan. 9**
| | | | |
|---|---|---|---|
| 1111 | A258 | 50h multicolored | .80 .35 |
| 1112 | A258 | 75h multicolored | 1.25 .45 |

## World Health Day — A259

**1990, Apr. 7    Litho.    Unwmk.    Perf. 12**
| | | | |
|---|---|---|---|
| 1113 | A259 | 75h multicolored | .90 .40 |
| 1114 | A259 | 150h multicolored | 1.75 .80 |

## Flowers — A262

**1990**
| | | |
|---|---|---|
| 1115 | Sheet of 21 | 10.00 |
| a.-u. | A262 50h any single | .50 .20 |
| 1116 | Sheet of 21 | 15.00 |
| a.-u. | A262 75h any single | .65 .35 |
| 1117 | Sheet of 21 | 54.00 |
| a.-u. | A262 150h any single | 1.25 .70 |
| | Nos. 1115-1117 (3) | 29.00 |

21 Different species pictured on the sheets. Issued: 50h, 75h, Feb. 6; 150h, Jan. 17. See No. 1292A.

## Islamic Conference, 20th Anniv. — A263

**1990, Feb. 7    Litho.    Perf. 12**
| | | | |
|---|---|---|---|
| 1118 | A263 | 75h blue & multi | .60 .30 |
| 1119 | A263 | 150h gray & multi | 1.25 .60 |

## Islamic Heritage A264

Designs: b, Arabic script in rectangle. c, Circular design. d, Mosque and minaret.

**1990, July 29**
| | | | |
|---|---|---|---|
| 1120 | Block of 4 | | 4.00 2.25 |
| | A264 | 75h any single | .95 .55 |

## Horses A265

### Color of Horse

**1990, Apr. 14**
| | | | |
|---|---|---|---|
| 1121 | | Block of 4 | 4.00 1.40 |
| a. | A265 | 50h white, red tassels on bridle | .95 .35 |
| b. | A265 | 50h black | .95 .35 |
| c. | A265 | 50h white, brown bridle | .95 .35 |
| d. | A265 | 50h chestnut | .95 .35 |
| 1122 | A265 | 50h like #1121d | .65 .35 |
| 1123 | A265 | 75h like #1121a | 1.00 .50 |
| 1124 | A266 | 100h like #1121b | 1.40 .65 |
| 1125 | A266 | 150h like #1121c | 2.00 1.00 |
| | | Nos. 1121-1125 (5) | 9.05 3.90 |

No. 1121 has white border on two sides. Nos. 1122-1125 have white border on four sides.

## Pilgrimage to Mecca — A266

**1990, June 28**
| | | | |
|---|---|---|---|
| 1126 | A266 | 75h multicolored | .90 .45 |
| 1127 | A266 | 150h multicolored | 1.90 .90 |

## Television Tower — A267

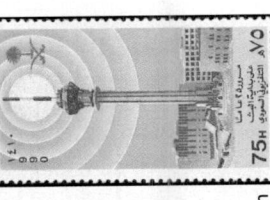

**1990, July 21**
| | | | |
|---|---|---|---|
| 1128 | A267 | 75h multicolored | .90 .45 |
| 1129 | A267 | 150h multicolored | 1.90 .90 |

## Saudi Arabian Airlines Route Map — A268

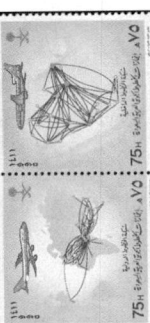

**1990, Sept. 3**
| | | | |
|---|---|---|---|
| 1130 | | 75h Global routes | .75 .40 |
| 1131 | | 75h Domestic routes | .75 .40 |
| a. | A268 | Pair, #1130-1131 | 1.50 .90 |
| 1132 | | 150h like #1130 | 1.50 .90 |
| 1133 | | 150h like #1131 | 1.50 .90 |
| a. | A268 | Pair, #1132-1133 | 3.00 1.90 |
| | | Nos. 1130-1133 (4) | 4.50 2.60 |

## World Food Day A269

**1990, Oct. 16    Litho.    Perf. 12**
| | | | |
|---|---|---|---|
| 1134 | A269 | 75h multicolored | .95 .50 |
| 1135 | A269 | 150h multicolored | 1.90 .95 |

## Organization of Petroleum Exporting Countries (OPEC), 30th Anniv. — A270

**1990, Sept. 26**
| | | | |
|---|---|---|---|
| 1136 | A270 | 75h multicolored | 1.25 .50 |
| 1137 | A270 | 150h multicolored | 2.40 .90 |

## Fifth Five Year Development Plan — A271

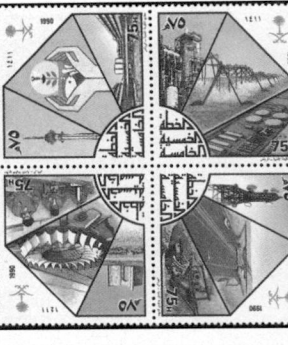

Designs: a, Oil refinery, irrigation, and oil storage tanks. b, Radio tower, highway, and

mine. c, Monument, sports stadium, and vocational training. d, Television tower, environmental protection, and modern architecture.

**1990, Oct. 30**
1138 A271 75h Block of 4, #a.-d.  4.50  1.75

Battle of Badr, 624— A272

**1991, Apr. 3    Litho.    Perf. 12**
1139 A272 75h org, dk grn & grn  .75  .40
1140 A272 150h blk, dk bl & grn  1.50  .75

A273

**1991, June 3    Perf. 12**
1149 A276 75h multicolored  .75  .40
1150 A276 150h multicolored  1.50  .75

A274

A277

**1991, Apr. 9**
1141 A273 75h multicolored  .70  .35
1142 A273 150h multicolored  1.40  .70
World Health Day.

**1991, May 11    Litho.    Perf. 12**
1151 A277 75h multicolored  .90  .55
1152 A277 150h multicolored  1.90  1.10
Liberation of Kuwait.

**1991    Litho.    Perf. 12**
Animals: a, k, Impala. b, l, Ibex. c, m, Oryx. d, n, Fox. e, o, Bat. f, p, Hyena. g, q, Cat. h, r, Dugong. i, s, Leopard.

**Blocks of 9**
1143 A274 25h Block, #a.-i.  3.50  1.75
1144 A274 50h Block, #a.-i.  6.50  3.50
1145 A274 75h Block, #a.-i.  10.00  5.25
1146 A274 100h Block, #a.-i.  13.00  6.50
1146J A274 150h Block, #a.-i.  20.00  10.00
  t.  Perf 14x13½  Block  #k.-s.  25.00  15.00
      53.00  32.00
Issued: #1143-1146, May 1: #1146J, Dec. 1.
Nos. 1143-1146J (5)
No. 1146J exists imperf.

**1991, Sept. 8    Litho.    Perf. 12**
1153 A278 75h blue & multi  1.25  .60
1154 A278 150h buff & multi  2.25  1.25
Literacy Day.

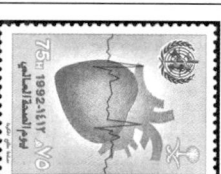

A279

A281

A280

**1991, Oct. 16    Litho.    Perf. 12**
1155 A279 75h green & multi  .80  .45
1156 A279 150h orange & multi  1.50  .90
World Food Day.

**1991    Litho.    Perf. 14**
1147 A275 75h blue & multi  .75  .40
1148 A275 150h green & multi  1.50  .75
Pilgrimage to Mecca — A275

**1991, Dec. 7    Litho.    Perf. 12**
1157 A280 75h green & multi  1.25  .60
1158 A280 150h dk blue & multi  2.40  1.25
Childrens' Day.

**1991, June 20**
World Telecommunications Day — A276

**1992, Apr. 8    Litho.    Perf. 12**
1159 A281 75h lt blue & multi  .90  .50
1160 A281 150h lt org & multi  1.75  .90
World Health Day.

**1992, Apr. 18    Litho.    Perf. 12**
1161 A282 75h lt org & grn  .80  .45
1162 A282 150h lt bl, dk bl & grn  1.50  .85
War Between the Arabs of Medina and Mecca, 624-630 A282

Pilgrimage to Mecca A283

**1992, June 9    Litho.    Perf. 12**
1163 A283 75h lt blue & multi  .90  .50
1164 A283 150h lt orange & multi  1.75  .90

Unwmk.

Population and Housing Census — A284

**1992, Sept. 26    Litho.    Perf. 14**
1165 A284 75h blue & multi  .55  .35
1166 A284 150h org yel & multi  1.10  .70

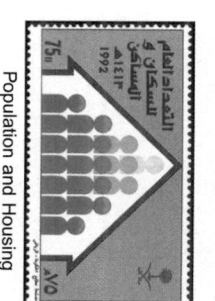

World Food Day A285

**1992, Oct. 17    Litho.    Perf. 12**
1167 A285 75h Vegetables  .95  .50
1168 A285 150h Fruits  1.90  .95

Consultative Council — A286

Document. d, g, 12 lines. e, h, 13 lines. f, i, 11 lines. 5r, Scrolls of 12, 11, & 13 lines.

**1992, Dec. 12    Litho.    Perf. 12**
1168A A286 75h Strip of 3, #a.-f.  2.00  1.10
1168B A286 150h Strip of 3, #g.-i.  4.00  2.25

**Size: 120x79mm    Imperf**
1168C A286 5r multicolored  22.50  11.00

Birds — A287

**1992-97    Blocks of 9    Perf. 14x13½**
a, k, Woodpecker. b, l, Arabian bustard. c, m, Lark. d, n, Turtle dove. e, o, Heron. f, p, Partridge. g, q, Hoopoe. h, r, Falcon. i, s, Houbara bustard. Illustration reduced.

1169 A287 25h #a.-i.  4.00  4.00
1170 A287 50h #a.-i.  8.00  8.00
1171 A287 75h #a.-i.  10.00  4.75
1172 A287 100h #a.-i.  20.00  10.00
1173 A287 150h #a.-i.  30.00  15.00
     Perf. 12 #k.-s.  13.00  6.50
Nos. 1169-1173 #k.-s.  72.00  33.75
Issued: 150h, 3/18/92; 75h, 7/14/92; 100h, 3/1/93; 25h, 50h, 116/94; #1171i, 1173i, 8/94; 169j; 1996; 117j; 1997(?).

**1993, Apr. 7    Litho.    Perf. 12**
1175 A288 75h red & multi  .70  .35
1175A A288 150h blue & multi  1.40  .70
World Health Day A288

King Fahd Championship Soccer Cup — A289

**1993, Mar. 15    Litho.**
1176 A289 75h green & multi  1.25  .60
1176A A289 150h rose red & multi  2.40  1.25

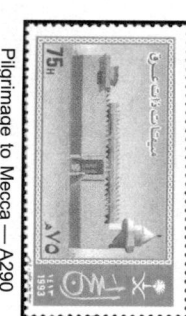

**1993, May 30    Litho.    Perf. 12**
1177 A290 75h green & multi  .70  .40
1178 A290 150h blue & multi  1.25  .80
Pilgrimage to Mecca — A290

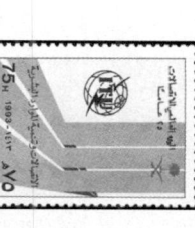

Intl. Telecommunications Day — A291

## Inscription Color

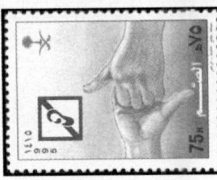

**1993, May 17**
| 1179 | A291 | 75h dark blue | .70 | .40 |
| 1180 | A291 | 150h red lilac | 1.25 | .80 |

## Battle of Alkandk A292

**1993, May 15**
| 1181 | A292 | 75h lt org & grn | .70 | .40 |
| 1182 | A292 | 150h lt bl, dk bl & grn | 1.25 | .80 |

## World Food Day — A293

**1993, Dec. 14    Litho.    Perf. 12**
| 1183 | A293 | 75h black & multi | .90 | .45 |
| 1184 | A293 | 150h red & multi | 1.90 | .90 |

## World Dental Health Day A294

**1994, Apr. 9    Litho.    Perf. 12**
| 1185 | A294 | 75h multicolored | .80 | .40 |
| 1186 | A294 | 160h multicolored | 1.50 | .80 |

## Intl. Olympic Committee, Cent. A295

**1994, Apr. 23    Litho.    Perf. 12**
| 1187 | A295 | 75h blue & multi | .95 | .50 |
| 1188 | A295 | 150h red & multi | 1.90 | .95 |

## Battle of Khaybar A296

**1994, June 14    Litho.    Perf. 12**
| 1189 | A296 | 75h bister & green | .80 | .40 |
| 1190 | A296 | 150h sil, bl & grn | 1.50 | .80 |

## Pilgrimage to Mecca — A297

**1994, May 14**
| 1191 | A297 | 75h green & multi | .65 | .40 |
| 1192 | A297 | 150h red & multi | 1.25 | .85 |

## Consultative Council — A298

Design: 150h, Different view of building, inscription tablet at right.

**1994, July 12    Litho.    Perf. 12**
| 1193 | A298 | 75h multicolored | .80 | .40 |
| 1194 | A298 | 150h multicolored | 1.50 | .80 |
| a. | | Souv. sheet of 2, #1193-1194, imperf. | 27.50 | |

No. 1194a sold for 5r.

A299

## 1994 World Soccer Cup Championships, U.S. — A300

**1994, June 18**
| 1195 | A299 | 75h multicolored | .80 | .40 |
| 1196 | A300 | 150h multicolored | 1.50 | .80 |

## King Abdul Aziz Port, Dammam — A301

**1994-95    Litho.    Perf. 12**
| 1198 | A301 | 25h multicolored | .50 | .25 |
| 1199 | A301 | 50h multicolored | .50 | .25 |
| 1200 | A301 | 75h multicolored | .70 | .35 |
| 1201 | A301 | 100h multicolored | .90 | .45 |
| 1202 | A301 | 150h multicolored | 1.40 | .70 |
| | | Nos. 1198-1202 (5) | 4.00 | 2.00 |

Issued: 75h, 8/22/94; 150h, 11/5/94; 100h, 3/11/95; 50h, 11/28/95; 25h, 12/27/95.

A304

## World Food Day A305

**1994, Oct. 16    Litho.    Perf. 12**
| 1212 | A304 | 75h Green house | 1.25 | .60 |
| 1213 | A305 | 150h Foods | 2.40 | 1.25 |

A306

## Arab League, 50th Anniv. A307

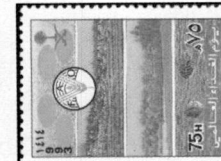

**1995, Mar. 25    Litho.    Perf. 12**
| 1214 | A306 | 75h multicolored | .70 | .40 |
| 1215 | A307 | 150h multicolored | 1.40 | .80 |

A308

## UN, 50th Anniv. — A309

| 1216 | A308 | 75h multicolored | .80 | .40 |
| 1217 | A309 | 150h multicolored | 1.50 | .80 |

**1995, Feb. 19**

## Refugee Care A310

**1995, Apr. 9    Litho.    Perf. 12**
| 1218 | A310 | 75h green & multi | .70 | .40 |
| 1219 | A310 | 150h tan & multi | 1.40 | .80 |

## Pilgrimage to Mecca A311

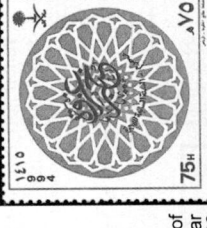

**1995, May 3    Litho.    Perf. 12**
| 1220 | A311 | 75h blue & multi | .70 | .40 |
| 1221 | A311 | 150h tan & multi | 1.40 | .80 |

## Deaf Week — A312

**1995, May 3    Litho.    Perf. 12**
| 1222 | A312 | 75h shown | .80 | .40 |
| 1223 | A312 | 150h Hand sign, ear | 1.50 | .80 |

## Saudi Arabian Airlines, 50th Anniv. A313

**1995, Aug. 21**
| 1224 | A313 | 75h Anniv. emblem, vert. | .80 | .40 |
| 1225 | A313 | 150h shown | 1.50 | .80 |

## FAO, 50th Anniv. — A314

**1995, Oct. 16    Litho.    Perf. 12**
| 1226 | A314 | 75h shown | 1.25 | .60 |
| 1227 | A314 | 150h Emblem over globe | 2.40 | 1.25 |

## Jeddah Port — A315

**1996    Litho.    Perf. 12**
| 1228 | A315 | 25h multicolored | .40 | .30 |
| 1229 | A315 | 50h multicolored | .80 | .40 |
| 1230 | A315 | 75h multicolored | 1.25 | .65 |
| 1230A | A315 | 100h multicolored | 2.00 | 2.00 |
| 1230B | A315 | 150h multicolored | 2.75 | 1.60 |

Issued: 25h and 50h, 1/27/96; 75h, 2/7/96; 100h, 11/25/96; 150h, 3/30/96.

## 1996 Summer Olympics, Atlanta A316

**1996, June 23**
| 1231 | A316 | 150h orange & multi | 1.90 | .95 |
| 1232 | A316 | 2r blue & multi | 2.50 | 1.25 |

## Pilgrimage to Mecca — A317

**1996, Apr. 21**
| 1233 | A317 | 150h black & multi | 1.60 | .85 |
| 1234 | A317 | 2r rose red & multi | 2.25 | 1.10 |
| 1235 | A317 | 3r green & multi | 3.25 | 1.60 |
| | | Nos. 1233-1235 (3) | 7.10 | 3.55 |

**World Health Organization A318**

**1996, July 21** Litho. Perf. 12
1236 A318 2r green & multi 1.90 1.00
1237 A318 3r red & multi 3.00 1.50

**FAO, 50th Anniv. A319**

**1996, Oct. 22** Litho. Perf. 12
1238 A319 2r blue & multi 3.00 1.40
1239 A319 3r red & multi 4.25 2.10

**UNICEF, 50th Anniv. A320**

**1996, Nov. 12** Litho. Perf. 12
1240 A320 150h buff & multi 1.60 .80
1241 A320 2r blue & multi 2.10 1.00

**King Abdul Aziz Research Center, 25th Anniv. A321**

**1996, Dec. 25** Litho. Perf. 12
1242 A321 150h brown & multi 1.60 .80
1243 A321 2r green & multi 2.10 1.10

**Rabigh Steam Power Plant A322**

**1996, Dec. 26**
1244 A322 150h multicolored 1.60 .80
1245 A322 2r multicolored 2.10 1.10
**Size: 51x26mm**
Designs: 150h, Power plant. 2r, Power plant, electrical power lines.

**Yanbu Port — A323**

**1996** Litho. Perf. 12
1245A A323 50h multicolored .90 .55
1246 A323 2r multicolored 3.50 1.75
Issued: 1245A, 12/21; 1246 11/25.
See No. 1273.

**Opening Mecca A324**

**1997, Jan. 30** Litho. Perf. 12
1247 A324 1r brt grn & multi 1.10 .50
1248 A324 2r lt yel grn & multi 2.10 1.10

**King Fahd Birthday A325**

**1997, Feb. 26**
1249 A325 100h green & multi 1.10 .50
1250 A325 150h pink & multi 1.50 .80
1251 A325 2r tan & multi 2.10 1.10
Nos. 1249-1251 (3) 4.70 2.40

An imperf souvenir sheet containing an enlarged version of design A325 exists. Sold for 5r. Value $15.

**Jubail Port — A326**

**1996-97**
1251A A326 50h multicolored .55 .30
1251B A326 100h multicolored .55 .25
1252 A326 150h multicolored .75 .40
1252A A326 2r multicolored 1.90 .95
1252B A326 4r multicolored 2.25 1.10
Nos. 1251A-1252B (5) 6.00 3.00
Issued: 50h, 10/17/96; 100h, 6/29/96; 150h, 7/8/96; 2r, 9/9/(?); 4r, 7/24/96.

**Campaign Against Illegal Use of Drugs A327**

**1997, Mar. 2** Litho. Perf. 12
1253 A327 150h blue & multi 2.50 1.25
1254 A327 2r red & multi 3.50 1.75

**Battle of Hunain A328**

**1997, Mar. 19** Litho. Perf. 12
1255 A328 150h multicolored 1.50 .80
1256 A328 2r multicolored 2.10 1.10

**World Health Day A329**

**King Fahd Natl. Library A332?**

**1997, June 24** Litho. Perf. 12
1261 A332 1r shown 1.10 .50
1262 A332 2r Open book 2.10 1.10

**Al-Hijjah A331**

**1997, Apr. 29** Litho. Perf. 12
1259 A330 150h multicolored 1.50 .80
1260 A331 2r multicolored 2.10 1.10

**A330**

**1997, May 9** Litho. Perf. 14
1257 A329 150h multicolored 1.50 .80
1258 A329 2r multicolored 2.10 1.10

**A333**

**1997, July 5** Litho. Perf. 12
1263 A333 150h Emblem, rays 1.90 .90
1264 A333 2r shown 2.50 1.25

**A334**

**1997, June 29** Litho. Perf. 12
1265 A334 1r red & multi 1.10 .55
1266 A334 2r green & multi 2.10 1.10
King Abdul Aziz Public Library.

Montreal Protocol on Substances that Deplete Ozone Layer, 10th anniv.

**3rd GCC Stamp Exhibition, Riyadh A335**

**1997, Sept. 28** Litho. Perf. 12
1267 A335 1r multicolored 1.25 .60

**Prince Salman Center — A336**

**1997, July 12** Litho. Perf. 12
1268 A336 1r multicolored 1.25 .60

**Battle of Tabuk A337**

**1997, Aug. 12** Litho. Perf. 12
1269 A337 1r multicolored 1.75 .80

**World Food Day — A338**

**1998, Feb. 9**
1270 A338 2r multicolored 2.25 1.25

**Disabled Persons Day — A339**

**1998, May 3** Litho. Perf. 12
1271 A339 1r multicolored .95 .50

**Al Hijjah — A340**

**1998, May 17** Litho. Perf. 12
1272 A340 2r multicolored 2.25 1.10

**Yanbu Port Type of 1997**

**1996, Sept. 3** Litho. Perf. 12
1273 A323 100h multicolored 1.75 .80
1273A A323 150h multicolored 2.75 1.75
1273B A323 4r multi 2.75 1.25
Issued: 150h, 8/28/96; 4r, 11/8/97.

**WHO, 50th Anniv. — A341**

**1998, May 31** Litho.
1274 A341 1r multicolored .95 .45

**Dam — A342**

**1998, May 17** Litho.
1275 A342 1r multicolored .95 .45

SAUDI ARABIA

**Consultative Council, 75th Anniv. — A360**

1.40 .90

**2000, June 7**
1298 A360 1r multi

**UN High Commissioner for Refugees, 50th Anniv. — A361**

1.75 .90

**2000, Sept. 23**
1299 A361 2r multi

**Jizan Port — A362**

*Perf. 14*
.45 .45
.90 .90
1.75 1.75

**Litho.**
**2000, Sept. 16**
1299A A362 50h multi
1299B A362
1300 A362 2r multi

King Abdul Aziz City for Science and Technology A363

.40 .40

**2000, Oct. 28**
1301 A363 1r multi

King Khalid University A364

*Perf. 14*
.90 .40

**2000, Dec. 5**
1302 A364 1r multi

**Buraydah — A365**

*Perf. 13¾x14*
.45 .45
.90 .90
1.75 1.75

**2000**
1303 A365 50h blue & multi
1304 A365 1r grn & multi
1305 A365 2r blk & multi

---

UPU, 125th Anniv. — A354

*Perf. 12*
2.00 .85

**Litho.**
**1999, Oct. 26**
1291 A354 1r multi

**World Meteorological Organization, 50th Anniv. — A355**

*Perf. 12*
1.10 .55

**Litho.**
**2000, Mar. 23**
1292 A355 1r multi

**Flowers Type of 1990**
Designs like Nos. 1115a-1115u.

*Perf. 12*
37.50

**2000, Feb. 1**
1292A Block of 21
b.-v. A262 1r Any single

Pilgrimage to Mecca A356

*Perf. 14x14¼*
.95 .50
1.75 .90

**2000, Mar. 11**
1293 A356 1r black & multi
1294 A356 2r red & multi

Scouting — A357

*Perf. 14*
.90 .40

**Litho.**
**2000, July 18**
1295 A357 1r multi

Riyadh, Arabian Cultural Capital, 2000 — A358

*Perf. 14*
1.40 .90

**Litho.**
**2000, July 4**
1296 A358 1r multi

Water Conservation A359

1.40 .90

**2000, June 18**
1297 A359 1r multi

---

World Food Day — A348a

*Perf. 12*
2.00 1.00

**Litho.**
**1999, Mar. 16**
1285 A348a 1r multicolored

Al-Hijjah — A349

*Perf. 12*
2.00 .95

**Litho.**
**1999, Mar. 18**
1286 A349 2r multicolored

A350

A351

**1999, Mar. 6**
1287 A350 1r multicolored     1.75 .85

Kingdom of Saudi Arabia, cent. Exists in an imperf. souvenir sheet of 1. It sold for 5r. Value $18.

*Perf. 12*
.90 .45

**Litho.**
**1999, May 22**
1288 A351 1r Traffic signals

Academy for Security Sciences — A352

*Perf. 12*
1.40 .70

**Litho.**
**1999, May 29**
1289 A352 150h multicolored

Intl. Holy Koran Competition — A353

*Perf. 12*
.90 .45

**Litho.**
**1999, Oct. 3**
1290 A353 1r multicolored

---

A343

A344

**1998, July 12**
1276 A343 1r multicolored

*Perf. 12*
.90 .45

**Litho.**

Islamic Organization for Education and Science.

**1998, Sept. 30**
1277 A344 2r multicolored     2.00 1.00

Arab Stamp Day.

A345

KSA, Cent. A346

Designs: No. 1278, Forts. No. 1279, Military equipment. No. 1280, Entrance to fort, vert. 2r, King Fahd, KSA emblem, outline of map of Saudi Arabia, vert.

**1999, Jan. 22     Litho.**     *Perf. 12*
1278 A345 1r multicolored     1.75 .90
1279 A346 1r multicolored     1.75 .90
1280 A345 1r multicolored     1.75 .90
1281 A345 2r multicolored     3.50 1.75
  Nos. 1278-1281 (4)     8.75 4.45

#1278-1279 exist imperf in souvenir sheets of 1. There are some color variations. #1280-1281 exist imperf in a souvenir sheet of 2. The three sheets sold for 5r each. Value, set of three sheets $50.

King Fahd Intl. Airport — A347

**1999, Feb. 6**
1282 A347 1r multicolored     .85 .45

**Size: 26x38mm**
1283 A347 2r Jet, control tower     1.75 .85

Development of Palace of Justice Area — A348

**1999, Jan. 22**
1284 A348 1r multicolored     1.75 .85

Exists imperf in a souvenir sheet of 1. It sold for 5r. Value $18.

Buraydah — A366

**2000-01**
| | | | | |
|---|---|---|---|---|
| 1306 | A366 | 50h blue & multi | .45 | .45 |
| 1307 | A366 | 1r grn & multi | .90 | .90 |
| 1308 | A366 | 2r blk & multi | 1.75 | 1.75 |

*Perf. 13¾x14*

No. 1308 issued 2/2/01.

King Fahd
Printing
Press
A367

Denomination color: 50h, Pink, 1r, Blue, 2r,
Black.

**2001, Apr. 25** Litho.
1309-1311 A367 Set of 3
*Perf. 14*
3.00 3.00

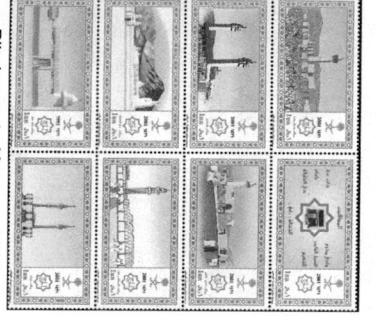

**2001, May 13**
1312 A368 1r multi
.90 .45

King Abdul Aziz
Center for Gifted
Care — A368

Pilgrimage to Mecca — A369

No. 1313: a, Mosque, tower at center, b,
Holy Ka'aba. c, Mosque, tower at left and
center. d, Mosque, tower and two men at left.
e, Mosque, tower at right, mountain in background. f, Mosque, tower and five pilgrims at
left. g, Mosque, tower at right. h, Mosque,
orange background.

**2001, Feb. 28**
1313 A369 1r Block of 8, #a-h
*Perf. 13¾x14*
7.25 7.25

Palestinian
Intifada
A370

**2001, May 30** Litho.
1314-1315 A370 Set of 2
*Perf. 14*
3.00 3.00

Designs: 1r, Map of Israel, Palestinian boy
and father. 2r, Barbed wire, boy and father,
vert.

A souvenir sheet containing an imperforate
49x36mm example of No. 1314 sold for 5r.

---

King Abdul Aziz Historical
Center — A371

No. 1316: a, Building with curved, pointed
wall. b, Building with one tree in front. c, Building with towers. d, Aerial view of building.
Illustration reduced.

**2001, June 25**
1316 A371 1r Block of 4, #a-d
3.50 3.50

World Teacher's
Day — A372

**2001, Oct. 6**
1317 A372 1r multi
.90 .90

**2001, Oct. 15**
1318 A373 1r Any single
a.-e. Horiz. strip of 5
.90 .90
4.50 4.50

Paintings
A373

No. 1318: a, Abstract cityscape in green and
yellow. b, Horse and geometric designs. c,
Building windows. d, Landscape in yellow,
orange and brown. e, Building with blue sky.

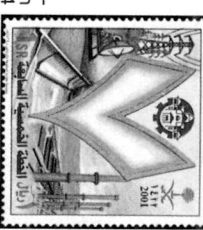

7th Five-
Year Plan
A374

**2002, Jan. 19**
1319 A374 1r multi
.90 .90

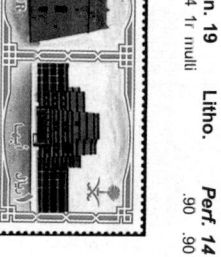

A375

Abha — A376

---

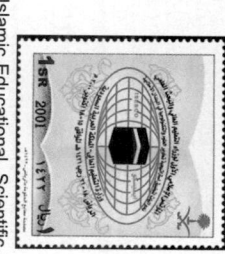

Islamic Educational, Scientific and
Cultural Organization — A377

**2002, Jan. 19**
1320 A375 1r blue & multi .75 .75
1321 A376 2r green & multi 1.50 1.50

Pilgrimage
to Mecca
A378

**2002, Jan. 29**
1322 A377 1r multi
.90 .90

**2002, Feb. 13**
1323 A378 1r multi
.90 .90

20 Years of
Achievements
Under King
Fahd — A379

**2002, Apr. 13**
**Litho. with Foil Application**
1324 A379 1r multi
.90 .90

An imperforate 3r souvenir sheet overprinted in gold and depicting an example of
No. 1324 and various other stamps, in whole
or in part, exists. Value $3.

King Fahd
Port, Yanbu
A380

**2002, May 26** Litho.
1325 A379 1r mult
*Perf. 14*
.90 .90

King Fahd
Port, Al
Jubail
A381

**2002, May 26**
1327 A381 1r black & multi .90 .90
1328 A381 2r multi 1.75 1.75
Issued: 1r, 7/13.

**2003, Feb. 7** Litho.
1329 A382 1r multi
Pilgrimage
to Mecca
A382
*Perf. 14*
.90 .90

---

Water Conservation — A383

**2003, Mar. 30** Litho.
1330-1331 A383 Set of 2
*Perf. 14*
1.75 1.75

Designs: No. 1330, 1r, Two water drops. No.
1331, 1r, One water drop, vert.

Civil
Defense
A384

Saudi
Arabian Red
Cresecent
Society
A385

**2003, Apr. 29**
1332 A384 1r multi
.90 .90

**2003, May 20**
1333 A385 1r multi
.75 .75

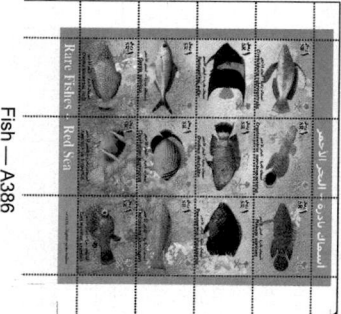

Fish — A386

**2003**
1334 A386 1r Sheet of 12, #a-l 9.00 9.00
1335 A386 2r Sheet of 12, #a-l 18.00 18.00
Issued: No. 1334, 5/26; No. 1335, 6/21.

Designs: Nos. 1334a, 1335a, Cirrhilabrus
rubriventralis. Nos. 1334b, 1335b, Cryptocentrus caeruleopunctatus. Nos. 1334c, 1335c,
Plesiops nigricans. Nos. 1334d, 1335d, Pomacanthus asfur. Nos. 1334f, 1335e, Chelilinus
abudjube. Nos. 1334f, 1335f, Pomacentrus
albicaudatus. Nos. 1334g, 1335g, Caesio
suevicus. Nos. 1334h, 1335h, Chaetodon austriacus. Nos. 1334i, 1335i, Thalassoma klunzingeri. Nos. 1334j, 1335j, Oxymonacanthus
halli. Nos. 1334k, 1335k, Amphiprion bicinctus. Nos. 1334l, 1335l, Canthigaster pygmaea.

Dialogue
Among
Civilizations
A387

**2003, July 1**
1336 A387 1r multi
.75 .75

World Summit on the Information Society A410

Perf. 14
.75 .75

**2004, Nov. 1**
1352 A410 1r multi

Tourism — A411

No. 1353: a, Sand dune. b, Funicular cars. c, Sea coast. d, Rock climbers. Illustration reduced.

**2004, Nov. 1**
1353 A411 2r Block of 4, #a-d    6.00 6.00

"Islam Is Peace" A412
1.50 1.50

**2004, Dec. 27**
1354 A412 2r multi

Pilgrimage to Mecca A413
.75 .75

**2005, Jan. 4**
1355 A413 1r multi

Municipal Elections — A414

Perf. 14    Litho.
.75 .75

**2005, Jan. 8**
1356 A414 1r multi

Tabouk — A403
.75 .75
1.50 1.50

**2004, Jan. 19**
1346 A403 1r blk & multi
1347 A403 2r red & multi

MD-11 A404
Boeing 747 — A405
Boeing 777 — A406
MD-90 A407

New airplanes of Saudi Arabian Airlines.

**2004, Jan. 19**
1348    Block of 4    3.00 3.00
a.    A404 1r multi    .75 .75
b.    A405 1r multi    .75 .75
c.    A406 1r multi    .75 .75
d.    A407 1r multi    .75 .75

Judicial Systems A408
Perf. 14    Litho.
.75 .75

**2004, Apr. 5**
1349 A408 1r multi

Hail — A409
Perf. 13¾x14    Litho.
.75 .75
1.50 1.50

**2004, Oct. 16**
1350 A409 1r blk & multi
1351 A409 2r red & multi

Electricity Conservation — A388
.75 .75

**2003, Sept. 27**
1337 A388 1r multi

World Post Day — A389
.75 .75

**2003, Oct. 9**
1338 A389 1r multi

Ninth Gulf Cooperation Council Stamp Exhibition — A390
.75 .75

**2003, Oct. 18**
1339 A390 1r multi

First Saudi Commemorative Stamp, 75th Islamic Year Anniv. — A391
.75 .75

**2003, Oct. 20**
1340 A391 1r No. 129

Supreme Council for Handicapped Affairs — A392
.75 .75

**2003, Nov. 11**
1341 A392 1r multi

King Abdul Aziz Equestrian Race Course, Janadriyah A393
.75 .75

**2003, Dec. 17**
1342 A393 1r multi

Pilgrimage to Mecca A394

**2003, Dec. 24**
1343 A394 1r multi    .75 .75
a.    Arabian "1" missing in denomination    —

Mosque, Buraydah A395
Mosque, Medina A396
Mosque, Riyadh A397
Mosque, Dammam A398
Mosque, Baha A399
Mosque, Khobar A400
Mosque, Taif — A401
Mosque, Najran A402

Mosques built in reign of King Fahd.

**2003, Dec. 24**
1344    Sheet of 8    6.00 6.00
a.    A395 1r brl & multi    .75 .75
b.    A396 1r brl & multi    .75 .75
c.    A397 1r brl & multi    .75 .75
d.    A398 1r brl & multi    .75 .75
e.    A399 1r brl & multi    .75 .75
f.    A400 1r brl & multi    .75 .75
g.    A401 1r brl & multi    .75 .75
h.    A402 1r brl & multi    .75 .75
1345    Sheet of 8    12.00 12.00
a.    A395 2r red & multi    1.50 1.50
b.    A396 2r red & multi    1.50 1.50
c.    A397 2r red & multi    1.50 1.50
d.    A398 2r red & multi    1.50 1.50
e.    A399 2r red & multi    1.50 1.50
f.    A400 2r red & multi    1.50 1.50
g.    A401 2r red & multi    1.50 1.50
h.    A402 2r red & multi    1.50 1.50

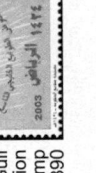

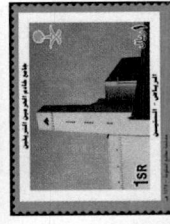

## 2005, Apr. 2
**Islamic Solidarity Games — A415**
1357 A415 1r multi .75 .75

**Anti-Terrorism Campaign A416**

1358 A416 1r multi

An imperf. souvenir sheet with simulated perfs sold for 3r.

## 2005, July 9 Litho. Perf. 14
**Arar A417**
1359 A417 1r multi .75 .75

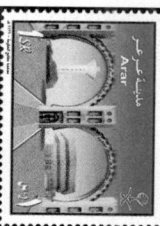

## 2005, July 16
1360 A418 1r multi
Ancient Artifacts — A418

**Ruins — A419**

1361 A419 2r multi

No. 1360: a, Bowl. b, Head of animal. c, Head of human. d, Inscribed tablet.
No. 1361: a, Ruin with two towers, walls in foreground, year in black. b, Building with one tower, year in white. c, Fort with towers at corners, year in white. d, Ruins on hilltop, year in black. Illustrations reduced.

## 2005, Aug. 20
1360 A418 1r Block of 4, #a-d 3.00 3.00
1361 A419 2r Block of 4, #a-d 6.00 6.00

---

## 2005, July 16 Litho. Perf. 14
**King Fahd (1923-2005) A421**
1362 A420 3r multi 2.25 2.25

**Mecca, Capital of Islamic Culture — A420**

## 2005, Dec. 21
1363-1364 A421
Denominations: 2r, 3r.

An imperf 105x80mm stamp with picture reversed sold for 5r.

**King Fahd (1923-2005) A421**
Set of 2 3.75 3.75

## 2005, Dec. 28
**Pilgrimage to Mecca A422**
1365 A422 2r multi 1.50 1.50

**King Abdullah — A423**
1366 A423 2r multi
**Crown Prince Sultan — A424**
1369 A424 3r multi

## 2006, Jan. 18 Litho. with Foil Application
1366 A423 2r multi 1.50 1.50
1367 A424 2r multi 1.50 1.50
1368 A423 3r multi 2.25 2.25
1369 A424 3r multi 2.25 2.25
Nos. 1366-1369 (4) 7.50 7.50

An installation of new king and crown prince. An imperf 105x80mm stamp depicting the new king and crown prince sold for 5r.

---

## AIR POST STAMPS

**Airspeed Ambassador Airliner — AP1**

## 1949-58 Unwmk. Typo. Perf. 11
| | | | | | |
|---|---|---|---|---|---|
| C1 | AP1 | 1g blue green | 3.75 | .40 |
| C2 | AP1 | 3g ultra | 4.75 | .40 |
| a. | | 3g dull ultra ('58) | 20.00 | 1.75 |
| C3 | AP1 | 4g orange | 4.75 | .40 |
| C4 | AP1 | 10g purple | 13.50 | .85 |
| C5 | AP1 | 20g vio ('58+) | 11.50 | 1.90 |
| a. | | 20g chocolate (49) | 22.50 | 2.40 |
| C6 | AP1 | 100g violet rose | 163.25 | 19.00 |
| | | Nos. C1-C6 (6) | 225.75 | 22.95 |

Imperfs. exist, not regularly issued. The 1st printings are on grayish paper and sell for more. No. C3 exists with pin-perf 6. + The date for No. C5 is not definite.

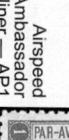

**Saudi Airlines Convair 440 — AP2**

## 1960-61 Photo. Perf. 14
Type I (Saud Cartouche)
(Illustrated over No. 286)

| | | | | |
|---|---|---|---|---|
| C7 | AP2 | 1p dull pur & grn | .65 | .25 |
| C8 | AP2 | 2p grn & dull pur | .65 | .25 |
| C9 | AP2 | 3p brn red & bl | .65 | .25 |
| C10 | AP2 | 4p bl & dull pur | .65 | .25 |
| C11 | AP2 | 6p & rose red | .65 | .25 |
| C12 | AP2 | 6p ocher & slate | 1.10 | .25 |
| C13 | AP2 | 8p & rose red | 1.25 | .25 |
| C14 | AP2 | 9p purple & gray ol | 1.25 | .25 |
| C15 | AP2 | 10p blue & dl red | 1.90 | .25 |
| C16 | AP2 | 15p grn & bis brn | 5.50 | .50 |
| C17 | AP2 | 20p bis brn & em- | 5.50 | .50 |
| | | er | | |
| C18 | AP2 | 30p sep & Prus | 5.50 | .40 |
| | | grn | | |
| C19 | AP2 | 50p green & indigo | 13.00 | 1.10 |
| C20 | AP2 | 100p gray & dk brn | 55.00 | .80 |
| C21 | AP2 | 200p dk vio & black | 199.50 | 10.40 |

Nos. C7-C18 exist imperf., probably not regularly issued.

## 1963-64 Photo. Wmk. 337
Size: 27½x22mm
| | | | | |
|---|---|---|---|---|
| C24 | AP2 | 1p lilac & grn | 2.75 | .25 |
| C25 | AP2 | 2p green & dull pur | 10.00 | .25 |
| C26 | AP2 | 4p blue & dull pur | 3.75 | .25 |
| C27 | AP2 | 6p ocher & slate | 10.00 | .80 |
| C28 | AP2 | 8p rose & rose red | 19.00 | .80 |
| C29 | AP2 | 9p pur & red brn | 13.00 | 1.10 |
| | | Nos. C24-C29 (6) | 58.50 | 4.25 |

## 1964 Redrawn Perf. 13½x13 Wmk. 337
Size: 28½x23mm Litho.
| | | | | |
|---|---|---|---|---|
| C30 | AP2 | 3p brn red & dull bl | 6.00 | .60 |
| C31 | AP2 | 10p bik & dk red brn | 9.50 | .90 |
| C32 | AP2 | 20p bis brn & emer | 20.00 | 2.00 |
| | | Nos. C30-C32 (3) | 35.50 | 3.50 |

Nos. C30-C32 are widely spaced in the sheet, producing large margins.

**Saudi Airline Boeing 720-B Jet — AP3**

## 1965-70 Unwmk. Litho. Perf. 14
Type I (Saud Cartouche)
(Illustrated over No. 286)
| | | | | |
|---|---|---|---|---|
| C33 | AP3 | 1p lilac & green | 80.00 | 1.50 |
| C34 | AP3 | 2p grn & dull pur | 80.00 | 2.75 |
| C35 | AP3 | 3p rose lil & dull | 90.00 | 90.00 |
| | | bl | | |
| C36 | AP3 | 4p blue & dull pur | 9.50 | .20 |
| C37 | AP3 | 6p ocher & slate | 1,800. | 400.00 |
| C38 | AP3 | 8p rose & ol gray | 100.00 | 1.75 |
| C39 | AP3 | 9p rose & red | 6.25 | .35 |
| C40 | AP3 | 10p bik & gray ol | 80.00 | 1.75 |
| C41 | AP3 | brn | | |
| C42 | AP3 | 10p bik & dk red | 5.25 | .30 |
| | | brn | 5.50 | |

**Falcon — AP4**

## 1968-71 Litho. Wmk. 361 Perf. 13½x14
| | | | | |
|---|---|---|---|---|
| C96 | AP4 | 1p green & red brn | 13.50 | .25 |
| C97 | AP4 | 4p dk red & red | 200.00 | 15.00 |
| | | brn | | |

---

## 1966-78 Unwmk. Litho. Perf. 14
Type II (Faisal Cartouche)
| | | | | |
|---|---|---|---|---|
| C45 | AP3 | 13p dk green & yel | 4.25 | .30 |
| C44 | AP3 | 12p orange & gray | 5.50 | .30 |
| C43 | AP3 | 11p green & bister | 18.00 | |
| | | | 80.00 | |
| C46 | AP3 | 14p dk blue & org | 140.00 | 6.25 |
| C47 | AP3 | 15p blue & bis brn | 4.25 | .35 |
| C48 | AP3 | 16p black & ultra | 75.00 | 5.50 |
| C49 | AP3 | 17p bister & sepia | 6.25 | .45 |
| C50 | AP3 | 19p car & dp org | 5.00 | .45 |
| C51 | AP3 | 20p ol brn & dul | 5.00 | .45 |
| | | | 5.00 | |
| C52 | AP3 | bis brn & em- | | |
| C53 | AP3 | 23p olive & bister | 150.00 | 6.25 |
| C54 | AP3 | 24p dk blue & sep | 6.25 | .45 |
| C55 | AP3 | 26p red brn & ol | 5.00 | .45 |
| C56 | AP3 | 27p ol brn & dul | 5.00 | .35 |
| C57 | AP3 | 31p car rose & | 7.25 | .45 |
| | | rose red | | |
| C58 | AP3 | 33p red & dull pur | 9.50 | .55 |
| C59 | AP3 | 1p dull pur & | 20.00 | .90 |
| | | grn | | |
| C60 | AP3 | 2p green & dull | 20.00 | 1.40 |
| | | ol | | |
| C61 | AP3 | 3p brn red & | 20.00 | .45 |
| | | dull bl | | |
| C62 | AP3 | 4p blue & dull | 10.00 | .25 |
| | | bl | | |
| C63 | AP3 | 6p & rose red | 1,800. | 450.00 |
| C64 | AP3 | 6p ocher & slate | 125.00 | 9.00 |
| C65 | AP3 | 7p grn & brn | 6.25 | |
| C66 | AP3 | 8p rose & gray | 57.50 | 6.25 |
| | | gray | | |
| C67 | AP3 | 9p purple & red | 77.50 | 11.00 |
| C68 | AP3 | 10p bik & dull red | 5.00 | .55 |
| C69 | AP3 | 11p green & bis- | 16.00 | .90 |
| | | ter | | |
| C70 | AP3 | 12p orange & | 12.00 | .45 |
| | | gray | | |
| C71 | AP3 | 13p dk grn & yel | 45.00 | 3.50 |
| C72 | AP3 | 14p dk blue & org | .90 | |
| C73 | AP3 | 15p blue & bis | 14.00 | 1.50 |
| C74 | AP3 | 16p black & ultra | 11.00 | .70 |
| C75 | AP3 | 17p bister & se- | 16.00 | 2.75 |
| | | pia | | |
| C76 | AP3 | 18p dk bik & yel | 14.00 | 1.40 |
| C77 | AP3 | 19p carmine & | 13.00 | 2.25 |
| | | rose red | | |
| C78 | AP3 | 20p brn & brt grn | 18.00 | .90 |
| C79 | AP3 | 23p olive & bister | 175.00 | 12.50 |
| C80 | AP3 | 24p dk blue & bik | 22.50 | 2.75 |
| C83 | AP3 | 31p car rose & | 27.50 | 2.75 |
| | | rose red | | |
| C84 | AP3 | 33p red & dull | — | |
| C85 | AP3 | 50p emer & ind | 11.00 | |
| C86 | AP3 | 100p gray & dk | 575.00 | .45 |
| C87 | AP3 | 200p dk vio & bik | 900.00 | 175.00 |
| | | | 775.00 | 275.00 |
| | | | 275.00 | 175.00 |

The existence of 26p and 27p denominations has been reported. The status of the 31p has been questioned. If it exists it may not have been issued.
Issue years: 1968, 9p, 20p; 1969, 7p; 1970, 8p, 9p, 12p, 14p, 33p; 1971, 4p, 50p, 200p; 1973, 12p, 14p, 15p, 16p; 1974, 50p, 200p; 1975, 13p, 17p, 19p, 24p; 1976, 18p; 1978, 31p, 100p; others, 1966.

## 1968-71 Wmk. 361 Litho. Perf. 14
| | | | | |
|---|---|---|---|---|
| C88 | AP3 | 1p lilac & green | 6.00 | .20 |
| C89 | AP3 | 2p green & lilac | 7.50 | .20 |
| C90 | AP3 | 3p rose lil & dull bl | 35.00 | 1.75 |
| C91 | AP3 | 4p blue & dull pur | 9.50 | 1.10 |
| C92 | AP3 | 7p rose & gray | 9.50 | 1.50 |
| C93 | AP3 | 8p red & gray ol | 37.50 | 6.00 |
| C94 | AP3 | 9p rose & red brn | 52.50 | 7.25 |
| C95 | AP3 | 10p bik & gray ol | | |
| | | brn | 32.50 | 3.50 |
| | | Nos. C88-C95 (8) | 190.00 | 21.50 |
| | | | 32.50 | 3.50 |

Issue years: 1969, 3p, 10p; 1970, 4p; 1971, 7p-9p; others, 1968.

**C98** AP4 10p blue & red brn 24.00 3.75
**C99** AP4 20p green & red brn ('71) 45.00 7.50
*Nos. C96-C99 (4)* *282.50 26.50*

Nine other denominations were printed but are not known to have been issued.

---

**HEJAZ POSTAGE DUE STAMPS**

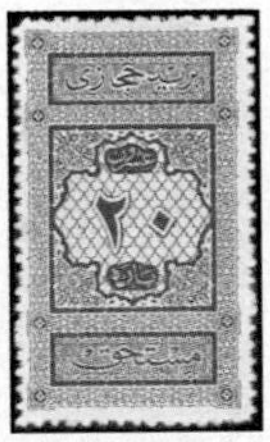

From Old Door at El Ashraf Barsbai in Shari el Ashrafiya, Cairo — D1

***Serrate Roulette 13***

**1917, June 27 Typo. Unwmk.**
**LJ1** D1 20pa red 3.25 2.00
**LJ2** D1 1pi blue 3.50 2.00
**LJ3** D1 2pi magenta 3.75 2.00
*Nos. LJ1-LJ3 (3)* 10.50 6.00

For overprints see Nos. LJ4-LJ10, LJ17-LJ25, J9,

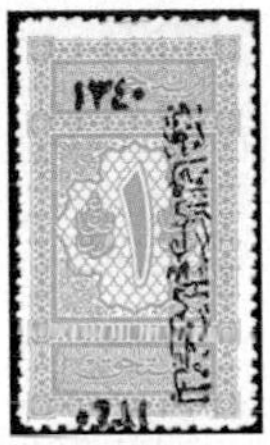

a

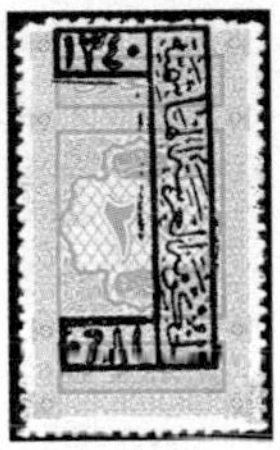

b

Nos. LJ1-LJ3 Overprinted Type "a" in Black or Red

**1921, Dec.**
**LJ4** D1 20pa red 20.00 2.75
*a.* Double overprint, one at left 140.00
*b.* Overprint at left 30.00 20.00
**LJ5** D1 1pi blue (R) 7.00 3.50
**LJ6** D1 1pi bl, ovpt. at left 30.00 18.00
*a.* Overprint at right 27.50 32.50
**LJ7** D1 2pi magenta 12.50 7.25
*a.* Double overprint, one at left 62.50
*b.* Overprint at left 27.50
*Nos. LJ4-LJ7 (4)* 69.50 31.50

Nos. LJ1-LJ3 Overprinted Type "b" in Black

**1922, Jan.**
**LJ8** D1 20pa red 25.00 27.50
*a.* Overprint at left 35.00
**LJ9** D1 1pi blue 5.00 3.25
*a.* Overprint at left 45.00
**LJ10** D1 2pi magenta 5.00 3.25
*a.* Overprint at left 32.50
*Nos. LJ8-LJ10 (3)* 35.00 34.00

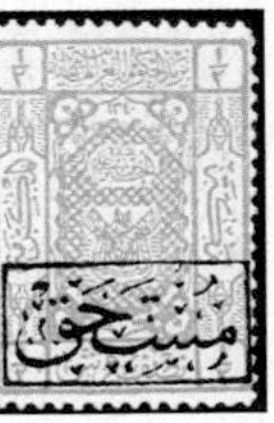

Regular issue of 1922 Overprinted

**Black Overprint**

**1923** ***Perf. 11½***
**LJ11** A7 ½pi red 4.25 1.40
*a.* Inverted overprint 50.00
**LJ12** A7 1pi dark blue 7.50 1.40
*a.* Inverted overprint 80.00
*b.* Double overprint 125.00
**LJ13** A7 2pi orange 5.00 1.75
*a.* Inverted overprint 47.50
*Nos. LJ11-LJ13 (3)* 16.75 4.55

**1924**

**Blue Overprint**

**LJ14** A7 ½pi red 17.50 2.75
*a.* Inverted overprint 80.00
**LJ15** A7 1pi dark blue 37.50 2.75
*a.* Inverted overprint 100.00
**LJ16** A7 2pi orange 27.50 4.50
*a.* Inverted overprint 80.00
*Nos. LJ14-LJ16 (3)* 82.50 10.00

This overprint reads "Mustahaq" (Due).

**Jedda Issues**

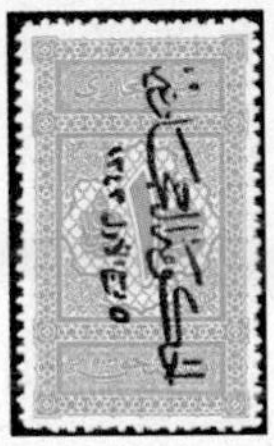

Nos. LJ1-LJ3 Overprinted in Red or Blue (Overprint reads up in illustration)

Jedda issues were also used in Medina and Yambo. **Used values for #L51-L186 and LJ17-LJ39 are for genuine cancels. Privately applied cancels exist for "Mekke" (Mecca, bilingual or all Arabic), Khartoum, Cairo, as well as for Jeddah. Many private cancels have wrong dates, some as early as 1916. These are worth half the used values.**

**1925, Jan.** ***Serrate Roulette 13***
**LJ17** D1 20pa red (R) 375.00 *350.00*
**LJ19** D1 1pi blue (R) 20.00 *18.00*
**LJ20** D1 1pi blue (Bl) 27.50 *25.00*
**LJ21** D1 2pi mag (Bl) 15.00 *14.00*

**Overprint Reading Down**

*LJ17a* D1 20pa *550.00 550.00*
**LJ18** D1 20pa red (Bl) *450.00*
*LJ19a* D1 1pi 18.00 *18.00*
*LJ20a* D1 1pi 67.50 *80.00*
*LJ21a* D1 2pi 60.00 *60.00*

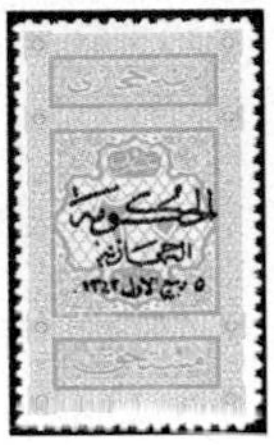

Nos. LJ1-LJ3 Overprinted in Blue or Red

**1925**
**LJ22** D1 20pa red (Bl) 450.00 *425.00*
*a.* Inverted overprint 325.00 *325.00*
**LJ24** D1 1pi blue (R) 25.00 *27.50*
*a.* Inverted overprint 32.50 *32.50*
**LJ25** D1 2pi magenta (Bl) 20.00 *18.00*
*a.* Inverted overprint 35.00 *45.00*
*b.* Double overprint 350.00

No. LJ2 with this overprint in blue is bogus.

Regular Issues of 1922-24 Overprinted

a

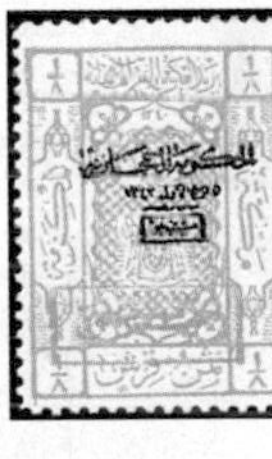

and Handstamped

b

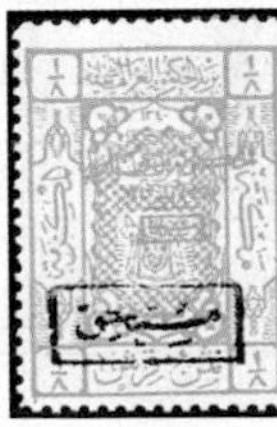

**1925** ***Perf. 11½***
**LJ26** A7 ⅛pi red brown 20.00 *18.00*
**LJ27** A7 ½pi red 27.50 *25.00*
**LJ28** A7 1pi dark blue 20.00 *18.00*
**LJ29** A7 1½pi violet 22.50 *18.00*
**LJ30** A7 2pi orange 25.00 *20.00*
**LJ31** A7 3pi olive brown 25.00 *20.00*
**LJ32** A7 3pi dull red 50.00 *45.00*
**LJ33** A7 5pi olive green 25.00 *20.00*
**LJ34** A7 10pi vio & dk brn 30.00 *25.00*
*Nos. LJ26-LJ34 (9)* 245.00 *209.00*

The printed overprint *(a)*, consisting of the three top lines of Arabic, was used alone for the first issue (Nos. LJ26a-LJ34a). The "postage due" box was so small and indistinct that its equivalent in larger characters was added by boxed handstamp *(b)* at bottom of each stamp for the second issue (Nos. LJ26-LJ34).

The handstamped overprint *(b)* is found double, inverted, etc. It is also known in dark violet.

Counterfeits exist of both overprint and handstamp.

**Without Boxed Handstamp "b"**

*LJ26a* A7 ⅛pi red brown 42.50
*LJ27a* A7 ½pi red 42.50
*LJ28a* A7 1pi dark blue 42.50
*LJ29a* A7 1½pi violet 42.50
*LJ30a* A7 2pi orange 42.50
*LJ31a* A7 3pi olive brown 42.50
*LJ32a* A7 3pi dull red 42.50
*LJ33a* A7 5pi olive green 55.00
*LJ34a* A7 10pi vio & dk brn 55.00
*Nos. LJ26a-LJ34a (9)* 407.50

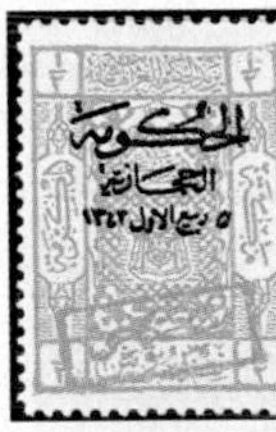

Regular Issue of 1922 Overprinted

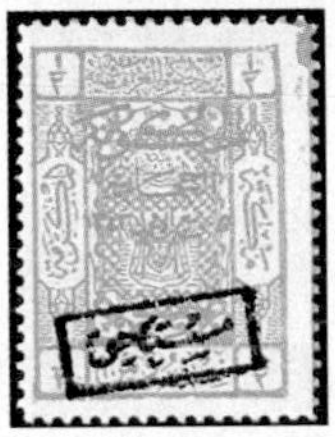

and Handstamped

**LJ35** A7 ½pi red *150.00 140.00*
**LJ36** A7 1½pi violet *150.00 140.00*
*a.* Overprint in red, boxed handstamp violet *1,400.*
**LJ37** A7 2pi orange *190.00 175.00*
**LJ38** A7 3pi olive brown *150.00 140.00*
**LJ39** A7 5pi olive green *150.00 140.00*
*Nos. LJ35-LJ39 (5)* *790.00 735.00*

Counterfeits exist of Nos. LJ4-LJ39.

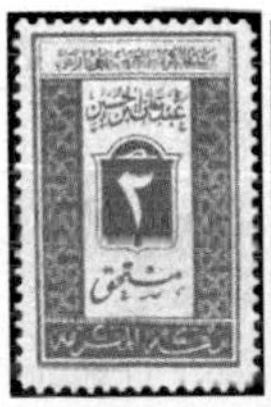

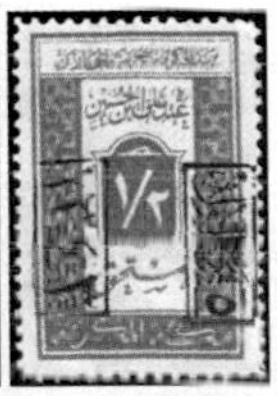

Arabic Numeral of Value
D2 D3

**1925, May-June** ***Perf. 11½***
**LJ40** D2 ½pi light blue 3.00
**LJ41** D2 1pi orange 3.00
**LJ42** D2 2pi lt brown 3.00
**LJ43** D2 3pi pink 3.00
*Nos. LJ40-LJ43 (4)* 12.00

Nos. LJ40-LJ43 exist imperforate. Impressions in colors other than issued are trial color proofs.

**Black Overprint**

**1925**
**LJ44** D3 ½pi light blue 3.00
**LJ45** D3 1pi orange 3.00
**LJ46** D3 2pi light brown 3.00
**LJ47** D3 3pi pink 3.75
*Nos. LJ44-LJ47 (4)* 12.75

Nos. LJ44-LJ47 exist with either Jedda or Cairo overprints and the tablets normally read upward. Values are for Cairo overprints; Jedda overprints sell for more.

**Red Overprint**

**LJ48** D3 ½pi light blue 3.75
**LJ49** D3 1pi orange 3.75
**LJ50** D3 2pi light brown 3.75
**LJ51** D3 3pi pink 3.75

**Blue Overprint**

**LJ52** D3 ½pi light blue 3.75
**LJ53** D3 1pi orange 3.75
**LJ54** D3 2pi light brown 3.75
**LJ55** D3 3pi pink 3.75
*Nos. LJ40-LJ55 (16)* 54.75

Red and blue overprints are from Cairo. Nos. LJ44-LJ55 exist imperf.

---

**NEJDI ADMINISTRATION OF HEJAZ POSTAGE DUE STAMPS**

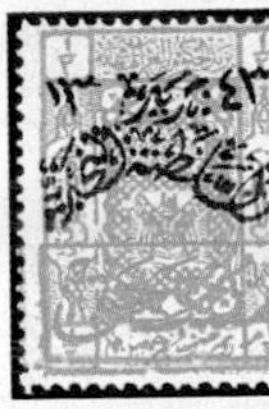

Nos. LJ11-LJ16 Handstamped in Blue, Red or Black

**1925, Apr.-June Unwmk.** ***Perf. 11½***
**J1** A7 ½pi red (Bl) 27.50 27.50
**J2** A7 1pi lt blue (R) 55.00 55.00
*a.* 1pi dark blue (R) 35.00 35.00
**J3** A7 2pi yel buff (Bl) 55.00 55.00
*a.* 2pi orange (Bl) 47.50 47.50
*Nos. J1-J3 (3)* 137.50 137.50

The original boxed overprint is printed on Nos. J1, J2a and J3a. Nos. J2-J3 are overprinted on a new printing of the basic stamps with handstamped boxed overprints.

**Same, with Postage Due Overprint in Blue**

**J4** A7 ½pi red (Bl) *140.00*
**J5** A7 1pi dk blue (R) —
**J6** A7 2pi orange (Bl) *175.00*

On Hejaz Stamps of 1922-24

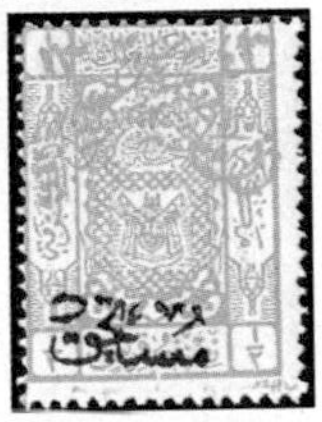

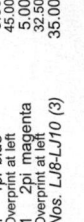

Handstamped in Blue

**J7** A7 ½pi red (Bl & Bl) 16.00 16.00
**J8** A7 3pi brn red (Bl & Bl) 19.00 19.00

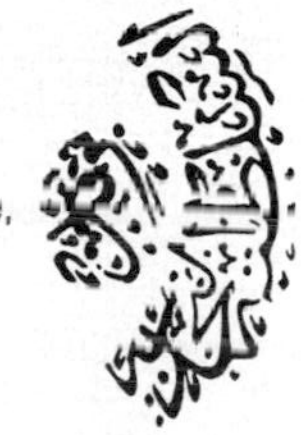

Handstamped in Blue, Black or Violet

**See note before No. 35.**

**On Hejaz No. LJ9**

***Serrate Roulette 13½***

**J9** D1 1pi blue (V) 60.00 27.50

Same Overprint on Hejaz Stamps of 1924 with additional Handstamp in Black, Blue or Red

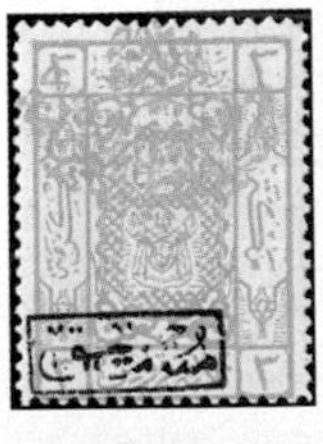

***Perf. 11½***
**J10** A7 3pi brn red (Bl & Bk) 11.00 11.00
**J11** A7 3pi brn red (Bk & Bl) 11.00 11.00

**Same Handstamps on Hejaz Railway Tax Stamps**

**J12** R3 1pi blue (Bk & R) 12.00 12.00
**J13** R3 2pi ocher (Bl & Bk) 12.00 12.00
**J14** R3 5pi green (Bk & R) 20.00 20.00
**J15** R3 5pi green (V & BK) 20.00 9.00
*Nos. J10-J15 (6)* 86.00 75.00

The second handstamp, which is struck on the lower part of the Postage Due Stamps, is the word Mustahaq (Due) in various forms.

#J13 exists with 2nd handstamp in blue.

### Hejaz-Nejd

D1

**1926** **Typo.** *Perf. 11*
**J16** D1 ½pi carmine 4.00 .65
**J17** D1 2pi orange 4.00 .65
**J18** D1 6pi light brown 4.00 .65
*Nos. J16-J18 (3)* 12.00 1.95

Nos. J16-J18 exist with perf. 14, 14x11 and 11x14, and imperf. These sell for six times the values quoted.

Nos. J16-J18 in colors other than listed (both perf. and imperf.) are proofs.

Counterfeit note after No. 80 also applies to Nos. J16-J21.

**Pan-Islamic Congress Issue**
Postage Due Stamps of 1926 Handstamped like Regular Issue

**J19** D1 ½pi carmine 5.50 4.50
**J20** D1 2pi orange 5.50 4.50
**J21** D1 6pi light brown 5.50 4.50
*Nos. J19-J21 (3)* 16.50 13.50

D2

**1927** *Perf. 11½*
**J22** D2 1pi slate 18.00 .45
*a.* Inscription reads "2 piastres" in upper right circle 175.00 100.00
**J23** D2 2pi dark violet 5.75 .45

**Saudi Arabia**

Saudi Arabia No. 161 Handstamped in Black

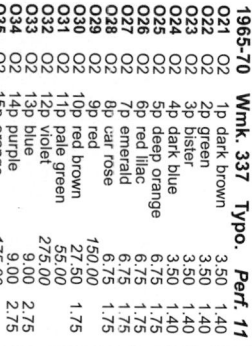

**1935**
**J24** A9 ½g dark carmine 225.00

Two types of overprint.

D3

**1937-39** **Unwmk.**
**J25** D3 ½g org brn ('39) 12.00 12.00
**J26** D3 1g light blue 12.00 12.00
**J27** D3 2g rose vio ('39) 17.00 8.00
*Nos. J25-J27 (3)* 41.00 32.00

**Catalogue values for unused stamps in this section, from this point to the end of the section, are for Never Hinged items.**

D4

**1961** **Litho.** *Perf. 13x13½*
**J28** D4 1p purple 5.00 5.00
**J29** D4 2p green 8.50 4.00
**J30** D4 4p rose red 10.00 10.00
*Nos. J28-J30 (3)* 23.50 19.00

The use of Postage Due stamps ceased in 1963.

### OFFICIAL STAMPS

Official stamps were normally used only on external correspondence.

O1

O2

**1939** **Unwmk.** **Typo.** *Perf. 11½*
**O1** O1 3g deep ultra 3.50 1.60

*Perf. 11, 11½*
**O2** O1 5g red violet 4.50 2.10

*Perf. 11*
**O3** O1 20g brown 9.50 4.25
**O4** O1 50g blue green 18.00 8.75
**O5** O1 100g olive grn 75.00 40.00
**O6** O1 200g purple 60.00 27.50
*Nos. O1-O6 (6)* 170.50 84.20

**Catalogue values for unused stamps in this section, from this point to the end of the section, are for Never Hinged items.**

**1961** **Litho.** *Perf. 13x13½*
**Size: 18x22-22½mm**
**O7** O2 1p black 1.10 .25
**O8** O2 2p dark green 1.90 .40
**O9** O2 3p bister 2.25 .45
**O10** O2 4p dark blue 2.75 .60
**O11** O2 5p rose red 3.50 .70
**O12** O2 10p maroon 6.00 2.25
**O13** O2 20p violet blue 10.50 4.00
**O14** O2 50p dull brown 29.00 11.50
**O15** O2 100p dull green 50.00 20.00
*Nos. O7-O15 (9)* 107.00 40.15

Nos. O8, O10-O15 exist imperf., probably not regularly issued.

**1964-65** **Wmk. 337** *Perf. 13½x13*
**Size: 21x26mm**
**O16** O2 1p black 1.25 .50
**O17** O2 2p green ('65) 2.50 1.00
**O18** O2 3p bister 8.75 3.50
**O19** O2 4p dark blue 6.25 2.50
**O20** O2 5p rose red 7.75 1.50
*Nos. O16-O20 (5)* 26.50 9.00

**1965-70** **Wmk. 337** **Typo.** *Perf. 11*
**O21** O2 1p dark brown 3.50 1.40
**O22** O2 2p green 3.50 1.40
**O23** O2 3p bister 3.50 1.40
**O24** O2 4p dark blue 3.50 1.40
**O25** O2 5p deep orange 6.75 1.75
**O26** O2 6p red lilac 6.75 1.75
**O27** O2 7p emerald 6.75 1.75
**O28** O2 8p car rose 6.75 1.75
**O29** O2 9p red *150.00*
**O30** O2 10p red brown 27.50 1.75
**O31** O2 11p pale green *55.00*
**O32** O2 12p violet *275.00*
**O33** O2 13p blue 9.00 2.75
**O34** O2 14p purple 9.00 2.75
**O35** O2 15p orange *175.00*
**O36** O2 16p black *175.00*
*a.* "19" instead of "16" *450.00*
**O37** O2 17p gray green *175.00*
**O38** O2 18p yellow *175.00*
**O39** O2 19p dp red lilac *175.00*
**O39A** O2 20p lt blue green
**O40** O2 23p ultra *225.00*
**O41** O2 24p yellow green *175.00*
**O42** O2 26p bister *175.00*
**O43** O2 27p pale lilac *175.00*
**O44** O2 31p pale salmon *225.00*
**O45** O2 33p yellow green *175.00*
**O46** O2 50p olive bister *350.00*
**O47** O2 100p ol gray ('70) *800.00*
*Nos. O21-O39,O40-O47 (27)* *3,741.*

Nos. O21-O28, O30 and O33-O34 were released to the philatelic trade in 1964. Nos. O21-O47 were printed from new plates; lines of the design are heavier. The numerals have been enlarged and the P's are smaller. Head of "P" 2mm wide on 1964-65 issue, 1mm wide on 1965-70 issue.

O3

**Wmk. 361, 337 (7p, 8p, 9p, 11p, 12p, 23p)**
**1970-72** **Litho.** *Perf. 13½x14*
**O48** O3 1p red brown 2.75 .90
**O49** O3 2p deep green 2.75 .90
**O50** O3 3p rose red 3.50 1.40
**O51** O3 4p bright blue 4.50 1.75
**O52** O3 5p brick red 4.50 1.75
**O53** O3 6p orange 4.50 1.75
*a.* Wmk. 337 *175.00* *45.00*
**O54** O3 7p deep salmon *175.00*
**O55** O3 8p violet
**O56** O3 9p dk blue grn
**O57** O3 10p blue 6.25 2.75
*a.* Wmk. 337
**O58** O3 11p olive green
**O58A** O3 12p black brown
**O59** O3 20p gray violet 14.00 4.50
*a.* Wmk. 337 *175.00* *90.00*
**O59B** O3 23p ocher ('72) *375.00*
**O60** O3 31p deep plum *45.00* *18.00*
**O61** O3 50p light brown *700.00*
**O62** O3 100p green *700.00*

Use of official stamps ceased in 1974.

### NEWSPAPER STAMPS

Nos. 8, 9 and 14 with Additional Overprint in Black

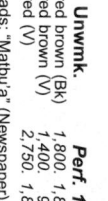

**1925** **Unwmk.** *Perf. 11½*
**P1** A7 ⅛pi red brown (Bk) *1,800.* *1,800.*
**P2** A7 ⅛pi red brown (V) *1,400.* *900.*
**P3** A7 ½pi red (V) *2,750.* *1,800.*

Overprint reads: "Matbu'a" (Newspaper), but these stamps were normally used for regular postage. Counterfeits exist.

The status of this set in question. The government may have declared it to be unauthorized.

### POSTAL TAX STAMPS

PT1

**1934, May 15** **Unwmk.** *Perf. 11½*
**RA1** PT1 ⅛g scarlet *175.00* 4.50

No. RA1 collected a "war tax" to aid wounded of the 1934 Saudi-Yemen war.

Nos. RA2-RA8 raised funds for the Medical Aid Society.

General Hospital, Mecca PT2

**1936, Oct.**
**Size: 37x20mm**
**RA2** PT2 ⅛g scarlet *625.00* 9.00

Type of 1936, Redrawn

**1937-42**
**Size: 30½x18mm**
**RA3** PT2 ⅛g scarlet 60.00 .90
*a.* ⅛g rose ('39) *110.00* *1.75*
*b.* ⅛g rose car, perf. 11 ('42) *175.00* *6.75*

General Hospital, Mecca — PT3

**1943** **Typo.** *Perf. 11½, 11*
**Grayish Paper**
**RA4** PT3 ⅛g car rose *35.00* .20
*a.* ⅛g scarlet *35.00* *.20*

The 1g green and 5g indigo were not for postal use.

See Nos. RA5-RA8.

Map of Saudi Arabia Type I — (Flag inscriptions intact) — PT4

Type II — (Flag inscriptions scratched out)

**1946** **Unwmk.** *Perf. 11½*
**RA4B** PT4 ½g magenta (II) 16.00 .90
*c.* Type I 55.00 .90
*d.* Type I, perf. 11 45.00 9.00
*e.* Type II, perf. 11 67.50

Return of King Ibn Saud from Egypt.

This stamp was required on all mail during Jan.-July.

Type of 1943, Redrawn

**1948-53** **Litho.** *Perf. 10*
**RA5** PT3 ⅛g rose brn ('53) *20.00* .20
*c.* Perf. 11x10 *27.50* 2.75

**Catalogue values for unused stamps in this section, from this point to the end of the section, are for Never Hinged items.**

**1950** *Rouletted*
**RA6** PT3 ⅛g red brown 5.50 .20
*a.* ⅛g rose 7.25 .20
*b.* ⅛g carmine 9.00 .25

All lines in lithographed design considerably finer; some shading in center eliminated.

Type of 1943

**1955-56** **Photo.** *Perf. 11*
**RA7** PT3 ⅛g rose car 8.00 .20
**RA8** PT3 ¼g car rose ('56) 4.75 .20

The tax on postal matter was discontinued in May, 1964.

Coat of Arms, Waves and View — PT5

**Wmk. 361**
**1974, Oct.** **Litho.** *Perf. 14*
**RA9** PT5 1r blue & multi *175.00*

Obligatory on all mailed entries in a government television contest during month of Ramadan in 1974 and 1975. The tax aided a benevolent society.

## SCHLESWIG

'shles-ˌwig

LOCATION — In the northern part of the former Schleswig-Holstein Province, in northern Germany.

Schleswig was divided into North and South Schleswig after the Versailles Treaty, and plebiscites were held in 1920. North Schleswig (Zone 1) voted

## SCHLESWIG (continued)

to join Denmark, South Schleswig to stay German.

100 Pfennig = 1 Mark
100 Øre = 1 Krone

**Watermark**

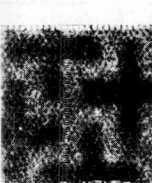

Wmk. 114 — Multiple Crosses

**Plebiscite Issue**

Arms — A11

View of Schleswig A12

**1920, Jan. 25**    **Perf. 14x15**    **Typo.**

| | | | | |
|---|---|---|---|---|
| 1 | A11 | 2½pf gray | .20 | .20 |
| 2 | A11 | 5pf green | .20 | .20 |
| 3 | A11 | 7½pf yellow brown | .20 | .20 |
| 4 | A11 | 10pf red violet | .20 | .25 |
| 5 | A11 | 15pf rose red | .20 | .25 |
| 6 | A11 | 20pf deep blue | .25 | .40 |
| 7 | A11 | 25pf orange | .40 | .65 |
| 8 | A11 | 35pf brown | .65 | 7.00 |
| 9 | A11 | 40pf violet | .65 | 2.50 |
| 10 | A11 | 75pf greenish blue | .30 | 3.75 |
| 11 | A11 | 1k dark brown | .40 | 7.00 |
| 12 | A12 | 2k deep blue | 2.50 | 25.00 |
| 13 | A12 | 5k green | 5.75 | 47.50 |
| 14 | A12 | 10k red | 16.20 | 127.90 |
| | | Nos. 1-14 (14) | 65.00 | |

Types of 1920 Overprinted in Blue

**1920, May 20**

| | | | | |
|---|---|---|---|---|
| 15 | A11 | 2½pf gray | .20 | 1.25 |
| 16 | A11 | 5pf green | .20 | .65 |
| 17 | A11 | 7o yellow brn | .20 | .75 |
| 18 | A11 | 10o rose red | .20 | 1.25 |
| 20 | A11 | 15o lilac rose | .20 | 4.25 |
| 21 | A11 | 20o dark blue | .20 | 7.00 |
| 22 | A11 | 25o orange | .65 | 7.00 |
| 23 | A11 | 35o brown | .30 | 3.75 |
| 24 | A11 | 40o violet | .40 | 7.00 |
| 25 | A11 | 75o greenish blue | 5.00 | 25.00 |
| 26 | A12 | 1k dark brown | 2.50 | 25.00 |
| 27 | A12 | 2k deep blue | 5.75 | 47.50 |
| 28 | A12 | 10k red | 16.20 | 127.90 |
| | | Nos. 15-28 (14) | 65.00 | |

Set, never hinged

### OFFICIAL STAMPS

Nos. 1-14 Overprinted   **C·I·S**

**1920**    **Perf. 14x15**

| | | | | |
|---|---|---|---|---|
| O1 | A11 | 2½pf gray | 50.00 | 72.50 |
| O2 | A11 | 5pf green | 50.00 | 85.00 |
| O3 | A11 | 7½pf yellow brn | | 72.50 |
| O4 | A11 | 10pf deep | 50.00 | 92.50 |
| O5 | A11 | 15pf red violet | 32.50 | 45.00 |
| O6 | A11 | 25pf dp blue | 50.00 | 52.50 |
| O7 | A11 | 40pf violet | 100.00 | 125.00 |
| | a. | Inverted overprint | 850.00 | |
| O8 | A11 | 35pf brown | 100.00 | 125.00 |
| O9 | A11 | 40pf violet | 85.00 | 80.00 |

**Wmk. 114**

| | | | | |
|---|---|---|---|---|
| O10 | A11 | 75pf grnsh blue | 100.00 | 200.00 |
| O11 | A12 | 1m dark brown | 100.00 | 200.00 |
| O12 | A12 | 2m deep blue | 150.00 | 210.00 |
| O13 | A12 | 5m green | 210.00 | 325.00 |
| O14 | A12 | 10m red | 400.00 | 500.00 |
| | | Nos. O1-O14 (14) | 1,527. | 2,185. |

The letters "C.I.S" are the initials of "Commission Interalliée Slesvig," under whose auspices the plebiscites took place. Counterfeit overprints exist.

---

# SENEGAL

se-ni-'gäl

LOCATION — West coast of Africa, bordering on the Atlantic Ocean
GOVT. — Republic
AREA — 76,000 sq. mi.
POP. — 10,051,930 (1999 est.)
CAPITAL — Dakar

The former French colony of Senegal became part of French West Africa in 1943. The Republic of Senegal was established Nov. 25, 1958. From Apr. 4, 1959, to June 20, 1960, the Republic of Senegal and the Sudanese Republic together formed the Mali Federation. After its breakup, Senegal resumed issuing its own stamps in 1960.

100 Centimes = 1 Franc

> **Catalogue values for unused stamps in this country are for Never Hinged items, beginning with Scott 195 in the regular postage section, Scott B16 in the semi-postal section, Scott C26 in the airpost section, Scott CB2 in the airpost semi-postal section, Scott J32 in the postage due section, and Scott O1 in the official section.**

French Colonies Nos. 48, 49, 51, 52, 55, Type A9, Surcharged:

**1887**    **Unwmk.**    **Perf. 14x13½**

Black Surcharge

| | | | | |
|---|---|---|---|---|
| 1 | (a) | 5c on 20c red, grn | 150.00 | 150.00 |
| | a. | Double surcharge | | |
| 2 | (b) | 5c on 20c red, grn | 200.00 | 200.00 |
| 3 | (d) | 5c on 20c red, grn | 725.00 | 725.00 |
| 4 | (d) | 5c on 20c red, grn | 175.00 | 175.00 |
| 5 | (a) | 5c on 30c brn, bis | 250.00 | 250.00 |
| 6 | (b) | 5c on 30c brn, bis | 225.00 | 250.00 |
| 7 | (b) | 5c on 30c brn, bis | 925.00 | 925.00 |
| 8 | (b) | 5c on 30c brn, bis | 325.00 | 325.00 |
| | | Nos. 1-8 (8) | 3,000. | 3,025. |

See Madagascar #6-7 for stamps with surcharge like "d" on 10c and 25c stamps.

Surcharged:

| | | | | |
|---|---|---|---|---|
| 9 | (f) | 10c on 4c cl, lav | 100.00 | 100.00 |
| 10 | (g) | 10c on 4c cl, lav | 140.00 | 140.00 |
| 11 | (h) | 10c on 4c cl, lav | 65.00 | 65.00 |
| | a. | "1" without top stroke | | |
| 12 | (f) | 10c on 20c red, grn | 450.00 | 450.00 |
| 13 | (g) | 10c on 20c red, grn | 525.00 | 525.00 |
| 14 | (h) | 10c on 20c red, grn | 450.00 | 450.00 |
| 15 | | 10c on 20c red, grn | 2,750. | 2,750. |
| 16 | | 10c on 20c red, grn | 525.00 | 525.00 |
| 17 | | 10c on 20c red, grn | 1,000. | 1,000. |
| 18 | (k) | 10c on 20c red, grn | 750.00 | 750.00 |
| 19 | (l) | 10c on 20c red, grn | 750.00 | 750.00 |
| 20 | (m) | 10c on 20c red, grn | 750.00 | 750.00 |
| 21 | (n) | 15c on 20c red, grn | 70.00 | 70.00 |
| 22 | (o) | 15c on 20c red, grn | 60.00 | 60.00 |
| 23 | (p) | 15c on 20c red, grn | 50.00 | 50.00 |
| 24 | | 15c on 20c red, grn | 92.50 | 92.50 |
| 25 | | 15c on 20c red, grn | 55.00 | 55.00 |
| 26 | | 15c on 20c red, grn | 55.00 | 55.00 |
| 27 | (s) | 15c on 20c red, grn | 160.00 | 160.00 |
| 28 | (t) | 15c on 20c red, grn | 47.50 | 47.50 |
| 29 | (u) | 15c on 20c red, grn | 65.00 | 65.00 |
| 30 | (w) | 15c on 20c red, grn | 275.00 | 275.00 |
| | | Nos. 21-30 (10) | 930.00 | 930.00 |

Counterfeits exist of Nos. 1-34.

**1892**    Black Surcharge

| | | | | |
|---|---|---|---|---|
| 31 | A9 | 75c on 15c blue | 325.00 | 325.00 |
| 32 | A9 | 1fr on 5c grn, grnsh | 325.00 | 325.00 |

"SENEGAL" in Red

| | | | |
|---|---|---|---|
| 33 | A9 | 75c on 15c blue | 10,500. |
| 34 | A9 | 1fr on 5c grn, grnsh | 4,600. |

4,000.
1,000.

Navigation and Commerce — A24

**1892-1900**    **Typo.**    **Perf. 14x13½**

Name of Colony in Blue or Carmine

| | | | | |
|---|---|---|---|---|
| 35 | A24 | 1c blk, lil bl | .85 | .80 |
| 36 | A24 | 2c brn, buff | 1.75 | 1.60 |
| 37 | A24 | 4c claret, lav | 1.75 | 1.25 |
| 38 | A24 | 5c grn, grnsh | 2.75 | 1.60 |
| 39 | A24 | 5c yel grn ('00) | 1.60 | .85 |
| 40 | A24 | 10c blk, lav | 5.75 | 4.75 |
| 41 | A24 | 10c red ('00) | 3.75 | 1.25 |
| 42 | A24 | 15c bl, quadrille paper | | 1.50 |
| 43 | A24 | 15c gray ('00) | 10.00 | 1.75 |
| 44 | A24 | 20c red, grn | 4.50 | 4.50 |
| 45 | A24 | 25c blk, rose | 8.00 | 5.00 |
| 46 | A24 | 25c blue ('00) | 13.00 | 13.00 |
| 47 | A24 | 30c brn, bis | 30.00 | 26.00 |
| 48 | A24 | 40c red, straw | 13.00 | 6.50 |
| 49 | A24 | 50c car, rose | 17.50 | 14.50 |
| 50 | A24 | 50c brn, az ('00) | 29.00 | 21.00 |
| 51 | A24 | 75c vio, org | 35.00 | 32.50 |
| 52 | A24 | 1fr brnz grn, straw | 14.50 | 14.50 |
| | | Nos. 35-52 (18) | 207.70 | 154.35 |

Perf. 13½x14 stamps are counterfeits.
For surcharges see Nos. 53-56, 73-78.

Stamps of 1892 Surcharged:

**1903**

| | | | | |
|---|---|---|---|---|
| 53 | A24 | 5c on 40c red, straw | 11.00 | 11.00 |
| 54 | A24 | 10c on 50c car, rose | 16.00 | 16.00 |
| 55 | A24 | 10c on 75c vio, org | 16.00 | 16.00 |
| 56 | A24 | 10c on 1fr brnz grn, straw | 65.00 | 60.00 |
| | | Nos. 53-56 (4) | 108.00 | 103.00 |

General Louis Faidherbe A25

Oil Palms — A26

Dr. Noel Eugène Ballay A27

**1906**    **Typo.**

"SÉNÉGAL" in Red or Blue

| | | | | |
|---|---|---|---|---|
| 57 | A25 | 1c slate | .90 | .90 |
| | a. | "SÉNÉGAL" omitted | 90.00 | 90.00 |
| 58 | A25 | 2c choc (R) | 1.10 | .90 |
| 58A | A25 | 2c choc (Bl) | 2.00 | 1.60 |
| 59 | A25 | 4c choc, gray bl | 1.75 | 1.25 |
| 60 | A25 | 5c green | 2.00 | .65 |
| 61 | A25 | 10c car (Bl) | 8.25 | .65 |
| | a. | "SÉNÉGAL" omitted | 340.00 | 340.00 |
| 62 | A25 | 15c violet | 5.25 | 3.00 |
| 63 | A26 | 20c blk, az | 6.50 | 3.50 |
| 64 | A26 | 20c bl, pnksh | 2.50 | 2.00 |
| 65 | A26 | 30c choc, prnksh | 6.00 | 4.25 |
| 66 | A26 | 35c blk, yellow | 22.50 | 2.00 |
| 67 | A26 | 40c car, az (Bl) | 8.00 | 5.00 |
| 67A | A26 | 45c choc, grnsh | 6.25 | 5.25 |
| 68 | A26 | 75c dp violet | 8.50 | 6.50 |
| 69 | A26 | 75c bl, org | 6.25 | 5.25 |
| 70 | A27 | 1fr blk, azure | 21.00 | 20.00 |
| 71 | A27 | 2fr blue, pink | 52.50 | 24.00 |
| 72 | A27 | 5fr car, straw (Bl) | 197.00 | 47.50 |
| | | Nos. 57-72 (18) | | 139.95 |

Stamps of 1892-1900 Surcharged in Carmine or Black

## 1912

| No. | Type | Description | Unused | Used |
|---|---|---|---|---|
| 73 | A24 | 5c on 15c gray (C) | .75 | .75 |
| 74 | A24 | 5c on 20c red, grn | 1.00 | 1.00 |
| 75 | A24 | 5c on 30c bis (C) | 1.00 | |
| 76 | A24 | 10c on 40c red, straw | .90 | .90 |
| 77 | A24 | 10c on 50c car, rose | 1.10 | 1.10 |
| 78 | A24 | 10c on 75c vio, org | 2.75 | 2.75 |
| | | Nos. 73-78 (6) | 4.25 | 4.25 |
| | | | 10.75 | 10.75 |

Two spacings between the surcharged numerals found on Nos. 73 to 78.

Senegalese Preparing Food — A28

## 1914-33   Typo.

| No. | Type | Description | Unused | Used |
|---|---|---|---|---|
| 79 | A28 | 1c ol brn & vio | .20 | .20 |
| 80 | A28 | 2c black & blue | .20 | .20 |
| 81 | A28 | 4c gray & brn | .20 | .20 |
| 82 | A28 | 5c yel grn & brn | .30 | .20 |
| 83 | A28 | 5c blk & rose ('22) | .20 | .20 |
| 84 | A28 | 10c org red & blue | .80 | |
| 85 | A28 | 10c yel grn & bl grn ('22) | .20 | .20 |
| 86 | A28 | 10c red brn & bl ('25) | .20 | .20 |
| 87 | A28 | 15c red org & brn vio ('22) | .20 | .20 |
| 88 | A28 | 25c brn & bl ('25) | .45 | .20 |
| 89 | A28 | 30c choc & blk | .40 | .20 |
| 90 | A28 | 20c grn & bl grn ('26) | .25 | .25 |
| 91 | A28 | 20c db & lt bl ('27) | .35 | .35 |
| 92 | A28 | 25c ultra & bl ('22) | .35 | .35 |
| 93 | A28 | 30c black & blk | .20 | .20 |
| 94 | A28 | 35c red & rose | .50 | .20 |
| 95 | A28 | 30c grn & bl ('28) | .45 | .20 |
| 96 | A28 | 30c dl grn & dp grn ('22) | .40 | .20 |
| 97 | A28 | 35c orange & vio | .50 | .35 |
| 98 | A28 | 35c choc & blk | | .35 |
| 99 | A28 | 40c violet & grn ('28) | .60 | .35 |
| 100 | A28 | 45c rose & bl ('22) | .25 | .25 |
| 101 | A28 | 45c red & ver ('28) | 1.75 | .25 |
| 102 | A28 | 45c ol brn & bl ('28) | 2.25 | 1.75 |
| 103 | A28 | 50c vio brn & bl | 1.25 | .85 |
| 104 | A28 | 50c ultra & bl ('22) | 1.50 | 1.40 |
| 105 | A28 | 50c red org & grn | | |
| 106 | A28 | 60c vio, prkish ('26) | .40 | .20 |
| 107 | A28 | 65c rose red & dp grn ('22) | .40 | .20 |
| 108 | A28 | 75c gray & bl ('28) | 1.25 | 1.10 |
| 109 | A28 | 75c dk bl & bl bl ('25) | .80 | .55 |
| 110 | A28 | 75c red vio ('30) | .70 | .55 |
| 111 | A28 | 90c brn red & rose ('30) | 1.25 | .45 |
| 112 | A28 | 1.25c dp grn & dp org ('33) | 4.00 | 3.50 |
| 113 | A28 | 1fr violet & blk | .85 | .85 |
| 114 | A28 | 1.50fr dk bl & bl ('30) | .70 | .55 |
| 115 | A28 | 1.10fr bl grn & blk | 1.25 | .45 |
| 116 | A28 | 90c brn red & rose ('30) | 3.00 | 3.00 |
| 117 | A28 | 1.50fr blue ('26) | .90 | .85 |
| 118 | A28 | 1.75fr dk brn & Prus bl ('33) | 2.10 | 2.00 |
| 119 | A28 | 2fr carmine & bl | 5.25 | |
| 120 | A28 | 2fr lt bl & bl grn ('22) | 2.50 | 1.90 |
| 121 | A28 | 3fr red vio ('30) | .65 | |
| 122 | A28 | 5fr green & vio | 3.25 | 1.60 |
| | | Nos. 79-122 (44) | 49.45 | 30.70 |

Nos. 79, 82, 84 and 97 are on both ordinary and chalky paper. For surcharges see Nos. 123-137, B1-B2.

## 1922-25

| No. | Type | Description | Unused | Used |
|---|---|---|---|---|
| 123 | A28 | 60c on 75c vio, prkish | .65 | .65 |
| 124 | A28 | 65c on 15c red org & dl vio ('25) | .85 | .85 |
| 125 | A28 | 15c red org & dl vio ('25) | | |
| 126 | A28 | 85c on 75c grn & vio ('25) | .90 | .90 |

No. 108 and Type of 1914 Surcharged:

No. 87 Surcharged in Various Colors

## 1922

Stamps and Type of 1914 Surcharged with New Value and Bars in Black or Red

| No. | Type | Description | Unused | Used |
|---|---|---|---|---|
| 127 | A28 | 1c on 15c (Bk) | .45 | .45 |
| 128 | A28 | 2c on 15c (Bl) | .45 | .45 |
| 129 | A28 | 2c on 15c (G) | .45 | .45 |
| 130 | A28 | 5c on 15c (V) | 5.05 | 5.05 |
| | | Nos. 123-130 (8) | | |

Common Design Types pictured following the introduction

## 1924-27

| No. | Type | Description | Unused | Used |
|---|---|---|---|---|
| 131 | A28 | 25c grn & vio | .60 | .60 |
| 132 | A28 | 90c on 75c brn red | .80 | .75 |
| a. | | Double surcharge | 90.00 | 90.00 |
| 133 | A28 | 1.25fr on 1fr bl & lt bl (R) ('26) | .85 | .75 |
| 134 | A28 | 1.50fr on 1fr bl & lt bl ultra ('27) | .75 | .60 |
| 135 | A28 | 3fr on 5fr mag & ol ('27) | 2.75 | .75 |
| 136 | A28 | 10fr on 5fr dk bl & red org ('27) | 6.00 | 2.25 |
| 137 | A28 | 20fr on 5fr vio & ol ('27) | 17.75 | 11.95 |
| | | Nos. 131-137 (7) | | |

## Colonial Exposition Issue

Common Design Types
Name of Country Typographed in Black

## 1931   Engr.   Perf. 12½

| No. | Type | Description | Unused | Used |
|---|---|---|---|---|
| 138 | CD70 | 40c deep green | 2.25 | 2.25 |
| 139 | CD71 | 50c violet | 2.25 | 2.25 |
| 140 | CD72 | 90c red orange | 2.25 | 2.25 |
| 141 | CD73 | 1.50fr dull blue | 2.25 | 2.25 |
| a. | | "SENEGAL" double | 100.00 | 100.00 |
| | | Nos. 138-141 (4) | 9.00 | 9.00 |

Faidherbe Bridge, St. Louis — A29

## 1935-40   Perf. 12½x12

| No. | Type | Description | Unused | Used |
|---|---|---|---|---|
| 142 | A29 | 1c violet blue | .20 | .20 |
| 143 | A29 | 2c brown | .20 | .20 |
| 144 | A29 | 3c violet | .40 | .20 |
| 145 | A29 | 4c gray blue | .20 | .20 |
| 146 | A29 | 4c orange red | .20 | .20 |
| 147 | A29 | 10c violet | .20 | .20 |
| 148 | A29 | 15c black | .20 | .20 |
| 149 | A29 | 20c dk carmine | .20 | .20 |
| 150 | A29 | 25c black brn | .20 | .20 |
| 151 | A29 | 30c green | .20 | .20 |
| 152 | A29 | 30c dk green | .20 | .20 |
| 153 | A29 | 40c rose car | .90 | .45 |
| 154 | A29 | 45c dk blue grn | .40 | .20 |
| 155 | A29 | 50c red orange | .25 | .20 |
| 156 | A29 | 60c dk blue ('40) | .25 | .20 |
| 157 | A29 | 65c dk violet | .40 | .20 |
| 158 | A29 | 70c red brn ('40) | .40 | .20 |
| 159 | A29 | 75c brown | .20 | .20 |
| 160 | A30 | 90c rose car | 2.50 | 1.25 |
| 161 | A30 | 1.25fr redsh brn | 10.00 | 10.00 |
| 162 | A30 | 1.25fr rose car ('39) | 1.50 | .75 |
| 163 | A30 | 1.40fr dk bl grn ('40) | .75 | .55 |
| 164 | A30 | 1.50fr dk bl grn ('40) | .75 | .55 |
| 165 | A30 | 1.60fr red brn ('40) | .65 | .55 |
| 166 | A30 | 1.75fr blue grn ('40) | .70 | .55 |
| 167 | A30 | 2fr Prus blue & red | .60 | .55 |
| 168 | A30 | 2fr dk ol brn & lake | .80 | .55 |
| 169 | A30 | 3fr grn & red vio | .90 | .55 |
| 170 | A30 | 5fr black brn | 1.75 | .85 |
| 171 | A30 | 10fr rose lake | 1.75 | .85 |
| 172 | A30 | 20fr grnsh slate | 7.30 | |
| | | Nos. 142-171 (30) | 28.10 | 12.80 |

Diourbel Mosque — A30

Nos. 143, 148 and 156 surcharged with new values are listed under French West Africa. For surcharges see Nos. B9, B11-B12.

## 1937   Colonial Arts Exhibition Issue

Common Design Types   Unwmk.   Perf. 13

| No. | Type | Description | Unused | Used |
|---|---|---|---|---|
| 172 | CD74 | 20c deep violet | .90 | .90 |
| 173 | CD75 | 30c dark green | .90 | .90 |
| 174 | CD76 | 40c dark rose | .90 | .90 |
| 175 | CD77 | 50c dark brown | .90 | .90 |
| 176 | CD78 | 90c red | .90 | .90 |
| 177 | CD79 | 1.50fr ultra | 1.60 | 1.60 |
| | | Nos. 172-177 (6) | 6.10 | 6.10 |

Souvenir Sheet   Imperf.

| No. | Type | Description | Unused | Used |
|---|---|---|---|---|
| 178 | CD76 | 3fr rose violet | 5.25 | 6.50 |

## 1938-40

Senegalese Woman — A31   Perf. 12½x12½, 12½x12

| No. | Type | Description | Unused | Used |
|---|---|---|---|---|
| 179 | A31 | 35c green | .45 | .45 |
| 180 | A31 | 55c chocolate | .45 | .45 |
| 181 | A31 | 80c violet | .85 | .45 |
| 182 | A31 | 90c lt rose vio ('39) | .85 | .45 |
| 183 | A31 | 1fr car lake | 1.75 | .85 |
| 184 | A31 | 1fr cop brn ('40) | .50 | .45 |
| 185 | A31 | 1.75fr ultra ('39) | .50 | .45 |
| 186 | A31 | 2.25fr ultra ('40) | .65 | .60 |
| 187 | A31 | 2.50fr dp ol brn ('40) | 1.00 | 1.00 |
| | | Nos. 179-187 (9) | 7.25 | 5.25 |

For surcharge see No. B10.

## 1939   Caillé Issue

Common Design Type   Engr.   Perf. 12½x12

| No. | Type | Description | Unused | Used |
|---|---|---|---|---|
| 188 | CD81 | 90c org brn & org | .55 | .55 |
| 189 | CD81 | 1fr brt vio | .75 | .75 |
| 190 | CD81 | 2.25fr ultra & dk bl | 2.15 | 2.15 |
| | | Nos. 188-190 (3) | | |

For No. 188 surcharged 20fr and 50fr, see French West Africa.

## New York World's Fair Issue

Common Design Type   Perf. 12½x12

| No. | Type | Description | Unused | Used |
|---|---|---|---|---|
| 191 | CD82 | 1.25fr car lake | .55 | .55 |
| 192 | CD82 | 2.25fr ultra | .55 | .55 |

## 1941

| No. | Type | Description | Unused | Used |
|---|---|---|---|---|
| 193 | A32 | 1fr green | .75 | .75 |
| 194 | A32 | 2.50fr blue | .75 | .75 |

Nos. 193-194 were issued by the German-controlled French government in France, but were not placed on sale in Senegal.

Diourbel Mosque and Marshal Pétain — A32

## 1943-44   Types of 1935-38 Without "RF"   Perf. 12½

| No. | Type | Description | Unused | Used |
|---|---|---|---|---|
| 194A | A29 | 40c rose lake | .60 | .60 |
| 194B | A30 | 1fr dk red vio & blk | 1.00 | 1.00 |
| 194C | A30 | 1.50fr bl grn & red | .60 | .60 |
| 194D | A30 | 2fr ultra, bis & grn | .80 | .80 |
| 194E | A30 | 3fr grn & red vio | .80 | .80 |
| 194F | A30 | 5fr car lake & claret | 1.00 | 1.00 |
| 194G | A30 | 45fr indigo & brn org | 1.50 | 1.50 |
| 194H | A30 | 20fr gray bl & red | 3.55 | 1.70 |
| | | Nos. 194A-194H (8) | | |

Nos. 194A-194H were issued by the Vichy government in France, but were not placed on sale in Senegal.

See French West Africa No. 69 for additional stamp inscribed "Senegal" and "Afrique Occidentale Française."

Catalogue values for unused stamps in this section, from this point to the end of the section, are for Never Hinged items.

# Republic

## 1960   Roan Antelope — A33   Unwmk.   Engr.   Perf. 13

| No. | Type | Description | Unused | Used |
|---|---|---|---|---|
| 195 | A33 | 5fr brn grn & claret | .70 | .20 |
| 196 | A33 | 10fr brn & brn | .45 | .20 |
| 197 | A33 | 15fr blk, claret & org brn | .55 | .20 |
| 198 | A33 | 20fr brn, grn & ocher & sal | | |
| 199 | A33 | 25fr brn, lt grn & org | 1.10 | .45 |
| 200 | A33 | 85fr brn, grn, olive & bis | 5.75 | 2.10 |
| | | Nos. 195-200 (6) | | |

Animals: 10fr, Savannah buffalo, horiz. 15fr, Wart hog. 20fr, Giant eland. 25fr, Bushbuck. 85fr, Defassa waterbuck.

### Imperforates

Most Senegal stamps from 1960 onward exist imperforate in issued and trial colors, and also in small presentation sheets in issued colors.

## Paris International Exposition Issue

Common Design Types   Perf. 13

## 1961, Apr. 4   Allegory of Independent State — A34

| No. | Type | Description | Unused | Used |
|---|---|---|---|---|
| 201 | A34 | 25fr bl, choc & grn | .80 | .20 |

Independence Day, Apr. 4.

## 1961, Sept. 30   Wrestling — A35   Perf. 13

| No. | Type | Description | Unused | Used |
|---|---|---|---|---|
| 202 | A35 | 50c ol, bl & choc | .20 | .20 |
| 203 | A35 | 1fr grn, bl & maroon | .20 | .20 |
| 204 | A35 | 1fr ultra, bis & sepia | .65 | .20 |
| 205 | A35 | 30fr carmine & claret | 1.00 | .60 |
| 206 | A35 | 45fr indigo & brn org | 3.55 | 1.70 |
| | | Nos. 202-206 (5) | | |

1fr, Pirogues racing. 2fr, Horse race. 30fr, Male tribal dance. 45fr, Lion game.

## 1962, Jan. 6   UN Headquarters, New York and Flag — A36   Engr.   Perf. 13

| No. | Type | Description | Unused | Used |
|---|---|---|---|---|
| 207 | A36 | 10fr grn, ocher & car | .35 | .25 |
| 208 | A36 | 30fr car, ocher & grn | .65 | .40 |
| 209 | A36 | 85fr grn, ocher & car | 2.25 | 1.30 |
| | | Nos. 207-209 (3) | | |

1st anniv. of Senegal's admission to the United Nations, Sept. 28, 1960.

Gorée
Sailboat
A53

Cashew — A54

Designs: 20fr, Large Seumbediou canoe.
30fr, Fadiouth one-man canoe. 45fr, One-man
canoe on Senegal River.

**1965, Aug. 7 Photo. *Perf. 12½x13***
| | | | |
|---|---|---|---|
| 253 | A53 | 10fr multi | .25 .20 |
| 254 | A53 | 20fr multi | .55 .20 |
| 255 | A53 | 30fr multi | 1.00 .30 |
| 256 | A53 | 45fr multi | 1.75 .60 |
| | | | 3.55 1.30 |

**1965 Photo.**
| | | | |
|---|---|---|---|
| 257 | A54 | 10fr shown | .25 .20 |
| 258 | A54 | 15fr Papaya | .45 .20 |
| 259 | A54 | 20fr Mango | .65 .30 |
| 260 | A54 | 30fr Peanuts | 1.25 .30 |
| | | | 2.60 1.00 |

Issued: 10fr, 15fr, 20fr, Nov. 6. 30fr, Dec. 18.

"Elegant
Man" — A55

Dolls of Gorée: 2fr. "Elegant Woman" 3fr.
Woman peddling fruit. 4fr. Woman pounding
grain.

**1966, Jan. 22 Engr. *Perf. 13***
| | | | |
|---|---|---|---|
| 261 | A55 | 1fr brn, rose car & ultra | .20 .20 |
| 262 | A55 | 2fr brn, bl & org | .20 .20 |
| 263 | A55 | 3fr brn, red & bl | .20 .20 |
| 264 | A55 | 4fr brn, lil & emer | .80 .80 |

Drummer and
Map of
Africa — A56

15fr, Sculpture; mother & child. #267,
Music; stringed instrument 75fr, Dance;
carved antelope headpiece (Bambara). 90fr,
Ideogram.

**1966**
| | | | |
|---|---|---|---|
| 265 | A56 | 15fr dk red brn, bl & ocher | .35 .20 |
| 266 | A56 | 30fr brn, red & grn | .70 .20 |
| 267 | A56 | 30fr red brn, bl & yel | 1.10 .60 |
| 268 | A56 | 75fr dk red brn, bl & blk | 1.75 .60 |
| 269 | A56 | 90fr dk red brn, org & sl grn | 2.10 .65 |
| a. | | Souv. sheet of 4, #265, 267-269 | 6.25 |
| | | | 6.00 2.25 |

Int. Negro Arts Festival, Dakar. Apr. 1-24.
Issued: #266, 2/5; others, 4/2. See #364.

Fish — A57

**1966, Feb. 26 Photo. *Perf. 12½x13***
| | | | |
|---|---|---|---|
| 270 | A57 | 20fr Tuna | .60 .20 |
| 271 | A57 | 30fr Merou | .60 .30 |
| 272 | A57 | 50fr Girella | 1.25 .65 |
| 273 | A57 | 100fr Parrot fish | 2.75 .85 |
| | | | 5.10 2.00 |

---

Leprosy Examination — A46

Leprosarium, Peycouk Village — A47

**1965, Jan. 30 Engr. *Perf. 13***
| | | | |
|---|---|---|---|
| 240 | A46 | 20fr brn red, grn & blk | .50 .30 |
| 241 | A47 | 65fr org, dk bl & grn | 1.50 .55 |

Issued to publicize the fight against leprosy.

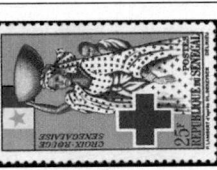

Upper Casamance Region — A48

Views: 30fr, Sangalkam. 45fr, Forest along
Senegal River.

**1965, Feb. 27 Unwmk. *Perf. 13***
| | | | |
|---|---|---|---|
| 242 | A48 | 25fr red brn, sl bl & grn | .55 .20 |
| 243 | A48 | 30fr indigo & lt brn | .65 .30 |
| 244 | A48 | 45fr yel grn, red brn & dk brn | 1.40 .50 |
| | | | 5.10 2.00 |

Nos. 242-244,C41 (4)

Abdoulaye Seck
A49

Berthon-Ader
Telephone
A51

General
Post Office,
Dakar
A50

**1965, Apr. 24 Unwmk. *Perf. 13***
| | | | |
|---|---|---|---|
| 245 | A49 | 10fr dk brn & blk | .35 .20 |
| 246 | A50 | 15fr brn & dk sl grn | .45 .20 |

**1965, May 17 Engr.**
Designs: 60fr, Cable laying ship "Alsace."
85fr, Picard's cable relay for submarine
telegraph.
| | | | |
|---|---|---|---|
| 247 | A51 | 50fr bl grn & org brn | .65 .30 |
| 248 | A51 | 60fr mag & dk bl | 1.25 .45 |
| 249 | A51 | 85fr ver, bl & red brn | 1.40 .50 |
| | | | 3.30 1.25 |

Nos. 247-249 (3)

ITU, centenary.

Plowing
with Ox
Team
A52

Designs: 60fr, Harvesting millet, vert. 85fr,
Men working in rice field.

**1965, July 3 Unwmk. *Perf. 13***
| | | | |
|---|---|---|---|
| 250 | A52 | 25fr dk ol grn, brn & pur | .55 .30 |
| 251 | A52 | 60fr ind, sl grn & dk brn | 1.25 .50 |
| 252 | A52 | 85fr dp car, sl grn & brt grn | 1.75 .55 |
| | | | 3.55 1.35 |

Nos. 250-252 (3)

---

Prof. Gaston Berger (1896-1960),
Philosopher, and Owl — A41

**1963, Nov. 13 *Perf. 12½x12***
| | | | |
|---|---|---|---|
| 227 | A41 | 25fr multi | .75 .30 |

Scales,
Globe,
Flag and
UNESCO
Emblem
A42

| | | | |
|---|---|---|---|
| | | | 1.25 .50 |

**1963, Dec. 10**
| | | | |
|---|---|---|---|
| 228 | A42 | 60fr multi | |

15th anniv. of the Universal Declaration of
Human Rights.

Flag, Mother and
Child — A43

**1963, Dec. 21 *Perf. 12x12½***
| | | | |
|---|---|---|---|
| 229 | A43 | 25fr multi | .80 .30 |

Issued for the Senegalese Red Cross.

Dredging of Titanium-bearing
Sand — A44

Designs: 10fr, Titanium extraction works.
15fr, Cement extraction at Rufisque. 20fr,
Phosphate quarry at Pallo. 25fr, Extraction of
phosphate ore at Taiba. 85fr, Mineral dock,
Dakar.

**1964, July 4 Engr. *Perf. 13***
| | | | |
|---|---|---|---|
| 230 | A44 | 5fr grnsh bl, car & dk brn | .20 .20 |
| 231 | A44 | 10fr ocher, grn & ind | .20 .20 |
| 232 | A44 | 15fr dk bl, brt grn & dk brn | .35 .20 |
| 233 | A44 | 20fr ultra, ol & pur | .55 .25 |
| 234 | A44 | 25fr dk bl, yel & blk | .70 .25 |
| 235 | A44 | 85fr bl, red & brn | 2.00 .85 |
| | | | 4.00 1.90 |

Nos. 230-235 (6)

**Cooperation Issue**
Common Design Type

**1964, Nov. 7 Engr. *Perf. 13***
| | | | |
|---|---|---|---|
| 236 | CD119 | 100fr dk grn, dk brn & car | 1.60 .85 |

St.
Theresa's
Church,
Dakar
A45

10fr, Mosque, Touba. 15fr, Mosque, Dakar,
vert.

**1964, Nov. 28 Unwmk. *Perf. 13***
| | | | |
|---|---|---|---|
| 237 | A45 | 5fr bl, grn & red brn | .20 .20 |
| 238 | A45 | 10fr dk bl, ocher & blk | .20 .20 |
| 239 | A45 | 15fr brn & sl grn | .90 .20 |
| | | | 1.35 .60 |

Nos. 237-239 (3)

---

Map of Africa, ITU Emblem and Man
with Telephone
A37

**1962, Jan. 22 Photo. *Perf. 12½x12***
| | | | |
|---|---|---|---|
| 210 | A37 | 25fr blk, grn, red & ocher | .80 .30 |

Meeting of the Commission for the Africa
Plan of the ITU, Dakar.

**African and Malgache Union Issue**
Common Design Type

**1962, Sept. 8 Unwmk.**
| | | | |
|---|---|---|---|
| 211 | CD110 | 30fr grn, bluish grn, red & gold | .80 .50 |

Boxing — A38

**Charaxes
Varanes — A40**

UPU
Monument,
Bern
A39

15fr, Diving, horiz. 20fr, High jump, horiz.
25fr, Soccer. 30fr, Basketball. 85fr, Running.

**1963, Apr. 11 Engr. *Perf. 13***
**Athletes in Dark Brown**
| | | | |
|---|---|---|---|
| 212 | A38 | 10fr ver & emer | .30 .20 |
| 213 | A38 | 15fr ver & bis | .40 .20 |
| 214 | A38 | 20fr dk bl & bl | .45 .20 |
| 215 | A38 | 25fr ver & dk bl | .65 .25 |
| 216 | A38 | 30fr ver & grn | 1.25 1.10 |
| 217 | A38 | 85fr vio bl | 2.75 2.45 |
| | | | 5.80 2.45 |

Nos. 212-217 (6)

**1963, June 14 Unwmk. *Perf. 13***
| | | | |
|---|---|---|---|
| 218 | A39 | 10fr grn & ver | .45 .20 |
| 219 | A39 | 15fr bl & red brn | .45 .25 |
| 220 | A39 | 85fr red brn & dk bl | 1.00 .40 |
| | | | 1.90 .85 |

Nos. 218-220 (3)

2nd anniv. of Senegal's admission to the
UPU.

**1963, July 20 Photo. *Perf. 12½x13***
**Butterflies in Natural Colors**
Butterflies: 45fr, Papilio nireus. 50fr, Colotis
danae. 85fr, Epiphora bauhiniae. 100fr,
Junonia hierta. 500fr, Danaus chrysippus.
| | | | |
|---|---|---|---|
| 221 | A40 | 30fr bl gray & blk | .90 .30 |
| 222 | A40 | 45fr org & blk | 1.25 .50 |
| 223 | A40 | 50fr brt yel & blk | 1.00 .65 |
| 224 | A40 | 85fr red & blk | 3.75 1.00 |
| 225 | A40 | 100fr bl & blk | 4.50 1.75 |
| 226 | A40 | 500fr emer & blk | 15.00 5.50 |
| | | | 26.80 9.70 |

Nos. 221-226 (6)

**Arms of Senegal — A58**

1966, July 2    Litho.    Perf. 13x12½
274  A58  30fr multi    .80  .20

**Flowers — A59**

ARGEMONE MEXICANA
ARGEMONE

1966, Nov. 19    Photo.    Perf. 11½
275  A59  45fr  Mexican poppy   1.10   .20
276  A59  55fr  Mimosa          1.10   .30
277  A59  60fr  Haemanthus      1.50   .40
278  A59  90fr  Baobab          2.00   .60
Nos. 275-278 (4)                5.70  1.50

**Harbor, Gorée Island — A60**

Designs: 25fr, S.S. France in roadstead, Dakar and seagulls. 30fr, Hotel and tourist village, N'Gor. 50fr, Hotel and bay, N'Gor.

1966, Dec. 25    Engr.    Perf. 13
279  A60  20fr  mar & vio bl       .25   .20
280  A60  25fr  red, grn & dk bl   2.00   .30
281  A60  30fr  dk red & dp bl      .40   .20
282  A60  50fr  brn, sl grn & emer  .65   .30
Nos. 279-282 (4)                   3.30  1.00

**Laying Urban Water Pipes — A61**

1967, Mar. 25    Engr.    Perf. 13
283  A61  10fr  org brn, grn & dk bl   .25   .20
284  A61  20fr  org bl & org brn       .65   .20

20fr, Cattle at water trough. 50fr, Village well.

**Symbolic Water Cycle — A62**

Typo.    Perf. 13x14
285  A62  30fr  sky bl, blk & org    .70   .20

Engr.    Perf. 13
286  A62  50fr  brn, red, brt bl & bis   1.50   .35
Nos. 283-286 (4)                        3.10   .95

Intl. Hydrological Decade (UNESCO), 1965-74.

**Lions Emblem — A63**

1967, May 27    Photo.    Perf. 12½x13
287  A63  30fr  lt ultra & multi    1.00   .40

50th anniversary of Lions International.

**Blaise Diagne — A64**

1967, June 10    Engr.    Perf. 13
288  A64  30fr  ocher, sl grn & dk red   .80   .30

Blaise Diagne (1872-1934), member of French Chamber of Deputies and Colonial Minister. For surcharge see No. 380.

**City Hall and Arms, Dakar — A65**

1967, June 10    Engr.    Perf. 13
289  A65  90fr  bl, dk grn & blk    1.75   .50

**Eagle and Antelope Carvings — A66**

150fr, Flags, maple leaf and EXPO '67 emblem.

1967, Sept. 2    Photo.    Perf. 13x12½
290  A66  90fr  red & blk        2.00   .50
291  A66  150fr  red & multi     2.50   .80

EXPO '67 Intl. Exhib., Montreal, 4/28-10/27.

**International Tourist Year Emblem — A67**

1967, Oct. 7    Typo.    Perf. 14x13
292  A67  50fr  blk & bl     .90   .40

**Tourist Photographing Hippopotamus and Simiti Hotel — A68**

Engr.    Perf. 13
293  A68  100fr  blk, sl grn & ocher    3.50   1.10

International Tourist Year.

**Monetary Union Issue**
**Common Design Type**

1967, Nov. 4    Engr.    Perf. 13
294  CD125  30fr  multi    .60   .20

West African Monetary Union, 5th anniv.

**Lyre-shaped Megalith, Kaffrine — A69**

70fr, Ancient covered bowl, Bandiala.

1967, Dec. 2    Engr.    Perf. 13
295  A69  30fr  grn, grnsh bl & red          1.25   .35
296  A69  70fr  red brn, ocher & brt bl      2.10   .85

**Nurse Feeding Child — A70**

1967, Dec. 23    Photo.    Perf. 13x12½
297  A70  50fr  bl grn, red & red brn    1.00   .40

Issued for the Senegalese Red Cross.

**Human Rights Flame — A71**

1968, Jan. 20    Photo.    Perf. 13x12½
298  A71  30fr  brt grn & gold    .80   .30

International Human Rights Year.

**Parliament, Dakar — A72**

1968, Apr. 16    Photo.    Perf. 12½x13
299  A72  30fr  car rose    .80   .20

Inter-Parliamentary Union Meeting, Dakar

**Pied Kingfisher — A73**

CERYLE RUDIS
MARTIN-PÊCHEUR PIE

**Goose Barnacles — A74**

MITELLA POLLICIPES
PIEDS DE BICHE

1968-69    Photo.    Perf. 11½
Dated "1968" or (70fr) "1969"
Granite Paper
300  A73  5fr   brn & multi        .25   .20
301  A73  10fr  red & multi        .35   .20
302  A73  15fr  yel & multi        .55   .20
303  A74  20fr  ultra & multi      .65   .20
304  A74  35fr  car rose & ol grn  1.75   .30
305  A73  70fr  Prus bl & multi    2.25   .85
306  A74  100fr  yel, grn & multi  5.75   1.00
Nos. 300-306 (7)                  11.55   3.00

Issued: 5fr, 7/13/68; 15fr, 12/21/68; 70fr, 4/26/69; others 5/18/68. See #C53-C57.

Designs: 10fr, Green lobster. 15fr, African jacana. 20fr, Sea cicada. 35fr, Shrimp. 70fr, African anhinga.

**Steer and Hypodermic Syringe — A75**

1968, Aug. 17    Engr.    Perf. 13
307  A75  30fr  dk grn, dp bl & brn    1.00   .40
red

Campaign against cattle plague.

**Boy and WHO Emblem — A76**

1968, Nov. 16    Engr.    Perf. 13
308  A76  30fr  blk, grn & car       .55   .30
309  A76  45fr  red brn, grn & blk   1.10   .30

WHO, 20th anniversary.

**Bambara Antelope Symbol — A77**

Design: 30fr, School of Medicine and Pharmacology, Dakar, horiz.

1969, Jan. 13    Engr.    Perf. 13
310  A77  30fr  emer, brt bl & ind      .80   .30
311  A77  50fr  red, gray ol & bl grn   .90   .30

6th Medical Meeting, Dakar, Jan. 13-18.

**Panet, Camels and Mogador-St. Louis Route — A78**

1969, Feb. 15    Engr.    Perf. 13
312  A78  75fr  ultra, Prus bl & brn    2.50   .80

Leopold Panet (1819-1859), first explorer of the Mauritanian Sahara.

**ILO Emblem — A79**

1969, May 3    Photo.    Perf. 12½x13
313  A79  30fr  blk & grnsh bl    .55   .20
314  A79  45fr  blk & multi       .80   .20

ILO, 50th anniversary.

**Arms of Casamance — A80**

1969, July 26    Litho.    Perf. 13½
315  A80  15fr  rose & multi   .25   .20
316  A80  20fr  bl & multi     .65   .20

Design: 20fr, Arms of Gorée Island.

1969, Sept. 10    Engr.    Perf. 13
317  CD130  30fr  gray, grn & ocher   .55   .20
318  CD130  45fr  grn, brn & ocher    .90   .20

**Development Bank Issue**
**Common Design Type**

**Mahatma Gandhi — A81**

1969, Oct. 2    Engr.    Perf. 13
319  A81  50fr  multi               1.50   .35
a.  Miniature sheet of 4            6.00   3.00

Mohandas K. Gandhi (1869-1948), leader in India's fight for independence.

Rotary Emblem and Symbolic Ship — A82

**1969, Nov. 29 Photo. *Perf. 12½x13***
**320** A82 30fr ultra, yel & blk .80 .30

Dakar Rotary Club, 30th anniversary.

**ASECNA Issue**
Common Design Type

**1969, Dec. 12 Engr. *Perf. 13***
**321** CD132 100fr dark gray 1.60 .50

Niokolo-Koba Campsite — A83

Tourism: 20fr, Cape Skiring, Casamance. 35fr, Elephants at Niokolo-Koba National Park. 45fr, Millet granaries, pigs and boats, Fadiouth Island.

**1969, Dec. 27**
**322** A83 20fr bl, red brn & ol .65 .20
**323** A83 30fr bl, red brn & ocher .90 .20
**324** A83 35fr grnsh bl, blk & ocher 3.50 .60
**325** A83 45fr vio bl & hn brn 1.60 .50
*Nos. 322-325 (4)* 6.65 1.50

Bottle-nosed Dolphins — A84

Lenin (1870-1924) — A85

**1970, Feb. 21 Photo. *Perf. 12x12½***
**326** A84 50fr dl bl, blk & red 6.75 1.25

**1970, Apr. 22 Photo. *Perf. 11½***
**327** A85 30fr brn, buff & ver 2.50 .65

**Souvenir Sheet**
***Perf. 12x11½***
**327A** A85 50fr brn, buff & ver 4.00 1.75

No. 327A contains one 32x48mm stamp.

**UPU Headquarters Issue**
Common Design Type

**1970, May 20 Engr. *Perf. 13***
**328** CD133 30fr dk red, ind & dp cl .55 .20
**329** CD133 45fr dl brn, dk car & bl grn 1.00 .30

Textile Plant, Thies — A86

Design: 45fr, Fertilizer plant, Dakar.

**1970, Nov. 21 Engr. *Perf. 13***
**330** A86 30fr grn, brt bl & brn red .65 .20
**331** A86 45fr brn red & brt bl 1.00 .30

Industrialization of Senegal.

Boy Scouts — A87

Three Heads and Sun — A88

Design: 100fr, Lord Baden-Powell, map of Africa with Dakar, and fleur-de-lis.

**1970, Dec. 11 Photo. *Perf. 11½***
**332** A87 30fr multi .55 .20
**333** A87 100fr multi 2.25 .60

1st African Boy Scout Conf., Dakar, Dec. 11-14.

**1970, Dec. 19 Engr. *Perf. 13***

Design: 40fr, African man and woman, globe with map of Africa.

**334** A88 25fr ultra, org & vio brn .65 .25
**335** A88 40fr brn ol, dk brn & org 1.00 .40

International Education Year.

Senegal Arms — A89

Refugees and UN Emblem — A90

**1970-76 Photo. *Perf. 12***
**336** A89 30fr yel grn & multi .50 .20
**336A** A89 35fr brt pink & multi ('71) .50 .20
*b.* Bklt. pane of 10 ('72) 5.00
**336C** A89 50fr bl & multi ('75) .50 .20
**336D** A89 65fr lil rose & multi ('76) .50 .20
*Nos. 336-336D (4)* 2.00 .80

The booklet pane has a control number in the margin.
See No. 654.

**1971, Jan. 16 *Perf. 12½x12***
**337** A90 40fr ver, blk, yel & grn 1.00 .30

High Commissioner for Refugees, 20th anniversary. See No. C94.

Mare "Mbayang" — A91

Horses: 25fr, Mare Madjiguene. 100fr, Stallion Pass. 125fr, Stallion Pepe.

**1971 Photo. *Perf. 11½***
**338** A91 25fr multi .70 .35
**339** A91 40fr multi 1.00 .50
**340** A91 100fr multi 2.75 1.50
**341** A91 125fr multi 3.25 1.25
*Nos. 338-341 (4)* 7.70 3.60

Improvements in horse breeding.
For surcharge see No. 392.

UN Emblem, Black and White Children — A92

Globe and Telephone — A94

UN Emblem, Four Races — A93

***Perf. 13x12½, 12½x11***
**1971, Mar. 21 Litho.**
**342** A92 30fr multi .60 .25
**343** A93 50fr multi .90 .40

Intl. Year against Racial Discrimination.

**1971, May 17 Engr. *Perf. 13***

Design: 40fr, Radar, satellite, orbits.

**344** A94 30fr pur, grn & brn .45 .20
**345** A94 40fr Prus bl, dk brn & red brn 1.10 .30

3rd World Telecommunications Day.

Drummer (Hayashida) — A95

50fr, Dwarf Japanese quince and grape hyacinth. 65fr, Judo. 75fr, Mt. Fuji.

**1971, Aug. 7 Photo. *Perf. 13½***
**346** A95 35fr lt ultra & multi 1.00 .25
**347** A95 50fr yel & multi 1.25 .40
**348** A95 65fr dp org & multi 2.00 .50
**349** A95 75fr grn & multi 2.50 .85
*Nos. 346-349 (4)* 6.75 2.00

13th Boy Scout World Jamboree, Asagiri Plain, Japan, Aug. 2-10.

Map of West Africa with Senegal, UNICEF Emblem — A97

100fr, Nurse, children, UNICEF emblem.

**1971, Oct. 30 *Perf. 12½***
**352** A97 35fr dl bl, org & blk .90 .35
**353** A97 100fr multi 3.00 .65

UNICEF, 25th anniv.

Basketball and Games' Emblem — A98

40fr, Basketball. 75fr, Emblem.

**1971, Dec. 24 Photo. *Perf. 13½x13***
**354** A98 35fr lt vio & multi .70 .20
**355** A98 40fr emer & multi 1.00 .30
**356** A98 75fr ocher & multi 1.60 .65
*Nos. 354-356 (3)* 3.30 1.15

6th African Basketball Championships, Dakar, Dec. 25, 1971-Jan. 2, 1972.

"The Exile of Albouri" — A99

Design: 40fr, "The Merchant of Venice."

**1972, Mar. 25 *Perf. 13x12½***
**357** A99 35fr dk red & multi .55 .30
**358** A99 40fr dk red & multi .90 .30

Intl. Theater Day. See No. C112.

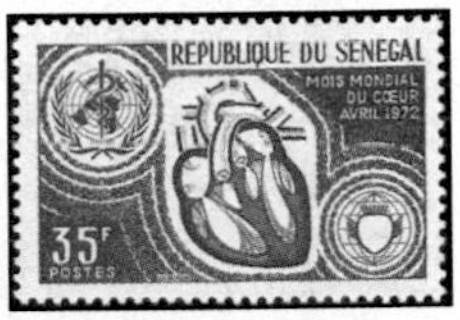

WHO Emblem and Heart — A100

Design: 40fr, Physician with patient, WHO emblem and electrocardiogram.

**1972, Apr. 7 Engr. *Perf. 13***
**359** A100 35fr brt bl & red brn .50 .20
**360** A100 40fr slate grn & brn 1.00 .25

"Your heart is your health," World Health Month.

Containment of the Desert, Environment Emblem — A101

**1972, June 3 Photo. *Perf. 13x12½***
**361** A101 35fr multi 1.00 .40

UN Conference on Human Environment, Stockholm, June 5-16. See No. C113.

Tartarin Shooting the Lion — A102

Design: 100fr, Alphonse Daudet.

**1972, June 24 Engr. *Perf. 13***
**362** A102 40fr brt grn, rose car & brn 1.25 .65
**363** A102 100fr Prus bl, bl & brn 1.60 .65

Alphonse Daudet (1840-1897), French novelist, and centenary of the publication of his "Tartarin de Tarascon."

## Souvenir Sheet

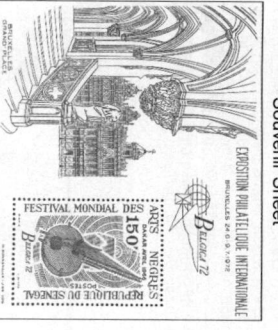

**1972, July 1    Engr.    Perf. 11½**
364  A103  150fr rose red    4.00  3.00

Belgica 72, Intl. Phil. Exhib. Brussels, June 24–July 9. No. 364 contains one stamp in design similar to No. 267.

Stringed Instrument — A103

**1972, July 22    Photo.    Perf. 14x13½**
365  A104  15fr shown    .35  .20
365  A104  20fr 100-meter dash    .80  .20
367  A104  100fr Basketball    2.50  .65
368  A104  125fr Judo    3.00  .65
Nos. 365–368 (4)    6.65  1.55

Wrestling, Olympic Rings — A104

### Souvenir Sheet
**Perf. 13½x14½**
369  A104  240fr Torchbearer and Munich    6.25  3.25

20th Olympic Games, Munich, 8/26–9/11.

Book Year Emblem, Children Reading A105

**1972, Sept. 16    Photo.    Perf. 13**
370  A105  50fr gray & multi    .90  .35

International Book Year.

Senegalese Fashion — A106

**1972–76**
371  A106  25fr black    .35  .20
        a.  Booklet pane of 5    2.00
365  A104  15fr shown    .35  .20
372  A106  40fr brt ultra    .50  .20
        a.  Booklet pane of 10    3.50
        b.  Booklet pane of 5    .50
372C  A106  60fr brt grn (76)    6.00
372D  A106  75fr lil rose    .50  .20
        a.  Booklet pane of 10    .50
        b.  Booklet pane of 5    1.85  .80

See Nos. 563–573, 1153–1164, 1249–1257D, 1345B.
Nos. 371–372D (4)

---

West African Monetary Union Issue
Common Design Type

**1972, Oct. 28    Photo.    Perf. 11½**
373  A107  100fr salmon & purple    3.00  .65

Aleksander Pushkin (1799–1837), Russian writer.

Aleksander Pushkin A107

Design: 40fr. African couple, city, village and commemorative coin.

Amphicra-sphedum Murrayanum A108

**1972, Nov. 2    Photo.    Perf. 13**
374  CD136  40fr ol brn, bl & gray    .50  .30

**1972–73    Photo.    Perf. 11½**
375  A108  5fr multi    .65  .20
376  A108  10fr multi    .65  .20
377  A108  15fr multi    1.60  .25
378  A108  20fr multi    2.10  .30
379  A108  30fr multi    5.55  .55

Marine Life: 10fr, Pterocanium tricolpum. 15fr, Ceratospyris polygona. 20fr, Cortiniscus typicus. 30fr, Theopera cortina.

Issued: #375–377, 11/25/72; #378–379, 7/28/73. Nos. 375–379, C115–C118 (9)    26.75  5.55

No. 288 Surcharged in Vermilion

**1972, Dec. 9    Engr.    Perf. 13**
380  A64  100fr on 30fr multi    2.25  .60

Blaise Diagne (1872–1934).

Melchior — A109

**1972, Dec. 23    Photo.    Perf. 13x13½**
381  A109  10fr shown    .25  .20
382  A109  15fr Caspar    .25  .20
383  A109  40fr Balthasar    .80  .35
384  A109  60fr Joseph    .85  .40
385  A109  100fr Virgin and Child    1.50  .65
        a.  Strip of 5, #381–385    5.25  2.00

Christmas. No. 385a has continuous design, showing traditional Gorée dolls.

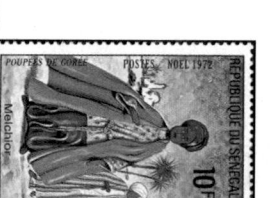

Black and White Men Carrying Emblem — A110

**1973, Jan. 20    Engr.    Perf. 13**
386  A110  65fr blk & grn    1.40  .40

Europafrica Issue

---

**1973, May 17    Engr.    Perf. 13**
387  A111  40fr multi    .80  .30

Radar Station, Gandoul A111

Phases of Solar Eclipse A112

**1973, June 30    Photo.    Perf. 13x14**
388  A112  35fr dk bl & multi    .65  .25
389  A112  65fr dk bl & multi    1.00  .40
390  A112  150fr dk bl & multi    2.25  .85
Nos. 388–390 (3)    3.90  1.50

Designs: 65fr, Moon between earth and sun casting shadow on earth. 150fr, Diagram of areas of partial and total eclipse, satellite in space.

Total solar eclipse over Africa, June 30.

Men Holding Torch over Africa — A113

**1973, July 7    Photo.    Perf. 12½x13**
391  A113  75fr multi    1.00  .40

Org. for African Unity, 10th anniv.

No. 338 Surcharged with New Value, 2 Bars, and Overprinted in Ultramarine: "SECHERESSE / SOLIDARITE AFRICAINE"

**1973, July 21    Photo.    Perf. 11½**
392  A91  100fr on 25fr multi    2.25  .85

African solidarity in drought emergency.

**1973, Sept. 12    Engr.    Perf. 13**
393  CD137  100fr dk grn, vio & dk red    1.60  .50

African Postal Union Issue
Common Design Type

Child, Map of Senegal, WMO Emblem A114

**1973, Sept. 22    Photo.**
394  A114  50fr multi    .80  .35

Intl. meteorological cooperation, cent.

INTERPOL Headquarters, Paris — A115

**1973, Oct. 6    Engr.    Perf. 13**
395  A115  75fr ultra, bis & slate grn    1.60  .50

50th anniv. of Intl. Criminal Police Org.

---

## Souvenir Sheet

John F. Kennedy (1917–1963) — A116

**1973, Nov. 22    Engr.    Perf. 13**
396  A116  150fr ultra    2.75  2.75

Victorious Athletes and Flag — A118

**1973, Dec. 15    Photo.    Perf. 12½x13**
397  A117  75fr multi    1.25  .40

Amilcar Cabral — A117

**1974, Apr. 6    Photo.    Perf. 12½x13**
398  A118  35fr shown    .80  .20
399  A118  40fr Folk theater    .80  .20

National Youth Week.

Amilcar Cabral (1924–1973), leader of anti-Portuguese guerrilla movement in Portuguese Guinea.

Soccer Cup, Yugoslavia-Brazil Game, Our Lady's Church, Munich — A119

**1974, June 29    Photo.    Perf. 13x14**
400  A119  25fr car & multi    .35  .20
401  A119  40fr car & multi    .80  .20
402  A119  65fr car & multi    .90  .30
403  A119  70fr car & multi    1.50  .40
Nos. 400–403 (4)    3.40  1.10

Soccer Cup and Games: 40fr, Australia-Hamburg. (Fed. Rep.) and Belltower, Hamburg. 65fr, Netherlands-Uruguay and Tower, Hanover. 70fr, Zaire-Italy and Church, Stuttgart.

World Cup Soccer Championship, Munich, June 13–July 7. For surcharge see No. 406.

A. G. Bell, Telephone, ITU Emblem — A134

**1976, Mar. 31    Litho.    Perf. 12½x13**
427   A134   175fr multi ............. 2.50  .80
Centenary of first telephone call by Alexander Graham Bell, Mar. 10, 1876.

Map of African French-speaking Countries — A135

**1976, Apr. 12    Litho.    Perf. 13½**
428   A135   60fr yel grn & multi ....... .80  .30
Scientific and Cultural Meeting of the African Dental Association, Dakar, Apr. 12-17.

Family and Graph — A136

**1976, Apr. 26    Photo.**
429   A136   65fr multi ............. 1.00  .40
1st population census in Senegal, Apr. 1976.

Thomas Jefferson and 13-star Flag — A137

**1976, June 19    Engr.    Perf. 13**
430   A137   50fr bl, red & blk ....... 1.00  .30
American Bicentennial.

Planting Seedlings — A138

**1976, Aug. 21    Litho.    Perf. 12**
431   A138   60fr yel & multi ....... 1.00  .25
Reclamation of Sahel region.

Campfire — A139

---

Staff of Aesculapius and African Mask — A130

**1975, Dec. 1    Photo.    Perf. 12½x13**
417   A130   50fr multi ............. .80  .30
40th French Medical Cong., Dakar, Dec. 1-3.

Map of Africa with Senegal and Namibia, UN Emblem A131

**1976, Jan. 5    Photo.**
418   A131   125fr vio bl & multi ..... 1.00  .35
International Human Rights and Namibia Conference, Dakar, Jan. 5-8.

Sailfish Fishing A132

200dr, Racing yachts & emblem.

**1976, Jan. 28    Photo.    Perf. 13½x13**
419   A132   140fr multi ............. 4.50  1.25
420   A132   200fr multi ............. 3.00  1.40
Oceanexpo 75, 1st Intl. Oceanographic Exhib., Okinawa, July 20, 1975-Jan. 1976.

Servals — A133

Designs: 3fr, Black-tailed godwits.    4fr, River hogs.   5fr, African fish eagles. No. 425, Okapis.   No. 426, Sitatungas.

**1976, Feb. 26    Photo.    Perf. 13**
421   A133   2fr gold & multi ......... .25  .20
422   A133   3fr gold & multi ......... .25  .20
423   A133   4fr gold & multi ......... .25  .20
424   A133   5fr gold & multi ......... .55  .20
425   A133   250fr gold & multi ....... 6.25  1.50
426   A133   250fr gold & multi ....... 6.25  1.50
   a.   Strip of 2, #425-426 + label  12.50
            Nos. 421-426 (6)         13.80  3.80
Basse Casamance National Park.
See Nos. 473-478.

---

Apollo of Belvedere, Arphila 75 Emblem, Stamps — A125

**1975, June 6    Engr.    Perf. 13**
411   A125   95fr dk brn, brn & bis ... 2.25  .80
Arphila 75 International Philatelic Exhibition, Paris, June 6-16.

Professional Instruction — A126

**1975, June 28    Engr.    Perf. 13**
412   A126   85fr multi ............. 1.25  .40

Dr. Albert Schweitzer (1875-1965), Medical Missionary, Lambarene Hospital — A127

**19/5, July 5**
413   A127   85fr grn & vio brn ....... 1.75  .65

Senegalese Soldier, Battalion Flag, Map of Sinai — A128

**1975, July 10    Litho.    Perf. 12½**
414   A128   100fr multi ............. 1.75  .50
Senegalese Battalion of the UN' Sinai Service, 1973-74.

Women and Child — A129

55fr, Women pounding grain, vert.

**1975, Oct. 18    Photo.    Perf. 13½**
415   A129   55fr silver & multi ...... 1.75  .35
416   A129   75fr silver & multi ...... 2.25  .50
International Women's Year.

---

UPU Emblem, Envelopes and Means of Transportation — A120

**1974, Oct. 9    Engr.    Perf. 13**
404   A120   100fr multi ............. 3.00  .85
Centenary of Universal Postal Union.

Fair Emblem — A121

**1974, Nov. 28    Engr.    Perf. 12½x13**
405   A121   100fr bl, org & dk brn ... 1.75  .50
Dakar International Fair.

No. 401 Surcharged in Black on Gold

**1975, Feb. 1    Photo.    Perf. 13x14**
406   A119   200fr on 40fr multi ...... 3.25  1.25
World Cup Soccer Championships, 1974, victory of German Federal Republic.

Pres. Senghor and King Baudouin — A122

**1975, Feb. 28    Photo.    Perf. 13x13½**
407   A122   65fr lil & dk bl ......... .80  .35
408   A122   100fr org & grn ......... 2.00  .50
Visit of King Baudouin of Belgium.

ILO Emblem A123

**1975, Apr. 30    Photo.    Perf. 13½x13**
409   A123   125fr multi ............. 1.75  .50
International Labor Festival.

Globe, Stamp, Letters, España 75 Emblem — A124

**1975, June 6    Engr.    Perf. 13**
410   A124   55fr indigo, grn & red ... 1.25  .40
Espana 75 Intl. Phil. Exhib., Madrid, 4/4-13.

**1976, Aug. 30    Litho.    Perf. 12½**

Jamboree Emblem, Map of Africa — A140

| 432 | A139 | 80fr multi | .90 | .40 |
| 433 | A140 | 100fr multi | 1.75 | .55 |

1st All Africa Scout Jamboree, Sherehills, Jos, Nigeria, Apr. 2-8, 1977.

A140a

1976 Summer Olympics, Montreal — A140b

**1976, Sept. 11    Litho.    Perf. 13½**

| 433A | A140a | 5fr Swimming | .20 | .20 |
| 433B | A140a | 10fr Weightlifting | .20 | .20 |
| 433C | A140a | 15fr Hurdles | .20 | .20 |
| 433D | A140a | 20fr Equestrian, horiz. | .25 | .20 |
| 433E | A140a | 25fr Steeplechase, horiz. | .25 | .20 |
| 433F | A140a | 50fr Wrestling | .35 | .20 |
| 433G | A140a | 60fr Field hockey | .70 | .20 |
| 433H | A140a | 65fr Track | .80 | .20 |
| 433I | A140a | 70fr Women's gymnastics | 1.00 | .40 |
| 433J | A140a | 100fr Cycling, horiz. | 1.25 | .50 |
| 433K | A140a | 400fr Boxing, horiz. | 4.50 | .95 |
| 433L | A140a | 500fr Judo | 5.75 | 1.10 |

**Litho. & Embossed**

**Souvenir Sheet**

| 433M | A140b | 1000fr Basketball | 9.00 | 3.75 |
| 433Q | A140b | 1000fr Boxers, city sky-line | 9.00 | 3.75 |

Nos. 433K-433Q are airmail.

Nos. 433A-433L (12)   15.80   4.55

**1976, Oct. 23    Photo.    Perf. 13**

Mechanized Tomato Harvest — A141

| 434 | A141 | 180fr multi | 3.00 | 1.25 |

Map of Dakar and Gorée A142

---

**1976, Oct. 9    Litho.    Perf. 13½x14**

Scroll with Map of Africa, Senegalese People — A143

| 435 | A142 | 40fr multi | .35 | .20 |
| 436 | A142 | 60fr multi | .50 | .20 |
| 437 | A142 | 70fr multi | 1.00 | .25 |
| 438 | A142 | 200fr multi | 4.60 | 1.50 |
| | | Nos. 435-438 (4) | 2.75 | .85 |

Designs: 60fr, Star over Africa. 70fr, Students in laboratory and library. 200fr, Handshake over world map, Pres. Senghor.

70th birthday of Pres. Leopold Sedar Senghor.

Joe Frazier and Muhammad Ali — A144

**1977, Jan. 8    Perf. 12½**

| 439 | A143 | 60fr multi | .80 | .30 |

Day of the Black People.

Dancer and Musician A145

**1977, Jan. 7    Photo.    Perf. 13x13½**

| 440 | A144 | 60fr blue & blk | .65 | .20 |
| 441 | A144 | 150fr emerald & blk | 2.25 | .60 |

Design: 60fr, Ali and Frazier in ring, vert.

World boxing champion Muhammad Ali.

**1977, Feb. 10    Litho.    Perf. 12½**

| 442 | A145 | 50fr yellow & multi | .55 | .20 |
| 443 | A145 | 75fr green & multi | 1.25 | .30 |
| 444 | A145 | 100fr rose & multi | 3.20 | 1.00 |
| | | Nos. 442-444 (3) | 1.40 | .50 |

Festival Emblem and: 75fr, Wood carving and masks. 100fr, Dancers and ancestor statuette.

2nd World Black and African Festival, Lagos, Nigeria, Jan. 15-Feb. 12.

Cogwheels and Symbols of Industry — A146

**1977, Mar. 28    Engr.    Perf. 13**

| 445 | A146 | 70fr yel grn & ocher | .80 | .30 |

Dakar Industrial Zone, 1st anniversary.

---

Burning Match and Burnt Trees — A147

**1977, Apr. 30    Litho.    Perf. 12½**

| 446 | A147 | 40fr green & multi | 1.00 | .35 |
| 447 | A147 | 60fr slate & multi | 1.75 | .55 |

60fr, Burnt trees and house, fire-truck, horiz.

Prevention of forest fires.

Drummer, Telephone, Agriculture and Industry — A148

**1977, May 17    Litho.    Perf. 13**

| 448 | A149 | 80fr multi | .80 | .40 |
| 449 | A149 | 100fr multi | 1.25 | .60 |

World Telecommunications Day.

Electronic Tree and ITU Emblem — A149

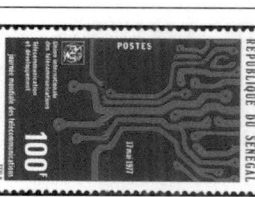

Symbol of Language Studies — A150

**1977, May 21    Litho.    Perf. 12x12½, 12½**

| 450 | A150 | 65fr multi | .65 | .20 |
| 451 | A151 | 250fr multi | 2.75 | 1.00 |

10th anniv. of Int'l French Language Council.

Sassenage Castle, Grenoble — A151

Woman in Boat, Wooden Shoe A152

---

Adult Reading Class A153

**1977, Sept. 10    Litho.    Perf. 12½**

| 454 | A153 | 65fr multi | .70 | .25 |
| 455 | A153 | 65fr multi | .70 | .25 |

Design: 65fr, Man learning to read.

National Literacy Week, Sept. 8-14.

**1977, June 4    Perf. 13½x14, 14x13½**

| 452 | A152 | 50fr blue grn & multi | .50 | .20 |
| 453 | A152 | 125fr ocher & multi | 1.50 | .45 |

Design: 125fr, Senegalese woman, symbolic tulip and stamp, vert.

Amphilex '77 International Philatelic Exhibition, Amsterdam, May 26-June 5.

A155

**1977, Nov.    Photo.    Perf. 13x13½**

| 456 | A154 | 20fr multi | .35 | .20 |
| 457 | A154 | 25fr multi | .35 | .20 |
| 458 | A154 | 40fr multi | .65 | .20 |
| 459 | A154 | 60fr multi | .85 | .35 |
| 460 | A154 | 65fr multi | 1.75 | .35 |
| 461 | A154 | 100fr multi | 4.30 | 1.80 |
| | | Nos. 456-461 (6) | | |

Paintings: 20fr, Mercury, by Rubens. 25fr, Daniel in the Lions' Den, by Peter Paul Rubens (1577-1640). 40fr, The Empress, by Titian (1477-1576). 60fr, Flora, by Titian. 65fr, Jo, the Beautiful Irish Woman, by Gustave Courbet (1819-1877). 100fr, The Painter's Studio, by Courbet.

A154

**1977, Dec. 22    Litho.    Perf. 12½**

| 462 | A155 | 20fr multi | .20 | .20 |
| 463 | A155 | 25fr multi | .30 | .20 |
| 464 | A155 | 40fr multi | .50 | .20 |
| 465 | A155 | 100fr multi | 2.00 | 1.10 |
| | | Nos. 462-465 (4) | 1.00 | .50 |

Christmas: 20fr, Adoration by People of Various Races. 25fr, Decorated arch and pro child. 40fr, Christmas tree, mother and child. 100fr, Adoration of the Kings, horiz.

Regatta at Soumbedioun A156

Tourism: 10fr, Senegalese wrestlers. 65fr, Regatta at Soumbedioun. 100fr, Dancers.

Soccer, Flags: Argentina, Hungary, France, Italy — A161

1978, June 24    Photo.    Perf. 13
481  A161  25fr multi        .25  .20
482  A161  40fr multi        .55  .20
483  A161  65fr multi        .80  .30
484  A161  100fr multi      1.50  .30
                            3.10 1.00

Soccer, Cup, Argentina '78 Emblem and Flags of: 40fr, No. 486a, Poland, German Democratic Rep., Tunisia, Mexico. 65fr, 125fr, Austria, Spain, Sweden, Brazil. 75fr, No. 484, Netherlands, Iran, Peru, Scotland. 150fr, like 25fr.

Souvenir Sheets
485                 Sheet of 2      2.75
  a. A161 75fr multi          .60
  b. A161 125fr multi        1.10
486                 Sheet of 2      2.75
  a. A161 100fr multi         .85
  b. A161 150fr multi        1.10

11th World Cup Soccer Championship, Argentina, June 1-25.

1978, June 27    Perf. 12
Design: 150fr, No. 489a, Martin Luther King. No. 489b, like 125fr.
487  A162  125fr multi     1.70  .35
488  A162  150fr multi     2.25  .60

Souvenir Sheet
489                 Sheet of 2      4.00
  a. A162 200fr multi        1.60
  b. A162 200fr multi        1.60

Mahatma Gandhi and Martin Luther King, advocates of non-violence.

Homes and Industry — A163

1978, Aug. 5    Litho.    Perf. 12½
490  A163  110fr multi     1.25  .40

3rd Intl. Fair, Dakar, Nov. 28-Dec. 10.

Wright Brothers and Flyer — A164

Designs: 150fr, like 75fr. 100fr, 250fr, Yuri Gagarin and spacecraft. 200fr, 300fr, US astronauts Frank Borman, William Anders, James Lovell Jr. and spacecraft.

1978, Sept. 25    Litho.    Perf. 13½x14
491  A164  75fr multi        .90  .25
492  A164  100fr multi      1.25  .20
493  A164  200fr multi      2.25  .85
                            4.40 1.50
Nos. 491-493 (3)

---

**Mahatma Gandhi — A162**

1978, Jan. 30    Photo.
470  A157  75fr multi        .80  .30

UNESCO campaign to save world's cultural heritage.

---

Acropolis, Athens, and African Buildings A157

1978, Jan. 7    Litho.    Perf. 12½
466  A156  10fr multi        .20  .20
467  A156  30fr multi        .35  .20
468  A156  65fr multi, horiz.  .80  .40
469  A156  100fr multi, horiz.  1.75  .50
                              3.10 1.30
Nos. 466-469 (4)

---

Solar-powered Pump, Field and Sheep — A158

Energy in Senegal: 95fr, Pylon bringing electricity to villages and factories.

1978, Feb. 25    Perf. 13
471  A158  50fr multi        .55  .20
472  A158  95fr multi       1.25  .40

Park Type of 1976

5fr, Caspian terns in flight, royal terns on ground. 10fr, Pink-backed pelicans. 15fr, Wart hog & gray heron. 20fr, Greater flamingoes, nests, eggs & young. #477, Gray heron & royal terns. #478, Abyssinian ground hornbill & wart hog.

1978, Apr. 22    Photo.    Perf. 13
473  A133  5fr  gold & multi     .25  .20
474  A133  10fr gold & multi     .35  .20
475  A133  15fr gold & multi    1.10  .25
476  A133  20fr gold & multi    1.25  .40
477  A133  150fr gold & multi   5.25 1.00
478  A133  150fr gold & multi   6.25 1.00
  a. Strip of 2, #477-478 + label  11.50
                                   13.65 3.05
Nos. 473-478 (6)

Salum Delta National Park.

Dome of the Rock, Jerusalem A159

1978, May 15    Litho.    Perf. 12½
479  A159  60fr multi        .80  .20

Palestinian fighters and their families.

1978, June 3
480  A160  60fr multi        .80  .35

Eradication of smallpox.

Vaccination, Dr. Jenner, WHO Emblem — A160

---

Souvenir Sheet
494                 Sheet of 3      6.25
  a. A164 150fr multi       1.60
  b. A164 250fr multi       1.40
  c. A164 300fr multi       2.00

75th anniv. of 1st powered flight; 10th anniv. of the death of Yuri Gagarin, first man in space; 10th anniv. of Apollo 8 flight around moon.

Henri Dunant (1828-1910), Founder of Red Cross, and Patients — A165

Design: 20fr, Henri Dunant, First Aid station, Red Cross flag.

1978, Oct. 28    Photo.    Perf. 11½
495  A165  5fr brt blue & red    .25  .20
496  A165  20fr multi            .45  .20

Bedside Lecture and Emblem — A166

100fr, Pollution, fish and mercury bottles.

1979, Jan. 15    Litho.    Perf. 13½x13
497  A166  50fr multi        .45  .20
498  A166  100fr multi      1.10  .30

9th Medical Days, Dakar, Jan. 15-20.

Map of Senegal with Shortwave Stations A167

60fr, Children on vacation, ambulance, soccer player. 65fr, Rural mobile post office.

1978, Dec. 27    Litho.    Perf. 13½x13
499  A167  5fr multi         .55  .20
500  A167  60fr multi        .55  .20
501  A167  65fr multi        .70  .20
                            1.80  .60
Nos. 499-501 (3)

Achievements of postal service.

Farmer A168

Design: 150fr, Factories, communication, transportation, fish, physician and worker.

1979, Feb. 17    Litho.    Perf. 12½
502  A168  30fr multi        .35  .20
503  A168  150fr multi      1.40  .50

Pride in workmanship.

Children's Village and Children — A169

Design: 60fr, Different view of village.

---

1979, Mar. 30    Perf. 12x12½
504  A169  40fr multi        .45  .20
505  A169  60fr multi        .70  .20

Children's SOS villages.

Infant, Physician Vaccinating Child, IYC Emblem — A170

65fr, Boys with book, globe, IYC emblem.

1979, Apr. 21    Litho.    Perf. 13½x13
506  A170  60fr multi        .65  .20
507  A170  65fr multi        .65  .20

International Year of the Child.

Drum, Carrier Pigeon, Satellite — A171

Design: 60fr, Baobab tree and flower. Independence monument with lion, vert.

1979, June 8    Size: 36x48mm
508  A171  60fr multi       1.75  .85

Perf. 12½    Size: 36x36mm
509  A171  150fr multi      3.50 1.50

Philexafrique II, Libreville, Gabon, June 8-17. Nos. 508, 509 each printed with labels showing UAPT '79 emblem.

People Walking through Open Book A172

1979, Sept. 15    Photo.    Perf. 11½x12
510  A172  250fr multi      2.50  .80

Intl. Bureau of Education, Geneva, 50th anniv.

Sir Rowland Hill (1795-1879), Originator of Penny Postage, Type AP3 with Exhibition Cancel — A173

1979, Oct. 9    Perf. 11½
511  A173  500fr multi      5.25 2.00

Black Trees, by Hundertwasser A174

Paintings by Friedensreich Hundertwasser, pseudonym of Friedrich Stowasser (b. 1928).

**1979, Dec. 10**    Litho. & Engr.    *Perf. 13½x14*
512 A174 60fr shown    4.50   1.50
513 A174 100fr Head of a
     man    175.00   175.00
514 A174 200fr Rainbow
a.   Souvenir sheet of 4
     windows   13.50   3.75
     Nos. 512-514 (3)   2.25

**1980, Jan. 14**    Litho.    *Perf. 13*
515 A175 20fr shown    .25   .20
516 A175 25fr Javelin    .25   .20
517 A175 50fr Relay race    .55   .20
518 A175 75fr Discus    2.30   1.05
     Nos. 515-518 (4)

1st African Athletic Championships.

Running,
Championship
Emblem
A175

**1980, Mar. 22**    Photo.    *Perf. 14*
519 A176 50fr shown    .45   .20
520 A176 100fr Dancers, festival
521 A176 200fr Drummer, danc-
     ers    1.00   .45
     Nos. 519-521 (3)   1.75   .85
     3.20   1.50

Mudra
Afrique
Arts
Festival
A176

**1980, May 17**    Litho.    *Perf. 13*
522 A177 100fr multi    1.10   .40

22nd Cong., Lions Intl. District 403, Dakar.

Lions
Emblem,
Map of
Dakar
Harbor
A177

Chimpanzees — A178

REPUBLIQUE DU SENEGAL

**1980, June 2**    Photo.    *Perf. 13½*
523 A178 40fr shown    .80   .35
524 A178 60fr Elephants    1.00   .35
525 A178 65fr Derby's elands    1.40   .35
526 A178 100fr Hyenas    2.00   .40
527    Pair    8.00   4.00
a.   A178 200fr Herd    4.00   .70
b.   A178 200fr Guest house    13.20   2.70
     Nos. 523-527 (5)

**Souvenir Sheet**
528
a.   A178 125fr like #523    8.00   8.00
b.   A178 125fr like #524    1.50   1.50
c.   A178 125fr like #525    1.50   1.50
d.   A178 125fr like #526    1.50   1.50
     1.50   1.50

Niokolo Koba National Park. No. 527
printed in continuous design with label showing location in park.

Tree Planting
Year — A179

**1980, June 27**    Litho.    *Perf. 13*
529 A179 60fr multi    .90   .40
530 A179 65fr multi    1.00   .40

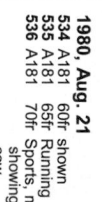

**1980, July 19**
531 A180 50fr multi    .35   .20
532 A180 100fr multi    .80   .35
533 A180 200fr multi    3.60   1.35
     Nos. 531-533 (3)

Rural women workers. 50fr, 200fr, horiz.

Rural Women
Workers
A180

**1980, Aug. 21**    *Perf. 14½*
534 A181 60fr shown    .45   .20
535 A181 65fr Running    .55   .30
536 A181 70fr Sports, map
     showing Mos-
     cow    .55   .30
537 A181 100fr Judo    .80   .40
538 A181 200fr Basketball    1.75   .80
     Nos. 534-538 (5)   4.10   2.00

**Souvenir Sheet**
539
a.   A181 75fr like #534    2.00   2.00
b.   A181 125fr like #535    .65   .65
**Sheet of 2**
540
a.   A181 75fr like #537    2.00   2.00
b.   A181 125fr like #538    .65   .35
     1.00   .35

Wrestling,
Moscow '80
Emblem — A181

22nd Summer Olympic Games, Moscow,
July 19-Aug. 3.

REPUBLIQUE DU SENEGAL

**1981, Jan. 31**    Litho.    *Perf. 14½x14*
541 A182 50fr multi    .30   .20
542 A182 70fr multi    .50   .45
543 A182 85fr multi    1.00   .45
544 A182 150fr multi    5.25   1.00
     Nos. 541-544 (4)   11.50   2.20

**Souvenir Sheet**
545
a.   A182 125fr like #541    16.00   16.00
b.   A182 125fr like #542    2.50   2.50
c.   A182 125fr like #543    2.50   2.50
d.   A182 125fr like #544    2.50   2.50
     2.50   2.50

National Park Wildlife. 70fr, Laughing gulls
and Hansel's tern, Barbarie Spit, 85fr, Turtle
and crab, Madeleine Islands. 150fr, Cormorant, Madeleine Islands.

Caspian
Tern and
Sea Gulls,
Kalissaye
Bird
Sanctuary
A182

Anti-Tobacco
Campaign — A183

**1981, June 20**    Litho.    *Perf. 13*
546 A183 75fr Healthy people    .70   .30
547 A183 80fr shown    .90   .30

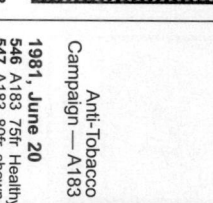  

**1981, Sept. 19**    Litho.    *Perf. 12½*
548 A184 80fr multi    .80   .30

4th Intl.
Dakar Fair,
Nov. 25-
Dec. 7
A184

**1982, Jan. 11**    Photo.    *Perf. 14*
549 A185 75fr Portrait, vert.    .55   .35
550 A185 500fr Battle    4.50   1.40

Natl.
Hero Lat
Dior
A185

**1982, Feb. 1**    *Perf. 11½*
551 A186 50fr Nymphaea lotus    .55   .20
552 A186 75fr Strophanthus
     sarmentosus    .90   .30
553 A186 200fr Crinum moorei    2.25   .65
554 A186 225fr Cochlospermum
     tinctorium    2.25   .85
     Nos. 551-554 (4)   5.95   2.00

Inscribed 1981.

Local
Flora — A186

**1982, Feb. 27**    Litho.    *Perf. 14*
555 A187 45fr shown    1.25   .35
556 A187 55fr Hypolimnas
     salinacis    1.75   .45
557 A187 75fr Cymothoe
     caenis    2.10   .55
558 A187 80fr Precis cebrene    2.40   .70
     Nos. 555-558 (4)   7.50   2.05

**Souvenir Sheet**
559
a.   A187 100fr like #555    16.00   16.00
b.   A187 150fr like #556    1.50   1.50
c.   A187 200fr like #557    3.50   3.50
d.   A187 250fr like #558    4.00   4.00

Euryphrene Senegalensis — A187

Destructive
Insects — A188

**1982, Apr. 7**    Litho.    *Perf. 14*
560 A188 75fr multi    1.50   .35
561 A188 80fr multi    3.00   .65
562 A188 100fr multi    2.25   .85
     Nos. 560-562 (3)   6.75   1.85

Various insects. 80fr, 100fr horiz.

PHILEXFRANCE
PARIS -82

Banner and
Stamp — A189

**1982, Dec. 30**    Photo.    *Perf. 13*
575 A189 100fr shown    .70   .35
576 A189 500fr Stamp, arrows    4.50   1.50

PHILEXFRANCE Intl. Stamp Exhibition,
Paris, June 11-21.

**1982-93**    Engr.    *Perf. 13*
563 A106 5fr Prus. blue    .20   .20
564 A106 10fr dull red    .20   .20
565 A106 15fr orange    .20   .20
566 A106 20fr dk purple    .20   .20
567 A106 30fr henna brn    .35   .20
568 A106 45fr orange yellow    .40   .20
569 A106 65fr bright magenta    .50   .20
570 A106 90fr brt carmine    .85   .35
571 A106 125fr ultramarine    .95   .30
572 A106 145fr orange    1.40   .70
573 A106 180fr gray blue    5.45   3.25
     Nos. 563-573 (11)

Issued: 5, 10, 15, 20, 30fr, 90fr, Apr. 30;
45fr, 1984; 180fr, 1991; 45, 50, 125fr, 1993;
145fr, 1995.

Fashion Type of 1972

Senegambia Confederation,
Feb. 1 — A190

**1982, Nov. 15**    Litho.    *Perf. 12½*
577 A190 225fr Map, flags    2.00   .65
578 A190 350fr Arms    2.75   1.00

Senegambia Confederation.

**1982, Dec. 1**    Photo.    *Perf. 11½*
579 A191 45fr Godwit    .55   .20
580 A191 50fr Jabiru    1.00   .30
581 A191 80fr Francolin    1.10   .50
582 A191 500fr Eagle    5.75   2.00
     Nos. 579-582 (4)   8.10   3.00

Local
Birds — A191

**1982, Dec. 11**    Litho.    *Perf. 12½x13*
583 A192 30fr Player    .55   .20
584 A192 50fr Player    .35   .20
585 A192 75fr Player, diff.    .80   .20
586 A192 80fr Cup    .90   .35
     Nos. 583-586 (4)   2.30   .95

**Souvenir Sheets**
587 A192 75fr like 30fr    .65   .65
588 A192 100fr like 50fr    .90   .90
589 A192 150fr like 75fr    1.25   1.25
590 A192 200fr like 80fr    1.75   1.75
     Nos. 587-590 (4)   4.55   4.55

Granite Paper

1982 World
Cup — A192

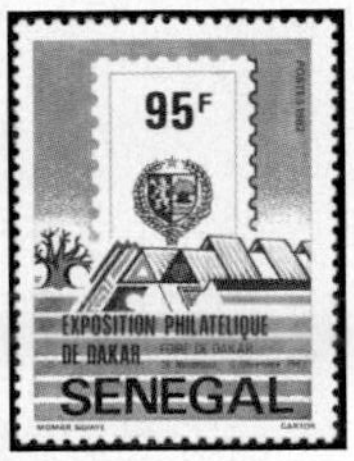

A193

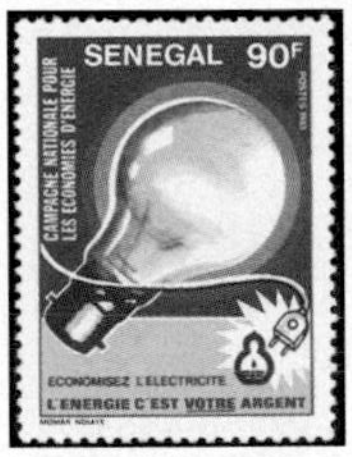

A194

Designs: 60fr, Exhibition poster, viewers, horiz. 70fr, Simulated butterfly stamps. 90fr, Simulated stamps under magnifying glass. 95fr, Coat of Arms over Exhibition Building.

**1983, Aug. 6** Litho. *Perf. 12½*
**591** A193 60fr multi .55 .20
**592** A193 70fr multi 1.40 .30
**593** A193 90fr multi 1.75 .30
**594** A193 95fr multi 1.75 .40
*Nos. 591-594 (4)* 5.45 1.20

Dakar '82 Stamp Exhibition.

**1983, Oct. 25** Litho. *Perf. 12½x13*
**595** A194 90fr Electricity .85 .40
**596** A194 95fr Gasoline 1.00 .45
**597** A194 260fr Coal, wood 2.25 .65
*Nos. 595-597 (3)* 4.10 1.50

Energy conservation.

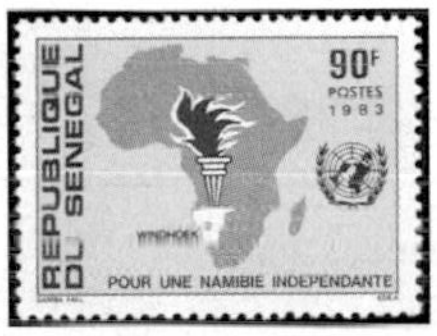

Namibia Day — A195

**1983, Nov. 14** Litho. *Perf. 13½x13*
**598** A195 90fr Torch .80 .35
**599** A195 95fr Chain, fist .90 .35
**600** A195 260fr Woman bearing torch 2.75 .65
*Nos. 598-600 (3)* 4.45 1.35

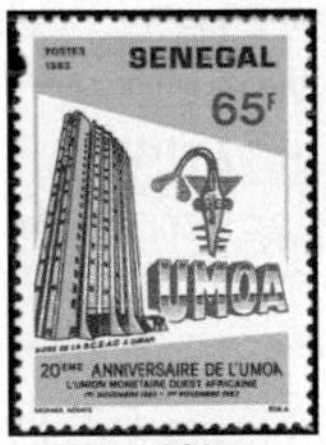

West African Monetary Union, 20th Anniv. — A196

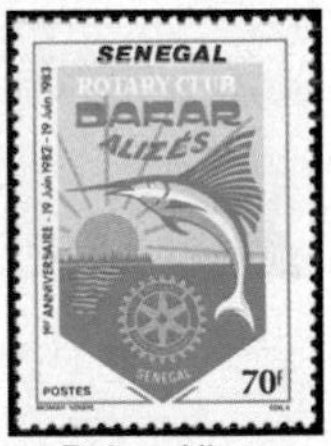

Dakar Alizes Rotary Club, First Anniv. — A197

Designs: 60fr, Mask emblem, Ziguinchor Agency building, Dakar, horiz. 65fr, Monetary Union headquarters, emblem.

*Perf. 13½x13, 13x13½*

**1983, Nov. 28**
**601** A196 60fr multi .65 .20
**602** A196 65fr multi .65 .20

**1983, Dec. 5** *Perf. 13x13½*
**603** A197 70fr green & multi .90 .35
**604** A197 500fr blue & multi 4.50 1.75

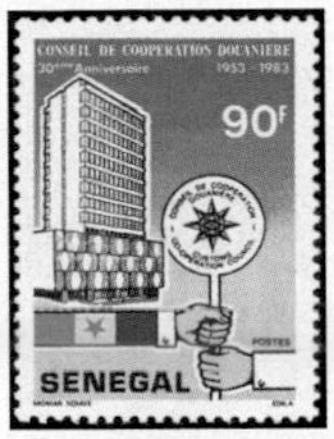

Customs Cooperation Council, 30th Anniv. — A198

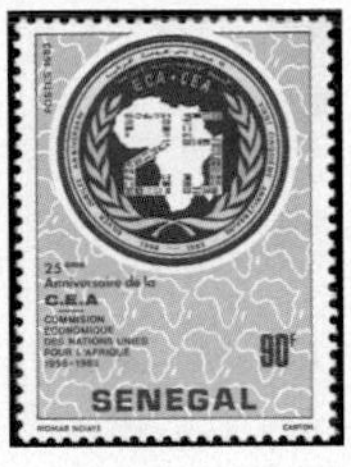

Economic Comm. for Africa, 25th Anniv. — A199

**1983, Dec. 23** *Perf. 12½x13*
**605** A198 90fr multi .65 .20
**606** A198 300fr multi 3.00 .80

**1984, Jan. 10** *Perf. 12½*
**607** A199 90fr multi .70 .35
**608** A199 95fr multi .90 .35

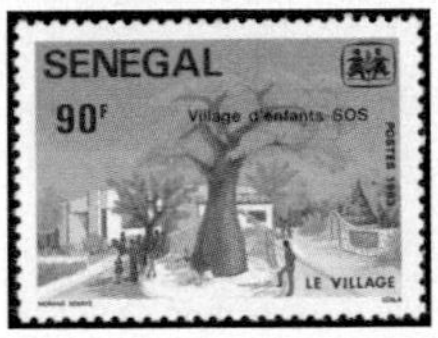

SOS Children's Village A200

**1984, Mar. 29** *Perf. 13½x13, 13x13½*
**609** A200 90fr Village .80 .25
**610** A200 95fr Mother & child, vert. 1.00 .40
**611** A200 115fr Brothers & sisters 1.10 .40
**612** A200 260fr House, vert. 2.50 .85
*Nos. 609-612 (4)* 5.40 1.90

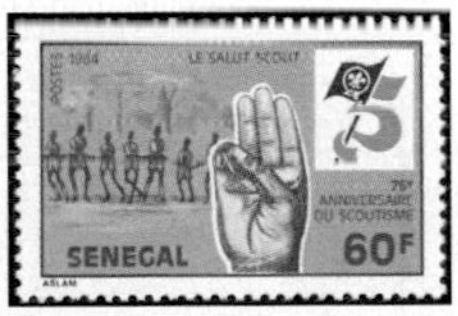

Scouting Year A201

**1984, May 28** Litho. *Perf. 13*
**613** A201 60fr Sign .55 .20
**614** A201 70fr Emblem .55 .20
**615** A201 90fr Scouts .70 .30
**616** A201 95fr Baden-Powell .90 .30
*Nos. 613-616 (4)* 2.70 1.00

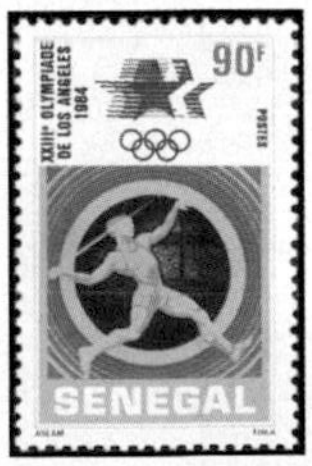

1984 Olympic Games — A202

**1984, July 28** Litho. *Perf. 13*
**617** A202 90fr Javelin .70 .20
**618** A202 95fr Hurdles .90 .35
**619** A202 165fr Soccer 1.50 .50
*Nos. 617-619 (3)* 3.10 1.05

**Souvenir Sheet**

*Perf. 13x12½*

**620** Sheet of 3 4.50 4.50
*a.* A202 125fr like 90fr .95 .95
*b.* A202 175fr like 95fr 1.50 1.50
*c.* A202 250fr like 165fr 1.75 1.75

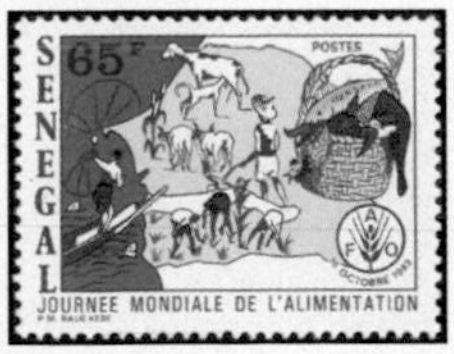

World Food Day A203

*Perf. 13x12½, 12½x13*

**1984, Dec. 16** Litho.
**621** A203 65fr Food production .55 .30
**622** A203 70fr Cooking, vert. .70 .30
**623** A203 225fr Dining 2.25 .85
*Nos. 621-623 (3)* 3.50 1.45

No. 612 Overprinted "AIDE AU SAHEL 84"

**1984, Dec.** *Perf. 13x13½*
**624** A200 260fr multi 2.25 1.25

Drought relief.

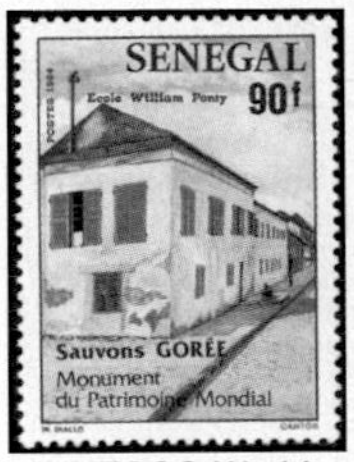

UNESCO World Heritage Campaign — A204

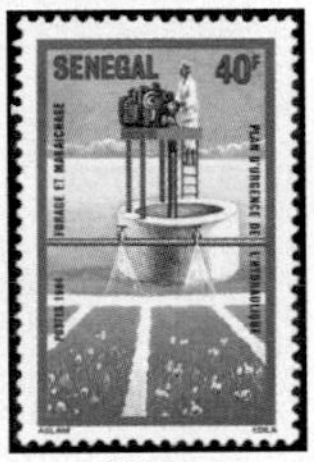

Water Emergency Plan — A205

**1984, Dec. 6** Litho. *Perf. 13½*
**625** A204 90fr William Ponty School .80 .35
**626** A204 95fr Island map, horiz. .80 .35
**627** A204 250fr History Museum 2.75 .85
**628** A204 500fr Slave Prison, horiz. 5.00 2.00
*Nos. 625-628 (4)* 9.35 3.55

**Souvenir Sheet**

*Perf. 13x12½, 12½x13*

**629** Sheet of 4 10.00 10.00
*a.* A204 125fr like No. 625 .75 .75
*b.* A204 150fr like No. 626 1.00 1.00
*c.* A204 325fr like No. 627 2.00 2.00
*d.* A204 675fr like No. 628 5.00 5.00

Restoration of historic sites, Goree Island.

**1985, Mar. 28** *Perf. 13x12½, 12½x13*
**630** A205 40fr Well and pump .50 .20
**631** A205 50fr Spigot and crops .65 .30
**632** A206 90fr Water tanks, livestock 1.10 .50
**633** A205 250fr Women at well 2.75 1.00
*Nos. 630-633 (4)* 5.00 2.00

Nos. 631-633 horiz.

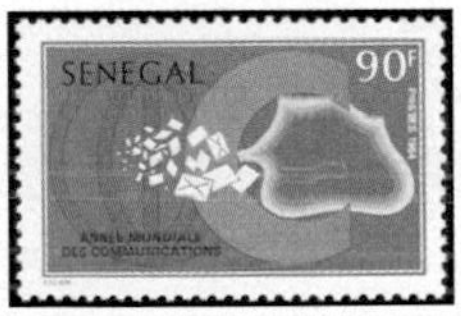

World Communications Year — A206

Designs: 95fr, Maps of Africa and Senegal, transmission tower. 350fr, Globe, pigeon with letter.

**1985, Apr. 13** Litho. *Perf. 13*
**634** A206 90fr multi .70 .35
**635** A206 95fr multi .90 .35
**636** A206 350fr multi 3.25 1.25
*Nos. 634-636 (3)* 4.85 1.95

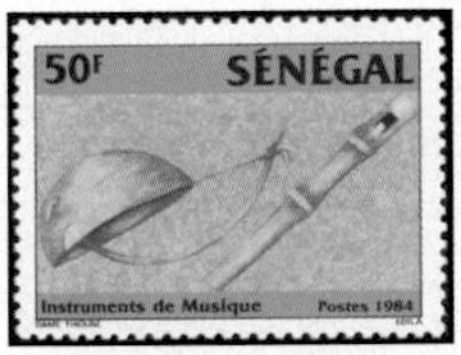

Traditional Musical Instruments — A207

50fr, Gourd fiddle, bamboo flute. 85fr, Drums, stringed instrument. 125fr, Musician playing balaphone, drums. 250fr, Rabab, shawm & single-string fiddles.

**1985, May 4** *Perf. 12½x13, 13x12½*
**637** A207 50fr multi .65 .20
**638** A207 85fr multi 1.00 .40
**639** A207 125fr multi 1.25 .50
**640** A207 250fr multi 2.50 .85
*Nos. 637-640 (4)* 5.40 1.95

Nos. 638-640 vert. For surcharge see No. 676.

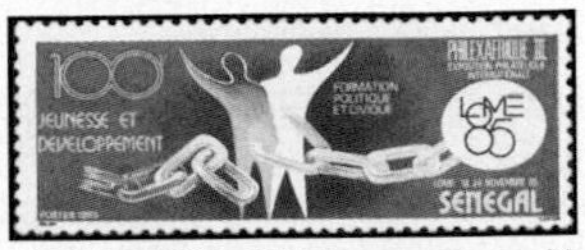

PHILEXAFRICA '85, Lome, Togo, Nov. 16-24 — A208

**1985, Oct. 21** *Perf. 13*
**641** A208 100fr Political and civic education .70 .25
**642** A208 125fr Vocational training 1.00 .40
**643** A208 150fr Culture, space exploration 1.25 .50
**644** A208 175fr Self-sufficiency in food production 2.25 .85
*Nos. 641-644 (4)* 5.20 2.00

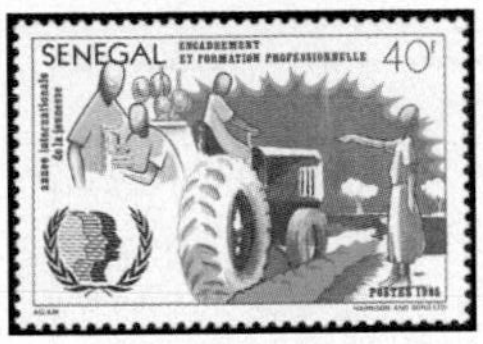

Intl. Youth Year A209

**1985, Nov. 30** *Perf. 14*
**645** A209 40fr Vocational training .35 .20
**646** A209 50fr Communications .45 .20
**647** A209 90fr World peace .80 .30
**648** A209 125fr Cultural exchange 1.25 .35
*Nos. 645-648 (4)* 2.85 1.05

Senegal Arms Type of 1970

**1985, Dec.** Litho. *Perf. 13*

**Background Color**

**654** A89 95fr bright orange .80 .20

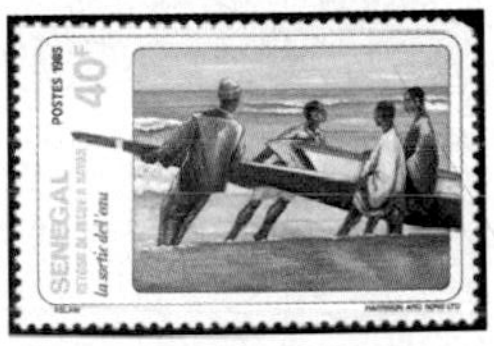

Fishing at Kayar A210

**1986, Jan. 28** Litho. *Perf. 14*
**659** A210 40fr Hauling boat .35 .20
**660** A210 50fr Women on beach .55 .20
**661** A210 100fr Fisherman, catch 1.00 .35
**662** A210 125fr Women buying fish 1.40 .50
**663** A210 150fr Unloading fish 1.60 .60
*Nos. 659-663 (5)* 4.90 1.85

Nos. 661-662 vert.

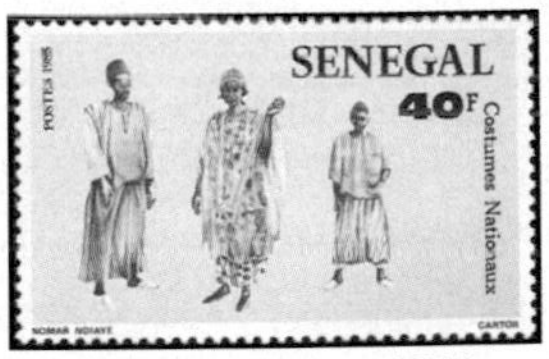

Folk Costumes — A211

**1985, Dec. 28** Litho. *Perf. 13½*
**664** A211 40fr multi .25 .20
**665** A211 95fr multi, vert., diff. .80 .30
**666** A211 100fr multi, vert., diff. .90 .30
**667** A211 150fr multi, vert., diff. 1.25 .50
*Nos. 664-667 (4)* 3.20 1.30

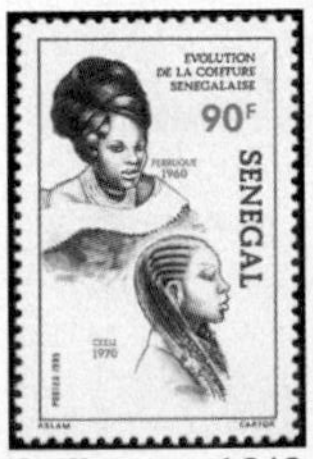

Coiffures — A212

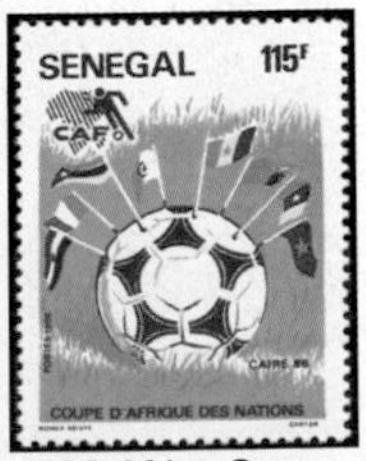

1986 Africa Soccer Cup, Cairo — A213

**1986, Mar. 3** *Perf. 13*
**668** A212 90fr Perruque, Ceeli .70 .35
**669** A212 125fr Ndungu, Kearly, Rasta 1.00 .40

     **SENEGAL**

670 A212 250fr Janono Kura, Kooraa 2.25 .75
671 A212 300fr Mbaram, Jeere 6.70 2.40
Nos. 668-671 (4)

**1986, Mar. 7**      *Perf. 13½*
672 A213 115fr Soccer ball, flags 1.00 .30
673 A213 125fr Athlete, map 1.00
674 A213 135fr Pyramid, heraldic lion 1.10 .40
675 A213 165fr Flag, lions, map 1.40 .50
Nos. 672-675 (4) 4.50 1.55

**1986, May 8**      *Perf. 13x12½*
676 A207 165fr on 85fr multi 1.40 .50

No. 638 Surcharged with Lions Intl. Emblem, Two Bars, and "Ve CONVENTION / MULTI-DISTRICT / 403 / 8-10 / MAI / 1986" in Dark Ultramarine

World Wildlife Fund — A214

**1986, June 30**      *Perf. 13*
677 A214 15fr multi .75 .20
678 A214 45fr multi 1.25 .25
679 A214 85fr multi 2.50 .60
680 A214 340fr multi 4.25 1.00
Nos. 677-680 (4) 8.75 2.05

Ndama gazelles.

 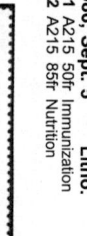

UN Child Survival Campaign — A215

**1986, Sept. 5**     Litho.      *Perf. 14*
681 A215 50fr Immunization .45 .20
682 A215 85fr Nutrition .70 .30

1986 World Cup Soccer Championships, Mexico — A216

Various plays, world cup and artifacts: 125fr, Ceremonial vase. 135fr, Mayan mask. Palenque. 165fr, Gold breastplate. 340fr, Porcelain head, Teotihuacan, 7th cent. B.C.

**1986, Nov. 17**      *Perf. 12½x12*
683 A216 125fr multi 1.00 .40
684 A216 135fr multi 1.10 .40
685 A216 165fr multi 1.40 .55
686 A216 340fr multi 2.75 1.10
Nos. 683-686 (4) 6.25 2.45

Designs of Nos. 683-686 Overprinted "ARGENTINE 3 / R.F.A. 2" in Scarlet

**1986, Nov. 17**
687 A216 125fr multi 1.00 .40
688 A216 135fr multi 1.10 .40
689 A216 165fr multi 1.40 .55
690 A216 340fr multi 2.75 1.10
Nos. 687-690 (4) 6.25 2.50

Guembeul Nature Reserve A217

---

**1986, Dec. 4**     Litho.      *Perf. 13½*
691 A217 50fr Ostriches 1.25 .25
692 A217 65fr Kob antelopes .45 .25
693 A217 85fr Girafes .60 .40
694 A217 100fr Ostrich, buffalo, kob, giraffe 2.00 .50
695 A217 150fr Buffaloes 1.25 .50
Nos. 691-695 (5) 5.55 1.95

**1986, Dec. 22**     Litho.      *Perf. 14*
696 A218 70fr Puppet, vert. .55 .20
697 A218 85fr Folk musicians .80 .25
698 A218 150fr Outdoor celebration 1.25 .50
699 A218 250fr Boy praying, creche 2.25 .85
Nos. 696-699 (4) 4.85 1.80
Inscribed 1985.

Christmas A218

Statue of Liberty, Cent. — A219

**1986, Dec. 30**     Litho.      *Perf. 12½*
700 A219 225fr multi 2.00 .65

Marine Life A220

**1987, Jan. 2**      *Perf. 14*
701 A220 50fr Jellyfish, coral 1.00 .25
702 A220 85fr Sea urchin, starfish 1.60 .50
703 A220 100fr Spiny lobster 2.10 .65
704 A220 150fr Dolphin 3.25 .90
705 A220 200fr Octopus 8.50 2.50
Nos. 701-705 (5)

Senegal Stamp Cent. — A221

**1987, Apr. 8**      *Perf. 13*
706 A221 100fr Intl. express mail 1.40 .30
707 A221 130fr #37 1.60 .40
708 A221 140fr Similar to #201 1.75 .40
709 A221 145fr Similar to #154 1.75 .50
710 A221 320fr #27 5.00 1.10
Nos. 706-710 (5) 11.50 2.70

Designs of Nos. 37, 151 and 27 same as originally released but perfs simulated. For overprint see No. 784.

Paris-Dakar Rally — A222

---

**1987, Jan. 22**      *Perf. 14*
711 A222 115fr Motorcycle, truck, vert. 1.25 .40
712 A222 125fr Official, race 1.75 .40
713 A222 135fr Sabine, truck 1.75 .55
714 A222 340fr Eiffel Tower, Dakar huts, vert. 3.25 1.25
Nos. 711-714 (4) 8.00 2.60

Homage to Thierry Sabine, Inscribed 1986.

Ferlo Nature Reserve — A223

**1987, Feb. 5**      *Perf. 13½*
715 A223 55fr Antelope .65 .25
716 A223 70fr Ostrich .85 .35
717 A223 85fr Warthog .85 .35
718 A223 90fr Elephant 1.00 .40
Nos. 715-718 (4) 3.35 1.35
Inscribed 1986.

Agena-Gemini 8 Link-up in Outer Space, 20th Anniv. — A224

**1987, Feb. 27**     Litho.      *Perf. 13*
719 A224 320fr multi 2.75 1.25

**Souvenir Sheet**      *Perf. 12½*
720 A224 500fr multi 6.25 6.25

Nos. 719-720 inscribed 1986 and have erroneous "10e Anniversaire" inscription.

Solidarity Against South African Apartheid — A225

**1987, July 31**     Litho.      *Perf. 13*
721 A225 130fr shown 1.00 .40
722 A225 140fr Mandela, hand, broken chain, vert. 1.10 .45
723 A225 145fr Mandela, dove, death 3.20 1.35
Nos. 721-723 (3)

130fr, Statue of saint, Fr. Daniel Brottier, vert.

Intelsat, 20th Anniv. A226

**1987, Aug. 31**      *Perf. 14*
724 A226 50fr Emblem .45 .20
725 A226 125fr Satellite 1.00 .40
726 A226 135fr Emblem, globe 1.10 .50
727 A226 200fr Earth, satellite in space 2.00 .70
Nos. 724-727 (4) 4.55 1.80
Inscribed 1985, Nos. 726-727 vert.

---

West African Union, 10th Anniv. — A227

Dakar Rotary Club, 45th Anniv. — A228

**1987, Sept. 7**      *Perf. 13*
728 A227 40fr shown .35 .20
729 A227 125fr Emblem, handshake 1.00 .45

**1987, Sept. 29**      *Perf. 13*
730 A228 500fr multi 4.50 1.75
Inscribed 1985.

United Nations, 40th Anniv. — A229

**1987, Oct. 8**      *Perf. 14*
731 A229 85fr Emblem, NYC office .90 .30
732 A229 95fr Mandela, emblem .90 .30
733 A229 150fr Hands, emblem 1.25 .55
Nos. 731-733 (3) 3.05 1.15
Inscribed 1985.

Cathedral of African Memory, 50th Anniv. A230

**1987, Oct. 16**    *Perf. 12½x13, 13x12½*
734 A230 130fr multi 1.00 .50
735 A230 140fr multi 1.00 .50
Inscribed 1986.

Lat Dior, King of Cayor (d. 1887) A231

**1987, Oct. 27**     Litho.      *Perf. 14*
736 A231 130fr Battle of Dekhele 1.25 .50
737 A231 160fr Lat Dior 1.25 .50

World Food Day A232

No. 710 Overprinted

RICCIONE 88  27-29-08-89

**1988, Aug. 27**   Litho.   *Perf. 13*
784  A221  320fr multi    2.75  1.25

Stamp Fair, Riccione, Aug. 27-29, 1988. Stamp incorrectly overprinted "89," instead of "88."

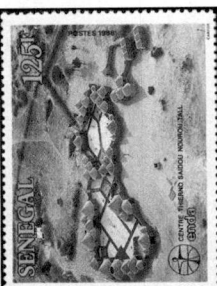

**1988**
785  A246  125fr  Thierno Saidou Nourou Tall Center    .80  .50

ENDA — A246

**1988 Summer Olympics, Seoul — A217**

**1988, Sept. 17**   Litho.   *Perf. 13*
786  A247   5fr shown    .20  .20
787  A247  75fr Running, swimming, soccer    .70  .35
788  A247  300fr Character trademark, torch    2.75  1.00
789  A247  410fr Emblems, running    3.50  1.40

*Nos. 786-789 (4)*    7.15  2.95

Industries — A248

LES F   EURS DU SE   EGAL
20fr

**Indigenous Flowers — A250**

Postcards, c. 1900 — A249

---

Mollusks — A242

**1988, Apr. 20**   *Perf. 12½*
771  A242   10fr Squid    .20  .20
772  A242   20fr Donax trunculus    .20  .20
773  A242  145fr Achatina fulica, vert.    .65  .85
774  A242  165fr Helix nemoralis    1.75  .65

*Nos. 771-774 (4)*    2.25  .85
    4.40  1.90

**1988 African Soccer Cup Championships, Rabat — A243**

**1988, May 10**   Litho.   *Perf. 13*
775  A243   80fr Cameroun (winner)    .70  .30
776  A243  100fr Kick, CAF emblem    .90  .35
777  A243  145fr Map, players, final score    1.25  .40
778  A243  180fr Trophy    1.75  .60

*Nos. 775-778 (4)*    4.60  1.65
*Nos. 776-778 vert.*

US Peace Corps in Senegal, 25th Anniv. — A244

**1988, May 11**   Litho.   *Perf. 13*
779  A244  190fr multi    1.50  .65

Marine Flora — A245

**1988, June 13**   Litho.   *Perf. 12½*
780  A245   10fr Dictyota atomaria    .20  .20
781  A245   65fr Agarum gmelini    .65  .25
782  A245  145fr Saccorrhiza bulbosa    1.40  .50
783  A245  180fr Rhodymenia palmetta    1.75  .65

*Nos. 780-783 (4)*    4.00  1.60
*Inscribed 1987.*

---

Noel 1987   SENEGAL   145F

Christmas — A237

Designs: 145fr, Youth dreaming of presents. 150fr, Madonna and child. 180fr, Holy Family, congregation praying. 200fr, Holy Family, candle and Christmas tree.

**1987, Dec. 24**   *Perf. 12½x13*
757  A237  145fr multi    1.25  .40
758  A237  150fr multi    1.25  .40
759  A237  180fr multi    1.75  .65
760  A237  200fr multi    2.00  .65

*Nos. 757-760 (4)*    6.25  2.10

Dakar Intl. Fair, 10th Anniv. (in 1985) — A238

**1988, Feb. 27**   Litho.   *Perf. 13*
761  A238  125fr multi    .90  .45

*Inscribed 1985.*

Fish — A239

**1988, Feb. 29**   Litho.
762  A239    5fr Ameiurus nebulosus    .20  .20
763  A239  100fr Heniochus acuminatus    1.10  .55
764  A239  145fr Anthias anthias    2.00  .70
765  A239  180fr Cyprinus carpin    3.50  1.25

*Nos. 762-765 (4)*    8.80  2.70

World Meteorology Day — A240

**1988, Mar. 15**   *Perf. 13½*
766  A240  145fr multi    1.25  .55

Paris-Dakar Rally, 10th Anniv. (in 1987) — A241

Various motorcycle and automobile entries in desert settings.

**1988**   *Perf. 13*
767  A241  145fr Motorcycle    1.25  .50
768  A241  180fr Race car    1.75  .55
769  A241  200fr Race car, truck    1.75  .80
770  A241  410fr Thierry Sabine    4.00  1.60

*Nos. 767-770 (4)*    8.75  3.45

*Inscribed 1987. For surcharge see No. 1051.*

---

**1987, Oct. 30**   Litho.   *Perf. 12½*
738  A232  130fr Earth storing grain, vert.    .90  .50
739  A232  140fr shown    1.00  .50
740  A232  145fr Emblem, vert.    3.15  1.50

*Inscribed 1986.*
*Nos. 738-740 (3)*

Fauna, Bassa Casamance Natl. Park — A234

**1987, Nov. 9**   *Perf. 13*
741  A233  115fr Felis servaline    1.00  .55
742  A233  135fr Galagoides demidovii    1.40  .60
743  A233  150fr Potamochoerus porcus    1.50  .65
744  A233  250fr Panthera pardus    2.75  1.25
745  A234  300fr Aigrette    12.50  3.75
746  A234  300fr Guepier    12.50  3.75
 a.   Pair, #745-746 + label    27.50  8.00
    31.65  10.55

Inscribed 1986. No. 745-746 has continuous design with corner label picturing map of Senegal with park highlighted.

Mollusks — A242

Fauna, Bassa Casamance Natl. Park — A234

Traditional Wrestling — A235

Various moves.

**1987, Nov. 30**   Litho.   *Perf. 14*
747  A235  115fr multi, horiz.    1.00  .40
748  A235  125fr multi, diff., horiz.    1.00  .45
749  A235  135fr multi, diff.    1.10  .50
750  A235  165fr multi, diff.    1.40  .65

*Nos. 747-750 (4)*    4.50  2.00

Birds in Djoudj Natl. Park — A236

**1987, Dec. 4**
751  A236  115fr Stork    1.75  .40
752  A236  125fr Pink flamingos, horiz.    2.00  .40
753  A236  135fr White pelicans, horiz.    2.50  .65
754  A236  300fr Pelicans in water    5.00  1.25
755  A236  350fr like 125fr, horiz.    5.25  1.75
756  A236  350fr like 135fr, horiz.    5.25  1.75
 a.   Pair, #755-756 + label    11.50  11.50
    21.75  6.20

**1988, Nov. 7** Litho. Perf. 13
| | | | | |
|---|---|---|---|---|
| 790 | A248 | 5fr Phosphate, Thies | .20 | .20 |
| 791 | A248 | 20fr I.C.S. | .20 | .20 |
| 792 | A248 | 145fr Seib Mill, | | .45 |
| 793 | A248 | 410fr Mbao refinery | 1.25 | .60 |
| | | Diourbel | 3.75 | 1.60 |
| | | Nos. 790-793 (4) | 5.40 | 2.45 |

**1988, Nov. 26**

20fr., Boys, Government Palace, 145fr., Wrestlers, St. Louis Great Mosque, 180fr., Dakar Depot, young woman in folk costume, 200fr., Governor's Residence; housewife using mortar & pestle.

| | | | | |
|---|---|---|---|---|
| 794 | A249 | 20fr red brn & blk | .20 | .20 |
| 795 | A249 | 145fr red brn & blk | 1.00 | .45 |
| 796 | A249 | 180fr red brn & blk | 1.40 | .65 |
| 797 | A249 | 200fr red brn & blk | 1.50 | .85 |
| | | Nos. 794-797 (4) | 4.10 | 2.15 |

11th Paris-Dakar Rally A251

**1988, Dec. 4**
| | | | | |
|---|---|---|---|---|
| 798 | A250 | 20fr Packia biglobosa | .20 | .20 |
| 799 | A250 | 60fr Euphorbia pulcherima | .55 | .20 |
| 800 | A250 | 65fr Cyrtosperma senegalense | .65 | .20 |
| 801 | A250 | 410fr Bombax costatum | 3.75 | 1.50 |
| | | Nos. 798-801 (4) | 5.15 | 2.10 |

**1989, Jan. 13** Litho. Perf. 13x12½
| | | | | |
|---|---|---|---|---|
| 802 | A251 | 10fr Mask, vehicle, Eiffel Tower | .20 | .20 |
| 803 | A251 | 145fr Helmet, desert scene | 1.50 | .50 |
| 804 | A251 | 180fr Turban, rallyist in desert | 1.75 | .65 |
| 805 | A251 | 220fr Thierry Sabine | 2.25 | .85 |
| | | Nos. 802-805 (4) | 5.70 | 2.20 |

For surcharge see No. 1050.

Tourism — A252

**1989, Feb. 15** Perf. 13
| | | | | |
|---|---|---|---|---|
| 806 | A252 | 10fr Teranga | .20 | .20 |
| 807 | A252 | 80fr Campement | .70 | .30 |
| 808 | A252 | 100fr Saly | .90 | .40 |
| 809 | A252 | 350fr Dior | 2.75 | 1.10 |
| | | Nos. 806-809 (4) | 4.55 | 2.00 |

Tourism — A253

**1989, Mar. 11**
| | | | | |
|---|---|---|---|---|
| 810 | A253 | 130fr Natl. tourism emblem, vert. | 1.00 | .40 |
| 811 | A253 | 140fr Visiting rural community | 1.10 | .45 |
| 812 | A253 | 145fr Sport fishing | 1.40 | .65 |
| 813 | A253 | 180fr Water skiing, polo | 1.40 | .80 |
| | | | 4.90 | 2.30 |
| | | Nos. 810-813 (4) | | |

Inscribed 1987.

French Revolution, Bicent. — A254

Designs: 180fr., Governor's Palace, St. Louis, 220fr., Declaration of Human Rights and Citizenship, vert. 300fr., Flag, revolutionaries.

**1989, May 24** Litho. Perf. 13
| | | | | |
|---|---|---|---|---|
| 814 | A254 | 180fr shown | 1.75 | 1.00 |
| 815 | A254 | 220fr multi | 2.00 | 1.00 |
| 816 | A254 | 300fr multi | 3.00 | 1.60 |
| | | Nos. 814-816 (3) | 6.75 | 3.60 |

PHILEXFRANCE '89 — A255

**1989, July 7** Litho. Perf. 13x12½
| | | | | |
|---|---|---|---|---|
| 817 | A255 | 10fr shown | .20 | .20 |
| 818 | A255 | 25fr Simulated stamp, map of France | .65 | .30 |
| 819 | A255 | 75fr Exhibit | 1.25 | .65 |
| 820 | A255 | 145fr Affixing stamp | 2.30 | 1.20 |
| | | Nos. 817-820 (4) | | |

Antoine de Saint-Exupery (1900-1944), French Aviator and Writer — A256

Scenes from novels: 180fr., Night Courier, 1929, 220fr., Night flier, 1931, 410fr., Southern Courier; Bomber pilot, 1942.

**1989, Aug. 30** Litho. Perf. 13
| | | | | |
|---|---|---|---|---|
| 821 | A256 | 180fr multi | 1.50 | .50 |
| 822 | A256 | 220fr multi | 1.75 | .85 |
| 823 | A256 | 410fr multi | 4.00 | 1.40 |
| | | Nos. 821-823 (3) | 7.25 | 2.75 |

**1989**
| | | | | |
|---|---|---|---|---|
| 824 | A246 | 555fr on 125fr multi | 4.00 | 1.25 |

No. 785 Surcharged in Bright Green
Litho. Perf. 13

3rd Francophone Summit on the Arts and Culture — A257

Designs: 5fr, Palette, quill pen in ink pot, dancer, vert. 30fr, Children reading; 100fr, Architecture, women, Earth, 200fr, Artist sketching, easel, gear wheels, chemist, computer operator.

**1989** Perf. 13x13½, 13½x13
| | | | | |
|---|---|---|---|---|
| 825 | A257 | 5fr multicolored | .20 | .20 |
| 826 | A257 | 30fr multicolored | .25 | .20 |
| 827 | A257 | 100fr multicolored | .70 | .40 |
| 828 | A257 | 200fr multicolored | 1.40 | .80 |
| | | Nos. 825-828 (4) | 2.55 | 1.60 |

Pottery A258

**1989, Nov. 1**
| | | | | |
|---|---|---|---|---|
| 829 | A258 | 15fr shown | .20 | .20 |
| 830 | A258 | 30fr Potter, three-handed urn | .30 | .20 |
| 831 | A258 | 75fr Vases | .60 | .30 |
| 832 | A258 | 145fr Woman carrying pottery | 1.10 | .40 |
| | | Nos. 829-832 (4) | 2.20 | 1.10 |

"30" Dakar Cancel — A259

**1989, Oct. 9** Perf. 13½
| | | | | |
|---|---|---|---|---|
| 833 | A259 | 25fr multicolored | .20 | .20 |
| 834 | A259 | 30fr multicolored | .25 | .20 |
| 835 | A259 | 180fr multicolored | 1.50 | .50 |
| 836 | A259 | 220fr multicolored | 1.75 | .65 |
| | | Nos. 833-836 (4) | 3.70 | 1.55 |

Conference of Postal and Telecommunication Administrations of West African Nations (CAPTEAO), 30th anniv.

30fr, Telephone handset, map. 180fr, Map, simulated stamp, phone handset. 220fr, Telecommunications satellite, globe, map.

Natl. Archives, 75th Anniv. — A260

**1989, Oct. 23** Perf. 11½
| | | | | |
|---|---|---|---|---|
| 837 | A260 | 15fr multicolored | .20 | .20 |
| 838 | A260 | 40fr multicolored | .30 | .20 |
| 839 | A260 | 180fr multicolored | 1.10 | .50 |
| 840 | A260 | 200fr multicolored | 1.25 | .60 |
| | | Nos. 837-840 (4) | 2.85 | 1.50 |

Designs: 15fr, Stacks, postal card of 1922. 40fr, Document, 1825. 145fr, Document, 180fr, Tome.

Jawaharlal Nehru, 1st Prime Minister of Independent India — A261

**1989, Nov. 14** Perf. 13
| | | | | |
|---|---|---|---|---|
| 841 | A261 | 220fr Portrait, vert. | 1.75 | .65 |
| 842 | A261 | 410fr shown | 3.75 | 1.40 |

Marine Life A262

**1989, Nov. 27**
| | | | | |
|---|---|---|---|---|
| 843 | A262 | 10fr Grapsus grapsus | .20 | .20 |
| 844 | A262 | 60fr Hippocampus guttulatus | .80 | .50 |
| 845 | A262 | 145fr Lepas anatifera | 1.60 | .50 |
| 846 | A262 | 220fr Beach flea | 1.75 | .80 |
| | | Nos. 843-846 (4) | 4.35 | 1.70 |

Children's March to the Sanctuary A263

**1989, Dec. 9** Litho. Perf. 13½
| | | | | |
|---|---|---|---|---|
| 847 | A263 | 145fr shown | 1.10 | .40 |
| 848 | A263 | 180fr Church | 1.50 | .60 |

Pilgrimage to Notre Dame de Popenguine, cent.

Birds A263a

Designs: 10fr, Phalacrocovax carbolucidus, Anhinga rufa. 45fr, Lavius circocephalus, 100fr, Dwarf bee-eater, Lophogetus occipitalis. 180fr, Egretta gularis.

**1989, Dec. 11** Perf. 13
| | | | | |
|---|---|---|---|---|
| 849 | A263a | 10fr multicolored | .20 | .20 |
| 850 | A263a | 45fr multicolored | .80 | .25 |
| 851 | A263a | 100fr multicolored | 1.60 | .50 |
| 852 | A263a | 180fr multicolored | 4.50 | .90 |
| | | Nos. 849-852 (4) | 7.10 | 1.85 |

Natl. parks: Djoudj (10fr), Langue de Barbarie (45fr), Basse Casamance (100fr) and Saloum (180fr).

Christmas A264

**1989, Dec. 22** Litho. Perf. 13
| | | | | |
|---|---|---|---|---|
| 853 | A264 | 10fr shown | .20 | .20 |
| 854 | A264 | 25fr Teddy bear | .20 | .20 |
| 855 | A264 | 30fr Manger | .25 | .20 |
| 856 | A264 | 200fr Mother and child | 1.75 | .80 |
| | | Nos. 853-856 (4) | 2.40 | 1.40 |

Joan of Arc Institute, 50th Anniv. A265

**1989, Dec. 26** Perf. 13½
| | | | | |
|---|---|---|---|---|
| 857 | A265 | 25fr shown | .25 | .20 |
| 858 | A265 | 500fr Institute | 4.25 | 1.40 |

Flight of the 1st Seaplane, Mar. 28, 1910 — A266

**1989, Dec. 30** Perf. 13x12½, 12½x13 Litho.
| | | | | |
|---|---|---|---|---|
| 859 | A266 | 10fr shown | .90 | .20 |
| 860 | A266 | 125fr Seaplane, Fabre | 1.00 | .30 |
| 861 | A266 | 475fr Fabre, schematic of aircraft, vert. | 3.75 | .85 |
| | | Nos. 859-861 (3) | 5.65 | 1.35 |

**Souvenir Sheet**
| | | | | |
|---|---|---|---|---|
| 862 | A266 | 700fr like 475fr, vert. | 5.25 | 3.50 |

Henri Fabre (1882-1984), aviator.

Designs: 125fr, Seaplane, schematic of aircraft. 475fr, Fabre.

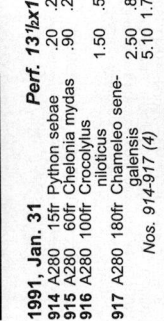

**1992 Summer Olympics, Barcelona — A267**

Various athletes and monuments or architecture.

Perf. 12½

1990, Jan. 8
| | | | | | |
|---|---|---|---|---|---|
| 863 | A267 | 10fr | Basketball | .20 | .20 |
| 864 | A267 | 130fr | High jump | .90 | .20 |
| 865 | A267 | 140fr | Discus | 1.25 | .30 |
| 866 | A267 | 190fr | Running | 1.50 | .40 |
| 867 | A267 | 315fr | Tennis | 2.25 | .50 |
| 868 | A267 | 475fr | Equestrian | 3.75 | .60 |
| | | Nos. 863-868 (6) | | 9.85 | 2.20 |

Souvenir Sheet

| | | | | | |
|---|---|---|---|---|---|
| 869 | A267 | 600fr | Soccer | 4.50 | 1.00 |

**Fight AIDS Worldwide A268**

Perf. 13½

1989, Dec. 1
| | | | | | |
|---|---|---|---|---|---|
| 870 | A268 | 5fr | shown | .20 | .20 |
| 871 | A268 | 100fr | Umbrella | .90 | .35 |
| 872 | A268 | 145fr | Fist crushing virus | 1.10 | .50 |
| 873 | A268 | 180fr | Hammering away at virus | 1.30 | .05 |
| | | Nos. 870-873 (4) | | 3.70 | 1.70 |

**12th Paris-Dakar Rally — A269**

Perf. 13

1990, Jan. 16
| | | | | | |
|---|---|---|---|---|---|
| 874 | A269 | 20fr | shown | .20 | .20 |
| 875 | A269 | 25fr | Motorcycle | .25 | .20 |
| 876 | A269 | 180fr | Trophy winner, crowd | 1.60 | .65 |
| 877 | A269 | 200fr | Thierry Sabine | 1.60 | .80 |
| | | Nos. 874-877 (4) | | 3.65 | 1.85 |

**1990 World Cup Soccer Championships, Italy — A270**

Various athletes and: 45fr, Trophy, the Piazza Della Signoria, Florence. 140fr, Piazza Navona, Rome. 180fr, The Virgin with St. Anne and the Infant Jesus, by Leonardo da Vinci. 220fr, Portrait of Giuseppe Garibaldi (1807-1882), Risorgimento Museum, Turin. 300fr, The Sistine Madonna, by Raphael. 415fr, The Virgin and Child, by Daniele da Volterra. 700fr, Columbus Monument, Milan.

Litho. Perf. 13x12½

1990, Jan. 31
| | | | | | |
|---|---|---|---|---|---|
| 878 | A270 | 45fr | multicolored | .35 | .20 |
| 879 | A270 | 140fr | multicolored | .85 | .30 |
| 880 | A270 | 180fr | multicolored | 1.25 | .40 |
| 881 | A270 | 220fr | multicolored | 1.40 | .50 |
| 882 | A270 | 300fr | multicolored | 2.10 | .65 |
| 883 | A270 | 415fr | multicolored | 2.75 | 1.00 |
| | | | | 8.70 | 3.05 |

Souvenir Sheet

Nos. 878-883 exist in souvenir sheets of 1.

| | | | | | |
|---|---|---|---|---|---|
| 884 | A270 | 700fr | multicolored | 5.00 | 1.40 |

**1990 African Soccer Cup Championships, Algeria — A271**

Litho. Perf. 13

1990, Mar. 2
| | | | | | |
|---|---|---|---|---|---|
| 885 | A271 | 20fr | shown | .20 | .20 |
| 886 | A271 | 60fr | Goalie | .55 | .25 |
| 887 | A271 | 100fr | Discus | | |
| 888 | A271 | 500fr | Ball, trophy | .90 / 4.50 | .40 / 1.75 |
| | | Nos. 885-888 (4) | | 6.15 | 2.60 |

**Postal Services — A272**

Litho. Perf. 13

1990, Apr. 30
| | | | | | |
|---|---|---|---|---|---|
| 889 | A272 | 5fr | Facsimile transmission | .20 | .20 |
| 890 | A272 | 15fr | Express mail | .20 | .20 |
| 891 | A272 | 100fr | Postal money orders | .75 | .30 |
| 892 | A272 | 180fr | CNE | 1.25 / 2.40 | .50 / 1.20 |
| | | Nos. 889-892 (4) | | | |

A273

A274

Perf. 13½

1990, May 31
| | | | | | |
|---|---|---|---|---|---|
| 893 | A273 | 145fr | shown | 1.00 | .40 |
| 894 | A273 | 180fr | Hand, wreath, envelope | 1.25 | .65 |

Multinational Postal School, 20th anniv.

1990, May 31
| | | | | | |
|---|---|---|---|---|---|
| 895 | A274 | 5fr | shown | .20 | .20 |
| 896 | A274 | 500fr | Family | 3.75 | 1.25 |

S.O.S. Children's Village appeal for aid.

**Boy Scouts A275**

Scouting emblems and: 30fr, Camping. 100fr, Hiking at lakeshore. 145fr, Following trail. 200fr, Scout, vert.

**Medicinal Plants — A276**

Litho. Perf. 11½

1990, Nov. 5
| | | | | | |
|---|---|---|---|---|---|
| 897 | A275 | 30fr | multicolored | .20 | .20 |
| 898 | A275 | 100fr | multicolored | .70 | .30 |
| 899 | A275 | 145fr | multicolored | 1.00 | .50 |
| 900 | A275 | 200fr | multicolored | 1.60 | .60 |
| | | Nos. 897-900 (4) | | 3.50 | 1.60 |

Perf. 13x13½

1990, Nov. 30
| | | | | | |
|---|---|---|---|---|---|
| 901 | A276 | 95fr | Cassia tora | 1.00 | .40 |
| 902 | A276 | 105fr | Tamarindus indica | 1.10 | .45 |
| 903 | A276 | 125fr | Cassia occidentalis | 1.40 | .55 |
| 904 | A276 | 175fr | Leptadenia hastata | 1.75 / 5.25 | .65 / 2.05 |
| | | Nos. 901-904 (4) | | | |

A277

A278

Christmas.

Litho. Perf. 13½

1990, Dec. 24
| | | | | | |
|---|---|---|---|---|---|
| 905 | A277 | 125fr | shown | .20 | .20 |
| 906 | A277 | 145fr | Angel, stars, people | 1.25 | .65 |
| 907 | A277 | 180fr | Adoration of the Magi | 1.60 | .65 |
| 908 | A277 | 200fr | Animals, baby in manger | 1.75 / 4.80 | .65 / 2.15 |
| | | Nos. 905-908 (4) | | | |

Intl. Red Cross, 125th Anniv. Senegalese Red Cross, 25th anniv. No. 909 inscribed 1988.

Litho. Perf. 13½x12½

1991, Jan. 2
| | | | | | |
|---|---|---|---|---|---|
| 909 | A278 | 180fr | multicolored | 1.50 | .65 |

**Paris-Dakar Rally — A279**

1991, Jan. 17
| | | | | | |
|---|---|---|---|---|---|
| 910 | A279 | 15fr | shown | .20 | .20 |
| 911 | A279 | 125fr | Car, motorcycle | .90 | .40 |
| 912 | A279 | 180fr | Car racing in water | 1.50 | .65 |
| 913 | A279 | 220fr | Two motorcycles, beach | 2.00 / 4.60 | .85 / 2.10 |
| | | Nos. 910-913 (4) | | | |

**Reptiles A280**

Perf. 13½x13

1991, Jan. 31
| | | | | | |
|---|---|---|---|---|---|
| 914 | A280 | 15fr | Python sebae | .20 | .20 |
| 915 | A280 | 60fr | Chelonia mydas | .90 | .20 |
| 916 | A280 | 100fr | Crocodylus niloticus | .50 | .50 |
| 917 | A280 | 180fr | Chameleo senegalensis | 1.50 / 2.50 | .50 / .85 |
| | | Nos. 914-917 (4) | | 5.10 | 1.75 |

Inscribed 1990.

**African Film Festival A281**

Designs: 30fr, Sphinx, slave house, cave paintings, tomb of Mohammed. 60fr, Dogon mask, mosque of Dioulasso, drawing of Osiris, man on camel. 100fr, Ruins, drum, statue of scribe, camels. 180fr, mask, mosque of Djenne, pyramids, Moroccan architecture.

Perf. 11½

1991, Feb. 23
| | | | | | |
|---|---|---|---|---|---|
| 918 | A281 | 30fr | org & multi | .25 | .20 |
| 919 | A281 | 60fr | org & multi | .50 | .25 |
| 920 | A281 | 100fr | org & multi | 1.00 | .45 |
| 921 | A281 | 180fr | org & multi | 1.75 / 3.50 | .65 / 1.55 |
| | | Nos. 918-921 (4) | | | |

**Alfred Nobel (1833-1896), Industrialist — A282**

Designs: 145fr, Drawing of Nobel.

Die Cut

Self-adhesive

Litho.

1991, Mar. 29
| | | | | | |
|---|---|---|---|---|---|
| 922 | A282 | 145fr | multi, vert. | 2.00 | .65 |
| 923 | A282 | 180fr | shown | 2.50 | .85 |

**Antelope — A283**

Litho. Perf. 13½x13

1991, Apr. 24
| | | | | | |
|---|---|---|---|---|---|
| 924 | A283 | 5fr | Ouerbia ourebi | .20 | .20 |
| 925 | A283 | 10fr | Gazella dorcas | .20 | .20 |
| 926 | A283 | 180fr | Kobos kob kob | 1.40 | .60 |
| 927 | A283 | 555fr | Alcelaphus bucelaphus major | 5.00 / 6.80 | 2.00 / 3.00 |
| | | Nos. 924-927 (4) | | | |

**Trees A284**

1991, May 30  Perf. 13½x13, 13x13½
| | | | | | |
|---|---|---|---|---|---|
| 928 | A284 | 90fr | Ancardium occidentalus | .75 | .40 |
| 929 | A284 | 100fr | Mangifera indica | 1.00 | .50 |
| 930 | A284 | 125fr | Borassus flabellifer, vert. | 1.00 | .50 |

931 A284 145fr Elaeis guineensis, vert. ............ 1.25 .60
*Nos. 928-931 (4)* ...... 4.00 2.00

Christopher Columbus — A285

100fr, Meeting Haitian natives, 145fr,
Columbus' personal coat of arms, vert. 180fr,
Santa Maria, Columbus. 200fr, 220fr, Colum-
bus, ships. 500fr, Details of voyages. 625fr,
Columbus at chart table.

**1991, July 8** **Litho.** **Perf. 13**
932 A285 100fr multicolored ....... .90 .40
a. Sheet of 1, perf. 12½ ....... .90 .40
933 A285 145fr multicolored ....... 1.25 .55
a. Sheet of 1, perf. 12½ ....... 1.25 .60
934 A285 180fr multicolored ....... 1.60 .60
a. Sheet of 1, perf. 12½ ....... 1.75 .75
935 A285 200fr multicolored ....... 1.75 .75
a. Sheet of 1, perf. 12½ ....... 1.75 .75
936 A285 220fr multicolored ....... 2.00 .80
a. Sheet of 1, perf. 12½ ....... 2.00 .80
937 A285 500fr multicolored ....... 4.50 1.90
a. Sheet of 1, perf. 12½ ....... 4.50 2.00
938 A285 625fr multicolored ....... 5.75 2.25
a. Sheet of 1, perf. 12½ ....... 5.75 2.50
*Nos. 932-938 (7)* ...... 17.75 7.30

Tourism
A286

**1991, July 30** **Litho.** **Perf. 13**
939 A286 10fr multicolored ....... .20 .20
940 A286 25fr multicolored ....... .20 .20
941 A286 30fr multicolored ....... .35 .20
942 A286 40fr multicolored ....... .35 .20
*Nos. 939-942 (4)* ...... 1.10 .80

Designs: 10fr, Canoe excursion, Basse-
Casamance. 25fr, Shore at Boufflers Hotel,
Goree Island. 30fr, Huts built on stilts,
Fadiouth Island. 40fr, Salt collecting on lake.

Dated 1989.

Louis Armstrong, Jazz Musician, 20th
Death Anniv. — A287

**1991, Oct. 7** **Perf. 13½**
943 A287 10fr shown ....... .20 .20
944 A287 145fr Singing ....... 1.25 .60
945 A287 180fr With trumpets ....... 1.50 .75
946 A287 220fr Playing trumpet ....... 1.75 .90
*Nos. 943-946 (4)* ...... 4.70 2.45

Yuri Gagarin, First Man in Space, 30th
Anniv. — A288

**1991, Nov. 25** **Litho.**
947 A288 15fr multicolored ....... .20 .20
948 A288 145fr multicolored ....... 1.25 .60
949 A288 180fr multicolored ....... 1.50 .75
950 A288 220fr multicolored ....... 1.75 .90
*Nos. 947-950 (4)* ...... 4.70 2.45

Various portraits of Gagarin with Vostok I in
Earth orbit.

---

Rural Water
Supply
Project — A289

**1991, Dec. 2** **Litho.** **Perf. 13½**
951 A289 30fr Bowl of water ....... .25 .20
952 A289 145fr Water faucet,
huts ....... 1.25 .65
953 A289 180fr Dripping faucet,
flags ....... 1.60 .80
954 A289 220fr Water tower, huts ....... 1.90 .95
*Nos. 951-954 (4)* ...... 5.00 2.60

6th Islamic
Summit — A290

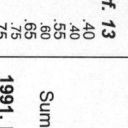

**1991, Dec. 9**
955 A290 15fr shown ....... .25 .20
956 A290 145fr Upraised hands ....... 1.25 .65
957 A290 180fr Congress Center,
Dakar ....... 1.60 .80
958 A290 220fr Grand Mosque,
Dakar ....... 1.90 .95
*Nos. 955-958 (4)* ...... 5.00 2.60

A291

**1991, Dec. 21** **Litho.** **Perf. 13½**
959 A291 125fr multicolored ....... 1.00 .50
960 A291 145fr multicolored ....... 1.25 .60
961 A291 180fr multicolored ....... 1.50 .75
962 A291 220fr multicolored ....... 1.75 .90
*Nos. 959-962 (4)* ...... 5.50 2.75

Basketball. Cent.: 145fr, Player dribbling
ball. 180fr, Couple holding trophy. 220fr, Lion,
basketball, trophies.

A292

**1991, Dec. 24** **Litho.** **Perf. 13½**
963 A292 5fr Jesus ....... .20 .20
964 A292 145fr Madonna and
Child ....... 1.25 .60
965 A292 160fr Angels ....... 1.40 .70
966 A292 220fr multicolored ....... 1.90 .95
*Nos. 963-966 (4)* ...... 4.75 2.45

Christmas. For surcharge see No. 975.

---

Jean Mermoz (1901-36), pilot.

Musical score and: 145fr, Bust of Mozart.
150fr, Mozart conducting. 180fr, Mozart at
piano. 220fr, Portrait.

**1991, Dec. 31** **Litho.**
967 A293 5fr multicolored ....... .20 .20
968 A293 150fr multicolored ....... 1.25 .65
969 A293 180fr multicolored ....... 1.60 .80
970 A293 220fr multicolored ....... 1.90 .95
*Nos. 967-970 (4)* ...... 5.00 2.60

Wolfgang Amadeus Mozart, death bicent.

**1991?** **Litho.** **Perf. 13½**
970A A293a 15fr multicolored ....... .20 .20
970B A293a 150fr multicolored ....... 1.00 .35
970C A293a 180fr multicolored ....... 1.50 .35
970D A293a 200fr multicolored ....... 2.00 .65

Mermoz and: 145fr, Outline maps of South
America, Africa. 180fr, Airplane. 200fr, Airplane
in flight.

Nos. 970A-970D exist in imperf. souvenir
sheets of 1.

**1992, Jan. 12** **Litho.** **Perf. 13½**
971 A294 10fr shown ....... .20 .20
972 A294 145fr Map, soccer balls ....... 1.25 .60
973 A294 200fr Lion, trophy ....... 1.60 .85
974 A294 220fr Players ....... 1.75 .90
*Nos. 971-974 (4)* ...... 4.80 2.55

18th African Soccer Cup Championships.

A293a

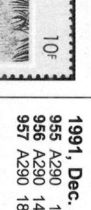

A294

---

Senegal's
Participation in
Gulf War — A296

Designs: 30fr, Oil wells, flag and missiles.
145fr, Oil wells, soldier. 180fr, Holy Ka'aba,
soldier with gun. 220fr, Peace dove with flag,
map.

**1992, Apr. 4** **Perf. 13½**
980 A296 30fr multicolored ....... .25 .20
981 A296 145fr multicolored ....... 1.25 .60
982 A296 180fr multicolored ....... 1.75 .90
983 A296 220fr multicolored ....... 4.75 2.45
*Nos. 980-983 (4)* ......

Fish
Industry
A297

Stylized designs: 5fr, Catching fish. 60fr,
Retail outlets. 100fr, Processing plant. 150fr,
Packaging.

**1992, Apr. 6** **Litho.** **Perf. 13½**
984 A297 5fr multicolored ....... .20 .20
985 A297 60fr multicolored ....... .55 .30
986 A297 100fr multicolored ....... .90 .45
987 A297 150fr multicolored ....... 1.25 .65
*Nos. 984-987 (4)* ...... 2.90 1.60

Tourism — A298

**1992, May 5** **Perf. 13½x13, 13x13½**
988 A298 5fr Niokolo complex ....... .20 .20
989 A298 10fr Casamance River ....... .20 .20
990 A298 150fr Dakar region ....... 1.25 .65
991 A298 200fr Saint-Louis excursion ....... 1.75 .95
*Nos. 988-991 (4)* ...... 3.40 2.00

---

National
Parks
A295

**1992, Mar. 20** **Perf. 13½x13**
976 A295 10fr Delta Du Saloum ....... .45 .20
977 A295 125fr Djoudj ....... 1.60 .50
978 A295 145fr Niokolo-Koba ....... 2.25 .60
979 A295 220fr Basse
Casamance ....... 2.75 .90
*Nos. 976-979 (4)* ...... 7.05 2.20

No. 965 Surcharged

**1992, Feb. 19** **Litho.** **Perf. 13½**
975 A292 180fr on 160fr ....... 2.00 1.00

Planting
Trees
A299

Various designs showing children planting
trees.

**1992, May 29** **Perf. 13½x13, 13x13½**
992 A299 145fr multi ....... 1.25 .65
993 A299 180fr multi ....... 1.60 .65
994 A299 200fr multi ....... 1.75 .90
995 A299 220fr multi, vert. ....... 1.90 1.10
*Nos. 992-995 (4)* ...... 6.50 3.30

Public
Works
Projects
A300

**1992, June 1** **Perf. 13½x13, 13x13½**
996 A300 25fr multi ....... .25 .20
997 A300 150fr multi ....... 1.25 .65
998 A300 180fr multi, vert. ....... 1.60 .80
999 A300 220fr multi, vert. ....... 2.00 1.00
*Nos. 996-999 (4)* ...... 5.10 2.65

Various scenes of people cleaning and
repairing public walkways.

**Environmental Protection — A314**

**Accident Prevention A315**

Designs: 20fr, Medical clinic. 25fr, Preventing industrial accidents. 145fr, Preventing chemical spills. 200fr, Red Cross helicopter, airline crash.

**1993, Mar. 22**    *Perf. 13 (#1052, 1055), 13½*    **Litho.**

| | | | | | |
|---|---|---|---|---|---|
| 1052 | A314 | 20fr | multicolored | .20 | .20 |
| 1053 | A315 | 25fr | multicolored | .20 | .20 |
| 1054 | A315 | 145fr | multicolored | 1.10 | .60 |
| 1055 | A314 | 200fr | multicolored | 1.60 | .80 |

Nos. 1052-1055 (4)    3.10 1.80

**Abdoulaye Seck Marie Parsine (1873-1931), PTT Director — A316**

**1993, Apr. 21**    **Litho.**    *Perf. 13½*

1056   A316   220fr multicolored   2.10   .90

**Wild Animals A317**

30fr, Crocuta crocuta. 50fr, Panthora leo. 70fr, Panthera pardus. 150fr, Giraffa camelopardalis peralta, vert. 100fr, Cervus.

**1993, Nov. 26**    **Litho.**    *Perf. 13½*

| | | | | | |
|---|---|---|---|---|---|
| 1057 | A317 | 30fr | multicolored | .20 | .20 |
| 1058 | A317 | 50fr | multicolored | .25 | .20 |
| 1059 | A317 | 70fr | multicolored | .55 | .20 |
| 1060 | A317 | 100fr | multicolored | 1.00 | .30 |
| 1061 | A317 | 150fr | multicolored | 1.60 | .35 |

Nos. 1057-1061 (5)    3.60 1.25

**Christmas A318**

Designs: 80fr, Two children seated by Christmas tree. 145fr, Santa holding presents, three children. 150fr, Girl, Santa with present.

**1993, Dec. 24**    **Litho.**    *Perf. 13x13½*

| | | | | | |
|---|---|---|---|---|---|
| 1062 | A318 | 5fr | multicolored | .20 | .20 |
| 1063 | A318 | 80fr | multicolored | .30 | .30 |
| 1064 | A318 | 145fr | multicolored | .55 | .30 |
| 1065 | A318 | 150fr | multicolored | .60 | .30 |

Nos. 1062-1065 (4)    1.65 1.00

---

15fr, Astronaut in spacesuit, flag, map, spacecraft, horiz. 145fr, American flag, Glenn, horiz. 180fr, Flag, lift-off of rocket, Glenn in spacesuit, horiz. 200fr, Astronaut in spacesuit, spacecraft.

**1992, Nov. 30**    **Litho.**    *Perf. 13½*

| | | | | | |
|---|---|---|---|---|---|
| 1036 | A310 | 15fr | multicolored | .20 | .20 |
| 1037 | A310 | 145fr | multicolored | 1.25 | .60 |
| 1038 | A310 | 180fr | multicolored | 1.60 | .70 |
| 1039 | A310 | 200fr | multicolored | 1.75 | .80 |

Nos. 1036-1039 (4)    4.80 2.30

**Maps Featuring Bakari II — A311**

100fr, Map from Spanish Atlas, 1375, 145fr, Stone head, Vera Cruz, Mexico, world map, 1413.

**1992, Dec. 2**    *Perf. 13*

1040   A311   100fr multicolored   1.50   .40
1041   A311   145fr multicolored   2.25   .60

No. 1041 issued only with black bar obliterating "Mecades."

**Biennial of Dakar — A312**

20fr, Picture frame. 50fr, Puppet head, stage. 145fr, Open book. 220fr, Musical instrument.

**1992, Dec. 14**    *Perf. 13½*

| | | | | | |
|---|---|---|---|---|---|
| 1042 | A312 | 20fr | multicolored | .20 | .20 |
| 1043 | A312 | 50fr | multicolored | .45 | .20 |
| 1044 | A312 | 145fr | multicolored | 1.25 | .60 |
| 1045 | A312 | 220fr | multicolored | 2.10 | .90 |

Nos. 1042-1045 (4)    4.00 1.90

**Christmas A313**

Designs: 15fr, Children dancing around large ornament, horiz. 145fr, Christmas tree. 180fr, Jesus Christ. 200fr, Santa Claus.

**1992, Dec. 24**    *Perf. 13½*

| | | | | | |
|---|---|---|---|---|---|
| 1046 | A313 | 15fr | multicolored | .20 | .20 |
| 1047 | A313 | 145fr | multicolored | 2.00 | .60 |
| 1048 | A313 | 180fr | multicolored | 2.50 | .70 |
| 1049 | A313 | 200fr | multicolored | 2.75 | .90 |

Nos. 1046-1049 (4)    7.45 2.40

**Nos. 770, 804 Surcharged in Red**

**1993, Jan. 17**    **Litho.**    *Perf. 13½*

1050   A251   145fr on 180fr #804   1.50   .85

         *Perf. 13*

1051   A241   220fr on 410fr #770   2.25 1.00

Size and location of surcharge varies.

---

**Corals A306**

Various coral formations.

     *Perf. 13½x13, 13x13½*

**1992, Sept. 18**    **Litho.**

| | | | | | |
|---|---|---|---|---|---|
| 1020 | A306 | 50fr | multicolored | .40 | .20 |
| 1021 | A306 | 100fr | multicolored | .85 | .40 |
| 1022 | A306 | 145fr | multi, vert. | 1.25 | .60 |
| 1023 | A306 | 220fr | multicolored | 4.25 | 2.10 |

Nos. 1020-1023 (4)

**Konrad Adenauer (1876-1967) — A307**

Designs: 5fr, Portrait, vert. 145fr, Schaumburg Palace, Bonn. 180fr, Hands clasped. 220fr, Map of West Germany.

     *Perf. 13x13½, 13½x13*

**1992, Sept. 30**    **Litho.**

| | | | | | |
|---|---|---|---|---|---|
| 1024 | A307 | 5fr | multicolored | .20 | .20 |
| 1025 | A307 | 145fr | multicolored | 1.25 | .60 |
| 1026 | A307 | 180fr | multicolored | 1.50 | .75 |
| 1027 | A307 | 220fr | multicolored | 1.75 | .90 |

Nos. 1024-1027 (4)    4.70 2.45

**Shellfish — A308**

**1992, Oct. 1**    **Litho.**    *Perf. 13½*

| | | | | | |
|---|---|---|---|---|---|
| 1028 | A308 | 20fr | Crab | .20 | .20 |
| 1029 | A308 | 30fr | Spider crab | .35 | .20 |
| 1030 | A308 | 180fr | Lobster | 1.75 | .70 |
| 1031 | A308 | 200fr | Shrimp | 2.10 | .75 |

Nos. 1028-1031 (4)    4.40 1.85

**Fruit-bearing Plants — A309**

**1992, Oct. 16**    **Litho.**    *Perf. 13x13½*

| | | | | | |
|---|---|---|---|---|---|
| 1032 | A309 | 10fr | Parkia biglobosa | .20 | .20 |
| 1033 | A309 | 50fr | Balanites aegyptiaca | .45 | .20 |
| 1034 | A309 | 200fr | Parinari macrophylla | 1.60 | .70 |
| 1035 | A309 | 220fr | Opuntiatuna | 1.75 | .90 |

Nos. 1032-1035 (4)    4.00 2.00

**John Glenn's Orbital Flight, 30th Anniv. — A310**

---

**Children's Rights — A301**

**1992, June 12**    *Perf. 13*

| | | | | | |
|---|---|---|---|---|---|
| 1000 | A301 | 20fr | Education | .20 | .20 |
| 1001 | A301 | 45fr | Guidance | .40 | .70 |
| 1002 | A301 | 165fr | Instruction | 1.40 | .80 |
| 1003 | A301 | 180fr | Health care | 1.60 | 1.90 |

Nos. 1000-1003 (4)    3.60

**African Integration A302**

**1992, June 29**    **Litho.**    *Perf. 13*

| | | | | | |
|---|---|---|---|---|---|
| 1004 | A302 | 10fr | Free trade | .20 | .20 |
| 1005 | A302 | 30fr | Youth activities | .25 | .20 |
| 1006 | A302 | 145fr | Communications | 1.25 | .60 |
| 1007 | A302 | 220fr | Women's movements | 2.00 | 1.00 |

Nos. 1004-1007 (4)    3.70 2.00

**1992 Summer Olympics, Barcelona A303**

**Blue Train — A304**

**1992, July 25**    **Litho.**    *Perf. 13½*

| | | | | | |
|---|---|---|---|---|---|
| 1008 | A303 | 145fr | Map, horiz. | 1.10 | .55 |
| 1009 | A303 | 145fr | Runner | 1.50 | .70 |
| 1010 | A303 | 300fr | Sprinter, horiz. | 2.75 | 1.10 |
| 1011 | A303 | 300fr | Torch bearer | 7.35 | 3.10 |

Nos. 1008-1011 (4)

**1992, Aug. 3**

| | | | | | |
|---|---|---|---|---|---|
| 1012 | A304 | 70fr | shown | .70 | .30 |
| 1013 | A304 | 145fr | Train yard | 1.40 | .55 |
| 1014 | A304 | 200fr | Train, passengers | 2.00 | .75 |
| 1015 | A304 | 220fr | Station | 2.10 | .85 |

Nos. 1012-1015 (4)    6.20 2.45

**Int'l. Maritime Heritage Year — A305**

25fr, Map of Antarctica. 100fr, Ocean, sea life. 180fr, Man addressing UN. 220fr, Hands holding globe, flags, ship, fish.

**1992, Sept. 4**

| | | | | | |
|---|---|---|---|---|---|
| 1016 | A305 | 25fr | multi, horiz. | .20 | .20 |
| 1017 | A305 | 100fr | multi | .90 | .35 |
| 1018 | A305 | 180fr | multi | 1.60 | .65 |
| 1019 | A305 | 220fr | multi | 2.00 | .80 |

Nos. 1016-1019 (4)    4.70 2.00

Paris-Dakar Rally, 16th Anniv. — A319

Designs: 145fr, Truck, car, motorcycle racing by tree. 180fr, Racing through desert, men with camel. 220fr, Car, truck, village.

**1994, Jan. 5**                   **Perf. 13½**
1066  A319  145fr  multicolored  .70  .30
1067  A319  180fr  multicolored  .90  .35
1068  A319  220fr  multicolored  1.00  .45
    Nos. 1066-1068 (3)  2.60  1.10

Assassination of John F. Kennedy, 30th Anniv. — A320

**1993, Dec. 31**   Litho.   **Perf. 13**
1069  A320  80fr  shown  .30  .20
1070  A320  555fr  Kennedy, White
    House  2.25  1.10

Fishing Industry A321

Design: 80fr, Drying eels. 90fr, Salting fish. 200fr, Sifting for shellfish. 100fr, Cooking fish.

**1994, Feb. 28**   Litho.
1071  A321  5fr  multicolored  .20  .20
1072  A321  90fr  multicolored  .35  .20
1073  A321  100fr  multicolored  .40  .20
1074  A321  200fr  multicolored  .80  .40
    Nos. 1071-1074 (4)  1.75  1.00

Flowers — A321a

Design: 80fr, Gloriosa superba. 100fr, Erythrina senegalensis. 145fr, Spathodea campanulata.

**Perf. 13¼x13½, 13½**
1074A  A321a  80fr  multi  4.00  —
1074B  A321a  100fr  multi  —  5.75
1074C  A321a  145fr  multi

No. 1074A dated 1993. Two additional stamps were issued in this set. Two additional stamps were issued in 1993. The editors would like to examine any examples.

Conservation of the Seashore — A322

Stylized designs: 5fr, Halting removal of sand. 75fr, Fight against drifting sand dunes. 100fr, Dams, dikes against beach erosion. 200fr, Healthy, aesthetic environment.

---

S.O.S. Elephant A323

**1994, Mar. 7**
1075  A322  5fr  multicolored  .20  .20
1076  A322  75fr  multicolored  .30  .20
1077  A322  100fr  multicolored  .55  .40
1078  A322  200fr  multicolored  .80  .60
    Nos. 1075-1078 (4)  1.85  1.40

**1994, Apr. 18**
1079  A323  30fr  shown  .20  .20
1080  A323  60fr  Elephant in "SOS"  .35  .20
1081  A323  90fr  Elephant form-
    ing "SOS"  .65  .25
1082  A323  145fr  Elephant, tusks  .85  .30
    Nos. 1079-1082 (4)  2.05  .95

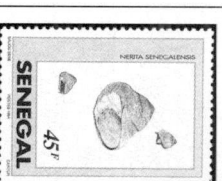

Arrival of Portuguese in Senegal, 550th Anniv. A324

**1994, Nov. 17**   Litho.   **Perf. 12**
1083  A324  175fr  multicolored  .80  .40

See Portugal No. 2036.

A326

Shells: 20fr, Murex saxatilis, horiz. 45fr, Nerita senegalensis. 75fr, Polymita picea, horiz. 175fr, Scalaria pretiosa. 215fr, Conus gloria maris.

**1994, Oct. 3**   Litho.   **Perf. 13½**
1084  A325  20fr  multicolored  .20  .20
1085  A325  45fr  multicolored  .20  .20
1086  A325  175fr  multi, horiz.  .75  .40
1087  A325  175fr  multicolored  .75  .40
1088  A325  215fr  multicolored  .95  .50
    Nos. 1084-1088 (5)  2.85  2.00

**1994, Nov. 4**
1089  A326  175fr  multi, horiz.  .75  .40
1090  A326  215fr  multi, horiz.  .95  .50
1091  A326  275fr  multicolored  1.25  .60
1092  A326  290fr  multi, diff.  1.25  .65
    Nos. 1089-1092 (4)  4.20  2.15

Intl. Olympic Committee, Cent.

---

African Children's Day A329

**1994, June 16**   Litho.   **Perf. 13½**
1100  A328  175fr  multicolored  .80  .40
1101  A328  215fr  multicolored  1.00  .50

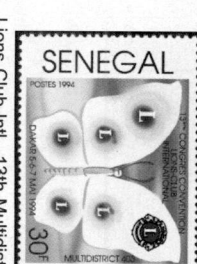

Lions Club Intl., 13th Multidistrict Convention, Dakar — A328

**1994, May 5**   Litho.   **Perf. 13½x13**
1098  A328  30fr  shown  .30  .20
1099  A328  60fr  Emblem, butter-
    fly  .30  .20
1100  A328  175fr  Emblem, "L's"  .85  .40
1101  A328  215fr  Colors, emblem  1.00  .50
    Nos. 1098-1101 (4)  2.35  1.30

1096  A327  175fr  Manis gigantea  .75  .40
1097  A327  215fr  Varanus niloticus  .95  .45
    Nos. 1093-1097 (5)  2.75  1.50

UNICEF emblem and: 175fr, Children playing. 215fr, Family, huts.

**1994, June 16**   Litho.   **Perf. 13½**
1102  A329  175fr  multicolored  2.00  1.00
1103  A329  215fr  multicolored  2.25  .50

1994 World Cup Soccer Championships, US — A330

Designs: 45fr, Flags of participants, soccer ball, vert. 75fr, Top of globe, bottom of soccer ball, vert. 215fr, Player. 665fr, Two players.

**1994, June 17**
1104  A330  45fr  multicolored  .20  .20
1105  A330  75fr  multicolored  .80  .50
1106  A330  215fr  multicolored  1.00  .50
1107  A330  665fr  multicolored  3.00  1.50
    Nos. 1104-1107 (4)  5.00  2.60

UPU Congress, Seoul — A331

**1994, Aug. 16**   Litho.   **Perf. 13½x13**
1108  A331  10fr  Rainbow  .20  .20

UPU Congress Type of 1994
**1994, Aug. 16**   Litho.   **Perf. 13½x13**
1110  A331  260fr  Stylized stamp  .50  .25

Two additional stamps were released in this set. The editors would like to examine them.

Intl. Year of the Family A333

---

**1994, Aug. 19**                   **Perf. 13½x13**
1113  A333  5fr  multicolored  .20  .20
1114  A333  175fr  multicolored  .80  .40
1115  A333  215fr  multicolored  1.00  .50
1116  A333  290fr  multicolored  1.40  .70
    Nos. 1113-1116 (4)  3.40  1.80

10th Toulouse to Saint-Louis Air Rally — A334

**1994, Apr. 10**                   **Perf. 13½**
1117  A334  100fr  Breguet 14  .50  .25
1118  A334  175fr  Guillaumet  .65  .35
1119  A334  185fr  Jean Mermoz  .85  .40
1120  A334  220fr  Saint-Exupery  1.00  .50
    Nos. 1117-1120 (4)  3.00  1.50

Dated 1993.

Christmas — A335

175fr, Santa Claus, children, presents. 215fr, Christmas scenes, religious scenes. 275fr, Magi, Christ Child. 290fr, Madonna & Child.

**1994, Nov. 24**   **Perf. 13x13½, 13½x13**
1121  A335  175fr  multi, vert.  .80  .40
1122  A335  215fr  multi, vert.  1.00  .65
1123  A335  275fr  multi  1.25  .70
1124  A335  290fr  multi, vert.  4.45  2.25
    Nos. 1121-1124 (4)  4.45  2.25

Historical Sites — A336

Designs: 100fr, Goree Chateau. 175fr, Soudan Mansion. 215fr, Goree Island. 275fr, Laprade fort, Sedhiou.

**1994, Mar. 20**   Litho.   **Perf. 13½x13**
1125  A336  100fr  multicolored  .45  .20
1126  A336  175fr  multicolored  .80  .40
1127  A336  215fr  multicolored  1.00  .65
1128  A336  275fr  multicolored  1.25  .65
    Nos. 1125-1128 (4)  3.50  1.75

Kalissaye Natl. Park A337

Water birds: 100fr, Ardea melanocephala, vert. 275fr, Sterna caspia, vert. 290fr, Egretta gularis, vert. 380fr, Pelecanus rufescens.

**1995, Feb. 2**                   **Perf. 13½**
1129  A337  100fr  multicolored  .45  .25
1130  A337  275fr  multicolored  1.25  .65
1131  A337  290fr  multicolored  1.40  .70
1132  A337  380fr  multicolored  1.75  .85
    Nos. 1129-1132 (4)  4.85  2.40

## Fashion Type of 1972

**1995, June 30**   **Perf. 13½x13**   **Size: 21x26mm**

| No. | Type | Denom. | Description | | |
|---|---|---|---|---|---|
| 1153 | A106 | 5fr | light brown | .20 | .20 |
| 1154 | A106 | 10fr | bright green | .20 | .20 |
| 1155 | A106 | 20fr | henna brown | .20 | .20 |
| 1156 | A106 | 25fr | olive | .20 | .20 |
| 1157 | A106 | 30fr | light olive | .20 | .20 |
| 1158 | A106 | 40fr | yellow green | .20 | .20 |
| 1159 | A106 | 100fr | slate blue | .50 | .50 |
| 1160 | A106 | 150fr | deep blue | .75 | .35 |
| 1161 | A106 | 175fr | dull brown | .90 | .45 |
| 1162 | A106 | 200fr | black | 1.00 | .50 |
| 1163 | A106 | 250fr | red | 1.25 | .60 |
| 1164 | A106 | 275fr | rose carmine | 1.40 | .80 |
|  |  |  | Nos. 1153-1164 (12) | 7.00 | 4.15 |

### Economic Community of West African States (ECOWAS), 20th Anniv. — A343

Designs: 175fr, Satellite dish, telephone, computer, map, dam, vert. 215fr, Flags of member nations, fruits, vegetables.

**1995, Sept. 11**   **Litho.**   **Perf. 13½**
| 1165 | A343 | 175fr | multicolored | .90 | .45 |
|---|---|---|---|---|---|
| 1166 | A343 | 215fr | multicolored | 1.10 | .55 |

### Louis Pasteur (1822-95) — A345

275fr, Holding vial. 500fr, In laboratory.

**1995, Sept. 28**   **Litho.**   **Perf. 11½**
| 1168 | A345 | 275fr | multicolored | 1.25 | .60 |
|---|---|---|---|---|---|
| 1169 | A345 | 500fr | multicolored | 2.25 | 1.25 |

### Motion Pictures, Cent. A346

Early developments by Lumiere Brothers: 100fr, Scene from "The Water Sprinkler." 200fr, First public showing of motion picture. 250fr, Auguste, Louis Lumiere watching picture of train arriving at station. 275fr, Demonstrating cinematography.

**1995, Oct. 2**   **Perf. 13½**
| 1170 | A346 | 100fr | multicolored | .45 | .20 |
|---|---|---|---|---|---|
| 1171 | A346 | 200fr | multicolored | 1.00 | .45 |
| 1172 | A346 | 250fr | multicolored | 1.25 | .55 |
| 1173 | A346 | 275fr | multicolored | 1.75 | .70 |
|  |  |  | Nos. 1170-1173 (4) | 4.45 | 1.90 |

### FAO, 50th Anniv. A347

Designs: 175fr, Farmer, oxen. 215fr, Technician, bringing water to arid regions. 260fr, Gathering fish. 275fr, Nutrition of infants.

**1995, Oct. 16**
| 1174 | A347 | 175fr | multicolored | .80 | .40 |
|---|---|---|---|---|---|
| 1175 | A347 | 215fr | multicolored | .95 | .50 |
| 1176 | A347 | 260fr | multicolored | 1.10 | .55 |
| 1177 | A347 | 275fr | multicolored | 1.25 | .60 |
|  |  |  | Nos. 1174-1177 (4) | 4.10 | 2.05 |

---

### UN, 50th anniv. A348

**1995, Nov. 2**
| 1178 | A348 | 275fr | shown | 1.25 | .60 |
|---|---|---|---|---|---|
| 1179 | A348 | 1000fr | Building | 4.25 | 2.00 |

### La Francophonie, 25th anniv. A349

| 1180 | A349 | 150fr | shown | .70 | .35 |
|---|---|---|---|---|---|
| 1181 | A349 | 500fr | Contestants | 2.25 | 1.10 |

### Wild Animals A350

Designs: a, 90fr, Syncerus nanus savanensis. b, 150fr, Phacochoerus aethiopicus. c, 175fr, Tragelaphus scriptus. d, 275fr, Goechelone sulcata. e, 300fr, Hystrix cristata.

**1995, Nov. 13**   **Perf. 13½**
| 1182 | A350 | Strip of 5, #a.-e. | 5.75 | 5.75 |
|---|---|---|---|---|

### Endangered Birds — A351

Designs: 45fr, Meganostoma eurydice. 100fr, Luehdorfia japonica. 200fr, Hebomoia glaucippe. 220fr, Aglais urticae.

**1995, Nov. 30**   **Perf. 13½x13**
| 1183 | A351 | 90fr | Hydroprogne caspia | .45 | .20 |
|---|---|---|---|---|---|
| 1184 | A351 | 145fr | Gelochelidon nilotica | .80 | .30 |
| 1185 | A351 | 150fr | Sterna maxima | 1.40 | .35 |
| 1186 | A351 | 180fr | Sterna hirunda | 1.75 | .55 |
|  |  |  | Nos. 1183-1186 (4) | 4.40 | 1.40 |

### Butterflies A352

**1995, Dec. 4**   **Perf. 13**
| 1187 | A352 | 45fr | multicolored | .35 | .20 |
|---|---|---|---|---|---|
| 1188 | A352 | 100fr | multicolored | .65 | .45 |
| 1189 | A352 | 200fr | multicolored | 1.60 | .45 |
| 1190 | A352 | 220fr | multicolored | 2.00 | .55 |
|  |  |  | Nos. 1187-1190 (4) | 4.60 | 1.40 |

### Tourism A353

---

## Dinosaurs A338

**1995, Jan. 27**
| 1133 | A338 | 100fr | Diplodocus | .45 | .20 |
|---|---|---|---|---|---|
| 1134 | A338 | 175fr | Brontosaurus | .75 | .40 |
| 1135 | A338 | 215fr | Triceratops | 1.00 | .50 |
| 1136 | A338 | 290fr | Stegosaurus | 1.40 | .70 |
| 1137 | A338 | 300fr | Tyrannosaurus | 1.40 | .70 |
|  |  |  | Nos. 1133-1137 (5) | 5.00 | 2.50 |

### House of Slaves, Goree A339

**1994**   **Litho.**   **Perf. 13½**
| 1138 | A339 | 500fr | multicolored | 2.50 | 1.25 |
|---|---|---|---|---|---|

### Flowers — A340

Designs: 30fr, Bombax costatum. 75fr, Allamanda cathartica. 100fr, Catharanthus roseus. 1000fr, Clerodendron speciossimum.

**1995, Apr. 9**
| 1139 | A340 | 30fr | multicolored | .20 | .20 |
|---|---|---|---|---|---|
| 1140 | A340 | 75fr | multicolored | .40 | .20 |
| 1141 | A340 | 100fr | multicolored | .50 | .20 |
| 1142 | A340 | 1000fr | multicolored | 5.00 | 2.50 |
|  |  |  | Nos. 1139-1142 (4) | 6.10 | 3.15 |

### A341 / A342

District 9100 Conference of Rotary, Intl.

**1995, May 11**   **Litho.**   **Perf. 11½**
| 1143 | A341 | 260fr | shown | 1.25 | .65 |
|---|---|---|---|---|---|
| 1144 | A341 | 275fr | Emblem, dove | 1.40 | .70 |

**1995, June 17**

Map of Africa with countries highlighted, native item or animal: 10fr, Sudan, musical instrument. 15fr, Dahomey (Benin), huts, canoes. 30fr, Ivory Coast, elephant. 70fr, Mauritania, camel. 175fr, Guinea, string instrument, bananas. 180fr, Upper Volta (Burkina Faso), ox, vegetables. 215fr, Niger, Cross of Agadès. 225fr, Senegal, lions.

| 1145 | A342 | 10fr | multicolored | .20 | .20 |
|---|---|---|---|---|---|
| 1146 | A342 | 15fr | multicolored | .20 | .20 |
| 1147 | A342 | 30fr | multicolored | .35 | .20 |
| 1148 | A342 | 70fr | multicolored | .90 | .45 |
| 1149 | A342 | 175fr | multicolored | .95 | .45 |
| 1150 | A342 | 180fr | multicolored | 1.10 | .55 |
| 1151 | A342 | 215fr | multicolored | 1.25 | .60 |
| 1152 | A342 | 225fr | multicolored | 5.15 | 2.85 |
|  |  |  | Nos. 1145-1152 (8) | | |

---

### Bassari Festival A354 / A355

**1995, Dec. 28**   **Perf. 13½**
| 1191 | A353 | 100fr | Baawnaan, vert. | .45 | .20 |
|---|---|---|---|---|---|
| 1192 | A353 | 175fr | Traditional huts | .80 | .40 |
| 1193 | A353 | 220fr | Turu | 1.00 | .50 |
| 1194 | A353 | 500fr | | 2.25 | 1.10 |
|  |  |  | Nos. 1191-1194 (4) | 4.50 | 2.20 |

Paris-Granada-Dakar Rally, 17th Anniv.: 215fr, Car, silhouettes of three people. 275fr, Man racing on motorcycle, vert. 290fr, Car under Eiffel Tower, car racing toward finish line. 665fr, Two cars going over hill.

**1996, Jan. 16**   **Litho.**   **Perf. 11½**
| 1195 | A354 | 215fr | multicolored | 1.10 | .60 |
|---|---|---|---|---|---|
| 1196 | A354 | 275fr | multicolored | 1.50 | .75 |
| 1197 | A354 | 290fr | multicolored | 1.60 | .80 |
| 1198 | A354 | 665fr | multicolored | 3.50 | 1.75 |
|  |  |  | Nos. 1195-1198 (4) | 7.70 | 3.90 |

**1996, Feb.2**

Flowers: 175fr, Gossypium barbadense. 275fr, Hibiscus sabdariffa. 290fr, Hibiscus asper. 500fr, Nymphaea lotus.

| 1199 | A355 | 175fr | multicolored | .95 | .45 |
|---|---|---|---|---|---|
| 1200 | A355 | 275fr | multicolored | 1.50 | .75 |
| 1201 | A355 | 290fr | multicolored | 1.60 | .80 |
| 1202 | A355 | 500fr | multicolored | 2.75 | 1.40 |
|  |  |  | Nos. 1199-1202 (4) | 6.80 | 3.40 |

### Sports A356

**1996, Mar. 29**   **Litho.**   **Perf. 11½**
| 1203 | A366 | 12fr | Boxing | .65 | .35 |
|---|---|---|---|---|---|
| 1204 | A356 | 215fr | Judo | 1.10 | .60 |
| 1205 | A356 | 275fr | Javelin | 1.50 | .75 |
| 1206 | A356 | 320fr | Discus | 1.75 | .90 |
|  |  |  | Nos. 1203-1206 (4) | 5.00 | 2.60 |

### Art by Serge Correa, Hall of Pearls A357

**1996, Apr. 18**
| 1207 | A357 | 260fr | Corridor 1 | 1.25 | .70 |
|---|---|---|---|---|---|
| 1208 | A357 | 320fr | Symphony 1 | 1.75 | .85 |

### National Parks A358

Designs: 175fr, Dolphin, flamingo, heron, Saloum Delta. 200fr, Chimpanze, giraffe, elephant, Niokolo-Koba. 220fr, Crustaceans, bird in cave, Madeleine Island. 275fr, Abyssinia hornbill, crocodile, hippopotamus, Basse Casamance.

**1996, Mar. 4**
| 1209 | A358 | 175fr | multicolored | .95 | .50 |
|---|---|---|---|---|---|
| 1210 | A358 | 200fr | multicolored | 1.10 | .55 |
| 1211 | A358 | 220fr | multicolored | 1.25 | .60 |
| 1212 | A358 | 275fr | multicolored | 1.50 | .75 |
|  |  |  | Nos. 1209-1212 (4) | 4.80 | 2.40 |

**1996, Dec. 11**

| | | |
|---|---|---|
| 1226 | A364 | 75fr shown |
| 1227 | A364 | 275fr Child, diff. |

UNICEF,
50th
Anniv.
A364

**Perf. 13½x13**
.30 .20
1.25 .60

---

Designs: 10fr, Cercopithecus aethiops. 30fr, Erthrocebus patas. 90fr, Cercopithecus campbelli. 215fr, Pantroglodytes verus. 260fr, Papio papio.

**1996, Nov. 29    Litho.    Perf. 13½x13½**

| | | |
|---|---|---|
| 1221 | A363 | 10fr multicolored | .20 .20 |
| 1222 | A363 | 30fr multicolored | .20 .20 |
| 1223 | A363 | 90fr multicolored | .35 .20 |
| 1224 | A363 | 215fr multicolored | .85 .45 |
| 1225 | A363 | 260fr multicolored | 1.00 .50 |
| a. | | Strip of 5, #1221-1225 | 3.50 2.00 |

Primates
A363

**1996, Oct. 21**

1220 A362 275fr multicolored

**Perf. 12½**
1.50 .75

Red Cross of
Senegal — A362

215fr, UN emblem, hand holding red stop sign, drug paraphernalia.

Decade of
UN Against
Illegal Drug
Abuse and
Trafficking
A361

**1996, June 21    Perf. 13½**

| | | |
|---|---|---|
| 1218 | A361 | 175fr multicolored | .95 .50 |
| 1219 | A361 | 215fr multicolored | 1.10 .60 |

**1996, July 15    Perf. 13**

| | | |
|---|---|---|
| 1214 | A360 | 10fr Swimming | .20 .20 |
| 1215 | A360 | 30fr Gymnastics | .40 .20 |
| 1216 | A360 | 175fr Running | 1.00 .50 |
| 1217 | A360 | 260fr Hurdles | 1.40 .70 |
| | | Nos. 1214-1217 (4) | 3.00 1.60 |

1996
Summer
Olympic
Games,
Atlanta
A360

**1996, July 1    Litho.    Perf. 12½**

1213 A359 215fr multicolored    1.25 .60

Intl.
Olympic
Committee,
Cent.
A359

Designs: 10fr, Mantis religiosa. 50fr, Forficula auricularia. 75fr, Schistocerca gregaria. 215fr, Cicindela lunulata. 220fr, Gryllus campestris.

**1997, Jan. 31    Perf. 13½x13**

| | | |
|---|---|---|
| 1241 | A368 | 10fr multicolored | .20 .20 |
| 1243 | A368 | 50fr multicolored | .30 .20 |
| 1244 | A368 | 75fr multicolored | .30 .20 |
| 1245 | A368 | 215fr multicolored | .90 .45 |
| 1246 | A368 | 220fr multicolored | .95 .45 |
| a. | | Strip of 5, #1241-1246 | 4.00 4.00 |

Insects
A368

25fr, Platalea leucorodia. 70fr, Lepitlos crumeniferus. 175fr, Balcarica pavonina. 215fr, Ephipiarnychus senegalensis. 220fr, Numenius arquata.

**1997, Feb. 28**

| | | |
|---|---|---|
| 1236 | A367 | 25fr multicolored | .20 .20 |
| 1237 | A367 | 70fr multicolored | .30 .20 |
| 1238 | A367 | 175fr multicolored | .75 .35 |
| 1239 | A367 | 215fr multicolored | .90 .45 |
| 1240 | A367 | 220fr multicolored | .95 .45 |
| a. | | Strip of 5, #1236-1240 | 5.00 5.00 |

Birds — A367

Designs: 90fr, Faidherbia albilda. 175fr, Eucalyptus. 220fr, Khaya senegalensis. 260fr, Casuarina equisetifolia.

**1997, Mar. 31**

| | | |
|---|---|---|
| 1232 | A366 | 90fr multicolored | .35 .20 |
| 1233 | A366 | 175fr multicolored | .75 .35 |
| 1234 | A366 | 220fr multicolored | .90 .45 |
| 1235 | A366 | 260fr multicolored | 1.00 .50 |
| | | Nos. 1232-1235 (4) | 3.00 1.50 |

Trees — A366

**1997, Jan. 19    Litho.    Perf. 13x13½**

| | | |
|---|---|---|
| 1228 | A365 | 25fr multicolored | .20 .20 |
| 1229 | A365 | 75fr multicolored | .30 .20 |
| 1230 | A365 | 215fr multicolored | .65 .65 |
| 1231 | A365 | 300fr multicolored | 1.25 .65 |
| | | Nos. 1228-1231 (4) | 2.65 1.50 |

25fr, Semi-truck. 75fr, Man pushing car, figure of man. 215fr, Race car. 300fr, Man on motorcycle.

19th Dakar-Agades-Dakar
Rally — A365

Diop: 175fr, and Egyptian hieroglyphs. Sphinx. 215fr, Performing carbon 14 test.

**1996, Feb. 26    Litho.    Perf. 13¾**

1247-1248 A369    Set of 2    3.50 1.50

Cheikh Anta Diop (1923-86),
Historian — A369

Postal officials in Senegal have declared Greenpeace sheets of nine with values of 250fr and 425fr "fake" and "illegal".


Designs: 20fr, Truck traveling across Sahel. 45fr, Motorcycle arriving at Lake Rose. 190fr, Sports utility vehicle crossing Mauritanian Desert. 240fr, Car at Senegal River.

**1998, Jan. 1    Litho.    Perf. 13½x13**

| | | |
|---|---|---|
| 1269 | A376 | 20fr multicolored | .20 .20 |
| 1270 | A376 | 45fr multicolored | .20 .20 |
| 1271 | A376 | 190fr multicolored | .80 .40 |
| 1272 | A376 | 240fr multicolored | 1.00 .50 |
| | | Nos. 1269-1272 (4) | 2.20 1.30 |

Dakar-Dakar Rally, 20th
Anniv. — A376

Design: 500fr, Hot air balloon in flight.

**1996, Apr. 13    Litho.    Perf. 13½**

| | | |
|---|---|---|
| 1258 | A370 | 215fr shown | .75 .40 |
| 1259 | A370 | 500fr multicolored | 1.75 .90 |

See Mali Nos. 812-813.

Third World
A370

Pictures of Senghor and: 175fr, Map of Senegal. 275fr, Quotation, vert.

**1996, Oct. 9    Litho.    Perf. 13¼**

1260-1261 A371    Set of 2    1.75 1.75

Pres.
Leopold
Senghor,
90th
Birthday
A371

**1997, May 30**

1268 A375 180fr multicolored    .75 .40

No. 1268 is dated 1992 and has word "alma-dies" obliterated.

Goree
Island
A375

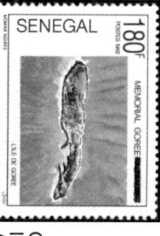

**1997, June 27**

1267 A374    Strip of 5, #a.-e.    4.00 4.00

Designs: a, 15fr, Cassis tesselata. b, 40fr, Cyprea mappa. d, 200fr, Natica adansoni. e, 300fr, Bulila miran.

**1997, Aug. 19**

1266 A373    Strip of 5, #a.-e.    4.00 4.00

Shells
A373

Designs: a, 25fr, African buffaloes. b, 90fr, Gazelles. c, 100fr, Gnu. d, 200fr, Wild dogs. e, 240fr, Cheetah.

**1996-97    Perf. 13½x13**

1249    A106    15fr green    .20 .20

Fashion Type of 1972
Size: 21x26mm
Engr.    Perf. 13½x14

| | | | |
|---|---|---|---|
| 1250 | A106 | 50fr green | |
| 1251 | A106 | 60fr olive grn | |
| 1251A | A106 | 60fr olive green | |
| 1252 | A106 | 70fr green | |
| 1253 | A106 | 80fr olive green | |
| 1254 | A106 | 190fr dark blue | .80 .40 |
| 1254A | A106 | 215fr dark blue | |
| 1255 | A106 | 225fr brown | |
| 1256 | A106 | 240fr brown | |
| 1256A | A106 | 260fr red brown | 1.00 .50 |
| 1256B | A106 | 300fr red brown | |
| 1257 | A106 | 320fr red lilac | |
| 1257B | A106 | 350fr rose lilac | |
| 1257C | A106 | 410fr lake | |
| 1257C | A106 | 410fr henna brown | |
| 1257C | A106 | 500fr brn violet | |
| 1257D | A100 | 1000fr carmine | |

Issued: 80fr, 225fr, 4/13/96. 50fr, 70fr, 215fr, 260fr, 4/13; 190fr, 240fr, 300fr, 350fr, 6/97.
Additional stamps were released in this set. The editors would like to examine them. Numbers will change if necessary.

Wild
Animals
A374

Designs: 30fr, Haliaetus vacifer. 90fr, Hippopotamus amphibius. 240fr, Loxindonta africana oxyotis. 300fr, Taurotragus derbianus.

**1997, July 21    Litho.    Perf. 13½x13**

| | | |
|---|---|---|
| 1262 | A372 | 30fr multicolored | .20 .20 |
| 1263 | A372 | 90fr multicolored | .65 .20 |
| 1264 | A372 | 240fr multicolored | .65 .65 |
| 1265 | A372 | 300fr multicolored | 1.25 .65 |
| | | Nos. 1262-1265 (4) | 3.55 1.55 |

Niokolo-Badiar Natl. Park — A372

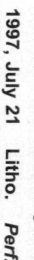

Designs: 50fr, Red buoy. 100fr, Mamelles Lighthouse. 190fr, Lighted buoy. 240fr, Port entrance lighthouse.

**1998, July 3**  *Perf. 12*
| 1322 | A391 | 50fr | multicolored | .20 | .20 |
| 1323 | A391 | 100fr | multicolored | .40 | .40 |
| 1324 | A391 | 190fr | multicolored | .70 | .35 |
| 1325 | A391 | 240fr | multicolored | .90 | .45 |
| | | *Nos. 1322-1325 (4)* | | 2.20 | 1.20 |

**21st Paris-Dakar Rally — A392**

Designs: 150fr, Race car broken down, hood up, helicopter, rescue van. 175fr, Man with shovels, vehicle stuck in sand, helicopter. 240fr, Motorcycles racing, one down, camel. 290fr, Motorcycle racing, man walking, vehicle broken down.

**1999, Jan. 17**  *Litho.*  *Perf. 11½*
| 1326 | A392 | 150fr | multicolored | .55 | .30 |
| 1327 | A392 | 175fr | multicolored | .65 | .35 |
| 1328 | A392 | 240fr | multicolored | .90 | .45 |
| 1329 | A392 | 290fr | multicolored | 1.00 | .50 |
| | | *Nos. 1326-1329 (4)* | | 3.10 | 1.60 |

**Women's Hair Styles, Headdresses A393**

Designs: 100fr, Long hair over shoulders. 240fr, Shorter hair. 300fr, Head wrapped.

**1998, Nov. 30**
| 1330 | A393 | 40fr | red brn & blk | .20 | .20 |
| 1331 | A393 | 100fr | brt grn & blk | .35 | .20 |
| 1332 | A393 | 240fr | violet & black | .90 | .45 |
| 1333 | A393 | 300fr | blue & black | 1.10 | .55 |
| | | *Nos. 1330-1333 (4)* | | 2.55 | 1.40 |

**Endangering Marine Fauna A394**

Designs: 50fr, Intensive net fishing. 100fr, Use of dynamite for fishing. 240fr, Sewage and pollutants in sea. 310fr, Oil slicks released from tanker ships.

**1998, Dec. 29**
| 1334 | A394 | 50fr | multicolored | .20 | .20 |
| 1335 | A394 | 100fr | multicolored | .35 | .20 |
| 1336 | A394 | 240fr | multicolored | 1.10 | .55 |
| 1337 | A394 | 365fr | multicolored | 1.25 | .65 |
| | | *Nos. 1334-1337 (4)* | | 2.90 | 1.60 |

**Intl. Year of the Ocean A395**

**1998, Oct. 30**  *Perf. 13x13½*
| 1338 | A395 | 190fr | shown | .70 | .35 |
| 1339 | A395 | 790fr | Sea life, diff. | 2.75 | 1.50 |

**Universal Declaration of Human Rights, 50th Anniv. A396**

**1998, Dec. 9**
| 1340 | A396 | 200fr | Prisoner | .75 | .40 |
| 1341 | A396 | 350fr | Free people | 1.25 | .65 |

---

**Souvenir Sheets**
| 1305 | A386 | 1000fr | Portrait | 4.25 | 2.10 |
| 1306 | A386 | 1500fr | With her sons | 6.25 | 3.25 |
| 1307 | A386 | 2000fr | Wearing tiara | 8.25 | 4.25 |

**1998 World Cup Soccer Cup Championships, France — A387**

Designs: 25fr, Soccer players. 50fr, Player's legs kicking ball. 150fr, Mascot, ball in air. 300fr, Country flags in shape of soccer players.

**1998, June 10**  *Litho.*  *Perf. 13x13½*
| 1308 | A387 | 25fr | multicolored | .20 | .20 |
| 1309 | A387 | 50fr | multicolored | .20 | .20 |
| 1310 | A387 | 150fr | multicolored | .60 | .25 |
| 1311 | A387 | 300fr | multicolored | 1.00 | .50 |
| | | *Nos. 1308-1311 (4)* | | 2.00 | 1.15 |

**Henriette Bathily Women's Museum A388**

**1998, May 16**  *Litho.*  *Perf. 13*
| 1312 | A388 | 190fr | shown | .75 | .35 |
| 1313 | A388 | 270fr | Emblem at right | 1.00 | .50 |

**Abolition of Slavery, 150th Anniv. — A389**

Designs: 20fr, Slavery Museum, Goree. 40fr, Frederick Douglass. 190fr, Mother, child. 290fr, Victor Schoelcher.

**1998, Apr. 27**
| 1314 | A389 | 20fr | multicolored | .20 | .20 |
| 1315 | A389 | 40fr | multicolored | .20 | .20 |
| 1316 | A389 | 190fr | multicolored | .70 | .35 |
| 1317 | A389 | 290fr | multicolored | 1.10 | .55 |
| | | *Nos. 1314-1317 (4)* | | 2.20 | 1.30 |

**SOS Children's Village — A390**

Children's drawings: 30fr, House, car. 50fr, shown. 180fr, Sun, flowers. 300fr, Lakes, trees.

**1998, June 16**
| 1318 | A390 | 30fr | multicolored | .20 | .20 |
| 1319 | A390 | 50fr | multicolored | .35 | .20 |
| 1320 | A390 | 180fr | multicolored | .70 | .35 |
| 1321 | A390 | 300fr | multicolored | 1.10 | .55 |
| | | *Nos. 1318-1321 (4)* | | 2.20 | 1.30 |

**Navigational Aids — A391**

---

**Musical Instruments A382**

**1997, Oct. 16**  *Perf. 13x13½*
| 1273 | A377 | 190fr | multicolored | .80 | .40 |
| 1274 | A377 | 200fr | multicolored | .85 | .45 |

**1997, Nov. 22**  Riiti
| 1290 | A382 | 125fr | Riiti | .75 | .25 |
| 1291 | A382 | 190fr | Kora | 1.00 | .40 |
| 1292 | A382 | 200fr | Fama | 1.25 | .45 |
| 1293 | A382 | 240fr | Dioung dioung | 1.50 | .50 |
| | | *Nos. 1290-1293 (4)* | | 4.50 | 1.60 |

**World Wildlife Fund A383**

Profelis aurata: 100fr, Climbing on tree limb. 240fr, Lying on tree limb. 300fr, Two cubs.

**1997, Dec. 24**  *Litho.*  *Perf. 11½*
| 1294 | A383 | 45fr | multicolored | .20 | .20 |
| 1295 | A383 | 100fr | multicolored | .35 | .20 |
| 1296 | A383 | 240fr | multicolored | .85 | .50 |
| 1297 | A383 | 300fr | multicolored | 1.00 | .65 |
| | | *Nos. 1294-1297 (4)* | | 2.40 | 1.55 |

**SOS Children's Village, Ziguinchor A384**

**1998, Jan. 14**  *Litho.*  *Perf. 11½*
| 1298 | A384 | 190fr | shown | .80 | .40 |
| 1299 | A384 | 240fr | Child, buildings | 1.00 | .50 |

**Club Aldiana, 25th Anniv. — A385**

Designs: 290fr, Hut, people at market, mother and baby. 320fr, People on boats, woman in traditional dress, fish in basket.

**1998, Jan. 12**  *Perf. 13½*
| 1300 | A385 | 290fr | multicolored | 2.25 | .60 |
| 1301 | A385 | 320fr | multicolored | 2.50 | .65 |

**Diana, Princess of Wales (1967-97) A386**

Various portraits.

**1998**
| 1302 | A386 | 240fr | like #1304g | 1.00 | .50 |
| | | **Sheets of 9** | | | |
| 1303 | A386 | 200fr | #a.-i. | 7.50 | 3.75 |
| 1304 | A386 | 250fr | #a.-i. | 9.50 | 4.75 |

a. Nos. 1303-1304 are continuous designs.

---

**Food Day A377**

190fr, Receiving grain through cereal bank. 200fr, Proper nutrition for women.

A378   A379

Masks: 45fr, Planche, Burkina Faso. 90fr, Kpelyehe, Ivory Coast. 200fr, Nimba, Guinea Bissau. 240fr, Walu, Mali. 300fr, Dogon, Mali.

**1997, Nov. 28**
| 1275 | A378 | 45fr | multicolored | .20 | .20 |
| 1276 | A378 | 90fr | multicolored | .45 | .20 |
| 1277 | A378 | 200fr | multicolored | .85 | .40 |
| 1278 | A378 | 240fr | multicolored | 1.00 | .50 |
| 1279 | A378 | 300fr | multicolored | 1.25 | .65 |
| a. | | Strip of 5, #1275-1279 | | 3.75 | 1.90 |

**1997**  *Perf. 11½*
| 1280 | A379 | 310fr | multicolored | 1.25 | .65 |

Heinrich von Stephan (1831-97).

**Vasco de Gama (1460-1524), Expedition Around Cape of Good Hope, 500th Anniv. A380**

De Gama and: 40fr, Route of spices. 75fr, Port of Zanzibar. 190fr, Caraval revolution. 200fr, Maps being printed.

**1997, Nov. 22**
| 1281 | A380 | 40fr | multicolored | .35 | .20 |
| 1282 | A380 | 75fr | multicolored | .35 | .20 |
| 1283 | A380 | 190fr | multicolored | 1.40 | .40 |
| 1284 | A380 | 200fr | multicolored | 1.40 | 1.20 |
| | | *Nos. 1281-1284 (4)* | | 3.50 | 1.20 |

**Trains A381**

Designs: 15fr, CC2400. 90fr, Loco-tractor. 100fr, Mountain train. 240fr, Maquinista. 310fr, Freight train, series 151-A.

**1997, Dec. 16**  *Perf. 13x13½*
| 1285 | A381 | 15fr | multicolored | .20 | .20 |
| 1286 | A381 | 90fr | multicolored | .40 | .25 |
| 1287 | A381 | 100fr | multicolored | .45 | .25 |
| 1288 | A381 | 240fr | multicolored | 1.00 | .50 |
| 1289 | A381 | 310fr | multicolored | 1.25 | .65 |
| a. | | Strip of 5, #1285-1289 | | 3.25 | 1.65 |

**1998, Nov. 6**  **Litho.**  **Perf. 13½x13**
Hotel Palm Beach, Voyages of Fram, 50th Anniv. — A397
1342  A397  240fr  multicolored  .90  .45
1343  A397  300fr  multicolored  1.10  .55

Designs: 240fr, Huts, trees, aerial view of hotel grounds. 300fr, Woman braiding another's hair, beach at hotel.

---

**1998, Oct. 23**  **Litho.**  **Perf. 13¾**
Italia '98 Int'l Philatelic Exhibition — A398a
1344  A398  290fr  multicolored  1.00  .50
1344A A398a  100fr  Sheet of 6, #b-g  3.50  3.50

Design: Leaning Tower of Pisa.
Souvenir Sheet

---

**1998, Oct. 23**  **Litho.**  **Perf. 13½**
Italia '98 Int'l Philatelic Exhibition — A398a
1345  A399  1000fr  multicolored  3.50  3.50

Ferrari Automobiles, 50th Anniv. — A399

No. 1344A — Race drivers and automobiles: b. Alberto Ascari. c. Giuseppe Farina. d. Ricardo Patrese. e. Michele Alboreto. f. Elio de Angelis. g. Andrea de Cesaris.

Souvenir Sheet

**1998**
Fashion Type of 1972
1345A  A106  125fr  dark olive  —  —
1345B  A106  290fr  violet  —  —
1345C  A106  310fr  purple brown  —  —

Engr.  Size: 21x26mm
Perf. 13½x13

---

**1998**  **Litho.**  **Perf. 13½x13**
De Tomaso Automobiles, 40th Anniv. — A400
1346  A400  250fr  Sheet of 4, #a-d  3.50  3.50

Automobile colors: a. black, shown. b, silver. c, black, diff. d, red.

Souvenir Sheet
Italia '98. Dated 1998.

---

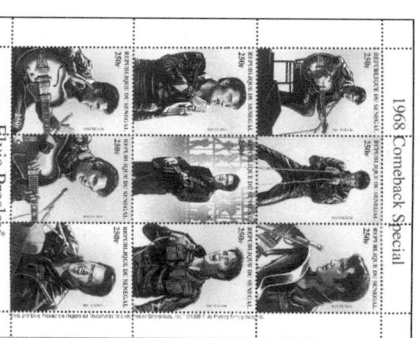

**1999, Feb. 28**  **Litho.**  **Perf. 13½**
1347  A401  200fr  Sheet of 9, #a-i.  6.00  6.00
1348  A401  1500fr  multicolored  5.00  5.00
1349  A401  2000fr  multicolored  6.75  6.75

Actors & Actresses — A401

No. 1347: a. Romy Schneider. b, Yves Montand. c, Catherine Deneuve. d, Gina Lollobrigida. e, Marcello Mastroianni. f, Sophia Loren. g, Frank Sinatra. h, Dean Martin. i, Marilyn Monroe.
Souvenir Sheets
Italia '98. Dated 1998.

---

**1999, Feb. 28**  **Litho.**  **Perf. 12½**
Chess Pieces and Scenes of the Crusades — A404
1353  A404  250fr  Sheet of 9, #a-i.  6.00  6.00
1354  A404  200fr  #a-i.  7.50  7.50
1355  A404  250fr  #a-i.  9.25  9.25
1356  A404  400fr  #a-i.  15.00  15.00

Designs: No. 1353, Pope Urban II, 1053. No. 1354: a, Muslim army. b, Bishopric of St. George. c, Army of Karbuqha. d, Muslim of Jerusalem. e, Christians. f, Baldwin I, King of Jerusalem. g, Third crusade. Richard the Lion-Hearted. h, Capture of Acre. 1191. i, Crusaders leave for Jaffa, 1191. No. 1355: a, Pope Urban II, diff. b, Peter the Hermit. c, Byzantine Emperor Alexius. d, People's Crusade, 1096. e, Godfrey of Bouillon. f, Crusaders at Constantinople, 1097. g, Knights of St. John. h, Crusaders cross Alps. i, Capture of Jerusalem. No. 1356: a, Chateau-gaillard of Richard the Lion-Hearted. b, Capture of Arsuf, 1191. c, Truce between Richard the Lion-Hearted and Saladin, 1192. d, Arrival of Louis IX at Damietta, 1248. e, Children's Crusade. f, Capture of Louis IX. g, Flood at El Mansurah. h, Treaty between Sultan al-Kamil and Frederick II. i, Monks record history of Crusades.

Sheets of 9

---

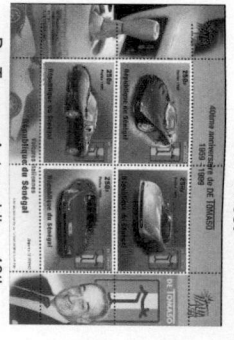

**1999, July 2**  **Litho.**  **Perf. 13**
PhilexFrance 99 — A403
1351  A403  240fr  multicolored  1.00  1.00

No. 1351 has a holographic image. Soaking in water may affect hologram.

---

**1999, July 16**  **Litho.**  **Perf. 13½**
Athletes — A405
1357  A405  250fr  multicolored  1.00  1.00
1358  A405  300fr  multicolored  1.25  1.25
1359  A405  250fr  #1357, 1359a-h.  .... ....
1360  A405  300fr  #1358, 1360a-h.  ...  ...

No. 1357, Jackie Robinson with bat behind back. No. 1358, Muhammad Ali, arm raised by referee. No. 1359: a-h, various portraits of Jackie Robinson. No. 1360: a-h, various portraits of Muhammad Ali.
Close-up of Jackie Robinson like No. 1359fr. 1000fr, Muhammad Ali in robe. 1500fr, Close-up of Jackie Robinson. No. 1363, Robinson at bat. No. 1364, Ali with both fists clenched.

Sheets of 9

---

**1999, July 23**  **Litho.**  **Perf. 13½**
Transportation — A406
1371  A406  250fr  multicolored  1.00  1.00
1372  A406  250fr  multicolored  1.25  1.25
1373  A406  300fr  multicolored  1.40  1.40
1374  A406  325fr  multicolored  1.40  1.40
1375  A406  350fr  multicolored  1.50  1.50
1376  A406  375fr  multicolored  2.00  2.00
1376A A406  500fr  multicolored  ....  ....
Nos. 1371-1376 (6)  ....  ....

Designs: 250fr, Sailboat of Sir Thomas Lipton. 300fr, Sinking of Titanic. 325fr, Bentley coupe. 350fr, Prussian locomotive. 375fr, Ducati Motorcycle. 500fr, Concorde.

---

**1999, Aug. 10**  **Litho.**
Souvenir Sheets
1361  A405a  1000fr  multicolored  4.25  4.25
1362  A405a  1500fr  multicolored  6.25  6.25
1363  A405  2000fr  multicolored  8.25  8.25
1364  A405  2000fr  multicolored  8.25  8.25

Sports — A405a
Nos. 1361-1364 each contain one 36x42mm stamp.

---

**1999, July 16**  **Litho.**  **Perf. 13**
1366  A405a  200fr  multi  7.50  7.50
1367  A405a  300fr  multi  11.00  11.00
1368  A405a  400fr  multi  15.00  15.00
1365-  A405a  Set of 3
1365B

Sheets of 9, #ai

1369  A405a  1500fr  multi  6.25  6.25
1370  A405a  1500fr  multi  8.00  8.00
1370A A405a  2000fr  multi  8.00  8.00

Souvenir Sheets

Designs: 200fr, Ayrton Senna, Formula 1 racing champion. 300fr, Ludger Beerbaum, equestrian competitor, vert. 400fr, Pete Sampras, tennis player, vert. No. 1366 — Formula 1 racing champions: a, Juan Manuel Fangio. b, Alberto Ascari. c, Graham Hill. d, Jim Clark. e, Jack Brabham. f, Jackie Stewart. g, Niki Lauda. h, Like No. 1365, no white margin. i, Alain Prost. No. 1367 — Equestrian competitors, vert.: a, Martin Schauadt. b, Klaus Balkenhol. c, Nadine Capelmann-Biffar. d, Walter Melliger. e, Like No. 1365A, without printer's name at LL. f, Ulrich Kirchhoff. g, Sally Clark. h, Bettina Overesch-Boker. i, Karen O'Conner. No. 1368 — Tennis and table tennis players, vert.: a, Liu Guoliang. b, Andre Agassi. c, Martina Hingis. d, Deng Yaping. e, Anna Kournikova. f, Jean-Philippe Gatien. g, Mikael Appelgren. h, Like No. 1365B, no white margin. i, Jan-Ove Waldner.
1500fr, German Equestrian jumping team. No. 1370, Ayrton Senna. No. 1370A, Table tennis players Vladimir Samsonov, Deng Yaping, Jörg Rosskopf.

---

**1998, Oct. 23**  **Litho.**  **Perf. 13¼**
1350  A402  250fr  Sheet of 9, #a-i.  7.75  7.75

Elvis Presley — A402
Various portraits.
1968 Comeback Special

No. 1350: a-i. A sheet similar to No. 1350 exists, are perf 13¼ and have Italia '98 logo. The top margins of the sheet are not inscribed.

---

**1999, Aug. 10**  **Litho.**
Intl. Year of Older Persons — A407
1377  A407  30fr  multicolored  .20  .20
1378  A407  150fr  multicolored  .60  .60
1379  A407  290fr  multicolored  1.10  1.10
1380  A407  300fr  multicolored  1.25  1.25
Nos. 1377-1380 (4)  3.15  3.15

30fr, Picture in book. 150fr, Man with mallet. 290fr, Musicians. 300fr, Scientists, vert.

See Nos. 1385-1399.

Perf. 13½x13, 13x13¼

## Mushrooms — A408

| | | Litho. | |
|---|---|---|---|
| **1999, Aug. 27** | | **Perf. 13½x13½** | |
| 1381 | A408 | 60fr multicolored | .25 .25 |
| 1382 | A408 | 175fr multicolored | .70 .70 |
| 1383 | A408 | 220fr multicolored | .90 .90 |
| 1384 | A408 | 250fr multicolored | 1.00 1.00 |
| | | *Nos. 1381-1384 (4)* | 2.85 2.85 |

Scouting emblem and: 60fr, "Amanite phalloïde." 175fr, Coprinus atramantarius. 220fr, "Amanite vireuse." 250fr, Agaricus campester.

## Transportation Type of 1999

No. 1385 — Boats and ships: a, France. b, United States. c, Finnjet. d, Chusan. e, Sheers. f, Vendredi 13. g, Like No. 1371 without white margin. h, Pen Duick 11. i, Jester.
No. 1386 — Titanic: a, Construction. b, Launching. c, Departing. d, At start of voyage. e, Collision with iceberg. f, Like No. 1372 without white margin. g, Exploration of wreckage. h, Bow, passengers. i, Captain Edward John Smith.
No. 1387 — Automobiles: a, Duryea. b, Menon. c, Petite Renault. d, Zero Fiat. e, Spa. f, Packard. g, Like No. 1373 without white margin. h, Mercedes-Benz. i, Morris Minor.
No. 1388 — Trains: a, Mikado. b, 241P. c, Ten-wheeler. d, The Milwaukee. e, Class 1.S. f, Prussian locomotive G12. g, Like No. 1374 without white margin. h, KK-SEB Series 310. i, Outrance.
No. 1389 — Motorcycles and bicycles: a, Brooklands. b, Moto Brough Superior. c, 1903 race. d, Like No. 1375 without inscription at LL. e, Dave Thorpe Moto-cross Yamaha. f, Kevin Schwantz Moto Suzuki. g, Michaux bicycle. h, Racing bicycle with helmeted rider. i, Women on bicycles.
No. 1390 — Rockets, vert.: a, R.D. 107, USSR. b, Soyuz, USSR. c, Proton, USSR. d, Atlas-Centaur, US. e, Atlas-Agena, US. f, Atlas-Mercury, US. g, Titan 2, US. h, Juno 2, US. i, Saturn 1, US.
No. 1391 — Express trains: a, Acela, US. b, Class 332, Great Britain. c, ICE, Germany. d, TEE, Luxembourg. e, Nevada Super Speed, US. f, Inter City 250, Great Britain. g, Korean High Speed, France. h, Eurostar, France & Great Britain. i, Thalys PBA, France.
No. 1392 — Supersonic aircraft or prototypes: a, SR-71. b, Magliffer. c, S.M. d, Super Concorde. e, TU-144. f, Roeing X. g, X-33. h, Like No. 1376 without white margin. i, X-34.
No. 1394, Marc Seguin, arrival of train at Mont Saint-Michel, vert. No. 1395, Walter P. Chrysler, 1924 Chrysler. No. 1396, Étienne Chambron, TGV trains, vert. No. 1397, Bobby Julich on racing bicycle. No. 1398, Concorde, diff. 2500fr, Neil Armstrong.

| | | Litho. | **Perf. 13½** |
|---|---|---|---|
| **1999, July 23** | | **Sheets of 9** | |
| 1385 | A406 | 250fr #a-i. | 9.25 9.25 |
| 1386 | A406 | 300fr #a-i. | 11.00 11.00 |
| 1387 | A406 | 325fr #a-i. | 12.00 12.00 |
| 1388 | A406 | 350fr #a-i. | 13.00 13.00 |
| 1389 | A406 | 375fr #a-i. | 14.00 14.00 |
| 1390 | A406 | 400fr #a-i. | 15.00 15.00 |
| 1391 | A406 | 450fr #a-i. | 17.00 17.00 |
| 1392 | A406 | 500fr #a-i. | 18.00 18.00 |
| | | **Souvenir Sheets** | |
| 1393 | A406 | 1000fr multicolored | 4.25 4.25 |
| 1394 | A406 | 1500fr multicolored | 5.50 5.50 |
| 1395 | A406 | 1500fr multicolored | 6.00 6.00 |
| 1396 | A406 | 2000fr multicolored | 8.25 8.25 |
| 1397 | A406 | 2000fr multicolored | 8.25 8.25 |
| 1398 | A406 | 2000fr multicolored | 8.25 8.25 |
| 1399 | A406 | 2500fr multicolored | 10.50 10.50 |

No. 1390 contains nine 35x50mm stamps. Nos. 1393, 1395, 1397-1399 each contain one 50x35 stamp. Nos. 1394 and 1396 each contain one 35x50mm stamp.

## UPU, 125th Anniv. — A409

## Mother Teresa — A411

UPU emblem and: 270fr, Rainbows, envelope. 350fr, "125."

| | | Litho. | **Perf. 11½x11¾** |
|---|---|---|---|
| **1999, Oct. 9** | | | |
| 1400 | A409 | 270fr multi | 1.10 1.10 |
| 1401 | A409 | 350fr multi | 1.40 1.40 |

## First Manned Moon Landing, 30th Anniv. — A410

Designs: 25fr, Two astronauts on moon, flag. 145fr, Neil Armstrong, flag, astronaut on moon, vert. 180fr, Astronaut, flag, rocket, vert. 500fr, Astronaut on moon, space shuttle, vert.

| | | | **Perf. 13½x13, 13x13½** |
|---|---|---|---|
| **1999, Oct. 9** | | | |
| 1402 | A410 | 25fr multi | .20 .20 |
| 1403 | A410 | 145fr multi | .60 .60 |
| 1404 | A410 | 180fr multi | .70 .70 |
| 1405 | A410 | 500fr multi | 2.00 2.00 |
| | | *Nos. 1402-1405 (4)* | 3.50 3.50 |

Mother Teresa and: 75fr, Child, facing away. 100fr, Three children. 290fr, Priest. 300fr, Child.

| | | | **Perf. 11½x11¾** |
|---|---|---|---|
| **1999, Oct. 9** | | | |
| 1406 | A411 | 75fr multi | .25 .25 |
| 1407 | A411 | 100fr multi | .40 .40 |
| 1408 | A411 | 290fr multi | 1.10 1.10 |
| 1409 | A411 | 300fr multi | 1.25 1.25 |
| | | *Nos. 1406-1409 (4)* | 3.00 3.00 |

Awarding of Nobel Peace Prize to Mother Teresa, 20th anniv.

## Fauna A412

Designs: 60fr, Hippotragus equinus. 90fr, Haematopus ostralegus. 300fr, Dendrocygna viduada. 320fr, Demochelys coriacea.

| | | | **Perf. 13½x13** |
|---|---|---|---|
| **1999, Oct. 9** | | | |
| 1410 | A412 | 60fr multi | .25 .25 |
| 1411 | A412 | 90fr multi | .35 .35 |
| 1412 | A412 | 300fr multi | 1.25 1.25 |
| 1413 | A412 | 320fr multi | 1.25 1.25 |
| | | *Nos. 1410-1413 (4)* | 3.10 3.10 |

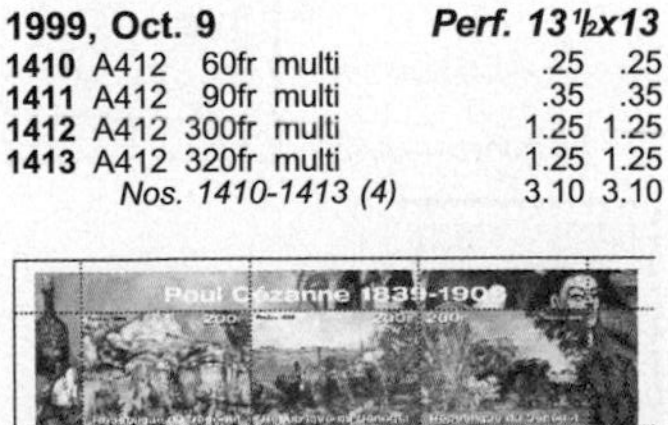

## Paintings by Paul Cézanne — A413

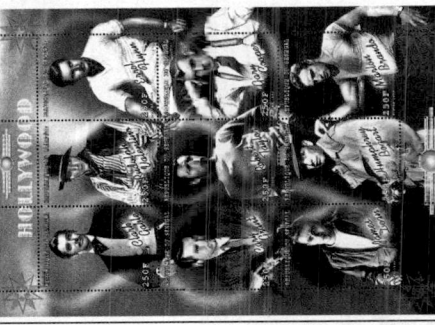

Various paintings.

| | | | **Perf. 13½** |
|---|---|---|---|
| **1999** | | | |
| 1414 | A413 | 200fr Sheet of 9, #a-i. | 8.00 8.00 |

## Betty Boop — A414

Designs: No. 1415, 250fr, With red guitar. No. 1416, 250fr, With microphone. b, With tambourine. c, Like #1415 (continuous design). d, With pink guitar. e, On piano keys. f, With drumsticks. g, With earphones. h, Like #1416 (continuous design). i, With purple jacket.
No. 1419, 400fr: a, With red dress. b, With flowers. c, With blue pants. d, With purple dress. e, Like #1417 (continuous design). f, With black pants. g, With ankh earrings. h, With black dress. i, With purple shirt and pants.
No. 1420, 1000fr, With saxophone. No. 1421, 1500fr, With red dress. No. 1422, 2000fr, With purple shirt.

| | | **Litho.** | **Perf. 13¾** |
|---|---|---|---|
| **1999** | | | |
| 1415-1417 | A414 | Set of 3 | 3.75 3.75 |
| | | **Sheets of 9, #a-i** | |
| 1418-1419 | A414 | Set of 2 | 24.00 24.00 |
| | | **Souvenir Sheets** | |
| 1420-1422 | A414 | Set of 3 | 12.00 12.00 |

## Actors and Actresses — A415

No. 1423, 250fr: a, Clark Gable. b, Rudolph Valentino. c, Errol Flynn. d, Cary Grant. e, Robert Taylor. f, Gary Cooper. g, James Dean. h, Humphrey Bogart. i, Marlon Brando.
No. 1424, 425fr: a, Grace Kelly. b, Marilyn Monroe. c, Audrey Hepburn. d, Greta Garbo. e, Jean Harlow. f, Loretta Young. g, Jane Russell. h, Dorothy Lamour. i, Veronica Lake.
No. 1425, 450fr: a, Ginger Rogers, Fred Astaire. b, Cary Grant, Katharine Hepburn. c, James Stewart. d, Melvyn Douglas, Greta Garbo. d, Vivien Leigh, Clark Gable. e, Burt Lancaster, Deborah Kerr. f, Humphrey Bogart, Lauren Bacall. g, Steve McQueen, Jacqueline Bisset. h, Gene Kelly, Rita Hayworth. i, Ingrid Bergman, Cary Grant.

| | | **Sheets of 9, #a-i** | |
|---|---|---|---|
| **1999** | | | |
| 1423-1425 | A415 | Set of 3 | 32.50 32.50 |

## I Love Lucy — A416

Designs: No. 1426, 300fr, Fred, Ethel and Lucy reading murder mystery, vert.

No. 1428: a, Ethel, Lucy holding box. b, Ricky, Lucy, Fred and Ethel. c, Fred, Ethel and Lucy standing. d, Lucy with chicks. e, Fred, Ethel, Lucy and Ricky at table. f, Ethel and Lucy bending over. g, Lucy, h, Lucy, Ethel and Fred at table.
No. 1429, vert. — Lucy with: a, Telephone. b, Green dress. c, Black vest. d, Black hair bow. e, Spoon and bottle. f, Salad. g, Lilac jacket. h, Tan coat.
No. 1430, 1000fr, Lucy holding box, vert. No. 1431, 2000fr, Lucy holding bag, vert.

| | | | |
|---|---|---|---|
| **1999** | | | |
| 1426-1427 | A416 | Set of 2 | 2.40 2.40 |
| 1428 | A416 | 300fr Sheet of 9, #1426, 1428a-1428h | 11.00 11.00 |
| 1429 | A416 | 300fr Sheet of 9, #1427, 1429a-1429h | 11.00 11.00 |
| | | **Souvenir Sheets** | |
| 1430-1431 | A416 | Set of 2 | 12.00 12.00 |

## The Three Stooges — A417

Designs: No. 1432, Larry with scissors, Curly, Moe with drill.
No. 1433: a, Larry and Moe on bed. b, Larry, Moe, Curly in police uniforms. c, Moe, Larry on telephone. d, Larry and Moe with scissors, Curly. e, Larry, Curly, Moe behind operating room equipment. f, Moe on floor, Larry, Curly. g, Moo, Curly, Larry with ladder. h, Moe with plank, Larry, Curly.
No. 1434, 1000fr, Moe with feathers in hair, Curly, vert. No. 1435, 1500fr, Curly with hat, vert.

| | | | |
|---|---|---|---|
| **1999** | | | |
| 1432 | A417 | 400fr multi | 1.60 1.60 |
| 1433 | A417 | 400fr Sheet of 9, #1433a-1433h | 14.50 14.50 |
| | | **Souvenir Sheets** | |
| 1434-1435 | A417 | Set of 2 | 10.00 10.00 |

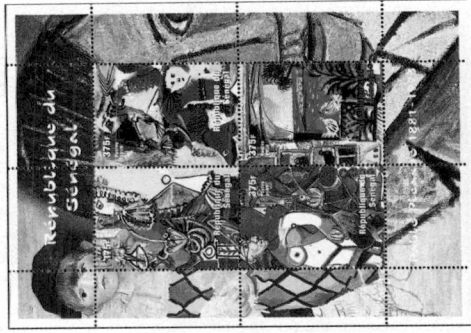

## Picasso Paintings — A418

No. 1436: a, Country name in yellow, denomination at UL. b, Country name in white. c, Country name in yellow, denomination at UR. d, Country name in red.

| | | | |
|---|---|---|---|
| **1999** | | | |
| 1436 | A418 | 375fr Sheet of 4, #a-d | 5.50 5.50 |

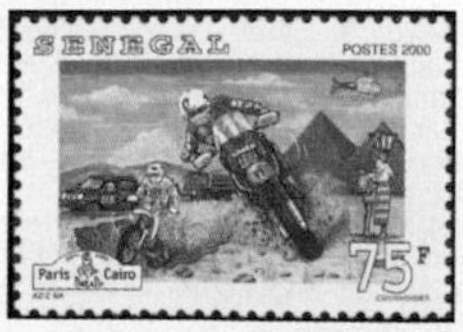

22nd Paris-Cairo-Dakar Rally — A419

Designs: 75fr, Motorcycles, car, truck, helicopter, Pyramids. 100fr, Cars, truck, Sphinx, Pyramid, camel and driver. 220fr, Motorcycle, truck, helicopter. 320fr, Camel and driver, motorcycle, car, Pyramids.

**2000 Litho. *Perf. 11¾x11½***
**1437-1440** A419 Set of 4 2.00 2.00

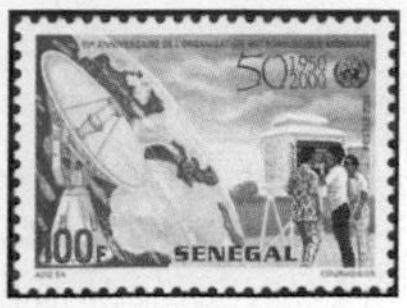

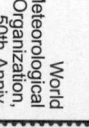

World Meteorological Organization, 50th Anniv. A420

Designs: 100fr, Satellite dish, map, weather station. 790fr, Weather measuring equipment, vert.

**2000 *Perf. 11¾x11½, 11½x11¾***
**1441-1442** A420 Set of 2 2.50 2.50

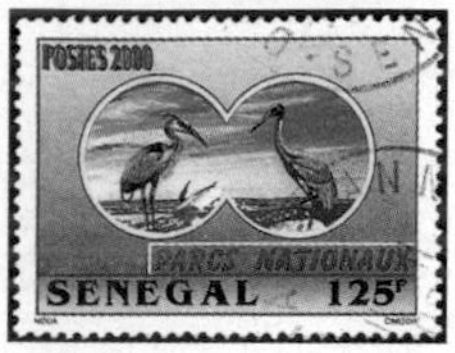

National Parks A420a

**2000 ? Litho. *Perf. 13¾x13½***
**1442A** A420a 125fr shown — —

The editors suspect other stamps were issued in this set and would like to examine any examples.

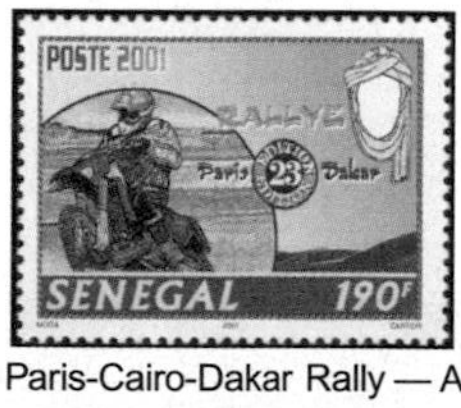

23rd Paris-Cairo-Dakar Rally — A421

Stylized head and: 190fr, Motorcyclist. 220fr, Facial features with text, vert. 240fr, Camel, vert. 790fr, Car.

***Perf. 13½x13¼, 13¼x13½***
**2001, Jan. 6**
**1443-1446** A421 Set of 4 4.00 4.00

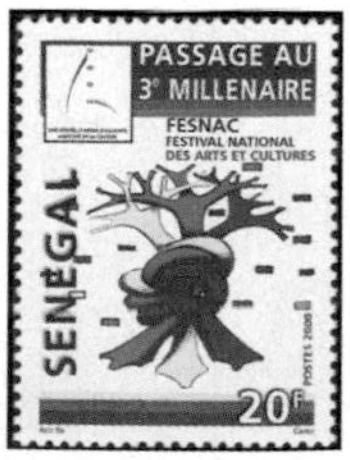

Advent of New Millennium A422

Millennium emblem and: 20fr, National Festival of Arts and Culture. 100fr, Pan-African Plastic Arts. 150fr, National Heritage Day. 300fr, Goree Memorial, horiz.

**2001, Feb. 13 *Perf. 13½x13, 13x13½***
**1447-1450** A422 Set of 4 1.60 1.60

Dated 2000.

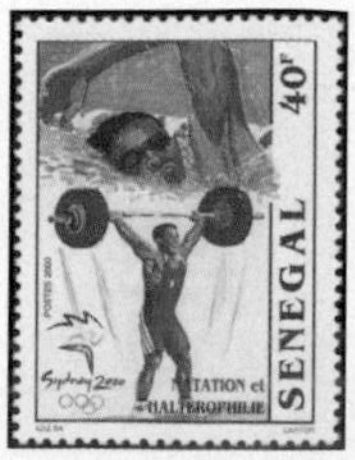

2000 Summer Olympics, Sydney — A423

Designs: 40fr, Swimming, weight lifting. 80fr, Taekwondo. 240fr, 200-meter race. 290fr, Handball.

**2001, Feb. 28 *Perf. 13¼x13½***
**1451-1454** A423 Set of 4 1.75 1.75

Dated 2000.

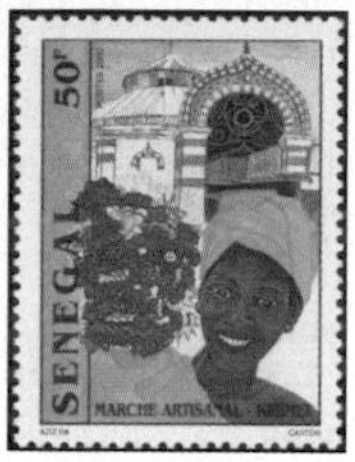

Kermel Artisan Market — A424

Building and: 50fr, Woman, flowers. 90fr, Mask, drum. 250fr, Masks, bowls, horiz. 350fr, Woman, carvings.

***Perf. 13¼x13½, 13½x13¼***
**2001, Mar. 15**
**1455-1458** A424 Set of 4 1.60 1.60

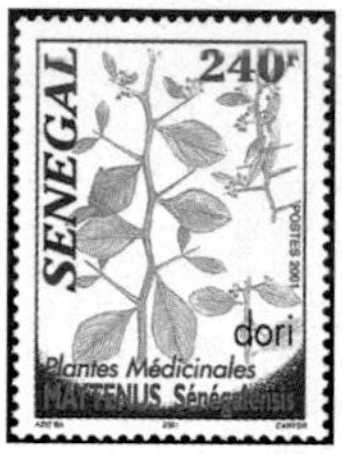

Medicinal Plants — A425

Designs: 240fr, Maytenus senegalensis. 320fr, Boscia senegalensis. 350fr, Euphorbia hirta. 500fr, Guierra senegalensis.

**2001, Apr. 16 Litho. *Perf. 13¼x13***
**1459-1462** A425 Set of 4 4.00 4.00

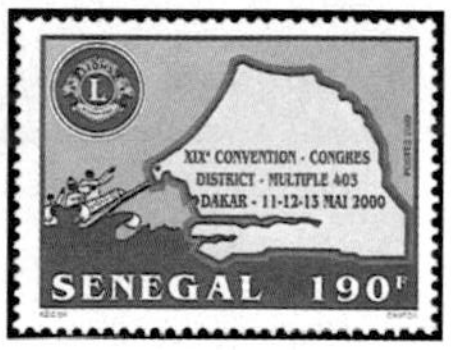

19th Lions Intl. Convention, Dakar A426

Lions Intl. emblem and: 190fr, People in canoe, map of Senegal. 300fr, Lion, vert.

***Perf. 13½x13¼, 13¼x13½***
**2001, May 21**
**1463-1464** A426 Set of 2 1.40 1.40

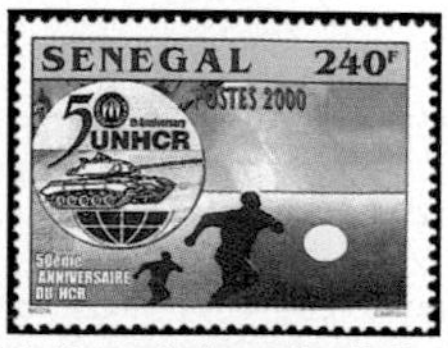

UN High Commissioner for Refugees, 50th Anniv. — A427

Emblem and: 240fr, Tank, refugees. 320fr, Refugee, globe, vert.

***Perf. 13½x13¼, 13¼x13½***
**2001, June 20**
**1465-1466** A427 Set of 2 1.60 1.60

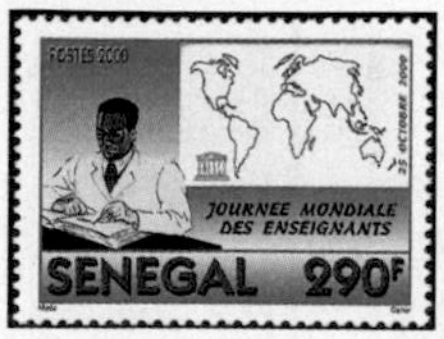

Intl. Teacher's Day — A428

UNESCO emblem and: 225fr, Book, teacher, vert. 290fr, Teacher, world map.

***Perf. 13¼x13, 13x13¼***
**2001, Oct. 5 Litho.**
**1467-1468** A428 Set of 2 1.50 1.50

Dated 2000.

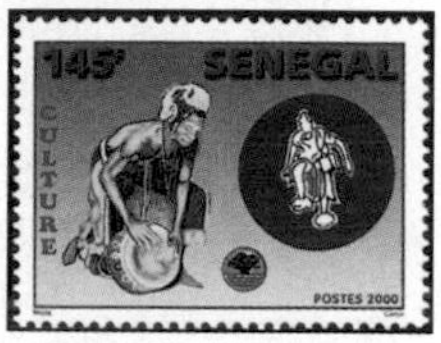

Tourism A430

Tourism emblem and: 145fr, Drummer and dancer. 290fr, Tree, windsurfer, person on air mattress, vert.

***Perf. 13x13¼, 13¼x13***
**2001, Dec. 3 Litho.**
**1473-1474** A430 Set of 2 1.25 1.25

Dated 2000.

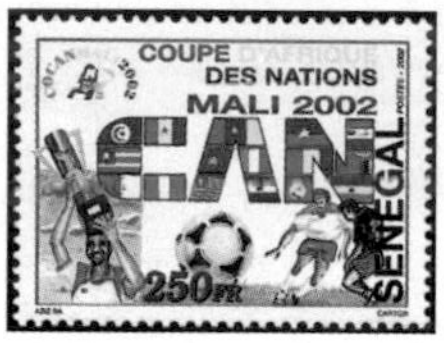

2002 African Cup Soccer Tournament, Mali A431

Tournament emblem and: 250fr, Flags, player holding cup, players and soccer ball. 380fr, Players near goal. 425fr, Players kicking ball at goal. 440fr, Player, cup, vert.

**2002, Jan. 9**
**1475-1478** A431 Set of 4 4.00 4.00

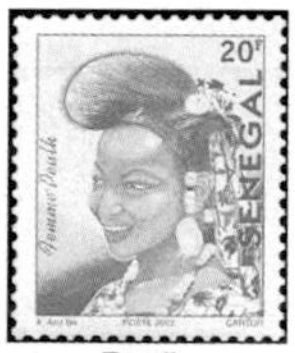

Peulh Woman — A433

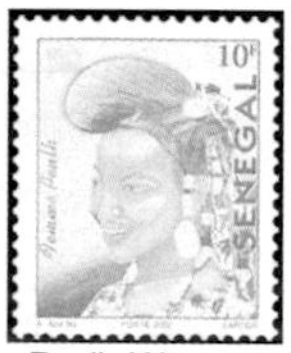

Peulh Woman — A433a

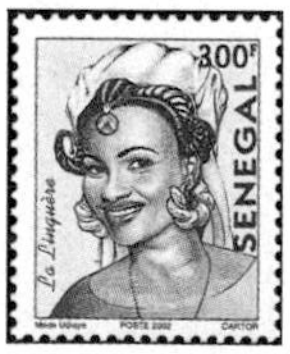

Linguère — A434

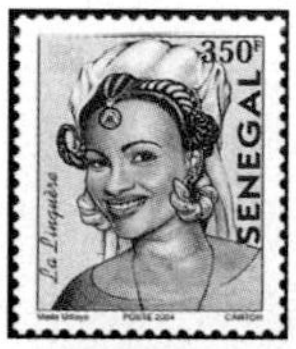

Linguère — A434a

On types A433a and A434a, the numerals in the denominations have thin serifs and zeroes that are thin at top and bottom. On types A433 and A434 the lines of these numerals are the same thickness.

**2002 Litho. *Perf. 13½x13***

| | | | | | |
|---|---|---|---|---|---|
| **1483** | A433 | 5fr | lilac rose | — | — |
| **1484** | A433 | 10fr | brt orange | — | — |
| **1484A** | A433a | 10fr | orange | — | — |
| **1485** | A433 | 20fr | orange | — | — |
| **1486** | A433 | 25fr | rose red | — | — |
| **1407** | A433 | 40fr | bright pink | — | — |
| **1488** | A433 | 50fr | light blue | — | — |
| **1488A** | A433a | 50fr | light blue | — | — |
| **1489** | A433 | 60fr | light blue green | — | — |
| **1490** | A433 | 70fr | light yel green | — | — |
| **1490A** | A433 | 75fr | dark green | — | — |
| **1491** | A433 | 100fr | brt yel grn | — | — |
| **1491A** | A433 | 125fr | silver | — | — |
| **1492** | A443 | 150fr | olive green | — | — |
| **1493** | A433 | 175fr | yellow brown | — | — |
| **1494** | A434 | 200fr | olive green | — | — |
| **1494A** | A434 | 225fr | lilac | — | — |
| **1495** | A434 | 250fr | ocher | — | — |
| **1496** | A434 | 290fr | red brown | — | — |
| **1497** | A434 | 300fr | brt rose lil | — | — |
| **1497A** | A434a | 350fr | brt rose lilac | — | — |
| **1498** | A434 | 360fr | violet | — | — |
| **1500** | A434 | 390fr | Prussian blue | — | — |
| **1500A** | A434 | 400fr | light brown | — | — |
| **1501** | A434 | 425fr | bright green | — | — |
| **1502** | A434 | 500fr | olive brown | — | — |
| **1502A** | A434a | 600fr | gray | — | — |
| **1502B** | A434a | 700fr | bright lilac | — | — |
| **1503** | A434 | 800fr | black | — | — |
| **1504** | A434 | 1000fr | brt blue | — | — |

Issued: 10fr (#1484), 10fr (#1484A), 50fr (#1488A), 75fr, 100fr, 300fr, 500fr, 1000fr, 2002; 5fr, 20fr, 25fr, 40fr, 50fr (#1488), 60fr, 150fr, 175fr, 200fr, 250fr, 290fr, 360fr, 390fr, 425fr, 800fr, 3/12/02; 225fr, 400fr, 2003; 125fr, 350fr, 600fr, 700fr, 4/5/04.

At least two additional stamps exist in this set. The editors would like to examine any examples.

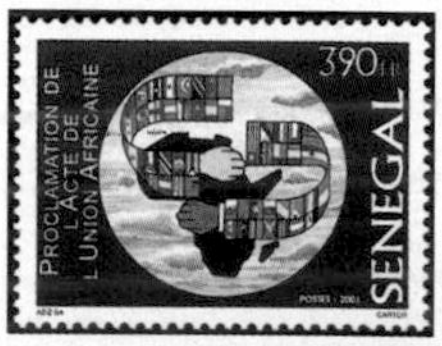

Proclamation of the Act of African Union — A435

Map of Africa and: 330fr, Handshake, vert. 390fr, Hands, flags.

**2002 Litho. *Perf. 13¼x13, 13x13¼***
**1505-1506** A435 Set of 2 2.00 2.00

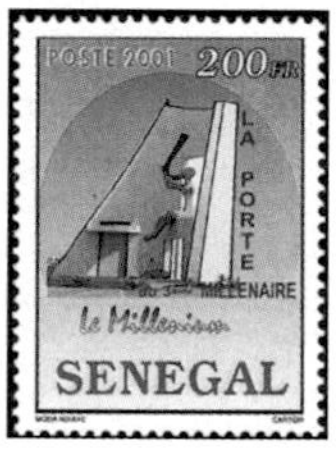

Door of the Third Millennium A436

Various depictions with frame colors of: 200fr, Orange. 290fr, Blue. 390fr, Olive green. 725fr, Rose pink.

**2002 *Perf. 13¼x13***
**1507-1510** A436 Set of 4 4.50 4.50

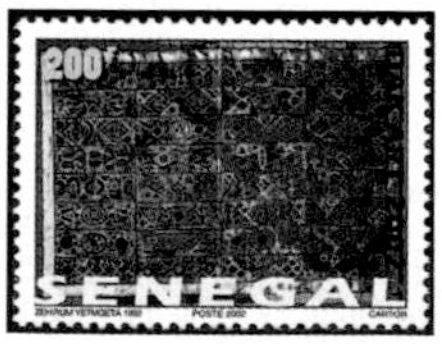

Dak'Art 2002 A437

Art by: 200fr, Zehirum Yetmgeta. 380fr, Moustapha Dime, vert. 400fr, Abdoulaye Konate. 425fr, Gora Mbengue.

**2002, Apr. 30 *Perf. 13x13¼, 13¼x13***
**1511-1514** A437 Set of 4 4.00 4.00

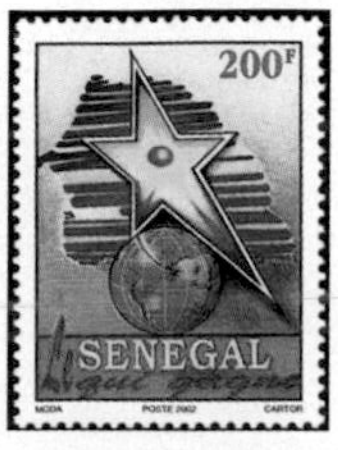

Star and Map of Senegal — A438

Denomination color: 200fr, Green. 380fr, Red.

**2002, May 15 *Perf. 13¼x13***
**1515-1516** A438 Set of 2 1.75 1.75

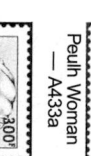

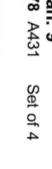

Stamps of 1935-38 Surcharged in Red or Black

**1941** **Perf. 12x12½, 12**
| | | | |
|---|---|---|---|
| B9 | A30 | 50c + 1fr red org | 1.60 |
| B10 | A31 | 80c + 2fr vio (R) | 4.25 |
| B11 | A30 | 1.50fr + 2fr dk bl | 4.25 |
| B12 | A30 | 2fr + 3fr blue | 4.25 |
| | | | 14.35 |

*Nos. B9-B12 (4)*

Common Design Type and

Colonial Soldier
SP2

Bambara Sharpshooter
SP1

**1941** **Photo.** **Perf. 13½**
| | | | |
|---|---|---|---|
| B13 | SP1 | 1fr + 1fr red | .80 |
| B14 | CD86 | 1.50fr + 3fr maroon | .80 |
| B15 | SP2 | 2.50fr + 1fr blue | .80 |
| | | | 2.40 |

*Nos. B13-B15 (3)*

The surtax was for the defense of the colonies.

Nos. B13-B15 were issued by the Vichy government, but it is doubtful whether they were placed in use in Senegal.

Nos. 193-194 Surcharged in Black or Red

Colonial Development Fund

**1944** **Engr.** **Perf. 12½x12**
| | | | |
|---|---|---|---|
| B15A | 50c + 1.50fr on 2.50fr deep blue (R) | | .55 |
| B15B | + 2.50fr on 1fr green | | .55 |

Nos. B15A-B15B were issued by the Vichy government in France, but were not placed on sale in Senegal.

Catalogue values for unused stamps in this section, from this point to the end of the section, are for Never Hinged items.

## Republic

Anti-Malaria Issue
Common Design Type

**Perf. 12½x12**
| | | | Engr. | Unwmk. |
|---|---|---|---|---|
| **1962, Apr. 7** | | | | |
| B16 | CD108 | 25fr + 5fr brt grn | 1.10 | .65 |

Freedom from Hunger Issue
Common Design Type

**Perf. 13**
| | | | |
|---|---|---|---|
| **1963, Mar. 21** | | | |
| B17 | CD112 | 25fr + 5fr dp vio, grn & brn | .80 | .50 |

SP3

---

Houses of Worship
A455

Designs: 200fr, Omarienne de Guédé Mosque. 225fr, Popenguine Basilica, vert. 250fr, Grand Mosque, Touba. 300fr, Grand Mosque, Tivaouane.

**Perf. 13x13¼, 13¼x13** **Litho.**
| | | | |
|---|---|---|---|
| **2004, Oct. 9** | | | 3.75 3.75 |
| 1567-1570 | A455 | Set of 4 | |

Locally Produced Crops — A456

Designs: 100fr, Millet. 150fr, Cowpeas, millet and corn, horiz. 200fr, Corn. 300fr, Rice.

**Perf. 13½x13¼, 13½x13** **Litho.**
| | | | |
|---|---|---|---|
| **2004, Dec. 6** | | | 3.00 3.00 |
| 1571-1574 | A456 | Set of 4 | |

27th Paris-Dakar Rally — A457

Designs: 45fr, Automobile, motorcycle and truck. 550fr, Motorcycle, vert.

**Perf. 13x13¼, 13¼x13** **Litho.**
| | | | |
|---|---|---|---|
| **2005, Jan. 16** | | | 4.00 4.00 |
| 1575-1576 | A457 | Set of 2 | |

## SEMI-POSTAL STAMPS

No. 84 Surcharged in Red

**1915** **Unwmk.** **Perf. 14x13½**
| | | | |
|---|---|---|---|
| B1 | A28 | 10c + 5c org rod & rose | 1.25 1.10 |

No. B1 is on both ordinary and chalky paper.

Same Surcharge on No. 87

**1918**
| | | | |
|---|---|---|---|
| B2 | A28 | 15c + 5c red org & brn vio | 1.25 1.10 |

Curie Issue
Common Design Type

**Perf. 13**
| | | | Engr. |
|---|---|---|---|
| **1938** | | | |
| B3 | CD80 | 1.75fr + 50c brt ultra | 8.50 9.75 |

French Revolution Issue
Common Design Type

Photo., Name & Value Typo. in Black

**1939**
| | | | |
|---|---|---|---|
| B4 | CD83 | 45c + 25c green | 8.00 8.00 |
| B5 | CD83 | 70c + 30c brown | 8.00 8.00 |
| B6 | CD83 | 90c + 35c red org | 8.00 8.00 |
| B7 | CD83 | 1.25fr + 1fr rose | 8.00 8.00 |
| | | pink | |
| B8 | CD83 | 2.25fr + 2fr blue | 40.00 40.00 |

*Nos. B4-B8 (5)*

---

Sculptures
A449

Designs: 200fr, Le Caïlcedrat Mort. 300fr, Tete d'un Sorcier. 380fr, Le Laardi. 440fr, Le Thioury.

**Perf. 13¼x13** **Litho.**
| | | | |
|---|---|---|---|
| **2003, July 16** | | | 11.50 11.50 |
| 1546-1549 | A449 | Set of 4 | |

26th Paris-Dakar Rally — A451

Designs: 390fr, Motorcyclists. 500fr, Motorcyclist and car.

**Perf. 13¼x13¼** **Litho.**
| | | | |
|---|---|---|---|
| **2004, Jan. 14** | | | 3.50 3.50 |
| 1553-1554 | A451 | Set of 2 | |

Dated 2003.

Intl. Cycling Union, Cent. (in 2000) A452

**Perf. 13¼x13**
| | | |
|---|---|---|
| **2004?** | A452 | Litho. |
| 1555 | A452 | 45fr multi |
| 1557 | A452 | 275frmulti |

Dated 2000.

Historic Sites A453

Designs: 240fr, Dakar Railroad Station. 370fr, Fort Podor. 390fr, Dakar City Hall. 500fr, Notre Dame des Victoires Cathedral.

**Perf. 13¼x13¼** **Litho.**
| | | | |
|---|---|---|---|
| **2004, Apr. 29** | | | 5.50 5.50 |
| 1559-1562 | A453 | Set of 4 | |

Dated 2003.

African Cup of Nations Soccer Tournament A454

Designs: 200fr, Cup, emblem. 300fr, Cup, soccer ball, stadium, television, horiz. 400fr, Emblems, players shaking hands, horiz. 425fr, Players in action, horiz.

**Perf. 13¼x13¼, 13x13¼** **Litho.**
| | | | |
|---|---|---|---|
| **2004** | | | 5.50 5.50 |
| 1563-1566 | A454 | Set of 4 | |

---

Horses A440

Designs: 30fr, Mbayar du Baol. 200fr, Mpar du Cayor. 250fr, Narougor. 300fr, Foutanke.

**Perf. 13x13¼** **Litho.**
| | | | |
|---|---|---|---|
| **2002, Dec. 20** | | | 2.50 2.50 |
| 1519-1522 | A440 | Set of 4 | |

New Partnership for African Development — A446

Designs: 260fr, Map of Africa, symbols of industry. 290fr, Map of Africa, bird, model of atom.

**Perf. 13¼x13, 13x13¼** **Litho.**
| | | | |
|---|---|---|---|
| **2003, June 22** | | | |
| 1533 | A444 | 200fr shown | .70 .70 |
| 1534 | A444 | 200fr multi | .85 .85 |
| 1535 | A445 | 250fr multi | .85 .85 |
| 1536 | A444 | 290fr multi | 1.00 1.00 |
| 1537 | A446 | 360fr shown | 1.25 1.25 |
| | | | 4.65 4.65 |

*Nos. 1533-1537 (5)*

Traditional Costumes — A447

Designs: 250fr, Goumbé Lébou. 360fr, Badiaranké. 390fr, Grand Boubou. 500fr, Bowede.

**Perf. 13¼x13** **Litho.**
| | | | |
|---|---|---|---|
| **2003, July 16** | | | 5.25 5.25 |
| 1538-1541 | A447 | Set of 4 | |

Marine Life A448

Designs: 290fr, Cymbium cymbium. 370fr, Herring. 380fr, Catfish. 400fr, Chelonia mydas.

**Perf. 13x13¼** **Litho.**
| | | | |
|---|---|---|---|
| **2003, July 16** | | | 5.00 5.00 |
| 1542-1545 | A448 | Set of 4 | |

## 2002 World Cup Soccer Championships, Japan and Korea — SP4

World Cup: 290fr+50fr, Soccer ball and stadium. 360fr+50fr, Soccer field and crowd.

**2002** **Litho.** **Perf. 13½**
| B18 | SP3 | 75fr +100fr shown | .55 | .55 |

**Perf. 13x13¼**
| B19 | SP4 | 200fr +100fr shown | .95 | .95 |
| B20 | SP4 | 290fr +50fr multi | 1.10 | 1.10 |
| B21 | SP4 | 360fr +50fr multi | 1.25 | 1.25 |

Nos. B18-B21 (4) 3.85 3.85

Value for No. B18 is for example with surrounding selvage.

## AIR POST STAMPS

Caravan AP2

Landscape AP1

**1935** **Engr.** **Perf. 12½x12, 12x12½**
| | | | Unwmk. | |
| C1 | AP1 | 25c dk brown | .20 | .20 |
| C2 | AP1 | 50c red orange | .45 | .35 |
| C3 | AP1 | 1fr rose lilac | .20 | .20 |
| C4 | AP1 | 1.25fr yellow grn | .20 | .20 |
| C5 | AP1 | 2fr blue | .20 | .20 |
| C6 | AP1 | 3fr olive grn | .35 | .20 |
| C7 | AP1 | 3.50fr violet | .35 | .20 |
| C8 | AP2 | 4.75fr orange | .75 | .35 |
| C9 | AP2 | 6.50fr dk blue | .85 | .75 |
| C10 | AP2 | 8fr black | 1.40 | 1.25 |
| C11 | AP2 | 15fr rose lake | 1.10 | .80 |

Nos. C1-C11 (11) 6.05 4.70

**1940** **Common Design Type** **Engr.** **Perf. 12½x12**
| C12 | CD85 | 1.90fr ultra | .35 | .35 |
| C13 | CD85 | 2.90fr dk red | .35 | .40 |
| C14 | CD85 | 4.50fr dk gray grn | .40 | .50 |
| C15 | CD85 | 4.90fr yellow bis | .95 | .85 |
| C16 | CD85 | 6.90fr dp orange | 2.70 | 3.40 |

Nos. C12-C16 (5)

**1942** **Common Design Types**
| C17 | CD88 | 50c car & bl | .20 | .20 |
| C18 | CD88 | 1fr brn & blk | .35 | .35 |
| C19 | CD88 | 2fr dk grn & red brn | .35 | .35 |
| C20 | CD88 | 3fr dk bl & scar | .80 | .80 |
| C21 | CD88 | 5fr vio & brn red | .55 | |

**Frame Engr., Center Typo.**
| C22 | CD89 | 10fr ultra, ind & hn | .55 | |
| C23 | CD89 | 20fr rose car, mag & choc | .80 | |
| C24 | CD89 | 50fr yel grn, dl grn & yel | 1.40 | 2.40 |

No. C8 surcharged "ENTR' AIDE FRANCAIS + 95f 25" in green, red violet or blue, was never issued in this colony.

## Republic

Abyssinian Roller — AP3

Designs: 50fr, Carmine bee-eater, vert. 200fr, Violet touraco, vert. 250fr, Red bishop, vert. 500fr, Fish eagle, vert.

**1960-63** **Photo.** **Unwmk.**
**Birds in Natural Colors**
**Perf. 12½x13, 13x12½**
| C26 | AP3 | 50fr blk & gray bl | 2.25 | |
| C27 | AP3 | 100fr blk, yel & lil ('61) | 4.00 | 1.00 |
| C28 | AP3 | 200fr blk, grn & bl ('61) | 9.00 | 2.50 |
| C29 | AP3 | 250fr blk & pale grn ('63) | 9.00 | 3.00 |
| C30 | AP3 | 500fr blk & bl ('63) | 25.00 | 5.25 |

Nos. C26-C30 (5) 49.25 12.25

**Common Design Type**
**Air Afrique Issue**
**1962, Feb. 17** **Engr.** **Perf. 13**
| C31 | CD107 | 25fr vio brn, sl grn & ocher | .80 | .30 |

**African Postal Union Issue**
**Common Design Type**
**1963, Sept. 8** **Photo.** **Perf. 12½**
| C32 | CD114 | 85fr choc, ocher & red | 1.75 | .50 |

**Air Afrique Issue, 1963**
**Common Design Type**
**1963, Nov. 19** **Unwmk.** **Perf. 13x12**
| C33 | CD115 | 50fr multicolored | 2.00 | .65 |

African Postal Union Issue
Common Design Type

**1964, Apr. 4** **Photo.** **Perf. 12x13**
| C34 | AP4 | 300fr ultra, tan, ocher & grn | 5.00 | 1.75 |

Independence Monument — AP4

Symbolic European and African Cities — AP5

**1964, Apr. 18** **Engr.** **Perf. 13**
| C35 | AP5 | 150fr grn, brn red & blk | 4.00 | 1.40 |

Congress of the Intl. Federation of Twin Cities, Dakar.

**Engr. & Photo.**
**Size: 47x26mm**
| C25 | CD88 | 100fr dk red & bl | 1.75 | 3.25 |

Nos. C17-C25 (9) 6.75

There is doubt whether Nos. C17 to C23 were officially placed in use.

**Catalogue values for unused stamps in this section, from this point to the end of the section, are for Never Hinged items.**

## Europafrica Issue, 1964

Europafrica — AP6

**1964, July 20** **Photo.** **Perf. 13x12**
| C36 | AP6 | 50fr multicolored | 2.00 | .60 |

See note after Madagascar No. 357.

Peanuts, Globe, Factory, Figures of "Africa," and "Europe" — AP6

Launching of Syncom 2 — AP8

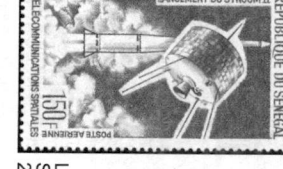

Communication through space.

**1964, Aug. 22** **Engr.** **Perf. 13**
| C37 | AP7 | 85fr shown | 2.50 | .65 |
| C38 | AP7 | 100fr Pole vault | 2.75 | 1.00 |

18th Olympic Games, Tokyo, Oct. 10-25.

**1964, Oct. 24** **Unwmk.** **Perf. 13**
| C39 | AP8 | 150fr grn, red brn & ul-tra | 3.00 | 1.00 |

Basketball AP7

Pres. John F. Kennedy (1917-1963) AP9

Mother and Child, Globe and Emblems AP10

**1964, Dec. 5** **Photo.** **Perf. 13**
| C40 | AP9 | 100fr brt yel, dk grn & brn red | 2.75 | 1.00 |

a. Souvenir sheet of 4 12.00 12.00

## A-1 Satellite and Earth — AP11

Scenic Type of Regular Issue, 1965
View: 100fr, Shore of Gambia River in Eastern Senegal.

**1965, Feb. 27** **Engr.** **Perf. 13**
**Size: 48x27mm**
| C41 | A48 | 100fr brn blk, grn & bis | 2.50 | 1.00 |

**1965, Sept. 25** **Unwmk.** **Perf. 13**
| C42 | AP10 | 50fr choc, brt bl & grn | 1.25 | .40 |

International Cooperation Year.

Designs: No. C44, Diamant rocket. 90fr, Scout rocket and FR-1 satellite.

**1966, Feb. 19** **Engr.** **Perf. 13**
| C43 | AP11 | 50fr yel brn, dk grn & blk | 1.00 | .40 |
| C44 | AP11 | 50fr Prus bl, lt red brn & car rose | 1.00 | .40 |
| C45 | AP11 | 90fr dk red brn, bl, gray & Prus bl | 2.50 | .85 |

Nos. C43-C45 (3) 4.50 1.65

French achievements in space.

## D-1 Satellite over Globe — AP12

**1966, June 11** **Engr.** **Perf. 13**
| C46 | AP12 | 100fr dk car, sl & vio | 2.50 | .80 |

Launching of the D-1 satellite at Hammaguir, Algeria, Feb. 17, 1966.

**Air Afrique Issue, 1966**
**Common Design Type**
**1966, Aug. 31** **Photo.** **Perf. 13**
| C47 | CD123 | 30fr red brn, blk & lem | .80 | .30 |

Jean Mermoz — AP14

Mermoz Plane "Arc-en-Ciel" — AP13

Designs: 35fr, Latecoère 300 "Croix du Sud." 100fr, Map showing last flight from Dakar to Brazil.

**1966, Dec. 7** **Engr.** **Perf. 13**
| C48 | AP13 | 20fr bl, rose lil & indigo | .80 | .20 |
| C49 | AP13 | 35fr slate, brn & grn | 1.00 | .20 |
| C50 | AP13 | 100fr grn, lt grn & mar | 1.75 | .50 |
| C51 | AP14 | 150fr blk, ultra & mar | 3.50 | 1.00 |

Nos. C48-C51 (4) 7.05 2.00

Jean Mermoz (1901-36), French aviator, on the 30th anniv. of his last flight.

René Maran, Martinique AP28

Portraits: 45fr, Marcus Garvey, Jamaica. 50fr, Dr. Price Mars, Haiti.

**1970, Mar. 21    Photo.    *Perf. 12½***
C76  AP28  30fr red brn, lt grn & blk    .35    .20
C77  AP28  45fr blue, pink & blk    1.00    .25
C78  AP28  50fr grn, buff & blk    1.10    .40
    *Nos. C76-C78 (3)*    2.45    .85

Issued to honor prominent Negro leaders.

"One People, One Purpose, One Faith" AP29

**1970, Apr. 3    Photo.    *Perf. 11½***
C79  AP29  500fr gold & multi    7.50    3.00
    *a.    Souvenir sheet*    10.00    10.00

10th anniv. of independence. No. C79 sold fu 000fr.

Bay of Naples and Dakar Post Office — AP30

**1970, May 2    Photo.    *Perf. 13x12½***
C80  AP30  100fr multicolored    2.00    .60

10th Europa Phil. Exhib., Naples. May 2-10.

Blue Cock, by Mamadou Niang AP31

Tapestries: 45fr, Fairy. 75fr, "Lunaris," by Jean Lurçat.

**1970, June 20    Photo.    *Perf. 12½'x12***
C81  AP31  30fr black & multi    .55    .35
C82  AP31  45fr dk red brn & multi    2.00    .50
C83  AP31  75fr yellow & multi    3.00    .65
    *Nos. C81-C83 (3)*    5.55    1.50

---

Pres. Lamine Gueye (1891-1968) AP23

Design: 45fr, Pres. Gueye wearing fez.

**1969, June 10    Photo.    *Perf. 12½***
C70  AP23  30fr brn, org & blk    .45    .20
C71  AP23  45fr brn, lt grnsh bl & blk    1.25    .30
    *a.    Min. sheet, 2 ea #C70-C71*    3.50    3.50

"Transmission of Thought" Tapestry by Ousmane Faye — AP24

Fari, Tapestry by Allaye N'Diaye — AP25

**1969, Oct. 26    Photo.    *Perf. 12½***
C72  AP24  25fr multicolored    .90    .35
    *Perf. 12x12½*
C73  AP25  50fr multicolored    2.00    .65

Europafrica Issue

Baila Bridge — AP26

**1969, Nov. 15    Photo.    *Perf. 13x12***
C74  AP26  100fr multicolored    2.00    .50

Emile Lécrivain, Plane and Toulouse-Dakar Route — AP27

**1970, Jan. 31    Engr.    *Perf. 13***
C75  AP27  50fr grn, slate & rose brn    1.25    .40

40th anniv. of the disappearance of the aviator Emile Lécrivain (1897-1929).

---

Weather Balloon, Vegetation and WMO Emblem — AP19

**1968, Feb. 17    Photo.    *Perf. 12½***
C61  AP18  100fr dk red, ol & blk    2.25    .60
    *a.    Souvenir sheet of 4*    10.00    10.00

Konrad Adenauer (1876-1967), chancellor of West Germany (1949-63).

**1968, Mar. 23    Engr.    *Perf. 13***
C62  AP19  50fr blk, ultra & bl grn    1.25    .40

8th World Meteorological Day, Mar. 23.

19th Olympic Games, Mexico City, Oct. 12-27 — AP20

**1968, Oct. 12    Engr.    *Perf. 13***
C63  AP20  20fr Hurdling    .55    .20
C64  AP20  30fr Javelin    .70    .30
C65  AP20  50fr Judn    1.40    .35
C66  AP20  75fr Basketball    2.25    .65
    *Nos. C63-C66 (4)*    4.90    1.50

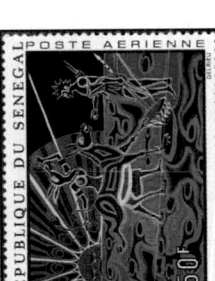

Young Woman Reading Letter, by Jean Raoux AP21

**1968, Oct. 26    Photo.    *Perf. 12½***
C67  AP21  100fr buff & multi    3.50    2.00

PHILEXAFRIQUE Issue

PHILEXAFRIQUE, Phil. Exhib. in Abidjan, Feb. 14-23, 1969. Printed with alternating buff label.

2nd PHILEXAFRIQUE Issue
Common Design Type

Senegal #160 and Boulevard, Dakar.

**1969, Feb. 14    Engr.    *Perf. 13***
C68  CD128  50fr grn, gray & pur    2.00    1.40

Tourist Emblem with Map of Africa and Dove — AP22

**1969    Photo.    *Perf. 13***
C69  AP22  100fr red, lt grn & lt bl    1.75    .50

Year of African Tourism, 1969.

---

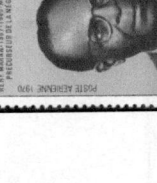

Dakar-Yoff Airport — AP15

**1967, Apr. 22    Engr.    *Perf. 13***
C52  AP15  200fr red brn, ind & brt bl    3.50    1.00

Knob-billed Goose — AP16

Flowers and Birds. 100fr, Mimosa. 150fr, Flowering cactus. 250fr, Village weaver. 500fr, Bateleur.

**1967-69    Photo.**
**Granite Paper**
**Dated "1967"**
C53  AP16  100fr gray, yel & grn    2.50    .80
C54  AP16  150fr multicolored    4.25    1.25
**Dated "1968"**
C55  AP16  250fr gray & multi    7.25    1.40
**Dated "1969"**
C56  AP16  300fr brt bl & multi    10.00    2.00
C57  AP16  500fr orange & multi    16.00    3.25
    *Nos. C53-C57 (5)*    40.00    8.70

Issued: 100fr, 150fr, 6/24/67; 500fr, 7/13/68; 300fr, 12/7/1'b8; 250fr, 4/26/69

The Girls from Avignon, by Picasso AP17

**1967, July 22    *Perf. 12x13***
C59  AP17  100fr multicolored    3.50    1.00

African Postal Union Issue, 1967
Common Design Type

**1967, Sept. 9    Engr.    *Perf. 13***
C60  CD124  100fr brt grn, vio & car lake    1.75    .50

Konrad Adenauer AP18

Head of the Courtesan Nagakawa, by Chobunsai Yeishi, and Mt. Fuji, by Hokusai — AP32

**1970, July 18**  **Engr.**  **Perf. 13**
EXPO Emblem and: 25fr, Woman Playing Guitar, by Hokusai, and Sun Tower, vert. 150fr, "One of the Present-day Beauties of Nanboku" by Katsukawa Shuncho, vert.

| | | | |
|---|---|---|---|
| C84 | AP32 | 25fr red & green | .65 .20 |
| C85 | AP32 | 75fr yel grn, dk bl & red brn | 1.75 .35 |
| C86 | AP32 | 150fr bl, red brn & ocher | 2.75 .80 |

Nos. C84-C86 (3)  5.15 1.35

EXPO '70 Intl. Exhib., Osaka, Japan, Mar. 15-Sept. 13.

---

Tuna, Processing Plant and Ship — AP33

Urban Development in Dakar — AP34

**1970, Aug. 22**  **Engr.**  **Perf. 13**
C87 AP33 30fr dl red, blk & brt bl 1.00 .20
C88 AP34 100fr chocolate & grn 1.75 .60

Progress in industrialization and urbanization in Dakar.

---

**1970, Sept. 26**  **Engr.**  **Perf. 13**
Design: 100fr, Beethoven holding quill.
C89 AP35 50fr ol, brn & ocher 2.25 .50
C90 AP35 100fr Prus grn & dp claret 4.50 1.10

Beethoven; Napoleon and Allegory of Eroica Symphony AP35

Ludwig van Beethoven (1770-1827), composer.

---

Globe, Scales and Women of Four Races — AP36

**1970, Oct. 24**  **Perf. 13**
C91 AP36 100fr grn, ocher & red 2.25 .80
25th anniversary of United Nations.

---

De Gaulle, Map of Africa, Symbols — AP37

---

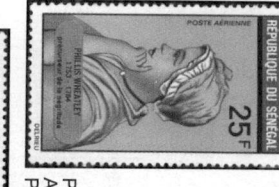

Phillis Wheatley, American Poet — AP39

**1970, Dec. 31**  **Photo.**  **Perf. 12½**
100fr, Charles de Gaulle & map of Senegal.
C92 AP37 50fr multicolored 1.75 .85
C93 AP37 100fr blue & multi 3.50 1.60

Honoring Pres. Charles de Gaulle as liberator of the colonies.

---

**1971, Jan. 16**
C94 AP38 100fr multicolored 1.75 .65
High Commissioner for Refugees, 20th anniv.

"A Roof for Every Refugee" — AP38

---

**1971, Apr. 10**  **Photo.**  **Perf. 12½**
Prominent Blacks: 40fr, James E. K. Aggrey, Methodist missionary, Ghana. 60fr, Alain Le Roy Locke, American educator. 100fr, Booker T. Washington, American educator.

| | | | |
|---|---|---|---|
| C95 | AP39 | 25fr multicolored | .25 .20 |
| C96 | AP39 | 40fr blk, bl & bis | .45 .30 |
| C97 | AP39 | 60fr blk, bl & emer | 1.00 .40 |
| C98 | AP39 | 100fr blk, bl & red | 1.50 .60 |

Nos. C95-C98 (4)  3.20 1.50

---

Napoleon as First Consul, by Ingres AP40

**1971, June 19**  **Photo.**  **Perf. 13**
Designs: 25fr, Napoleon in 1809, by Robert Lefevre. 35fr, Napoleon on his death bed, by Georges Rouget. 50fr, Awakening into Immortality, sculpture by Francois Rude.

| | | | |
|---|---|---|---|
| C99 | AP40 | 15fr gold & multi | .70 .40 |
| C100 | AP40 | 25fr gold & multi | 1.00 .50 |
| C101 | AP40 | 35fr gold & multi | 1.40 .60 |
| C102 | AP40 | 50fr gold & multi | 1.75 1.00 |

Nos. C99-C102 (4)  5.85 2.50

Napoleon Bonaparte (1769-1821).

---

Gamal Abdel Nasser — AP41

Alfred Nobel — AP41a

**1971, July 17**  **Perf. 12½**
C103 AP41 50fr multicolored 1.00 .30
Nasser (1918-1970), President of Egypt.

**1971, Sept. 25**  **Photo.**  **Perf. 13½x13**
C103A AP41a 100fr multicolored 2.25 .60
Alfred Nobel (1833-1896), inventor of dynamite who established the Nobel Prizes.

---

Iranian Flag and Senegal Coat of Arms — AP42

**1971, Oct. 15**  **Perf. 13x12½**
C104 AP42 200fr multicolored 3.00 1.00
2500th anniversary of the founding of the Persian empire by Cyrus the Great.

---

**African Postal Union Issue, 1971**
Common Design Type

**1971, Nov. 13**  **Perf. 13x13½**
C105 CD135 100fr blue & multi 1.60 .50

Design: 100fr, Arms of Senegal and UAMPT Building, Brazzaville, Congo.

---

Sapporo Olympic Emblem and Speed Skating — AP44

**1972, Jan. 22**  **Photo.**  **Perf. 13**
Sapporo '72 Emblem and: 10fr, Bobsledding. 125fr, Skiing.
C107 AP44 5fr multicolored .25 .20
C108 AP44 10fr multicolored .25 .20
C109 AP44 125fr multicolored 2.75 .60

Nos. C107-C109 (3)  3.25 1.00

11th Winter Olympic Games, Sapporo, Japan, Feb. 3-13.

---

Louis Armstrong (1900-1971), American Jazz Musician — AP43

**1971, Nov. 27**  **Photo.**  **Perf. 12½**
C106 AP43 150fr gold & dk brn 6.75 1.60

---

Fonteghetto della Farina, by Canaletto — AP45

**1972, Feb. 26**  **Photo.**  **Perf. 12½x12½**
Design: 100fr, San Giorgio Maggiore, by Giovanni Antonio Guardi, vert.
C110 AP45 50fr gold & multi 1.25 .65
C111 AP45 100fr gold & multi 2.50 1.25

UNESCO campaign to save Venice.

**1972, Mar. 25**  **Photo.**  **Perf. 12½x13**
Theater Type of Regular Issue
150fr, Daniel Sorano as Shylock, vert.
C112 A99 150fr multicolored 4.00 1.50

**1972, June 3**  **Photo.**  **Perf. 13½x13**
Environment Type of Regular Issue
100fr, Protection of the ocean (oil slick).
C113 A101 100fr multicolored 2.25 .60

---

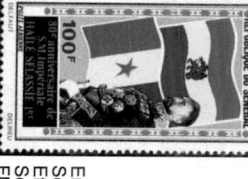

Emperor Haile Selassie, Ethiopian and Senegalese Flags — AP46

**1972, July 23**  **Photo.**  **Perf. 13½x13**
C114 AP46 100fr gold & multi 1.75 .60
80th birthday of Emperor Haile Selassie of Ethiopia.

---

Swordfish — AP47

**1972-73**  **Photo.**  **Perf. 11½**
Designs: 65fr, Killer whale. 75fr, Rhinocodon. 125fr, Common rorqual (whale).

| | | | |
|---|---|---|---|
| C115 | AP47 | 50fr multi | 3.00 .65 |
| C116 | AP47 | 65fr multi | 4.00 1.00 |
| C117 | AP47 | 75fr multi | 6.25 1.25 |
| C118 | AP47 | 125fr multi | 7.25 1.40 |

Nos. C115-C118 (4)  20.50 4.30

Issued: #C115, C118, 11/25/72; #C116-C117, 7/28/73.

---

Palace of the Republic — AP48

**1973, Apr. 3**  **Photo.**  **Perf. 13**
C119 AP48 100fr multi 1.75 .60

Spaceship and Control Room — AP62

**1977, June 25    Litho.    Perf. 12½**
C144 AP62 300fr multi    3.25 1.25
Viking space mission to Mars.

No. C143 Overprinted in Red:
"22.11.77 / PARIS NEW-YORK"

**1977, Nov. 22    Perf. 13**
C145 AP61 300fr multi    4.00 2.00
Concorde, 1st commercial flight, Paris-New York.

Evolution of Fishing — AP62a

Designs: 10fr, Fishermen hauling in netted catch. 15fr, Two fishermen in canoe. 20fr, Ship, man holding fish. 25fr, Fisherman holding net.

**1977    Litho.    Perf. 12¾**
C145A AP62a 5fr shown    — —
C145B AP62a 10fr multi    — —
C116C AP62a 15fr multi    — —
C145D AP62a 20fr multi    — —
C145E AP62a 25fr multi    — —

**Philexafrique II-Essen Issue**
**Common Design Types**

Designs: No. C146, Lion & Senegal #C28. No. C147, Caporalulé & Schleswig Holstein #1.

**1978, Nov. 1    Litho.    Perf. 12½**
C146 CD138 100fr multi    2.00 1.50
C147 CD139 100fr multi    2.00 1.50
a.    Pair, #C146-C147    10.00 4.00

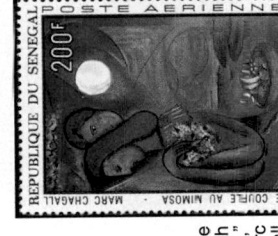

J. Dabry, L. Gimie, and J. Mermoz, Airplane, Map of Route (St. Louis-Natal) — AP63

**1980, Dec.    Photo.    Perf. 13**
C148 AP63 300fr multi    3.25 1.00
1st airmail crossing of So. Atlantic, 50th anniv.

1st Transatlantic Commercial Airmail Flight, 55th Anniv. — AP64

**1985, May 12    Litho.    Perf. 13**
C149 AP64 250fr multi    2.75 1.00

---

Soyuz and Apollo, Space Docking Emblem — AP58

**1975, May 23    Engr.    Perf. 13**
C138 AP58 125fr multi    2.00 .60
US-USSR space cooperation.
For overprint see No. C140.

Senegal Type D6, Tuscany Type A1, Map of Italy AP59

**1975, Aug. 23    Engr.    Perf. 13**
C139 AP59 125fr org, vio & dk red    2.00 .65
Intl. Phil. Exhib., Riccione 1975.

No. C138 Overprinted: "JONCTION / 17 Juil. 1975"

**1975, Oct. 21    Engr.    Perf. 13**
C140 AP58 125fr multi    2.00 .60
Apollo-Soyuz link-up in space, July 17, 1975.

Boston Massacre — AP60

Design: 500fr, Lafayette, Washington, Rochambeau and Battle of Yorktown.

**1975, Dec. 20    Perf. 13**
C141 AP60 250fr ultra, red & brn    3.00 1.10
C142 AP60 500fr bl & ver    6.75 2.50
American Bicentennial.

Concorde and Map — AP61

**1976, Jan. 21    Litho.    Perf. 13**
C143 AP61 300fr multi    4.00 2.00
First commercial flight of supersonic jet Concorde, Paris to Rio de Janeiro, Jan. 21.
For overprint see No. C145.

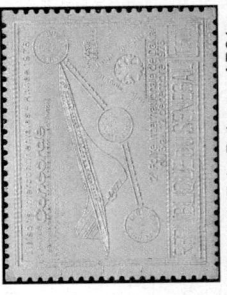

2nd Intl. Fair, Dakar — AP61a

**1976, Dec. 3    Embossed    Perf. 10½**
C143A AP61a 500fr silver    6.50 6.50
C143B AP61a 1500fr gold    27.50 27.50

---

**1973, Dec. 15    Photo.    Perf. 13½**
65fr, Human Rights flame and drummer.
C126 AP54 35fr grn & multi    .70 .25
C127 AP54 65fr org & multi    1.00 .40
25th anniv. of the Universal Declaration of Human Rights.

Men of Four Races, Arms of Dakar, Congress Emblem — AP55

50fr, Key joining twin cities & emblem, vert.

**1973, Dec. 26    Photo.**
C128 AP55 50fr org & multi    .90 .35
C129 AP55 125fr red & multi    1.75 .50
8th Congress of the World Federation of Twin Cities, Dakar, Dec. 26-29.

Finfoots — AP56

**1974, Feb. 9    Photo.    Perf. 13**
C130 AP56 1fr shown    .20 .20
C131 AP56 2fr Swoumbillo    .20 .20
C132 AP56 3fr Crested cranes    .25 .20
C133 AP56 4fr Egrets    .25 .20
C134 AP56 250fr Flamingos    6.25 1.50
C135 AP56 250fr Flamingos    6.25 1.50
a.    Strip of 2 + label    12.50
Nos. C130-C135 (6)    13.40 3.80
Djoudj Park bird sanctuary. Denomination in gold on No. C134, in black on No. C135.

Tiger Attacking Wild Horse, by Delacroix — AP57

Design: 200fr, Tiger Hunt, by Eugéne Delacroix (1798-1863).

**1974, Mar. 23    Photo.    Perf. 13**
C136 AP57 150fr gold & multi    3.00 .80
C137 AP57 200fr gold & multi    3.75 1.25

Intl. Fair, Dakar — AP57a

**1974, Nov. 28    Embossed    Perf. 10½**
C137A AP57a 350fr silver    5.75 4.50
C137B AP57a 1500fr gold    27.50 18.00

---

Hotel Teranga, Dakar — AP49

**1973, May 26    Photo.    Perf. 13**
C120 AP49 100fr multi    1.75 .60

Emblem of African Lions Club — AP50

**1973, June 2    Perf. 13**
C121 AP50 150fr multi    2.50 .80
15th Congress of Lions Intl., District 403, Dakar, June 1-2.

"Couple with Mimosa," by Marc Chagall AP51

**1973, Aug. 11    Photo.    Perf. 13**
C122 AP51 200fr multi    5.25 2.10

Map of Italy with Riccione AP52

**1973, Aug. 25    Engr.**
C123 AP52 100fr dk grn, red & pur    2.25 .60
Intl. Phil. Exhib., Riccione 1973.

Human Rights Flame and People AP54

Raoul Follereau and World Map — AP53

**1973, Dec. 22    Engr.    Perf. 13**
100fr, Dr. Armauer G. Hansen & leprosy bacilli.
C124 AP53 40fr sl grn, pur & red brn    .90 .20
C125 AP53 100fr sl grn, mag & plum    1.75 .60
Centenary of the discovery of the Hansen bacillus, the cause of leprosy.

Clement Ader (1841-1926), Engineer and Aviation Pioneer — AP65

Ader and: 145fr, Automobile, microphone, 180fr, 615fr, 940fr, Bat-winged steam powered airplane.

**1991, June 7 — Litho. — Perf. 13**

| | | | |
|---|---|---|---|
| C150 | AP65 | 145fr multicolored | 2.00 .40 |
| C151 | AP65 | 180fr multicolored | 2.25 .60 |
| C152 | AP65 | 615fr multi, vert. | 7.50 2.25 |
| | | Nos. C150-C152 (3) | 11.75 3.30 |

**Souvenir Sheet**

| | | | |
|---|---|---|---|
| C153 | AP65 | 940fr multi, vert. | 7.00 3.50 |

## AIR POST SEMI-POSTAL STAMPS

**1939 French Revolution Issue**
Common Design Type
Unwmk. Photo. Perf. 13

| | | | |
|---|---|---|---|
| CB1 | CD83 | 4.75 + 4fr brn blk | 10.00 11.00 |

Surtax used for the defense of the colonies.

Dahomey types SPAP1-SPAP3 inscribed Senegal

Perf. 13½x12½, 13 (#CB4)

**1942, June 22 — Photo, Engr. (#CB4)**

| | | | |
|---|---|---|---|
| CB2 | SPAP1 | 1.50fr + 3.50fr green | .66 4.00 |
| CB3 | SHAP2 | 2fr + 6fr brown | .65 4.00 |
| CB4 | SPAP3 | 3fr + 9fr car red | .65 4.00 |
| | | Nos. CB2-CB4 (3) | 1.95 12.00 |

Native children's welfare fund.

**Colonial Education Fund**
Common Design Type

**1942, June 22 — Perf. 12½x13½**

| | | | |
|---|---|---|---|
| CB5 | CD8a | 1.20fr + 1.80fr blue & red | .45 4.00 |

**1964, Mar. 7 — Engr. — Perf. 13**

| | | | |
|---|---|---|---|
| CB6 | SPAP1 | 25fr + 5fr Prus bl, red brn & si grn | 1.60 .65 |

UNESCO campaign to save historic monuments in Nubia.

Nile Gods Uniting Upper and Lower Egypt (Abu Simbel) — SPAP1

Catalogue values for unused stamps in this section, from this point to the end of the section, are for Never Hinged items.

## POSTAGE DUE STAMPS

Postage Due Stamps of French Colonies Surcharged

**1903 — Unwmk.**

| | | | |
|---|---|---|---|
| J1 | D1 | 10c on 50c lilac | 62.50 62.50 |
| J2 | D1 | 10c on 60c brown, buff | 65.00 65.00 |
| J3 | D1 | 10c on 1fr rose, buff | 350.00 375.00 |
| | | Nos. J1-J3 (3) | 475.00 505.00 |

### Republic

**1906 — Typo. — Perf. 14x13½**

| | | | |
|---|---|---|---|
| J4 | D2 | 5c green, grnsh | 4.50 3.25 |
| J5 | D2 | 10c red brown | 4.00 4.00 |
| J6 | D2 | 15c dark blue | 6.75 7.50 |
| J7 | D2 | 20c black, yellow | 7.25 4.50 |
| J8 | D2 | 30c red, straw | 9.00 9.00 |
| J9 | D2 | 50c violet | 10.00 10.00 |
| J10 | D2 | 1fr black, buff | 13.50 14.50 |
| J11 | D2 | 1fr black, pinkish | 20.00 20.00 |
| | | Nos. J4-J11 (8) | 77.25 72.75 |

**1914**

| | | | |
|---|---|---|---|
| J12 | D3 | 5c green, grnsh | .35 .35 |
| J13 | D3 | 10c rose | .35 .35 |
| J14 | D3 | 15c gray | .55 .55 |
| J15 | D3 | 20c brown | .65 .65 |
| J16 | D3 | 30c blue | 1.10 .85 |
| J17 | D3 | 60c orange | 1.50 1.10 |
| J18 | D3 | 60c orange | 1.60 1.40 |
| J19 | D3 | 1fr violet | 7.35 6.40 |
| | | Nos. J12-J19 (8) | |

**1927 — Type of 1914 Issue Surcharged**

| | | | |
|---|---|---|---|
| J20 | D3 | 2fr on 1fr lilac rose | 5.00 5.00 |
| J21 | D3 | 3fr on 1fr orange brown | 5.00 5.00 |

Design D4

**1935 — Engr. — Perf. 12½x12**

| | | | |
|---|---|---|---|
| J22 | D4 | 5c yellow green | .20 .20 |
| J23 | D4 | 10c red orange | .20 .20 |
| J24 | D4 | 15c violet | .20 .20 |
| J25 | D4 | 20c olive green | .20 .20 |
| J26 | D4 | 30c reddish brown | .20 .20 |
| J27 | D4 | 50c rose lilac | .75 .75 |
| J28 | D4 | 60c orange | 1.00 1.00 |
| J29 | D4 | 1fr black | 1.00 1.00 |
| J30 | D4 | 2fr dark blue | .75 .75 |
| J31 | D4 | 3fr dark carmine | 5.25 5.25 |
| | | Nos. J22-J31 (10) | |

Design D5

**1961, Feb. 20 — Typo. — Perf. 14x13**

| | | | |
|---|---|---|---|
| J32 | D5 | 1fr orange & red | .20 .20 |
| J33 | D5 | 2fr yel brn & red | .20 .20 |
| J34 | D5 | 5fr red lilac & black | .20 .20 |
| J35 | D5 | 5fr brown & red | .60 .60 |
| J36 | D5 | 25fr red lilac & red | 1.25 1.25 |
| | | Nos. J32-J36 (5) | 2.45 2.45 |

Lion in Gold

Lion — D6

**1966-83 — Typo. — Perf. 14x13**

| | | | |
|---|---|---|---|
| J37 | D6 | 1fr red & black | .20 .20 |
| J38 | D6 | 2fr yel brn & black | .20 .20 |
| J39 | D6 | 5fr red lilac & black | .20 .20 |
| J40 | D6 | 10fr brt blue & black | .40 .40 |
| J41 | D6 | 20fr emerald & black | .40 .40 |
| J42 | D6 | 30fr gray & black | .80 .80 |
| J43 | D6 | 60fr blue & black | .40 .40 |
| J44 | D6 | 90fr rose & black | .60 .60 |
| | | Nos. J37-J44 (8) | 3.00 2.80 |

Issued: 1fr-30fr, 12/1/66; others, 10/1983.

## OFFICIAL STAMPS

Catalogue values for unused stamps in this section are for Never Hinged items.

Arms — O1

Baobab Tree — O2

**1961, Sept. 18 — Typo. — Perf. 14x13½**
Denominations in Black

| | | | |
|---|---|---|---|
| O1 | O1 | 1fr sepia & bl | .20 .20 |
| O2 | O1 | 2fr dk bl & org | .20 .20 |
| O3 | O1 | 5fr maroon & grn | .20 .20 |
| O4 | O1 | 10fr ver & bl | .20 .20 |
| O5 | O1 | 25fr vio bl & ver | .65 .20 |
| O6 | O1 | 85fr ver & org | 1.00 .60 |
| O7 | O1 | 100fr ver & yel grn | 1.00 .45 |
| O8 | O1 | 100fr lilac & org | 2.75 1.10 |
| | | Nos. O1-O8 (8) | 7.20 3.15 |

**1966-77 — Typo. — Perf. 14x13**

| | | | |
|---|---|---|---|
| O9 | O2 | 1fr yel & blk | .20 .20 |
| O10 | O2 | 5fr org & blk | .20 .20 |
| O11 | O2 | 10fr red & blk | .20 .20 |
| O12 | O2 | 20fr dp red lil & blk | .25 .20 |
| O13 | O2 | 25fr dp lil & blk (75) | .45 .20 |
| O14 | O2 | 30fr bl & blk | .45 .20 |
| O15 | O2 | 35fr bl & blk (73) | .55 .20 |
| O16 | O2 | 40fr grnsh bl & blk (75) | .55 .20 |
| O17 | O2 | 55fr emer & blk | 1.00 .55 |
| O18 | O2 | 55fr ver & blk (77) | 1.00 .45 |
| O19 | O2 | 60fr emer & blk | .55 .25 |
| O20 | O2 | 90fr dk bl grn & blk | 1.40 .25 |
| O21 | O2 | 100fr brn & blk | 1.75 .25 |
| | | Nos. O9-O20 (12) | 7.55 2.75 |

**1969**

| | | | |
|---|---|---|---|
| O21 | O2 | 60fr emer & blk | 1.75 .20 |

No. O17 Surcharged with New Value and Two Bars

**1983, Oct. — Typo. — Perf. 14x13**

| | | | |
|---|---|---|---|
| O22 | O2 | 90fr dk grn & blk | .60 .20 |

"90F" is shorter and wider than on Nos. O9-O22.

**1991 — Litho. — Perf. 13**

| | | | |
|---|---|---|---|
| O23 | O2 | 50fr red & blk | 1.00 1.00 |
| O24 | O2 | 145fr brt grn & blk | 2.75 2.75 |
| O25 | O2 | 180fr org yel & blk | 3.25 3.25 |
| | | Nos. O23-O25 (3) | 7.00 7.00 |

See Nos. O22-O25.
This is an expanding set. Numbers will change if necessary.

## SENEGAMBIA & NIGER

se-nə-'gam-bē-ə and 'nī-jər

A French Administrative unit for the Senegal and Niger possessions in Africa during the period when the French possessions in Africa were being definitively divided into colonies and protectorates. The name was dropped in 1904 when this territory was consolidated with part of French Sudan, under the name Upper Senegal and Niger.

100 Centimes = 1 Franc

Navigation and Commerce — A1

**1903 — Unwmk. Typo. — Perf. 14x13½**
Name of Colony in Blue or Carmine

| | | | |
|---|---|---|---|
| 1 | A1 | 1c black, lil bl | 1.40 1.40 |
| 2 | A1 | 2c brown, buff | 1.40 1.40 |
| 3 | A1 | 4c claret, lav | 4.50 4.50 |
| 4 | A1 | 5c yel grn | 4.50 4.50 |
| 5 | A1 | 5c gray | 5.25 5.25 |
| 6 | A1 | 10c red | 10.00 10.00 |
| 7 | A1 | 20c red, green | 8.50 8.50 |
| 8 | A1 | 25c blue | 13.50 8.50 |
| 9 | A1 | 30c brn, bister | 11.50 11.50 |
| 10 | A1 | 40c red, straw | 16.00 16.00 |
| 11 | A1 | 50c brn, azure | 32.50 32.50 |
| 12 | A1 | 75c deep vio, org | 35.00 35.00 |
| 13 | A1 | 1fr bronze grn, straw | 188.55 188.55 |
| | | Nos. 1-13 (13) | 188.55 188.55 |

Perf. 13½x14 stamps are counterfeits.

Catalogue values for unused stamps in this section, from this point to the end of the section, are for Never Hinged items.

# SERBIA

'sar-bē-ə

LOCATION — In southeastern Europe, bounded by Romania and Bulgaria on the east, the former Austro-Hungarian Empire on the north, Greece on the south, and Albania and Montenegro on the west
GOVT. — Kingdom
AREA — 18,650 sq. mi.
POP. — 2,911,701 (1910)
CAPITAL — Belgrade

Following World War I, Serbia united with Montenegro, Bosnia and Herzegovina, Croatia, Dalmatia and Slovenia to form the kingdom (later republic) of Yugoslavia.

100 Paras = 1 Dinar

Coat of Arms — A1

**1866    Unwmk.    Typo.    Imperf.**
Paper colored Through

| 1 | A1 | 1p dk green, dk vio rose | 45.00 | |
|---|----|--------------------------|-------|---|

Surface Colored Paper, Thin or Thick

| 2 | A1 | 1p dk green, lil rose | 50.00 | |
| a. | | 1p olive green, rose | 50.00 | |
| b. | | 1p yel grn, pale rose (thick paper) | 300.00 | |
| 3 | A1 | 2p red brown, lilac | 60.00 | |
| b. | | 2p red brn, lil gray (thick paper) | 250.00 | |
| c. | | 1p ol grn, lil gray (thick paper) | 800.00 | |
| | | Nos. 1-3 (3) | 156.00 | |

Vienna Printing
Perf. 12

| 4 | A2 | 10p orange | 750.00 | 500.00 |
| 5 | A2 | 20p rose | 425.00 | 17.50 |
| 6 | A2 | 40p ultra | 475.00 | 125.00 |
| a. | | 40p ultra | 1,650. | 642.50 |

Belgrade Printing
Perf. 9½

| 7 | A2 | 1p green | 15.00 | |
| 8 | A2 | 2p bister brn | 22.50 | |
| 9 | A2 | 20p rose | 15.00 | |
| a. | | Pair, imperf. between | 160.00 | 175.00 |
| 10 | A2 | 40p ultra | 212.50 | |
| a. | | Half used as 20p on cover | | |

| 11 | A2 | 10p orange | 65.00 | 70.00 |
| 12 | A2 | 20p rose | 60.00 | 8.75 |
| 13 | A2 | 40p ultra | 35.00 | 25.00 |
| a. | | Pair, imperf. between | | |
| b. | | Half used as 20p on cover | 160.00 | 103.75 |

Nos. 1-3, 7-8, 14-16, 25-26 were used only as newspaper tax stamps.

**1868-69    Ordinary Paper    Imperf.**

| 14 | A2 | 1p green | 35.00 | |
| a. | | 1p olive green (69) | 2,000. | |
| 15 | A2 | 2p brown | 50.00 | |
| a. | | 2p bister brown (69) | 160.00 | |

Counterfeits of type A2 are common.

Prince Michael (Obrenovich III) — A2

Prince Milan (Obrenovich IV) A4

**Perf. 9½, 12 and Compound**
1869-78

| 16 | A3 | 1p yellow | 3.75 | 95.00 |
| 17 | A3 | 10p red brown | 7.50 | 3.75 |
| a. | | 10p yellow brown | 350.00 | 35.00 |
| 18 | A3 | 10p orange (78) | 1.25 | 3.25 |
| 19 | A3 | 15p orange | 85.00 | 15.00 |
| 20 | A3 | 20p gray blue | 1.50 | 2.50 |
| a. | | 20p ultramarine | | 3.25 |
| b. | | Half used as 10p on cover | | |
| 21 | A3 | 25p rose | 1.50 | 5.75 |
| 22 | A3 | 35p lt green | 3.00 | 3.50 |
| 23 | A3 | 40p violet | 1.50 | 2.75 |
| a. | | Half used as 20p on cover | | |
| 24 | A3 | 50p blue green | 5.00 | 3.75 |
| | | | 110.00 | 135.25 |

The first setting, which included all values except No. 18, had the stamps 2-2½mm apart. A new setting, introduced in 1878, had the stamps 3-4mm apart, providing wider margins. Only Nos. 17, 18, 20 and 21 exist in this new setting, which differs also in shades from the earlier setting.
The narrow-spaced Nos. 17, 20 and 21 are rarer, especially unused, as are the early shades of Nos. 23 and 24.
All values except Nos. 19 and 24 are known in various partly perforated varieties. Counterfeits exist.
See No. 25.

King Milan I — A5

**1872-79    Imperf.**

| 25 | A3 | 1p yellow | 4.50 | 8.75 |
| a. | | Tête bêche pair | | |
| 26 | A4 | 2p blk, thin paper ('79) | .50 | .50 |
| a. | | Thick paper (73) | 1.50 | 10.00 |

Used value of No. 26 is for canceled-to-order.

King Alexander (Obrenovich V) — A6

**1880    Perf. 13x13½**

| 27 | A5 | 5p green | .50 | .20 |
| a. | | 5p olive green | 475.00 | 2.00 |
| 28 | A5 | 10p rose | 1.50 | .20 |
| 29 | A5 | 20p orange | .50 | 1.25 |
| a. | | 20p yellow | 3.00 | .75 |
| 30 | A5 | 25p ultra | 1.00 | .75 |
| a. | | 25p blue | 1.25 | .75 |
| 31 | A5 | 50p brown | 1.00 | 3.75 |
| a. | | 50p brown violet | | 8.00 |
| 32 | A5 | 1d violet | 6.75 | 11.00 |
| | | | 11.25 | 11.10 |
| | | Nos. 27-32 (6) | | |

**1890    Perf. 13x13½**

| 33 | A6 | 5p green | .20 | .20 |
| 34 | A6 | 15p rose red | .50 | .20 |
| 35 | A6 | 15p red violet | .50 | .20 |
| 36 | A6 | 20p orange | .50 | .20 |
| 37 | A6 | 25p blue | .35 | .60 |
| 38 | A6 | 50p brown | 2.00 | 2.00 |
| 39 | A6 | 1d dull lilac | 7.50 | 6.25 |
| | | | 11.65 | 9.30 |
| | | Nos. 33-39 (7) | | |

King Alexander — A7

**1894-96    Granite Paper**

| 40 | A7 | 5p green | 3.25 | .20 |
| | | Perf. 11½ | | |
| 41 | A7 | 10p car rose | 3.50 | .40 |
| | | Perf. 11½ | | |
| 42 | A7 | 15p violet | 45.00 | .75 |
| 43 | A7 | 30p brown | 5.00 | .20 |
| a. | | Half used as 10p on cover | 52.50 | .50 |
| 44 | A7 | 25p blue | 10.50 | .50 |
| 45 | A7 | 50p brown | 11.00 | .45 |
| 46 | A7 | 1d dk green | 1.50 | 2.50 |
| 47 | A7 | 1d red brn, bl ('96) | 11.00 | 3.75 |
| | | | 98.25 | 8.00 |
| | | Nos. 40-47 (8) | | |

**1898-1900    Ordinary Paper    Imperf.**
Perf. 13x13½, 11½

| 48 | A7 | 1p dull red | .25 | .25 |
| 49 | A7 | 5p green | 1.50 | .20 |
| 50 | A7 | 15p violet | 42.50 | .20 |
| 51 | A7 | 15p violet | 7.00 | .25 |
| 52 | A7 | 25p deep blue | 6.25 | .20 |
| 53 | A7 | 50p deep blue | 7.00 | .30 |
| 54 | A7 | 50p bister | 12.50 | 3.00 |
| | | | 77.00 | 4.40 |
| | | Nos. 48-54 (7) | | |

Nos. 49-51, 53 exist imperf. and 56-57 exist with perf. 13x13½x11½x13½.

Type of 1900 Stamp Surcharged

**1900**

| 56 | A7 | 10p on 20p rose | 2.50 | .20 |

Same, Surcharged

**1901**

| 57 | A7 | 10p on 20p rose | 1.75 | .20 |
| 58 | A7 | 15p on 1d red brn, rose | 3.75 | 1.00 |
| b. | | Inverted surcharge | 100.00 | 110.00 |

King Alexander (Obrenovich V) A8, A9

**1901-03    Typo.    Perf. 11½**

| 59 | A8 | 5p green | .20 | .20 |
| 60 | A8 | 10p rose | .20 | .20 |
| 61 | A8 | 15p red violet | .20 | .20 |
| 62 | A8 | 20p orange | .20 | .20 |
| 63 | A8 | 25p ultra | .20 | .20 |
| 64 | A8 | 50p bister | .70 | .60 |
| 65 | A8 | 1d brt rose | .75 | .75 |
| 66 | A9 | 3d brt rose | 6.75 | 5.75 |
| 67 | A9 | 5d deep violet | 5.25 | 5.25 |
| | | | 13.90 | 13.30 |
| | | Nos. 59-67 (9) | | |

Counterfeits of Nos. 66-67 exist Nos. 59-67 imperf. value of set of pairs, $100.

Arms of Serbia on Head of King Alexander — A10

Two Types of the Overprint

Type I — Overprint 12mm wide. Bottom of mantle defined by a single line. Wide crown above shield.
Type II — Overprint 10mm wide. Double line at bottom of mantle. Smaller crown above shield.

Arms Overprinted in Blue, Black, Red and Red Brown

**1903-04    Type I    Perf. 13½**

| 68 | A10 | 1p red lil & blk (Bl) | .50 | .50 |
| a. | | Inverted overprint | 10.00 | |
| 69 | A10 | 5p yel grn & blk (Bl) | .35 | .20 |
| 70 | A10 | 10p car & blk (Bk) | 8.75 | .20 |
| 71 | A10 | 15p of gray & blk (Bk) | 8.75 | |
| a. | | Double overprint | .25 | .20 |
| 72 | A10 | 20p org & blk (Bk) | .25 | .20 |
| 73 | A10 | 25p bl & blk (Bk) | 10.00 | |
| a. | | Double overprint | 2.50 | .65 |
| 74 | A10 | 50p gray & blk (R) | | |

There were two printings of the type I overprint on Nos. 68-74, one typographed and one lithographed.

**Type II    Perf. 11½**

| 75 | A10 | 1d bl grn & blk (Bk) | 7.50 | 2.50 |

#68-75 with overprint omitted, value, set $75.

**Type I**

| 75A | A10 | 5p (Bl) | .25 | .35 |
| 75B | A10 | 50p (R) | .75 | 2.00 |
| 75C | A10 | 1d (Bk) | 1.50 | 4.00 |

**Type II    Perf. 13½**

| 76 | A10 | 3d vio & blk (R Br) | 1.50 | 1.75 |
| | | | 90.00 | 90.00 |

Perf. 11½
**Type I**

| 77 | A10 | 5d lt brn & blk (Bl) | 1.50 | 2.00 |

Karageorge and Peter I — A11

Insurgents, 1804 A12

**1904    Typo.**

| 79 | A11 | 5p yellow green | .20 | .20 |
| 80 | A11 | 10p rose red | .20 | .30 |
| 81 | A11 | 15p rod violet | .35 | .30 |
| 82 | A11 | 20p blue | .50 | .35 |
| 83 | A11 | 25p gray brown | .60 | .60 |
| 84 | A12 | 1d bister | .60 | 1.25 |
| 85 | A12 | 3d blue green | 1.00 | 3.50 |
| 86 | A12 | 5d violet | 2.50 | 4.00 |
| | | | 7.35 | 10.40 |
| | | Nos. 79-86 (8) | | |

Centenary of the Karageorgevich dynasty and the coronation of King Peter. Counterfeits of Nos. 79-86 exist.

King Peter I Karageorgevich A13, A14

**1905    Perf. 11½, 12x11½**
Wove Paper

| 87 | A13 | 1p gray & blk | .20 | .20 |
| 88 | A13 | 5p yel grn & blk | .50 | .20 |
| 89 | A13 | 10p red & blk | 1.50 | .20 |
| 90 | A13 | 15p red lil & blk | 1.75 | .20 |
| 91 | A13 | 20p yellow & blk | 3.00 | .20 |
| 92 | A13 | 25p ultra & blk | 4.25 | .20 |
| 93 | A13 | 30p sl grn & blk | 2.50 | .20 |
| 94 | A13 | 50p dk brown & blk | 3.00 | .70 |
| 95 | A13 | 1d bister & blk | .60 | .25 |
| 96 | A13 | 3d blue grn & blk | .60 | .60 |
| 97 | A13 | 5d slate blk | 20.40 | 4.35 |
| | | Nos. 87-97 (11) | | |

Counterfeits of Nos. 87-97 abound.
The stamps of this issue may be found on both thick and thin paper.

**1908    Laid Paper**

| 98 | A13 | 1p gray & blk | .25 | .20 |
| 99 | A13 | 5p yel grn & blk | 2.25 | .20 |
| 100 | A13 | 10p red & blk | 6.75 | .20 |
| 101 | A13 | 15p red lilac & blk | 6.75 | .20 |
| 102 | A13 | 20p yellow & blk | 7.25 | .20 |
| 103 | A13 | 25p ultra & blk | 6.75 | .20 |
| 104 | A13 | 30p grn & blk | 10.00 | .20 |
| 105 | A13 | 50p dk brn & blk | 13.00 | .60 |
| | | | 53.00 | 2.00 |
| | | Nos. 98-105 (8) | | |

Nos. 90, 98-100, 102-104 are known imperforate but are not believed to have been issued in this condition.
Values of Nos. 98-105 are for horizontally laid paper. Four values also exist on vertically laid paper (1p, 5p, 10p, 30p).

**1911-14    Thick Wove Paper**

| 108 | A14 | 1p slate green | .20 | .20 |
| 109 | A14 | 5p dark violet | .20 | .20 |
| 110 | A14 | 5p green | .20 | .20 |
| 111 | A14 | 5p pale yel grm ('14) | .20 | .20 |
| 112 | A14 | 10p carmine | .20 | .20 |
| 113 | A14 | 10p red ('14) | .20 | .20 |
| 114 | A14 | 15p red violet | .20 | .20 |
| 115 | A14 | 15p slate blk ('14) | .20 | .20 |
| a. | | 15p red (error) | | |
| 116 | A14 | 20p yellow | .20 | .20 |
| 117 | A14 | 20p brown ('14) | .40 | .20 |
| 118 | A14 | 25p deep blue | .30 | .20 |

SERBIA

| | | | | |
|---|---|---|---|---|
| 119 | A14 | 25p indigo ('14) | .20 | .20 |
| 120 | A14 | 30p blue green ('14) | .20 | .20 |
| 121 | A14 | 50p olive grn ('14) | .20 | .20 |
| 122 | A14 | 50p dk brown | .20 | .20 |
| 123 | A14 | 50p brn red ('14) | .20 | .20 |
| 124 | A14 | 1d orange | 15.00 | 25.00 |
| 125 | A14 | 1d slate ('14) | 2.00 | 2.75 |
| 126 | A14 | 3d lake | 27.50 | 475.00 |
| 127 | A14 | 3d violet ('14) | 77.50 | 42.50 |
| 128 | A14 | 5d dk violet ('14) | 2.00 | 14.00 |
| 129 | A14 | 5d dk violet ('14) | 155.00 | 639.95 |

Nos. 108-129 (22)

Counterfeits exist.

King Peter and Military Staff — A15

**1915** **Perf. 11½**

| | | | |
|---|---|---|---|
| 132 | A15 | 5p yellow green | .20 |
| 133 | A15 | 10p scarlet | — |
| 134 | A15 | 15p slate | 3.75 |
| 135 | A15 | 20p brown | .60 |
| 136 | A15 | 25p blue | 7.50 |
| 137 | A15 | 30p olive green | 5.00 |
| 138 | A15 | 50p orange brown | 37.25 |

Nos. 132-138 (7)

## POSTES SERBES

Stamps of France, 1900-1907, with this handstamped control were used in 1916-1918 by the Serbian Postal Bureau, in the Island of Corfu. On the 1c to 35c, the handstamp covers 2 or 3 stamps. It was applied after the stamps were on the cover.

Nos. 134-138 were prepared but not issued for postal use. Instead they were permitted to be used as wartime emergency currency. Some are known imperf. The 15p also exists in blue from an erroneous cliche in the 25p plate; value $250.

King Peter and Prince Alexander — A16

**1918-20** **Typo.** **Perf. 11, 11½**

| | | | | |
|---|---|---|---|---|
| 155 | A16 | 1p black | .20 | .20 |
| 133 | A16 | 2p olive brown | .20 | .20 |
| 157 | A16 | 5p apple green | .20 | .20 |
| 158 | A16 | 10p red | .20 | .20 |
| 159 | A16 | 15p black brown | .20 | .20 |
| 160 | A16 | 20p brown | .20 | .20 |
| 161 | A16 | 25p violet ('20) | 1.10 | .60 |
| 162 | A16 | 30p deep blue | .20 | .20 |
| 163 | A16 | 50p olive green | .20 | .20 |
| 164 | A16 | 1d violet brown | .20 | .20 |
| 165 | A16 | 1d black brown | .25 | .60 |
| 166 | A16 | 3d slate green | .75 | .60 |
| 167 | A16 | 5d red brown | 1.25 | 4.00 |

#157-160, 164 exist imperf. Value each $6.

Nos. 155-167 (13)

**1920**

| | | | | |
|---|---|---|---|---|
| 169 | A16 | 1p black | .20 | .20 |
| 170 | A16 | 2p olive brown | .20 | .20 |

**Pelure Paper** **Perf. 11½**

---

## SERBIA & MONTENEGRO

100 Paras = 1 Dinar

Yugoslavia became Serbia & Montenegro Feb. 4, 2003, with each section of the country maintaining and operating their own postal service, and each having their own currency. After Feb. 4, 2006, both Serbia and Montenegro will have the right to vote for independence.

The listings below contain stamps bearing the dinar currency, for use in Serbia, or those bearing both the dinar and euro currencies, which were for use in either Serbia or Montenegro. Stamps inscribed in euro currency only were used in Montenegro and may be found in listings for that country.

Council of Europe — A20

**2003, Apr. 3** **Litho.** **Perf. 13¾**

180-181 A20 Set of 2

Map color: 16d, Red violet. 28.70d, Blue.
1.50 1.50

Religious paintings: 12d, From 16th cent. 16d, By D. Bacevic. 26.20d, From 1616. 28.70d, By Giovanni Bellini.

Easter — A21

**2003, Apr. 18**

182-185 A21 Set of 4
3.00 3.00

Belgrade Choral Society, 150th Anniv. A22

**2003, Apr. 22** **Perf. 13¼ Syncopated**

186 A22 16d multi .55 .55

Europa — A23

**2003, May 9**

187-188 A23 Set of 2
**Perf. 13¾**
2.75 2.75

Man pasting poster on: 28.70d, Pillar; 50d, Wall.

Flowers — A24

**2003, May 13**

189 Horiz. strip of 4 + central label

| | | | | |
|---|---|---|---|---|
| a. | A24 | 16d Galanthus nivalis | 3.25 | 3.25 |
| b. | A24 | 24d Erythronium dens-canis | .55 | .80 |
| c. | A24 | 26.20d Hepatica nobilis | .80 | .90 |
| d. | A24 | 28.70d Anemone ranunculoides | .90 | .90 |
| | | | 1.00 | 1.00 |

**2003, May 20**

190 A25 16d Sheet of 8, #a-h, + 8 labels
4.50 4.50

No. 190: a, Ilija Stanojevic (1859-1930). b, Dobrivoje Dobrica Milutinovic (1880-1956). c, Zivana Zanka Stokic (1887-1947). d, Ljubinka Bobic (1897-1978). e, Radomir-Rasa Plaovic (1899-1977). f, Milivoje Zivanovic (1900-76). g, Miloslav Mija Aleksic (1923-95). h, Zoran Radmilovic (1933-85).

Actors and Actresses — A25

First Automobile in Belgrade, Cent. — A26

**2003, June 3** **Perf. 13¼ Syncopated**

191 A26 16d multi .55 .55

Views of Zasavica Nature Reserve: 28.70d, River; 50d, Swamp, vert.

Nature Protection A27

**2003, June 12** Set of 2

192-193 A27
2.75 2.75

Yugoslavia No. F1 and Type of Yugoslavia No. 2258 Surcharged

| | | | | |
|---|---|---|---|---|
| 194 | A75i | 1d on (R) ultra | .20 | .20 |
| 195 | A751 | 12d on 20p lil rose & pale vio | .40 | .40 |

**2003, July 3** **Litho.** **Perf. 12½**

**2003** **Litho.**

| | | | | |
|---|---|---|---|---|
| 196 | A28 | 1d multi | .20 | .20 |
| 197 | A29 | 8d multi | .25 | .25 |
| 198 | A30 | 12d multi | .40 | .40 |
| 199 | A31 | 16d multi | .55 | .55 |
| 200 | A32 | 32d multi | 2.50 | 2.50 |

Nos. 196-200 (5)

Military Museum, Belgrade, 125th Anniv. — A33

**2003, Aug. 27**

201 A33 16d (25c) multi
**Perf. 13x13¾**
.55 .55

**2003, Aug. 28**

202 A34 16d (25c) multi
.55 .55

Serbian Women's Circle, Cent. — A34
**Perf. 13¼ Syncopated**

**2003, Sept. 10**

203-204 A35 Set of 2
1.10 1.10

Serbian and Montenegrin States, 125th Anniv. — A35

Designs: No. 203, 16d (25c), Serbian arms, denomination at UR. No. 204, 16d (25c), Montenegrin arms, denomination at UL.

**2003, Sept. 12**

205 A36 16d (25c) multi
**Perf. 13x13¾**
.55 .55

Ninth European Model Rocketry Championship, Sremska Mitrovica A36

**2003, Sept. 17**

206-207 A37 Set of 2
1.10 1.10

Carved rocks with: No. 206, 16d (25c), Denomination at UL. No. 207, 16d (25c), Denomination at UR.

Second Danube Countries Conference on Art and Culture — A37

Nos. 206-207 were each printed in sheets of 8 + label.

No. 189b Under Magnifying Glass — A28

Postal Van and Parcels — A29

Woman With Headset A30

Postal Van A31

Cable Television System — A32

## Serbiafila XIII Philatelic Exhibition — A38

**Souvenir Sheet**

No. 208: a, Belgrade in the 17th century. b, Sculpture.

**Perf. 13½**

**2003, Sept. 22**
208 A38 32d (50c) Sheet of 2, #a-b   2.25 2.25

## Joy of Europe — A39

Children's drawings: 28.70d (50c), Man, woman, bird and flower. 50d (80c), Rabbit, flowers, horiz.

**Perf. 13¼**

**2003, Oct. 14**   Set of 2
209-210 A39   2.75 2.75

## Vecernje Novosti Newspaper, 50th Anniv. — A40

**2003, Oct. 16**
211 A40 32d (50c) multi   1.10 1.10

## Stamp Day — A41

**2003, Oct. 24**
212 A41 16d (25c) multi   .55 .55

## Association of Applied Artists and Designers, 50th Anniv. — A42

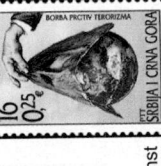

**2003, Oct. 29**
213 A42 16d (25c) multi   .55 .55

## National Theater of Montenegro, 50th Anniv. — A43

**Perf. 13¾x13**

**2003, Nov. 1**
214 A43 32d (50c) multi   1.10 1.10

## City of Pancevo, 850th Anniv. — A44

**Perf. 13x13¾**

**2003, Nov. 12**
215 A44 32d (50c) multi   1.25 1.25

## Christmas — A45

Designs: 10d, Santa Claus and reindeer. 13.50d, Ornaments. 26.20d, Snowflakes.

**Perf. 13¼**

**2003, Nov. 24**   Set of 3   1.75 1.75
216-218 A45
  Complete booklet, 10 #216   3.75
  Complete booklet, 10 #217   4.75

## Serbian Orthodox Church Museum Exhibits — A46

No. 219: a, Painting of St. John the Baptist, 1645. b, Cross, 1602. c, Miter, 15th cent. d, Tabernacle, 1550-51.

**Perf. 13¾x13**

**2003, Nov. 26**
219 Horiz. strip of 4 + central label   3.50 3.50
  a. A46 16d (25c) multi   .60 .60
  b. A46 24d (35c) multi   .85 .85
  c. A46 26.20d (40c) multi   .95 .95
  d. A46 28.70d (50c) multi   1.00 1.00

## Christmas A47

Religious paintings: 12d (20c), Nativity, 1983. 16d (25c), Nativity, 18th cent. 26.20d (40c), Madonna and Child, 2000. 28.70d (50c), Adoration of the Magi, by Albrecht Durer.

**Perf. 13x13¾**

**2003, Dec. 2**   Set of 4   3.00 3.00
220-223 A47

## Submarine Units, 75th Anniv. A48

**Perf. 13¼**

**2003, Dec. 10**
224 A48 32d (50c) multi   1.25 1.25
Printed in sheets of 8 + label.

## Powered Flight, Cent. — A49

Designs: 16d (25c), Wright Brothers and airplane. 28.70d (50c), Airplane in flight, horse-drawn carriages.

**2003, Dec. 17**
225-226 A49   Set of 2   1.75 1.75

## Politika Newspaper, Cent. — A50

Centenary emblem and: No. 227, 16d (25c), Typewriter. No. 228, 16d, (25c), Office building, vert.

**2004, Jan. 21**
227-228 A50   Set of 2   1.25 1.25

## Worldwide Fund for Nature (WWF) A51

**Perf. 13¼**

No. 229 — Insects: a, Parnassius apollo. b, Rosalia alpina. c, Aeshna viridis. d, Saga pedo.

**2004, Jan. 30**
229 Horiz. strip of 4 + central label   3.00 3.00
  a. A51 12d (20c) multi   .45 .45
  b. A51 16d (25c) multi   .60 .60
  c. A51 26.20d (40c) multi   .95 .95
  d. A51 28.70d (50c) multi   1.00 1.00

## First Serbian Rebellion, Bicent. — A52

Bicentennial emblem and: No. 230, 16d (25c), Flag, Karageorge (George Petrovic). No. 231, 16d (25c), Children and map of Europe.

**Perf. 13x13¾**

**2004, Feb. 13**
230 231 A52   Set of 2   1.10 1.10

## Flora and Butterflies — A53

No. 232: a, Ramonda serbica. b, Ramonda nathaliae. c, Heodes virgaureae. d, Lysandra bellargus.

**Perf. 13¾x13**

**2004, Feb. 16**
232 Horiz. strip of 4 + central label   3.50 3.50
  a. A53 16d (25c) multi   .60 .60
  b. A53 24d (35c) multi   .85 .85
  c. A53 26.20d (40c) multi   .95 .95
  d. A53 28.70d (50c) multi   1.00 1.00

## 2004 Summer Olympics, Athens — A54

Serbia and Montenegro Olympic Committee emblem and: 32d (50c), Runner. 56d (80c), Wrestlers.

**Perf. 13¾x13¾**

**2004, Feb. 27**
233-234 A54   Set of 2   3.25 3.25

## First Serbian Rebellion, Bicent. A55

Designs: 12d, Rebels. 16d, Flag, gun, vert. 28.70d, Karageorge (George Petrovic), vert. 32d, Children, globe, vert.

**2004, Mar. 1**   Litho.   **Perf. 13¼**
235-238 A55   Set of 4   3.25 3.25

## Campaign Against Terrorism — A56

**2004, Mar. 12**
239 A56 16d (25c) multi   .60 .60

## Easter — A57

**Perf. 13¾x13**

Designs: 16d (25c), The Crucifixion. 28.70d (50c), The Resurrection, by Klemens Katounakis.

**2004, Mar. 15**
240-241 A57   Set of 2   1.60 1.60

## Milutin Milankovic (1879-1958), Climatologist A58

**2004, Mar. 22**
242 A58 16d (25c) multi   .60 .60

## Albert Einstein (1879-1955), Physicist — A59

**Perf. 13¾x13**

**2004, Mar. 31**
243 A59 16d (25c) multi   .60 .60
Printed in sheets of 8 + label.

## Selection of Kotor as World Heritage Site, 25th Anniv. — A60

**2004, Apr. 7**
244 A60 16d (25c) multi   .60 .60

**Perf. 13¾**

**2004, Apr. 29**

245 A61 16d (25c) multi .60 .60

Printing of First History of Montenegro, by Vasilije Petrovic, 250th Anniv. — A61

**Europa — A62**

Designs: 16d (25c), Paragliders. No. 247, 56d (80c), Sailboat, swimmer, horiz. No. 248: a, 32d (50c), Sailboats, paragliders, horiz. b, 56d (80c), Rowboats, horiz.

**Souvenir Sheet**

**2004, May 5**   **Perf. 13¾x13, 13x13¾**
246-247 A62 Set of 2 2.50 2.50
248 A62 Sheet of 2, #a-b 3.00 3.00

Church of St. Sava, Belgrade — A63

**2004, May 10**   **Perf. 13¾x13, 13x13¾**
249-250 A63 Set of 2 1.60 4.60

Designs: 16d (25c), Church, statue of St. Sava, horiz.

Michael Pupin (1854-1935), Inventor — A64

**2004, May 13**   **Engr.**   **Perf. 13¾**
251 A64 16d (25c) violet .55 .55

**2004, May 21**   **Litho.**   **Perf. 13x13¾**
252 A65 28.70d (50c) multi 1.00 1.00

FIFA (Fédération Internationale de Football Association), Cent. — A65

Nature Protection A66

**2004, June 10**   Set of 2
253-254 A66 3.00 3.00

Designs: 32d (50c), Ravnjak River. 56d (80c), Sara National Park.
Each stamp printed in sheet of 8 + label.

---

**Souvenir Sheet**

JUFIZ XII Philatelic Exhibition, Belgrade — A67

**2004, June 21**   **Perf. 13¾**
255 A67 32d (50c) Sheet of 2, #a-b 2.25 2.25

No. 255: a, Lion from Terazije Fountain. b, Entire fountain.

2004 Summer Olympics, Athens — A68

**2004, June 24**   **Perf. 13x13¾**
256-259 A68 Set of 4 4.75 4.75

Athens Olympics emblem, ancient Greek ruins and: 16d (25c), Runners. 28.70d (50c), Runners, diff. 32d (50c), Long jumper. 57.40d (80c), Hurdlers.
Each stamp printed in sheets of 8 + label.

Yugoslavia Nos. 2255-2256 Surcharged

**Methods and Perfs as Before**

**2004, June 25**
260 A751 12d on 1p #2255 .45 .45
261 A751 32d on 5p #2256 1.10 1.10

See Yugoslavia No. 2577 for stamp similar to No. 260, but with violet surcharge.

Volujica Telegraph Station, Cent. — A69

**2004, Aug. 3**   **Litho.**   **Perf. 13x13¾**
262 A69 16d (25c) multi .55 .55

Joy of Europe — A70

**2004, Oct. 2**   Set of 2
263-264 A70 **Perf. 13¾** 3.00 3.00

Children's drawings: 32d (50c), Bridge and city skyline. 56d (80c), City buildings, vert.
Each stamp printed in sheets of 8 + label.

---

Port of Bar, 125th Anniv. — A71

**2004, Oct. 12**
265 A71 32d (50c) multi 1.10 1.10

Stamp Day — A72

**2004, Oct. 22**   **Perf. 13¾x13**
266 A72 16d (25c) multi .55 .55

Designs: 16d (25c), Bank building. 32d (50c), Bank building, George Valjerta.

National Bank of Serbia, 120th Anniv. — A73

**2004, Oct. 28**   **Perf. 13¼ Syncopated**

**Engr.**
267-268 A73 Set of 2 1.75 1.75

Silver Objects From 1899 — A74

**2004, Nov. 2**   **Litho.**   **Perf. 13¾x13**
269 A74 16d (25c) label

a. A74 16d (25c) Plate on pedestal 3.25 3.25
b. A74 24d (35c) Box .55 .55
c. A74 26.2d (40c) Bowl .80 .80
d. A74 28.70d (50c) Bowl with lid 1.00 1.00

Buildings A75

**2004, Nov. 15**   Horiz. strip of 4 + central label
270 **Perf. 13x13¾** 3.25 3.25

a. A75 16d (25c) Lombardic Palace .55 .55
b. A75 24d (35c) Pima Palace .80 .80
c. A75 26.2d (40c) Girgirina Palaoo .90 .90
d. A75 28.70d (50c) Bizanit Palace 1.00 1.00

Christmas A76

Designs: 16d (25c), Nativity, by Vasilis Leurac. 28.70d (50c), Nativity, by Ememija Profeta.

**2004, Dec. 1**   Set of 2
271-272 A76 1.60 1.60

---

Endangered Birds — A77

**2005, Jan. 31**   **Litho.**   **Perf. 13¼**
273 Horiz. strip of 4 + central label 4.50 4.50

a. A77 16.50d (25c) Egretta alba .90 .90
b. A77 33d (40c) Podiceps nigricollis 1.00 1.00
c. A77 41.50d (50c) Aythya nyroca 1.40 1.40
d. A77 49.50d (60c) Ciconia nigra 1.60 1.60

Yugoslavia No. F1, Serbia Nos. 199, 200 Surcharged in Blue or Black

**2005, Feb. 3**   **Litho.**
274 RL1 50p on R #F1 (Bl) .20 .20
275 A31 16.50d on R #199 .55 .55
276 A32 33d on 32d #200 1.10 1.10
Nos. 274-276 (3) 1.85 1.85

Surcharge styles differ.

Stamp Collecting — A78

**2005, Feb. 3**   **Litho.**   **Perf. 12½**
277 A78 50p multi .20 .20

Flora and Fauna — A79

**2005, Feb. 16**   Horiz. strip of 4 + central label
278 **Perf. 13x13¾**

a. A79 16.50d (25c) Capparis spinosa .55 .55
b. A79 33d (40c) Mustela erminea 1.10 1.10
c. A79 41.50d (50c) Trollus europaeus 1.40 1.40
d. A79 49.50d (60c) Rupicapra rupicapra 1.60 1.60

Montenegrin Table Tennis Assoc., 50th Anniv. — A80

**2005, Feb. 28**
279 A80 16.50d (25c) multi .55 .55

## Joy of Europe — A98

**2005, Sept. 21**    *Perf. 13¾x13, 13x13¾*
312 A97 41.50d (50c) multi   1.25   1.25
313 A98 58d (70c) multi   1.75   1.75
Each stamp printed in sheets of 8 + label.

## World Youth Day — A99

**2005, Sept. 30**
314 A99 41.50d (50c) multi   1.25   1.25
Printed in sheets of 8 + label.

## Start of European Union Accession Negotiations — A100

**2005, Oct. 10**    *Perf. 13¾x13*
315 A100 10.50d (26c) multi   .50   .50

## Intl. Airline Federation, Cent. — A101

Emblem and: 49.50d (60c), Alberto Santos-Dumont's 14-bis airplane. 58d (70c), Parachute, glider, ultra-light aircraft.
**2005, Oct. 14**    *Perf. 13¾x13¾*
316-317 A101 Set of 2   3.00   3.00
Each stamp printed in sheets of 8 + label.

## Stamp Day — A102

**2005, Oct. 24**
318 A102 16.50d (25c) multi   .50   .50

---

## Souvenir Sheet
## Danube Regatta, 50th Anniv. — A91

No. 303: a, 41.50d (50c), Rowers in boats. b, 49.50d (60c), Rowers in boats, map.
**2005, June 6**
303 A91   Sheet of 2, #a-b   2.75   2.75

## Intl. Year of Physics A92

**2005, June 10**
304 A92 41.50d (50c) multi   1.25   1.25
305 A93 58d (70c) multi   1.75   1.75

## Theory of Relativity, Cent. — A93

## European Nature Protection A94

Various views of Koviljsko-Petrovaradinski Rit Special Nature Reserve: 41.50d (50c), 58d (70c).
**2005, June 20**
306-307 A94   Set of 2   3.00   3.00

## European Volleyball Championships, Belgrade and Rome — A95

**2005, Sept. 2**   *Litho.*   *Perf. 13x13¾*
310 A95 16.50d (25c) multi   .50   .50
Printed in sheets of 8 + label.

## European Basketball Championships, Serbia & Montenegro — A96

**2005, Sept. 16**
311 A96 16.50d (25c) multi   .50   .50
Printed in sheets of 8 + label.

---

289 A85 16.50d (25c) blue   .55   .55
   a.   Souvenir sheet, #286-289   2.25   2.25
290 A85 41.50d (50c) claret   1.40   1.40
291 A85 41.50d (50c) olive gray   1.40   1.40
292 A85 41.50d (50c) blue   1.40   1.40
293 A85 41.50d (50c) orange   1.40   1.40
   a.   Souvenir sheet, #290-293   5.75   5.75
    Nos. 286-293 (8)   7.80   7.80
Europa stamps, 50th anniv. (in 2006).

## Hans Christian Andersen (1805-75), Author — A86

Silhouette of Andersen and: 41.50d (50c), The Snow Queen.
**2005, Apr. 1**   Set of 2
294-295 A86   *Perf. 13¾x13*   3.25   3.25

## Europa — A87

Designs: No. 296, 41.50d (50c), Dumplings and rolls. No. 297, 73d (90c), Fish dish, tomato, lettuce, garlic, oil cruet, pepper mill. No. 298: a, 41.50d (50c), Cake, flower, cup of coffee. b, 73d (90c), Slice of pie, apples.
**2005, May 5**   Set of 2
296-297 A87   *Perf. 13¾x13¾*   3.75   3.75

## Souvenir Sheet
298 A07   Sheet of 2, #a-b   3.75   3.75

## Captains and Their Ships A88

**2005, May 13**   *Perf. 13¾*
299   Horiz. strip of 4 + central label   4.25   4.25
   a.   A88 16.50d (25c) Marko Ivanovic   .50   .50
   b.   A88 33d (40c) Petar Zelalic   1.00   1.00
   c.   A88 41.50d (50c) Matija Balovic   1¼   1.25
   d.   A88 49.50d (60c) Ivan Bronza   1.50   1.50

## Emblem of Red Star Sports Club — A89
## Emblem of Partisan Sports Club — A90

No. 302 — Knight with shield with emblem of: a, Red Star. b, Partisan.
**2005, May 23**   *Perf. 13¾x13¾*
300 A89 16.50d (25c) multi   .50   .50
301 A90 16.50d (25c) multi   .50   .50

## Souvenir Sheet
302   Sheet of 2   1.00   1.00
   a.   A89 16.50d (25c) multi   .50   .50
   b.   A90 16.50d (25c) multi   .50   .50

---

## Easter — A81

Designs: 16.50d (25c), Fresco, 18th cent. 28.70d (50c), Crucifixion, 1602.
**2005, Mar. 1**   Set of 2
280-281 A81   1.50   1.50

## Mountain Scenes — A82

**2005, Mar. 7**   *Litho.*   *Perf. 12½*
282 A82 16.50d Zlatibor   .55   .55
283 A82 33d Kopaonik   1.10   1.10

## Serbian Law University, Cent. — A83

**2005, Mar. 12**   *Perf. 13¾x13*
284 A83 16.50d (25c) multi   .55   .55

## Miniature Sheet
## Theater Celebrities — A84

No. 285: a, Jovan Djordjevic (1826-1900). b, Milan Predic (1881-1972). c, Milan Grol (1876-1952). d, Mira Trailovic (1924-89). e, Soja Jovanovich (1922-2002). f, Hugo Klajn (1894-1981). g, Mata Milosevic (1901-97). h, Bojan Stupica (1910-70).
**2005, Mar. 25**   *Perf. 13¾x13*
285 A84 16.50d (25c) multi, Sheet of 8, #a-d, + central label   4.25   4.25

## European Philatelic Cooperation, 50th Anniv. (in 2006) — A85

Elements of Europa common design types (CD) or Yugoslavian stamps: No. 286, CD12. No. 287, CD13. No. 288, CD14. No. 289, CD15. No. 290, CD16. No. 291, Yugoslavia #1206. No. 292, Yugoslavia #1678. No. 293, CD13, CD15 and Yugoslavia #1678.
**2005, Mar. 31**   *Perf. 13x13¾*   **Background Color**
286 A85 16.50d (25c) green   .55   .55
287 A85 16.50d (25c) blue   .55   .55
288 A85 16.50d (25c) claret   .55   .55

**2005, Oct. 24**
319 A103 16.50d (25c) multi ... .50 .50

United Nations, 60th Anniv. A103

**2005, Oct. 28**
320 A104 16.50d (25c) multi ... .50 .50

St. Petar of Cetinje (1782-1830), Montenegrin Leader A104

**2005, Nov. 14**
321 A105 16.50d (25c) multi ... .45 .45

First Montenegrin Constitution, Cent. — A105

**2005, Nov. 23**
322 A106 16.50d (25c) multi ... .45 .45

**Perf. 13¼**

Stevan Sremac (1855-1906), Humorist — A106

**2005, Nov. 28**
**323**
No. 323: a. Studenica Monastery, by Djordje Krstic. b. Sopocani Monastery, by Paja Jovanovic. c. Zica Monastery, by Krstic. d. Gracanica Monastery, by Milan Milanovic.

Horiz. strip of 4 + central label
a. A107 16.50d (25c) multi ... 4.00 4.00
b. A107 33d (40c) multi ... .45 .45
c. A107 41.50d (50c) multi ... 1.25 .90
d. A107 49.50d (60c) multi ... 1.40 1.25

Paintings of Monasteries A107

**2005, Dec. 9**
**324**
No. 324: a. Girl with a Blue Ribbon, by F. X. Winterhalter. b. Adoration of the Child, by Andrea Alovidi. c. Madonna and Child with Saints, by Biagio d'Antonio. d. Remorse, by Vlaho Bukovac.

Horiz. strip of 4 + central label
a. A108 16.50d (26c) multi ... 4.00 4.00
b. A108 33d (40c) multi ... .90 .45
c. A108 41.50d (50c) multi ... 1.25 .90
d. A108 49.50d (60c) multi ... 1.40 1.25

Paintings in Museums A108

Christmas A109

**2005, Dec. 12**
325-326 A109 Set of 2 ... 1.75 1.75
Designs: 16.50d (25c), Nativity, diff.

Stevan Stojanovic Mokranjac (1856-1914), Composer A110

**2006, Jan. 9**
327 A110 46d (50c) multi ... 1.25 1.25
**Perf. 13x13¾**

Jovan Sterija Popovic (1806-56), Writer — A111

**2006, Jan. 13**
328 A111 33d (40c) multi ... .90 .90

2006 Winter Olympics, Turin — A112

**2006, Feb. 10**
329-330 A112 Set of 2 ... 3.50 3.50
**Perf. 13x13¾**
Designs: 53d (60c), Ski jumping. 73d (80c), Downhill skiing.

---

## POSTAGE DUE STAMPS

Coat of Arms
D1   D2

**1895 Unwmk. Typo. Perf. 13x13½**
**Granite Paper**
J1 D1 5p red lilac ... 2.50 .80
J2 D1 10p blue ... 2.50 .80
J3 D1 20p orange brown ... 30.00 .20
J4 D1 30p green ... .30 .35
J5 D1 50p rose ... 75.00 5.00
a. Cliché of 5p in plate of 50p ... .30 .40
Nos. J1-J5 (5) ... 35.50 6.75

No. J1 exists imperf. Value $35.

## NEWSPAPER STAMPS

N1

Overprinted with Crown-topped Shield in Black

**1911 Unwmk. Typo. Perf. 11½**
P1 N1 1p gray ... .45 .45
P2 N1 5p green ... .45 .45
P3 N1 10p orange ... .45 .45
a. Cliché of 1p in plate of 10p ... 200.00
P4 N1 15p violet ... .45 .45
P5 N1 20p yellow ... .45 .45
a. Cliché of 50p in plate of
P6 N1 25p blue ... .50 .50
P7 N1 30p slate ... .50 .50
P8 N1 50p brown ... 75.00 125.00
P9 N1 1d bister ... 4.50 4.50
P10 N1 3d rose red ... 4.50 4.50
P11 N1 5d gray vio ... 26.00 26.00
Nos. P1-P11 (11) ...

---

# SERBIA

**1898-1904 Ordinary Paper**
**1906 Laid Paper**
**1909 Granite Paper**
**Perf. 11½**

D1
J9 D1 5p magenta ... 5.25 1.00

**1906**
J6 D1 5p magenta ('04) ... 3.00 .70
J7 D1 10p pale blue ... 3.00 .40
J8 D1 20p pale brown ... 6.70 2.10
Nos. J6-J8 (3) ...

**1909**
J10 D1 5p magenta ... .60 .60
J11 D1 10p pale blue ... 3.00 1.60
J12 D1 20p pale brown ... 4.00 2.60
Nos. J10-J12 (3) ...

**1914 White Wove Paper**
J13 D1 5p rose ... .25 .50
J14 D1 10p deep blue ... 3.75 6.25
**Perf. 11**

**1918-20**
J15 D1 5p red ... .40 .85
J16 D1 5p red brown ('20) ... .40 .85
J17 D1 10p yellow green ... .40 .85
J18 D1 10p olive brown ... .40 .85
J19 D1 30p slate green ... .40 1.25
J20 D1 50p chocolate ... .80 2.80
Nos. J15-J20 (6) ... 2.80 5.50

---

## ISSUED UNDER AUSTRIAN OCCUPATION

**1916**
Stamps of Bosnia, 1912-14, Overprinted

100 Heller = 1 Krone

**Unwmk.   Typo.   Perf. 12½**
1N1 A23 1h olive green ... 1.60 1.60
1N2 A23 2h brt blue ... 1.60 2.25
1N3 A23 3h claret ... 1.60 1.75
1N4 A23 3h green ... .45 .45
1N5 A23 6h dk gray ... .80 .80
1N6 A23 10h rose carmine ... .80 1.50
1N7 A23 15h ultra ... .50 .80
1N8 A23 25h orange brown ... .50 .90
1N9 A23 30h orange red ... .50 1.50
1N10 A23 35h myrtle grn ... .50 .80
1N11 A23 40h olive brown ... .50 .80
1N12 A23 45h olive violet ... .50 .80
1N13 A23 50h dk brown ... .50 .80
1N14 A23 60h olive green ... .50 .80
1N15 A23 72h slate blue ... .50 .80
1N16 A23 80h olive green ... .80 .80
1N17 A23 50h brown violet ... .70 .80
1N18 A23 72h dark blue ... .50 .80
1N19 A23 1k brn vio, straw ... .70 .80
1N20 A23 5k dk vio, gray ... 10.00 19.00
1N21 A23 10k dk ultra, gray ... 24.50 40.40
Nos. 1N1-1N21 (21) ...

**1916**
Stamps of Bosnia, 1912-14, Overprinted "SERBIEN" Horizontally at Bottom

Nos. 1N22-1N42 were prepared in 1914, at the time of the 1st Austrian occupation of Serbia. They were not issued at that time because of the retreat. The stamps were put on sale in 1916, at the same time as Nos. 1N1-1N21.

1N22 A23 1h olive green ... 6.75 8.00
1N23 A23 2h bright blue ... 6.75 8.00
1N24 A23 3h claret ... 6.75 8.00
1N25 A23 3h green ... .50 .65
1N26 A23 6h dark gray ... 6.75 8.00
1N27 A23 10h rose carmine ... .65
1N28 A23 12h dp olive grn ... 6.75 8.00
1N29 A23 15h ultra ... 6.75 8.00
1N30 A23 25h orange brn ... 6.75 8.00
1N31 A23 30h orange red ... 6.75 8.00
1N32 A23 35h myrtle green ... 6.75 8.00
1N33 A23 40h dark violet ... 6.75 8.00
1N34 A23 45h olive brown ... 6.75 8.00
1N35 A23 50h slate blue ... 6.75 8.00
1N36 A23 60h brown violet ... 6.75 8.00
1N37 A23 72h dark blue ... 6.75 8.00
1N38 A23 1k brn vio, bl ... 14.00 19.00
1N40 A24 3k dk gray, bl ... 18.00 19.00
1N41 A24 5k dk carmine, gray ... 27.50 30.00
1N42 A25 10k dk ultra, gray ... 42.50 45.00
Nos. 1N22-1N42 (21) ... 213.50 245.30

---

## ISSUED UNDER GERMAN OCCUPATION

In occupied Serbia, authority was ostensibly in the hands of a government created by the former Yugoslav General, Milan Nedich, supported by Serbian Chetniks, a nationalist organization which turned fascist. Actually the German military ran the country.

**1941**
Types of Yugoslavia, 1939-40, Overprinted in Black

**Unwmk.   Typo.   Perf. 12½**
2N1 A16 25p blk (lt grn) ... 5.00 .20
2N2 A16 50p org (lt grn) ... .75 .20
2N3 A16 1d yel grn (lt grn) ... 1.00 1.75
2N4 A16 1.50d red (pink) ... 1.25 1.75
2N5 A16 2d dp mag (grn) ... .20 1.75
2N6 A16 3d dl red brn (grn) ... .20 1.75
2N7 A16 4d ultra (lt grn) ... .90 .20
2N8 A16 5d dk bl (lt grn) ... .45 3.25
2N9 A16 5.50d dk brn (grn) ... .75 10.00
2N10 A16 6d sep (lt grn) ... .20 10.00
2N11 A16 8d sl bl (lt grn) ... .75 10.00
2N12 A16 12d brt vio (lt grn) ... 1.00 16.00
2N13 A16 16d dl vio (pink) ... 1.25 16.00
2N14 A16 20d bl (lt grn) ... 1.50 55.00
2N15 A16 30d brt pink (lt grn) ... 2.40 800.00
Nos. 2N1-2N15 (15) ...

**1941 Unwmk. Typo. Perf. 12½**
**Paper with colored network**
2N16 A16 25p blk ... .20 16.00
2N17 A16 50p org (lt grn) ... .35 3.25
2N18 A16 1d yel grn (lt grn) ... .20 3.25
2N19 A16 1.50d red (pink) ... 1.25
2N20 A16 2d dp mag ... .55
2N21 A16 3d dl red brn ... .35
2N22 A16 4d ultra (lt grn) ... .20
2N24 A16 5.50d dk brn (grn) ... .70 13.50
2N25 A16 6d sl bl (pink) ... .70 13.50

Double overprints exist on 50p, 1d, 5d, 5.50d and 12d. Value, each $125 to $250.

Stamps of Yugoslavia, 1939-40, Overprinted in Black

Set, never hinged
Nos. 2N1-2N15 (15) ...

**2N26** A16 8d sep *(lt grn)* 1.10 *20.00*
**2N27** A16 12d brt vio *(lt grn)* 1.75 *20.00*
**2N28** A16 16d dl vio *(pink)* 1.75 *65.00*
**2N29** A16 20d bl *(lt grn)* 1.75 *200.00*
**2N30** A16 30d brt pink *(lt grn)* 8.50 *675.00*
*Nos. 2N16-2N30 (15)* 18.50 *1,059.*
Set, never hinged 26.00

Lazaritza Monastery — OS1

Ruins of Manassia Monastery OS4

Designs: 1d, Kalenica Monastery. 1.50d, Ravanica Monastery. 3d, Ljubostinja Monastery. 4d, Sopocane Monastery. 7d, Tsitsa Monastery. 12d, Goriak Monastery. 16d, Studenica Monastery.

**1942-43** **Typo.** ***Perf. 11½***
**2N31** OS1 50p brt violet .20 *.25*
**2N32** OS1 1d red .20 *.20*
**2N33** OS1 1.50d red brn .75 *3.25*
**2N34** OS1 1.50d green ('43) .20 *.35*
**2N35** OS4 2d dl rose violet .20 *.25*
**2N36** OS4 3d brt blue .75 *3.25*
**2N37** OS4 3d rose pink ('43) .20 *.20*
**2N38** OS4 4d ultra .20 *.25*
**2N39** OS4 7d dk slate grn .20 *.25*
**2N40** OS1 12d lake .20 *1.60*
**2N41** OS1 16d grnsh blk 1.00 *2.00*
*Nos. 2N31-2N41 (11)* 4.10 *11.85*
Set, never hinged 4.25

For surcharges see Nos. 2NB29-2NB37.

Post Rider — OS10

Post Wagon — OS11

9d, Mail train. 30d, Mail truck. 50d, Mail plane.

**1943, Oct. 15** **Photo.** ***Perf. 12½***
**2N42** OS10 3d copper red & gray lilac .45 *3.25*
**2N43** OS11 8d vio rose & gray .45 *3.25*
**2N44** OS10 9d dk bl grn & sep .45 *3.25*
**2N45** OS10 30d chnt & sl grn .45 *3.25*
**2N46** OS10 50d dp bl & red brn .45 *3.25*
*Nos. 2N42-2N46 (5)* 2.25 *16.25*
Set, never hinged 5.00

Centenary of postal service in Serbia. Printed in sheets of 24 containing 4 of each stamp and 4 labels.

## OCCUPATION SEMI-POSTAL STAMPS

Smederevo Fortress on the Danube OSP1

Refugees OSP2

***Perf. 11½x12½***
**1941, Sept. 22** **Typo.** **Unwmk.**
**2NB1** OSP1 50p + 1d dk brn .25 *1.40*
**2NB2** OSP2 1d + 2d dk gray grn .25 *1.60*
**2NB3** OSP2 1.50d + 3d dp cl .40 *3.00*
*a.* Perf. 12½ 3.00 *13.50*
Never hinged 6.50
**2NB4** OSP1 2d + 4d dk bl .60 *4.00*
*Nos. 2NB1-2NB4 (4)* 1.50 *10.00*
Set, never hinged 3.25

### Souvenir Sheets

**2NB5** Sheet of 2 32.50 *300.00*
Never hinged 72.50
*a.* OSP2 1d + 49d rose lake 6.75 *30.00*
*b.* OSP1 2d + 48d gray 6.75 *30.00*

***Imperf***

**2NB6** Sheet of 2 32.50 *300.00*
Never hinged 72.50
*a.* OSP2 1d + 49d gray 6.75 *30.00*
*b.* OSP1 2d + 48d rose lake 6.75 *30.00*

The surtax aided the victims of an explosion at Smederevo and was used for the reconstruction of the town.

Christ and Virgin Mary — OSP4

a

b

**1941, Dec. 5** **Photo.** ***Perf. 11½***
**With Rose Burelage**
**2NB7** OSP4 50p + 1.50d brn red .25 *5.25*
**2NB8** OSP4 1d + 3d sl grn .25 *5.25*
**2NB9** OSP4 2d + 6d dp red .25 *5.25*
**2NB10** OSP4 4d + 12d dp bl .25 *5.25*
*Nos. 2NB7-2NB10 (4)* 1.00 *21.00*
Set, never hinged 2.00

### With Symbol "a" Outlined in Cerise

*2NB7a* OSP4 50p 7.50 *60.00*
*2NB8a* OSP4 1d 7.50 *60.00*
*2NB9a* OSP4 2d 7.50 *60.00*
*2NB10a* OSP4 4d 7.50 *60.00*
*Nos. 2NB7a-2NB10a (4)* 30.00 *240.00*
Set, never hinged 65.00

### With Symbol "b" Outlined in Cerise

*2NB7b* OSP4 50p 7.50 *60.00*
*2NB8b* OSP4 1d 7.50 *60.00*
*2NB9b* OSP4 2d 7.50 *60.00*
*2NB10b* OSP4 4d 7.50 *60.00*
*Nos. 2NB7b-2NB10b (4)* 30.00 *240.00*
Set, never hinged 65.00

### Without Burelage

*2NB7c* OSP4 50p 1.25 *16.00*
*2NB8c* OSP4 1d 1.25 *16.00*
*2NB9c* OSP4 2d 1.25 *16.00*
*2NB10c* OSP4 4d 1.25 *16.00*
*Nos. 2NB7c-2NB10c (4)* 5.00 *64.00*
Set, never hinged 10.00

These stamps were printed in sheets of 50, in 2 panes of 25. In the panes, #8, 12, 13, 14, 18, forming a cross, are without burelage. #7, 17 are type "a," #9, 19 type "b." 16 of the 25 stamps have overall burelage.

Surtax aided prisoners of war.

**1942, Mar. 26**
**Thicker Paper, Without Burelage**
**2NB11** OSP4 50p + 1.50d brn .60 *3.25*
**2NB12** OSP4 1d + 3d bl grn .60 *3.25*
**2NB13** OSP4 2d + 6d mag .60 *3.25*
**2NB14** OSP4 4d + 12d ultra .60 *3.25*
*Nos. 2NB11-2NB14 (4)* 2.40 *13.00*
Set, never hinged 5.25

OSP5

OSP6

OSP7

OSP8

Designs: Anti-Masonic symbolisms.

**1942, Jan. 1**
**2NB15** OSP5 50p + 50p yel brn .20 *3.00*
**2NB16** OSP6 1d + 1d dk grn .20 *3.00*
**2NB17** OSP7 2d + 2d rose car .25 *5.25*
**2NB18** OSP8 4d + 4d indigo .30 *5.25*
*Nos. 2NB15-2NB18 (4)* .95 *16.50*
Set, never hinged 1.75

Anti-Masonic Exposition of Oct. 22, 1941. The surtax was used for anti-Masonic propaganda.

Mother and Children — OSP9

**1942**
**2NB19** OSP9 2d + 6d brt pur 3.00 *8.50*
**2NB20** OSP9 4d + 8d dp bl 3.00 *8.50*
**2NB21** OSP9 7d + 13d dk bl grn 3.00 *8.50*
**2NB22** OSP9 20d + 40d dp rose lake 3.00 *8.50*
*Nos. 2NB19-2NB22 (4)* 12.00 *34.00*
Set, never hinged 26.00

Nos. 2NB19-2NB22 were issued in sheets of 16 consisting of a block of four of each denomination. The surtax aided war orphans.

Broken Sword — OSP10

Wounded Flag-bearer OSP11

Designs: 1.50d+48.50d, Broken sword. 3d+5d, 2d+48d, Wounded soldier. 3d+47d, Wounded flag-bearer. 4d+10d, 4d+46d, Tending casualty.

**1943**
**2NB23** OSP10 1.50d + 1.50d dk brn .45 *2.00*
**2NB24** OSP11 2d + 3d dk bl grn .45 *2.00*
**2NB25** OSP11 3d + 5d dp rose vio .90 *3.25*
**2NB26** OSP10 4d + 10d dp bl 1.25 *4.50*
*Nos. 2NB23-2NB26 (4)* 3.05 *11.75*
Set, never hinged 6.50

### Souvenir Sheets
**Thick Paper**

**2NB27** Sheet of 2 30.00 *2,300.*
Never hinged 65.00
*a.* OSP10 1.50d + 48.50d dk brn 7.50 *300.00*
*b.* OSP10 4d + 46d dp bl 7.50 *300.00*
**2NB28** Sheet of 2 35.00 *2,300.*
Never hinged 80.00
*a.* OSP11 2d + 48d dk bl grn 7.50 *300.00*
*b.* OSP11 3d + 47d dp rose vio 7.50 *300.00*

The sheets measure 150x110mm. The surtax aided war victims.

Stamps of 1942-43 Surcharged in Black

**1943, Dec. 11**
**Pale Green Burelage**
**2NB29** OS1 50p + 2d brt vio .20 *32.50*
**2NB30** OS1 1d + 3d red .20 *32.50*
**2NB31** OS1 1.50d + 4d dp grn .20 *32.50*
**2NB32** OS4 2d + 5d dl rose vio .20 *32.50*
**2NB33** OS4 3d + 7d rose pink .20 *32.50*
**2NB34** OS4 4d + 9d ultra .20 *32.50*
**2NB35** OS4 7d + 15d dk sl grn .35 *32.50*
**2NB36** OS1 12d + 25d lake .35 *160.00*
**2NB37** OS1 16d + 33d grnsh blk .75 *260.00*
*Nos. 2NB29-2NB37 (9)* 2.65 *647.50*
Set, never hinged 4.25

The surtax aided victims of the bombing of Nisch.

# OCCUPATION AIR POST STAMPS

Types of Yugoslavia, 1937-40, Overprinted in Carmine or Maroon

Nos. 2NC1-2NC3, 2NC5-2NC7, 2NC9 Overprinted in Carmine or Maroon

Nos. 2NC4, 2NC8, 2NC10

**SERBIEN**

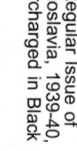 

## 1941 — Unwmk. — Perf. 12½

| | | | | |
|---|---|---|---|---|
| 2NC1 | AP6 | 50p brown | 1.75 | 125.00 |
| 2NC2 | AP7 | 1d yellow grn | 2.50 | 100.00 |
| 2NC3 | AP8 | 2d blue gray | 2.50 | 100.00 |
| 2NC4 | AP9 | 2.50dose red | 2.50 | 100.00 |
| 2NC6 | AP7 | 5d brown vio | 2.50 | 100.00 |
| 2NC7 | AP8 | 10d dk green | 2.50 | 100.00 |
| 2NC9 | AP10 | 40d Prus grn & pale grn (C) | 6.00 | 500.00 |
| | | (M) | 9.00 | 925.00 |
| 2NC10 | AP11 | 50d sl bl & gray (C) | 35.00 | 2,225. |
| | | | 72.50 | |

Set, never hinged
Nos. 2NC1-2NC10 (10)

Nos. 2NC1-2NC2 exist without network.

## 1941 — Unwmk. — Perf. 12½
### Paper with colored network

| | | | | |
|---|---|---|---|---|
| 2NC11 | AP7 | 1d on 10d | 1.75 | 125.00 |
| 2NC12 | AP8 | 4d on 20d | 1.75 | 125.00 |
| 2NC13 | AP9 | 6d on 30d | 1.75 | 125.00 |
| 2NC14 | AP10 | 8d on 40d | 3.50 | 650.00 |
| 2NC15 | AP11 | 12d on 50d | 6.00 | 660.00 |

Set, never hinged
Nos. 2NC11-2NC15 (5) 14.75 / 32.50 — 1,325

Same Surcharged in Maroon or Carmine with New Values and Bars
**Without colored network**

Regular Issue of Yugoslavia, 1939-40, Surcharged in Black

## 1942
### Green Network

| | | | | |
|---|---|---|---|---|
| 2NC16 | A16 | 2d on 2d dp mag | .20 | 1.60 |
| 2NC17 | A16 | 4d on 4d ultra | .20 | 1.60 |
| 2NC18 | A16 | 6d on 12d brt vio | .20 | 3.25 |
| 2NC19 | A16 | 8d on 40d | .35 | 13.50 |
| 2NC20 | A16 | 20d on 30d brt pink | 1.15 | 23.20 |

Set, never hinged
Nos. 2NC16-2NC20 (5) 1.90

## 1942 — Perf. 12½

OD3 OD4

| | | | | |
|---|---|---|---|---|
| 2NJ9 | OD3 | 1d maroon & grn | .90 | 5.25 |
| 2NJ10 | OD3 | 2d dk blue & red | .90 | 8.00 |
| 2NJ11 | OD3 | 3d vermilion & bl | .90 | 8.00 |
| 2NJ12 | OD4 | 4d blue & red | 1.25 | 12.00 |
| 2NJ13 | OD4 | 5d orange & bl | 1.25 | 16.00 |
| 2NJ14 | OD4 | 10d violet & red | 6.00 | 65.00 |
| 2NJ15 | OD4 | 20d green & red | 12.10 / 26.00 | 119.50 |

Set, never hinged
Nos. 2NJ9-2NJ15 (7)

## OCCUPATION POSTAGE DUE STAMPS

Types of Yugoslavia Similar to OD3-OD4 Overprinted

### 1941 — Typo. — Perf. 12½
#### Watermark

| | | | | |
|---|---|---|---|---|
| 2NJ1 | OD3 | 50p violet | .55 | 32.50 |
| 2NJ2 | OD3 | 1d violet | .55 | 32.50 |
| 2NJ3 | OD3 | 2d lake | .55 | 32.50 |
| 2NJ4 | OD3 | 3d red | .75 | 50.00 |
| 2NJ5 | OD3 | 4d dark blue | .90 | 75.00 |
| 2NJ6 | OD3 | 4d lt blue | .90 | 125.00 |
| 2NJ7 | OD4 | 5d orange | 1.90 | 300.00 |
| 2NJ8 | OD4 | 10d violet | 5.00 | 800.00 |

Set, never hinged
Nos. 2NJ1-2NJ8 (8) 11.10 / 24.00 — 1,497.

## OCCUPATION OFFICIAL STAMP

OD5

### 1942

| | | | | |
|---|---|---|---|---|
| 2NJ16 | OD5 | 50p black | .45 | 3.25 |
| 2NJ17 | OD5 | 1d red | .45 | 3.25 |
| 2NJ18 | OD5 | 3d violet | .45 | 3.25 |
| 2NJ19 | OD5 | 5d dk slate grn | .90 | 13.50 |
| 2NJ20 | OD5 | 10d red | 3.00 | 32.50 |
| 2NJ21 | OD5 | 10d orange | 6.30 | 69.00 |
| 2NJ22 | OD5 | 20d ultra | 13.50 | |

Set, never hinged
Nos. 2NJ16-2NJ22 (7)

OOS1

### 1943
2NO1 OOS1 3d red lilac
Never hinged — Unwmk. — Typo. — Perf. 12½
OOS1 3d red lilac .50 1.50 / 1.10

---

# SEYCHELLES
sā-shel´z

LOCATION—A group of islands in the Indian Ocean, off the coast of Africa north of Madagascar.
GOVT.—Republic
AREA—175 sq. mi.
POP.—79,164 (1999 est.)
CAPITAL—Victoria

The islands were attached to the British colony of Mauritius from 1810 to 1903, when they became a separate colony. Seychelles achieved internal self-government in October 1975 and independence on June 29, 1976.

100 Cents = 1 Rupee

Catalogue values for unused stamps in this country are for Never Hinged items, beginning with Scott 149 in the regular postage section and Scott J1 in the postage due section.

Wmk. 380 — "POST OFFICE"

Queen Victoria — A1

Two dies of 2c, 4c, 8c, 10c, 13c, 16c:
Die I — Shading lines at right of diamond in tiara band.
Die II — No shading lines in this rectangle.

## 1890-1900 — Typo. — Wmk. 2 — Perf. 14

| | | | | |
|---|---|---|---|---|
| 1 | A1 | 2c grn & rose (I) | 3.00 | 1.00 |
| a. | | Die I | 3.50 | 10.50 |
| 2 | A1 | 2c org brn & grn ('93) | 2.25 | 3.50 |
| a. | | Die I | 3.00 | 10.50 |
| 3 | A1 | 3c dk vio ('93) | 1.75 | .60 |
| 4 | A1 | 4c car rose & grn (II) | 3.00 | 1.10 |
| a. | | Die I | 29.00 | 4.00 |
| 5 | A1 | 6c car rose ('00) | 1.10 | .60 |
| 6 | A1 | 8c brn vio & ultra (II) | 8.00 | 2.00 |
| a. | | Die I | 29.00 | 4.00 |
| 7 | A1 | 10c ultra & brn (I) | 9.25 | 3.75 |
| a. | | 10c dl ultra ('00) | | 7.50 |
| 8 | A1 | 12c ol gray & grn ('93) | 3.00 | 3.00 |
| 9 | A1 | 13c slate & blk (II) | .70 | 2.00 |
| a. | | Die I | 3.75 | 12.50 |
| 10 | A1 | 15c ol grn & vio | 2.25 | |
| a. | | Die I | 3.75 | 7.00 |
| 11 | A1 | 15c ultra ('00) | 5.25 | 3.75 |
| 12 | A1 | 16c org brn & bl (I) | 6.25 | 4.75 |
| a. | | 16c org brn & ultra (II) | 4.75 | 12.50 |
| 13 | A1 | 18c ultra ('97) | 47.50 | .60 |
| 14 | A1 | 36c brn & rose ('97) | 5.00 | 1.10 |
| 15 | A1 | 45c brn & rose ('97) | 27.50 | 5.25 |
| 16 | A1 | 48c ocher & green ('93) | 26.00 | 40.00 |
| 17 | A1 | 75c yel & pur ('00) | 22.50 | 13.50 |
| 18 | A1 | 96c violet & car ('00) | 62.50 | 80.00 |
| 19 | A1 | 1r red ('97) | 57.50 | 55.00 |
| 20 | A1 | 1.50r blk & rose | 15.00 | 5.00 |
| 21 | A1 | 2.25r vio & grn ('00) | 80.00 | 97.50 |
| | | ('00) | 110.00 | 97.50 |

Nos. 1-21 (21) 460.75 418.75

Numerals of 75c, 1r, 1.50r and 2.25r of type A1 are in color on plain tablet.
For surcharges see Nos. 22-37.

Surcharged in Black

## 1893

| | | | | |
|---|---|---|---|---|
| 22 | A1 | 3c on 4c car rose & green | 1.25 | 1.75 |
| a. | | Double surcharge | 350.00 | |
| b. | | Inverted surcharge | 550.00 | 425.00 |
| c. | | Surcharge, one without surcharge | 9,750. | |
| 23 | A1 | 12c on 16c org brn | 1.75 | 4.25 |
| a. | | Double surcharge | | 3.00 |
| 24 | A1 | 15c on 16c org brn | 12.50 | 3.00 |
| a. | | "15c" on 16c org brn & ultra (II) | | 1.75 |
| b. | | Double surcharge | 525.00 | 5,250 |
| c. | | Inverted surcharge | | |
| d. | | Double surcharge (II) | | |
| e. | | Triple surcharge (II) | | |
| f. | | "45c" on 45c ocher | | |
| 25 | A1 | 45c on 48c ocher & grn | 26.00 | 6.25 |
| 26 | A1 | 90c on 96c vio & car | 57.50 | 37.50 |

Nos. 22-26 (5) 112.25 52.00

## 1896

| | | | | |
|---|---|---|---|---|
| 27 | A1 | 18c on 45c brn & rose | 8.00 | 3.25 |
| a. | | Double surcharge | 2,300 | 1,600. |
| 28 | A1 | 36c on 45c brn & rose | 9.25 | 57.50 |
| a. | | Double surcharge | 1,850. | |

Surcharged in Black:

 "3 cents"

No. 15 Surcharged in Black

 "18 CENTS"

## 1901

| | | | | |
|---|---|---|---|---|
| 29 | A1 | 3c on 10c bl & brn | 1.40 | .70 |
| 30 | A1 | 3c on 16c org brn & ultra (II) | 3.00 | 4.50 |
| a. | | "3 cents" omitted (II) | 750.00 | |
| 31 | A1 | 3c on 36c brn & | 625.00 | 575.00 |
| a. | | Without bars | 850.00 | |
| b. | | Inverted surcharge (I) | 750.00 | |
| c. | | "3 cents" omitted | 750.00 | 800.00 |
| 32 | A1 | 6c on 8c brn vio & ultra (II) | 1.10 | 3.50 |
| a. | | Inverted surcharge | 875.00 | |

Nos. 29-32 (4) 6.10 9.60

Surcharged in Black:

 "3 cents"

## 1902, June

| | | | | |
|---|---|---|---|---|
| 33 | A1 | 2c on 4c car rose & grn | 1.90 | 3.25 |
| 34 | A1 | 30c on 75c yel & | 4.50 | 52.50 |
| 35 | A1 | 30c on 1r vio & | 1.75 | 4.50 |
| a. | | Narrow "0" in "30" | | 11.50 |
| 36 | A1 | 45c on 1r vio & red | 5.50 | 30.00 |
| a. | | Double surcharge | 1,600. | |
| 37 | A1 | 45c on 2.25r vio & grn | 4.25 | 32.50 |
| a. | | Narrow "5" in "45" | 47.50 | 47.50 |

Nos. 33-37 (5) 60.90 167.75

Stamps of 1890-1900 Surcharged

King Edward VII — A6

Numerals of 75c, 1.50r and 2.25r of type A6 are in color on plain tablet.

## 1903, May 26 — Typo. — Wmk. 2

| | | | | |
|---|---|---|---|---|
| 38 | A6 | 2c red brn & grn | 2.00 | 2.25 |
| 39 | A6 | 3c green | 1.10 | 1.50 |
| 40 | A6 | 6c carmine rose | 3.25 | 1.50 |
| 41 | A6 | 12c ol gray & grn | 4.50 | 3.00 |
| 42 | A6 | 15c ultra | 4.50 | 4.50 |
| 43 | A6 | 18c pale yel grn & rose | 4.75 | 7.50 |
| 44 | A6 | 30c purple & grn | 8.00 | 12.50 |
| 45 | A6 | 45c brown & rose | 8.00 | 12.50 |
| 46 | A6 | 75c yel & pur | 11.50 | 32.50 |
| 47 | A6 | 1.50r black & grn | 47.50 | 80.00 |
| 48 | A6 | 2.25r red vio & grn | 128.85 | 253.75 |

Nos. 38-48 (11)

**1903**
**49** A6 3c on 15c 1.10 *3.50*
**50** A6 3c on 18c 3.25 *42.50*
**51** A6 3c on 45c 3.50 *3.50*
*Nos. 49-51 (3)* 7.85 *49.50*

Type of 1903

**1906** **Wmk. 3**
**52** A6 2c red brn & grn 1.60 *4.75*
**53** A6 3c green 1.60 1.60
**54** A6 6c car rose 2.25 .90
**55** A6 12c ol gray & grn 3.50 3.50
**56** A6 15c ultra 3.50 *2.25*
**57** A6 18c pale yel grn & rose 3.50 *7.25*
**58** A6 30c purple & grn 6.75 *9.00*
**59** A6 45c brown & rose 3.50 *7.25*
**60** A6 75c yellow & pur 9.50 *62.50*
**61** A6 1.50r black & rose 57.50 *67.50*
**62** A6 2.25r red vio & grn 35.00 *67.50*
*Nos. 52-62 (11)* 128.20 *234.00*

King George V
A7 A8

Numerals of 75c, 1.50r and 2.25r of type A7 are in color on plain tablet.

**1912** ***Perf. 14***
**63** A7 2c org brn & grn .75 *5.75*
**64** A7 3c green 2.25 .50
**65** A7 6c car rose 4.75 .65
**66** A7 12c ol gray & grn 1.40 *4.50*
**67** A7 15c ultra 4.00 .70
**68** A7 18c pale yel grn & rose 3.50 *6.00*
**69** A7 30c purple & grn 5.75 1.40
**70** A7 45c brown & rose 3.00 *40.00*
**71** A7 75c yellow & pur 3.25 *6.00*
**72** A7 1.50r black & rose 8.50 1.10
**73** A7 2.25r violet & grn 55.00 2.75
*Nos. 63-73 (11)* 92.15 69.35

Die I

For description of dies I and II see Dies of British Colonial Stamps in the Table of Contents.

The 5c of type A8 has a colorless numeral on solid color tablet. Numerals of 9c, 20c, 25c, 50c, 75c, and 1r to 5r of type A8 are in color on plain tablet.

**1917-20**
**74** A8 2c org brn & grn .55 *3.00*
**75** A8 3c green 2.25 *1.40*
**76** A8 5c brown ('20) 2.50 *7.25*
**77** A8 6c carmine rose 2.25 1.60
**78** A8 12c gray 1.10 *1.10*
**79** A8 15c ultra 1.90 1.60
**80** A8 18c violet, *yel* 4.00 *25.00*
*a.* Die II ('20) 1.90 *14.00*
**81** A8 25c blk & red, *yel* ('20) 1.90 *35.00*
*a.* Die II ('20) 1.50 *9.00*
**82** A8 30c dull vio & ol grn 1.60 *9.50*
**83** A8 45c dull vio & org 3.50 *40.00*
**84** A8 50c dull vio & blk ('20) 6.00 *27.50*
**85** A8 75c blk, *bl grn*, ol back 1.75 *17.00*
*a.* 75c blk, *emer* (Die II) ('20) 5.00 *17.50*
**86** A8 1r dl vio & red ('20) 12.50 *50.00*
**87** A8 1.50r vio & bl, *bl* 12.50 *57.00*
*a.* Die II ('20) 10.00 *30.00*
**88** A8 2.25r gray grn & dp vio 55.00 *150.00*
**89** A8 5r gray grn & ultra ('20) 90.00 *250.00*
*Nos. 74-89 (16)* 199.30 *676.95*

Die II

**1921-32** **Wmk. 4**

**Ordinary Paper**

**91** A8 2c org brn & grn .25 .20
**92** A8 3c green 1.75 .20
**93** A8 3c black ('22) 1.10 .35
**94** A8 4c green ('22) 1.10 *2.75*
**95** A8 4c ol grn & rose red ('28) 7.25 *19.00*
**96** A8 5c dk brown 1.25 *6.00*
**97** A8 6c car rose 3.00 *10.00*
**98** A8 6c violet ('22) .70 .20
**99** A8 9c rose red ('27) 3.50 *4.75*
**100** A8 12c gray 3.00 .20
*a.* Die I ('32) 7.50 .65
**101** A8 12c carmine ('22) 1.10 .25
**102** A8 15c ultra 2.25 *60.00*
**103** A8 15c yellow ('22) 1.10 *3.00*
**104** A8 18c violet, *yel* 2.75 *13.50*
**105** A8 20c ultra ('22) 1.60 .25

**Chalky Paper**

**106** A8 25c blk & red, *yel* ('22) 3.00 *16.00*
**107** A8 30c dull vio & ol grn 1.40 *17.00*
**108** A8 45c dull vio & org 1.40 *5.75*
**109** A8 50c dull vio & blk 2.75 *2.50*
**110** A8 75c blk, *emerald* 9.00 *24.00*
**111** A8 1r dull vio & red 14.50 *20.00*
*a.* Die I ('32) 11.00 *30.00*
**112** A8 1.50r vio & bl, *bl* 16.00 *25.00*
**113** A8 2.25r green & vio 12.00 *16.00*
**114** A8 5r green & ultra 80.00 *175.00*
*Nos. 91-114 (24)* 171.75 *421.90*

Common Design Types pictured following the introduction.

**Silver Jubilee Issue**
Common Design Type

**1935, May 6** **Engr.** ***Perf. 11x12***
**118** CD301 6c black & ultra .55 *1.40*
**119** CD301 12c indigo & green 1.60 1.00
**120** CD301 20c ultra & brown 1.40 1.40
**121** CD301 1r brn vio & indigo 4.00 *8.75*
*Nos. 118-121 (4)* 7.55 *12.55*
Set, never hinged 14.50

**Coronation Issue**
Common Design Type

**1937, May 12** ***Perf. 11x11½***
**122** CD302 6c olive green .20 .20
**123** CD302 12c deep orange .25 *.35*
**124** CD302 20c deep ultra .35 *.75*
*Nos. 122-124 (3)* .80 1.30
Set, never hinged 1.25

Coco-de-mer Palm — A9

Seychelles Giant Tortoise — A10

Fishing Canoe — A11

***Perf. 13½x14½, 14½x13½***
**1938-41** **Photo.** **Wmk. 4**
**125** A9 2c violet brown .35 .20
**126** A10 3c green 4.25 1.40
**127** A10 3c orange .40 .25
**128** A11 6c orange 4.25 2.75
**129** A11 6c green 1.00 .25
**130** A9 9c rose red 5.00 *2.25*
**131** A9 9c peacock blue 2.50 .50
**132** A10 12c violet 20.00 1.50
**133** A10 15c copper red 3.00 .20
**134** A9 18c rose lake 2.50 .75
**135** A11 20c bright blue 21.00 5.50
**136** A11 20c ocher 1.60 .35
**137** A9 25c ocher 25.00 15.00
**138** A10 30c rose lake 25.00 10.00
**139** A9 30c bright blue 1.60 .40
**140** A11 45c brown 3.50 .60
**141** A9 50c dull violet 1.50 .30
**142** A10 75c gray blue 42.50 42.50
**143** A10 75c dull violet 2.25 .45
**144** A11 1r yellow green 50.00 55.00
**145** A11 1r gray 2.75 .60
**146** A9 1.50r ultra 5.00 2.75
**147** A10 2.25r olive bister 8.00 6.50
**148** A11 5r copper red 5.50 *7.00*
*Nos. 125-148 (24)* 238.45 157.00
Set, never hinged 525.00

Issued: #126, 128, 132, 135, 137, 1/1; #125, 130, 138, 140-142, 144, 146-148, 2/10; others, 8/8/41.
See Nos. 158-169, 174-188.

**Catalogue values for unused stamps in this section, from this point to the end of the section, are for Never Hinged items.**

**Peace Issue**
Common Design Type
***Perf. 13½x14***

**1946, Sept. 23** **Engr.** **Wmk. 4**
**149** CD303 9c light blue .20 .20
**150** CD303 30c dark blue .20 .20

**Silver Wedding Issue**
Common Design Types

**1948, Nov. 11** **Photo.** ***Perf. 14x14½***
**151** CD304 9c bright ultra .20 .20

**Engraved; Name Typographed**
***Perf. 11½x11***
**152** CD305 5r rose carmine 13.00 *27.50*

**UPU Issue**
Common Design Types
***Perf. 13½, 11x11½***

**1949, Oct. 10** **Engr.**
**153** CD306 18c red violet .20 .20
**154** CD307 50c dp rose violet 1.75 .75
**155** CD308 1r gray .35 .35
**156** CD309 2.25r olive .45 *.75*
*Nos. 153-156 (4)* 2.75 2.05

Types of 1938-41 Redrawn and

Sailfish — A12

Map — A13

***Perf. 14½x13½, 13½x14½***
**1952, Mar. 3** **Photo.** **Wmk. 4**
**157** A12 2c violet .50 .55
**158** A10 3c orange .50 .25
**159** A9 9c peacock blue .50 *1.00*
**160** A11 15c yellow green .35 *.60*
**161** A13 18c rose lake 1.00 .25
**162** A11 20c ocher 1.00 .60
**163** A10 25c bright red .65 .80
**164** A12 40c ultra .75 *.75*
**165** A11 45c violet brown .65 .25
**166** A9 50c brt violet 1.10 .55
**167** A13 1r gray 2.50 1.90
**168** A9 1.50r brt blue 5.50 *8.25*
**169** A10 2.25r olive bister 8.00 *8.25*
**170** A13 5r copper red 8.50 *10.00*
**171** A12 10r green 16.00 *21.00*
*Nos. 157-171 (15)* 47.50 55.00

The redrawn design shows a new portrait of King George VI surmounted by crown, as on type A12.
Nos. 157-170 exist with watermark 4a.

**Coronation Issue**
Common Design Type

**1953, June 2** **Engr.** ***Perf. 13½x13***
**172** CD312 9c dark blue & blk .50 .60

Types of 1938-52 with Portrait of Queen Elizabeth II
***Perf. 14½x13½, 13½x14½***

**1954-56** **Photo.**
**173** A12 2c violet .20 .20
**174** A10 3c orange .20 .20
**175** A9 9c peacock blue .20 .20
**176** A9 10c blue ('56) .55 *1.40*
**177** A11 15c yellow grn .25 .20
**178** A13 18c rose lake .20 .20
**179** A11 20c ocher .55 1.10
**180** A10 25c bright red .70 1.10
**181** A13 35c mag ('56) 3.00 1.25
**182** A12 40c ultra .25 .25
**183** A11 45c violet brn .20 .20
**184** A9 50c brt violet .25 .20
**185** A11 70c vio brn ('56) 5.75 1.50
**186** A13 1r gray .60 .60
**187** A9 1.50r brt blue 3.75 *4.50*
**188** A10 2.25r olive bister 3.75 *4.50*
**189** A13 5r copper red 20.00 11.50
**190** A12 10r green 30.00 25.00
*Nos. 173-190 (18)* 70.40 54.10

Issued: 10c, 35c, 70c, 9/15/56; others, 2/1/54.
For surcharge see No. 193.

"Stone of Possession" A14

Flying Fox A15

***Perf. 14½x14***
**1956, Nov. 15** **Wmk. 4**
**191** A14 40c ultra .20 .20
**192** A14 1r gray black .30 .30

Bicentenary of French colonization.

No. 183 Surcharged "5 cents" and Bars

**1957, Sept. 16** ***Perf. 13½x14½***
**193** A11 5c on 45c violet brn .25 .25
*a.* Double surcharge *325.00*
*b.* Thick bars omitted *650.00*

The "c," "e" or "s" of surcharge may be found in italic.

**1957, Oct. 25** ***Perf. 14½x13½***
**194** A15 5c light violet .60 .20

Mauritius Stamp of 1859 with Seychelles "B64" Cancellation A16

**Engr. & Typo.**
***Perf. 11½x11***

**1961, Dec. 11** **Wmk. 314**
**Stamp in Dull Blue & Black**
**195** A16 10c lilac .20 .20
**196** A16 35c dull green .30 .30
**197** A16 2.25r orange brown 1.10 1.10
*Nos. 195-197 (3)* 1.60 1.60

1st post office in Victoria, Seychelles, cent.

Black Parrot — A17

Anse Royal Bay — A18

Designs: 10c, Vanilla. 15c, Fisherman. 20c, Denis Island Lighthouse. 25c, Clock Tower, Victoria. 30c, 35c, Anse Royal Bay. 40c, Government House. 45c, Fishing boat. 50c, Cascade Church. 60c, Flying fox. 70c, 85c, Sailfish. 75c, Coco-de-mer palm. 1r, Cinnamon. 1.50r, Copra. 2.25r, Map of Indian Ocean. 3.50r, Settlers' homes. 5r, Regina Mundi Convent. 10r, Badge of Seychelles.

***Perf. 14½x13½, 13½x14½***
**1962-69** **Photo.** **Wmk. 314**
**Size: 24x31mm, 31x24mm**
**198** A17 5c multicolored 2.00 .20
*a.* Wmkd. sideways ('67) .20 .20
**199** A17 10c multicolore 1.10 .20
*a.* Wmkd. sideways ('68) .20 .20
**200** A17 15c multicolored .20 .20
**201** A17 20c multicolored .20 .20
**202** A17 25c multicolored .20 .20
**202A** A18 30c multicolored 3.00 *3.50*
**203** A18 35c multicolored 1.40 1.75
**204** A18 40c multicolored .20 *.85*
**204A** A18 45c multicolore 2.75 *3.50*
**205** A17 50c multicolored .35 .20
*b.* Wmkd. sideways ('69) .80 .80
**205A** A17 60c multicolored 1.40 .40
**206** A17 70c multicolored 4.75 2.50
**206A** A17 75c multicolored 1.75 *3.25*
**206B** A17 85c multicolored .70 .35
**207** A18 1r multicolored .25 .20
**208** A18 1.50r multicolored 4.25 *5.25*

**209** A18 2.25r multicolored 4.25 4.25
**210** A18 3.50r multicolored 1.75 *4.50*
**211** A18 5r multicolored 2.75 2.00

***Perf. 13x14***

**Size: 22½x39mm**

**212** A17 10r multicolored 10.25 4.00
*Nos. 198-212 (20)* 43.50 37.50

Issued: 45c, 75c, 8/1/66; #198a, 2/7/67; 30c, 60c, 85c, 7/15/68; others 2/21/62.

The 60c and 85c have watermark sideways.

For surcharges and overprints see Nos. 216-217, 233-236, 241-243.

**Freedom from Hunger Issue**
Common Design Type

**1963, June 4** ***Perf. 14x14½***
**213** CD314 70c lilac .75 .35

**Red Cross Centenary Issue**
Common Design Type

**1963, Sept. 2 Litho.** ***Perf. 13***
**214** CD315 10c black & red .20 .20
**215** CD315 75c ultra & red .70 .60

Nos. 203 and 206 Surcharged with New Value and Bars

***Perf. 14x14½, 14½x14***

**1965, Apr. Photo. Wmk. 314**
**216** A18 45c on 35c .20 .20
**217** A17 75c on 70c .30 .30

**ITU Issue**
Common Design Type

***Perf. 11x11½***

**1965, June 1 Litho. Wmk. 314**
**218** CD317 5c orange & vio bl .20 .20
**219** CD317 1.50r red lil & apple grn .70 .35

**Intl. Cooperation Year Issue**
Common Design Type

**1965, Oct. 25** ***Perf. 14½***
**220** CD318 5c blue grn & claret .20 .20
**221** CD318 40c lt violet & green .40 .30

**Churchill Memorial Issue**
Common Design Type

**1966, Jan. 24 Photo.** ***Perf. 14***

**Design in Black, Gold and Carmine Rose**

**222** CD319 5c bright blue .20 .20
**223** CD319 15c green .20 .20
**224** CD319 75c brown .60 .25
**225** CD319 1.50r violet 1.40 .75
*Nos. 222-225 (4)* 2.40 1.40

**World Cup Soccer Issue**
Common Design Type

**1966, July 1 Litho.** ***Perf. 14***
**226** CD321 15c multicolored .20 .20
**227** CD321 1r multicolored .30 .30

**WHO Headquarters Issue**
Common Design Type

**1966, Sept. 20 Litho.** ***Perf. 14***
**228** CD322 20c multicolored .20 .20
**229** CD322 50c multicolored .55 .30

**UNESCO Anniversary Issue**
Common Design Type

**1966, Dec. 1 Litho.** ***Perf. 14***
**230** CD323 15c "Education" .20 .20
**231** CD323 1r "Science" .40 .40
**232** CD323 5r "Culture" 1.60 1.60
*Nos. 230-232 (3)* 2.20 2.20

Nos. 200, 204A, 206A and 210 Overprinted: "UNIVERSAL / ADULT / SUFFRAGE / 1967"

***Perf. 14½x14, 14x14½***

**1967, Sept. 18 Photo. Wmk. 314**
**233** A17 15c multicolored .20 .20
**234** A18 45c brt blue & yel .20 .20
**235** A17 75c multicolored .20 .20
**236** A18 3.60r multicolored .40 *.50*
*Nos. 233-236 (4)* 1.00 1.10

Cowries: Tiger, Mole, Money
A19

Sea Shells (ITY Emblem and): 40c, Textile, betulinus and virgin cones. 1r, Arthritic spidor conch. 2.25r, Triton and subulate auger.

***Perf. 14x13½***

**1967, Dec. 4 Photo. Wmk. 314**
**237** A19 15c multicolored .20 .20
**238** A19 40c multicolored .25 .25
**239** A19 1r multicolored .40 .40
**240** A19 2.25r multicolored .65 .65
*Nos. 237-240 (4)* 1.50 1.50

Issued for International Tourist Year, 1967.

Nos. 204, 204A and 206A Surcharged

***Perf. 14x14½, 14½x14***

**1968, Apr. 16 Photo. Wmk. 314**
**241** A18 30c on 40c multicolored .20 .20
**242** A18 60c on 45c blue & yel .20 .20
**243** A17 85c on 75c multicolored .25 .25
*Nos. 241-243 (3)* .65 .65

The surcharge on No. 241 includes 2 bars; on Nos. 242-243 it includes 3 bars and "CENTS."

Family, Rising Sun and Human Rights Flame
A20

***Perf. 14½x14***

**1968, Sept. 2 Litho. Wmk. 314**
**244** A20 20c chocolate & multi .20 .20
**245** A20 50c vio blue & multi .20 .20
**246** A20 85c black & multi .20 .20
**247** A20 2.25r brown & multi .25 *.75*
*Nos. 244-247 (4)* .85 1.35

International Human Rights Year.

First Landing on Praslin Island — A21

Designs: 50c, La Digue and La Curieuse at anchor, vert. 85c, Coco-de-mer and black parrot, vert. 2.25r, La Digue and La Curieuse under sail.

**Litho.; Head Embossed in Gold**

***Perf. 14x14½***

**1968, Dec. 30 Wmk. 314**
**248** A21 20c multicolored .20 .20
**249** A21 50c dk blue, blk & red .25 .25
**250** A21 85c rose red & multi .45 .45
**251** A21 2.25r ultra & multi 2.25 2.25
*Nos. 248-251 (4)* 3.15 3.15

Landing on Praslin Island of the Chevalier Marion Dufresne expedition, 200th anniv.

Separation of Rocket and Spacecraft — A22

5c, Launching of Apollo XI, vert. 50c, Landing module & men on the moon. 85c, Seychelles tracking station. 2.25r, Moonscape & earth.

**1969, Sept. 9 Litho.** ***Perf. 13½***
**252** A22 5c multicolored .20 .20
**253** A22 20c multicolored .20 .20
**254** A22 50c multicolored .25 .20
**255** A22 85c multicolored .35 .35
**256** A22 2.25r multicolored .60 *1.25*
*Nos. 252-256 (5)* 1.60 2.20

See note after US No. C76.

Lazare Picault Landing in 1741 — A23

History of Seychelles: 10c, US satellite tracking station. 15c, German cruiser Königsberg at Aldabra, 1915. 20c, British fleet refueling, St. Anne, 1939-45. 25c, Ashanti King Prempeh in exile, 1896. 30c, 40c, Stone of Possession placed, 1756. 50c, 65c, Pirates. 60c, Corsairs. 85c, 95c, Jet and airport. 1r, First capitulation of the French to the British, 1794. 1.50r, Battle between the sailing vessels Sybille and Chiffone, 1801. 3.50r, Visit of Duke of Edinburgh, 1956. 5r, Chevalier Queau de Quincy. 10r, Map of Indian Ocean, 1574. 15r, Seychelles coat of arms.

***Perf. 13x12½***

**1969-72 Litho. Wmk. 314**
**257** A23 5c multicolored .20 .20
**258** A23 10c multicolored .20 .20
**259** A23 15c multicolored 1.90 1.75
**260** A23 20c multicolored 1.10 .20
**261** A23 25c multicolored .20 .20
**262** A23 30c multicolored .95 *3.00*
**262A** A23 40c multicolored 1.75 1.10
**263** A23 50c multicolored .25 .25
**264** A23 60c multicolored .95 *1.10*
**264A** A23 65c multicolored 5.25 *6.25*
**265** A23 85c multicolored 1.90 1.60
**265A** A23 95c multicolored 5.50 3.75
**266** A23 1r multicolored .25 .20
**267** A23 1.50r multicolored 1.60 *1.75*
**268** A23 3.50r multicolored .95 *2.00*
**269** A23 5r multicolored .95 *2.40*
**270** A23 10r multicolored 2.40 *5.50*
**271** A23 15r multicolored 3.50 *9.00*
*Nos. 257-271 (18)* 29.80 40.45

Issued: 40, 65, 95c, 12/11/72; others, 11/3/69.

For overprints & surcharges see Nos. 294-298, 323-330, 361-369.

St. Anne Island, Ship and Gulls
A24

Designs: 50c, Flying fish, island and ship. 85c, Map of Seychelles and compass rose. 3.50r, Anchor, chain on sea bottom.

**1970, Apr. 27** ***Perf. 14***
**272** A24 20c multicolored .75 .75
**273** A24 50c multicolored .50 .50
**274** A24 85c multicolored .50 .50
**275** A24 3.50r multicolored .75 .75
*Nos. 272-275 (4)* 2.50 2.50

Bicentenary of first settlement on St. Anne.

Girl and Eye Chart
A25

Designs: 50c, Infant on scales and milk bottles. 85c, Mother and child, vert. 3.50r, Red Cross branch headquarters.

**1970, Aug. 4 Litho. Wmk. 314**
**276** A25 20c lt blue & multi .20 .20
**277** A25 50c multicolored .40 .40
**278** A25 85c multicolored .65 .65
**279** A25 3.50r multicolored 1.75 1.75
*Nos. 276-279 (4)* 3.00 3.00

Centenary of British Red Cross Society.

Pitcher Plant — A26

Flowers: 50c, Wild vanilla. 85c, Tropic-bird flower. 3.50r, Vare hibiscus.

**1970, Dec. 29** ***Perf. 14½***
**280** A26 20c multicolored .20 .20
**281** A26 50c multicolored .45 .45
**282** A26 85c multicolored .85 .85

**283** A26 3.50r multicolored 4.25 4.25
*a.* Souvenir sheet of 4, #280-283 8.00 *10.00*
*Nos. 280-283 (4)* 5.75 5.75

Souvenir Sheet

Map Showing Location of Seychelles — A27

***Perf. 13½x14***

**1971, Apr. 20 Litho. Wmk. 314**
**284** A27 5r yellow grn & multi 5.00 *6.00*

Issued to publicize Seychelles' location.

Consolidated Catalina Amphibian — A28

Designs: 5c, Piper Navajo, vert. 20c, Westland Wessex, vert. 60c, Grumman Albatross amphibian, vert. 85c, "G" class Short Brothers flying boat. 3.50r, Vickers supermarine "Walrus" amphibian.

***Perf. 14x14½, 14½x14***

**1971, June 28 Litho. Wmk. 314**
**285** A28 5c orange & multi .20 .20
**286** A28 20c purple & multi .20 .20
**287** A28 50c olive & multi .55 .20
**288** A28 60c sepia & multi .70 .25
**289** A28 85c brown & multi .95 .35
**290** A28 3.50r blue & multi 7.00 2.00
*Nos. 285-290 (6)* 9.60 3.20

Completion of Seychelles Airport.

Santa Claus, by Jean-Claude Waye Hive — A29

Christmas (Children's Drawings): 15c, Santa Claus riding a tortoise, by Edison Thérésine. 3.50r, Santa Claus on the seashore, by Isabelle Tirant.

**1971, Oct. 12** ***Perf. 13½***
**291** A29 10c dark blue & multi .20 .20
**292** A29 15c dark green & multi .20 .20
**293** A29 3.50r violet & multi .60 *.85*
*Nos. 291-293 (3)* 1.00 1.25

Nos. 262, 264-265 Surcharged with New Value and 5 Bars

**1971, Dec. 21** ***Perf. 13x12½***
**294** A23 40c on 30c multicolored .25 *.40*
**295** A23 65c on 60c multicolored .35 *.75*
**296** A23 95c on 85c multicolored .40 *1.00*
*Nos. 294-296 (3)* 1.00 2.15

Nos. 260, 269 Overprinted in Black or Gold: "ROYAL VISIT 1972"

**1972, Mar. 21 Litho. Wmk. 314**
**297** A23 20c multicolored .20 .20
**298** A23 5r multicolored (G) 1.40 *2.00*

Visit of Elizabeth II and Prince Philip.

**Seychelles Sunbird — A40**

**1976, Nov. 8    Wmk. 373    Litho.    Perf. 14½**

| | | | | |
|---|---|---|---|---|
| 357 | A40 | 20c multicolored | .20 | .20 |
| 358 | A40 | 1.25r multicolored | .95 | .65 |
| 359 | A40 | 1.50r multicolored | 1.25 | .85 |
| 360 | A40 | 5r multicolored | 3.00 | 3.00 |
| | | Souvenir sheet of 4, #357-360 | 7.75 | 8.00 |
| | | Nos. 357-360 (4) | 5.40 | 4.70 |

Seychelles Birds (James R. Mancham, Congress Emblem and): 20c, Paradise flycatcher, vert. 1.50r, Gray white-eye. 5r, Black parrot, vert.

4th Pan-African Ornithological Cong., Mahe Beach Hotel, Nov. 6-13.

Nos. 260, 262, 263, 265A-266, 268-271, 264A Overprinted or Surcharged: "Independence / 1976"

**1976, Nov. 22    Perf 13x12½    Litho.**

| | | | | |
|---|---|---|---|---|
| 361 | A23 | 20c multicolored | .80 | 1.75 |
| 362 | A23 | 50c multicolored | .75 | 2.10 |
| 363 | A23 | 95c multicolored | 2.25 | 2.10 |
| 364 | A23 | 1r multicolored | .70 | 2.10 |
| 365 | A23 | 3.50r multicolored | 3.50 | 4.25 |
| 366 | A23 | 5r multicolored | 3.00 | 6.00 |
| 367 | A23 | 10r multicolored | 4.00 | 11.50 |
| 368 | A23 | 15r multicolored | 4.50 | 11.50 |
| 369 | A23 | 25r on 65c multi | 5.50 | 18.00 |
| | | Nos. 361-369 (9) | 25.00 | 59.30 |

**Washington's Inauguration — A41**

American Bicentennial: 2c, Jefferson and map of Louisiana Purchase. 3c, Seward and map of Alaska Purchase. 4c, Pony Express, 1860. 5c, Lincoln's Emancipation Proclamation, 1863. 1.50r, Completion of Transcontinental Railroad, 1000. 0.60r, Wright Brothers' 1st flight, 1903. 5r, Ford assembly line, 1913. 10r, Kennedy and Apollo 11 moon landing, 1969. 25r, Declaration of Independence, 1770.

**SILVER JUBILEE**

**1976, Dec. 21    Perf. 14x13½**

| | | | | |
|---|---|---|---|---|
| 370 | A41 | 1c rose & plum | .20 | .20 |
| 371 | A41 | 2c lilac & vio | .20 | .20 |
| 372 | A41 | 3c blue & vio bl | .20 | .20 |
| 373 | A41 | 4c yellow & brn | .20 | .20 |
| 374 | A41 | 5c brt yel & grn | .20 | .20 |
| 375 | A41 | 1.50r brt brn & brn | .30 | .30 |
| 376 | A41 | 3.50r brt grn & bl grn | .75 | .75 |
| 377 | A41 | 5r yellow & brn | 1.10 | 1.10 |
| 378 | A41 | 10r dull bl & dk bl | 2.25 | 2.25 |
| | | Nos. 370-378 (9) | 5.40 | 5.40 |

**Souvenir Sheet**

| | | | | |
|---|---|---|---|---|
| 379 | A41 | 25r lilac rose & pur | 4.75 | 4.75 |

**Seychelles Islands and Arms — A42**

**The Orb — A43**

---

**Praslin Map and Grand Anse Postmark, 1907 — A36**

**First Landing, 1609, and James Mancham — A37**

**1976, Mar. 30    Wmk. 373    Perf. 14**

| | | | | |
|---|---|---|---|---|
| 339 | A36 | 20c lt blue & multi | .20 | .20 |
| 340 | A36 | 65c lt blue & multi | .30 | .30 |
| 341 | A36 | 1r lt blue & multi | .40 | .40 |
| 342 | A36 | 1.50r lt blue & multi | .60 | .60 |
| a. | | Souvenir sheet of 4, #339-342 | 2.50 | 3.00 |
| | | Nos. 339-342 (4) | 1.50 | 1.50 |

Rural posts of Seychelles.

**1976, June 29    Perf. 14**

| | | | | |
|---|---|---|---|---|
| 343 | A37 | 20c rose & multi | .20 | .20 |
| 344 | A37 | 25c yellow & multi | .20 | .20 |
| 345 | A37 | 40c lilac & multi | .20 | .20 |
| 346 | A37 | 75c green & multi | .35 | .35 |
| 347 | A37 | 1r salmon & multi | .55 | .55 |
| 348 | A37 | 1.25r multicolored | .60 | .60 |
| 349 | A37 | 1.50r ocher & multi | .80 | .80 |
| 350 | A37 | 3.50r blue & multi | 1.75 | 1.75 |
| | | Nos. 343-350 (8) | 4.65 | 4.65 |

Designs: 25c, Stone of Possession. 40c, Arrival of 1st settlers, 1770 (ship). 75c, Le Chevalier Queau de Quincy. 1r, Sir Bickham Sweet Escott. 1.25r, Government House. 1.50r, Coat of arms of Internal Self-government. 3.50r, Seychelles flag.

Seychelles' independence, June 29, 1976.

**Flags of Seychelles and US — A38**

**1976, July 12    Litho.**

| | | | | |
|---|---|---|---|---|
| 351 | A38 | 1r blue & multi | .25 | .25 |
| 352 | A38 | 10r red & multi | 1.75 | 2.50 |

US bicent.: 10r, State House, Seychelles, and Independence Hall, Philadelphia.

**Swimming — A39**

**1976, July 26    Perf. 14½**

| | | | | |
|---|---|---|---|---|
| 353 | A39 | 20c vio blue & blk | .20 | .20 |
| 354 | A39 | 65c dk grn, yel grn & blk | .40 | .35 |
| 355 | A39 | 1r brown, grn & blk | .60 | 1.50 |
| 356 | A39 | 3.50r car rose & blk | 1.60 | 2.10 |
| | | Nos. 353-356 (4) | 4.20 | 4.70 |

Designs (Olympic Rings and): 65c, Hockey. 1r, Basketball. 3.50r, Soccer.

21st Olympic Games, Montreal, Canada, July 17-Aug. 1.

---

**1974, Oct. 9    Perf. 12½x12    Wmk. 314**

| | | | | |
|---|---|---|---|---|
| 317 | A33 | 20c multicolored | .20 | .20 |
| 318 | A33 | 50c multicolored | .30 | .30 |
| 319 | A33 | 95c multicolored | .50 | .50 |
| 320 | A33 | 1.50r multicolored | 1.20 | 1.20 |
| | | Nos. 317-320 (4) | | |

**Winston Churchill A34**

Design: 1.50r, Churchill, different portrait.

**1974, Nov. 30    Perf. 14½    Litho.**

| | | | | |
|---|---|---|---|---|
| 321 | A34 | 95c lt blue & multi | .35 | .35 |
| 322 | A34 | 1.50r lt green & multi | .60 | 1.25 |
| a. | | Souvenir sheet of 2, #321-322 | | |

Sir Winston Churchill (1874-1965).

**VISIT OF Q.E. II**

Nos. 260, 263, 265A and 267 Overprinted in Black or Silver

**1975, Feb. 8    Perf. 13x12½    Wmk. 314**

| | | | | |
|---|---|---|---|---|
| 323 | A23 | 20c multi (B) | .20 | .20 |
| 324 | A23 | 50c multi (B) | .20 | .20 |
| 325 | A23 | 65c multi (S) | .25 | .25 |
| 326 | A23 | 1.50r multi (B) | .35 | .75 |
| | | Nos. 323-326 (4) | 1.00 | 1.40 |

Visit of cruise ship Queen Elizabeth II, Mahe, Seychelles.

**1975, Oct. 1    Litho.    Wmk. 314**

| | | | | |
|---|---|---|---|---|
| 327 | A23 | 20c multicolored | .20 | .20 |
| 328 | A23 | 65c multicolored | .25 | .35 |
| 329 | A23 | 1r multicolored | .45 | .35 |
| 330 | A23 | 3.50r multicolored | 1.50 | 1.10 |
| | | Nos. 327-330 (4) | 2.40 | 1.90 |

Nos. 260, 264A, 266, 268 Overprinted in Gold

**Queen Elizabeth I A35**

**1975, Dec. 15    Wmk. 314    Litho.    Perf. 13½**

| | | | | |
|---|---|---|---|---|
| 331 | A35 | 10c dp brown & multi | .20 | .20 |
| 332 | A35 | 15c dk brown & multi | .20 | .20 |
| 333 | A35 | 20c dk green & multi | .20 | .20 |
| 334 | A35 | 25c purple & multi | .20 | .20 |
| 335 | A35 | 65c dk blue & multi | .40 | .35 |
| 336 | A35 | 1r Prus blue & multi | .60 | .55 |
| 337 | A35 | 1.50r dp violet & multi | .80 | 1.00 |
| 338 | A35 | 3.50r dk violet & multi | 1.60 | 1.50 |
| | | Nos. 331-338 (8) | 4.20 | 4.70 |

Portraits: 15c, Gladys Aylward. 20c, Elizabeth Fry. 25c, Emmeline Pankhurst. 65c, Florence Nightingale. 1r, Amy Johnson. 1.50r, Joan of Arc. 3.50r, Eleanor Roosevelt.

International Women's Year.

---

**Brush Warbler — A30**

**Fireworks — A31**

**1972, July 15    Perf. 14x13½**

| | | | | |
|---|---|---|---|---|
| 299 | A30 | 5c shown | 1.00 | .50 |
| 300 | A30 | 20c Scops owl | 2.00 | .50 |
| 301 | A30 | 50c Blue pigeons | 2.25 | .50 |
| 302 | A30 | 65c Magpie robin | 2.75 | .65 |
| 303 | A30 | 95c Paradise flycatcher | 3.75 | 2.25 |
| 304 | A30 | 3.50r Kestrel | 8.00 | 11.00 |
| a. | | Souvenir sheet of 6, #299-304 | 35.00 | 35.00 |
| | | Nos. 299-304 (6) | 19.75 | 15.50 |

Seychelles Festival 1972.

**1972, Sept. 18    Litho.    Perf. 14**

| | | | | |
|---|---|---|---|---|
| 305 | A31 | 10c shown | .20 | .20 |
| 306 | A31 | 15c Canoe race, horiz. | .20 | .20 |
| 307 | A31 | 25c Women in local costumes | | |
| 308 | A31 | 5r Water-skiing, horiz. | .70 | .70 |
| | | Nos. 305-308 (4) | 1.30 | 1.30 |

**Silver Wedding Issue, 1972**

**Common Design Type**

Design: Queen Elizabeth II, Prince Philip, giant tortoise and leaping sailfish.

**1972, Nov. 20    Photo.    Perf. 14x14½**

| | | | | |
|---|---|---|---|---|
| 309 | CD324 | 95c multicolored | .50 | .50 |
| 310 | CD324 | 1.50r multicolored | .50 | .50 |

**Princess Anne's Wedding Issue**

**Common Design Type**

**1973, Nov. 14    Litho.    Perf. 14**

| | | | | |
|---|---|---|---|---|
| 311 | CD325 | 95c ocher & multi | .30 | .30 |
| 312 | CD325 | 1.50r slate & multi | .30 | .30 |

**Soldierfish — A32**

**1974, Mar. 5    Wmk. 314    Litho.**

| | | | | |
|---|---|---|---|---|
| 313 | A32 | 20c shown | .20 | .20 |
| 314 | A32 | 50c Filefish | .35 | .60 |
| 315 | A32 | 95c Butterflyfish | .70 | .60 |
| 316 | A32 | 1.50r Gaterin | 1.75 | 1.75 |
| | | Nos. 313-316 (4) | 3.00 | 2.75 |

**Envelope and Globe — A33**

UPU. cent.: 50c, Globe with location of Seychelles and radio tower. 95c, Cancellation and globe. 1.50r, "UPU" with emblems.

Coral Reef — A44

**1977, Sept. 5 — Litho. — Perf. 14**

| | | | | |
|---|---|---|---|---|
| 380 | A42 | 20c multicolored | .20 | .20 |
| 381 | A42 | 40c multicolored | .20 | .20 |
| 382 | A42 | 50c multicolored | .20 | .20 |
| 383 | A42 | 1r multicolored | .20 | .20 |
| 384 | A43 | 1.25r multicolored | .20 | .20 |
| 385 | A43 | 1.50r multicolored | .20 | .20 |
| 386 | A42 | 5r multicolored | .35 | .35 |
| 387 | A42 | 10r multicolored | .65 | .65 |
| a. | | Souv. sheet of 4, #380, 382, 383, 387 | 1.10 | 1.25 |
| | | Nos. 380-387 (8) | 2.20 | 2.20 |

25th anniv. of reign of Elizabeth II.

**1977, Nov. 7 — Unwmk. — Perf. 12**

| | | | | |
|---|---|---|---|---|
| 404 | A45 | 1.50r, red, black & gold | .65 | .50 |
| a. | | Souvenir sheet | 1.40 | 1.40 |

60th anniv. of Russian Oct. Revolution.

**Perf. 14, 14x14½ (40c, 1, 1.25, 1.50r)**
**1977-91 — Litho. — Wmk. 373**
Sizes: 40c, 1, 1.25, 1.50r, 30x25mm
Others 28x23mm

| | | | | |
|---|---|---|---|---|
| 388 | A44 | 5c Reef fish | .20 | .20 |
| 389 | A44 | 10c Hawksbill turtle | .20 | .20 |
| 390 | A44 | 15c Coco de mer | .20 | .20 |
| 391 | A44 | 20c Wild vanilla | 1.20 | .20 |
| 392 | A44 | 25c Butterfly | .25 | .20 |
| 393 | A44 | 40c Coral reef | .25 | .20 |
| 394 | A44 | 50c Giant tortoise | .25 | .30 |
| a. | | Wmk. 384, perf. 14x14½ | .30 | .30 |
| 395 | A44 | 75c Crayfish | .30 | .25 |
| 396 | A44 | 1r Madagascar cardinal | .35 | .30 |
| 397 | A44 | 1.25r Fairy tern | 1.00 | .40 |
| 398 | A44 | 1.50r Flying fox | 1.00 | .45 |
| 398A | A44 | 3r like #399 Wmk. 384 | 2.00 | 1.75 |
| 399 | A44 | 3.50r Green gecko | 1.25 | 2.50 |

Size: 27x35mm

| | | | | |
|---|---|---|---|---|
| 400 | A44 | 5r Octopus, vert. | 1.90 | 1.60 |
| 401 | A44 | 10r Tiger cowrie, vert. | 3.75 | 3.25 |
| 402 | A44 | 15r Pitcher plant, vert. | 5.25 | 3.25 |
| 403 | A44 | 20r Arms, vert. | 5.75 | 5.75 |
| | | Nos. 388-403 (17) | 26.00 | 20.25 |

Issued: 40c, 1r, 1.25r, 1.50r, 10/31/77; #394a, 398A, 11/1991; others, 1978. Reissued dated "1979" below design: 10, 15, 25, 40, 50, 75c, 1r, 1.50r. Dated "1981": 40c. For surcharge and overprint see #446, 605.

**1981, Jan. 6 — Perf. 14x14½, 14 (1.10r)**
Denomination "R" instead of "Re." or "Rs."
Sizes: 1.10r, 28x23mm Others, 30x25mm

| | | | | |
|---|---|---|---|---|
| 403A | A44 | 1r like No. 396 | .30 | .30 |
| 403B | A44 | 1.10r like No. 399 | .35 | .35 |
| 403C | A44 | 1.25r like No. 397 | .40 | .40 |
| 403D | A44 | 1.50r like No. 398 | .45 | .45 |

**Perf. 13**

| | | | | |
|---|---|---|---|---|
| 403E | A44 | 5r like No. 400 | 1.60 | 1.60 |
| j. | | ("90") | | |
| 403F | A44 | 10r like No. 401 | 2.00 | 2.00 |
| 403G | A44 | 15r like No. 402 | 4.75 | 4.75 |
| 403H | A44 | 20r like No. 403 | 6.50 | 6.50 |
| | | Nos. 403A-403H | 17.60 | 17.60 |

Reissued dated "1981" below design: 1.50r. Dated "1982": 1r, 1.50r. Dated "1986": 1r. Dated "1991": 1r, 1.50r. Dated "1985": 5r. "1990": 1r. See No. 576 for No. 403C with commemorative inscription.

Designs: 40c, 5r, 10r, similar to 20c, 1r. St. Edward's Crown, 1.25r, Ampulla and Spoon, 1.50r, Scepter with Cross.

Cruiser Aurora, Star and Flag — A45

---

Christmas: 1r, Anglican Cathedral, Victoria, 1.50r, R. C. Cathedral, Victoria, 5r, St. Mark's Anglican Church, Praslin.

St. Roch Roman Catholic Church, Bel Ombre — A46

**1977, Dec. 5 — Perf. 13½x14 — Wmk. 373**

| | | | | |
|---|---|---|---|---|
| 405 | A46 | 20c multicolored | .20 | .20 |
| 406 | A46 | 1r multicolored | .20 | .20 |
| 407 | A46 | 1.50r multicolored | .40 | .40 |
| 408 | A46 | 5r multicolored | 1.00 | 1.00 |
| | | Nos. 405-408 (4) | | |

Calendar Page, June 5, 1977 — A47

**1978, June 5 — Litho. — Wmk. 373 — Perf. 14x13½**

| | | | | |
|---|---|---|---|---|
| 409 | A47 | 40c multicolored | .20 | .20 |
| 410 | A47 | 1.25r multicolored | .20 | .20 |
| 411 | A47 | 1.50r multicolored | .20 | .20 |
| 412 | A47 | 5r multicolored | .50 | .50 |
| | | Nos. 409-412 (4) | 1.10 | 1.10 |

First anniversary of Liberation Day.

Edward VII, George V, George VI — A48

**1978, Aug. 21 — Litho. — Perf. 14**

1.25r, Hands holding rifle, torch & Seychelles flag. 1.50r, Fisherman & farmer holding hands. 5r, Soldiers & waving children.

| | | | | |
|---|---|---|---|---|
| 413 | A48 | 40c multicolored | .20 | .20 |
| 414 | A48 | 1.25r multicolored | .20 | .20 |
| 415 | A48 | 1.50r multicolored | .20 | .20 |
| 416 | A48 | 5r multicolored | .35 | .35 |
| a. | | Souvenir sheet of 4, #413-416 | 1.00 | 1.00 |
| | | Nos. 413-416 (4) | | |

25th anniv. of coronation of Elizabeth II.

Designs: 1.50r, Queens Victoria and Elizabeth II. 3r, Queen Victoria Monument, Seychelles. 5r, Queen's Building, Victoria, Seychelles.

Gardenia from Aride Island — A49

Designs (Coat of Arms and): 1.25r, Magpie robin from Fregate Island. 1.50r, Seychelles paradise flycatchers. 5r, Green turtle.

---

**1978, Oct. 16 — Perf. 13½x14 — Litho. — Wmk. 373**

| | | | | |
|---|---|---|---|---|
| 417 | A49 | 40c multicolored | .20 | .20 |
| 418 | A49 | 1.25r multicolored | .60 | .60 |
| 419 | A49 | 1.50r multicolored | 1.75 | 1.50 |
| 420 | A49 | 5r multicolored | 5.45 | 2.90 |
| | | Nos. 417-420 (4) | | |

"Stone of Possession" — A50

Bicentennary of the founding of Victoria.

**1978, Dec. 15 — Litho. — Perf. 13½**

| | | | | |
|---|---|---|---|---|
| 421 | A50 | 20c shown | .20 | .20 |
| 422 | A50 | 1r multicolored | .20 | .20 |
| 423 | A50 | 1.50r Map, 1782 | .40 | .40 |
| 424 | A50 | 5r Clock tower | 1.00 | 1.00 |
| | | Nos. 421-424 (4) | | |

5r, Pierre Poivre, St. Pierre Island.

Seychelles Fody — A51

Birds: No. 426, Green-backed heron. No. 427, Seychelles bulbul. No. 428, Seychelles cave swiftlets. No. 429, Grayheaded lovebirds.

**1979, Feb. 27 — Litho. — Perf. 14**

| | | | | |
|---|---|---|---|---|
| 425 | A51 | 2r multicolored | .80 | .80 |
| 426 | A51 | 2r multicolored | .80 | .80 |
| 427 | A51 | 2r multicolored | .80 | .80 |
| 428 | A51 | 2r multicolored | .80 | .80 |
| 429 | A51 | 2r multicolored | .80 | .80 |
| a. | | Strip of 5, #425-429 | 4.00 | 4.00 |
| | | Nos. 425-429 (5) | 4.00 | 4.00 |

Patrice Lumumba — A52

African Liberation Heroes: 2r, Kwame Nkrumah. 2.25r, Dr. Eduardo Mondlane. 5r, Amilcar Cabral.

**1979, June 5 — Litho. — Perf. 14½**

| | | | | |
|---|---|---|---|---|
| 430 | A52 | 40c violet & blk | .20 | .20 |
| 431 | A52 | 2r dark blue & blk | .25 | .25 |
| 432 | A52 | 2.25r orange brn & blk | .45 | .45 |
| 433 | A52 | 5r olive grn & blk | 1.10 | 1.10 |
| | | Nos. 430-433 (4) | | |

Coat of Arms, Rowland Hill, Seychelles No. 412 — A53

**1979, Aug. 27 — Litho. — Perf. 14x14½**

Coat of Arms, Hill, Seychelles stamps: 2.25r, No. 301. 3r, No. 205. 5r, No. 4.

| | | | | |
|---|---|---|---|---|
| 434 | A53 | 40c multicolored | .20 | .20 |
| 435 | A53 | 2.25r multicolored | .35 | .35 |
| 436 | A53 | 5r multicolored | .45 | .45 |
| | | Nos. 434-436 (3) | 1.00 | 1.00 |

**Souvenir Sheet**

| | | | | |
|---|---|---|---|---|
| 437 | A53 | 5r multicolored | .90 | .90 |

Sir Rowland Hill (1795-1879), originator of penny postage.

---

IYC Emblem and: 2.25r, Children, 3r, Girl with ball, vert. 5r, Girl with puppet, vert.

Schoolboy, IYC Emblem — A54

**1979, Oct. 25 — Perf. 14½x14, 14x14½ — Litho.**

| | | | | |
|---|---|---|---|---|
| 438 | A54 | 40c multicolored | .20 | .20 |
| 439 | A54 | 2.25r multicolored | .20 | .20 |
| 440 | A54 | 3r multicolored | .25 | .25 |
| 441 | A54 | 5r multicolored | .35 | .35 |
| | | Nos. 438-441 (4) | 1.00 | 1.00 |

International Year of the Child.

Three Kings Bearing Gifts — A55

Christmas (Stained Glass Windows): 20c, Angel, vert. 2.25r, Virgin and Child, vert. 5r, Flight into Egypt.

**1979, Dec. 3 — Litho. — Perf. 14½**

| | | | | |
|---|---|---|---|---|
| 442 | A55 | 20c multicolored | .20 | .20 |
| 443 | A55 | 2.25r multicolored | .35 | .35 |
| 444 | A55 | 3r multicolored | .45 | .45 |
| | | Nos. 442-444 (3) | 1.00 | 1.00 |

**1979, Dec. 7 — Wmk. 373 — Perf. 14**

No. 399 Surcharged

| | | | | |
|---|---|---|---|---|
| 445 | A55 | 5r multicolored | .85 | .86 |

**Souvenir Sheet**

| | | | | |
|---|---|---|---|---|
| 446 | A44 | 1.10r on 3.50r multicolored | .35 | .35 |

Seychelles Kestrel — A56

**1980, Feb. 29 — Litho. — Perf. 14**

Seychelles Kestrel: a. shown. b. Pair. c. Female, eggs. d. Mother and chick. e. Chicks nesting.

| | | | | |
|---|---|---|---|---|
| 447 | A56 | 5.25 | 5.25 |
| a.-e. | | A56 2r any single | 1.00 | 1.00 |
| | | Strip of 5 | | |

See Nos. 468, 483.

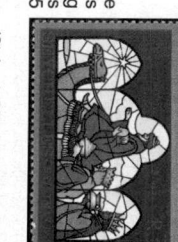

50-Rupee Bank Note, London 1980 Emblem — A57

Sprinting, Moscow '80 Emblem — A58

New Currency: 40c, 1.50r, horiz.

Denis Isld.
Lighthouse,
1910 — A71

**Perf. 14x13½**

**1983, July 14**
| | | | | |
|---|---|---|---|---|
| 515 | A71 | 40c shown | .20 | .20 |
| 516 | A71 | 2.75r Seychelles Hospital, 1924 | .30 | .30 |
| 517 | A71 | 3.50r Supreme Court, 1894 | .45 | .45 |
| 518 | A71 | 7r State House, 1911 | .80 | .80 |
| a. | | Souvenir sheet of 4, #515-518 | 1.75 | 1.75 |
| | | Nos. 515-518 (4) | | |

 with text image showing "40c SEYCHELLES" — Manned Flight Bicentenary — A72

**Perf. 14**

**1983, Sept. 15**
| | | | | |
|---|---|---|---|---|
| 519 | A72 | 40c Royal Vauxhall balloon, 1836 | .20 | .20 |
| 520 | A72 | 1.75r DeHavilland D.H.-50j | .50 | .50 |
| 521 | A72 | 2.75r Grumman Albatross | .75 | .75 |
| 522 | A72 | 7r Sweavingen Merlin | 1.90 | 1.90 |
| | | Nos. 519-522 (4) | 3.35 | 3.35 |

Air Seychelles
R2

First Intl. Air Seychelles Flight — A73

**Litho.**

**1983, Oct. 26**
| | | | | |
|---|---|---|---|---|
| 523 | A73 | 2r DC10 aircraft | 2.25 | 2.25 |

SEYCHELLES
40c

Paintings, Marianne North — A74

**Perf. 14   Litho.**

**1983, Nov. 17**
| | | | | |
|---|---|---|---|---|
| 524 | A74 | 40c Swamp Plant and Moorhen | .20 | .20 |
| 525 | A74 | 1.75r Wormia flagellaria | .35 | .35 |
| 526 | A74 | 2.75r Asiatic Pancratium | .55 | .55 |
| 527 | A74 | 7r Pitcher Plant | 1.40 | 1.40 |
| a. | | Souvenir sheet of 4, #524-527 | 6.00 | 6.00 |
| | | Nos. 524-527 (4) | 2.50 | 2.50 |

**Nos. 469-474 Surcharged**

**Wmk. 380**

**Perf. 14**

**1983, Dec. 28   Litho.**
| | | | | |
|---|---|---|---|---|
| 528 | A61b | 50c on 1.50r multi | .20 | .20 |
| 529 | A61b | 50c on 1.50r multi | .20 | .20 |
| 530 | A61b | 2.25r on 5r multi | 1.10 | 1.10 |
| 531 | A61b | 2.25r on 5r multi | 1.10 | 1.10 |
| 532 | A61b | 3.75r on 10r multi | 1.90 | 1.90 |
| 533 | A61b | 3.75r on 10r multi | 1.90 | 1.90 |
| | | Souvenir sheet of 4, #528-533 (6) | 6.40 | 6.40 |

SEYCHELLES
50c

Handicrafts — A75

---

SEYCHELLES
40c

5th Anniv. of Liberation A66

**Perf. 14**

**1982, June 5**
| | | | | |
|---|---|---|---|---|
| 491 | A66 | 40c Bookmobile | .20 | .20 |
| 492 | A66 | 1.75r Mobile dental clinic | .35 | .35 |
| 493 | A66 | 2.75r Farming | 1.25 | 1.25 |
| 494 | A66 | 7r Construction site | 4.25 | 4.25 |
| a. | | Souvenir sheet of 4, #491-494 | 2.00 | 2.00 |
| | | Nos. 491-494 (4) | | |

R1.75
Seychelles

Tourist Board Emblem A67

Tourism: Hotels.

**1982, Sept. 1**
| | | | | |
|---|---|---|---|---|
| 495 | A67 | 1.75r Northolme | .40 | .40 |
| 496 | A67 | 1.75r Reef | .40 | .40 |
| 497 | A67 | 1.75r Barbarons Beach | .40 | .40 |
| 498 | A67 | 1.75r Coral Strand | .40 | .40 |
| 499 | A67 | 1.75r Beau Vallon Bay | .40 | .40 |
| 500 | A67 | 1.75r Fisherman's Cove | .40 | .40 |
| 501 | A67 | 1.75r Mahe Beach, shown | .40 | .40 |
| 502 | A67 | 1.75r Island scene | 3.20 | 3.20 |
| | | Nos. 495-502 (8) | | |

Seychelles 20c

Tata Bus A68

**Perf. 14**

**Wmk. 373   Litho.**

**1982, Nov. 18**
| | | | | |
|---|---|---|---|---|
| 503 | A68 | 20c shown | .20 | .20 |
| 504 | A68 | 1.75r Mini moke | .35 | .35 |
| 505 | A68 | 2.25r Ox cart | .55 | .55 |
| 506 | A68 | 7r Truck | 1.40 | 1.40 |
| | | Nos. 503-506 (4) | 2.50 | 2.50 |

Seychelles
40c

World Communications Year — A69

**1983, Feb. 25**
| | | | | |
|---|---|---|---|---|
| 507 | A69 | 40c Radio control room | .20 | .20 |
| 508 | A69 | 2.75r Satellite earth station | .45 | .45 |
| 509 | A69 | 3.50r TV control room | .55 | .55 |
| 510 | A69 | 5r Postal services | .80 | .80 |
| | | Nos. 507-510 (4) | 2.00 | 2.00 |

SEYCHELLES
40c

Commonwealth Day — A70

**1983, Mar. 14**
| | | | | |
|---|---|---|---|---|
| 511 | A70 | 40c Agricultural research | .20 | .20 |
| 512 | A70 | 2.75r Food processing plant | .30 | .30 |
| 513 | A70 | 3.50r Fishing industry | 1.10 | 1.10 |
| 514 | A70 | 7r Flag | 2.00 | 2.00 |
| | | Nos. 511-514 (4) | | |

---

SEYCHELLES
R1.50
Royal Wedding

Prince Charles and Lady Diana — A61b

Illustration A61b is reduced.

**Wmk. 380**

**Perf. 14**

**1981, June 23   Litho.**
| | | | | |
|---|---|---|---|---|
| 469 | A61a | 1.50r Couple, Victoria & Albert I | .20 | .20 |
| a. | | Bklt. pane of 4, perf. 12 | 1.00 | |
| 470 | A61b | 1.50r Couple | .40 | .40 |
| 471 | A61a | 5r Cleveland | 1.50 | 1.50 |
| 472 | A61b | 5r like #470 | 1.60 | |
| a. | | Bklt. pane of 2, perf. 12 | 1.25 | 1.25 |
| 473 | A61a | 10r Britannia | 3.00 | 3.00 |
| 474 | A61b | 10r like #470 | 6.85 | 6.85 |
| | | Nos. 469-474 (6) | | |

Each denomination issued in sheets of 7 (6 type A61a, 1 type A61b).
For surcharges see Nos. 528-533.

Souvenir Sheet

**Perf. 12**

**1981   Litho.**
| | | | |
|---|---|---|---|
| 474A | A61a | 7.50r Couple | 2.10 | 2.10 |

Seychelles
R5

Seychelles Intl. Airport, 10th Anniv. — A62

**Wmk. 373   Litho.**

**Perf. 14½**

**1981, July 27**
| | | | | |
|---|---|---|---|---|
| 475 | A62 | 40c Britten-Norman Islander | .20 | .20 |
| 476 | A62 | 2.25r Britten-Norman Trislander | .55 | .55 |
| 477 | A62 | 3.50r Vickers VC-10 | .80 | .80 |
| 478 | A62 | 5r Boeing 747 | 1.10 | 1.10 |
| | | Nos. 475-478 (4) | 2.65 | 2.65 |

Silhouette Island
SEYCHELLES
40c

La Dique
A65

A63

A64

Designs: Various flying foxes.

**Perf. 14   Litho.**

**1981, Oct. 9**
| | | | | |
|---|---|---|---|---|
| 479 | A63 | 40c multicolored | .20 | .20 |
| 480 | A63 | 2.25r multicolored | .35 | .35 |
| 481 | A63 | 3r multicolored | .50 | .50 |
| 482 | A63 | 5r multicolored | .95 | .95 |
| a. | | Souvenir sheet, #479-482 (4) | 3.50 | 3.50 |
| | | Nos. 479-482 (4) | 2.00 | 2.00 |

Bird Type of 1980

**Wmk. 373**

**Perf. 14**

**1982, Feb. 4   Litho.**
| | | | |
|---|---|---|---|
| 483 | | Strip of 5 | 14.50 | 14.50 |
| a.-e. | A56 | 3r any single | 2.75 | 2.75 |

Map of Silhouette Island and La Digue

**1982, Apr. 22   Perf. 14½**
| | | | | |
|---|---|---|---|---|
| 487 | A65 | 40c Map of Silhouette Island and La Digue | .20 | .20 |
| 488 | A65 | 1.50r Denis & Bird Islds. | .30 | .30 |
| 489 | A65 | 2.75r Curieuse Isld., Praslin | .60 | .60 |
| 490 | A65 | 7r Mahe | 1.40 | 1.40 |
| a. | | Souvenir sheet of 4, #487-490 (4) | 3.75 | 3.75 |
| | | Nos. 487-490 (4) | 2.50 | 2.50 |

---

L'Éducation
SEYCHELLES
40c

**Perf. 14**

**1980, Apr. 18   Litho.**
| | | | | |
|---|---|---|---|---|
| 448 | A57 | 40c multicolored | .20 | .20 |
| 449 | A57 | 1.50r multicolored | .30 | .30 |
| 450 | A57 | 2.25r multicolored | .40 | .40 |
| 451 | A57 | 5r multicolored | .75 | .75 |
| a. | | Souvenir sheet of 4, #448-451 | 1.65 | 1.65 |
| | | Nos. 448-451 (4) | | |

London 1980 Intl. Stamp Exhib., May 6-14.

**Perf. 14½**

**1980, June 13**
| | | | | |
|---|---|---|---|---|
| 452 | A58 | 40c shown | .20 | .20 |
| 453 | A58 | 2.25r Weight lifting | .25 | .25 |
| 454 | A58 | 3r Boxing | .35 | .35 |
| 455 | A58 | 5r Yachting | .85 | .85 |
| a. | | Souvenir sheet of 4, #452-455 | 2.25 | 2.25 |
| | | Nos. 452-455 (4) | 1.65 | 1.65 |

22nd Summer Olympic Games, Moscow, July 19-Aug. 3.

Boeing 747
A59

SEYCHELLES
40c

**Perf. 14**

**1980, Aug. 22   Litho.**
| | | | | |
|---|---|---|---|---|
| 456 | A59 | 40c shown | .20 | .20 |
| 457 | A59 | 2.25r Tour bus | .30 | .30 |
| 458 | A59 | 3r Ocean liner, pirogue | .45 | .45 |
| 459 | A59 | 5r Tour motor boat | .75 | .75 |
| a. | | Souvenir sheet of 4, #456-459 (4) | 1.70 | 1.70 |

World Tourism Conf., Manila, Sept. 27.

Female Coco-de-Mer Palm Tree — A60

SEYCHELLES
40c

**Perf. 14**

**1980, Oct. 31   Litho.**
| | | | | |
|---|---|---|---|---|
| 460 | A60 | 40c shown | .20 | .20 |
| 461 | A60 | 2.25r Male tree | .35 | .35 |
| 462 | A60 | 3r Bowls | .50 | .50 |
| 463 | A60 | 5r Gourds, canoes | .75 | .75 |
| a. | | Souvenir sheet of 4, #460-463 (4) | 2.75 | 2.75 |
| | | Nos. 460-463 (4) | 1.80 | 1.80 |

Female Palm
SEYCHELLES
40c

Vasco da Gama's San Gabriel, 1497 A61

SEYCHELLES
40c

**Wmk. 373**

**1981, Feb.   Litho.**
| | | | | |
|---|---|---|---|---|
| 464 | A61 | 40c shown | .20 | .20 |
| 465 | A61 | 2.25r Mascarenhas' Caravel, 1505 | .35 | .35 |
| 466 | A61 | 3.50r Darwin's Beagle, 1831 | .55 | .55 |
| 467 | A61 | 5r Queen Elizabeth 2, 1968 | .75 | .75 |
| a. | | Souvenir sheet of 4, #464-467 (4) | 3.25 | 3.25 |
| | | Nos. 464-467 (4) | 2.45 | 2.45 |

Bird Type of 1980

**Perf. 14**

**1981, Apr. 10   Litho.**
| | | | | |
|---|---|---|---|---|
| 468 | | Strip of 5, multi | 6.00 | 6.00 |
| a. | A56 | 2r Male fairy tern | 1.10 | 1.10 |
| b. | A56 | 2r Pair | 1.10 | 1.10 |
| c. | A56 | 2r Female | 1.10 | 1.10 |
| d. | A56 | 2r Female, diff. | 1.10 | 1.10 |
| e. | A56 | 2r Adult bird, chick | 1.10 | 1.10 |

Royal Wedding R1.50
SEYCHELLES

Prince Charles, Lady Diana, Royal Yacht Charlotte A61a

## Lloyd's List Issue
### Common Design Type

**1984, Feb. 29** — Wmk. 373 · **1984, May 21** Litho. Perf. 14½x14

| | | | | |
|---|---|---|---|---|
| 534 | A75 | 50c Coconut kettle | .20 | .20 |
| 535 | A75 | 2r Scarf, doll | .35 | .60 |
| 536 | A75 | 2r Coconut-fiber roses | .55 | .90 |
| 537 | A75 | 10r Carved fishing boat, doll | 1.90 | 2.75 |
| | | Nos. 534-537 (4) | 3.00 | 4.45 |

### SEYCHELLES / 30th Anniversary of SPUP — A76

**1984, May 21** People's United Party, 20th. Anniv. Common Design Type

| | | | | |
|---|---|---|---|---|
| 538 | CD335 | 50c Port Victoria | .60 | .60 |
| 539 | CD335 | 2r Steamship, 1930s | .90 | .90 |
| 540 | CD335 | 3r Cruise liner | 2.75 | 2.75 |
| 541 | CD335 | 10r Ennerdale | 4.45 | 4.45 |
| | | Nos. 538-541 (4) | | |

### People's United Party, 20th. Anniv. A76

**1984, June 2** Litho. Perf. 14

| | | | | |
|---|---|---|---|---|
| 542 | A76 | 50c Original headquarters | .20 | .20 |
| 543 | A76 | 2r Liberation statue, vert. | .40 | .40 |
| 544 | A76 | 2r New headquarters | .60 | .60 |
| 545 | A76 | 10r Pres. Rene, vert. | 1.60 | 1.60 |
| | | Nos. 542-545 (4) | 2.80 | 2.80 |

### 19TH CONGRESS OF THE UNIVERSAL POSTAL UNION HAMBURG

Souvenir Sheet

### UPU Congress — A77

**1984, June 18** Perf. 14½

| | | | | |
|---|---|---|---|---|
| 546 | A77 | 5r No. 156 | 2.00 | 2.00 |

### 1984 Summer Olympics A78

**1984, July 28** Perf. 14

| | | | | |
|---|---|---|---|---|
| 547 | A78 | 50c Long jump | .20 | .20 |
| 548 | A78 | 2r Boxing | .40 | .40 |
| 549 | A78 | 3r Diving | .55 | .55 |
| 550 | A78 | 10r Weight lifting | 2.00 | 2.00 |
| a. | | Souvenir sheet of 4, #547-550 | 3.75 | 3.75 |
| | | Nos. 547-550 (4) | 3.15 | 3.15 |

### Scuba Diving A79

**1984, Sept. 24**

| | | | | |
|---|---|---|---|---|
| 551 | A79 | 50c shown | .20 | .20 |
| 552 | A79 | 2r Paragliding | .80 | .80 |
| 553 | A79 | 3r Sailing | 1.25 | 1.25 |
| 554 | A79 | 10r Water skiing | 4.00 | 4.00 |
| | | Nos. 551-554 (4) | 6.25 | 6.25 |

### Whale Conservation — A80

**1984, Nov.** Litho.

| | | | | |
|---|---|---|---|---|
| 555 | A80 | 50c Humpback whale | 2.00 | 2.00 |
| 556 | A80 | 2r Sperm whale | 4.00 | 4.00 |
| 557 | A80 | 3r Right whale | 4.50 | 4.50 |
| 558 | A80 | 10r Blue whale | 8.50 | 8.50 |
| | | Nos. 555-558 (4) | 19.00 | 19.00 |

### Audubon Birth Bicent. — A81

**1985, Mar. 11** Litho. Perf. 14

| | | | | |
|---|---|---|---|---|
| 559 | A81 | 50c multicolored | 2.25 | 2.25 |
| 560 | A81 | 2r multicolored | 3.25 | 3.25 |
| 561 | A81 | 3r multicolored | 3.50 | 3.50 |
| 562 | A81 | 10r multicolored | 6.75 | 6.75 |
| | | Nos. 559-562 (4) | 15.75 | 15.75 |

Bare-legged scops owls.

### EXPO '85, Tsukuba — A82

**1985, Mar. 15** Wmk. 373 Litho. Perf. 14

| | | | | |
|---|---|---|---|---|
| 563 | A82 | 50c Giant tortoise | .30 | .30 |
| 564 | A82 | 2r Fairy tern | 1.40 | 1.40 |
| 565 | A82 | 3r Wind surfing | 1.90 | 1.90 |
| 566 | A82 | 10r multicolored | 3.25 | 3.25 |
| a. | | Souvenir sheet of 4, #563-566 | 6.75 | 6.75 |
| | | Nos. 563-566 (4) | 7.75 | 7.75 |

See No. 604.

### Queen Mother 85th Birthday
### Common Design Type

**1985, June 7** Litho. Wmk. 384 Perf. 14½x14

| | | | | |
|---|---|---|---|---|
| 567 | CD336 | 50c Queen Elizabeth, 1930 | .20 | .20 |
| 568 | CD336 | 2r With grandchildren, 1930 | .30 | .30 |
| 569 | CD336 | 3r 75th birthday celebration | .60 | .60 |
| 570 | CD336 | 5r Holding Prince Henry | .95 | .95 |
| | | Nos. 567-570 (4) | 1.25 | 1.25 |

Souvenir Sheet

| | | | | |
|---|---|---|---|---|
| 571 | CD336 | 10r Exiting from helicopter | 4.00 | 4.00 |

### 2nd Indian Ocean Islands Games A83

**1985, Aug. 24** Perf. 14

| | | | | |
|---|---|---|---|---|
| 572 | A83 | 50c Boxing | .20 | .20 |
| 573 | A83 | 2r Soccer | .70 | .70 |
| 574 | A83 | 3r Swimming | 1.10 | 1.10 |
| 575 | A83 | 10r Wind surfing | 3.75 | 3.75 |
| | | Nos. 572-575 (4) | 5.75 | 5.75 |

### A84

**1985, Nov. 1** Wmk. 384

| | | | | |
|---|---|---|---|---|
| 576 | A83a | 1.25r Fairy tern | 2.75 | 2.75 |

Air Seychelles 1st Airbus.

**1985, Nov. 28**

| | | | | |
|---|---|---|---|---|
| 577 | A84 | 50c Agriculture | .20 | .20 |
| 578 | A84 | 2r Construction | .60 | .60 |
| 579 | A84 | 3r Carpentry | .95 | .95 |
| 580 | A84 | 10r Science education | 3.25 | 3.25 |
| | | Nos. 577-580 (4) | 5.00 | 5.00 |

Int. Youth Year.

### Vintage Cars A85

**1985, Dec. 18**

| | | | | |
|---|---|---|---|---|
| 581 | A85 | 50c 1919 Ford Model T | .25 | .25 |
| 582 | A85 | 2r 1922 Austin Seven | 1.25 | 1.25 |
| 583 | A85 | 3r 1924 Morris Bull-nose Oxford | 1.50 | 1.50 |
| 584 | A85 | 10r 1929 Humber Coupe | 5.25 | 5.25 |
| | | Nos. 581-584 (4) | 8.25 | 8.25 |

### Halley's Comet — A86

**1986, Feb. 3** Wmk. 384 Perf. 14x14½

| | | | | |
|---|---|---|---|---|
| 585 | A86 | 50c Transit instrument | .20 | .20 |
| 586 | A86 | 2r Quadrant | .80 | .80 |
| 587 | A86 | 3r Trajectory diagram | 1.25 | 1.25 |
| 588 | A86 | 10r Edmond Halley | 4.00 | 4.00 |
| | | Nos. 585-588 (4) | 6.25 | 6.25 |

**1986, Apr. 4** Wmk. 384 Litho. Perf. 14

| | | | | |
|---|---|---|---|---|
| 589 | A87 | 2r Heroine | .75 | .75 |
| 590 | A87 | 3r Hero | 1.25 | 1.25 |

Souvenir Sheet

| | | | | |
|---|---|---|---|---|
| 591 | A87 | 10r United | 3.75 | 3.75 |

First ballet performed in the Seychelles. Giselle, Performed by the Ballet Louvre, Apr. 4-8 — A87

### Queen Elizabeth II 60th Birthday
### Common Design Type

Designs: 50c, Marrying the Duke of Edinburgh, 1947. 1.25r, Silver Jubilee celebration. 2r, Greeting child aboard the Britannia, Qatar Harbor. 3r, State opening of Parliament, 1982. 5r, Visiting Crown Agents' offices, 1983.

**1986, Apr. 21** Perf. 14½

| | | | | |
|---|---|---|---|---|
| 592 | CD337 | 50c scarlet, blk & sil | .20 | .20 |
| 593 | CD337 | 1.25r ultra & multi | .25 | .25 |
| 594 | CD337 | 2r green & multi | .40 | .40 |
| 595 | CD337 | 3r violet & multi | 1.00 | 1.00 |
| 596 | CD337 | 5r rose vio & multi | 2.45 | 2.45 |
| | | Nos. 592-596 (5) | | |

For overprints see Nos. 625-629.

### AMERIPEX '86, Inter-island Communications — A88

**1986, May 22** Wmk. 384 Litho. Perf. 14

| | | | | |
|---|---|---|---|---|
| 597 | A88 | 50c La Digue Ferry | .20 | .20 |
| 598 | A88 | 2r Phone booth, vert. | 1.25 | 1.25 |
| 599 | A88 | 3r Victoria P.O., vert. | 2.00 | 2.00 |
| 600 | A88 | 7r Air Seychelles tris-lander | 4.75 | 4.75 |
| | | Nos. 597-600 (4) | 8.30 | 8.30 |

### Coptic Catholic Knights of Malta Celebration Day — A89

**1986, June 7** Litho. Wmk. 384 Perf. 14½x14

| | | | | |
|---|---|---|---|---|
| 601 | A89 | 5r Nat. arms, assoc. emblem | 3.50 | 3.50 |
| a. | | Souvenir sheet of 1 | 1.50 | 1.50 |

### Royal Wedding Issue, 1986
### Common Design Type

**1986, July 23** Litho. Perf. 14

| | | | | |
|---|---|---|---|---|
| 602 | CD338 | 2r multicolored | .50 | .50 |
| 603 | CD338 | 10r multicolored | 2.75 | 2.75 |

2r, Informal portrait. 10r, Andrew, helicopter.

### Tsukuba Expo Type of 1985
### Souvenir Sheet

**1986, July 12** Wmk. 384 Litho. Perf. 14

| | | | | |
|---|---|---|---|---|
| 604 | | Sheet of 4 | 4.75 | 4.75 |
| a. | A82 | 50c multicolored | .20 | .20 |
| b. | A82 | 2r multicolored | .90 | .90 |
| c. | A82 | 3r multicolored | 1.25 | 1.25 |
| d. | A82 | 10r multicolored | 2.75 | 2.75 |

No. 604 inscribed "Seychelles Philatelic Exhibition-Tokyo-1986" and printed without stamps. Nos. 604a-604d inscribed on margin or on individual stamps. Nos. 604a-604d inscribed "1986."

### State Visit of Pope John Paul II — A90

**1986, Oct. 28** Wmk. 373 Perf. 14½x14

| | | | | |
|---|---|---|---|---|
| 605 | A44 | 1r multicolored | 3.00 | 3.00 |

Int. Creole Day.

No. 396 Overprinted

Pope and: 50c, Seychelles Airport. 2r, Cathedral. 3r, Baie Lazare parish church. 10r, People's Stadium.

## 1986, Dec. 1   Wmk. 384   Litho.   *Perf. 14½*
| 606 | A90 | 50c multicolored | .20 | .20 |
|---|---|---|---|---|
| 607 | A90 | 2r multicolored | 1.60 | 1.60 |
| 608 | A90 | 3r multicolored | 2.25 | 2.25 |
| 609 | A90 | 10r multicolored | 7.25 | 7.25 |
| | | | 16.00 | 16.00 |
| a. | | Souvenir sheet of 4, #606-609 | 11.30 | 11.30 |

Nos. 606-609 (4)

Butterflies — A91

## 1987, Feb. 18   Litho.   *Perf. 14½*
| 610 | A91 | 1r Melanitis leda | .85 | .85 |
|---|---|---|---|---|
| 611 | A91 | 2r Phalanta phaliberti | 1.60 | 1.60 |
| 612 | A91 | 3r Danaus chrysippus | 2.75 | 2.75 |
| | | | 7.50 | 7.50 |
| 613 | A91 | 10r Euploea mitra | 12.20 | 12.20 |

Nos. 610-613 (4)

Seashells — A92

## 1987, May 7   Wmk. 373
| 614 | A92 | 1r Gloripallium pallium | 1.00 | 1.00 |
|---|---|---|---|---|
| 615 | A92 | 2r Spondylus aurantius | 1.90 | 1.90 |
| 616 | A92 | 3r Harpa ventricosa, Lioconcha ornata | 2.75 | 2.75 |
| 617 | A92 | 10r Strombus lentiginosus | 8.75 | 8.75 |
| | | | 14.40 | 14.40 |

Nos. 614-617 (4)

*Perf. 14x14½, 14½x14*

Liberation, 10th Anniv. — A93

## 1987, June 5   Wmk. 384
| 618 | A93 | 1r Liberation monument | .25 | .25 |
|---|---|---|---|---|
| 619 | A93 | 2r Hospital, horiz. | .40 | .40 |
| 620 | A93 | 3r Orphanage, horiz. | .60 | .60 |
| 621 | A93 | 10r Fish monument | 1.75 | 1.75 |
| | | | 3.00 | 3.00 |

Nos. 618-621 (4)

Natl. Banking Cent. — A94

## 1987, June 25   *Perf. 14½x14*
| 622 | A94 | 1r Savings Bank, Praslin | .25 | .25 |
|---|---|---|---|---|
| 623 | A94 | 3r Development Bank | .35 | .35 |
| 624 | A94 | 10r Central Bank | 1.50 | 1.50 |
| | | | 2.10 | 2.10 |

Nos. 622-624 (3)

Nos. 592-596 Ovptd. in Silver

---

Fishing Industry A95

## 1987, Dec. 9   Wmk. 384   Litho.   *Perf. 14½*
| 625 | A95 | 50c scar, blk & sil | .20 | .20 |
|---|---|---|---|---|
| 626 | CD337 | 1.25r ultra & multi | .25 | .25 |
| 627 | CD337 | 2r green & multi | .45 | .45 |
| 628 | CD337 | 3r violet & multi | .65 | .65 |
| 629 | CD337 | 5r rose vio & multi | 1.10 | 1.10 |
| | | | 2.65 | 2.65 |

Nos. 625-629 (5)

## 1987, Dec. 11   Wmk. 384   Litho.   *Perf. 14*
| 630 | A95 | 1r Tuna cannery | .20 | .20 |
|---|---|---|---|---|
| 631 | A95 | 2r Fishing trawler | .65 | .65 |
| 632 | A95 | 3r Weighing fish | 1.00 | 1.00 |
| 633 | A95 | 10r Hauling catch from net | 3.50 | 3.50 |
| | | | 5.35 | 5.35 |

Nos. 630-633 (4)

Beach Scenes A96

## 1988, Feb. 9   Wmk. 384   Litho.   *Perf. 14½*
| 634 | A96 | 1r Para-sailing, windsurfing, kayaks | .40 | .40 |
|---|---|---|---|---|
| 635 | A96 | 2r Boating | 1.00 | 1.00 |
| 636 | A96 | 3r Yacht at anchor | 1.40 | 1.40 |
| 637 | A96 | 10r Hotel, cabanas | 4.50 | 4.50 |
| | | | 7.30 | 7.30 |

Nos. 634-637 (4)

Green Turtles — A97   A98

## 1988, Apr. 22   Wmk. 373
| 638 | A97 | 3r multicolored | 2.00 | 2.00 |
|---|---|---|---|---|
| 639 | A97 | 3r multicolored | 2.00 | 2.00 |
| 640 | A97 | 3r multicolored | 2.75 | 2.75 |
| 641 | A97 | 3r multicolored | 2.75 | 2.75 |
| | | | 9.50 | 9.50 |

Nos. 638-641 (4)

No. 638, Newly hatched turtles headed toward ocean. No. 639, Offspring hatching. No. 640, Female emerging from ocean. No. 641, Female laying eggs in sand. Stamps of same denomination printed se-tenant in a continuous design.

## 1988, July 29   Wmk. 384   *Perf. 14½*

| 642 | A98 | 1r multicolored | .30 | .30 |
|---|---|---|---|---|
| 643 | A98 | 3r multicolored | .60 | .60 |
| 644 | A98 | 3r multicolored | .90 | .90 |
| 645 | A98 | 4r multicolored | 1.25 | 1.25 |
| 646 | A98 | 5r multicolored | 1.40 | 1.40 |
| | | | 3.00 | 3.00 |
| 647 | | Strip of 5 | 3.00 | 3.00 |
| a.-e. | A98 | 2r any single | 7.45 | 7.45 |

Nos. 642-647 (6)

Designs: 1r, No. 647a, Shot put. Nos. 643, 647b, High jump. 3r, No. 647c. Medal winner, grandstand and flags. 4r, No. 647d, Running. 5r, No. 647e, Javelin. 10r, Tennis.

---

### Souvenir Sheet   Wmk. 373
| 648 | A98 | 10r multicolored | 6.50 | 6.50 |
|---|---|---|---|---|

No. 647 has a continuous design. 1988 Summer Olympics, Seoul, (1r-5r). Intl. Tennis Fed., 75th anniv. (10r). No. 648 contains one stamp, size: 28x39mm.

### Lloyds of London, 300th Anniv.
Common Design Type

Designs: 1r, Leadenhall Street, London, 1928. 2r, Cinq Juin, horiz. 3r, Queen Elizabeth II, horiz. 10r, Explosion of the Hindenburg, Lakehurst, New Jersey, 1937.

## 1988, Sept. 30   Wmk. 384   *Perf. 14*
| 649 | CD341 | 1r multicolored | .85 | .85 |
|---|---|---|---|---|
| 650 | CD341 | 2r multicolored | 1.00 | 1.00 |
| 651 | CD341 | 3r multicolored | 2.00 | 3.00 |
| 652 | CD341 | 10r multicolored | 7.25 | 7.25 |
| | | | 11.10 | 12.10 |

Nos. 649-652 (4)

Defense Forces Day, 1st Anniv. A99

## 1988, Nov. 25   Wmk. 373   Litho.
| 653 | A99 | 1r Motorcycle police | 1.10 | 1.10 |
|---|---|---|---|---|
| 654 | A99 | 3r Air force helicopter | 2.10 | 2.10 |
| 655 | A99 | 5r Navy patrol boat | 3.25 | 3.25 |
| 656 | A99 | 10r Tank | 11.50 | 11.50 |
| | | | 17.95 | 17.95 |

Nos. 653-656 (4)

Christmas A100

Illustrations by local artists.

## 1988, Dec. 1   Litho.   Wmk. 373
| 657 | A100 | 50c Selwyn Hoareau | .20 | .20 |
|---|---|---|---|---|
| 658 | A100 | 2r Robin Leste | .70 | .70 |
| 659 | A100 | 3r France Anacoura | 1.10 | 1.10 |
| 660 | A100 | 10r Andre McGaw | 3.75 | 3.75 |
| | | | 5.75 | 5.75 |

Nos. 657-660 (4)

Orchids A101

## 1988, Dec. 21   Wmk. 384   Litho.   *Perf. 14*
| 661 | A101 | 1r Dendrobium, vert. | .55 | .55 |
|---|---|---|---|---|
| 662 | A101 | 2r Arachnis hybrid | 1.10 | 1.10 |
| 663 | A101 | 3r Vanda caerulea, vert. | 1.50 | 1.50 |
| 664 | A101 | 10r Dendrobium phalaenopsis | 5.25 | 5.25 |
| | | | 8.40 | 8.40 |

Nos. 661-664 (4)

Jawaharlal Nehru (1889-1964), 1st Prime Minister of Independent India A102

## 1989, Mar. 30   *Perf. 13½*
| 665 | A102 | 2r India Type A409 | 1.00 | 1.00 |
|---|---|---|---|---|
| 666 | A102 | 10r Portrait | 5.25 | 5.25 |

---

People's United Party (SPUP), 25th Anniv. — A103

### *Perf. 14*
| 667 | A103 | 1r Rally, old office | .30 | .30 |
|---|---|---|---|---|
| 668 | A103 | 2r Maison Du Peuple | .55 | .55 |
| 669 | A103 | 3r Pres. Rene, banner, torch | .85 | .85 |
| 670 | A103 | 10r Torch, flag, Rene | 2.75 | 2.75 |
| | | | 4.45 | 4.45 |

Nos. 667-670 (4)

### Moon Landing, 20th Anniv.
Common Design Type

Apollo 15: 1r, Saturn 5 lift-off. 2r, David R. Scott, Alfred M. Worden and James B. Irwin. 3r, Mission emblem. 5r, Irwin salutes flag in front of the Hadley Delta. 10r, Buzz Aldrin about to step onto the Moon, Apollo 11 mission.

## 1989, July 20   Size of Nos. 677-678: 29x29mm
| 676 | CD342 | 1r multicolored | .40 | .40 |
|---|---|---|---|---|
| 677 | CD342 | 2r multicolored | .95 | .95 |
| 678 | CD342 | 3r multicolored | 1.50 | 1.50 |
| 679 | CD342 | 5r multicolored | 2.40 | 2.40 |
| | | | 5.25 | 5.25 |

Nos. 676-679 (4)

### Souvenir Sheet
| 680 | CD342 | 10r multicolored | 7.75 | 7.75 |
|---|---|---|---|---|

Intl. Red Cross and Red Crescent Organizations, 125th Anniv. — A104

### *Perf. 14½*
| 681 | A104 | 1r Ambulance, 18/70 | 1.10 | 1.10 |
|---|---|---|---|---|
| 682 | A104 | 2r H.M. Hospital Ship Liberty, 1914-18 | 2.40 | 2.40 |
| 683 | A104 | 3r Sunbeam Standard Army Ambulance, 1914-18 | 4.00 | 4.00 |
| 684 | A104 | 10r The White Train, 1899-1902 | 12.50 | 12.50 |
| | | | 20.00 | 20.00 |

Nos. 681-684 (4)

Island Birds — A105

## 1989, Oct. 16   *Perf. 14½x14*
| 685 | A105 | 50c Black parrot | .25 | .25 |
|---|---|---|---|---|
| 686 | A105 | 2r Sooty tern | 2.75 | 2.75 |
| 687 | A105 | 3r Magpie robin | 4.00 | 4.00 |
| 688 | A105 | 5r Roseate tern | 6.75 | 6.75 |
| | | | 16.00 | 16.00 |
| a. | | Souvenir sheet of 4, #685-688 | 13.75 | 13.75 |

Nos. 685-688 (4)

French Revolution Bicent., World Stamp Expo '89 — A106

## 1989, Nov. 17   *Perf. 14*
| 689 | A106 | 2r Flags | 1.50 | 1.50 |
|---|---|---|---|---|
| 690 | A106 | 5r Storming of the Bastille | 4.00 | 4.00 |

## African Development Bank, 25th Anniv. — A107

### 1989, Dec. 29 — Wmk. 384

| | | | | |
|---|---|---|---|---|
| 692 | A107 | 1r multicolored | .80 | .80 |
| 693 | A107 | 2r multicolored | 1.60 | 1.60 |
| 694 | A107 | 3r multicolored | 2.50 | 2.50 |
| 695 | A107 | 10r multicolored | 8.75 | 8.75 |
| | | Nos. 692-695 (4) | 13.65 | 13.65 |

1r, Beau Vallon School, horiz. 2r, Fishing Authority headquarters, horiz. 3r, Variola. 10r, Deneb.

## Orchids — A108

### 1990, Jan. 26

| | | | | |
|---|---|---|---|---|
| 696 | A108 | 1r Disperis tripeta-loides | 1.00 | 1.00 |
| 697 | A108 | 2r Vanilla phalae-nopsis | 2.25 | 2.25 |
| 698 | A108 | 3r Angraecum eburneum | 3.25 | 3.25 |
| 699 | A108 | 10r Polystachya con-creta | 18.00 | 18.00 |
| | | Nos. 696-699 (4) | 11.50 | 11.50 |

Designs: 2r, Fumiyo Sako. 3r, Coco-de-mer, male and female plants. 5r, Pitcher plant, Aldabra lily. 7r, Gardenia, Arms of Seychelles.

## Expo '90 (International Garden & Greenery Exposition), Japan — A109

### 1990, June 8 — Litho. — Wmk. 373

| | | | | |
|---|---|---|---|---|
| 700 | A109 | 2r multicolored | 1.25 | 1.25 |
| 701 | A109 | 3r multicolored | 1.75 | 1.75 |
| 702 | A109 | 5r multicolored | 3.00 | 3.00 |
| 703 | A109 | 7r multicolored | 4.25 | 4.25 |
| a. | | Souvenir sheet of 4, #700-703 | 11.00 | 11.00 |
| | | Nos. 700-703 (4) | 10.25 | 10.25 |

## Penny Black 150th Anniv., Stamp World London '90. A110

### 691 A106 10r Raising French flag, Seychelles, 1791 — 8.25 8.25

**Souvenir Sheet**

Exhibition emblem and stamps on stamps: 1r, Seychelles #38, Great Britain #80 canceled. 2r, Seychelles #81, Great Britain #64 canceled. 3r, Seychelles #74, Great Britain #62 canceled. 5r, Seychelles #2, Great Britain #3 canceled. 10r, Seychelles #197, Great Britain #1 canceled.

### 1990, May 3

| | | | | |
|---|---|---|---|---|
| 704 | A110 | 1r multicolored | .85 | .85 |
| 705 | A110 | 2r multicolored | 1.75 | 1.75 |
| 706 | A110 | 3r multicolored | 2.40 | 2.40 |
| 707 | A110 | 5r multicolored | 4.25 | 4.25 |
| | | Nos. 704-707 (4) | 9.25 | 9.25 |

**Souvenir Sheet — Perf. 12½**

| | | | | |
|---|---|---|---|---|
| 708 | A110 | 10r multicolored | 10.50 | 10.50 |

## Boeing 767-200ER A111

### 1990, July 27 — Litho. — Wmk. 384 — Perf. 14½x14½

| | | | | |
|---|---|---|---|---|
| 709 | A111 | 3r multicolored | 3.50 | 3.50 |

## Queen Mother, 90th Birthday — Common Design Types

### 1990, Aug. 4 — Wmk. 384 — Perf. 14x15

| | | | | |
|---|---|---|---|---|
| 710 | CD343 | 2r Queen Elizabeth in coronation robes, 1937 | 1.00 | 1.00 |
| 711 | CD344 | 10r Visiting work-shops, 1947 | 5.00 | 5.00 |

Printed in panes of 10 (2 strips of 5 separated by pictorial gutter).

## Int'l Literacy Year. A112, A113

### 1990, Sept. 8 — Wmk. 373 — Perf. 14

| | | | | |
|---|---|---|---|---|
| 712 | A112 | 1r Blackboard | .80 | .80 |
| 713 | A112 | 2r Reading mail | 1.60 | 1.60 |
| 714 | A112 | 3r Reading direc-tions | 2.25 | 2.25 |
| 715 | A112 | 10r Crossword puz-zle | 8.00 | 8.00 |
| | | Nos. 712-715 (4) | 12.65 | 12.65 |

| | | | | |
|---|---|---|---|---|
| 716 | | Strip of 5 | 12.00 | 12.00 |
| a.-e. | A113 | 2r any single | 2.25 | 2.25 |

Various Sega Dancers: a, Pink and white skirt, white blouse. b, Yellow dress. c, Blue, sky blue and pink dress. d, Yellow, green and pink dress. e, White and pink skirt, green blouse.

### 1990, Oct. 27 — Perf. 13½x14

Festival Kreol 1990.

## First Regional Seminar, Indian Ocean Petroleum Exploration A114

### 1990, Dec. 10 — Wmk. 384 — Perf. 14½

| | | | | |
|---|---|---|---|---|
| 717 | A114 | 3r Beach | 2.50 | 2.50 |
| 718 | A114 | 10r Geological map | 8.25 | 8.25 |

## Orchids — A115

### 1991, Feb. 1 — Perf. 14

| | | | | |
|---|---|---|---|---|
| 719 | A115 | 1r Bulbophyllum in-tertextum | .95 | .95 |
| 720 | A115 | 2r Agrostophyllum occidentale | 1.90 | 1.90 |
| 721 | A115 | 3r Vanilla planifolia | 3.00 | 3.00 |
| 722 | A115 | 10r Malaxis seychel-larum | 9.50 | 9.50 |
| | | Nos. 719-722 (4) | 15.35 | 15.35 |

## Elizabeth & Philip, Birthdays — Common Design Types

### 1991, June 17 — Perf. 14½

| | | | | |
|---|---|---|---|---|
| 723 | CD345 | 4r multicolored | 1.50 | 1.50 |
| 724 | CD346 | 4r multicolored | 1.50 | 1.50 |
| a. | | Pair, #723-724 + label | 4.00 | 4.00 |

## Butterflies A116

### 1991, Nov. 15 — Litho. — Wmk. 373 — Perf. 14½x14

| | | | | |
|---|---|---|---|---|
| 725 | A116 | 1.50r Precis rhadama | 1.50 | 1.50 |
| 726 | A116 | 3r Lampides boeticus | 3.00 | 3.00 |
| 727 | A116 | 3.50r Zizeeria knys-na | 4.00 | 4.00 |
| 728 | A116 | 10r Phalanta pha-lanta aethiopica | 11.50 | 11.50 |
| | | Nos. 725-728 (4) | 20.00 | 20.00 |

**Souvenir Sheet**

| | | | | |
|---|---|---|---|---|
| 729 | A116 | 3r Eagris sabadius | 11.00 | 11.00 |

Phila Nippon '91.

## Christmas A117

### 1991, Dec. 2 — Wmk. 384 — Perf. 14

| | | | | |
|---|---|---|---|---|
| 730 | A117 | 50c multicolored | .65 | .65 |
| 731 | A117 | 1r multicolored | .90 | .90 |
| 732 | A117 | 2r multicolored | 1.90 | 1.90 |
| 733 | A117 | 7r multicolored | 7.25 | 7.25 |
| | | Nos. 730-733 (4) | 10.80 | 10.80 |

Woodcuts: 50c, The Holy Virgin, Joseph, the Holy Child and St. John by Raphael, engraved by S. Vouillemont. 1r, The Holy Virgin, the Child and an Angel by Van Dyck, engraved by A. Blooting. 2r, The Holy Family, St. John and St. Anna by Rubens, engraved by Lucas Vorsterman. 7r, The Holy Family, an Angel and St. Catherine, painting and engraving by Cornelius Bloemaert.

## Queen Elizabeth II's Accession to the Throne, 40th Anniv. — Common Design Type

### 1992, Feb. 6 — Wmk. 373

| | | | | |
|---|---|---|---|---|
| 734 | CD349 | 1r multicolored | .65 | .65 |
| 735 | CD349 | 1.50r multicolored | .90 | .90 |
| 736 | CD349 | 2r multicolored | 1.90 | 1.90 |
| 737 | CD349 | 3r multicolored | 2.10 | 2.10 |
| 738 | CD349 | 5r multicolored | 3.25 | 3.25 |
| | | Nos. 734-738 (5) | 8.80 | 8.80 |

## Flora and Fauna A118

### 1993, Mar. 1 — Litho. — Perf. 13½

| | | | | |
|---|---|---|---|---|
| 739 | A118 | 10c multicolored | .20 | .20 |
| 740 | A118 | 25c multicolored | .20 | .20 |
| 741 | A118 | 50c multicolored | .20 | .20 |
| 742 | A118 | 1r multicolored | .35 | .35 |
| 743 | A118 | 1.50r multicolored | .55 | .55 |
| 744 | A118 | 2r multicolored | .80 | .80 |
| 745 | A118 | 3r multicolored | .55 | .55 |
| 746 | A118 | 3.50r multicolored | 1.10 | 1.10 |
| a. | A118 | 3.50r multicolored | 1.40 | 1.40 |
| 747 | A118 | 4r multicolored | — | — |
| 748 | A118 | 5r multicolored | 1.90 | 1.90 |
| 749 | A118 | 10r multicolored | 3.75 | 3.75 |
| 750 | A118 | 15r multicolored | 5.75 | 5.75 |
| 751 | A118 | 25r multicolored | 9.50 | 9.50 |
| 752 | A118 | 50r multicolored | 18.00 | 18.00 |
| | | Nos. 739-752 (14) | 45.20 | 45.20 |

Perf. 14x13½

Designs: 10c, Brush warbler. 25c, Bronze gecko. 50c, Seychelles tree frog. 1r, Seychelles splendid palm, vert. 1.50r, Seychelles skink, vert. 2r, Giant tenebrionid beetle. 3r, Seychelles sunbird. 3.50r, Seychelles killifish. 4r, Magpie robin. 5r, Seychelles vanilla, vert. 10r, Tiger chameleon. 15r, Coco-de-mer, vert. 25r, Paradise flycatcher, vert. 50r, Giant tortoise.

#742, 748-749, 751-752 exist inscribed "1994;" #739-741, 750 "1996;" #1998;" #739, 741-743, 745-46 "2000." #745, No. 746a is dated 2000.

## First Visit to Seychelles by Archbishop of Canterbury — A119

### 1993, June 8 — Perf. 13½

| | | | | |
|---|---|---|---|---|
| 753 | A119 | 3r multicolored | 2.25 | 1.10 |
| 754 | A119 | 10r multicolored | 7.50 | 3.75 |

Archbishop and: 3r, Anglican Cathedral, Victoria. 10r, Air France, Air Seychelles.

## 4th Indian Ocean Island Games — A120

### 1993, Aug. 21 — Perf. 14½

| | | | | |
|---|---|---|---|---|
| 755 | A120 | 1.50r Running | .85 | .85 |
| 756 | A120 | 1.50r Soccer | .85 | .85 |
| 757 | A120 | 2r Cycling | 1.90 | 1.90 |
| 758 | A120 | 3.50r Sailing | 5.25 | 5.25 |
| | | Nos. 755-758 (4) | 9.50 | 9.50 |

## Telecommunications, Cent. — A121

Designs: 10c, Cable ship Scotia, Victoria, 1893. 3r, Eastern Telegraph Company's Office, Victoria, 1904. 4r, HF Transmitting Station, operational 1971. 10r, New Telecoms House, Victoria, 1993.

### 1993, Nov. 12 — Perf. 13

| | | | | |
|---|---|---|---|---|
| 759 | A121 | 1r multicolored | .75 | .75 |
| 760 | A121 | 3r multicolored | 2.25 | 2.25 |
| 761 | A121 | 4r multicolored | 3.25 | 3.25 |
| 762 | A121 | 10r multicolored | 8.00 | 8.00 |
| | | Nos. 759-762 (4) | 14.25 | 14.25 |

## Zil Elwannyen Sesel Nos. 59, 61, 63, 64 Surcharged

### 1994, Feb. 18 — Perf. 14x14½

| | | | | |
|---|---|---|---|---|
| 763 | A9 | 1r on 2.10r #59 | .50 | .50 |
| 764 | A9 | 1.50r on 2.10r #61 | .75 | .75 |
| 765 | A9 | 3.50r on 7r #63 | 1.75 | 1.75 |
| 766 | A9 | 5r on 7r #64 | 7.75 | 7.75 |
| | | Nos. 763-766 (4) | 4.75 | 4.75 |

Hong Kong '94. Size and location of surcharge varies.

**Birds — A127**

**1996, Nov. 11    Wmk. 373    Litho.**

| | | | |
|---|---|---|---|
| 786 | 3r multicolored | 1.25 | 1.25 |
| 787 | 3r multicolored | 1.25 | 1.25 |
| a. | A127 Pair, #786-787 | 2.50 | 2.50 |
| 788 | 3r multicolored | 1.25 | 1.25 |
| 789 | 3r multicolored | 1.25 | 1.25 |
| a. | A127 Pair, #788-789 | 2.50 | 2.50 |
| 790 | 3r multicolored | 1.25 | 1.25 |
| 791 | 3r multicolored | 1.25 | 1.25 |
| a. | A127 Pair, #790-791 | 2.50 | 2.50 |
| 792 | 3r multicolored | 1.25 | 1.25 |
| 793 | 3r multicolored | 1.25 | 1.25 |
| a. | A127 Pair, #792-793 | 2.50 | 2.50 |
| | Nos. 786-793 (8) | 10.00 | 10.00 |

#786, Aldabra souimanga sunbird. #787, Seychelles sunbird. #788, Aldabra blue pigeon. #789, Seychelles blue pigeon. #790, Aldabra red headed fody. #791, Seychelles fody. #792, Aldabra white-eye. #793, Seychelles white-eye.

**Zil Elwannyen Sesel No. 58 Surcharged**

**1997, Feb. 12    Perf. 14x14½**

| | | | |
|---|---|---|---|
| 794 | A9 1.50r on 2r | 1.60 | 1.60 |

Hong Kong '97.

**Queen Elizabeth II and Prince Philip, 50th Wedding Anniv. — A128**

**1997, Nov. 20    Wmk. 373    Litho.**

| | | | |
|---|---|---|---|
| 795 | 1r multicolored | .75 | .75 |
| 796 | 1r multicolored | .75 | .75 |
| a. | A128 Pair, #795-796 | 1.50 | 1.50 |
| 797 | 1.50r multicolored | 11.50 | 11.50 |
| 798 | 1.50r multicolored | 1.00 | 1.00 |
| a. | A128 Pair, #797-798 | 2.00 | 2.00 |
| 799 | 3r multicolored | 2.10 | 2.10 |
| 800 | 3r multicolored | 2.10 | 2.10 |
| a. | A128 Pair, #799-800 | 4.25 | 4.25 |
| | Nos. 795-800 (6) | 7.70 | 7.70 |

**Souvenir Sheet**

| | | | |
|---|---|---|---|
| 801 | A128 10r multicolored | 6.25 | 6.25 |

Designs: a, In red dress. b, Wearing white blouse, printed vest. c, In blue dress, flowers. d, Wearing white dress.

Designs: No. 795, Queen in red & white dress. No. 796, Prince driving four-in-hand team. No. 797, Prince in business suit. No. 798, Queen, horse. No. 799, Prince Charles, Princess Anne. No. 800, Prince, Queen. 10r, Queen and Prince in open carriage, horiz.

**Diana, Princess of Wales (1961-97) Common Design Type**

**Butterflies A122**

**1994, Aug. 16    Wmk. 384    Perf. 14**

| | | | |
|---|---|---|---|
| 767 | A122 1.50r Eurema floricola | 1.25 | 1.25 |
| 768 | A122 3r Coeliades forestan | 2.75 | 2.75 |
| 769 | A122 3.50r Borbo borbonica | 3.00 | 3.00 |
| 770 | A122 10r Zizula hylax | 9.00 | 9.00 |
| | Nos. 767-770 (4) | 16.00 | 16.00 |

**A124**

**1995, Sept. 26    Wmk. 373**

| | | | |
|---|---|---|---|
| 771 | A123 Age 9 | .85 | .85 |
| 772 | A123 1.50r Running | 1.60 | 1.60 |
| 773 | A123 3.50r Wedding day | 1.75 | 1.75 |
| 774 | A123 1936 Portrait | | |
| | 1975 Photograph | 5.00 | 5.00 |
| a. | A123 Strip of 4, #771-774 | 9.20 | 9.20 |
| | Nos. 771-774 (4) | 7.25 | 7.25 |

Queen Mother, 95th birthday.

**Black Paradise Flycatcher**

**1996, July 12    Wmk. 384    Litho.**

| | | | |
|---|---|---|---|
| 775 | A124 1r Female on branch | .90 | .90 |
| 776 | A124 1r Male in flight | .90 | .90 |
| 777 | A124 1r Male on branch | .90 | .90 |
| 778 | A124 1r Female, young | .90 | .90 |
| a. | A124 Strip of 4, #775-778 | 4.00 | 4.00 |

**Souvenir Sheet**

| | | | |
|---|---|---|---|
| 779 | A124 10r Female, male birds | 7.25 | 7.25 |

World Wildlife Fund.
Stamps in No. 778a may be out of Scott number sequence.

**A126**

**1996, July 15    Wmk. 373    Litho.    Perf. 14**

| | | | |
|---|---|---|---|
| 780 | A125 50c Swimming | .20 | .20 |
| 781 | A125 1.50r Running | .90 | .90 |
| 782 | A125 3r Sailing | 1.90 | 1.90 |
| 783 | A125 5r Boxing | 3.00 | 3.00 |
| | Nos. 780-783 (4) | 6.00 | 6.00 |

Modern Olympic Games, cent.

**1996, Aug. 19    Wmk. 373    Litho.    Perf. 14**

| | | | |
|---|---|---|---|
| 784 | A126 3r shown | 1.75 | 1.75 |
| 785 | A126 10r Portrait up close | 5.50 | 5.50 |

Archbishop Makarios of Cyprus, Exiled in Seychelles, 40th anniv.

national sales being donated to designated local charity.

**Intl. Year of the Ocean — A129**

**1998    Litho.    Perf. 14**

| | | | |
|---|---|---|---|
| 803 | A129 3r Strip of 6, #a.-f. | 7.25 | 7.25 |
| | Complete booklet, #803 | 15.00 | |

Designs: a, Blue and yellow fish. b, School of gold-colored fish. c, Lionfish. d, Various small fish. e, Anemones. f, Turtle.

**Australia '99, World Stamp Expo A130**

**1999    Litho.    Wmk. 384    Perf. 14**

| | | | |
|---|---|---|---|
| 804 | A130 1.50r multicolored | .60 | .60 |
| 805 | A130 3r multicolored | 1.25 | 1.25 |
| 806 | A130 3.50r multicolored | 1.40 | 1.40 |
| 807 | A130 10r multicolored | 4.00 | 4.00 |
| | Nos. 804-807 (4) | 7.25 | 7.25 |

**Souvenir Sheet**

| | | | |
|---|---|---|---|
| 808 | A130 20r multicolored | 8.75 | 8.75 |

18th Cent. ships: 1.50r, Vierge du Cap, 1721. 3r, Elizabeth, 1741. 3.50r, Curieuse, 1768. 10r, Le Fleche, 1801. Souvenir sheet, 20r, The Cheval Marin, 1774, vert.

Nos. 804-807 each issued with se-tenant label.

**Wedding of Prince Edward and Sophie Rhys-Jones A131**

**1999, Sept. 1    Wmk. 373    Litho.    Perf. 13½**

| | | | |
|---|---|---|---|
| 809 | A131 3r shown | 1.75 | 1.75 |
| 810 | A131 15r In carriage | 6.00 | 6.00 |

**Christmas and Millennium A132**

1r, Cathedral of the Immaculate Conception. 1.50r, Fairy tern. 2.50r, Dolphin. 10r, Comet.

**1999, Dec. 14    Wmk. 373    Litho.    Perf. 14x14½**

| | | | |
|---|---|---|---|
| 811 | A132 1r multi | .40 | .40 |
| 812 | A132 1.50r multi | .65 | .65 |
| 813 | A132 2.50r multi | 1.10 | 1.10 |
| 814 | A132 10r multi | 4.25 | 4.25 |
| | Nos. 811-814 (4) | 6.40 | 6.40 |

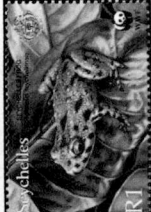

**Queen Mother, 100th Birthday — A133**

Designs: 3r, As child. 5r, As young woman. 7r, With King George VI. 10r, As old woman.

**2000, Aug. 4    Wmk. 373    Litho.    Perf. 14½**

| | | | |
|---|---|---|---|
| 815 | A133 3r multi | 1.10 | 1.10 |
| 816 | A133 5r multi | 1.75 | 1.75 |
| 817 | A133 7r multi | 2.50 | 2.50 |
| 818 | A133 10r multi | 3.50 | 3.50 |
| | Nos. 815-818 (4) | 8.85 | 8.85 |

**Anniversaries — A134**

Designs: 1r, Arrival of the Jacobin deportees, 200th anniv. 1.50r, Victoria as capital of Seychelles, 160th anniv. 3r, Arrival of Father Leon Des Avanchers, 150th anniv. 3.50r, Victoria Fountain, cent., vert. 5r, Botanical Gardens, cent. 10r, Independence, 25th anniv., vert.

**2001, July 25    Wmk. 373    Litho.    Perf. 14**

| | | | |
|---|---|---|---|
| 819-824 | A134 | 6.00 | 6.00 |

Nos. 819 and 824 lack Age of Victoria emblem.

**Ducks A135**

Designs: No. 825, 3r, Garganey. No. 826, 3r, Northern shoveler. No. 827, 3r, Ruddy shelduck. No. 828, 3r, White faced whistling duck.

**2001, Oct. 4    Wmk. 384    Litho.**

| | | | |
|---|---|---|---|
| 825-828 | A135 | Set of 4 | 5.25 5.25 |

**Birdlife International World Bird Festival — A136**

Seychelles Scops owl: a, In flight. b, In tree. c, Standing on branch, vert. d, Standing on tip of broken branch, vert. e, Standing on branch.

**2001, Oct. 4    Perf. 14½x14¼, 14½x14¼**

| | | | |
|---|---|---|---|
| 829 | A136 3r Sheet of 5, #a-e | 5.25 | 5.25 |

**Queen Mother Elizabeth (1900-2002) Common Design Type Souvenir Sheet**

No. 830: a, 5r, As young woman, without hat. b, 10r, As old woman, wearing hat.

**2002, Aug. 5    Perf. 14½x14¼    Wmk. 373    Litho.    Without Purple Frames**

| | | | |
|---|---|---|---|
| 830 | Sheet of 2, #a- | 5.50 | 5.50 |
| | CD361 | b | 5.50 5.50 |

**Worldwide Fund for Nature (WWF) A137**

Frogs: No. 831, 1r, Seychelles frog. No. 832, 1r, Palm frog. No. 833, 1r, Thomasset's frog. No. 834, 1r, Gardiner's frog. No. 20r, Seychelles tree frog.

## SEYCHELLES

**2003, Feb. 3**   Wmk. 373   Litho.   Perf. 14
831-834 A137   Set of 4   2.00 2.00
835 A137   20r multi   Souvenir Sheet   7.25 7.25

Fish — A138

**2003, Nov. 3**   Wmk. 373   Litho.   Perf. 14
836 A138 10c multi .20 .20
837 A138 50c multi .20 .20
838 A138 50c multi .40 .40
839 A138 1r multi .60 .60
840 A138 1.50r multi 1.10 1.10
841 A138 3r multi 1.90 1.90
842 A138 5r multi 19.00 19.00
Nos. 836-842 (7) 23.40 23.40

Designs: 10c, Seychelles blenny. 50c, Seychelles anemonefish. 1r, Indian butterflyfish. 1.50r, Goldbar wrasse. 3r, Seychelles squirrelfish. 5r, Greenthroat parrotfish. 50r, Whale shark.

SITCC
La Commission de l'Océan Indien a 20 ans

**2004, Feb. 16**   Wmk. 373   Litho.   Perf. 13½
843 A139 15r multi   6.00 6.00

Indian Ocean Commission, 20th Anniv. — A139

Nos. 743, 745, 748-752 Surcharged

**2004, July 1**   Wmk. 373
Methods and Perfs As Before
844 A118 1r on 1.50r #743 .40 .40
845 A118 2r on 3r #745 .75 .75
846 A118 3.50r on 5r #748 .40 .40
847 A118 3.50r on 5r #749 1.40 1.40
848 A118 3.50r on 5r #750 1.40 1.40
849 A118 4r on 25r #751 1.50 1.50
850 A118 4r on 50r #752 1.50 1.50
Nos. 844-850 (7) 8.35 8.35

Pope John Paul II (1920-2005) — A140

**2005, Aug. 18**   Wmk. 373   Litho.   Perf. 14
851 A140 5r multi   1.90 1.90

Fish Type of 2003

**2005, Oct. 3**   Wmk. 373   Perf. 14
852 A138 25c multi .20 .20
853 A138 50c multi .75 .75
854 A138 2r multi 1.40 1.40
855 A138 4r multi 1.50 1.50
856 A138 10r multi 3.75 3.75

Designs: 25c, African pygmy angelfish. 2r, Picasso triggerfish. 3.50r, Palette surgeonfish. 4r, Longfin batfish. 10r, Masked rabbitfish. 15r, Lyretail grouper. 25r, Emperor snapper.

---

857 A138 15r multi 5.50 5.50
858 A138 25r multi 9.25 9.25
Nos. 852-858 (7) 22.35 22.35

## POSTAGE DUE STAMPS

Catalogue values for unused stamps in this section are for Never Hinged items.

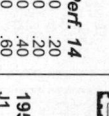
D1

**1951, Mar. 1**   Wmk. 4   Perf. 11½
Engr.: Denomination Typo. in Carmine
J1 D1 2c carmine 1.90 4.25
J2 D1 3c blue green 1.90 4.25
J3 D1 6c ocher 1.25 4.00
J4 D1 9c brown orange 1.60 6.50
J5 D1 15c purple 1.90 8.00
J6 D1 18c deep blue 2.40 9.00
J7 D1 30c black brown 3.00 10.50
J8 D1 30c red brown 16.45 58.00
Nos. J1-J8 (8)

**1964-65**   Engr.; Denomination Typo.
Wmk. 314
J9 D1 2c carmine .80 8.00
J10 D1 3c green & red 2.50 24.00
Issue dates: July 7, 1964, Sept. 14, 1965.

**1980**   Dated "1980"   Litho.   Perf. 14
J11 D1 5c lilac rose & red .20 1.00
J12 D1 10c dk green & red .20 1.00
J13 D1 15c bister & red .20 1.00
J14 D1 20c brown & red .20 1.00
J15 D1 25c violet & red 1.00 1.00
J16 D1 75c dk red brown & red .25 1.00
J17 D1 80c dk blue & red .30 1.10
J18 D1 1r claret & red 1.85 8.20
Nos. J11-J18 (8)

## ZIL ELWANNYEN SESEL

LOCATION — South of Seychelles

The islands of Aldabra, Farquhar and Des Roches. Formerly part of the British Indian Ocean Territory.

Catalogue values for unused stamps in this country are for Never Hinged items.

Type of Seychelles, 1977-78
**1980-81**   Perf. 14, 14¼x14 (40c, 1r, 1.25r, 1.50r)
Size: 30x26mm (40c, 1r, 1.25r, 1.50r)   Litho.   Wmk. 373
1 A44 5c Reef fish .20 .20
2 A44 10c Hawksbill turtle .20 .20
3 A44 10c Coco-de-mer .20 .25
4 A44 20c Wild vanilla .20 .25
5 A44 25c Butterfly 1.00 .25
6 A44 40c Coral reef .25 .25
7 A44 50c Giant tortoise .35 .35
8 A44 75c Crayfish .45 .25
9 A44 1r Madagascar fody .25 .25
10 A44 1.10r Green gecko .50 .50
11 A44 1.25r Fairy tern .65 .60
12 A44 1.50r Flying fox .60 .60

Size: 27x35mm
13 A44 5r Octopus, vert. .85 1.10
14 A44   a. Perf. 13 (8½) 1.25
14 A44 10r Giant tiger cowrie, vert. 1.00 1.90
15 A44 15r Pitcher plant, vert. 2.00 2.00
  a. Perf. 13 (8½)
16 A44 20r Nat'l arms, vert. 11.20 14.35
  a. Perf. 13 (8½)
Nos. 1-16 (16)
Nos. 1-12 exist with 1981 imprint.

**1980, Oct. 24**

Marine Life — A2
20 A2 50c Yellowfin Tuna .30 .30
21 A2 1.50r Blue marlin .75 .75
22 A2 5r Sperm whale 1.40 1.40
Nos. 20-22 (3)

**1981, June 23**   Wmk. 380   Perf. 14
23 A3 40c Royal Escape .20 .20
Souvenir Sheet   Perf. 12½x12
24 A3 7.50r like #24 2.00 2.00

Royal Wedding Types of Seychelles
**1981, Dec. 11**   Wmk. 373   Perf. 14
30 A3 1.40r Wright's skink .20 .20
31 A3 2.25r Tree frog .25 .25
32 A3 5r Robber crab .45 .45
Nos. 30-32 (3) .90 .90

Wildlife A3

TREE FROG

**1982, Mar. 11**   Wmk. 373   Perf. 14x14½
33 A4 1.75r Cinq Juin .50 .40
34 A4 2.10r Junon .60 .60
35 A4 5r Diamond M. Dragon 1.80 1.50
Nos. 33-35 (3)
Workboats — A4

**1982, July 22**   Wmk. 373   Perf. 14
36 A5 40c Paulette .35 .25
37 A5 1.75r Janette .50 .50
38 A5 2.75r Lady Esme .65 .70
39 A5 3.50r Cinq Juin 2.20 2.30
Nos. 36-39 (4)
Mailboats A5

Beto Lopo Lokal Local Mail Vessels

**1983, July 13**   Wmk. 373   Perf. 14x14½
50 A9 5c Barred ground dove .20 .20
51 A9 10c Barred ground dove .20 .20
52 A9 15c Aldabra nightjar .20 .20
53 A9 20c Malagasy grass warbler .20 .20
54 A9 25c Aldabra white-eye .20 .20
55 A9 40c Aldabra fody .20 .20
56 A9 50c Aldabra rail .25 .25
57 A9 75c Aldabra bulbul .25 .25
58 A9 2r Dimorphic little egret .85 .85
59 A9 2.10r Aldabra sunbird .90 .95
60 A9 2.50r Aldabra turtle dove 1.10 1.10
61 A9 2.75r Aldabra sacred ibis 1.25 1.40
62 A9 3.50r Aldabra coucal 1.50 1.60
63 A9 15r Aldabra kestrel 3.25 3.50
64 A9 20r Aldabra blue pigeon 7.00 7.25
65 A9 20r Greater flamingo 8.75 9.00
Nos. 50-65 (16) 26.25 27.30
Birds — A9

BARRED GROUND DOVE

Nos. 62-65 vert. See Nos. 96-100. For surcharges see Seychelles Nos. 763-766.

---

ZIL ELWAGNE SESEL SEYCHELLES
Traveling Post Office A1

**1980, Oct. 24**   Perf. 14
17 A1 1.50r Cinq Juin .20 .20
18 A1 2.10r Canceling letters .35 .35
19 A1 5r Map .75 .75
Nos. 17-19 (3)

The 5r showing Agalega as part of the Seychelles was not issued.

Aldabra, World Heritage Site — A6

**1982, Nov. 19**   Wmk. 373   Perf. 14x14½
40 A6 40c Birds flying over island .20 .20
41 A6 2.75r Map .35 .35
42 A6 7r Giant tortoises .80 .80
Nos. 40-42 (3) 1.35 1.35

BLACK TERRAPIN
ZIL ELWAGNE SESEL SEYCHELLES
Wildlife A7

**1983, Feb. 25**   Wmk. 373   Perf. 14x14½
43 A7 1.75r Red land crab .30 .30
44 A7 2.75r Black terrapin .50 .50
45 A7 7r Madagascar green gecko 2.05 2.05
Nos. 43-45 (3) 1.25 1.25

World Tourism Day A10

**1983, Apr. 27**   Perf. 14½
46 A8 40c Poivre Island, Ile du Sud .20 .20
47 A8 1.50r Ile des Roches .45 .45
48 A8 2.75r Astove Island 1.25 1.25
49 A8 7r Coetivy Island 3.50 3.50
  a. Souvenir sheet of 4, #46-49 2.10 2.10
Nos. 46-49 (4)
Maps — A8

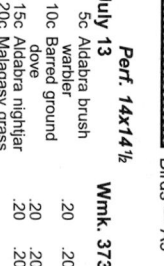

**1983, Sept. 27** — Perf. 14

| | | | | | |
|---|---|---|---|---|---|
| 66 | A10 | 50c | Windsurfing | .20 | .20 |
| 67 | A10 | 2r | Hotel | .25 | .25 |
| 68 | A10 | 3r | Beach | .40 | .40 |
| 69 | A10 | 10r | Sunset | 1.25 | 2.10 |

Nos. 66-69 (4)

**1983** — Wmk. 380 — Perf. 14

| | | | | | |
|---|---|---|---|---|---|
| 70 | A61a | 30c on 40c multi | | .30 | .30 |
| 71 | A61b | 30c on 40c multi | | .30 | .30 |
| 72 | A61a | 2r on 5r multi | | 1.25 | 1.25 |
| 73 | A61b | 2r on 5r multi | | 1.25 | 1.25 |
| 74 | A61a | 3r on 10r multi | | 1.75 | 1.75 |
| 75 | A61b | 3r on 10r multi | | 1.75 | 1.75 |

Nos. 70-75 (6) 6.60 6.60

Each denomination issued in sheets of 7 (6 type A61a, 1 type A61b).

Aldabra Post Office, Reopening — A11

**1984, Mar. 30** — Wmk. 373 — Perf. 14

| | | | | | |
|---|---|---|---|---|---|
| 76 | A11 | 50c | Map, postmark | .20 | .20 |
| 77 | A11 | 2.75r | Aldabra rail | .85 | .85 |
| 78 | A11 | 5r | Giant tortoise | 2.75 | 2.75 |
| 79 | A11 | 10r | Red-footed booby | 4.55 | 4.55 |

Nos. 76-79 (4)

Game Fishing A12

**1984, May 31**

| | | | | | |
|---|---|---|---|---|---|
| 80 | A12 | 50c | Fishing boat | .20 | .20 |
| 81 | A12 | 2r | Hooked fish, vert. | .50 | .50 |
| 82 | A12 | 3r | Weighing catch, | .70 | .00 |
| 83 | A12 | 10r | Fishing boat, stern view | 2.50 | 2.50 |
| | | | | 3.90 | 3.20 |

Nos. 80-83 (4)

Crabs A13

**1984, Aug. 24** — Perf. 14½

| | | | | | |
|---|---|---|---|---|---|
| 84 | A13 | 50c | Giant hermit crab | .20 | .20 |
| 85 | A13 | 2r | Fiddler crabs | .60 | .60 |
| 86 | A13 | 3r | Ghost crab | .80 | .80 |
| 87 | A13 | 10r | Spotted pebble crab | 3.00 | 3.00 |
| | | | | 4.60 | 4.60 |

Nos. 84-87 (4)

Constellations A14

**1984, Oct. 16**

| | | | | | |
|---|---|---|---|---|---|
| 88 | A14 | 50c | Orion | .20 | .20 |
| 89 | A14 | 2r | Cygnus | .55 | .55 |
| 90 | A14 | 3r | Virgo | .75 | .75 |
| 91 | A14 | 10r | Scorpio | 2.50 | 2.50 |
| | | | | 3.20 | |

Nos. 88-91 (4)

Mushrooms A15

**1985, Jan. 31** — Wmk. 373 — Litho. — Perf. 14

| | | | | | |
|---|---|---|---|---|---|
| 92 | A15 | 50c | Lenzites elegans | .20 | .20 |
| 93 | A15 | 2r | Xylaria telfairei | 1.25 | 1.75 |
| 94 | A15 | 3r | Lentinus sajor-caju | 1.75 | 1.75 |
| 95 | A15 | 10r | Hexagonia tenuis | 6.00 | 6.00 |
| | | | | 9.20 | 9.20 |

Nos. 92-95 (4)


Bird Type of 1983
Inscribed "Zil Elwannyen Sesel"
Wmk. 373, 384 (5c)
Perf. 14x14½

**1985-88** — Perf. 14x14½

| | | | | | |
|---|---|---|---|---|---|
| 96 | A9 | 5c | Like #50 ('08) | .20 | .20 |
| 97 | A9 | 10c | Like #51 | .20 | .20 |
| 98 | A9 | 25c | Like #54 | .20 | .20 |
| | a. | Wmk. 384 (88) | | | |
| 99 | A9 | 50c | Like #56 ('87) | .20 | .20 |
| | a. | Wmk. 384 (88) | | .55 | .55 |
| 100 | A9 | 2r | Like #58 | .55 | .55 |
| | a. | Wmk. 384 (88) | | 1.35 | 1.35 |

Nos. 96-100 (5)

No. 97 exists with 1987 imprint, No. 100a with 1990 imprint.

Common Design Types pictured following the introduction.

Queen Mother 85th Birthday
Common Design Type
Perf. 14½x14

**1985, June 1** — Wmk. 384

| | | | | | |
|---|---|---|---|---|---|
| 101 | CD336 | 1r | Coronation portrait | .25 | .25 |
| 102 | CD336 | 2r | With Princess Anne | .55 | .55 |
| 103 | CD336 | 3r | Wearing tiara | .80 | .80 |
| 104 | CD336 | 5r | Holding Prince Henry | 1.40 | 1.40 |
| | | | | 3.00 | 3.00 |

Nos. 101-104 (4)

Souvenir Sheet

105 CD336 10r In river taxi, Venice 3.00 3.00

World Wildlife Fund A16

**1985, Sept. 27** — Perf. 14

| | | | | | |
|---|---|---|---|---|---|
| 106 | A16 | 50c | Giant tortoise | 6.50 | 2.50 |
| 107 | A16 | 75c | Tortoises crossing stream | 7.25 | .80 |
| 108 | A16 | 1r | Three tortoises | 7.75 | 3.25 |
| 109 | A16 | 2r | Tortoise facing right | 10.50 | 4.30 |
| | | | | 32.00 | 11.05 |

Nos. 106-109 (4)

Souvenir Sheet — Perf. 13x13½

110 A16 10r Two tortoises 22.50 22.50

See Nos. 131-134.

Famous Visitors A17

**1985, Oct. 25** — Wmk. 373 — Perf. 14

| | | | | | |
|---|---|---|---|---|---|
| 111 | A17 | 50c | scar, blk & sil | .25 | .25 |
| 112 | A17 | 2r | multicolored | 1.25 | 1.25 |
| 113 | A17 | 10r | multicolored | 5.75 | 5.75 |
| | | | | 7.25 | 7.25 |

Nos. 111-113 (3)

Visitors and their ships: 50c, Phoenician trader, 600 B.C. 2r, Sir Hugh Scott, HMS Sealark, 1908. 10r, Vasco de Gama, Sao Gabriel, 1502.

Queen Elizabeth II, 60th Birthday
Common Design Type

Designs: 75c, As princess. 1r, With Prince Philip. 1.50r, Wearing blue cape. 3.75r, Portrait. 5r, Wearing red hat.

**1986, Apr. 21** — Perf. 14½x14

| | | | | | |
|---|---|---|---|---|---|
| 114 | CD337 | 75c | scar, blk & sil | .20 | .20 |
| 115 | CD337 | 1r | blue & multi | .25 | .25 |
| 116 | CD337 | 1.50r | grn & multi | .30 | .30 |
| 117 | CD337 | 3.75r | vio & multi | .55 | .55 |
| 118 | CD337 | 5r | rose vio & multi | .85 | .85 |
| | | | | 2.10 | 2.10 |

Nos. 114-118 (5)

For overprints see Nos. 135-139.

Royal Wedding
Common Design Type


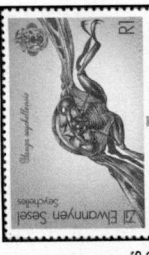

**1986, July 23**

| | | | | | |
|---|---|---|---|---|---|
| 119 | CD338 | 3r | multicolored | .70 | .70 |
| 120 | CD338 | 7r | multicolored | 1.60 | 1.60 |

Perf. 14

Coral — A18   Flowers — A19

Continuous design: a, Acropora palifera, Tubastraea coccinea. b, Echinopora lamellosa, Favia pallida. c, Sarcophyton sp, Porites lutea. d, Goniopora sp, Goniastrea retiformis. e, Tubipora musica, Fungia fungites.

**1986, Sept. 17**

121 A18 2r Strip of 5, #a.-e. 12.00 12.00

**1986, Nov. 12**

| | | | | | |
|---|---|---|---|---|---|
| 122 | A19 | 50c | Hibiscus tiliaceus | .25 | .25 |
| 123 | A19 | 2r | Crinum angustum | 1.25 | 1.25 |
| 124 | A19 | 3r | Phalus tetragonus | 2.00 | 2.00 |
| 125 | A19 | 10r | Rothmannia annae | 6.50 | 6.50 |
| | | | | 10.00 | 10.00 |

Nos. 122-125 (4)

Fish — A20   Trees — A21

Continuous design: a, Chaetodon unimaculatus. b, Cheilinus fleurieu. c, Platax orbicularis. d, abudefduf annulatus. e, Chaetodon lineolatus.

**1987, Mar. 26**

126 A20 2r Strip of #126a-126e 8.00 8.00

Perf. 14½

**1987, Aug. 26**

| | | | | | |
|---|---|---|---|---|---|
| 127 | A21 | 1r | Coconut | .75 | .75 |
| 128 | A21 | 2r | Mangrove | 1.75 | 1.75 |
| 129 | A21 | 3r | Pandanus palm | 2.75 | 2.75 |
| 130 | A21 | 5r | Indian almond | 4.50 | 4.50 |
| | | | | 9.75 | 9.75 |

Nos. 127-130 (4)

Nos. 106-110 Redrawn
World Wildlife Fund Emblem without Circle

**1987, Sept. 9** — Wmk. 384 — Perf. 14

| | | | | | |
|---|---|---|---|---|---|
| 131 | A16 | 50c | multicolored | 7.00 | 4.00 |
| 132 | A16 | 75c | multicolored | 9.00 | 5.00 |
| 133 | A16 | 1r | multicolored | 11.00 | 6.00 |
| 134 | A16 | 2r | multicolored | 41.00 | 23.00 |

Nos. 131-134 (4)

Nos. 114-118 Ovptd. in Silver
"40TH WEDDING ANNIVERSARY"

**1987, Dec. 9** — Perf. 14½x14

| | | | | | |
|---|---|---|---|---|---|
| 135 | CD337 | 75c | scar, blk & multi | .25 | .25 |
| 136 | CD337 | 1r | blue & multi | .30 | .30 |
| 137 | CD337 | 1.50r | grn & multi | .50 | .50 |
| 138 | CD337 | 3.75r | vio & multi | 1.25 | 1.25 |
| 139 | CD337 | 5r | rose vio & multi | 1.75 | 1.75 |
| | | | | 4.00 | 4.00 |

Nos. 135-139 (5)

Mai Valley Tropical Forest — A22

Continuous design: b, Trunk of palm tree at right. c, Bamboo.

**1987, Dec. 16** — Perf. 14

140 A22 3r Strip of 3, #a.-c. 9.00 9.00


Insects A23

**1988, July 28** — Wmk. 373

| | | | | | |
|---|---|---|---|---|---|
| 141 | A23 | 1r | Yanga seychellensis | 1.75 | 1.75 |
| 142 | A23 | 2r | Belenois aldabraensis | 3.00 | 3.00 |
| 143 | A23 | 3r | Polyspilota seychelliana | 3.50 | 3.50 |
| 144 | A23 | 5r | Polposipus herculeanus | 4.25 | 4.25 |
| | | | | 12.50 | 12.50 |

Nos. 141-144 (4)

Souvenir Sheet

1988 SEOUL OLYMPICS 1988   R10

1988 Summer Olympics, Seoul — A24

**1988, Aug. 31** — Wmk. 384

145 A24 10r multicolored 5.25 5.25

Lloyds' of London, 300th Anniv.
Common Design Type

Designs: 1r, Lloyd's building, 1988. 2r, Cable ship Retriever, horiz. 3r, Chantel, horiz. 5r, Torrey Canyon aground off Cornwall, 1967.

**1988, Oct. 28** — Wmk. 373

| | | | | | |
|---|---|---|---|---|---|
| 146 | CD341 | 1r | multicolored | 1.00 | 1.00 |
| 147 | CD341 | 2r | multicolored | 1.75 | 1.75 |
| 148 | CD341 | 3r | multicolored | 2.75 | 2.75 |
| 149 | CD341 | 5r | multicolored | 4.50 | 4.50 |
| | | | | 10.00 | 10.00 |

Nos. 146-149 (4)

Christmas — A25

Perf. 13½x14, 14x13½ — Wmk. 384

**1988, Nov. 1R**

| | | | | | |
|---|---|---|---|---|---|
| 150 | A25 | 1r | Santa, toys in canoe | .40 | .40 |
| 151 | A25 | 2r | Church, vert. | .75 | .75 |
| 152 | A25 | 3r | Santa riding bird, vert. | 1.10 | 1.10 |
| 153 | A25 | 5r | Sleigh over island | 1.75 | 1.75 |
| | | | | 4.00 | 4.00 |

Nos. 150-153 (4)

Moon Landing, 20th Anniv.
Common Design Type

Apollo 18: 1r, Firing room, Launch Control Center. 2r, Astronauts Slayton, Stafford, Brand and cosmonauts Leonov and Kubasov. 3r, Mission emblem. 5r, Apollo and Soyuz docking in space. 10r, Apollo 11 lifted aboard USS Hornet.

**1989, July 20** — Perf. 14x13½, 14 (#155-156)
Size of Nos. 155-156: 29x29mm

| | | | | | |
|---|---|---|---|---|---|
| 154 | CD342 | 1r | multicolored | 1.00 | 1.00 |
| 155 | CD342 | 2r | multicolored | 1.75 | 1.75 |
| 156 | CD342 | 3r | multicolored | 2.75 | 2.75 |
| 157 | CD342 | 5r | multicolored | 4.25 | 4.25 |
| | | | | 9.75 | 9.75 |

Nos. 154-157 (4)

Souvenir Sheet

158 CD342 10r multicolored 12.50 12.50

Poisonous Plants — A26

1044 SEYCHELLES — Zil Elwannyen Sesel — SHANGHAI

**1989, Oct. 9** *Perf. 14*
**159** A26 1r Dumb cane 1.25 1.25
**160** A26 2r Star of Bethlehem 2.75 2.75
**161** A26 3r Indian licorice 4.00 4.00
**162** A26 5r Black nightshade 6.25 6.25
*Nos. 159-162 (4)* 14.25 14.25

See Nos. 173-176.

Creole Cooking — A27

**1989, Dec. 18**
**163** A27 1r Tec-tec broth 1.25 1.25
**164** A27 2r Pilaf a la Seychelloise 2.50 2.50
**165** A27 3r Mullet grilled in banana leaves 3.50 3.50
**166** A27 5r Daube 5.75 5.75
*a.* Souvenir sheet of 4, #163-166 13.00 13.00
*Nos. 163-166 (4)* 13.00 13.00

No. 166a has continuous design.

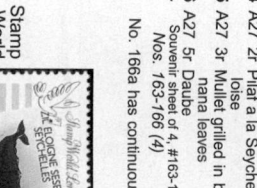

Stamp World London '90 A28

Designs: 1r, #22. 2r, #13. 3r, #61. 5r, #32.

**Wmk. 373**
**1990, May 3 Litho.** *Perf. 12½*
**167** A28 1r multicolored 1.25 1.25
**168** A28 2r multicolored 2.75 2.75
**169** A28 3r multicolored 3.75 3.75
**170** A28 5r multicolored 6.75 6.75
*a.* Souvenir sheet of 4, #167-170 14.50 14.50
*Nos. 167-170 (4)* 14.50 14.50

**Queen Mother 90th Birthday**
Common Design Types

Designs: 2r, As Duchess of York with infant Elizabeth. 10r, With King George VI viewing bomb-damaged London, 1940.

**1990, Aug. 4 Wmk. 384** *Perf. 14x15*
**171** CD343 2r multi 1.25 1.25
*Perf. 14½*
**172** CD344 10r yel brn & blk 6.75 6.75

Poisonous Plants Type of 1989

**Wmk. 373**
**1990, Nov. 5 Litho.** *Perf. 12½*
**173** A26 1r Ordeal plant 1.25 1.25
**174** A26 2r Thorn apple 2.50 2.50
**175** A26 3r Strychnine tree 3.50 3.50
**176** A26 5r Bwa zasmen 6.25 6.25
*Nos. 173-176 (4)* 13.50 13.50

**Elizabeth & Philip, Birthdays**
Common Design Types

**Wmk. 384**
**1991, June 17 Litho.** *Perf. 14½*
**177** CD345 4r multicolored 2.50 2.50
**178** CD346 4r multicolored 2.50 2.50
*a.* Pair, #177-178 + label 5.50 5.50

Shipwrecks — A29

**Wmk. 373**
**1991, Oct. 28 Litho.** *Perf. 14*
**179** A29 1.50r St. Abbs, 1860 2.00 2.00
**180** A29 3r Norden, 1862 3.50 3.50
**181** A29 3.50r Clan Mackay, 1894 4.00 4.00
**182** A29 10r Glenlyon, 1905 10.00 10.00
*Nos. 179-182 (4)* 19.50 19.50

**Queen Elizabeth II's Accession to the Throne, 40th Anniv.**
Common Design Type

**1992, Feb. 6**
**183** CD349 1r multicolored .70 .70
**184** CD349 1.50r multicolored .95 .95
**185** CD349 3r multicolored 1.75 1.75
**186** CD349 3.50r multicolored 2.10 2.10
**187** CD349 5r multicolored 3.25 3.25
*Nos. 183-187 (5)* 8.75 8.75

Aldabra World Heritage Site, 10th Anniv. — A30

Designs: 1.50r, Lomatopyllum aldabrense. 3r, Dryolimnas cuvieri aldabranus. 3.50r, Birgus latro. 10r, Dicrurus aldabranus.

**1992, Nov. 19** *Perf. 14½*
**188** A30 1.50r multicolored 1.50 1.50
**189** A30 3r multicolored 3.00 3.00
**190** A30 3.50r multicolored 3.50 3.50
**191** A30 10r multicolored 9.50 9.50
*Nos. 188-191 (4)* 17.50 17.50

## SHANGHAI

shaŋ-'hī

LOCATION — A city on the Whangpoo River, Kiangsu Province, China
POP. — 3,489,998

A British settlement was founded there in 1843 and by agreement with China settlements were established by France and the United States. Special areas were set aside for the foreign settlements and a postal system independent of China was organized which was continued until 1898.

16 Cash = 1 Candareen
100 Candareens = 1 Tael
100 Cents = 1 Dollar (1890)

**Watermark**

Wmk. 175 — Kung Pu (Municipal Council)

Dragon — A1

**1865-66 Unwmk. Typo.** *Imperf.*
**Antique Numerals**
**Roman "I" in "16"**
**"Candareens" Plural**
**Wove Paper**

**1** A1 2ca black 325.00 2,250.
*a.* Pelure paper 475.00
**2** A1 4ca yellow 325.00 3,250.
*a.* Pelure paper 650.00 —
*b.* Double impression —
**3** A1 8ca green 325.00 3,750.
*a.* 8ca yellow green 375.00 —
**4** A1 16ca scarlet 750.00 5,000.
*a.* 16ca vermilion 675.00
*b.* Pelure paper 875.00
*Nos. 1-4 (4)* 1,725.

**No. 1: top character of three in left panel as illustrated. No. 5: top character is two horiz. lines.**

**Nos. 2, 3: center character of three in left panel as illustrated. Nos. 6, 7: center character much more complex.**

**Antique Numerals**
**"Candareens" Plural**
**Pelure Paper**

**5** A1 2ca black 325.00
*a.* Wove paper 275.00
**6** A1 4ca yellow 550.00 —
**7** A1 8ca deep green 550.00 —
*Nos. 5-7 (3)* 1,425.

**Antique Numerals**
**"Candareen" Singular**
**Laid Paper**

**8** A1 1ca blue 325.00 4,000.
**9** A1 2ca black 3,250.
**10** A1 4ca yellow 750.00
*Nos. 8-10 (3)* 4,325.

**Wove Paper**

**11** A1 1ca blue 300.00 5,000.
**12** A1 2ca black 625.00 3,250.
**13** A1 4ca yellow 550.00 —
**14** A1 8ca olive green 550.00 —
**15** A1 16cavermilion 300.00 —
*a.* "1" of "16" omitted —
*Nos. 11-15 (5)* 2,325.

**Roman "I," Antique "2"**
**"Candareens" Plural Except on 1ca**
**Wove Paper**

**16** A1 1ca blue 650.00 3,250.
**17** A1 12cafawn 375.00
**18** A1 12cachocolate 375.00
*Nos. 16-18 (3)* 1,400.

**Antique Numerals**
**"Candareens" Plural Except on 1ca**
**Wove Paper**

**19** A1 1ca indigo, pelure paper 275.00 2,250.
*a.* 1ca blue, wove paper 3,750.
**20** A1 3ca orange brown 250.00 2,000.
*a.* Pelure paper 325.00
**21** A1 6ca red brown 150.00
**22** A1 6ca fawn 450.00 —
**23** A1 6ca vermilion 225.00
**24** A1 12caorange brown 125.00
**25** A1 16cavermilion 150.00 775.00
*a.* "1" of "16" omitted 500.00
*Nos. 19-25 (7)* 1,625.

Examples of No. 22 usually have the straight lines cutting through the paper.

**Antique Numerals**
**Roman "I"**
**"Candareens" Plural Except on 1ca**
**Laid Paper**

**26** A1 1ca blue —
**27** A1 2ca black 5,000.
**28** A1 3ca red brown —

Examples of No. 28 usually have the straight lines cutting through the paper.

**Modern Numerals**
**"Candareen" Singular**

**29** A1 1ca slate blue 225.00 2,250.
*a.* 1ca dark blue 160.00 —
**30** A1 3ca red brown 140.00

**"Candareens" Plural Except the 1c**

**31** A1 2ca gray 190.00
**32** A1 3ca red brown 160.00 2,250.

**Coarse Porous Wove Paper**

*33a* A1 1ca blue 160.00
*34a* A1 2ca black 210.00
*b.* Grayish paper 275.00
*35a* A1 3ca red brown 140.00
*36a* A1 4ca yellow 325.00
*37a* A1 6ca olive green 190.00 —
*38a* A1 8ca emerald 225.00 —
*39a* A1 12ca orange vermilion 160.00 —
*40a* A1 16ca red 250.00 875.00
*41a* A1 16ca red brown 190.00 875.00
*Nos. 33a-41a (9)* 1,850.

Chinese characters change on same denomination stamps.

Nos. 1, 2, 11 and 32 exist on thicker paper, usually toned. Most authorities consider these four stamps and Nos. 33a-41a to be official reprints made to present sample sets to other post offices. The tone in this paper is an acquired characteristic, due to various causes. Many shades and minor varieties exist of Nos. 1-41a.

A2

A3

A4

A5

**1866 Litho.** *Perf. 12*
**42** A2 2c rose 11.50 *14.00*
**43** A3 4c lilac 25.00 25.00
**44** A4 8c gray blue 27.50 *30.00*
**45** A5 16c green 60.00 *70.00*
*Nos. 42-45 (4)* 124.00 139.00

Nos. 42-45 imperf. are proofs. See No. 50. For surcharges see Nos. 51-61, 67.

A6

A7

A8

A9

**1866** *Perf. 15*
**46** A6 10ca brown 6.00 5.50
*a.* "CANDS" 55.00 50.00
**47** A7 3ca orange 25.00 *30.00*
**48** A8 6ca slate 25.00 *30.00*
**49** A9 12ca olive gray 60.00 *65.00*
*Nos. 46-49 (4)* 116.00 130.50

See Nos. 69-77. For surcharges see Nos. 62-66, 68, 78-83.

**1872**
**50** A2 2c rose 85.00 *110.00*

Handstamp Surcharged in Blue, Red or Black

a

**1873** *Perf. 12*
**51** A2 1ca on 2c rose 37.50 *50.00*
**52** A3 1ca on 4c lilac 16.00 *18.00*
**53** A3 1ca on 4c lilac (R) *1,750. 1,750.*
**54** A3 1ca on 4c lilac (Bk) 20.00 *27.50*
**55** A4 1ca on 8c gray bl 25.00 *27.50*
**56** A4 1ca on 8c gray bl (R) *3,500. 3,500.*
**57** A5 1ca on 16c green *2,750. 2,750.*
**58** A5 1ca on 16c green (R) *4,000. 3,750.*

*Perf. 15*
**59** A2 1ca on 2c rose 37.50 *42.50*

**1875** *Perf. 12*
**60** A2 3ca on 2c rose 70.00 70.00
**61** A5 3ca on 16c green *1,100. 1,100.*

*Perf. 15*
**62** A7 1ca on 3ca orange *4,000. 4,000.*
**63** A8 1ca on 6ca slate 275.00 275.00
**64** A8 1ca on 6ca slate (R) *2,500. 2,500.*
**65** A9 1ca on 12ca ol gray 250.00 250.00
**66** A9 1ca on 12ca ol gray (R) *2,500. 2,500.*
**67** A2 3ca on 2c rose 225.00 225.00
**68** A9 3ca on 12ca olive gray *6,000. 6,000.*

Counterfeits exist of Nos. 51-68.

Types of 1866

**1875** *Perf. 15*
**69** A6 1ca yel, *yel* 22.50 22.50
**70** A7 3ca rose, *rose* 20.00 22.50

*Perf. 11½*
**71** A6 1ca yel, *yel* 350.00 350.00

**1876** *Perf. 15*
72 A6 1ca yellow 10.00 *12.50*
73 A7 3ca rose 50.00 *60.00*
74 A8 6ca green 65.00 *75.00*
75 A9 9ca blue 95.00 95.00
76 A9 12ca light brown 120.00 120.00
*Nos. 72-76 (5)* 340.00 362.50

**1877** **Engr.** *Perf. 12½*
77 A6 1ca rose 1,000. *1,100.*

Stamps of 1875-76 Surcharged type "a" in Blue or Red

**1877** **Litho.** *Perf. 15*
78 A7 1ca on 3ca rose, *rose* 250.00 250.00
79 A7 1ca on 3ca rose 42.50 42.50
80 A8 1ca on 6ca green 60.00 60.00
81 A9 1ca on 9ca blue 190.00 190.00
82 A9 1ca on 12ca lt brn 1,200. 1,000.
83 A9 1ca on 12ca lt brn (R) *3,250.* *3,250.*

Counterfeits exist of Nos. 78-83.

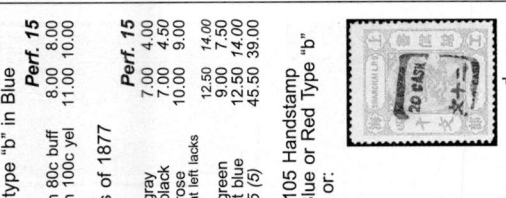

A11

A12

A13

A14

**1877** *Perf. 15*
84 A11 20 cash blue violet 10.00 *12.00*
*a.* 20 cash violet 9.00 9.00
85 A12 40 cash rose 12.50 11.00
86 A13 60 cash green 12.50 12.50
87 A14 80 cash blue 22.50 20.00
88 A14 100 cash brown 17.50 *25.00*
*Nos. 84-88 (5)* 75.00 00.50

Handstamp Surcharged in Blue

b

**1879** *Perf. 15*
89 A12 20 cash on 40c rose 19.00 19.00
90 A14 60 cash on 80c blue 25.00 *32.50*
91 A14 60 cash on 100c brn 25.00 *32.50*
*Nos. 89-91 (3)* 69.00 84.00

Types of 1877

**1880** *Perf. 11½*
92 A11 20 cash violet 8.00 *9.00*
93 A12 40 cash rose 9.00 8.00
94 A13 60 cash green 7.50 *9.00*
95 A14 80 cash blue 10.00 *12.50*
96 A14 100 cash brown 11.50 *14.00*

*Perf. 15x11½*
97 A11 20 cash lilac 50.00 *70.00*
*Nos. 92-97 (6)* 96.00 122.50

Surcharged type "b" in Blue

**1884** *Perf. 11½*
98 A12 20 cash on 40c rose 15.00 11.00
99 A14 60 cash on 80c blue 17.50 *20.00*
100 A14 60 cash on 100c brn 22.50 22.50
*Nos. 98-100 (3)* 55.00 53.50

Types of 1877

**1884**
101 A11 20 cash green 8.00 *9.00*

**1885** *Perf. 15*
102 A11 20 cash green 4.00 3.50
103 A12 40 cash brown 5.50 *6.00*
104 A13 60 cash violet 9.00 *10.50*
*a.* 60 cash red violet 12.50 *20.00*
105 A14 80 cash buff 8.00 7.00
106 A14 100 cash yellow 9.50 *11.50*

*Perf. 11½x15*
107 A11 20 cash green 9.00 6.50
108 A13 60 cash red vio 10.00 9.00
*Nos. 102-108 (7)* 55.00 54.00

Surcharged type "b" in Blue

**1886** *Perf. 15*
109 A14 40 cash on 80c buff 8.00 8.00
110 A14 60 cash on 100c yel 11.00 10.00

Types of 1877

**1888** *Perf. 15*
111 A11 20 cash gray 7.00 4.00
112 A12 40 cash black 7.00 *4.50*
113 A13 60 cash rose 10.00 9.00
*a.* Third character at left lacks dot at top 12.50 *14.00*
114 A14 80 cash green 9.00 7.50
115 A14 100 cash lt blue 12.50 *14.00*
*Nos. 111-115 (5)* 45.50 39.00

#106, 103, 105 Handstamp Surcharged in Blue or Red Type "b" or:

c

d

**1888** *Perf. 15*
116 A14(b) 40 cash on 100c 8.00 *9.00*
117 A14(b) 40 cash on 100c (R) 12.50 *14.00*
118 A12(c) 20 cash on 40c 17.50 17.50
119 A14(c) 20 cash on 80c 7.50 7.50
120 A12(d) 20 cash on 40c 15.00 *17.50*
*Nos. 116-120 (5)* 60.50 65.50

Inverted surcharges exist on Nos. 116-120; double on Nos. 116, 119, 120; omitted surcharges paired with normal stamp on Nos. 116, 119.

Handstamp Surcharged in Black and Red (100 cash) or Red (20 cash)

e

**1889** **Unwmk.**
121 A14(e) 100 cash on 20c on 100c yel 55.00 45.00
*a.* Without the surcharge "100 cash" 300.00
*b.* Blue & red surcharge —
122 A14(c) 20 cash on 80c grn 10.00 10.00
123 A14(c) 20 cash on 100c bl 10.00 10.00
*Nos. 121-123 (3)* 75.00 65.00

Counterfeits exist of Nos. 116-123.

**1889** **Wmk. 175** *Perf. 15*
124 A11 20 cash gray 3.50 3.50
125 A12 40 cash black 5.00 5.00
126 A13 60 cash rose 10.00 *11.00*
*a.* Third character at left lacks dot at top 15.00 *15.00*

*Perf. 12*
127 A14 80 cash green 7.00 *8.00*
128 A14 100 cash dk bl 9.50 8.50
*Nos. 124-128 (5)* 35.00 36.00

Nos. 124-126 are sometimes found without watermark. This is caused by the sheet being misplaced in the printing press, so that the stamps are printed on the unwatermarked margin of the sheet.

Shield with Dragon Supporters — A20

**1890** **Unwmk.** **Litho.** *Perf. 15*
129 A20 2c brown 3.00 *3.75*
130 A20 5c rose 8.00 5.00
131 A20 15c blue 12.50 12.50

Nos. 129-131 imperforate are proofs.

**Wmk. 175**
132 A20 10c black 10.00 8.00
133 A20 15c blue 12.00 12.00
134 A20 20c violet 10.00 10.00
*Nos. 129-134 (6)* 55.50 51.25

See Nos. 135-141. For surcharges and overprints see Nos. 142-152, J1-J13.

**1891** *Perf. 12*
135 A20 2c brown 2.00 2.00
136 A20 5c rose 6.00 6.00

**1892**
137 A20 2c green 2.50 2.25
138 A20 5c red 6.50 6.00
139 A20 10c orange 12.00 *13.50*
140 A20 15c violet 10.00 8.00
141 A20 20c brown 11.00 11.00
*Nos. 137-141 (5)* 42.00 40.75

No. 130 Handstamp Surcharged in Blue

f

**1892** **Unwmk.** *Perf. 15*
142 A20 2c on 5c rose 55.00 45.00

Counterfeits exist of Nos. 142-152.

Stamps of 1892 Handstamp Surcharged in Blue:

g

h

**1893** **Wmk. 175** *Perf. 12*
143 A20 ½c on 15c violet 10.00 8.00
144 A20 1c on 20c brown 10.00 8.00
*a.* ½c on 20c brown (error) *5,000.*

Surcharged in Blue or Red (#152) on Halves of #136 (#145-147), #138 (#148-150), #135 (#151), #137 (#152)

**½Ct.** **½Ct.** **½Ct.** **1Ct.**
*i* *j* *k* *m*

145 A20(i) ½c on half of 5c 7.50 6.50
146 A20(j) ½c on half of 5c 9.00 8.00
147 A20(k) ½c on half of 5c 80.00 70.00
148 A20(i) ½c on half of 5c 7.50 6.50
149 A20(j) ½c on half of 5c 8.50 6.50
150 A20(k) ½c on half of 5c 80.00 70.00
151 A20(m) 1c on half of 2c 3.00 2.50
*c.* Dbl. surch., one in green *350.00*
*d.* Dbl. surch., one in black *350.00*
152 A20(m) 1c on half of 2c 11.00 10.00
*Nos. 145-152 (8)* 206.50 180.00

The ½c surcharge setting of 20 (2x10) covers a vertical strip of 10 unsevered stamps, with horizontal gutter midway. This setting has 11 of type "i," 8 of type "j" and 1 of type "k." Nos. 145-152 are perforated vertically down the middle.

Inverted surcharges exist on Nos. 145-151. Double surcharges, one inverted, are also found in this issue.

Handstamped provisionals somewhat similar to Nos. 145-152 were issued in Foochow by the Shanghai Agency.

Coat of Arms — A24

Typo. (Dot)

Litho. (No Dot)

**1893** **Litho.** *Perf. 13½x14*
**Frame Inscriptions in Black**
153 A24 ½c orange, typo. .40 .30
*a.* ½c orange, litho. 5.00 5.00
154 A24 1c brown, typo. .40 .30
*a.* 1c brown, litho. 5.00 5.00
155 A24 2c vermilion 8.00 5.00
*a.* Imperf., pair 100.00
156 A24 5c blue .75 .50
*a.* Black inscriptions inverted 800.00

157 A24 10c grn, typo. & litho. 2.50 *3.00*
*a.* 10c green, litho. 8.00 *10.00*
158 A24 15c yellow .80 .75
159 A24 20c lil, typo. & litho. 2.75 *3.50*
*a.* 20c lilac, litho. 6.50 6.50
*Nos. 153-159 (7)* 15.60 13.35

On Nos. 157 and 159, frame inscriptions are lithographed, rest of design typographed.

See Nos. 170-172. For overprints and surcharges see Nos. 160-166, 168-169.

Stamps of 1893 Overprinted in Black

**1893, Dec. 14**
160 A24 ½c orange & blk .40 .40
161 A24 1c brown & blk .60 .60
*a.* Double overprint 27.50 27.50
162 A24 2c vermilion & blk .75 .75
*a.* Inverted overprint 57.50
163 A24 5c blue & black 3.00 *3.50*
*a.* Inverted overprint 120.00
164 A24 10c green & blk 7.00 *8.00*
165 A24 15c yellow & blk 4.00 4.00
166 A24 20c lilac & blk 6.00 *6.50*
*Nos. 160-166 (7)* 21.75 23.75

50th anniv. of the first foreign settlement in Shanghai.

Mercury — A26

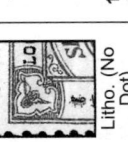

**1893, Nov. 11** **Litho.** *Perf. 13½*
167 A26 2c vermilion & black .80 .80

Nos. 158 and 159 Handstamp Surcharged in Black

**1896** *Perf. 13½x14*
168 A24 4c on 15c yellow & blk 7.00 6.00
169 A24 6c on 20c lilac & blk (#159) 7.00 6.00
*a.* On #159a 50.00 25.00

Surcharge occurs inverted or double on Nos. 168-169.

Arms Type of 1893

**1896**
170 A24 2c scarlet & blk .30 *1.25*
*a.* Black inscriptions inverted 150.00
171 A24 4c orange & blk, *yel* 3.00 *3.25*
172 A24 6c car & blk, *rose* 2.50 *3.75*
*Nos. 170-172 (3)* 5.80 8.25

## POSTAGE DUE STAMPS

Postage Stamps of 1890-92 Handstamped in Black, Red or Blue

**1892** **Unwmk.** *Perf. 15*
J1 A20 2c brown (Bk) 275.00 *300.00*
J2 A20 5c rose (Bk) 7.00 *7.50*
J3 A20 15c blue (Bk) 27.50 27.50

**Wmk. 175**
J4 A20 10c black (R) 17.50 *20.00*
J5 A20 15c blue (Bk) 15.00 *20.00*
J6 A20 20c violet (Bk) 12.50 *15.00*
*Nos. J1-J6 (6)* 354.50 390.00

**1892-93** *Perf. 12*
J7 A20 2c brown (Bk) 3.00 3.00
J8 A20 2c brown (Bl) 2.50 *3.00*
J9 A20 5c rose (Bl) 10.00 8.00

| J10 | A20 | 10c orange (Bk) | 70.00 | 75.00 |
| J11 | A20 | 10c orange (Bl) | 11.50 | 9.00 |
| J12 | A20 | 15c violet (R) | 20.00 | 20.00 |
| J13 | A20 | 20c brown (R) | 17.50 | 17.50 |

Nos. J7-J13 (7)   134.50   135.50

**1893**

| J14 | D2 | ½c orange & blk | .55 | .55 |

**Litho.   Perf. 14x13½**

| J15 | D2 | 1c brown & black | .55 | .55 |
| J16 | D2 | 2c vermilion & black | .60 | .55 |
| J17 | D2 | 5c blue & black | .90 | .90 |
| J18 | D2 | 10c green & black | 5.00 | 2.00 |
| J19 | D2 | 15c yellow & black | 4.00 | 4.00 |
| J20 | D2 | 20c violet & black | 1.50 | 1.50 |

Nos. J14-J20 (7)   13.15   10.05

D2

Stamps of Shanghai were discontinued in 1898.

---

# SHARJAH & DEPENDENCIES

shär-je

LOCATION — Oman Peninsula, Arabia, on Persian Gulf
GOVT. — Sheikdom under British protection
POP. — 5,000 (estimated)
CAPITAL — Sharjah

The dependencies on the Gulf of Oman are Dhiba, Khor Fakkan, and Kalba.

Sharjah is one of six Persian Gulf sheikdoms to join the United Arab Emirates which proclaimed independence Dec. 2, 1971. See United Arab Emirates.

100 Naye Paise = 1 Rupee

**Catalogue values for all unused stamps in this country are for Never Hinged items.**

Sheik Saqr bin Sultan al Qasimi, Flag and Map — A1

**1963, July 10   Photo.   Unwmk.**
Black Portrait and Inscriptions;
Rose Flag   Lilac

| 1 | A1 | 1np lt bl grn & pink | .20 | .20 |
| 2 | A1 | 2np grnsh bl & sal | .20 | .20 |
| 3 | A1 | 3np violet & yel | .20 | .20 |
| 4 | A1 | 4np emerald & gray | .20 | .20 |
| 5 | A1 | 5np aqua & lt grn | .20 | .20 |
| 6 | A1 | 6np dl grn & brt yel | .20 | .20 |

Malaria Eradication Emblem — A2

**1963, Aug. 8**

| 7 | A1 | 8np Prus bl & tan | .20 | .20 |
| 8 | A1 | 10np aqua & tan | .20 | .20 |
| 9 | A1 | 16np ultra & bis | .25 | .20 |
| 10 | A1 | lt vio & bis | .30 | .20 |
| 11 | A1 | 30np rose lil & brt yel grn | .40 | .25 |
| 12 | A1 | 40np dk bl & yel grn | .45 | .30 |
| 13 | A1 | 50np green & fawn | .60 | .40 |
| 14 | A1 | 75np ultra & lawn | .70 | .50 |
| 15 | A1 | 100np ol bis & rose | 1.00 | .75 |

Nos. 1-15 (15)   6.10   4.30

**Miniature Sheet**
**Imperf**

| 16-20 | A1 | | | |
| 16 | A1 | 1np yellow brown | .30 | .20 |
| 17 | A1 | 2np dull blue | .30 | .20 |
| 18 | A1 | 3np violet blue | .60 | .40 |
| 19 | A1 | 4np emerald | 1.10 | .75 |
| 20 | A1 | 90np carmine | 1.40 | .75 |

Nos. 16-20 (5)   3.65   1.80

| 21 | A2 | 100np bright blue | 3.75 | 2.00 |

WHO drive to eradicate malaria. No. 21 contains one 39x67mm stamp. See Nos. 35, C1-C6, C7-C12, O1-O9. For surcharge and overprints see Nos. 22-27.

Red Crescent and Sheik — A3

**1963, Aug. 25   Perf. 14x14½**

| 22 | A3 | 1np purple & red | .20 | .20 |
| 23 | A3 | 2np brt green & red | .20 | .20 |
| 24 | A3 | 3np dark blue & red | .20 | .20 |
| 25 | A3 | 4np dark green & red | .20 | .20 |
| 26 | A3 | 5np dark brown & red | .20 | .20 |
| 27 | A3 | 85np dark brown & red | 1.75 | 1.75 |

Nos. 22-27 (6)   2.75   1.75

**Miniature Sheet**
**Imperf**

| 28 | A3 | 100np plum & red | 3.25 | 2.00 |

Cent. of the Intl. Red Cross. Imperfs. exist, set $5. No. 28 contains one 67x39mm. stamp.

Nos. 29-34

No. 35

**1963, Oct. 6   Photo.   Perf. 14½x14**

| 29 | A4 | 10np on 1np brt grn | .30 | .30 |
| 30 | A4 | 20np on 2np red brn | .60 | .50 |
| 31 | A4 | 30np on 3np dl grn | 1.00 | .75 |
| 32 | A4 | 75np on 4np dp ultra | 1.25 | 1.00 |
| 33 | A4 | 40np on 4np lt grn | 1.50 | 1.25 |
| 34 | A4 | 80np on 90np carmine | 1.75 | 1.50 |
| 35 | A2 | 1r on 90np carmine | 2.25 | 1.75 |

Nos. 29-35 (7)   8.65   7.05

Due to a stamp shortage the surcharged set appeared before the commemorative issue.

Wheat Emblem and Hands with Broken Chains — A4

**Nos. 36-40 and No. 20 Surcharged**

**1963, Oct. 15   Perf. 14½x14**

| 36 | A4 | 1np brt green | .20 | .20 |
| 37 | A4 | 2np red brown | .20 | .20 |
| 38 | A4 | 3np olive green | .20 | .20 |
| 39 | A4 | 4np deep ultra | .20 | .20 |
| 40 | A4 | 90np carmine | 2.00 | .40 |

Nos. 36-40 (5)   2.80   1.20

**Miniature Sheet**
**Imperf**

| 41 | A4 | 100np purple | 2.25 | 1.75 |

"Freedom from Hunger" campaign of the FAO. Imperfs. exist. No. 41 contains one 39x67mm stamp. For surcharges see Nos. 29-34.

Orbiting Astronomical Observatory — A5

**1964, Feb. 5   Photo.   Perf. 14**

| 42 | A5 | 1np blue | .20 | .20 |
| 43 | A5 | 2np red brn & yel grn | .20 | .20 |
| 44 | A5 | 3np blk & grnsh bl | .20 | .20 |
| 45 | A5 | 4np lemon & blk | .20 | .20 |
| 46 | A5 | 5np brt pur & lem | .20 | .20 |
| 47 | A5 | 35np grnsh bl & pur | .75 | .60 |
| 48 | A5 | 50np ol grn & redsh brn | 1.50 | .90 |

Nos. 42-48 (7)   3.25   2.50

Space research. A 100np imperf. souvenir sheet shows various satellites, the Earth and stars. Colors: dark blue, gold, green & pink. Size: 112x80mm. Value $5.00.

Satellites: 2np, Nimbus weather satellite. 3np, Pioneer V space probe. 4np, Explorer XII, 35np, Relay satellite. 5np, Explorer XII. 50np, Orbiting Solar Observatory.

Runner — A6

**1964, Mar. 3   Photo.   Unwmk.**

| 49 | A6 | 1np shown | .20 | .20 |
| 50 | A6 | 2np Discus | .20 | .20 |
| 51 | A6 | 3np Hurdler | .20 | .20 |
| 52 | A6 | 4np Shot put | .20 | .20 |
| 53 | A6 | 20np High jump | .40 | .20 |
| 54 | A6 | 30np Weight lifting | .70 | .40 |
| 55 | A6 | 40np Javelin | .90 | .30 |
| 56 | A6 | 1r Diving | 1.75 | 1.00 |

Nos. 49-56 (8)   4.55   2.55

18th Olympic Games, Tokyo, Oct. 10-25, 1964. An imperf. souvenir sheet contains one 1r stamp similar to No. 56. Size of sheet:

Girl Scouts A7

**1964, June 30   Perf. 14x14½**

| 57 | A7 | 1np grnsh gray | .20 | .20 |
| 58 | A7 | 2np emerald | .20 | .20 |
| 59 | A7 | 3np brt blue | .25 | .20 |
| 60 | A7 | 4np brt violet | .20 | .20 |
| 61 | A7 | 5np carmine rose | .30 | .20 |
| 62 | A7 | 2r dark red brown | 3.95 | 2.25 |

Nos. 57-62 (6)   3.75   1.25

An imperf. souvenir sheet contains one 2r bright red stamp. Size of sheet: 102½x76mm. Value $4.00.

67x67mm, size of sheet: 102x102mm. Value $6.50.

Sharjah Boy Scout — A8

**1964, June 30   Perf. 14x14, 14x14½**

| 63 | A8 | 1np gray green | .20 | .20 |
| 64 | A8 | 2np emerald | .20 | .20 |
| 65 | A8 | 3np brt blue | .20 | .20 |
| 66 | A8 | 4np brt violet | .20 | .20 |
| 67 | A9 | 5np brt carmine rose | .50 | .40 |
| 68 | A8 | 2r dk red brn | 3.50 | 2.55 |

Nos. 63-68 (6)   2.00   1.25

Issued to honor the Sharjah Boy Scouts. An imperf. souvenir sheet exists with one 2r bright red stamp in design of No. 68. Size of sheet: 77x103mm.

Designs: 3np, 2r, Boy Scout portrait.

Marching Scouts With Drummers — A9

Olympic Torch and Rings — A10

**1964, Oct. 15   Litho.   Perf. 14**

| 69 | A10 | 1np olive green | .20 | .20 |
| 70 | A10 | 2np ultra | .20 | .20 |
| 71 | A10 | 3np orange brown | .20 | .20 |
| 72 | A10 | 4np blue green | .20 | .20 |
| 73 | A10 | 5np dark violet | .30 | .20 |
| 74 | A10 | 40np brt blue | .50 | .30 |
| 75 | A10 | 50np dark red brown | .80 | .40 |
| 76 | A10 | 2r bister | 4.40 | 2.95 |

Nos. 69-76 (8)   6.75   4.40

18th Olympic Games, Tokyo, Oct. 10-25, 1964. An imperf. souvenir sheet exists with one 2r bright red stamp in design of No. 76. Size of sheet: 107x76mm. Value $6.75.

## Early Telephone — A11

Designs: No. 78, Modern telewriter. No. 79, 1895 car. No. 80, American automobile. No. 81, Early X-ray. No. 82, Modern X-ray. No. 83, Mail coach. No. 84, Telstar and Delta rocket. No. 85, Sailing vessel. No. 86, Nuclear ship "Savannah." No. 87, Early astronomers. No. 88, Jodrell Bank telescope. No. 89, Greek messengers. No. 90, Relay satellite, Delta rocket and globe. No. 91, Early flying machine. No. 92, Caravelle plane. No. 93, Persian water wheel. No. 94, Hydroelectric dam. No. 95, Old steam locomotive. No. 96, Diesel locomotive.

**1965, Apr. 23    Unwmk.    Litho.    Perf. 14**

| | | | | |
|---|---|---|---|---|
| 77 | A11 | 1np rose red & blk | .20 | .20 |
| 78 | A11 | 1np rose red & blk | .20 | .20 |
| 79 | A11 | 2np orange & indigo | .20 | .20 |
| 80 | A11 | 2np orange & indigo | .20 | .20 |
| 81 | A11 | 3np dk brn & emer | .20 | .20 |
| 82 | A11 | 3np emer & dk brn | .20 | .20 |
| 83 | A11 | 4np yel grn & dk yel grn | .20 | .20 |
| 84 | A11 | 4np dk vio & yel grn | .20 | .20 |
| 85 | A11 | 5np bl grn & brn | .25 | .20 |
| 86 | A11 | 5np bl grn & brn | .25 | .20 |
| 87 | A11 | 30np gray & bl | .30 | .20 |
| 88 | A11 | 30np blue & gray | .30 | .20 |
| 89 | A11 | 40np vio bl & yel | .30 | .20 |
| 90 | A11 | 40np vio bl & yel | .40 | .20 |
| 91 | A11 | 50np blue & sepia | .50 | .30 |
| 92 | A11 | 50np blue & sepia | .60 | .30 |
| 93 | A11 | 75np brt grn & dk brn | .60 | .30 |
| 94 | A11 | 75np brt grn & dk brn | .75 | 1.00 |
| 95 | A11 | 1r yellow & vio bl | 1.75 | 1.00 |
| 96 | A11 | 1r yellow & vio bl | 8.50 | 5.80 |

*Nos. 77-96 (20)*

Issued to show progress in science, transport and communications. Each two stamps of same denomination are printed se-tenant. Two imperf. souvenir sheets exist. One contains one each of Nos. 89-90 and the other, of Nos. 95-96. Sizes: 102x75mm.

Stamps of Sharjah & Dependencies were replaced in 1972 by those of United Arab Emirates.

## AIR POST STAMPS

Type of Regular Issue, 1963 with Flying Hawk and "Air Mail" in English and Arabic Added

**1963, July 10    Photo.    Unwmk.    Perf. 14½x14**

Black Portrait and Inscriptions; Lilac
### Rose Flag

| | | | | |
|---|---|---|---|---|
| C1 | A1 | 1r ultra & fawn | .60 | .40 |
| C2 | A1 | 2r violet & lemon | 1.10 | .70 |
| C3 | A1 | 3r dl grn & brt yel | 1.25 | 1.00 |
| C4 | A1 | 4r grnsh bl & sal | 2.10 | 1.40 |
| C5 | A1 | 5r emerald & gray | 2.75 | 1.60 |
| C6 | A1 | 10r olive bis & rose | 6.50 | 3.50 |

*Nos. C1-C6 (6)* | | 14.30 | 8.60 |

Nos. C1-C6 Overprinted

**1964, Apr. 7**
Black Portrait and Inscriptions; Lilac
### Rose Flag

| | | | | |
|---|---|---|---|---|
| C7 | A1 | 1r ultra & fawn | 2.75 | 2.75 |
| C8 | A1 | 2r lt violet & lem | 5.50 | 5.50 |
| C9 | A1 | 3r dull grn & brt yel | 9.00 | 9.00 |
| C10 | A1 | 4r grnsh blue & sal | 10.00 | 10.00 |

| | | | | |
|---|---|---|---|---|
| C11 | A1 | 5r emerald & gray | 15.00 | 15.00 |
| C12 | A1 | 10r olive bis & rose | 22.50 | 22.50 |
| | | | 64.75 | 64.75 |

*Pres. John F. Kennedy (1917-63).*

### World Map and Flame — AP1

**1964, Apr. 15    Perf. 14x14½**

| | | | | |
|---|---|---|---|---|
| C13 | AP1 | 50np red brown | 1.00 | .45 |
| C14 | AP1 | 1r purple | 2.00 | 1.00 |
| C15 | AP1 | 150np Prus green | 3.50 | 1.70 |

*Nos. C13-C15 (3)*

Issued for Human Rights Day. An imperf. souvenir sheet contains one 3r carmine rose stamp. Size of stamp: 67x40mm. Value of sheet: 89x64mm. Value $3.50.

### View of Khor Fakkan — AP2

Designs: 20np, Beni Qatab Bedouin camp near Dhaid. 30np, Oasis of Dhaid. 40np, Kalba Castle. 75np, Sharjah street with wind tower. 100np, Sharjah Fortress.

**1964, Aug. 13    Photo.    Perf. 14½x14**

| | | | | |
|---|---|---|---|---|
| | | | **Unwmk.** | |
| C16 | AP2 | 10np multi | .20 | .20 |
| C17 | AP2 | 20np multi | .25 | .20 |
| C18 | AP2 | 30np multi | .30 | .25 |
| C19 | AP2 | 40np multi | .30 | .25 |
| C20 | AP2 | 75np multi | 1.00 | .35 |
| C21 | AP2 | 100np multi | 3.10 | 1.80 |

*Nos. C16-C21 (6)*

### Rock Dove — AP5

ROCK DOVE

**1964, Nov. 22    Perf. 14x13½**

| | | | | |
|---|---|---|---|---|
| C25 | AP4 | 40np multicolored | 1.50 | .85 |
| C26 | AP4 | 60np multicolored | 1.75 | .85 |
| C27 | AP4 | 100np multicolored | 5.00 | 2.55 |

*Nos. C25-C27 (3)*

Pres. John F. Kennedy. A souvenir sheet contains one each of Nos. C25-C27, imperf. Size: 107x76mm. Value $9.50.

Birds: 40np, 2r, Red jungle fowl. 75np, 3r, Hoopoe.

**1965, Feb. 20    Photo.    Perf. 14x14½**

| | | | | |
|---|---|---|---|---|
| | | | **Unwmk.** | |
| C28 | AP5 | 30np gray & multi | .75 | .25 |
| C29 | AP5 | 40np multicolored | .90 | .30 |
| C30 | AP5 | 75np brt blue & multi | 1.25 | .35 |
| C31 | AP5 | 150np blue & multi | 2.00 | .40 |
| C32 | AP5 | 2r multicolored | 2.25 | .80 |
| C33 | AP5 | 3r red & multi | 5.00 | 1.25 |
| | | | 12.15 | 3.30 |

*Nos. C28-C33 (6)*

## OFFICIAL STAMPS

### ON STATE SERVICE

Nos. 7-15 Overprinted

| | | |
|---|---|---|
| O1 | A1 | 8np multi |
| O2 | A1 | 10np multi |
| O3 | A1 | 10np multi |
| O4 | A1 | 20np multi |
| O5 | A1 | 30np multi |
| O6 | A1 | 40np multi |
| O7 | A1 | 50np multi |
| O8 | A1 | 75np multi |
| O9 | A1 | 100np multi |

**1965, Jan. 13    Photo.    Perf. 14½x14    Unwmk.**

| O1 | .20 | .20 |
|---|---|---|
| O2 | .20 | .20 |
| O3 | .20 | .20 |
| O4 | .20 | .20 |
| O5 | .20 | .20 |
| O6 | .30 | .20 |
| O7 | .85 | .65 |
| O8 | 2.00 | 1.60 |
| O9 | 4.50 | 3.00 |
| | 8.70 | 6.50 |

*Nos. O1-O9 (9)*

Unisphere and Sheik Sqar — AP3

J. F. Kennedy, Statue of Liberty — AP4

20np, Offshore oil rig. 1r, New York skyline.

**1964, Sept. 5    Photo.    Perf. 14½x14**

Size: 26x45mm

| | | | **Unwmk.** | |
|---|---|---|---|---|
| C22 | AP3 | 20np multi | .40 | .20 |
| C23 | AP3 | 40np multi | .75 | .25 |

Size: 86x45mm

| C24 | AP3 | 1r multi, horiz. | 2.00 | .60 |
|---|---|---|---|---|
| | | Strip of 3, Nos. C22-C24 | 3.50 | 3.50 |

New York World's Fair, 1964-65. An imperf. souvenir sheet exists with one 40np stamp in AP3 design. Size of stamp: 40x68mm. Size of sheet: 76x108mm. Value $3.

## SIBERIA
sī-'bir-ē-ə

LOCATION — A vast territory of Russia lying between the Ural Mountains and the Pacific Ocean.

The anti-Bolshevist provisional government set up at Omsk under Adm. Aleksandr V. Kolchak issued Nos. 1-10 in 1919. The monarchist, anti-Soviet government in Priamur province issued Nos. 51-118 in 1921-22. (Stamps of the Czechoslovak Legion are listed under Czechoslovakia.)

100 Kopecks = 1 Ruble

Russian Stamps of 1909-18 Surcharged

On Stamps of 1909-12
**1919    Unwmk.    Perf. 14x14½**
Wove Paper
Lozenges of Varnish on Face

| | | | | |
|---|---|---|---|---|
| 1 | A14(a) | 35k on 2k dull | .55 | 3.00 |
| a. | Inverted surcharge | | 35.00 | |
| b. | "5" omitted | | 80.00 | |
| c. | Double surcharge | | | |

| | | | | |
|---|---|---|---|---|
| 2 | A14(a) | 50k on 3k car | .55 | 2.75 |
| a. | Inverted surcharge | | 40.00 | |
| 3 | A14(a) | 70k on 1k dl org | .80 | 5.50 |
| a. | A14(a) 70k on 1k dl org yel | .90 | 35.00 | |
| 4 | | Inverted surcharge | | 110.00 | |
| | a. | 1r... on 4k car | 2.75 | 10.00 | |
| | b. | Dbl. surch., one inverted | | 110.00 | |
| 4 | A15(b) | 1r... on 4k car | .90 | 2.75 |
| a. | Inverted surcharge | | 55.00 | |
| b. | Double surcharge | | 80.00 | |
| 5 | A14(b) | 3r on 7k bl10 | 1.50 | 5.50 |
| a. | Pair, one without surcharge | | 35.00 | 30.00 |
| c. | Inverted surcharge | | 30.00 | 25.00 |
| d. | "3" omitted | | — | |
| 6 | A11(b) | 5r on 14k dk bl & car | 3.00 | 14.00 |
| a. | Double surcharge | | 30.00 | 30.00 |
| b. | Inverted surcharge | | 30.00 | 30.00 |

### On Stamps of 1917
Imperf

| | | | | |
|---|---|---|---|---|
| 7 | A14(a) | 35k on 2k gray grn | .90 | 5.50 |
| a. | Inverted surcharge | | 80.00 | |
| 8 | A14(a) | 50k on 3k red | .90 | 5.50 |
| a. | Double surcharge | | 100.00 | |
| b. | Inverted surcharge | | — | |
| 9 | A14(a) | 70k on 1k orange | .75 | 5.50 |
| a. | Inverted surcharge | | 40.00 | |
| b. | Dbl. surch., one inverted | | | |
| 10 | A15(b) | 1r on 4k car | 4.50 | 7.75 |
| a. | Nos. 1-10 (10) | | 14.35 | 57.75 |

Nos. 1-10, were first issued in Omsk during the regime of Admiral Kolchak. Later they were used along the line of the Trans-Siberian railway to Vladivostok.

Some experts question the postal use of most off-cover canceled copies of Nos. 1-10.

## 25 P 1-

Similar surcharges, handstamped as above are bogus.

### Priamur Government Issues
Nikolaevsk Issue

A5        A7

### Russian Stamps Handstamp Surcharged or Overprinted On Stamps of 1909-17

**1921    Unwmk.    Perf. 14x14½, 13½**

| | | | |
|---|---|---|---|
| 51 | A5 | 10k on 4k carmine | 110.00 |
| 52 | A5 | 10k on 10k dark blue | 1,200. |
| 53 | A6 | 15k on 14k dk blue & car | 125.00 |
| 54 | A6 | 15k on 15k red brn & dp bl | 70.00 |
| 55 | A6 | 15k on 35k red brn & grn | 80.00 |
| 56 | A6 | 15k on 50k brn vio & grn | 75.00 |
| 57 | A6 | 15k on 70k brn & red org | 200.00 |
| 58 | A7 | 15k on 1r brn & org | 175.00 |
| 59 | A5 | on 20k dl bl & dk car | 175.00 |
| 60 | A5 | on 20k on 14k dk bl & car (error) (#118) | 160.00 |
| a. | 15k on 20k on 14k dk bl | — | |
| 61 | A7 | 20k on 3½r mar & lt grn | 200.00 |
| 62 | A7 | 20k on 5r ind, grn & lt bl | 850.00 |
| 63 | A7 | 20k on 7r dk grn & pink | 400.00 |

Nos. 59-60 are overprinted with initials but original denominations remain. A 10k on 5k claret (Russia No. 77) and a 15k on 20k blue & carmine (Russia Nn. 82a) were not officially issued. Some authorities consider them bogus.

No evidence found of genuine usage of #51-72.

*Reprints exist.*

**On Semi-Postal Stamp of 1914**

64 SP6 20k on 3k mar & gray grn, *pink* *775.00*

On Stamps of 1917

***Imperf***

65 A5 10k on 1k orange *55.00*
66 A5 10k on 2k gray green *60.00*
67 A5 10k on 3k red *60.00*
68 A5 10k on 5k claret *700.00*
69 A6 15k on 1r pale brn, brn & red org *80.00*
70 A7 20k on 1r pale brn, brn & red org *140.00*
71 A7 20k on 3½r mar & lt grn *260.00*
72 A7 20k on 7r dk grn & pink *500.00*

The letters of the overprint are the initials of the Russian words for "Nikolaevsk on Amur Priamur Provisional Government."

As the surcharges on Nos. 51-72 are handstamped, a number exist inverted or double.

A 20k blue & carmine (Russia No. 126) with Priamur overprint and a 15k on 20k (Russia No. 126) were not officially issued. Some authorities consider them bogus.

No evidence found of genuine usage of #51-72.

Stamps of Far Eastern Republic Overprinted

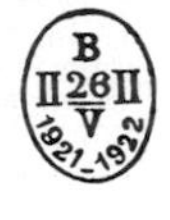

**1922**

78 A2 2k gray green 25.00 25.00
a. Inverted overprint 125.00
79 A2a 4k rose 25.00 25.00
a. Inverted overprint *110.00*
80 A2 5k claret 25.00 25.00
81 A2a 10k blue 25.00 25.00
*Nos. 78-81 (4)* 100.00 100.00

Anniv. of the overthrow of the Bolshevik power in the Priamur district.

The letters of the overprint are the initials of "Vremeno Priamurski Pravitel'stvo" i.e. Provisional Priamur Government, 26th May.

Russian Stamps of 1909-21 Overprinted in Dark Blue or Vermilion

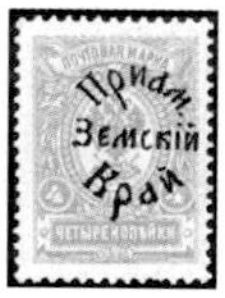

On Stamps of 1909-18

**1922** ***Perf. 14x14½***

85 A14 1k dull org yel 45.00 50.00
86 A14 2k dull green 80.00 65.00
87 A14 3k carmine 25.00 30.00
88 A15 4k carmine 12.50 15.00
89 A14 5k dk claret 25.00 27.50
90 A14 7k blue (V) 25.00 27.50
91 A15 10k dark blue (V) 35.00 40.00
92 A11 14k dk bl & car 45.00 55.00
93 A11 15k red brn & dp bl 12.50 15.00
94 A8 20k dl bl & dk car 12.50 15.00
95 A11 20k on 14k dk bl & car 100.00 100.00
96 A11 25k dl grn & dk vio (V) 25.00 30.00
97 A11 35k red brn & grn 7.50 10.00
a. Inverted overprint 80.00
98 A8 50k brn vio & grn 12.50 15.00
99 A11 70k brn & red org 25.00 30.00
*Nos. 85-99 (15)* 487.50 525.00

On Stamps of 1917

***Imperf***

100 A14 1k orange 4.25 5.00
a. Inverted overprint 65.00 85.00
101 A14 2k gray green 9.00 9.00
102 A14 3k red 12.00 12.00
103 A15 4k carmine 65.00 65.00
104 A14 5k claret 19.00 15.00
105 A11 15k red brn & dp bl 110.00 100.00
106 A8 20k blue & car 47.50 40.00
107 A9 1r pale brn, brn & red org 14.00 15.00
*Nos. 100-107 (8)* 280.75 261.00

On Stamps of Siberia, 1919

***Perf. 14½x15***

108 A14 35k on 2k green 60.00 60.00

***Imperf***

109 A14 70k on 1k orange 85.00 85.00

**On Stamps of Far Eastern Republic, 1921**

110 A2 2k gray green 6.00 5.50
111 A2a 4k rose 6.00 5.50
112 A2 5k claret 6.00 5.50
a. Inverted overprint 100.00
113 A2a 10k blue (R) 4.00 3.50
*Nos. 109-113 (5)* 107.00 105.00

**Same, Surcharged with New Values**

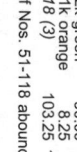

114 A2 1k on 2k gray grn 4.00 3.50
115 A2a 3k on 4k rose 4.00 3.50

The overprint is in a rectangular frame on stamps of 1k to 10k and 1r; on the other values the frame is omitted. It is larger on the 1 ruble than on the smaller stamps.

The overprint reads "Priamurski Zemski Krai," Priamur Rural Province.

Far Eastern Republic Nos. 30-32 Overprinted in Blue

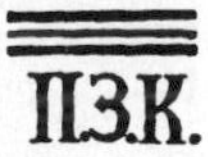

***Perf. 14½x15***

116 A14 35k on 2k green 5.00 6.50

***Imperf***

117 A14 35k on 2k green 90.00 110.00
118 A14 70k on 1k orange 8.25 11.50
*Nos. 116-118 (3)* 103.25 128.00

Counterfeits of Nos. 51-118 abound.

## SIERRA LEONE

sē-ˌer-ə lē-ˈōn

LOCATION — West coast of Africa, between Guinea and Liberia
GOVT. — Republic in British Commonwealth
AREA — 27,925 sq. mi.
POP. — 5,296,651 (1999 est.)
CAPITAL — Freetown

Sierra Leone was a British colony and protectorate. In 1961 it became fully independent, remaining within the Commonwealth. It became a republic April 19, 1971.

12 Pence = 1 Shilling
20 Shillings = 1 Pound
100 Cents = 1 Leone (1964)

**Catalogue values for unused stamps in this country are for Never Hinged items, beginning with Scott 186 in the regular postage section and Scott C1 in the air post section.**

**Watermark**

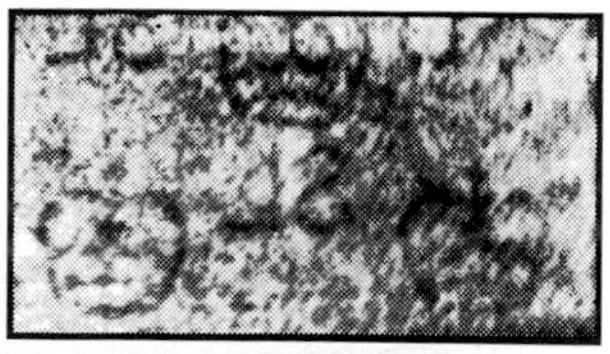

Wmk. 336 — St. Edwards Crown & SL, Multiple

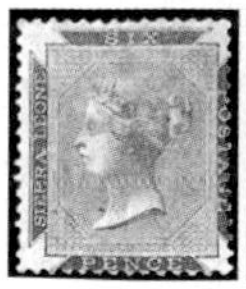
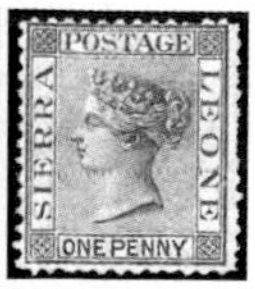

Queen Victoria
A1 A2

**1859-74 Unwmk. Typo. *Perf. 14***

1 A1 6p bright violet ('74) 55.00 30.00
a. 6p dull violet ('59) 220.00 55.00
b. 6p gray lilac ('65) 300.00 45.00

**1872** ***Perf. 12½***

5 A1 6p violet 425.00 70.00

**1872 Wmk. 1 Sideways *Perf. 12½***

6 A2 1p rose 85.00 40.00
8 A2 3p yellow buff 150.00 40.00
9 A2 4p blue 200.00 45.00
10 A2 1sh yellow green 500.00 62.50

**1873 Wmk. 1 Upright**

6a A2 1p 140.00 35.00
7 A2 2p magenta 140.00 55.00
8a A2 3p 525.00 95.00
9a A2 4p 275.00 57.50
10a A2 1sh 450.00 110.00

**1876-96 Wmk. 1 Upright *Perf. 14***

11 A2 ½p bister 2.75 8.00
12 A2 1p rose 52.50 15.00
13 A2 1½p violet ('77) 50.00 9.00
14 A2 2p magenta 67.50 4.50
15 A2 3p yellow buff 52.50 4.75
16 A2 4p blue 175.00 7.25
17 A1 6p brt violet ('85) 62.50 26.00
a. Half used as 3p on cover 2,750.
18 A1 6p violet brn ('90) 13.50 16.00
19 A1 6p brown vio ('96) 2.25 7.25
20 A2 1sh green 57.50 7.25
*Nos. 11-20 (10)* 536.00 105.00

For surcharge see No. 32.

**1883-93 Wmk. Crown and C A (2)**

21 A2 ½p bister 25.00 57.50
22 A2 ½p dull green ('84) 2.75 1.75
23 A2 1p carmine ('84) 4.50 1.10
a. 1p rose carmine 32.50 9.50
b. 1p rose 225.00 40.00
24 A2 1½p violet ('93) 3.25 7.25
25 A2 2p magenta 57.50 9.50
26 A2 2p slate ('84) 35.00 2.75
27 A2 2½p ultra ('91) 9.50 1.00
28 A2 3p org yel ('92) 3.25 11.00
29 A2 4p blue 1,000. 30.00
30 A2 4p bister ('84) 1.90 1.60
31 A2 1sh org brn ('88) 21.00 12.00
*Nos. 21-28,30-31 (10)* 163.65 105.45

For surcharge see No. 33.

Nos. 13 and 24 Surcharged in Black

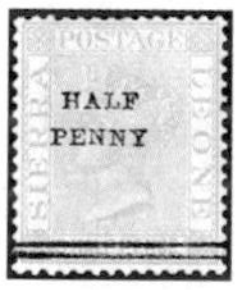

**1893 Wmk. 1**

32 A2 ½p on 1½p violet 525.00 *800.00*
a. "PFNNY" 3,000. *4,000.*

**Wmk. 2**

33 A2 ½p on 1½p violet 4.00 3.50
a. "PFNNY" 80.00 *80.00*
b. Inverted surcharge 110.00 110.00
c. Same as "a," inverted 2,500. *5,500.*
d. Double surcharge *1,100.*

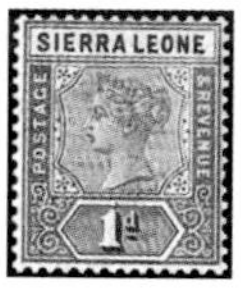

A4

**1896-97**

34 A4 ½p lilac & grn ('97) 2.25 3.25
35 A4 1p lilac & car 3.25 2.00
36 A4 1½p lilac & blk ('97) 4.50 20.00
37 A4 2p lilac & org 2.75 5.50
38 A4 2½p lilac & ultra 2.50 1.40
39 A4 3p lilac & sl ('97) 9.00 8.00
40 A4 4p lilac & car ('97) 11.00 15.00
41 A4 5p lilac & blk 15.00 15.00
42 A4 6p lilac ('97) 9.00 22.50
43 A4 1sh green & blk 7.00 20.00
44 A4 2sh green & ultra 28.00 60.00
45 A4 5sh green & car 67.50 200.00
46 A4 £1 violet, *red* 175.00 475.00
*Nos. 34-46 (13)* 336.75 847.65

Numerals of Nos. 39-46 of type A4 are in color on plain tablet.

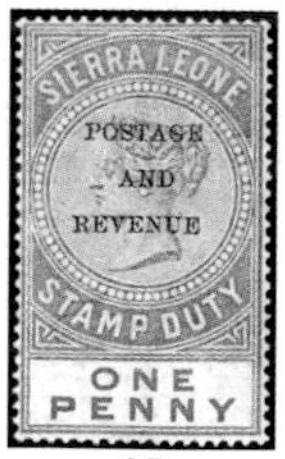

A5

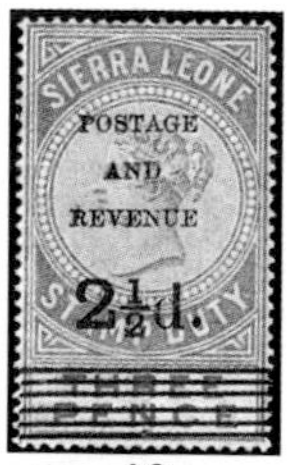

A6

2½d.

a

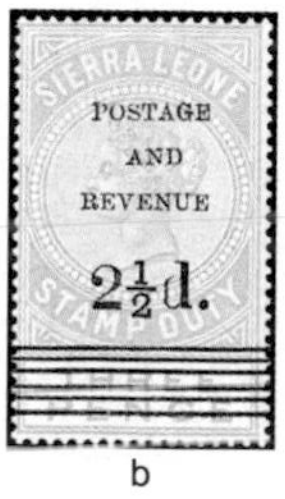

b

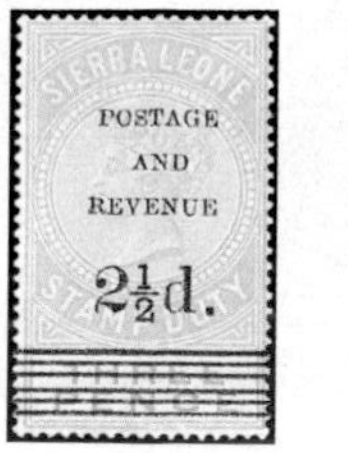

c

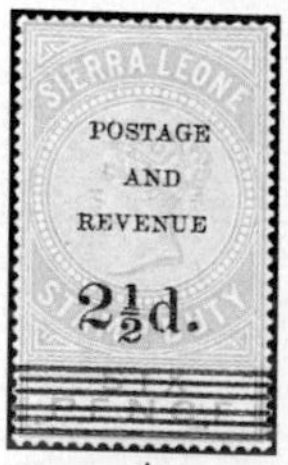

d

2½d.

e

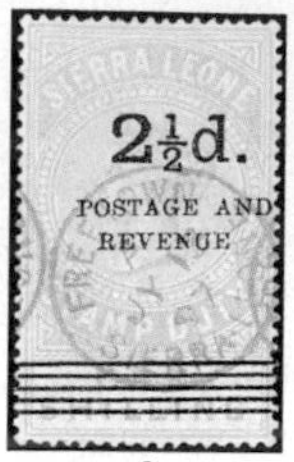

f

**1897 Wmk. C A over Crown (46)**

47 A5 1p lilac & grn 4.00 3.00
a. Double overprint *15,500.* *15,500.*
48 A6(a) 2½p on 3p lil & grn 12.50 *14.00*
a. Double surcharge *20,000.*
49 A6(b) 2½p on 3p 62.50 *70.00*
50 A6(c) 2½p on 3p 175.00 *200.00*
51 A6(d) 2½p on 3p 350.00 *450.00*
52 A6(a) 2½p on 6p lil & grn 10.00 *15.00*
53 A6(b) 2½p on 6p 47.50 *60.00*
54 A6(c) 2½p on 6p 125.00 140.00
55 A6(d) 2½p on 6p 275.00 *350.00*
56 A6(a) 2½p on 1sh lilac 95.00 75.00
57 A6(b) 2½p on 1sh lilac 1,100. 1,100.
58 A6(c) 2½p on 1sh lilac 475.00 475.00
59 A6(e) 2½p on 1sh lilac 1,750. 2,000.
59A A6(f) 2½p on 1sh lilac 1,450. 1,350.
60 A6(a) 2½p on 2sh lilac 1,800. 2,100.
61 A6(b) 2½p on 2sh lilac *16,000.*
62 A6(c) 2½p on 2sh lilac *9,000.* *10,000*
63 A6(e) 2½p on 2sh lilac *36,000.* *42,500*
63A A6(f) 2½p on 2sh lilac *36,000.* *42,500*

The words "POSTAGE AND REVENUE" on Nos. 56-63A are set in two lines and overprinted below instead of above "2½d."

The "d" in type "f" is 3½mm wide; that in type "a" is 3mm.

Very fine examples of Nos. 47-63A will have perforations touching the frameline on one or more sides.

Nos. 56-59A are often found discolored. Such copies sell for about half the values quoted.

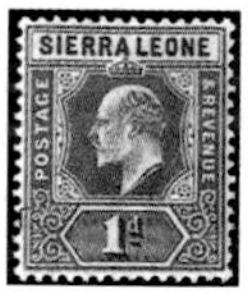

King Edward VII — A7

Numerals of 3p to £1 of type A7 are in color on plain tablet.

**1903 Wmk. Crown and C A (2)**

64 A7 ½p violet & grn 3.25 *5.00*
65 A7 1p violet & car 2.25 1.10
66 A7 1½p violet & blk 1.50 *11.00*
67 A7 2p violet & brn org 4.50 *17.50*
68 A7 2½p violet & ultra 5.00 *9.00*
69 A7 3p violet & gray 11.00 *15.00*
70 A7 4p violet & car 8.00 *16.00*
71 A7 5p violet & blk 9.00 *35.00*
72 A7 6p violet & dull vio 12.50 *17.50*
73 A7 1sh green & blk 18.00 *67.50*
74 A7 2sh green & ultra 50.00 *67.50*
75 A7 5sh green & car 80.00 *110.00*
76 A7 £1 violet, *red* 225.00 275.00
*Nos. 64-76 (13)* 430.00 647.10

**1904-05 Wmk. 3**

**Chalky Paper**

77 A7 ½p violet & grn 5.75 5.25
78 A7 1p violet & car 4.50 1.75
79 A7 1½p violet & blk 3.50 *15.00*
80 A7 2p violet & brn org 4.75 4.50
81 A7 2½p violet & ultra 5.25 2.25
82 A7 3p violet & gray 40.00 4.00
83 A7 4p violet & car 8.00 8.00
84 A7 5p violet & blk 14.00 *30.00*
85 A7 6p violet & dl vio 4.50 *3.50*
86 A7 1sh green & blk 8.50 *10.00*
87 A7 2sh green & ultra 25.00 30.00
88 A7 5sh green & car 35.00 57.50
89 A7 £1 violet, *red* 240.00 260.00
*Nos. 77-89 (13)* 398.75 431.75

The 1p also exists on ordinary paper. Value, unused $1.75, used $1.00.

**1907-10**

**Ordinary Paper**

| | | | | | |
|---|---|---|---|---|---|
| **90** | A7 | ½p green | 1.00 | .60 |
| **91** | A7 | 1p carmine | 6.25 | .80 |
| **92** | A7 | 1½p orange ('10) | 1.40 | 2.25 |
| **93** | A7 | 2p gray | 1.40 | 1.75 |
| **94** | A7 | 2½p ultra | 4.00 | 3.25 |

**Chalky Paper**

| | | | | |
|---|---|---|---|---|
| **95** | A7 | 3p violet, *yel* | 8.50 | *3.25* |
| **96** | A7 | 4p blk & red, *yel* | 2.60 | 1.75 |
| **97** | A7 | 5p vio & ol grn | 9.00 | 5.75 |
| **98** | A7 | 6p vio & red vio | 10.00 | 9.00 |
| **99** | A7 | 1sh black, *green* | 6.25 | 5.75 |
| **100** | A7 | 2sh vio & bl, *bl* | 17.50 | 22.50 |
| **101** | A7 | 5sh grn & red, *yel* | 47.50 | 62.50 |
| **102** | A7 | £1 vio & blk, *red* | 300.00 | 210.00 |
| | | *Nos. 90-102 (13)* | 415.40 | 329.15 |

The 3p also exists on ordinary paper. Value, unused $12.50, used $15.

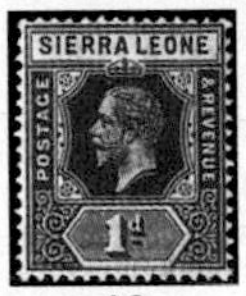

A8

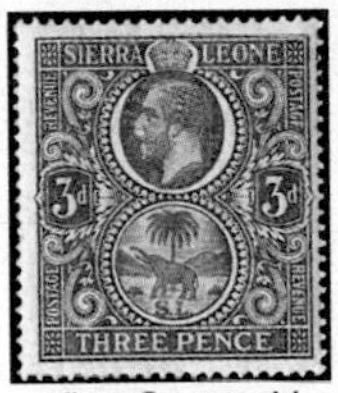

King George V and Seal of the Colony — A9

Die I

For description of dies I and II see front of this volume.

Numerals of 3p, 4p, 5p, 6p and 10p of type A8 are in color on plain tablet. Numerals of 7p and 9p are on solid-color tablet.

**1912-24** **Ordinary Paper** **Wmk. 3**

| | | | | |
|---|---|---|---|---|
| **103** | A8 | ½p green | 2.50 | *2.50* |
| **104** | A8 | 1p scarlet | 4.00 | .80 |
| *a.* | | 1p carmine | 2.00 | .45 |
| **105** | A8 | 1½p orange | 2.25 | *2.75* |
| **106** | A8 | 2p gray | 1.50 | .25 |
| **107** | A8 | 2½p ultra | 1.25 | 1.00 |

**Chalky Paper**

| | | | | |
|---|---|---|---|---|
| **108** | A9 | 3p violet, *yel* | 3.50 | *3.75* |
| **109** | A8 | 4p blk & red, *yel* | 3.25 | *9.50* |
| *a.* | | Die II ('24) | 5.00 | *6.00* |
| **110** | A8 | 5p violet & ol grn | 1.50 | *7.00* |
| **111** | A8 | 6p vio & red vio | 3.75 | *0.75* |
| **112** | A8 | 7p violet & org | 3.50 | *9.50* |
| **113** | A8 | 9p violet & blk | 5.75 | *14.00* |
| **114** | A8 | 10p violet & red | 3.50 | *20.00* |
| **115** | A9 | 1sh black, *green* | 5.00 | *5.25* |
| *a.* | | 1sh black, *emerald* | | *190.00* |
| **116** | A9 | 2sh vio & ultra, *bl* | 15.00 | 6.25 |
| **117** | A9 | 5sh grn & red, *yel* | 15.00 | *30.00* |
| **118** | A9 | 10sh grn & red, *grn* | 80.00 | *140.00* |
| **119** | A9 | £1 vio & blk, *red* | 175.00 | *260.00* |
| **120** | A9 | £2 violet & ultra | 575.00 | *775.00* |
| **121** | A9 | £5 gray grn & org | *1,400.* | *2,000.* |
| | | *Nos. 103-119 (17)* | 326.25 | 519.30 |

The status of #115a has been questioned.

Die II

**1921-27** **Wmk. 4**

**Ordinary Paper**

| | | | | |
|---|---|---|---|---|
| **122** | A8 | ½p green | 1.40 | 1.10 |
| **123** | A8 | 1p violet ('26) | 3.50 | .20 |
| *a.* | | Die I ('24) | 1.75 | *2.50* |
| **124** | A8 | 1½p scarlet | 2.00 | 1.50 |
| **125** | A8 | 2p gray ('22) | 1.10 | .20 |
| **126** | A8 | 2½p ultra | 1.40 | *9.00* |
| **127** | A8 | 3p ultra ('22) | 1.40 | 1.40 |
| **128** | A8 | 4p blk & red, *yel* | 2.00 | *3.75* |
| **129** | A8 | 5p vio & ol grn | 1.40 | 1.40 |

**Chalky Paper**

| | | | | |
|---|---|---|---|---|
| **130** | A8 | 6p dp vio & red vio | 1.40 | *2.75* |
| **131** | A8 | 7p vio & org ('27) | 3.25 | *22.50* |
| **132** | A8 | 9p dl vio & blk ('22) | 3.25 | *16.00* |
| **133** | A8 | 10p violet & red | 4.00 | *30.00* |
| **134** | A9 | 1sh blk, *emerald* | 9.00 | 8.00 |
| **135** | A9 | 2sh vio & ultra, *bl* | 11.00 | 11.50 |
| **136** | A9 | 5sh grn & red, *yel* | 11.00 | *57.50* |
| **137** | A9 | 10sh grn & red, *grn* | 105.00 | *200.00* |
| **138** | A9 | £2 violet & ultra | 550.00 | *750.00* |
| **139** | A9 | £5 gray grn & org | *1,300.* | *2,000.* |
| | | *Nos. 122-137 (16)* | 162.10 | 366.80 |

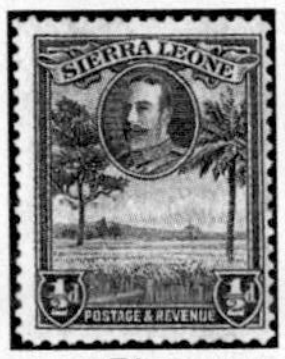

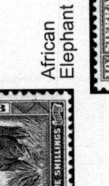

Rice Field — A10

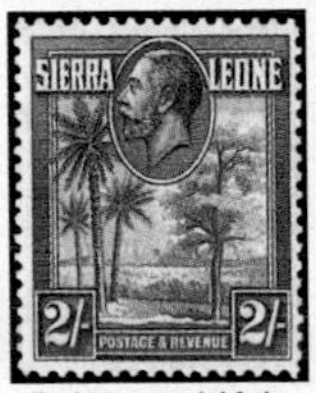

Palms and Kola Tree — A11

**1932, Mar. 1** **Engr.** ***Perf. 12½***

| | | | | |
|---|---|---|---|---|
| **140** | A10 | ½p green | .20 | .20 |
| **141** | A10 | 1p dk violet | .30 | .20 |
| **142** | A10 | 1½p rose car | .35 | *1.40* |
| **143** | A10 | 2p yellow brn | .35 | .20 |
| **144** | A10 | 3p ultra | .75 | *2.00* |
| **145** | A10 | 4p orange | .75 | *8.00* |
| **146** | A10 | 5p olive green | 1.00 | *3.50* |
| **147** | A10 | 6p light blue | .75 | *3.50* |
| **148** | A10 | 1sh red brown | 2.75 | *6.50* |

***Perf. 12***

| | | | | |
|---|---|---|---|---|
| **149** | A11 | 2sh dk brown | 6.00 | *8.25* |
| **150** | A11 | 5sh indigo | 14.00 | *22.50* |
| **151** | A11 | 10sh deep green | 70.00 | *140.00* |
| **152** | A11 | £1 deep violet | 120.00 | *225.00* |
| | | *Nos. 140-152 (13)* | 217.20 | 421.25 |

**Wilberforce Issue**

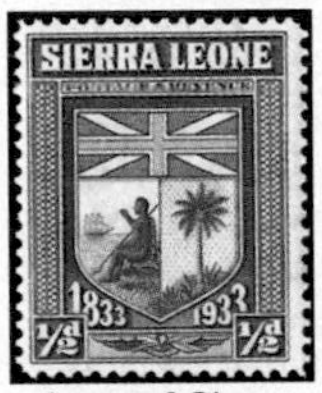

Arms of Sierra Leone — A12

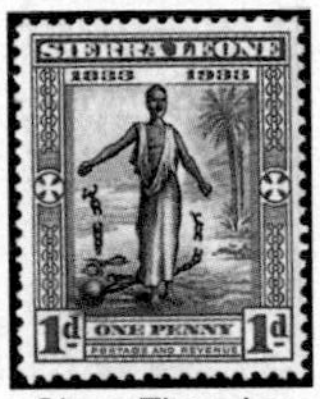

Slave Throwing Off Shackles — A13

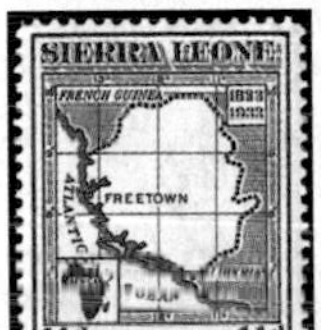

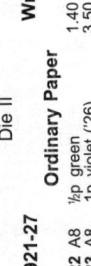

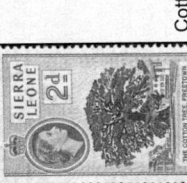

Map of Sierra Leone — A14

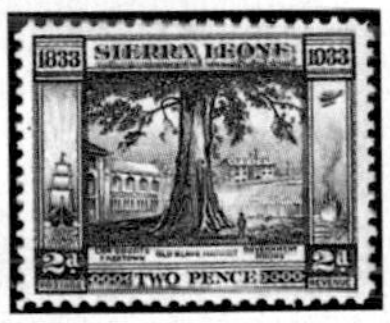

Old Slave Market, Freetown A15

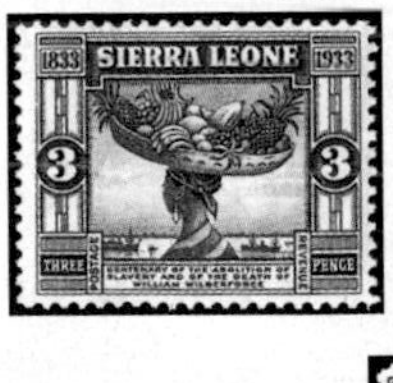

Fruit Seller — A16

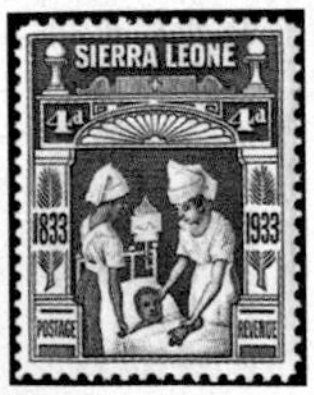

Government Sanatorium — A17

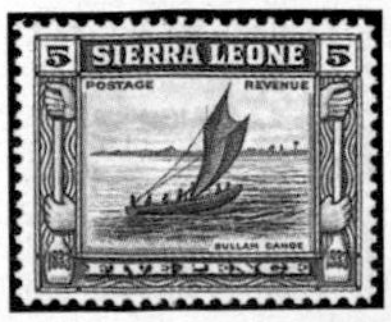

Bullom Canoe — A18

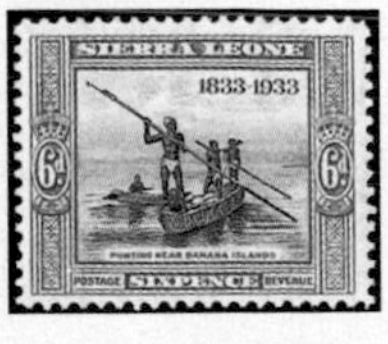

Punting near Banana Islands — A19

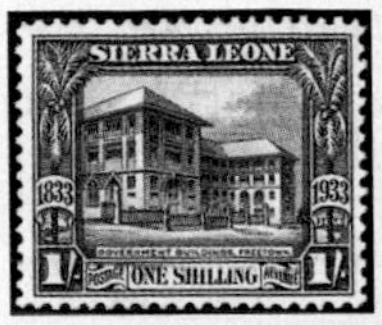

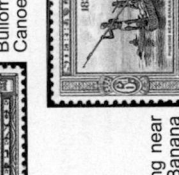

Government Buildings, Freetown A20

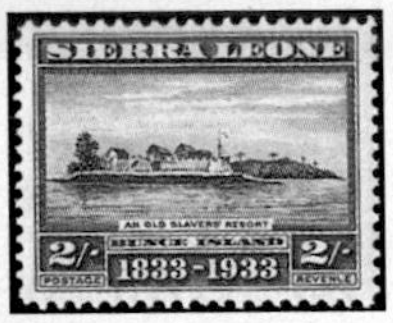

Old Slavers' Resort, Bunce Island — A21

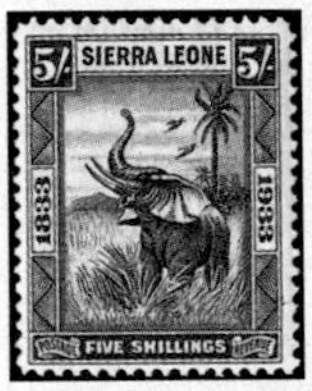

African Elephant — A22

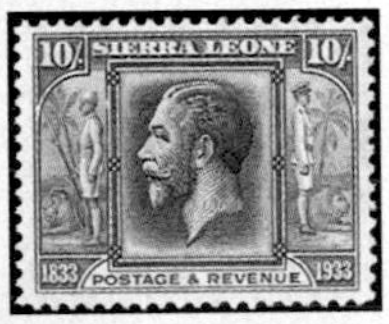

George V A23

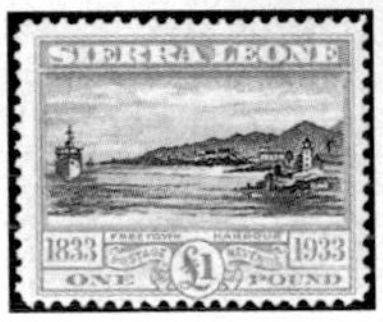

Freetown Harbor — A24

**1933, Oct. 2**

| | | | | |
|---|---|---|---|---|
| **153** | A12 | ½p deep green | .80 | *1.40* |
| **154** | A13 | 1p brown & blk | .70 | .20 |
| **155** | A14 | 1½p orange brn | 5.25 | 5.25 |
| **156** | A15 | 2p violet | 3.50 | .20 |
| **157** | A16 | 3p ultra | 3.50 | 2.10 |
| **158** | A17 | 4p dk brown | 7.50 | *11.50* |
| **159** | A18 | 5p red brn & sl grn | 8.00 | *15.00* |
| **160** | A19 | 6p dp org & blk | 9.00 | 9.00 |
| **161** | A20 | 1sh dk violet | 5.50 | *21.00* |
| **162** | A21 | 2sh bl & dk brn | 25.00 | *45.00* |
| **163** | A22 | 5sh red vio & blk | 175.00 | *190.00* |
| **164** | A23 | 10sh green & blk | 200.00 | *275.00* |
| **165** | A24 | £1 yel & dk vio | 400.00 | *475.00* |
| | | *Nos. 153-165 (13)* | 843.75 | *1,050.* |

Abolition of slavery in the British colonies and cent. of the death of William Wilberforce, English philanthropist and agitator against the slave trade.

Common Design Types pictured following the introduction.

**Silver Jubilee Issue**

Common Design Type

**1935, May 6** ***Perf. 11x12***

| | | | | |
|---|---|---|---|---|
| **166** | CD301 | 1p black & ultra | .85 | *2.50* |
| **167** | CD301 | 3p ultra & brown | .90 | *9.50* |
| **168** | CD301 | 5p indigo & green | 1.25 | *12.50* |
| **169** | CD301 | 1sh brown vio & ind | 5.00 | 5.50 |
| | | *Nos. 166-169 (4)* | 8.00 | 30.00 |
| | | Set, never hinged | 12.50 | |

**Coronation Issue**

Common Design Type

**1937, May 12** ***Perf. 11x11½***

| | | | | |
|---|---|---|---|---|
| **170** | CD302 | 1p deep orange | .40 | .40 |
| **171** | CD302 | 2p dark violet | .60 | .45 |
| **172** | CD302 | 3p deep ultra | .80 | 2.25 |
| | | *Nos. 170-172 (3)* | 1.80 | 3.10 |
| | | Set, never hinged | 3.00 | |

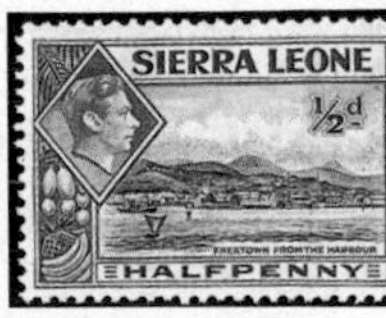

Freetown Harbor A25

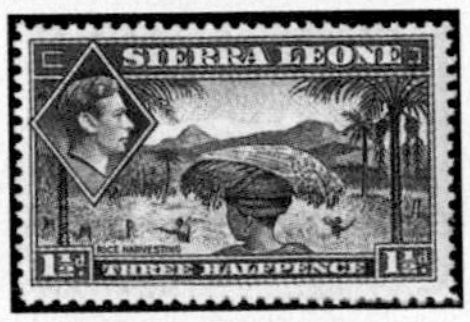

Rice Harvesting A26

**1938-44** ***Perf. 12½***

| | | | | |
|---|---|---|---|---|
| **173** | A25 | ½p green & blk | .20 | .40 |
| **174** | A25 | 1p dp cl & blk | .25 | .60 |
| **175** | A26 | 1½p rose red | 15.00 | 1.00 |
| **175A** | A26 | 1½p red vio ('41) | .20 | *.60* |
| **176** | A26 | 2p red violet | 30.00 | 2.50 |
| **176A** | A26 | 2p dark red ('41) | .20 | *1.75* |
| **177** | A25 | 3p ultra & blk | .25 | *.50* |
| **178** | A25 | 4p red brn & blk | .50 | *4.75* |
| **179** | A26 | 5p olive green | 3.50 | 3.75 |
| **180** | A26 | 6p gray | .50 | .50 |
| **181** | A25 | 1sh ol grn & blk | 1.25 | .75 |
| **181A** | A26 | 1sh3p org yel ('44) | .25 | .50 |
| **182** | A25 | 2sh sepia & blk | 3.25 | 3.00 |
| **183** | A26 | 5sh red brown | 7.00 | 8.00 |
| **184** | A26 | 10sh emerald | 12.50 | 9.50 |
| **185** | A25 | £1 dk blue | 12.50 | *22.50* |
| | | *Nos. 173-185 (16)* | 87.35 | 60.60 |
| | | Set, never hinged | 120.00 | |

**Catalogue values for unused stamps in this section, from this point to the end of the section, are for Never Hinged items.**

**Peace Issue**

Common Design Type

***Perf. 13½x14***

**1946, Oct. 1** **Engr.** **Wmk. 4**

| | | | | |
|---|---|---|---|---|
| **186** | CD303 | 1½p lilac | .20 | .20 |
| **187** | CD303 | 3p bright ultra | .20 | .20 |

**Silver Wedding Issue**

Common Design Types

**1948, Dec. 1** **Photo.** ***Perf. 14x14½***

| | | | | |
|---|---|---|---|---|
| **188** | CD304 | 1½p brt red violet | .20 | .20 |

**Engraved; Name Typographed**

***Perf. 11½x11***

| | | | | |
|---|---|---|---|---|
| **189** | CD305 | £1 dark blue | 19.00 | *17.50* |

**UPU Issue**

Common Design Types

**Engr.; Name Typo. on 3p, 6p**

**1949, Oct. 10** ***Perf. 13½, 11x11½***

| | | | | |
|---|---|---|---|---|
| **190** | CD306 | 1½p rose violet | .20 | .25 |
| **191** | CD307 | 3p indigo | .35 | 1.25 |
| **192** | CD308 | 6p gray | .60 | 1.50 |
| **193** | CD309 | 1sh olive | 1.00 | .75 |
| | | *Nos. 190-193 (4)* | 2.15 | 3.75 |

**Coronation Issue**

Common Design Type

**1953, June 2** **Engr.** ***Perf. 13½x13***

| | | | | |
|---|---|---|---|---|
| **194** | CD312 | 1½p purple & black | .25 | .25 |

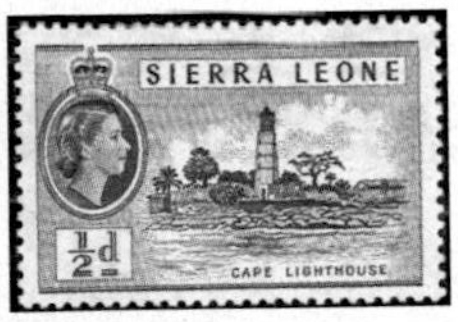

Cape Lighthouse A27

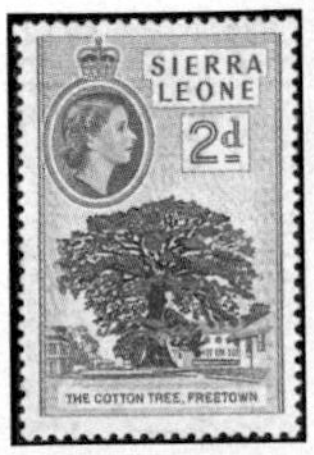

Cotton Tree, Freetown — A28

1p, Queen Elizabeth II Quay. 1½d, Piassava workers. 3p, Rice harvesting. 4p, Iron ore production, Marampa. 6p, Whale Bay, York Village. 1sh, Bullom boat. 1sh3p, Map of Sierra Leone & plane. 2sh6p, Orugu Bridge. 5sh, Kuranko chief. 10sh, Law Courts, Freetown. £1, Government House.

***Perf. 13 (A27), 13½ (A28)***

**1956, Jan. 2** **Engr.** **Wmk. 4**

**Center in Black**

| | | | | |
|---|---|---|---|---|
| **195** | A27 | ½p lt violet | .70 | 1.00 |
| **196** | A27 | 1p reseda | .70 | .20 |
| **197** | A27 | 1½p ultra | 1.25 | 2.50 |
| **198** | A28 | 2p lt brown | .55 | .20 |
| **199** | A28 | 3p ultra | .95 | .20 |
| *a.* | | Perf 13x13½ | 1.40 | 6.00 |

200 A27 4p gray blue 1.90 .65
201 A27 6p violet .75 .20
202 A28 1sh carmine .95 .20
203 A27 1sh3p gray brown .20 .20
204 A28 2sh6p brown org 10.50 4.00
205 A28 5sh green 1.75 1.25
206 A27 10sh green 2.75 1.90
207 A27 £1 orange 40.00 24.50
Nos. 195-207 (13) 40.00 24.50

For surcharges and overprints see Nos. 242-247, 251-253, 255-256, 319, 322, C1-C7, C13.

## Independent State

Carrying Oil Palm Fruit — A29

Diamond Miner and Badge A30

Badge and: 1½p, 5sh, Bundu mask. 2p, 10sh, Bishop Crowther and Old Fourah Bay College. 3p, 6p, Sir Milton Margai. 4p, 1sh3p, Lumley Beach, Freetown. £1, Bugler.

**1961, Apr. 27    Engr.    Wmk. 336**

208 A29 ½p blue grn & dk brn .20 .20
209 A30 1p gray grn & brn .20 .20

*Perf. 13x13½, 13½x13*

210 A29 1½p green & blk .20 .20
211 A29 2p vio blue & blk .20 .20
212 A30 3p brn org & ultra .20 .20
213 A30 4p rose red & grnsh brn .20 .20
214 A30 6p lilac & gray 1.25 .30
215 A29 1sh org & dk brn .30 .20
216 A30 1sh3p vio & grnsh bl .30 .20
217 A30 2sh6p black & grn 2.75 .30
218 A29 5sh rose red & grn 1.00 1.25
219 A29 10sh emerald & yel 1.00 1.25
220 A29 £1 carmine & yel 15.55 11.60
Nos. 208-220 (13) 7.00

Sierra Leone's Independence. See Nos. 254, 274, 279-280, 285-286, 290-291, 294, 296, 299, C10, C29-C31, C132-C133.

---

Royal Charter, 1799 — A31

House of Representatives, Freetown, 1924 — A32

Designs: 4p, King's Yard Gate, Freetown, 1817. 1sh3p, Yacht "Britannia."

**1961, Nov. 25    Engr.    Wmk. 336**

221 A31 3p vermilion & blk .25 .20
222 A31 4p violet & blk .25 .20
223 A32 6p orange & blk .30 .30
224 A32 1sh3p blue & blk .60 .60
Nos. 221-224 (4) 1.35 1.35

Visit of Elizabeth II to Sierra Leone, 1961.
For overprints and surcharges see Nos. 272, 273, C8-C9, C11-C12.

---

**1962, Apr. 7    Perf. 11x11½**

225 A33 3p crimson .20 .20
226 A33 1sh3p green .40 .40

WHO drive to eradicate malaria.

Malaria Eradication Emblem — A33

---

Fireball Lily — A34

Jina Gbo — A35

**1963, Jan. 1    Photo.    Perf. 14**

**Flowers in Natural Colors**

227 A34 ½p olive brown .20 .20
228 A35 1p org ver & dk red .20 .20
229 A34 1½p green .20 .20
230 A35 2p lemon .20 .20
231 A34 3p dark green .20 .20
232 A35 4p lt violet blue .20 .20
233 A34 5p brt yel grn & indigo .20 .20
234 A35 1sh brt grn & red .40 .25
235 A35 1sh3p dk yellow grn .50 .25
236 A34 2sh6p dk gray 1.00 .70
237 A35 5sh deep violet 1.50 1.25
238 A34 10sh red lilac 3.25 2.75
239 A35 £1 bright blue 8.50 6.75
Nos. 227-239 (13) 16.55 13.35

Plants: 1½p, Stereospermum. 2p, Black-eyed Susan. 3p, Beniseed. 4p, Blushing hibiscus. 6p, Climbing lily. 1sh, Beautiful crinum. 1sh3p, Bluebells. 2sh6p, Broken hearts. 5sh, Ra-ponthi. 12sh, Blue plumbago. £1, African tulip tree.

For surcharges see Nos. 271, 273, 276-277, 283-284, 289, 295, 300-305, 317-318, 320-321, 329-332, C37-C41, C57-C60, C134.

---

**1962, Apr. 7    Perf. 11x11½**

225 A33 3p crimson .20 .20
226 A33 1sh3p green .40 .40

WHO drive to eradicate malaria.

---

On A28

**1963, Apr. 27    Center in Black**
**Perf. 13, 13½    Wmk. 4**

242 A27 3p on ½p lt vio (R) .20 .20
243 A27 4p on 1½p ultra (Br) .20 .20
244 A27 6p on 1½p vio (O) .20 .20
245 A28 10p on 3p ultra (V) .30 .30
246 A28 1sh6p on 3p ultra (V) .40 .40
247 A28 3sh6p on 3p ultra (Bl) .85 .85
Nos. 242-247 (6) 2.15 2.15

Type "a" exists in two settings, varying in the width of the line "19 Progress 63" in each sheet of 60; this line measures 19½-21mm on 55 stamps, and 17½-18mm on 5 stamps. See Nos. 242-247 (6).

---

Centenary Emblem — A37

**1963, Nov. 1    Engr.    Perf. 11x11½**

248 A37 3p purple & red .20 .20
249 A37 6p black & red .20 .20
250 A37 1sh3p dark green & red .30 .30
Nos. 248-250 (3) .70 .70

Centenary of International Red Cross. For surcharge see No. C56.

---

Nos. 199, 197, 216 and 195 Overprinted or Surcharged in Pink, Red, Violet or Brown

**1963, Nov. 4    Perf. 13, 13½, 13½x13**
**Center in Black except No. 254    Engr. Wmk. 254**

251 A28 1p (P) .20 .20
252 A27 4p on 1½p .20 .20
253 A27 5p on 1½p .20 .20
254 A30 1sh on 1sh3p .20 .20
255 A27 1sh6p on ½p (R) .30 .30
256 A28 2sh6p on ½p (Br) .35 .35
Nos. 251-256,C8-C13 (12) 12.75 12.75

Oldest postal service (1st stamps in 1859) and the newest GPO in West Africa. Overprint in 5 lines on Nos. 251 and 256. A number of surcharge varieties and errors exist.

---

On A27

**1963, Mar. 21    Perf. 11½x11**
**Engr.    Wmk. 336**

240 A36 3p orange yel & blk .20 .20
241 A36 1sh3p green & blk .40 .40

FAO "Freedom from Hunger" campaign. For surcharges see Nos. 275, C28.

Wheat Emblem, Grain Bin and Threshing Machine A36

Nos. 195, 197 and 199 Surcharged in Red, Brown, Orange, Violet or Blue:

1sh3p, Bullom woman examining onion crop.

---

Map and Lion of Sierra Leone — A38

**1964, Feb. 10    Self-adhesive**
**Engraved and Lithographed   Unwmk.   Die Cut**

257 A38 1p multicolored .20 .20
258 A38 3p multicolored .20 .20
259 A38 4p multicolored .20 .20
260 A38 6p multicolored .20 .20
261 A38 1sh multicolored .20 .20

---

"John F. Kennedy, American Patriot, World Humanitarian" A39

**1964, May 11    Self-adhesive**

262 A38 2sh multicolored .30 .30
263 A38 5sh multicolored .80 .80
Nos. 257-263,C14-C20 (14) 5.85 5.85

New York World's Fair, 1964-65. For surcharges see Nos. 288, 297, 335 and note under No. 299.

**1964, Aug. 4    Self-adhesive**

264 A39 1p multicolored .20 .20
265 A39 3p multicolored .20 .20
266 A39 4p multicolored .20 .20
267 A39 6p multicolored .20 .20
268 A39 1sh multicolored .20 .20
269 A39 2sh multicolored .35 .35
270 A39 5sh multicolored .95 .95
Nos. 264-270,C21-C27 (14) 6.80 6.80

Issues of 1961-63 Surcharged in Red, Black, Dark Blue, Violet or Orange

**1965, Jan. 20**

271 A35 1c on 6p (#233) (R) .20 .20
272 A31 3c on 3p (#221) .20 .20
273 A34 3c on 3p (#231) .20 .20
274 A29 5c on ½p (#208) (DB) .20 .20
275 A36 5c on 3p (#240) (R) .20 .20
276 A35 10c on 3p (#235) (R) .30 .25
277 A34 15c on 1sh3p (#234) .40 .35
278 A32 25c on 6p (#223) (V) .60 .60
279 A39 5sh multicolored 1.20 1.20
Nos. 271-279,C28-C31 (13) 5.70 5.65

Issues of 1961-64 Surcharged in Black or Gold

**1965, Jan. 20**

280 A30 1c on 3p (#212) .20 .20
281 A39 2c on 1p (#264) .20 .20
282 A30 4c on 3p (#259) .20 .20
283 A35 5c on 2p (#230) .20 .20
284 A34 1 le on 5sh (#237) (G) 2.50 2.50
285 A29 2 le on £1 (#220) 5.25 5.25
Nos. 280-285 (6) 8.55 8.55

The surcharges on Nos. 284-285 are given in numerals and spelled out in two lines; numeral on Nos. 280-283.

Issues of 1961-64 Surcharged in Red, Black, Orange, Blue or Pink

**1965, Apr.**

286 A29 1c on 1½p (#210) .20 .20
287 A39 1c on 3p (#265) .20 .20
288 A38 2c on 2sh (#259) .20 .20
289 A39 3c on 4p (#266) .20 .20
290 A29 3c on 2p (#211) (O) .20 .20
291 A30 5c on 2p (#216) .20 .20
292 A39 15c on 6p (#267) .95 .95
293 A39 15c on 1sh (#268) .95 .95
294 A30 20c on 6p (#214) 1.65 1.65
295 A35 20c on 6p (#265) (O) .40 .40
296 A35 50c on 6p (#233) (R) .55 .55
297 A38 50c on 5sh (#263) (B) 1.10 1.10
298 A38 60c on 1sh (#228) (B) 2.50 2.50
299 A29 2 le on 4p (#220) (Bl) 3.25 3.25
Nos. 286-299 (14) 17.60 17.60

Additional surcharges exist: "1c" on Nos. 260, 262, 269-270. See note after No. C41 for airmails. Value $4 each. For surcharges see Nos. 333, 335-336.

---

Designs of Surcharge: Nos. 301, 304, Sir Milton Margai. Nos. 302, 305, Sir Winston Churchill.

**Wmk. 336**

**1965, May 19 Photo. *Perf. 14***

**300** A35 2c on 1p multi .20 .20
**301** A34 3c on 3p multi .20 .20
**302** A34 10c on 1sh multi .30 .30
**303** A35 20c on 1sh3p multi .55 .55
**304** A34 50c on 4p multi 1.25 1.25
**305** A34 75c on 5sh multi 2.25 2.25
*Nos. 300-305,C37-C41 (11)* 14.35 14.35

For surcharges see Nos. 329-332.

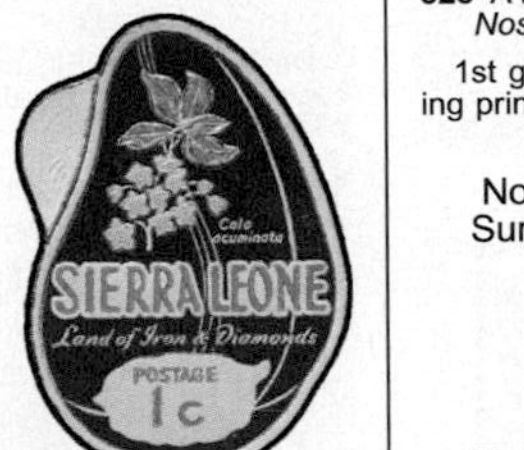

Cola Nut and Plant — A40

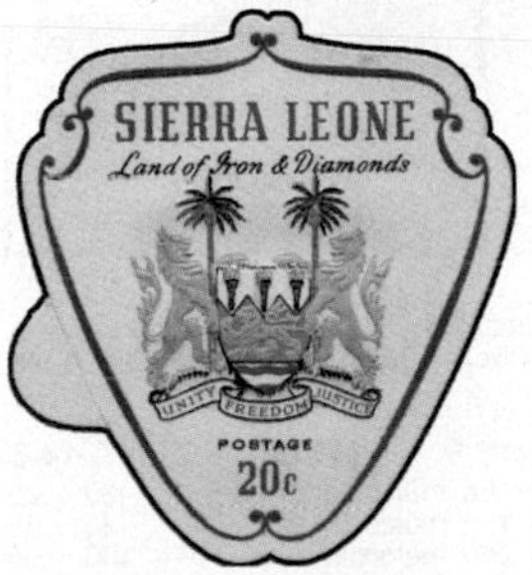

Coat of Arms A41

**Typographed; Embossed on Silver Foil**

**1965 Unwmk. *Die Cut***

**Self-adhesive**

**310** A40 1c multicolored .20 .20
**311** A40 2c multicolored .20 .20
**312** A40 3c multicolored .20 .20
**313** A40 4c multicolored .30 .30
**314** A40 5c multicolored .30 .30

**Engr.; Embossed on Paper**

**315** A41 20c multi, *cream* .75 .00
**316** A41 50c multi, *cream* 2.00 1.75
*Nos. 310-316,C53-C55 (10)* 6.80 6.40

Various advertisements printed on peelable paper backing. Nos. 310-316 have side tabs for handling and come packed in boxes of 100. Nos. 310-312 and 314 were released during November due to a stamp shortage; official release date for set, Dec. 17, 1965. See #338-356, C67, C97. For surcharges see #334, 337, 364-368.

Nos. 197-198, and 232-234, 236 Surcharged with New Value in Black or Ultramarine and Overprinted: "FIVE YEARS / INDEPENDENCE / 1961-1966"

**1966, Apr. 27 Wmk. 4, 336**

**317** A35 1c on 6p multi .20 .20
**318** A34 2c on 4p multi .20 .20
**319** A27 3c on 1½p ultra & blk (U) .20 .20
**320** A34 8c on 1sh multi (U) .20 .20
**321** A34 10c on 2sh6p multi (U) .20 .20
**322** A28 20c on 2p lt brown (U) .40 .40
*Nos. 317-322,C56-C60 (11)* 6.10 6.10

5th anniv. of independence. The surcharge on No. 317 includes an "X" over old denomination.

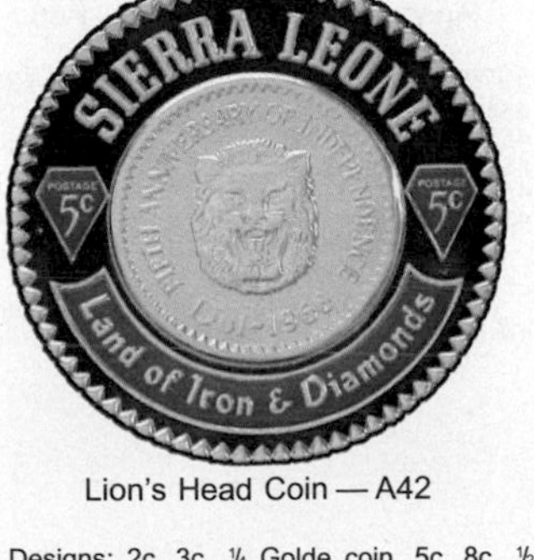

Lion's Head Coin — A42

Designs: 2c, 3c, ¼ Golde coin. 5c, 8c, ½ Golde coin. 25c, 1 le, 1 Golde coin. (3c, 8c, 1 le, Map of Sierra Leone.)

**Litho.; Embossed on Gilt Foil**

**1966, Nov. 12 Unwmk. *Die Cut***

**Self-adhesive**

**Diameter: 2c, 3c, 38mm; 5c, 8c, 54mm; 25c, 1 le, 82mm**

**323** A42 2c orange & dp plum .20 .20
**324** A42 3c red lilac & emerald .20 .20
**325** A42 5c vio blue & red org .20 .20
**326** A42 8c black & Prus blue .20 .20
**327** A42 25c emerald & violet .35 .35
**328** A42 1 le red & orange 1.75 1.75
*Nos. 323-328,C61-C66 (12)* 8.40 8.40

1st gold coinage of Sierra Leone. Advertising printed on paper backing.

Nos. 297-298, 303-305 and 316 Surcharged in Red, Silver, Violet, Green, Blue or Black:

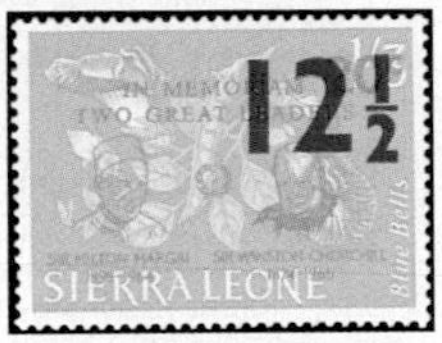

on A34, A35

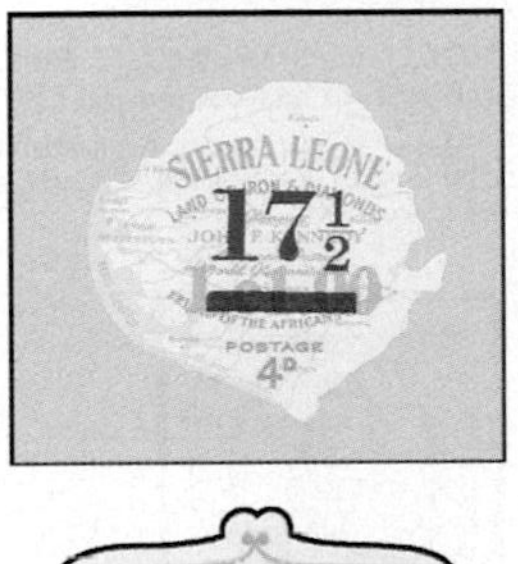

on A38, A39

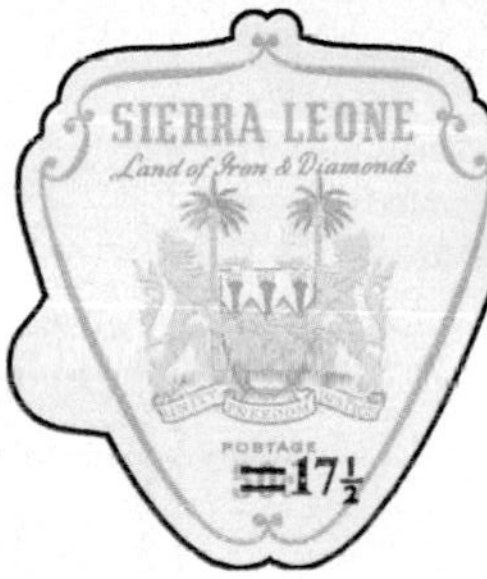

on A41

**1967, Dec. 2**

**329** A34 6½c on 75c on 5sh (R) .30 .30
**330** A34 7½c on 75c on 5sh (S) .30 .30
**331** A34 9½c on 50c on 4p (G) .40 .40
**332** A35 12½c on 20c on 1sh3p (V) .50 .50
**333** A39 17½c on 1 le on 4p (Bl) 3.50 3.50
**334** A41 17½c on 50c 3.50 3.50
**335** A38 18½c on 60c on 5sh 10.00 10.00
**336** A39 18½c on 1 le on 4p 3.50 3.50
**337** A41 25c on 50c 1.00 1.00
*Nos. 329-337,C67-C69 (12)* 24.90 24.90

Self-adhesive & Die Cut

Nos. 338-421 are self-adhesive and die cut.

Cola Nut Type of 1965

**Typographed; Embossed on White Paper**

**1967-68 Unwmk.**

**White Numeral Tablet**

**338** A40 ½c brt car, grn & yel .20 .20
**339** A40 1c brt car, grn & yel .20 .20
**340** A40 1½c orange, grn & yel .20 .20
**341** A40 2c brt car, grn & yel .25 .25
**342** A40 2½c emer, bl grn & yel .40 .40
**343** A40 3c brt car, grn & yel .25 .25
**344** A40 3½c olive, rose & ultra .25 .25
**345** A40 4½c gray ol, grn & yel .40 .40
**346** A40 5c brt car, grn & yel .40 .40
**347** A40 5½c red brn, grn & yel .45 .45
*Nos. 338-347 (10)* 3.00 3.00

Advertisements printed on peelable backing except on the 2c, 3c, 3½c and 5c.

**Colored Numeral Tablet**

**348** A40 ½c brt car, grn & yel .20 .20
**349** A40 1c brt car, grn & yel .20 .20
**350** A40 2c pink, brn & car .20 .20
**351** A40 2c brt car, grn & yel .75 .60
**352** A40 2½c bl grn, vio & org 1.00 .75
**353** A40 2½c emer, bl grn & yel .30 .20
**354** A40 3c brt car, grn & yel .20 .20
**355** A40 3½c lilac rose, grn & yel .30 .30
**356** A40 4c brt car, grn & yel .25 .25
*Nos. 348-356 (9)* 3.40 2.90

Nos. 344, 348-354 issued in 1968. Advertisements printed on peelable backing on the 3½c and 4c.

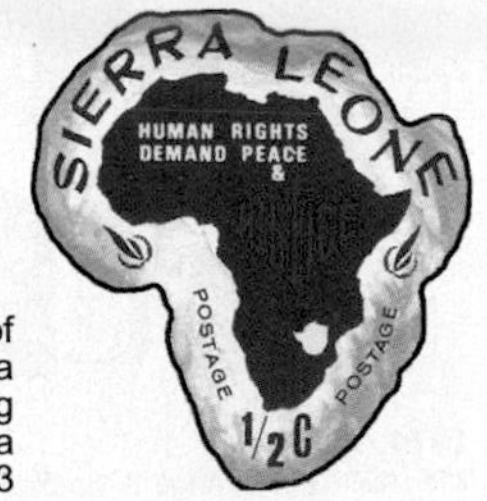

Map of Africa Showing Rhodesia A43

Each denomination shows map of Africa with map of one of the following countries—Portuguese Guinea, South Africa, Mozambique, Rhodesia, South West Africa or Angola.

**1968, Sept. 25 Unwmk. Litho.**

**357** A43 ½c multicolored .20 .20
**358** A43 2c multicolored .20 .20
**359** A43 2½c multicolored .20 .20
**360** A43 3½c multicolored .20 .20
**361** A43 10c multicolored .40 .40
**362** A43 11½c multicolored .45 .45
**363** A43 15c multicolored .60 .60
*Nos. 357-363 (7)* 2.25 2.25
7 Strips of 6 (1 of each design) (42) 11.40

Intl. Human Rights Year. Sheets of 30 have 5 horizontal rows containing one stamp of each design. Advertisements printed on peelable backing.

See #C72-C78. For surcharges see #C106-C111.

No. 316 Surcharged

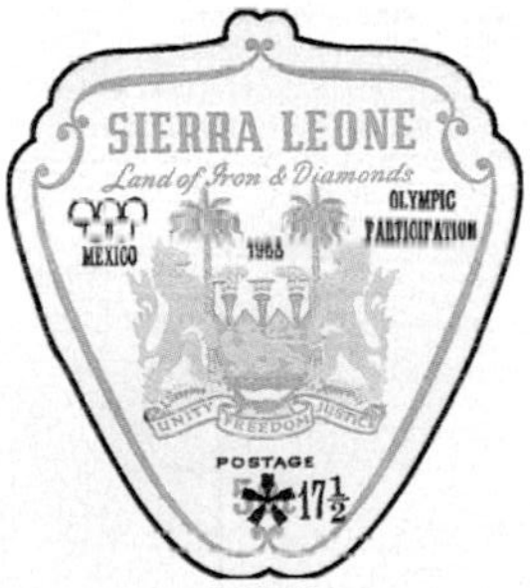

**Engraved; Embossed on Paper**

**1968, Nov. 30**

**364** A41 6½c on 50c multi .20 .20
**365** A41 17½c on 50c multi .30 .30
**366** A41 22½c on 50c multi .40 .40
**367** A41 28½c on 50c multi .50 .50
**368** A41 50c on 50c multi .85 .85
*Nos. 364-368,C79-C83 (10)* 4.65 4.65

19th Olympic Games, Mexico City, 10/12-27.

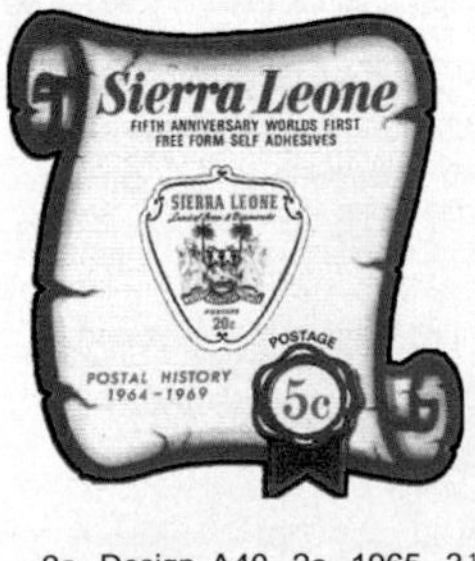

Sierra Leone Type A1, 1859 A44

2c, Design A40, 2c, 1965. 3½c, #220. 5c, #315. 12½c, #189. 1 le, Design A9, #2, 1912.

**1969, Mar. 1 Litho.**

**369** A44 1c multicolored .20 .20
**370** A44 2c multicolored .20 .20
**371** A44 3½c multicolored .20 .20
**372** A44 5c multicolored .20 .20
**373** A44 12½c multicolored .40 .40
**374** A44 1 le multicolored 4.75 4.75
*Nos. 369-374,C84-C89 (12)* 25.25 25.25

5th anniv. of free-form self-adhesive postage stamps. Various advertisements printed on peelable paper backing. No. 369 has side tab for handling and comes packed in boxes of 50. Nos. 370-374 are without side tabs and come 20 stamps attached to one sheet.

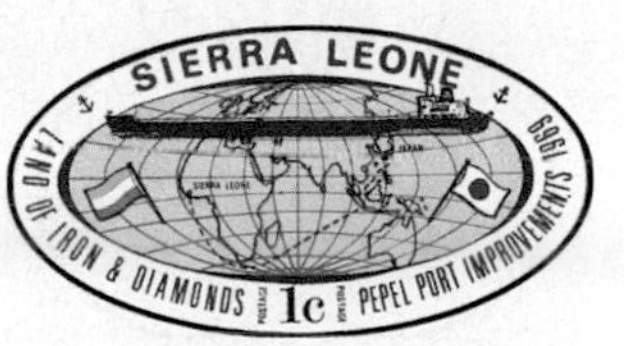

Globe, Freighter, Flags of Sierra Leone and Japan — A45

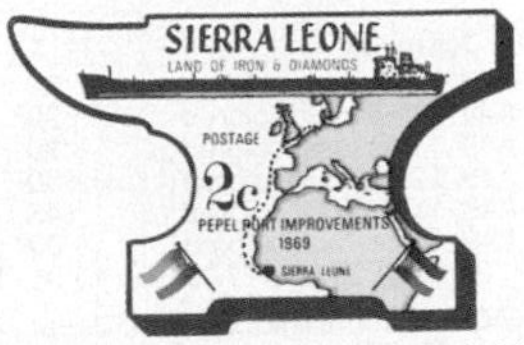

Map of Europe and Africa, Freighter, Flags of Sierra Leone and Netherlands — A46

Anvil Shape with Flags of Sierra Leone and: 3½c, Union Jack. 10c, 50c, West Germany. 18½c, Netherlands.

**1969, July 10**

**375** A45 1c multicolored .20 .20
**376** A46 2c multicolored .20 .20
**377** A46 3½c multicolored .20 .20
**378** A46 10c multicolored .20 .20
**379** A46 18½c multicolored .30 .30
**380** A46 50c multicolored .80 .80
*Nos. 375-380,C90-C95 (12)* 7.80 7.80

Completion of the Pepel Port iron ore carrier terminal. Various advertisements printed on peelable paper backing. No. 375 has side tab for handling and comes packed in boxes of 50. Nos. 376-380 are without side tabs and come 20 stamps attached to one sheet.

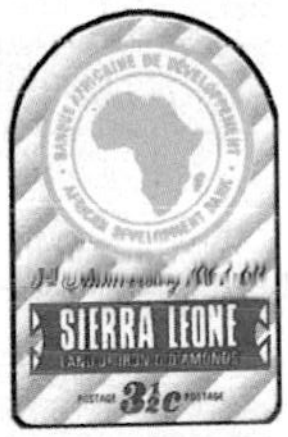

African Development Bank Emblem — A47

**Lithographed; Gold Impressed**

**1969, Sept. 10**

**381** A47 3½c lt blue, grn & gold .30 .30

5th anniv. of the African Development Bank. Advertising printed on peelable paper backing, 20 imperf. stamps to a sheet of backing, roulette 10. See No. C96.

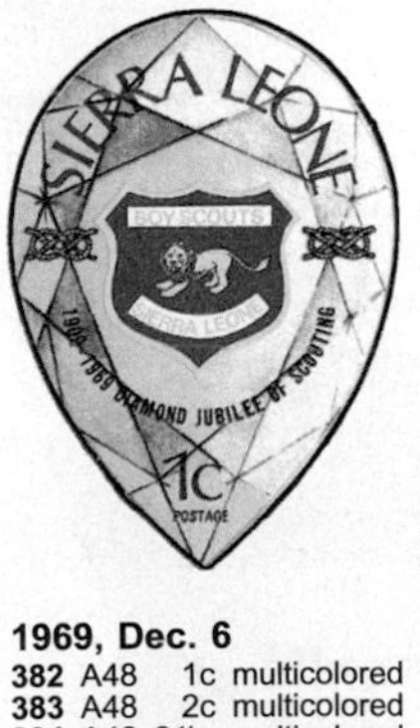

Diamond and Boy Scout Emblem A48

**1969, Dec. 6 Litho.**

**382** A48 1c multicolored .20 .20
**383** A48 2c multicolored .20 .20
**384** A48 3½c multicolored .20 .20
**385** A48 4½c multicolored .25 .20
**386** A48 5c multicolored .30 .30
**387** A48 75c multicolored 10.00 8.00
*Nos. 382-387,C100-C105 (12)* 123.50 91.20

60th anniv. of the Sierra Leone Boy Scouts. Various advertising printed on peelable paper backing. No. 382 has side tab for handling and comes packed in boxes of 100. Nos. 383-387 are without side tabs and come 20 stamps attached to one sheet.

**EXPO '70 Emblems, Torii, Maps of Sierra Leone and Japan — A49**

| | | | |
|---|---|---|---|
| 388 | A49 | 2c multicolored | .20 .20 |
| 389 | A49 | 3½c multicolored | .20 .20 |
| 390 | A49 | 10c multicolored | .20 .20 |
| 391 | A49 | 12½c multicolored | .30 .30 |
| 392 | A49 | 20c multicolored | .45 .45 |
| 393 | A49 | 45c multicolored | .45 .45 |

Nos. 388-393,C112-C117 (12) 13.05 13.05

EXPO '70 Int'l. Exhib., Osaka, Japan, Mar. 15-Sept. 13. Various advertising printed on peelable paper backing.

**1970, June 22**

| | | | |
|---|---|---|---|
| 413 | A52 | 40c multicolored | 3.25 1.35 |
| 414 | A52 | 1 le multicolored | 14.00 10.00 |

Nos. 409-414,C125-C130 (12) 68.65 44.55

Diamond industry. Advertisement printed on peelable paper backing. Sheets of 20.

Palm
Kernel — A51

Diamond
A50

**1971, Mar. 1 Litho.**

| | | | |
|---|---|---|---|
| 415 | A53 | 3½c orange & vio blue | .25 .25 |

Right hand traffic change-over. See No. C131. Advertisements printed on peelable paper backing.

Traffic
Pattern — A53

**Lithographed and Embossed**
**1970, Oct. 3 Unwmk.**

Light Blue Background

| | | | |
|---|---|---|---|
| 394 | A50 | 1c carmine & blk | .20 .20 |
| 395 | A50 | 1½c brt green & car | .20 .20 |
| 396 | A50 | 2c lilac & yel grn | .20 .20 |
| 397 | A50 | 4c orange | .20 .20 |
| 398 | A50 | 9c lilac | .20 .20 |
| 399 | A50 | 10c dark blue | .25 .25 |
| 400 | A50 | 3½c vio bl & org red | .25 .25 |
| 401 | A50 | 3c vio bl & grn | .30 .30 |
| 402 | A50 | 4c olive & ultra | .30 .30 |
| 403 | A50 | 5c black & lilac | .30 .30 |

Orange Brown Background

| | | | |
|---|---|---|---|
| 402 | A51 | 6c bright green | .30 .30 |
| 403 | A51 | 7c rose lilac | .45 .45 |
| 404 | A51 | 8½c orange | .50 .50 |
| 405 | A51 | 9c orange | .50 .50 |
| 406 | A51 | 10c dark blue | .55 .55 |
| 407 | A51 | 11½c blue | .75 .75 |
| 408 | A51 | 18½c yellow green | 1.10 1.10 |

Nos. 394-408,C118-C124 (22) 28.60 24.80

Advertisements printed on peelable paper backing. Packed in boxes of 500.

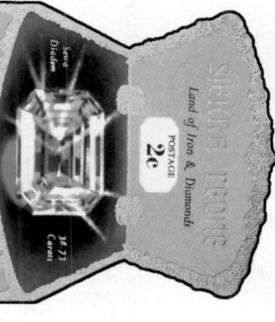

Sewa Diadem in Jewelry Box — A52

**1970, Dec. 30**

| | | | |
|---|---|---|---|
| 409 | A52 | 2c multicolored | .50 .20 |
| 410 | A52 | 3½c multicolored | .50 .20 |
| 411 | A52 | 10c multicolored | .90 .35 |
| 412 | A52 | 12½c multicolored | 1.00 .45 |

**Litho.; Embossed in Silver**
**1971, Apr. 27**

| | | | |
|---|---|---|---|
| 416 | A54 | 2c multicolored | .20 .20 |
| 417 | A54 | 3½c multicolored | .20 .20 |
| 418 | A54 | 10c multicolored | .20 .20 |
| 419 | A54 | 12½c multicolored | .20 .20 |
| 420 | A54 | 40c multicolored | .80 .80 |
| 421 | A54 | 1 le multicolored | 1.75 1.75 |

Nos. 416-421,C137-C142 (12) 12.20 12.20

10th anniversary of independence. Advertisements printed on peelable paper backing. Stamps are in shape of Sierra Leone map.

Flag and
Lion's
Head — A54

**1975, Oct. 3 Litho. Perf. 13x13½**

| | | | |
|---|---|---|---|
| 438 | A58 | 4c multicolored | 1.40 1.40 |

Mano River Union Agreement between Liberia and Sierra Leone, signed Oct. 3, 1973. See No. C145.

Pres. Tolbert and Stevens, Hands across Mano River — A58

**1975, Aug. 24 Litho. Perf. 13x13½**

| | | | |
|---|---|---|---|
| 437 | A57 | 5c multicolored | 11.00 11.00 |

Congo Bridge opening and Pres. Siaka Stevens' 70th birthday. See No. C144.

Pres. Siaka Stevens and Opening of Congo Bridge — A57

**1972 Litho.**

| | | | |
|---|---|---|---|
| 422 | A55 | 1c pink & multi | .20 .20 |
| 423 | A55 | 2c violet & multi | .20 .20 |
| 424 | A55 | 4c lt ultra & multi | .20 .20 |
| 425 | A55 | 5c buff & multi | .20 .20 |
| 426 | A55 | 7c rose & multi | .20 .20 |
| 427 | A55 | 10c olive & multi | .20 .20 |
| 428 | A55 | 15c emerald & multi | .25 .25 |
| 429 | A55 | 18c yellow & multi | .25 .25 |
| 430 | A55 | lt blue & multi | .35 .35 |
| 431 | A55 | 25c orange & multi | .40 .40 |
| 432 | A55 | 50c brt green & multi | .90 .90 |
| 433 | A55 | 1 le multicolored | 1.60 1.60 |
| 434 | A55 | 2 le red org & multi | 3.25 3.25 |
| 435 | A55 | 5 le multicolored | 16.75 16.75 |

Nos. 422-435 (14) 28.50 28.50

Pres. Siaka
Stevens — A55

Shades from later printings are found on several denominations including 1c, 2c, 7c, 10c, 1 le, 2 le.

**1977, Jan. 28 Litho. Perf. 13 rough**

| | | | |
|---|---|---|---|
| 439 | A59 | 30c multicolored | .80 .80 |

Mohammed Ali Jinnah (1876-1948), First Governor General of Pakistan.

Mohammed Ali Jinnah, Flags of Sierra Leone and Pakistan — A59

**1977, Nov. 28 Litho. Perf. 12½x12**

| | | | |
|---|---|---|---|
| 440 | A60 | 5c multicolored | .20 .20 |
| 441 | A60 | 1 le multicolored | 1.40 1.40 |

25th anniv. of the reign of Elizabeth II.

Elizabeth II — A60

**1975, Jan. 14 Litho. Perf. 13½**

| | | | |
|---|---|---|---|
| 436 | A56 | 4c multicolored | 125.00 82.50 |

African Development Bank, 10th anniversary. See No. C143.

Guma Valley Dam and Bank Emblem — A56

**1977, Dec. 19 Litho.**

| | | | |
|---|---|---|---|
| 442 | A61 | 5c multicolored | .20 .20 |
| 443 | A61 | 20c multicolored | .35 .35 |

Fourah Bay College, Mt. Aureol, Freetown, founded 1827.

Design: 20c, Old College, vert.

Fourah Bay College — A61

**1978, Sept. 14 Litho. Perf. 14½x14**

| | | | |
|---|---|---|---|
| 444 | A62 | 5c multicolored | .20 .20 |
| 445 | A62 | 50c multicolored | .60 .60 |
| 446 | A62 | 1 le multicolored | 1.90 1.90 |

Nos. 444-446 (3) 1.10 1.10

25th anniv. of coronation of Elizabeth II.

Designs: 50c, Elizabeth II in coronation coach, 1 le, Elizabeth II and Prince Philip on coronation day.

St. Edward's Crown and Scepters — A62

**1979, Apr. 9 Litho. Perf. 14½**

| | | | |
|---|---|---|---|
| 447 | A63 | 5c multicolored | .20 .20 |
| 448 | A63 | 15c multicolored | .35 .35 |
| 449 | A63 | 25c multicolored | .60 .60 |
| 450 | A63 | 1 le multicolored | 3.65 3.65 |

Nos. 447-450 (4) 2.50 2.50

Butterflies: 15c, Narrow blue-banded swallowtail. 25c, Pirate. 1 le, African giant swallowtail.

Fig Tree
Blue
A63

**1979, Aug. 13 Litho. Wmk. 373**

| | | | |
|---|---|---|---|
| 451 | A64 | 5c multicolored | .20 .20 |
| 452 | A64 | 27c multicolored | 2.25 2.25 |
| 453 | A64 | 1 le multicolored | 3.00 3.00 |
| a. | | Souvenir sheet of 1 | 2.50 2.50 |

Nos. 451-453 (3) 3.00 3.00

Int'l. Year of the Child and 30th anniv. of SOS villages (villages for homeless children).

Designs (Emblems and): 27c, Girl and infant. 1 le, Mother and infant.

Child, IYC and SOS Emblems — A64

**1979, Oct. 3 Litho. Perf. 13½**

| | | | |
|---|---|---|---|
| 454 | A65 | 5c multicolored | .20 .20 |
| 455 | A65 | 22c multicolored | .30 .30 |
| 456 | A65 | 27c multicolored | .40 .40 |
| 457 | A65 | 35c multicolored | .45 .45 |
| 458 | A65 | 1 le multicolored | 1.40 1.40 |
| a. | | Souvenir sheet of 1 | 2.75 2.75 |

Nos. 454-458 (5) 2.75 2.75

Mano River Union, 5th anniv.; Postal Union, 1st anniv.

Presidents Stevens and Tolbert, Pigeon Post, Mano River — A65

Sierra Leone No. 9, Hill — A66

**1979, Dec. 19 Litho. *Perf. 14½x14***
**459** A66 10c Grt. Britain #6 .20 .20
**460** A66 15c shown .25 .25
**461** A66 50c Sierra Leone #220 .90 .90
*Nos. 459-461 (3)* 1.35 1.35

**Souvenir Sheet**

**462** A66 1 le Sierra Leone #119 1.25 1.25

Sir Rowland Hill (1795-1879), originator.

Touraco A67

**1980, Jan. 29 *Perf. 14***
**463** A67 1c shown .20 .20
**464** A67 2c Olive-bellied sunbird .20 .20
**465** A67 3c Black-headed oriole .20 .20
**466** A67 5c Spur-winged goose .20 .20
**467** A67 7c White-bellied didric cuckoo .20 .20
**468** A67 10c Gray parrot, vert. .20 .20
**469** A67 15c African blue quail, vert. .45 .45
**470** A67 20c West African wood owl, vert. .60 .60
**471** A67 30c Blue plantain eater, vert. .90 .90
**472** A67 40c Nigerian blue-breasted kingfisher, vert. 1.10 1.10
**473** A67 50c Black crake, vert. 1.60 1.60
**474** A67 1 le Hartlaub's duck 3.00 3.00
**475** A67 2 le Black bee-eater 6.00 6.00
**476** A67 5 le Denham's bustard 15.00 15.00
*Nos. 463-476 (14)* 29.85 29.85

Reissues: Nos. 464-476 inscribed 1982. Nos. 463-464, 466, 468-473, 475-476 inscribed 1983.
For surcharges see Nos. 632-636. For overprints see Nos. 637-638.

Rotary Intl., 75th Anniv. A68

**1980, Feb. 23 *Perf. 14***
**477** A68 5c orange & multi .20 .20
**478** A68 27c red & multi .50 .50
**479** A68 50c green & multi 1.00 1.00
**480** A68 1 le blue & multi 2.10 2.10
*Nos. 477-480 (4)* 3.80 3.80

Mail Ship "Maria," 1884, London '80 Emblem A69

**1980, May 6 Litho. *Perf. 14***
**481** A69 6c shown .20 .20
**482** A69 31c "Tarquah," 1902 .45 .45
**483** A69 50c "Aureol," 1951 .75 .75
**484** A69 1 le "Africa Palm," 1974 1.50 1.50
*Nos. 481-484 (4)* 2.90 2.90

London 80 Intl. Stamp Exhib., May 6-14.

Conf. Emblem — A70

Small Striped Swordtail — A71

**1980, July 1 Litho. *Perf. 14½***
**485** A70 20c multicolored .25 .25
**486** A70 1 le multicolored 1.25 1.25

17th African Summit Conf., Freetown, July 1-4.

**1980, Oct. 6 Litho. *Perf. 14***
**487** A71 5c shown .20 .20
**488** A71 27c Pearl charaxes .45 .45
**489** A71 35c White barred charaxes .55 .55
**490** A71 1 le Zaddach's forester 1.65 1.65
*Nos. 487-490 (4)* 2.85 2.85

Freetown Airport — A72

**1980, Dec. 5 Litho. *Perf. 13½***
**491** A72 6c shown .20 .20
**492** A72 26c Mammy Yoko Hotel .30 .30
**493** A72 31c Freetown Cotton Tree .35 .35
**494** A72 40c Beindomgo Falls .50 .50
**495** A72 50c Water skiing .60 .60
**496** A72 1 le Elephant 1.25 1.25
*Nos. 491-496 (6)* 3.20 3.20

Servals — A73

Cats and Kittens: No. 498, Serval kittens. No. 500a, African golden cats. No. 502a, Leopards. No. 504a, Lions. Pairs have continuous design.

**1981, Feb. 23 Litho. *Perf. 14***
**497** A73 6c multicolored .20 .20
**498** A73 6c multicolored .20 .20
*a.* Pair, #497-498 .20 .20
**499** A73 31c multicolored .55 .55
**500** A73 31c multicolored .55 .55
*a.* Pair, #499-500 1.10 1.10
**501** A73 50c multicolored .90 .90
**502** A73 50c multicolored .90 .90
*a.* Pair, #501-502 1.90 1.90
**503** A73 1 le multicolored 1.90 1.90
**504** A73 1 le multicolored 1.90 1.90
*a.* Pair, #503-504 4.00 4.00
*Nos. 497-504 (8)* 7.10 7.10

Ambulance Clinic — A74

**Wmk. 373**

**1981, Apr. 18 Litho. *Perf. 14½***
**505** A74 6c Soldiers, vert. .40 .40
**506** A74 31c shown 1.25 1.25
**507** A74 40c Traffic policeman, vert. 1.75 1.75
**508** A74 1 le Coast Guard ship 4.00 4.00
*Nos. 505-508 (4)* 7.40 7.40

Anniv.: independence, 20th; republic, 10th.

**Royal Wedding Issue**
Common Design Type

**1981 Litho. *Perf. 12, 14***
**509** CD331 31c Bouquet .60 .60
**510** CD331 35c Sandringham .70 .70
**511** CD331 45c Charles .95 .95
**512** CD331 60c Charles 1.25 1.25
**513** CD331 70c like 35c 1.50 1.50
**514** CD331 1 le Couple 2.00 2.00
**515** CD331 1.30 le Charles 2.50 2.50
**516** CD331 1.50 le Couple 3.00 3.00
**517** CD331 2 le Couple 4.00 4.00
*Nos. 509-517 (9)* 16.50 16.50

**Souvenir Sheet**

**518** CD331 3 le Royal landau 5.00 5.00

31c, 45c, 1 le, 3 le issued July 22, perf. 14. 35c, 60c, 1.50 le issued in sheets of 5 plus label; perf. 12, Sept. 9. 70c, 1.30 le, 2 le issued in booklets only, perf. 14.
For surcharges see #540-546, 714, 716, 721.

Soccer Player — A75

**Wmk. 373**

**1981, Sept. 30 Litho. *Perf. 14***
**519** A75 6c shown .20 .20
**520** A75 31c Boys planting trees .45 .45
**521** A75 1 le Duke of Edinburgh 1.50 1.50
**522** A75 1 le Pres. Stevens 1.50 1.50
*Nos. 519-522 (4)* 3.65 3.65

Duke of Edinburgh's Awards and Pres. Steven's Awards, 25th anniv.

Pineapples — A76

Woman Tending Rice Plants — A77

***Perf. 14, 14½ (A77)***

**1981 Litho. Wmk. 373**
**523** A76 6c shown .20 .20
**524** A77 6c Peanuts for export .20 .20
**525** A76 31c Peanuts .50 .50
**526** A77 31c Crushing, eating cassava .50 .50
**527** A76 50c Cassava fruits .85 .85
**528** A77 50c shown .85 .85
**529** A76 1 le Rice plants 1.60 1.60
**530** A77 1 le Men tending pineapple plants 1.60 1.60
*Nos. 523-530 (8)* 6.30 6.30

World Food Day. Issue dates: Nos. 523, 525, 527, 529, Oct. 16; others, Nov. 2.

**Princess Diana Issue**
Common Design Type

**1982, July Litho. *Perf. 14½***
**531** CD332 31c Caernarvon Castle .50 .50
**532** CD332 50c Honeymoon .85 .85
**533** CD332 2 le Wedding 3.00 3.00
*Nos. 531-533 (3)* 4.35 4.35

**Souvenir Sheet**

**534** CD332 3 le Diana 4.75 4.75

Also issued in sheetlets of 5 + label.
For overprints and surcharges see Nos. 552-555, 713, 715, 717-720, 722-723.

Scouting Year A78

**1982, Aug. 23 *Perf. 14***
**535** A78 20c Studying animal husbandry .30 .30
**536** A78 50c Botanical study .85 .85
**537** A78 1 le Baden-Powell 1.60 1.60
**538** A78 2 le Fishing at campsite 3.00 3.00
*Nos. 535-538 (4)* 5.75 5.75

**Souvenir Sheet**

**539** A78 3 le Raising flag 4.75 4.75

For surcharges see Nos. 694-698.

Nos. 509-512, 514, 516, 518 Surcharged

**1982, Aug. 30 Wmk. 373**
**540** CD331 50c on 31c 1.60 1.60
**541** CD331 50c on 35c 1.60 1.60
**542** CD331 50c on 45c 1.60 1.60
**543** CD331 50c on 60c 1.60 1.60
**544** CD331 90c on 1 le 2.75 2.75
**545** CD331 2 le on 1.50 le 6.00 6.00
*Nos. 540-545 (6)* 15.15 15.15

**Souvenir Sheet**

**546** CD331 3.50 le on 3 le 6.00 6.00

1982 World Cup — A79

Designs: Various soccer players.

**1982, Sept. 7**
**547** A79 20c multicolored .45 .45
**548** A79 30c multicolored .65 .65
**549** A79 1 le multicolored 2.25 2.25
**550** A79 2 le multicolored 4.25 4.25
*Nos. 547-550 (4)* 7.60 7.60

**Souvenir Sheet**

**551** A79 3 le multicolored 6.00 6.00

For overprints see Nos. 561-565.

Nos. 531-534 Overprinted: "ROYAL BABY/ 21.6.82"

**1982, Oct. 15 Litho. *Perf. 14½***
**552** CD332 31c multicolored .50 .50
**553** CD332 50c multicolored .85 .85
**554** CD332 2 le multicolored 3.00 3.00
*Nos. 552-554 (3)* 4.35 4.35

**Souvenir Sheet**

**555** CD332 3 le multicolored 4.75 4.75

Birth of Prince William of Wales, June 21.
Also issued in sheetlets of 5 + label.
For surcharges see #715, 719-720, 723.

**George Washington — A80**

**1982, Oct. 30          Litho.          Perf. 14**

| | | | |
|---|---|---|---|
| 556 | A80 | 6c multicolored | .20  .20 |
| 557 | A80 | 31c multicolored | .45  .45 |
| 558 | A80 | 50c multicolored | .75  .75 |
| 559 | A80 | 1 le multicolored | 1.50  1.50 |
| | | Nos. 556-559 (4) | 2.90  2.90 |

*Souvenir Sheet*

| 560 | A80 | 2 le multicolored | 3.00  3.00 |
|---|---|---|---|

Various paintings of Washington. 31c, 1 le, vert.

**1982, Nov. 9          Perf. 14**

| 561 | A79 | 20c multicolored | .30  .30 |
|---|---|---|---|
| 562 | A79 | 30c multicolored | .45  .45 |
| 563 | A79 | 1 le multicolored | 1.50  1.50 |
| 564 | A79 | 2 le multicolored | 2.75  2.75 |
| | | Nos. 561-564 (4) | 5.00  5.00 |

*Souvenir Sheet*

| 565 | A79 | 3 le multicolored | 4.25  4.25 |
|---|---|---|---|

Nos. 547-551 Overprinted with Finalists and Score
Italy's victory in 1982 World Cup.

**Christmas — A81**

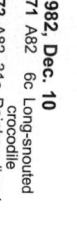

**1982, Nov. 18          Perf. 14**

| 566 | A81 | 6c Temptation of Christ | .20  .20 |
|---|---|---|---|
| 567 | A81 | 31c Baptism of Christ | .45  .45 |
| 568 | A81 | 50c Annunciation | .75  .75 |
| 569 | A81 | 1 le Nativity | 1.50  1.50 |
| | | Nos. 566-569 (4) | 2.90  2.90 |

*Souvenir Sheet*

| 570 | A81 | 2 le Mary and Joseph | 3.00  3.00 |
|---|---|---|---|

Stained-glass Windows, St. George's Cathedral, Freetown.

**Charles Darwin (1809-82) — A82**

**1982, Dec. 10**

| 571 | A82 | 6c Long-snouted crocodile | .50  .50 |
|---|---|---|---|
| 572 | A82 | 31c Rainbow lizard | 1.50  1.50 |
| 573 | A82 | 50c River turtle | 2.75  2.75 |
| 574 | A82 | 1 le Chameleon | 5.25  5.25 |
| | | Nos. 571-574 (4) | 10.00  10.00 |

*Souvenir Sheet*

| 575 | A82 | 2 le Royal python, vert. | 3.75  3.75 |
|---|---|---|---|

**500th Birth Anniv. of Raphael — A83**

School of Athens, Fresco, Vatican. Nos. 576-579 show details.

**1983, Jan. 28          Litho.          Perf. 14**

| 576 | A83 | 6c Diogenes | .20  .20 |
|---|---|---|---|
| 577 | A83 | 31c Euclid, Ptolemy | .45  .45 |
| 578 | A83 | 50c Euclid and his Students | .75  .75 |
| 579 | A83 | 1 le Pythagoras, Heraclitus | 1.50  1.50 |
| | | Nos. 576-579 (4) | |

*Souvenir Sheet*

| 580 | A83 | 3 le Entire painting | 4.50  4.50 |
|---|---|---|---|

**1983, Mar. 14          Litho.          Perf. 14**

| 581 | A83a | 6c Agricultural training | .20  .20 |
|---|---|---|---|
| 582 | A83a | 10c Tourism development | .20  .20 |
| 583 | A83a | 50c Broadcast training | .75  .75 |
| 584 | A83a | 1 le Airport services | 1.50  1.50 |
| | | Nos. 581-584 (4) | 2.65  2.65 |

Commonwealth Day.

**25th Anniv. of Economic Commission for Africa — A84**

**1983, Apr. 29          Litho.          Perf. 13½x13**

| 585 | A84 | 1 le multicolored | 1.40  1.40 |
|---|---|---|---|

**1983, May          Litho.          Perf. 14**

| 586 | A85 | 6c multicolored | 2.00  2.00 |
|---|---|---|---|
| 587 | A85 | 10c multicolored | 2.00  2.00 |
| 588 | A85 | 31c multicolored | 4.25  4.25 |
| 589 | A85 | 60c multicolored | 7.00  7.00 |
| | | Nos. 586-589 (4) | 15.75  15.75 |

*Souvenir Sheet*

| 590 | A84 | 3 le Elephants | 5.50  5.50 |
|---|---|---|---|

**Endangered Chimpanzees, World Wildlife Fund Emblem — A85**

Various chimpanzees from Outamba-Kilimi Natl. Park. 10c, 31c, vert.

**World Communications Year — A86**

**1983, July 14          Perf. 14**

| 591 | A86 | 6c Traditional communications | .20  .20 |
|---|---|---|---|
| 592 | A86 | 10c Mano River mail | .20  .20 |
| 593 | A86 | 20c Satellite ground station | .30  .30 |
| 594 | A86 | 1 le English packet, 1805 | 1.50  1.50 |
| | | Nos. 591-594 (4) | 2.20  2.20 |

*Souvenir Sheet*

| 595 | A86 | 2 le Map, phone, envelope | 3.00  3.00 |
|---|---|---|---|

**Manned Flight Bicentenary — A87**

**1983, Aug. 31          Litho.          Perf. 14**

| 596 | A87 | 6c Montgolfiere, 1783, vert. | .30  .30 |
|---|---|---|---|
| 597 | A87 | 20c Deutschland blimp, 1897 | .70  .70 |
| 598 | A87 | 50c Norge I blimp, North Pole, 1926 | 1.60  1.60 |
| 599 | A87 | 1 le Cape Sierra sport balloon, Freetown, 1983, vert. | 3.25  3.25 |
| | | Nos. 596-599 (4) | 5.85  5.85 |

*Souvenir Sheet*

| 600 | A87 | 2 le Futuristic airship | 5.00  5.00 |
|---|---|---|---|

**Walt Disney, Space Ark Fantasy — A88**

**1983, Nov.          Litho.          Perf. 14**

| 601 | A88 | 1c Hippopotamus, Huey, Dewey and Louie | .20  .20 |
|---|---|---|---|
| 602 | A88 | 1c Mickey Mouse and Snake | .20  .20 |
| 603 | A88 | 3c Elephant and Donald Duck | .20  .20 |
| 604 | A88 | 3c Zebra and Goofy | .20  .20 |
| 605 | A88 | 10c Lion and Ludwig von Drake | .20  .20 |
| 606 | A88 | 10c Rhinoceros and Goofy | .20  .20 |
| 607 | A88 | 2 le Giraffe and Mickey Mouse | 1.75  1.75 |
| 608 | A88 | 3 le Monkey and Donald Duck | 2.50  2.50 |
| | | Nos. 601-608 (8) | 5.45  5.45 |

*Souvenir Sheet*

| 609 | A88 | 5 le Mickey Mouse and animals | 4.50  4.50 |
|---|---|---|---|

**10th Anniv. of Mano River Union A89**

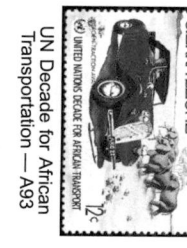

**1984, Feb. 8          Litho.          Perf. 15**

| 610 | A89 | 6c Teaching Program graduates | .20  .20 |
|---|---|---|---|
| 611 | A89 | 25c Emblem | .20  .20 |
| 612 | A89 | 31c Map, presidents | .25  .25 |
| 613 | A89 | 41c Guinea Accession signing | .35  .35 |
| | | Nos. 610-613 (4) | 1.00  1.00 |
| a. | | Souvenir sheet of 1 | 1.00  1.00 |

**23rd Olympic Games, Los Angeles, July 28-Aug. 12 — A90**

**1984, Mar. 15          Perf. 14**

| 614 | A90 | 90c Gymnastics | .65  .65 |
|---|---|---|---|
| 615 | A90 | 1 le Hurdles | .70  .70 |
| 616 | A90 | 3 le Javelin | 2.25  2.25 |
| | | Nos. 614-616 (3) | 3.60  3.60 |

*Souvenir Sheet*

| 617 | A90 | 7 le Boxing | 5.25  5.25 |
|---|---|---|---|

For surcharges see Nos. 699-702.

**Apollo 11, 15th Anniv. — A91**

**1984, May 14          Litho.          Perf. 14**

| 618 | A91 | 50c Lift off | .40  .40 |
|---|---|---|---|
| 619 | A91 | 75c Lunar landing | .60  .60 |
| 620 | A91 | 1.25 le 1st step on moon | 1.00  1.00 |
| 621 | A91 | 2.50 le Walking on moon | 2.00  2.00 |
| | | Nos. 618-621 (4) | 4.00  4.00 |

*Souvenir Sheet*

| 622 | A91 | 5 le TV transmission, horiz. | 4.00  4.00 |
|---|---|---|---|

**UPU Congress A92**

**1984, June 19          Perf. 14**

| 623 | A92 | 4 le Concorde | 4.25  4.25 |
|---|---|---|---|
| 624 | A92 | 4 le UPU emblem, von Stephan | 3.25  3.25 |

*Souvenir Sheet*

**UN Decade for African Transportation — A93**

Various cars.

**1984, July 16          Perf. 14½x15**

| 625 | A93 | 1.50 le Citroen | .95  .95 |
|---|---|---|---|
| 626 | A93 | 60c Locomobile | .60  .60 |
| 627 | A93 | 60c AC Ace | .75  .75 |
| 628 | A93 | 1 le Vauxhall Prince Henry | .95  .95 |
| 629 | A93 | 1.50 le Delahaye-185 | 1.90  1.90 |
| 630 | A93 | 2 le Mazda | 1.90  1.90 |
| | | Nos. 625-630 (6) | 5.90  5.90 |

*Souvenir Sheet*

| 631 | A93 | 6 le Volkswagon Beetle | 5.00  5.00 |
|---|---|---|---|

**1984, Aug. 3          Litho.          Perf. 14**

| 632 | A67 | 25c on 10c multi | .20  .20 |
|---|---|---|---|
| 633 | A67 | 40c on 10c multi | .30  .30 |
| 634 | A67 | 60c on 10c multi | .30  .30 |
| 635 | A67 | 70c on 5c multi | .55  .55 |
| 636 | A67 | 10 le on 5c multi | 8.00  8.00 |
| | | Nos. 632-636 (5) | 9.55  9.55 |

#473, 476 Ovptd: "AUSIPEX 84"

**1984, Aug. 22          Litho.          Perf. 14**

| 637 | A67 | 50c multicolored | 2.50  2.50 |
|---|---|---|---|
| 638 | A67 | 5 le multicolored | 27.50  27.50 |

Nos. 466, 468, 475 Surcharged

**Portuguese Caravel Da Sintra — A94**

**1984          Wmk. 373**

| 639 | A94 | 2c shown | .80  1.50 |
|---|---|---|---|
| 640 | A94 | 5c Merlin of Bristol | .80  .80 |
| 641 | A94 | 10c Golden Hind | 1.25  .60 |
| 642 | A94 | 15c Interloper Mordaunt | .60  .60 |

643 A94 20c Navy Board Transport Atlantic 1.50 .60
644 A94 25c Navy Vessel Lapwing 1.50 .60
645 A94 30c Brig Traveller 1.50 .60
646 A94 40c Schooner Amistad 1.60 .90
647 A94 50c Teazer 1.75 1.10
648 A94 70c Cable Ship Scotia 2.00 1.60
649 A94 1 le Alecto 2.50 2.25
650 A94 2 le Blonde 5.00 4.50
651 A94 5 le Fox 14.00 12.00
652 A94 10 le Mail ship Accra 24.00 24.00
*Nos. 639-652 (14)* 60.20 51.65

Issued: #639-649, 9/5; #650-651, 10/9; 10 le, 11/7.

See #739-740. For surcharges see #809-812.

**1985** *Perf. 12½x12*

| | | | | |
|---|---|---|---|---|
| *639a* | A94 | 2c | .20 | .20 |
| *640a* | A94 | 5c | .20 | .20 |
| *641a* | A94 | 10c | .20 | .20 |
| *643a* | A94 | 20c | .20 | .20 |
| *644a* | A94 | 25c | .20 | .20 |
| *645a* | A94 | 30c | .20 | .20 |
| *646a* | A94 | 40c | .20 | .20 |
| *647a* | A94 | 50c | .20 | .20 |
| *648a* | A94 | 70c | .20 | .20 |
| *649a* | A94 | 1 le | 1.10 | 1.10 |
| *650a* | A94 | 2 le | 2.10 | 2.10 |
| *651a* | A94 | 5 le | 5.25 | 5.25 |
| *652a* | A94 | 10 le | 10.50 | 10.50 |
| | *Nos. 639a-652a (13)* | | 20.75 | 20.75 |

125th Anniv. of Sierra Leone Postage Stamps A95

**1984, Oct. 9**
653 A95 50c Mail messenger, No. 2 .35 .35
654 A95 2 le Post Master receiving letters, No. 2 1.50 1.50
655 A95 3 le Cover 2.40 2.40
*Nos. 653-655 (3)* 4.25 4.25

**Souvenir Sheet**

656 A95 5 le Penny Black, No. 2 3.25 3.25

50th Anniv. of Donald Duck — A95a

**1984, Nov. Litho.** *Perf. 14x13½*
657 A95a 1c Wise Little Hen .20 .20
658 A95a 2c Boat Builders .20 .20
659 A95a 3c Three Caballeros .20 .20
660 A95a 4c Mathematic Land .20 .20
661 A95a 5c Mickey Mouse Club .20 .20
662 A95a 10c On Parade .20 .20
663 A95a 1 le Don Donald 1.10 1.10
663A A95a 2 le Donald gets drafted, p. 12½x12 2.25 2.25
664 A95a 4 le Tokyo Disneyland 4.50 4.50
*Nos. 657-664 (9)* 9.05 9.05

**Souvenir Sheet**

665 A95a 5 le Sketches 7.25 7.25

Christmas — A96

Mother and Child paintings.

**1984, Nov. 28** *Perf. 14*
666 A96 20c Pisanello .95 .95
667 A96 1 le Memling 2.25 2.25
668 A96 2 le Raphael 3.25 3.25
669 A96 3 le van der Werff 7.25 7.25
*Nos. 666-669 (4)* 13.70 13.70

**Souvenir Sheet**

670 A96 6 le Picasso 4.25 4.25

Songbirds A97

**1985, Jan. 31** **Litho.**
671 A97 40c Straw-tailed whydah .40 .40
672 A97 90c Spotted flycatcher .95 .95
673 A97 1.30 le Garden warbler 1.40 1.40
674 A97 3 le Speke's weaver 3.00 3.00
*Nos. 671-674 (4)* 5.75 5.75

**Souvenir Sheet**

675 A97 5 le Great gray shrike 5.00 5.00

International Youth Year — A98

**1985, Feb. 14** **Litho.**
676 A98 1.15 le Fishing 1.10 1.10
677 A98 1.50 le Timber 1.40 1.40
678 A98 2.15 le Rice farming 2.00 2.00
*Nos. 676-678 (3)* 4.50 4.50

**Souvenir Sheet**

679 A98 5 le Diamond polishing 4.50 4.50

Intl. Civil Aviation Org., 40th Anniv. A100

Early aviators and their aircraft: 70c, Eddie Rickenbacker, Spad XIII (1918). 1.25 le, Samuel P. Langley, Aerodrome No. 5. 1.30 le, Orville and Wilbur Wright, Flyer 1. 2 le, Charles Lindbergh, Spirit of St. Louis.

**1985, Feb. 28 Litho.** *Perf. 14*
680 A100 70c multicolored 1.25 1.25
681 A100 1.25 le multicolored 2.25 2.25
682 A100 1.30 le multicolored 2.25 2.25
683 A100 2 le multicolored 4.00 4.00
*Nos. 680-683 (4)* 9.75 9.75

**Souvenir Sheet**

684 A100 5 le Jet over Freetown 4.50 4.50

Easter A101

Religious paintings: Nos. 685, 687, 689 by Botticelli (1445-1510). Nos. 686, 688 by Velazquez (1599-1660).

**1985, Apr. 29**
685 A101 45c The Temptation of Christ .20 .20
686 A101 70c Christ at the Column .35 .35
687 A101 1.55 le Pieta .80 .80
688 A101 10 le Christ on the Cross 6.00 6.00
*Nos. 685-688 (4)* 7.35 7.35

**Souvenir Sheet**

689 A101 12 le Man of Sorrows 6.00 6.00

Queen Mother, 85th Birthday — A102

Designs: 1 le, Queen Mother at St. Peter's Cathedral, London, vert. 1.70 le, With Double Star at Sandown Racetrack. 10 le, Attending the gala ballet at Covent Garden, 1971, vert. 12 le, With Princess Anne at Ascot, vert.

**1985, July 8 Litho.** *Perf. 14*
690 A102 1 le multicolored .30 .30
691 A102 1.70 le multicolored .60 .60
692 A102 10 le multicolored 3.25 3.25
*Nos. 690-692 (3)* 4.15 4.15

**Souvenir Sheet**

693 A102 12 le multicolored 4.00 4.00

Nos. 535-539 Surcharged "75th Anniversary / of Girl Guides," Black Bar and New Value

**1985, July 25**
694 A78 70c on 20c multi .90 .90
695 A78 1.30 le on 50c multi 1.90 1.90
696 A78 5 le on 1 le multi 1.25 1.25
697 A78 7 le on 2 le multi 2.50 2.50
*Nos. 694-697 (4)* 6.55 6.55

**Souvenir Sheet**

698 A78 15 le on 3 le multi 5.50 5.50

Nos. 614-617 Surcharged with Winners Names, Country, "Gold Medal," Black Bar and New Value

**1985, July 25**
699 A90 2 le on 90c Ma Yanhonjg, China .80 .80
700 A90 4 le on 1 le E. Moses, USA 1.50 1.50
701 A90 8 le on 3 le A. Haerkoenen, Finland 3.00 3.00
*Nos. 699-701 (3)* 5.30 5.30

**Souvenir Sheet**

702 A90 15 le on 7 le M. Taylor, USA 5.50 5.50

1905 Chater-Lea, Hill Station House — A103

Designs: 2 le, Honda XR 350 R, QE II Quay. 4 le, Kawasaki Vulcan, Bo Clock Tower. 5 le, Harley-Davidson Electra-Glide, Makeni. 12 le, 1893 Millet.

**1985, Aug. 15**
703 A103 1.40 le multicolored 1.10 1.10
704 A103 2 le multicolored 1.50 1.50
705 A103 4 le multicolored 3.00 3.00
706 A103 5 le multicolored 3.75 3.75
*Nos. 703-706 (4)* 9.35 9.35

**Souvenir Sheet**

707 A103 12 le multicolored 4.00 4.00

Motorcycle cent., Decade for African Transport.

A104

Christmas — A105

**1985, Sept. 3**
708 A104 70c Viola pomposa .50 .50
709 A104 3 le Spinet 2.00 2.00
710 A104 4 le Lute 2.50 2.50
711 A104 5 le Oboe 3.25 3.25
*Nos. 708-711 (4)* 8.25 8.25

**Souvenir Sheet**

712 A104 12 le Portrait 6.50 6.50

Johann Sebastian Bach (1685-1750), composer. Nos. 708-712 show music from "Clavier Ubang."

Nos. 510, 512, 516, 531-534, 552-555 Surcharged

**1985, Sept. 30** ***Perfs. as Before***
**Designs CD331-CD332**
713 70c on 31c #531 .50 .50
714 1.30 le on 60c #512 .90 .90
715 1.30 le on 31c #552 .90 .90
716 2 le on 35c #510 1.25 1.25
717 4 le on 50c #532 2.75 2.75
718 5 le on 2 le #533 3.25 3.25
719 5 le on 50c #553 3.25 3.25
720 7 le on 2 le #554 4.50 4.50
721 8 le on 1.50 le #516 5.50 5.50
*Nos. 713-721 (9)* 22.80 22.80

**Souvenir Sheets**

722 15 le on 3 le #534 7.00 7.00
723 15 le on 3 le #555 7.00 7.00

**1985, Oct. 18 Litho.** *Perf. 14*

Madonna and child paintings by: 70c, Carlo Crivelli (c. 1430-1494). 3 le, Dirk Bouts (c. 1400-1475). 4 le, Antonello de Messina (c. 1430-1479). 5 le, Stefan Lochner (c. 1400-1451). 12 le, Miniature from the Book of Kells, 9th cent., Ireland.

724 A105 70c multicolored .25 .25
725 A105 3 le multicolored 1.00 1.00
726 A105 4 le multicolored 1.25 1.25
727 A105 5 le multicolored 1.60 1.60
*Nos. 724-727 (4)* 4.10 4.10

**Miniature Sheet**

728 A105 12 le multicolored 4.00 4.00

Jacob and Wilhelm Grimm, Fabulists — A106

Mark Twain, American Humorist A107

Walt Disney characters acting out Twain quotes (A107) or in Rumpelstiltskin (A106).

**1985, Oct. 30 Litho.** *Perf. 14*
729 A106 70c multicolored .35 .35
730 A106 1.30 le multicolored .55 .55
731 A107 1.50 le multicolored .60 .60
732 A106 2 le multicolored .75 .75
733 A107 3 le multicolored 1.10 1.10
734 A107 4 le multicolored 1.75 1.75
735 A107 5 le multicolored 1.90 1.90
736 A106 10 le multicolored 3.75 3.75
*Nos. 729-736 (8)* 10.75 10.75

**Souvenir Sheets**

737 A106 15 le multicolored 8.75 8.75
738 A107 15 le multicolored 7.25 7.25

Nos. 731, 733-735 bear the Intl. Youth Year emblem.

Ship Type of 1984

**1985, Nov. 15**
739 A94 15 le Favourite 4.50 4.50
740 A94 25 le Euryalus 7.50 7.50

# SIERRA LEONE

UN, 40th Anniv. A108

Stamps of UN and famous men: 2 le, No. 30, Kennedy; 4 le, No. 59, Einstein. 7 le, No. 44, Maimonides (1135-1204), medieval Judaic scholar. 12 le, Martin Luther King, Jr. (1929-1968), civil rights leader, vert.

15c, Johannes Kepler (1571-1630), German astronomer, & Paris Observatory. 50c, US space shuttle landing, 1985. 70c, Bayeux Tapestry (detail), 1066 sighting. 10 le, Arthurian Comet over Sierra Leone.

**1985, Nov. 28**    Litho.    Perf. 14½
- 741 A108 2 le multicolored   1.25   1.25
- 742 A108 4 le multicolored   2.40   2.40
- 743 A108 7 le multicolored   4.25   4.25
- Nos. 741-743 (3)   7.90   7.90

**Souvenir Sheet**
- 744 A108 12 le multicolored   4.00   4.00

1986 World Cup Soccer Championships A109

Various soccer plays.

**1986, Mar. 3**    Litho.    Perf. 14
- 745 A109 70c multicolored   .40   .40
- 746 A109 3 le multicolored   1.40   1.40
- 747 A109 4 le multicolored   1.90   1.90
- 748 A109 5 le multicolored   2.50   2.50
- Nos. 745-748 (4)   6.20   6.20

**Souvenir Sheet**
- 749 A109 12 le multicolored   4.50   4.50

For overprints and surcharges see Nos. 788-792.

Statue of Liberty, Cent. — A110

**1986, Mar. 11**
- 750 A110 40c multicolored   .20   .20
- 751 A110 70c multicolored   .45   .45
- 752 A110 1 le multicolored   .45   .45
- 753 A110 10 le multicolored   3.00   3.00
- Nos. 750-753 (4)   3.85   3.85

**Souvenir Sheet**
- 754 A110 12 le multicolored   4.00   4.00

New York City: 40c, Times Square, 1905. 70c, Times Square, 1986. 1 le, Tally Ho Coach, c. 1880, horiz. 10 le, Statue of Liberty. 12 le, Statue of Liberty.

Halley's Comet — A112

HALLEY'S COMET 1985-6 SIERRA LEONE Le.12    A111

---

**1986, Apr. 1**    Litho.
- 755 A111 15c multicolored   .20   .20
- 756 A111 50c multicolored   .30   .30
- 757 A111 70c multicolored   .30   .30
- 758 A111 10 le multicolored   4.70   4.70
- Nos. 755-758 (4)   5.50   5.50

**Souvenir Sheet**
- 759 A112 12 le multicolored   2.75   2.75

For overprints and surcharges see Nos. 813-817.

Queen Elizabeth II, 60th Birthday
Common Design Type

**1986, Apr. 21**
- 760 CD339 10c Cranwell, 1951   .20   .20
- 761 CD339 1.70 le Garter Ceremony   .50   .50
- 762 CD339 10 le Braemar Games, 1970   2.50   2.50
- Nos. 760-762 (3)   3.20   3.20

**Souvenir Sheet**
- 763 CD339 12 le Windsor Castle, 1943   2.50   2.50

For surcharges see Nos. 793-795.

AMERIPEX '86 — A113

Locomotives.

**1986, May 22**
- 764 A113 50c Hiawatha, Milwaukee   .20   .20
- 765 A113 2 le The Rocket, Rock Is.   1.10   1.10
- 766 A113 4 le Prospector, Rio Grande   2.00   2.00
- 767 A113 7 le Daylight, So. Pacific   3.00   3.00
- Nos. 764-767 (3)   3.75   3.75

**Souvenir Sheet**
- 768 A113 12 le Broadway, Pennsylvania   5.00   5.00

Royal Wedding Issue, 1986
Common Design Type

Designs: 10c, Prince Andrew and Sarah Ferguson. 1.70 le, Andrew with shotgun. 10 le, Andrew saluting. 12 le, Couple, diff.

**1986, July 23**
- 769 CD340 10c multi   .20   .20
- 770 CD340 1.70 le multi   .35   .35
- 771 CD340 10 le multi   1.60   1.60
- Nos. 769-771 (3)   2.15   2.15

**Souvenir Sheet**
- 772 CD340 12 le multi   2.75   2.75

For surcharges see Nos. 796-798.

Indigenous Flowers — A114

**1986, Aug. 25**    Litho.    Perf. 15
- 773 A114 70c Monodora myristica   .20   .20
- 774 A114 1.50 le Gloriosa simplex   1.00   1.00
- 775 A114 4 le Mussaenda erythrophylla   .45   .45
- 776 A114 6 le Crinum ornatum   .70   .70
- 777 A114 8 le Bauhinia purpurea   .80   .80
- 778 A114 10 le Bombax costatum   1.00   1.00
- 779 A114 20 le Hibiscus rosa-sinensis   1.75   1.75
- 780 A114 30 le Cassia fistula   2.25   2.25
- Nos. 773-780 (8)   8.15   8.15

**Souvenir Sheets**
- 781 A114 40 le Clitoria ternatea   3.75   3.75
- 782 A114 40 le Plumbago auriculata   3.75   3.75

US Peace Corps in Sierra Leone, 25th Anniv. A115

SIERRA LEONE PARTNERS FOR PROGRESS 25th ANNIVERSARY Le.10

**1986, Aug. 26**    Litho.    Perf. 14
- 783 A115 10 le multi   1.10   1.10

Int'l Peace Year A116

**1986, Sept. 1**
- 784 A116 1 le Transportation   .40   .40
- 785 A116 2 le Education   .55   .55
- 786 A116 5 le Communications   1.00   1.00
- 787 A116 10 le Fishing   1.90   1.90
- Nos. 784-787 (4)   3.85   3.85

Nos. 745-749 Ovptd. or Surcharged "WINNERS / Argentina 3 / West Germany 2" in Gold

**1986, Sept. 15**
- 788 A109 1 le multi   .40   .40
- 789 A109 3 le multi   .90   .90
- 790 A109 4 le multi   .95   .95
- 791 A109 40 le on 5 le multi   8.00   8.00
- Nos. 788-791 (4)   10.25   10.25

**Souvenir Sheet**
- 792 A109 40 le on 12 le multi   4.50   4.50

Nos. 760, 762-763 Surcharged in Silver or Black

**1986, Sept. 15**
- 793 CD339 70c on 10c multi   .50   .50
- 794 CD339 45 le on 10 le multi   4.00   4.00

**Souvenir Sheet**
- 795 CD339 50 le on 12 le multi (B)   3.25   3.25

Nos. 769, 771-772 Surcharged in Silver

**1986, Sept. 15**
- 796 CD340 70c on 10c multi   .20   .20
- 797 CD340 45 le on 10 le multi   2.50   2.50

**Souvenir Sheet**
- 798 CD340 50 le on 12 le multi   3.75   3.75

STOCKHOLMIA '86 — A117

Disney characters in Mother Goose fairy tales.

**1986, Sept. 22**    Perf. 11
- 799 A117 70c Jack and Jill   .20   .20
- 800 A117 1 le Wee Willie Winkie   .20   .20
- 801 A117 2 le Little Miss Muffet   .20   .20
- 802 A117 2 le Old King Cole   .55   .55
- 803 A117 5 le Mary Quite Contrary   .75   .75
- 804 A117 10 le Little Bo Peep   1.10   1.10
- 805 A117 25 le Polly Put the Kettle On   2.75   2.75
- 806 A117 35 le Rub-a-Dub-Dub   3.75   3.75
- Nos. 799-806 (8)   9.50   9.50

**Souvenir Sheets**
- 807 A117 40 le Old Woman in the Shoe   4.75   4.75
- 808 A117 40 le Simple Simon   4.75   4.75

---

HALLEY'S COMET 1985-6 SIERRA LEONE 50c    A112

Nos. 755-759 Ovptd. or Surcharged with Halley's Comet Emblem in Black or Silver

**1986, Oct. 15**
- 809 A94 30 le on 2c multi   2.75   2.75
- 810 A94 40 le on 30c multi   3.00   3.00
- 811 A94 45 le on 40c multi   3.50   3.50
- 812 A94 50 le on 70c multi   3.50   3.50
- Nos. 809-812 (4)   12.75   12.75

Nos. 639, 645-646 and 648 Surcharged

**1986, Oct. 15**
- 813 A111 50c multi   .20   .20
- 814 A111 70c multi   .20   .20
- 815 A111 1.50 le on 15c multi   3.00   3.00
- 816 A111 45 le on 10 le multi   6.50   6.50
- Nos. 813-816 (4)   7.10   7.10

**Souvenir Sheet**
- 817 A112 50 le on 12 le multi (S)   5.25   5.25

Paintings by Titian: 70c, Virgin and Child with St. Dorothy. $1.50, The Holy Family. 20 le, The Gypsy Madonna, vert. 20 le, Virgin and Child in an Evening Landscape, vert. 40 le, Madonna with the Pesaro Family.

VIRGIN and CHILD with St DOROTHY TITIAN / Christmas 1986 SIERRA LEONE 70c

Christmas A118

**1986, Nov. 17**    Litho.    Perf. 14
- 818 A118 70c multi   .20   .20
- 819 A118 1.50 le multi   .20   .20
- 820 A118 20 le multi   3.00   3.00
- 821 A118 20 le multi   3.75   3.75
- Nos. 818-821 (4)   7.15   7.15

**Souvenir Sheet**
- 822 A118 40 le multi   11.00   11.00

Statue of Liberty, Cent. A119

100TH ANNIVERSARY STATUE OF LIBERTY SIERRA LEONE Le1.50    A119

Pictures of the statue by Peter B. Kaplan before and after renovation. Nos. 823, 825-826, 828-829, 831, vert.

**1987, Jan. 2**    Perf. 14
- 823 A119 70c Torch assembly   .20   .20
- 824 A119 1.50 le Liberty holding torch   .20   .20
- 825 A119 2 le Torch assembly, diff.   .20   .20
- 826 A119 3 le Man, torch   .20   .20
- 827 A119 4 le Crown   .20   .20
- 828 A119 5 le Lighting of the statue   .25   .25
- 829 A119 10 le Lighting, diff.   .25   .25
- 830 A119 25 le Liberty Is.   1.25   1.25
- 831 A119 30 le Face   1.50   1.50
- Nos. 823-831 (9)   4.50   4.50

UNICEF, 40th Anniv. A120

**1987, Mar. 18**    Litho.    Perf. 14
- 832 A120 10 le multi   .80   .80

## Nomoli Soapstone Sculpture — A121

## Tall Ship in Harbor, Freetown — A122

"An early view of Freetown"

| 1987, Jan. 2 | | Perf. 15 | |
|---|---|---|---|
| 833 | A121 | 2 le shown | .20 | .20 |
| 834 | A121 | 5 le King's Yard Gate, 1817 | .30 | .30 |

**Souvenir Sheet**

| 835 | A122 | 60 le shown | 4.00 | 4.00 |
|---|---|---|---|---|

First settlement of liberated slaves returned to the African continent by the British, Freetown, bicent.

## Works of Art by Marc Chagall (1887-1985) — A128

100th ANNIVERSARY · CHAGALL — SIERRA LEONE Le 3

| 1987, Aug. 17 | | | Perf. 14 | |
|---|---|---|---|---|
| 879 | A128 | 3 le The Quarrel, 1911-1912 | .20 | .20 |
| 880 | A128 | 5 le Rebecca Giving Abraham's Servant a Drink | .25 | .50 |
| 881 | A128 | 10 le The Village | .25 | .50 |
| 882 | A128 | 20 le Ida at the Window, 1924 | .85 | .85 |
| 883 | A128 | 25 le Promenade, 1913 | 1.25 | 1.25 |
| 884 | A128 | 45 le Peasants | 2.75 | 2.75 |
| 885 | A128 | 50 le Turquoise Plate | 3.25 | 3.25 |
| 886 | A128 | 75 le Cemetery Gate, 1917 | 4.50 | 4.50 |
| | | Nos. 879-886 (8) | 13.55 | 13.55 |

Size: 111x95mm

**Imperf**

| 887 | A128 | 100 le Wedding Feast, Stravinsky's Ballet, 1945 | 7.25 | 7.25 |
|---|---|---|---|---|
| 888 | A128 | 100 le The Falling Angel | 7.25 | 7.25 |

Nos. 879-886 printed in sheets of 10 (5x2). Stamp selvage inscribed with name of painting.

## CAPEX '87 — A125

| 1987, June 15 | | | Perf. 11 | |
|---|---|---|---|---|
| 849 | A125 | 2 le Parliament | .20 | .20 |
| 850 | A125 | 5 le Totem poles | .45 | .45 |
| 851 | A125 | 10 le Perce Rock | .75 | .75 |
| 852 | A125 | 20 le Canadian Rockies | 1.25 | 1.25 |
| 853 | A125 | 25 le Old Quebec City | 1.50 | 1.50 |
| 854 | A125 | 45 le Aurora Borealis | 2.25 | 2.25 |
| 855 | A125 | 50 le Yukon P.O. | 2.50 | 2.50 |
| 856 | A125 | 75 le Niagara Falls | 4.25 | 4.25 |
| | | Nos. 849-856 (8) | 13.15 | 13.15 |

**Souvenir Sheets**

| 857 | A125 | 100 le Exploring Newfoundland | 5.50 | 5.50 |
|---|---|---|---|---|
| 858 | A125 | 100 le Calgary Exhibition and Stampede | 5.50 | 5.50 |

OLYMPIC GAMES 1988 — SIERRA LEONE Le 5

## Butterflies — A126

Sierra Leone 10c — BLUE SALAMIS

## 1988 Summer Olympics, Seoul — A127

| 1987, Aug. 4 | | | Perf. 14 | |
|---|---|---|---|---|
| 859 | A126 | 10c Blue salamis | 1.75 | .60 |
| 860 | A126 | 20c Pale-tailed blue | 1.75 | .60 |
| 861 | A126 | 40c Acraea swallowtail | 1.75 | .60 |
| 862 | A126 | 1 le Broad blue-banded swallowtail | 1.75 | .60 |
| 863 | A126 | 2 le Giant blue swallowtail | 1.75 | .60 |
| 864 | A126 | 3 le Blood-red cymothoe | 2.10 | .90 |
| 865 | A126 | 5 le Green-spotted swallowtail | 2.10 | .90 |
| 866 | A126 | 10 le Small-striped swordtail | 3.50 | 1.25 |
| 867 | A128 | 20 le Congo long-tailed blue | 6.50 | 3.00 |
| 868 | A126 | 25 le Blue monarch | 6.75 | 3.75 |
| 869 | A126 | 30 le Black and yellow swallowtail | | |
| 870 | A126 | 45 le Western blue charaxes | 6.75 | 4.00 |
| 871 | A126 | 60 le Violet-washed charaxes | 11.50 | 5.50 |
| 872 | A126 | 75 le Orange admiral | 2.76 | 4.50 |
| 873 | A126 | 100 le Blue-patched judy | 3.25 | 4.00 |
| | | | 4.75 | 7.50 |
| | | Nos. 859-873 (15) | 58.70 | 38.30 |

Nos. 859-864 exist with 1989 date. No. 871 with 1990. See Nos. 1257-1260, 1332A-1332I.

**Perf. 12x12½**

| 1988-89 | | | | |
|---|---|---|---|---|
| 859a | A126 | 10c | .60 | .20 |
| 860a | A126 | 20c | .90 | .20 |
| 861a | A126 | 40c | .90 | .20 |
| 862a | A126 | 1 le | .90 | .20 |
| 863a | A126 | 2 le | 1.10 | .40 |
| 864a | A126 | 3 le | 1.10 | .40 |
| 865a | A126 | 5 le | 1.10 | .80 |
| 866a | A126 | 10 le | 1.40 | 1.25 |
| 867a | A126 | 20 le | 1.40 | 1.60 |
| 868a | A126 | 25 le | 1.75 | 1.75 |
| 869a | A126 | 30 le | 5.00 | 5.00 |
| 870a | A126 | 100 le | 6.25 | 6.25 |
| 873a | A126 | | 20.00 | 11.60 |
| | | Nos. 859a-873a (13) | | |

Nos. 859a-873a exist.

| 1987, Aug. 10 | | | | |
|---|---|---|---|---|
| 874 | A127 | 5 le Cycling | .25 | .25 |
| 875 | A127 | 10 le Equestrian | .55 | .55 |
| 876 | A127 | 45 le Running | 2.50 | 2.50 |
| 877 | A127 | 50 le Tennis | 2.75 | 2.75 |
| | | Nos. 874-877 (4) | 6.05 | 6.05 |

**Souvenir Sheet**

| 878 | A127 | 100 le Gold medal, map | 6.50 | 6.50 |
|---|---|---|---|---|

## America's Cup — A123

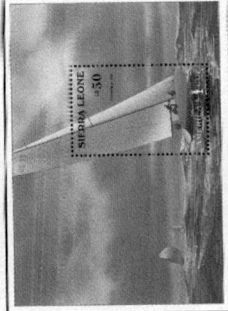

SIERRA LEONE 1 le — AMERICA'S CUP

## Constellation, 1964 — A124

| 1987, June 15 | | Litho. | Perf. 14 | |
|---|---|---|---|---|
| 836 | A123 | 1 le USA, 1987 | .20 | .20 |
| 837 | A123 | 1.50 le New Zealand, 1987 | .20 | .20 |
| 838 | A123 | 2.50 le French Kiss, 1987 | .20 | .20 |
| 839 | A123 | 10 le Stars & Stripes, 1987 | 1.10 | 1.10 |
| 840 | A123 | 15 le Australia II, 1983 | 1.50 | 1.50 |
| 841 | A123 | 25 le Freedom, 1980 | 1.50 | 1.50 |
| 842 | A123 | 30 le Kookaburra III, 1987 | 2.40 | 2.40 |
| | | Nos. 836-842 (7) | 8.00 | 8.00 |

**Souvenir Sheet**

| 843 | A124 | 50 le shown | 3.50 | 3.50 |
|---|---|---|---|---|

Nos. 837, 839 and 842 horiz.

For overprint see No. 964.

SIERRA LEONE Le 2

Disney characters, Canadian sights.

---

SIERRA LEONE Le 2

## Wimbledon Tennis Champions — A130

2 le, Evonne Goolagong, Australia. 5 le, Martina Navratilova, US-Czechoslovakia. 10 le, Jimmy Connors, US. 15 le, Bjorn Borg, Sweden. 30 le, Boris Becker, West Germany. 40 le, John McEnroe, US. 50 le, Chris Evert Lloyd, US. 75 le, Virginia Wade, Great Britain. #907, Steffi Graf, German Open 1986. #908, Boris Becker.

| 1987, Sept. 4 | | | Perf. 14 | |
|---|---|---|---|---|
| 899 | A130 | 2 le multicolored | .25 | .25 |
| 900 | A130 | 5 le multicolored | .60 | .60 |
| 901 | A130 | 10 le multicolored | .90 | .90 |
| 902 | A130 | 15 le multicolored | 1.25 | 1.25 |
| 903 | A130 | 30 le multicolored | 2.50 | 2.50 |
| 904 | A130 | 40 le multicolored | 2.75 | 2.75 |
| 905 | A130 | 50 le multicolored | 3.00 | 3.00 |
| 906 | A130 | 75 le multicolored | 4.00 | 4.00 |
| | | Nos. 899-906 (8) | 15.25 | 15.25 |

**Souvenir Sheets**

| 907 | A130 | 100 le multicolored | 7.00 | 7.00 |
|---|---|---|---|---|
| 908 | A130 | 100 le multicolored | 7.00 | 7.00 |

For overprints see Nos. 965, 1023-1024.

## Discovery of America, 500th Anniv. (in 1992) A131

SIERRA LEONE Le 5 — Christopher Columbus 1437-1506, Santa Maria — Ducats

5 le, Ducats, Santa Maria, Issac Abravanel (1437-1508), fund raiser. 10 le, Astrolabe, Pinta, Abraham Zacuto (1452-1515), astronomer. 45 le, Maravedis (coins), Nina, Luis de Santangel (1448-1498), fund raiser. 50 le, Tobacco leaves, plant, Luis de Torres (1453-1522), translator.

| 1987, Sept. 11 | | | | |
|---|---|---|---|---|
| 909 | A131 | 5 le multicolored | .90 | .90 |
| 910 | A131 | 10 le multicolored | 1.10 | 1.00 |
| 911 | A131 | 45 le multicolored | 3.50 | 3.50 |
| 912 | A131 | 50 le multicolored | 4.00 | 4.00 |
| | | Nos. 909-912 (4) | 9.50 | 9.40 |

**Souvenir Sheet**

| 913 | A131 | 100 le Columbus, map | 5.25 | 5.25 |
|---|---|---|---|---|

For overprint see No. 966.

## Fauna and Flora — A132

Le 3 — Cotton Tree, Gambia Museum — SIERRA LEONE

| 1987, Sept. 15 | | | | |
|---|---|---|---|---|
| 914 | A132 | 3 le Cotton tree | .20 | .20 |
| 915 | A132 | 5 le Dwarf crocodile | .20 | .20 |
| 916 | A132 | 10 le Kudu | .65 | .65 |
| 917 | A132 | 20 le Yellowbells | 1.40 | 1.40 |
| 918 | A132 | 25 le Hippopotamus | 1.75 | 1.75 |
| 919 | A132 | 45 le Comet orchid | 3.00 | 3.00 |
| 920 | A132 | 50 le Baobab tree | 3.25 | 3.25 |
| 921 | A132 | 75 le Elephant | 5.25 | 5.25 |
| | | Nos. 914-921 (8) | 15.70 | 15.70 |

**Souvenir Sheets**

| 922 | A132 | 100 le Banana, papaya, coconut, pineapple | 4.50 | 4.50 |
|---|---|---|---|---|
| 923 | A132 | 100 le Leopard | 4.50 | 4.50 |

## 16th World Scout Jamboree, Australia, 1987-88 — A133

AYERS ROCK — 16th WORLD SCOUT JAMBOREE — SIERRA LEONE LE 5

Scouts, jamboree emblem, map of Australia and: 5 le, Ayers Rock. 15 le, Sailing. 40 le, Sydney skyline. 50 le, Sydney harbor bridge.

## Transportation Innovations — A129

Le 5 — Blanchard's Balloon, First US Balloon Flight — SIERRA LEONE

| 1987, Aug. 28 | | | Perf. 15 | |
|---|---|---|---|---|
| 889 | A129 | 3 le Apollo 8, 1968, vert. | .20 | .20 |
| 890 | A129 | 5 le Blanchard's Balloon, 1793 | .20 | .20 |
| 891 | A129 | 10 le Lockheed Vega, 1932 | .50 | .50 |
| 892 | A129 | 15 le Vicker's Vimy, 1919 | .80 | .80 |
| 893 | A129 | 20 le Tank Mk1, c. 1918 | 1.10 | 1.10 |
| 894 | A129 | 25 le Sikorsky VS-300, 1939 | 1.25 | 1.25 |
| 895 | A129 | 30 le Flyer XI, 1903 | 1.60 | 1.60 |
| 896 | A129 | 35 le Bleriot XI, 1909 | 1.75 | 1.75 |
| 897 | A129 | 40 le Paraplane, 1983, vert. | 2.10 | 2.10 |
| 898 | A129 | 50 le Daimler's motorcycle, 1885 | 2.50 | 2.50 |
| | | Nos. 889-898 (10) | 12.00 | 12.00 |

## Rhinegold Express, Ireland (1st Electric Railroad, 1884) — A129a

SIERRA LEONE LE 100

| 1987, Aug. 28 | | Litho. | Perf. 15 | |
|---|---|---|---|---|
| 898A | A129a | 100 le multi | 6.25 | 6.25 |

opera house, 100 le, Flags of Sierra Leone, Australia and Scouts.

**1987, Oct. 5**  **Litho.**  **Perf. 15**
924 A133 5 le multicolored .35 .35
925 A133 15 le multicolored .75 .75
926 A133 40 le multicolored 1.60 1.60
927 A133 50 le multicolored 2.75 2.75
Nos. 924-927 (4) 5.45 5.45

**Souvenir Sheet**
928 A133 100 le multicolored 5.00 5.00

1.50 le stamps like the 50 le were printed but not issued.

## US Constitution Bicentennial — A134

Designs: 5 le, White House, 10 le, George Washington, 30 le, Patrick Henry, 65 le, New Hampshire state flag. 100 le, John Jay.

**1987, Nov. 9**  **Perf. 14**
929 A134 5 le multi .20 .20
930 A134 10 le multi .70 .70
931 A134 30 le multi, vert. 1.10 1.10
932 A134 65 le multi, vert. 2.25 2.25
Nos. 929-932 (4) 4.25 4.25

**Souvenir Sheet**
933 A134 100 le multi, vert. 4.50 4.50

The Annunciation (Detail)
CHRISTMAS 1987 SIERRA LEONE Le 2

**1987, Dec. 9**
Paintings by Titian: 2 le, The Annunciation. 10 le, Madonna and Child with Saints. 20 le, Madonna of the Cherries. 65 le, Pesaro Altarpiece, vert.

**1987, Dec. 9**  **Litho.**
934 A135 20c Space Mountain .20 .20
935 A135 40c Country Bear Jamboree .20 .20
936 A135 80c Mickey Mouse Review .20 .20
937 A135 1 le Mark Twain's River Boat .20 .20
938 A135 2 le Western River Railroad .20 .20
939 A135 3 le Pirates of the Caribbean .20 .20
940 A135 10 le Big Thunder Mountain train .70 .70
941 A135 20 le It's a Small World .70 .70
942 A135 30 le Park entrance 2.25 2.25
Nos. 934-942 (9) 5.75 5.75

**Souvenir Sheet**
943 A135 65 le Cinderella's Castle 9.00 9.00

Mickey Mouse, 60th anniv.

Disney animated characters and attractions at Tokyo Disneyland.

Tokyo Disneyland, 5th Anniv.—A135

**1987, Dec. 21**
944 A136 2 le multicolored .25 .25
945 A136 10 le multicolored .95 .95
946 A136 20 le multicolored 1.60 1.60
947 A136 35 le multicolored 2.75 2.75
Nos. 944-947 (4) 5.55 5.55

**Souvenir Sheet**
948 A136 65 le multicolored 6.00 6.00

Paintings by Titian: 2 le, The Annunciation. 10 le, Madonna and Child with Saints. 20 le, Brigid. 35 le, Madonna of the Cherries. 65 le, Pesaro Altarpiece, vert.

Christmas—A136

---

SIERRA LEONE

**1988, Feb. 15**  **Litho.**  **Perf. 14**
949 A137 2 le Ceremony, 1947 .25 .25
950 A137 3 le Elizabeth, Charles, 1948 .25 .25
951 A137 10 le Elizabeth, Anne, Charles, c. 1950 .60 .60
952 A137 50 le Elizabeth, c. 1970 3.00 3.00
Nos. 949-952 (4) 4.10 4.10

**Souvenir Sheet**
953 A137 65 le Wedding portrait 4.00 4.00

40th Wedding Anniv. of Queen Elizabeth II and Prince Philip A137

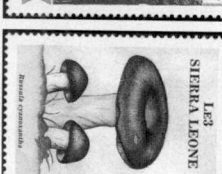
Mushrooms A138

**1988, Feb. 29**
954 A138 3 le Russula cyanoxantha .20 .20
955 A138 10 le Lycoperdon perlatum 1.40 1.40
956 A138 20 le Lactarius deliciosus 2.75 2.75
957 A138 30 le Boletus edulis 4.25 4.25
Nos. 954-957 (4) 8.60 8.60

**Miniature Sheet**
958 A138 65 le Amanita muscaria 7.25 7.25

Fish A139

**1988, Apr. 13**  **Perf. 15**
959 A139 3 le Golden pheasant .30 .30
960 A139 10 le Banded toothcarp .60 .60
961 A139 20 le Jewel fish 1.00 1.00
962 A139 35 le Butterfly fish 1.50 1.50
Nos. 959-962 (4) 3.50 3.50

**Miniature Sheet**
963 A139 65 le African longfin 4.00 4.00

Nos. 841, 903 and 911 Ovptd. for Philatelic Exhibitions in Black

SIERRA LEONE
OLYMPHILEX 88 Le 45

SIERRA LEONE Le
Christopher Columbus 1451-1506

SIERRA LEONE
AMERICA'S CUP
INDEPENDENCE 40 Le 25

a
b
c

**1988, Apr. 19**  **Litho.**  **Perf. 14**
964 A123(a) 25 le multicolored 1.60 1.60
965 A130(b) 30 le multicolored 1.90 1.90
966 A131(c) 45 le multicolored 2.50 2.50
Nos. 964-966 (3) 6.00 6.00

---

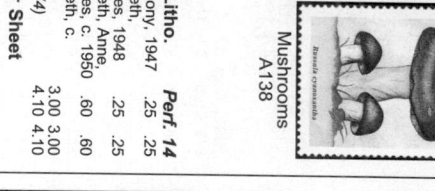
SIERRA LEONE Le3 Basketball

1988 Summer Olympics, Seoul—A141

**1988, June 15**
970 A141 3 le Basketball .20 .20
971 A141 10 le Judo .50 .50
972 A141 20 le Gymnastics .65 .65
973 A141 45 le Synchronized swimming 1.90 1.90
Nos. 970-973 (4) 3.25 3.25

**Souvenir Sheet**
974 A141 66 le Torch-bearer 2.75 2.75

**1988, June 25**
975 A142 3 le Swallow-tailed bee-eater 1.00 1.00
976 A142 5 le Tooth-billed barbet 1.25 1.25
977 A142 8 le African golden oriole 1.60 1.60
978 A142 10 le Red bishop 1.90 1.90
979 A142 12 le Red-billed shrike 1.60 1.60
980 A142 20 le European bee-eater 2.50 2.50
981 A142 35 le Barbary shrike 1.60 1.60
982 A142 40 le Black-headed oriole 3.00 3.00
Nos. 975-982 (8) 14.45 14.45

**Souvenir Sheets**
983 A142 65 le Saddlebill stork 3.00 3.00
984 A142 65 le Purple heron 3.00 3.00

Birds—A142

SIERRA LEONE Le3 AUREOL

**1988, July 1**
985 A143 3 le Aureol .80 .80
986 A143 10 le Dunkwa 2.10 2.10
987 A143 15 le Melampus 2.75 2.75
988 A143 30 le Dumbaia 3.50 3.50
Nos. 985-988 (4) 9.15 9.15

**Souvenir Sheet**
989 A143 65 le Loading containers 3.25 3.25

Merchant Marine A143

Paintings by Titian A144

SIERRA LEONE Le1
THE CONCERT (Detail) TITIAN, 1488-1576

1 le, The Concert, 1512. 2 le, Philip II of Spain, c. 1550-51. 3 le, St. Sebastian, c. 1520-22. 5 le, Martyrdom of St. Peter Martyr, c.

---

SIERRA LEONE Le 3

Int'l. Fund for Agricultural Development (IFAD), 10th Anniv. — A140

**1988, May 3**  **Litho.**  **Perf. 14**
967 A140 3 le Cocoa, coffee .20 .20
968 A140 15 le Tropical fruit .95 .95
969 A140 25 le Harvest 1.75 1.75
Nos. 967-969 (3) 2.90 2.90

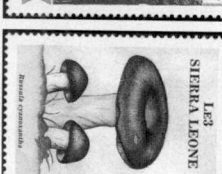
SIERRA LEONE
SWALLOW-TAILED BEE-EATER Le3

John F. Kennedy A145

Kennedy half-dollar and space achievements: 3 le, Recovery of Mercury capsule by the US Navy. 5 le, Splashdown and recovery of Liberty Bell 7, July 21, 1961, piloted by "Gus" Grissom, vert. 15 le, Launch of Freedom 7, piloted by Alan B. Shephard, May 5, 1961, vert. 40 le, Friendship 7 in orbit, piloted by John Glenn, Feb. 20, 1962. 65 le, Kennedy, speech excerpt.

**1988, Aug. 22**  **Litho.**  **Perf. 13½x14**
990 A144 1 le multicolored .20 .20
991 A144 2 le multicolored .25 .25
992 A144 3 le multicolored .40 .40
993 A144 5 le multicolored .50 .50
994 A144 15 le multicolored 1.25 1.25
995 A144 40 le multicolored 1.40 1.40
996 A144 25 le multicolored 1.75 1.75
997 A144 30 le multicolored 2.00 2.00
Nos. 990-997 (8) 7.55 7.55

**Souvenir Sheets**
998 A144 50 le multicolored 3.25 3.25
999 A144 50 le multicolored 3.25 3.25

1528-30, 15 le, St. Jerome, 1560. 20 le, St. Mark Enthroned with Saints Cosmas and Damian, Roch & Sebastian, c. 1508-09. 25 le, Portrait of a Young Man, 1506. 30 le, St. Jerome in Penitence, 1555. #998, Self-portrait, 1567. #999, Orpheus and Eurydice, 1508.

SIERRA LEONE Le3

**1988, Sept. 26**  **Litho.**  **Perf. 14**
1000 A145 3 le multicolored .25 .25
1001 A145 5 le multicolored .40 .40
1002 A145 15 le multicolored 1.25 1.25
1003 A145 40 le multicolored 3.50 3.50
Nos. 1000-1003 (4) 5.40 5.40

**Souvenir Sheet**
1004 A145 65 le multicolored 3.50 3.50

Int'l. Red Cross and Red Crescent Organizations, 125th Anniv.—A146

SIERRA LEONE Le3
Africa food relief

**1988, Nov. 1**
1005 A146 3 le Africa food relief .75 .75
1006 A146 10 le Battle of Solferino 2.50 2.50
1007 A146 20 le WWII Pacific 3.25 3.25
1008 A146 40 le WWII Europe 4.25 4.25
Nos. 1005-1008 (4) 10.75 10.75

**Souvenir Sheet**
**Size: 41x28mm**
1009 A146 65 le multicolored horiz., Alfred Nobel, Dunant, 3.75 3.75

Mickey's Christmas Dance

Wait Disney characters dancing: No. 1010a, Huey, Dewey and Louie. No. 1010b, Clarabelle Cow. No. 1010c, Goofy. No. 1010d, Scrooge McDuck and Grandma Duck. No. 1010e, Donald Duck. No. 1010f, Daisy Duck. No. 1010g, Minnie Mouse. No. 1010h, Mickey Mouse. No. 1010i, Mickey Mouse. No. 1011, Dance, c. 1920. No. 1012, Dance, c. 1950.

Christmas, Mickey Mouse 60th Anniv.—A147

**Miniature Sheet**

**1988, Dec. 1** *Perf. 13½x14*
**1010** A147 Sheet of 8 8.25 8.25
*a.-h.* 10 le any single .80 .80

**Souvenir Sheets**

**1011** A147 70 le multicolored 5.25 5.25
**1012** A147 70 le multicolored 5.25 5.25

Christmas A148

Paintings by Rubens (details): 3 le, Adoration of the Magi (Virgin and Child). 3.60 le, Adoration of the Shepherds (shepherds and child). 5 le, Adoration of the Magi (Magi). 10 le, Adoration of the Shepherds (Virgin and Child). 20 le, Virgin and Child Surrounded by Flowers. 40 le, St. Gregory the Great and Other Saints (Virgin and Child). 60 le, Adoration of the Magi, (Virgin, Child and Magi), diff. 80 le, Madonna and Child with Saints. No. 1021, St. Gregory the Great and Other Saints. No. 1022, Virgin and Child Enthroned with Saints.

**1988, Dec. 15** **Litho.** *Perf. 13½x14*
**1013** A148 3 le multicolored .20 .20
**1014** A148 3.60 le multicolored .20 .20
**1015** A148 5 le multicolored .40 .40
**1016** A148 10 le multicolored .60 .60
**1017** A148 20 le multicolored 1.10 1.10
**1018** A148 40 le multicolored 2.25 2.25
**1019** A148 60 le multicolored 3.25 3.25
**1020** A148 80 le multicolored 4.25 4.25
*Nos. 1013-1020 (8)* 12.25 12.25

**Souvenir Sheets**

**1021** A148 100 le multicolored 5.50 5.50
**1022** A148 100 le multicolored 5.50 5.50

No. 907 Ovptd. "GRAND SLAM WINNER" in Gold

**1989, Jan. 16** *Perf. 14*

**Souvenir Sheets**

**1023A-1023D** A130 100 le Set of 4 20.00 20.00

Gold marginal overprints: No. 1023A, "AUSTRALIAN OPEN / JANUARY 11-24, 1988 / GRAF v EVERET / 6-1 / 7-6." 1023B, "FRENCH OPEN / MAY 23-JUNE 5, 1988 / GRAF v ZVEREVA / 6-0 / 6-0." 1023C, "WIMBLEDON / JUNE 20 JULY 4, 1988 / GRAF v NAVRATILOVA / 5-7 / 6-2 / 6-1." 1023D, "U.S. OPEN / AUGUST 29-SEPTEMBER 11, 1988 / GRAF v SABATINI / 6-3 / 3-6 / 6-1."

No. 907 Ovptd. "GOLD MEDALIST" in Gold

**1989, Jan. 16** **Litho.** *Perf. 14*
**1024** A130 100 le multi 5.00 5.00

Marginal overprint: "SEOUL OLYMPICS 1988 / GRAF v SABATINI / 6-3 / 6-3."

Medalists of the 1988 Summer Olympics, Seoul A149

Designs: 3 le, Christian Schenk, German Democratic Republic, decathlon. 6 le, Hitoshi Saito, Japan, heavyweight judo. 10 le, Jutta Niehaus, Federal Republic of Germany, women's road race. 15 le, Tomas Lange, German Democratic Republic, single sculls. 20 le, Matthew Biondi, US, 50m and 100m freestyle. 30 le, Carl Lewis, US, 100m sprint. 40 le, Nicole Uphoff, Federal Republic of Germany, individual dressage. 50 le, Andras Sike, Hungary, 126-pound Greco-Roman wrestling. No. 1033, Gold medal, five-ring emblem. No. 1034, Torch, five-ring emblem.

**1989, Apr. 28** **Litho.** *Perf. 14*
**1025** A149 3 le multicolored .70 .70
**1026** A149 6 le multicolored .90 .90
**1027** A149 10 le multicolored 1.50 1.50
**1028** A149 15 le multicolored 1.50 1.50
**1029** A149 20 le multicolored 1.50 1.50
**1030** A149 30 le multicolored 1.90 1.90
**1031** A149 40 le multicolored 2.25 2.25
**1032** A149 50 le multicolored 2.25 2.25
*Nos. 1025-1032 (8)* 12.50 12.50

**Souvenir Sheets**

**1033** A149 100 le multicolored 5.25 5.25
**1034** A149 100 le multicolored 5.25 5.25

Name of athlete not inscribed on No. 1031.

1990 World Cup Soccer Championships, Italy — A150

**1989, May 8**
**1035** A150 3 le Brazil vs. Sweden .20 .20
**1036** A150 6 le Germany vs. Hungary .50 .50
**1037** A150 8 le England vs. Germany .65 .65
**1038** A150 10 le Argentina vs. The Netherlands .80 .80
**1039** A150 12 le Brazil vs. Czechoslovakia .95 .95
**1040** A150 20 le Germany vs. The Netherlands 1.60 1.60
**1041** A150 30 le Italy vs. Germany 2.40 2.40
**1042** A150 40 le Brazil vs. Italy 3.25 3.25
*Nos. 1035-1042 (8)* 10.35 10.35

**Souvenir Sheets**

**1043** A150 100 le Uruguay vs. Brazil 4.00 4.00
**1044** A150 100 le Argentina vs. Germany 4.00 4.00

Mano River Union, 15th Anniv. A151

Designs: 1 le, Sierra Leone-Guinea postal service. 3 le, Presidents Momoh, Conte of Guinea and Doe of Liberia. 10 le, Freetown-Monrovia Highway under construction. 15 le, Presidents signing the Communique at a 1988 summit.

**1989, May 19** *Perf. 14*
**1045** A151 1 le multicolored .75 .75
**1046** A151 3 le multicolored 1.25 1.25
**1047** A151 10 le multicolored 2.00 2.00
*Nos. 1045-1047 (3)* 4.00 4.00

**Souvenir Sheet**

**1048** A151 15 le multicolored 3.50 3.50

Ahmadiyya Muslim Centenary Thanksgiving Celebrations A152

**1989, June 8**
**1049** A152 3 le black & brt blue .50 .50

Miniature Sheets

Shakespeare's 425th Birth Anniv. — A153

Scenes from the playwright's works.
No. 1050: a, Richard III. b, Othello (Desdemona and two men). c, The Two Gentlemen of Verona. d, Macbeth (chamber). e, Hamlet. f, Taming of the Shrew (scene with dog). g, The Merry Wives of Windsor. h, Henry IV (assembly room).
No. 1051: a, Macbeth (horsemen). b, Romeo and Juliet. c, Merchant of Venice. d, As You Like It. e, Taming of the Shrew (ruined meal). f, King Lear. g, Othello (death scene). h, Henry IV (street scene).

**1989, May 30** *Perf. 13*
**1050** Sheet of 8 + label 7.00 7.00
*a.-h.* A153 15 le any single .80 .80
**1051** Sheet of 8 + label 7.00 7.00
*a.-h.* A153 15 le any single .80 .80

**Souvenir Sheets**

**1052** A153 100 le Portrait 7.00 7.00
**1053** A153 100 le Portrait, coat of arms 7.00 7.00

Nos. 1050-1051 contain center label picturing Shakespeare's portrait (No. 1050) or his birthplace in Stratford (No. 1051).

Paintings by Takeuchi Seiho (1864-1942) — A154

Designs: 3 le, Lapping Waves. 6 le, Hazy Moon, vert. 8 le, Passing Spring, vert. 10 le, Mackerels. 12 le, Calico Cat. 30 le, The First Time To Be a Model, vert. 40 le, Kingly Lion. 75 le, After a Shower, vert. No. 1062, Domesticated Monkeys and Rabbits. No. 1063, Dozing in the Midst of All the Chirping, vert.

*Perf. 14x13½, 13½x14*

**1989, July 3** **Litho.**
**1054** A154 3 le multicolored .20 .20
**1055** A154 6 le multicolored .25 .25
**1056** A154 8 le multicolored .40 .40
**1057** A154 10 le multicolored .50 .50
**1058** A154 12 le multicolored .55 .55
**1059** A154 30 le multicolored 1.40 1.40
**1060** A154 40 le multicolored 2.00 2.00
**1061** A154 75 le multicolored 3.75 3.75
*Nos. 1054-1061 (8)* 9.05 9.05

**Souvenir Sheets**

**1062** A154 150 le multicolored 6.50 6.50
**1063** A154 150 le multicolored 6.50 6.50

Hirohito (1901-89) and enthronement of Akihito as emperor of Japan.
See Nos. 1098-1129.

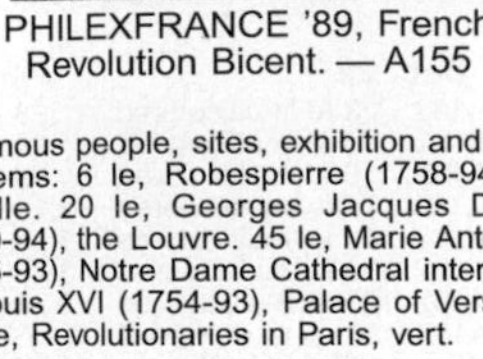

PHILEXFRANCE '89, French Revolution Bicent. — A155

Famous people, sites, exhibition and anniv. emblems: 6 le, Robespierre (1758-94), the Bastille. 20 le, Georges Jacques Danton (1759-94), the Louvre. 45 le, Marie Antoinette (1755-93), Notre Dame Cathedral interior. 80 le, Louis XVI (1754-93), Palace of Versailles. 150 le, Revolutionaries in Paris, vert.

**1989, July 14** **Litho.** *Perf. 14*
**1064** A155 6 le multicolored .60 .60
**1065** A155 20 le multicolored 1.10 1.10
**1066** A155 45 le multicolored 2.00 2.00
**1067** A155 80 le multicolored 3.50 3.50
*Nos. 1064-1067 (4)* 7.20 7.20

**Souvenir Sheet**

**1068** A155 150 le multicolored 5.75 5.75

Miniature Sheets

Space Exploration — A156

Satellites, probes and spacecraft.
No. 1069: a, Sputnik, 1957. b, Telstar, 1962. c, Rendezvous of Gemini 6 and 7, 1965. d, Yuri Gagarin, 1st man in space, 1961. e, Mariner, 1964. f, Surveyor on Mars, 1966. g, US-Canadian Alouette satellite, 1962. h, Edward White, 1st American to walk in space, 1965. i, OGO-4 satellite, 1967.
No. 1070: a, Buzz Aldrin on the Moon, Apollo 11 mission, 1969. b, Apollo 15 mission lunar rover. c, Apollo 15 crew member. d, Conducting experiments on the lunar surface. e, Splitrock, Valley of Taurus-Littrow. f, Saluting the flag, Apollo 15 lunar module. g, Solar wind experiment. h, Lunar rover, diff. i, Apollo command module.
No. 1071: a, Module separation. b, Docking maneuvers. c, Lunar module in space. d, Second stage separation. e, Module transposition. f, Lunar module controlled descent, Moon's surface. g, Apollo 11 liftoff, 1969. h, Lunar module separates from command module. i, Neil Armstrong's first step on the Moon.
No. 1072: a, Mariner-Mars, 1971. b, Mariner 10, 1973. c, Viking, 1975. d, Skylab, 1974. e, Soyuz-Salyut, 1974. f, Viking robot craft, 1974. g, Pioneer 2, 1973. h, Apollo-Soyuz, 1975. i, Pioneer-Venus, 1978.
No. 1073: a, Apollo 17 lunar module, 1972. b, Command module jettison of service module before reentry. c, Soyuz 11, 1971. d, Lunar module liftoff. e, U.S. Navy recovery operation. f, Mars 2, 1971. g, Command module in docking position. h, Luna 17, 1970. i, Mars 3, 1971.
No. 1074: a, Voyager 1 and 2, 1977. b, Columbia space shuttle, 1981. c, Mir space station, 1986. d, IUE-Ultraviolet Explorer, US, U.K. and the European Space Agency, 1078. e, Astronaut operating out of shuttle cargo bay, 1983. f, Magellan, 1989. g, Soyuz-Salyut, 1978. h, STS-10, 1984. i, Shuttle, space telescope, 1989.
No. 1075, Spacelab. No. 1076, Future space station. No. 1077, Voyager.

**1989, July 20** **Litho.** *Perf. 14*
**1069** Sheet of 9 4.75 4.75
*a.-i.* A156 10 le any single .50 .50
**1070** Sheet of 9 4.75 4.75
*a.-i.* A156 10 le any single .50 .50
**1071** Sheet of 9 4.75 4.75
*a.-i.* A156 10 le any single .50 .50
**1072** Sheet of 9 7.00 7.00
*a.-i.* A156 15 le any single .75 .75
**1073** Sheet of 9 7.00 7.00
*a.-i.* A156 15 le any single .75 .75
**1074** Sheet of 9 7.00 7.00
*a.-i.* A156 15 le any single .75 .75

**Souvenir Sheets**

**1075** A156 100 le multicolored 6.50 6.50
**1076** A156 100 le multicolored 6.50 6.50
**1077** A156 100 le multicolored 6.50 6.50

Nos. 1069f is incorrectly inscribed "Mars" instead of "Moon."

Orchids — A157

Butterflies — A158

**1989, Sept. 8** **Litho.** *Perf. 14*
**1078** A157 3 le Bulbophyllum barbigerum .75 .75
**1079** A157 6 le Bulbophyllum falcatum 1.10 1.10
**1080** A157 12 le Habenaria macrara 1.60 1.60

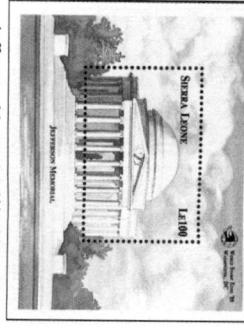

Jefferson Memorial, Washington, DC — A159

**1989, Nov. 17**    **Litho.**    **Perf. 14**
1136 A159 100 le multicolored   2.00 2.00
World Stamp Expo '89.

| | | |
|---|---|---|
| 1081 | A157 | 20 le Eurychone rothschildi- |
| | | christy- | 2.00 2.00 |
| 1082 | A157 | 50 le Calyp- |
| | | anum | 3.00 3.00 |
| 1083 | A157 | 60 le Bulbophyl- |
| | | lum distans | 3.00 3.00 |
| 1084 | A157 | 70 le Eulophia |
| | | guineensis | 3.50 3.50 |
| 1085 | A157 | 80 le Diapha- |
| | | nanthe pel- |
| | | lu-cida | 3.50 3.50 |

Nos. 1078-1085 (8) | 19.45 19.45

**Souvenir Sheets**
| | | | |
|---|---|---|---|
| 1086 | A157 | 100 le Cyrtorchis arcuata | 11.00 11.00 |
| 1087 | A157 | 100 le Butterflies, Eulophia cucullata | 11.00 11.00 |

**1989, Sept. 11**
| | | | |
|---|---|---|---|
| 1088 | A158 | 6 le Salamis temora | 1.25 1.25 |
| 1089 | A158 | 12 le Pseudacraea lucretia | 1.60 1.60 |
| 1090 | A158 | 18 le Charaxes boueti | 2.10 2.10 |
| 1091 | A158 | 30 le Graphium antheus | 3.00 3.00 |
| 1092 | A158 | 40 le Colotis protomedia | 3.75 3.75 |
| 1093 | A158 | 60 le Asterope | 4.25 4.25 |
| 1094 | A158 | 72 le Coenura pechueli | 4.75 4.75 |
| 1095 | A158 | 80 le Precis octa- aurantiaca | 4.75 4.75 |

Nos. 1088-1095 (8) | 25.45 25.45

**Souvenir Sheets**
| | | | |
|---|---|---|---|
| 1096 | A158 | 100 le Charaxes cithaeron | 11.00 11.00 |
| 1097 | A158 | 100 le Euphaedra themis | 11.00 11.00 |

Nos. 1088-1090, 1095 and 1097 horiz.

Art Type of 1989

Paintings by Hiroshige in the series Fifty-three Stations on the Tokaido: No. 1098, Coolies Warming Themselves at Hamamatsu, No. 1099, Imakiri Ford at Maisaka, No. 1100, Pacific Ocean Seen from Shirasuka, No. 1101, Futakawa Street Singers, No. 1102, Repairing Yoshida Castle, No. 1103, The Inn at Akasaka, No. 1104, The Bridge to Okazaki, No. 1105, Samurai's Wife Entering Narumi, No. 1106, Harbour at Kuwana, No. 1107, Autumn in Ishiyakushi, No. 1108, Snowfall at Kameyama, No. 1109, The Frontier Station of Seki, No. 1110, Teahouse at Sakanoshita, No. 1111, Kansai Houses at Minakushi, No. 1112, Kusatsu Station, No. 1113, Ferry to Kawasaki, No. 1114, The Hilly Town of Hodogaya, No. 1115, Lute Players at Fujisawa, No. 1116, Mild Rainstorm at Oiso, No. 1117, Lake Ashi and Mountains of Hakone, No. 1118, Twilight at Numazu, No. 1119, Mount Fuji From Hara, No. 1120, Samurai's Children Riding Through Yoshiwara, No. 1121, Mountain Pass at Yui, No. 1122, Harbour at Ejiri, No. 1123, Stopping at Fujieda, No. 1124, Misty Kanaya on the Oi River, No. 1125, The Bridge to Kakegawa, No. 1126, Teahouse at Kuwana, No. 1127, The Ford at Mistuke, No. 1128, Sanjo Bridge in Kyoto, No. 1129, Nibonbashi Bridge in Edo.

**1989, Nov. 13**    **Litho.**    **Perf. 14x13½**
1096-1127 A154 25 le Set of 30   35.00 35.00

**Souvenir sheets**
1128-1129 A154 120 le each   6.50 6.50

Hirohito (1901-1989) and enthronement of Akihito as emperor of Japan.

---

Endangered Species — A160

**1989, Nov. 29**    **Perf. 14**
| | | | |
|---|---|---|---|
| 1137 | A160 | 6 le Humpback whale | .20 .20 |
| 1138 | A160 | 9 le Formosan sika deer | .25 .25 |
| 1139 | A160 | 16 le Spanish lynx | .60 .60 |
| 1140 | A160 | 20 le Goitered ga- zelle | .85 .85 |
| 1141 | A160 | 30 le Japanese sea lion | 1.25 1.25 |
| 1142 | A160 | 50 le Long-eared owl | 2.10 2.10 |
| 1143 | A160 | 70 le Chinese copper pheasant | 3.00 3.00 |
| 1144 | A160 | 100 le Siberian ti- ger | 4.25 4.25 |

Nos. 1137-1144 (8) | 12.50 12.50

**Souvenir Sheets**
| | | | |
|---|---|---|---|
| 1145 | A160 | 150 le Mauritius kestrel fal- cap. | 7.25 7.25 |
| 1146 | A160 | 150 le Crested ibis | 7.25 7.25 |

World Stamp Expo '89.

Christmas — A161

Disney characters and classic automobiles: 3 le, 1934 Phantom II Rolls-Royce Roadstar. 6 le, 1935 Mercedes-Benz 500K. 10 le, 1938 Jaguar SS-100. 12 le, 1941 Jeep. 20 le, 1937 Buick Roadmaster Sedan Model 91. 30 le, 1948 Tucker. 40 le, 1933 Alfa Romeo. 50 le, 1937 Cord. No. 1155, 1938 Fiat Topolino. 60 le, 1931 Pontiac Model 401, 1929 Pontiac Landau.

**1989, Dec. 18**    **Perf. 14x13½**
| | | | |
|---|---|---|---|
| 1147 | A161 | 3 le multicolored | .80 .80 |
| 1148 | A161 | 6 le multicolored | 1.00 1.00 |
| 1149 | A161 | 10 le multicolored | 1.25 1.25 |
| 1150 | A161 | 12 le multicolored | 1.40 1.40 |
| 1151 | A161 | 20 le multicolored | 2.00 2.00 |
| 1152 | A161 | 30 le multicolored | 2.25 2.25 |
| 1153 | A161 | 40 le multicolored | 2.25 2.25 |
| 1154 | A161 | 50 le multicolored | 2.75 2.75 |

Nos. 1147-1154 (8) | 13.95 13.95

**Souvenir Sheets**
| | | | |
|---|---|---|---|
| 1155 | A161 | 100 le multicolored | 5.50 5.50 |
| 1156 | A161 | 100 le multicolored | 5.50 5.50 |

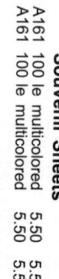

Christmas — A162

Religious paintings by Rembrandt: 3 le, Adoration of the Magi. 6 le, The Holy Family with a Cat. 10 le, The Holy Family with Angels. 15 le, Simeon in the Temple. 30 le, The Circumcision. 90 le, The Holy Family. 100 le, Visitation. 120 le, The Flight into Egypt. No. 1165, The Adoration of the Shepherds. No. 1166, The Presentation of Jesus in the Temple.

**1989, Dec. 22**    **Perf. 14**
| | | | |
|---|---|---|---|
| 1157 | A162 | 3 le multicolored | .55 .55 |
| 1158 | A162 | 6 le multicolored | .70 .70 |
| 1159 | A162 | 15 le multicolored | .95 .95 |
| 1160 | A162 | 30 le multicolored | 1.10 1.10 |
| 1161 | A162 | 90 le multicolored | 1.75 1.75 |
| 1162 | A162 | 100 le multicolored | 3.25 3.25 |
| 1163 | A162 | 120 le multicolored | 3.25 3.25 |
| 1164 | A162 | 120 le multicolored | 3.25 3.25 |

Nos. 1157-1164 (8) | 14.80 14.80

---

Exploration of Mars — A163

No. 1167: a, Kepler. b, Galileo. c, Drawings by Huygens in 1672 and Schiaparelli in 1886. d, Sir W. Herschel. e, Percival Lowell in Arizona, 1896-1907. f, Mars. g, Mariner 4, 1965. h, Mars 2, 1971. i, Mars 3, 1971.

No. 1168: a, Mariner 9, 1971. b, Mariner 9. Phobos. c, Cydonia Region. d, South polar cap. e, Profile of Mars. f, Polar cap, diff. g, Nix Olympica. h, Grand Canyon of Mars. i, North Pole.

No. 1169: a, Olympus Mons. b, Viking 1, July 1976. c, Viking 2 releases Lander, Sept. 1976. d, Lander entering Mars's atmosphere. e, Parachute deployed. f, Terminal descent. g, Viking Lander on Mars. h, Soil Sampler (robotic arm). i, Space station.

No. 1170: a, Martian dusk. b, Project Deimos. c, Exploration of Mars (astronauts surveying land). d, Return to Rombus. e, US rocket bound for Mars. f, Spacecraft bound for Mars. g, Spacecraft in Martian orbit. h, Mission to Mars (astronauts weightless in spacecraft cabin). i, Space station.

**1990**    **Litho.**    **Perf. 14**
| | | | |
|---|---|---|---|
| 1167 | A163 | Sheet of any single | 25.00 25.00 |
| a.-f. | A163 | 175 le any single | 2.75 2.75 |
| 1168 | A163 | Sheet of 9 | 25.00 25.00 |
| a.-f. | A163 | 175 le any single | 2.75 2.75 |
| 1169 | A163 | Sheet of 9 | 25.00 25.00 |
| a.-f. | A163 | 175 le any single | 2.75 2.75 |
| 1170 | A163 | Sheet of 9 | 25.00 25.00 |
| a.-f. | A163 | 175 le any single | 2.75 2.75 |

**Souvenir Sheet**
| | | | |
|---|---|---|---|
| 1171 | A163 | 150 le multicolored | 6.00 6.00 |
| 1171A | A163 | 150 le Space station | 6.00 6.00 |

Issued: No. 1171A, Dec. 24; others, Jan. 15. Extreme speculation exists about this issue, centered around No. 1171, the face on Mars stamp.

USAF aircraft.

**1990, Feb. 5**    **Litho.**    **Perf. 14**
| | | | |
|---|---|---|---|
| 1172 | A164 | 1 le Doolittle Raid B-25 | .20 .20 |
| 1173 | A164 | 2 le B-24 Libera- tor | .20 .20 |
| 1174 | A164 | 3 le A-20 Boston | .20 .20 |
| 1175 | A164 | 9 le P-38 Light- ning | .40 .40 |
| 1176 | A164 | 12 le B-26 | .40 .45 |
| 1178 | A164 | 16 le B-17 F | .65 .65 |
| 1179 | A164 | 50 le B-25 D | |
| 1180 | A164 | 80 le Boeing B-29 | 2.00 2.00 |
| 1181 | A164 | 90 le B-17 G | 3.00 3.00 |
| 1182 | A164 | 100 le The Enola Gay | 3.50 3.50 |

Nos. 1172-1181 (10) | 14.60 14.60

**Souvenir Sheets**
| | | | |
|---|---|---|---|
| 1182 | A164 | 150 le B-25 Mitchell | 4.00 4.00 |
| 1183 | A164 | 150 le B-17 G Hornet | 5.00 5.00 |

World War II — A164

Stage and Screen Roles Played by Sir Laurence Olivier (1907-1989) — A165

---

Souvenir Sheets
1165 A162 150 le multicolored   4.25 4.25
1166 A162 150 le multicolored   4.25 4.25

Miniature Sheets

Exploration of Mars — A163

Walt Disney Characters, Settings in Sierra Leone — A166

**1990, Apr. 23**
| | | | |
|---|---|---|---|
| 1194 | A166 | 3 le Bauxite mine | .20 .20 |
| 1195 | A166 | 6 le Panning for gold | .20 .20 |
| 1196 | A166 | 10 le Lungi Intl. Airport | .25 .25 |
| 1197 | A166 | 12 le Old Fourah Bay Col- lege | .30 .30 |
| 1198 | A166 | 16 le Mining baux- ite | .40 .40 |
| 1199 | A166 | 20 le Rice harvest | .50 .50 |
| 1200 | A166 | 30 le The Cotton Tree | .75 .75 |
| 1201 | A166 | 100 le Rutile Mine | 2.50 2.50 |
| 1202 | A166 | 200 le Fishing at Goderich | 5.00 5.00 |
| 1203 | A166 | 225 le Bintumani Hotel | 5.50 5.50 |
| 1204 | A166 | 250 le Market Place, King Jimmy | 5.50 5.50 |
| 1205 | A166 | 250 le Diamond mining | 5.00 5.00 |

Nos. 1194-1203 (10) | 15.60 15.60

**Souvenir Sheets**

---

Souvenir Sheets
1184 A165 3 le Antony & Cleopatra, 1951   .20
| 1185 | A165 | 6 le Henry V, 1943 | .20 |
| 1186 | A165 | 9 le Oedipus, 1945 | .20 |
| 1187 | A165 | 20 le Wuthering Heights, 1939 | .40 |
| 1188 | A165 | 30 le Marathon Man, 1976 | .50 |
| 1189 | A165 | 70 le Othello, 1964 | .70 |
| 1190 | A165 | 175 le Beau Geste, 1929 | 4.25 |
| 1191 | A165 | 200 le Richard III, 1956 | 4.75 |

Nos. 1184-1191 (8) | 12.60 12.60

**Souvenir Sheets**
| | | | |
|---|---|---|---|
| 1192 | A165 | 250 le The Battle of Britain, 1969 | 5.00 5.00 |
| 1193 | A165 | 250 le Hamlet, 1947 | 5.00 5.00 |

World Cup Soccer Championships, Italy — A168

Team photographs.

**1990, May 3**    **Perf. 14**
| | | | |
|---|---|---|---|
| 1206 | A167 | 50 le deep ultra | 1.75 1.75 |
| 1207 | A167 | 100 le violet brown | 4.50 4.50 |

**Souvenir Sheet**
1208 A167 250 le black   6.00 6.00

Penny Black, 150th Anniv. — A167

Penny Black, 150th Anniversary.

**1990, May 11 Litho. *Perf. 14***

**1209** A168 15 le Colombia .50 .50
**1210** A168 15 le United Arab Emirates .50 .50
**1211** A168 15 le South Korea .50 .50
**1212** A168 15 le Cameroun .50 .50
**1213** A168 15 le Costa Rica .50 .50
**1214** A168 15 le Romania .50 .50
**1215** A168 15 le Yugoslavia .50 .50
**1216** A168 15 le Egypt .50 .50
**1217** A168 30 le Netherlands 1.00 1.00
**1218** A168 30 le Uruguay 1.00 1.00
**1219** A168 30 le USSR 1.00 1.00
**1220** A168 30 le Czechoslova-kia 1.00 1.00
**1221** A168 30 le Scotland 1.00 1.00
**1222** A168 30 le Belgium 1.00 1.00
**1223** A168 30 le Austria 1.00 1.00
**1224** A168 30 le Sweden 1.00 1.00
**1225** A168 45 le W. Germany 1.50 1.50
**1226** A168 45 le England 1.50 1.50
**1227** A168 45 le United States 1.50 1.50
**1228** A168 45 le Ireland 1.50 1.50
**1229** A168 45 le Spain 1.50 1.50
**1230** A168 45 le Brazil 1.50 1.50
**1231** A168 45 le Italy 1.50 1.50
**1232** A168 45 le Argentina 1.50 1.50
*Nos. 1209-1232 (24)* 24.00 24.00

No. 1209 spelled "Columbia," No. 1218 "Uraguay," No. 1220 "Czecheslovakia" on stamps.

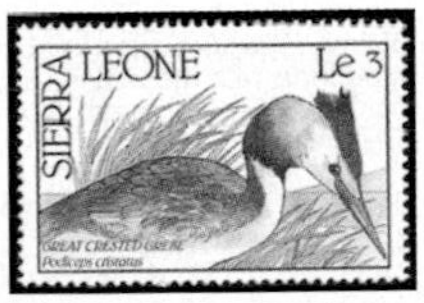

Great Crested Grebe A169

**1990, June 4**

**1233** A169 3 le shown .20 .20
**1234** A169 6 le Green wood-hoopoe .20 .20
**1235** A169 10 le African jacana .20 .20
**1236** A169 12 le Avocet .20 .20
**1237** A169 20 le African finfoot .40 .40
**1238** A169 80 le Glossy ibis 1.50 1.50
**1239** A169 150 le Hamerkop 2.75 2.75
**1240** A169 200 le Greater honey guide 3.50 3.50
*Nos. 1233-1240 (8)* 8.95 8.95

**Souvenir Sheets**

**1241** A169 250 le Painted snipe 5.00 5.00
**1242** A169 250 le Palm swift 5.00 5.00

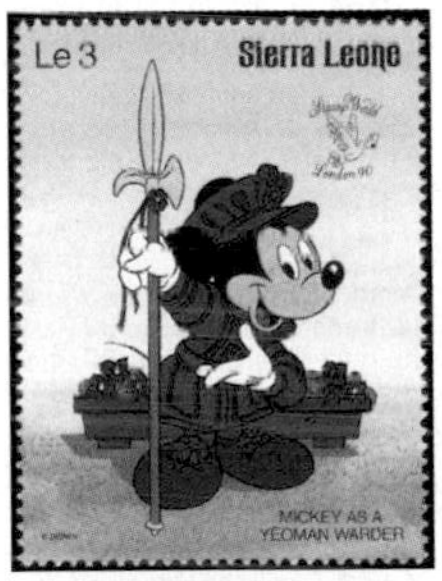

Mickey as Yeoman Warder A170

Disney characters: 6 le, Scrooge as lamplighter. 12 le, Knight Goofy. 15 le, Clarabell as Anne Boleyn. 75 le, Minnie Mouse as Queen Elizabeth I. 100 le, Donald Duck as chimney sweep. 125 le, Pete as King Henry VIII. 150 le, May dancers in Salisbury. No. 1251, Boadicea, Queen of the Iceni. No. 1252, Lawyers at Parliament House.

**1990, June 6 *Perf. 13½x14***

**1243** A170 3 le multicolored .20 .20
**1244** A170 6 le multicolored .20 .20
**1245** A170 12 le multicolored .20 .20
**1246** A170 15 le multicolored .25 .25
**1247** A170 75 le multicolored 1.90 1.90
**1248** A170 100 le multicolored 2.50 2.50
**1249** A170 125 le multicolored 3.25 3.25
**1250** A170 150 le multicolored 3.75 3.75
*Nos. 1243-1250 (8)* 12.25 12.25

**Souvenir Sheets**

**1251** A170 250 le multicolored 5.00 5.00
**1252** A170 250 le multicolored 5.00 5.00

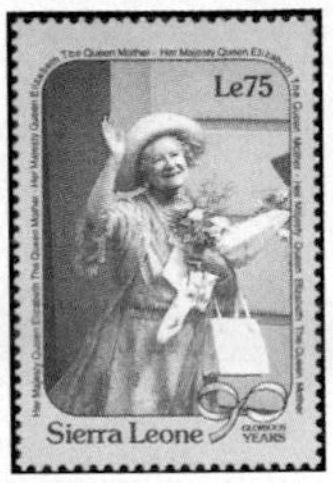

Queen Mother, 90th Birthday — A171

**1990, July 5 *Perf. 14***

**1253** 75 le shown 1.25 1.25
**1254** 75 le Wearing black hat 1.25 1.25
**1255** 75 le Wearing yellow hat 1.25 1.25
*a.* A171 Strip of 3, #1253-1255 3.75 3.75
*Nos. 1253-1255 (3)* 3.75 3.75

**Souvenir Sheet**

**1256** A171 250 le Like No. 1252 4.50 4.50

Butterfly Type of 1987

**1990 *Perf. 12½x11½***

**1257** A126 3 le like No. 861 .20 .20
**1258** A126 9 le like No. 864 .20 .20
**1259** A126 12 le like No. 859 .20 .20
**1260** A126 16 le like No. 860 .30 .30
*Nos. 1257-1260 (4)* .90 .90

Inscribed 1989.

Miniature Sheet

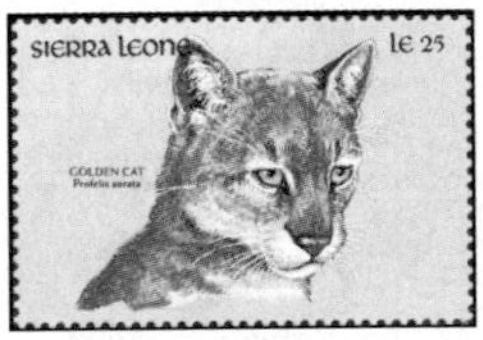

Wildlife A172

Designs: No. 1261a, Golden cat. b, White-backed night heron. c, Bateleur eagle. d, Marabou stork. e, White-faced whistling duck. f, Aardvark. g, Royal antelope. h, Pygmy hippopotamus. i, Leopard. j, Sacred ibis. k, Mona monkey. l, Darter. m, Chimpanzee. n, African elephant. o, Potto. p, African manatee. q, African fish eagle. r, African spoonbill.

**1990, Sept. 24 Litho. *Perf. 14***

**1261** Sheet of 18 13.50 13.50
*a.-r.* A172 25 le any single .70 .70

**Souvenir Sheet**

**1262** A172 150 le Crowned eagle, vert. 9.00 9.00

No. 1261 printed in continuous design showing map of Sierra Leone in background.

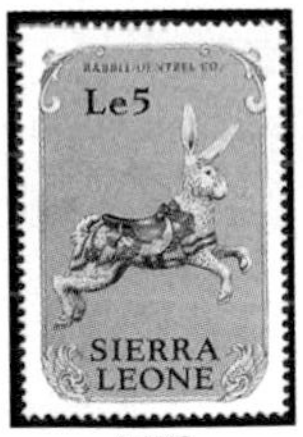

A173

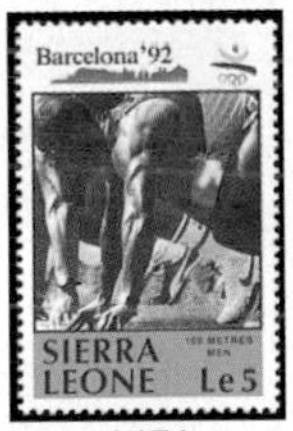

A174

Carousel animals.

**1990, Oct. 22 Litho. *Perf. 14***

**1263** A173 5 le Rabbit .20 .20
**1264** A173 10 le Horse with panther saddle .20 .20
**1265** A173 20 le Ostrich .30 .30
**1266** A173 30 le Zebra .50 .50
**1267** A173 50 le White horse .80 .80
**1268** A173 80 le Sea monster 1.25 1.25
**1269** A173 100 le Giraffe 1.60 1.60
**1270** A173 150 le Armored horse 2.40 2.40
**1271** A173 200 le Camel 3.25 3.25
*Nos. 1263-1271 (9)* 10.50 10.50

**Souvenir Sheets**

**1272** A173 300 le Centaur, Lord Baden-Powell 5.50 5.50
**1273** A173 300 le Horse head 5.50 5.50

**1990, Nov. 12 Litho. *Perf. 14***

**1274** A174 5 le Men's 100-meter race .20 .20
**1275** A174 10 le Men's 4x400-meter relay .20 .20
**1276** A174 20 le Men's 100-meter race, diff. .35 .35
**1277** A174 30 le Weight lifting .55 .55
**1278** A174 40 le Freestyle wrestling .70 .70
**1279** A174 80 le Water polo 1.40 1.40
**1280** A174 150 le Women's gymnastics 2.50 2.50
**1281** A174 200 le Cycling 3.50 3.50
*Nos. 1274-1281 (8)* 9.40 9.40

**Souvenir Sheets**

**1282** A174 400 le Boxing 6.50 6.50
**1283** A174 400 le Olympic flag 6.50 6.50

1992 Summer Olympics, Barcelona.

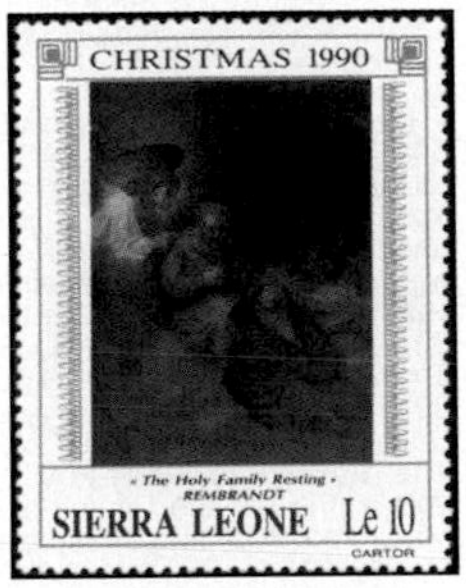

Christmas A175

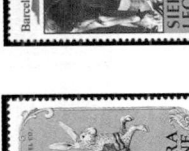

Paintings: 10 le, The Holy Family Resting by Rembrandt. 20 le, The Holy Family with St. Elizabeth by Andrea Mantegna. 30 le, Virgin and Child with an Angel by Correggio. 50 le, The Annunciation by Bernardo Strozzi. 100 le, Madonna and Child Appearing to St. Anthony by Filippino Lippi. 175 le, Virgin and Child by Giovanni Boltraffio. 200 le, The Esterhazy Madonna by Raphael. 300 le, Coronation of Mary by Orcagna. No. 1292, Adoration of the Shepherds by Bronzino. No. 1293, Adoration of the Shepherds by Gerard David.

**1990, Dec. 17 *Perf. 13***

**1284** A175 10 le multicolored .20 .20
**1285** A175 20 le multicolored .30 .30
**1286** A175 30 le multicolored .50 .50
**1287** A175 50 le multicolored .80 .80
**1288** A175 100 le multicolored 1.60 1.60
**1289** A175 175 le multicolored 2.75 2.75
**1290** A175 200 le multicolored 3.25 3.25
**1291** A175 300 le multicolored 4.75 4.75
*Nos. 1284-1291 (8)* 14.15 14.15

**Souvenir Sheets**

**1292** A175 400 le multicolored 6.50 6.50
**1293** A175 400 le multicolored 6.50 6.50

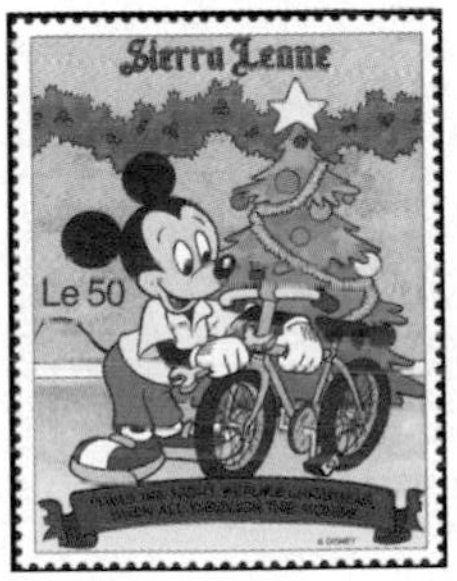

Christmas A176

Walt Disney characters in "The Night Before Christmas."

No. 1294a, 'Twas the night. . . b, Not a creature. . . c, The stockings were hung. . . d, And Mama in her kerchief. . . e, When out on the lawn. . . f, I sprang from my bed. . . g, Away to the window. . . h, Tore open the shutter. . .

No. 1295a, The moon on the breast. . . b, When what to my wondering. . . c, With a little old driver. . . d, More rapid than eagles. . . e, To the top of the porch. . . f, And then in a twinkling. . . g, As I drew in my head. . . h, He was dressed. . .

No. 1296a, A bundle of toys. . . b, The stump of a pipe. . . c, He had a broad face. . . d, He was chubby and plump. . . e, A wink of his eye. . . f, Then turned with a jerk. . . g, And giving a nod. . . h, He sprang to his sleigh. . .

No. 1297, The children were nestled. . . No. 1298, His eyes, how they twinkled. . . No. 1299, He spoke not a word. . . No. 1300, And he whistled. . . No. 1301, As dry leaves. . . No. 1302, But I heard him exclaim. . .

**1990, Dec. 17 Litho. *Perf. 13***

**Miniature Sheets of 8**

**1294** A176 50 le #a.-h. 5.75 5.75
**1295** A176 75 le #a.-h. 8.75 8.75
**1296** A176 100 le #a.-h. 11.50 11.50

**Souvenir Sheets**

**1297** A176 400 le multi 4.50 4.50
**1298** A176 400 le multi, horiz. 4.50 4.50
**1299** A176 400 le multi 4.50 4.50
**1300** A176 400 le multi, horiz. 4.50 4.50
**1301** A176 400 le multi, horiz. 4.50 4.50
**1302** A176 400 le multi 4.50 4.50

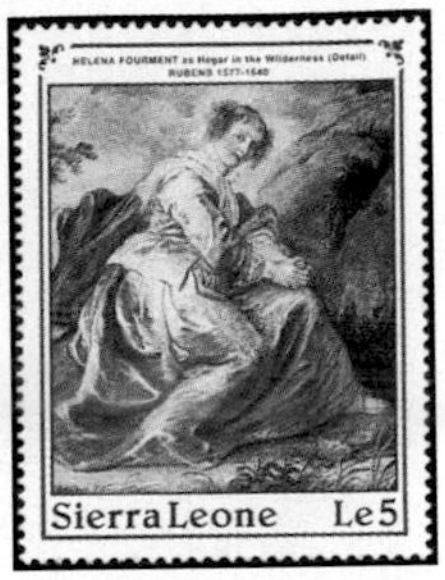

Peter Paul Rubens (1577-1640), Painter A177

Entire paintings or different details from: 5 le, Helena Fourment as Hagar in the Wilderness. 10 le, Isabella Brant. 20 le, 60 le, Countess of Arundel and Her Party. 80 le, Nicolaas Rockox. 100 le, Adriana Perez. 150 le, George Villiers, Duke of Buckingham. 300 le, Countess of Buckingham. No. 1311, Veronica Spinola Dorio. No. 1312, Giovanni Carlo Dorio.

**1990, Dec. 24 *Perf. 14***

**1303** A177 5 le multicolored .20 .20
**1304** A177 10 le multicolored .20 .20
**1305** A177 20 le multicolored .30 .30
**1306** A177 60 le multicolored .95 .95
**1307** A177 80 le multicolored 1.25 1.25
**1308** A177 100 le multicolored 1.60 1.60
**1309** A177 150 le multicolored 2.40 2.40
**1310** A177 300 le multicolored 4.75 4.75
*Nos. 1303-1310 (8)* 11.65 11.65

**Souvenir Sheets**

**1311** A177 350 le multicolored 5.50 5.50
**1312** A177 350 le multicolored 5.50 5.50

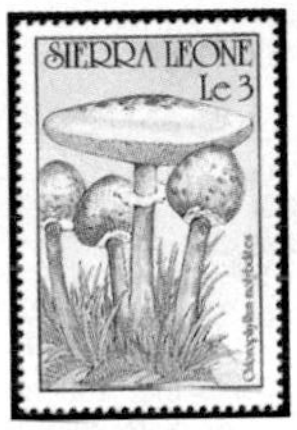

Mushrooms — A178

Designs: 3 le, Chlorophyllum molybdites. 5 le, Lepista nuda. 10 le, Clitocybe nebularis. 15 le, Cyathus striatus. 20 le, Bolbitius vitellinus. 25 le, Leucoagaricus naucinus. 30 le, Suillus luteus. 40 le, Podaxis pictillaris. 50 le, Oudemansiella radicata. 60 le, Phallus indusiatus. 80 le, Macrolepiota rhacodes. 100 le, Mycona pura 150 le, Volvariella volvacea. 175 le, Omphalotus olearius. 200 le, Sphaerobolus stellatus. 250 le, Schizophyllum commune. No. 1329, Agaricus campestris. No. 1330, Hypholama fasciculare. No. 1331, Suillus granulatus. No. 1332, Psilocybe coprophila.

**1990, Dec. 31 *Perf. 14***

**1313** A178 3 le multicolored .20 .20
**1314** A178 5 le multicolored .20 .20
**1315** A178 10 le multicolored .20 .20
**1316** A178 15 le multicolored .25 .25
**1317** A178 20 le multicolored .35 .35
**1318** A178 25 le multicolored .50 .50
**1319** A178 30 le multicolored .60 .60
**1320** A178 40 le multicolored .80 .80
**1321** A178 50 le multicolored .95 .95
**1322** A178 60 le multicolored 1.10 1.10
**1323** A178 80 le multicolored 1.50 1.50
**1324** A178 100 le multicolored 1.90 1.90
**1325** A178 150 le multicolored 2.75 2.75
**1326** A178 175 le multicolored 3.25 3.25
**1327** A178 200 le multicolored 4.00 4.00
**1328** A178 250 le multicolored 4.75 4.75
*Nos. 1313-1328 (16)* 23.30 23.30

**Souvenir Sheets**

**1329-1332** A178 350 le each 5.50 5.50

Butterfly Type of 1987 "Sierra Leone" in Blue

**1990(?) Litho.**

**1332A** A126 50c like #861 .20 .20
**1332B** A126 2 le like #863
**1332C** A126 5 le like #865
**1332D** A126 10 le like #866
**1332E** A126 30 le like #864
**1332F** A126 50 le like No. 859
**1332G** A126 60 le like #871
**1332H** A126 80 le like No. 860
**1332I** A126 100 le like #873 — —
**1332J** A126 300 le like No. 869

Issued: 2, 5, 10, 30, 60 le, 1990(?), perf. 14; 50c, 50, 80, 300 le, Aug. 1991, perf. 12½x11½.

Nos. 1332A, 1332F, 1332H-1332J inscribed 1990.

1062 SIERRA LEONE

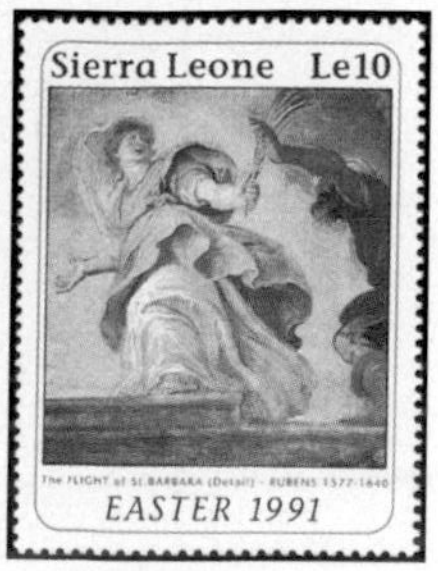
Sierra Leone Le10
EASTER 1991

Easter A179

Entire works or details from paintings by Rubens: 10 le, Flight of St. Barbara. 20 le, No. 1341, The Last Judgement. 30 le, St. Gregory of Nazianzus. 50 le, Doubting Thomas. 80 le, No. 1342, The Way to Calvary. 100 le, St. Gregory with Sts. Domitilla, Maurus and Papianus. 175 le, Sts. Gregory, Maurus and Papianus. 300 le, Christ and the Penitent Sinners.

**1991, Apr. 8 Litho. *Perf. 13½x14***

**1333** A179 10 le multicolored .20 .20
**1334** A179 20 le multicolored .30 .30
**1335** A179 30 le multicolored .50 .50
**1336** A179 50 le multicolored .80 .80
**1337** A179 80 le multicolored 1.25 1.25
**1338** A179 100 le multicolored 1.60 1.60
**1339** A179 175 le multicolored 2.75 2.75
**1340** A179 300 le multicolored 4.75 4.75
*Nos. 1333-1340 (8)* 12.15 12.15

**Souvenir Sheets**

**1341-1342** A179 400 le each 6.50 6.50

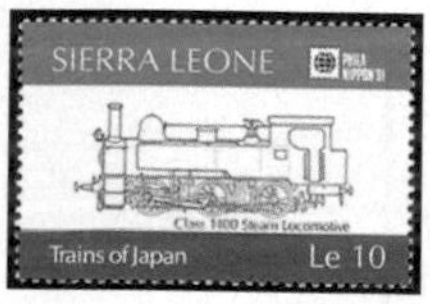
SIERRA LEONE
Trains of Japan Le 10

Phila Nippon '91 — A180

Japanese locomotives: 10 le, Class 1400 steam. 20 le, Streamlined C55 steam. 30 le, ED17 electric. 60 le, EF13 electric. 100 le, Baldwin Mikado steam. 150 le, C62 steam. 200 le, KiHa 81 class diesel. 300 le, Class 8550 steam. No. 1351, Hikari bullet train. No. 1352, Class 7000 electric. No. 1353, D51 steam. No. 1354, Class 9600 steam.

**1991, May 13 Litho. *Perf. 14***

**1343** A180 10 le multicolored .20 .20
**1344** A180 20 le multicolored .30 .30
**1345** A180 30 le multicolored .50 .50
**1346** A180 60 le multicolored .95 .95
**1347** A180 100 le multicolored 1.60 1.60
**1348** A180 150 le multicolored 2.40 2.40
**1349** A180 200 le multicolored 3.25 3.25
**1350** A180 300 le multicolored 4.75 4.75
*Nos. 1343-1350 (8)* 13.95 13.95

**Souvenir Sheets**

**1351-1354** A180 400 le each 6.50 6.50

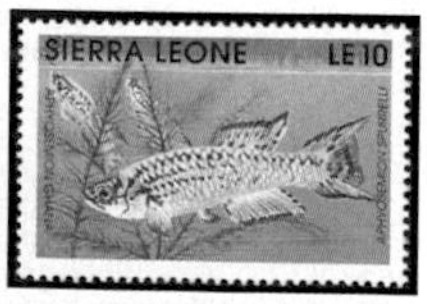
SIERRA LEONE LE10

Fish — A181

**1991, June 3 Litho. *Perf. 14***

**1355** A181 10 le Aphyosemion ghana .20 .20
**1356** A181 20 le Black-lipped panchax .25 .25
**1357** A181 30 le Peter's killie .50 .50
**1358** A181 60 le Micro-walkeri killie .95 .95
**1359** A181 100 le Butterfly fish 1.75 1.75
**1360** A181 150 le Green panchax 2.40 2.40
**1361** A181 200 le Six-barred panchax 3.25 3.25
**1362** A181 300 le Banded puffer 4.75 4.75
*Nos. 1355-1362 (8)* 14.05 14.05

**Souvenir Sheets**

**1363** A181 400 le Spotfin synodontis 6.00 6.00
**1364** A181 400 le Two-striped panchax 6.00 6.00

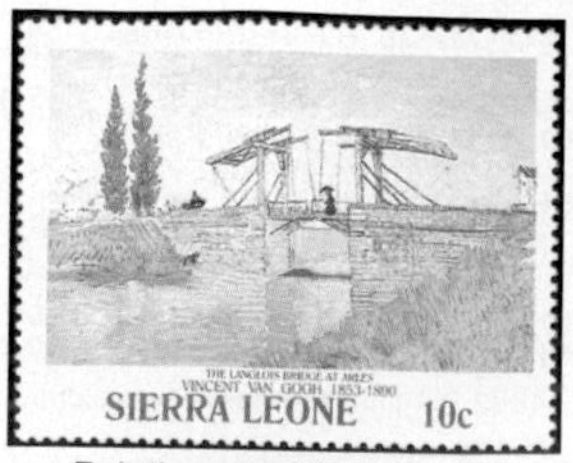
SIERRA LEONE 10c

Paintings by Vincent Van Gogh — A182

Designs: 10c, The Langlois Bridge at Arles. 50c, Trees in the Garden of Saint-Paul Hospital, vert. 1 le, Wild Flowers and Thistles in a Vase, vert. 2 le, Still Life: Vase with Oleanders and Books. 5 le, Farmhouses in a Wheat Field Near Arles. 10 le, Self-Portrait, Sept. 1889, vert. 20 le, Portrait of Patience Escalier, vert. 30 le, Portrait of Doctor Felix Rey, vert. 50 le, The Iris, vert. 60 le, The Shepherdess, vert. 80 le, Vincent's House in Arles (The Yellow House). 100 le, The Road Menders. 150 le, The Garden of Saint-Paul Hospital, vert. 200 le, View of the Church of Saint-Paul-De-Mausole. 250 le, Seascape at Saintes-Maries. 300 le, Pieta, vert. No. 1381, Church at Auvers Sur Dise, vert. No. 1382, Vineyards with a View of Auvers. No. 1383, The Trinquetaille Bridge. No. 1384, Two Poplars on a Road Through the Hills, vert. No. 1385, Haystacks in Provence. No. 1386, The Garden of Saint-Paul Hospital, diff.

**1991, June 28 Litho. *Perf. 13½***

**1365** A182 10c multicolored .20 .20
**1366** A182 50c multicolored .20 .20
**1367** A182 1 le multicolored .20 .20
**1368** A182 2 le multicolored .20 .20
**1369** A182 5 le multicolored .20 .20
**1370** A182 10 le multicolored .20 .20
**1371** A182 20 le multicolored .25 .25
**1372** A182 30 le multicolored .40 .40
**1373** A182 50 le multicolored .70 .70
**1374** A182 60 le multicolored .80 .80
**1375** A182 80 le multicolored 1.10 1.10
**1376** A182 100 le multicolored 1.40 1.40
**1377** A182 150 le multicolored 2.00 2.00
**1378** A182 200 le multicolored 2.75 2.75
**1379** A182 250 le multicolored 3.50 3.50
**1380** A182 300 le multicolored 4.00 4.00
*Nos. 1365-1380 (16)* 18.10 18.10

**Size: 102x76mm**

***Imperf***

**1381-1386** A182 400 le each 4.75 4.75

**Royal Family Birthday, Anniversary**

Common Design Type

**1991, July 5 Litho. *Perf. 14***

**1387** CD347 10 le multi .20 .20
**1388** CD347 20 le multi .30 .30
**1389** CD347 30 le multi .50 .50
**1390** CD347 80 le multi 1.25 1.25
**1391** CD347 100 le multi 1.60 1.60
**1392** CD347 200 le multi 3.25 3.25
**1393** CD347 250 le multi 4.00 4.00
**1394** CD347 300 le multi 4.75 4.75
*Nos. 1387-1394 (8)* 15.85 15.85

**Souvenir Sheets**

**1395** CD347 400 le Elizabeth, Philip 6.50 6.50
**1396** CD347 400 le Charles, Diana, sons 6.50 6.50

10 le, 30 le, 200 le, 250 le, No. 1395, Queen Elizabeth II, 65th birthday. Others, Charles and Diana, 10th wedding anniversary.

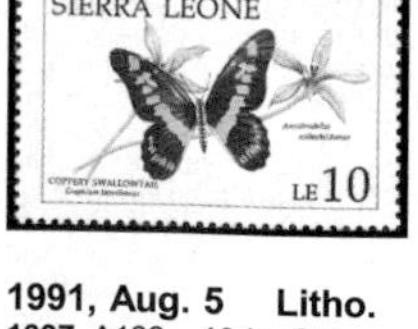
SIERRA LEONE
LE10

Butterflies A183

**1991, Aug. 5 Litho. *Perf. 14x13½***

**1397** A183 10 le Coppery swallowtail .20 .20
**1398** A183 30 le Orange forester .75 .75
**1399** A183 50 le Large striped swordtail 1.25 1.25
**1400** A183 60 le Lilac beauty 1.50 1.50
**1401** A183 80 le African leaf 1.90 1.90
**1402** A183 100 le Blue diadem 2.50 2.50
**1403** A183 200 le Beautiful monarch 5.00 5.00
**1404** A183 300 le Veined swallowtail 7.00 7.00
*Nos. 1397-1404 (8)* 20.10 20.10

**Souvenir Sheets**

***Perf. 13x12***

**1405** A183 400 le Blue banded nymph 6.25 6.25
**1406** A183 400 le Western red charaxes 3.50 3.50
**1407** A183 400 le Broad-bordered grass yellow 3.50 3.50
**1408** A183 400 le African clouded yellow 4.25 4.25

While numbers 1406-1407 have the same issue date as Nos. 1397-1405, the dollar value of Nos. 1406-1407 was lower when they were released. While No. 1408 has the same issue date as Nos. 1397-1407, the value of No. 1408 was different when released.

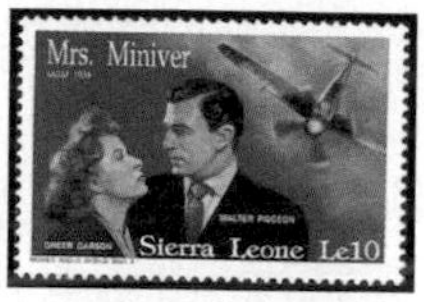
Mrs. Miniver
Sierra Leone Le10

World War II Motion Pictures A184

Designs: 2 le, To Hell and Back, Audie Murphy. 5 le, Attack, Jack Palance. 10 le, Mrs. Miniver, Greer Garson and Walter Pidgeon. 20 le, The Guns of Navarone. 30 le, The Great Dictator, Paulette Goddard and Charlie Chaplin. 50 le, The Train. 60 le, The Diary of Anne Frank. 80 le, The Bridge on the River Kwai, William Holden. 100 le, Lifeboat, Alfred Hitchcock, Tallulah Bankhead. 200 le, Sands of Iwo Jima, John Wayne. 300 le, Thirty Seconds Over Tokyo, Van Johnson and Spencer Tracy. 350 le, Casablanca, Humphrey Bogart and Ingrid Bergman. No. 1421, Twelve O'Clock High, Gregory Peck. No. 1422, Tora! Tora! Tora!. No. 1423, Patton, George C. Scott.

**1991, Oct. 14 Litho. *Perf. 14***

**1409** A184 2 le multicolored .20 .20
**1410** A184 5 le multicolored .20 .20
**1411** A184 10 le multicolored .20 .20
**1412** A184 20 le multicolored .25 .25
**1413** A184 30 le multicolored .40 .40
**1414** A184 50 le multicolored .70 .70
**1415** A184 60 le multicolored .80 .80
**1416** A184 80 le multicolored 1.10 1.10
**1417** A184 100 le multicolored 1.40 1.40
**1418** A184 200 le multicolored 2.75 2.75
**1419** A184 300 le multicolored 4.00 4.00
**1420** A184 350 le multicolored 4.75 4.75
*Nos. 1409-1420 (12)* 16.75 16.75

**Souvenir Sheets**

**1421** A184 450 le multicolored 5.50 5.50
**1422** A184 450 le multicolored 5.50 5.50
**1423** A184 450 le multicolored 5.50 5.50

Miniature Sheets

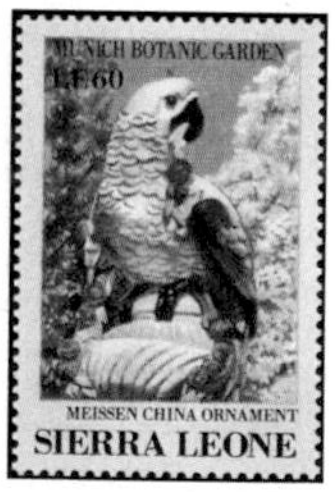
MUNICH BOTANIC GARDEN
LE60
MEISSEN CHINA ORNAMENT
SIERRA LEONE

Botanic Gardens — A185

Munich Botanic Garden: No. 1424a, Meissen China ornament. b, Masdevallia. c, White Egyptian lotus. d, French marigold. e, Pitcher plant. f, The Palm House. g, Dog's tooth violet. h, Passion flower. i, Hedge rose. j, Sensitive plant. k, Pitcher plant, diff. l, Trillium. m, Wild plantain. n, German primrose. o, Tulip. p, Spring walk.

Kyoto Botanic Garden: No. 1425a, Flowering cherry. b, Gardenia. c, The Domed Conservatory. d, Chrysanthemums. e, Bleeding heart. f, Hibiscus. g, Hiryu azalea. h, Sweet honeysuckle. i, Goldband lily. j, Non-traditional garden art. k, Viburnum. l, Japanese iris. m, Orchid. n, Hydrangea. o, View of Kyoto Botanic Garden. p, Camelia.

Brooklyn Botanic Garden: No. 1426a, The Palm House. b, Kurume azalea. c, Southern magnolia. d, Oleander. e, Chinese wisteria. f, Sourwood tree. g, Cattleya orchid. h, Gingko tree. i, Japanese Hill and Pond Garden. j, Rose. k, German iris. l, East Indian lotus. m, Speciosum lily. n, Lilac. o, Rose bay. p, Cranford Rose Garden.

No. 1427, Rhododendron, Munich, horiz. No. 1428, Chrysanthemum, Kyoto, horiz. No. 1429, Magnolia soulangeana, Brooklyn, horiz.

**1991, Oct. 28**

**Sheets of 16**

**1424** A185 60 le #a.-p. 11.50 11.50
**1425** A185 60 le #a.-p. 11.50 11.50
**1426** A185 60 le #a.-p. 11.50 11.50

**Souvenir Sheets**

**1427-1429** A185 600 le each 7.25 7.25

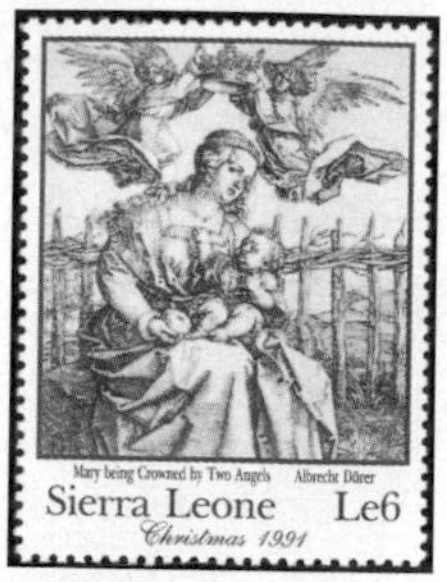
Sierra Leone Le6
Christmas 1991

Christmas A186

Details from paintings or engravings by Albrecht Durer: 6 le, Mary being Crowned by Two Angels. 60 le, St. Christopher. 80 le, Virgin and Child. 100 le, Madonna and Child (Virgin with the Pear). 200 le, Madonna and Child. 300 le, The Virgin in Half-Length. 700 le, The Madonna with the Siskin. No. 1437, The Feast of the Rose Garlands. No. 1438, Virgin and Child with St. Anne.

**1991, Dec. 9 Litho. *Perf. 12***

**1430** A186 6 le pink & black .20 .20
**1431** A186 60 le blue & black .50 .50
**1432** A186 80 le multicolored .65 .65
**1433** A186 100 le multicolored .80 .80
**1434** A186 200 le multicolored 1.60 1.60
**1435** A186 300 le multicolored 2.40 2.40
**1436** A186 700 le multicolored 5.50 5.50
*Nos. 1430-1436 (7)* 11.65 11.65

**Souvenir Sheets**

***Perf. 14½***

**1437-1438** A186 600 le each 4.75 4.75

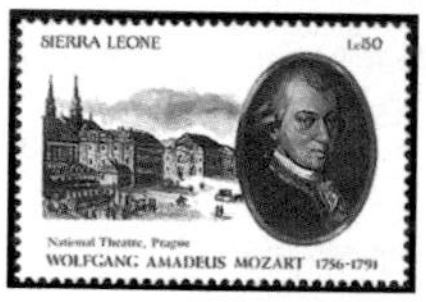
SIERRA LEONE
WOLFGANG AMADEUS MOZART 1756-1791

Wolfgang Amadeus Mozart, Death Bicent. A187

Mozart and: 50 le, National Theatre, Prague. 100 le, St. Peter's Abbey, Salzburg. 500 le, Scene from opera, "Idomeneo."

**1991, Dec. 20 *Perf. 14***

**1439** A187 50 le multicolored .45 .45
**1440** A187 100 le multicolored .90 .90
**1441** A187 500 le multicolored 4.50 4.50
*Nos. 1439-1441 (3)* 5.85 5.85

**Souvenir Sheet**

**1442** A187 600 le Bust, vert. 7.00 7.00

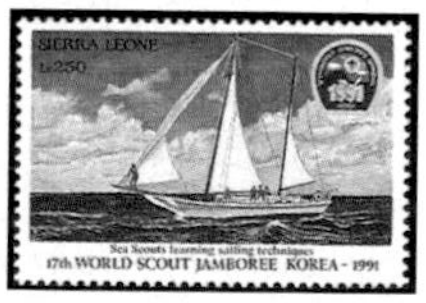
SIERRA LEONE

17th World Scout Jamboree, Korea A188

Designs: 250 le, Scouts learning to sail. 300 le, Lord Robert Baden-Powell, founder. 400 le, Scouts playing baseball. 750 le, Jamboree emblem, vert.

**1991, Dec. 20**

**1443** A188 250 le multicolored 2.00 2.00
**1444** A188 300 le multicolored 2.40 2.40
**1445** A188 400 le multicolored 3.25 3.25
*Nos. 1443-1445 (3)* 7.65 7.65

**Souvenir Sheet**

**1446** A188 750 le multicolored 7.25 7.25

Miniature Sheet

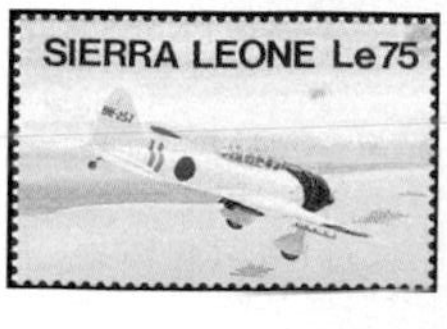
SIERRA LEONE Le75

Attack on Pearl Harbor, 50th Anniv. A189

Designs: a, Japanese D3A1 Val dive bomber. b, Plane amid rising smoke over Ford Island. c, Battleships ablaze. d, Naval station, three planes. e, Drydock ablaze, tank farm. f,

Two Vals over water, ships. g, USS Utah and Ford Island installations ablaze, ship underway. h, Installations on Ford Island ablaze. i, US P-40 Warhawk fighter plane. j, Two Japanese torpedo bombers, plane on fire falling from sky. k, Three Japanese bombers over Pearl City. l, Two Japanese bombers diving on four ships, one burning ship. m, Japanese plane on fire. n, Two Japanese planes. o, One Japanese plane over Waipio Peninsula.

**1991, Dec. 20** *Perf. 14½x15*
**1447** A189 75 le Sheet of 15, #a.-o. 12.50 12.50

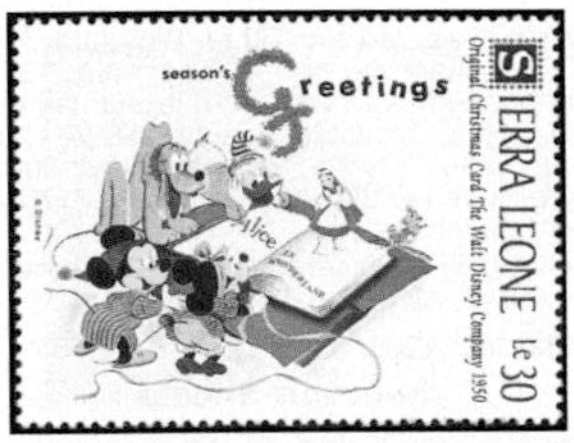


Walt Disney Christmas Cards — A190

Designs and year of issue: 12 le, Mickey and Donald decorating tree, 1952. 30 le, Characters surrounding book with "Alice in Wonderland", 1950. 60 le, Dwarf asleep with hare and tortoise, 1938. 75 le, Minnie, Donald, Mickey and Pluto mailing Christmas card, 1936. 100 le, Costumed characters in front of Magic Kingdom, 1984. 125 le, Mickey singing, Donald's nephews and Pluto reading 20,000 Leagues Under the Sea, 1954. 150 le, 101 Dalmations with season's greetings, 1960. 200 le, Donald and Mickey among gifts, 1948. 300 le, Mickey, Minnie at home for Christmas, 1983. 400 le, Donald and ducks preparing for Christmas watching Mickey Mouse Club, 1956. Characters on parade with Christmas cheer. 500 le, Disney characters, 50th birthday of Walt Disney Productions, 1972. No. 1460, Map of Magic Kingdom, 1955, vert. No. 1461, Seven dwarfs in bobsled, 1959, vert. No. 1462, Alice in Wonderland at tea party, 1950, vert.

**1991, Dec. 24** **Litho.** *Perf. 14x13½*
**1448** A190 12 le multicolored .20 .20
**1449** A190 30 le multicolored .20 .20
**1450** A190 60 le multicolored .40 .40
**1451** A190 75 le multicolored .45 .45
**1452** A190 100 le multicolored .65 .65
**1453** A190 125 le multicolored .90 .90
**1454** A190 150 le multicolored 1.00 1.00
**1455** A190 200 le multicolored 1.40 1.40
**1456** A190 300 le multicolored 2.00 2.00
**1457** A190 400 le multicolored 2.50 2.50
**1458** A190 500 le multicolored 3.25 3.25
**1459** A190 600 le multicolored 3.75 3.75
*Nos. 1448-1459 (12)* 16.70 16.70

**Souvenir Sheets**
*Perf. 13½x14*
**1460-1462** A190 900 le each 5.25 5.25

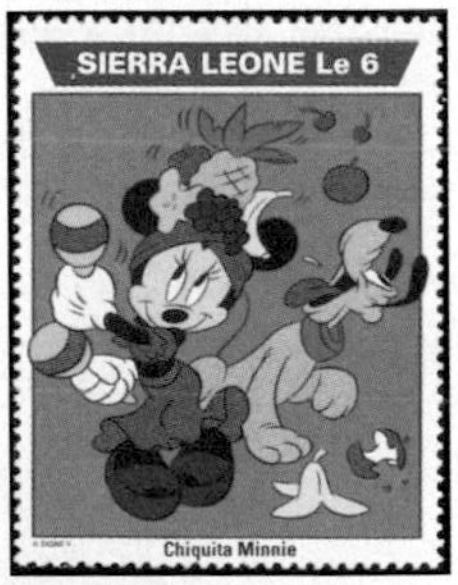


Disney Characters on World Tour A192

Designs: 6 le, Chiquita Minnie in Central America. 10 le, Gold Medal Goofy in Ancient Greece. 20 le, Donald, Daisy having Flamenco Fun in Spain. 30 le, Goofy guarding Donald at London's Buckingham Palace. 50 le, Mickey and Minnie dressed in Paris originals. 100 le, Goofy with mountain goat in Switzerland. 200 le, Daisy, Minnie as luau ladies in Hawaii. 350 le, Mickey, Donald and Goofy as ancient Egyptian comic strips, horiz. 500 le, Daisy and Minnie as can-can dancers in Paris, horiz. No. 1479, Mickey playing bagpipes in Scotland. No. 1480, Goofy fishes from Donald's gondola in Venice, Italy. No. 1481, Mickey and Goofy taking crash course in Greek.

*Perf. 13x13½, 13½x13*
**1992, Feb.** **Litho.**
**1470** A192 6 le multicolored .20 .20
**1471** A192 10 le multicolored .20 .20
**1472** A192 20 le multicolored .20 .20
**1473** A192 30 le multicolored .25 .25
**1474** A192 50 le multicolored .40 .40
**1475** A192 100 le multicolored .80 .80
**1476** A192 200 le multicolored 1.60 1.60
**1477** A192 350 le multicolored 2.75 2.75
**1478** A192 500 le multicolored 4.00 4.00
*Nos. 1470-1478 (9)* 10.40 10.40

**Souvenir Sheets**
**1479-1481** A192 700 le each 5.50 5.50

**Queen Elizabeth II's Accession to the Throne, 40th Anniv.**
Common Design Type

**1992, Feb. 6** **Litho.** *Perf. 14*
**1482** CD348 60 le multicolored .50 .50
**1483** CD348 100 le multicolored .80 .80
**1484** CD348 300 le multicolored 2.40 2.40
**1485** CD348 400 le multicolored 3.25 3.25
*Nos. 1482-1485 (4)* 6.95 6.95

**Souvenir Sheets**
**1486** CD348 700 le Queen, hillside 5.50 5.50
**1487** CD348 700 le Queen, houses 5.50 5.50

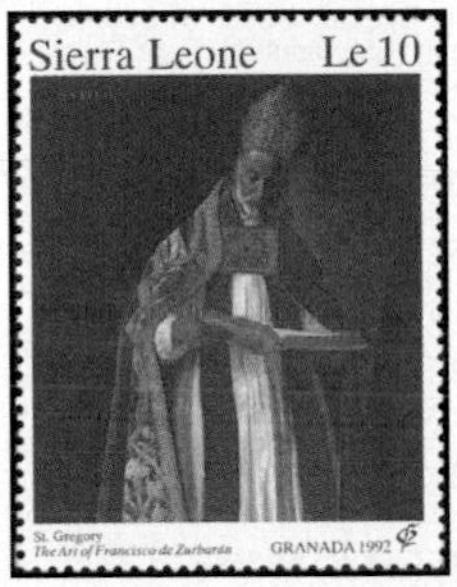


Spanish Art — A193

Paintings by Francisco de Zurbaran: 1 le, The Visit of St. Thomas Aquinas to St. Bonaventure. 10 le, St. Gregory. 30 le, St. Andrew. 50 le, St. Gabriel the Archangel. 60 le, The Blessed Henry Suso. 100 le, St. Lucy. 300 le, St. Casilda. 400 le, St. Margaret of Antioch. 500 le, St. Apollonia. 600 le, St. Bonaventure at the Council of Lyons. 700 le, St. Bonaventure on His Bier. 800 le, The Martyrdom of St. James (detail). No. 1496, St. Hugh in the Refectory, horiz. No. 1497, The Martyrdom of St. James. No. 1497A, The Young Virgin.

**1992, May 25** **Litho.** *Perf. 13*
**1487A** A193 1 le multi .20 .20
**1488** A193 10 le multi .20 .20
**1489** A193 30 le multi .25 .25
**1490** A193 50 le multi .40 .40
**1491** A193 60 le multi .45 .45
**1491A** A193 100 le multi .50 .50
**1491B** A193 300 le multi 1.50 1.50
**1492** A193 400 le multi 3.00 3.00
**1493** A193 500 le multi 4.00 4.00
**1494** A193 600 le multi 4.75 4.75
**1495** A193 700 le multi 3.50 3.50
**1495A** A193 800 le multi 4.00 4.00

**Size: 120x95mm**
*Imperf*
**1496** A193 900 le multi 7.25 7.25
**1497** A193 900 le multi 6.75 6.75
**1497A** A193 900 le multi 4.75 4.75
*Nos. 1487A-1497A (15)* 41.50 41.50

Granada '92.
While Nos. 1487A-1497A all have the same issue date, the dollar value of Nos. 1487A, 1489-1490, 1491A-1491B, 1492, 1495, 1497-1497A was lower when they were released.

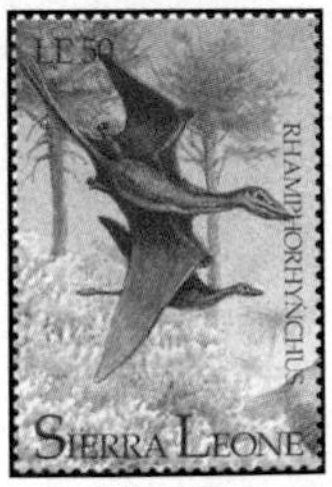


Prehistoric Animals — A194

Designs: No. 1498a, Rhamphorhynchus. b, Pteranodon. c, Dimorphodon. d, Pterodactyl. e, Archaeopteryx. f, Iguanodon. g, Hypsilophodon. h, Nothosaurus. i, Brachiosaurus. j, Kentrosaurus. k, Plesiosaurus. l, Trachodon. m, Hesperornis. n, Henodus. o, Steneosaurus. p, Stenopterygius. q, Eurhinosaurus r, Placodus. s, Mosasaurus. t, Mixosaurus. No. 1499, Herperornis, diff.

**1992, June 8** *Perf. 14*
**1498** A194 50 le Sheet of 20, #a.-t. 8.00 8.00

**Souvenir Sheet**
**1499** A194 50 le multicolored .40 .40
"Sierra Leone" is 22mm wide on No. 1499.

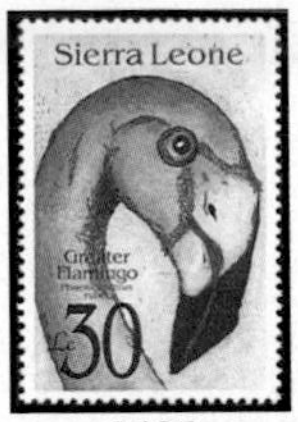


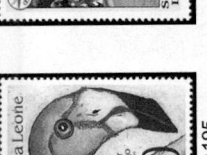

A195

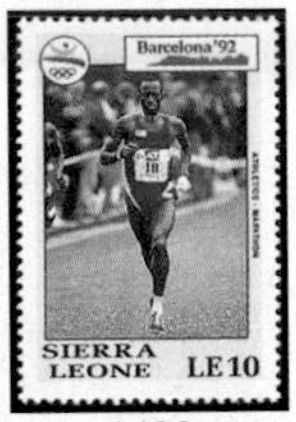


A196

Tropical Birds: 30 le, Greater flamingo. 50 le, White-crested hornbill. 100 le, Verreaux's touraco. 170 le, Yellow-spotted barbet. 200 le, African spoonbill. 250 le, Saddlebill stork. 300 le, Red-headed lovebird. 600 le, Yellow-billed barbet. No. 1508, Fire-bellied woodpecker. No. 1509, Swallow-tailed bee-eater.

**1992, July 20** **Litho.** *Perf. 14*
**1500** A195 30 le multi .25 .25
**1501** A195 50 le multi .40 .40
**1502** A195 100 le multi .50 .50
**1503** A195 170 le multi .90 .90
**1504** A195 200 le multi 1.50 1.50
**1505** A195 250 le multi 1.25 1.25
**1506** A195 300 le multi 1.60 1.60
**1507** A195 600 le multi 4.75 4.75
*Nos. 1500-1507 (8)* 11.15 11.15

**Souvenir Sheets**
**1508** A195 1000 le multi 7.75 7.75
**1509** A195 1000 le multi 5.25 5.25

While Nos. 1500-1509 all have the same release date, the value of Nos. 1502-1503, 1505-1506, 1509 was lower when they were released.

**1992** **Litho.** *Perf. 14*

1992 Summer Olympics, Barcelona: 10 le, Marathon. 20 le, Gymnastics, parallel bars. 30 le, Discus. 50 le, 110-meter hurdles, horiz. 60 le, Women's long jump. 100 le, Gymnastics floor exercise, horiz. 200 le, Windsurfing. 300 le, Road race cycling. 400 le, Weight lifting. 900 le, Soccer, horiz.

**1510** A196 10 le multicolored .20 .20
**1511** A196 20 le multicolored .20 .20
**1512** A196 30 le multicolored .25 .25
**1513** A196 50 le multicolored .35 .35
**1514** A196 60 le multicolored .45 .45
**1515** A196 100 le multicolored .75 .75
**1516** A196 200 le multicolored 1.50 1.50
**1517** A196 300 le multicolored 2.25 2.25
**1518** A196 400 le multicolored 3.00 3.00
*Nos. 1510-1518 (9)* 8.95 8.95

**Souvenir Sheet**
**1519** A196 900 le multicolored 6.75 6.75

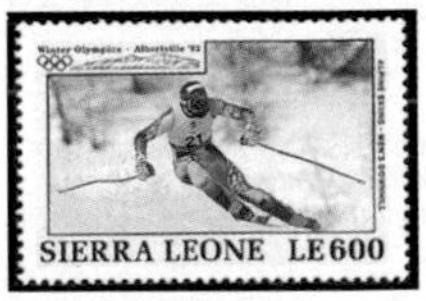


1992 Winter Olympics, Albertville A197

Designs: 250 le, Women's biathlon, vert. 500 le, Speed skating, vert. 600 le, Men's downhill skiing. No. 1523, Men's single luge. No. 1524, Ice dancing, vert.

**1992, Sept. 8** **Litho.** *Perf. 14*
**1520** A197 250 le multicolored 1.25 1.25
**1521** A197 500 le multicolored 2.60 2.60
**1522** A197 600 le multicolored 3.00 3.00
*Nos. 1520-1522 (3)* 6.85 6.85

**Souvenir Sheets**
**1523-1524** A197 900 le each 4.75 4.75

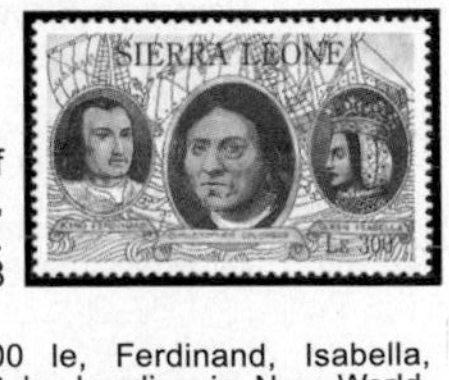


Discovery of America, 500th Anniv. A198

Designs: 300 le, Ferdinand, Isabella, Columbus. 500 le, Landing in New World. 900 le, Columbus, vert.

**1992, Oct.** **Litho.** *Perf. 14*
**1525** A198 300 le multicolored 1.60 1.60
**1526** A198 500 le multicolored 2.60 2.60

**Souvenir Sheet**
**1527** A198 900 le multicolored 4.75 4.75

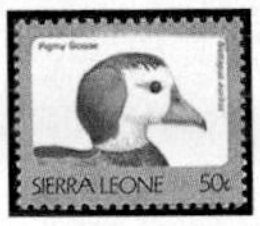


Birds — A199

Designs: 50c, Pygmy goose. 1 le, Spotted eagle owl. 2 le, Verreaux's touraco. 5 le, Saddlebill stork. 10 le, African golden oriole. 20 le, Malachite kingfisher. 30 le, Fire-crowned bishop. 40 le, Fire-bellied woodpecker. 50 le, Red-billed fire-finch. 80 le, Blue fairy flycatcher. 100 le, Crested malimbe. 150 le, Vitelline masked weaver. 170 le, Blue plantain-eater. 200 le, Superb sunbird. 250 le, Swallow-tailed bee-eater. 300 le, Cabani's yellow bunting. 500 le, Crocodile bird. 750 le, White-faced owl. 1000 le, Blue cuckoo-shrike. 2000 le, Bare-headed rock-fowl. 3000 le, Red-tailed buzzard.

**1992-93** **Litho.** *Perf. 14x15*
**1528** A199 50c multi .20 .20
**1529** A199 1 le multi .20 .20
**1530** A199 2 le multi .20 .20
**1531** A199 5 le multi .20 .20
**1532** A199 10 le multi .20 .20
**1533** A199 20 le multi .20 .20
**1534** A199 30 le multi .20 .20
**1535** A199 40 le multi .20 .20
**1536** A199 50 le multi .25 .25
**1537** A199 80 le multi .40 .40
**1538** A199 100 le multi .50 .50
**1539** A199 150 le multi .80 .80
**1540** A199 170 le multi .90 .90
**1541** A199 200 le multi 1.00 1.00
**1542** A199 250 le multi 1.25 1.25
**1543** A199 300 le multi 1.60 1.60
**1544** A199 500 le multi 2.75 2.75
**1545** A199 750 le multi 4.00 4.00
**1546** A199 1000 le multi 5.25 5.25
**1546A** A199 2000 le multi 16.00 16.00
**1546B** A199 3000 le multi 15.75 15.75
*Nos. 1528-1546B (21)* 52.05 52.05

#1536, 1538-1539, 1541, 1543 exist inscribed 1994; #1538, 1541, 1543-1544, 1546, 1546B inscribed 1996; #1536, 1538, 1541-1544 inscribed 1997; #1538, 1541, 1543, 1546 inscribed 1999; #1538, 1541-1546B 2000; #1542, 1544, 1546, 1546A, 1546B inscribed 2002.
Issued: #1528-1546, 9/92; #1546A-1546B, 1993.
See Nos. 2152-2155.

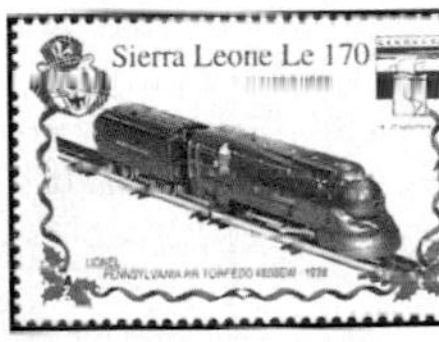


Model Trains A200

Lionel models: No. 1547a, Pennsylvania RR GG-1 electric #6-18306, O gauge, 1992. b, Wabash RR Hudson #8610, O gauge, 1985. c, Locomotive #1911, standard gauge, 1911. d, Chesapeake & Ohio 4-4-2 #6-18627, O gauge, 1992. e, Gang car #50, O gauge, 1954. f, #8004, 1980 model of Rock Island & Peoria RR engine built for Columbian Exposition of 1893, O gauge. g, Western Maryland RR Shay #6-18023, O gauge, 1992. h, (Kenner-Parker) Boston & Albany Hudson #784, O gauge, 1986. i, Locomotive #6, standard gauge, 1906.

No. 1548a, Pennsylvania RR Torpedo #238EW, O gauge, 1936. b, Denver & Rio Grande Western Alco Pa No. 6-18107, O gauge, 1992. c, #408E Locomotive, standard gauge, 1930. d, Mickey Mouse 60th birthday boxcar No. 19241, O gauge, 1991. e, Polished brass locomotive, No. 54, standard gauge, 1913. f, Broadway limited #392E, standard gauge, 1936. g, Great Northern RR EP-5 #18302, O gauge, 1988. h, 4-4-0 Locomotive #6, standard gauge, 1918. i, 4-4-4 Locomotive No. 400E, standard gauge, 1933.

No. 1549a, Special F-3 diesel engine, O gauge, 1947. b, Pennsylvania RR GE 44-ton switcher #6-18905, O gauge, 1992. c, #1 trolley, standard gauge, 1913. d, Seaboard RR freight diesel, O gauge, 1958. e, Pennsylvania S-2 turbine, O gauge, 1991. f, Western Pacific RR GP-9 diesel #6-18822, O gauge, 1992. g, #10 with Ives plates transition model, standrad gauge, 1929. h, 4-4-4 locomotive #400E, standard gauge, 1931. i, #384E, standard gauge, 1928.

No. 1550, Hudson No. 8210 Special, O gauge. No. 1551, #381E, standard gauge, 1928. No. 1552, 2-Rail electric model #300 trolley with converse body, 2⅞-inch gauge.

1064 SIERRA LEONE

**1992, Nov. 23 Litho. *Perf. 14***
**Sheets of 9**

**1547** A200 150 le #a.-i. 7.00 7.00
**1548** A200 170 le #a.-i. 8.00 8.00
**1549** A200 170 le #a.-i. 8.00 8.00

**Souvenir Sheets**
***Perf. 13***

**1550-1552** A200 1000 le each 5.25 5.25

Genoa '92 (#1547-1549). Nos. 1550-1552 contains one 51x39mm stamp.

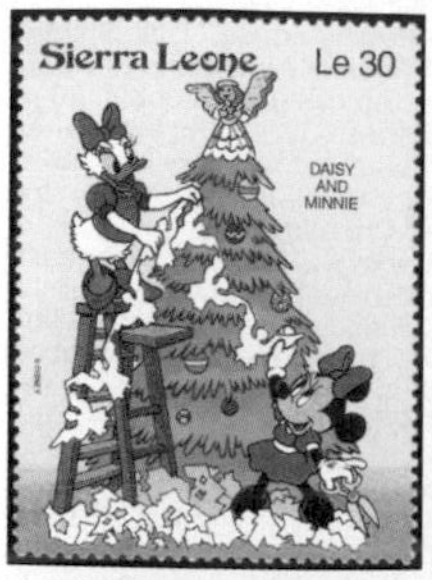
Sierra Leone Le 30
DAISY AND MINNIE
Walt Disney Characters in Christmas Scenes A201

**1992, Nov. 16 *Perf. 13½x14***

**1553** A201 10 le Minnie & Chip .20 .20
**1554** A201 20 le Goofy as Santa .20 .20
**1555** A201 30 le Daisy, Minnie .20 .20
**1556** A201 50 le Mickey, Goofy .25 .25
**1557** A201 80 le Pete .40 .40
**1558** A201 100 le Donald Duck .50 .50
**1559** A201 150 le Morty & Ferdie .80 .80
**1560** A201 200 le Mickey 1.00 1.00
**1561** A201 300 le Goofy with ornament 1.60 1.60
**1562** A201 500 le Chip & Dale 2.00 2.00
**1563** A201 600 le Donald & Dale 3.25 3.25
**1564** A201 800 le Huey, Dewey & Louie 4.25 4.25
*Nos. 1553-1564 (12)* 15.25 15.25

**Souvenir Sheets**

**1565** A201 900 le Mickey Mouse 4.75 4.75

***Perf. 14x13½***

**1566** A201 900 le Angel with Chip, horiz. 4.75 4.75
**1567** A201 900 le Mickey & Minnie, horiz. 4.75 4.75

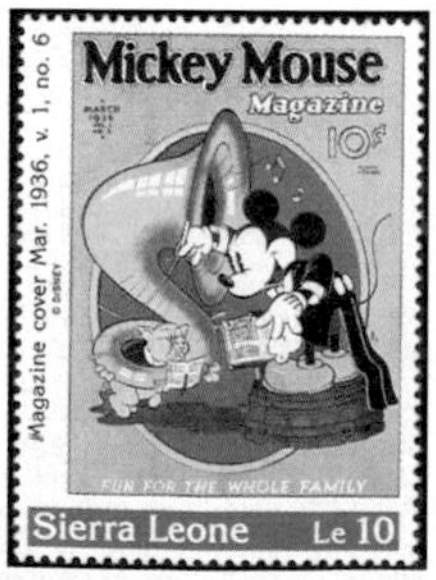
Mickey Mouse Magazine
Magazine cover Mar. 1936, v. 1, no. 6
FUN FOR THE WHOLE FAMILY
Sierra Leone Le 10
Mickey Mouse Magazines and Books A202

10 le, Magazine cover, Mar. 1936, v. 1, #6. 20 le, Magazine cover, June 1936, v. 1, #9. 30 le, Magazine cover, Nov. 1936, v. 2, #2. 40 le, Magazine cover, Aug. 1937, v. 2, #11. 50 le, Magazine cover, Oct. 1937, v. 2, #13. 60 le, Magazine cover, Dec. 1937, v. 3, #3. 70 le, Magazine cover, Jan. 1938, v. 3, #4. 150 le, Cover, Big Book #4062, 1935. 170 le, Story book cover, 1936. 200 le, Comic book cover, unnumbered. 300 le, Comic book cover, No. 181. 400 le, Comic book cover #194. 500 le, Story book cover, Book 1, 1931. No. 1581, Boys' and Girls' March of Comics cover, 1948. No. 1582, First Mickey Mouse Magazine cover for June-Aug. 1935, v. 1, #1, horiz. No. 1583, Cover of early Mickey Mouse story book published in England, 1933, horiz.

**1992 *Perf. 13½x14***

**1568** A202 10 le multicolored .20 .20
**1569** A202 20 le multicolored .20 .20
**1570** A202 30 le multicolored .20 .20
**1571** A202 40 le multicolored .20 .20
**1572** A202 50 le multicolored .30 .30
**1573** A202 60 le multicolored .35 .35
**1574** A202 70 le multicolored .40 .40
**1575** A202 150 le multicolored .80 .80
**1576** A202 170 le multicolored .90 .90
**1577** A202 200 le multicolored 1.00 1.00
**1578** A202 300 le multicolored 1.60 1.60
**1579** A202 400 le multicolored 2.00 2.00
**1580** A202 500 le multicolored 2.75 2.75
*Nos. 1568-1580 (13)* 10.90 10.90

**Souvenir Sheets**

**1581** A202 900 le multicolored 4.75 4.75

***Perf. 14x13½***

**1582** A202 900 le multicolored 4.75 4.75
**1583** A202 900 le multicolored 4.75 4.75

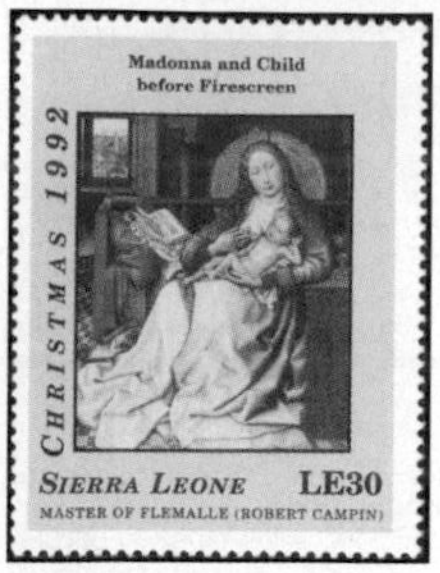
Madonna and Child before Firescreen
CHRISTMAS 1992
SIERRA LEONE LE30
MASTER OF FLEMALLE (ROBERT CAMPIN)
Christmas A203

Details or entire paintings: 1 le, Virgin and Child, by Fiorenzo di Lorenzo. 10 le, Madonna and Child on a Wall, by Circle of Dirk Bouts. 20 le, Virgin and Child with the Flight into Egypt, by Master of Hoogstraeten. 30 le, Madonna and Child before Firescreen, by Master of Flemalle. 50 le, Mary in a Rose Garden, by Hans Memling. 100 le, Virgin Mary and Child, by Lucas Cranach the Elder. 170 le, Virgin and Child, by Rogier van der Weyden. 200 le, Madonna and Saints, by Perugino. 250 le, Madonna Enthroned with Saints Catherine and Barbara, by Master of Hoogstraeten. 300 le, The Virgin in a Rose Arbor, by Stefan Lochner. 500 le, Madonna and Child with Angels, by Sandro Botticelli. 1000 le, Madonna and Child with Young St. John the Baptist, by Fra Bartolommeo. No. 1596, The Virgin with the Green Cushion, by Andrea Solario. No. 1597, The Virgin and Child, by Jan Gossaert. No. 1598, The Virgin and Child, by Lucas Cranach the Younger.

**1992, Dec. 7 Litho. *Perf. 13½x14***

**1584** A203 1 le multi .20 .20
**1585** A203 10 le multi .20 .20
**1586** A203 20 le multi .20 .20
**1587** A203 30 le multi .20 .20
**1588** A203 50 le multi .30 .30
**1589** A203 100 le multi .50 .50
**1590** A203 170 le multi .90 .90
**1591** A203 200 le multi 1.00 1.00
**1592** A203 250 le multi 1.25 1.25
**1593** A203 300 le multi 1.60 1.60
**1594** A203 500 le multi 2.75 2.75
**1595** A203 1000 le multi 5.25 5.25
*Nos. 1584-1595 (12)* 14.35 14.35

**Souvenir Sheets**

**1596-1598** A203 900 le each 4.75 4.75

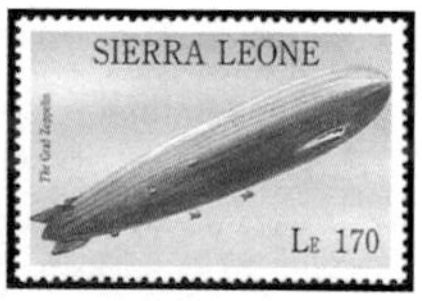
SIERRA LEONE
Le 170
Anniversaries and Events A204

150 le, Emblems of FAO, ICN, WHO. #1600, Graf Zeppelin. #1601, Cow, emblems, grain stalk. 200 le, Starving child. #1603, Lions Intl. emblem, map. #1604, Cottonwood tree. 300 le, African elephant. 600 le, Space Shuttle. 700 le, Graf Zeppelin LZ 127, specifications. #1608, Astronaut. #1609, Count Zeppelin.

**1992, Dec. Litho. *Perf. 14***

**1599** A204 150 le multicolored .80 .80
**1600** A204 170 le multicolored .90 .90
**1601** A204 170 le multicolored .90 .90
**1602** A204 200 le multicolored 1.00 1.00
**1603** A204 250 le multicolored 1.25 1.25
**1604** A204 250 le multicolored 1.25 1.25
**1605** A204 300 le multicolored 1.60 1.60
**1606** A204 600 le multicolored 3.25 3.25
**1607** A204 700 le multicolored 3.65 3.65
*Nos. 1599-1607 (9)* 14.60 14.60

**Souvenir Sheets**

**1608-1609** A204 900 le each 4.75 4.75

Intl. Conference on Nutrition, Rome (#1599, 1601). Count Zeppelin, 75th anniv. of death (#1600, 1607, 1609). World Health Organization (#1602). Lions Intl., 75th anniv. (#1603). Earth Summit, Rio de Janeiro (#1604-1605). Intl. Space Year (#1606, 1608).

Miniature Sheet

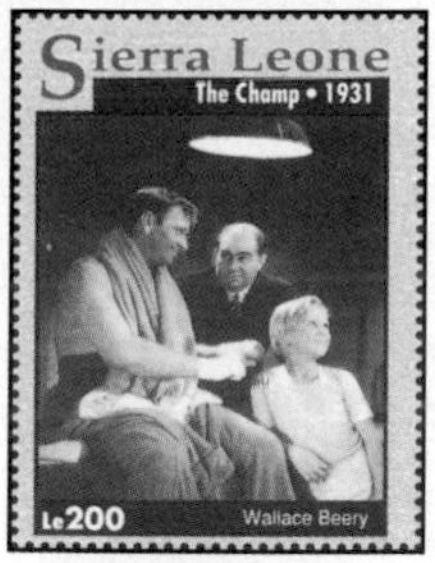
Sierra Leone
The Champ • 1931
Le200
Wallace Beery
Boxing A205

Boxing movies, stars: No. 1610a, The Champ, Wallace Beery. b, Golden Boy, William Holden. c, Body and Soul, John Garfield. d, Champion, Kirk Douglas. e, The Set-Up, Robert Ryan. f. Requiem for a Heavyweight, Anthony Quinn. g, Kid Galahad, Elvis Presley. h, Fat City, Jeff Bridges.

No. 1612, Gentlemen Jim, Errol Flynn. No. 1614, Rocky III, Sylvester Stallone.

Boxing champions: No. 1611a, Joe Louis. b, Archie Moore. c, Muhammad Ali. d, George Foreman. e, Joe Frazier. f, Marvin Hagler. g, Sugar Ray Leonard. h, Evander Holyfield.

No. 1613, Muhammad Ali, diff.

**1993, Feb. 8 Litho. *Perf. 13½x14***

**1610** A205 200 le Sheet of 8, #a.-h. 8.50 8.50
**1611** A205 200 le Sheet of 8, #a.-h. 8.50 8.50

**Souvenir Sheets**

**1612-1614** A205 1000 le each 5.25 5.25

Miniature Sheets

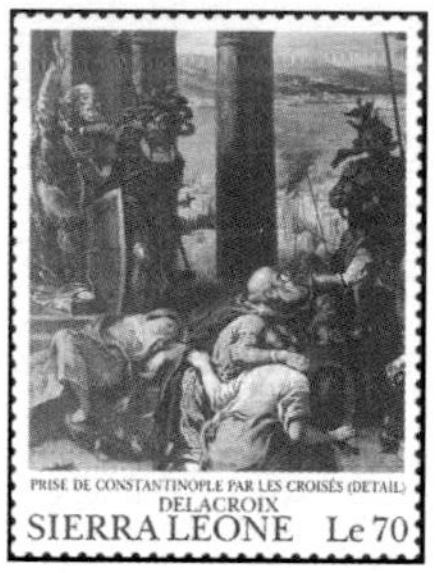
PRISE DE CONSTANTINOPLE PAR LES CROISÉS (DETAIL)
DELACROIX
SIERRA LEONE Le70
Louvre Museum, Bicent. A206

Details or entire paintings by Eugene Delacroix (1798-1863): Nos. 1615a-1615b, Entry of the Crusaders into Constantinople (left, right). c-d, Jews Purchasing Brides in Morocco (left, right). e-f, The Death of Sardanapalus (left, right). g-h, Liberty Guiding the People (left, right).

No. 1616a, An Orphan at the Cemetery. b-c, Women of Algiers in their Apartment (left, right). d, Dante and Virgil in the Infernal Regions. e, Self-Portrait. f-g, Massacre at Chios (left, right). h, Frederic Chopin.

No. 1617, Rape of the Sabine Women, by Jacques-Louis David (1748-1825).

**1993, Mar. 8 Litho. *Perf. 12x12½***

**1615** A206 70 le Sheet of 8, #a.-h. + label 3.00 3.00
**1616** A206 70 le Sheet of 8, #a.-h. + label 3.00 3.00

**Souvenir Sheet**
***Perf. 14½***

**1617** A206 900 le multicolored 4.75 4.75

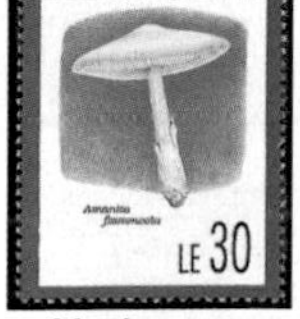
SIERRA LEONE
LE 30
Mushrooms A207

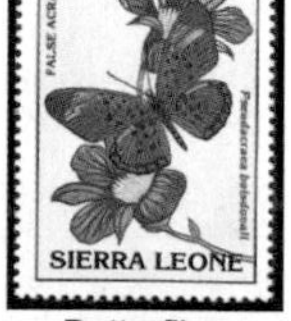
Le20
FALSE ACRAEA
SIERRA LEONE
Butterflies A208

Designs: 30 le, Amanita flammeola. 50 le, Cantharellus pseudocibarius. 100 le, Volvariella volvacea. 200 le, Termitomyces microcarpus. 300 le, Auricularia auricula. 400 le, Pleurotus tuberregium. 500 le, Schizophyllum commune. 600 le, Termitomyces robustus. No. 1626, Phallus rubicundus. No. 1627, Daldina concentrica.

**1993, May 5 *Perf. 14***

**1618** A207 30 le multi .20 .20
**1619** A207 50 le multi .30 .30
**1620** A207 100 le multi .50 .50
**1621** A207 200 le multi 1.00 1.00
**1622** A207 300 le multi 1.50 1.50
**1623** A207 400 le multi 2.10 2.10
**1624** A207 500 le multi 2.75 2.75
**1625** A207 600 le multi 3.25 3.25
*Nos. 1618-1625 (8)* 11.60 11.60

**Souvenir Sheets**

**1626-1627** A207 1000 le each 5.25 5.25

**1993, May 5**

20 le, False acraea. 30 le, Blue temora. 50 le, Foxy charaxes. 100 le, Leaf blue. 150 le, Blue-banded swallowtail. 170 le, African monarch. 200 le, Mountain beauty. 250 le, Gaudy commodore. 300 le, Palla butterfly. 500 le, Pirate butterfly. 600 le, Painted lady. 700 le, Gold-banded forester.

#1640, Blue diadem. #1641, Blue swallowtail. #1642, African leaf butterfly.

**1628-1639** A208 Set of 12 16.50 16.50

**Souvenir Sheets**

**1640-1642** A208 1000 le Set of 3 15.50 15.50

Miniature Sheets

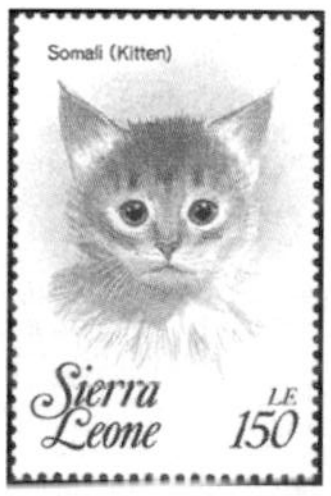
Somali (Kitten)
Sierra Leone LE 150
Cats A209

Designs: No. 1643a, Somali. b, Egyptian Mau smoke. c, Chocolate-point Siamese. d, Mi-Ke Japanese bobtail. e, Chinchilla. f, Red Burmese. g, British shorthair brown tabby. h, Blue Persian. i, British silver classic tabby. j, Oriental ebony. k, Red Persian. l, British calico shorthair.

No. 1644a, Black Persian. b, Blue-point Siamese. c, American wirehair. d, Birman. e, Scottish fold (silver tabby). f, American shorthair red tabby. g, Blue & white Persian bicolor. h, Havana brown. i, Norwegian forest cat. j, Brown tortie Burmese. k. Angora. l, Exotic shorthair.

No. 1645, American shorthair blue tabby, horiz. No. 1646, Seal-point colorpoint, horiz.

**1993, May 17 Litho. *Perf. 14***

**1643** A209 150 le Sheet of 12, #a.-l. 9.50 9.50
**1644** A209 150 le Sheet of 12, #a.-l. 9.50 9.50

**Souvenir Sheets**

**1645-1646** A209 1000 le each 5.25 5.25

Nos. 1643-1646 Ovptd. with Hong Kong '94 Emblem

**1994 Litho. *Perf. 14***

*1643m* On #1643b & in sheet margin 9.50 9.50
*1644m* On #1644b & in sheet margin 9.50 9.50
*1645a* Ovptd. in sheet margin 5.25 5.25
*1646a* Ovptd. in sheet margin 5.25 5.25

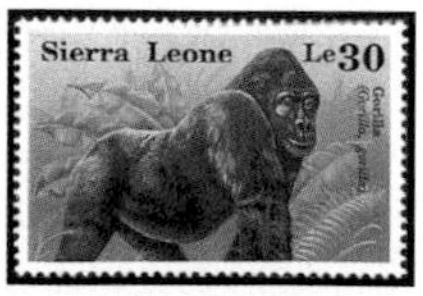
Sierra Leone Le30
Wild Animals A210

**1993, June 17**

**1647** A210 30 le Gorilla .20 .20
**1648** A210 100 le Bongo .50 .50
**1649** A210 150 le Potto .80 .80
**1650** A210 170 le Chimpanzee .90 .90
**1651** A210 200 le Dwarf galago 1.00 1.00
**1652** A210 300 le African linsang 1.60 1.60
**1653** A210 500 le Banded duiker 2.75 2.75
**1654** A210 750 le Diana monkey 4.00 4.00
*Nos. 1647-1654 (8)* 11.75 11.75

**Souvenir Sheets**

**1655** A210 1200 le Leopard 6.25 6.25
**1656** A210 1200 le Elephant 6.25 6.25

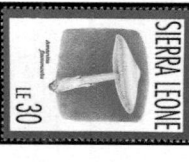

## Flowers — A211

30 le, Bleeding-heart vine. 40 le, Passion vine. 50 le, Hydrangea. 60 le, Wax begonia. 100 le, Hibiscus. 150 le, Crape-myrtle. 170 le, Bougainvillea. 200 le, Leadwort. 250 le, Gerbera daisy. 300 le, Black-eyed susan. 500 le, Gloriosa lily, diff. #1669, #1670, Sweet violet. #1669, #1671, Hibiscus, diff.

**1993, July 15    Litho.    Perf. 14**

| No. | Type | Denom. | | | |
|---|---|---|---|---|---|
| 1657 | A211 | 30 le multi | .20 | .20 |
| 1658 | A211 | 40 le multi | .25 | .25 |
| 1659 | A211 | 50 le multi | .25 | .25 |
| 1660 | A211 | 60 le multi | .30 | .30 |
| 1661 | A211 | 100 le multi | .50 | .50 |
| 1662 | A211 | 150 le multi | .80 | .80 |
| 1663 | A211 | 170 le multi | .90 | .90 |
| 1664 | A211 | 200 le multi | 1.00 | 1.00 |
| 1665 | A211 | 250 le multi | 1.25 | 1.25 |
| 1666 | A211 | 300 le multi | 1.50 | 1.50 |
| 1667 | A211 | 500 le multi | 2.50 | 2.50 |
| 1668 | A211 | 900 le multi | 3.00 | 3.00 |
| | | Nos. 1657-1668 (12) | 12.40 | 12.40 |

**Souvenir Sheets**

1669-1671 A211 1200 le each  6.25  6.25

## Coronation of Queen Elizabeth II, 40th Anniv. — A212

100 le, Queen, Princess Anne. 200 le, Coronation procession. 600 le, Official coronation photograph. 1500 le, Portrait, by Pietro Annigoni, 1954-55.

**1993, Oct.   Litho.   Perf. 14**

| 1672 | A212 | 100 le multicolored | .50 | .50 |
|---|---|---|---|---|
| 1673 | A212 | 200 le black | 1.00 | 1.00 |
| 1674 | A212 | 600 le multicolored | 3.25 | 3.25 |
| | | Nos. 1672-1674 (3) | 4.75 | 4.75 |

**Souvenir Sheet**

1675 A212 1500 le multicolored  7.75  7.75

## Copernicus (1473-1543) — A213

250 le, Early telescope. 800 le, Moon's surface.

**1993, Oct.**

1676 A213 250 le multicolored  1.25  1.25
1677 A213 800 le multicolored  4.25  4.25

## Picasso (1881-1973) — A214

**1993, Oct.**

Sculpture: 170 le, Woman with Hat, 1961. Paintings: 200 le, Buste de Femme, 1958. 800 le, Maya with a Doll, 1938. 1000 le, Women of Algiers (after Delacroix), 1955.

1678 A214 170 le multicolored  .90  .90
1679 A214 200 le multicolored  1.00  1.00
1680 A214 800 le multicolored  4.25  4.25
Nos. 1678-1680 (3)  6.15  6.15

**Souvenir Sheet**

1681 A214 1000 le multicolored  5.25  5.25

## Christmas — A215

Details or entire paintings, by Raphael: 50 le, 100 le, No. 1690, Madonna of the Fish. 150 le, Madonna & Child Enthroned with Five Saints. 800 le, The Holy Family with the Lamb. Details or entire woodcuts, by Durer: 200 le, 250 le, 300 le, The Circumcision. 500 le, No. 1691, Holy Clan with Saints and Two Angels Playing Music.

**1993, Dec.    Perf. 13½x14**

| 1682 | A215 | 50 le multi | .25 | .25 |
|---|---|---|---|---|
| 1683 | A215 | 100 le multi | .50 | .50 |
| 1684 | A215 | 150 le multi | .80 | .80 |
| 1685 | A215 | 200 le multi | 1.00 | 1.00 |
| 1686 | A215 | 250 le multi | 1.25 | 1.25 |
| 1687 | A215 | 300 le multi | 1.50 | 1.50 |
| 1688 | A215 | 500 le multi | 2.50 | 2.50 |
| 1689 | A215 | 800 le multi | 4.25 | 4.25 |
| | | Nos. 1682-1689 (8) | 12.05 | 12.05 |

**Souvenir Sheets**

1690-1691 A215 1200 le each  6.25  6.25

## Christmas — A216

Disney characters celebrate Christmas: different: #1700, Santa. #1701, Elves, horiz. #1702, Santa, horiz. #1703, Mickey, Minnie, horiz.

**1993, Dec. 17    Perf. 13½x14, 14x13½**

| 1692 | A216 | 50 le multi | .25 | .25 |
|---|---|---|---|---|
| 1693 | A216 | 100 le multi | .50 | .50 |
| 1694 | A216 | 170 le multi | .90 | .90 |
| 1695 | A216 | 200 le multi | 1.00 | 1.00 |
| 1696 | A216 | 250 le multi | 1.25 | 1.25 |
| 1697 | A216 | 500 le multi | 2.50 | 2.50 |
| 1698 | A216 | 600 le multi | 3.00 | 3.00 |
| 1699 | A216 | 800 le multi | 4.25 | 4.25 |
| | | Nos. 1692-1699 (8) | 13.65 | 13.65 |

**Souvenir Sheets**

**Perf. 13½x14, 14x13½**

1700-1703 A216 1200 le each  6.25  6.25

## 1994 World Cup Soccer Championships, US — A217

Players, country: 30 le, Jose Luis Brown (R), Argentina. 50 le, Gary Lineker, England. 100 le, Carlos Valderrama, Colombia. 250 le, Skuhravy, Czechoslovakia; Marchena, Costa Rica. 300 le, Butragueno, Spain. 400 le, Roger Milla, Cameroun. 500 le, Roberto Donadoni, Italy. 700 le, Enzo Scifo, Belgium. No. 1712, 1200 le, Socrates, Brazil. No. 1713, 1200 le, Wright, England; Demol, Belgium.

**1993    Perf. 13½x14**

1704-1711 A217  Set of 8  10.00  10.00

**Souvenir Sheets**

1712-1713 A217 1200 le each  6.25  6.25

## Hong Kong '94 — A219

Stamps and: No. 1714, Hong Kong #455, pagoda, Tiger Baum Garden. No. 1715, Ai Par Garden, #1084.

Carved lacquer, Qing Dynasty: No. 1716a, Bowl with "Wan-Sui-Ch'ang-Chun." b, Four-wheeled box. c, Flower container. d, Box with human figure design. e, Shishi dog (not lacquer), f, Persimmon.

**1994, Feb. 18    Litho.    Perf. 14**

1714 A218 200 le multicolored  1.00  1.00
1715 A218 200 le multicolored  1.00  1.00
a.  Pair, #1714-1715  2.00  2.00

**Miniature Sheet**

1716 A219 100 le Sheet of 6, #a.-f.  3.25  3.25

Nos. 1714-1715 issued in sheets of 5 pairs. No. 1715a is a continuous design. New Year 1994 (Year of the Dog) (#1716e).

## New Year 1994 (Year of the Dog) — A220

a, 100 le, Pekingese. b, 150 le, Doberman pinscher. c, 200 le, Tibetan terrier. d, 250 le, Weimaraner. e, 400 le, Rottweiler. f, 500 le, Akita. g, 600 le, Schnauzer. h, 1000 le, Tibetan spaniel. No. 1718, Wire-haired pointing Griffon. No. 1719, Shih Tzu.

**1994, June 20    Litho.    Perf. 14**

1717 A220  Sheet of 8, #a.-h.  13.00  13.00

**Souvenir Sheets**

1718-1719 A220 1200 le each  4.75  4.75

## D Day, 50th Anniv. — A221

Designs: 500 le, British paratroops drop behind enemy lines. 750 le, US paratrooper jumps from C47 transport. 1000 le, C47 Douglas Dakota, paratroops.

**1994, July 11    Litho.    Perf. 14**

1720 A221 500 le multicolored  2.00  2.00
1721 A221 750 le multicolored  3.00  3.00

**Souvenir Sheet**

1722 A221 1000 le multicolored  4.00  4.00

A222

## PHILAKOREA '94 — A223

100 le, Traditional wedding, Korea House, Seoul. 400 le, Royal tombs, Koryo Dynasty, Kaesong. 600 le, Terraced farm land, near Chungmu.

Tiger paintings, Choson Dynasty: No. 1726: a, Tiger, cubs. 19th cent. b, Munsa-pasal seated on lion. c, Extinct Korean tiger. d, Tiger, bamboo. e, Tiger guarding 3 cubs. 4 magpies. f, Tiger, 19th cent. g, Mountain Spirit. h, Tiger, bird in tree.

No. 1727, Wall painting of mounted hunters from Tomb of the Dancers of Kungnaesong, Koguryo period.

**1994, July 11    Perf. 14, 13½ (#1726)    Litho.**

1723-1725 A222  Set of 3  4.50  4.50

**Miniature Sheet of 8**

1726 A223 200 le #a.-h.  6.50  6.50

**Souvenir Sheet**

1727 A222 1200 le multicolored  4.75  4.75

**Miniature Sheets of 6**

## First Manned Moon Landing, 25th Anniv. — A224

No. 1728: a, Edwin E. Aldrin, Jr. b, Michael Collins. c, Neil A. Armstrong. d, Apollo 11 liftoff. e, Aldrin descending to lunar surface. f, Armstrong, lunar module Eagle reflected in Aldrin's face shield.

No. 1729: a, Aldrin gathering soil samples. b, Eagle with Aldrin deploying solar wind experiment. c, Aldrin, ALSEP & Eagle at Tranquility Base. d, US flag, Aldrin. e, Plaque on moon. f, Apollo 11 crew, stamp ceremony. 1000 le, First footprint on moon.

**1994, July 11    Perf. 14**

1728-1729 A224 200 le #a, ea  4.75  4.75

**Souvenir Sheet**

1730 A224 1000 le multicolored  4.00  4.00

**Miniature Sheet of 6**

A225

## 1994 World Cup Soccer Championships, U.S. — A226

Players: No. 1731a, Kim Ho, South Korea. b, Cobi Jones, U.S. c, Claudio Suarez, Mexico. d, Tomas Brolin, Sweden. e, Ruud Gullit, Netherlands. f, Andreas Herzog, Austria. No. 1732, Sierra Leone team. No. 1733, Giants Stadium, New Jersey.

**1994, July 15**

1731 A225 250 le #a.-f.  6.00  6.00

**Souvenir Sheets**

1732-1733 A226 1500 le each  6.00  6.00

## Birds — A227

No. 1739, Greater flamingo, vert.

250 le, Black kite, 300 le, Superb sunbird. 500 le, Martial eagle, 800 le, Red bishop. White-necked picathartes: No. 1738a, 50 le, Feeding young. b, 100 le, On brown tree limb. c, 150 le, Two at nest. d, On gray limb, green leaves.

No. 1739, Greater flamingo, vert. No. 1740, White-necked picathartes up close, vert.

**1994, Aug. 10**

| | | | |
|---|---|---|---|
| 1734-1737 | A227 | Set of 4 | |
| 1738 | A227 | 3 each, #a.-d. | |

**Miniature Sheet of 12**
| | | | |
|---|---|---|---|
| | | 11.00 | 11.00 |
| | | 11.00 | 11.00 |

**Souvenir Sheets**
| | | | |
|---|---|---|---|
| 1739-1740 | A227 | 1200 le each | 5.75 5.75 |

World Wildlife Fund (#1738).

## Orchids — A228

Designs: 50 le, Aerangis kotschyana. 100 le, Brachycorythis kalbreyeri. 150 le, Diaphananthe pellucida. 200 le, Eulophia guineensis. 300 le, Eurychone rothschildiana. 500 le, Tridactyle tridactylites. 750 le, Cyrtorchis arcuata. 900 le, Ancistrochilus rothschildianus.

No. 1749, Plectrelminthus caudatus. No. 1750, Polystachaya affinis.

**1994, Sept. 1**

| | | | |
|---|---|---|---|
| 1741-1748 | A228 | Set of 8 | |
| | | 12.00 | 12.00 |

**Souvenir Sheets**
| | | | |
|---|---|---|---|
| 1749-1750 | A228 | 1500 le each | 6.00 6.00 |

## Christmas — A229

The Birth of the Virgin, Christmas 1994, Murillo

Details or entire paintings: 50 le, The Birth of the Virgin, by Murillo. 100 le, Education of the Virgin, by Murillo. 150 le, Annunciation, by Filippino Lippi. 200 le, Marriage of the Virgin, by Bernard van Orley. 250 le, The Visitation, by Nicolas Vleughels. 300 le, Holy infant from Castelfranco altarpiece, by Giorgione. 400 le, Adoration of the Magi, Workshop of Bartholome Zeitblom. 600 le, Presentation of Infant Jesus in the Temple, by Memling. No. 1759, Nativity Altarpiece, by Lorenzo Monaco. No. 1760, Allendale Nativity, by Giorgione.

**1994, Dec. 1**

| | | | |
|---|---|---|---|
| 1751-1758 | A229 | Set of 8 | |

**Litho. Perf. 13¼x14**
| | | | |
|---|---|---|---|
| | | 6.75 | 6.75 |

**Souvenir Sheets**
| | | | |
|---|---|---|---|
| 1759-1760 | A229 | 1500 le each | 5.00 5.00 |

**1994, Dec. 20    Litho.    Perf. 14**

| | | | |
|---|---|---|---|
| 1761 | A230 | 300 le Working in field | 1.00 1.00 |
| 1762 | A230 | 350 le At beach | 1.10 1.10 |

Int'l Year of the Family A230

---

## Disney Christmas — A231

Designs: 50 le, Mickey's Christmas cat. 100 le, Goofy's Christmas tree, vert. 150 le, Daisy's Christmas gift. 200 le, Minnie's Christmas surprise, vert. 250 le, Minnie's Christmas flight. 300 le, Goofy's Christmas letters, vert. 400 le, Goofy's Christmas snowball, vert. 500 le, Mickey's Christmas sled ride, vert. 600 le, Mickey's Christmas snowman. 800 le, Pluto's Christmas treat, vert.

No. 1773, Goofy hanging outdoor lights. No. 1774, Mickey asleep in chair, vert.

**1995, Jan. 23    Perf. 14x13½, 13½x14**

| | | | |
|---|---|---|---|
| 1763-1772 | A231 | Set of 10 | |
| | | 5.00 | 5.00 |

**Souvenir Sheets**
| | | | |
|---|---|---|---|
| 1773-1774 | A231 | 1500 le each | 5.00 5.00 |

## Donald Duck's Gallery of Old Masters — A232

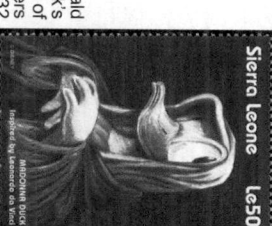

Name of painting, inspiration: 50 le, Madonna Duck, Leonardo da Vinci. 100 le, Portrait of a Venetian Duck, Tintoretto. 150 le, Duck with a Glove, Frans Hals. 200 le, Duck with a Pink, Quentin Massys. 250 le, Daisy, Sir Thomas Lawrence. 300 le, Donald Whistling Mother, Whistler. 400 le, Pinkie El Greco. 500 le, The Noble Snob, Rembrandt. 600 le, The Blue Duck, by Gainsborough. 800 le, Modern Quack, Picasso. No. 1785, Soup's On, Brueghel. No. 1786, Duck Dancers, Degas, horiz.

**1995, Jan. 23    Perf. 13½x14, 14x13½**

| | | | |
|---|---|---|---|
| 1775-1784 | A232 | Set of 10 | |
| | | 5.00 | 5.00 |

**Souvenir Sheets**
| | | | |
|---|---|---|---|
| 1785-1786 | A232 | 1500 le each | 5.00 5.00 |

## Olympic Medal Winners — A233

Summer Olympics: No. 1787a, Ragnar Lundberg, 1952 men's pole vault. b, Karin Janz, 1972 all-round gymnastics. c, Matthias Volz, 1936 gymnastics. d, Carl Lewis, 1988 long jump. e, Sara Simeoni, 1976 high jump. f, Daley Thompson, 1980 decathlon. g, Japan vs. Britain, 1964 soccer. h, Gabriella Dorio, 1984 1500-meters run. i, Daniela Hunger, 1988 200-meters individual medley swimming. j, Kyoko Iwasaki, 1992 200-meters breast stroke. k, Italian team member, 1960 water polo. l, David Wilkie, 1976 200-meters breast stroke.

1994 Winter Olympics, Lillehammer: No. 1788a, Katja Seizinger, downhill skiing. b, Hot air balloon (no medalist). c, Elvis Stojko, figure skating. d, Jens Weissflog, individual large hill ski jump. e, Bjorn Daehlie, 10K cross-country skiing. f, Germany, four-man bobsled. g, Markus Wasmeier, men's super giant slalom. h, Georg Hackl, luge. i, Trovill & Dean, ice dancing. j, Bonnie Blair, speed skating. k, Nancy Kerrigan, figure skating. l, Team Sweden, hockey.

No. 1789, torchbearer, horiz. No. 1790, Okeana Baiul, Nancy Kerrigan, Chen Lu, 1994 figure skating, horiz.

**1995, Feb. 6    Litho.    Perf. 14**

| | | | |
|---|---|---|---|
| 1787 | A233 | 75 le #a.-l. | 3.00 3.00 |
| 1788 | A233 | 200 le #a.-l. | 8.00 8.00 |

**Souvenir Sheets**
| | | | |
|---|---|---|---|
| 1789-1790 | A233 | 1000 le each | 3.50 3.50 |

---

## Dinosaurs — A234

No. 1791: a, Ceratosaurus. b, Brachiosaurus. c, Pteranodon. d, Stegoceras. e, Saurolophus. f, Ornithomimus. g, Compsognathus. h, Deinonychus. i, Ornitholestes. j, Archaeopteryx. k, Heterodontosaurus. l, Lesothosaurus.

No. 1792: a, 100 le, Triceratops. b, 250 le, 800 le, Styracosaurus. c, 400 le, Protoceratops (c). i, 400 le, Monoclonius (b). No. 1793, Deinonychus. No. 1794, Rhamphorynchus.

**1995, May 4    Litho.    Perf. 14**

| | | | |
|---|---|---|---|
| 1791 | A234 | 200 le Sheet of 12 | 8.00 8.00 |
| | | #a.-l. | |
| 1792 | A234 | Sheet of 4, | 5.25 5.25 |
| | | #a.-d. | |

**Souvenir Sheets**
| | | | |
|---|---|---|---|
| 1793-1794 | A234 | 2500 le each | 8.25 8.25 |

Sierra Club, Cent. A235

## Miniature Sheets of 9

No. 1795, vert: a, L'Hoest's guenon. b, Black-footed cat. c, Colobus monkey up close, forward. d, Colobus monkey in tree. e, Mandrill facing forward. f, Bonobo lying down. g, Bonobo lying down. h, Mandrill facing right. i, Colobus monkey standing.

No. 1796: a, Black-faced impala facing forward. b, Herd of black-faced impala. c, Black-faced impala drinking. d, Bonobo. e, Black-footed impala. f, Black-footed cat up close. g, L'Hoest's guenon. h, L'Hoest's guenon seated. i, Mandrills.

**1995, May 10**

| | | | |
|---|---|---|---|
| 1795-1796 | A235 | 150 le #a.-i., ea | 4.50 4.50 |

## New Year 1995 (Year of the Boar) A236

Stylized boars: No. 1797a, red & multi, facing left. b, green & multi, facing right. c, green & multi, facing left. d, red & multi, facing right. No. 1798, Two boars, vert.

**1995, May 8    Litho.    Perf. 14**

| | | | |
|---|---|---|---|
| 1797 | A236 | 100 le Block of 4, #a.- | 4.00 4.00 |

**Souvenir Sheet**
| | | | |
|---|---|---|---|
| 1798 | A236 | 500 le multicolored | 1.25 1.25 |

## Miniature Sheets of 9

Marine life: No. 1799a, Pufferfish. b, Coral grouper. c, Hawksbill turtle. d, Hogfish. e, Emperor angelfish. f, Butterflyfish. g, Lemon butterflyfish. h, Parrotfish. i, Moray eel. Water birds, marine life: No. 1800a, Cape pigeons. b, Pelican. c, Puffin. d, Humpback whale. e, Greater shearwater. f, Bottlenose dolphin. g, Gurnard. h, Salmon. i, John dory, dolphin. g, Gurnard. h, Surgeonfish. #1802, Angelfish, vert.

Singapore '95 — A237

**1995    Litho.    Perf. 14**

| | | | |
|---|---|---|---|
| 1799-1800 | A237 | 300 le #a.-i., each | 9.00 9.00 |

**Souvenir Sheets**
| | | | |
|---|---|---|---|
| 1801-1802 | A237 | 1500 le each | 5.00 5.00 |

---

## End of World War II, 50th Anniv. A239

No. 1803: a, USS Idaho. b, HMS Ark Royal. c, Admiral Graf Spee. d, Destroyer. e, HMS Nelson. f, PT 109. g, USS Iowa. h, Bismark. No. 1804: a, B-17. b, B-25. c, B-24 Liberator. d, USS Missouri. e, A-20 Boston. f, Pennsylvania. Colorado. Louisville, Portland, Columbia enter Lingayen Gulf.

No. 1805, HMS Indomitable launching aircraft. No. 1806, B-29 bomber.

**1995, July 10**

| | | | |
|---|---|---|---|
| 1803 | A238 | 250 le #a.-h. + label | 6.75 6.75 |
| 1804 | A239 | 300 le #a.-f. + label | 6.00 6.00 |

**Souvenir Sheets**
| | | | |
|---|---|---|---|
| 1805 | A238 | 1500 le multicolored | 5.00 5.00 |
| 1806 | A239 | 1500 le multicolored | 5.00 5.00 |

No. 1805 contains one 67x42mm stamp.

## UN, 50th Anniv. — A240

No. 1807: a, 300 le, Dais, UN General Assembly. 400 le, Sec. Gen. U. Thant. 500 le, UN building, dove. 1500 le, Sec. Gen. Dag Hammarskjold.

**1995, July 10    Litho.    Perf. 14**

| | | | |
|---|---|---|---|
| 1807 | A240 | Strip of 3, #a.-c. | 4.00 4.00 |

**Souvenir Sheet**
| | | | |
|---|---|---|---|
| 1808 | A240 | 1500 le multicolored | 5.00 5.00 |

No. 1807 is a continuous design.

## 1995 Boy Scout Jamboree, Holland A241

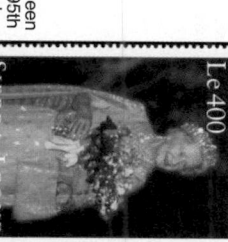

No. 1809: a, 400 le, Natl. flag. b, 500 le, Lord Baden-Powell. c, 600 le, Scout salute. 1500 le, Scout sign.

**1995, July 10**

| | | | |
|---|---|---|---|
| 1809 | A241 | Strip of 3, #a.-c. | 5.00 5.00 |

**Souvenir Sheet**
| | | | |
|---|---|---|---|
| 1810 | A241 | 1500 le multicolored | 5.00 5.00 |

## Queen Mother, 95th Birthday A242

# SIERRA LEONE

No. 1811: a, Drawing. b, Holding bouquet of flowers. c, Formal portrait. d, Without hat.

**1995, July 10**    *Perf. 13½x14*
1811 A242 400 le Block or strip of 4, #a.-d.   5.25 5.25
**Souvenir Sheet**
1812 A242 1500 le multicolored   5.00 5.00
No. 1811 was issued in sheets of 8 stamps.

**FAO, 50th Anniv. A243**

No. 1813: a, 300 le, Man working with sack of food. b, 400 le, Boy carrying bundle of sticks on head. c, 500 le, Woman holding bowl of fruit.
1500 le, Woman holding baby, vert.

**1995, July 10**    *Perf. 14*
1813 A243 Strip of 3, #a.-c.   4.00 4.00
**Souvenir Sheet**
1814 A243 1500 le multicolored   5.00 5.00

**Rotary Intl., 90th Anniv. A244**

Designs: 500 le, Natl. flag, Rotary emblem. 1000 le, Paul Harris, Rotary emblem.

**1995, July 10**    *Perf. 14*
1815 A244 500 le multicolored   1.75 1.75
**Souvenir Sheet**
1816 A244 1000 le multicolored   3.50 3.50
**Miniature Sheets of 8**

Flora & fauna: No. 1817a, African tulip tree. b, Senegal bush locust. c, Killifish d, Bird of paradise. e, Mandrill. f, Painted reed frog. g, Large spotted acraea. h, Carmine bee-eater.
No. 1818: a, Flame lilly. b, Giants gazelle. c, Dogbane. d, Gold-banded forester. e, Horned chameleon. f, Malachite kingfisher. g, Leaf beetle. I, Acanthuo.
No. 1819, Lion. No. 1820, African elephant.

**1995, Sept. 5**    *Litho.*    *Perf. 14*
1817-1818 A245 300 le #a.-h., each   8.00 8.00
**Souvenir Sheets**
1819-1820 A245 1500 le each   5.00 5.00

**Singapore '95 — A245**

**Third UN Decade for Advancement of Women — A246**

Designs: 300 le, Development. 500 le, Peace. 700 le, Equality.

**1995**    *Litho.*    *Perf. 14*
1821-1823 A246 Set of 3   5.00 5.00

---

Wiesel, peace, 1986. h, Bertha von Suttner, peace, 1905. i, Dalai Lama, peace, 1989. No. 1846: a, Richard Zsigmondy, chemistry, 1925. b, Robert Huber, chemistry, 1988. c, Wilhelm Ostwald, chemistry, 1909. d, Johann Deisenhofer, chemistry, 1988. e, Heinrich Wieland, chemistry, 1927. f, Gerhard Herzberg, chemistry, 1971. g, Hans von Euler-Chelpin, chemistry, 1929. h, Richard Willstätter, chemistry, 1915. i, Fritz Haber, chemistry, 1918.
No. 1847, Albert Einstein, physics, 1921. No. 1848, Wilhelm Röentgen, physics, 1901. No. 1849, Sin-Itiro Tomonaga, physics, 1965.

**Sierra Leone Grammar School, 150th Anniv. A247**

**1995, Sept. 27**    *Litho.*    *Perf. 14*
1824 A247 300 le multicolored   1.00 1.00

**Christmas A248**

Details or entire paintings: 50 le, Holy Family, by Beccafumi. 100 le, Rest on Flight into Egypt, by Barocci. 150 le, La Vierge, by Bellini. 200 le, The Flight, by d'Arpino. 600 le, Adoration of the Magi, by Francken. 800 le, The Annunciation, by da Conogliano. No. 1831, Virgin and child, by Cranach. No. 1832, Madonna and Child, by Berlinghiero.

**1995, Dec. 1**    *Litho.*    *Perf. 13½x14*
1825-1830 A248 Set of 6   6.50 6.50
**Souvenir Sheets**
1831-1832 A248 1500 le each   5.00 5.00

**Disney Christmas A249**

Antique Disney toys: 5 le, Mickey Mouse doll. 10 le, Donald rag drum major. 15 le, Donald wind up. 20 le, Toothbrush holder. 25 le, Mickey telephone. 30 le, Walking wind-up. 800 le, Movie projector. 1000 le, Goofy tricycle.
No. 1841, Black Mickey Mouse. No. 1842, First Mickey book.

**1995, Dec. 4**    *Perf. 13½x14*
1833-1840 A249 Set of 8   6.50 6.50
**Souvenir Sheets**
1841-1842 A249 1500 le each   5.00 5.00
**Miniature Sheets of 9**

**Nobel Prize Fund Established, Cent. — A250**

Recipients: No. 1843a, Andrew Huxley, medicine, 1963. b, Nelson Mandela, peace, 1993. c, Gabriela Mistral, literature, 1945. d, Otto Diels, chemistry, 1950. e, Hannes Alfven, physics, 1970. f, Wole Soyinka, literature, 1986. g, Hans G. Dehmelt, physics, 1989. h, Desmond Tutu, peace, 1984. i, Leo Esaki, physics, 1973.
No. 1844: a, Maria Goeppert Mayer, physics, 1963. b, Irène Joliot-Curie, chemistry, 1935. c, Mother Teresa, peace, 1979. d, Selma Lagerlöf, literature, 1909. e, Rosalyn Yalow, medicine, 1977. f, Dorothy Hodgkin, chemistry, 1964. g, Rita Levi-Montalcini, medicine, 1986. h, Mairead Corrigan, peace, 1976. i, Betty Williams, peace, 1976. No. 1845: a, Tobias Asser, peace, 1911. b, Andrei Sakharov, peace, 1975. c, Frederic Passy, peace, 1901. d, Dag Hammarskjöld, peace, 1961. e, Aung San Suu Kyi, peace, 1991. f, Ludwig Quidde, peace, 1927. g, Elie

**1995, Dec. 29**    *Litho.*    *Perf. 14*
1843-1846 A250 250 le #a.-l. each   7.50 7.50
**Souvenir Sheets**
1847-1849 A250 1500 le each   5.00 5.00
**Miniature Sheets of 12**

**Railways of the World A251**

---

No. 1850: a, Denver and Rio Grande Western. b, Central of Georgia. c, Seaboard Air Line. d, Missouri Pacific Lines. e, Atchison, Topeka and Santa Fe. f, Chicago, Milwaukee, St. Paul and Pacific. g, Texas and Pacific. h, Minneapolis, St. Paul & Sault Saint Marie (Soo Line). i, Western Pacific. j, Great Northern. k, Baltimore & Ohio. l, Chicago, Rock Island and Pacific.
No. 1851: a, Southern Pacific 4-8-4 "Daylight" express. b, US. b, Belgian National 4-4-2 express. c, Indian Railways 4-6-2 "WP" express. d, South Australian 4-8-4 express. e, Union Pacific 4-8-8-4 "Big Boy." US. f, UK 4-6-2 "Royal Scot" streamlined. g, German Federal, class 052 2-10-0. h, Japanese National 4-6-4 express. i, Pennsylvania, 4-4-4-4 streamlined. US. j, East African 4-8-2+2-8-4 Beyer-Garratt. k, Milwaukee Road 4-6-4 "Hiawatha" express. US. l, Paris-Orleans, 4-6-2 Pacific, France.
No. 1852: a, "Eurostar" express. b, ETR 401 Pendolino four-car tilting train, Italy. c, HST 125 inter-city high speed train, UK. d, "Virgin" B-B class high speed diesel-hydraulic express, Spain. e, French Natl. Railways TGV. f, Amtrak "Southwest Chief," US. g, TGV "Atlantique," France. h, "Peloponnese Express," Greece. i, "Shin-Kansen" high-speed electric train, Japan. j, Canadian Natl. turbo train. k, XPT high-speed diesel-electric train, Australia. l, SS1 Co-Co electric locomotive, China.
No. 1853: a, Canadian Natl. U1-F. b, Central Pacific No. 119 at Promontory, US. c, LNER "A4" class streamlined 4-6-2, UK. d, New York Central J32 "Empire State Express," US. e, Canadian 4-6-2 express, Australia. g, Canadian Pacific 4-6-2 express, Australia. g, Southern "West Country" class 4-6-2, UK. i, Norfolk & Western Class J 4-8-4, US. j, RM Class 4-6-0 Pacific, China. k, P 36 class 4-8-4 express, USSR. l, Great Western "King" class 4-6-0, UK. No. 1853M, British Railways Jubilee class 4-6-0, No. 45627 named "Sierra Leone." No. 1853N, Denver & Rio Grande Western "California Zephyr," US. No. 1853O, 1st train to cross newly opened bridge over Yangtze River, 1968, China. No. 1853P, Beijing-Shanghai, Express, China. No. 1853Q, China Railways, "QJ" class 2-10-2.

**1995, May 23**    *Litho.*    *Perf. 14*
1850-1851 A251 200 le #a.-l., each   8.00 8.00
1852 A251 250 le #a.-l.   10.00 10.00
1853 A251 300 le #a.-l.   12.00 12.00
**Souvenir Sheets**
1853M-1853Q A251 1500 le each 5.00 5.00
Nos. 1853M-1853Q each contain one 56x43mm stamp. No. 1850 exists with two different top margin inscriptions, "THE COLOURFUL RAILROADS OF NORTH AMERICA" and "THE COLOURFUL RAILROADS OF THE WORLD."

**New Year 1996 (Year of the Rat) A252**

Different stylized rats: No. 1854a, Facing left, purple & multi. b, Facing right, blue green & multi. c, Facing left, blue green & multi. d, Facing right, blue & multi. No. 1856, Rat, vert.

---

**1996, Jan. 6**
**Miniature Sheet of 4**
1854 A252 200 le Block of 4, #a.- d.   2.00 2.00
1855 A252 200 le #1854a-1854d   2.00 2.00
**Souvenir Sheet**
1856 A252 500 le multicolored   1.25 1.25
No. 1854 was issued in sheets of 16 stamps.

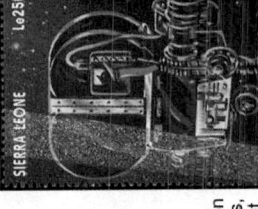

**Disney Characters as Circus Performers A253**

Designs: 100 le, Mickey, the magician. 200 le, Clarabelle Cow, the tightrope walker. 250 le, The clowns, Donald and Huey, Dewey and Louie. 300 le, Donald, the lion tamer. 800 le, Minnie, the bareback rider. 1000 le, Goofy and Minnie, the trapeze artists. #1863, Mickey, horiz. #1864, Pluto, horiz.

**1996, Jan. 29**    *Litho.*    *Perf. 14x13½*
1857-1862 A253 Set of 6   6.50 6.50
**Souvenir Sheets**    *Perf. 13½x14½*
1863-1864 A253 1500 le each   3.75 3.75
**Miniature Sheets of 9**

**Motion Pictures, Cent. A254**

No. 1865: a, Film projector. b, Pete. c, Silver. d, Rin-Tin-Tin. e, King Kong. f, Flipper. g, Jaws. h, Elsa. i, Moby Dick.
Directors or stars, scene from movie: No. 1866: a, Lumière Brothers. b, George Méliès. c, Toshiro Mifune d, Clark Gable. Vivian Leigh, David O. Selznick e, Fritz Lang, Metropolis. f, Marlene Dietrich. i, Steven Spielberg, ET. #1867, Lassie. #1868, Cecil B. de Mille.

**1996, Feb. 26**    *Litho.*    *Perf. 14*
1865-1866 A254 250 le #a.-i.   7.50 7.50
**Souvenir Sheets**
1867-1868 A254 1500 le each   3.75 3.75
**Sheets of 8 + label**

**Paintings from Metropolitan Museum of Art — A255**

Entire paintings or details: No. 1869: a, Honfleur, by Jongkind. b, A Boat on the Shore, by Courbet. c, Barges at Pontoise, by Pissarro. d, The Dead Christ with Angels, by Manet. e, Salisbury Cathedral, by Constable. f, A Lady with a Setter Dog, by Eakins. g, Tahitian Women Bathing, by Gauguin. h, Majas on a Balcony, by Goya. By Renoir: No. 1870: a, In the Meadow. b, By the Seashore. c, Still Life with Peaches and Grapes. d, Marguerite (Margot) Bérard. e,

Young Girl in Pink and Black Hat. f, A Waitress at Duval's Restaurant. g, A Road in Louveciennes. h, Two Young Girls at the Piano.

No. 1871: a, Morning, an Overcast Day, Rouen. b, Pissarro. c, The Horse Fair, by Bonheur. c, High Tide: the Bathers, by Homer, d, The Dance Class, by Degas. e, The Brioche, by Manet. f, The Grand Canal, Venice, by Turner. g, St. Tecia Interceding for Plaguestricken Este, by G. B. Tiepolo. h, Bridge at Villeneuve, by Sisley.

No. 1872: a, Madame Charpentier, by Renoir. b, Head of Christ, by Rembrandt. c, The Standard-Bearer, by Rembrandt. d, Girl Asleep, by Vermeer. e, Lady with a Lute, by Vermeer. f, Portrait of a Woman, by Rembrandt. g, La Grenouillère, by Monet. h, Woman with Chrysanthemums, by Degas.

No. 1873, The Death of Socrates, by J.L. David. No. 1874, Battle of Constantine and Licinius, by Rubens. No. 1875, Samson and Delilah, by Rubens. No. 1876, The Emblem of Christ Appearing to Constantine, by Rubens.

Sierra Leone

H.M. QUEEN ELIZABETH II

**1996**
Summer
Olympic
Games,
Atlanta
A256

100 le, 1932 Olympic Stadium, Los Angeles. 150 le, Archery. 500 le, Pole vault (gymnastics). 600 le, Field hockey. b, Swimming. c, Equestrian. d, Boxing. e, Pommel horse. f, 100-meter dash.

**1996, June 11     Litho.     Perf. 14**
1877-1880 A256   Set of 4      3.40 3.40
1881 A256   300 le     4.50 4.50
1882 A256   1500 le   Souvenir Sheet

**Souvenir Sheet**
3.75 3.75

**1996, July 15     Litho.     Perf. 13½x14**
1886 A257   600 le   Strip of 3,     4.50 4.50
#a.-c.
1887 A257   1500 le multicolored     3.75 3.75
No. 1886 was issued in sheets of 9 stamps.

**1996**
Summer
Olympic
Games,
Atlanta
A255

**1996     Litho.     Perf. 13½x14**
1869-1872 A255   200 le #a.-h.,     4.00 4.00
each

**Souvenir Sheets**
**Perf. 14**
1873-1876 A255   1500 le each     3.75 3.75
Nos. 1873-1876 each contain one 85x57mm.
Nos. 1874-1876 are not in the Metropolitan.

ABYSSINIAN

SIERRA LEONE   Le200

Cats — A259

No. 1892: a, Abyssinian. b, British tabby. c, Norwegian forest. d, Maine coon. e, Bengal. f, Asian. g, American curl. h, Devon rex. i, Tonkinese. j, Egyptian mau. k, Burmese. l, Siamese.

No. 1893: a, British shorthair. b, Tiffany. c, Birman. d, Somali. e, Malayan. f, Japanese bobtail. g, Himalayan. h, Tortoiseshell. i, Oriental. j, Ocicat. k, Chartreux. l, Ragdoll. No. 1894, Persian. No. 1895, Burmilla.

**1996, June 17**
1892-1893 A259   200 le #a.-l.,     6.00 6.00
each

**Souvenir Sheets**
1894-1895 A259   2000 le each     5.00 5.00

SIERRA LEONE

Le 150

**Butterflies**
A262

Designs: 150 le, Charaxes pleione. 200 le, Eurema brigitta. 300 le, Charaxes ameliae. 500 le, Kallimoides rumia.

No. 1910: a, Precis orithya. b, Palla ussheri. c, Junonia orithya. d, Cymothoe sangaris. e, Cyrestis camillus. f, Precis madama. g, Precis

SIERRA LEONE

Le300

**Mushrooms — A260**

50 le, Cinnabar-red chanterelle. 300 le, Larch suillus. 400 le, Yellow morel. 500 le, Variable cort.

No. 1900: a, African driver ant, Indigo milky. Marshall's false monarch (e). b, Scally inky cap. c, Pyxie cup (d). d, Barometer earthstar (c). rainbow grasshopper (h). e, Felt-ringed agaricus, long-horned longhorn. f, Spotted mycena. g, Orange latex milky. h, Tawny grisset amanita fulva, lamellicorn larva.

No. 1901: a, Millar tiger, little nest polymore. b, Coral slime. c, Red-gilled cort. d, Parasitic volvamella, veined tiger. e, Onion-stalked lepiota. f, Blusher. g, Orange mock oyster. h, Lizard claw, red and yellow barbel.

No. 1903, Netted modotus. No. 1904, Parasitic psathyriella.

**1996, June 17**
1896-1899 A260   200 le #a.-h.     3.25 3.25
**Sheets of 8, #a.-h.**
1900-1901 A260   250 le each     4.00 4.00
**Souvenir Sheets**
1902-1903 A260   1500 le each     3.75 3.75

SIERRA LEONE

**Space Exploration — A261**

Designs: a, Pioneer-Venus orbiter, 1986-92. b, Hubble space telescope. c, Voyager probe. d, Space Shuttle Challenger in orbit. e, Pioneer II. f, Mars-Viking 1 lander.

1500 le, Shuttle Challenger landing.

**1996**
1904 A261   300 le   Sheet of 6,     4.50 4.50
#a.-f.
1905 A261   1500 le multicolored     3.75 3.75
**Souvenir Sheet**

**Fantasies of the Sea — A267**

#1934, Sea Dragon's Daughter. #1935, Homo Aquaticus. #1936, Chinese Sea Fairy. #1937, Sea Totem. #1938, The Turtle, horiz. #1939, Mermaid, horiz. #1940, How the Whale Got its Throat, horiz. #1941, Killer Whale Crest. #1942, Aphrodite. #1943, Ship Figurehead. #1944, Lilith. #1945, Queen of the Orkney Islands. #1946, Haida Eagle. #1947, Captain Ahab. #1948, Waskos. #1949, Jonah. #1950, Odysseus. #1951, The Little Mermaid. #1952, Squamish Indians. #1953, Boy on a Dolphin. #1954, Airship to Atlantis. #1955, Sea Bishop. #1956, 20,000 Leagues Under the Sea. #1957, Whale Song. #1958, Arion. #1959, Dragonrider of Pern. #1960, Kelpie. #1961, Natsilane. #1962, Merman. #1963, Albatross. #1964, City under polar ice melt. #1965, Tom Swift. #1966, The Flying Dutchman, horiz. #1967, Sea Centaur. #1968, Lang Serpent. #1969, Triton. #1970, Sea man, horiz. #1971, Arthropod sea monster (dragon), horiz. #1972, The Ancient Mariner. #1973, Poseidon.

**1996, Dec. 19     Litho.     Perf. 14**
1934-1973 A267   1500 le each     3.75 3.75

Sheets of 12

SIERRA LEONE

Le150

**Chinese
Lunar
Calendar
A264**

Year of the: a, Rat. b, Ox. c, Tiger. d, Hare. e, Dragon. f, Snake. g, Horse. h, Sheep. i, Monkey. j, Rooster. k, Dog. l, Pig.

**1996, July 15     Litho.     Perf. 13½x14**
1921 A264   150 le   Sheet of 12,     4.50 4.50
#a.-l.

SIERRA LEONE   Le150

**New Year
1997
(Year of
the Ox)
A268**

Various stylized oxen, background color: claret.
Nos. 1975-1976: a, purple. b, green. c, blue. d, claret.

**1997, Jan. 8     Litho.     Perf. 14**
1975 A268   150 le   Block of 4, #a.-     1.50 1.50
d.
1976 A268   250 le   Block of 4,     2.50 2.50
#a.-d.
**Souvenir Sheet**
1977 A268   800 le multicolored     2.00 2.00
No. 1975 was issued in sheets of 16 stamps.

UNICEF,
50th Anniv.
A258

Designs: 300 le, Children reading, 400 le, Young man, woman reading, 500 le, Children in class. 1500 le, Children's faces.

**1996, July 15     Perf. 14**
1888-1890 A258   Set of 3     3.00 3.00
1891 A258   1500 le multicolored     3.75 3.75

**Souvenir Sheet**

Queen
Elizabeth II,
70th
Birthday
A257

**Souvenir Sheet**
1882 A256   1500 le   Runner     3.75 3.75

Ships
A265

No. 1922: a, Clipper ship, "Cutty Sark." 19th cent. b, SS Great Britain, 1846. c, "Dreadnaught," 1906. d, RMS Queen Elizabeth, 1940-72. e, Ocean-going racing yacht, 1962. f, SS United States, 1952. g, Nuclear powered submarine, 1950's. h, Super tanker, 1960's. i, USS Enterprise, 1980s.

No. 1923: a, Greek war galley, 4th cent BC. b, Roman war galley, 50AD. c, Viking ship, 9th cent. d, Flemish carrack, 15th cent. e, Merchant man, 16th cent. f, Tudor warship, 16th cent. g, Elizabethan galleon, 17th cent. h, Dutch Man of War, 17th cent. i, Maltese galley, 18th cent.

No. 1924, Cruise ship "Legend of the Seas," 1996. Panama Canal. No. 1925, Egyptian ocean-going ship, 1480BC.

**1996, Dec.**

cebrene. h, Hypolimnas misippus. i, Colotis danae.
No. 1911, Charaxes bohemani. No. 1912, Papilio antimachus.

**1996, Aug. 15     Litho.     Perf. 14**
1906-1909 A262   250 le   Sheet of 9,     3.00 3.00
#a.-i.
1910 A262   250 le   Sheet of 9,     5.50 5.50
#a.-i.
**Souvenir Sheets**
1911-1912 A262   1500 le each     3.75 3.75

Tulipa 'Margetta'

SIERRA LEONE   Le150

**Flowers — A263**

Details or entire paintings, by Filippo Lippi: 200 le, Madonna of Humility, 250 le, Coronation of the Virgin. 400 le, Corona. 600 le, Barbadori Altarpiece. 800 le, Coronation of the Virgin, diff.

Designs: 150 le, Tulipa. 200 le, Helichrysum bracteatum. 400 le, Viola. 500 le, Phalaenopsis. No. 1917: a, Fountain. b, Begonia multiflora. c, Narcissus. d, Crocus speciosus. e, Chrysanthemum frutescens. Petunia. f, Cosmos pipinnatus. g, Anemone coronaria. h, Convolvulus minor.

No. 1918: a, Paphiopedilum. d, Miltonia. e, "Peach bloom." c, Sailboat. d, Miltonia. e, Parides gundalachianus. f, Laeliocatt leya. g, Lycaste aromatica. h, Brassolaelocatt teuilia. Cymbidium "Southern Lace." Catastica teuilia. No. 1919, "Helianthus annuus. No. 1920, Cymbidium "Lucifer."

**1996, Aug. 19**
1913-1916 A263   Set of 4     3.25 3.25
1917 A263   200 le   Sheet of 9,     4.50 4.50
#a.-i.
1918 A263   300 le   Sheet of 9,     6.75 6.75
#a.-i.
**Souvenir Sheets**
1919-1920 A263   1500 le each     3.75 3.75

**1996, Dec. 12     Litho.     Perf. 13½x14**
1926-1931 A266   Set of 6     6.75 6.75
**Souvenir Sheets**
1932-1933 A266   2000 le each     5.00 5.00

SierraLeone Le200

Madonna of Humility
Christmas 1996
Filippo Lippi

**Christmas
A266**

**1996, Oct. 29     Litho.     Perf. 14**
1922-1923 A265   300 le #a.-i.,     6.75 6.75
each
**Sheets of 9**
1924-1925 A265   1500 le each     3.75 3.75
Nos. 1924-1925 each contain one 56x43mm stamp.
**Souvenir Sheets**

Designs: 10 le, Aladdin, Jasmine. 15 le, Santa, Genie. 20 le, Aladdin, Jasmine on magic carpet. 25 le, Genie as Christmas tree. 30 le, Aladdin, Genie "Santa." 100 le, Jasmine, Aladdin, Genie. 800 le, Genie's letter to Santa.

No. 1986, Aladdin, Abu. No. 1987, Jasmine, Aladdin, horiz.

**1997, Jan. 27**    **Perf. 14x13½**
1978-1985 A269   Set of 8    5.00   5.00

**Souvenir Sheets**

**Perf. 14x13½, 13½x14**
1986-1987 A269 2000 le each   5.00   5.00

---

Disney's Aladdin in Christmas Scenes — A269

---

Hong Kong — A270

Panoramic view of Hong Kong: No. 1088, in daytime. No. 1089, at night.

**1997, Feb. 12**    **Litho.**

**Sheets of 4**

**Perf. 14x13½, 13½x14**
1988-1989 A270 500 le #a.-d., each    5.25   5.25

---

UNESCO, 50th Anniv. A271

World Heritage Sites: 60 le, Town of Kizhi Pogost, Russia. 200 le, Durmitor Natl. Park, Yugoslavia. 250 le, City of Nessebar, Bulgaria. 400 le, City of Bukhara, Uzbekistan. 500 le, Monastery of Kiev-Pechersk, Ukraine. 700 le, Mountain Walks, Vilkolinec, Slovakia.

No. 1996: a, Town of Roros, Norway. b, City of Warsaw, Poland. c, Cathedral of Notre Dame, Luxembourg. d, City of Vilnius, Lithuania. e, Jelling, Denmark. f, Old Church of Petäjävesi, Finland. g, Sweden. h, Cathedral City of Bern, Switzerland.

No. 1997: a, Area surrounding Mt. Kilimanjaro, Tanzania. b, Monument, Fasil Ghebbi, Ethiopia. c, Natl. Park, Mt. Ruwenzori, Uganda. d, Abu Simbel, Egypt. e, Tsingy Bemaraha Strict Nature Reserve, Madagascar. f, House, Djenne, Mali. g, Traditional house construction, Ghana. h, Large house, Aromey.

Various views of Himeji-Jo, Japan, vert: No. 1998: a, b, c, d, e.
No. 1999, Natl. Bird Sanctuary, Djudj, Senegal, horiz. No. 2000, Acropolis, Athens, Greece, horiz.

**1997, Mar. 24**    **Litho.**    **Perf. 13½x14**
1990-1995 A271   Set of 6    5.50   5.50

**Sheets of 8 + Label**
1996-1997 A271 300 le #a.-h., + Label each    6.00   6.00

**Sheet of 5 + Label**
1998   A271 500 le #a.-e.    6.25   6.25

**Souvenir Sheets**
1999-2000 A271 2000 le each    5.00   5.00

---

Paintings by Hiroshige (1797-1858) A272

No. 2001: a, Hatsune Riding Grounds, Bakuro-cho. b, Mannen Bridge, Fukagawa. c, Ryogoku Bridge and the Great Riverbank. d, Asakusa River, Great Riverbank, Miyato River. e, Silk-goods Lane, Odenma-cho. f, Mokuboji Temple, Uchigawa Inlet, Gozensaihata.
No. 2002, Tsukudajima from Eitai Bridge. No. 2003, Nihonbashi Bridge and Edobashi Bridge.

**1997**    **Litho.**    **Perf. 13½x14**
2001   A272   400 le   Sheet of 6, #a.-f.    6.50   6.50

**Souvenir Sheets**
2002-2003 A272 1500 le each    3.75   3.75

---

Chernobyl Disaster, 10th Anniv. A273

Designs: 1000 le, UNESCO. 1500 le, Chabad's Children of Chernobyl.

**1997, June 23**
2004   A273 1000 le multicolored    2.75   2.75
2005   A273 1500 le multicolored    4.00   4.00

---

Queen Elizabeth II and Prince Philip, 50th Wedding Anniv. A274

No. 2006: a, Queen. b, Royal arms. c, Black & white photograph, Prince in dress uniform. d, Black & white photograph, Prince in tuxedo, bow tie. e, Palace of Holyroodhouse. f, Prince in hat guiding horses.

**1997, June 23**    **Perf. 14**
2006   A274   400 le   Sheet of 6, #a.-f.    6.50   6.50

**Souvenir Sheet**
2007   A274 1500 le multicolored    4.00   4.00

---

Return of Hong Kong to China — A275

Designs: 400 le, Flag of China, map of China, Hong Kong, Victoria at night. 500 le, 650 le, Flag of China, July 1, 1997, city scene le, Flag of China, Victoria harbor inside letters spelling "Hong Kong." 550 le, 600 le, Flag of China, "Hong Kong '97." 800 le, Victoria harbor, Deng Xiaoping (1904-97).

**1997, June 23**
2008-2013 A275   Set of 6    9.50   9.50

Nos. 2008-2013 were each issued in sheets of 3.

---

**Souvenir Sheets**

Mother Goose — A276

Designs: No. 2014, Three Blind Mice. No. 2015, Woman holding out full skirt as "Myself."

**1997, June 23**    **Perf. 14**
2014-2015 A276 1500 le each    4.00   4.00

---

1998 Winter Olympic Games, Nagano A277

Designs: 250 le, Stadium, Calgary, 1988, American Indian. 300 le, Freestyle aerial skiing, vert. 500 le, Ice hockey, vert. 800 le, Dan Jansen, 1000-meter speed skater, vert.
No. 2022, vert: a, Peggy Fleming, figure skating. b, Japanese ski jumper, Nordic combined. c, 2-man luge, Germany. d, Frank-Peter Roetsch, biathlon, E. Germany.
No. 2023, Jamaican bobsled team, vert. No. 2024, Johann Olav Koss, Norway, vert.

**1997, July 16**    **Litho.**    **Perf. 14**
2018-2021 A277   Set of 4    5.00   5.00
2022   A276 300 le   Strip of 4, #a.-d.    3.25   3.25

**Souvenir Sheets**
2023-2024 A277 1500 le each    4.00   4.00

No. 2022 was issued in sheets of 8 stamps.

---

1998 World Cup Soccer Championships, France — A278

Players: 100 le, Stabile, Uruguay. 150 le, Schiavio, Italy. 200 le, Kocsis, Hungary. 250 le, Nejedly, Czechoslovakia. 500 le, Leonidas, Brazil. 600 le, Ademir, Brazil.
No. 2031: a, Dwight Yorke, Trinidad & Tobago. b, Dennis Bergkamp, Holland. c, Steve McManaman, England. d, Ryan Giggs, Wales. e, Romario, Brazil. f, Faustino Asprilla, Colombia. g, Roy Keane, Ireland. h, Peter Schmeichel, Denmark.
No. 2032, Pele, Brazil, horiz. No. 2033, Lato, Poland, horiz.

**1997, July 23**   **Perf. 13½x14, 14x13½**
2025-2030 A278   Set of 6    4.75   4.75

**Sheet of 8**
2031   A278 300 le #a.-h. + 2 labels    6.50   6.50

**Souvenir Sheets**
2032-2033 A278 1500 le each    4.00   4.00

---

Classic Horror Movies — A279

Lead character, movie: No. 2034: a, Lon Chaney, "Phantom of the Opera," 1934. b, Boris Karloff, "The Mummy," 1932. c, Fredric March, "Dr. Jekyll & Mr. Hyde," 1932. d, Lon Chaney, Jr., "The Wolf Man," 1941. e, Charles Laughton, "Island of Lost Souls," 1933. f, Lionel Atwill, "Mystery of the Wax Museum," 1933. g, Bela Lugosi, "Dracula," 1931. h, Vincent Price, "The Haunted Palace," 1963. i, Elsa Lanchester, "Bride of Frankenstein," 1935.
3000 le, Bela Lugosi, Boris Karloff, "Son of Frankenstein," 1939.

**1997, Aug. 15**    **Perf. 14**
2034   A279   300 le   Sheet of 9, #a.-i.    7.25   7.25

**Souvenir Sheet**
2035   A279 3000 le multicolored    8.00   8.00

---

Domestic Cats — A280

Designs: 150 le, American short hair tabby. 200 le, British short hair. 500 le, Turkish angora. c, Chartreux. b, Abyssinian. c, Burmese. d, White angora. e, Japanese bobtail. f, Cymric.
1500 le, Egyptian mau.

**1997, Aug. 29**
2036-2038 A280   Set of 3    2.25   2.25
2039   A280   400 le   Sheet of 6, #a.-f.    8.50   6.50

**Souvenir Sheet**
2040   A280 1500 le multicolored    4.00   4.00

No. 2040 contains one 64x32mm stamp.

---

Butterflies A281

Orchids A282

Designs: 150 le, Vindula erota. 200 le, Pereutel leucodrosime. 250 le, Dynstor napolean. 800 le, Thauria aliris. 600 le, Papilio aegeus. 800 le, Amblypodia anita. 1500 le, Kallimoides rumia. 2000 le, Papilio dardanas.
No. 2049: a, Lycaena dispar. b, Graphium sarpedon. c, Euploe core. d, Papilio cresphontes. e, Colotis danae. f, Battus philenor.
No. 2050: a, Mylothris chloris. b, Argynnis lathonia. c, Elymnias agondas. d, Palla ussheri. e, Papilio glaucus. f, Cercyonis pegala.
No. 2051, Hebomoia glaucippe, horiz. No. 2052, Colias eurytheme, horiz.

Designs: 150 le, Huey, Dewey, & Louie, 200 le, Mickey's kids, 250 le, Daisy Duck, 300 le, Minnie, 400 le, Mickey, 500 le, Goofy, 600 le, Pluto, 800 le, Donald Duck.

**Disney Christmas Stamps A285**

**1997, Aug. 1**  Litho.  **Perf. 14'**
2041-2048 A281  Set of 8  15.00 15.00
**Sheets of 6**
2049  A281  500 le  #a.-f.  8.00 8.00
2050  A281  600 le  #a.-f.  9.75 9.75

**1997, Sept. 1**

Designs: 150 le, Ansellia africana, 200 le, Maxillaria praestans, 250 le, Cymbidium minivitellina, 800 le, Epidendrum prismatocarpum, 300 le, Dendrobium bigibbum, 500 le, Encyclia ... a, Laelia anceps, b, Paphiopedilum fairrieanum, c, Restrepia lansberghi, d, Yamadara cattleya, e, Cleistes divaricata, f, Calypso bulbosa, ... Odontoglossum schlieperianum. No. 2061, Paphiopedilum tonsum.

2051-2052 A281 3000 le each  8.00 8.00
**Souvenir Sheets**
2053-2058 A282  Set of 6  6.00 6.00
2059 A282 400 le #a.-f.  3.25 3.25
2060-2061 A282 1500 le each  4.00 4.00

---

Designs: 100 le, Shetland sheep dog, 250 le, Alaskan husky, 600 le, Jack Russell terrier, St. Bernard. d, Basset hound. b, Irish setter. c, German shepherd. e, Dalmatian. f, Cocker spaniel. Boxer.

**Dogs — A284**

**1997, Aug. 15**  Litho.  **Perf. 14**
2062 A283 350 le  Sheet of 9, #a.-i.  8.50 8.50
2063 A283 1500 le multicolored  4.00 4.00
**Souvenir Sheet**

**1997, Aug. 29**
2064-2066 A284  Set of 3  2.50 2.50
2067 A284 400 le Sheet of 6, #a.-f.  6.50 6.50
2068 A284 1500 le multicolored  4.00 4.00
**Souvenir Sheet**
No. 2068 contains one 31x63mm stamp.

---

No. 2062: a, Ray Milland in "Dial M for Murder." b, James Stewart, Kim Novak in "Vertigo." c, Cary Grant, Ingrid Bergman in "Notorious." d, John Dall, James Stewart in "Rope." e, Cary Grant in "North by Northwest." f, Grace Kelly, James Stewart in "Rear Window." g, Joan Fontaine, Laurence Olivier in "Rebecca." h, Tippi Hedren in "The Birds." i, Janet Leigh in "Psycho." 1500 le, Alfred Hitchcock.

**Motion Pictures Directed by Alfred Hitchcock A283**

**1997, Oct. 1**  **Perf. 13½x14, 14x13½**
2069-2076 A285  Set of 8  8.50 8.50
2077 A285 50 le Sheet of 6, #a.-f.  1.60 1.60

**1997, Oct. 6**
2078-2079 A285 2000 le multi  5.25 5.25
**Souvenir Sheets**
For overprints see Nos. 2117-2119.

No. 2078, Mickey in sleigh. No. 2079, Mickey, Donald, Daisy in Santa suits, horiz.

No. 2077: a, like #2071. b, like #2069. c, like #2074. d, like #2072. e, like #2070. f, like #2073.

---

No. 2080: a, SUD Caravelle 6. b, DeHavilland comet. c, Boeing 707. d, Airbus industrie A-300.
No. 2080E: f, Benoist Type XIV. g, Junkers JU52/3m. h, Douglas DC-3. i, Sikorsky S-42. 1649A Starliner. #2081, Concorde. #2081A, Lockheed L-1649A Starliner.

**Civilian Airliners A286**

**1997, Oct. 6**  **Perf. 14**
2080 A286 600 le Sheet of 4, #a.-d. + label  6.50 6.50
2080E A286 600 le Sheet of 4, #f.-i. + label  6.50 6.50
2081-2081A A286 2000 le each  5.25 5.25
**Souvenir Sheets**
Nos. 2081-2081A contain one 91x34mm stamp.

---

Entire paintings or details: 100 le, 150 le, The Annunciation, by Titian (diff. details), 200 le, Madonna of Foligno, by Raphael, 250 le, The Annunciation, by Michelino, 500 le, The Prophet Isaiah, by Michelangelo, 600 le, Three Angels, by Master of the Rhenish Housebook. No. 2088, The Fall of the Rebel Angels, by Peter Bruegel the Elder, horiz. No. 2089, Unidentified painting of Angel pointing hand in air, man with book, horiz.

**Christmas A287**

**1997, Dec. 24**  Litho.  **Perf. 14**
2082-2087 A287  Set of 6  4.75 4.75
2088-2089 A287 2000 le each  5.25 5.25
**Souvenir Sheets**

---

Various portraits, color of sheet margin: No. 2090, Pale pink. No. 2091, Pale yellow. No. 2092, Pale yellow. No. 2093, Wearing wide-brimmed hat. No. 2094, With Prince Harry (in margin). No. 2095, Helping to feed needy.

**Diana, Princess of Wales (1961-97) — A288**

**1998, Jan. 12**  Litho.  **Perf. 14**
2090-2092 A288  400 le each  6.50 6.50
2093-2095 A288 1600 le each  4.00 4.00
**Souvenir Sheets**

---

Various stylized tigers in: No. 2096: a, purple, b, maroon, c, bright lilac rose, d, orange, 800 le, maroon, maroon.

**New Year 1998 (Year of the Tiger) A289**

**1998, Jan. 26**  Litho.  **Perf. 14**
2096 A289 250 le Sheet of 4, #a.-d.  2.75 2.75
2097 A289 800 le red org & multi  2.25 2.25
**Souvenir Sheet**

---

Designs: 200 le, Metagyrphus nitens, vert. 250 le, Lord Derby's parakeet, vert. 300 le, Narcissus, vert. 400 le, Barbus tetrazona, 500 le, Agalychnis callidryas. 600 le, ...
No. 2104: a, Japanese white-eyes. b, Rhododendron. c, Slow loris. d, Violet flowers. e, Wolverine.
No. 2105: a, Cheetah. b, Ornithogalum thyrsoides. c, Ostrich. d, Common chameleon. e, Orthetrum albistylum. f, Coluber jugularis.
No. 2106, Tricolored heron, vert. No. 2107, Fennec fox. f, Junonia hierta cebrene.
No. 2105, Arthieris squamiger.

**Flora and Fauna A290**

**1998, Aug. 4**  Litho.  **Perf. 14**
2098-2103 A290  Set of 6  4.50 4.50
2104-2105 A290 450 le each  6.50 6.50
2106-2107 A290 2000 le each  4.00 4.00
**Sheets of 6, #a.-f.**
**Souvenir Sheets**

---

Designs: 200 le, Hypsilophodon, vert. 400 le, Lambeosaurus, vert. 500 le, Corythosaurus, vert. 600 le, Stegosaurus, vert. 800 le, Antrodemus.
No. 2113: a, Plateosaurus. b, Tyrannosaurus. c, Brachiosaurus. d, Iguanodon. e, Styracosaurus. f, Hadrosaurus.
No. 2114: a, Tyrannosaurus. b, Tenontosaurus. c, Deinonychus. d, Triceratops. e, Maiasaura. f, Struthiomimus. No. 2115, Tyrannosaurus. No. 2116, Triceratops.

**Dinosaurs A291**

**1998, Aug. 18**  Litho.  **Perf. 14**
2108-2112 A291  Set of 5  5.00 5.00
2113-2114 A291 500 le Sheets of 6, #a.-f.  6.00 6.00
2115-2116 A291 2000 le each  4.00 4.00
**Souvenir Sheets**

---

Nos. 2077-2079 Ovptd.

Emblem and "MICKEY & MINNIE — 70TH ANNIVERSARY" appear in sheet margin on Nos. 2118-2119.

**1998, Aug. 31**  **Perf. 13½x14, 14x13½**
2117 A285 50 le Sheet of 6, #a.-f.  .60 .60
2118-2119 A285 2000 le each  4.00 4.00

---

No. 2120: a, Phoenician, 8th cent. BC. b, Drakkar, 6th cent. c, Carrack, 14th cent. d, Venetian Galley, 16th cent. e, Galeasse, 17th cent. f, Chebeck, 17th cent.
No. 2121: a, Junk, 19th cent. b, HMS Victory, 19th cent. c, Savanna, 19th cent. d, Gaissa, 19th cent. e, Warrior, 19th cent. f, Preussen, 20th cent.
No. 2122, Santa Maria, 1492. No. 2123, Titanic, 1912.

**Ships of the World A292**

**1998, Sept. 1**  **Perf. 14**
2120-2121 A292 300 le Sheets of 6, #a.-f.  3.50 3.50
2122-2123 A292 2000 le each  4.00 4.00
**Souvenir Sheets**
Nos. 2122-2123 each contain one 57x43mm stamp.

---

No. 2124: a, Kiara (with bird). b, Pumbaa. c, Kiara & Kovu. d, Kovu. e, Kiara & Kovu (red background). f, Timon (orange background).
No. 2125: a, Kiara (with butterfly). b, Timon & Pumbaa. c, Kiara. d, Kiara & Kovu (green background). e, Kovu (with bird). f, Kiara & Kovu (with bird). f, Kiara & Kovu (pink background). No. 2126, Pumbaa & Timon. No. 2127, Kiara & Kovu, horiz.

**Disney's The Lion King, Simba's Pride A293**

**1998, Sept. 15**  **Perf. 13½x14, 14x13½**
2124-2125 A293 500 le each  6.00 6.00
2126-2127 A293 2500 le each  5.00 5.00
**Sheets of 6, #a.-f.**
**Souvenir Sheets**

---

Paintings: 400 le, Man with Straw Hat and Ice Cream Cone, 1938, 600 le, Woman in Red Armchair, 1932. 800 le, Nude in a Garden, 1934. 2000 le, Child Holding a Dove, 1901.

**Paintings by Picasso — A294**

**1998, Dec. 15**  Litho.  **Perf. 14½**
2128-2130 A294  Set of 3  3.75 3.75
2131 A294 2000 le multicolored  4.00 4.00
**Souvenir Sheet**

**Gandhi — A295**

**1998, Dec. 15**  **Perf. 14**
2132 A295  600 le Portrait  1.25 1.25
2133 A295 2000 le Close-up  4.00 4.00
**Souvenir Sheet**

SIERRA LEONE

**Royal Air Force, 80th Anniv. A296**

No. 2134: a, McDonnell Douglas Phantom FRG2. b, Two Panavia Tornado GR1. c, Jaguar GR1A. d, Hercules C-130. e, Lysander, Eurofighter.

**1998, Dec. 15**
2134  A296  800 le  Sheet of 4,  6.50 6.50
  #a.-d.
**Souvenir Sheets**
2135-2136  A296  2000 le each  4.00 4.00

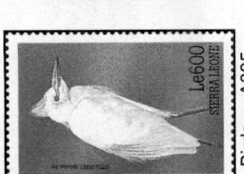

**19th World Scouting Jamboree, Chile A297**

No. 2137: a, Dan Beard, Robert Baden-Powell, 1937. b, Kuwaiti Scouts. c, Scout locator bottle feeding bear cub.
No. 2138, vert.: a, William D. Boyce, Lone Scouts founder. b, Guion S. Bluford. c, Ellison S. Onizuka.
No. 2140, Bear cub drinking from bottle.

**1998, Dec. 15**
**Sheets of 3, #a.-c.**
2137-2138  A297  1500 le each  9.00 9.00
**Souvenir Sheets**
2139-2140  A297  3000 le each  6.00 6.00

**Diana, Princess of Wales (1961-97) — A299**

*Perf. 14½x14*
2147  A299  600 le multicolored  .90 .90
No. 2147 was issued in sheets of 6.

**New Year 1999 (Year of the Rabbit) A300**

Color of stylized rabbits — #2148: a, red. b, red violet. c, blue. d, light violet. 1500 le, Rabbit, vert.

**1998, Dec. 24**  *Perf. 14*
2148  A300  700 le  Sheet of 4,  4.25 4.25
  #a.-d.
**Souvenir Sheet**
2149  A300  1500 le multicolored  2.50 2.50

**Paintings by Eugène Delacroix (1798-1863) — A301**

Designs: a, Rocks and a Small Valley. b, Jewish Musicians from Magador. c, Moroccans Traveling. d, Women of Algiers in their Apartment. e, Moroccan Military Exercises f, Arabs Skirmishing in the Mountains. g, Arab Chieftain Reclining on a Carpet. h, Procession in Tangier.
No. 2151, Chopin, vert.

**1998**
2150  A301  400 le  Sheet of 8,  5.00 5.00
  #a.-h.
**Souvenir Sheet**
2151  A301  400 le multicolored  .65 .65

**Bird Type of 1992**

Designs: 4000 le, Gray-headed bush-shrike. 5000 le, Black-backed puffback. 6000 le, Crimson-breasted shrike. 10,000 le, Northern shrike.

**1999**  **Litho.**  *Perf. 14x15*
2152  A199  4000 le multi  5.25 5.25
2153  A199  5000 le multi  6.50 6.50
2154  A199  6000 le multi  7.75 7.75
2155  A199  10,000 le multi  13.00 13.00
  Nos. 2152-2155 (4)  32.50 32.50
Issued: 4000 le, 5000 le, 2/18/99.
No. 2153 exists dated 2002.

**Birds, Marine Life — A302**

150 le, Powder blue surgeon. 250 le, Frilled anemone. 600 le, Red beard sponge. 800 le, Red-finned batfish.
No. 2160: a, Eastern reef egret. b, Dolphins. c, Sailing ship, Humpback whale. d, Red and green macaw. e, Blue tangs. f, Guitarfish. g, Manatees. h, Hammerhead shark. i, Blue shark. j, Lemon goby, moorish idol. k, Ribbon eels. l, Loggerhead turtle.
Sharks — #2161: a, Blue shark. b, Tiger shark. c, Bull shark. d, Great white. e, Scalloped hammerhead. f, Oceanic whitetip. g, Zebra shark. h, Leopard shark. i, Horn shark.
Dolphins, whales — #2162: a, Hector's dolphin. b, Tucuxi. c, Hourglass dolphin. d, Bottlenose dolphin. e, Gray's beaked whale. f, Bowhead whale. g, Fin whale. h, Gray whale. i, Blue whale.

No. 2163, Purple firefish. No. 2164, Spotted eagle ray. No. 2165, Leatherback turtle.

**1999, Feb. 22**  *Perf. 14*
2156-2159  A302  Set of 4  2.25 2.25
2160  A302  400 le  Sheet of 12,  6.25 6.25
  #a.-l.
**Souvenir Sheets**
2161-2162  A302  500 le each  4.00 4.00
2163-2165  A302  3000 le each  5.75 5.75
Int'l Year of the Ocean (#2160-2162, #2164-2165).

**Airplanes A303**

200 le, Grumman X-29. 300 le, Rocket-powered Bell X-1. 400 le, MiG-21 Fishbed, 1956, USSR. 500 le, Blériot X1 Monoplane, 1909. 800 le, Southern Cross, Fokker F.VII, 1928. 1500 le, Supermarine S.6B.
No. 2172: a, Grumman F3F-1, 1940. b, North American F-86A Sabre Jet, 1949. c, Cessna 377 Super Skymaster. d, F-16 Fighting Falcon, 1973. e, Voyager, Experimental Aircraft, Dick Rutan, Jeana Yeager. f, Fairchild A10A Thunderbolt II, 1975. g, Lockheed Vega, 1933. h, Lockheed Vega, 1930.
No. 2173: a, Sopwith Tabloid, 1914, UK. b, Vickers F.B.5 Gun Bus, 1915. c, Savoia Marchetti S.M. 79-II Sparviero, 1940. d, Mitsubishi A6M3 Zero Sen, 1942. e, Morane-Saulnier L, 1915. f, Shorts 360. g, Tupolev TU-160, 1988. h, Mikoyan-Gurevich MiG-15, 1948.
No. 2174: a, Nieuport 11C. 1, 1915. b, D.H. Vampire N.F. 10, 1951. c, Aerospatiale-Aeritalia ATR 72. d, Fiat CR.32, 1933. e, Curtiss P-6E Hawk, 1932. f, Saab JA 37 Viggen, 1977. g, Piper Pa-46 Malibu. h, F-14 Tomcat. No. 2175, Spirit of St. Louis. No. 2176, Canadair CL-215.

**1999, Mar. 22**  **Litho.**  *Perf. 14*
2166-2171  A303  Set of 6  5.50 5.50
**Sheets of 8, #a.-h.**
2172-2174  A303  600 le each  6.75 6.75
**Souvenir Sheets**
2175-2176  A303  3000 le each  4.50 4.50

**Australia '99 World Stamp Expo A304**

Flowers: 150 le, Geranium wallchianum. 200 le, Osmanthus x burkwoodu. 250 le, Iris pallida, vert. 500 le, Rhododendron, vert. 600 le, Rose, vert. 800 le, Papoose, vert. 1500 le, Viola labradorica, vert. 2000 le, Rosa banksiae, vert.
No. 2185: a, Jack snipe. b, Alstroemeria ligtu. c, Lilium (yellow). d, Marjorie fair. e, Aemone coranaria. f, Clematis ranncu.
No. 2186: a, Aquilegiea olympica. b, Lilium (orange). c, Magnolia grandiflora. d, Polygonatum x hybridum. e, Clematis montana. f, Vinca minor.
No. 2187: a, Colchicum speciosum. b, Scandere. c, Helianthus annuus. d, Lady Kerkrade. e, Clematix x durandil. f, Lilium regale. No. 2188, vert.: a, Clematis hybrida. b, Cardiospermum halicacabum. c, Fritillaria imperialis. d, Iris ibetidisima. e, Pyracantina. f, Hepatica transsilvanica.
No. 2189, Clerodendrum trichotomum. No. 2190, Holbollia. No. 2191, Crocus angustifolius, vert. No. 2192, Rubus fruitcosus, vert.

**1999, Apr. 14**
2177-2184  A304  Set of 8  8.50 8.50
**Sheets of 6, #a.-f.**
2185-2188  A304  600 le each  5.00 5.00
**Souvenir Sheets**
2189-2192  A304  4000 le each  5.75 5.75

**Fauna — A306**

**Birds — A305**

No. 2193: a, Cattle egret. b, White-fronted bee-eater. c, African gray parrot. d, Cinnamon-chested bee-eater. e, Malachite kingfisher. f, White-throated bee-eater. g, Yellow-billed stork. h, Hildebrandt's starling.
No. 2194: a, Great white pelican. b, Superb starling. c, Red-throated bee-eater. d, Woodland kingfisher. e, Purple swamphen. f, Pied kingfisher. g, African spoonbill. h, Crocodile bird.
No. 2195, African fish-eagle. No. 2196, Richenow's weaver.

**1999, May 18**  **Litho.**
**Sheets of 8, #a.-h.**
2193-2194  A305  600 le each  6.50 6.50
**Souvenir Sheets**
2195-2196  A305  3000 le each  4.00 4.00

**1999, May 31**  **Litho.**
Designs: 300 le, Diana monkey. 400 le, Red-vented malimbe. 500 le, Eurasian kestrel. 600 le, Little owl. 800 le, Bush pig. 1500 le, Lion.
No. 2203: a, Flap-necked chameleon. b, Golden oriole (c). c, European bee-eater. d, Leopard. e, Lion (d). f, Chimpanzee (e).
No. 2204: a, Senegal galago. b, Hoopoe. c, Long-tailed pangolin (f). d, Hippopotamus. e, African elephant (d). f, West African linsang. No. 2205, West African linsang. No. 2206, Gray parrot.

2197-2202  A306  Set of 6  6.25 6.25
**Sheets of 6, #a.-f.**
2203-2204  A306  900 le each  7.25 7.25
**Souvenir Sheets**
2205-2206  A306  3000 le each  4.50 4.50

**Trains — A308**

**Queen Mother (b. 1900) — A307**

No. 2207: a, With Duke of York and Princess Elizabeth, 1926. b, In 1979. c, In Nairobi, 1959. d, In 1991. 4000 le, With crown, 1937.

**1999, Aug. 4**  **Litho.**  *Perf. 14*
**Gold Frames**
2207  A307  1300 le  Sheet of 4,  6.75 6.75
  #a.-d. + label
**Souvenir Sheet**  *Perf. 13½*
2208  A307  4000 le multicolored  5.75 5.75
No. 2208 contains one 38x51mm stamp. See Nos. 2512-2513.

**1999, Aug. 4**  *Perf. 14*
Designs: 100 le, Rocket. 150 le, Benguela Railway, horiz. 200 le, Sudan Railways 310 2-8-2, horiz. 250 le, Chicago, Burlington & Quincy Railroad, horiz. 300 le, Terrier, horiz. 400 le, Dublin-Cork Express, horiz. 500 le, Shay, horiz. 600 le, George Stephenson, horiz. 1500 le, South Wind, horiz. No. 2218, horiz.: a, American. b, Flying Scotsman. c, Lord Nelson idol. d, Mallard. e, Evening Star. f, Britannia. No. 2219, horiz.: a, Class 19D 4-8-2. b, Double-headed train. c, Egyptian Railways Bo-Bo. d, GMAM Garratt 4-8-2+2-8-4. e, Passenger train, Rabat. f, Rhodesian Railway 14A Class 2-2 Garratt.

**Christmas A298**

Entire paintings or details: 200 le, Penitent of Mary Magdalen, by Titian. 500 le, Lamentation of Christ, by Veronese. 1500 le, The Building of Noah's Ark, by Guido Reni. 2000 le, Abraham and Isaac, by Rembrandt. No. 2145, Adoration of the Shepherds, by Bartolomé Estéban Murillo. No. 2146, The Assumption of the Virgin, by Murillo.

**1998, Dec. 14**  **Litho.**  *Perf. 14*
2141-2144  A298  Set of 4  6.50 6.50
**Souvenir Sheets**
2145-2146  A298  3000 le each  4.50 4.50

**Ferrari Automobiles — A298a**

No. 2146A: c, 400 Superamerica. d, 250 GT Lusso. e, 342 America. 2000 le, 330 GTC. Illustration reduced.

**1998, Dec. 15**  **Litho.**  *Perf. 14*
2146A  A298a  800 le  Sheet of 3,  3.00 3.00
  #a.-c.
**Souvenir Sheet**
2146B  A298a  2000 le multi  2.60 2.60
No. 2146A contains three 39x25mm stamps.

No. 2220, Mountain Class Garratt. No. 2221, Royal train.

**2209-2217** A308 Set of 9 4.25 4.25

**Sheets of 6, #a.-f.**

**2218-2219** A308 800 le each 5.00 5.00

**Souvenir Sheets**

**2220-2221** A308 3000 le each 3.25 3.25

Inscription on No. 2218f is misspelled.

---

**Paintings of Fu Baoshi (1904-65) — A309**

No. 2222: a. Interpretation of a Poem of Shi-Tao. b. Autumn of Ho-Pao. c. Landscape in Rain (bridge). d. Landscape in Rain, diff. e. Landscape in Rain (house on mountain). f. Portrait of To-Fu. g. Classic Lady (trees with leaves). h. Portrait of Li-Pai. i. Sprite of the Mountain. j. Classic Lady (bare trees).

No. 2223: a. 800 le, Four Seasons - Winter, horiz. b. 1500 le, Four Seasons - Summer, horiz.

**1999, Aug. 4**

**2222** A309 400 le Sheet of 10, #a.-j. 5.25 5.25

**Perf. 12½**

**Sheet of 2, #a.-b.**

**2223** A309 3.00 3.00

China 1999 World Philatelic Exhibition. No. 2223 contains 51x38mm stamps.

---

**1999 Return of Macao to People's Republic of China — A310**

THE HANGING CLOUD BRIDGE
SIERRA LEONE LE1200

Illustration reduced.

**1999, Aug. 4**

**2224** A310 1200 le multi 1.60 1.60

Issued in sheets of 3 stamps.

---

**Hokusai Paintings — A311**

SIERRA LEONE LE1000

**1999, Aug. 4**

**Sheets of 6, #a.-f.**

**2225-2226** A311 1000 le each 6.50 6.50

**2227-2228** A311 3000 le each 3.25 3.25

**Perf. 13¾**

No. 2225: a. Hanging Cloud Bridge. b. Timber Yard by the Tate River. c. Bird Drawings (owl). d. As "c." (ducks). e. Travelers Crossing the Oi River. f. Travelers on the Tokaido Road at Hodogaya.

No. 2226: a. People Admiring Mount Fuji from a Tea House. b. People on a Temple Balcony. c. Sea Life (crustacean). d. Sea Life (clam). e. Pontoon Bridge at Sano in Winter. f. A Shower Below the Summit.

No. 2227, A View of Mount Fuji and Travelers by a Bridge, vert. No. 2228, A Sudden Gust of Wind at Ejiri, vert.

---

**Johann Wolfgang von Goethe (1749-1832), German Poet — A312**

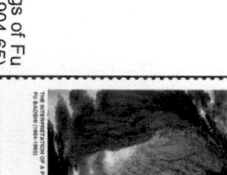

THE INTERPRETATION OF A POEM OF SHI-TAO
SIERRA LEONE Le400
A309

No. 2229: a. Witch besieges faust. b. Goethe and Friedrich von Schiller. c. Margaret places flowers before the niche of Mater Dolorosa.

No. 2230: a. Helena with her chorus. b. Faust takes a seat beside Helena.

#2231, Angelic spirit. #2232, Ariel, vert.

**1999, Aug. 4**

**Sheets of 3**

**2229** A312 1600 le #a.-c. 5.00 5.00

**2230** A312 1600 le #a.-b, 2229b 5.00 5.00

**Souvenir Sheets**

**2231-2232** A312 3000 le each 3.25 3.25

---

**PhilexFrance '99 — A313**

SIERRA LEONE

Designs: No. 2234, De Glehn compound with Lemaitre front end 4-4-2. No. 2233, Crampton locomotive.

**1999, Aug. 4**

**2233-2234** A313 3000 le each 3.25 3.25

**Perf. 13¾**

---

**IBRA '99 — A314**

Le1500
SIERRA LEONE

**1999**

**2235** A314 1500 le Class 4-4-0 1.60 1.60

**2236** A314 2000 le Class 05 2.10 2.10

**Perf. 14x14½**

---

**Rights of the Child — A315**

SIERRA LEONE
Le1600

No. 2237: a. Girl holding candle. b. Two children. c. Girl, diff.

**1999, Aug. 4**

**Litho.**

**2237** A315 1600 le Sheet of 3, #a.-c. 5.25 5.25

**Souvenir Sheet**

**2238** A315 3000 le multicolored 3.25 3.25

---

**Wedding of Prince Edward and Sophie Rhys-Jones A316**

SOPHIE Rhys-JONES
SIERRA LEONE

No. 2239: a. Sophie, close-up. b. Sophie, diff. d. Edward, diff. 4000 le, Couple.

**1999, Aug. 4**

**2239** A316 2000 le Sheet of 4, #a.-d. 8.50 8.50

**Souvenir Sheet**

**2240** A316 4000 le multicolored 4.25 4.25

**Perf. 13¼x13¾**

---

**Birds of Africa A317**

Le600
SIERRA LEONE

No. 2241: a. African paradise monarch. b. Lilac-breasted roller. c. Common Scops owl. d. African emerald cuckoo. e. Blue monarch. f. African golden oriole. g. White-throated bee eater. h. Black-bellied seedcracker. i. Hoopoe.

No. 2242: a. White-faced whistling duck. b. Black-headed heron. c. Black-headed gonolek. d. Malachite kingfisher. e. Fish eagle. f. African spoonbill. g. African skimmer. h. Black heron. i. Allen's gallinule.

No. 2243: a. Schmitarbill. b. Bateleur. c. Black-headed weaver. d. Variable sunbird. e. Blue swallow. f. Black-winged red bishop. g. Namaqua dove. h. Golden-breasted bunting. i. Hartlaub's bustard.

No. 2244: a. Montagu's harrier. b. Booted eagle. c. Yellow crested helmet-shrike. d. Scarlet-tufted malachite sunbird. e. Pin-tailed whydah. f. Red-headed malimbe. g. Western violet-backed sunbird. h. Yellow white eye. i. African pygmy kingfisher, vert. No. 2247, Gray crowned crane, vert. No. 2248, Shoebill, vert.

**1999**

**Litho.**

**Sheets of 9, #a.-i.**

**2241-2244** A317 600 le each 5.75 5.75

**Souvenir Sheets**

**2245-2248** A317 4000 le each 4.25 4.25

**Perf. 14**

---

**New Year 2000 (Year of the Dragon) A318**

No. 2249: a. Brown red. b. Blue green. c. Bright red. d. Lilac.

No. 2249 (dragon color): a. Brown red. b. Blue green. c. Bright red. d. Lilac. 4000 le, Red dragon, vert.

**2000, Feb. 5**

**Litho.**

**Perf. 14**

**2249** A318 1500 le Sheet of 4, #a.-d. 6.25 6.25

**Souvenir Sheet**

**2250** A318 4000 le multi 4.25 4.25

---

**Sammy Davis, Jr. — A319**

SIERRA LEONE
Le 1,000

No. 2251: a. As child. b. With motorcycle. c. With red checked shirt. d. With microphone. e. With leg on chair. f. Holding cigarette. 5000 le, With other people.

---

**Various flowers making up a photomosaic of Princess Diana.**

**Flowers — A320**

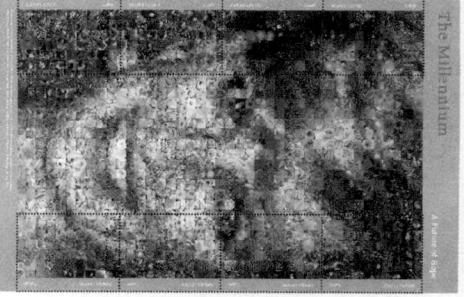

**2000, Mar. 28**

**2252** A319 5000 le multi 5.25 5.25

**Souvenir Sheet**

**2253** A320 800 le Sheet of 8, #a.-h. 6.50 6.50

See Nos. 2359-2360.

**2000, Mar. 8**

**2251** A319 1000 le Sheet of 6, #a.-f. 6.25 6.25

**Souvenir Sheet**

**Perf. 13¾**

---

**Millennium — A321**

The Millennium
1600-1650

Highlights of 1600-1650: a. Election of Michael Romanov as Russian tsar. b. William Shakespeare publishes "Hamlet." c. Kung Hsien paints "Thousand Peaks and Myriad Ravines." d. Francis Bacon publishes his works. e. Founding of Jamestown, Virginia. f. Reign of Louis XIV of France. g. Founding of Quebec. h. Birth of Isaac Newton. i. Nicholas Poussin paints "Rape of the Sabine Women." j. Johannes Kepler publishes "The New Astronomy." k. The Mayflower arrives in America. l. King James Bible is published. m. Dutch East India Company introduces tea to Europe. n. René Descartes develops his philosophy. o. Galileo defends Copernican system. p. Queen Elizabeth I dies (60x40mm). q. Miguel de Cervantes publishes "Don Quixote."

**2000, Mar. 28**

**2254** A321 400 le Sheet of 17, #a.-q, + label 6.75 6.75

**Perf. 12¾x12½**

## BETTY BOOP™

**Betty Boop — A330**

No. 2288: a, Wearing flowered dress. b, Carrying shopping bags. c, Wearing baseball cap. d, Holding shoes. e, Sitting in chair. f, Wearing jacket. g, Playing guitar. h, Holding lasso. i, Holding flower.
No. 2289, Pointing at dog. No. 2290, Riding bicycle.

**2000, Mar. 8**    **Litho.**    **Perf. 13¾**
2288 A330 800 le Sheet of 9,   8.25   8.25
    #a-i
**Souvenir Sheets**
2289-2290 A330 5000 le each   5.75   5.75
Illustration reduced.

**I Love Lucy — A331**

No. 2291 — Lucy: a, Wearing blue cap. b, With arms in front, with Vitameatavegamin bottle. c, Wearing pink nightgown. d, Wearing pink nightgown, sticking out tongue. e, Wearing blue cap on television screen. f, Holding blue cap on television near table. g, With arms at side, with bottle. h, Holding bottle near cheek. i, Pouring out liquid in bottle.
No. 2292, Wearing blue cap on television, Desi touching television. No. 2293, Lucy and Fred Mertz.
Illustration reduced.

**2000, Mar. 8**
2291 A331 800 le Sheet of 9,   8.25   8.25
    #a-i
**Souvenir Sheets**
2292-2293 A331 5000 le each   5.75   5.75

**Prince William, 18th Birthday — A327**

Various photos.
Illustration reduced.

**2000, May 29**    **Perf. 14**
2283 A327 1100 le Sheet of 4,   5.00   5.00
    #a-d
**Souvenir Sheet**    **Perf. 13¾**
2284 A327 5000 le multi   5.50   5.50
No. 2284 contains one 38x50mm stamp.

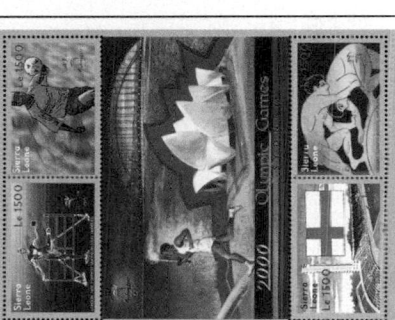

**2000 Summer Olympics, Sydney — A328**

Designs: a, Hurdler. b, Soccer player. c, Finnish flag, Helsinki Stadium. d, Auckland, Greek wrestlers.
Illustration reduced.

**2000, May 29**    **Perf. 14**
2285 A328 1500 le Sheet of 4.   6.75   6.75
    #a-d

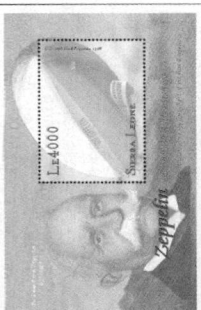

**First Zeppelin Flight, Cent. — A329**

No. 2286: a, LZ-129. b, LZ-4. c, LZ-6.
4000 le, LZ-127.
Illustration reduced.

**2000, May 29**    **Perf. 14**
2286 A329 2000 le Sheet of 3,   6.75   6.75
    #a-c
**Souvenir Sheet**    **Perf. 14½**
2287 A329 4000 le multi   4.50   4.50
Size of stamps: No. 2286, 38x24mm.

**Scenes from "The Little Colonel" with Shirley Temple — A324**

Temple — No. 2267: a, With Colonel Lloyd (Lionel Barrymore), standing. b, With Walker (Bill Robinson). c, With two children. d, With soldiers. e, With mother (Evelyn Venable). Becky (Hattie McDaniel). f, Hugging Colonel Lloyd.
No. 2268: a, With Becky and Walker. b, With Walker, diff. c, Alone. d, Tugging Colonel Lloyd's coat.
No. 2269, Holding chair.
Illustration reduced.

**2000, Mar. 28**
**Sheets of 6 and 4**
2267 A324 1200 le #a-f   8.00   8.00
2268 A324 1500 le #a-d   6.75   6.75
**Souvenir Sheet**
2269 A324 5000 le multi   5.50   5.50

**Parrots — A325**

Designs: 200 le, African gray parrot. 1500 le, Rufus-crested turaco, horiz.
No. 2272: a, Monk parakeet. b, Citron-crested cockatoo. c, Queen-of-Bavaria conure. d, Budgerigar. e, Yellow-chevroned parakeet. f, Cockatiel. g, Amazon parrot. h, Sun conure. i, Malabar parakeet.
No. 2273: a, Grand eclectus parrot. b, Sun parakeet. c, Red fan parakeet. d, Fischer's lovebird. e, Blue masked lovebird. f, White belly rosella. g, Plum-headed parakeet. h, Striated lorikeet. i, Gold-mantled rosella.
4000 le, Blue and gold macaw.

**2000, May 16**   **Perf. 13¾x14, 14x13¾**
2270-2271 A325    Set of 2   1.90   1.90
**Sheets of 9, #a-i**
2272-2273 A325 800 le each   8.00   8.00
**Souvenir Sheet**
2274 A325 4000 le multi   4.50   4.50
The Stamp Show 2000, London (Nos. 2272-2274). Size of stamps: Nos. 2272-2273, 28x42mm; No. 2274, 38x50mm.

**Orchids A326**

Designs: 300 le, Aeranthes henrici. 500 le, Ophrys apifera. 600 le, Disa crassicornis. 2000 le, Aeranthes grandiflora.
No. 2279: a, Oeleoclades maculata. b, Polystachya campyloglossa. c, Polystachya pubescens. d, Tridactyle bicaudata. e, Angraecum veitcii. f, Sobennikoffia robusta.
No. 2280: a, Aerangis curnowiana. b, Aerangis fastudsa. c, Angraecum magdalenae. d, Angraecum sororium. e, Eulophia speciosa. f, Ansellia africana.
No. 2281, Angraecum compactum. No. 2282, Angraecum eburneum.

**2000, May 16**    **Perf. 14**
2275-2278 A326   Set of 4   3.75   3.75
**Sheets of 6, #a-f**
2279-2280 A326 1100 le each   7.50   7.50
**Souvenir Sheets**
2281-2282 A326 4000 le each   4.50   4.50

**Paintings of Anthony Van Dyck — A322**

No. 2255: a, Portrait of a Man. b, Anna Wake, Wife of Peter Stevens. c, Peter Stevens. d, Adriaen Stevens. e, Maria Bosschaerts, Wife of Adriaen Stevens. f, Portrait of a Woman.
No. 2256: a, Self-portrait, 1617-18. b, Self-portrait, 1620-21. c, Self-portrait, 1622-23. d, Andromeda Chained to the Rock. e, Self-portrait, late 1620s-early 1630s. f, Mary Ruthven.
No. 2257: a, The Betrayal of Judas (detail of The Taking of Christ). b, Ecce Homo, 1625-26. c, Christ Carrying the Cross (showing woman with blue garment). d, The Raising of Christ on the Cross. e, The Crucifixion, c. 1627 f, The Lamentation, c. 1616 (actually the "Mocking of Christ").
No. 2258: a, The Taking of Christ. b, The Mocking of Christ. c, Ecce Homo, 1628-32. d, Christ Carrying the Cross (showing poleax). e, The Crucifixion, c. 1629-30. f, The Lamentation 1618-20.
No. 2258G: h, The Duchess of Crow With Her Son. i, Susanna Fourment and Her Daughter. j, Geronima Brignolo Sale With Her Daughter Maria Aurelia. k, A Woman With Her Daughter. l, A Genoese Noblewoman With Her Child. m, A Genoese Noblewoman (Paola Adorno) and Her Son.
No. 2259, Self portrait With a Sunflower. No. 2260, Self-portrait with Endymion Porter. No. 2261, Young Woman With a Child. No. 2262, Porzia Imperiale With Her Daughter Maria Franscesca. No. 2263, Portrait of a Mother and Her Daughter. No. 2264, A Woman and a Child, horiz.

**2000, Apr. 10**    **Perf. 13¾**
**Sheets of 6, #a-f.**
2255-2258G A322 1000 le each   6.25   6.25
**Souvenir Sheets**
2259-2264 A322 5000 le each   5.25   5.25
Easter (Nos. 2257-2258).

**Mario Andretti — A323**

No. 2265: a, Behind wheel. b, With helmet, facing left. c, In pits. d, In crash. e, Inspecting tire. f, With white shirt. g, Without shirt. h, In car #50.
No. 2266, With others in front of old car. 5000 le, With white shirt.
Illustration reduced.

**2000, Mar. 28**    **Litho.**    **Perf. 13¾**
2265 A323 600 le Sheet of 8,   5.50   5.50
    #a-h
**Souvenir Sheet**
2266 A323 5000 le multi   5.50   5.50

# SIERRA LEONE

## Berlin Film Festival, 50th Anniv. — A332

No. 2294: a, Las Palabras de Max. b, Ascendancy. c, Deprisa Deprisa. d, Die Sehnsucht der. Veronika Voss. e, Heartland. f, La Colmena.

No. 2294, a, Las Palabras de Max, b, 5000 le, Las Truchas. Illustration reduced.

**2000, May 16**    **Litho.**    **Perf. 14**
2298-2301 A335   Set of 4    3.75   3.75
2302-2303 A335 1000 le each    6.00   6.00

**Sheets of 6, #a-f**
2304-2305 A335 5000 le each    5.00   5.00

## Sea Birds — A335

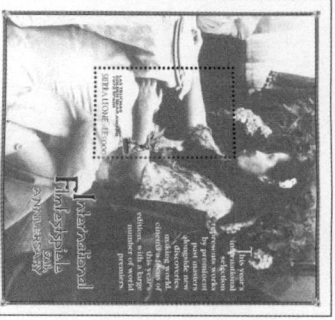

Designs: 400 le, Herring gull. 600 le, Caspian tern. 800 le, Red phalarope. 2000 le, Magnificent frigatebird.

No. 2302: a, Caspian tern, diff. b, Glaucous gull. c, Northern gannet. d, Long-tailed jaeger. e, Brown pelican. f, Great skua.

No. 2303: a, Wandering albatross. b, Fork-tailed storm petrel. c, Great shearwater. d, Blue-footed booby. e, Great cormorant. f, Atlantic puffin.

No. 2304, Brown booby, diff. No. 2305, Red-tailed tropicbird, diff.

*Sierra Leone Le6000 souvenir sheet*

## Richard Petty, Stock Car Racer — A336

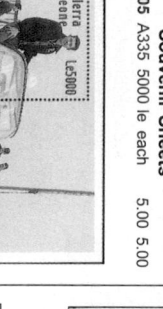

No. 2306: a, Car in pits. b, With family. c, Wearing red jacket. d, Wearing Pontiac cap. e, Wearing white hat, uniform with two STP logos. f, Wearing STP cap. g, Standing in car. h, Profile, wearing STP logos on shoulder. i, Wearing headphones.

No. 2307: a, Holding trophy. b, Wearing Winston cap. c, Wearing black hat. d, Hatless, blue background. e, Wearing shirt with red collar. f, Holding helmet. g, Leaning on blue and red car. h, With arm in car. i, Leaning head out of car.

No. 2308: a, Wearing red shirt, white hat. b, Hatless, orange background. c, Wearing Pontiac cap. d, Strapped in car, without helmet. e, Holding timer. f, Wearing red and blue helmet. g, Wearing white hat, blue uniform. h, With trophy, wearing STP cap. i, With white hat, reclining.

No. 2309, Standing in car, diff. No. 2310, In race, horiz. Illustration reduced.

**2000, Aug. 15**    **Perf. 13¾**
**Sheets of 9, #a-i**
2306-2308 A336   800 le each    7.00   7.00

**Souvenir Sheets**
2309-2310 A336 5000 le each    5.00   5.00

## Monarchs — A338

No. 2313, Nicholas IV (1288-92), diff. No. 2314, Clement XI (1700-21), Illustration reduced.

**2000, Aug. 21**
2311-2312 A337 1100 le each    6.50   6.50

**Sheets of 6, #a-f**
2313-2314 A337 5000 le each    5.00   5.00

No. 2315: a, Emperor Hung Wu of China. b, Emperor Hsuan Te of China. c, King Sejong of Korea. d, Emperor Tung Chih of China. e, Emperor Tai Tsu (Chao Kuang-yin) of Chin. f, Empress Yung Ching of China.

No. 2316, Kublai Khan of China. Illustration reduced.

**2000, Aug. 21**
2315 A338 1100 le Sheet of 6, #a-f    6.50   6.50

**Souvenir Sheet**
2316 A338 5000 le multi    5.00   5.00

## Apollo-Soyuz Mission, 25th Anniv. — A341

No. 2326, vert.: a, Apollo 18. b, Soyuz 19. c, Apollo and Soyuz docked. Illustration reduced.

No. 2327, Apollo and Soyuz docking. Illustration reduced.

**2000, May 29**
2326 A341 1200 le Sheet of 3, #a-c    3.50   3.50

**Souvenir Sheet**
2327 A341 5000 le multi    5.00   5.00

**2000, May 29**    **Litho.**    **Perf. 14**
2325 A340 5000 le multi    5.00   5.00

---

## Public Railways, 175th Anniv. — A333

No. 2296: a, Locomotion No. 1, George Stephenson. b, James Watt's original design for a separate condenser engine. Illustration reduced.

**2000, May 29**
2296 A333 3000 le Sheet of 2, #a-b    7.00   7.00

## Johann Sebastian Bach (1685-1750) — A334

**2000, May 29**
2297 A334 5000 le multi    5.75   5.75

No. 2294, a, Las Palabras de Max. b,

**2000, May 29**
2294 A332 1100 le Sheet of 6, #a-f    7.50   7.50

**Souvenir Sheet**
2295 A332 5000 le multi    5.75   5.75

## Popes — A337

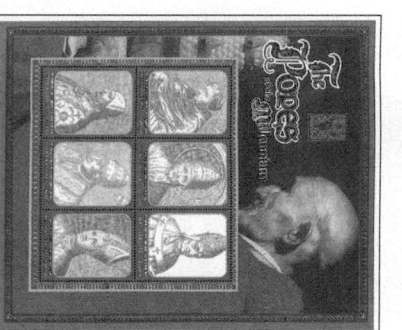

No. 2311: a, Gregory VI (1045-46). b, Celestine V (1294). c, Honorius IV (1285-87). d, Innocent IV (1243-54). e, Innocent VI (1404-06). f, John XXII (1316-34).

No. 2312: a, Martin IV (1281-85). b, Nicholas II (1059-61). c, Nicholas IV (1288-92). d, Urban IV (1261-64). e, Urban V (1362-70). f, Urban VI (1378-89).

## European Soccer Championships — A339

No. 2317 — Germany: a, Worms. b, Team photo. c, Babbel. d, Franz Beckenbauer. e, Selessin Stadium, Liege, Belgium. f, Stefan Kuntz.

No. 2318 — Italy: a, Walter Zenga. b, Team photo. c, Roberto Bettega. d, Totti. e, Philips Stadium, Eindhoven, Netherlands. f, Vieri.

No. 2319 — Portugal: a, Dimas. b, Team photo. c, Pinto. d, Santos. e, Gelredome Stadium, Arnhem, Netherlands. f, Sousa.

No. 2320 — Romania: a, Munteanu. b, Team photo. c, Petre. d, Petrescu. e, Popescu. vert. No. 2321, German coach Erich Ribbeck, vert. No. 2322, Italian coach Dino Zoff, vert. No. 2323, Portuguese coach Humberto Coelho, vert. No. 2324, Romanian coach Emerich Jenei, vert. Illustration reduced.

**2000, Aug. 21**
**Sheets of 6, #a-f (#2317-2319);
Sheet of 6 #a-e, #2319e (#2320)**
2317-2320 A339 1300 le each    7.75   7.75

**Souvenir Sheets**
2321-2324 A339 5000 le each    5.00   5.00

## Queen Mother, 100th Birthday — A342

**2000, Aug. 4**
**Litho. & Embossed
Die Cut Perf. 8¾
Without Gum**
2328 A342 18,000 le gold & multi

## Albert Einstein (1879-1955) — A340

**Souvenir Sheet**

## Dogs and Cats — A343

500 le, Bulldog. 800 le, Brown tabby. 1500 le, Burmese. 2000 le, Dachshund. No. 2333, 1000 le: a, Beagle. b, Scottish terrier. c, Bloodhound. d, Greyhound. e, German shepherd. f, Cocker spaniel.

No. 2334, 1000 le: a, Red tabby stumpy Manx. b, Red self. c, Maine Coon cat. d, Black smoke. e, Chinchilla. f, Russian Blue.

No. 2335, 1100 le: a, Pointer. b, Doberman pinscher. c, Collie. d, Chihuahua. e, Afghan hound. f, Boxer.

No. 2336, 1100 le: a, Singapura. b, Himalayan. c, Abyssinian. d, Black cat. e, Siamese. f, North African wild cat.

No. 2337, 5000 le, Fox terrier, vert. No. 2338, 5000 le, Calico, vert.

**2000, Oct. 2**    **Litho.**    **Perf. 14**
2329-2332 A343   Set of 4    5.00   5.00

**Sheets of 6, #a-f**
2333-2336 A343   Set of 4    26.00   26.00

**Souvenir Sheets**
2337-2338 A343   Set of 2    10.50   10.50

# SIERRA LEONE

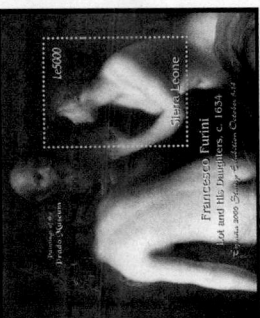

Francesco Furini
Lot and His Daughters, c. 1634

## Paintings from the Prado — A344

No. 2339, 1000 le: a, The Transport of Mary Magdalen, by José Antolínez. b, The Holy Family, by Francisco de Goya. c, Our Lady of the Immaculate Conception, by Antolínez. d, Charles IV as Prince, by Anton Raphael Mengs. e, Louis XIII of France, by Philippe de Champaigne. f, Prince Ferdinand VI by Jean Ranc.

No. 2340, 1000 le: a, Adam, by Albrecht Dürer. b, Moor, by Manuel Benedito Vives. c, Eve, by Dürer. d, A Gypsy, by Raimundo Madrazo y Garreta. e, María Guerrero, by Joaquín Sorolla y Bastida. f, The Model Aline Masson with a White Mantilla, by Madrazo y Garreta.

No. 2341, 1000 le: a, Figure in yellow robe from Madonna and Child Between Saints Catherine and Ursula, by Giovanni Bellini. b, Madonna and Child from Madonna and Child Between Saints Catherine and Ursula. c, Figure in red robe from Madonna and Child Between Saints Catherine and Ursula. d, Giovanni Mateo Ghiberti, by Bernardino India. e, The Marchioness of Santa Cruz, by Agustín Esteve. f, Self-portrait, by Orazio Borgianni.

No. 2342, 1000 le: a, Mary from The Holy Family with a Bird, by Bartolomé Esteban Murillo. b, Jesus from The Holy Family with a Bird. c, Joseph, from The Holy Family with a Bird. d, Cardinal Carlos de Borja, by Andrea Procaccini. e, St. Dominic de Guzmán, by Claudio Coello. f, St. Paul Supported by an Angel, by Alonso Cano.

No. 2343, 1000 le: a, Woman from The Seller of Fans, by José del Castillo. b, Allegory of Summer, by Mariano Salvador Maella. c, Man with basket from The Seller of Fans. d, Portrait of a Girl, by Carlos Luis de Ribera y Fieve. e, The Poultry Keeper, by Pensionante del Saraceni. f, The Death of Cleopatra, by Guido Reni.

No. 2344, 1000 le: a, Feliciana Bayeu, by Francisco Bayeu y Subías. b, Tomás de Iriarte by Joaquín Inza. c, St. Elizabeth of Portugal, by Francisco de Zurbarán. d, Christ from The Vision of St. Francis at Porziuncola, by Murillo. e, Monk from The Vision of St. Francis at Porziuncola. f, Woman from The Vision of St. Francis at Porziuncola.

No. 2345, 5000 le, Lot and His Daughters, by Francesco Furini. No. 2346, 5000 le, the Execution of Torrijos and His Companions, by Antonio Gisbert Pérez. No. 2347, 5000 le, the Concert, by Vicente Palmaroli y González. No. 2348, 5000 le, The Finding of Joseph's Cup in Benjamin's Bag, by Jacopo Amiconi. No. 2349, 5000 le, Vulcan's Forge, by Diego Velázquez. No. 2350, 5000 le, The Two Friends, by Joaquín Agrasot y Juan, horiz.
Illustration reduced.

**2000, Oct. 6**    **Perf. 12x12¼, 12¼x12**
#### Sheets of 6, #a-f
2339-2344   A344   Set of 6    37.50   37.50
#### Souvenir Sheets
2345-2350   A344   Set of 6    32.50   32.50
Espana 2000 Intl. Philatelic Exhibition.

Sierra Leone
Tuberous Polypore
Ifibonus Polypore Hypora lutescere

## Mushrooms — A345

Designs: 600 le, Tuberous polyphore. 900 le, Cultivated agaricus. 1200 le, Scarlet wax cap. 2500 le, Blue-green psilocybe. No. 2355, 1000 le, erect. a, Armed stinkhorn. b, Red-staining inocybe. c, Amanitopsis vaginata. d, Inocybe jurana. e, Xerula longipes. f, Tricholoma matsutake. No. 2356, 1000 le: a, Orange-staining mycena. b, Russula amoema. c, Cinnabar chanterelle. d, Calodon aurantiacum. e, Lentinus lepidus. f, Gomphidius roseus. No. 2357, 5000 le, Orange latex lactarius. No. 2358, 5000 le, Common morel, vert.

---

**2000, Oct. 30**    **Litho.**    **Perf. 14**
2351-2354   A345   Set of 4    5.50   5.50
#### Sheets of 6, #a-f
2355-2356   A345   Set of 2    12.50   12.50
#### Souvenir Shoots
2357-2358   A345   Set of 2    10.50   10.50

## Flower Photomosaic Type of 2000

No. 2359, 800 le: Various flowers making up a photomosaic of the Queen Mother. No. 2360, 900 le: Various photographs of religious scenes making up a photomosaic of Pope John Paul II.

**2000, Oct. 30**    **Perf. 13¾**
#### Sheets of 8, #a-h
2359-2360   A320   Set of 2    14.50   14.50

## Massacre of Israeli Olympic Athletes, 1972 — A346

No. 2361, horiz.: a, Kahat Shor. b, Andrei Schpitzer. c, Joseph Romano. d, Yaakov Springer. e, Eliazer Halfin. f, Amitsur Shapira. g, Moshe Weinberg. h, Mark Slavin. i, Torchbearer, Israeli flag. j, Joseph Gottfreund. k, Ze'ev Friedman. l, David Berger.

**2000, Nov. 9**    **Perf. 14**
2361   A346   Sheet of 12, #a-l    6.25   6.25
#### Souvenir Sheet
2362   A346   5000 le Torchbearer    5.25   5.25

Le800
Tightrope Rider
SIERRA LEONE

## Circus A347

Designs: 800 le, Tightrope rider. 1000 le, Rear and ball. 1500 le, Tiger on ball. 2000 le, Camels.

No. 2367, 1100 le: a, Polar bear on roller. b, Ape. c, Clown, green background. d, Tightrope walker. e, Seals. f, Camel.

No. 2368, 1100 le: a, Clown, brown background. b, Tiger on wires. c, Monkey. d, Dogs. e, Bear on skates. f, Trapeze artists.

No. 2369, 1100 le: a, Acrobat. b, Elephant. c, Bear on poles. d, Elephant. e, Horse. f, Fire eater.

No. 2370, 5000 le, Trainer on elephant's trunk, vert. No. 2371, 5000 le, Tiger jumping through flaming hoop, vert. No. 2372, 5000 le, Cannon flyer, vert.

**2000, Dec. 1**    **Litho.**
2363-2366   A347   Set of 4    5.75   5.75
#### Sheets of 6, #a-f
2367-2369   A347   Set of 3    21.00   21.00
#### Souvenir Sheets
2370-2372   A347   Set of 3    16.00   16.00

SIERRA LEONE
LE 1100
THE QUEEN MOTHER

## Queen Mother, 100th Birthday — A348

**2000, Dec. 18**
2373   A348   1100 le multi    1.10   1.10
Issued in sheets of 6.

---

THE HISTORY OF THE ORIENT EXPRESS

## History of the Orient Express — A350

No. 2376, 1000 le: a, First sleeping car, 1872. b, Dining car #193, 1886. c, Dining car #2422, 1913. d, Sleeping car Type S1. e, Metal sleeping car #2645. f, Metal sleeping car #2644, 1922.

No. 2377, 1000 le: a, Dining car, Series #8341. b, Dining car, Series #3342. c, Sleeping car, Series #3312 Type Z. d, Sleeping car, Series #3879, 1950. e, Sleeping car, Series #3311 Type Z. f, Dining rar, Series #3785, 1932.

No. 2378, 1100 le: a, Ostend-Vienna. b, Engine East 230, #3175. c, Dual cylinder locomotivo. d, Simplon Orient Express, 1919. e, Engine East 220, #2405. f, Caboose of Simplon Express, c. 1906.

No. 2379, 1100 le: a, Sleeping car #507, 1897. b, Sleeping car #438, 1894. c, Sleeping car #313, 1880. d, Sleeping car #190, 1886. e, Sleeping car #102, 1882. f, Sleeping car #77, 1881.

No. 2380, 5000 le, Locomotive, vert. No. 2381, 5000 le, Georges Nagelmackers, vert. No. 2382, 5000 le, Mata Hari, vert. No. 2383, 5000 le, Agatha Christie, vert.

**2001, Jan. 15**    **Perf. 14**
#### Sheets of 6, #a-f
2376-2379   A350   Set of 4    26.00   26.00
#### Souvenir Sheets
2380-2383   A350   Set of 4    21.00   21.00

LE £00
SIERRA LEONE

## Reptiles A351

Designs: 250 le, Natal Mixands dwarf chameleon. 400 le, Cape cobra. 500 le, Western sand lizard. 600 le, Pan-hinged terrapin. 800 le, Many-horned adder. 1500 le, Hawequa flat gecko.

No. 2390, 1200 le: a, Reticulated desert lizard. b, Ball python. c, Gaboon viper. d, Dumeril's boa. e, Common egg-eater. f, Helmet turtle.

No. 2391, 1200 le: a, Asian saw-scaled viper. b, Namibian sand snake. c, Angolan garter snake. d, Striped skaapsteker. e, Brown house snake. f, Shield-nosed cobra.

No. 2392, 5000 le, Green water snake. No. 2393, 5000 le, Flap-necked chameleon.

**2001, Jan. 15**
2384-2389   A351   Set of 6    4.25   4.25
#### Sheets of 6, #a-f
2390-2391   A351   Set of 2    15.00   15.00
#### Souvenir Sheets
2392-2393   A351   Set of 2    10.50   10.50

## New Year 2001 (Year of the Snake) — A349

No. 2374, horiz.: a, Blue snake. b, Red snake. c, Purple snake. d, Green snake.

**2001, Jan. 2**
2374   A349   800 le Sheet of 4, #a-d    3.50   3.50
#### Souvenir Sheet
2375   A349   2500 le Green snake    2.60   2.60

---

Rijksmuseum, Amsterdam, Bicent. (in 2000) — A352

No. 2394, 1100 le, vert.: a, Gentleman Writing a Letter, by Gabriel Metsu. b, Self-portrait, by Carel Fabritius. c, The Windmill at Wijk bij Duurstede, by Jacob van Ruisdael. d, Bentheim Castle, by van Ruisdael. e, Ships on a Stormy Sea, by Willem van de Velde, the Younger. f, David from David Playing the Harp, by Jan de Bray.

No. 2395, 1100 le, vert.: a, St. Paul from St. Paul Healing the Cripple at Lystra, by Karel Dujardin. b, Two hatless men form The Meagre Company, by Frans Hals and Pieter Codde. c, Man from Elegant Couple in an Interior, by Eglon van der Neer. d, Laid Table with Cheese and Fruit, by Floris van Dijck. e, Bacchanal, by Moses van Uyttenbroeck. f, Kneeling woman from St. Paul Healing the Cripple at Lystra.

No. 2396, 1100 le, vert.: a, Lady Reading a Letter, by Metsu. b, Portrait of Titus, by Rembrandt. c, Portrait of Gerard de Lairesse, by Rembrandt. d, Portrait of a Family in an Interior, by Emanuel de Witte. e, The Letter, by Gerard Terborch. f, Three Women and a Man in a Courtyard Behind a House, by Pieter de Hooch.

No. 2397, 1100 le, vert.: a, Candlebearors from David Playing the Harp. b, Hand of St. Paul from St. Paul Healing the Cripple at Lystra. c, Two men, one with hat, from The Meagre Company. d, The Gray, by Ohilips Wouwerman. e, Couple from Elegant Couple in an Interior. f, The Hut, by Adriaen van de Velde.

No. 2398, 5000 le, Road in the Dunes With a Passenger Coach, by Salomon van Ruysdael. No. 2399, 5000 le, Cows in the Meadow, by Albert Gerard Bilders. No. 2400, 5000 le, Lot and His Daughters, by Hendrick Goltzius. No. 2401, 5000 le, Arrival of Queen Wilhelmina at the Frederiksplein in Amsterdam, by Otto Eerelman.

**2001, Jan. 15**    **Perf. 13¾**
#### Sheets of 6, #a-f
2394-2397   A352   Set of 4    27.50   27.50
#### Souvenir Sheets
2398-2401   A352   Set of 4    21.00   21.00

Battle of Britain, 60th Anniv. — A353

No. 2402, 1000 le: a, Bombed village near London. b, The Underground as a bomb shelter. c, Firemen. d, Home Guard. e, Setting lights out time. f, Pilots resting between flights. g, Brendan "Paddy" Finucane, ace pilot. h, Hawk 75.

No. 2403, 1000 le: a, St. Paul's Cathedral. b, Eastenders leaving London. c, Winston Churchill being cheered by British crew. d, Rescue pilot. e, Boy Scouts helping children. f, Big gunners, 1940. g, Plane spotter lights. h, Survey watchers.

No. 2404, 1000 le: a, Post Office Engineer, WAFF. b, Women munitions workers. c, Churchill as prime minister and defense minister. d, German Dornier DO17. e, Church fires from Nazi bombs, London, 1940. f, All-night raid on London, 1940. g, Lunchtime in the

Underground, h, People in the Underground, 1940.
No. 2405, 1000 le: a, London Bridge, b, Surrey Home Guard, c, British Cruiser tank MK III. d, Newfoundland men at the guns, 1940. e, Lady Astor's Constituency hit, 1940. f, Churchill worried with war, 1940. g, Bomb blast at Parliament, h, Development of radar, 1940.
No. 2406, 6000 le, Churchill and wife inspecting harbor damage. No. 2407, 6000 le, London, 1940. No. 2408, 6000 le, British Supermarine Spitfire. No. 2409, 6000 le, Bombing crew preparing for flight, 1940, vert.

**2001, Jan. 30**     **Perf. 14**

| | | | |
|---|---|---|---|
| 2402-2405 | A353 | Set of 4 | 35.00 35.00 |
| | | **Sheets of 8, #a-h** | |
| 2406-2409 | A353 | Set of 4 | 25.00 25.00 |

The Bible According to **Rembrandt**

Biblical Scenes by Rembrandt — A354

No. 2410, 1000 le: a, The Song of Simeon. b, Study for Adoration of the Magi. c, Mary With the Child by a Window. d, Flight Into Egypt. e, The Circumcision. f, The Shepherds Worship the Child.
No. 2411, 1000 le: a, The Angel Rises Up in the Flame of Manoah's Sacrifice. b, Tobias Frightened by the Fish. c, The Angel of the Lord Stands in Balaam's Path. d, The Angel Appears to Hagar in the Desert. e, Jacob's Dream. f, The Healing of Tobit.
No. 2412, 5000 le, Simeon's Prophecy to Mary. No. 2413, 5000 le, The Angel Prevents the Sacrifice of Isaac. No. 2414, 5000 le, The Angel Leaves Tobit and His Family, vert. No. 2415, 5000 le, The Adoration of the Magi, vert.

**2001, Feb. 13**     **Perf. 13¾**

| | | | |
|---|---|---|---|
| 2410-2411 | A354 | **Sheets of 6, #a-f** | |
| | | Set of 2 | 12.50 12.50 |
| | | **Souvenir Sheets** | |
| 2412-2415 | A354 | Set of 4 | 21.00 21.00 |

Racehorses A355

Designs: 200 le, Native Dancer. 500 le, Citation. 1500 le, Spectre 2000 le, Carbine.
No. 2420, 1200 le: a, Arkle. b, Golden Miller. c, Phar Lap. d, Battleship. e, Kelso. f, Nijinsky.
No. 2421, 1200 le: a, Red Rum. b, Sir Ken. c, War Admiral. d, Troytown. e, Shergar. f, Allez France.
No. 2422, 5000 le, Cigar. No. 2423, 5000 le, Desert Orchid. No. 2424, 5000 le, Trophy. No. 2425, 5000 le, Horses on turf track, horiz.

**2001, Feb. 27**     **Perf. 14**

| | | | |
|---|---|---|---|
| 2416-2419 | A355 | Set of 4 | 4.50 4.50 |
| | | **Sheets of 6, #a-f** | |
| 2420-2421 | A355 | Set of 2 | 15.00 15.00 |
| | | **Souvenir Sheets** | |
| 2422-2425 | A355 | Set of 4 | 21.00 21.00 |

---

Automobiles — A356

Butterflies A357

No. 2426, 1000 le: a, 1898 Benz Velo. b, 1909 Rolls-Royce Silver Ghost, c, 1912 Ford Model T. d, 1937 Duesenberg SJ. e, 1938-40 Grosser Mercedes. f, 1938 Citroen Light 15.
No. 2427, 1000 le: a, 1939 Lincoln Zephyr. b, 1947 Volkswagen Beetle, c, 1959 Jaguar Mark II. d, 1968 Ford Shelby Mustang GT500. e, 1987-94 Opel/Vauxhall Senator. f, 2002 Mercedes Maybach.
No. 2428, 5000 le, 1928 Bentley 3-liter short chassis Tourer. No. 2429, 5000 le, 1999 Ferrari 360 Modena.

**2001, Apr. 30**     **Perf. 13¾**

| | | | |
|---|---|---|---|
| 2426-2427 | A356 | **Sheets of 6, #a-f** | |
| | | Set of 2 | 12.50 12.50 |
| | | **Souvenir Sheets** | |
| 2428-2429 | A356 | Set of 2 | 10.50 10.50 |

Designs: 250 le, Euroma fluricula. 400 le, Papilio dardanus. 800 le, Amauris nossima. 1500 le, Gideona lucasi.
No. 2434, 1100 le: a, Papilio dardanus. b, Cymothoe sangaris. c, Epiphora albida. d, African giant swallowtail. e, Papilio nobilis. f, Charaxes hadranus.
No. 2435, 1100 le: a, Charaxes lucretia. b, Euxanthe clossliex. c, Charaxes phenix. d, Charaxes acraeades. e, Charaxes protoclea azota. f, Charaxes lydiae.
No. 2436, 5000 le, Clotis zoe, No. 2437, 5000 le, Acraea ranauaiona, vert.

**2001, Apr. 30**     **Perf. 13¼x13½, 13¾x13¾**

| | | | |
|---|---|---|---|
| 2430-2433 | A357 | Set of 4 | 3.25 3.25 |
| | | **Litho.** | |
| 2434-2435 | A357 | **Sheets of 6, #a-f** | |
| | | Set of 2 | 14.50 14.50 |
| | | **Souvenir Sheets** | |
| 2436-2437 | A357 | Set of 2 | 11.00 11.00 |

H.M. Queen Elizabeth II

Queen Elizabeth II, 75th Birthday — A358

No. 2438: a, Wearing hat. b, With infant. c, Wearing crown. d, Wearing black blouse.

**2001, June 18**     **Litho.**     **Perf. 14**

| | | | |
|---|---|---|---|
| 2438 | A358 | Sheet of 4, #a-d | 8.25 8.25 |
| | | **Souvenir Sheet** | |
| | | **Perf. 13¾** | |
| 2439 | A358 | 5000 le As older woman | 5.25 5.25 |

No. 2438 contains four 28x42mm stamps.

---

Japanese Art — A359

Legends of Hollywood

Marlene Dietrich — A360

Designs: 50 le, Izu Chiruki No Hi, by Hokkei, horiz. 100 le, A Visit to Enoshima, by Kiyonaga Torii, horiz. 150 le, Inn on a Harbor, by Sadahide, horiz. 200 le, Entrance to Foreigner's Establishment by Sadahide, horiz. 250 le, Courtesans at Cherry Blossom Time, by Kiyonaga, horiz. 300 le, Cherry Blossom Viewing at Ueno, by Toyohara Chikanobu, horiz. 400 le, A Summer Evening at a Restaurant by the Sumida River, by Torii, horiz. 500 le, Ichikana Yaozo I As Samurai, by Torii, horiz. 600 le, The Actor Nakamura Nosihoi II as a Street Walker, by Shunzan Katsukawa. 800 le, Arashi Sangoro II, by Shokosai. 1500 le, bando Mitsugoro I, by Shunko. No. 2451, 2000 le, Matsumoto Koshiro II, by Masanobu.
No. 2452, 2000 le: a, Nakamura Shikan II and Nakamura Baiko, by Shigeharu. b, Women Making Rice Cakes, by Shunsho. c, Youth Sending Letter by Arrow, by Harushige. d, Woman with green sash from Six Girls, by Eisho.
No. 2453, 2000 le: a, Woman with checked kimono, from Six Girls. b, Courtesan on a Bench, by Eiri. c, Courtesan and Her Two Kamuro, by Suzuki Harunobu. d, Clearing Weather at Awazu, by Shigemasa.
No. 2454, 2000 le: a, Promenade. b, Wine Tasters. c, Rain in May, all Lovers by the Wall.
No. 2455, 2000 le — Paintings by Harunobu: a, Young Woman Attended by Maid. b, Lovers by Lespedeza Bush. c, Girl Contemplating a Landscape. d, Young Man Unrolling a Hanging Scroll.
No. 2456, 5000 le, Searching for the Hermit, by Harunobu. No. 2457, 5000 le, Courtesan and Two Kamuro, by Harunobu. No. 2458, 5000 le, Drying Clothes, by Harunobu. No. 2459, 5000 le, Komachi Praying For Rain, by Harunobu. No. 2460, 5000 le, Girl Contemplating Landscape, by Harunobu.

**2001, July 2**     **Perf. 13½**

| | | | |
|---|---|---|---|
| 2440-2451 | A359 | Set of 12 | 7.25 7.25 |
| | | **Sheets of 4, #a-d** | |
| 2452-2455 | A359 | Set of 4 | 32.50 32.50 |
| | | **Souvenir Sheets** | |
| 2456-2460 | A359 | Set of 5 | 26.00 26.00 |

Phila Nippon '01, Japan (#2452-2460).

No. 2461: a, Looking over shoulder. b, Wearing necklace. c, Wearing coat with flower. d, Holding cigarette.

**2001, June 18**     **Litho.**     **Perf. 13¾**

| | | | |
|---|---|---|---|
| 2461 | A360 | Sheet of 4, #a-d | 8.25 8.25 |

---

Toulouse-Lautrec Paintings — A361

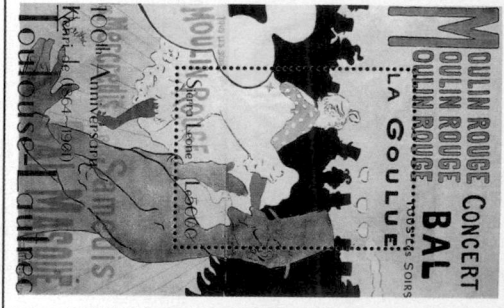

75th Anniversary

Monet Paintings — A362

No. 2462, horiz.: a, A La Mie. b, A Corner of the Moulin de la Gallete. c, The Start of the Quadrille.
No. 2463, horiz.: a, At the Moulin Rouge, 5000 le, La Goulue.

**2001, June 18**

| | | | |
|---|---|---|---|
| 2462 | A361 | 2200 le Sheet of 3, #a-c | 7.00 7.00 |
| | | **Souvenir Sheet** | |
| 2463 | A361 | 5000 le multi | 5.25 5.25 |

No. 2464, horiz.: a, The Road to Vetheuil, Winter. b, The Church at Vetheuil, Snow. c, Breakup of the Ice Near Vetheuil, d, The Boulevard de Pontoise at Argenteuil, Snow.
No. 2465, 5000 le, Irises by the Pond.

**2001, June 18**

| | | | |
|---|---|---|---|
| 2464 | A362 | 1500 le Sheet of 4, #a-d | 6.25 6.25 |
| | | **Souvenir Sheet** | |
| 2465 | A362 | 5000 le multi | 5.25 5.25 |

Giuseppe Verdi

Giuseppe Verdi (1813-1901), Opera Composer — A363

No. 2466: a, Vladimir Popov. b, Enrico Caruso. c, Rudolf Bockelmann. d, Stage 5000 le, Aprile Millo and Barseq Tumayan.

**SIERRA LEONE**

Designs: 100 le, 2001 360 Challenge. 500 le, 1971 712 Can Am. 600 le, 1970 512M. 1000 le, 1988 F40. 1500 le, 1982 365 GT4/BB. 2000 le, 1972 365 GTB/4.

2001, Oct. 8    *Perf. 13¾*
2495-2500 A371 Set of 6   6.00   6.00

**Souvenir Sheets**

**Horses — A372**

**Chinese Character for Horse — A373**

No. 2501: a, Green background. b, Blue background.
No. 2502 — "2002" in: a, Green. b, Red. c, Orange. d, Purple.

2001, Nov. 29    *Perf. 13*
2501 A372 1200 le Sheet of 2, #a-b   2.50   2.50

*Perf. 13x13¼*
2502 A373 1200 le Sheet of 4, #a-d   5.00   5.00

New Year 2002 (Year of the Horse).

**2002 World Cup Soccer Championships, Japan and Korea — A374**

No. 2503, 1400 le: a, Newspaper article, 1950. b, Jules Rimet, 1954. c, Pele and teammates, 1958. d, Vava and Schroiff, 1962. e, Bobby Charlton, 1966. f, Pele, 1970.
No. 2504, 1400 le: a, Daniel Passarella, 1978. b, Karl-Heinz Rummenigge, 1982. c, Diego Maradona, 1986. d, Roger Milla, 1990. e, Romario, 1994. f, Zinedine Zidane, 1998.
No. 2505, 5000 le, Head from Jules Rimet trophy, 1930. No. 2506, 5000 le, Head and globe from World Cup trophy, 2002.

2001, Dec. 7    *Perf. 13¾x14¼*
2503-2504 A374 Set of 2   17.00   17.00
   Sheets of 6, #a-f

*Perf. 14½x14½*
2505-2506 A374 Set of 2   10.00   10.00

**Souvenir Sheets**

**Christmas A375**

Paintings by Filippo Lippi: 300 le, Madonna of Humility. 600 le, Annunciation. 1500 le,

---

*Butterflies of the World*

**Butterflies — A368**

No. 2486, 1100 le: a, Teinopalpus imperialis. b, Swallowtail. c, Doris. d, Northern Jezebel. e, Beautiful monarch. f, Gaudy commodore.
No. 2487, 1100 le: a, Plain tiger. b, Tiger. c, Morpho cypris. d, Castnia litus. e, Dismorphia nemesis. f, Blue and yellow butterfly (inscribed African violets).
No. 2488, 5000 le, Scarce swallowtail. No. 2489, 5000 le, Clouded yellow, vert.

2001, Apr. 30    *Perf. 14*
   **Sheets of 6, #a-f**
2486-2487 A368 Set of 2   14.50   14.50

**Souvenir Sheets**
2488-2489 A368 Set of 2   11.00   11.00

**Photomosaic of Queen Elizabeth II — A369**

*Perf. 14*
2001, June 18
2490 A369 1000 le multi   1.10   1.10

Printed in sheets of 8.

**Mao Zedong (1893-1976) — A370**

No. 2492, 1100 le — Map of China and Mao: a, Without hat. b, With green cap. c, With blue cap.
No. 2493, 1100 le — Red frame and Mao with: a, Uniform. b, Shirt with open collar. c, Cap.
No. 2493, 5000 le, Mao wearing black suit. No. 2494, 5000 le, Mao in white.

2001, June 18
   **Sheets of 3, #a-c**
2491-2492 A370 Set of 2   7.00   7.00

**Souvenir Sheets**
2493-2494 A370 Set of 2   10.50   10.50

**Ferrari Automobiles — A371**

---

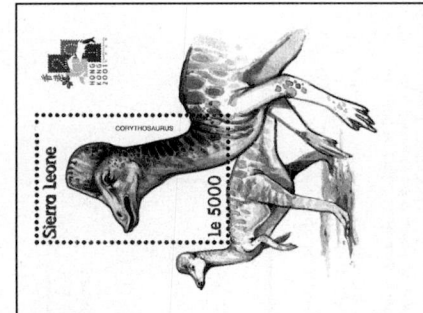

**Dinosaurs — A367**

No. 2482, 1000 le: a, Acrocanthosaurus. b, Edmontosaurus. c, Archaeopteryx. d, Hadrosaurus. e, Mongolian avimimus. f, Pachyrhinosaurus. g, Iguanodons (with tree trunk). h, Iguanodons, diff.
No. 2483, 1000 le, horiz.: a, Albertosaurus. b, Pteranodon ingens. c, Asiatic iguanodon. d, Sordes. e, Coelophysis. f, Saichania. g, Barctosaurus. h, Triceratops.
No. 2484, 5000 le, Corythosaurus. No. 2485, 5000 le, Stenonychosaurus.

2001, Mar. 1    *Perf. 13½*
   **Sheets of 8, #a-h**
2482-2483 A367 Set of 2   17.00   17.00

**Souvenir Sheets**
2484-2485 A367 Set of 2   10.50   10.50

Hong Kong 2001 Stamp Exhibition.

 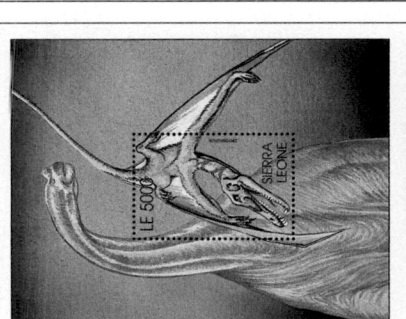

**Souvenir Sheets**

**Dinosaurs — A367a**

Designs: No. 2485A, 5000 le, Dryosaurus. No. 2485B, 5000 le, Diplodocids. No. 2485C, 5000 le, Allosaurus.

2001, Mar. 1   Litho.   *Perf. 13½*
2485A- A367a   3   15.00   15.00
2485C

Nos. 2485A-2485C were not available in the marketplace until 2002.

---

Red Pony, by John Steinbeck. e, Black Stallion, by Walter Farley. f, Misty of Chincoteague, by Marguerite Henry. No. 2479, 1100 le: a, Arvak Alsvid. b, Pegasus. c, Sleipnir. d, Veillanfif. e, Grani. f, Galathe, from Troilus and Cressida, by William Shakespeare.
No. 2480, 5000 le, Rosinante, from Don Quixote, by Miguel de Cervantes. No. 2481, 5000 le, Xanthus and Balius.

2001, Feb. 27   Litho.   *Perf. 14*
   **Sheets of 6, #a-f**
2478-2479 A366 Set of 2   14.00   14.00

**Souvenir Sheets**
2480-2481 A366 Set of 2   10.50   10.50

---

2001, June 18    *Perf. 14*
2466 A363 1700 le Sheet of 4, #a-d   7.00   7.00

**Souvenir Sheet**
2467 A363 5000 le multi   5.25   5.25

**Royal Navy Submarines, Cent. — A364**

No. 2468: a, C Class submarine. b, HMS Spartan. c, HMS Exeter. d, HMS Chatham. e, HMS Verdun. f, HMS Marlborough.

2001, June 18   Sheet of 6, #a-f
2468 A364 1100 le multi   7.00   7.00

**Souvenir Sheet**
2469 A364 5000 le multi   5.25   5.25

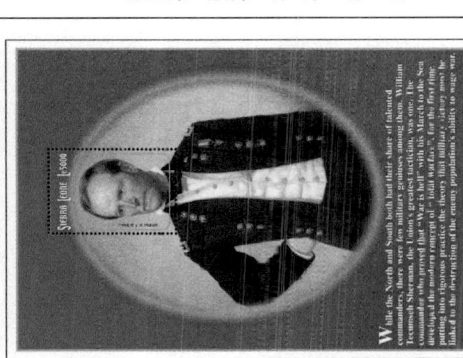

**U.S. Civil War — A365**

No. 2470, 2000 le — Generals: a, Ulysses S. Grant. b, John Bell Hood. c, Jeb Stuart. d, Robert E. Lee.
No. 2471, 2000 le: a, Gen. Joshua Chamberlain. b, Gen. Stonewall Jackson. c, Gen George McClellan. d, Adm. David Farragut.
No. 2472, 2000 le — Battle scenes: a, Shiloh. b, Bull Run. c, Fair Oaks. d, Chattanooga.
No. 2473, 2000 le — Battle scenes: a, Fredericksburg. b, Gettysburg. c, Mobile Bay. d, Fort Sumter.
No. 2474, 5000 le, Gen. William Tecumseh Sherman. No. 2475, 5000 le, Gen. George A. Custer. No. 2476, 5000 le, Battle of Vicksburg. No. 2477, 5000 le, Battle of Antietam.

2001, Aug. 27   **Sheets of 4, #a-d**
2470-2473 A365 Set of 4   32.50   32.50

**Souvenir Sheets**
2474-2477 A365 Set of 4   21.00   21.00

**Horses in Literature and Mythology — A366**

No. 2478, 1100 le: a, Piebald, from National Velvet, by Enid Bagnold. b, Strider, by Leo Tolstoy. c, Black Beauty, by Anna Sewell. d,

Annunciation, vert. 2000 le, Adoration of the Child and Saints, vert.

**2001, Dec. 26**
2507-2510 A375    Set of 4    4.50 4.50
5000 le, Barbadori Altarpiece, vert.
2511 A375 5000 le multi    5.00 5.00

**2001, Dec.**    **Perf. 14**
**Souvenir Sheet**

**Queen Mother Type of 1999**
**Redrawn**

No. 2512: a. With Duke of York and Princess Elizabeth, 1926. b. In 1979. c. In Nairobi, 1959. d. In 1991.
4000 le, With crown, 1937.

**2001, Dec.**    **Perf. 14**
**Yellow Orange Frames**

2512 A307 1300 le Sheet of 4,
#a-d, + label 5.25 5.25
**Souvenir Sheet**    **Perf. 13¾**

Queen Mother's 101st birthday. No. 2513 contains one 38x51mm stamp with a slightly darker backdrop than that found on No. 2208. Sheet margins of Nos. 2512-2513 lack embossing and gold arms and frames found on Nos. 2207-2208.

2513 A307 4000 le multi    4.00 4.00

**2002, Jan. 24**
2514 A376 2000 le multi

**2002, Jan. 24**    **Perf. 14**
**Souvenir Sheet**    2.00 2.00

SOS Children's
Village — A376

Sierra Leone
1958 Steam Locomotive
Le 5000

The Century of Steam Ends and

**The Century of Steam Ends and
Their Inventors — A377**

Steam and Electric Inventions and
Their Inventors — A377

No. 2515, 1100 le: a. The Rocket steam locomotive, 1829. b. High-speed electric passenger train. c. 1863 Steam pumper. d. Early electric trolley. e. 1893 Steam automobile. f. Early Electric monorail.

No. 2516, 1100 le: a. Early steam pumper. b. Telephone. c. Steam liner. d. Battery and light bulb. e. 1770 Steam carriage. f. Electric passenger train.

No. 2517, 1100 le: a. Robert Fulton and steamboat. b. Thomas Edison and light bulb. c. 1899 T9 steam locomotive. d. Radio and antennae. e. James Watt, and steam engine diagram. f. Alexander Graham Bell and telephone.

No. 2518, 5000 le, 1899 Steam locomotive.
No. 2519, 5000 le, Telephone, radio and light bulb. No. 2520, 5000 le, Benjamin Franklin, vert.

**2002, Jan. 24**
**Perf. 13¼x13½, 13½x13¾**
2515-2517 A377    Set of 3    15.00 15.00
**Sheets of 6, #a-f**
2518-2520 A377    Set of 3    20.00 20.00
**Souvenir Sheets**

Sierra Leone
Le 400

Sierra
Leone
Le 400

Designs: 400 le, Jerusalem artichoke, 500 le, Painted trillium. 600 le, Bluebells. 1000 le, Rough fruited cinquefoil. 1500 le, Wake robin. 2000 le, Seashore mallow.
No. 2532, 1300 le, horiz.: a. Hepatica. b. Star of Bethlehem. c. Wood lily. d. Wild geranium. e. Hedge bindweed. f. Gloxinias.

Flowers — A381

**2002, Jan. 24**
2521 A378 2000 le multi

SIERRA LEONE
Le2000
UNITED WE STAND

**2002, Feb. 6**
**United We**
**Stand — A378**

2521 A378 2000 le multi

**2002, Feb. 6**    **Perf. 13½x13¾**
**Souvenir Sheet**
2526-2531 A381    Set of 6    6.00 6.00

GOLDEN JUBILEE - 6th February, 2002
50th Anniversary of the Majesty Queen Elizabeth II's Accession

**Reign of Queen Elizabeth II, 50th
Anniv. — A379**

No. 2522: a. With young Prince Charles and Princess Anne. b. Wearing tiara and stole, looking forward. c. Wearing tiara and stole, looking right. d. Wearing hat.
5000 le, Wearing hat and gloves.

**2002, Feb. 6**    **Perf. 14¼**
2522 A379 2000 le Sheet of 4,
#a-d    9.00 9.00
**Souvenir Sheet**
2523 A379 5000 le multi    5.50 5.50

CELEBRATE HUMANITY
2002 WINTER OLYMPICS
SALT LAKE CITY
LE2000
Sierra Leone

**2002**
**Winter**
**Olympics**
**Salt Lake**
**City**
**A380**

Designs: Nos. 2524, 2525, 2000 le, Curling. Nos. 2524A, 2525A, 2000 le, Ice hockey.

**2002, Apr. 22    Litho.    Perf. 14**
**Olympic Rings in Color**
2524  A380    Set of 2
2524A    4.00 4.00
Souvenir sheet #2524-    4.00 4.00
2524Ab
**Olympic Rings in White on Black
Background**
**Perf. 13¼x13½**
2525  A380    Set of 2
2525A    4.00 4.00
Souvenir sheet, #2525-    4.00 4.00
2525Ab

No. 2533, 1300 le, horiz.: a. Leevigata iris. b. Dietes. c. Day lily. d. Cardinal flower. e. Mountain pink. f. Seaside gentian.
No. 2534, 5000 le, Dame's rocket. No. 2535, 5000 le, Pinxter flower.

**2002, Apr. 29    Litho.    Perf. 14x14½**
2532-2533 A381    Set of 6    6.00 6.00
**Sheets of 6, #a-f**
2534-2535 A381    Set of 2    15.00 15.00
**Souvenir Sheets**
Nos. 2532-2533 contain six 42x38mm stamps. Nos. 2534-2535 contain one 38x42mm stamp.

Gazde Giraffe Camelopardalis
Sierra
Leone
Le 200

**Wildlife — A382**

Designs: 200 le, Giraffe. 400 le, L'Host's guenon. 1500 le, Jentik's duiker.
No. 2539, 1100 le, horiz.: a. Kudu. b. Caracal. c. Oribi. d. Aardwolf. e. Bushpig. f. Suricates.
No. 2540, 1100 le, horiz.: a. African buffalo. b. Wild dog. c. Black-backed jackal. d. Aardvark. e. Impala. f. Waterbuck.
No. 2541, 8000 le, Vervet monkey. No. 2542, 8000 le, Springbok.

**2002, Apr. 29**    **Perf. 14**
2536-2538 A382    Set of 3    2.10 2.10
**Sheets of 6, #a-f**
2539-2540 A382    Set of 2    13.00 13.00
**Souvenir Sheets**
2541-2542 A382    Set of 2    16.00 16.00

Sierra Leone
LE2000
CHIUNE/SUGIHARA

**Chiune Sugihara,**
**Japanese Diplomat**
**Who Saved Jews**
**in World War**
**II — A383**

**2002, July 1    Litho.    Perf. 14**
2543 A383 2000 le multi    2.00 2.00
Printed in sheets of 4.

SIERRA LEONE
LE 800

Nos. 1811-
1812
Surcharged

**Methods & Perfs, As Before**

**2002, July 1**
2544 A242    800 le on 400 le
Block or
strip of 4,
#a-d
**Souvenir Sheet**
2545 A242 5000 le on 1500 le    3.25 3.25
multi    5.00 5.00

Queen Mother Elizabeth (1900-2002). No. 2544 was issued in sheets of eight stamps. Sheet margins of 2544-2544 were overprinted with black border and "In Memoriam / 1900-2002."

**2002, July 1    Litho.    Perf. 14**
2546 A384 1300 le Sheet of 6,
#a-f    7.75 7.75
**Souvenir Sheet**
2547 A384 5000 le multi    5.00 5.00

Int'l Year of Ecotourism — A384

No. 2546: a. Bullom boats. b. Dinkongor Falls. c. Rokel River. d. Pygmy hippopotamus. e. Hills of Soa Chiefdom. f. Long Beach.
5000 le, Photo safari.

Sierra Leone
eco-tourism
Int'l YEAR OF ECO-TOURISM
UNITED NATIONS · YEAR OF ECO TOURISM

75th Anniversary of the first solo
Trans-Atlantic Flight
CHARLES AUGUSTUS LINDBERGH (1902-1974)

**First Non-stop Solo Transatlantic**
**Flight, 75th Anniv. — A385**

No. 2548, horiz.: a. The Spirit of St. Louis. b. Being towed from Ryan Airlines factory. c. Taking off, May 20, 1927.
No. 2549, Charles Lindbergh.

**2002, July 1**
2548 A385 2500 le Sheet of 3,
#a-c    7.50 7.50
**Souvenir Sheet**
2549 A385 2500 le multi    2.50 2.50

SIERRA LEONE
Le 800

**Shirley Temple Movie Type of 2000**

Temple in scenes from "Wee Willie Winkie" — No. 2550: a. With woman, man in army uniform, two men wearing turbans. b. Resting head near mirror. c. With boy wearing army uniform and kilt. d. With man wearing turban. e. With man in army uniform. f. Giving note to man in prison.
No. 2551, vert. a. With man wearing turban. b. With man wearing turban. c. With woman and man. d. With man in army uniform. e. With woman and man. f. With man in army uniform, vert.

**2002, July 1**    **Perf. 12½**
2550 A324 1100 le Sheet of 6,
#a-f    6.50 6.50
2551 A324 1300 le Sheet of 4,
#a-d    5.25 5.25
**Souvenir Sheet**
2552 A324 5000 le multi    5.00 5.00

Pres. Ronald Reagan — A395

No. 2582, 1700 le — Country name in black: a, Wearing brown tie. b, Wearing red tie. No. 2583, 1700 le — Country name in white: a, Wearing spotted tie. b, Wearing striped tie.

**Litho.**

2002, Dec. 30

2582-2583  A395  Set of 2  6.75  6.75

**Pairs, #a-b**  5.75  5.75

Nos. 2582-2583 each were printed in sheets containing two pairs.

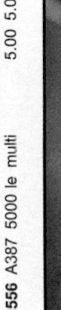

*Portraits of a President*

Pres. John F. Kennedy (1917-63) — A396

No. 2584, 1700 le: a, Wearing red tie. b, With newspaper. c, In front on brown curtain. d, In front of brown and tan background. No. 2585, 1700 le — John and Jacqueline: a, In formal wear greeting man. b, With purple background. c, Playing with child. d, At Love Field, Nov. 22, 1963.

**Perf. 14**

2002, Dec. 30

2584-2585  A396  Set of 2  13.50  13.50

**Sheets of 4, #a-d**  13.50  13.50

Princess Diana (1961-97) — A397

Designs: No. 2586, 1700 le, Wearing black dress. No. 2587, 1700 le, Wearing blue dress and tiara.

2002, Dec. 30

2586-2587  A397  Set of 2  3.50  3.50

Nos. 2586-2587 each were printed in sheets of 4.

---

No. 2563: a, Wearing flowered shirt. b, Wearing jacket, holding light-colored guitar. c, Seated in chair. d, Wearing sweater. e, With arms raised. f, With black guitar.

**Litho.**

2002, Oct. 7

2563  A392  1000 le  Sheet of 6, #a-f  5.75  5.75

2002 World Cup Soccer Championships, Japan and Korea — A393

No. 2564, 1400 le — Germany vs. Paraguay: a, Michael Ballack. b, Oliver Kahn. c, Miroslav Klose. d, Diego Gacilan. e, Jose Luis Chilavert. f, Guido Alvarenga.
No. 2565, 1400 le — Denmark vs. England: a, Jesper Gronkjaer. b, Thomas Helveg. c, Dennis Rommedahl. d, Michael Owen. e, David Seaman. f, Rio Ferdinand.
No. 2566, 1400 le — Mexico vs. U.S.: a, Rafael Marquez. b, Oscar Perez. c, Jared Borgetti. d, Landon Donovan. e, Brad Friedel. f, DaMarcus Beasley.
No. 2567, 1400 le — Japan vs. Turkey: a, Ryuzo Morioka. b, Kazuyuki Toda. c, Atsushi Yanagisawa. d, Fatih Akyel. e, Yildiray Basturk. f, Umit Davala.
No. 2568, 2500 le — Germany: a, Coach Rudi Voeller. b, Dietmar Hamann.
No. 2569, 2500 le — Paraguay: a, Julio Cesar Caceres. b, Coach Cesare Maldini.
No. 2570, 2500 le — Denmark: a, Coach Morten Olsen. b, Jon Dahl Tomasson.
No. 2571, 2500 le — England: a, David Beckham. b, Coach Sven Goran Eriksson.
No. 2572, 2500 le — Mexico: a, Coach Javier Aguirre. b, Jesus Arellano.
No. 2573, 2500 le — United States: a, Brian McBride. b, Coach Bruce Arena.
No. 2574, 2500 le — Japan: a, Coach Philippe Troussier. b, Junichi Inamoto.
No. 2575, 2500 le — Turkey: a, Vildiray Basturk. b, Coach Senol Gunes.

**Perf. 13¼**

2002, Nov. 18

**Sheets of 6, #a-f**

2564-2567  A393  Set of 4  40.00  40.00

**Souvenir Sheets of 2, #a-b**

2568-2575  A393  Set of 8  47.50  47.50

Christmas — A394

Designs: 50 le, Madonna and Child Between Saints John the Baptist and Catherine of Alexandria, by Perugino. 100 le, Madonna and Child Enthroned Between Angels and Saints, by Domenico Ghirlandaio. 150 le, The Virgin, by Giovanni Bellini. 500 le, Stories of the Virgin Birth of Mary, by Ghirlandaio. 5000 le, Adoration of the Magi, by Ghirlandaio. 6000 le, Madonna Enthroned with Saints, by Ghirlandaio.

**Perf. 14**

2002, Nov. 18

2576-2580  A394  Set of 5  6.75  6.75

**Souvenir Sheet**

2581  A394  6000 le  multi  7.00  7.00

---

Popeye in New York — A389

No. 2559, vert. — Popeye and: a, And Olive Oyl on river tour. b, And Olive Oyl in Central Park. c, And Olive Oyl near Brooklyn Bridge. d, Statue of Liberty. e, Flatiron Building. f, Empire State Building.
5000 le, Popeye and Olive Oyl skating at Rockefeller Center.

**Perf. 12¼**

2002, Aug. 26

2559  A389  1300 le  Sheet of 6, #a-f  8.00  8.00

**Souvenir Sheet**

2560  A389  5000 le  multi  5.25  5.25

No. 2559 contains six 38x50mm stamps.

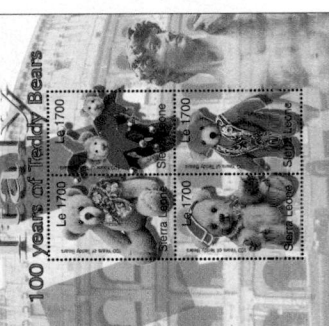

A390

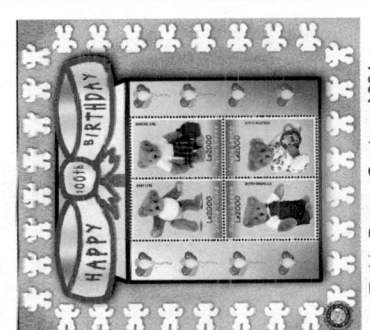

Teddy Bears, Cent. — A391

No. 2561: a, Bear with green bow. b, Bears with harlequin costumes. c, Bear with red headdress. d, Bear with black and gold neckband.
No. 2562: a, Baby girl bear. b, School girl bear. c, Bear in overalls. d, Bear in pajamas.

**Perf. 14**

2002, Sept. 23

2561  A390  1700 le  Sheet of 4, #a-d  6.50  6.50

2562  A391  2000 le  Sheet of 4, #a-d  7.75  7.75

Elvis Presley (1935-77) — A392

---

20th World Scout Jamboree, Thailand — A386

No. 2553: a, Boys on rocks fishing. b, Scouts without caps. c, Scouts in water holding fish. d, Scouts with caps.
5000 le, Scouts in sailboat.

**Perf. 14**

2002, July 1

2553  A386  2000 le  Sheet of 4, #a-d  8.00  8.00

**Souvenir Sheet**

2554  A386  5000 le  multi  5.00  5.00

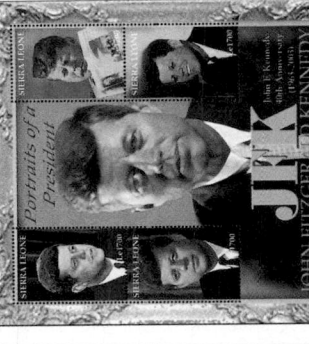

Intl. Year of Mountains — A387

No. 2555: a, Mt. Etna, Italy. b, Cotopaxi, Ecuador. c, Mt. Everest, Nepal. d, Mt. Popocatepetl, Mexico.
5000 le, Mt. Machhapuchare, Nepal.

2002, July 1

2555  A387  2000 le  Sheet of 4, #a-d  8.00  8.00

**Souvenir Sheet**

2556  A387  5000 le  multi  5.00  5.00

Pokémon — A388

No. 2557, vert.: a, Sudowoodo. b, Aipom. c, Shuckle. d, Miltank. e, Hitmontop. f, Ledian.
5000 le, Lugia.

**Perf. 13¾**

2002, Aug. 26

2557  A388  1500 le  Sheet of 6, #a-f  9.25  9.25

**Souvenir Sheet**

2558  A388  5000 le  multi  5.25  5.25

## Birds, Flowers and Insects of Africa — A398

No. 2588, 1300 le — Birds: a. Great blue turaco. b. Helmet vanga. c. Scarlet-tufted malachite sunbird. d. African pitta. e. African jacana. f. Southern carmine bee-eater.

No. 2589, 1300 le — Flowers: a. Ancistrochilus rothschildianus. b. Oeceoclades maculata. c. Eulophia guineensis. d. Angraecum distichum. e. Disa uniflora. f. Vanilla imperialis.

No. 2590, 1300 le — Insects: a. Panther-spotted grasshopper. b. Basker moth. c. Charaxes samegdalis. d. Carpenter ant. e. Worker bee. f. Ten-spot dragonfly.

**2003, Jan. 13**
2588-2590  A398  Set of 3  25.00 25.00
  Souvenir Sheets
2591-2593  A398  Set of 3  16.00 16.00

## Astronauts Killed in Space Shuttle Columbia Accident — A400

No. 2595: a. Mission Specialist 1 David M. Brown. b. Commander Rick D. Husband. c. Mission Specialist 4 Laurel Blair Salton Clark. d. Mission Specialist 4 Kalpana Chawla. e. Payload Commander Michael P. Anderson. f.

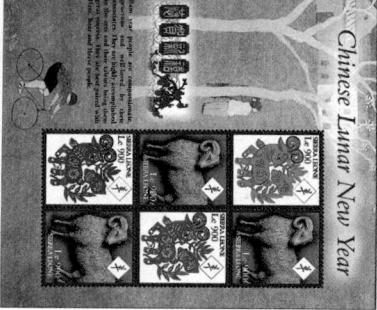

## Chinese Lunar New Year

New Year 2003 (Year of the Ram) — A399

No. 2594 — Color of ram: a. Green. b. Orange. c. Red violet. d. Orange brown.

**2003, Feb. 10**
2594  A399  900 le Sheet of 6, #a-c, 3 #d  5.75 5.75

### Sheets of 6, #a-f
2003, ...

---

Pilot William C. McCool. g. Payload Specialist 4 Ilan Ramon.

**2003, Apr. 7**
2595  A400  1000 le Sheet of 7, #a-g  6.25 6.25

## Teddy Bears, Cent. — A402

No. 2596, vert.: a. Bear with umbrella. b. Bear with horn. c. Bear in automobile. d. Bear with belt. c. Bear with pink dress. d. Bear with flower.

**2003**
2596  A401  1500 le Sheet of 4, #a-d  5.25 5.25
  Souvenir Sheet
2597  A401  5000 le multi  4.25 4.25
  Embroidered
  Imperf
2598  A402  12,000 le multi  10.50 10.50

Issued: Nos. 2596, 2597, 7/1; No. 2598, Apr. No. 2598 issued in sheets of 4.

Coronation of Queen Elizabeth II, 50th Anniv. — A404

Designs: No. 2599, 1500 le, Crowning of the Queen. No. 2600, 1500 le, Queen signs the oath. No. 2601, 1500 le, Sovereign's orb. No. 2602, 1500 le, Anointing of the Queen. No. 2603, 1500 le, Queen presented with Holy Bible. No. 2604, 1500 le, Royal onlookers. No. 2605, 1500 le, Ampulla and spoon. No. 2606, 1500 le, Orb and scepter.

**2003**
2599-2606  A403  Set of 8  10.50 10.50
  Souvenir Sheet
2607  A403  5000 le multi  4.25 4.25
  Miniature Sheet
  Litho. & Embossed

Queen with crown. 15,000 le, Queen with hat.

2608  A404  15,000 le multi  13.00 13.00

Issued: Nos. 2599-2607, 7/1: No. 2608, 4/7. No. 2607 contains one 37x50mm stamp.

## Japanese Art — A406

Designs: 800 le, Priest Raigo Transformed Into a Rat, by Yoshitoshi Tsukioka. 1000 le, The Spirit of Tamichi as a Great Snake, by Yoshitoshi Tsukioka. 1500 le, The Gathering and Gossiping of Various Tools, by Kuniyoshi Utagawa. 2500 le, Caricatures of Actors as

## Rembrandt Paintings — A405

Designs: 800 le, Young Man with Pointed Beard. 1000 le, Old Man with Book. 1200 le, The Shipbuilder Jan Rijcksen and His Wife, Griet Jans, horiz. 2000 le, Portrait of a Young Jew.

No. 2613: a. Juno. b. Bellona, Goddess of War. c. Artemesia. d. Esther Preparing to Intercede with Ahasuerus.

**2003, May 13**
2609-2612  A405  Set of 4  4.50 4.50
2613  A405  1700 le Sheet of 4, #a-d  6.00 6.00
  Souvenir Sheet
  Litho.
2614  A405  5000 le multi  4.50 4.50

---

Three Animals Playing Ken, by Kuniyoshi Utagawa.

No. 2619 — Paintings by Yoshitoshi Tsukioka: a. The Fox Woman Leaving Her Child. b. Fox Cry. c. The Lucky Teakettle of Morin Temple. d. The Ghost of Okiku.

5000 le, Fox in a Thunderstorm, by Kunisada Utagawa.

**2003, May 13**
2615-2618  A406  Set of 4  5.25 5.25
2619  A406  2000 le Sheet of 4, #a-d  7.25 7.25
  Souvenir Sheet
2620  A406  5000 le multi  4.50 4.50

## Paintings by Pablo Picasso — A407

Designs: 400 le, Glass, Pipe and Playing Card. 500 le, Still-Life on a Pedestal in front of a Window. 600 le, Woman in a Feathered Hat. 700 le, Pedestal and Guitar. 1000 le, Bread Carrier. 3000 le, Female Acrobat. No. 2627: a. Portrait of a Woman. b. Woman in a Red Armchair. c. Seated Woman with Crossed Hands. d. Woman with Small Round Hat (Dora Maar). d. Woman with Crossed Hands.

No. 2628, Boy in Black Shorts. No. 2629, Bathers, horiz.

**2003, May 13**
2621-2626  A407  Set of 6  5.50 5.50
2627  A407  2000 le Sheet of 4, #a-d  7.25 7.25
  Imperf
  Size: 82x105mm
2628  A407  5000 le multi  4.50 4.50
  Size: 103x82mm
2629  A407  5000 le multi  4.50 4.50

## Painting of Mona Lisa, 500th Anniv. — A408

No. 2629A, 500th Anniversary of Mona Lisa (complete painting).
No. 2630 — Inscribed: a. Chartier: Mona Lisa — Mistress of Francis I. b. Copy of Mona Lisa, Cheramy Collection.
5000 le, 500th Anniversary of Mona Lisa (face).

**2003, July 1**
2629A  A408  2000 le multi  1.75 1.75
2630  A408  2000 le Sheet of 3, #a-b, No. 2629A  5.25 5.25
  Souvenir Sheet
  Perf. 14
2631  A408  5000 le multi  4.25 4.25

No. 2629A was issued in two sheets of six with different selvage in 2004.

---

## H.M. Queen Elizabeth II 50th Anniversary of the Coronation

Sierra Leone  Le150

A403

No. 2590, vert.: ... Litho. Imperf. Perf. 14¼ ... 4.25 4.25

Litho.  **Perf. 14¼**

Litho.  **Perf. 13¼**

**Perf. 14¼, 13¼ (#2613)**

**Perf. 13¼x13¾**

**Perf. 13½x13¾**

**500th Anniversary of the Mona Lisa**

100th Birthday Celebration

## Chiao Ping-chen
(1689-1726)

*Sierra Leone Le5000*

Paintings of Chiao Ping-chen (1689-1726) — A418

No. 2665: a, Untitled painting depicting courtyard. b, Untitled landscape. c, Court Ladies (woman with purple robe at LR). d, Court Ladies (woman with purple robe at center).

5000 le, The Beauty of Traditional Chinese Architecture in Painting.

**2004, Jan. 21** *Perf. 13¼*
2665 A418 2000 le  Sheet of 4,
#a-d                    6.50  6.50
*Imperf*
2666 A418 5000 le shown        4.25  4.25
No. 2665 contains four 38x50mm stamps.

*Le 500*
BRITISH COUNCIL
Go Years Working with Sierra Leone
SIERRA LEONE

British Council, 60th Anniv. A419

Frame mnrs; 500 le, Gray green. 1000 le, Dull green. 2000 le, Purple. 3000 le, Red.

**2004, Jan. 29** *Perf. 14*
2667-2670 A419  Set of 4   5.50  5.50

Map & Lion Type of 1964 Redrawn *Die Cut*
**2001, Feb. 4** *Self-Adhesive*
2671 A38 1000 le multi        .85   .85
Printed in sheets of 10.

*SIERRA LEONE*
*1894-1978 25th ANNIVERSARY*

Paintings by Norman Rockwell — A420

No. 2672: a, Ice Cream Carrier. b, The Voyeur. c, Teacher's Birthday. d, Fisk Tires Advertisement.
5000 le, Cousin Reginald Plays Pirate.

**2004, Feb. 24** *Litho.* *Perf. 13½*
2672 A420 2000 le  Sheet of 4,
#a-d                    6.50  6.50
**Souvenir Sheet**
2673 A420 5000 le multi        4.25  4.25

---

No. 2647, 5000 le, Bobet, 1953-55. No. 2648, 5000 le, Anquetil, 1957, diff. No. 2649, 5000 le, Bernard Hinault, 1978.

**2003, July 14** *Perf. 13¼*
**Sheets of 4, #a-d**
2644-2646 A414  Set of 3   15.50  15.50
**Souvenir Sheets**
2647-2649 A414  Set of 3   13.00  13.00

*Le300*
*T. SMITHSON LONDON 1908*
*Sierra Leone*

Olympic Medalists A415

Designs: 300 le, Forrest Smithson, 1908. 400 le, Hannes Kolehmainen, 1912. 500 le, Larissa Latynina, 1964. 800 le, Klaus Dibiasi, 1976. 1000 le, Archie Hahn, 1904. 1500 le. M. Hurley, 2000 le, Ray Ewry, 1900. 3000 le, Henry Taylor, 1908.

**2003, Nov. 17** *Perf. 13¼*
2650-2657 A415  Set of 8   7.75  .75

Inscription on No. 2655 is incorrect as there were no cycling events in 1904 and no cycling medalists in any year named Hurley.

*Xmas 2003  Le 100*
*DETAIL: MADONNA & CHILD WITH ST. ANNE & FOUR SAINTS*
*SIERRA LEONE*

Christmas A416

Paintings by Pontormo Rosso Fiorentino: 100 le, Madonna and Child with St. Anno and Four Saints. 150 le, Madonna and Child with Two Saints. 500 le, Madonna and Child Enthroned with Four Saints (Ognissanti Altarpicco). 4000 le, Madonna Enthroned Between Two Saints.
5000 le, Madonna with Saints.

**2003, Nov. 17** *Perf. 14¼*
2658-2661 A416  Set of 4   4.00  4.00
**Souvenir Sheet**
2662 A416 5000 le multi        4.25  4.25

*SIERRA LEONE*

New Year 2004 (Year of the Monkey) — A417

No. 2663 — Background color: a, Yellow orange. b, Blue. c, Rose pink. d, Dark orange. 2500 le, Pink.

**2004, Jan. 15** *Perf. 13¾*
2663 A417 1200 le  Sheet of 4,
#a-d                    4.00  4.00
**Souvenir Sheet** *Perf. 14*
2664 A417 2500 le multi        2.10  2.10
No. 2664 contains one 42x28mm stamp.

---

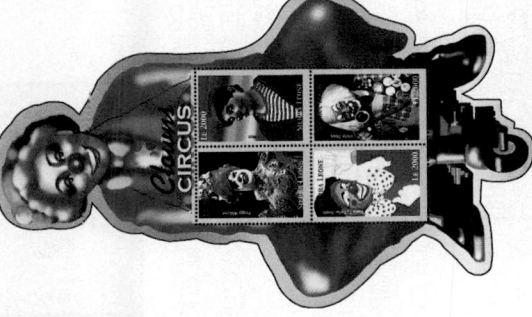

*CIRCUS  SIERRA LEONE*

Circus Performers — A412

No. 2638, 2000 le: a, Peggy Williams. b, Nico. c, Steve T. J. Tatter Smith. d, Uncle Dippy.
No. 2639, 2000 le: a, Caracal. b, Chairs. c, Elena Panova. d, Chinese Circus.

**2003, July 1** *Litho.*
**Sheets of 4, #a-d**
2638-2639 A412  Set of 2   13.50  13.50

*SIERRA LEONE  Le5000*

Powered Flight, Cont. — A413

No. 2640, 1500 le: a, Wright Brothers first plane (gray background). b, Volsin-Farmin (blue background). c, Levavasseur Antoinette (pink background). d, Nieuport (numbered 345).
No. 2641, 1500 le: a, Wright Brothers first plane (blue background). b, Voisin-Farmin (gray background). c, Levavasseur Antoinette (blue background). d, Nieuport (no number on plane).
No. 2642, 5000 le, Henri Farmin Crossing Finish Line in Voisin-Farmin plane. No. 2643, 5000 le, Roland Garros and others around airplane.

**2003, July 14**
**Sheets of 4, #a-d**
2640-2641 A413  Set of 2   10.50  10.50
**Souvenir Sheets**
2642-2643 A413  Set of 2   8.50   8.50
Inscriptions on No. 2640 are incorrect.

*SIERRA LEONE  Le5000*

Tour de France Bicycle Race, Cent. — A414

No. 2644, 1500 le: a, Ferdinand Kubler, 1950. b, Hugo Koblet, 1951. c, Fausto Coppi, 1952. d, Louison Bobet, 1953.
No. 2645, 1500 le: a, Bobet, 1954. b, Bobet, 1955. c, Roger Walkowiak, 1956. d, Jacques Anquetil, 1957.
No. 2646, 1500 le: a, Eddy Merckx, 1970. b, Merckx, 1971. c, Merckx, 1972. d, Luis Ocana, 1973.

---

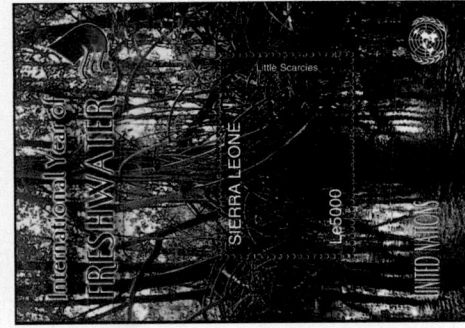

*International Year of FRESHWATER*
*SIERRA LEONE  Le5000  Little Scarcies*
*UNITED NATIONS*

Intl. Year of Fresh Water — A409

No. 2632 a, Waterfalls of Mount Tonkoui. b, Tagbaladougou Falls. c, Cascades d'Ouzoud.
5000 le, Little Scarcies.

**2003, July 1**
2632 A409 2000 le  Sheet of 3,
#a-c                    5.25  5.25
**Souvenir Sheet**
2633 A409 5000 le multi        4.25  4.25

*40th Anniversary of the Rotary Club Sierra Leone*

Rotary Club of Sierra Leone, 40th Anniv. — A410

No. 2634 — Rotarians and: a, People in canoe. b, Cacheted first day cover envelope, Sierra Leone natives. c, Girl with flowers.
6000 le, Bhichai Rattakul, Rotary President.

**2003, July 1**
2634 A410 2600 le  Sheet of 3,
#a-c                    6.50  6.50
**Souvenir Sheet**
2635 A410 6000 le multi        5.25  5.25

*21st Birthday of H.R.H. Prince William*
*Sierra Leone  Le5000*

Prince William, 21st Birthday — A411

No. 2636: a, Wearing solid shirt. b, Wearing striped shirt. c, Wearing sweater.
5000 le, Wearing plaid shirt.

**2003, July 1**
2636 A411 2500 le  Sheet of 3,
#a-c                    6.50  6.50
**Souvenir Sheet**
2637 A411 5000 le multi        4.25  4.25

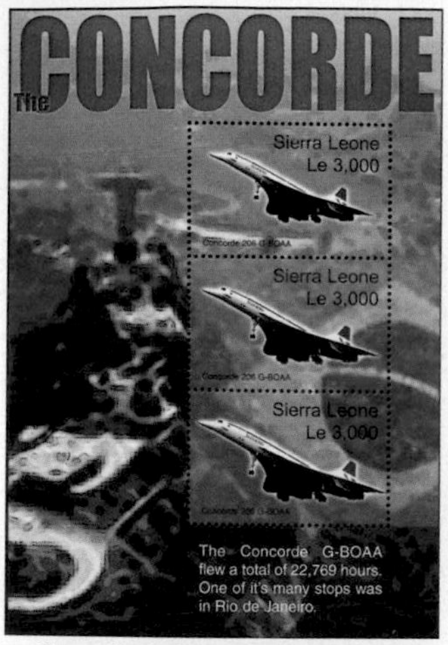
The CONCORDE
Sierra Leone
Le 3,000
The Concorde G-BOAA flew a total of 22,769 hours. One of it's many stops was in Rio de Janeiro.

Cessation of Concorde Flights in 2003 — A421

No. 2674, 3000 le — Concorde 206-G BOAA and: a, Blue background. b, Top half of Brazilian flag. b, Bottom half of Brazilian flag.
No. 2675, 3000 le — Concorde G-AXDN and: a, Pink background. b, Top half of Egyptian flag (red stripe). c, Bottom half of Egyptian flag.
No. 2676, 3000 le — Concorde G-ADXN Aircraft 101 and: a, City skyline. b, Top half of Kenyan flag (black stripe). c, Bottom half of Kenyan flag.

**2004, Feb. 24** *Perf. 13¼x13½*
**Sheets of 3, #a-c**
**2674-2676** A421 Set of 3 22.50 22.50

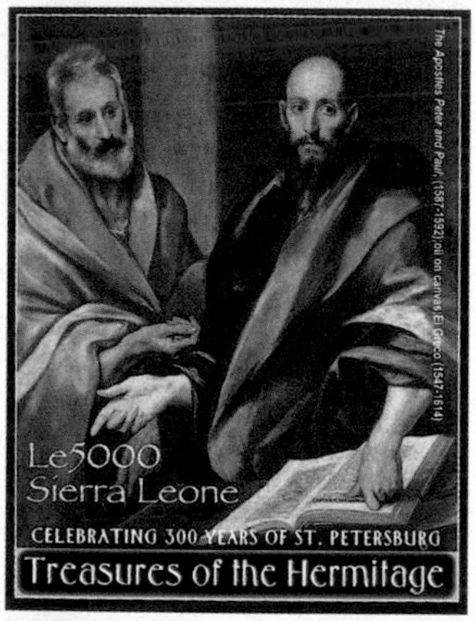
Le5000
Sierra Leone
CELEBRATING 300 YEARS OF ST. PETERSBURG
Treasures of the Hermitage

Paintings from the Hermitage, St. Petersburg, Russia — A422

No. 2677: a, The Birth of St. John the Baptist, by Jacopo Tintoretto. b, Penitent Mary Magdalene, by Titian. c, The Death of St. Petronilla, by Simone Pignoni. d, The Assumption of the Virgin, by Bartolomé Esteban Murillo. e, St. Jerome Hears the Trumpet, by Jusepe de Ribera. f, St. George and the Dragon, by Tintoretto.
No. 2678 — Paintings by Elisabeth Vigée-Lebrun: a, Countess A. S. Stroganova and Her Son. b, Count G. I. Chernyshev Holding a Mask. c, Self-portrait. d, Baron G. A. Stroganov.
No. 2679, The Apostles Peter and Paul, by El Greco. No. 2680, A Visit to the Priest, by Jean-Baptiste Greuze, horiz.

**2004, Feb. 24** **Litho.** *Perf. 13¼*
**2677** A422 1400 le Sheet of 6, #a-f 7.00 7.00
**2678** A422 2000 le Sheet of 4, #a-d 6.50 6.50

***Imperf***
**2679** A422 5000 le shown 4.25 4.25

**Size: 100x69mm**
**2680** A422 5000 le multi 4.25 4.25

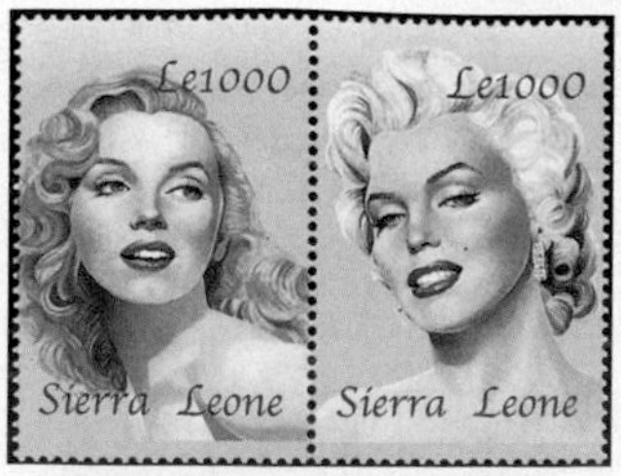
Le1000
Sierra Leone

Marilyn Monroe (Larger Final Zero) — A423

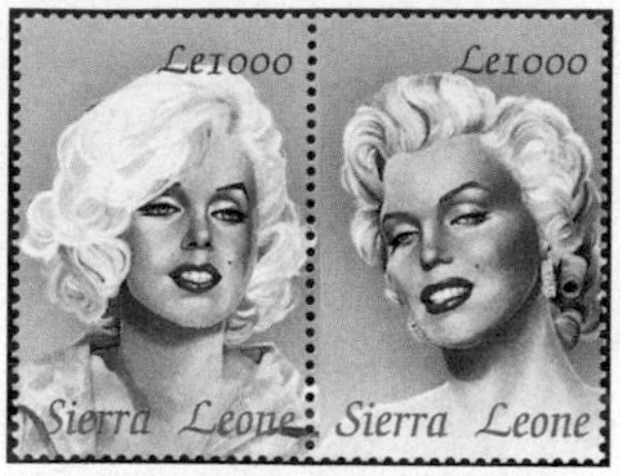
Le1000
Sierra Leone

Marilyn Monroe (Zeroes Same Size) — A424

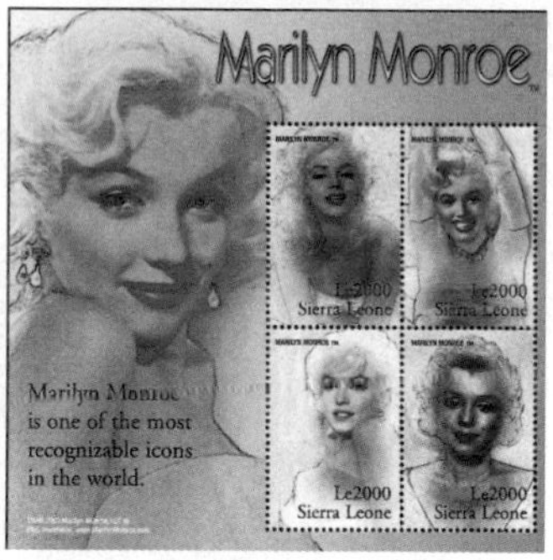
Marilyn Monroe
Marilyn Monroe is one of the most recognizable icons in the world.
Le2000
Sierra Leone

Marilyn Monroe — A425

**2004, May 3** *Perf. 14*
**2681** A423 1000 le Pair, #a-b 1.60 1.60

*Perf. 13½x13¼*
**2682** A424 1000 le Pair, #a-b 1.60 1.60
**2683** A425 2000 le Sheet of 4, #a-d 6.50 6.50

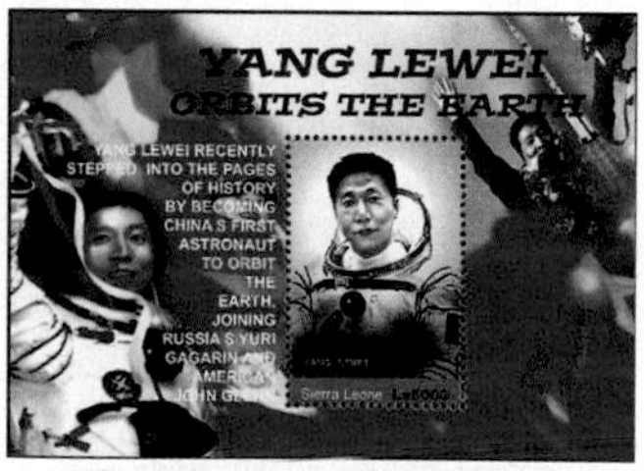
YANG LEWEI
ORBITS THE EARTH

First Orbiting Astronauts of China, US and Russia — A426

No. 2684, horiz. — Yang Lewei: a, Wearing flight jumpsuit. b, Wearing uniform. c, Wearing space suit. d, Wearing space suit, giving hand gesture.
No. 2685: a, Vostok 1. b, John Glenn. c, Friendship 7. d, Yuri Gagarin. e, Shenzhou 5. f, Yang Lewei, diff.
No. 2686, 5000 le, Yang Lewei, diff. No. 2687, 5000 le, Glenn, diff.

**2004, May 10** *Perf. 13¼x13½*
**2684** A426 900 le Horiz. strip of 4, #a-d 2.75 2.75

*Perf. 13½x13¼*
**2685** A426 1200 le Sheet of 6, #a-f 5.50 5.50

**Souvenir Sheets**
**2686-2687** A426 Set of 2 7.75 7.75

No. 2684 printed in sheets containing two strips.

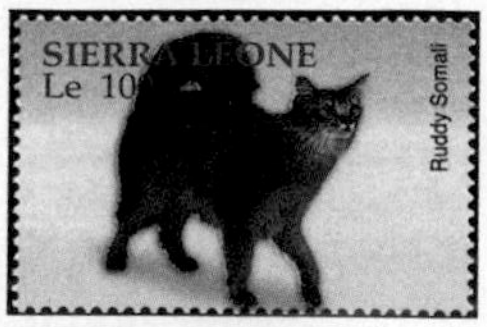
SIERRA LEONE
Ruddy Somali

Cats
A427

Designs: 100 le, Ruddy Somali. 800 le, Bombay. 1200 le, Burmese. 3000 le, Blue British Shorthair.
No. 2692, vert.: a, Persian. b, Colorpoint Shorthair. c, Cornish Rex. d, Blue Point Balinese.
5000 le, Devon Rex.

*Perf. 13¼x13½, 13½x13¼*
**2004, May 17**
**2688-2691** A427 Set of 4 4.25 4.25
**2692** A427 1700 le Sheet of 4, #a-d 5.50 5.50

**Souvenir Sheet**
**2693** A427 5000 le multi 4.00 4.00

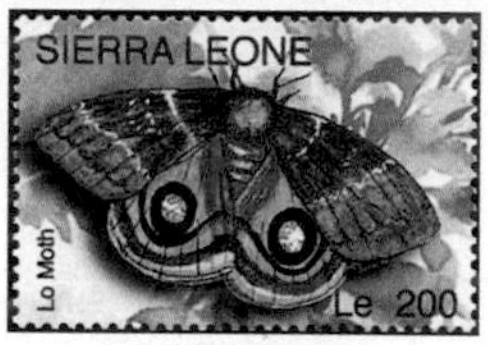
SIERRA LEONE
Lo Moth
Le 200

Moths and Butterflies
A428

Designs: 200 le, Io moth. 300 le, Hackberry butterfly. 400 le, Red admiral butterfly. 4000 le, Spangled fritillary butterfly.
No. 2698: a, Pearl crescent butterfly. b, Pipevine swallowtail butterfly. c, Alfalfa looper moth. d, Tiger swallowtail butterfly.
5000 le, Cecropia moth.

**2004, May 17** *Perf. 13¼x13½*
**2694-2697** A428 Set of 4 4.00 4.00
**2698** A428 1700 le Sheet of 4, #a-d 5.50 5.50

**Souvenir Sheet**
**2699** A428 5000 le multi 4.00 4.00

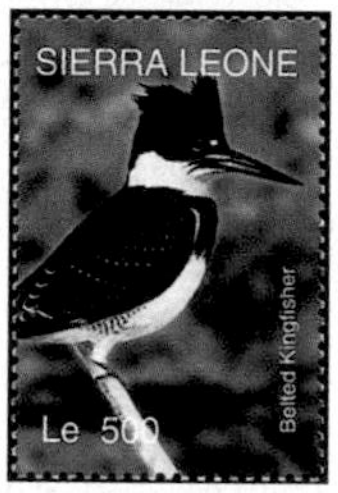
SIERRA LEONE
Belted Kingfisher

Birds — A429

Designs: 500 le, Belted kingfisher. 1000 le, Burrowing owl. 1500 le, Crested caracara. 2000 le, Red-headed finch.
No. 2704, horiz.: a, Snail kite. b, Avocet. c, Greater flamingo. d, Bald eagle.
5000 le, Ring-necked pheasant, horiz.

*Perf. 13½x13¼, 13¼x13½*
**2004, May 17**
**2700-2703** A429 Set of 4 4.00 4.00
**2704** A429 1700 le Sheet of 4, #a-d 5.50 5.50

**Souvenir Sheet**
**2705** A429 5000 le multi 4.00 4.00

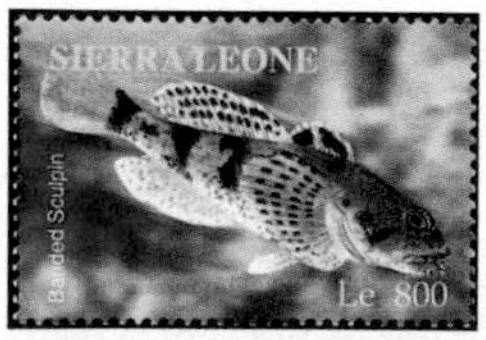
SIERRA LEONE
Banded Sculpin
Le 800

Fish
A430

Designs: 800 le, Banded sculpin. 1100 le, Black durgon. No. 2708, 1400 le, Atlantic spadefish. No. 2709, 1400 le, Queen triggerfish.
No. 2710: a, Peacock flounder. b, Northern puffer. c, Sea raven. d, Tiger shark.
5000 le, Sea lamprey, vert.

*Perf. 13¼x13½, 13½x13¼*
**2004, May 17**
**2706-2709** A430 Set of 4 4.00 4.00
**2710** A430 1700 le Sheet of 4, #a-d 5.50 5.50

**Souvenir Sheet**
**2711** A430 5000 le multi 4.00 4.00

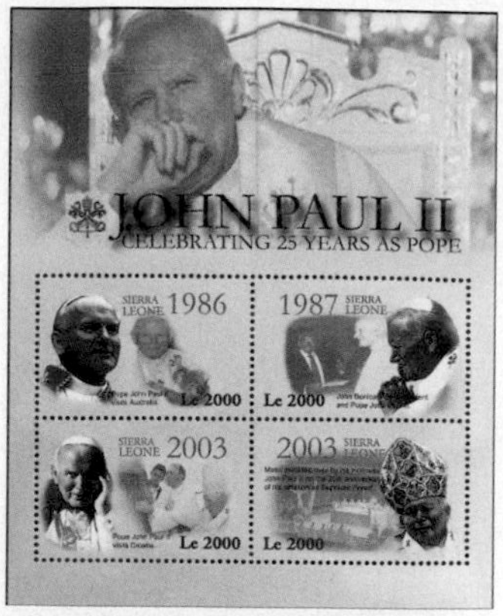
JOHN PAUL II
CELEBRATING 25 YEARS AS POPE
1986
1987
2003
Le 2000

Election of Pope John Paul II, 25th Anniv. (in 2003) — A431

No. 2712 — Pope John Paul II: a, Visiting Australia, 1986. b, With John Bonica, 1987. c, Visiting Croatia, 2003. d, Celebrating 25th anniversary mass, 2003.

**2004, May 24** *Perf. 13¼x13½*
**2712** A431 2000 le Sheet of 4, #a-d 6.50 6.50

Souvenir Sheet

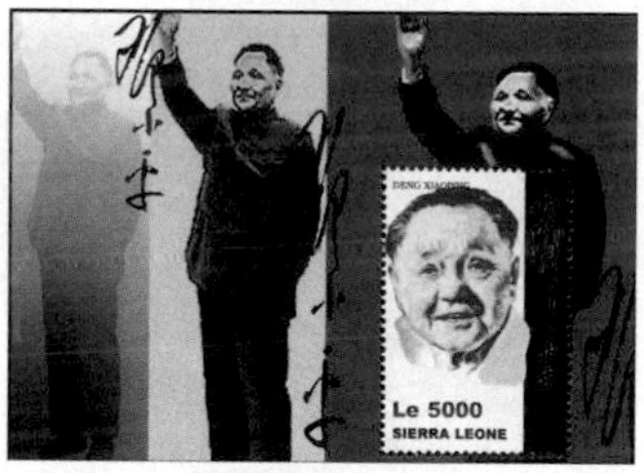
Le 5000
SIERRA LEONE

Deng Xiaoping (1904-97), Chinese Leader — A432

**2004, June 1** *Perf. 14*
**2713** A432 5000 le multi 4.00 4.00

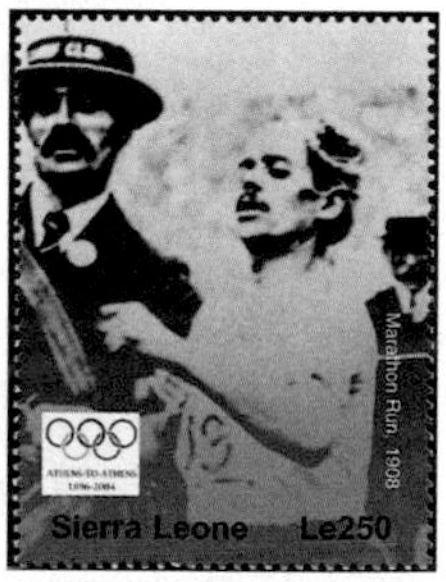
Sierra Leone
Le250
Marathon Run, 1908

2004 Summer Olympics, Athens
A433

Designs: 250 le, Marathon, 1908. 300 le, Dimitrios Vikelas, first president of Intl. Olympic Committee. 1500 le, 1896 Olympic medal. 2000 le, Discus thrower.

**2004, June 6** *Perf. 14¼*
**2714-2717** A433 Set of 4 3.25 3.25

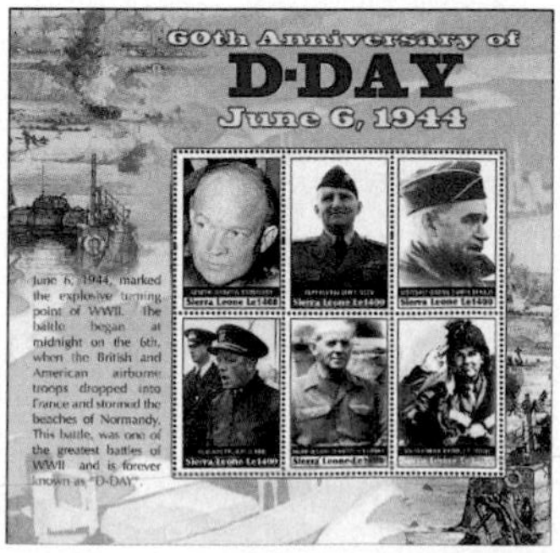
60th Anniversary of
D-DAY
June 6, 1944

A434

# SIERRA LEONE

*Sequoyah and the Cherokee Alphabet*

Sequoyah's mother was the daughter of a Cherokee Chief; his father was a Virginia fur trader.

Sequoyah created 86 symbols for the Cherokee language. With this system, thousands of Cherokees learned to read and write in a very short time.

**American Indians — A438**

No. 2730: a, Arapaho pipe bag. b, Apache basket. c, Blackfoot parfleche. d, Crow elkhide robe. e, Iroquois moccasins. f, Hopi canteen. g, Sioux parfleche. h, Navajo rug. i, Nez Perce cradle.

No. 2731 — Ioway chiefs and warriors: a, Ne-O-Mon-Ne. b, Ma-Has-Kah. c, Moa-Na-Hon-Ga. d, Tah-Ro-Hon. e, Not-Chi-Mi-Ne. f, Shau-Hau-Napo-Tinia.

No. 2732, horiz. — Paintings by Charles Russell: a, Medicine Man. b, War Party. c, Signal Smoke.

**2004, July 5**        *Perf. 14*

| | | | |
|---|---|---|---|
| 2730 A437 1000 le Sheet of 9, #a-i | | 7.50 | 7.50 |
| 2731 A438 1500 le Sheet of 6, #a-f | | 7.50 | 7.50 |
| 2732 A438 3000 le Sheet of 3, #a-c | | 7.50 | 7.50 |
| | | 22.50 | 22.50 |

**Souvenir Sheet**

Nos. 2730-2732 (3)

| | |
|---|---|
| 2733 A438 5000 le multi | 4.00 4.00 |

Explore a world of **Prehistoric Animals**

Sierra Leone Le500U

**Prehistoric Animals — A439**

No. 2734, 2000 le: a, Apatosaurus. b, Styracosaurus. c, Plateosaurus. d, Pachyrhinosaurus.

No. 2735, 2000 le, horiz.: a, Camarasaurus. b, Iystrosaurus. c, Ankylosaurus. d, Herrerasaurus.

No. 2736, 5000 le, Dunklosteus. No. 2737, 5000 le, Archaeopteryx, horiz.

**2004**        *Perf. 14*

**Sheets of 4, #a-d**

| | |
|---|---|
| 2734-2735 A439 | Set of 2   13.00 13.00 |
| | 13.00 13.00 |

**Souvenir Sheets**

| | |
|---|---|
| 2736-2737 A439 | Set of 2   8.25 8.25 |
| | 8.25 8.25 |

No. 2734 has two labels.

SIERRA LEONE

**Orchids — A440**

Designs: 150 le, Catasetum pileatum. No. 2739, 400 le, Cattleya araguainsis. No. 2740, 400 le, Barkeria spectabilis. 3500 le, Catasetum fimbriatum.

No. 2742: a, Odontonia vesta. b, Ancistrorhschidianus. c, Ansellia africana. d, Aspasia epidendroides.

5000 le, Bulbophyllum lobbii.

---

**D-Day, 60th Anniv. — A435**

No. 2718: a, Gen. Dwight D. Eisenhower. b, Rear Adm. Don P. Moon. c, Lt. Gen. Omar N. Bradley. d, Rear Adm. Alan G. Kirk. e, Maj. Gen. Clarence R. Huebner. f, Maj. Gen. Maxwell D. Taylor.

No. 2719, 950 le: a, LST landing craft. b, M4 Sherman tank. c, M4 Sherman tank and soldier. d, Tank cannon. e, 70th Tank Battalion patch. f, Soldier with rifle. g, 743rd Tank Battalion patch. h, 741st Tank Battalion patch.

No. 2720, 1100 le: a, P-51 Mustang over battle. b, Paratroopers. map. c, Map. d, P-38 Lightning. e, M4 Sherman tank. diff. f, Soldiers. g, LCM landing craft, map. h, US light cruiser, map with numbers.

No. 2721, 1000 le: a, P-47 Thunderbolt. b, Paratroopers, airplanes, map. c, Tank, map. d, Soldier with rifle, map. e, US heavy cruiser. f, US light cruiser, map. g, Ships. h, US destroyer escorts.

No. 2722, 1000 le: a, Spitfire. b, Typhoon. c, Tail of Typhoon, wing of P-38 Lightning. other airplane. d, P-51 Mustang. e, C-47 Skytrain. f, Wing of Typhoon, fuselage of C-47 Skytrain, other airplane. g, P-38 Lightning. h, US Air Force patch.

No. 2723, 1100 le: a, US light cruiser, blimps. b, LST landing craft, blimps. c, Landing craft with door open. d, LST landing craft. e, US armored car. f, Soldiers, tank. g, US medical transport vehicle. h, US armored car leaving landing craft.

No. 2724, 1100 le: a, Soldier with rifle, map. diff. b, Paratrooper, 101st Airborne Division patch. c, Paratrooper, tail of plane. d, Nose of airplane. e, Gen. Eisenhower. f, Gen. Bernard Montgomery. g, Paratrooper, 82nd Airborne Division patch. h, Two paratroopers, C-47 Skytrain.

**2004, June 1**        *Perf. 14*

| | | | |
|---|---|---|---|
| 2718 A434 1400 le Sheet of 6, #a-f | | 7.00 | 7.00 |

**Sheets of 8, #a-h**

| | |
|---|---|
| 2719-2724 A435 | Set of 6   40.00 40.00 |

Le1800

Sierra Leone

**British Lighthouses A436**

Designs: 1800 le, Smalls Lighthouse. 2000 le, Needles Rocks Lighthouse. 2500 le, St. John's Point Lighthouse. 3500 le, Bell Rock Lighthouse. 4000 le, Eddystone Lighthouse.

**2004, June 17**        *Perf. 14¾x14*

| | |
|---|---|
| 2725-2729 A436 | Set of 5   11.50 11.50 |

**American Indian Decorative Artifacts**

**American Indian Artifacts — A437**

---

**2004, May 17**     *Litho.*     *Perf. 12½*

| | | | |
|---|---|---|---|
| 2738-2741 A440 | Set of 4 | 3.75 | 3.75 |
| 2742 A440 1700 le Sheet of 4, #a-d | | 5.50 | 5.50 |
| | | 4.25 | 4.25 |

**Souvenir Sheet**

| | |
|---|---|
| 2743 A440 5000 le multi | 4.25 4.25 |

SIERRA LEONE   Le 250

Great Pyrenees

**Dogs — A441**

Designs: 250 le, Great Pyrenees. 600 le, Kerry Blue terrier. 1300 le, Mastiff. 1800 le, English sheepdog.

No. 2748: a, Sealyham terrier. b, Norwich terrier. c, Wheaton terrier. d, Bull terrier. 5000 le, Greyhound.

**2004, May 17**

| | | | |
|---|---|---|---|
| 2744-2747 A441 | Set of 4 | 3.25 | 3.25 |
| 2748 A441 1700 le Sheet of 4, #a-d | | 5.50 | 5.50 |

**Souvenir Sheet**

| | |
|---|---|
| 2749 A441 5000 le multi | 4.25 4.25 |

**Souvenir Sheet**

United Nations **International Year of Peace**

**Intl. Year of Peace — A442**

No. 2750 — Position of olive branch carried by dove: a, Below last two zeros of denomination. b, Below three and first two zeros of denomination. c, Covered by last two zeros of denomination.

**2004, June 1**        *Perf. 14*

| | | | |
|---|---|---|---|
| 2750 A442 3000 le Sheet of 3, #a-c | | 7.50 | 7.50 |

**Powered Flight Type of 2003**

No. 2751: a, Curtiss Triad. b, Avro Biplane. c, Curtiss America. d, Farnborought Be-2.

**2004, July 17**

| | | | |
|---|---|---|---|
| 2751 A413 1500 le Sheet of 4, #a-d | | 5.00 | 5.00 |

SIERRA LEONE Le 1000   MONKEY   WWF

**Worldwide Fund for Nature (WWF) — A443**

No. 2752 — Patas monkey: a, Monkey grooming another. b, Monkeys and flower. c, Adult and juvenile. d, Head of monkey. Illustration reduced.

**2004, Oct. 11**     *Perf. 13¼x13½*

| | | | |
|---|---|---|---|
| 2752 A443 1000 le Block of 4, #a-d | | 3.50 | 3.50 |
| e. Miniature sheet, 2 each #2752a-2752d | | 7.25 | 7.25 |

LAKERS   KOBE BRYANT   Sierra Leone Le700

**National Basketball Association Players — A444**

---

Designs: No. 2753, 700 le, Kobe Bryant, Los Angeles Lakers. No. 2754, 700 le, Carmelo Anthony, Denver Nuggets. No. 2755, 700 le, Yao Ming, Houston Rockets. No. 2756, 700 le, Jermaine O'Neal, Indiana Pacers. No. 2757, 700 le, Leandro Barbosa, Phoenix Suns. 2000 le, Vlade Divac, Sacramento Kings.

**2004**        *Perf. 14*

| | | | |
|---|---|---|---|
| 2753-2758 A444 | Set of 6 | 4.50 | 4.50 |

Issued: Nos. 2753, 2758, 11/2; No. 2754, 11/4; Nos. 2755-2756, 11/6; No. 2757, 12/13. Each stamp printed in a sheet of 12.

Babe Ruth (1895-1948)   Le 500   Sierra Leone

George Herman "Babe" Ruth (1895-1948) Baseball Player — A445

**2004, Dec. 13**

| | |
|---|---|
| 2759 A445 500 le multi | .40 .40 |

Printed in sheet of 16.

Sierra Leone Le2000   National Football Team

**National Soccer Team — A446**

**2004, Dec. 13**        *Perf. 12*

| | |
|---|---|
| 2760 A446 2000 le multi | 1.75 1.75 |

Sierra Leone

**Pres. Ronald Reagan and Queen Elizabeth II — A447**

No. 2761, Reagan and Queen: a, With spouses. b, Making a toast. Illustration reduced.

**2004, Dec. 13**     *Perf. 13½*

| | |
|---|---|
| 2761 A447 2000 le Horiz. pair, #a-b | 3.25 3.25 |

Printed in sheets containing three each of Nos. 2761a and 2761b.

SIERRA LEONE   Paris   Le 600

**Ocean Liners A448**

Designs: 600 le, Paris. 800 le, Statendam. 1000 le, Stavengerford. 1500 le, Campania. 2000 le, Drottningholm. 3000 le, Lusitania. 5000 le, United States, horiz.

**2004, Dec. 13**     *Perf. 14¼*

| | | | |
|---|---|---|---|
| 2762-2767 A448 | Set of 6 | 7.25 | 7.25 |

**Souvenir Sheet**

| | |
|---|---|
| 2768 A448 5000 le multi | 4.25 4.25 |

Christmas
A449

Designs: 1000 le, Nativity with the Annunciation to the Shepherds, by Follower of Jan Joest. 1500 le, Christmas Snow, by Norman Rockwell. 2000 le, The Christmas Tree, by E. Osborn. 5000 le, The Spirit of Christmas, by Rockwell. 8000 le, Madonna and Child Enthroned with Two Angels, by Fra Filippo Lippi.

**2004, Dec. 13**    **Perf. 12½x12**
2769-2772 A449    Set of 4
2773   A449   8000 le multi

**Souvenir Sheet**

7.75 7.75
6.50 6.50

**Miniature Sheet**

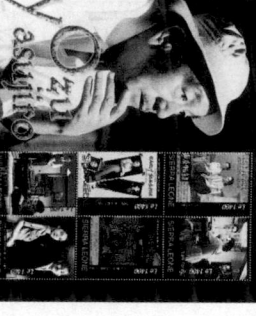  

Yasujiro Ozu (1903-63), Film Director — A450

No. 2774 — Posters or scenes from: a, Tokyo Story. b, Late Spring. c, Early Summer. d, Equinox Flower. e, Good Morning. f, An Autumn Afternoon.

**2004, Dec. 13**    **Perf. 13¼**
2774 A450 1400 le Sheet of 6,
    #a-f     7.00 7.00

Elvis Presley (1935-77) — A452

Various depictions of Presley.

**2004, Dec. 13**
2775 A451 2000 le Sheet of 4,
    #a-d     6.50 6.50
2776 A452 2000 le Sheet of 4,
    #a-d     6.50 6.50

---

FIFA (Fédération Internationale de Football Association), Cent. — A453

No. 2777: a, Diego Simeone. b, Careca. c, Oliver Bierhoff. d, Kevin Keegan. e, 5000 le, David Ginola.

**2004, Dec. 13**    **Perf. 12¾x12½**
2777 A453 2000 le Sheet of 4,
    #a-d     6.50 6.50

**Souvenir Sheet**

2778 A453 5000 le multi     4.25 4.25

Locomotives, 200th Anniv. — A454

No. 2779, 1000 le: a, Stephenson's Rocket. b, Indonesian State Railway B50 class 2-4-0. c, Eurostar Paris-London train. d, China Railways SY Class 2-8-2. e, Baldwin 0-6-0. f, Hungaie 0-4-2T. g, Bagnall 0-6-0 ST Progress. h, North British-built 4-8-2T. i, Baldwin 0-6-2I.

No. 2780, 1000 le, vert.: a, GWR Mogul, 2-6-0. c, China Railways SL7 Class Pacific. d, Severn Valley Railway. b, Kitson Meyer 0-6-6-0. e, USATC 0-6-0T. f, China Railways ZP Pacific. Class Pacific. d, Indian Railways McArthur 2-8-2. e, Baldwin 0-6-0. f, China Railways KD6 2-8-0. g, Polish Feldbahn 0-8-0T. h, Indian Railways Mawd 2-8-2. i, North British 2-10-0.

No. 2781, 1000 le, vert.: a, LMS 8F 2-8-0. Great Central Railway. b, Rhodesia Railways 12 Class 4-8-2. c, DR German Railways 01 Class. d, Bagnall 0-4-0. e, Ledo Brickworks. f, Indian sugar mill. g, Tangshan Locomotive Works. China. h, Crane loading timber on train car, Lanxiang. i, Worker carrying clay to train at Ledo Brickworks.

No. 2782, 1000 le, vert.: a, GWR Mogul. 0. c, China Railways SL7 Class Pacific. d, Severn Valley Railway. b, Kitson Meyer 0-6-6-0. e, Lookout man with flag. f, Workers filling sandboxes. g, Indian Railways locomotive taking water. h, Man on Indian Railways ZP Pacific Pulgeon. i, Worker cleaning smokebox.

b, Uruguay Railways Beyer Peacock Mogul 2-6-0. c, Ghana Railways Diesel-electric locomotive. d, Bagnall 0-4-0. e, Ledo Brickworks. Upper Assam. f, Train at Indian sugar mill. g, Carbon converter, Tangshan Locomotive Works, China. h, Crane loading timber on train car, Lanxiang, China. i, Worker carrying clay to train at Ledo Brickworks.
No. 2783, 5000 le, Ghan. No. 2784, 5000 le, Hudson Line. No. 2785, 5000 le, Blue Train. No. 2786, 5000 le, Bullet Train.

**2004, Dec. 13**    **Perf. 13½x13½, 13½x13¾**
2779-2782 A454   Sheets of 9, #a-i
2783-2786 A454   Set of 4    30.00 30.00

**Souvenir Sheets**

16.50 16.50

New Year 2005 (Year of the Rooster) — A455

No. 2787, a, Country name in blue. b, Country name in red.

**2005, Feb. 23**    **Perf. 12**
2787 A455 600 le Pair, #a-b    1.00 1.00
Printed in sheets containing two pairs.

---

SIERRA LEONE

**2005, May 24**    **Litho.**    **Perf. 13½x13¼**
2788 A456 1800 le multi    1.60 1.60
Printed in sheet of 6.

Pope John Paul II (1920-2005) and French President Jacques Chirac — A456

Maimonides (1135-1204), Philosopher — A457

**2005, May 24**    **Perf. 12**
2789 A457 2000 le multi    1.75 1.75
Printed in sheets of 4.

Rotary International, Cent. — A458

No. 2790: a, Map, handshake. b, Map, people. "Service Above Self." c, Emblem. d, Founder Paul P. Harris.

**2005, May 24**    **Perf. 12¾**
2790 A458 1800 le Sheet of 4,
    #a-d     6.25 6.25

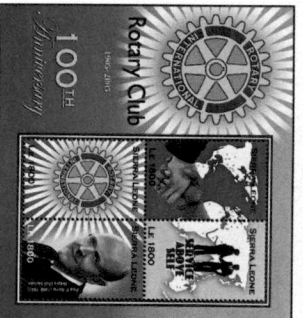

Nature's Wisdom

No. 2791: a, Glacial polish, Toiyabe National Forest, Nevada. b, African gorilla. c, Rock climber, Yosemite Valley, California. d, Nassau grouper spawning, Caribbean Sea. e, Ladybug swarm. f, Evolution Valley, California.

Expo 2005, Aichi, Japan — A459

**2005, May 24**    **Perf. 12**
2791 A459 1500 le Sheet of 6,
    #a-f     7.75 7.75

---

Hans Christian Andersen (1805-75), Author — A460

No. 2792: a, Little Claus and Big Claus. b, Little Ida's Flowers. c, The Tinderbox. d, The Princess and the Pea.

**2005, May 24**    **Perf. 12¾**
2792 A460 3000 le Sheet of 3,
    #a-c     7.75 7.75

**Souvenir Sheet**

2793 A460 5000 le multi    4.25 4.25
No. 2792 contains three 42x28mm stamps.

Friedrich von Schiller (1759-1805), Writer — A461

No. 2794: a, Statue of Schiller, Berlin. b, Statue of Schiller, Munich. c, Statue of Schiller and Johann Wolfgang von Goethe, 5000 le, Schiller.

**2005, May 24**    **Perf. 12¾**
2794 A461 3000 le Sheet of 3,
    #a-c     7.75 7.75

**Souvenir Sheet**

2795 A461 5000 le multi    4.25 4.25

Jules Verne (1828-1905), Writer — A462

No. 2796: a, Verne's tomb, Amiens, France. b, Michael Arden, From the Earth to the Moon. c, Verne, Moon.

**2005, May 24**
2796 A462 3000 le Sheet of 3,
    #a-c     7.75 7.75

**Souvenir Sheet**

2797 A462 5000 le multi    4.25 4.25

Battle of Trafalgar, Bicent. — A463

Paintings of various battle scenes: 500 le, 1000 le, 2000 le, 5000 le, 8000 le, Battle scene, diff.

**2005, May 24** *Perf. 12¾*
**2798-2801** A463 Set of 4 7.25 7.25

**Souvenir Sheet**
*Perf. 12*

**2802** A463 8000 le multi 7.00 7.00

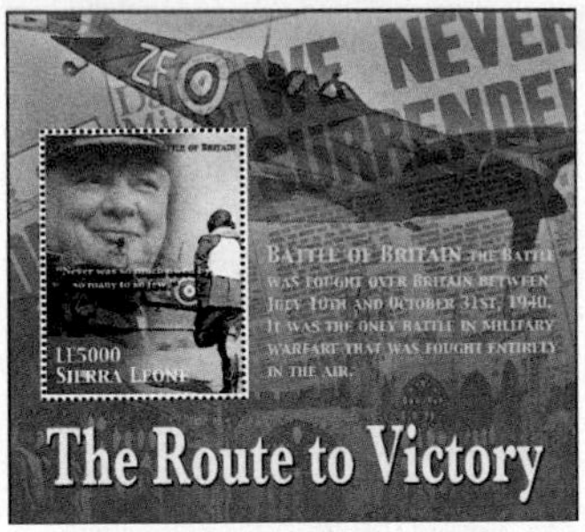
NEVER SURRENDER
BATTLE OF BRITAIN
LE5000
SIERRA LEONE
The Route to Victory

World War II Battles — A464

No. 2803, 2000 le, horiz. — Battle of Britain: a, Luftwaffe launches air strikes on Britain. b, Civilians take cover on underground station platform. c, Pilots race to planes. d, War in the sky.

No. 2804, 2000 le, horiz. — Battle of Stalingrad: a, Russians counterattack. b, Destroyed German tank. c, End of the German 6th Army. d, German prisoners of war.

No. 2805, 5000 le, Winston Churchill. No. 2806, 5000 le, Russian victory at Stalingrad, horiz.

**2005, May 24** *Perf. 13¼*

**Sheets of 4, #a-d**

**2803-2804** A464 Set of 2 14.00 14.00

**Souvenir Sheets**

**2805-2806** A464 Set of 2 8.50 8.50

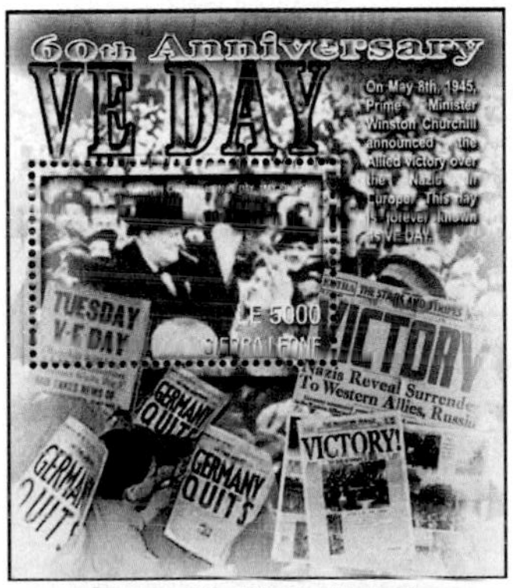
60th Anniversary
VE DAY
TUESDAY V-E DAY
LE 5000
SIERRA LEONE
VICTORY
GERMANY QUITS

End of World War II, 60th Anniv. — A465

No. 2807, 2000 le: a, Franklin D. Roosevelt, Winston Churchill. b, Secretary of Defense Louis Johnson, Generals Douglas MacArthur and Omar Bradley. c, Meeting of Allied Expeditionary Force commanders. d, Winston Churchill.

No. 2808, 2000 le: a, Roosevelt's address to Congress after Pearl Harbor attack. b, "Little Boy" atomic bomb. c, "Fat Man" atomic bomb. d, Japanese surrender ceremony.

No. 2809, 5000 le, Winston Churchill on V-E Day. No. 2810, 5000 le, Women reading newspapers.

**2005, May 24** *Perf. 12¾*

**Sheets of 4, #a-d**

**2807-2808** A465 Set of 2 14.00 14.00

**Souvenir Sheets**

**2809-2810** A465 Set of 2 8.50 8.50

The picture used for No. 2807b is not from the World War II era as Johnson was not Secretary of Defense until 1949.

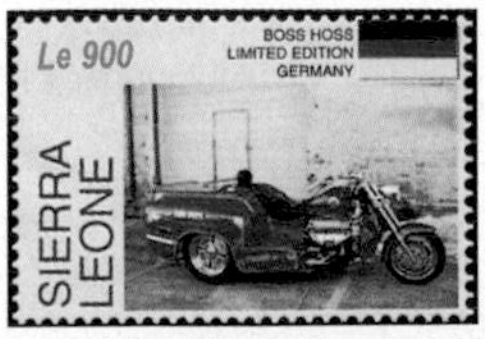
Le 900
BOSS HOSS LIMITED EDITION GERMANY
SIERRA LEONE

Fire Fighting Apparatus — A466

Designs: 900 le, Boss Hoss Limited Edition fire motorcycle, German flag. 1200 le, Pumper 8 by 10, Austrian flag. 1500 le, Hydraulic platform truck, Germay, Ireland flag. 1800 le, Scania fire appliance, Australian flag.

No. 2815, 2000 le — Trucks from: a, Japan. b, Germany. c, Canada. d, Ireland.

No. 2816, 2000 le: a, Mercedes-Benz 2635 Thoma, Germany. b, 1997 Dennis Sabre water tender, Ireland. c, Microscopic fire truck, Japan. d, Scania fire appliance, Australia, diff.

No. 2817, 2000 le: a, 1935 Chevrolet fire truck. b, 1914 International fire truck. c, 1885 Chemical fire engine. d, 1963 Mason FD1.

No. 2818, 5000 le, Fire engine, US flag. No. 2819, 5000 le, 1890 horse-driven fire wagon, British flag.

**2005, May 24** *Perf. 12¾*
**2811-2814** A466 Set of 4 4.75 4.75

**Sheets of 4, #a-d**

**2815-2817** A466 Set of 3 21.00 21.00

**Souvenir Sheets**

**2818-2819** A466 Set of 2 8.50 8.50

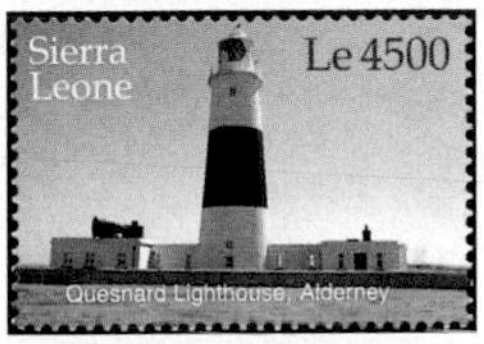
Sierra Leone
Le 4500
Quesnard Lighthouse, Alderney

Quesnard Lighthouse, Alderney — A467

**2005, June 17**
**2820** A467 4500 le multi 4.00 4.00

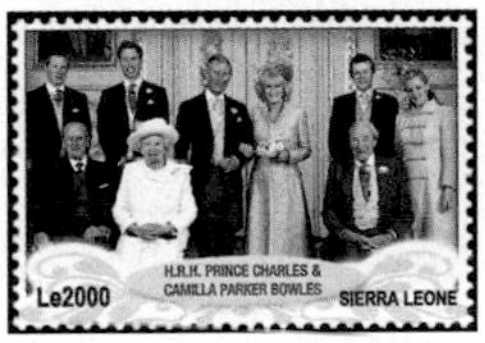
H.R.H. PRINCE CHARLES & CAMILLA PARKER BOWLES
Le2000
SIERRA LEONE

Wedding of Prince Charles and Camilla Parker Bowles A468

Designs: No. 2821, 2000 le, Families of bride and groom. No. 2822, 2000 le, Charles and Camilla, vert. No. 2823, 2000 le, Charles, Camilla and bookstand, vert.

*Perf. 13¼x13½, 13½x13¼*

**2005, Sept. 22** **Litho.**
**2821-2823** A468 Set of 3 5.25 5.25

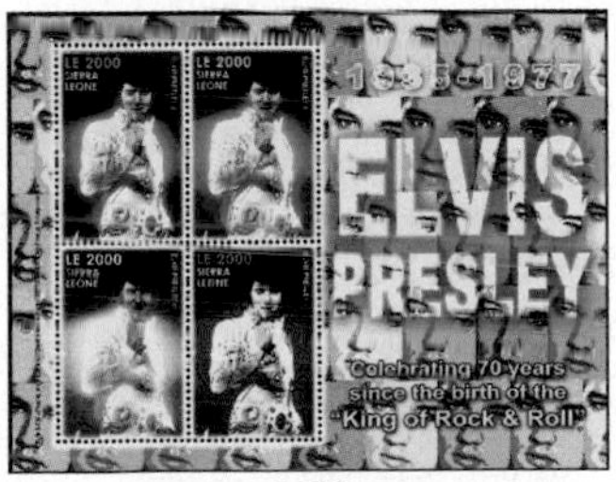
1935-1977
ELVIS PRESLEY
Celebrating 70 years since the birth of the King of Rock & Roll

A469

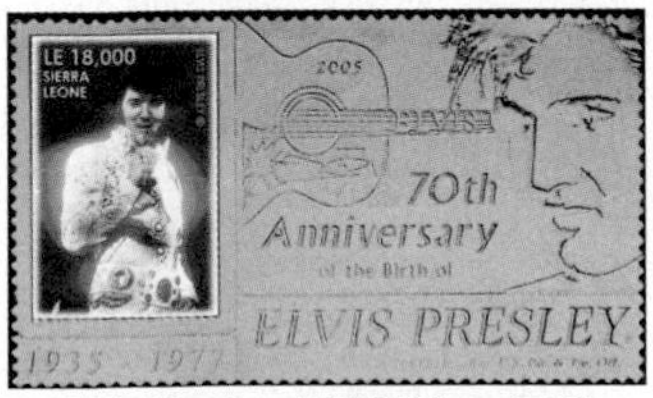
LE 18,000
SIERRA LEONE
2005
70th Anniversary of the Birth of
ELVIS PRESLEY
1935 - 1977

Elvis Presley (1935-70) — A470

No. 2824, 2000 le — Elvis with microphone with background colors of: a, Blue. b, Dark green. c, Yellow green. d, Red and violet.

No. 2825, 2000 le — Elvis: a, Playing guitar, blue denomination. b, Holding guitar, pale olive denomination. c, Holding guitar, pink denomination. d, Playing guitar, lilac denomination.

Illustrations reduced.

**2005, Dec. 1** **Litho.** *Perf. 13¼*

**Sheets of 4, #a-d**

**2824-2825** A469 Set of 2 13.50 13.50

**Litho. & Embossed**

***Serpentine Die Cut 8¾***

**2826** A470 18,000 le gold & multi 15.50 15.50

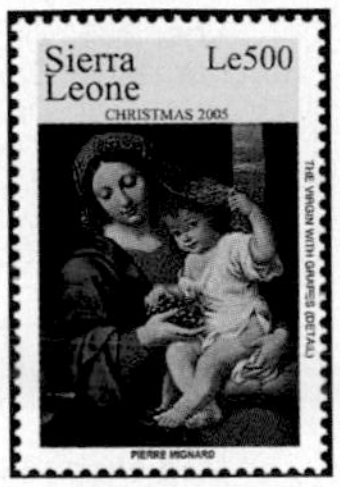
Sierra Leone
Le500
CHRISTMAS 2005

Christmas — A471

Paintings: 500 le, The Virgin with Grapes, by Pierre Mignard. 1500 le, Adoration of the Shepherds, by Bartolomé Esteban Murillo. 2000 le, Madonna with the Child, by Murillo. 3000 le, Fountain of Life, by Hans Holbein, the Elder.

6000 le, Adoration of the Shepherds, by Murillo, diff.

**2005, Dec. 13** **Litho.** *Perf. 12½*
**2827-2830** A471 Set of 4 6.00 6.00

**Souvenir Sheet**

**2831** A471 6000 le multi 5.25 5.25

Souvenir Sheet

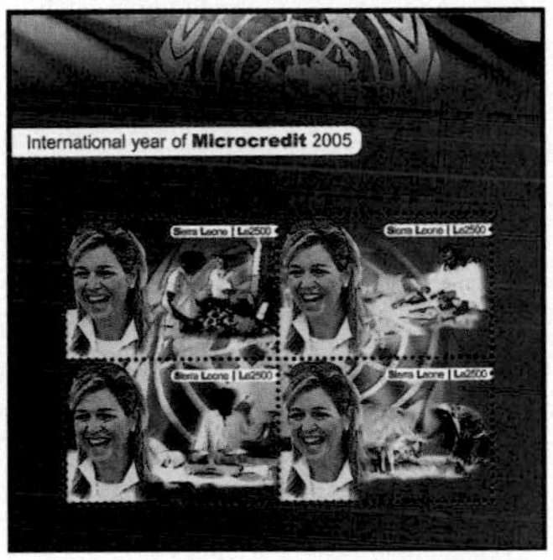
International year of Microcredit 2005

Intl. Year of Microcredit — A472

No. 2832 — Woman at left and: a, Man and woman. b, Man holding stick. c, Man with scales. d, Woman and cow.

**2005**
**2832** A472 2500 le Sheet of 4, #a-d 8.50 8.50

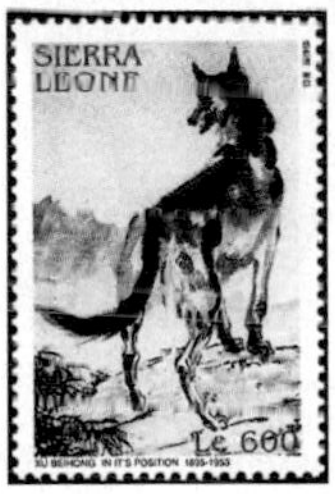
SIERRA LEONE
Le 600

New Year 2006 (Year of the Dog) — A473

In its Position, by Xu Beihong: 600 le, Detail. 2000 le, Entire painting.

**2006** *Perf. 13¼*
**2833** A473 600 le multi .50 .50

**Souvenir Sheet**

*Perf. 11¼x11½*

**2834** A473 2000 le multi 1.75 1.75

No. 2833 printed in sheets of 4. No. 2834 contains one 26x60mm stamp.

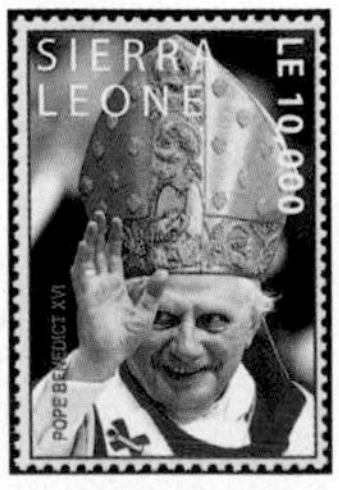
SIERRA LEONE
LE 10,000
POPE BENEDICT XVI

Pope Benedict XVI — A474

**2006, Jan. 24** *Perf. 13¼*
**2835** A474 10,000 le multi 8.50 8.50

Printed in sheets of 4.

Miniature Sheet

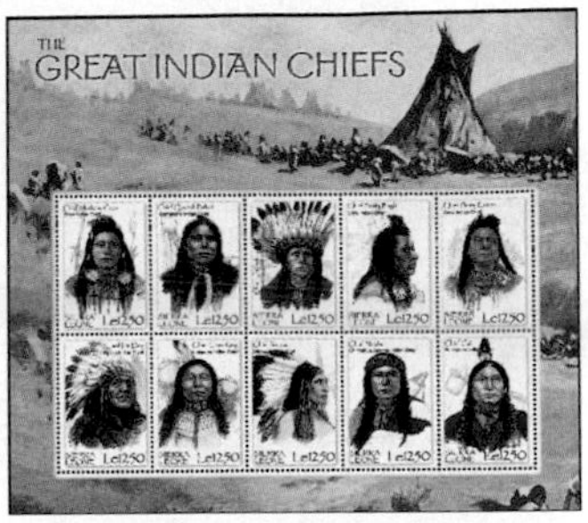
THE GREAT INDIAN CHIEFS

Indian Chiefs — A475

No. 2836 — Chief and tribe: a, Medicine Crow, Crow. b, Quanah Parker, Comanche. c, Garfield, Jicarilla. d, Pretty Eagle, Crow. e, Plenty Coups, Crow. f, He Dog, Oglala. g, Crow King, Hunkpapa. h, Pontiac, Ottawa. i, Naiche, Chiricahua. j, Gall, Hunkpapa.

**2006, Jan. 31**
**2836** A475 1250 le Sheet of 10, #a-j 11.00 11.00

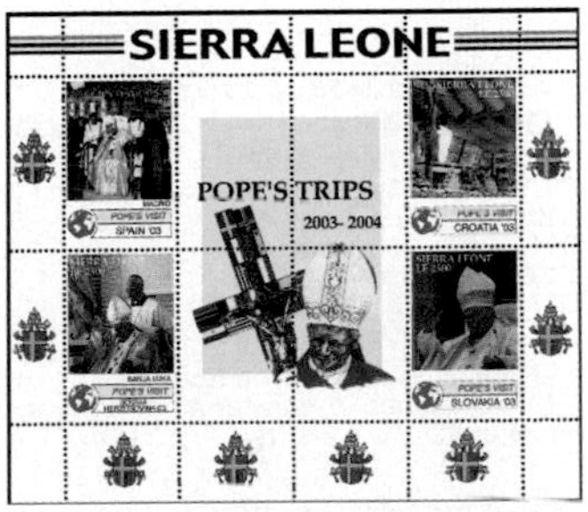
SIERRA LEONE
POPE'S TRIPS
2003- 2004

Travels of Pope John Paul II in 2003-04 — A476

No. 2837, 2500 le: a, Madrid, Spain. b, Croatia. c, Banja Luka, Bosnia & Herzegovina. d, Slovakia.

No. 2838, 2500 le: a, Pompeii, Italy. b, Bern Switzerland. c, Lourdes, France. d, Loreto, Italy.

**2006, Feb. 27** *Perf. 13½*

**Sheets of 4, #a-d, + 4 Labels**

**2837-2838** A476 Set of 2 17.00 17.00

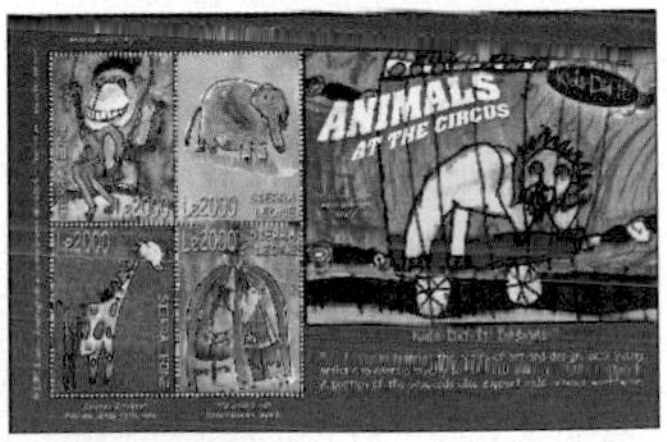
ANIMALS AT THE CIRCUS

Children's Art — A477

No. 2839, 2000 le — Circus animals: a, Monkey. b, Red-toed elephant. c, Colored giraffe. d, Colored bird.

No. 2840, 2000 le — Reptiles: a, Green gecko. b, Frog. c, Spotted lizard. d, Orange lizard.

No. 2841, 2000 le — Flowers: a, Yellow flowers. b, Poppies. c, Orange flowers. d, Lilies.

**2006** *Perf. 13¼*

**Sheets of 4, #a-d**

**2839-2841** A477 Set of 3 21.00 21.00

---

**AIR POST STAMPS**

**Catalogue values for unused stamps in this section are for Never Hinged items.**

**Independence — Progress Issue**

Nos. 197, 199, 204 and 206 Surcharged Like Nos. 242-247 plus "AIRMAIL" in Carmine, Red, Violet, Blue or Orange

*Perf. 13, 13½*

**1963, Apr. 27 Wmk. 4 Engr.**

**Center in Black**

**C1** A27 7p on 1½p (C) .20 .20
**C2** A27 1sh3p on 1½p (R) .20 .20
**C3** A28 2sh6p brn org (V) .40 .40
**C4** A28 3sh on 3p (Bl) .40 .40
**C5** A28 6sh on 3p (O) .50 .50
**C6** A27 11sh on 10sh (C) 1.60 1.60
**C7** A27 11sh on £1 (C) 500.00 175.00
*Nos. C1-C6 (6)* 3.30 3.30

Nos. 221, 224, 213, 223 and 207 Surcharged or Overprinted in Brown, Red, Black, Violet, Ultramarine or Orange

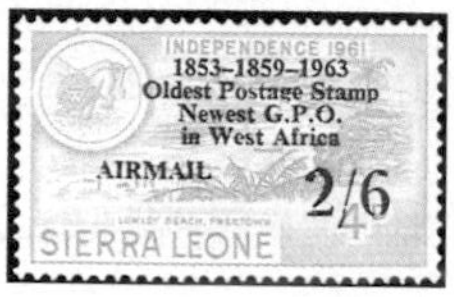


*Perf. 13x13½, 13½x13, 13*

**1963, Nov. 4 Wmk. 4, 336**

**C8** A31 7p on 3p (Br) .20 .20
**C9** A32 1sh3p blue & blk (R) .25 .25
**C10** A30 2sh6p on 4p (Bk) .50 .50
**C11** A31 3sh on 3p (V) .60 .60
**C12** A32 6sh on 6p (U) 1.25 1.25
**C13** A27 £1 org & blk (O) 8.50 8.50
*Nos. C8-C13 (6)* 11.30 11.30

Overprint is in 6 lines on Nos. C8, C11 and C12. A number of surcharge varieties and errors exist.

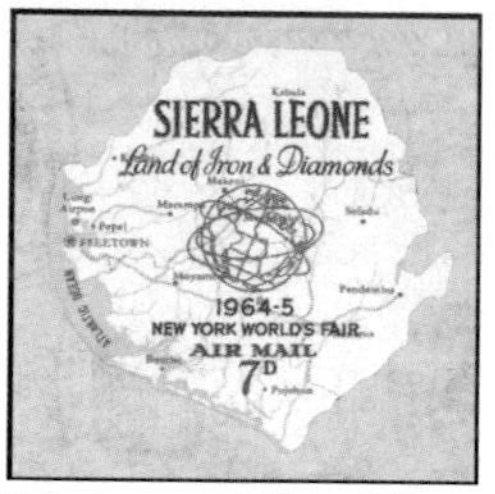


Unisphere and Map of Sierra Leone — AP1

**Engraved and Lithographed**

**1964, Feb. 10 Unwmk. *Die Cut***

**Self-adhesive**

**C14** AP1 7p multicolored .20 .20
**C15** AP1 9p multicolored .20 .20
**C16** AP1 1sh3p multicolored .20 .20
**C17** AP1 2sh6p multicolored .35 .35
**C18** AP1 3sh6p multicolored .50 .50
**C19** AP1 6sh multicolored .90 .90
**C20** AP1 11sh multicolored 1.40 1.40
*Nos. C14-C20 (7)* 3.75 3.75

New York World's Fair, 1964-65.
For surcharge see No. C33.

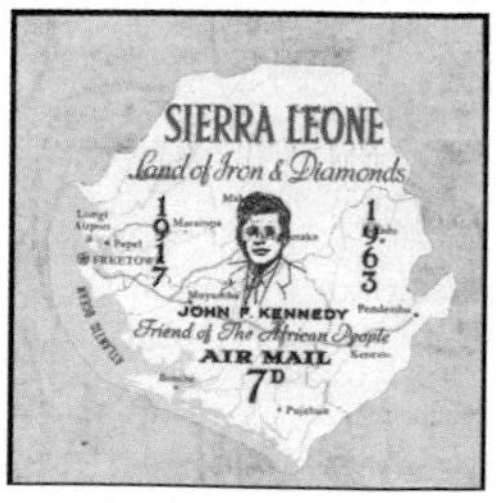


John F. Kennedy AP2

**1964, May 11**

**Self-adhesive**

**C21** AP2 7p multicolored .20 .20
**C22** AP2 9p multicolored .20 .20
**C23** AP2 1sh3p multicolored .25 .25
**C24** AP2 2sh6p multicolored .40 .40
**C25** AP2 3sh6p multicolored .60 .60
**C26** AP2 6sh multicolored 1.10 1.10
**C27** AP2 11sh multicolored 1.75 1.75
*Nos. C21-C27 (7)* 4.50 4.50

For surcharges see Nos. C32, C34-C36.

Nos. 241, 213, 219 and 218 Surcharged in Dark Blue, Black, Red or Violet Blue

*Perf. 11½x11, 13½x13, 13x13½*

**1964, Aug. 4 Engr. Wmk. 336**

**C28** A36 7c on 1sh3p (#241) (DB) .25 .25
**C29** A30 20c on 4p (#213) .40 .40
**C30** A29 30c on 10sh (#219) (R) .70 .70
**C31** A29 40c on 5sh (#218) (VB) .85 .85
*Nos. C28-C31 (4)* 2.20 2.20

Map-shaped Issues of 1964 Surcharged in Red or Black

**Engraved and Lithographed**

**1964-65 Unwmk. *Die Cut***

**C32** AP2 7c on 7p (#C21) (R) .20 .20
**C33** AP1 7c on 9p (#C15) .85 .85
**C34** AP2 60c on 9p (#C22) 1.25 1.25
**C35** AP2 1 le on 1sh3p (#C23) (R) 2.00 2.00
**C36** AP2 2 le on 11sh (#C27) 4.25 4.25
*Nos. C32-C36 (5)* 8.55 8.55

Issue dates: Aug. 4, 1964, Nos. C35-C36. Jan. 20, 1965, Nos. C32, C34. April, 1965, No. C33.

Regular Issue of 1963 Surcharged like Nos. 300-305 with "AIRMAIL" added

**Wmk. 336**

**1965, May 19 Photo. *Perf. 14***

Designs of Surcharge: No. C37, C39-C40, Sir Milton Margai and Sir Winston Churchill. No. C38, Margai. No. C41, Churchill.

**C37** A35 7c on 2p (#230) .20 .20
**C38** A34 15c on ½p (#227) .40 .40
**C39** A35 30c on 6p (#233) .75 .75
**C40** A35 1 le on £1 (#239) 2.75 2.75
**C41** A34 2 le on 10sh (#238) 5.50 5.50
*Nos. C37-C41 (5)* 9.60 9.60

The portraits and inscription on No. C39 are white, the denomination and "AIRMAIL" are orange.

Ten more surcharges were issued Nov. 9, 1965: "2c" on Nos. C16, C23 and C25. "3c" on Nos. C14 and C22. "5c" on Nos. C17-C19, C24, and C26. Value $4 each.

One further surcharge was issued Jan. 28, 1966: "TWO/Leones" on No. C39. Value $10.

Type of Regular Issue and

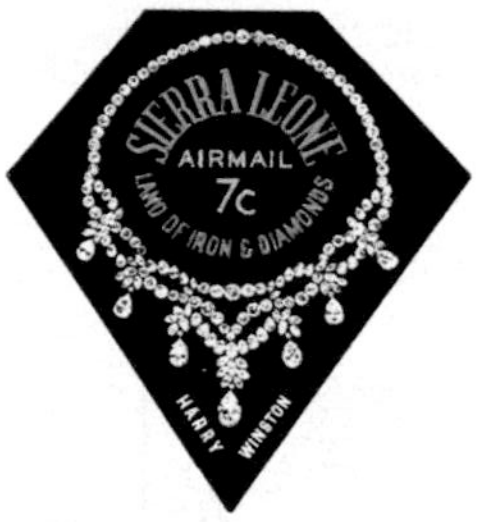


Diamond Necklace AP3

**Litho.; Reversed Embossing**

**1965, Dec. 17 Unwmk. *Die Cut***

**Self-adhesive**

**C53** AP3 7c blk, grn, gold & bl .35 .35
**C54** AP3 15c blk, brnz, car & bl .75 .75

**Engr. and Embossed on Paper**

**C55** A41 40c multi, *cream* 1.75 1.75
*Nos. C53-C55 (3)* 2.85 2.85

Various advertisements printed on peelable paper backing. Nos. C54-C55 have side tabs for handling and come packed in boxes of 100. No. C53 is without side tab and comes 25 stamps attached to one sheet.

For overprints and surcharges see Nos. C68-C69, C79-C83.

Nos. 248, 229, 232, 234 and 236 Surcharged and Overprinted: "AIRMAIL/FIVE YEARS/INDEPENDENCE/1961-1966"

**1966, Apr. 27 Wmk. 336**

**C56** A37 7c on 3p pur & red .20 .20
**C57** A34 15c on 1sh multi .35 .35
**C58** A34 25c on 2sh6p multi .55 .55
**C59** A34 50c on 1½p multi 1.10 1.10
**C60** A34 1 le on 4p multi 2.50 2.50
*Nos. C56-C60 (5)* 4.70 4.70

The denomination on No. C60 is spelled out "One Leone."

Self-adhesive & Die Cut

Nos. C61-C131, C135-C142 are self-adhesive and die cut.

Gold Coin Type of Regular Issue

Designs: 7c, 10c, ¼ Golde coin. 15c, 30c, ½ Golde coin. 50c, 2 le, 1 Golde coin. (7c, 15c, 50c, Map of Sierra Leone. 10c, 30c, 2 le, Lion's head.)

Diameter: 7c, 10c, 38mm; 15c, 30c, 54mm; 50c, 2 le, 82mm.

**Lithographed; Embossed on Gilt Foil**

**1966, Nov. 12 Unwmk.**

**C61** A42 7c red & orange .20 .20
**C62** A42 10c dull blue & red .20 .20
**C63** A42 15c red & orange .20 .20
**C64** A42 30c black & rose lilac .40 .40
**C65** A42 50c rose lilac & emer .75 .75
**C66** A42 2 le green & black 3.75 3.75
*Nos. C61-C66 (6)* 5.50 5.50

Advertising printed on paper backing.

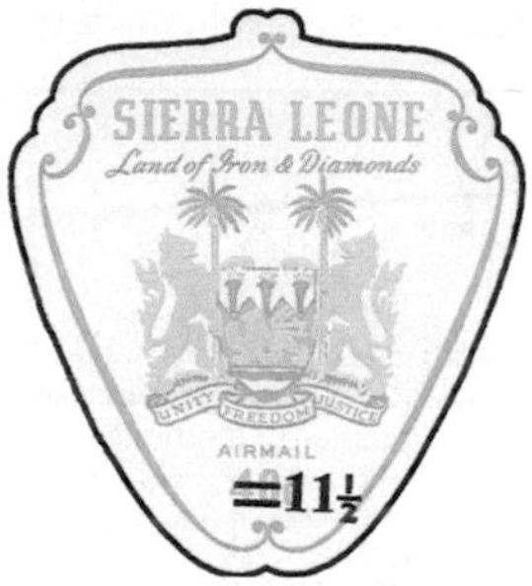


Type of Regular Issue, 1965 and No. C55 Surcharged

**1967, Dec. 2 Engr. & Embossed**

**C67** A41 10c multi (red frame), *cream* .50 .50
a. Black frame .50 .50
**C68** A41 11½c on 40c multi, *cr* .40 .40
**C69** A41 25c on 40c multi, *cr* 1.00 1.00
*Nos. C67-C69 (3)* 1.90 1.90

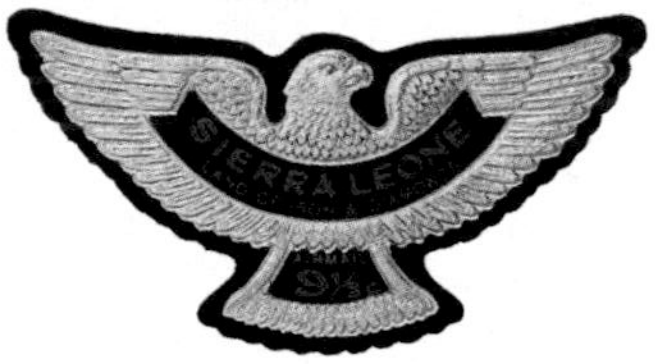


Eagle — AP4

**Embossed Foil on Black Paper**

**1967, Dec. 2 Unwmk.**

**C70** AP4 9½c black, gold & red .75 .75
**C71** AP4 15c black, gold & grn .90 .90

Various advertisements printed on peelable paper backing. See Nos. C98-C99, C118-C124.

Map Type of Regular Issue

Designs: Each denomination shows map of Africa with map of one of the following countries — Portuguese Guinea, South Africa, Mozambique, Rhodesia, South West Africa or Angola. Sheets of 30 (6x5) have 5 horizontal rows containing one stamp of each design.

**1968, Sept. 25 Litho.**

**C72** A43 7½c multicolored .30 .30
**C73** A43 9½c multicolored .45 .45
**C74** A43 14½c multicolored .65 .65
**C75** A43 18½c multicolored .75 .75
**C76** A43 25c multicolored 1.25 1.25
**C77** A43 1 le multicolored 7.50 7.50
**C78** A43 2 le multicolored 17.50 17.50
*Nos. C72-C78 (7)* 28.40 28.40
7 Strips of 6, 1 of each design (42) 170.40

No. C55 Overprinted and Surcharged in Red Similar to Nos. 364-368

**Engraved and Embossed on Paper**

**1968, Nov. 30**

**C79** A41 6½c on 40c multi .20 .20
**C80** A41 17½c on 40c multi .40 .40
**C81** A41 22½c on 40c multi .40 .40
**C82** A41 28½c on 40c multi .55 .55
**C83** A41 40c multicolored .85 .85
*Nos. C79-C83 (5)* 2.40 2.40

Scroll Type of Regular Issue

7½c, #C54. 9½c, #C70. 20c, #C16. 30c, #C26. 50c, #165. 2 le, #207 with "2nd Year of Independence" overprint. All are horiz.

**1969, Mar. 1 Litho.**

**C84** A44 7½c multicolored .25 .25
**C85** A44 9½c multicolored .30 .30
**C86** A44 20c multicolored .60 .60
**C87** A44 30c multicolored .90 .90
**C88** A44 50c multicolored 2.25 2.25
**C89** A44 2 le multicolored 15.00 15.00
*Nos. C84-C89 (6)* 19.30 19.30

Various advertisements printed on peelable paper backing. No. C84 has side tab for handling and comes packed in boxes of 50. Nos. C85-C89 are without side tabs and come 20 stamps attached to one sheet.

For surcharges see Nos. C135-C136.

Pepel Port Types of Regular Issue

Designs: 7½c, 15c, Globe, tanker, flags of Sierra Leone and Japan. Anvil Shape with Flags of Sierra Leone and: 9½c, 2 le, Union Jack. 25c, Netherlands. 1 le, West Germany.

**1969, July 10**

**C90** A45 7½c multicolored .20 .20
**C91** A46 9½c multicolored .20 .20
**C92** A45 15c multicolored .25 .25
**C93** A46 25c multicolored .40 .40
**C94** A46 1 le multicolored 1.60 1.60
**C95** A46 2 le multicolored 3.25 3.25
*Nos. C90-C95 (6)* 5.90 5.90

Various advertisements printed on peelable paper backing. No. C90 has side tab for handling and comes packed in boxes of 50. Nos. C91-C95 are without side tabs and come 20 stamps attached to one sheet.

Bank Type of Regular Issue

**Lithographed; Gold Impressed**

**1969, Sept. 10**

**C96** A47 9½c yel grn, vio & gold .90 .90

Advertising printed on peelable paper backing; 20 imperf. stamps to a sheet of backing, roulette 10.

Cola Nut Type of Regular Issue and Type of 1967

**Typo.; Embossed on White Paper**

**1969, Sept. 10**

**C97** A40 7c yel, mar & car .40 .40

**Embossed Foil on Black Paper**

**C98** AP4 9½c blk, gold & bl .50 .50
**C99** AP4 15c blk, gold & red .75 .75
*Nos. C97-C99 (3)* 1.65 1.65

No. C97 has side tab for handling and comes packed in boxes of 100. Nos. C98-C99 have advertisements printed on peelable paper backing, side tabs and come packed in boxes of 50.

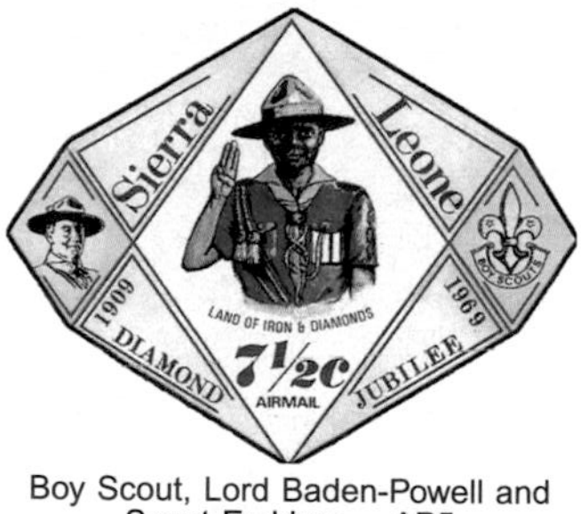


Boy Scout, Lord Baden-Powell and Scout Emblem — AP5

**1969, Dec. 6 Litho.**

**C100** AP5 7½c multicolored .50 .40
**C101** AP5 9½c multicolored .60 .50
**C102** AP5 15c multicolored 1.25 .80
**C103** AP5 22c multicolored 2.00 1.40
**C104** AP5 55c multicolored 8.00 6.50
**C105** AP5 3 le multicolored 100.00 72.50
*Nos. C100-C105 (6)* 112.35 82.10

60th anniv. of the Sierra Leone Boy Scouts. Various advertising printed on peelable paper backing. No. C100 has side tab for handling and comes packed in boxes of 100. Nos. C101-C105 are without side tabs and come 20 stamps attached to one sheet.

No. 357 Surcharged "AIRMAIL" and New Denomination in Metallic Emerald, Lilac, Blue, Green, Bronze or Silver

**1970, Mar 28**

**C106** A43 7½c on ½c (E) .30 .30
**C107** A43 9½c on ½c (L) .40 .40
**C108** A43 15c on ½c (Bl) .55 .55
**C109** A43 28c on ½c (G) 1.00 1.00
**C110** A43 40c on ½c (Br) 1.75 1.75
**C111** A43 2 le on ½c (S) 9.00 9.00
*Nos. C106-C111 (6)* 13.00 13.00

See design paragraph over No. 357.

# STOCKBOOKS

Stockbooks are a classic and convenient storage alternative for many collectors. These German-made stockbooks feature heavyweight archival quality paper with 9 pockets on each page. The 8 1⁄2" x 11 5⁄8" pages are bound inside a handsome leatherette grain cover and include glassine interleaving between the pages for added protection. The Value Priced Stockbooks are available in two page styles, the white page stockbooks feature glassine pockets while the black page variety includes clear acetate pockets

## Black Page Stockbooks
### Acetate Pockets

| ITEM | COLOR | PAGES | RETAIL |
|------|-------|-------|--------|
| ST16RD | Red | 16 pages | $10.95 |
| ST16GR | Green | 16 pages | $10.95 |
| ST16BL | Blue | 16 pages | $10.95 |
| ST16BK | Black | 16 pages | $10.95 |
| ST32RD | Red | 32 pages | $16.95 |
| ST32GR | Green | 32 pages | $16.95 |
| ST32BL | Blue | 32 pages | $16.95 |
| ST32BK | Black | 32 pages | $16.95 |
| ST64RD | Red | 64 pages | $29.95 |
| ST64GR | Green | 64 pages | $29.95 |
| ST64BL | Blue | 64 pages | $29.95 |
| ST64BK | Black | 64 pages | $29.95 |

Available from your favorite dealer or direct from:

---

## EXPO Type of Regular Issue

Maps of Sierra Leone and Japan.

**1970, June 22**    Litho.

| | | | |
|---|---|---|---|
| C112 | A49 | 7 1⁄2c multicolored | .20 .20 |
| C113 | A49 | 9 1⁄2c multicolored | .20 .20 |
| C114 | A49 | 15c multicolored | .35 .35 |
| C115 | A49 | 25c multicolored | .70 .70 |
| C116 | A49 | 50c multicolored | 1.50 1.50 |
| C117 | A49 | 3 le multicolored | 7.75 7.75 |
| | | Nos. C112-C117 (6) | 10.70 10.70 |

Various advertising printed on peelable paper backing.

### Eagle Type of 1967

**1970, Oct. 3**    Embossed Foil

| | | | |
|---|---|---|---|
| C118 | AP4 | 7 1⁄2c crim & gold | .45 .45 |
| C119 | AP4 | 9 1⁄2c emer & cop. | .55 .50 |
| C120 | AP4 | 15 1⁄2c grnsh bl & sil | .85 .65 |
| C121 | AP4 | 25c brt red lil & gold | 1.10 1.10 |
| C122 | AP4 | 50c gold & emer | 2.75 2.25 |
| C123 | AP4 | 1 le silver & dk bl | 5.50 4.50 |
| C124 | AP4 | 2 le gold & brt bl | 11.00 9.25 |
| | | Nos. C118-C124 (7) | 22.50 18.70 |

Advertisements printed on peelable paper backing. Issued in sheets of 10.

"Treasure of Sierra Leone" Diamond — AP6

### Lithographed and Embossed

**1970, Dec. 30**

| | | | |
|---|---|---|---|
| C125 | AP6 | 7 1⁄2c multicolored | .75 .20 |
| C126 | AP6 | 9 1⁄2c multicolored | 1.00 .30 |
| C127 | AP6 | 15c multicolored | 1.25 .50 |
| C128 | AP6 | 25c multicolored | 2.00 .50 |
| C129 | AP6 | 75c multicolored | 8.50 5.50 |
| C130 | AP6 | 2 le multicolored | 35.00 25.00 |
| | | Nos. C125-C130 (6) | 48.50 32.00 |

Diamond industry. Advertisement printed on peelable paper backing. Sheets of 20.

### Traffic Type of Regular Issue

**1971, Mar. 1**    Litho.

| | | | |
|---|---|---|---|
| C131 | A53 | 9 1⁄2c vio blue & org | .75 .75 |

Advertisements printed on peelable paper backing.

---

**Unwmk.**

Litho.

| | | | |
|---|---|---|---|
| C135 | A44(b) | 70c on 30c (DB) | 2.75 2.50 |
| C136 | A44(b) | 1 le on 30c (Bk) | 4.00 3.25 |
| | | Nos. C132-C136 (5) | 9.55 8.20 |

**Imperf.**

Lion's Head and Bugles
AP7

### Lithographed and Embossed (Gold)

**1971, Apr. 27**

| | | | |
|---|---|---|---|
| C137 | AP7 | 7 1⁄2c multicolored | .20 .20 |
| C138 | AP7 | 9 1⁄2c multicolored | .20 .20 |
| C139 | AP7 | 15c multicolored | .25 .25 |
| C140 | AP7 | 25c multicolored | .45 .45 |
| C141 | AP7 | 75c multicolored | 1.75 1.75 |
| C142 | AP7 | 2 le multicolored | 6.00 6.00 |
| | | Nos. C137-C142 (6) | 8.85 8.85 |

10th anniversary of independence. Advertisements printed on peelable paper backing. Stamps are in shape of Sierra Leone map and in flag colors.

Guma Valley Dam and Bank Emblem — AP8

**1975, Jan. 14**    Litho.    Perf. 13 1⁄2

| | | | |
|---|---|---|---|
| C143 | AP8 | 15c multicolored | 1.00 1.00 |

African Development Bank, 10th anniv.

Congo River Type of 1975

**1975, Aug. 24**    Litho.    Perf. 13x13 1⁄2

| | | | |
|---|---|---|---|
| C144 | A57 | 20c multicolored | .75 .75 |

Mano River Type of 1975

**1975, Oct. 3**    Perf. 13x13 1⁄2

| | | | |
|---|---|---|---|
| C145 | A58 | 15c multicolored | .60 .60 |

---

**Wmk. 336**

| | | | |
|---|---|---|---|
| C132 | A29(a) | 10c on 2p (DR) | .35 .30 |
| C133 | A29(a) | 20c on 1sh (DB) | .70 .65 |

**Engr.**

Nos. 211, 215, 228 and C87 Surcharged in Dark Red, Dark Blue or Black

a

b

**1971, Mar. 1**    Engr.    Perf. 14

**Photo.**

| | | | |
|---|---|---|---|
| C134 | A35(a) | 50c on 1p (Bk) | 1.75 1.50 |

# SINGAPORE

'sip-ə-,por

**LOCATION** — An island just off the southern tip of the Malay Peninsula, south of Johore.

**GOVT.** — Republic in British Commonwealth

**AREA** — 250 sq. mi.

**POP.** — 3,531,600 (1999 est.)

**CAPITAL** — Singapore

100 Cents = 1 Dollar

Singapore, Malacca and Penang were the British settlements which, together with the Federated Malay States, composed the former colony of Straits Settlements. On April 1, 1946, Singapore became a separate colony when the Straits Settlements colony was dissolved. Malacca and Penang joined the Malayan Union, which was renamed the Federation of Malaya in 1948. In 1959 Singapore became a state with internal self-government. Singapore joined the Federation of Malaysia in 1963 and withdrew in 1965.

**Catalogue values for all unused stamps in this country are for Never Hinged items.**

## Watermark

Wmk. 366 — S multiple

## King George VI — A1

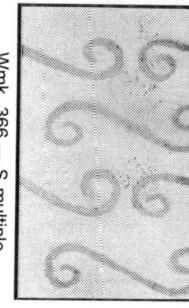

### 1948 Wmk. 4 Typo. Perf. 14

| | | | | | |
|---|---|---|---|---|---|
| 1 | A1 | 1c black | .20 | 1.00 |
| 2 | A1 | 2c orange | .25 | .50 |
| 3 | A1 | 3c green | .35 | .80 |
| 4 | A1 | 4c chocolate | .35 | 1.25 |
| 6 | A1 | 6c gray | .35 | .85 |
| 7 | A1 | 8c rose red | .40 | .85 |
| 9 | A1 | 10c ultra | .45 | .20 |
| 11 | A1 | 15c plum | 11.00 | .40 |
| 12 | A1 | 20c dk green & blk | 7.00 | .40 |
| 14 | A1 | 25c org & rose lilac | 1.50 | .20 |
| 16 | A1 | 40c dk vio & rose red | 13.00 | .20 |
| 17 | A1 | 50c org & rose red | 8.50 | .25 |
| 18 | A1 | $1 vio brn & ultra | 72.50 | 4.00 |
| 19 | A1 | $2 rose red & emer | 150.00 | 6.00 |
| 20 | A1 | $5 chocolate & emer | 278.35 | 30.50 |

Set, hinged 150.00

### 1949-52 Perf. 18

| | | | | | |
|---|---|---|---|---|---|
| 1a | A1 | 1c black ('52) | .70 | 3.00 |
| 2a | A1 | 2c orange | 1.00 | 1.25 |
| 4a | A1 | 4c chocolate | 1.90 | .85 |
| 5 | A1 | 5c rose violet ('52) | 4.00 | .20 |
| 6a | A1 | 6c gray ('52) | 1.60 | 1.25 |
| 8 | A1 | 8c green ('52) | 9.00 | 3.00 |
| 9a | A1 | 10c ultra | .55 | .20 |
| 10 | A1 | 12c plum ('52) | 7.00 | .20 |
| 12a | A1 | 20c dk green & blk | 9.50 | .40 |
| 14a | A1 | 25c org & rose lil ('52) | 6.50 | .75 |
| 15 | A1 | 35c dk vio & rose red | 1.10 | .20 |
| 16a | A1 | 40c nk vio & rose red ('52) | 6.00 | 3.00 |
| 17a | A1 | 50c ultra & black ('50) | 40.00 | 15.00 |
| 18a | A1 | $1 violet brown & ultra ('50) | 9.50 | .20 |
| 19a | A1 | $2 rose red & emer ('51) | 6.000 | .75 |
| 20a | A1 | $5 choc & emerald ('51) | 235.00 | 3.00 |

Nos. 1a-20a (18) 487.85 48.85
Set, hinged 275.00

**b.** Wmk. 4a (error) 120.00
**b.** Wmk. 4a (error) 19.00
**b.** Wmk. 4a (error) 6.000

Common Design Types pictured following the introduction.

## Silver Wedding Issue
Common Design Types
Inscribed: "Singapore"

### 1948, Oct. 25 Photo. Perf. 14x14½
21 CD304 10c purple 1.00 .20

**Engraved; Name Typographed Perf. 11½x11**
22 CD305 $5 light brown 130.00 45.00

## UPU Issue
Common Design Types
Inscribed: "Malaya-Singapore"

### 1949, Oct. 10 Perf. 14x14½, 11x11½ Wmk. 4
| | | | | |
|---|---|---|---|---|
| 23 | CD306 | 10c rose violet | .75 | .25 |
| 24 | CD307 | 15c indigo | 7.25 | .75 |
| 25 | CD308 | 25c orange | 7.25 | 1.25 |
| 26 | CD309 | 50c slate | 22.50 | 4.25 |

Nos. 23-26 (4) 6.50

## Coronation Issue
Common Design Type

### 1953, June 2 Engr. Perf. 13½x13
27 CD312 10c magenta & black 2.00 .20

Sir Stamford Raffles Statue — A3

Singapore River — A4

Chinese Sampans — A2

### 1955, Sept. 4 Photo. Wmk. 4
**Perf. 13½x14, 14x13½**

| | | | | |
|---|---|---|---|---|
| 28 | A2 | 1c sepia | .20 | .80 |
| 29 | A2 | 2c rose red | .60 | 1.00 |
| 30 | A2 | 4c orange yellow | 1.50 | .20 |
| 31 | A2 | 5c orange brown | .80 | 1.00 |
| 32 | A2 | 6c gray blue | .40 | .30 |
| 33 | A2 | 8c aqua | .40 | .50 |
| 34 | A2 | 10c dark purple | .95 | .75 |
| 35 | A2 | 12c rose red | .50 | .20 |

**Perf. 13½x14½**

| | | | | |
|---|---|---|---|---|
| 36 | A2 | 20c violet blue | 2.00 | .80 |
| 37 | A2 | 25c orange & purple | 2.25 | .20 |
| 38 | A2 | 30c purple & plum | 3.00 | .20 |
| 39 | A2 | 50c bright blue | 2.00 | .20 |

**Engr.**
| | | | | |
|---|---|---|---|---|
| 40 | A3 | $1 blue & purple | 30.00 | .30 |
| 41 | A4 | $2 blue green & red | 42.50 | 1.75 |

**Perf. 13x14½**
42 A3 $5 multicolored 45.00 4.00
Nos. 28-42 (15) 138.50 13.10

**Engr.; Arms Typo.**

Designs: 2c, Malay kolek. 4c, Twa-kow. 5c, Lombok sloop. 6c, Malay pinas. 8c, Palari. 10c, Trengganu pinas. 12c, Hylam trader. 20c, Timber tongkong. 25c, Cocos-Keeling schooner. 30c, Liner Argonaut plane. 50c, Oil tanker. 50c, Liner (M.S. Chusan). $5, Arms of Singapore.

Sea Horse — A8

Malayan Fish: 4c, Tiger barb, horiz. 5c, Anemone fish, horiz. 6c, Archerfish. 10c, Harlequin fish, horiz. 20c, Butterflyfish. 25c, Two-spot gourami, horiz.

### 1962, Mar. 31 Perf. 14½x13½, 13½x14½ Wmk. 314
| | | | | |
|---|---|---|---|---|
| 53 | A8 | 2c lt grn & red brn | .40 | 1.00 |
| 54 | A8 | 4c red orange & blk | .40 | .60 |
| | a. | Black omitted | 550.00 | |
| 55 | A8 | 5c gray & red org | .20 | .20 |
| | a. | Red orange omitted | 550.00 | |
| | b. | Wmk. sideways ('67) | 3.25 | |
| 56 | A8 | 6c yellow & blk | .65 | .20 |
| 57 | A8 | 10c dk gray & red org | .60 | .20 |
| | a. | Red orange omitted | 400.00 | |
| | b. | Wmk. sideways ('67) | .50 | |
| 58 | A8 | 20c blue & orange | 1.60 | .50 |
| | a. | Orange omitted | 600.00 | |
| 59 | A8 | 25c orange & black | 1.25 | .20 |
| | a. | Black omitted | 100.00 | |
| | b. | Wmk. sideways ('67) | .85 | .25 |

Nos. 53-59 (7) 4.90 3.00
For surcharge see No. 370.

## Government Housing Project — A12

### 1963, June 3 Perf. 12½
| | | | | |
|---|---|---|---|---|
| 70 | A12 | 4c multicolored | 1.25 | .30 |
| 71 | A12 | 10c multicolored | 1.75 | .45 |

Issued for National Day, June 3, 1963.

Singapore Lion and Administrative Center — A5

### 1959, June 1 Photo. Wmk. 314
**Perf. 11½x12**
| | | | | |
|---|---|---|---|---|
| 43 | A5 | 4c deep rose red | .70 | .65 |
| 44 | A5 | 10c magenta | 1.00 | .35 |
| 45 | A5 | 20c ultra | 2.50 | .25 |
| 46 | A5 | 25c yellow green | 2.75 | 2.25 |
| 47 | A5 | 30c bright violet | 2.75 | 3.00 |
| 48 | A5 | 50c bluish gray | 3.75 | 3.00 |

Nos. 43-48 (6) 13.45 12.00
New Constitution of Singapore.

## Lion in Gold — A6

### 1960, June 3 Litho. Perf. 13½
| | | | | |
|---|---|---|---|---|
| 49 | A6 | 4c blue, red & yellow | 1.50 | .50 |
| 50 | A6 | 10c gray, red & yellow | 2.50 | .75 |

Issued for National Day, June 3, 1960.

## Hands and Map of Singapore A7

### 1961, June 3 Photo.
| | | | | |
|---|---|---|---|---|
| 51 | A7 | 4c brown, yellow & gray | 1.60 | .30 |
| 52 | A7 | 10c green, yellow & gray | 2.00 | .45 |

Issued for National Day, June 3, 1961.

## State Flag of Singapore A6

### 1960, June 3 Unwmk. Perf. 11½
*(listing appears separately)*

## Symbolic of Labor's Role in Building the Nation — A9

### 1962, June 3 Unwmk. Perf. 11½
| | | | | |
|---|---|---|---|---|
| 60 | A9 | 4c brt rose, blk & yel | 1.25 | .35 |
| 61 | A9 | 10c brt blue, blk & yel | 2.25 | .65 |

Issued for National Day, June 3, 1962.

## Yellow-Breasted Sunbird — A11

Vanda Tan Chay Yan — A10

Designs: 1c, Arachnis Maggie Oei, horiz. 12c, Grammatophyllum speciosum. 30c, Vanda Miss Joaquim. 50c, Shama. $1, White-breasted kingfisher, horiz. $5, White-tailed sea eagle.

### 1963, Mar. 10 Photo. Wmk. 314
## Flowers and Birds in Natural Colors
**Size: 37x26mm, 26x37mm**

| | | | | |
|---|---|---|---|---|
| 62 | A10 | 1c brt pink & ultra | .30 | .20 |
| | a. | Wmkd. sideways ('66) | .20 | |
| 63 | A10 | 8c lt blue & mag | .50 | .55 |
| 64 | A10 | 12c salmon & brown | 1.50 | .20 |
| 65 | A10 | 30c tan & ol green | 110.00 | |
| | a. | tan omitted | | |

**Size: 35½x25½mm, 25½x35½mm**

| | | | | |
|---|---|---|---|---|
| 66 | A11 | 50c yel green & blk | 1.50 | .20 |
| | a. | Wmkd. sideways ('66) | 6.00 | 6.00 |
| 67 | A11 | $1 yellow & blk | 6.00 | 2.00 |
| | a. | Wmkd. sideways ('67) | 24.00 | |
| 68 | A11 | $2 dull blue & blk | 14.50 | 1.10 |
| 69 | A11 | $5 pale blue & blk | 30.00 | 2.75 |

Nos. 62-69 (8) 74.80 5.50
See No. 76.

**Perf. 12½, 13½x13 (50c, $1), 13x13½ ($2, $5)**

Workers, Factory and Apartment House A14

### 1963, Aug. 8 Photo. Perf. 14x14½
72 A13 5c multicolored 1.10 1.10
Southeast Asia Cultural Festival.

Folk Dancers — A13

dance, 75c, Tarian Kuda Kepang, Javanese dance, $1, Yao Chi, Chinese opera mask.

**Wmk. 314 (30c), Unwmd. (15, 20c)**
**1966, Aug. 9 Photo.** *Perf. 12½x13*
| | | | | |
|---|---|---|---|---|
| 73 | A14 | 15c ultra & multi | 1.10 | .25 |
| 74 | A14 | 20c red & multi | 1.40 | 1.00 |
| 75 | A14 | 30c yellow & multi | 2.00 | 1.50 |
| | | | 4.50 | 2.75 |
| | | Nos. 73-75 (3) | | |

First anniversary of the Republic.

Bird Type of 1963

Design: 15c, Black-naped tern (sterna).

**1966, Nov. 9 Wmk. 314** *Perf. 12½*
**Bird in Natural Colors**
**Size: 26x37mm**
| | | | | |
|---|---|---|---|---|
| 76 | A11 | 15c blue & black | 2.75 | |
| a. | | Orange (eye) omitted | 45.00 | .20 |

Marching Women, Chinese
Inscription — A15

15c, Malay inscription. 50c, Tamil inscription.

**1967, Aug. 9** *Perf. 14x14½*
| | | **Photo.** | **Unwmk.** | |
|---|---|---|---|---|
| 77 | A15 | 6c lt brown, gray & red | .55 | .65 |
| 78 | A15 | 15c multicolored | .75 | .20 |
| 79 | A15 | 50c multicolored | 1.75 | 1.40 |
| | | | 3.05 | 2.25 |
| | | Nos. 77-79 (3) | | |

"Build a Vigorous Singapore" campaign.

Buildings and Map of Africa and Southeast Asia — A16

**1967, Oct. 7** *Perf. 14x13½*
| | | | **Black Overprint** | |
|---|---|---|---|---|
| 80 | A16 | 10c multicolored | .35 | .25 |
| 81 | A16 | 25c multicolored | .85 | .90 |
| 82 | A16 | 50c multicolored | 1.50 | 1.25 |
| | | | 2.70 | 2.40 |
| | | Nos. 80-82 (3) | | |

2nd Afro-Asian Housing Cong., Oct. 7-15.
No. 80 exists without overprint.

Sword Dance — A18

Map of Singapore and Symbolic Worker — A17

Stamps are inscribed "Work for Prosperity" in English and: 6c, Chinese. 15c, Malay. 50c, Tamil.

**1968, Aug. 9** *Perf. 13½x14½*
| | | **Photo.** | **Unwmk.** | |
|---|---|---|---|---|
| 83 | A17 | 6c red, black & gold | .20 | .20 |
| 84 | A17 | 15c red, blk yel grn, blk & gold | .40 | .35 |
| 85 | A17 | 50c brt blue, blk & gold | 1.40 | 1.25 |
| | | | 2.00 | 1.80 |
| | | Nos. 83-85 (3) | | |

Issued for National Day, 1968.

**Wmk. Rectangles (334)**
**1968 Photo.** *Perf. 14*

Designs: 6c, Lion dance. 10c, Bharatha Natyam, Indian dance. 15c, Tari Payong, Sumatran dance. 20c, Kathak Kali, Indian dance mask. 25c, Lu Chih Shen and Lin Chung, Chinese opera masks. 30c, Dragon dance, horiz. 50c, Tari Lilin, Malayan candle

---

strings, vert. $5, Vina, Indian, 7 strings. $10, Ta Ku, Chinese drum.

**1969 Photo. Wmk. 366** *Perf. 13*
| | | | | |
|---|---|---|---|---|
| 107 | A22 | 1c multicolored | .20 | 2.25 |
| 108 | A22 | 4c multicolored | .80 | 2.75 |
| 109 | A22 | $2 multicolored | 4.00 | 1.00 |
| 110 | A22 | $5 multicolored | 14.00 | 1.50 |
| 111 | A22 | $10 multicolored | 40.00 | 12.50 |
| | | | 59.00 | 22.50 |
| | | Nos. 107-111 (5) | | |

Issued: 1c, 4c, $2, $5, Nov. 10; $10, Dec. 6.

Sea Shells — A23

Designs: 30c, Tropical fish. 75c, Greater flamingo and helmeted hornbill. $1, Orchids.

**1970, Mar. 15** *Perf. 13½*
| | | | **Unwmk.** | |
|---|---|---|---|---|
| 112 | A23 | 15c pale vio & multi | .85 | .25 |
| 113 | A23 | 30c lt blue & multi | 2.50 | 1.00 |
| 114 | A23 | 75c yellow & multi | 6.50 | 4.25 |
| 115 | A23 | $1 lt green & multi | 7.75 | 7.00 |
| | | | 17.60 | 12.50 |
| a. | | Souvenir sheet of 4, #112-115 | 29.00 | 29.00 |
| | | Nos. 112-115 (4) | | |

EXPO 70 International Exposition, Osaka, Japan, Mar. 15-Sept. 13.

Child Playing (Kindergarten) — A24

50c, Sports activities. 75c, Cultural activities.

**1970, July Unwmk.** *Perf. 13½*
| | | | | |
|---|---|---|---|---|
| 116 | A24 | 15c deep orange & blk | .85 | .25 |
| 117 | A24 | 50c orange, blk & vio | 2.75 | 2.25 |
| 118 | A24 | 75c blk & dp lilac rose | 4.25 | 3.50 |
| | | | 7.85 | 6.00 |
| | | Nos. 116-118 (3) | | |

People's Association, 10th anniversary.

---

Soldier and Map of Singapore — A25

Map and soldiers in various positions.

**1970, Aug. 9 Litho. Unwmk.**
| | | | | |
|---|---|---|---|---|
| 119 | A25 | 15c emerald, blk & org | 1.60 | .20 |
| 120 | A25 | 50c org, blk & brt mag | 4.75 | 3.00 |
| 121 | A25 | $1 brt mag, blk & emer | 6.25 | 7.00 |
| | | | 12.60 | 10.20 |
| | | Nos. 119-121 (3) | | |

National military service.

Runners A26

**1970, Aug. 23 Photo.** *Perf. 13*
| | | | | |
|---|---|---|---|---|
| 122 | A26 | 10c shown | 2.00 | 2.00 |
| 123 | A26 | 15c Swimmers | 2.50 | 2.50 |
| 124 | A26 | 25c Badminton | 2.75 | 2.75 |
| 125 | A26 | 50c Automobile race | 3.25 | 3.25 |
| | | | 13.75 | 13.75 |
| a. | | Strip of 4, #122-125 | | |

1970 Festival of Sports.

Ship and Emblem of National Line (Neptune Oriental Lines) — A27

Designs: 30c, Ship in first container berth. 75c, Ship repairing and ship building.

**1970, Nov. 1 Litho.** *Perf. 12*
| | | | | |
|---|---|---|---|---|
| 126 | A27 | 15c vio bl, lem & red | 3.75 | 2.75 |
| 127 | A27 | 30c dp ultra & lemon | 7.75 | 5.75 |
| 128 | A27 | 75c red & lemon | 13.00 | 9.50 |
| | | | 24.50 | 18.00 |
| | | Nos. 126-128 (3) | | |

Singapore shipping industry.

---

Plane over Docks of Singapore A21

**1969, July 20 Litho.** *Perf. 13x13½*
| | | | **Unwmk.** | |
|---|---|---|---|---|
| 99 | A20 | 25c emerald & black | 1.00 | .70 |
| 100 | A20 | 50c dark blue & black | 1.50 | 1.25 |

1960-69 building program of the Housing and Development Board.

"Homes for the People" A20

**1969, Apr. 15 Unwmk.** *Perf. 13*
| | | | | |
|---|---|---|---|---|
| 96 | A19 | 15c blue, black & silver | .50 | .25 |
| 97 | A19 | 30c red, black & silver | 1.10 | .65 |
| 98 | A19 | 75c violet, black & silver | 2.25 | 2.00 |
| | | | 3.85 | 2.90 |
| | | Nos. 96-98 (3) | | |

25th Plenary Session of the Economic Commission for Asia and the Far East (ECAFE), Singapore, Apr. 15-28.

Cogwheel and Emblem A19

**1969, Aug. 9** *Perf. 14x14½*
| | | | | |
|---|---|---|---|---|
| 101 | A21 | 15c yel, blk & org | .50 | |
| 102 | A21 | 30c brt blue & multi | 2.75 | 1.50 |
| 103 | A21 | 75c orange & multi | 6.00 | 1.75 |
| 104 | A21 | $1 red & black | 11.00 | 8.75 |
| 105 | A21 | $5 gray, blk & red | 40.00 | 47.50 |
| 106 | A21 | $10 emerald & blk | 52.50 | 50.00 |
| | | | 115.00 | 110.00 |
| a. | | Souv. sheet of 6, #101-106 | 600.00 | 600.00 |
| | | Nos. 101-106 (6) | | |

30c, UN emblem and map of Singapore. 75c, Flags and map of Malaya and Borneo. $1, Uplifted hands and Singapore flag. $5, Tail of Japanese plane and searchlights. $10, Statue of Sir Thomas Stamford Raffles.

**1973** *Perf. 13*
| | | | | |
|---|---|---|---|---|
| 86a | A18 | 5c yellow & multi | 7.75 | 9.00 |
| 88a | A18 | 10c blue green & multi | 14.00 | 7.25 |
| 90a | A18 | 20c brown & multi | 11.00 | 12.50 |
| 91a | A18 | 25c deep car & multi | 7.00 | 10.50 |
| 92a | A18 | 30c pink & multi | 12.00 | 14.50 |
| 93a | A18 | 50c brown org & multi | 13.00 | 22.50 |
| 95a | A18 | $1 olive green & multi | 21.00 | 18.00 |
| | | | 85.75 | 94.25 |
| | | Nos. 86a-95a (7) | | |

Mirudhangam, South Indian Drum — A22

Musical Instruments: 4c, Pi Pa, Chinese, 4 strings, vert. $2, Rebab, Malay violin, 3

---

dance. 75c, Tarian Kuda Kepang, Javanese dance. $1, Yao Chi, Chinese opera mask.

| | | | | |
|---|---|---|---|---|
| 86 | A18 | 5c yellow & multi | .65 | .20 |
| 87 | A18 | 6c orange & multi | 1.40 | .20 |
| 88 | A18 | 10c blue green & multi | | .30 |
| 89 | A18 | 15c lt brown & multi | .25 | |
| | | | .70 | .30 |
| a. | | Booklet pane of 4 ('69) | 42.50 | |
| 90 | A18 | 20c brown & multi | .75 | .30 |
| 91 | A18 | 25c dp car & multi | 1.25 | .50 |
| 92 | A18 | 30c pink & multi | .45 | .50 |
| 93 | A18 | 50c brown org & multi | 3.50 | 1.00 |
| 94 | A18 | 75c brt rose & multi | | 1.50 |
| 95 | A18 | $1 olive grn & multi | 4.50 | 2.00 |
| | | | 14.15 | 6.70 |
| | | Nos. 86-95 (10) | | |

Issue dates: 6c, 20c, 30c, 50c, 75c, Dec. 1; 5c, 10c, 15c, 25c, $1, Dec. 29.

ECAFE Emblem

## Flags of Commonwealth Nations — A28

Designs: 15c, Circular arrangement of names of Commonwealth members, 30c, Flags arranged in circle, $1, Flags (different arrangement).

**1971, Jan. 14**            **Perf. 15x14½**

**Size: 46½x31mm**

| | | | |
|---|---|---|---|
| 131 | A28 | 15c gold & multi | .75 .75 |
| 130 | A28 | 30c gold & multi | 1.75 1.75 |
| 132 | A28 | $1 gold & multi | 10.00 10.00 |
| | | Nos. 129-132 (4) | 4.25 4.25 |

Commonwealth Heads of Government Meeting, Singapore, Jan. 12-14.

## Cycle Rickshaws A29

**1971, Apr. 4       Unwmk.**

**Size: 67x31mm       Perf. 14**

| | | | |
|---|---|---|---|
| 133 | A29 | 15c shown | .80 .20 |
| 134 | A29 | 20c Sampans | 1.25 .55 |
| 135 | A29 | 30c Market place | 3.50 1.25 |

**Perf. 13x13½       Litho.**

| | | | |
|---|---|---|---|
| 136 | A30 | 50c Waterfront | 4.25 5.00 |
| 137 | A30 | 75c shown | 7.75 6.50 |
| | | Nos. 133-137 (5) | 17.55 13.50 |

Tourist publicity.

## Houses of Worship in Singapore — A30

Chinese New Year — A31

**1971, Aug. 9       Litho.       Perf. 14**

| | | | |
|---|---|---|---|
| 138 | A31 | 15c multicolored | 1.40 1.40 |
| 139 | A31 | 30c multicolored | 3.75 3.75 |
| 140 | A31 | 40c multicolored | 4.75 4.75 |
| 141 | A31 | 50c multicolored | 6.50 6.50 |
| a. | | Souvenir sheet of 4, #138- | |
| | | 141 | 120.00 120.00 |
| | | Nos. 138-141 (4) | 16.40 16.40 |

Singapore Festivals: 30c, Hari Raya Puasa (Moslem). 50c, Deepavali (Hindu). 75c, Christmas.

Satellite Earth Station, Sentosa Island—A32

---

## Views of Singapore, from 19th century art works: 15c, The Padang, 1851. 20c, Waterfront, 1848-1849. 35c, View from Fort Canning, 1846. 50c, View from Mount Wallich, 1857. $1, Waterfront with ships, from the sea, 1861.

**1971, Dec. 5   Unwmk.   Perf. 13x12½**

**Size: 52x45mm**

| | | | |
|---|---|---|---|
| 144 | A33 | 10c gold & multi | 3.00 .75 |
| 145 | A33 | 15c gold & multi | 4.25 4.25 |
| 146 | A33 | 20c gold & multi | 5.50 5.50 |
| 147 | A33 | 35c gold & multi | 11.00 11.00 |

**Perf. 12½x13**

**Size: 68x47mm**

| | | | |
|---|---|---|---|
| 148 | A33 | 50c gold & multi | 16.00 16.00 |
| 149 | A33 | $1 gold & multi | 20.00 20.00 |
| | | Nos. 144-149 (6) | 59.75 59.75 |

## George V 1c Copper Coin, 1920 A34

Singapore Coins: 35c, Silver dollar, 1969. $1, Gold $150, 1969 commemorative coin for sesquicentennial of founding of Singapore.

**1972, June 4              Litho.       Perf. 13½**

| | | | |
|---|---|---|---|
| 150 | A34 | 15c dk grn, dp org & blk | 1.75 1.75 |
| 151 | A34 | 35c red & black | 3.75 3.75 |
| 152 | A34 | $1 ultra, yellow & blk | 9.00 9.00 |
| | | Nos. 150-152 (3) | |

## "Moon Festival," by Seah Kim Joo — A35

Paintings by Singapore Artists: 35c, "Complimentary Force," by Thomas Yeo. 50c, "Rhythm in Blue," by Yusman Aman. $1, "Gibbons," by Chen Wen Hsi.

**1972, July 9              Litho.       Perf. 12½**

**Size: 40x43½mm**

| | | | |
|---|---|---|---|
| 153 | A35 | 15c brown org & multi | .65 .65 |
| 154 | A35 | 35c blue green & multi | 1.90 1.90 |
| 155 | A35 | 50c dull violet & multi | 2.75 2.75 |
| 156 | A35 | $1 bister & multi | 7.25 7.25 |
| | | Nos. 153-156 (4) | 12.55 12.55 |

---

## Singapore River and Fort Canning, 1843-1847 — A33

**1971, Oct. 23       Unwmk.       Perf. 13½**

| | | | |
|---|---|---|---|
| 142 | A32 | 15c red & multi | 6.50 1.50 |
| 143 | A32 | Block of 4 | 58.50 40.00 |
| a. | | 30c (yellow numeral) | 14.50 10.00 |
| b. | | 30c (green numeral) | 14.50 10.00 |
| c. | | 30c (rose numeral) | 14.50 10.00 |
| d. | | 30c (orange numeral) | 14.50 10.00 |

No. 143 as 15c, enlarged to cover 4 stamps.

Establishment of Singapore's satellite earth station, Sentosa Island.

## Chinese New Year — A36

Festivals: 35c, Hari Raya Puasa (candles and ornament). 50c, Deepavali (incense and teapot). 75c, Christmas (candle and stained glass window).

**1972, Aug. 9       Litho.       Perf. 13x12½**

| | | | |
|---|---|---|---|
| 157 | A36 | 15c deep rose & multi | .70 .70 |
| 158 | A36 | 35c violet & multi | 1.75 1.75 |
| 159 | A36 | 50c green & multi | 2.25 2.25 |
| 160 | A36 | 75c blue & multi | 3.50 3.50 |
| | | Nos. 157-160 (4) | 8.20 8.20 |

## Technical and Scientific Training — A37

Designs: 35c, Sport. $1, Art and culture.

**1972, Oct. 1       Photo.       Perf. 12**

| | | | |
|---|---|---|---|
| 161 | A37 | 15c orange & multi | 1.50 1.50 |
| 162 | A37 | 35c blue & multi | 2.75 2.75 |
| 163 | A37 | $1 orange & multi | 4.25 4.25 |
| | | Nos. 161-163 (3) | 8.50 8.50 |

Youth of Singapore.

## Neptune Ruby A38

**1972, Dec. 17       Litho.       Perf. 14x14½**

**Size: 42x28½mm**

| | | | |
|---|---|---|---|
| 164 | A38 | 15c shown | .65 .65 |

## Maria Rickmers A38

**Size: 29½x28½mm**

| | | | |
|---|---|---|---|
| 165 | A38 | 15c gold & multi | 4.50 4.50 |
| 166 | A38 | 75c gold & multi | 14.50 14.50 |
| a. | | Souvenir sheet of 3, #164-166 | 57.50 57.50 |
| | | Nos. 164-166 (3) | 19.65 19.65 |

Singapore shipping industry.

## Quality and Reliability Emblem — A39

15c, Emblem & initials of participating organizations: Singapore Institute of Standards & Industrial Research, Singapore Manufacturers' Association, Natl. Trades Union Congress. 75c, Emblem & "Prosperity through Quality & Reliability" in multiple rows. $1, Quality & Reliability emblem.

**1973, Feb. 25       Litho.       Perf. 14½x14**

| | | | |
|---|---|---|---|
| 167 | A39 | 15c gold & multi | .75 .75 |
| 168 | A39 | 30c gold & multi | 2.10 2.10 |
| 169 | A39 | 75c gold & multi | 2.40 2.40 |
| 170 | A39 | $1 gold & multi | 7.65 7.65 |
| | | Nos. 167-170 (4) | |

Prosperity through Quality and Reliability campaign.

---

## Airline Emblems A41

35c, Emblem of Singapore Airlines and intl. destinations. 75c, SIA emblem on stylized tail of Boeing jet. $1, SIA emblems circling globe.

**1973, Apr. 29       Perf. 12½**

| | | | |
|---|---|---|---|
| 171 | A40 | 15c vermilion & blk | 1.00 1.00 |
| 172 | A40 | 35c dull green & blk | 2.25 2.25 |
| 173 | A40 | 50c brown & blk | 3.00 3.00 |
| 174 | A40 | $1 dark violet & blk | 4.75 4.75 |
| | | Nos. 171-174 (4) | 11.00 11.00 |

Singapore Intl. Airport at Paya Lebar.

## Entertainers A42

Landmarks: 35c, Dancers. National Theater. 50c, City Hall and ballplayers. $1, Singapore River with boats and buildings.

**1973, June 24       Litho.       Perf. 13½**

| | | | |
|---|---|---|---|
| 175 | A41 | 10c multicolored | .70 .70 |
| 176 | A41 | 35c multicolored | 1.90 1.90 |
| 177 | A41 | 75c multicolored | 2.25 2.25 |
| 178 | A41 | $1 multicolored | 7.85 7.85 |
| | | Nos. 175-178 (4) | |

## Running, Judo, Boxing — A43

Composite of various forms of entertainment.

**1973, Aug. 9       Litho.       Perf. 13½x14**

| | | | |
|---|---|---|---|
| 179 | A42 | 10c black & orange | 2.00 2.00 |
| 180 | A42 | 35c black & orange red | 2.75 2.75 |
| 181 | A42 | 50c black & orange red | 2.75 2.75 |
| 182 | A42 | 75c black & orange | 3.00 3.00 |
| a. | | Block of 4, #179-182 | 12.75 12.75 |

National Day 1973.

## Birds, Jurong Bird Park — A40

Designs: 15c, Bicycling, weight lifting, pistol shoot, yachting. 25c, Various balls. 35c, Tennis racket, ball, hockey stick. 50c, Swimming. $1, Singapore National Stadium.

**1973, Sept. 1       Photo.       Perf. 14**

**Size: 25x25mm**

| | | | |
|---|---|---|---|
| 183 | A43 | 10c gold silver & ind | .65 .65 |
| 184 | A43 | 15c gold & dk brown | 2.10 2.10 |
| 185 | A43 | 25c silver, gold & blk | 1.90 1.90 |
| 186 | A43 | 35c gold, silver & dk pur | 3.50 3.50 |

**Size: 40½x25mm**

| | | | |
|---|---|---|---|
| 187 | A43 | 50c gold & multi | 2.50 2.50 |
| 188 | A43 | $1 sil, vio bl & emer | 4.25 4.25 |
| a. | | Souvenir sheet of 6, #183-188 | 45.00 45.00 |
| | | Nos. 183-188 (6) | 14.90 14.90 |

7th South East Asia (SEAP) Games, Singapore.

## Agave A44

## Mangosteen A45

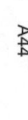

Designs: Stylized flowers and fruit.

## 1973 Photo. Perf. 13

| | | | | | |
|---|---|---|---|---|---|
| 189 | A44 | 1c | shown | .20 | .20 |
| 190 | A44 | 5c | Coleus blumei | .20 | .20 |
| a. | | | Booklet pane of 10 (4 #190, 4 #191 + 2 #193) | 15.00 | |
| 191 | A44 | 10c | Madagascar periwinkle | .20 | .20 |
| 192 | A44 | 15c | Sunflower | .20 | .20 |
| 193 | A44 | 20c | Dwarf palm | .50 | .20 |
| 194 | A44 | 25c | Yellow daisy | .55 | .40 |
| 195 | A44 | 35c | Chrysanthemum | .90 | .40 |
| 196 | A44 | 50c | Costus | 1.25 | .70 |
| 197 | A44 | $1 | shown | 1.75 | .20 |
| 198 | A45 | $1 | shown | 2.40 | .75 |
| 199 | A45 | $2 | Jackfruit | 5.00 | .75 |
| 200 | A45 | $5 | Coconuts | 12.50 | 5.50 |
| 201 | A45 | $10 | Pineapple | 24.00 | 11.50 |
| | | | Nos. 189-201 (13) | 49.65 | 20.45 |

Nos. 189-201 have fluorescent underprint "Singapore" in multiple rows.

Tiger and Orangutans — A46

Tropical Fish — A47

## 1973, Dec. 16 Litho. Perf. 13

| | | | | | |
|---|---|---|---|---|---|
| 202 | A46 | 5c | shown | .75 | .75 |
| 203 | A46 | 10c | Leopard and deer | .40 | .40 |
| 204 | A46 | 35c | Panther and stag | 5.50 | 5.50 |
| 205 | A46 | 75c | White horse & lion | 8.50 | 8.50 |
| | | | Nos. 202-205 (4) | 15.15 | 15.15 |

Opening of Singapore Zoo.

## 1974, Apr. 21 Litho. Perf. 13½x14

Designs: Various poecilia reticulata fish.

| | | | | | |
|---|---|---|---|---|---|
| 206 | A47 | 5c | apple green & multi | 1.00 | 1.00 |
| 207 | A47 | 10c | pink & multi | 1.00 | 1.00 |
| 208 | A47 | 35c | brt blue & multi | 3.50 | 3.50 |
| 209 | A47 | 75c | brt green & multi | 6.25 | 6.25 |
| | | | Nos. 206-209 (4) | 11.75 | 11.75 |

Scout Conference Emblem A48

## 1974, June 9 Perf. 13½x14½

| | | | | | |
|---|---|---|---|---|---|
| 210 | A48 | 10c | multicolored | 1.00 | 1.00 |
| 211 | A48 | 75c | multicolored | 2.00 | 2.00 |
| | | | Nos. 210-211 | | |

9th Asia-Pacific Boy Scout Conf., Singapore.

UPU Emblem, Circle and "Centenary" Multiple — A49

UPU, cent.: 35c, Circle and UN emblems, multiple. 75c, Circle and pigeons, multiple.

## 1974, July 7 Litho. Perf. 14½x13½

| | | | | | |
|---|---|---|---|---|---|
| 212 | A49 | 10c | orange brn & multi | .20 | .20 |
| 213 | A49 | 35c | blue & multi | .60 | .60 |
| 214 | A49 | 75c | emerald & multi | 1.40 | 1.40 |
| | | | Nos. 212-214 (3) | 2.20 | 2.20 |

Family — A50

## 1974, Aug. 9 Litho. Perf. 13x13½

| | | | | | |
|---|---|---|---|---|---|
| 215 | A50 | 10c | shown | .30 | .30 |
| 216 | A50 | 35c | Symbols for male & female | 1.00 | 1.00 |

---

| | | | | | |
|---|---|---|---|---|---|
| 217 | A50 | 75c | World map and WPY emblem | 2.25 | 2.25 |
| | | | | 3.55 | 3.55 |
| | | | Nos. 215-217 (3) | | |

Natl. Day and World Population Year 1974.

"Sun and Tree" — A51

Children's Drawings: 10c, "My Daddy and Mommy." 35c, "A Dump Truck." 50c, "My Aunt."

## 1974, Oct. 1 Photo. Perf. 14x13½

| | | | | | |
|---|---|---|---|---|---|
| 218 | A51 | 5c | multicolored | .40 | .40 |
| 219 | A51 | 10c | multicolored | .40 | .40 |
| 220 | A51 | 35c | multicolored | 2.40 | 2.40 |
| 221 | A51 | 50c | multicolored | 2.50 | 2.50 |
| a. | | | Souv. sheet, #218-221, perf 13 | 27.50 | 27.50 |
| | | | Nos. 218-221 (4) | 5.70 | 5.70 |

Children's drawings for Children's Day (UNICEF).

Alfresco Dining A52

Tourist publicity: 20c, Singapore River. $1, "Kelong" fish traps.

## 1975, Jan. 26 Litho. Perf. 14

| | | | | | |
|---|---|---|---|---|---|
| 222 | A52 | 15c | multicolored | .90 | .90 |
| 223 | A52 | 20c | multicolored | 1.75 | 1.75 |
| 224 | A52 | $1 | multicolored | 5.75 | 5.75 |
| | | | Nos. 222-224 (3) | 8.40 | 8.40 |

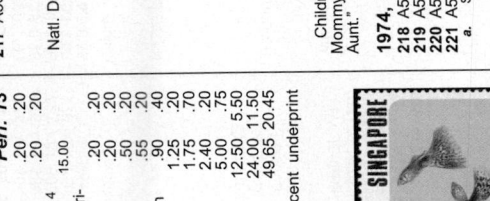

Prows of Barges and Wave Design A53

25c, Cargo ships & ship's wheel. 50c, Tanker & signal flags. $1, Container ship & propellers.

## 1975, Mar. 10 Litho. Perf. 13½

| | | | | | |
|---|---|---|---|---|---|
| 225 | A53 | 10c | multicolored | .25 | .25 |
| 226 | A53 | 25c | multicolored | 2.10 | 2.10 |
| 227 | A53 | 50c | multicolored | 2.75 | 2.75 |
| 228 | A53 | $1 | multicolored | 4.00 | 4.00 |
| | | | Nos. 225-228 (4) | 9.10 | 9.10 |

9th Biennial Conf. of the Intl. Assoc. of Ports and Harbors, Singapore, Mar. 8-15.

Satellite Earth Stations, Sentosa Island — A54

Oil Refinery — A55

Science and Industry: 75c, Brain surgery, Medical Center, Jurong.

## 1975, June 29 Photo. Perf. 13½

| | | | | | |
|---|---|---|---|---|---|
| 229 | A54 | 10c | multicolored | .25 | .25 |
| 230 | A55 | 35c | multicolored | 2.50 | 2.50 |
| 231 | A54 | 75c | multicolored | 2.75 | 2.75 |
| | | | Nos. 229-231 (3) | 5.50 | 5.50 |

---

Crowned Cranes — A57

"10" and "Homes and Gardens for the People" — A56

Tenth Natl. Day ("10" and): 35c, "Shipping and ship building." 75c, "Communications and technology." $1, "Trade, commerce and industry."

## 1975, Aug. 9 Litho. Perf. 13½

| | | | | | |
|---|---|---|---|---|---|
| 232 | A56 | 10c | multicolored | .35 | .35 |
| 233 | A56 | 35c | multicolored | .90 | .90 |
| 234 | A56 | 75c | multicolored | 2.25 | 2.50 |
| 235 | A56 | $1 | multicolored | 6.00 | 6.00 |
| | | | Nos. 232-235 (4) | 2.50 | 2.50 |

## 1975, Oct. 5 Litho. Perf. 14½x13½

Birds: 10c, Great hornbill. 35c, White-breasted and white-collared kingfishers. $1, Sulphur-crested cockatoo and blue and yellow macaw.

| | | | | | |
|---|---|---|---|---|---|
| 236 | A57 | 5c | emerald & multi | 2.00 | 2.00 |
| 237 | A57 | 10c | emerald & multi | 2.00 | 2.00 |
| 238 | A57 | 35c | emerald & multi | 10.50 | 10.50 |
| 239 | A57 | $1 | emerald & multi | 16.00 | 16.00 |
| | | | Nos. 236-239 (4) | 30.50 | 30.50 |

IWY Emblem, Peace Dove as "Equality" — A58

IWY Emblem: 35c, Peace dove with eggs in basket, symbolizing "Development." 75c, Peace dove & young, symbolizing "Peace."

## 1975, Dec. 7 Litho. Perf. 13½

| | | | | | |
|---|---|---|---|---|---|
| 240 | A58 | 10c | blk, blue & pink | .20 | .20 |
| 241 | A58 | 35c | orange & multi | 2.25 | 2.25 |
| 242 | A58 | 75c | dp violet & multi | 2.75 | 2.75 |
| a. | | | Souvenir sheet of 3, #240-242 | 20.00 | 20.00 |
| | | | Nos. 240-242 (3) | 5.20 | 5.20 |

International Women's Year 1975.

Aranda Hybrid — A60

Yellow Flame — A59

Wayside Trees: 35c, Cabbage tree. 50c, Rose of India. 75c, Variegated coral tree.

## 1976, Apr. 18 Litho. Perf. 14

| | | | | | |
|---|---|---|---|---|---|
| 243 | A59 | 10c | multicolored | .60 | .60 |
| 244 | A59 | 35c | multicolored | 1.75 | 1.75 |
| 245 | A59 | 50c | multicolored | 2.75 | 2.75 |
| 246 | A59 | 75c | multicolored | 5.00 | 5.00 |
| | | | Nos. 243-246 (4) | 10.10 | 10.10 |

## 1976, June 20 Litho. Perf. 14

Designs: Varieties of aranda orchids.

| | | | | | |
|---|---|---|---|---|---|
| 247 | A60 | 10c | black & multi | 1.50 | 1.50 |
| 248 | A60 | 35c | black & multi | 4.50 | 4.50 |
| 249 | A60 | 50c | black & multi | 5.50 | 5.50 |
| 250 | A60 | 75c | black & multi | 6.50 | 6.50 |
| | | | Nos. 247-250 (4) | 18.00 | 18.00 |

"10" and Children's Band A61

---

35c, Running boys. 75c, Dancing children.

## 1976, Aug. 9 Litho. Perf. 12½

| | | | | | |
|---|---|---|---|---|---|
| 251 | A61 | 10c | multicolored | .25 | .25 |
| 252 | A61 | 35c | multicolored | 1.50 | 1.50 |
| 253 | A61 | 75c | multicolored | 1.75 | 1.75 |
| | | | Nos. 251-253 (3) | 3.50 | 3.50 |

Singapore Youth Festival, 10th anniversary.

Queen Elizabeth Walk — A62

Paintings of Old Singapore, c. 1905-10: 50c, The Padang. $1, Raffles Place.

## 1976, Nov. 14 Litho.

| | | | | | |
|---|---|---|---|---|---|
| 254 | A62 | 10c | multicolored | .75 | .75 |
| 255 | A62 | 50c | multicolored | 2.75 | 2.75 |
| 256 | A62 | $1 | multicolored | 5.50 | 5.50 |
| a. | | | Souvenir sheet of 3, #254-256, perf 13½ | 25.00 | 25.00 |
| | | | Nos. 254-256 (3) | 9.00 | 9.00 |

Chinese Bridal Costume — A63

Radar, Surface to Air Missile, Soldiers — A64

Designs: 35c, Indian bridal costume. 75c, Malay bridal costume.

## 1976, Dec. 19 Litho. Perf. 14½

| | | | | | |
|---|---|---|---|---|---|
| 257 | A63 | 10c | lt green & multi | .55 | .55 |
| 258 | A63 | 35c | lilac & multi | 1.90 | 1.90 |
| 259 | A63 | 75c | yellow & multi | 4.00 | 4.00 |
| | | | Nos. 257-259 (3) | 6.45 | 6.45 |

## 1977, Mar. 12 Litho. Perf. 14½

| | | | | | |
|---|---|---|---|---|---|
| 260 | A64 | 10c | multicolored | .75 | .75 |
| 261 | A64 | 50c | multicolored | 3.00 | 3.00 |
| 262 | A64 | 75c | multicolored | 4.25 | 4.25 |
| | | | Nos. 260-262 (3) | 8.00 | 8.00 |

50c, Infantry soldiers and tank. 75c, Jet fighter, pilot, telecommunications center.

National Service, 10th anniversary.

---

Lyrate Cockle A65

Spotted Hermit Crab A66

Sea Shells: 5c, Folded scallop. 10c, Marble cone. 15c, Scorpion conch. 20c, Amplustre bubble. 25c, Spiral Babylon. 35c, Regal thorny oyster. 50c, Winged frog shell. 75c, Troschel's murex.

Marine Life: $2, Stingray. $5, Cuttlefish. $10, Lionfish.

## 1977

| | | | | | |
|---|---|---|---|---|---|
| 263 | A65 | 1c | orange & multi | 1.00 | 1.50 |
| 264 | A65 | 1c | orange & multi | .20 | .20 |
| a. | | | Bklt. pane, 4 #264, 8 #265 | 14.00 | |
| 265 | A65 | 10c | orange & multi | .20 | .20 |
| 266 | A65 | 15c | orange & multi | 1.00 | .20 |
| 267 | A65 | 20c | orange & multi | 1.00 | .25 |
| 268 | A65 | 25c | orange & multi | 1.25 | 2.00 |
| 269 | A65 | 35c | orange & multi | 1.50 | .25 |
| 270 | A65 | 50c | orange & multi | 2.00 | 1.25 |
| 271 | A65 | 75c | orange & multi | 3.00 | .90 |

Symbols of Life Sciences — A71

**Perf. 14**
272 A66 $1 multicolored 2.50 .25
273 A66 $2 multicolored 2.50 .65
274 A66 $5 multicolored 6.50 2.00
275 A66 $10 multicolored 26.15 13.65
Nos. 263-275 (13)

No. 264a has a large inscribed selvage, the size of 6 stamps. Issued: #263-271, Apr. 9; others, June 4.

Singapore Harbor Improvements A67

**1977, May 1    Litho.    Perf. 13x12½**
Labor Day: 50c, Construction workers. 75c, Road workers.
276 A67 10c multicolored .40 .40
277 A67 50c multicolored 1.50 1.50
278 A67 75c multicolored 2.25 2.25
Nos. 276-278 (3) 4.15 4.15

"Key to Savings" — A68

**1977, July 16    Litho.    Perf. 13, 14**
Designs: 35c, "On-line Banking Service." 75c, "GIRO Service."
279 A68 10c multicolored .20 .20
280 A68 35c multicolored .90 .90
281 A68 75c multicolored 2.50 2.50
Nos. 279-281 (3) 3.60 3.60

Centenary of Post Office Savings Bank.

Grain and Cattle — A69

**1977, Aug. 8    Litho.    Perf. 14**
282 A69 10c multicolored .40 .40
283 A69 35c multicolored .95 .95
284 A69 75c multicolored 3.85 3.85
Nos. 282-284 (3)

Association of South East Asian Nations (ASEAN), 10th anniversary. Flags of founding members: Thailand, Indonesia, Singapore, Malaysia, Philippines. 75c, Steel, oil & chemical industries.

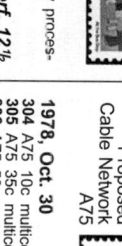

Bus Stop — A70

**1977, Oct. 1**
Children's Drawings: 10c, Chingay procession, veil. 75c, Playground.
285 A70 10c multicolored .35 .20
286 A70 35c multicolored 1.00 .65
287 A70 75c multicolored 3.25 1.50
a. Souvenir sheet of 3, #285-287 17.50 17.50
Nos. 285-287 (3) 4.60 2.35

Botanical Gardens — A72

**1977, Dec. 10    Litho.    Perf. 14½x14**
Singapore Science Center: 35c, "Physical sciences." 75c, "Science and technology." $1, Science Center.
288 A71 10c multicolored .20 .20
289 A71 35c multicolored .55 .55
290 A71 75c multicolored 1.25 1.20
291 A71 $1 multicolored 2.10 2.10
Nos. 288-291 (4) 4.10 4.10

**1978, Apr. 22    Litho.    Perf. 14½**
Singapore Parks and Gardens: 10c, Jurong Bird Park. 35c, East Coast Lagoon and Park.
292 A72 10c multicolored .20 .20
293 A72 35c multicolored 1.20 1.20
294 A72 75c multicolored 1.75 1.75
Nos. 292-294 (3) 2.75 2.75

Red-whiskered Bulbul — A73

**1978, July 1    Litho.    Perf. 13½**
Songbirds: 35c, White eyes, White-rumped shama. 75c, White-crested laughing thrush.
295 A73 10c multicolored .75 .75
296 A73 35c multicolored 2.10 2.10
297 A73 50c multicolored 2.25 2.25
298 A73 75c multicolored 2.75 2.75
Nos. 295-298 (4) 7.85 7.85

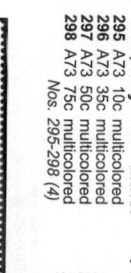

Thian Hock Keng Temple — A74

**1978, Aug. 9**
National Monuments: No. 303a, like No. 299. Nos. 300, 303b, Hajjah Fatimah Mosque. Nos. 301, 303c, Armenian Church. Nos. 302, 303d, Sri Mariamman Temple.
299 A74 10c tan & multi .60 .60
300 A74 10c green & multi .60 .60
301 A74 10c blue & multi .60 .60
302 A74 10c lilac & multi .60 .60

**Souvenir Sheet**
303 Sheet of 4 7.00 7.00
a. A74 10c tan & multi 1.10
b. A74 10c green & multi 1.10
c. A74 10c blue & multi 1.10
d. A74 10c lilac & multi 1.10
Nos. 299-302 (4) 2.40 2.40

Map of Proposed Cable Network A75

**1978, Oct. 30    Litho.    Perf. 14**
ASEAN Submarine Cable Network. Nos. 304-307 printed in sheets of 100. Stamps have perforations around design and around edges. See No. 429a.
304 A75 10c multicolored .20 .20
305 A75 35c multicolored .80 .80
306 A75 50c multicolored 1.10 1.10
307 A75 75c multicolored 1.90 1.90
Nos. 304-307 (4) 4.00 4.00

Neptune Spinel — A76

Neptune Orient Shipping Lines, 10th anniv.

**1978, Nov. 18    Litho.    Perf. 13½x14**
Ships: 35c, Neptune Aries. 50c, Arno Temasek. 75c, Neptune Pearl.
308 A76 10c multicolored .90 .90
309 A76 35c multicolored 2.25 2.25
310 A76 50c multicolored 2.40 2.40
311 A76 75c multicolored 3.00 3.00
Nos. 308-311 (4) 8.55 8.55

Concorde A77

**1978, Dec. 16    Litho.    Perf. 13½**
Aviation Development: 35c, Vickers-Vimy, 1st aircraft to land in Singapore. 50c, Boeing 747B. 75c, Wright Brothers Flyer I.
312 A77 10c yellow green & blk 1.40 1.40
313 A77 35c blue & black 1.40 1.40
314 A77 50c carmine & black 2.00 2.00
315 A77 75c brown & black 2.25 2.25
Nos. 312-315 (4) 7.05 7.05

75th anniversary of 1st powered flight.

Distance Marker in Kilometers — A78

**1979, Jan. 24    Litho.    Perf. 13x13½**
Designs: 35c, Tape measure in centimeters. 75c, Scales in grams and kilograms.
316 A78 10c multicolored .25 .25
317 A78 35c multicolored .50 .50
318 A78 75c multicolored 1.75 1.75
Nos. 316-318 (3) 2.40 2.40

Introduction of metric system.

Vanda Orchids — A79

**1979, Apr. 14    Litho.    Perf. 14½x14, 14x14½**
Varieties of vanda hybrids: 10c, 35c, horiz.
319 A79 10c multicolored .20 .20
320 A79 35c multicolored .70 .70
321 A79 50c multicolored 1.10 1.10
322 A79 75c multicolored 1.40 1.40
Nos. 319-322 (4) 3.40 3.40

Envelope Addressed to Postmaster A80

**1979, July 1    Litho.    Perf. 12½x13**
50c, Envelope addressed to Philatelic Bureau.
323 A80 10c orange & multi .20 .20
324 A80 50c dark blue & multi .80 .80

Singapore's postal code system.

Old Phone, Telephone Lines — A81

Designs: 35c, Dial, world map. 50c, Push-button phone, skyline. 75c, Line network.

**1979, Oct. 5    Litho.    Perf. 13½**
325 A81 10c multicolored .20 .20
326 A81 35c multicolored .30 .30
327 A81 50c multicolored .45 .45
328 A81 75c multicolored .65 .65
Nos. 325-328 (4) 1.60 1.60

Telephone service centenary.

IYC Emblem, Lanterns Festival A82

**1979, Nov. 10    Litho.    Perf. 13**
IYC Emblem, Children's Drawings: 35c, Singapore Harbor. 50c, "Use Your Hands." 75c, Soccer.
329 A82 10c multicolored .20 .20
330 A82 35c multicolored .35 .35
331 A82 50c multicolored .35 .35
332 A82 75c multicolored .55 .55
a. Souvenir sheet of 4, #329-332 6.75 6.75
Nos. 329-332 (4) 1.35 1.35

International Year of the Child.

Botanic Gardens, 120th Anniversary — A83

**1979, Dec. 15    Litho.    Perf. 13½**
333 A83 10c shown .20 .20
334 A83 50c Gazebo .85 .85
335 A83 $1 Greenhouse 1.75 1.75
Nos. 333-335 (3) 2.80 2.80

Hainan Junk — A84

**1980    Litho.    Perf. 14**
336 A84 1c shown .20 .20
337 A84 5c Clipper .20 .20
338 A84 10c Fujian junk .20 .20
a. Booklet pane of 10 1.00
339 A84 15c Golekkan .20 .20
340 A84 20c Palari .20 .20
341 A84 25c East Indiaman .20 .20
342 A84 35c Galleon .35 .35
343 A84 50c Caravel .55 .55
344 A84 75c Jiangsu trader .80 .80

**Size: 41½x24½mm**
345 A84 $1 Coaster 1.10 .30
346 A84 $2 Oil tanker 2.10 .50
347 A84 $5 Screw steamer 5.50 1.50
348 A84 $10 Paddle wheel steamer 11.00 5.00
22.60 9.20
Nos. 336-348 (13)

Issued: #336-344, Apr. 26; others, Apr. 5.

Straits Settlements No. 1, Old Singapore Map, London 1980 Emblem — A85

London 1980 Emblem and: 35c, Straits Settlements No. 146, letter. $1, Singapore No. 19, map of Straits. $2, Singapore No. 106, letter, 1819.

# SINGAPORE

**1980, May 6    Litho.    Perf. 13**
349 A85 10c multicolored    .20 .20
350 A85 35c multicolored    .35 .35
351 A85 $1 multicolored    .70 .70
352 A85 $2 multicolored    1.25 1.25
 a. Souvenir sheet of 4, #349-352    3.50 3.50
Nos. 349-352 (4)    2.50 2.50

London 1980 Intl. Stamp Exhib., May 6-14.

Fund Board Emblem, Keys to Retirement — A86

**1980, July 1    Litho.    Perf. 13**
353 A86 10c shown    .20 .20
354 A86 50c Home ownership savings    .35 .35
355 A86 $1 Old age savings    .70 .70
Nos. 353-355 (3)    1.25 1.25

Central Provident Fund Board, 25th anniv.

Map Showing Singapore-Indonesia Cable Route — A87

**1980, Aug. 8    Litho.    Perf. 14**
356 A87 10c multicolored    .20 .20
357 A87 35c multicolored    .80 .80
358 A87 50c multicolored    1.10 1.10
359 A87 75c multicolored    1.75 1.75
Nos. 356-359 (4)    3.85 3.85

ASEAN Submarine Cable Network extension. Stamps perforated around design and around edges. See No. 429a.

Fair Emblem A88

**1980, Oct. 3    Litho.    Perf. 13**
360 A88 10c multicolored    .20 .20
361 A88 35c multicolored    .40 .40
362 A88 75c multicolored    .90 .90
Nos. 360-362 (3)    1.50 1.50

Asean Trade Fair, Oct. 3-12.

**1980, Nov. 2    Litho.    Perf. 13½**
363 A89 10c Flame of the wood    .20 .20
364 A89 35c Golden trumpet    .40 .40
365 A89 50c Sky vine    .50 .50
366 A89 75c Bougainvillea    .80 .80
Nos. 363-366 (4)    1.90 1.90

**1981, Jan. 24    Litho.    Perf. 14x14½**
367 A90 10c multicolored    .20 .20
368 A90 35c multicolored    .30 .30
369 A90 $1 multicolored    .60 .60
Nos. 367-369 (3)    1.10 1.10

Monetary Authority of Singapore, 10th anniv.

No. 54 Surcharged

**Perf. 13½x14½    Photo.    Wmk. 314**
**1981, Mar. 5**
370 A8 10c on 4c red org & blk    .30 .30

**1981, Apr. 11    Unwmk.    Litho.    Perf. 13**
371 A91 10c Technical Training (Woodworking)    .20 .20
372 A91 35c Building construction    .30 .30
373 A91 50c Electronics    .45 .45
374 A91 75c Precision machinery    .55 .55
Nos. 371-374 (4)    1.50 1.50

**1981, Aug. 25    Litho.    Perf. 14**
375 A92 10c multicolored    .45 .45
376 A92 35c multicolored    3.00 3.00
377 A92 $1 multicolored    3.50 3.50
Nos. 375-377 (3)    6.95 6.95

Sports For All: Various sports.

**1981, Nov. 24    Litho.    Perf. 14½**
378 A93 10c Man in wheelchair    .20 .20
379 A93 35c Group    .40 .40
380 A93 50c Teacher, student    .60 .60
381 A93 75c Blind communications worker    .80 .80
Nos. 378-381 (4)    2.00 2.00

Intl. Year of the Disabled.

**1981, Dec. 29    Litho.    Perf. 14x13½**
382 A94 10c multicolored    .20 .20
383 A94 35c multicolored    .30 .30
384 A94 50c multicolored    .45 .45
385 A94 75c multicolored    .60 .60
386 A94 $1 multicolored    .70 .70
 a. Souvenir sheet of 5, #382-386    4.25 4.25
Nos. 382-386 (5)    2.25 2.25

Changi airport opening.

**1982, Mar. 3    Litho.    Perf. 14x14½**
387 A95 10c Clipper    .50 .50
388 A95 50c Blue grassy tiger    1.50 1.50
389 A95 $1 Raja Brooke's birdwing    2.00 2.00
Nos. 387-389 (3)    4.00 4.00

**1982, June 14    Litho.    Perf. 14**
390 A96 10c multicolored    .20 .20
391 A96 35c multicolored    .60 .60
392 A96 50c multicolored    .75 .75
393 A96 75c multicolored    1.00 1.00
Nos. 390-393 (4)    2.55 2.55

15th ASEAN Ministerial meeting.

**1982, July 9    Litho.    Perf. 12**
394 A97 10c multicolored    .20 .20
395 A97 75c multicolored    1.10 1.10
396 A97 $1 multicolored    1.90 1.90
Nos. 394-396 (3)    3.20 3.20

1982 World Cup.

Sultan Shoal Lighthouse, 1896 — A98

**1982, Aug. 7**
397 A98 10c shown    .60 .60
398 A98 75c Horsburgh, 1851    1.90 1.90
399 A98 $1 Raffles, 1855    2.25 2.25
 a. Souvenir sheet of 3, #397-399    5.00 5.00
Nos. 397-399 (3)    4.75 4.75

10th Anniv. of PSA Container Terminal A99

**1982, Sept. 15    Litho.    Perf. 13½**
400 A99 10c Yard gantry cranes    .20 .20
401 A99 35c Computer    .45 .45
402 A99 50c Freightlifter    .60 .60
403 A99 75c Straddle carrier    .95 .95
Nos. 400-403 (4)    2.20 2.20

Scouting Year — A100

**1982, Oct. 15    Litho.    Perf. 14x13½**
404 A100 10c Color guard    .20 .20
405 A100 35c Hiking    .65 .65
406 A100 50c Building tower    .90 .90
407 A100 75c Kayaking    1.40 1.40
Nos. 404-407 (4)    3.15 3.15

Productivity Movement A101

**1982, Nov. 17    Perf. 13½**
408 A101 10c Text    .20 .20
409 A101 35c Housing    .45 .45
410 A101 50c Quality control meeting    .65 .65
411 A101 75c Participation    1.00 1.00
Nos. 408-411 (4)    2.30 2.30

Commonwealth Day — A102

**1983, May 14    Litho.**
412 A102 10c multicolored    .20 .20
413 A102 35c multicolored    .40 .40
414 A102 50c multicolored    .75 .75
415 A102 $1 multicolored    1.00 1.00
Nos. 412-415 (4)    2.35 2.35

12th Southeast Asia Games — A103

**Perf. 13½x13**

**1983, May 28    Litho.**
416 A103 10c Soccer    .20 .20
417 A103 35c Racket games    .40 .40
418 A103 75c Athletics    .90 .90
419 A103 $1 Swimming    1.25 1.25
Nos. 416-419 (4)    2.75 2.75

Neighborhood Watch Safety Campaign A104

**Perf. 14x13½**

**1983, June 24    Perf. 14    Litho.**
420 A104 10c Family    .20 .20
421 A104 35c Children    .75 .75
422 A104 75c Community    1.75 1.75
Nos. 420-422 (3)    2.70 2.70

BANGKOK '83 Intl. Stamp Show. Aug. 4-13 — A105

**1983, Aug. 4    Litho.    Perf. 14x14½**
423 A105 10c multicolored    .20 .20
424 A105 35c multicolored    .65 .65
425 A105 $1 multicolored    2.00 2.00
 a. Souvenir sheet of 3, #423-425    4.25 4.25
Nos. 423-425 (3)    2.85 2.85

10c, #282-284, statue of King Chulalongkorn (1868-1910). 35c, #304-307, map of southeast Asia. $1, #390-393, Declaration of ASEAN (Assoc. of South East Asian Nations) signatures, 1976.

ASEAN Submarine Cable Network A106

**1983, Sept. 27 Litho. *Perf. 14***
**426** A106 10c multicolored .30 .30
**427** A106 35c multicolored 1.00 1.00
**428** A106 50c multicolored 1.40 1.40
**429** A106 75c multicolored 2.10 2.10
*a.* Souv. sheet of 6, #304, 359, 426-429 7.25 7.25
*Nos. 426-429 (4)* 4.80 4.80

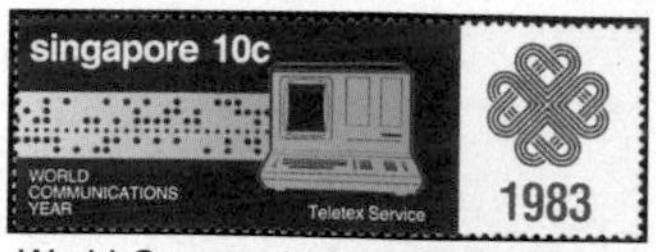

World Communications Year — A107

**1983, Nov. 10 Litho. *Perf. 13***
**430** A107 10c Telex service .30 .30
**431** A107 35c Telephone numbering plan .75 .75
**432** A107 75c Satellite transmission 1.60 1.60
**433** A107 $1 Sea communications 2.25 2.25
*Nos. 430-433 (4)* 4.90 4.90

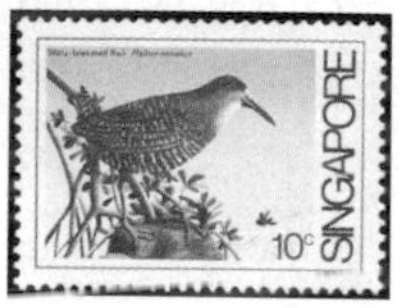

Coastal Birds — A108

***Perf. 14½x13½***
**1984, Mar. 15 Litho.**
**434** A108 10c Slaty-breasted rail .25 .25
**435** A108 35c Black bittern 1.50 1.50
**436** A108 50c Brahminy kite 2.25 2.25
**437** A108 75c Common moorhens 3.25 3.25
*Nos. 434-437 (4)* 7.25 7.25

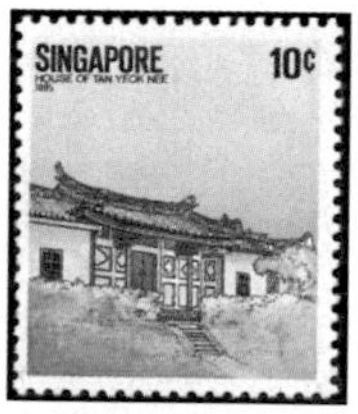

Natl. Monuments A109

10c, House of Tan Yeok Nee (merchant), 1885. 35c, Thong Chai Building (former hospital), 1892. 50c, Telok Ayer Market, 1894. $1, Nagore Durgha Muslim Shrine, 1828.

**1984, June 7 Litho. *Perf. 12***
**438** A109 10c multicolored .20 .20
**439** A109 35c multicolored .60 .60
**440** A109 50c multicolored .90 .90
**441** A109 $1 multicolored 1.90 1.90
*Nos. 438-441 (4)* 3.60 3.60

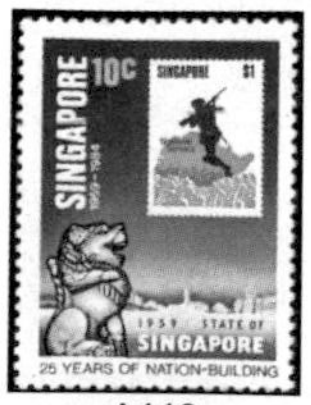

A110

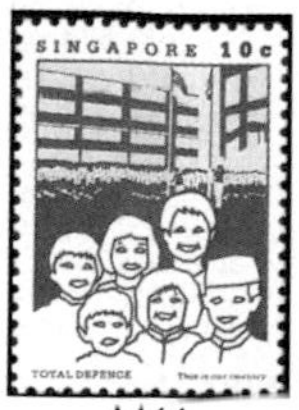

A111

**1984, Aug. 9 Litho. *Perf. 14***
**442** A110 10c No. 121 .20 .20
**443** A110 35c No. 377 .55 .55
**444** A110 50c No. 99 .75 .75
**445** A110 75c No. 243 1.10 1.10
**446** A110 $1 No. 386 1.50 1.50
**447** A110 $2 No. 367 3.00 3.00
*a.* Souvenir sheet of 6, #442-447 10.00 10.00
*Nos. 442-447 (6)* 7.10 7.10

25th anniv. of self-government.

**1984, Oct. 26 Litho. *Perf. 12***

Total Defense: a, This is our country. b, We are one. c, We work together. d, We are prepared. e, We are ready.

**448** Strip of 5 1.00 1.00
*a.-e.* A111 10c any single .20 .20

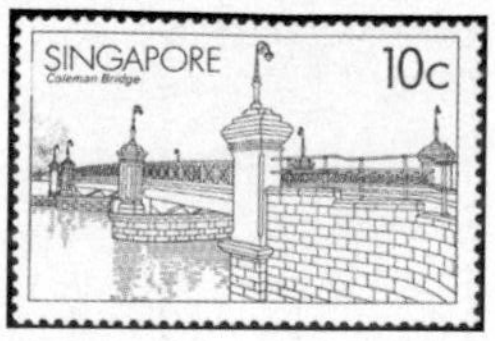

Bridges A112

**1985, Mar. 15 Engr. *Perf. 14½x14***
**449** A112 10c Coleman .20 .20
**450** A112 35c Cavenagh .50 .50
**451** A112 75c Elgin 1.25 1.25
**452** A112 $1 Benjamin Sheares 1.75 1.75
*Nos. 449-452 (4)* 3.70 3.70

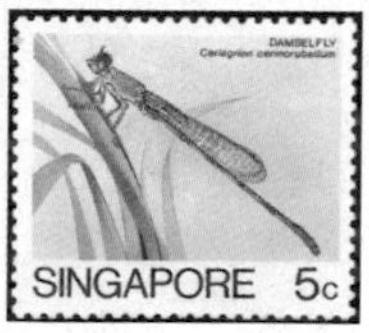

Insects — A113

**1985 Litho. *Perf. 13x13½***
**453** A113 5c Ceriagrion cerinorubellum .20 .20
**454** A113 10c Apis javana .20 .20
**455** A113 15c Delta arcuata .20 .20
**456** A113 20c Xylocopa caerulea .20 .20
**457** A113 25c Donacia javana .25 .25
**458** A113 35c Heteroneda reticulata .50 .50
**459** A113 50c Catacanthus nigripes .75 .75
**460** A113 75c Chremistica pontianaka 1.10 1.10

**Litho. & Engr.**
**Size: 35x30mm**

**461** A113 $1 Homoeoxipha lycoides 1.50 1.50
**462** A113 $2 Traulia azureipennis 3.00 3.00
**463** A113 $5 Trithemis aurora 7.25 7.25
**464** A113 $10 Scambophyllum sangiunolentum 15.00 15.00
*Nos. 453-464 (12)* 30.15 30.15

Issued: #453-460, 4/24; #461-464, 6/5.

Redrawn

**1986 *Perf. 13x13½***
*453a* A113 5c 5.50 5.50
*454a* A113 10c 10.50 10.50
*455a* A113 15c 16.00 16.00
*456a* A113 20c 22.50 22.50
*457a* A113 25c 27.50 27.50
*458a* A113 35c 37.50 37.50
*459a* A113 50c 57.50 57.50
*460a* A113 75c 82.50 82.50
*Nos. 453a-460a (8)* 259.50 259.50

Singapore is 20½mm long on Nos. 453a-454a; 21mm long on Nos. 453-454. Rock is 1½mm from bottom right on No. 455; 2½mm on No. 455a. Pink flower touches frame on No. 456; is clear of the frame on No. 456a. Feelers indistinct and left one touches frame on No. 457; feelers sharp and left one ends just below frame on No. 457a.

Vein of leaf at lower left stops short of frame on No. 458; vein touches frame on No. 458a. Leaf at top touches frame on No. 459; leaf is below frame on No. 459a. Wing ends 1½mm above frame on No. 460; wing touches frame at bottom on No. 460a.

Other differences exist in the position and sharpness of the design and colors.

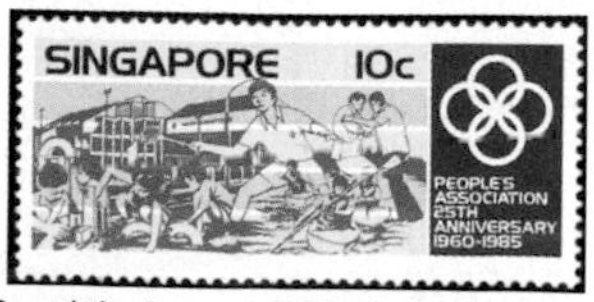

People's Assoc., 25th Anniv. — A114

Montage of public services.

**1985, July 1 *Perf. 13½x14***
**465** A114 10c multicolored .20 .20
**466** A114 35c multicolored .50 .50
**467** A114 50c multicolored .85 .85
**468** A114 75c multicolored 1.10 1.10
*Nos. 465-468 (4)* 2.65 2.65

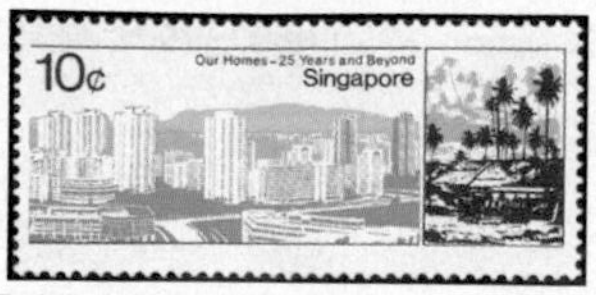

Public Housing, 25th Anniv. — A115

Modern housing developments.

**1985, Aug. 9**
**469** A115 10c multicolored .20 .20
**470** A115 35c multicolored .50 .50
**471** A115 50c multicolored .65 .65
**472** A115 75c multicolored 1.00 1.00
*a.* Souv. sheet of 4, #469-472 5.75 5.75
*Nos. 469-472 (4)* 2.35 2.35

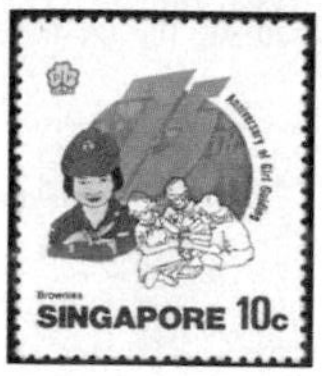

Girl Guides, 75th Anniv. — A116

Activities.

**1985, Nov 6 *Perf. 14½x14***
**473** A116 10c Brownies .20 .20
**474** A116 35c Guides .45 .45
**475** A116 50c Seniors .65 .65
**476** A116 75c Guide leaders 1.10 1.10
*Nos. 473-476 (4)* 2.40 2.40

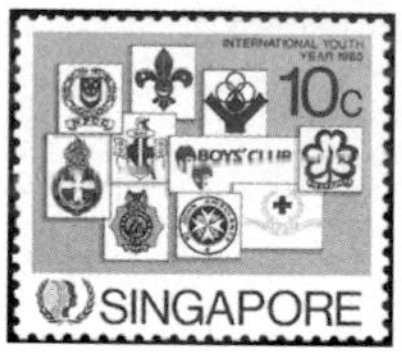

Intl. Youth Year — A117

**1985, Dec. 18 *Perf. 13***
**477** A117 10c Youth assoc. emblems .20 .20
**478** A117 75c Hand, sapling 1.25 1.25
**479** A117 $1 Dove, stick figures 1.60 1.60
*Nos. 477-479 (3)* 3.05 3.05

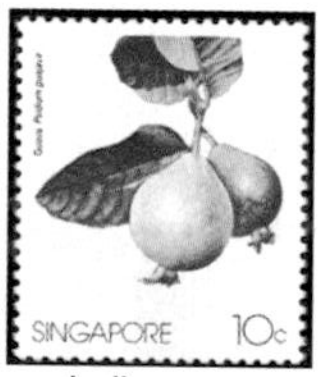

Indigenous Fruit — A118

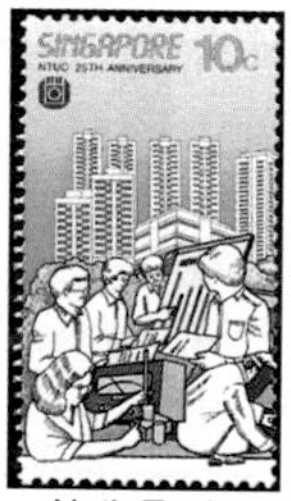

Natl. Trade Unions Cong., 25th Anniv. — A119

**1986, Feb. 26 Litho. *Perf. 14½x14***
**480** A118 10c Psidium guajava .20 .20
**481** A118 35c Eugenia aquea 1.25 1.25
**482** A118 50c Nephelium lappaceum 1.60 1.60
**483** A118 75c Manilkara zapota 2.50 2.50
*Nos. 480-483 (4)* 5.55 5.55

**1986, May 1 *Perf. 13½***

Progress: a, Science and technology. b, Communications. c, Industry. d, Education.

**484** Strip of 4 2.40 2.40
*a.-d.* A119 10c any single .20 .20

**Souvenir Sheet**

**485** Sheet of 4 6.00 6.00
*a.-d.* A119 35c any single .50 .50

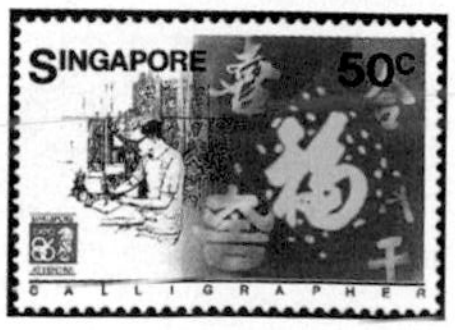

EXPO '86, Vancouver A120

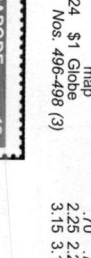

**1986, May 2 *Perf. 14½x14***
**486** Strip of 3 3.75 3.75
*a.* A120 50c Calligraphy .80 .80
*b.* A120 75c Garland making 1.10 1.10
*c.* A120 $1 Batik printing 1.60 1.60

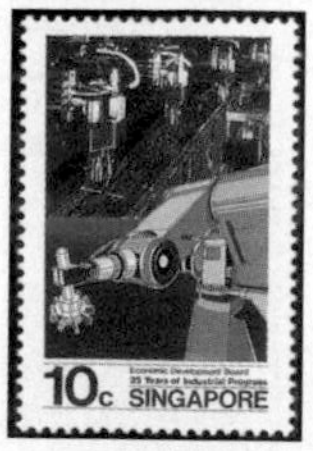

Economic Development Board, 25th Anniv. — A121

**1986, Aug. 1 *Perf. 15***
**487** A121 10c Automation .20 .20
**488** A121 35c Precision engineering .40 .40
**489** A121 50c Electronics .60 .60
**490** A121 75c Biotechnology .95 .95
*Nos. 487-490 (4)* 2.15 2.15

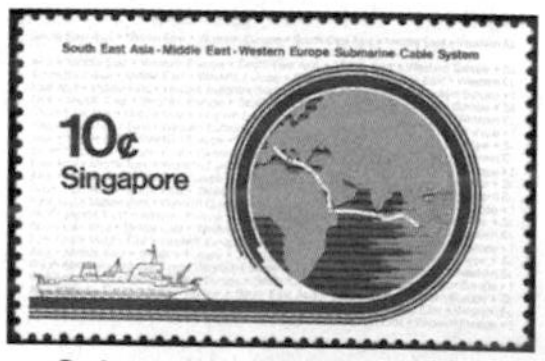

Submarine Cable — A122

**1986, Sept. 8 *Perf. 13½***
**491** A122 10c multicolored .20 .20
**492** A122 35c multicolored 1.10 1.10
**493** A122 50c multicolored 1.40 1.40
**494** A122 75c multicolored 2.00 2.00
*Nos. 491-494 (4)* 4.70 4.70

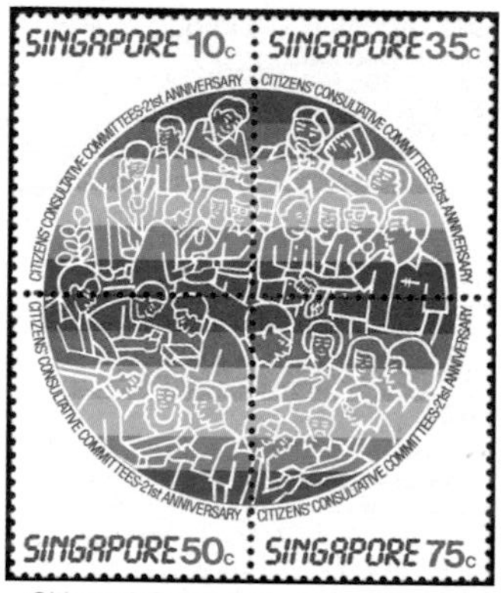

Citizens' Consultative Committees, 21st Anniv. — A123

**1986, Oct 15 *Perf. 12***
**495** A123 Block of 4 2.75 2.75
*a.* 10c multicolored .20 .20
*b.* 35c multicolored .50 .50
*c.* 50c multicolored .75 .75
*d.* 75c multicolored 1.10 1.10

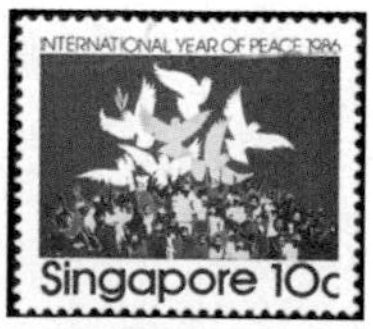

Intl. Peace Year — A124

**1986, Dec. 17 Litho. *Perf. 14x13½***
**496** A124 10c People .20 .20
**497** A124 35c Southeast Asia map .70 .70
**498** A124 $1 Globe 2.25 2.25
*Nos. 496-498 (3)* 3.15 3.15

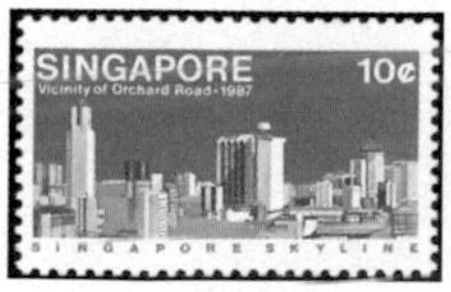

Views of Singapore A125

**1986, Feb. 25 *Perf. 12x12½***
**499** A125 10c Orchard Road .20 .20
**500** A125 50c Central business district .95 .95

**501** A125 75c Marina Center, Raffles City 1.25 1.25
*Nos. 499-501 (3)* 2.40 2.40

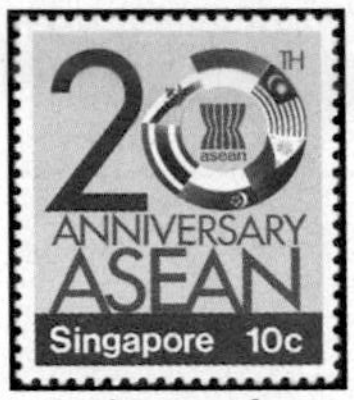

Assoc. of Southeast Asian Nations (ASEAN), 20th Anniv. A126

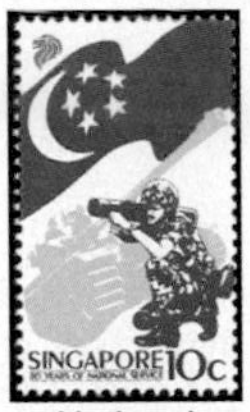

National Service, 20th Anniv. A127

**1987, June 15** ***Perf. 12***
**502** A126 10c multicolored .20 .20
**503** A126 35c multicolored .45 .45
**504** A126 50c multicolored .70 .70
**505** A126 75c multicolored 1.10 1.10
*Nos. 502-505 (4)* 2.45 2.45

**1987, July 1** ***Perf. 15x14***

Designs: a, Army. b, Navy. c, Air Force. d, Pledge of Allegiance. e, Singapore Lion.

**506** Strip of 4 2.25 2.25
***a.-d.*** A127 10c any single .20 .20
**507** Sheet of 5 6.00 6.00
***a.-e.*** A127 35c any single .40 .40

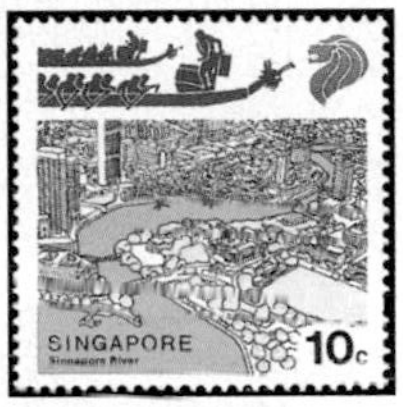

River Life — A128

**1987, Sept. 2** ***Perf. 14***
**508** A128 10c Singapore River .20 .20
**509** A128 50c Kallang Basin 1.25 1.25
**510** A128 $1 Kranji Reservoir 2.75 2.75
*Nos. 508-510 (3)* 4.20 4.20

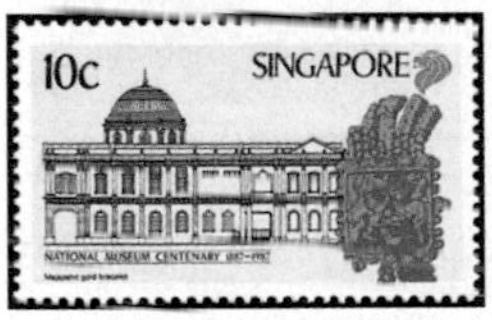

Natl. Museum Cent. A129

Views of the museum and artifacts: 10c, Majapahis gold bracelet, 14th-15th cent. 75c, Ming fluted kendi (water jar). $1, Seventeen-wave kris (sword with silver hilt, sheath), property of Sultan Abdul Jalil Sabat, 1699.

**1987, Oct. 12** **Litho.** ***Perf. 13½x14***
**511** A129 10c multicolored .20 .20
**512** A129 75c multicolored 1.90 1.90
**513** A129 $1 multicolored 2.25 2.25
*Nos. 511-513 (3)* 4.35 4.35

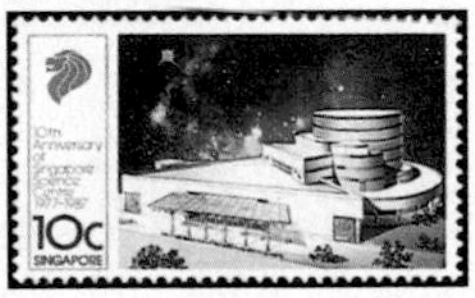

Singapore Science Center, 10th Anniv. A130

Attractions.

**1987, Dec. 10** ***Perf. 14½***
**514** A130 10c Omni Theater .30 .30
**515** A130 35c Omni Planetarium .80 .80
**516** A130 75c Cellular model 1.75 1.75
**517** A130 $1 Science exhibits 2.25 2.25
*Nos. 514-517 (4)* 5.10 5.10

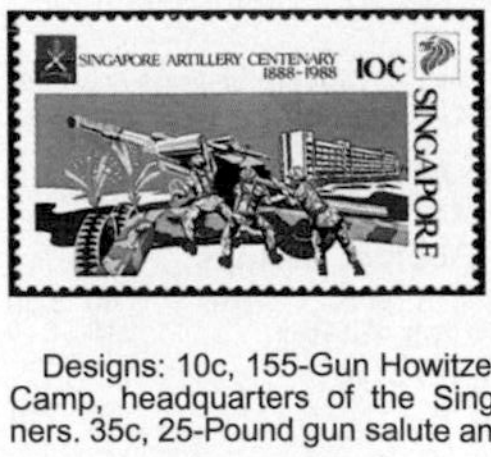

Artillery, Cent. A131

Designs: 10c, 155-Gun Howitzer and Khatib Camp, headquarters of the Singapore Gunners. 35c, 25-Pound gun salute and Singapore City Hall. 50c, 4.5-inch Howitzer and Singapore Cricket Club, c. 1928. $1, Ft. Fullerton Drill Hall, c. 1893, and .405 Maxim gun.

**1988, Feb. 22** **Litho.** ***Perf. 13½x14***
**518** A131 10c multicolored .50 .50
**519** A131 35c multicolored 1.25 1.25
**520** A131 50c multicolored 2.00 2.00
**521** A131 $1 multicolored 3.75 3.75
*Nos. 518-521 (4)* 7.50 7.50

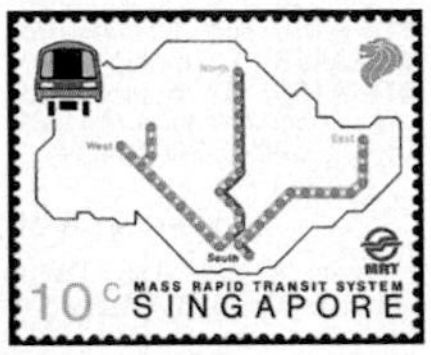

Mass Transit A132

**1988, Mar. 12** ***Perf. 14***
**522** A132 10c Rail car, map .40 .40
**523** A132 50c Elevated train 1.90 1.90
**524** A132 $1 Urban subway 4.00 4.00
*Nos. 522-524 (3)* 6.30 6.30

See No. 1064.

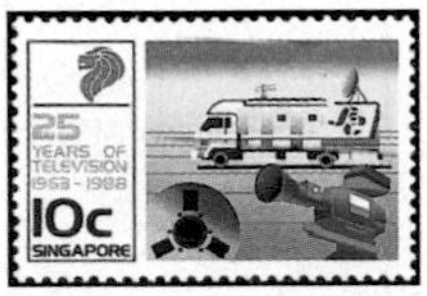

Natl. Television Broadcast System, 25th Anniv. A133

**1988, Apr. 4** **Litho.** ***Perf. 13½x14***
**525** A133 10c shown .30 .30
**526** A133 35c Studio .70 .70
**527** A133 75c Television, transmission tower 1.50 1.50
**528** A133 $1 Screen, satellite dish 2.00 2.00
*Nos. 525-528 (4)* 4.50 4.50

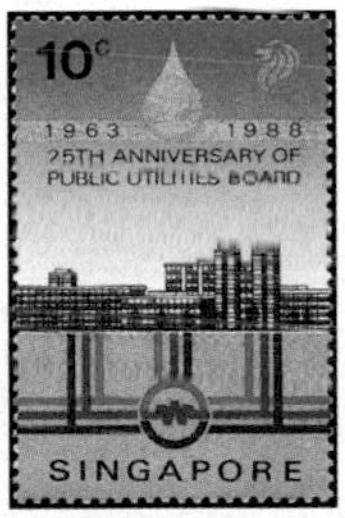

Public Utilities Board, 25th Anniv. — A134

**1988, May 4** **Litho.** ***Perf. 13½***
**529** A134 10c Water works .20 .20
**530** A134 50c Electric company 1.25 1.25
**531** A134 $1 Fossil fuels 2.50 2.50
***a.*** Souvenir sheet of 3, #529-531 6.00 6.00
*Nos. 529-531 (3)* 3.95 3.95

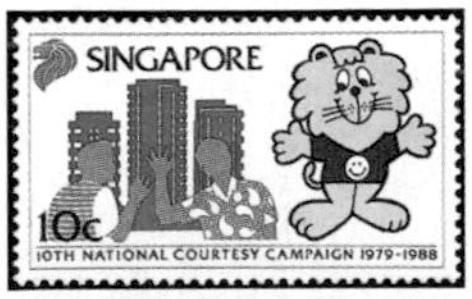

Courtesy Campaign, 10th Anniv. — A135

Singa the lion (character trademark) and: 10c, Neighbors. 30c, Store service counter. $1, Helping the elderly.

**1988, July 6** **Litho.** ***Perf. 14½***
**532** A135 10c multicolored .20 .20
**533** A135 30c multicolored .65 .65
**534** A135 $1 multicolored 2.10 2.10
*Nos. 532-534 (3)* 2.95 2.95

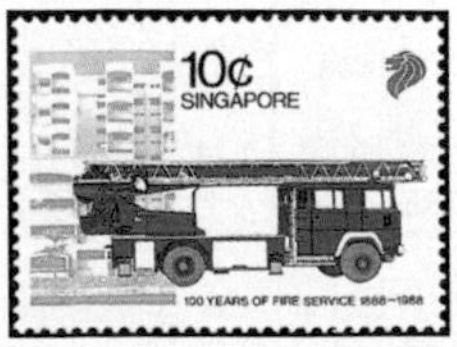

Fire Service, Cent. A136

**1988, Nov. 1** **Litho.** ***Perf. 13½***
**535** A136 10c Turntable ladder truck .30 .30
**536** A136 $1 1890s Steam pump 5.50 5.50

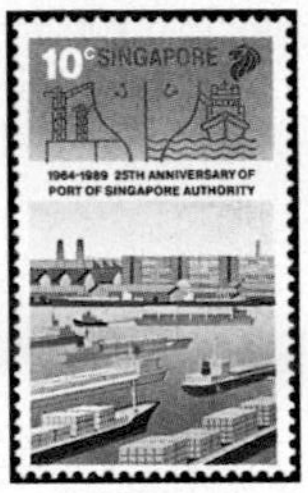

Port Authority, 25th Anniv. — A137

Various facilities.

**1989, Apr. 3** **Litho.** ***Perf. 14x13½***
**537** A137 10c multicolored .20 .20
**538** A137 30c multi, diff. .80 .80
**539** A137 75c multi, diff. 2.00 2.00
**540** A137 $1 multi, diff. 2.75 2.75
*Nos. 537-540 (4)* 5.75 5.75

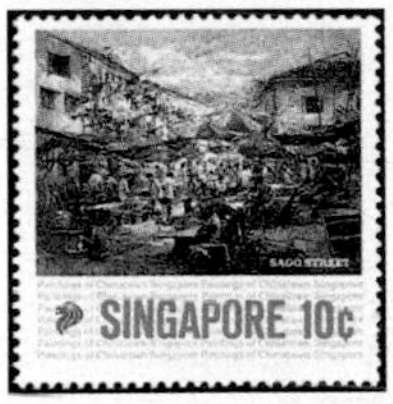

Old Chinatown A138

**1989, May 17** **Litho.** ***Perf. 14½***
**541** A138 10c Sago St. .40 .40
**542** A138 35c Pagoda St. 1.40 1.40
**543** A138 75c Trengganu St. 2.75 2.75
**544** A138 $1 Temple St. 3.50 3.50
*Nos. 541-544 (4)* 8.05 8.05

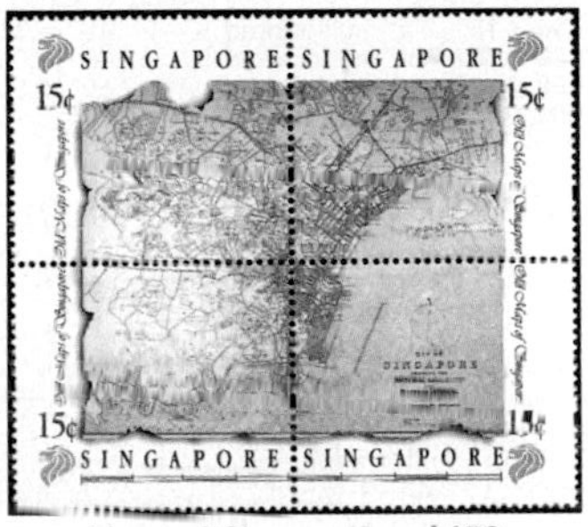

Maps of Singapore — A139

Early 19th cent. map Singapore Showing Principal Residences and Places of Interest: No. 545a, Upper left. No. 545b, Upper right. No. 545c, Lower left. No. 545d, Lower right. (Illustration reduced).

**1989, July 26** **Litho.** ***Perf. 14½***
**545** A139 Block of 4 3.50 3.50
***a.-d.*** 15c any single .20 .20

**Size: 33x31mm**

***Perf. 12½x13***

**546** A139 50c Singapore and Dependencies 3.00 3.00
**547** A139 $1 Plan of the British Settlement 6.00 6.00
*Nos. 545-547 (3)* 12.50 12.50

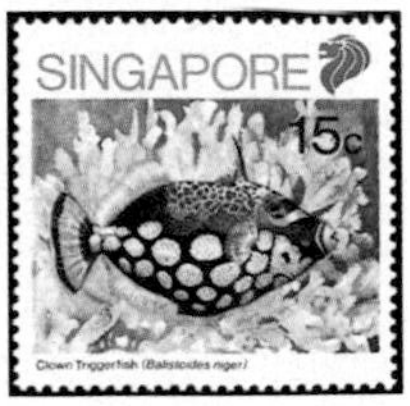

Fish — A140

**1989, Sept. 6** ***Perf. 14***
**548** A140 15c Clown triggerfish .80 .80
**549** A140 30c Majestic angelfish 1.50 1.50
**550** A140 75c Emperor angelfish 4.00 4.00
**551** A140 $1 Royal empress angelfish 3.50 3.50
*Nos. 548-551 (4)* 9.80 9.80

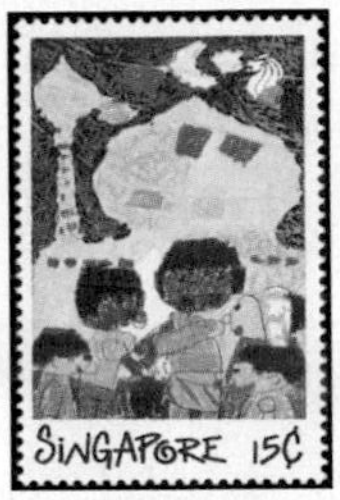

Festivals — A141

Children's drawings: 15c, *Hari Raya Puasa,* by Loke Yoke Yen. 35c, *Chinese New Year,* by Simon Koh. 75c, *Thaipusam,* by Henry Setiono. $1, *Christmas,* by Wendy Ang Lin.

**1989, Oct. 25** **Litho.** ***Perf. 14½***
**552** A141 15c multicolored .30 .30
**553** A141 35c multicolored .95 .95
**554** A141 75c multicolored 1.90 1.90
**555** A141 $1 multicolored 2.75 2.75
***a.*** Souv. sheet of 4, #552-555, perf. 14 6.50 6.50
*Nos. 552-555 (4)* 5.90 5.90

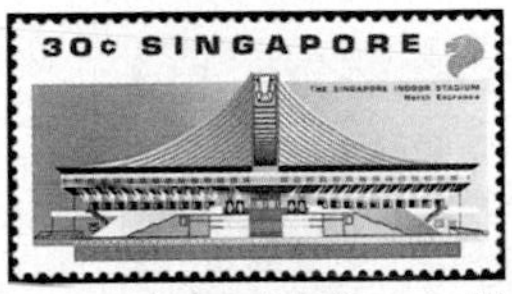

Singapore Indoor Stadium — A142

**1989, Dec. 27** **Litho.** ***Perf. 14½***
**556** A142 30c North entrance 1.00 1.00
**557** A142 75c Interior 2.25 2.25
**558** A142 $1 East entrance 3.25 3.25
***a.*** Souvenir sheet of 3, #556-558 7.25 7.25
*Nos. 556-558 (3)* 6.50 6.50

Sports issue.

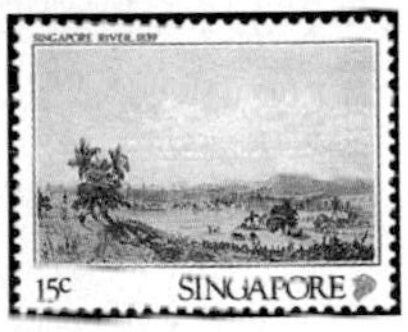

Lithographs of 19th Cent. Singapore A143

**1990, Feb. 21** **Litho.** ***Perf. 13***
**559** A143 15c Singapore River, 1839 .45 .45
**560** A143 30c Chinatown, 1837 .90 .90
**561** A143 75c Waterfront, 1837 2.40 2.40
**562** A143 $1 View from Ft. Canning, 1824 3.25 3.25
*Nos. 559-562 (4)* 7.00 7.00

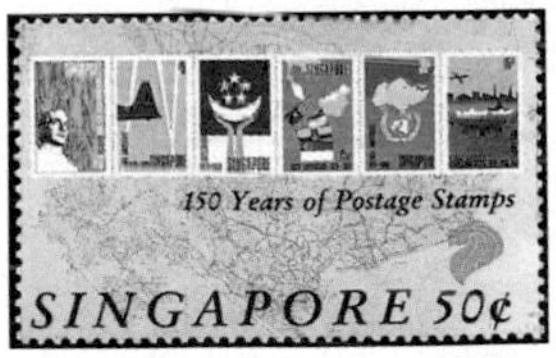

First Postage Stamps, 150th Anniv. — A144

Maps and: 50c, Nos. 101-106. 75c, Cover to Scotland. $1, Cover to Ireland $2, Great Britain Nos. 1, 2.

**1990, May 3** **Litho.** ***Perf. 13½***
**563** A144 50c multicolored 1.10 1.10
**564** A144 75c multicolored 1.75 1.75
**565** A144 $1 multicolored 2.40 2.40
**566** A144 $2 multicolored 4.75 4.75
***a.*** Souvenir sheet of 4, #563-566 12.50 12.50
*Nos. 563-566 (4)* 10.00 10.00

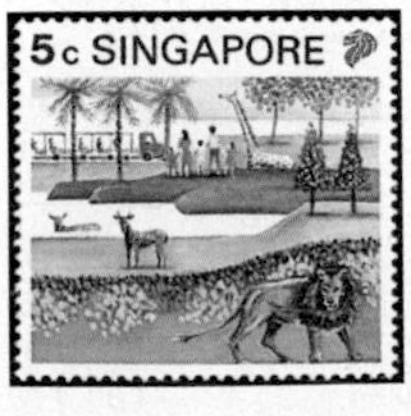

Tourism A145

**1990, July 4** ***Perf. 14½***
**567** A145 5c Zoo .20 .20
**568** A145 15c Resort .20 .20
***a.*** Booklet pane of 10 1.60

**569** A145 20c City .25 .25
**570** A145 25c Dragon boat race .30 .30
**571** A145 30c Hotel .35 .35
**572** A145 35c Caged birds .40 .40
**573** A145 40c Park .45 .45
**574** A145 50c Festival .55 .55
**575** A145 75c Building, diff. .85 .85
*Nos. 567-575 (9)* 3.55 3.55

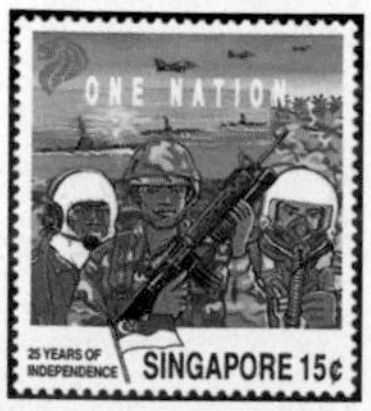


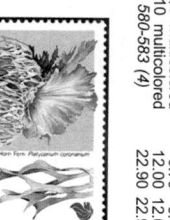

Independence, 25th Anniv. — A146

**1990, Aug. 16 Litho. *Perf. 14x14½***
**576** A146 15c shown .40 .40
  a. Booklet pane of 10 1.60
**577** A146 35c One Singapore 1.10 1.10
**578** A146 75c One hope 2.40 2.40
**579** A146 $1 One people 3.25 3.25
*Nos. 576-579 (4)* 7.15 7.15

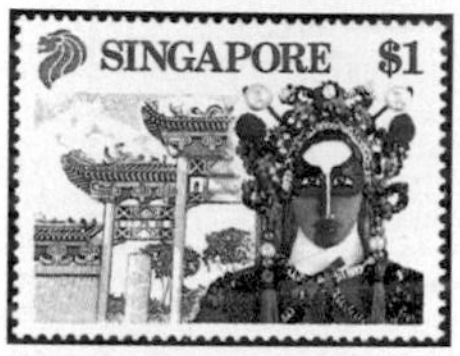


Tourism A147

$1, Chinese opera singer, Siong Lim Temple. $2, Malay dancer, Sultan Mosque. $5, Indian dancer, Sri Mariamman Temple. $10, Ballet dancer, Victoria Memorial Hall.

**Photo. & Engr.**

**1990, Oct. 10 *Perf. 15x14***
**580** A147 $1 multicolored 1.40 1.40
**581** A147 $2 multicolored 2.75 2.75
**582** A147 $5 multicolored 6.75 6.75
**583** A147 $10 multicolored 12.00 12.00
*Nos. 580-583 (4)* 22.90 22.90

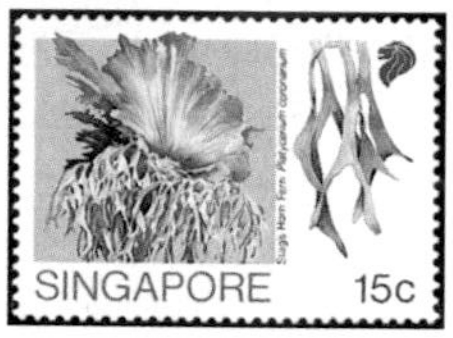


Ferns A148

**1990, Nov. 14 Litho. *Perf. 14***
**584** A148 15c Stag's horn .35 .35
**585** A148 35c Maiden hair .90 .90
**586** A148 75c Bird's nest 1.90 1.90
**587** A148 $1 Rabbit's foot 2.50 2.50
*Nos. 584-587 (4)* 5.65 5.65

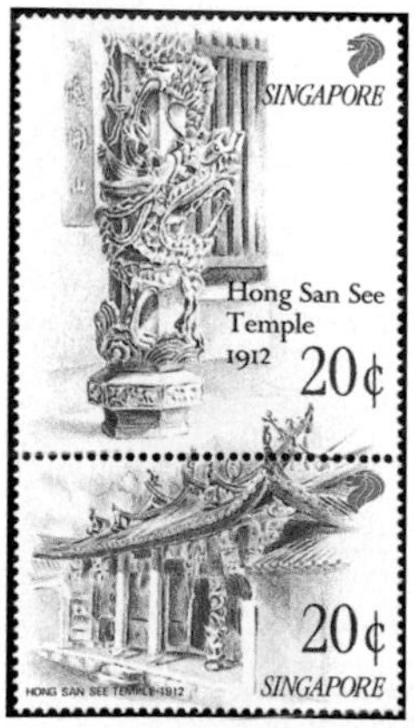


Houses of Worship A149

Designs: 20c, Hong San See Temple, 1912. 50c, Abdul Gattoor Mosque, 1910. 75c, Sri Perumal Temple, 1961. $1, St. Andrew's Cathedral, 1863.

**1991, Jan. 23 Litho. *Perf. 14½***
**588** 20c multicolored .40 .40
**589** 20c multicolored .40 .40
  a. A149 Pair, #588-589 .80 .80
**590** 50c multicolored 1.00 1.00
**591** 50c multicolored 1.00 1.00
  a. A149 Pair, #590-591 2.00 2.00
**592** 75c multicolored 1.50 1.50
**593** 75c multicolored 1.50 1.50
  a. A149 Pair, #592-593 3.00 3.00

**594** $1 multicolored 2.00 2.00
**595** $1 multicolored 2.00 2.00
  a. A149 Pair, #594-595 4.00 4.00
*Nos. 588-595 (8)* 9.80 9.80

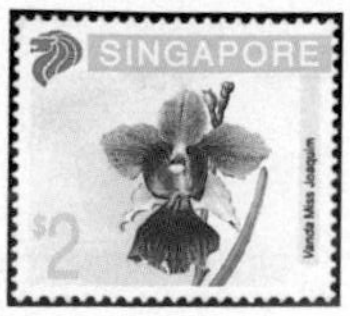


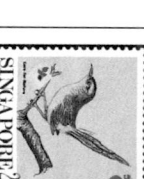

Vanda Miss Joaquim — A151

Design: No. 597, Dendrobium Anocha.

**1991, Apr. 24 Litho. *Perf. 14***
**596** A151 $2 multicolored 4.25 4.25
**597** A151 $2 multicolored 4.25 4.25
  a. Pair, #596-597 + label 8.50 8.50
  b. Souvenir sheet, #596-597 8.50 8.50

Singapore '95 Intl. Philatelic Exhibition.
See Nos. 615-616, 664-665, 685-686, 716-717.

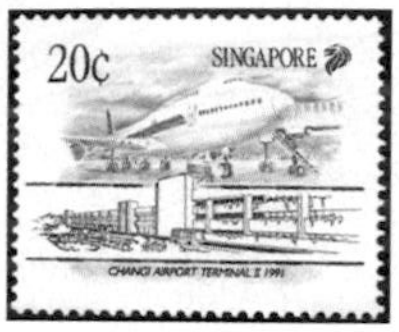


Civilian Airports A152

Designs: 20c, Boeing 747, Changi Terminal II, 1991. 75c, Boeing 747, Changi Terminal I, 1981. $1, Concorde, Paya Lebar, 1955-1981. $2, DC-3, Kallang, 1937-1955.

***Perf. 13½x14½***

**1991, July 1 Litho. & Engr.**
**598** A152 20c multicolored .45 .45
**599** A152 75c multicolored 2.00 2.00
**600** A152 $1 multicolored 2.50 2.50
**601** A152 $2 multicolored 5.25 5.25
*Nos. 598-601 (4)* 10.20 10.20

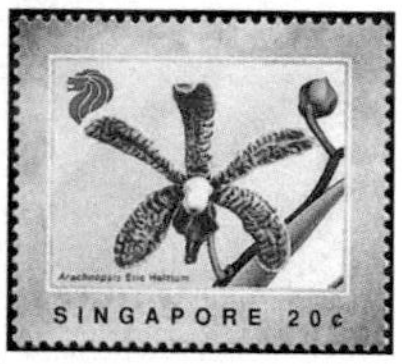


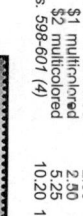

Arachnopsis Eric Holttum A153

Orchids: 30c, Cattleya Meadii. $1, Calanthe vestita.

**1991, Aug. 8 Litho. *Perf. 14½x13½***
**602** A153 20c multicolored .95 .95
**603** A153 30c multicolored 1.40 1.40
**604** A153 $1 multicolored 4.25 4.25
*Nos. 602-604 (3)* 6.60 6.60

Birds — A154

Designs: 20c, Common tailorbird. 35c, Scarlet-backed flowerpecker. 75c, Black-naped oriole. $1, Common tora.

**1991, Sept. 19 *Perf. 14***
**605** A154 20c multicolored .25 .25
  a. Booklet pane of 10 2.50 2.50
**606** A154 35c multicolored .60 .60
**607** A154 75c multicolored 2.00 2.00
**608** A154 $1 multicolored 6.00 6.00
*Nos. 605-608 (4)* 8.85 8.85

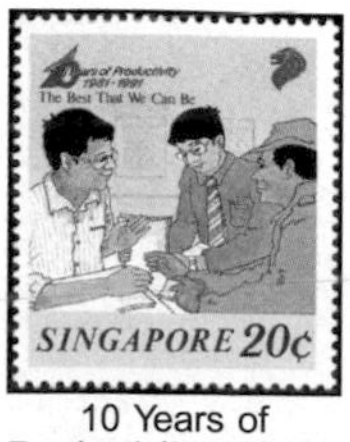


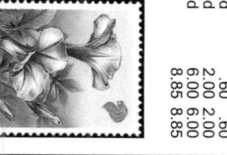

10 Years of Productivity — A155

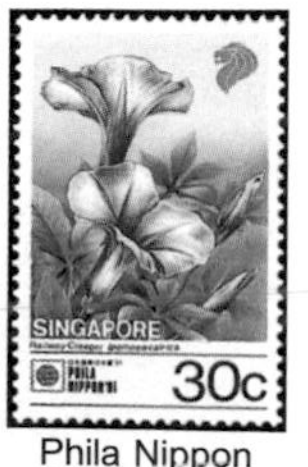


Phila Nippon '91 — A156

**1991, Nov. 1 Litho. *Perf. 14x14½***
**609** A155 20c shown .30 .30
**610** A155 $1 Construction engineers 1.90 1.90

**1991, Nov. 16 *Perf. 14½x14***

Flowers: 30c, Railway creeper. 75c, Asystasia. $1, Singapore rhododendron. $2, Coat buttons.

**611** A156 30c multicolored .60 .60
**612** A156 75c multicolored 1.50 1.50
**613** A156 $1 multicolored 2.00 2.00
**614** A156 $2 multicolored 4.00 4.00
  a. Souvenir sheet of 4, #611-614 9.50 9.50
*Nos. 611-614 (4)* 8.10 8.10

**Flower Type of 1991**

Designs: No. 615, Dendrobium Sharifah Fatimah. No. 616, Phalaenopsis Shim Beauty.

**1992, Jan. 22 Litho. *Perf. 14***
**615** A151 $2 multicolored 3.75 3.75
**616** A151 $2 multicolored 3.75 3.75
  a. Pair, #615-616 + label 7.75 7.75
  b. Souvenir sheet of 2, #615-616 9.50 9.50

Singapore '95 Intl. Philatelic Exhibition.

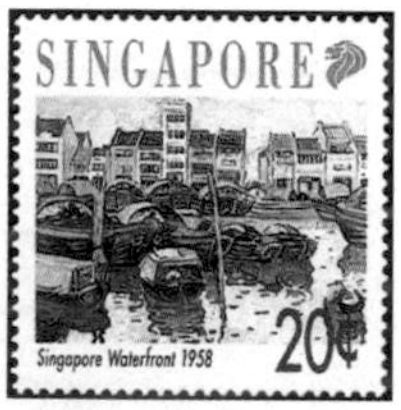


Paintings A157

**1992, Mar. 11 Litho. *Perf. 14***
**617** A157 20c Singapore Waterfront, 1958 .35 .35
**618** A157 75c Kampung Hut, 1973 1.50 1.50
**619** A157 $1 Bridge, 1983 2.00 2.00
**620** A157 $2 Singapore River, 1984 4.00 4.00
*Nos. 617-620 (4)* 7.85 7.85

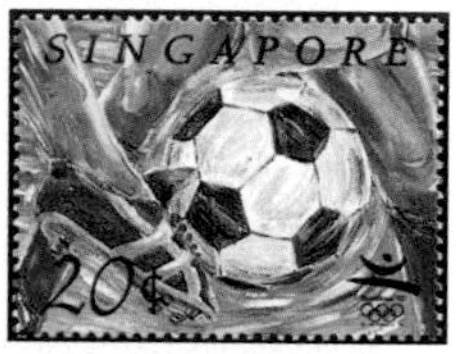


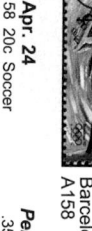

1992 Summer Olympics, Barcelona A158

**1992, Apr. 24 *Perf. 14***
**621** A158 20c Soccer .35 .35
**622** A158 35c Relay races .60 .60
**623** A158 50c Swimming .75 .75
**624** A158 75c Basketball 1.25 1.25
**625** A158 $1 Tennis 1.75 1.75
**626** A158 $2 Sailing 3.50 3.50
  a. Souvenir sheet of 6, #621-626 9.50 9.50
*Nos. 621-626 (6)* 8.20 8.20

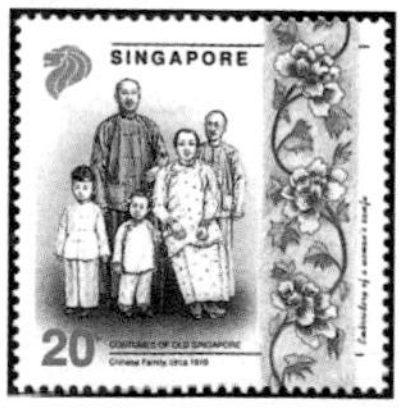


Costumes, 1910 — A159

**1992, Apr. 24 Litho. *Perf. 14½***
**627** A159 20c Chinese family .30 .30
**628** A159 35c Malay family .60 .60
**629** A159 75c Indian family 1.25 1.25
**630** A159 $2 Straits Chinese family 3.00 3.00
*Nos. 627-630 (4)* 5.15 5.15

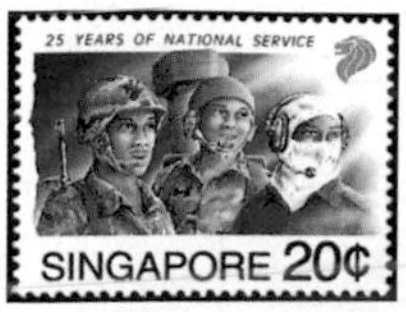


Natl. Military Forces, 25th Anniv. — A160

Designs: 35c, Frogman with gun, fighter plane, artillery. $1, Fighter, tank, ship.

**1992, July 1**
**631** A160 20c multicolored .35 .35
**632** A160 35c multicolored 1.25 1.25
**633** A160 $1 multicolored 2.75 2.75
*Nos. 631-633 (3)* 4.35 4.35

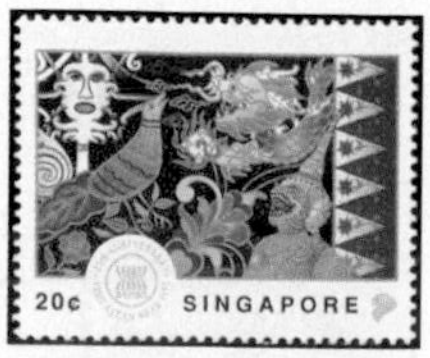


Visit ASEAN Year, 25th Anniv. A161

Designs: 20c, Mask, bird, sea life. 35c, Costumed women. $1, Outdoor scenery.

**1992, Aug. 8**
**634** A161 20c multicolored .35 .35
**635** A161 35c multicolored 1.00 1.00
**636** A161 $1 multicolored 2.50 2.50
*Nos. 634-636 (3)* 3.85 3.85

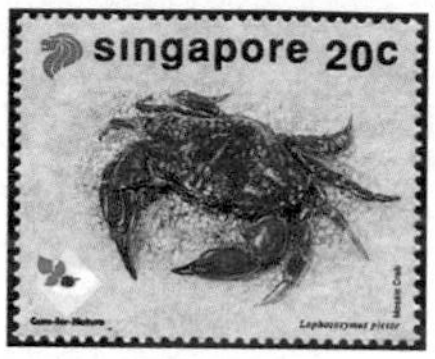


Crabs A162

Designs: 20c, Mosaic crab. 50c, Johnson's freshwater crab. 75c, Singapore freshwater crab. $1, Swamp forest crab.

**1992, Aug. 21 *Perf. 14½x15***
**637** A162 20c multicolored .35 .35
  a. Booklet pane of 10 3.50
**638** A162 50c multicolored 1.25 1.25
**639** A162 75c multicolored 1.75 1.75
**640** A162 $1 multicolored 2.50 2.50
*Nos. 637-640 (4)* 5.85 5.85

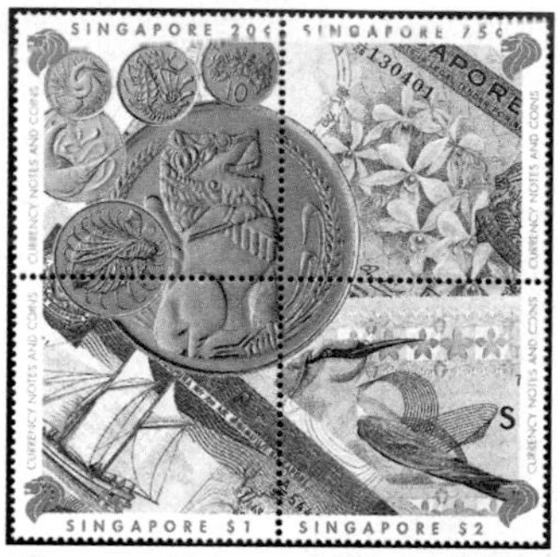


Currency, Notes and Coins — A163

**1992, Oct. 2 Litho. *Perf. 14½***
**641** 20c Coins .40 .40
**642** 75c Coin, flowers on note 1.60 1.60
**643** $1 Boat on note, coins 2.00 2.00
**644** $2 Bird on note 4.00 4.00
  a. A163 Block of 4, #641-644 8.00 8.00

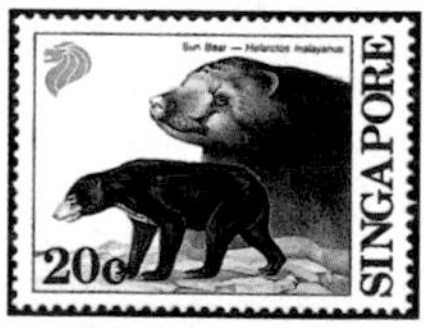


Wild Animals A164

**1993, Jan. 13 Litho. *Perf. 14½x15***
**645** A164 20c Sun bear .35 .35
**646** A164 30c Orangutan .50 .50
**647** A164 75c Slow loris 1.25 1.25
**648** A164 $2 Large mouse deer 3.75 3.75
*Nos. 645-648 (4)* 5.85 5.85

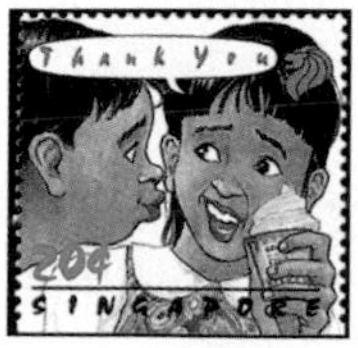


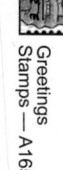

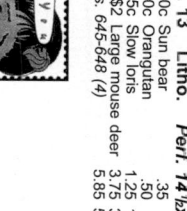

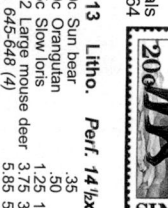

Greetings Stamps — A165

a, Thank you. b, Congratulations. c, Best wishes. d, Happy birthday. e, Get well soon.

***Perf. 14½x14 on 3 Sides***

**1993, Feb. 10**

**Booklet Stamps**

**649** A165 20c Strip of 5, #a.-e. 3.00 3.00
  f. Booklet pane of 2 #649 6.00 6.00

## Preservation of Tanjong Pagar — A166

SINGAPORE 20¢ — Conservation (Tanjong Pagar)

**1993, Mar. 10    Litho.    Perf. 14**

| | | | | |
|---|---|---|---|---|
| 650 | A166 | 20c shown | .30 | .30 |
| 651 | A166 | 30c Building facade, tower | .70 | .70 |
| 652 | A166 | $2 Aerial view | 5.00 | 5.00 |
| | | Nos. 650-652 (3) | 6.00 | 6.00 |

A167 — 20¢

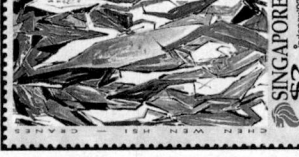

CHEN WEN HSI — FISH HSI CRANES — SINGAPORE $2

**1993, May 29    Perf. 12x11½**

| | | | | |
|---|---|---|---|---|
| 653 | A167 | $2 Cranes, by Chen Wen Hsi | 3.25 | 3.25 |

Indopex '93.

A168

20¢

**1993, June 12    Litho.    Perf. 14**

| | | | | |
|---|---|---|---|---|
| 654 | A168 | 20c Soccer | .30 | .30 |
| 655 | A168 | 35c Basketball | .50 | .50 |
| 656 | A168 | 50c Badminton | .70 | .70 |
| 657 | A168 | 75c Running | 1.00 | 1.00 |
| 658 | A168 | $1 Water polo | 1.50 | 1.50 |
| 659 | A168 | $2 Yachting | 3.25 | 3.25 |
| | | Nos. 654-659 (6) | 7.25 | 7.25 |

17th Sea Games, Singapore.

## Butterflies — A169

SINGAPORE 20¢ — THE PLAIN TIGER

**1993, Aug. 21    Litho.    Perf. 14½**

| | | | | |
|---|---|---|---|---|
| 660 | A169 | 20c Plain tiger | .30 | .30 |
| a. | | Booklet pane of 10 | 3.00 | |
| 661 | A169 | 50c Malay lacewing | .75 | .75 |
| 662 | A169 | 75c Palm king | 1.25 | 1.25 |
| 663 | A169 | $1 Banded swallowtail | 1.60 | 1.60 |
| | | Nos. 660-663 (4) | 3.90 | 3.90 |

### Flower Type of 1991

**Size: 26x34mm**

**1993, Aug. 13**

| | | | | |
|---|---|---|---|---|
| 664 | A151 | $2 Phalaenopsis amabilis | 4.00 | 4.00 |
| 665 | A151 | $2 Vanda sumatrana | 8.00 | 8.00 |
| a. | | Pair, #664-665 + label | 8.00 | 8.00 |
| b. | | Souvenir sheet of 2, #664-665, perf. 15x14½ | | |

Singapore '95 World Stamp Exhibition and Taipei '93, Asian Intl. Invitation Stamp Exhibition (#665b).

## Fruits — A170

SINGAPORE 20¢

**1993, Oct. 1    Litho.    Perf. 14½x14**

| | | | | |
|---|---|---|---|---|
| 666 | A170 | 20c Papaya | .30 | .30 |
| 667 | A170 | 35c Pomegranate | .55 | .55 |
| 668 | A170 | 75c Starfruit | 1.25 | 1.25 |
| 669 | A170 | $2 Durian | 3.00 | 3.00 |
| a. | | Souvenir sheet of 4, #666-669 | 6.00 | 6.00 |
| | | Nos. 666-669 (4) | 5.10 | 5.10 |

Bangkok '93 (#669a).

## Chinese Egrets — A171

SINGAPORE 20¢

**1993, Nov. 10    Litho.    Perf. 13½x14**

| | | | | |
|---|---|---|---|---|
| 670 | A171 | 20c multicolored | .75 | .75 |
| 671 | A171 | 25c multicolored | .85 | .85 |
| 672 | A171 | 30c multicolored | 1.00 | 1.00 |
| 673 | A171 | 35c multicolored | 1.50 | 1.50 |
| a. | | Strip of 4, #670-673 | 4.75 | 4.75 |

World Wildlife Fund.

Designs: 20c, Two, one with bill in water. 25c, Two, one with fish in mouth. 30c, Two facing opposite directions. 35c, In flight.

Palm Tree — A171a — **Die Cut**

Palm Tree — SINGAPORE — For Local Addresses Only

**1993, Nov. 24    Photo.    Self-Adhesive Booklet Stamp**

| | | | | |
|---|---|---|---|---|
| 673B | A171a | (20c) multicolored | .45 | .45 |
| c. | | Booklet pane of 6 | 6.75 | 6.75 |

By its nature, No. 673c is a complete booklet. The peelable backing serves as a booklet cover.

## Marine Life — A172

SINGAPORE 5¢ — TREE CORAL

**1994    Perf. 13x13½, 13½x14 (#675B)    Litho.**

| | | | | |
|---|---|---|---|---|
| 674 | A172 | 5c Tiger cowrie | .20 | .20 |
| 675 | A172 | 20c Sea fan | .25 | .25 |
| 675B | A172 | (20c) Blue-spotted stingray | 2.50 | |
| a. | | Booklet pane of 10 | | |
| 676 | A172 | 25c Tunicate | .30 | .30 |
| 677 | A172 | 30c Clownfish | .35 | .35 |
| 678 | A172 | 35c Nudibranch | .40 | .40 |
| 679 | A172 | 40c Sea urchin | .45 | .45 |
| 680 | A172 | 50c Soft coral | .50 | .50 |
| 681 | A172 | 75c Pin cushion star | .95 | .95 |

**Litho. & Embossed**

**Perf. 14 Syncopated Type A (2 Sides)**

| | | | | |
|---|---|---|---|---|
| 682 | A172 | $1 Knob coral | 1.40 | 1.40 |
| 683 | A172 | $2 Mushroom coral | 2.75 | 2.75 |
| 684 | A172 | $5 Bubble coral | 7.00 | 7.00 |
| 684A | A172 | $10 Octopus coral | 14.00 | 14.00 |
| | | Nos. 674-684A (13) | 29.20 | 29.20 |

**Self-Adhesive**

**Die Cut Perf. 8½**

| | | | | |
|---|---|---|---|---|
| 684B | A172 | (20c) Blue-spotted stingray | .30 | .30 |
| c. | | Booklet pane of 10 | 3.00 | |

Nos. 675B, 684B inscribed "FOR LOCAL ADDRESSES ONLY." By its nature, No. 684c is a complete booklet. The peelable paper backing serves as a booklet cover.

Issued: 5c-75c, 1/12/94; $1-$10, 3/23/94; #675B, 684B, 11/16/94.

See Nos. 816-824.

### Flower Type of 1991

SINGAPORE 20¢

**1994, Feb. 18    Size: 26x35mm    Perf. 14½**

| | | | | |
|---|---|---|---|---|
| 685 | A151 | $2 multicolored | 5.00 | 5.00 |
| 686 | A151 | $2 multicolored | 5.00 | 5.00 |
| a. | | Pair, #685-686 + label | 10.00 | 10.00 |
| b. | | Souvenir sheet of 2, #685-686 | 10.00 | 10.00 |

Singapore '95 and Hong Kong '94 (#686b).

Designs: No. 685, Paphiopedilum vicotriaregina. No. 686, Dendrobium similileae.

## Spring Festival — A173

SINGAPORE 20¢

**1994, May 18    Litho.    Perf. 13½**

| | | | | |
|---|---|---|---|---|
| 687 | A173 | 20c Ballet | .40 | .40 |
| 688 | A173 | 30c Mime, puppets | .50 | .50 |
| 689 | A173 | 50c Musicians | 1.90 | 1.90 |
| 690 | A173 | $1 Crafts | 3.80 | 3.80 |
| | | Nos. 687-690 (4) | | |

## Operationally Ready Natl. Servicemen, 25th Anniv. — A174

SINGAPORE 20¢

**1994, July 1    Litho.    Perf. 13½**

| | | | | |
|---|---|---|---|---|
| 691 | A174 | 20c multicolored | .90 | .90 |
| 692 | A174 | 30c multicolored | 1.00 | 1.00 |
| 693 | A174 | 45c multicolored | 2.25 | 2.25 |
| 694 | A174 | 75c multicolored | 4.65 | 4.65 |
| | | Nos. 691-694 (4) | | |

Civilian-soldiers: 20c, Saluting flag, aiming anti-tank missile. 30c, With family, on jungle patrol with automatic rifle. 35c, Reading newspaper, aiming machine gun. 75c, Working with computer, and as commander, looking through binoculars.

## Herons — A175

SINGAPORE 20c  50c  75c  $1

**1994, Aug. 16    Litho.    Perf. 14**

| | | | | |
|---|---|---|---|---|
| 695 | A175 | 20c Black-crowned night heron | .35 | .35 |
| a. | | Booklet pane of 10 | 3.50 | |
| 696 | A175 | 50c Little heron | .80 | .80 |
| 697 | A175 | 75c Purple heron | 1.00 | 1.00 |
| 698 | A175 | $1 Gray heron | 1.50 | 1.50 |
| a. | A175 | Block of 4, #695-698 | 3.75 | 3.75 |
| | | Nos. 695-698 (4) | 3.65 | 3.65 |

### Greetings Stamps — A175a

**1994, Sept. 14    Die Cut Perf. 11½    Litho.**

**Self-Adhesive Booklet Stamps**

| | | | | |
|---|---|---|---|---|
| 698B | A175a | (20c) multicolored | .45 | .45 |
| 698C | A175a | (20c) multicolored | .45 | .45 |
| 698D | A175a | (20c) multicolored | .45 | .45 |
| 698E | A175a | (20c) multicolored | .45 | .45 |
| 698F | A175a | (20c) multicolored | .45 | .45 |
| g. | | Bklt. pane, 2 ea #698B-698F (5) | 2.25 | 2.25 |

Nos. 698B-693F inscribed "For Local Addresses Only." By its nature, No. 698Fg is a complete booklet. The peelable paper backing serves as a booklet cover. The outside of the cover contains 10 peelable labels.

#698B, Birthday cake. #698C, Bouquet of flowers. #698D, Gift-wrapped present. #698E, Fireworks. #698F, Balloons.

## Modern Singapore, 175th Anniv. — A176

SINGAPORE

**1994, Sept. 30    Perf. 13½x14**

| | | | | |
|---|---|---|---|---|
| 699 | A176 | 20c multicolored | .40 | .40 |
| 700 | A176 | 50c multicolored | .75 | .75 |
| 701 | A176 | 75c multicolored | 1.25 | 1.25 |
| 702 | A176 | $1 multicolored | 1.75 | 1.75 |
| a. | | Souvenir sheet of 4, #699-702 | 4.25 | 4.25 |
| | | Nos. 699-702 (4) | 4.15 | 4.15 |

Early, modern scenes: 20c, Schoolchildren reading, graduating seniors. 50c, Horse-drawn carriages, high-speed train. 75c, Small boats, container ship dock. $1, Skyline.

## ICAO, 50th Anniv. — A177

SINGAPORE 20¢ — 50

Designs: 35c, Control tower, passenger jet. 75c, Terminal, Concord jet. $2, Control tower, communication satellite, passenger jet.

**1994, Oct. 5    Litho.**

| | | | | |
|---|---|---|---|---|
| 703 | A177 | 20a multicolored | .30 | .30 |
| 704 | A177 | 35c multicolored | .50 | .50 |
| 705 | A177 | 75c multicolored | 1.10 | 1.10 |
| 706 | A177 | $2 multicolored | 3.00 | 3.00 |
| | | Nos. 703-706 (4) | 4.90 | 4.90 |

## Love Stamps — A178

SINGAPORE — Love LOVE Love — For local addresses only

**1995, Feb. 8    Die Cut Perf. 11½    Litho.**

**Self-Adhesive Booklet Stamps**

| | | | | |
|---|---|---|---|---|
| 707 | A178 | (20c) multicolored | .50 | .50 |
| 708 | A178 | (20c) multicolored | .50 | .50 |
| 709 | A178 | (20c) multicolored | .50 | .50 |
| 710 | A178 | (20c) multicolored | .50 | .50 |
| 711 | A178 | (20c) multicolored | .50 | .50 |
| a. | | Booklet pane, 2 each #707-711 (5) | 2.50 | 2.50 |
| | | Nos. 707-711 (5) | | |

#707, "Love" in three different inscriptions. #708, Spiral of "Love." #709, "Love" on two lines. #710, "Love" in different languages. #711, Geometrical "Love."

Nos. 707-711 inscribed "FOR LOCAL ADDRESSES ONLY." By its nature, No. 711a is a complete booklet. The peelable paper backing serves as a complete booklet. The peelable paper backing serves as a booklet cover. The outside of the cover contains 10 peelable labels.

## Meet in Singapore — A179

SINGAPORE

Scenes in Suntec City: (20c), Intl. Convention & Exhibition Center. 75c, High rise buildings. $1, Temasek Boulevard. $2, Fountain Terrace.

**1995, Jan. 11** *Perf. 13½x14*

**712** A179 (20c) multicolored .30 .30
**713** A179 75c multicolored 1.10 1.10
**714** A179 $1 multicolored 1.50 1.50
**715** A179 $2 multicolored 3.00 3.00
*Nos. 712-715 (4)* 5.90 5.90

Singapore '95. No. 712 inscribed "FOR LOCAL ADDRESSES ONLY."

**Souvenir Sheets of 2, #712, 715 Inscribed:**

*715a* FIP DAY 8.00 8.00
*715b* OLYMPIC DAY-YOUTH 8.00 8.00
*715c* FIAP DAY 8.00 8.00
*715d* LETTER WRITING DAY 8.00 8.00
*715e* STAMP COLLECTING DAY 8.00 8.00
*715f* SINGAPORE '95 DAY 8.00 8.00
*715g* PHILATELIC MUSEUM DAY 8.00 8.00
*715h* SINGAPORE POST DAY 8.00 8.00
*715i* AWARDS DAY 8.00 8.00
*715j* THEMATIC PHILATELY DAY 8.00 8.00

**Flower Type of 1991**

Designs: No. 716, Vanda Marlie Dolera, No. 717, Vanda limbata.

**1995, Mar. 15** **Litho.** *Perf. 14*

**716** A151 $2 multicolored 3.00 3.00
**717** A151 $2 multicolored 3.00 3.00
*a.* Pair, #716-717 + label 6.00 6.00
*b.* Souvenir sheet, #716-717 6.00 6.00
*c.* Souvenir sheet, #716-717 6.00 6.00

Singapore '95 (#717a-717c).
The margin of No. 717b pictures a chimpanzee in the jungle and No. 717c pictures a fish.
Three limited edition sheets were issued 9/1/95 at the show. They sold for 50, 12.5 and 2.9 times face. Values, $550, $220, $350.

Independence, 30th Anniv. — A180

"My Singapore, My Country, Happy Birthday" in various languages and: 20c, "30" formed in ribbon, vert. 50c, #471, flower. 75c, #598, Music sheet. $1, Natl. flag, #489, music sheets, vert.

*Perf. 14x13½, 13½x14*

**1995, Apr. 19** **Litho.**

**718** A180 (20c) multicolored .30 .30
**719** A180 50c multicolored .75 .75
**720** A180 75c multicolored 1.25 1.25
**721** A180 $1 multicolored 1.25 1.25
*a.* Souvenir sheet of 4, #718-721 4.50 4.50
*Nos. 718-721 (4)* 3.55 3.55

No. 718 inscribed "For Local Addresses Only." No. 721a is a continuous design.

End of World War II, 50th Anniv. A181

Designs: (20c), Crowd celebrating, Straits Settlements #271, vert. 60c, Lord Mountbatten receiving Japanese surrender of Singapore, Straits Settlements #265, vert. 70c, Food kitchen. $2, Police road block.

*Perf. 14x13½, 13½x14*

**1995, June 21** **Litho.**

**723** A181 (20c) multicolored .30 .30
**724** A181 60c multicolored .90 .90
**725** A181 70c multicolored 1.00 1.00
**726** A181 $2 multicolored 3.00 3.00
*Nos. 723-726 (4)* 5.20 5.20

No. 723 inscribed "For Local Addresses Only" and sold for 20c on day of issue.

New Six Digit Postal Code A182

**1995, Sept. 1** **Litho.** *Perf. 14x14½*

**727** A182 (20c) shown .30 .30
**728** A182 $2 Six boxes, numbers 3.00 3.00

No. 728 inscribed "For Local Addresses Only."

Philatelic Museum, Singapore A183

Museum building, various stamps, featuring: 20c, #12. 50c, #157. 60c, #661. $2, Displays of stamps.

**1995, Aug. 19** *Perf. 13x13½*

**729** A183 (20c) multicolored .30 .30
**730** A183 50c multicolored .80 .80
**731** A183 60c multicolored .90 .90
**732** A183 $2 multicolored 3.00 3.00
*Nos. 729-732 (4)* 5.00 5.00

No. 729 inscribed "For Local Addresses Only."

Fish A184

**1995, July 19** **Litho.** *Perf. 13½x14*

**733** A184 (20c) Yellow-faced angelfish .30 .30
Complete booklet, 10 #733 3.00
**734** A184 60c Harlequin sweetlips .90 .90
**735** A184 70c Lionfish 1.00 1.00
**736** A184 $1 Longfin bannerfish 1.50 1.50
*Nos. 733-736 (4)* 3.70 3.70

No. 733 inscribed "For Local Addresses Only."

Paintings in Singapore Art Museum A185

Designs: (20c), Tropical Fruits, by Georgette Chen. 30c, Bali Beach, by Cheong Soo Pieng. 70c, Gibbons, by Chen Wen Hsi. $2, Shi (Lion), by Pan Shou (calligraphy).

**1995, Oct. 20** **Litho.** *Perf. 12½*

**737** A185 (20c) multicolored .30 .30
**738** A185 30c multicolored .45 .45
**739** A185 70c multicolored 1.00 1.00

*Perf. 13½x13*

**740** A185 $2 multicolored 3.00 3.00
*Nos. 737-740 (4)* 4.75 4.75

No. 737 inscribed "For Local Addresses Only." No. 740 is 22½x39mm.

New Year 1996 (Year of the Rat) — A186

**1996, Feb. 9** **Litho.** *Perf. 12*

**741** A186 (20c) shown .25 .25
**742** A186 $2 Rat with orange 3.25 3.25

**Souvenir Sheet**

**742A** A186 Sheet of 2, #742, 742Ab 10.00 10.00
*b.* 22c like #741 .25 .25
*c.* As #742A, diff. sheet margin 10.00 10.00
*d.* As #742A, diff. sheet margin 12.00 12.00

No. 741 inscribed "For Local Addresses Only."
Sheet margins contain exhibition emblems for: #742A: Indonesia '96; #742Ac, China '96; #742Ad, CAPEX '96.
Issued: #742A, 3/21; #742Ac, 5/18; #742Ad, 6/8.

Architectural Styles — A187

Designs: (20c), Bukit Pasoh, Chinatown. 35c, Jalan Sultan, Kampong Glam. 70c, Dalhousie Lane, Little India. $1, Supreme Court, Civic District.

**1996, Jan. 17** *Perf. 13½x14*

**743** A187 (20c) multicolored .30 .30
**744** A187 35c multicolored .55 .55
**745** A187 70c multicolored 1.00 1.00
**746** A187 $1 multicolored 1.50 1.50
*Nos. 743-746 (4)* 3.35 3.35

No. 743 inscribed "For Local Addresses Only."

Old Maps of Singapore A188

Designs: (20c), Old Straits. 60c, Detail of town. $1, Part of Malay Penisula, Singapore. $2, Town and entrance.

**1996, Mar. 13** **Litho.** *Perf. 12*

**747** A188 (20c) multicolored .30 .30
**748** A188 60c multicolored .90 .90
**749** A188 $1 multicolored 1.50 1.50
**750** A188 $2 multicolored 3.00 3.00
*Nos. 747-750 (4)* 5.70 5.70

No. 747 inscribed "For Local Addresses Only."

Greetings Stamps — A189

Children's drawings about courtesy: (22c), #755Bc, Child telling another to be quiet in library. 35c, Children helping elderly during outdoor activities. 50c, Giving seat at bus stop to expectant mother. 60c, Sharing umbrella. $1, Giving up seat on bus to senior citizen.

*Die Cut Perf. 11*

**1996, July 10** **Litho.**

**Self-Adhesive Booklet Stamps**

**751** A189 (22c) multicolored .30 .30
*a.* Booklet pane of 10 3.00
**752** A189 35c multicolored .55 .55
**753** A189 50c multicolored .75 .75
**754** A189 60c multicolored .90 .90
**755** A189 $1 multicolored 1.50 1.50
*a.* Booklet pane of 10, 5 #751, 2 #752, 1 each #753-755 5.75
*Nos. 751-755 (5)* 4.00 4.00

**Souvenir Sheet**

**755B** A189 Sheet of 5, #752-755, 755Bc 4.00 4.00
*c.* 22c multicolored .30 .30

No. 751 inscribed "For Local Addresses Only." By their nature Nos. 751a and 755a are complete booklets. The peelable paper backing serves as a booklet cover. The outside of the cover contains 10 peelable labels.

1996 Summer Olympic Games, Atlanta — A190

Designs: (22c), #759Ab, Board, dinghy sailing. 60c, Soccer, tennis. 70c, Pole vault, hurdles. $2, Diving, swimming.

**1996, July 19** **Litho.** *Perf. 14½*

**756** A190 (22c) multicolored .30 .30
**757** A190 60c multicolored .90 .90
**758** A190 70c multicolored 1.00 1.00
**759** A190 $2 multicolored 3.00 3.00
*Nos. 756-759 (4)* 5.20 5.20

**Souvenir Sheet**

**759A** A190 Sheet of 4, #757-759, 759Ab 5.25 5.25
*b.* 22c multicolored .30 .30

No. 756 inscribed "For Local Addresses Only."

Asian Civilizations Museum — A191

(22c), Calligraphy in Caoshu, Ming Dynasty, 17th cent. 60c, Javanese Divination manuscript, Surkarta (Solo), Indonesia, 1842. 70c, Temple hanging, Tamilnadu, South India, 19th cent. $2, Calligraphic implements, Persia and Turkey, 17th-19th cent.

**1996, June 5** **Litho.** *Perf. 13½x14*

**760** A191 (22c) multicolored .30 .30
**761** A191 60c multicolored .90 .90
**762** A191 70c multicolored 1.00 1.00
**763** A191 $2 multicolored 3.00 3.00
*Nos. 760-763 (4)* 5.20 5.20

No. 760 inscribed "For Local Addresses Only."

Care for Nature — A192

Native trees: (22c), Cinnamomum iners. 60c, Hibiscus tiliaceus. 70c, Parkia speciosa. $1, Terminalia catappa.

**1996, Sept. 11** **Litho.** *Perf. 13½*

**764** A192 (22c) multicolored .30 .30
*a.* Booklet pane of 10 3.00
Complete booklet, #764a 3.00
**765** A192 60c multicolored .90 .90
**766** A192 70c multicolored 1.00 1.00
**767** A192 $1 multicolored 1.50 1.50
*Nos. 764-767 (4)* 3.70 3.70

No. 764 inscribed "For Local Addresses Only."

Panmen, Suzhou, China — A193

Design: 60c, Singapore waterfront.

**1996, Oct. 9** Litho. **Perf. 13x13½**
768 A193 (22c) multicolored .30 .30
769 A193 60c multicolored .90 .90
**Souvenir Sheet**
769A A193 Sheet of 2, #769, 769Ab 2.00 2.00
b. 22c like #768 .30 .30
c. As #769A, ovptd. in sheet margin 2.00 2.00
No. 768 inscribed "For Local Addresses Only."
No. 769Ac is ovptd. in sheet margin with violet on gold Singapore-China Stamp Exhibition emblem.
See People's Republic of China Nos. 2733-2734.

First World Trade Organization Ministerial Conference — A194

Illustration reduced.

**1996, Nov. 20** Litho. **Perf. 14**
770 A194 (22c) pink, vio & multi .35 .35
771 A194 60c ver, grn & multi .90 .90
772 A194 $1 bl, yel org & multi 1.50 1.50
773 A194 $2 grn, car & multi 3.00 3.00
Nos. 770-773 (4) 5.75 5.75
No. 770 inscribed "For Local Addresses Only."

New Year 1997 (Year of the Ox) A195

Nos. 774, 775, Different stylized oxen.

**1997, Jan. 10** Litho. **Perf. 13½x14**
774 A195 (22c) multicolored .35 .35
775 A195 $2 multicolored 3.00 3.00
a. Sheet, 9 each #775d 32.50
b. As "b," diff. sheet margin 8.00 8.00
c. As #774 8.00
d. As "b," diff. sheet margin .35 .35
Souvenir sheet of 4, #776-779 3.30 3.30
Nos. 776-779 (4)
Sheet margin contains exhibition emblem: #775b Hong Kong '97; #775c Pacific '97; #775e Shanghai 1997.
Issued: #775b, 2/12/97; #775c, 5/29/97; #775e, 11/19/97.

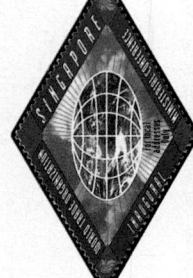

Traditional Games A196

**1997, Feb. 21** Litho. **Perf. 14½**
776 A196 (22c) multicolored .35 .35
777 A196 35c Marbles .55 .55
778 A196 70c Tops .90 .90
779 A196 $1 Fivestones 1.50 1.50
779a Souvenir sheet of 4, #776-779 3.30 3.30
Nos. 776-779 (4)
No. 776 inscribed "For Local Addresses Only." Singpex '97 (#779a).

Ground Transportation A197

**1997, Mar. 19** **Perf. 13½**
780 A197 5c Bullock cart .20 .20
781 A197 20c Bicycle .30 .30
782 A197 (22c) Rickshaw .35 .35
783 A197 30c Electric tram .45 .45
784 A197 35c Trolley bus .55 .55

785 A197 40c Trishaw .60 .60
786 A197 50c Vintage car .75 .75
787 A197 60c Horse-drawn carriage .90 .90
788 A197 70c Fire engine 1.00 1.00
Nos. 780-788 (9) 5.10 5.10
**Souvenir Sheet**
788A A197 Sheet, #780-781, 783-788, 788Ab 5.00 5.00
b. 22c like #782 .35 .35

**Self-Adhesive**
**Serpentine Die Cut Perf. 11½**
**Booklet Stamp**
789 A197 (22c) multicolored .35 .35
a. Booklet pane of 10 3.50
Nos. 782, 789 are inscribed "For Local Addresses Only." Nos. 780, 783-784, 787-788 are horiz.
By its nature No. 789a is a complete booklet. The peelable paper backing serves as a booklet cover.

**1997, Apr. 23** Litho. & Engr. **Perf. 13**
Size: 28x35mm (#790, 792), 43x24mm (#791, 793)
790 A197 $1 multicolored 1.50 1.50
791 A197 $3 multicolored 3.00 3.00
792 A197 $5 multicolored 7.50 7.50
793 A197 $10 multicolored 15.00 15.00
a. Souvenir sheet, #790-793 27.50 27.50
Nos. 790-793 (4) 27.00 27.00
$1, Taxi. $3, Bus, horiz. $5, Mass rapid transit system. $10, Light rapid transit system, horiz.

Greetings Stamps — A198

Word "Friends" used in making designs: #794, Man's head, #795, Sharing umbrella; #796, Penguins, #797, Butterflies, hand. #798, Coffee cup. #799, Flower. #800, Candle. #801, Tree. #802, Jar holding stars. #803, Two cans connected by string.

**Serpentine Die Cut 14½**
**Self-Adhesive**
**Booklet Stamps**
**1997, May 14**
794 A198 (22c) multicolored .35 .35
795 A198 (22c) multicolored .35 .35
796 A198 (22c) multicolored .35 .35
797 A198 (22c) multicolored .35 .35
798 A198 (22c) multicolored .35 .35
a. Booklet pane, 2 each #794-798 3.50
Nos. 794-798 (5) 1.75 1.75
799 A198 (22c) multicolored .35 .35
800 A198 (22c) multicolored .35 .35
801 A198 (22c) multicolored .35 .35
802 A198 (22c) multicolored .35 .35
803 A198 (22c) multicolored .35 .35
a. Booklet pane, 2 each #799-803 3.50
Nos. 799-803 (5) 1.75 1.75
Nos. 794-803 are inscribed "For Local Addresses Only." By their nature Nos. 798a and 803a are complete booklets. The peelable paper backing serves as a booklet cover. The outside cover contains 10 peelable labels.

Upgrading of Public Housing — A199

Designs: (22c), New look for the precinct. 30c, Outdoor facilities. 70c, Landscaped gardens. $1, Additional space, balcony.

**1997, July 16** Litho. **Perf. 14**
804 A199 (22c) multicolored .30 .30
805 A199 30c multicolored .40 .40
806 A199 70c multicolored .90 .90
807 A199 $1 multicolored 1.40 1.40
Nos. 804-807 (4) 3.00 3.00
No. 804 is inscribed "For Local Addresses Only."

ASEAN, 30th Anniv. — A200

Designs: (22c), 30 years of "dates," globe, hands clasped, sky. 35c, Southeast Asian cultures. 60c, Satellite dish, circuit board, map of Southeast Asia, sky. $1, Tourist attractions in ASEAN countries.

**1997, Aug. 8** Litho. **Perf. 14**
808 A200 (22c) multicolored .30 .30
809 A200 35c multicolored .50 .50
810 A200 60c multicolored .80 .80
811 A200 $1 multicolored 1.40 1.40
Nos. 808-811 (4) 3.00 3.00
No. 808 is inscribed "For Local Addresses Only."
Value is for copy with surrounding selvage.

Protection of the Environment — A201

(22c), Clean Environment. 60c, Clean waters. 70c, Clean air. $1, Clean homes.

**1997, Sept. 13** Litho. **Perf. 14x13½**
812 A201 (22c) multicolored .30 .30
a. Complete booklet, #812a 3.00
Booklet pane of 10
813 A201 60c multicolored .80 .80
814 A201 70c multicolored .90 .90
815 A201 $1 multicolored 1.30 1.30
Nos. 812-815 (4) 3.30 3.30
No. 812 is inscribed "For Local Addresses Only."

Marine Life Type of 1994
**Photo.** **Perf. 13x13½**
**1997**
816 A172 5c like #674 .20 .20
816A A172 (20c) like #675B .30 .30
817 A172 (22c) like #677 .30 .30
818 A172 30c like #678 .40 .40
819 A172 35c like #679 .45 .45
820 A172 40c like #679 .50 .50
821 A172 50c like #680 .65 .65
821A A172 75c like #681 1.25 1.25

**Photo. & Embossed** **Type A (2 Sides)**
**Perf. 14 Syncopated**
822 A172 $1 like #682 1.25 1.25
822A A172 $2 like #683 3.25 3.25
823 A172 $5 like #684 6.25 6.25
824 A172 $10 like #684A 12.50 12.50
Nos. 816-824 (12) 27.35 27.35
No. 816A is inscribed "For Local Addresses Only."
Nos. 822-824 have embossed logo in center of stamp and denomination and country are white. Nos. 682, 684, 684A have embossed lettering for country name and denomination.

Shells of Singapore and Thailand A202

Designs: (22c), Drupa morum. 35c, Nerita chamaeleon. 60c, Littoraria melanostoma. $1, Cryptospira elegans.

**1997, Oct. 9** Litho. **Perf. 13x14**
825 A202 (22c) multicolored .30 .30
826 A202 35c multicolored .45 .45
827 A202 60c multicolored .75 .75
828 A202 $1 multicolored 1.25 1.25
Nos. 825-828 (4) 2.75 2.75

**Souvenir Sheet**
828A A202 Sheet of 4, #826-828, 828Ab 2.75 2.75
b. 22c like #825 .30 .30
No. 825 inscribed "For Local Addresses Only."
See Thailand Nos. 1771-1774.

New Year 1998 (Year of the Tiger) A203

Different stylized tigers.

**1998, Jan. 9** Litho. **Perf. 13x14**
829 A203 (22c) multicolored .25 .25
830 A203 $2 multicolored 2.50 2.50
a. Horiz. or vert. pair, #829-830 2.75 2.75
b. Sheet of 9 each #829-830 27.50 27.50
**Souvenir Sheet**
830C A203 Sheet of 2, #830, 830Cd 2.75 2.75
d. 22c like #829 .30 .30
e. As #830C, diff. inscription 2.75 2.75
Israel '98 (#830C). Italia '98 (#830Ce). No. 829 inscribed "For Local Addresses Only."
Stamps in No. 830b are arranged in a checkerboard fashion.
Issued: #830Ce, 10/23/98.

Dinosaurs — A204

**Self-Adhesive**
831 A204 (22c) Pentaceratops .30 .30
832 A204 (22c) Apatosaurus .30 .30
833 A204 (22c) Albertosaurus .30 .30
a. Pane, 5 each #831-833 4.50 4.50
Nos. 831-833 (3) .90 .90

Songbirds: (22c), Lesser green leafbird. 60c, Magpie robin. 70c, Straw-headed bulbul. $2, Yellow-bellied prinia.

A205

**1998, May 6** **Photo.** **Granite Paper** **Perf. 11½**
834 A205 (22c) multicolored .25 .25
835 A205 60c multicolored .75 .75
836 A205 70c multicolored .85 .85
837 A205 $2 multicolored 2.40 2.40
Nos. 834-837 (4) 4.25 4.25
No. 834 is inscribed "For Local Addresses Only."

A206

**Serpentine Die Cut 11** Litho.
**Self-Adhesive**
**Booklet Stamps**
**1998, May 20**
"Hello" stamps.
838 A206 (22c) yellow & multi .25 .25
839 A206 (22c) orange & multi .25 .25
840 A206 (22c) green & multi .25 .25

**841** A206 (22c) blue & multi .25 .25
**842** A206 (22c) black & multi .25 .25
*a.* Booklet pane, 2 each #838-842 2.50

Nos. 838-842 are inscribed "For Local Addresses Only."

By its nature No. 842a is a complete booklet. The peelable paper backing serves as a booklet cover. The outside cover contains 10 peelable labels.

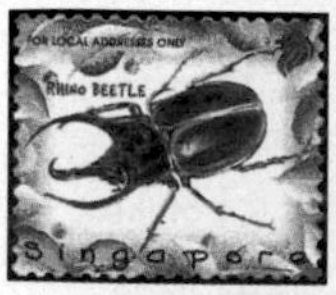
FOR LOCAL ADDRESSES ONLY
RHINO BEETLE
Singapore

Fauna from "Fragile Forest," Singapore Zoological Gardens — A207

***Serpentine Die Cut 11½***

**1998, June 5** **Litho.**

**Self-Adhesive**

**Booklet Stamps**

**843** A207 (22c) Rhino beetle .30 .30
**844** A207 (22c) Surinam horned frog .30 .30
**845** A207 (22c) Atlas moth .30 .30
**846** A207 (22c) Green iguana .30 .30
**847** A207 (22c) Giant scorpion .30 .30
*a.* Booklet, 2 each #843-847 3.00
**848** A207 (22c) Hissing cockroach .30 .30
**849** A207 (22c) Two-toed sloth .30 .30
**850** A207 (22c) Archer fish .30 .30
**851** A207 (22c) Cobalt blue tarantula .30 .30
**852** A207 (22c) Greater mousedeer .30 .30
*a.* Booklet, 2 each #848-852 3.00

Nos. 843-852 are inscribed "For Local Addresses Only."

The peelable paper backing of Nos. 847a & 852a serves as a booklet cover. In the margins of Nos. 847a & 852a there is a leaf-shapped scratch-off that reveals an animal.

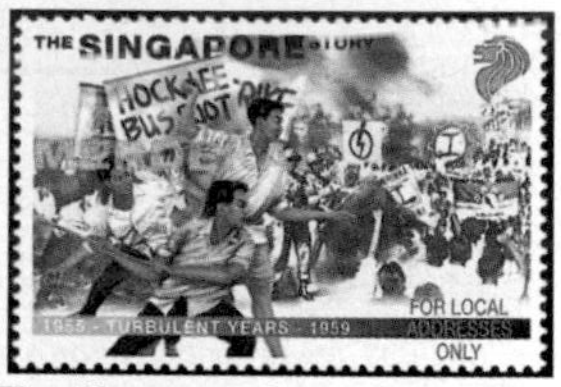
THE SINGAPORE STORY
1955 - TURBULENT YEARS - 1959
FOR LOCAL ADDRESSES ONLY

The Singapore Story (Moments in History) — A208

(22c), 22c, "Turbulent years," 1955-59. 60c, "Self-government," 1959-63. $1, "Towards merger and independence," 1961-65. $2, "A nation is born," 1965.

**1998** ***Perf. 13x13½***

**853** A208 (22c) multicolored .30 .30
**854** A208 60c multicolored .75 .75
**855** A208 $1 multicolored 1.25 1.25
**856** A208 $2 multicolored 2.50 2.50
*Nos. 853-856 (4)* 4.80 4.80

**Souvenir Sheet**

**857** Souvenir sheet of 4 9.00 9.00
*a.* 22c multicolored .50 .50
*b.* 60c multicolored 1.40 1.40
*c.* $1 multicolored 2.25 2.25
*d.* $2 multicolored 4.50 4.50

Issued: #853-856, 7/7/98; #857, 7/23/98.

No. 853 is inscribed "For Local Addresses Only." No. 857 has a UV varnish producing a shiny effect on portions of the design. No. 857 sold for $7.

Singpex '98 (#857).

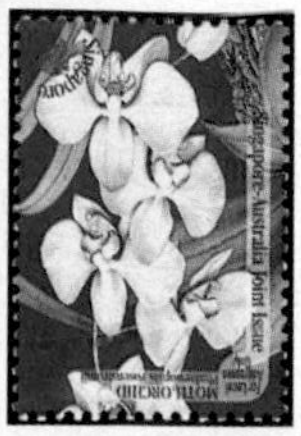

Orchids of Singapore and Australia — A209

**1998, Aug. 6** **Photo.** ***Perf. 11½***

**858** A209 (22c) Moth orchid .30 .30
**859** A209 70c Bamboo orchid .85 .85
**860** A209 $1 Tiger orchid 1.25 1.25
**861** A209 $2 Cooktown orchid 2.60 2.60
*Nos. 858-861 (4)* 5.00 5.00

**Souvenir Sheet**

**861A** A209 Sheet of 4, #859-861, #861Ab 5.00 5.00
*b.* 22c like #858 .30 .30

No. 858 is inscribed "For Local Addresses Only."

See Australia Nos. 1681-1684.

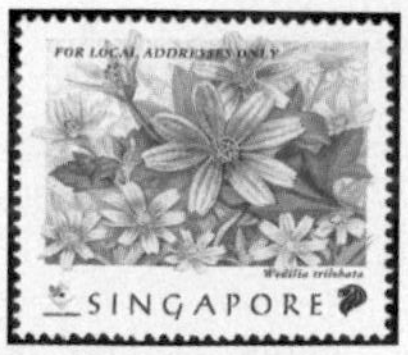
SINGAPORE

Flowers A210

Designs: No. 862, Wedilia trilobata. No. 863, Dillenia suffruticosa. No. 864, Canna hybrid. No. 865, Caesalpinia pulcherrima.

No. 866, Zephyranthes rosea. No. 867, Cassia alata. No. 868, Heliconia rostrata. No. 869, Allamanda cathartica.

**1998, Sept. 9** **Litho.** ***Perf. 14***

**862** A210 (22c) multicolored .30 .30
**863** A210 (22c) multicolored .30 .30
**864** A210 (22c) multicolored .30 .30
**865** A210 (22c) multicolored .30 .30
*a.* Strip of 4, #862-865 1.25 1.25
*b.* Booklet pane, 3 each #864-865, 2 each #862-863 3.00
Complete booklet, #865b 3.00
**866** A210 35c multicolored .40 .40
**867** A210 35c multicolored .40 .40
**868** A210 60c multicolored .70 .70
**869** A210 60c multicolored .70 .70
*a.* Strip of 4, #866-869 2.25 2.25
*b.* Souvenir sheet of 8, #862-869 3.40 3.40

Stamps in #869b are in pairs, #864-863, 862/865 horiz., #866-867, 868, 869 vert.

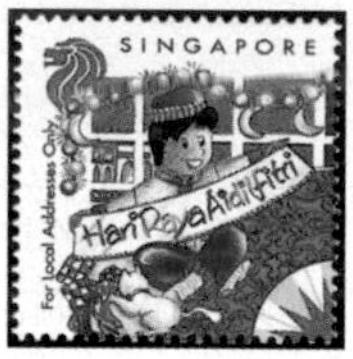
SINGAPORE
For Local Addresses Only

A211

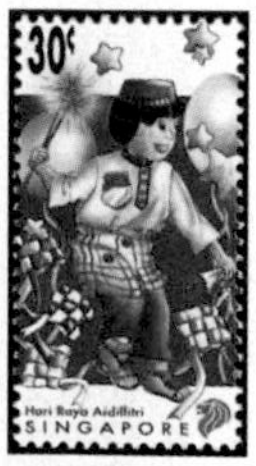
30c
SINGAPORE

Festivals — A212

#870, 874 Eid al-Fitr. #871, 875, Christmas. #872, 876, Chinese New Year. #873, 877, Deepavali.

**1998, Oct. 7** **Litho.** ***Perf. 13x14***

**870** A211 (22c) multicolored .30 .30
**871** A211 (22c) multicolored .30 .30
**872** A211 (22c) multicolored .30 .30
**873** A211 (22c) multicolored .30 .30
*a.* Block of 4, #870-873 1.25 1.25
**874** A212 30c multicolored .35 .35
**875** A212 30c multicolored .35 .35
**876** A212 30c multicolored .35 .35
**877** A212 30c multicolored .35 .35
*Nos. 870-877 (8)* 2.60 2.60

Nos. 870-873 are inscribed "For Local Addresses Only."

***Serpentine Die Cut***

**878** A211 (22c) like #870 .30 .30
**879** A211 (22c) like #871 .30 .30
**880** A211 (22c) like #872 .30 .30
**881** A211 (22c) like #873 .30 .30
*Nos. 878-881 (4)* 1.20 1.20

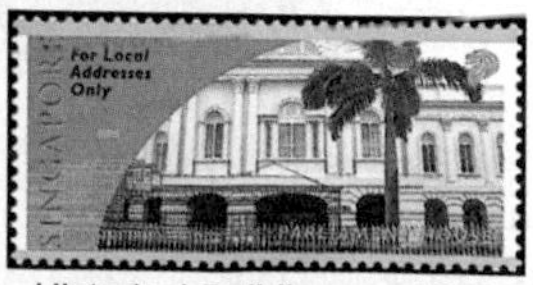
For Local Addresses Only
SINGAPORE

Historical Buildings — A213

(22c), Parliament House. 70c, Former Convent of the Holy Infant Jesus Chapel. $1, Hill Street Building. $2, Sun Yat Sen Nanyang Memorial Hall.

**1998, Nov. 4** ***Perf. 13½***

**882** A213 (22c) multicolored .30 .30
**883** A213 70c multicolored .90 .90
**884** A213 $1 multicolored 1.25 1.25
**885** A213 $2 multicolored 2.50 2.50
*Nos. 882-885 (4)* 4.95 4.95

No. 882 inscribed "For Local Addresses Only."

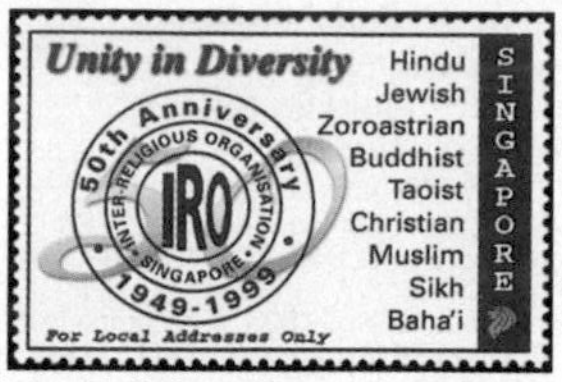
Unity in Diversity
50th Anniversary
IRO
1949-1999
Hindu
Jewish
Zoroastrian
Buddhist
Taoist
Christian
Muslim
Sikh
Baha'i
SINGAPORE
For Local Addresses Only

Inter-Religious Organization, 50th Anniv. — A214

**1999, Jan. 15** **Litho.** ***Perf. 13x13½***

**886** A214 (22c) white & multi .25 .25
**887** A214 60c pink & multi .70 .70
**888** A214 $1 blue & multi 1.25 1.25
*Nos. 886-888 (3)* 2.20 2.20

No. 886 is inscribed "For Local Addresses Only."

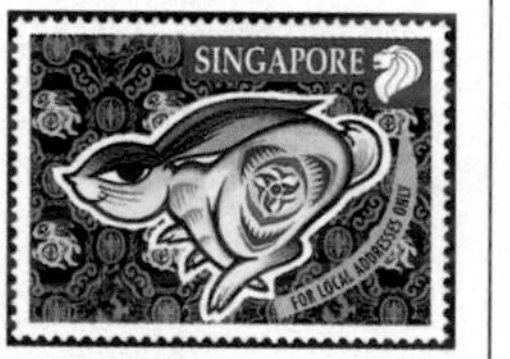
SINGAPORE

New Year 1999 (Year of the Rabbit) A215

Various stylized rabbits.

**1999, Jan. 15** ***Perf. 14***

**889** A215 (22c) multicolored .25 .25
**890** A215 $2 multicolored 2.40 2.40
*a.* Horiz. or vert. pair, #889-890 2.75 2.75
*b.* Sheet, 9 each #829-830 25.00

**Souvenir Sheet**

**890C** Sheet of 2, #890 & 890Cd 2.75 2.75
*d.* A215 22c like #889 .30 .30
*e.* As #890C, with PhilexFrance 99 margin 2.75 2.75
*f.* As #890C, with China 1999 World Phil. Exhib. margin 2.75 2.75

No. 889 is inscribed "For Local Addresses Only."

No. 890C was issued 4/27 for IBRA '99, World Philatelic Exhibition, Nuremberg.

Issued: #890Ce, 7/2/99; #890Cf, 8/21/99.

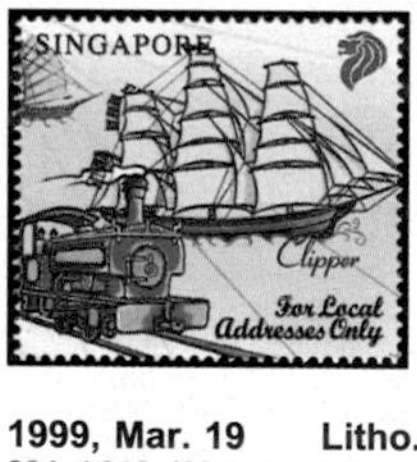
SINGAPORE
Clipper
For Local Addresses Only

19th Century Sailing Ships — A216

**1999, Mar. 19** **Litho.** ***Perf. 14½***

**891** A216 (22c) Clipper .25 .25
**892** A216 70c Twakow, vert. .80 .80
**893** A216 $1 Fujian junk, vert. 1.25 1.25
**894** A216 $2 Golekkan 2.40 2.40
*Nos. 891-894 (4)* 4.70 4.70

**Souvenir Sheet**

**894A** A216 Sheet of 4, #892-894, #894Ab 4.50 4.50
*b.* 22c like #891 .25 .25

Australia '99 World Stamp Expo (#894A).

No. 891 is inscribed "For Local Address Only."

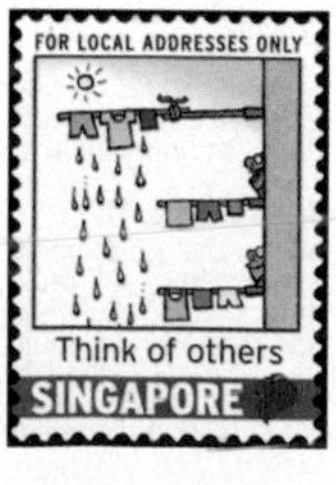
FOR LOCAL ADDRESSES ONLY
Think of others
SINGAPORE

Greetings Stamps — A217

Expressions of kindness: a, "Think of others." b, "Do not litter." c, "Be kind to animals." d, "Be considerate." e, "Be generous."

***Serpentine Die Cut 9½***

**1999, May 12** **Litho.**

**Self-Adhesive**

**Booklet Stamps**

**895** A217 (22c) Booklet pane, 2 each #a.-e. 2.60 2.60

Nos. 895a-895e are inscribed "For Local Addresses Only."

No. 895 is a complete booklet. The peelable paper backing serves as a booklet cover. Stamps are printed 2 each #895a-895c on one side, 2 each #895d-895e on the other with 3 labels on each side.

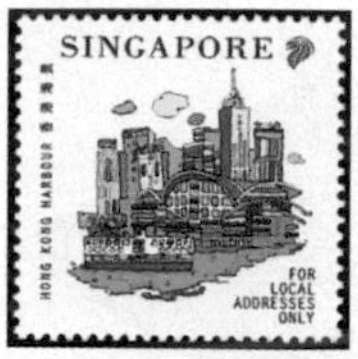
SINGAPORE
FOR LOCAL ADDRESSES ONLY

Hong Kong and Singapore Tourism — A218

(22c), Hong Kong Harbor. 35c, Skyline of Singapore. 50c, Giant Buddha, Hong Kong. 60c, Merlion Sentosa Island, Singapore. 70c, Hong Kong Street scene. $1, Bugis Junction, Singapore.

**1999, July 1** **Litho.** ***Perf. 13½x13¼***

**896** A218 (22c) multicolored .25 .25
**897** A218 35c multicolored .40 .40
**898** A218 50c multicolored .60 .60
**899** A218 60c multicolored .70 .70
**900** A218 70c multicolored .85 .85
**901** A218 $1 multicolored 1.25 1.25
*Nos. 896-901 (6)* 4.05 4.05

**Souvenir Sheet**

**902** Sheet of 6, #897-901, #902a 4.00 4.00
*a.* A218 22c like #896 .25 .25

No. 896 is inscribed for "For Local Addresses Only."

See Hong Kong Nos. 849-854.

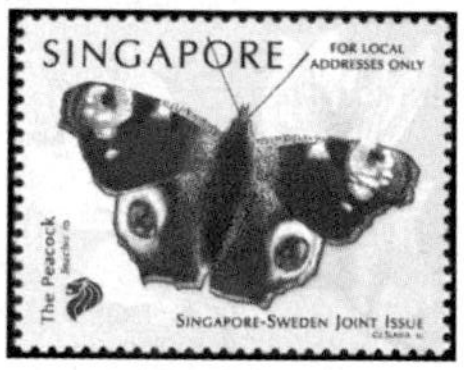
SINGAPORE
FOR LOCAL ADDRESSES ONLY
The Peacock
SINGAPORE-SWEDEN JOINT ISSUE

Butterflies A219

***Perf. 12½x12¾***

**1999, Aug. 12** **Litho. & Engr.**

**903** A219 (22c) Peacock .25 .25
**904** A219 70c Blue pansy .85 .85
**905** A219 $1 Great egg-fly 1.25 1.25
**906** A219 $2 Red admiral 2.40 2.40
*Nos. 903-906 (4)* 4.75 4.75

**Souvenir Sheet**

**907** A219 Sheet of 4, #904-906, #907a 4.75 4.75
*a.* A219 22c like #903 .25 .25

No. 903 is inscribed "For Local Addresses Only."

See Sweden No. 2356.

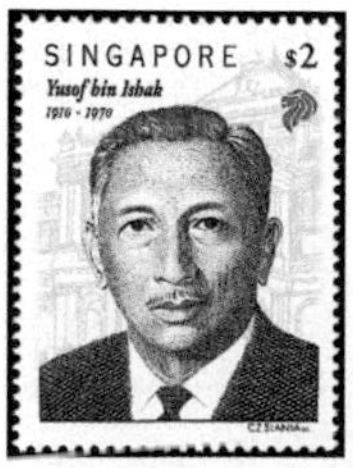
SINGAPORE $2
Yusof bin Ishak

Yusof bin Ishak (1910-70), First President of Singapore A220

***Perf. 13¼x13¾***

**1999, Sept. 9** **Litho. & Engr.**

**908** A220 $2 multicolored 2.40 2.40

Issued in sheets of 4.

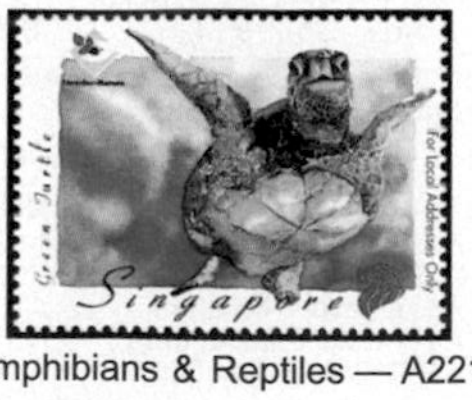
Green Turtle
Singapore

Amphibians & Reptiles — A221

**1999, Oct. 13 Litho. *Perf. 14***

**909** A221 (22c) Green turtle .25 .25
Complete booklet, 10 #909 2.50
**910** A221 60c Green crested lizard .75 .75
**911** A221 70c Copper-cheeked frog .85 .85
**912** A221 $1 Water monitor 1.25 1.25
*Nos. 909-912 (4)* 3.10 3.10

No. 909 inscribed "For Local Addresses Only."

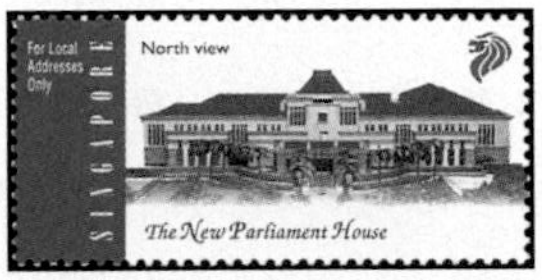


New Parliament House — A222

***Perf. 13¼x13¾***

**1999, Nov. 17 Litho.**

**913** A222 (22c) North view .30 .30
**914** A222 60c Northeast view .75 .75
**915** A222 $1 Southeast view 1.25 1.25
**916** A222 $2 West view 2.50 2.50
*Nos. 913-916 (4)* 4.80 4.80

#913 inscribed "For Local Address Only."

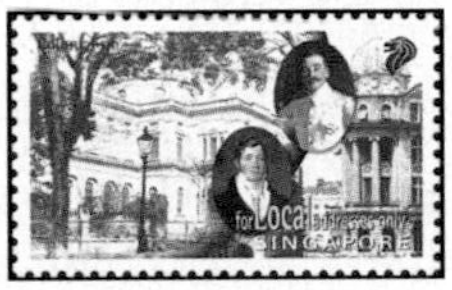

Singapore in the 20th Century A223

No. 917: a, Colonialism. b, Education. c, Immigration. d, Government. e, Japanese occupation. f, National service. g, Transportation. h, Tourism. i, Housing. j, Economic progress.

***Perf. 13¼x12½***

**1999, Dec. 31 Litho.**

**917** Sheet of 10 + 5 labels 7.00 7.00
*a.-b.* A223 (22c) Any single .25 .25
*c.-d.* A223 35c Any single .40 .40
*e.-f.* A223 60c Any single .70 .70
*g.-h.* A223 70c Any single .85 .85
*i.-j.* A223 $1 Any single 1.25 1.25

Nos. 917a-917b inscribed "For Local Addresses Only."

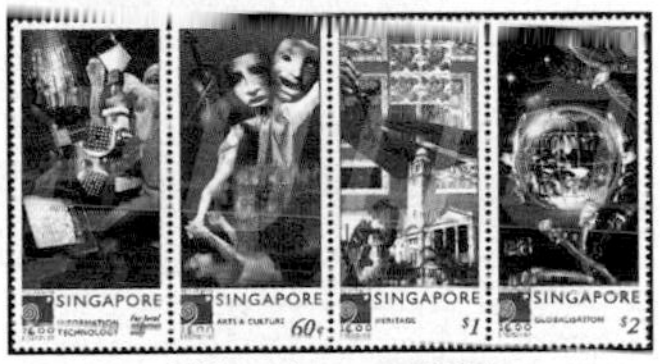

Millennium — A224

No. 918: a, (22c), Information technology. b, 60c, Arts and culture. c, $1, Heritage. d, $2, Globalization.
Illustration reduced.

**2000, Jan. 1 Photo. *Perf. 14¼x14¾***
**Granite Paper**

**918** A224 Horiz. strip of 4, #a-d 4.75 4.75
*e.* Souvenir sheet, #918 4.75 4.75

No. 918a inscribed "For Local Addresses Only."

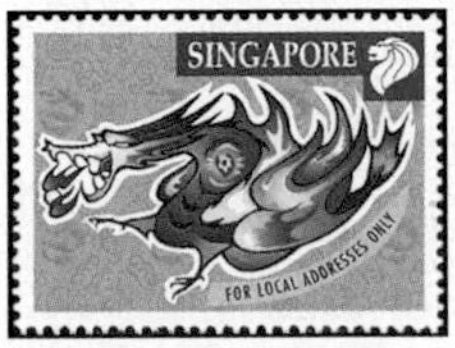


New Year 2000 (Year of the Dragon) A225

Dragon: (22c), 22c, Facing left. $2, $10, Facing right.

**2000 Litho. *Perf. 13x13¼***

**919** A225 (22c) multi .25 .25
**920** A225 $2 multi 2.40 2.40
*a.* Horiz. pair, #919-920 2.75 2.75
*b.* Souvenir sheet, #920a 2.75 2.75

**Souvenir Sheets**

**921** Sheet of 2, #920, 922a, with Bangkok 2000 margin 2.75 2.75
*a.* A225 22c multi .25 .25
*b.* As No. 921, with The Stamp Show 2000 margin 2.75 2.75
*c.* As No. 921, with Naba 2000 margin 2.75 2.75

**Litho. & Embossed**

**922** A225 $10 gold & multi 12.00 12.00

Issued: No. 920b, 10/30; No. 921, 3/25; No. 921b, 5/22, No. 921c, 6/21; others, 1/1. No. 919 inscribed "For Local Addresses Only."

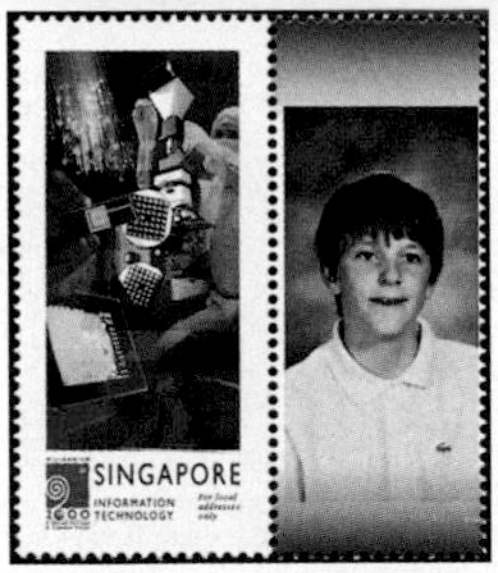

Millennium Personalized Stamp — A225a

**2000, Mar. 8 Litho. *Perf. 14x14¼***

**923** A225a (22c) multi + label 1.25 1.25

No. 923 printed in sheets of 20 stamps + labels that could be personalized. Sheets sold for $20 for the first sheet with additional sheets available for $10. The design on No. 923 is similar to that on No. 918a, but is 19x46mm and lacks frame.

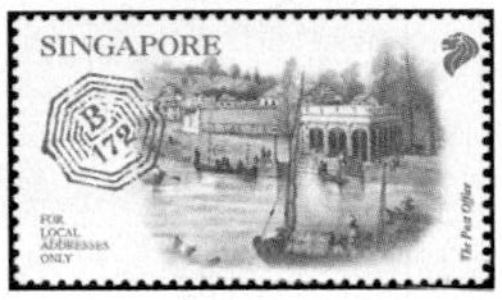


Post Offices and Cancels A226

Designs: (22c), Original post office, B172 cancel. 60c, General Post Office, c. 1873, 1875 cancel. $1, General Post Office, 1928, 1935 cancel. $2, Singapore Post Center, 1998 cancel.

**2000, Mar. 8 Litho. *Perf. 13½***

**935** A226 (22c) multi .25 .25
**936** A226 60c multi .70 .70
*a.* Booklet pane, 4 #935, 2 #936 2.40
**937** A226 $1 multi 1.10 1.10
**938** A226 $2 multi 2.40 2.40
*a.* Booklet pane, 4 #937, 2 #938 9.25
Complete bklt., #936a, 938a 12.00
*Nos. 935-938 (4)* 4.45 4.45

**Souvenir Sheet**

**939** A226 Sheet of 4, #936-938, 939a 4.50 4.50
*a.* A226 22c like No. 935 .25 .25

No. 935 is inscribed "For Local Addresses Only."

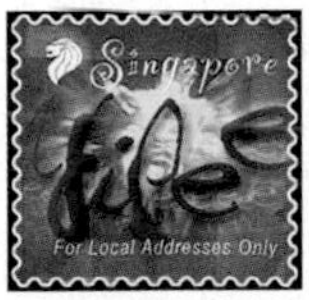


Celebrations A227

Designs: No. 940, (22c), Yipee. No. 940A, (22c), Yeah. No. 940B, (22c), Hurray. No. 940C, (22c), Yes. No. 941, (22c), Happy.

***Serpentine Die Cut 9½***

**2000, May 10 Litho.**
**Self-Adhesive**

**940-941** A227 Set of 5 1.40 1.40
*941a* Booklet, 2 each #940-941 2.80

Nos. 940-941 are inscribed "For Local Addresses Only." Eight self-adhesive die cut labels are affixed to the opposite side of the peelable backing paper.

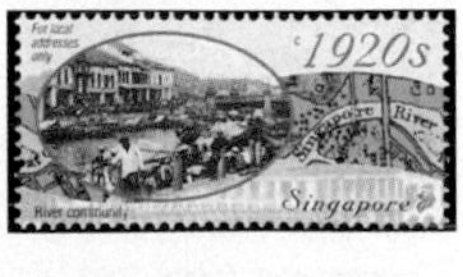


Singapore River A228

No. 942: a, River community, 1920s. b, South Boat Quay, 1930s. c, Social gathering, 1950s. d, Changing skyline, 1980s. e, River Regatta, 1990s. f, At the river mouth, 1900s. g, Stevedores, 1910s. h, Lighters, 1940s. i, Men at work, 1960s. j, Working with cranes, 1970s.

**2000, June 21 *Perf. 14***

**942** Sheet of 10 5.00 5.00
*a.-e.* A228 (22c) Any single .25 .25
*f.-j.* A228 60c Any single .75 .75

Nos. 942a-942e are inscribed "For Local Addresses Only."

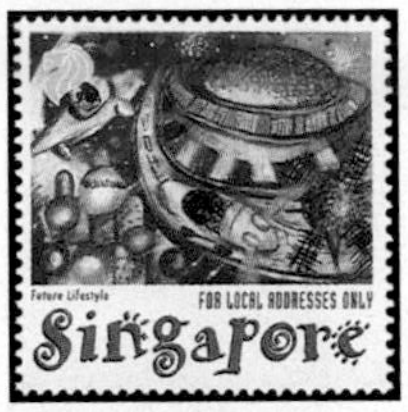


Stampin' the Future A229

Children's Stamp Design Contest Winners: (22c), Future lifestyle, art by Liu Jiang Wen. 60c, Future homes, art by Shaun Yew Chuan Bin. $1, Home automation, art by Gwendolyn Soh Shihui. $2, Floating city, art by Dawn Koh.

**2000, July 7 Litho. *Perf. 14x12¾***

**943-946** A229 Set of 4 4.75 4.75
*946a* Souvenir sheet, #943-946 4.75 4.75

World Stamp Expo 2000, Anaheim (No. 946a). No. 943 is inscribed "For Local Addresses Only."

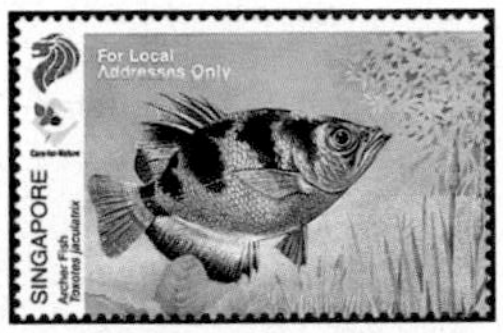


Care for Nature A230

No. 947: a, Archer fish. b, Smooth otter. c, Collared kingfisher. d, Orange fiddler crab.

**2000, Aug. 11 Photo. *Perf. 14½***
**Granite Paper**

**947** Block of 4 3.00 3.00
*a.-b.* A230 (22c) Any single .25 .25
*c.-d.* A230 $1 Any single 1.25 1.25
*e.* Booklet pane, 5 each #947a, 947b 7.50
Booklet, #947e 7.50
*f.* Souv. sheet, #947, 947 imperf 6.00 6.00

Nos. 947a-947b are inscribed "For Local Addresses Only."
No. 947f sold for $5.

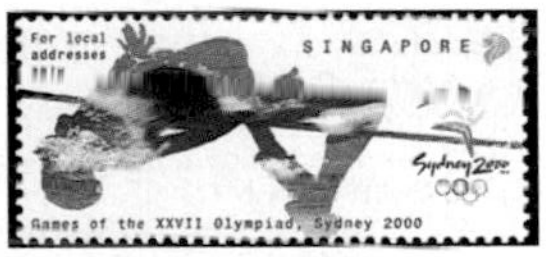


2000 Summer Olympics, Sydney — A231

Designs: (22c), Swimming and high jump. 60c, Badminton and discus. $1, Soccer and hurdles. $2, Table tennis and gymnastics.

**2000, Sept. 15 Litho. *Perf. 13½***

**948-951** A231 Set of 4 4.75 4.75

No. 948 is inscribed "For Local Addresses Only."

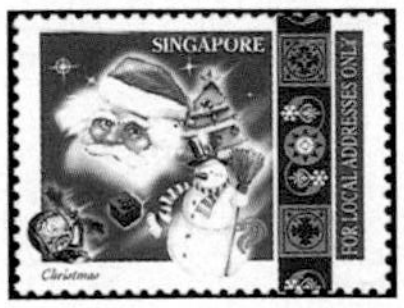


A232

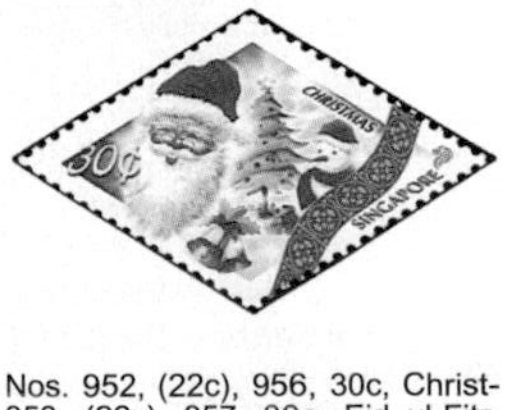


Festivals and Holidays A233

Designs: Nos. 952, (22c), 956, 30c, Christmas. Nos. 953, (22c), 957, 30c, Eid ul-Fitr. Nos. 954, (22c), 958, 30c, Chinese New Year. Nos. 955, (22c), 959, 30c, Deepavali.

**2000, Oct. 11 Litho. *Perf. 13***

**952-955** A232 Set of 4 1.00 1.00
**956-959** A233 Set of 4 1.40 1.40

Nos. 952-955 are inscribed "For Local Addresses Only."

**Festivals and Holidays Type of 2000**

Designs: No. 960, (22c), Christmas. No. 961, (22c), Eid ul-Fitr. No. 962, (22c), Chinese New Year. No. 963, (22c), Deepavali.

***Serpentine Die Cut 12¾x13¼***

**2000, Oct. 11 Litho.**
**Self-Adhesive**

**960-963** A232 Set of 4 1.00 1.00

Nos. 960-963 inscribed "For Local Addresses Only."

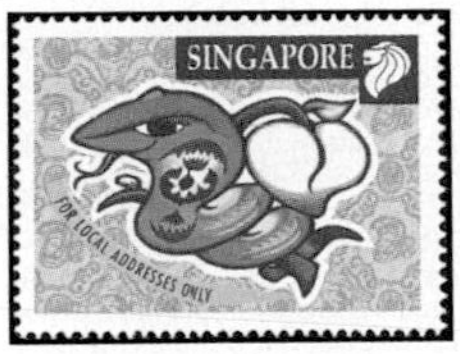


New Year 2001 (Year of the Snake) A234

Designs: (22c), Snake and branch. $2, Two snakes.

**2001, Jan. 12 *Perf. 14½x14***

**964** A234 (22c) multi .25 .25
**965** A234 $2 multi 2.40 2.40
*a.* Horiz. pair, #964-965 2.75 2.75
*b.* Souvenir sheet, #964-965, with Hong Kong 2001 margin 2.75 2.75
*c.* Souvenir sheet, #964-965, with Belgica 2001 margin 2.75 2.75
*d.* Souvenir sheet, #964-965, with Phila Nippon '01 margin 2.75 2.75

Issued: No. 965c, 6/9; No. 965d, 7/1.

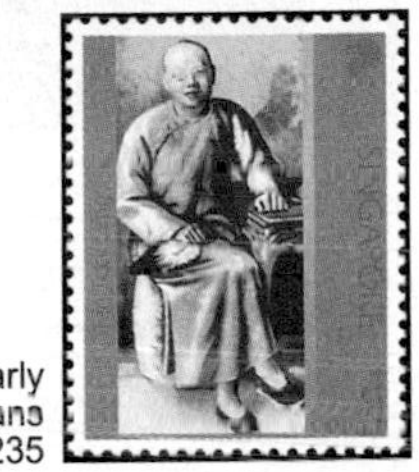

Early Singaporeans A235

Designs: No. 966, $1, Tan Tock Seng (1798-1850), philanthropist. No. 967, $1, P. Govindasamy Pillai (1887-1980), businessman. No. 968, $1, Edwin John Tessensohn (1857-1926), politician. No. 969, $1, Eunos bin Abdullah (1876-1941), politician.

**2001, Feb. 28 Photo. *Perf. 11¾***
**Granite Paper**

**966-969** A235 Set of 4 4.75 4.75

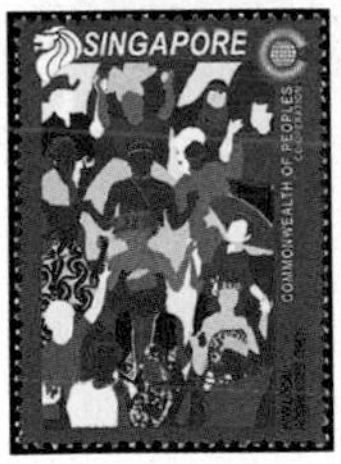


Commonwealth Day, 25th Anniv. — A236

Designs: (22c), Co-operation. 60c, Education. $1, Sports. $2, Arts and culture.

**2001, Mar. 12 Litho. *Perf. 14x14¼***

**970-973** A236 Set of 4 4.25 4.25

No. 970 inscribed "For Local Addresses Only."

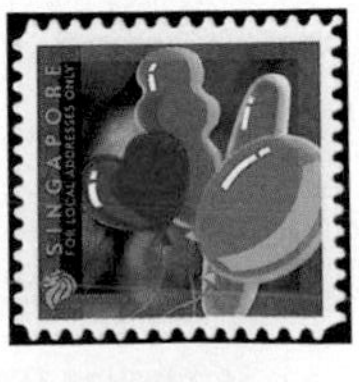


Greetings — A237

***Serpentine Die Cut 10***

**2001, Apr. 25** **Litho.**

**Self-Adhesive**

**974** A237 (22c) Balloons .25 .25
**975** A237 (22c) Fireworks .25 .25
**976** A237 (22c) Roses .25 .25
**977** A237 (22c) Gifts .25 .25
**978** A237 (22c) Musical instruments .25 .25
*a.* Booklet, 2 each #974-978 + 10 labels 2.50
*Nos. 974-978 (5)* 1.25 1.25

Nos. 974-978 inscribed "For Local Addresses Only."

**Greetings Type of 2001**

**2001, Apr. 25** **Litho.** ***Perf. 14***

**Water-Activated Gum**

**978B** A237 (22c) Fireworks .60 .60
**978C** A237 (22c) Musical instruments .60 .60
**978D** A237 (22c) Roses .60 .60
**978E** A237 (22c) Balloons .60 .60
**978F** A237 (22c) Gifts .60 .60
*g.* Vert. strip, #978B-978F + 5 labels 3.00 3.00

Nos. 978B-978F were printed in sheets containing four of each stamp and 20 labels that could be personalized. Sheets sold for $11 for the first sheet with additional sheets available for $10.

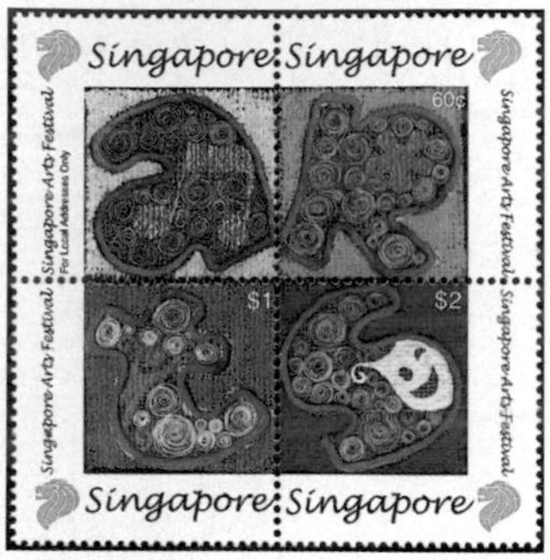

Singapore Arts Festival — A238

No. 979: a, (22c), "a." b, 60c, "r." c, $1, "t." d, $2, "s."

**2001, May 16** ***Perf. 14***

**979** A238 Block of 4, #a-d 4.25 4.25

No. 979a inscribed "For Local Addresses Only."

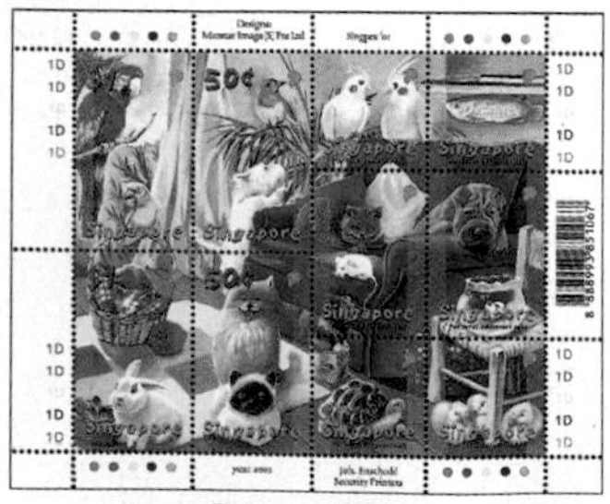

Pets — A239

No. 980: a, Fish. b, Cockatoos. c, Chicks. d, Turtle. e, Dog and fish. f, Cat and mice. g, Bird and dog. h, Dog and cat. i, Parrots. j, Cat and rabbit.

**2001, July 26** ***Perf. 13½***

**980** A239 Sheet of 10 5.00 5.00
*a.-d.* (22c) Any single, 25x25mm .25 .25
*e.-f.* (22c) Any single, 25x35mm .25 .25
*g.-h.* 50c Any single, 25x42mm .60 .60
*i.-j.* $1 Any single, 25x42mm 1.10 1.10

Nos. 980a-980f are inscribed "For Local Addresses Only." Singpex '01.

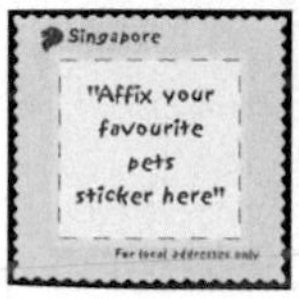

Frame — A240

***Serpentine Die Cut 15x14½***

**2001, July 26**

**Self-Adhesive**

**981** A240 (22c) multi .25 .25

**Size: 24x34mm**

**982** A240 (22c) multi .25 .25
*a.* Pane, 6 #981, 4 #982 +16 labels 2.50

Nos. 981-982 inscribed "For Local Addresses Only." No. 982a contains three examples of No. 982 with differing white paw prints, and one example without paw print. Singpex '01.

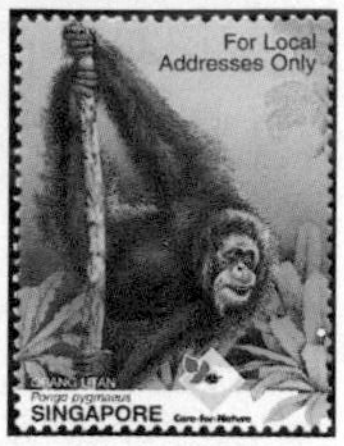

Care for Nature — A241

Orangutans: (22c), Adult hanging on tree. 60c, Two adults. No. 983c, Adult and child. No. 983d, Two adults and child.

**2001, Sept. 5** ***Perf. 13½x13***

**983** Horiz. strip of 4 3.25 3.25
*a.* A241 (22c) multi .25 .25
*b.* A241 60c multi .70 .70
*c.-d.* A241 $1 Any single 1.10 1.10
*e.* Souvenir sheet, #983 4.50 4.50
*f.* Sheet, 2 each #983c-983d, + 8 labels, perf. 12¾ ('05) 7.50 7.50

**Self-Adhesive**

**Booklet Stamp**

***Serpentine Die Cut 12½***

**984** A241 (22c) multi .25 .25
*a.* Booklet of 10 2.50

Nos. 983a, 984 inscribed "For Local Addresses Only."

No. 983e sold for $3.90, with 50c of that donated to the Care for Nature Trust Fund.

No. 983f issued 5/1/05. No. 983f sold for $6.

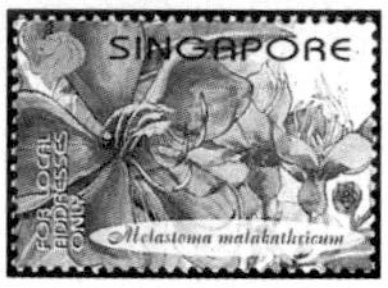

Flowers A242

Designs: (22c), Melastoma malabathricum. 60c, Leontopodium alpinum. $1, Saraca cauliflora. $2, Gentiana clusii.

**2001, Sept. 20** ***Perf. 13¼x12¾***

**985-988** A242 Set of 4 4.50 4.50
*988a* Souvenir sheet, #985-988 4.50 4.50

No. 985 inscribed "For Local Addresses Only." See Switzerland No. 1107.

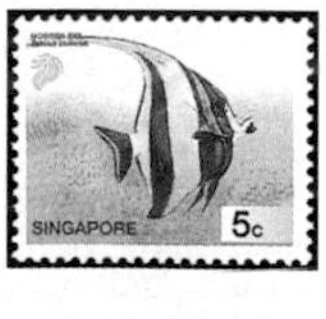

Tropical Fish — A243

Designs: 5c, Moorish idol. 20c, Threadfin butterflyfish. (22c), Copperband butterflyfish. (23c), Copperband butterflyfish. 30c, Pearlscale butterflyfish. 31c, Eight-banded butterflyfish. 40c, Rainbow butterflyfish. 50c, Yellow-faced angelfish. 60c, Emperor angelfish. 70c, Striped sailfin tang. 80c, Palette tang.

**2001-05** ***Perf. 13x13¼***

**989** A243 5c multi .20 .20
**990** A243 20c multi .20 .20
**991** A243 (22c) multi .25 .25
**992** A243 30c multi .35 .35
**992A** A243 31c multi .40 .40
**992B** A243 (31c) multi .40 .40
**993** A243 40c multi .45 .45
**994** A243 50c multi .55 .55
**995** A243 60c multi .65 .65
**996** A243 70c multi .75 .75
**997** A243 80c multi .85 .85
*a.* Sheet of 9, #989-997 4.25 4.25
*Nos. 989-997 (11)* 5.05 5.05

**Self-Adhesive**

***Serpentine Die Cut 12½***

**998** A243 (22c) multi .25 .25
*a.* Booklet of 10 2.50
**998B** A243 (23c) multi .30 .30
*c.* Booklet pane of 10 3.00

Issued: Nos. 989-992, 993-998 issued 10/24/01. 31c, 2/3/04; (23c), 7/7/04; No. 992B, 3/18/05.

Nos. 991, 998 inscribed "For Local Addresses Only." No. 998B is inscribed "1st Local." No. 992B is inscribed "2nd Local."

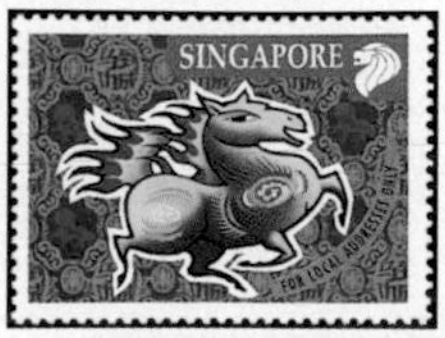

New Year 2002 (Year of the Horse) A244

Designs: Nos. 999, 1001a, (22c), One horse. Nos. 1000, 1001b, $2, Two horses.

**Litho., Litho & Embossed with Foil Application (#1001a, 1001b)**

**2002, Jan. 10** ***Perf. 13½x13¼***

**999-1000** A244 Set of 2 2.50 2.50
*1000a* Souvenir sheet, #999-1000, perf. 13x13¼ 2.50 2.50
**1001** Sheet, #1001a-1001b, 8 each #999-1000 22.50 22.50
*a.* A244 (22c) silver & multi .25 .25
*b.* A244 $2 gold & multi 2.25 2.25

A souvenir sheet containing one each of Nos. 1001a and 1001b exists. It was sold only in year sets.

No. 1000a issued 8/2/02, for Philakorea.

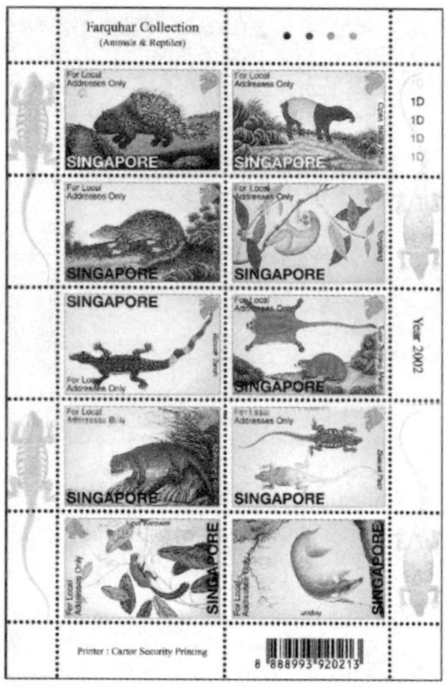

William Farquhar Collection of Natural History Drawings — A245

No. 1002, (22c) — Animals and Reptiles: a, Landak raya. b, Cipan, Badak murai. c, Landak kelubu. d, Kongkang. e, Biawak tanah. f, Tupai terbang merah. g, Memerang kecil. h, Biawak pasir. i, Tupai kerawak, vert. j, Napuh, vert.

No. 1003, (22c) — Fruits and Plants: a, Buah rumenia. b, Manggis hutan. c, Cempedak. d, Bunga dedap. e, Jeringau, vert. f, Rotang, vert. g, Tuba, vert. h, Tebu gagak, vert. i, Temu kunci, vert. j, Rambutan, vert.

No. 1004, (22c) — Birds: a, Burung gaji-gaji. b, Kuau cermin. c, Ayam kolam. d, Kelengking. e, Burung kuang. f, Puhung. g, Burung kunyit, vert. h, Burung pacat sayap biru, vert. i, Burung mural, vert. j, Burung berek-berek, vert.

No. 1005, (22c) — Fish: a, Ikan tenggiri papan. b, Ikan kertang. c, Ikan kakatua. d, Ikan bambangan. e, Ikan parang. f, Ikan buntai pisang. g, Ikan ketang. h, Pari hitam. i, Telinga gajah. j, Ikan babi.

***Perf. 13¼x13¾, 13¾x13¼***

**2002** **Litho.**

**Sheets of 10, #a-j**

**1002-1005** A245 Set of 4 10.00 10.00

Issued: Nos. 1002-1003, 2/20; Nos. 1004-1005, 3/20.

**Farquhar Collection Type of 2002**

Designs: No. 1006, Like No. 1002. No. 1007, Like No. 1003. No. 1008, Like No. 1004. No. 1009, Like No. 1005.

***Serpentine Die Cut 12½***

**2002** **Litho.**

**Sheets of 10, #a-j**

**Self-Adhesive**

**1006-1009** A245 Set of 4 10.00 10.00

Issued: Nos. 1006-1007, 2/20; Nos. 1008-1009, 3/20. Nos. 1002-1009 inscribed "For Local Addresses Only."

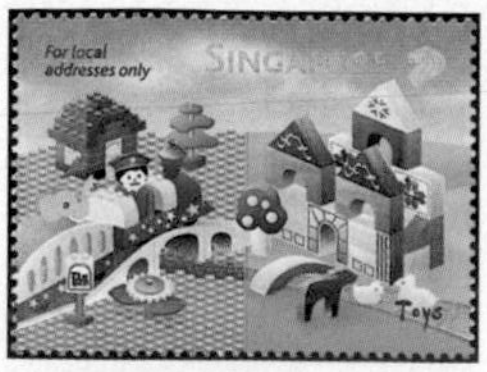

Toys A246

Designs: (22c), Lego blocks. 60c, Cowboys and Indians, robot. 70c, Dolls. $1, Racing cars.

**2002, May 22** ***Perf. 14½x14***

**1010-1013** A246 Set of 4 3.00 3.00

No. 1010 inscribed "For local addresses only."

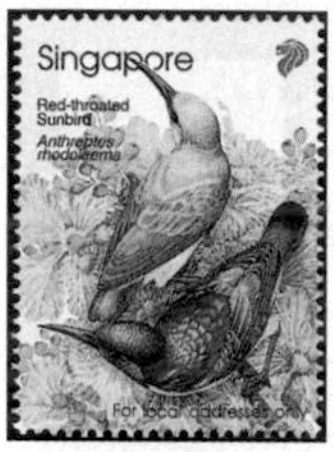

Tropical Birds — A247

Designs: (22c), Red-throated sunbird. 40c, Asian fairy bluebird. $1, Black-naped oriole. $2, White-bellied woodpecker.

**2002, June 27** ***Perf. 13¼x14***

**1014-1017** A247 Set of 4 4.25 4.25
*1017a* Souvenir sheet, #1014-1017 4.25 4.25

No. 1014 inscribed "For local addresses only." See Malaysia Nos. 886-888.

**Fish Type of 2001**

Discus fish: $1, Blue turquoise. $2, Brown discus. $5, Red alenquer. $10, Red turquoise.

**2002, July 24** ***Perf. 13½x13¼***

**Size: 29x25mm**

**1018** A243 $1 multi 1.10 1.10
**1019** A243 $2 multi 2.25 2.25
**1020** A243 $5 multi 5.75 5.75
**1021** A243 $10 multi 11.50 11.50
*a.* Souvenir sheet, #1018-1021 21.00 21.00
*Nos. 1018-1021 (4)* 20.60 20.60

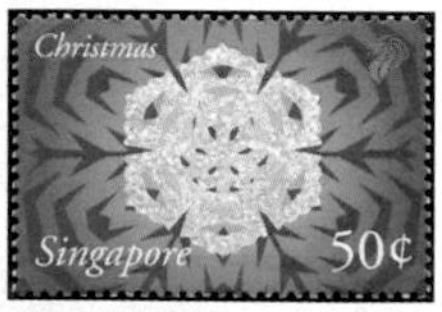

A248

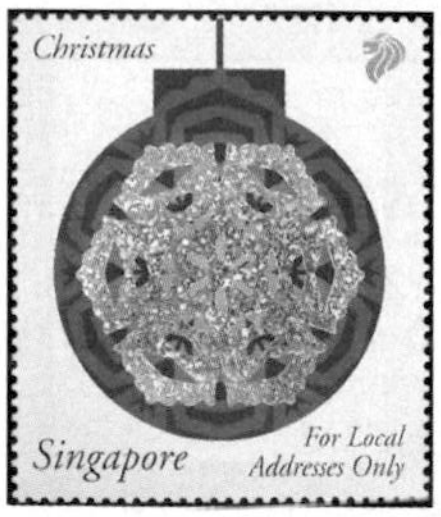

Festivals and Holidays A249

Designs: Nos. 1022, 50c; 1026, 1030, (22c), Christmas. Nos. 1023, 50c; 1027, 1031, (22c), Chinese New Year. Nos. 1024, 50c; 1028, 1032, (22c), Deepavali. Nos. 1025, 50c; 1029, 1033, (22c), Eid ul-Fitr.

**Litho. with Hologram Affixed**

**2002, Aug. 21** ***Perf. 13¼x13¾***

**1022-1025** A248 Set of 4 2.25 2.25
**1026-1029** A249 Set of 4 1.00 1.00

**Self-Adhesive**

***Serpentine Die Cut 13¼x13¾***

**1030-1033** A249 Set of 4 1.00 1.00

Nos. 1026-1033 are inscribed "For Local Addresses Only."

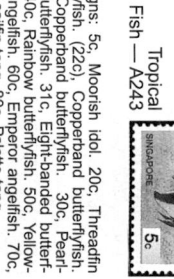

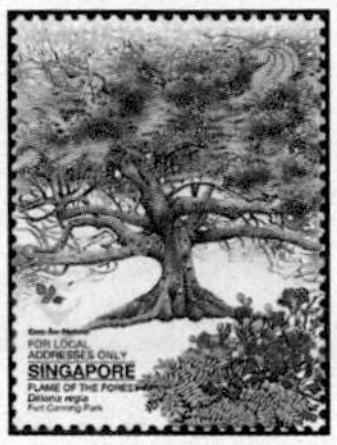


Trees — A250

Designs: Nos. 1034, 1038, (22c), Flame of the forest. 60c, Rain tree. No. 1036, $1, Tembusu. No. 1037, $1, Kapok tree.

**2002, Sept. 25 Litho. *Perf. 13½x13***
**1034-1037** A250 Set of 4 3.25 3.25

**Self-Adhesive**
**Booklet Stamp**
***Serpentine Die Cut 12½***

**1038** A250 (22c) multi .25 .25
*a.* Booklet of 10 2.50

Nos. 1034, 1038 are inscribed "For Local Addresses Only."

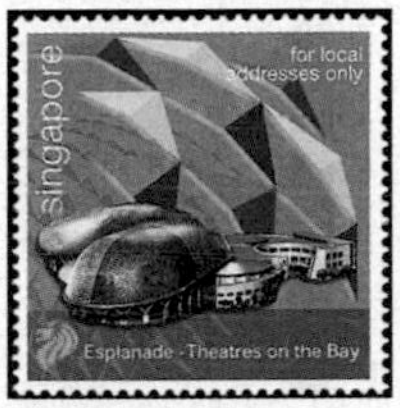


Opening of Esplanade Performing Arts Center A251

Various views of complex with background colors of: (22c), Orange. 60c, Brown. $1, Blue green. $2, Dark blue.

**2002, Oct. 12 Litho. *Perf. 13¼x13¾***
**1039-1042** A251 Set of 4 4.25 4.25
*1042a* Souvenir sheet, #1039-1042 4.25 4.25

No. 1039 is inscribed "For local addresses only."

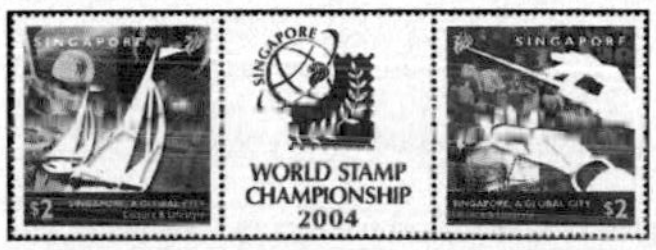


Singapore, A Global City — A252

No. 1043: a, Sailboats. b, Conductor's hands.
Illustration reduced.

**2002-04 *Perf. 14¼x14***
**1043** A252 $2 Horiz. pair, #a-b + central label 4.50 4.50
*1043c* Souvenir sheet, #1043a-1043b, + American Express label 4.50 4.50
*d.* As "c," with Coca-Cola label 4.50 4.50
*e.* As "c," with McDonald's label 4.50 4.50
*f.* As "c," with Reader's Digest label 4.50 4.50
*g.* As "c," with Swatch label 4.50 4.50
*h.* As "c," ovptd. in margin with World Stamp Championship emblem in silver 5.50 5.50
*i.* As "d," ovptd. in margin with World Stamp Championship emblem in silver 5.50 5.50
*j.* As "e," ovptd. in margin with World Stamp Championship emblem in silver 5.50 5.50
*k.* As "f," ovptd. in margin with World Stamp Championship emblem in silver 5.50 5.50
*l.* As "g," ovptd. in margin with World Stamp Championship emblem in silver 5.50 5.50

Issued: Nos. 1043-1043g, 11/20/02. Nos. 1043h-1043l, 6/23/04. Nos. 1043h-1043l sold for $4.53 each.

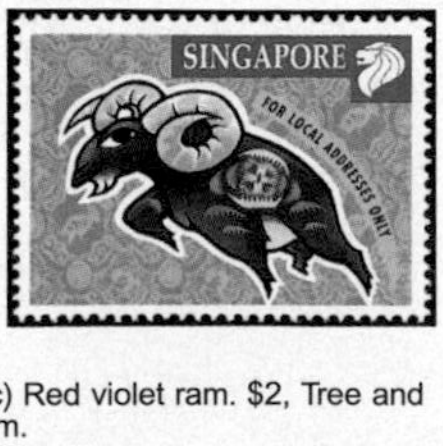


New Year 2003 (Year of the Ram) A253

Designs: (22c) Red violet ram. $2, Tree and yellow green ram.

**2003, Jan. 10 Litho. *Perf. 13x13½***
**1044-1045** A253 Set of 2 2.60 2.60
*1045a* Sheet, 9 each #1044-1045 24.00 24.00
*1045b* Souvenir sheet, #1044-1045, with Bangkok 2003 margin 2.60 2.60
*1045c* Souvenir sheet, #1044-1045, with China 2003 margin 2.60 2.60

No. 1044 inscribed "For Local Addresses Only."
Issued: No. 1045b, 10/4; No. 1045c, 11/20.

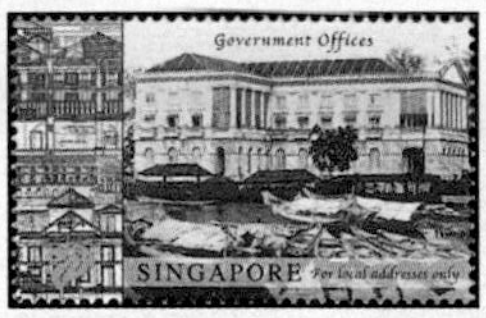


History of Empress Place Building A254

Designs: (22c), Government offices. 60c, Government offices, diff. $1, Empress Place Museum. $2, Asian Civilizations Museum.

**2003, Feb. 26 *Perf. 14½***
**1046-1049** A254 Set of 4 4.50 4.50

No. 1046 inscribed "For local addresses only."

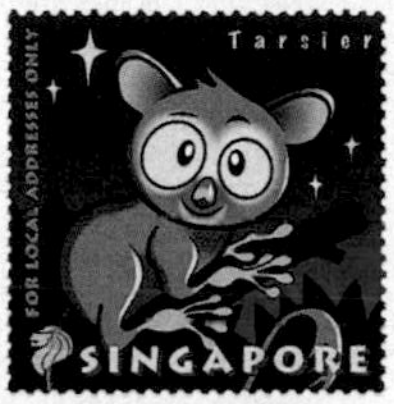


Nocturnal Animals A255

Designs: (22c), Tarsier. 40c, Barn owl. $1, Babirusa. $2, Clouded leopard.

**2003, Mar. 20 Litho. *Perf. 13¼***
**1050-1053** A255 Set of 4 4.25 4.25
*1053a* Souvenir sheet, #1050-1053 4.25 4.25

No. 1050 inscribed "For Local Addresses Only." Glow-in-the-dark ink was applied to portions of No. 1053a by silk-screening.

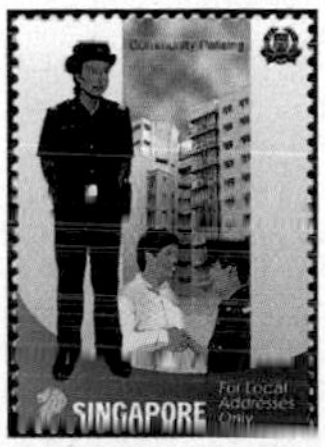


Singapore Police Force — A256

Designs: (22c), Community policing. 40c, Traffic policing. $1, Maritime policing. $2, International peacekeeping.

**2003, Apr. 23 Litho. *Perf. 13¼x13***
**1054-1057** A256 Set of 4 4.25 4.25

No. 1054 inscribed "For Local Addresses Only."

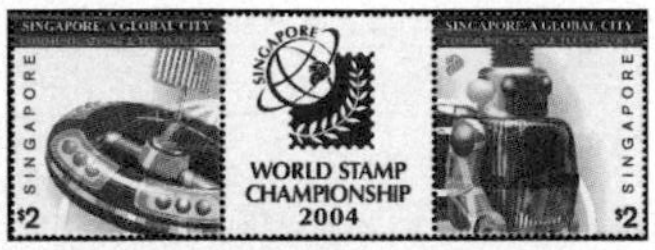


Singapore, A Global City — A257

No. 1058: a, Spacecraft. b, Robot.
Illustration reduced.

**2003, May 21 Litho. *Perf. 14¼x14***
**1058** A257 $2 Horiz. pair, #a-b + central label 4.75 4.75
*c.* Souvenir sheet, #1058a-1058b + CNN label 4.75 4.75
*d.* As "c," with Creative Technology label 4.75 4.75
*e.* As "c," with Microsoft label 4.75 4.75
*f.* As "c," with Siemens label 4.75 4.75
*g.* As "c," with Singapore Airlines label 4.75 4.75
*h.* As "c," ovptd. in margin with World Stamp Championship emblem in silver 5.50 5.50
*i.* As "d," ovptd. in margin with World Stamp Championship emblem in silver 5.50 5.50
*j.* As "e," ovptd. in margin with World Stamp Championship emblem in silver 5.50 5.50
*k.* As "f," ovptd. in margin with World Stamp Championship emblem in silver 5.50 5.50
*l.* As "g," ovptd. in margin with World Stamp Championship emblem in silver 5.50 5.50

Issued: Nos. 1058-1058g, 5/21/03. Nos. 1058h-1058l, 6/23/04. Nos. 1058h-1058l sold for $4.53 each.

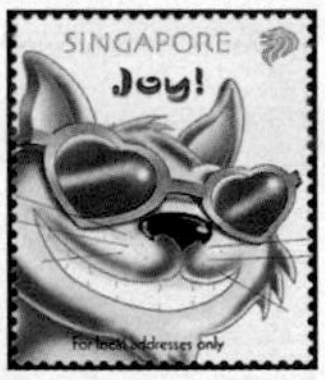


Joy and Caring — A258

Designs and inscriptions: Nos. 1059a, 1060a, Cat (Joy). Nos. 1059b, 1060b, Running heart (Joy). Nos. 1059c, 1060c, Teddy bear (Joy). Nos. 1059d, 1060d, Laughing man (Joy). Nos. 1059e, 1060e, Ostrich head (Joy). Nos. 1059f, 1060f, Apple (Caring). Nos. 1059g, 1060g, Hand and heart (A helping hand). Nos. 1059h, 1060h, Hearts (Togetherness). Nos. 1059i, 1060i, Flower (Beauty of a caring heart). Nos. 1059j, 1060j, Stars (Keeping in touch keeps us going).

**2003, June 25 *Perf. 14½***
**1059** Sheet of 10 + 2 labels 2.50 2.50
*a.-j.* A258 (22c) Any single .25 .25
*k.* Sheet, 10 each #1059c, 1059h + 20 labels 9.00 9.00
*l.* Sheet of 20 #1059i + 20 labels 9.25 9.25
*m.* Sheet, 10 each #1059c, 1059h + 20 labels 10.00 10.00

**Self-Adhesive**
***Serpentine Die Cut 10x9¾***

**1060** Booklet of 10 + 6 labels 2.50 2.50
*a.-j.* A258 (22c) Any single .25 .25

Inscribed "For Local Addresses Only." Labels on No. 1059k could be personalized for an additional fee.
Issued: No. 1059l, 8/8; No. 1059m, 11/25/04. Nos. 1059l and 1059m each sold for $8. See Nos. 1119-1121.

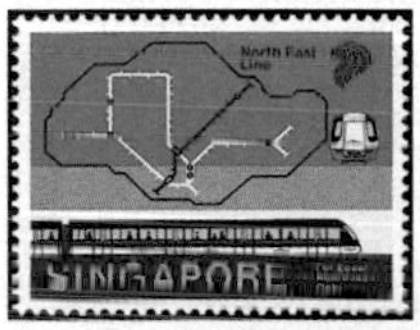


Opening of North East Line of Rapid Transit System A259

Designs: (22c), Map of Rapid Transit System, train. 60c, Entrance gates, station cross-section, train. $2, System control room, train.
No. 1064: a, (22c), Like No. 522. b, 60c, Like No. 523. c, $2, Like No. 524.

**2003, July 18 *Perf. 13¾***
**1061-1063** A259 Set of 3 3.25 3.25

**Souvenir Sheet**

**1064** A259 Sheet of 6, #1061-1063, 1064a-1064c 6.50 6.50

Nos. 1061, 1064a are inscribed "For Local Addresses Only."

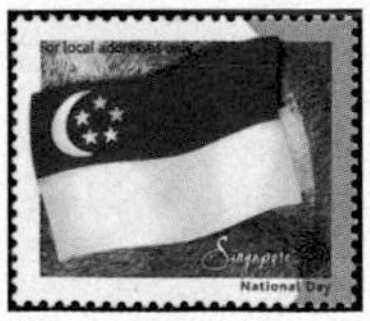


National Day — A260

Designs: (22c), Flag. 60c, National flower, Vanda Miss Joaquim orchid. $1, Merlion and buildings. $2, People of Singapore.

**2003, Aug. 9 *Perf. 13¼x13½***
**1065-1068** A260 Set of 4 4.50 4.50
*1065a* Sheet of 20 + 20 labels 9.50 9.50
*1068a* Souvenir sheet, #1065-1068 4.50 4.50
*c.* A260 60c Like #1066, 35x28mm 1.10 1.10
*d.* A260 $1 Like #1067, 35x28mm 2.00 2.00
**1068B** Sheet, 3 #1068Bc, 2#1068Bd + 10 labels 7.50 7.50

No. 1065 is inscribed "For local addresses only."
No. 1065a sold for $8. Labels could be personalized.
Size of Nos. 1066-1067: 33x28mm. No. 1068B sold for $6.

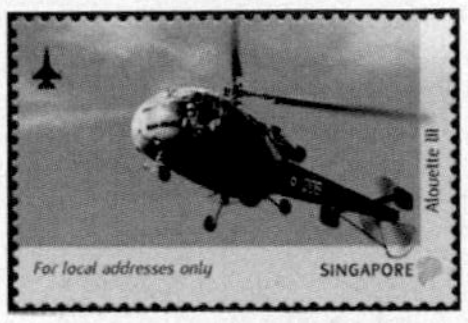


Aircraft A261

No. 1069 — Military aircraft: a, Alouette III helicopter. b, E-2C Hawkeye. c, Hawker Hunter. d, Super Puma AS-332M helicopter. e, Hercules C-130H. f, F-16 C/D Fighting Falcon. g, AH-64D Apache helicopter. h, KC-135R Stratotanker. i, Cessna 172. j, F-5E Tiger II.
No. 1070 — Civil aircraft: a, Airbus 340-500. b, Boeing 747-400. c, Boeing 777-200. d, Boeing 747-400 Freighter. e, Airbus 320. f, Concorde. g, Boeing 737-100. h, Comet IV. i, Viscount. j, Airspeed Consul.

**2003, Sept. 3 *Perf. 13¼x13½***
**1069** Sheet of 10 2.50 2.50
*a.-j.* A261 (22c) Any single .25 .25
**1070** Sheet of 10 2.50 2.50
*a.-j.* A261 (22c) Any single .25 .25
*k.* Sheet of 20, #1069a-1069j, 1070a-1070j 5.00 5.00

**Self-Adhesive**
***Serpentine Die Cut 12½***

**1071** Sheet of 10 2.50
*a.-j.* A261 (22c) Any single .25 .25
**1072** Sheet of 10 2.50
*a.-j.* A261 (22c) Any single .25 .25

Inscribed "For local addresses only." Powered flight, cent.; Singapore Air Force, 35th anniv.

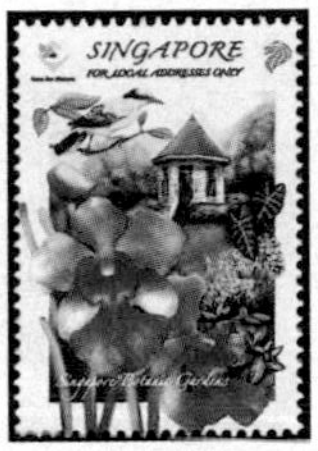


Singapore, A Garden City — A262

Designs: Nos. 1073, 1077, (22c), Singapore Botanic Gardens. 60c, Fort Canning Park. No. 1075, $1, Marina City Park. No. 1076, $1, Sungei Buloh Wetland Reserve.

**2003, Oct. 22 Litho. *Perf. 13½***
**1073-1076** A262 Set of 4 3.25 3.25

**Booklet Stamp**
**Self-Adhesive**
***Serpentine Die Cut 10x9½***

**1077** A262 (22c) multi .25 .25
*a.* Booklet pane of 10 2.50 2.50

Nos. 1073, 1077 are inscribed "For Local Addresses Only."

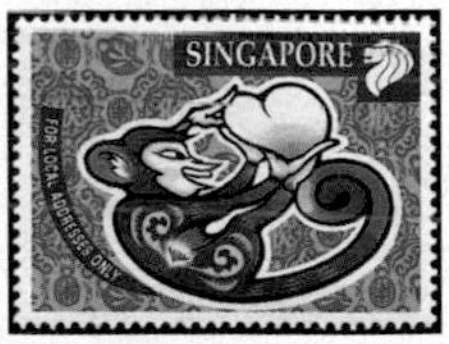


New Year 2004 (Year of the Monkey) A263

Designs: (22c), Monkey and heart. $2, Two monkeys.

**2004, Jan. 9 *Perf. 14x13¼***
**1078-1079** A263 Set of 2 2.60 2.60
*1079a* Sheet, 9 each #1078-1079 23.50 23.50
*1079b* Souvenir sheet, #1078-1079, with Hong Kong 2004 Stamp Expo margin 2.60 2.60

No. 1078 is inscribed "For Local Addresses Only." No. 1079a is reserved.

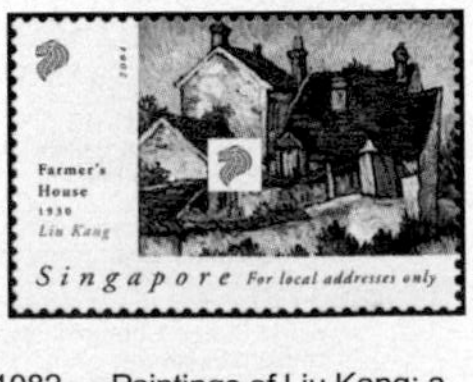


Paintings A264

Nos. 1080, 1082 — Paintings of Liu Kang: a, Farmer's House. b, Artist and Model. c, Lanterns Galore. d, Enjoying a Smoke, Kashmir. e, Life by the River. f, Tenth Trip Up to Huangshan. g, My Young Wife, vert. h, Kek Lok Si, Penang, vert. i, Souri, vert. j, Siesta in Bali, vert.

Nos. 1081, 1083 — Paintings of Ong Kim Seng: a, Kampong Tengah, Singapore. b, Gyantse Market. c, Sebatu Spring, Bali. d, Jetty, Bangkok. e, Resort, Bali. f, Dance Studio, Bali. g, Telok Ayer Market. h, Kathmandu, Nepal. i, Portofino, Italy, vert. j, Boats at Rest, vert.

***Perf. 13¼x13½, 13½x13¼ (Vert. stamps)***

**2004, Feb. 18**

**1080** Sheet of 10 2.75 2.75
*a.-j.* A264 (23c) Any single .25 .25
**1081** Sheet of 10 2.75 2.75
*a.-j.* A264 (23c) Any single .25 .25

**Self-Adhesive**

***Serpentine Die Cut 12½x12¼, 12¼x12½ (Vert. stamps)***

**1082** Sheet of 10 2.75 2.75
*a.-j.* A264 (23c) Any single .25 .25
**1083** Sheet of 10 2.75 2.75
*a.-j.* A264 (23c) Any single .25 .25
*Nos. 1080-1083 (4)* 11.00 11.00

Inscribed "For local addresses only."

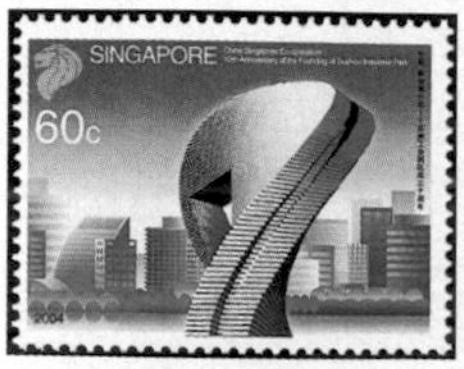
SINGAPORE
60c

Suzhou, China Industrial Park, 10th Anniv. A265

**2004, Mar. 1 Litho.** ***Perf. 13x13½***

**1084** A265 60c multi .70 .70
*a.* Sheet of 8 5.75 5.75

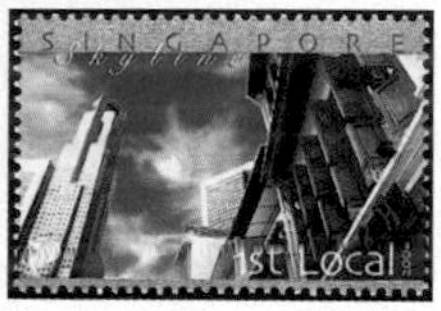
SINGAPORE
1st Local

Singapore Skyline A266

Designs: (23c), Buildings as seen from street level. 60c, Fountain. 70c, Buildings as seen from distance.

$1, Singapore, circa 1900. $5, Singapore, 2004.

***Perf. 14¼x14½***

**2004, Mar. 24 Litho.**

**1085-1087** A266 Set of 3 1.90 1.90
*1087a* Sheet, 3 #1086, 2 #1087, + 10 labels, perf. 12¾x13 ('05) 7.50 7.50

**Souvenir Sheets**

***Perf. 14¼x14***

**1088** A266 $1 multi 1.25 1.25

**Litho. & Engr.**

**1089** A266 $5 multi 6.00 6.00

No. 1085 is inscribed "1st Local." Nos. 1088 and 1089 each contain one 95x35mm stamp

No. 1087a issued 5/1/05. No. 1087a sold for $6.

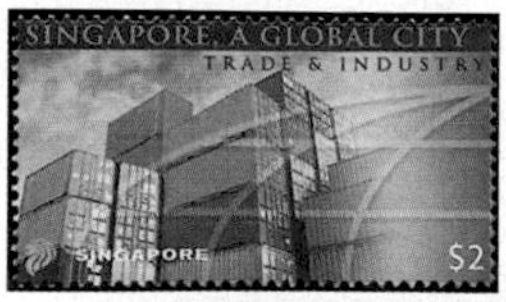
SINGAPORE, A GLOBAL CITY
TRADE & INDUSTRY
SINGAPORE
$2

Singapore, A Global City — A267

No. 1090: a, Cargo containers. b, Gas tanks.

**2004 Litho.** ***Perf. 14½x14¼***

**1090** Horiz. pair with central label 4.75 4.75
*a.-b.* A267 $2 Either single 2.25 2.25
*c.* Souvenir sheet, #1090a-1090b + AIA label 4.75 4.75
*d.* As "c," with GlaxoSmithKline label 4.75 4.75
*e.* As "c," with HSBC label 4.75 4.75
*f.* As "c," with Shell Oil label 4.75 4.75
*g.* As "c," with Sony label 4.75 4.75
*h.* As "c," ovptd. in margin with World Stamp Championship emblem in silver 5.50 5.50
*i.* As "d," ovptd. in margin with World Stamp Championship emblem in silver 5.50 5.50
*j.* As "e," ovptd. in margin with World Stamp Championship emblem in silver 5.50 5.50
*k.* As "f," ovptd. in margin with World Stamp Championship emblem in silver 5.50 5.50
*l.* As "g," ovptd. in margin with World Stamp Championship emblem in silver 5.50 5.50
*m.* Souvenir sheet, #1043a, 1043b, 1058a, 1058b, 1090a, 1090b 15.00 15.00

Issued: Nos. 1090, 1090c-1090g, 4/21; 1090h-1090l, 6/23; No. 1090m, 8/28. Nos. 1090h-1090l sold for $4.53 each. No. 1090m sold for $12.60 and exists imperf.

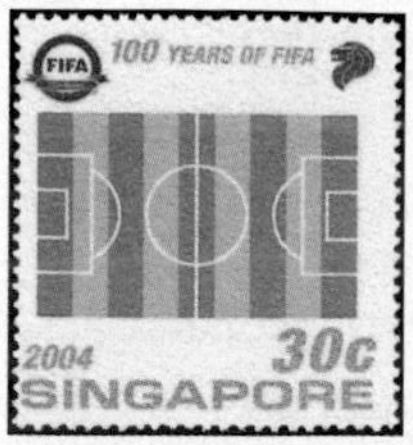
100 YEARS OF FIFA
2004
30c
SINGAPORE

FIFA (Fédération Internationale de Football Association), Cent. — A268

FIFA emblem and: 30c, Soccer field. 60c, Soccer ball. $1, Player's shirt. $2, World map.

**Litho. & Embossed**

**2004, May 21** ***Perf. 13***

**Flocked Paper**

**1091-1094** A268 Set of 4 4.75 4.75

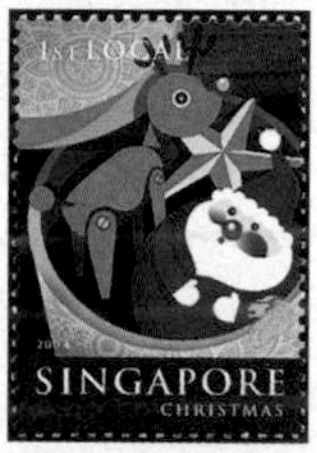
1st LOCAL
SINGAPORE
CHRISTMAS

Festivals and Holidays — A269

Designs: Nos. 1095, 1103, (23c), Santa Claus, reindeer (Christmas). Nos. 1096, 1104, (23c), Flowers, fruit (Chinese New Year). Nos. 1097, 1105, (23c), Candles (Deepavali). Nos. 1098, 1106, Candle (Eid ul-Fitr). No. 1099, 50c, Carolers (Christmas). No. 1100, 50c, Woman (Chinese New Year). No. 1101, 50c, Woman and candle (Deepavali). No. 1102, 50c, Child with sparkler (Eid ul-Fitr).

**2004, July 7 Litho.** ***Perf. 13***

**1095-1102** A269 Set of 8 3.50 3.50
*1095a* Perf. 12¾x13 + label .25 .25
*1099a* Perf. 12¾x13 + label .55 .55
*1102a* Sheet, #1099-1102, + 8 labels, perf. 12¾x13 7.50 7.50

**Self-Adhesive**

***Serpentine Die Cut 12½***

**1103-1106** A269 Set of 4 1.10 1.10

Nos. 1103-1106 were each printed in sheets of 10. Nos. 1095-1098, 1103-1106 are inscribed "1st Local."

Nos. 1095a, 1099a issued 11/7/05. Nos. 1095a, 1099a issued in sheets of 8 + 8 labels.

No. 1102a issued 5/1/05. No. 1102a sold for $6.

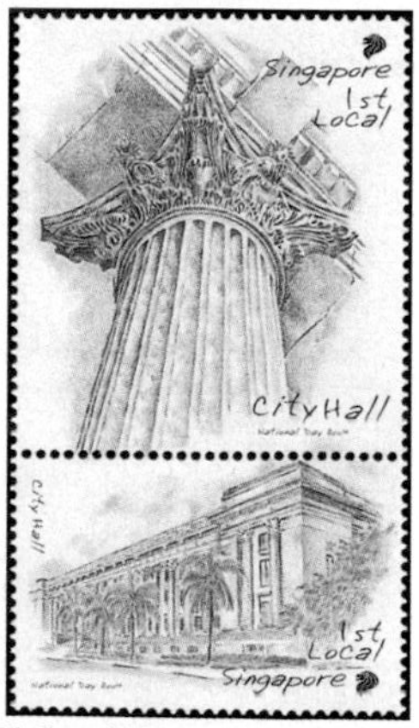
Singapore
1st
Local
City Hall
1st
Local
Singapore

National Monuments — A270

No. 1107, (23c): a, Column, City Hall. b, City Hall.

No. 1108, 30c: a, Tower, Victoria Theater and Concert Hall. b, Victoria Theater and Concert Hall.

No. 1109, 60c: a, Dome, Supreme Court. b, Supreme Court.

No. 1110, $1: a, Decoration, Istana (President's residence). b, Istana.

Sizes: Nos. 1107a-1110a, 41x46mm. Nos. 1107b-1110b, 41x27mm.

**2004, Aug. 9** ***Perf. 13¼x13¾***

**Vert. Pairs, #a-b**

**1107-1110** A270 Set of 4 5.00 5.00
*1110c* Souvenir sheet, #1107b, 1108b, 1109b, 1110b 2.50 2.50

No. 1107 is inscribed "1st Local."

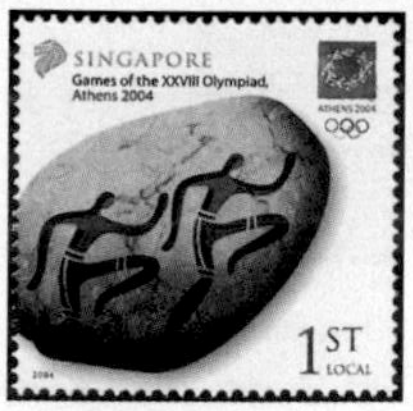
SINGAPORE
Games of the XXVIII Olympiad, Athens 2004
1ST
LOCAL

2004 Summer Olympics, Athens A271

Carved rocks with stylized: (23c), Runners. 30c, Swimmers. $1, Weight lifter. $2, Sailor.

**2004, Aug. 13** ***Perf. 13¾***

**1111-1114** A271 Set of 4 4.25 4.25

No. 1111 is inscribed "1st Local."

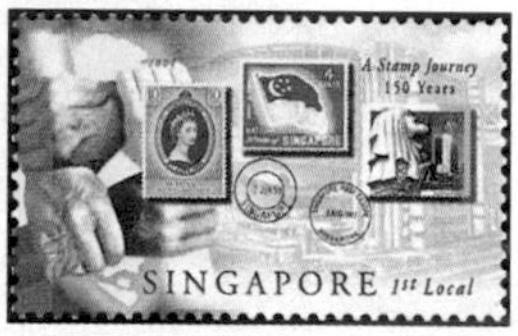
A Stamp Journey 150 Years
SINGAPORE 1st Local

Use of Postage Stamps in Singapore, 150th Anniv. — A272

Cancels, buildings, stamp vignettes and: (23c), Singapore #27, 49, 1067. 60c, Straits Settlements #N27, 271, Singapore #11. $1, Straits Settlements #124, 167, 251. $2, India #6, Straits Settlements #1, 18.

**2004, Aug. 28** ***Perf. 12¼x11¾***

**1115-1118** A272 Set of 4 4.50 4.50
*1115a* Sheet of 15 + 15 labels 7.25 7.25
*1118a* Souvenir sheet, #1115-1118 4.50 4.50

No. 1115a sold for $6 and labels could be personalized for an additional fee.

**Joy and Caring Type of 2003 Inscribed "1st Local"**

Designs: No. 1119, Flower (Beauty of a Caring Heart). No. 1120, Hearts (Togetherness). No. 1121, Teddy bear (Joy).

**2004 Litho.** ***Perf. 14½***

**1119** A258 (23c) multi + label 1.75 1.75
**1120** A258 (23c) multi + label .50 .50
*a.* Pair, #1119-1120 + 2 labels 3.50 3.50
**1121** A258 (23c) multi + label .50 .50
*a.* Pair, #1120-1121 + 2 labels 1.00 1.00
*Nos. 1119-1121 (3)* 2.75 2.75

Issued: Nos. 1119, 1120, 8/28; No. 1121, 8/30. Nos. 1119 and 1120 were printed in a sheet containing five of each stamp and ten labels that sold for $15. Nos. 1120 and 1121 were printed in a sheet containing ten of each stamp and 20 labels that sold for $8.

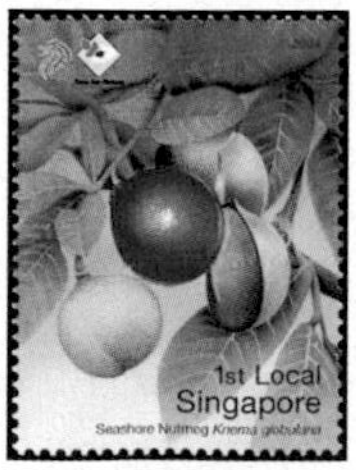
1st Local
Singapore

Care For Nature — A273

Designs: Nos. 1122a, 1123 Seashore nutmeg. Nos. 1122b, 1124, Oriental pied hornbill. No. 1122c, Knobby sea star. No. 1122d, Common seahorse.

**2004, Oct. 20** ***Perf. 14***

**1122** Horiz. strip of 4 3.00 3.00
*a.-b.* A273 (23c) Either single .30 .30
*c.-d.* A273 $1 Either single 1.10 1.10

**Booklet Stamps**

**Self-Adhesive**

***Serpentine Die Cut 10¼x9½***

**1123** A273 (23c) multi .30 .30
**1124** A273 (23c) multi .30 .30
*a.* Booklet pane, 5 each #1123-1124 3.00

Nos. 1122a-1122b, 1123-1124 are inscribed "1st Local."

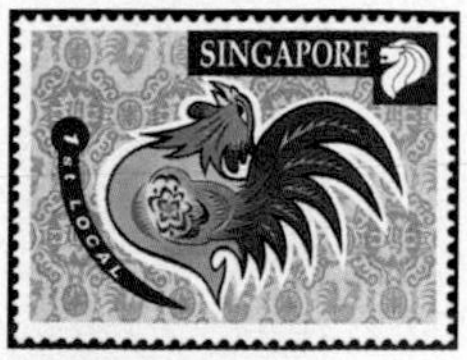
SINGAPORE
1st LOCAL

New Year 2005 (Year of the Rooster) A274

Designs: (23c), Rooster. $2, Rooster and hen.

**2005, Jan. 14** ***Perf. 13¼x13½***

**1125-1126** A274 Set of 2 2.75 2.75
*1126a* Sheet, 9 each #1125-1126 25.00 25.00
*1126b* Souvenir sheet, #1125-1126, perf. 12¾, with Pacific Explorer emblem in margin 2.75 2.75
*1126c* Souvenir sheet, #1125-1126, perf. 12¾, with Taipei 2005 emblem in margin 2.75 2.75

No. 1125 is inscribed "1st Local."

No. 1126b issued 4/21; No. 1126c, 8/19.

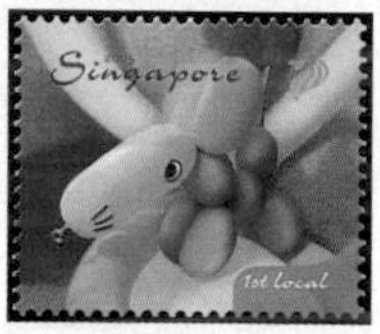
Singapore
1st Local

Greetings A275

Designs: Nos. 1127a, 1132, Balloon animal. Nos. 1127a, 1131, Orchid. Nos. 1127c, 1130, Gift. Nos. 1127d, 1129, Flowers and teddy bears. Nos. 1127e, 1128, Candle and goblets.

**2005, Feb. 23** ***Perf. 13½x13¾***

**1127** Vert. strip of 5 1.50 1.50
*a.-e.* A275 (23c) Any single .30 .30

**Booklet Stamps**

**Self-Adhesive**

***Serpentine Die Cut 11¼***

**1128** A275 (23c) multi .30 .30
**1129** A275 (23c) multi .30 .30
**1130** A275 (23c) multi .30 .30
**1131** A275 (23c) multi .30 .30
**1132** A275 (23c) multi .30 .30
*a.* Booklet pane, 2 each #1128-1132 3.00

Inscribed "1st Local."

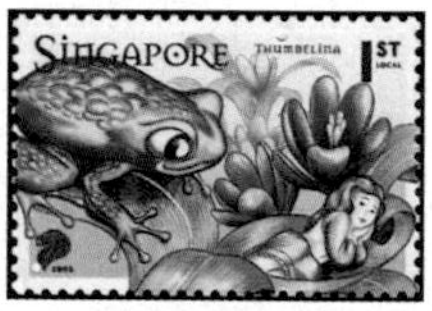
SINGAPORE
THUMBELINA
1ST

Hans Christian Andersen (1805-75), Author A276

Stories: (23c), Thumbelina. 60c, The Ugly Duckling. $1, The Emperor's New Clothes. $2, The Little Mermaid.

**2005, Mar. 30 Litho.** ***Perf. 13x12¾***

**1133-1136** A276 Set of 4 4.75 4.75
*1136a* Souvenir sheet, #1133-1136 4.75 4.75

No. 1133 is inscribed "1st Local."

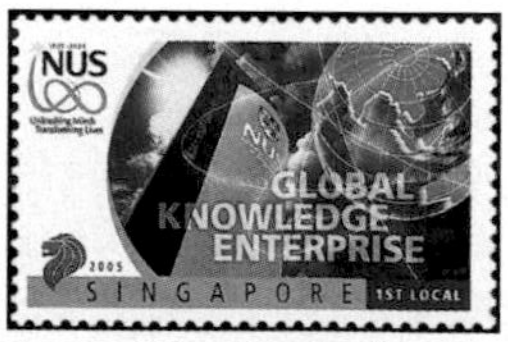
NUS
GLOBAL
KNOWLEDGE
ENTERPRISE
SINGAPORE
1ST LOCAL

University Education in Singapore, Cent. — A277

Designs: (23c), Global knowledge enterprise. 60c, Quality education. 70c, Artistic and cultural hub. $1, Research excellence.

**2005, Apr. 20** ***Perf. 12¼***

**1137-1140** A277 Set of 4 3.25 3.25

No. 1137 is inscribed "1st Local."

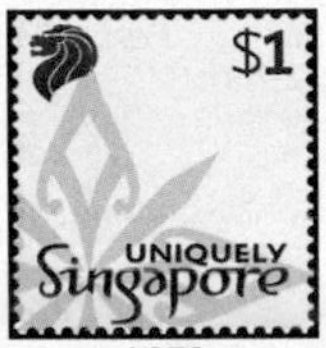
A278

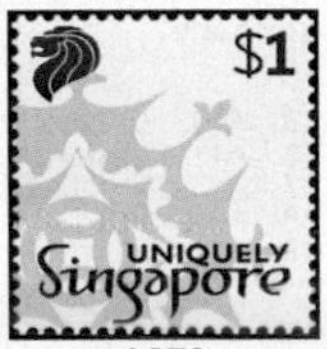
A279

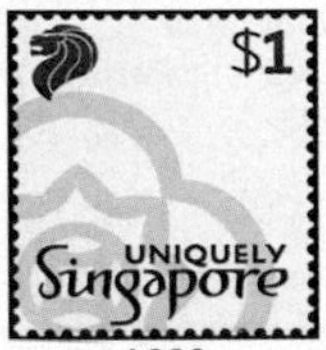
A280

A281

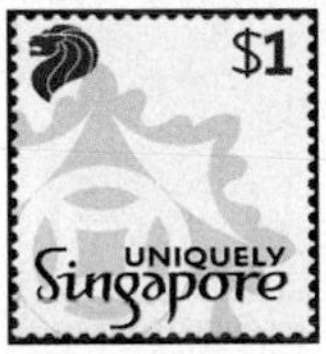
"Uniquely Singapore" — A282

**2005, May 1** *Perf. 12¾*

**1141** Miniature sheet of 5 + 10 labels 7.50 7.50
- *a.* A278 $1 multi 1.50 1.50
- *b.* A279 $1 multi 1.50 1.50
- *c.* A280 $1 multi 1.50 1.50
- *d.* A281 $1 multi 1.50 1.50
- *e.* A282 $1 multi 1.50 1.50

No. 1141 sold for $6. Labels could be personalized.

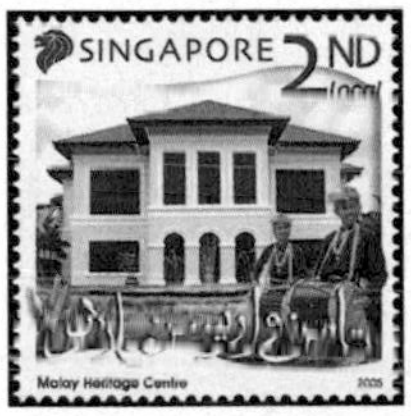
Malay Heritage Center A283

Designs: (31c), Building, drummers. 60c, Fountain pen, seal, manuscript. $1, Stringed instrument, man and woman. $2, Sailor, boat.

**2005, May 31** *Perf. 13¾*

**1142-1145** A283 Set of 4 4.75 4.75

No. 1142 is inscribed "2nd Local."

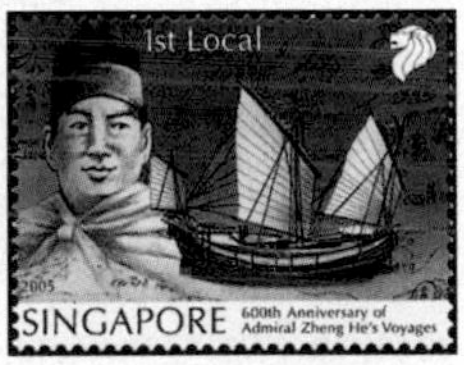
Admiral Zheng He's Voyages, 600th Anniv. A284

Map and: No. 1146, (23c), Admiral Zheng He, ship. No. 1147 (23c), Ships. 60c, Ships, diff. $1, Ships, diff.

**2005, June 28** *Perf. 13¼x13½*

**1146-1149** A284 Set of 4 2.50 2.50
*1147a* Sheet, 5 each #1146-1147, perf. 12¾ 2.75 2.75

Nos. 1146 and 1147 are inscribed "1st Local."

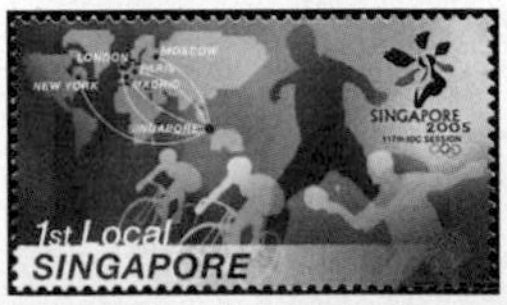
117th International Olympic Committee Session, Singapore — A285

Emblem, world map showing Singapore and candidates for hosting 2012 Olympics and: (23c), Cycling, running, table tennis. 50c, Running, basketball, tennis. 60c, Soccer, tennis, javelin. $1, Gymnastics, weight lifting.

**2005, July 5** *Perf. 14¼*

**Size: 44x25mm**

**1150-1153** A285 Set of 4 2.75 2.75

*Perf. 12¼*

**1154** Miniature sheet, #1154a-1154b, 2 each #1154c-1154d, + 6 labels 7.25 7.25
- *a.* A285 (23c) multi, 44x28mm .45 .45
- *b.* A285 50c multi, 44x28mm .95 .95
- *c.* A285 60c multi, 44x28mm 1.10 1.10
- *d.* A285 $1 multi, 44x28mm 1.75 1.75

Nos. 1150, 1154a are inscribed "1st Local." No. 1154 sold for $6, and labels could be personalized.

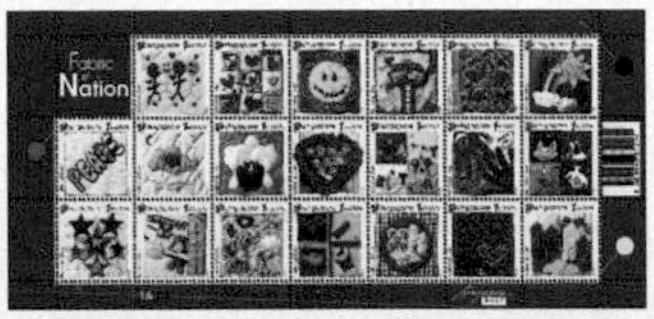
A286

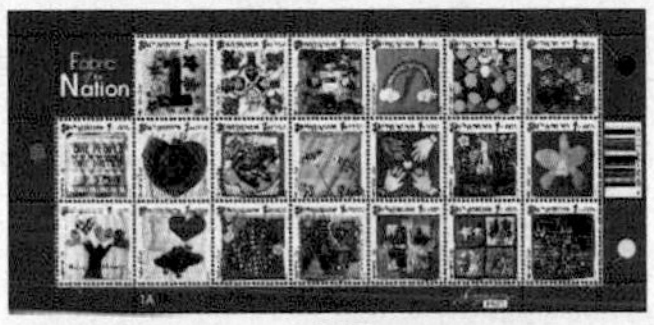
A287

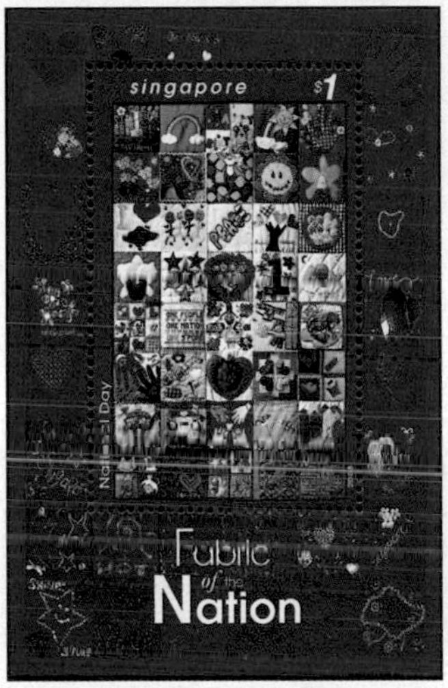
National Day — A288

Nos. 1155 and 1157 — Patchwork quilt blocks depicting: a, Stylized people, nine hearts. b, Hearts in a block of nine. c, Flower with face. d, Tower and hearts. e, Red orchid on green patterned background. f, Sun and rainbow. g, "Peace." h, Crescent and heart on Singapore map. i, White and purple orchid. j, Heart with red lace border. k, "Happy Birthday." l, Hands, "One Singapore," and "United We Stand." m, Cats and dog, "Singapore Is Our Home Too." n, Five stars around large star. o, Clothes on line, "One Nation Many Colors." p, Airplane, clouds. q, Love, star, dove, smiling face, "Love, Hope, Peace, Joy." r, Plate of food. s, Hearts and "Many Hearts One Nation." t, Stylized buildings and trees.

Nos. 1156 and 1158 — Patchwork quilt blocks depicting: a, "1" and flowers. b, Children with arms raised, "Home. . . Everyone Fits In!" c, Heads around flag. d, Rainbow and clouds. e, Person looking up, butterflies. f, Sun, butterflies, flowers, "Love Singapore." g, "One People, One Nation, One S'pore." h, Heart and durian. i, Frog on lily pad. j, Bird kites and flowers, "Flying High, My Singapore." k, Hands and heart. l, Singapore skyline, "Singapore My Home." m, Yellow, purple and green orchid on red background. n, Tree, hearts, "Racial Harmony." o, "I", heart, map of Singapore. p, Hand with buttons, child. q, Heart, stars, "Singapore." r, Four hearts in squares. s, Stars, hearts, stylized people in block of four. t, The Pledge.

$1, Entire quilt.

**2005, Aug. 9** *Perf. 14¼x14½*

**1155** A286 (23c) Sheet of 20, #a-t, + label 3.00 3.00
**1156** A287 (23c) Sheet of 20, #a-t, + label 3.00 3.00

**Self-Adhesive (#1157-1158)**

***Serpentine Die Cut 10x9½***

**1157** A286 (23c) Sheet of 20, #a-t, + label 3.00 3.00
**1158** A287 (23c) Sheet of 20, #a-t, + label 3.00 3.00

**Souvenir Sheet**

***Perf. 14***

**1159** A288 $1 multi 1.25 1.25
- *a.* Sheet of 4 #1159 6.75 6.75

Each stamp on Nos. 1155-1158 inscribed "1st Local." No. 1159a sold for $5.50.

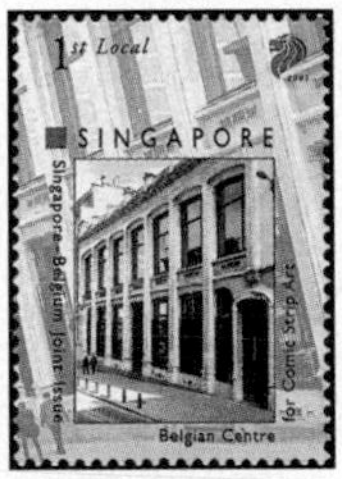
Buildings in Belgium and Singapore A289

Designs: (23c), Belgian Center for Comic Strip Art, Brussels. 60c, Shop on Kandahar Street, Singapore. $1, Shops on Bukit Pasoh Road, Singapore. $2, Museum of Musical Instruments, Brussels.

**2005, Sept. 9** *Perf. 12¾*

**1160-1163** A289 Set of 4 4.75 4.75
- *1160a* Perf. 13½x13¼ + label .70 .70
- *1161a* Perf. 13½x13¼ + label 1.00 1.00
- *1162a* Perf. 13½x13¼ + label 1.60 1.60
- *1163a* Souvenir sheet, #1160-1163 4.75 4.75

No. 1160 is inscribed "1st Local." See Belgium Nos. 2104-2107.

Nos. 1160a, 1161a, 1162a issued 11/7/05. Nos. 1160a issued in sheets of 8 + 8 labels that sold for $5. Nos. 1161a and 1162a were issued in sheets containing four of each stamp + eight labels that sold for $9.

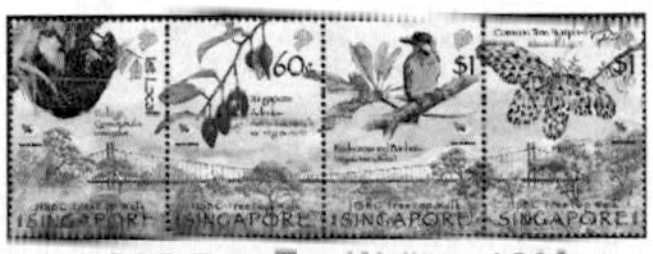
HSBC Tree Top Walk A290

No. 1164: a, (23c), Colugo. b, 60c, Adenia. c, $1, Red-crowned barbet. d, $1, Common tree nymph butterfly.

Illustration reduced.

**2005, Oct. 19** *Perf. 14*

**1164** A290 Horiz. strip of 4, #a-d 3.50 3.50

**Booklet Stamp**

**Self-Adhesive**

***Serpentine Die Cut 10x9½***

**1165** A290 (23c) Like #1164a .30 .30
- *a.* Booklet pane of 10 3.00 3.00

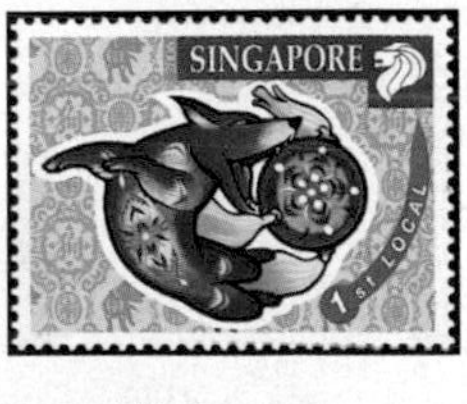
New Year 2006 (Year of the Dog) A291

Designs: (23c), Dog. $2, Two dogs.

**2006, Jan. 6** **Litho.** *Perf. 13x13¼*

**1167-1168** A291 Set of 2 2.75 2.75
*1168a* Sheet, 9 each #1167-1168 25.00 25.00

No. 1167 is inscribed "1st Local."

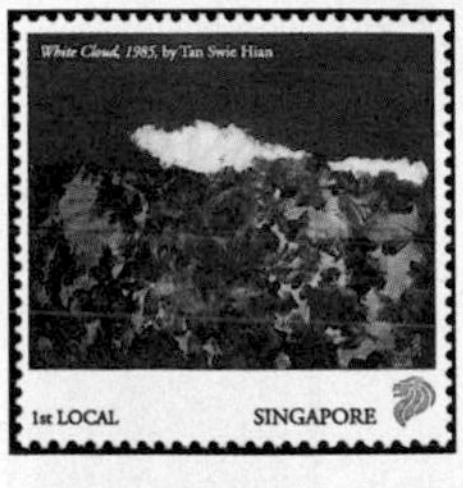
Art by Tan Swie Hian A292

No. 1169: a, White Cloud. b, Ganges. c, Soaring over the Flower Field. d, Kuta is a Song. e, The Winged Steed.

No. 1170, vert.: a, Black Panther (Pine). b, Ginkgo (Male). c, White Elephant. d, Summer Lotus. e, Water Dhyana.

$2, Calligraphy, vert.

**2006, Feb. 22** *Perf. 12*

**1169** Horiz. strip of 5 1.40 1.40
- *a.-e.* A292 (23c) Any single .25 .25

*Perf. 12¾*

**Size: 27x57mm**

**1170** Horiz. strip of 5 3.25 3.25
- *a.-e.* A292 50c Any single .65 .65

**Souvenir Sheet**

**1171** A292 $2 multi 2.50 2.50

Nos. 1169a-1169e are inscribed "1st Local." No. 1171 contains one 40x60mm stamp.

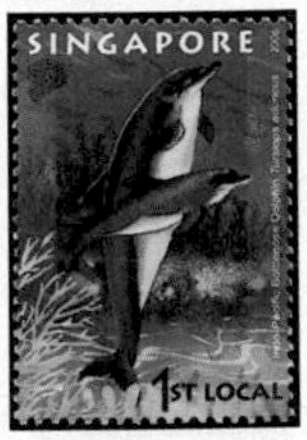
Marine Mammals — A293

Designs: (23c), Indo-Pacific bottlenose dolphin. (31c), Indo-Pacific humpbacked dolphin. $1, Finless porpoise. $2, Dugong.

**2006, Mar. 22** *Perf. 13¼*

**1172-1175** A293 Set of 4 4.50 4.50
*1175a* Sheet, #1172-1175 4.50 4.50

No. 1172 is inscribed "1st Local;" No. 1173, "2nd Local."

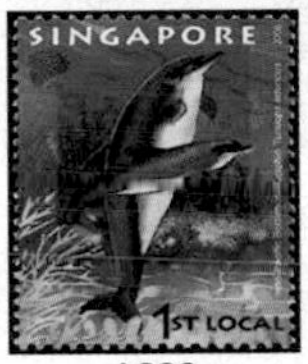
A293

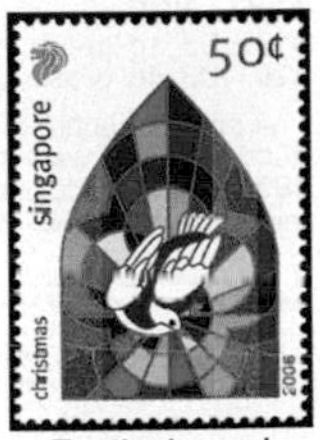
Festivals and Holidays — A294

Designs: Nos. 1176, 1184, (23c), Dove (Christmas). Nos. 1177, 1185, (23c), Fruit (Chinese New Year). Nos. 1178, 1186, (23c), Candle (Deepavali). Nos. 1179, 1187 (23c), Crescent and star (Eid ul-Fitr).

No. 1180, 50c, Dove (Christmas), diff. No. 1181, 50c, Fruit (Chinese New Year), diff. No. 1182, 50c, Candle (Deepavali), diff. No. 1183, 50c, Crescent and star (Eid ul-Fitr), diff.

**2006, Apr. 19** *Perf. 14½x14*

**1176-1179** A293 Set of 4 1.25 1.25
**1180-1183** A294 Set of 4 2.50 2.50

**Self-Adhesive**

***Die Cut Perf. 14½x14***

**1184-1187** A293 Set of 4 1.25 1.25

Nos. 1176-1179, 1184-1187 are inscribed "1st Local." Nos. 1184-1187 were each issued in sheets of 10.

## POSTAGE DUE STAMPS

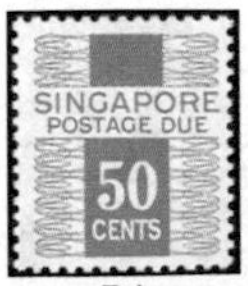
D1

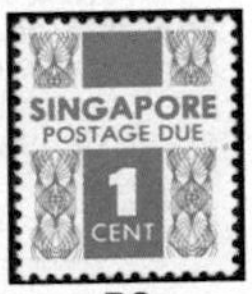
D2

**Wmk. 314**

**1968, Feb. 1** **Litho.** *Perf. 9*

| | | | | |
|---|---|---|---|---|
| **J1** | D1 | 1c emerald | .25 | .25 |
| **J2** | D1 | 2c red org | .45 | .45 |
| **J3** | D1 | 4c yel org | .90 | .90 |
| **J4** | D1 | 8c brown | 1.10 | 1.10 |
| **J5** | D1 | 10c rose mag | 2.75 | 2.75 |
| **J6** | D1 | 12c dl vio | 1.50 | 1.50 |
| **J7** | D1 | 20c brt bl | 3.25 | 3.25 |
| **J8** | D1 | 50c gray grn | 7.75 | 7.75 |
| | | *Nos. J1-J8 (8)* | 17.95 | 17.95 |

## SINGAPORE (Postage Due)

1 CENT — POSTAGE DUE — D3

**1973-77**  Perf. 13x13½

| | | | | |
|---|---|---|---|---|
| J7a | D1 | 1c | Unwmkd. (77) | 72.50  72.50 |
| J5a | D1 | 10c | Unwmkd. (77) | 72.50  72.50 |
| J8a | D1 | 50c | Unwmkd. (77) | 77.50  77.50 |
| | | | | 85.00  85.00 |
| | | | | 11.50  11.50 |
| | | | | 100.00  100.00 |

**1978, Sept. 25**  Perf. 12x11½

| | | | | |
|---|---|---|---|---|
| J9 | D2 | 1c emerald | | .20  .20 |
| J10 | D2 | 4c orange | | .20  .20 |
| J11 | D2 | 10c carmine | | 1.25  1.25 |
| J12 | D2 | 20c light blue | | 1.25  1.25 |
| J13 | D2 | 50c light yellow green | | 4.65  4.65 |
| | | Nos. J9-J13 (5) | | |

**1981**  Unwmk.  Perf. 12x11½

| | | | |
|---|---|---|---|
| J9a | D2 | 1c | .20  .20 |
| J10a | D2 | 4c | 1.25  1.25 |
| J11a | D2 | 10c | 1.25  1.25 |
| J12a | D2 | 20c | 1.75  1.75 |
| J13a | D2 | 50c | 4.65  4.65 |

**1989, July 12**  Litho.  Perf. 13x13½

| | | | |
|---|---|---|---|
| J14 | D3 | 5c red lilac | .20  .20 |
| J15 | D3 | 10c red | .20  .20 |
| J16 | D3 | 20c light blue | .25  .25 |
| J17 | D3 | 50c yellow green | .80  .80 |
| J18 | D3 | $1 brown | 1.75  1.75 |
| | | | 3.20  3.20 |

Issued: $1, 4/30/93; others, 7/12/89.

**1997, Nov. 7**  Litho.  Perf. 13x13½

| | | | |
|---|---|---|---|
| J19 | D3 | 1c green | 75.00  — |
| J20 | D3 | 4c brown orange | 75.00  — |

A small quantity of Nos. J19-J20 were produced, which was sold locally only, in late 1997. Postage due stamps were replaced by machine-generated labels on Dec. 31, 1997.

## SLOVAKIA

slō-vä-kē-a

LOCATION — Central Europe
GOVT. — Republic
AREA — 18,932 sq. mi.
POP. — 5,396,193 (1999 est.)
CAPITAL — Bratislava

100 Halierov = 1 Koruna

Formerly a province of Czechoslovakia, Slovakia declared its independence in Mar. 1939. A treaty was immediately concluded with Germany guaranteeing Slovakian independence but providing for German "protection" for 25 years. In 1945 the republic ended and Slovakia again became a part of Czechoslovakia.

On January 1, 1993 Czechoslovakia split into the Czech Republic and Slovakia.

Catalogue values for unused stamps in this country are for never hinged items, beginning with Scott 26 in the regular postage section, Scott B1 in the semi-postal section, Scott C1 in the airmail section, Scott EX1 in the personal delivery section, Scott J1 in the postage due section, and Scott P10 in the newspaper section.

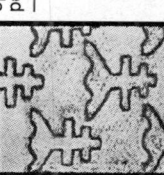

Watermark — Wmk. 263 — Double-Barred Cross Multiple

Catalogue values for unused stamps in this section, from this point to the end of the section, are for Never Hinged items.

### Stamps of Czechoslovakia, 1928-39, Overprinted in Red or Blue

**1939**  Perf. 10, 12½, 12x12½
Size: 30x23¾mm

| | | | |
|---|---|---|---|
| 2 | A29 | 5h dk ultra | 1.00  1.00 |
| 3 | A29 | 10h brown | .90  .20 |
| 4 | A29 | 20h red (Bl) | .20  .20 |
| 5 | A29 | 25h green | 5.00  4.00 |
| 6 | A66 | 50h dk brn | .20  .20 |
| 7 | A61a | 60h red (Bl) | .20  .20 |
| 8 | A68 | 90h dark blue | 1.00  1.00 |
| 9 | A73 | 1k dk vio (Bl) | .20  .20 |
| 10 | A69a | 1k dk violet | .20  .20 |
| 11 | A63 | dull blue | 8.00  8.75 |
| 12 | A60 | 1k rose lake | .20  .20 |

Overprinted Diagonally

| | | | |
|---|---|---|---|
| 13 | A64 | 1.20k rose III (Bl) | 1.00  1.00 |
| 14 | A29 | 1.50k carmine (Bl) | 1.00  1.00 |
| 15 | A79 | 1.60k ol grn (Bl) | 1.75  2.50 |
| 16 | A29 | 2k dk grn | 2.50  2.50 |
| 17 | A67 | 3k brown | 1.75  1.00 |
| 18 | A68 | 3.50k dark blue | .20  .20 |
| 19 | A69 | 3.50k dk violet | 22.50  22.50 |
| 20 | A70 | 5k deep green | 30.00  30.00 |
| 21 | A70 | dull violet | 15.00  10.00 |
| 22 | A71 | 5k green | 125.00  125.00 |
| 23 | A72 | 10k blue | 225.60  226.75 |

Nos. 2-23 (22)

Excellent counterfeit overprints exist.

### 1939, May

Size: 25x20mm  Perf. 12½

| | | | |
|---|---|---|---|
| 34 | A3 | 40h dk blue | .90 |
| 35 | A3 | 60h slate green | .90 |
| 36 | A3 | 1k gray violet | .90 |
| 37 | A3 | 2k bl vio & sepia | 1.25  3.95 |
| | | Nos. 34-37 (4) | |

20th anniv. of the death of Gen. Milan Stefánik, but not issued.

Girl Embroidering — A5
Woodcutter — A6

**1939**  Unwmk.

| | | | |
|---|---|---|---|
| 38 | A4 | 60h purple | .25  .20 |
| 39 | A4 | 1.20k slate black | .25  .30 |

10th anniv. of the death of Rev. Josef Murgas. See No. 65.

Stiavnica — A15

Spissky Hrad — A17

Lietava — A18
Bojnice — A16

### 1940-43  Wmk. 263  Perf. 12½
Size: 17x21mm
Hlinka Type of 1939

| | | | |
|---|---|---|---|
| 45 | A10 | 5h dk olive grn | .25  .20 |
| 46 | A10 | 10h deep brown | .25  .20 |
| 47 | A11 | 20h blue black | .60  .20 |
| 48 | A12 | 30h olive brown | .45  .20 |
| 49 | A13 | 25h chestnut brown | .45  .25 |
| a. | A14 | 30h ('43) | 2.50  1.00 |
| | | | 1.40  1.10 |

Nos. 45-49 (5)

See Nos. 84-87, 103-107.

### 1940-42  Wmk. 263  Perf. 12½
Hlinka Type of 1939

| | | | |
|---|---|---|---|
| 55 | A2 | 1k dk car rose | .80  .60 |
| 56 | A2 | 2.50k brt blue ('42) | 1.00  .75 |
| 57 | A2 | 3k black brn ('41) | 1.00  .60 |
| a. | | Perf. 10½ | 1.00  .90 |

On Nos. 56 and 57 a pearl frame surrounds the medallion.

### 1941  Perf. 12½

| | | | |
|---|---|---|---|
| 58 | A15 | 1.20k rose lake | .25  .20 |
| 59 | A15 | 1.50k rose pink | .25  .20 |
| 60 | A16 | 1.60k royal blue | .25  .20 |
| 61 | A18 | 2k dk gray green | 1.00  .80 |

Nos. 58-61 (4)

Slovakian Castles.

S. M. Daxner and Stefan Moyses — A19

### 1941, May 26  Photo.  Wmk. 263  Perf. 12½

| | | | |
|---|---|---|---|
| 62 | A19 | 50h olive green | 2.25  1.50 |
| 63 | A19 | 1k slate blue | 6.00  5.00 |
| 64 | A19 | 2k dk blue | 13.25  10.50 |

Nos. 62-64 (3)

80th anniv. of the Memorandum of the Slovak Nation.

Andrej Hlinka — A20

### 1941  Wmk. 263
| | | | |
|---|---|---|---|
| 65 | A4 | 60h purple | .40  .20 |

Murgas Type of 1939

### 1942  Wmk. 263
| | | | |
|---|---|---|---|
| 69 | A20 | 1.30k dark purple | .45  .20 |

Post Horn and Miniature Stamp — A21

Rev. Josef Murgas and Radio Towers — A4

General Stefánik and Memorial Tomb — A3

Andrej Hlinka A2

### 1939, Apr.  Unwmk.  Perf. 12½
Overprinted in Red or Blue

| | | | |
|---|---|---|---|
| 24 | A1 | 50h dark green (R) | .40  .40 |
| 25 | A1 | 1k dk car rose (Bl) | 4.00  2.00 |
| a. | | Perf. 10½x12½ | 20.00  10.00 |
| b. | | Never hinged | .60 |

### 1939  Unwmk.  Perf. 12½

| | | | |
|---|---|---|---|
| 26 | A2 | 5h brt ultra | .50  .45 |
| 27 | A2 | 10h olive green | .65  .45 |
| a. | | Perf. 10½x12½ | 80.00 |
| b. | | Never hinged | |
| 28 | A2 | 20h orange red | 80.00 |
| a. | | Imperf | 175.00 |
| 29 | A2 | 30h dp violet | .80 |
| a. | | Perf. 10½x12½ | .85 |
| b. | | Never hinged | .80 |
| 30 | A2 | 50h dk green | 1.00 |
| a. | | Perf. 10½x12½ | 25.00 |
| 31 | A2 | 1k dk carmine rose | 1.00 |
| 32 | A2 | 2.50k blue | .80 |
| a. | | Perf. 10½x12½ | 1.00 |
| 33 | A2 | 3k black brown | 3.00 |
| | | Nos. 26-33 (8) | 8.70 |

On Nos. 32 and 33 a pearl frame surrounds the medallion. See Nos. 55-57, 69.

Dr. Josef Tiso — A8

Presidential Residence — A9

### 1939-44  Wmk. 263  Perf. 12½

| | | | |
|---|---|---|---|
| 43 | A8 | 50h slate green | .45  .30 |
| 43A | A8 | 70h dk red brn ('42) | .50  .20 |
| b. | | Perf. 10½ ('44) | .50  .35 |

See No. 88.

### 1939-44  Photo.

| | | | |
|---|---|---|---|
| 40 | A5 | 2k dk blue green | 6.25  .50 |
| 41 | A6 | 4k copper brown | 1.40  1.50 |
| 42 | A7 | 5k orange red | 1.25  1.00 |
| a. | | Perf. 10 ('44) | 1.00  1.00 |
| | | Nos. 40-42 (3) | 8.65  2.00 |

Girl at Spring — A7

### 1940, Mar. 14
| | | | |
|---|---|---|---|
| 44 | A9 | 10k deep blue | 1.00  .75 |

Tatra Mountains — A10
Krivan Peak — A11

Edelweiss in the Tatra Mountains — A12
Chamois — A13

Church at Javorina — A14

## Philatelist — A22
## Philatelist — A23

**1942, May 23**

| | | | | |
|---|---|---|---|---|
| 70 | A21 | 30h dark green | 1.00 | .80 |
| 71 | A22 | 70h dk car rose | 1.00 | .80 |
| 72 | A23 | 80h purple | 1.00 | .80 |
| 73 | A21 | 1.30k dark brown | 4.00 | 3.20 |

Nos. 70-73 (4)

Natl. Philatelic Exhibition at Bratislava. On No. 70 the miniature stamp bears the coat-of-arms of Bratislava; on No. 73 it shows the National arms of Slovakia.

## St. Stephen's Cathedral, Vienna — A24

**1942, Oct. 12**    *Perf. 14*

| | | | | |
|---|---|---|---|---|
| 74 | A24 | 70h blue green | .65 | .75 |
| 75 | A24 | 1.30k olive green | 1.10 | 1.75 |
| 76 | A24 | 2k sapphire | 1.75 | 2.50 |
| | | | 3.50 | 5.00 |

Nos. 74-76 (3)

European Postal Congress held in Vienna.

## Slovakian Educational Society — A25

**1942, Dec. 14**

| | | | | |
|---|---|---|---|---|
| 77 | A25 | 70h black | .20 | .20 |
| 78 | A25 | 1k rose red | .20 | .20 |
| 79 | A25 | 1.30k sapphire | .20 | .20 |
| 80 | A25 | 2k chestnut brown | .25 | .20 |
| 81 | A25 | 3k olive green | .35 | .30 |
| 82 | A25 | 4k dull purple | .35 | .30 |

Nos. 77-82 (6)

Slovakian Educational Soc., 150th anniv.

## Andrej Hlinka — A26

**1943**    *Wmk. 263*

| | | | | |
|---|---|---|---|---|
| 83 | A26 | 1.30k brt ultra | .40 | .25 |

See Nos. 93-94A.

## Types of 1939-40

**1943**    *Unwmk.*    *Perf. 12½*

| | | | | |
|---|---|---|---|---|
| 84 | A11 | 10h deep brown | .25 | .20 |
| 85 | A12 | 20h blue black | .70 | .50 |
| 86 | A13 | 25h olive brown | .70 | .50 |
| 87 | A14 | 70h chestnut brown | .35 | .35 |
| 88 | A8 | 70h dk red brown | .85 | .95 |
| | | | 3.00 | 2.50 |

Nos. 84-88 (5)

## Presov Church — A27
## Railway Tunnel A29
## Locomotive A28
## Viaduct — A30

**1943, Sept. 5**    *Perf. 14*

| | | | | |
|---|---|---|---|---|
| 89 | A27 | 70h dk rose violet | .45 | .40 |
| 90 | A28 | 80h sapphire | .45 | .40 |
| 91 | A29 | 1.30k black | .45 | .40 |
| 92 | A30 | 2k dk violet brn | 1.80 | 1.60 |

Nos. 89-92 (4)

Inauguration of the new railroad line between Presov and Strazske.

## Hlinka Type of 1943 and
## Ludovit Stur — A31
## Martin Razus — A32

**1944**    *Unwmk.*

| | | | | |
|---|---|---|---|---|
| 93 | A31 | 80h slate green | .25 | .20 |
| 94 | A31 | 1k brown red | .20 | .20 |
| 94A | A26 | 1.30k brt ultra | .70 | .60 |

Nos. 93-94A (3)

## Prince Pribina — A33
## Prince — A33

Designs: 70h, Prince Mojmir. 80h, Prince Ratislav. 1.30k, King Svatopluk. 2k, Kocel. 3k, Prince Mojmir II. 5k, Prince Svatopluk II. 10k, Prince Braslav.

**1944, Mar. 14**    *Perf. 14*

| | | | | |
|---|---|---|---|---|
| 95 | A33 | 50h dark green | .20 | .20 |
| 96 | A33 | 70h lilac rose | .20 | .20 |
| 97 | A33 | 80h red brown | .20 | .20 |
| 98 | A33 | 1.30k red violet | .20 | .20 |
| 99 | A33 | 2k Prus blue | .45 | .30 |
| 100 | A33 | 3k dark brown | .95 | .70 |
| 101 | A33 | 5k violet | 2.50 | .70 |
| 102 | A33 | 50k Bratislava | 4.90 | 4.00 |

Nos. 95-102 (8)

## Scenic Types of 1940

**1944, Apr. 1**    *Perf. 14*

Size: 18x23mm

| | | | | |
|---|---|---|---|---|
| 103 | A11 | 10h bright carmine | .20 | .20 |
| 104 | A12 | 20h bright blue | .20 | .20 |
| 105 | A13 | 25h brown red | .20 | .20 |
| 106 | A14 | 30h red violet | .20 | .20 |
| 107 | A10 | 50h deep green | 1.00 | 1.00 |

Nos. 103-107 (5)

5th anniv. of Slovakia's independence.

## Symbolic of National Protection A41
## President Josef Tiso — A42

**1944, Oct. 6**    *Wmk. 263*

| | | | | |
|---|---|---|---|---|
| 108 | A41 | 2k green | .40 | .60 |
| 109 | A41 | 3.80k red violet | .40 | .90 |

**1945**    *Unwmk.*

| | | | | |
|---|---|---|---|---|
| 110 | A42 | 1k orange | .55 | .40 |
| 111 | A42 | 1.50k brown | .20 | .40 |
| 112 | A42 | 2k green | .20 | .40 |
| 113 | A42 | 4k rose red | .90 | .55 |
| 114 | A42 | 5k sapphire | .80 | .40 |

*Wmk. 263*

| | | | | |
|---|---|---|---|---|
| 115 | A42 | 10k red violet | .60 | .40 |
| | | | 3.25 | 2.35 |

Nos. 110-115 (6)

6th anniv. of the Republic of Slovakia's declaration of independence, Mar. 14, 1939.

## Natl. Arms — A50

**1993**    *Photo. & Engr.*    *Perf. 11½*

| | | | | |
|---|---|---|---|---|
| 150 | A50 | 3k multicolored | .50 | .30 |

*Engr.*    *Perf. 12*

Size: 30x44mm

| | | | | |
|---|---|---|---|---|
| 151 | A50 | 8k multicolored | 4.00 | 3.00 |

Issued: 3k, Jan. 2; 8k, Jan. 1. No. 151 does not have black frameline.
No. 151 was issued in sheets of 6.

## Castles & Churches — A51

#152-155 are churches; #156-157 castles.

*Perf. 11½x12, 12x11½*

**1993-95**    *Photo. & Engr.*

| | | | | |
|---|---|---|---|---|
| 152 | A51 | 2k Nitra | .20 | .20 |
| 153 | A51 | 3k Banska Bystrica | .25 | .20 |
| 154 | A51 | 5k Ruzomberok, horiz. | .40 | .20 |
| 155 | A51 | 10k Kosice | .80 | .40 |
| 156 | A51 | 30k Zvolen, horiz. | 2.50 | 1.25 |
| 157 | A51 | 50k Bratislava | 6.50 | 3.25 |
| | | | 10.65 | 5.50 |

Nos. 152-157 (6)

Issued: 5k, 10k, 1993; 30k, 9/12/93; 50k, 12/31/93; 3k, 11/15/94; 2k, 3/15/95.
See Nos. 218-227.

## St. John Nepomuk, 600th Death Anniv. A57

**1993, Mar. 11**    *Photo. & Engr.*    *Perf. 12x11½*

| | | | | |
|---|---|---|---|---|
| 158 | A57 | 8k multicolored | .75 | .40 |

See Czech Republic #2880; Germany #1776.

## President Michal Kovac

**1993**    *Engr.*    *Perf. 12x11½*

| | | | | |
|---|---|---|---|---|
| 159 | A58 | 2k dark gray blue | .20 | .20 |
| 159A | A58 | 3k red brown & red | .25 | .20 |

Issued: 2k, 3/2/93; 3k, 11/3/93.

**1993, May 14**    *Photo. & Engr.*    *Perf. 11½*

Trees.

| | | | | |
|---|---|---|---|---|
| 160 | A59 | 3k Quercus robur | .25 | .20 |
| 161 | A59 | 4k Carpinus betulus | .35 | .20 |
| 162 | A59 | 10k Pinus silvestris | .85 | .40 |
| | | | 1.45 | .80 |

Nos. 160-162 (3)

Famous Men: 5k, Jan Levoslav Bella (1843-1936), composer. 8k, Alexander Dubcek (1921-92), politician. 20k, Jan Kollar (1793-1852), writer.

**1993, May 20**    *Photo. & Engr.*    *Perf. 12x11½*

| | | | | |
|---|---|---|---|---|
| 163 | A60 | 5k red brown & blue | .75 | .40 |
| 164 | A60 | 8k brown & lilac red | 1.25 | .60 |
| 165 | A60 | 20k gray blue & orange | 3.00 | 1.50 |
| | | | 3.00 | 2.50 |

Nos. 163-165 (3)

**1993, May 31**    *Engr.*    *Perf. 12*

Woman with Pitcher, by Marian Cunderlik.

| | | | | |
|---|---|---|---|---|
| 166 | A61 | 14k multicolored | 6.00 | 5.00 |

Europa. Issued in sheets of 4.

## Literary Slovak Language, 150th Anniv. A62

Design: 8k, Arrival of St. Cyril and St. Methodius, 1130th Anniv.

**1993, June 22**    *Photo. & Engr.*    *Perf. 12x11½*

| | | | | |
|---|---|---|---|---|
| 167 | A62 | 2k multicolored | .20 | .20 |
| 168 | A62 | 8k multicolored | .75 | .40 |

See Czech Republic No. 2886.

Arms of Dubnica nad Vahom.

**1993, July 8**    *Photo. & Engr.*    *Perf. 12x11½*

| | | | | |
|---|---|---|---|---|
| 169 | A63 | 1k multicolored | .20 | .20 |

**1993, Sept. 2**    *Photo. & Engr.*    *Perf. 11½*

The Big Pets, by Lane Smith.

| | | | | |
|---|---|---|---|---|
| 170 | A64 | 5k multicolored | .45 | .20 |

Bratislava Biennial of Illustrators.

Gavcikovo Dam — A65

**1993, Nov. 12**   **Photo. & Engr.**
172 A65 10k multicolored   1.25   .60
No. 172 issued se-tenant with label.

**1993, Dec. 1**   **Photo. & Engr.**   **Perf. 11½**
173 A66 2k multicolored   .30   .20
Christmas.

Souvenir Sheet

**1993, Dec. 17**   **Engr.**   **Perf. 11½x12**
174 A67 16k multicolored   2.00   1.00

Monument to Gen. Milan
Stefanik — A67

Art from Bratislava Natl.
Gallery — A68

**1993, Dec. 31**
175 A68 9k multicolored   1.50   1.00
Issued in sheets of 4.
See Nos. 199-200, 237-238, 255.

Sculpture: 9k, Plough of Springtime, by
Josef Kostka.

**1994, Jan. 26**   **Photo. & Engr.**   **Perf. 11x11½**
176 A69 2k multicolored   .50   .20
Complete booklet, 10 #176   6.00
1994 Winter Olympics, Lillehammer.

Jan Andrej Segner
(1704-77),
Physicist — A71

**1994, Apr. 29**   **Photo. & Engr.**
177 A70 3k multicolored   .25   .20
Complete booklet, 5 #177   1.75
Int. Year of the Family.

Design: 9k, Antoine de Saint-Exupery
(1900-44), aviator, author.

**1994, May 25**   **Photo. & Engr.**   **Perf. 11½x11**
178 A71 8k red brown & blue   .80   .40
179 A71 9k black, blue & pink   .90   .45
See Nos. 196-198.

Josef Murgas
(1864-1929),
Inventor of Radio
Transmitters — A72

**1994, May 27**   **Engr.**   **Perf. 11½**
180 A72 28k multicolored   2.25   1.10
Europa. Issued in sheets of 4.

**1994, May 31**   **Photo. & Engr.**   **Perf. 11½x11**
181 A73 3k multicolored   .25   .20
Int. Stop Smoking Day.

**1994, June 10**   **Photo. & Engr.**   **Perf. 11½**
182 A74 2k blue, black & green   .50   .20
1994 World Cup Soccer Championships, US.

Int. Olympic
Committee,
Cent. — A75

**1994, June 23**
183 A75 3k multicolored   .40   .20
No. 183 issued with se-tenant label.

Raptors — A76

**1994, July 4**   **Photo. & Engr.**   **Perf. 11½x12**
184 A76 4k Aquila chrysaetos   .40   .20
185 A76 5k Falco peregrinus   .50   .25
186 A76 7k Bubo bubo   .70   .35
Nos. 184-186 (3)   1.60   .80

Prince Svatopluk of Moravia (870-
894) — A77

**1994, July 20**   **Engr.**   **Perf. 12**
187 A77 12k red brn, buff & blk   1.25   .60
Issued in sheets of 4.

**1994, Aug. 1**   **Photo. & Engr.**
188 A78 8k multicolored   .55   .30

Slovak Uprising, 50th Anniv. — A79

**1994, Aug. 27**   **Photo. & Engr.**   **Perf. 12x11½**
189 A79 6k multicolored   .75   .40
190 A79 8k multicolored   .75   .40
Nos. 189-190 printed with se-tenant label.
Designs: 6k, Gen. Rudolf Viest, Gen. Jan
Golian. 8k, French Volunteers' Memorial,
Strecno hill.

UPU, 120th
Anniv. — A78

**1994, Sept. 1**   **Photo. & Engr.**
191 A80 34k multicolored   3.25   1.60
Design: 34k, Matuska, woman with pitcher,
verse of "A Well She Dug."

Souvenir Sheet

Janko
Matuska,
Lyricist,
150th
Death
Anniv.
A80

**1994, Oct. 18**   **Photo. & Engr.**   **Perf. 11½x12**
192 A81 12k multicolored   1.25   .60

Comenius University,
75th Anniv. — A81

St. George's
Church,
Kostolany pod
Tribecom — A83

**1994, Nov. 8**   **Photo. & Engr.**
194 A83 20k multicolored   1.90   .95

Christmas — A84

**1994, Nov. 29**   **Photo. & Engr.**   **Perf. 11½**
195 A84 2k multicolored   .35   .20

**Personalities Type of 1994**
**1994, Dec. 12**   **Perf. 11½x11**
196 A71 5k multicolored   .50   .25
Complete booklet, 5 #196   7.50
197 A71 6k multicolored   .60   .30
198 A71 10k multicolored   1.00   .50
Nos. 196-198 (3)   2.10   1.05
Designs: 5k, Chatam Sofer (1762-1839),
rabbi. 6k, Wolfgang Kempelen (1734-1804),
polytechnician. 10k, Stefan Banic (1870-
1941), inventor of aviation parachute.

Bratislava Art Type of 1993

**1994, Dec. 15**   **Perf. 12x11½, 11½x12**
199 A68 7k multicolored   .70   .35
200 A68 14k multicolored   1.40   .70
Designs: 7k, Girls, by Janko Alexy, horiz.
14k, The Bulls, by Vincent Hloznik.

Ships — A85

**1994, Dec. 30**   **Photo. & Engr.**   **Perf. 12x11½**
201 A85 5k multicolored   .50   .25
202 A85 8k multicolored   .75   .40
203 A85 10k multicolored   1.00   .50
Nos. 201-203 (3)   2.25   1.15
5k, Cargo ship, NL EMS. 8k, Cargo ship,
Ryn. 10k, 400-passenger cruise ship.

Samuel Jurkovic,
Founder of
Landlords Assoc.,
1845 — A86

**1995, Feb. 8**   **Photo. & Engr.**   **Perf. 11½**
204 A86 9k multicolored   .65   .35

European Nature
Conservation
Year — A87

**1995, Feb. 28**   **Engr.**
205 A87 2k multicolored   .20   .20
Complete booklet, 10 #205   12.50
Protected plants: 2k, Ciminalis clusii. 3k,
Pulsatilla slavica. 8k, Onosma tornense.

Mojmirovce
Horse Race,
180th Anniv.
A82

**1994, Oct. 25**   **Perf. 12x11½**
193 A82 2k multicolored   .20   .20

**Souvenir Sheet**

**Year for the Eradication of Poverty — A117**

**1996, Apr. 15** **Engr.** **Perf. 12**
243 A117 7k multicolored 1.00 .70

A118

A119

Europa: a, Holding thistle, carduus texturie anus marg. b, Portrait, daphne cneorum.

**1996, May 3** **Engr.** **Perf. 11½**
244 A118 8k Pair, #a.-b. 1.00 .50

Izabela Textorisová (1866-1949), Slovakia's 1st female botanist. Issued in sheets of 4.

**Souvenir Sheet**

Motion Pictures, Cent.: Two frames from 1936 film, Jánosik.

**1996, May 15** **Perf. 11½x12**
245 A119 16k multicolored 1.00 .50
Printed se-tenant with label.

**Round Slovakia Cycle Race — A120**

**1996, May 30** **Engr.** **Perf. 11½**
246 A120 3k multicolored .20 .20
Complete booklet, 10 #246 2.00

---

**Photo. & Engr.** **Perf. 11½**
**1995, Sept. 5**
232 A109 2k multicolored .20 .20
Complete booklet, 10 #232 1.50
233 A109 3k multicolored .20 .20
Complete booklet, 10 #233 2.00

**St. Adalbert Assoc.**

**1995, Sept. 14**
234 A110 4k multicolored .30 .20

**The Cleveland Agreement, 80th Anniv. A111**

**1995, Oct. 20** **Photo. & Engr.** **Perf. 12x11½**
235 A111 5k multicolored .40 .20

**UN, 50th Anniv. A112**

**1995, Oct. 24** **Engr.** **Perf. 11½x12**
235A A112 8k multicolored .60 .30
Issued in sheets of 8 + 2 labels.

**Christmas A113**

**1995, Oct. 27** **Photo. & Engr.** **Perf. 11½x12**
236 A113 2k multicolored .20 .20

**Bratislava Art Type of 1993**
Designs: 4k The Ilohovoo Nativity. 16k, Two Women, by Mikuláš Galanda.

**1995, Nov. 30** **Photo. & Engr.** **Perf. 11½x12**
237 A68 8k multicolored .55 .30
238 A68 16k multicolored 1.10 .55
Issued in sheets of 4 + 2 labels.

**Olympic Games, Cent. A115**

**Jozef Ciger-Hronsky (1896-1960) A114**

**1996, Feb. 15** **Photo. & Engr.** **Perf. 11½**
239 A114 3k multicolored .20 .20
240 A114 4k multicolored .25 .20

4k, Jozef L'udovit Holuby (1836-1923). See Nos. 293-295, 320-322.

**1996, Feb. 15**
241 A115 9k multicolored .60 .30

**Folk Traditions — A116**
Easter tradition of dousing women with water

---

**Visit of Pope John Paul II — A95**

**1995, May 29** **Engr.** .20 .20
216 A95 3k red 2.00
Complete booklet, 10 #216

**Organized Philately in Slovakia, Cent. — A96**

**1995, June 1** **Perf. 11½x12**
217 A96 3k blue, black & gray .20 .20
a. Souv. sheet of 2 .40 .40
Dunafila '95. 2.00

**Castles & Churches — A100**

**Perf. 11¾x11¼, 11½x11¾ (#218, 225-226)**

**1995-2001** **Photo. & Engr.**
218 A100 50h Bardejov, horiz. .20 .20
219 A100 4k Nova Bana .30 .20
220 A100 4k Presov .30 .20
221 A100 5k Tmava .30 .20
222 A100 7k Martin .40 .20
223 A100 8k Trencin Castle .55 .30
224 A100 9k Zelina .55 .55
225 A100 20k Roznava, horiz. .85 .40
226 A100 40k Piestany, horiz. 1.60 .80
227 A100 50k Komarno 2.10 1.00
Nos. 218-227 (10) 7.03 3.00

Issued: 4k (#219), 6/15/95; 8k, 9/12/95. 9k, 4/15/97. 7k., 7/17/97. 5k. 9/12/98. 4k (#220), 11/3/98. 50h, 2/11/00. 20k, 7/26/00. 40k, 5/25/01. 50k 4/26/01.
See Nos. 421-425.

**UNESCO World Heritage Sites A107**

**1995, July 19** **Perf. 11½x12, 12x11½** **Photo. & Engr.**
228 A107 7k Banska Stiavnica, vert. .50 .25
229 A107 10k Spissky Hrad .70 .35
230 A107 15k Vikolinec 1.00 .50
Nos. 228-230 (3) 2.20 1.10

**Volleyball, Cent. — A108**

**1995, Aug. 16** **Perf. 11½**
231 A108 9k multicolored .60 .30

A109

A110

Bratislava Biennial of Illustrators: 2k, Clown, by Lorenzo Mattotti, Italy. 3k, Two characters, by Dusan Kallay, Slovakia.

---

206 A87 3k multicolored .20 .20
Complete booklet, 5 #206 12.50
207 A87 8k multicolored .60 .30
Nos. 205-207 (3) 1.00 .70

**Slovak Natl. Theatre, 75th Anniv. A88**

**1995, Feb. 28** **Perf. 12x11½**
208 A88 10k multicolored .70 .35

**1995 Group B World Cup Ice Hockey Championships, Bratislava — A89**

**1995, Mar. 29** **Perf. 11½**
209 A89 5k blue & yellow .35 .20

**Bela Bartok (1881-1945), Composer A90**

**1995, Apr. 20** **Perf. 12x11½**
210 A90 3k multicolored .20 .20
211 A90 6k multicolored .40 .20

6k, Jan Bahyl (1856-1916), inventor.

**Souvenir Sheet**
**Ludovit Stur (1815-56), Writer — A91**

**1995, Apr. 20** **Perf. 11½**
212 A91 16k multicolored 1.10 .55

**Europa A92**

**1995, May 5** **Perf. 12**
213 A92 8k multicolored 1.00 .80

**Liberation of the Concentration Camps, 50th Anniv. — A93**

**1995, May 5** **Perf. 11**
214 A93 12k multicolored .80 .40

**Slovak Scouting — A94**

**1995, May 18** **Perf. 11½x11**
215 A94 5k multicolored 1.00 .30

**1996, May 30**

247 A121 18k multicolored 1.10 .55

Slovak Perspectives, 150th Anniv.—A121

A121

A122

**1996, June 14**

248 A122 6k Coat of arms .40 .20

Town of Senica.

**Photo. & Engr. Perf. 12x11½**

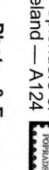

A123

**1996, July 16 Perf. 11½x12**

249 A123 4k multicolored .30 .30
Complete booklet, 10 #249 3.00
250 A123 4k multicolored .30 .30
Complete booklet, 10 #250 3.00
251 A123 4k multicolored .30 .30
Complete booklet, 10 #251 3.00
Nos. 249-251 (3) .90 .60

Nature protection: No. 249, Ovis musimon. No. 250, Bison bonasus. No. 251, Rupicapra rupicapra.

Splendors of Homeland—A124

A124

**1996, Sept. 25 Perf. 11½x12**

252 A124 4k Popradské Lake .30 .20
253 A124 8k Skalnaté Lake .30 .20
254 A124 12k Štrbské Lake .90 .45
Nos. 252-254 (3) 1.80 .95

**Photo. & Engr.**

**1996, Oct. 5 Engr. Perf. 11**

255 A68 14k multicolored 1.00 .50

See Czech Republic #2995, Sweden #2199. The Baroque Chair, by Endre Nemes (1909-85).

Bratislava Art Type of 1993

A125

**1996, Oct. 15 Perf. 11**

256 A125 4k multicolored .30 .20
257 A125 6k multicolored .45 .25
Complete booklet, 10 #256 3.00
Complete booklet, 10 #257 4.50

4k, Bratislava-Trnava horse-drawn railway. 6k, Andrej Kvasz's (1883-1974) airplane.

**Photo. & Engr.**

Technological Advances A125

---

Queen Ntombi Twala, by Andy Warhol (1928-87)—A126

A126

**1996 Engr. Perf. 11½**

258 A126 7k multicolored .45 .20
259 A126 10k multicolored .65 .30

Each issued in sheets of 4.
Issued: 7k, 11/13/96; 10k, 10/5/96.
See #284-286, 311, 314-315, 340-341.

Design: 10k. Suppressed Laughter, by Franz Xaver Messerschmidt (1736-83).

Christmas, Kysuce Village—A127

A127

**1996, Nov. 5 Photo. & Engr. Perf. 11½**

260 A127 2k multicolored .20 .20

Michael Martikén, Olympic Gold Medalist, Canoeing A128

A128

**1996, Dec. 18 Photo. & Engr. Perf. 12x11½**

261 A128 3k brown & yellow .20 .20

Stamp Day—A129

A129

**1996, Dec. 18**

262 A129 3k violet & buff .20 .20
Complete booklet, 9 #262 9.00

No. 262 was printed se-tenant with label.

Designs: Unexecuted 1938 stamp design of a woman with patriarchal cross, dove, Martin Benka, stamp designer.

Bishop Stefan Moyses (1797-1869)—A130

A130

**1997, Jan. 16 Photo. & Engr. Perf. 11½**

263 A130 3k multicolored .25 .20
264 A130 4k multicolored .30 .20

Design: 4k, Svetozar Hurban Vajansky (1847-1916), politician.

---

A131

**1997, Jan. 31 Photo. & Engr. Perf. 11½**

265 A131 6k multicolored .35 .20

1997 World Biathlon Championships, Osrblie.

A132

**1997, Feb. 15 Photo. & Engr. Perf. 11½**

266 A132 3k multicolored .20 .20
Complete booklet, 10 #266 2.00

Folk Tradition of collecting dew.

Franciscan Church, Bratislava, 700th Anniv.—A133

**1997, Mar. 25 Photo. & Engr. Perf. 11½x12**

267 A133 16k multicolored 1.00 .50

Radio, Cent. A135

A135

**1997, Apr. 15 Perf. 12x11½**

269 A135 10k multicolored .60 .30

Europa (Stories and Legends): Miraculous rain near Hron.

A136

**1997, May 5 Engr. Perf. 12x11½**

270 A136 9k multicolored .55 .30

Issued in sheets of 7 + 3 labels.

A137

**1997, June 12 Engr. Perf. 12x11½**

271 A137 6k multicolored .35 .20
272 A137 8k multicolored .50 .25

Nos. 271-272 issued in sheets of 8 + label.

Limestone Formations: 6k, Domica Cavern, Silická. 8k, Aragonit Cavern, Ochtiná.

---

Folklore Festival, Vychodná—A138

**1997, June 12 Photo. & Engr. Perf. 12x11½**

273 A138 11k multicolored .65 .35

Triennale of Naive Art, Bratislava A139

A138

**1996, June 26 Photo. & Engr. Perf. 12x11½**

274 A139 3k multicolored .20 .20
Complete booklet, 10 #274 2.00

Souvenir Sheet

A139

World Year of Slovaks A140

**1997, July 17 Perf. 11½**

276 A140 9k multicolored .50 .25

A140

Bratislava Biennale of Illustrators A141

**1997, Aug. 5 Photo. & Engr. Perf. 11½**

277 A141 3k multicolored .20 .20
Complete booklet, 10 #277 2.00

A141

Water Mill, Jelka—A142

**1997, Aug. 5**

278 A142 4k multicolored .25 .20
Complete booklet, 10 #278 2.50

A142

A143

**1997, Sept. 1 Photo. & Engr. Perf. 11½**

279 A143 4k multicolored .25 .20

Constitution, 5th anniv.

A144

**1997, Sept. 17 Photo. & Engr. Perf. 11½**

280 A144 9k multicolored .55 .30

6th Half Marathon World Championships, Kosice.

**Mushrooms — A145**

Designs: #281, Boletus aereus. #282, Morchella esculenta. #283, Catathelasma imperiale.

**1997, Sept. 17**   **Perf. 12**
281 A145 9k multicolored .55 .30
282 A145 9k multicolored .55 .30
283 A145 9k multicolored .55 .30
a. Souvenir sheet, #281-283 1.75 .90
Nos. 281-283 (3) 1.65 .90

**Art Type of 1996**

Designs: 9k, Self-portrait, by Ján Kupecky (1667-1740). 10k, Bojnice Altar, St. Peter and St. Lucia, by Nardo Di Cione, 14th cent., horiz. 12k, Towards the Goal (The Miners), by Koloman Sokol (b. 1902).

**1997, Oct. 15**   **Engr.**   **Perf. 11½**
284 A126 9k multicolored .55 .30
285 A126 10k multicolored .70 .40
286 A126 12k multicolored 1.85 1.00
Nos. 284-286 (3)

**Cernova 1907**
A146

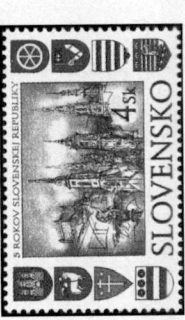

**1997, Oct. 24**   **Photo. & Engr.**   **Perf. 11½x12**
287 A146 4k Lamenting woman, church .30 .20

**Christmas**
A147

**1997, Nov. 3**   **Perf. 11½**
288 A147 3k Nativity .25 .20

**Ondrej Nepela, Figure Skater—A148**

289 A148 5k multicolored .60 .20

**1997, Dec. 1**   **Photo. & Engr.**   **Perf. 11½**
290 A149 4k Resurrection of Christ .25 .20
Complete booklet, 10 #290 2.50
Spiritual renewal. See #301, 327.

**Stamp Day — A150**

**1997, Dec. 18**
291 A150 4k dark brown & blue .50 .20
Complete booklet, 9 #291 + 12 labels 6.00
No. 291 was printed se-tenant with label.

**Slovak Republic, 5th Anniv. — A151**

**Photo. & Engr.**   **Perf. 11½**
**1998, Jan. 1** .25 .20
292 A151 4k multicolored
Complete booklet, 10 #292 2.50

**Personality Type of 1996**

Writers: No. 293, Martin Rázus (1888-1937), politician. No. 294, Ján Smrek (1898-1982), poet. No. 295, Jozef Skultéty (1853-1948), linguist, editor.

**1998, Jan. 19**
293 A114 4k multicolored .25 .20
294 A114 4k multicolored .25 .20
295 A114 4k multicolored .75 .60
Nos. 293-295 (3)

**1998 Winter Olympic Games, Nagano A152**

**1998, Jan. 19**   **Perf. 12x11½**
296 A152 19k Hockey player 2.00 .55

**Folk Tradition, Banishing of Winter — A153**

**Perf. 11½**
**1998, Mar. 3** .20 .20
297 A153 11k multicolored
Complete booklet, 10 #297 2.00

**Castles A154**

**1998, Mar. 3**
298 A154 6k Budatin .35 .20
299 A154 11k Krásna Horka .65 .30

**Souvenir Sheet**
300 A154 18k Nitra 1.00 .50

**Spiritual Renewal Type of 1997**

Design: Descent of the Holy Spirit, flames above peoples' heads.

**Photo. & Engr.**   **Perf. 11½**
**1998, May 5** .25 .20
301 A149 4k multicolored
Complete booklet, 10 #301 2.50

**Folklore Festivals — A155**

**1998, May 5** .70 .35
302 A155 12k Tekov wedding
Europa. Issued in sheet of 8 + label.

A157

A156

**Photo. & Engr.**   **Perf. 11½**
**1998, June 1** .20 .20
303 A156 3k Child's drawing
Complete booklet, 10 #303 2.00
The Children's Center, Ruzomberok.

**1998, June 1**
Design: Viktor Kolibik (1890-1918), wireworker, leader of revolt.
304 A157 3k multicolored .20 .20
Mutiny at Kragujevac, 80th anniv.

**Slovak Uprising of 1848-49 A158**

**1998, June 1**
305 A158 4k multi, with 1 or 2 labels 1.50 .40

**Railways in Slovakia, Cent. — A159**

Designs: 4k, Atlier steam locomotive. 10k, Lubochna-Mucidla electrified narrow-gauge trolley. 15k, Diesel locomotive.

**Photo. & Engr.**   **Perf. 11½**
**1998, Aug. 20**
306 A159 4k multicolored .50 .20
307 A159 10k multicolored .60 .30
308 A159 15k multicolored .85 .50
Nos. 306-308 (3) 1.95 1.00

**Fish A160**

Designs: a, 4k, Umbra krameri. b, 11k, Zingel zingel. c, 16k, Cyprinus carpio.

**Sheet of 3**
**1998, Sept. 7**
309 A160 #a.-c. + label 1.75 .90

**Art Type of 1996**   **Perf. 11½x12**
1564 Wooden "Pieta" statue, by unknown artist, Sastin.
**1998, Sept. 14** 1.00 .50
311 A126 18k multicolored
Issued in sheets of 4.

**"No" to Drugs — A161**

**Photo. & Engr.**   **Perf. 11x11½**
**1998, Oct. 5** .20 .20
312 A161 3k multicolored

**Ektopfilm, Ecology-Related Film Festival, 25th Anniv. — A162**

**1998, Oct. 5**   **Perf. 11**
313 A162 4k multicolored .20 .20
Complete booklet, 10 #313 2.00

**Art Type of 1996**

Designs: 10k, Terchova Landscape, by Martin Benka (1888-1971). 12k, Fishermen, by L'udovit Fulla (1902-80).

**1998, Oct. 15**   **Engr.**   **Perf. 11½x12**
314 A126 10k multicolored .55 .30
315 A126 12k multicolored .65 .35

**Adoration of the Magi — A163**

**1998, Nov. 3**   **Perf. 11x11½** .20 .20
317 A163 3k Christmas 1.50
Complete booklet, 10 #317

**Stamp Day — A164**

**Photo. & Engr.**   **Perf. 12x11½**
**1998, Dec. 18** .50 .20
318 A164 4k multi, with 1 or 2 labels 6.00
Complete booklet, 9 #318 + 12 labels

**19th World Winter Universiad Games, 4th European Youth Olympic Days — A165**

**Photo. & Engr.**   **Perf. 12x11½**
**1999, Jan. 12** 1.00 .30
319 A165 12k multicolored
No. 319 is printed se-tenant with 2 labels.

**Personality Type of 1996**

Designs: 3k, Matej Bel (1684-1749), teacher, pastor. 4k, Juraj Haulik (1788-1869), 1st cardinal of Croatia. 11k, Pavol Országh-Hviezdoslav (1849-1921), poet, dramatist.

**1999, Jan. 28**   **Perf. 11½**
320 A114 3k multicolored .20 .20
321 A114 4k multicolored .20 .20
322 A114 11k multicolored .60 .30
Nos. 320-322 (3) 1.00 .70
See Croatia 388.

A167

**UPU, 125th Anniv. — A166**

**Photo. & Engr.**   **Perf. 11½**
**1999, Mar. 12** .20 .20
323 A166 4k multicolored 2.00
Complete booklet, 10 #323

**Litho. & Engr.**

**1999, Mar. 12**
Traditional bonnets.
Perf. 11½x12
324 A167 4k Cajkov .20 .20
325 A167 15k Helpa .75 .35
326 A167 18k Madunice .90 .45
Nos. 324-326 (3) 1.85 1.00

Nos. 324-326 were each issued in sheets of 10.

Astronaut Ivan Bella, First Slovak in Space — A172

Illustration reduced.

**1999, June 15**
333 A172 12k multicolored
Perf. 11¾x11½
.55 .30

A170

A171

Council of Europe, 50th Anniv. A169

Souvenir Sheet

Int'l. Year of Older Persons.

**1999, June 15**
332 A171 5k multicolored Perf. 11½ .25 .20

**1999, June 15**
331 A170 4k multicolored Perf. 11½x11¾ .20 .20

Slovak Philharmonic Orchestra, 50th anniv.

**1999, May 5** **Engr.**
330 A169 16k multicolored Perf. 12x11½ .75 .75
a. Souvenir sheet of 1 .75 .75

**1999, May 5** **Engr.**
328 A168 9k shown .40 .20
329 A168 11k Mountains, diff. .50 .25
a. Pair, #328-329 .90 .45

Europa No. 329a is a continuous design. Issued in sheets of 8 + label.

Tatra National Park A168

**Spiritual Renewal Type of 1997**
Design: "Transfiguration," by Vincent Hloznik, depicting ascension of Christ.

**1999, May 5** **Photo. & Engr.**
327 A149 5k multicolored Perf. 11½ .25 .20
Complete booklet, 10 #327 2.50

A174

A175

**1999, July 15** **Photo. & Engr.**
334 A173 12k Zilina University .55 .30
335 A173 16k Globe .75 .75

UPU, 125th Anniv. — A173

**1999, Sept. 3** **Photo. & Engr.**
336 A174 4k multicolored Perf. 11½x11¾ .20 .20
Bratislava Univ. of Fine Arts, 50th anniv.
337 A175 5k multicolored Perf. 11½x11¾ .25 .20
Complete booklet, 10 #337 2.50
Bratislava Biennale of Illustrators.

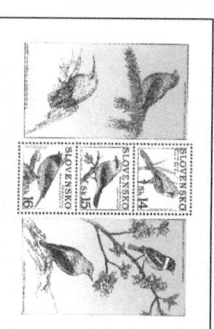

Birds — A177

**1999, Sept. 21** **Litho. & Engr.**
339 A177 Sheet of 3, #a-c. 2.25 1.10
a, 14k, Panurus biarmicus. b, 15k, Lanius collurio. c, 16k, Phoenicurus phoenicurus.

Souvenir Sheet

**1999, Sept. 21**
338 A176 7k sepia & yellow Perf. 11x11¾ .35 .20

Mine Water Pump Invented By Jozef Hell (1713-89) A176

**1999, Oct. 5** **Engr.**
340 A126 13k multicolored .65 .30
341 A126 14k multicolored .70 .35

Each issued in sheets of 4.

**Art Type of 1996**
Designs: 13k, Malatiná, by Milos Alexander Bazovsky (1899-1968), horiz. 14k, Study of the Blacksmith, by Dominik Skutecky.

**1999, Nov. 3** **Photo. & Engr.**
342 A178 4k multicolored Perf. 11¾x11¼ .20 .20
Complete booklet, 10 #342 2.00

Christmas — A178

Ceramic Urns, Museum of Jewish Culture — A180

**1999, Nov. 23** **Litho. & Engr.**
344 A180 12k urn .55 .30
345 A180 18k 1734 urn .85 .40
a. Pair, #344-345 1.40 .70
Issued in sheets of 8.
See Israel #1380-1381.

**1999, Nov. 17**
343 A179 5k multicolored Perf. 12x11¾ .25 .20

Czechoslovakia's "Velvet Revolution," 10th Anniv. — A179

**1999, Dec. 18** **Photo. & Engr.**
346 A181 5k multicolored Perf. 12x11¾ .50 .20
Complete booklet, 9 #346 6.00

Albin Brunovsky (1935-97), Stamp Designer A181

**2000, Jan. 1** **Litho. & Engr.**
347 A182 Pair, #a-b. 1.00 .50

Designs: a, 10k, Dunajec. b, 12k, Váh.
Issued in sheets of 8.

Rivers and Gaps — A182

**2000, Jan. 11** **Photo. & Engr.**
348 A183 4k multi .20 .20
349 A183 5k multi .25 .20

Famous People — A183

4k, Hana Meličkova (1900-78), actress. 5k, Štefan Anián Jedlik (1800-95), inventor.

**2000, Feb. 15** **Photo. & Engr.**
351 A184 4k multi Perf. 11¾x11½ .20 .20
Ruzomberok team, 1999 European Women's Basketball League champions.

Basketball A184

**2000, Feb. 15** **Photo. & Engr.**
352 A185 5k multi Perf. 11¾x11½ .25 .20
Juraj Hronec (1881-1959), Stefan Schwarz (1914-96), mathematicians.

World Mathematics Year — A185

**2000, Feb. 15**
353 A186 4k brown Perf. 11½x11¾ .20 .20
Complete booklet, 10 #353 2.00

Easter A186

**2000, Mar. 24** **Photo. & Engr.**
354 A187 5.50k multi Perf. 11½x11¾ .25 .20

Ján Hollý (1785-1849), Poet — A187

**2000, May 9** Europa, 2000 Common Design Type **Litho. & Engr.**
355 CD17 12k multi Perf. 11¾ .55 .30

**2000, June 1** **Photo. & Engr.**
356 A188 5.50k multi Perf. 11½x11¾ .25 .20

UNICEF A188

Postman and Austria design A1.
First postage stamp used in Slovakia, 150th anniv.

**2000, June 1** **Photo. & Engr.**
357 A189 10k multi Perf. 11½x11¾ .45 .25

A189

A190

**2000, June 15** **Engr.**
358 A190 5.50k multi Perf. 11¾x11¼ .25 .20

Pres. Rudolf Schuster

Souvenir Sheet

No. 381: a, 14k, Ursus arctos. b, 15k, Canis lupus. c, 16k, Lynx lynx.

**Wild Animals — A207**

**Perf. 11¾x11½**
2.00 1.00
**2001, July 10**
381 A207 Sheet of 3, #a-c

**Dobro Resonator Guitar and US Map — A208**

**Photo. & Engr.**
**Perf. 11¾x11¼**
.85 .40
**2001, Aug. 1**
382 A208 19k multi

**Bratislava Biennale of Illustrators A209**

**Perf. 11½x11¾**
.30 .20
3.00
**2001, Aug. 15**
383 A209 7k multi
Booklet, 10 #383

The Righteous Among Nations A210

**Perf. 11¾x11¼**
.60 .30
**2001, Sept. 9**
384 A210 14k multi

Souvenir Sheet

Alexander Dubcek (1921-92), Czechoslovakian Communist Leader — A211

---

**Traditional Costumes — A203**

Designs: 5.50k, Man from Detva. 6k, Woman and child from Detva.

**Perf. 11½x11¾**
.25 .20
2.50
.25 .20
2.50
**2001, Feb. 22**
374 A203 5.50k multi
Booklet, 10 #374
375 A203 6k multi
Booklet, 10 #375

**Archaeological Sites — A204**

No. 376: a, 12k. Havránok. b, 15k, Ducové. Illustration reduced.

**Perf. 11¾**
1.10 .55
**2001, Apr. 10**
376 A204 Horiz. pair, #a-b

**Engr.**

**Europa A205**

**Perf. 11¾**
.75 .35
**2001, May 5**
379 A205 18k multi

Souvenir Sheet

**Princes of Great Moravia — A206**

No. 380: a, 6k, Pribina. b, 9k, Rastislav. c, 11k, Kocel. d, 14k, Svatopluk.

**Litho. & Engr.**
**Perf. 11¾**
1.75 .90
**2001, July 4**
380 A206 Sheet of 4, #a-d

---

**Art Type of 1996**

Designs: 18k, Nativity, from church in Spisska Stara Ves. 20k, Crucifixion, from church in Kocelovce, horiz.

**Perf. 11½x11¾, 11¾x11½**
1.75 .85
**2000, Oct. 17**
366-367 A126 Set of 2

**Stamp Day — A197**

Illustration reduced.

**Photo. & Engr.**
**Perf. 11¾x11½**
.50 .20
6.00
**2000, Dec. 18**
368 A197 5.50k multi + label
Booklet, 9 #368
POFIS, 50th Anniv.

**History of Postal Law A198**

**Engr.**
**Perf. 11¾**
2.50 1.50
**2000, Dec. 18**
369 A198 20k multi
Issued in sheets of 4.

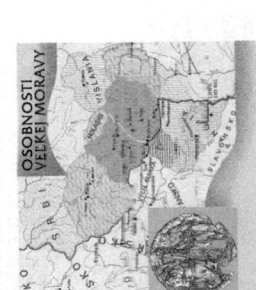

**Mantel Clock, c. 1780 — A199**

**Photo. & Engr.**
**Perf. 11¾x11½**
.55 .30
**2001, Jan. 1**
370 A199 13k multi

**Janko Blaho (1901-81), Singer — A200**

.25 .20
**2001, Jan. 15**
371 A200 5.50k multi

**2001 European Figure Skating Championships, Bratislava — A201**

.70 .35
**2001, Jan. 16**
372 A201 16k multi

**Agricultural Control Institute, 50th Anniv. — A202**

**Perf. 11¾x11¼**
.50 .25
**2001, Feb. 22**
373 A202 12k multi

---

**2000 Summer Olympics, Sydney — A191**

**Photo. & Engr.**
**Perf. 11¾x11¾**
1.50 1.00
**2000, June 27**
359 A191 18k multi + label

**Organization for Security and Cooperation in Europe, 25th Anniv. — A192**

**Perf. 11½x11¼**
.20 .20
**2000, Aug. 18**
361 A192 4k black & blue

**Wooden Bridge, Klukava A193**

**Perf. 11¾**
.50 .20
**2000, Sept. 14**
362 A193 6k multi

Souvenir Sheet

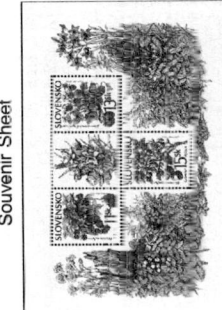

**Berries — A194**

No. 363: a, 11k, Rubus idaeus. b, 13k, Fragaria vesca. c, 15k, Vaccinium myrtillus.

**Litho. & Engr.**
**Perf. 11¾**
1.60 .80
**2000, Sept. 14**
363 A194 Sheet of 3, #a-c

**Holy Year 2000 — A195**

**Photo. & Engr.**
**Perf. 11½x11½**
.20 .20
2.00
**2000, Oct. 5**
364 A195 4k multi
Booklet, 10 #364

**Postal Agreement with Sovereign Military Order of Malta — A196**

**Perf. 11¼x11¾**
.45 .20
**2000, Oct. 13**
365 A196 10k multi

**Litho. & Engr.**

**2001, Sept. 18** *Perf. 11¾*
**385** A211 18k multi .80 .40

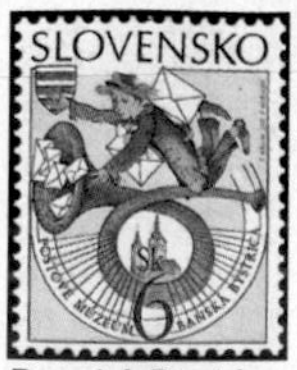


Banská Bystrica Postal Museum A212

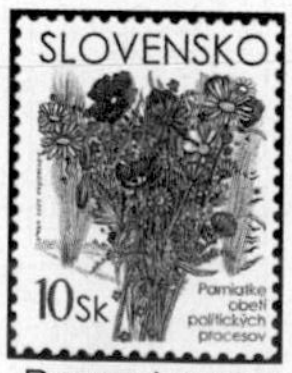


Remembrance of Political Trial Victims A213

**Photo. & Engr.**

**2001, Oct. 9** *Perf. 11¼x11½*
**386** A212 6k multi .25 .20

**2001, Oct. 9**
**387** A213 10k multi .45 .20

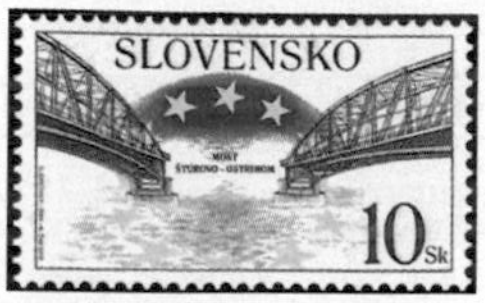


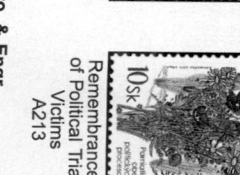

Maria Valeria Bridge Reconstruction — A214

**2001, Oct. 11** *Perf. 11¾x11¼*
**388** A214 10k multi .45 .20

See Hungary No. 3776.

**Art Type of 1996**

Designs: 16k, Raftsman's Dream, by Imrich Woiner-Král'. 10k, Light of the Soul, by Albín Brunovsky. 20k, St. Michael the Archangel with Saints, by unknown artist.

**2001, Oct. 15 Engr.** *Perf. 11¾*
**389-391** A126 Set of 3 2.40 1.25

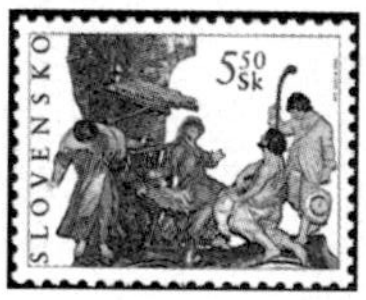


Christmas A215

**Photo. & Engr.**

**2001, Oct. 15** *Perf. 11½x11¼*
**392** A215 5.50k multi .25 .20
Booklet, 10 #392 2.50

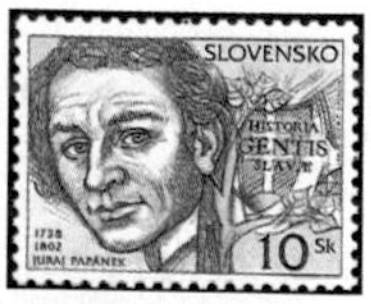


Famous Men — A216

Designs: 10k, Juraj Papánek (1738-1802), historian. 14k, Bjornsterne Bjornson (1832-1910), 1903 Nobel laureate for Literature.

**2002, Jan. 15**
**393-394** A216 Set of 2 1.00 .50

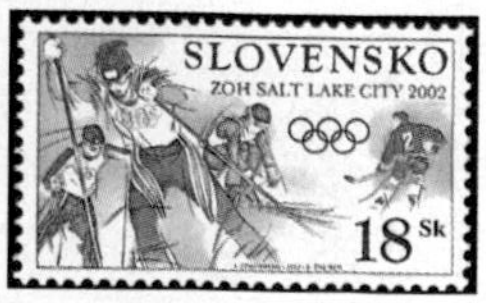


2002 Winter Olympics, Salt Lake City A217

**2002, Jan. 25** *Perf. 11¾x11¼*
**395** A217 18k multi .80 .40

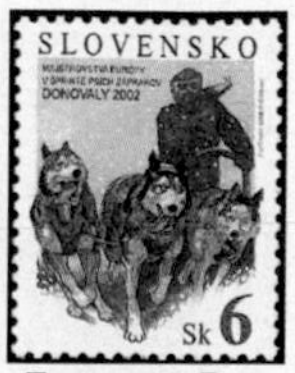


European Dog Sled Championships A218

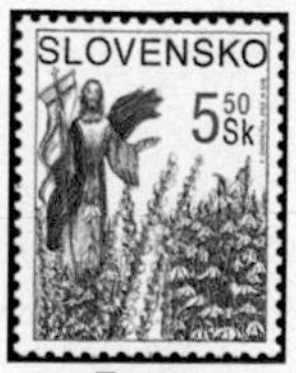


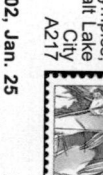

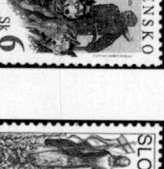

Easter A219

**2002, Feb. 8** *Perf. 11¼x11½*
**396** A218 6k multi .50 .20

**2002, Feb. 15**
**397** A219 5.50k multi .25 .20
Booklet, 10 #397 2.50

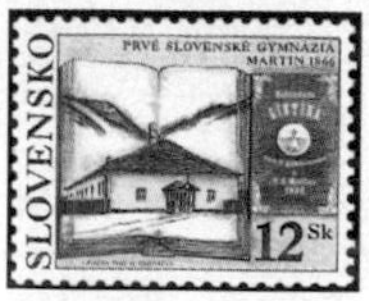


First Slovakian High Schools — A220

Designs: 12k, Martin, 1866. 13k, Revuca, 1862. 15k, Klástor pod Znievom, 1869.

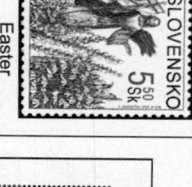

**2002, Mar. 20** *Perf. 11½x11¼*
**398-400** A220 Set of 3 1.75 .90

**Castles and Churches Type of 1995**

***Perf. 11¾x11¼, 11¼x11¾***

**2002 Photo. & Engr.**
**401** A100 10k Kezmarok .45 .20
**402** A100 16k Levoca, horiz. .70 .35

Issued: 10k, 5/6; 16k, 4/18.

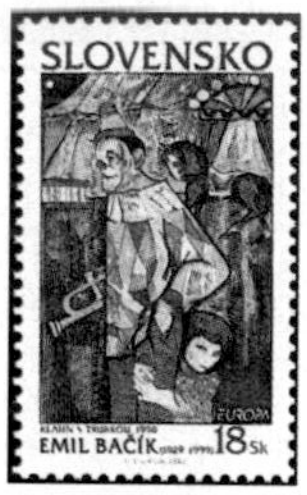


Europa — A221

**2002, May 6 Engr.** *Perf. 11¾*
**403** A221 18k multi .80 .40

Issued in sheets of 8.

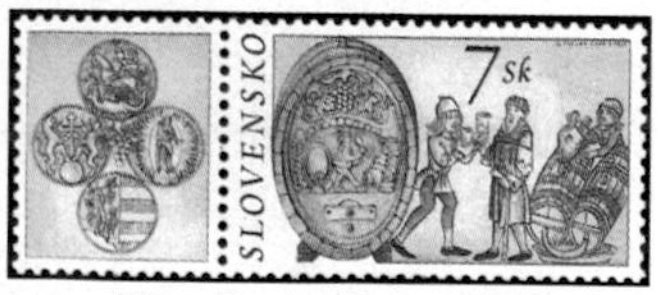


Wine Production — A222

Designs: 7k, Barrels. 9k, Wine press. Illustration reduced.

**Photo. & Engr.**

**2002, June 24** *Perf. 11¾x11¼*

**Stamps + labels**

**404-405** A222 Set of 2 1.50 .40

Souvenir Sheet

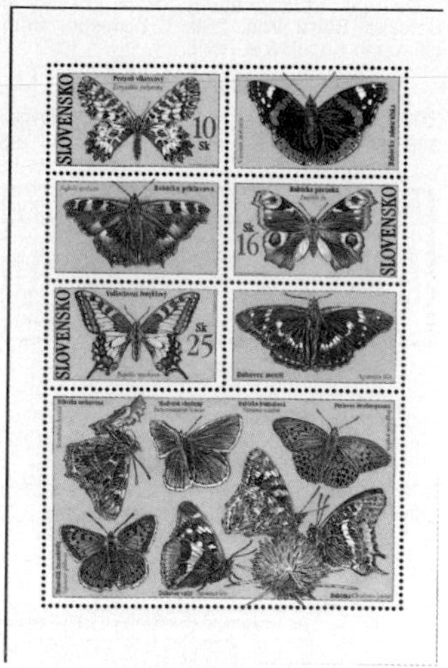


Butterflies — A223

No. 406: a, 10k, Zerynthia polyxena. b, 16k, Inachis io. c, 25k, Papilio machaon.

**Litho. & Engr.**

**2002, June 26** *Perf. 11¾*
**406** A223 Sheet of 3, #a-c, + 4 labels 2.25 1.10

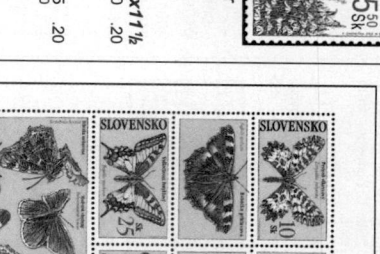

Souvenir Sheet

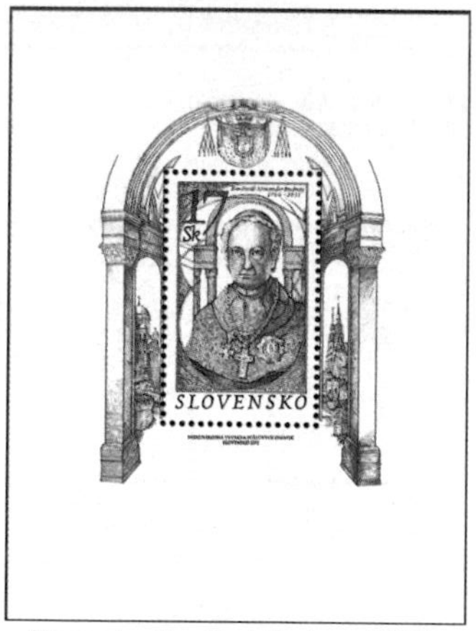


Alexander Cardinal Rudnay (1760-1831) — A224

**2002, July 4 Engr.**
**407** A224 17k multi .75 .35

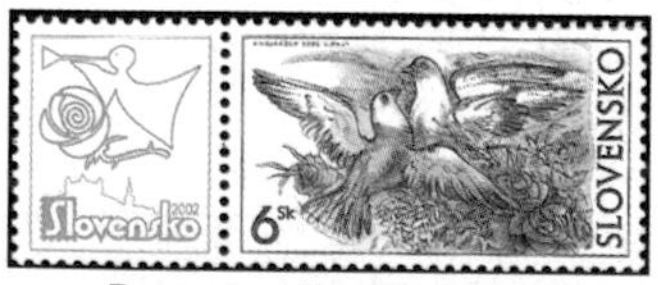


Doves and Roses — A225

Illustration reduced.

**Photo. & Engr.**

**2002, July 4** *Perf. 11¾x11¼*
**408** A225 6k multi + label .30 .20

Issued in sheets of 12 stamps + 12 labels which could be personalized.

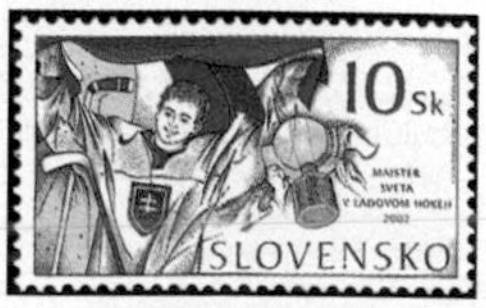


Victory at 2002 World Ice Hockey Championships — A226

**2002, July 4**
**409** A226 10k multi .50 .25

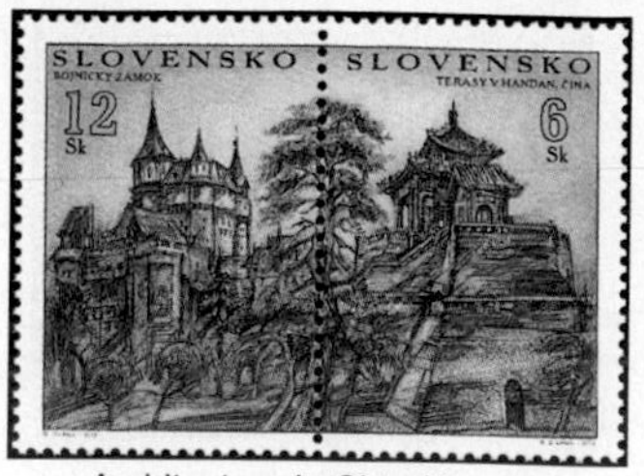


Architecture in Slovakia and China — A227

No. 410: a, 6k, Handan Congtai Pavilion, People's Republic of China. b, 12k, Bojnice Castle, Slovakia.
Illustration reduced.

**2002, Oct. 12** *Perf. 11¾x11½*
**410** A227 Horiz. pair, #a-b .90 .45

Issued in sheets of 4.
See People's Republic of China No. 3239.

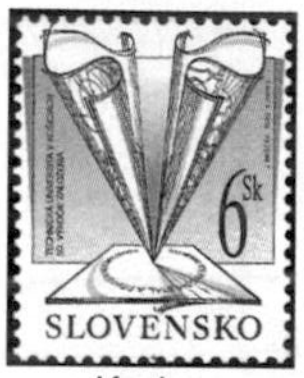


Kosice Technological University, 50th Anniv. A228

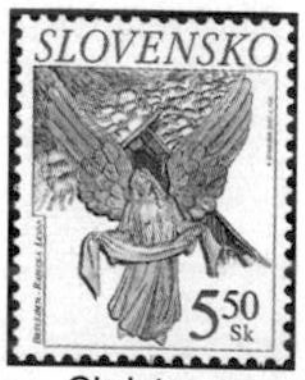


Christmas A229

**Photo. & Engr.**

**2002, Oct. 17** *Perf. 11¼x11½*
**411** A228 6k multi .30 .20

**2002, Nov. 8**
**412** A229 5.50k multi .30 .20
Complete booklet, 10 #412 3.00

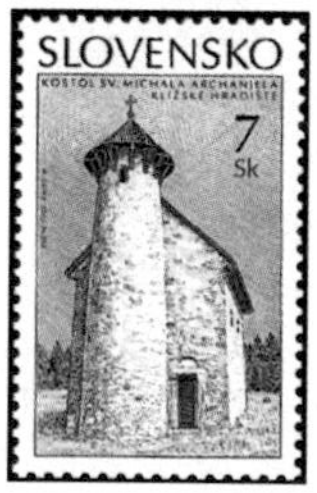


Churches — A230

Designs: 7k, St. Michael's Church, Klizske Hradiste. 14k, St. George's Rotunda, Skalica. 22k, St. Martin's Cathedral, Spisska Kapitula.

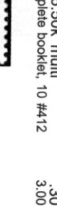

**2002, Nov. 15 Engr.** *Perf. 11¾x11½*
**413-415** A230 Set of 3 2.25 1.10

Issued in sheets of 10.

Miniature Sheet

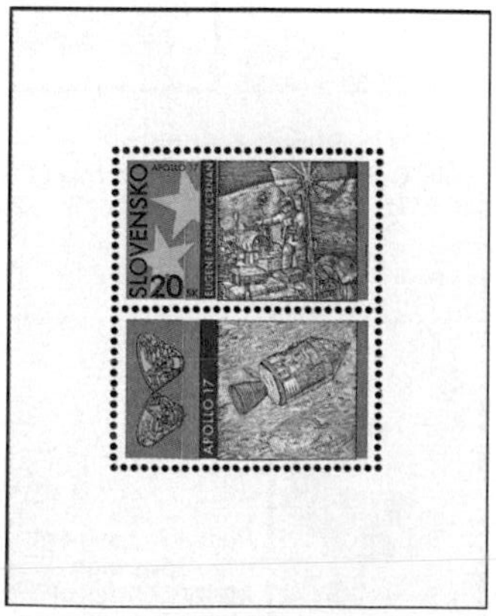


Astronaut Eugene Cernan and Lunar Rover — A231

**Photo. & Engr.**

**2002, Dec. 6** *Perf. 11¾x11¼*
**416** A231 20k multi + label 1.00 .50

Apollo 17 mission, 30th anniv.

**Art Type of 1996**

Designs: 20k, The Beheading of St. John the Baptist, by Master Pavol of Levoca. 23k, In the Studio, by Koloman Sokol.

**2002** **Engr.** *Perf. 11¾*
**417-418** A126 Set of 2 2.25 1.10

Issued: 20k, 12/18; 23k, 12/12.

Stamp Day — A232

Illustration reduced.

**Photo. & Engr.**

**2002, Dec. 18** *Perf. 11¾x11¼*
**419** A232 10k multi + 2 labels .50 .25

Nitrafila Stamp Exhibition, Nitra.

Independent Slovakia, 10th Anniv. — A233

*Perf. 11¾x11½*

**2003, Jan. 1** **Litho. & Engr.**
**420** A233 20k multi 1.00 .50

**Pres. Schuster Type of 2000**

**2003, Feb. 5** **Engr.** *Perf. 11¾x11¼*
**421** A190 7k blue .40 .20

Roses — A234

**Photo. & Engr.**

**2003, Feb. 14** *Perf. 11½x11¼*
**422** A234 7k multi .40 .20
**a.** Sheet of 8 + 8 labels 12.00 6.00

No. 422a issued 4/30. Labels on No. 422a could be personalized.

Easter — A235

**2003, Mar. 10** *Perf. 11¼x11½*
**423** A235 7k multi .40 .20
Booklet, 10 #423 4.00

**Churches and Castles Type of 1995-2001**

**Photo. & Engr.**

**2003** *Perf. 11¾x11¼*
**424** A100 18k Kremnica .90 .45
**425** A100 100k Pezinok 5.50 2.75

Issued: 18k, 3/20, 100k, 9/18.

Souvenir Sheet

Saints Cyril and Methodius — A236

No. 426: a, 17k, St. Cyril. b, 22k, St. Methodius.

**Litho. & Engr.**

**2003, Apr. 6** *Perf. 11¾*
**426** A236 Sheet of 2, #a-b, + 2 labels 2.10 1.10

Ludwig van Beethoven (1770-1827), Composer A237

**Photo. & Engr.**

**2003, Apr. 24** *Perf. 11½x11¼*
**427** A237 15k multi .85 .40

Milan Stefánik (1880-1919), Czechoslovakian General — A238

**Litho. & Engr.**

**2003, May 3** *Perf. 11¾*
**428** A238 14k multi .80 .40

Issued in sheets of 8.
See France No. 2942.

Europa — A239

**2003, May 9**
**429** A239 14k multi .80 .40

Issued in sheets of 10.

**Art Type of 1996**

Design: The Brook, by Ladislav Mednansky, horiz.

**2003, May 9** **Engr.** *Perf. 11¾*
**430** A126 18k multi 1.00 .50

Issued in sheets of 4.

Sts. Benedict and Andrej Svorad — A240

**Photo. & Engr.**

**2003, May 16** *Perf. 11½x11¼*
**431** A240 13k multi .75 .35

Third Place Finish of Slovakian Ice Hockey Team at World Championships, Finland — A241

**2003, May 30** **Litho.** *Perf. 13½*
**432** A241 20k multi 1.10 .55

Issued in sheets of 4.

Matko and Kubko — A242

**Photo. & Engr.**

**2003, June 1** *Perf. 11¼x11½*
**433** A242 7k multi .40 .20
Complete booklet, 10 #433 4.00

Intl. Children's Day.

Worldwide Fund for Nature (WWF) — A243

Various views of Felis silvestris silvestris: a, 13k. b, 14k. c, 16k. d, 18k.

**Litho. & Engr.**

**2003, June 25** *Perf. 11¾*
**434** A243 Sheet of 4, #a-d 5.00 3.00

World Swimming Championships, Barcelona A244

**Photo. & Engr.**

**2003, July 7** *Perf. 11½x11¼*
**435** A244 11k multi .60 .30

Banska Stiavnica Reservoirs — A245

No. 436: a, 9k, Lake Klinger. b, 12k, Rozgrund Reservoir.
Illustration reduced.

**2003, July 15** **Engr.** *Perf. 11¾*
**436** A245 Pair, #a-b 1.10 .55

Issued in sheets of 4 pairs + 1 label.

Bratislava Biennale of Illustrators — A246

**Photo. & Engr.**

**2003, Aug. 15** *Perf. 11¼x11½*
**437** A246 12k multi .65 .30
Complete booklet, 10 # 437 6.50

Visit of Pope John Paul II — A247

*Die Cut Perf. 14¾x14½*

**2003, Sept. 7** **Litho.**

**Self-Adhesive**

**438** A247 12k violet .65 .35

Issued in sheets of 4.

Father Ján Baltazár Magin (1681-1734), Poet — A248

**Photo. & Engr.**

**2003, Sept. 17** *Perf. 11½x11¼*
**439** A248 8k multi .45 .20

Christmas A249

**2003, Oct. 30**
**440** A249 7k multi .40 .20
Complete booklet, 10 #440 4.00

Bronze Buttons, Sword Hilt and Cross A250

**2003, Nov. 17** *Perf. 11¾x11¼*
**441** A250 18k multi 1.10 .55

"Travel of History" exhibit of archaeological treasures.

Powered Flight, Cent. — A251

**2003, Nov. 17** *Perf. 11½x11¼*
**442** A251 18k multi 1.10 .55

**Art Type of 1996**

Designs: 14k, St. Catherine, by Simon Vouet. 16k, Bagpipes, by Rudolf Krivos, horiz. 21k, The Annunciation, by Master Jan.

**2003, Nov. 28** **Engr.** *Perf. 11¾*
**443-445** A126 Set of 3 3.00 1.50

Marginal Design from Czechoslovakia No. 2517 Sheet, by Josef Baláz — A252

**Photo. & Engr.**

**2003, Nov. 28** *Perf. 11¾x11¼*
**446** A252 12k multi + label .70 .35

Stamp Day.

## Castles and Churches Type of 1995-2001

**2004, Jan. 30   Litho.   Perf. 14¼x14**
447  A100  9k Liptovský Mikuláš, horiz.   .55   .25

St. Valentine's Day — A253

**2004, Jan. 30   Litho. & Embossed**
448  A253  8k multi   .50   .25

Lilium Royal Parade — A254

**2004, Feb. 12**   **Perf. 11¾**
449  A254  8k multi   .50   .25

Tulip Kaufmanniana — A255

Illustration reduced.

**2004, Feb. 12**   **Perf. 14¼x14½ Syncopated**   **Litho.**
450  A255  9k multi + label   .55   .25
a.   Booklet pane of 10   5.50

Printed in sheets of 8 + 8 labels which could be personalized.

Easter Egg — A256

**2004, Mar. 10   Die Cut Perf. 14½**
**Self-Adhesive**
451  A256  8k multi   .50   .25

Wedding Clothing From Pata — A257

**2004, Apr. 16**   **Perf. 13¾**
452-453  A257  Set of 2   2.60   1.25

Designs: 15k, Groom. 26k, Bride.

Europa — A258

**2004, Apr. 23**   **Perf. 14x14½ Syncopated**
454  A258  20k multi   1.25   .60

**2004, May 1**   **Perf. 13½**
455  A259  18k multi   1.10   .55

Admission Into European Union A259

Admission Into NATO — A260

**2004, May 1**
456  A260  60k multi   3.50   1.75

Grandfather, From Evening Tales Television Program — A261

**2004, May 21**   **Perf. 14**
457  A261  8k multi   .50   .25

Granite Paper

2004 Paralympics, Athens — A262

**2004, May 31**   **Perf. 13¼x13½**
458  A262  34k multi   2.10   1.10

Granite Paper

Pres. Ivan Gasparovic — A263

**2004, June 15**   **Perf. 13**
459  A263  8k multi   .50   .25

Granite Paper

Dobroc Forest A264

**2004, June 17**   **Perf. 14**
460  A264  12k multi   .75   .35

Granite Paper

Tatra Omnibus, 1904-06 A265

**2004, June 30**   **Perf. 13¼x13½**
461  A265  14k multi   .90   .45

Granite Paper

**2004, June 30**   **Granite Paper**
462  A266  24k multi   1.50   .75

Spania Valley Mining Water System A266

**2004, Sept. 3**   **Perf. 13¼x13**
463  A267  21k multi   1.40   .70

Dunajec River Raftsmen — A267

See Poland No. 3752.

Roman Legions in Trencín — A268

**2004, Oct. 15**   **Perf. 13**
464  A268  2Rk multi   1.00   .80

## Art Type of 1996

Designs: 33k, Cock Fight, by Jakub Bogdan, horiz. 35k, Don Quixote, by Július Jakoby.

**2004, Oct. 20**   **Litho. & Engr.**
465-466  A126  Set of 2   4.50   2.25   **Perf. 11¾**

Christmas A269

**2004, Nov. 5**   **Litho.**   **Perf. 13**
467  A269  8k multi   .55   .25
Complete booklet, 10 #467   5.50

Medalists at 2004 Summer Olympics — A270

**2004, Nov. 5**   **Self-Adhesive**   **Litho.**
468   Serpentine Die Cut 12½
  a.-b.   A270  8k Either single   5.50   .25
  c.-d.   A270  14k Either single   .95   .45
  e.-f.   A270  20k Either single   1.25   .65

No. 468: a, Jozef Gonci, air rifle bronze medalist. b, Kayak 1000-meter fours team, bronze medalists. c, Jozef Krnac, 66-kilogram judo silver medalist. d, Michal Martikán, men's canoe slalom silver medalist. e, Elena Kaliská, women's canoe slalom gold medalist. f, Pavol and Peter Hochschorner, canoe slalom doubles gold medalists.

Stamp Day — A271

**2004, Dec. 18**   **Perf. 13**
469  A271  9k multi   .65   .30

St. Valentine's Day — A272

**2005, Jan. 31**   **Litho.**   **Perf. 13½**
470  A272  9k multi   .65   .30

Family — A273

**2005, Feb. 14**   **Perf. 13½x13**
471  A273  9k multi   .65   .30

Banska Bystrica, 760th Anniv. A274

**2005, Feb. 14**   **Perf. 13½**
472  A274  16k multi   1.25   .60

Summit Meeting of Presidents George W. Bush and Vladimir Putin A275

**2005, Feb. 24**   **Perf. 13**
473  A275  25k multi   1.75   .90

Easter — A276

**2005, Mar. 10**   **Litho.**   **Perf. 13½**
474  A276  9k multi   .65   .30
Complete booklet, 10 #474   6.50

# SLOVAKIA

Mother and Child — SP3

Soldier and Hlinka Youth — SP4

**1941, Dec. 10**
| | | | | |
|---|---|---|---|---|
| B5 | SP3 | 50h + 50h dull green | .95 | .85 |
| B6 | SP3 | 1k + 1k brown | .95 | .85 |
| B7 | SP3 | 2k + 1k violet | 2.85 | 2.55 |

*Nos. B5-B7 (3)*

Surtax for the benefit of child welfare.

**1942, Mar. 14**
| | | | | |
|---|---|---|---|---|
| B8 | SP4 | 70h + 1k brown org | .35 | .25 |
| B9 | SP4 | 1.30k + 1k brt blue | .35 | .25 |
| B10 | SP4 | 2k + 1k rose red | 1.10 | 1.00 |
| | | | 1.80 | 1.50 |

*Nos. B8-B10 (3)*

The surtax aided the Hlinka Youth Society "Hlinkova Mládez."

70h+1Ks SP6

80h+2Ks National Costumes — SP7

50+50h SP5

**Perf. 14**

**1943**
| | | | | |
|---|---|---|---|---|
| B11 | SP5 | 50h + 50h dk slato grn | .25 | .20 |
| B12 | SP6 | 70h + 1k dp carmine | .25 | .20 |
| B13 | SP7 | 80h + 2k dark blue | .35 | .35 |
| | | | .85 | .75 |

*Nos. B11-B13 (3)*

The surtax was for the benefit of children, the Red Cross and winter relief of the Slovakian popular party.

Infantrymen — SP8

70h+2Ks Aviator — SP9

Tank and Gun Crew SP10

---

Stamp Day — A290

**Perf. 13½x13½** .95 .45

Illustration reduced.

**2005, Nov. 25**
491 A290 15k multi + label

Karol Kuzmány (1806-66), Writer — A291

**Perf. 13½** 1.00 .50

**2006, Feb. 3**
492 A291 16k multi

2006 Winter Olympics, Turin — A292

**Perf. 13½x13½** 1.40 .70

Illustration reduced.

**2006, Feb. 3**
493 A292 21k multi + label

Poprad and Town Arms — A293

**Perf. 13¼** 1.50 .75

**2006, Feb. 3**
494 A293 23k multi

## SEMI-POSTAL STAMPS

**Catalogue values for unused stamps in this section are for Never Hinged items.**

Josef Tiso — SP1

**Perf. 12½  Wmk. 263  Photo.**

**1939, Nov. 6**
B1 SP1 2.50k + 2.50k royal blue 3.25 3.50

The surtax was used for Child Welfare.

Medical Corpsman and Wounded Soldier — SP2

**1941, Nov. 10**
| | | | | |
|---|---|---|---|---|
| B2 | SP2 | 50h + 50h dull green | .45 | .45 |
| B3 | SP2 | 1k + 1k rose lake | .45 | .45 |
| B4 | SP2 | 2k + 1k brt blue | 1.60 | 1.25 |
| | | | 2.50 | 2.15 |

*Nos. B2-B4 (3)*

---

Intl. Year of Physics A282

**Perf. 13½** 1.25 .60

**2005, May 16  Litho.**
480 A282 18k multi

Fish — A283

**Perf. 13¼** .60 .30

**2005, May 23  Litho.**
481 A283 9k multi  6.00
Complete booklet, 10 #481

Biennale of Children's Book Illustrations, Bratislava — A284

1.90 .95

**2005, May 23**
482 A284 30k multi

Pres. Ivan Gasparovic A286

**Perf. 13¾x13** 1.40 .70

**2005, June 3  Litho.**
483 A285 22k multi

Holic and Town Arms A285

**Perf. 11¾x11¼  Litho. & Engr.** .60 .30

**2005, June 15**
484 A286 9k brn & buff

Locomotives — A288

Designs: 24k, Ciernohronska Railroad. 33k, Vychylovka.

**2005, Sept. 22  Litho. & Engr.  Perf. 11¾**
486-487 A288 Set of 2 3.75 1.90

**Art Type of 1996**

Designs: 28k, Supper at Emmaus, by Rembrandt. 35k, Magic of Still Life Paintings V. by Karol Baron, horiz.

**2005, Oct. 20  Engr.**
488-489 A126 Set of 2 4.00 2.00

Christmas — A289

**Perf. 13¼** .55 .30

**2005, Nov. 16  Litho.**
490 A289 9k multi  5.50
Complete booklet, 10 #490

---

## Souvenir Sheet

Beatification of Sister Zdenka Schelingová — A277

**Perf. 13x13¼** 2.50 1.25

**2005, Mar. 10**
475 A277 34k multi

Cycling for the Handicapped A278

**Perf. 13½** 1.50 .75

**2005, Mar. 30**
476 A278 22k multi

Poor Mother, by Frantisek Studeny — A279

**Perf. 11¾x11½  Litho. & Engr.** 1.75 .85

**2005, Mar. 30**
477 A279 25k blk & lt grn

An unstated portion of the receipts were donated to UNICEF for relief works for the Dec. 26, 2004 tsunami.

Europa A280

**Perf. 13¾** 1.25 .60

**2005, Apr. 22  Litho.**
478 A280 19k multi

Peace of Bratislava (Pressburg), Bicent. — A281

**Perf. 13½** 1.50 .75

**2005, Apr. 29**
479 A281 23k multi

## 1943, July 28
| | | | |
|---|---|---|---|
| B14 | SP8 | 70h + 2k rose brown | .75 .90 |
| B15 | SP9 | 1.30k + 2k sapphire | .75 .90 |
| B16 | SP10 | 2k + 2k olive green | .90 |
| | | Nos. B14-B16 (3) | 2.25 2.70 |

The surtax was for soldiers' welfare.

"The Slovak Language Is Our Life" — L'. Stur — SP11

Slovakian National Museum SP12

Slovakian Foundation SP13

## 1943, Oct. 16
| | | | |
|---|---|---|---|
| B17 | SP11 | 30h + 1k brown red | .45 .35 |
| B18 | SP12 | 70h + 1k slate green | .60 .55 |
| B19 | SP13 | 80h + 2k slate blue | .45 .35 |
| B20 | SP14 | 1.30k + 2k dull brown | .50 .35 |
| | | Nos. B17-B20 (4) | 2.00 1.60 |

The surtax was for the benefit of Slovakian cultural institutions.

Peasant — SP14

Skier — SP16

Soccer Player — SP15

Diver — SP17

Relay Race — SP18

## 1944, Apr. 30
| | | | |
|---|---|---|---|
| B21 | SP15 | 70h + 70k slate grn | .75 .75 |
| B22 | SP16 | 1k + 1k violet | .75 .75 |
| B23 | SP17 | 1.30k + 1.30k rose blue | .75 .75 |
| B24 | SP18 | 2k + 2k chnt brn | 3.00 3.00 |
| | | Nos. B21-B24 (4) | |

Children — SP20

## 1944, Oct. 6 — Wmk. 263
| | | | |
|---|---|---|---|
| B25 | SP19 | 70h + 4h sapphire | .75 .75 |
| B26 | SP19 | 1.30k + 4k red brown | .75 .75 |

The surtax was to aid social work for Slovak youth.

## 1944, Dec. 18
| | | | |
|---|---|---|---|
| B27 | SP20 | 2k + 4k light blue | 3.00 4.00 |
| a. | | Sheet of 8 + Label | 50.00 70.00 |

The surtax was for the benefit of social institutions.

Red Cross — SP21

## 1993, Nov. 15 — Photo. & Engr.
| | | | |
|---|---|---|---|
| B28 | SP21 | 3k +1k red & gray | .30 .30 |

Perf. 11x11½

## 1996, May 15 — Photo. & Engr. — Perf. 12x11½
| | | | |
|---|---|---|---|
| B29 | SP22 | 12k +2k multi | .80 .80 |

Surcharge for Slovak Olympic Committee.

1996 Summer Olympics, Atlanta — SP22

Souvenir Sheet

---

## AIR POST STAMPS

Catalogue values for unused stamps in this section are for Never Hinged items.

Planes over Tatra Mountains AP1, AP2

### 1939, Nov. 20 — Photo. — Perf. 12½
**Unwmk.**
| | | | |
|---|---|---|---|
| C1 | AP1 | 30h dark violet | .35 .35 |
| C2 | AP1 | 50h dark green | .35 .35 |
| C3 | AP1 | 1k vermilion | .55 .55 |
| C4 | AP2 | 2k grnsh black | .55 .55 |
| C5 | AP2 | 3k dark brown | .80 .80 |
| C6 | AP2 | 4k slate blue | 4.00 4.00 |
| | | Nos. C1-C6 (6) | |

Plane in Flight — AP3

### 1940, Nov. 30 — Wmk. 263 — Perf. 12½
| | | | |
|---|---|---|---|
| C7 | AP3 | 5k dk violet brn | 1.40 1.40 |
| C8 | AP3 | 10k gray black | 1.60 1.60 |
| C9 | AP3 | 20k myrtle green | 2.00 2.00 |
| | | Nos. C7-C9 (3) | 5.00 5.00 |

### 1944, Sept. 15 — Wmk. 263
| | | | |
|---|---|---|---|
| C10 | AP1 | 1k vermilion | 1.00 1.00 |

Type of 1939
See No. C10.

---

## PERSONAL DELIVERY STAMPS

Catalogue values for unused stamps in this section are for Never Hinged items.

### 1940 — Wmk. 263 — Photo. — Imperf.
| | | | |
|---|---|---|---|
| EX1 | PD1 | 50h indigo & blue | .90 1.60 |
| EX2 | PD1 | 50h carmine & rose | .90 1.60 |

PD1

---

## POSTAGE DUE STAMPS

Catalogue values for unused stamps in this section are for Never Hinged items.

D1

Letter, Post Horn — D2

### 1939 — Unwmk. — Photo. — Perf. 12½
| | | | Unwmk. | Wmk. 263 |
|---|---|---|---|---|
| J1 | D1 | 5h bright blue | 1.00 | .55 |
| J2 | D1 | 10h bright blue | .55 | .30 |
| J3 | D1 | 20h bright blue | .50 | .30 |
| J4 | D1 | 30h bright blue | 3.00 | .50 |
| J5 | D1 | 40h bright blue | 1.00 | .75 |
| J6 | D1 | 50h bright blue | .70 | .75 |
| J7 | D1 | 60h bright blue | 2.00 | .80 |
| J8 | D1 | 1k dark carmine | 2.50 | .80 |
| J9 | D1 | 2k dark carmine | 14.00 | 8.25 |
| J10 | D1 | 5k dark carmine | 14.00 | 14.00 |
| J11 | D1 | 10k dark carmine | 8.00 | 14.00 |
| J12 | D1 | 20k dark carmine | 18.00 | 2.50 |
| | | Nos. J1-J12 (12) | 119.20 | 35.00 |

### 1940-41
| | | | |
|---|---|---|---|
| J13 | D1 | 5h bright blue | |
| J14 | D1 | 10h bright blue ('41) | |
| J15 | D1 | 20h bright blue ('41) | |
| J16 | D1 | 30h bright blue ('41) | |
| J17 | D1 | 40h bright blue ('41) | |
| J18 | D1 | 50h bright blue ('41) | |

### 1942 — Perf. 14
**Unwmk. — Imperf.**
| | | | |
|---|---|---|---|
| J19 | D1 | 60h bright blue | .90 .95 |
| J20 | D1 | 1k dark carmine | .90 1.10 |
| J21 | D1 | 2k dark carmine | 20.00 9.00 |
| J22 | D1 | 2k dark carmine ('41) | 4.00 2.75 |
| J23 | D1 | 10k dark carmine ('41) | 3.00 3.25 |
| | | Nos. J13-J23 (11) | 35.70 21.70 |

| | | | Perf. 14 | Imperf. |
|---|---|---|---|---|
| J24 | D2 | 10h deep brown | .20 | .20 |
| J25 | D2 | 20h deep brown | .40 | .40 |
| J26 | D2 | 40h deep brown | .30 | .30 |
| J27 | D2 | 60h deep brown | .30 | .40 |
| J28 | D2 | 80h deep brown | .60 | .20 |
| J29 | D2 | 1k deep brown | .30 | .30 |
| J30 | D2 | 1.10k rose red | .30 | .30 |
| J31 | D2 | 1.30k rose red | .60 | .70 |
| J32 | D2 | 1.60k rose red | .70 | .20 |
| J33 | D2 | 2k rose red | .50 | .20 |
| J34 | D2 | 2.60k rose red | 1.25 | 1.00 |
| J35 | D2 | 3k rose red | 7.75 | 6.50 |
| J36 | D2 | 3.50k rose red | 2.25 | 2.75 |
| J37 | D2 | 5k rose red | 3.25 | 20.00 |
| J38 | D2 | 10k rose red | 20.00 | 15.50 |
| | | Nos. J24-J38 (15) | | |

---

## NEWSPAPER STAMPS

Newspaper Stamps of Czechoslovakia, 1937, Overprinted in Red or Blue

### 1939, Apr. — Unwmk. — Imperf.
| | | | |
|---|---|---|---|
| P1 | N2 | 2h bister brn (Bl) | .30 .40 |
| P2 | N2 | 5h dull blue (R) | .30 .40 |
| P3 | N2 | 7h red org (Bl) | .30 .40 |
| P4 | N2 | 9h emerald (R) | .30 .40 |
| P5 | N2 | 10h deep brown | .30 .30 |
| P6 | N2 | 12h ultra (R) | .30 .40 |
| P7 | N2 | 15h henna brn (R) | .30 .40 |
| P8 | N2 | 20h dk brown (Bl) | .65 .85 |
| P9 | N2 | 1k dark brown (R) | 2.00 2.50 |
| | | Nos. P1-P9 (9) | 14.40 17.75 |

Excellent counterfeits exist of Nos. P1-P9.

Arms of Slovakia N1

Type Block "N" (for "Noviny" — Newspaper) N2

### 1939 — Photo.
**Unwmk. — Typo.**
| | | | |
|---|---|---|---|
| P10 | N1 | 2h ocher | .20 .20 |
| P11 | N1 | 5h ultra | .25 .40 |
| P12 | N1 | 7h red orange | .20 .20 |
| P13 | N1 | 9h emerald | .20 .30 |
| P14 | N1 | 10h henna brown | .95 1.10 |
| P15 | N1 | 12h dk ultra | .60 .35 |
| P16 | N1 | 15h grnsh gray | .95 1.10 |
| P17 | N1 | 20h dark green | 1.10 1.10 |
| P18 | N1 | 50h grnsh gray | 5.15 6.10 |
| | | Nos. P10-P18 (9) | |

### 1940-41
| | | | |
|---|---|---|---|
| P20 | N1 | 2h ocher | .20 .20 |
| P23 | N1 | 5h ultra | .20 .20 |
| P24 | N1 | 7h brt purple ('41) | .20 .20 |
| P25 | N1 | 10h brt brown ('41) | .20 .30 |
| P26 | N1 | 15h dark green ('41) | .20 .35 |
| P28 | N1 | 20h emerald | .35 .35 |
| P29 | N1 | 40h It blue ('41) | .95 1.10 |
| P30 | N1 | 50h chocolate | .60 .55 |
| | | 2k emerald ('41) | 1.25 1.40 |
| | | Nos. P20-P30 (9) | 4.10 4.15 |

### 1943 — Photo.
**Unwmk.**
| | | | |
|---|---|---|---|
| P31 | N2 | 10h green | .20 .20 |
| P32 | N2 | 20h green | .20 .30 |
| P33 | N2 | 50h ultra | .30 .30 |
| P34 | N2 | 1k slate green | .40 .60 |
| P35 | N2 | 2k intense blue | .60 .60 |
| P36 | N2 | | 2.00 2.00 |
| | | Nos. P31-P36 (6) | |

Catalogue values for unused stamps in this section, from this point to the end of the section, are for Never Hinged items.

# SLOVENIA

slō-vē-nē-ə

LOCATION — Southeastern Europe
GOVT. — Independent state
AREA — 7,819 sq. mi.
POP. — 1,970,570 (1999 est.)
CAPITAL — Ljubljana

A constituent republic of Yugoslavia since 1945, Slovenia declared its independence on June 25, 1991.

100 Paras = 1 Dinar
100 Stotin = 1 Tolar

**Catalogue values for unused stamps in this country are for Never Hinged items, beginning with Scott 100 in the regular postage section and Scott RA1 in the postal tax section.**

Declaration of Independence
A18

**1991, June 26    Litho.    Perf. 10½**
100  A18  5d Parliament building   .60  .60

National Arms
A19      A20      **Perf. 14**

**1991-92**
**Background Color**

| | | | | | |
|---|---|---|---|---|---|
| 101 | A19 | 1t | brown | .20 | .20 |
| 102 | A20 | 1t | brown | .20 | .20 |
| 103 | A20 | 2t | lilac rose | .20 | .20 |
| 104 | A19 | 4t | green | .20 | .20 |
| 105 | A20 | 4t | green | .20 | .20 |
| 106 | A19 | 5t | salmon | .20 | .20 |
| 107 | A20 | 5t | salmon | .20 | .25 |
| 108 | A20 | 6t | yellow | .25 | .25 |
| 109 | A19 | 11t | orange | .40 | .35 |
| 110 | A19 | 11t | orange | .25 | .25 |
| 111 | A20 | 11t | orange | .30 | .25 |
| 112 | A20 | 15t | blue | .55 | .55 |
| 113 | A20 | 20t | purple | .75 | .75 |
| 114 | A20 | 50t | dark green | 1.25 | 1.25 |
| | | 100t | gray | 5.15 | 5.00 |

Nos. 101-114 (14)

Issued: #107, 3/6/91; #101, 104, 106, 109, 12/26/91; #102, 6t, 20t, 50t, 100t, 2/12/92; 2t, 15t, #105, 110, 3/16/92.

1992 Winter Olympics, Albertville — A21

**1992, Feb. 8**
134 A21 Pair, #a.-b., + 1 or 2 labels   3.50 3.50
a, 30t, Ski jumper. b, 50t, Alpine skier.
Rhomboid stamps issued in sheets of 3 #134 plus 4 labels. See No. 143.

Ljubljana Opera House, Cent. A22

**1992, Mar. 31**
135 A22 20t multicolored   .60 .60

Giuseppe Tartini (1692-1770), Italian Violinist and Composer A23

**1992, Apr. 8**
136 A23 27t multicolored   .65 .65

Discovery of America, 500th Anniv. A24

Designs: a, 27t, Map of northwestern Mexico and Gulf of California, Marko Anton Kappus preaching to natives. b, 47t, Map of parts of North and South America, sailing ship.

**1992, Apr. 21**
137 A24 Pair, #a.-b.   4.25 4.25
Issued in sheets containing 6 No. 137.

Intl. Conference of Interior Designers, Ljubljana — A25

**1992, May 17**
138 A25 41t multicolored   .65 .65

A. M. Slomsek (1800-1862), Bishop of Maribor — A26

**1992, May 29**
139 A26 6t multicolored   .25 .25

Mountain Rescue Service, 80th Anniv. — A27

**1992, June 12**
140 A27 41t multicolored   .65 .65

A28

A29

**1992, June 20**
141 A28 6t multicolored   .25 .25
Ljubljana Boatmen's Competition, 900th anniv.

**1992, June 25**
142 A29 41t multicolored   .65 .65
Independence, 1st anniv.

**Olympic Type of 1992**
a, 40t, Leon Stukelj, triple medalist in 1924, 1928. b, 46t, Olympic rings, three heads of Apollo.

**1992, July 25**
143 A21 Pair, #a.-b. +1 or 2 labels   1.75 1.75
1992 Summer Olympics, Barcelona. Rhomboid stamps issued in sheets of 3 #143 plus 4 labels.

World Championship of Registered Dogs, Ljubljana — A30

**1992, Sept. 4**
144 A30 40t Slovenian sheep dug   .70 .65

Marij Kogoj (1892-1956), Composer A31

Self-Portrait, by Matevz Langus (1792-1855), Painter — A32

**1992, Sept. 30**
145 A31 40t multicolored   .70 .65

**1992, Oct. 30**
146 A32 40t multicolored   .70 .65

Christmas
A33

Designs: 6t, 7t, Nativity Scene, Ljubljana. 41t, Stained glass window of Madonna and Child, St. Mary's Church, Bovec, vert.

**1992**
147  A33  6t multicolored   .20 .20
147A A33  7t multicolored   .20 .20
148  A33  41t multicolored  .70 .70
Nos. 147-148 (3)   1.10
Issued: 6t, 41t, Nov. 20. 7t, Dec. 15.

Herman Potocnik, Theoretician of Geosynchronous Satellite Orbit, Birth Cent. — A34

**1992, Nov. 27    Litho.    Perf. 14**
149 A34 46t multicolored   .70 .60

Prezihov Voranc (1893-1950), Writer — A35

**1993, Jan. 22    Litho.**
150 A35 7t multicolored   .20

Rihard Jakopic (1869-1943), Painter — A36

**1993, Jan. 22**
151 A36 44t multicolored   .65 .60

Jozef Stefan (1835-93), Physicist A37

**1993, Jan. 22**
152 A37 51t multicolored   .75 .65

A38

Designs: 1t, Early cake. 2t, Pan pipes. 5t, Kozolec. 6t, Early building. 7t, Zither. 8t, Water mill. 9t, Sled. 10t, Lonceni bajs. 11t, Kraski kos. 12t, Statue of boy on horseback. Ribnica. 20t, Cross-section of house. 44t, Stone building. 50t, Wind-powered pump. 100t, Potica.

## 1993-94

| | | | | |
|---|---|---|---|---|
| 153 | A38 | 1t multicolored | .20 | .20 |
| 154 | A38 | 2t multicolored | .20 | .20 |
| 155 | A38 | 5t multicolored | .20 | .20 |
| 156 | A38 | 6t multicolored | .20 | .20 |
| 157 | A38 | 7t multicolored | .20 | .20 |
| 158 | A38 | 8t multicolored | .20 | .20 |
| 159 | A38 | 9t multicolored | .20 | .20 |
| 160 | A38 | 10t multicolored | .20 | .20 |
| 160A | A38 | 11t multicolored | .20 | .20 |
| 160B | A38 | 12t multicolored | .20 | .20 |
| 161 | A38 | 20t multicolored | .30 | .30 |
| 162 | A38 | 30t multicolored | .30 | .30 |
| 163 | A38 | 40t multicolored | .60 | .60 |
| 163 | A38 | 50t multicolored | 1.10 | 1.10 |
| 164 | A38 | 100t multicolored | 4.45 | 4.20 |

Issued: 1t, 6t, 7t, 44t, 2/18/93; 2t, 5t, 10t, 7/8/94; 5/14/93; 8t, 9t, 8/25/93; 11t, 12t, 7/8/94.
Nos. 153-164 (14)
For surcharge see #371.
See #208A-220, 370, 373-379, 616-623.

**Mountain Climbers A39**

**1993, Feb. 27**
| | | | | |
|---|---|---|---|---|
| 165 | A39 | 7t shown | .20 | .20 |
| 166 | A39 | 44t Route map, mountain | .50 | .45 |

Slovenian Alpine Club, centennial (#165). Joza Cop (1893-1975), mountain climber (#166).

**A40**

**1993, Mar. 19**
| | | | | |
|---|---|---|---|---|
| 167 | A40 | 7t multicolored | .20 | .20 |

Slovenian Post Office, 75th anniv.

**A41**

**1993, Apr. 9**    **Litho.**    **Perf. 14**
| | | | | |
|---|---|---|---|---|
| 168 | A41 | 7t multicolored | .20 | .20 |
| 169 | A41 | 44t multicolored | .55 | .55 |

Collegiate Church of Novo Mesto, 500th anniv.

**Contemporary Art—A42**

Europa: 44t, Round Table of Pompeii, by Marij Pregelj (1913-1967), 159t, Little Girl at Play, by Gabrijel Stupica (1913-1990).

**1993, Apr. 29**    **Litho.**
| | | | | |
|---|---|---|---|---|
| 170 | | 44t multicolored | 1.00 | 1.00 |
| 171 | | 159t multicolored | 2.50 | 2.50 |
| a. | A42 | Pair, #170-171 | 3.50 | 3.50 |

---

**Schwagerina Carniolica — A43**

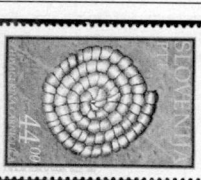

**1993, May 7**
| | | | | |
|---|---|---|---|---|
| 172 | A43 | 44t multicolored | .60 | .60 |

**Admission of Slovenia to UN, 1st Anniv. A44**

**1993, May 21**    **Litho.**    **Perf. 14**
| | | | | |
|---|---|---|---|---|
| 173 | A44 | 62t multicolored | .90 | .90 |

**Mediterranean Youth Games, Agde, France — A45**

**1993, June 8**
| | | | | |
|---|---|---|---|---|
| 174 | A45 | 36t multicolored | .45 | .45 |

**Battle of Sisak, 400th Anniv. A46**

**1993, June 22**    **Litho.**    **Perf. 14**
| | | | | |
|---|---|---|---|---|
| 175 | A46 | 49t multicolored | .60 | .60 |

**Aphaenopidius Kamnikensis — A47**

**1993, July 12**    **Litho.**    **Perf. 14**
| | | | | |
|---|---|---|---|---|
| 176 | A47 | 7t multicolored | .20 | .20 |
| 177 | A47 | 40t multicolored | .40 | .40 |
| 178 | A47 | 44t multicolored | .60 | .60 |
| 179 | A47 | 65t multicolored | .80 | .80 |
| | | Nos. 176-179 (4) | 2.00 | 2.00 |

Designs: 7t, Monolistra spinosissima. 55t, Proteus anguinus. 65t, Zospeum spelaeum.

**A48**

---

**A49**

**1993, July 30**
| | | | | |
|---|---|---|---|---|
| 180 | A48 | 65t multicolored | .75 | .75 |

World dressage competition.

**1993, Oct. 29**    **Litho.**    **Perf. 14**
| | | | | |
|---|---|---|---|---|
| 181 | A49 | 9t multicolored | .20 | .20 |
| 182 | A49 | 65t multicolored | .75 | .75 |

Coats of Arms: 9t, Janez Vajkard Valvasor. 65t, Citizen's Academy of Ljubljana.

**Christmas A50**

**1993, Nov. 15**
| | | | | |
|---|---|---|---|---|
| 183 | A50 | 9t multicolored | .20 | .20 |
| 184 | A50 | 65t multicolored | .75 | .75 |

Designs: 9t, Slovenian Family Viewing Nativity, by Maxim Gaspari (1883-1960), 65t, Archbishop Joze Pogacnik (1902-80), writer.

**Famous People — A51**

**1994, Jan. 14**    **Litho.**    **Perf. 14**
| | | | | |
|---|---|---|---|---|
| 185 | A51 | 8t multicolored | .20 | .20 |
| 186 | A51 | 9t multicolored | .20 | .20 |
| 187 | A51 | 55t multicolored | .60 | .60 |
| 188 | A51 | 65t multicolored | .65 | .65 |
| | | Nos. 185-188 (4) | 1.65 | 1.65 |

Works by: 8t, Josip Jurcic (1844-81), writer. 9t, Simon Gregorcic (1844-1906), poet. 55t, Stanislav Skrabec (1844-1918), linguist. 65t, Jernej Kopitar (1780-1844), linguist.

**Love — A52**

**1994, Jan. 25**
| | | | | |
|---|---|---|---|---|
| 189 | A52 | 9t multicolored | .20 | .20 |

**1994 Winter Olympics, Lillehammer — A53**

**1994, Feb. 4**
| | | | | |
|---|---|---|---|---|
| 190 | A53 | 9t Cross-country skiing | .20 | .20 |
| 191 | A53 | 65t Slalom skiing | .60 | .60 |
| a. | | Pair, #190-191 | .75 | .75 |

---

**J. V. VALVASOR 300 LET — SLOVENIJA #9**

**World Ski Jumping Championships, Planica — A54**

**1994, Mar. 11**    **Litho.**    **Perf. 14**
| | | | | |
|---|---|---|---|---|
| 192 | A54 | 70t multicolored | .75 | .75 |

**City of Ljubljana, 850th Anniv. A55**

**1994, Mar. 25**    **Litho.**    **Perf. 14**
| | | | | |
|---|---|---|---|---|
| 193 | A55 | 9t multicolored | | .20 |

**Europa — A56**

**1994, Apr. 22**
| | | | | |
|---|---|---|---|---|
| 194 | A56 | 70t multicolored | .75 | .75 |
| 195 | A56 | 215t multicolored | 1.90 | 1.90 |
| a. | | Pair, #194-195 | 2.75 | 2.75 |

Designs: 70t, Janez Puhar, camera, 215t, Moon, Jurij Vega.

**Flowers of Slovenia — A57**
**Miniature Sheet**

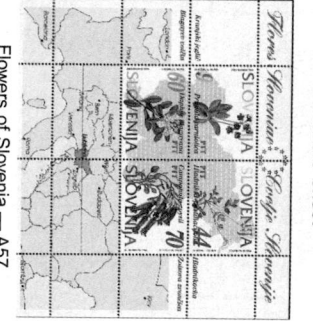

**1994, May 20**    **Litho.**    **Perf. 14**
| | | | | |
|---|---|---|---|---|
| 196 | A57 | Sheet of 4 + 2 labels | 1.75 | 1.75 |

Designs: a, 9t, Primula carniolica. b, 44t, Hladnikia pastinacifolia. c, 60t, Daphne blagayana. d, 70t, Campanula zoysii.

**1994 World Cup Soccer Championships, U.S. — A58**

**1994, June 10**
| | | | | |
|---|---|---|---|---|
| 197 | A58 | 44t multicolored | .45 | .45 |

**Intl. Olympic Committee, Cent. A59**

**1994, June 10**
| | | | | |
|---|---|---|---|---|
| 198 | A59 | 100t multicolored | 1.00 | 1.00 |

## Mt. Ojstrica — A60 / Max Pletersnik, Professors — A61

**Perf. 14**
**1994, July 1 Litho.**
199 A60 12t multicolored .20 .20
**1994, July 22**
200 A61 70t multicolored .60 .60
First Slovenian-German dictionary published by Max Pletersnik (1840-1932), cent.

## Battle of the Frigidus, 1600th Anniv. A62

**Perf. 14** .55 .55
**1994, Sept. 1 Litho.**
201 A62 60t multicolored

## Maribor Post Office, Cent. A63

**Perf. 14** .60 .60
**1994, Sept. 23 Litho.**
202 A63 70t multicolored

## Ljubljana-Novo Mesto Railway, Cent. — A64

**Perf. 14** .60 .60
**1994, Sept. 24 Litho.**
203 A64 70t Locomotive 5722, 1893
See Nos. 233, 243, 291, 325, 363.

## Philharmonic Assoc., Bicent. — A65

Designs: 12t, Building, Ljubljana. 70t, Beethoven, Brahms, Dvorak, Haydn, Paganini.
**1994, Oct. 20**
204 A65 12t multicolored .20 .20
205 A65 70t multicolored .55 .55

## Black Madonna of Loreto, 700th Anniv. — A66

**1994, Nov. 18**
206 A66 70t multicolored .60 .60

## Christmas — A67 / Intl. Year of the Family — A68

**1994, Nov. 18**
207 A67 12t multicolored .20 .20
**1994, Nov. 18**
208 A68 70t multicolored .60 .60

## Type of 1993

13t, Wind rattle, Prlekija. 14t, Sentjernej pottery cock. 15t, Blast furnace, Zelezniki. 16t, Windmill, Stara Gora. 17t, Corn storage building. 55t, Easter eggs, Bela Krajina. 65t, Cobbler's lamp with glass spheres, Trzic. 70t, Snow skis. 75t, 1812 Iron window lattice, Srednja vas, Bohinj. 80t, Palm Sunday bundle. 90t, Boehive. 300t, "Zajec," insect-shaped booIjJack, Dvor. 300t, Siamnali doznjek. 400t, Wine press. 500t, Kumer family's table, Koprivna, Carinthia.

**1994-99 Litho. Size 25x34mm Perf. 14**

| No. | Type | Value | | |
|---|---|---|---|---|
| 208A | A38 | 13t multicolored | .40 | .20 |
| 208B | A38 | 14t multicolored | .20 | .20 |
| 209 | A38 | 15t multicolored | .20 | .20 |
| 210 | A38 | 16t multicolored | .20 | .20 |
| 210A | A38 | 17t multicolored | .20 | .20 |
| 211 | A38 | 55t multicolored | .40 | .40 |
| 212 | A38 | 65t multicolored | .50 | .50 |
| 213 | A38 | 70t multicolored | .60 | .55 |
| 214 | A38 | 75t multicolored | .55 | .55 |
| 215 | A38 | 80t multicolored | .55 | .55 |
| 216 | A38 | 90t multicolored | .60 | .60 |
| 217 | A38 | 300t multicolored | 1.90 | 1.90 |
| 218 | A38 | 300t brown | 4.25 | 4.25 |
| 219 | A38 | 400t brown & lake | 6.25 | 6.25 |
| 220 | A38 | 500t multicolored | 5.75 | 5.75 |
| | | Nos. 208A-220 (15) | 22.55 | 22.35 |

Issued: 300t, 400t, 11/7/94; 70t, 11/16/95; 55t, 90t, 75t, 3/22/96; 80t, 3/20/97; 13t, 14t, 8/8/97; 90t, 5/30/97; 16t, 6/23/98; 200t, 500t, 11/12/98; 16t, 2/5/99; 17t, 5/7/99.

## Ljubljana University, 75th Anniv. — A69

Design: 70t, Provincial palace buildings, founders, I. Hribar, M. Rostohar, D. Majaron.
**Perf. 14** .60 .60
**1994, Dec. 3 Litho.**
221 A69 70t multicolored

## Postal Service Emblem — A70

**1995, Jan. 27**
222 A70 13t multicolored .20 .20

## Love — A71

## Famous People — A72

**1995, Feb. 7**
223 A71 20t multicolored .25 .20

**1995, Feb. 7**
Works by: 20t, Anton Tomaz Linhart (1756-95), playwright, horiz. No. 225, Ivan Vurnik (1884-1971), architect. No. 226, Lili Novy (1885-1958), poet, horiz.
224 A72 20t multicolored .20 .20
225 A72 70t multicolored .55 .55
226 A72 70t multicolored .55 .55
Nos. 224-226 (3) 1.30 1.30

## A73 / A74

**Perf. 14** .20 .20
**1995, Mar. 20 Litho.**
227 A73 13t multicolored
End of World War II, 50th anniv.

**1995, Mar. 29**
228 A74 70t Karavankina schellwieni .60 .60

## Liberation of the Concentration Camps, 50th Anniv. — A75

Europa: 60t, Skeleton of Death lying on bride. 70t, Nike going from dark to light.
**1995, Mar. 29**
229 A75 60t multicolored .60 .60
230 A75 70t multicolored .75 .75
a. Pair, #229-230 2.40
#230a was issued in sheets of 4.

## European Nature Conservation Year — A76

**1995, Mar. 29**
231 A76 70t Triglav Natl. Park .60 .60

## Town of Radovljica, 500th Anniv. A77

**Perf. 14** .40 .40
**1995, June 8 Litho.**
232 A77 44t multicolored

## Railways Type of 1994

Design: 70t, Locomotive KRB 37, Podnart.
**1995, June 8**
233 A64 70t multicolored .60 .60
Ljubljana-Jesenice Line, 125th anniv.

## Aljaz Tower, Cent. — A78

**Perf. 13½** .85 .85
**1995, June 8**
234 A78 100t multicolored
Portions of the design on No. 234 were applied by a thermographic process producing a shiny, raised effect.

## Endangered Birds — A79

Designs: a, 13t, Falco naumanni. b, 60t, Coracias garrulus. c, 70t, Lanius minor. d, 215t, Burhinus oedicnemus.
**Perf. 14**
**1995, June 8**
235 A79 Block of 4, #a.-d. 3.25 3.25

## Slovenian Boy Scouts A80

**1995, Sept. 26 Litho.**
236 A80 70t multicolored .60 .60

## Comtemporary Art, by France Kralj — A81

**Perf. 14**
**1995, Sept. 26**
237 A81 60t Death of a Genius, 1921 .50 .50
238 A81 70t Family of Horses, 1959 .60 .60
a. Pair, #237-238 1.10 1.10

A82

A83

UN, FAO, 50th Anniv.: No. 239, Stylized pictures of food products, faces of people from many nations. No. 240, Black & white figures touching hands, faces of people from many nations.

**1995, Sept. 26**
239 A82 70t multicolored .50 .50
240 A82 70t multicolored .50 .50
a. Pair, #239-240 1.25 1.25
Issued in miniature sheets of 4 stamps.

**1995, Nov. 16**
Christmas (Paintings): 13t, Winter, by Marlenka Stupica. 70t, St. Mary of Succour, Brezje, by Leopold Layer.
241 A83 13t multicolored .20 .20
a. Booklet pane of 10 + 2 labels 1.50 1.50
Complete booklet 6.00
242 A83 70t multicolored .60 .60
a. Booklet pane of 10 + 2 labels 6.00 6.00
Complete booklet 6.00

**Railways Type of 1994**
Design: 70t, Locomotive "Aussee."
**1996, Jan. 31** Litho. **Perf. 14**
243 A64 70t multicolored .60 .60
The Graz-Celje Line, 150th anniv.

**1996, Jan. 31** Litho. **Perf. 14**
244 A84 13t multicolored .20 .20

St. Gregory's Day—A84

Carnival Costumes A85

**1996, Jan. 31**
245 A85 13t, Ptujsko region .20 .20
246 A85 70t, Dravsko region .50 .50
See Nos. 281-282, 384-385.

**1996, Jan. 31**
Emys Orbicularis A86
247 A86 13t, Peeking head out of water. b, 50t, Two young. c, 60t, Adult crawling through water. d, 70t, Laying eggs.
247 A86 Strip of 4, #a.-d. 3.75 3.75
No. 247 printed in sheets of 4, vertical or horizontal strips, each having a different order.
World Wildlife Fund: a, 13t, Peeking head out of water. b, 50t, Two young. c, 60t, Adult crawling through water. d, 70t, Laying eggs.

Fran Saleski Finžgar (1871-1962), Writer, Priest.—A87

**1996, Apr. 18** Litho. **Perf. 14**
248 A87 13t multicolored .20

A88

**1996, Apr. 18**
249 A88 65t multicolored .50 .50
UNICEF, 50th anniv.

A89

**1996, Apr. 18**
Paintings: 65t, Children on Grass (detail). 75t, Bouquet of Dahlias.
250 A89 65t multicolored .45 .45
251 A89 75t multicolored .55 .55
a. Pair, Nos. 250-251 1.00 1.00
Issued in sheets of 8 stamps. Europa.

Ita Rina (1907-79), Film Actress A90

**1996, Apr. 18**
252 A90 100t multicolored .75 .75

**1996, Apr. 18**
253 A91 75t multicolored .50 .50
254 A91 200t multicolored 1.50 1.50

**Souvenir Sheet**

Visit of Pope John Paul II, May 17-19—A91

255 A92 24t Gallenberg Castle .25 .25
City of Zagorje ob Savi, 700th Anniv. A92

**1996, June 6** Litho. **Perf. 14**
255 A92 24t Gallenberg Castle .25 .25

World Junior Cycling Championships, Novo Mesto—A93

**1996, June 21**
256 A93 55t multicolored .45 .45

Mushrooms—A95

**1996, June 6**
Designs: a, 65t, Cantharellus cibarius. b, 75t, Boletus aestivalis.
258 A95 Sheet of 2, #a.-b. 1.40 1.40

257 A94 75t multicolored .60 .60
Independence, 5th Anniv.—A94

**1996, June 6**
257 A94 75t multicolored .60 .60

Modern Olympic Games, Cent., 1996 Summer Olympics, Atlanta—A96

**1996, June 6**
259 A96 75t multicolored .60 .60
260 A96 100t multicolored .80 .80
a. Pair, #259-260+label 1.50 1.50
Designs: 75t, Iztok Cop, rower; Fredja Marsic, kayaker. 100t, Britta Bilac, high jumper; Brigita Bukovec, hurdler.
No. 260a issued in sheets of 6 stamps + 3 labels. Two versions of the sheet exist. One with white, red & blue flag, the other with white, blue & red flag.

Emys Orbicularis A86

**1996, June 6**
275 A105 55t multicolored

A97 A98 A99 A100

Idrijan Lace A101 A102

**1996, June 21** Litho. **Perf. 14**
261 A97 11t shown .20 .20
262 A97 11t olive gray, diff. .20 .20
263 A98 21t shown .20 .20
264 A98 21t carmine, diff. .20 .20
265 A99 5t shown .20 .20
266 A99 5t square .20 .20
267 A100 12t shown .20 .20
268 A100 12t diamond .20 .20
269 A101 13t shown .30 .30
270 A101 13t red, diff. .20 .20
271 A102 50t shown .30 .30
272 A102 50t lilac, diff. .40 .40
a. Pair, #261-262 .40 .40
a. Pair, #263-264 .40 .40
a. Pair, #265-266 .40 .40
a. Pair, #267-268 .20 .20
a. Pair, #269-270 .30 .30
a. Pair, #271-272 .80 .80
Nos. #272-272 2.80 2.80

The background of the designs on Nos. 261-272 contain "1996," posthorn, and security lettering that appear under UV light. Nos. 264a, 266a exist with date appears under UV light. Nos. 264a, 266a exist with date "1997" that appears under UV light. See Nos. 297-304.

Grammar School, Novo Mesto, 250th Anniv.—A104

**1996, Sept. 6**
274 A104 55t multicolored .55 .35

Modern Cardiology, Cent.—A103

**1996, Sept. 6** Litho. **Perf. 14**
273 A103 12t multicolored .20 .20

Škocjan Caves, Karst Region, UNESCO World Heritage Site A105

**1996, Sept. 6**
275 A105 55t multicolored .55 .35

Moscon Family Portrait, by Jozef Tominc (1790-1866)—A106

**1996, Sept. 6**
276 A106 65t multicolored .75 .50

A107

A108

**1996, Oct. 18**    **Litho.**    *Perf. 14*
277 A107 100t multicolored    1.00  .65
Post Office, Ljubljana, cent.

**1996, Oct. 20**
278 A108 12t multicolored    .20  .20
Introduction of automatic letter sorting machines, Maribor.

A109

**Christmas**
A110

**1996, Nov. 20**    **Litho.**    *Perf. 14*
279 A109 12t Children sledding    .20  .20
a.   Booklet pane of 10    1.40
  Complete booklet, #279a    1.40
280 A110 66t Nativity    .65  .50
a.   Booklet pane of 10    6½
  Complete booklet, #280a    6.75

**Carnival Costumes Type of 1996**
From Cerkno region: 20t, "Ta terjast." 80t, "Pust."

**1997, Jan. 21**    **Litho.**    *Perf. 14*
281 A85 20t multicolored    .20  .20
282 A85 80t multicolored    .80  .55

Love
A111

**1997, Jan. 21**    **Litho.**    *Perf. 14*
283 A111 15t multicolored    .20  .20

Sneznik Mountain
A112

**1997, Jan. 21**
284 A112 20t multicolored    .20  .20

A113

A114

**1997, Mar. 27**    **Litho.**    *Perf. 14*
285 A113 80t Legend of the Goldenhorn    .80  .50
Europa.

**1997, Mar. 27**
286 A114 80t Wulfenite    .80  .50

**Endangered Fish—A115**

**1997, Mar. 27**
287 A115 12t Salmo marmoratus    .20  .20
288 A115 13t Zingel streber    .20  .20
289 A115 80t Vimba vimba    .80  .60
290 A115 90t Umbra krameri    .95  .60
a.   Souvenir sheet, #287-290    2.00 2.00
Nos. 287-290 (4)    2.15 1.50

**Railways Type of 1994**
Design: 80t, Locomotive SZ 03-002, Ljubljana-Trieste Railway Line, 110th anniv.

**1997, May 30**    **Litho.**    *Perf. 14*
291 A64 80t multicolored    .80  .50

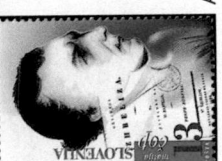

A116

A117

**1997, May 30**
292 A116 70t multicolored    .65  .45
Volunteer fire fighting brigades in Slovenia.

**1997, May 30**
Famous People: 13t, Matija Cop (1797-1835), literary expert. 24t, Sigismundus Zois (1747-1819), economist, natural scientist. 80t, Bishop Frederic Baraga (1797-1868), missionary, linguist.

293 A117 13t multicolored    .20  .20
294 A117 24t multicolored    .25  .20
295 A117 80t multicolored    .80  .50
Nos. 293-295 (3)    1.25  .90

**4th Meeting of the Presidents of Central European Countries, Piran—A118**

Designs: a, 100t, Tartini Square. b, 200t, Coats of arms from eight countries.

**1997, June 6**
296 A118 Sheet of 2, #a.-b.    3.00 3.00

**Idrijan Lace Type of 1996**
Shape of lace: No. 297, Flower in center of oval. No. 298, Circular outside with swirl at bottom. No. 299, Butterfly. No. 300, Diamond. No. 301, Square. No. 302, Circle. No. 303, Leaves. No. 304, Tulip.

**1997, June 20**    **Litho.**    *Perf. 14*
297 A97 10t magenta    .20  .20
298 A97 10t magenta    .20  .20
a.   Pair, #297-298    .25  .25
299 A97 20t violet    .20  .20
300 A97 20t violet    .20  .20
a.   Pair, #299-300    .40  .40
301 A97 44t bright blue    .45  .30
302 A97 44t bright blue    .45  .30
a.   Pair, #301-302    .90  .90
303 A97 100t gray brown    1.00  .60
304 A97 100t gray brown    1.00  .60
a.   Pair, #303-304    2.00 2.00
Nos. 299-304 (6)    3.30 2.20

A119

A120

**1997, Sept. 9**
305 A119 14t multicolored    .20  .20
Children's Week.

**1997, Sept. 9**
306 A120 50t multicolored    .50  .35
Return of Primorska, 50th anniv.

France Gorse (1897-1986), Sculptor—A121

**1997, Sept. 9**
307 A121 70t "Bashful Armor"    .70  .45
308 A121 80t "Peasant Woman"    .80  .55
a.   Pair, #307-308    1.50 1.50

A122

A123

**1997, Sept. 9**
309 A122 90t multicolored    .90  .60
MEJP '97, European Youth Judo Championship.

**1997, Nov. 18**    **Litho.**    *Perf. 14*
310 A123 90t multicolored    .90  .60
Golden Fox World Cup Ski Competition for Women, 35th anniv.

**Christmas & New Year**
A124

Designs: 14t, Children watching birds and snow outside window. 90t, Sculptured Nativity scene, by Liza Hribar (1913-96).

**1997, Nov. 18**
311 A124 14t multicolored    .20  .20
312 A124 90t multicolored    .80  .55
a.   Booklet pane of 8, 5 #311, 3 #312    3.50
  Complete booklet, #312a    3.50

New Mail Center, Ljubljana—A125

**1997, Nov. 28**
313 A125 30t multicolored    .30  .20

Borovo Gostúvanje (Pine Wedding)—A126

20t, Participating "players," top of pine tree. 80t, Participants, "bride & groom," top of pine tree.

**1998, Jan. 22**    **Litho.**    *Perf. 14*
314 A126 20t multicolored    .25  .20
315 A126 80t multicolored    .75  .50
a.   Pair, #314-315    1.00 1.00
See Nos. 338-339.

1998 Winter Olympic Games, Nagano
A127

**1998, Jan. 22**
316 A127 70t Woman skater    .65  .45
317 A127 90t Biathlete    .90  .55
a.   Vert. pair, #316-317 + label    1.60 1.60

Issued in sheets of 6 stamps + 3 labels.

**1998, Jan. 22**
318 A128 90t multicolored .90 .60

EUROCONTROL (European Organization for Safety of Air Navigation), 35th Anniv. — A128

**1998, Mar. 25** Litho. Perf. 14
319 A129 26t multicolored .25 .20
320 A129 90t multicolored .85 .55

90t, Francesco Robba (1698-1757), sculptor.

Louis Adamic (1898-1951), Writer — A129

**1998, Mar. 25**
321 A130 90t multicolored .90 .60

Jurjevanje (Green George's Festival) A130

Europa.

**1998, June 10**
326 A132 14t multicolored .20 .20

Boc Mountain, Pulsatilla Grandis — A132

**1998, June 10** Litho. Perf. 14
325 A64 80t multicolored .80 .50

Design: Steam locomotive SZ 06-018.

Railways Type of 1994

**1998, Mar. 25**
322 A131 14t Fox .20 .20
323 A131 105t Turtle 1.00 .65
324 A131 118t Wolf 1.10 .70
a. Sheet, 2 each #322-324 4.50 4.50
Nos. 322-324 (3) 2.30 1.55

Comic Strip Characters, by Miki Muster — A131

---

**1998, June 10**
327 A133 Sheet of 4, #a-d. 2.00 2.00

Conifers: a. 14t, Picea abies. b, 15t, Juniperus communis. c, 80t, Larix decidua. d, 90t, Pinus nigra.

A133

**1998, June 23** Litho. Perf. 14
328 A134 15t multicolored .20 .20

Committee for the Protection of Human Rights, 10th anniv.

A134

**1998, June 23**
329 A135 80t multicolored .80 .50

Cistercian Order, 900th Anniv. and Sticna Revival, Cent. A136

**1998, Sept. 11**
330 A136 14t multicolored .20 .20

United Slovenia, 150th Anniv. A135

**1998, Sept. 11**
331 A137 50t Cuckoo .50 .30

Radio Ljubljana, 70th Anniv. A137

**1998, Sept. 11**
332 A138 70t multicolored .65 .45
333 A138 80t multicolored .75 .55
a. Pair, #332-333 1.40 1.40

Designs: 70t, Abstract painting, "Banker." 80t, Sculpture, "El."

Avgust Cernigoj (1898-1985), Artist — A138

---

A133

A134

juniperus communis
14
SLOVENIJA

**1998, Sept. 11**
334 A139 100t multicolored .95 .65

Universal Declaration of Human Rights, 50th Anniv. — A139

Christmas A140

**1998, Nov. 12** Litho. Perf. 14
335 A140 15t multicolored .20 .20
336 A140 90t multicolored .85 .55
a. Booklet pane of 10 1.60
Complete booklet, #335a 4.50
Bklt. pane, 6 #335, 4 #336 4.50
Complete booklet, #336a 4.50

Designs: 15t, Children walking through snow, candle. 90t, Fresco of "Bow of the Three Wise Men of the East," Church of St. Nicholas, Mace, 1476.

**1998, Nov. 12**
337 A141 100t Sheet of 3, #a-c. 3.00 3.00

Leon Stukelj, Olympic Gymnastics Champion, 100th Birthday — A141

Designs: a. Portrait, b As a gymnast, c, With IOC Pres. Juan Antonio Samaranch, horiz. (58x40mm).

**1998, Nov. 12**
337 A141 100t Sheet of 3, #a-c. 3.00 3.00

Wedding, Festival Type of 1998

**1999, Jan. 22** Litho. Perf. 14
338 A126 20t multicolored .25 .20
339 A126 80t multicolored .75 .50
a. Pair, #338-339 1.00 1.00

Skoromati carnival mask characters: 20t, Wearing tall hats. Skopit character in black. 80t, Skopit character blowing horn.

**1999, Jan. 22**
340 A142 15t multicolored .20 .20

Greetings A142

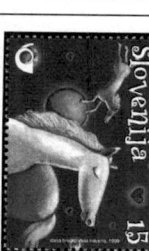

**1999, Jan. 22**
341 A143 14t multicolored .20 .20
342 A143 15t multicolored .20 .20
343 A143 70t multicolored .65 .40
344 A143 80t multicolored .75 .50
Nos. 341-344 (4) 1.80 1.30

14t, Peter Kozler (1824-79), geographer. 15t, Bozidar Lavric (1899-1961), surgeon. 70t, Rudolf Maister (1874-1934), general, poet. 80t, France Preseren (1800-49), poet.

Famous Men — A143

---

**1999, Mar. 23**
345 A144 15t multicolored .20 .20

Golica Mountain, Narcissus Flowers A144

**1999, Mar. 23**
346 A145 16t Yugoslavia #3L5 & #305 .20 .20

Slovenian Philatelic Assoc., 50th Anniv. — A145

**1999, Mar. 23**
347 A146 80t multicolored .90 .45

Mercury & Cinnabar, Idrija Mine A146

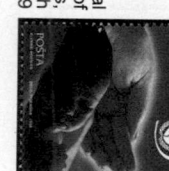

**1999, Mar. 23**
348 A147 80t multicolored .90 .45

Council of Europe, 50th Anniv. A147

Triglav Natl Park A148

**1999, Mar. 23**
349 A148 90t multicolored 1.00 .50

Europa.

**1999, May 21** Litho. Perf. 14
350 A149 80t multicolored .90 .45

5th Rescue Dog World Championships — A149

UPU, 125th Anniv. — A150

Designs: 30t, Early postman with backpack. 90t, Astronaut on moon with backpack.

SLOVENIA

**1999, May 21**
351 A150 30t multicolored .60 .30
352 A150 90t multicolored 1.00 .50
a. Pair, #351-352 1.60 .80

Horses — A151

Designs: 60t, Slovenian cold-blooded horse. 70t, Ljutomer trotter. 120t, Slovenian warm-blooded horse (show jumper). 350t, Lipizzaner.

**1999, May 21**
353 A151 60t multicolored .65 .35
354 A151 70t multicolored .75 .40
355 A151 120t multicolored 1.25 .65
356 A151 350t multicolored 3.75 1.90
a. Sheet of 4, #353-356 6.50 3.50
Nos. 353-356 (4) 6.40 3.30

Millennium — A155

Christmas — A156

**1999, Nov. 18** **Litho.** **Perf. 14**
365 A155 17t multicolored .20 .20
a. Booklet pane of 10 2.00
Complete booklet, #365a 2.00
366 A155 18t multicolored .20 .20
367 A156 80t multicolored .80 .40
a. Booklet pane, 5 #365, 3 #367 + 2 labels 3.50
Complete booklet, #367a 3.50
368 A156 90t multicolored .90 .45
a. Complete booklet (4) 2.10 1.25

#365 and 367 were issued only in booklets.

A159

A160

**2000, Jan. 20**
384 A85 34t multi .35 .20
385 A85 80t multi .80 .40

**2000, Jan. 20**
386 A159 64t multi .65 .30

Tone Seliškar (1900-69), poet.

**2000, Jan. 20**
387 A160 120t multi 1.25 .60

Elvira Kralj (1900-78), actress.

Postal Service in Slovenia, 500th Anniv. — A161

**2000, Jan. 20**
388 A161 500t multi 5.00 2.50

Mt. Storžič A162

**2000, Mar. 21** **Litho.** **Perf. 14**
389 A162 18t multi .20 .20

Return of World War II Exiles A163

**2000, Mar. 21**
390 A163 25t multi .25 .20

Characters from Children's Books — A164

**2000, Mar. 21** **Perf. 14**
391 A164 20t multi .20 .20
392 A164 20t multi .20 .20
393 A164 20t multi .20 .20

#391, 394, Pedeniped. #392, 395, Mojca Pokrajculja. #393, 396, Macek Muri.

---

Towards A New Millennium — A152

Designs: 20t, Balanced objects. 70t, Roadway, earth. 80t, Cogwheels. 90t, Tree.

**1999, Sept. 16** **Litho.** **Perf. 13¾**
357 A152 20t multicolored .20 .20
358 A152 70t multicolored .80 .40
359 A152 80t multicolored .90 .45
360 A152 90t multicolored 1.00 .50
a. Block of 4, #357-360 3.00 1.50

Božidar Jakac (1899-1989), Painter — A153

Self-portraits and: 70t, Girl drawing curtain. 80t, Landscape.

**1999, Sept. 16**
361 A153 70t multicolored .80 .40
362 A153 80t multicolored .90 .45
a. Pair, #361-362 1.75 .85

Railway type of 1994

**1999, Sept. 16**
363 A64 80t multicolored .90 .45

Rail Line to Ljubljana, 150th anniv.

Bishop Anton M. Slomšek (1800-62) — A154

**1999, Sept. 16**
364 A154 90t multicolored 1.00 .50

Love — A158

**2000, Jan. 20** **Litho.** **Perf. 14**
383 A158 34t multi .35 .20

**Carnival Costume Type of 1996**

Pustovi masks: 34t, Two masks, horiz. 80t, Four masks, horiz.

---

Types of 1993-94 and No. 210A Surcharged

Design: 18t, Accordion. No. 373, Easter eggs. A, Post office door, Zgornji Otok. No. 375, Fishing boat. No. 375A, Miner's house. Trbovlje. C, Juvile. No. 378, Ljubljana Palm Sunday bundle. No. 379, Fishing boat and oars.

**1999-2004** **Litho.** **Size 25x34mm**
370 A38 18t multi .20 .20
371 A38 19t on 17t multi .20 .20
373 A3R A multi .25 .25
374 A38 A multi .40 .40
375 A38 B multi .45 .45
375A A38 B multi .50 .50
376 A38 C multi 1.00 .50
377 A38 C multi .85 .45
378 A38 D multi 1.10 .55
379 A38 D multi 1.10 .55
Nos. 370-378 (9) 4.95 2.80

Issued: 18t, 12/17/99. No. 371, 2000. B, D, 2/28/02. Nos. 374, 375, 376, 378, 11/19/03. Nos. 375A, 7/3/04. No. 379, 9/22/04. Nos. 373 and 377 sold for 31t and 107t respectively on day of issue. Nos. 374, 375, 376 and 378 sold for 38t, 44t, 95t and 107t respectively on day of issue. No. 375A sold for 48t on day of issue. No. 379 sold for 107t on day of issue.

This is an continuing set. Numbers may change.

Issued: No. 371, 4/20/00.

---

**Booklet Stamps**
**Self-Adhesive**
**Serpentine Die Cut 7½**
394 A164 20t multi .20 .20
395 A164 20t multi .20 .20
396 A164 20t multi .20 .20
a. Booklet pane, 3 each #394-396 + 9 labels 1.90
Nos. 391-396 (6) 1.20 1.20

No. 396a is a complete booklet.

Fossils and Minerals A165

**2000, Mar. 21** **Perf. 14**
397 A165 80t Trilobite .75 .35
398 A165 90t Dravite .85 .45

See Nos. 453-454, 517.

Souvenir Sheet

CHRISTUS HERI HODIE SEMPER

Holy Year 2000 — A166

Illustration reduced.

**2000, Mar. 21**
399 A166 2000t multi 27.50 21.00

Castles — A167

**2000-04** **Litho.** **Size 23x32mm**
400 A167 1t Predjama .20 .20
401 A167 1t Velenje .20 .20
a. Pair, #400-401 .20
404 A167 A Ptuj .20 .20
405 A167 A Otocec .25 .25
a. Pair, #404-405 .35
406 A167 B Zuzemberk .20 .20
407 A167 B Turjak .30 .30
a. Pair, #406-407 .35
410 A167 C Dobrovo .80 .40
411 A167 C Breziski .80 .40
a. Pair, #410-411 .80
411B A167 C Gewerkenegg 1.10 .55
412 A167 100t Podsreda .90 .45
413 A167 100t Bled .90 .45
a. Pair, #412-413 1.90
414 A167 D Olimje .85 .45
415 A167 D Murska Sobota .85 .45
a. Pair, #414-415 1.75 1.10

**Size: 38x26mm**
415B A167 1000t Kamen 9.25 4.50
Nos. 400-415B (14) 16.65 8.85

Nos. 404-405 each sold for 20t; Nos. 406-407 for 21t; Nos. 410-411 for 95t; Nos. 411B sold for 95t on day of issue; Nos. 414-415 for 107t on day of issue; A, B, 6/23; Nos. 410-411, 414-415, 10/4/01. No. 1000t, Nos. 1000t.

3/24/03. No. 411B; 11/18/04. This is an expanding set. See Nos. 624-628.

## Fruits, Blossoms and Insects — A168

Designs: No. 416, Apple blossom weevil. No. 417, Apple blossom. No. 418, Apple.

**2000, Apr. 20    Litho.    Perf. 13¾**
Vignette Frame Size 20x26½mm

| | | | |
|---|---|---|---|
| 416 | A168 | 10t multi | .20 .20 |
| 417 | A168 | 10t multi | .20 .20 |
| 418 | A168 | 10t multi | .20 .20 |
| a. | | Strip, #416-418 | .25 .20 |

Printed in sheets of 15 stamps + 5 labels.
See Nos. 426-428, 464-466, 502-504, 528-530, 568-570, 606-608, 629-646.

**2000, May 9    Perf. 14**

| | | | |
|---|---|---|---|
| 419 | A169 | 20t multi | .20 .20 |

Amateur Radio A169

---

**Meteorology A173**

**2000, May 9    Litho.    Perf. 13¾**

| | | | |
|---|---|---|---|
| 425 | A173 | 150t multi | 1.40 .70 |

Issued in sheets of 9 + 1 label.

 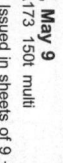

## Fruits, Blossoms and Insects Type of 2000

**2000, June 23    Litho.    Perf. 13¾**
Vignette Frame Size 20x26½mm

| | | | |
|---|---|---|---|
| 426 | A168 | 5t multi | .20 .20 |
| 427 | A168 | 5t multi | .20 .20 |
| 428 | A168 | 5t multi | .20 .20 |
| a. | | Strip, #426-428 | .20 .20 |

Printed in sheets of 15 stamps + 5 labels.

#426, Cherry blossom. #427, European cherry fruit fly. #428, Cherries.

---

**First Book Printed in Slovenian, 450th Anniv. — A177**

**2000, Nov. 21**

| | | | |
|---|---|---|---|
| 436 | A177 | 50t multi | .45 .20 |

---

## Slovenian Team Qualification for European Soccer Championships A170

**2000, May 9    Perf. 14**

| | | | |
|---|---|---|---|
| 420 | A170 | 40t multi | .35 .20 |

---

## Paintings by Tone Kraji (1900-75) — A174

**2000, Sept. 15    Litho.    Perf. 14**

| | | | |
|---|---|---|---|
| 429 | | | 1.25 .65 |
| a. | A174 | 70t multi, Horiz. pair | .60 .30 |
| b. | A174 | 80t multi, diff. | .65 .35 |

## Grape Varieties — A175

**2000, Sept. 15    Litho.**

| | | | |
|---|---|---|---|
| 430-433 | A175 | Set of 4 | 2.25 1.10 |
| a. | | Souvenir sheet, #430-433 | 2.25 1.10 |

Designs: 20t, Zelen. 40t, Zametovka. 130t, Ranfol. 80t, Rumeni Plavec.

---

**Christmas A178**

Designs: B, Children in snow. 90t, Christ in manger.

**2000, Nov. 21**

| | | | |
|---|---|---|---|
| 437 | A178 | B multicolored | .20 .20 |
| 438 | A178 | 90t multicolored | .80 .40 |

**Serpentine Die Cut 7¼**
**Booklet Stamps**
**Self-Adhesive**

| | | | |
|---|---|---|---|
| 439 | A178 | B multi | .20 .20 |
| a. | | Booklet of 10 + 2 labels | 2.00 |
| 440 | A178 | 90t multi | .80 .40 |
| a. | | Booklet, 6 #439, 4 #440 + 2 labels | 4.50 |
| | | Nos. 437-440 (4) | 2.00 1.20 |

Nos. 437 and 439 sold for 211 on day of issue.

---

## 2000 Summer Olympics, Sydney A171

**2000, May 9**

| | | | |
|---|---|---|---|
| 421 | A171 | 80t Sailboats | .70 .35 |
| 422 | A171 | 90t Sydney Opera House | .80 .40 |
| a. | | Pair, #421-422 | 1.50 .75 |

## World Environment Day — A172

**2000, May 9**

| | | | |
|---|---|---|---|
| 423 | A172 | 90t multi | .80 .40 |

Issued in sheets of 10 + 5 labels.

## Europa, 2000 Common Design Type

**2000, May 9    Litho.    Perf. 14**

| | | | |
|---|---|---|---|
| 424 | CD17 | 90t multi | .80 .40 |

Issued in sheets of 8 + 1 label.

## Gold Medalists at 2000 Summer Olympics A176

**2000, Oct. 16**

| | | | |
|---|---|---|---|
| 434-435 | A176 | Set of 2 | .35 .20 |

Winners and events: No. 434, 21t, Iztok Čop, Luka Špik, double sculls. No. 435, 21t, Rajmond Debevec, Men's three-position rifle.

---

## Advent of New Millennium — A179

**2000, Nov. 21    Litho.    Perf. 14**

| | | | |
|---|---|---|---|
| 441 | A179 | 40t multi | .35 .20 |

## Wedding Greetings A180

**2001, Jan. 19    Litho.    Perf. 14**

| | | | |
|---|---|---|---|
| 442 | A180 | B multi | .25 .20 |

No. 442 sold for 25t on day of issue.

---

## Comic Strip Characters by Bozo Kos — A184

**2001, Mar. 21**

| | | | |
|---|---|---|---|
| 449 | A184 | B multicolored | .20 .20 |
| 450 | A184 | B multicolored | .20 .20 |

**Serpentine Die Cut 7¼**
**Booklet Stamps**
**Self-Adhesive**

| | | | |
|---|---|---|---|
| 451 | A184 | B multi | .20 .20 |
| 452 | A184 | B multicolored | .20 .20 |
| a. | | Booklet, 4 each #451-452 | .80 .80 |
| | | Nos. 449-452 (4) | .80 .80 |

Nos. 449-452 each sold for 25t on day of issue.

Designs: Nos. 449, 451, Cowboy. Nos. 450, 452, Indian.

---

## Writers — A182

**2001, Jan. 19**

| | | | |
|---|---|---|---|
| 445-447 | A182 | Set of 3 | 2.00 1.00 |

Objects symbolic of writer's works: A, Bucket (Dragotin Kette, 1876-99); 95t, Flowers in jar (Ivan Tavcar, 1851-1923); 107t, Coffee cup (Ivan Cankar, 1876-1918).

No. 445 sold for 24t on day of issue.

## Mt. Jalovec and Triglav Flowers — A183

**2001, Mar. 21    Litho.    Perf. 14**

| | | | |
|---|---|---|---|
| 448 | A183 | B multi | .20 .20 |

No. 448 sold for 25t on day of issue.

---

## Carnival Masks, Dobrepolje — A181

**2001, Jan. 19**

| | | | |
|---|---|---|---|
| 443-444 | A181 | Set of 2 | 1.25 .65 |

Mask wearers including: 50t, Woman with flowers. 95t, Woman in box on cart.

## Fossil and Mineral Type of 2000

**2001, Mar. 21    Litho.    Perf. 14**

| | | | |
|---|---|---|---|
| 453 | A165 | 21t multi | 1.60 .80 |
| a.-b. | | Horiz. pair | .80 .40 |
| 453 | | Any single | .90 .45 |
| 454 | A165 | 107t Starfish fossil | |

No. 453 — Stereoscopic image of fluorite crystal with arrow at: a, Right. b, Left.

## Europe Day A185

**2001, Mar. 21**

| | | | |
|---|---|---|---|
| 455 | A185 | 221t multi | 1.90 .95 |

**Souvenir Sheet**

Apiculture — A192

No. 462: a, 24t, Bee on flower. b, 48t, Queen and drones. c, 95t, Worker bees. d, 170t, Hive and apiary.

2.75 1.40

**2001, May 23**
462 A192 Sheet of 4, #a-d

Flags of US and Russia, Dragon Bridge, Ljubljana — A193

.85 .45
.85 .45

**2001, June 14**
463 A193 107t multi
a. Souvenir sheet of 1

First meeting of US Pres. George W. Bush and Russian Pres. Vladimir Putin, Brdo Castle, June 16.

**Fruit, Blossoms and Insects Type of 2000**

*Perf. 13¾*

**Vignette Frame Size 20x26mm**

Designs: Nn. 464, Peach blossom. No. 465, Green peach aphid. No. 466, Peach.

**2001, July 21**
464 A168 50t multi   .40 .20
465 A168 50t multi   .40 .20
466 A168 50t multi   .40 .20
a. Strip, #464-466   1.20 .60

Printed in sheets of 15 strips + 5 labels.

Mohorjeve Druzbe Publishing House, 150th Anniv. — A194

*Perf. 14*

.25 .20

**2001, Sept. 4**
467 A194 B multi

No. 467 sold for 27t on day of issue.

Foundation of First Technical High School, Cent. A195

.20 .20

**2001, Sept. 21**
468 A195 A multi

No. 468 sold for 26t on day of issue.

---

**World Animal Day — A196**

.90 .45

**2001, Sept. 21**
469 A196 107t multi

Year of Dialogue Among Civilizations A197

*Litho.*   *Perf. 14*

.90 .45

**2001, Sept. 21**
470 A197 107t multi

Composers — A198

Designs: 95t, Blaz Arnic (1901-70). 107t, Lucijan Marija Skerjanc (1900-73).

*Litho.*   *Perf. 14*

1.75 .85

Set of 2

**2001, Sept. 21**
471-472 A198

New Year's Greetings A199

Christmas A200

*Litho.*   *Perf. 14*

.25 .20
.90 .45

**Self-Adhesive, Serpentine Die Cut 7¼**

**Booklet Stamps**

**2001, Nov. 16**
473 A199 B multi   .25 .20
474 A200 D multi   .90 .45
475 A199 B multi   .20
a. Booklet pane of 12   3.00
476 A200 D multi   .45
a. Booklet pane, 6 each #475-476   7.00

Nos. 473 and 475 sold for 31t. Nos. 474 and 476 for 107t on day of issue.

Love — A201

*Litho.*   *Perf. 14*

.25 .20

**2002, Jan. 23**
477 A201 B multi

No. 477 sold for 31t on day of issue.

---

Masks — A202

Designs: 56t, Rusa. 95t, Picek.

1.25 .60

**2002, Jan. 23**
478-479 A202   Set of 2

Famous Slovenians — A203

Designs: 95t, Joze Plecnik (1872-1957), architect. 107t, Janko Kersnik (1852-97), poet.

1.60 .80

**2002, Jan. 23**
480-481 A203   Set of 2

2002 Winter Olympics, Salt Lake City — A204

No. 482: a, 95t, Sledder. b, 107t, Skier. Illustration reduced.

1.60 .80

**2002, Jan. 23**
482 A204   Horiz. pair, #a-b, + label

No. 482 printed in sheets of three pairs. Labels, which have different designs, appear at left and center in other pairs on the sheet.

Insect Fossil A205

.75 .40

**2002, Mar. 21**
485 A205 C multi

No. 485 sold for 95t on day of issue.

Kostanjevica on the Krka, 750th Anniv. A206

.85 .45

**2002, Mar. 21**
486 A206 D multi

No. 486 sold for 107t on day of issue.

Intl. Year of Mountains A207

---

Solkan, 1000th Anniv. — A186

2.25 1.10

**2001, Mar. 21**
456 A186 261t multi

Formation of Liberation Front, 60th Anniv. — A187

*Litho.*   *Perf. 14*

.20 .20

**2001, Apr. 24**
457 A187 24t multi

Independence, 10th Anniv. — A188

.80 .40

**2001, May 23**
458 A188 100t multi

Issued in sheets of 10 + 2 labels.

Europa — A189

.90 .45

**2001, May 23**
459 A189 107t multi

Issued in sheets of 8 + 1 label.

Ljubljana Tram System, Cent. A190

.85 .45

**2001, May 23**
460 A190 113t multi

6th World Maxi Basketball Championships, Ljubljana — A191

2.10 1.10

**2001, May 23**
461 A191 261t multi

**2002, Mar. 21**
487-488 A207 Set of 2 ... 1.10 .55

Flowers and mountains: A, Clematis alpina and Martuljek Group. D, Lilium carniolicum and Mt. Špik.
Nos. 487-488 sold for 30t and 107t respectively on day of issue.

SLOVENIJA B

Martin Krpan from Vrh, by Fran Levstik — A208

**2002, Mar. 21**
489-491 A208 Set of 3 ... .75 .35

Designs: No. 489, B, Krpan carrying horse. No. 490, B, Krpan at blacksmith's shop. No. 491, B, Krpan in Ljubljana. No. 492, B, Like #489. No. 493, B, Like #490. No. 494, B, Like No. 491.

**Self-Adhesive, Serpentine Die Cut 7¼**
**Booklet Stamps**

| | | Perf. 14 | |
|---|---|---|---|
| 492-494 | A208 | Set of 3 | .75 .35 |
| 494a | | Booklet pane, 3 each #492-494 | 2.25 |

Nos. 489-494 each sold for 31t on day of issue.

**2002, May 22**
495 A209 D multi ... .90 .45

No. 495 sold for 107t on day of issue.

Europa — A209

SLOVENIJA

**2002, May 22**
496 A210 D multi ... .90 .45

No. 496 sold for 107t on day of issue.

2002 World Cup Soccer Championships, Japan and Korea — A210

**2002, May 22**
497-499 A211 Set of 3 ... 1.40 .70

**Souvenir Sheet**
500 A211 D multi ... .90 .45

Designs: A, Rosa canina. B, Chamomilla recutita. C, Valeriana officinalis. D, Viola odorata.
Nos. 497-500 each sold for 30t, 31t, 95t and 107t respectively on day of issue.

ŠIPEK Rosa canina
SLOVENIJA A

Medicinal Plants — A211

**2002, May 22**
501 A212 Sheet of 2, #a-b ... 1.90 .95

Nos. 501a and 501b each sold for 107t on day of issue.

Designs: No. 501: a, D, Bled Island in map of Europe. b, D, Map of Europe, Brdo Castle.

**Souvenir Sheet**

9th Summit of Presidents of Central European States, Bled — A212

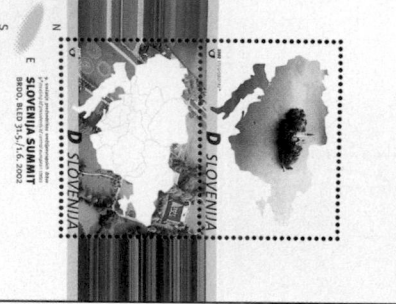

SLOVENIJA SUMMIT

**Fruit, Blossoms and Insects Type of 2000**

Designs: No. 502, Bilberry blossoms, No. 503, Winter moth. No. 504, Bilberries.

MATIJA JAMA
SLOVENIJA

Paintings by Matija Jama (1872-1947) — A213

**2002, July 19**
**Vignette Frame Size 20x26mm**

| | | | Perf. 13¾ | |
|---|---|---|---|---|
| 502 | A168 | 150t multi | 1.25 | .65 |
| 503 | A168 | 150t multi | 1.25 | .65 |
| 504 | A168 | 150t multi | 1.75 | 1.00 |
| a. | | Horiz. strip, #502-504 | 3.75 | 2.00 |

**2002, Sept. 19**
505-506 A213 Set of 2 ... 2.75 1.40

Designs: 95t, Kolo - A National Dance. 214t, A Village in Winter.

**Souvenir Sheet**

**2002, Sept. 19**
507 A214 Sheet of 2, #a-b ... 1.75 .85

35th Chess Olympiad, Bled — A214

35ᵗʰ Chess Olympiad Bled 2002
35. šahovska olimpiada Bled 2002
Slovenija Slovenija

Designs: 95t: a, C, Horse, Bled Castle. b, D, Fields in checkerboard pattern.
Nos. 507a and 507b each sold for 95t and 107t respectively on day of issue.

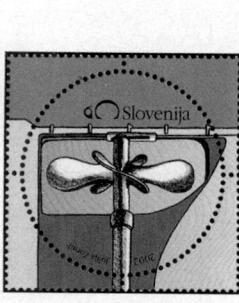

Slovenija

**2002, Nov. 15** Litho. Perf. 13¾
508 A215 C multi ... .85 .40

Screw Propeller Invented by Josef Ressel (1793-1857) — A215

No. 508 sold for 95t on day of issue. Values are for stamps with surrounding selvage.

Slovenija
SLOVENSKA ISTRA
A

Christmas and New Year's Greetings — A216

**2002, Nov. 15** Litho. Perf. 14
509 A216 B multi ... .35 .20
510 A216 D multi ... .95 .45

Designs: Nos. 509, 511, Snowman. Nos. 510, 512, Girl with evergreen branch.

**Booklet Stamps**
**Self-Adhesive**
**Serpentine Die Cut 7¼**

| | | | | |
|---|---|---|---|---|
| 511 | A216 | B multi | .35 | .20 |
| 512 | A216 | D multi | .95 | .45 |
| a. | | Booklet, 6 each #511-512 | 8.00 | |
| | | Nos. 509-512 (4) | 2.60 | 1.30 |

Nos. 509 and 511 each sold for 36t, and Nos. 510 and 512 each sold for 107t on day of issue.

**2003, Jan. 21** Litho. Perf. 14
513 A217 A multi ... .35 .20

Traditional Istrian Clothing A217

No. 513 sold for 38t on day of issue.

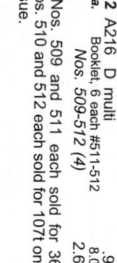

180 SLOVENIJA

Love A218

**2003, Jan. 21** Perf. 11
514 A218 180t multi ... 1.75 .85

No. 514 is impregnated with a rose scent. Values are for examples with surrounding selvage.

107 SLOVENIJA

Famous Men A219

**2003, Jan. 21** Set of 2 ... 3.25 1.60
515-516 A219

Designs: 107t, Ferdinand Avgustin Hallerstein (1703-724), astronomer and Chinese missionary. 221t, Alfonz Paulin, (1853-1942), director of Ljubljana Botanical Gardens.

**Mineral Type of 2000**
**2003, Mar. 24**
517 A165 D Barite ... 1.00 .50

No. 517 sold for 107t on day of issue.

SLOVENIJA

Vilenica Cave — A220

**2003, Mar. 24**
518 A220 D multi ... 1.00 .50

No. 518 sold for 107t on day of issue.

Slovenija B

Fairy Tales A221

**Fairy Tale Type of 2003**
**2003, Mar. 24** Perf. 14
519-520 A221 Set of 2 ... .80 .40

Designs: No. 519, B, The Three Vixens. No. 520, B, The Golden Bird, vert.
Nos. 519-520 each sold for 44t on day of issue.

**Booklet Stamps**
**Self-Adhesive**
**Serpentine Die Cut 7¼**
**2003, Mar. 24** Litho.

| | | | | |
|---|---|---|---|---|
| 521 | A221 | B Like #519 | .40 | .20 |
| 522 | A221 | B Like #520 | .40 | .20 |
| a. | | Booklet, 4 each #521-522 | 3.75 | |

Nos. 521-522 each sold for 44t on day of issue.

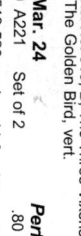

SLOVENIJA
EUROPA D

Europa — A222

**2003, May 22** Litho. Perf. 14
523 A222 D multi ... 1.10 .55

No. 523 sold for 107t on day of issue. Printed in sheets of 8 + 1 label.

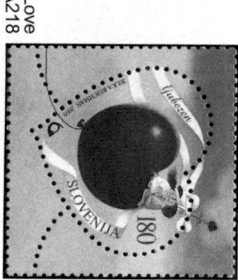
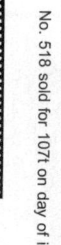

Kresnik, Mythological Character — A223

**2003, May 22**
524 A223 110t multi     1.10 .55

No. 531 sold for 38t on day of issue.

Souvenir Sheet

Slavko and Vilko Avsenik, Musicians — A224

**2003, May 22**
525 A224 180t multi     1.90 .95

European Water Polo Championships, Kranj and Ljubljana — A225

**2003, May 22**
526 A225 180t multi     1.90 .95

Painted Beehive Panel A226

**2003, May 22**
527 A226 218t multi     2.25 1.10

**Fruit, Blossom and Insect Type of 2000**

Designs: No. 528, Olive blossom. No. 529, Olive fruit fly. No. 530, Olives on branch.

**2003, Sept. 18**    *Perf. 13³⁄₄x14*
**Vignette Frame Size 20x26¹⁄₂mm**
528 A168 B multi     .45 .20
529 A168 B multi     .45 .20
530 A168 B multi     .45 .20
a.   Horiz. strip, #528-530   1.35 .60

Nos. 528-530 each sold for 44t on day of issue.

Stampless Covers, 1830 A227

**2003, Sept. 18**    *Perf. 14*
531 A227 A multi     .40 .20

No. 531 sold for 38t on day of issue.

---

Illustration from the Tournament Book of Gasper Lamberger — A228

Jousting contest: a, 76t, Riderless horse. b, 570t, Horse with rider. Illustration reduced.

**2003, Sept. 18**    *Perf. 13³⁄₄*
532 A228   Horiz. pair, #a-b   6.25 3.25

Farm Animals A229

Designs: 95t, Krsko Polje pig. 107t, Cika cattle. 148t, Jezersko-Solcava sheep. 368t, Styrian hen and rooster, vert.

**2003, Sept. 18**    *Perf. 14*
533-535 A229   Set of 3   3.50 1.75
**Souvenir Sheet**
536 A229 368t multi     3.50 1.75

Opening of Mail Sorting and Logistics Center, Maribor A230

**Litho. with Hologram Applied**
**2003, Nov. 11**    *Perf. 13³⁄₄x14¹⁄₄*
537 A230 221t multi     2.25 1.10

Franja Partisan Hospital, 60th Anniv. A231

**2003, Nov. 19**    *Litho.*
538 A231 76t brown & bronze   .80 .40

Wooden Cart A232

**2003, Nov. 19**
539 A232 221t multi     2.25 1.10

Christmas A233

**2003, Nov. 19**    *Perf. 14*
540 A233 D multi     1.10 .55
**Serpentine Die Cut 7¹⁄₄**
**Booklet Stamp**
**Self-Adhesive**
541 A233 D multi     1.10 .55
a.   Booklet pane of 12   13.50

No. 540 and 541 each sold for 107t on day of issue.

---

New Year's Greetings A234

**2003, Nov. 19**    *Perf. 14*
542 A234 B multi     .45 .25
**Serpentine Die Cut 7¹⁄₄**
**Booklet Stamp**
**Self-Adhesive**
543 A233 B multi     .45 .25
a.   Booklet pane of 12   5.50

No. 542 and 543 each sold for 44t on day of issue.

Traditional Clothing from Vipava Valley — A235

**2004, Jan. 22**    *Litho.*    *Perf. 13³⁄₄*
544 A235 A multi     .40 .20

No. 544 sold for 38t on day of issue.

March of IIIe 14Ii Division to the Styria, 60th Anniv. A236

**2004, Jan. 22**    *Perf. 14*
545 A236 B multi     .45 .25

Edvard Kocbek (1904-81), Writer A237

**2004, Jan. 22**
546 A237 D multi     1.10 .55

No. 546 sold for 107t on day of issue.

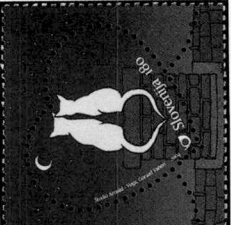

Love A238

**2004, Jan. 22**    *Perf. 11*
547 A238 180t multi     1.90 .95

Values are for examples with surrounding selvage.

Srecko Kosovel (1904-26), Writer A239

**2004, Jan. 22**    *Perf. 14*
548 A239 221t black & red   2.40 1.25

---

Sixth Men's European Handball Championships A240

**2004, Jan. 22**
549 A240 221t multi     2.40 1.25

**Fossil Type of 2000**

**2004, Mar. 24**    *Litho.*    *Perf. 14*
550 A165 D Fish     1.10 .55

No. 541 sold for 107t on day of issue.

European Men's Gymnastic Championships, Ljubljana — A241

**2004, Mar. 24**
551 A241 D multi     1.10 .55

No. 551 sold for 107t on day of issue.

Bled, 1000th Anniv. — A242

**2004, Mar. 24**
552 A242 218t multi     2.25 1.10

Kekec, the Shepherd Boy, by Josip Vandot — A243

Designs: No. 553, B, Kekec. No. 554, B, Pehta. No. 555, B, Kosobrin.

**2004, Mar. 24**    *Perf. 14*
553-555 A243   Set of 3   1.40 .70

Nos. 553-555 each sold for 44t on day of issue.

**Kekec, the Shepherd Boy Type of 2004**

Designs: No. 556, B, Kekec. No. 557, B, Pehta. No. 558, B, Kosobrin.

**Serpentine Die Cut 7¹⁄₄**    *Litho.*
**Booklet Stamps**

**2004, Mar. 24**
556-558 A243   Set of 3   1.40 .70
558a   Booklet pane, 3 each #556-558   4.25

Nos. 556-558 each sold for 44t on day of issue.

SLOVENIA

**2004, Apr. 2    Litho.    Perf. 14**
559  A244  D multi    1.10  .55
No. 559 sold for 107t on day of issue.

Admission to NATO
A244

**2004, May 1**
560  A245  95t multi    .95  .50

Admission to the European Union — A245

Laurenz Koschier (1804-79), Proposer of Postage Stamps
A246

**2004, May 21**
561  A246  B multi    .50  .25
No. 561 sold for 48t on day of issue.

SLOVENIJA

**2004, May 21**
562  A247  B multi    .50  .25
a.    Booklet pane of 8    4.00
No. 562 sold for 48t on day of issue.

Serpentine Die Cut 12½

**2004, May 21**
563  A248  D multi    1.10  .55
No. 563 sold for 107t on day of issue.

Booklet Stamp
Self-Adhesive
Posthorns — A247

Europa — A248

**2004, May 21**
564  A249  110t multi

Puch Bicycle, Chainwheel and Chain — A249

---

2004 Summer Olympics, Athens — A251

**2004, May 21**
566  A251    2.10  1.00
No. 566: a, C, Discus thrower, silhouette of gymnast. b, C, Long jumper, silhouette of pole vaulter.
No. 566a sold for 95t; No. 566b sold for 107t on day of issue.

Souvenir Sheet

Slovenija
VIADUKT ČRNIKAL
95 m

Opening of Crni Kal Viaduct — A252

**2004, Sept. 15    Litho.    Perf. 14**
567  A252  95t multi    1.00  .50

**2004, Sept. 22**
568  A168  A multi    .50  .25
569  A168  A multi    .50  .25
570  A168  A multi    1.50  .75
a.    Horiz. strip, #568-570
Nos. 568-570 each sold for 45t on day of issue.
Designs: No. 568, Pear blossom, No. 570, Pear psylla; No. 570, Pear.

Fruit, Blossoms and Insect Type of 2000

**2004, Sept. 22**
Vignette Frame Size 19x26½mm    Perf. 13¾

First Mention of Town of Maribor in Document, 750th Anniv.
A253

**2004, Sept. 22**
571  A253  C multi    1.00  .50
No. 571 sold for 95t on day of issue.

Epipactis palustris

Designs: B, Epipactis palustris, holosericea. D, Ophrys

Orchids
A254

---

SLOVENIJA
218

**2004, May 21**
565  A250  218t multi    2.25  1.10

Painted Beehive Panel and Bee
A250

Nos. 572 and 573 sold for 52t and 107t respectively on day of issue.

Illuminated Manuscripts — A255
"Q." No. 574: a, Illuminated "P." b, Illuminated Illustration reduced.

**2004, Sept. 22**
574  A255  107t Pair, #a-b    2.25  1.10

Souvenir Sheet

**2004, Sept. 22**
575  A256  221t multi    2.40  1.25

Signing of Second London Memorandum, 50th Anniv. — A256

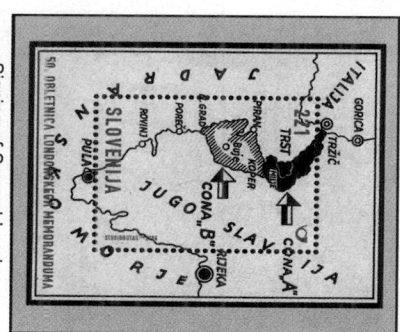

ITALIA
SLOVENIJA
JUGOSLAVIJA

**2004, Nov. 18**
576  A257  C multi    1.10  .55
577  A257  C multi    1.10  .55
a.    Booklet pane of 12    13.50
Nos. 576 and 577 each sold for 95t on day of issue.

Booklet Stamp
Self-Adhesive
Serpentine Die Cut 7¼

Slovenija
MARPVRG

**2004, Sept. 22**
572  A254  B multi    .55  .25
573  A254  D multi    1.10  .55

Souvenir Sheet

Slovenija

Christmas
A257

---

Slovenija
52

Native Dishes — A259
No. 580 — Map and cuisine of the Prekmurje region: a, Prekmurska gibanica (pie). b, Bograc, bujta repa (goulash, pickled turnips).

**2004, Nov. 18**
580  A259  52t Pair, #a-b    1.25  .60

Birth Fairies Rojenice and Sojenice — A260

**2004, Nov. 18**
581  A260  180t multi    2.10  1.00

Slovenija
POHORJE IN KOBANSKO
A

Traditional Clothing From Pohorje and Kobansko Areas
A261

**2005, Jan. 21    Perf. 11½x11¾**
582  A261  A multi    .50  .25
No. 582 sold for 45t on day of issue.

Posthorn Type of 2004

**2005, Jan. 21    Perf. 14, 11½x11¾ (#583A)**
583  A247  83t multi    .90  .45
583A  A247  83t multi    .90  .45
Issued: No. 583, 1/21; No. 583A, 4/2. Size of No. 583: 25x34mm.

SLOVENIJA
107

Janez Sigismund Valentin Popovic (1705-74), Linguist, Scientist — A262

**2005, Jan. 21    Perf. 11½x11¾**
584  A262  107t multi    1.25  .60

SLOVENIJA
B
EUROPA
D

Europa — A248

**2004, May 21    Perf. 14**
564  A248  D multi    1.10  .55

**2004, Nov. 18**
578  A258  A multi    .50  .25
579  A258  A multi    .50  .25
a.    Booklet pane of 12    6.00
Nos. 578 and 579 each sold for 45t on day of issue.

Booklet Stamp
Self-Adhesive
Serpentine Die Cut 7¼
New Year's Greetings — A258

Love
A263

**2005, Jan. 21** *Perf. 11*
**585** A263 180t multi 2.00 1.00

Values are for stamps with surrounding selvage.

Janez Trdina (1830-1905), Writer — A264

**2005, Jan. 21** *Perf. 11¼x11¾*
**586** A264 221t multi 2.40 1.25

Return of Slovenian Exiles, 60th Anniv. A265

**2005, Mar. 18** *Perf. 11¾x11¼*
**587** A265 A multi .55 .25

No. 587 sold for 49t on day of issue.

Victory in World War II, 60th Anniv. A266

**2005, Mar. 18**
**588** A266 B multi .65 .30

No. 588 sold for 57t on day of issue.

Souvenir Sheet

National Tourist Association, Cent. — A267

**2005, Mar. 18** *Perf. 11¼*
**589** A267 100t multi 1.10 .55

Zoisite
A268

**2005, Mar. 18** *Perf. 11¾x11¼*
**590** A268 D multi 1.25 .60

No. 590 sold for 107t on day of issue.

Folk Tales — A269

Designs: No. 591, A, The Golden Fish. No. 592, A, The Grateful Bear.

**2005, Mar. 18** *Perf. 11¼x11¾*
**591-592** A269 Set of 2 1.10 .55

Nos. 591 and 592 each sold for 49t on day of issue.

**Folk Tales Type of 2005**
***Serpentine Die Cut 7¼***
**2005, Mar. 18** **Litho.**
**Booklet Stamps**
**Self-Adhesive**

**593** A269 A Like #591 .55 .25
**594** A269 A Like #592 .55 .25
*a.* Booklet pane, 4 each #593, 594 4.50

Nos. 593 and 594 each sold for 49t on day of issue.

Child and Sunflower — A270

***Die Cut Perf. 12½x12¼***
**2005, May 20** **Litho.**
**Self-Adhesive**

**595** A270 A multi .50 .25

No. 595 sold for 49t on day of issue.

1910 Puch Motorcycle A271

**2005, May 20** *Perf. 11¾x11¼*
**596** A271 98t multi 1.00 .50

Europa
A272

**2005, May 20**
**597** A272 D multi 1.10 .55

No. 597 sold for 107t on day of issue.

Postal Wagon and Mail Box — A273

**2005, May 20**
**598** A273 107t multi 1.10 .55

Vesna, Goddess of Spring — A274

**2005, May 20** *Perf. 11¼x11¾*
**599** A274 180t multi 1.90 .95

**Painted Beehive Panel Type of 2004**
**2005, May 20** *Perf. 11¾x11¼*
**600** A250 221t Hunter and bird 2.25 1.10

Bishop Anton Jeglic and St. Stanislav's Institute A275

**2005, May 20**
**601** A275 221t multi 2.25 1.10

St. Stanislav's Institute, cent.

European Philatelic Cooperation, 50th Anniv. (in 2006) — A276

Magnifying glass and details from Slovenian stamps: No. 602, 60t, #495 (circus elephant). No. 603, 60t, #285 (ram), and stamp tongs. No. 604, 60t, #349 (river). #605, 60t, #195 (Jurij Vega).

**2005, May 20** *Perf. 14x13½*
**602-605** A276 Set of 4 2.50 1.25
*605a* Souvenir sheet, #602-605, perf. 14 2.50 1.25

**Fruit, Blossoms and Insects Type of 2000**

Designs: No. 606, Apricot blossom. No. 607, Apricots on branch. No. 608, San José scale on branch.

**2005, July 5** *Perf. 11¾x11¼*
**Size 19x23mm**

**606** A168 D multi 1.10 .55
**607** A168 D multi 1.10 .55
**608** A168 D multi 1.10 .55
*a.* Horiz. strip, #606-608 3.30 1.65

Nos. 606-608 each sold for 107t on day of issue.

**Orchids Type of 2004**

Designs: B, Dactylorhiza sambucina. D, Platanithera bifolia.

**2005, Sept. 23** *Perf. 11¾x11¼*
**Size: 37x26mm**

**609** A254 B multi .60 .30

**Souvenir Sheet**

**610** A254 D multi 1.10 .55

No. 609 sold for 57t and No. 610 sold for 107t on day of issue. No. 610 contains one 41x28mm stamp.

Dance of Death Fresco, by Janez of Kastav — A277

No. 611: a, Denomination in gray. b, Denomination in brown.
Illustration reduced.

**Litho. & Embossed**
**2005, Sept. 23** *Perf. 13½x13¾*
**611** A277 107t Horiz. pair, #a-b 2.25 1.10

Dogs
A278

Designs: A, Posavec hound. B, Istrian rough-coated hound. C, Slovenian mountain hound.
D, Istrian smooth-coated hound, vert.

**2005, Sept. 23** *Perf. 11¾x11¼*
**612-614** A278 Set of 3 2.00 1.00

**Souvenir Sheet**
*Perf. 11¼*

**615** A278 D multi 1.10 .55

On day of issue, No. 612 sold for 49t, No. 613, 57t, No. 614, 95t, and No. 615, 107t. No. 615 contains one 28x41mm stamp.

**Types of 1993 Redrawn**
**2005** **Litho.** *Perf. 11¼x11¾*
**Size: 26x36mm**

**616** A38 A Like #374 .55 .25
**617** A38 B Like #373 .65 .30
**618** A38 B Like #375 .65 .30
**619** A38 B Like #375A .65 .30
**620** A38 90t Like #216 1.00 .50
**621** A38 C Like #376 1.00 .50
**622** A38 D Like #378 1.25 .60
**623** A38 D Like #379 1.25 .60
*Nos. 616-623 (8)* 7.00 3.35

Issued: Nos. 616-617, 3/18; Nos. 618, 622, 4/2; Nos. 619-621, 623, 5/4. On day of issue No. 616 sold for 49t, Nos. 618-619 each sold for 57t, No. 621 sold for 95t, and Nos. 622-623 each sold for 107t.
Size of Nos. 216, 373-375, 375A, 376, 378-379: 25x34mm.

**Castles Type of 2000-04 Redrawn**
**2005** **Litho.** *Perf. 11¼x11¾*
**Size: 24x34mm**

**624** A167 1t Predjama .20 .20
**625** A167 1t Velenje .20 .20
*a.* Pair, #624-625 .20 .20
**626** A167 C Gewerkenegg 1.00 .50
**627** A167 100t Podsreda 1.10 .55
**628** A167 100t Bled 1.10 .55
*a.* Pair, #626-627 2.20 1.10
*Nos. 624-628 (5)* 3.60 2.00

Issued: Nos. 626, 4/2, others 5/4. No. 626 sold for 95t on day of issue.
Size of Nos. 400-401, 411B, 412-413: 23x32mm.

**Fruits, Blossoms and Insects Type of 2000 Redrawn**
**2005** **Litho.** *Perf. 11¾x11¼*
**Vignette Frame Size: 19x23mm**

**629** A168 5t Like #426 .20 .20
**630** A168 5t Like #427 .20 .20
**631** A168 5t Like #428 .20 .20
*a.* Strip of 3, #629-631 .20 .20
**632** A168 10t Like #416 .20 .20
**633** A168 10t Like #417 .20 .20
**634** A168 10t Like #418 .20 .20
*a.* Strip of 3, #632-634 .35 .20
**635** A168 A Like #568 .50 .25
**636** A168 A Like #569 .50 .25
**637** A168 A Like #570 .50 .25
*a.* Strip of 3, #635-637 1.50 .75
**638** A168 50t Like #464 .55 .25
**639** A168 50t Like #465 .55 .25
**640** A168 50t Like #466 .55 .25
*a.* Strip of 3, #638-640 1.65 .75
**641** A168 B Like #528 .60 .30
**642** A168 B Like #529 .60 .30
**643** A168 B Like #530 .60 .30
*a.* Strip of 3, #641-643 1.80 .90
**644** A168 150t Like #502 1.50 .75
**645** A168 150t Like #503 1.50 .75
**646** A168 150t Like #504 1.50 .75
*a.* Strip of 3, #644-646 4.50 2.25
*Nos. 629-646 (18)* 10.65 5.85

Issued: Nos. 629-631, 638-640, 5/4; Nos. 632-634, 4/2; Nos. 635-637, 7/22; Nos. 641-643, 6/30; Nos. 644-646, 7/5. On day of issue Nos. 635-637 each sold for 49t; Nos. 641-643 each sold for 57t.
Sizes of vignette frames of Nos. 426-428, 416-418, 568-570, 464-466, 528-530, and 502-504 vary from 19 to 20x26 to 26½mm. Some designs extend beyond vignette frames.

SLOVENIA

**2005, Nov. 18**    **Perf. 11¾x11¾**
647 A279 107t multi    1.10 .55

Slovenian Chairmanship of Organization for Security and Cooperation in Europe — A279

---

Traditional Foods — A280

**2005, Nov. 18**
648 A280 107t Pair, #a-b    2.10 1.10

No. 648: a, Prieska Gibanica and Ajdov Krapec. b, Prieska Tunka (bread, meat, lard and onion on wooden barrel).
Illustration reduced.

---

Christmas A281

**2005, Nov. 18**    **Perf. 11¾x11¾**
649 A281 A multi    .50 .25
650 A281 A multi    .50 .25
   a. Booklet pane of 12    6.00

**Size: 40x28mm**
**Serpentine Die Cut 7¼**
**Self-Adhesive**

Nos. 649-650 each sold for 49t on day of issue.

---

New Year's Day — A282

**2005, Nov. 18**    **Perf. 11¾x11¾**
651 A282 C multi    .95 .45
652 A282 C multi    .95 .45

**Size: 40x28mm**
**Serpentine Die Cut 7¼**
**Self-Adhesive**

   a. Booklet pane of 12    11.50

Nos. 651-652 each sold for 95t on day of issue.

---

Traditional Carinthian Clothing A283

**2006, Jan. 20**    **Perf. 14**
653 A283 A multi    .50 .25

No. 653 sold for 49t on day of issue.

---

Love A284

**2006, Jan. 20**    **Perf. 11**
654 A284 B multi    .60 .30

No. 654 sold for 57t on day of issue. Values are for stamps with surrounding selvage.

---

Dr. Anton Trstenjak (1906-96), Psychologist — A285

**2006, Jan. 20**    **Perf. 14**
655 A285 B multi    .60 .30

No. 655 sold for 57t on day of issue.

---

Ponikve Carnival — A286

**2006, Jan. 20**
656 A286 420t multi    4.25 2.10

---

2006 Winter Olympics, Turin — A287

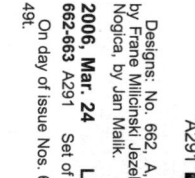

**2006, Jan. 20**
657 A287    2.10 1.10
   a. Horiz. pair, #a-b, + label at right

No. 657: a, 95t, Ski jumper. b, 107t, Snowboarder.
Printed in sheets containing 3 pairs and labels.

---

Pericnik Waterfall — A288

**2006, Mar. 24**
658 A288 D multi    1.10 .55

No. 658 sold for 107t on day of issue.

---

Pereiraea Gervaisi Fossil — A289

**2006, Mar. 24**
659 A289 D multi    1.10 .55

No. 659 sold for 107t on day of issue.

---

Butterflies A290

**2006, Mar. 24**
660 A290 B multi    .60 .30

**Souvenir Sheet**
**Perf. 14x14x13x14**
661 A290 D multi    1.10 .55

Designs: B, Erannis ankeraria. D, Erebia calcaria.
On day of issue No. 660 sold for 57t; No. 661 for 107t.

---

Children's Book Characters A291

Zvezdica Zaspanka: Frane Milčinski - Ježek

**2006, Mar. 24**    **Perf. 14**
662-663 A291    Set of 2    1.00 .50

Designs: No. 662, A, Zvezdica Zaspanka, by Frane Milicinski Jiezek. No. 663, A, Zogica Nogica, by Jan Malik.
On day of issue Nos. 662-663 each sold for 49t.

---

## POSTAL TAX STAMPS

Catalogue values for unused stamps in this section are for Never Hinged items.

---

Red Cross — PT1

**1992, May 8**    **Litho.**
RA1 PT1 3t blue, black & red    .50 .50

---

Red Cross — PT2

**1992, June 2**    **Perf. 14½x14**
RA2 PT2 3t multicolored    .30 .30

Red Cross, Solidarity.

---

**1992, Sept. 14**    **Litho.**
RA3 PT3 3t multicolored    .25 .25

Stop Smoking Week, Sept. 14-21.

---

Red Cross — PT4

**1993, May 8**    **Litho.**
RA4 PT4 3.50t blue, black & red    .20 .20

Rescue Team — PT5

**1993, June 1**    **Litho.**
RA5 PT5 3.50t multicolored    .20 .20

---

Anti-Smoking Campaign PT6

**1993, Sept. 14**    **Litho.**
RA6 PT6 4.50t multicolored    .20 .20

---

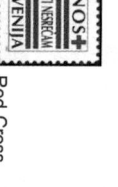

**1994, May 8**    **Litho.**
RA7 PT7 4.50t multicolored    .20 .20

Obligatory on mail May 8-15.

---

Red Cross Worker, Child — PT8

**1994, June 1**
RA8 PT8 4.50t multicolored    .20 .20

Obligatory on mail June 1-7.

---

PT9

Red Cross, Solidarity PT10

**1995, May 8** *Perf. 14*
RA9 PT9 6.50t multicolored   .20   .20
Obligatory on mail May 8-15.

**1995, June 1** *Perf. 14*
RA10 PT10 6.50t multicolored   .20   .20
Obligatory on mail June 1-7.

Red Cross, Solidarity — PT11

**1996, May 8** *Perf. 14*
RA11 PT11 7t multicolored   .20   .20
Obligatory on mail May 8-15.

Red Cross, Solidarity PT12

**1996, June 1** *Perf. 14*
RA12 PT12 7t multicolored   .20   .20
Obligatory on mail June 1-7.

Red Cross, Solidarity PT13

**1997, May 8** *Perf. 14*
RA13 PT13 7t multicolored   .20   .20
Obligatory on mail May 8-14.

Red Cross, Solidarity PT14

**1997, June 1** *Perf. 14*
RA14 PT14 7t multicolored   .20   .20
Obligatory on mail June 1-7.

PT15

**1998, May 8** *Perf. 14*
RA15 PT15 7t black & red   .20   .20
Obligatory on mail May 8-14.

Red Cross, Solidarity — PT16

**1998, June 1**
Design: No. RA16a, "7" at lower left. No. RA16b, "7" at upper right.
RA16 PT16 7t Pair, #a-b.   .20   .20
Obligatory on mail June 1-7.

Red Cross — PT17

**1999, May 8** *Perf. 14*
RA17 PT17 8t black & red   .20   .20
Obligatory on mail May 8-15.

**Solidarity Type of 1998**
a, 9t at LL. b, 9t at UR.

**1999, Nov. 1** *Perf. 14*
RA18 PT16 9t Pair, #a-b.   .20   .20
Obligatory on mail Nov. 1-7.

Red Cross — PT19

**2000, May 8** *Perf. 14*
RA19 PT19 10t blk & red   .20   .20
Obligatory on mail May 8-15.

**Red Cross Solidarity Type of 1998**
No. RA20: a, 10 at LL. b, 10 at UR.

**2000, Nov. 1** *Perf. 14*
RA20 PT16 10t Horiz. pair, #a-b   .20   .20
Obligatory on mail Nov. 1-7.

Red Cross — PT20

**2001, May 8**
RA21 PT20 12t multi   .20   .20
Obligatory on mail May 8-15.

Red Cross Solidarity Week — PT21

**2001, Nov. 1** *Perf. 14*
RA22 PT21 13t multi   .20   .20
Obligatory on mail Nov. 1-7.

Red Cross Week — PT22

**2002, May 8**
RA23 PT22 15t multi   .20   .20
Obligatory on mail May 8-15.

Red Cross Solidarity Week — PT23

**2002, Nov. 1**
RA24 PT23 15t multi   .20   .20
Obligatory on mail Nov. 1-7.

Red Cross Week — PT24

**2003, May 8** *Perf. 14*
RA25 PT24 19t multi   .20   .20

**Self-Adhesive**
*Imperf*
RA25A PT24 19t multi   .20   .20
Obligatory on mail May 8-15.

Red Cross — PT26

No. RA27: a, Blood droplet. b, Girl. c, Injured boy. d, Old woman. Illustration reduced.

**2004, May 8** *Perf. 14*
RA27 PT26 19t Block of 4, #a-d   .75   .40
Obligatory on mail May 8-15.

Red Cross Solidarity Week — PT27

No. RA28: a, Airplane dropping aid packages. b, House on fire. c, Aid packages landing on ground. d, Damaged building. Illustration reduced.

**2004, Nov. 1** *Perf. 14*
RA28 PT27 23t Block of 4, #a-d   1.00   .50
Obligatory on mail Nov. 1-7.

Red Cross Solidarity — PT29

No. RA30: a, House in flood. b, Flood gauge.

**2005, Nov. 1** *Perf. 14*
RA30 PT29 25t Horiz. pair, #a-b   .50   .25
Obligatory on mail Nov. 1-7.

# Vol. 5 Number Additions, Deletions & Changes

**Philippines**

| Number in 2006 Catalogue | Number in 2007 Catalogue |
|---|---|
| new | 24A |
| new | 27A |
| new | 2213a |
| new | 2218a |
| 2218A | 2218b |
| 2220a | 2218c |
| 2220 | 2220 |
| 2220 | 2220i |
| new | 2463B |
| new | 2466A |
| new | 2467A |
| new | 2468A |
| new | 2469A |
| new | 2545A |

**Qatar**

| Number in 2006 Catalogue | Number in 2007 Catalogue |
|---|---|
| 750 | 748 |
| 752 | 749 |
| 754 | 750 |
| 756 | 751 |
| 759 | 752 |
| 770 | 769 |
| 772 | 770 |
| 773 | 771 |
| 774 | 772 |
| 775 | 773 |
| 776 | 774 |

**Ruanda-Urundi**

| Number in 2006 Catalogue | Number in 2007 Catalogue |
|---|---|
| new | 7a |
| new | 14a |

**Russia**

| Number in 2006 Catalogue | Number in 2007 Catalogue |
|---|---|
| new | 5984a |
| 6016B | 6016Bc |
| new | 6016B |
| 6113 | 6112 |
| 6114 | 6113 |
| 6115 | 6114 |
| 6118 | 6115 |
| 6119 | 6116 |
| 6120 | 6117 |
| 6121 | 6118 |
| 6122 | 6119 |
| 6123 | 6120 |
| 6124 | 6121 |
| 6125 | 6122 |
| 6125A | 6123 |
| new | 6124 |
| new | C76Da |

**Singapore**

| Number in 2006 Catalogue | Number in 2007 Catalogue |
|---|---|
| new | 279a |
| new | 280a |
| new | 281a |

**Slovenia**

| Number in 2006 Catalogue | Number in 2007 Catalogue |
|---|---|
| 105 | 104 |
| 106 | 105 |
| 107 | 106 |
| 108 | 107 |
| 109 | 108 |
| 114 | 109 |
| 115 | 110 |
| 119 | 111 |
| 123 | 112 |
| 126 | 113 |
| 131 | 114 |
| 415A | 415B |

**Saar**

| Number in 2006 Catalogue | Number in 2007 Catalogue |
|---|---|
| O21 | deleted |
| new | O21b |
| O22 | deleted |
| new | O22b |
| O24 | deleted |
| new | O24b |
| O25 | deleted |
| new | O25b |

**St. Christopher**

| Number in 2006 Catalogue | Number in 2007 Catalogue |
|---|---|
| new | AR1-AR6 |

**St. Helena**

| Number in 2006 Catalogue | Number in 2007 Catalogue |
|---|---|
| new | 23c |

**St. Kitts-Nevis**

| Number in 2006 Catalogue | Number in 2007 Catalogue |
|---|---|
| 12 | deleted |
| new | 12a |
| 14 | deleted |
| new | 14a |
| 43 | deleted |
| new | 43a |

**Saudi Arabia**

| Number in 2006 Catalogue | Number in 2007 Catalogue |
|---|---|
| new | 872b |

# Illustrated Identifier

This section pictures stamps or parts of stamp designs that will help identify postage stamps that do not have English words on them.

Many of the symbols that identify stamps of countries are shown here as well as typical examples of their stamps.

See the Index and Identifier on the previous pages for stamps with inscriptions such as "sen," "posta," "Baja Porto," "Helvetia," "K.S.A.," etc.

*Linn's Stamp Identifier* is now available. The 144 pages include more 2,000 inscriptions and over 500 large stamp illustrations. Available from Linn's Stamp News, P.O. Box 29, Sidney, OH 45365-0029.

## 1. HEADS, PICTURES AND NUMERALS

### GREAT BRITAIN

Great Britain stamps never show the country name, but, except for postage dues, show a picture of the reigning monarch.

Victoria

Edward VII

George V

Edward VIII

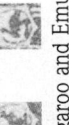

George VI

George VI

Elizabeth II

Some George VI and Elizabeth II stamps are surcharged in annas, new paisa or rupees. These are listed under Oman.

*Grandpa Dickson* 10P

Silhouette (sometimes facing right, generally at the top of stamp)

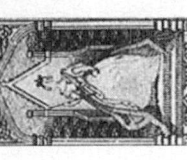

The Bicentennial of American Independence 1776-1976

*Benjamin Franklin* 11P

The silhouette indicates this is a British stamp. It is not a U.S. stamp.

### VICTORIA

Queen Victoria

### INDIA

Other stamps of India show this portrait of Queen Victoria and the words "Service" and "Annas."

### AUSTRIA

### YUGOSLAVIA

### BOSNIA & HERZEGOVINA

(Also BOSNIA & HERZEGOVINA if imperf.)

### HUNGARY

Denominations also appear in top corners instead of bottom corners.

Another stamp has posthorn facing left

### BRAZIL

### AUSTRALIA

Kangaroo and Emu

### GERMANY

Mecklenburg-Vorpommern

## SWITZERLAND

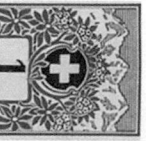   

## PALAU

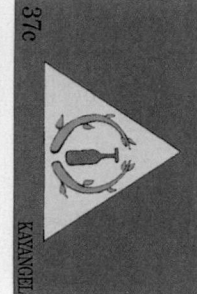

37c

KAYANGEL

# 2. ORIENTAL INSCRIPTIONS

## CHINA

中

Any stamp with this one character is from China (Imperial, Republic or People's Republic). This character appears in a four-character overprint on stamps of Manchukuo. These stamps are local provisionals, which are unlisted. Other overprinted Manchukuo stamps show this character, but have more than four characters in the overprints. These are listed in People's Republic of China.

 Some Chinese stamps show the Sun.

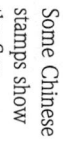

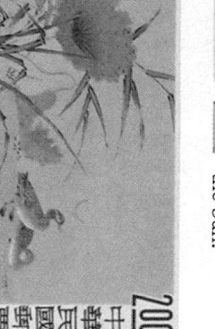

Most stamps of Republic of China show this series of characters.

中華民國郵票

Stamps with the China character and this character are from People's Republic of China. 人

## REPUBLIC OF CHINA
### Chinese stamps without China character

  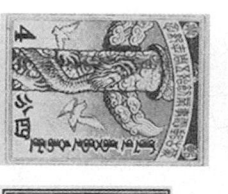 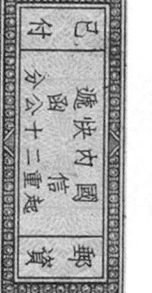  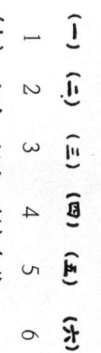 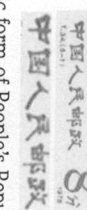 

Calligraphic form of People's Republic of China

| (一) | (二) | (三) | (四) | (五) | (六) |
|---|---|---|---|---|---|
| 1 | 2 | 3 | 4 | 5 | 6 |
| (七) | (八) | (九) | (十) | (十一) | (十二) |
| 7 | 8 | 9 | 10 | 11 | 12 |

## PEOPLE'S REPUBLIC OF CHINA

## PHILIPPINES (Japanese Occupation)

比島郵便 — Country Name

## NORTH BORNEO (Japanese Occupation)

大日本帝国郵便 — Indicates Japanese Occupation

北ボルネオ — Country Name

## MALAYA (Japanese Occupation)

大日本帝国郵便 — Indicates Japanese Occupation

マライ — Country Name

## BURMA
### Union of Myanmar

## Union of Myanmar (Japanese Occupation)

大日本帝国郵便 — Indicates Japanese Occupation

シャン — Country Name

國滿洲帝 — The last 3 characters are common to other Manchukuo stamps.

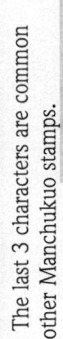

Manchukuo stamp without these elements

Orchid Crest

## JAPAN

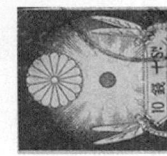

日本郵便 — Country Name

Chrysanthemum Crest

Japanese stamps without these elements

The number of characters in the center and the design of dragons on the sides will vary.

## RYUKYU ISLANDS

琉球郵便 — Country Name

## MANCHUKUO

Mao Tse-tung

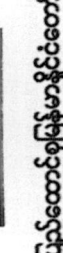

Emperor Pu-Yi

Temple

The first 3 characters are common to many Manchukuo stamps.

Other Burma Japanese Occupation stamps without these elements

## KOREA

Burmese Script

These two characters, in any order, are common to stamps from the Republic of Korea (South Korea) or of the People's Democratic Republic of Korea (North Korea).

This series of four characters can be found on the stamps of both Koreas. Most stamps of the Democratic People's Republic of Korea (North Korea) have just this inscription.

Indicates Republic of Korea (South Korea)

South Korean postage stamps issued after 1952 do not show currency expressed in Latin letters. Stamps with "HW," "HWAN," "WON," "WN," "W" or "W" with two lines through it, if not illustrated in listings of stamps before this date, are revenues. North Korean postage stamps do not have currency expressed in Latin letters.

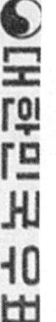

## THAILAND

Yin Yang appears on some stamps.

Country Name

King Chulalongkorn

King Prajadhipok and Chao P'ya Chakri

## 3. CENTRAL AND EASTERN ASIAN INSCRIPTIONS

### INDIA - FEUDATORY STATES

#### Alwar

#### Bhor

#### Bundi

Similar stamps come with different designs in corners and differently drawn daggers (at center of circle).

#### Dhar

#### Faridkot

#### Hyderabad

Similar stamps exist with straight line frame around stamp, and also with different central design which is inscribed "Postage" or "Post & Receipt."

#### Indore

#### Jhalawar

A similar stamp has the central figure in an oval.

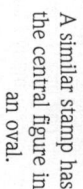

## ARMENIA

Country Name

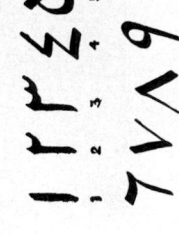

The four characters are found somewhere on pictorial stamps. On some stamps only the middle two are found.

## 4. AFRICAN INSCRIPTIONS

### ETHIOPIA

## 5. ARABIC INSCRIPTIONS

١ ٢ ٣ ٤ ٥
١ ٢ ٣ ٤ ٥
٦ ٧ ٨ ٩ ٠

## NEPAL

Similar stamps are smaller, have squares in upper corners and have five or nine characters in central bottom panel.

## ISRAEL

## TANNU TUVA

## GEORGIA

This inscription is found on other pictorial stamps.

## Nandgaon

## Nowanuggur

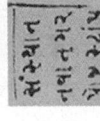

## Poonch

Similar stamps exist in various sizes

## Soruth

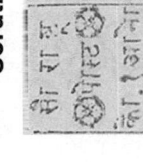

## Rajpeepla

## BANGLADESH

Country Name

## AFGHANISTAN

Many early Afghanistan stamps show Tiger's head, many of these have ornaments protruding from outer ring, others show inscriptions in black.

Arabic Script

Mosque Gate & Crossed Cannons
The four characters are found somewhere on pictorial stamps. On some stamps only the middle two are found.

## EGYPT

POSTAGE
M
20
OM KOLTHOUM
L. ELSAWAF
P.P.M. CAIRO
A.R. EGYPT
1975

15

Postage

## BAHRAIN

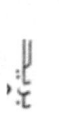

# LIBYA

Country Name in various styles

Other Libya stamps show Eagle and Shield (head facing either direction) or Red, White and Black Shield (with or without eagle in center).

## SAUDI ARABIA

Without Country Name

---

Symbol

## IRAQ

## JORDAN

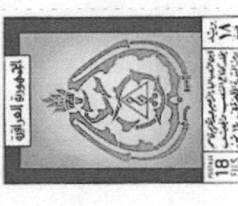

## LEBANON

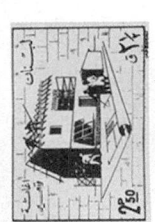

Similar types have denominations at top and slightly different design.

---

# INDIA - FEUDATORY STATES

## Jammu & Kashmir

Text and thickness of ovals vary. Some stamps have flower devices in corners.

## India-Hyderabad

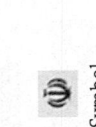

## IRAN

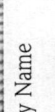
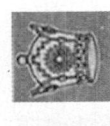

Country Name

Royal Crown

Lion with Sword

**SYRIA**

Palm Tree and Swords

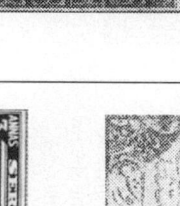

Tughra (Central design)

**PAKISTAN - BAHAWALPUR**

Country Name in top panel, star and crescent

**TURKEY**

Star & Crescent is a device found on many Turkish stamps, but is also found on stamps from other Arabic areas (see Pakistan-Bahawalpur)

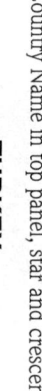

**PAKISTAN**

**THRACE**

**YEMEN**

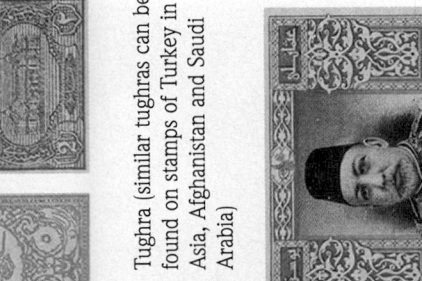

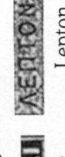
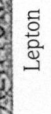

Other forms of Country Name

No country name

**CRETE**

Country Name

**TURKEY IN ASIA**

Tughra (similar tughras can be found on stamps of Turkey in Asia, Afghanistan and Saudi Arabia)

Mohammed V

Mustafa Kemal

Plane, Star and Crescent

Other Turkey in Asia pictorials show star & crescent.

Other stamps show tughra shown under Turkey.

**6. GREEK INSCRIPTIONS**

**GREECE**

Country Name in various styles
(Some Crete stamps overprinted with the Greece country name are listed in Crete.)

Lepta

Lepton

ΔΡΑΧΜΗ Drachma

ΔΡΑΧΜΑΙ Drachmas

ΛΕΠΤΟΝ Lepton

Abbreviated Country Name

# 7. CYRILLIC INSCRIPTIONS

These words are on other stamps

Crete stamps with a surcharge that have the year "1922" are listed under Greece.

Grosion

**EPIRUS**

**IONIAN IS.**

Country Name

**RUSSIA**

Postage Stamp

Imperial Eagle

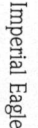

**почта** Russian

почта

*почта* Postage in various styles

**Почта**

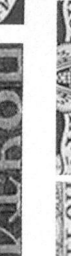

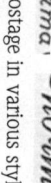

**коп** Abbreviation for Kopeck

**руб** Abbreviation for Ruble

**россія** Russian

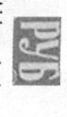

---

Abbreviation for Russian Soviet Federated Socialist Republic RSFSR stamps were overprinted (see below)

Abbreviation for Union of Soviet Socialist Republics

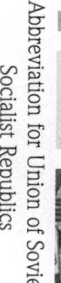

**RUSSIA - Army of the North**

This item is footnoted in Latvia

**RUSSIA - Wenden**

"OKCA"

---

## RUSSIAN OFFICES IN THE TURKISH EMPIRE

These letters appear on other stamps of the Russian offices.

The unoverprinted version of this stamp and a similar stamp were overprinted by various countries (see below).

**ARMENIA**

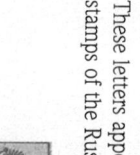

**BELARUS**

Country Name

**FAR EASTERN REPUBLIC**

## UKRAINE

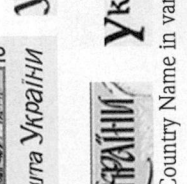

*Пошта України*

*Украї́ни*

*Украї́ни* A. БЕНДЕР

*Украïни*

Country Name in various forms

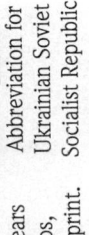

**VC PP**

Abbreviation for Ukrainian Soviet Socialist Republic

The trident appears on many stamps, usually as an overprint.

## WESTERN UKRAINE

Abbreviation for Country Name

## AZERBAIJAN

## AZƏRBAYCAN

Country Name

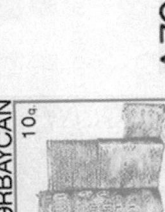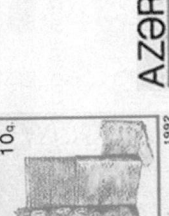

---

## TRANSCAUCASIAN FEDERATED REPUBLICS

**З.С.Ф.С.Р.**

Abbreviation for Country Name

## KAZAKHSTAN

## КАЗАКСТАН

Country Name

## KYRGYZSTAN

## КЫРГЫЗСТАН

Country Name

## ROMANIA

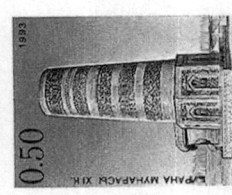

## TADJIKISTAN

**Тоҷикистон**

**Тадж.**

Country Name & Abbreviation

---

## SOUTH RUSSIA

Country Name

## FINLAND

Circles and Dots on stamps similar to Imperial Russia issues

## BATUM

Forms of Country Name

**А.С.С.Р.**
Abbreviation for Azerbaijan
Soviet Socialist Republic

**MONTENEGRO**

**ЦРНА ГОРА**

Country Name in various forms

**ПРΙΟΡΕ**
Abbreviation
for country
name

No country name
(A similar Montenegro
stamp without country
name has same vignette.)

**SERBIA**

**СРБИЈА**

Country Name in various forms

Abbreviation for country name

---

No country name

**SERBIA & MONTENEGRO**

**YUGOSLAVIA**

Showing country name

**ЈУГОСЛАВИЈА**

**MACEDONIA**

No Country Name

**МАКЕДОНИЈА**

Country Name

---

**BOSNIA & HERZEGOVINA
(Serb Administration)**

Different form of Country Name

**МАКЕДОНСКИ**
Different form of Country Name

**РЕПУБЛИКА СРПСКА**

Country Name

**РЕПУБЛИКЕ СРПСКЕ**
Different form of Country Name

No Country Name

Mung
in Mongolian

Tugrik
in Mongolian

No Country Name

Arms

No country name

Abbreviation for
Lev, leva

**MONGOLIA**

Country name in
one word

тθгрθг
Tugrik in Cyrillic

мθнгθ
Mung in Cyrillic

Country name in
two words

**BULGARIA**

Country Name

Postage

Stotinka

Stotinki (plural)

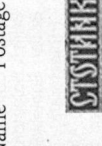

Abbreviation for
Stotinki

Country Name in various forms and styles

НР България

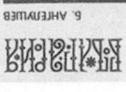

**INDEX AND IDENTIFIER**

All page numbers shown are those in this Volume 5.

Postage stamps that do not have English words on them are shown in the Identifier which begins on page 1135.

# Scottmounts

For stamp presentation unequaled in beauty and clarity, insist on ScottMounts. Made of 100% inert polystyrol foil, ScottMounts protect your stamps from the harmful effects of dust and moisture. Available in your choice of clear or black backs, ScottMounts are center-split across the back for easy insertion of stamps and feature crystal clear mount faces. Double layers of gum assure stay-put bonding on the album page. Discover the quality and value ScottMounts have to offer. ScottMounts are available from your favorite stamp dealer or direct from:

Discover the quality and value ScottMounts have to offer. For a complete list of ScottMount sizes call or write Scott Publishing Co.

**SCOTT®**

Scott Publishing Co.
1-800-572-6885
P.O. Box 828 Sidney OH 45365-0828
www.amosadvantage.com

**AMOS**
HOBBY PUBLISHING

Publishers of:
Coin World, Linn's Stamp News and Scott Publishing Co.

# Pronunciation Symbols

ə .... banana, collide, abut

ˈə, ˌə .... humdrum, abut

ə .... immediately preceding \l\, \n\, \m\, \ŋ\, as in battle, mitten, eaten, and sometimes open \ˈō-pᵊm\, lock and key \ˈläk-ᵊn-; immediately following \l\, \m\, \r\, as often in French table, prisme, titre

ər .... further, merger, bird

ˈər-  
ˌə-r } .... as in two different pronunciations of hurry \ˈhər-ē, ˈhə-rē\

a .... mat, map, mad, gag, snap, patch

ā .... day, fade, date, aorta, drape, cape

ä .... bother, cot, and, with most American speakers, father, car

à .... father as pronounced by speakers who do not rhyme it with bother; French patte

aù .... now, loud, out

b .... baby, rib

ch .... chin, nature \ˈnā-chər\

d .... did, adder

e .... bet, bed, peck

ˈē, ˌē .... beat, nosebleed, evenly, easy

ē .... easy, mealy

f .... fifty, cuff

g .... go, big, gift

h .... hat, ahead

hw .... whale as pronounced by those who do not have the same pronunciation for both whale and wail

i .... tip, banish, active

ī .... site, side, buy, tripe

j .... job, gem, edge, join, judge

k .... kin, cook, ache

k̲ .... German ich, Buch; one pronunciation of loch

l .... lily, pool

m .... murmur, dim, nymph

n .... no, own

n .... indicates that a preceding vowel or diphthong is pronounced with the nasal passages open, as in French un bon vin blanc \œⁿ-bōⁿ-vaⁿ-bläⁿ\

ŋ .... sing \ˈsiŋ\, singer \ˈsiŋ-ər\, finger \ˈfiŋ-gər\, ink \ˈiŋk\

ō .... bone, know, beau

ȯ .... saw, all, gnaw, caught

œ .... French boeuf, German Hölle

œ̄ .... French feu, German Höhle

ȯi .... coin, destroy

p .... pepper, lip

r .... red, car, rarity

s .... source, less

sh .... as in shy, mission, machine, special (actually, this is a single sound, not two); with a hyphen between, two sounds as in grasshopper \ˈgras-ˌhä-pər\

t .... tie, attack, late, later, latter

th .... as in thin, ether (actually, this is a single sound, not two); with a hyphen between, two sounds as in knighthood \ˈnīt-ˌhud\

th .... then, either, this (actually, this is a single sound, not two)

ü .... rule, youth, union \ˈyün-yən\, few \ˈfyü\

u̇ .... pull, wood, book, curable \ˈkyu̇r-ə-bəl\, fury \ˈfyu̇r-ē\

ᵫ .... German füllen, hübsch

ᵫ̄ .... French rue, German fühlen

v .... vivid, give

w .... we, away

y .... yard, young, cue \ˈkyü\, mute \ˈmyüt\, union \ˈyün-yən\

y .... indicates that during the articulation of the sound represented by the preceding character the front of the tongue has substantially the position it has for the articulation of the first sound of yard, as in French digne \dēnʸ\

z .... zone, raise

zh .... as in vision, azure \ˈa-zhər\ (actually, this is a single sound, not two); with a hyphen between, two sounds as in hogshead \ˈhȯgz-ˌhed, ˈhägz-\

\ .... slant line used in pairs to mark the beginning and end of a transcription: \ˈpen\

ˈ .... mark preceding a syllable with primary (strongest) stress: \ˈpen-mən-ˌship\

ˌ .... mark preceding a syllable with secondary (medium) stress: \ˈpen-mən-ˌship\

- .... mark of syllable division

( ) .... indicate that what is symbolized between is present in some utterances but not in others: factory \ˈfak-t(ə-)rē\

÷ .... indicates that many regard as unacceptable the pronunciation variant immediately following: cupola \ˈkyü-pə-lə, ÷-ˌlō\

# value priced **stockbooks**

Stockbooks are a classic and convenient storage alternative for many collectors. These German-made stockbooks feature heavyweight archival quality paper with 9 pockets on each page. The 8½" x 11⅝" pages are bound inside a handsome leatherette grain cover and include glassine interleaving between the pages for added protection. The Value Priced Stockbooks are available in two page styles, the white page stockbooks feature glassine pockets while the black page stockbooks feature glassine pockets while the black page variety includes clear acetate pockets

## BLACK PAGE STOCKBOOKS ACETATE POCKETS

| ITEM | COLOR | PAGES | RETAIL |
|---|---|---|---|
| ST16RD | Red | 16 pages | $10.95 |
| ST16GR | Croon | 16 pages | $10.95 |
| ST16BL | Blue | 16 pages | $10.95 |
| ST16RK | Black | 16 pages | $10.95 |
| ST32RD | Red | 32 pages | $16.95 |
| ST32GR | Green | 32 pages | $16.95 |
| ST32BL | Blue | 32 pages | $16.95 |
| ST32BK | Black | 32 pages | $16.95 |
| ST64RD | Red | 64 pages | $29.95 |
| ST64GR | Green | 64 pages | $29.95 |
| ST64BL | Blue | 64 pages | $29.95 |
| ST64BK | Black | 64 pages | $29.95 |

## WHITE PAGE STOCKBOOKS GLASSINE POCKETS

| ITEM | DESCRIPTION | | RETAIL |
|---|---|---|---|
| SW16BL | Blue | 16 pages | $6.95 |
| SW16GR | Green | 16 pages | $6.95 |
| SW16RD | Red | 16 pages | $6.95 |

Scott Value Priced Stockbooks are available from your favorite dealer or direct from:

**SCOTT**®

**AMOS** HOBBY PUBLISHING

P.O. Box 828
Sidney OH 45365-0828
www.amosadvantage.com
1-800-572-6885

# INDEX TO ADVERTISERS 2007 VOLUME 5

# 2007
# VOLUME 5
# DEALER DIRECTORY
# YELLOW PAGE LISTINGS

This section of your Scott Catalogue contains advertisements to help you conveniently find what you need, when you need it...!

## Accessories

**BROOKLYN GALLERY COIN & STAMP, INC.**
8725 4th Ave.
Brooklyn, NY 11209
PH: 718-745-5701
FAX: 718-745-2775
info@brooklyngallery.com
www.brooklyngallery.com

## Albums

**THE KEEPING ROOM**
PO Box 257
Trumbull, CT 06611
PH: 203-372-8436

## Asia

**MICHAEL ROGERS, INC.**
Mailing Address:
336 Grove Ave.
Suite B
Winter Park, FL 32789-3602
Walk-in Address:
Ranch Mall
325 S. Orlando Ave.
Suite 14
Winter Park, FL 32789-3608
PH: 407-644-2290
PH: 800-843-3751
FAX: 407-645-4434
Stamps@michaelrogersinc.com
www.michaelrogersinc.com

## Auctions

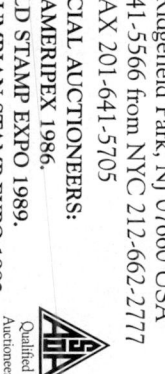

**JACQUES C. SCHIFF, JR., INC.**
195 Main St.
Ridgefield Park, NJ 07660
PH: 201-641-5566
From NYC: PH: 212-662-2777
FAX: 201-641-5705

## Auctions

**R. MARESCH & SON LTD.**
5th Floor - 6075 Yonge St.
Toronto, ON M2M 3W2
CANADA
PH: 416-363-7777
FAX: 416-363-6511
www.maresch.com

**THE STAMP CENTER**
**DUTCH COUNTRY AUCTIONS**
4115 Concord Pike
Wilmington, DE 19803
PH: 302-478-8740
FAX: 302-478-8779
scdca@dol.net
www.thestampcenter.com

## Auctions - Public

**ALAN BLAIR STAMPS/ AUCTIONS**
5405 Lakeside Ave.
Suite 1
Richmond, VA 23228
PH/FAX: 800-689-5602
alanblair@prodigy.net

## Austria

**JOSEPH EDER**
PO Box 185529
Hamden, CT 06518
PH: 203-281-0742
FAX: 203-230-2410
j.eder@worldnet.att.net
www.ederstamps.com

## British Commonwealth

## British Commonwealth

**ARON R. HALBERSTAM PHILATELISTS, LTD.**
PO Box 150168
Van Brunt Station
Brooklyn, NY 11215-0168
PH: 718-788-3978
PH: 718-788-3099
arh@arhstamps.com
www.arhstamps.com

**EMPIRE STAMP CO.**
PO Box 8337
Calabasa, CA 91372-8337
PH: 800-616-7278
PH: 818-225-1181
FAX: 818-225-1182
info@empirestamps.com
www.empirestamps.com

## Central America

**GUY SHAW**
PO Box 10025
Bakersfield, CA 93389
PH/FAX: 661-834-7135
guyshaw@guyshaw.com
www.guyshaw.com

## China

**MICHAEL ROGERS, INC.**
Mailing Address:
336 Grove Ave.
Suite B
Winter Park, FL 32789-3602
Walk-in Address:
Ranch Mall
325 S. Orlando Ave.
Suite 14
Winter Park, FL 32789-3608
PH: 407-644-2290
PH: 800-843-3751
FAX: 407-645-4434
Stamps@michaelrogersinc.com
www.michaelrogersinc.com

## Collections

**HENRY GITNER PHILATEL-ISTS, INC.**
PO Box 3077-S
Middletown, NY 10940
PH: 845-343-5151
PH: 800-947-8267
FAX: 845-343-0068
hgitner@hgitner.com
www.hgitner.com

## Ducks

**MICHAEL JAFFE**
PO Box 61484
Vancouver, WA 98666
PH: 360-695-6161
PH: 800-782-6770
FAX: 360-695-1616
mjaffe@brookmanstamps.com
www.brookmanstamps.com

## Europe

**WWW.WORLDSTAMPS.COM**
242 West Saddle River Road
Suite C
Upper Saddle River, NJ 07458
PH: 201-236-8122
FAX: 201-236-8133
by mail:
Frank Geiger Philatelists
info@WorldStamps.com
www.WorldStamps.com

## Europe-Western

**CURTIS GIDDING STAMP STORE**
2003 Sunview Dr.
Suite 101
Champaign, IL 61821
PH: 217-359-4017
curtstamp@aol.com
www.stores.ebay.com/curtisgiddingstampstore

## France

**JOSEPH EDER**
PO Box 185529
Hamden, CT 06518
PH: 203-281-0742
FAX: 203-230-2410
j.eder@worldnet.att.net
www.ederstamps.com

## German Colonies

**COLONIAL STAMP COMPANY**
$1 million photo price list,
$5.00
(refundable against purchase)
5757 Wilshire Blvd. PH #8
Los Angeles, CA 90036
PH: 323-933-9435
FAX: 323-939-9930
Toll Free in North America
PH: 877-272-6693
FAX: 877-272-6694
info@colonialstampcompany.com
www.colonialstampcompany.com

## German Occupation

**JOSEPH EDER**
PO Box 185529
Hamden, CT 06518
PH: 203-281-0742
FAX: 203-230-2410
j.eder@worldnet.att.net
www.ederstamps.com

## Germany

**JOSEPH EDER**
PO Box 185529
Hamden, CT 06518
PH: 203-281-0742
FAX: 203-230-2410
j.eder@worldnet.att.net
www.ederstamps.com

## Germany-Third Reich

**JOSEPH EDER**
PO Box 185529
Hamden, CT 06518
PH: 203-281-0742
FAX: 203-230-2410
j.eder@worldnet.att.net
www.ederstamps.com

## Great Britain

**COLONIAL STAMP COMPANY**
5757 Wilshire Blvd. PH #8
Los Angeles, CA 90036
PH: 323-933-9435
FAX: 323-939-9930
Toll Free in North America
PH: 877-272-6693
FAX: 877-272-6694
info@colonialstampcompany.com
www.colonialstampcompany.com

## Insurance

**COLLECTIBLES INSURANCE AGENCY**
PO Box 1200 SSC
Westminster, MD 21158
PH: 888-837-9537
FAX: 410-876-9233
info@insurecollectibles.com
www.collectinsure.com

## Japan

**MICHAEL ROGERS, INC.**
Mailing Address:
336 Grove Ave.
Suite B
Winter Park, FL 32789-3602
Walk-in Address:
Ranch Mall
325 S. Orlando Ave.
Suite 14
Winter Park, FL 32789 3608
PH: 407-644-2290
PH: 800-843-3751
FAX: 407-645-4434
Stamps@michaelrogersinc.com
www.michaelrogersinc.com

## Korea

**MICHAEL ROGERS, INC.**
Mailing Address:
336 Grove Ave.
Suite B
Winter Park, FL 32789-3602
Walk-in Address:
Ranch Mall
325 S. Orlando Ave.
Suite 14
Winter Park, FL 32789-3608
PH: 407-644-2290
PH: 800-843-3751
FAX: 407-645-4434
Stamps@michaelrogersinc.com
www.michaelrogersinc.com

## Latin America

**GUY SHAW**
PO Box 10025
Bakersfield, CA 93389
PH/FAX: 661-834-7135
guyshaw@guyshaw.com
www.guyshaw.com

## Manchukuo

**MICHAEL ROGERS, INC.**
Mailing Address:
336 Grove Ave.
Suite B
Winter Park, FL 32789-3602
Walk-in Address:
Ranch Mall
325 S. Orlando Ave.
Suite 14
Winter Park, FL 32789-3608
PH: 407-644-2290
PH: 800-843-3751
FAX: 407-645-4434
Stamps@michaelrogersinc.com
www.michaelrogersinc.com

## New Issues

**DAVIDSON'S STAMP SERVICE**
PO Box 36355
Indianapolis, IN 46236-0355
PH: 317-826-2620
davidson@in.net
www.newstampissues.com

## New Issues-Wholesale

**BOMBAY PHILATELIC INC.**
PO Box 480009
Delray Beach, FL 33448
PH: 561-499-7990
FAX: 561-499-7553
sales@bombaystamps.com
www.bombaystamps.com

## Papua New Guinea

**COLONIAL STAMP COMPANY**
5757 Wilshire Blvd. PH #8
Los Angeles, CA 90036
PH: 323-933-9435
FAX: 323-939-9930
Toll Free in North America
PH: 877-272-6693
FAX: 877-272-6694
info@colonialstampcompany.com
www.colonialstampcompany.com

## Poland

**HENRY GITNER PHILATEL-ISTS, INC.**
PO Box 3077-S
Middletown, NY 10940
PH: 845-343-5151
PH: 800-947-8267
FAX: 845-343-0068
hgitner@hgitner.com
www.hgitner.com

**WWW.WORLDSTAMPS.COM**
242 West Saddle River Road
Suite C
Upper Saddle River, NJ 07458
PH: 201-236-8122
FAX: 201-236-8133
by mail:
Frank Geiger Philatelists
info@WorldStamps.com
www.WorldStamps.com

## Portugal & Colonies

**AMEEN STAMPS**
8831 Long Point Road
Suite 201
Houston, TX 77055
PH: 713-468-0644
FAX: 713-468-2420
rameen@ev1.net or
rameen03@sbcglobal.net

## Proofs & Essays

**HENRY GITNER PHILATEL-ISTS, INC.**
PO Box 3077-S
Middletown, NY 10940
PH: 845-343-5151
PH: 800-947-8267
FAX: 845-343-0068
hgitner@hgitner.com
www.hgitner.com

## Rhodesia

**COLONIAL STAMP COMPANY**
5757 Wilshire Blvd. PH #8
Los Angeles, CA 90036
PH: 323-933-9435
FAX: 323-939-9930
Toll Free in North America
PH: 877-272-6693
FAX: 877-272-6694
info@colonialstampcompany.com
www.colonialstampcompany.com

## Russia

**AMEEN STAMPS**
8831 Long Point Road
Suite 204
Houston, TX 77055
PH: 713-468-0644
FAX: 713-468-2420
rameen@ev1.net or
rameen03@sbcglobal.net

**WWW.WORLDSTAMPS.COM**
242 West Saddle River Road
Suite C
Upper Saddle River, NJ 07458
PH: 201-236-8122
FAX: 201-236-8133
by mail:
Frank Geiger Philatelists
info@WorldStamps.com
www.WorldStamps.com

## Ryukyus

**HENRY GITNER PHILATEL-ISTS, INC.**
PO Box 3077-S
Middletown, NY 10940
PH: 845-343-5151
PH: 800-947-8267
FAX: 845-343-0068
hgitner@hgitner.com
www.hgitner.com

## St. Christopher

**COLONIAL STAMP COMPANY**
5757 Wilshire Blvd. PH #8
Los Angeles, CA 90036
PH: 323-933-9435
FAX: 323-939-9930
Toll Free in North America
PH: 877-272-6693
FAX: 877-272-6694
info@colonialstampcompany.com
www.colonialstampcompany.com

## St. Helena

**COLONIAL STAMP COMPANY**
5757 Wilshire Blvd. PH #8
Los Angeles, CA 90036
PH: 323-933-9435
FAX: 323-939-9930
Toll Free in North America
PH: 877-272-6693
FAX: 877-272-6694
info@colonialstampcompany.com
www.colonialstampcompany.com

## St. Kitts & Nevis

**COLONIAL STAMP COMPANY**
5757 Wilshire Blvd. PH #8
Los Angeles, CA 90036
PH: 323-933-9435
FAX: 323-939-9930
Toll Free in North America
PH: 877-272-6693
FAX: 877-272-6694
info@colonialstampcompany.com
www.colonialstampcompany.com

## St. Lucia

**COLONIAL STAMP COMPANY**
5757 Wilshire Blvd. PH #8
Los Angeles, CA 90036
PH: 323-933-9435
FAX: 323-939-9930
Toll Free in North America
PH: 877-272-6693
FAX: 877-272-6694
info@colonialstampcompany.com
www.colonialstampcompany.com

## St. Vincent

**COLONIAL STAMP COMPANY**
5757 Wilshire Blvd. PH #8
Los Angeles, CA 90036
PH: 323-933-9435
FAX: 323-939-9930
Toll Free in North America
PH: 877-272-6693
FAX: 877-272-6694
info@colonialstampcompany.com
www.colonialstampcompany.com

## Samoa

**COLONIAL STAMP COMPANY**
5757 Wilshire Blvd. PH #8
Los Angeles, CA 90036
PH: 323-933-9435
FAX: 323-939-9930
Toll Free in North America
PH: 877-272-6693
FAX: 877-272-6694
info@colonialstampcompany.com
www.colonialstampcompany.com

## Sarawak

**COLONIAL STAMP COMPANY**
5757 Wilshire Blvd. PH #8
Los Angeles, CA 90036
PH: 323-933-9435
FAX: 323-939-9930
Toll Free in North America
PH: 877-272-6693
FAX: 877-272-6694
info@colonialstampcompany.com
www.colonialstampcompany.com

## Seychelles

**COLONIAL STAMP COMPANY**
5757 Wilshire Blvd. PH #8
Los Angeles, CA 90036
PH: 323-933-9435
FAX: 323-939-9930
Toll Free in North America
PH: 877-272-6693
FAX: 877-272-6694
info@colonialstampcompany.com
www.colonialstampcompany.com

## Sierra Leone

**COLONIAL STAMP COMPANY**
5757 Wilshire Blvd. PH #8
Los Angeles, CA 90036
PH: 323-933-9435
FAX: 323-939-9930
Toll Free in North America
PH: 877-272-6693
FAX: 877-272-6694
info@colonialstampcompany.com
www.colonialstampcompany.com

## South America

**AMEEN STAMPS**
8831 Long Point Road
Suite 204
Houston, TX 77055
PH: 713-468-0644
FAX: 713-468-2420
rameen@ev1.net or
rameen03@sbcglobal.net

**WWW.WORLDSTAMPS.COM**
242 West Saddle River Road
Suite C
Upper Saddle River, NJ 07458
PH: 201-236-8122
FAX: 201-236-8133
by mail:
Frank Geiger Philatelists
info@WorldStamps.com
www.WorldStamps.com

**GUY SHAW**
PO Box 10025
Bakersfield, CA 93389
PH/FAX: 661-834-7135
guyshaw@guyshaw.com
www.guyshaw.com

## STAMP STORES

## Arizona

**B.J.'S STAMPS**
Barbara J. Johnson
6342 W. Bell Road
Glendale, AZ 85308
PH: 623-878-2080
FAX: 623-412-3456
info@bjstamps.com
www.bjstamps.com

## California

**BROSIUS STAMP & COIN**
2105 Main St.
Santa Monica, CA 90405
PH: 310-396-7480
FAX: 310-396-7455

**COLONIAL STAMP CO./ BRITISH EMPIRE SPECIALIST**
(by appt.)
5757 Wilshire Blvd. PH #8
Los Angeles, CA 90036
PH: 323-933-9435
FAX: 323-939-9930
Toll Free in North America
PH: 877-272-6693
FAX: 877-272-6694
info@colonialstampcompany.com
www.colonialstampcompany.com

**FISCHER-WOLK PHILATELICS**
24771 "G" Alicia Parkway
Laguna Hills, CA 92653
PH: 949-837-2932
fischerwolk@earthlink.net

**NATICK STAMPS & HOBBIES**
405 S. Myrtle Ave.
Monrovia, CA 91016
PH: 626-305-7333
natickco@earthlink.net

# STAMP STORES

## California

**STANLEY M. PILLER & ASSOCIATES**
(HOURS BY APPT. ONLY)
800 S. Broadway
Suite 201
Walnut Creek, CA 94596
PH: 925-938-8290
FAX: 925-938-8812
stmpdlr@aol.com
www.smpiller.com

## Colorado

**ACKLEY'S ROCKS & STAMPS**
3230 N. Stone Ave.
Colorado Springs, CO 80907
PH: 719-633-1153
ackl9@aol.com

**SHOWCASE STAMPS**
3865 Wadsworth
Wheat Ridge, CO 80033
PH: 303-425-9252
kbeiner@colbi.net
www.showcasestamps.com

## Connecticut

**SILVER CITY COIN & STAMP**
41 Colony Street
Meriden, CT 06451
PH: 203-235-7634
FAX: 203-237-4915

## Florida

**R.D.C. STAMPS**
7,381 SW 24th St.
Miami, FL 33155-1402
PH: 305-264-4213
FAX: 305-262-2919
rdcstamps@aol.com

**WINTER PARK STAMP SHOP**
Ranch Mall (17-92)
325 S. Orlando Ave.
Suite 11
Winter Park, FL 32789-3608
PH: 407-628-1120
PH: 800-845-1819
FAX: 407-628-0091
stamps@winterparkstampshop.com
www.winterparkstampshop.com

## Georgia

**STAMPS UNLIMITED OF GEORGIA, INC.**
133 Carnegie Way
Room 250
Atlanta, GA 30303
PH: 404-688-9161

## Illinois

**DR. ROBERT FRIEDMAN & SONS**
2029 W. 75th St.
Woodridge, IL 60517
PH: 800-588-8100
FAX: 630-985-1588
drbobstamps@yahoo.com
www.drbobfriedmanstamps.com

## Indiana

**KNIGHT STAMP & COIN CO.**
237 Main St.
Hobart, IN 46342
PH: 219-942-4341
PH: 800-634-2646
knight@knightcoin.com
www.knightcoin.com

## Massachusetts

**KAPPY'S COINS & STAMPS**
534 Washington St.
Norwood, MA 02062
PH: 781-762-5552
FAX: 781-762-3292
kappyscoins@aol.com

## Maryland

**BULLDOG STAMP COMPANY**
4641 Montgomery Ave.
Bethesda, MD 20814
PH: 301-654-1138

## Michigan

**THE MOUSE AND SUCH**
696 N. Mill Street
Plymouth, MI 48170
734-454-1515
weluvstamps@hotmail.com

## New Jersey

**AALLSTAMPS**
38 N. Main St.
PO Box 249
Milltown, NJ 08850
PH: 732-247-1093
FAX: 732-247-1094
mail@aallstamps.com
www.aallstamps.com

## Stamp Shows

## New Jersey

**BERGEN STAMPS & COLLECTIBLES**
717 American Legion Dr.
Teaneck, NJ 07666
PH: 201-836-8987

**RON RITZER STAMPS INC.**
Millburn Mall
2933 Vauxhall Rd.
Vauxhall, NJ 07088
PH: 908-687-0007
FAX: 908-687-0795
rritzer@comcast.net

**TRENTON STAMP & COIN CO.**
Thomas DeLuca
Store: Forest Glen Plaza
1804 Route 33
Hamilton Square, NJ 08690
Mail: PO Box 8574
Trenton, NJ 08650
PH: 800-446-8664
PH: 609-584-8100
FAX: 609-587-8664
TOMD4TSC@aol.com

## New York

**CHAMPION STAMP CO., INC.**
432 W. 54th St.
New York, NY 10019
PH: 212-489-8130
FAX: 212-581-8130
championstamp@aol.com
www.championstamp.com

## Ohio

**HILLTOP STAMP SERVICE**
Richard A. Peterson
PO Box 626
Wooster, OH 41691
PH: 330-262-8907
PH: 330-262-5378
hilltop@bright.net

**THE LINK STAMP CO.**
3461 E. Livingston Ave.
Columbus, OH 43227
PH/FAX: 614-237-4125
PH/FAX: 800-546-5726

## Tennessee

**HERRON HILL, INC.**
5007 Black Road
Suite 140
Memphis, TN 38117
PH: 901-683-9644

## Virginia

**KENNEDY'S STAMPS & COINS, INC.**
7059 Brookfield Plaza
Springfield, VA 22150
PH: 703-569-7300
FAX: 703-569-7644
j.w.kennedy@verizon.net

**LATHEROW & CO., INC.**
5054 Lee Hwy.
Arlington, VA 22207
PH: 703-538-2727
PH: 800-647-4624
FAX: 703-538-5210

## Topicals

**E. JOSEPH McCONNELL**
PO Box 683
Monroe, NY 10949
PH: 845-496-5916
FAX: 845-782-0347
ejstamps@gmail.com
www.EJMcConnell.com

## Topicals-Columbus

**MR. COLUMBUS**
PO Box 1492
Fennville, MI 49408
PH: 269-543-4755
columbus@accn.org

## Topicals-Miscellaneous

**HENRY GITNER PHILATEL-ISTS, INC.**
PO Box 3077-S
Middletown, NY 10940
PH: 845-343-5151
FAX: 800-947-8267
FAX: 845-343-0068
hgitner@hgitner.com
www.hgitner.com

## United States

**BROOKMAN STAMP CO.**
PO Box 90
Vancouver, WA 98666
PH: 360-695-1391
PH: 800-545-4871
FAX: 360-695-1616
dave@brookmanstamps.com
www.brookmanstamps.com

## Topicals

## U.S.-Collections Wanted

**DR. ROBERT FRIEDMAN & SONS**
2029 W. 75th St.
Woodridge, IL 60517
PH: 800-588-8100
FAX: 630-985-1588
drbobstamps@yahoo.com
www.drbobfriedmanstamps.com

## Want Lists

**BROOKMAN INTERNATIONAL**
PO Box 450
Vancouver, WA 98666
PH: 360-695-1391
PH: 800-545-4871
FAX: 360-695-1616
dave@brookmanstamps.com

**CHARLES P. SCHWARTZ**
PO Box 165
Mora, MN 55051
PH: 320-679-4705
charlesp@ecenet.com

## Want Lists-British Empire 1840-1935 German Cols./Offices

**COLONIAL STAMP COMPANY**
5757 Wilshire Blvd PH #8
Los Angeles, CA 90036
PH: 323-933-9435
FAX: 323-939-9930
Toll Free in North America
PH: 877-272-6693
FAX: 877-272-6694
info@colonialstampcompany.com
www.colonialstampcompany.com

## Wanted-U.S. Collections

**THE STAMP CENTER**
**DUTCH COUNTRY AUCTIONS**
4115 Concord Pike
Wilmington, DE 19803
PH: 302-478-8740
FAX: 302-478-8779
scdca@dol.net
www.thestampcenter.com

## Wanted-Worldwide Collections

**DR. ROBERT FRIEDMAN & SONS**
2029 W. 75th St.
Woodridge, IL 60517
PH: 800-588-8100
FAX: 630-985-1588
drbobstamps@yahoo.com
www.drbobfriedmanstamps.com

**THE STAMP CENTER**
**DUTCH COUNTRY AUCTIONS**
4115 Concord Pike
Wilmington, DE 19803
PH: 302-478-8740
FAX: 302-478-8779
scdca@dol.net
www.thestampcenter.com

## Websites

**ARON R. HALBERSTAM PHILATELISTS, LTD.**
PO Box 150168
Van Brunt Station
Brooklyn, NY 11215-0168
PH: 718-788-3978
FAX: 718-965-3099
arh@arhstamps.com
www..arhstamps.com

## Wholesale

**HENRY GITNER PHILATEL- ISTS, INC.**
PO Box 3077-S
Middletown, NY 10940
PH: 845-343-5151
PH: 800-947-8267
FAX: 845-343-0068
hgitner@hgitner.com
www.hgitner.com

## Worldwide Stamps

**METROPOLITAN STAMP CO., INC.**
PO Box 657
Park Ridge, IL 60068-0657
PH: 815-439-0142
FAX: 815-439-0143
metrostamp@aol.com
www.metropolitanstamps.com

## Worldwide-Year Sets

**WWW.WORLDSTAMPS.COM**
242 West Saddle River Road
Suite C
Upper Saddle River, NJ 07458
PH: 201-236-8122
FAX: 201-236-8133
by mail:
Frank Geiger Philatelists
info@WorldStamps.com
www.WorldStamps.com

# Specialty Series

Scott Publishing Co. produces album pages for more than 120 countries. Scott Specialty pages are renowned for their quality and detail. There are spaces for every major variety of postage stamp within each country or specialty area.

Each space is identified by Scott number and many of the spaces are illustrated. Pages are printed on one side only on chemically neutral paper that will not harm your stamps.

Scott Specialty series pages are sold as page units only. Binders and slipcases are sold separately.

For more information on the entire line of Scott products visit your favorite stamp dealer or go online at:

**www.amosadvantage.com**

S·C·O·T·T®

P.O. Box 828, Sidney OH 45365-0828
1-800-572-6885

AMOS
HOBBY PUBLISHING